GB Rail Timetable

Sunday 22 May 2011 to Saturday 10 December 2011

Britain's national railway network and stations are owned by Network Rail. Passenger services are operated by the Train Companies included in this Timetable, who work together closely to provide a co-ordinated *National Rail* network offering a range of travel opportunities. Details and identification codes are shown on the Train Operator pages.

This Timetable contains rail services operated over the National R… h rail and shipping connections with Ireland, the Isle of Man, the Isle of Wight and the Channel I… aged stations however the remainder are operated on their behalf by the Train Operat… n Index. The Timetable Network Map shows the number of the individual t…

CW01261094

Contents

Services on Public Holidays

An amended service will operate on many parts of the rail network during Public Holidays and you are strongly advised to confirm your journey details if travelling around a holiday period. For more information, visit nationalrail.co.uk/holidays

Engineering Work

It is sometimes necessary to carry out essential Engineering Work which means that services may be changed, particularly late at night or at weekends to allow this work to be carried out. Engineering Work is usually planned many weeks in advance and details of changes to train times can be obtained from the National Rail Enquiries website – www.nationalrail.co.uk/engineering

National Rail Conditions of Carriage

Details of the conditions against which all National Rail tickets are issued, including the conditions which apply to the carriage of luggage and cycles can be obtained from the National Rail Enquiries website – www.nationalrail.co.uk/nrcc

What's New?

Welcome to the GB Rail Timetable valid from Sunday 22 May 2011 to Saturday 10 December 2011.

Chiltern Railways

Following a £250 million investment in improved infrastructure between Birmingham Moor Street and London Marylebone, Chiltern Railways are launching a completely revised 'Mainline' Timetable with much faster journeys to London. The fastest journey from Birmingham Moor Street to London Marylebone will now be just 90 minutes, and just 70 minutes non-stop from Warwick Parkway. Most other main stations along the route will also have journey times around 20% faster. This new service will start on 4 September 2011.

East Coast

The new East Coast Timetable will bring fantastic benefits, such as:
19 new train services per weekday, Improved frequency and pattern of train services and many faster typical journeys

New services will be introduced, including:
A return service from London King's Cross and Harrogate, a return service between Lincoln and London King's Cross and a new 'Flying Scotsman' early morning service from Edinburgh to London King's Cross in just four hours, stopping at Newcastle only and arriving in London at 0940.

East Midland Trains

Newark Northgate to Lincoln and Grimsby services will be altered to accommodate the changes on the East Coast Mainline.

Sunday services on the Robin Hood Line will only run from Nottingham to Mansfield Woodhouse and vice versa.

During the period of the Timetable, the 1352 Liverpool to Nottingham service will be extended to Norwich.

An additional HST (high speed train) will operate on Saturdays between Derby and Skegness at 0753. It returns from Skegness at 1126.

From the start of the Timetable until 10 September 2011, the 0637 London to York Saturday service will run through to Scarborough. It will return at 1703.

First Capital Connect

There are no major changes to services, however weekend and evening services will continue to be affected by engineering work. Many of these alterations are included in these Timetables, however you are advised to check for additional alterations before travelling.

First Great Western

1948 SX London Paddington to Cheltenham Spa will be extended to run through to Worcester Shrub Hill
0553 and 0729 Cheltenham Spa to London Paddington will start back from Worcester Shrub Hill
1706 SX London Paddington to Westbury is diverted after Pewsey, thus ceasing to call at Westbury, but now runs through to Bristol Temple Meads calling additionally at Trowbridge, Bradford-on-Avon, Bath Sap and Bristol Temple Meads
0608 SX Westbury to London Paddington starts back from Bristol Temple Meads calling additionally at Bradford-on-Avon and Trowbridge.

Additional train - 1436 Fridays only London Paddington to Exeter St Davids from 8 July to 26 August 2011 inclusive calling at Reading, Westbury, Castle Cary, Taunton and Tiverton Parkway.
Additional train - 1820 Fridays only Exeter St Davids to London Paddington from 8 July to 26 August 2011 inclusive calling at Taunton and London Paddington only.
Additional train - 1553 SX Bristol Parkway to Bath Spa

All train services between Oxford and Bicester Town will be operated by Chiltern Railways.

LOROL (London Overground)

There are new services as well as frequency increases between Richmond / Clapham Junction and Stratford as below:
Mondays to Fridays: (Peak only: 0700-1000 and 1600-1900)
Between Richmond and Stratford services increase to run to every 15 minutes
Between Clapham Junction and Stratford services increase to run to every 15 minutes
The above changes will result in services between Willesden Junction and Stratford increasing to run to every 7-8 minutes

Mondays to Fridays (Off-peak) and all day at weekends

Between Richmond and Stratford services increase to run about every 15 minutes

Between Clapham Junction and Willesden Junction services increase to run every 15 minutes - every other train will continue to / from Stratford

The above changes will result in services between Willesden Junction and Stratford increasing to run every 10 minutes

In February 2011 London Overground has extended one of its lines northbound, from Dalston Junction to Highbury & Islington via Canonbury.

Services to / from both Crystal Palace and West Croydon have been extended to Highbury & Islington (running daily on each branch up to every 15 minutes)

Services from New Cross branch will continue to terminate at Dalston Junction (running daily up to every 15 minutes)

Services between Gospel Oak and Barking will be enhanced on Sundays, with trains running up to every 15 minutes, matching the frequency on Mondays to Saturdays

Services between Watford Junction and Euston will be enhanced on Sundays, with trains running up to every 20 minutes, matching the frequency on Mondays to Saturdays

NYMR (North Yorkshire Moors Railway)

The heritage train operator, the North Yorkshire Moors Railway, will now be running trains every day between Pickering and Whitby (apart from Summer Sundays when no track capacity is available) until the end of their daily service on 30 October 2011.

Northern Rail

From May 2011 Blackpool North – Liverpool Lime Street services will be extended to run through to Liverpool South Parkway on Mondays to Saturdays during the off-peak period.

Customers on the Leeds – Settle – Carlisle route will benefit from earlier through journey opportunities (Mondays to Fridays). The first southbound train from Carlisle arrives in Leeds before 0845 and the first northbound train from Leeds arrives in Carlisle before 0845.

There are a significant number of small changes to Northern services operating to and from stations on the ECML. A standard pattern is now in place between Darlington, Middlesbrough and Saltburn. Changes between York, Selby and Hull are designed to provide customers with better connections with services on the ECML north of York.

ScotRail

The Edinburgh to Oban direct service returns, running for an extended period this summer, all Edinburgh to Dunbar services will now call at Musselburgh and we will also launch the full Helensburgh/Milngavie – Edinburgh via Airdrie and Bathgate service.

Southeastern Railway

A new High Speed train service has been introduced for Maidstone West to provide the people of Maidstone with an alternative way of getting to and from London, during the morning and evening peak periods. It will also help improve the reliability and punctuality of services along the North Kent and Sidcup lines into London.

The new service will consist of three departures Mondays to Fridays from Maidstone West in the morning at 0656, 0726 and 0756, with return journeys departing from St Pancras International at 1714, 1744 and 1814. The new services will call at Strood, Gravesend, Stratford International and St Pancras International with journey times of approximately 50 minutes.

There will also be one service in the morning departing St Pancras International at 0625 to Maidstone West and in the evening one service departing at 1913 from Maidstone West to St Pancras International.

Existing High Speed services to and from Rochester and Faversham will be diverted. To ensure that Rochester receives the same number of trains, the current Broadstairs High Speed services will call additionally at Rochester and will be increased to 12 carriages to accommodate additional passengers.

How to use this Timetable

Some tables are self-contained (such as Table 1 London–Shoeburyness) showing every train running between any two stations on the route. Train journey-lengths vary from the under-three-quarters-of-a-mile Stourbridge Town – Stourbridge Junction shuttle to the 703 mile Penzance–Dundee service. To show details of longer-distance services in a single table, short-distance services are omitted, these appearing in separate 'composite' tables.

WHICH TABLE?

General Layout of the Timetable

There are several ways of finding the correct table(s) for a journey. Tables start with the north bank of the Thames and radiate anti-clockwise around London as far as the south bank (Table 212, London-Faversham-Margate) with non-London tables (like the Cardiff Valleys) placed close to the appropriate London route. Internal Scottish routes follow from Table 216. Tables numbered 400-406 cover domestic Sleeper services. Once used to this geographic layout, required tables can usually be found with relative ease, but there are more precise methods:

Using the Index

Look up your destination. If it appears in up to five tables, those tables are listed (for example Hilsea appears in Tables 156, 157, 158, 165 and 188). If it appears in six or more then there may be sub-divisions. If your destination is sub-divided in this way and your origin is NOT shown (for example Shipley is not shown under Lancaster) then look up the origin instead as it probably has fewer tables. Alongside the station name is shown a two character code indicating which operator is responsible for operating the facilities at that station (see also Train Operator pages).

Using the Timetable Network Map

If your journey is more complicated and involves several changes between tables, the Timetable Network Map will be very useful. For example, to plan a journey from North Berwick to Pontypridd one would not expect to find both in the same table. The map makes it clear that one has to change at Edinburgh and Cardiff and, as there is no through service between North Berwick and Pontypridd, allows one to look up possible routes, for example, via Crewe and Shrewsbury (Tables 65 and 131), Crewe and Birmingham (Tables 57 and 65) or York and Birmingham (Tables 51 and 57).

Using Route/Network Diagrams

For many tables a Route or Network Diagram is also provided. Route Diagrams are generally used for longer distance tables (for example Table 26) and show the route and stations served in diagrammatic form as well as the principal connecting links. Network Diagrams (for example Tables 152–154) are generally used where there is a dense network of shorter distance routes and show *all* stations and routes in the area concerned in diagrammatic form.

Using the Table

Having found the table you require make sure you look at the correct set of pages: Mondays to Fridays, Mondays to Saturdays, Saturdays, Sundays plus any relevant dates. Look for the station from which you will leave, read across until you find a suitable train, then read down to see when you will arrive at your destination.

↪ indicates the train is continued **in** a later column.

↩ indicates the train is continued **from** an earlier column.

Bold times denote through trains whilst light, *italic*, times are connections (Please read carefully the section on the "Connections" page). Check if there is a column-heading and if there is, refer to the foot of the table for an explanation.

Because of the large number of services that 'cross' Midnight, a Railway Timetable needs to be precise in the meaning of 'a day'. Trains starting their journeys before Midnight are shown towards the end of a table – but if you are looking for the 'last' train do not stop there, as there may be later ones at the start of the table!

A train crossing Midnight will be shown in full at the END of a table and any column heading denoting the day of the week applies to the day the train STARTS. For example a 2350 train headed 'SO' (see the general notes on inside front cover) commences 2350 Saturday and runs into Sunday. The train will also be shown at the front of the Sunday table with the times prior to Midnight shown with note 'p', e.g. 23p50, to indicate that they refer to the previous night.

Do not worry about the ambiguity as to which day Midnight itself belongs, for, to avoid this problem, all times skip from 2359 to 0001 and neither 0000 nor 2400 is ever used!

A two character code is shown at the head of each train column indicating which operator is providing the train service (see also Train Operator pages).

How to use this Timetable (continued)

Mileages between stations served (but not those shown for connecting purposes) are shown on the first page of each Timetable

Unique Timetable Number (as shown on the Insert Map and in the Index to Stations)

Stations served

Catering Information

Indicates the Operating Company of the train concerned

Indicates the days of the week (and in some cases dates) on which the Timetable operates

Table 97

Colne, Burnley, Accrington and Blackburn—Preston—Blackpool

Mondays to Saturdays

Miles	Miles		NT	NT	NT	NT	NT		NT	NT	NT	NT	NT	NT	NT	NT
																SO
			◇	◇						◇	◇			◇	◇	◇
							J									K
			⌶	⌶						⌶	⌶			⌶	⌶	
0	—	**Colne** d			09 25							10 16				
2	—	Nelson d			09 31							10 22				
3½	—	Briefield d			09 34							10 25				
5½	—	**Burnley Central** 98 d			09 39							10 30				
6	—	Burnley Barracks 98 d										10 32				
—	—	Leeds 39 d	08 18							09 18				10 18		
—	—	Burnley Manchester Road 39 d	09 21							10 21				11 21		
7	—	Rose Grove d			09 44						10 36					
8½	—	Hapton d										10 39				
10	—	Huncoat d										10 42				
11½	—	Accrington d	09 31		09 51					10 31		10 46		11 31		
12½	—	Church & Oswaldtwistle d			09 54							10 49				
14½	—	Rishton d			09 58							10 52				
18	—	**Blackburn** a	09 39		10 03					10 39		10 57		11 39		
—	—	Manchester Victoria 94 a	*10 39*		*11 06*							*12 06*				
—	—	Clitheroe 94 d								*09 58*				*10 58*		
—	—	**Blackburn** d	09 39		10 03					10 39		10 59		11 39		
19½	—	Mill Hill (Lancashire) d			10 06							11 02				
20	—	Cherry Tree d			10 08							11 04				
21	—	Pleasington d										11 06				
26	—	Bamber Bridge d			10 16							11 13				
27½	—	Lostock Hall d			10 19							11 15				
30	—	**Preston** 10 a	09 56		10 26					10 56		11 24		11 56		
—	—	London Euston 65 a	*12c 55*							*14c 75*				*14g 49*		
—	—	London Euston 65 d							*07f 40*			*08f 40*				
—	0	**Preston** 10 d	09 58	10 02	10 27	10 32	10 38		10 50	10 58	11 02	11 26	11 45	11 58	12 02	12 21
35½	5½	Salwick d														
37½	7½	Kirkham & Wesham d			10 36				10 59			11 35	11 54			
41	—	Moss Side d										11 40				
43½	—	Lytham d			10 44							11 44				
44½	—	Ansdell & Fairhaven d			10 47							11 47				
46½	—	St Annes-on-the-Sea d			10 51							11 51				
48½	—	Squires Gate d			10 54							11 54				
49½	—	Blackpool Pleasure Beach d			10 57							11 57				
50	—	**Blackpool South** a			11 02							12 02				
—	14½	Poulton-le-Fylde d	10 14	10 18					11 07	11 14	11 18		12 02	12 14	12 18	
—	16½	Layton d							11 10				12 06			
—	17½	Blackpool North a	10 24	10 28		10 57	11 04		11 18	11 24	11 28		12 13	12 24	12 28	12 50

For general notes see front of timetable

J Mondays to Fridays until 1 November and from 31 March, also Saturdays until 2 November and from 1 March
K Until 2 November
c Saturdays arr. 10 minutes later
f Saturdays dep. 10 minutes earlier
g Saturdays arr. 1500

Principal stations on the route are shown in **bold**

For non-connecting stations only - indicates that additional services between these stations are included on other Timetables (see also below 'Route Diagrams')

Indicates the minimum interchange time (in minutes) that should be allowed when connecting between trains. Where no figure is shown, a minimum of 5 minutes should be allowed

For connecting stations only - indicates the Timetables on which the full service to and from the connecting station can be found (see also below under Route Diagrams)

Train times indicate that the train stops at the station concerned. Arrival times are denoted by **'a'** against the station name and departure times by **'d'**. Where there is no time shown against a station then the train concerned does not serve that station

Train runs on **S**aturdays **O**nly (see also page called 'References and Symbols used in this Timetable')

Seat Reservations symbols

Train time in ***italics*** indicate connecting times. The letter **'a'** alongside a connecting station indicates the arrival time at that station. Conversely, the letter **'d'** indicates the departure time

Intra-time letter indicating note at foot of page

A wavy line indicates that the train does not run on all dates included in the Timetable. In all such cases an additional headnote (in this case 'J') will be used to provide full details

Route/Network Diagrams (see previous page): For many tables a Route/Network Diagram is also provided to show the routes and stations served in diagrammatic form. Where this is the case, a reference to the Route/Network Diagram will be provided at the top of each page of the Timetable concerned. Timetable numbers for connecting or alternative services will not be included within the Table itself; instead this will be indicated on the accompanying Route/Network Diagram

General Information

Smoking Policy

Smoking is not permitted on any National Rail service or in any station. In England and Wales, this includes all covered and uncovered concourses, ticket halls, platforms, footbridges and subways at station premises.

Left Luggage Facilities

Details of Left Luggage Facilities at individual stations are available at www.nationalrail.co.uk/stations

Penalty Fares

Penalty Fares are charged by Train Companies at some stations and on some trains. Where this is the case, warning notices will be displayed. Those stations at which Penalty Fares are in operation are indicated in the Station Index and the individual Table numbers section (see also Train Operator pages). Please be aware that at some stations where Penalty Fare Schemes are in place not all Train Operator services calling at that station are included in the scheme.

If you cannot produce a valid ticket for your entire journey when asked to do so, you may be charged a Penalty Fare. This will be either twice the full single fare to the next station at which the train is due to stop, or £20 (£50 on Transport for London services and stations, reducing to £25 if paid within 21 days), whichever is the greater. Any travel beyond the next station will be charged at the full single fare.

To avoid paying a Penalty Fare, you must purchase a valid ticket to your destination, before starting your journey. If the ticket office is closed and you cannot buy the ticket you need from a self service ticket machine, you must buy a Permit to Travel paying as much of your fare as possible. This permit must be exchanged for a valid ticket at the first opportunity.

More information is available at nationalrail.co.uk/penaltyfares.

Timetable Accuracy, Contents, Presentation

Every effort is made to ensure that the information contained in this Timetable is correct, however errors can still occur. If you have any questions or queries about the train services shown in this Timetable, please contact the appropriate operator shown in the Directory of Train Operators.

General comments about this publication should be addressed to:–

TSO,

PO Box 29,

Norwich,

NR3 1GN.

Additional Amendments

A facility is available whereby details of any train service alterations introduced subsequent to the production of the GB Rail Timetable may be accessed through the Network Rail website

(see http:networkrail.co.uk). Follow the link to the "Electronic National Rail Timetable" in the "For Passengers" section. For up to date timetables, incorporating any changes to services please select the 'Route index / Timetable links' document link.

From time to time, further alterations may apply at short notice and details of these may be found at http://www.nationalrail.co.uk/service_disruptions/currentAndFuture.html.

Other National Rail Timetables

Regional and route specific Timetables are available from individual train companies. Please contact the relevant train company to request the latest version of the Timetable you require.

National Rail Enquiries offers an online 'Pocket Timetable' service which gives you the flexibility to create a customised Timetable based around your origin and destination, your own time requirements and the days of the week that you intend to travel. Visit www.nationalrail.co.uk/pockettimetables for more details.

Connections

Bold type times in vertical columns in the timetable show direct trains. In a few cases, where one train overtakes another, the times appear in more than one column and arrow symbols indicate where the train continues in the Timetable.

Many more journey opportunities are possible by changing trains. To help plan such journeys, times in light italic type are shown in some of the Timetables for departures (if the time is earlier than the bold type times for the station below in the column at which you should change trains) or arrivals (if they are later than the bold type times for the station above in the column at which you should change trains).

Where light type italic times are not shown you may have to refer to other tables in the book to work out your connecting services. In order to find the right table to reference, first look at the Route/Network Diagram that covers the table you are working from. This will show the principal connecting links and their table references, which may include the destination you are searching for. If your journey is not covered, follow the advice given on 'How to use this Timetable' under the headings 'Using the Timetable Network Map' and 'Using the Index'.

Connections between trains cannot be guaranteed. The nature of the integrated operation of railway passenger services means that to delay one train to await customers from a late running train arriving at a station may cause significant disruption to many other customers when they make connections at other stations along the route. Every endeavour is made to minimise the total disruption and particular attention is given to services operating infrequently and the last train services each day.

The aim of all Train Operating Companies is to run punctually; inevitably some disruption occurs from time to time. When planning a journey you may wish to consider the effects which any disruption could have and to allow some contingency margin when planning connections.

Minimum Interchange Times at Stations

Unless a connection is shown by times printed in light type, you should generally allow a minimum of five minutes between arrival and departure.

The exceptions to this rule are indicated by minimum interchange times (e.g. **15**) alongside the station name in the tables. In certain cases the minimum interchange time is different according to the Train Operators involved.

These are detailed below:-

STATION AND 'STANDARD' MINIMUM CONNECTIONAL ALLOWANCE (Minutes)		***EXCEPTIONS** Showing the Train Operator(s) and minimum connectional allowance applicable*	
Barnham	5	*SN*	2
Bournemouth	5	*SW*	3
Brighton	10	*SN*	4
Cardiff Central	7	*AW*	3*
Clapham Junction	10	*SN*	5
Gatwick Airport	10	*SN*	5
Guildford	5	*GW*	4
Leatherhead	5	*SN*	3
London Blackfriars	3	SE	5
London Victoria	15	*SE, SN*	10
Luton	10	*FC*	4
Luton Airport Parkway	7	*FC*	4
Redhill	5	*SN*	3
St. Denys	5	*SW*	3
Southampton Central	5	*SN, SW*	4
Tulse Hill	3	FC	4
Wimbledon	6	*SN, FC*	5

Example

At Barnham a different minimum connectional allowance applies for Train Operator SN. This means that if your journey involves changing between two trains *both of which* are operated by SN, you need only allow 2 minutes. If, however, one or both trains are provided by any other Operator then the minimum of 5 minutes (as shown after the station name) applies.

* Applicable to Valley Lines services only (table 130).

Train Information

National Rail Enquiries

Timetable and Fares are available 24 hours a day at www.nationalrail.co.uk or, if you are on the move, at mobile.nationalrail.co.uk

National Rail Enquiries provides up-to-the-minute advice on all aspects of journey planning, fares and buying tickets, live train running updates and other useful information.

08457 48 49 50 **24 Hours Daily**

(calls may be recorded for training purposes)

0845 60 40 500 **Welsh Language**

0845 60 50 600 **Textphone – 0600 - 2100 Daily**

TrainTracker

For live train times for today and train Timetables for the next three months call TrainTracker™ Text on:

0871 200 49 50

Average calls to TrainTracker cost 10p a minute from a BT Landline. Charges from other operators may vary. Calls may be recorded for training purposes.

TrainTracker Text

For live departure and arrival times direct to your mobile text station name to TrainTracker™ on:

8 49 50

TrainTracker texts cost 25p for each successful response (plus usual text costs)

Train company numbers for disabled passengers requiring assistance:–

Company	Telephone	Textphone
Arriva Trains Wales	08453 003 005	0845 605 0600
c2c	01702 357640	08457 125 988
Chiltern Railways	08456 005 165	08457 078051
CrossCountry	0844 811 0125	0844 811 0126
East Coast	08457 225 225	08451 202 067
East Midlands Trains	08457 125 678	08457 078 051
Eurostar	08705 186 186	Not available
First Capital Connect	0800 058 2844	0800 975 1052
First Great Western	0800 197 1329/0845 600 5604	0800 294 9209
First Hull Trains	08450 710 222	08456 786 967
First TransPennine Express	0800 107 2149	0800 107 2061
Gatwick Express	0800 138 1016	0800 138 1018
Grand Central	0844 811 0072	0845 305 6815
Heathrow Connect	0845 678 6975	0800 294 9209
Heathrow Express	0845 600 1515	Not available
Island Line	0800 528 2100	0800 692 0792
London Midland	0800 0924260	0844 811 0134
London Overground	0845 601 4867	Not available
Merseyrail	0151 702 2071	0870 0552 681
National Express East Anglia	0800 028 28 78	0845 606 7245
Northern	0808 1561606	08456 045 608
ScotRail	0800 912 2 901	18001 0800 912 2 901
South West Trains	0800 52 82 100	0800 692 0792
Southeastern	0800 783 4524	0800 783 4548
Southern	0800 138 1016	0800 138 1018
Virgin Trains	08457 443366	08457 443367

Train Information (continued)

London Travel Information

0843 222 1234	24 hours (Daily)	www.tfl.gov.uk

Services to Europe on Eurostar via the Channel Tunnel

08432 186 186	0800-1900 (Daily)	www.eurostar.com

Ireland

NI Railways 028 90 66 6630	0700-2000 (M-F) 0800-1800 (S+S)	www.translink.co.uk
Iarnrod Eireann (IE) (Irish Rail) 00 353 183 66 222		www.irishrail.ie

Transport Direct

Plan journeys by car, bus, train, tube, coach, plane at www.transportdirect.info. Transport Direct is the first door-to-door on-line journey planner for Great Britain.

It's free to use; simply enter your departure point, destination and time of travel and Transport Direct will offer a number of options by different modes of transport - both public and private. Journey plans are presented as step-by-step instructions supported by detailed maps including bus stops and other points of interest to travellers. Tickets for rail and coach journeys can be booked via retail web sites without the need to re-enter journey details. Transport Direct includes live travel news for rail and car users. The car journey planner gives route information that takes account of historical traffic level data, offering the user the choice to travel at a different time, or choose public transport. When travelling by public transport, users can adjust their expected walking speed to plan rail, coach and bus connections more efficiently. You can also access Transport Direct via mobile phone and PDA to find out when your next train is due or to check road conditions.

Bus Information in Great Britain

For details of buses within Greater London ring the Transport for London line: 0843 222 1234 (24-hours).

Bus information for the rest of Great Britain is available nationally from 'Traveline' which is run by local authorities and bus operators. There are regional call centres all of which share the same telephone number and any centre will switch calls pertaining to another part of the country through to the relevant centre. Alternatively codes for reaching the appropriate centre direct can be obtained from www.traveline.info/powercodes.html

The number is 0871 200 22 33 (calls from landlines cost 10p per minute) and centres are open at least between the hours of 0800 and 2000 daily (except Christmas Day and Boxing Day). Website: www.traveline.info

PlusBus

PlusBus is an easy-to-use add-on to your train ticket which gives unlimited bus travel on most bus services around the whole urban area of your origin or destination town or city. ***PlusBus*** is available to many towns and cities across Great Britain with season tickets also available for most ***PlusBus*** destinations. For more information visit www.plusbus.info

Traintaxi

Taxi symbols on the Station index pages

Where appears against any station that has sub-entries, there will be a taxi rank outside the station from which taxis should usually be available. This also applies to Basingstoke, Bournemouth, Chelmsford, Cheltenham, Colchester, Lincoln, Middlesbrough, Milton Keynes, Northampton, Sunderland and Swindon.

Where appears against any other station, there will be a taxi rank or a cab office within 100 metres of the station. However, you are advised to check availability before travelling, and to pre-book if necessary. Indication of a rank or office is no guarantee of cabs being available.

Visit **www.traintaxi.co.uk** for information on cab firms serving **all** train, tram, metro and underground stations in Great Britain, and all bus and ferry destinations listed in this *GB Rail Timetable.*

Rail Travel for Disabled Passengers

All train operators are able to carry disabled passengers and can provide additional assistance for boarding and alighting and information during train journeys.

If using a wheelchair, it is recommended that passengers book assistance in advance as space on trains for wheelchair users is limited.

National Rail produce a booklet called 'Rail Travel Made Easy' which details the provisions Train Companies make for disabled people. The booklet is available from major stations or can be obtained by writing to: Rail Travel Made Easy, PO Box 11631, Laurence Kirk AB30 9AA. Alternatively, you can download a copy by visiting www.nationalrail.co.uk/passenger_services/disabled_passengers/

You can also see what facilities and services are available at stations throughout the UK, including stop-free routes by visiting www.nationalrail.co.uk

Seat Reservations, Luggage, Cycles and Animals

Seat Reservations

You can reserve seats on any train marked 🅁, 🆁, ◇ or ∝ at the top of the column in the timetable pages. Further detailed information is shown in the Directory of Train Operators.

Reservations can normally be made from about 12 weeks in advance of the day of travel, up to about 2 hours before the train departs from its start point, or, for early morning trains, up to 1600 hours the previous evening.

Where and How to Reserve

You can reserve either by visiting a station identified in the Index pages by ◇, or a rail appointed travel agent or by calling one of the telephone booking facilities listed on each Train Operator's page. Telephone reservations are only available when made in conjunction with purchasing a ticket. When reserving you will need to tell your station or agent:

1. Starting and finishing point of your journey.
2. Date of travel (Take care if your departure is soon after Midnight – see "How to use this Timetable").
3. Departure time of train.
4. Number of seats required.
5. You may be able to specify other preferences such as facing or back to direction of travel*, window seat, seat in Restaurant Car where available, seats round a table or airline style with fold down table where available.
   *Customers should note that some trains reverse their direction of travel during the journey.
6. First Class or Standard Accommodation (if you do not specify class of travel it will be assumed that you require Standard Accommodation).

Names on Seats

Your name can be included in your seat reservation label or on the electronic display above your seat, if you wish, when travelling First Class on some East Coast, East Midlands Trains and National Express East Anglia services or First and Standard Class on CrossCountry, First Great Western, First TransPennine Express, ScotRail and Virgin Trains services.

Connecting Reservations

If your journey involves changing between trains on which seats are reservable (including journeys crossing London or other major cities), through reservations on both services are available.

Children

Seats may be reserved for children, however, for a child under 5 years of age a seat may be reserved only if an appropriate child rail ticket is held.

Reservations Recommended

Trains shown 🆁 at the head of a column in the Timetable pages are expected to be very busy. Seat Reservations are therefore recommended for a comfortable journey and will consequently be provided free of charge to holders of valid travel tickets.

Seat Reservations, Luggage, Cycles and Animals (continued)

Reservations Compulsory

On trains shown [R] at the head of a column, Seat Reservations are compulsory and are available free of charge. Passengers may not be able to board the train if they do not have a reservation.

Trains For Weekends Away

Most long distance services after 1400 on Fridays and on Saturday mornings, also trains arriving in London on Sunday evenings and Monday mornings can be extremely busy.

Customers are advised to reserve seats in advance if planning to travel at these times.

Travelling at Peak Holiday Periods

Trains are usually extremely busy immediately before and after Bank Holidays and in some cases access to trains is only by reservation and/or boarding pass. Customers are advised to reserve seats as early as possible.

Cycles by Train

You can take your cycle on many National Rail services, however reservations may be required and restrictions may apply for peak services. Folded cycles can be carried on most train services. More information is shown in the Directory of Train Operators, the National Rail 'Cycling by Train' leaflet and online at www.nationalrail.co.uk/cycling. Cycle storage is also available at many stations.

Weekend First

Weekend First is available on many CrossCountry, East Coast*, East Midlands Trains, First Great Western, First TransPennine Express*, Grand Central*, National Express East Anglia, ScotRail*, South West Trains* and Virgin Trains services on Saturdays, Sundays and Bank Holidays. If you hold a ticket for travel in Standard Class, you may be able to upgrade to the added comfort of First Class Accommodation on payment of an additional fare. On some services a 'Weekend First' ticket allows you to upgrade to First Class at weekends and Bank Holidays. Holders of Annual Gold Cards may also be able to upgrade on off-peak services for a small amount. Costs vary depending on the journey you are making.

*may only be purchased on trains at time of travel

More information can be found at www.nationalrail.co.uk/firstclass

Customers' Luggage and Animals

Customers may take up to 3 items of personal luggage free of charge; this includes 2 large items (such as suitcases or rucksacks) and 1 item of smaller hand luggage (such as a briefcase). Folded prams, non-folding prams and carrycots are also able to be carried. Full details of the free allowances are available at stations. Excess luggage and certain more bulky items (such as skis) may be carried, subject to available space, at an extra charge. On Gatwick Express services, bulky items such as skis are conveyed free in the luggage van. There is plenty of space on board for other luggage.

Passengers may take dogs, cats and other small animals (maximum two per passenger), free of charge and subject to certain conditions, provided they do not endanger or inconvenience other passengers or staff.

ScotRail allows dogs to accompany able-bodied passengers in Sleeper Services subject to a charge for cleaning of the compartment. The booking must be First Class, Standard Class with two people travelling together, or a Solo supplement is payable for exclusive use of a twin-berth cabin. First Great Western do **not** allow animals (except Guide Dogs) to travel in Sleeper Accommodation. There is no charge for Guide Dogs.

More information can be found at www.nationalrail.co.uk/luggageandanimals

Directory of Train Operators

The following pages contain details of the Train Operating Companies who operate trains included in this Timetable and indicate the services they provide.

Each operator is identified by a two character code listed below. The codes are displayed in the index alongside the station name indicating which operator is responsible for operating the facilities at that station. The code is also shown at the head of each train column in the timetable pages indicating which operator is providing the train service.

18 stations are the operating responsibility of Network Rail and are shown in the index by the code NR and information about Network Rail is shown at the end of the Train Operating Company pages.

Page No	Train Company Name	Code
13	Arriva Trains Wales	AW
14	c2c	CC
15	CrossCountry	XC
16	Chiltern Railways	CH
17	Devon & Cornwall Railway	DC
18	East Coast	GR
19	East Midlands Trains	EM
20	First Capital Connect	FC
21	First Great Western	GW
22	First Hull Trains	HT
23	First TransPennine Express	TP
24	Gatwick Express	GX
25	Grand Central	GC
26	Heathrow Connect	HC
27	Heathrow Express	HX
28	Island Line	IL
29	London Midland	LM
30	London Overground	LO
31	Merseyrail	ME
32	National Express East Anglia	LE
33	North Yorkshire Moors Railway	NY
34	Northern	NT
35	ScotRail	SR
36	South West Trains	SW
37	Southeastern	SE
38	Southern	SN
39	Virgin Trains	VT
40	West Coast Railway Co.	WR

AW Arriva Trains Wales AW

ADDRESS

St Mary's House
47 Penarth Road
Cardiff CF10 5DJ
Telephone: 0845 6061 660
Website: www.arrivatrainswales.co.uk
Email: customer.relations@arrivatrainswales.co.uk

MANAGING DIRECTOR

Tim Bell

RESERVATIONS AND TICKETS BY TELEPHONE AND ONLINE

Tickets may be booked in advance and seats reserved, by telephone, from the following numbers (0800–2000 daily):

0870 9000 773 for Great Britain, tickets and reservations. 0870 9000 767 for Group and 0845 300 3005 for Disabled travel arrangements. Textphone 0845 758 5469 Please allow 5 days for delivery.

RESERVATION DETAILS

All seat reservations are free to ticket holders.

CATERING ON TRAINS

At-seat catering service of cold snacks, sandwiches and hot and cold drinks on all services marked ⊼, for all or part of the journey.

Complimentary meal service for first class and a counter service of hot and cold snacks for standard class on trains with ⌧.

Train catering on Arriva Trains Wales services is provided by:

At Seat Catering (2003) Ltd
St Mary's House
47 Penarth Road
Cardiff
CF10 5DJ

CYCLES

See Cycling by Train leaflet, a guide to Arriva Trains Wales services for full details.

LOST PROPERTY

Contact Arriva Trains Wales Customer Relations on 0845 6061 660.

TRAIN SERVICE UPDATE

Please consult our website at www.arrivatrainswales.co.uk for real time service updates.

PENALTY FARES

Penalty Fares are not in force on Arriva Trains Wales services. Customers are reminded that they must have a valid ticket when boarding at a staffed station, if not it will be necessary to charge you the full single/return fare for the journey.

DISABLED PEOPLE'S PROTECTION POLICY

Address as above.

CODE OF PRACTICE FOR COMMENTS, COMPLAINTS AND SUGGESTIONS

Address as above.

ALCOHOL POLICY

Arriva Trains Wales have prohibited the consumption of alcohol on all services and stations between Caerphilly - Rhymney, and Pontypridd - Treherbert/Merthr Tydfil/Aberdare

c2c

A member of the National Express Group plc

ADDRESS	2nd Floor Cutlers Court 115 Houndsditch London EC3A 7BR Telephone: 0845 601 4873 Fax: 01603 214517 Website: www.c2c-online.co.uk
MANAGING DIRECTOR	Julian Drury
RESERVATIONS AND TICKETS BY TELEPHONE AND ONLINE	Tickets may be booked in advance by telephoning 08457 44 44 22 - 0800 to 2000 daily.
RESERVATION DETAILS	Reservations are not available.
CATERING ON TRAINS	Not available.
CYCLES	Cycles can be taken on off-peak trains free-of-charge when accompanied by a fare-paying passenger, subject to space availability. Bicycles are not permitted, Mondays to Fridays on services that arrive in London between 0715 and 0945, or those which leave London between 1630 and 1840. To comply with safety regulations, all cycles, with the exception of folding cycles which are completely enclosed in a container or case throughout the journey, must be conveyed in the designated area on trains. During engineering work, cycles cannot be accommodated on replacement bus services.
LOST PROPERTY	Telephone: 01702 357 699
TRAIN SERVICE UPDATE	Up to date train running information is available on the c2c website www.c2c-online.co.uk, the National Rail Enquiries website at nationalrail.co.uk or on ceefax page 433.
PENALTY FARES	If you travel without a valid ticket you may be charged a penalty fare of £20 or twice the full single fare, whichever is the greater.
DISABLED PEOPLE'S PROTECTION POLICY	Available from:- Customer Relations c2c FREEPOST ADM3968 Southend SS1 1ZS Telephone: 0845 601 4873 - 0830 to 1700 Monday to Friday
CODE OF PRACTICE FOR COMMENTS, COMPLAINTS AND SUGGESTIONS	Available from Customer Relations at above address or telephone 0845 601 4873.

CrossCountry

XC

ADDRESS

CrossCountry
5th Floor, Cannon House,
18 Priory Queensway, Birmingham B4 6BS
Telephone: 08447 369 123
Textphone: 0121 200 6420
Fax: 0121 200 6005
Website: www.crosscountrytrains.co.uk
Email: customer.relations@crosscountrytrains.co.uk

MANAGING DIRECTOR

Andy Cooper

RESERVATIONS AND TICKETS BY TELEPHONE AND ONLINE

On-line at crosscountrytrains.co.uk is the easiest way to purchase your tickets.

If you prefer, you can also make telephone bookings on 0844 811 0124 between 0800 and 2200 daily. Parties of 10 or more should contact Group Travel on 0871 244 2388 between 0800 and 1800 weekdays

RESERVATION DETAILS

You are strongly advised to make a seat reservation in advance; especially when travelling on trains shown with the ▣ symbol in timetables. Seat reservations are free of charge.

CATERING ON TRAINS

Catering is available on most CrossCountry trains.

In First Class, on weekdays between 0630 and 1830 customers can enjoy complimentary light refreshments including hot and soft drinks, served at seat. In Standard Class we offer a range of quality snacks, sandwiches and hot drinks plus soft and alcoholic beverages between 0600 and 2000. For more information on the Nottingham - Cardiff and Birmingham - Stansted Airport routes please refer to our timetables.

CYCLES

We do not charge to carry your cycle. However, as space is very limited you will need to reserve in advance on nearly all our services. Please enquire before travelling. We are unable to accept powered cycles, tricycles, tandems or trailers on any of our services.

LOST PROPERTY

Contact Customer Relations on 08447 369 123 between 0800 and 2000 Monday to Saturday; or email lost.property@crosscountrytrains.co.uk

TRAIN SERVICE UPDATE

Details of major disruption to services and weekend engineering work are summarised on BBC Ceefax and BBCi on digital TV. Live travel updates are available on-line at crosscountrytrains.co.uk and details of all service disruptions can be found at nationalrail.co.uk/disruption/

PENALTY FARES

A Penalty Fares scheme is not currently in operation on CrossCountry trains. Visit crosscountrytrains.co.uk for the most up to date information. Should you board one of our trains without a valid ticket you will be charged the full Single or Return fare for your journey unless the ticket office is closed and a self-service ticket machine is not available.

DISABLED PEOPLE'S PROTECTION POLICY

We provide a Journey Care service for the disabled, elderly and infirm. By phoning our team on 0844 811 0125, textphone 0844 811 0126, beforehand we will, where possible, arrange help for your journey. Our Disabled People's Protection Policy is available on-line at crosscountrytrains.co.uk

CODE OF PRACTICE FOR COMMENTS, COMPLAINTS AND SUGGESTIONS

Copies of our Complaints Handling Procedure and Passenger's Charter are available on-line at crosscountrytrains.co.uk

Chiltern Railways

CH

ADDRESS

Customer Services
Banbury ICC
Merton Street
Banbury
Oxfordshire OX16 4RN
Telephone: 08456 005 165 (Mondays to Fridays 0830-1730)
Fax: 01926 729 914
Website: www.chilternrailways.co.uk

MANAGING DIRECTOR

Adrian Shooter (Acting)

RESERVATIONS AND TICKETS BY TELEPHONE AND ONLINE

Telephone 08456 005 165 (0700-2000, 7 days a week)

RESERVATION DETAILS

Reservations are not available.

CATERING ON TRAINS

We aim to provide an at-seat trolley catering service on many of our most popular longer distance trains. The trains providing this service change from time to time depending on circumstances and expected demand. If your train does not have a trolley do not forget that our main stations offer excellent catering facilities. For more details check our website. Please allow enough time to purchase your refreshments before boarding your train.

CYCLES

On Mondays to Fridays we are unable to convey cycles on our busiest trains. These are trains arriving at London Marylebone or Birmingham Snow Hill between 0745 and 1000 and trains departing London Marylebone or Birmingham Snow Hill between 1630 and 1930. These restrictions apply even if you are only travelling for part of the journey. Tandems are not carried at any time on Chiltern Railways. There are no restrictions on folding bikes. Bikes are not allowed on rail replacement buses.

LOST PROPERTY

If we find any item of lost property, we will always do our best to contact the owner if they can be identified. Items can be collected from London Marylebone up to 3 months after they have been handed in - we charge a collection fee to cover our administration costs.

If you lose something on one of our trains or stations you can report it by:

* Using the online form on our website

* Using a Lost Property Form available at any Chiltern Railways ticket office, and returning it to a member of Chiltern Railways Staff.

* By phone, fax or post using the contact details below:

Phone: 08456 005 165
Fax: 020 7333 3002
Write to: Chiltern Railways Lost Property
Marylebone Station
London NW1 6JJ.

Lost Property Office Operating Hours: Mondays to Fridays 1200 to 2000. Please allow up to 2 weeks for processing lost items. If you do not hear from us in that period, you should assume the item has not been found.

TRAIN SERVICE UPDATE

Visit our website www.chilternrailways.co.uk for current train running information and details of changes to train times because of engineering work or other special events.

PENALTY FARES

If you do not have a valid rail ticket for the journey you are making, you will have to pay a Penalty Fare of £20 or twice the single fare, whichever is the greater, for the journey you are making on Chiltern Railways services. For full details write to the above address, or see our website.

DISABLED PEOPLE'S PROTECTION POLICY

Copies of the Disabled People's Protection Policy can be obtained from the above address, or from our website.

CODE OF PRACTICE FOR COMMENTS, COMPLAINTS AND SUGGESTIONS

If you have any comments, complaints or suggestions regarding Chiltern Railways services, please write to the address shown above or telephone 08456 005 165 (0830-1730 Mondays to Fridays), Fax 01926 729 914. Alternatively you can use the 'Contact Us' option on our website.

Devon & Cornwall Railway

DC

ADDRESS

MANAGING DIRECTOR

RESERVATIONS AND TICKETS BY TELEPHONE AND ONLINE

RESERVATION DETAILS

New operator due to commence operation during this Timetable – for full details see National Rail website nearer the time

CATERING ON TRAINS

CYCLES

LOST PROPERTY

TRAIN SERVICE UPDATE

PENALTY FARES

DISABLED PEOPLE'S PROTECTION POLICY

CODE OF PRACTICE FOR COMMENTS, COMPLAINTS AND SUGGESTIONS

East Coast

ADDRESS	Freepost RRZG-ZZZX-LKXK Newcastle upon Tyne NE1 5DN Telephone: 08457 225 333 Open 0830-1700 Monday-Friday Fax: 0191 227 5986 Website: www.eastcoast.co.uk Email: customers@eastcoast.co.uk
MANAGING DIRECTOR	Karen Boswell
RESERVATIONS AND TICKETS BY TELEPHONE AND ONLINE	Internet — Purchase tickets via the internet 24 hours a day at www.eastcoast.co.uk Self service ticket machines are available at all East Coast stations. Purchase tickets for today or collect pre-booked tickets. Telephone — 08457 225 225 Telesales — Open 0800-2000 Monday-Saturday, 1000-2000 Sunday Business Travel — Open 0800-1800 Monday-Friday For corporate credit card and account holder bookings. Group Travel — Open 0900-1800 Monday-Friday Discounts may be available for groups of 10 or more people. Assisted Travel — Open 0800-2000 Monday-Saturday, 1000-2000 Sunday The minimum transaction is £10. Please allow 7 days from the time of booking for tickets to reach you through the post.
RESERVATION DETAILS	Seat Reservations can usually be made on any East Coast train up to ten weeks in advance. They are available to any ticket holder upon request, and are compulsory with some ticket types. Only one reservation can be made per single journey.
CATERING ON TRAINS	Passengers travelling in First Class will receive complimentary food and drink on board. For shorter journeys, you will be offered non-alcoholic drinks and snacks, while on longer trips you can look forward to something a little more substantial. Passengers in Standard Class can enjoy a wide range of refreshments from our caféBAR. An at-seat trolley service will also be available on selected services.
CYCLES	Bicycles are welcome on East Coast trains. A reservation must be made and bookings are subject to space being available. Reservations can be made by calling 08457 225 225 or at any East Coast ticket office.
LOST PROPERTY	If you lose something on a East Coast train or at a station please speak to a member of staff or contact us on 08457 225 333. Please note that charges are normally made for returning items of lost property and that we are unable to forward items of lost property on train services.
TRAIN SERVICE UPDATE	Visit www.eastcoast.co.uk or call National Rail Enquiries on 08457 48 49 50 (calls may be recorded for training purposes).
PENALTY FARES	East Coast does not operate a Penalty Fares scheme. However, you should always purchase a ticket valid for travel before you board any East Coast service as only full fare tickets are sold on our trains. The only exception being Disabled Railcard holders who will be sold appropriate discounted tickets on-board.
DISABLED PEOPLE'S PROTECTION POLICY	A copy of our DPPP can be obtained free of charge from the address at the top of this page. Our Assisted Travel Team can help you plan your journey and organise tickets, assistance and Seat Reservations. To ensure the best possible levels of assistance we recommend that you contact us no later than 1800 the day before you intend to travel. Telephone 08457 225 225 or textphone 08457 202 067* (open 0800-2000 Monday-Saturday, 1000-2000 Sunday). * Please note that this number should only be used to contact the Assisted Travel Team. For all other enquiries please telephone 08457 225 225.
CODE OF PRACTICE FOR COMMENTS, COMPLAINTS AND SUGGESTIONS	Our Passenger's Charter is available from all East Coast stations or from our website www.eastcoast.co.uk. All correspondence should be sent using the address at the top of this page.

East Midlands Trains

EM

ADDRESS	Customer Relations East Midlands Trains FREEPOST RSAK-GETK-BSJX Nottingham NG2 3DQ Telephone: 08457 125 678 Website: eastmidlandstrains.co.uk Email: getintouch@eastmidlandstrains.co.uk
MANAGING DIRECTOR	Tim Shoveller
RESERVATIONS AND TICKETS BY TELEPHONE AND ONLINE	Buy your tickets online at eastmidlandstrains.co.uk. You can buy tickets for all rail journeys (within Great Britain) with us. Alternatively call 08457 125 678 between 0800-2000 (7 days a week).
RESERVATION DETAILS	Seat Reservations on East Midlands Trains services are free. Just book in advance when you buy your ticket. We advise that you always make a reservation, as seats cannot be guaranteed without one. On our Local Services reservations are available on the Liverpool to Norwich services.
CATERING ON TRAINS	On our East Midlands London Services (to/from St Pancras International), we offer a range of delicious food options, plus snacks and hot and cold drinks. A trolley service is available on selected East Midlands Local Services (denoted by a symbol within the Timetable).
CYCLES	Two bicycles per train are accepted for free on all East Midlands Trains services; however reservations must be made in advance on reservable Services subject to availability.
LOST PROPERTY	Please allow a minimum of 24 hours for the items to be received at a lost property office. If your item is located you may be charged for the return of it and will be advised of this cost. To enquire about lost property, please call our Lost Property office, ideally between the hours of 1000 and 1600 Monday to Saturday on 0115 9576525.
TRAIN SERVICE UPDATE	Details of services and real time running information, including travel alerts by email are available through our website. Visit eastmidlandstrains.co.uk. Alternatively, call National Rail Enquiries on 08457 48 49 50 (calls may be recorded for training purposes).
PENALTY FARES	You should always buy a ticket in advance of boarding your train. Penalty Fares may be in operation on your service.
DISABLED PEOPLE'S PROTECTION POLICY	We aim to make travelling with us accessible to all our customers. If you require assistance in travelling, have special needs or mobility problems please call our team on 08457 125 678 to arrange help for your journey. A text direct service is also available on 18001 08457 125 678 (for people with hearing problems).
CODE OF PRACTICE FOR COMMENTS, COMPLAINTS AND SUGGESTIONS	Our Customer Relations team is available to receive your comments, complaints or suggestions. Please write to Customer Relations at the above address, or email getintouch@eastmidlandstrains.co.uk

FC First Capital Connect FC

A member of the First Rail Division

ADDRESS

Freepost, RRBR-REEJ-KTKY
First Capital Connect
Customer Relations Department
PO Box 443
Plymouth PL4 6WP
Telephone: 0845 026 4700 (open 7 days a week 0700-2200 with the exception of Christmas Day)
Fax: 0845 676 9904
Website: www.firstcapitalconnect.co.uk
Email: customer.relations.fcc@firstgroup.com

MANAGING DIRECTOR

Neal Lawson

RESERVATIONS AND TICKETS BY TELEPHONE AND ONLINE

First Capital Connect does not offer telesales, however tickets can be booked at www.firstcapitalconnect.co.uk

RESERVATION DETAILS

Reservations are not available.

CATERING ON TRAINS

None.

CYCLES

We welcome passengers with bicycles on services where they can be safely accommodated, however restrictions apply, bicycles cannot be carried on:

- trains that are scheduled to arrive at a London terminal between 0700 and 1000;
- trains that are scheduled to depart from a London terminal between 1600 and 1900;
- trains running between Drayton Park and Moorgate;
- services between Royston and Ely that depart or arrive at Cambridge between 0745 and 0845, with the exception of the 0715 and 0745 departures from King's Cross;
- replacement bus services unless stated otherwise in any associated publicity; and
- any train where a member of our staff asks you to remove your bicycle.
- Bicycles cannot be conveyed within Travelcard Zone 1 in any direction between the hours of 0700-1000 and 1600-1900 Monday to Friday

Compact, folding bicycles can be carried on any service at any time.

LOST PROPERTY

In order to trace lost property please contact our Customer Relations department on 0845 026 4700, between 0700 - 2200 Monday to Sunday.

TRAIN SERVICE UPDATE

For current train information call National Rail enquiries on 08457 48 49 50 (calls may be recorded for training purposes) or check our website at: www.firstcapitalconnect.co.uk/live-info

PENALTY FARES

First Capital Connect operates a Penalty Fares System. If you do not have a valid ticket or permit to travel, you will be liable to pay a penalty fare. This is £20 or twice the appropriate single fare to the next station stop, whichever is greater. This does not apply for travel from Crews Hill.

If you do not buy a ticket, you could also be prosecuted and this can lead to a Criminal Conviction.

DISABLED PEOPLE'S PROTECTION POLICY

Our Disabled People's Protection Policy is available from Customer Relations, and is also available on our website and available at all staffed stations. First Capital Connect operates a dedicated telephone and textphone service for disabled or mobility impaired customers, the contact details are:

Telephone: 0800 058 2844

Textphone: 0800 975 1052

These are available 0700 - 2200, Monday to Sunday, with the exception of Christmas Day.

CODE OF PRACTICE FOR COMMENTS, COMPLAINTS AND SUGGESTIONS

Our Passenger's Charter details our code of practice and is available from all staffed stations and from our Customer Relations Department. The Customer Relations Department will be happy to assist with any comments, complaints or suggestions and can be contacted using the contact details above.

GW First Great Western GW

A member of the First Rail Division

ADDRESS

Milford House
1 Milford Street
Swindon SN1 1HL
Telephone: 01793 499400
Fax: 01793 499460
Website: www.firstgreatwestern.co.uk. On our website you can create and print your own personalised timetables, download complete timetable booklets, find departure and arrival times for specific journeys, buy tickets, obtain live timetable updates specific to individual stations, check any late alterations to our services, view promotions and contact us with your comments.

MANAGING DIRECTOR

Mark Hopwood

RESERVATIONS AND TICKETS BY TELEPHONE AND ONLINE

Tickets may be booked in advance using credit and debit cards and seats reserved by ringing **08457 000 125** (open 0700-2200 Mondays to Fridays and 0700-2100 Saturdays and Sundays). Allow at least 5 working days for postal delivery. A next day delivery can be arranged at £5 per transaction. Arrangements can be made for tickets to be collected from Fast Ticket machines (the credit or debit card used for purchase will be needed at many stations). For Group Travel call **08457 000 125**.

RESERVATION DETAILS

One seat reservation per single journey when purchasing a ticket, additional reservations, including those made by season ticket holders, will be subject to a £5 fee.

CATERING ON TRAINS

Most First Great Western high speed services offer an Express Café service with freshly brewed coffee, hot baguettes and paninis and a wide range of drinks and snacks.

A Travelling Chef is available on many weekday services, preparing meals and snacks to order for both First and Standard Class customers. On a small number of weekday services, a Pullman restaurant provides à la carte dining to First and Standard Class customers, subject to availability.

First Class customers also enjoy additional complimentary services:

- An at-seat trolley service offering light refreshments (available on most Monday to Friday services between 0700-1900), including hot and cold drinks and light snacks appropriate to the time of day. The trolley also offers a range of items for sale from our Express Café.
- At the weekend and on weekdays after 1900, complimentary refreshments are available from the Express Cafe on production of valid travel tickets.

CYCLES

First Great Western welcomes customers with bicycles on services where they can be safely accommodated. However it is not possible to carry bicycles on some services particularly during peak periods. For full details of when bicycles cannot be carried or when reservations are required, please visit our website or pick up a leaflet at any of our staffed stations.

LOST PROPERTY

Customers who have left property on First Great Western services should contact our Customer Services team on **08457 000 125**.

TRAIN SERVICE UPDATE

For current train information including details of engineering work please visit our website: www.firstgreatwestern.co.uk

PENALTY FARES

These operate on most of our services. A penalty fare of £20 or twice the appropriate single fare to the next station stop (whichever is the greater) will be charged to anybody who is unable to produce a valid ticket or other authority when required to do so. For further information, pick up a leaflet about Penalty Fares from any staffed station.

DISABLED PEOPLE'S PROTECTION POLICY

Available from Customer Services Team
First Great Western
PO Box 313
Plymouth PL4 6YD
Tel: 08457 000 125
Email: fgwfeedback@firstgroup.com
Opening hours 0700-2200 daily

Customers requiring assistance should contact 0800 197 1329 (18001 0800 197 1329 textphone service), if possible giving 24 hours notice of travel plans.

CODE OF PRACTICE FOR COMMENTS, COMPLAINTS AND SUGGESTIONS

Your views leaflets and copies of the Passenger's Charter are available to download from our website www.firstgreatwestern.co.uk, at all staffed First Great Western stations or alternatively from the Customer Services Team at the address above.

HT First Hull Trains HT

ADDRESS	First Hull Trains Customer Services Freepost RLYY-XSTG-YXCK 4th Floor Europa House 184 Ferensway Hull HU1 3UT Telephone: 08456 76 99 05 Website: www.hulltrains.co.uk Email: customer.services@hulltrains.co.uk
MANAGING DIRECTOR	Cath Bellamy
RESERVATIONS AND TICKETS BY TELEPHONE AND ONLINE	First Hull Trains tickets can be booked in advance and seats reserved by ringing 08450 710 222 (0700 to 2200 Monday to Friday and 0800 to 1900 Saturday and Sunday). Please allow five working days for delivery. Tickets on departure are available.
RESERVATION DETAILS	Seat Reservations are free for First and Standard Class ticket holders. Season Ticket holders may reserve seats at a cost of £2 for First Class and £1 for Standard Class.
CATERING ON TRAINS	First Hull Trains provides a buffet on all services, and a comprehensive catering package for First Class passengers. Catering is subject to availability and may be limited when services are disrupted by engineering works or Bank Holidays.
CYCLES	Cycles and tandems are carried free of charge, however, a reservation is compulsory. Please telephone 08450 710 222
LOST PROPERTY	Please contact Customer Services.
TRAIN SERVICE UPDATE	Available at www.hulltrains.co.uk, or by telephone on 08450 710222.
PENALTY FARES	Penalty Fares are not in force on any Hull Trains Service
DISABLED PEOPLE'S PROTECTION POLICY	Available at: www.hulltrains.co.uk. Alternatively, a copy can be requested from Customer Services.
CODE OF PRACTICE FOR COMMENTS, COMPLAINTS AND SUGGESTIONS	First Hull Trains' Passenger's Charter is available at www.hulltrains.co.uk. Alternatively, any comments, complaints or suggestions can be sent to Customer Services

TP First TransPennine Express TP

A joint venture between First and Keolis

ADDRESS	7th Floor Bridgewater House 60 Whitworth Street Manchester M1 6LT Telephone: 08700 005151 Website: www.tpexpress.co.uk
MANAGING DIRECTOR	Vernon Barker
RESERVATIONS AND TICKETS BY TELEPHONE AND ONLINE	Reservations and tickets are available at www.tpexpress.co.uk and from all local staffed stations.
RESERVATION DETAILS	Seat Reservations are available at staffed stations. Seat Reservations for travel on First TransPennine Express services can be booked up until the day before travel. There is no charge for making a Seat Reservation if you have a rail ticket, or buy one at the same time.
CATERING ON TRAINS	Catering trolley services are available between 0700 and 1900 Monday to Friday on First TransPennine Express trains between Manchester Piccadilly and York, Manchester Piccadilly and Doncaster and Manchester Piccadilly and Preston. In addition to the above, all services between Manchester Airport, Manchester Piccadilly, Carlisle, Glasgow Central and Edinburgh convey a trolley service for the whole journey. This facility is also provided at weekends.
CYCLES	Customers may take their bicycle with them on First TransPennine Express trains at no extra cost. As space is limited to two bicycles per train, reservations for cycle space should be made at least 24 hours before the journey.
LOST PROPERTY	Customers who have left their property on First TransPennine Express trains or stations should contact 0845 600 1672.
TRAIN SERVICE UPDATE	For current train information call National Rail Enquiries on 0845 48 49 50 (calls may be recorded for monitoring purposes) or check our website at: www.tpexpress.co.uk/travelupdates
PENALTY FARES	Penalty Fares are not applicable on First TransPennine Express services. Customers are reminded that they must have a valid ticket when they travel. If not it will be necessary to charge the full Open Single or Return Fare for the journey.
DISABLED PEOPLE'S PROTECTION POLICY	Available online at www.tpexpress.co.uk and also from: Customer Relations First TransPennine Express ADMAIL 3878 Freepost Manchester M1 9YB Customers who have special needs and require customer assistance should contact us on 0800 107 2149. A textphone service is available on 0800 107 2061.
CODE OF PRACTICE FOR COMMENTS, COMPLAINTS AND SUGGESTIONS	Feedback leaflets and copies of the Passenger's Charter are available from all stations served by First TransPennine Express services or alternatively contact: Customer Relations, First TransPennine Express, ADMAIL 3878, Freepost, Manchester M1 9YB. Telephone: 0845 600 1671 Email: tpecustomer.relations@firstgroup.com

Gatwick Express

ADDRESS	Southern Customer Services PO Box 3021 Bristol BS2 2BS Telephone: 0845 850 1530 Fax: 020 8929 8687 (Overseas: +44 208 9298687) Website: www.gatwickexpress.com Email: comments@southernrailway.com
MANAGING DIRECTOR	Chris Burchell
RESERVATIONS AND TICKETS BY TELEPHONE AND ONLINE	Reservations are not necessary on Gatwick Express services. For information and telesales please call 0845 850 1530. Tickets can also be purchased through our website at www.gatwickexpress.com
RESERVATION DETAILS	Reservations are not available.
CATERING ON TRAINS	An at-seat trolley service of drinks and light refreshments is available throughout the day.
CYCLES	Cycles and other bulky items such as skis are conveyed free in the luggage van of the Gatwick Expresss trains that do not run to/from Brighton. On the following trains, cycles are not permitted unless they are standard size folding cycles provided they are folded, Brighton depart 0632, 0640, 0656, 0715, 0730, 0744, Gatwick Airport depart 0705, 0720, 0735, 0750, 0805, 0820, London Victoria depart 1730, 1745, 1800, 1815, 1830, 1845.
LOST PROPERTY	Please call our Lost Property Office on 0845 850 15 30, select option 2.
TRAIN SERVICE UPDATE	Journey time is 30 minutes (35 minutes on Sundays). First Class and Express Class accommodation is available. From London Victoria at 0330, 0430, 0500 then every 15 minutes (15, 30, 45, 00 minutes past each hour) until 0001, 0030. From Gatwick Airport at 0435, 0520, 0550 then every 15 minutes (05, 20, 35, 50 minutes past each hour) until 0050, 0135. For current train information call 0845 850 15 30, select option 2.
PENALTY FARES	Penalty Fares will be applied for passengers without the correct ticket between Brighton and Gatwick Airport. The only passengers permitted to buy a ticket on the train are those travelling between Gatwick Airport and London Victoria in either direction.
DISABLED PEOPLE'S PROTECTION POLICY	Customers requiring assistance can book this prior to travel. Arrangements can be made by calling 0845 138 1016, textphone available 0800 138 1018. It is advisable to give 24 hours notice of travel plans, although customers will be given assistance if they arrive at the stations without notice but please allow a little extra time.
CODE OF PRACTICE FOR COMMENTS, COMPLAINTS AND SUGGESTIONS	Initially comments or issues requiring immediate attention should be addressed to any member of Gatwick Express staff on the train or platforms. Additionally Customer Comments forms and our Passenger's Charter are available at Gatwick Express ticket offices. Alternatively you may write to the address above.

Grand Central

GC

ADDRESS

Grand Central Railway Company Ltd
River House
17 Museum Street
York YO1 7DJ
Telephone: 0845 603 4852
Fax: 01904 466066
Website: www.grandcentralrail.com
Email: customer.services@grandcentralrail.com

MANAGING DIRECTOR

Tom Clift

RESERVATIONS AND TICKETS BY TELEPHONE AND ONLINE

Reservations are strongly advised on Friday afternoons, at weekends and Bank Holidays. Tickets and Seat Reservations are available in advance on our website www.grandcentralrail.com or over the phone by calling 0844 811 0071 (0800-2200 7 days a week). You can book tickets for all rail journeys within Great Britain with us. Tickets booked in advance can be sent by post (allow 5 working days), collected from self service ticket machines at certain stations or sent electronically by text message or email to print at home. Tickets can be purchased from the staff on the train at no extra cost. For group bookings, business travel and Carnet tickets please call 0845 603 4852

RESERVATION DETAILS

Complimentary Seat Reservations are available; these must be booked at least 24 hours in advance. To guarantee a seat we advise that you always make a reservation. Reservations are strongly advised on Friday afternoons, at weekends and Bank Holidays.

CATERING ON TRAINS

A buffet service is available on all services. In First Class customers enjoy complimentary light refreshments including hot and cold drinks, served at-seat. A complimentary light breakfast is served for customers travelling to or from London before 1000 Monday to Friday. Daily and weekend newspapers are provided. In Standard Class a buffet is available offering a selection of fair trade and locally sourced products, including hot, soft and alcoholic drinks, sandwiches, crisps and a large selection of other snacks. A standard class trolley service is provided on selected trains.

CYCLES

Normal sized cycles are conveyed free of charge subject to room being available, cycle reservations can be made by calling 0845 603 4852 or at any station ticket office. Passengers wishing to travel with larger sized cycles (Tandems etc) should call 0845 603 4852 in advance of travelling. During engineering work cycles cannot be accommodated on replacement bus services.

LOST PROPERTY

For trains travelling towards Sunderland or Bradford, please contact Northern Rail's Lost Property office on 0845 00 00 125. For trains travelling towards London, please contact King's Cross Lost Property Office on 0207 837 4334.

TRAIN SERVICE UPDATE

For live travel updates contact National Rail Enquiries on 08457 48 49 50, visit www.nationalrail.co.uk or call Train Tracker on 0871 200 4950. You can also text your station to 8 49 50 for live departures.

Details of weekend engineering work will be available on our website www.grandcentralrail.com or by calling 0845 603 4852.

PENALTY FARES

Grand Central does not operate a Penalty Fares System. Passengers can purchase tickets on the train at the same price as if purchased in advance or at stations.

DISABLED PEOPLE'S PROTECTION POLICY

Assisted travel can be booked by calling 0844 811 0072 (0800-2200 7 days a week) or using our text phone service on 0845 305 6815 please call at least 48 hours in advance. Our full Disabled People's Protection Policy is available on our website, by calling 0845 603 4852 or by writing to us at the address above. Copies are also available at staffed stations on our route.

CODE OF PRACTICE FOR COMMENTS, COMPLAINTS AND SUGGESTIONS

Copies of our Complaint Handling Guide, Passenger's Charter and comments forms are available from the above address or on our website. Customer Services can be contacted on 0845 603 4852.

Copies of comments forms are available at staffed stations on our route and from any member of Grand Central staff.

Heathrow Connect

HC

A joint venture between First Rail Division and BAA (Heathrow Express)

ADDRESS

Freepost RLRZ-TZXE-BYKY
Heathrow Connect
6th Floor, 50 Eastbourne Terrace
London W2 6LG
Telephone: 0845 678 6975
Fax: 020 8750 6615
Website: www.heathrowconnect.com
Email: web_customer_correspondence@baa.com

MANAGING DIRECTORS

Heathrow Connect is a joint venture between First Great Western and BAA (Heathrow Express).
Mark Hopwood (First Great Western)
Richard Robinson (Heathrow Express)

RESERVATIONS AND TICKETS BY TELEPHONE AND ONLINE

Reservations are not necessary. Tickets can be booked by telephone on 0845 700 0125. Open 0700-2200 (0800-1900 Saturdays and Sundays). Allow 3 working days for delivery. A next day delivery can be arranged at £5 per transaction. Tickets may also be purchased through our website www.heathrowconnect.com

RESERVATION DETAILS

Reservations are not available.

CATERING ON TRAINS

Catering on trains is not available.

CYCLES

Cycles are carried free of charge, but are not allowed on trains timed to arrive at London Paddington between 0745-0945, or depart London Paddington between 1630-1830 Mondays to Fridays. In the interest of safety and customer comfort, we reserve the right to limit the number of cycles at other times.

LOST PROPERTY

Property lost at Paddington Station is collected by Network Rail, who can be contacted on 020 7313 1514.

For items lost at Heathrow Airport call 020 8745 7727.

For items lost on Heathrow Express trains, please ask our Customer Service Representatives, or alternatively email Heathrow Airport Lost Property at lrh.lostproperty@bagport.co.uk

TRAIN SERVICE UPDATE

For current train information call 0845 678 6975.
Website: www.heathrowconnect.com

PENALTY FARES

Penalty Fares apply at stations between Hayes & Harlington and Paddington (incl). Customers are liable to a Penalty Fare of £20 to the next station stop.

DISABLED PEOPLE'S PROTECTION POLICY

This is available from Customer Relations at the above address and telephone number.

CODE OF PRACTICE FOR COMMENTS, COMPLAINTS AND SUGGESTIONS

It is our aim to try and resolve any issues or grievances on the spot. All our Customer Services Representative have a supply of comment forms and our Customer Care Line on 0845 604 15 15 can deal with any issues over the telephone or submit any comments to web_customer_correspondance@baa.com. If you wish to write with a suggestion or complain, please write to Customer Relations at the address at the top of this page, or through our website www.heathrowexpress.com

Heathrow Express

HX

ADDRESS

Heathrow Express
Customer Relations
FREEPOST
London W2 6LG
Telephone: 0845 604 1515 (call centre)
Fax: 020 8750 6615
Website: www.heathrowexpress.com
Email: web_customer_correspondence@baa.com

MANAGING DIRECTOR

Richard Robinson

RESERVATIONS AND TICKETS BY TELEPHONE AND ONLINE

Reservations are not necessary on Heathrow Express services. Tickets may be purchased online and from www.heathrowexpress.com as well as our ticket offices at Heathrow Airport, Paddington station and travel other appointed outlets. For details call our Customer Services team on 0845 600 1515 (24 hour service - local rate call) or visit www.heathrowexpress.com

RESERVATION DETAILS

Reservations are not available.

CATERING ON TRAINS

As the overall journey time is only 15 minutes, or 21 minutes to Terminal 5, there is currently no catering on Heathrow Express services.

CYCLES

Limited accommodation is available for cycles on Heathrow Express services, for passengers flying with their cycles from the airport. Heathrow Express reserve the right to limit the number of cycles conveyed on each train to no more than three at busy times. Cyclists not travelling onwards by air may use the service to and from Heathrow Terminals, subject to space being available for airline passengers.

LOST PROPERTY

Property lost at Paddington station is collected by Network Rail, who can be contacted on 020 7313 1514. For items lost at Heathrow Airport call 020 8745 7727. For items lost on Heathrow Express trains, please ask our Customer Service Representatives, or alternatively write to: Excess Baggage Co., Heathrow Airport, Middlesex UB3 5AP or email to heathrow.lostproperty@excess-baggage.com

TRAIN SERVICE UPDATE

For current information on train services please contact our customer care line on 0845 604 15 15, or through our website www.heathrowexpress.com

PENALTY FARES

Penalty Fares do not apply on Heathrow Express services, therefore customers may join the train without having first purchased a ticket or authority to travel. Customer Service Representatives on every train will accept cash, debit and credit cards, for ticket purchase. Please note however for tickets purchased on board there is a £5.00 premium to pay. Only full fare tickets are available to purchase on board the train. (However Disabled Railcard is accepted on board).

DISABLED PEOPLE'S PROTECTION POLICY

Heathrow Express trains have been specially designed with the needs of the disabled in mind. Platforms at all our stations give level access into the trains and there is space for wheelchairs on all trains. For further information on facilities for the disabled, call the Customer Care Line on 0845 604 15 15, or write to the Managing Director at the address at the top of this page.

CODE OF PRACTICE FOR COMMENTS, COMPLAINTS AND SUGGESTIONS

It is our aim to try and resolve any issues or grievances on the spot. All our Customer Service Representatives have a supply of comment forms and our Customer Care Line on 0845 604 15 15 can deal with any issues over the telephone or submit any comments at web_customer_correspondence@baa.com. If you wish to write with a suggestion or complaint, please write to the Managing Director at the address at the top of this page, or through our website www.heathrowexpress.com

Island Line Trains

ADDRESS	Friars Bridge Court 41–45 Blackfriars Road London SE1 8NZ Telephone: 08700 005151 Fax: 020 7620 5177 Website: www.southwesttrains.co.uk Email: customerrelations@swtrains.co.uk
MANAGING DIRECTOR	Andy Pitt
RESERVATIONS AND TICKETS BY TELEPHONE AND ONLINE	Reservations are not required on Island Line Trains services. Group travel information can be obtained by calling 023 8072 8162.
RESERVATION DETAILS	Reservations are not available.
CATERING ON TRAINS	There are no catering facilities on trains.
CYCLES	A maximum of 4 cycles may be carried in the Shanklin end of all trains at no extra charge. For the safety and comfort of our passengers, the guard may refuse to carry any further cycles on the train.
LOST PROPERTY	All items of lost property are retained at Ryde Esplanade Ticket Office. If you have lost an item please telephone the Ticket Office on 01983 562492 (0900-1700 Daily). A charge may be applicable on collection.
TRAIN SERVICE UPDATE	For current train information, please call our helpline on 0845 6000 650 or visit www.islandlinetrains.co.uk
PENALTY FARES	Penalty Fares are not in force on any Island Line Trains services.
DISABLED PEOPLE'S PROTECTION POLICY	Island Line Trains is committed to making travel easier for customers with disabilities including wheelchair users. For travel on the mainland, please call our Assisted Travel line on 0800 5282 100 (textphone 0800 692 0792), giving 24 hours notice before travelling. Please note that scooters cannot be conveyed on any Island Line Trains Service. For journeys wholly within Island Line Trains, please telephone 01983 812591 giving 24 hours notice if assistance is required.
CODE OF PRACTICE FOR COMMENTS, COMPLAINTS AND SUGGESTIONS	Feedback leaflets are available at Ryde Esplanade or Shanklin Ticket Offices. Copies of Island Line Trains' and South West Trains' Passenger's Charters are available from any staffed station or by writing to: Customer Service Centre South West Trains Overline House Southampton SO15 1GW Telephone 0845 6000 650 Fax 023 8072 8187 Email: customerrelations@swtrains.co.uk The Passenger's Charter is also featured on the website www.islandlinetrains.co.uk and www.southwesttrains.co.uk

London Midland

LM

ADDRESS	PO Box 4323 Birmingham B2 4JB Telephone: 0844 811 0133 Website: www.londonmidland.com Email: comments@londonmidland.com
MANAGING DIRECTOR	Mike Hodson
RESERVATIONS AND TICKETS BY TELEPHONE AND ONLINE	Tickets can be booked in advance on-line at www.londonmidland.com or by ringing 0844 811 0133, 0800-2000 Monday to Sunday, please allow 5 days for delivery.
RESERVATION DETAILS	Reservations are not available. Group travel enquiries and bookings can also be made on 0844 811 0133.
CATERING ON TRAINS	A trolley service of drinks and light refreshments is available on a number of our Birmingham–Liverpool, Birmingham–London and Crewe–London trains, as indicated on our website.
CYCLES	Cycles are carried free of charge on most off-peak services, however, advance reservations are required for our Birmingham–Liverpool and Crewe–London services. Cycles cannot be conveyed on trains arriving into London Euston between 0700 and 0959 and departing London Euston between 1600 and 1859 on Mondays to Fridays (excluding Bank Holidays). Folding cycles, completely folded down, are regarded as accompanied luggage and carried free.
LOST PROPERTY	Enquiries can be made at your nearest staffed station or by ringing Customer Relations on 0844 811 0133.
TRAIN SERVICE UPDATE	Available from National Rail Enquiries on 08457 48 49 50 (calls may be recorded for training purposes).
PENALTY FARES	A Penalty Fares System is in place across most of the London Midland network. If you board a service from a staffed station without a valid ticket or permit to travel, you will be liable to a £20 penalty fare or twice the standard single fare to the next station whichever is the greater. You can only purchase a ticket on-train when travelling from an unstaffed station. Details of the scheme are available at www.londonmidland.com or by writing to Customer Relations at the address below.
DISABLED PEOPLE'S PROTECTION POLICY	Available from Customer Relations London Midland PO Box 4323 Birmingham B2 4JB Telephone: 0844 811 0133
CODE OF PRACTICE FOR COMMENTS, COMPLAINTS AND SUGGESTIONS	Available from Customer Relations at the above address.

LO London Overground LO

Operated by London Overground Rail Operations Ltd. (LOROL)
on behalf of Rail for London Ltd., a subsidiary of TfL

ADDRESS	125 Finchley Road London NW3 6HY Telephone: 0845 601 4867 Website: www.tfl.gov.uk/overground Email: overgroundinfo@tfl.gov.uk
MANAGING DIRECTOR	Steve Murphy
RESERVATIONS AND TICKETS BY TELEPHONE AND ONLINE	Tickets may be booked in advance and seats reserved on many long distance national rail services from most London Overground ticket offices. Oyster tickets may be purchased online from https://oyster.tfl.gov.uk
RESERVATION DETAILS	Reservations are not available.
CATERING ON TRAINS	Catering is not provided on London Overground services.
CYCLES	London Overground allows folding bicycles free of charge on all trains at all times, provided it is safe to do so. Non-folding bicycles are also accepted free of charge but due to space constraints they are not permitted on the following routes between the times shown: • Willesden Junction (High Level) and Gospel Oak in both directions Mondays to Fridays (except Public Holidays) 0800-1000 and 1630-1830 • Gospel Oak and Blackhorse Road in both directions Mondays to Fridays (except Public Holidays) 0800-1000 and 1630-1830 • Watford Junction and Euston Mondays to Fridays (except Public Holidays) on services timed to arrive at Euston 0700-1000 or depart from Euston 1630-1900 • Highbury & Islington/Dalston Junction and New Cross/Crystal Palace/ West Croydon in both directions Mondays to Fridays (except Public Holidays) 0700-1000 and 1600-1900 Only one bicycle is allowed per customer within a limit of one bicycle per vestibule area. Tandems and three-wheeled vehicles cannot be accomodated on any London Overground train. Only folding bicycles can be carried on buses that replace trains due to engineering work.
LOST PROPERTY	Please contact the TfL Lost Property Office at Baker Street on 0845 330 9882 or our Customer Services Team on 0845 601 4867.
TRAIN SERVICE UPDATE	Information about London Overground services and fares can be obtained by telephoning either: • London Travel Information on 0843 222 1234 (Textphone 020 7918 3015) • National Rail Enquiries 08457 48 49 50 (calls may be recorded for training purposes). (Textphone 08456 050 600, 0800-2000 daily) A wide range of information about London Overground is also available from our website: www.tfl.gov.uk/overground
PENALTY FARES	London Overground operates a Penalty Fares Scheme. If you cannot produce, on request, a valid ticket for your entire journey or, when using Oyster to Pay as you Go, your Oyster card containing a record of the start of your Pay as you Go journey, you will be liable to pay a Penalty Fare.
DISABLED PEOPLE'S PROTECTION POLICY	This can be obtained at any London Overground station or from our Customer Services Team at the above address.
CODE OF PRACTICE FOR COMMENTS, COMPLAINTS AND SUGGESTIONS	For a copy of the London Overground Customer Charter leaflet please ask at any London Overground Station or contact our Customer Services Team at the above address.

Merseyrail

A Serco/Abellio company

ADDRESS	Rail House Lord Nelson Street Liverpool L1 1JF Telephone: 0151 702 2534 Fax: 0151 702 3074
MANAGING DIRECTOR	Bart Schmeink
RESERVATIONS AND TICKETS BY TELEPHONE AND ONLINE	Tickets may be booked in advance and seats reserved from most Merseyrail stations for National Rail Services.
RESERVATION DETAILS	Reservations are not available.
CATERING ON TRAINS	Catering is not available.
CYCLES	Cycles carried free of charge at any time, subject to sufficient space being available.
LOST PROPERTY	Please contact:- Lost Property Office James Street Station James Street Liverpool L2 7PQ Phone: 0151 702 2951
TRAIN SERVICE UPDATE	For current train information please call 08457 48 49 50 (calls may be recorded for training purposes). ***For details of Bank Holiday services see also the boxed note immediately preceding Table 103.***
PENALTY FARES	Please refer to notices displayed at stations for details of the Penalty Fare Scheme in operation.
DISABLED PEOPLE'S PROTECTION POLICY	Available from:– Customer Relations Merseyrail Rail House Lord Nelson Street Liverpool L1 1JF Phone : 0151 702 2071 (Textphone 0870 0552 681) Fax : 0151 702 2413
CODE OF PRACTICE FOR COMMENTS, COMPLAINTS AND SUGGESTIONS	Available from above address

National Express East Anglia (NXEA)

LE

ADDRESS	Customer Relations National Express East Anglia Norwich Station Station Approach Norwich NR1 1EF Telephone: 0845 600 7245 Fax: 01603 214567 Website: www.nationalexpresseastanglia.com Email: nxea.customerrelations@nationalexpress.com
MANAGING DIRECTOR	Andrew Chivers
RESERVATIONS AND TICKETS BY TELEPHONE AND ONLINE	Tickets may be booked in advance by telephoning 0845 600 7245 between 0800 and 2200 (Mondays to Fridays) and 0900 and 1800 (weekends and Bank Holidays). For Business Travel, please telephone 0845 850 9080
RESERVATION DETAILS	NXEA offers Seat Reservations on services between London Liverpool Street and Norwich at a charge of £2.50 per seat (£1 for season ticket holders).
CATERING ON TRAINS	Hot and cold drinks, sandwiches and light snacks are generally available on main line services between Norwich and London Liverpool Street and on Stansted Express services.
CYCLES	Accompanied bicycles are conveyed free of charge on most NXEA services, but are not permitted on Stansted Express services at any time or on weekday peak services to and from London. A similar restriction also applies at Cambridge. On main line and rural services, the number of bicycles per train is limited, so a free reservation is recommended. For further details, please call NXEA customer services on 0845 600 7245.
LOST PROPERTY	If you have lost an item of property on one of our trains or stations, please contact NXEA customer services on 0845 600 7245 or email us at nxea.lostproperty@nationalexpress.com
TRAIN SERVICE UPDATE	For current train service information, please contact NXEA customer services on 0845 600 7245 or call our recorded information line on 020 7247 5488.
PENALTY FARES	NXEA operates a Penalty Fares System on most of its network, except on designated 'paytrain' routes and from certain specified stations without ticket issuing facilities. Stations within the Penalty Fares area are identified by warning notices at each entrance. When travelling from these stations, you must have a valid ticket for your journey. For journeys where Oyster Pay as you Go (PAYG) is accepted, you must hold a valid Oyster card which has been touched in at the start of your journey. Oyster PAYG is not valid for travel outside the area where PAYG is accepted. If you cannot present a valid ticket for the journey you are making, you may be liable for a Penalty Fare (minimum £20).
DISABLED PEOPLE'S PROTECTION POLICY	Available from: Customer Relations, National Express East Anglia, Norwich Station, Station Approach, Norwich NR1 1EF. Customers who require assistance are recommended to book at least 24 hours in advance on 0800 028 28 78 or Textphone 0845 606 7245.
CODE OF PRACTICE FOR COMMENTS, COMPLAINTS AND SUGGESTIONS	Available from: Customer Relations, National Express East Anglia, Norwich Station, Station Approach, Norwich NR1 1EF. The NXEA Passenger's Charter is also available from the same address.

NY North Yorkshire Moors Railway NY

(Operators of steam and heritage services between Whitby, Grosmont, Goathland and Pickering)

ADDRESS	Pickering Station Pickering North Yorkshire YO18 7AJ Telephone: 01751-472508 (Customer Services and Information) Fax: 01751-476048 Website: www.nymr.co.uk Email: info@nymr.co.uk
GENERAL MANAGER	Philip Benham
RESERVATIONS AND TICKETS BY TELEPHONE AND ONLINE	Telephone: 01751-472508 Hours of operation: 26 March to 30 October and other operating dates: 0930-1630 (Monday - Friday), 1000-1430 (Saturday and Sunday); All other times: 1000-1430 (Monday - Friday). At least 7 days should be allowed for receipt of tickets purchased by telephone. National Rail tickets can be booked in advance from our office in Whitby – telephone 01947 605872.
RESERVATION DETAILS	Reservations are not available on normal services. They can be made for groups of 20 or more passengers and are required on North Yorkshire Moors Railways dining train services (between Pickering and Grosmont).
CATERING ON TRAINS	An at-seat trolley service of drinks and snacks is provided on most trains.
CYCLES	Cycles and dogs are carried for a charge of £2 (subject to space being available).
LOST PROPERTY	Enquiries about lost property should be made to Pickering Station at the above, or by telephone 01751-472508.
TRAIN SERVICE UPDATE	Updated train service information on all North Yorkshire Moors Railway is available on the website (see address above). A 'talking timetable' is also available giving current details of all North Yorkshire Moors Railway services by telephoning 01751-473535.
PENALTY FARES	Penalty Fares are not in force on any North Yorkshire Moors Railway service.
DISABLED PEOPLE'S PROTECTION POLICY	Available from the address above, or Pickering and Grosmont Stations.
CODE OF PRACTICE FOR COMMENTS, COMPLAINTS AND SUGGESTIONS	North Yorkshire Moors Railway welcomes comments from passengers. Comments/suggestion cards are available from stations and on-board staff, or alternatively please write to the General Manager. Details of the company's policy are available from the above address, or Pickering and Grosmont Stations.

NT **Northern** NT

Northern

A joint venture between Serco and Abellio

ADDRESS	Northern Rail Ltd Northern House 9 Rougier Street York YO1 6HZ Telephone: 08700 005151 Website: www.northernrail.org
MANAGING DIRECTOR	Ian Bevan
RESERVATIONS AND TICKETS BY TELEPHONE AND ONLINE	Reservations and tickets are available from all local staffed stations.
RESERVATION DETAILS	Reservations are not available on normal services, however they can be made for groups of 10 or more travelling together, telephone 0845 124 3345 or fax 0845 124 3346. For groups of 10 or more travelling on the Leeds-Settle-Carlisle line telephone 0800 9800 766, between 0900 and 1700 on Mondays to Fridays to make a booking. All accommodation on Northern trains is Standard Class.
CATERING ON TRAINS	On most Leeds-Settle-Carlisle services, food and drink can be purchased from the trolley which will pass through the train.
CYCLES	Up to two cycles can be carried on each service. This is subject to space being available, however, and cannot be booked in advance. For further details telephone 0845 000 0125.
LOST PROPERTY	Call 0845 000 0125, contact your nearest staffed station or write to Northern at the address below.
TRAIN SERVICE UPDATE	Information about Northern services and fares can be obtained by telephoning: **08457 48 49 50** (calls may be recorded for training purposes) or access the website on www.nationalrail.co.uk For more information on our services, please visit our website on www.northernrail.org The latest information on train running is available by phoning TrainTracker™ from National Rail Enquiries on 0871 200 4915 or by texting TrainTracker™. Text to 84950.
PENALTY FARES	Penalty Fares are not in force on any Northern service.
DISABLED PERSON'S PROTECTION POLICY	If you would like a copy of Northern's Policy or wish to arrange assistance for your journey, please phone: 0808 1561606. (Textphone 0845 604 5608) or by writing to Customer Relations, Northern, FREEPOST (RLSL-ABEC-BGUU), Leeds LS1 4DY or email: assistance@northernrail.org
CODE OF PRACTICE FOR COMMENTS, COMPLAINTS AND SUGGESTIONS	Please contact our Customer Helpline on 0845 000 0125, a textphone is available on 0845 604 5608. Alternatively you can write to us at: Customer Relations, Northern, FREEPOST (RLSL-ABEC-BGUU), Leeds LS1 4DY. If you would like a copy of the Northern Passenger's Charter, or Northern's Guide for Customers with Disabilities please contact our Customer Relations team.

ScotRail

SR

A member of the First Rail Division

ADDRESS

1st Floor
Atrium Court
50 Waterloo Street
Glasgow G2 6HQ
Telephone: 08700 00 51 51
Fax: 0141 335 4592
Website: www.scotrail.co.uk
Email: scotrailcustomer.relations@firstgroup.com

MANAGING DIRECTOR

Steve Montgomery

RESERVATIONS AND TICKETS BY TELEPHONE AND ONLINE

Tickets may be purchased in advance and Sleepers or seats reserved, by telephone, using a debit/credit card from the following number: 08457 550033 (opening hours 0700-2200)

Please allow 3 days for tickets by post, tickets on departure arrangements available at selected stations. Tickets can also be purchased through the website - www.scotrail.co.uk

ScotRail customers can buy selected Caledonian Sleeper tickets online - and have the ticket confirmation sent to their mobile phone. Passengers simply turn up for their train, show the text message to train staff and hop on board. A confirmatory email is sent as a back-up. This free SMS service is available for 'Bargain Berth' tickets on the Caledonian Sleeper, which connects Scottish cities to Central London. Tickets can be booked up to 12 weeks in advance of travel - and right up until Midday on the day of travel, subject to availability. The berths start from just £19.

RESERVATION DETAILS

Seat Reservations are free and can be made from 12 weeks in advance up to approximately two hours prior to the departure of the train.

CATERING ON TRAINS

A Lounge Car is provided on all Caledonian Sleeper services offering a wide range of drinks, snacks and hot meals. A trolley service is available on many longer-distance services as indicated in the timetable.

CYCLES

Cycles are carried free on all ScotRail services subject to availability. Reservations are required on Caledonian Sleeper services and on longer distance routes. Tandems, tricycles, cycle trailers, motorcycles, mopeds or motorised cycles are not carried on any ScotRail service.

LOST PROPERTY

Please phone 0141 335 3276 (0700-1900 Mon-Sat)

TRAIN SERVICE UPDATE

Register with JourneyCheck/JourneyAlert on our website: www.scotrail.co.uk

PENALTY FARES

Penalty Fares are not in force on any ScotRail services.

DISABLED PEOPLE'S PROTECTION POLICY

Available from ScotRail Customer, PO Box 7031, Fort William PH33 6WW. Tel: 0800 912 2 901 or 18001 0800 912 2 901 Fax: 0141 335 4611

Travel arrangements may be made for disabled people by calling 0800 912 2 901*. A light travel scooter, length 104cm, width 56cm with a turning radius of 99cm and combined weight of 300kg can be conveyed. Details of station facilities and information on accessibility are available at www.nationalrail.co.uk or www.scotrail.co.uk.

*For assisted travel, an advance notice of up to 24 hours notice is appreciated.

CODE OF PRACTICE FOR COMMENTS, COMPLAINTS AND SUGGESTIONS

ScotRail welcomes comments on the services we provide. A leaflet is available at all staffed ScotRail stations and also from the Customer Relations Manager at the address above. Tel: 0845 601 5929

South West Trains

SW

ADDRESS	Friars Bridge Court 41–45 Blackfriars Road London SE1 8NZ Telephone: 08700 005151 Fax: 020 7620 5177 Website: www.southwesttrains.co.uk Email: customerrelations@swtrains.co.uk
MANAGING DIRECTOR	Andy Pitt
RESERVATIONS AND TICKETS BY TELEPHONE AND ONLINE	Tickets may be booked in advance by telephone, on the following number: 0845 6000 650. Tickets may also be purchased via the South West Trains website (see above). When ordering, please allow 5 working days for ticket delivery.
RESERVATION DETAILS	Reservations are not available.
CATERING ON TRAINS	Catering on South West Trains is provided on those services marked with the symbol T for all or part of the journey. Catering may be provided from a buffet area, at seat trolley service or a combination of both according to the route and time of day. Comments on the service should be sent to the Customer Service Centre at the address below.
CYCLES	A limited number of cycles can be carried on most of our services except during the Monday to Friday peak periods. Restrictions apply on certain routes into and out of London Waterloo between 0715 and 1000 and between 1645 and 1900. At all times some services require advance reservations, as space is limited. To obtain full details of South West Trains Cycling Policy and full details of routes and times when cycles are not carried visit www.southwesttrains.co.uk, pick up a leaflet from stations served by South West Trains or contact our Customer Service Centre at the address shown. Cycles that can be folded to a size which allows them to be carried safely in the luggage racks on our services may be carried folded at all times. For reasons of safety and comfort of our passengers, if the available identified cycle spaces on the train are already taken, the guard has the right to refuse to carry any further cycles on that train.
LOST PROPERTY	A lost property helpline is available between 0730-1900 Mondays to Fridays by calling 020 7401 7861
TRAIN SERVICE UPDATE	For current train information, please call our helpline on 0845 6000 650 or visit www.southwesttrains.co.uk
PENALTY FARES	South West Trains has a duty to its fare paying passengers to ensure no-one travels for free. To this end South West Trains operates a Penalty Fares Scheme across its network, with the only exceptions being Dean, Mottisfont & Dunbridge and Romsey. Passengers travelling to and from stations within the penalty fares area without a valid ticket may be liable to a penalty of £20 or twice the single fare to the next station at which their train stops (whichever is the greater).
DISABLED PEOPLE'S PROTECTION POLICY	For a copy of this publication, please contact the Customer Service Centre at the address below. Assistance for mobility impaired passengers can be arranged by telephoning 0800 5282 100 between 0600 - 2200 daily. Please give at least 24 hours notice. A textphone facility is available on 0800 6920 792 (calls are charged at local rates).
CODE OF PRACTICE FOR COMMENTS, COMPLAINTS AND SUGGESTIONS	Copies of South West Trains Passenger's Charter are available from any staffed station or by writing to: Customer Service Centre, South West Trains, Overline House, Blechynden Terrace, Southampton SO15 1GW Telephone 0845 6000 650. Fax 023 8072 8187 Email: customerrelations@swtrains.co.uk The Passenger's Charter is also available on our website www.southwesttrains.co.uk

Southeastern

SE

ADDRESS

Southeastern Customer Services
PO Box 63428
London SE1P 5FD
Telephone: 0845 000 2222
Assisted Travel: 0800 783 4524 (Textphone 0800 783 4548)
Fax: 0845 678 6976
Textphone: 0800 783 4548

Website: southeasternrailway.co.uk

Southeastern Customer Services is staffed 24 hours a day, seven days a week (closed Christmas Day). Comments and complaints are dealt with here by post, fax, and website as well as on the telephone.

MANAGING DIRECTOR

Charles Horton

RESERVATIONS AND TICKETS BY TELEPHONE AND ONLINE

Group travel (parties of 10 persons or more) on Southeastern services must be booked at least seven days in advance so that space can be allocated. To order, go to southeasternrailway.co.uk, select tickets, then group, then complete the online form.

Customers can renew their Season Tickets for one month or longer by completing the Season Ticket application form at their local ticket office or online at southeasternrailway.co.uk (photocard required). Payment may be made by debit card and by most major credit and charge cards.

For new monthly season ticket purchases, please complete an application form available at local stations or online at southeasternrailway.co.uk.

RESERVATIONS

Reservations are not available. Reservations are only needed on Southeastern services for Group Travel and mobility impaired customers who require assistance.

CATERING ON TRAINS

Catering is not available.

CYCLES

Cycles are not permitted on peak time services, which are those timed to arrive in London terminals between 0700 and 0959, and those timed to leave between 1600 and 1859. Folding cycles are permitted provided they are folded.

LOST PROPERTY

Customers who have lost property on a train or at a station should contact Southeastern Customer Services on 0845 000 2222.

TRAIN SERVICE UPDATE

For current train running information contact Southeastern Customer Services on 0845 000 2222

Information is also available from national and local radio station travel updates on Ceefax page 433, and from our website: southeasternrailway.co.uk, select journey.

PENALTY FARES

Penalty Fares are not in force on any Southeastern service.

DISABLED PEOPLE'S PROTECTION POLICY

Copies of the Disabled People's Protection Policy are available from Southeastern Customer Services.

If you have any special needs and would like help with planning your journey anywhere in Great Britain please call 0800 783 4524 or use the Textphone 0800 783 4548 - open 24 hours a day.

The Southeastern Assisted Travel team will offer advice and make any special arrangements you need. If at least 24 hours' notice can be given, this will be very much appreciated.

CODE OF PRACTICE FOR COMMENTS, COMPLAINTS AND SUGGESTIONS

Southeastern Passengers' Charter leaflets are available at any Southeastern sales point or Southeastern Customer Services at the address shown above.

Southern

SN

ADDRESS

Southern Customer Services
PO Box 3021
Bristol BS2 2BS
Telephone: 08451 27 29 20 (Customer Services)
Fax: 08451 27 29 30 (Customer Services)
Website: www.southernrailway.com
Email: comments@southernrailway.com

MANAGING DIRECTOR

Chris Burchell

RESERVATIONS AND TICKETS BY TELEPHONE AND ONLINE

Discounted Advance Tickets are available from the Southern website.

RESERVATION DETAILS

Reservations are only required for Advance tickets. These reservations authorise the holder to travel on the specified train but do not identify individual seats.

CATERING ON TRAINS

A light refreshment of food and drinks is available on trains marked with ☕ in the timetable.

CYCLES

Standard size folding cycles are welcome on all Southern trains (as long as they are folded) Non-folding cycles are not permitted on Monday – Friday trains scheduled to arrive between 0700 and 1000 to, or depart between 1600 and 1900 from London Bridge, London Victoria, Kensington Olympia or Brighton.

LOST PROPERTY

Please call Southern Customer Services on 08451 27 29 20.

TRAIN SERVICE UPDATE

For current train information call Customer Services on 08451 27 29 20 or check our website at www.southernrailway.com

PENALTY FARES

Southern operate a Penalty Fares Scheme on all routes. You must buy a valid ticket (or permit to travel) for your journey before boarding a train. If you do not have a valid ticket or permit to travel, you may have to pay a Penalty Fare of £20.00 or twice the single fare, whichever is the greater. Please pick up a Penalty Fare leaflet from a staffed station for your information.

DISABLED PEOPLE'S PROTECTION POLICY

Available from Southern Customer Services at
PO Box 3021
Bristol BS2 2BS.

To get advice about accessible travel or to book assistance please call 0800 136 1016; Minicom/textphone – 0800 138 1018, Fax – 0800 138 1017

CODE OF PRACTICE FOR COMMENTS, COMPLAINTS AND SUGGESTIONS

Write to Southern Customer Services at the above address.

Copies of Southern Passenger's charter are available from any staffed station.

You can also obtain a copy by contacting Customer Services or from Southern's website.

VT Virgin Trains VT

The trading name of West Coast Trains Ltd

ADDRESS	Virgin Trains 85 Smallbrook Queensway Birmingham B5 4HA Telephone: 0845 000 8000 Textphone: 0121 654 7528 Website: www.virgintrains.com Email: customer.relations@virgintrains.co.uk
CHIEF EXECUTIVE	Tony Collins
MANAGING DIRECTOR	Chris Gibb
RESERVATIONS AND TICKETS BY TELEPHONE AND ONLINE	Buy tickets for Virgin Trains and any other train company in Great Britain on the internet at www.virgintrains.com or by calling 0871 977 4222 (calls to this number cost 10p a minute from a BT landline; calls from other operators may vary and cost more) - between 0800 and 2200 7 days a week. If you have a disability or have specific needs and wish to arrange assistance on your journey call the Virgin Trains JourneyCare service on 08457 44 33 66 (Textphone 08457 44 33 67) between 0800 and 2200 every day except Christmas Day or Boxing Day.
RESERVATION DETAILS	You are strongly advised to make a Seat Reservation in advance. Reservations can be made for the Quiet Zone carriage, where customers should refrain from using mobile phones or creating unnecessary noise. On routes to and from London, Standard Class Quiet Zone is in coach A and in coach H for First Class. On other routes, Quiet Zone is located in Standard Class, coach F. Seat reservations are free of charge.
CATERING ON TRAINS	In First Class on a Pendolino from Monday to Friday customers can enjoy a selection of snacks throughout the day, including a cooked breakfast on many morning peak services. In addition, Fairtrade tea, Fairtrade coffee, soft drinks and alcoholic drinks (alcohol is not offered with breakfast services) are served at seat throughout the day. A complimentary newspaper is also available. In First Class on Super Voyager from Monday to Friday customers can enjoy complimentary light refreshments, including Fairtrade tea, Fairtrade coffee, soft drinks and a newspaper with an at-seat service available, on most services. In Standard, we have a wide range of snacks and sandwiches, Fairtrade teas, fresh ground Fairtrade coffee, soft and alcoholic drinks and a selection of non-food items available at our onboard shop. The shop is generally open throughout. Pendolinos offer an at-seat trolley service to standard customers on Mondays to Fridays. For more information about our onboard service pick up a copy of Travelling with Virgin Trains.
CYCLES	Subject to availability of space cycles can be carried on all trains. Most trains can carry 3 cycles, and on journeys to and from London Euston, Pendolinos can carry tandems (however, tandems are not carried on Voyager services). An advance reservation is required for all journeys.
LOST PROPERTY	Call Customer Relations on 0845 000 8000 – 0830 to 1800 Mondays to Fridays, 0900 to 1600 Saturdays, answerphone available at all other times.
TRAIN SERVICE UPDATE	Details of any disruption to services or weekend engineering work are summarised on BBC Ceefax and on BBCi on digital TV. Details of Engineering work can also be found at www.virgintrains.com.
PENALTY FARES	Penalty Fares are not applicable on any Virgin Trains service.
DISABLED PEOPLE'S PROTECTION POLICY	Our Customer Relations Manager (at the address above) will be pleased to supply a free copy of the Disabled People's Protection Policy. It can also be downloaded at www.virgintrains.com. For information on station accessibility and to arrange special help please contact Virgin Trains JourneyCare (details above).
CODE OF PRACTICE FOR COMMENTS, COMPLAINTS AND SUGGESTIONS	We want you to tell us what you think of our service, good or bad. A copy of our Code of Practice for handling comments, complaints and suggestions together with Virgin Trains Passenger's Charter is available free on request from our Customer Relations Manager at the above address.

West Coast Railway Company

WR

(Operators of the 'Jacobite' and 'Cambrian' Steam Services)

ADDRESS	Jesson Way Carnforth Lancashire LA5 9UR Telephone: 01524 737751/737753 Fax: 01524 735518 Website: www.westcoastrailways.co.uk Email: jacobite@wcrc.co.uk
GENERAL MANAGER	Mrs Pat Marshall
COMMERCIAL MANAGER	James Shuttleworth
RESERVATIONS AND TICKETS BY TELEPHONE AND ONLINE	Advance bookings are recommended and can be made on line, at www.westcoastrailways.co.uk, by post (enclose SAE) to the Carnforth Office (address above) or by telephone, on 01524 737751/737753, during normal office hours. Credit cards accepted. Tickets can also be purchased from the WCR Guard/Train Manager, on the train, on the day of travel (subject to availablility).
RESERVATION DETAILS	Phone 01524 737751/737753
CATERING ON TRAINS	A buffet service, serving hot and cold drinks and cold snacks, is available on all trains.
CYCLES	Cycles carried free of charge, subject to space.
LOST PROPERTY	Telephone: 01524 737751/737753
PENALTY FARES	Penalty Fares are not in force on any West Coast Railway Company service.
TRAIN SERVICE UPDATE	For current train information please phone 08457 48 49 50 (calls may be recorded for training purposes).
DISABLED PEOPLE'S PROTECTION POLICY	Available from the above address.
CODE OF PRACTICE FOR COMMENTS, COMPLAINTS AND SUGGESTIONS	West Coast Railway Company welcomes comments on services provided. Write to Carnforth office (address above).

Network Rail

ADDRESS	King's Place Yorkway London N1 9AG Telephone: 020 7557 8000 Fax: 020 7557 9000 Website: www.networkrail.co.uk
CHIEF EXECUTIVE	David Higgins

Network Rail is responsible for operating 18 managed stations, indicated in the index by the code **NR**. Details of facilities provided, including the Disabled Peoples Protection Policy, are obtainable from the Network Rail Station Manager at the following station addresses:–

London Bridge	Network Rail Offices, Platform 14, London Bridge Station, Station Approach, London SE1 9SP
London Cannon Street	Cannon Street Station, Cannon Street, London EC4N 6AP
London Charing Cross	Network Rail Offices, Charing Cross Station, The Strand, London WC2 5HS
London Euston	Room 430, Stephenson Room, East Colonnade, Euston, London NW1 2RT
London Fenchurch Street	Network Rail Office, Fenchurch Place, London EC3M 4AJ
London King's Cross	Room 304, West Side Offices, King's Cross Station, London N1 9AP
London Liverpool Street	Network Rail Station Reception, Platform 10, Liverpool Street Station, London EC2M 7PY
London Paddington	Room B115, Tournament House, Paddington Station, London W2 1FT
London Victoria	3rd Floor, Kent Side Offices, Victoria Station, London SW1V 1JU
London Waterloo	CP2-4-G General Offices, Waterloo Station, London SE1 8SW
Birmingham New Street	Reception, Network Rail Offices, Station Forecourt, Birmingham New Street Station, Birmingham B2 4ND
Edinburgh Waverley	Room 255, North Block, Waverley Station, Edinburgh EH1 1BB
Gatwick Airport	Gatwick Airport Station, Gatwick Airport, Sussex RH6 0RD
Glasgow Central	Glasgow Central Station, Gordon Street, Glasgow G1 3SL
Leeds City	Room 405, Administration Block, Leeds City Station, Leeds LS1 4DY
Manchester Piccadilly	9th Floor, Piccadilly Tower, Piccadilly Station, Manchester M60 7RA
Liverpool Lime Street	Station Manager, The Barrier Line Building, Liverpool Lime Street Station, Liverpool L1 1JF
St Pancras International	Station Reception, St Pancras International Station, Pancras Road, London NW1 2QP

Staffed Left Luggage facilities, offering maximum security, are available at all Network Rail Stations.

If you wish to raise any issue concerning the rail infrastructure or the 18 managed stations operated by Network Rail (excluding matters concerning the running of trains or ticket purchase) please call the national 24 hour Helpline:- **08457 11 41 41**

Other Addresses

Department for Transport

Great Minster House, 76 Marsham Street, London SW1P 4DR

Telephone: 0300 330 3000

Email: rail@dft.gsi.gov.uk

Office of Rail Regulation

One Kemble Street, London WC2B 4AN

Telephone: 020 7282 2000

Fax: 020 7282 2040

Chair of the Board: Anna Walker
Chief Executive: Bill Emery

The main areas of the Regulator's statutory functions are:

- the issue, modification and enforcement of licences to operate trains, networks, stations and light maintenance depots;
- the approval of agreements for access by operators of railway assets to track, stations and light maintenance depots;
- the enforcement of domestic competition law; and consumer protection including a duty under the Railways Act 1993 in relation to the protection of the interests of users of railway services, including the disabled.

Publications are available from:

Sue MacSwan, The Library, ORR, 1 Waterhouse Square, 138–142 Holborn, London EC1N 2TQ

Telephone: 020 7282 2001

Email: rail.library@orr.gsi.gov.uk

Association of Train Operating Companies (ATOC)

3rd Floor, 40 Bernard Street, London WC1N 1BY

Telephone: 020 7841 8000

Chief Executive: Michael Roberts

ATOC represents the interests of most of the national and international passenger Train Operating Companies whose services are shown in this timetable. It manages a range of network services, products and responsibilities on behalf of these train operators including:

- the National Rail Conditions of Carriage (the passenger's contract with the train operators)
- the National Rail Enquiries Service
- the licensing of rail appointed travel agents
- National Railcards, the London Travelcard and Network Railcard.

London Underground Limited

Head Office

55 Broadway, London SW1H 0BD

Telephone: 020 7222 5600

Responsible for the operation of stations indicated in the index by the code **LT**

How to Cross London

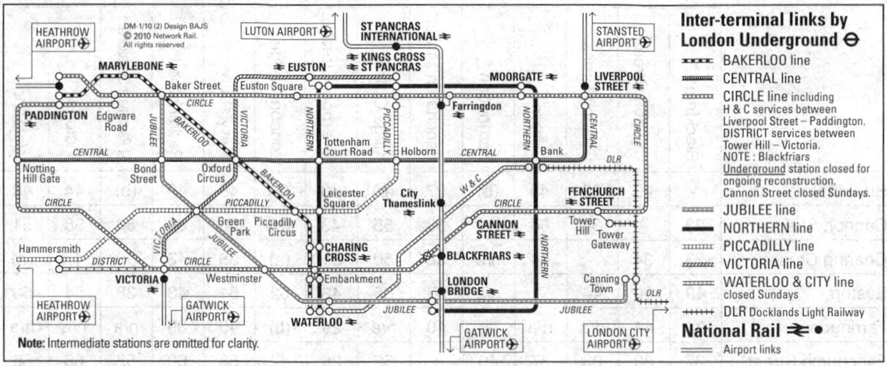

Note: Intermediate stations are omitted for clarity.

Introduction

The time taken to travel between London's stations will vary from journey to journey dependent on distance, mode of transport, time of day and the need to change en route. The quickest way to cross London is usually by the Underground network with frequent services operating between the following hours*:

- 0530 to 0015 on Monday to Friday
- 0630 to 0115 on Saturday
- 0700 to 0001 on Sunday

(* Times shown are approximate)

Buses also link many of London's main terminal stations including an extensive network of Night Bus services.

Ticket & Fares

Rail tickets for journeys routed via London are valid for transfer by London Underground or First Capital Connect services between London terminal stations, and other designated interchange stations* appropriate to the route of the through journey being made, at no extra cost. For example a Brighton to Leeds ticket is valid on London Underground services from Victoria to Kings Cross (Victoria Line), or alternatively on First Capital Connect services to St Pancras International. A Chelmsford to Southampton ticket is valid on London Underground services to Waterloo via either Liverpool Street (Circle Line) or Stratford (Jubilee Line).

(*NB. check which cross London routes your ticket is valid before you travel. A break of journey is permitted at an intermediate Underground station, but a further ticket must be purchased in order to continue the journey)

London's Fare Zones – National Rail, Underground and Docklands Light Railway (DLR) stations within the Greater London area are in one of nine Fare Zones. Single and return tickets are available for through journeys to and from all Underground and DLR stations with prices determined by the number of zones crossed or travelled through.

A range of day and longer period Travelcards are also available and provide unlimited travel on National Rail, London Underground, Docklands Light Railway and Tramlink services within the Fare Zones for which they are valid. All Travelcards, irrespective of the zones for which they are issued, can also be used on any London bus displaying this sign ⊖.

For information on ticket prices and availability contact your local staffed station, call National Rail Enquiries anytime on **08457 48 49 50*** (Textphone **0845 60 50 600**), or visit www.nationalrail.co.uk. * Calls may be recorded for training purposes.

More detailed information about London's Underground and Bus services, also Docklands Light Railway and Croydon Tramlink is available anytime from London Travel Information on **0843 222 1234** (textphone **020 7918 3015**) or visit **www.tfl.gov.uk**.

First Capital Connect and Southeastern

First Capital Connect operates fast, direct services from Bedford, Luton and St Albans via Central London to East Croydon, Gatwick Airport and Brighton and stopping trains between Luton, St Albans, North London, the City, Streatham, Wimbledon and Sutton. There are nine Central London First Capital Connect stations with Underground connections. First Capital Connect connects with East Midlands Trains at Luton, Luton Airport Parkway, London St Pancras and Bedford – see Tables 52 and 53.

Southeastern, in partnership with First Capital Connect also operate trains between Kentish Town, the City and Sevenoaks and at peak times between Bedford, Luton, the City and various destinations in Kent.

London Overground

Trains run daily between Clapham Junction, Imperial Wharf, West Brompton, Kensington (Olympia), Shepherd's Bush and Willesdon Junction - see Table 186.

Southern Services

Direct trains are provided between East Croydon, South London, Clapham Junction and stations to Watford Junction and Milton Keynes Central. These trains also stop at Imperial Wharf, West Brompton, Kensington (Olympia) and Shepherd's Bush. See table 176.

These trains provide connections to most of the Southern network at Clapham Junction.

Passengers requiring step free interchange for Southern main line trains to Gatwick Airport and the Sussex Coast should change at East Croydon, and step free interchange for Southern Metro trains is usually available at Balham.

Interchange for the West Midlands and North West is available at either Watford Junction or Milton Keynes.

Cross London Transfer Times (in minutes)

	Blackfriars **	Cannon Street	Charing Cross	Euston	Farringdon	Fenchurch Street*	Kings Cross	Liverpool Street	London Bridge	Marylebone	Paddington	St Pancras International †	Victoria	Waterloo
Blackfriars **	–	23	23	49	(b)	27	(b)	40	(b)	45	49	(b)	44	40
Cannon Street	23	–	34	60	44	30	55	43	(a)	56	60	58	55	51
Charing Cross	23	34	–	44	n/a	38	50	51	(a)	38	43	52	47	(a)
Euston	49	60	44	–	n/a	57	35	43	52	51	43	38	54	53
Farringdon	(b)	44	n/a	n/a	–	40	n/a	29	(b)	45	39	n/a	n/a	n/a
Fenchurch Street*	27	30	38	57	40	–	52	26	47	68	60	52	68	56
Kings Cross	(b)	55	50	35	n/a	52	–	41	50	50	45	30	56	55
Liverpool Street	40	43	51	43	29	26	41	–	49	56	55	41	126	62
London Bridge	(b)	(a)	(a)	52	(b)	47	50	49	–	58	62	60	n/a	(a)
Marylebone	45	56	38	51	45	68	50	56	58	–	32	53	58	47
Paddington	49	60	43	43	39	60	45	55	62	32	–	45	62	51
St Pancras International †	(b)	58	52	38	n/a	52	30	41	60	53	45	–	56	61
Victoria	44	55	47	54	n/a	68	56	126	n/a	58	62	56	–	124
Waterloo	40	51	(a)	53	n/a	56	55	62	(a)	47	51	61	124	–

All times are based on use of London Underground services and are shown as a guide only – extra time should be allowed during the early morning/late evening and on Sundays.

* Tower Hill Underground Station
† An additional 35 minutes should be allowed for Eurostar Connections
(a) Direct train services available (operated by Southeastern)
(b) Direct train services available (operated by First Capital Connect)
n/a Transfer not likely to be required as part of a through rail journey

** Blackfriars Underground Station is closed until 2011 to allow for major reconstruction work as part of the Thameslink improvement programme. During the period of closure, passengers are advised to use St Pancras, Farringdon or Elephant and Castle to connect with the Underground network. You should allow extra time for these connections

Some other useful transfers

If your journey requires a transfer between any of the following pairs of stations, you should allow a margin of at least the number of minutes shown when planning connections. All transfers are assumed to be by foot unless otherwise stated.

Ash Vale – North Camp	19
Bicester North – Town	30
Burnley Central – Manchester Rd	25
Burscough Bridge – Junction	20
Canterbury East – West	25
Catford – Bridge	10
Clock House – Kent House	15
Dorchester South – West	15
Dorking – Deepdene	9
East Croydon – West Croydon	25
Edenbridge – Town	20
Enfield Chase – Town	29
Falkirk High – Grahamston	44
Farnborough Main – North	24
Forest Gate – Wanstead Park	13
Gainsborough Central – Lea Rd	33
Hackney Central – Downs	14
Harringay – Green Lanes	14
Heath High Level – Low Level	10
Hertford North – East	34
Maidstone Barracks – East	16
New Mills Central – Newtown	25
Penge East – West	19
Purley Oaks – Sanderstead	10
Seven Sisters – South Tottenham	14
Southend Central – Victoria	17
Upper Warlingham – Whyteleafe	10
Walthamstow Central – Queen's Rd	14
West Hampstead – Thameslink	11
Windsor & Eton Central – Riverside	14
Yeovil Junction – Yeovil Pen Mill	30*

* This runs half-hourly approximately 0700–1900 Monday to Saturday.

Airport Links

Aberdeen Airport

Aberdeen Airport is close to Dyce station, from where trains operate to Aberdeen, Elgin and Inverness. There are also some direct trains to Glasgow and Edinburgh. A shuttle bus runs between Dyce station and the airport, connecting with most trains during the day.

For full bus timetable information, call **0871 200 22 33**, or visit **www.travelinescotland.com**

Birmingham International Airport

Birmingham Airport is alongside Birmingham International station. The free Air-Rail Link transit system operates to the passenger terminals about every 2 minutes with a journey time of less than 2 minutes. Birmingham International station is served by direct trains from London Euston and Manchester Piccadilly. In addition a frequent service operates between Birmingham New Street and Birmingham International providing connections at Birmingham New Street to and from all parts of the country. (See Tables 65, 66, 68, 71, 74 and 116). Regular buses operated by National Express West Midlands (966) also run from Solihull station (see Tables 71 and 115) and through fares are available by purchasing a PlusBus ticket. The journey time is approximately 20 minutes and through ticketing is available. Solihull is served by Chiltern Railways services from London Marylebone, Gerrards Cross, Beaconsfield, High Wycombe, Princes Risborough, Haddenham & Thame Parkway, Bicester North, Banbury, Leamington Spa and Warwick and by London Midland local services.

Bournemouth (Hurn) International Airport

Bournemouth (Hurn) International Airport now has an hourly bus service to and from Bournemouth station. See www.bournemouth-airport-shuttle.co.uk or phone 01202 557007 for details.

Bristol International Airport

The Bristol Airport Flyer is the only express link between Bristol Temple Meads station, Bristol Bus Station, Clifton and Bristol Airport. The journey time to the city centre is approximately 30 minutes with services operating (every 10 minutes at Peak times) daily between 0230 and 0045.

Cardiff International Airport

The airport is served by a free bus link from Rhoose Cardiff International Rail Station to/from the airport operated by New Adventure Travel. Full details of the timetable and further information can be obtained from Traveline on **0871 200 22 33** or visit **www.traveline.info.**

The airport is also served by bus service X45 which is operated by EST Bus on Monday to Saturday with an hourly daytime frequency to/from Barry Rail Station, and bus service X5 which is operated by Veolia Transport Cymru on a Sunday with a two hourly frequency. In addition Cardiff Bus service X91 also operates from Cardiff Central Bus Station (Stand F1) directly to the airport. Journey time is approximately 30 minutes and through ticketing is available from any rail station.

Coventry Airport

Coventry Airport is accessible from Coventry rail station by a scheduled bus service (No. 737). A combined discounted bus and rail ticket can be purchased for travel to the airport.

For bus times call **0871 200 22 33** or visit **www.traveline.info.**

Durham Tees Valley Airport

Darlington Railway station is situated just 5 miles away. Passengers should use the Arriva service 12 between Darlington and the airport. Visit **www.durhamteesvalleyairport.com.**

East Midlands Airport

The most convenient way to get to East Midlands Airport is via East Midlands Parkway Station, served by East Midlands Trains.

A taxi transfer service operates between East Midlands Parkway and the Airport. To guarantee a great price, book your taxi in advance at www.eastmidlandstrains.co.uk/taxi and fill out a booking form. Please ensure that you book at least 12 hours or more in advance of the taxi being required.

Edinburgh Airport

There are two ways to get to Edinburgh Airport by rail and bus:

- If you are travelling from Fife, Dundee and other areas north, you should catch a train to Inverkeithing – from here a frequent bus service operates to Edinburgh Airport
- If you are travelling from other parts of Scotland, including the Glasgow area, you should catch a train to Haymarket or Edinburgh Waverley – a frequent bus service operates to Edinburgh Airport from both these stations

For full bus timetable information, call **0871 200 22 33**, or visit **www.travelinescotland.com**

Exeter International Airport

Stagecoach operates an hourly daytime service (56 Monday - Saturday, 379 Sundays) from Exeter St. Davids station forecourt direct to Exeter Airport. For more information call Traveline on **0871 200 22 33** or visit **www.traveline.info.**

Airport Links (continued)

Glasgow Airport

There are three ways to get to Glasgow Airport by rail and bus:

- If you are travelling from Ayrshire or Inverclyde, you should catch a train to Paisley Gilmour Street – a frequent bus service operates from here to Glasgow Airport
- If you are travelling from north west Glasgow, Milngavie, Dumbarton, Helensburgh and the West Highlands, you should catch a train to Partick – from here a frequent bus service operates to Glasgow Airport
- If you are travelling from other parts of Scotland, including Edinburgh and the central belt, you should catch a train to Glasgow Central or Glasgow Queen Street – a frequent bus service operates to Glasgow Airport from both these stations

For full bus timetable information, call **0871 200 22 33**, or visit **www.travelinescotland.com**

Leeds Bradford International Airport

Leeds Bradford International Airport is located to the north of the cities of Bradford and Leeds, to the south of the spa town of Harrogate and to the west of the historic city of York. For more information on Leeds Bradford International Airport visit **www.lbia.co.uk**

From Leeds a direct bus service, MetroConnect 757, operates half hourly throughout the day Mondays to Saturdays (hourly early mornings, evenings and Sundays) every day from Stand S8 from outside Leeds Rail Station (Leeds Station Interchange). The journey time is approximately 40 minutes. Through ticketing is available.

From Bradford a half hourly direct bus service, MetroConnect 747, operates throughout the day Mondays to Saturdays (hourly evenings and Sundays) from Bradford Interchange and Forster Square rail stations. The journey time from Bradford is approximately 40 minutes. Through ticketing is available with a PlusBus ticket.

From Harrogate a direct bus service, Bus2Jet 767, operates daily from Harrogate, from Stand 11 in the Bus Station, to the airport. The journey time from Harrogate is approximately 35 minutes. Through ticketing is available with a PlusBus ticket.

For further information on the above services please telephone MetroLine **0113 245 7676** or visit **www.wymetro.com**.

Liverpool John Lennon Airport

Regular bus services operate between Liverpool John Lennon Airport and the Liverpool South Parkway station; journey time is 10 minutes. Liverpool South Parkway is served by direct services from North, South and East Liverpool, Leeds, York, Sheffield, Nottingham, Manchester, Warrington, Southport, Crewe, Stafford, Wolverhampton and Birmingham.

The airport is located to the south of the city centre. A direct bus service operates between Lime Street, Moorfields and James Street stations to the airport seven days a week. Buses run every 30 minutes between 0600 & 0100 hours from the Liverpool City Centre Stations to the Airport, and between 0515 and 0015 from the Airport to the Liverpool City Centre Stations. Journey time is approximately 45 minutes.

For further information please contact **0871 200 22 33,** or visit **www.traveline.info**.

London City Airport

London City Airport is located in London's Docklands, to the east of the capital. There are no National Rail services direct to the airport.

Access to the airport is available via the Docklands Light Railway to and from London City Airport Station which is located next to the terminal building. Between Central London and the airport, passengers can travel on the London Underground Jubilee Line and change at Canning Town for the Docklands Light Railway. Connections between National Rail and the Docklands Light Railway are available at Greenwich, Lewisham, Limehouse, Stratford and Woolwich Arsenal.

For further information on London City Airport telephone **020 7646 0088** or visit **www.londoncityairport.com**.

London Gatwick Airport

Gatwick has its own railway station underneath the South Terminal. Access to the North Terminal is via a free transit.

Airport to/from London

Gatwick Express operate a dedicated non-stop service every 15 minutes throughout most of the day between London Victoria and Gatwick Airport (See Table 186).

Southern provides frequent trains throughout the day and hourly throughout the night between London Victoria and Gatwick Airport (See Table 186).

First Capital Connect operate direct services throughout the day between London St Pancras International, Farringdon, City Thameslink, London Blackfriars, London Bridge and Gatwick Airport (generally every 15 mins, See Table 52), a reduced frequency operates throughout the night. The most convenient connection option is Victoria. Overnight and at weekends it may be necessary to use London bus or Tube services to travel to/from stations north of London Bridge. Your rail ticket will be valid.

Airport to/from Reading

First Great Western operate a direct rail service between Reading and Gatwick – (See Table 148). Customers using this route should allow at least 7 minutes at Reading to make a connection.

Other direct services to/from Airport

Southern also operates direct services to/from Hastings, Southampton, Portsmouth and intermediate stations on the South Coast (See Tables 186, 187, 188, 189) Clapham Jn and East Croydon (SeeTable 186).

First Great Western operate services from Wokingham, North Camp and Guildford (See Table 148).

First Capital Connect provide regular direct services from Gatwick Airport to St. Albans, Luton, Bedford, East Croydon, Haywards Heath and Brighton (See Table 52). At Luton Airport Parkway, Luton and Bedford, they also offer convenient connections with East Midlands Trains to Leicester, Derby, Nottingham and Sheffield (See Table 53).

Airport Links (continued)

London Heathrow Airport

Airport to/from Central London

Heathrow Express operates a direct high-speed rail service from the Airport to London Paddington. Stations are located in all Heathrow terminals - Heathrow Central (Terminals 1, 2 & 3), Terminal 4 and Terminal 5. Journey time is 15 minutes between Paddington and Terminals 1, 2 and 3, with a further 6 minutes to Terminal 5. Trains run every 15 minutes. A free transfer service operates to Terminal 4 from Heathrow Central, departing every 15 minutes and arriving in 4 minutes.

- 0510 to 2325 from Paddington
- 0507 to 2342 from Heathrow Terminal 5 (0503 to 2348 on Sundays)
- 0512 to 2348 from Heathrow Terminal 1, 2 and 3 (0508 to 2353 on Sundays)

For further details see Table 118.

Through tickets can be purchased from any National Rail or London Underground Station to the airport via Heathrow Express.

For further information visit **www.heathrowexpress.com**.

Heathrow Connect operates a local rail service every 30 minutes between Heathrow Central and London Paddington, calling at Hayes & Harlington, Southall, Hanwell, West Ealing and Ealing Broadway. For details see Table 117.

Through tickets are available from most stations.

The London Underground Piccadilly Line connects central London with all five terminals (Terminal 1/2/3, Terminal 4 and Terminal 5).

Through single and return tickets can be issued to customers travelling via a Rail terminus in Zone 1. Sample journey time from Piccadilly Circus to the Airport is approximately one hour.

Airport to/from Reading

RailAir coaches leave from Reading railway station every 20 minutes during the daytime on Mondays to Fridays (every 30 minutes early weekday mornings and evenings, on weekends and public holidays). The luxury, air-conditioned coaches run non-stop to Terminals 1, 2 and 3 in 40-50 minutes. On the return journey from Heathrow Airport they only pick up passengers at Heathrow Central Bus Station (stands one and two) and not the terminals. Customers travelling to/from Terminal 4 should use Heathrow Connect from Terminal 1.

Follow the RailAir signs from your platform at Reading station. You can buy your ticket in the RailAir lounge, or combined rail and coach tickets are also available from many stations. You should allow 15 minutes at Reading to transfer between train and coach.

For further information telephone **0118 957 9425** or visit **www.RailAir.com.**

Airport to/from Woking

Coaches leave at half-hourly intervals throughout most of the day to/from Terminal 5 and Heathrow Central Bus Station (for Terminals 1, 2 and 3) (see Table 158A).

Customers travelling to Heathrow should exit on platform 5 and the coach leaves from outside the station.

On arrival at Woking customers should allow at least 10 minutes to transfer to your train after the arrival of the coach at the station. Combined rail and coach tickets are available from most National Rail stations and from the Railair sales points at the airport. Tickets may also be booked at **www.nationalexpress.com** or by calling **08717 818 181**. For through trains and coach times, telephone **08457 48 49 50.** (calls may be recorded for training purposes)

Airport to/from Feltham

London Buses operates frequent bus services from Feltham Station to Heathrow Airport. Route 285 operates to Hatton Cross and Heathrow Central Bus Station for Terminals 1, 2 and 3. Buses operate every 10 minutes during the day, 15 minutes in the evenings and on Sundays and 30 minutes throughout the night.

Route 490 operates to Hatton Cross and Terminals 4 and 5. Buses operate every 12 minutes during the day, 20 minutes in the evenings and on Sundays.

Customers should allow 10 minutes at Feltham to transfer between train and bus from the station forecourt adjoining platform 1.

Other direct services to/from Airport

A coach service, Green Line 724, runs throughout the day between Heathrow, West Drayton, Uxbridge, Rickmansworth, Watford, St. Albans, Hatfield, Welwyn Garden City, Hertford and Harlow. Tickets can only be purchased on the coach. A frequent bus service (route 140) runs 24 hours between Hayes & Harlington and Heathrow Airport (Central Bus Station).

For further information telephone **0870 608 7261** (Green Line Travel Information)

London Luton Airport

A frequent dedicated shuttle bus links Luton Airport with Luton Airport Parkway station – journey time 5 minutes. Luton Airport Parkway is served by frequent First Capital Connect services direct to Bedford, Central London, South London, Gatwick Airport and Brighton – see Table 52 for details. East Midlands Trains services link Luton Airport Parkway with St Pancras International and Leicester, Derby, Nottingham and Sheffield – see Table 53 for details.

In addition a coach link operates between the Airport, Luton railway station and town centre and Milton Keynes Central railway station and town centre (see Table 65B for details).

Airport Links (continued)

London Stansted Airport

Stansted Airport has its own railway station right in the heart of the airport terminal building.

The Stansted Express is a dedicated rail service operating between London Liverpool Street and Stansted Airport station (See Table 22). Trains run every 15 minutes throughout the day, seven days per week.

Typical journey time is 46 minutes including an intermediate stop at Tottenham Hale to enable transfer onto the Victoria Line (London Underground) for the West End.

CrossCountry operates an hourly express service seven days a week between Birmingham and Stansted Airport calling at Leicester, Peterborough and Cambridge – see Table 49 – offering connections with services to Yorkshire and the North East. Customers should be advised to arrive at the airport 1 hour 45 minutes prior to their latest check-in time.

The airport is also served by the X22 limited stop coach service, operated by Tellings Golden Miller. This links the airport with Colchester and Marks Tey rail stations and also serves Braintree Bus Park and the University of Essex campus. Coaches generally run every two hours, including during the night.

For further information telephone **0871 200 22 33** or visit **www.traveline.info**

London Southend Airport

Southend Airport station, which is adjacent to the airport, is due to open during the validity of this timetable. It will be served by trains on the London Liverpool Street to Southend Victoria line (Table 5), generally every 20 minutes. Journey times will be up to 55 minutes on weekdays and Saturdays and up to 66 minutes on Sundays.

Manchester Airport

The airport railway station is right in the heart of the airport complex, linked by covered travellators. The station is served by up to 8 trains per hour from Manchester Piccadilly and direct services operate between Middlesbrough, Newcastle, York, Leeds, Huddersfield, Cleethorpes, Doncaster, Sheffield, Edinburgh, Glasgow, Carlisle, Barrow-in-Furness, Windermere, Lancaster, Preston, Liverpool and the Airport. Additional regular services operate during the day, to/from many stations which can be found under the entry for Manchester Airport in the index in this timetable.

Newcastle Airport

A frequent Tyne and Wear Metro service runs between Newcastle Central Station and Newcastle Airport providing links with Northern, East Coast, First TransPennine Express and CrossCountry services. Inclusive 'Train and Metro' tickets are available at discount prices.

Metro journey time approximately 20 minutes.

Metro frequency up to 6 trains each way each hour. Service operates between approx. 0600 and 2300.

Connections are available at Sunderland station between Grand Central services and Tyne and Wear Metro services direct to the airport.

Prestwick International Airport

Prestwick International Airport has its own rail station, served by fast and frequent trains from Glasgow, Paisley, Ayr and intermediate stations.

See Table 221 for details.

Robin Hood Airport

Doncaster Airport, Doncaster Sheffield

Robin Hood Airport, the UK's newest purpose built international airport, is built on the site of the former RAF Finningley airbase. It is situated 7 miles south of Doncaster. For more information on Robin Hood Airport visit **www.robinhoodairport.com**

From Doncaster a dedicated bus service, The Airport Arrow 707, operates hourly throughout the day from the Frenchgate Interchange (Stand A1) adjacent to Doncaster Rail Station from 0535 to 2235. The journey takes under 25 minutes.

The Airport Arrow 707 service runs alongside other local bus services which link to Robin Hood Airport, including service X19 from Barnsley.

For further information on the above services please telephone Travel South Yorkshire **01709 515151** or visit **www.travelsouthyorkshire.com**

Southampton Airport

Southampton Airport (Parkway) station is adjacent to Southampton Airport.

South West Trains operate up to 3 trains per hour between London Waterloo, Winchester and Southampton Airport with up to 2 direct services to Bournemouth, Poole, Wareham and Weymouth and most intermediate stations (See Table 158).

CrossCountry services link Southampton Airport Parkway with Bournemouth, Reading, Oxford and Manchester (see Table 51).

Saturdays Southern operate trains every two hours between Brighton, Worthing, Chichester, Havant, Cosham, Fareham and Southampton Airport, at other times use Southern regular trains to Southampton Central and connecting train to Southampton Airport.

Station index and table numbers

[10] Connection time
Ⓟ Station Car Park
🚲 Bicycle storage facility
◇ Seat reservations can be made at this station
⚠ Penalty Fare Schemes in operation on some or all services from this station
🚕 Taxi rank or cab office at station, or signposted and within 100 metres
Ⓤ Unstaffed station
[ ] Station Operator Code

A

Abbey Wood [SE] Ⓟ 🚲 ◇ ⚠ 🚕 200
Aber [AW] Ⓟ 130
Abercynon [AW] Ⓤ 130
Aberdare [AW] [3] Ⓟ ◇ 130
Aberdeen [SR] Ⓟ 🚲 ◇ 🚕
- Birmingham 51, 65
- Blackpool 65
- Bournemouth 51
- Bristol 51
- Cambridge 26
- Cardiff 51
- Carlisle 65
- Crewe 65, *Sleepers* 402
- Darlington 26
- Derby 51
- Doncaster 26
- Dundee 229
- Dyce 240
- Edinburgh 229
- Elgin 240
- Exeter 51
- Glasgow 229
- Grantham 26
- Inverkeithing 229
- Inverness 240
- Inverurie 240
- Kirkcaldy 229
- Leeds 26
- Liverpool 65
- London 26, *Sleepers* 402
- Manchester 65
- Newcastle 26
- Newport (South Wales) 51
- Norwich 26
- Oxenholme Lake District 65
- Oxford 51
- Paignton 51
- Penzance 51
- Perth 229
- Peterborough 26
- Plymouth 51
- Preston 65, *Sleepers* 402
- Reading 51
- Sheffield 26
- Southampton 51
- Stirling 229
- Torquay 51
- Watford 65
- York 26

Aberdour [SR] Ⓟ 🚲 242
Aberdovey [AW] 🚲 Ⓤ 75
Abererch [AW] Ⓤ 75
Abergavenny [AW] Ⓟ 🚲 ◇ 🚕 131
Abergele & Pensarn [AW] Ⓟ Ⓤ 81
Aberystwyth [AW] Ⓟ ◇ 🚕 75
Abingdon Stratton Way *Bus* 116B
Accrington [NT] Ⓟ ◇ 🚕 41, 97
Achanalt [SR] Ⓟ 🚲 Ⓤ 239
Achnasheen [SR] Ⓟ 🚲 Ⓤ 239
Achnashellach [SR] Ⓟ 🚲 Ⓤ 239
Acklington [NT] Ⓟ 🚲 Ⓤ 48
Acle [LE] Ⓟ 🚲 Ⓤ 15
Acocks Green [LM] Ⓟ ⚠ 71
Acton Bridge [LM] Ⓟ Ⓤ 91
Acton Central [LO] 🚲 ⚠ 59
Acton Main Line [GW] ⚠ 117
Acton, South [LO] (see South Acton)
Adderley Park [LM] ◇ ⚠ 68
Addiewell [SR] Ⓟ 🚲 Ⓤ 225
Addlestone [SW] ⚠ 🚕 149
Adisham [SE] Ⓟ ⚠ Ⓤ 212
Adlington (Cheshire) [NT] Ⓟ Ⓤ 84
Adlington (Lancashire) [NT] Ⓟ 82
Adwick [NT] Ⓟ 🚲 Ⓤ 29, 31
Agbrigg [NT] (See Sandal & Agbrigg)
Aigburth [ME] Ⓟ ⚠ 103
Ainsdale [ME] Ⓟ ⚠ 103
Aintree [ME] Ⓟ ⚠ 103
Airbles [SR] Ⓟ 🚲 Ⓤ 226
Airdrie [SR] Ⓟ 🚲 ◇ 🚕 226
Albany Park [SE] ◇ ⚠ 200
Albrighton [LM] Ⓟ Ⓤ 74
Alderley Edge [NT] Ⓟ 🚲 84
Aldermaston [GW] Ⓟ Ⓤ 116
Aldershot [SW] Ⓟ 🚲 ◇ ⚠ 🚕 149, 155
Aldrington [SN] ⚠ Ⓤ 188
Alexandra Palace [FC] 🚲 ⚠ 🚕 24
Alexandra Parade [SR] 🚲 Ⓤ 226
Alexandria [SR] Ⓟ 🚲 226
Alfreton [EM] Ⓟ ◇ ⚠ 🚕 34, 49, 53
Allens West [NT] 🚲 Ⓤ 44
Alloa [SR] Ⓟ 🚲 Ⓤ 230
Alness [SR] Ⓟ 🚲 Ⓤ 239
Alnmouth for Alnwick [NT] Ⓟ 🚲 ◇ 26, 48, 51
Alresford [LE] 🚲 ⚠ 11
Alsager [EM] Ⓤ 50, 67
Althorne [LE] Ⓟ 🚲 Ⓤ 5
Althorpe [NT] Ⓤ 29
Altnabreac [SR] 🚲 Ⓤ 239
Alton [SW] Ⓟ 🚲 ◇ ⚠ 🚕 155
Altrincham [NT] Ⓟ 🚲 ◇ 🚕 88
Alvechurch [LM] Ⓟ ⚠ Ⓤ 69
Ambergate [EM] Ⓟ Ⓤ 56
Amberley [SN] 🚲 ⚠ Ⓤ 188
Amersham [LT] Ⓟ 🚲 ⚠ 🚕 114
Ammanford [AW] Ⓤ 129
Ancaster [EM] Ⓟ Ⓤ 19
Anderston [SR] 🚲 226
Andover [SW] Ⓟ 🚲 ⚠ ◇ 🚕 160
Anerley [LO] 🚲 ⚠ 178
Angel Road [LE] ⚠ Ⓤ 22
Angmering [SN] [3] Ⓟ 🚲 ◇ ⚠ 🚕 188
Annan [SR] Ⓟ 🚲 Ⓤ 216
Anniesland [SR] 🚲 🚕 226, 232
Ansdell & Fairhaven [NT] Ⓤ 97
Appleby [NT] Ⓟ ◇ 36
Appledore (Kent) [SN] Ⓤ 189
Appleford [GW] Ⓤ 116
Appley Bridge [NT] Ⓟ Ⓤ 82
Apsley [LM] Ⓟ 66
Arbroath [SR] Ⓟ 🚲 ◇ 🚕 26, 51, 229, *Sleepers* 402
Ardgay [SR] Ⓟ 🚲 Ⓤ 239
Ardlui [SR] 🚲 Ⓤ 227, *Sleepers* 404
Ardrossan Harbour [SR] Ⓟ 🚲 Ⓤ 221, *Ship* 221A
Ardrossan South Beach [SR] Ⓟ 🚲 221
Ardrossan Town [SR] 🚲 Ⓤ 221
Ardwick [NT] Ⓤ 78, 79
Argyle Street [SR] 226
Arisaig [SR] Ⓟ 🚲 Ⓤ 227
Arlesey [FC] Ⓟ 🚲 ⚠ 25
Armadale [SR] Ⓟ 🚲 Ⓤ 226
Armadale (Skye) *Ship* 227A
Armathwaite [NT] Ⓟ Ⓤ 36
Arnside [TP] Ⓤ 82
Arram [NT] Ⓤ 43
Arrochar & Tarbet [SR] Ⓟ 🚲 Ⓤ 227, *Sleepers* 404
Arundel [SN] Ⓟ 🚲 ◇ ⚠ 🚕 188
Ascot [SW] [3] Ⓟ 🚲 ◇ ⚠ 🚕 149
Ascott-under-Wychwood [GW] Ⓤ 126
Ash [SW] Ⓟ 🚲 ◇ ⚠ 148, 149
Ash Vale [SW] 🚲 ◇ ⚠ 149, 155
Ashburys [NT] Ⓤ 78, 79
Ashchurch for Tewkesbury [GW] Ⓟ 🚲 Ⓤ 57
Ashfield [SR] 🚲 Ⓤ 232
Ashford International [SE] Ⓟ 🚲 ◇ ⚠ 🚕 189, 194, 196, 207
Ashford (Surrey) [SW] Ⓟ 🚲 ◇ ⚠ 149
Ashley [NT] Ⓟ Ⓤ 88
Ashtead [SN] Ⓟ 🚲 ◇ ⚠ 152, 182
Ashton-under-Lyne [NT] Ⓟ 🚲 39
Ashurst [SN] Ⓟ ⚠ Ⓤ 184
Ashurst New Forest [SW] Ⓟ 🚲 ⚠ Ⓤ 158
Ashwell & Morden [FC] Ⓟ 🚲 ⚠ 25
Askam [NT] Ⓟ Ⓤ 100
Aslockton [EM] Ⓟ Ⓤ 19
Aspatria [NT] Ⓟ Ⓤ 100
Aspley Guise [LM] Ⓤ 64
Aston [LM] ⚠ 69, 70
Atherstone [LM] Ⓟ Ⓤ 67
Atherton [NT] Ⓟ 🚲 82
Attadale [SR] 🚲 Ⓤ 239
Attenborough [EM] ⚠ Ⓤ 56, 57

【10】 Connection time
Ⓟ Station Car Park
🚲 Bicycle storage facility
◇ Seat reservations can be made at this station
⚠ Penalty Fare Schemes in operation on some or all services from this station
🚕 Taxi rank or cab office at station, or signposted and within 100 metres
Ⓤ Unstaffed station
[ ] Station Operator Code

Station index and table numbers

Attleborough [LE] Ⓟ Ⓤ 17
Auchinleck [SR] Ⓟ 🚲 Ⓤ 216
Audley End [LE] Ⓟ 🚲 ⚠ 🚕 22, 49
Aughton Park [ME] ⚠ 103
Aviemore [SR] Ⓟ 🚲 ◇ 🚕 229, *Sleepers* 403
Avoncliff [GW] Ⓤ 123
Avonmouth [GW] 【2】 Ⓟ 🚲 Ⓤ 133
Axminster [SW] Ⓟ 🚲 ◇ 🚕 160
Aylesbury [CH] Ⓟ 🚲 ◇ ⚠ 🚕 114, 115
Aylesbury Vale Parkway [CH] Ⓟ 🚲 ◇ ⚠ 114
Aylesford [SE] ⚠ Ⓤ 208
Aylsham [SE] Ⓟ ◇ ⚠ 212
Ayr [SR] Ⓟ 🚲 ◇ 🚕 218, 221

B

Bache [ME] Ⓤ 106
Backwell [GW] (see Nailsea)
Baglan [AW] Ⓟ 🚲 Ⓤ 128
Bagshot [SW] Ⓟ 🚲 ◇ ⚠ 149
Baildon [NT] Ⓟ Ⓤ 38
Baillieston [SR] 🚲 Ⓤ 220
Balcombe [SN] ◇ ⚠ 52, 186
Baldock [FC] Ⓟ ⚠ 25
Balham [SN] 【4】 ◇ ⚠ 🚕 176, 177, 178, 182
Balloch [SR] 🚲 🚕 226
Balmossie [SR] 🚲 Ⓤ 229
Bamber Bridge [NT] Ⓟ Ⓤ 97
Bamford [NT] Ⓟ Ⓤ 78
Banavie [SR] Ⓟ 🚲 Ⓤ 227
Banbury [CH] Ⓟ 🚲 ◇ ⚠ 🚕 51, 71, 75, 115, 116
Bangor (Gwynedd) [AW] Ⓟ ◇ 🚕 65, 81, 131
Bank Hall [ME] ⚠ 103
Banstead [SN] ⚠ Ⓤ 182
Barassie [SR] Ⓟ 🚲 Ⓤ 221
Bardon Mill [NT] Ⓟ Ⓤ 48
Bare Lane [NT] Ⓟ Ⓤ 36, 98
Bargeddie [SR] Ⓟ 🚲 Ⓤ 220
Bargoed [AW] 🚕 130
Barking [CC] ◇ ⚠ 🚕 1, 62
Barlaston Orchard Place *Bus* 67
Barming [SE] Ⓟ ◇ ⚠ 196
Barmouth [AW] 🚲 75
Barnehurst [SE] 【4】 Ⓟ ◇ ⚠ 🚕 200
Barnes [SW] 🚲 ◇ ⚠ 149
Barnes Bridge [SW] 🚲 ◇ ⚠ Ⓤ 149
Barnetby [TP] Ⓟ Ⓤ 27, 29, 30
Barnham [SN] Ⓟ 🚲 ◇ ⚠ 🚕 123, 188
Barnhill [SR] 🚲 Ⓤ 226
Barnsbury [LO] (see Caledonian Road)
Barnsley [NT] Ⓟ 🚲 ◇ 🚕 30, 34
Barnstaple [GW] Ⓟ 🚲 ◇ 🚕 136
Barnt Green [LM] Ⓟ ⚠ Ⓤ 69, 71
Barrhead [SR] Ⓟ 🚲 🚕 222
Barrhill [SR] Ⓟ 🚲 218
Barrow Haven [NT] Ⓤ 29
Barrow-in-Furness [TP] Ⓟ ◇ 🚕 65, 82, 100
Barrow Upon Soar [EM] ⚠ Ⓤ 53
Barry [AW] 【3】 Ⓟ ◇ 🚕 130
Barry Docks [AW] Ⓟ 130
Barry Island [AW] Ⓤ 130
Barry Links [SR] 🚲 Ⓤ 229
Barton-on-Humber [NT] Ⓟ Ⓤ 29
Basildon [CC] 🚲 ◇ ⚠ 🚕 1
Basingstoke [SW] Ⓟ 🚲 ◇ ⚠ 🚕
Aberdeen 51
Bath 160
Birmingham 51
Bournemouth 158
Bristol 160
Brockenhurst 158
Clapham Junction 155
Coventry 51
Crewe 51
Derby 51
Dorchester 158
Dundee 51
Eastleigh 158
Edinburgh 51
Exeter 160
Fareham 158
Farnborough 158
Glasgow 51
Leeds 51
London 155
Lymington 158
Manchester 51
Newcastle 51
Oxford 51
Poole 158
Portsmouth 158
Preston 51
Reading 122
Salisbury 160
Sheffield 51
Southampton 158
Southampton Airport 158
Stoke-on-Trent 51
Surbiton 155
Weymouth 158
Weybridge 155
Wimbledon 155
Winchester 158
Woking 155
Wolverhampton 51
Yeovil 160
York 51
Bat & Ball [SE] Ⓟ ⚠ Ⓤ 52, 195
Bath Spa [GW] 【7】 Ⓟ 🚲 ◇ ⚠ 🚕 123, 125, 132, 135, 160
Bathgate [SR] Ⓟ 🚲 ◇ 🚕 226
Batley [NT] Ⓟ 🚲 Ⓤ 39
Battersby [NT] Ⓤ 45
Battersea Park [SN] 【4】 ◇ ⚠ 177, 178
Battle [SE] Ⓟ ◇ ⚠ 🚕 206
Battlesbridge [LE] Ⓟ 🚲 Ⓤ 5
Bayford [FC] Ⓟ ⚠ Ⓤ 24
Beaconsfield [CH] Ⓟ 🚲 ◇ ⚠ 🚕 115
Bearley [LM] Ⓟ ⚠ Ⓤ 115
Bearsden [SR] Ⓟ 🚲 🚕 226
Bearsted [SE] Ⓟ 🚲 ◇ ⚠ 196
Beasdale [SR] 🚲 Ⓤ 227
Beaulieu Road [SW] 🚲 ⚠ Ⓤ 158
Beauly [SR] Ⓟ 🚲 Ⓤ 239
Bebington [ME] Ⓟ ⚠ 🚕 106
Beccles [LE] Ⓟ 🚲 Ⓤ 13
Beckenham Hill [SE] 🚲 ◇ ⚠ 52, 195
Beckenham Junction [SE] 【4】 Ⓟ 🚲 ◇ ⚠ 🚕 177, 195
Bedford [FC] 【7】 Ⓟ 🚲 ◇ ⚠ 🚕
Barnsley 53
Bletchley 64
Brighton 52, 186
Chesterfield 53
Derby 53
Doncaster 53
East Croydon 52
Gatwick Airport 52, 186
Haywards Heath 52, 186
Herne Hill 52
Hove 186
Kettering 53
Leeds 53
Leicester 53
London 52
Luton 52
Luton Airport Parkway 52
Meadowhall 53
Milton Keynes Central *Bus* 65C
Nottingham 53
Redhill 52, 186
St Albans 52
Sheffield 53
Sutton (Surrey) 52
Wakefield 53
Wellingborough 53
Wimbledon 52
York 53
Bedford Bus Station 🚕 *Bus* 65C
Bedford St Johns [LM] Ⓤ 64
Bedhampton [SW] 🚲 ◇ ⚠ 156, 157, 188
Bedminster [GW] Ⓤ 134
Bedworth [LM] Ⓟ Ⓤ 67
Bedwyn [GW] Ⓟ 🚲 Ⓤ 116
Beeston [EM] Ⓟ 🚲 ◇ ⚠ 53, 56, 57
Bekesbourne [SE] Ⓟ ⚠ Ⓤ 212
Belfast
Port *Catamaran/Ship* (via Stranraer Harbour) 218
Belle Vue [NT] Ⓤ 78
Bellgrove [SR] 🚲 Ⓤ 226

Station index and table numbers

- [10] Connection time
- Ⓟ Station Car Park
- 🚲 Bicycle storage facility
- ◇ Seat reservations can be made at this station
- ⚠ Penalty Fare Schemes in operation on some or all services from this station
- 🚕 Taxi rank or cab office at station, or signposted and within 100 metres
- Ⓤ Unstaffed station
- [ ] Station Operator Code

Bellingham [SE] 🚲 ◇ ⚠ 52, 195
Bellshill [SR] Ⓟ 🚲 225, 226
Belmont [SN] ⚠ Ⓤ 182
Belper [EM] ⚠ Ⓤ 56
Beltring [SE] ⚠ Ⓤ 208
Belvedere [SE] ◇ ⚠ 200
Bempton [NT] Ⓤ 43
Ben Rhydding [NT] Ⓟ Ⓤ 38
Benfleet [CC] Ⓟ 🚲 ◇ ⚠ 🚕 1
Bentham [NT] Ⓟ Ⓤ 36
Bentley [SW] Ⓟ 🚲 ◇ ⚠ 155
Bentley (S. Yorks.) [NT] Ⓟ 🚲 Ⓤ 29, 31
Bere Alston [GW] Ⓟ Ⓤ 139
Bere Ferrers [GW] Ⓟ 🚲 Ⓤ 139
Berkhamsted [LM] Ⓟ 🚲 ◇ ⚠ 🚕 66, 176
Berkswell [LM] Ⓟ 🚲 ⚠ 68
Berney Arms [LE] 🚲 Ⓤ 15
Berry Brow [NT] Ⓤ 34
Berrylands [SW] Ⓟ 🚲 ◇ ⚠ 152
Berwick [SN] Ⓟ 🚲 ◇ ⚠ 189
Berwick-upon-Tweed [GR] Ⓟ 🚲 ◇ 🚕 26, 26K, 51
Bescar Lane [NT] Ⓤ 82
Bescot Stadium [LM] Ⓟ ◇ ⚠ 70
Betchworth [GW] Ⓤ 148
Bethnal Green [LE] 🚲 ⚠ Ⓤ 20, 21, 22
Betws-y-Coed [AW] Ⓤ 102
Beverley [NT] Ⓟ ◇ 🚕 43
Bexhill [SN] [4] ◇ ⚠ 🚕 189
Bexley [SE] Ⓟ ◇ ⚠ 🚕 200
Bexleyheath [SE] Ⓟ 🚲 ◇ ⚠ 🚕 200
Bicester (Bure Place) *Bus* 65A
Bicester North [CH] [8] Ⓟ 🚲 ◇ ⚠ 🚕 115
Bicester Town [GW] Ⓟ 🚲 Ⓤ 116
Bickley [SE] [4] Ⓟ ◇ ⚠ 52, 195
Bidston [ME] Ⓟ ⚠ 101, 106
Biggleswade [FC] Ⓟ 🚲 ⚠ 25
Bilbrook [LM] Ⓤ 74
Billericay [LE] Ⓟ 🚲 ⚠ 🚕 5
Billingham [NT] 🚲 🚕 Ⓤ 44
Billingshurst [SN] Ⓟ 🚲 ◇ ⚠ 🚕 188
Bingham [EM] Ⓟ Ⓤ 19
Bingley [NT] Ⓟ 🚲 ◇ 36
Birchgrove [AW] Ⓤ 130
Birchington-on-Sea [SE] Ⓟ 🚲 ◇ ⚠ 🚕 194, 212
Birchwood [TP] Ⓟ 🚲 🚕 39, 89
Birkbeck [SN] ⚠ Ⓤ 177
Birkdale [ME] Ⓟ ⚠ 103
Birkenhead Central [ME] ⚠ 106
Birkenhead North [ME] ⚠ 106
Birkenhead Park [ME] ⚠ 106
Birmingham International [VT] (for National Exhibition Centre and Airport) Ⓟ 🚲 ◇ ⚠ 🚕
  Aberdeen 65
  Aberystwyth 75
  Banbury 71
  Bangor (Gwynedd) 65, 81
  Basingstoke 51
  Birmingham 68
  Blackpool 65
  Bournemouth 51
  Carlisle 65
  Chester 65, 75, 81
  Clapham Junction 66
  Coventry 68
  Crewe 65, 81
  Derby 51
  Dundee 65
  East Croydon 66
  Edinburgh 51, 65
  Glasgow 51, 65
  Holyhead 65, 75, 81
  Inverness 65
  Leamington Spa 71
  Leeds 51
  Liverpool 65
  London 66, 116
  Manchester 65
  Manchester Airport 65
  Milton Keynes Central 66
  Newcastle 51
  Northampton 66
  Nottingham 51
  Oxenholme Lake District 65
  Oxford 51
  Preston 65
  Pwllheli 75
  Reading 51
  Rugby 66
  Sheffield 51
  Shrewsbury 75
  Southampton 51
  Stafford 68
  Stoke-on-Trent 65
  Watford 66
  Wolverhampton 68
  Wrexham 75
  York 51
Birmingham
  Moor Street [CH] ◇ ⚠ 🚕
  New Street [NR] [12] 🚲 ◇ ⚠ 🚕
  Snow Hill [LM] Ⓟ ◇ ⚠
  Aberdeen 51, 65
  Aberystwyth 75
  Banbury 71
  Bangor (Gwynedd) 65, 81
  Barmouth 75
  Barrow-in-Furness 65
  Basingstoke 51
  Birmingham International 68
  Blackpool 65
  Bournemouth 51
  Bristol 57
  Bromsgrove 71
  Burton-on-Trent 57
  Cambridge 49
  Cardiff 57
  Carlisle 65
  Cheltenham Spa 57
  Chester 75, 81
  Clapham Junction 66
  Coventry 68
  Crewe 65
  Darlington 51
  Derby 57
  Douglas (IOM) 98A
  Dundee 51, 65
  East Croydon 66
  Edinburgh 51, 65
  Ely 49
  Exeter 51
  Glasgow 51, 65
  Gloucester 57
  Hereford 71
  Holyhead 65, 81
  Inverness 65
  Kidderminster 71
  Leamington Spa 71
  Leeds 51
  Leicester 57
  Lichfield 69
  Liverpool 65, 91
  Llandudno 81
  London 66, 115, 116
  Longbridge 69
  Manchester 65, 84
  Manchester Airport 65, 84
  Milton Keynes Central 66
  Newcastle 51
  Newport (South Wales) 57
  Northampton 66
  Norwich 49
  Nottingham 57
  Nuneaton 57
  Oxenholme Lake District 65
  Oxford 116
  Paignton 135
  Penzance 135
  Peterborough 49
  Plymouth 135
  Preston 65
  Reading 116
  Redditch 69
  Rugby 66
  Rugeley 70
  Sheffield 51
  Shrewsbury 74
  Solihull 71
  Southampton 51
  Stafford 68
  Stansted Airport 49
  Stockport 65
  Stoke-on-Trent 65
  Stourbridge 71
  Stratford-upon-Avon 71
  Telford 74
  Torquay 135
  Walsall 70
  Warrington 65
  Warwick 71
  Watford 66
  Wigan 65
  Wolverhampton 68
  Worcester 71
  Wrexham 75

Station index and table numbers

10 Connection time
Ⓟ Station Car Park
🚲 Bicycle storage facility
◇ Seat reservations can be made at this station
⚠ Penalty Fare Schemes in operation on some or all services from this station
🚕 Taxi rank or cab office at station, or signposted and within 100 metres
Ⓤ Unstaffed station
[ ] Station Operator Code

York 51
Birnam [SR] (see Dunkeld)
Bishop Auckland [NT] Ⓟ 🚕 Ⓤ 44
Bishopbriggs [SR] 🚲 228, 230
Bishops Lydeard Hithermead *Bus* 135E
Bishops Stortford [LE] Ⓟ 🚲 ◇ ⚠ 🚕 22
Bishopstone [SN] Ⓤ 189
Bishopton [SR] Ⓟ 🚲 219
Bitterne [SW] Ⓟ 🚲 ⚠ Ⓤ 165
Blackburn [NT] Ⓟ ◇ 🚕 41, 94, 97
Blackfriars [FC] (see London)
Blackheath [SE] **4** ◇ ⚠ 🚕 200
Blackhorse Road [LT] ⚠ 62
Blackpool
North [NT] Ⓟ ◇ 🚕
Pleasure Beach [NT] Ⓤ
South [NT] 🚕 Ⓤ
Birmingham 65
Birmingham International 65
Blackburn 97
Bolton 82
Bradford 41
Burnley 97
Colne 97
Coventry 65
Crewe 65
Lancaster 65
Leeds 41
Liverpool 65, 90
London 65
Manchester 82
Manchester Airport 82
Milton Keynes Central 65
Preston 97
Rugby 65
St Helens 90
Stafford 65
Stockport 82
Warrington 65
Watford 65
Wigan 65
Wolverhampton 65
York 41
Blackridge [SR] Ⓟ 🚲 Ⓤ 226
Blackrod [NT] Ⓤ 82
Blackwater [GW] Ⓟ Ⓤ 148
Blaenau Ffestiniog [AW] Ⓤ 102
Blair Atholl [SR] Ⓟ 🚲 229, *Sleepers* 403
Blairhill [SR] Ⓟ 🚲 🚕 226
Blake Street [LM] Ⓟ ⚠ 69
Blakedown [LM] Ⓟ ⚠ Ⓤ 71
Blantyre [SR] Ⓟ 🚲 226
Blaydon [NT] Ⓤ 48
Bleasby [EM] Ⓤ 27
Bledlow, Village Hall *Bus* 115A
Bletchley [LM] Ⓟ 🚲 ◇ ⚠ 🚕 64, 66, 176
Bloxwich [LM] ⚠ Ⓤ 70
Bloxwich North [LM] ⚠ Ⓤ 70
Bluewater [SE] (see Greenhithe for Bluewater)
Blundellsands & Crosby [ME] Ⓟ ⚠ 103
Blythe Bridge [EM] Ⓟ Ⓤ 50
Bodmin Mount Folly *Bus* 135C
Bodmin Parkway [GW] Ⓟ 🚲 ◇ 🚕 51, 135, *Bus* 135C, *Sleepers* 406
Bodorgan [AW] Ⓟ Ⓤ 81
Bognor Regis [SN] Ⓟ 🚲 ◇ ⚠ 🚕 188
Bogston [SR] 🚲 Ⓤ 219
Bolton [NT] 🚲 ◇ 🚕 65, 82, 94
Bolton-upon-Dearne [NT] Ⓟ Ⓤ 31
Bookham [SW] Ⓟ 🚲 ◇ ⚠ 🚕 152, 182
Bootle [NT] Ⓤ 100
Bootle New Strand [ME] ⚠ 🚕 103
Bootle Oriel Road [ME] Ⓟ ⚠ 103
Bordesley [LM] ⚠ Ⓤ 71
Borehamwood [FC] (see Elstree)
Borough Green & Wrotham [SE] Ⓟ ◇ ⚠ 🚕 196
Borth [AW] Ⓟ Ⓤ 75
Bosham [SN] 🚲 ⚠ 188
Boston [EM] Ⓟ 🚲 ◇ 🚕 19
Botley [SW] Ⓟ 🚲 ⚠ Ⓤ 158
Bottesford [EM] Ⓟ Ⓤ 19
Bourne End [GW] **3** Ⓟ 🚲 ⚠ 120
Bournemouth [SW] Ⓟ 🚲 ◇ ⚠ 🚕 51, 158
Bournville [LM] ⚠ 69
Bow Brickhill [LM] Ⓤ 64
Bowes Park [FC] ⚠ 24
Bowling [SR] Ⓟ 🚲 Ⓤ 226
Boxhill & Westhumble [SN] Ⓟ ⚠ Ⓤ 152, 182
Bracknell [SW] Ⓟ 🚲 ◇ ⚠ 🚕 149
Bradford
Forster Square [NT] Ⓟ 🚲 ◇ 🚕
Interchange [NT] 🚲 ◇ 🚕
Blackpool 41
Blackburn 41
Brighouse 41
Cambridge 26
Carlisle 36
Grantham 26
Halifax 41
Huddersfield 41
Ilkley 38
Lancaster 36
Leeds 37
London 26
Manchester 41
Morecambe 36
Newark 26
Norwich 26
Peterborough 26
Preston 41
Retford 26
Rochdale 41
Selby 40
Settle 36
Shipley 37
Skipton 36
York 40
Bradford-on-Avon [GW] Ⓟ 🚲 ◇ 🚕 123, 160
Brading [IL] Ⓟ Ⓤ 167
Braintree [LE] Ⓟ 🚲 ⚠ 🚕 11
Braintree Freeport [LE] 🚲 ⚠ Ⓤ 11
Bramhall [NT] 84
Bramley (Hants) [GW] ⚠ 122
Bramley [NT] Ⓟ Ⓤ 37, 41
Brampton (Cumbria) [NT] Ⓟ Ⓤ 48
Brampton (Suffolk) [LE] Ⓤ 13
Branchton [SR] Ⓟ 🚲 Ⓤ 219
Brandon [LE] Ⓟ Ⓤ 17
Branksome [SW] Ⓟ 🚲 ◇ ⚠ 158
Braystones [NT] Ⓤ 100
Bredbury [NT] Ⓟ 🚲 78
Breich [SR] 🚲 Ⓤ 225
Brentford [SW] Ⓟ 🚲 ◇ 🚕 149
Brentwood [LE] Ⓟ 🚲 ⚠ 🚕 5
Bricket Wood [LM] Ⓤ 61
Bridge of Allan [SR] Ⓟ 🚲 Ⓤ 230
Bridge of Orchy [SR] Ⓟ 🚲 Ⓤ 227, *Sleepers* 404
Bridgend [AW] Ⓟ 🚲 ◇ 🚕 125, 128, 130
Bridgeton [SR] 🚲 🚕 226
Bridgwater [GW] Ⓟ ◇ 134, 135
Bridlington [NT] Ⓟ 🚲 ◇ 🚕 43
Brierfield [NT] Ⓟ Ⓤ 97
Brigg [NT] Ⓟ Ⓤ 30
Brighouse [NT] Ⓟ Ⓤ 26, 32, 41
Brighton [SN] **10** Ⓟ 🚲 ◇ ⚠ 🚕
Ashford International 189
Bath Spa 123
Bedford 52
Bognor Regis 188
Bristol 123
Cardiff 123
Chichester 188
Eastbourne 189
East Croydon 176, 186
Elstree & Borehamwood 52
Gatwick Airport 186
Hastings 189
Haywards Heath 186
Hove 188
Isle of Wight 167
Kensington (Olympia) 176
Lewes 189
Littlehampton 188
London 186
Luton 52
Luton Airport Parkway 52
Mill Hill Broadway 52
Milton Keynes Central 176
Portsmouth 188
Radlett 52

Station index and table numbers

■10 Connection time
Ⓟ Station Car Park
🚲 Bicycle storage facility
◇ Seat reservations can be made at this station
⚠ Penalty Fare Schemes in operation on some or all services from this station
🚕 Taxi rank or cab office at station, or signposted and within 100 metres
Ⓤ Unstaffed station
[ ] Station Operator Code

Station index and table numbers

⟦10⟧ Connection time
Ⓟ Station Car Park
🚲 Bicycle storage facility
◇ Seat reservations can be made at this station
⚠ Penalty Fare Schemes in operation on some or all services from this station
🚕 Taxi rank or cab office at station, or signposted and within 100 metres
Ⓤ Unstaffed station
[ ] Station Operator Code

Station index and table numbers

❿ Connection time
Ⓟ Station Car Park
🚲 Bicycle storage facility
◇ Seat reservations can be made at this station
⚠ Penalty Fare Schemes in operation on some or all services from this station
🚕 Taxi rank or cab office at station, or signposted and within 100 metres
Ⓤ Unstaffed station
[ ] Station Operator Code

Chalfont & Latimer [LT] Ⓟ 🚲 ⚠ 🚕 114
Chalkwell [CC] 🚲 ◇ ⚠ 🚕 1
Chandlers Ford [SW] Ⓟ 🚲 ◇ 158
Chapel-en-le-Frith [NT] Ⓟ Ⓤ 86
Chapelton [GW] Ⓟ Ⓤ 136
Chapeltown [NT] Ⓤ 34
Chappel & Wakes Colne [LE] 🚲 Ⓤ 10
Charing [SE] Ⓟ ◇ ⚠ 196
Charing Cross (Glasgow) **[SR]** 🚲 226
Charing Cross [NR] (see London)
Charlbury [GW] Ⓟ 🚲 126
Charlton [SE] ❹ ◇ ⚠ 200
Chartham [SE] ⚠ Ⓤ 207
Chassen Road [NT] 89
Chatelherault [SR] 🚲 Ⓤ 226
Chatham [SE] ❹ Ⓟ ◇ ⚠ 🚕 194, 200, 212
Chathill [NT] Ⓟ Ⓤ 48
Cheadle Hulme [NT] Ⓟ 🚲 84
Cheam [SN] Ⓟ 🚲 ◇ ⚠ 🚕 182
Cheddington [LM] Ⓟ 66
Chelford [NT] Ⓟ 🚲 Ⓤ 84
Chelmsford [LE] ❸ Ⓟ 🚲 ◇ ⚠ 🚕 11
Chelsfield [SE] ❸ Ⓟ ◇ ⚠ 🚕 204
Cheltenham Spa [GW] Ⓟ 🚲 ◇ 🚕 51, 57, 125
Chepstow [AW] Ⓟ 132
Cherry Tree [NT] Ⓟ Ⓤ 97
Chertsey [SW] Ⓟ 🚲 ◇ ⚠ 🚕 149
Cheshunt [LE] Ⓟ 🚲 ⚠ 🚕 21, 22
Chessington North [SW] Ⓟ 🚲 ◇ ⚠ 🚕 152
Chessington South [SW] Ⓟ 🚲 ◇ ⚠ 152
Chester [AW] Ⓟ ◇ 🚕
- Altrincham 88
- Bangor (Gwynedd) 81
- Birmingham 75, 81
- Cardiff 75, 81, 131
- Crewe 81
- Hereford 131
- Holyhead 81
- Liverpool 106
- Llandudno 81
- Llandudno Junction 81
- London 65
- Manchester 81, 88
- Newport (South Wales) 131
- Northwich 88
- Rhyl 81
- Runcorn East 81
- Shrewsbury 75, 131
- Stafford 65
- Stockport 88
- Warrington 81
- Wolverhampton 65, 75
- Wrexham 75

Chester Road [LM] Ⓟ ⚠ 69
Chesterfield [EM] Ⓟ 🚲 ◇ ⚠ 🚕 34, 49, 51, 53
Chester-le-Street [NT] Ⓟ 🚲 ◇ 🚕 Ⓤ 26, 39, 44, 51
Chestfield & Swalecliffe [SE] ◇ ⚠ 212
Chetnole [GW] Ⓤ 123
Chichester [SN] ❹ Ⓟ 🚲 ◇ ⚠ 🚕 123, 165, 188
Chilham [SE] Ⓟ ⚠ Ⓤ 207
Chilworth [GW] Ⓤ 148
Chingford [LE] Ⓟ 🚲 ⚠ 🚕 20
Chinley [NT] Ⓟ Ⓤ 78
Chinnor, Estover Way *Bus* 115A
Chinnor, Lower Road *Bus* 115A
Chinnor, The Red Lion *Bus* 115A
Chinnor, The Wheatsheaf *Bus* 115A
Chippenham [GW] Ⓟ 🚲 ◇ ⚠ 🚕 123, 125
Chipping Norton West Street *Bus* 126A
Chipstead [SN] Ⓟ ⚠ 181
Chirk [AW] Ⓟ Ⓤ 75
Chislehurst [SE] Ⓟ ◇ ⚠ 🚕 204
Chiswick [SW] Ⓟ 🚲 Ⓤ 149
Cholsey [GW] Ⓟ 🚲 116
Chorley [NT] Ⓟ ◇ 82
Chorleywood [LT] Ⓟ 🚲 ⚠ 🚕 114
Christchurch [SW] Ⓟ 🚲 ◇ ⚠ 🚕 158
Christs Hospital [SN] Ⓟ 🚲 ◇ ⚠ 188
Church Fenton [NT] Ⓟ 🚲 Ⓤ 33, 40
Church & Oswaldtwistle [NT] Ⓤ 97
Church Stretton [AW] Ⓟ Ⓤ 129, 131
Cilmeri [AW] Ⓤ 129
City Thameslink [FC] (see London)
Clacton-on-Sea [LE] Ⓟ 🚲 ◇ ⚠ 🚕 11
Clandon [SW] Ⓟ 🚲 ◇ ⚠ 152
Clapham High Street [SN] 🚲 ⚠ Ⓤ 178
Clapham Junction [SW] ❿ ◇ ⚠
- Alton 155
- Andover 160
- Ascot 149
- Basingstoke 155, 158
- Bexhill 189
- Birmingham 66
- Birmingham International 66
- Bognor Regis 188
- Bournemouth 158
- Brighton 186
- Bristol 160
- Chertsey 149
- Chessington 152
- Chichester 188
- Coventry 66
- Crystal Palace 177, 178
- Dorking 152, 182
- Eastbourne 189
- East Croydon 175, 176
- East Grinstead 184
- Effingham Junction 152
- Epsom 152, 182
- Epsom Downs 182
- Exeter 160
- Gatwick Airport 186
- Guildford 152, 156
- Hampton Court 152
- Hastings 189
- Haywards Heath 186
- Horsham 186
- Hounslow 149
- Hove 186
- Kensington (Olympia) 66, 176, 186
- Kingston 149, 152
- Lewes 189
- London
  - Victoria 175, 177
  - Waterloo 149, 152
- Milton Keynes Central 66, 176
- Northampton 66
- Oxted 184
- Portsmouth 156, 158, 188
- Purley 175
- Reading 149
- Redhill 186
- Rugby 66
- Salisbury 160
- Shepperton 152
- Southampton 158, 188
- Staines 149
- Surbiton 152
- Sutton (Surrey) 182
- Tattenham Corner 181
- Twickenham 149
- Uckfield 184
- Watford Junction 66, 176, 186
- West Croydon 177
- Weybridge 155
- Willesden Junction 176, 186
- Wimbledon 152
- Windsor 149
- Woking 155
- Worthing 188
- Yeovil Junction 160

Clapham (Nth Yorkshire) [NT] Ⓟ Ⓤ 36
Clapton [LE] ⚠ 20, 22
Clarbeston Road [AW] Ⓤ 128
Clarkston [SR] 🚲 222
Claverdon [LM] ⚠ Ⓤ 115
Claygate [SW] Ⓟ 🚲 ◇ ⚠ 🚕 152
Cleethorpes [TP] Ⓟ 🚲 ◇ 🚕 27, 29, 30
Cleland [SR] Ⓟ 🚲 Ⓤ 225
Clifton [NT] Ⓤ 82
Clifton Down [GW] Ⓟ Ⓤ 133
Clitheroe [NT] Ⓟ 94
Clock House [SE] 🚲 ◇ ⚠ 🚕 203

Station index and table numbers

[10] Connection time
Ⓟ Station Car Park
🚲 Bicycle storage facility
◇ Seat reservations can be made at this station
⚠ Penalty Fare Schemes in operation on some or all services from this station
🚕 Taxi rank or cab office at station, or signposted and within 100 metres
Ⓤ Unstaffed station
[ ] Station Operator Code

Clunderwen [AW] Ⓟ Ⓤ 128
Clydebank [SR] 🚲 🚕 226
Coatbridge Central [SR] Ⓟ 🚲 🚕 Ⓤ 224, 226
Coatbridge Sunnyside [SR] Ⓟ 🚲 226
Coatdyke [SR] Ⓟ 🚲 Ⓤ 226
Cobham & Stoke d'Abernon [SW] Ⓟ 🚲 ◇ ⚠ 🚕 152
Cockermouth (Main Street) *Bus* 65F
Codsall [LM] Ⓟ Ⓤ 74
Cogan [AW] Ⓟ Ⓤ 130
Colchester [LE] [4] Ⓟ 🚲 ◇ ⚠ 🚕 10, 11, 14
Colchester Town [LE] Ⓟ 🚲 ⚠ 11
Coleshill Parkway [LM] Ⓟ 🚲 ◇ 🚕 49, 57
Coll *Ship* 227B
Collingham [EM] Ⓤ 27
Collington [SN] ⚠ Ⓤ 189
Colne [NT] Ⓟ Ⓤ 97
Colonsay *Ship* 227B
Colwall [LM] Ⓟ ⚠ Ⓤ 71, 126
Colwyn Bay [AW] Ⓟ ◇ 🚕 81
Combe [GW] Ⓤ 126
Commondale [NT] Ⓤ 45
Congleton [NT] Ⓟ ◇ 51, 65, 84
Conisbrough [NT] Ⓟ Ⓤ 29
Connel Ferry [SR] Ⓟ 🚲 Ⓤ 227
Cononley [NT] Ⓟ Ⓤ 36
Conway Park [ME] 106
Conwy [AW] Ⓤ 81
Cooden Beach [SN] Ⓟ 🚲 ◇ ⚠ 189
Cookham [GW] Ⓟ 120
Cooksbridge [SN] Ⓟ ⚠ Ⓤ 189
Coombe Junction Halt [GW] Ⓤ 140
Copplestone [GW] Ⓟ Ⓤ 136
Corbridge [NT] Ⓟ Ⓤ 48
Corby [EM] ⚠ 53
Corby George Street *Bus* 26B
Corkerhill [SR] 🚲 Ⓤ 217
Corkickle [NT] Ⓤ 100
Corpach [SR] Ⓟ 🚲 Ⓤ 227
Corrour [SR] 🚲 Ⓤ 227, *Sleepers* 404
Coryton [AW] Ⓤ 130
Coseley [LM] Ⓟ ⚠ 68
Cosford [LM] Ⓟ Ⓤ 74, 75
Cosham [SW] Ⓟ 🚲 ◇ ⚠ 🚕 123, 158, 165, 188
Cottingham [NT] Ⓟ 🚕 Ⓤ 43
Cottingley [NT] Ⓤ 39
Coulsdon South [SN] Ⓟ ⚠ 🚕 186
Coventry [VT] Ⓟ 🚲 ◇ ⚠ 🚕
- Aberdeen 65
- Barrow-in-Furness 65
- Banbury 71
- Basingstoke 51
- Birmingham 68
- Birmingham International 68
- Blackpool 65
- Bournemouth 51
- Brighton 66
- Carlisle 65
- Clapham Junction 66
- Crewe 65
- Derby 51
- Dundee 65
- East Croydon 66
- Edinburgh 51, 65
- Gatwick Airport 66
- Glasgow 51, 65
- Holyhead 65
- Inverness 65
- Leamington Spa 71
- Leeds 51
- Liverpool 65
- London 66
- Manchester 65
- Manchester Airport 65
- Milton Keynes Central 66
- Newcastle 51
- Northampton 66
- Nuneaton 67
- Oxenholme Lake District 65
- Oxford 51
- Preston 65
- Reading 51
- Rugby 66
- Sheffield 51
- Southampton 51
- Stafford 67, 68
- Stoke-on-Trent 65
- Watford 66
- Wolverhampton 68
- York 51

Cowden [SN] Ⓟ ⚠ Ⓤ 184
Cowdenbeath [SR] 🚲 ◇ 242
Cradley Heath [LM] Ⓟ 🚲 ◇ ⚠ 71, 115
Craigendoran [SR] Ⓟ 🚲 Ⓤ 226
Craignure *Ship* 227B
Cramlington [NT] Ⓟ 🚲 Ⓤ 48
Craven Arms [AW] Ⓟ Ⓤ 129, 131
Crawley [SN] Ⓟ 🚲 ◇ ⚠ 🚕 186, 188
Crayford [SE] Ⓟ ◇ ⚠ 200
Crediton [GW] Ⓟ 🚲 Ⓤ 136
Cressing [LE] 🚲 ⚠ Ⓤ 11
Cressington [ME] Ⓟ ⚠ 103
Creswell [EM] Ⓤ 55
Crewe [VT] [10] Ⓟ 🚲 ◇ 🚕
- Aberdeen 65, *Sleepers* 402
- Bangor (Gwynedd) 81
- Barrow-in-Furness 65
- Birmingham 65
- Birmingham International 65
- Blackpool 65
- Bournemouth 51
- Bristol 51
- Cardiff 131
- Carlisle 65
- Cheltenham Spa 51
- Chester 81
- Coventry 65, 67
- Derby 50
- Douglas (IOM) 98A
- Dundee 65, *Sleepers* 402
- Edinburgh 65
- Exeter 51
- Fort William *Sleepers* 404
- Glasgow 65
- Hartford 91
- Hereford 131
- Holyhead 81
- Inverkeithing *Sleepers* 402
- Inverness 65, *Sleepers* 403
- Kirkcaldy *Sleepers* 402
- Lancaster 65
- Liverpool 91
- Liverpool South Parkway 91
- Llandudno 81
- London 65, 67
- Manchester 84
- Manchester Airport 84
- Milton Keynes Central 65, 67
- Newport (South Wales) 131
- Northampton 67
- Oxenholme Lake District 65
- Oxford 51
- Paignton 51
- Penzance 51
- Perth 65, *Sleepers* 403
- Plymouth 51
- Preston 65
- Reading 51
- Rugby 65, 67
- Runcorn 91
- Shrewsbury 131
- Southampton 51
- Stafford 65, 67
- Stirling *Sleepers* 403
- Stockport 84
- Stoke-on-Trent 50
- Torquay 51
- Watford 65
- Wilmslow 84
- Wolverhampton 65

Crewkerne [SW] Ⓟ 🚲 ◇ 160
Crews Hill [FC] ⚠ Ⓤ 24
Crianlarich [SR] Ⓟ 🚲 Ⓤ 227, *Sleepers* 404
Criccieth [AW] Ⓟ 🚲 Ⓤ 75
Cricklewood [FC] 🚲 ◇ ⚠ 52
Croftfoot [SR] 🚲 223
Crofton Park [SE] ◇ ⚠ 52, 195
Cromer [LE] Ⓟ 🚲 Ⓤ 16
Cromford [EM] Ⓟ Ⓤ 54, 56
Crompton [NT] (see Shaw)
Crookston [SR] 🚲 Ⓤ 217
Crosby [ME] (see Blundellsands)
Crossflatts [NT] Ⓟ 🚲 Ⓤ 36
Cross Gates [NT] Ⓟ 40
Cross Keys [AW] Ⓤ 127
Crosshill [SR] 223
Crossmyloof [SR] 🚲 Ⓤ 222
Croston [NT] Ⓟ Ⓤ 99
Crouch Hill [LO] ⚠ 62
Crowborough [SN] Ⓟ 🚲 ◇ ⚠ 184

Station index and table numbers

▪10 Connection time
Ⓟ Station Car Park
🚲 Bicycle storage facility
◇ Seat reservations can be made at this station
⚠ Penalty Fare Schemes in operation on some or all services from this station
🚕 Taxi rank or cab office at station, or signposted and within 100 metres
Ⓤ Unstaffed station
[ ] Station Operator Code

Crowhurst [SE] Ⓟ ⚠ 206
Crowle [NT] Ⓤ 29
Crowthorne [GW] Ⓟ 🚲 148
Croy [SR] ▪3 Ⓟ 🚲 228, 230
Croydon
see East Croydon
see South Croydon
see West Croydon
Crystal Palace [LO] ▪4 Ⓟ ⚠ 🚕 177, 178
Cuddington [NT] Ⓟ Ⓤ 88
Cuffley [FC] Ⓟ 🚲 ⚠ 🚕 24
Culham [GW] Ⓟ 🚲 Ⓤ 116
Culrain [SR] 🚲 Ⓤ 239
Cumbernauld [SR] Ⓟ 🚲 🚕 224
Cupar [SR] Ⓟ 🚲 ◇ 51, 229
Curriehill [SR] Ⓟ 🚲 Ⓤ 225
Cuxton [SE] Ⓟ ⚠ Ⓤ 208
Cwmbach [AW] Ⓟ Ⓤ 130
Cwmbran [AW] Ⓟ 🚲 ◇ 🚕 131
Cynghordy [AW] Ⓤ 129

D

Dagenham Dock [CC] Ⓟ 🚲 ◇ ⚠ 1
Daisy Hill [NT] Ⓟ 🚲 82
Dalgety Bay [SR] Ⓟ 🚲 🚕 Ⓤ 242
Dalmally [SR] Ⓟ 🚲 Ⓤ 227
Dalmarnock [SR] 226
Dalmeny [SR] Ⓟ 🚲 242
Dalmuir [SR] Ⓟ 🚲 226, 227, *Sleepers* 404
Dalreoch [SR] Ⓟ 🚲 226
Dalry [SR] Ⓟ 🚲 Ⓤ 221
Dalston [NT] Ⓟ Ⓤ 100
Dalston Junction [LO] ⚠ 178
Dalston Kingsland [LO] ⚠ 59
Dalton [NT] Ⓟ Ⓤ 82
Dalwhinnie [SR] Ⓟ 🚲 Ⓤ 229, *Sleepers* 403
Danby [NT] Ⓟ Ⓤ 45
Danescourt [AW] Ⓤ 130
Danzey [LM] Ⓟ ⚠ Ⓤ 71
Darlington [GR] ▪7 Ⓟ 🚲 ◇ 🚕
Aberdeen 26
Birmingham 51
Bishop Auckland 44
Bournemouth 51
Bristol 51
Cambridge 26
Cardiff 51
Catterick Garrison *Bus* 26H
Derby 51
Doncaster 26
Durham 26
Dundee 26
Edinburgh 26
Exeter 51
Glasgow 26
Grantham 26
Huddersfield 39
Leeds 26
Liverpool 39
London 26
Manchester 39
Manchester Airport 39
Middlesbrough 44
Newark 26
Newcastle 26
Newport (South Wales) 51
Norwich 26
Northallerton 26
Oxford 51
Paignton 51
Penzance 51
Peterborough 26
Plymouth 51
Reading 51
Redcar 44
Retford 26
Richmond *Bus* 26H
Saltburn 44
Sheffield 26
Southampton 51
Stansted Airport 26
Sunderland 26, 44
Torquay 51
Whitby 45
York 26
Darnall [NT] Ⓤ 30
Darnley [SR] (see Priesthill)
Darsham [LE] Ⓟ 🚲 Ⓤ 13
Dartford [SE] ▪4 Ⓟ ◇ ⚠ 🚕 200, 212
Darton [NT] Ⓟ Ⓤ 34
Darwen [NT] Ⓤ 94
Datchet [SW] 🚲 ◇ ⚠ 149
Davenport [NT] Ⓟ 86
Dawlish [GW] Ⓟ ◇ 🚕 51, 135
Dawlish Warren [GW] Ⓟ 🚲 Ⓤ 135
Deal [SE] Ⓟ 🚲 ◇ ⚠ 🚕 207
Dean [GW] 🚲 Ⓤ 158
Deansgate [NT] 82, 84, 85, 86, 89
Deganwy [AW] Ⓤ 81, 102
Deighton [NT] Ⓤ 39
Delamere [NT] Ⓟ Ⓤ 88
Denby Dale [NT] Ⓟ Ⓤ 34
Denham [CH] Ⓟ 🚲 ◇ ⚠ 🚕 115
Denham Golf Club [CH] ⚠ Ⓤ 115
Denmark Hill [SE] ▪4 ◇ ⚠ 52, 178, 195, 200
Dent [NT] Ⓟ Ⓤ 36
Denton [NT] Ⓤ 78
Deptford [SE] ◇ ⚠ 200
Derby [EM] ▪6 Ⓟ 🚲 ◇ ⚠ 🚕
Barnsley 53
Bedford 53
Belper 53, 56
Birmingham 57
Birmingham International 51
Bournemouth 51
Bristol 57
Burton-on-Trent 57
Cardiff 57
Chesterfield 53
Coventry 51
Crewe 50
Doncaster 53
Edinburgh 51
Exeter 51
Gloucester 57
Kettering 53
Leeds 53
Leicester 53
London 53
Long Eaton 56
Loughborough 53
Luton 53
Market Harborough 53
Matlock 56
Meadowhall 53
Newcastle 51
Newport (South Wales) 57
Nottingham 56
Oxford 51
Paignton 51
Penzance 51
Plymouth 51
Reading 51
Sheffield 53
Southampton 51
Stoke-on-Trent 50
Wakefield 53
Wellingborough 53
York 53
Derby Road [LE] 🚲 Ⓤ 13
Dereham 🚕 *Bus* 26A
Devonport [GW] Ⓟ 🚲 Ⓤ 135, 139
Dewsbury [TP] Ⓟ 🚲 ◇ 🚕 39, 41
Didcot Parkway [GW] Ⓟ 🚲 ◇ ⚠ 🚕 116, 125
Digby & Sowton [GW] Ⓟ Ⓤ 136
Dilton Marsh [GW] Ⓤ 123
Dinas Powys [AW] Ⓤ 130
Dinas Rhondda [AW] Ⓟ Ⓤ 130
Dingle Road [AW] Ⓤ 130
Dingwall [SR] Ⓟ 🚲 ◇ 🚕 239
Dinsdale [NT] Ⓤ 44
Dinting [NT] ▪3 Ⓟ 🚲 79
Disley [NT] Ⓟ 86
Diss [LE] Ⓟ 🚲 ◇ 🚕 11
Dockyard [GW] Ⓤ 135, 139
Dodworth [NT] Ⓟ Ⓤ 34
Dolau [AW] 🚲 Ⓤ 129
Doleham [SN] Ⓤ 189
Dolgarrog [AW] Ⓤ 102
Dolwyddelan [AW] Ⓟ Ⓤ 102
Doncaster [GR] ▪7 Ⓟ 🚲 ◇ 🚕
Aberdeen 26
Bedford 53
Birmingham 51
Bournemouth 51
Bristol 51
Cambridge 26
Cleethorpes 29
Darlington 26

Station index and table numbers

- **10** Connection time
- Ⓟ Station Car Park
- 🚲 Bicycle storage facility
- ◇ Seat reservations can be made at this station
- ⚠ Penalty Fare Schemes in operation on some or all services from this station
- 🚕 Taxi rank or cab office at station, or signposted and within 100 metres
- Ⓤ Unstaffed station
- [ ] Station Operator Code

E

Station index and table numbers

[10] Connection time
Ⓟ Station Car Park
🚲 Bicycle storage facility
◇ Seat reservations can be made at this station
⚠ Penalty Fare Schemes in operation on some or all services from this station
🚕 Taxi rank or cab office at station, or signposted and within 100 metres
Ⓤ Unstaffed station
[ ] Station Operator Code

East Midlands Parkway [EM] ⚠ 53
East Tilbury [CC] ◇ ⚠ 1
East Worthing [SN] ⚠ Ⓤ 188
Eastbourne [SN] [4] Ⓟ 🚲 ◇ ⚠ 🚕 189
Eastbrook [AW] Ⓟ Ⓤ 130
Easterhouse [SR] Ⓟ 🚲 226
Eastham Rake [ME] Ⓟ 🚲 ⚠ 106
Eastleigh [SW] [3] Ⓟ 🚲 ◇ ⚠ 🚕 158
Eastrington [NT] Ⓤ 29
Ebbsfleet International [SE] ◇ ⚠ 🚕 194, 196, 200, 207, 212
Ebbw Vale Parkway [AW] Ⓟ Ⓤ 127
Eccles [NT] Ⓟ 90
Eccles Road [LE] Ⓟ Ⓤ 17
Eccleston Park [NT] 90
Edale [NT] Ⓟ Ⓤ 78
Eden Camp *Bus* 26G
Eden Park [SE] ◇ ⚠ 203
Eden Project *Bus* 135B
Edenbridge [SN] Ⓟ ⚠ Ⓤ 186
Edenbridge Town [SN] Ⓟ 🚲 ◇ ⚠ 🚕 184
Edge Hill [NT] Ⓟ 89, 90, 91
Edinburgh [NR] [10] Ⓟ 🚲 ◇ 🚕
Aberdeen 229
Bathgate 226
Birmingham New Street 51, 65
Birmingham International 51, 65
Blackpool 65
Bournemouth 51
Bristol 51
Cambridge 26
Cardiff 51
Carlisle 65
Carstairs 225
Cowdenbeath 242
Crewe 65
Croy 228
Darlington 26
Derby 51
Doncaster 26
Dunbar 238
Dunblane 230
Dundee 229
Dunfermline 242
Dyce 229
Edinburgh Park 226, 230
Exeter 51
Falkirk 228, 230
Fort William 227
Glasgow 225, 228
Glenrothes with Thornton 242
Grantham 26
Inverkeithing 242
Inverness 229
Inverurie 229
Kirkcaldy 242
Lancaster 65
Larbert 230
Leeds 26
Linlithgow 230
Liverpool 65
Livingston 225, 226
London 26, *Sleepers* 400
Mallaig 227
Manchester 65
Manchester Airport 65
Markinch 229
Motherwell 225
Newcastle 26
Newcraighall 242
Newport (South Wales) 51
North Berwick 238
Oban 227
Oxenholme Lake District 65
Oxford 51
Paignton 51
Penzance 51
Perth 229
Peterborough 26
Plymouth 51
Polmont 230
Preston 65
Reading 51
Sheffield 26
Shotts 225
Southampton 51
Stafford 65
Stirling 230
Thurso 239
Torquay 51
Warrington 65
Watford 65, *Sleepers* 400
West Calder 225
Western Isles *Ship* 239B
Wigan 65
York 26
Edinburgh Park [SR] 🚲 Ⓤ 226, 230
Edmonton Green [LE] ⚠ 21
Effingham Junction [SW] [6] Ⓟ 🚲 ◇ ⚠ 152, 182
Eggesford [GW] Ⓟ Ⓤ 136
Egham [SW] Ⓟ 🚲 ◇ ⚠ 🚕 149
Egton [NT] Ⓤ 45
Eigg *Ship* 227A
Elephant & Castle [FC] 🚲 ◇ ⚠
Ashford 196
Bromley South 195
Canterbury 212
Catford 195
Chatham 212
Dover 212
East Croydon 177
Faversham 212
London 52, 177
Luton 52
Maidstone 196
Margate 212
Ramsgate 212
Rochester 212
St Albans 52
St Pancras International 52, 177
Sevenoaks 195
Streatham 177
Sutton (Surrey) 179
Swanley 195
Wimbledon 179
Elgin [SR] Ⓟ 🚲 ◇ 🚕 240
Ellesmere Port [ME] 🚕 106, 109
Elmers End [SE] [4] Ⓟ 🚲 ◇ ⚠ 203
Elmstead Woods [SE] Ⓟ ◇ ⚠ 🚕 204
Elmswell [LE] 🚲 Ⓤ 14
Elsecar [NT] Ⓤ 34
Elsenham [LE] 🚲 ⚠ 22
Elstree & Borehamwood [FC] Ⓟ 🚲 ◇ ⚠ 🚕 52
Eltham [SE] Ⓟ 🚲 ◇ ⚠ 🚕 200
Elton (Ches.) **[NT]** (see Ince & Elton)
Elton & Orston [EM] Ⓟ Ⓤ 19
Ely [LE] [6] Ⓟ 🚲 ◇ ⚠ 🚕 14, 17, 49
Emerson Park [LE] 🚲 ⚠ Ⓤ 4
Emsworth [SN] Ⓟ 🚲 ◇ ⚠ 188
Enfield Chase [FC] Ⓟ 🚲 ⚠ 24
Enfield Lock [LE] 🚲 ⚠ 22
Enfield Town [LE] ⚠ 🚕 21
Entwistle [NT] Ⓤ 94
Epsom [SN] [3] 🚲 ◇ ⚠ 🚕 152, 182
Epsom Downs [SN] ⚠ Ⓤ 182
Erdington [LM] ⚠ 69
Eridge [SN] 🚲 ◇ ⚠ 184
Erith [SE] ◇ ⚠ 🚕 200
Esher [SW] Ⓟ 🚲 ◇ ⚠ 🚕 155
Eskdale [NT] (see Ravenglass)
Essex Road [FC] 🚲 ⚠ 24
Etchingham [SE] Ⓟ 🚲 ◇ ⚠ 206
Eton (see Windsor)
Euston [NR] (see London)
Euxton Balshaw Lane [NT] Ⓟ Ⓤ 90
Evesham [GW] Ⓟ 🚲 🚕 126
Ewell East [SN] Ⓟ 🚲 ◇ ⚠ 182
Ewell West [SW] Ⓟ 🚲 ◇ ⚠ 152
Exeter
Central [GW] Ⓟ 🚲 ◇
St Davids [GW] [6] Ⓟ 🚲 ◇ ⚠ 🚕
St Thomas [GW] Ⓤ
Aberdeen 51
Andover 160
Barnstaple 136
Basingstoke 160
Birmingham 51
Bristol 135
Bude Strand *Bus* 135D
Cardiff 135
Carlisle 51
Clapham Junction 160
Crewe 51
Derby 51
Dundee 51
Edinburgh 51
Exmouth 136
Glasgow 51
Holsworthy *Bus* 135D
Leeds 51

Station index and table numbers

[10] Connection time
Ⓟ Station Car Park
🚲 Bicycle storage facility
◇ Seat reservations can be made at this station
⚠ Penalty Fare Schemes in operation on some or all services from this station
🚕 Taxi rank or cab office at station, or signposted and within 100 metres
Ⓤ Unstaffed station
[ ] Station Operator Code

London 135, 160, *Sleepers* 406
Manchester 51
Newcastle 51
Newport (South Wales) 135
Newquay 135
Newton Abbot 135
Nottingham 51
Okehampton *Summer only* 136
Okehampton West Street *Bus* 135D
Paignton 135
Penzance 135
Plymouth 135
Preston 51
Reading 135, *Sleepers* 406
Salisbury 160
Sheffield 51
Taunton 135
Torquay 135
Truro 135
Weston-super-Mare 135
Wolverhampton 51
York 51
Exhibition Centre [SR] 🚲 226
Exmouth [GW] Ⓟ 🚲 ◇ 135, 136
Exton [GW] Ⓟ 🚲 Ⓤ 136
Eynsford [SE] Ⓟ ◇ ⚠ 52, 195
Eynsham Church *Bus* 116C

F

Fairbourne [AW] Ⓟ Ⓤ 75
Fairfield [NT] Ⓤ 78
Fairhaven [NT] (see Ansdell)
Fairlie [SR] Ⓟ 🚲 Ⓤ 221
Fairwater [AW] Ⓤ 130
Falconwood [SE] ◇ ⚠ 🚕 200
Falkirk Grahamston [SR] Ⓟ 🚲 ◇ 🚕 224, 230, *Sleepers* 403
Falkirk High [SR] Ⓟ 🚲 ◇ 🚕 228
Falls of Cruachan [SR] Ⓤ *Summer only* 227
Falmer [SN] Ⓟ 🚲 ⚠ 189
Falmouth Docks [GW] Ⓟ Ⓤ 143
Falmouth Town [GW] Ⓤ 143
Fambridge [LE] (North Fambridge)
Fareham [SW] Ⓟ 🚲 ◇ ⚠ 🚕 123, 158, 165, 188
Farnborough (Main) [SW] Ⓟ 🚲 ◇ ⚠ 🚕 155,158
Farnborough North [GW] Ⓟ Ⓤ 148
Farncombe [SW] Ⓟ 🚲 ◇ ⚠ 156
Farnham [SW] Ⓟ 🚲 ◇ ⚠ 🚕 155
Farningham Road [SE] Ⓟ ◇ ⚠ 212
Farnworth [NT] 82
Farringdon [LT] (see London)
Fauldhouse [SR] Ⓟ 🚲 Ⓤ 225
Faversham [SE] [2] Ⓟ 🚲 ◇ ⚠ 🚕 194, 212
Faygate [SN] ⚠ Ⓤ 186
Fazakerley [ME] ⚠ 103
Fearn [SR] Ⓟ 🚲 Ⓤ 239
Featherstone [NT] Ⓤ 32
Felixstowe [LE] 🚲 🚕 Ⓤ 13
Feltham [SW] Ⓟ 🚲 ◇ ⚠ 149
Fenchurch Street [NR] (see London)
Feniton [SW] Ⓟ 🚲 ◇ 160
Fenny Stratford [LM] Ⓤ 64
Fernhill [AW] Ⓤ 130
Ferriby [NT] Ⓟ 🚲 Ⓤ 29
Ferryside [AW] Ⓤ 128
Ffairfach [AW] Ⓤ 129
Filey [NT] Ⓟ 🚕 Ⓤ 43
Filton Abbey Wood [GW] Ⓟ 🚲 123, 132, 134, 135
Finchley Road & Frognal [LO] ⚠ 59
Finsbury Park [FC] ⚠ 🚕 24, 25
Finstock [GW] Ⓤ 126
Fishbourne (Sussex) [SN] ⚠ Ⓤ 188
Fishersgate [SN] ⚠ Ⓤ 188
Fishguard Harbour [AW] Ⓤ 128
Fiskerton [EM] Ⓟ Ⓤ 27
Fitzwilliam [NT] Ⓟ Ⓤ 31
Five Ways [LM] ⚠ 69
Flamingo Land *Bus* 26G
Fleet [SW] Ⓟ 🚲 ◇ ⚠ 🚕 155, 158
Flimby [NT] Ⓤ 100
Flint [AW] Ⓟ ◇ 81
Flitwick [FC] Ⓟ 🚲 ◇ ⚠ 🚕 52
Flixton [NT] 🚲 89
Flowery Field [NT] Ⓤ 79
Folkestone Central [SE] Ⓟ 🚲 ◇ ⚠ 🚕 194, 207
Folkestone West [SE] Ⓟ ◇ ⚠ 194, 207
Ford [SN] [4] 🚲 ◇ ⚠ 188
Forest Gate [LE] 🚲 ⚠ 5
Forest Hill [LO] [4] Ⓟ 🚲 ◇ ⚠ 🚕 178
Formby [ME] Ⓟ 🚲 ⚠ 103
Forres [SR] Ⓟ 🚲 ◇ 🚕 240
Forsinard [SR] Ⓟ 🚲 Ⓤ 239
Fort Matilda [SR] Ⓟ 🚲 Ⓤ 219
Fort William [SR] Ⓟ 🚲 ◇ 🚕 227, *Ship* 227A, *Sleepers* 404
Four Oaks [LM] Ⓟ ⚠ 69
Foxfield [NT] Ⓤ 100
Foxton [FC] ⚠ Ⓤ 25
Frant [SE] Ⓟ ◇ ⚠ 206
Fratton [SW] Ⓟ 🚲 ◇ ⚠ 🚕 123, 156, 157, 158, 165, 188
Freshfield [ME] Ⓟ 🚲 ⚠ 103
Freshford [GW] Ⓟ Ⓤ 123
Frimley [SW] Ⓟ 🚲 ◇ ⚠ 149
Frinton-on-Sea [LE] Ⓟ 🚲 ⚠ 11
Frizinghall [NT] Ⓟ Ⓤ 36, 37, 38
Frodsham [AW] Ⓟ Ⓤ 81
Frognal [LO] (see Finchley Road)
Frome [GW] Ⓟ 🚲 🚕 123
Fulwell [SW] 🚲 ◇ ⚠ 149, 152
Furness Vale [NT] Ⓤ 86
Furze Platt [GW] 120

G

Gainsborough Central [NT] Ⓟ Ⓤ 30
Gainsborough Lea Road [EM] Ⓟ 🚲 Ⓤ 18, 30
Galton Bridge (Smethwick) [LM] (see Smethwick Galton Bridge)
Garelochhead [SR] Ⓟ 🚲 Ⓤ 227, *Sleepers* 404
Garforth [NT] Ⓟ 🚲 39, 40
Gargrave [NT] Ⓤ 36
Garrowhill [SR] 🚲 226
Garscadden [SR] 🚲 226
Garsdale [NT] Ⓟ Ⓤ 36
Garston (Hertfordshire) [LM] Ⓤ 61
Garswood [NT] Ⓟ 90
Gartcosh [SR] Ⓟ 🚲 Ⓤ 224
Garth (Powys) [AW] Ⓤ 129
Garth (Mid Glamorgan) [AW] Ⓤ 128
Garve [SR] Ⓟ 🚲 Ⓤ 239
Gateshead [NT] (see Metrocentre)
Gathurst [NT] Ⓟ 🚲 Ⓤ 82
Gatley [NT] Ⓟ 85
Gatwick Airport [NR] [10] ◇ ⚠ 🚕
Bedford 52
Bognor Regis 188
Brighton 186
Chichester 188
City Thameslink 52, 186
Clapham Junction 176, 186
Eastbourne 189
East Croydon 176, 186
Elstree & Borehamwood 52
Guildford 148
Hastings 189
Haywards Heath 186
Hove 186
Kensington (Olympia) 176
Lewes 189
London 186
Luton 52, 186
Luton Airport Parkway 52
Mill Hill Broadway 52
Milton Keynes Central 176
Portsmouth 188
Radlett 52
Reading 148
St Albans 52
St Pancras International 52
Southampton Central 188
Watford Junction 176
West Hampstead Thameslink

Station index and table numbers

[10] Connection time
℗ Station Car Park
🚲 Bicycle storage facility
◇ Seat reservations can be made at this station
⚠ Penalty Fare Schemes in operation on some or all services from this station
🚕 Taxi rank or cab office at station, or signposted and within 100 metres
ⓤ Unstaffed station
[ ] Station Operator Code

■10 Connection time
Ⓟ Station Car Park
🚲 Bicycle storage facility
◇ Seat reservations can be made at this station
⚠ Penalty Fare Schemes in operation on some or all services from this station
🚕 Taxi rank or cab office at station, or signposted and within 100 metres
⊕ Unstaffed station
[ ] Station Operator Code

Station index and table numbers

Great Coates [NT] ⊕ 29
Great Malvern [LM] Ⓟ ◇ ⚠ 🚕 71, 126
Great Missenden [CH] Ⓟ 🚲 ◇ ⚠ 🚕 114
Great Yarmouth [LE] Ⓟ 🚲 ◇ 🚕 15
Green Lane [ME] ⚠ 106
Green Road [NT] Ⓟ ⊕ 100
Greenbank [NT] Ⓟ ⊕ 88
Greenfaulds [SR] Ⓟ 🚲 ⊕ 224
Greenfield [NT] 🚲 39
Greenford [LT] Ⓟ ⚠ 🚕 117
Greenhithe for Bluewater [SE] ◇ ⚠ 200, 212
Greenock Central [SR] Ⓟ 🚲 219
Greenock West [SR] 🚕 219
Greenwich [SE] ■4 ◇ ⚠ 200
Gretna Green [SR] Ⓟ 🚲 ⊕ 216
Grimsby Docks [NT] ⊕ 29
Grimsby Town [TP] Ⓟ 🚲 ◇ 🚕 26, 27, 29, 30
Grindleford [NT] ⊕ 78
Grosmont [NT] [NY] Ⓟ ⊕ 45
Grove Park [SE] ■4 ◇ ⚠ 🚕 204
Guide Bridge [NT] Ⓟ 78, 79
Guildford [SW] Ⓟ 🚲 ◇ ⚠ 🚕
  Ascot 149
  Birmingham 51
  Clapham Junction 152, 155, 156
  Gatwick Airport 148
  London 152, 155, 156
  Portsmouth 156
  Reading 148
  Surbiton 152
  West Croydon 182
Guiseley [NT] Ⓟ 🚲 ◇ 38
Gunnersbury [LT] 59
Gunnislake [GW] Ⓟ 🚲 ⊕ 139
Gunton [LE] Ⓟ 🚲 ⊕ 16
Gwersyllt [AW] Ⓟ ⊕ 101
Gypsy Lane [NT] 🚲 ⊕ 45

H

Habrough [NT] Ⓟ ⊕ 27, 29, 30
Hackbridge [SN] Ⓟ ◇ ⚠ 52, 179, 182
Hackney Central [LO] 🚲 ⚠ 🚕 59
Hackney Downs [LE] 🚲 ⚠ 20, 21, 22
Hackney Wick [LO] ⚠ 59
Haddenham & Thame Parkway [CH] Ⓟ 🚲 ◇ ⚠ 🚕 115
Haddiscoe [LE] Ⓟ 🚲 ⊕ 15
Hadfield [NT] Ⓟ 🚲 79
Hadley Wood [FC] ⚠ 24
Hag Fold [NT] 82
Haggerston [LO] ⚠ 178
Hagley [LM] Ⓟ ⚠ 71
Hairmyres [SR] Ⓟ 🚲 ⊕ 222
Hale [NT] Ⓟ 88
Halesworth [LE] Ⓟ 🚲 ⊕ 13
Halewood [NT] 89
Halifax [NT] Ⓟ 🚲 ◇ 🚕 26, 32, 41
Hall Green [LM] Ⓟ ⚠ 71
Hall I' Th' Wood [NT] ⊕ 94
Hall Road [ME] 🚲 ⚠ 103
Halling [SE] ⚠ ⊕ 208
Haltwhistle [NT] Ⓟ 🚲 ⊕ 48
Ham Street [SN] Ⓟ ◇ ⚠ 189
Hamble [SW] 🚲 ⚠ ⊕ 165
Hamilton Central [SR] Ⓟ 🚲 ◇ 🚕 226
Hamilton Square [ME] ◇ ⚠ 🚕 106
Hamilton West [SR] Ⓟ 🚲 🚕 226
Hammerton [NT] Ⓟ ⊕ 35
Hampden Park [SN] ■4 ◇ ⚠ 189
Hampstead Heath [LO] 🚲 ⚠ 59
Hampstead (South) [LO] (see South Hampstead)
Hampstead (West) (see West Hampstead) (see West Hampstead Thameslink)
Hampton [SW] 🚲 ⚠ 152
Hampton-in-Arden [LM] Ⓟ ⚠ 68
Hampton Court [SW] Ⓟ 🚲 ◇ ⚠ 152
Hampton Wick [SW] 🚲 ⚠ 149, 152
Hamstead [LM] ⚠ 70
Hamworthy [SW] 🚲 ◇ ⚠ 158
Hanborough [GW] Ⓟ 🚲 ⊕ 126
Handforth [NT] 🚲 84
Hanley Bus Station *Bus* 67
Hanwell [GW] 🚲 ⚠ 117
Hapton [NT] ⊕ 97
Harlech [AW] Ⓟ 🚲 ⊕ 75
Harlesden [LT] 60
Harling Road [LE] Ⓟ 🚲 ⊕ 17
Harlington (Beds.) **[FC]** Ⓟ 🚲 ◇ ⚠ 🚕 52
Harlington (Middx.) **[GW]** (see Hayes & Harlington)
Harlow Mill [LE] Ⓟ 🚲 ⚠ 22
Harlow Town [LE] Ⓟ 🚲 ◇ ⚠ 🚕 22
Harold Wood [LE] Ⓟ 🚲 ⚠ 🚕 5
Harpenden [FC] Ⓟ 🚲 ◇ ⚠ 🚕 52
Harrietsham [SE] Ⓟ ◇ ⚠ 196
Harringay [FC] ⚠ 24
Harringay Green Lanes [LO] ⚠ 62
Harrington [NT] Ⓟ ⊕ 100
Harrogate [NT] Ⓟ 🚲 ◇ 🚕 26, 35
Harrow & Wealdstone [LT] Ⓟ ⚠ 🚕 60, 66, 176, 177
Harrow Road [CH] (see Sudbury & Harrow Road)
Harrow Sudbury Hill [CH] (see Sudbury Hill Harrow)
Harrow-on-the-Hill [LT] ■3 Ⓟ 🚲 ⚠ 🚕 114
Hartford [LM] Ⓟ ◇ 65, 91
Hartlebury [LM] Ⓟ ⚠ ⊕ 71
Hartlepool [NT] Ⓟ 🚲 ◇ 🚕 26, 44
Hartwood [SR] Ⓟ 🚲 ⊕ 225
Harwich International [LE] 🚲 ◇ 11, 14
Harwich Town [LE] 🚲 ⊕ 11
Haslemere [SW] ■4 Ⓟ 🚲 ◇ ⚠ 🚕 156
Hassocks [SN] ■4 Ⓟ 🚲 ◇ ⚠ 🚕 52, 186
Hastings [SE] ■4 Ⓟ ◇ ⚠ 🚕 189, 206
Hatch End [LO] Ⓟ 🚲 ⚠ 🚕 60
Hatfield [FC] Ⓟ 🚲 ⚠ 🚕 24, 25
Hatfield & Stainforth [NT] Ⓟ ⊕ 29
Hatfield Peverel [LE] Ⓟ 🚲 ⚠ 11
Hathersage [NT] Ⓟ ⊕ 78
Hattersley [NT] ⊕ 79
Hatton (Derbyshire) **[EM]** (see Tutbury & Hatton)
Hatton (Warwickshire) **[CH]** Ⓟ ⚠ ⊕ 71, 115
Havant [SW] Ⓟ 🚲 ◇ ⚠ 🚕 123, 156, 157, 165, 188
Havenhouse [EM] ⊕ 19
Haverfordwest [AW] Ⓟ ◇ 🚕 128
Hawarden [AW] Ⓟ ⊕ 101
Hawarden Bridge [AW] ⊕ 101
Hawkhead [SR] 🚲 ⊕ 217
Haydon Bridge [NT] Ⓟ 🚲 ⊕ 48
Haydons Road [FC] Ⓟ ⚠ 52, 179
Hayes & Harlington [GW] ■3 Ⓟ 🚲 ◇ ⚠ 🚕 117
Hayes (Kent) [SE] Ⓟ 🚲 ◇ ⚠ 🚕 203
Hayle [GW] Ⓟ ⊕ 51, 135, *Sleepers* 406
Haymarket (Edinburgh) **[SR]** Ⓟ 🚲 ◇ 🚕
  Aberdeen 229
  Bathgate 226
  Birmingham 51, 65
  Birmingham International 51, 65
  Blackpool 65
  Bournemouth 51
  Bristol 51
  Cambridge 26
  Carlisle 65
  Carstairs 225
  Cowdenbeath 242
  Crewe 65
  Croy 228
  Darlington 26
  Derby 51
  Doncaster 26
  Dunblane 230
  Dundee 229
  Dunfermline 242

Station index and table numbers

[10] Connection time
Ⓟ Station Car Park
🚲 Bicycle storage facility
◇ Seat reservations can be made at this station
⚠ Penalty Fare Schemes in operation on some or all services from this station
🚕 Taxi rank or cab office at station, or signposted and within 100 metres
Ⓤ Unstaffed station
[ ] Station Operator Code

- Edinburgh Park 226
- Exeter 51
- Glasgow 225, 228
- Inverness 229
- Lancaster 65
- Larbert 230
- Leeds 26
- Liverpool 65
- Livingston 225, 226
- London 26, 65
- Manchester 65
- Manchester Airport 65
- Motherwell 225
- Newcastle 26
- Newcraighall 242
- North Berwick 238
- Oxenholme Lake District 65
- Oxford 51
- Paignton 51
- Penzance 51
- Perth 229
- Peterborough 26
- Plymouth 51
- Preston 65
- Reading 51
- Sheffield 26
- Southampton 51
- Stirling 230
- Torquay 51
- York 26

Haywards Heath [SN] [3] Ⓟ 🚲 ◇ ⚠ 🚕
- Bedford 52
- Brighton 186
- Clapham Junction 186
- Eastbourne 189
- East Croydon 186
- Gatwick Airport 186
- Hastings 189
- Hove 188
- Lewes 189
- London 186
- Littlehampton 188
- Luton 52, 186
- Portsmouth 188
- St Albans 52
- Seaford 189
- Southampton Central 188
- West Hampstead Thameslink 52
- Worthing 188

Hazel Grove [NT] Ⓟ 🚲 78, 82, 86
Headcorn [SE] Ⓟ ◇ ⚠ 🚕 207
Headingley [NT] Ⓟ Ⓤ 35
Headstone Lane [LO] ⚠ 60
Heald Green [NT] Ⓟ 🚲 82, 85
Healing [NT] Ⓤ 29
Heath High Level [AW] Ⓤ 130
Heath Low Level [AW] Ⓤ 130
Heathrow London Airport [HX] ◇ 🚕 117, 118, *Bus* 125A, *Bus* 158A
Heaton Chapel [NT] 🚲 84, 86
Hebden Bridge [NT] Ⓟ 🚲 ◇ 41
Heckington [EM] Ⓟ 🚲 Ⓤ 19
Hedge End [SW] Ⓟ 🚲 ◇ ⚠ 158
Hednesford [LM] Ⓟ ⚠ Ⓤ 70
Heighington [NT] Ⓟ Ⓤ 44
Helensburgh Central [SR] Ⓟ 🚲 ◇ 🚕 226
Helensburgh Pier *Ship* 219A
Helensburgh Upper [SR] 🚲 Ⓤ 227, *Sleepers* 404
Hellifield [NT] Ⓟ Ⓤ 36
Helmsdale [SR] Ⓟ 🚲 Ⓤ 239
Helsby [AW] Ⓟ Ⓤ 81, 109
Helston Coinagehall Street *Bus* 135A
Hemel Hempstead [LM] Ⓟ ◇ ⚠ 🚕 66, 176
Hendon [FC] Ⓟ 🚲 ◇ ⚠ 52
Hengoed [AW] Ⓟ Ⓤ 130
Henley-in-Arden [LM] Ⓟ ⚠ Ⓤ 71
Henley-on-Thames [GW] Ⓟ 🚲 🚕 121
Hensall [NT] Ⓤ 32
Hereford [AW] [7] Ⓟ 🚲 ◇ 🚕 71, 126, 131
Herne Bay [SE] Ⓟ 🚲 ◇ ⚠ 194, 212
Herne Hill [SE] [4] 🚲 ◇ ⚠ 52, 177, 179, 195
Hersham [SW] 🚲 ◇ ⚠ 155
Hertford East [LE] Ⓟ 🚲 ⚠ 🚕 22
Hertford North [FC] Ⓟ 🚲 ⚠ 🚕 24, 25
Hessle [NT] Ⓤ 29
Heswall [AW] Ⓟ Ⓤ 101
Hever [SN] Ⓟ 🚲 ⚠ Ⓤ 184
Heworth [NT] Ⓟ 🚲 🚕 Ⓤ 44
Hexham [NT] Ⓟ 🚲 ◇ 🚕 44, 48
Heyford [GW] Ⓟ Ⓤ 116
Heysham Port [NT] Ⓤ 98, 98A
High Brooms [SE] Ⓟ ◇ ⚠ 207
High Street (Glasgow) **[SR]** 226
High Wycombe [CH] [1] Ⓟ 🚲 ◇ ⚠ 🚕 115
Higham [SE] Ⓟ ◇ ⚠ 200
Highams Park [LE] Ⓟ 🚲 ⚠ 20
Highbridge & Burnham [GW] Ⓟ 🚲 Ⓤ 134
Highbury & Islington [LT] ⚠ 24, 59, 176
Hightown [ME] 🚲 ⚠ 103
Hildenborough [SE] Ⓟ 🚲 ◇ ⚠ 204
Hillfoot [SR] Ⓟ 🚲 🚕 Ⓤ 226
Hillington East [SR] 🚲 219
Hillington West [SR] 🚲 219
Hillside [ME] ⚠ 103
Hilsea [SW] ⚠ 156, 157, 158, 165, 188
Hinchley Wood [SW] 🚲 ◇ ⚠ 152
Hinckley [EM] Ⓟ ◇ 🚕 57
Hindley [NT] Ⓟ 82
Hinton Admiral [SW] Ⓟ 🚲 ◇ ⚠ 158
Hitchin [FC] [4] Ⓟ 🚲 ◇ ⚠ 🚕 24, 25
Hither Green [SE] [4] ◇ ⚠ 199, 200, 204
Hockley [LE] Ⓟ 🚲 ⚠ 🚕 5
Hollingbourne [SE] Ⓟ ⚠ Ⓤ 196
Holmes Chapel [NT] Ⓟ 🚲 84
Holmwood [SN] 🚲 ⚠ Ⓤ 182
Holsworthy *Bus* 135D
Holton Heath [SW] Ⓟ 🚲 ⚠ Ⓤ 158
Holyhead [AW] ◇ 🚕 65, 81, 81A, 131
Holytown [SR] Ⓟ 🚲 Ⓤ 225, 226
Homerton [LO] 🚲 ⚠ 59
Honeybourne [GW] Ⓟ Ⓤ 126
Honiton [SW] Ⓟ 🚲 ◇ 🚕 160
Honley [NT] Ⓤ 34
Honor Oak Park [LO] 🚲 ⚠ 178
Hook [SW] Ⓟ 🚲 🚕 155
Hooton [ME] Ⓟ 🚲 ⚠ 106
Hope (Derbyshire) [NT] Ⓟ Ⓤ 78
Hope (Flintshire) [AW] Ⓤ 101
Hopton Heath [AW] Ⓤ 129
Horley [SN] [4] 🚲 ◇ ⚠ 186, 188
Hornbeam Park [NT] Ⓟ Ⓤ 35
Hornsey [FC] 🚲 ⚠ 24
Horsforth [NT] Ⓟ 🚲 ◇ 35
Horsham [SN] [4] Ⓟ 🚲 ◇ ⚠ 🚕 182, 186, 188
Horsley [SW] Ⓟ 🚲 ◇ ⚠ 🚕 152
Horton-in-Ribblesdale [NT] Ⓟ Ⓤ 36
Horwich Parkway [NT] Ⓟ 🚲 82
Hoscar [NT] Ⓤ 82
Hough Green [NT] Ⓟ 89
Hounslow [SW] Ⓟ 🚲 ◇ ⚠ 🚕 149
Hove [SN] [2] Ⓟ 🚲 ◇ ⚠ 🚕 123, 186, 188
Hoveton & Wroxham [LE] Ⓟ 🚲 🚕 Ⓤ 16
Howden [NT] Ⓟ 🚲 Ⓤ 29, 39
How Wood (Herts) **[LM]** Ⓤ 61
Howwood (Renfrewshire) **[SR]** Ⓟ 🚲 Ⓤ 221
Hoxton [LO] ⚠ 178
Hoylake [ME] Ⓟ 🚲 ⚠ 106
Hubberts Bridge [EM] Ⓤ 19
Hucknall [EM] Ⓟ Ⓤ 55
Huddersfield [TP] Ⓟ 🚲 ◇ 🚕
- Barnsley 34
- Bradford 41
- Brighouse 41
- Darlington 39
- Durham 39
- Halifax 41
- Hull 39
- Leeds 39
- Liverpool 39
- London 26
- Manchester 39
- Manchester Airport 39
- Meadowhall 34
- Middlesbrough 39

Station index and table numbers

10 Connection time
Ⓟ Station Car Park
🚲 Bicycle storage facility
◇ Seat reservations can be made at this station
⚠ Penalty Fare Schemes in operation on some or all services from this station
🚕 Taxi rank or cab office at station, or signposted and within 100 metres
ⓤ Unstaffed station
[ ] Station Operator Code

Station index and table numbers

【10】 Connection time
Ⓟ Station Car Park
🚲 Bicycle storage facility
◇ Seat reservations can be made at this station
⚠ Penalty Fare Schemes in operation on some or all services from this station
🚕 Taxi rank or cab office at station, or signposted and within 100 metres
Ⓤ Unstaffed station
[ ] Station Operator Code

Keyham [GW] Ⓤ 135, 139
Keynsham [GW] Ⓟ 🚲 123, 132
Kidbrooke [SE] Ⓟ 🚲 ◇ ⚠ 200
Kidderminster [LM] Ⓟ ◇ ⚠ 🚕 71, 115
Kidsgrove [EM] Ⓟ ◇ 50, 67, 84
Kidwelly [AW] Ⓤ 128
Kilburn High Road [LO] ⚠ 60
Kilcreggan *Ship* 219A
Kildale [NT] Ⓟ Ⓤ 45
Kildonan [SR] Ⓟ 🚲 Ⓤ 239
Kilgetty [AW] Ⓤ 128
Kilmarnock [SR] 【3】 Ⓟ 🚲 ◇ 🚕 216, 218, 222
Kilmaurs [SR] Ⓟ 🚲 Ⓤ 222
Kilpatrick [SR] Ⓟ 🚲 Ⓤ 226
Kilwinning [SR] Ⓟ 🚲 🚕 218, 221
Kinbrace [SR] Ⓟ 🚲 Ⓤ 239
Kingham [GW] Ⓟ 🚲 126, *Bus* 126A
Kinghorn [SR] 🚲 242
Kings Cross [NR] (see London)
Kings Langley [LM] Ⓟ 🚲 🚕 66
Kings Lynn [FC] Ⓟ 🚲 ◇ ⚠ 🚕 17, *Bus* 17A
Kings Lynn Bus Station 🚕 *Bus* 26A
Kings Norton [LM] Ⓟ ◇ ⚠ 69
Kings Nympton [GW] Ⓟ Ⓤ 136
Kings Park [SR] 🚲 223
Kings Sutton [CH] ⚠ Ⓤ 115, 116
Kingsknowe [SR] 🚲 Ⓤ 225
Kingston [SW] ◇ ⚠ 🚕 149, 152
Kingswood [SN] Ⓟ ◇ ⚠ 181
Kingussie [SR] Ⓟ 🚲 229, *Sleepers* 403
Kintbury [GW] Ⓟ 🚲 Ⓤ 116
Kirby Cross [LE] 🚲 ⚠ Ⓤ 11
Kirkby [ME] Ⓟ ⚠ 🚕 82, 103
Kirkby in Ashfield [EM] Ⓟ Ⓤ 55
Kirkby-in-Furness [NT] Ⓤ 100
Kirkby Stephen [NT] Ⓟ Ⓤ 36
Kirkcaldy [SR] Ⓟ 🚲 ◇ 🚕
Aberdeen 229
Birmingham 51
Bournemouth 51
Bristol 51
Carlisle 51
Crewe *Sleepers* 402
Derby 51
Dundee 229
Edinburgh 242
Inverness 229
London 26, *Sleepers* 402
Newcastle 26
Oxford 51
Penzance 51
Perth 229
Plymouth 51
Preston 51, *Sleepers* 402
Reading 51
Sheffield 51
Southampton 51
York 26
Kirkconnel [SR] Ⓟ 🚲 Ⓤ 216
Kirkdale [ME] ⚠ 103
Kirkham & Wesham [NT] Ⓟ ◇ 82, 97
Kirk Sandall [NT] Ⓟ Ⓤ 29
Kirkhill [SR] Ⓟ 🚲 Ⓤ 223
Kirknewton [SR] Ⓟ 🚲 Ⓤ 225
Kirkoswald [NT] (see Lazonby)
Kirkwood [SR] Ⓤ 220
Kirton Lindsey [NT] Ⓟ Ⓤ 30
Kiveton Bridge [NT] Ⓤ 30
Kiveton Park [NT] Ⓟ 🚲 Ⓤ 30
Knaresborough [NT] Ⓟ Ⓤ 35
Knebworth [FC] Ⓟ 🚲 ⚠ 24, 25
Knighton [AW] Ⓤ 129
Knockholt [SE] Ⓟ ◇ ⚠ 204
Knottingley [NT] Ⓟ Ⓤ 32
Knucklas [AW] Ⓤ 129
Knutsford [NT] Ⓟ 88
Kyle of Lochalsh [SR] Ⓟ 🚲 ◇ 239, *Ship* 239B

L

Ladybank [SR] Ⓟ 🚲 51, 229
Ladywell [SE] 🚲 ◇ ⚠ 203
Laindon [CC] Ⓟ 🚲 ◇ ⚠ 🚕 1
Lairg [SR] Ⓟ 🚲 Ⓤ 239
Lake [IL] (IOW) Ⓤ 167
Lake District [VT] (see Oxenholme)
Lakenheath [LE] Ⓤ 17
Lamphey [AW] Ⓤ 128
Lanark [SR] Ⓟ 🚲 🚕 226
Lancaster [VT] 【6】 Ⓟ 🚲 ◇ 🚕
Aberdeen 65
Barrow-in-Furness 82
Birmingham 65
Blackpool 65
Bolton 82
Bournemouth 51
Bradford 36
Bristol 51
Carlisle 65
Chorley 82
Crewe 65
Douglas (IOM) 98A
Edinburgh 65
Exeter 51
Glasgow 65
Heysham Port 98
Leeds 36
Liverpool 65
London 65
Manchester 82
Manchester Airport 82
Millom 100
Milton Keynes Central 65
Morecambe 98
Oxenholme Lake District 65
Oxford 51
Paignton 51
Penzance 51
Plymouth 51
Preston 65
Reading 51
Skipton 36
Southampton 51
Stafford 65
Torquay 51
Warrington 65
Whitehaven 100
Wigan 65
Windermere 65
Workington 100
Lancing [SN] Ⓟ 🚲 ◇ ⚠ 🚕 188
Landywood [LM] Ⓟ ⚠ Ⓤ 70
Langbank [SR] Ⓟ 🚲 Ⓤ 219
Langho [NT] Ⓟ Ⓤ 94
Langley [GW] Ⓟ 🚲 ⚠ 🚕 117
Langley Green [LM] Ⓟ ⚠ 71
Langley Mill [EM] Ⓤ 34, 49, 53
Langside [SR] 🚲 Ⓤ 223
Langwathby [NT] Ⓤ 36
Langwith - Whaley Thorns [EM] Ⓤ 55
Lapford [GW] Ⓤ 136
Lapworth [CH] Ⓟ ⚠ Ⓤ 71, 115
Larbert [SR] Ⓟ 🚲 ◇ 🚕 229, 230
Largs [SR] Ⓟ 🚲 🚕 221
Larkhall [SR] 🚲 Ⓤ 226
Latimer [LT] (see Chalfont & Latimer)
Laurencekirk [SR] Ⓟ 🚲 Ⓤ 229
Lawrence Hill [GW] Ⓤ 133, 134
Layton [NT] Ⓟ Ⓤ 82, 97
Lazonby & Kirkoswald [NT] Ⓤ 36
Lea Green [NT] Ⓟ 🚲 90
Lea Hall [LM] Ⓟ ⚠ 68
Leagrave [FC] Ⓟ 🚲 ◇ ⚠ 🚕 52
Lealholm [NT] Ⓤ 45
Leamington Spa [CH] 【8】 Ⓟ 🚲 ◇ ⚠ 🚕 51, 71, 75, 115, 116
Leasowe [ME] Ⓟ ⚠ 106
Leatherhead [SN] Ⓟ 🚲 ◇ ⚠ 🚕 152, 182
Ledbury [LM] Ⓟ ⚠ Ⓤ 71, 126
Lee [SE] Ⓟ ◇ ⚠ 200
Leeds [NR] 【10】 Ⓟ 🚲 ◇ 🚕
Barnsley 34
Bedford 53
Birmingham 51
Birmingham International 51
Blackburn 41
Blackpool 41
Bournemouth 51
Bradford 37
Brighouse 41
Bristol 51
Burnley 41
Cambridge 26
Cardiff 51
Carlisle 36
Carnforth 36
Chesterfield 53

■10 Connection time
Ⓟ Station Car Park
🚲 Bicycle storage facility
◇ Seat reservations can be made at this station
⚠ Penalty Fare Schemes in operation on some or all services from this station
🚕 Taxi rank or cab office at station, or signposted and within 100 metres
® Unstaffed station
[ ] Station Operator Code

Station index and table numbers

Darlington 26
Derby 53
Dewsbury 39
Doncaster 31
Edinburgh 26
Exeter 51
Glasgow 26
Goole 32
Grantham 26
Halifax 41
Harrogate 35
Huddersfield 39, 41
Hull 39
Ilkley 38
Keighley 36
Knaresborough 35
Lancaster 36
Leicester 53
Liverpool 39, 41
London 26, 53
Luton 53
Manchester 39, 41
Manchester Airport 39
Meadowhall 31
Morecambe 36
Newark 26
Newcastle 26
Newport (South Wales) 51
Norwich 26
Nottingham 53
Oxford 51
Paignton 51
Penzance 51
Peterborough 26
Plymouth 51
Preston 41
Reading 51
Retford 26
Rochdale 41
Scarborough 39
Selby 40
Settle 36
Sheffield 31
Shipley 37
Skipton 36
Stansted Airport 26
Southampton 51
Torquay 51
Wakefield 31
Warrington 39
York 35, 40

Leicester [EM] Ⓟ 🚲 ◇ ⚠ 🚕 49, 53, 57
Leigh (Kent) [SN] ⚠ ® 186
Leigh-on-Sea [CC] Ⓟ 🚲 ◇ ⚠ 🚕 1
Leighton Buzzard [LM] Ⓟ 🚲 ◇ ⚠ 🚕 66, 176
Lelant [GW] Ⓟ ® 144
Lelant Saltings [GW] Ⓟ ® 144
Lenham [SE] Ⓟ ◇ ⚠ 196
Lenzie [SR] ■3 Ⓟ 🚲 🚕 228, 230
Leominster [AW] Ⓟ 131
Letchworth Garden City [FC] 🚲 ⚠ 🚕 24, 25
Leuchars [SR] ■3 Ⓟ 🚲 ◇ 🚕 26, 51, 229, *Sleepers* 402
Levenshulme [NT] 84, 86
Levisham [NY] 🚲 45
Lewes [SN] ■4 Ⓟ 🚲 ◇ ⚠ 🚕 186, 189
Lewisham [SE] ■4 Ⓟ 🚲 ◇ ⚠ 🚕
Bexleyheath 200
Dartford 200
Gillingham (Kent) 200
Gravesend 200
Hayes (Kent) 203
London 195, 199
Orpington 199, 204
Sidcup 200
Woolwich Arsenal 200

Leyland [NT] Ⓟ ◇ 🚕 82, 90
Leyton Midland Road [LO] 🚲 ⚠ 62
Leytonstone High Road [LO] 🚲 ⚠ 62
Lichfield City [LM] Ⓟ ◇ ⚠ 🚕 69
Lichfield Trent Valley [LM] Ⓟ ◇ ⚠ 65, 67, 69
Lidlington [LM] ® 64
Limehouse [CC] ⚠ 1
Lincoln [EM] Ⓟ 🚲 ◇ 🚕 18, 27, 30, 53
Lincoln [GR] 🚲 🚕
Lingfield [SN] Ⓟ 🚲 ◇ ⚠ 🚕 184
Lingwood [LE] Ⓟ 🚲 ® 15
Linlithgow [SR] Ⓟ 🚲 ◇ 228, 230
Liphook [SW] Ⓟ 🚲 ◇ ⚠ 🚕 156
Liskeard [GW] ■6 Ⓟ 🚲 ◇ 51, 135, 140, *Sleepers* 406
Lismore *Ship* 227B
Liss [SW] Ⓟ 🚲 ◇ ⚠ 156
Lisvane & Thornhill [AW] Ⓟ ® 130
Litherland [ME] (see Seaforth & Litherland)
Little Kimble [CH] ⚠ ® 115
Little Sutton [ME] ® 106
Littleborough [NT] Ⓟ 41
Littlehampton [SN] ■4 Ⓟ 🚲 ◇ ⚠ 🚕 188
Littlehaven [SN] ◇ ⚠ 186
Littleport [FC] 🚲 ⚠ ® 17
Liverpool
Central [ME] ■10 ⚠ 🚕
James Street [ME] ◇ ⚠
Lime Street (Main Line) **[NR]** ■10 Ⓟ 🚲 ◇ 🚕
Lime Street (Low Level) **[ME]** ■10 ◇ ⚠ 🚕
Moorfields [ME] ■10 ⚠
Aberdeen 65
Barrow-in-Furness 65
Birkenhead 106
Birmingham 65
Birmingham International 65
Blackpool 65, 90
Bolton 82
Cambridge 49
Carlisle 65
Chester 106
Coventry 65
Crewe 91
Darlington 39
Douglas (IOM) 98A
Dundee 65
Durham 39
Edinburgh 65
Ellesmere Port 106
Ely 49
Gatwick Airport 65
Glasgow 65
Hartford 91
Hooton 106
Huddersfield 39
Hull 39
Hunts Cross 89, 103
Inverness 65
Kirkby 103
Lancaster 65
Leeds 39
Liverpool South Parkway 91
London 65
Manchester 89, 90
Manchester Airport 89
Middlesbrough 39
Milton Keynes Central 65
Mossley Hill 91
Motherwell 65
New Brighton 106
Newcastle 39
Norwich 49
Nottingham 49
Nuneaton 65
Ormskirk 103
Oxenholme Lake District 65
Peterborough 49
Preston 90
Rhyl 81
Rochdale 95
Rock Ferry 106
Rugby 65
Runcorn 91
St Helens 90
Scarborough 39
Sheffield 89
Southport 103
Stafford 65
Stansted Airport 49
Stockport 89
Wakefield 39
Warrington 89, 90
Watford 65
West Kirby 106
Wigan 82, 90
Windermere 65
Wolverhampton 65
York 39

Liverpool Landing Stage *Ship* 98A
Liverpool South Parkway [ME] ■7 Ⓟ 🚲 ⚠ 🚕 39,49, 65, 89, 91, 103
Liverpool Street [NR] (see London)

Station index and table numbers

■10 Connection time
Ⓟ Station Car Park
🚲 Bicycle storage facility
◇ Seat reservations can be made at this station
⚠ Penalty Fare Schemes in operation on some or all services from this station
🚕 Taxi rank or cab office at station, or signposted and within 100 metres
Ⓤ Unstaffed station
[ ] Station Operator Code

Livingston North [SR] Ⓟ 🚲 Ⓤ 226
Livingston South [SR] Ⓟ 🚲 Ⓤ 225
Llanaber [AW] Ⓤ 75
Llanbedr [AW] Ⓤ 75
Llanbister Road [AW] Ⓤ 129
Llanbradach [AW] Ⓟ Ⓤ 130
Llandaf [AW] Ⓟ 130
Llandanwg [AW] Ⓤ 75
Llandecwyn [AW] Ⓤ 75
Llandeilo [AW] Ⓟ Ⓤ 129
Llandovery [AW] Ⓟ Ⓤ 129
Llandrindod [AW] Ⓟ ◇ 129
Llandudno [AW] ◇ 🚕 81, 102
Llandudno Junction [AW] Ⓟ ◇ 🚕 65, 81, 102, 131
Llandybie [AW] Ⓟ Ⓤ 129
Llanelli [AW] ◇ 128, 129
Llanfairfechan [AW] Ⓟ Ⓤ 81
Llanfairpwll [AW] Ⓟ Ⓤ 81
Llangadog [AW] Ⓤ 129
Llangammarch [AW] Ⓤ 129
Llangennech [AW] Ⓤ 129
Llangynllo [AW] Ⓤ 129
Llanharan [AW] Ⓟ Ⓤ 128
Llanhilleth [AW] Ⓟ Ⓤ 127
Llanishen [AW] Ⓟ Ⓤ 130
Llanrwst [AW] Ⓤ 102
Llansamlet [AW] Ⓟ Ⓤ 128
Llantwit Major [AW] Ⓟ 🚲 Ⓤ 130
Llanwrda [AW] Ⓤ 129
Llanwrtyd [AW] Ⓟ Ⓤ 129
Llwyngwril [AW] Ⓤ 75
Llwynypia [AW] Ⓟ Ⓤ 130
Loch Awe [SR] Ⓟ 🚲 Ⓤ 227
Loch Eil Outward Bound [SR] 🚲 Ⓤ 227
Lochailort [SR] Ⓟ 🚲 Ⓤ 227
Lochboisdale *Ship* 227C
Locheilside [SR] Ⓟ 🚲 Ⓤ 227
Lochgelly [SR] Ⓟ 🚲 Ⓤ 242
Lochluichart [SR] Ⓟ Ⓤ 239
Lochmaddy *Ship* 239B
Lochwinnoch [SR] Ⓟ 🚲 Ⓤ 221
Lockerbie [SR] Ⓟ 🚲 ◇ 🚕 51, 65
Lockwood [NT] Ⓟ Ⓤ 34
London
- **Blackfriars [FC]** ■3 ◇ ⚠ 🚕
- **Cannon Street [NR]** ■4 ◇ ⚠ 🚕
- **Charing Cross [NR]** ■4 ◇ ⚠ 🚕
- **City Thameslink [FC]** ■3 ◇ ⚠ 🚕
- **Euston [NR]** ■15 Ⓟ 🚲 ◇ ⚠ 🚕
- **Farringdon [LT]** ■3 ⚠
- **Fenchurch Street [NR]** ■7 ◇ ⚠ 🚕
- **Kings Cross [NR]** ■15 Ⓟ 🚲 ◇ ⚠ 🚕
- **Liverpool Street [NR]** ■15 🚲 ◇ ⚠ 🚕
- **London Bridge [NR]** ■4 🚲 ◇ ⚠ 🚕
- **Marylebone [CH]** ■10 🚲 ◇ ⚠ 🚕
- **Moorgate [LT]** ⚠
- **Paddington [NR]** ■15 Ⓟ 🚲 ◇ ⚠ 🚕
- **St Pancras International [NR]** ■15 Ⓟ ◇ ⚠ 🚕
- **Victoria [NR]** ■15 Ⓟ 🚲 ◇ ⚠ 🚕
- **Waterloo [NR]** ■15 Ⓟ 🚲 ◇ ⚠ 🚕
- **Waterloo East [SE]** ■4 ⚠

Aberdeen 26, *Sleepers* 402
Aldershot 149, 155
Alexandra Palace 24
Alnmouth 26
Alton 155
Amersham 114
Arbroath 26, *Sleepers* 402
Ascot 149
Ashford International 196, 207
Aviemore *Sleepers* 403
Aylesbury 114, 115
Balham 177, 178
Banbury 115, 116
Bangor (Gwynedd) 65
Barking 1
Barnsley 53
Barrow-in-Furness 65
Basingstoke 155, 158
Bath Spa 125, 160
Beckenham Junction 177, 195
Bedford 52
Belper 53
Berwick-upon-Tweed 26
Bexhill 189
Bicester 115, 116
Birmingham 66, 115, 116
Birmingham International 66
Bishops Stortford 22
Blackburn 97
Blackpool 65
Bletchley 66
Bodmin Parkway 135, *Sleepers* 406
Bognor Regis 188
Bourne End 120
Bournemouth 158
Bradford 26
Braintree 11
Brighton 186
Bristol 125, 160
Bromley North 204
Bromley South 195
Broxbourne 22
Camborne 135, *Sleepers* 406
Cambridge 22, 25
Canterbury 207, 212
Cardiff 125
Carlisle 65, *Sleepers* 400, 401
Carstairs 65, *Sleepers* 401
Carmarthen 128
Caterham 181
Chatham 200, 212
Chelmsford 11
Cheltenham Spa 125
Chertsey 149
Chessington 152
Chester 65
Chesterfield 53
Chichester 188
Chingford 20
Clacton-on-Sea 11
Clapton 20, 22
Cleethorpes 29
Colchester 11
Coventry 66
Crewe 65
Cromer 16
Crystal Palace 177, 178
Darlington 26
Dartford 200
Derby 53
Didcot 116
Doncaster 26, 53
Dorking 152, 182
Douglas (IOM) 98A
Dover 207, 212
Dundee 26, *Sleepers* 402
Durham 26
Eaglescliffe 26
Eastbourne 189
East Croydon 175
East Grinstead 184
Edinburgh 26, *Sleepers* 400
Effingham Junction 152
Ely 17
Enfield Town 21
Epsom 152, 182
Epsom Downs 182
Exeter 135, 160, *Sleepers* 406
Fareham 158, 188
Felixstowe 13
Finsbury Park 24, 25
Folkestone 207
Fort William *Sleepers* 404
Gatwick Airport 186
Gillingham (Kent) 200, 212
Glasgow 26, 65, *Sleepers* 401
Gloucester 125
Grantham 26
Gravesend 200
Grays 1
Great Yarmouth 15
Greenford 117
Grove Park 204
Guildford 152, 155, 156
Halifax 26
Hampton Court 152
Harrogate 26
Harrow (Sudbury Hill) 115
Harrow & Wealdstone 60, 66
Harrow-on-the-Hill 114
Hartlepool 26
Harwich 11
Haslemere 156
Hastings 189, 206
Hatfield 24

Station index and table numbers

10 Connection time
℗ Station Car Park
🚲 Bicycle storage facility
◇ Seat reservations can be made at this station
⚠ Penalty Fare Schemes in operation on some or all services from this station
🚕 Taxi rank or cab office at station, or signposted and within 100 metres
Ⓤ Unstaffed station
[ ] Station Operator Code

Station index and table numbers

10 Connection time
Ⓟ Station Car Park
🚲 Bicycle storage facility
◇ Seat reservations can be made at this station
⚠ Penalty Fare Schemes in operation on some or all services from this station
🚕 Taxi rank or cab office at station, or signposted and within 100 metres
Ⓤ Unstaffed station
[ ] Station Operator Code

London Heathrow Airport [HX] (see Heathrow Airport)
London Luton Airport (see also Luton Airport Parkway) 🚕 *Bus* 65B
London Southend Airport [LE] 5
London Road (Brighton) [SN] ◇ ⚠ 189
London Road (Guildford) [SW] Ⓟ 🚲 ◇ ⚠ 🚕 152
London Stansted Airport [LE] (see Stansted Airport)
Long Buckby [LM] Ⓟ 68
Long Eaton [EM] Ⓟ 🚲 ◇ ⚠ 53, 56, 57
Long Preston [NT] Ⓟ Ⓤ 36
Longbeck [NT] 🚲 Ⓤ 44
Longbridge [LM] ◇ ⚠ 69
Longcross [SW] ⚠ Ⓤ 149
Longfield [SE] Ⓟ ◇ ⚠ 🚕 212
Longniddry [SR] Ⓟ 🚲 Ⓤ 238
Longport [EM] Ⓟ Ⓤ 50, 84
Longton [EM] Ⓟ Ⓤ 50
Looe [GW] Ⓟ 🚲 Ⓤ 140
Lostock [NT] Ⓟ 82
Lostock Gralam [NT] Ⓟ Ⓤ 88
Lostock Hall [NT] Ⓟ Ⓤ 97
Lostwithiel [GW] Ⓟ Ⓤ 51,135, *Sleepers* 406
Loughborough [EM] Ⓟ 🚲 ◇ ⚠ 🚕 53
Loughborough Junction [FC] 🚲 ◇ ⚠ 52, 177, 179, 195
Lowdham [EM] Ⓟ Ⓤ 27
Lower Sydenham [SE] 🚲 ◇ ⚠ 203
Lowestoft [LE] Ⓟ 🚲 ◇ 🚕 13, 15
Ludlow [AW] Ⓟ ◇ 131
Luton [FC] **10** Ⓟ 🚲 ◇ ⚠ 🚕 52, *Bus* 52A, 53, *Bus* 65B
Luton Airport (see London Luton Airport)
Luton Airport Parkway [FC] **7** Ⓟ 🚲 ◇ ⚠ 🚕 52, 53, 177, 179, 186
Luxulyan [GW] Ⓟ Ⓤ 142
Lydney [AW] Ⓟ Ⓤ 132
Lye [LM] Ⓟ ⚠ 71
Lymington Pier [SW] 🚲 ⚠ Ⓤ 158
Lymington Town [SW] Ⓟ 🚲 ◇ ⚠ 158
Lympstone Commando [GW] Ⓤ 136
Lympstone Village [GW] Ⓟ 🚲 Ⓤ 136
Lytham [NT] Ⓤ 97

M

Macclesfield [VT] Ⓟ 🚲 ◇ 🚕 51, 65, 84
Machynlleth [AW] **4** Ⓟ ◇ 75
Maesteg [AW] Ⓟ Ⓤ 128, *Bus* 128A
Maesteg (Ewenny Road) [AW] Ⓤ 128
Maghull [ME] Ⓟ 🚲 ⚠ 🚕 103
Maidenhead [GW] **3** Ⓟ 🚲 ◇ ⚠ 🚕 116, 117, 120
Maiden Newton [GW] Ⓟ Ⓤ 123
Maidstone Barracks [SE] ⚠ Ⓤ 208
Maidstone East [SE] **4** Ⓟ ◇ ⚠ 🚕 196
Maidstone West [SE] **4** Ⓟ ◇ ⚠ 🚕 207, 208
Malden Manor [SW] Ⓟ 🚲 ◇ ⚠ 152
Mallaig [SR] 🚲 ◇ 227, *Ship* 227A
Malton [TP] Ⓟ 🚲 ◇ 🚕 39
Malvern Link [LM] Ⓟ ◇ ⚠ 71, 126
Manchester
Oxford Road [NT] ◇ 🚕
Piccadilly [NR] **10** Ⓟ 🚲 ◇ 🚕
Victoria [NT] ◇ 🚕
Aberdeen 65
Altrincham 88
Bangor (Gwynedd) 81
Barrow-in-Furness 82
Birmingham 65
Birmingham International 65
Blackpool 82
Bolton 82
Bournemouth 51
Bradford 41
Bristol 51
Burnley 97
Buxton 86
Cambridge 49
Cardiff 131
Carlisle 65
Carmarthen 128
Cheadle Hulme 84
Chester 81, 88
Chinley 78
Cleethorpes 29
Clitheroe 94
Coventry 65
Crewe 84
Darlington 39
Doncaster 29
Douglas (IOM) 98A
Dundee 65
Durham 39
Edinburgh 65
Exeter 51
Glasgow 65
Glossop 79
Grimsby 29
Guide Bridge 78
Hadfield 79
Heysham Port 98A
Holyhead 81
Huddersfield 39
Hull 29, 39
Inverness 65
Kirkby 82
Lancaster 82
Leeds 39, 41
Liverpool 89, 90
Liverpool South Parkway 89
Llandudno 81
London 65
Macclesfield 84
Manchester Airport 85
Marple 78
Middlesbrough 39
Milford Haven 128
Milton Keynes Central 65
Motherwell 65
Newcastle 39
New Mills 78, 86
Newport (South Wales) 131
Northwich 88
Nottingham 49
Oxenholme Lake District 65
Oxford 51
Paignton 51
Penzance 51
Peterborough 49
Plymouth 51
Preston 82
Reading 51
Rhyl 81
Rochdale 41
Rose Hill Marple 78
Rugby 65
St Helens 90
Salford 82
Scarborough 39
Sheffield 78
Shrewsbury 131
Southampton 51
Southport 82
Stafford 84
Stalybridge 39
Stansted Airport 49
Stockport 84
Stoke-on-Trent 84
Swansea 131
Tenby 128
Torquay 51
Wakefield 39
Warrington 89, 90
Watford 65
Wigan 82
Wilmslow 84
Windermere 82
Wolverhampton 65
York 39
Manchester Airport [TP] ◇
Bangor (Gwynedd) 81
Barrow-in-Furness 82
Birmingham 65

Station index and table numbers

[10] Connection time
Ⓟ Station Car Park
🚲 Bicycle storage facility
◇ Seat reservations can be made at this station
⚠ Penalty Fare Schemes in operation on some or all services from this station
🚕 Taxi rank or cab office at station, or signposted and within 100 metres
Ⓤ Unstaffed station
[ ] Station Operator Code

Birmingham International 65
Blackburn 94
Blackpool 82
Bolton 82
Carlisle 65
Coventry 65
Crewe 84
Darlington 39
Doncaster 29
Durham 39
Edinburgh 65
Glasgow 65
Huddersfield 39
Hull 29, 39
Holyhead 81
Lancaster 82
Leeds 39
Liverpool 89
London 65
Manchester 85
Middlesbrough 39
Motherwell 65
Newcastle 39
Oxenholme Lake District 82
Penrith North Lakes 65
Preston 82
St Helens 90
Salford 82
Scarborough 39
Sheffield 78
Southport 82
Stafford 65, 84
Wakefield 39
Warrington 89
Watford 65
Wigan 82
Wilmslow 84
Windermere 82
Wolverhampton 65
York 39

Manea [LE] Ⓤ 14, 17
Manningtree [LE] [2] Ⓟ 🚲 ⚠ 🚕 11, 14
Manor Park [LE] 🚲 ⚠ 5
Manor Road [ME] 🚲 ⚠ 106
Manorbier [AW] Ⓤ 128
Manors [NT] Ⓤ 48
Mansfield [EM] Ⓟ 🚲 🚕 55
Mansfield Woodhouse [EM] Ⓟ Ⓤ 55
March [LE] Ⓟ ◇ 🚕 14, 17, 49
Marden [SE] Ⓟ ◇ ⚠ 207
Margate [SE] [4] Ⓟ 🚲 ◇ ⚠ 🚕 194, 207, 212
Market Harborough [EM] Ⓟ 🚲 ◇ ⚠ 🚕 53
Market Rasen [EM] Ⓟ 🚲 Ⓤ 27
Markinch [SR] Ⓟ 🚲 🚕 51, 229
Marks Tey [LE] [2] Ⓟ 🚲 ⚠ 10, 11
Marlow [GW] 🚲 Ⓤ 120
Marple [NT] Ⓟ 🚲 78
Marsden [NT] Ⓟ Ⓤ 39
Marske [NT] 🚲 Ⓤ 44
Marston Green [LM] Ⓟ ◇ ⚠ 68
Martin Mill [SE] Ⓟ ⚠ 207
Martins Heron [SW] Ⓟ 🚲 ◇ ⚠ 149
Marton [NT] Ⓟ 🚲 Ⓤ 45
Maryhill [SR] 🚲 Ⓤ 232
Maryland [LE] 🚲 ⚠ 🚕 5
Marylebone [CH] (see London)
Maryport [NT] Ⓟ Ⓤ 100
Matlock [EM] Ⓟ Ⓤ 56
Matlock Bath [EM] Ⓟ Ⓤ 56
Mauldeth Road [NT] 85
Maxwell Park [SR] 🚲 Ⓤ 223
Maybole [SR] Ⓟ 🚲 Ⓤ 218
Maze Hill [SE] ◇ ⚠ 200
Meadowhall [NT] Ⓟ 🚲 ◇
Barnsley 34
Castleford 34
Cleethorpes 29
Doncaster 29
Gainsborough 30
Grimsby 29
Huddersfield 34
Hull 29
Leeds 31
Lincoln 30
Manchester 29
Manchester Airport 29
Penistone 34
Pontefract 33
Retford 30
Rotherham 29
Scunthorpe 29
Sheffield 29
Wakefield 31
Worksop 30
York 29, 33
Meldreth [FC] Ⓟ 🚲 ⚠ 25
Melksham [GW] Ⓟ Ⓤ 123
Melrose *Bus* 26K
Melton [LE] Ⓟ 🚲 🚕 Ⓤ 13
Melton Mowbray [EM] Ⓟ 🚲 ◇ 🚕 49, 53
Menheniot [GW] Ⓟ Ⓤ 135
Menston [NT] Ⓟ 🚲 ◇ 38
Meols [ME] Ⓟ 🚲 ⚠ 🚕 106
Meols Cop [NT] Ⓤ 82
Meopham [SE] Ⓟ ◇ ⚠ 🚕 212
Merryton [SR] 🚲 Ⓤ 226
Merstham [SN] Ⓟ 🚲 ◇ ⚠ 🚕 186
Merthyr Tydfil [AW] Ⓟ ◇ 130
Merthyr Vale [AW] Ⓤ 130
Metheringham [EM] Ⓟ 🚲 Ⓤ 18
Metrocentre [NT] Ⓤ 44, 48
Mexborough [NT] Ⓟ 🚲 ◇ 29
Micheldever [SW] Ⓟ 🚲 ◇ ⚠ 158
Micklefield [NT] Ⓟ 🚲 Ⓤ 40
Middlesbrough [TP] Ⓟ 🚲 ◇ 🚕 26, 39, 44, 45
Middlewood [NT] Ⓤ 86
Midgham [GW] Ⓟ Ⓤ 116
Milford Haven [AW] Ⓟ 🚕 Ⓤ 128
Milford (Surrey) [SW] Ⓟ 🚲 ⚠ 156
Millbrook (Bedfordshire) [LM] Ⓤ 64
Millbrook (Hants.) [SW] 🚲 ⚠ Ⓤ 158
Mill Hill Broadway [FC] Ⓟ 🚲 ◇ ⚠ 52
Mill Hill (Lancashire) [NT] Ⓤ 97
Milliken Park [SR] 🚲 Ⓤ 221
Millom [NT] Ⓟ Ⓤ 100
Mills Hill [NT] Ⓟ Ⓤ 41
Milngavie [SR] Ⓟ 🚲 226
Milton Keynes Central [LM] Ⓟ 🚲 ◇ ⚠ 🚕
Bedford *Bus* 65C
Bicester *Bus* 65A
Birmingham International 66
Birmingham New Street 66
Blackpool 65
Bletchley 66
Brighton 66
Buckingham *Bus* 65A
Cambridge *Bus* 65C
Coventry 66, 67
Crewe 65, 67
Edinburgh 65
Gatwick Airport 66
Glasgow 65
Lancaster 65
Liverpool 65
London 67
Luton *Bus* 65B
Luton Airport *Bus* 65B
Manchester 65
Northampton 66, 67
Oxenholme Lake District 65
Preston 65
Rugby 66, 67
St Neots *Bus* 65C
Stafford 65, 67
Stockport 65
Stoke-on-Trent 65, 67
Tring 66
Warrington 65
Watford Junction 66, 176, 177
Wembley Central 66, 176, 177
Wigan 65
Wolverhampton 66
Milton Keynes City Centre *Bus* 65B
Minehead Bancks Street *Bus* 135E
Minehead Butlins *Bus* 135E
Minehead Parade *Bus* 135E
Minffordd [AW] Ⓤ 75
Minster [SE] [4] Ⓟ ⚠ Ⓤ 207
Mirfield [NT] Ⓟ 🚲 Ⓤ 39, 41
Mistley [LE] 🚲 Ⓤ 11
Mitcham Eastfields [SN] ◇ ⚠ 52, 179, 182
Mitcham Junction [SN] Ⓟ 🚲 ◇ ⚠ 52, 179, 182
Mobberley [NT] Ⓤ 88
Monifieth [SR] 🚲 Ⓤ 229
Monks Risborough [CH] ⚠ Ⓤ 115
Montpelier [GW] 🚲 Ⓤ 133

Station index and table numbers

- **10** Connection time
- Ⓟ Station Car Park
- 🚲 Bicycle storage facility
- ◇ Seat reservations can be made at this station
- ⚠ Penalty Fare Schemes in operation on some or all services from this station
- 🚕 Taxi rank or cab office at station, or signposted and within 100 metres
- Ⓤ Unstaffed station
- [ ] Station Operator Code

Montrose [SR] Ⓟ 🚲 ◇ 🚕 26, 51, 229, *Sleepers* 402
Moorfields [ME] (see Liverpool)
Moorgate [LT] ⚠ 24
Moorside [NT] 82
Moorthorpe [NT] Ⓟ Ⓤ 31, 33
Morar [SR] Ⓟ 🚲 Ⓤ 227
Morchard Road [GW] Ⓟ Ⓤ 136
Morden (Herts) **[FC]** (see Ashwell & Morden)
Morden South [FC] ⚠ Ⓤ 52, 179
Morecambe [NT] Ⓟ 🚲 ◇ 36, 98, 98A
Moreton (Dorset) [SW] Ⓟ 🚲 Ⓤ 158
Moreton (Merseyside) [ME] 🚲 ⚠ 🚕 106
Moreton-in-Marsh [GW] Ⓟ 🚲 ◇ 126
Morfa Mawddach [AW] Ⓤ 75
Morley [NT] Ⓟ Ⓤ 39
Morpeth [NT] Ⓟ 🚲 ◇ 🚕 26, 48, 51
Mortimer [GW] Ⓟ 122
Mortlake [SW] Ⓟ 🚲 ◇ ⚠ 149
Moses Gate [NT] Ⓤ 82
Moss Side [NT] Ⓤ 97
Mossley (Greater Manchester) [NT] Ⓟ 🚲 39
Mossley Hill [NT] Ⓟ 89, 91
Mosspark [SR] 🚲 Ⓤ 217
Moston [NT] Ⓤ 41
Motherwell [SR] Ⓟ 🚲 ◇ 🚕
Birmingham 51, 65
Bournemouth 51
Bristol 51
Crewe 65
Cumbernauld 224
Darlington 26
Doncaster 26
Edinburgh 225
Exeter 51
Glasgow 225, 226
Liverpool 65
London 26, 65, *Sleepers* 401
Manchester 65
Manchester Airport 65
Newcastle 26
Oxenholme Lake District 65
Oxford 51
Paignton 51
Penzance 51
Peterborough 26
Plymouth 51
Reading 51
Southampton 51
Torquay 51
Watford 65, *Sleepers* 401
York 26
Motspur Park [SW] ◇ ⚠ 152
Mottingham [SE] Ⓟ ◇ ⚠ 200
Mottisfont & Dunbridge [GW] Ⓤ 158
Mouldsworth [NT] Ⓟ Ⓤ 88
Moulsecoomb [SN] ◇ ⚠ 189
Mount Florida [SR] 🚲 223
Mount Vernon [SR] 🚲 Ⓤ 220
Mountain Ash [AW] Ⓟ Ⓤ 130
Muck *Ship* 227A
Muir of Ord [SR] Ⓟ 🚲 Ⓤ 239
Muirend [SR] 🚲 223
Musselburgh [SR] Ⓟ 🚲 Ⓤ 238
Mytholmroyd [NT] Ⓤ 41

N

Nafferton [NT] Ⓤ 43
Nailsea & Backwell [GW] Ⓟ 🚲 134
Nairn [SR] Ⓟ 🚲 ◇ 🚕 240
Nantwich [AW] Ⓤ 131
Narberth [AW] Ⓤ 128
Narborough [EM] Ⓟ 57
National Exhibition Centre [VT] (see Birmingham International)
Navigation Road [NT] Ⓤ 88
Neath [AW] Ⓟ 🚲 ◇ 🚕 125, 128
Needham Market [LE] Ⓤ 11, 14
Neilston [SR] Ⓟ 🚲 🚕 223
Nelson [NT] Ⓟ 97
Neston [AW] Ⓟ Ⓤ 101
Netherfield [EM] Ⓤ 19
Nethertown [NT] Ⓟ Ⓤ 100
Netley [SW] Ⓟ 🚲 ◇ 165
New Barnet [FC] Ⓟ 🚲 ⚠ 24
New Beckenham [SE] **4** Ⓟ 🚲 ◇ ⚠ 203
New Brighton [ME] ⚠ 106
New Clee [NT] Ⓤ 29
New Cross [SE] **4** 🚲 ◇ ⚠ 178, 199, 200, 203, 204
New Cross Gate [LO] **4** 🚲 ⚠ 175, 178, 181, 182, 186
New Cumnock [SR] Ⓟ 🚲 Ⓤ 216
New Eltham [SE] Ⓟ ◇ ⚠ 200
New Haw [SW] (see Byfleet & New Haw)
New Holland [NT] 🚲 Ⓤ 29
New Hythe [SE] ⚠ Ⓤ 208
New Inn [AW] (see Pontypool and New Inn)
New Lane [NT] Ⓤ 82
New Malden [SW] **6** Ⓟ 🚲 ◇ ⚠ 🚕 152
New Mills Central [NT] 78
New Mills Newtown [NT] Ⓟ 🚲 86
New Milton [SW] Ⓟ 🚲 ◇ ⚠ 🚕 158
New Pudsey [NT] Ⓟ 🚲 ◇ 37, 41
New Southgate [FC] Ⓟ ⚠ 24
Newark Castle [EM] Ⓟ 🚲 Ⓤ 27
Newark North Gate [GR] **7** Ⓟ 🚲 ◇ 🚕 26, 27
Newbridge [AW] Ⓟ Ⓤ 127
Newbury [GW] Ⓟ 🚲 ◇ 🚕 116, 135
Newbury Racecourse [GW] Ⓤ 116
Newcastle [GR] **8** Ⓟ 🚲 ◇ 🚕
Aberdeen 26
Alnmouth 26
Arbroath 26
Berwick-upon-Tweed 26
Birmingham 51
Birmingham International 51
Bournemouth 51
Bradford 39
Bristol 51
Cambridge 26
Cardiff 51
Carlisle 48
Chathill 48
Darlington 26
Derby 51
Doncaster 26
Dundee 26
Edinburgh 26
Exeter 51
Glasgow 26, 216
Grantham 26
Haltwhistle 48
Hartlepool 44
Hexham 48
Huddersfield 39
Hull 26
Leeds 26
Liverpool 39
London 26
Manchester 39
Manchester Airport 39
MetroCentre 48
Middlesbrough 44
Morpeth 48
Newark 26
Newport (South Wales) 51
Northallerton 26
Norwich 26
Oxford 51
Paignton 51
Penzance 51
Peterborough 26
Plymouth 51
Preston 39
Reading 51
Retford 26
Sheffield 26
Southampton 51
Stansted Airport 26
Stockton 44
Sunderland 44
Torquay 51
Whitby 45
York 26
Newcraighall [SR] Ⓟ 🚲 Ⓤ 242
Newhaven Harbour [SN] ◇ Ⓤ 189
Newhaven Town [SN] 🚲 ⚠ 189
Newington [SE] Ⓟ ⚠ 212
Newmarket [LE] Ⓟ 🚲 Ⓤ 14
Newport (Essex) [LE] Ⓟ 🚲 ⚠ 22

Station index and table numbers

10 Connection time
Ⓟ Station Car Park
🚲 Bicycle storage facility
◇ Seat reservations can be made at this station
⚠ Penalty Fare Schemes in operation on some or all services from this station
🚕 Taxi rank or cab office at station, or signposted and within 100 metres
Ⓤ Unstaffed station
[ ] Station Operator Code

Station index and table numbers

■10 Connection time
Ⓟ Station Car Park
🚲 Bicycle storage facility
◇ Seat reservations can be made at this station
⚠ Penalty Fare Schemes in operation on some or all services from this station
🚕 Taxi rank or cab office at station, or signposted and within 100 metres
Ⓤ Unstaffed station
[ ] Station Operator Code

Nunhead [SE] ■4 ◇ ⚠ 52, 195, 200
Nunthorpe [NT] Ⓟ 🚲 Ⓤ 45
Nutbourne [SN] ⚠ Ⓤ 188
Nutfield [SN] ⚠ Ⓤ 186

O

Oakengates [LM] Ⓟ Ⓤ 74
Oakham [EM] Ⓟ ◇ 🚕 49, 53
Oakleigh Park [FC] ⚠ 🚕 24
Oban [SR] Ⓟ 🚲 ◇ 🚕 227, *Ship* 227B, 227C
Ockendon [CC] Ⓟ 🚲 ◇ ⚠ 🚕 1
Ockley [SN] Ⓟ ⚠ Ⓤ 182
Okehampton 136
Okehampton West Street *Bus* 135D
Old Hill [LM] Ⓟ ⚠ 71
Old Roan [ME] ⚠ 103
Old Street [LT] ⚠ 24
Oldfield Park [GW] 🚲 123, 132
Olton [LM] Ⓟ ⚠ 71
Ore [SN] Ⓤ 189, 206
Ormskirk [ME] Ⓟ 🚲 ◇ ⚠ 🚕 99, 103
Orpington [SE] ■4 Ⓟ ◇ ⚠ 🚕 195, 199, 204, 206, 207
Orrell [NT] Ⓤ 82
Orrell Park [ME] ⚠ 103
Orston [EM] (see Elton & Orston)
Oswaldtwistle [NT] (see Church & Oswaldtwistle)
Otford [SE] ■4 Ⓟ ◇ ⚠ 52, 195, 196
Oulton Broad North [LE] Ⓟ 🚲 Ⓤ 15
Oulton Broad South [LE] Ⓟ 🚲 Ⓤ 13
Oundle (Market Place) *Bus* 26B
Outwood [NT] Ⓟ 🚲 Ⓤ 31
Overpool [ME] Ⓤ 106
Overton [SW] Ⓟ 🚲 ◇ ⚠ 160
Oxenholme Lake District [VT] Ⓟ 🚲 ◇ 🚕 51, 65, 82, 83
Oxford [GW] Ⓟ 🚲 ◇ 🚕 51, 116,*Bus* 116B, 126
Oxford Frideswide Square *Bus* 116C
Oxshott [SW] Ⓟ 🚲 ◇ ⚠ 🚕 152
Oxted [SN] ■3 Ⓟ 🚲 ◇ ⚠ 🚕 184

P

Paddington [NR] (see London)
Paddock Wood [SE] ■4 Ⓟ 🚲 ◇ ⚠ 🚕 207, 208
Padgate [NT] Ⓟ Ⓤ 89
Padstow Old Rly Station *Bus* 135C
Paignton [GW] Ⓟ 🚲 ◇ 🚕 51, 135
Paisley Canal [SR] 🚲 Ⓤ 217
Paisley Gilmour Street [SR] Ⓟ 🚲 ◇ 🚕
Ayr 221
Ardrossan 221
Belfast *Catamaran/Ship* 218
Clyde Coast *Ship* 219A, 219B, 221A
Glasgow 219, 221
Gourock 219
Largs 221
Stranraer 218
Wemyss Bay 219
Paisley St James [SR] 🚲 Ⓤ 219
Palmers Green [FC] Ⓟ ⚠ 24
Pangbourne [GW] Ⓟ 🚲 116
Pannal [NT] Ⓟ 🚲 Ⓤ 35
Pantyffynnon [AW] Ⓤ 129
Par [GW] Ⓟ ◇ 51, 135, 142, *Sleepers* 406
Parbold [NT] 82
Park Street [LM] Ⓤ 61
Parkhouse [SR] (see Possilpark & Parkhouse)
Parkstone (Dorset) [SW] Ⓟ 🚲 ◇ 158
Parson Street [GW] Ⓤ 134
Partick [SR] 🚲 226
Parton [NT] Ⓟ Ⓤ 100
Patchway [GW] Ⓟ Ⓤ 132
Patricroft [NT] Ⓤ 90
Patterton [SR] Ⓟ 🚲 Ⓤ 223
Peartree [EM] Ⓤ 50
Peckham Rye [SN] ■4 🚲 ◇ ⚠ 52, 177, 178, 179, 195, 200
Pegswood [NT] Ⓤ 48
Pemberton [NT] Ⓤ 82
Pembrey & Burry Port [AW] Ⓟ Ⓤ 128
Pembroke [AW] Ⓟ Ⓤ 128
Pembroke Dock [AW] Ⓟ Ⓤ 128
Penally [AW] Ⓤ 128
Penarth [AW] Ⓟ ◇ 🚕 130
Pencoed [AW] Ⓟ Ⓤ 128
Pengam [AW] Ⓟ Ⓤ 130
Penge East [SE] Ⓟ 🚲 ◇ ⚠ 195
Penge West [LO] 🚲 ⚠ 178
Penhelig [AW] Ⓤ 75
Penistone [NT] Ⓟ 🚲 Ⓤ 34
Penketh [NT] (see Sankey for Penketh)
Penkridge [LM] Ⓟ Ⓤ 65, 68
Penmaenmawr [AW] Ⓤ 81
Penmere [GW] Ⓟ 🚲 Ⓤ 143
Penrhiwceiber [AW] Ⓤ 130
Penrhyndeudraeth [AW] Ⓟ 🚲 Ⓤ 75
Penrith North Lakes [VT] Ⓟ 🚲 ◇ 🚕 51, 65, *Bus* 65F
Penryn [GW] 🚲 Ⓤ 143
Pensarn (Gwynedd) **[AW]** Ⓤ 75
Penshurst [SN] ⚠ Ⓤ 186
Pentre-bach [AW] Ⓤ 130
Pen-y-bont [AW] Ⓟ Ⓤ 129
Penychain [AW] Ⓤ 75
Penyffordd [AW] Ⓟ Ⓤ 101
Penzance [GW] Ⓟ 🚲 ◇ 🚕 51, 135, 144, *Sleepers* 406
Perranwell [GW] Ⓟ 🚲 Ⓤ 143
Perry Barr [LM] ◇ ⚠ 70
Pershore [GW] Ⓟ 🚲 Ⓤ 126
Perth [SR] Ⓟ 🚲 ◇ 🚕 26, 65, 229, *Sleepers* 403
Peterborough [GR] ■8 Ⓟ 🚲 ◇ ⚠ 🚕
Aberdeen 26
Birmingham 49
Bradford 26
Cambridge 17
Corby George Street *Bus* 26B
Darlington 26
Dereham *Bus* 26A
Doncaster 26
Dundee 26
Edinburgh 26
Ely 17
Grantham 26
Grimsby 26
Hitchin 25
Hull 26
Huntingdon 25
Ipswich 17
Kettering Library *Bus* 26B
Kings Lynn *Bus* 26A
Leeds 26
Leicester 49
Lincoln 18, 26
Liverpool 49
London 14, 25
Manchester 49
March 17
Newark 26
Newcastle 26
Norwich 17
Nottingham 49
Nuneaton 49
Oundle (Market Place) *Bus* 26B
Retford 26
Sheffield 49
Spalding 18
Stansted Airport 49
Stevenage 25
Stockport 49
Swaffham *Bus* 26A
Wakefield 26
York 26
Petersfield [SW] Ⓟ 🚲 ◇ ⚠ 🚕 156
Petts Wood [SE] ■4 Ⓟ ◇ ⚠ 🚕 195, 199, 204
Pevensey & Westham [SN] Ⓟ 🚲 ⚠ 189
Pevensey Bay [SN] Ⓤ 189
Pewsey [GW] Ⓟ 🚲 ◇ ⚠ 135
Pickering [NY] Ⓟ 🚲 45
Pickering Eastgate *Bus* 26G
Pilning [GW] Ⓟ Ⓤ 132
Pinhoe [SW] Ⓤ 160

Station index and table numbers

[10] Connection time
Ⓟ Station Car Park
🚲 Bicycle storage facility
◇ Seat reservations can be made at this station
⚠ Penalty Fare Schemes in operation on some or all services from this station
🚕 Taxi rank or cab office at station, or signposted and within 100 metres
ⓤ Unstaffed station
[ ] Station Operator Code

Pitlochry [SR] Ⓟ 🚲 🚕 229, *Sleepers* 403
Pitsea [CC] Ⓟ 🚲 ◇ ⚠ 🚕 1
Pleasington [NT] Ⓟ ⓤ 97
Pleasure Beach [NT] (see Blackpool)
Plockton [SR] Ⓟ 🚲 ⓤ 239
Pluckley [SE] Ⓟ 🚲 ◇ ⚠ 207
Plumley [NT] Ⓟ ⓤ 88
Plumpton [SN] Ⓟ ◇ ⚠ 189
Plumstead [SE] ◇ ⚠ 200
Plymouth [GW] Ⓟ 🚲 ◇ ⚠ 🚕
Aberdeen 51
Birmingham 51, 135
Bristol 135
Cardiff 135
Carlisle 51
Crewe 51
Derby 51
Dundee 51
Edinburgh 51
Exeter 135
Glasgow 51
Gunnislake 139
Leeds 51
London 135, *Sleepers* 406
Manchester 51
Newcastle 51
Newton Abbot 135
Nottingham 51
Paignton 135
Penzance 135
Preston 51
Reading 135, *Sleepers* 406
Sheffield 51
Taunton 135
Torquay 135
Wolverhampton 51
York 51
Pokesdown [SW] 🚲 ◇ ⚠ 158
Polegate [SN] Ⓟ 🚲 ◇ ⚠ 🚕 189
Polesworth [LM] Ⓟ ⓤ 67
Pollokshaws East [SR] 🚲 ⓤ 223
Pollokshaws West [SR] 🚲 ⓤ 222
Pollokshields East [SR] 🚲 223
Pollokshields West [SR] 🚲 ⓤ 223
Polmont [SR] [3] Ⓟ 🚲 ◇ 🚕 228, 230
Polsloe Bridge [GW] ⓤ 136
Ponders End [LE] ⚠ 22
Pontarddulais [AW] Ⓟ ⓤ 129
Pontefract Baghill [NT] Ⓟ ⓤ 33
Pontefract Monkhill [NT] Ⓟ ⓤ 26, 31, 32
Pontefract Tanshelf [NT] Ⓟ ⓤ 32
Pontlottyn [AW] Ⓟ ⓤ 130
Pont-y-Pant [AW] ⓤ 102
Pontyclun [AW] Ⓟ ⓤ 128
Pontypool & New Inn [AW] Ⓟ ⓤ 131
Pontypridd [AW] [3] 🚲 ◇ 🚕 130
Poole [SW] [4] Ⓟ 🚲 ◇ ⚠ 🚕 158
Poppleton [NT] Ⓟ 🚲 ⓤ 35
Portchester [SW] 🚲 ⚠ 158, 165, 188
Port Glasgow [SR] 🚲 🚕 219
Porth [AW] Ⓟ ◇ 130
Porthmadog [AW] ⓤ 75
Portlethen [SR] Ⓟ 🚲 ⓤ 229
Portslade [SN] Ⓟ 🚲 ◇ ⚠ 188
Portsmouth Arms [GW] Ⓟ ⓤ 136
Portsmouth
Harbour [SW] 🚲 ◇ ⚠ 🚕
& Southsea [SW] Ⓟ 🚲 ◇ ⚠ 🚕
Bognor Regis 188
Brighton 188
Bristol 123
Cardiff 123
Chichester 188
Crawley 188
East Croydon 188
Exeter 160
Fareham 165
Gatwick Airport 188
Guildford 156
Haslemere 156
Havant 157
Horsham 188
Littlehampton 188
London 156, 158, 188
Reading
via Eastleigh 158
via Guildford 156
Redhill 188
Ryde 167
Salisbury 123
Sandown 167
Shanklin 167
Southampton Central 165
Winchester 158
Worthing 188
Port Sunlight [ME] 🚲 ⚠ 106
Port Talbot Parkway [AW] Ⓟ 🚲 ◇ 🚕 125, 128
Possilpark & Parkhouse [SR] 🚲 ⓤ 232
Potters Bar [FC] Ⓟ ◇ ⚠ 🚕 24, 25
Poulton-le-Fylde [NT] Ⓟ ◇ 🚕 41, 82, 97
Poynton [NT] Ⓟ 84
Prees [AW] ⓤ 131
Prescot [NT] Ⓟ 90
Prestatyn [AW] ◇ 🚕 ⓤ 81
Prestbury [NT] Ⓟ ⓤ 84
Preston [VT] [8] Ⓟ 🚲 ◇ 🚕
Aberdeen 65, *Sleepers* 402
Barrow-in-Furness 82
Birmingham 65
Birmingham International 65
Blackburn 97
Blackpool 97
Bolton 82
Bournemouth 51
Bradford 41
Bristol 51
Burnley 97
Carlisle 65
Chorley 82
Clitheroe 94, 97
Colne 97
Coventry 65
Crewe 65
Douglas (IOM) 98A
Dundee 65, *Sleepers* 402
Edinburgh 65
Exeter 51
Fort William *Sleepers* 404
Glasgow 65
Inverkeithing *Sleepers* 402
Inverness 65, *Sleepers* 403
Kirkcaldy *Sleepers* 402
Lancaster 65
Leeds 41
Liverpool 90
London 65
Manchester 82
Manchester Airport 82
Milton Keynes Central 65
Ormskirk 99
Oxenholme Lake District 65
Oxford 51
Paignton 51
Penzance 51
Perth 65, *Sleepers* 403
Plymouth 51
Reading 51
Rugby 65
Southampton 51
Stafford 65
Stirling *Sleepers* 403
Stockport 82
Torquay 51
Warrington 65
Watford 65
Wigan 65
Windermere 65
Wolverhampton 65
York 41
Preston Park [SN] ◇ ⚠ 52, 186, 188
Preston (Fishergate) *Bus* 65E
Prestonpans [SR] Ⓟ 🚲 ⓤ 238
Prestwick International Airport 🚕 ⓤ 218, 221
Prestwick Town [SR] Ⓟ 🚲 🚕 218, 221
Priesthill & Darnley [SR] 🚲 ⓤ 222
Princes Risborough [CH] [2] Ⓟ 🚲 ◇ ⚠ 🚕 115, 115A
Prittlewell [LE] Ⓟ 🚲 ⚠ 5
Prudhoe [NT] Ⓟ 🚲 ⓤ 48
Pulborough [SN] Ⓟ 🚲 ◇ ⚠ 🚕 188
Purfleet [CC] Ⓟ 🚲 ◇ ⚠ 1
Purley [SN] [4] Ⓟ ◇ ⚠ 🚕 175, 181, 186
Purley Oaks [SN] Ⓟ ⚠ 175, 181
Putney [SW] 🚲 ◇ ⚠ 149

Station index and table numbers

⟦10⟧ Connection time
Ⓟ Station Car Park
🚲 Bicycle storage facility
◇ Seat reservations can be made at this station
⚠ Penalty Fare Schemes in operation on some or all services from this station
🚕 Taxi rank or cab office at station, or signposted and within 100 metres
Ⓤ Unstaffed station
[ ] Station Operator Code

Pwllheli [AW] 🚲 🚕 75
Pyle [AW] Ⓟ 🚲 Ⓤ 128

Q

Quakers Yard [AW] Ⓤ 130
Queenborough [SE] Ⓟ ◇ ⚠ 212
Queens Park (Glasgow) **[SR]** 🚲 223
Queen's Park (London) **[LT]** 60
Queens Road, Peckham [SN] 🚲 ◇ ⚠ 177, 178, 179
Queen's Road, Walthamstow [LO] (see Walthamstow Queen's Road)
Queenstown Road (Battersea) [SW] ⚠ Ⓤ 149
Quintrell Downs [GW] Ⓤ 142

R

Radcliffe (Notts.) **[EM]** Ⓟ Ⓤ 19
Radlett [FC] Ⓟ 🚲 ◇ ⚠ 🚕 52
Radley [GW] Ⓟ Ⓤ 116
Radyr [AW] ⟦3⟧ Ⓟ 🚲 ◇ 130
Rainford [NT] Ⓟ Ⓤ 82
Rainham (Essex) **[CC]** Ⓟ 🚲 ◇ ⚠ 1
Rainham (Kent) [SE] Ⓟ ◇ ⚠ 🚕 194, 212
Rainhill [NT] 90
Ramsgate [SE] ⟦4⟧ Ⓟ 🚲 ◇ ⚠ 🚕 194, 207, 212
Ramsgreave & Wilpshire [NT] Ⓟ Ⓤ 94
Rannoch [SR] Ⓟ 🚲 Ⓤ 227, *Sleepers* 404
Rauceby [EM] Ⓤ 19
Ravenglass for Eskdale [NT] Ⓤ 100
Ravensbourne [SE] ◇ ⚠ 52, 195
Ravensthorpe [NT] Ⓤ 39
Rawcliffe [NT] Ⓤ 32
Rayleigh [LE] Ⓟ 🚲 ⚠ 🚕 5
Raynes Park [SW] ⟦6⟧ 🚲 ◇ ⚠ 🚕 152
Reading [GW] ⟦7⟧ Ⓟ 🚲 ◇ ⚠ 🚕
- Aberdeen 51
- Ascot 149
- Banbury 116
- Basingstoke 122
- Bath Spa 125
- Birmingham 116
- Bodmin Parkway 135, *Sleepers* 406
- Bournemouth 158
- Bristol 125
- Camborne 135, *Sleepers* 406
- Cardiff 125
- Carlisle 51
- Cheltenham Spa 125
- Clapham Junction 149
- Coventry 51
- Crewe 51
- Derby 51
- Didcot 116
- Dundee 51
- Edinburgh 51
- Exeter 135, *Sleepers* 406
- Gatwick Airport 148
- Glasgow 51
- Gloucester 125
- Guildford 148
- Hayle 135, *Sleepers* 406
- Heathrow Airport *Bus* 125A
- Henley-on-Thames 121
- Hereford 126
- Leamington Spa 116
- Leeds 51
- Liskeard 135, *Sleepers* 406
- London 116, 117, 149
- Lostwithiel 135, *Sleepers* 406
- Manchester 51
- Milford Haven 128
- Moreton-in-Marsh 126
- Newbury 116
- Newcastle 51
- Newport (South Wales) 125
- Newton Abbot 135, *Sleepers* 406
- Oxford 116
- Paignton 135
- Par 135, *Sleepers* 406
- Penzance 135, *Sleepers* 406
- Plymouth 135, *Sleepers* 406
- Poole 158
- Portsmouth
  - via Basingstoke 158
  - via Guildford 156
- Preston 51
- Redhill 148
- Redruth 135, *Sleepers* 406
- Rosslare Harbour 128
- Sheffield 51
- Slough 117
- Southampton 158
- St Austell 135, *Sleepers* 406
- St Erth 135, *Sleepers* 406
- Staines 149
- Swansea 125
- Swindon 125
- Taunton 135
- Torquay 135
- Truro 135, *Sleepers* 406
- Wallingford *Bus* 116A
- Weston-super-Mare 125
- Weymouth 158
- Winchester 158
- Wolverhampton 51
- Worcester 126
- York 51

Reading West [GW] ⟦3⟧ 116, 122
Rectory Road [LE] ⚠ 21
Redbridge [SW] Ⓟ ⚠ Ⓤ 158
Redcar British Steel [NT] Ⓤ 44
Redcar Central [NT] Ⓟ 🚲 ◇ 🚕 44
Redcar East [NT] 🚲 Ⓤ 44
Reddish North [NT] Ⓟ 🚲 78
Reddish South [NT] Ⓤ 78
Redditch [LM] Ⓟ ◇ ⚠ 69
Redhill [SN] Ⓟ 🚲 ◇ ⚠ 🚕 148, 186, 188
Redland [GW] 🚲 Ⓤ 133
Redruth [GW] Ⓟ 🚲 ◇ 🚕 51, 135, *Sleepers* 406
Reedham (Norfolk) [LE] Ⓟ 🚲 Ⓤ 15
Reedham (Surrey) **[SN]** ⚠ 181
Reigate [SN] Ⓟ 🚲 ◇ ⚠ 148, 186
Renton [SR] 🚲 Ⓤ 226
Retford [GR] ⟦10⟧ Ⓟ 🚲 ◇ 🚕 26, 30
Rhiwbina [AW] Ⓤ 130
Rhoose Cardiff Int. Airport [AW] Ⓟ 🚲 Ⓤ 130
Rhosneigr [AW] Ⓤ 81
Rhyl [AW] ◇ 🚕 81
Rhymney [AW] ⟦3⟧ Ⓟ 🚕 Ⓤ 130
Ribblehead [NT] Ⓟ Ⓤ 36
Rice Lane [ME] ⚠ 103
Richmond (Greater London) **[SW]** Ⓟ 🚲 ◇ ⚠ 🚕 59, 149
Richmond (Market) 🚕 *Bus* 26H
Rickmansworth [LT] Ⓟ 🚲 ⚠ 114
Riddlesdown [SN] 🚲 ◇ ⚠ 184
Ridgmont [LM] Ⓤ 64
Riding Mill [NT] Ⓟ 🚲 Ⓤ 48
Risca & Pontymister [AW] Ⓟ Ⓤ 127
Rishton [NT] Ⓟ 🚲 Ⓤ 97
Robin Hood Airport 🚕 *Bus* 26F
Robertsbridge [SE] Ⓟ ◇ ⚠ 206
Roby [NT] 90
Rochdale [NT] Ⓟ ◇ 🚕 41, 82
Roche [GW] Ⓤ 142
Rochester [SE] ⟦4⟧ Ⓟ ◇ ⚠ 🚕 194, 200, 212
Rochford [LE] Ⓟ 🚲 ⚠ 🚕 5
Rock Ferry [ME] Ⓟ 🚲 ◇ ⚠ 🚕 106
Rogart [SR] Ⓟ 🚲 Ⓤ 239
Rogerstone [AW] Ⓟ Ⓤ 127
Rolleston [EM] Ⓤ 27
Roman Bridge [AW] Ⓤ 102
Romford [LE] 🚲 ◇ ⚠ 🚕 4, 5, 11
Romiley [NT] Ⓟ 🚲 78
Romsey [GW] Ⓟ 🚲 123, 158
Roose [NT] Ⓟ Ⓤ 82
Rose Grove [NT] Ⓤ 97
Rose Hill Marple [NT] Ⓟ 🚲 ◇ 78
Rosslare Harbour *Ship* 128
Rosyth [SR] Ⓟ Ⓤ 242
Rotherham Central [NT] Ⓟ ◇ 🚕 29, 31, 33
Rotherhithe [LO] ⚠ 178
Rothesay *Ship* 219B
Roughton Road [LE] 🚲 Ⓤ 16

Station index and table numbers

〔10〕 Connection time
Ⓟ Station Car Park
🚲 Bicycle storage facility
◇ Seat reservations can be made at this station
⚠ Penalty Fare Schemes in operation on some or all services from this station
🚕 Taxi rank or cab office at station, or signposted and within 100 metres
Ⓤ Unstaffed station
[ ] Station Operator Code

Rowlands Castle [SW] Ⓟ 🚲 ◇ ⚠ 156
Rowley Regis [LM] Ⓟ ◇ ⚠ 71, 115
Roy Bridge [SR] 🚲 Ⓤ 227, *Sleepers* 404
Roydon [LE] Ⓟ ⚠ 22
Royston [FC] Ⓟ 🚲 ◇ ⚠ 🚕 25
Ruabon [AW] Ⓟ Ⓤ 75
Rufford [NT] Ⓟ Ⓤ 99
Rugby [VT] Ⓟ 🚲 ◇ 🚕 65, 66, 67, 68
Rugeley Town [LM] Ⓟ Ⓤ 70
Rugeley Trent Valley [LM] Ⓤ 67, 70
Ruislip [CH] (see South and West Ruislip)
Rum *Ship* 227A
Runcorn [VT] Ⓟ 🚲 ◇ 🚕 65, 91
Runcorn East [AW] Ⓟ 81
Ruskington [EM] Ⓟ 🚲 Ⓤ 18
Ruswarp [NT] Ⓤ 45
Rutherglen [SR] 🚲 226
Ryde Esplanade [IL] ◇ 🚕 167
Ryde Pier Head [IL] Ⓟ 🚲 ◇ 167
Ryde St. Johns Road [IL] Ⓟ 🚲 Ⓤ 167
Ryder Brow [NT] Ⓤ 78
Rye [SN] Ⓟ ⚠ 🚕 189
Rye House [LE] ⚠ 22

S

St Albans [FC] Ⓟ 🚲 ◇ ⚠ 🚕 52, 186
St Albans Abbey [LM] Ⓟ Ⓤ 61
St Andrews Bus Station *Bus* 229
St Andrews Road [GW] Ⓟ 🚲 Ⓤ 133
St Annes-on-the-Sea [NT] Ⓟ ◇ 🚕 97
St Austell [GW] Ⓟ 🚲 ◇ 🚕 51, 135, *Bus* 135B, *Sleepers* 406
St Bees [NT] Ⓟ Ⓤ 100
St Budeaux Ferry Road [GW] Ⓤ 135, 139
St Budeaux Victoria Road [GW] Ⓤ 139
St Columb Road [GW] Ⓟ Ⓤ 142
St Denys [SW] Ⓟ 🚲 ◇ ⚠ 158, 165
St Erth [GW] Ⓟ ◇ 51, 135, 144, *Sleepers* 406
St Germans [GW] Ⓤ 135
St Helens Central [NT] Ⓟ ◇ 🚕 90
St Helens Junction [NT] Ⓟ 90
St Helier (Surrey) **[FC]** 🚲 ⚠ Ⓤ 52, 179
St Ives [GW] Ⓟ Ⓤ 144
St James' Park [GW] Ⓤ 136
St James Street [LE] 🚲 ⚠ 20
St Johns [SE] ◇ ⚠ 199, 200, 203, 204
St Keyne Wishing Well Halt [GW] Ⓤ 140
St Leonards Warrior Square [SE] 〔4〕 Ⓟ ◇ ⚠ 🚕 189, 206
St Margarets (Herts.) [LE] Ⓟ ⚠ 🚕 22
St Margarets (Greater London) **[SW]** 🚲 ◇ ⚠ 🚕 149
St Mary Cray [SE] Ⓟ ◇ ⚠ 52, 195, 196, 212
St Michaels [ME] Ⓟ ⚠ 103
St Neots [FC] Ⓟ 🚲 ⚠ 🚕 25
St Neots Cambridge Street *Bus* 65C
St Neots Square *Bus* 65C
St Pancras International (see London)
Salford Central [NT] 82, 94
Salford Crescent [NT] 82, 94
Salfords [SN] ◇ ⚠ 186
Salhouse [LE] Ⓟ 🚲 Ⓤ 16
Salisbury [SW] Ⓟ 🚲 ◇ ⚠ 🚕 123, 158, 160
Saltaire [NT] Ⓤ 36
Saltash [GW] Ⓟ 🚲 Ⓤ 135
Saltburn [NT] Ⓤ 44
Saltcoats [SR] Ⓟ 🚲 🚕 221
Saltmarshe [NT] Ⓟ Ⓤ 29
Salwick [NT] Ⓤ 97
Sampford Courtenay Ⓤ 136
Sandal & Agbrigg [NT] Ⓟ 🚲 Ⓤ 31
Sandbach [NT] Ⓟ 🚲 84
Sanderstead [SN] Ⓟ ◇ ⚠ 🚕 184
Sandhills [ME] ⚠ 103
Sandhurst [GW] Ⓤ 148
Sandling [SE] Ⓟ ◇ ⚠ 207
Sandown [IL] Ⓟ 🚲 Ⓤ 167
Sandplace [GW] Ⓤ 140
Sandringham Norwich Gates *Bus* 17A
Sandringham Visitor Centre *Bus* 17A
Sandwell & Dudley [LM] Ⓟ 🚲 ◇ ⚠ 🚕 66, 68, 74
Sandwich [SE] Ⓟ ◇ ⚠ 207
Sandy [FC] Ⓟ 🚲 ⚠ 25
Sankey for Penketh [NT] Ⓟ 89
Sanquhar [SR] Ⓟ 🚲 Ⓤ 216
Sarn [AW] Ⓟ Ⓤ 128
Saundersfoot [AW] Ⓤ 128
Saunderton [CH] Ⓟ 🚲 ⚠ Ⓤ 115
Sawbridgeworth [LE] Ⓟ ⚠ 22
Saxilby [EM] Ⓟ 🚲 Ⓤ 18, 30
Saxmundham [LE] Ⓟ 🚲 Ⓤ 13
Scarborough [TP] Ⓟ 🚲 ◇ 🚕 26, 39, 43
Scotscalder [SR] Ⓟ 🚲 Ⓤ 239
Scotstounhill [SR] Ⓟ 🚲 226
Scrabster *Ship* 239A
Scunthorpe [TP] Ⓟ ◇ 🚕 29
Sea Mills [GW] 🚲 Ⓤ 133
Seaford [SN] Ⓟ 🚲 ◇ ⚠ 🚕 189
Seaforth & Litherland [ME] ⚠ 🚕 103
Seaham [NT] Ⓟ Ⓤ 44
Seamer [TP] Ⓟ Ⓤ 39, 43
Seascale [NT] Ⓟ Ⓤ 100
Seaton Carew [NT] Ⓟ 🚲 Ⓤ 44
Seer Green [CH] Ⓟ 🚲 ⚠ 115
Selby [TP] Ⓟ 🚲 ◇ 🚕 26, 29, 39, 40, 41
Selhurst [SN] 〔4〕 🚲 ◇ ⚠ 176, 177
Selkirk *Bus* 65G
Sellafield [NT] Ⓟ Ⓤ 100
Selling [SE] Ⓟ ⚠ Ⓤ 212
Selly Oak [LM] Ⓟ 🚲 ◇ ⚠ 69
Settle [NT] Ⓟ ◇ 36
Seven Kings [LE] 🚲 ⚠ 5
Seven Sisters [LE] ⚠ 21, 22
Sevenoaks [SE] 〔4〕 Ⓟ ◇ ⚠ 🚕 52, 195, 204, 206, 207
Severn Beach [GW] 🚲 Ⓤ 133
Severn Tunnel Junction [AW] Ⓟ 🚲 ◇ 123, 132
Shadwell [LO] ⚠ 178
Shalford [GW] Ⓟ Ⓤ 148
Shanklin [IL] Ⓟ 🚲 ◇ 🚕 167
Shawford [SW] Ⓟ 🚲 Ⓤ 158
Shawlands [SR] 🚲 Ⓤ 223
Sheerness-on-Sea [SE] 🚲 ◇ ⚠ 🚕 212
Sheffield [EM] 〔7〕 Ⓟ 🚲 ◇ ⚠ 🚕
Barnsley 34
Birmingham 51
Bournemouth 51
Bristol 51
Cambridge 49
Cardiff 51
Chesterfield 53
Cleethorpes 29
Darlington 26
Derby 53
Doncaster 29
Edinburgh 26
Exeter 51
Glasgow 26
Goole 29
Grimsby 29
Huddersfield 34
Hull 29
Leeds 31
Leicester 53
Lincoln 30
Liverpool 89
London 53
Luton 53
Manchester 78
Manchester Airport 78
Meadowhall 29, 35
Newcastle 26
New Mills 78
Newport (South Wales) 51
Norwich 49
Nottingham 53
Oxford 51

Station index and table numbers

■10 Connection time
Ⓟ Station Car Park
🚲 Bicycle storage facility
◇ Seat reservations can be made at this station
⚠ Penalty Fare Schemes in operation on some or all services from this station
🚕 Taxi rank or cab office at station, or signposted and within 100 metres
Ⓤ Unstaffed station
[ ] Station Operator Code

Paignton 51
Penistone 34
Penzance 51
Peterborough 49
Plymouth 51
Reading 51
Retford 30
Rotherham 29
Scunthorpe 29
Southampton 51
Stockport 78
Torquay 51
Wakefield 31
Warrington 89
York 29
Shelford [LE] ⚠ 22
Shenfield [LE] ■3 Ⓟ 🚲 ◇ ⚠ 🚕 5, 11
Shenstone [LM] Ⓟ ⚠ 69
Shepherd's Bush [LO] ⚠ 66, 176, 177
Shepherds Well [SE] Ⓟ ⚠ 212
Shepley [NT] Ⓤ 34
Shepperton [SW] Ⓟ 🚲 ◇ ⚠ 🚕 152
Shepreth [FC] Ⓟ 🚲 ⚠ Ⓤ 25
Sherborne [SW] Ⓟ 🚲 ◇ 🚕 160
Sherburn-in-Elmet [NT] Ⓤ 33
Sheringham [LE] Ⓟ 🚲 Ⓤ 16
Shettleston [SR] Ⓟ 🚲 🚕 226
Shieldmuir [SR] 🚲 Ⓤ 226
Shifnal [LM] Ⓟ Ⓤ 74
Shildon [NT] Ⓤ 44
Shiplake [GW] Ⓟ Ⓤ 121
Shipley [NT] Ⓟ 🚲 ◇ 26, 36, 37, 38
Shippea Hill [LE] Ⓟ Ⓤ 17
Shipton [GW] Ⓤ 126
Shirebrook [EM] Ⓤ 55
Shirehampton [GW] Ⓟ 🚲 Ⓤ 133
Shireoaks [NT] Ⓤ 30
Shirley [LM] Ⓟ 🚲 ◇ ⚠ 71
Shoeburyness [CC] Ⓟ 🚲 ◇ ⚠ 🚕 1
Sholing [SW] 🚲 ⚠ Ⓤ 165
Shoreditch High Street [LO] ⚠ 178
Shoreham (Kent) [SE] Ⓟ ⚠ Ⓤ 52, 195
Shoreham-by-Sea (Sussex) **[SN]** Ⓟ 🚲 ◇ ⚠ 🚕 188
Shortlands [SE] ■4 Ⓟ 🚲 ◇ ⚠ 52, 195
Shotton [AW] Ⓟ 🚕 81
Shotton High Level [AW] Ⓟ 🚕 101
Shotts [SR] Ⓟ 🚲 225
Shrewsbury [AW] Ⓟ ◇ 🚕
Aberystwyth 75
Bangor (Gwynedd) 131
Barmouth 75
Birmingham 74
Cardiff 131
Chester 75, 131
Crewe 131
Hereford 131
Holyhead 131
Llandudno Junction 131
Llandrindod 129
Llanelli 129
Machynlleth 75
Manchester 131
Newport (South Wales) 131
Pwllheli 75
Swansea 129
Telford Central 74
Whitchurch (Salop) 131
Wrexham 75
Wolverhampton 74
Sidcup [SE] ■4 Ⓟ ◇ ⚠ 🚕 200
Sileby [EM] ⚠ Ⓤ 53
Silecroft [NT] Ⓤ 100
Silsden [NT] (see Steeton & Silsden)
Silkstone Common [NT] Ⓟ Ⓤ 34
Silverdale [NT] Ⓤ 82
Silver Street [LE] ⚠ 21
Singer [SR] 🚲 🚕 226
Sittingbourne [SE] ■4 Ⓟ ◇ ⚠ 🚕 194, 212
Skegness [EM] 🚲 ◇ 🚕 19
Skewen [AW] Ⓟ Ⓤ 128
Skipton [NT] Ⓟ 🚲 ◇ 🚕 26, 36
Slade Green [SE] ■4 Ⓟ ◇ ⚠ 200
Slaithwaite [NT] Ⓟ Ⓤ 39
Slateford [SR] 🚲 Ⓤ 225
Sleaford [EM] Ⓟ 🚲 ◇ 🚕 18, 19
Sleights [NT] Ⓟ Ⓤ 45
Slough [GW] ■3 Ⓟ 🚲 ◇ ⚠ 🚕 116, 117, 119, 125, 135
Small Heath [LM] ⚠ 71
Smallbrook Junction [IL] Ⓤ 167
Smethwick Galton Bridge [LM] ■7 ◇ ⚠ 68, 71, 74, 75
Smethwick Rolfe Street [LM] ⚠ 68
Smitham (Coulsdon Town) [SN] Ⓟ ⚠ 181
Smithy Bridge [NT] Ⓟ Ⓤ 41
Snaith [NT] Ⓟ Ⓤ 32
Snodland [SE] Ⓟ ⚠ 🚕 Ⓤ 208
Snowdown [SE] ⚠ Ⓤ 212
Sole Street [SE] Ⓟ ◇ ⚠ 212
Solihull [LM] Ⓟ 🚲 ◇ ⚠ 71, 115
Somerleyton [LE] Ⓟ 🚲 Ⓤ 15
South Acton [LO] 🚲 ⚠ 59
South Bank [NT] 🚲 Ⓤ 44
South Bermondsey [SN] ◇ ⚠ 177, 178, 179
South Croydon [SN] ■4 Ⓟ ◇ ⚠ 175, 176, 181, 184
South Elmsall [NT] Ⓟ 🚲 Ⓤ 31
South Greenford [GW] Ⓤ 117
South Gyle [SR] Ⓟ 🚲 Ⓤ 242
South Hampstead [LO] ⚠ 60
South Kenton [LT] 60
South Merton [FC] ⚠ Ⓤ 52, 179
South Milford [NT] Ⓟ Ⓤ 39, 40
South Ruislip [CH] Ⓟ 🚲 ⚠ 🚕 115
South Tottenham [LO] ⚠ 62
South Wigston [EM] Ⓤ 57
South Woodham Ferrers [LE] Ⓟ 🚲 🚕 5
Southall [GW] ⚠ 117
Southampton Airport Parkway [SW] Ⓟ 🚲 ◇ ⚠ 🚕 51, 158
Southampton Central [SW] Ⓟ 🚲 ◇ ⚠ 🚕
Aberdeen 51
Basingstoke 158
Bath Spa 123
Birmingham 51
Bognor Regis 188
Bournemouth 158
Brighton 188
Bristol 123
Brockenhurst 158
Cardiff 123
Carlisle 51
Chichester 188
Clapham Junction 158, 188
Crawley 188
Crewe 51
Derby 51
Dorchester 158
Dundee 51
East Croydon 188
Eastleigh 158
Edinburgh 51
Exeter 160
Fareham 165, 188
Gatwick Airport 188
Glasgow 51
Havant 165, 188
Horsham 188
Leeds 51
Littlehampton 188
London 158, 188
Lymington Pier 158
Manchester 51
Newcastle 51
Newport (South Wales) 123
Oxford 51
Poole 158
Portsmouth 165
Preston 51
Reading 158
Redhill 188
Romsey 123
Ryde 167
Salisbury 123
Shanklin 167
Sheffield 51
Swindon 123
Westbury (Wilts.) 123
Weymouth 158
Winchester 158
Woking 158
Wolverhampton 51
Worthing 188
Yarmouth (IOW) 158
Yeovil 160

Station index and table numbers

[10] Connection time
Ⓟ Station Car Park
🚲 Bicycle storage facility
◇ Seat reservations can be made at this station
⚠ Penalty Fare Schemes in operation on some or all services from this station
🚕 Taxi rank or cab office at station, or signposted and within 100 metres
Ⓤ Unstaffed station
[ ] Station Operator Code

York 51
Southbourne [SN] ◇ ⚠ 188
Southbury [LE] ⚠ 21
Southease [SN] Ⓤ 189
Southend Central [CC] Ⓟ 🚲 ◇ ⚠ 🚕 1
Southend East [CC] Ⓟ 🚲 ◇ ⚠ 1
Southend Victoria [LE] 🚲 ◇ ⚠ 🚕 5
Southminster [LE] Ⓟ 🚲 Ⓤ 5
Southport [ME] 🚲 ◇ ⚠ 🚕 82, 103
Southsea [SW] (see Portsmouth & Southsea)
Southwick [SN] 🚲 ◇ ⚠ 188
Sowerby Bridge [NT] Ⓟ 🚲 Ⓤ 41
Sowton [GW] (see Digby & Sowton)
Spalding [EM] Ⓟ 🚲 🚕 18
Spean Bridge [SR] Ⓟ 🚲 Ⓤ 227, *Sleepers* 404
Spital [ME] 🚲 ⚠ 106
Spondon [EM] ⚠ Ⓤ 56
Spooner Row [LE] Ⓤ 17
Spring Road [LM] ⚠ 71
Springburn [SR] 🚲 224, 226
Springfield [SR] 🚲 Ⓤ 229
Squires Gate [NT] Ⓤ 97
Stafford [VT] Ⓟ 🚲 ◇ 🚕
Bangor (Gwynedd) 65
Birmingham 68
Blackpool 65
Bournemouth 51
Bristol 51
Carlisle 65
Chester 65
Coventry 67, 68
Crewe 65
Edinburgh 65
Exeter 51
Glasgow 65
Holyhead 65
Lichfield 67
Liverpool 65
London 65
Manchester 84
Manchester Airport 84
Nuneaton 67
Oxenholme Lake District 65
Oxford 51
Paignton 51
Penzance 51
Plymouth 51
Preston 65
Reading 51
Rugby 65
Southampton 51
Stockport 84
Stoke-on-Trent 65, 68A
Tamworth 67
Torquay 51
Watford 65
Wolverhampton 68
Staines [SW] Ⓟ 🚲 ◇ ⚠ 🚕 149
Stainforth [NT] (see Hatfield & Stainforth)
Stallingborough [NT] Ⓤ 29
Stalybridge [TP] Ⓟ 🚲 ◇ 39
Stamford [EM] Ⓟ ◇ 49
Stamford Hill [LE] ⚠ 21
Stanford-le-Hope [CC] Ⓟ 🚲 ◇ ⚠ 1
Stanlow & Thornton [NT] Ⓤ 109
Stansted Airport [LE] 🚲 ◇ ⚠ 🚕 17, 22, 26, 49
Stansted Mountfitchet [LE] Ⓟ 🚲 ⚠ 🚕 22
Staplehurst [SE] Ⓟ 🚲 ◇ ⚠ 🚕 207
Stapleton Road [GW] 🚲 Ⓤ 133, 134
Starbeck [NT] 🚲 Ⓤ 35
Starcross [GW] 🚲 Ⓤ 135
Staveley [TP] Ⓤ 83
Stechford [LM] ⚠ 68
Steeton & Silsden [NT] Ⓟ 🚲 Ⓤ 36
Stepps [SR] Ⓟ 🚲 Ⓤ 224
Stevenage [FC] [4] Ⓟ 🚲 ◇ ⚠ 🚕 24, 25, 26
Stevenston [SR] 🚲 Ⓤ 221
Stewartby [LM] Ⓤ 64
Stewarton [SR] Ⓟ 🚲 Ⓤ 222
Stirling [SR] Ⓟ 🚲 ◇ 🚕 26, 229, 230, *Sleepers* 403
Stockport [VT] Ⓟ 🚲 ◇ 🚕
Altrincham 88
Birmingham 65
Birmingham International 65
Blackpool 82
Bolton 82
Bournemouth 51
Bristol 51
Buxton 86
Cambridge 49
Cardiff 131
Chester 88
Coventry 65
Crewe 84
Doncaster 29
Ely 49
Exeter 51
Hazel Grove 86
Hull 29
Liverpool 89
London 65
Macclesfield 84
Manchester 84
Newport (South Wales) 131
Northwich 88
Norwich 49
Nottingham 49
Oxford 51
Paignton 51
Penzance 51
Peterborough 49
Plymouth 51
Preston 82
Reading 51
Rugby 65
Salford Crescent 82
Sheffield 78
Southampton 51
Stafford 84
Stoke-on-Trent 84
Torquay 51
Watford 65
Wigan 82
Wolverhampton 65
Stocksfield [NT] Ⓟ 🚲 Ⓤ 48
Stocksmoor [NT] Ⓟ 🚲 Ⓤ 34
Stockton [NT] 🚲 🚕 Ⓤ 44
Stoke d'Abernon [SW] (see Cobham)
Stoke Mandeville [CH] Ⓟ 🚲 ⚠ 114
Stoke Newington [LE] ⚠ 21
Stoke-on-Trent [VT] Ⓟ 🚲 ◇ 🚕 50, 51, 65, 67, 84
Stone [LM] 67
Stone Crown Street *Bus* 67
Stone Granville Square *Bus* 67
Stone Crossing [SE] ◇ ⚠ 200
Stonebridge Park [LT] 60
Stonegate [SE] Ⓟ 🚲 ◇ ⚠ 206
Stonehaven [SR] Ⓟ 🚲 ◇ 26, 51, 229, *Sleepers* 402
Stonehouse [GW] Ⓟ 125
Stoneleigh [SW] 🚲 ◇ ⚠ 152
Stornoway *Ship* 239B
Stourbridge Junction [LM] [2] Ⓟ ◇ ⚠ 71, 72, 115
Stourbridge Town [LM] ⚠ 72
Stowmarket [LE] Ⓟ 🚲 ◇ 🚕 11, 14
Stranraer [SR] 🚲 ◇ 218
Stranraer Harbour *Ship and Catamaran* 218
Stratford (London) **[LE]** [7] ⚠ 🚕
Barking 1
Basildon 1
Bishops Stortford 22
Braintree 11
Broxbourne 22
Bury St. Edmunds 14
Cambridge 14
Chelmsford 11
Cheshunt 22
Clacton-on-Sea 11
Colchester 11
Ely 14
Gospel Oak 59, 176
Hackney 59
Harlow 22
Harwich 11
Hertford East 22
Highbury & Islington 59, 176
Ilford 5
Ipswich 11
London 5
Manningtree 11
Norwich 11
Peterborough 14
Richmond 59

Station index and table numbers

❿ Connection time
Ⓟ Station Car Park
🚲 Bicycle storage facility
◇ Seat reservations can be made at this station
⚠ Penalty Fare Schemes in operation on some or all services from this station
🚕 Taxi rank or cab office at station, or signposted and within 100 metres
Ⓤ Unstaffed station
[ ] Station Operator Code

Romford 5
Shenfield 5
Shoeburyness 1
Southend 1, 5
Southminster 5
Stansted Airport 22
Stowmarket 11
Tottenham Hale 22
Upminster 1
Walton-on-the-Naze 11
West Hampstead 59, 176
Wickford 5
Willesden Junction 59
Witham 11
Stratford International [SE] ⚠ 194, 196, 200, 207, 212
Stratford-upon-Avon [LM] Ⓟ 🚲 ◇ ⚠ 🚕 71, 115
Strathcarron [SR] Ⓟ 🚲 Ⓤ 239
Strawberry Hill [SW] 🚲 ◇ ⚠ 149, 152
Streatham [SN] ❹ ◇ ⚠ 52, 177, 179
Streatham Common [SN] ❹ Ⓟ 🚲 ◇ ⚠ 176, 177
Streatham Hill [SN] ◇ ⚠ 🚕 177, 178
Streatley [GW] (see Goring & Streatley)
Streethouse [NT] Ⓟ Ⓤ 32
Strines [NT] Ⓟ Ⓤ 78
Stromeferry [SR] Ⓟ 🚲 Ⓤ 239
Stromness 🚕 *Ship* 239A
Strood [SE] ❹ Ⓟ 🚲 ◇ ⚠ 🚕 194, 200, 208, 212
Stroud [GW] Ⓟ 🚲 ◇ 🚕 125
Sturry [SE] ⚠ 207
Styal [NT] Ⓟ Ⓤ 84
Sudbury (Suffolk) **[LE]** 🚲 Ⓤ 10
Sudbury & Harrow Road [CH] ⚠ Ⓤ 115
Sudbury Hill Harrow [CH] ⚠ Ⓤ 115
Sugar Loaf [AW] Ⓤ 129
Summerston [SR] Ⓤ 232
Sunbury [SW] Ⓟ 🚲 ◇ ⚠ 152
Sunderland [NT] ◇ 🚕 26, 44, 48
Sundridge Park [SE] Ⓟ ◇ ⚠ 204
Sunningdale [SW] Ⓟ 🚲 ◇ ⚠ 🚕 149
Sunnymeads [SW] ⚠ Ⓤ 149
Surbiton [SW] ❻ Ⓟ 🚲 ◇ ⚠ 🚕 152, 155
Surrey Quays [LO] ⚠ 178
Sutton Coldfield [LM] Ⓟ 🚲 ◇ ⚠ 69
Sutton Common [FC] ⚠ Ⓤ 52, 179
Sutton Parkway [EM] Ⓟ Ⓤ 55
Sutton (Surrey) [SN] ❹ Ⓟ 🚲 ◇ ⚠ 🚕 52, 179, 182
Swaffham *Bus* 26A
Swale [SE] ⚠ Ⓤ 212
Swalecliffe [SE] (see Chestfield & Swalecliffe)
Swanley [SE] ❹ Ⓟ ◇ ⚠ 🚕 52, 195, 196, 212
Swanscombe [SE] ◇ ⚠ 200
Swansea [AW] Ⓟ 🚲 ◇ 🚕
Bristol 128
Cardiff 128
Camarthen 128
Crewe 131
Derby 57
Fishguard Harbour 128
Gloucester 57
Hereford 131
Llandrindod 129
London 125, 128
Manchester 128, 131
Pembroke Dock 128
Portsmouth 128
Reading 125, 128
Rosslare Harbour 128
Shrewsbury 129
Slough 125
Tenby 128
Swanwick [SW] Ⓟ 🚲 ◇ ⚠ 🚕 165, 188
Sway [SW] Ⓟ 🚲 ◇ ⚠ 158
Swaythling [SW] Ⓟ 🚲 ◇ ⚠ 158
Swinderby [EM] Ⓤ 27
Swindon [GW] Ⓟ 🚲 ◇ ⚠ 🚕 123, 125
Swineshead [EM] Ⓤ 19
Swinton (Gtr. Manchester) **[NT]** 82
Swinton (S. Yorks.) [NT] Ⓟ 🚲 ◇ 29, 31, 33
Sydenham [LO] Ⓟ ◇ ⚠ 🚕 178
Sydenham Hill [SE] Ⓟ ⚠ 195
Syon Lane [SW] 🚲 ⚠ Ⓤ 149
Syston [EM] Ⓟ ⚠ Ⓤ 53

T

Tackley [GW] Ⓤ 116
Tadworth [SN] ◇ ⚠ 181
Taffs Well [AW] ❸ Ⓟ Ⓤ 130
Tain [SR] Ⓟ Ⓤ 239
Talsarnau [AW] Ⓤ 75
Talybont [AW] Ⓤ 75
Tal-y-Cafn [AW] Ⓤ 102
Tame Bridge Parkway [LM] Ⓟ 🚲 ◇ ⚠ 70, 75
Tamworth [LM] Ⓟ ◇ 🚕 51, 57, 65, 67
Taplow [GW] Ⓟ 🚲 ⚠ 🚕 117
Tarbert *Ship* 239B
Tattenham Corner [SN] Ⓟ ◇ ⚠ 181
Taunton [GW] Ⓟ 🚲 ◇ ⚠ 🚕 51, 134, 135, *Bus* 135E
Taynuilt [SR] Ⓟ 🚲 Ⓤ 227
Teddington [SW] 🚲 ◇ ⚠ 149, 152
Tees-side Airport [NT] Ⓤ 44
Teignmouth [GW] Ⓟ 🚲 ◇ 🚕 51, 135
Telford Central [LM] Ⓟ ◇ 🚕 74, 75
Templecombe [SW] Ⓟ 🚲 ◇ 160
Tenby [AW] Ⓟ Ⓤ 128
Tewkesbury [GW] (see Ashchurch)
Teynham [SE] Ⓟ ◇ ⚠ 212
Thame [CH] (see Haddenham & Thame Parkway)
Thames Ditton [SW] 🚲 ⚠ 152
Thatcham [GW] Ⓟ 🚲 116, 135
Thatto Heath [NT] Ⓟ 90
The Hawthorns [LM] Ⓟ ⚠ 71
The Lakes (Warwickshire) **[LM]** ⚠ Ⓤ 71
Theale [GW] Ⓟ 🚲 116, 135
Theobalds Grove [LE] ⚠ 21
Thetford [LE] Ⓟ ◇ 🚕 17, 49
Thirsk [TP] Ⓟ ◇ 26, 39
Thornaby [TP] Ⓟ 🚲 ◇ 🚕 39, 44
Thorne North [NT] Ⓟ 🚲 29
Thorne South [NT] Ⓟ Ⓤ 29
Thornford [GW] Ⓤ 123
Thornhill [AW] (see Lisvane)
Thornliebank [SR] 🚲 Ⓤ 222
Thornton (Ches.) **[NT]** (see Stanlow & Thornton)
Thornton (Fife) **[SR]** (see Glenrothes With Thornton)
Thornton Abbey [NT] Ⓤ 29
Thorntonhall [SR] 🚲 Ⓤ 222
Thornton Heath [SN] 🚲 ◇ ⚠ 🚕 176, 177
Thorpe Bay [CC] Ⓟ 🚲 ◇ ⚠ 🚕 1
Thorpe Culvert [EM] Ⓟ Ⓤ 19
Thorpe-le-Soken [LE] ❶ Ⓟ 🚲 ⚠ 11
Three Bridges [SN] ❹ Ⓟ 🚲 ◇ ⚠ 🚕 52, 186, 188
Three Oaks [SN] Ⓤ 189
Thurgarton [EM] Ⓤ 27
Thurnscoe [NT] Ⓟ Ⓤ 31
Thurso [SR] Ⓟ 🚲 ◇ 🚕 239, *Ship* 239A
Thurston [LE] Ⓟ 🚲 Ⓤ 14
Tilbury Riverside [CC] Ⓤ *Bus* 1A
Tilbury Town [CC] ❸ 🚲 ◇ ⚠ 1, *Bus* 1A
Tile Hill [LM] Ⓟ ⚠ 68
Tilehurst [GW] Ⓟ 🚲 116
Tipton [LM] Ⓟ ⚠ 68
Tiree *Ship* 227B
Tir-phil [AW] Ⓟ Ⓤ 130
Tisbury [SW] Ⓟ 🚲 ◇ 160
Tiverton Parkway [GW] Ⓟ 🚲 ◇ ⚠ 🚕 51, 135
Todmorden [NT] Ⓟ 🚲 🚕 41
Tolworth [SW] Ⓟ 🚲 ◇ ⚠ 🚕 152
Tonbridge [SE] ❹ Ⓟ 🚲 ◇ ⚠ 🚕 186, 204, 206, 207, 208

■10 Connection time
Ⓟ Station Car Park
🚲 Bicycle storage facility
◇ Seat reservations can be made at this station
⚠ Penalty Fare Schemes in operation on some or all services from this station
🚕 Taxi rank or cab office at station, or signposted and within 100 metres
Ⓤ Unstaffed station
[ ] Station Operator Code

Station index and table numbers

Ton Pentre [AW] Ⓤ 130
Tondu [AW] Ⓟ Ⓤ 128
Tonfanau [AW] Ⓤ 75
Tonypandy [AW] Ⓤ 130
Tooting [FC] ◇ ⚠ 52, 179
Topsham [GW] Ⓟ 🚲 Ⓤ 136
Torquay [GW] Ⓟ 🚲 ◇ 🚕 51, 135
Torre [GW] Ⓟ Ⓤ 135
Totley [NT] (see Dore & Totley)
Totnes [GW] Ⓟ 🚲 ◇ ⚠ 🚕 51, 135, *Sleepers* 406
Tottenham Hale [LE] ⚠ 🚕 22
Tottenham South [LO] (see South Tottenham)
Totton [SW] Ⓟ 🚲 ◇ ⚠ 158
Town Green [ME] Ⓟ ⚠ 103
Trafford Park [NT] 🚕 Ⓤ 89
Treforest [AW] Ⓟ ◇ 130
Treforest Estate [AW] Ⓤ 130
Trehafod [AW] Ⓟ Ⓤ 130
Treherbert [AW] Ⓤ 130
Treorchy [AW] Ⓟ Ⓤ 130
Trimley [LE] Ⓟ 🚲 Ⓤ 13
Tring [LM] Ⓟ 🚲 ⚠ 🚕 66, 176
Troed-y-rhiw [AW] Ⓤ 130
Troon [SR] Ⓟ 🚲 🚕 218, 221
Trowbridge [GW] Ⓟ 🚲 ◇ 🚕 123, 160
Truro [GW] Ⓟ 🚲 ◇ 🚕 51, 135, 143, *Sleepers* 406
Tulloch [SR] Ⓟ 🚲 Ⓤ 227, *Sleepers* 404
Tulse Hill [SN] ■3 ◇ ⚠ 52, 177, 179, 182
Tunbridge Wells [SE] ■4 Ⓟ 🚲 ◇ ⚠ 🚕 206
Turkey Street [LE] ⚠ 21
Tutbury & Hatton [EM] Ⓤ 50
Twickenham [SW] Ⓟ 🚲 ◇ ⚠ 149
Twyford [GW] ■3 Ⓟ 🚲 ⚠ 🚕 116, 117, 121
Ty Croes [AW] Ⓤ 81
Ty Glas [AW] Ⓤ 130
Tygwyn [AW] Ⓟ Ⓤ 75
Tyndrum Lower [SR] Ⓟ 🚲 Ⓤ 227
Tyndrum Upper [SR] (see Upper Tyndrum)
Tyseley [LM] ⚠ 71
Tywyn [AW] 🚲 Ⓤ 75

U

Uckfield [SN] Ⓟ 🚲 ◇ ⚠ 184
Uddingston [SR] Ⓟ 🚲 🚕 225, 226
Uig *Ship* 239B
Ulceby [NT] Ⓤ 29
Ullapool *Ship* 239B
Ulleskelf [NT] Ⓤ 33, 40
Ulverston [TP] ◇ 82
Umberleigh [GW] Ⓟ Ⓤ 136
University [LM] ◇ ⚠ 69, 71
Uphall [SR] Ⓟ 🚲 Ⓤ 226
Upholland [NT] Ⓤ 82
Upminster [CC] Ⓟ 🚲 ◇ ⚠ 🚕 1, 4
Upper Halliford [SW] ◇ ⚠ 152
Upper Holloway [LO] ⚠ 62
Upper Tyndrum [SR] Ⓟ 🚲 Ⓤ 227, *Sleepers* 404
Upper Warlingham [SN] Ⓟ 🚲 ◇ ⚠ 🚕 184
Upton [AW] Ⓤ 101
Upwey [SW] Ⓟ 🚲 ⚠ Ⓤ 123, 158
Urmston [NT] Ⓟ 🚲 89
Uttoxeter [EM] Ⓟ Ⓤ 50

V

Valley [AW] Ⓟ Ⓤ 81
Vauxhall (London) **[SW]** ◇ ⚠ 149, 152, 155
Victoria [NR] (see London)
Virginia Water [SW] Ⓟ 🚲 ◇ ⚠ 🚕 149

W

Waddon [SN] ◇ ⚠ 182
Wadebridge Bus Station *Bus* 135C
Wadhurst [SE] Ⓟ ◇ ⚠ 206
Wainfleet [EM] Ⓟ 🚲 Ⓤ 19
Wakefield
Kirkgate [NT] ■4 Ⓟ 🚲 Ⓤ
Westgate [GR] ■7 Ⓟ 🚲 ◇ 🚕
Barnsley 34
Bedford 53
Birmingham 51
Bournemouth 51
Bristol 51
Cambridge 26
Derby 53
Doncaster 31
Exeter 51
Huddersfield 39
Knottingley 32
Leeds 31
Leicester 53
Liverpool 39
London 26, 53
Luton 53
Manchester 39
Manchester Airport 39
Meadowhall 31
Newquay 51
Norwich 26
Nottingham 53
Paignton 51
Penzance 51
Plymouth 51
Pontefract 32
Sheffield 31
Southampton 51
Torquay 51
Wakes Colne [LE] (see Chappel & Wakes Colne)
Walkden [NT] 82
Wallasey Grove Road [ME] Ⓟ ⚠ 106
Wallasey Village [ME] ⚠ 106
Wallingford Market Place *Bus* 116A
Wallingford Town Hall *Bus* 116A
Wallington [SN] Ⓟ ◇ ⚠ 🚕 182
Wallyford [SR] Ⓟ 🚲 Ⓤ 238
Walmer [SE] Ⓟ ◇ ⚠ 🚕 207
Walsall [LM] ◇ ⚠ 70
Walsden [NT] Ⓤ 41
Waltham Cross [LE] Ⓟ ⚠ 🚕 22
Walthamstow Central [LE] Ⓟ 🚲 ⚠ 🚕 20
Walthamstow Queen's Road [LO] 🚲 ⚠ 62
Walton (Merseyside) [ME] ⚠ 103
Walton-on-the-Naze [LE] 🚲 ⚠ 11
Walton-on-Thames [SW] Ⓟ 🚲 ◇ ⚠ 🚕 155
Wanborough [SW] ⚠ Ⓤ 148, 149
Wandsworth Common [SN] Ⓟ 🚲 ◇ ⚠ 🚕 176, 177, 178
Wandsworth Road [SN] ⚠ Ⓤ 176, 178
Wandsworth Town [SW] 🚲 ◇ ⚠ 149
Wanstead Park [LO] 🚲 ⚠ 62
Wapping [LO] ⚠ 178
Warblington [SN] ⚠ Ⓤ 188
Ware [LE] Ⓟ 🚲 ⚠ 🚕 22
Wareham [SW] Ⓟ 🚲 ◇ ⚠ 🚕 158
Wargrave [GW] Ⓟ 🚲 Ⓤ 121
Warminster [GW] Ⓟ 🚲 ◇ 🚕 123, 160
Warnham [SN] ⚠ Ⓤ 182
Warrington
Bank Quay [VT] Ⓟ ◇ 🚕
Central [TP] Ⓟ 🚲 ◇ 🚕
Aberdeen 65
Bangor (Gwynedd) 81
Birmingham 65
Bournemouth 51
Bristol 51
Cambridge 49
Carlisle 65
Chester 81
Crewe 65
Dundee 65
Edinburgh 65
Ellesmere Port 109
Exeter 51

Station index and table numbers

[10] Connection time
Ⓟ Station Car Park
🚲 Bicycle storage facility
◇ Seat reservations can be made at this station
⚠ Penalty Fare Schemes in operation on some or all services from this station
🚕 Taxi rank or cab office at station, or signposted and within 100 metres
Ⓤ Unstaffed station
[ ] Station Operator Code

Station index and table numbers

❿ Connection time
Ⓟ Station Car Park
🚲 Bicycle storage facility
◇ Seat reservations can be made at this station
⚠ Penalty Fare Schemes in operation on some or all services from this station
🚕 Taxi rank or cab office at station, or signposted and within 100 metres
Ⓤ Unstaffed station
[ ] Station Operator Code

Whifflet [SR] Ⓟ 🚕 Ⓤ 220, 224, 226
Whimple [SW] Ⓟ 🚲 Ⓤ 160
Whinhill [SR] 🚲 Ⓤ 219
Whiston [NT] Ⓟ 90
Whitby [NT] Ⓟ ◇ 🚕 45
Whitby Bus Station 🚕 *Bus* 26G
Whitchurch (Cardiff) [AW] Ⓤ 130
Whitchurch (Hants.) [SW] Ⓟ 🚲 ◇ ⚠ 160
Whitchurch (Shrops) [AW] Ⓟ Ⓤ 131
White Hart Lane [LE] ⚠ 21
White Notley [LE] 🚲 ⚠ Ⓤ 11
Whitechapel [LT] 178
Whitecraigs [SR] Ⓟ 🚲 223
Whitehaven [NT] Ⓟ ◇ 100
Whitland [AW] Ⓟ Ⓤ 128
Whitley Bridge [NT] Ⓟ Ⓤ 32
Whitlock's End [LM] ⚠ Ⓤ 71
Whitstable [SE] Ⓟ ◇ ⚠ 🚕 194, 212
Whittlesea [LE] Ⓟ Ⓤ 14, 17
Whittlesford Parkway [LE] Ⓟ 🚲 ⚠ 22
Whitton [SW] 🚲 ◇ ⚠ 149
Whitwell [EM] Ⓤ 55
Whyteleafe [SN] Ⓟ 🚲 ◇ ⚠ 181
Whyteleafe South [SN] Ⓟ 🚲 ◇ ⚠ 181
Wick [SR] Ⓟ 🚲 ◇ 🚕 239
Wickford [LE] ❷ Ⓟ 🚲 ⚠ 🚕 5
Wickham Market [LE] Ⓟ 🚲 Ⓤ 13
Widdrington [NT] Ⓟ 🚲 Ⓤ 48
Widnes [NT] Ⓟ 🚕 49, 89
Widney Manor [LM] Ⓟ ⚠ 71
Wigan
  North Western [VT] Ⓟ ◇ 🚕
  Wallgate [NT] 🚲 🚕
 Barrow-in-Furness 65
 Birmingham 65
 Blackpool 90
 Bolton 82
 Bournemouth 51
 Bristol 51
 Carlisle 65
 Crewe 65
 Edinburgh 65
 Exeter 51
 Glasgow 65
 Kirkby 82
 Lancaster 65
 Liverpool 82, 90
 London 65
 Manchester 82
 Milton Keynes Central 65
 Manchester Airport 82
 Paignton 51
 Penzance 51
 Plymouth 51
 Preston 65
 Oxenholme Lake District 65
 Oxford 51
 Reading 51
 St Helens 90
 Southampton 51
 Southport 82
 Stafford 65
 Stockport 82
 Torquay 51
 Warrington 65
 Wolverhampton 65
 Windermere 65
Wigton [NT] Ⓟ 🚕 Ⓤ 100
Wildmill [AW] Ⓤ 128
Willesden Junction [LO] 🚲 ⚠ 59, 60, 176
Williamwood [SR] 🚲 223
Willington [EM] Ⓤ 57
Wilmcote [LM] ⚠ Ⓤ 71, 115
Wilmslow [NT] Ⓟ 🚲 ◇ 🚕 51, 65, 84, 85, 131
Wilnecote [LM] Ⓤ 57
Wilpshire [NT] (see Ramsgreave and Wilpshire)
Wimbledon [SW] ❻ Ⓟ 🚲 ◇ ⚠ 🚕 52, 152, 155, 179, 182
Wimbledon Chase [FC] ⚠ Ⓤ 52, 179
Winchelsea [SN] Ⓤ 189
Winchester [SW] Ⓟ 🚲 ◇ ⚠ 🚕 51, 158
Winchfield [SW] Ⓟ 🚲 ◇ ⚠ 155
Winchmore Hill [FC] ⚠ 24
Windermere [TP] Ⓟ ◇ 🚕 65, 82, 83
Windsor & Eton Central [GW] ⚠ 🚕 119
Windsor & Eton Riverside [SW] Ⓟ 🚲 ◇ ⚠ 🚕 149
Winnersh [SW] 🚲 ◇ ⚠ 149
Winnersh Triangle [SW] ◇ ⚠ 149
Winsford [LM] Ⓟ ◇ 91
Wisbech *Bus* 🚕 26A
Wishaw [SR] Ⓟ 🚲 226
Witham [LE] ❷ Ⓟ 🚲 ◇ ⚠ 🚕 11
Witley [SW] Ⓟ 🚲 ⚠ 156
Witney Market Place *Bus* 116C
Witton [LM] ⚠ 70
Wivelsfield [SN] ❹ 🚲 ◇ ⚠ 52, 186, 189
Wivenhoe [LE] ❸ Ⓟ 🚲 ⚠ 🚕 11
Woburn Sands [LM] Ⓤ 64
Woking [SW] Ⓟ 🚲 ◇ ⚠ 🚕
 Aldershot 155
 Basingstoke 155
 Bournemouth 158
 Bristol 160
 Exeter 160
 Fareham 158
 Guildford 156
 Heathrow Airport *Bus* 158A
 London 149, 155, 156
 Portsmouth 156
 Salisbury 160
 Southampton 158
 Surbiton 155
 Weymouth 158
Wokingham [SW] Ⓟ 🚲 ◇ ⚠ 🚕 148, 149
Woldingham [SN] Ⓟ 🚲 ◇ ⚠ 184
Wolverhampton [VT] ❼ Ⓟ 🚲 ◇ ⚠ 🚕
 Bangor (Gwynedd) 65
 Birmingham 68
 Birmingham International 68
 Bournemouth 51
 Bristol 51
 Carlisle 65
 Chester 65, 75
 Coventry 68
 Crewe 65
 Edinburgh 65
 Exeter 51
 Glasgow 65
 Holyhead 65
 Liverpool 65
 London 66
 Macclesfield 84
 Manchester 65
 Manchester Airport 65
 Oxenholme Lake District 65
 Oxford 51
 Paignton 51
 Penzance 51
 Plymouth 51
 Preston 65
 Reading 51
 Rugby 66
 Shrewsbury 74
 Southampton 51
 Stafford 68
 Stockport 65
 Stoke-on-Trent 65
 Torquay 51
 Walsall 70
 Watford 66
 Wrexham 75
Wolverton [LM] Ⓟ 🚲 66
Wombwell [NT] Ⓟ Ⓤ 34
Wood End [LM] ⚠ Ⓤ 71
Wood Street [LE] ⚠ 20
Woodbridge [LE] Ⓟ 🚲 🚕 Ⓤ 13
Woodgrange Park [LO] 🚲 ⚠ 62
Woodhall [SR] 🚲 219
Woodham Ferrers [LE] (South Woodham Ferrers)
Woodhouse [NT] Ⓟ Ⓤ 30
Woodlesford [NT] Ⓟ 🚲 Ⓤ 32, 34
Woodley [NT] Ⓟ Ⓤ 78
Woodmansterne [SN] ⚠ 181
Woodsmoor [NT] 86
Wool [SW] Ⓟ 🚲 ◇ ⚠ 🚕 158
Woolston [SW] Ⓟ 🚲 ◇ ⚠ 165
Woolwich Arsenal [SE] ❹ Ⓟ ◇ ⚠ 🚕 200
Woolwich Dockyard [SE] ◇ ⚠ 200
Wootton Wawen [LM] ⚠ Ⓤ 71

Station index and table numbers

10 Connection time
Ⓟ Station Car Park
🚲 Bicycle storage facility
◇ Seat reservations can be made at this station
⚠ Penalty Fare Schemes in operation on some or all services from this station
🚕 Taxi rank or cab office at station, or signposted and within 100 metres
Ⓤ Unstaffed station
[ ] Station Operator Code

Worcester Foregate Street [LM] **7** ◇ ⚠ 🚕 71, 126
Worcester Shrub Hill [LM] **7** Ⓟ ◇ ⚠ 🚕 57, 71, 125, 126
Worcester Park [SW] Ⓟ 🚲 ◇ ⚠ 🚕 152
Workington [NT] Ⓟ ◇ 100
Workington (Bus Station) *Bus* 65F
Worksop [NT] Ⓟ ◇ 30, 55
Worle [GW] Ⓟ 🚲 Ⓤ 134
Worplesdon [SW] Ⓟ 🚲 ◇ ⚠ 155, 156
Worstead [LE] Ⓟ 🚲 Ⓤ 16
Worthing [SN] **4** Ⓟ 🚲 ◇ ⚠ 🚕 123, 188
Wrabness [LE] Ⓟ 🚲 Ⓤ 11
Wraysbury [SW] Ⓟ ⚠ Ⓤ 149
Wrenbury [AW] Ⓟ Ⓤ 131
Wressle [NT] Ⓤ 29
Wrexham Central [AW] Ⓤ 101
Wrexham General [AW] Ⓟ ◇ 🚕 65, 75, 101
Wrotham [SE] (see Borough Green & Wrotham)
Wroxham [LE] (see Hoveton & Wroxham)
Wye [SE] Ⓟ ◇ ⚠ 207
Wylam [NT] Ⓟ 🚲 Ⓤ 48
Wylde Green [LM] Ⓟ ⚠ 69
Wymondham [LE] Ⓟ 🚕 17
Wythall [LM] ⚠ 71

Y

Yalding [SE] Ⓟ ⚠ Ⓤ 208
Yardley Wood [LM] Ⓟ ⚠ 71
Yarm [TP] Ⓟ Ⓤ 39
Yarmouth (IOW) *Ship* 🚕 158
Yate [GW] Ⓟ 🚲 134
Yatton [GW] Ⓟ 🚲 134
Yeoford [GW] Ⓤ 136
Yeovil Junction [SW] Ⓟ 🚲 ◇ 🚕 160
Yeovil Pen Mill [GW] Ⓟ ◇ 123
Yetminster [GW] Ⓟ Ⓤ 123
Ynyswen [AW] Ⓤ 130
Yoker [SR] 🚲 Ⓤ 226
York [GR] **8** Ⓟ 🚲 ◇ 🚕
Aberdeen 26
Bedford 53
Birmingham 51
Birmingham International 51
Blackpool 41
Bournemouth 51
Bradford 40
Bristol 51
Cambridge 26
Cardiff 51
Darlington 26
Derby 53
Doncaster 26
Dundee 26
Eden Camp *Bus* 26G
Edinburgh 26
Exeter 51
Flamingo Land *Bus* 26G
Glasgow 26
Grantham 26
Halifax 41
Harrogate 35
Hartlepool 26
Huddersfield 39
Hull 33
Knaresborough 35
Leeds 35, 40
Leicester 53
Liverpool 39
London 26
Luton 53
Manchester 39
Manchester Airport 39
Middlesbrough 26
Newark 26
Newcastle 26
Newport (South Wales) 51
Newton Abbot 51
Norwich 26
Nottingham 53
Oxford 51
Paignton 51
Penzance 51
Peterborough 26
Pickering Eastgate *Bus* 26G
Plymouth 51
Preston 41
Reading 51
Retford 26
Scarborough 39
Selby 33
Sheffield 29
Stansted Airport 26
Southampton 51
Sunderland 26
Torquay 51
Whitby *Bus* 26G
Yorton [AW] Ⓟ Ⓤ 131
Ystrad Mynach [AW] **3** Ⓟ ◇ 130
Ystrad Rhondda [AW] Ⓟ Ⓤ 130

Network Diagram for Tables 1, 4

DM-1/06
Design BAJS

© Network Rail OPSU 2006.
All rights reserved

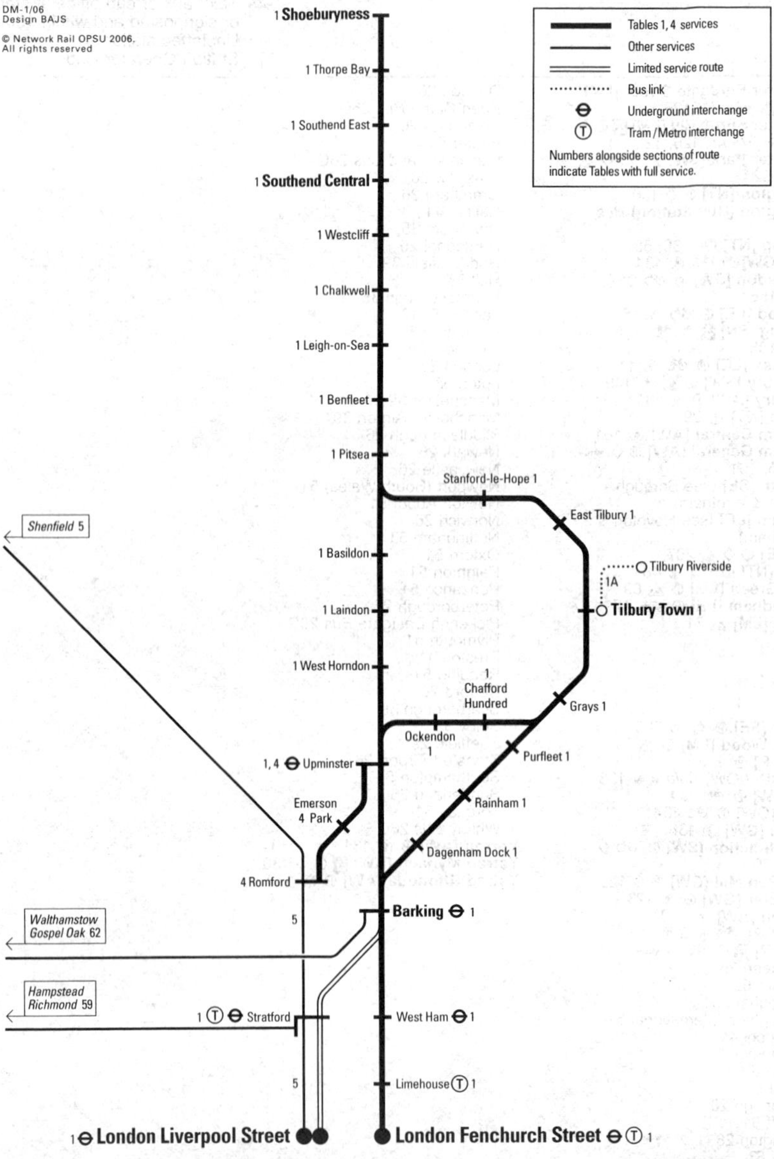

Table I

London - Southend Central and Shoeburyness

Miles	Miles	Miles			CC MO	CC MX	CC MX	CC MO	CC MX	CC MX	CC MO	CC MX	CC MX		CC MX	CC MX	CC MO	CC MX	CC MX	CC MX	CC MX	CC MO	CC MX		CC MX
0	0	—	**London Fenchurch St** 7 ⊖	d	22p50	22p50	23p00			23p05	23p10	23p10			23p20	23p35	23p40	23p40	23p50	00 01		00 10	00 15		00 25
1¾	1¾	—	Limehouse	d	22p54	22p54				23p09	23p14	23p14			23p24	23p39	23p44	23p44	23p54			00 14	00 19		00 29
4¾	4¾	—	West Ham ⊖	d	22p59	22p59	23p08			23p14	23p19	23p19			23p29	23p44	23p49	23p49	23p59	00 09		00 19	00 24		00 34
—	—	—	**London Liverpool St** 15 ⊖	d																					
—	—	—	Stratford 7 ⊖	d																					
7½	7½	—	Barking ⊖	d	23p04	23p05	23p14			23p20	23p24	23p25			23p35	23p50	23p54	23p55	00 05	00 15		00 24	00 30		00 40
15¼	—	0	Upminster ⊖	d	23p12	23p14	23p23				23p32	23p34			23p44		00 02	00 04	00 14	00 24		00 32			00 49
—	—	3	Ockendon	d	23p18	23p19									23p49				00 19						
—	—	5	Chafford Hundred	d	23p21	23p23									23p53				00 23						
19¼	—	—	West Horndon	d							23p37	23p39					00 07	00 09				00 37			00 54
22¾	—	—	Laindon	d			23p31				23p42	23p44					00 12	00 16		00 32		00 42			00 59
24½	—	—	Basildon	d			23p34				23p45	23p47					00 15	00 19		00 35		00 45			01 02
—	10½	—	Dagenham Dock	d						23p25						23p55							00 35		
—	12¾	—	Rainham	d						23p29						23p59							00 39		
—	16	—	Purfleet	d						23p34						00 04							00 44		
—	19¾	7½	Grays	d	23p25	23p27				23p42					23p57	00a10			00 27				00a50		
—	21½	—	**Tilbury Town** 3	d	23p28	23p30				23p45					00 01				00 30						
—	25¼	—	East Tilbury	d	23p34	23p36				23p51					00 06				00 36						
—	27¼	—	Stanford-le-Hope	d	23p37	23p40				23p55			←		00 10				00 40						
26½	32¼	—	Pitsea	d	23p45	23p48		←	←	00 06	23p49	23p52	00 06		00 18		00 19	00 22	00 48		←	00 49			01 06
29¼	35	—	Benfleet	d	23p49	23p52	23p41	23p49	23p52	→	23p52	23p56	00 10		00 22		00 22	00 26	00 52	00 42	00 52	00 52			01 10
32½	38¼	—	Leigh-on-Sea	d	→	→	23p45	23p53	23p56		23p57	23p59	00 15		00 27		00 27	00 31	→	00 46	00 56	00 57			01 14
34	39¾	—	Chalkwell	d			23p48	23p56	23p59		23p59	00 03	00 18		00 30		00 29	00 34		00 49	00 59	00 59			01 17
34¾	40½	—	Westcliff	d			23p51	23p58	00 02		00 02	00 06	00 20		00 32		00 32	00 36		00 52	01 02	01 02			01 20
35¾	41½	—	**Southend Central**	a			23p54	00 01	00 05		00 05	00 09	00 23		00 35		00 35	00 39		00 55	01 05	01 05			01 23
—	—	—		d			23p54	00 01	00 05		00 06	00 09	00 23		00 35		00 36	00 40		00 55	01 05	01 06			01 23
36½	42¼	—	Southend East	d			23p56	00 03	00 07		00 08	00 11	00 26		00 38		00 38	00 42		00 57	01 07	01 08			01 25
38	43¾	—	Thorpe Bay	d			23p59	00 06	00 11		00 10	00 15	00 29		00 41		00 40	00 46		01 01	01 11	01 10			01 29
39½	45¼	—	**Shoeburyness**	a			00 06	00 13	00 17		00 18	00 21	00 36		00 48		00 48	00 52		01 07	01 17	01 18			01 35

		CC	CC	CC	CC	CC	CC	CC	CC		CC	CC	CC	CC	CC	CC	CC	CC	CC		CC	CC	CC	CC	CC
London Fenchurch St 7 ⊖	d		05 10	05 40					06 10		06 20	06 40		06 44	06 50	07 00	07 09	07 13	07 17		07 30	07 40	07 42	07 48	07 52
Limehouse	d		05 14	05 44					06 14		06 24	06 44		06 48	06 54		07 13					07 44			07 56
West Ham ⊖	d		05 19	05 49					06 19		06 29	06 49		06 53	06 59	07 08	07 18		07 25		07 38	07 49	07 52		08 01
London Liverpool St 15 ⊖	d																								
Stratford 7 ⊖	d																								
Barking ⊖	d		05 25	05 55	05 45		06 05		06 25		06 35	06 55	06 52	07 00	07 05	07 14	07 24	07 26	07 31		07 44	07 55	07 57		08 07
Upminster ⊖	d	05 32	05 34	06 04		06 07		06 10	06 34			07 04		07 11		07 23	07 33		07 41		07 53	08 04		08 10	08 16
Ockendon	d	05 37				06 12		06a15						07 16					07 47					08 19	
Chafford Hundred	d	05 41				06 16								07 20					07 51					08 23	
West Horndon	d		05 39	06 09					06 39			07 09					07 38					08 09			08 21
Laindon	d		05 44	06 14					06 44			07 14					07 45					08 14			08a27
Basildon	d		05 47	06 17					06 47			07 17				07 33	07 48				08 03	08 17			
Dagenham Dock	d				05 50		06 10				06 40		06 57		07 10			07 31					08 02		
Rainham	d				05 54		06 14				06 44		07 01		07 14			07 35					08 06		
Purfleet	d				05 59		06 19				06 49		07 06		07 19			07 40					08 12		
Grays	d	05a45			06 05	06a21	06 25				06 55		07 12	07a24	07 27			07 46	07 55				08 17	08 27	
Tilbury Town 3	d				06 08		06 28				06 58		07 15		07 30				07 59				08 21		
East Tilbury	d				06 14		06 34				07 04		07 21		07 36				08 05				08 27		
Stanford-le-Hope	d				06 18		06 38				07 08		07 25		07 40			07 56	08 09				08 31	08 37	
Pitsea	d		05 51	06 21	06 27		06a46		06 51		07 16	07 21	07a33		07a47		07 52	08a03	08a16			08 21	08 41	08a45	
Benfleet	d		05 55	06 25	06 32				06 55		07 20	07 25				07 39	07 56				08 09	08 25	08 45		
Leigh-on-Sea	d		06 00	06 30	06 36				07 00		07 24	07 29				07 44	08 00				08 14	08 30	→		
Chalkwell	d		06 03	06 33	06 39				07 03		07 27	07 32				07 47	08 03				08 17	08 33			
Westcliff	d		06 05	06 35	06 42				07 05		07 30	07 35				07 49	08 06				08 19	08 35			
Southend Central	a		06 08	06 38	06 44				07 08		07 32	07 37				07 52	08 08				08 22	08 38			
	d		06 08	06 38	06 44				07 08		07 33	07 37				07 52	08 08				08 22	08 38			
Southend East	d		06 10	06 40	06 46				07 10		07 35	07 39				07 54	08 10				08 24	08 40			
Thorpe Bay	d		06 14	06 44	06 50				07 14		07 38	07 43				07 58	08 14				08 28	08 44			
Shoeburyness	a		06 18	06 48	06 54				07 18		07 43	07 47				08 02	08 18				08 32	08 48			

		CC	CC	CC	CC		CC	CC	CC	CC	CC	CC	CC	CC	CC		CC	CC	CC	CC	CC	CC	CC	CC	CC
London Fenchurch St 7 ⊖	d	08 00		08 05	08 10		08 15	08 20	08 30		08 40	08 50	08 54	09 00			09 10	09 16	09 20	09 30		09 35	09 40		09 50
Limehouse	d			08 09	08 14			08 24			08 44	08 54					09 14	09 20	09 24			09 39	09 44		09 54
West Ham ⊖	d	08 08			08 19			08 29	08 38		08 49	08 59		09 08			09 19	09 25	09 29	09 38		09 44	09 49		09 59
London Liverpool St 15 ⊖	d																								
Stratford 7 ⊖	d																								
Barking ⊖	d	08 14		08 18	08 25		08 29	08 37	08 45		08 55	09 07	09 09	09 16			09 25	09 31	09 35	09 44		09 50	09 55		10 05
Upminster ⊖	d	08 23			08 34		08 41		08 54		09 04		09 18	09 25			09 34		09 45	09 53			10 04		10 14
Ockendon	d						08 46						09 23						09 50						10 19
Chafford Hundred	d						08 50						09 27						09 54						10 23
West Horndon	d				08 39						09 09						09 39						10 09		
Laindon	d	08 31			08 44				09 03		09 14			09 34			09 44			10 01			10 14		
Basildon	d	08 34			08 47				09 06		09 17			09 37			09 47			10 04			10 17		
Dagenham Dock	d			08 23				08 42				09 12						09 36				09 55			
Rainham	d			08 27				08 46				09 16						09 40				09 59			
Purfleet	d			08 33				08 52				09 21						09 45				10 04			
Grays	d			08 38			08a54	08 57				09 27	09a31					09 51	09 58			10a10			10 27
Tilbury Town 3	d			08 42				09 01				09 30						09 54	10 02						10 30
East Tilbury	d			08 48				09 07				09 36						10 00	10 08						10 36
Stanford-le-Hope	d			08 52				09 11		←		09 40						10 04	10 12					←	10 40
Pitsea	d	08 38	←	08a59	08 51			09 18	09 09	09 18	09 21	09 48			←		09 51	10 12	10 25		←		10 21	10 25	10 48
Benfleet	d	08 42	08 45		08 55			→	09 13	09 22	09 26	09 52		09 43	09 52		09 55	10 16	→	10 11	10 16		10 25	10 29	10 52
Leigh-on-Sea	d	08 46	08 50		09 00				09 18	09 27	09 30	→		09 48	09 57		10 00	→		10 15	10 20		10 30	10 34	→
Chalkwell	d	08 49	08 53		09 03				09 21	09 30	09 33			09 51	10 00		10 03			10 18	10 23		10 33	10 37	
Westcliff	d	08 52	08 55		09 05				09 23	09 32	09 36			09 53	10 02		10 05			10 21	10 26		10 35	10 39	
Southend Central	a	08 54	08 58		09 08				09 26	09 35	09 38			09 56	10 05		10 08			10 23	10 29		10 38	10 42	
	d	08 55			09 08				09 26		09 38			09 56			10 08			10 23			10 38		
Southend East	d	08 57			09 10				09 28		09 40			09 58			10 10			10 25			10 40		
Thorpe Bay	d	09 00			09 14				09 32		09 44			10 02			10 14			10 29			10 44		
Shoeburyness	a	09 05			09 18				09 36		09 48			10 06			10 18			10 33			10 48		

Table I

Mondays to Fridays

London - Southend Central and Shoeburyness

Station			CC	CC	CC	CC	CC	CC	CC	CC	CC		CC	CC	CC	CC	CC	CC	CC	CC	CC		CC	CC	CC
London Fenchurch St 7	⊖ d		10 00		10 05	10 10	10 20	10 30		10 35	10 40		10 50	11 00		11 05	11 10	11 20	11 30		11 35		11 40	11 50	12 00
Limehouse	d				10 09	10 14	10 24			10 39	10 44		10 54			11 09	11 14	11 24			11 39		11 44	11 54	
West Ham	⊖ d		10 08		10 14	10 19	10 29	10 38		10 44	10 49		10 59	11 08		11 14	11 19	11 29	11 38		11 44		11 49	11 59	12 08
London Liverpool St 15	⊖ d																								
Stratford 7	⊖ d																								
Barking	⊖ d		10 14		10 20	10 25	10 35	10 44		10 50	10 55		11 05	11 14		11 20	11 25	11 35	11 44		11 50		11 55	12 05	12 14
Upminster	⊖ d		10 23			10 34	10 44	10 53			11 04		11 14	11 23			11 34	11 44	11 53				12 04	12 14	12 23
Ockendon	d						10 49						11 19					11 49						12 19	
Chafford Hundred	d						10 53						11 23					11 53						12 23	
West Horndon	d					10 39					11 09						11 39						12 09		
Laindon	d		10 31			10 44		11 01			11 14			11 31			11 44		12 01				12 14		12 31
Basildon	d		10 34			10 47		11 04			11 17			11 34			11 47		12 04				12 17		12 34
Dagenham Dock	d				10 25					10 55						11 25					11 55				
Rainham	d				10 29					10 59						11 29					11 59				
Purfleet	d				10 34					11 04						11 34					12 04				
Grays	d				10a40		10 57			11a10			11 27			11a40		11 57			12a10			12 27	
Tilbury Town 3	d						11 00						11 30					12 00						12 30	
East Tilbury	d						11 06						11 36					12 06						12 36	
Stanford-le-Hope	d						11 10						11 40					12 10						12 40	
Pitsea	d			←		10 51	11 18		←		11 21		11 48		←		11 51	12 18		←			12 21	12 48	
Benfleet	d		10 41	10 52		10 55	11 22	11 11	11 22		11 25		11 52	11 41	11 52		11 55	12 22	12 11	12 22			12 25	12 52	12 41
Leigh-on-Sea	d		10 45	10 56		11 00	→	11 15	11 26		11 30		→	11 45	11 57		12 00	→	12 15	12 26			12 30	→	12 45
Chalkwell	d		10 48	10 59		11 03		11 18	11 29		11 33			11 48	12 00		12 03		12 18	12 29			12 33		12 48
Westcliff	d		10 51	11 02		11 05		11 21	11 32		11 35			11 51	12 02		12 05		12 21	12 32			12 35		12 51
Southend Central	a		10 53	11 05		11 08		11 23	11 35		11 38			11 53	12 05		12 08		12 23	12 35			12 38		12 53
	d		10 53			11 08		11 23			11 38			11 53			12 08		12 23				12 38		12 53
Southend East	d		10 55			11 10		11 25			11 40			11 55			12 10		12 25				12 40		12 55
Thorpe Bay	d		10 59			11 14		11 29			11 44			11 59			12 14		12 29				12 44		12 59
Shoeburyness	a		11 03			11 18		11 33			11 48			12 03			12 18		12 33				12 48		13 03

Station		CC	CC	CC	CC	CC	CC		CC	CC	CC	CC	CC	CC	CC	CC	CC		CC	CC	CC	CC	CC	CC	CC
London Fenchurch St 7	⊖ d		12 05	12 10	12 20	12 30			12 35	12 40	12 50	13 00		13 05	13 10	13 20	13 30			13 35	13 40	13 50	14 00		14 05
Limehouse	d		12 09	12 14	12 24				12 39	12 44	12 54			13 09	13 14	13 24				13 39	13 44	13 54			14 09
West Ham	⊖ d		12 14	12 19	12 29	12 38			12 44	12 49	12 59	13 08		13 14	13 19	13 29	13 38			13 44	13 49	13 59	14 08		14 14
London Liverpool St 15	⊖ d																								
Stratford 7	⊖ d																								
Barking	⊖ d		12 20	12 25	12 35	12 44			12 50	12 55	13 05	13 14		13 20	13 25	13 35	13 44			13 50	13 55	14 05	14 14		14 20
Upminster	⊖ d			12 34	12 44	12 53				13 04	13 14	13 23			13 34	13 44	13 53				14 04	14 14	14 23		
Ockendon	d				12 49						13 19					13 49						14 19			
Chafford Hundred	d				12 53						13 23					13 53						14 23			
West Horndon	d			12 39						13 09					13 39						14 09				
Laindon	d			12 44		13 01				13 14		13 31			13 44		14 01				14 14		14 31		
Basildon	d			12 47		13 04				13 17		13 34			13 47		14 04				14 17		14 34		
Dagenham Dock	d		12 25						12 55					13 25						13 55					14 25
Rainham	d		12 29						12 59					13 29						13 59					14 29
Purfleet	d		12 34						13 04					13 34						14 04					14 34
Grays	d		12a40		12 57				13a10		13 27			13a40		13 57				14a10		14 27			14a40
Tilbury Town 3	d				13 00						13 30					14 00						14 30			
East Tilbury	d				13 06						13 36					14 06						14 36			
Stanford-le-Hope	d				13 10						13 40					14 10						14 40			
Pitsea	d	←		12 51	13 18		←			13 21	13 48		←		13 51	14 18			←		14 21	14 48		←	
Benfleet	d	12 52		12 55	13 22	13 11	13 22			13 25	13 52	13 41	13 52		13 55	14 22	14 11		14 22		14 25	14 52	14 41	14 52	
Leigh-on-Sea	d	12 57		13 00	→	13 15	13 27			13 30	→	13 45	13 57		14 00	→	14 15		14 26		14 30	→	14 45	14 56	
Chalkwell	d	13 00		13 03		13 18	13 30			13 33		13 48	14 00		14 03		14 18		14 29		14 33		14 48	14 59	
Westcliff	d	13 02		13 05		13 21	13 32			13 35		13 51	14 02		14 05		14 21		14 32		14 35		14 51	15 02	
Southend Central	a	13 05		13 08		13 23	13 35			13 38		13 53	14 05		14 08		14 23		14 35		14 38		14 53	15 05	
	d			13 08		13 23				13 38		13 53			14 08		14 23				14 38		14 53		
Southend East	d			13 10		13 25				13 40		13 55			14 10		14 25				14 40		14 55		
Thorpe Bay	d			13 14		13 29				13 44		13 59			14 14		14 29				14 44		14 59		
Shoeburyness	a			13 18		13 33				13 48		14 03			14 18		14 33				14 48		15 03		

Station		CC	CC		CC	CC	CC	CC	CC	CC	CC	CC	CC		CC	CC	CC	CC	CC	CC	CC	CC	CC		CC
London Fenchurch St 7	⊖ d	14 10	14 20		14 30		14 35	14 40	14 50	15 00		15 05	15 10		15 20	15 25	15 30	15 35	15 40		15 50	15 55	16 00		16 10
Limehouse	d	14 14	14 24				14 39	14 44	14 54			15 09	15 14		15 24			15 39	15 44		15 54	15 59			16 14
West Ham	⊖ d	14 19	14 29		14 38		14 44	14 49	14 59	15 08		15 14	15 19		15 29	15 33	15 38	15 44	15 49		15 59	16 04	16 08		16 19
London Liverpool St 15	⊖ d																								
Stratford 7	⊖ d																								
Barking	⊖ d	14 25	14 35		14 44		14 50	14 55	15 05	15 14		15 20	15 25		15 35	15 39	15 44	15 50	15 54		16 05	16 10	16 14		16 25
Upminster	⊖ d	14 34	14 44		14 53			15 04	15 14	15 23			15 34		15 44	15 48	15 53		16 02		16 14		16 23		16 34
Ockendon	d		14 49						15 19						15 49						16 19				
Chafford Hundred	d		14 53						15 23						15 53						16 23				
West Horndon	d	14 39						15 09					15 39						16 07						16 39
Laindon	d	14 44			15 01			15 14		15 31			15 44			15 56	16 01		16 12						16 44
Basildon	d	14 47			15 04			15 17		15 34			15 47			15 59	16 04		16 15				16 33		16 47
Dagenham Dock	d						14 55					15 25						15 55				16 15			
Rainham	d						14 59					15 29						15 59				16 19			
Purfleet	d						15 04					15 34						16 04				16 25			
Grays	d		14 57				15a10		15 27			15a40			15 57			16a10			16 27	16a33			
Tilbury Town 3	d		15 00						15 30						16 00						16 30				
East Tilbury	d		15 06						15 36						16 06						16 36				
Stanford-le-Hope	d		15 10						15 40						16 10					←	16 40				
Pitsea	d	14 51	15 18			←		15 21	15 48		←		15 51		16 22	16 03			16 19	16 22	16a48				16 51
Benfleet	d	14 55	15 22		15 11	15 22		15 25	15 52	15 41	15 52		15 55		→	16 07	16 11		16 22	16 26			16 40		16 55
Leigh-on-Sea	d	15 00	→		15 15	15 26		15 30	→	15 45	15 56		16 00			16a12	16 15		16 27	16 30			16 45		17 00
Chalkwell	d	15 03			15 18	15 29		15 33		15 48	15 59		16 03				16 18		16 29	16 33			16 48		17 03
Westcliff	d	15 05			15 21	15 32		15 35		15 51	16 02		16 05				16 21		16 32	16 36			16 50		17 05
Southend Central	a	15 08			15 23	15 35		15 38		15 53	16 05		16 08				16 23		16 34	16 41			16 53		17 08
	d	15 08			15 23			15 38		15 53			16 08				16 23		16 35				16 53		17 08
Southend East	d	15 10			15 25			15 40		15 55			16 10				16 25		16 37				16 55		17 10
Thorpe Bay	d	15 14			15 29			15 44		15 59			16 14				16 29		16 39				16 59		17 14
Shoeburyness	a	15 18			15 33			15 48		16 03			16 20				16 33		16 44				17 05		17 20

London - Southend Central and Shoeburyness

		CC	CC	CC	CC	CC	CC	CC	CC		CC	CC	CC	CC	CC	CC	CC	CC	CC		CC	CC	CC	CC	CC
London Fenchurch St [7] ⊖	d	16 13	16 20	16 28	16 30	16 33	16 37	16 45	16 48		16 54	17 00	17 02	17 05	17 07	17 11	17 15	17 18	17 20		17 22	17 26	17 30	17 32	17 35
Limehouse	d	16 17	16 24		16 34	16 37	16 41	16 49	16 52		16 58			17 09	17 12	17 16	17 19		17 24		17 27	17 30			17 39
West Ham ⊖	d	16 22	16 29	16 36	16 39	16 42	16 46		16 57		17 03				17 17						17 32				
London Liverpool St [15] ⊖	d																								
Stratford [7] ⊖	d																								
Barking ⊖	d	16 28	16 35		16 45	16 48	16 52	16 59	17 03		17 09		17 15	17 19	17 22	17 25			17 34		17 37	17 40		17 45	17 49
Upminster ⊖	d		16 45		16 55		17 02	17 07	17 13				17 24		17 31		17 36	17 39			17 46			17 54	
Ockendon	d		16 50				17 08						17 29											18 00	
Chafford Hundred	d		16 54				17 12						17 34											18 04	
West Horndon	d				17 00				17 18						17 36						17 51				
Laindon	d			16 56	17a08			17 16	17a26					17 35	17a43				17 50		17a58				18 05
Basildon	d			16 59				17 19						17 39				17 50	17 54						18 08
Dagenham Dock	d	16 33				16 53					17 14					17 30						17 45			
Rainham	d	16 37				16 57					17 18					17 34						17 49			
Purfleet	d	16 43				17 03					17 24					17 39						17 54			
Grays	d	16 49	16 59			17 09	17a18				17 30		17a40			17 48						18 00		18a10	
Tilbury Town [3]	d	16 52	17 02			17 12					17 33					17 51						18 04			
East Tilbury	d	16 58	17 08			17 18					17 39					17 57						18 10			
Stanford-le-Hope	d	17 02	17a15			17 22					17 43					18 01						18 14			
Pitsea	d	17a12				17a32		17 23			17a53			17 42		18a11		17 53	17 57			18a23			18 12
Benfleet	d			17 06				17 27				17 33		17 46			17 52	17 58	18 02				18 07		18 16
Leigh-on-Sea	d			17 11				17 32				17 38		17 51			17 56	18 02	18 06				18 11		18 21
Chalkwell	d			17 14				17 34				17 41		17 53			17 59	18 05	18 09				18 14		18 24
Westcliff	d			17 16				17 37				17 43		17 56			18 02	18 08	18 12				18 17		18 26
Southend Central	a			17 19				17 39				17 46		17 58			18 04	18 13	18 14				18 19		18 29
	d			17 19				17 39				17 46		17 58			18 04		18 15				18 19		18 29
Southend East	d			17 21				17 41				17 48		18 00			18 06		18 17				18 21		18 31
Thorpe Bay	d			17 24				17 44				17 50		18 03			18 10		18 20				18 25		18 34
Shoeburyness	a			17 31				17 51				17 57		18 11			18 16		18 28				18 31		18 41

		CC	CC	CC	CC		CC	CC	CC	CC	CC	CC	CC	CC	CC		CC	CC	CC	CC	CC	CC	CC	CC	CC
London Fenchurch St [7] ⊖	d	17 37	17 41	17 45	17 47		17 50	17 53	17 56	18 00	18 02	18 06	18 09		18 12		18 20		18 22	18 25	18 30	18 33	18 40	18 45	18 51
Limehouse	d	17 42	17 45	17 49	17 52			17 57	18 00		18 06	18 10	18 13		18 16				18 26	18 29	18 34	18 37		18 50	18 55
West Ham ⊖	d	17 47					17 58			18 08			18 18		18 21					18 34			18 48	18 55	19 00
London Liverpool St [15] ⊖	d																								
Stratford [7] ⊖	d																								
Barking ⊖	d	17 52	17 55					18 07	18 10		18 16	18 20	18 24		18 28					18 40	18 45	18 47		19 00	19 06
Upminster ⊖	d	18 01			18 09		18 12				18 26		18 33						18 43	18 50		18 56		19 09	
Ockendon	d				18 14						18 32								18 48			19 03			
Chafford Hundred	d				18 18						18 36								18 52			19 08			
West Horndon	d	18 06						18 20					18 38							18 55				19 14	
Laindon	d	18a13						18 25				18 36	18 42				18 46			19 00				19 19	
Basildon	d						18 23	18 29		18 33		18 40	18 46				18 50			19 04			19 10	19 22	
Dagenham Dock	d		18 00						18 15						18 33						18 50				19 11
Rainham	d		18 04						18 19						18 37						18 54				19 15
Purfleet	d		18 09						18 24						18 42						18 59				19 21
Grays	d		18 18		18a24				18 32		18 41				18 48				18 57		19 05	19a14			19 27
Tilbury Town [3]	d		18 21						18 35		18 44				18 52				19 00		19 09				19 30
East Tilbury	d		18 27						18 41		18 50				18 58				19 06		19 15				19 36
Stanford-le-Hope	d		18 31						18 46		18 54			←	19 02				19 10		19 19				19 40
Pitsea	d		18a41				18 26	18 32	18 56	18 37	19a04	18 43	18 49	18 56	19a11			←	19a22	19 08	19a28			19 26	19 48
Benfleet	d			18 22			18 31	18 37	→	18 41		18 48	18 53	19 01			18 57	19 01		19 12			19 17	19 30	→
Leigh-on-Sea	d			18 26			18 35	18 41		18 46		18 52	18 58	→			19 02	19 05		19 16			19 22	19 34	
Chalkwell	d			18 29			18 38	18 44		18 49		18 55	19 00				19 05	19 08		19 19			19 25	19 37	
Westcliff	d			18 32			18 41	18 47		18 51		18 58	19 03				19 07	19 11		19 22			19 27	19 39	
Southend Central	a			18 34			18 43	18 49		18 54		19 00	19 05				19 10	19 16		19 24			19 30	19 42	
	d			18 34			18 43	18 49		18 54		19 00	19 06				19 10			19 24			19 30	19 42	
Southend East	d			18 36			18 45	18 51		18 56		19 02	19 08				19 12			19 26			19 32	19 44	
Thorpe Bay	d			18 40			18 49	18 55		18 59		19 06	19 10				19 15			19 30			19 35	19 46	
Shoeburyness	a			18 48			18 55	19 01		19 06		19 12	19 17				19 24			19 36			19 42	19 53	

			CC	CC	CC	CC	CC	CC	CC	CC	CC		CC	CC	CC	CC	CC	CC	CC	CC	CC		CC	CC	CC
London Fenchurch St ■ ⊖	d		19 00	19 02	19 05		19 08	19 11	19 20	19 30			19 32	19 35	19 40	19 50	20 00		20 05	20 10	20 20		20 30		
Limehouse	d				19 09		19 12	19 15	19 24				19 36	19 39	19 44	19 54			20 09	20 14	20 24		20 34		
West Ham ⊖	d			19 10			19 17	19 20	19 29				19 41	19 44	19 49	19 59	20 08		20 14	20 19	20 29		20 39		
London Liverpool St [15] ⊖	d																								20 35
Stratford ■ ⊖	d																								20 42
Barking ⊖	d			19 16	19 19		19 23	19 26	19 35				19 47	19 50	19 55	20 05	20 14		20 20	20 25	20 35		20 45		20 50
Upminster ⊖	d			19 26	19 30			19 35	19 44	19 50			19 56		20 04	20 14	20 23			20 34	20 44		20 54		
Ockendon	d			19 33					19 49							20 19					20 49				
Chafford Hundred	d			19 39					19 53							20 23					20 53				
West Horndon	d							19 40					20 01		20 09					20 39					
Laindon	d		19 26					19 45					20a07		20 14		20 31			20 44			21 02		
Basildon	d				19 40			19 48		20 00					20 17		20 34			20 47			21 05		
Dagenham Dock	d						19 28							19 55					20 25						20 55
Rainham	d						19 32							19 59					20 29						20 59
Purfleet	d						19 37							20 04					20 34						21 04
Grays	d			19 46			19a43		19 57					20a10		20 27			20a40		20 57				21a12
Tilbury Town [3]	d			19 50					20 00							20 30					21 00				
East Tilbury	d			19 56					20 06							20 36					21 06				
Stanford-le-Hope	d			20 00		←			20 10							20 40					21 10				
Pitsea	d			20a07	19 44	19 48		19 52	20 18		←				20 21	20 48		←		20 51	21 18			←	
Benfleet	d		19 33		19 48	19 52		19 56	20 22	20 06	20 22				20 26	20 52	20 41	20 52		20 55	21 22		21 12	21 22	
Leigh-on-Sea	d		19 38		19 52	19 56		20 00	→	20 11	20 27				20 30	→	20 45	20 56		21 00	→		21 16	21 26	
Chalkwell	d		19 41		19 55	19 59		20 03		20 14	20 30				20 33		20 48	20 59		21 03			21 19	21 29	
Westcliff	d		19 43		19 58	20 02		20 06		20 16	20 32				20 36		20 51	21 02		21 05			21 22	21 32	
Southend Central	a		19 46		20 00	20 07		20 08		20 19	20 35				20 38		20 53	21 05		21 08			21 24	21 35	
	d		19 46		20 00			20 08		20 19					20 38		20 53			21 08			21 24		
Southend East	d		19 48		20 02			20 10		20 21					20 40		20 55			21 10			21 26		
Thorpe Bay	d		19 50		20a06			20 14		20 25					20 44		20 59			21 14			21 30		
Shoeburyness	a		19 57					20 18		20 29					20 48		21 03			21 18			21 34		

Table 1

Mondays to Fridays

London - Southend Central and Shoeburyness

Station		CC	CC	CC	CC	CC	CC		CC	CC	CC	CC	CC	CC	CC	CC	CC		CC	CC	CC	CC	CC	CC	CC
London Fenchurch St 7 ⊖	d	20 40	20 50	21 00		21 05	21 10		21 20	21 30			21 40	21 50	22 00		22 05		22 10	22 20	22 35	22 40	22 50	23 00	
Limehouse	d	20 44	20 54			21 09	21 14		21 24	21 34			21 44	21 54			22 09		22 14	22 24	22 39	22 44	22 54		
West Ham ⊖	d	20 49	20 59	21 08		21 14	21 19		21 29	21 39			21 49	21 59	22 08		22 14		22 19	22 29	22 44	22 49	22 59	23 08	
London Liverpool St 15 ⊖	d											21 35													
Stratford 7 ⊖	d											21 42													
Barking ⊖	d	20 55	21 05	21 14		21 20	21 25		21 35	21 45		21 50	21 55	22 05	22 14		22 20		22 25	22 35	22 50	22 55	23 05	23 14	
Upminster ⊖	d	21 04	21 14	21 23			21 34		21 44	21 54			22 04	22 14	22 23				22 34	22 44		23 04	23 14	23 23	
Ockendon	d		21 19						21 49					22 19						22 49			23 19		
Chafford Hundred	d		21 23						21 53					22 23						22 53			23 23		
West Horndon	d	21 09					21 39						22 09						22 39			23 09			
Laindon	d	21 14		21 31			21 44			22 02			22 14		22 31				22 44			23 14		23 31	
Basildon	d	21 17		21 34			21 47			22 05			22 17		22 34				22 47			23 17		23 34	
Dagenham Dock	d					21 25						21 55					22 25				22 55				
Rainham	d					21 29						21 59					22 29				22 59				
Purfleet	d					21 34						22 04					22 34				23 04				
Grays	d		21 27			21a40			21 57			22a12		22 27			22a40			22 57	23a10		23 27		
Tilbury Town 3	d		21 30						22 00					22 30						23 00			23 30		
East Tilbury	d		21 36						22 06					22 36						23 06			23 36		
Stanford-le-Hope	d		21 40						22 10					22 40						23 10			23 40		
Pitsea	d	21 21	21 48		←		21 51		22 18		←		22 21	22 48		←			22 51	23 18		23 22	23 48		←
Benfleet	d	21 25	21 52	21 41	21 52		21 55		22 22	22 12	22 22		22 25	22 52	22 41	22 52			22 55	23 22		23 26	23 52	23 41	23 52
Leigh-on-Sea	d	21 30	→	21 45	21 56		22 00		→	22 16	22 26		22 30	→	22 45	22 56			23 00	23 26		23 30	→	23 45	23 56
Chalkwell	d	21 33		21 48	21 59		22 03			22 19	22 29		22 33		22 48	22 59			23 03	23 29		23 33		23 48	23 59
Westcliff	d	21 35		21 51	22 02		22 05			22 22	22 32		22 35		22 51	23 02			23 05	23 32		23 36		23 51	00 02
Southend Central	a	21 38		21 53	22 05		22 08			22 24	22 35		22 38		22 53	23 05			23 08	23 35		23 39		23 54	00 05
	d	21 38		21 53			22 08			22 24			22 38		22 53	23 05			23 08	23 35		23 39		23 54	00 05
Southend East	d	21 40		21 55			22 10			22 26			22 40		22 55	23 07			23 10	23 37		23 41		23 56	00 07
Thorpe Bay	d	21 44		21 59			22 14			22 30			22 44		22 59	23 10			23 14	23 41		23 45		23 59	00 11
Shoeburyness	a	21 48		22 03			22 18			22 34			22 48		23 03	23 15			23 18	23 47		23 51		00 06	00 17

Station		CC	CC		CC	CC	CC	CC	CC
London Fenchurch St 7 ⊖	d	23 05	23 10			23 20	23 35	23 40	23 50
Limehouse	d	23 09	23 14			23 24	23 39	23 44	23 54
West Ham ⊖	d	23 14	23 19			23 29	23 44	23 49	23 59
London Liverpool St 15 ⊖	d								
Stratford 7 ⊖	d								
Barking ⊖	d	23 20	23 25			23 35	23 50	23 55	00 05
Upminster ⊖	d		23 34			23 44		00 04	00 14
Ockendon	d					23 49			00 19
Chafford Hundred	d					23 53			00 23
West Horndon	d		23 39					00 09	
Laindon	d		23 44					00 16	
Basildon	d		23 47					00 19	
Dagenham Dock	d	23 25					23 55		
Rainham	d	23 29					23 59		
Purfleet	d	23 34					00 04		
Grays	d	23 42				23 57	00a10		00 27
Tilbury Town 3	d	23 45				00 01			00 30
East Tilbury	d	23 51				00 06			00 36
Stanford-le-Hope	d	23 55			←	00 10			00 40
Pitsea	d	00 06	23 52		00 06	00 18		00 22	00 48
Benfleet	d	→	23 56		00 10	00 22		00 26	00 52
Leigh-on-Sea	d		23 59		00 15	00 27		00 31	00 56
Chalkwell	d		00 03		00 18	00 30		00 34	00 59
Westcliff	d		00 06		00 20	00 32		00 36	01 02
Southend Central	a		00 09		00 23	00 35		00 39	01 05
	d		00 09		00 23	00 35		00 40	01 05
Southend East	d		00 11		00 26	00 38		00 42	01 07
Thorpe Bay	d		00 15		00 29	00 41		00 46	01 11
Shoeburyness	a		00 21		00 36	00 48		00 52	01 17

Saturdays

Station		CC	CC	CC	CC	CC	CC	CC	CC	CC		CC	CC	CC	CC	CC	CC	CC	CC	CC		CC	CC	CC	CC
London Fenchurch St 7 ⊖	d	22p50	23p00		23p05	23p10		23p20	23p35	23p40		23p50	00 01		00 15	00 25			05 10	05 35		05 50	06 05	06 10	06 20
Limehouse	d	22p54			23p09	23p14		23p24	23p39	23p44		23p54			00 19	00 29			05 14	05 39		05 54	06 09	06 14	06 24
West Ham ⊖	d	22p59	23p08		23p14	23p19		23p29	23p44	23p49		23p59	00 09		00 24	00 34			05 19	05 44		05 59	06 14	06 19	06 29
London Liverpool St 15 ⊖	d																								
Stratford 7 ⊖	d																								
Barking ⊖	d	23p05	23p14		23p20	23p25		23p35	23p50	23p55		00 05	00 15		00 30	00 40			05 24	05 49		06 04	06 19	06 24	06 34
Upminster ⊖	d	23p14	23p23			23p34		23p44		00 04		00 14	00 24			00 49	05 05	05 27	05 32			06 12		06 32	06 42
Ockendon	d	23p19						23p49				00 19					05a12	05 32				06 18			06 48
Chafford Hundred	d	23p23						23p53				00 23						05 36				06 21			06 51
West Horndon	d					23p39				00 09						00 54			05 37					06 37	
Laindon	d		23p31			23p44				00 16			00 32			00 59			05 42					06 42	
Basildon	d		23p34			23p47				00 19			00 35			01 02			05 45					06 45	
Dagenham Dock	d				23p25				23p55						00 35					05 54			06 24		
Rainham	d				23p29				23p59						00 39					05 57			06 27		
Purfleet	d				23p34				00 04						00 44					06 03			06 33		
Grays	d	23p27			23p42			23p57	00a10			00 27			00a50			05a42		06a12		06 25	06a42		06 55
Tilbury Town 3	d	23p30			23p45			00 01				00 30										06 28			06 58
East Tilbury	d	23p36			23p51			00 06				00 36										06 34			07 04
Stanford-le-Hope	d	23p40			23p55		←	00 10				00 40										06 37			07 07
Pitsea	d	23p48		←	00 06	23p52	00 06	00 18		00 22		00 48		←		01 06			05 50			06 45		06 49	07 15
Benfleet	d	23p52	23p41	23p52	→	23p56	00 10	00 22		00 26		00 52	00 42	00 52		01 10			05 54			06 49		06 52	07 19
Leigh-on-Sea	d	→	23p45	23p56		23p59	00 15	00 27		00 31		→	00 46	00 56		01 14			05 58			06 53		06 57	07 23
Chalkwell	d		23p48	23p59		00 03	00 18	00 30		00 34			00 49	00 59		01 17			06 01			06 56		06 59	07 26
Westcliff	d		23p51	00 02		00 06	00 20	00 32		00 36			00 52	01 02		01 20			06 03			06 58		07 02	07 28
Southend Central	a		23p54	00 05		00 09	00 23	00 35		00 39			00 55	01 05		01 23			06 06			07 04		07 05	07 34
	d		23p54	00 05		00 09	00 23	00 35		00 40			00 55	01 05		01 23			06 07					07 06	
Southend East	d		23p56	00 07		00 11	00 26	00 38		00 42			00 57	01 07		01 25			06 09					07 08	
Thorpe Bay	d		23p59	00 11		00 15	00 29	00 41		00 46			01 01	01 11		01 29			06 12					07 10	
Shoeburyness	a		00 06	00 17		00 21	00 36	00 48		00 52			01 07	01 17		01 35			06 19					07 18	

Table I

Saturdays

London - Southend Central and Shoeburyness

		CC	CC	CC	CC	CC		CC	CC	CC	CC	CC	CC	CC	CC	CC		CC	CC	CC	CC	CC	CC	CC	
London Fenchurch St 7 ⊖	d	06 35	06 40	06 50	07 05	07 10		07 20	07 35	07 40	07 50	08 05	08 10	08 20	08 35	08 40		08 50	09 00		09 05	09 10	09 20	09 30	
Limehouse	d	06 39	06 44	06 54	07 09	07 14		07 24	07 39	07 44	07 54	08 09	08 14	08 24	08 39	08 44		08 54			09 09	09 14	09 24		
West Ham ⊖	d	06 44	06 49	06 59	07 14	07 19		07 29	07 44	07 49	07 59	08 14	08 19	08 29	08 44	08 49		08 59	09 08		09 14	09 19	09 29	09 38	
London Liverpool St 15 ⊖	d																								
Stratford 7 ⊖	d																								
Barking ⊖	d	06 49	06 54	07 04	07 19	07 24		07 34	07 49	07 54	08 04	08 19	08 24	08 34	08 49	08 54		09 04	09 13		09 19	09 24	09 34	09 43	
Upminster ⊖	d		07 02	07 12		07 32		07 42		08 02	08 12		08 32	08 42		09 02		09 12	09 21			09 32	09 42	09 51	
Ockendon	d			07 18				07 48			08 18			08 48				09 18					09 48		
Chafford Hundred	d			07 21				07 51			08 21			08 51				09 21					09 51		
West Horndon	d		07 07			07 37				08 07			08 37			09 07						09 37			
Laindon	d		07 12			07 42				08 12			08 42			09 12			09 29			09 42		09 59	
Basildon	d		07 15			07 45				08 15			08 45			09 15			09 32			09 45		10 02	
Dagenham Dock	d	06 54			07 24				07 54			08 24			08 54						09 24				
Rainham	d	06 57			07 27				07 57			08 27			08 57						09 27				
Purfleet	d	07 03			07 33				08 03			08 33			09 03						09 33				
Grays	d	07a12		07 25	07a42			07 55	08a12		08 25	08a42		08 55	09a12			09 25			09a42		09 55		
Tilbury Town 3	d			07 28				07 58			08 28			08 58				09 28					09 58		
East Tilbury	d			07 34				08 04			08 34			09 04				09 34					10 04		
Stanford-le-Hope	d			07 37				08 07			08 37			09 07				09 37					10 07		
Pitsea	d		07 19	07 45		07 49		08 15		08 19	08 45		08 49	09 15		09 19		09 45		←		09 49	10 15		
Benfleet	d		07 22	07 49		07 52		08 19		08 22	08 49		08 52	09 19		09 22		09 49	09 38	09 49		09 52	10 19	10 08	
Leigh-on-Sea	d		07 27	07 53		07 57		08 23		08 27	08 53		08 57	09 23		09 27		→	09 42	09 53		09 57	→	10 12	
Chalkwell	d		07 29	07 56		07 59		08 26		08 29	08 56		08 59	09 26		09 29			09 45	09 56		09 59		10 15	
Westcliff	d		07 32	07 58		08 02		08 28		08 32	08 58		09 02	09 28		09 32			09 47	09 58		10 02		10 17	
Southend Central	a		07 35	08 04		08 05		08 34		08 35	09 04		09 05	09 34		09 35			09 50	10 04		10 05		10 20	
	d		07 36			08 06				08 36			09 06			09 36			09 50			10 06		10 20	
Southend East	d		07 38			08 08				08 38			09 08			09 38			09 52			10 08		10 22	
Thorpe Bay	d		07 40			08 10				08 40			09 10			09 40			09 55			10 10		10 25	
Shoeburyness	a		07 48			08 18				08 48			09 18			09 48			10 02			10 18		10 32	

		CC		CC		CC	CC	CC	CC	CC	CC	CC	CC	CC		CC	CC	CC	CC	CC	CC	CC	CC	CC
London Fenchurch St 7 ⊖	d					19 35	19 40	19 50	20 00		20 05	20 10	20 20	20 35		20 40	20 50	21 00		21 05	21 10	21 20	21 35	21 40
Limehouse	d					19 39	19 44	19 54			20 09	20 14	20 24	20 39		20 44	20 54			21 09	21 14	21 24	21 39	21 44
West Ham ⊖	d					19 44	19 49	19 59	20 08		20 14	20 19	20 29	20 44		20 49	20 59	21 08		21 14	21 19	21 29	21 44	21 49
London Liverpool St 15 ⊖	d																							
Stratford 7 ⊖	d																							
Barking ⊖	d					19 49	19 54	20 04	20 13		20 19	20 24	20 34	20 49		20 54	21 04	21 13		21 19	21 24	21 34	21 49	21 54
Upminster ⊖	d						20 02	20 12	20 21			20 32	20 42			21 02	21 12	21 21			21 32	21 42		22 02
Ockendon	d							20 18					20 48				21 18					21 48		
Chafford Hundred	d							20 21					20 51				21 21					21 51		
West Horndon	d						20 07					20 37				21 07					21 37			22 07
Laindon	d		and at				20 12		20 29			20 42				21 12		21 29			21 42			22 12
Basildon	d		the same				20 15		20 32			20 45				21 15		21 32			21 45			22 15
Dagenham Dock	d		minutes			19 54					20 24			20 54						21 24			21 54	
Rainham	d		past			19 57					20 27			20 57						21 27			21 57	
Purfleet	d		each			20 03					20 33			21 03						21 33			22 03	
Grays	d		hour until			20a12		20 25			20a42		20 55	21a12			21 25			21a42		21 55	22a12	
Tilbury Town 3	d							20 28					20 58				21 28					21 58		
East Tilbury	d							20 34					21 04				21 34					22 04		
Stanford-le-Hope	d							20 37					21 07				21 37					22 07		
Pitsea	d	←		←			20 19	20 45		←		20 49	21 15			21 19	21 45		←		21 49	22 15		22 19
Benfleet	d	10 19		20 19			20 22	20 49	20 38	20 49		20 52	21 19			21 22	21 49	21 38	21 49		21 52	22 19		22 22
Leigh-on-Sea	d	10 23		20 23			20 27	→	20 42	20 53		20 57	21 23			21 27	→	21 42	21 53		21 57	22 23		22 27
Chalkwell	d	10 26		20 26			20 29		20 45	20 56		20 59	21 26			21 29		21 45	21 56		21 59	22 26		22 29
Westcliff	d	10 28		20 28			20 32		20 47	20 58		21 02	21 28			21 32		21 47	21 58		22 02	22 28		22 32
Southend Central	a	10 34		20 34			20 35		20 50	21 04		21 05	21 34			21 35		21 50	22 04		22 05	22 34		22 35
	d						20 36		20 50			21 06				21 36		21 50			22 06			22 36
Southend East	d						20 38		20 52			21 08				21 38		21 52			22 08			22 38
Thorpe Bay	d						20 40		20 55			21 10				21 40		21 55			22 10			22 40
Shoeburyness	a						20 48		21 02			21 18				21 48		22 02			22 18			22 48

			CC	CC	CC	CC	CC	CC	CC	CC	CC		CC	CC	CC	CC	CC	CC	CC	CC					
London Fenchurch St 7 ⊖	d		21 50	22 00		22 05	22 10	22 20	22 35	22 40	22 50		23 05	23 10		23 20	23 35	23 40		23 50					
Limehouse	d		21 54			22 09	22 14	22 24	22 39	22 44	22 54		23 09	23 14		23 24	23 39	23 44		23 54					
West Ham ⊖	d		21 59	22 08		22 14	22 19	22 29	22 44	22 49	22 59		23 14	23 19		23 29	23 44	23 49		23 59					
London Liverpool St 15 ⊖	d																								
Stratford 7 ⊖	d																								
Barking ⊖	d		22 04	22 13		22 19	22 24	22 34	22 49	22 54	23 04		23 19	23 24		23 34	23 49	23 54		00 04					
Upminster ⊖	d		22 12	22 21			22 32	22 42		23 02	23 12			23 32		23 42		00 02		00 12					
Ockendon	d		22 18					22 48			23 18					23 48				00 18					
Chafford Hundred	d		22 21					22 51			23 21					23 51				00 21					
West Horndon	d						22 37			23 07				23 37				00 07							
Laindon	d			22 29			22 42			23 12				23 42				00 12							
Basildon	d			22 32			22 45			23 15				23 45				00 15							
Dagenham Dock	d					22 24			22 54				23 24				23 54								
Rainham	d					22 27			22 57				23 27				23 57								
Purfleet	d					22 33			23 03				23 33				00 03								
Grays	d		22 25			22a42		22 55	23a12		23 25		23 38			23 55	00 08			00 25					
Tilbury Town 3	d		22 28					22 58			23 28		23 41			23 58	00 11			00 28					
East Tilbury	d		22 34					23 04			23 34		23 47			00 04	00 17			00 34					
Stanford-le-Hope	d		22 37					23 07			23 37		23 50		←	00 07	00 20		←	00 37					
Pitsea	d		22 45		←		22 49	23 15		23 19	23 45		23 58	23 49	23 58	00 15	00 28	00 19	00 28	00 45					
Benfleet	d		22 49	22 38	22 49		22 52	23 19		23 22	23 49		→	23 52	00 01	00 19	→	00 22	00 31	00 49					
Leigh-on-Sea	d		→	22 42	22 53		22 57	23 23		23 27	23 53			23 57	00 06	00 23		00 27	00 36	00 53					
Chalkwell	d			22 45	22 56		22 59	23 26		23 29	23 56			23 59	00 08	00 26		00 29	00 38	00 56					
Westcliff	d			22 47	22 58		23 02	23 28		23 32	23 58			00 02	00 11	00 28		00 32	00 41	00 58					
Southend Central	a			22 50	23 04		23 05	23 31		23 35	00 01			00 05	00 14	00 31		00 35	00 44	01 01					
	d			22 50			23 06	23 31		23 36	00 01			00 06	00 14	00 31		00 36	00 44	01 01					
Southend East	d			22 52			23 08	23 34		23 38	00 04			00 08	00 16	00 34		00 38	00 46	01 04					
Thorpe Bay	d			22 55			23 10	23 36		23 41	00 06			00 11	00 19	00 36		00 41	00 49	01 06					
Shoeburyness	a			23 02			23 18	23 43		23 48	00 13			00 18	00 26	00 43		00 48	00 56	01 13					

Table 1

Sundays

London - Southend Central and Shoeburyness

		CC A	CC A	CC A	CC A	CC A	CC A	CC A	CC A	CC A	CC	CC	CC	CC	CC	CC	CC	CC	CC	CC	CC	CC	CC
London Fenchurch St 7 ⊖	d	22p50	23p05	23p10		23p20	23p35	23p40		23p50	00 10	00 40	06 40		07 10	07 40	07 50	08 10			08 40	08 50	09 10
Limehouse	d	22p54	23p09	23p14		23p24	23p39	23p44		23p54	00 14	00 44	06 44		07 14	07 44	07 54	08 14			08 44	08 54	09 14
West Ham ⊖	d	22p59	23p14	23p19		23p29	23p44	23p49		23p59	00 19	00 49	06 49		07 19	07 49	07 59	08 19			08 49	08 59	09 19
London Liverpool St 15 ⊖	d																						
Stratford 7 ⊖	d																						
Barking ⊖	d	23p04	23p19	23p24		23p34	23p49	23p54		00 04	00 24	00 54	06 54	07 04	07 24	07 54	08 04	08 24	08 29	08 34	08 54	09 04	09 24
Upminster ⊖	d	23p12		23p32		23p42		00 02		00 12	00 32	01 02	07 02	07 12	07 32	08 02	08 12	08 32		08 42	09 02	09 12	09 32
Ockendon	d	23p18				23p48				00 18				07 18			08 18			08 48		09 18	
Chafford Hundred	d	23p21				23p51				00 21				07 21			08 21			08 51		09 21	
West Horndon	d			23p37				00 07			00 37	01 07	07 07		07 37	08 07		08 37			09 07		09 37
Laindon	d			23p42				00 12			00 42	01 12	07 12		07 42	08 12		08 42			09 12		09 42
Basildon	d			23p45				00 15			00 45	01 15	07 15		07 45	08 15		08 45			09 15		09 45
Dagenham Dock	d		23p24				23p54												08 33				
Rainham	d		23p27				23p57												08 37				
Purfleet	d		23p33				00 03												08 42				
Grays	d	23p25	23p38			23p55	00 08			00 25				07 25			08 25		08a50	08 55		09 25	
Tilbury Town 3	d	23p28	23p41			23p58	00 11			00 28				07 28			08 28			08 58		09 28	
East Tilbury	d	23p34	23p47			00 04	00 17			00 34				07 34			08 34			09 04		09 34	
Stanford-le-Hope	d	23p37	23p50		←	00 07	00 20		←	00 37				07 37			08 37			09 07		09 37	
Pitsea	d	23p45	23p58	23p49	23p58	00 15	00 28	00 19	00 28	00 45	00 49	01 19	07 19	07 45	07 49	08 19	08 45	08 49		09 15	09 19	09 45	09 49
Benfleet	d	23p49	→	23p52	00 01	00 19	→	00 22	00 31	00 49	00 52	01 22	07 22	07 49	07 52	08 22	08 49	08 52		09 19	09 22	09 49	09 52
Leigh-on-Sea	d	23p53		23p57	00 06	00 23		00 27	00 36	00 53	00 57	01 27	07 27	07 53	07 57	08 27	08 53	08 57		09 23	09 27	09 53	09 57
Chalkwell	d	23p56		23p59	00 08	00 26		00 29	00 38	00 56	00 59	01 29	07 29	07 56	07 59	08 29	08 56	08 59		09 26	09 29	09 56	09 59
Westcliff	d	23p58		00 02	00 11	00 28		00 32	00 41	00 58	01 02	01 32	07 32	07 58	08 02	08 32	08 58	09 02		09 28	09 32	09 58	10 02
Southend Central	a	00 01		00 05	00 14	00 31		00 35	00 44	01 01	01 05	01 35	07 34	08 04	08 05	08 34	09 04	09 05		09 34	09 35	10 04	10 05
	d	00 01		00 06	00 14	00 31		00 36	00 44	01 01	01 06	01 36	07 36		08 06	08 36		09 06			09 36		10 06
Southend East	d	00 04		00 08	00 16	00 34		00 38	00 46	01 04	01 08	01 38	07 38		08 08	08 38		09 08			09 38		10 08
Thorpe Bay	d	00 06		00 11	00 19	00 36		00 41	00 49	01 06	01 11	01 41	07 40		08 10	08 40		09 10			09 40		10 10
Shoeburyness	a	00 13		00 18	00 26	00 43		00 48	00 56	01 13	01 18	01 48	07 48		08 18	08 48		09 18			09 48		10 18

		CC	CC	CC	CC	CC	CC	CC		CC	CC	CC	CC	CC	CC	CC	CC	CC	CC	CC	CC	CC
London Fenchurch St 7 ⊖	d			09 40	09 50	10 10		10 20		20 20	20 40	20 50	21 10		21 20	21 40	21 50	22 10	22 40	22 50	23 10	23 40
Limehouse	d			09 44	09 54	10 14		10 24		20 24	20 44	20 54	21 14		21 24	21 44	21 54	22 14	22 44	22 54	23 14	23 44
West Ham ⊖	d			09 49	09 59	10 19		10 29		20 29	20 49	20 59	21 19		21 29	21 49	21 59	22 19	22 49	22 59	23 19	23 49
London Liverpool St 15 ⊖	d																					
Stratford 7 ⊖	d																					
Barking ⊖	d	09 29	09 34	09 54	10 04	10 24	10 29	10 34		20 34	20 54	21 04	21 24	21 29	21 34	21 54	22 04	22 24	22 54	23 04	23 24	23 54
Upminster ⊖	d		09 42	10 02	10 12	10 32		10 42		20 42	21 02	21 12	21 32		21 42	22 02	22 12	22 32	23 02	23 12	23 32	00 02
Ockendon	d		09 48		10 18			10 48		20 48		21 18			21 48		22 18			23 18		
Chafford Hundred	d		09 51		10 21			10 51		20 51		21 21			21 51		22 21			23 21		
West Horndon	d			10 07		10 37					21 07		21 37			22 07		22 37	23 07		23 37	00 07
Laindon	d			10 12		10 42			and at		21 12		21 42			22 12		22 42	23 12		23 42	00 12
Basildon	d			10 15		10 45			the same		21 15		21 45			22 15		22 45	23 15		23 45	00 15
Dagenham Dock	d	09 33					10 33		minutes					21 33								
Rainham	d	09 37					10 37		past					21 37								
Purfleet	d	09 42					10 42		each					21 42								
Grays	d	09a50	09 55		10 25		10a50	10 55	hour until	20 55		21 25		21a50	21 55		22 25			23 25		
Tilbury Town 3	d		09 58		10 28			10 58		20 58		21 28			21 58		22 28			23 28		
East Tilbury	d		10 04		10 34			11 04		21 04		21 34			22 04		22 34			23 34		
Stanford-le-Hope	d		10 07		10 37			11 07		21 07		21 37			22 07		22 37			23 37		
Pitsea	d		10 15	10 19	10 45	10 49		11 15		21 15	21 19	21 45	21 49		22 15	22 19	22 45	22 49	23 19	23 45	23 49	00 19
Benfleet	d		10 19	10 22	10 49	10 52		11 19		21 19	21 22	21 49	21 52		22 19	22 22	22 49	22 52	23 22	23 49	23 52	00 22
Leigh-on-Sea	d		10 23	10 27	10 53	10 57		11 23		21 23	21 27	21 53	21 57		22 23	22 27	22 53	22 57	23 27	23 53	23 57	00 27
Chalkwell	d		10 26	10 29	10 56	10 59		11 26		21 26	21 29	21 56	21 59		22 26	22 29	22 56	22 59	23 29	23 56	23 59	00 29
Westcliff	d		10 28	10 32	10 58	11 02		11 28		21 28	21 32	21 58	22 02		22 28	22 32	22 58	23 02	23 32	23 58	00 02	00 32
Southend Central	a		10 34	10 35	11 04	11 05		11 34		21 34	21 35	22 04	22 05		22 31	22 35	23 01	23 05	23 35	00 01	00 05	00 35
	d			10 36		11 06					21 36		22 06		22 31	22 36	23 01	23 06	23 36	00 01	00 06	00 36
Southend East	d			10 38		11 08					21 38		22 08		22 33	22 38	23 03	23 08	23 38	00 03	00 08	00 38
Thorpe Bay	d			10 40		11 10					21 40		22 10		22 36	22 40	23 06	23 10	23 40	00 06	00 10	00 40
Shoeburyness	a			10 48		11 18					21 48		22 18		22 43	22 48	23 13	23 18	23 48	00 13	00 18	00 48

A not 22 May

Shoeburyness and Southend Central - London

Miles	Miles	Miles			CC MX	CC MX	CC MX	CC	CC	CC	CC	CC	CC		CC	CC	CC	CC	CC	CC	CC	CC	CC		CC
0	0	—	**Shoeburyness**	d			23p05		04 20		04 40	04 59			05 13	05 24		05 28			05 45				05 58
1½	1½	—	Thorpe Bay	d			23p09		04 24		04 44	05 03			05 17	05 28		05 32			05 49		05 58		06 02
3	3	—	Southend East	d			23p12		04 27		04 47	05 06			05 20	05 31		05 35			05 52		06 01		06 05
3¾	3¾	—	**Southend Central**	a			23p14		04 29		04 49	05 08			05 22	05 33		05 37			05 54		06 03		06 07
—	—	—		d	22p50		23p15		04 29		04 50	05 09			05 23	05 34		05 38		05 47	05 55		06 04		06 08
4¾	4¾	—	Westcliff	d	22p53		23p17		04 31		04 52	05 11			05 25	05 36		05 40		05 49	05 57		06 06		06 10
5½	5½	—	Chalkwell	d	22p55		23p19		04 34		04 54	05 13			05 27	05 38		05 42		05 51	05 59		06 08		06 12
7	7	—	Leigh-on-Sea	d	22p58		23p22		04 37		04 57	05 16			05 30	05 41		05 45		05 54	06 02		06 11		06 15
10¼	10¼	—	Benfleet	d	23p03		23p27		04 41		05 02	05 21			05 35	05 46		05 50		05 59	06 07		06 16		06 20
13	13	—	Pitsea	d	23p07		23p32		04 45		05 06	05 25			05 39	05 50		05 54		06 04	06 11		06 24		
—	18	—	Stanford-le-Hope	d	23p14			04 29			05 14				05 46			06 01		06 11			06 31		
—	20	—	East Tilbury	d	23p18			04 33			05 18				05 50			06 05		06 15			06 35		
—	23¾	—	**Tilbury Town** 3	d	23p24			04 39			05 24				05 56			06 11		06 21			06 41		
—	25½	0	Grays	d	23p27	23p31		04 42		05 12	05 27		05 50		06 00			06 15		06 25		06 29	06 45		
—	29¼	—	Purfleet	d		23p36					05 33				06 05			06 20				06 34	06 51		
—	32½	—	Rainham	d		23p41					05 38				06 10			06 25				06 40	06 56		
—	34¾	—	Dagenham Dock	d		23p45					05 41				06 14			06 29				06 43	07 00		
15	—	—	Basildon	d			23p36		04 50			05 29				05 54					06 16				06 27
16¾	—	—	Laindon	d			23p39		04 53			05 32				05 57					06 19				06 31
20¼	—	—	West Horndon	d			23p44		04 58			05 37				06 02					06 24				
—	—	2½	Chafford Hundred	d	23p31			04 46		05 16			05 54							06 30					
—	—	4½	Ockendon	d	23p35			04 50		05 20			05 58						06 19	06 37					
24¼	—	7½	Upminster	⊖ d	23p42		23p50	04 57	05 04	05a25		05 42	06 03			06 08	←		06a24	06 44	06 30				06 40
32	37¾	—	Barking	⊖ d	23p50	23p51	23p59	05 06	05 13		05 47	05 51	06 12		06 20	06 16	06 20	06 35		→	06 38	06 50	07 06		
—	—	—	Stratford 7	⊖ a		23p58		05 14							→								→		
—	—	—	**London Liverpool St** 15	⊖ a		00 11		05 27																	
35	40¾	—	West Ham	⊖ d	23p56		00 04		05 18		05 53	05 57	06 17			06 22	06 26	06 41			06 44	06 56			
37¾	43½	—	Limehouse	d	00 01		00 09		05 23		05 58	06 02	06 22			06 27	06 31	06 46			06 49	07 01			06 57
39½	45¼	—	**London Fenchurch St** 7	⊖ a	00 05		00 14		05 30		06 04	06 08	06 29			06 31	06 37	06 52			06 53	→			07 03

		CC	CC	CC	CC	CC	CC	CC	CC		CC	CC	CC	CC	CC	CC	CC	CC	CC		CC	CC	CC	CC	CC
Shoeburyness	d			06 04			06 13		06 17			06 28			06 32	06 46								06 53	
Thorpe Bay	d			06 08		06 13	06 17		06 21			06 32			06 36	06 50								06 57	
Southend East	d			06 11		06 16	06 20		06 24			06 35			06 39	06 53								07 00	
Southend Central	a			06 13		06 18	06 22		06 26			06 37			06 41	06 55								07 02	
	d			06 14		06 19	06 23		06 27			06 38			06 42	06 56								07 03	
Westcliff	d			06 16		06 21	06 25		06 29			06 40			06 44	06 58								07 05	
Chalkwell	d			06 18		06 23	06 27		06 31			06 42			06 46	07 00								07 07	
Leigh-on-Sea	d			06 21		06 26	06 30		06 34			06 45			06 49	07 03								07 10	
Benfleet	d			06 26		06 31	06 35		06 39			06 50			06 54	07 08								07 15	
Pitsea	d			06 30		06 39			06 43					06 55	06 58				07 02				07 15	07 19	
Stanford-le-Hope	d					06 46								07 02					07 09				07 22		
East Tilbury	d					06 50								07 06					07 13				07 26		
Tilbury Town 3	d					06 56								07 12					07 20				07 32		
Grays	d				06 51	07 00								07 16					07 24		07 32		07 36		
Purfleet	d					07 05								07 21							07 37				
Rainham	d					07 11								07 27							07 43				
Dagenham Dock	d					07 14								07 30							07 46				
Basildon	d			06 35			06 42		06 48			06 57			07 03	07 15								07 24	
Laindon	d			06 38					06 51						07 06			07 22				07 39		07 27	
West Horndon	d			06 43					06 56						07 11			07 27				07 44			
Chafford Hundred	d				06 55														07 28				07 40		
Ockendon	d		←		07 00						←								07 32				07 48		
Upminster	⊖ d		06 44	06 49	07 06			←	07 02		07 06	07 10	←		07 17		←	07 32	07 39			07 49	07 56		←
Barking	⊖ d			06 58	→	07 21	07 01	07 06	07 11		07 15		07 21	07 37	07 27		07 37	07 41	07 48		07 54	07 58		07 45	07 48
Stratford 7	⊖ a					→								→					→		→	→			
London Liverpool St 15	⊖ a																								
West Ham	⊖ d	←	06 59	07 03			07 07	07 12			07 20	07 23	07 26					07 46							
Limehouse	d	07 01	07 04					07 17	07 20		07 25		07 32		07 36		07 46	07 51						07 54	
London Fenchurch St 7	⊖ a	07 07	07 10	07 14			07 17	07 23	07 26		07 32	07 34	07 38		07 42	07 46	07 52	07 58					08 19	08 00	08 03

		CC	CC	CC	CC		CC	CC	CC	CC	CC	CC	CC	CC	CC		CC	CC	CC	CC	CC	CC	CC	CC	CC
Shoeburyness	d		07 05					07 20						07 24			07 35							07 50	
Thorpe Bay	d		07 09				07 14	07 24						07 28			07 39				07 43			07 54	
Southend East	d		07 12				07 17	07 27						07 31			07 42				07 46			07 57	
Southend Central	a		07 14				07 19	07 29						07 33			07 44				07 48			07 59	
	d	07 10	07 15				07 20	07 30						07 34			07 45				07 49			08 00	
Westcliff	d	07 12	07 17				07 22	07 32						07 36			07 47				07 51			08 02	
Chalkwell	d	07 14	07 19				07 24	07 34						07 38			07 49				07 53			08 04	
Leigh-on-Sea	d	07 18	07 22				07 27	07 37						07 41			07 52				07 56			08 07	
Benfleet	d	07 22	07 27				07 32	07 42						07 46			07 57				08 01			08 12	
Pitsea	d	07 27					07 36					07 42	07 49	07 50						07 54	08 05				
Stanford-le-Hope	d	07 34									07 44	07 49	07 56							08 02					
East Tilbury	d	07 38										07 53								08 06					
Tilbury Town 3	d	07 44										07 59								08 12					
Grays	d	07 48									07 54	08 03	08 07							08 16					
Purfleet	d	07 53										08 08								08 21					
Rainham	d	07 59										08 14								08 27					
Dagenham Dock	d	08 02										08 17								08 30					
Basildon	d		07 34				07 41							07 55							08 10				
Laindon	d						07 44			07 52				07 58					08 08		08 13				08 23
West Horndon	d									07 57									08 13						08 28
Chafford Hundred	d										07 59		08 11												
Ockendon	d										08 03		08 18									←			
Upminster	⊖ d			←	←				←	08 03	08 10		08 25		←		08 14	←	08 18			08 25	←	08 29	08 33
Barking	⊖ d	08 09		07 54	07 58		08 01		08 09	08 12	08 19	08 24	→	08 15	08 19			08 24	08 27	08 37	08 30		08 37		08 43
Stratford 7	⊖ a	→									→	→								→					
London Liverpool St 15	⊖ a																								
West Ham	⊖ d				08 03					08 17									08 32						08 48
Limehouse	d		08 00	08 03	08 08		08 10	08 16	08 19	08 22				08 25			08 31	08 34	08 37		08 39		08 46	08 48	08 53
London Fenchurch St 7	⊖ a		08 07	08 10	08 14		08 17	08 22	08 25	08 28				08 32	08 34		08 37	08 40	08 43		08 46	08 48	08 52	08 55	08 59

Shoeburyness and Southend Central - London

			CC	CC	CC	CC	CC	CC	CC	CC	CC		CC	CC	CC	CC	CC	CC	CC	CC	CC		CC	CC	CC
Shoeburyness	d				07 54		08 05						08 10		08 25					08 40					
Thorpe Bay	d				07 58		08 09						08 14		08 29					08 44					
Southend East	d				08 01		08 12						08 17		08 32					08 47					
Southend Central	a				08 03		08 14						08 19		08 34					08 49					
	d				08 04		08 15						08 20		08 34					08 50				09 06	
Westcliff	d				08 06		08 17						08 22		08 36					08 52				09 08	
Chalkwell	d				08 08		08 19						08 24		08 39					08 54				09 11	
Leigh-on-Sea	d				08 11		08 22						08 27		08 42					08 57				09 14	
Benfleet	d				08 16		08 27						08 32		08 47					09 02				09 19	
Pitsea	d			08 13	08 20						08 34		08 36		08 51				08 54	09 06					09 08
Stanford-le-Hope	d		08 12	08 20						08 32	08 41								09 01						09 16
East Tilbury	d		08 16	08 24						08 36	08 45								09 05						09 20
Tilbury Town 3	d		08 22	08 30						08 42	08 51								09 11						09 26
Grays	d		08 26	08 34						08 46	08 56						09 03		09 15						09 29
Purfleet	d			08 40						08 51							09 08		09 20						
Rainham	d			08 45						08 57							09 13		09 26						
Dagenham Dock	d			08 49						09 00							09 17		09 29						
Basildon	d				08 25								08 41		08 55					09 11				09 26	
Laindon	d				08 28				08 38				08 44					09 04		09 14			09 17	09 29	
West Horndon	d								08 43									09 10					09 22		
Chafford Hundred	d		08 30								09 01														09 34
Ockendon	d		08 34								09 05					←									09 38
Upminster	⊖ d		08 41			←		←	08 49		09 11		08 54	←	09 06	09 11		09 16			←		09 28	09 38	09 45
Barking	⊖ d		08 51	08 55	08 47	08 51		08 55	08 58	09 07	→		09 03	09 07		09 20	09 23	09 25	09 35	09 30	09 35		09 37	09 47	09 54
Stratford 7	⊖ a		→	→						→									→						
London Liverpool St 15	⊖ a																								
West Ham	⊖ d							09 01	09 04				09 08			09 25	09 29	09 31					09 43	09 52	09 59
Limehouse	d				08 56			09 06	09 09				09 14	09 17	09 23	09 30	09 34	09 36			09 44			09 57	10 04
London Fenchurch St 7	⊖ a				09 02	09 06	09 08	09 12	09 15				09 20	09 26	09 29	09 38	09 40	09 43		09 45	09 51		09 53	10 04	10 09

		CC	CC	CC	CC	CC	CC		CC	CC	CC	CC		CC	CC	CC		CC	CC	CC	CC	CC	CC	CC
Shoeburyness	d	09 05			09 20		09 35				09 50				15 05				15 20		15 35			15 50
Thorpe Bay	d	09 09			09 24		09 39				09 54				15 09				15 24		15 39			15 54
Southend East	d	09 12			09 27		09 42				09 57				15 12				15 27		15 42			15 57
Southend Central	a	09 14			09 29		09 44				09 59				15 14				15 29		15 44			15 59
	d	09 15		09 20	09 30		09 45			09 50	10 00				15 15			15 20	15 30		15 45		15 48	16 00
Westcliff	d	09 17		09 23	09 32		09 47			09 53	10 02				15 17			15 23	15 32		15 47		15 50	16 02
Chalkwell	d	09 19		09 25	09 34		09 49			09 55	10 04				15 19			15 25	15 34		15 49		15 53	16 04
Leigh-on-Sea	d	09 22		09 28	09 37		09 52			09 58	10 07				15 22			15 28	15 37		15 52		15 56	16 07
Benfleet	d	09 27		09 33	09 42		09 57			10 03	10 12				15 27			15 33	15 42		15 57		16 00	16 12
Pitsea	d	09 32		09 37			10 02			10 07					15 32			15 37			16 02		16 04	
Stanford-le-Hope	d			09 44						10 14			and at the same minutes past each hour until					15 44					16 11	
East Tilbury	d			09 48						10 18								15 48					16 15	
Tilbury Town 3	d			09 54						10 24								15 54					16 21	
Grays	d		09 46	09 57					10 16	10 27						15 46		15 57				16 16	16 26	
Purfleet	d		09 51						10 21							15 51						16 21		
Rainham	d		09 56						10 26							15 56						16 26		
Dagenham Dock	d		10 00						10 30							16 00						16 30		
Basildon	d	09 36			09 49		10 06				10 19				15 36				15 49		16 06			16 19
Laindon	d	09 39			09 52		10 09				10 22				15 39				15 52		16 09			16 22
West Horndon	d	09 44					10 14								15 44						16 14			
Chafford Hundred	d			10 01						10 31								16 01					16 30	
Ockendon	d			10 05		←				10 35		←		←				16 05		←			16 34	
Upminster	⊖ d	09 50		10 12	10 02	10 12	10 20			10 42	10 32	10 42		15 42	15 50			16 12	16 02	16 12	16 20		16 41	16 30
Barking	⊖ d	09 58	10 06	→	10 10	10 20	10 28		10 36	→	10 40	10 50		15 50	15 58	16 06		→	16 10	16 20	16 28	16 36	→	16 38
Stratford 7	⊖ a																							
London Liverpool St 15	⊖ a																							
West Ham	⊖ d	10 04	10 11		10 16	10 26	10 34		10 41		10 46	10 56		15 56	16 04	16 11			16 17	16 26	16 34			16 44
Limehouse	d	10 09	10 16			10 31	10 39		10 46			11 01		16 01	16 09	16 16				16 31	16 39			
London Fenchurch St 7	⊖ a	10 13	10 21		10 24	10 35	10 43		10 51		10 54	11 05		16 05	16 13	16 21			16 26	16 36	16 43	16 48		16 52

		CC	CC		CC	CC	CC	CC	CC	CC	CC	CC	CC		CC	CC	CC	CC	CC	CC	CC	CC	CC		CC
Shoeburyness	d		16 05					16 15			16 28					16 49		16 56							17 10
Thorpe Bay	d		16 09					16 19			16 32					16 53		17 00							17 14
Southend East	d		16 12					16 22			16 35					16 56		17 03							17 17
Southend Central	a		16 14					16 24			16 37					16 58		17 05							17 19
	d		16 15				16 19	16 25	16 31		16 38				16 54	16 59		17 06							17 19
Westcliff	d		16 17				16 21	16 27	16 33		16 40				16 56	17 01		17 08							17 21
Chalkwell	d		16 19				16 23	16 29	16 35		16 42				16 59	17 03		17 10							17 24
Leigh-on-Sea	d		16 22				16 26	16 32	16 38		16 45				17 02	17 06		17 13							17 27
Benfleet	d		16 27				16 31	16 37	16 43		16 50				17 06	17 11		17 18							17 32
Pitsea	d		16 31				16 35		16 47		16 54		16 57		17 10	17 15		17 22					17 24		17 36
Stanford-le-Hope	d						16 42						17 04							17 19			17 32		
East Tilbury	d						16 46						17 08							17 23			17 36		
Tilbury Town 3	d						16 52						17 14							17 29			17 42		
Grays	d				16 39	16 52	16 57						17 19				17 22			17 32	17 44		17 50		
Purfleet	d				16 44	16 57											17 27			17 38	17 49				
Rainham	d				16 49	17 02											17 32			17 43	17 54				
Dagenham Dock	d				16 53	17 06											17 36			17 46	17 58				
Basildon	d		16 35					16 43	16 51		16 58				17 14	17 19		17 26							17 40
Laindon	d		16 38								17 01				17 17							17 47			17 44
West Horndon	d		16 43								17 06				17 22							17 52			
Chafford Hundred	d						17 01						17 23										17 54		
Ockendon	d	←					17 07					←	17 30						←				17 59		
Upminster	⊖ d	16 41	16 48				17 15	16 54		←	17 11	17 15	17 39		17 28	17 31			17 39			17 58	18 06		
Barking	⊖ d	16 49	16 57		17 00	17 16	→	17 03		17 16	17 20	17 25	→		17 36	17 40	17 42		17 47	17 52	18 04	18 06	18 14		
Stratford 7	⊖ a					→																			
London Liverpool St 15	⊖ a																								
West Ham	⊖ d		17 02					17 09		17 22		17 31						17 49		17 58	18 09	18 12			
Limehouse	d		17 08		17 10			17 14			17 29									18 03		18 17			
London Fenchurch St 7	⊖ a	17 03	17 12		17 15			17 18	17 24	17 30	17 33	17 39			17 49	17 52	17 54	17 58	18 00	18 09	18 18	18 21	18 27		18 11

Shoeburyness and Southend Central - London

		CC	CC	CC	CC	CC	CC	CC	CC		CC	CC	CC	CC	CC	CC	CC	CC	CC		CC	CC	CC	CC	CC
Shoeburyness	d		17 30		17 45				18 05			18 20			18 35			18 50			19 05			19 20	
Thorpe Bay	d		17 34		17 49				18 09			18 24			18 39			18 54			19 09			19 24	
Southend East	d		17 37		17 52				18 12			18 27			18 42			18 57			19 12			19 27	
Southend Central	a		17 39		17 54				18 14			18 29			18 44			18 59			19 15			19 29	
	d		17 40		17 55				18 15		18 20	18 30			18 45		18 49	19 00			19 15		19 20	19 30	
Westcliff	d		17 42		17 57				18 17		18 23	18 32			18 47		18 51	19 02			19 17		19 23	19 32	
Chalkwell	d		17 44		17 59				18 19		18 25	18 34			18 49		18 53	19 04			19 19		19 25	19 34	
Leigh-on-Sea	d		17 47		18 02				18 22		18 28	18 37			18 52		18 56	19 07			19 22		19 28	19 37	
Benfleet	d		17 52		18 07				18 27		18 33	18 42			18 57		19 01	19 12			19 27		19 33	19 42	
Pitsea	d	17 43	17 56	17 59	18 11			18 31	18 32		18 37				19 02		19 05				19 32		19 37		
Stanford-le-Hope	d	17 50		18 06				18 38			18 44						19 12						19 44		
East Tilbury	d	17 54		18 10				18 42			18 48						19 16						19 48		
Tilbury Town 3	d	18 00		18 16				18 48			18 54						19 22						19 54		
Grays	d	18 04		18 20			18 28	18 54			18 57					19 18	19 25					19 48	19 57		
Purfleet	d	18 09					18 33				19 04					19 23						19 53			
Rainham	d	18 14					18 38				19 09					19 28						19 58			
Dagenham Dock	d	18 18					18 42				19 12					19 32						20 02			
Basildon	d		18 00		18 15				18 36			18 49			19 06			19 19			19 36			19 49	
Laindon	d		18 05		18 18				18 39			18 52			19 09			19 22			19 39			19 52	
West Horndon	d		18 10		18 23				18 44						19 14						19 44				
Chafford Hundred	d			18 25				18 59									19 29						20 01		
Ockendon	d			18 31		←		19 04						←			19 34		←				20 05		
Upminster ⊖	d		18 15	18 38	18 30	18 38		19 10	18 50			19 02	←	19 10	19 20		19 40	19 32	19 40		19 50		20 12	20 02	←
Barking ⊖	d	18 26	18 24	→	18 38		18 48	→	18 58		19 18	19 10	19 18	19 20	19 28	19 37	→	19 40	19 50		19 58	20 12	→	20 10	20 12
Stratford 7 ⊖	a										→											→			20 21
London Liverpool St 15 ⊖	a																								20 33
West Ham ⊖	d	18 32	18 29		18 44		18 53		19 04			19 16		19 26	19 34	19 43		19 46	19 56		20 04			20 16	
Limehouse	d	18 37			18 49		18 58		19 09				19 27		19 39	19 48			20 01		20 09				
London Fenchurch St 7 ⊖	a	18 41	18 38		18 53	19 00	19 03		19 13			19 24	19 32	19 36	19 43	19 53		19 55	20 05		20 13			20 25	

		CC	CC	CC	CC		CC	CC	CC	CC	CC	CC	CC	CC	CC		CC	CC	CC	CC	CC	CC	CC	CC	CC
Shoeburyness	d		19 35				19 50			20 05			20 20		20 35				21 05			21 20		21 35	
Thorpe Bay	d		19 39				19 54			20 09			20 24		20 39				21 09			21 24		21 39	
Southend East	d		19 42				19 57			20 12			20 27		20 42				21 12			21 27		21 42	
Southend Central	a		19 44				19 59			20 14			20 29		20 44				21 14			21 29		21 45	
	d		19 45		19 50		20 00			20 15		20 20	20 30		20 45			20 50	21 15		21 20	21 30		21 45	
Westcliff	d		19 47		19 53		20 02			20 17		20 23	20 32		20 47			20 53	21 17		21 23	21 32		21 47	
Chalkwell	d		19 49		19 55		20 04			20 19		20 25	20 34		20 49			20 55	21 19		21 25	21 34		21 49	
Leigh-on-Sea	d		19 52		19 58		20 07			20 22		20 28	20 37		20 52			20 58	21 22		21 28	21 37		21 52	
Benfleet	d		19 57		20 03		20 12			20 27		20 33	20 42		20 57			21 03	21 27		21 33	21 42		21 57	
Pitsea	d		20 02		20 07					20 32		20 37			21 02			21 07	21 32		21 37			22 02	
Stanford-le-Hope	d				20 14							20 44						21 14			21 44				
East Tilbury	d				20 18							20 48						21 18			21 48				
Tilbury Town 3	d				20 24							20 54						21 24			21 54				
Grays	d			20 16	20 27						20 46	20 57					21 16	21 27		21 46	21 57				22 16
Purfleet	d			20 21							20 51						21 21			21 51					22 21
Rainham	d			20 26							20 56						21 26			21 56					22 26
Dagenham Dock	d			20 30							21 00						21 30			22 00					22 30
Basildon	d		20 06				20 19			20 36			20 49		21 06				21 36			21 49		22 06	
Laindon	d		20 09				20 22			20 39			20 52		21 09				21 39			21 52		22 09	
West Horndon	d		20 14							20 44					21 14				21 44					22 14	
Chafford Hundred	d				20 31							21 01						21 31			22 01				
Ockendon	d	←			20 35			←				21 05		←				21 35			22 05		←		
Upminster ⊖	d	20 12	20 20		20 42		20 32	20 42		20 50		21 12	21 02	21 12	21 20			21 42	21 50		22 12	22 02	22 12	22 20	
Barking ⊖	d	20 20	20 28	20 36	→		20 40	20 50	20 51	20 58	21 06	→	21 10	21 20	21 28		21 36	21 50	21 58	22 06	→	22 10	22 20	22 28	22 36
Stratford 7 ⊖	a								21 00		21 15														
London Liverpool St 15 ⊖	a								21 12		21 26														
West Ham ⊖	d	20 26	20 34	20 41			20 46	20 56		21 04			21 16	21 26	21 34		21 41	21 56	22 04	22 11		22 16	22 26	22 34	22 41
Limehouse	d	20 31	20 39	20 46				21 01		21 09				21 31	21 39		21 46	22 01	22 09	22 16			22 31	22 39	22 46
London Fenchurch St 7 ⊖	a	20 35	20 43	20 51			20 54	21 05		21 13			21 24	21 35	21 43		21 52	22 05	22 13	22 21		22 24	22 35	22 43	22 52

			CC	CC	CC	CC	CC	CC	CC	CC
Shoeburyness	d			22 05			22 35			23 05
Thorpe Bay	d			22 09			22 39			23 09
Southend East	d			22 12			22 42			23 12
Southend Central	a			22 14			22 44			23 14
	d		21 50	22 15		22 20	22 45	22 50		23 15
Westcliff	d		21 53	22 17		22 23	22 47	22 53		23 17
Chalkwell	d		21 55	22 19		22 25	22 49	22 55		23 19
Leigh-on-Sea	d		21 58	22 22		22 28	22 52	22 58		23 22
Benfleet	d		22 03	22 27		22 33	22 57	23 03		23 27
Pitsea	d		22 07	22 32		22 37	23 02	23 07		23 32
Stanford-le-Hope	d		22 14			22 44		23 14		
East Tilbury	d		22 18			22 48		23 18		
Tilbury Town 3	d		22 24			22 54		23 24		
Grays	d		22 27		22 46	22 57		23 27	23 31	
Purfleet	d				22 51				23 36	
Rainham	d				22 56				23 41	
Dagenham Dock	d				23 00				23 45	
Basildon	d			22 36			23 06			23 36
Laindon	d			22 39			23 09			23 39
West Horndon	d			22 44			23 14			23 44
Chafford Hundred	d		22 31			23 01		23 31		
Ockendon	d		22 35			23 05		23 35		
Upminster ⊖	d		22 42	22 50		23 12	23 20	23 42		23 50
Barking ⊖	d		22 50	22 58	23 06	23 20	23 28	23 50	23 51	23 59
Stratford 7 ⊖	a								23 58	
London Liverpool St 15 ⊖	a								00 11	
West Ham ⊖	d		22 56	23 04	23 11	23 26	23 34	23 56		00 04
Limehouse	d		23 01	23 09	23 16	23 31	23 39	00 01		00 09
London Fenchurch St 7 ⊖	a		23 05	23 13	23 21	23 35	23 43	00 05		00 14

Table 1

Saturdays

Shoeburyness and Southend Central - London

		CC	CC	CC	CC	CC	CC	CC	CC	CC		CC	CC	CC	CC	CC	CC	CC	CC	CC		CC	CC	CC	CC
Shoeburyness	d			23p05		04 20		05 05				05 35			06 05			06 35				07 05			07 35
Thorpe Bay	d			23p09		04 23		05 08				05 38			06 08			06 38				07 08			07 38
Southend East	d			23p12		04 26		05 11				05 41			06 11			06 41				07 11			07 41
Southend Central	a			23p14		04 28		05 13				05 43			06 13			06 43				07 13			07 43
	d	22p50		23p15		04 29		05 14		05 20		05 44		05 50	06 14		06 20	06 44		06 50		07 14		07 20	07 44
Westcliff	d	22p53		23p17		04 31		05 16		05 23		05 46		05 53	06 16		06 23	06 46		06 53		07 16		07 23	07 46
Chalkwell	d	22p55		23p19		04 33		05 18		05 25		05 48		05 55	06 18		06 25	06 48		06 55		07 18		07 25	07 48
Leigh-on-Sea	d	22p58		23p22		04 36		05 21		05 28		05 51		05 58	06 21		06 28	06 51		06 58		07 21		07 28	07 51
Benfleet	d	23p03		23p27		04 40		05 25		05 32		05 55		06 02	06 25		06 32	06 55		07 02		07 25		07 32	07 55
Pitsea	d	23p07		23p32		04 44		05 29		05 36		05 59		06 06	06 29		06 36	06 59		07 06		07 29		07 36	07 59
Stanford-le-Hope	d	23p14			04 29					05 42				06 12			06 42			07 12				07 42	
East Tilbury	d	23p18			04 32					05 45				06 15			06 45			07 15				07 45	
Tilbury Town 3	d	23p24			04 38					05 51				06 21			06 51			07 21				07 51	
Grays	d	23p27	23p31		04 41				05 48	05 54			06 18	06 24		06 48	06 54		07 18	07 24			07 48	07 54	
Purfleet	d		23p36						05 53				06 23			06 53			07 23				07 53		
Rainham	d		23p41						05 58				06 28			06 58			07 28				07 58		
Dagenham Dock	d		23p45						06 02				06 32			07 02			07 32				08 02		
Basildon	d			23p36		04 47		05 32				06 02			06 32			07 02				07 32			08 02
Laindon	d			23p39		04 50		05 35				06 05			06 35			07 05				07 35			08 05
West Horndon	d			23p44		04 55		05 40				06 10			06 40			07 10				07 40			08 10
Chafford Hundred	d	23p31			04 45					05 59				06 29			06 59			07 29				07 59	
Ockendon	d	23p35			04 49		05 16			06 02				06 32			07 02			07 32				08 02	
Upminster ⊖	d	23p42		23p50	04a57	05 02	05a23	05 46		06 09		06 16		06 39	06 46		07 09	07 16		07 39		07 46		08 09	08 16
Barking ⊖	d	23p50	23p51	23p59		05 10		05 54	06 08	06 17		06 24	06 38	06 47	06 54	07 08	07 17	07 24	07 38	07 47		07 54	08 08	08 17	08 24
Stratford 7 ⊖	a		23p58																						
London Liverpool St 15 ⊖	a		00 11																						
West Ham ⊖	d	23p56		00 04		05 16		06 00	06 14	06 23		06 30	06 44	06 53	07 00	07 14	07 23	07 30	07 44	07 53		08 00	08 14	08 23	08 30
Limehouse	d	00 01		00 09		05 21		06 05	06 19	06 28		06 35	06 49	06 58	07 05	07 19	07 28	07 35	07 49	07 58		08 05	08 19	08 28	08 35
London Fenchurch St 7 ⊖	a	00 05		00 14		05 27		06 12	06 26	06 34		06 42	06 56	07 04	07 12	07 26	07 34	07 42	07 56	08 04		08 12	08 26	08 34	08 42

		CC	CC	CC	CC	CC		CC	CC	CC	CC	CC	CC	CC	CC	CC		CC	CC	CC	CC	CC	CC	CC	CC
Shoeburyness	d			07 50				08 05			08 20			08 35				08 50			09 05			09 20	
Thorpe Bay	d			07 53				08 08			08 23			08 38				08 53			09 08			09 23	
Southend East	d			07 56				08 11			08 26			08 41				08 56			09 11			09 26	
Southend Central	a			07 58				08 13			08 28			08 43				08 58			09 13			09 28	
	d		07 50	07 59				08 14		08 20	08 29			08 44		08 50		08 59			09 14		09 20	09 29	
Westcliff	d		07 53	08 01				08 16		08 23	08 31			08 46		08 53		09 01			09 16		09 23	09 31	
Chalkwell	d		07 55	08 03				08 18		08 25	08 33			08 48		08 55		09 03			09 18		09 25	09 33	
Leigh-on-Sea	d		07 58	08 06				08 21		08 28	08 36			08 51		08 58		09 06			09 21		09 28	09 36	
Benfleet	d		08 02	08 10				08 25		08 32	08 40			08 55		09 02		09 10			09 25		09 32	09 40	
Pitsea	d		08 06					08 29		08 36				08 59		09 06					09 29		09 36		
Stanford-le-Hope	d		08 12							08 42						09 12							09 42		
East Tilbury	d		08 15							08 45						09 15							09 45		
Tilbury Town 3	d		08 21							08 51						09 21							09 51		
Grays	d	08 18	08 24						08 48	08 54					09 18	09 24						09 48	09 54		
Purfleet	d	08 23							08 53						09 23							09 53			
Rainham	d	08 28							08 58						09 28							09 58			
Dagenham Dock	d	08 32							09 02						09 32							10 02			
Basildon	d			08 16				08 32			08 46			09 02				09 16			09 32			09 46	
Laindon	d			08 19				08 35			08 49			09 05				09 19			09 35			09 49	
West Horndon	d							08 40						09 10							09 40				
Chafford Hundred	d		08 29							08 59						09 29							09 59		
Ockendon	d		08 32			←				09 02			←			09 32				←			10 02		
Upminster ⊖	d		08 39	08 28	←	08 39		08 46		09 09	08 58	←	09 09	09 16		09 39		09 28	←	09 39	09 46		10 09	09 58	←
Barking ⊖	d	08 38	→	08 36	08 38	08 47		08 54	09 08	→	09 06	09 08	09 17	09 24	09 38	→		09 36	09 38	09 47	09 54	10 08	→	10 06	10 08
Stratford 7 ⊖	a	↪							↪						↪							↪			
London Liverpool St 15 ⊖	a																								
West Ham ⊖	d			08 42	08 44	08 53		09 00			09 12	09 14	09 23	09 30				09 42	09 44	09 53	10 00			10 12	10 14
Limehouse	d				08 49	08 58		09 05				09 19	09 28	09 35					09 49	09 58	10 05				10 19
London Fenchurch St 7 ⊖	a			08 53	08 56	09 04		09 12			09 23	09 26	09 34	09 42				09 53	09 56	10 04	10 12			10 23	10 26

		CC		CC	CC	CC	CC	CC	CC	CC	CC	CC		CC	CC	CC	CC	CC	CC	CC	CC	CC		CC	CC
Shoeburyness	d			09 35			09 50			10 05				10 20			10 35			10 50				11 05	
Thorpe Bay	d			09 38			09 53			10 08				10 23			10 38			10 53				11 08	
Southend East	d			09 41			09 56			10 11				10 26			10 41			10 56				11 11	
Southend Central	a			09 43			09 58			10 13				10 28			10 43			10 58				11 13	
	d			09 44		09 50	09 59			10 14		10 20		10 29			10 44		10 50	10 59				11 14	
Westcliff	d			09 46		09 53	10 01			10 16		10 23		10 31			10 46		10 53	11 01				11 16	
Chalkwell	d			09 48		09 55	10 03			10 18		10 25		10 33			10 48		10 55	11 03				11 18	
Leigh-on-Sea	d			09 51		09 58	10 06			10 21		10 28		10 36			10 51		10 58	11 06				11 21	
Benfleet	d			09 55		10 02	10 10			10 25		10 32		10 40			10 55		11 02	11 10				11 25	
Pitsea	d			09 59		10 06				10 29		10 36					10 59		11 06					11 29	
Stanford-le-Hope	d					10 12						10 42							11 12						
East Tilbury	d					10 15						10 45							11 15						
Tilbury Town 3	d					10 21						10 51							11 21						
Grays	d				10 18	10 24					10 48	10 54						11 18	11 24						11 48
Purfleet	d				10 23						10 53							11 23							11 53
Rainham	d				10 28						10 58							11 28							11 58
Dagenham Dock	d				10 32						11 02							11 32							12 02
Basildon	d			10 02			10 16			10 32				10 46			11 02			11 16				11 32	
Laindon	d			10 05			10 19			10 35				10 49			11 05			11 19				11 35	
West Horndon	d			10 10						10 40							11 10							11 40	
Chafford Hundred	d					10 29						10 59							11 29						
Ockendon	d	←				10 32		←				11 02				←			11 32			←			
Upminster ⊖	d	10 09		10 16		10 39	10 28	←	10 39	10 46		11 09		10 58	←	11 09	11 16		11 39	11 28	←	11 39		11 46	
Barking ⊖	d	10 17		10 24	10 38	→	10 36	10 38	10 47	10 54	11 08	→		11 06	11 08	11 17	11 24	11 38	→	11 36	11 38	11 47		11 54	12 08
Stratford 7 ⊖	a				↪						↪							↪							↪
London Liverpool St 15 ⊖	a																								
West Ham ⊖	d	10 23		10 30			10 42	10 44	10 53	11 00				11 12	11 14	11 23	11 30			11 42	11 44	11 53		12 00	
Limehouse	d	10 28		10 35				10 49	10 58	11 05					11 19	11 28	11 35				11 49	11 58		12 05	
London Fenchurch St 7 ⊖	a	10 34		10 42			10 53	10 56	11 04	11 12				11 23	11 26	11 34	11 42			11 53	11 56	12 04		12 12	

Table 1

Saturdays

Shoeburyness and Southend Central - London

		CC	CC	CC	CC	CC	CC	CC		CC	CC	CC	CC	CC	CC	CC	CC	CC		CC	CC	CC	CC	CC	CC
Shoeburyness	d		11 20			11 35				11 50			12 05			12 20				12 35			12 50		
Thorpe Bay	d		11 23			11 38				11 53			12 08			12 23				12 38			12 53		
Southend East	d		11 26			11 41				11 56			12 11			12 26				12 41			12 56		
Southend Central	a		11 28			11 43				11 58			12 13			12 28				12 43			12 58		
	d	11 20	11 29			11 44		11 50		11 59			12 14		12 20	12 29				12 44		12 50	12 59		
Westcliff	d	11 23	11 31			11 46		11 53		12 01			12 16		12 23	12 31				12 46		12 53	13 01		
Chalkwell	d	11 25	11 33			11 48		11 55		12 03			12 18		12 25	12 33				12 48		12 55	13 03		
Leigh-on-Sea	d	11 28	11 36			11 51		11 58		12 06			12 21		12 28	12 36				12 51		12 58	13 06		
Benfleet	d	11 32	11 40			11 55		12 02		12 10			12 25		12 32	12 40				12 55		13 02	13 10		
Pitsea	d	11 36				11 59		12 06					12 29		12 36					12 59		13 06			
Stanford-le-Hope	d	11 42						12 12							12 42							13 12			
East Tilbury	d	11 45						12 15							12 45							13 15			
Tilbury Town 3	d	11 51						12 21							12 51							13 21			
Grays	d	11 54					12 18	12 24						12 48	12 54						13 18	13 24			
Purfleet	d						12 23							12 53							13 23				
Rainham	d						12 28							12 58							13 28				
Dagenham Dock	d						12 32							13 02							13 32				
Basildon	d		11 46			12 02				12 16			12 32			12 46				13 02			13 16		
Laindon	d		11 49			12 05				12 19			12 35			12 49				13 05			13 19		
West Horndon	d					12 10							12 40							13 10					
Chafford Hundred	d	11 59						12 29							12 59							13 29			
Ockendon	d	12 02			←			12 32				←			13 02			←				13 32			←
Upminster ⊖	d	12 09	11 58	←	12 09	12 16		12 39		12 28	←	12 39	12 46		13 09	12 58	←	13 09		13 16		13 39	13 28	←	13 39
Barking ⊖	d	→	12 06	12 08	12 17	12 24	12 38	→		12 36	12 38	12 47	12 54	13 08	→	13 06	13 08	13 17		13 24	13 38	→	13 36	13 38	13 47
Stratford 7 ⊖	a						→							→							→				
London Liverpool St 15 ⊖	a																								
West Ham ⊖	d		12 12	12 14	12 23	12 30				12 42	12 44	12 53	13 00			13 12	13 14	13 23		13 30			13 42	13 44	13 53
Limehouse	d			12 19	12 28	12 35					12 49	12 58	13 05				13 19	13 28		13 35				13 49	13 58
London Fenchurch St 7 ⊖	a		12 23	12 26	12 34	12 42				12 53	12 56	13 04	13 12			13 23	13 26	13 34		13 42			13 53	13 56	14 04

		CC	CC	CC		CC	CC	CC	CC	CC	CC	CC	CC	CC		CC	CC	CC	CC	CC	CC	CC	CC	CC	
Shoeburyness	d	13 05				13 20			13 35			13 50				14 05			14 20			14 35			
Thorpe Bay	d	13 08				13 23			13 38			13 53				14 08			14 23			14 38			
Southend East	d	13 11				13 26			13 41			13 56				14 11			14 26			14 41			
Southend Central	a	13 13				13 28			13 43			13 58				14 13			14 28			14 43			
	d	13 14		13 20		13 29			13 44		13 50	13 59				14 14		14 20	14 29			14 44		14 50	
Westcliff	d	13 16		13 23		13 31			13 46		13 53	14 01				14 16		14 23	14 31			14 46		14 53	
Chalkwell	d	13 18		13 25		13 33			13 48		13 55	14 03				14 18		14 25	14 33			14 48		14 55	
Leigh-on-Sea	d	13 21		13 28		13 36			13 51		13 58	14 06				14 21		14 28	14 36			14 51		14 58	
Benfleet	d	13 25		13 32		13 40			13 55		14 02	14 10				14 25		14 32	14 40			14 55		15 02	
Pitsea	d	13 29		13 36					13 59		14 06					14 29		14 36				14 59		15 06	
Stanford-le-Hope	d			13 42							14 12							14 42						15 12	
East Tilbury	d			13 45							14 15							14 45						15 15	
Tilbury Town 3	d			13 51							14 21							14 51						15 21	
Grays	d		13 48	13 54						14 18	14 24						14 48	14 54					15 18	15 24	
Purfleet	d		13 53							14 23							14 53						15 23		
Rainham	d		13 58							14 28							14 58						15 28		
Dagenham Dock	d		14 02							14 32							15 02						15 32		
Basildon	d	13 32				13 46			14 02			14 16				14 32			14 46			15 02			
Laindon	d	13 35				13 49			14 05			14 19				14 35			14 49			15 05			
West Horndon	d	13 40							14 10							14 40						15 10			
Chafford Hundred	d			13 59							14 29							14 59						15 29	
Ockendon	d			14 02				←			14 32			←				15 02			←			15 32	
Upminster ⊖	d	13 46		14 09		13 58	←	14 09	14 16		14 39	14 28	←	14 39		14 46		15 09	14 58	←	15 09	15 16		15 39	
Barking ⊖	d	13 54	14 08	→		14 06	14 08	14 17	14 24	14 38	→	14 36	14 38	14 47		14 54	15 08	→	15 06	15 08	15 17	15 24	15 38	→	
Stratford 7 ⊖	a		→							→							→						→		
London Liverpool St 15 ⊖	a																								
West Ham ⊖	d	14 00				14 12	14 14	14 23	14 30			14 42	14 44	14 53		15 00			15 12	15 14	15 23	15 30			
Limehouse	d	14 05					14 19	14 28	14 35				14 49	14 58		15 05				15 19	15 28	15 35			
London Fenchurch St 7 ⊖	a	14 12				14 23	14 26	14 34	14 42			14 53	14 56	15 04		15 12			15 23	15 26	15 34	15 42			

		CC	CC	CC	CC	CC	CC	CC	CC	CC		CC	CC	CC	CC	CC	CC	CC	CC	CC		CC	CC	CC	CC
Shoeburyness	d	14 50			15 05			15 20				15 35			15 50			16 05				16 20			16 35
Thorpe Bay	d	14 53			15 08			15 23				15 38			15 53			16 08				16 23			16 38
Southend East	d	14 56			15 11			15 26				15 41			15 56			16 11				16 26			16 41
Southend Central	a	14 58			15 13			15 28				15 43			15 58			16 13				16 28			16 43
	d	14 59			15 14		15 20	15 29				15 44		15 50	15 59			16 14		16 20		16 29			16 44
Westcliff	d	15 01			15 16		15 23	15 31				15 46		15 53	16 01			16 16		16 23		16 31			16 46
Chalkwell	d	15 03			15 18		15 25	15 33				15 48		15 55	16 03			16 18		16 25		16 33			16 48
Leigh-on-Sea	d	15 06			15 21		15 28	15 36				15 51		15 58	16 06			16 21		16 28		16 36			16 51
Benfleet	d	15 10			15 25		15 32	15 40				15 55		16 02	16 10			16 25		16 32		16 40			16 55
Pitsea	d				15 29		15 36					15 59		16 06				16 29		16 36					16 59
Stanford-le-Hope	d						15 42							16 12						16 42					
East Tilbury	d						15 45							16 15						16 45					
Tilbury Town 3	d						15 51							16 21						16 51					
Grays	d					15 48	15 54						16 18	16 24					16 48	16 54					
Purfleet	d					15 53							16 23						16 53						
Rainham	d					15 58							16 28						16 58						
Dagenham Dock	d					16 02							16 32						17 02						
Basildon	d	15 16			15 32			15 46				16 02			16 16			16 32				16 46			17 02
Laindon	d	15 19			15 35			15 49				16 05			16 19			16 35				16 49			17 05
West Horndon	d				15 40							16 10						16 40							17 10
Chafford Hundred	d						15 59							16 29						16 59					
Ockendon	d			←			16 02			←				16 32			←			17 02				←	
Upminster ⊖	d	15 28	←	15 39	15 46		16 09	15 58	←	16 09		16 16		16 39	16 28	←	16 39	16 46		17 09		16 58	←	17 09	17 16
Barking ⊖	d	15 36	15 38	15 47	15 54	16 08	→	16 06	16 08	16 17		16 24	16 38	→	16 36	16 38	16 47	16 54	17 08	→		17 06	17 08	17 17	17 24
Stratford 7 ⊖	a					→							→						→						
London Liverpool St 15 ⊖	a																								
West Ham ⊖	d	15 42	15 44	15 53	16 00			16 12	16 14	16 23		16 30			16 42	16 44	16 53	17 00				17 12	17 14	17 23	17 30
Limehouse	d		15 49	15 58	16 05				16 19	16 28		16 35				16 49	16 58	17 05					17 19	17 28	17 35
London Fenchurch St 7 ⊖	a	15 53	15 56	16 04	16 12			16 23	16 26	16 34		16 42			16 53	16 56	17 04	17 12				17 23	17 26	17 34	17 42

Table I

Shoeburyness and Southend Central - London

		CC	CC	CC	CC	CC		CC	CC	CC	CC	CC	CC	CC	CC	CC		CC	CC	CC	CC	CC	CC	CC	CC
Shoeburyness	d			16 50				17 05			17 20			17 35				17 50			18 05			18 20	
Thorpe Bay	d			16 53				17 08			17 23			17 38				17 53			18 08			18 23	
Southend East	d			16 56				17 11			17 26			17 41				17 56			18 11			18 26	
Southend Central	a			16 58				17 13			17 28			17 43				17 58			18 13			18 28	
	d		16 50	16 59				17 14		17 20	17 29			17 44		17 50		17 59			18 14		18 20	18 29	
Westcliff	d		16 53	17 01				17 16		17 23	17 31			17 46		17 53		18 01			18 16		18 23	18 31	
Chalkwell	d		16 55	17 03				17 18		17 25	17 33			17 48		17 55		18 03			18 18		18 25	18 33	
Leigh-on-Sea	d		16 58	17 06				17 21		17 28	17 36			17 51		17 58		18 06			18 21		18 28	18 36	
Benfleet	d		17 02	17 10				17 25		17 32	17 40			17 55		18 02		18 10			18 25		18 32	18 40	
Pitsea	d		17 06					17 29		17 36				17 59		18 06					18 29		18 36		
Stanford-le-Hope	d		17 12							17 42						18 12							18 42		
East Tilbury	d		17 15							17 45						18 15							18 45		
Tilbury Town 3	d		17 21							17 51						18 21							18 51		
Grays	d	17 18	17 24						17 48	17 54					18 18	18 24						18 48	18 54		
Purfleet	d	17 23							17 53						18 23							18 53			
Rainham	d	17 28							17 58						18 28							18 58			
Dagenham Dock	d	17 32							18 02						18 32							19 02			
Basildon	d			17 16				17 32			17 46			18 02				18 16			18 32			18 46	
Laindon	d			17 19				17 35			17 49			18 05				18 19			18 35			18 49	
West Horndon	d							17 40						18 10							18 40				
Chafford Hundred	d		17 29							17 59						18 29							18 59		
Ockendon	d		17 32			←				18 02			←			18 32				←			19 02		
Upminster ⊖	d		17 39	17 28	←	17 39		17 46		18 09	17 58	←	18 09	18 16		18 39		18 28	←	18 39	18 46		19 09	18 58	←
Barking ⊖	d	17 38	→	17 36	17 38	17 47		17 54	18 08	→	18 06	18 08	18 17	18 24	18 38	→		18 36	18 38	18 47	18 54	19 08	→	19 06	19 08
Stratford 7 ⊖	a	↪							↪						↪							↪			
London Liverpool St 15 ⊖	a																								
West Ham ⊖	d			17 42	17 44	17 53		18 00			18 12	18 14	18 23	18 30				18 42	18 44	18 53	19 00			19 12	19 14
Limehouse	d				17 49	17 58		18 05				18 19	18 28	18 35					18 49	18 58	19 05				19 19
London Fenchurch St 7 ⊖	a			17 53	17 56	18 04		18 12			18 23	18 26	18 34	18 42				18 53	18 56	19 04	19 12			19 23	19 26

		CC		CC	CC	CC	CC	CC	CC	CC	CC	CC		CC	CC	CC	CC	CC	CC	CC	CC	CC		CC	CC
Shoeburyness	d			18 35			18 50			19 05				19 20			19 35			19 50				20 05	
Thorpe Bay	d			18 38			18 53			19 08				19 23			19 38			19 53				20 08	
Southend East	d			18 41			18 56			19 11				19 26			19 41			19 56				20 11	
Southend Central	a			18 43			18 58			19 13				19 28			19 43			19 58				20 13	
	d			18 44		18 50	18 59			19 14		19 20		19 29			19 44		19 50	19 59				20 14	
Westcliff	d			18 46		18 53	19 01			19 16		19 23		19 31			19 46		19 53	20 01				20 16	
Chalkwell	d			18 48		18 55	19 03			19 18		19 25		19 33			19 48		19 55	20 03				20 18	
Leigh-on-Sea	d			18 51		18 58	19 06			19 21		19 28		19 36			19 51		19 58	20 06				20 21	
Benfleet	d			18 55		19 02	19 10			19 25		19 32		19 40			19 55		20 02	20 10				20 25	
Pitsea	d			18 59		19 06				19 29		19 36					19 59		20 06					20 29	
Stanford-le-Hope	d					19 12						19 42							20 12						
East Tilbury	d					19 15						19 45							20 15						
Tilbury Town 3	d					19 21						19 51							20 21						
Grays	d				19 18	19 24					19 48	19 54						20 18	20 24						20 48
Purfleet	d				19 23						19 53							20 23							20 53
Rainham	d				19 28						19 58							20 28							20 58
Dagenham Dock	d				19 32						20 02							20 32							21 02
Basildon	d			19 02			19 16			19 32				19 46			20 02			20 16				20 32	
Laindon	d			19 05			19 19			19 35				19 49			20 05			20 19				20 35	
West Horndon	d			19 10						19 40							20 10							20 40	
Chafford Hundred	d					19 29						19 59							20 29						
Ockendon	d	←				19 32			←			20 02				←			20 32			←			
Upminster ⊖	d	19 09		19 16		19 39	19 28	←	19 39	19 46		20 09		19 58	←	20 09	20 16		20 39	20 28	←	20 39		20 46	
Barking ⊖	d	19 17		19 24	19 38	→	19 36	19 38	19 47	19 54	20 08	→		20 06	20 08	20 17	20 24	20 38	→	20 36	20 38	20 47		20 54	21 08
Stratford 7 ⊖	a				↪						↪							↪							
London Liverpool St 15 ⊖	a																								
West Ham ⊖	d	19 23		19 30			19 42	19 44	19 53	20 00				20 12	20 14	20 23	20 30			20 42	20 44	20 53		21 00	21 14
Limehouse	d	19 28		19 35				19 49	19 58	20 05					20 19	20 28	20 35				20 49	20 58		21 05	21 19
London Fenchurch St 7 ⊖	a	19 34		19 42			19 53	19 56	20 04	20 12				20 23	20 26	20 34	20 42			20 53	20 56	21 04		21 12	21 26

		CC	CC	CC	CC	CC	CC	CC		CC	CC	CC	CC	CC	CC	CC	CC	CC		CC	CC	CC	CC	CC	
Shoeburyness	d		20 35			20 50				21 05			21 35			22 05				22 35			23 05		
Thorpe Bay	d		20 38			20 53				21 08			21 38			22 08				22 38			23 08		
Southend East	d		20 41			20 56				21 11			21 41			22 11				22 41			23 11		
Southend Central	a		20 43			20 58				21 13			21 43			22 13				22 43			23 13		
	d	20 20	20 44		20 50	20 59				21 14		21 20	21 44		21 50	22 14		22 20		22 44		22 50	23 14	23 20	
Westcliff	d	20 23	20 46		20 53	21 01				21 16		21 23	21 46		21 53	22 16		22 23		22 46		22 53	23 16	23 23	
Chalkwell	d	20 25	20 48		20 55	21 03				21 18		21 25	21 48		21 55	22 18		22 25		22 48		22 55	23 18	23 25	
Leigh-on-Sea	d	20 28	20 51		20 58	21 06				21 21		21 28	21 51		21 58	22 21		22 28		22 51		22 58	23 21	23 28	
Benfleet	d	20 32	20 55		21 02	21 10				21 25		21 32	21 55		22 02	22 25		22 32		22 55		23 02	23 25	23 32	
Pitsea	d	20 36	20 59		21 06					21 29		21 36	21 59		22 06	22 29		22 36		22 59		23 06	23 29	23 36	
Stanford-le-Hope	d	20 42			21 12							21 42			22 12			22 42				23 12		23 42	
East Tilbury	d	20 45			21 15							21 45			22 15			22 45				23 15		23 45	
Tilbury Town 3	d	20 51			21 21							21 51			22 21			22 51				23 21		23 51	
Grays	d	20 54		21 18	21 24						21 48	21 54		22 18	22 24		22 48	22 54			23 18	23 24		23 54	
Purfleet	d			21 23							21 53			22 23			22 53				23 23				
Rainham	d			21 28							21 58			22 28			22 58				23 28				
Dagenham Dock	d			21 32							22 02			22 32			23 02				23 32				
Basildon	d		21 02			21 16				21 32			22 02			22 32				23 02			23 32		
Laindon	d		21 05			21 19				21 35			22 05			22 35				23 05			23 35		
West Horndon	d		21 10							21 40			22 10			22 40				23 10			23 40		
Chafford Hundred	d	20 59			21 29							21 59			22 29			22 59				23 29		23 59	
Ockendon	d	21 02			21 32		←					22 02			22 32			23 02				23 32		00 02	
Upminster ⊖	d	21 09	21 16		21 39	21 28	←	21 39		21 46		22 09	22 16		22 39	22 46		23 09		23 16		23 39	23 46	00 08	
Barking ⊖	d	21 17	21 24	21 38	→	21 36	21 38	21 47		21 54	22 08	22 17	22 24	22 38	22 47	22 54	23 08	23 17		23 24	23a39	23 47	23 55	00a18	
Stratford 7 ⊖	a			↪																					
London Liverpool St 15 ⊖	a																								
West Ham ⊖	d	21 23	21 30			21 42	21 44	21 53		22 00	22 14	22 23	22 30	22 44	22 53	23 00	23 14	23 23		23 30		23 53	00 01		
Limehouse	d	21 28	21 35				21 49	21 58		22 05	22 19	22 28	22 35	22 49	22 58	23 05	23 19	23 28		23 35		23 58	00 06		
London Fenchurch St 7 ⊖	a	21 34	21 42			21 53	21 56	22 04		22 12	22 26	22 34	22 42	22 56	23 04	23 12	23 26	23 34		23 42		00 04	00 12		

Table I

Sundays

Shoeburyness and Southend Central - London

		CC A	CC A	CC A	CC	CC	CC	CC	CC	CC		CC	CC	CC	CC	CC	CC		CC		CC	CC	CC	CC
Shoeburyness	d		23p05		05 35	06 05	06 11	06 35	07 05	07 11		07 35	08 05			08 35					21 05			21 35
Thorpe Bay	d		23p08		05 38	06 08	06 14	06 38	07 08	07 14		07 38	08 08			08 38					21 08			21 38
Southend East	d		23p11		05 41	06 11	06 17	06 41	07 11	07 17		07 41	08 11			08 41					21 11			21 41
Southend Central	a		23p13		05 43	06 13	06 19	06 43	07 13	07 19		07 43	08 13			08 43					21 13			21 43
	d	22p50	23p14	23p20	05 44	06 14	06 20	06 44	07 14	07 20		07 44	08 14	08 20		08 44	08 50		20 50		21 14	21 20		21 44
Westcliff	d	22p53	23p16	23p23	05 46	06 16	06 23	06 46	07 16	07 23		07 46	08 16	08 23		08 46	08 53		20 53		21 16	21 23		21 46
Chalkwell	d	22p55	23p18	23p25	05 48	06 18	06 25	06 48	07 18	07 25		07 48	08 18	08 25		08 48	08 55		20 55		21 18	21 25		21 48
Leigh-on-Sea	d	22p58	23p21	23p28	05 51	06 21	06 28	06 51	07 21	07 28		07 51	08 21	08 28		08 51	08 58		20 58		21 21	21 28		21 51
Benfleet	d	23p02	23p25	23p32	05 55	06 25	06 32	06 55	07 25	07 32		07 55	08 25	08 32		08 55	09 02		21 02		21 25	21 32		21 55
Pitsea	d	23p06	23p29	23p36	05 59	06 29	06 36	06 59	07 29	07 36		07 59	08 29	08 36		08 59	09 06		21 06		21 29	21 36		21 59
Stanford-le-Hope	d	23p12		23p42			06 42			07 42				08 42			09 12	and at	21 12			21 42		
East Tilbury	d	23p15		23p45			06 45			07 45				08 45			09 15	the same	21 15			21 45		
Tilbury Town 3	d	23p21		23p51			06 51			07 51				08 51			09 21	minutes	21 21			21 51		
Grays	d	23p24		23p54			06 54			07 54				08 54	08 59		09 24	past	21 24			21 54	21 59	
Purfleet	d														09 04			each					22 04	
Rainham	d														09 09			hour until					22 09	
Dagenham Dock	d														09 13								22 13	
Basildon	d		23p32		06 02	06 32		07 02	07 32			08 02	08 32			09 02					21 32			22 02
Laindon	d		23p35		06 05	06 35		07 05	07 35			08 05	08 35			09 05					21 35			22 05
West Horndon	d		23p40		06 10	06 40		07 10	07 40			08 10	08 40			09 10					21 40			22 10
Chafford Hundred	d	23p29		23p59			06 59			07 59				08 59			09 29		21 29			21 59		
Ockendon	d	23p32		00 02			07 02			08 02				09 02			09 32		21 32			22 02		
Upminster ⊖	d	23p39	23p46	00 08	06 16	06 46	07 09	07 16	07 46	08 09		08 16	08 46	09 09		09 16	09 39		21 39		21 46	22 09		22 16
Barking ⊖	d	23p47	23p55	00a18	06 25	06 55	07 17	07 25	07 55	08 17		08 25	08 55	09 17	09a20	09 25	09 47		21 47		21 55	22 17	22a20	22 25
Stratford 7 ⊖	a																							
London Liverpool St 15 ⊖	a																							
West Ham ⊖	d	23p53	00 01		06 31	07 01	07 23	07 31	08 01	08 23		08 31	09 01	09 23		09 31	09 53		21 53		22 01	22 23		22 31
Limehouse	d	23p58	00 06		06 36	07 06	07 28	07 36	08 06	08 28		08 36	09 06	09 28		09 36	09 58		21 58		22 06	22 28		22 36
London Fenchurch St 7 ⊖	a	00 04	00 12		06 42	07 12	07 34	07 42	08 12	08 34		08 42	09 12	09 34		09 42	10 04		22 04		22 12	22 34		22 42

		CC	CC	CC
Shoeburyness	d	22 05		22 35
Thorpe Bay	d	22 08		22 38
Southend East	d	22 11		22 41
Southend Central	a	22 13		22 43
	d	22 14	22 20	22 44
Westcliff	d	22 16	22 23	22 46
Chalkwell	d	22 18	22 25	22 48
Leigh-on-Sea	d	22 21	22 28	22 51
Benfleet	d	22 25	22 32	22 55
Pitsea	d	22 29	22 36	22 59
Stanford-le-Hope	d		22 42	
East Tilbury	d		22 45	
Tilbury Town 3	d		22 51	
Grays	d		22 54	
Purfleet	d			
Rainham	d			
Dagenham Dock	d			
Basildon	d	22 32		23 02
Laindon	d	22 35		23 05
West Horndon	d	22 40		23 10
Chafford Hundred	d		22 59	
Ockendon	d		23 02	
Upminster ⊖	d	22 46	23 09	23 16
Barking ⊖	d	22 55	23 17	23 25
Stratford 7 ⊖	a			
London Liverpool St 15 ⊖	a			
West Ham ⊖	d	23 01	23 23	23 31
Limehouse	d	23 06	23 28	23 36
London Fenchurch St 7 ⊖	a	23 12	23 34	23 42

A not 22 May

Table 1A

Mondays to Fridays

Tilbury Town - Tilbury Riverside

Bus Service

		CC	CC	CC	CC	CC	CC	CC	CC	CC	CC	CC	CC	CC	CC	CC	CC	CC	CC	CC	CC	CC	CC
Tilbury Town ■	d	05 40	06 18	06 50	07 18	07 45	08 13	08 38	09 03	09 33	10 03	10 33	11 03	11 33	12 03	12 33	13 03	13 33	14 03	14 33	15 03	15 33	16 03
Tilbury Riverside	a	05 47	06 25	06 57	07 25	07 52	08 20	08 45	09 10	09 40	10 10	10 40	11 10	11 40	12 10	12 40	13 10	13 40	14 10	14 40	15 10	15 40	16 10

		CC	CC	CC	CC	CC		CC
Tilbury Town ■	d	16 33	17 03	17 33	18 00	18 30		19 00
Tilbury Riverside	a	16 40	17 10	17 40	18 07	18 37		19 07

Saturdays

		CC	CC	CC	CC	CC	CC	CC	CC	CC	CC	CC	CC	CC	CC	CC	CC	CC	CC	CC	CC	CC	CC
Tilbury Town ■	d	05 40	06 15	07 01	07 31	08 01	08 31	09 01	09 31	10 01	10 31	11 01	11 31	12 01	12 31	13 01	13 31	14 01	14 31	15 01	15 31	16 01	16 31
Tilbury Riverside	a	05 47	06 22	07 08	07 38	08 08	08 38	09 08	09 38	10 08	10 38	11 08	11 38	12 08	12 38	13 08	13 38	14 08	14 38	15 08	15 38	16 08	16 38

		CC	CC	CC	CC	CC
Tilbury Town ■	d	17 01	17 31	18 01	18 31	19 01
Tilbury Riverside	a	17 08	17 38	18 08	18 38	19 08

Table 1A

Mondays to Fridays

Tilbury Riverside - Tilbury Town

Bus Service

		CC	CC	CC	CC	CC	CC	CC	CC	CC	CC	CC	CC	CC	CC	CC	CC	CC	CC	CC	CC	CC	CC
Tilbury Riverside	d	05 50	06 30	07 00	07 30	07 55	08 23	08 50	09 12	09 42	10 12	10 42	11 12	11 42	12 12	12 42	13 12	13 42	14 12	14 42	15 12	15 42	16 12
Tilbury Town ■	a	05 57	06 37	07 07	07 37	08 02	08 30	08 57	09 19	09 49	10 19	10 49	11 19	11 49	12 19	12 49	13 19	13 49	14 19	14 49	15 19	15 49	16 19

		CC	CC	CC	CC	CC		CC
Tilbury Riverside	d	16 40	17 15	17 45	18 15	18 40		19 10
Tilbury Town ■	a	16 47	17 22	17 52	18 22	18 47		19 17

Saturdays

		CC	CC	CC	CC	CC	CC	CC	CC	CC	CC	CC	CC	CC	CC	CC	CC	CC	CC	CC	CC	CC	CC
Tilbury Riverside	d	05 50	06 30	07 10	07 50	08 09	08 39	09 09	09 39	10 09	10 39	11 09	11 39	12 09	12 39	13 09	13 39	14 09	14 39	15 09	15 39	16 09	16 39
Tilbury Town ■	a	05 57	06 37	07 17	07 57	08 16	08 46	09 16	09 46	10 16	10 46	11 16	11 46	12 16	12 46	13 16	13 46	14 16	14 46	15 16	15 46	16 16	16 46

		CC	CC	CC	CC	CC
Tilbury Riverside	d	17 09	17 39	18 09	18 39	19 09
Tilbury Town ■	a	17 16	17 46	18 16	18 46	19 16

No Sunday Service

Table 4

Mondays to Fridays

Romford - Upminster

Miles			LE	LE	LE	LE	LE	LE	LE		LE
0	**Romford**	d	06 12	06 42	07 06	07 30	07 54	08 18	08 42	and every 30 minutes until	19 42
2	Emerson Park	d	06 16	06 46	07 10	07 34	07 58	08 22	08 46		19 46
3½	**Upminster** ⊖	a	06 20	06 50	07 14	07 38	08 02	08 26	08 50		19 50

Saturdays

		LE		LE
Romford	d	06 12	and every 30 minutes until	19 42
Emerson Park	d	06 16		19 46
Upminster ⊖	a	06 20		19 50

No Sunday Service

Table 4

Mondays to Fridays

Upminster - Romford

Miles			LE	LE	LE	LE	LE	LE	LE		LE
0	**Upminster** ⊖	d	06 24	06 54	07 18	07 42	08 06	08 30	08 54	and every 30 minutes until	19 54
1½	Emerson Park	d	06 28	06 58	07 22	07 46	08 10	08 34	08 58		19 58
3½	**Romford**	a	06 32	07 02	07 26	07 50	08 14	08 38	09 02		20 02

Saturdays

		LE		LE
Upminster ⊖	d	06 24	and every 30 minutes until	19 54
Emerson Park	d	06 28		19 58
Romford	a	06 32		20 02

No Sunday Service

Network Diagram for Tables 5, 10, 11

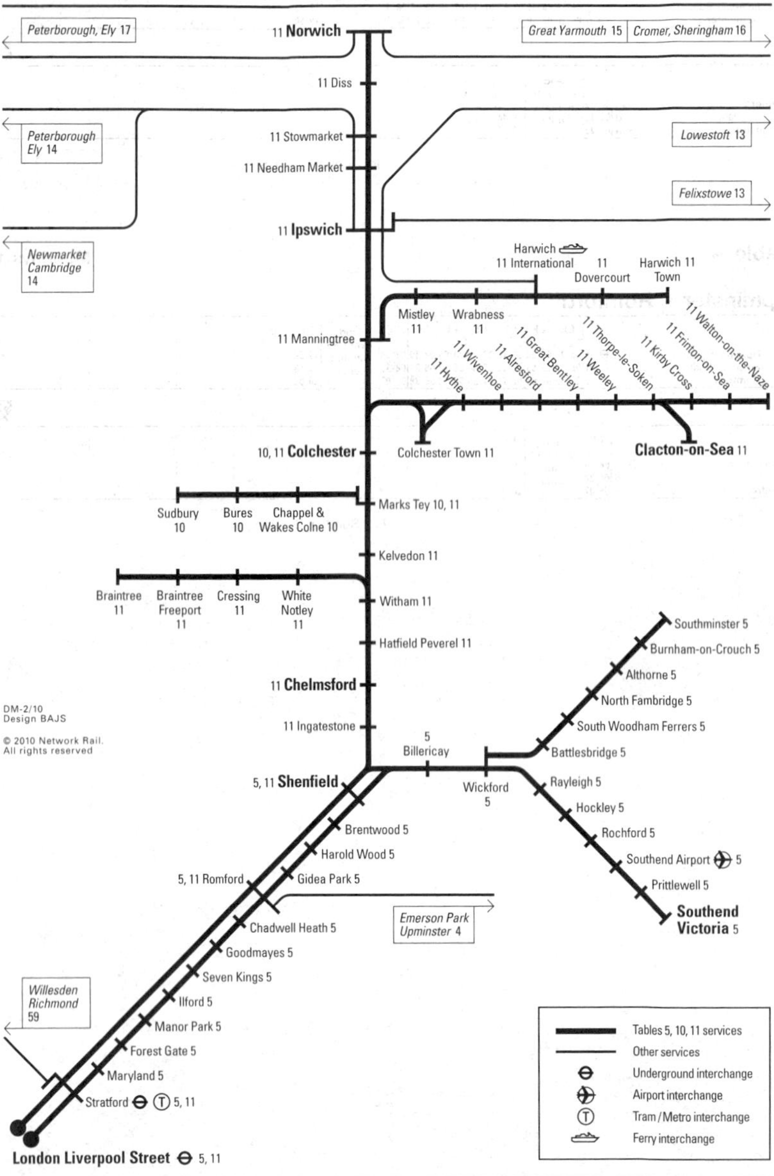

Table 5

Mondays to Fridays

London - Shenfield, Southminster and Southend Victoria

Miles	Miles			LE MX	LE MO	LE MX	LE MO	LE MX	LE MX	LE MO	LE MX	LE MX	LE MX	LE MO	LE MO	LE MX	LE MO	LE MX	LE MX	LE MX	LE MO	LE MO	LE MX
				[1]	[1]				[1]	[1]	[1]			[1]		[1]	[1]	[1]				[1]	[1]
0	—	**London Liverpool Street** [15] ⊖	d	23p15	23p15	23p20	23p35	23p35	23p45	23p45	23p48	23p50	00 01	00 02	00 05	00 15	00 15	00 18	00 20	00 32	00 35	00 45	00 46
4	—	Stratford [7] ⊖	d	23p22	23p22	23p27	23p42	23p42	23p52	23p52	23p55	23p57	00 08	00 09	00 12	00 22	00 22	00 25	00 27	00 39	00 42	00 52	00 53
4½	—	Maryland	d			23p29	23p43	23p44				23p59	00 10		00 13				00 29	00 41	00 43		
5¼	—	Forest Gate	d			23p31	23p45	23p46				00 01	00 12		00 15				00 31	00 43	00 45		
6¼	—	Manor Park	d			23p33	23p47	23p48				00 03	00 14		00 17				00 33	00 45	00 47		
7¼	—	Ilford [2]	d			23p36	23p50	23p51				00 06	00 17		00 20				00 36	00 48	00 50		
8½	—	Seven Kings	d			23p38	23p53	23p53				00 08	00 19		00 23				00 38	00 50	00 53		
9¼	—	Goodmayes	d			23p40	23p55	23p55				00 10	00 21		00 25				00 40	00 52	00 55		
10	—	Chadwell Heath	d			23p42	23p57	23p57				00 12	00 23		00 27				00 42	00 54	00 57		
12½	—	Romford	d		23p33	23p46	23p59	00 02		00 03		00 16	00 27		00 30	00 32	00 33		00 46	00 58	01 00	01 03	
13½	—	Gidea Park [2]	d		23p37	23p50	00 04	00 05		00 07		00 20	00a31		00a36		00 37		00 50	01a02	01a06	01 07	01 07
15	—	Harold Wood	d		23p40	23p53	00 07	00 08		00 10		00 23					00 40		00 53			01 10	
18¼	—	Brentwood	d		23p44	23p57	00 11	00 12		00 14		00 27					00 44		00 57			01 14	
—	—	**Shenfield** [3]	a	23p38	23p50	00 03	00 18	00 18	00 08	00 20	00 10	00 33		00 30		00 44	00 50	00 47	01 03			01 20	01 17
20¼	—	**Shenfield** [3]	d	23p39	23p50				00 09	00 20						00 45	00 50					01 20	
24¼	—	Billericay	d	23p45	23p56				00 15	00 26						00 51	00 56					01 26	
29	0	**Wickford** [2]	d	23p51	00 01				00 21	00 31						00 56	01 01					01 31	
—	2½	Battlesbridge	d																				
—	5	South Woodham Ferrers	d																				
—	8¼	North Fambridge	d																				
—	11¼	Althorne	d																				
—	14¼	Burnham-on-Crouch	d																				
—	16½	**Southminster**	a																				
33	—	Rayleigh	d	23p56	00 06				00 26	00 36						01 01	01 06					01 36	
36	—	Hockley	d	00 01	00 11				00 31	00 41						01 06	01 11					01 41	
38¾	—	Rochford	d	00 04	00 14				00 34	00 44						01 09	01 14					01 44	
39¾	—	Southend Airport ✈	d	00 07	00 17				00 37	00 47						01 12	01 17					01 47	
41	—	Prittlewell	d	00 10					00 40							01 15							
41½	—	**Southend Victoria**	a	00 18	00 27				00 48	00 57						01 23	01 27					01 57	

		LE MX	LE	LE	LE	LE	LE	LE	LE	LE	LE	LE	LE	LE	LE	LE	LE	LE	LE	LE	LE	LE	LE
		[1]		[1]	[1]	[1]			[1]	[1]		[1]	[1]		[1]	[1]			[1]	[1]		[1]	
London Liverpool Street [15] ⊖	d	00 50	00 55		05 23		05 28	05 37	05 52	05 55	06 00	06 02		06 10	06 12	06 15	06 20	06 30	06 35	06 38	06 40	06 48	06 50
Stratford [7] ⊖	d	00 57	01 02		05 30		05 35	05 44	06a01	06 02	06 07	06 09		06 17	06 19	06 22	06 27	06 37	06 42	06 45	06 47	06 55	06 57
Maryland	d		01 04					05 46			06 09			06 19			06 29	06 39			06 49		06 59
Forest Gate	d		01 06					05 48			06 11			06 21			06 31	06 41			06 51		07 01
Manor Park	d		01 08					05 50			06 13			06 23			06 33	06 43			06 53		07 03
Ilford [2]	d		01 11				05 40	05 53			06 16			06 26			06 36	06 46			06 56		07 06
Seven Kings	d		01 13				05 42	05 55			06 18			06 28			06 38	06 48			06 58		07 08
Goodmayes	d		01 15					05 57			06 20			06 30			06 40	06 50			07 00		07 10
Chadwell Heath	d		01 17					05 59			06 22			06 32			06 42	06 52			07 02		07 12
Romford	d	01 08	01 21		05 38		05 48	06 03			06 26			06 36			06 46	06 56			07 06		07 16
Gidea Park [2]	d		01 25				05 51	06 07			06 30			06 40			06 50	07 00			07 10		07 20
Harold Wood	d		01 28				05 54	06 10			06 33			06 43			06 53	07 03			07 13		07 23
Brentwood	d		01 32				05 59	06 14			06 37			06 47			06 57	07 07			07 17		07 27
Shenfield [3]	a	01 20	01 38		05 47		06 04	06 20		06 18	06 43	06 24		06 53	06 35	06 38	07 03	07 13	06 58	07 00	07 23	07 11	07 33
Shenfield [3]	d	01 20				05 56	06 04			06 19			06 33			06 39			06 59				
Billericay	d	01 26				06 02	06 10			06 25			06 39			06 45			07 05				
Wickford [2]	d	01 31		05 16		06 09	06 16			06 31			06 46			06 51			07 11				
Battlesbridge	d			05 20		06 13							06 50										
South Woodham Ferrers	d			05 24		06 17							06 54										
North Fambridge	d			05 41		06 25							07 03										
Althorne	d			05 46		06 30							07 08										
Burnham-on-Crouch	d			05 51		06 35							07 13										
Southminster	a			05 57		06 41							07 19										
Rayleigh	d	01 36					06 21			06 36						06 56			07 16				
Hockley	d	01 41					06 26			06 41						07 01			07 21				
Rochford	d	01 44					06 29			06 44						07 04			07 24				
Southend Airport ✈	d	01 47					06 32			06 47						07 07			07 27				
Prittlewell	d	01 50					06 35			06 50						07 10			07 30				
Southend Victoria	a	01 58					06 39			06 55						07 14			07 34				

		LE	LE	LE	LE	LE	LE	LE	LE	LE	LE	LE	LE	LE	LE	LE	LE	LE	LE	LE	LE	LE
		[1]		◇[1]	[1]	[1]		[1]	[1]	[1]			[1]	[1]		[1]		[1]	[1]		[1]	
London Liverpool Street [15] ⊖	d	06 55	07 00	07 00	07 02	07 08	07 10		07 13	07 18	07 20	07 30	07 35	07 38	07 40	07 48	07 50		07 55	08 00	08 02	08 10
Stratford [7] ⊖	d	07 02	07 07		07 09	07 15	07 17		07 20	07 25	07 27	07 37	07 42	07 45	07 47	07 55	07 57		08 02	08 07	08 09	08 17
Maryland	d		07 09				07 19				07 29	07 39			07 49		07 59			08 09		08 19
Forest Gate	d		07 11				07 21				07 31	07 41			07 51		08 01			08 11		08 21
Manor Park	d		07 13				07 23				07 33	07 43			07 53		08 03			08 13		08 23
Ilford [2]	d		07 16				07 26				07 36	07 46			07 56		08 06			08 16		08 26
Seven Kings	d		07 18				07 28				07 38	07 48			07 58		08 08			08 18		08 28
Goodmayes	d		07 20				07 30				07 40	07 50			08 00		08 10			08 20		08 30
Chadwell Heath	d		07 22				07 32				07 42	07 52			08 02		08 12			08 22		08 32
Romford	d		07 26				07 36		07 28		07 46	07 56			08 06		08 16			08 26		08 36
Gidea Park [2]	d		07 30				07 40				07 50	08 00			08 10		08 20			08 30		08 40
Harold Wood	d		07 33				07 43				07 53	08 03			08 13		08 23			08 33		08 43
Brentwood	d		07 37				07 47				07 57	08 07			08 17		08 27			08 37		08 47
Shenfield [3]	a	07 18	07 43		07 24	07 30	07 53		07 38	07 40	08 03	08 13	07 58	08 00	08 23	08 10	08 33		08 18	08 43	08 24	08 53
Shenfield [3]	d	07 19							07 39				07 59						08 19			
Billericay	d	07 25							07 45				08 05						08 25			
Wickford [2]	d	07 31						07 36	07 51				08 11					08 16	08 31			
Battlesbridge	d							07 40										08 20				
South Woodham Ferrers	d							07 44										08 24				
North Fambridge	d							07 53										08 31				
Althorne	d							07 58										08 36				
Burnham-on-Crouch	d							08 03										08 41				
Southminster	a							08 09										08 47				
Rayleigh	d	07 36							07 56				08 16						08 36			
Hockley	d	07 41							08 01				08 21						08 41			
Rochford	d	07 44							08 04				08 24						08 44			
Southend Airport ✈	d	07 47							08 07				08 27						08 47			
Prittlewell	d	07 50							08 10				08 30						08 50			
Southend Victoria	a	07 54							08 14				08 34						08 54			

London - Shenfield, Southminster and Southend Victoria

		LE 1		LE 1	LE	LE	LE 1	LE 1	LE	LE 1		LE	LE 1	LE	LE 1	LE	LE 1	LE 1	LE 1	LE		LE	LE 1	LE 1	LE
London Liverpool Street 15 ⊖	d	08 14		08 17	08 20	08 30	08 32	08 36	08 40	08 48		08 50	08 55	09 00	09 02	09 10		09 13	09 18	09 20		09 30	09 35	09 38	09 40
Stratford 7 ⊖	d	08 22		08 25	08 27	08 37	08 42	08 45	08 47	08 55		08 57	09 02	09 07	09 09	09 17		09 21	09 25	09 27		09 37	09 42	09 45	09 47
Maryland	d				08 29	08 39			08 49			08 59		09 09		09 19				09 29		09 39			09 49
Forest Gate	d				08 31	08 41			08 51			09 01		09 11		09 21				09 31		09 41			09 51
Manor Park	d				08 33	08 43			08 53			09 03		09 13		09 23				09 33		09 43			09 53
Ilford 2	d				08 36	08 46			08 56			09 06		09 16		09 26				09 36		09 46			09 56
Seven Kings	d				08 38	08 48			08 58			09 08		09 18		09 28				09 38		09 48			09 58
Goodmayes	d				08 40	08 50			09 00			09 10		09 20		09 30				09 40		09 50			10 00
Chadwell Heath	d				08 42	08 52			09 02			09 12		09 22		09 32				09 42		09 52			10 02
Romford	d				08 46	08 56			09 06			09 16		09 26		09 36				09 46		09 56		09 53	10 06
Gidea Park 2	d				08 50	09 00			09 10			09 20		09 30		09 40				09 50		10 00			10 10
Harold Wood	d				08 53	09 03			09 13			09 23		09 33		09 43				09 53		10 03			10 13
Brentwood	d				08 57	09 07			09 17			09 27		09 37		09 47				09 57		10 07			10 17
Shenfield 3	a	08 39		08 41	09 03	09 13	08 59	09 01	09 23	09 11		09 33	09 18	09 43	09 24	09 53		09 38	09 40	10 03		10 13	09 58	10 02	10 23
Shenfield 3	d	08 39					08 59						09 19					09 39					09 59		
Billericay	d	08 45					09 05						09 25					09 45					10 05		
Wickford 2	d	08 55	08 58				09 11						09 31				09 36	09 51					10 11		
Battlesbridge	d		09 02														09 40								
South Woodham Ferrers	d		09 06														09 44								
North Fambridge	d		09 12														09 51								
Althorne	d		09 17														09 56								
Burnham-on-Crouch	d		09 22														10 01								
Southminster	a		09 28														10 07								
Rayleigh	d	09 00					09 16						09 36					09 56					10 16		
Hockley	d	09 04					09 21						09 41					10 01					10 21		
Rochford	d	09 08					09 24						09 44					10 04					10 24		
Southend Airport ✈	d	09 10					09 27						09 47					10 07					10 27		
Prittlewell	d	09 13					09 30						09 50					10 10					10 30		
Southend Victoria	a	09 17					09 34						09 54					10 14					10 34		

		LE 1	LE	LE 1	LE 1	LE		LE 1	LE	LE 1	LE 1	LE	LE	LE 1	LE 1	LE 1		LE	LE 1	LE	LE 1	LE	LE 1	LE	LE 1
London Liverpool Street 15 ⊖	d	09 48	09 50		09 55	10 00		10 02	10 10	10 13	10 18	10 20	10 30		10 35	10 38		10 40	10 48	10 50	10 55	11 00	11 02	11 10	
Stratford 7 ⊖	d	09 55	09 57		10 02	10 07		10 09	10 17	10 20	10 25	10 27	10 37		10 42	10 45		10 47	10 55	10 57	11 02	11 07	11 09	11 17	
Maryland	d		09 59			10 09			10 19			10 29	10 39					10 49		10 59		11 09		11 19	
Forest Gate	d		10 01			10 11			10 21			10 31	10 41					10 51		11 01		11 11		11 21	
Manor Park	d		10 03			10 13			10 23			10 33	10 43					10 53		11 03		11 13		11 23	
Ilford 2	d		10 06			10 16			10 26			10 36	10 46					10 56		11 06		11 16		11 26	
Seven Kings	d		10 08			10 18			10 28			10 38	10 48					10 58		11 08		11 18		11 28	
Goodmayes	d		10 10			10 20			10 30			10 40	10 50					11 00		11 10		11 20		11 30	
Chadwell Heath	d		10 12			10 22			10 32			10 42	10 52					11 02		11 12		11 22		11 32	
Romford	d		10 16			10 26			10 36	10 28		10 46	10 56			10 53		11 06		11 16		11 26		11 36	
Gidea Park 2	d		10 20			10 30			10 40			10 50	11 00					11 10		11 20		11 30		11 40	
Harold Wood	d		10 23			10 33			10 43			10 53	11 03					11 13		11 23		11 33		11 43	
Brentwood	d		10 27			10 37			10 47			10 57	11 07					11 17		11 27		11 37		11 47	
Shenfield 3	a	10 11	10 33		10 18	10 43		10 24	10 53	10 38	10 40	11 03	11 13		10 58	11 02		11 23	11 11	11 33	11 18	11 43	11 24	11 53	
Shenfield 3	d				10 19					10 39					10 59						11 19				
Billericay	d				10 25					10 45					11 05						11 25				
Wickford 2	d			10 16	10 31					10 51				10 56	11 11						11 31				11 36
Battlesbridge	d			10 20										11 00											11 40
South Woodham Ferrers	d			10 24										11 04											11 44
North Fambridge	d			10 31										11 11											11 51
Althorne	d			10 36										11 16											11 56
Burnham-on-Crouch	d			10 41										11 21											12 01
Southminster	a			10 47										11 27											12 07
Rayleigh	d				10 36					10 56					11 16						11 36				
Hockley	d				10 41					11 01					11 21						11 41				
Rochford	d				10 44					11 04					11 24						11 44				
Southend Airport ✈	d				10 47					11 07					11 27						11 47				
Prittlewell	d				10 50					11 10					11 30						11 50				
Southend Victoria	a				10 54					11 14					11 34						11 54				

		LE 1		LE 1	LE	LE	LE 1	LE 1	LE	LE 1	LE	LE 1		LE 1	LE	LE 1	LE	LE 1	LE 1	LE	LE	LE 1		LE 1	LE 1
London Liverpool Street 15 ⊖	d	11 13		11 18	11 20	11 30	11 35	11 38	11 40	11 48	11 50			11 55	12 00	12 02	12 10	12 13	12 18	12 20	12 30			12 35	12 38
Stratford 7 ⊖	d	11 20		11 25	11 27	11 37	11 42	11 45	11 47	11 55	11 57			12 02	12 07	12 09	12 17	12 20	12 25	12 27	12 37			12 42	12 45
Maryland	d				11 29	11 39			11 49		11 59				12 09		12 19			12 29	12 39				
Forest Gate	d				11 31	11 41			11 51		12 01				12 11		12 21			12 31	12 41				
Manor Park	d				11 33	11 43			11 53		12 03				12 13		12 23			12 33	12 43				
Ilford 2	d				11 36	11 46			11 56		12 06				12 16		12 26			12 36	12 46				
Seven Kings	d				11 38	11 48			11 58		12 08				12 18		12 28			12 38	12 48				
Goodmayes	d				11 40	11 50			12 00		12 10				12 20		12 30			12 40	12 50				
Chadwell Heath	d				11 42	11 52			12 02		12 12				12 22		12 32			12 42	12 52				
Romford	d	11 28			11 46	11 56		11 53	12 06		12 16				12 26		12 36	12 28		12 46	12 56				12 53
Gidea Park 2	d				11 50	12 00			12 10		12 20				12 30		12 40			12 50	13 00				
Harold Wood	d				11 53	12 03			12 13		12 23				12 33		12 43			12 53	13 03				
Brentwood	d				11 57	12 07			12 17		12 27				12 37		12 47			12 57	13 07				
Shenfield 3	a	11 38		11 40	12 03	12 13	11 58	12 02	12 23	12 11	12 33			12 18	12 43	12 24	12 53	12 38	12 40	13 03	13 13			12 58	13 02
Shenfield 3	d	11 39					11 59							12 19				12 39						12 59	
Billericay	d	11 45					12 05							12 25				12 45						13 05	
Wickford 2	d	11 51					12 11					12 16		12 31				12 51				12 56		13 11	
Battlesbridge	d											12 20										13 00			
South Woodham Ferrers	d											12 24										13 04			
North Fambridge	d											12 31										13 11			
Althorne	d											12 36										13 16			
Burnham-on-Crouch	d											12 41										13 21			
Southminster	a											12 47										13 27			
Rayleigh	d	11 56					12 16							12 36				12 56						13 16	
Hockley	d	12 01					12 21							12 41				13 01						13 21	
Rochford	d	12 04					12 24							12 44				13 04						13 24	
Southend Airport ✈	d	12 07					12 27							12 47				13 07						13 27	
Prittlewell	d	12 10					12 30							12 50				13 10						13 30	
Southend Victoria	a	12 14					12 34							12 54				13 14						13 34	

London - Shenfield, Southminster and Southend Victoria

		LE	LE 1	LE	LE 1	LE	LE 1	LE		LE 1	LE 1	LE 1	LE	LE	LE 1	LE 1	LE	LE 1		LE	LE 1	LE 1	LE	LE 1	LE
London Liverpool Street 15 ⊖	d	12 40	12 48	12 50	12 55	13 00	13 02	13 10			13 13	13 18	13 20	13 30	13 35	13 38	13 40	13 48		13 50		13 55	14 00	14 02	14 10
Stratford 7 ⊖	d	12 47	12 55	12 57	13 02	13 07	13 09	13 17			13 20	13 25	13 27	13 37	13 42	13 45	13 47	13 55		13 57		14 02	14 07	14 09	14 17
Maryland	d	12 49		12 59		13 09		13 19					13 29	13 39			13 49			13 59			14 09		14 19
Forest Gate	d	12 51		13 01		13 11		13 21					13 31	13 41			13 51			14 01			14 11		14 21
Manor Park	d	12 53		13 03		13 13		13 23					13 33	13 43			13 53			14 03			14 13		14 23
Ilford 2	d	12 56		13 06		13 16		13 26					13 36	13 46			13 56			14 06			14 16		14 26
Seven Kings	d	12 58		13 08		13 18		13 28					13 38	13 48			13 58			14 08			14 18		14 28
Goodmayes	d	13 00		13 10		13 20		13 30					13 40	13 50			14 00			14 10			14 20		14 30
Chadwell Heath	d	13 02		13 12		13 22		13 32					13 42	13 52			14 02			14 12			14 22		14 32
Romford	d	13 06		13 16		13 26		13 36			13 28		13 46	13 56		13 53	14 06			14 16			14 26		14 36
Gidea Park 2	d	13 10		13 20		13 30		13 40					13 50	14 00			14 10			14 20			14 30		14 40
Harold Wood	d	13 13		13 23		13 33		13 43					13 53	14 03			14 13			14 23			14 33		14 43
Brentwood	d	13 17		13 27		13 37		13 47					13 57	14 07			14 17			14 27			14 37		14 47
Shenfield 3	a	13 23	13 11	13 33	13 18	13 43	13 24	13 53			13 38	13 40	14 03	14 13	13 58	14 02	14 23	14 11		14 33		14 18	14 43	14 24	14 53
Shenfield 3	d				13 19						13 39				13 59							14 19			
Billericay	d				13 25						13 45				14 05							14 25			
Wickford 2	d				13 31					13 36	13 51				14 11						14 16	14 31			
Battlesbridge	d									13 40											14 20				
South Woodham Ferrers	d									13 44											14 24				
North Fambridge	d									13 51											14 31				
Althorne	d									13 56											14 36				
Burnham-on-Crouch	d									14 01											14 41				
Southminster	a									14 07											14 47				
Rayleigh	d				13 36						13 56				14 16							14 36			
Hockley	d				13 41						14 01				14 21							14 41			
Rochford	d				13 44						14 04				14 24							14 44			
Southend Airport ✈	d				13 47						14 07				14 27							14 47			
Prittlewell	d				13 50						14 10				14 30							14 50			
Southend Victoria	a				13 54						14 14				14 34							14 54			

		LE 1	LE 1	LE		LE	LE 1	LE 1	LE 1	LE	LE 1	LE	LE 1	LE		LE 1	LE	LE 1	LE 1	LE 1	LE	LE	LE 1	LE 1	
London Liverpool Street 15 ⊖	d	14 13	14 18	14 20		14 30		14 35	14 38	14 40	14 48	14 50	14 55	15 00		15 02	15 10		15 13	15 18	15 20	15 30	15 35	15 38	
Stratford 7 ⊖	d	14 20	14 25	14 27		14 37		14 42	14 45	14 47	14 55	14 57	15 02	15 07		15 09	15 17		15 20	15 25	15 27	15 37	15 42	15 45	
Maryland	d			14 29		14 39				14 49		14 59		15 09			15 19				15 29	15 39			
Forest Gate	d			14 31		14 41				14 51		15 01		15 11			15 21				15 31	15 41			
Manor Park	d			14 33		14 43				14 53		15 03		15 13			15 23				15 33	15 43			
Ilford 2	d			14 36		14 46				14 56		15 06		15 16			15 26				15 36	15 46			
Seven Kings	d			14 38		14 48				14 58		15 08		15 18			15 28				15 38	15 48			
Goodmayes	d			14 40		14 50				15 00		15 10		15 20			15 30				15 40	15 50			
Chadwell Heath	d			14 42		14 52				15 02		15 12		15 22			15 32				15 42	15 52			
Romford	d	14 28		14 46		14 56			14 53	15 06		15 16		15 26			15 36		15 28		15 46	15 56		15 53	
Gidea Park 2	d			14 50		15 00				15 10		15 20		15 30			15 40				15 50	16 00			
Harold Wood	d			14 53		15 03				15 13		15 23		15 33			15 43				15 53	16 03			
Brentwood	d			14 57		15 07				15 17		15 27		15 37			15 47				15 57	16 07			
Shenfield 3	a	14 38	14 40	15 03		15 13		14 58	15 02	15 23	15 11	15 33	15 18	15 43		15 24	15 53		15 38	15 40	16 03	16 13	15 58	16 02	
Shenfield 3	d	14 39						14 59					15 19						15 39				15 59		
Billericay	d	14 45						15 05					15 25						15 45				16 05		
Wickford 2	d	14 51					14 56	15 11					15 31					15 36	15 51				16 11		
Battlesbridge	d						15 00											15 40							
South Woodham Ferrers	d						15 04											15 44							
North Fambridge	d						15 11											15 51							
Althorne	d						15 16											15 56							
Burnham-on-Crouch	d						15 21											16 01							
Southminster	a						15 27											16 07							
Rayleigh	d	14 56						15 16					15 36						15 56				16 16		
Hockley	d	15 01						15 21					15 41						16 01				16 21		
Rochford	d	15 04						15 24					15 44						16 04				16 24		
Southend Airport ✈	d	15 07						15 27					15 47						16 07				16 27		
Prittlewell	d	15 10						15 30					15 50						16 10				16 30		
Southend Victoria	a	15 14						15 34					15 54						16 14				16 34		

		LE	LE 1	LE	LE 1	LE 1	LE	LE 1	LE	LE 1		LE 1	LE 1	LE	LE 1	LE	LE 1	LE 1	LE	LE		LE 1	LE 1	LE	LE 1
London Liverpool Street 15 ⊖	d	15 40	15 48	15 50		15 55	16 00	16 02	16 10	16 10		16 14	16 17	16 20	16 24	16 28	16 32	16 34	16 37	16 40			16 40	16 47	16 47
Stratford 7 ⊖	d	15 47	15 55	15 57		16 02	16 07	16 09	16 17	16 18		16 22	16 25	16 27	16 32	16 35		16 42	16 44	16 47			16 48	16 54	16 55
Maryland	d	15 49		15 59			16 09		16 19					16 29		16 37				16 49					
Forest Gate	d	15 51		16 01			16 11		16 21					16 31		16 39				16 51					
Manor Park	d	15 53		16 03			16 13		16 23					16 33		16 41				16 53					
Ilford 2	d	15 56		16 06			16 16		16 26					16 36		16 44			16 50	16 56				17 00	
Seven Kings	d	15 58		16 08			16 18		16 28					16 38		16 47			16 52					17 02	
Goodmayes	d	16 00		16 10			16 20		16 30					16 40		16 49			16 54					17 04	
Chadwell Heath	d	16 02		16 12			16 22		16 32					16 42		16 51			16 56	17 00				17 06	
Romford	d	16 06		16 16			16 26		16 36					16 46		16 55			17 00	17 04				17 10	
Gidea Park 2	d	16 10		16 20			16 30		16 40					16 50		17a00			17 04	17a10				17 14	
Harold Wood	d	16 13		16 23			16 33		16 43					16 53					17 07					17 17	
Brentwood	d	16 17		16 27			16 37		16 47					16 57					17 11					17 21	
Shenfield 3	a	16 23	16 11	16 33		16 18	16 43	16 24	16 53	16 34		16 38	16 41	17 03	16 49		16 54	16 58	17 19				17 04	17 29	17 11
Shenfield 3	d					16 19				16 34					16 49								17 04		
Billericay	d					16 25				16 41					16 56								17 11		
Wickford 2	d				16 14	16 31				16 48					17 03							17 06	17 18		
Battlesbridge	d				16 18																	17 10			
South Woodham Ferrers	d				16 22																	17 14			
North Fambridge	d				16 29																	17 21			
Althorne	d				16 34																	17 26			
Burnham-on-Crouch	d				16 39																	17 31			
Southminster	a				16 45																	17 37			
Rayleigh	d					16 36				16 53					17 08								17 23		
Hockley	d					16 41				16 57					17 12								17 27		
Rochford	d					16 44				17 01					17 16								17 31		
Southend Airport ✈	d					16 47				17 03					17 18								17 33		
Prittlewell	d					16 50				17 06					17 21								17 36		
Southend Victoria	a					16 54				17 15					17 27								17 42		

London - Shenfield, Southminster and Southend Victoria

		LE	LE [1]	LE	LE	LE ◇[1]		LE [1]	LE	LE [1]	LE	LE [1]	LE [1]	LE	LE [1]	LE		LE [1]	LE [1]	LE [1]	LE	LE	LE [1]	LE [1]	LE
London Liverpool Street [15] ⊖	d	16 50	16 54	16 57	17 00	17 02		17 04	17 07	17 08	17 10	17 12	17 15	17 17	17 18	17 20		17 20	17 22	17 25	17 27	17 30	17 32	17 34	17 36
Stratford [7] ⊖	d	16 57	17 02	17 04	17 07	17 10		17 13	17 14	17a16	17 17	17a20	17 23	17 24	17a26	17 27				17 34	17 34	17 37	17a40	17 43	17 43
Maryland	d	16 59			17 09						17 19					17 29						17 39			17 45
Forest Gate	d	17 01			17 11						17 21					17 31						17 41			
Manor Park	d	17 03			17 13						17 23					17 33						17 43			
Ilford [2]	d	17 06		17 10	17 16				17 20		17 26			17 30		17 36					17 40	17 46			17 50
Seven Kings	d			17 12					17 22					17 32							17 42				17 52
Goodmayes	d			17 14					17 24					17 34							17 44				17 54
Chadwell Heath	d	17 10		17 16	17 20				17 26		17 30			17 36		17 40					17 46	17 50			17 56
Romford	d	17 14		17 20	17 24				17 30		17 34			17 40		17 44					17 50	17 54			18 00
Gidea Park [2]	d	17a20		17 24	17a30				17 34		17a40			17 44		17a50					17 54	18a00			18 04
Harold Wood	d			17 27					17 37					17 47							17 57				18 07
Brentwood	d			17 31					17 41					17 51							18 01				18 11
Shenfield [3]	a		17 19	17 39		17 26		17 30	17 49				17 39	17 59				17 45		17 51	18 09			17 59	18 19
Shenfield [3]	d		17 19					17 30					17 39							17 52				17 59	
Billericay	d		17 26					17 37					17 46							17 58				18 06	
Wickford [2]	d		17 33					17 44					17 53						18 00	18 05				18 13	
Battlesbridge	d																		18 04						
South Woodham Ferrers	d																		18 08						
North Fambridge	d																		18 14						
Althorne	d																		18 19						
Burnham-on-Crouch	d																		18 24						
Southminster	a																		18 32						
Rayleigh	d		17 38					17 49					17 58							18 10				18 18	
Hockley	d		17 42					17 53					18 02							18 15				18 22	
Rochford	d		17 46					17 57					18 06							18 18				18 26	
Southend Airport ✈	d		17 48					17 59					18 08							18 21				18 28	
Prittlewell	d		17 51					18 02					18 11							18 24				18 31	
Southend Victoria	a		17 57					18 08					18 17							18 30				18 37	

		LE [1]		LE	LE [1]	LE	LE [1]	LE	LE	LE	LE [1]	LE [1]		LE	LE [1]	LE	LE [1]	LE	LE [1]	LE [1]	LE	LE		LE	LE [1]
London Liverpool Street [15] ⊖	d	17 38		17 39	17 40	17 42	17 45	17 46	17 49	17 52	17 52	17 54		17 56	17 58	17 59	18 00	18 02	18 02	18 05		18 07		18 10	18 12
Stratford [7] ⊖	d	17a46		17 46		17 49	17 53	17 53	17 56	17 59	18a00	18 03		18 03	18a06	18 06	18 09	18 09	18 11	18 14		18 14		18 17	18a20
Maryland	d							17 55						18 05										18 19	
Forest Gate	d					17 52				18 02								18 12						18 21	
Manor Park	d			17 50					18 00							18 10								18 23	
Ilford [2]	d			17 53		17 56		18 00	18 03	18 06				18 10		18 13		18 16				18 20		18 26	
Seven Kings	d			17 56		17 59		18 02	18 06	18 09				18 12		18 16		18 19				18 22			
Goodmayes	d			17 58		18 01		18 04	18 08	18 11				18 14		18 18		18 21				18 24			
Chadwell Heath	d			18 00		18 03		18 06	18 10	18 13				18 16		18 20		18 23				18 26		18 30	
Romford	d			18 04		18 07		18 10	18 14	18 17				18 20		18 24		18 27				18 30		18 34	
Gidea Park [2]	d			18a09		18a12		18 14	18 18	18a22				18 24		18a29		18a32				18 34		18a40	
Harold Wood	d							18 17	18 21					18 27								18 37			
Brentwood	d							18 21	18 25					18 31							←	18 41			
Shenfield [3]	a				18 05		18 09	18 29	18 33			18 19		18 39			18 25			18 31	18 33	18 49			
Shenfield [3]	d						18 09		18 36			18 19								18 31	18 36				
Billericay	d						18 16		→			18 26								18 38	18 42				
Wickford [2]	d						18 23					18 33							18 40	18 45	18 49				
Battlesbridge	d																		18 44						
South Woodham Ferrers	d																		18 48						
North Fambridge	d																		18 54						
Althorne	d																		18 59						
Burnham-on-Crouch	d																		19 04						
Southminster	a																		19 12						
Rayleigh	d						18 28					18 38								18 50	18 54				
Hockley	d						18 32					18 42								18 55	18 59				
Rochford	d						18 36					18 46								18 58	19 02				
Southend Airport ✈	d						18 38					18 48								19 01	19 05				
Prittlewell	d						18 41					18 51								19 04	19 08				
Southend Victoria	a						18 47					18 57								19 10	19 14				

		LE [1]	LE	LE [1]	LE	LE [1]	LE [1]	LE		LE	LE [1]	LE [1]	LE	LE [1]	LE	LE [1]	LE [1]	LE		LE [1]	LE	LE [1]	LE	LE	LE [1]
London Liverpool Street [15] ⊖	d	18 14	18 17	18 18	18 20	18 20	18 25	18 27		18 30	18 32	18 35	18 37	18 38	18 40	18 41	18 45	18 47		18 48	18 50	18 55	18 57	19 00	19 02
Stratford [7] ⊖	d	18 23	18 24	18a26	18 27	18 29	18 33	18 34		18 37	18a40	18 43	18 44	18 46	18 47	18 49	18 53	18 54		18a56	18 57	19 03	19 04	19 07	19 09
Maryland	d				18 29					18 39					18 49						18 59			19 09	
Forest Gate	d				18 31					18 41					18 51						19 01			19 11	
Manor Park	d				18 33					18 43					18 53						19 03			19 13	
Ilford [2]	d		18 30		18 36			18 40		18 46			18 50		18 56			19 00			19 06		19 10	19 16	
Seven Kings	d		18 32					18 42					18 52					19 02					19 12	19 18	
Goodmayes	d		18 34					18 44					18 54					19 04					19 14	19 20	
Chadwell Heath	d		18 36		18 40			18 46		18 50			18 56		19 00			19 06			19 10		19 16	19 22	
Romford	d		18 40		18 44			18 50		18 54			19 00		19 04			19 10			19 14		19 20	19 26	
Gidea Park [2]	d		18 44		18a50			18 54		19a00			19 04		19 08			19 14			19a20		19 24	19 30	
Harold Wood	d		18 47					18 57					19 07		19 11			19 17					19 27	19 33	
Brentwood	d		18 51					19 01					19 11		19 15			19 21					19 31	19 37	
Shenfield [3]	a	18 40	18 59			18 45	18 50	19 09				18 59	19 19	19 02	19 23		19 10	19 29				19 20	19 39	19 43	19 24
Shenfield [3]	d	18 40					18 50					18 59					19 10					19 20			
Billericay	d	18 47					18 57					19 06					19 17					19 27			
Wickford [2]	d	18 54					19 04					19 13				19 19	19 24					19 34			
Battlesbridge	d															19 23									
South Woodham Ferrers	d															19 27									
North Fambridge	d															19 34									
Althorne	d															19 39									
Burnham-on-Crouch	d															19 44									
Southminster	a															19 52									
Rayleigh	d	18 59					19 09					19 18					19 29					19 39			
Hockley	d	19 03					19 13					19 22					19 33					19 43			
Rochford	d	19 07					19 17					19 26					19 37					19 47			
Southend Airport ✈	d	19 09					19 19					19 28					19 39					19 49			
Prittlewell	d	19 12					19 22					19 31					19 42					19 52			
Southend Victoria	a	19 18					19 28					19 37					19 48					19 58			

Table 5

London - Shenfield, Southminster and Southend Victoria

		LE 1	LE	LE 1		LE 1	LE	LE	LE 1	LE 1	LE	LE 1	LE	LE 1		LE 1	LE	LE 1	LE	LE 1	LE 1	LE	LE	CC	
London Liverpool Street 15 ⊖	d	19 08	19 10	19 15		19 18	19 20	19 30	19 35	19 38	19 40	19 48	19 50			19 55	20 00	20 02	20 10	20 13	20 18	20 20	20 30	20 35	
Stratford 7 ⊖	d	19a15	19 17	19 22		19 25	19 27	19 37	19 42	19 45	19 47	19 55	19 57			20 02	20 07	20 09	20 17	20 20	20 25	20 27	20 37	20a42	
Maryland	d		19 19				19 29	19 39			19 49		19 59				20 09		20 19			20 29	20 39		
Forest Gate	d		19 21				19 31	19 41			19 51		20 01				20 11		20 21			20 31	20 41		
Manor Park	d		19 23				19 33	19 43			19 53		20 03				20 13		20 23			20 33	20 43		
Ilford 2	d		19 26				19 36	19 46			19 56		20 06				20 16		20 26			20 36	20 46		
Seven Kings	d		19 28				19 38	19 48			19 58		20 08				20 18		20 28			20 38	20 48		
Goodmayes	d		19 30				19 40	19 50			20 00		20 10				20 20		20 30			20 40	20 50		
Chadwell Heath	d		19 32				19 42	19 52			20 02		20 12				20 22		20 32			20 42	20 52		
Romford	d		19 36				19 46	19 56			20 06		20 16				20 26		20 36	20 28		20 46	20 56		
Gidea Park 2	d		19 40				19 50	20 00			20 10		20 20				20 30		20 40			20 50	21 00		
Harold Wood	d		19 43				19 53	20 03			20 13		20 23				20 33		20 43			20 53	21 03		
Brentwood	d		19 47				19 57	20 07			20 17		20 27				20 37		20 47			20 57	21 07		
Shenfield 3	a		19 53	19 38		19 40	20 03	20 13	19 58	20 00	20 23	20 11	20 33			20 18	20 43	20 24	20 53	20 38	20 40	21 03	21 13		
Shenfield 3	d			19 39					19 59							20 19				20 39					
Billericay	d			19 45					20 05							20 25				20 45					
Wickford 2	d			19 51					20 11					20 16		20 31				20 51					
Battlesbridge	d													20 20											
South Woodham Ferrers	d													20 24											
North Fambridge	d													20 31											
Althorne	d													20 36											
Burnham-on-Crouch	d													20 41											
Southminster	a													20 47											
Rayleigh	d			19 56					20 16							20 36				20 56					
Hockley	d			20 01					20 21							20 41				21 01					
Rochford	d			20 04					20 24							20 44				21 04					
Southend Airport ✈	d			20 07					20 27							20 47				21 07					
Prittlewell	d			20 10					20 30							20 50				21 10					
Southend Victoria	a			20 14					20 34							20 54				21 14					

		LE 1	LE 1	LE 1	LE	LE 1	LE	LE 1	LE	LE 1		LE	LE 1	LE 1	LE 1	LE	LE	LE 1	CC	LE 1		LE	LE 1	LE	LE 1
London Liverpool Street 15 ⊖	d		20 35	20 38	20 40	20 48	20 50	20 55	21 00	21 02		21 10		21 13	21 18	21 20	21 30	21 35	21 35	21 38		21 40	21 48	21 50	
Stratford 7 ⊖	d		20 42	20 45	20 47	20 55	20 57	21 02	21 07	21 09		21 17		21 20	21 25	21 27	21 37	21 42	21a42	21 45		21 47	21 55	21 57	
Maryland	d				20 49		20 59		21 09			21 19				21 29	21 39					21 49		21 59	
Forest Gate	d				20 51		21 01		21 11			21 21				21 31	21 41					21 51		22 01	
Manor Park	d				20 53		21 03		21 13			21 23				21 33	21 43					21 53		22 03	
Ilford 2	d				20 56		21 06		21 16			21 26				21 36	21 46					21 56		22 06	
Seven Kings	d				20 58		21 08		21 18			21 28				21 38	21 48					21 58		22 08	
Goodmayes	d				21 00		21 10		21 20			21 30				21 40	21 50					22 00		22 10	
Chadwell Heath	d				21 02		21 12		21 22			21 32				21 42	21 52					22 02		22 12	
Romford	d			20 53	21 06		21 16		21 26			21 36		21 28		21 46	21 56			21 53		22 06		22 16	
Gidea Park 2	d				21 10		21 20		21 30			21 40				21 50	22 00					22 10		22 20	
Harold Wood	d				21 13		21 23		21 33			21 43				21 53	22 03					22 13		22 23	
Brentwood	d				21 17		21 27		21 37			21 47				21 57	22 07					22 17		22 27	
Shenfield 3	a		20 58	21 02	21 23	21 11	21 33	21 18	21 43	21 24		21 53		21 38	21 40	22 03	22 13	21 58		22 02		22 23	22 11	22 33	
Shenfield 3	d		20 59					21 19						21 39				21 59							
Billericay	d		21 05					21 25						21 45				22 05							
Wickford 2	d	20 56	21 11					21 31					21 36	21 51				22 11							22 16
Battlesbridge	d	21 00											21 40												22 20
South Woodham Ferrers	d	21 04											21 44												22 24
North Fambridge	d	21 11											21 51												22 31
Althorne	d	21 16											21 56												22 36
Burnham-on-Crouch	d	21 21											22 01												22 41
Southminster	a	21 27											22 07												22 47
Rayleigh	d		21 16					21 36						21 56				22 16							
Hockley	d		21 21					21 41						22 01				22 21							
Rochford	d		21 24					21 44						22 04				22 24							
Southend Airport ✈	d		21 27					21 47						22 07				22 27							
Prittlewell	d		21 30					21 50						22 10				22 30							
Southend Victoria	a		21 34					21 54						22 14				22 34							

		LE 1	LE 1	LE	LE 1	LE 1		LE	LE	LE 1	LE 1	LE 1	LE	LE 1	LE	LE 1		LE 1	LE	LE	LE 1	LE 1	LE		
London Liverpool Street 15 ⊖	d	21 55	22 02	22 05	22 13	22 18		22 20	22 35	22 38		22 45	22 50	23 02	23 05	23 15		23 18	23 20	23 35	23 45	23 48	23 50		
Stratford 7 ⊖	d	22 02	22 09	22 12	22 20	22 25		22 27	22 42	22 45		22 52	22 57	23 09	23 12	23 22		23 25	23 27	23 42	23 52	23 55	23 57		
Maryland	d			22 14				22 29	22 44				22 59		23 14				23 29	23 44			23 59		
Forest Gate	d			22 16				22 31	22 46				23 01		23 16				23 31	23 46			00 01		
Manor Park	d			22 18				22 33	22 48				23 03		23 18				23 33	23 48			00 03		
Ilford 2	d			22 21				22 36	22 51				23 06		23 21				23 36	23 51			00 06		
Seven Kings	d			22 23				22 38	22 53				23 08		23 23				23 38	23 53			00 08		
Goodmayes	d			22 25				22 40	22 55				23 10		23 25				23 40	23 55			00 10		
Chadwell Heath	d			22 27				22 42	22 57				23 12		23 27				23 42	23 57			00 12		
Romford	d			22 31	22 28			22 46	23 01				23 16		23 31				23 46	00 02			00 16		
Gidea Park 2	d			22 35				22 50	23 05				23 20		23 35				23 50	00 05			00 20		
Harold Wood	d			22 38				22 53	23 08				23 23		23 38				23 53	00 08			00 23		
Brentwood	d			22 42				22 57	23 12				23 27		23 42				23 57	00 12			00 27		
Shenfield 3	a	22 18	22 24	22 48	22 38	22 40		23 03	23 18	23 00		23 08	23 33	23 24	23 48	23 38		23 40	00 03	00 18	00 08	00 10	00 33		
Shenfield 3	d	22 19			22 39							23 09				23 39					00 09				
Billericay	d	22 25			22 45							23 15				23 45					00 15				
Wickford 2	d	22 31			22 51						22 56	23 21				23 51					00 21				
Battlesbridge	d										23 00														
South Woodham Ferrers	d										23 04														
North Fambridge	d										23 11														
Althorne	d										23 16														
Burnham-on-Crouch	d										23 21														
Southminster	a										23 27														
Rayleigh	d	22 36			22 56							23 26				23 56					00 26				
Hockley	d	22 41			23 01							23 31				00 01					00 31				
Rochford	d	22 44			23 04							23 34				00 04					00 34				
Southend Airport ✈	d	22 47			23 07							23 37				00 07					00 37				
Prittlewell	d	22 50			23 10							23 40				00 10					00 40				
Southend Victoria	a	22 54			23 14							23 48				00 18					00 48				

Table 5

Saturdays

London - Shenfield, Southminster and Southend Victoria

		LE 1	LE	LE	LE 1	LE 1	LE	LE	LE 1	LE 1		LE	LE	LE 1	LE 1	LE	LE 1	LE 1	LE 1	LE 1		LE	LE 1	LE	LE 1
London Liverpool Street [15] ⊖	d	23p15	23p20	23p35	23p45	23p48	23p50	00 01	00 15	00 18		00 20	00 32	00 46	00 50	00 55	05 23			05 28		05 28	05 30	05 40	06 02
Stratford [7] ⊖	d	23p22	23p27	23p42	23p52	23p55	23p57	00 08	00 22	00 25		00 27	00 39	00 53	00 57	01 02	05a32			05 35		05a37	05 37	05 47	06 09
Maryland	d		23p29	23p44			23p59	00 10				00 29	00 41			01 04								05 49	
Forest Gate	d		23p31	23p46			00 01	00 12				00 31	00 43			01 06								05 51	
Manor Park	d		23p33	23p48			00 03	00 14				00 33	00 45			01 08								05 53	
Ilford [2]	d		23p36	23p51			00 06	00 17				00 36	00 48			01 11				05 40				05 56	
Seven Kings	d		23p38	23p53			00 08	00 19				00 38	00 50			01 13				05 42				05 58	
Goodmayes	d		23p40	23p55			00 10	00 21				00 40	00 52			01 15								06 00	
Chadwell Heath	d		23p42	23p57			00 12	00 23				00 42	00 54			01 17								06 02	
Romford	d		23p46	00 02			00 16	00 27	00 32			00 46	00 58		01 08	01 21				05 48			05 45	06 06	
Gidea Park [2]	d		23p50	00 05			00 20	00a31				00 50	01a02	01 07		01 25				05 51				06 10	
Harold Wood	d		23p53	00 08			00 23					00 53				01 28				05 54				06 13	
Brentwood	d		23p57	00 12			00 27					00 57				01 32				05 59				06 17	
Shenfield [3]	a	23p38	00 03	00 18	00 08	00 10	00 33		00 44	00 47		01 03		01 17	01 20	01 38				06 04			05 54	06 23	06 24
Shenfield [3]	d	23p39			00 09				00 45						01 20					06 04					
Billericay	d	23p45			00 15				00 51						01 26					06 10					
Wickford [2]	d	23p51			00 21				00 56						01 31			05 36	06 12	06 16					
Battlesbridge	d																	05 40	06 16						
South Woodham Ferrers	d																	05 44	06 20						
North Fambridge	d																	05 51	06 31						
Althorne	d																	05 56	06 36						
Burnham-on-Crouch	d																	06 01	06 41						
Southminster	a																	06 07	06 47						
Rayleigh	d	23p56			00 26				01 01						01 36					06 22					
Hockley	d	00 01			00 31				01 06						01 41					06 26					
Rochford	d	00 04			00 34				01 09						01 44					06 30					
Southend Airport ✈	d	00 07			00 37				01 12						01 47					06 32					
Prittlewell	d	00 10			00 40				01 15						01 50					06 35					
Southend Victoria	a	00 18			00 48				01 23						01 58					06 39					

		LE 1	LE	LE 1	LE 1	LE 1		LE 1	LE 1	LE	LE 1	LE 1	LE	LE 1	LE	LE 1		LE 1	LE 1	LE	LE	LE 1	LE 1	LE	LE 1
London Liverpool Street [15] ⊖	d	06 05	06 10	06 18	06 23			06 35	06 38	06 40	06 48	06 55	07 00	07 02	07 10			07 13	07 18	07 20	07 30	07 35	07 38	07 40	07 48
Stratford [7] ⊖	d	06 12	06 17	06 25	06a32			06 42	06 45	06 47	06 55	07 02	07 07	07 09	07 17			07 20	07 25	07 27	07 37	07 42	07 45	07 47	07 55
Maryland	d		06 19							06 49			07 09		07 19					07 29	07 39			07 49	
Forest Gate	d		06 21							06 51			07 11		07 21					07 31	07 41			07 51	
Manor Park	d		06 23							06 53			07 13		07 23					07 33	07 43			07 53	
Ilford [2]	d		06 26							06 56			07 16		07 26					07 36	07 46			07 56	
Seven Kings	d		06 28							06 58			07 18		07 28					07 38	07 48			07 58	
Goodmayes	d		06 30							07 00			07 20		07 30					07 40	07 50			08 00	
Chadwell Heath	d		06 32							07 02			07 22		07 32					07 42	07 52			08 02	
Romford	d		06 36						06 53	07 06			07 26		07 36			07 28		07 46	07 56		07 53	08 06	
Gidea Park [2]	d		06 40							07 10			07 30		07 40					07 50	08 00			08 10	
Harold Wood	d		06 43							07 13			07 33		07 43					07 53	08 03			08 13	
Brentwood	d		06 47							07 17			07 37		07 47					07 57	08 07			08 17	
Shenfield [3]	a	06 30	06 53	06 40				06 58	07 02	07 23	07 11	07 18	07 43	07 24	07 53			07 38	07 40	08 03	08 13	07 58	08 02	08 23	08 11
Shenfield [3]	d	06 30						06 59				07 19						07 39				07 59			
Billericay	d	06 36						07 05				07 25						07 45				08 05			
Wickford [2]	d	06 43				06 56		07 11				07 31				07 36		07 51				08 11			
Battlesbridge	d					07 00										07 40									
South Woodham Ferrers	d					07 04										07 44									
North Fambridge	d					07 11										07 51									
Althorne	d					07 16										07 56									
Burnham-on-Crouch	d					07 21										08 01									
Southminster	a					07 27										08 07									
Rayleigh	d	06 48						07 16				07 36						07 56				08 16			
Hockley	d	06 53						07 21				07 41						08 01				08 21			
Rochford	d	06 56						07 24				07 44						08 04				08 24			
Southend Airport ✈	d	06 59						07 27				07 47						08 07				08 27			
Prittlewell	d	07 02						07 30				07 50						08 10				08 30			
Southend Victoria	a	07 05						07 34				07 54						08 14				08 34			

		LE		LE 1	LE 1	LE	LE 1	LE	LE 1	LE 1	LE	LE		LE 1	LE 1	LE 1	LE	LE 1	LE	LE 1	LE	LE 1		LE	LE 1
London Liverpool Street [15] ⊖	d	07 50			07 55	08 00	08 02	08 10	08 13	08 18	08 20	08 30			08 35	08 38	08 40	08 48	08 50	08 55	09 00	09 02		09 10	
Stratford [7] ⊖	d	07 57			08 02	08 07	08 09	08 17	08 20	08 25	08 27	08 37			08 42	08 45	08 47	08 55	08 57	09 02	09 07	09 09		09 17	
Maryland	d	07 59				08 09		08 19			08 29	08 39					08 49		08 59		09 09			09 19	
Forest Gate	d	08 01				08 11		08 21			08 31	08 41					08 51		09 01		09 11			09 21	
Manor Park	d	08 03				08 13		08 23			08 33	08 43					08 53		09 03		09 13			09 23	
Ilford [2]	d	08 06				08 16		08 26			08 36	08 46					08 56		09 06		09 16			09 26	
Seven Kings	d	08 08				08 18		08 28			08 38	08 48					08 58		09 08		09 18			09 28	
Goodmayes	d	08 10				08 20		08 30			08 40	08 50					09 00		09 10		09 20			09 30	
Chadwell Heath	d	08 12				08 22		08 32			08 42	08 52					09 02		09 12		09 22			09 32	
Romford	d	08 16				08 26		08 36	08 28		08 46	08 56				08 53	09 06		09 16		09 26			09 36	
Gidea Park [2]	d	08 20				08 30		08 40			08 50	09 00					09 10		09 20		09 30			09 40	
Harold Wood	d	08 23				08 33		08 43			08 53	09 03					09 13		09 23		09 33			09 43	
Brentwood	d	08 27				08 37		08 47			08 57	09 07					09 17		09 27		09 37			09 47	
Shenfield [3]	a	08 33			08 18	08 43	08 24	08 53	08 38	08 40	09 03	09 13			08 58	09 02	09 23	09 11	09 33	09 18	09 43	09 24		09 53	
Shenfield [3]	d				08 19				08 39						08 59					09 19					
Billericay	d				08 25				08 45						09 05					09 25					
Wickford [2]	d			08 16	08 31				08 51					08 56	09 11					09 31					09 36
Battlesbridge	d			08 20										09 00											09 40
South Woodham Ferrers	d			08 24										09 04											09 44
North Fambridge	d			08 31										09 11											09 51
Althorne	d			08 36										09 16											09 56
Burnham-on-Crouch	d			08 41										09 21											10 01
Southminster	a			08 47										09 27											10 07
Rayleigh	d				08 36				08 56						09 16					09 36					
Hockley	d				08 41				09 01						09 21					09 41					
Rochford	d				08 44				09 04						09 24					09 44					
Southend Airport ✈	d				08 47				09 07						09 27					09 47					
Prittlewell	d				08 50				09 10						09 30					09 50					
Southend Victoria	a				08 54				09 14						09 34					09 54					

Table 5

Saturdays

London - Shenfield, Southminster and Southend Victoria

		LE 1	LE 1	LE	LE	LE 1	LE 1	LE		LE 1	LE	LE 1	LE 1	LE	LE 1	LE	LE 1	LE 1		LE	LE	LE 1	LE 1	LE 1	LE
London Liverpool Street 15 ⊖	d	09 13	09 18	09 20	09 30	09 35	09 38	09 40		09 48	09 50		09 55	10 00	10 02	10 10	10 13	10 18		10 20	10 30		10 35	10 38	10 40
Stratford 7 ⊖	d	09 20	09 25	09 27	09 37	09 42	09 45	09 47		09 55	09 57		10 02	10 07	10 09	10 17	10 20	10 25		10 27	10 37		10 42	10 45	10 47
Maryland	d			09 29	09 39			09 49			09 59			10 09		10 19				10 29	10 39				10 49
Forest Gate	d			09 31	09 41			09 51			10 01			10 11		10 21				10 31	10 41				10 51
Manor Park	d			09 33	09 43			09 53			10 03			10 13		10 23				10 33	10 43				10 53
Ilford 2	d			09 36	09 46			09 56			10 06			10 16		10 26				10 36	10 46				10 56
Seven Kings	d			09 38	09 48			09 58			10 08			10 18		10 28				10 38	10 48				10 58
Goodmayes	d			09 40	09 50			10 00			10 10			10 20		10 30				10 40	10 50				11 00
Chadwell Heath	d			09 42	09 52			10 02			10 12			10 22		10 32				10 42	10 52				11 02
Romford	d	09 28		09 46	09 56		09 53	10 06			10 16			10 26		10 36	10 28			10 46	10 56			10 53	11 06
Gidea Park 2	d			09 50	10 00			10 10			10 20			10 30		10 40				10 50	11 00				11 10
Harold Wood	d			09 53	10 03			10 13			10 23			10 33		10 43				10 53	11 03				11 13
Brentwood	d			09 57	10 07			10 17			10 27			10 37		10 47				10 57	11 07				11 17
Shenfield 3	a	09 38	09 40	10 03	10 13	09 58	10 02	10 23		10 11	10 33		10 18	10 43	10 24	10 53	10 38	10 40		11 03	11 13		10 58	11 02	11 23
Shenfield 3	d	09 39				09 59							10 19				10 39						10 59		
Billericay	d	09 45				10 05							10 25				10 45						11 05		
Wickford 2	d	09 51				10 11						10 16	10 31				10 51					10 56	11 11		
Battlesbridge	d											10 20										11 00			
South Woodham Ferrers	d											10 24										11 04			
North Fambridge	d											10 31										11 11			
Althorne	d											10 36										11 16			
Burnham-on-Crouch	d											10 41										11 21			
Southminster	a											10 47										11 27			
Rayleigh	d	09 56				10 16							10 36				10 56						11 16		
Hockley	d	10 01				10 21							10 41				11 01						11 21		
Rochford	d	10 04				10 24							10 44				11 04						11 24		
Southend Airport ✈	d	10 07				10 27							10 47				11 07						11 27		
Prittlewell	d	10 10				10 30							10 50				11 10						11 30		
Southend Victoria	a	10 14				10 34							10 54				11 14						11 34		

		LE 1	LE	LE 1		LE	LE 1	LE	LE 1	LE 1	LE 1	LE	LE	LE 1		LE 1	LE	LE 1	LE	LE 1	LE 1	LE	LE 1	LE	
London Liverpool Street 15 ⊖	d	10 48	10 50	10 55		11 00	11 02	11 10		11 13	11 18	11 20	11 30	11 35		11 38	11 40	11 48	11 50		11 55	12 00	12 02	12 10	
Stratford 7 ⊖	d	10 55	10 57	11 02		11 07	11 09	11 17		11 20	11 25	11 27	11 37	11 42		11 45	11 47	11 55	11 57		12 02	12 07	12 09	12 17	
Maryland	d		10 59			11 09		11 19				11 29	11 39				11 49		11 59			12 09		12 19	
Forest Gate	d		11 01			11 11		11 21				11 31	11 41				11 51		12 01			12 11		12 21	
Manor Park	d		11 03			11 13		11 23				11 33	11 43				11 53		12 03			12 13		12 23	
Ilford 2	d		11 06			11 16		11 26				11 36	11 46				11 56		12 06			12 16		12 26	
Seven Kings	d		11 08			11 18		11 28				11 38	11 48				11 58		12 08			12 18		12 28	
Goodmayes	d		11 10			11 20		11 30				11 40	11 50				12 00		12 10			12 20		12 30	
Chadwell Heath	d		11 12			11 22		11 32				11 42	11 52				12 02		12 12			12 22		12 32	
Romford	d		11 16			11 26		11 36		11 28		11 46	11 56			11 53	12 06		12 16			12 26		12 36	
Gidea Park 2	d		11 20			11 30		11 40				11 50	12 00				12 10		12 20			12 30		12 40	
Harold Wood	d		11 23			11 33		11 43				11 53	12 03				12 13		12 23			12 33		12 43	
Brentwood	d		11 27			11 37		11 47				11 57	12 07				12 17		12 27			12 37		12 47	
Shenfield 3	a	11 11	11 33	11 18		11 43	11 24	11 53		11 38	11 40	12 03	12 13	11 58		12 02	12 23	12 11	12 33		12 18	12 43	12 24	12 53	
Shenfield 3	d			11 19						11 39				11 59							12 19				
Billericay	d			11 25						11 45				12 05							12 25				
Wickford 2	d			11 31					11 36	11 51				12 11						12 16	12 31				
Battlesbridge	d								11 40											12 20					
South Woodham Ferrers	d								11 44											12 24					
North Fambridge	d								11 51											12 31					
Althorne	d								11 56											12 36					
Burnham-on-Crouch	d								12 01											12 41					
Southminster	a								12 07											12 47					
Rayleigh	d			11 36						11 56				12 16							12 36				
Hockley	d			11 41						12 01				12 21							12 41				
Rochford	d			11 44						12 04				12 24							12 44				
Southend Airport ✈	d			11 47						12 07				12 27							12 47				
Prittlewell	d			11 50						12 10				12 30							12 50				
Southend Victoria	a			11 54						12 14				12 34							12 54				

		LE 1	LE 1	LE	LE	LE 1	LE 1	LE 1	LE	LE 1		LE	LE 1	LE	LE 1	LE	LE 1	LE 1	LE 1	LE		LE	LE 1	LE 1	LE
London Liverpool Street 15 ⊖	d	12 13	12 18	12 20	12 30		12 35	12 38	12 40	12 48		12 50	12 55	13 00	13 02	13 10		13 13	13 18	13 20		13 30	13 35	13 38	13 40
Stratford 7 ⊖	d	12 20	12 25	12 27	12 37		12 42	12 45	12 47	12 55		12 57	13 02	13 07	13 09	13 17		13 20	13 25	13 27		13 37	13 42	13 45	13 47
Maryland	d			12 29	12 39				12 49			12 59		13 09		13 19				13 29		13 39			13 49
Forest Gate	d			12 31	12 41				12 51			13 01		13 11		13 21				13 31		13 41			13 51
Manor Park	d			12 33	12 43				12 53			13 03		13 13		13 23				13 33		13 43			13 53
Ilford 2	d			12 36	12 46				12 56			13 06		13 16		13 26				13 36		13 46			13 56
Seven Kings	d			12 38	12 48				12 58			13 08		13 18		13 28				13 38		13 48			13 58
Goodmayes	d			12 40	12 50				13 00			13 10		13 20		13 30				13 40		13 50			14 00
Chadwell Heath	d			12 42	12 52				13 02			13 12		13 22		13 32				13 42		13 52			14 02
Romford	d	12 28		12 46	12 56			12 53	13 06			13 16		13 26		13 36		13 28		13 46		13 56		13 53	14 06
Gidea Park 2	d			12 50	13 00				13 10			13 20		13 30		13 40				13 50		14 00			14 10
Harold Wood	d			12 53	13 03				13 13			13 23		13 33		13 43				13 53		14 03			14 13
Brentwood	d			12 57	13 07				13 17			13 27		13 37		13 47				13 57		14 07			14 17
Shenfield 3	a	12 38	12 40	13 03	13 13		12 58	13 02	13 23	13 11		13 33	13 18	13 43	13 24	13 53		13 38	13 40	14 03		14 13	13 58	14 02	14 23
Shenfield 3	d	12 39					12 59						13 19					13 39					13 59		
Billericay	d	12 45					13 05						13 25					13 45					14 05		
Wickford 2	d	12 51				12 56	13 11						13 31				13 36	13 51					14 11		
Battlesbridge	d					13 00											13 40								
South Woodham Ferrers	d					13 04											13 44								
North Fambridge	d					13 11											13 51								
Althorne	d					13 16											13 56								
Burnham-on-Crouch	d					13 21											14 01								
Southminster	a					13 27											14 07								
Rayleigh	d	12 56					13 16						13 36					13 56					14 16		
Hockley	d	13 01					13 21						13 41					14 01					14 21		
Rochford	d	13 04					13 24						13 44					14 04					14 24		
Southend Airport ✈	d	13 07					13 27						13 47					14 07					14 27		
Prittlewell	d	13 10					13 30						13 50					14 10					14 30		
Southend Victoria	a	13 14					13 34						13 54					14 14					14 34		

Table 5

Saturdays

London - Shenfield, Southminster and Southend Victoria

Station		LE 1	LE	LE 1	LE 1	LE		LE 1	LE	LE 1	LE 1	LE	LE	LE 1	LE 1	LE 1		LE	LE 1	LE	LE 1	LE	LE 1	LE	LE 1
London Liverpool Street 15 ⊖	d	13 48	13 50		13 55	14 00		14 02	14 10	14 13	14 18	14 20	14 30		14 35	14 38		14 40	14 48	14 50	14 55	15 00	15 02	15 10	
Stratford 7 ⊖	d	13 55	13 57		14 02	14 07		14 09	14 17	14 20	14 25	14 27	14 37		14 42	14 45		14 47	14 55	14 57	15 02	15 07	15 09	15 17	
Maryland	d		13 59			14 09			14 19			14 29	14 39					14 49		14 59		15 09		15 19	
Forest Gate	d		14 01			14 11			14 21			14 31	14 41					14 51		15 01		15 11		15 21	
Manor Park	d		14 03			14 13			14 23			14 33	14 43					14 53		15 03		15 13		15 23	
Ilford 2	d		14 06			14 16			14 26			14 36	14 46					14 56		15 06		15 16		15 26	
Seven Kings	d		14 08			14 18			14 28			14 38	14 48					14 58		15 08		15 18		15 28	
Goodmayes	d		14 10			14 20			14 30			14 40	14 50					15 00		15 10		15 20		15 30	
Chadwell Heath	d		14 12			14 22			14 32			14 42	14 52					15 02		15 12		15 22		15 32	
Romford	d		14 16			14 26			14 36	14 28		14 46	14 56			14 53		15 06		15 16		15 26		15 36	
Gidea Park 2	d		14 20			14 30			14 40			14 50	15 00					15 10		15 20		15 30		15 40	
Harold Wood	d		14 23			14 33			14 43			14 53	15 03					15 13		15 23		15 33		15 43	
Brentwood	d		14 27			14 37			14 47			14 57	15 07					15 17		15 27		15 37		15 47	
Shenfield 3	a	14 11	14 33		14 18	14 43		14 24	14 53	14 38	14 40	15 03	15 13		14 58	15 02		15 23	15 11	15 33	15 18	15 43	15 24	15 53	
Shenfield 3	d				14 19					14 39					14 59						15 19				
Billericay	d				14 25					14 45					15 05						15 25				
Wickford 2	d			14 16	14 31					14 51				14 56	15 11						15 31				15 36
Battlesbridge	d			14 20										15 00											15 40
South Woodham Ferrers	d			14 24										15 04											15 44
North Fambridge	d			14 31										15 11											15 51
Althorne	d			14 36										15 16											15 56
Burnham-on-Crouch	d			14 41										15 21											16 01
Southminster	a			14 47										15 27											16 07
Rayleigh	d				14 36					14 56					15 16						15 36				
Hockley	d				14 41					15 01					15 21						15 41				
Rochford	d				14 44					15 04					15 24						15 44				
Southend Airport ✈	d				14 47					15 07					15 27						15 47				
Prittlewell	d				14 50					15 10					15 30						15 50				
Southend Victoria	a				14 54					15 14					15 34						15 54				

Station		LE 1		LE 1	LE	LE	LE 1	LE 1	LE	LE 1	LE	LE 1		LE 1	LE	LE 1	LE	LE 1	LE 1	LE	LE	LE 1		LE 1	LE 1
London Liverpool Street 15 ⊖	d	15 13		15 18	15 20	15 30	15 35	15 38	15 40	15 48	15 50			15 55	16 00	16 02	16 10	16 13	16 18	16 20	16 30			16 35	16 38
Stratford 7 ⊖	d	15 20		15 25	15 27	15 37	15 42	15 45	15 47	15 55	15 57			16 02	16 07	16 09	16 17	16 20	16 25	16 27	16 37			16 42	16 45
Maryland	d				15 29	15 39			15 49		15 59				16 09		16 19			16 29	16 39				
Forest Gate	d				15 31	15 41			15 51		16 01				16 11		16 21			16 31	16 41				
Manor Park	d				15 33	15 43			15 53		16 03				16 13		16 23			16 33	16 43				
Ilford 2	d				15 36	15 46			15 56		16 06				16 16		16 26			16 36	16 46				
Seven Kings	d				15 38	15 48			15 58		16 08				16 18		16 28			16 38	16 48				
Goodmayes	d				15 40	15 50			16 00		16 10				16 20		16 30			16 40	16 50				
Chadwell Heath	d				15 42	15 52			16 02		16 12				16 22		16 32			16 42	16 52				
Romford	d	15 28			15 46	15 56		15 53	16 06		16 16				16 26		16 36	16 28		16 46	16 56				16 53
Gidea Park 2	d				15 50	16 00			16 10		16 20				16 30		16 40			16 50	17 00				
Harold Wood	d				15 53	16 03			16 13		16 23				16 33		16 43			16 53	17 03				
Brentwood	d				15 57	16 07			16 17		16 27				16 37		16 47			16 57	17 07				
Shenfield 3	a	15 38		15 40	16 03	16 13	15 58	16 02	16 23	16 11	16 33			16 18	16 43	16 24	16 53	16 38	16 40	17 03	17 13			16 58	17 02
Shenfield 3	d	15 39					15 59							16 19				16 39						16 59	
Billericay	d	15 45					16 05							16 25				16 45						17 05	
Wickford 2	d	15 51					16 11					16 16		16 31				16 51				16 56		17 11	
Battlesbridge	d											16 20										17 00			
South Woodham Ferrers	d											16 24										17 04			
North Fambridge	d											16 31										17 11			
Althorne	d											16 36										17 16			
Burnham-on-Crouch	d											16 41										17 21			
Southminster	a											16 47										17 27			
Rayleigh	d	15 56					16 16							16 36				16 56						17 16	
Hockley	d	16 01					16 21							16 41				17 01						17 21	
Rochford	d	16 04					16 24							16 44				17 04						17 24	
Southend Airport ✈	d	16 07					16 27							16 47				17 07						17 27	
Prittlewell	d	16 10					16 30							16 50				17 10						17 30	
Southend Victoria	a	16 14					16 34							16 54				17 14						17 34	

Station		LE	LE 1	LE	LE 1	LE	LE 1	LE		LE 1	LE 1	LE 1	LE	LE	LE 1	LE 1	LE	LE 1		LE	LE 1	LE 1	LE	LE 1	LE
London Liverpool Street 15 ⊖	d	16 40	16 48	16 50	16 55	17 00	17 02	17 10			17 13	17 18	17 20	17 30	17 35	17 38	17 40	17 48		17 50		17 55	18 00	18 02	18 10
Stratford 7 ⊖	d	16 47	16 55	16 57	17 02	17 07	17 09	17 17			17 20	17 25	17 27	17 37	17 42	17 45	17 47	17 55		17 57		18 02	18 07	18 09	18 17
Maryland	d	16 49		16 59		17 09		17 19					17 29	17 39			17 49			17 59			18 09		18 19
Forest Gate	d	16 51		17 01		17 11		17 21					17 31	17 41			17 51			18 01			18 11		18 21
Manor Park	d	16 53		17 03		17 13		17 23					17 33	17 43			17 53			18 03			18 13		18 23
Ilford 2	d	16 56		17 06		17 16		17 26					17 36	17 46			17 56			18 06			18 16		18 26
Seven Kings	d	16 58		17 08		17 18		17 28					17 38	17 48			17 58			18 08			18 18		18 28
Goodmayes	d	17 00		17 10		17 20		17 30					17 40	17 50			18 00			18 10			18 20		18 30
Chadwell Heath	d	17 02		17 12		17 22		17 32					17 42	17 52			18 02			18 12			18 22		18 32
Romford	d	17 06		17 16		17 26		17 36			17 28		17 46	17 56		17 53	18 06			18 16			18 26		18 36
Gidea Park 2	d	17 10		17 20		17 30		17 40					17 50	18 00			18 10			18 20			18 30		18 40
Harold Wood	d	17 13		17 23		17 33		17 43					17 53	18 03			18 13			18 23			18 33		18 43
Brentwood	d	17 17		17 27		17 37		17 47					17 57	18 07			18 17			18 27			18 37		18 47
Shenfield 3	a	17 23	17 11	17 33	17 18	17 43	17 24	17 53			17 38	17 40	18 03	18 13	17 58	18 02	18 23	18 11		18 33		18 18	18 43	18 24	18 53
Shenfield 3	d				17 19						17 39				17 59							18 19			
Billericay	d				17 25						17 45				18 05							18 25			
Wickford 2	d				17 31					17 36	17 51				18 11						18 16	18 31			
Battlesbridge	d									17 40											18 20				
South Woodham Ferrers	d									17 44											18 24				
North Fambridge	d									17 51											18 31				
Althorne	d									17 56											18 36				
Burnham-on-Crouch	d									18 01											18 41				
Southminster	a									18 07											18 47				
Rayleigh	d				17 36						17 56				18 16							18 36			
Hockley	d				17 41						18 01				18 21							18 41			
Rochford	d				17 44						18 04				18 24							18 44			
Southend Airport ✈	d				17 47						18 07				18 27							18 47			
Prittlewell	d				17 50						18 10				18 30							18 50			
Southend Victoria	a				17 54						18 14				18 34							18 54			

Table 5

Saturdays

London - Shenfield, Southminster and Southend Victoria

		LE 1	LE 1	LE		LE	LE 1	LE 1	LE 1	LE	LE 1	LE	LE 1	LE		LE 1	LE	LE 1	LE 1	LE 1	LE	LE	LE 1	LE 1	
London Liverpool Street 15 ⊖	d	18 13	18 18	18 20		18 30		18 35	18 38	18 40	18 48	18 50	18 55	19 00		19 02	19 10		19 13	19 18	19 20	19 30	19 35	19 38	
Stratford 7 ⊖	d	18 20	18 25	18 27		18 37		18 42	18 45	18 47	18 55	18 57	19 02	19 07		19 09	19 17		19 20	19 25	19 27	19 37	19 42	19 45	
Maryland	d			18 29		18 39				18 49		18 59		19 09			19 19				19 29	19 39			
Forest Gate	d			18 31		18 41				18 51		19 01		19 11			19 21				19 31	19 41			
Manor Park	d			18 33		18 43				18 53		19 03		19 13			19 23				19 33	19 43			
Ilford 2	d			18 36		18 46				18 56		19 06		19 16			19 26				19 36	19 46			
Seven Kings	d			18 38		18 48				18 58		19 08		19 18			19 28				19 38	19 48			
Goodmayes	d			18 40		18 50				19 00		19 10		19 20			19 30				19 40	19 50			
Chadwell Heath	d			18 42		18 52				19 02		19 12		19 22			19 32				19 42	19 52			
Romford	d	18 28		18 46		18 56			18 53	19 06		19 16		19 26			19 36		19 28		19 46	19 56		19 53	
Gidea Park 2	d			18 50		19 00				19 10		19 20		19 30			19 40				19 50	20 00			
Harold Wood	d			18 53		19 03				19 13		19 23		19 33			19 43				19 53	20 03			
Brentwood	d			18 57		19 07				19 17		19 27		19 37			19 47				19 57	20 07			
Shenfield 3	a	18 38	18 40	19 03		19 13		18 58	19 02	19 23	19 11	19 33	19 18	19 43		19 24	19 53		19 38	19 40	20 03	20 13	19 58	20 02	
Shenfield 3	d	18 39						18 59					19 19						19 39				19 59		
Billericay	d	18 45						19 05					19 25						19 45				20 05		
Wickford 2	d	18 51					18 56	19 11					19 31					19 36	19 51				20 11		
Battlesbridge	d						19 00											19 40							
South Woodham Ferrers	d						19 04											19 44							
North Fambridge	d						19 11											19 51							
Althorne	d						19 16											19 56							
Burnham-on-Crouch	d						19 21											20 01							
Southminster	a						19 27											20 07							
Rayleigh	d	18 56						19 16					19 36						19 56				20 16		
Hockley	d	19 01						19 21					19 41						20 01				20 21		
Rochford	d	19 04						19 24					19 44						20 04				20 24		
Southend Airport ✈	d	19 07						19 27					19 47						20 07				20 27		
Prittlewell	d	19 10						19 30					19 50						20 10				20 30		
Southend Victoria	a	19 14						19 34					19 54						20 14				20 34		

		LE	LE 1	LE	LE 1	LE 1	LE	LE 1	LE	LE 1		LE 1	LE	LE	LE 1	LE 1	LE 1	LE	LE 1	LE		LE 1	LE 1	LE	LE 1
London Liverpool Street 15 ⊖	d	19 40	19 48	19 50		19 55	20 00	20 02	20 10	20 13		20 18	20 20	20 30		20 35	20 38	20 40	20 48	20 50		20 55	21 02	21 05	
Stratford 7 ⊖	d	19 47	19 55	19 57		20 02	20 07	20 09	20 17	20 20		20 25	20 27	20 37		20 42	20 45	20 47	20 55	20 57		21 02	21 09	21 12	
Maryland	d	19 49		19 59			20 09		20 19				20 29	20 39				20 49		20 59				21 14	
Forest Gate	d	19 51		20 01			20 11		20 21				20 31	20 41				20 51		21 01				21 16	
Manor Park	d	19 53		20 03			20 13		20 23				20 33	20 43				20 53		21 03				21 18	
Ilford 2	d	19 56		20 06			20 16		20 26				20 36	20 46				20 56		21 06				21 21	
Seven Kings	d	19 58		20 08			20 18		20 28				20 38	20 48				20 58		21 08				21 23	
Goodmayes	d	20 00		20 10			20 20		20 30				20 40	20 50				21 00		21 10				21 25	
Chadwell Heath	d	20 02		20 12			20 22		20 32				20 42	20 52				21 02		21 12				21 27	
Romford	d	20 06		20 16			20 26		20 36	20 28			20 46	20 56			20 53	21 06		21 16				21 31	
Gidea Park 2	d	20 10		20 20			20 30		20 40				20 50	21 00				21 10		21 20				21 35	
Harold Wood	d	20 13		20 23			20 33		20 43				20 53	21 03				21 13		21 23				21 38	
Brentwood	d	20 17		20 27			20 37		20 47				20 57	21 07				21 17		21 27				21 42	
Shenfield 3	a	20 23	20 11	20 33		20 18	20 43	20 24	20 53	20 38		20 40	21 03	21 13		20 58	21 02	21 23	21 11	21 33		21 18	21 24	21 48	
Shenfield 3	d					20 19				20 39						20 59						21 19			
Billericay	d					20 25				20 45						21 05						21 25			
Wickford 2	d				20 16	20 31				20 51					20 56	21 11						21 31			21 36
Battlesbridge	d				20 20										21 00										21 40
South Woodham Ferrers	d				20 24										21 04										21 44
North Fambridge	d				20 31										21 11										21 51
Althorne	d				20 36										21 16										21 56
Burnham-on-Crouch	d				20 41										21 21										22 01
Southminster	a				20 47										21 27										22 07
Rayleigh	d					20 36				20 56						21 16						21 36			
Hockley	d					20 41				21 01						21 21						21 41			
Rochford	d					20 44				21 04						21 24						21 44			
Southend Airport ✈	d					20 47				21 07						21 27						21 47			
Prittlewell	d					20 50				21 10						21 30						21 50			
Southend Victoria	a					20 54				21 14						21 34						21 54			

		LE 1	LE 1	LE	LE 1	LE		LE 1	LE 1	LE	LE 1	LE 1	LE 1	LE	LE 1	LE 1		LE	LE	LE 1	LE 1	LE 1	LE	LE 1	LE
London Liverpool Street 15 ⊖	d	21 13	21 18	21 20	21 35	21 35		21 38	21 48	21 50		21 55	22 02	22 05	22 13	22 18		22 20	22 35	22 38		22 45	22 50	23 02	23 05
Stratford 7 ⊖	d	21 20	21 25	21 27	21 42	21 42		21 45	21 55	21 57		22 02	22 09	22 12	22 20	22 25		22 27	22 42	22 45		22 52	22 57	23 09	23 12
Maryland	d			21 29		21 44				21 59				22 14				22 29	22 44				22 59		23 14
Forest Gate	d			21 31		21 46				22 01				22 16				22 31	22 46				23 01		23 16
Manor Park	d			21 33		21 48				22 03				22 18				22 33	22 48				23 03		23 18
Ilford 2	d			21 36		21 51				22 06				22 21				22 36	22 51				23 06		23 21
Seven Kings	d			21 38		21 53				22 08				22 23				22 38	22 53				23 08		23 23
Goodmayes	d			21 40		21 55				22 10				22 25				22 40	22 55				23 10		23 25
Chadwell Heath	d			21 42		21 57				22 12				22 27				22 42	22 57				23 12		23 27
Romford	d	21 28		21 46		22 01		21 53		22 16				22 31	22 28			22 46	23 01	22 53			23 16		23 31
Gidea Park 2	d			21 50		22 05				22 20				22 35				22 50	23 05				23 20		23 35
Harold Wood	d			21 53		22 08				22 23				22 38				22 53	23 08				23 23		23 38
Brentwood	d			21 57		22 12				22 27				22 42				22 57	23 12				23 27		23 42
Shenfield 3	a	21 38	21 40	22 03	21 57	22 18		22 02	22 11	22 33		22 18	22 24	22 48	22 38	22 40		23 03	23 18	23 02		23 08	23 33	23 24	23 48
Shenfield 3	d	21 39			21 59							22 19			22 39							23 09			
Billericay	d	21 45			22 05							22 25			22 45							23 15			
Wickford 2	d	21 51			22 11						22 16	22 31			22 51						22 56	23 21			
Battlesbridge	d										22 20										23 00				
South Woodham Ferrers	d										22 24										23 04				
North Fambridge	d										22 31										23 11				
Althorne	d										22 36										23 16				
Burnham-on-Crouch	d										22 41										23 21				
Southminster	a										22 47										23 27				
Rayleigh	d	21 56			22 16							22 36			22 56							23 26			
Hockley	d	22 01			22 21							22 41			23 01							23 31			
Rochford	d	22 04			22 24							22 44			23 04							23 34			
Southend Airport ✈	d	22 07			22 27							22 47			23 07							23 37			
Prittlewell	d	22 10			22 30							22 50			23 10							23 40			
Southend Victoria	a	22 14			22 34							22 54			23 14							23 48			

Table 5

Saturdays

London - Shenfield, Southminster and Southend Victoria

		LE [1]		LE [1]	LE	LE	LE [1]	LE [1]	LE
London Liverpool Street [15] ⊖	d	23 15		23 18	23 20	23 35	23 45	23 48	23 50
Stratford [7] ⊖	d	23 22		23 25	23 27	23 42	23 52	23 55	23 57
Maryland	d				23 29	23 44			23 59
Forest Gate	d				23 31	23 46			00 01
Manor Park	d				23 33	23 48			00 03
Ilford [2]	d				23 36	23 51			00 06
Seven Kings	d				23 38	23 53			00 08
Goodmayes	d				23 40	23 55			00 10
Chadwell Heath	d				23 42	23 57			00 12
Romford	d				23 46	00 02			00 16
Gidea Park [2]	d				23 50	00 05			00 20
Harold Wood	d				23 53	00 08			00 23
Brentwood	d				23 57	00 12			00 27
Shenfield [3]	a	23 38		23 40	00 03	00 18	00 08	00 10	00 33
Shenfield [3]	d	23 39					00 09		
Billericay	d	23 45					00 15		
Wickford [2]	d	23 51					00 21		
Battlesbridge	d								
South Woodham Ferrers	d								
North Fambridge	d								
Althorne	d								
Burnham-on-Crouch	d								
Southminster	a								
Rayleigh	d	23 56					00 26		
Hockley	d	00 01					00 31		
Rochford	d	00 04					00 34		
Southend Airport ✈	d	00 07					00 37		
Prittlewell	d	00 10					00 40		
Southend Victoria	a	00 18					00 48		

Table 5

Sundays

London - Shenfield, Southminster and Southend Victoria

		LE 1 A	LE A	LE A	LE 1 A	LE 1 A	LE A	LE	LE 1	LE 1	LE	LE	LE 1	LE	LE	LE	LE 1	LE 1	LE	LE 1	LE 1	LE 1	LE
London Liverpool Street 15 ⊖	d	23p15	23p20	23p35	23p45	23p48	23p50	00 01	00 15	00 18	00 20	00 32	00 50	00 55	06 35	07 05		07 15	07 35		07 45	08 02	08 05
Stratford 7 ⊖	d	23p22	23p27	23p42	23p52	23p55	23p57	00 08	00 22	00 25	00 27	00 39	00 57	01 02	06 42	07 12		07 22	07 42		07 52	08 09	08 12
Maryland	d		23p29	23p44			23p59	00 10			00 29	00 41		01 04	06 43	07 13			07 43				08 13
Forest Gate	d		23p31	23p46			00 01	00 12			00 31	00 43		01 06	06 45	07 15			07 45				08 15
Manor Park	d		23p33	23p48			00 03	00 14			00 33	00 45		01 08	06 47	07 17			07 47				08 17
Ilford 2	d		23p36	23p51			00 06	00 17			00 36	00 48		01 11	06 50	07 20			07 50				08 20
Seven Kings	d		23p38	23p53			00 08	00 19			00 38	00 50		01 13	06 53	07 23			07 53				08 23
Goodmayes	d		23p40	23p55			00 10	00 21			00 40	00 52		01 15	06 55	07 25			07 55				08 25
Chadwell Heath	d		23p42	23p57			00 12	00 23			00 42	00 54		01 17	06 57	07 27			07 57				08 27
Romford	d		23p46	00 02			00 16	00 27	00 32		00 46	00 58	01 08	01 21	07 00	07 30		07 33	08 00		08 03		08 30
Gidea Park 2	d		23p50	00 05			00 20	00a31			00 50	01a02		01 25	07 04	07 34		07 37	08 04		08 07		08 34
Harold Wood	d		23p53	00 08			00 23				00 53			01 28	07 07	07 37		07 40	08 07		08 10		08 37
Brentwood	d		23p57	00 12			00 27				00 57			01 32	07 11	07 41		07 44	08 11		08 14		08 41
Shenfield 3	a	23p38	00 03	00 18	00 08	00 10	00 33		00 44	00 47	01 03		01 20	01 38	07 18	07 48		07 50	08 18		08 20	08 30	08 48
Shenfield 3	d	23p39			00 09				00 45				01 20					07 50			08 20		
Billericay	d	23p45			00 15				00 51				01 26					07 56			08 26		
Wickford 2	d	23p51			00 21				00 56				01 31				07 30	08 01		08 05	08 31		
Battlesbridge	d																07 34			08 09			
South Woodham Ferrers	d																07 38			08 13			
North Fambridge	d																07 44			08 20			
Althorne	d																07 49			08 25			
Burnham-on-Crouch	d																07 54			08 30			
Southminster	a																08 00			08 36			
Rayleigh	d	23p56			00 26				01 01				01 36					08 06			08 36		
Hockley	d	00 01			00 31				01 06				01 41					08 11			08 41		
Rochford	d	00 04			00 34				01 09				01 44					08 14			08 44		
Southend Airport ✈	d	00 07			00 37				01 12				01 47					08 17			08 47		
Prittlewell	d	00 10			00 40				01 15				01 50										
Southend Victoria	a	00 18			00 48				01 23				01 58					08 25			08 55		

		LE 1	LE 1	LE	LE 1	LE 1	LE	LE 1	LE	LE 1	LE		LE	LE 1	LE	LE 1	LE 1	LE	LE 1	LE 1	LE	LE 1
London Liverpool Street 15 ⊖	d	08 15	08 32	08 35		08 45	08 47	09 02	09 05	09 15	09 17	and at the same minutes past each hour until	20 17	20 32	20 35		20 45	20 47	21 00	21 02	21 05	21 15
Stratford 7 ⊖	d	08 22	08 39	08 42		08 52	08 54	09 09	09 12	09 22	09 24		20 24	20 39	20 42		20 52	20 54		21 09	21 12	21 22
Maryland	d			08 43					09 13						20 43						21 13	
Forest Gate	d			08 45			08 57		09 15		09 27		20 27		20 45			20 57			21 15	
Manor Park	d			08 47			08 59		09 17		09 29		20 29		20 47			20 59			21 17	
Ilford 2	d			08 50			09 02		09 20		09 32		20 32		20 50			21 02			21 20	
Seven Kings	d			08 53			09 04		09 23		09 34		20 34		20 53			21 04			21 23	
Goodmayes	d			08 55			09 06		09 25		09 36		20 36		20 55			21 06			21 25	
Chadwell Heath	d			08 57			09 08		09 27		09 38		20 38		20 57			21 08			21 27	
Romford	d	08 33		09 00		09 03	09 12		09 30	09 33	09 42		20 42		21 00		21 03	21 12			21 30	21 33
Gidea Park 2	d	08 37		09 04		09 07	09a17		09 34	09 37	09a47		20a47		21 04		21 07	21a17			21 34	21 37
Harold Wood	d	08 40		09 07		09 10			09 37	09 40					21 07		21 10				21 37	21 40
Brentwood	d	08 44		09 11		09 14			09 41	09 44					21 11		21 14				21 41	21 44
Shenfield 3	a	08 50	09 00	09 18		09 20		09 30	09 48	09 50				21 00	21 18		21 20		21 27	21 30	21 48	21 50
Shenfield 3	d	08 50				09 20				09 50							21 20					21 50
Billericay	d	08 56				09 26				09 56							21 26					21 56
Wickford 2	d	09 01			09 05	09 31				10 01						21 05	21 31					22 01
Battlesbridge	d				09 09											21 09						
South Woodham Ferrers	d				09 13											21 13						
North Fambridge	d				09 20											21 20						
Althorne	d				09 25											21 25						
Burnham-on-Crouch	d				09 30											21 30						
Southminster	a				09 36											21 36						
Rayleigh	d	09 06				09 36				10 06							21 36					22 06
Hockley	d	09 11				09 41				10 11							21 41					22 11
Rochford	d	09 14				09 44				10 14							21 44					22 14
Southend Airport ✈	d	09 17				09 47				10 17							21 47					22 17
Prittlewell	d																					
Southend Victoria	a	09 25				09 55				10 25							21 55					22 25

A not 22 May

		LE	LE 1	LE	LE 1	LE 1	LE	LE 1	LE	LE 1	LE	LE 1	LE	LE 1	LE 1	LE	LE 1	LE 1	LE	LE 1
London Liverpool Street 15 ⊖	d	21 17	21 32	21 35		21 45	21 47	22 02	22 05	22 15	22 17	22 32	22 35	22 45	23 02	23 05	23 15	23 32	23 35	23 45
Stratford 7 ⊖	d	21 24	21 39	21 42		21 52	21 54	22 09	22 12	22 22	22 24	22 39	22 42	22 52	23 09	23 12	23 22	23 39	23 42	23 52
Maryland	d			21 43					22 13				22 43			23 13			23 43	
Forest Gate	d	21 27		21 45			21 57		22 15		22 27		22 45			23 15			23 45	
Manor Park	d	21 29		21 47			21 59		22 17		22 29		22 47			23 17			23 47	
Ilford 2	d	21 32		21 50			22 02		22 20		22 32		22 50			23 20			23 50	
Seven Kings	d	21 34		21 53			22 04		22 23		22 34		22 53			23 23			23 53	
Goodmayes	d	21 36		21 55			22 06		22 25		22 36		22 55			23 25			23 55	
Chadwell Heath	d	21 38		21 57			22 08		22 27		22 38		22 57			23 27			23 57	
Romford	d	21 42		22 00		22 03	22 12		22 30	22 33	22 42		23 00	23 03		23 30	23 33		23 59	00 03
Gidea Park 2	d	21a47		22 04		22 07	22a17		22 34	22 37	22a47		23 04	23 07		23 34	23 37		00 04	00 07
Harold Wood	d			22 07		22 10			22 37	22 40			23 07	23 10		23 37	23 40		00 07	00 10
Brentwood	d			22 11		22 14			22 41	22 44			23 11	23 14		23 41	23 44		00 11	00 14
Shenfield 3	a		22 00	22 18		22 20		22 30	22 48	22 50		23 00	23 18	23 20	23 30	23 48	23 50	23 59	00 18	00 20
Shenfield 3	d					22 20				22 50				23 20			23 50			00 20
Billericay	d					22 26				22 56				23 26			23 56			00 26
Wickford 2	d				22 05	22 31				23 01				23 31			00 01			00 31
Battlesbridge	d				22 09															
South Woodham Ferrers	d				22 13															
North Fambridge	d				22 20															
Althorne	d				22 25															
Burnham-on-Crouch	d				22 30															
Southminster	a				22 36															
Rayleigh	d					22 36				23 06				23 36			00 06			00 36
Hockley	d					22 41				23 11				23 41			00 11			00 41
Rochford	d					22 44				23 14				23 44			00 14			00 44
Southend Airport ✈	d					22 47				23 17				23 47			00 17			00 47
Prittlewell	d																			
Southend Victoria	a					22 55				23 27				23 57			00 27			00 57

Southend Victoria, Southminster and Shenfield - London

Miles	Miles			LE	LE	LE	LE	CC	LE	LE	LE	CC		LE	LE	LE	LE	LE	LE	LE	LE	LE		LE	LE
				MX	MX	MX	MO	MX	MO	MX															
				◇1		1	◇1									1			1		1	1		1	◇1
0	—	**Southend Victoria**	d								04 00				04 30				05 00			05 20			
0½	—	Prittlewell	d								04 02				04 32				05 02			05 22			
1¾	—	Southend Airport ✈	d								04 05				04 35				05 05			05 25			
2¾	—	Rochford	d								04 08				04 38				05 08			05 28			
5½	—	Hockley	d								04 12				04 42				05 11			05 31			
8¼	—	Rayleigh	d								04 16				04 46				05 16			05 36			
—	0	**Southminster**	d			22p56																		05 26	
—	2¼	Burnham-on-Crouch	d			23p00																		05 30	
—	5¼	Althorne	d			23p05																		05 35	
—	8¼	North Fambridge	d			23p11																		05 41	
—	11½	South Woodham Ferrers	d			23p16																		05 46	
—	14	Battlesbridge	d			23p20																		05 50	
12½	16½	**Wickford 2**	d			23p26					04 21				04 51				05 21			05 41		05a56	
17¼	—	Billericay	d			23p32					04 28				04 58				05 27			05 47			
—	—	**Shenfield 3**	a			23p39					04 39				05 09				05 35			05 55			
21¼	—	**Shenfield 3**	d		23p29	23p39			23p43	23p44	04 39				05 09	05 24		05 29	05 35	05 44	05 53	05 55			
23¼	—	Brentwood	d		23p32				23p46	23p47	04 42				05 12			05 32		05 47					
26½	—	Harold Wood	d		23p37				23p51	23p52	04 47				05 17			05 37		05 52					
28	—	Gidea Park 2	d		23p41				23p55	23p56	04 51				05 21	05 31		05 41		05 56					
29	—	Romford	d		23p43	23p47			23p57	23p58	04 53				05 23			05 43		05 58					
31½	—	Chadwell Heath	d		23p47				00 01	00 02	04 57				05 27			05 47		06 02					
32¼	—	Goodmayes	d		23p49				00 03	00 04	04 59				05 29			05 49		06 04					
33	—	Seven Kings	d		23p51				00 05	00 06	05 01				05 31	05 36		05 51		06 06					
34¼	—	Ilford 2	d		23p54				00 08	00 09	05 04			05 09	05 34		05 39	05 54		06 09					
35¼	—	Manor Park	d		23p57				00 10	00 12				05 11			05 41	05 57		06 12					
36¼	—	Forest Gate	d		23p59				00 12	00 14				05 14			05 44	05 59		06 14					
37	—	Maryland	d		00 01				00 14	00 16				05 16			05 46	06 01		06 16					
37½	—	Stratford 7 ⊖	d	23b52	00 04	23p56	23b57	23p58	00 16	00 19	05 10	05 14		05 18	05 40	05 42	05 48	06 04	05 49	06 19	06 07	06 10			
41½	—	**London Liverpool Street 15** ⊖	a	00 02	00 12	00 05	00 08	00 11	00 26	00 27	05 18	05 27		05 26	05 48	05 55	05 56	06 12	05 58	06 27	06 16	06 19			06 34

		LE	LE	LE	LE	LE	LE	LE		LE	LE	LE	LE	LE	LE	LE	LE	LE		LE	LE	LE	LE	LE	LE
																					R				
					1		1	◇1			1	1			1	1				1	1				1
								☕													☕				
Southend Victoria	d				05 40						06 00				06 11							06 26			
Prittlewell	d				05 42						06 02				06 13							06 28			
Southend Airport ✈	d				05 45						06 05				06 16							06 31			
Rochford	d				05 48						06 08				06 19							06 34			
Hockley	d				05 51						06 11				06 22							06 38			
Rayleigh	d				05 56						06 16				06 27							06 42			
Southminster	d																			06 10					
Burnham-on-Crouch	d																			06 14					
Althorne	d																			06 19					
North Fambridge	d																			06 26					
South Woodham Ferrers	d																			06 32					
Battlesbridge	d																			06 36					
Wickford 2	d				06 01						06 21				06 32					06 42		06 47			
Billericay	d				06 07						06 27				06 39					06 49		06 54			
Shenfield 3	a				06 15						06 35				06 45					06 55		07 01			
Shenfield 3	d		06 04	06 14	06 15	06 24	06 25			06 34	06 35	06 41		06 44	06 45	06 52		06 54		06 55		07 01		07 04	07 09
Brentwood	d		06 07	06 17		06 27				06 37				06 47				06 57						07 07	
Harold Wood	d		06 12	06 22		06 32				06 42				06 52				07 02						07 12	
Gidea Park 2	d	06 06	06 16	06 26		06 36				06 45			06 49	06 55			06 59	07 05					07 09	07 15	
Romford	d	06 08	06 18	06 28		06 38				06 48			06 51	06 58			07 01	07 08					07 11	07 18	
Chadwell Heath	d	06 12	06 22	06 32		06 42				06 52			06 55	07 02			07 05	07 12					07 15	07 22	
Goodmayes	d	06 14	06 24	06 34		06 44							06 57				07 07						07 17		
Seven Kings	d	06 16	06 26	06 36		06 46							06 59				07 09						07 19		
Ilford 2	d	06 19	06 29	06 39		06 49				06 57			07 02	07 07			07 12	07 17					07 22	07 27	
Manor Park	d	06 22	06 32	06 42		06 52							07 05				07 15						07 25		
Forest Gate	d	06 24	06 34	06 44		06 54							07 07				07 17						07 27		
Maryland	d	06 26	06 36	06 46		06 56							07 09				07 19						07 29		
Stratford 7 ⊖	d	06 29	06 39	06 49	06 29	06 59	06 39			07 03	06 49	06s57	07 12	07 15	07s02	07s08	07 22	07 25		07s12		07s19	07 32	07 35	07s25
London Liverpool Street 15 ⊖	a	06 37	06 47	06 57	06 40	07 07	06 48	06 54		07 13	06 58	07 09	07 22	07 25	07 14	07 20	07 32	07 35		07 23	07 27	07 30	07 42	07 45	07 37

b Previous night, stops to set down only

		LE	LE	LE		LE	LE	LE	LE	LE	LE	LE	LE	LE		LE	LE	LE	LE	LE	LE	LE	LE	LE	
		1				1	1	1			1	1	1				1	1	1			1	1	1	
Southend Victoria	d					06 41					06 51		07 03									07 13			
Prittlewell	d					06 43					06 53		07 05									07 15			
Southend Airport ✈	d					06 46					06 56		07 08									07 18			
Rochford	d					06 49					06 59		07 11									07 21			
Hockley	d					06 52					07 02		07 14									07 24			
Rayleigh	d					06 57					07 07		07 19									07 29			
Southminster	d											06 48													
Burnham-on-Crouch	d											06 52													
Althorne	d											06 57													
North Fambridge	d											07 04													
South Woodham Ferrers	d											07 10													
Battlesbridge	d											07 14													
Wickford 2	d					07 02					07 12	07 19	07 24									07 34			
Billericay	d					07 09					07 19	07 26	07 31									07 41			
Shenfield 3	a					07 15					07 25	07 32										07 47			
Shenfield 3	d			07 14		07 15	07 19			07 24	07 25	07 32				07 34	07 39	07 42			07 44	07 47	07 50		
Brentwood	d			07 17						07 27						07 37					07 47				
Harold Wood	d			07 22						07 32						07 42					07 52				
Gidea Park 2	d		07 19	07 25					07 29	07 35				07 39		07 45				07 49	07 55				
Romford	d		07 21	07 28					07 31	07 38				07 41		07 48				07 51	07 58				
Chadwell Heath	d		07 25	07 32					07 35	07 42				07 45		07 52				07 55	08 02				
Goodmayes	d		07 27	07 34					07 37	07 44				07 47		07 54				07 57	08 04				
Seven Kings	d		07 29	07 36					07 39	07 46				07 49		07 56				07 59	08 06				
Ilford 2	d		07 32	07 39					07 42	07 49				07 52		07 59				08 02	08 09				
Manor Park	d		07 35						07 45					07 55						08 05					
Forest Gate	d		07 37						07 47					07 57						08 07					
Maryland	d		07 39						07 49					07 59						08 09					
Stratford 7 ⊖	d		07 42	07 45		07s32	07s35		07 52	07 55	07s42		07s52	08 02		08 05	07s55	07s58		08 12	08 15	08s04			
London Liverpool Street 15 ⊖	a	07 40	07 52	07 55		07 43	07 47	07 50	08 02	08 05	07 53	08 01	08 03	08 12		08 15	08 08	08 10	08 13	08 22	08 25	08 16	08 19	08 21	

Southend Victoria, Southminster and Shenfield - London

		LE	LE	LE	LE	LE	LE	LE	LE	LE		LE	LE	LE	LE	LE	LE	LE	LE	LE		LE	LE	LE	LE
						[1]		[1]	[1]	[1]		[1]	◇[1]				[1]	[1]					[1]	[1]	[1]
Southend Victoria	d				07 18	07 23				07 32							07 42								07 53
Prittlewell	d				07 20	07 25				07 34							07 44								07 55
Southend Airport ✈	d				07 23	07 28				07 37							07 47								07 58
Rochford	d				07 26	07 31				07 40							07 50								08 01
Hockley	d				07 30	07 34				07 43							07 53								08 04
Rayleigh	d				07 34	07 39				07 48							07 58								08 09
Southminster	d																	07 37							
Burnham-on-Crouch	d																	07 41							
Althorne	d																	07 46							
North Fambridge	d																	07 52							
South Woodham Ferrers	d																	07 59							
Battlesbridge	d																								
Wickford [2]	d				07 39	07 44				07 53							08 03	08 07							08 14
Billericay	d				07 46	07 51				08 00							08 10	08 14							08 21
Shenfield [3]	a				07 53	07 57				08 06							08 16								08 27
Shenfield [3]	d		07 50		07 54	07 57	08 00	08 01		08 06		08 09				08 10	08 16					08 20	08 21	08 24	08 27
Brentwood	d		07 53		07 57		08 03									08 13						08 23			
Harold Wood	d		07 58		08 02		08 08									08 18						08 28			
Gidea Park [2]	d	07 59	08 02	08 05	08 09		08 12							08 15	08 19	08 22				08 29		08 32			
Romford	d	08 01	08 04	08 07	08 11		08 14							08 17	08 21	08 24				08 31		08 34			
Chadwell Heath	d	08 05	08 08	08 11	08 15		08 18							08 21	08 25	08 28				08 35		08 38			
Goodmayes	d	08 07	08 10	08 13	08 17		08 20							08 23	08 27	08 30				08 37		08 40			
Seven Kings	d	08 09	08 12	08 15	08 19		08 22							08 25	08 29	08 32				08 39		08 42			
Ilford [2]	d	08 12	08 15	08 18	08 22		08 25							08 28	08 32	08 35			08 38	08 42		08 45			
Manor Park	d			08 21										08 31					08 41						
Forest Gate	d			08 23										08 33					08 43						
Maryland	d			08 25										08 35					08 45						
Stratford [7] ⊖	d	08 18	08 21	08 28	08 31		08 34	08s17		08s23		08 26		08 38	08 41	08 44		08s36	08 48	08 51		08 54	08s38	08s42	08s44
London Liverpool Street [15] ⊖	a	08 28	08 31	08 38	08 41	08 25	08 43	08 29	08 33	08 36		08 38	08 40	08 48	08 51	08 53	08 45	08 48	08 58	09 01		09 03	08 50	08 54	08 56

		LE	LE	LE	LE	LE		LE	LE	LE	LE	LE	LE	LE	LE	LE		LE	LE	LE	LE	LE	LE	LE	LE
		[1]	[1]					[1]	[1]	R [1]			[1]		[1]			[1]	[1]	[1]	[1]	◇[1]			[1]
Southend Victoria	d							08 02					08 10							08 30					
Prittlewell	d							08 04					08 12							08 32					
Southend Airport ✈	d							08 07					08 15							08 35					
Rochford	d							08 10					08 18							08 38					
Hockley	d							08 13					08 21							08 41					
Rayleigh	d							08 18					08 26							08 46					
Southminster	d																		08 16						
Burnham-on-Crouch	d																		08 20						
Althorne	d																		08 25						
North Fambridge	d																		08 31						
South Woodham Ferrers	d																		08 37						
Battlesbridge	d																		08 41						
Wickford [2]	d							08 23					08 31						08 46	08 51					
Billericay	d							08 30					08 38						08 53	08 58					
Shenfield [3]	a							08 36					08 44						08 59	09 04					
Shenfield [3]	d	08 30				08 30		08 36	08 39				08 44	08 44	08 51	08 54		08 55	08 59	09 04			09 04	09 14	09 21
Brentwood	d					08 33								08 47		08 57							09 07	09 17	
Harold Wood	d					08 38								08 52		09 02							09 12	09 22	
Gidea Park [2]	d				08 39	08 42						08 49		08 56		09 06							09 16	09 26	
Romford	d				08 41	08 44						08 51	08 53	08 58		09 08							09 18	09 28	
Chadwell Heath	d				08 45	08 48						08 55		09 02		09 12							09 22	09 32	
Goodmayes	d				08 47	08 50						08 57		09 04		09 14							09 24	09 34	
Seven Kings	d				08 49	08 52						08 59		09 06		09 16							09 26	09 36	
Ilford [2]	d			08 48	08 52	08 55					08 58	09 02		09 09		09 19							09 29	09 39	
Manor Park	d			08 51							09 01			09 12		09 22							09 32	09 42	
Forest Gate	d			08 53							09 03			09 14		09 24							09 34	09 44	
Maryland	d			08 55							09 05			09 16		09 26							09 36	09 46	
Stratford [7] ⊖	d	08s47		08 58	09 01	09 04			08s55		09 08	09 11	09s03	09 19	09s07	09 29			09s16	09s21			09 39	09 49	09s37
London Liverpool Street [15] ⊖	a	08 59	09 01	09 08	09 11	09 13		09 03	09 08	09 10	09 18	09 21	09 14	09 27	09 19	09 37		09 21	09 28	09 32	09 36	09 40	09 47	09 57	09 49

		LE		LE	LE	LE	LE	LE	LE	LE	LE	LE		LE	LE	LE	LE	LE	LE	LE	LE	LE		LE	LE
				[1]	[1]	[1]	R [1]		[1]		[1]	[1]				[1]	[1]	[1]		[1]		[1]		R [1]	
Southend Victoria	d				08 52						09 10					09 30						09 50			
Prittlewell	d				08 54						09 12					09 32						09 52			
Southend Airport ✈	d				08 57						09 15					09 35						09 55			
Rochford	d				09 00						09 18					09 38						09 58			
Hockley	d				09 03						09 21					09 41						10 01			
Rayleigh	d				09 08						09 26					09 46						10 06			
Southminster	d					08 56											09 36								
Burnham-on-Crouch	d					09 00											09 40								
Althorne	d					09 05											09 45								
North Fambridge	d					09 12											09 51								
South Woodham Ferrers	d					09 17											09 56								
Battlesbridge	d					09 21											10 00								
Wickford [2]	d				09 13	09a27					09 31					09 51	10a06					10 11			
Billericay	d				09 20						09 37					09 57						10 17			
Shenfield [3]	a				09 27						09 45					10 05						10 25			
Shenfield [3]	d	09 24		09 25	09 27			09 34	09 38	09 44	09 45	09 51		09 54	10 04	10 05		10 08	10 14	10 20	10 24	10 25			10 34
Brentwood	d	09 27						09 37		09 47				09 57	10 07				10 17		10 27				10 37
Harold Wood	d	09 32						09 42		09 52				10 02	10 12				10 22		10 32				10 42
Gidea Park [2]	d	09 36						09 46		09 56				10 06	10 16				10 26		10 36				10 46
Romford	d	09 38						09 48		09 58	09 53			10 08	10 18				10 28	10 28	10 38				10 48
Chadwell Heath	d	09 42						09 52		10 02				10 12	10 22				10 32		10 42				10 52
Goodmayes	d	09 44						09 54		10 04				10 14	10 24				10 34		10 44				10 54
Seven Kings	d	09 46						09 56		10 06				10 16	10 26				10 36		10 46				10 56
Ilford [2]	d	09 49						09 59		10 09				10 19	10 29				10 39		10 49				10 59
Manor Park	d	09 52						10 02		10 12				10 22	10 32				10 42		10 52				11 02
Forest Gate	d	09 54						10 04		10 14				10 24	10 34				10 44		10 54				11 04
Maryland	d	09 56						10 06		10 16				10 26	10 36				10 46		10 56				11 06
Stratford [7] ⊖	d	09 59		09s41	09s43			10 09	09 52	10 19	10 01	10 05		10 29	10 39	10 19		10 22	10 49	10 36	10 59	10 39			11 09
London Liverpool Street [15] ⊖	a	10 07		09 53	09 55		09 58	10 17	10 01	10 27	10 10	10 14		10 37	10 47	10 28		10 31	10 57	10 45	11 07	10 48		10 55	11 17

Southend Victoria, Southminster and Shenfield - London

		LE 1	LE	LE 1	LE 1	LE 1	LE	LE		LE 1	LE 1	LE	LE 1	LE	LE 1	LE 1		LE		LE 1	LE	LE 1	LE 1	LE	LE
Southend Victoria	d			10 10						10 30					10 50							11 10			
Prittlewell	d			10 12						10 32					10 52							11 12			
Southend Airport ✈	d			10 15						10 35					10 55							11 15			
Rochford	d			10 18						10 38					10 58							11 18			
Hockley	d			10 21						10 41					11 01							11 21			
Rayleigh	d			10 26						10 46					11 06							11 26			
Southminster	d				10 16											10 56									
Burnham-on-Crouch	d				10 20											11 00									
Althorne	d				10 25											11 05									
North Fambridge	d				10 31											11 11									
South Woodham Ferrers	d				10 36											11 16									
Battlesbridge	d				10 40											11 20									
Wickford 2	d			10 31	10a46					10 51					11 11	11a26						11 31			
Billericay	d			10 37						10 57					11 17							11 37			
Shenfield 3	a			10 45						11 05					11 25							11 45			
Shenfield 3	d	10 38	10 44	10 45		10 51	10 54	11 04		11 05	11 08	11 14	11 20	11 24	11 25			11 34		11 38	11 44	11 45	11 51	11 54	12 04
Brentwood	d		10 47				10 57	11 07				11 17		11 27				11 37			11 47			11 57	12 07
Harold Wood	d		10 52				11 02	11 12				11 22		11 32				11 42			11 52			12 02	12 12
Gidea Park 2	d		10 56				11 06	11 16				11 26		11 36				11 46			11 56			12 06	12 16
Romford	d		10 58	10 53			11 08	11 18				11 28	11 28	11 38				11 48			11 58	11 53		12 08	12 18
Chadwell Heath	d		11 02				11 12	11 22				11 32		11 42				11 52			12 02			12 12	12 22
Goodmayes	d		11 04				11 14	11 24				11 34		11 44				11 54			12 04			12 14	12 24
Seven Kings	d		11 06				11 16	11 26				11 36		11 46				11 56			12 06			12 16	12 26
Ilford 2	d		11 09				11 19	11 29				11 39		11 49				11 59			12 09			12 19	12 29
Manor Park	d		11 12				11 22	11 32				11 42		11 52				12 02			12 12			12 22	12 32
Forest Gate	d		11 14				11 24	11 34				11 44		11 54				12 04			12 14			12 24	12 34
Maryland	d		11 16				11 26	11 36				11 46		11 56				12 06			12 16			12 26	12 36
Stratford 7 ⊖	d	10 52	11 19	11 01		11 05	11 29	11 39		11 19	11 22	11 49	11 36	11 59	11 39			12 09		11 52	12 19	12 01	12 05	12 29	12 39
London Liverpool Street 15 ⊖	a	11 01	11 27	11 10		11 14	11 37	11 47		11 28	11 31	11 57	11 45	12 07	11 48			12 17		12 01	12 27	12 10	12 14	12 37	12 47

		LE 1	LE 1	LE 1		LE	LE 1	LE	LE 1		LE	LE 1	LE	LE 1		LE 1	LE 1	LE	LE	LE 1	LE 1	LE	LE 1	LE	
Southend Victoria	d	11 30							11 50					12 10						12 30					
Prittlewell	d	11 32							11 52					12 12						12 32					
Southend Airport ✈	d	11 35							11 55					12 15						12 35					
Rochford	d	11 38							11 58					12 18						12 38					
Hockley	d	11 41							12 01					12 21						12 41					
Rayleigh	d	11 46							12 06					12 26						12 46					
Southminster	d		11 36													12 16									
Burnham-on-Crouch	d		11 40													12 20									
Althorne	d		11 45													12 25									
North Fambridge	d		11 51													12 31									
South Woodham Ferrers	d		11 56													12 36									
Battlesbridge	d		12 00													12 40									
Wickford 2	d	11 51	12a06						12 11					12 31		12a46				12 51					
Billericay	d	11 57							12 17					12 37						12 57					
Shenfield 3	a	12 05							12 25					12 45						13 05					
Shenfield 3	d	12 05		12 08		12 14	12 20	12 24	12 25		12 34	12 38	12 44	12 45			12 51	12 54	13 04	13 05	13 08	13 14	13 20	13 24	
Brentwood	d					12 17		12 27			12 37		12 47					12 57	13 07			13 17		13 27	
Harold Wood	d					12 22		12 32			12 42		12 52					13 02	13 12			13 22		13 32	
Gidea Park 2	d					12 26		12 36			12 46		12 56					13 06	13 16			13 26		13 36	
Romford	d					12 28	12 28	12 38			12 48		12 58	12 53				13 08	13 18			13 28	13 28	13 38	
Chadwell Heath	d					12 32		12 42			12 52		13 02					13 12	13 22			13 32		13 42	
Goodmayes	d					12 34		12 44			12 54		13 04					13 14	13 24			13 34		13 44	
Seven Kings	d					12 36		12 46			12 56		13 06					13 16	13 26			13 36		13 46	
Ilford 2	d					12 39		12 49			12 59		13 09					13 19	13 29			13 39		13 49	
Manor Park	d					12 42		12 52			13 02		13 12					13 22	13 32			13 42		13 52	
Forest Gate	d					12 44		12 54			13 04		13 14					13 24	13 34			13 44		13 54	
Maryland	d					12 46		12 56			13 06		13 16					13 26	13 36			13 46		13 56	
Stratford 7 ⊖	d	12 19		12 22		12 49	12 36	12 59	12 39		13 09	12 52	13 19	13 01			13 05	13 29	13 39	13 19	13 22	13 49	13 36	13 59	
London Liverpool Street 15 ⊖	a	12 28		12 31		12 57	12 45	13 07	12 48		13 17	13 01	13 27	13 10			13 14	13 37	13 47	13 28	13 31	13 57	13 45	14 07	

		LE 1	LE 1		LE	LE 1	LE	LE 1	LE 1	LE		LE	LE 1	LE 1	LE 1	LE	LE 1	LE	LE 1			LE	LE 1	LE	LE 1
Southend Victoria	d	12 50						13 10					13 30						13 50						14 10
Prittlewell	d	12 52						13 12					13 32						13 52						14 12
Southend Airport ✈	d	12 55						13 15					13 35						13 55						14 15
Rochford	d	12 58						13 18					13 38						13 58						14 18
Hockley	d	13 01						13 21					13 41						14 01						14 21
Rayleigh	d	13 06						13 26					13 46						14 06						14 26
Southminster	d		12 56											13 36											
Burnham-on-Crouch	d		13 00											13 40											
Althorne	d		13 05											13 45											
North Fambridge	d		13 11											13 51											
South Woodham Ferrers	d		13 16											13 56											
Battlesbridge	d		13 20											14 00											
Wickford 2	d	13 11	13a26					13 31					13 51	14a06					14 11						14 31
Billericay	d	13 17						13 37					13 57						14 17						14 37
Shenfield 3	a	13 25						13 45					14 05						14 25						14 45
Shenfield 3	d	13 25			13 34	13 38	13 44	13 45	13 51	13 54		14 04	14 05		14 08	14 14	14 20	14 24	14 25			14 34	14 38	14 44	14 45
Brentwood	d				13 37		13 47			13 57		14 07				14 17		14 27				14 37		14 47	
Harold Wood	d				13 42		13 52			14 02		14 12				14 22		14 32				14 42		14 52	
Gidea Park 2	d				13 46		13 56			14 06		14 16				14 26		14 36				14 46		14 56	
Romford	d				13 48		13 58	13 53		14 08		14 18				14 28	14 28	14 38				14 48		14 58	14 53
Chadwell Heath	d				13 52		14 02			14 12		14 22				14 32		14 42				14 52		15 02	
Goodmayes	d				13 54		14 04			14 14		14 24				14 34		14 44				14 54		15 04	
Seven Kings	d				13 56		14 06			14 16		14 26				14 36		14 46				14 56		15 06	
Ilford 2	d				13 59		14 09			14 19		14 29				14 39		14 49				14 59		15 09	
Manor Park	d				14 02		14 12			14 22		14 32				14 42		14 52				15 02		15 12	
Forest Gate	d				14 04		14 14			14 24		14 34				14 44		14 54				15 04		15 14	
Maryland	d				14 06		14 16			14 26		14 36				14 46		14 56				15 06		15 16	
Stratford 7 ⊖	d	13 39			14 09	13 52	14 19	14 01	14 05	14 29		14 39	14 19		14 22	14 49	14 36	14 59	14 39			15 09	14 52	15 19	15 01
London Liverpool Street 15 ⊖	a	13 48			14 17	14 01	14 27	14 10	14 14	14 37		14 47	14 28		14 31	14 57	14 45	15 07	14 48			15 17	15 01	15 27	15 10

Southend Victoria, Southminster and Shenfield - London

	LE 1	LE 1	LE	LE	LE 1		LE 1	LE	LE 1	LE	LE 1	LE 1		LE	LE 1		LE	LE 1	LE 1	LE	LE	LE 1	LE 1	LE 1
Southend Victoria d					14 30						14 50							15 10				15 30		
Prittlewell d					14 32						14 52							15 12				15 32		
Southend Airport ✈ d					14 35						14 55							15 15				15 35		
Rochford d					14 38						14 58							15 18				15 38		
Hockley d					14 41						15 01							15 21				15 41		
Rayleigh d					14 46						15 06							15 26				15 46		
Southminster d	14 16											14 56											15 36	
Burnham-on-Crouch d	14 20											15 00											15 40	
Althorne d	14 25											15 05											15 45	
North Fambridge d	14 31											15 11											15 51	
South Woodham Ferrers d	14 36											15 16											15 56	
Battlesbridge d	14 40											15 20											16 00	
Wickford 2 d	14a46				14 51						15 11	15a26						15 31				15 51	16a06	
Billericay d					14 57						15 17							15 37				15 57		
Shenfield 3 a					15 05						15 25							15 45				16 05		
Shenfield 3 d		14 51	14 54	15 04	15 05		15 08	15 14	15 20	15 24	15 25			15 34	15 38		15 44	15 45	15 51	15 54	16 04	16 05		16 08
Brentwood d			14 57	15 07				15 17		15 27				15 37			15 47			15 57	16 07			
Harold Wood d			15 02	15 12				15 22		15 32				15 42			15 52			16 02	16 12			
Gidea Park 2 d			15 06	15 16				15 26		15 36				15 46			15 56			16 06	16 16			
Romford d			15 08	15 18				15 28	15 28	15 38				15 48			15 58	15 53		16 08	16 18			
Chadwell Heath d			15 12	15 22				15 32		15 42				15 52			16 02			16 12	16 22			
Goodmayes d			15 14	15 24				15 34		15 44				15 54			16 04			16 14	16 24			
Seven Kings d			15 16	15 26				15 36		15 46				15 56			16 06			16 16	16 26			
Ilford 2 d			15 19	15 29				15 39		15 49				15 59			16 09			16 19	16 29			
Manor Park d			15 22	15 32				15 42		15 52				16 02			16 12			16 22	16 32			
Forest Gate d			15 24	15 34				15 44		15 54				16 04			16 14			16 24	16 34			
Maryland d			15 26	15 36				15 46		15 56				16 06			16 16			16 26	16 36			
Stratford 7 ⊖ d		15 05	15 29	15 39	15 19		15 22	15 49	15 36	15 59	15 39			16 09	15 52		16 19	16 01	16 05	16 29	16 39	16 19		16 22
London Liverpool Street 15 ⊖ a		15 14	15 37	15 47	15 28		15 31	15 57	15 45	16 07	15 48			16 17	16 01		16 27	16 11	16 14	16 37	16 47	16 29		16 31

	LE		LE 1	LE	LE 1		LE	LE 1	LE	LE 1	LE 1		LE 1	LE	LE	LE 1	LE 1	LE	LE 1	LE	LE		LE 1	LE 1
Southend Victoria d					15 50					16 10						16 30							16 50	
Prittlewell d					15 52					16 12						16 32							16 52	
Southend Airport ✈ d					15 55					16 15						16 35							16 55	
Rochford d					15 58					16 18						16 38							16 58	
Hockley d					16 01					16 21						16 41							17 01	
Rayleigh d					16 06					16 26						16 46							17 06	
Southminster d											16 14													
Burnham-on-Crouch d											16 18													
Althorne d											16 23													
North Fambridge d											16 29													
South Woodham Ferrers d											16 34													
Battlesbridge d											16 38													
Wickford 2 d					16 11					16 31	16a44					16 51							17 11	
Billericay d					16 17					16 37						16 57							17 17	
Shenfield 3 a					16 25					16 45						17 05							17 25	
Shenfield 3 d	16 14		16 20	16 24	16 25		16 34	16 38	16 44	16 45			16 51	16 54	17 04	17 05	17 08	17 14	17 22		17 24		17 25	17 28
Brentwood d	16 17			16 27			16 37		16 47					16 57	17 07			17 17			17 27			
Harold Wood d	16 22			16 32			16 42		16 52					17 02	17 12			17 22			17 32			
Gidea Park 2 d	16 26			16 36			16 46		16 56					17 06	17 16			17 26		17 32	17 36			
Romford d	16 28			16 38			16 48		16 58					17 08	17 18			17 28		17 34	17 38			
Chadwell Heath d	16 32			16 42			16 52		17 02					17 12	17 22			17 32			17 42			
Goodmayes d	16 34			16 44			16 54		17 04					17 14	17 24			17 34			17 44			
Seven Kings d	16 36			16 46			16 56		17 06					17 16	17 26			17 36			17 46			
Ilford 2 d	16 39			16 49			16 59		17 09					17 19	17 29			17 39		17 42	17 49			
Manor Park d	16 42			16 52			17 02		17 12					17 22	17 32					17 45				
Forest Gate d	16 44			16 54			17 04		17 14					17 24	17 34					17 47				
Maryland d	16 46			16 56			17 06		17 16					17 26	17 36					17 49				
Stratford 7 ⊖ d	16 49		16 34	16 59	16 39		17 09	16 52	17 19	16 59			17 05	17 29	17 39	17 19	17 22	17 45	17 36	17 52	17 55		17 39	17 42
London Liverpool Street 15 ⊖ a	16 57		16 44	17 07	16 48		17 17	17 03	17 27	17 13			17 16	17 37	17 47	17 29	17 34	17 53	17 46	18 00	18 03		17 49	17 53

		LE	LE	LE 1	LE	LE	LE 1		LE 1	LE 1	LE	LE	LE 1	LE	LE	LE 1	LE 1		LE	LE	LE 1	LE	LE	LE 1
Southend Victoria d							17 10						17 25				17 35							17 50
Prittlewell d							17 12						17 27				17 37							17 52
Southend Airport ✈ d							17 15						17 30				17 40							17 55
Rochford d							17 18						17 33				17 43							17 58
Hockley d							17 21						17 36				17 46							18 01
Rayleigh d							17 26						17 41				17 51							18 06
Southminster d									17 06															
Burnham-on-Crouch d									17 10															
Althorne d									17 15															
North Fambridge d									17 21															
South Woodham Ferrers d									17 26															
Battlesbridge d									17 30															
Wickford 2 d							17 31		17 37				17 46				17 56							18 11
Billericay d							17 37						17 52				18 02							18 17
Shenfield 3 a							17 45		17 48				18 00				18 10							18 25
Shenfield 3 d			17 34	17 38		17 44	17 45		17 49	17 51		17 54	18 00		18 04	18 08	18 10			18 14	18 20		18 24	18 25
Brentwood d			17 37			17 47						17 57			18 07					18 17			18 27	
Harold Wood d			17 42			17 52						18 02			18 12					18 22			18 32	
Gidea Park 2 d		17 42	17 46		17 52	17 56					18 02	18 06		18 12	18 16				18 22	18 26		18 32	18 36	
Romford d		17 44	17 48		17 54	17 58					18 04	18 08		18 14	18 18				18 24	18 28	18 28	18 34	18 38	
Chadwell Heath d			17 52			18 02						18 12			18 22					18 32			18 42	
Goodmayes d			17 54			18 04						18 14			18 24					18 34			18 44	
Seven Kings d			17 56			18 06						18 16			18 26					18 36			18 46	
Ilford 2 d		17 52	17 59		18 02	18 09					18 12	18 19		18 22	18 29				18 32	18 39		18 42	18 49	
Manor Park d		17 55			18 05						18 15			18 25					18 35			18 45	18 52	
Forest Gate d		17 57			18 07						18 17			18 27					18 37			18 47	18 54	
Maryland d		17 59			18 09						18 19			18 29					18 39			18 49	18 56	
Stratford 7 ⊖ d		18 02	18 05	17 52	18 12	18 15	17 59		18 08	18 06	18 22	18 25	18 14	18 32	18 35	18 22	18 25		18 42	18 45	18 36	18 52	18 59	18 39
London Liverpool Street 15 ⊖ a		18 10	18 13	18 01	18 20	18 23	18 11		18 17	18 15	18 30	18 33	18 24	18 40	18 43	18 31	18 35		18 50	18 53	18 45	19 00	19 07	18 48

Table 5

Mondays to Fridays

Southend Victoria, Southminster and Shenfield - London

Station		LE [1]	LE	LE [1]	LE [1]	LE [1]	LE	LE [1]	LE	LE [1]	LE	LE [1]	LE [1]	LE [1]	LE	LE [1]	LE	LE [1]	LE [1]	LE
Southend Victoria	d				18 05					18 20		18 30						18 50		
Prittlewell	d				18 07					18 22		18 32						18 52		
Southend Airport ✈	d				18 10					18 25		18 35						18 55		
Rochford	d				18 13					18 28		18 38						18 58		
Hockley	d				18 16					18 31		18 41						19 01		
Rayleigh	d				18 21					18 36		18 46						19 06		
Southminster	d					17 56													18 36	
Burnham-on-Crouch	d					18 00													18 40	
Althorne	d					18 05													18 45	
North Fambridge	d					18 14													19 01	
South Woodham Ferrers	d					18 19													19 06	
Battlesbridge	d					18 23													19 10	
Wickford [2]	d				18 26	18a29				18 41		18 51						19 11	19 17	
Billericay	d				18 32					18 47		18 57						19 17	19 23	
Shenfield [3]	a				18 40					18 55		19 05						19 25	19 33	
Shenfield [3]	d	18 27	18 34	18 38	18 40		18 44	18 51	18 54	18 57	19 04	19 05	19 08	19 14	19 14	19 20	19 24	19 25		19 34
Brentwood	d		18 37				18 47		18 57		19 07				19 17		19 27			19 37
Harold Wood	d		18 42				18 52		19 02		19 12				19 22		19 32			19 42
Gidea Park [2]	d		18 46				18 56		19 06		19 16				19 26		19 36			19 46
Romford	d		18 48				18 58		19 08		19 18				19 28	19 28	19 38			19 48
Chadwell Heath	d		18 52				19 02		19 12		19 22				19 32		19 42			19 52
Goodmayes	d		18 54				19 04		19 14		19 24				19 34		19 44			19 54
Seven Kings	d		18 56				19 06		19 16		19 26				19 36		19 46			19 56
Ilford [2]	d		18 59				19 09		19 19		19 29				19 39		19 49			19 59
Manor Park	d		19 02				19 12		19 22		19 32				19 42		19 52			20 02
Forest Gate	d		19 04				19 14		19 24		19 34				19 44		19 54			20 04
Maryland	d		19 06				19 16		19 26		19 36				19 46		19 56			20 06
Stratford [7] ⊖	d	18 42	19 09	18 52	18 55		19 19	19 05	19 29	19 11	19 39	19 19	19 22	19 28	19 49	19 36	19 59	19 39		20 09
London Liverpool Street [15] ⊖	a	18 51	19 17	19 01	19 04		19 27	19 14	19 37	19 20	19 47	19 28	19 31	19 37	19 57	19 45	20 07	19 48		20 17

Station		LE [1]	LE	LE [1]	LE [1]	LE [1]	LE	LE	LE [1]	LE [1]	CC	LE [1]	LE	LE [1]	LE	LE [1]	LE	LE [1]	CC	LE	LE [1]	LE [1]
Southend Victoria	d			19 10					19 30							19 50					20 10	
Prittlewell	d			19 12					19 32							19 52					20 12	
Southend Airport ✈	d			19 15					19 35							19 55					20 15	
Rochford	d			19 18					19 38							19 58					20 18	
Hockley	d			19 21					19 41							20 01					20 21	
Rayleigh	d			19 26					19 46							20 06					20 26	
Southminster	d									19 17												20 16
Burnham-on-Crouch	d									19 21												20 20
Althorne	d									19 26												20 25
North Fambridge	d									19 33												20 31
South Woodham Ferrers	d									19 38												20 36
Battlesbridge	d									19 42												20 40
Wickford [2]	d			19 31					19 51	19 55						20 11					20 31	20a46
Billericay	d			19 37					19 57							20 17					20 37	
Shenfield [3]	a			19 45					20 05	20 07						20 25					20 45	
Shenfield [3]	d	19 38	19 44	19 45	19 51		19 54	20 04	20 05			20 08	20 14	20 20	20 24	20 25	20 34	20 38		20 44	20 45	
Brentwood	d		19 47				19 57	20 07					20 17		20 27		20 37			20 47		
Harold Wood	d		19 52				20 02	20 12					20 22		20 32		20 42			20 52		
Gidea Park [2]	d		19 56				20 06	20 16					20 26		20 36		20 46			20 56		
Romford	d		19 58	19 53			20 08	20 18					20 28	20 28	20 38		20 48			20 58	20 53	
Chadwell Heath	d		20 02				20 12	20 22					20 32		20 42		20 52			21 02		
Goodmayes	d		20 04				20 14	20 24					20 34		20 44		20 54			21 04		
Seven Kings	d		20 06				20 16	20 26					20 36		20 46		20 56			21 06		
Ilford [2]	d		20 09				20 19	20 29					20 39		20 49		20 59			21 09		
Manor Park	d		20 12				20 22	20 32					20 42		20 52		21 02			21 12		
Forest Gate	d		20 14				20 24	20 34					20 44		20 54		21 04			21 14		
Maryland	d		20 16				20 26	20 36					20 46		20 56		21 06			21 16		
Stratford [7] ⊖	d	19 52	20 19	20 01	20 05	20 14	20 29	20 39	20 19		20 21	20 22	20 49	20 36	20 59	20 39	21 09	20 52	21 00	21 19	21 01	
London Liverpool Street [15] ⊖	a	20 01	20 27	20 10	20 14	20 23	20 37	20 47	20 28		20 33	20 31	20 57	20 45	21 07	20 48	21 17	21 01	21 12	21 27	21 10	

Station		LE [1]	LE [1]	CC	LE	LE	LE [1]	LE [1]	LE	LE	LE [1]	LE [1]	LE [1]	LE	LE [1]	LE	LE [1]	LE [1]	LE	LE [1]	LE [1]	LE [1]
Southend Victoria	d						20 30				20 50						21 10			21 30		
Prittlewell	d						20 32				20 52						21 12			21 32		
Southend Airport ✈	d						20 35				20 55						21 15			21 35		
Rochford	d						20 38				20 58						21 18			21 38		
Hockley	d						20 41				21 01						21 21			21 41		
Rayleigh	d						20 46				21 06						21 26			21 46		
Southminster	d											20 56									21 36	
Burnham-on-Crouch	d											21 00									21 40	
Althorne	d											21 05									21 45	
North Fambridge	d											21 11									21 51	
South Woodham Ferrers	d											21 16									21 56	
Battlesbridge	d											21 20									22 00	
Wickford [2]	d						20 51				21 11	21a26					21 31			21 51	22a07	
Billericay	d						20 57				21 17						21 37			21 57		
Shenfield [3]	a						21 05				21 25						21 45			22 05		
Shenfield [3]	d	20 47	20 53		20 54	21 04	21 05	21 08	21 14	21 24	21 25		21 27	21 34	21 38	21 44	21 45	21 51	21 59	22 05		22 08
Brentwood	d				20 57	21 07			21 17	21 27				21 37		21 47			22 02			
Harold Wood	d				21 02	21 12			21 22	21 32				21 42		21 52			22 07			
Gidea Park [2]	d				21 06	21 16			21 26	21 36				21 46		21 56			22 11			
Romford	d				21 08	21 18			21 28	21 38				21 48		21 58	21 53		22 13			
Chadwell Heath	d				21 12	21 22			21 32	21 42				21 52		22 02			22 17			
Goodmayes	d				21 14	21 24			21 34	21 44				21 54		22 04			22 19			
Seven Kings	d				21 16	21 26			21 36	21 46				21 56		22 06			22 21			
Ilford [2]	d				21 19	21 29			21 39	21 49				21 59		22 09			22 24			
Manor Park	d				21 22	21 32			21 42	21 52				22 02		22 12			22 27			
Forest Gate	d				21 24	21 34			21 44	21 54				22 04		22 14			22 29			
Maryland	d				21 26	21 36			21 46	21 56				22 06		22 16			22 31			
Stratford [7] ⊖	d		21 07	21 15	21 29	21 39	21 19	21 22	21 49	21 59	21 39		21 42	22 09	21 52	22 19	22 01	22 05	22 34	22 19		22 22
London Liverpool Street [15] ⊖	a	21 12	21 16	21 26	21 37	21 47	21 28	21 31	21 57	22 07	21 48		21 51	22 17	22 01	22 27	22 10	22 14	22 42	22 28		22 31

Southend Victoria, Southminster and Shenfield - London

		LE	LE	LE	LE	LE	LE	LE	LE	LE	LE	LE	LE	LE	LE	LE	LE	LE	LE	CC	LE
			1	◇1		1	1	1	1		1		1	1		1		1	1		
Southend Victoria	d					22 00							22 30					23 00			
Prittlewell	d					22 02							22 32					23 02			
Southend Airport ✈	d					22 05							22 35					23 05			
Rochford	d					22 08							22 38					23 08			
Hockley	d					22 11							22 41					23 11			
Rayleigh	d					22 16							22 46					23 16			
Southminster	d						22 16												22 56		
Burnham-on-Crouch	d						22 20												23 00		
Althorne	d						22 25												23 05		
North Fambridge	d						22 31												23 11		
South Woodham Ferrers	d						22 36												23 16		
Battlesbridge	d						22 40												23 20		
Wickford 2	d					22 21	22a46						22 51					23 21	23 26		
Billericay	d					22 27							22 57					23 27	23 32		
Shenfield 3	a					22 35							23 05					23 35	23 39		
Shenfield 3	d	22 14	22 20		22 29	22 35		22 38		22 44	22 51	22 59	23 05	23 08	23 14	23 20	23 29	23 35	23 39		23 44
Brentwood	d	22 17			22 32					22 47		23 02			23 17		23 32				23 47
Harold Wood	d	22 22			22 37					22 52		23 07			23 22		23 37				23 52
Gidea Park 2	d	22 26			22 41					22 56		23 11			23 26		23 41				23 56
Romford	d	22 28	22 28		22 43					22 58		23 13			23 28	23 28	23 43		23 47		23 58
Chadwell Heath	d	22 32			22 47					23 02		23 17			23 32		23 47				00 02
Goodmayes	d	22 34			22 49					23 04		23 19			23 34		23 49				00 04
Seven Kings	d	22 36			22 51					23 06		23 21			23 36		23 51				00 06
Ilford 2	d	22 39			22 54					23 09		23 24			23 39		23 54				00 09
Manor Park	d	22 42			22 57					23 12		23 27			23 42		23 57				00 12
Forest Gate	d	22 44			22 59					23 14		23 29			23 44		23 59				00 14
Maryland	d	22 46			23 01					23 16		23 31			23 46		00 01				00 16
Stratford 7 ⊖	d	22 49	22 36		23 04	22 49		22 52	23 05	23 19	23 05	23 34	23 19	23 22	23 49	23 36	00 04	23 49	23 56	23 58	00 19
London Liverpool Street 15 ⊖	a	22 57	22 45	22 55	23 12	22 58		23 01	23 14	23 27	23 15	23 42	23 28	23 31	23 57	23 45	00 12	23 58	00 05	00 11	00 27

Southend Victoria, Southminster and Shenfield - London

		LE	LE	LE	CC	LE	LE	LE	LE	LE		LE	LE	LE	LE	LE	LE	LE	LE	LE			LE	LE	LE
		◇1		1			1		1	1			1	1		1	1			1				1	1
Southend Victoria	d						04 00		04 30				05 00				05 30							06 00	
Prittlewell	d						04 02		04 32				05 02				05 32							06 02	
Southend Airport ✈	d						04 05		04 35				05 05				05 35							06 05	
Rochford	d						04 08		04 38				05 08				05 38							06 08	
Hockley	d						04 12		04 42				05 11				05 41							06 11	
Rayleigh	d						04 16		04 46				05 16				05 46							06 16	
Southminster	d			22p56																					06 16
Burnham-on-Crouch	d			23p00																					06 20
Althorne	d			23p05																					06 25
North Fambridge	d			23p11																					06 31
South Woodham Ferrers	d			23p16																					06 36
Battlesbridge	d			23p20																					06 40
Wickford 2	d			23p26			04 21		04 51				05 21				05 51							06 21	06a46
Billericay	d			23p32			04 28		04 58				05 27				05 57							06 27	
Shenfield 3	a			23p39			04 39		05 09				05 35				06 05							06 35	
Shenfield 3	d		23p29	23p39		23p44	04 39		05 09	05 24			05 35		05 44	05 53	06 05		06 14	06 24				06 35	
Brentwood	d		23p32			23p47	04 42		05 12						05 47				06 17						
Harold Wood	d		23p37			23p52	04 47		05 17						05 52				06 22						
Gidea Park 2	d		23p41			23p56	04 51		05 21	05 31					05 56			06 16	06 26				06 36		
Romford	d		23p43	23p47		23p58	04 53		05 23				05 43		05 58			06 18	06 28				06 38	06 43	
Chadwell Heath	d		23p47			00 02	04 57		05 27						06 02			06 22	06 32				06 42		
Goodmayes	d		23p49			00 04	04 59		05 29						06 04			06 24	06 34				06 44		
Seven Kings	d		23p51			00 06	05 01		05 31	05 36					06 06			06 26	06 36				06 46		
Ilford 2	d		23p54			00 09	05 04	05 09	05 34			05 39			06 09			06 29	06 39				06 49		
Manor Park	d		23p57			00 12		05 11				05 41			06 12			06 32	06 42				06 52		
Forest Gate	d		23p59			00 14		05 14				05 44			06 14			06 34	06 44				06 54		
Maryland	d		00 01			00 16		05 16				05 46			06 16			06 36	06 46				06 56		
Stratford 7 ⊖	d	23b52	00 04	23p56	23p58	00 19	05 10	05 18	05 40	05 42		05 48	05 51	06 05	06 19	06 07	06 19	06 39	06 49	06 38			06 59	06 51	
London Liverpool Street 15 ⊖	a	00 02	00 12	00 05	00 11	00 27	05 18	05 26	05 48	05 55		05 56	06 00	06 14	06 27	06 16	06 28	06 47	06 57	06 47			07 07	07 00	

		LE	LE	LE	LE	LE		LE	LE	LE	LE	LE	LE	LE		LE		LE	LE	LE	LE	LE	LE	LE	LE
				1				1	1		1		1	1				1		1	1			1	1
Southend Victoria	d							06 30					06 50							07 10				07 30	
Prittlewell	d							06 32					06 52							07 12				07 32	
Southend Airport ✈	d							06 35					06 55							07 15				07 35	
Rochford	d							06 38					06 58							07 18				07 38	
Hockley	d							06 41					07 01							07 21				07 41	
Rayleigh	d							06 46					07 06							07 26				07 46	
Southminster	d													06 56											07 36
Burnham-on-Crouch	d													07 00											07 40
Althorne	d													07 05											07 45
North Fambridge	d													07 11											07 51
South Woodham Ferrers	d													07 16											07 56
Battlesbridge	d													07 20											08 00
Wickford 2	d							06 51					07 11	07a26						07 31				07 51	08a06
Billericay	d							06 57					07 17							07 37				07 57	
Shenfield 3	a							07 05					07 25							07 45				08 05	
Shenfield 3	d		06 44	06 51		07 04		07 05	07 08	07 14	07 20	07 24	07 25			07 34		07 38	07 44	07 45	07 51	07 54	08 04	08 05	
Brentwood	d		06 47			07 07				07 17		07 27				07 37			07 47			07 57	08 07		
Harold Wood	d		06 52			07 12				07 22		07 32				07 42			07 52			08 02	08 12		
Gidea Park 2	d	06 46	06 56		07 06	07 16				07 26		07 36				07 46			07 56			08 06	08 16		
Romford	d	06 48	06 58		07 08	07 18				07 28	07 28	07 38				07 48			07 58	07 53		08 08	08 18		
Chadwell Heath	d	06 52	07 02		07 12	07 22				07 32		07 42				07 52			08 02			08 12	08 22		
Goodmayes	d	06 54	07 04		07 14	07 24				07 34		07 44				07 54			08 04			08 14	08 24		
Seven Kings	d	06 56	07 06		07 16	07 26				07 36		07 46				07 56			08 06			08 16	08 26		
Ilford 2	d	06 59	07 09		07 19	07 29				07 39		07 49				07 59			08 09			08 19	08 29		
Manor Park	d	07 02	07 12		07 22	07 32				07 42		07 52				08 02			08 12			08 22	08 32		
Forest Gate	d	07 04	07 14		07 24	07 34				07 44		07 54				08 04			08 14			08 24	08 34		
Maryland	d	07 06	07 16		07 26	07 36				07 46		07 56				08 06			08 16			08 26	08 36		
Stratford 7 ⊖	d	07 09	07 19	07 05	07 29	07 39		07 19	07 22	07 49	07 36	07 59	07 39			08 09		07 52	08 19	08 01	08 05	08 29	08 39	08 19	
London Liverpool Street 15 ⊖	a	07 17	07 27	07 14	07 37	07 47		07 28	07 31	07 57	07 45	08 07	07 48			08 17		08 01	08 27	08 10	08 14	08 37	08 47	08 28	

b Previous night, stops to set down only

		LE		LE	LE	LE	LE		LE	LE	LE	LE		LE	LE	LE	LE	LE	LE	LE	LE	LE		LE	LE
		1			1		1			1		1		1	1			1	1		1			1	1
Southend Victoria	d						07 50					08 10						08 30						08 50	
Prittlewell	d						07 52					08 12						08 32						08 52	
Southend Airport ✈	d						07 55					08 15						08 35						08 55	
Rochford	d						07 58					08 18						08 38						08 58	
Hockley	d						08 01					08 21						08 41						09 01	
Rayleigh	d						08 06					08 26						08 46						09 06	
Southminster	d													08 16											08 56
Burnham-on-Crouch	d													08 20											09 00
Althorne	d													08 25											09 05
North Fambridge	d													08 31											09 11
South Woodham Ferrers	d													08 36											09 16
Battlesbridge	d													08 40											09 20
Wickford 2	d						08 11					08 31		08a46				08 51						09 11	09a26
Billericay	d						08 17					08 37						08 57						09 17	
Shenfield 3	a						08 25					08 45						09 05						09 25	
Shenfield 3	d	08 08		08 14	08 20	08 24	08 25		08 34	08 38	08 44	08 45			08 51	08 54	09 04	09 05	09 08	09 14	09 20	09 24		09 25	
Brentwood	d			08 17		08 27			08 37		08 47					08 57	09 07			09 17		09 27			
Harold Wood	d			08 22		08 32			08 42		08 52					09 02	09 12			09 22		09 32			
Gidea Park 2	d			08 26		08 36			08 46		08 56					09 06	09 16			09 26		09 36			
Romford	d			08 28	08 28	08 38			08 48		08 58	08 53				09 08	09 18			09 28	09 28	09 38			
Chadwell Heath	d			08 32		08 42			08 52		09 02					09 12	09 22			09 32		09 42			
Goodmayes	d			08 34		08 44			08 54		09 04					09 14	09 24			09 34		09 44			
Seven Kings	d			08 36		08 46			08 56		09 06					09 16	09 26			09 36		09 46			
Ilford 2	d			08 39		08 49			08 59		09 09					09 19	09 29			09 39		09 49			
Manor Park	d			08 42		08 52			09 02		09 12					09 22	09 32			09 42		09 52			
Forest Gate	d			08 44		08 54			09 04		09 14					09 24	09 34			09 44		09 54			
Maryland	d			08 46		08 56			09 06		09 16					09 26	09 36			09 46		09 56			
Stratford 7 ⊖	d	08 22		08 49	08 36	08 59	08 39		09 09	08 52	09 19	09 01			09 05	09 29	09 39	09 19	09 22	09 49	09 36	09 59		09 39	
London Liverpool Street 15 ⊖	a	08 31		08 57	08 45	09 07	08 48		09 17	09 01	09 27	09 10			09 14	09 37	09 47	09 28	09 31	09 57	09 45	10 07		09 48	

Table 5

Saturdays

Southend Victoria, Southminster and Shenfield - London

			LE	LE 1	LE	LE 1	LE 1	LE		LE	LE 1	LE 1	LE 1	LE	LE 1	LE	LE 1			LE	LE 1	LE	LE 1	LE 1	LE 1
Southend Victoria	d					09 10					09 30						09 50						10 10		
Prittlewell	d					09 12					09 32						09 52						10 12		
Southend Airport ✈	d					09 15					09 35						09 55						10 15		
Rochford	d					09 18					09 38						09 58						10 18		
Hockley	d					09 21					09 41						10 01						10 21		
Rayleigh	d					09 26					09 46						10 06						10 26		
Southminster	d											09 36												10 16	
Burnham-on-Crouch	d											09 40												10 20	
Althorne	d											09 45												10 25	
North Fambridge	d											09 51												10 31	
South Woodham Ferrers	d											09 56												10 36	
Battlesbridge	d											10 00												10 40	
Wickford 2	d					09 31					09 51	10a06					10 11						10 31	10a46	
Billericay	d					09 37					09 57						10 17						10 37		
Shenfield 3	a					09 45					10 05						10 25						10 45		
Shenfield 3	d		09 34	09 38	09 44	09 45	09 51	09 54		10 04	10 05		10 08	10 14	10 20	10 24	10 25			10 34	10 38	10 44	10 45		10 51
Brentwood	d		09 37		09 47			09 57		10 07				10 17		10 27				10 37		10 47			
Harold Wood	d		09 42		09 52			10 02		10 12				10 22		10 32				10 42		10 52			
Gidea Park 2	d		09 46		09 56			10 06		10 16				10 26		10 36				10 46		10 56			
Romford	d		09 48		09 58	09 53		10 08		10 18				10 28	10 28	10 38				10 48		10 58	10 53		
Chadwell Heath	d		09 52		10 02			10 12		10 22				10 32		10 42				10 52		11 02			
Goodmayes	d		09 54		10 04			10 14		10 24				10 34		10 44				10 54		11 04			
Seven Kings	d		09 56		10 06			10 16		10 26				10 36		10 46				10 56		11 06			
Ilford 2	d		09 59		10 09			10 19		10 29				10 39		10 49				10 59		11 09			
Manor Park	d		10 02		10 12			10 22		10 32				10 42		10 52				11 02		11 12			
Forest Gate	d		10 04		10 14			10 24		10 34				10 44		10 54				11 04		11 14			
Maryland	d		10 06		10 16			10 26		10 36				10 46		10 56				11 06		11 16			
Stratford 7 ⊖	d		10 09	09 52	10 19	10 01	10 05	10 29		10 39	10 19		10 22	10 49	10 36	10 59	10 39			11 09	10 52	11 19	11 01		11 05
London Liverpool Street 15 ⊖	a		10 17	10 01	10 27	10 10	10 14	10 37		10 47	10 28		10 31	10 57	10 45	11 07	10 48			11 17	11 01	11 27	11 10		11 14

		LE	LE	LE 1		LE 1	LE	LE 1	LE	LE 1	LE 1		LE	LE 1		LE	LE 1	LE 1	LE	LE	LE 1	LE 1	LE 1	LE	
Southend Victoria	d			10 30						10 50							11 10				11 30				
Prittlewell	d			10 32						10 52							11 12				11 32				
Southend Airport ✈	d			10 35						10 55							11 15				11 35				
Rochford	d			10 38						10 58							11 18				11 38				
Hockley	d			10 41						11 01							11 21				11 41				
Rayleigh	d			10 46						11 06							11 26				11 46				
Southminster	d										10 56											11 36			
Burnham-on-Crouch	d										11 00											11 40			
Althorne	d										11 05											11 45			
North Fambridge	d										11 11											11 51			
South Woodham Ferrers	d										11 16											11 56			
Battlesbridge	d										11 20											12 00			
Wickford 2	d			10 51						11 11	11a26						11 31				11 51	12a06			
Billericay	d			10 57						11 17							11 37				11 57				
Shenfield 3	a			11 05						11 25							11 45				12 05				
Shenfield 3	d	10 54	11 04	11 05		11 08	11 14	11 20	11 24	11 25			11 34	11 38		11 44	11 45	11 51	11 54	12 04	12 05		12 08	12 14	
Brentwood	d	10 57	11 07				11 17		11 27				11 37			11 47			11 57	12 07				12 17	
Harold Wood	d	11 02	11 12				11 22		11 32				11 42			11 52			12 02	12 12				12 22	
Gidea Park 2	d	11 06	11 16				11 26		11 36				11 46			11 56			12 06	12 16				12 26	
Romford	d	11 08	11 18				11 28	11 28	11 38				11 48			11 58	11 53		12 08	12 18				12 28	
Chadwell Heath	d	11 12	11 22				11 32		11 42				11 52			12 02			12 12	12 22				12 32	
Goodmayes	d	11 14	11 24				11 34		11 44				11 54			12 04			12 14	12 24				12 34	
Seven Kings	d	11 16	11 26				11 36		11 46				11 56			12 06			12 16	12 26				12 36	
Ilford 2	d	11 19	11 29				11 39		11 49				11 59			12 09			12 19	12 29				12 39	
Manor Park	d	11 22	11 32				11 42		11 52				12 02			12 12			12 22	12 32				12 42	
Forest Gate	d	11 24	11 34				11 44		11 54				12 04			12 14			12 24	12 34				12 44	
Maryland	d	11 26	11 36				11 46		11 56				12 06			12 16			12 26	12 36				12 46	
Stratford 7 ⊖	d	11 29	11 39	11 19		11 22	11 49	11 36	11 59	11 39			12 09	11 52		12 19	12 01	12 05	12 29	12 39	12 19		12 22	12 49	
London Liverpool Street 15 ⊖	a	11 37	11 47	11 28		11 31	11 57	11 45	12 07	11 48			12 17	12 01		12 27	12 10	12 14	12 37	12 47	12 28		12 31	12 57	

		LE 1	LE	LE 1		LE	LE 1	LE	LE 1	LE 1		LE 1	LE	LE	LE 1	LE 1	LE	LE 1	LE	LE 1		LE 1		LE	LE 1
Southend Victoria	d			11 50					12 10						12 30					12 50					
Prittlewell	d			11 52					12 12						12 32					12 52					
Southend Airport ✈	d			11 55					12 15						12 35					12 55					
Rochford	d			11 58					12 18						12 38					12 58					
Hockley	d			12 01					12 21						12 41					13 01					
Rayleigh	d			12 06					12 26						12 46					13 06					
Southminster	d									12 16												12 56			
Burnham-on-Crouch	d									12 20												13 00			
Althorne	d									12 25												13 05			
North Fambridge	d									12 31												13 11			
South Woodham Ferrers	d									12 36												13 16			
Battlesbridge	d									12 40												13 20			
Wickford 2	d			12 11					12 31	12a46					12 51					13 11		13a26			
Billericay	d			12 17					12 37						12 57					13 17					
Shenfield 3	a			12 25					12 45						13 05					13 25					
Shenfield 3	d	12 20	12 24	12 25		12 34	12 38	12 44	12 45			12 51	12 54	13 04	13 05	13 08	13 14	13 20	13 24	13 25				13 34	13 38
Brentwood	d		12 27			12 37		12 47					12 57	13 07			13 17		13 27					13 37	
Harold Wood	d		12 32			12 42		12 52					13 02	13 12			13 22		13 32					13 42	
Gidea Park 2	d		12 36			12 46		12 56					13 06	13 16			13 26		13 36					13 46	
Romford	d	12 28	12 38			12 48		12 58	12 53				13 08	13 18			13 28	13 28	13 38					13 48	
Chadwell Heath	d		12 42			12 52		13 02					13 12	13 22			13 32		13 42					13 52	
Goodmayes	d		12 44			12 54		13 04					13 14	13 24			13 34		13 44					13 54	
Seven Kings	d		12 46			12 56		13 06					13 16	13 26			13 36		13 46					13 56	
Ilford 2	d		12 49			12 59		13 09					13 19	13 29			13 39		13 49					13 59	
Manor Park	d		12 52			13 02		13 12					13 22	13 32			13 42		13 52					14 02	
Forest Gate	d		12 54			13 04		13 14					13 24	13 34			13 44		13 54					14 04	
Maryland	d		12 56			13 06		13 16					13 26	13 36			13 46		13 56					14 06	
Stratford 7 ⊖	d	12 36	12 59	12 39		13 09	12 52	13 19	13 01			13 05	13 29	13 39	13 19	13 22	13 49	13 36	13 59	13 39				14 09	13 52
London Liverpool Street 15 ⊖	a	12 45	13 07	12 48		13 17	13 01	13 27	13 10			13 14	13 37	13 47	13 28	13 31	13 57	13 45	14 07	13 48				14 17	14 01

Table 5

Saturdays

Southend Victoria, Southminster and Shenfield - London

		LE	LE 1	LE 1	LE	LE		LE 1	LE 1	LE 1	LE	LE 1	LE	LE 1		LE		LE 1	LE	LE 1	LE 1	LE 1	LE	LE	LE 1
Southend Victoria	d		13 10					13 30						13 50						14 10					14 30
Prittlewell	d		13 12					13 32						13 52						14 12					14 32
Southend Airport ✈	d		13 15					13 35						13 55						14 15					14 35
Rochford	d		13 18					13 38						13 58						14 18					14 38
Hockley	d		13 21					13 41						14 01						14 21					14 41
Rayleigh	d		13 26					13 46						14 06						14 26					14 46
Southminster	d								13 36												14 16				
Burnham-on-Crouch	d								13 40												14 20				
Althorne	d								13 45												14 25				
North Fambridge	d								13 51												14 31				
South Woodham Ferrers	d								13 56												14 36				
Battlesbridge	d								14 00												14 40				
Wickford 2	d		13 31					13 51	14a06					14 11						14 31	14a46				14 51
Billericay	d		13 37					13 57						14 17						14 37					14 57
Shenfield 3	a		13 45					14 05						14 25						14 45					15 05
Shenfield 3	d	13 44	13 45	13 51	13 54	14 04		14 05		14 08	14 14	14 20	14 24	14 25		14 34		14 38	14 44	14 45		14 51	14 54	15 04	15 05
Brentwood	d	13 47			13 57	14 07					14 17		14 27			14 37			14 47				14 57	15 07	
Harold Wood	d	13 52			14 02	14 12					14 22		14 32			14 42			14 52				15 02	15 12	
Gidea Park 2	d	13 56			14 06	14 16					14 26		14 36			14 46			14 56				15 06	15 16	
Romford	d	13 58	13 53		14 08	14 18					14 28	14 28	14 38			14 48			14 58	14 53			15 08	15 18	
Chadwell Heath	d	14 02			14 12	14 22					14 32		14 42			14 52			15 02				15 12	15 22	
Goodmayes	d	14 04			14 14	14 24					14 34		14 44			14 54			15 04				15 14	15 24	
Seven Kings	d	14 06			14 16	14 26					14 36		14 46			14 56			15 06				15 16	15 26	
Ilford 2	d	14 09			14 19	14 29					14 39		14 49			14 59			15 09				15 19	15 29	
Manor Park	d	14 12			14 22	14 32					14 42		14 52			15 02			15 12				15 22	15 32	
Forest Gate	d	14 14			14 24	14 34					14 44		14 54			15 04			15 14				15 24	15 34	
Maryland	d	14 16			14 26	14 36					14 46		14 56			15 06			15 16				15 26	15 36	
Stratford 7 ⊖	d	14 19	14 01	14 05	14 29	14 39		14 19		14 22	14 49	14 36	14 59	14 39		15 09		14 52	15 19	15 01		15 05	15 29	15 39	15 19
London Liverpool Street 15 ⊖	a	14 27	14 10	14 14	14 37	14 47		14 28		14 31	14 57	14 45	15 07	14 48		15 17		15 01	15 27	15 10		15 14	15 37	15 47	15 28

		LE 1		LE	LE 1	LE	LE 1	LE 1		LE	LE 1	LE		LE 1	LE 1	LE	LE	LE 1	LE 1	LE 1	LE	LE 1		LE	LE 1
Southend Victoria	d						14 50							15 10				15 30							15 50
Prittlewell	d						14 52							15 12				15 32							15 52
Southend Airport ✈	d						14 55							15 15				15 35							15 55
Rochford	d						14 58							15 18				15 38							15 58
Hockley	d						15 01							15 21				15 41							16 01
Rayleigh	d						15 06							15 26				15 46							16 06
Southminster	d							14 56											15 36						
Burnham-on-Crouch	d							15 00											15 40						
Althorne	d							15 05											15 45						
North Fambridge	d							15 11											15 51						
South Woodham Ferrers	d							15 16											15 56						
Battlesbridge	d							15 20											16 00						
Wickford 2	d						15 11	15a26						15 31				15 51	16a06						16 11
Billericay	d						15 17							15 37				15 57							16 17
Shenfield 3	a						15 25							15 45				16 05							16 25
Shenfield 3	d	15 08		15 14	15 20	15 24	15 25			15 34	15 38	15 44		15 45	15 51	15 54	16 04	16 05		16 08	16 14	16 20		16 24	16 25
Brentwood	d			15 17		15 27				15 37		15 47				15 57	16 07				16 17			16 27	
Harold Wood	d			15 22		15 32				15 42		15 52				16 02	16 12				16 22			16 32	
Gidea Park 2	d			15 26		15 36				15 46		15 56				16 06	16 16				16 26			16 36	
Romford	d			15 28	15 28	15 38				15 48		15 58		15 53		16 08	16 18				16 28	16 28		16 38	
Chadwell Heath	d			15 32		15 42				15 52		16 02				16 12	16 22				16 32			16 42	
Goodmayes	d			15 34		15 44				15 54		16 04				16 14	16 24				16 34			16 44	
Seven Kings	d			15 36		15 46				15 56		16 06				16 16	16 26				16 36			16 46	
Ilford 2	d			15 39		15 49				15 59		16 09				16 19	16 29				16 39			16 49	
Manor Park	d			15 42		15 52				16 02		16 12				16 22	16 32				16 42			16 52	
Forest Gate	d			15 44		15 54				16 04		16 14				16 24	16 34				16 44			16 54	
Maryland	d			15 46		15 56				16 06		16 16				16 26	16 36				16 46			16 56	
Stratford 7 ⊖	d	15 22		15 49	15 36	15 59	15 39			16 09	15 52	16 19		16 01	16 05	16 29	16 39	16 19		16 22	16 49	16 36		16 59	16 39
London Liverpool Street 15 ⊖	a	15 31		15 57	15 45	16 07	15 48			16 17	16 01	16 27		16 10	16 14	16 37	16 47	16 28		16 31	16 57	16 45		17 07	16 48

			LE	LE 1	LE	LE 1	LE 1	LE 1		LE	LE	LE 1	LE 1	LE	LE 1	LE	LE 1	LE 1			LE	LE 1	LE 1	LE	LE 1
Southend Victoria	d					16 10						16 30					16 50						17 10		
Prittlewell	d					16 12						16 32					16 52						17 12		
Southend Airport ✈	d					16 15						16 35					16 55						17 15		
Rochford	d					16 18						16 38					16 58						17 18		
Hockley	d					16 21						16 41					17 01						17 21		
Rayleigh	d					16 26						16 46					17 06						17 26		
Southminster	d						16 16											16 56							
Burnham-on-Crouch	d						16 20											17 00							
Althorne	d						16 25											17 05							
North Fambridge	d						16 31											17 11							
South Woodham Ferrers	d						16 36											17 16							
Battlesbridge	d						16 40											17 20							
Wickford 2	d					16 31	16a46					16 51					17 11	17a26					17 31		
Billericay	d					16 37						16 57					17 17						17 37		
Shenfield 3	a					16 45						17 05					17 25						17 44		
Shenfield 3	d		16 34	16 38	16 44	16 45		16 51		16 54	17 04	17 05	17 08	17 14	17 20	17 24	17 25				17 34	17 38	17 45	17 44	17 51
Brentwood	d		16 37		16 47					16 57	17 07			17 17		17 27					17 37			17 47	
Harold Wood	d		16 42		16 52					17 02	17 12			17 22		17 32					17 42			17 52	
Gidea Park 2	d		16 46		16 56					17 06	17 16			17 26		17 36					17 46			17 56	
Romford	d		16 48		16 58	16 53				17 08	17 18			17 28	17 28	17 38					17 48		17 53	17 58	
Chadwell Heath	d		16 52		17 02					17 12	17 22			17 32		17 42					17 52			18 02	
Goodmayes	d		16 54		17 04					17 14	17 24			17 34		17 44					17 54			18 04	
Seven Kings	d		16 56		17 06					17 16	17 26			17 36		17 46					17 56			18 06	
Ilford 2	d		16 59		17 09					17 19	17 29			17 39		17 49					17 59			18 09	
Manor Park	d		17 02		17 12					17 22	17 32			17 42		17 52					18 02			18 12	
Forest Gate	d		17 04		17 14					17 24	17 34			17 44		17 54					18 04			18 14	
Maryland	d		17 06		17 16					17 26	17 36			17 46		17 56					18 06			18 16	
Stratford 7 ⊖	d		17 09	16 52	17 19	17 01		17 05		17 29	17 39	17 19	17 22	17 49	17 36	17 59	17 39				18 09	17 52	18 01	18 19	18 05
London Liverpool Street 15 ⊖	a		17 17	17 01	17 27	17 10		17 14		17 37	17 47	17 28	17 31	17 57	17 45	18 07	17 48				18 17	18 01	18 10	18 27	18 14

Table 5

Southend Victoria, Southminster and Shenfield - London

		LE	LE	LE 1		LE 1	LE 1	LE	LE 1	LE	LE 1	LE ◇1	LE	LE 1		LE	LE 1	LE 1	LE 1	LE	LE	LE 1	LE 1	LE	
Southend Victoria	d			17 30							17 50						18 10					18 30			
Prittlewell	d			17 32							17 52						18 12					18 32			
Southend Airport ✈	d			17 35							17 55						18 15					18 35			
Rochford	d			17 38							17 58						18 18					18 38			
Hockley	d			17 41							18 01						18 21					18 41			
Rayleigh	d			17 46							18 06						18 26					18 46			
Southminster	d					17 36												18 16							
Burnham-on-Crouch	d					17 40												18 20							
Althorne	d					17 45												18 25							
North Fambridge	d					17 51												18 31							
South Woodham Ferrers	d					17 56												18 36							
Battlesbridge	d					18 00												18 40							
Wickford 2	d			17 51		18a06					18 11						18 31	18a46				18 51			
Billericay	d			17 57							18 17						18 37					18 57			
Shenfield 3	a			18 05							18 25						18 45					19 05			
Shenfield 3	d	17 54	18 04	18 05			18 08	18 14	18 20	18 24	18 25		18 34	18 38		18 44	18 45		18 51	18 54	19 04	19 05	19 08	19 14	
Brentwood	d	17 57	18 07					18 17		18 27			18 37			18 47				18 57	19 07			19 17	
Harold Wood	d	18 02	18 12					18 22		18 32			18 42			18 52				19 02	19 12			19 22	
Gidea Park 2	d	18 06	18 16					18 26		18 36			18 46			18 56				19 06	19 16			19 26	
Romford	d	18 08	18 18					18 28	18 28	18 38			18 48			18 58	18 53			19 08	19 18			19 28	
Chadwell Heath	d	18 12	18 22					18 32		18 42			18 52			19 02				19 12	19 22			19 32	
Goodmayes	d	18 14	18 24					18 34		18 44			18 54			19 04				19 14	19 24			19 34	
Seven Kings	d	18 16	18 26					18 36		18 46			18 56			19 06				19 16	19 26			19 36	
Ilford 2	d	18 19	18 29					18 39		18 49			18 59			19 09				19 19	19 29			19 39	
Manor Park	d	18 22	18 32					18 42		18 52			19 02			19 12				19 22	19 32			19 42	
Forest Gate	d	18 24	18 34					18 44		18 54			19 04			19 14				19 24	19 34			19 44	
Maryland	d	18 26	18 36					18 46		18 56			19 06			19 16				19 26	19 36			19 46	
Stratford 7 ⊖	d	18 29	18 39	18 19			18 22	18 49	18 36	18 59	18 39		19 09	18 52		19 19	19 01		19 05	19 29	19 39	19 19	19 22	19 49	
London Liverpool Street 15 ⊖	a	18 37	18 47	18 28			18 31	18 57	18 45	19 07	18 48	18 55	19 17	19 01		19 27	19 10		19 14	19 37	19 47	19 28	19 31	19 57	

		LE 1	LE	LE 1	LE 1		LE	LE 1	LE	LE 1		LE 1	LE	LE	LE 1	LE 1	LE 1	LE	LE 1	LE		LE 1		LE	LE 1
Southend Victoria	d			18 50						19 10					19 30							19 50			
Prittlewell	d			18 52						19 12					19 32							19 52			
Southend Airport ✈	d			18 55						19 15					19 35							19 55			
Rochford	d			18 58						19 18					19 38							19 58			
Hockley	d			19 01						19 21					19 41							20 01			
Rayleigh	d			19 06						19 26					19 46							20 06			
Southminster	d				18 56											19 36									
Burnham-on-Crouch	d				19 00											19 40									
Althorne	d				19 05											19 45									
North Fambridge	d				19 11											19 51									
South Woodham Ferrers	d				19 16											19 56									
Battlesbridge	d				19 20											20 00									
Wickford 2	d			19 11	19a26					19 31					19 51	20a06						20 11			
Billericay	d			19 17						19 37					19 57							20 17			
Shenfield 3	a			19 25						19 45					20 05							20 25			
Shenfield 3	d	19 20	19 24	19 25			19 34	19 38	19 44	19 45		19 51	19 54	20 04	20 05		20 08	20 14	20 20	20 24		20 25		20 34	20 38
Brentwood	d		19 27				19 37		19 47				19 57	20 07				20 17		20 27				20 37	
Harold Wood	d		19 32				19 42		19 52				20 02	20 12				20 22		20 32				20 42	
Gidea Park 2	d		19 36				19 46		19 56				20 06	20 16				20 26		20 36				20 46	
Romford	d	19 28	19 38				19 48		19 58	19 53			20 08	20 18				20 28	20 28	20 38				20 48	
Chadwell Heath	d		19 42				19 52		20 02				20 12	20 22				20 32		20 42				20 52	
Goodmayes	d		19 44				19 54		20 04				20 14	20 24				20 34		20 44				20 54	
Seven Kings	d		19 46				19 56		20 06				20 16	20 26				20 36		20 46				20 56	
Ilford 2	d		19 49				19 59		20 09				20 19	20 29				20 39		20 49				20 59	
Manor Park	d		19 52				20 02		20 12				20 22	20 32				20 42		20 52				21 02	
Forest Gate	d		19 54				20 04		20 14				20 24	20 34				20 44		20 54				21 04	
Maryland	d		19 56				20 06		20 16				20 26	20 36				20 46		20 56				21 06	
Stratford 7 ⊖	d	19 36	19 59	19 39			20 09	19 52	20 19	20 01		20 05	20 29	20 39	20s19		20 22	20 49	20 36	20 59		20 39		21 09	20 52
London Liverpool Street 15 ⊖	a	19 45	20 07	19 48			20 17	20 01	20 27	20 10		20 14	20 37	20 47	20 28		20 31	20 57	20 45	21 07		20 48		21 17	21 01

		LE	LE 1	LE 1	LE 1	LE		LE 1	LE 1	LE	LE 1	LE 1	LE 1		LE	LE 1		LE	LE 1	LE 1	LE	LE 1	LE 1	LE 1	LE
Southend Victoria	d		20 10					20 30				20 50							21 10			21 30			
Prittlewell	d		20 12					20 32				20 52							21 12			21 32			
Southend Airport ✈	d		20 15					20 35				20 55							21 15			21 35			
Rochford	d		20 18					20 38				20 58							21 18			21 38			
Hockley	d		20 21					20 41				21 01							21 21			21 41			
Rayleigh	d		20 26					20 46				21 06							21 26			21 46			
Southminster	d			20 16									20 56										21 36		
Burnham-on-Crouch	d			20 20									21 00										21 40		
Althorne	d			20 25									21 05										21 45		
North Fambridge	d			20 31									21 11										21 51		
South Woodham Ferrers	d			20 36									21 16										21 56		
Battlesbridge	d			20 40									21 20										22 00		
Wickford 2	d		20 31	20a46				20 51				21 11	21a26						21 31			21 51	22a06		
Billericay	d		20 37					20 57				21 17							21 37			21 57			
Shenfield 3	a		20 45					21 05				21 25							21 45			22 05			
Shenfield 3	d	20 44	20 45		20 51	20 59		21 05	21 08	21 14	21 20	21 25			21 29	21 38		21 44	21 45	21 51	21 59	22 05		22 08	22 14
Brentwood	d	20 47				21 02				21 17					21 32			21 47			22 02				22 17
Harold Wood	d	20 52				21 07				21 22					21 37			21 52			22 07				22 22
Gidea Park 2	d	20 56				21 11				21 26					21 41			21 56			22 11				22 26
Romford	d	20 58	20 53			21 13				21 28	21 28				21 43			21 58	21 53		22 13				22 28
Chadwell Heath	d	21 02				21 17				21 32					21 47			22 02			22 17				22 32
Goodmayes	d	21 04				21 19				21 34					21 49			22 04			22 19				22 34
Seven Kings	d	21 06				21 21				21 36					21 51			22 06			22 21				22 36
Ilford 2	d	21 09				21 24				21 39					21 54			22 09			22 24				22 39
Manor Park	d	21 12				21 27				21 42					21 57			22 12			22 27				22 42
Forest Gate	d	21 14				21 29				21 44					21 59			22 14			22 29				22 44
Maryland	d	21 16				21 31				21 46					22 01			22 16			22 31				22 46
Stratford 7 ⊖	d	21 19	21 01		21 05	21 34		21 19	21 22	21 49	21 36	21 39			22 04	21 52		22 19	22 01	22 05	22 34	22 19		22 22	22 49
London Liverpool Street 15 ⊖	a	21 27	21 10		21 14	21 42		21 28	21 31	21 57	21 45	21 48			22 12	22 01		22 27	22 10	22 14	22 42	22 28		22 31	22 57

Table 5

Saturdays

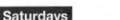

Southend Victoria, Southminster and Shenfield - London

		LE 1			LE	LE 1	LE 1	LE 1	LE 1	LE	LE 1	LE		LE 1	LE 1	LE	LE 1	LE	LE 1	LE 1	LE				
Southend Victoria	d					22 00								22 30					23 00						
Prittlewell	d					22 02								22 32					23 02						
Southend Airport ✈	d					22 05								22 35					23 05						
Rochford	d					22 08								22 38					23 08						
Hockley	d					22 11								22 41					23 11						
Rayleigh	d					22 16								22 46					23 16						
Southminster	d						22 16													22 56					
Burnham-on-Crouch	d						22 20													23 00					
Althorne	d						22 25													23 05					
North Fambridge	d						22 31													23 11					
South Woodham Ferrers	d						22 36													23 16					
Battlesbridge	d						22 40													23 20					
Wickford 2	d					22 21	22a46							22 51					23 21	23 26					
Billericay	d					22 27								22 57					23 27	23 32					
Shenfield 3	a					22 35								23 05					23 35	23 39					
Shenfield 3	d	22 20			22 29	22 35		22 38		22 44	22 51	22 59		23 05	23 08	23 14	23 20	23 29	23 35	23 39	23 44				
Brentwood	d				22 32					22 47		23 02				23 17		23 32			23 47				
Harold Wood	d				22 37					22 52		23 07				23 22		23 37			23 52				
Gidea Park 2	d				22 41					22 56		23 11				23 26		23 41			23 56				
Romford	d	22 28			22 43					22 58		23 13				23 28	23 28	23 43		23 47	23 58				
Chadwell Heath	d				22 47					23 02		23 17				23 32		23 47			00 02				
Goodmayes	d				22 49					23 04		23 19				23 34		23 49			00 04				
Seven Kings	d				22 51					23 06		23 21				23 36		23 51			00 06				
Ilford 2	d				22 54					23 09		23 24				23 39		23 54			00 09				
Manor Park	d				22 57					23 12		23 27				23 42		23 57			00 12				
Forest Gate	d				22 59					23 14		23 29				23 44		23 59			00 14				
Maryland	d				23 01					23 16		23 31				23 46		00 01			00 16				
Stratford 7 ⊖	d	22 36			23 04	22 49		22 52	23 05	23 19	23 05	23 34		23 19	23 22	23 49	23 36	00 04	23 49	23 56	00 19				
London Liverpool Street 15 ⊖	a	22 46			23 12	22 58		23 01	23 17	23 27	23 14	23 42		23 28	23 31	23 57	23 45	00 12	23 58	00 05	00 27				

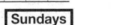

Sundays

		LE ◇1 A	LE A	LE 1 A	LE A	LE	LE	LE	LE 1	LE		LE 1	LE	LE 1	LE	LE 1	LE	LE 1	LE	LE 1		LE	LE 1	LE 1	LE 1
Southend Victoria	d								06 15					06 45				07 15						07 49	
Prittlewell	d																								
Southend Airport ✈	d								06 19					06 49				07 19						07 53	
Rochford	d								06 22					06 52				07 22						07 56	
Hockley	d								06 25					06 55				07 25						07 59	
Rayleigh	d								06 30					07 00				07 30						08 04	
Southminster	d			22p56																					08 05
Burnham-on-Crouch	d			23p00																					08 09
Althorne	d			23p05																					08 14
North Fambridge	d			23p11																					08 20
South Woodham Ferrers	d			23p16																					08 25
Battlesbridge	d			23p20																					08 29
Wickford 2	d			23p26					06 35					07 05				07 35						08 09	08a35
Billericay	d			23p32					06 41					07 11				07 41						08 15	
Shenfield 3	a			23p39					06 52					07 22				07 52						08 22	
Shenfield 3	d		23p29	23p39	23p44			06 43	06 53			07 07	07 13	07 23		07 37	07 43	07 53		08 07		08 13	08 20	08 23	
Brentwood	d		23p32	⌇	23p47			06 46	06 56				07 16	07 26			07 46	07 56				08 16		08 26	
Harold Wood	d		23p37	⌇	23p52			06 51	07 01				07 21	07 31			07 51	08 01				08 21		08 31	
Gidea Park 2	d		23p41	⌇	23p56	05 55	06 25	06 55	07 05	07 11			07 25	07 35	07 41		07 55	08 05	08 11			08 25		08 35	
Romford	d		23p43	23p47	23p58	05 57	06 27	06 57	07 07	07 13			07 27	07 37	07 43		07 57	08 07	08 13			08 27		08 37	
Chadwell Heath	d		23p47	⌇	00 02	06 01	06 31	07 01		07 17			07 31		07 47		08 01		08 17			08 31			
Goodmayes	d		23p49	⌇	00 04	06 03	06 33	07 03		07 19			07 33		07 49		08 03		08 19			08 33			
Seven Kings	d		23p51	⌇	00 06	06 05	06 35	07 05		07 21			07 35		07 51		08 05		08 21			08 35			
Ilford 2	d		23p54	⌇	00 09	06 08	06 38	07 08		07 24			07 38		07 54		08 08		08 24			08 38			
Manor Park	d		23p57	⌇	00 12	06 10	06 40	07 10		07 26			07 40		07 56		08 10		08 26			08 40			
Forest Gate	d		23p59	⌇	00 14	06 12	06 42	07 12		07 28			07 42		07 58		08 12		08 28			08 42			
Maryland	d		00 01	⌇	00 16	06 14	06 44	07 14					07 44				08 14					08 44			
Stratford 7 ⊖	d	23b52	00 04	23p56	00 19	06 16	06 46	07 16	07 19	07 31		07s34	07 46	07 49	08 01	08s04	08 16	08 19	08 31	08s34		08 46	08s49	08 49	
London Liverpool Street 15 ⊖	a	00 02	00 12	00 05	00 27	06 26	06 56	07 26	07 27	07 41		07 42	07 56	07 57	08 11	08 12	08 26	08 27	08 41	08 42		08 56	08 59	08 59	

A not 22 May

b Previous night, stops to set down only

		LE	LE 1	LE	LE 1	LE		LE 1	LE	LE 1	LE 1	LE	LE 1	LE	LE 1	LE		LE 1	LE	LE 1	LE 1	LE	LE 1	LE	
Southend Victoria	d				08 19					08 49					09 19					09 49					
Prittlewell	d																								
Southend Airport ✈	d				08 23					08 53					09 23					09 53					
Rochford	d				08 26					08 56					09 26					09 56					
Hockley	d				08 29					08 59					09 29					09 59					
Rayleigh	d				08 34					09 04					09 34					10 04					
Southminster	d										09 05										10 05				
Burnham-on-Crouch	d										09 09										10 09				
Althorne	d										09 14										10 14				
North Fambridge	d										09 20										10 20				
South Woodham Ferrers	d										09 25										10 25				
Battlesbridge	d										09 29										10 29				
Wickford 2	d				08 39					09 09	09a35				09 39					10 09	10a35				
Billericay	d				08 45					09 15					09 45					10 15					
Shenfield 3	a				08 52					09 22					09 52					10 22					
Shenfield 3	d		08 41	08 43	08 53			09 11	09 13	09 23			09 41	09 43	09 53			10 11	10 13	10 23			10 41	10 43	
Brentwood	d			08 46	08 56				09 16	09 26				09 46	09 56				10 16	10 26				10 46	
Harold Wood	d			08 51	09 01				09 21	09 31				09 51	10 01				10 21	10 31				10 51	
Gidea Park 2	d	08 41		08 55	09 05	09 11			09 25	09 35		09 41		09 55	10 05	10 11			10 25	10 35		10 41		10 55	
Romford	d	08 43		08 57	09 07	09 13			09 27	09 37		09 43		09 57	10 07	10 13			10 27	10 37		10 43		10 57	
Chadwell Heath	d	08 47		09 01		09 17			09 31			09 47		10 01		10 17			10 31			10 47		11 01	
Goodmayes	d	08 49		09 03		09 19			09 33			09 49		10 03		10 19			10 33			10 49		11 03	
Seven Kings	d	08 51		09 05		09 21			09 35			09 51		10 05		10 21			10 35			10 51		11 05	
Ilford 2	d	08 54		09 08		09 24			09 38			09 54		10 08		10 24			10 38			10 54		11 08	
Manor Park	d	08 56		09 10		09 26			09 40			09 56		10 10		10 26			10 40			10 56		11 10	
Forest Gate	d	08 58		09 12		09 28			09 42			09 58		10 12		10 28			10 42			10 58		11 12	
Maryland	d			09 14					09 44					10 14					10 44					11 14	
Stratford 7 ⊖	d	09 01	09s04	09 16	09 19	09 31		09s34	09 46	09 49		10 01	10s04	10 16	10 21	10 31		10s34	10 46	10 49		11 01	11s04	11 16	
London Liverpool Street 15 ⊖	a	09 11	09 12	09 26	09 29	09 41		09 42	09 56	09 59		10 11	10 12	10 26	10 31	10 41		10 42	10 56	10 59		11 11	11 12	11 26	

Table 5

Sundays

Southend Victoria, Southminster and Shenfield - London

		LE 1		LE 1		LE	LE 1	LE	LE 1	LE 1	LE	LE 1	LE	LE 1		LE	LE 1	LE	LE 1	LE 1	LE	LE 1	LE	LE 1
Southend Victoria	d	10 19		16 19					16 49					17 19					17 49					18 19
Prittlewell	d																							
Southend Airport ✈	d	10 23		16 23					16 53					17 23					17 53					18 23
Rochford	d	10 26		16 26					16 56					17 26					17 56					18 26
Hockley	d	10 29		16 29					16 59					17 29					17 59					18 29
Rayleigh	d	10 34		16 34					17 04					17 34					18 04					18 34
Southminster	d									17 05										18 05				
Burnham-on-Crouch	d									17 09										18 09				
Althorne	d									17 14										18 14				
North Fambridge	d									17 20										18 20				
South Woodham Ferrers	d		and at							17 25										18 25				
Battlesbridge	d		the same							17 29										18 29				
Wickford 2	d	10 39	minutes	16 39					17 09	17a35				17 39					18 09	18a35				18 39
Billericay	d	10 45	past	16 45					17 15					17 45					18 15					18 45
Shenfield 3	a	10 52	each	16 52					17 22					17 52					18 22					18 52
Shenfield 3	d	10 53	hour until	16 53			17 11	17 13	17 23			17 41	17 43	17 53			18 11	18 13	18 23			18 41	18 43	18 53
Brentwood	d	10 56		16 56				17 16	17 26				17 46	17 56				18 16	18 26				18 46	18 56
Harold Wood	d	11 01		17 01				17 21	17 31				17 51	18 01				18 21	18 31				18 51	19 01
Gidea Park 2	d	11 05		17 05		17 11		17 25	17 35		17 41		17 55	18 05		18 11		18 25	18 35		18 41		18 55	19 05
Romford	d	11 07		17 07		17 13		17 27	17 37		17 43		17 57	18 07		18 13		18 27	18 37		18 43		18 57	19 07
Chadwell Heath	d					17 17		17 31			17 47		18 01			18 17		18 31			18 47		19 01	
Goodmayes	d					17 19		17 33			17 49		18 03			18 19		18 33			18 49		19 03	
Seven Kings	d					17 21		17 35			17 51		18 05			18 21		18 35			18 51		19 05	
Ilford 2	d					17 24		17 38			17 54		18 08			18 24		18 38			18 54		19 08	
Manor Park	d					17 26		17 40			17 56		18 10			18 26		18 40			18 56		19 10	
Forest Gate	d					17 28		17 42			17 58		18 12			18 28		18 42			18 58		19 12	
Maryland	d							17 44					18 14					18 44					19 14	
Stratford 7 ⊖	d	11 19		17 19		17 31	17s34	17 46	17 49		18 01	18s04	18 16	18 19		18 31	18s34	18 46	18 49		19 01	19s04	19 16	19 19
London Liverpool Street 15 ⊖	a	11 29		17 29		17 41	17 42	17 56	17 59		18 11	18 12	18 26	18 31		18 41	18 42	18 56	18 59		19 11	19 12	19 26	19 29

			LE	LE 1	LE	LE 1	LE 1	LE	LE 1	LE	LE 1		LE	LE 1	LE	LE 1	LE 1	LE	LE 1	LE	LE 1		LE	LE 1	LE
Southend Victoria	d					18 49					19 19					19 49					20 19				
Prittlewell	d																								
Southend Airport ✈	d					18 53					19 23					19 53					20 23				
Rochford	d					18 56					19 26					19 56					20 26				
Hockley	d					18 59					19 29					19 59					20 29				
Rayleigh	d					19 04					19 34					20 04					20 34				
Southminster	d						19 05										20 05								
Burnham-on-Crouch	d						19 09										20 09								
Althorne	d						19 14										20 14								
North Fambridge	d						19 20										20 20								
South Woodham Ferrers	d						19 25										20 25								
Battlesbridge	d						19 29										20 29								
Wickford 2	d					19 09	19a35				19 39					20 09	20a35				20 39				
Billericay	d					19 15					19 45					20 15					20 45				
Shenfield 3	a					19 22					19 52					20 22					20 52				
Shenfield 3	d			19 11	19 13	19 23			19 41	19 43	19 53			20 11	20 13	20 23			20 41	20 43	20 53			21 11	21 13
Brentwood	d				19 16	19 26				19 46	19 56				20 16	20 26				20 46	20 56				21 16
Harold Wood	d				19 21	19 31				19 51	20 01				20 21	20 31				20 51	21 01				21 21
Gidea Park 2	d		19 11		19 25	19 35		19 41		19 55	20 05		20 11		20 25	20 35		20 41		20 55	21 05		21 11		21 25
Romford	d		19 13		19 27	19 37		19 43		19 57	20 07		20 13		20 27	20 37		20 43		20 57	21 07		21 13		21 27
Chadwell Heath	d		19 17		19 31			19 47		20 01			20 17		20 31			20 47		21 01			21 17		21 31
Goodmayes	d		19 19		19 33			19 49		20 03			20 19		20 33			20 49		21 03			21 19		21 33
Seven Kings	d		19 21		19 35			19 51		20 05			20 21		20 35			20 51		21 05			21 21		21 35
Ilford 2	d		19 24		19 38			19 54		20 08			20 24		20 38			20 54		21 08			21 24		21 38
Manor Park	d		19 26		19 40			19 56		20 10			20 26		20 40			20 56		21 10			21 26		21 40
Forest Gate	d		19 28		19 42			19 58		20 12			20 28		20 42			20 58		21 12			21 28		21 42
Maryland	d				19 44					20 14					20 44					21 14					21 44
Stratford 7 ⊖	d		19 31	19s34	19 46	19 49		20 01	20s04	20 16	20 19		20 31	20s34	20 46	20 49		21 01	21s04	21 16	21 19		21 31	21s34	21 46
London Liverpool Street 15 ⊖	a		19 41	19 42	19 56	19 59		20 11	20 12	20 26	20 29		20 41	20 42	20 56	20 59		21 11	21 12	21 26	21 29		21 41	21 42	21 56

		LE 1	LE 1	LE 1	LE 1	LE	LE 1		LE 1	LE	LE 1	LE 1	LE 1	LE	LE 1	LE 1	LE 1		LE	LE 1	LE 1	LE			
Southend Victoria	d	20 49					21 19				21 49				22 19					22 49					
Prittlewell	d																								
Southend Airport ✈	d	20 53					21 23				21 53				22 23					22 53					
Rochford	d	20 56					21 26				21 56				22 26					22 56					
Hockley	d	20 59					21 29				21 59				22 29					22 59					
Rayleigh	d	21 04					21 34				22 04				22 34					23 04					
Southminster	d		21 05									22 05									22 45				
Burnham-on-Crouch	d		21 09									22 09									22 49				
Althorne	d		21 14									22 14									22 54				
North Fambridge	d		21 20									22 20									23 00				
South Woodham Ferrers	d		21 25									22 25									23 05				
Battlesbridge	d		21 29									22 29									23 09				
Wickford 2	d	21 09	21a35				21 39				22 09	22a35			22 39					23 09	23 15				
Billericay	d	21 15					21 45				22 15				22 45					23 15					
Shenfield 3	a	21 22					21 52				22 22				22 52					23 22	23 26				
Shenfield 3	d	21 23		21 26	21 41	21 43	21 53		22 11	22 13	22 23		22 41	22 43	22 53		23 11		23 13	23 23		23 43			
Brentwood	d	21 26				21 46	21 56			22 16	22 26			22 46	22 56				23 16	23 26		23 46			
Harold Wood	d	21 31				21 51	22 01			22 21	22 31			22 51	23 01				23 21	23 31		23 51			
Gidea Park 2	d	21 35				21 55	22 05			22 25	22 35			22 55	23 05				23 25	23 35		23 55			
Romford	d	21 37				21 57	22 07			22 27	22 37			22 57	23 07				23 27	23 37		23 57			
Chadwell Heath	d					22 01				22 31				23 01					23 31			00 01			
Goodmayes	d					22 03				22 33				23 03					23 33			00 03			
Seven Kings	d					22 05				22 35				23 05					23 35			00 05			
Ilford 2	d					22 08				22 38				23 08					23 38			00 08			
Manor Park	d					22 10				22 40				23 10					23 40			00 10			
Forest Gate	d					22 12				22 42				23 12					23 42			00 12			
Maryland	d					22 14				22 44				23 14					23 44			00 14			
Stratford 7 ⊖	d	21 49		21s51	22s04	22 16	22 19		22s34	22 46	22 49		23s04	23 16	23 19	23 22	23s34		23 46	23 49		00 16			
London Liverpool Street 15 ⊖	a	21 59		21 59	22 12	22 26	22 29		22 42	22 56	22 59		23 12	23 26	23 31	23 36	23 42		23 56	23 59		00 26			

Table 10

Mondays to Fridays

Marks Tey - Sudbury

Miles			LE	LE	LE	LE	LE	LE	LE	LE	LE	LE	LE	LE	LE	LE	LE	LE	LE	LE
0	**Colchester 4**	d					09 51													
5	Marks Tey 2	d	06 01	06 53	07 40	08 27	10 01	11 01	12 01	13 01	14 01	15 01	16 01	17 07	18 05	19 11	20 05	21 01	22 01	23 01
8½	Chappel & Wakes Colne	d	06 07	06 59		08 33	10 07	11 07	12 07	13 07	14 07	15 07	16 07	17 13	18 11	19 17	20 11	21 07	22 07	23 07
11¾	Bures	d	06 13	07 05		08 39	10 13	11 13	12 13	13 13	14 13	15 13	16 13	17 19	18 17	19 23	20 17	21 13	22 13	23 13
16¾	**Sudbury**	a	06 21	07 13	07 56	08 47	10 21	11 21	12 21	13 21	14 21	15 21	16 21	17 27	18 25	19 31	20 25	21 21	22 21	23 21

Saturdays

		LE	LE	LE	LE	LE	LE	LE	LE	LE	LE	LE	LE	LE	LE	LE	LE	LE	LE
Colchester 4	d	05 50																	
Marks Tey 2	d	06 01	07 01	08 01	09 01	10 01	11 01	12 01	13 01	14 01	15 01	16 01	17 01	18 01	19 01	20 01	21 01	22 01	23 01
Chappel & Wakes Colne	d	06 07	07 07	08 07	09 07	10 07	11 07	12 07	13 07	14 07	15 07	16 07	17 07	18 07	19 07	20 07	21 07	22 07	23 07
Bures	d	06 13	07 13	08 13	09 13	10 13	11 13	12 13	13 13	14 13	15 13	16 13	17 13	18 13	19 13	20 13	21 13	22 13	23 13
Sudbury	a	06 21	07 21	08 21	09 21	10 21	11 21	12 21	13 21	14 21	15 21	16 21	17 21	18 21	19 21	20 21	21 21	22 21	23 21

Sundays

		LE	LE	LE	LE	LE	LE	LE	LE	LE	LE	LE	LE	LE	LE	LE
Colchester 4	d	07 07														
Marks Tey 2	d	07 15	08 15	09 15	10 15	11 15	12 15	13 15	14 15	15 15	16 15	17 15	18 15	19 15	20 15	21 15
Chappel & Wakes Colne	d	07 21	08 21	09 21	10 21	11 21	12 21	13 21	14 21	15 21	16 21	17 21	18 21	19 21	20 21	21 21
Bures	d	07 27	08 27	09 27	10 27	11 27	12 27	13 27	14 27	15 27	16 27	17 27	18 27	19 27	20 27	21 27
Sudbury	a	07 35	08 35	09 35	10 35	11 35	12 35	13 35	14 35	15 35	16 35	17 35	18 35	19 35	20 35	21 35

Table 10

Mondays to Fridays

Sudbury - Marks Tey

Miles			LE	LE	LE	LE	LE	LE	LE	LE	LE	LE	LE	LE	LE	LE	LE	LE	LE	LE	LE
0	**Sudbury**	d	05 30	06 30	07 17	08 00	08 55	10 26	11 26	12 26	13 26	14 26	15 26	16 32	17 32	18 37	19 37	20 32	21 26	22 26	23 26
5	Bures	d	05 37	06 37	07 24	08 07	09 02	10 33	11 33	12 33	13 33	14 33	15 33	16 39	17 39	18 44	19 44	20 39	21 33	22 33	23 33
8¼	Chappel & Wakes Colne	d	05 43	06 43	07 30	08 13	09 08	10 39	11 39	12 39	13 39	14 39	15 39	16 45	17 45	18 50	19 50	20 45	21 39	22 39	23 39
11¾	Marks Tey 2	a	05 49	06 49	07 36	08 19	09 14	10 45	11 45	12 45	13 45	14 45	15 45	16 51	17 51	18 56	19 56	20 51	21 45	22 45	23 45
16¾	**Colchester 4**	a					09 28														23 59

Saturdays

		LE	LE	LE	LE	LE	LE	LE	LE	LE	LE	LE	LE	LE	LE	LE	LE	LE	LE
Sudbury	d	06 26	07 26	08 26	09 26	10 26	11 26	12 26	13 26	14 26	15 26	16 26	17 26	18 26	19 26	20 26	21 26	22 26	23 26
Bures	d	06 33	07 33	08 33	09 33	10 33	11 33	12 33	13 33	14 33	15 33	16 33	17 33	18 33	19 33	20 33	21 33	22 33	23 33
Chappel & Wakes Colne	d	06 39	07 39	08 39	09 39	10 39	11 39	12 39	13 39	14 39	15 39	16 39	17 39	18 39	19 39	20 39	21 39	22 39	23 39
Marks Tey 2	a	06 45	07 45	08 45	09 45	10 45	11 45	12 45	13 45	14 45	15 45	16 45	17 45	18 45	19 45	20 45	21 45	22 45	23 45
Colchester 4	a																		23 59

Sundays

		LE	LE	LE	LE	LE	LE	LE	LE	LE	LE	LE	LE	LE	LE	LE
Sudbury	d	07 40	08 40	09 40	10 40	11 40	12 40	13 40	14 40	15 40	16 40	17 40	18 40	19 40	20 40	21 40
Bures	d	07 47	08 47	09 47	10 47	11 47	12 47	13 47	14 47	15 47	16 47	17 47	18 47	19 47	20 47	21 47
Chappel & Wakes Colne	d	07 53	08 53	09 53	10 53	11 53	12 53	13 53	14 53	15 53	16 53	17 53	18 53	19 53	20 53	21 53
Marks Tey 2	a	07 59	08 59	09 59	10 59	11 59	12 59	13 59	14 59	15 59	16 59	17 59	18 59	19 59	20 59	21 59
Colchester 4	a															22 08

London - Chelmsford, Colchester, Walton-on-Naze, Clacton, Harwich, Ipswich and Norwich

Miles	Miles	Miles	Miles	Miles			LE MX ◇■1 🛏	LE MO ◇■1 🛏	LE MO ■1	LE MX ■1	LE MO ■1	LE MX ■1	LE MX ◇■1 🛏	LE MO ◇■1	LE MX ■1		LE MO ■1	LE MX ■1	LE MO ■1	LE MX ■1	LE	LE ■1	LE ◇■1	LE ■1	LE ■1
0	—	—	—	—	**London Liverpool Street** 15 ⊖	d	22p30	22p30	22p32	23p02	23p02	23p18	23p30	23p30			23p32	23p48	00 02	00 18					
4	—	—	—	—	Stratford 7 ⊖	d	22b38		22p39	23p09	23p09	23p25	23b38				23p39	23p55	00 09	00 25					
12¼	—	—	—	—	Romford	d																			
20¼	—	—	—	—	Shenfield 3	d			23p01	23p25	23p31	23p41					00 01	00 11	00 31	00 47					
23½	—	—	—	—	Ingatestone	d					23p35	23p45						00 15	00 35	00 51					
29¾	—	—	—	—	**Chelmsford** 3	d	23p03		23p10	23p34	23p42	23p52	00 03				00 10	00 22	00 42	00 58					
36	—	—	—	—	Hatfield Peverel	d				23p40	23p48							00 28	00 48	01 04					
38½	0	—	—	—	**Witham** 2	d			23p21	23p47	23p55	00 03			00 05		00 21	00 35	00 55	01 11		05 21			
—	3	—	—	—	White Notley	d									00 12							05 28			
—	4¼	—	—	—	Cressing	d									00 14							05 30			
—	5½	—	—	—	Braintree Freeport	d									00 17							05 33			
—	6¼	—	—	—	**Braintree**	a									00 21							05 37			
42¼	—	—	—	—	Kelvedon	d				23p51	23p59							00 39	00 59	01 15					
46¾	—	—	—	—	Marks Tey 2	d			23p28	23p57	00 05						00 28	00 45	01 05	01 21					
51¾	—	—	—	—	**Colchester** 4	a	23p22	23p23	23p36	00 04	00 12	00 15	00 22	00 27			00 39	00 57	01 18	01 41					
—	0	0	—	—	**Colchester** 4	d	23p23	23p23	23p36	00 04	00 12	00 16	00 23	00 27									05 40		
—	—	2¼	—	—	Colchester Town	a																			
—	—	—	—	—		d																			
—	2¾	3¼	—	—	Hythe	d																			
—	—	5¾	—	—	Wivenhoe 3	d			23p44			00 23													
—	—	7½	—	—	Alresford (Essex)	d			23p47			00 27													
—	—	9¾	—	—	Great Bentley	d			23p51			00 31													
—	—	12½	—	—	Weeley	d																			
—	—	14¾	0	—	Thorpe-le-Soken 1	a			23p58			00 38													
—	—	—	—	—		d			23p58			00 38													06 03
—	—	—	4¾	—	**Clacton-on-Sea**	a			00 07			00 51													
—	—	17¼	—	—	Kirby Cross	d																			06 12
—	—	18½	—	—	Frinton-on-Sea	d																			06 15
—	—	19¾	—	—	**Walton-on-the-Naze**	a																			06 19
59½	—	—	—	0	Manningtree 2	d	23p31	23p31		00 12	00 20		00 31	00 35									05 49	05 56	
—	—	—	—	1¾	Mistley	d																		06 00	
—	—	—	—	5¾	Wrabness	d																		06 05	
—	—	—	—	9½	Harwich International	d																		06 13	
—	—	—	—	10¾	Dovercourt	d																		06 16	
—	—	—	—	11¼	**Harwich Town**	a																		06 18	
68¾	—	—	—	—	**Ipswich**	a	23p43	23p43		00 28	00 36		00 43	00 47									05 59		
—	—	—	—	—		d	23p44	23p44					00 44	00 48							05 10		06 00		
77	—	—	—	—	Needham Market	d															05 20				
80¾	—	—	—	—	Stowmarket	d	23p55	23p55					00 55	00 59							05a26		06 12		
—	—	—	—	—	**Peterborough** 8	a																	07 38		
95	—	—	—	—	Diss	d	00 08	00 08					01 08	01 12											
115	—	—	—	—	**Norwich**	a	00 39	00 41					01 43	01 45											

		LE ■1	LE ■1	LE ■1	LE ■1	LE ■1	LE ■1	LE ■1	LE ■1	LE ■1		LE ■1	LE ■1	LE ◇■1	LE ■1	LE ■1	LE ■1	LE ■1	LE ◇■1	LE ■1		LE ■1	LE ■1	LE ■1
London Liverpool Street 15 ⊖	d						05 23							06 00	06 02	06 12			06 25				06 38	06 48
Stratford 7 ⊖	d						05 30								06 09	06 19			06u33				06 45	06 55
Romford	d						05 38																	
Shenfield 3	d						05 48								06 25	06 36							07 01	07 11
Ingatestone	d						05 52									06 40								07 15
Chelmsford 3	d						05 59								06 34	06 47			06 58				07 10	07 22
Hatfield Peverel	d						06 05									06 53								
Witham 2	d						06 12	06 16							06 45	07 03			07 09				07 21	07 33
White Notley	d							06 23								07 10								
Cressing	d							06 25								07 12								
Braintree Freeport	d							06 28								07 15								
Braintree	a							06 32								07 19								
Kelvedon	d						06 16								06 49								07 25	
Marks Tey 2	d						06 22								06 55								07 31	07 40
Colchester 4	a						06 29							06 46	07 02				07 22				07 38	07 47
Colchester 4	d		05 58		06 15		06 29		06 35					06 47	07 02		07 10		07 23			07 26	07 43	07 48
Colchester Town	a								06 42													07 34		07 56
	d																					07 38		
Hythe	d														07 07							07 42		
Wivenhoe 3	d						06 37								07 11							07 46		
Alresford (Essex)	d														07 14							07 50		
Great Bentley	d														07 18							07 54		
Weeley	d														07 22									
Thorpe-le-Soken 1	a						06 50								07 28							08 01		
	d					06 31	06 50					06 56			07 28					07 38		08 01		
Clacton-on-Sea	a						06 59								07 37							08 10		
Kirby Cross	d					06 39						07 06								07 47				
Frinton-on-Sea	d					06 42						07 09								07 50				
Walton-on-the-Naze	a					06 46						07 13								07 54				
Manningtree 2	d		06 07	06 16	06 23									06 55			07 18	07 22	07 31				07 51	
Mistley	d			06 20														07 26					07 55	
Wrabness	d			06 25														07 31					08 01	
Harwich International	d			06 33														07 39					08 10	
Dovercourt	d			06 36														07 42					08 13	
Harwich Town	a			06 38														07 44					08 15	
Ipswich	a		06 21		06 34									07 07			07 30		07 42					
	d	06 16								06 39			06 56	07 08					07 44					
Needham Market	d	06 25											07 05											
Stowmarket	d	06a30								06 51			07a10	07 19					07 55					
Peterborough 8	a																							
Diss	d									07 04				07 32					08 08					
Norwich	a									07 24				07 51					08 27					

b Previous night, stops to pick up only

London - Chelmsford, Colchester, Walton-on-Naze, Clacton, Harwich, Ipswich and Norwich

		LE 1	LE ◇1	LE 1	LE 1	LE 1	LE 1		LE 1	LE 1	LE ◇1 ☕	LE 1	LE 1		LE ◇1 ☕	LE 1	LE 1		LE 1	LE 1	LE 1	LE	LE 1	LE ◇1 ☕	LE 1
London Liverpool Street 15 ⊖	d		07 00	07 02			07 08		07 18		07 30	07 38	07 48		08 00				08 02	08 17				08 30	08 36
Stratford 7 ⊖	d			07 09			07 15		07 25		07u38	07 45	07 55						08 09	08 25				08u38	08 45
Romford	d																								
Shenfield 3	d		07u22	07 25			07 31		07 41			08 01	08 11						08 25	08 41					09 03
Ingatestone	d								07 45			08 05							08 29	08 45					
Chelmsford 3	d			07 34			07 40		07 52		08 03	08 12	08 20						08 36	08 52				09 03	09 12
Hatfield Peverel	d			07 40															08 42						
Witham 2	d			07 48			07 51		08 03			08 23	08 35	08 38					08 49	09 03					09 23
White Notley	d			07 55									08 42												
Cressing	d			07 57									08 44												
Braintree Freeport	d			08 00									08 47												
Braintree	a			08 04									08 51												
Kelvedon	d						07 55					08 27							08 53						09 27
Marks Tey 2	d						08 01					08 33							08 59			09 19			09 33
Colchester 4	a		07 50				08 08		08 15		08 22	08 40		08 53	08 48				09 06	09 15		09 28		09 22	09 40
Colchester 4	d		07 51			07 56	08 08		08 16		08 23	08 41		08 56	08 48				09 06	09 16			09 20	09 23	09 41
Colchester Town	a					08 03						08 49		09 03									09 27		09 49
	d					08 07								09 07											
Hythe	d					08 11			08 20					09 11											
Wivenhoe 3	d					08 15			08 24					09 15						09 23					
Alresford (Essex)	d					08 19								09 19											
Great Bentley	d					08 23								09 23											
Weeley	d					08 26				←				09 26							←				
Thorpe-le-Soken 1	a					08 31			08 35	08 31				09 31						09 35	09 31				
	d					08 37			08 35	08 37				09 37						09 35	09 37				
Clacton-on-Sea	a					→			08 45					→						09 44					
Kirby Cross	d									08 42											09 42				
Frinton-on-Sea	d									08 45											09 45				
Walton-on-the-Naze	a									08 49											09 49				
Manningtree 2	d		07 59				08 16				08 31				08 56	09 02			09 14					09 31	
Mistley	d				08 02											09 06									
Wrabness	d															09 11									
Harwich International	d															09 19									
Dovercourt	d															09 22									
Harwich Town	a															09 24									
Ipswich	a		08 11		08 17		08 29				08 43				09 08				09 26					09 43	
	d	08 03	08 12		08 19						08 44				09 09		09 19							09 44	
Needham Market	d				08 28												09 28								
Stowmarket	d	08 15	08 23		08a33						08 55						09a33							09 55	
Peterborough 8	a	09 39																							
Diss	d		08 36								09 08				09 30									10 08	
Norwich	a		08 55								09 27				09 49									10 27	

		LE 1	LE 1		LE ◇1 ☕	LE 1	LE 1	LE 1	LE 1	LE 1	LE 1	LE 1	LE ◇1 ☕		LE 1	LE 1	LE ◇1 ☕	LE 1	LE 1	LE 1	LE 1	LE 1	LE 1		LE 1
London Liverpool Street 15 ⊖	d	08 48			09 00				09 02	09 18			09 30		09 38	09 48	10 00				10 02	10 18			
Stratford 7 ⊖	d	08 55							09 09	09 25			09u38		09 45	09 55					10 09	10 25			
Romford	d														09 53										
Shenfield 3	d	09 11							09 25	09 41					10 03	10 11					10 25	10 41			
Ingatestone	d	09 15								09 45						10 15						10 45			
Chelmsford 3	d	09 22							09 34	09 52			10 03		10 12	10 22					10 34	10 52			
Hatfield Peverel	d								09 40												10 40				
Witham 2	d	09 35							09 47	10 03					10 23	10 34					10 47	11 03			
White Notley	d	09 42														10 41									
Cressing	d	09 44														10 43									
Braintree Freeport	d	09 47														10 46									
Braintree	a	09 51														10 50									
Kelvedon	d								09 51						10 27						10 51				
Marks Tey 2	d								09 57						10 33						10 57				
Colchester 4	a				09 46				10 04	10 15			10 22		10 40		10 46				11 04	11 15			
Colchester 4	d				09 47			09 56	10 04	10 16		10 20	10 23		10 41		10 47			10 56	11 04	11 16			11 20
Colchester Town	a							10 03				10 27			10 49					11 03					11 27
	d							10 07												11 07					
Hythe	d							10 11												11 11					
Wivenhoe 3	d							10 15		10 23										11 15		11 23			
Alresford (Essex)	d							10 19												11 19					
Great Bentley	d							10 23												11 23					
Weeley	d							10 26			←									11 26			←		
Thorpe-le-Soken 1	a							10 31		10 35	10 31									11 31		11 35	11 31		
	d							10 37		10 35	10 37									11 37		11 35	11 37		
Clacton-on-Sea	a							→		10 44										→		11 44			
Kirby Cross	d										10 42												11 42		
Frinton-on-Sea	d										10 45												11 45		
Walton-on-the-Naze	a										10 49												11 49		
Manningtree 2	d				09 55	10 00			10 12				10 31				10 55	11 00			11 12				
Mistley	d					10 04												11 04							
Wrabness	d					10 09												11 09							
Harwich International	d					10 17												11 17							
Dovercourt	d					10 20												11 20							
Harwich Town	a					10 22												11 22							
Ipswich	a				10 07				10 25				10 43				11 07				11 25				
	d		10 00		10 08		10 19						10 44				11 08		11 19						
Needham Market	d						10 28												11 28						
Stowmarket	d		10 12				10a33						10 55						11a33						
Peterborough 8	a		11 37																						
Diss	d				10 29								11 08				11 29								
Norwich	a				10 48								11 27				11 48								

London - Chelmsford, Colchester, Walton-on-Naze, Clacton, Harwich, Ipswich and Norwich

		LE ◇1 ⊏	LE 1	LE 1	LE 1	LE ◇1 ⊏	LE 1	LE 1	LE 1		LE 1	LE 1	LE 1	LE 1	LE ◇1 ⊏	LE 1	LE 1	LE ◇1 ⊏	LE 1		LE 1	LE 1	LE 1	LE 1	LE 1
London Liverpool Street 15 ⊖	d	10 30	10 38	10 48		11 00					11 02	11 18			11 30	11 38	11 48	12 00					12 02	12 18	
Stratford 7 ⊖	d	10u38	10 45	10 55							11 09	11 25			11u38	11 45	11 55						12 09	12 25	
Romford	d		10 53													11 53									
Shenfield 3	d		11 03	11 11							11 25	11 41				12 03	12 11						12 25	12 41	
Ingatestone	d			11 15								11 45					12 15							12 45	
Chelmsford 3	d	11 03	11 12	11 22							11 34	11 52			12 03	12 12	12 22						12 34	12 52	
Hatfield Peverel	d										11 40												12 40		
Witham 2	d		11 23	11 34							11 47	12 03				12 23	12 34						12 47	13 03	
White Notley	d			11 41													12 41								
Cressing	d			11 43													12 43								
Braintree Freeport	d			11 46													12 46								
Braintree	a			11 50													12 50								
Kelvedon	d		11 27								11 51					12 27							12 51		
Marks Tey 2	d		11 33								11 57					12 33							12 57		
Colchester 4	a	11 22	11 40			11 46					12 04	12 15			12 22	12 40		12 46					13 04	13 15	
Colchester 4	d	11 23	11 41			11 47			11 56		12 04	12 16		12 20	12 23	12 41		12 47				12 56	13 04	13 16	
Colchester Town	a		11 49						12 03					12 27		12 49						13 03			
	d								12 07													13 07			
Hythe	d								12 11													13 11			
Wivenhoe 3	d								12 15			12 23										13 15		13 23	
Alresford (Essex)	d								12 19													13 19			
Great Bentley	d								12 23													13 23			
Weeley	d								12 26				←									13 26			←
Thorpe-le-Soken 1	a								12 31			12 35	12 31									13 31		13 35	13 31
	d								12 37			12 35	12 37									13 37		13 35	13 37
Clacton-on-Sea	a								↪			12 44										↪		13 44	
Kirby Cross	d												12 42												13 42
Frinton-on-Sea	d												12 45												13 45
Walton-on-the-Naze	a												12 49												13 49
Manningtree 2	d	11 31				11 55	12 00				12 12				12 31			12 55	13 00				13 12		
Mistley	d						12 04												13 04						
Wrabness	d						12 09												13 09						
Harwich International	d						12 17												13 17						
Dovercourt	d						12 20												13 20						
Harwich Town	a						12 22												13 22						
Ipswich	a	11 43				12 07					12 25				12 43			13 07					13 25		
	d	11 44			12 00	12 08		12 19							12 44			13 08			13 19				
Needham Market	d							12 28													13 28				
Stowmarket	d	11 55			12 12			12a33							12 55						13a33				
Peterborough 8	a				13 37																				
Diss	d	12 08				12 29									13 08			13 29							
Norwich	a	12 27				12 48									13 27			13 48							

		LE 1	LE ◇1 ⊏	LE 1	LE 1		LE 1	LE ◇1 ⊏	LE 1	LE 1	LE 1	LE 1	LE 1	LE 1	LE 1		LE ◇1 ⊏	LE 1	LE 1	LE ◇1 ⊏	LE 1	LE 1	LE 1	LE 1	LE 1
London Liverpool Street 15 ⊖	d		12 30	12 38	12 48			13 00				13 02	13 18				13 30	13 38	13 48	14 00				14 02	14 18
Stratford 7 ⊖	d		12u38	12 45	12 55							13 09	13 25				13u38	13 45	13 55					14 09	14 25
Romford	d			12 53														13 53							
Shenfield 3	d			13 03	13 11							13 25	13 41					14 03	14 11					14 25	14 41
Ingatestone	d				13 15								13 45						14 15						14 45
Chelmsford 3	d		13 03	13 12	13 22							13 34	13 52				14 03	14 12	14 22					14 34	14 52
Hatfield Peverel	d											13 40												14 40	
Witham 2	d			13 23	13 34							13 47	14 03					14 23	14 34					14 47	15 03
White Notley	d				13 41														14 41						
Cressing	d				13 43														14 43						
Braintree Freeport	d				13 46														14 46						
Braintree	a				13 50														14 50						
Kelvedon	d			13 27								13 51						14 27						14 51	
Marks Tey 2	d			13 33								13 57						14 33						14 57	
Colchester 4	a		13 22	13 40				13 46				14 04	14 15				14 22	14 40		14 46				15 04	15 15
Colchester 4	d	13 20	13 23	13 41				13 47			13 56	14 04	14 16		14 20		14 23	14 41		14 47			14 56	15 04	15 16
Colchester Town	a	13 27		13 49							14 03				14 27			14 49					15 03		
	d										14 07												15 07		
Hythe	d										14 11												15 11		
Wivenhoe 3	d										14 15		14 23										15 15		15 23
Alresford (Essex)	d										14 19												15 19		
Great Bentley	d										14 23												15 23		
Weeley	d										14 26			←									15 26		
Thorpe-le-Soken 1	a										14 31		14 35	14 31									15 31		15 35
	d										14 37		14 35	14 37									15 37		15 35
Clacton-on-Sea	a										↪		14 44										↪		15 44
Kirby Cross	d													14 42											
Frinton-on-Sea	d													14 45											
Walton-on-the-Naze	a													14 49											
Manningtree 2	d		13 31					13 55	14 00			14 12					14 31			14 55	15 00			15 12	
Mistley	d								14 04												15 04				
Wrabness	d								14 09												15 09				
Harwich International	d								14 17												15 17				
Dovercourt	d								14 20												15 20				
Harwich Town	a								14 22												15 22				
Ipswich	a		13 43					14 07				14 25					14 43			15 07				15 25	
	d		13 44				14 00	14 08		14 19							14 44			15 08		15 19			
Needham Market	d									14 28												15 28			
Stowmarket	d		13 55				14 12			14a33							14 55					15a33			
Peterborough 8	a						15 37																		
Diss	d		14 08					14 29									15 08			15 29					
Norwich	a		14 27					14 48									15 27			15 48					

London - Chelmsford, Colchester, Walton-on-Naze, Clacton, Harwich, Ipswich and Norwich

		LE	LE	LE	LE	LE	LE	LE	LE	LE	LE	LE	LE	LE	LE	LE	LE	LE	LE	LE	LE	LE
																	R				R	
		1	1	◇1	1	1	1	◇1	1	1	1	1	1	1	1	1	1	1	1	1	1	1
				☕				☕									☕				☕	
London Liverpool Street 15 ⊖	d			14 30	14 38	14 48		15 00				15 02		15 18			15 30		15 38	15 48	16 00	
Stratford 7 ⊖	d			14u38	14 45	14 55						15 09		15 25					15 45	15 55		
Romford	d				14 53														15 53			
Shenfield 3	d				15 03	15 11						15 25		15 41					16 03	16 11		
Ingatestone	d					15 15								15 45				16 00		16 15		
Chelmsford 3	d			15 03	15 12	15 22						15 34		15 52			16 00	16 07	16 12	16 22		
Hatfield Peverel	d											15 40						16 13				
Witham 2	d				15 23	15 35						15 47		16 03				16 20	16 24	16 35		
White Notley	d					15 42														16 42		
Cressing	d					15 44														16 44		
Braintree Freeport	d					15 47														16 47		
Braintree	a					15 51														16 51		
Kelvedon	d				15 27							15 51						16 24	16 28			
Marks Tey 2	d				15 33							15 57						16 30	16 34			
Colchester 4	a			15 22	15 40			15 46				16 04		16 15			16 21	16 38	16 41		16 46	
Colchester 4	d		15 20	15 23	15 41			15 47			15 56	16 04	16 14	16 16		16 20	16 21		16 42		16 47	
Colchester Town	a		15 27		15 49						16 03					16 27			16 50			
	d										16 07											
Hythe	d										16 11											
Wivenhoe 3	d										16 15			16 23								
Alresford (Essex)	d										16 19											
Great Bentley	d										16 23											
Weeley	d	←									16 26				←							
Thorpe-le-Soken 1	a	15 31									16 31			16 35	16 31							
	d	15 37									16 37			16 35	16 37							
Clacton-on-Sea	a										→			16 44								
Kirby Cross	d	15 42													16 42							
Frinton-on-Sea	d	15 45													16 45							
Walton-on-the-Naze	a	15 49													16 49							
Manningtree 2	d			15 31				15 55	16 00			16 12	16 23				16 29				16 55	17 00
Mistley	d								16 04				16 27									17 04
Wrabness	d								16 09				16 32									17 09
Harwich International	d								16 17				16 41									17 17
Dovercourt	d								16 20				16 44									17 20
Harwich Town	a								16 22				16 46									17 22
Ipswich	a			15 43				16 07				16 25					16 40				17 07	
	d			15 44			16 00	16 08		16 19							16 41				17 08	
Needham Market	d									16 28												
Stowmarket	d			15 55			16 12			16a33							16 52				17 19	
Peterborough 8	a						17 37															
Diss	d			16 08				16 29									17 05				17 32	
Norwich	a			16 27				16 48									17 24				17 53	

Table 11

Mondays to Fridays

London - Chelmsford, Colchester, Walton-on-Naze, Clacton, Harwich, Ipswich and Norwich

		LE	LE	LE	LE	LE	LE		LE		LE	LE	LE	LE	LE	LE			LE	LE	LE	LE	LE	LE	LE
												R									R				
		1	1	1	1	1	1		1		1	1	1	1	1	1			1	1	1	1	1	◇1	1
																					A				
												☕									☕				
London Liverpool Street 15 ⊖	d			16 02					16 14		16 17	16 30	16 32	16 34		16 45			16 47		17 00			17 02	
Stratford 7 ⊖	d			16 09					16 22		16 25			16 42					16 55					17 10	
Romford	d																								
Shenfield 3	d			16 25							16 41		16 54	16 58					17 11					17 26	
Ingatestone	d										16 46								17 16						
Chelmsford 3	d			16 34					16 45		16 53		17 04	17 08		17 15			17 23					17 36	
Hatfield Peverel	d			16 40										17 14											
Witham 2	d			16 47							17a06		17 14	17 21					17a36					17 46	
White Notley	d													17 28											
Cressing	d													17 30											
Braintree Freeport	d													17 33											
Braintree	a													17 39											
Kelvedon	d			16 51					16 57							17 26								17 51	
Marks Tey 2	d			16 57					17 02							17 32								17 56	
Colchester 4	a			17 04					17 10			17 16	17 26			17 39								18 03	
Colchester 4	d		16 56	17 04	17 09				17 14	17 24		17 17	17 27			17 43	17 47						17 56	18 04	
Colchester Town	a		17 03		17 16					17 33													18 03		
	d		17 07							17 37													18 07		
Hythe	d		17 11						17 18	17 41													18 11		
Wivenhoe 3	d		17 15						17 22	17 45						17 50							18 15		
Alresford (Essex)	d		17 19							17 49						17 54							18 19		
Great Bentley	d		17 23							17 53						17 58							18 23		
Weeley	d		17 26			←				17 56					←								18 26		←
Thorpe-le-Soken 1	a		17 31			17 31			17 35	18 01					18 01	18 05							18 31		18 31
	d		17 37			17 37			17 35	18 09					18 09	18 05							18 37		18 37
Clacton-on-Sea	a		→						17 46	→						18 16							→		
Kirby Cross	d					17 42									18 14										18 42
Frinton-on-Sea	d					17 45									18 17										18 45
Walton-on-the-Naze	a					17 49									18 21										18 49
Manningtree 2	d			17 12			17 24						17 35				17 57							18 12	
Mistley	d						17 28										18 01								
Wrabness	d						17 33										18 06								
Harwich International	d						17 41										18 15								
Dovercourt	d						17 44										18 18								
Harwich Town	a						17 46										18 22								
Ipswich	a			17 27								17 34	17 49								17 59			18 23	
	d	17 19										17 36								17 49	18 00	18 16		18 24	
Needham Market	d	17 28																		17 58		18 25			
Stowmarket	d	17a33										17 47								18 04		18a30		18 35	
Peterborough 8	a																			19 38					
Diss	d											18 00									18 21			18 47	
Norwich	a											18 22									18 42			19 09	

A The East Anglian

London - Chelmsford, Colchester, Walton-on-Naze, Clacton, Harwich, Ipswich and Norwich

		LE 1			LE 1	LE 1	LE 1	LE R 1 ⊏P	LE 1	LE 1	LE 1	LE 1	LE 1		LE 1	LE R 1 ⊏P	LE 1	LE 1	LE 1	LE 1	LE 1	LE R 1 ⊏P	LE 1		LE 1
London Liverpool Street 15 ⊖	d	17 08			17 12	17 18	17 20	17 30	17 32		17 38				17 40	17 50	17 52			17 58	18 00	18 10			18 12
Stratford 7 ⊖	d	17 16			17 20	17 26			17 40		17 46						18 00			18 06	18 09				18 20
Romford	d																								
Shenfield 3	d						17 45								18 05						18 25				
Ingatestone	d						17 49								18 09						18 29				
Chelmsford 3	d	17 40			17 44	17 50	17 57		18 05		18 12				18 17		18 25				18 37				18 46
Hatfield Peverel	d				17 50				18 11								18 31								18 52
Witham 2	d	17 50			17a59		18 10		18 17						18 31		18 37			18 41	19 01				18 58
White Notley	d						18 17														→				
Cressing	d						18 19																		
Braintree Freeport	d						18 22																		
Braintree	a						18 28																		
Kelvedon	d	17 55				18 02					18 25				18 37					18 46					
Marks Tey 2	d	18 00							18 25								18 46								19 06
Colchester 4	a	18 08				18 12			18 32		18 36				18 48	18 42	18 53			18 56		19 00			19 13
Colchester 4	d	18 12	18 16			18 12			18 32		18 36		18 40		18 49	18 43	18 54			18 57		19 02	19 06		19 14
Colchester Town	a		18 26												18 59								19 13		
	d																						19 19		
Hythe	d	18 16											18 44				18 58						19 23		19 18
Wivenhoe 3	d	18 20							18 40				18 48				19 02						→		19 27
Alresford (Essex)	d	18 24											18 52												19 31
Great Bentley	d	18 28											18 56												19 35
Weeley	d												18 59												19 38
Thorpe-le-Soken 1	a	18 35							18 51				19 04				19 13								19 43
	d	18 35							18 51			18 53	19 04				19 13								19 43
Clacton-on-Sea	a	18 46							19 02				19 13				19 24								19 52
Kirby Cross	d											19 01													
Frinton-on-Sea	d											19 04													
Walton-on-the-Naze	a											19 08													
Manningtree 2	d					18 20		18 27		18 35	18 44					18 52		19 00		19 05		19 11			
Mistley	d									18 39								19 04							
Wrabness	d									18 44								19 09							
Harwich International	d									18 52								19 17							
Dovercourt	d									18 55								19 20							
Harwich Town	a									18 57								19 22							
Ipswich	a					18 35		18 37			18 59					19 03				19 19		19 21			
	d							18 39								19 04			19 14			19 23			
Needham Market	d																		19 23						
Stowmarket	d							18 50								19 16			19a28			19 34			
Peterborough 8	a																								
Diss	d							19 03								19 29						19 47			
Norwich	a							19 25								19 50						20 09			

Table 11

Mondays to Fridays

London - Chelmsford, Colchester, Walton-on-Naze, Clacton, Harwich, Ipswich and Norwich

		LE	LE	LE	LE	LE	LE	LE	LE		LE	LE		LE	LE	LE	LE	LE	LE		LE	LE	LE	LE	LE
						R											R								
		1	1	1	1	1	1	1	1		1	1		1	1	1	1	1	1		1	1	1	1	1
						P											P								
London Liverpool Street 15 ⊖	d		18 18		18 20	18 30						18 32		18 38	18 48		19 00	19 02					19 08	19 18	
Stratford 7 ⊖	d		18 26		18 29							18 40		18 46	18 56			19 09					19 15	19 25	
Romford	d																								
Shenfield 3	d				18 45									19 02				19 25						19 41	
Ingatestone	d				18 49									19 07										19 45	
Chelmsford 3	d		18 52		18 57							19 05		19 14	19 20			19 34					19 38	19 52	
Hatfield Peverel	d	←										19 11						19 40							
Witham 2	d	19 01			19 11							19 17		19 24	19 30			19 49					19 50	20 03	
White Notley	d	19 08																19 56							
Cressing	d	19 10																19 58							
Braintree Freeport	d	19 13																20 01							
Braintree	a	19 19																20 05							
Kelvedon	d		19 06		19 17							19 22											19 55		
Marks Tey 2	d				19 23									19 32									20 00		
Colchester 4	a		19 16		19 30	19 21						19 33		19 39	19 43		19 47						20 07	20 15	
Colchester 4	d		19 17	19 20	19 30	19 23						19 37	19 39	19 39	19 44		19 47					19 56	20 08	20 16	
Colchester Town	a			19 27				←					19 50									20 03			
	d																					20 07			
Hythe	d							19 23							19 48							20 11			
Wivenhoe 3	d							19 27				19 44			19 52							20 15		20 23	
Alresford (Essex)	d							19 31				19 48										20 19			
Great Bentley	d							19 35				19 52										20 23			
Weeley	d							19 38				19 55				←						20 26			←
Thorpe-le-Soken 1	a							19 43				20 00			20 04	20 00						20 31		20 35	20 31
	d						19 35	19 43				20 08			20 04	20 08						20 37		20 35	20 37
Clacton-on-Sea	a							19 52				→			20 15							→		20 44	
Kirby Cross	d						19 40									20 13									20 42
Frinton-on-Sea	d						19 43									20 16									20 45
Walton-on-the-Naze	a						19 47									20 22									20 49
Manningtree 2	d		19 25		19 40	19 32			19 38					19 47			19 55		20 00				20 16		
Mistley	d								19 42										20 04						
Wrabness	d								19 47										20 09						
Harwich International	d				20a01				19 55										20 17						
Dovercourt	d								19 58										20 20						
Harwich Town	a								20 00										20 22						
Ipswich	a		19 39			19 42								20 04			20 07						20 28		
	d					19 44					20 00						20 08				20 19				
Needham Market	d																				20 28				
Stowmarket	d					19 55					20 12						20 19				20a33				
Peterborough 8	a										21 39														
Diss	d					20 08											20 32								
Norwich	a					20 30											20 51								

Table 11

Mondays to Fridays

London - Chelmsford, Colchester, Walton-on-Naze, Clacton, Harwich, Ipswich and Norwich

		LE R 1 ☕	LE 1	LE 1	LE 1		LE 1	LE ◇1 ☕	LE 1	LE	LE 1	LE 1	LE 1	LE 1	LE 1		LE ◇1 ☕	LE 1	LE 1	LE 1	LE ◇1 ☕	LE 1	LE	LE 1	LE 1
London Liverpool Street 15 ⊖	d	19 30		19 38	19 48			20 00				20 02	20 18				20 30	20 38	20 48		21 00				21 02
Stratford 7 ⊖	d			19 45	19 55							20 09	20 25				20u38	20 45	20 55						21 09
Romford	d																	20 53							
Shenfield 3	d			20 01	20 11							20 25	20 41					21 03	21 11						21 25
Ingatestone	d				20 15								20 45						21 15						
Chelmsford 3	d	20 00		20 10	20 22							20 34	20 52				21 03	21 12	21 22						21 34
Hatfield Peverel	d			20 16								20 40													21 40
Witham 2	d			20 23	20 34							20 47	21 03					21 23	21 34						21 47
White Notley	d				20 41														21 41						
Cressing	d				20 43														21 43						
Braintree Freeport	d				20 46														21 46						
Braintree	a				20 50														21 50						
Kelvedon	d			20 27								20 51						21 27							21 51
Marks Tey 2	d			20 33								20 57						21 33							21 57
Colchester 4	a	20 19		20 40				20 46				21 04	21 15				21 22	21 40			21 46				22 04
Colchester 4	d	20 20	20 20	20 41				20 47			20 56	21 04	21 16		21 20		21 23	21 41			21 47			21 56	22 04
Colchester Town	a		20 27	20 49							21 03				21 27			21 49						22 03	
	d										21 07													22 07	
Hythe	d										21 11													22 11	
Wivenhoe 3	d										21 15		21 23											22 15	
Alresford (Essex)	d										21 19													22 19	
Great Bentley	d										21 23													22 23	
Weeley	d										21 26			←										22 26	
Thorpe-le-Soken 1	a										21 31		21 35	21 31										22 31	
	d										21 37		21 35	21 37										22 37	
Clacton-on-Sea	a										↦		21 44											↦	
Kirby Cross	d													21 42											
Frinton-on-Sea	d													21 45											
Walton-on-the-Naze	a													21 49											
Manningtree 2	d	20 28					20 36	20 55	21 00			21 12					21 31				21 55	22 00			22 12
Mistley	d						20 40		21 04													22 04			
Wrabness	d						20 45		21 09													22 09			
Harwich International	d						20 53		21 17											21 38		22 17			22a28
Dovercourt	d						20 56		21 20													22 20			
Harwich Town	a						20 58		21 22													22 22			
Ipswich	a	20 40						21 07				21 25					21 43			22 03	22 07				
	d	20 41						21 08		21 16							21 44				22 08		22 16		
Needham Market	d									21 26													22 26		
Stowmarket	d	20 52						21 19		21a32							21 55				22 19		22a32		
Peterborough 8	a																								
Diss	d	21 05						21 32									22 08				22 32				
Norwich	a	21 24						21 51									22 27				22 51				

			LE 1	LE 1	LE ◇1 ☕	LE 1	LE 1	LE 1	LE 1	LE 1	LE 1		LE 1	LE 1	LE ◇1 ☕	LE 1	LE 1	LE 1	LE	LE 1	LE 1		LE ◇1 ☕	LE 1	
London Liverpool Street 15 ⊖	d		21 18		21 30	21 38	21 48	22 00	22 02				22 18		22 30	22 38				23 02	23 18		23 30	23 48	
Stratford 7 ⊖	d		21 25		21u38	21 45	21 55		22 09				22 25		22u38	22 45				23 09	23 25		23u38	23 55	
Romford	d					21 53																			
Shenfield 3	d		21 41			22 03	22 11		22 25				22 41			23 01				23 25	23 41			00 11	
Ingatestone	d		21 45				22 15						22 45			23 05					23 45			00 15	
Chelmsford 3	d		21 52		22 03	22 12	22 22	22 28	22 34				22 52		23 03	23 12				23 34	23 52		00 03	00 22	
Hatfield Peverel	d								22 40											23 40				00 28	
Witham 2	d		22 03			22 23	22 34		22 47				23 03			23 23	23 25			23 47	00 03			00 35	
White Notley	d						22 41										23 32								
Cressing	d						22 43										23 34								
Braintree Freeport	d						22 46										23 37								
Braintree	a						22 50										23 41								
Kelvedon	d					22 27			22 51							23 27				23 51				00 39	
Marks Tey 2	d					22 33			22 57							23 33			23 46	23 57				00 45	
Colchester 4	a		22 15		22 22	22 40		22 47	23 05				23 15		23 22	23 45			23 59	00 04	00 15		00 22	00 57	
Colchester 4	d		22 16		22 23	22 41		22 47			22 56		23 16		23 23					00 04	00 16		00 23		
Colchester Town	a					22 49					23 03														
	d										23 07														
Hythe	d										23 11														
Wivenhoe 3	d		22 23								23 15		23 23								00 23				
Alresford (Essex)	d										23 19										00 27				
Great Bentley	d										23 23										00 31				
Weeley	d			←							23 26			←											
Thorpe-le-Soken 1	a		22 35	22 31							23 31		23 35	23 31							00 38				
	d		22 35	22 37							23 37		23 35	23 37							00 38				
Clacton-on-Sea	a		22 44								↦		23 44								00 51				
Kirby Cross	d			22 42										23 42											
Frinton-on-Sea	d			22 45										23 45											
Walton-on-the-Naze	a			22 49										23 49											
Manningtree 2	d				22 31			22 55		23 00					23 31			23 36		00 12			00 31		
Mistley	d									23 04								23 40							
Wrabness	d									23 09								23 45							
Harwich International	d									23 17								23 53							
Dovercourt	d									23 20								23 56							
Harwich Town	a									23 22								23 58							
Ipswich	a				22 43			23 08							23 43					00 28			00 43		
	d				22 44										23 44								00 44		
Needham Market	d																								
Stowmarket	d				22 55										23 55								00 55		
Peterborough 8	a																								
Diss	d				23 08										00 08								01 08		
Norwich	a				23 27										00 39								01 43		

Table 11

Saturdays

London - Chelmsford, Colchester, Walton-on-Naze, Clacton, Harwich, Ipswich and Norwich

		LE ◇1 ☕	LE 1	LE 1	LE ◇1 ☕	LE 1	LE 1	LE 1	LE	LE 1		LE ◇1	LE 1	LE 1	LE 1	LE 1	LE 1	LE 1	LE 1	LE 1		LE ◇1 ☕	LE 1	LE 1	LE 1
London Liverpool Street 15 ⊖	d	22p30	23p02	23p18	23p30		23p48	00 18									05 30								06 02
Stratford 7 ⊖	d	22b38	23p09	23p25	23b38		23p55	00 25									05 37								06 09
Romford	d																05 45								
Shenfield 3	d		23p25	23p41			00 11	00 47									05 55								06 25
Ingatestone	d			23p45			00 15	00 51									05 59								
Chelmsford 3	d	23p03	23p34	23p52	00 03		00 22	00 58									06 06								06 34
Hatfield Peverel	d		23p40				00 28	01 04									06 12								06 40
Witham 2	d		23p47	00 03		00 05	00 35	01 11		05 34							06 19	06 34							06 47
White Notley	d					00 12				05 41								06 41							
Cressing	d					00 14				05 43								06 43							
Braintree Freeport	d					00 17				05 46								06 46							
Braintree	a					00 21				05 50								06 50							
Kelvedon	d		23p51				00 39	01 15									06 24								06 51
Marks Tey 2	d		23p57				00 45	01 21									06 29								06 57
Colchester 4	a	23p22	00 04	00 15	00 22		00 57	01 41									06 36								07 04
Colchester 4	d	23p23	00 04	00 16	00 23							05 40	05 52		06 20	06 24	06 37							06 56	07 04
Colchester Town	a														06 27									07 03	
	d																							07 07	
Hythe	d																							07 11	
Wivenhoe 3	d			00 23																				07 15	
Alresford (Essex)	d			00 27																				07 19	
Great Bentley	d			00 31																				07 23	
Weeley	d																							07 26	
Thorpe-le-Soken 1	a			00 38																				07 31	
	d			00 38															06 37					07 37	
Clacton-on-Sea	a			00 51																				→	
Kirby Cross	d																		06 42						
Frinton-on-Sea	d																		06 45						
Walton-on-the-Naze	a																		06 49						
Manningtree 2	d	23p31	00 12		00 31							05 49	06 00			06 32	06 45			07 00					07 12
Mistley	d												06 04							07 04					
Wrabness	d												06 09							07 09					
Harwich International	d												06 17							07 17					
Dovercourt	d												06 20							07 20					
Harwich Town	a												06 22							07 22					
Ipswich	a	23p43	00 28		00 43							05 59				06 44	06 56								07 25
	d	23p44			00 44				05 10			06 00		06 16								07 10	07 19		
Needham Market	d								05 20					06 25									07 28		
Stowmarket	d	23p55			00 55				05a26			06 12		06a30								07 21	07a33		
Peterborough 8	a											07 38													
Diss	d	00 08			01 08																	07 34			
Norwich	a	00 39			01 43																	07 53			

		LE 1	LE 1	LE ◇1 ☕	LE 1	LE 1		LE 1	LE 1	LE ◇1 ☕	LE 1	LE 1	LE 1	LE 1	LE 1	LE 1		LE 1	LE ◇1 ☕	LE 1	LE 1	LE ◇1 ☕	LE 1	LE 1	LE 1
London Liverpool Street 15 ⊖	d	06 18		06 30	06 38	06 48				07 00				07 02	07 18				07 30	07 38	07 48	08 00			
Stratford 7 ⊖	d	06 25		06u38	06 45	06 55								07 09	07 25				07u38	07 45	07 55				
Romford	d				06 53															07 53					
Shenfield 3	d	06 41			07 03	07 11								07 25	07 41					08 03	08 11				
Ingatestone	d	06 45				07 15									07 45						08 15				
Chelmsford 3	d	06 52		07 03	07 12	07 22								07 34	07 52				08 03	08 12	08 22				
Hatfield Peverel	d													07 40											
Witham 2	d	07 03			07 23	07 34								07 47	08 03					08 23	08 34				
White Notley	d					07 41															08 41				
Cressing	d					07 43															08 43				
Braintree Freeport	d					07 46															08 46				
Braintree	a					07 50															08 50				
Kelvedon	d				07 27									07 51						08 27					
Marks Tey 2	d				07 33									07 57						08 33					
Colchester 4	a	07 15		07 22	07 40					07 46				08 04	08 15				08 22	08 40		08 46			
Colchester 4	d	07 16		07 23	07 40			07 44		07 47			07 56	08 04	08 16			08 20	08 23	08 41		08 47			08 56
Colchester Town	a							07 51					08 03					08 27		08 49					09 03
	d												08 07												09 07
Hythe	d												08 11												09 11
Wivenhoe 3	d	07 23											08 15		08 23										09 15
Alresford (Essex)	d												08 19												09 19
Great Bentley	d												08 23												09 23
Weeley	d		←										08 26			←									09 26
Thorpe-le-Soken 1	a	07 35	07 31										08 31		08 35	08 31									09 31
	d	07 35	07 37										08 37		08 35	08 37									09 37
Clacton-on-Sea	a	07 44											→		08 44										→
Kirby Cross	d		07 42													08 42									
Frinton-on-Sea	d		07 45													08 45									
Walton-on-the-Naze	a		07 49													08 49									
Manningtree 2	d			07 31	07 48					07 55		08 00		08 12					08 31			08 55	09 00		
Mistley	d										08 02	08 04											09 04		
Wrabness	d											08 09											09 09		
Harwich International	d				08a09							08 17											09 17		
Dovercourt	d											08 20											09 20		
Harwich Town	a											08 22											09 22		
Ipswich	a			07 43						08 07	08 17			08 25					08 43			09 07			
	d			07 44					08 00	08 08	08 19								08 44			09 08		09 19	
Needham Market	d										08 28													09 28	
Stowmarket	d			07 55					08 12		08a33								08 55					09a33	
Peterborough 8	a								09 38																
Diss	d			08 08						08 29									09 08			09 29			
Norwich	a			08 27						08 48									09 27			09 48			

b Previous night, stops to pick up only

Table 11

Saturdays

London - Chelmsford, Colchester, Walton-on-Naze, Clacton, Harwich, Ipswich and Norwich

		LE	LE	LE	LE	LE	LE	LE	LE	LE	LE	LE	LE	LE	LE	LE	LE	LE	LE	LE	LE
		1	1	1	1	◇1	1	1	1	◇1	1	1	1	1	1	1	1	◇1	1	1	◇1
																					A
						☕				☕								☕			☕
London Liverpool Street 15 ⊖	d	08 02	08 18			08 30	08 38	08 48		09 00				09 02	09 18			09 30	09 38	09 48	10 00
Stratford 7 ⊖	d	08 09	08 25			08u38	08 45	08 55						09 09	09 25			09u38	09 45	09 55	
Romford	d						08 53												09 53		
Shenfield 3	d	08 25	08 41				09 03	09 11						09 25	09 41				10 03	10 11	
Ingatestone	d		08 45					09 15							09 45					10 15	
Chelmsford 3	d	08 34	08 52			09 03	09 12	09 22						09 34	09 52			10 03	10 12	10 22	
Hatfield Peverel	d	08 40												09 40							
Witham 2	d	08 47	09 03				09 23	09 34						09 47	10 03				10 23	10 34	
White Notley	d							09 41												10 41	
Cressing	d							09 43												10 43	
Braintree Freeport	d							09 46												10 46	
Braintree	a							09 50												10 50	
Kelvedon	d	08 51					09 27							09 51					10 27		
Marks Tey 2	d	08 57					09 33							09 57					10 33		
Colchester 4	a	09 04	09 15			09 22	09 40			09 46				10 04	10 15			10 22	10 40		10 46
Colchester 4	d	09 04	09 16		09 20	09 23	09 41			09 47			09 56	10 04	10 16		10 20	10 23	10 41		10 47
Colchester Town	a				09 27		09 49						10 03				10 27		10 49		
	d												10 07								
Hythe	d												10 11								
Wivenhoe 3	d		09 23										10 15		10 23						
Alresford (Essex)	d												10 19								
Great Bentley	d												10 23								
Weeley	d			←									10 26			←					
Thorpe-le-Soken 1	a		09 35	09 31									10 31		10 35	10 31					
	d		09 35	09 37									10 37		10 35	10 37					
Clacton-on-Sea	a		09 44										↦		10 44						
Kirby Cross	d			09 42												10 42					
Frinton-on-Sea	d			09 45												10 45					
Walton-on-the-Naze	a			09 49												10 49					
Manningtree 2	d	09 12				09 31				09 55	10 00			10 12				10 31			10 55
Mistley	d										10 04										
Wrabness	d										10 09										
Harwich International	d										10 17										
Dovercourt	d										10 20										
Harwich Town	a										10 22										
Ipswich	a	09 25				09 43				10 07				10 25				10 43			11 07
	d					09 44			10 00	10 08		10 19						10 44			11 08
Needham Market	d											10 28									
Stowmarket	d					09 55			10 12			10a33						10 55			
Peterborough 8	a								11 37												
Diss	d					10 08				10 29								11 08			11 29
Norwich	a					10 27				10 48								11 27			11 48

Table 11

Saturdays

London - Chelmsford, Colchester, Walton-on-Naze, Clacton, Harwich, Ipswich and Norwich

		LE	LE	LE	LE	LE	LE	LE		LE	LE	LE	LE	LE	LE	LE	LE	LE		LE	LE	LE	LE	LE	LE
		1	1	1	1	1	1	1		◇1 ☕	1	1	1	◇1 ☕	1	1	1	1		1	1	1	◇1 ☕	1	1
London Liverpool Street 15 ⊖	d				10 02	10 18				10 30	10 38	10 48		11 00				11 02		11 18			11 30	11 38	11 48
Stratford 7 ⊖	d				10 09	10 25				10u38	10 45	10 55						11 09		11 25			11u38	11 45	11 55
Romford	d										10 53													11 53	
Shenfield 3	d				10 25	10 41					11 03	11 11						11 25		11 41				12 03	12 11
Ingatestone	d					10 45						11 15								11 45					12 15
Chelmsford 3	d				10 34	10 52				11 03	11 12	11 22						11 34		11 52			12 03	12 12	12 22
Hatfield Peverel	d				10 40													11 40							
Witham 2	d				10 47	11 03					11 23	11 34						11 47		12 03				12 23	12 34
White Notley	d											11 41													12 41
Cressing	d											11 43													12 43
Braintree Freeport	d											11 46													12 46
Braintree	a											11 50													12 50
Kelvedon	d				10 51						11 27							11 51						12 27	
Marks Tey 2	d				10 57						11 33							11 57						12 33	
Colchester 4	a				11 04	11 15				11 22	11 40			11 46				12 04		12 15			12 22	12 40	
Colchester 4	d			10 56	11 04	11 16		11 20		11 23	11 41			11 47			11 56	12 04		12 16		12 20	12 23	12 41	
Colchester Town	a			11 03				11 27			11 49						12 03					12 27		12 49	
	d			11 07													12 07								
Hythe	d			11 11													12 11								
Wivenhoe 3	d			11 15		11 23											12 15			12 23					
Alresford (Essex)	d			11 19													12 19								
Great Bentley	d			11 23													12 23								
Weeley	d			11 26			←										12 26				←				
Thorpe-le-Soken 1	a			11 31		11 35	11 31										12 31			12 35	12 31				
	d			11 37		11 35	11 37										12 37			12 35	12 37				
Clacton-on-Sea	a			→		11 44											→			12 44					
Kirby Cross	d						11 42														12 42				
Frinton-on-Sea	d						11 45														12 45				
Walton-on-the-Naze	a						11 49														12 49				
Manningtree 2	d	11 00			11 12					11 31				11 55	12 00			12 12					12 31		
Mistley	d	11 04													12 04										
Wrabness	d	11 09													12 09										
Harwich International	d	11 17													12 17										
Dovercourt	d	11 20													12 20										
Harwich Town	a	11 22													12 22										
Ipswich	a				11 25					11 43				12 07				12 25					12 43		
	d		11 19							11 44			12 00	12 08		12 19							12 44		
Needham Market	d		11 28													12 28									
Stowmarket	d		11a33							11 55			12 12			12a33							12 55		
Peterborough 8	a												13 37												
Diss	d									12 08				12 29									13 08		
Norwich	a									12 27				12 48									13 27		

Table 11

Saturdays

London - Chelmsford, Colchester, Walton-on-Naze, Clacton, Harwich, Ipswich and Norwich

		LE	LE	LE	LE	LE	LE	LE	LE	LE	LE	LE	LE	LE	LE	LE	LE	LE	LE	LE	LE
										R											
		◇1	1	1	1	1	1	1	1	◇1	1	1	1	◇1	1	1	1	1	1	1	1
										B											
		☕								☕				☕							
London Liverpool Street 15 ⊖	d	12 00				12 02	12 18			12 30	12 38	12 48		13 00				13 02	13 18		
Stratford 7 ⊖	d					12 09	12 25			12u38	12 45	12 55						13 09	13 25		
Romford	d										12 53										
Shenfield 3	d					12 25	12 41				13 03	13 11						13 25	13 41		
Ingatestone	d						12 45					13 15							13 45		
Chelmsford 3	d					12 34	12 52			13 03	13 12	13 22						13 34	13 52		
Hatfield Peverel	d					12 40												13 40			
Witham 2	d					12 47	13 03				13 23	13 34						13 47	14 03		
White Notley	d											13 41									
Cressing	d											13 43									
Braintree Freeport	d											13 46									
Braintree	a											13 50									
Kelvedon	d					12 51					13 27							13 51			
Marks Tey 2	d					12 57					13 33							13 57			
Colchester 4	a	12 46				13 04	13 15			13 22	13 40			13 46				14 04	14 15		
Colchester 4	d	12 47			12 56	13 04	13 16		13 20	13 23	13 41			13 47			13 56	14 04	14 16		14 20
Colchester Town	a				13 03				13 27		13 49						14 03				14 27
	d				13 07												14 07				
Hythe	d				13 11												14 11				
Wivenhoe 3	d				13 15		13 23										14 15		14 23		
Alresford (Essex)	d				13 19												14 19				
Great Bentley	d				13 23												14 23				
Weeley	d				13 26			←									14 26			←	
Thorpe-le-Soken 1	a				13 31		13 35	13 31									14 31		14 35	14 31	
	d				13 37		13 35	13 37									14 37		14 35	14 37	
Clacton-on-Sea	a				→		13 44										→		14 44		
Kirby Cross	d							13 42												14 42	
Frinton-on-Sea	d							13 45												14 45	
Walton-on-the-Naze	a							13 49												14 49	
Manningtree 2	d	12 55	13 00			13 12				13 31				13 55	14 00			14 12			
Mistley	d		13 04												14 04						
Wrabness	d		13 09												14 09						
Harwich International	d		13 17												14 17						
Dovercourt	d		13 20												14 20						
Harwich Town	a		13 22												14 22						
Ipswich	a	13 07				13 25				13 43				14 07				14 25			
	d	13 08		13 19						13 44			14 00	14 08		14 19					
Needham Market	d			13 28												14 28					
Stowmarket	d			13a33						13 55			14 12			14a33					
Peterborough 8	a												15 37								
Diss	d	13 29								14 08				14 29							
Norwich	a	13 48								14 27				14 48							

Table 11

Saturdays

London - Chelmsford, Colchester, Walton-on-Naze, Clacton, Harwich, Ipswich and Norwich

		LE ◇1 🍴	LE 1	LE 1	LE ◇1 🍴	LE 1	LE 1	LE 1	LE 1	LE 1		LE 1	LE 1	LE ◇1 🍴	LE 1	LE 1	LE 1	LE ◇1 🍴	LE 1	LE 1		LE 1	LE 1	LE 1	LE 1
London Liverpool Street [15] ⊖	d	13 30	13 38	13 48	14 00				14 02	14 18				14 30	14 38	14 48		15 00					15 02	15 18	
Stratford [7] ⊖	d	13u38	13 45	13 55					14 09	14 25				14u38	14 45	14 55							15 09	15 25	
Romford	d		13 53												14 53										
Shenfield [3]	d		14 03	14 11					14 25	14 41					15 03	15 11							15 25	15 41	
Ingatestone	d			14 15						14 45						15 15								15 45	
Chelmsford [3]	d	14 03	14 12	14 22					14 34	14 52				15 03	15 12	15 22							15 34	15 52	
Hatfield Peverel	d								14 40														15 40		
Witham [2]	d		14 23	14 34					14 47	15 03					15 23	15 34							15 47	16 03	
White Notley	d			14 41												15 41									
Cressing	d			14 43												15 43									
Braintree Freeport	d			14 46												15 46									
Braintree	a			14 50												15 50									
Kelvedon	d		14 27						14 51						15 27								15 51		
Marks Tey [2]	d		14 33						14 57						15 33								15 57		
Colchester [4]	a	14 22	14 40		14 46				15 04	15 15				15 22	15 40			15 46					16 04	16 15	
Colchester [4]	d	14 23	14 41		14 47			14 56	15 04	15 16			15 20	15 23	15 41			15 47				15 56	16 04	16 16	
Colchester Town	a		14 49					15 03					15 27		15 49							16 03			
	d							15 07														16 07			
Hythe	d							15 11														16 11			
Wivenhoe [3]	d							15 15		15 23												16 15		16 23	
Alresford (Essex)	d							15 19														16 19			
Great Bentley	d							15 23														16 23			
Weeley	d							15 26				←										16 26			←
Thorpe-le-Soken [1]	a							15 31		15 35		15 31										16 31		16 35	16 31
	d							15 37		15 35		15 37										16 37		16 35	16 37
Clacton-on-Sea	a							→		15 44												→		16 44	
Kirby Cross	d											15 42													16 42
Frinton-on-Sea	d											15 45													16 45
Walton-on-the-Naze	a											15 49													16 49
Manningtree [2]	d	14 31			14 55	15 00			15 12					15 31				15 55	16 00				16 12		
Mistley	d					15 04													16 04						
Wrabness	d					15 09													16 09						
Harwich International	d					15 17													16 17						
Dovercourt	d					15 20													16 20						
Harwich Town	a					15 22													16 22						
Ipswich	a	14 43			15 07				15 25					15 43				16 07					16 25		
	d	14 44			15 08		15 19							15 44			16 00	16 08		16 19					
Needham Market	d						15 28													16 28					
Stowmarket	d	14 55					15a33							15 55			16 12			16a33					
Peterborough [8]	a																17 37								
Diss	d	15 08			15 29									16 08				16 29							
Norwich	a	15 27			15 48									16 27				16 48							

		LE 1	LE ◇1 🍴	LE 1	LE 1	LE ◇1 🍴		LE 1	LE 1	LE 1	LE 1	LE 1	LE 1	LE 1	LE ◇1 🍴	LE 1		LE 1	LE 1	LE ◇1 🍴	LE 1	LE 1	LE 1	LE 1	LE 1
London Liverpool Street [15] ⊖	d		15 30	15 38	15 48	16 00					16 02	16 18			16 30	16 38		16 48		17 00				17 02	17 18
Stratford [7] ⊖	d		15u38	15 45	15 55						16 09	16 25			16u38	16 45		16 55						17 09	17 25
Romford	d			15 53												16 53									
Shenfield [3]	d			16 03	16 11						16 25	16 41				17 03		17 11						17 25	17 41
Ingatestone	d				16 15							16 45						17 15							17 45
Chelmsford [3]	d		16 03	16 12	16 22						16 34	16 52			17 03	17 12		17 22						17 34	17 52
Hatfield Peverel	d										16 40													17 40	
Witham [2]	d			16 23	16 34						16 47	17 03				17 23		17 34						17 47	18 03
White Notley	d				16 41													17 41							
Cressing	d				16 43													17 43							
Braintree Freeport	d				16 46													17 46							
Braintree	a				16 50													17 50							
Kelvedon	d			16 27							16 51					17 27								17 51	
Marks Tey [2]	d			16 33							16 57					17 33								17 57	
Colchester [4]	a		16 22	16 40		16 46					17 04	17 15			17 22	17 40				17 46				18 04	18 15
Colchester [4]	d	16 20	16 23	16 41		16 47				16 56	17 04	17 16		17 20	17 23	17 41				17 47			17 56	18 04	18 16
Colchester Town	a	16 27		16 49						17 03				17 27		17 49							18 03		
	d									17 07													18 07		
Hythe	d									17 11													18 11		
Wivenhoe [3]	d									17 15		17 23											18 15		18 23
Alresford (Essex)	d									17 19													18 19		
Great Bentley	d									17 23													18 23		
Weeley	d									17 26			←										18 26		
Thorpe-le-Soken [1]	a									17 31		17 35	17 31										18 31		18 35
	d									17 37		17 35	17 37										18 37		18 35
Clacton-on-Sea	a									→		17 44											→		18 44
Kirby Cross	d												17 42												
Frinton-on-Sea	d												17 45												
Walton-on-the-Naze	a												17 49												
Manningtree [2]	d		16 31			16 55		17 00			17 12				17 31					17 55	18 00			18 12	
Mistley	d							17 04													18 04				
Wrabness	d							17 09													18 09				
Harwich International	d							17 17													18 17				
Dovercourt	d							17 20													18 20				
Harwich Town	a							17 22													18 22				
Ipswich	a		16 43			17 07					17 25				17 43					18 07				18 25	
	d		16 44			17 08			17 19						17 44				18 00	18 08		18 19			
Needham Market	d								17 28													18 28			
Stowmarket	d		16 55			17 19			17a33						17 55				18 12			18a33			
Peterborough [8]	a																		19 38						
Diss	d		17 08			17 32									18 08					18 29					
Norwich	a		17 27			17 51									18 27					18 48					

Table 11

Saturdays

London - Chelmsford, Colchester, Walton-on-Naze, Clacton, Harwich, Ipswich and Norwich

		LE 1		LE 1	LE ◇1 ☕	LE 1	LE 1	LE ◇1 ☕	LE 1	LE 1	LE 1	LE 1		LE 1	LE 1	LE 1	LE ◇1 ☕	LE 1	LE 1	LE 1	LE ◇1 ☕	LE 1		LE 1	LE 1
London Liverpool Street 15 ⊖	d				17 30	17 38	17 48	18 00				18 02		18 18			18 30	18 38	18 48		19 00				
Stratford 7 ⊖	d				17u38	17 45	17 55					18 09		18 25			18u38	18 45	18 55						
Romford	d					17 53												18 53							
Shenfield 3	d					18 03	18 11					18 25		18 41				19 03	19 11						
Ingatestone	d						18 15							18 45					19 15						
Chelmsford 3	d				18 03	18 12	18 22					18 34		18 52			19 03	19 12	19 22						
Hatfield Peverel	d											18 40													
Witham 2	d					18 23	18 34					18 47		19 03				19 23	19 34						
White Notley	d						18 41												19 41						
Cressing	d						18 43												19 43						
Braintree Freeport	d						18 46												19 46						
Braintree	a						18 50												19 50						
Kelvedon	d					18 27						18 51						19 27							
Marks Tey 2	d					18 33						18 57						19 33							
Colchester 4	a				18 22	18 40		18 46				19 04		19 15			19 22	19 40			19 46				
Colchester 4	d			18 20	18 23	18 41		18 47			18 56	19 04		19 16		19 20	19 23	19 41			19 47				19 56
Colchester Town	a			18 27		18 49					19 03					19 27		19 49							20 03
	d										19 07														20 07
Hythe	d										19 11														20 11
Wivenhoe 3	d										19 15			19 23											20 15
Alresford (Essex)	d										19 19														20 19
Great Bentley	d										19 23														20 23
Weeley	d	←									19 26				←										20 26
Thorpe-le-Soken 1	a	18 31									19 31			19 35	19 31										20 31
	d	18 37									19 37			19 35	19 37										20 37
Clacton-on-Sea	a										↪			19 44											↪
Kirby Cross	d	18 42													19 42										
Frinton-on-Sea	d	18 45													19 45										
Walton-on-the-Naze	a	18 49													19 49										
Manningtree 2	d				18 31			18 55	19 00			19 12					19 31				19 55	20 00			
Mistley	d								19 04													20 04			
Wrabness	d								19 09													20 09			
Harwich International	d								19 17													20 17			
Dovercourt	d								19 20													20 20			
Harwich Town	a								19 22													20 22			
Ipswich	a				18 43			19 07				19 25					19 43				20 07				
	d				18 44			19 08		19 19							19 44			20 00	20 08			20 19	
Needham Market	d									19 28														20 28	
Stowmarket	d				18 55					19a33							19 55			20 12				20a33	
Peterborough 8	a																			21 37					
Diss	d				19 08			19 29									20 08				20 29				
Norwich	a				19 27			19 48									20 27				20 48				

		LE 1	LE 1	LE 1	LE 1	LE ◇1 ☕	LE 1	LE 1		LE ◇1 ☕	LE 1	LE	LE 1	LE 1	LE 1	LE 1	LE 1	LE ◇1 ☕		LE 1	LE 1	LE 1	LE 1	LE 1	LE
London Liverpool Street 15 ⊖	d	19 02	19 18			19 30	19 38	19 48		20 00				20 02	20 18			20 30		20 38	20 48		21 00		
Stratford 7 ⊖	d	19 09	19 25			19u38	19 45	19 55						20 09	20 25			20u38		20 45	20 55				
Romford	d						19 53													20 53					
Shenfield 3	d	19 25	19 41				20 03	20 11						20 25	20 41					21 03	21 11				
Ingatestone	d		19 45					20 15							20 45						21 15				
Chelmsford 3	d	19 34	19 52			20 03	20 12	20 22						20 34	20 52			21 03		21 12	21 22				
Hatfield Peverel	d	19 40												20 40											
Witham 2	d	19 47	20 03				20 23	20 34						20 47	21 03					21 23	21 34				
White Notley	d							20 41													21 41				
Cressing	d							20 43													21 43				
Braintree Freeport	d							20 46													21 46				
Braintree	a							20 50													21 50				
Kelvedon	d	19 51					20 27							20 51						21 27					
Marks Tey 2	d	19 57					20 33							20 57						21 33					
Colchester 4	a	20 04	20 15			20 22	20 40			20 46				21 04	21 15			21 22		21 40			21 46		
Colchester 4	d	20 04	20 16		20 20	20 23	20 41			20 47			20 56	21 04	21 16		21 20	21 23		21 41			21 47		
Colchester Town	a				20 27		20 49						21 03				21 27			21 49					
	d												21 07												
Hythe	d												21 11												
Wivenhoe 3	d		20 23										21 15		21 23										
Alresford (Essex)	d												21 19												
Great Bentley	d												21 23												
Weeley	d			←									21 26			←									
Thorpe-le-Soken 1	a		20 35	20 31									21 31		21 35	21 31									
	d		20 35	20 37									21 37		21 35	21 37									
Clacton-on-Sea	a		20 44										↪		21 44										
Kirby Cross	d			20 42												21 42									
Frinton-on-Sea	d			20 45												21 45									
Walton-on-the-Naze	a			20 49												21 49									
Manningtree 2	d	20 12				20 31				20 55	21 00			21 12				21 31					21 55	22 00	
Mistley	d										21 04													22 04	
Wrabness	d										21 09													22 09	
Harwich International	d										21 17											21 38		22 17	
Dovercourt	d										21 20													22 20	
Harwich Town	a										21 22													22 22	
Ipswich	a	20 25				20 43				21 07				21 25				21 43				22 03	22 08		
	d					20 44				21 08		21 16						21 44							22 16
Needham Market	d											21 26													22 26
Stowmarket	d					20 55						21a32						21 55							22a32
Peterborough 8	a																								
Diss	d					21 08				21 29								22 08							
Norwich	a					21 27				21 48								22 27							

Table 11

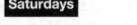

London - Chelmsford, Colchester, Walton-on-Naze, Clacton, Harwich, Ipswich and Norwich

		LE	LE	LE		LE	LE	LE	LE	LE	LE	LE	LE	LE		LE	LE	LE	LE	LE	LE	LE	LE	LE
		1	1	1		1	◇1 ⊏P	1	1	1	1	1	1	1		1	◇1 ⊏P	1	1	1		1	1	◇1 ⊏P
London Liverpool Street 15 ⊖	d		21 02	21 18			21 30	21 38	21 48	22 00	22 02			22 18			22 30	22 38				23 02	23 18	23 30
Stratford 7 ⊖	d		21 09	21 25			21u38	21 45	21 55		22 09			22 25			22u38	22 45				23 09	23 25	23u38
Romford	d							21 53										22 53						
Shenfield 3	d		21 25	21 41				22 03	22 11		22 25			22 41				23 03				23 25	23 41	
Ingatestone	d			21 45					22 15					22 45									23 45	
Chelmsford 3	d		21 34	21 52			22 03	22 12	22 22	22 28	22 34			22 52			23 03	23 12				23 34	23 52	00 03
Hatfield Peverel	d		21 40								22 40											23 40		
Witham 2	d		21 47	22 03				22 23	22 34		22 47			23 03				23 23	23 25			23 47	00 03	
White Notley	d								22 41										23 32					
Cressing	d								22 43										23 34					
Braintree Freeport	d								22 46										23 37					
Braintree	a								22 50										23 41					
Kelvedon	d		21 51					22 27			22 51							23 27				23 51		
Marks Tey 2	d		21 57					22 33			22 57							23 33			23 46	23 57		
Colchester 4	a		22 04	22 15			22 22	22 40		22 47	23 05			23 15			23 22	23 45			23 59	00 04	00 15	00 22
Colchester 4	d	21 56	22 04	22 16			22 23	22 41		22 48			22 56	23 16			23 23					00 04	00 16	00 23
Colchester Town	a	22 03						22 49					23 03											
	d	22 07											23 07											
Hythe	d	22 11											23 11											
Wivenhoe 3	d	22 15		22 23									23 15	23 23									00 23	
Alresford (Essex)	d	22 19											23 19										00 27	
Great Bentley	d	22 23											23 23										00 31	
Weeley	d	22 26				⟵							23 26			⟵								
Thorpe-le-Soken 1	a	22 31		22 35		22 31							23 31	23 35		23 31							00 38	
	d	22 37		22 35		22 37							23 37	23 35		23 37							00 38	
Clacton-on-Sea	a	⟶		22 44									⟶	23 44									00 51	
Kirby Cross	d					22 42										23 42								
Frinton-on-Sea	d					22 45										23 45								
Walton-on-the-Naze	a					22 49										23 49								
Manningtree 2	d		22 12				22 31			22 56		23 00					23 31			23 36		00 12		00 31
Mistley	d											23 04								23 40				
Wrabness	d											23 09								23 45				
Harwich International	d		22a28									23 17								23 53				
Dovercourt	d											23 20								23 56				
Harwich Town	a											23 22								23 58				
Ipswich	a						22 43			23 08							23 43					00 28		00 43
	d						22 44										23 44							00 44
Needham Market	d																							
Stowmarket	d						22 55										23 55							00 55
Peterborough 8	a																							
Diss	d						23 08										00 08							01 08
Norwich	a						23 27										00 27							01 31

		LE
		1
London Liverpool Street 15 ⊖	d	23 48
Stratford 7 ⊖	d	23 55
Romford	d	
Shenfield 3	d	00 11
Ingatestone	d	00 15
Chelmsford 3	d	00 22
Hatfield Peverel	d	00 28
Witham 2	d	00 35
White Notley	d	
Cressing	d	
Braintree Freeport	d	
Braintree	a	
Kelvedon	d	00 39
Marks Tey 2	d	00 45
Colchester 4	a	00 57
Colchester 4	d	
Colchester Town	a	
	d	
Hythe	d	
Wivenhoe 3	d	
Alresford (Essex)	d	
Great Bentley	d	
Weeley	d	
Thorpe-le-Soken 1	a	
	d	
Clacton-on-Sea	a	
Kirby Cross	d	
Frinton-on-Sea	d	
Walton-on-the-Naze	a	
Manningtree 2	d	
Mistley	d	
Wrabness	d	
Harwich International	d	
Dovercourt	d	
Harwich Town	a	
Ipswich	a	
	d	
Needham Market	d	
Stowmarket	d	
Peterborough 8	a	
Diss	d	
Norwich	a	

Table 11

Sundays

London - Chelmsford, Colchester, Walton-on-Naze, Clacton, Harwich, Ipswich and Norwich

		LE	LE	LE	LE	LE	LE	LE	LE	LE		LE	LE	LE	LE	LE	LE	LE	LE	LE		LE	LE	LE	LE
		◇[1]	[1]	[1]	◇[1]	[1]	[1]	[1]	[1]	[1]		[1]	[1]		[1]	[1]	[1]	[1]	[1]	[1]		◇[1]	◇[1]	[1]	[1]
		A	A	A	A	A			B																
		☕			☕																				
London Liverpool Street [15] ⊖	d	22p30	23p02	23p18	23p30	23p48	00 18											08 02				08 30		08 32	
Stratford [7] ⊖	d	22b38	23p09	23p25	23b38	23p55	00 25											08 09						08 39	
Romford	d																								
Shenfield [3]	d		23p25	23p41		00 11	00 47											08 31						09 01	
Ingatestone	d			23p45		00 15	00 51											08 35							
Chelmsford [3]	d	23p03	23p34	23p52	00 03	00 22	00 58											08 42						09 10	
Hatfield Peverel	d		23p40			00 28	01 04											08 48							
Witham [2]	d		23p47	00 03		00 35	01 11	07 34					08 24					08 55						09 21	09 24
White Notley	d							07 41					08 31												09 31
Cressing	d							07 43					08 33												09 33
Braintree Freeport	d							07 46					08 36												09 36
Braintree	a							07 50					08 40												09 40
Kelvedon	d		23p51			00 39	01 15											08 59							
Marks Tey [2]	d		23p57			00 45	01 21											09 05						09 28	
Colchester [4]	a	23p22	00 04	00 15	00 22	00 57	01 32											09 12				09 23		09 36	
Colchester [4]	d	23p23	00 04	00 16	00 23					07 40		08 12				08 18	08 36	09 12				09 23	09 32	09 36	
Colchester Town	a																								
	d																								
Hythe	d																								
Wivenhoe [3]	d			00 23													08 44							09 44	
Alresford (Essex)	d			00 27													08 47							09 47	
Great Bentley	d			00 31													08 51							09 51	
Weeley	d																								
Thorpe-le-Soken [1]	a			00 38													08 58							09 58	
	d			00 38													08 58		09 00					09 58	
Clacton-on-Sea	a			00 51													09 07							10 07	
Kirby Cross	d																		09 05						
Frinton-on-Sea	d																		09 08						
Walton-on-the-Naze	a																		09 12						
Manningtree [2]	d	23p31	00 12		00 31					07 48		08 20				08 26		09 20		09 26		09 31	09 40		
Mistley	d															08 30				09 30					
Wrabness	d															08 35				09 35					
Harwich International	d														08 30	08 43				09 43					
Dovercourt	d															08 46				09 46					
Harwich Town	a															08 48				09 48					
Ipswich	a	23p43	00 28		00 43					08 00		08 32			08 53			09 32				09 43	09 51		
	d	23p44			00 44				07 55					08 45	09 02							09 44	09 55		
Needham Market	d														09 12										
Stowmarket	d	23p55			00 55				08 07					08a59	09a17							09 55	10 07		
Peterborough [8]	a								09 36														11 36		
Diss	d	00 08			01 08																	10 08			
Norwich	a	00 27			01 31																	10 29			

A not 22 May

B until 11 September

b Previous night, stops to pick up only

Table 11

Sundays

London - Chelmsford, Colchester, Walton-on-Naze, Clacton, Harwich, Ipswich and Norwich

		LE 1	LE 1	LE 1	LE ◇1 ☕	LE 1		LE 1	LE 1	LE 1	LE 1	LE 1	LE ◇1 ☕	LE 1	LE 1	LE 1		LE 1	LE 1	LE 1	LE ◇1 ☕	LE 1	LE 1	LE 1	LE 1
London Liverpool Street 15 ⊖	d	09 02			09 30	09 32					10 02		10 30	10 32				11 02			11 30	11 32			
Stratford 7 ⊖	d	09 09				09 39					10 09			10 39				11 09				11 39			
Romford	d																								
Shenfield 3	d	09 31				10 01					10 31			11 01				11 31				12 01			
Ingatestone	d	09 35									10 35							11 35							
Chelmsford 3	d	09 42				10 10					10 42			11 10				11 42				12 10			
Hatfield Peverel	d	09 48									10 48							11 48							
Witham 2	d	09 55				10 21		10 24			10 55			11 21	11 24			11 55				12 21	12 24		
White Notley	d							10 31							11 31								12 31		
Cressing	d							10 33							11 33								12 33		
Braintree Freeport	d							10 36							11 36								12 36		
Braintree	a							10 40							11 40								12 40		
Kelvedon	d	09 59									10 59							11 59							
Marks Tey 2	d	10 05				10 28					11 05			11 28				12 05				12 28			
Colchester 4	a	10 12			10 23	10 36					11 12		11 23	11 36				12 12			12 23	12 36			
Colchester 4	d	10 12			10 23	10 36					11 12		11 23	11 36				12 12			12 23	12 36			
Colchester Town	a																								
	d																								
Hythe	d																								
Wivenhoe 3	d					10 44								11 44								12 44			
Alresford (Essex)	d					10 47								11 47								12 47			
Great Bentley	d					10 51								11 51								12 51			
Weeley	d																								
Thorpe-le-Soken 1	a					10 58								11 58								12 58			
	d		10 00			10 58			11 00					11 58					12 00			12 58		13 00	
Clacton-on-Sea	a					11 07								12 07								13 07			
Kirby Cross	d		10 05						11 05										12 05					13 05	
Frinton-on-Sea	d		10 08						11 08										12 08					13 08	
Walton-on-the-Naze	a		10 12						11 12										12 12					13 12	
Manningtree 2	d	10 20		10 26	10 31						11 20	11 26	11 31					12 20		12 26	12 31				
Mistley	d			10 30								11 30								12 30					
Wrabness	d			10 35								11 35								12 35					
Harwich International	d			10 43								11 43								12 43					
Dovercourt	d			10 46								11 46								12 46					
Harwich Town	a			10 48								11 48								12 48					
Ipswich	a	10 32			10 43						11 32		11 43					12 32			12 43				
	d				10 44					11 02			11 44			11 55					12 44				13 02
Needham Market	d									11 12															13 12
Stowmarket	d				10 55					11a18			11 55			12 07					12 55				13a18
Peterborough 8	a															13 31									
Diss	d				11 08								12 08								13 08				
Norwich	a				11 29								12 29								13 29				

		LE 1		LE 1	LE ◇1 ☕	LE 1	LE 1	LE 1	LE 1	LE 1	LE 1	LE ◇1 ☕		LE 1	LE 1	LE 1	LE 1	LE 1	LE 1	LE ◇1 ☕	LE 1	LE 1		LE 1	LE 1
London Liverpool Street 15 ⊖	d	12 02			12 30	12 32			13 02			13 30		13 32				14 02		14 30	14 32				15 02
Stratford 7 ⊖	d	12 09				12 39			13 09					13 39				14 09			14 39				15 09
Romford	d																								
Shenfield 3	d	12 31				13 01			13 31					14 01				14 31			15 01				15 31
Ingatestone	d	12 35							13 35									14 35							15 35
Chelmsford 3	d	12 42				13 10			13 42					14 10				14 42			15 10				15 42
Hatfield Peverel	d	12 48							13 48									14 48							15 48
Witham 2	d	12 55				13 21	13 24		13 55					14 21	14 24			14 55			15 21	15 24			15 55
White Notley	d						13 31								14 31							15 31			
Cressing	d						13 33								14 33							15 33			
Braintree Freeport	d						13 36								14 36							15 36			
Braintree	a						13 40								14 40							15 40			
Kelvedon	d	12 59							13 59									14 59							15 59
Marks Tey 2	d	13 05				13 28			14 05					14 28				15 05			15 28				16 05
Colchester 4	a	13 12			13 23	13 36			14 12			14 23		14 36				15 12		15 23	15 36				16 12
Colchester 4	d	13 12			13 23	13 36			14 12			14 23		14 36				15 12		15 23	15 36				16 12
Colchester Town	a																								
	d																								
Hythe	d																								
Wivenhoe 3	d					13 44								14 44							15 44				
Alresford (Essex)	d					13 47								14 47							15 47				
Great Bentley	d					13 51								14 51							15 51				
Weeley	d																								
Thorpe-le-Soken 1	a					13 58								14 58							15 58				
	d					13 58				14 00				14 58		15 00					15 58				
Clacton-on-Sea	a					14 07								15 07							16 07				
Kirby Cross	d									14 05						15 05									
Frinton-on-Sea	d									14 08						15 08									
Walton-on-the-Naze	a									14 12						15 12									
Manningtree 2	d	13 20		13 26	13 31				14 20		14 26	14 31						15 20	15 26	15 31					16 20
Mistley	d			13 30							14 30								15 30						
Wrabness	d			13 35							14 35								15 35						
Harwich International	d			13 43							14 43								15 43						
Dovercourt	d			13 46							14 46								15 46						
Harwich Town	a			13 48							14 48								15 48						
Ipswich	a	13 32			13 43				14 32			14 43						15 32		15 43					16 32
	d				13 44			13 55				14 44					15 02			15 44				15 55	
Needham Market	d																15 12								
Stowmarket	d				13 55			14 07				14 55					15a18			15 55				16 07	
Peterborough 8	a							15 31																17 31	
Diss	d				14 08							15 08								16 08					
Norwich	a				14 29							15 29								16 29					

Table 11

Sundays

London - Chelmsford, Colchester, Walton-on-Naze, Clacton, Harwich, Ipswich and Norwich

		LE	LE	LE	LE	LE	LE	LE		LE	LE	LE	LE	LE	LE	LE	LE	LE		LE	LE	LE	LE	LE	LE
		1	1	◇1 ☕	1	1	1	1		1	1	◇1 ☕	1	1	1	1	1	1		◇1 ☕	1	1	1	1	1
London Liverpool Street 15 ⊖	d			15 30	15 32					16 02		16 30	16 32			17 02				17 30	17 32				18 02
Stratford 7 ⊖	d				15 39					16 09			16 39			17 09					17 39				18 09
Romford	d																								
Shenfield 3	d				16 01					16 31			17 01			17 31					18 01				18 31
Ingatestone	d									16 35						17 35									18 35
Chelmsford 3	d				16 10					16 42			17 10			17 42					18 10				18 42
Hatfield Peverel	d									16 48						17 48									18 48
Witham 2	d				16 21	16 24				16 55			17 21	17 24		17 55					18 21	18 24			18 55
White Notley	d					16 31								17 31								18 31			
Cressing	d					16 33								17 33								18 33			
Braintree Freeport	d					16 36								17 36								18 36			
Braintree	a					16 40								17 40								18 40			
Kelvedon	d									16 59						17 59									18 59
Marks Tey 2	d				16 28					17 05			17 28			18 05					18 28				19 05
Colchester 4	a			16 23	16 36					17 12		17 23	17 36			18 12				18 23	18 36				19 12
Colchester 4	d			16 23	16 36					17 12		17 23	17 36			18 12				18 23	18 36				19 12
Colchester Town	a																								
	d																								
Hythe	d																								
Wivenhoe 3	d				16 44								17 44								18 44				
Alresford (Essex)	d				16 47								17 47								18 47				
Great Bentley	d				16 51								17 51								18 51				
Weeley	d																								
Thorpe-le-Soken 1	a				16 58								17 58								18 58				
	d	16 00			16 58		17 00						17 58				18 00				18 58		19 00		
Clacton-on-Sea	a				17 07								18 07								19 07				
Kirby Cross	d	16 05					17 05										18 05						19 05		
Frinton-on-Sea	d	16 08					17 08										18 08						19 08		
Walton-on-the-Naze	a	16 12					17 12										18 12						19 12		
Manningtree 2	d		16 26	16 31						17 20	17 26	17 31				18 20		18 26		18 31					19 20
Mistley	d		16 30								17 30							18 30							
Wrabness	d		16 35								17 35							18 35							
Harwich International	d		16 43								17 43							18 43							
Dovercourt	d		16 46								17 46							18 46							
Harwich Town	a		16 48								17 48							18 48							
Ipswich	a			16 43						17 32		17 43				18 32				18 43					19 32
	d			16 44				17 02				17 44			17 55					18 44				19 02	
Needham Market	d							17 12																19 12	
Stowmarket	d			16 55				17a18				17 55			18 07					18 55				19a18	
Peterborough 8	a														19 32										
Diss	d			17 08								18 08								19 08					
Norwich	a			17 29								18 30								19 29					

		LE	LE	LE		LE	LE	LE	LE	LE	LE	LE	LE	LE		LE	LE	LE	LE	LE	LE	LE	LE	LE	
		1	◇1 ☕	1		◇1 ☕	1	1	1	1	◇1 ☕	1	1	1			1	1	1	◇1 ☕	1	1	1		
London Liverpool Street 15 ⊖	d		18 30	18 32		19 00		19 02			19 30	19 32					20 02			20 30	20 32		21 00		
Stratford 7 ⊖	d			18 39				19 09				19 39					20 09				20 39				
Romford	d																								
Shenfield 3	d			19 01				19 31				20 01					20 31				21 01		21 27		
Ingatestone	d							19 35									20 35								
Chelmsford 3	d			19 10		19 37		19 42				20 10					20 42				21 10		21 37		
Hatfield Peverel	d							19 48									20 48								
Witham 2	d			19 21			19 24	19 55				20 21	20 24				20 55				21 21	21 24	21 48		
White Notley	d						19 31						20 31									21 31			
Cressing	d						19 33						20 33									21 33			
Braintree Freeport	d						19 36						20 36									21 36			
Braintree	a						19 40						20 40									21 40			
Kelvedon	d							19 59									20 59								
Marks Tey 2	d			19 28				20 05				20 28					21 05				21 28			22 00	
Colchester 4	a		19 23	19 36		19 56		20 12			20 23	20 36					21 12			21 23	21 36		22 00	22 08	
Colchester 4	d		19 23	19 36		19 56		20 12			20 23	20 36					21 12			21 23	21 36		22 00		
Colchester Town	a																								
	d																								
Hythe	d																								
Wivenhoe 3	d			19 44								20 44									21 44				
Alresford (Essex)	d			19 47								20 47									21 47				
Great Bentley	d			19 51								20 51									21 51				
Weeley	d																								
Thorpe-le-Soken 1	a			19 58								20 58									21 58				
	d			19 58					20 00			20 58		21 00							21 58				
Clacton-on-Sea	a			20 07								21 07									22 07				
Kirby Cross	d								20 05					21 05											
Frinton-on-Sea	d								20 08					21 08											
Walton-on-the-Naze	a								20 12					21 12											
Manningtree 2	d	19 26	19 31			20 04		20 20		20 26	20 31						21 20		21 26	21 31			22 08		
Mistley	d	19 30								20 30									21 30						
Wrabness	d	19 35								20 35									21 35						
Harwich International	d	19 43								20 43								21 10	21 43				22a28		
Dovercourt	d	19 46								20 46									21 46						
Harwich Town	a	19 48								20 48									21 48						
Ipswich	a		19 43			20 16		20 32			20 43						21 32	21 36		21 43					
	d		19 44			20 17					20 44					21 02				21 44					
Needham Market	d															21 12									
Stowmarket	d		19 55			20 28					20 55					21a18				21 55					
Peterborough 8	a																								
Diss	d		20 08			20 41					21 08									22 08					
Norwich	a		20 29			21 02					21 29									22 29					

Table 11

Sundays

London - Chelmsford, Colchester, Walton-on-Naze, Clacton, Harwich, Ipswich and Norwich

		LE	LE	LE	LE	LE	LE	LE	LE	LE		LE	LE	LE	LE	LE
		[1]	[1]	[1]	◇[1]	[1]	[1]	[1]	◇[1]	[1]		[1]	[1]	[1]	◇[1]	[1]
					☕				☕							
London Liverpool Street [15] ⊖	d	21 02			21 30	21 32		22 02	22 30			22 32		23 02	23 30	23 32
Stratford [7] ⊖	d	21 09				21 39		22 09				22 39		23 09		23 39
Romford	d															
Shenfield [3]	d	21 31				22 01		22 31				23 01		23 31		00 01
Ingatestone	d	21 35						22 35						23 35		
Chelmsford [3]	d	21 42				22 10		22 42				23 10		23 42		00 10
Hatfield Peverel	d	21 48						22 48						23 48		
Witham [2]	d	21 55				22 21	22 24	22 55				23 21	23 24	23 55		00 21
White Notley	d						22 31						23 31			
Cressing	d						22 33						23 33			
Braintree Freeport	d						22 36						23 36			
Braintree	a						22 40						23 40			
Kelvedon	d	21 59						22 59						23 59		
Marks Tey [2]	d	22 05				22 28		23 05				23 28		00 05		00 28
Colchester [4]	a	22 12			22 23	22 36		23 12	23 23			23 36		00 12	00 27	00 39
Colchester [4]	d	22 12			22 23	22 36		23 12	23 23			23 36		00 12	00 27	
Colchester Town	a															
	d															
Hythe	d															
Wivenhoe [3]	d					22 44						23 44				
Alresford (Essex)	d					22 47						23 47				
Great Bentley	d					22 51						23 51				
Weeley	d															
Thorpe-le-Soken [1]	a					22 58						23 58				
	d		22 00			22 58				23 00		23 58				
Clacton-on-Sea	a					23 07						00 07				
Kirby Cross	d		22 05							23 05						
Frinton-on-Sea	d		22 08							23 08						
Walton-on-the-Naze	a		22 12							23 12						
Manningtree [2]	d	22 20		22 26	22 31			23 20	23 31					00 20	00 35	
Mistley	d			22 30												
Wrabness	d			22 35												
Harwich International	d			22 43												
Dovercourt	d			22 46												
Harwich Town	a			22 48												
Ipswich	a	22 32			22 43			23 32	23 43					00 36	00 47	
	d				22 44				23 44						00 48	
Needham Market	d															
Stowmarket	d				22 55				23 55						00 59	
Peterborough [8]	a															
Diss	d				23 08				00 08						01 12	
Norwich	a				23 29				00 41						01 45	

Table 11

Mondays to Fridays

Norwich, Ipswich, Harwich, Clacton, Walton-on-Naze, Colchester and Chelmsford - London

Miles	Miles	Miles	Miles	Miles			LE MX	LE MO	LE MX	LE MO	LE MX	LE	LE	LE	LE	LE	LE	LE	LE	LE	LE	LE	LE	LE
							◇1	◇1			1	1	◇1	1	1	1	◇1 ☕	1	1	1	1	1	1	■ 1 ☕
0	—	—	—	—	**Norwich**	d	22p00	22p00									05 00							05 30
20	—	—	—	—	Diss	d	22p17	22p17									05 18							05 48
—	—	—	—	—	**Peterborough 8**	d																		
34¼	—	—	—	—	Stowmarket	d	22p29	22p29	23p47	00 06							05 30		05 54					06 00
38	—	—	—	—	Needham Market	d			23p52	00 11									05 59					
46¼	—	—	—	—	**Ipswich**	a	22p41	22p41	00 05	00 23							05 42		06 09					06 12
—	—	—	—	—		d	22p43	22p43					05 14				05 44							06 14
—	0	—	—	—	**Harwich Town**	d								05 24										
—	0½	—	—	—	Dovercourt	d								05 26										
—	1¾	—	—	—	Harwich International	d								05 29										
—	5½	—	—	—	Wrabness	d								05 35										
—	9½	—	—	—	Mistley	d								05 41										
55½	11¼	—	—	—	Manningtree 2	d	22p53	22p53					05 25	05a46			05 54							06 24
—	—	0	—	—	**Walton-on-the-Naze**	d												05 35				06 05		
—	—	1¼	—	—	Frinton-on-Sea	d												05 38				06 08		
—	—	2½	—	—	Kirby Cross	d												05 41				06 11		
—	—	—	0	—	**Clacton-on-Sea**	d										05 20					05 43			
—	—	5	4¾	—	Thorpe-le-Soken 1	a										05 28		05 47			05 51	06 17		
—	—	—	—	—		d										05 28					05 51			
—	—	7¼	—	—	Weeley	d															05 55			
—	—	10	—	—	Great Bentley	d															05 58			
—	—	12¼	—	—	Alresford (Essex)	d															06 02			
—	—	14	—	—	Wivenhoe 3	d										05 38					06 06			
—	—	16½	—	—	Hythe	d															06 10			
—	—	18	—	—	Colchester Town	a																		
—	—	—	—	—		d																	06 19	
63¼	—	—	—	—	**Colchester 4**	a	23p02	23p02					05 34			05 46	06 03				06 16		06 26	06 33
—	0	19¾	—	—	**Colchester 4**	d	23p03	23p03				05 12	05 35			05 47	06 05				06 17		06 27	06 35
68¼	—	—	—	—	Marks Tey 2	d						05 18				05 53							06 33	
72¾	—	—	—	—	Kelvedon	d						05 23				05 59					06 27			
—	—	—	—	0	**Braintree**	d					00 25				05 45									
—	—	—	—	0¾	Braintree Freeport	d					00 27				05 47									
—	—	—	—	2	Cressing	d					00 30				05 50									
—	—	—	—	3¼	White Notley	d					00 33				05 53									
76½	—	—	—	6¼	**Witham 2**	d	23p16	23p16			00a41	05 29	05 48		06a02	06 05				06 18	06 33		06 48	
79	—	—	—	—	Hatfield Peverel	d						05 33								06 22				
85¼	—	—	—	—	**Chelmsford 3**	d	23p25	23p25				05 40	05 58			06 14				06 29	06 42		06 57	
91½	—	—	—	—	Ingatestone	d						05 47								06 36			07 04	
94¾	—	—	—	—	Shenfield 3	a	23b36	23b36				05 52				06 24				06 41	06 52		07 08	
102¾	—	—	—	—	Romford	a																		
111¾	—	—	—	—	Stratford 7 ⊖	a	23b52	23b57				06 07	06s22			06 39	06s44			06s57	07s08		07s25	07s15
115	—	—	—	—	**London Liverpool Street 15 ⊖**	a	00 02	00 08				06 16	06 34			06 48	06 54			07 09	07 20		07 37	07 27

b Previous night, stops to set down only

Norwich, Ipswich, Harwich, Clacton, Walton-on-Naze, Colchester and Chelmsford - London

		LE	LE	LE	LE	LE	LE	LE	LE	LE	LE	LE	LE	LE	LE	LE	LE	LE	LE	LE	LE	LE
							R									R						
		1	1	1	1	1	1	1	1	1	1		1	1	1	1	1	1	1	1	1	◇1
							☕									☕						
Norwich	d						06 00									06 25						
Diss	d						06 18									06 43						
Peterborough 8	d																					
Stowmarket	d						06 30					06 44				06 55						07 05
Needham Market	d											06 49										
Ipswich	a						06 42					07 01				07 07						07 18
	d			06 29			06 44				06 52					07 09						07 18
Harwich Town	d				06 24								06 52									
Dovercourt	d				06 26								06 54									
Harwich International	d				06 29								06 57									
Wrabness	d				06 35								07 03									
Mistley	d				06 41								07 09									
Manningtree 2	d			06 39	06a46		06 54				07 02		07a14			07 19						07 28
Walton-on-the-Naze	d								06 32									06 59				
Frinton-on-Sea	d								06 35									07 02				
Kirby Cross	d								06 38									07 05				
Clacton-on-Sea	d	06 10						06 28		06 38					06 49		06 53				07 05	
Thorpe-le-Soken 1	a	06 18						06 36	06 44	06 46					06 57		07 01	07 11			07 13	
	d	06 18						06 36		06 46					06 57		07 01				07 13	
Weeley	d							06 40									07 05					
Great Bentley	d							06 43									07 08					
Alresford (Essex)	d							06 47									07 12					
Wivenhoe 3	d	06 29						06 51		06 57					07 08		07 16				07 24	
Hythe	d	06 33						06 55		07 01							07 20					
Colchester Town	a							06 59									07 24					
	d					06 49		07 03									07 28					
Colchester 4	a	06 39		06 48		06 56	07 03	07 13		07 07	07 12				07 16	07 28	07 36				07 32	07 37
Colchester 4	d	06 40		06 49		06 57	07 05	→		07 08	07 13				07 17	07 30					07 33	07 38
Marks Tey 2	d			06 55		07 03					07 19				07 23							07 44
Kelvedon	d	06 50		07 00						07 18					07 29							07 49
Braintree	d		06 42																	07 27		
Braintree Freeport	d		06 44																	07 29		
Cressing	d		06 47																	07 32		
White Notley	d		06 50																	07 35		
Witham 2	d		06 58	07 06		07 18								07 29	07 35					07 43	07 50	07 55
Hatfield Peverel	d		07 02											07 33						07 47		
Chelmsford 3	d	07 04	07 09	07 15		07 27				07 31	07 35			07 40					07 49	07 55	07 59	
Ingatestone	d					07 34					07 42								07 56			
Shenfield 3	a		07 19			07 39				07 42				07 50					08 01		08 09	
Romford	a																					
Stratford 7 ⊖	a	07s28	07s35	07s39		07s55				07s58	08s01				08s10				08s17	08s20		08s28
London Liverpool Street 15 ⊖	a	07 40	07 47	07 50		08 08	07 58			08 10	08 13			08 19	08 21	08 23			08 29	08 32	08 38	08 40

Norwich, Ipswich, Harwich, Clacton, Walton-on-Naze, Colchester and Chelmsford - London

		LE	LE	LE	LE	LE	LE	LE	LE	LE	LE	LE	LE	LE	LE	LE	LE	LE	LE	LE	LE	LE	LE
				R					R						R								
		1	1	1	1	1	1	1	1		1	1	1	1	1	1	1	◇1	1	1	1	1	1
															A								
				☕					☕						☕								
Norwich	d			06 50					07 10						07 40								
Diss	d			07 08					07 28						07 58								
Peterborough 8	d																						
Stowmarket	d			07 20					07 40	07 45								08 11					
Needham Market	d									07 50													
Ipswich	a			07 32					07 52	08 03					08 18			08 24					
	d			07 34			07 39		07 54						08 20			08 26					
Harwich Town	d				07 16											07 58			08 28				
Dovercourt	d				07 18											08 00			08 30				
Harwich International	d		07 15		07 21											08 03			08 33				
Wrabness	d				07 27											08 09			08 39				
Mistley	d				07 33											08 15			08 45				
Manningtree 2	d		07 32	07 44	07 38		07 49		08 04							08 20		08 36	08a50				
Walton-on-the-Naze	d																08 00				07 40		
Frinton-on-Sea	d																08 03				07 43		
Kirby Cross	d																08 06				07 46		
Clacton-on-Sea	d					07 16							07 45										08 15
Thorpe-le-Soken 1	a					07 24							07 53				08 11				07 52		08 23
	d					07 24							07 53				08 12				07 57		08 23
Weeley	d					07 28															08 01		
Great Bentley	d					07 31															08 04		08 28
Alresford (Essex)	d					07 35								←							08 08		08 32
Wivenhoe 3	d					07 39							08 03	08 12			08 22				08 12		08 36
Hythe	d					07 43								08 16			08 26				↪		
Colchester Town	a													08 20								←	
	d											08 00		08 32									
Colchester 4	a		07 41		07 47	07 50	07 58		08 13			08 09	08 16	08 40		08 29	08 35	08 45				08 40	08 46
Colchester 4	d		07 42		07 54		07 59		08 15			08 18		08 48		08 37		08 45				08 48	08 48
Marks Tey 2	d		07 48				08 05					08 24		↪								08 54	08 54
Kelvedon	d				08 04		08 10					08 30										09 00	09 00
Braintree	d										08 12												
Braintree Freeport	d										08 14												
Cressing	d										08 17												
White Notley	d										08 20												
Witham 2	d		08 03		08 11		08 16				08 28	08 36				08 50				08 58		09 06	09 06
Hatfield Peverel	d		08 07								08 32									09 02			
Chelmsford 3	d	08 09	08 15		08 20			08 27			08 39	08 45				08 59		09 04		09 09		09 15	09 15
Ingatestone	d	08 16						08 34			08 46									09 16			
Shenfield 3	a	08 21	08 24		08 30			08 39			08 51	08 55								09 21		09 25	09 25
Romford	a																						
Stratford 7 ⊖	a	08s38	08s42		08s47		08s50	08s55	08s58		09s07					09s24		09s28		09s37		09s41	09s41
London Liverpool Street 15 ⊖	a	08 50	08 54	08 42	08 59		09 01	09 08	09 10		09 19	09 21			09 24	09 36		09 40		09 49		09 53	09 53

A The East Anglian

Norwich, Ipswich, Harwich, Clacton, Walton-on-Naze, Colchester and Chelmsford - London

		LE R 1 ☕	LE 1	LE 1		LE 1	LE 1	LE R 1 ☕	LE 1	LE 1	LE 1	LE 1	LE 1	LE		LE 1	LE R 1 ☕	LE 1	LE 1	LE 1	LE 1	LE ◇1 ☕	LE 1	LE 1	
Norwich	d	08 00						08 30									09 00					09 30			
Diss	d	08 17						08 47									09 17					09 47			
Peterborough 8	d								07 45																
Stowmarket	d	08 29		08 44					09 14								09 29				09 44				
Needham Market	d			08 49																	09 49				
Ipswich	a	08 41		09 00				09 08	09 28								09 41				10 02	10 08			
	d	08 43				08 48		09 09									09 43			09 52		10 09			
Harwich Town	d									09 28													10 28		
Dovercourt	d									09 30													10 30		
Harwich International	d									09 33													10 33		
Wrabness	d									09 39													10 39		
Mistley	d									09 45													10 45		
Manningtree 2	d	08 53				08 58		09 19		09a50							09 53			10 02		10 19	10a50		
Walton-on-the-Naze	d										09 00													10 00	
Frinton-on-Sea	d										09 03													10 03	
Kirby Cross	d										09 06													10 06	
Clacton-on-Sea	d											09 05													
Thorpe-le-Soken 1	a										09 12	09 13												10 12	
	d										09 17	09 13												10 17	
Weeley	d										09 21													10 21	
Great Bentley	d										09 24													10 24	
Alresford (Essex)	d										09 28					←								10 28	
Wivenhoe 3	d										09 32	09 23				09 32								10 32	
Hythe	d										→					09 36								→	
Colchester Town	a															09 40									
	d						08 58						09 35			09 44		10 00							
Colchester 4	a	09 02				09 08	09 05	09 28				09 31	09 42			09 52	10 02	10 07		10 11		10 28			
Colchester 4	d	09 03					09 12	09 30				09 33	09 43	09 51			10 03			10 12		10 30			
Marks Tey 2	d						09 18						09 49	10a00						10 18					
Kelvedon	d						09 23						09 54							10 23					
Braintree	d		09 00																10 00						
Braintree Freeport	d		09 02																10 02						
Cressing	d		09 05																10 05						
White Notley	d		09 08																10 08						
Witham 2	d		09 16				09 29					09 46	10 00						10 16	10 29					
Hatfield Peverel	d						09 33													10 33					
Chelmsford 3	d	09 21	09 26				09 40					09 56	10 09				10 21		10 26	10 40					
Ingatestone	d		09 32									10 02							10 32						
Shenfield 3	a		09 38				09 50					10 08	10 19						10 38	10 50					
Romford	a												10 28												
Stratford 7 ⊖	a	09s46	09 52				10 05					10 22	10 36				10s45		10 52	11 05					
London Liverpool Street 15 ⊖	a	09 58	10 01				10 14	10 17				10 31	10 45				10 55		11 01	11 14		11 17			

		LE 1	LE 1	LE 1	LE ◇1 ☕	LE 1	LE 1	LE 1	LE 1	LE ◇1 ☕		LE 1	LE 1	LE 1	LE 1	LE 1	LE 1	LE ◇1 ☕	LE 1	LE 1		LE 1	LE 1	LE ◇1 ☕	LE 1
Norwich	d				10 00					10 30								11 00						11 30	
Diss	d				10 17					10 47								11 17						11 47	
Peterborough 8	d											09 45													
Stowmarket	d				10 29				10 44			11 14						11 29					11 44		
Needham Market	d								10 49														11 49		
Ipswich	a				10 41				11 00	11 08		11 28						11 41					12 00	12 08	
	d				10 43			10 52		11 09								11 43				11 52		12 09	
Harwich Town	d												11 28												12 28
Dovercourt	d												11 30												12 30
Harwich International	d												11 33												12 33
Wrabness	d												11 39												12 39
Mistley	d												11 45												12 45
Manningtree 2	d				10 53			11 02		11 19			11a50					11 53				12 02		12 19	12a50
Walton-on-the-Naze	d													11 00											
Frinton-on-Sea	d													11 03											
Kirby Cross	d													11 06											
Clacton-on-Sea	d	10 05													11 05										
Thorpe-le-Soken 1	a	10 13												11 12	11 13										
	d	10 13												11 17	11 13										
Weeley	d													11 21											
Great Bentley	d													11 24											
Alresford (Essex)	d			←										11 28			←								
Wivenhoe 3	d	10 23		10 32										11 32	11 23		11 32								
Hythe	d			10 36										→			11 36								
Colchester Town	a			10 40													11 40								
	d		10 35	10 44		11 00										11 35	11 44		12 00						
Colchester 4	a	10 31	10 42	10 52	11 02	11 07		11 11		11 28					11 31	11 42	11 52	12 02	12 07			12 11		12 28	
Colchester 4	d	10 33	10 43		11 03			11 12		11 30					11 33	11 43		12 03				12 12		12 30	
Marks Tey 2	d		10 49					11 18								11 49						12 18			
Kelvedon	d		10 54					11 23								11 54						12 23			
Braintree	d						11 00													12 00					
Braintree Freeport	d						11 02													12 02					
Cressing	d						11 05													12 05					
White Notley	d						11 08													12 08					
Witham 2	d	10 46	11 00				11 16	11 29							11 46	12 00				12 16		12 29			
Hatfield Peverel	d							11 33														12 33			
Chelmsford 3	d	10 56	11 09		11 21		11 26	11 40							11 56	12 09		12 21		12 26		12 40			
Ingatestone	d	11 02					11 32								12 02					12 32					
Shenfield 3	a	11 08	11 19				11 38	11 50							12 08	12 19				12 38		12 50			
Romford	a		11 28													12 28									
Stratford 7 ⊖	a	11 22	11 36		11s45		11 52	12 05							12 22	12 36		12s45		12 52		13 05			
London Liverpool Street 15 ⊖	a	11 31	11 45		11 55		12 01	12 14		12 17					12 31	12 45		12 55		13 01		13 14		13 17	

Norwich, Ipswich, Harwich, Clacton, Walton-on-Naze, Colchester and Chelmsford - London

		LE	LE	LE	LE	LE		LE	LE	LE	LE	LE	LE	LE	LE	LE		LE	LE	LE	LE	LE	LE	LE	LE
		1	1	1	1	◇1 ☕		1	1	1	1	◇1 ☕	1	1	1	1		1	1	◇1 ☕	1	1	1	1	◇1 ☕
Norwich	d					12 00						12 30								13 00					13 30
Diss	d					12 17						12 47								13 17					13 47
Peterborough 8	d												11 45												
Stowmarket	d					12 29					12 44		13 13							13 29				13 44	
Needham Market	d										12 49													13 49	
Ipswich	a					12 41					13 00	13 08	13 28							13 41				14 00	14 08
	d					12 43				12 52		13 09								13 43			13 52		14 09
Harwich Town	d													13 28											
Dovercourt	d													13 30											
Harwich International	d													13 33											
Wrabness	d													13 39											
Mistley	d													13 45											
Manningtree 2	d					12 53				13 02		13 19		13a50						13 53			14 02		14 19
Walton-on-the-Naze	d	12 00													13 00										
Frinton-on-Sea	d	12 03													13 03										
Kirby Cross	d	12 06													13 06										
Clacton-on-Sea	d		12 05													13 05									
Thorpe-le-Soken 1	a	12 12	12 13												13 12	13 13									
	d	12 17	12 13												13 17	13 13									
Weeley	d	12 21													13 21										
Great Bentley	d	12 24													13 24										
Alresford (Essex)	d	12 28			←										13 28				←						
Wivenhoe 3	d	12 32	12 23		12 32										13 32	13 23			13 32						
Hythe	d	↦			12 36										↦				13 36						
Colchester Town	a				12 40														13 40						
	d			12 35	12 44			13 00										13 35	13 44		14 00				
Colchester 4	a		12 31	12 42	12 52	13 02		13 07		13 11		13 28				13 31		13 42	13 52	14 02	14 07		14 11		14 28
Colchester 4	d		12 33	12 43		13 03				13 12		13 30				13 33		13 43		14 03			14 12		14 30
Marks Tey 2	d			12 49						13 18								13 49					14 18		
Kelvedon	d			12 54						13 23								13 54					14 23		
Braintree	d								13 00													14 00			
Braintree Freeport	d								13 02													14 02			
Cressing	d								13 05													14 05			
White Notley	d								13 08													14 08			
Witham 2	d		12 46	13 00					13 16	13 29						13 46		14 00				14 16	14 29		
Hatfield Peverel	d									13 33													14 33		
Chelmsford 3	d		12 56	13 09		13 21			13 26	13 40						13 56		14 09		14 21		14 26	14 40		
Ingatestone	d		13 02						13 32							14 02						14 32			
Shenfield 3	a		13 08	13 19					13 38	13 50						14 08		14 19				14 38	14 50		
Romford	a			13 28														14 28							
Stratford 7 ⊖	a		13 22	13 36		13s45			13 52	14 05						14 22		14 36		14s45		14 52	15 05		
London Liverpool Street 15 ⊖	a		13 31	13 45		13 55			14 01	14 14		14 17				14 31		14 45		14 55		15 01	15 14		15 17

		LE		LE	LE	LE	LE	LE	LE	LE	LE	LE		LE	LE	LE	LE	LE	LE	LE	LE	LE		LE	LE
		1		1	1	1	1	◇1 ☕	1	1	1	1		◇1 ☕	1	1	1	1	1	1	◇1 ☕	1		1	1
Norwich	d							14 00						14 30							15 00				
Diss	d							14 17						14 47							15 17				
Peterborough 8	d														13 45										
Stowmarket	d							14 29				14 44			15 13						15 29				
Needham Market	d											14 49													
Ipswich	a							14 41				15 00		15 08	15 28						15 41				
	d							14 43			14 52			15 09							15 43				15 52
Harwich Town	d	14 28														15 28									
Dovercourt	d	14 30														15 30									
Harwich International	d	14 33														15 33									
Wrabness	d	14 39														15 39									
Mistley	d	14 45														15 45									
Manningtree 2	d	14a50						14 53			15 02			15 19		15a50					15 53				16 02
Walton-on-the-Naze	d			14 00													15 00								
Frinton-on-Sea	d			14 03													15 03								
Kirby Cross	d			14 06													15 06								
Clacton-on-Sea	d				14 05													15 05							
Thorpe-le-Soken 1	a			14 12	14 13												15 12	15 13							
	d			14 17	14 13												15 17	15 13							
Weeley	d			14 21													15 21								
Great Bentley	d			14 24													15 24								
Alresford (Essex)	d			14 28			←										15 28			←					
Wivenhoe 3	d			14 32	14 23		14 32										15 32	15 23		15 32					
Hythe	d			↦			14 36										↦			15 36					
Colchester Town	a						14 40													15 40					
	d					14 35	14 44		15 00										15 35	15 44		16 00			
Colchester 4	a				14 31	14 42	14 52	15 02	15 07		15 11			15 28				15 31	15 42	15 52	16 02	16 07			16 11
Colchester 4	d				14 33	14 43		15 03			15 12			15 30				15 33	15 43		16 03				16 12
Marks Tey 2	d					14 49					15 18								15 49						16 18
Kelvedon	d					14 54					15 23								15 54						16 23
Braintree	d									15 00														16 00	
Braintree Freeport	d									15 02														16 02	
Cressing	d									15 05														16 05	
White Notley	d									15 08														16 08	
Witham 2	d				14 46	15 00				15 16	15 29							15 46	16 00					16 16	16 29
Hatfield Peverel	d										15 33														16 33
Chelmsford 3	d				14 56	15 09		15 21		15 26	15 40							15 56	16 09		16 21			16 26	16 40
Ingatestone	d				15 02					15 32								16 02						16 32	
Shenfield 3	a				15 08	15 19				15 38	15 50							16 08	16 19					16 38	16 50
Romford	a					15 28																			
Stratford 7 ⊖	a				15 22	15 36		15s45		15 52	16 05							16 22	16 34		16s45			16 52	17 05
London Liverpool Street 15 ⊖	a				15 31	15 45		15 55		16 01	16 14			16 17				16 31	16 44		16 55			17 03	17 16

Norwich, Ipswich, Harwich, Clacton, Walton-on-Naze, Colchester and Chelmsford - London

		LE ■1	LE ◇■1 ☕	LE ■1	LE ■1	LE ■1	LE ■1	LE ■1		LE ■1	LE ◇■1 ☕	LE ■1	LE ■1	LE ■1	LE ■1	LE ■1	LE ◇■1 ☕	LE ■1		LE ■1	LE ■1	LE ■1	LE ■1	LE ■1	LE ■1
Norwich	d		15 30								16 00						16 30								
Diss	d		15 47								16 17						16 47								
Peterborough ■8	d																	15 45							
Stowmarket	d	15 44									16 29				16 44			17 13							
Needham Market	d	15 49													16 49										
Ipswich	a	16 00	16 08								16 41				17 00		17 08	17 28							
	d		16 09								16 43			16 52			17 09								17 33
Harwich Town	d			16 28												16 53									
Dovercourt	d			16 30												16 55									
Harwich International	d			16 33												16 58									
Wrabness	d			16 39												17 04									
Mistley	d			16 45												17 10									
Manningtree ■2	d		16 19	16a50							16 53			17 02		17a15	17 19								17 43
Walton-on-the-Naze	d				16 00															17 00					
Frinton-on-Sea	d				16 03															17 03					
Kirby Cross	d				16 06															17 06					
Clacton-on-Sea	d					16 05															17 05				
Thorpe-le-Soken ■1	a				16 12	16 13														17 12	17 13				
	d				16 17	16 13														17 17	17 13				
Weeley	d				16 21															17 21					
Great Bentley	d				16 24															17 24					
Alresford (Essex)	d				16 28					←										17 28				←	
Wivenhoe ■3	d				16 32	16 23				16 32										17 32	17 23			17 32	
Hythe	d				→					16 36										→				17 36	
Colchester Town	a									16 40														17 40	
	d						16 35			16 44		16 56											17 30	17 44	
Colchester ■4	a		16 28			16 31	16 42			16 54	17 02	17 05		17 11			17 28				17 31		17 37	17 52	17 52
Colchester ■4	d		16 30			16 33	16 43	16 53			17 03			17 12			17 30				17 33		17 48		
Marks Tey ■2	d							16 59						17 18									17 54		
Kelvedon	d						16 52							17 23									17 59		
Braintree	d												17 00									17 44			
Braintree Freeport	d												17 02									17 46			
Cressing	d												17 05									17 49			
White Notley	d												17 08									17 52			
Witham ■2	d					16 46	16 58	17 08					17 16	17 29							17 46	18 00	18 05		
Hatfield Peverel	d						17 02							17 33									18 09		
Chelmsford ■3	d					16 56	17 09	17 17			17 21		17 26	17 40							17 56	18 09	18 16		
Ingatestone	d					17 02							17 32								18 02				
Shenfield ■3	a					17 08	17 19	17 27					17 38	17 50							18 08	18 19	18 26		
Romford	a																					18 28			
Stratford ■7 ⊖	a					17 22	17 36	17 42			17s45		17 52	18 06							18 22	18 36	18 42		
London Liverpool Street ■15 ⊖	a		17 19			17 34	17 46	17 53			17 58		18 01	18 15			18 17				18 31	18 45	18 51		

		LE ■1	LE ◇■1 ☕	LE ■1		LE ■1	LE ■1	LE ■1	LE ◇■1 ☕	LE ■1	LE ■1	LE ■1	LE ■1	LE ■1		LE ■1	LE ■1	LE ■1	LE ■1	LE ■1	LE ◇■1 ☕	LE ■1	LE ■1	LE ■1	
Norwich	d		17 00						17 30												18 00				
Diss	d		17 17						17 47												18 17				
Peterborough ■8	d																								
Stowmarket	d		17 29	17 45					17 59												18 29			18 45	
Needham Market	d			17 50																				18 50	
Ipswich	a		17 41	18 04					18 11												18 41			19 02	
	d		17 43						18 13							18 22					18 43		18 47		
Harwich Town	d	17 28				18 00												18 26							
Dovercourt	d	17 30				18 02												18 28							
Harwich International	d	17 33				18 05												18 31							
Wrabness	d	17 39				18 11												18 37							
Mistley	d	17 45				18 17												18 43							
Manningtree ■2	d	17a50	17 53			18a22										18 33		18a48			18 53		18 57		
Walton-on-the-Naze	d									17 56			18 33						18 54						
Frinton-on-Sea	d									17 59			18 36						18 57						
Kirby Cross	d									18 02			18 42						19 00						
Clacton-on-Sea	d										18 05														
Thorpe-le-Soken ■1	a									18 08	18 13		18 48						19 08						
	d									18 17	18 13								19 17						
Weeley	d									18 21									19 21						
Great Bentley	d									18 24									19 24						
Alresford (Essex)	d									18 28							←		19 28						
Wivenhoe ■3	d									18 32	18 23						18 32		19 32						
Hythe	d									→							18 36		→						
Colchester Town	a																18 40								
	d											18 32					18 44								
Colchester ■4	a		18 02						18 28		18 31	18 39				18 42	18 52				19 02		19 06		
Colchester ■4	d		18 03					18 12	18 30		18 33					18 43				18 55	19 03		19 12		
Marks Tey ■2	d							18 18								18 49				19 01			19 18		
Kelvedon	d							18 23								18 54							19 23		
Braintree	d													18 34											
Braintree Freeport	d													18 36											
Cressing	d													18 39											
White Notley	d													18 42											
Witham ■2	d						18 16	18 29			18 46			18 50		19 00				19 16			19 29		
Hatfield Peverel	d							18 33						18 54								←	19 33		
Chelmsford ■3	d		18 21				18 26	18 40			18 56			19 01		19 09				19 26	19 21	19 26	19 40		
Ingatestone	d						18 32				19 02									→		19 32			
Shenfield ■3	a						18 38	18 50			19 08			19 13		19 19						19 38	19 50		
Romford	a															19 28									
Stratford ■7 ⊖	a		18s45				18 52	19 05			19 22			19 27		19 36					19s45	19 52	20 05		
London Liverpool Street ■15 ⊖	a		18 55				19 01	19 14	19 17		19 31			19 36		19 45					19 55	20 01	20 14		

Norwich, Ipswich, Harwich, Clacton, Walton-on-Naze, Colchester and Chelmsford - London

		LE 1	LE ◇1 ⊡	LE 1	LE 1	LE 1	LE 1	LE 1	LE 1	LE 1	LE 1	LE 1	LE 1	LE ◇1 ⊡	LE 1	LE 1	LE 1	LE 1	LE 1	LE ◇1	LE 1	LE 1	LE 1
Norwich	d		18 30											19 00						19 30			
Diss	d		18 47											19 17						19 47			
Peterborough 8	d										17 45												
Stowmarket	d										19 13			19 29					19 44				
Needham Market	d																		19 49				
Ipswich	a		19 08								19 28			19 41					20 00	20 09			
	d		19 09						19 23			19 35		19 43				19 49		20 09			
Harwich Town	d			19 05									19 28								20 05		
Dovercourt	d			19 07									19 30								20 07		
Harwich International	d			19 10									19 33								20 10		
Wrabness	d			19 16									19 39								20 16		
Mistley	d			19 22									19 45								20 22		
Manningtree 2	d		19 19	19a27					19 36			19 45	19a50	19 53				20 02		20 19	20a27		
Walton-on-the-Naze	d						19 15															19 55	
Frinton-on-Sea	d						19 18															19 58	
Kirby Cross	d						19 21															20 01	
Clacton-on-Sea	d					19 02																	20 05
Thorpe-le-Soken 1	a					19 10	19 27															20 07	20 13
	d					19 10																20 17	20 13
Weeley	d																					20 21	
Great Bentley	d																					20 24	
Alresford (Essex)	d									←												20 28	
Wivenhoe 3	d					19 23				19 32												20 32	20 23
Hythe	d									19 36												→	
Colchester Town	a									19 40													
	d	19 12						19 35		19 44						20 00							
Colchester 4	a	19 20	19 28			19 31		19 42	19 46	19 52		19 54		20 02		20 07		20 11		20 29			20 31
Colchester 4	d		19 30			19 33		19 43				19 55		20 03				20 12		20 30			20 33
Marks Tey 2	d							19 49				20 01						20 18					
Kelvedon	d							19 54										20 23					
Braintree	d				19 26												20 11						
Braintree Freeport	d				19 28												20 13						
Cressing	d				19 31												20 16						
White Notley	d				19 34												20 19						
Witham 2	d				19 42	19 46		20 00				20 16					20 27	20 31					20 46
Hatfield Peverel	d														←			20 35					
Chelmsford 3	d				19 51	19 56		20 09				20 26		20 21	20 26		20 36	20 42					20 56
Ingatestone	d					20 02						→			20 32								21 02
Shenfield 3	a					20 08		20 19							20 38		20 46	20 52					21 08
Romford	a							20 28															
Stratford 7 ⊖	a				20 14	20 22		20 36						20s45	20 52			21 07					21 22
London Liverpool Street 15 ⊖	a		20 17		20 23	20 31		20 45						20 55	21 01		21 12	21 16		21 18			21 31

		LE 1	LE 1	LE 1	LE 1	LE 1	LE ◇1 ⊡	LE 1	LE 1	LE 1	LE 1	LE ◇1	LE 1	LE 1	LE 1	LE ◇1	LE 1	LE 1	LE ◇1 ⊡	LE 1	LE 1	LE 1	LE 1
Norwich	d						20 00					20 30							21 00				
Diss	d						20 17					20 47							21 17				
Peterborough 8	d															19 45							
Stowmarket	d						20 29				20 44					21 11			21 29	21 44			
Needham Market	d										20 49									21 49			
Ipswich	a						20 41				21 00	21 08				21 25			21 41	22 00			
	d	20 20					20 43				21 00	21 09				21 26			21 43				
Harwich Town	d		20 28															21 28					
Dovercourt	d		20 30															21 30					
Harwich International	d		20 33							20 45	21a29							21 33					
Wrabness	d		20 39															21 39					
Mistley	d		20 45															21 45					
Manningtree 2	d	20 33	20a50				20 53			20 58		21 19				21 37		21a50	21 53				
Walton-on-the-Naze	d			20 33									21 00										22 00
Frinton-on-Sea	d			20 36									21 03										22 03
Kirby Cross	d			20 42									21 06										22 06
Clacton-on-Sea	d													21 05									
Thorpe-le-Soken 1	a			20 48									21 12	21 13									22 12
	d												21 17	21 13									22 17
Weeley	d												21 21										22 21
Great Bentley	d												21 24										22 24
Alresford (Essex)	d					←							21 28				←						22 28
Wivenhoe 3	d					20 32							21 32	21 23			21 32						22 32
Hythe	d					20 36							→				21 36						→
Colchester Town	a					20 40											21 40						
	d				20 35	20 44		21 00							21 35		21 44					22 00	
Colchester 4	a	20 45			20 42	20 52	21 02	21 07		21 07		21 28		21 31	21 42	21 48	21 52		22 02			22 07	
Colchester 4	d				20 50		21 03			21 12		21 30		21 33	21 43				22 03			22 12	
Marks Tey 2	d				20 56					21 18					21 49							22 18	
Kelvedon	d				21 01					21 23					21 54							22 23	
Braintree	d								21 00												22 00		
Braintree Freeport	d								21 02												22 02		
Cressing	d								21 05												22 05		
White Notley	d								21 08												22 08		
Witham 2	d				21 07				21 16	21 29				21 46	22 00						22 16	22 29	
Hatfield Peverel	d									21 33												22 33	
Chelmsford 3	d				21 16		21 21		21 26	21 40				21 56	22 09				22 21		22 26	22 40	
Ingatestone	d								21 32					22 02							22 32		
Shenfield 3	a				21 26				21 38	21 50				22 08	22 19						22 38	22 50	
Romford	a														22 28								
Stratford 7 ⊖	a				21 42		21s45		21 52	22 05				22 22	22 36				22s45		22 52	23 05	
London Liverpool Street 15 ⊖	a				21 51		21 55		22 01	22 14		22 17		22 31	22 45				22 55		23 01	23 15	

Table 11

Mondays to Fridays

Norwich, Ipswich, Harwich, Clacton, Walton-on-Naze, Colchester and Chelmsford - London

		LE 1		LE 1	LE 1	LE 1	LE 1	LE ◇1	LE 1	LE 1	LE 1	LE 1		LE 1	LE ◇1	LE 1	LE 1	LE 1	LE
Norwich	d							22 00								23 05			
Diss	d							22 17								23 22			
Peterborough 8	d														21 45				
Stowmarket	d							22 29	22 44						23 06	23 34			23 47
Needham Market	d								22 49										23 52
Ipswich	a							22 41	23 00						23 18	23 48			00 05
	d			22 23				22 43				23 15			23 19				
Harwich Town	d					22 28											23 28		
Dovercourt	d					22 30											23 30		
Harwich International	d					22 33											23 33		
Wrabness	d					22 39											23 39		
Mistley	d					22 45											23 45		
Manningtree 2	d			22 33		22a50		22 53				23 25			23 29		23 50		
Walton-on-the-Naze	d										23 00								
Frinton-on-Sea	d										23 03								
Kirby Cross	d										23 06								
Clacton-on-Sea	d	22 05												23 05					
Thorpe-le-Soken 1	a	22 13									23 12			23 13					
	d	22 13												23 13					
Weeley	d													23 17					
Great Bentley	d													23 20					
Alresford (Essex)	d				←									23 24					
Wivenhoe 3	d	22 23			22 32									23 28					
Hythe	d				22 36									23 32					
Colchester Town	a				22 40														
	d				22 44					23 00									
Colchester 4	a	22 31		22 42	22 52			23 02		23 07		23 35		23 38	23 40		23 59		
Colchester 4	d	22 33		22 43				23 03											
Marks Tey 2	d			22 49															
Kelvedon	d			22 54															
Braintree	d						22 56											23 45	
Braintree Freeport	d						22 58											23 47	
Cressing	d						23 01											23 50	
White Notley	d						23 04											23 53	
Witham 2	d	22 46		23 00			23a12	23 16										00a01	
Hatfield Peverel	d																		
Chelmsford 3	d	22 56		23 09				23 25											
Ingatestone	d	23 02																	
Shenfield 3	a	23 08		23 19				23s36											
Romford	a			23 28															
Stratford 7 ⊖	a	23 22		23 36				23s52											
London Liverpool Street 15 ⊖	a	23 31		23 45				00 02											

Saturdays

		LE ◇1	LE	LE 1	LE 1	LE 1	LE	LE 1	LE ◇1	LE 1		LE 1	LE ◇1	LE 1	LE 1	LE 1	LE 1	LE 1	LE ◇1	LE 1		LE 1	LE	LE ◇1	LE 1
Norwich	d	22p00							05 00				05 30						06 00					06 30	
Diss	d	22p17							05 17				05 47						06 17					06 47	
Peterborough 8	d																								
Stowmarket	d	22p29	23p47						05 29										06 29				06 44		
Needham Market	d		23p52																				06 49		
Ipswich	a	22p41	00 05						05 41				06 08						06 41				07 02	07 08	
	d	22p43							05 43				06 09						06 43			06 52		07 09	
Harwich Town	d													06 28											
Dovercourt	d													06 30											
Harwich International	d													06 33											
Wrabness	d													06 39											
Mistley	d													06 45											
Manningtree 2	d	22p53							05 53				06 19	06a50					06 53			07 02		07 19	
Walton-on-the-Naze	d														06 00										07 00
Frinton-on-Sea	d														06 03										07 03
Kirby Cross	d														06 06										07 06
Clacton-on-Sea	d							05 30								06 05									
Thorpe-le-Soken 1	a							05 38							06 12	06 13									07 12
	d							05 38							06 17	06 13									07 17
Weeley	d														06 21										07 21
Great Bentley	d														06 24										07 24
Alresford (Essex)	d														06 28			←							07 28
Wivenhoe 3	d							05 48							06 32	06 23		06 32							07 32
Hythe	d														→			06 36							→
Colchester Town	a																	06 40							
	d																06 35	06 44							
Colchester 4	a	23p02						05 57	06 02				06 28			06 31	06 42	06 52	07 02			07 11		07 28	
Colchester 4	d	23p03			05 12	05 43	05 50		06 03			06 12	06 30			06 33	06 43		07 03			07 12		07 30	
Marks Tey 2	d				05 18	05 49	05a57					06 18					06 49					07 18			
Kelvedon	d				05 23	05 54						06 23					06 54					07 23			
Braintree	d			00 25						06 00										07 00					
Braintree Freeport	d			00 27						06 02										07 02					
Cressing	d			00 30						06 05										07 05					
White Notley	d			00 33						06 08										07 08					
Witham 2	d	23p16		00a41	05 29	06 00				06a16		06 29				06 46	07 00			07 16		07 29			
Hatfield Peverel	d				05 33	06 04						06 33										07 33			
Chelmsford 3	d	23p25			05 40	06 11			06 21			06 40				06 56	07 09		07 21	07 26		07 40			
Ingatestone	d				05 47	06 18										07 02				07 32					
Shenfield 3	a	23b36			05 52	06 23						06 50				07 08	07 19			07 38		07 50			
Romford	a																07 28								
Stratford 7 ⊖	a	23b52			06 07	06 38			06s45			07 05				07 22	07 36		07s45	07 52		08 05			
London Liverpool Street 15 ⊖	a	00 02			06 16	06 47			06 55			07 14	07 17			07 31	07 45		07 55	08 01		08 14		08 17	

b Previous night, stops to set down only

Table 11

Saturdays

Norwich, Ipswich, Harwich, Clacton, Walton-on-Naze, Colchester and Chelmsford - London

		LE	LE	LE	LE	LE		LE	LE	LE	LE	LE	LE	LE	LE	LE		LE	LE	LE	LE	LE	LE	LE	LE
		1	1	1	1	◇1 ☕		1	1	1		◇1 ☕	1	1	1	1		1	◇1 ☕	1	1	1	1	◇1 ☕	1
Norwich	d					07 00						07 30							08 00					08 30	
Diss	d					07 17						07 47							08 17					08 47	
Peterborough 8	d																								07 45
Stowmarket	d					07 29					07 45								08 29				08 44		09 13
Needham Market	d										07 50												08 49		
Ipswich	a					07 41					08 03	08 08							08 41				09 00	09 08	09 28
	d					07 43				07 52		08 09							08 43			08 52		09 09	
Harwich Town	d				07 28								08 28												
Dovercourt	d				07 30								08 30												
Harwich International	d		07 20		07 33								08 33												
Wrabness	d				07 39								08 39												
Mistley	d				07 45								08 45												
Manningtree 2	d		07 33		07a50	07 53				08 02		08 19	08a50						08 53			09 02		09 19	
Walton-on-the-Naze	d													08 00											
Frinton-on-Sea	d													08 03											
Kirby Cross	d													08 06											
Clacton-on-Sea	d	07 05													08 05										
Thorpe-le-Soken 1	a	07 13												08 12	08 13										
	d	07 13												08 17	08 13										
Weeley	d													08 21											
Great Bentley	d													08 24											
Alresford (Essex)	d			←										08 28				←							
Wivenhoe 3	d	07 23		07 32										08 32	08 23			08 32							
Hythe	d			07 36										→				08 36							
Colchester Town	a			07 40														08 40							
	d			07 44				08 00								08 35		08 44		09 00					
Colchester 4	a	07 31	07 42	07 52		08 02		08 07		08 11		08 28			08 31	08 42		08 52	09 02	09 07		09 11		09 28	
Colchester 4	d	07 33	07 43			08 03				08 12		08 30			08 33	08 43			09 03			09 12		09 30	
Marks Tey 2	d		07 49							08 18						08 49						09 18			
Kelvedon	d		07 54							08 23						08 54						09 23			
Braintree	d								08 00												09 00				
Braintree Freeport	d								08 02												09 02				
Cressing	d								08 05												09 05				
White Notley	d								08 08												09 08				
Witham 2	d	07 46	08 00						08 16	08 29					08 46	09 00					09 16	09 29			
Hatfield Peverel	d									08 33												09 33			
Chelmsford 3	d	07 56	08 09			08 21			08 26	08 40					08 56	09 09			09 21		09 26	09 40			
Ingatestone	d	08 02							08 32						09 02						09 32				
Shenfield 3	a	08 08	08 19						08 38	08 50					09 08	09 19					09 38	09 50			
Romford	a		08 28													09 28									
Stratford 7 ⊖	a	08 22	08 36			08s45			08 52	09 05					09 22	09 36			09s45		09 52	10 05			
London Liverpool Street 15 ⊖	a	08 31	08 45			08 55			09 01	09 14		09 17			09 31	09 45			09 55		10 01	10 14		10 17	

		LE		LE	LE	LE	LE	LE	LE	LE	LE	LE		LE	LE	LE	LE	LE	LE	LE	LE	LE		LE	LE
		1		1	1	1	1	◇1 ☕	1	1	1	1		◇1 ☕	1	1	1	1	1	◇1 ☕	1	1		1	1
Norwich	d							09 00						09 30						10 00					
Diss	d							09 17						09 47						10 17					
Peterborough 8	d																								
Stowmarket	d							09 29				09 44								10 29					10 44
Needham Market	d											09 49													10 49
Ipswich	a							09 41				10 00		10 08						10 41					11 00
	d							09 43			09 52			10 09						10 43				10 52	
Harwich Town	d	09 28													10 28										
Dovercourt	d	09 30													10 30										
Harwich International	d	09 33													10 33										
Wrabness	d	09 39													10 39										
Mistley	d	09 45													10 45										
Manningtree 2	d	09a50						09 53			10 02			10 19	10a50					10 53				11 02	
Walton-on-the-Naze	d			09 00												10 00									
Frinton-on-Sea	d			09 03												10 03									
Kirby Cross	d			09 06												10 06									
Clacton-on-Sea	d				09 05												10 05								
Thorpe-le-Soken 1	a			09 12	09 13											10 12	10 13								
	d			09 17	09 13											10 17	10 13								
Weeley	d			09 21												10 21									
Great Bentley	d			09 24												10 24									
Alresford (Essex)	d			09 28			←									10 28			←						
Wivenhoe 3	d			09 32	09 23		09 32									10 32	10 23		10 32						
Hythe	d			→			09 36									→			10 36						
Colchester Town	a						09 40												10 40						
	d					09 35	09 44		10 00									10 35	10 44		11 00				
Colchester 4	a				09 31	09 42	09 52	10 02	10 07		10 11			10 28			10 31	10 42	10 52	11 02	11 07			11 11	
Colchester 4	d				09 33	09 43		10 03			10 12			10 30			10 33	10 43		11 03				11 12	
Marks Tey 2	d					09 49					10 18							10 49						11 18	
Kelvedon	d					09 54					10 23							10 54						11 23	
Braintree	d									10 00												11 00			
Braintree Freeport	d									10 02												11 02			
Cressing	d									10 05												11 05			
White Notley	d									10 08												11 08			
Witham 2	d				09 46	10 00				10 16	10 29						10 46	11 00				11 16		11 29	
Hatfield Peverel	d										10 33													11 33	
Chelmsford 3	d				09 56	10 09		10 21		10 26	10 40						10 56	11 09		11 21		11 26		11 40	
Ingatestone	d				10 02					10 32							11 02					11 32			
Shenfield 3	a				10 08	10 19				10 38	10 50						11 08	11 19				11 38		11 50	
Romford	a					10 28												11 28							
Stratford 7 ⊖	a				10 22	10 36		10s45		10 52	11 05						11 22	11 36		11s45		11 52		12 05	
London Liverpool Street 15 ⊖	a				10 31	10 45		10 55		11 01	11 14			11 17			11 31	11 45		11 55		12 01		12 14	

Table 11

Saturdays

Norwich, Ipswich, Harwich, Clacton, Walton-on-Naze, Colchester and Chelmsford - London

		LE	LE	LE	LE	LE	LE	LE		LE	LE	LE	LE	LE		LE	LE	LE		LE	LE	LE	LE	LE	LE
																R									
		◇1	1	1	1	1	1	1		◇1	1	1	1	1		◇1	1	1		1	1	1	◇1	1	1
																B									
		☕								☕						☕							☕		
Norwich	d	10 30								11 00						11 30							12 00		
Diss	d	10 47								11 17						11 47							12 17		
Peterborough 8	d		09 46																						
Stowmarket	d		11 06							11 29				11 44									12 29		
Needham Market	d													11 49											
Ipswich	a	11 08	11 20							11 41				12 00		12 08							12 41		
	d	11 09								11 43			11 52			12 09							12 43		
Harwich Town	d			11 28													12 28								
Dovercourt	d			11 30													12 30								
Harwich International	d			11 33													12 33								
Wrabness	d			11 39													12 39								
Mistley	d			11 45													12 45								
Manningtree 2	d	11 19		11a50						11 53			12 02			12 19	12a50						12 53		
Walton-on-the-Naze	d				11 00													12 00							
Frinton-on-Sea	d				11 03													12 03							
Kirby Cross	d				11 06													12 06							
Clacton-on-Sea	d					11 05														12 05					
Thorpe-le-Soken 1	a				11 12	11 13												12 12		12 13					
	d				11 17	11 13												12 17		12 13					
Weeley	d				11 21													12 21							
Great Bentley	d				11 24													12 24							
Alresford (Essex)	d				11 28			←										12 28				←			
Wivenhoe 3	d				11 32	11 23		11 32										12 32		12 23		12 32			
Hythe	d				→			11 36										→				12 36			
Colchester Town	a							11 40														12 40			
	d						11 35	11 44			12 00										12 35	12 44		13 00	
Colchester 4	a	11 28				11 31	11 42	11 52		12 02	12 07		12 11			12 28				12 31	12 42	12 52	13 02	13 07	
Colchester 4	d	11 30				11 33	11 43			12 03			12 12			12 30				12 33	12 43		13 03		
Marks Tey 2	d						11 49						12 18								12 49				
Kelvedon	d						11 54						12 23								12 54				
Braintree	d											12 00													13 00
Braintree Freeport	d											12 02													13 02
Cressing	d											12 05													13 05
White Notley	d											12 08													13 08
Witham 2	d					11 46	12 00					12 16	12 29							12 46	13 00				13 16
Hatfield Peverel	d												12 33												
Chelmsford 3	d					11 56	12 09			12 21		12 26	12 40							12 56	13 09		13 21		13 26
Ingatestone	d					12 02						12 32								13 02					13 32
Shenfield 3	a					12 08	12 19					12 38	12 50							13 08	13 19				13 38
Romford	a						12 28														13 28				
Stratford 7 ⊖	a					12 22	12 36			12s45		12 52	13 05							13 22	13 36		13s45		13 52
London Liverpool Street 15 ⊖	a	12 17				12 31	12 45			12 55		13 01	13 14			13 17				13 31	13 45		13 55		14 01

Table 11

Saturdays

Norwich, Ipswich, Harwich, Clacton, Walton-on-Naze, Colchester and Chelmsford - London

		LE	LE	LE		LE	LE	LE	LE	LE	LE	LE	LE	LE		LE	LE	LE	LE	LE	LE	LE	LE
		1	1	◇1		1	1	1	1	1	1	◇1	1	1		1	1	◇1	1	1	1	1	1
				☕								☕						☕					
Norwich	d			12 30								13 00						13 30					
Diss	d			12 47								13 17						13 47					
Peterborough 8	d					11 45																	
Stowmarket	d		12 44			13 13						13 29					13 44						
Needham Market	d		12 49														13 49						
Ipswich	a		13 00	13 08		13 28						13 41					14 00	14 08					
	d	12 52		13 09								13 43				13 52		14 09					
Harwich Town	d						13 28												14 28				
Dovercourt	d						13 30												14 30				
Harwich International	d						13 33												14 33				
Wrabness	d						13 39												14 39				
Mistley	d						13 45												14 45				
Manningtree 2	d	13 02		13 19			13a50					13 53				14 02		14 19	14a50				
Walton-on-the-Naze	d							13 00												14 00			
Frinton-on-Sea	d							13 03												14 03			
Kirby Cross	d							13 06												14 06			
Clacton-on-Sea	d								13 05												14 05		
Thorpe-le-Soken 1	a							13 12	13 13											14 12	14 13		
	d							13 17	13 13											14 17	14 13		
Weeley	d							13 21												14 21			
Great Bentley	d							13 24												14 24			
Alresford (Essex)	d							13 28			←									14 28			←
Wivenhoe 3	d							13 32	13 23		13 32									14 32	14 23		14 32
Hythe	d							↪			13 36									↪			14 36
Colchester Town	a										13 40												14 40
	d									13 35	13 44		14 00									14 35	14 44
Colchester 4	a	13 11		13 28					13 31	13 42	13 52	14 02	14 07			14 11		14 28			14 31	14 42	14 52
Colchester 4	d	13 12		13 30					13 33	13 43		14 03				14 12		14 30			14 33	14 43	
Marks Tey 2	d	13 18								13 49						14 18						14 49	
Kelvedon	d	13 23								13 54						14 23						14 54	
Braintree	d													14 00									
Braintree Freeport	d													14 02									
Cressing	d													14 05									
White Notley	d													14 08									
Witham 2	d	13 29							13 46	14 00				14 16		14 29					14 46	15 00	
Hatfield Peverel	d	13 33														14 33							
Chelmsford 3	d	13 40							13 56	14 09		14 21		14 26		14 40					14 56	15 09	
Ingatestone	d								14 02					14 32							15 02		
Shenfield 3	a	13 50							14 08	14 19				14 38		14 50					15 08	15 19	
Romford	a									14 28												15 28	
Stratford 7 ⊖	a	14 05							14 22	14 36		14s45		14 52		15 05					15 22	15 36	
London Liverpool Street 15 ⊖	a	14 14		14 17					14 31	14 45		14 55		15 01		15 14		15 17			15 31	15 45	

Table 11

Saturdays

Norwich, Ipswich, Harwich, Clacton, Walton-on-Naze, Colchester and Chelmsford - London

		LE	LE	LE	LE	LE	LE	LE	LE	LE		LE	LE	LE	LE	LE	LE	LE	LE	LE		LE	LE	LE	LE
		◇1	1	1	1	1	◇1	1	1	1		1	1	1	◇1	1	1	1	1	◇1		1	1	1	1
		☐P					☐P								☐P					☐P					
		R																							
Norwich	d	14 00					14 30								15 00					15 30					
Diss	d	14 17					14 47								15 17					15 47					
Peterborough 8	d							13 45																	
Stowmarket	d	14 29				14 44		15 13							15 29				15 44						
Needham Market	d					14 49													15 49						
Ipswich	a	14 41				15 00	15 08	15 28							15 41				16 00	16 08					
	d	14 43			14 52		15 09								15 43			15 52		16 09					
Harwich Town	d								15 28													16 28			
Dovercourt	d								15 30													16 30			
Harwich International	d								15 33													16 33			
Wrabness	d								15 39													16 39			
Mistley	d								15 45													16 45			
Manningtree 2	d	14 53			15 02		15 19		15a50						15 53			16 02		16 19		16a50			
Walton-on-the-Naze	d									15 00													16 00		
Frinton-on-Sea	d									15 03													16 03		
Kirby Cross	d									15 06													16 06		
Clacton-on-Sea	d											15 05												16 05	
Thorpe-le-Soken 1	a									15 12		15 13											16 12	16 13	
	d									15 17		15 13											16 17	16 13	
Weeley	d									15 21													16 21		
Great Bentley	d									15 24													16 24		
Alresford (Essex)	d									15 28				←									16 28		
Wivenhoe 3	d									15 32		15 23		15 32									16 32	16 23	
Hythe	d									→				15 36									→		
Colchester Town	a													15 40											
	d		15 00										15 35	15 44		16 00									16 35
Colchester 4	a	15 02	15 07		15 11		15 28					15 31	15 42	15 52	16 02	16 07		16 11		16 28				16 31	16 42
Colchester 4	d	15 03			15 12		15 30					15 33	15 43		16 03			16 12		16 30				16 33	16 43
Marks Tey 2	d				15 18								15 49					16 18							16 49
Kelvedon	d				15 23								15 54					16 23							16 54
Braintree	d			15 00													16 00								
Braintree Freeport	d			15 02													16 02								
Cressing	d			15 05													16 05								
White Notley	d			15 08													16 08								
Witham 2	d			15 16	15 29							15 46	16 00				16 16	16 29						16 46	17 00
Hatfield Peverel	d				15 33													16 33							
Chelmsford 3	d	15 21		15 26	15 40							15 56	16 09		16 21		16 26	16 40						16 56	17 09
Ingatestone	d			15 32								16 02					16 32							17 02	
Shenfield 3	a			15 38	15 50							16 08	16 19				16 38	16 50						17 08	17 19
Romford	a												16 28												17 28
Stratford 7 ⊖	a	15s45		15 52	16 05							16 22	16 36		16s45		16 52	17 05						17 22	17 36
London Liverpool Street 15 ⊖	a	15 55		16 01	16 14		16 17					16 31	16 45		16 55		17 01	17 14		17 17				17 31	17 45

Norwich, Ipswich, Harwich, Clacton, Walton-on-Naze, Colchester and Chelmsford - London

Station		LE 1	LE ◇1 ☕	LE 1	LE 1	LE 1		LE 1	LE ◇1 ☕	LE 1	LE 1	LE 1	LE 1
Norwich	d		16 00						16 30				
Diss	d		16 17						16 47				
Peterborough 8	d									15 45			
Stowmarket	d		16 29					16 44		17 13			
Needham Market	d							16 49					
Ipswich	a		16 41					17 00	17 08	17 28			
	d		16 43			16 52			17 09				
Harwich Town	d										17 28		
Dovercourt	d										17 30		
Harwich International	d										17 33		
Wrabness	d										17 39		
Mistley	d										17 45		
Manningtree 2	d		16 53			17 02			17 19		17a50		
Walton-on-the-Naze	d											17 00	
Frinton-on-Sea	d											17 03	
Kirby Cross	d											17 06	
Clacton-on-Sea	d												17 05
Thorpe-le-Soken 1	a											17 12	17 13
	d											17 17	17 13
Weeley	d											17 21	
Great Bentley	d											17 24	
Alresford (Essex)	d	←										17 28	
Wivenhoe 3	d	16 32										17 32	17 23
Hythe	d	16 36										→	
Colchester Town	a	16 40											
	d	16 44		17 00									
Colchester 4	a	16 52	17 02	17 07		17 11			17 28				17 31
Colchester 4	d		17 03			17 12			17 30				17 33
Marks Tey 2	d					17 18							
Kelvedon	d					17 23							
Braintree	d				17 00								
Braintree Freeport	d				17 02								
Cressing	d				17 05								
White Notley	d				17 08								
Witham 2	d				17 16	17 29							17 46
Hatfield Peverel	d					17 33							
Chelmsford 3	d		17 21		17 26	17 40							17 56
Ingatestone	d				17 32								18 02
Shenfield 3	a				17 38	17 50							18 08
Romford	a												
Stratford 7 ⊖	a		17s45		17 52	18 05							18 22
London Liverpool Street 15 ⊖	a		17 55		18 01	18 14			18 17				18 31

Station		LE 1	LE 1	LE ◇1 ☕		LE 1	LE 1	LE 1	LE 1	LE ◇1 ☕	LE 1	LE 1	LE 1
Norwich	d			17 00						17 30			
Diss	d			17 17						17 47			
Peterborough 8	d												
Stowmarket	d			17 29					17 45	17 59			
Needham Market	d								17 50				
Ipswich	a			17 41					18 01	18 11			
	d			17 43				17 52		18 13			
Harwich Town	d										18 28		
Dovercourt	d										18 30		
Harwich International	d										18 33		
Wrabness	d										18 39		
Mistley	d										18 45		
Manningtree 2	d			17 53				18 02			18a50		
Walton-on-the-Naze	d											18 00	
Frinton-on-Sea	d											18 03	
Kirby Cross	d											18 06	
Clacton-on-Sea	d												18 05
Thorpe-le-Soken 1	a											18 12	18 13
	d											18 17	18 13
Weeley	d											18 21	
Great Bentley	d											18 24	
Alresford (Essex)	d		←									18 28	
Wivenhoe 3	d		17 32									18 32	18 23
Hythe	d		17 36									→	
Colchester Town	a		17 40										
	d	17 35	17 44			18 00							
Colchester 4	a	17 42	17 52	18 02		18 07		18 11		18 28			18 31
Colchester 4	d	17 43		18 03				18 12		18 30			18 33
Marks Tey 2	d	17 49						18 18					
Kelvedon	d	17 54						18 23					
Braintree	d						18 00						
Braintree Freeport	d						18 02						
Cressing	d						18 05						
White Notley	d						18 08						
Witham 2	d	18 00					18 16	18 29					18 46
Hatfield Peverel	d							18 33					
Chelmsford 3	d	18 09		18 21			18 26	18 40					18 56
Ingatestone	d						18 32						19 02
Shenfield 3	a	18 19					18 38	18 50					19 08
Romford	a	18 28											
Stratford 7 ⊖	a	18 36		18s45			18 52	19 05					19 22
London Liverpool Street 15 ⊖	a	18 45		18 55			19 01	19 14		19 17			19 31

Station		LE 1		LE 1	LE ◇1 ☕	LE 1	LE 1	LE 1	LE 1	LE ◇1 ☕	LE 1	LE 1	
Norwich	d				18 00					18 30			
Diss	d				18 17					18 47			
Peterborough 8	d										17 45		
Stowmarket	d				18 29				18 45		19 13		
Needham Market	d								18 50				
Ipswich	a				18 41				19 01	19 08	19 28		
	d				18 43			18 52		19 09			
Harwich Town	d											19 28	
Dovercourt	d											19 30	
Harwich International	d											19 33	
Wrabness	d											19 39	
Mistley	d											19 45	
Manningtree 2	d				18 53			19 02		19 19		19a50	
Walton-on-the-Naze	d												
Frinton-on-Sea	d												
Kirby Cross	d												
Clacton-on-Sea	d												
Thorpe-le-Soken 1	a												
	d												
Weeley	d												
Great Bentley	d												
Alresford (Essex)	d			←									
Wivenhoe 3	d			18 32									
Hythe	d			18 36									
Colchester Town	a			18 40									
	d	18 35		18 44		19 00							
Colchester 4	a	18 42		18 52	19 02	19 07		19 11		19 28			
Colchester 4	d	18 43			19 03			19 12		19 30			
Marks Tey 2	d	18 49						19 18					
Kelvedon	d	18 54						19 23					
Braintree	d						19 00						
Braintree Freeport	d						19 02						
Cressing	d						19 05						
White Notley	d						19 08						
Witham 2	d	19 00					19 16	19 29					
Hatfield Peverel	d							19 33					
Chelmsford 3	d	19 09			19 21		19 26	19 40					
Ingatestone	d						19 32						
Shenfield 3	a	19 19					19 38	19 50					
Romford	a	19 28											
Stratford 7 ⊖	a	19 36			19s45		19 52	20 05					
London Liverpool Street 15 ⊖	a	19 45			19 55		20 01	20 14		20 17			

Station		LE 1	LE 1	LE 1	LE 1	LE ◇1 ☕	LE 1	LE 1	LE 1	LE 1		LE 1	LE 1
Norwich	d					19 00							
Diss	d					19 17							
Peterborough 8	d												
Stowmarket	d					19 29				19 44			
Needham Market	d									19 49			
Ipswich	a					19 41				20 00			
	d					19 43			19 52			20 09	
Harwich Town	d												20 28
Dovercourt	d												20 30
Harwich International	d												20 33
Wrabness	d												20 39
Mistley	d												20 45
Manningtree 2	d					19 53			20 02			20 20	20a50
Walton-on-the-Naze	d	19 00											
Frinton-on-Sea	d	19 03											
Kirby Cross	d	19 06											
Clacton-on-Sea	d		19 05										
Thorpe-le-Soken 1	a	19 12	19 13										
	d	19 17	19 13										
Weeley	d	19 21											
Great Bentley	d	19 24											
Alresford (Essex)	d	19 28			←								
Wivenhoe 3	d	19 32	19 23		19 32								
Hythe	d	→			19 36								
Colchester Town	a				19 40								
	d			19 35	19 44		20 00						
Colchester 4	a		19 31	19 42	19 52	20 02	20 07		20 11			20 29	
Colchester 4	d		19 33	19 43		20 03			20 12			20 30	
Marks Tey 2	d			19 49					20 18				
Kelvedon	d			19 54					20 23				
Braintree	d							20 00					
Braintree Freeport	d							20 02					
Cressing	d							20 05					
White Notley	d							20 08					
Witham 2	d		19 46	20 00				20 16	20 29				
Hatfield Peverel	d								20 33				
Chelmsford 3	d		19 56	20 09		20 21		20 26	20 40				
Ingatestone	d		20 02					20 32					
Shenfield 3	a		20 08	20 19				20 38	20 50				
Romford	a			20 28									
Stratford 7 ⊖	a		20 22	20 36		20s45		20 52	21 05				
London Liverpool Street 15 ⊖	a		20 31	20 45		20 55		21 01	21 14			21 17	

Table 11

Saturdays

Norwich, Ipswich, Harwich, Clacton, Walton-on-Naze, Colchester and Chelmsford - London

		LE	LE	LE	LE	LE	LE	LE		LE	LE	LE	LE	LE	LE	LE	LE	LE		LE	LE	LE	LE	LE	LE
		1	1	1	1	◇1 🍽	1	1		1	1	1	1	1	1	◇1	1	1		◇1 🍽	1	1	1	1	1
Norwich	d					20 00														21 00					
Diss	d					20 17														21 17					
Peterborough 8	d															19 45									
Stowmarket	d					20 29					20 44					21 09				21 29				21 44	
Needham Market	d										20 49													21 49	
Ipswich	a					20 41					21 00					21 22				21 41				22 00	
	d					20 43					21 00	21 09				21 25				21 43			21 52		
Harwich Town	d																	21 28							
Dovercourt	d																	21 30							
Harwich International	d									20 45	21a29							21 33							
Wrabness	d																	21 39							
Mistley	d																	21 45							
Manningtree 2	d					20 53				20 58		21 19				21 35		21a50		21 53			22 02		
Walton-on-the-Naze	d	20 00											21 00												22 00
Frinton-on-Sea	d	20 03											21 03												22 03
Kirby Cross	d	20 06											21 06												22 06
Clacton-on-Sea	d		20 05											21 05											
Thorpe-le-Soken 1	a	20 12	20 13										21 12	21 13											22 12
	d	20 17	20 13										21 17	21 13											22 17
Weeley	d	20 21											21 21												22 21
Great Bentley	d	20 24											21 24												22 24
Alresford (Essex)	d	20 28			←								21 28				←								22 28
Wivenhoe 3	d	20 32	20 23		20 32								21 32	21 23			21 32								22 32
Hythe	d	→			20 36								→				21 36								→
Colchester Town	a				20 40												21 40								
	d			20 35	20 44		21 00								21 35		21 44				22 00				
Colchester 4	a		20 31	20 42	20 52	21 02	21 07			21 07		21 28		21 31	21 42	21 46	21 52			22 02	22 07		22 11		
Colchester 4	d		20 33	20 43		21 03				21 12		21 30		21 33	21 43					22 03			22 12		
Marks Tey 2	d			20 49						21 18					21 49								22 18		
Kelvedon	d			20 54						21 23					21 54								22 23		
Braintree	d							21 00														22 00			
Braintree Freeport	d							21 02														22 02			
Cressing	d							21 05														22 05			
White Notley	d							21 08														22 08			
Witham 2	d		20 46	21 00				21 16		21 29				21 46	22 00							22 16	22 29		
Hatfield Peverel	d									21 33													22 33		
Chelmsford 3	d		20 56	21 09		21 21		21 26		21 40				21 56	22 09					22 21		22 26	22 40		
Ingatestone	d		21 02					21 32						22 02								22 32			
Shenfield 3	a		21 08	21 19				21 38		21 50				22 08	22 19							22 38	22 50		
Romford	a			21 28											22 28										
Stratford 7 ⊖	a		21 22	21 36		21s45		21 52		22 05				22 22	22 36					22s45		22 52	23 05		
London Liverpool Street 15 ⊖	a		21 31	21 45		21 55		22 01		22 14		22 17		22 31	22 46					22 55		23 01	23 14		

		LE	LE	LE		LE	LE	LE	LE	LE	LE	LE	LE	LE		LE	LE	LE	LE						
		1	1	1		1	1	◇1	1	1	1	1	1	◇1		1	1	1							
Norwich	d							22 00								23 05									
Diss	d							22 17								23 22									
Peterborough 8	d													21 45											
Stowmarket	d							22 29	22 44					23 06		23 36			23 47						
Needham Market	d								22 49										23 52						
Ipswich	a							22 41	23 00					23 18		23 50			00 05						
	d		22 23					22 43				23 15		23 19											
Harwich Town	d					22 28											23 28								
Dovercourt	d					22 30											23 30								
Harwich International	d					22 33											23 33								
Wrabness	d					22 39											23 39								
Mistley	d					22 45											23 45								
Manningtree 2	d		22 33			22a50		22 53				23 25		23 29			23 50								
Walton-on-the-Naze	d										23 00														
Frinton-on-Sea	d										23 03														
Kirby Cross	d										23 06														
Clacton-on-Sea	d	22 05											23 05												
Thorpe-le-Soken 1	a	22 13									23 12		23 13												
	d	22 13											23 13												
Weeley	d												23 17												
Great Bentley	d												23 20												
Alresford (Essex)	d			←									23 24												
Wivenhoe 3	d	22 23		22 32									23 28												
Hythe	d			22 36									23 32												
Colchester Town	a			22 40																					
	d			22 44						23 00															
Colchester 4	a	22 31	22 42	22 52				23 02		23 07		23 35	23 38	23 40			23 59								
Colchester 4	d	22 33	22 43					23 03																	
Marks Tey 2	d		22 49																						
Kelvedon	d		22 54																						
Braintree	d						22 56											23 45							
Braintree Freeport	d						22 58											23 47							
Cressing	d						23 01											23 50							
White Notley	d						23 04											23 53							
Witham 2	d	22 46	23 00				23a12	23 16										00a01							
Hatfield Peverel	d																								
Chelmsford 3	d	22 56	23 09					23 25																	
Ingatestone	d	23 02																							
Shenfield 3	a	23 08	23 19					23s36																	
Romford	a		23 28																						
Stratford 7 ⊖	a	23 22	23 36					23s52																	
London Liverpool Street 15 ⊖	a	23 31	23 45					00 02																	

Table 11

Sundays

Norwich, Ipswich, Harwich, Clacton, Walton-on-Naze, Colchester and Chelmsford - London

		LE ◇1 A	LE A	LE 1	LE 1	LE 1	LE	LE 1	LE 1	LE ◇1 ☕	LE 1	LE 1	LE 1	LE ◇1 ☕	LE 1	LE 1	LE 1	LE 1	LE 1	LE ◇1 ☕	LE 1	LE 1	LE 1
Norwich	d	22p00								07 00				08 00						09 00			
Diss	d	22p17								07 17				08 17						09 17			
Peterborough 8	d	⟆																					
Stowmarket	d	22p29	23p47							07 29				08 29						09 29			
Needham Market	d	⟆	23p52																				
Ipswich	a	22p41	00⟆05							07 41				08 41						09 41			
	d	22p43								07 43			08 09	08 43					09 09	09 43			
Harwich Town	d	⟆														08 53						09 53	
Dovercourt	d	⟆														08 55						09 55	
Harwich International	d	⟆							07 20							08 58						09 58	
Wrabness	d	⟆														09 04						10 04	
Mistley	d	⟆														09 10						10 10	
Manningtree 2	d	22p53							07 33	07 53			08 19	08 53		09a15			09 19	09 53		10a15	
Walton-on-the-Naze	d	⟆													08 30						09 30		
Frinton-on-Sea	d	⟆													08 33						09 33		
Kirby Cross	d	⟆													08 36						09 36		
Clacton-on-Sea	d	⟆										07 36						08 36					
Thorpe-le-Soken 1	a	⟆										07 44			08 42			08 44			09 42		
	d	⟆										07 44						08 44					
Weeley	d	⟆																					
Great Bentley	d	⟆										07 49						08 49					
Alresford (Essex)	d	⟆										07 53						08 53					
Wivenhoe 3	d	⟆										07 57						08 57					
Hythe	d	⟆																					
Colchester Town	a	⟆																					
	d	⟆																					
Colchester 4	a	23p02							07 42	08 02		08 05	08 29	09 02				09 05	09 29	10 02			
Colchester 4	d	23p03				06 56	07 07	07 26	07 43	08 03		08 06	08 30	09 03				09 06	09 30	10 03			
Marks Tey 2	d	⟆				07 02	07a14	07 32	07 49			08 12	08 36					09 12	09 36				
Kelvedon	d	⟆				07 07		07 37	07 54				08 41						09 41				
Braintree	d	⟆		00 25							08 00						09 00						10 00
Braintree Freeport	d	⟆		00 27							08 02						09 02						10 02
Cressing	d	⟆		00 30							08 05						09 05						10 05
White Notley	d	⟆		00 33							08 08						09 08						10 08
Witham 2	d	23p16		00a41		07 13		07 43	08 00		08a16	08 21	08 47				09a16	09 21	09 47				10a16
Hatfield Peverel	d	⟆				07 17		07 47					08 51						09 51				
Chelmsford 3	d	23p25			06 54	07 24		07 54	08 09			08 30	08 58					09 30	09 58				
Ingatestone	d	⟆			07 01	07 31		08 01					09 05						10 05				
Shenfield 3	a	23b36			07 06	07 36		08 06	08 19			08 40	09 10					09 40	10 10				
Romford	a	⟆																					
Stratford 7 ⊖	a	23b52			07s34	08s04		08s34	08s49			09s04	09s34					10s04	10s34				
London Liverpool Street 15 ⊖	a	00⟆02			07 42	08 12		08 42	08 59	09 03		09 12	09 42	10 01				10 12	10 42	11 01			

A not 22 May

b Previous night, stops to set down only

Table 11

Sundays

Norwich, Ipswich, Harwich, Clacton, Walton-on-Naze, Colchester and Chelmsford - London

		LE 1	LE 1	LE	LE ◇1 ☕	LE 1		LE 1	LE 1	LE 1	LE 1	LE 1 A	LE ◇1 ☕	LE 1	LE 1	LE 1		LE 1	LE 1	LE 1	LE ◇1 ☕	LE 1	LE 1	LE 1	LE 1
Norwich	d				10 00								11 00								12 00				
Diss	d				10 17								11 17								12 17				
Peterborough 8	d											09 45													
Stowmarket	d			10 18	10 29							11 13	11 29							12 18	12 29				
Needham Market	d			10 23																12 23					
Ipswich	a			10 35	10 41							11 28	11 41							12 35	12 41				
	d		10 09		10 43						11 09		11 43						12 09		12 43				
Harwich Town	d							10 53							11 53								12 53		
Dovercourt	d							10 55							11 55								12 55		
Harwich International	d							10 58							11 58								12 58		
Wrabness	d							11 04							12 04								13 04		
Mistley	d							11 10							12 10								13 10		
Manningtree 2	d		10 19		10 53			11a15			11 19		11 53		12a15				12 19		12 53		13a15		
Walton-on-the-Naze	d					10 30								11 30								12 30			
Frinton-on-Sea	d					10 33								11 33								12 33			
Kirby Cross	d					10 36								11 36								12 36			
Clacton-on-Sea	d	09 36								10 36								11 36							12 36
Thorpe-le-Soken 1	a	09 44				10 42				10 44				11 42				11 44				12 42			12 44
	d	09 44								10 44								11 44							12 44
Weeley	d																								
Great Bentley	d	09 49								10 49								11 49							12 49
Alresford (Essex)	d	09 53								10 53								11 53							12 53
Wivenhoe 3	d	09 57								10 57								11 57							12 57
Hythe	d																								
Colchester Town	a																								
	d																								
Colchester 4	a	10 05	10 29		11 02					11 05	11 29		12 02					12 05	12 29		13 02				13 05
Colchester 4	d	10 06	10 30		11 03					11 06	11 30		12 03					12 06	12 30		13 03				13 06
Marks Tey 2	d	10 12	10 36							11 12	11 36							12 12	12 36						13 12
Kelvedon	d		10 41								11 41								12 41						
Braintree	d								11 00							12 00								13 00	
Braintree Freeport	d								11 02							12 02								13 02	
Cressing	d								11 05							12 05								13 05	
White Notley	d								11 08							12 08								13 08	
Witham 2	d	10 21	10 47						11a16	11 21	11 47					12a16		12 21	12 47					13a16	13 21
Hatfield Peverel	d		10 51								11 51								12 51						
Chelmsford 3	d	10 30	10 58							11 30	11 58							12 30	12 58						13 30
Ingatestone	d		11 05								12 05								13 05						
Shenfield 3	a	10 40	11 10							11 40	12 10							12 40	13 10						13 40
Romford	a																								
Stratford 7 ⊖	a	11s04	11s34							12s04	12s34							13s04	13s34						14s04
London Liverpool Street 15 ⊖	a	11 12	11 42		12 01					12 12	12 42		13 01					13 12	13 42		14 01				14 12

		LE 1		LE 1	LE ◇1 ☕	LE 1	LE 1	LE 1	LE 1	LE 1	LE 1	LE ◇1 ☕		LE 1	LE 1	LE 1	LE 1	LE 1	LE 1	LE ◇1 ☕	LE 1	LE 1		LE 1	LE 1
Norwich	d				13 00							14 00								15 00					
Diss	d				13 17							14 17								15 17					
Peterborough 8	d			11 45															13 46						
Stowmarket	d			13 13	13 29						14 18	14 29							15 13	15 29					
Needham Market	d										14 23														
Ipswich	a			13 28	13 41						14 35	14 41							15 28	15 41					
	d	13 09			13 43					14 09		14 43						15 09		15 43					
Harwich Town	d						13 53								14 53							15 53			
Dovercourt	d						13 55								14 55							15 55			
Harwich International	d						13 58								14 58							15 58			
Wrabness	d						14 04								15 04							16 04			
Mistley	d						14 10								15 10							16 10			
Manningtree 2	d	13 19			13 53		14a15			14 19		14 53			15a15			15 19		15 53		16a15			
Walton-on-the-Naze	d					13 30								14 30							15 30				
Frinton-on-Sea	d					13 33								14 33							15 33				
Kirby Cross	d					13 36								14 36							15 36				
Clacton-on-Sea	d								13 36								14 36								15 36
Thorpe-le-Soken 1	a					13 42			13 44					14 42			14 44				15 42				15 44
	d								13 44								14 44								15 44
Weeley	d																								
Great Bentley	d								13 49								14 49								15 49
Alresford (Essex)	d								13 53								14 53								15 53
Wivenhoe 3	d								13 57								14 57								15 57
Hythe	d																								
Colchester Town	a																								
	d																								
Colchester 4	a	13 29			14 02				14 05	14 29		15 02					15 05	15 29		16 02					16 05
Colchester 4	d	13 30			14 03				14 06	14 30		15 03					15 06	15 30		16 03					16 06
Marks Tey 2	d	13 36							14 12	14 36							15 12	15 36							16 12
Kelvedon	d	13 41								14 41								15 41							
Braintree	d							14 00								15 00								16 00	
Braintree Freeport	d							14 02								15 02								16 02	
Cressing	d							14 05								15 05								16 05	
White Notley	d							14 08								15 08								16 08	
Witham 2	d	13 47						14a16	14 21	14 47						15a16	15 21	15 47						16a16	16 21
Hatfield Peverel	d	13 51								14 51								15 51							
Chelmsford 3	d	13 58							14 30	14 58							15 30	15 58							16 30
Ingatestone	d	14 05								15 05								16 05							
Shenfield 3	a	14 10							14 40	15 10							15 40	16 10							16 40
Romford	a																								
Stratford 7 ⊖	a	14s34							15s04	15s34							16s04	16s34							17s04
London Liverpool Street 15 ⊖	a	14 42			15 01				15 12	15 42		16 01					16 12	16 42		17 01					17 12

A until 11 September

Table 11

Sundays

Norwich, Ipswich, Harwich, Clacton, Walton-on-Naze, Colchester and Chelmsford - London

		LE	LE	LE	LE	LE	LE	LE		LE	LE	LE	LE	LE	LE	LE	LE	LE		LE	LE	LE	LE	LE	LE
		1	1	R 1 ☕	1	1	1	1		◇1 ☕	1	1	◇1 ☕	1	1	1	1	1		1	◇1 ☕	1	1	1	1
Norwich	d			16 00						16 20			17 00								18 00				
Diss	d			16 17						16 37			17 17								18 17				
Peterborough 8	d											15 45													
Stowmarket	d		16 18	16 29						16 49		17 13	17 29							18 18	18 29				
Needham Market	d		16 23																	18 23					
Ipswich	a		16 35	16 41						17 01		17 28	17 41							18 35	18 41				
	d	16 09		16 43						17 03	17 09		17 43					18 09			18 43				
Harwich Town	d					16 53									17 53								18 53		
Dovercourt	d					16 55									17 55								18 55		
Harwich International	d					16 58									17 58								18 58		
Wrabness	d					17 04									18 04								19 04		
Mistley	d					17 10									18 10								19 10		
Manningtree 2	d	16 19		16 53		17a15					17 19		17 53		18a15			18 19			18 53		19a15		
Walton-on-the-Naze	d				16 30									17 30								18 30			
Frinton-on-Sea	d				16 33									17 33								18 33			
Kirby Cross	d				16 36									17 36								18 36			
Clacton-on-Sea	d							16 36									17 36								18 36
Thorpe-le-Soken 1	a				16 42			16 44						17 42			17 44					18 42			18 44
	d							16 44									17 44								18 44
Weeley	d																								
Great Bentley	d							16 49									17 49								18 49
Alresford (Essex)	d							16 53									17 53								18 53
Wivenhoe 3	d							16 57									17 57								18 57
Hythe	d																								
Colchester Town	a																								
	d																								
Colchester 4	a	16 29		17 02				17 05		17 18	17 29		18 02				18 05	18 29			19 02				19 05
Colchester 4	d	16 30		17 03				17 06		17 21	17 30		18 03				18 06	18 30			19 03				19 06
Marks Tey 2	d	16 36						17 12			17 36						18 12	18 36							19 12
Kelvedon	d	16 41									17 41							18 41							
Braintree	d						17 00									18 00								19 00	
Braintree Freeport	d						17 02									18 02								19 02	
Cressing	d						17 05									18 05								19 05	
White Notley	d						17 08									18 08								19 08	
Witham 2	d	16 47					17a16	17 21			17 47					18a16	18 21	18 47						19a16	19 21
Hatfield Peverel	d	16 51									17 51							18 51							
Chelmsford 3	d	16 58						17 30			17 58						18 30	18 58							19 30
Ingatestone	d	17 05									18 05							19 05							
Shenfield 3	a	17 10						17 40			18 10						18 40	19 10							19 40
Romford	a																								
Stratford 7 ⊖	a	17s34						18s04			18s34						19s04	19s34							20s04
London Liverpool Street 15 ⊖	a	17 42		18 01				18 12		18 28	18 42		19 01				19 12	19 42			20 01				20 12

		LE	LE	LE		LE	LE	LE	LE	LE	LE	LE	LE	LE		LE	LE	LE	LE	LE	LE	LE	LE	LE	
		1	◇1	◇1 ☕		1	1	1	1	1	1	1	1	◇1 ☕		1	1	1	1	◇1	◇1	1	1	1	
Norwich	d			19 00										20 00							21 00				
Diss	d			19 17										20 17							21 17				
Peterborough 8	d		17 45																	19 45					
Stowmarket	d		19 13	19 29									20 18	20 29						21 06	21 29				
Needham Market	d												20 23												
Ipswich	a		19 28	19 41									20 35	20 41						21 18	21 41				
	d	19 09	19 28	19 43						20 09			20 35	20 43					21 09	21 19	21 43				
Harwich Town	d						19 53									20 53							21 53		
Dovercourt	d						19 55									20 55							21 55		
Harwich International	d						19 58					20 35	21a04			20 58							21 58		
Wrabness	d						20 04									21 04							22 04		
Mistley	d						20 10									21 10							22 10		
Manningtree 2	d	19 19	19 38	19 53			20a15			20 19		20 48		20 53		21a15			21 19	21 29	21 53		22a15		
Walton-on-the-Naze	d					19 30					20 30											21 30			
Frinton-on-Sea	d					19 33					20 33											21 33			
Kirby Cross	d					19 36					20 36											21 36			
Clacton-on-Sea	d								19 36									20 36							
Thorpe-le-Soken 1	a					19 42			19 44		20 42							20 44				21 42			
	d								19 44									20 44							
Weeley	d																								
Great Bentley	d								19 49									20 49							
Alresford (Essex)	d								19 53									20 53							
Wivenhoe 3	d								19 57									20 57							
Hythe	d																								
Colchester Town	a																								
	d																								
Colchester 4	a	19 29	19 49	20 02					20 05	20 29		20 57		21 02				21 05	21 29	21 40	22 02				
Colchester 4	d	19 30		20 03					20 06	20 30		20 57		21 03				21 06	21 30		22 03				
Marks Tey 2	d	19 36							20 12	20 36								21 12	21 36						
Kelvedon	d	19 41								20 41									21 41						
Braintree	d							20 00									21 00							22 00	
Braintree Freeport	d							20 02									21 02							22 02	
Cressing	d							20 05									21 05							22 05	
White Notley	d							20 08									21 08							22 08	
Witham 2	d	19 47						20a16	20 21	20 47							21a16	21 21	21 47					22a16	
Hatfield Peverel	d	19 51								20 51									21 51						
Chelmsford 3	d	19 58							20 30	20 58		21 15						21 30	21 58						
Ingatestone	d	20 05								21 05									22 05						
Shenfield 3	a	20 10							20 40	21 10		21 25						21 40	22 10						
Romford	a																								
Stratford 7 ⊖	a	20s34							21s04	21s34		21s51						22s04	22s34						
London Liverpool Street 15 ⊖	a	20 42		21 01					21 12	21 42		21 59		22 01				22 12	22 42		23 01				

Table 11

Sundays

Norwich, Ipswich, Harwich, Clacton, Walton-on-Naze, Colchester and Chelmsford - London

		LE 1	LE 1	LE 1	LE 1	LE 1	LE 1	LE ◇1	LE 1
Norwich	d							22 00	
Diss	d							22 17	
Peterborough 8	d								
Stowmarket	d				22 18			22 29	
Needham Market	d				22 23				
Ipswich	a				22 35			22 41	
	d		22 09					22 43	
Harwich Town	d								22 53
Dovercourt	d								22 55
Harwich International	d								22 58
Wrabness	d								23 04
Mistley	d								23 10
Manningtree 2	d		22 19					22 53	23 15
Walton-on-the-Naze	d			22 16					
Frinton-on-Sea	d			22 19					
Kirby Cross	d			22 22					
Clacton-on-Sea	d	21 36				22 22			
Thorpe-le-Soken 1	a	21 44		22 28		22 30			
	d	21 44				22 30			
Weeley	d								
Great Bentley	d	21 49							
Alresford (Essex)	d	21 53							
Wivenhoe 3	d	21 57				22 40			
Hythe	d								
Colchester Town	a								
	d								
Colchester 4	a	22 05	22 29			22 48		23 02	23 24
Colchester 4	d	22 06	22 30					23 03	
Marks Tey 2	d	22 12	22 36						
Kelvedon	d		22 41						
Braintree	d						22 56		
Braintree Freeport	d						22 58		
Cressing	d						23 01		
White Notley	d						23 04		
Witham 2	d	22 21	22 47				23a12	23 16	
Hatfield Peverel	d		22 51						
Chelmsford 3	d	22 30	22 58					23 25	
Ingatestone	d		23 05						
Shenfield 3	a	22 40	23 10					23s36	
Romford	a								
Stratford 7 ⊖	a	23s04	23s34					23s57	
London Liverpool Street 15 ⊖	a	23 12	23 42					00 08	

Network Diagram for Tables 13, 14, 15, 16, 17

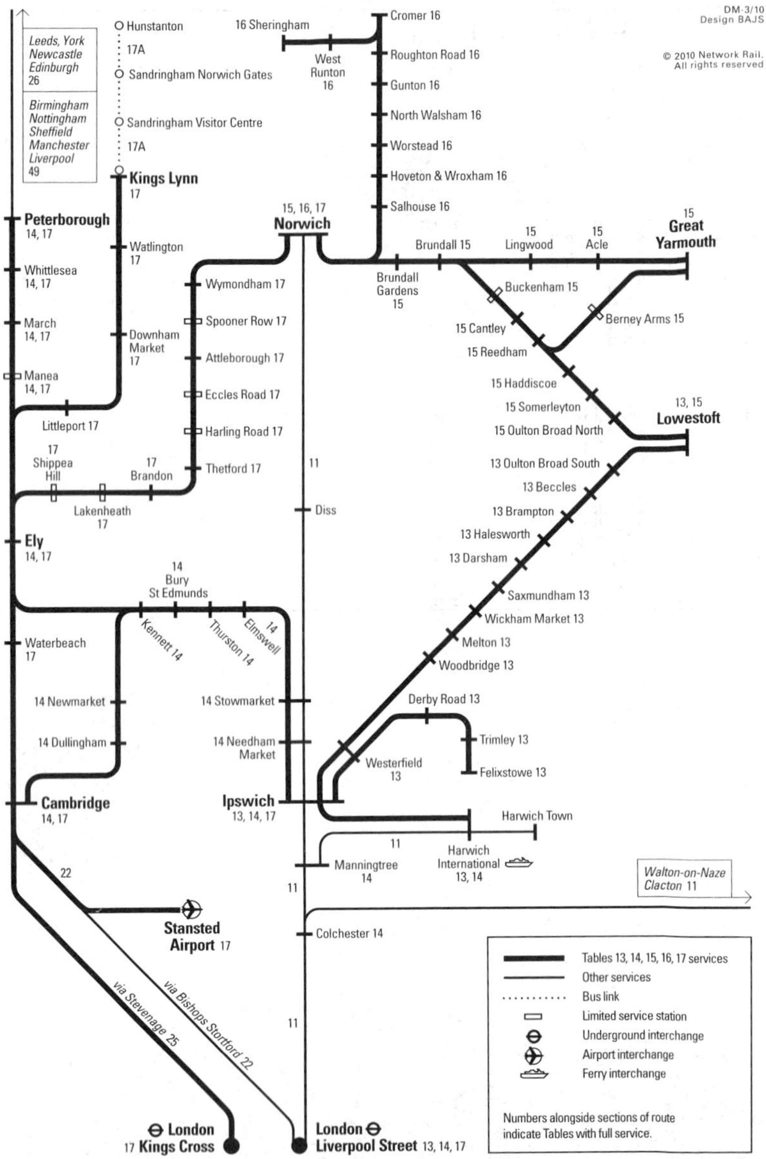

Table 13

Mondays to Fridays

Ipswich - Felixstowe and Lowestoft

Miles	Miles			LE	LE	LE	LE 1	LE	LE	LE	LE 1	LE		LE	LE 1	LE	LE	LE	LE 1	LE	LE	LE		LE 1	LE
—	—	London Liverpool Street 15 ⊖	d				06 38																		
—	—	Harwich International	d				08a09				07 50														
0	—	**Ipswich**	d	05 04	06 04	06 20		07 14		07 35	08a17	08 25		08 58	09 13	09 58	10 13	10 58	11 13	11 58	12 13	12 58		13 13	13 58
3½	0	Westerfield	d	05 10	06 10	06 27		07 20		07 42		08 31		09 04	09 20	10 04	10 20	11 04	11 20	12 04	12 20	13 04		13 20	14 04
—	2½	Derby Road	d	05 15	06 15			07 25				08 36		09 09		10 09		11 09		12 09		13 09			14 09
—	10½	Trimley	d	05 24	06 24			07 34				08 45		09 18		10 18		11 18		12 18		13 18			14 18
—	12¼	**Felixstowe**	a	05 30	06 30			07 40				08 51		09 24		10 24		11 24		12 24		13 24			14 24
10¼	—	Woodbridge	d			06 39				07 54					09 32		10 32		11 32		12 32			13 32	
11½	—	Melton	d			06 43				07 58					09 36		10 36		11 36		12 36			13 36	
15¾	—	Wickham Market	d			06 49				08 04					09 42		10 42		11 42		12 42			13 42	
22½	—	Saxmundham	d			07a00			07 45	08 16					09 54		10a53		11 54		12a53			13 54	
26¾	—	Darsham	d						07 52	08 22					10 00				12 00					14 00	
32	—	Halesworth	d						08 02	08 32					10 10				12 10					14 10	
36	—	Brampton (Suffolk)	d						08 09	08 39					10 17				12 17					14 17	
40¼	—	Beccles	d						08 17	08 47					10 25				12 25					14 25	
46¾	—	Oulton Broad South	d						08 27	08 57					10 35				12 35					14 35	
49	—	**Lowestoft**	a						08 35	09 06					10 44				12 44					14 44	

		LE	LE	LE 1	LE	LE	LE 1	LE		LE 1	LE	LE	LE 1	LE	LE	LE	LE	LE 1		LE 1	LE
London Liverpool Street 15 ⊖	d						16 45														
Harwich International	d						18a15													21 38	
Ipswich	d	14 13	14 58	15 13	15 54	15 58		16 58		17 13	17 58	18 13	18 54	18 58	19 58	20 13	20 58	21 13		22e13	22 28
Westerfield	d	14 20	15 04	15 20	16 01	16 04		17 04		17 20	18 04	18 20	19 01	19 04	20 04	20 20	21 04	21 20		22 20	22 37
Derby Road	d		15 09			16 09		17 09			18 09			19 09	20 09		21 09				22 42
Trimley	d		15 18			16 18		17 18			18 18			19 18	20 18		21 18				22 51
Felixstowe	a		15 24			16 24		17 24			18 24			19 24	20 24		21 24				22 57
Woodbridge	d	14 32		15 32	16 20					17 32		18 32	19 13			20 32		21 32		22 32	
Melton	d	14 36		15 36	16 24					17 36		18 36	19 17			20 36		21 36		22 36	
Wickham Market	d	14 42		15 42	16 30					17 42		18 42	19 23			20 42		21 42		22 42	
Saxmundham	d	14a53		15 54	16a41					17 54		18 54	19 35			20a53		21 54		22 54	
Darsham	d			16 00						18 00		19 00	19 41					22 00		23 00	
Halesworth	d			16 10						18 10		19 22	19 51					22 10		23 10	
Brampton (Suffolk)	d			16 17						18 17		19 29	19 58					22 17		23 17	
Beccles	d			16 25						18 25		19 37	20 06					22 25		23 25	
Oulton Broad South	d			16 35						18 35		19 47	20 16					22 35		23 35	
Lowestoft	a			16 44						18 44		19 56	20 25					22 44		23 44	

Saturdays

		LE	LE	LE	LE 1	LE	LE	LE	LE 1	LE		LE	LE	LE 1	LE	LE	LE	LE 1	LE	LE		LE	LE 1	LE	LE
London Liverpool Street 15 ⊖	d																								
Harwich International	d				07 50																				
Ipswich	d	05 58	06 58	07 13	08a17	07 58	08 13	08 58	09 13	09 58		10 13	10 58	11 13	11 58	12 13	12 58	13 13	13 58	14 13		14 58	15 13	15 58	16 13
Westerfield	d	06 04	07 04	07 20		08 04	08 20	09 04	09 20	10 04		10 20	11 04	11 20	12 04	12 20	13 04	13 20	14 04	14 20		15 04	15 20	16 04	16 20
Derby Road	d	06 09	07 09			08 09		09 09		10 09			11 09		12 09		13 09		14 09			15 09		16 09	
Trimley	d	06 18	07 18			08 18		09 18		10 18			11 18		12 18		13 18		14 18			15 18		16 18	
Felixstowe	a	06 24	07 24			08 24		09 24		10 24			11 24		12 24		13 24		14 24			15 24		16 24	
Woodbridge	d			07 32			08 32		09 32			10 32		11 32		12 32		13 32		14 32			15 32		16 32
Melton	d			07 36			08 36		09 36			10 36		11 36		12 36		13 36		14 36			15 36		16 36
Wickham Market	d			07 42			08 42		09 42			10 42		11 42		12 42		13 42		14 42			15 42		16 42
Saxmundham	d			07 54			08a53		09 54			10a53		11 54		12a53		13 54		14a53			15 54		16a53
Darsham	d			08 00					10 00					12 00				14 00					16 00		
Halesworth	d			08 10					10 10					12 10				14 10					16 10		
Brampton (Suffolk)	d			08 17					10 17					12 17				14 17					16 17		
Beccles	d			08 25					10 25					12 25				14 25					16 25		
Oulton Broad South	d			08 35					10 35					12 35				14 35					16 35		
Lowestoft	a			08 44					10 44					12 44				14 44					16 44		

		LE	LE 1	LE	LE	LE		LE 1	LE	LE	LE	LE 1	LE 1	LE
London Liverpool Street 15 ⊖	d													
Harwich International	d												21 38	
Ipswich	d	16 58	17 13	17 58	18 13	18 58		19 13	19 58	20 13	20 58	21 13	22 13	22 28
Westerfield	d	17 04	17 20	18 04	18 20	19 04		19 20	20 04	20 20	21 04	21 20	22 20	22 34
Derby Road	d	17 09		18 09		19 09			20 09		21 09			22 39
Trimley	d	17 18		18 18		19 18			20 18		21 18			22 48
Felixstowe	a	17 24		18 24		19 24			20 24		21 24			22 54
Woodbridge	d		17 32		18 32			19 32		20 32		21 32	22 32	
Melton	d		17 36		18 36			19 36		20 36		21 36	22 36	
Wickham Market	d		17 42		18 42			19 42		20 42		21 42	22 42	
Saxmundham	d		17 54		18a53			19 54		20a53		21 54	22 54	
Darsham	d		18 00					20 00				22 00	23 00	
Halesworth	d		18 10					20 10				22 10	23 10	
Brampton (Suffolk)	d		18 17					20 17				22 17	23 17	
Beccles	d		18 25					20 25				22 25	23 25	
Oulton Broad South	d		18 35					20 35				22 35	23 35	
Lowestoft	a		18 44					20 44				22 44	23 44	

Table 13

Sundays

Ipswich - Felixstowe and Lowestoft

		LE 1	LE A	LE 1	LE	LE	LE 1	LE	LE	LE
London Liverpool Street 15 ⊖	d									
Harwich International	d	08 30								
Ipswich	d	08a53	09 55	10 00	10 55	11 55	12 00	12 55	13 55	14 00
Westerfield	d		10 01	10 07	11 01	12 01	12 07	13 01	14 01	14 07
Derby Road	d		10 06		11 06	12 06		13 06	14 06	
Trimley	d		10 15		11 15	12 15		13 15	14 15	
Felixstowe	a		10 21		11 21	12 21		13 21	14 21	
Woodbridge	d			10 19			12 19			14 19
Melton	d			10 23			12 23			14 23
Wickham Market	d			10 29			12 29			14 29
Saxmundham	d			10 41			12 41			14 41
Darsham	d			10 47			12 47			14 47
Halesworth	d			10 57			12 57			14 57
Brampton (Suffolk)	d			11 04			13 04			15 04
Beccles	d			11 12			13 12			15 12
Oulton Broad South	d			11 22			13 22			15 22
Lowestoft	a			11 31			13 31			15 31

		LE	LE	LE 1	LE	LE	LE 1	LE	LE	LE	LE 1	LE 1
London Liverpool Street 15 ⊖	d											
Harwich International	d										21 10	
Ipswich	d	14 55	15 55	16 00	16 55	17 55	18 00	18 55	19 55	20 00	21a36	22 00
Westerfield	d	15 01	16 01	16 07	17 01	18 01	18 07	19 01	20 01	20 07		22 07
Derby Road	d	15 06	16 06		17 06	18 06		19 06	20 06			
Trimley	d	15 15	16 15		17 15	18 15		19 15	20 15			
Felixstowe	a	15 21	16 21		17 21	18 21		19 21	20 21			
Woodbridge	d			16 19			18 19			20 19		22 19
Melton	d			16 23			18 23			20 23		22 23
Wickham Market	d			16 29			18 29			20 29		22 29
Saxmundham	d			16 41			18 41			20 41		22 41
Darsham	d			16 47			18 47			20 47		22 47
Halesworth	d			16 57			18 57			20 57		22 57
Brampton (Suffolk)	d			17 04			19 04			21 04		23 04
Beccles	d			17 12			19 12			21 12		23 12
Oulton Broad South	d			17 22			19 22			21 22		23 22
Lowestoft	a			17 31			19 31			21 31		23 31

A until 11 September

Table 13

Lowestoft and Felixstowe - Ipswich

Miles	Miles			LE	LE [1]	LE	LE [1]	LE [1]	LE	LE	LE	LE		LE [1]	LE	LE	LE	LE [1]	LE	LE	LE	LE [1]		LE	LE
0	—	**Lowestoft**	d		05 25		06 11	06 42		07 27				09 08				11 08				13 08			
2¼	—	Oulton Broad South	d		05 32		06 18	06 49		07 34				09 15				11 15				13 15			
8½	—	Beccles	d		05 41		06 27	06 58		07 43				09 24				11 24				13 24			
13	—	Brampton (Suffolk)	d		05 49		06 35	07 06		07 51				09 32				11 32				13 32			
17	—	Halesworth	d		05 57		06 43	07 14		07 59				09 40				11 40				13 40			
22¼	—	Darsham	d		06 05		06 51	07 22		08 07				09 48				11 48				13 48			
26½	—	Saxmundham	d		06 14		07 05	07 31		08 18				09 57		10 57		11 57		12 57		13 57			14 57
33¼	—	Wickham Market	d		06 23		07 14	07 40		08 27				10 06		11 06		12 06		13 06		14 06			15 06
37¼	—	Melton	d		06 30		07 21	07 47		08 34				10 13		11 13		12 13		13 13		14 13			15 13
38¾	—	Woodbridge	d		06 35		07 26	07 52		08 39				10 18		11 18		12 18		13 18		14 18			15 18
—	0	**Felixstowe**	d	05 34		06 38			07 48		08 54	09 28			10 28		11 28		12 28		13 28			14 28	
—	1¾	Trimley	d	05 37		06 41			07 51		08 57	09 31			10 31		11 31		12 31		13 31			14 31	
—	9¾	Derby Road	d	05 47		06 51			08 01		09 10	09 41			10 41		11 41		12 41		13 41			14 41	
45½	12¼	Westerfield	d	05 52	06 46	06 56	07 37	08 03	08 07	08 50	09 15	09 46		10 29	10 46	11 29	11 46	12 29	12 46	13 29	13 46	14 29		14 46	15 29
49	—	**Ipswich**	a	06 00	06 53	07 04	07 44	08 10	08 15	08 57	09 25	09 54		10 36	10 54	11 36	11 54	12 36	12 54	13 36	13 54	14 36		14 54	15 36
—	—	Harwich International	a		07 26																				
—	—	London Liverpool Street 15 ⊖	a																						

		LE	LE [1]	LE	LE	LE	LE [1]	LE		LE	LE [1]	LE	LE	LE	LE	LE
Lowestoft	d		15 08				17 08				18 49				21 08	
Oulton Broad South	d		15 15				17 15				18 56				21 15	
Beccles	d		15 24				17 24				19 05				21 24	
Brampton (Suffolk)	d		15 32				17 32				19 13				21 32	
Halesworth	d		15 40				17 40				19 21				21 40	
Darsham	d		15 48				17 48				19 29				21 48	
Saxmundham	d		15 57		17 09		17 57				19 38		20 57		21 57	
Wickham Market	d		16 06		17 18		18 06				19 47		21 06		22 06	
Melton	d		16 13		17 25		18 13				19 54		21 13		22 13	
Woodbridge	d		16 18		17 30		18 18				19 59		21 18		22 18	
Felixstowe	d	15 28		16 28		17 28		18 28		19 28		20 28		21 28		23 01
Trimley	d	15 31		16 31		17 31		18 31		19 31		20 31		21 31		23 04
Derby Road	d	15 41		16 41		17 41		18 41		19 41		20 41		21 41		23 14
Westerfield	d	15 46	16 29	16 46	17 41	17 46	18 29	18 46		19 46	20 10	20 46	21 29	21 46	22 29	23 19
Ipswich	a	15 54	16 36	16 54	17 49	17 54	18 36	18 54		19 54	20 20	20 54	21 36	21 54	22 36	23 27
Harwich International	a															
London Liverpool Street 15 ⊖	a															

Saturdays

		LE	LE [1]	LE	LE [1]	LE	LE	LE	LE [1]	LE		LE	LE	LE [1]	LE	LE	LE	LE [1]	LE	LE		LE	LE [1]	LE	LE
Lowestoft	d		06 08		07 08				09 08					11 08				13 08					15 08		
Oulton Broad South	d		06 15		07 15				09 15					11 15				13 15					15 15		
Beccles	d		06 24		07 24				09 24					11 24				13 24					15 24		
Brampton (Suffolk)	d		06 32		07 32				09 32					11 32				13 32					15 32		
Halesworth	d		06 40		07 40				09 40					11 40				13 40					15 40		
Darsham	d		06 48		07 48				09 48					11 48				13 48					15 48		
Saxmundham	d		06 57		07 57		08 57		09 57			10 57		11 57		12 57		13 57		14 57			15 57		16 57
Wickham Market	d		07 06		08 06		09 06		10 06			11 06		12 06		13 06		14 06		15 06			16 06		17 06
Melton	d		07 13		08 13		09 13		10 13			11 13		12 13		13 13		14 13		15 13			16 13		17 13
Woodbridge	d		07 18		08 18		09 18		10 18			11 18		12 18		13 18		14 18		15 18			16 18		17 18
Felixstowe	d	06 28		07 28		08 28		09 28		10 28			11 28		12 28		13 28		14 28			15 28		16 28	
Trimley	d	06 31		07 31		08 31		09 31		10 31			11 31		12 31		13 31		14 31			15 31		16 31	
Derby Road	d	06 41		07 41		08 41		09 41		10 41			11 41		12 41		13 41		14 41			15 41		16 41	
Westerfield	d	06 46	07 29	07 46	08 29	08 46	09 29	09 46	10 29	10 46		11 29	11 46	12 29	12 46	13 29	13 46	14 29	14 46	15 29		15 46	16 29	16 46	17 29
Ipswich	a	06 54	07 36	07 54	08 36	08 54	09 36	09 54	10 36	10 54		11 36	11 54	12 36	12 54	13 36	13 54	14 36	14 54	15 36		15 54	16 36	16 54	17 36
Harwich International	a																								
London Liverpool Street 15 ⊖	a																								

		LE	LE [1]	LE	LE	LE		LE [1]	LE	LE	LE	LE	LE
Lowestoft	d		17 08					19 08				21 08	
Oulton Broad South	d		17 15					19 15				21 15	
Beccles	d		17 24					19 24				21 24	
Brampton (Suffolk)	d		17 32					19 32				21 32	
Halesworth	d		17 40					19 40				21 40	
Darsham	d		17 48					19 48				21 48	
Saxmundham	d		17 57		18 57			19 57		20 57		21 57	
Wickham Market	d		18 06		19 06			20 06		21 06		22 06	
Melton	d		18 13		19 13			20 13		21 13		22 13	
Woodbridge	d		18 18		19 18			20 18		21 18		22 18	
Felixstowe	d	17 28		18 28		19 28			20 28		21 28		22 58
Trimley	d	17 31		18 31		19 31			20 31		21 31		23 01
Derby Road	d	17 41		18 41		19 41			20 41		21 41		23 11
Westerfield	d	17 46	18 29	18 46	19 29	19 46		20 29	20 46	21 29	21 46	22 29	23 16
Ipswich	a	17 54	18 36	18 54	19 36	19 54		20 36	20 54	21 36	21 54	22 36	23 24
Harwich International	a												
London Liverpool Street 15 ⊖	a												

Table 13

Sundays

Lowestoft and Felixstowe - Ipswich

		LE	LE	LE	LE	LE	LE	LE	LE	LE		LE	LE	LE	LE	LE	LE	LE	LE	LE					
		1		1						1				1						1					
			A																						
Lowestoft	d	08 05		10 05			12 05			14 05				16 05			18 05			20 05					
Oulton Broad South	d	08 12		10 12			12 12			14 12				16 12			18 12			20 12					
Beccles	d	08 21		10 21			12 21			14 21				16 21			18 21			20 21					
Brampton (Suffolk)	d	08 29		10 29			12 29			14 29				16 29			18 29			20 29					
Halesworth	d	08 37		10 37			12 37			14 37				16 37			18 37			20 37					
Darsham	d	08 45		10 45			12 45			14 45				16 45			18 45			20 45					
Saxmundham	d	08 54		10 54			12 54			14 54				16 54			18 54			20 54					
Wickham Market	d	09 03		11 03			13 03			15 03				17 03			19 03			21 03					
Melton	d	09 10		11 10			13 10			15 10				17 10			19 10			21 10					
Woodbridge	d	09 15		11 15			13 15			15 15				17 15			19 15			21 15					
Felixstowe	d		10 25		11 25	12 25		13 25	14 25			15 25	16 25		17 25	18 25		19 25	20 25						
Trimley	d		10 28		11 28	12 28		13 28	14 28			15 28	16 28		17 28	18 28		19 28	20 28						
Derby Road	d		10 38		11 38	12 38		13 38	14 38			15 38	16 38		17 38	18 38		19 38	20 38						
Westerfield	d	09 26	10 43	11 26	11 43	12 43	13 26	13 43	14 43	15 26		15 43	16 43	17 26	17 43	18 43	19 26	19 43	20 43	21 26					
Ipswich	a	09 33	10 50	11 33	11 50	12 50	13 33	13 50	14 50	15 33		15 50	16 50	17 33	17 50	18 50	19 33	19 50	20 50	21 33					
Harwich International	a																								
London Liverpool Street 15 ⊖	a																								

A until 11 September

Ipswich - Bury St. Edmunds, Cambridge, Ely and Peterborough

Miles	Miles	Miles			LE	XC	LE	LE	LE	LE	LE	LE	LE		LE	LE	LE	LE	LE	LE	LE	LE	LE		LE
						◇1	◇1	1	1	1	1	1	1		1	1	1	1	1	1	1	1	1		1
—	—	—	London Liverpool Street 15 ⊖	d																					
—	—	—	Colchester	d			05 40																		
—	—	—	Manningtree	d			05 49																		
—	—	0	Harwich International	d							07 50														
0	—	18	**Ipswich**	d	05 10		06 00	06 16	06 56	08 03	08 19	09 19	10 00		10 19	11 19	12 00	12 19	13 19	14 00	14 19	15 19	16 00		16 19
8¼	—	—	Needham Market	d	05 20			06 25	07 05		08 28	09 28			10 28	11 28		12 28	13 28		14 28	15 28			16 28
12	—	—	Stowmarket	d	05 26		06 12	06 31	07 11	08 15	08 34	09 34	10 12		10 34	11 34	12 12	12 34	13 34	14 12	14 34	15 34	16 12		16 34
17¾	—	—	Elmswell	d	05 35			06 39	07 19		08 42	09 42			10 42	11 42		12 42	13 42		14 42	15 42			16 42
22¼	—	—	Thurston	d	05 41			06 45	07 25		08 48	09 48			10 48	11 48		12 48	13 48		14 48	15 48			16 48
—	—	—	**Bury St Edmunds**	a	05 48		06 28	06 51	07 31	08 31	08 54	09 54	10 28		10 54	11 54	12 28	12 54	13 54	14 28	14 54	15 54	16 28		16 54
26¼	—	—	**Bury St Edmunds**	d	05 49		06 29	06 53	07 32	08 31	08 56	09 56	10 29		10 56	11 56	12 29	12 56	13 56	14 29	14 56	15 56	16 29		16 56
36	0	—	Kennett	d	06 00			07 03	07 42			10 06				12 06			14 06			16 06			17 06
41	—	—	Newmarket	d	06 09			07 13	07 51		09 15	10 16			11 15	12 16		13 15	14 16		15 15	16 16			17 16
44¼	—	—	Dullingham	d	06 14			07 18	08 00		09 20				11 20			13 20			15 20				
55¼	—	—	**Cambridge**	a	06 36			07 39	08 19		09 39	10 39			11 39	12 39		13 39	14 39		15 39	16 39			17 38
70	14¾	—	**Ely 6**	a			06 59			09 00			10 58				12 58			14 58			16 58		
—	—	—		d		05 30	07 00			09 00			10 58				12 58			14 58			16 59		
79¾	—	—	Manea	d																					
85¼	—	—	March	d		05 46	07 16			09 17			11 15				13 15			15 15			17 15		
93¼	—	—	Whittlesea	d		05 58	07 27			09 28			11 26				13 26			15 26			17 27		
99¼	—	—	**Peterborough 8**	a		06 08	07 38			09 39			11 37				13 37			15 37			17 37		

		LE	LE	LE	LE	LE	LE	LE	LE
		1	1	1	1	1	1		
London Liverpool Street 15 ⊖	d								
Colchester	d								
Manningtree	d								
Harwich International	d								
Ipswich	d	17 19	17 49	18 16	19 10	20 00	20 19	21 16	22 16
Needham Market	d	17 28	17 58	18 25	19 19		20 28	21 26	22 26
Stowmarket	d	17 34	18 04	18 31	19 25	20 12	20 34	21 32	22 32
Elmswell	d	17 42	18 12	18 39	19 33		20 42	21 41	22 41
Thurston	d	17 48	18 18	18 45	19 39		20 48	21 47	22 47
Bury St Edmunds	a	17 54	18 24	18 51	19 45	20 28	20 54	21 54	22 54
Bury St Edmunds	d	17 56	18 25	18 56	19 56	20 29	20 56	21 55	
Kennett	d	18 06			20 06			22 06	
Newmarket	d	18 16		19 15	20 16		21 15	22 16	
Dullingham	d			19 20			21 20	22 22	
Cambridge	a	18 39		19 39	20 39		21 39	22 39	
Ely 6	a		18 52			21 00			
	d		19 00			21 00			
Manea	d								
March	d		19 16			21 17			
Whittlesea	d		19 28			21 28			
Peterborough 8	a		19 38			21 39			

Saturdays

		LE	XC	LE	LE	LE	LE	LE	LE	LE		LE	LE	LE	LE	LE	LE	LE	LE	LE		LE	LE	LE	LE
			◇1	◇1	1	1	1	1	1	1		1	1	1	1	1	1	1	1	1		1	1	1	1
London Liverpool Street 15 ⊖	d																								
Colchester	d			05 40																					
Manningtree	d			05 49																					
Harwich International	d							07 50																	
Ipswich	d	05 10		06 00	06 16	07 19	08 00	08 19	09 19	10 00		10 19	11 19	12 00	12 19	13 19	14 00	14 19	15 19	16 00		16 19	17 19	18 00	18 19
Needham Market	d	05 20			06 25	07 28		08 28	09 28			10 28	11 28		12 28	13 28		14 28	15 28			16 28	17 28		18 28
Stowmarket	d	05 26		06 12	06 31	07 34	08 12	08 34	09 34	10 12		10 34	11 34	12 12	12 34	13 34	14 12	14 34	15 34	16 12		16 34	17 34	18 12	18 34
Elmswell	d	05 35			06 39	07 42		08 42	09 42			10 42	11 42		12 42	13 42		14 42	15 42			16 42	17 42		18 42
Thurston	d	05 41			06 45	07 48		08 48	09 48			10 48	11 48		12 48	13 48		14 48	15 48			16 48	17 48		18 48
Bury St Edmunds	a	05 48		06 28	06 51	07 54	08 28	08 54	09 54	10 28		10 54	11 54	12 28	12 54	13 54	14 28	14 54	15 54	16 28		16 54	17 54	18 28	18 54
Bury St Edmunds	d	05 49		06 29	06 53	07 56	08 29	08 56	09 56	10 29		10 56	11 56	12 29	12 56	13 56	14 29	14 56	15 56	16 29		16 56	17 56	18 29	18 56
Kennett	d	06 00			07 03	08 06			10 06				12 06			14 06			16 06			17 06	18 06		
Newmarket	d	06 09			07 13	08 16		09 15	10 16			11 15	12 16		13 15	14 16		15 15	16 16			17 16	18 16		19 15
Dullingham	d	06 14			07 18	08 21		09 20				11 20			13 20			15 20							19 20
Cambridge	a	06 36			07 39	08 39		09 39	10 39			11 39	12 39		13 39	14 39		15 39	16 39			17 39	18 39		19 39
Ely 6	a			06 59			08 58			10 58				12 58			14 58			16 58				18 58	
	d		05 30	07 00			08 58			10 58				12 58			14 58			16 58				19 00	
Manea	d																								
March	d		05 46	07 16			09 15			11 15				13 15			15 15			17 15				19 16	
Whittlesea	d		05 58	07 27			09 26			11 26				13 26			15 26			17 26				19 28	
Peterborough 8	a		06 08	07 38			09 38			11 37				13 37			15 37			17 37				19 38	

Table 14

Saturdays

Ipswich - Bury St. Edmunds, Cambridge, Ely and Peterborough

		LE 1	LE 1	LE 1	LE	LE
London Liverpool Street 15 ⊖	d					
Colchester	d					
Manningtree	d					
Harwich International	d					
Ipswich	d	19 19	20 00	20 19	21 16	22 16
Needham Market	d	19 28		20 28	21 26	22 26
Stowmarket	d	19 34	20 12	20 34	21 32	22 32
Elmswell	d	19 42		20 42	21 41	22 41
Thurston	d	19 48		20 48	21 47	22 47
Bury St Edmunds	a	19 54	20 28	20 54	21 54	22 54
Bury St Edmunds	d	19 56	20 29	20 56	21 55	
Kennett	d	20 06			22 06	
Newmarket	d	20 16		21 15	22 16	
Dullingham	d			21 20	22 22	
Cambridge	a	20 39		21 39	22 39	
Ely 6	a		20 58			
	d		20 59			
Manea	d					
March	d		21 15			
Whittlesea	d		21 27			
Peterborough 8	a		21 37			

Sundays

		LE 1 A	LE	LE 1	LE ◇1	LE 1	LE 1	LE 1	LE 1	LE 1	LE 1	LE 1	LE 1	LE 1	LE
London Liverpool Street 15 ⊖	d														
Colchester	d				09 32										
Manningtree	d				09 40										
Harwich International	d			08 30											
Ipswich	d	07 55	08 45	09 02	09 55	11 02	11 55	13 02	13 55	15 02	15 55	17 02	17 55	19 02	21 02
Needham Market	d			09 12		11 12		13 12		15 12		17 12		19 12	21 12
Stowmarket	d	08 07	08 59	09 18	10 07	11 18	12 07	13 18	14 07	15 18	16 07	17 18	18 07	19 18	21 18
Elmswell	d			09 27		11 27		13 27		15 27		17 27		19 27	21 27
Thurston	d			09 33		11 33		13 33		15 33		17 33		19 33	21 33
Bury St Edmunds	a	08 23	09 17	09 40	10 23	11 40	12 23	13 40	14 23	15 40	16 23	17 40	18 23	19 40	21 40
Bury St Edmunds	d	08 24		09 41	10 24	11 41	12 24	13 41	14 24	15 41	16 24	17 41	18 24	19 41	21 41
Kennett	d			09 52		11 52		13 52		15 52		17 52		19 52	21 52
Newmarket	d			10 01		12 01		14 01		16 01		18 01		20 01	22 01
Dullingham	d			10 06		12 06		14 06		16 06		18 06		20 06	22 06
Cambridge	a			10 24		12 24		14 25		16 25		18 25		20 24	22 24
Ely 6	a	08 51			10 51		12 51		14 51		16 51		18 51		
	d	08 52			10 52		12 52		14 52		16 52		18 52		
Manea	d														
March	d	09 09			11 09		13 09		15 09		17 09		19 09		
Whittlesea	d	09 20			11 20		13 20		15 20		17 20		19 20		
Peterborough 8	a	09 36			11 36		13 31		15 31		17 31		19 32		

A until 11 September

Peterborough, Ely, Cambridge and Bury St. Edmunds - Ipswich

Miles	Miles	Miles			LE MX	LE MO	LE 1	LE	LE	LE 1	LE 1	LE 1	LE 1	LE 1	LE 1	LE 1	LE 1	LE 1	LE 1	LE 1	LE 1	LE 1	LE 1
0	—	—	**Peterborough 8**	d							07 45			09 45			11 45			13 45			15 45
6	—	—	Whittlesea	d							07 53			09 53			11 53			13 53			15 53
14	—	—	March	d							08 04			10 04			12 04			14 04			16 04
19¼	—	—	Manea	d																			
29¼	0	—	**Ely 6**	a							08 31			10 25			12 29			14 29			16 29
—	—	—		d							08 31			10 32			12 31			14 31			16 31
45	—	—	**Cambridge**	d	22p43	23p00			06 41	07 43		08 43	09 43		10 43	11 43		12 43	13 43		14 43	15 43	
56	—	—	Dullingham	d	22p59	23p16				07 59			09 59			11 59			13 59			15 59	
58¼	—	—	Newmarket	d	23p05	23p22			07 01	08 04		09 03	10 04		11 03	12 04		13 03	14 04		15 03	16 04	
63¼	14¾	—	Kennett	d	23p13	23p30			07 09			09 11			11 11			13 11			15 11		
—	—	—	**Bury St Edmunds**	a	23p25	23p42			07 22	08 22	08 57	09 23	10 22	10 58	11 23	12 22	12 57	13 23	14 22	14 57	15 23	16 22	16 57
73¼	—	—	**Bury St Edmunds**	d	23p26	23p43	05 33	06 23	07 23	08 23	08 58	09 23	10 23	10 58	11 23	12 23	12 57	13 23	14 23	14 57	15 23	16 23	16 57
77¼	—	—	Thurston	d	23p32	23p49	05 39	06 29	07 29	08 29		09 29	10 29		11 29	12 29		13 29	14 29		15 29	16 29	
81¼	—	—	Elmswell	d	23p38	23p55	05 45	06 36	07 36	08 35		09 35	10 35		11 35	12 35		13 35	14 35		15 35	16 35	
87¼	—	—	Stowmarket	d	23p47	00 06	05 54	06 44	07 45	08 44	09 14	09 44	10 44	11 14	11 44	12 44	13 13	13 44	14 44	15 13	15 44	16 44	17 13
90¾	—	—	Needham Market	d	23p52	00 11	05 59	06 49	07 50	08 49		09 49	10 49		11 49	12 49		13 49	14 49		15 49	16 49	
99¼	—	0	**Ipswich**	a	00 05	00 23	06 09	07 01	08 03	09 00	09 28	10 02	11 00	11 28	12 00	13 00	13 28	14 00	15 00	15 28	16 00	17 00	17 28
—	—	18	Harwich International	a																			
—	—	—	Manningtree	a																			
—	—	—	Colchester	a																			
—	—	—	London Liverpool Street 15 ⊖	a																			

		LE 1	LE 1	LE 1	LE 1	LE 1	LE ◇1	LE 1	LE 1	LE ◇1	LE
Peterborough 8	d			17 45			19 45			21 45	
Whittlesea	d			17 53			19 53			21 53	
March	d			18 04			20 04			22 04	
Manea	d										
Ely 6	a			18 28			20 28			22 23	
	d			18 31			20 28			22 23	
Cambridge	d	16 43	17 43		18 43	19 43		20 43	21 43		22 43
Dullingham	d	16 59	17 59			19 59			21 59		22 59
Newmarket	d	17 04	18 04		19 03	20 04		21 03	22 04		23 05
Kennett	d	17 12	18 12		19 11			21 11			23 13
Bury St Edmunds	a	17 24	18 24	18 57	19 23	20 22	20 54	21 23	22 22	22 49	23 25
Bury St Edmunds	d	17 25	18 25	18 57	19 23	20 23	20 55	21 23	22 23	22 50	23 26
Thurston	d	17 31	18 31		19 29	20 29		21 29	22 29		23 32
Elmswell	d	17 37	18 37		19 35	20 35		21 35	22 35		23 38
Stowmarket	d	17 45	18 45	19 13	19 44	20 44	21 11	21 44	22 44	23 06	23 47
Needham Market	d	17 50	18 50		19 49	20 49		21 49	22 49		23 52
Ipswich	a	18 04	19 02	19 28	20 00	21 00	21 25	22 00	23 00	23 18	00 05
Harwich International	a					21 29					
Manningtree	a						21 36			23 29	
Colchester	a						21 48			23 40	
London Liverpool Street 15 ⊖	a										

Saturdays

		LE	LE	LE	LE 1	LE 1	LE 1	LE 1	LE 1	LE 1	LE 1	LE 1	LE 1	LE 1	LE 1	LE 1	LE 1	LE 1	LE 1	LE 1	LE 1	LE 1	LE 1
Peterborough 8	d					07 45			09 46			11 45			13 45			15 45			17 45		
Whittlesea	d					07 53			09 54			11 53			13 53			15 53			17 53		
March	d					08 04			10 05			12 04			14 04			16 04			18 04		
Manea	d																						
Ely 6	a					08 22			10 24			12 28			14 28			16 28			18 28		
	d					08 31			10 24			12 31			14 31			16 31			18 31		
Cambridge	d	22p43		06 41	07 43		08 43	09 43		10 43	11 43		12 43	13 43		14 43	15 43		16 43	17 43		18 43	19 43
Dullingham	d	22p59			07 59			09 59			11 59			13 59			15 59		16 59	17 59			19 59
Newmarket	d	23p05		07 01	08 04		09 03	10 04		11 03	12 04		13 03	14 04		15 03	16 04		17 04	18 04		19 03	20 04
Kennett	d	23p13		07 09			09 11			11 11			13 11			15 11			17 12	18 12		19 11	
Bury St Edmunds	a	23p25		07 22	08 22	08 57	09 23	10 22	10 50	11 23	12 22	12 57	13 23	14 22	14 57	15 23	16 22	16 57	17 24	18 24	18 57	19 23	20 22
Bury St Edmunds	d	23p26	06 23	07 23	08 23	08 57	09 23	10 23	10 50	11 23	12 23	12 57	13 23	14 23	14 57	15 23	16 23	16 57	17 25	18 25	18 57	19 23	20 23
Thurston	d	23p32	06 29	07 29	08 29		09 29	10 29		11 29	12 29		13 29	14 29		15 29	16 29		17 31	18 31		19 29	20 29
Elmswell	d	23p38	06 36	07 36	08 35		09 35	10 35		11 35	12 35		13 35	14 35		15 35	16 35		17 37	18 37		19 35	20 35
Stowmarket	d	23p47	06 44	07 45	08 44	09 13	09 44	10 44	11 06	11 44	12 44	13 13	13 44	14 44	15 13	15 44	16 44	17 13	17 45	18 45	19 13	19 44	20 44
Needham Market	d	23p52	06 49	07 50	08 49		09 49	10 49		11 49	12 49		13 49	14 49		15 49	16 49		17 50	18 50		19 49	20 49
Ipswich	a	00 05	07 02	08 03	09 00	09 28	10 00	11 00	11 20	12 00	13 00	13 28	14 00	15 00	15 28	16 00	17 00	17 28	18 01	19 01	19 28	20 00	21 00
Harwich International	a																						21 29
Manningtree	a																						
Colchester	a																						
London Liverpool Street 15 ⊖	a																						

Table 14

Saturdays

Peterborough, Ely, Cambridge and Bury St. Edmunds - Ipswich

		LE ◇1	LE 1	LE 1	LE ◇1	LE
Peterborough 8	d	19 45			21 45	
Whittlesea	d	19 53			21 53	
March	d	20 04			22 04	
Manea	d					
Ely 6	a	20 26			22 23	
	d	20 27			22 23	
Cambridge	d		20 43	21 43		22 43
Dullingham	d			21 59		22 59
Newmarket	d		21 03	22 04		23 05
Kennett	d		21 11			23 13
Bury St Edmunds	a	20 53	21 23	22 22	22 49	23 25
Bury St Edmunds	d	20 53	21 23	22 23	22 50	23 26
Thurston	d		21 29	22 29		23 32
Elmswell	d		21 35	22 35		23 38
Stowmarket	d	21 09	21 44	22 44	23 06	23 47
Needham Market	d		21 49	22 49		23 52
Ipswich	a	21 22	22 00	23 00	23 18	00 05
Harwich International	a					
Manningtree	a	21 35			23 29	
Colchester	a	21 46			23 40	
London Liverpool Street 15 ⊖	a					

Sundays

		LE A	LE	LE 1 B	LE 1	LE 1	LE 1	LE 1	LE 1	LE 1	LE 1	LE ◇1	LE 1	LE ◇1	LE 1	LE
Peterborough 8	d			09 45		11 45		13 46		15 45		17 45		19 45		
Whittlesea	d			09 53		11 53		13 55		15 53		17 53		19 53		
March	d			10 04		12 04		14 06		16 04		18 04		20 04		
Manea	d															
Ely 6	a			10 28		12 28		14 29		16 23		18 23		20 23		
	d			10 31		12 31		14 31		16 31		18 31		20 23		
Cambridge	d	22p43			11 12		13 12		15 12		17 12		19 12		21 12	23 00
Dullingham	d	22p59			11 28		13 28		15 28		17 28		19 28		21 28	23 16
Newmarket	d	23p05			11 34		13 34		15 34		17 34		19 34		21 34	23 22
Kennett	d	23p13			11 42		13 42		15 42		17 42		19 42		21 42	23 30
Bury St Edmunds	a	23p25		10 57	11 54	12 57	13 54	14 57	15 54	16 57	17 54	18 57	19 54	20 49	21 54	23 42
Bury St Edmunds	d	23p26	09 55	10 57	11 55	12 57	13 55	14 57	15 55	16 57	17 55	18 57	19 55	20 50	21 55	23 43
Thurston	d	23p32	10 01		12 01		14 01		16 01		18 01		20 01		22 01	23 49
Elmswell	d	23p38	10 07		12 07		14 07		16 07		18 07		20 07		22 07	23 55
Stowmarket	d	23p47	10 18	11 13	12 18	13 13	14 18	15 13	16 18	17 13	18 18	19 13	20 18	21 06	22 18	00 06
Needham Market	d	23p52	10 23		12 23		14 23		16 23		18 23		20 23		22 23	00 11
Ipswich	a	00 05	10 35	11 28	12 35	13 28	14 35	15 28	16 35	17 28	18 35	19 28	20 35	21 18	22 35	00 23
Harwich International	a												21 04			
Manningtree	a											19 38		21 29		
Colchester	a											19 49		21 40		
London Liverpool Street 15 ⊖	a															

A not 22 May

B until 11 September

Table 15

Norwich - Great Yarmouth and Lowestoft

Miles	Miles	Miles			LE	LE	LE	LE	LE	LE 1	LE	LE	LE		LE	LE	LE	LE	LE	LE	LE	LE	LE		LE
—	—	—	London Liverpool Street 15 ⊖	d																					
0	0	0	**Norwich**	d	05 10	05 40	06 21	06 30	06 50	07 00	07 36		08 00		08 09	08 36	09 06	09 36	10 06	10 36	11 06	11 36	12 06		12 36
4¾	4¾	4¾	Brundall Gardens	d		05 47	06 28		06 57				08 07			08 43		09 43		10 43		11 43			12 43
5¾	5¾	5¾	Brundall	d	05 19	05 50	06 31	06 39	07 00	07 09	07 45		08 10			08 46		09 46	10 15	10 46		11 46	12 15		12 46
8	—	—	Lingwood	d			06 36		07 05						08 21	08 51		09 51		10 51					12 51
10½	—	—	Acle	d			06 43		07 13						08 28	08 58		09 56		10 56					12 56
—	7¾	7¾	Buckenham	d																					
—	10	10	Cantley	d		05 56				07 15	07 51		08 16						10 21			11 52	12 21		
—	12¼	12¼	Reedham (Norfolk)	d		06 00		06 47		07 19	07 55		08 21						10 25			11 57	12 25		
—	16	—	Berney Arms	d							08x01											12x03			
18¼	20½	—	**Great Yarmouth**	a	05 40		06 56		07 26		08 12				08 41	09 11		10 09		11 09		12 13			13 09
—	—	16¼	Haddiscoe	d		06 09				07 28			08 29						10 34				12 34		
—	—	18	Somerleyton	d		06 13				07 32			08 33						10 38				12 38		
—	—	22	Oulton Broad North	d		06 19		07 02		07 38			08 40				09 36		10 44		11 36		12 44		
—	—	23½	**Lowestoft**	a		06 26		07 09		07 45		08 35	08 46				09 43		10 51		11 43		12 51		

		LE	LE	LE	LE	LE	LE	LE	LE 1		LE	LE	LE	LE	LE 1	LE	LE	LE	LE		LE	LE	LE	LE	LE
London Liverpool Street 15 ⊖	d																								
Norwich	d	13 06	13 36	14 06	14 36	15 06	15 36	15 50	16 40		16 58	17 06	17 36	17 50	18 06	18 40	18 58	19 33	20 06		20 40	21 06	21 40	22 06	22 40
Brundall Gardens	d		13 43		14 43		15 43		16 47			17 13	17 43		18 13	18 47		19 40			20 47		21 47		
Brundall	d		13 46	14 15	14 46		15 46	15 59	16 50		17 07	17 16	17 46	17 59	18 16	18 50	19 07	19 43	20 15		20 50	21 15	21 50	22 15	22 49
Lingwood	d		13 51		14 51		15 51		16 55			17 21	17 51		18 21	18 55		19 48			20 55		21 55		
Acle	d		13 56		14 56		15 56		17 00			17 28	17 56		18 28	19 00		19 53			21 00		22 00		
Buckenham	d																								
Cantley	d			14 21		15 18		16 05			17 13			18 05			19 13		20 21			21 21		22 21	22 55
Reedham (Norfolk)	d			14 25		15 23		16 09			17 17			18 09			19 17		20 25			21 25		22 25	22 59
Berney Arms	d																								
Great Yarmouth	a		14 09		15 09		16 09		17 13			17 41	18 09		18 41	19 13		20 06			21 13		22 13		
Haddiscoe	d			14 34				16 18			17 26			18 18			19 26		20 34					22 34	23 08
Somerleyton	d			14 38				16 22			17 30			18 22			19 30		20 38					22 38	23 12
Oulton Broad North	d	13 36		14 44		15 38		16 28			17 36			18 28			19 36		20 44			21 40		22 44	23 18
Lowestoft	a	13 43		14 51		15 44		16 35			17 43			18 35			19 43		20 51			21 47		22 51	23 25

		LE
London Liverpool Street 15 ⊖	d	
Norwich	d	23 00
Brundall Gardens	d	
Brundall	d	23 09
Lingwood	d	23 14
Acle	d	23 18
Buckenham	d	
Cantley	d	
Reedham (Norfolk)	d	
Berney Arms	d	
Great Yarmouth	a	23 31
Haddiscoe	d	
Somerleyton	d	
Oulton Broad North	d	
Lowestoft	a	

Saturdays

		LE	LE	LE	LE	LE	LE	LE 1	LE	LE		LE A	LE	LE	LE	LE A	LE B	LE A	LE	LE A		LE B	LE R 1 A	LE B	LE A
London Liverpool Street 15 ⊖	d																						10 00		
Norwich	d	05 30	05 40	06 36	06 50	07 06	07 36	07 50	08 09	08 36		08 55	09 06	09 36	10 06	10 24	10 36	10 36	11 06	11 36		11 36	12 03	12 06	12 10
Brundall Gardens	d		05 47	06 43		07 13		07 57		08 43				09 43			10 43	10 43		11 43		11 43			
Brundall	d	05 39	05 50	06 46	06 59	07 16	07 45	08 00		08 46				09 46	10 15		10 46	10 46		11 46		11 46		12 15	12 19
Lingwood	d			06 51		07 21			08 21	08 51				09 51			10 51			11 51					
Acle	d			06 56		07 28			08 28	08 58				09 56			10 56			11 56					
Buckenham	d														10x19										
Cantley	d		05 56		07 05		07 51	08 06							10 23			10 52				11 52		12 21	12 25
Reedham (Norfolk)	d	05 47	06 01		07 09		07 55	08 11							10 27			10 57				11 57		12 25	12 29
Berney Arms	d						08x01											11x03				12x03			
Great Yarmouth	a	06 02		07 09		07 41	08 12		08 41	09 11		09 24		10 09		10 53	11 09	11 13		12 09		12 13	12 40		
Haddiscoe	d		06 09		07 18			08 19							10 36									12 34	12 38
Somerleyton	d		06 13		07 22			08 23							10 40									12 38	12 42
Oulton Broad North	d		06 20		07 28			08 30					09 36		10 46				11 36					12 44	12 48
Lowestoft	a		06 26		07 35			08 36					09 43		10 53				11 43					12 51	12 55

A until 24 September

B from 1 October

Table 15

Saturdays

Norwich - Great Yarmouth and Lowestoft

		LE	LE	LE A	LE	LE B		LE A	LE	LE R 1 A	LE	LE A	LE	LE	LE	LE		LE	LE	LE	LE	LE	LE	LE	LE
London Liverpool Street 15 ⊖	d									12 30															
Norwich	d	12 36	13 06	13 18	13 36	14 06		14 10	14 36	14 50	15 06	15 18	15 36	15 50	16 40	16 58		17 06	17 36	17 50	18 06	18 40	18 58	19 33	20 06
Brundall Gardens	d	12 43			13 43				14 43				15 43		16 47			17 13	17 43		18 13	18 47		19 40	
Brundall	d	12 46			13 46	14 15		14 19	14 46				15 46	15 59	16 50	17 07		17 16	17 46	17 59	18 16	18 50	19 07	19 43	20 15
Lingwood	d	12 51			13 51				14 51				15 51		16 55			17 21	17 51		18 21	18 55		19 48	
Acle	d	12 56			13 56				14 56				15 56		17 00			17 28	17 56		18 28	19 00		19 53	
Buckenham	d																								
Cantley	d					14 21		14 25			15 18			16 05		17 13				18 05			19 13		20 21
Reedham (Norfolk)	d					14 26		14 30			15 23			16 09		17 17				18 09			19 17		20 25
Berney Arms	d																								
Great Yarmouth	a	13 09		13 47	14 09				15 09	15 28		15 47	16 09		17 13			17 41	18 09		18 41	19 13		20 06	
Haddiscoe	d					14 34		14 38						16 18		17 26				18 18			19 26		20 34
Somerleyton	d					14 38		14 42						16 22		17 30				18 22			19 30		20 38
Oulton Broad North	d		13 36			14 45		14 49			15 38			16 28		17 36				18 28			19 36		20 44
Lowestoft	a		13 43			14 51		14 55			15 44			16 35		17 43				18 35			19 43		20 51

		LE		LE	LE	LE	LE	LE
London Liverpool Street 15 ⊖	d							
Norwich	d	20 40		21 06	21 40	22 06	22 40	23 00
Brundall Gardens	d	20 47			21 47			
Brundall	d	20 50		21 15	21 50	22 15	22 49	23 09
Lingwood	d	20 55			21 55			23 14
Acle	d	21 00			22 00			23 18
Buckenham	d							
Cantley	d			21 21		22 21	22 55	
Reedham (Norfolk)	d			21 25		22 25	22 59	
Berney Arms	d							
Great Yarmouth	a	21 13			22 13			23 31
Haddiscoe	d					22 34	23 08	
Somerleyton	d					22 38	23 12	
Oulton Broad North	d			21 40		22 44	23 18	
Lowestoft	a			21 47		22 51	23 25	

Sundays

		LE 1	LE	LE	LE	LE	LE	LE	LE	LE		LE 1	LE	LE	LE 1	LE C	LE D	LE	LE D	LE C		LE	LE	LE 1	LE
London Liverpool Street 15 ⊖	d																								
Norwich	d	07 25	07 36	08 45	08 57	09 36	10 45	10 57	11 36	12 45		12 57	13 36	14 45	14 57	15 36	15 36	16 45	16 57	16 57		17 36	18 45	18 57	19 36
Brundall Gardens	d			08 52			10 52			12 52				14 52				16 52					18 52		
Brundall	d		07 45	08 55	09 06	09 45	10 55	11 06	11 45	12 55		13 06	13 45	14 55	15 06	15 45	15 45	16 55	17 06	17 06		17 45	18 55	19 06	19 45
Lingwood	d			09 00			11 00			13 00				15 00				17 00					19 00		
Acle	d			09 05			11 05			13 05				15 05				17 05					19 05		
Buckenham	d					09x49			11x49							15x49	15x49		17x10						
Cantley	d		07 51		09 12	09 53		11 12	11 53			13 12	13 51		15 12	15 53	15 53		17 14	17 14		17 51		19 12	19 51
Reedham (Norfolk)	d		07 55		09 16	09 57		11 16	11 57			13 16	13 55		15 16	15 57	15 57		17 18	17 18		17 55		19 16	19 55
Berney Arms	d		08x01			10x03			12x03				14x01				16x03								
Great Yarmouth	a		08 12	09 18		10 14	11 18		12 14	13 18			14 12	15 18		16 14	16 14	17 18				18 10	19 18		20 10
Haddiscoe	d				09 25			11 25				13 25			15 25				17 27	17 27				19 25	
Somerleyton	d				09 29			11 29				13 29			15 29				17 31	17 31				19 29	
Oulton Broad North	d	07 53			09 35			11 35				13 35			15 35				17 37	17 37				19 35	
Lowestoft	a	08 00			09 42			11 42				13 42			15 42				17 44	17 44				19 42	

		LE	LE 1	LE	LE
London Liverpool Street 15 ⊖	d				
Norwich	d	20 45	20 57	21 36	22 36
Brundall Gardens	d	20 52			22 43
Brundall	d	20 55	21 06	21 45	22 46
Lingwood	d	21 00			22 51
Acle	d	21 05			22 56
Buckenham	d				
Cantley	d		21 12	21 51	
Reedham (Norfolk)	d		21 16	21 55	
Berney Arms	d				
Great Yarmouth	a	21 18		22 10	23 09
Haddiscoe	d		21 25		
Somerleyton	d		21 29		
Oulton Broad North	d		21 35		
Lowestoft	a		21 42		

A until 24 September
B from 1 October
C from 18 September
D until 11 September

Table 15

Lowestoft and Great Yarmouth - Norwich

Miles	Miles	Miles			LE MX	LE MX	LE MO 1	LE	LE 1	LE	LE	LE	LE		LE 1	LE 1	LE	LE	LE	LE	LE	LE	LE		LE
0	—	—	**Lowestoft**	d		23p30	23p35		05 42		06 35				07 35	07 55			08 50		09 50		11 00		
1½	—	—	Oulton Broad North	d		23p34	23p39		05 46		06 39				07 39	07 59			08 54		09 54		11 04		
5½	—	—	Somerleyton	d					05 52		06 45				07 45				09 00		10 00				
7¼	—	—	Haddiscoe	d					05 56		06 49				07 49				09 04		10 04				
—	0	0	**Great Yarmouth**	d	23p34			05 47		06 32		07 02	07 35				08 17	08 47		09 17		10 17			11 17
—	—	4½	Berney Arms	d																					
11¼	—	8¼	Reedham (Norfolk)	d	23p47	23p52	23p54		06 05		06 58				07 58	08 14			09 13		10 13				
13½	—	10½	Cantley	d		23p56			06 09		07 02				08 02	08 19			09 17		10 17				
15¾	—	12¾	Buckenham	d																					
—	8	—	Acle	d				05 58		06 43		07 13	07 46				08 28	08 58		09 28		10 28			11 28
—	10½	—	Lingwood	d				06 03		06 48		07 18	07 51				08 33	09 03		09 33		10 33			11 33
17¾	12¾	14¾	Brundall	d	23p55	00 03	00 03	06 07	06 16	06 52	07 09	07 22	07 55		08 09		08 37		09 24	09 37	10 24	10 37			11 37
18¾	13¾	15¾	Brundall Gardens	d				06 10		06 55		07 25	07 58				08 40			09 40		10 40			11 40
23½	18½	20½	**Norwich**	a	00 07	00 14	00 13	06 20	06 27	07 05	07 20	07 35	08 08		08 20	08 34	08 50	09 17	09 35	09 50	10 35	10 50	11 35		11 50
—	—	—	London Liverpool Street 15 ⊖	a																					

		LE	LE	LE	LE	LE	LE	LE	LE		LE	LE	LE	LE 1	LE A	LE B	LE	LE	LE		LE	LE	LE	LE	LE 1
Lowestoft	d	11 50		13 00		13 50		15 00			15 50		16 50				17 50				18 55		19 55		21 00
Oulton Broad North	d	11 54		13 04		13 54		15 04			15 54		16 54				17 54				18 59		19 59		21 04
Somerleyton	d	12 00				14 00					16 00		17 00				18 00				19 05		20 05		
Haddiscoe	d	12 04				14 04					16 04		17 04				18 04				19 09		20 09		
Great Yarmouth	d		12 17		13 17		14 17		15 13			16 17		17 17	17 47	17 47		18 17	18 47			19 17		20 17	
Berney Arms	d								15x20						17x54										
Reedham (Norfolk)	d	12 13				14 13			15 28		16 13		17 13		18 01	18 01	18 13		19 01		19 18		20 18		
Cantley	d	12 17				14 17			15 32		16 17		17 17		18 05	18 05	18 17		19 05		19 22		20 22		
Buckenham	d																								
Acle	d		12 28		13 28		14 28					16 28		17 28				18 28				19 28		20 28	
Lingwood	d		12 33		13 33		14 33					16 33		17 33				18 33				19 33		20 33	
Brundall	d	12 24	12 37		13 37	14 24	14 37		15 38		16 24	16 37	17 24	17 37	18 12	18 12	18 24	18 37	19 12		19 29	19 37	20 29	20 37	
Brundall Gardens	d		12 40		13 40		14 40		15 41			16 40		17 40				18 40				19 40		20 40	
Norwich	a	12 35	12 50	13 35	13 50	14 35	14 50	15 35	15 50		16 35	16 50	17 35	17 50	18 23	18 23	18 35	18 50	19 23		19 40	19 50	20 40	20 50	21 35
London Liverpool Street 15 ⊖	a																								

		LE	LE	LE	LE 1		LE	LE
Lowestoft	d		21 50		22 50			23 30
Oulton Broad North	d		21 54		22 54			23 34
Somerleyton	d		22 00		23 00			
Haddiscoe	d		22 04		23 04			
Great Yarmouth	d	21 17		22 17			23 34	
Berney Arms	d							
Reedham (Norfolk)	d		22 13		23 13		23 47	23 52
Cantley	d		22 17		23 17			23 56
Buckenham	d							
Acle	d	21 28		22 28				
Lingwood	d	21 33		22 33				
Brundall	d	21 37	22 24	22 37	23 24		23 55	00 03
Brundall Gardens	d	21 40		22 40				
Norwich	a	21 50	22 35	22 50	23 35		00 07	00 14
London Liverpool Street 15 ⊖	a							

Saturdays

		LE	LE	LE	LE	LE	LE	LE	LE	LE		LE	LE	LE C	LE	LE	LE R 1 D ☕	LE	LE	LE C		LE	LE	LE	LE R 1 D ☕
Lowestoft	d		23p30		06 38			07 40				08 50			09 50			11 00				11 50		13 00	
Oulton Broad North	d		23p34		06 42			07 44				08 54			09 54			11 04				11 54		13 04	
Somerleyton	d				06 48			07 50				09 00			10 00							12 00			
Haddiscoe	d				06 52			07 54				09 04			10 04							12 04			
Great Yarmouth	d	23p34		06 17		07 17	07 45		08 17	08 47			09 17	09 55		10 17	10 40		11 17	11 55			12 17		13 10
Berney Arms	d																								
Reedham (Norfolk)	d	23p47	23p52		07 01			08 03				09 13			10 13							12 13			
Cantley	d		23p56		07 05			08 07				09 17			10 17							12 17			
Buckenham	d																								
Acle	d			06 28		07 28	07 56		08 28	08 58			09 28			10 28			11 28				12 28		
Lingwood	d			06 33		07 33	08 01		08 33	09 03			09 33			10 33			11 33				12 33		
Brundall	d	23p55	00 03	06 37	07 12	07 37	08 05	08 14	08 37			09 24	09 37		10 24	10 37			11 37			12 24	12 37		
Brundall Gardens	d			06 40		07 40	08 08		08 40				09 40			10 40			11 40				12 40		
Norwich	a	00 07	00 14	06 50	07 24	07 50	08 18	08 25	08 50	09 17		09 35	09 50	10 23	10 35	10 50	11 10	11 35	11 50	12 23		12 35	12 50	13 35	13 44
London Liverpool Street 15 ⊖	a																13 17								15 55

A until 23 September
B from 26 September
C until 24 September
D until 24 September. ☕ from Norwich

Table 15

Saturdays

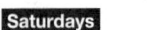

Lowestoft and Great Yarmouth - Norwich

		LE	LE	LE	LE	LE	LE	LE	LE	LE	LE	LE	LE	LE	LE	LE	LE	LE	LE	LE	LE	LE	LE
					A		B	A	A					A	B								[1]
Lowestoft	d		13 50			15 00				15 50		16 50				17 50			18 55		19 55		21 00
Oulton Broad North	d		13 54			15 04				15 54		16 54				17 54			18 59		19 59		21 04
Somerleyton	d		14 00							16 00		17 00				18 00			19 05		20 05		
Haddiscoe	d		14 04							16 04		17 04				18 04			19 09		20 09		
Great Yarmouth	d	13 17		14 17	14 55		15 13	15 13	15 55		16 17		17 17	17 47	17 47		18 17	18 47		19 17		20 17	
Berney Arms	d						15x20	15x20						17x54									
Reedham (Norfolk)	d		14 13				15 28	15 28		16 13		17 13		18 01	18 01	18 13		19 01	19 18		20 18		
Cantley	d		14 17				15 32	15 32		16 17		17 17		18 05	18 05	18 17		19 05	19 22		20 22		
Buckenham	d									16x21													
Acle	d	13 28		14 28							16 28		17 28				18 28			19 28		20 28	
Lingwood	d	13 33		14 33							16 33		17 33				18 33			19 33		20 33	
Brundall	d	13 37	14 24	14 37			15 38	15 38		16 24	16 37	17 24	17 37	18 12	18 12	18 24	18 37	19 12	19 29	19 37	20 29	20 37	
Brundall Gardens	d	13 40		14 40			15 41	15 41			16 40		17 40				18 40			19 40		20 40	
Norwich	a	13 52	14 35	14 50	15 23	15 35	15 50	15 51	16 23	16 35	16 50	17 35	17 50	18 23	18 23	18 35	18 50	19 23	19 40	19 50	20 40	20 50	21 35
London Liverpool Street [15] ⊖	a																						

		LE	LE	LE	LE	LE	LE
					[1]		
Lowestoft	d		21 50		22 50		23 30
Oulton Broad North	d		21 54		22 54		23 34
Somerleyton	d		22 00		23 00		
Haddiscoe	d		22 04		23 04		
Great Yarmouth	d	21 17		22 17		23 34	
Berney Arms	d						
Reedham (Norfolk)	d		22 13		23 13	23 47	23 52
Cantley	d		22 17		23 17		23 56
Buckenham	d						
Acle	d	21 28		22 28			
Lingwood	d	21 33		22 33			
Brundall	d	21 37	22 24	22 37	23 24	23 55	00 03
Brundall Gardens	d	21 40		22 40			
Norwich	a	21 50	22 35	22 50	23 35	00 07	00 14
London Liverpool Street [15] ⊖	a						

Sundays

		LE	LE	LE	LE	LE	LE	LE	LE	LE	LE	LE	LE	LE	LE	LE	LE	LE	LE	LE	LE	LE	LE
									[1]			[1]							[1]			[1]	
		C	C													D	E						
Lowestoft	d		23p30			09 50			11 50			13 50			15 50				17 50			19 50	
Oulton Broad North	d		23p34			09 54			11 54			13 54			15 54				17 54			19 54	
Somerleyton	d					10 00			12 00			14 00			16 00				18 00			20 00	
Haddiscoe	d					10 04			12 04			14 04			16 04				18 04			20 04	
Great Yarmouth	d	23p34		08 20	09 22		10 18	11 22		12 18	13 22		14 20	15 22		16 18	16 18	17 22		18 18	19 22		20 20
Berney Arms	d			08x27			10x25			12x25			14x27				16x25						
Reedham (Norfolk)	d	23p47	23p52	08 34		10 13	10 32		12 13	12 32		14 13	14 34		16 13	16 32	16 32		18 13	18 31		20 13	20 33
Cantley	d		23p56	08 38		10 17	10 36		12 17	12 36		14 17	14 38		16 17	16 36	16 36		18 17	18 35		20 17	20 37
Buckenham	d					10x21	10x40			12x40							16x40						
Acle	d				09 33			11 33			13 33			15 33				17 33			19 33		
Lingwood	d				09 38			11 38			13 38			15 38				17 38			19 38		
Brundall	d	23p55	00 03	08 45	09 42	10 24	10 44	11 42	12 24	12 44	13 42	14 24	14 45	15 42	16 24	16 44	16 44	17 42	18 24	18 41	19 42	20 24	20 43
Brundall Gardens	d				09 45			11 45			13 45			15 45				17 45			19 45		
Norwich	a	00 07	00 14	08 55	09 55	10 35	10 55	11 55	12 35	12 55	13 55	14 35	14 55	15 55	16 35	16 55	16 55	17 55	18 35	18 52	19 55	20 35	20 55
London Liverpool Street [15] ⊖	a																						

		LE	LE	LE	LE	LE
			[1]			[1]
Lowestoft	d		21 50			23 35
Oulton Broad North	d		21 54			23 39
Somerleyton	d		22 00			
Haddiscoe	d		22 04			
Great Yarmouth	d	21 22		22 20	23 20	
Berney Arms	d					
Reedham (Norfolk)	d		22 13	22 33	23 33	23 54
Cantley	d		22 17	22 37	23 37	
Buckenham	d					
Acle	d	21 33				
Lingwood	d	21 38				
Brundall	d	21 42	22 24	22 43	23 43	00 03
Brundall Gardens	d	21 45			23 46	
Norwich	a	21 55	22 35	22 55	23 55	00 13
London Liverpool Street [15] ⊖	a					

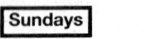

A until 24 September
B from 1 October
C not 22 May
D from 18 September
E until 11 September

Table 16

Mondays to Saturdays

Norwich - Cromer and Sheringham

Miles			LE SX	LE SO	LE SO	LE SX	LE	LE	LE	LE	LE	LE	LE	LE	LE	LE	LE	LE	LE	LE	LE
0	**Norwich**	d	05 15	05 20	05 45	05 45	07 15	08 21	09 45	10 45	11 45	12 45	13 45	14 45	15 45	16 45	17 45	18 51	19 55	21 15	22 45
6	Salhouse	d			05 55	05 55	07 25	08 31	09 55		11 55		13 55		15 55	16 55	17 55		20 05	21 25	22 55
8¾	Hoveton & Wroxham	d	05 30	05 34	06 00	06 00	07 30	08 36	10 00	10 59	12 00	12 59	14 00	14 59	16 00	17 00	18 00	19 05	20 10	21 30	23 00
13	Worstead	d			06 07	06 07	07 37	08 43		11 05		13 05		15 05	16 07	17 07	18 07	19 11	20 17	21 37	23 07
—	**North Walsham**	a	05 40	05 44	06 12	06 12	07 42	08 48	10 10	11 11	12 10	13 11	14 10	15 11	16 12	17 12	18 12	19 17	20 22	21 42	23 12
16	**North Walsham**	d	05 40	05 44	06 13	06 15	07 45	08 51	10 13	11 13	12 13	13 13	14 13	15 13	16 15	17 15	18 17	19 20	20 25	21 43	23 13
19¾	Gunton	d			06 19	06 21	07 51	08 57	10 19		12 19		14 19		16 21	17 21	18 23	19 26	20 31	21 49	23 19
23½	Roughton Road	d			06 25	06 28	07 57	09 04		11 24		13 24		15 24	16 27	17 27	18 30	19 33	20 38	21 55	23 25
—	**Cromer**	a	05 55	05 59	06 31	06 33	08 03	09 09	10 30	11 30	12 30	13 30	14 30	15 30	16 33	17 33	18 36	19 39	20 43	22 01	23 31
26½	**Cromer**	d	06 02	06 01	06 36	06 46	08 05	09 12	10 32	11 32	12 32	13 32	14 32	15 32	16 35	17 35	18 38	19 41	20 46	22 03	23 33
28¾	West Runton	d	06 06	06 06	06 40	06 50	08 10	09 16	10 37	11 37	12 37	13 37	14 37	15 37	16 40	17 40	18 43	19 46	20 50	22 08	23 38
30½	**Sheringham**	a	06 13	06 12	06 46	06 56	08 15	09 22	10 43	11 43	12 43	13 43	14 43	15 43	16 46	17 46	18 49	19 52	20 56	22 14	23 44

Sundays

until 11 September

		LE	LE	LE	LE	LE	LE	LE	LE	LE	LE	LE	LE	LE
Norwich	d	08 36	09 45	10 36	11 45	12 36	13 45	14 36	15 45	16 36	17 45	18 36	19 45	20 36
Salhouse	d	08 46		10 46		12 46		14 46		16 46		18 46		20 46
Hoveton & Wroxham	d	08 51	09 59	10 51	11 59	12 51	13 59	14 51	15 59	16 51	17 59	18 51	19 59	20 51
Worstead	d	08 58		10 58		12 58		14 58		16 58		18 58		20 58
North Walsham	a	09 03	10 09	11 03	12 09	13 03	14 09	15 03	16 09	17 03	18 09	19 03	20 09	21 03
North Walsham	d	09 04	10 11	11 06	12 11	13 06	14 11	15 06	16 11	17 06	18 11	19 06	20 11	21 06
Gunton	d	09 10		11 12		13 12		15 12		17 12		19 12		21 12
Roughton Road	d	09 16		11 19		13 19		15 19		17 19		19 19		21 19
Cromer	a	09 22	10 26	11 24	12 26	13 24	14 26	15 24	16 26	17 24	18 26	19 24	20 26	21 24
Cromer	d	09 25	10 29	11 27	12 29	13 27	14 29	15 27	16 29	17 27	18 29	19 27	20 29	21 27
West Runton	d	09 30		11 31		13 31		15 31		17 31		19 31		21 31
Sheringham	a	09 36	10 38	11 38	12 38	13 38	14 38	15 38	16 38	17 38	18 38	19 38	20 38	21 38

from 18 September

		LE	LE	LE	LE	LE	LE	LE
Norwich	d	08 36	10 36	12 36	14 36	16 36	18 36	20 36
Salhouse	d	08 46	10 46	12 46	14 46	16 46	18 46	20 46
Hoveton & Wroxham	d	08 51	10 51	12 51	14 51	16 51	18 51	20 51
Worstead	d	08 58	10 58	12 58	14 58	16 58	18 58	20 58
North Walsham	a	09 03	11 03	13 03	15 03	17 03	19 03	21 03
North Walsham	d	09 04	11 06	13 06	15 06	17 06	19 06	21 06
Gunton	d	09 10	11 12	13 12	15 12	17 12	19 12	21 12
Roughton Road	d	09 16	11 19	13 19	15 19	17 19	19 19	21 19
Cromer	a	09 22	11 24	13 24	15 24	17 24	19 24	21 24
Cromer	d	09 25	11 27	13 27	15 27	17 27	19 27	21 27
West Runton	d	09 30	11 31	13 31	15 31	17 31	19 31	21 31
Sheringham	a	09 36	11 38	13 38	15 38	17 38	19 38	21 38

Table 16

Mondays to Saturdays

Sheringham and Cromer - Norwich

Miles			LE MX	LE SX	LE SO	LE SX	LE	LE	LE	LE	LE	LE	LE	LE	LE	LE	LE	LE	LE	LE	LE	LE
0	**Sheringham**	d	23p47		06 22	06 32	07 16	08 23	09 46	10 46	11 46	12 46	13 46	14 46	15 46	16 49	17 49	18 55	19 57	21 10	22 17	23 47
1¾	West Runton	d	23p51		06 26	06 36	07 20	08 27	09 50	10 50	11 50	12 50	13 50	14 50	15 50	16 53	17 53	18 59	20 01	21 14	22 21	23 51
—	**Cromer**	a	23p55		06 30	06 40	07 24	08 31	09 54	10 54	11 54	12 54	13 54	14 54	15 54	16 57	17 57	19 03	20 05	21 18	22 25	23 55
4	**Cromer**	d	23p58	05 58	06 33	06 43	07 27	08 34	09 57	10 57	11 57	12 57	13 57	14 57	15 57	17 00	18 00	19 06	20 08	21 21	22 28	23 58
7	Roughton Road	d		06 04	06 39	06 49	07 33	08 40	10 03		12 03		14 03	15 03	16 03		18 06		20 14	21 27	22 34	
10¾	Gunton	d		06 10	06 45	06 55	07 39	08 46		11 08		13 08			16 09		18 12		20 20	21 33	22 40	
—	**North Walsham**	a	00 12	06 15	06 50	07 00	07 45	08 51	10 13	11 13	12 13	13 13	14 13	15 13	16 15	17 15	18 17	19 20	20 25	21 38	22 45	00 12
14½	**North Walsham**	d	00 13	06 16	06 51	07 01	07 45	08 52	10 13	11 14	12 13	13 14	14 13	15 14	16 15	17 15	18 18	19 21	20 26	21 43	22 46	00 13
17½	Worstead	d		06 21	06 56	07 06	07 50	08 57	10 18		12 18		14 18		16 20		18 23		20 31	21 48	22 51	
21¾	Hoveton & Wroxham	d	00 22	06 28	07 03	07 13	07 57	09 04	10 25	11 24	12 25	13 24	14 25	15 24	16 27	17 25	18 30	19 31	20 38	21 55	22 58	00 22
24½	Salhouse	d		06 32	07 07	07 17	08 02	09 08		11 28		13 28		15 28	16 32		18 34		20 42	21 59	23 02	
30½	**Norwich**	a	00 37	06 45	07 20	07 30	08 14	09 21	10 41	11 41	12 41	13 41	14 41	15 41	16 44	17 41	18 47	19 46	20 55	22 12	23 15	00 37

Sundays

until 11 September

		LE A	LE	LE	LE	LE	LE	LE	LE	LE	LE	LE	LE	LE	LE
Sheringham	d	23p47	09 42	10 42	11 42	12 42	13 42	14 42	15 42	16 42	17 42	18 42	19 42	20 42	21 42
West Runton	d	23p51	09 46		11 46		13 46		15 46		17 46		19 46		21 46
Cromer	a	23p55	09 50	10 48	11 50	12 48	13 50	14 48	15 50	16 48	17 50	18 48	19 50	20 48	21 50
Cromer	d	23p58	09 54	10 52	11 54	12 52	13 54	14 52	15 54	16 52	17 54	18 52	19 54	20 52	21 54
Roughton Road	d		10 00		12 00		14 00		16 00		18 00		20 00		22 00
Gunton	d		10 06		12 06		14 06		16 06		18 06		20 06		22 06
North Walsham	a	00 12	10 11	11 06	12 11	13 06	14 11	15 06	16 11	17 06	18 11	19 06	20 11	21 06	22 11
North Walsham	d	00 13	10 12	11 07	12 12	13 07	14 12	15 07	16 12	17 07	18 12	19 07	20 12	21 07	22 12
Worstead	d		10 17		12 17		14 17		16 17		18 17		20 17		22 17
Hoveton & Wroxham	d	00 22	10 24	11 17	12 24	13 17	14 24	15 17	16 24	17 17	18 24	19 17	20 24	21 17	22 24
Salhouse	d		10 28		12 28		14 28		16 28		18 28		20 28		22 28
Norwich	a	00 37	10 40	11 31	12 40	13 31	14 40	15 31	16 40	17 31	18 40	19 31	20 40	21 31	22 40

from 18 September

		LE	LE	LE	LE	LE	LE	LE	LE
Sheringham	d	23p47	09 42	11 42	13 42	15 42	17 42	19 42	21 42
West Runton	d	23p51	09 46	11 46	13 46	15 46	17 46	19 46	21 46
Cromer	a	23p55	09 50	11 50	13 50	15 50	17 50	19 50	21 50
Cromer	d	23p58	09 54	11 54	13 54	15 54	17 54	19 54	21 54
Roughton Road	d		10 00	12 00	14 00	16 00	18 00	20 00	22 00
Gunton	d		10 06	12 06	14 06	16 06	18 06	20 06	22 06
North Walsham	a	00 12	10 11	12 11	14 11	16 11	18 11	20 11	22 11
North Walsham	d	00 13	10 12	12 12	14 12	16 12	18 12	20 12	22 12
Worstead	d		10 17	12 17	14 17	16 17	18 17	20 17	22 17
Hoveton & Wroxham	d	00 22	10 24	12 24	14 24	16 24	18 24	20 24	22 24
Salhouse	d		10 28	12 28	14 28	16 28	18 28	20 28	22 28
Norwich	a	00 37	10 40	12 40	14 40	16 40	18 40	20 40	22 40

A not 22 May

London, Norwich and Cambridge - Ely, Kings Lynn and Peterborough

Miles	Miles			LE MX	FC	FC	XC	XC	LE	FC	EM	LE		XC	FC	LE	LE	EM	FC	XC	FC	LE		EM	FC
				[1]	[1]	[1]	◇[1]	◇[1]	[1]	[1]	◇	◇[1]		◇[1]	[1]	[1]	[1]	◇	[1]	◇[1]	[1]	[1]		◇	[1]
					A	B																			
—	—	**London Liverpool Street**	d																						
—	0	**London Kings Cross**	d		23p10	23p15									05 45				06 45		07 15				07 45
—	—	Ipswich	d									06 00													
—	—	Stansted Airport	d					05 15						06 06						07 21					
—	—	**Norwich**	d	22p40					05 33		05 50					06 33		06 52				07 37		07 57	
10¾	—	Wymondham	d	22p52					05 45		06 02					06 45						07 49			
12¾	—	Spooner Row	d																						
16	—	Attleborough	d	22p59					05 52		06 09					06 52						07 56			
19¾	—	Eccles Road	d																						
22¾	—	Harling Road	d																						
30½	—	Thetford	d	23p13					06 06		06 23					07 06		07 20				08 10		08 24	
37¾	—	Brandon	d	23p21					06 14							07 14						08 18			
41½	—	Lakenheath	d																						
47	—	Shippea Hill	d																						
—	58	**Cambridge**	d		00 13	00 13		05 55		06 18				06 52	06 57		07 22		07 35	08 00	08 04				08 38
—	63¼	Waterbeach	d		00 19	00 19				06 24					07 03				07 41		08 10				08 44
53	72¾	**Ely** [6]	a	23p38	00 29	00 29			06 31	06 33	06 45	06 59			07 12	07 31	07 38	07 41	07 51		08 19	08 37		08 46	08 53
—	—	**Cambridge**	a	00 02			05d15	05 53	06 51					06 37		07 52				07 58		08 59			
—	—	**Ely** [6]	d				05 30	06 10		06 33	06 51	07 00		07 08	07 12			07 45	07 51	08 15	08 21			08 50	08 53
—	78¼	Littleport	d							06 43					07 19				07 58		08 28				09 01
—	88½	Downham Market	d							06 54					07 28				08 07		08 37				09 10
—	93¼	Watlington	d							07 00					07 34				08 13		08 43				09 16
—	99¼	**Kings Lynn**	a							07 09					07 44				08 22		08 53				09 25
62¾	—	Manea	d					06x20																	
68¼	—	March	d				05 46	06 28			07 07	07 16		07 26				08 01		08 31				09 07	
76¼	—	Whittlesea	d				05 58	06 39				07 27		07 39				08 13							
82¼	—	**Peterborough** [8]	a				06 08	06 50			07 25	07 38		07 51				08 24		08 50				09 25	

		LE	XC	LE	EM	FC	XC	LE		EM	FC	LE	XC	LE	FC	EM	XC	LE		EM	FC	EM	LE	XC	LE
		[1]	◇[1]	[1]	◇	[1]	◇[1]	[1]		◇	[1]	[1]	◇[1]	[1]	[1]	◇	◇[1]	[1]		◇	[1]	◇	[1]	◇[1]	[1]
London Liverpool Street	d																								
London Kings Cross	d					08 45					09 45				10 45						11 45				
Ipswich	d	08 03										10 00											12 00		
Stansted Airport	d		08 21				09 21						10 21				11 25							12 25	
Norwich	d			08 40	08 57			09 40		09 57				10 40		10 57		11 40		11 57					12 40
Wymondham	d			08 52				09 52						10 52				11 52							12 52
Spooner Row	d																								
Attleborough	d			08 59				09 59						10 59				11 59							12 59
Eccles Road	d																								
Harling Road	d																								
Thetford	d			09 13	09 24			10 13		10 24				11 13		11 24		12 13		12 24					13 13
Brandon	d			09 21				10 21						11 21				12 21							13 21
Lakenheath	d																								
Shippea Hill	d																								
Cambridge	d		09 00			09 38	10 00				10 37		11 00		11 33		12 00				12 33			13 00	
Waterbeach	d					09 44					10 43				11 39						12 39				
Ely [6]	a	09 00		09 38	09 47	09 53		10 38		10 48	10 52	10 58		11 38	11 48	11 48		12 38		12 47	12 48		12 58		13 38
Cambridge	a		08 58	09 59			09 58	10 59					10 58	11 59			11 58	12 59				←		12 58	13 59
Ely [6]	d	09 00	09 15		09 52	09 55	10 15			10 52	10 52	10 58	11 15		11 48	11 52	12 15			12 52	12 48	12 52	12 58	13 15	
Littleport	d					10 01					10 59				11 55					→	12 55				
Downham Market	d					10 10					11 08				12 04						13 04				
Watlington	d					10 16					11 14				12 10						13 10				
Kings Lynn	a					10 25					11 23				12 20						13 20				
Manea	d																								
March	d	09 17	09 31				10 31					11 15	11 31				12 31						13 15	13 31	
Whittlesea	d	09 28										11 26											13 26		
Peterborough [8]	a	09 39	09 50		10 26		10 50			11 25		11 37	11 50			12 24	12 50					13 25	13 37	13 50	

A MO from 8 August until 12 September

B until 5 August, MX from 9 August until 9 September, from 13 September

London, Norwich and Cambridge - Ely, Kings Lynn and Peterborough

		FC 1	EM ◇	XC ◇1	LE 1	EM ◇	FC 1	EM ◇	LE 1	XC ◇1	LE 1	FC 1	EM ◇	FC 1	EM ◇	XC ◇1	FC 1	LE 1	EM ◇	FC 1	LE 1	LE 1
London Liverpool Street	d																					15 58
London Kings Cross	d	12 45					13 45							14 45						15 44		
Ipswich	d								14 00												16 00	
Stansted Airport	d			13 25						14 25						15 25						
Norwich	d		12 57		13 40	13 57					14 40		14 57					15 40	15 52			
Wymondham	d				13 52						14 52							15 52				
Spooner Row	d																					
Attleborough	d				13 59						14 59							15 59	16 09			
Eccles Road	d																		16 14			
Harling Road	d																		16 18			
Thetford	d		13 24		14 13	14 24					15 13		15 24					16 13	16 27			
Brandon	d				14 21						15 21							16 21				
Lakenheath	d																					
Shippea Hill	d																					
Cambridge	d	13 33		14 00			14 35			15 00		15 24		15 35		16 00	16 15			16 39		17 22
Waterbeach	d	13 39					14 41					15 30		15 41			16 21			16 46		17 28
Ely 6	a	13 48	13 49		14 39	14 47	14 50		14 58		15 38	15 40	15 47	15 50			16 30	16 39	16 48	16 55	16 58	17 38
Cambridge	a			13 58	14 59			←		14 58	15 59				←	15 58		16 59				
Ely 6	d	13 48	13 52	14 15		14 52	14 50	14 52	14 58	15 15			15 52	15 50	15 52	16 15	16 30		16 52	16 56	16 59	
Littleport	d	13 55				→	14 57						→	15 57			16 37			17 03		
Downham Market	d	14 04					15 06							16 06			16a47			17 12		
Watlington	d	14 10					15 12							16 11						17 20		
Kings Lynn	a	14 20					15 21							16 20						17 28		
Manea	d																					
March	d			14 31					15 15	15 31						16 31					17 15	
Whittlesea	d								15 26												17 27	
Peterborough 8	a		14 25	14 50				15 27	15 37	15 50					16 27	16 50			17 24		17 37	

		XC ◇1	LE 1	EM ◇	FC 1	FC 1	XC ◇1	LE 1	LE 1	LE 1	EM ◇	LE 1	FC 1	LE 1	XC ◇1	FC 1	LE 1	LE 1	EM ◇	FC 1	XC ◇1	LE 1	LE 1
London Liverpool Street	d							16 58									17 58					18 58	
London Kings Cross	d				16 44	17 14							17 44			18 14				18 44			
Ipswich	d											17 49											
Stansted Airport	d	16 25					17 18								18 21						19 21		
Norwich	d		16 38	16 57					17 35		17 54							18 40	18 57				19 40
Wymondham	d		16 50	17 09					17 47		18 06							18 52					19 52
Spooner Row	d		16x54																				
Attleborough	d		16 59						17 54		18 13							18 59					19 59
Eccles Road	d								17 59														
Harling Road	d								18 03														
Thetford	d		17 13	17 27					18 13		18 27							19 13	19 24				20 13
Brandon	d		17 21						18 21									19 21					20 21
Lakenheath	d																						
Shippea Hill	d																						
Cambridge	d	17 00			17 40	18 04	17 51	18 14		18 24			18 39		19 00	19 08	19 19			19 39	20 00	20 15	
Waterbeach	d				17 46			18 20		18 30			18 45				19 25			19 45		20 21	
Ely 6	a		17 38	17 48	17 56	18 19		18 30	18 39	18 40	18 48	18 52	18 55				19 34	19 38	19 48	19 55		20 30	20 38
Cambridge	a	16 58	17 59				17 49		18 59					←	18 58	19 07		19 59			19 58		20 59
Ely 6	d	17 15		17 52	17 56		18 06	18 30			18 52	19 00	18 56	19 00	19 15	19 22	19 35		19 52	19 56	20 15	20 31	
Littleport	d				18 03			18 37				→	19 03				19 42			20 03		20 38	
Downham Market	d				18 13			18 47					19 12			19 37	19 52			20 12		20 47	
Watlington	d				18 18			18 53					19 18				19 58			20 18		20 53	
Kings Lynn	a				18 29			19 05					19 28			19 52	20 10			20 28		21 05	
Manea	d						18x17																
March	d	17 31					18 25				19 08			19 16	19 31						20 31		
Whittlesea	d													19 28									
Peterborough 8	a	17 51		18 25			18 50				19 26			19 38	19 50				20 26		20 50		

		FC 1	LE 1	XC ◇1	FC 1	FC 1	LE 1	FC 1	FC 1	LE 1	FC FO 1	FC FX 1
London Liverpool Street	d											
London Kings Cross	d	19 45			20 15	20 45		21 15	22 15		23 15	23 15
Ipswich	d		20 00									
Stansted Airport	d			20 21								
Norwich	d						21 15			22 40		
Wymondham	d						21 27			22 52		
Spooner Row	d											
Attleborough	d						21 34			22 59		
Eccles Road	d											
Harling Road	d											
Thetford	d						21 48			23 13		
Brandon	d						21 56			23 21		
Lakenheath	d											
Shippea Hill	d											
Cambridge	d	20 41		21 00	21 11	21 35		22 08	23 08		00 13	00 13
Waterbeach	d	20 47			21 17	21 41		22 14	23 14		00 19	00 19
Ely 6	a	20 56	21 00		21 26	21 52	22 14	22 23	23 23	23 38	00 28	00 29
Cambridge	a			20 59			22 34			00 02		
Ely 6	d	20 56	21 00	21 15	21 26	21 53		22 23	23 23		00 29	
Littleport	d	21 03			21 33	22 00		22 30	23 30		00 36	
Downham Market	d	21 12			21 42	22 09		22 39	23 39		00 45	
Watlington	d	21 18			21 48	22 15		22 45	23 45		00 50	
Kings Lynn	a	21 27			21 57	22 24		22 54	23 54		01 00	
Manea	d											
March	d		21 17	21 31								
Whittlesea	d		21 28									
Peterborough 8	a		21 39	21 51								

Table 17

Saturdays

until 18 June

London, Norwich and Cambridge - Ely, Kings Lynn and Peterborough

		LE	FC	XC	XC	LE	EM	FC	EM	LE		XC	LE	EM	FC	EM	LE	XC	LE	EM		FC	EM	LE	XC
		1	1	◇ 1	◇ 1	1	◇	1	◇	◇ 1		◇ 1	1	◇	1	◇	1	◇ 1	1	◇		1	◇	1	◇ 1
London Liverpool Street	d																06 58								
London Kings Cross	d		23p15												06 44							07 44			
Ipswich	d									06 00														08 00	
Stansted Airport	d				05 25							06 25						07 25							08 25
Norwich	d	22p40				05 37	05 52						06 40	06 53					07 40	07 57					
Wymondham	d	22p52				05 49	06 04						06 52						07 52						
Spooner Row	d																								
Attleborough	d	22p59				05 56	06 11						06 59						07 59						
Eccles Road	d																								
Harling Road	d																								
Thetford	d	23p13				06 10	06 25						07 13	07 22					08 13	08 24					
Brandon	d	23p21				06 18							07 21						08 21						
Lakenheath	d																								
Shippea Hill	d																								
Cambridge	d		00 13		05 55			06 32				06 56			07 35		08 20	08 00				08 35			09 00
Waterbeach	d		00 19					06 38							07 41		08 26					08 41			
Ely 6	a	23p38	00 28			06 35	06 46	06 47		06 59			07 38	07 45	07 50		08 36		08 38	08 47		08 50		08 58	
Cambridge	a	00 02		05d15	05 54	06 56			←			06 55	07 59			←		07 55	08 59				←		08 58
Ely 6	d		00 29	05 30	06 10		06 51	06 47	06 51	07 00		07 11		07 53	07 50	07 53		08 15		08 54		08 50	08 54	08 58	09 15
Littleport	d		00 36				→	06 54						→	07 57					→		08 57			
Downham Market	d		00 45					07 03							08 06							09 06			
Watlington	d		00 50					07 08							08 11							09 11			
Kings Lynn	a		01 00					07 20							08 21							09 20			
Manea	d				06x20																				
March	d			05 46	06 28				07 07	07 16		07 29				08 08		08 31					09 11	09 15	09 31
Whittlesea	d			05 58	06 39					07 27		07 40				08 19								09 26	
Peterborough 8	a			06 08	06 50				07 25	07 38		07 50				08 31		08 50					09 28	09 38	09 50

		LE	EM	FC	EM	XC		LE	EM	FC	EM	LE	XC	LE	EM	FC		EM	XC	LE	EM	FC	EM	LE	XC
		1	◇	1	◇	◇ 1		1	◇	1	◇	1	◇ 1	1	◇	1		◇	◇ 1	1	◇	1	◇	1	◇ 1
London Liverpool Street	d																								
London Kings Cross	d			08 44						09 44						10 44						11 44			
Ipswich	d											10 00												12 00	
Stansted Airport	d					09 25							10 25						11 25						12 25
Norwich	d	08 40	08 57					09 40	09 57					10 40	10 57					11 40	11 57				
Wymondham	d	08 52						09 52						10 52						11 52					
Spooner Row	d																								
Attleborough	d	08 59						09 59						10 59						11 59					
Eccles Road	d																								
Harling Road	d																								
Thetford	d	09 13	09 24					10 13	10 24					11 13	11 24					12 13	12 24				
Brandon	d	09 21						10 21						11 21						12 21					
Lakenheath	d							10x26																	
Shippea Hill	d																								
Cambridge	d			09 35		10 00				10 35			11 00			11 35			12 00			12 35			13 00
Waterbeach	d			09 41						10 41						11 41						12 41			
Ely 6	a	09 39	09 48	09 50				10 39	10 47	10 50		10 58		11 38	11 48	11 50				12 38	12 47	12 50		12 58	
Cambridge	a	09 59			←	09 58		10 59			←		10 58	11 59				←	11 58	12 59			←		12 58
Ely 6	d		09 51	09 50	09 51	10 15			10 53	10 50	10 53	10 58	11 15		11 53	11 50		11 53	12 15		12 54	12 50	12 54	12 58	13 15
Littleport	d		→	09 57					→	10 57					→	11 57					→	12 57			
Downham Market	d			10 06						11 06						12 06						13 06			
Watlington	d			10 11						11 11						12 11						13 11			
Kings Lynn	a			10 20						11 20						12 20						13 20			
Manea	d																								
March	d					10 31						11 15	11 31						12 31					13 15	13 31
Whittlesea	d											11 26												13 26	
Peterborough 8	a				10 25	10 50					11 24	11 37	11 50					12 24	12 50				13 26	13 37	13 50

		LE		EM	FC	EM	XC	LE	EM	FC	EM	LE		XC	LE	EM	FC	EM	XC	LE	EM	FC		EM	LE
		1		◇	1	◇	◇ 1	1	◇	1	◇	1		◇ 1	1	◇	1	◇	◇ 1	1	◇	1		◇	1
London Liverpool Street	d																								
London Kings Cross	d				12 44					13 44							14 44					15 44			
Ipswich	d											14 00													16 00
Stansted Airport	d						13 25							14 25					15 25						
Norwich	d	12 40		12 57				13 40	13 57						14 40	14 57				15 35	15 52				
Wymondham	d	12 52						13 52							14 52					15 47					
Spooner Row	d																								
Attleborough	d	12 59						13 59							14 59					15 54	16 09				
Eccles Road	d																			15 59					
Harling Road	d																			16 03					
Thetford	d	13 13		13 24				14 13	14 24						15 13	15 24				16 13	16 23				
Brandon	d	13 21						14 21							15 21					16 21					
Lakenheath	d																								
Shippea Hill	d																								
Cambridge	d				13 35		14 00			14 35				15 00			15 35		16 00			16 35			
Waterbeach	d				13 41					14 41							15 41					16 41			
Ely 6	a	13 38		13 47	13 50			14 38	14 47	14 50		14 58			15 38	15 48	15 50			16 38	16 47	16 50			16 58
Cambridge	a	13 59				←	13 58	14 59			←			14 58	15 59			←	15 58	16 59				←	
Ely 6	d			13 53	13 50	13 53	14 15		14 53	14 50	14 53	14 58		15 15		15 52	15 50	15 52	16 15		16 52	16 50		16 52	16 58
Littleport	d			→	13 57				→	14 57						→	15 57				→	16 57			
Downham Market	d				14 06					15 06							16 06					17 06			
Watlington	d				14 11					15 11							16 11					17 11			
Kings Lynn	a				14 20					15 20							16 20					17 20			
Manea	d																								
March	d						14 31					15 15		15 31					16 31						17 15
Whittlesea	d											15 26													17 26
Peterborough 8	a					14 25	14 50				15 25	15 37		15 50				16 25	16 50					17 26	17 37

Table 17

Saturdays
until 18 June

London, Norwich and Cambridge - Ely, Kings Lynn and Peterborough

		XC ◇1	LE 1	EM ◇	FC 1	EM ◇	XC ◇1	LE 1		EM ◇	FC 1	EM ◇	LE 1	XC ◇1	FC 1	LE 1	EM ◇	FC 1		XC ◇1	LE 1	FC 1	LE 1	LE 1	FC 1
London Liverpool Street	d																								
London Kings Cross	d				16 44						17 44				18 15			18 45				19 45			20 45
Ipswich	d												18 00										20 00		
Stansted Airport	d	16 25					17 25							18 25						19 25					
Norwich	d		16 38	16 57				17 35		17 54						18 40	18 57				19 40			20 40	
Wymondham	d		16 50	17 09				17 47		18 06						18 52					19 52			20 52	
Spooner Row	d		16x54																						
Attleborough	d		16 59					17 54		18 13						18 59					19 59			20 59	
Eccles Road	d							17 59																	
Harling Road	d							18 03																	
Thetford	d		17 13	17 27				18 13		18 27						19 13	19 24				20 13			21 13	
Brandon	d		17 21					18 21								19 21					20 21			21 21	
Lakenheath	d																								
Shippea Hill	d															19x29									
Cambridge	d	17 00			17 35		18 00				18 35			19 00	19 04			19 41		20 00		20 41			21 41
Waterbeach	d				17 41						18 41							19 47				20 47			21 47
Ely 6	a		17 38	17 48	17 50			18 38		18 48	18 50		18 58			19 39	19 47	19 56			20 38	20 56	20 58	21 38	21 56
Cambridge	a	16 58	17 59			←	17 58	18 59				←		18 58	19 01	19 59				19 58	20 59			21 59	
Ely 6	d	17 15		17 52	17 50	17 52	18 15			18 53	18 50	18 53	19 00	19 15	19 19		19 53	19 56		20 15		20 56	20 59		21 56
Littleport	d			↪	17 57					↪	18 57							20 03				21 03			22 03
Downham Market	d				18 06						19 06				19 35			20 12				21 12			22 12
Watlington	d				18 11						19 11				19 44			20 18				21 18			22 18
Kings Lynn	a				18 20						19 20				19 52			20 26				21 26			22 26
Manea	d						18x25																		
March	d	17 31					18 33					19 09	19 16	19 31						20 31			21 15		
Whittlesea	d												19 28										21 27		
Peterborough 8	a	17 50				18 25	18 50					19 27	19 38	19 50			20 25			20 50			21 37		

		FC 1	LE 1	FC 1
London Liverpool Street	d			
London Kings Cross	d	22 15		23 15
Ipswich	d			
Stansted Airport	d			
Norwich	d		22 40	
Wymondham	d		22 52	
Spooner Row	d			
Attleborough	d		22 59	
Eccles Road	d			
Harling Road	d			
Thetford	d		23 13	
Brandon	d		23 21	
Lakenheath	d			
Shippea Hill	d			
Cambridge	d	23 11		00 15
Waterbeach	d	23 17		00 21
Ely 6	a	23 26	23 38	00 30
Cambridge	a		23 59	
Ely 6	d	23 26		00 30
Littleport	d	23 33		00 37
Downham Market	d	23 43		00 46
Watlington	d	23 48		00 52
Kings Lynn	a	23 58		01 01
Manea	d			
March	d			
Whittlesea	d			
Peterborough 8	a			

Table 17

Saturdays

25 June to 30 July

London, Norwich and Cambridge - Ely, Kings Lynn and Peterborough

		LE [1]	FC [1]	XC ◇[1]	XC ◇[1]	LE [1]	EM ◇	FC [1]	EM ◇	LE ◇[1]		XC ◇[1]	LE [1]	EM ◇	FC [1]	EM ◇	LE [1]	XC ◇[1]	LE [1]	EM ◇		FC [1]	EM ◇	LE [1]	XC ◇[1]
London Liverpool Street	d																06 58								
London Kings Cross	d		23p15												06 44							07 44			
Ipswich	d									06 00														08 00	
Stansted Airport	d				05 25							06 25						07 25							08 25
Norwich	d	22p40				05 37	05 52						06 40	06 53					07 40	07 57					
Wymondham	d	22p52				05 49	06 04						06 52						07 52						
Spooner Row	d																								
Attleborough	d	22p59				05 56	06 11						06 59						07 59						
Eccles Road	d																								
Harling Road	d																								
Thetford	d	23p13				06 10	06 25						07 13	07 22					08 13	08 24					
Brandon	d	23p21				06 18							07 21						08 21						
Lakenheath	d																								
Shippea Hill	d																								
Cambridge	d		00 13		05 55			06 32				06 56			07 35		08 20	08 00				08 35			09 00
Waterbeach	d		00 19					06 38							07 41		08 26					08 41			
Ely [6]	a	23p38	00 28			06 35	06 46	06 47		06 59			07 38	07 45	07 50		08 36		08 38	08 47		08 50		08 58	
Cambridge	a	00 02		05d15	05 54	06 56			←			06 55	07 59			←		07 55	08 59				←		08 58
Ely [6]	d		00 29	05 30	06 10		06 51	06 47	06 51	07 00		07 11		07 53	07 50	07 53		08 15		08 54		08 50	08 54	08 58	09 15
Littleport	d		00 36				→	06 54						→	07 57					→		08 57			
Downham Market	d		00 45					07 03							08 06							09 06			
Watlington	d		00 50					07 08							08 11							09 11			
Kings Lynn	a		01 00					07 20							08 21							09 20			
Manea	d				06x20																				
March	d			05 46	06 28				07 07	07 16		07 29				08 08		08 31					09 11	09 15	09 31
Whittlesea	d			05 58	06 39					07 27		07 40				08 19								09 26	
Peterborough [8]	a			06 08	06 50				07 25	07 38		07 50				08 31		08 50					09 28	09 38	09 50

		LE [1]	EM ◇	FC [1]	EM ◇	XC ◇[1]		LE [1]	EM ◇	FC [1]	EM ◇	LE [1]	XC ◇[1]	LE [1]	EM ◇	FC [1]		EM ◇	XC ◇[1]	LE [1]	EM ◇	FC [1]	EM ◇	LE [1]	XC ◇[1]
London Liverpool Street	d																								
London Kings Cross	d			08 44						09 44						10 44						11 44			
Ipswich	d											10 00												12 00	
Stansted Airport	d					09 25							10 25						11 25						12 25
Norwich	d	08 40	08 57					09 40	09 57					10 40	10 57					11 40	11 57				
Wymondham	d	08 52						09 52						10 52						11 52					
Spooner Row	d																								
Attleborough	d	08 59						09 59						10 59						11 59					
Eccles Road	d																								
Harling Road	d																								
Thetford	d	09 13	09 24					10 13	10 24					11 13	11 24					12 13	12 24				
Brandon	d	09 21						10 21						11 21						12 21					
Lakenheath	d							10x26																	
Shippea Hill	d																								
Cambridge	d			09 35		10 00				10 35			11 00			11 35			12 00			12 35			13 00
Waterbeach	d			09 41						10 41						11 41						12 41			
Ely [6]	a	09 39	09 48	09 50				10 39	10 47	10 50		10 58		11 38	11 48	11 50				12 38	12 47	12 50		12 58	
Cambridge	a	09 59			←	09 58		10 59			←		10 58	11 59				←	11 58	12 59			←		12 58
Ely [6]	d		09 51	09 50	09 51	10 15			10 53	10 50	10 53	10 58	11 15		11 53	11 50		11 53	12 15		12 54	12 50	12 54	12 58	13 15
Littleport	d		→	09 57					→	10 57					→	11 57					→	12 57			
Downham Market	d			10 06						11 06						12 06						13 06			
Watlington	d			10 11						11 11						12 11						13 11			
Kings Lynn	a			10 20						11 20						12 20						13 20			
Manea	d																								
March	d					10 31						11 15	11 31						12 31					13 15	13 31
Whittlesea	d											11 26												13 26	
Peterborough [8]	a				10 25	10 50					11 24	11 37	11 50					12 24	12 50				13 26	13 37	13 50

		LE [1]		EM ◇	FC [1]	EM ◇	XC ◇[1]	LE [1]	EM ◇	FC [1]	EM ◇	LE [1]		XC ◇[1]	LE [1]	EM ◇	FC [1]	EM ◇	XC ◇[1]	LE [1]	EM ◇	FC [1]		EM ◇	LE [1]
London Liverpool Street	d																								
London Kings Cross	d				12 44					13 44							14 44					15 44			
Ipswich	d											14 00													16 00
Stansted Airport	d						13 25							14 25					15 25						
Norwich	d	12 40		12 57				13 40	13 57						14 40	14 57				15 35	15 52				
Wymondham	d	12 52						13 52							14 52					15 47					
Spooner Row	d																								
Attleborough	d	12 59						13 59							14 59					15 54	16 09				
Eccles Road	d																			15 59					
Harling Road	d																			16 03					
Thetford	d	13 13		13 24				14 13	14 24						15 13	15 24				16 13	16 23				
Brandon	d	13 21						14 21							15 21					16 21					
Lakenheath	d																								
Shippea Hill	d																								
Cambridge	d				13 35		14 00			14 35				15 00			15 35		16 00			16 35			
Waterbeach	d				13 41					14 41							15 41					16 41			
Ely [6]	a	13 38		13 47	13 50			14 38	14 47	14 50		14 58			15 38	15 48	15 50			16 38	16 47	16 50			16 58
Cambridge	a	13 59				←	13 58	14 59			←			14 58	15 59			←	15 58	16 59				←	
Ely [6]	d			13 53	13 50	13 53	14 15		14 53	14 50	14 53	14 58		15 15		15 52	15 50	15 52	16 15		16 52	16 50		16 52	16 58
Littleport	d			→	13 57				→	14 57						→	15 57				→	16 57			
Downham Market	d				14 06					15 06							16 06					17 06			
Watlington	d				14 11					15 11							16 11					17 11			
Kings Lynn	a				14 20					15 20							16 20					17 20			
Manea	d																								
March	d						14 31					15 15		15 31					16 31						17 15
Whittlesea	d											15 26													17 26
Peterborough [8]	a					14 25	14 50				15 25	15 37		15 50				16 25	16 50					17 26	17 37

Table 17

Saturdays

25 June to 30 July

London, Norwich and Cambridge - Ely, Kings Lynn and Peterborough

		XC ◇1	LE 1	EM ◇	FC 1	EM ◇	XC ◇1	LE 1		EM ◇	FC 1	EM ◇	LE 1	XC ◇1	FC 1	LE 1	EM ◇	FC 1		XC ◇1	LE 1	FC 1	LE 1	LE 1	FC 1
London Liverpool Street	d																								
London Kings Cross	d				16 44						17 44				18 15			18 45				19 45			
Ipswich	d												18 00										20 00		
Stansted Airport	d	16 25					17 25							18 25						19 25					
Norwich	d		16 38	16 57				17 35		17 54						18 40	18 57				19 40			20 40	
Wymondham	d		16 50	17 09				17 47		18 06						18 52					19 52			20 52	
Spooner Row	d		16x54																						
Attleborough	d		16 59					17 54		18 13						18 59					19 59			20 59	
Eccles Road	d							17 59																	
Harling Road	d							18 03																	
Thetford	d		17 13	17 27				18 13		18 27						19 13	19 24				20 13			21 13	
Brandon	d		17 21					18 21								19 21					20 21			21 21	
Lakenheath	d																								
Shippea Hill	d															19x29									
Cambridge	d	17 00			17 35		18 00				18 35			19 00	19 04			19 41		20 00		20 41			21 41
Waterbeach	d				17 41						18 41							19 47				20 47			21 47
Ely 6	a		17 38	17 48	17 50			18 38		18 48	18 50		18 58			19 39	19 47	19 56			20 38	20 56	20 58	21 38	21 56
Cambridge	a	16 58	17 59			←	17 58	18 59				←		18 58	19 01	19 59				19 58	20 59			21 59	
Ely 6	d	17 15		17 52	17 50	17 52	18 15			18 53	18 50	18 53	19 00	19 15	19 19		19 53	19 56		20 15		20 56	20 59		21 56
Littleport	d			→	17 57					→	18 57							20 03				21 03			22 03
Downham Market	d				18 06						19 06				19 35			20 12				21 12			22 12
Watlington	d				18 11						19 11				19 44			20 18				21 18			22 18
Kings Lynn	a				18 20						19 20				19 52			20 26				21 26			22 28
Manea	d						18x25																		
March	d	17 31					18 33					19 09	19 16	19 31						20 31			21 15		
Whittlesea	d												19 28										21 27		
Peterborough 8	a	17 50				18 25	18 50					19 27	19 38	19 50			20 25			20 50			21 37		

		FC 1	LE 1	FC 1
London Liverpool Street	d			
London Kings Cross	d			23 15
Ipswich	d			
Stansted Airport	d			
Norwich	d		22 40	
Wymondham	d		22 52	
Spooner Row	d			
Attleborough	d		22 59	
Eccles Road	d			
Harling Road	d			
Thetford	d		23 13	
Brandon	d		23 21	
Lakenheath	d			
Shippea Hill	d			
Cambridge	d	23 11		00 15
Waterbeach	d	23 17		00 21
Ely 6	a	23 26	23 38	00 30
Cambridge	a		23 59	
Ely 6	d	23 26		00 30
Littleport	d	23 33		00 37
Downham Market	d	23 43		00 46
Watlington	d	23 48		00 52
Kings Lynn	a	23 58		01 01
Manea	d			
March	d			
Whittlesea	d			
Peterborough 8	a			

Table 17

Saturdays
from 6 August

London, Norwich and Cambridge - Ely, Kings Lynn and Peterborough

		LE ■1	FC ■1	XC ◇■1	XC ◇■1	LE ■1	EM ◇	FC ■1	EM ◇	LE ◇■1		XC ◇■1	LE ■1	EM ◇	FC ■1	EM ◇	LE ■1	XC ◇■1	LE ■1	EM ◇		FC ■1	EM ◇	LE ■1	XC ◇■1
London Liverpool Street	d																06 58								
London Kings Cross	d		23p15												06 44							07 44			
Ipswich	d									06 00														08 00	
Stansted Airport	d				05 25							06 25						07 25							08 25
Norwich	d	22p40				05 37	05 52						06 40	06 53					07 40	07 57					
Wymondham	d	22p52				05 49	06 04						06 52						07 52						
Spooner Row	d																								
Attleborough	d	22p59				05 56	06 11						06 59						07 59						
Eccles Road	d																								
Harling Road	d																								
Thetford	d	23p13				06 10	06 25						07 13	07 22					08 13	08 24					
Brandon	d	23p21				06 18							07 21						08 21						
Lakenheath	d																								
Shippea Hill	d																								
Cambridge	d		00 13		05 55			06 32				06 56			07 35		08 20	08 00				08 35			09 00
Waterbeach	d		00 19					06 38							07 41		08 26					08 41			
Ely ■6	a	23p38	00 28			06 35	06 46	06 47		06 59			07 38	07 45	07 50		08 36		08 38	08 47		08 50		08 58	
Cambridge	a	00 02		05d15	05 54	06 56			←			06 55	07 59			←		07 55	08 59				←		08 58
Ely ■6	d		00 29	05 30	06 10		06 51	06 47	06 51	07 00		07 11		07 53	07 50	07 53		08 15		08 54		08 50	08 54	08 58	09 15
Littleport	d		00 36				→	06 54						→	07 57					→		08 57			
Downham Market	d		00 45					07 03							08 06							09 06			
Watlington	d		00 50					07 08							08 11							09 11			
Kings Lynn	a		01 00					07 20							08 21							09 20			
Manea	d				06x20																				
March	d			05 46	06 28				07 07	07 16		07 29				08 08		08 31					09 11	09 15	09 31
Whittlesea	d			05 58	06 39					07 27		07 40				08 19								09 26	
Peterborough ■8	a			06 08	06 50				07 25	07 38		07 50				08 31		08 50					09 28	09 38	09 50

		LE ■1	EM ◇	FC ■1	EM ◇	XC ◇■1		LE ■1	EM ◇	FC ■1	EM ◇	LE ■1	XC ◇■1	LE ■1	EM ◇	FC ■1		EM ◇	XC ◇■1	LE ■1	EM ◇	FC ■1	EM ◇	LE ■1	XC ◇■1
London Liverpool Street	d																								
London Kings Cross	d			08 44						09 44						10 44						11 44			
Ipswich	d											10 00												12 00	
Stansted Airport	d					09 25							10 25						11 25						12 25
Norwich	d	08 40	08 57					09 40	09 57					10 40	10 57					11 40	11 57				
Wymondham	d	08 52						09 52						10 52						11 52					
Spooner Row	d																								
Attleborough	d	08 59						09 59						10 59						11 59					
Eccles Road	d																								
Harling Road	d																								
Thetford	d	09 13	09 24					10 13	10 24					11 13	11 24					12 13	12 24				
Brandon	d	09 21						10 21						11 21						12 21					
Lakenheath	d							10x26																	
Shippea Hill	d																								
Cambridge	d			09 35		10 00				10 35			11 00			11 35			12 00			12 35			13 00
Waterbeach	d			09 41						10 41						11 41						12 41			
Ely ■6	a	09 39	09 48	09 50				10 39	10 47	10 50		10 58		11 38	11 48	11 50				12 38	12 47	12 50		12 58	
Cambridge	a	09 59			←	09 58		10 59			←		10 58	11 59				←	11 58	12 59			←		12 58
Ely ■6	d		09 51	09 50	09 51	10 15			10 53	10 50	10 53	10 58	11 15		11 53	11 50		11 53	12 15		12 54	12 50	12 54	12 58	13 15
Littleport	d		→	09 57					→	10 57					→	11 57					→	12 57			
Downham Market	d			10 06						11 06						12 06						13 06			
Watlington	d			10 11						11 11						12 11						13 11			
Kings Lynn	a			10 20						11 20						12 20						13 20			
Manea	d																								
March	d					10 31						11 15	11 31						12 31					13 15	13 31
Whittlesea	d											11 26												13 26	
Peterborough ■8	a				10 25	10 50					11 24	11 37	11 50					12 24	12 50				13 26	13 37	13 50

		LE ■1		EM ◇	FC ■1	EM ◇	XC ◇■1	LE ■1	EM ◇	FC ■1	EM ◇	LE ■1		XC ◇■1	LE ■1	EM ◇	FC ■1	EM ◇	XC ◇■1	LE ■1	EM ◇	FC ■1		EM ◇	LE ■1
London Liverpool Street	d																								
London Kings Cross	d				12 44					13 44							14 44					15 44			
Ipswich	d											14 00													16 00
Stansted Airport	d						13 25							14 25					15 25						
Norwich	d	12 40		12 57				13 40	13 57						14 40	14 57				15 35	15 52				
Wymondham	d	12 52						13 52							14 52					15 47					
Spooner Row	d																								
Attleborough	d	12 59						13 59							14 59					15 54	16 09				
Eccles Road	d																			15 59					
Harling Road	d																			16 03					
Thetford	d	13 13		13 24				14 13	14 24						15 13	15 24				16 13	16 23				
Brandon	d	13 21						14 21							15 21					16 21					
Lakenheath	d																								
Shippea Hill	d																								
Cambridge	d				13 35		14 00			14 35				15 00			15 35		16 00			16 35			
Waterbeach	d				13 41					14 41							15 41					16 41			
Ely ■6	a	13 38		13 47	13 50			14 38	14 47	14 50		14 58			15 38	15 48	15 50			16 38	16 47	16 50			16 58
Cambridge	a	13 59				←	13 58	14 59			←			14 58	15 59			←	15 58	16 59				←	
Ely ■6	d			13 53	13 50	13 53	14 15		14 53	14 50	14 53	14 58		15 15		15 52	15 50	15 52	16 15		16 52	16 50		16 52	16 58
Littleport	d			→	13 57				→	14 57						→	15 57				→	16 57			
Downham Market	d				14 06					15 06							16 06					17 06			
Watlington	d				14 11					15 11							16 11					17 11			
Kings Lynn	a				14 20					15 20							16 20					17 20			
Manea	d																								
March	d						14 31					15 15		15 31					16 31						17 15
Whittlesea	d											15 26													17 26
Peterborough ■8	a					14 25	14 50				15 25	15 37		15 50				16 25	16 50					17 26	17 37

Table 17

Saturdays
from 6 August

London, Norwich and Cambridge - Ely, Kings Lynn and Peterborough

		XC ◇1	LE 1	EM ◇	FC 1	EM ◇	XC ◇1	LE 1		EM ◇	FC 1	EM ◇	LE 1	XC ◇1	FC 1	LE 1	EM ◇	FC 1		XC ◇1	LE 1	FC 1	LE 1	LE 1	FC 1
London Liverpool Street	d																								
London Kings Cross	d				16 44						17 44				18 15			18 45				19 45			20 45
Ipswich	d												18 00										20 00		
Stansted Airport	d	16 25					17 25							18 25						19 25					
Norwich	d		16 38	16 57				17 35		17 54						18 40	18 57				19 40			20 40	
Wymondham	d		16 50	17 09				17 47		18 06						18 52					19 52			20 52	
Spooner Row	d		16x54																						
Attleborough	d		16 59					17 54		18 13						18 59					19 59			20 59	
Eccles Road	d							17 59																	
Harling Road	d							18 03																	
Thetford	d		17 13	17 27				18 13		18 27						19 13	19 24				20 13			21 13	
Brandon	d		17 21					18 21								19 21					20 21			21 21	
Lakenheath	d																								
Shippea Hill	d															19x29									
Cambridge	d	17 00			17 35		18 00				18 35			19 00	19 04			19 41		20 00		20 41			21 41
Waterbeach	d				17 41						18 41							19 47				20 47			21 47
Ely 6	a		17 38	17 48	17 50			18 38		18 48	18 50		18 58			19 39	19 47	19 56			20 38	20 56	20 58	21 38	21 56
Cambridge	a	16 58	17 59			←	17 58	18 59				←		18 58	19 01	19 59				19 58	20 59			21 59	
Ely 6	d	17 15		17 52	17 50	17 52	18 15			18 53	18 50	18 53	19 00	19 15	19 19		19 53	19 56		20 15		20 56	20 59		21 56
Littleport	d			→	17 57					→	18 57							20 03				21 03			22 03
Downham Market	d				18 06						19 06				19 35			20 12				21 12			22 12
Watlington	d				18 11						19 11				19 44			20 18				21 18			22 18
Kings Lynn	a				18 20						19 20				19 52			20 26				21 26			22 26
Manea	d						18x25																		
March	d	17 31					18 33					19 09	19 16	19 31						20 31			21 15		
Whittlesea	d												19 28										21 27		
Peterborough 8	a	17 50				18 25	18 50					19 27	19 38	19 50			20 25			20 50			21 37		

		FC 1	LE 1	FC 1 A
London Liverpool Street	d			
London Kings Cross	d	22 15		23 15
Ipswich	d			
Stansted Airport	d			
Norwich	d		22 40	
Wymondham	d		22 52	
Spooner Row	d			
Attleborough	d		22 59	
Eccles Road	d			
Harling Road	d			
Thetford	d		23 13	
Brandon	d		23 21	
Lakenheath	d			
Shippea Hill	d			
Cambridge	d	23 11		00 15
Waterbeach	d	23 17		00 21
Ely 6	a	23 26	23 38	00 30
Cambridge	a		23 59	
Ely 6	d	23 26		00 30
Littleport	d	23 33		00 37
Downham Market	d	23 43		00 46
Watlington	d	23 48		00 52
Kings Lynn	a	23 58		01 01
Manea	d			
March	d			
Whittlesea	d			
Peterborough 8	a			

A from 17 September

Table 17

Sundays

29 May to 19 June

London, Norwich and Cambridge - Ely, Kings Lynn and Peterborough

		FC [1]	LE [1]	FC [1]	LE [1]	FC [1]	EM ◇	LE ◇[1]	XC ◇[1]	LE [1]		FC [1]	EM ◇	XC ◇[1]	LE [1]	FC [1]	LE [1]	XC ◇[1]	LE [1]	FC [1]		XC ◇[1]	LE [1]	FC [1]	EM ◇
London Liverpool Street	d																								
London Kings Cross	d	23p15		07 53		09 15						10 15				11 15				12 15				13 15	
Ipswich	d		07 55					09 55									11 55								
Stansted Airport	d								10 25					11 25				12 25				13 25			
Norwich	d				09 03		09 33			10 03			10 47		11 03				12 03				13 03		13 49
Wymondham	d				09 15					10 15					11 15				12 15				13 15		
Spooner Row	d																								
Attleborough	d				09 22					10 22					11 22				12 22				13 22		
Eccles Road	d																								
Harling Road	d																								
Thetford	d				09 36		10 00			10 36			11 14		11 36				12 36				13 36		14 16
Brandon	d				09 44					10 44					11 44				12 44				13 44		
Lakenheath	d				09x49										11x49										
Shippea Hill	d																								
Cambridge	d	00 15		09 05		10 06			11 00			11 06		12 00		12 06		13 00		13 06		14 00		14 05	
Waterbeach	d	00 21		09 11		10 12						11 12				12 12				13 12				14 11	
Ely [6]	a	00 30	08 51	09 20	10 08	10 21	10 23	10 51		11 06		11 21	11 35		12 08	12 21	12 51		13 01	13 21			14 01	14 20	14 42
Cambridge	a				10 27				10 58	11 25				11 57	12 27			12 58	13 22			13 58	14 22		
Ely [6]	d	00 30	08 52	09 20		10 21	10 32	10 52	11 15			11 21	11 39	12 15		12 21	12 52	13 15		13 21		14 15		14 20	14 45
Littleport	d	00 37		09 27		10 28						11 28				12 28				13 28				14 27	
Downham Market	d	00 46		09 36		10 37						11 37				12 37				13 37				14 36	
Watlington	d	00 52		09 41		10 42						11 42				12 42				13 42				14 41	
Kings Lynn	a	01 01		09 50		10 51						11 51				12 51				13 51				14 51	
Manea	d																								
March	d		09 09					11 09	11 31					12 31			13 09	13 31				14 31			
Whittlesea	d		09 20					11 20									13 20								
Peterborough [8]	a		09 36				11 09	11 36	11 50				12 16	12 50			13 31	13 50				14 50			15 24

		LE [1]	XC ◇[1]	LE [1]	FC [1]	EM ◇		XC ◇[1]	LE [1]	FC [1]	LE [1]	XC ◇[1]	LE [1]	FC [1]	EM ◇	XC ◇[1]		LE [1]	FC [1]	EM ◇	LE [1]	XC ◇[1]	LE [1]	FC [1]	EM ◇
London Liverpool Street	d																								
London Kings Cross	d				14 15					15 15				16 15					17 15					18 15	
Ipswich	d	13 55									15 55										17 55				
Stansted Airport	d		14 25					15 25				16 25				17 25						18 25			
Norwich	d			14 03		14 49			15 03				16 03		16 53			17 03		17 53			18 03		18 56
Wymondham	d			14 15					15 15				16 15					17 15					18 15		
Spooner Row	d																								
Attleborough	d			14 22					15 22				16 22					17 22					18 22		
Eccles Road	d																								
Harling Road	d																								
Thetford	d			14 36		15 16			15 36				16 36		17 20			17 36		18 20			18 36		19 23
Brandon	d			14 44					15 44				16 44					17 44					18 44		
Lakenheath	d								15x49																
Shippea Hill	d																								
Cambridge	d		15 00		15 05			16 00		16 05		17 00		17 05		18 00			18 05			19 00		19 07	
Waterbeach	d				15 12					16 11				17 11					18 11					19 13	
Ely [6]	a	14 51		15 01	15 20	15 42			16 03	16 20	16 51		17 01	17 20	17 44			18 01	18 20	18 44	18 51		19 01	19 22	19 44
Cambridge	a		14 57	15 22				15 58	16 22			16 58	17 22			17 58		18 22				18 58	19 22		
Ely [6]	d	14 52	15 15		15 20	15 48		16 15		16 20	16 52	17 15		17 20	17 48	18 15			18 20	18 48	18 52	19 15		19 22	19 48
Littleport	d				15 27					16 27				17 27					18 27					19 29	
Downham Market	d				15 36					16 36				17 36					18 36					19 38	
Watlington	d				15 41					16 41				17 41					18 41					19 44	
Kings Lynn	a				15 51					16 51				17 51					18 52					19 52	
Manea	d																								
March	d	15 09	15 31					16 31			17 09	17 31				18 31					19 09	19 31			
Whittlesea	d	15 20									17 20										19 20				
Peterborough [8]	a	15 31	15 50			16 22		16 50			17 31	17 50			18 25	18 50				19 24	19 32	19 50			20 29

		XC ◇[1]		FC [1]	LE [1]	FC [1]	EM ◇	FC [1]	LE [1]	FC [1]	FC [1]
London Liverpool Street	d										
London Kings Cross	d			19 15		20 15		21 15		22 15	23 15
Ipswich	d										
Stansted Airport	d	19 25									
Norwich	d				20 03		20 52		22 03		
Wymondham	d				20 15				22 15		
Spooner Row	d										
Attleborough	d				20 22				22 22		
Eccles Road	d										
Harling Road	d										
Thetford	d				20 36		21 19		22 36		
Brandon	d				20 44				22 44		
Lakenheath	d										
Shippea Hill	d										
Cambridge	d	20 00		20 05		21 05		22 06		23 08	00 13
Waterbeach	d			20 11		21 11		22 12		23 14	00 19
Ely [6]	a			20 20	21 01	21 20	21 40	22 21	23 01	23 23	00 29
Cambridge	a	19 58			21 22				23 22		
Ely [6]	d	20 15		20 20		21 20	21 44	22 21		23 23	
Littleport	d			20 27		21 27		22 28		23 30	
Downham Market	d			20 36		21 36		22 37		23 39	
Watlington	d			20 41		21 41		22 43		23 44	
Kings Lynn	a			20 51		21 51		22 50		23 53	
Manea	d										
March	d	20 31									
Whittlesea	d										
Peterborough [8]	a	20 50					22 20				

Table 17

Sundays

26 June to 31 July

London, Norwich and Cambridge - Ely, Kings Lynn and Peterborough

		FC	LE	FC	LE	FC	EM	LE	XC	LE		FC	EM	XC	LE	FC	LE	XC	LE	FC		XC	LE	FC	EM
		1	1	1	1	1	◇	◇1	◇1	1		1	◇	◇1	1	1	1	◇1	1	1		◇1	1	1	◇
London Liverpool Street	d																								
London Kings Cross	d	23p15																						13 15	
Ipswich	d		07 55					09 55									11 55								
Stansted Airport	d								10 25					11 25				12 25				13 25			
Norwich	d				09 03		09 33			10 03			10 47		11 03				12 03				13 03		13 49
Wymondham	d				09 15					10 15					11 15				12 15				13 15		
Spooner Row	d																								
Attleborough	d				09 22					10 22					11 22				12 22				13 22		
Eccles Road	d																								
Harling Road	d																								
Thetford	d				09 36		10 00			10 36			11 14		11 36				12 36				13 36		14 16
Brandon	d				09 44					10 44					11 44				12 44				13 44		
Lakenheath	d				09x49										11x49										
Shippea Hill	d																								
Cambridge	d	00 15		09 05		10 05			11 00			11 05		12 00		12 05		13 00		13 05		14 00		14 05	
Waterbeach	d	00 21		09 11		10 11						11 11				12 11				13 11				14 11	
Ely 6	a	00 30	08 51	09 20	10 08	10 20	10 23	10 51		11 06		11 20	11 35		12 08	12 20	12 51		13 01	13 20			14 01	14 20	14 42
Cambridge	a				10 27				10 58	11 25				11 57	12 27			12 58	13 22			13 58	14 22		
Ely 6	d	00 30	08 52	09 20		10 20	10 32	10 52	11 15			11 20	11 39	12 15		12 20	12 52	13 15		13 20		14 15		14 20	14 45
Littleport	d	00 37		09 27		10 27						11 27				12 27				13 27				14 27	
Downham Market	d	00 46		09 36		10 36						11 36				12 36				13 36				14 36	
Watlington	d	00 52		09 41		10 41						11 41				12 41				13 41				14 41	
Kings Lynn	a	01 01		09 50		10 51						11 51				12 51				13 51				14 51	
Manea	d																								
March	d		09 09					11 09	11 31					12 31			13 09	13 31				14 31			
Whittlesea	d		09 20					11 20									13 20								
Peterborough 8	a		09 36				11 09	11 36	11 50				12 16	12 50			13 31	13 50				14 50			15 24

		LE	XC	LE	FC	EM		XC	LE	FC	LE	XC	LE	FC	EM	XC		LE	FC	EM	LE	XC	LE	FC	EM
		1	◇1	1	1	◇		◇1	1	1	1	◇1	1	1	◇	◇1		1	1	◇	1	◇1	1	1	◇
London Liverpool Street	d																								
London Kings Cross	d				14 15					15 15				16 15					17 15					18 15	
Ipswich	d	13 55									15 55										17 55				
Stansted Airport	d		14 25					15 25				16 25				17 25						18 25			
Norwich	d			14 03		14 49			15 03				16 03		16 53			17 03		17 53			18 03		18 56
Wymondham	d			14 15					15 15				16 15					17 15					18 15		
Spooner Row	d																								
Attleborough	d			14 22					15 22				16 22					17 22					18 22		
Eccles Road	d																								
Harling Road	d																								
Thetford	d			14 36		15 16			15 36				16 36		17 20			17 36		18 20			18 36		19 23
Brandon	d			14 44					15 44				16 44					17 44					18 44		
Lakenheath	d								15x49																
Shippea Hill	d																								
Cambridge	d		15 00		15 05			16 00		16 05		17 00		17 05		18 00			18 05			19 00		19 07	
Waterbeach	d				15 12					16 11				17 11					18 11					19 13	
Ely 6	a	14 51		15 01	15 20	15 42			16 03	16 20	16 51		17 01	17 20	17 44			18 01	18 20	18 44	18 51		19 01	19 22	19 44
Cambridge	a		14 57	15 22				15 58	16 22			16 58	17 22			17 58		18 22				18 58	19 22		
Ely 6	d	14 52	15 15		15 20	15 48		16 15		16 20	16 52	17 15		17 20	17 48	18 15			18 20	18 48	18 52	19 15		19 22	19 48
Littleport	d				15 27					16 27				17 27					18 27					19 29	
Downham Market	d				15 36					16 36				17 36					18 36					19 38	
Watlington	d				15 41					16 41				17 41					18 41					19 44	
Kings Lynn	a				15 51					16 51				17 51					18 52					19 52	
Manea	d																								
March	d	15 09	15 31					16 31			17 09	17 31				18 31					19 09	19 31			
Whittlesea	d	15 20									17 20										19 20				
Peterborough 8	a	15 31	15 50			16 22		16 50			17 31	17 50			18 25	18 50				19 24	19 32	19 50			20 29

		XC		FC	LE	FC	EM	FC	LE	FC	FC
		◇1		1	1	1	◇	1	1	1	1
London Liverpool Street	d										
London Kings Cross	d			19 15		20 15		21 15		22 15	23 15
Ipswich	d										
Stansted Airport	d	19 25									
Norwich	d				20 03		20 52		22 03		
Wymondham	d				20 15				22 15		
Spooner Row	d										
Attleborough	d				20 22				22 22		
Eccles Road	d										
Harling Road	d										
Thetford	d				20 36		21 19		22 36		
Brandon	d				20 44				22 44		
Lakenheath	d										
Shippea Hill	d										
Cambridge	d	20 00		20 05		21 05		22 06		23 08	00 13
Waterbeach	d			20 11		21 11		22 12		23 14	00 19
Ely 6	a			20 20	21 01	21 20	21 40	22 21	23 01	23 23	00 29
Cambridge	a	19 58			21 22				23 22		
Ely 6	d	20 15		20 20		21 20	21 44	22 21		23 23	
Littleport	d			20 27		21 27		22 28		23 30	
Downham Market	d			20 36		21 36		22 37		23 39	
Watlington	d			20 41		21 41		22 43		23 44	
Kings Lynn	a			20 51		21 51		22 50		23 53	
Manea	d										
March	d	20 31									
Whittlesea	d										
Peterborough 8	a	20 50					22 20				

Sundays

7 August to 11 September

London, Norwich and Cambridge - Ely, Kings Lynn and Peterborough

		LE 1	FC 1	LE 1	FC 1	EM ◇	LE ◇1	XC ◇1	LE 1	FC 1		EM ◇	XC ◇1	LE 1	FC 1	LE 1	XC ◇1	LE 1	FC 1 A	FC 1 B		XC ◇1	LE 1	FC 1	EM ◇
London Liverpool Street	d																								
London Kings Cross	d		07 50		09 10					10 10					11 10				12 10	12 15				13 10	
Ipswich	d	07 55					09 55									11 55									
Stansted Airport	d							10 25					11 25				12 25					13 25			
Norwich	d			09 03		09 33			10 03			10 47		11 03				12 03					13 03		13 49
Wymondham	d			09 15					10 15					11 15				12 15					13 15		
Spooner Row	d																								
Attleborough	d			09 22					10 22					11 22				12 22					13 22		
Eccles Road	d																								
Harling Road	d																								
Thetford	d			09 36		10 00			10 36			11 14		11 36				12 36					13 36		14 16
Brandon	d			09 44					10 44					11 44				12 44					13 44		
Lakenheath	d			09x49										11x49											
Shippea Hill	d																								
Cambridge	d		09 05		10 06			11 00		11 07			12 00		12 06		13 00		13 06	13 06		14 00		14 05	
Waterbeach	d		09 11		10 12					11 13					12 12				13 12	13 12				14 11	
Ely 6	a	08 51	09 20	10 08	10 21	10 23	10 51		11 06	11 22		11 35		12 08	12 21	12 51		13 01	13 21	13 21			14 01	14 20	14 42
Cambridge	a			10 27				10 58	11 25				11 57	12 27			12 58	13 22				13 58	14 22		
Ely 6	d	08 52	09 20		10 21	10 32	10 52	11 15		11 22		11 39	12 15		12 21	12 52	13 15		13 21	13 21		14 15		14 20	14 45
Littleport	d		09 27		10 28					11 29					12 28				13 28	13 28				14 27	
Downham Market	d		09 36		10 37					11 38					12 37				13 37	13 37				14 36	
Watlington	d		09 41		10 42					11 44					12 42				13 42	13 42				14 41	
Kings Lynn	a		09 50		10 51					11 53					12 51				13 51	13 51				14 51	
Manea	d																								
March	d	09 09					11 09	11 31					12 31			13 09	13 31					14 31			
Whittlesea	d	09 20					11 20									13 20									
Peterborough 8	a	09 36				11 09	11 36	11 50				12 16	12 50			13 31	13 50					14 50			15 24

		LE 1	XC ◇1	LE 1	FC 1	EM ◇		XC ◇1	LE 1	FC 1	LE 1	XC ◇1	LE 1	FC 1	EM ◇	XC ◇1		LE 1	FC 1	EM ◇	LE 1	XC ◇1	LE 1	FC 1	EM ◇
London Liverpool Street	d																								
London Kings Cross	d				14 10					15 15				16 10					17 10					18 10	
Ipswich	d	13 55									15 55										17 55				
Stansted Airport	d		14 25					15 25				16 25				17 25						18 25			
Norwich	d			14 03		14 49			15 03				16 03		16 53			17 03		17 53			18 03		18 56
Wymondham	d			14 15					15 15				16 15					17 15					18 15		
Spooner Row	d																								
Attleborough	d			14 22					15 22				16 22					17 22					18 22		
Eccles Road	d																								
Harling Road	d																								
Thetford	d			14 36		15 16			15 36				16 36		17 20			17 36		18 20			18 36		19 23
Brandon	d			14 44					15 44				16 44					17 44					18 44		
Lakenheath	d								15x49																
Shippea Hill	d																								
Cambridge	d		15 00		15 05			16 00		16 05		17 00		17 05		18 00			18 05			19 00		19 07	
Waterbeach	d				15 12					16 11				17 11					18 11					19 13	
Ely 6	a	14 51		15 01	15 20	15 42			16 03	16 20	16 51		17 01	17 20	17 44			18 01	18 20	18 44	18 51		19 01	19 22	19 44
Cambridge	a		14 57	15 22				15 58	16 22			16 58	17 22			17 58		18 22				18 58	19 22		
Ely 6	d	14 52	15 15		15 20	15 48		16 15		16 20	16 52	17 15		17 20	17 48	18 15			18 20	18 48	18 52	19 15		19 22	19 48
Littleport	d				15 27					16 27				17 27					18 27					19 29	
Downham Market	d				15 36					16 36				17 36					18 36					19 38	
Watlington	d				15 41					16 41				17 41					18 41					19 44	
Kings Lynn	a				15 51					16 51				17 51					18 52					19 52	
Manea	d																								
March	d	15 09	15 31					16 31			17 09	17 31				18 31					19 09	19 31			
Whittlesea	d	15 20									17 20										19 20				
Peterborough 8	a	15 31	15 50			16 22		16 50			17 31	17 50			18 25	18 50				19 24	19 32	19 50			20 29

A not 28 August

B 28 August

Table 17

Sundays
7 August to 11 September

London, Norwich and Cambridge - Ely, Kings Lynn and Peterborough

		XC	FC	LE	FC	EM	FC	LE	FC	FC
		◇1	1	1	1	◇	1	1	1	1
London Liverpool Street	d									
London Kings Cross	d		19 10		20 10		21 10		22 10	23 10
Ipswich	d									
Stansted Airport	d	19 25								
Norwich	d			20 03		20 52		22 03		
Wymondham	d			20 15				22 15		
Spooner Row	d									
Attleborough	d			20 22				22 22		
Eccles Road	d									
Harling Road	d									
Thetford	d			20 36		21 19		22 36		
Brandon	d			20 44				22 44		
Lakenheath	d									
Shippea Hill	d									
Cambridge	d	20 00	20 05		21 05		22 06		23 08	00 13
Waterbeach	d		20 11		21 11		22 12		23 14	00 19
Ely 6	a		20 20	21 01	21 20	21 40	22 21	23 01	23 23	00 29
Cambridge	a	19 58		21 22				23 22		
Ely 6	d	20 15	20 20		21 20	21 44	22 21		23 23	
Littleport	d		20 27		21 27		22 28		23 30	
Downham Market	d		20 36		21 36		22 37		23 39	
Watlington	d		20 41		21 41		22 43		23 44	
Kings Lynn	a		20 51		21 51		22 50		23 53	
Manea	d									
March	d	20 31								
Whittlesea	d									
Peterborough 8	a	20 50				22 20				

Sundays
from 18 September

		FC	FC	LE	FC	LE	XC	LE	FC	EM	XC	LE	FC	LE	XC	LE	FC	XC	LE	FC	EM	LE	XC
		1	1	1	1	◇1	◇1	1	1	◇	◇1	1	1	1	◇1	1	1	◇1	1	1	◇	1	◇1
London Liverpool Street	d																						
London Kings Cross	d	23p15	07 53		09 15				10 15				11 15				12 15			13 15			
Ipswich	d					09 55								11 55								13 55	
Stansted Airport	d						10 25				11 25				12 25			13 25					14 25
Norwich	d			09 03				10 03		10 47		11 03				12 03			13 03		13 49		
Wymondham	d			09 15				10 15				11 15				12 15			13 15				
Spooner Row	d																						
Attleborough	d			09 22				10 22				11 22				12 22			13 22				
Eccles Road	d																						
Harling Road	d																						
Thetford	d			09 36				10 36		11 14		11 36				12 36			13 36		14 16		
Brandon	d			09 44				10 44				11 44				12 44			13 44				
Lakenheath	d			09x49								11x49											
Shippea Hill	d																						
Cambridge	d	00 15	09 05		10 06		11 00		11 06		12 00		12 06		13 00		13 06	14 00		14 05			15 00
Waterbeach	d	00 21	09 11		10 12				11 12				12 12				13 12			14 11			
Ely 6	a	00 30	09 20	10 08	10 21	10 51		11 06	11 21	11 35		12 08	12 21	12 51		13 01	13 21		14 01	14 20	14 42	14 51	
Cambridge	a			10 27			10 58	11 25			11 57	12 27			12 58	13 22		13 58	14 22				14 57
Ely 6	d	00 30	09 20		10 21	10 52	11 15		11 21	11 39	12 15		12 21	12 52	13 15		13 21	14 15		14 20	14 45	14 52	15 15
Littleport	d	00 37	09 27		10 28				11 28				12 28				13 28			14 27			
Downham Market	d	00 46	09 36		10 37				11 37				12 37				13 37			14 36			
Watlington	d	00 52	09 41		10 42				11 42				12 42				13 42			14 41			
Kings Lynn	a	01 01	09 50		10 51				11 51				12 51				13 51			14 51			
Manea	d																						
March	d					11 09	11 31				12 31			13 09	13 31			14 31				15 09	15 31
Whittlesea	d					11 20								13 20								15 20	
Peterborough 8	a					11 36	11 50			12 16	12 50			13 31	13 50			14 50			15 24	15 31	15 50

Table 17

Sundays

from 18 September

London, Norwich and Cambridge - Ely, Kings Lynn and Peterborough

		LE ■1	FC ■1	EM ◇	XC ◇■1	LE ■1		FC ■1	LE ■1	XC ◇■1	LE ■1	FC ■1	EM ◇	XC ◇■1	LE ■1	FC ■1		EM ◇	LE ■1	XC ◇■1	LE ■1	FC ■1	EM ◇	XC ◇■1	FC ■1
London Liverpool Street	d																								
London Kings Cross	d		14 15					15 15				16 15				17 15						18 15			19 15
Ipswich	d								15 55										17 55						
Stansted Airport	d				15 25					16 25				17 25						18 25				19 25	
Norwich	d	14 03		14 49		15 03					16 03		16 53		17 03			17 53			18 03		18 56		
Wymondham	d	14 15				15 15					16 15				17 15						18 15				
Spooner Row	d																								
Attleborough	d	14 22				15 22					16 22				17 22						18 22				
Eccles Road	d																								
Harling Road	d																								
Thetford	d	14 36		15 16		15 36					16 36		17 20		17 36			18 20			18 36		19 23		
Brandon	d	14 44				15 44					16 44				17 44						18 44				
Lakenheath	d					15x49																			
Shippea Hill	d																								
Cambridge	d		15 05		16 00			16 05		17 00		17 05		18 00		18 05				19 00		19 07		20 00	20 05
Waterbeach	d		15 12					16 11				17 11				18 11						19 13			20 11
Ely 6	a	15 01	15 20	15 42		16 03		16 20	16 51		17 01	17 20	17 44		18 01	18 20		18 44	18 51		19 01	19 22	19 44		20 20
Cambridge	a	15 22			15 58	16 22				16 58	17 22			17 58	18 22					18 58	19 22			19 58	
Ely 6	d		15 20	15 48	16 15			16 20	16 52	17 15		17 20	17 48	18 15		18 20		18 48	18 52	19 15		19 22	19 48	20 15	20 20
Littleport	d		15 27					16 27				17 27				18 27						19 29			20 27
Downham Market	d		15 36					16 36				17 36				18 36						19 38			20 36
Watlington	d		15 41					16 41				17 41				18 41						19 44			20 41
Kings Lynn	a		15 51					16 51				17 51				18 52						19 52			20 51
Manea	d																								
March	d				16 31				17 09	17 31				18 31					19 09	19 31				20 31	
Whittlesea	d								17 20										19 20						
Peterborough 8	a			16 22	16 50				17 31	17 50			18 25	18 50				19 24	19 32	19 50			20 29	20 50	

		LE ■1		FC ■1	EM ◇	FC ■1	LE ■1	FC ■1	FC ■1
London Liverpool Street	d								
London Kings Cross	d			20 15		21 15		22 15	23 15
Ipswich	d								
Stansted Airport	d								
Norwich	d	20 03			20 52		22 03		
Wymondham	d	20 15					22 15		
Spooner Row	d								
Attleborough	d	20 22					22 22		
Eccles Road	d								
Harling Road	d								
Thetford	d	20 36			21 19		22 36		
Brandon	d	20 44					22 44		
Lakenheath	d								
Shippea Hill	d								
Cambridge	d			21 05		22 06		23 08	00 13
Waterbeach	d			21 11		22 12		23 14	00 19
Ely 6	a	21 01		21 20	21 40	22 21	23 01	23 23	00 29
Cambridge	a	21 22					23 22		
Ely 6	d			21 20	21 44	22 21		23 23	
Littleport	d			21 27		22 28		23 30	
Downham Market	d			21 36		22 37		23 39	
Watlington	d			21 41		22 43		23 44	
Kings Lynn	a			21 51		22 50		23 53	
Manea	d								
March	d								
Whittlesea	d								
Peterborough 8	a				22 20				

Peterborough, Kings Lynn and Ely - Cambridge, Norwich and London

Miles	Miles			FC MO	FC MX	LE MX	FC	LE	LE	FC	FC	LE		EM	LE	FC	LE	FC	XC	LE	EM	FC		LE	LE
				1	1	1	1	1	1	1	1	1		◇	1	1	1	1	◇1	1	◇	1		1	1
0	—	**Peterborough 8**	d											06 27					07 12		07 35				07 45
6	—	Whittlesea	d																07 21						07 53
14	—	March	d											06 43					07 32		07 51				08 04
19¼	—	Manea	d																07x39						
—	0	**Kings Lynn**	d	22p28	22p28		04 56	05 19		05 51		06 18				06 51		07 18				07 54			
—	6	Watlington	d	22p35	22p35		05 03	05 26		05 58		06 25				06 58		07 25				08 01			
—	10¾	Downham Market	d	22p41	22p41		05 09	05 33		06 04		06 32				07 04		07 31				08 07			
—	21	Littleport	d	22p50	22p50		05 18	05 42		06 13		06 41				07 13		07 40				08 16			
29¼	26½	**Ely 6**	a	22p58	22p58		05 26	05 51		06 21		06 49		07 01		07 21		07 47	07 53		08 11	08 24			08 31
—	—	**Cambridge**	d			22p55			06 05						07 04				08 10					08 12	
—	—	**Ely 6**	d	22p58	22p58	23p10	05 26	05 52	06 20	06 21	06 47	06 50		07 05	07 19	07 21	07 30	07 47		08 02	08 15	08 25		08 29	08 31
—	36	Waterbeach	d	23p07	23p07		05 35	06 01		06 31		06 59				07 31		07 57		08 11		08 34			
—	41¼	**Cambridge**	a	23p14	23p14		05 44	06 10		06 38	07 05	07 08				07 39	07 47	08 06	08 09	08 20		08 42			
35¼	—	Shippea Hill	d												07x28										
40¾	—	Lakenheath	d																						
44½	—	Brandon	d			23p26			06 36					07 20	07 38									08 45	
51¾	—	Thetford	d			23p34			06 44					07 29	07 47						08 37			08 53	
59½	—	Harling Road	d						06 53						07 55										
62½	—	Eccles Road	d						06 58						08 00										
66¼	—	Attleborough	d			23p49			07 04					07 43	08 06						08 51			09 08	
69½	—	Spooner Row	d												08x11										
72	—	Wymondham	d			23p57			07 11					07 50	08 16						08 58			09 16	
82¼	—	**Norwich**	a			00 11			07 27					08 13	08 30						09 13			09 30	
—	—	Stansted Airport	a																08 39						
—	—	Ipswich	a																						09 28
—	99¼	**London Kings Cross**	a	00 33	00 42		06 38			07 42	08 06					08 39		09 10				09 43			
—	—	London Liverpool Street	a					07 34				08 34					09 19			09 49					

		XC	FC	LE	FC	EM	XC	EM		LE	LE	FC	XC	EM	FC	LE	XC	EM		FC	LE	LE	XC	EM	FC
		◇1	1	1	1	◇	◇1	◇		1	1	1	◇1	◇	1	1	◇1	◇		1	1	1	◇1	◇	1
Peterborough 8	d	08 18				08 59	09 18	09 40			09 45		10 18	10 44			11 18	11 41				11 45	12 18	12 43	
Whittlesea	d										09 53											11 53			
March	d	08 34					09 34				10 04		10 34				11 34					12 04	12 34		
Manea	d																								
Kings Lynn	d		08 27		08 59							09 59			10 56					11 56					12 56
Watlington	d		08 34		09 06							10 06			11 03					12 03					13 03
Downham Market	d		08 40		09 12							10 12			11 09					12 09					13 09
Littleport	d		08 49		09 21							10 21			11 18					12 18					13 18
Ely 6	a	08 52	08 57		09 29	09 41	09 51	10 13			10 25	10 29	10 52	11 16	11 26		11 52	12 14		12 26		12 29	12 52	13 16	13 26
Cambridge	d	09 10		09 12			10 10			10 12			11 10			11 12	12 10				12 12		13 10		
Ely 6	d		08 57	09 27	09 29	09 44		10 17		10 27	10 32	10 29		11 19	11 26	11 27		12 18		12 26	12 27	12 31		13 19	13 26
Waterbeach	d		09 07		09 38							10 38			11 35					12 35					13 35
Cambridge	a	09 08	09 15		09 47		10 08					10 45	11 08		11 44		12 08			12 44			13 08		13 44
Shippea Hill	d																								
Lakenheath	d																								
Brandon	d			09 43						10 43						11 43					12 43				
Thetford	d			09 51		10 05		10 41		10 51				11 41		11 51		12 39			12 51			13 40	
Harling Road	d																								
Eccles Road	d																								
Attleborough	d			10 06						11 06						12 06					13 06				
Spooner Row	d			10x11																					
Wymondham	d			10 16						11 14						12 14					13 14				
Norwich	a			10 30		10 44		11 14		11 30				12 13		12 30		13 13			13 30			14 09	
Stansted Airport	a	09 38					10 45						11 45				12 45						13 45		
Ipswich	a										11 28											13 28			
London Kings Cross	a		10 15		10 47							11 44			12 35					13 34					14 34
London Liverpool Street	a																								

		LE	XC	EM		FC	LE	LE	XC	EM	FC	LE	XC	FC		EM	FC	LE	LE	XC	FC	EM	FC	LE	
		1	◇1	◇		1	1	1	◇1	◇	1	1	◇1	1		◇	1	1	1	◇1	1	◇	1	1	
Peterborough 8	d		13 18	13 41				13 45	14 18	14 41			15 18			15 40			15 45	16 18		16 41			
Whittlesea	d							13 53											15 53						
March	d		13 34					14 04	14 34				15 34						16 04	16 34					
Manea	d																								
Kings Lynn	d					13 56					14 56						15 54				16 35				
Watlington	d					14 03					15 03						16 01				16 42				
Downham Market	d					14 09					15 09						16 07				16 48				
Littleport	d					14 18					15 18						16 16				16 57				
Ely 6	a		13 52	14 14		14 26		14 29	14 52	15 14	15 26		15 52			16 13	16 24		16 29	16 52	17 05	17 14			
Cambridge	d	13 12	14 10				14 12		15 10			15 12	16 10					16 12		17 10				17 12	
Ely 6	d	13 27		14 17		14 26	14 27	14 31		15 17	15 26	15 27		16 06		16 16	16 24	16 27	16 31		17 06	17 17	17 24	17 27	
Waterbeach	d					14 35					15 35			16 16			16 33				17 16		17 33		
Cambridge	a		14 08			14 44			15 08		15 44		16 08	16 22			16 43			17 08	17 22		17 43		
Shippea Hill	d																								
Lakenheath	d																								
Brandon	d	13 43					14 43					15 43						16 43						17 43	
Thetford	d	13 51		14 38			14 51			15 38		15 51				16 37		16 51				17 38		17 51	
Harling Road	d																								
Eccles Road	d																								
Attleborough	d	14 06					15 06					16 06						17 06						18 06	
Spooner Row	d																								
Wymondham	d	14 14					15 14					16 14						17 14						18 14	
Norwich	a	14 30		15 13			15 30			16 14		16 30				17 13		17 28				18 13		18 28	
Stansted Airport	a		14 45						15 45				16 45							17 39					
Ipswich	a							15 28											17 28						
London Kings Cross	a					15 34					16 34			17 32			17 35				18 32		18 35		
London Liverpool Street	a																								

Peterborough, Kings Lynn and Ely - Cambridge, Norwich and London

		XC	FC	EM	LE	LE	XC	FC	EM	LE		XC	XC	FC	EM	LE	LE	XC	FC	LE		XC	FC	EM	LE
		◇1	1	◇	1	1	◇1	1	◇	1		◇1	◇1	1	◇	◇1	1	◇1	1	1		◇1	1	◇	◇1
				A																					
Peterborough 8	d	17 18		17 42		17 45	18 18		18 45			19 00	19 19		19 40	19 45		20 18				21 19		21 38	21 45
Whittlesea	d	17 26				17 53										19 53									21 53
March	d	17 37				18 04	18 34		19 01			19 16	19 35			20 04		20 35				21 35			22 04
Manea	d	17x44																							
Kings Lynn	d		17 35					18 35						19 36					20 36				21 36		
Watlington	d		17 42					18 42						19 43					20 43				21 43		
Downham Market	d		17 48					18 48						19 49					20 49				21 49		
Littleport	d		17 57					18 57						19 58					20 58				21 58		
Ely 6	a	17 58	18 05	18 16		18 28	18 52	19 05	19 24			19 33	19 53	20 08	20 13	20 28		20 53	21 08			21 53	22 08	22 11	22 23
Cambridge	d	18 18			18 09		19 10			19 25		19a51	20 10				20 20	21 10		21 15		22 11			
Ely 6	d		18 06	18 20	18 24	18 31		19 06	19 27	19 40				20 08	20 16	20 28	20 37		21 08	21 30			22 08	22 15	22 23
Waterbeach	d		18 15					19 15						20 17					21 17				22 17		
Cambridge	a	18 16	18 23				19 08	19 22					20 08	20 26				21 08	21 26			22 09	22 24		
Shippea Hill	d																								
Lakenheath	d																								
Brandon	d				18 44					19 56							20 53			21 46					
Thetford	d			18 42	18 53				19 50	20 04					20 37		21 01			21 55				22 36	
Harling Road	d																								
Eccles Road	d																								
Attleborough	d				19 08					20 19							21 16			22 10				22 50	
Spooner Row	d																								
Wymondham	d				19 15					20 27							21 24			22 17				22 57	
Norwich	a			19 15	19 30				20 22	20 41					21 14		21 38			22 31				23 18	
Stansted Airport	a	18 45					19 42						20 45					21 45				22 54			
Ipswich	a					19 28										21 25									23 18
London Kings Cross	a		19 35					20 32						21 32					22 32				23 31		
London Liverpool Street	a																								

		XC	FC	LE
		◇1	1	1
Peterborough 8	d	22 18		
Whittlesea	d			
March	d	22 35		
Manea	d			
Kings Lynn	d		22 28	
Watlington	d		22 35	
Downham Market	d		22 41	
Littleport	d		22 50	
Ely 6	a	22 54	22 58	
Cambridge	d	23a11		22 55
Ely 6	d		22 58	23 10
Waterbeach	d		23 07	
Cambridge	a		23 14	
Shippea Hill	d			
Lakenheath	d			
Brandon	d			23 26
Thetford	d			23 34
Harling Road	d			
Eccles Road	d			
Attleborough	d			23 49
Spooner Row	d			
Wymondham	d			23 57
Norwich	a			00 11
Stansted Airport	a			
Ipswich	a			
London Kings Cross	a		00 42	
London Liverpool Street	a			

A from 1 August

Table 17

Saturdays
until 18 June

Peterborough, Kings Lynn and Ely - Cambridge, Norwich and London

		FC [1]	LE [1]	FC [1]	LE [1]	FC [1]	EM ◇	LE [1]	FC [1]	XC ◇[1]		EM ◇	LE [1]	FC [1]	LE [1]	XC ◇[1]	LE [1]	FC [1]	LE [1]	EM ◇		XC ◇[1]	FC [1]	EM ◇	LE [1]
Peterborough [8]	d						06 27			07 13		07 35	07 45			08 18				09 00		09 18		09 43	09 46
Whittlesea	d									07 21			07 53												09 54
March	d						06 43			07 32		07 51	08 04			08 34						09 34			10 05
Manea	d									07x39															
Kings Lynn	d	22p28				05 56			06 56					07 56				08 56					09 30		
Watlington	d	22p35				06 03			07 03					08 03				09 03							
Downham Market	d	22p41				06 09			07 09					08 09				09 09					09 41		
Littleport	d	22p50				06 18			07 18					08 18				09 18							
Ely [6]	a	22p58				06 26	07 01		07 26	07 52		08 11	08 22	08 26		08 52		09 26		09 33		09 52	09 58	10 14	10 24
Cambridge	d		22p55		06 08			07 00		08 10					08 12	09 10			09 12			10 10	10 15		
Ely [6]	d	22p58	23p10	05 26	06 23	06 26	07 06	07 15	07 26			08 14	08 31	08 26	08 27		09 11	09 26	09 30	09 39				10 17	10 24
Waterbeach	d	23p07		05 35		06 35			07 35					08 35			09 20	09 35							
Cambridge	a	23p14		05 42		06 44			07 44	08 08				08 44		09 07	09 28	09 44				10 07	10 13		
Shippea Hill	d							07x24																	
Lakenheath	d																								
Brandon	d		23p26		06 39		07 22	07 34							08 43				09 46						
Thetford	d		23p34		06 48		07 30	07 42				08 36			08 51				09 55	10 04				10 40	
Harling Road	d				06 56			07 51																	
Eccles Road	d				07 01			07 56																	
Attleborough	d		23p49		07 07		07 44	08 02				08 50			09 06				10 10						
Spooner Row	d							08x07																	
Wymondham	d		23p57		07 15		07 51	08 12				08 57			09 14				10 17						
Norwich	a		00 11		07 29		08 13	08 30				09 15			09 30				10 31	10 43				11 15	
Stansted Airport	a									08 45						09 45						10 45			
Ipswich	a												09 28												11 20
London Kings Cross	a	00 42		06 39		07 36			08 36					09 38				10 34					11 03		
London Liverpool Street	a																10 43								

		FC [1]	LE [1]	XC ◇[1]	EM ◇	FC [1]		LE [1]	XC ◇[1]	EM ◇	FC [1]	LE [1]	LE [1]	XC ◇[1]	EM ◇	FC [1]		LE [1]	XC ◇[1]	EM ◇	FC [1]	LE [1]	LE [1]	XC ◇[1]	EM ◇
Peterborough [8]	d			10 18	10 41				11 18	11 41			11 45	12 18	12 40				13 18	13 41			13 45	14 18	14 43
Whittlesea	d												11 53										13 53		
March	d			10 34					11 34				12 04	12 34					13 34				14 04	14 34	
Manea	d																								
Kings Lynn	d	09 56				10 56					11 56					12 56					13 56				
Watlington	d	10 03				11 03					12 03					13 03					14 03				
Downham Market	d	10 09				11 09					12 09					13 09					14 09				
Littleport	d	10 18				11 18					12 18					13 18					14 18				
Ely [6]	a	10 26		10 52	11 17	11 26			11 52	12 12	12 26		12 28	12 52	13 13	13 26			13 52	14 14	14 26		14 28	14 52	15 14
Cambridge	d		10 12	11 10				11 12	12 10			12 12		13 10				13 12	14 10			14 12		15 10	
Ely [6]	d	10 26	10 29		11 22	11 26		11 29		12 15	12 26	12 27	12 31		13 17	13 26		13 27		14 17	14 26	14 27	14 31		15 17
Waterbeach	d	10 35				11 35					12 35					13 35					14 34				
Cambridge	a	10 44		11 07		11 44			12 07		12 44			13 07		13 44			14 07		14 44			15 07	
Shippea Hill	d																								
Lakenheath	d																								
Brandon	d		10 45					11 45				12 43						13 43				14 43			
Thetford	d		10 54		11 44			11 54		12 39		12 51			13 39			13 51		14 38		14 51			15 40
Harling Road	d																								
Eccles Road	d																								
Attleborough	d		11 09					12 09				13 06						14 06				15 06			
Spooner Row	d																								
Wymondham	d		11 16					12 16				13 14						14 14				15 14			
Norwich	a		11 30		12 18			12 30		13 13		13 30			14 13			14 30		15 13		15 30			16 15
Stansted Airport	a			11 45					12 45					13 45					14 45					15 45	
Ipswich	a												13 28										15 28		
London Kings Cross	a	11 34				12 34					13 34					14 34					15 34				
London Liverpool Street	a																								

		FC [1]		LE [1]	XC ◇[1]	EM ◇	FC [1]	LE [1]	LE [1]	XC ◇[1]	EM ◇	FC [1]		LE [1]	XC ◇[1]	FC [1]	LE [1]	LE [1]	XC ◇[1]	FC [1]	EM ◇	LE [1]		XC ◇[1]	FC [1]
Peterborough [8]	d				15 18	15 41			15 45	16 18	16 41				17 18			17 45	18 18		18 45			19 18	
Whittlesea	d								15 53						17 27			17 53							
March	d				15 34				16 04	16 34					17 38			18 04	18 34		19 04			19 34	
Manea	d														17x45										
Kings Lynn	d	14 56					15 56					16 56				17 56				18 35					19 35
Watlington	d	15 03					16 03					17 03				18 03				18 42					19 42
Downham Market	d	15 09					16 09					17 09				18 09				18 48					19 48
Littleport	d	15 18					16 18					17 18				18 18				18 57					19 57
Ely [6]	a	15 26			15 52	16 14	16 26		16 28	16 52	17 13	17 26			17 59	18 26		18 28	18 52	19 05	19 22			19 51	20 05
Cambridge	d			15 12	16 10			16 12		17 10				17 12	18 20		18 12		19 10			19 12		20 10	
Ely [6]	d	15 26		15 27		16 17	16 26	16 27	16 31		17 17	17 26		17 27		18 26	18 27	18 31		19 05	19 26	19 29			20 05
Waterbeach	d	15 35					16 35					17 35				18 35				19 15					20 15
Cambridge	a	15 44			16 07		16 44			17 07		17 44			18 16	18 44			19 08	19 21				20 07	20 21
Shippea Hill	d																								
Lakenheath	d			15x40																					
Brandon	d			15 45				16 43						17 43			18 43					19 45			
Thetford	d			15 54		16 38		16 51			17 40			17 51			18 51				19 47	19 54			
Harling Road	d																								
Eccles Road	d																								
Attleborough	d			16 09				17 06						18 06			19 06					20 09			
Spooner Row	d																								
Wymondham	d			16 16				17 14						18 14			19 14					20 16			
Norwich	a			16 30		17 13		17 30			18 18			18 30			19 30				20 21	20 30			
Stansted Airport	a				16 45					17 45					18 53				19 45					20 45	
Ipswich	a								17 28									19 28							
London Kings Cross	a	16 34					17 34					18 35				19 34				20 31					21 31
London Liverpool Street	a																								

Table 17

Saturdays
until 18 June

Peterborough, Kings Lynn and Ely - Cambridge, Norwich and London

		EM ◇	LE ◇1	LE 1	XC ◇1	FC 1	LE 1	XC ◇1		FC 1	EM ◇	LE ◇1	LE 1	XC ◇1	FC 1
Peterborough 8	d	19 41	19 45		20 18			21 18			21 38	21 45		22 18	
Whittlesea	d		19 53									21 53			
March	d		20 04		20 34			21 34				22 04		22 34	
Manea	d														
Kings Lynn	d					20 35				21 35					23 10
Watlington	d					20 42				21 42					23 17
Downham Market	d					20 48				21 48					23 23
Littleport	d					20 57				21 57					23 32
Ely 6	a	20 14	20 26		20 51	21 05		21 51		22 05	22 12	22 23		22 53	23 41
Cambridge	d			20 12	21 10		21 12	22 10					22 30	23a10	
Ely 6	d	20 16	20 27	20 27		21 05	21 27			22 05	22 18	22 23	22 45		23 43
Waterbeach	d					21 15				22 15					23 52
Cambridge	a				21 07	21 21		22 07		22 21					23 59
Shippea Hill	d														
Lakenheath	d														
Brandon	d			20 43			21 43						23 01		
Thetford	d	20 37		20 51			21 51				22 41		23 09		
Harling Road	d														
Eccles Road	d														
Attleborough	d			21 06			22 06				22 55		23 24		
Spooner Row	d														
Wymondham	d			21 14			22 14				23 02		23 32		
Norwich	a	21 14		21 30			22 30				23 20		23 46		
Stansted Airport	a				21 45			22 45							
Ipswich	a		21 22									23 18			
London Kings Cross	a					22 31				23 31					
London Liverpool Street	a														

Saturdays
25 June to 30 July

		FC 1	LE 1	FC 1	LE 1	FC 1	EM ◇	LE 1	FC 1	XC ◇1		EM ◇	LE 1	FC 1	LE 1	XC ◇1	LE 1	FC 1	LE 1	EM ◇		XC ◇1	FC 1	EM ◇	LE 1
Peterborough 8	d						06 27			07 13		07 35	07 45			08 18				09 00		09 18		09 43	09 46
Whittlesea	d									07 21			07 53												09 54
March	d						06 43			07 32		07 51	08 04			08 34						09 34			10 05
Manea	d									07x39															
Kings Lynn	d	22p28				05 56			06 56					07 56				08 56					09 30		
Watlington	d	22p35				06 03			07 03					08 03				09 03							
Downham Market	d	22p41				06 09			07 09					08 09				09 09					09 41		
Littleport	d	22p50				06 18			07 18					08 18				09 18							
Ely 6	a	22p58				06 26	07 01		07 26	07 52		08 11	08 22	08 26		08 52		09 26		09 33		09 52	09 58	10 14	10 24
Cambridge	d		22p55		06 08			07 00		08 10					08 12	09 10			09 12			10 10	10 15		
Ely 6	d	22p58	23p10	05 26	06 23	06 26	07 06	07 15	07 26			08 14	08 31	08 26	08 27		09 11	09 26	09 30	09 39				10 17	10 24
Waterbeach	d	23p07		05 35		06 35			07 35					08 35			09 20	09 35							
Cambridge	a	23p14		05 42		06 44			07 44	08 08				08 44		09 07	09 28	09 44				10 07	10 13		
Shippea Hill	d							07x24																	
Lakenheath	d																								
Brandon	d		23p26		06 39		07 22	07 34							08 43				09 46						
Thetford	d		23p34		06 48		07 30	07 42				08 36			08 51				09 55	10 04				10 40	
Harling Road	d				06 56			07 51																	
Eccles Road	d				07 01			07 56																	
Attleborough	d		23p49		07 07		07 44	08 02				08 50			09 06				10 10						
Spooner Row	d							08x07																	
Wymondham	d		23p57		07 15		07 51	08 12				08 57			09 14				10 17						
Norwich	a		00 11		07 29		08 13	08 30				09 15			09 30				10 31	10 43				11 15	
Stansted Airport	a									08 45						09 45						10 45			
Ipswich	a												09 28												11 20
London Kings Cross	a	00 42		06 39		07 36			08 36					09 38				10 34					11 03		
London Liverpool Street	a																10 43								

		FC 1	LE 1	XC ◇1	EM ◇	FC 1		LE 1	XC ◇1	EM ◇	FC 1	LE 1	LE 1	XC ◇1	EM ◇	FC 1		LE 1	XC ◇1	EM ◇	FC 1	LE 1	LE 1	XC ◇1	EM ◇
Peterborough 8	d			10 18	10 41				11 18	11 41			11 45	12 18	12 40				13 18	13 41			13 45	14 18	14 43
Whittlesea	d												11 53										13 53		
March	d			10 34					11 34				12 04	12 34					13 34				14 04	14 34	
Manea	d																								
Kings Lynn	d	09 56				10 56					11 56					12 56					13 56				
Watlington	d	10 03				11 03					12 03					13 03					14 03				
Downham Market	d	10 09				11 09					12 09					13 09					14 09				
Littleport	d	10 18				11 18					12 18					13 18					14 18				
Ely 6	a	10 26		10 52	11 17	11 26			11 52	12 12	12 26		12 28	12 52	13 13	13 26			13 52	14 14	14 26		14 28	14 52	15 14
Cambridge	d		10 12	11 10				11 12	12 10			12 12		13 10				13 12	14 10			14 12		15 10	
Ely 6	d	10 26	10 29		11 22	11 26		11 29		12 15	12 26	12 27	12 31		13 17	13 26		13 27		14 17	14 26	14 27	14 31		15 17
Waterbeach	d	10 35				11 35					12 35					13 35					14 34				
Cambridge	a	10 44		11 07		11 44			12 07		12 44			13 07		13 44			14 07		14 44			15 07	
Shippea Hill	d																								
Lakenheath	d																								
Brandon	d		10 45					11 45				12 43						13 43				14 43			
Thetford	d		10 54		11 44			11 54		12 39		12 51			13 39			13 51		14 38		14 51			15 40
Harling Road	d																								
Eccles Road	d																								
Attleborough	d		11 09					12 09				13 06						14 06				15 06			
Spooner Row	d																								
Wymondham	d		11 16					12 16				13 14						14 14				15 14			
Norwich	a		11 30		12 18			12 30		13 13		13 30			14 13			14 30		15 13		15 30			16 15
Stansted Airport	a			11 45					12 45					13 45					14 45					15 45	
Ipswich	a												13 28										15 28		
London Kings Cross	a	11 34				12 34					13 34					14 34					15 34				
London Liverpool Street	a																								

Table 17

Saturdays
25 June to 30 July

Peterborough, Kings Lynn and Ely - Cambridge, Norwich and London

		FC 1		LE 1	XC ◇1	EM ◇	FC 1	LE 1	LE 1	XC ◇1	EM ◇	FC 1		LE 1	XC ◇1	FC 1	LE 1	LE 1	XC ◇1	FC 1	EM ◇	LE 1		XC ◇1	FC 1
Peterborough 8	d				15 18	15 41			15 45	16 18	16 41				17 18			17 45	18 18		18 45			19 18	
Whittlesea	d								15 53						17 27			17 53							
March	d				15 34				16 04	16 34					17 38			18 04	18 34		19 04			19 34	
Manea	d														17x45										
Kings Lynn	d	14 56					15 56					16 56				17 56				18 35					19 35
Watlington	d	15 03					16 03					17 03				18 03				18 42					19 42
Downham Market	d	15 09					16 09					17 09				18 09				18 48					19 48
Littleport	d	15 18					16 18					17 18				18 18				18 57					19 57
Ely 6	a	15 26			15 52	16 14	16 26		16 28	16 52	17 13	17 26			17 59	18 26		18 28	18 52	19 05	19 22			19 51	20 05
Cambridge	d			15 12	16 10			16 12		17 10				17 12	18 20		18 12		19 10			19 12		20 10	
Ely 6	d	15 26		15 27		16 17	16 26	16 27	16 31		17 17	17 26		17 27		18 26	18 27	18 31		19 05	19 26	19 29			20 05
Waterbeach	d	15 35					16 35					17 35				18 35				19 15					20 15
Cambridge	a	15 44			16 07		16 44			17 07		17 44			18 16	18 44			19 08	19 21				20 07	20 21
Shippea Hill	d																								
Lakenheath	d			15x40																					
Brandon	d			15 45				16 43						17 43			18 43					19 45			
Thetford	d			15 54		16 38		16 51			17 40			17 51			18 51				19 47	19 54			
Harling Road	d																								
Eccles Road	d																								
Attleborough	d			16 09				17 06						18 06			19 06					20 09			
Spooner Row	d																								
Wymondham	d			16 16				17 14						18 14			19 14					20 16			
Norwich	a			16 30		17 13		17 30			18 18			18 30			19 30				20 21	20 30			
Stansted Airport	a				16 45					17 45					18 53				19 45					20 45	
Ipswich	a								17 28									19 28							
London Kings Cross	a	16 34					17 34					18 35				19 34				20 31					
London Liverpool Street	a																								

		EM ◇	LE ◇1	LE 1	XC ◇1	FC 1	LE 1	XC ◇1		FC 1	EM ◇	LE ◇1	LE 1	XC ◇1	FC 1
Peterborough 8	d	19 41	19 45		20 18			21 18			21 38	21 45		22 18	
Whittlesea	d		19 53									21 53			
March	d		20 04		20 34			21 34				22 04		22 34	
Manea	d														
Kings Lynn	d					20 35				21 35					23 10
Watlington	d					20 42				21 42					23 17
Downham Market	d					20 48				21 48					23 23
Littleport	d					20 57				21 57					23 32
Ely 6	a	20 14	20 26		20 51	21 05		21 51		22 05	22 12	22 23		22 53	23 41
Cambridge	d			20 12	21 10		21 12	22 10					22 30	23a10	
Ely 6	d	20 16	20 27	20 27		21 05	21 27			22 05	22 18	22 23	22 45		23 43
Waterbeach	d					21 15				22 15					23 52
Cambridge	a				21 07	21 21		22 07		22 21					23 59
Shippea Hill	d														
Lakenheath	d														
Brandon	d			20 43			21 43						23 01		
Thetford	d	20 37		20 51			21 51				22 41		23 09		
Harling Road	d														
Eccles Road	d														
Attleborough	d			21 06			22 06				22 55		23 24		
Spooner Row	d														
Wymondham	d			21 14			22 14				23 02		23 32		
Norwich	a	21 14		21 30			22 30				23 20		23 46		
Stansted Airport	a				21 45			22 45							
Ipswich	a		21 22									23 18			
London Kings Cross	a														
London Liverpool Street	a														

Saturdays
from 6 August

		FC 1	LE 1	FC 1	LE 1	FC 1	EM ◇	LE 1	FC 1	XC ◇1		EM ◇	LE 1	FC 1	LE 1	XC ◇1	LE 1	FC 1	LE 1	EM ◇		XC ◇1	FC 1	EM ◇	LE 1
Peterborough 8	d						06 27			07 13		07 35	07 45			08 18				09 00		09 18		09 43	09 46
Whittlesea	d									07 21			07 53												09 54
March	d						06 43			07 32		07 51	08 04			08 34						09 34			10 05
Manea	d									07x39															
Kings Lynn	d	22p28				05 56			06 56					07 56				08 56					09 30		
Watlington	d	22p35				06 03			07 03					08 03				09 03							
Downham Market	d	22p41				06 09			07 09					08 09				09 09					09 41		
Littleport	d	22p50				06 18			07 18					08 18				09 18							
Ely 6	a	22p58				06 26	07 01		07 26	07 52		08 11	08 22	08 26		08 52		09 26		09 33		09 52	09 58	10 14	10 24
Cambridge	d		22p55		06 08			07 00		08 10					08 12	09 10			09 12			10 10	10 15		
Ely 6	d	22p58	23p10	05 26	06 23	06 26	07 06	07 15	07 26			08 14	08 31	08 26	08 27		09 11	09 26	09 30	09 39				10 17	10 24
Waterbeach	d	23p07		05 35		06 35			07 35					08 35			09 20	09 35							
Cambridge	a	23p14		05 42		06 44			07 44	08 08				08 44		09 07	09 28	09 44				10 07	10 13		
Shippea Hill	d							07x24																	
Lakenheath	d																								
Brandon	d		23p26		06 39		07 22	07 34							08 43				09 46						
Thetford	d		23p34		06 48		07 30	07 42				08 36			08 51				09 55	10 04				10 40	
Harling Road	d				06 56			07 51																	
Eccles Road	d				07 01			07 56																	
Attleborough	d		23p49		07 07		07 44	08 02				08 50			09 06				10 10						
Spooner Row	d							08x07																	
Wymondham	d		23p57		07 15		07 51	08 12				08 57			09 14				10 17						
Norwich	a		00 11		07 29		08 13	08 30				09 15			09 30				10 31	10 43				11 15	
Stansted Airport	a									08 45						09 45						10 45			
Ipswich	a												09 28												11 20
London Kings Cross	a	00 42		06 39		07 36			08 36					09 38				10 34					11 03		
London Liverpool Street	a																10 43								

Table 17

Saturdays
from 6 August

Peterborough, Kings Lynn and Ely - Cambridge, Norwich and London

		FC	LE	XC	EM	FC		LE	XC	EM	FC	LE	LE	XC	EM	FC		LE	XC	EM	FC	LE	LE	XC	EM
		1	1	◇1	◇	1		1	◇1	◇	1	1	1	◇1	◇	1		1	◇1	◇	1	1	1	◇1	◇
Peterborough 8	d			10 18	10 41				11 18	11 41			11 45	12 18	12 40				13 18	13 41			13 45	14 18	14 43
Whittlesea	d												11 53										13 53		
March	d			10 34					11 34				12 04	12 34					13 34				14 04	14 34	
Manea	d																								
Kings Lynn	d	09 56				10 56					11 56					12 56					13 56				
Watlington	d	10 03				11 03					12 03					13 03					14 03				
Downham Market	d	10 09				11 09					12 09					13 09					14 09				
Littleport	d	10 18				11 18					12 18					13 18					14 18				
Ely 6	a	10 26		10 52	11 17	11 26			11 52	12 12	12 26		12 28	12 52	13 13	13 26			13 52	14 14	14 26		14 28	14 52	15 14
Cambridge	d		10 12	11 10				11 12	12 10			12 12		13 10				13 12	14 10			14 12		15 10	
Ely 6	d	10 26	10 29		11 22	11 26		11 29		12 15	12 26	12 27	12 31		13 17	13 26		13 27		14 17	14 26	14 27	14 31		15 17
Waterbeach	d	10 35				11 35					12 35					13 35					14 34				
Cambridge	a	10 44		11 07		11 44			12 07		12 44			13 07		13 44			14 07		14 44			15 07	
Shippea Hill	d																								
Lakenheath	d																								
Brandon	d		10 45					11 45				12 43						13 43				14 43			
Thetford	d		10 54		11 44			11 54		12 39		12 51			13 39			13 51		14 38		14 51			15 40
Harling Road	d																								
Eccles Road	d																								
Attleborough	d		11 09					12 09				13 06						14 06				15 06			
Spooner Row	d																								
Wymondham	d		11 16					12 16				13 14						14 14				15 14			
Norwich	a		11 30		12 18			12 30		13 13		13 30			14 13			14 30		15 13		15 30			16 15
Stansted Airport	a			11 45					12 45					13 45					14 45					15 45	
Ipswich	a												13 28										15 28		
London Kings Cross	a	11 34				12 34					13 34					14 34					15 34				
London Liverpool Street	a																								

		FC		LE	XC	EM	FC	LE	LE	XC	EM	FC		LE	XC	EM	FC	LE	LE	XC	FC	EM		LE	XC
		1		1	◇1	◇	1	1	1	◇1	◇	1		1	◇1	◇	1	1	1	◇1	1	◇		1	◇1
Peterborough 8	d				15 18	15 41			15 45	16 18	16 41				17 18	17 41			17 45	18 18		18 45			19 18
Whittlesea	d								15 53						17 27				17 53						
March	d				15 34				16 04	16 34					17 38				18 04	18 34		19 04			19 34
Manea	d														17x45										
Kings Lynn	d	14 56					15 56					16 56					17 56				18 35				
Watlington	d	15 03					16 03					17 03					18 03				18 42				
Downham Market	d	15 09					16 09					17 09					18 09				18 48				
Littleport	d	15 18					16 18					17 18					18 18				18 57				
Ely 6	a	15 26			15 52	16 14	16 26		16 28	16 52	17 13	17 26			17 59	18 14	18 26		18 28	18 52	19 05	19 22			19 51
Cambridge	d			15 12	16 10			16 12		17 10				17 12	18 20			18 12		19 10				19 12	20 10
Ely 6	d	15 26		15 27		16 17	16 26	16 27	16 31		17 17	17 26		17 27		18 17	18 26	18 27	18 31		19 05	19 26		19 29	
Waterbeach	d	15 35					16 35					17 35					18 35				19 15				
Cambridge	a	15 44			16 07		16 44			17 07		17 44			18 16		18 44			19 08	19 21				20 07
Shippea Hill	d																								
Lakenheath	d			15x40																					
Brandon	d			15 45				16 43						17 43				18 43						19 45	
Thetford	d			15 54		16 38		16 51			17 40			17 51		18 39		18 51				19 47		19 54	
Harling Road	d																								
Eccles Road	d																								
Attleborough	d			16 09				17 06						18 06				19 06						20 09	
Spooner Row	d																								
Wymondham	d			16 16				17 14						18 14				19 14						20 16	
Norwich	a			16 30		17 13		17 30			18 18			18 30		19 21		19 30				20 21		20 30	
Stansted Airport	a				16 45					17 45					18 53					19 45					20 45
Ipswich	a								17 28										19 28						
London Kings Cross	a	16 34					17 34					18 35					19 34				20 31				
London Liverpool Street	a																								

		FC	EM	LE	LE	XC	FC	LE		XC	FC	EM	LE	LE	XC	FC
		1	◇	◇1	1	◇1	1	1		◇1	1	◇	◇1	1	◇1	1
Peterborough 8	d		19 41	19 45		20 18				21 18		21 38	21 45		22 18	
Whittlesea	d			19 53									21 53			
March	d			20 04		20 34				21 34			22 04		22 34	
Manea	d															
Kings Lynn	d	19 35					20 35				21 35					23 10
Watlington	d	19 42					20 42				21 42					23 17
Downham Market	d	19 48					20 48				21 48					23 23
Littleport	d	19 57					20 57				21 57					23 32
Ely 6	a	20 05	20 14	20 26		20 51	21 05			21 51	22 05	22 12	22 23		22 53	23 41
Cambridge	d				20 12	21 10		21 12		22 10				22 30	23a10	
Ely 6	d	20 05	20 16	20 27	20 27		21 05	21 27			22 05	22 18	22 23	22 45		23 43
Waterbeach	d	20 15					21 15				22 15					23 52
Cambridge	a	20 21				21 07	21 21			22 07	22 21					23 59
Shippea Hill	d															
Lakenheath	d															
Brandon	d				20 43			21 43						23 01		
Thetford	d		20 37		20 51			21 51				22 41		23 09		
Harling Road	d															
Eccles Road	d															
Attleborough	d				21 06			22 06				22 55		23 24		
Spooner Row	d															
Wymondham	d				21 14			22 14				23 02		23 32		
Norwich	a		21 14		21 30			22 30				23 20		23 46		
Stansted Airport	a					21 45				22 45						
Ipswich	a			21 22									23 18			
London Kings Cross	a	21 31					22 31				23 31					
London Liverpool Street	a															

Table 17

Sundays
until 19 June

Peterborough, Kings Lynn and Ely - Cambridge, Norwich and London

		FC	LE	FC	LE	FC	LE	EM	FC	LE		LE	FC	LE	EM	XC	FC	LE	EM	LE		XC	FC	LE	EM
		■1	■1	■1	■1	■1	■1	◇	■1	■1		■1	■1	■1	◇	◇■1	■1	■1	◇	■1		◇■1	■1	■1	◇
Peterborough ■	d				09 45			11 09				11 45			12 53	13 18			13 43	13 46		14 18			14 53
Whittlesea	d				09 53							11 53								13 55					
March	d				10 04			11 25				12 04				13 34				14 06		14 34			
Manea	d																								
Kings Lynn	d	08 28		09 28		10 28			11 28				12 28				13 28						14 28		
Watlington	d	08 35		09 35		10 35			11 35				12 35				13 35						14 35		
Downham Market	d	08 41		09 41		10 41			11 41				12 41				13 41						14 41		
Littleport	d	08 50		09 50		10 50			11 50				12 50				13 50						14 50		
Ely ■	a	08 58		09 58	10 28	10 58		11 48	11 58			12 28	12 58		13 32	13 52	13 58		14 16	14 29		14 52	14 58		15 29
Cambridge	d		08 48				10 48			11 52				12 52		14 10		13 52				15 10		14 52	
Ely ■	d	08 58	09 03	09 58	10 31	10 58	11 03	11 59	11 58	12 07		12 31	12 58	13 07	13 36		13 58	14 07	14 24	14 31			14 58	15 07	15 33
Waterbeach	d	09 07		10 07		11 07			12 07				13 07				14 07						15 07		
Cambridge	a	09 14		10 14		11 14			12 14				13 14			14 08	14 16					15 08	15 16		
Shippea Hill	d																								
Lakenheath	d		09x17				11x17							13x20											
Brandon	d		09 22				11 22	12 15		12 23				13 25				14 23	14 42					15 23	
Thetford	d		09 31				11 31	12 23		12 31				13 34	13 57			14 31	14 50					15 31	15 54
Harling Road	d																								
Eccles Road	d																								
Attleborough	d		09 46				11 46	12 37		12 46				13 49				14 46	15 04					15 46	
Spooner Row	d																								
Wymondham	d		09 53				11 53	12 44		12 54				13 56				14 54	15 11					15 54	
Norwich	a		10 13				12 13	13 06		13 13				14 13	14 35			15 13	15 30					16 13	16 35
Stansted Airport	a															14 43						15 43			
Ipswich	a				11 28							13 28								15 28					
London Kings Cross	a	10 08		11 08		12 08			13 08				14 08				15 08						16 08		
London Liverpool Street	a																								

		XC	FC	LE	LE	EM		XC	FC	LE	EM	XC	FC	LE	LE	FC		EM	XC	FC	LE	EM	XC	FC	LE
		◇■1	■1	■1	■1	◇		◇■1	■1	■1	◇	◇■1	■1	■1	◇■1	■1		◇	◇■1	■1	■1	◇	◇■1	■1	■1
Peterborough ■	d	15 18			15 45	16 03		16 18			16 59	17 18			17 45			17 56	18 18			18 48	19 18		
Whittlesea	d				15 53										17 53										
March	d	15 34			16 04			16 34				17 34			18 04			18 12	18 34				19 34		
Manea	d																								
Kings Lynn	d		15 28						16 28				17 28			17 58				18 28				19 28	
Watlington	d		15 35						16 35				17 35			18 05				18 35				19 35	
Downham Market	d		15 41						16 41				17 41			18 11				18 41				19 41	
Littleport	d		15 50						16 50				17 50			18 20				18 50				19 50	
Ely ■	a	15 52	15 58		16 23	16 38		16 52	16 58		17 32	17 52	17 58		18 23	18 29		18 31	18 52	18 58		19 21	19 52	19 58	
Cambridge	d	16 10		15 52				17 10		16 52		18 10		17 52					19 10		18 52		20 10		19 52
Ely ■	d		15 58	16 07	16 31	16 41			16 58	17 07	17 37		17 58	18 07	18 31	18 29		18 35		18 58	19 07	19 26		19 58	20 07
Waterbeach	d		16 07						17 07				18 07			18 38				19 07				20 07	
Cambridge	a	16 08	16 16					17 07	17 14			18 07	18 15			18 45			19 07	19 15			20 07	20 15	
Shippea Hill	d																								
Lakenheath	d			16x20																					
Brandon	d			16 25						17 23				18 23							19 23				20 23
Thetford	d			16 34		17 02				17 31	17 58			18 31				18 56			19 31	19 50			20 31
Harling Road	d																								
Eccles Road	d																								
Attleborough	d			16 49						17 46				18 46							19 46				20 46
Spooner Row	d																								
Wymondham	d			16 56						17 54				18 54							19 54				20 54
Norwich	a			17 13		17 35				18 13	18 31			19 10				19 29			20 13	20 29			21 10
Stansted Airport	a	16 43						17 43				18 43							19 43				20 43		
Ipswich	a				17 28										19 28										
London Kings Cross	a		17 08						18 08				19 10			19 38				20 11				21 10	
London Liverpool Street	a																								

		LE		EM	XC	FC	XC	FC	LE	EM	XC	FC
		◇■1		◇	◇■1	■1	◇■1	■1	■1	◇	◇■1	■1
Peterborough ■	d	19 45		19 58	20 18		21 18			21 51	22 18	
Whittlesea	d	19 53										
March	d	20 04			20 34		21 34				22 34	
Manea	d											
Kings Lynn	d					20 28		21 28				22 28
Watlington	d					20 35		21 35				22 35
Downham Market	d					20 41		21 41				22 41
Littleport	d					20 50		21 50				22 50
Ely ■	a	20 23		20 31	20 52	20 58	21 52	21 58		22 24	22 52	22 58
Cambridge	d				21 10		22 10		21 52		23a07	
Ely ■	d	20 23		20 35		20 58		21 58	22 07	22 27		22 58
Waterbeach	d					21 07		22 07				23 07
Cambridge	a				21 07	21 15	22 07	22 15				23 14
Shippea Hill	d											
Lakenheath	d											
Brandon	d								22 23			
Thetford	d			20 56					22 31	22 48		
Harling Road	d											
Eccles Road	d											
Attleborough	d			21 10					22 46	23 02		
Spooner Row	d											
Wymondham	d			21 17					22 54	23 09		
Norwich	a			21 35					23 13	23 28		
Stansted Airport	a				21 43		22 43					
Ipswich	a	21 18										
London Kings Cross	a					22 10		23 08				00 33
London Liverpool Street	a											

Table 17

Sundays

26 June to 31 July

Peterborough, Kings Lynn and Ely - Cambridge, Norwich and London

		FC 1	LE 1	FC 1	LE 1	FC 1	LE 1	EM ◇	FC 1	LE 1		LE 1	FC 1	LE 1	EM ◇	XC ◇1	FC 1	LE 1	EM ◇	LE 1		XC ◇1	FC 1	LE 1	EM ◇
Peterborough 8	d				09 45			11 09				11 45			12 53	13 18			13 43	13 46		14 18			14 53
Whittlesea	d				09 53							11 53								13 55					
March	d				10 04			11 25				12 04				13 34				14 06		14 34			
Manea	d																								
Kings Lynn	d	08 28		09 28		10 28			11 28				12 28				13 28						14 28		
Watlington	d	08 35		09 35		10 35			11 35				12 35				13 35						14 35		
Downham Market	d	08 41		09 41		10 41			11 41				12 41				13 41						14 41		
Littleport	d	08 50		09 50		10 50			11 50				12 50				13 50						14 50		
Ely 6	a	08 58		09 58	10 28	10 58		11 48	11 58			12 28	12 58		13 32	13 52	13 58		14 16	14 29		14 52	14 58		15 29
Cambridge	d		08 48				10 48			11 52				12 52		14 10		13 52				15 10		14 52	
Ely 6	d	08 58	09 03	09 58	10 31	10 58	11 03	11 59	11 58	12 07		12 31	12 58	13 07	13 36		13 58	14 07	14 24	14 31			14 58	15 07	15 33
Waterbeach	d	09 07		10 07		11 07			12 07				13 07				14 07						15 07		
Cambridge	a	09 15		10 15		11 15			12 15				13 14			14 08	14 16					15 08	15 16		
Shippea Hill	d																								
Lakenheath	d		09x17				11x17							13x20											
Brandon	d		09 22				11 22	12 15		12 23				13 25				14 23	14 42					15 23	
Thetford	d		09 31				11 31	12 23		12 31				13 34	13 57			14 31	14 50					15 31	15 54
Harling Road	d																								
Eccles Road	d																								
Attleborough	d		09 46				11 46	12 37		12 46				13 49				14 46	15 04					15 46	
Spooner Row	d																								
Wymondham	d		09 53				11 53	12 44		12 54				13 56				14 54	15 11					15 54	
Norwich	a		10 13				12 13	13 06		13 13				14 13	14 35			15 13	15 30					16 13	16 35
Stansted Airport	a															14 43						15 43			
Ipswich	a				11 28							13 28								15 28					
London Kings Cross	a												14 08				15 08						16 08		
London Liverpool Street	a																								

		XC ◇1	FC 1	LE 1	LE 1	EM ◇		XC ◇1	FC 1	LE 1	EM ◇	XC ◇1	FC 1	LE 1	LE ◇1	FC 1		EM ◇	XC ◇1	FC 1	LE 1	EM ◇	XC ◇1	FC 1	LE 1
Peterborough 8	d	15 18			15 45	16 03		16 18			16 59	17 18			17 45			17 56	18 18			18 48	19 18		
Whittlesea	d				15 53										17 53										
March	d	15 34			16 04			16 34				17 34			18 04			18 12	18 34				19 34		
Manea	d																								
Kings Lynn	d		15 28						16 28				17 28			17 58				18 28				19 28	
Watlington	d		15 35						16 35				17 35			18 05				18 35				19 35	
Downham Market	d		15 41						16 41				17 41			18 11				18 41				19 41	
Littleport	d		15 50						16 50				17 50			18 20				18 50				19 50	
Ely 6	a	15 52	15 58		16 23	16 38		16 52	16 58		17 32	17 52	17 58		18 23	18 29		18 31	18 52	18 58		19 21	19 52	19 58	
Cambridge	d	16 10		15 52				17 10		16 52		18 10		17 52					19 10		18 52		20 10		19 52
Ely 6	d		15 58	16 07	16 31	16 41			16 58	17 07	17 37		17 58	18 07	18 31	18 29		18 35		18 58	19 07	19 26		19 58	20 07
Waterbeach	d		16 07						17 07				18 07			18 38				19 07				20 07	
Cambridge	a	16 08	16 16					17 07	17 14			18 07	18 15			18 45			19 07	19 15			20 07	20 15	
Shippea Hill	d																								
Lakenheath	d			16x20																					
Brandon	d			16 25						17 23				18 23							19 23				20 23
Thetford	d			16 34		17 02				17 31	17 58			18 31				18 56			19 31	19 50			20 31
Harling Road	d																								
Eccles Road	d																								
Attleborough	d			16 49						17 46				18 46							19 46				20 46
Spooner Row	d																								
Wymondham	d			16 56						17 54				18 54							19 54				20 54
Norwich	a			17 13		17 35				18 13	18 31			19 10				19 29			20 13	20 29			21 10
Stansted Airport	a	16 43						17 43				18 43							19 43				20 43		
Ipswich	a				17 28										19 28										
London Kings Cross	a		17 08						18 08				19 10			19 38				20 11				21 10	
London Liverpool Street	a																								

		LE ◇1		EM ◇	XC ◇1	FC 1	XC ◇1	FC 1	LE 1	EM ◇	XC ◇1	FC 1
Peterborough 8	d	19 45		19 58	20 18		21 18			21 51	22 18	
Whittlesea	d	19 53										
March	d	20 04			20 34		21 34				22 34	
Manea	d											
Kings Lynn	d					20 28		21 28				22 28
Watlington	d					20 35		21 35				22 35
Downham Market	d					20 41		21 41				22 41
Littleport	d					20 50		21 50				22 50
Ely 6	a	20 23		20 31	20 52	20 58	21 52	21 58		22 24	22 52	22 58
Cambridge	d				21 10		22 10		21 52		23a07	
Ely 6	d	20 23		20 35		20 58		21 58	22 07	22 27		22 58
Waterbeach	d					21 07		22 07				23 07
Cambridge	a				21 07	21 15	22 07	22 15				23 14
Shippea Hill	d											
Lakenheath	d											
Brandon	d								22 23			
Thetford	d			20 56					22 31	22 48		
Harling Road	d											
Eccles Road	d											
Attleborough	d			21 10					22 46	23 02		
Spooner Row	d											
Wymondham	d			21 17					22 54	23 09		
Norwich	a			21 35					23 13	23 28		
Stansted Airport	a				21 43		22 43					
Ipswich	a	21 18										
London Kings Cross	a					22 10		23 08				00 33
London Liverpool Street	a											

Table 17

Sundays

7 August to 11 September

Peterborough, Kings Lynn and Ely - Cambridge, Norwich and London

		FC 1	LE 1	FC 1	LE 1	FC 1	LE 1	EM ◇	LE 1	LE 1		FC 1	LE 1	EM ◇	XC ◇1	FC 1	LE 1	EM ◇	LE 1	XC ◇1		FC 1	LE 1	EM ◇	XC ◇1
Peterborough 8	d				09 45			11 09		11 45				12 53	13 18			13 43	13 46	14 18				14 53	15 18
Whittlesea	d				09 53					11 53									13 55						
March	d				10 04			11 25		12 04					13 34				14 06	14 34					15 34
Manea	d																								
Kings Lynn	d	08 28		09 28		10 28						12 28				13 28						14 28			
Watlington	d	08 35		09 35		10 35						12 35				13 35						14 35			
Downham Market	d	08 41		09 41		10 41						12 41				13 41						14 41			
Littleport	d	08 50		09 50		10 50						12 50				13 50						14 50			
Ely 6	a	08 58		09 58	10 28	10 58		11 48		12 28		12 58		13 32	13 52	13 58		14 16	14 29	14 52		14 58		15 29	15 52
Cambridge	d		08 48				10 48		11 52				12 52		14 10		13 52			15 10			14 52		16 10
Ely 6	d	08 58	09 03	09 58	10 31	10 58	11 03	11 59	12 07	12 31		12 58	13 07	13 36		13 58	14 07	14 24	14 31			14 58	15 07	15 33	
Waterbeach	d	09 07		10 07		11 07						13 07				14 07						15 07			
Cambridge	a	09 14		10 14		11 14						13 14			14 08	14 16				15 08		15 16			16 08
Shippea Hill	d																								
Lakenheath	d		09x17				11x17						13x20												
Brandon	d		09 22				11 22	12 15	12 23				13 25				14 23	14 42					15 23		
Thetford	d		09 31				11 31	12 23	12 31				13 34	13 57			14 31	14 50					15 31	15 54	
Harling Road	d																								
Eccles Road	d																								
Attleborough	d		09 46				11 46	12 37	12 46				13 49				14 46	15 04					15 46		
Spooner Row	d																								
Wymondham	d		09 53				11 53	12 44	12 54				13 56				14 54	15 11					15 54		
Norwich	a		10 13				12 13	13 06	13 13				14 13	14 35			15 13	15 30					16 13	16 35	
Stansted Airport	a														14 43					15 43					16 43
Ipswich	a				11 28					13 28									15 28						
London Kings Cross	a	10 08		11 08		12 08						14 08				15 08						16 08			
London Liverpool Street	a																								

		FC 1	LE 1	LE 1	EM ◇	XC ◇1		FC 1	LE 1	EM ◇	XC ◇1	FC 1	LE 1	LE ◇1	FC 1	EM ◇		XC ◇1	FC 1	LE 1	EM ◇	XC ◇1	FC 1	LE 1	LE ◇1
Peterborough 8	d			15 45	16 03	16 18				16 59	17 18			17 45		17 56		18 18			18 48	19 18			19 45
Whittlesea	d			15 53										17 53											19 53
March	d			16 04		16 34					17 34			18 04		18 12		18 34				19 34			20 04
Manea	d																								
Kings Lynn	d	15 28						16 28				17 28			17 58				18 28				19 28		
Watlington	d	15 35						16 35				17 35			18 05				18 35				19 35		
Downham Market	d	15 41						16 41				17 41			18 11				18 41				19 41		
Littleport	d	15 50						16 50				17 50			18 20				18 50				19 50		
Ely 6	a	15 58		16 23	16 38	16 52		16 58		17 32	17 52	17 58		18 23	18 29	18 31		18 52	18 58		19 21	19 52	19 58		20 23
Cambridge	d		15 52			17 10			16 52		18 10		17 52					19 10		18 52		20 10		19 52	
Ely 6	d	15 58	16 07	16 31	16 41			16 58	17 07	17 37		17 58	18 07	18 31	18 29	18 35			18 58	19 07	19 26		19 58	20 07	20 23
Waterbeach	d	16 07						17 07				18 07			18 38				19 07				20 07		
Cambridge	a	16 16				17 07		17 14			18 07	18 15			18 45			19 07	19 15			20 07	20 15		
Shippea Hill	d																								
Lakenheath	d		16x20																						
Brandon	d		16 25						17 23				18 23							19 23				20 23	
Thetford	d		16 34		17 02				17 31	17 58			18 31			18 56				19 31	19 50			20 31	
Harling Road	d																								
Eccles Road	d																								
Attleborough	d		16 49						17 46				18 46							19 46				20 46	
Spooner Row	d																								
Wymondham	d		16 56						17 54				18 54							19 54				20 54	
Norwich	a		17 13		17 35				18 13	18 31			19 10			19 29				20 13	20 29			21 10	
Stansted Airport	a					17 43					18 43							19 43				20 43			
Ipswich	a			17 28										19 28											21 18
London Kings Cross	a	17 08						18 08				19 10			19 38				20 11				21 10		
London Liverpool Street	a																								

		EM ◇		XC ◇1	FC 1	XC ◇1	FC 1	LE 1	EM ◇	XC ◇1	FC 1
Peterborough 8	d	19 58		20 18		21 18			21 51	22 18	
Whittlesea	d										
March	d			20 34		21 34				22 34	
Manea	d										
Kings Lynn	d				20 28		21 28				22 28
Watlington	d				20 35		21 35				22 35
Downham Market	d				20 41		21 41				22 41
Littleport	d				20 50		21 50				22 50
Ely 6	a	20 31		20 52	20 58	21 52	21 58		22 24	22 52	22 58
Cambridge	d			21 10		22 10		21 52		23a07	
Ely 6	d	20 35			20 58		21 58	22 07	22 27		22 58
Waterbeach	d				21 07		22 07				23 07
Cambridge	a			21 07	21 15	22 07	22 15				23 14
Shippea Hill	d										
Lakenheath	d										
Brandon	d							22 23			
Thetford	d	20 56						22 31	22 48		
Harling Road	d										
Eccles Road	d										
Attleborough	d	21 10						22 46	23 02		
Spooner Row	d										
Wymondham	d	21 17						22 54	23 09		
Norwich	a	21 35						23 13	23 28		
Stansted Airport	a			21 43		22 43					
Ipswich	a										
London Kings Cross	a				22 10		23 08				00 33
London Liverpool Street	a										

Table 17

Sundays

from 18 September

Peterborough, Kings Lynn and Ely - Cambridge, Norwich and London

		FC 1	LE 1	FC 1	FC 1	LE 1	LE 1	LE 1	FC 1	LE 1		XC ◇1	FC 1	LE 1	EM ◇	LE 1	XC ◇1	FC 1	LE 1	EM ◇		XC ◇1	FC 1	LE 1	LE 1
Peterborough 8	d							11 45				13 18			13 43	13 46	14 18			14 53		15 18			15 45
Whittlesea	d							11 53								13 55									15 53
March	d							12 04				13 34				14 06	14 34					15 34			16 04
Manea	d																								
Kings Lynn	d	08 28		09 28	10 28				12 28				13 28					14 28					15 28		
Watlington	d	08 35		09 35	10 35				12 35				13 35					14 35					15 35		
Downham Market	d	08 41		09 41	10 41				12 41				13 41					14 41					15 41		
Littleport	d	08 50		09 50	10 50				12 50				13 50					14 50					15 50		
Ely 6	a	08 58		09 58	10 58			12 28	12 58			13 52	13 58		14 16	14 29	14 52	14 58		15 29		15 52	15 58		16 23
Cambridge	d		08 48			10 48	11 52			12 52		14 10		13 52			15 10		14 52			16 10		15 52	
Ely 6	d	08 58	09 03	09 58	10 58	11 03	12 07	12 31	12 58	13 07			13 58	14 07	14 24	14 31		14 58	15 07	15 33			15 58	16 07	16 31
Waterbeach	d	09 07		10 07	11 07				13 07				14 07					15 07					16 07		
Cambridge	a	09 14		10 14	11 14				13 14			14 08	14 16				15 08	15 16				16 08	16 16		
Shippea Hill	d																								
Lakenheath	d		09x17			11x17				13x20														16x20	
Brandon	d		09 22			11 22	12 23			13 25				14 23	14 42				15 23					16 25	
Thetford	d		09 31			11 31	12 31			13 34				14 31	14 50				15 31	15 54				16 34	
Harling Road	d																								
Eccles Road	d																								
Attleborough	d		09 46			11 46	12 46			13 49				14 46	15 04				15 46					16 49	
Spooner Row	d																								
Wymondham	d		09 53			11 53	12 54			13 56				14 54	15 11				15 54					16 56	
Norwich	a		10 13			12 13	13 13			14 13				15 13	15 30				16 13	16 35				17 13	
Stansted Airport	a											14 43					15 43					16 43			
Ipswich	a							13 28								15 28									17 28
London Kings Cross	a	10 08		11 08	12 08				14 08				15 08					16 08					17 08		
London Liverpool Street	a																								

		EM ◇	XC ◇1	FC 1	LE 1	EM ◇		XC ◇1	FC 1	LE 1	LE ◇1	FC 1	EM ◇	XC ◇1	FC 1	LE 1		EM ◇	XC ◇1	FC 1	LE 1	LE ◇1	EM ◇	XC ◇1	FC 1
Peterborough 8	d	16 03	16 18			16 59		17 18			17 45		17 56	18 18				18 48	19 18			19 45	19 58	20 18	
Whittlesea	d										17 53											19 53			
March	d		16 34					17 34			18 04		18 12	18 34					19 34			20 04		20 34	
Manea	d																								
Kings Lynn	d			16 28					17 28			17 58			18 28					19 28					20 28
Watlington	d			16 35					17 35			18 05			18 35					19 35					20 35
Downham Market	d			16 41					17 41			18 11			18 41					19 41					20 41
Littleport	d			16 50					17 50			18 20			18 50					19 50					20 50
Ely 6	a	16 38	16 52	16 58		17 32		17 52	17 58		18 23	18 29	18 31	18 52	18 58			19 21	19 52	19 58		20 23	20 31	20 52	20 58
Cambridge	d		17 10		16 52			18 10		17 52				19 10		18 52			20 10		19 52			21 10	
Ely 6	d	16 41		16 58	17 07	17 37			17 58	18 07	18 31	18 29	18 35		18 58	19 07		19 26		19 58	20 07	20 23	20 35		20 58
Waterbeach	d			17 07					18 07			18 38			19 07					20 07					21 07
Cambridge	a		17 07	17 14				18 07	18 15			18 45		19 07	19 15				20 07	20 15				21 07	21 15
Shippea Hill	d																								
Lakenheath	d																								
Brandon	d				17 23					18 23						19 23					20 23				
Thetford	d	17 02			17 31	17 58				18 31			18 56			19 31		19 50			20 31		20 56		
Harling Road	d																								
Eccles Road	d																								
Attleborough	d				17 46					18 46						19 46					20 46		21 10		
Spooner Row	d																								
Wymondham	d				17 54					18 54						19 54					20 54		21 17		
Norwich	a	17 35			18 13	18 31				19 10			19 29			20 13		20 29			21 10		21 35		
Stansted Airport	a		17 43					18 43						19 43					20 43					21 43	
Ipswich	a										19 28											21 18			
London Kings Cross	a			18 08					19 10			19 38			20 11					21 10					22 10
London Liverpool Street	a																								

		XC ◇1		FC 1	LE 1	EM ◇	XC ◇1	FC 1
Peterborough 8	d	21 18				21 51	22 18	
Whittlesea	d							
March	d	21 34					22 34	
Manea	d							
Kings Lynn	d			21 28				22 28
Watlington	d			21 35				22 35
Downham Market	d			21 41				22 41
Littleport	d			21 50				22 50
Ely 6	a	21 52		21 58		22 24	22 52	22 58
Cambridge	d	22 10			21 52		23a07	
Ely 6	d			21 58	22 07	22 27		22 58
Waterbeach	d			22 07				23 07
Cambridge	a	22 07		22 15				23 14
Shippea Hill	d							
Lakenheath	d							
Brandon	d				22 23			
Thetford	d				22 31	22 48		
Harling Road	d							
Eccles Road	d							
Attleborough	d				22 46	23 02		
Spooner Row	d							
Wymondham	d				22 54	23 09		
Norwich	a				23 13	23 28		
Stansted Airport	a	22 43						
Ipswich	a							
London Kings Cross	a			23 08				00 33
London Liverpool Street	a							

Kings Lynn - Sandringham and Hunstanton

Bus Service

		FC	FC	FC	FC	FC	FC	FC	FC	FC		FC	FC	FC	FC	FC	FC	FC	FC	FC		FC	FC	FC	FC
Kings Lynn	d	06 25	06 55	07 28	08 35	08 50	09 05	09 20	09 35	09 50		10 05	10 20	10 35	10 50	11 05	11 20	11 35	11 50	12 05		12 20	12 35	12 50	13 05
Sandringham Visitor Centre	a					09 12		09 42		10 12			10 42		11 12		11 42		12 12			12 42		13 12	
Sandringham Norwich Gates	a			07 51		09 14		09 44		10 14			10 44		11 14		11 44		12 14			12 44		13 14	
Hunstanton Bus Station	a	07 14	07 44	08 21	09 25	09 44	09 55	10 14	10 25	10 44		10 55	11 14	11 25	11 44	11 55	12 14	12 25	12 44	12 55		13 14	13 25	13 44	13 55

		FC	FC	FC	FC	FC		FC	FC	FC	FC	FC	FC	FC	FC	FC		FC	FC	FC	FC	FC	FC	FC	FC
Kings Lynn	d	13 20	13 35	13 50	14 05	14 20		14 30	15 05	15 35	15 50	16 05	16 20	16 35	16 50	17 05		17 20	17 35	17 50	18 20	19 00	20 00	21 30	23 00
Sandringham Visitor Centre	a	13 42		14 12		14 42			15 27		16 12		16 42		17 12			17 42		18 12					
Sandringham Norwich Gates	a	13 44		14 14		14 44			15 29		16 14		16 44		17 14			17 44		18 14					
Hunstanton Bus Station	a	14 14	14 25	14 44	14 55	15 14		15 20	15 59	16 25	16 44	16 55	17 14	17 25	17 44	17 55		18 14	18 25	18 41	19 03	19 40	20 40	22 10	23 40

Saturdays

		FC	FC	FC	FC	FC	FC	FC	FC	FC		FC	FC	FC	FC	FC	FC	FC	FC	FC		FC	FC	FC	FC
Kings Lynn	d	06 35	07 35	08 35	08 50	09 05	09 20	09 35	09 50	10 05		10 20	10 35	10 50	11 05	11 20	11 35	11 50	12 05	12 20		12 35	12 50	13 05	13 20
Sandringham Visitor Centre	a				09 12		09 42		10 12			10 42		11 12		11 42		12 12		12 42			13 12		13 42
Sandringham Norwich Gates	a				09 14		09 44		10 14			10 44		11 14		11 44		12 14		12 44			13 14		13 44
Hunstanton Bus Station	a	07 25	08 25	09 25	09 44	09 55	10 14	10 25	10 44	10 55		11 14	11 25	11 44	11 55	12 14	12 25	12 44	12 55	13 14		13 25	13 44	13 55	14 14

		FC	FC	FC	FC	FC		FC	FC	FC	FC	FC	FC	FC	FC	FC		FC	FC	FC	FC	FC	FC	FC	FC
Kings Lynn	d	13 35	13 50	14 05	14 20	14 35		14 50	15 05	15 20	15 35	15 50	16 05	16 20	16 35	16 50		17 05	17 20	17 35	17 50	18 20	19 00	20 00	21 30
Sandringham Visitor Centre	a		14 12		14 42			15 12	15 27	15 42		16 12		16 42		17 12			17 42		18 12				
Sandringham Norwich Gates	a		14 14		14 44			15 14	15 29	15 44		16 14		16 44		17 14			17 44		18 14				
Hunstanton Bus Station	a	14 25	14 44	14 55	15 14	15 25		15 44	15 59	16 14	16 25	16 44	16 55	17 14	17 25	17 44		17 55	18 14	18 25	18 41	19 03	19 40	20 40	22 10

		FC
Kings Lynn	d	23 00
Sandringham Visitor Centre	a	
Sandringham Norwich Gates	a	
Hunstanton Bus Station	a	23 40

Sundays

		FC	FC	FC	FC	FC	FC	FC	FC	FC		FC	FC	FC	FC
Kings Lynn	d	08 50	09 50	10 50	11 50	12 50	13 50	14 50	15 50	16 50		17 50	20 00	21 30	23 00
Sandringham Visitor Centre	a	09 12	10 12	11 12	12 12	13 12	14 12	15 12	16 12	17 12		18 12			
Sandringham Norwich Gates	a	09 14	10 14	11 14	12 14	13 14	14 14	15 14	16 14	17 14		18 14			
Hunstanton Bus Station	a	09 42	10 42	11 42	12 42	13 42	14 42	15 42	16 42	17 42		18 42	20 40	22 10	23 40

Hunstanton and Sandringham - Kings Lynn

Bus Service

		FC	FC	FC	FC	FC	FC	FC	FC	FC	FC	FC	FC	FC	FC	FC	FC	FC	FC	FC	FC	FC	FC
Hunstanton Bus Station	d	23p44	06 30	07 16	07 48	08 33	08 48	09 03	09 18	09 33	09 48	10 03	10 18	10 33	10 48	11 03	11 18	11 33	11 48	12 03	12 18	12 33	12 48
Sandringham Norwich Gates	d	-	06 55	07 43	-	-	09 15	-	09 45	-	10 15	-	10 45	-	11 15	-	11 45	-	12 15	-	12 45	-	13 15
Sandringham Visitor Centre	d	-	-	-	-	-	09 17	-	09 47	-	10 17	-	10 47	-	11 17	-	11 47	-	12 17	-	12 47	-	13 17
Kings Lynn	a	00 22	07 20	08 10	08 40	09 25	09 44	09 55	10 14	10 25	10 44	10 55	11 14	11 25	11 44	11 55	12 14	12 25	12 44	12 55	13 14	13 25	13 44

		FC	FC	FC	FC	FC	FC	FC	FC	FC	FC	FC	FC	FC	FC	FC	FC	FC	FC	FC	FC	FC	FC
Hunstanton Bus Station	d	13 03	13 18	13 33	13 48	14 03	14 18	14 33	14 48	15 18	15 25	16 03	16 18	16 33	16 48	17 08	17 18	17 33	17 48	18 03	18 44	19 14	19 44
Sandringham Norwich Gates	d	-	13 45	-	14 15	-	14 45	-	15 15	15 45	15 56	-	16 45	-	17 15	-	17 45	-	18 15	-	-	-	-
Sandringham Visitor Centre	d	-	13 47	-	14 17	-	14 47	-	15 17	15 47	15 58	-	16 47	-	17 17	-	17 47	-	18 17	-	-	-	-
Kings Lynn	a	13 55	14 14	14 25	14 44	14 55	15 14	15 25	15 44	16 14	16 25	16 55	17 14	17 25	17 44	18 00	18 14	18 25	18 44	18 55	19 22	19 52	20 22

		FC	FC	FC
Hunstanton Bus Station	d	20 44	22 14	23 44
Sandringham Norwich Gates	d	-	-	-
Sandringham Visitor Centre	d	-	-	-
Kings Lynn	a	21 22	22 52	00 22

Saturdays

		FC	FC	FC	FC	FC	FC	FC	FC	FC	FC	FC	FC	FC	FC	FC	FC	FC	FC	FC	FC	FC	FC
Hunstanton Bus Station	d	23p44	06 30	07 30	08 33	08 48	09 03	09 18	09 33	09 48	10 03	10 18	10 33	10 48	11 03	11 18	11 33	11 48	12 03	12 18	12 33	12 48	13 03
Sandringham Norwich Gates	d	-	06 55	07 55	-	09 15	-	09 45	-	10 15	-	10 45	-	11 15	-	11 45	-	12 15	-	12 45	-	13 15	-
Sandringham Visitor Centre	d	-	-	-	-	09 17	-	09 47	-	10 17	-	10 47	-	11 17	-	11 47	-	12 17	-	12 47	-	13 17	-
Kings Lynn	a	00 22	07 20	08 20	09 25	09 44	09 55	10 14	10 25	10 44	10 55	11 14	11 25	11 44	11 55	12 14	12 25	12 44	12 55	13 14	13 25	13 44	13 55

		FC	FC	FC	FC	FC	FC	FC	FC	FC	FC	FC	FC	FC	FC	FC	FC	FC	FC	FC	FC	FC	FC
Hunstanton Bus Station	d	13 18	13 33	13 48	14 03	14 18	14 33	14 48	15 03	15 18	15 33	15 48	16 03	16 18	16 33	16 48	17 03	17 18	17 33	17 48	18 03	18 44	19 14
Sandringham Norwich Gates	d	13 45	-	14 15	-	14 45	-	15 15	-	15 45	-	16 15	-	16 45	-	17 15	-	17 45	-	18 15	-	-	-
Sandringham Visitor Centre	d	13 47	-	14 17	-	14 47	-	15 17	-	15 47	-	16 17	-	16 47	-	17 17	-	17 47	-	18 17	-	-	-
Kings Lynn	a	14 14	14 25	14 44	14 55	15 14	15 25	15 44	15 55	16 14	16 25	16 44	16 55	17 14	17 25	17 44	17 55	18 14	18 25	18 44	18 55	19 22	19 52

		FC	FC	FC	FC
Hunstanton Bus Station	d	19 44	20 44	22 14	23 44
Sandringham Norwich Gates	d	-	-	-	-
Sandringham Visitor Centre	d	-	-	-	-
Kings Lynn	a	20 22	21 22	22 52	00 22

Sundays

		FC A	FC	FC	FC	FC	FC	FC	FC	FC	FC	FC	FC	FC	FC
Hunstanton Bus Station	d	23p44	09 47	10 47	11 47	12 47	13 47	14 47	15 47	16 47	17 47	18 47	20 44	22 14	23 44
Sandringham Norwich Gates	d	}	10 14	11 14	12 14	13 14	14 14	15 14	16 14	17 14	18 14	19 14	-	-	-
Sandringham Visitor Centre	d	}	10 16	11 16	12 16	13 16	14 16	15 16	16 16	17 16	18 16	-	-	-	-
Kings Lynn	a	00 22	10 40	11 40	12 40	13 40	14 40	15 40	16 40	17 40	18 40	19 38	21 22	22 52	00 22

A not 22 May

Network Diagram for Tables 18, 19, 27, 29, 30

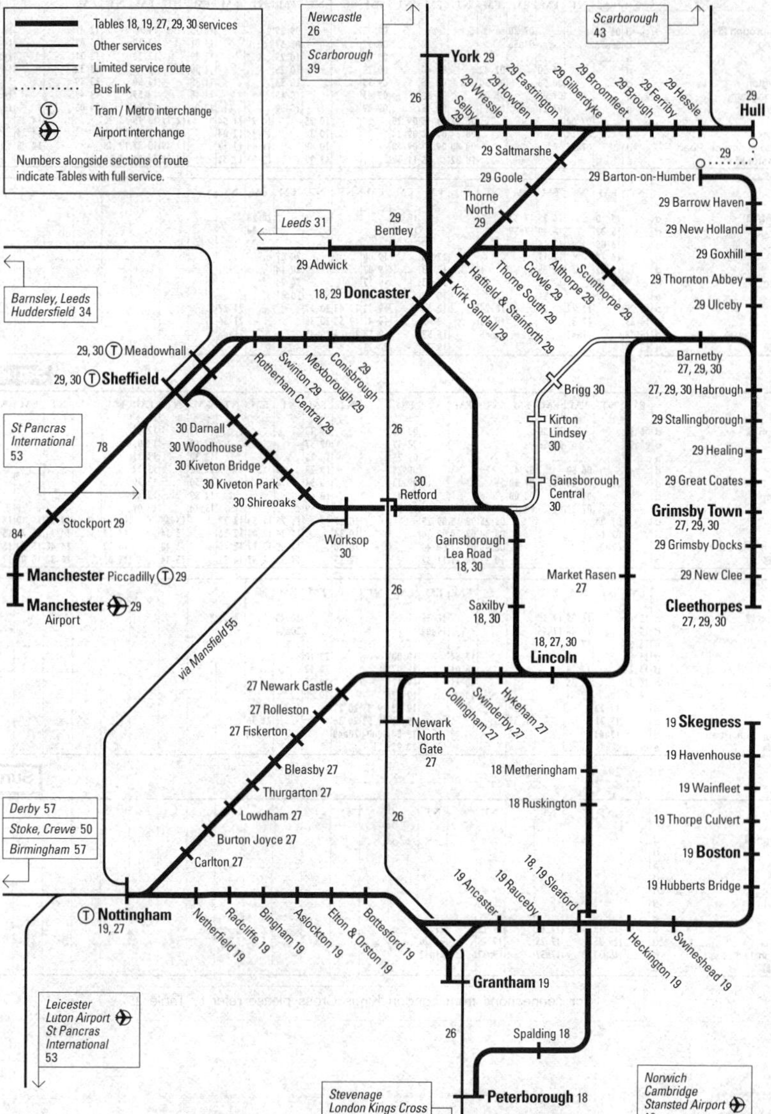

DM-2/08
Design BAJS

© Network Rail OPSU 2008. All rights reserved

Peterborough - Sleaford, Lincoln and Doncaster

Mondays to Fridays

Miles			EM	NT	EM	EM	EM	NT	EM	NT	EM		NT	EM	NT	EM	EM	NT	EM	NT	EM		NT	EM	NT
0	**Peterborough** 8	d	06 30			07 30					08 33			09 35			10 38		11 48		12 41			13 40	
16½	Spalding	d	06a56			07a56					08 57			09 57			11 01		12 10		13 03			14 02	
35½	Sleaford	a									09 25			10 25			11 29		12 38		13 31			14 30	
—		d			06 50		07 42		08 40		09 25			10 25			11 30		12 42		13 32			14 32	
40	Ruskington	d			06 58		07 50		08 48		09 33			10 33			11 38		12 50		13 39			14 39	
47½	Metheringham	d			07 08		08 00		08 58		09 43			10 43			11 48		12 59		13 49			14 49	
56¾	**Lincoln**	a			07 21		08 13		09 13		09 59			10 59			12 04		13 14		14 05			15 05	
—		d		07 04				08 25	09 15	09 25			10 25		11 25	11 54		12 27	13 15	13 26			14 25		15 24
62¾	Saxilby	d		07 14				08 34	09 24	09 34			10 34		11 34	12 04		12 36	13 24	13 35			14 34		15 33
72¼	Gainsborough Lea Road	d		07a26				08 48	09 37	09 48			10 48		11 48	12 17		12 49	13 37	13 48			14 48		15 48
93½	**Doncaster** 7	a						10 32	10 05	11 32			12 32		13 33	12 47		14 32	14 06	15 33			16 32		17 32

		NT	EM	NT	EM	EM	NT		EM	EM	EM	NT	NT	EM	EM	NT
Peterborough 8	d		15 10		16 25	17 32				18 36					20 28	
Spalding	d		15 32		16 48	17a58				19a02					20a54	
Sleaford	a		16 00		17 16											
	d		16 14		17 17				17 56		19 00			20 07		
Ruskington	d		16 22		17 25				18 03		19 07			20 14		
Metheringham	d		16 32		17 35				18 13		19 17			20 24		
Lincoln	a		16 47		17 51				18 29		19 32			20 41		
	d	16 25		17 22			18 24		18 31		19 32	19 43	20 27			21 27
Saxilby	d	16 35		17 31			18 33		18 42		19 41	19 52	20 36			21 36
Gainsborough Lea Road	d	16 48		17a43			18a45		18 57		19 53	20a04	20a48			21a48
Doncaster 7	a	18 35							19 25		20 23					

Saturdays

		EM	NT	EM	EM	EM	NT	EM	NT	EM		NT	EM	NT	EM	NT	EM	NT	EM	EM		NT	EM	NT	NT
Peterborough 8	d	06 30			07 30					08 33			09 33				11 48		12 41						
Spalding	d	06a56			07a56					08 57			09 57				12 10		13 03						
Sleaford	a									09 25			10 25				12 38		13 31						
	d			06 50		07 42				09 25			10 25				12 42		13 32						
Ruskington	d			06 58		07 50				09 33			10 33				12 50		13 39						
Metheringham	d			07 08		08 00				09 43			10 43				12 59		13 49						
Lincoln	a			07 21		08 13				09 59			10 59				13 14		14 07						
	d		07 04				08 25	09 15	09 25			10 25		11 25	11 54	12 27		13 25		14 10		14 25	15 10	15 24	16 25
Saxilby	d		07 14				08 34	09 24	09 34			10 34		11 34	12 04	12 36		13 34		14 19		14 34	15 20	15 33	16 35
Gainsborough Lea Road	d		07a26				08 48	09 37	09 48			10 48		11 48	12 17	12 49		13 48		14 32		14 48	15 32	15 48	16 48
Doncaster 7	a						10 32	10 11	11 32			12 33		13 32	12 47	14 32		15 34		15 01		16 32	16 02	17 32	18 38

		EM	NT	EM	EM	NT		EM	EM	EM	NT	NT	EM	EM	NT
Peterborough 8	d	15 11		16 25	17 30				18 36					20 28	
Spalding	d	15 33		16 48	17a56				19a02					20a54	
Sleaford	a	16 02		17 16											
	d	16 14		17 17				17 54		19 00			20 10		
Ruskington	d	16 22		17 25				18 01		19 07			20 17		
Metheringham	d	16 32		17 35				18 11		19 17			20 27		
Lincoln	a	16 48		17 51				18 27		19 32			20 40		
	d		17 22			18 24				19 32	19 43	20 27			21 27
Saxilby	d		17 31			18 33				19 41	19 52	20 36			21 36
Gainsborough Lea Road	d		17a43			18a45				19 54	20a04	20a48			21a48
Doncaster 7	a									20 23					

Sundays

			NT		NT		NT		NT
Peterborough 8	d								
Spalding	d								
Sleaford	a								
	d								
Ruskington	d								
Metheringham	d								
Lincoln	a								
	d		15 15		17 15		19 15		21 10
Saxilby	d		15 25		17 25		19 25		21 20
Gainsborough Lea Road	d		15a37		17a37		19a37		21a32
Doncaster 7	a								

For connections from London Kings Cross please refer to Table 25

Doncaster, Lincoln and Sleaford - Peterborough

Mondays to Fridays

Miles			NT	EM	EM	EM	EM	NT	NT	EM	NT		EM	NT	EM	EM	NT	EM	NT	EM	EM		NT	EM	NT
0	**Doncaster** 7	d												09 01		10 24	10 04		11 04		13 05		12 03		13 02
21¼	Gainsborough Lea Road	d	06 25					07 38	08 24		09 38			10 38		10 52	11 38		12 38		13 31		13 39		14 38
30¾	Saxilby	d	06 37					07 51	08 37		09 51			10 51		11 05	11 51		12 51		13 44		13 52		14 51
36¾	**Lincoln**	a	06 53					08 06	08 52		10 06			11 06		11 17	12 06		13 06		13 55		14 06		15 06
—		d			07 05		08 00			09 10			10 15		11 10			12 10		13 30				14 41	
46¼	Metheringham	d			07 17		08 12			09 22			10 27		11 23			12 22		13 43				14 53	
53½	Ruskington	d			07 27		08 22			09 32			10 37		11 33			12 32		13 53				15 03	
58	Sleaford	a			07 36		08 31			09 41			10 50		11 42			12 41		14 02				15 13	
—		d					08 34			09 42			10 50		11 42			12 42		14 03				15 16	
77	Spalding	d		07 00		08 00	09 02			10 07			11 16		12 07			13 07		14 28				15 43	
93½	**Peterborough** 8	a		07 25		08 25	09 27			10 31			11 42		12 33			13 32		14 53				16 09	

		EM	EM	EM	NT	NT	EM		NT	EM	EM	NT	EM	NT	EM	EM	EM		NT	EM	EM
Doncaster 7	d		14 27		14 03	15 04			16 03			17 01			19 34					20 33	
Gainsborough Lea Road	d		14 54		15 38	16 38			17 38			18 38		19 39	20 00				20 42	21 00	
Saxilby	d		15 07		15 51	16 51			17 51			18 51		19 52	20 13				20 55	21 14	
Lincoln	a		15 18		16 10	17 06			18 06			19 07		20 06	20 25				21 10	21 26	
	d	15 12		16 01			17 20				18 10		19 10				20 48				
Metheringham	d	15 24		16 14			17 33				18 23		19 22				21 01				
Ruskington	d	15 34		16 24			17 42				18 33		19 32				21 10				
Sleaford	a	15 43		16 34			17 51				18 42		19 41				21 19				
	d			16 34																	
Spalding	d			16 59						18 02						19 56					21 00
Peterborough 8	a			17 25						18 27						20 21					21 26

Saturdays

		NT	EM	EM	EM	EM	NT	NT	NT	EM		NT	EM	EM	NT	NT	EM	EM	NT	EM		NT	EM	EM	NT
Doncaster 7	d											09 03		10 24	10 04	11 04		13 05	12 03			13 04	15 07		14 01
Gainsborough Lea Road	d	06 25					07 38	08 24	09 38			10 38		10 52	11 38	12 38		13 31	13 37			14 36	15 33		15 40
Saxilby	d	06 37					07 51	08 37	09 51			10 51		11 05	11 51	12 51		13 44	13 50			14 49	15 46		15 53
Lincoln	a	06 53					08 06	08 52	10 06			11 06		11 16	12 06	13 06		13 55	14 07			15 06	15 57		16 10
	d			07 05		08 00				10 15			11 10				13 30			14 41				16 01	
Metheringham	d			07 17		08 12				10 27			11 23				13 43			14 53				16 14	
Ruskington	d			07 27		08 22				10 37			11 33				13 53			15 03				16 24	
Sleaford	a			07 36		08 31				10 50			11 42				14 02			15 13				16 34	
	d					08 34				10 50			11 42				14 03			15 16				16 34	
Spalding	d		07 00		08 00	09 02				11 16			12 07				14 28			15 41				16 59	
Peterborough 8	a		07 25		08 25	09 27				11 42			12 33				14 53			16 07				17 25	

		NT	EM	EM	NT	EM		EM	EM	NT	NT	EM	EM	NT	EM	EM
Doncaster 7	d	15 04		16 27	16 01					17 00	18 02				20 33	
Gainsborough Lea Road	d	16 38		16 56	17 38					18 38	19 39			20 42	21 00	
Saxilby	d	16 51		17 09	17 51					18 51	19 52			20 55	21 14	
Lincoln	a	17 06		17 20	18 06					19 07	20 06			21 10	21 26	
	d		17 15					18 10	19 05				20 49			
Metheringham	d		17 28					18 23	19 17				21 02			
Ruskington	d		17 38					18 33	19 27				21 11			
Sleaford	a		17 47					18 42	19 36				21 20			
	d															
Spalding	d					18 02						19 56				20 58
Peterborough 8	a					18 27						20 21				21 23

Sundays

			NT		NT		NT		NT
Doncaster 7	d								
Gainsborough Lea Road	d		14 26		16 35		18 35		20 24
Saxilby	d		14 39		16 48		18 48		20 37
Lincoln	a		14 54		17 02		19 03		20 51
	d								
Metheringham	d								
Ruskington	d								
Sleaford	a								
	d								
Spalding	d								
Peterborough 8	a								

For connections to London Kings Cross please refer to Table 25

Table 19

Mondays to Fridays

until 15 July

Skegness - Grantham and Nottingham

Miles	Miles			EM	EM	EM	EM	EM	EM	EM	EM	EM	EM	EM	EM	EM	EM	EM	EM	EM	EM	EM	EM
							◇		◇		◇		◇		◇		◇		◇		◇		◇
0	—	**Skegness**	d					07 09		08 10		09 06		10 15		11 15		12 15		13 15		14 15	
3¼	—	Havenhouse	d					07 15															
5	—	Wainfleet	d					07 19		08 18		09 14		10 23		11 23		12 23		13 23		14 23	
7	—	Thorpe Culvert	d					07 23															
23¾	—	**Boston**	d		06 14			07 46		08 45		09 41		10 50		11 50		12 50		13 50		14 50	
27½	—	Hubberts Bridge	d					07 52															
30¾	—	Swineshead	d					07 57															
35¾	—	Heckington	d		06 28			08 02		08 59		09 55		11 04		12 04		13 04		14 04		15 04	
40¼	—	**Sleaford**	d		06 36	06 50		08 11		09 07		10 03		11 12		12 12		13 12		14 13		15 12	
42½	—	Rauceby	d					08 15															
46¼	0	Ancaster	d		06 45			08 21						11 21									
57¾	—	**Grantham** 7	a		07 04			08 42		09 35		10 31		11 41		12 41		13 41		14 42		15 41	
—	—		d	06 10	07 10		07 58	08 45	08 55	09 40	09 58	10 36	11 00	11 45	11 58	12 45	12 58	13 45	13 58	14 45	14 58	15 45	16 01
65¼	12¾	Bottesford	d	06 21	07 21		08 11			09 52				11 56				13 56				15 56	
67¾	—	Elton & Orston	d	06 25																			
69½	—	Aslockton	d	06 29	07 27		08 18	09 00				10 52				13 00				15 00			
71¾	—	Bingham	d	06 33	07 31		08 22	09 05		10 00		10 57		12 04		13 04		14 04		15 05		16 04	
75¼	—	Radcliffe (Notts)	d	06 39	07 37		08 28							12 09									
77	—	Netherfield	d		07 42		08 33																
80¼	—	**Nottingham** 8	a	06 54	07 54	08 30	08 40	09 20	09 36	10 18	10 36	11 14	11 35	12 23	12 36	13 23	13 36	14 23	14 36	15 23	15 36	16 22	16 36

		EM	EM	EM	EM	EM	EM	EM	EM	EM	EM	EM	EM
			◇		◇		◇		◇		◇		
Skegness	d	15 09		16 11		17 30		18 14		19 14		20 15	21 02
Havenhouse	d			16 17									
Wainfleet	d	15 17		16 21		17 38		18 22		19 22		20 23	21 10
Thorpe Culvert	d			16 25									
Boston	d	15 44		16 48		18 05		18 49		19 49		20 50	21 37
Hubberts Bridge	d	15 50											
Swineshead	d	15 55											
Heckington	d	16 01		17 04		18 19		19 04		20 05		21 04	21 51
Sleaford	d	16 10		17 13		18 27		19 13		20 13		21 12	22 00
Rauceby	d	16 14											
Ancaster	d	16 20											
Grantham 7	a	16 41		17 42				19 41		20 40		21 43	
	d	16 45	17 00	17 45	17 58		18 58	19 45	19 59	20 44	20 59	21 47	
Bottesford	d			17 56				19 56				21 58	
Elton & Orston	d												
Aslockton	d			18 02				20 02				22 04	
Bingham	d	17 02		18 07		19 03	19 15	20 06		21 01		22 08	22 35
Radcliffe (Notts)	d							20 12					
Netherfield	d							20 16					
Nottingham 8	a	17 20	17 36	18 22	18 36	19 22	19 36	20 25	20 32	21 21	21 35	22 25	22 54

Mondays to Fridays

18 July to 16 September

		EM	EM	EM	EM	EM	EM	EM	EM	EM	EM	EM	EM	EM	EM	EM	EM	EM	EM	EM	EM	EM	EM
					◇		◇		◇		◇		◇		◇		◇		◇		◇		◇
Skegness	d					07 09		08 10		09 06		10 15		11 15		12 15		13 15		14 15		15 09	
Havenhouse	d					07 15																	
Wainfleet	d					07 19		08 18		09 14		10 23		11 23		12 23		13 23		14 23		15 17	
Thorpe Culvert	d					07 23																	
Boston	d		06 14			07 46		08 45		09 41		10 50		11 50		12 50		13 50		14 50		15 44	
Hubberts Bridge	d					07 52																15 50	
Swineshead	d					07 57																15 55	
Heckington	d		06 28			08 02		08 59		09 55		11 04		12 04		13 04		14 04		15 04		16 01	
Sleaford	d		06 36	06 50		08 11		09 07		10 03		11 12		12 12		13 12		14 13		15 12		16 10	
Rauceby	d					08 15																16 14	
Ancaster	d		06 45			08 21						11 21										16 20	
Grantham 7	a		07 04			08 42		09 35		10 31		11 41		12 41		13 41		14 42		15 41		16 41	
	d	06 10	07 10		07 58	08 45	08 55	09 40	09 58	10 36	11 00	11 45	11 58	12 45	12 58	13 45	13 58	14 45	14 58	15 45	16 01	16 45	17 00
Bottesford	d	06 21	07 21		08 11			09 52				11 56				13 56				15 56			
Elton & Orston	d	06 25																					
Aslockton	d	06 29	07 27		08 18	09 00				10 52				13 00				15 00					
Bingham	d	06 33	07 31		08 22	09 05		10 00		10 57		12 04		13 04		14 04		15 05		16 04		17 02	
Radcliffe (Notts)	d	06 39	07 37		08 28							12 09											
Netherfield	d		07 42		08 33																		
Nottingham 8	a	06 54	07 54	08 30	08 40	09 20	09 36	10 18	10 36	11 14	11 35	12 23	12 36	13 23	13 36	14 23	14 36	15 23	15 36	16 22	16 36	17 20	17 36

For connections to London Kings Cross please refer to Table 26

Table 19

Skegness - Grantham and Nottingham

Mondays to Fridays

18 July to 16 September

		EM	EM ◇	EM	EM ◇	EM	EM ◇	EM	EM ◇	EM	EM A	EM B	EM A
Skegness	d	16 11		17 30		18 14		19 14		20 15	20 35	21 02	
Havenhouse	d	16 17											
Wainfleet	d	16 21		17 38		18 22		19 22		20 23	20 52	21 10	
Thorpe Culvert	d	16 25											
Boston	d	16 48		18 05		18 49		19 49		20 50	21a27	21 37	21 37
Hubberts Bridge	d												
Swineshead	d												
Heckington	d	17 04		18 19		19 04		20 05		21 04		21 51	21 51
Sleaford	d	17 13		18 27		19 13		20 13		21 12		22 00	22 00
Rauceby	d												
Ancaster	d												
Grantham 7	a	17 42				19 41		20 40		21 43			
	d	17 45	17 58		18 58	19 45	19 59	20 44	20 59	21 47			
Bottesford	d	17 56				19 56				21 58			
Elton & Orston	d												
Aslockton	d	18 02				20 02				22 04			
Bingham	d	18 07		19 03	19 15	20 06		21 01		22 08		22 35	22 35
Radcliffe (Notts)	d					20 12							
Netherfield	d					20 16							
Nottingham 8	a	18 22	18 36	19 22	19 36	20 25	20 32	21 21	21 35	22 25		22 54	22 54

Mondays to Fridays

12 September to 23 September

		EM	EM	EM	EM ◇	EM	EM ◇	EM	EM ◇	EM	EM ◇	EM
Skegness	d					07 09		08 10		09 06		10 15
Havenhouse	d					07 15						
Wainfleet	d					07 19		08 18		09 14		10 23
Thorpe Culvert	d					07 23						
Boston	d		06 14			07 46		08 45		09 41		10 50
Hubberts Bridge	d					07 52						
Swineshead	d					07 57						
Heckington	d		06 28			08 02		08 59		09 55		11 04
Sleaford	d		06 36	06 50		08 11		09 07		10 03		11 12
Rauceby	d					08 15						
Ancaster	d		06 45			08 21						11 21
Grantham 7	a		07 04			08 42		09 35		10 31		11 41
	d	06 10	07 10		07 58	08 45	08 55	09 40	09 58	10 36	11 00	11 45
Bottesford	d	06 21	07 21		08 11			09 52				11 56
Elton & Orston	d	06 25										
Aslockton	d	06 29	07 27		08 18	09 00				10 52		
Bingham	d	06 33	07 31		08 22	09 05		10 00		10 57		12 04
Radcliffe (Notts)	d	06 39	07 37		08 28							12 09
Netherfield	d		07 42		08 33							
Nottingham 8	a	06 54	07 54	08 30	08 40	09 20	09 36	10 18	10 36	11 14	11 35	12 23

		EM ◇	EM	EM ◇	EM	EM ◇	EM	EM ◇	EM	EM ◇	EM	EM ◇
Skegness	d		11 15		12 15		13 15		14 15		15 09	
Havenhouse	d											
Wainfleet	d		11 23		12 23		13 23		14 23		15 17	
Thorpe Culvert	d											
Boston	d		11 50		12 50		13 50		14 50		15 44	
Hubberts Bridge	d										15 50	
Swineshead	d										15 55	
Heckington	d		12 04		13 04		14 04		15 04		16 01	
Sleaford	d		12 12		13 12		14 13		15 12		16 10	
Rauceby	d										16 14	
Ancaster	d										16 20	
Grantham 7	a		12 41		13 41		14 42		15 41		16 41	
	d	11 58	12 45	12 58	13 45	13 58	14 45	14 58	15 45	16 01	16 45	17 00
Bottesford	d				13 56				15 56			
Elton & Orston	d											
Aslockton	d		13 00				15 00					
Bingham	d		13 04		14 04		15 05		16 04		17 02	
Radcliffe (Notts)	d											
Netherfield	d											
Nottingham 8	a	12 36	13 23	13 36	14 23	14 36	15 23	15 36	16 22	16 36	17 20	17 36

		EM	EM ◇	EM	EM ◇	EM	EM ◇	EM	EM ◇	EM	EM C	EM FO	EM C
Skegness	d	16 11		17 30		18 14		19 14		20 15	20 35	21 02	
Havenhouse	d	16 17											
Wainfleet	d	16 21		17 38		18 22		19 22		20 23	20 52	21 10	
Thorpe Culvert	d	16 25											
Boston	d	16 48		18 05		18 49		19 49		20 50	21a27	21 37	21 37
Hubberts Bridge	d												
Swineshead	d												
Heckington	d	17 04		18 19		19 04		20 05		21 04		21 51	21 51
Sleaford	d	17 13		18 27		19 13		20 13		21 12		22 00	22 00
Rauceby	d												
Ancaster	d												
Grantham 7	a	17 42				19 41		20 40		21 43			
	d	17 45	17 58		18 58	19 45	19 59	20 44	20 59	21 47			
Bottesford	d	17 56				19 56				21 58			
Elton & Orston	d												
Aslockton	d	18 02				20 02				22 04			
Bingham	d	18 07		19 03	19 15	20 06		21 01		22 08		22 35	22 35
Radcliffe (Notts)	d					20 12							
Netherfield	d					20 16							
Nottingham 8	a	18 22	18 36	19 22	19 36	20 25	20 32	21 21	21 35	22 25		22 54	22 54

A from 12 September until 15 September **B** not from 12 September until 15 September **C** not 16 September, 23 September

For connections to London Kings Cross please refer to Table 26

Mondays to Fridays

from 26 September

Skegness - Grantham and Nottingham

		EM	EM	EM	EM	EM	EM	EM	EM	EM	EM	EM	EM	EM	EM	EM	EM	EM	EM	EM	EM	EM	EM
					◇		◇		◇		◇		◇		◇		◇		◇		◇		◇
Skegness	d					07 09		08 10		09 06		10 15		11 15		12 15		13 15		14 15		15 09	
Havenhouse	d					07 15																	
Wainfleet	d					07 19		08 18		09 14		10 23		11 23		12 23		13 23		14 23		15 17	
Thorpe Culvert	d					07 23																	
Boston	d		06 14			07 46		08 45		09 41		10 50		11 50		12 50		13 50		14 50		15 44	
Hubberts Bridge	d					07 52																15 50	
Swineshead	d					07 57																15 55	
Heckington	d		06 28			08 02		08 59		09 55		11 04		12 04		13 04		14 04		15 04		16 01	
Sleaford	d		06 36	06 50		08 11		09 07		10 03		11 12		12 12		13 12		14 13		15 12		16 10	
Rauceby	d					08 15																16 14	
Ancaster	d		06 45			08 21						11 21										16 20	
Grantham 7	a		07 04			08 42		09 35		10 31		11 41		12 41		13 41		14 42		15 41		16 41	
	d	06 10	07 10		07 58	08 45	08 55	09 40	09 58	10 36	11 00	11 45	11 58	12 45	12 58	13 45	13 58	14 45	14 58	15 45	16 01	16 45	17 00
Bottesford	d	06 21	07 21		08 11			09 52				11 56				13 56				15 56			
Elton & Orston	d	06 25																					
Aslockton	d	06 29	07 27		08 18	09 00				10 52				13 00				15 00					
Bingham	d	06 33	07 31		08 22	09 05		10 00		10 57		12 04		13 04		14 04		15 05		16 04		17 02	
Radcliffe (Notts)	d	06 39	07 37		08 28							12 09											
Netherfield	d		07 42		08 33																		
Nottingham 8	a	06 54	07 54	08 32	08 40	09 20	09 36	10 18	10 36	11 14	11 35	12 23	12 36	13 23	13 36	14 23	14 36	15 23	15 36	16 22	16 36	17 20	17 36

		EM	EM	EM	EM	EM	EM	EM	EM	EM	EM FX	EM FO	EM FX
			◇		◇		◇		◇		bus		
Skegness	d	16 11		17 30		18 14		19 14		20 15	20 35	21 02	
Havenhouse	d	16 17											
Wainfleet	d	16 21		17 38		18 22		19 22		20 23	20 52	21 10	
Thorpe Culvert	d	16 25											
Boston	d	16 48		18 05		18 49		19 49		20 50	21a27	21 37	21 37
Hubberts Bridge	d												
Swineshead	d												
Heckington	d	17 04		18 19		19 04		20 05		21 04		21 51	21 51
Sleaford	d	17 13		18 27		19 13		20 13		21 12		22 00	22 00
Rauceby	d												
Ancaster	d												
Grantham 7	a	17 42				19 41		20 40		21 43			
	d	17 45	17 58		18 58	19 45	19 59	20 44	20 59	21 47			
Bottesford	d	17 56				19 56				21 58			
Elton & Orston	d												
Aslockton	d	18 02				20 02				22 04			
Bingham	d	18 07		19 03	19 15	20 06		21 01		22 08		22 35	22 35
Radcliffe (Notts)	d					20 12							
Netherfield	d					20 16							
Nottingham 8	a	18 22	18 36	19 22	19 36	20 25	20 32	21 21	21 35	22 25		22 54	22 54

Saturdays

until 16 July

		EM	EM	EM	EM	EM	EM	EM	EM	EM	EM	EM	EM	EM	EM	EM	EM	EM	EM	EM	EM	EM	EM
					◇		◇		◇		◇		◇		◇		◇		◇		◇		◇
Skegness	d					07 09		08 15		09 15		10 15		11 15		12 15		13 15		14 15		15 09	
Havenhouse	d					07 15																	
Wainfleet	d					07 19		08 23		09 23		10 23		11 23		12 23		13 23		14 23		15 17	
Thorpe Culvert	d					07 23																	
Boston	d		06 14			07 46		08 50		09 50		10 50		11 50		12 50		13 50		14 50		15 44	
Hubberts Bridge	d					07 52																15 50	
Swineshead	d					07 57																15 55	
Heckington	d		06 28			08 02		09 04		10 05		11 04		12 04		13 04		14 04		15 04		16 01	
Sleaford	d		06 36	06 50		08 11		09 12		10 14		11 12		12 12		13 12		14 13		15 12		16 10	
Rauceby	d					08 15																16 14	
Ancaster	d		06 45			08 21						11 21										16 20	
Grantham 7	a		07 06			08 42		09 41		10 43		11 41		12 41		13 41		14 42		15 41		16 41	
	d	06 10	07 10		07 58	08 45	09 07	09 45	09 58	10 45	10 58	11 45	11 58	12 45	12 58	13 45	13 58	14 45	14 58	15 45	15 58	16 45	16 58
Bottesford	d	06 21	07 21		08 11			09 56				11 56				13 56				15 56			
Elton & Orston	d	06 25																					
Aslockton	d	06 29	07 27		08 17	09 00				11 01				13 00				15 00					
Bingham	d	06 33	07 31		08 21	09 05		10 04		11 06		12 04		13 04		14 04		15 05		16 04		17 02	
Radcliffe (Notts)	d	06 39	07 37		08 27							12 09											
Netherfield	d		07 41		08 31																		
Nottingham 8	a	06 54	07 53	08 30	08 39	09 20	09 41	10 22	10 40	11 24	11 35	12 23	12 36	13 23	13 36	14 23	14 36	15 23	15 36	16 22	16 36	17 20	17 36

For connections to London Kings Cross please refer to Table 26

Table 19

Skegness - Grantham and Nottingham

Saturdays
until 16 July

		EM	EM	EM	EM	EM		EM	EM	EM	EM	EM	EM
			◇		◇			◇		◇			
Skegness	d	16 11		17 30		18 14			19 19		20 15		21 02
Havenhouse	d	16 17											
Wainfleet	d	16 21		17 38		18 22			19 27		20 23		21 10
Thorpe Culvert	d	16 25											
Boston	d	16 48		18 05		18 49			19 54		20 50		21 37
Hubberts Bridge	d												
Swineshead	d												
Heckington	d	17 04		18 19		19 04			20 10		21 04		21 51
Sleaford	d	17 13		18 27		19 13			20 18		21 12		22 00
Rauceby	d												
Ancaster	d												
Grantham 7	a	17 42				19 41			20 45		21 43		
	d	17 45	18 03		18 58	19 45		20 03	20 48	20 58	21 47	22 02	
Bottesford	d	17 56				19 56					21 58		
Elton & Orston	d												
Aslockton	d	18 02				20 02					22 04		
Bingham	d	18 07		19 03	19 15	20 06			21 05		22 08		22 35
Radcliffe (Notts)	d					20 12							
Netherfield	d					20 16							
Nottingham 8	a	18 22	18 36	19 22	19 36	20 25		20 37	21 24	21 32	22 25	22 32	22 54

Saturdays
23 July to 10 September

		EM	EM	EM	EM	EM	EM	EM	EM	EM		EM	EM
					◇		◇		◇			◇	
Skegness	d					07 09		08 15		09 10			10 15
Havenhouse	d					07 15							
Wainfleet	d					07 19		08 23		09 18			10 23
Thorpe Culvert	d					07 23							
Boston	d		06 14			07 46		08 50		09 50			10 50
Hubberts Bridge	d					07 52							
Swineshead	d					07 57							
Heckington	d		06 28			08 02		09 04		10 05			11 04
Sleaford	d		06 36	06 50		08 11		09 12		10 14			11 12
Rauceby	d					08 15							
Ancaster	d		06 45			08 21							11 21
Grantham 7	a		07 06			08 42		09 41		10 43			11 41
	d	06 10	07 10		07 58	08 45	09 07	09 45	09 58	10 45		10 58	11 45
Bottesford	d	06 21	07 21		08 11			09 56					11 56
Elton & Orston	d	06 25											
Aslockton	d	06 29	07 27		08 17	09 00				11 01			
Bingham	d	06 33	07 31		08 21	09 05		10 04		11 06			12 04
Radcliffe (Notts)	d	06 39	07 37		08 27								12 09
Netherfield	d		07 41		08 31								
Nottingham 8	a	06 54	07 53	08 30	08 39	09 20	09 41	10 22	10 40	11 24		11 35	12 23

		EM	EM	EM	EM	EM	EM	EM		EM	EM	EM	EM
		◇		◇			◇			◇		◇	
Skegness	d		11 15		11 26	12 15		13 15			14 15		15 09
Havenhouse	d												
Wainfleet	d		11 23			12 23		13 23			14 23		15 17
Thorpe Culvert	d												
Boston	d		11 50		12 25	12 50		13 50			14 50		15 44
Hubberts Bridge	d												15 50
Swineshead	d												15 55
Heckington	d		12 04			13 04		14 04			15 04		16 01
Sleaford	d		12 12		12 47	13 12		14 13			15 12		16 10
Rauceby	d												16 14
Ancaster	d												16 20
Grantham 7	a		12 41			13 41		14 42			15 41		16 41
	d	11 58	12 45	12 58		13 45	13 58	14 45		14 58	15 45	15 58	16 45
Bottesford	d					13 56					15 56		
Elton & Orston	d												
Aslockton	d		13 00					15 00					
Bingham	d		13 04			14 04		15 05			16 04		17 02
Radcliffe (Notts)	d												
Netherfield	d												
Nottingham 8	a	12 36	13 23	13 36	13 42	14 23	14 36	15 23		15 36	16 22	16 36	17 20

		EM	EM	EM	EM	EM		EM	EM	EM	EM	EM	EM	EM
		◇		◇		◇			◇		◇			
Skegness	d		16 11		17 30			18 14		19 19		20 15		21 02
Havenhouse	d		16 17											
Wainfleet	d		16 21		17 38			18 22		19 27		20 23		21 10
Thorpe Culvert	d		16 25											
Boston	d		16 48		18 05			18 49		19 54		20 50		21 37
Hubberts Bridge	d													
Swineshead	d													
Heckington	d		17 04		18 19			19 04		20 10		21 04		21 51
Sleaford	d		17 13		18 27			19 13		20 18		21 12		22 00
Rauceby	d													
Ancaster	d													
Grantham 7	a		17 42					19 41		20 45		21 43		
	d	16 58	17 45	18 03		18 58		19 45	20 03	20 48	20 58	21 47	22 02	
Bottesford	d		17 56					19 56				21 58		
Elton & Orston	d													
Aslockton	d		18 02					20 02				22 04		
Bingham	d		18 07		19 03	19 15		20 06		21 05		22 08		22 35
Radcliffe (Notts)	d							20 12						
Netherfield	d							20 16						
Nottingham 8	a	17 36	18 22	18 36	19 22	19 36		20 25	20 37	21 24	21 32	22 25	22 32	22 54

For connections to London Kings Cross please refer to Table 26

Table 19

Saturdays

17 September to 24 September

Skegness - Grantham and Nottingham

		EM	EM	EM	EM	EM	EM	EM	EM	EM	EM	EM	EM	EM	EM	EM	EM	EM	EM	EM	EM	EM	EM
					◇		◇		◇		◇		◇		◇		◇		◇		◇		◇
Skegness	d					07 09		08 15		09 15		10 15		11 15		12 15		13 15		14 15		15 09	
Havenhouse	d					07 15																	
Wainfleet	d					07 19		08 23		09 23		10 23		11 23		12 23		13 23		14 23		15 17	
Thorpe Culvert	d					07 23																	
Boston	d		06 14			07 46		08 50		09 50		10 50		11 50		12 50		13 50		14 50		15 44	
Hubberts Bridge	d					07 52																15 50	
Swineshead	d					07 57																15 55	
Heckington	d		06 28			08 02		09 04		10 05		11 04		12 04		13 04		14 04		15 04		16 01	
Sleaford	d		06 36	06 50		08 11		09 12		10 14		11 12		12 12		13 12		14 13		15 12		16 10	
Rauceby	d					08 15																16 14	
Ancaster	d		06 45			08 21						11 21										16 20	
Grantham 7	a		07 06			08 42		09 41		10 43		11 41		12 41		13 41		14 42		15 41		16 41	
	d	06 10	07 10		07 58	08 45	09 07	09 45	09 58	10 45	10 58	11 45	11 58	12 45	12 58	13 45	13 58	14 45	14 58	15 45	15 58	16 45	16 58
Bottesford	d	06 21	07 21		08 11			09 56				11 56				13 56				15 56			
Elton & Orston	d	06 25																					
Aslockton	d	06 29	07 27		08 17	09 00				11 01				13 00				15 00					
Bingham	d	06 33	07 31		08 21	09 05		10 04		11 06		12 04		13 04		14 04		15 05		16 04		17 02	
Radcliffe (Notts)	d	06 39	07 37		08 27							12 09											
Netherfield	d		07 41		08 31																		
Nottingham 8	a	06 54	07 53	08 30	08 39	09 20	09 41	10 22	10 40	11 24	11 35	12 23	12 36	13 23	13 36	14 23	14 36	15 23	15 36	16 22	16 36	17 20	17 36

		EM	EM	EM	EM	EM	EM	EM	EM	EM	EM	EM
			◇		◇		◇		◇			
Skegness	d	16 11		17 30		18 14		19 19		20 15		21 02
Havenhouse	d	16 17										
Wainfleet	d	16 21		17 38		18 22		19 27		20 23		21 10
Thorpe Culvert	d	16 25										
Boston	d	16 48		18 05		18 49		19 54		20 50		21 37
Hubberts Bridge	d											
Swineshead	d											
Heckington	d	17 04		18 19		19 04		20 10		21 04		21 51
Sleaford	d	17 13		18 27		19 13		20 18		21 12		22 00
Rauceby	d											
Ancaster	d											
Grantham 7	a	17 42				19 41		20 45		21 43		
	d	17 45	18 03		18 58	19 45	20 03	20 48	20 58	21 47	22 02	
Bottesford	d	17 56				19 56				21 58		
Elton & Orston	d											
Aslockton	d	18 02				20 02				22 04		
Bingham	d	18 07		19 03	19 15	20 06		21 05		22 08		22 35
Radcliffe (Notts)	d					20 12						
Netherfield	d					20 16						
Nottingham 8	a	18 22	18 36	19 22	19 36	20 25	20 37	21 24	21 32	22 25	22 32	22 54

Saturdays

from 1 October

		EM	EM	EM	EM	EM	EM	EM	EM	EM	EM	EM	EM	EM	EM	EM	EM	EM	EM	EM	EM	EM	EM
					◇		◇		◇		◇		◇		◇		◇		◇		◇		◇
Skegness	d					07 09		08 15		09 15		10 15		11 15		12 15		13 15		14 15		15 09	
Havenhouse	d					07 15																	
Wainfleet	d					07 19		08 23		09 23		10 23		11 23		12 23		13 23		14 23		15 17	
Thorpe Culvert	d					07 23																	
Boston	d		06 14			07 46		08 50		09 50		10 50		11 50		12 50		13 50		14 50		15 44	
Hubberts Bridge	d					07 52																15 50	
Swineshead	d					07 57																15 55	
Heckington	d		06 28			08 02		09 04		10 05		11 04		12 04		13 04		14 04		15 04		16 01	
Sleaford	d		06 36	06 50		08 11		09 12		10 14		11 12		12 12		13 12		14 13		15 12		16 10	
Rauceby	d					08 15																16 14	
Ancaster	d		06 45			08 21						11 21										16 20	
Grantham 7	a		07 06			08 42		09 41		10 43		11 41		12 41		13 41		14 42		15 41		16 41	
	d	06 10	07 10		07 58	08 45	09 07	09 45	09 58	10 45	10 58	11 45	11 58	12 45	12 58	13 45	13 58	14 45	14 58	15 45	15 58	16 45	16 58
Bottesford	d	06 21	07 21		08 11			09 56				11 56				13 56				15 56			
Elton & Orston	d	06 25																					
Aslockton	d	06 29	07 27		08 17	09 00				11 01				13 00				15 00					
Bingham	d	06 33	07 31		08 21	09 05		10 04		11 06		12 04		13 04		14 04		15 05		16 04		17 02	
Radcliffe (Notts)	d	06 39	07 37		08 27							12 09											
Netherfield	d		07 41		08 31																		
Nottingham 8	a	06 54	07 53	08 32	08 39	09 20	09 41	10 22	10 40	11 24	11 35	12 23	12 36	13 23	13 36	14 23	14 36	15 23	15 36	16 22	16 36	17 20	17 36

For connections to London Kings Cross please refer to Table 26

Table 19

Skegness - Grantham and Nottingham

Saturdays
from 1 October

		EM	EM ◇	EM	EM ◇	EM	EM ◇	EM	EM ◇	EM	EM	EM
Skegness	d	16 11		17 30		18 14		19 19		20 15		21 02
Havenhouse	d	16 17										
Wainfleet	d	16 21		17 38		18 22		19 27		20 23		21 10
Thorpe Culvert	d	16 25										
Boston	d	16 48		18 05		18 49		19 54		20 50		21 37
Hubberts Bridge	d											
Swineshead	d											
Heckington	d	17 04		18 19		19 04		20 10		21 04		21 51
Sleaford	d	17 13		18 27		19 13		20 18		21 12		22 00
Rauceby	d											
Ancaster	d											
Grantham 7	a	17 42				19 41		20 45		21 43		
	d	17 45	18 03		18 58	19 45	20 03	20 48	20 58	21 47	22 02	
Bottesford	d	17 56				19 56				21 58		
Elton & Orston	d											
Aslockton	d	18 02				20 02				22 04		
Bingham	d	18 07		19 03	19 15	20 06		21 05		22 08		22 35
Radcliffe (Notts)	d					20 12						
Netherfield	d					20 16						
Nottingham 8	a	18 22	18 36	19 22	19 36	20 25	20 37	21 24	21 32	22 25	22 32	22 54

Sundays
29 May to 11 September

		EM	EM	EM ◇	EM	EM ◇	EM	EM	EM ◇	EM	EM ◇	EM	EM ◇	EM ◇	EM	EM ◇	EM	EM ◇	EM	EM ◇
Skegness	d		10 14		11 08		12 27	14 10		15 04		16 22			18 07		19 15		20 43	
Havenhouse	d																			
Wainfleet	d		10 22		11 16		12 35	14 18		15 12		16 30			18 15		19 23		20 51	
Thorpe Culvert	d																			
Boston	d	09 06	10 49		11 43		13 02	14 45		15 40		16 57			18 42		19 50		21 18	
Hubberts Bridge	d																			
Swineshead	d																			
Heckington	d	09 20	11 03		11 57		13 16	14 59		15 54		17 11			18 56		20 04		21 32	
Sleaford	d	09 28	11 11		12 05		13 24	15 07		16 03		17 19			19 04		20 12		21 41	
Rauceby	d																			
Ancaster	d																			
Grantham 7	a	09 57	11 40		12 34			15 35		16 32					19 33		20 41		22 10	
	d	10 01	11 45	11 56	12 39	12 54		15 40	15 59	16 36	16 56		17 55	18 58	19 37	19 57	20 45	21 03	22 13	22 55
Bottesford	d		11 56			13 05														
Elton & Orston	d																			
Aslockton	d		12 02			13 11														
Bingham	d	10 18	12 06		12 56	13 16	14 00	15 57		16 53		17 55	18 14		19 54		21 02		22 30	
Radcliffe (Notts)	d		12 12			13 21														
Netherfield	d		12 16			13 25														
Nottingham 8	a	10 37	12 27	12 29	13 15	13 33	14 19	16 17	16 28	17 13	17 25	18 11	18 29	19 33	20 14	20 31	21 21	21 35	22 49	23 29

Sundays
from 18 September

		EM ◇	EM	EM	EM ◇	EM ◇	EM	EM ◇	EM ◇	EM	EM ◇	EM	EM ◇	EM	EM ◇
Skegness	d			14 10			16 17			18 07		19 15			
Havenhouse	d														
Wainfleet	d			14 18			16 25			18 15		19 23			
Thorpe Culvert	d														
Boston	d		12 13	14 45			16 52			18 42		19 50			
Hubberts Bridge	d														
Swineshead	d														
Heckington	d		12 27	14 59			17 06			18 56		20 04			
Sleaford	d		12 35	15 07			17 14			19 04		20 12		21 41	
Rauceby	d														
Ancaster	d														
Grantham 7	a		13 04	15 35			17 43			19 33		20 41		22 10	
	d	12 54		15 40	15 59	16 56	17 47	17 55	18 58	19 37	19 57	20 45	21 03	22 13	22 55
Bottesford	d	13 05													
Elton & Orston	d														
Aslockton	d	13 11													
Bingham	d	13 16		15 57			18 04	18 14		19 54		21 02		22 30	
Radcliffe (Notts)	d	13 21													
Netherfield	d	13 25													
Nottingham 8	a	13 33		16 17	16 28	17 25	18 23	18 29	19 33	20 14	20 31	21 21	21 35	22 49	23 29

For connections to London Kings Cross please refer to Table 26

Table 19

Nottingham and Grantham - Skegness

Mondays to Fridays

until 15 July

Miles	Miles			EM	EM	EM	EM	EM	EM	EM	EM	EM		EM	EM	EM	EM	EM	EM	EM	EM	EM		EM	EM
										◇	◇			◇		◇		◇		◇		◇			◇
0	—	**Nottingham** 8 ⛴	d	05 10		05 50	06 45	06 53	07 34	07 52	08 34	08 50		09 34	09 55	10 34	10 45	11 34	11 45	12 34	12 45	13 34		13 45	14 34
4½	—	Netherfield	d									08 56													
5	—	Radcliffe (Notts)	d									09 01									12 55				
8½	—	Bingham	d	05 24		06 04	06 59		07 48			09 07			10 09		10 59		11 59		13 01			13 59	
10¾	—	Aslockton	d	05 28					07 52			09 11					11 03							14 03	
14½	—	Elton & Orston	d																						
15	0	Bottesford	d	05 35		06 13	07 08		07 59			09 17					11 10				13 09				
22½	—	**Grantham** 7	a	05 49		06 27	07 22		08 12	08 23	09 07	09 31		10 06		11 07	11 23	12 07	12 19	13 07	13 23	14 05		14 21	15 07
—	—		d			06 31	07 26		08 16			09 36					11 27		12 25		13 27			14 27	
34	12¾	Ancaster	d						08 34												13 45				
37¾	—	Rauceby	d						08 40																
40	—	**Sleaford**	d			06 57	07 52	08a31	08 45			10 04			10 44		11 53		12 50		13 55			14 52	
44½	—	Heckington	d			07 04	07 59		08 52			10 11			10 51		12 00		12 57		14 02			14 59	
49½	—	Swineshead	d				08 05																		
52¾	—	Hubberts Bridge	d				08 10																		
56½	—	**Boston**	d		06 25	07 24	08 20		09 12			10 28			11 11		12 19		13 15		14 21			15 17	
73¼	—	Thorpe Culvert	d			07 46																			
75¼	—	Wainfleet	d		06 49	07 51	08 45		09 36			10 52			11 35		12 44		13 40		14 46			15 42	
77	—	Havenhouse	d			07 54																			
80¼	—	**Skegness**	a		07 03	08 05	08 59		09 49			11 05			11 50		12 58		13 54		15 00			15 56	

		EM	EM	EM	EM	EM	EM	EM		EM	EM	EM	EM	EM
			◇				◇			◇		◇		
Nottingham 8 ⛴	d	14 45	15 34	15 45	16 14	16 45	17 34	17 45		18 35	18 45	20 34		20 51
Netherfield	d			15 51		16 51								
Radcliffe (Notts)	d			15 56		16 56		17 55						21 01
Bingham	d	14 59		16 02		17 02	17 48	18 01			18 59			21 07
Aslockton	d			16 06		17 06	17 52	18 05			19 03			21 11
Elton & Orston	d					17 10								
Bottesford	d	15 08		16 12		17 14		18 12			19 10			21 17
Grantham 7	a	15 22	16 08	16 25		17 28	18 09	18 25		19 07	19 23	21 07		21 32
	d	15 26		16 29		17 32		18 29			19 26			21 36
Ancaster	d					17 50					19 44			
Rauceby	d					17 56					19 50			
Sleaford	d	15 52		16 55	17a51	18 01		18 55			19 55		21 20	22 01
Heckington	d	15 59		17 02		18 08		19 02			20 02		21 28	22 08
Swineshead	d	16 05												
Hubberts Bridge	d	16 10											21 43	
Boston	d	16 20		17 21		18 26		19 21			20 19		21a53	22a29
Thorpe Culvert	d			17 43										
Wainfleet	d	16 45		17 48		18 51		19 46			20 43			
Havenhouse	d			17 51										
Skegness	a	16 59		18 00		19 05		20 00			20 57			

Mondays to Fridays

18 July to 16 September

		EM	EM	EM	EM	EM	EM	EM	EM	EM		EM	EM	EM	EM	EM	EM	EM	EM	EM		EM	EM	EM	EM
								◇	◇			◇		◇		◇		◇		◇			◇		◇
Nottingham 8 ⛴	d	05 10		05 50	06 45	06 53	07 34	07 52	08 34	08 50		09 34	09 55	10 34	10 45	11 34	11 45	12 34	12 45	13 34		13 45	14 34	14 45	15 34
Netherfield	d									08 56															
Radcliffe (Notts)	d									09 01									12 55						
Bingham	d	05 24		06 04	06 59		07 48			09 07			10 09		10 59		11 59		13 01			13 59		14 59	
Aslockton	d	05 28					07 52			09 11					11 03							14 03			
Elton & Orston	d																								
Bottesford	d	05 35		06 13	07 08		07 59			09 17					11 10				13 09					15 08	
Grantham 7	a	05 49		06 27	07 22		08 12	08 23	09 07	09 31		10 06		11 07	11 23	12 07	12 19	13 07	13 23	14 05		14 21	15 07	15 22	16 08
	d			06 31	07 26		08 16			09 36					11 27		12 25		13 27			14 27		15 26	
Ancaster	d						08 34												13 45						
Rauceby	d						08 40																		
Sleaford	d			06 57	07 52	08a31	08 45			10 04			10 44		11 53		12 50		13 55			14 52		15 52	
Heckington	d			07 04	07 59		08 52			10 11			10 51		12 00		12 57		14 02			14 59		15 59	
Swineshead	d				08 05																			16 05	
Hubberts Bridge	d				08 10																			16 10	
Boston	d		06 25	07 24	08 20		09 12			10 28			11 11		12 19		13 15		14 21			15 17		16 20	
Thorpe Culvert	d			07 46																					
Wainfleet	d		06 49	07 51	08 45		09 36			10 52			11 35		12 44		13 40		14 46			15 42		16 45	
Havenhouse	d			07 54																					
Skegness	a		07 03	08 05	08 59		09 49			11 05			11 50		12 58		13 54		15 00			15 56		16 59	

For connections from London Kings Cross please refer to Table 26

Table 19

Nottingham and Grantham - Skegness

Mondays to Fridays

18 July to 16 September

		EM	EM	EM	EM	EM	EM	EM	EM	EM	EM	EM	EM	EM
				◇		◇		◇				◇		
				A					B	C	C 🚌			
Nottingham 8	d	15 45	16 14	16 34	16 45	17 34	17 45	18 35	18 45	18 45		20 34		20 51
Netherfield	d	15 51			16 51									
Radcliffe (Notts)	d	15 56			16 56		17 55							21 01
Bingham	d	16 02			17 02	17 48	18 01		18 59	18 59				21 07
Aslockton	d	16 06			17 06	17 52	18 05		19 03	19 03				21 11
Elton & Orston	d				17 10									
Bottesford	d	16 12			17 14		18 12		19 10	19 10				21 17
Grantham 7	a	16 25		17 08	17 28	18 09	18 25	19 07	19 23	19 23		21 07		21 32
	d	16 29			17 32		18 29		19 26	19 26				21 36
Ancaster	d				17 50				19 44	19 44				
Rauceby	d				17 56				19 50	19 50				
Sleaford	d	16 55	17a51		18 01		18 55		19 55	19 55			21 20	22 01
Heckington	d	17 02			18 08		19 02		20 02	20 02			21 28	22 08
Swineshead	d													
Hubberts Bridge	d												21b43	
Boston	d	17 21			18 26		19 21		20 19	20a20	20 30		21a53	22a29
Thorpe Culvert	d	17 43												
Wainfleet	d	17 48			18 51		19 46		20 43		21 06			
Havenhouse	d	17 51												
Skegness	a	18 00			19 05		20 00		20 57		21 21			

Mondays to Fridays

12 September to 23 September

		EM	EM	EM	EM	EM	EM	EM	EM	EM	EM	EM	EM	EM	EM	EM	EM	EM	EM	EM	EM	EM	EM
								◇	◇		◇		◇	◇		◇	◇				◇		◇
Nottingham 8	d	05 10		05 50	06 45	06 53	07 34	07 52	08 34	08 50	09 34	09 55	10 34	10 45	11 34	11 45	12 34	12 45	13 34	13 45	14 34	14 45	15 34
Netherfield	d									08 56													
Radcliffe (Notts)	d									09 01								12 55					
Bingham	d	05 24		06 04	06 59		07 48			09 07		10 09		10 59		11 59		13 01		13 59		14 59	
Aslockton	d	05 28					07 52			09 11				11 03						14 03			
Elton & Orston	d																						
Bottesford	d	05 35		06 13	07 08		07 59			09 17				11 10				13 09				15 08	
Grantham 7	a	05 49		06 27	07 22		08 12	08 23	09 07	09 31	10 06		11 07	11 23	12 07	12 19	13 07	13 23	14 05	14 21	15 07	15 22	16 08
	d			06 31	07 26		08 16			09 36				11 27		12 25		13 27		14 27		15 26	
Ancaster	d						08 34											13 45					
Rauceby	d						08 40																
Sleaford	d			06 57	07 52	08a31	08 45			10 04		10 44		11 53		12 50		13 55		14 52		15 52	
Heckington	d			07 04	07 59		08 52			10 11		10 51		12 00		12 57		14 02		14 59		15 59	
Swineshead	d				08 05																	16 05	
Hubberts Bridge	d				08 10																	16 10	
Boston	d		06 25	07 24	08 20		09 12			10 28		11 11		12 19		13 15		14 21		15 17		16 20	
Thorpe Culvert	d			07 46																			
Wainfleet	d		06 49	07 51	08 45		09 36			10 52		11 35		12 44		13 40		14 46		15 42		16 45	
Havenhouse	d			07 54																			
Skegness	a		07 03	08 05	08 59		09 49			11 05		11 50		12 58		13 54		15 00		15 56		16 59	

		EM	EM	EM	EM	EM	EM	EM	EM FO	EM	EM	EM	EM	EM
				◇		◇		◇				◇		
										D	D 🚌			
Nottingham 8	d	15 45	16 14	16 34	16 45	17 34	17 45	18 35	18 45	18 45		20 34		20 51
Netherfield	d	15 51			16 51									
Radcliffe (Notts)	d	15 56			16 56		17 55							21 01
Bingham	d	16 02			17 02	17 48	18 01		18 59	18 59				21 07
Aslockton	d	16 06			17 06	17 52	18 05		19 03	19 03				21 11
Elton & Orston	d				17 10									
Bottesford	d	16 12			17 14		18 12		19 10	19 10				21 17
Grantham 7	a	16 25		17 08	17 28	18 09	18 25	19 07	19 23	19 23		21 07		21 32
	d	16 29			17 32		18 29		19 26	19 26				21 36
Ancaster	d				17 50				19 44	19 44				
Rauceby	d				17 56				19 50	19 50				
Sleaford	d	16 55	17a51		18 01		18 55		19 55	19 55			21 20	22 01
Heckington	d	17 02			18 08		19 02		20 02	20 02			21 28	22 08
Swineshead	d													
Hubberts Bridge	d												21 43	
Boston	d	17 21			18 26		19 21		20 19	20a20	20 30		21a53	22a29
Thorpe Culvert	d	17 43												
Wainfleet	d	17 48			18 51		19 46		20 43		21 06			
Havenhouse	d	17 51												
Skegness	a	18 00			19 05		20 00		20 57		21 21			

A from 1 August until 16 September
B not from 12 September until 15 September
C from 12 September until 15 September
D not 16 September, 23 September

For connections from London Kings Cross please refer to Table 26

Table 19

Mondays to Fridays

from 26 September

Nottingham and Grantham - Skegness

		EM	EM	EM	EM	EM	EM	EM	EM	EM	EM	EM	EM	EM	EM	EM	EM	EM	EM	EM	EM	EM	EM
								◇	◇		◇		◇		◇		◇		◇		◇		◇
Nottingham 8	d	05 10		05 50	06 45	06 53	07 34	07 52	08 34	08 50	09 34	09 55	10 34	10 45	11 34	11 45	12 34	12 45	13 34	13 45	14 34	14 45	15 34
Netherfield	d									08 56													
Radcliffe (Notts)	d									09 01								12 55					
Bingham	d	05 24		06 04	06 59		07 48			09 07		10 09		10 59		11 59		13 01		13 59		14 59	
Aslockton	d	05 28					07 52			09 11				11 03						14 03			
Elton & Orston	d																						
Bottesford	d	05 35		06 13	07 08		07 59			09 17				11 10				13 09				15 08	
Grantham 7	a	05 49		06 27	07 22		08 12	08 23	09 07	09 31	10 06		11 07	11 23	12 07	12 19	13 07	13 23	14 05	14 21	15 07	15 22	16 08
	d			06 31	07 26		08 16			09 36				11 27		12 25		13 27		14 27		15 26	
Ancaster	d						08 34											13 45					
Rauceby	d						08 40																
Sleaford	d			06 57	07 52	08a31	08 45			10 04		10 44		11 53		12 50		13 55		14 52		15 52	
Heckington	d			07 04	07 59		08 52			10 11		10 51		12 00		12 57		14 02		14 59		15 59	
Swineshead	d				08 05																	16 05	
Hubberts Bridge	d				08 10																	16 10	
Boston	d		06 25	07 24	08 20		09 12			10 28		11 11		12 19		13 15		14 21		15 17		16 20	
Thorpe Culvert	d			07 46																			
Wainfleet	d		06 49	07 51	08 45		09 36			10 52		11 35		12 44		13 40		14 46		15 42		16 45	
Havenhouse	d			07 54																			
Skegness	a		07 03	08 05	08 59		09 49			11 05		11 50		12 58		13 54		15 00		15 56		16 59	

		EM	EM	EM	EM	EM	EM	EM	EM	EM	EM	EM	EM	EM
									FO	FX	FX			
				◇		◇		◇				◇		
											🚌			
Nottingham 8	d	15 45	16 14	16 34	16 45	17 34	17 45	18 35	18 45	18 45		20 34		20 51
Netherfield	d	15 51			16 51									
Radcliffe (Notts)	d	15 56			16 56		17 55							21 01
Bingham	d	16 02			17 02	17 48	18 01		18 59	18 59				21 07
Aslockton	d	16 06			17 06	17 52	18 05		19 03	19 03				21 11
Elton & Orston	d				17 10									
Bottesford	d	16 12			17 14		18 12		19 10	19 10				21 17
Grantham 7	a	16 25		17 08	17 28	18 09	18 25	19 07	19 23	19 23		21 07		21 32
	d	16 29			17 32		18 29		19 26	19 26				21 36
Ancaster	d				17 50				19 44	19 44				
Rauceby	d				17 56				19 50	19 50				
Sleaford	d	16 55	17a51		18 01		18 55		19 55	19 55			21 20	22 01
Heckington	d	17 02			18 08		19 02		20 02	20 02			21 28	22 08
Swineshead	d													
Hubberts Bridge	d												21 43	
Boston	d	17 21			18 26		19 21		20 19	20a20	20 30		21a53	22a29
Thorpe Culvert	d	17 43												
Wainfleet	d	17 48			18 51		19 46		20 43		21 06			
Havenhouse	d	17 51												
Skegness	a	18 00			19 05		20 00		20 57		21 21			

Saturdays

until 16 July

		EM	EM	EM	EM	EM	EM	EM	EM	EM	EM	EM	EM	EM	EM	EM	EM	EM	EM	EM	EM	EM	EM
								◇	◇		◇		◇		◇		◇		◇		◇		◇
Nottingham 8	d	05 10		05 50	06 45	06 55	07 28	07 45	08 32	08 45	09 34	09 55	10 34	10 45	11 34	11 45	12 34	12 45	13 34	13 45	14 34	14 45	15 34
Netherfield	d									08 51													
Radcliffe (Notts)	d									08 56								12 55					
Bingham	d	05 24		06 04	06 59		07 42			09 02		10 09		10 59		11 59		13 01		13 59		14 59	
Aslockton	d	05 28					07 46			09 06				11 03						14 03			
Elton & Orston	d																						
Bottesford	d	05 35		06 13	07 08		07 53			09 12				11 10				13 09				15 08	
Grantham 7	a	05 49		06 27	07 22		08 07	08 15	09 02	09 26	10 07		11 06	11 23	12 06	12 19	13 07	13 25	14 05	14 21	15 07	15 22	16 06
	d			06 31	07 26		08 16			09 30				11 27		12 25		13 29		14 27		15 26	
Ancaster	d						08 34																
Rauceby	d						08 40																
Sleaford	d			06 57	07 52	08a31	08 45			09 56		10 44		11 53		12 50		13 55		14 52		15 52	
Heckington	d			07 04	07 59		08 52			10 03		10 51		12 00		12 57		14 02		14 59		15 59	
Swineshead	d				08 05																	16 05	
Hubberts Bridge	d				08 10																	16 10	
Boston	d		06 25	07 24	08 20		09 11			10 22		11 11		12 19		13 15		14 21		15 17		16 20	
Thorpe Culvert	d			07 46																			
Wainfleet	d		06 49	07 51	08 45		09 35			10 47		11 35		12 44		13 40		14 46		15 42		16 45	
Havenhouse	d			07 54																			
Skegness	a		07 03	08 05	08 59		09 48			11 00		11 50		12 58		13 54		15 00		15 56		16 59	

For connections from London Kings Cross please refer to Table 26

Table 19

Nottingham and Grantham - Skegness

Saturdays

until 16 July

		EM	EM	EM	EM	EM	EM	EM	EM	EM
				◇		◇		◇		
Nottingham 8 ⛴	d	15 45	16 45	17 34	17 45	18 34	18 45	20 34		20 51
Netherfield	d	15 51	16 51							
Radcliffe (Notts)	d	15 56	16 56		17 55					21 01
Bingham	d	16 02	17 02	17 48	18 01		18 59			21 07
Aslockton	d	16 06	17 06	17 52	18 05		19 03			21 11
Elton & Orston	d		17 10							
Bottesford	d	16 12	17 14		18 12		19 10			21 17
Grantham 7	a	16 25	17 28	18 10	18 25	19 07	19 23	21 05		21 31
	d	16 29	17 32		18 29		19 26			21 36
Ancaster	d		17 50				19 44			
Rauceby	d		17 56				19 50			
Sleaford	d	16 55	18 01		18 55		19 55		21 21	22 01
Heckington	d	17 02	18 08		19 02		20 02		21 29	22 08
Swineshead	d									
Hubberts Bridge	d								21 43	
Boston	d	17 21	18 26		19 21		20 19		21a53	22a29
Thorpe Culvert	d	17 43								
Wainfleet	d	17 48	18 51		19 46		20 43			
Havenhouse	d	17 51								
Skegness	a	18 00	19 05		20 00		20 57			

Saturdays

23 July to 10 September

		EM	EM	EM	EM	EM	EM	EM	EM	EM	EM	EM
								◇		◇		◇
Nottingham 8 ⛴	d	05 10		05 50	06 45	06 55	07 28	07 45	08 24	08 32	08 45	09 34
Netherfield	d										08 51	
Radcliffe (Notts)	d										08 56	
Bingham	d	05 24		06 04	06 59		07 42				09 02	
Aslockton	d	05 28					07 46				09 06	
Elton & Orston	d											
Bottesford	d	05 35		06 13	07 08		07 53				09 12	
Grantham 7	a	05 49		06 27	07 22		08 07	08 15		09 02	09 26	10 07
	d			06 31	07 26		08 16				09 30	
Ancaster	d						08 34					
Rauceby	d						08 40					
Sleaford	d			06 57	07 52	08a31	08 45		09 14		09 56	
Heckington	d			07 04	07 59		08 52				10 03	
Swineshead	d				08 05							
Hubberts Bridge	d				08 10							
Boston	d		06 25	07 24	08 20		09 11		09 44		10 22	
Thorpe Culvert	d			07 46								
Wainfleet	d		06 49	07 51	08 45		09 35				10 47	
Havenhouse	d			07 54								
Skegness	a		07 03	08 05	08 59		09 48		10 44		11 00	

		EM	EM	EM	EM	EM	EM	EM	EM	EM	EM	EM
			◇		◇		◇		◇		◇	
Nottingham 8 ⛴	d	09 55	10 34	10 45	11 34	11 45	12 34	12 45	13 34	13 45	14 34	14 45
Netherfield	d											
Radcliffe (Notts)	d							12 55				
Bingham	d	10 09		10 59		11 59		13 01		13 59		14 59
Aslockton	d			11 03						14 03		
Elton & Orston	d											
Bottesford	d			11 10				13 09				15 08
Grantham 7	a		11 06	11 23	12 06	12 19	13 07	13 25	14 05	14 21	15 07	15 22
	d			11 27		12 25		13 29		14 27		15 26
Ancaster	d											
Rauceby	d											
Sleaford	d	10 44		11 53		12 50		13 55		14 52		15 52
Heckington	d	10 51		12 00		12 57		14 02		14 59		15 59
Swineshead	d											16 05
Hubberts Bridge	d											16 10
Boston	d	11 11		12 19		13 15		14 21		15 17		16 20
Thorpe Culvert	d											
Wainfleet	d	11 35		12 44		13 40		14 46		15 42		16 45
Havenhouse	d											
Skegness	a	11 50		12 58		13 54		15 00		15 56		16 59

		EM	EM	EM	EM	EM	EM	EM	EM	EM	EM	EM
		◇		◇		◇		◇		◇		
				A								
Nottingham 8 ⛴	d	15 34	15 45	16 34	16 45	17 34	17 45	18 34	18 45	20 34		20 51
Netherfield	d		15 51		16 51							
Radcliffe (Notts)	d		15 56		16 56		17 55					21 01
Bingham	d		16 02		17 02	17 48	18 01		18 59			21 07
Aslockton	d		16 06		17 06	17 52	18 05		19 03			21 11
Elton & Orston	d				17 10							
Bottesford	d		16 12		17 14		18 12		19 10			21 17
Grantham 7	a	16 06	16 25	17 07	17 28	18 10	18 25	19 07	19 23	21 05		21 31
	d		16 29		17 32		18 29		19 26			21 36
Ancaster	d				17 50				19 44			
Rauceby	d				17 56				19 50			
Sleaford	d		16 55		18 01		18 55		19 55		21 21	22 01
Heckington	d		17 02		18 08		19 02		20 02		21 29	22 08
Swineshead	d											
Hubberts Bridge	d										21 43	
Boston	d		17 21		18 26		19 21		20 19		21a53	22a29
Thorpe Culvert	d		17 43									
Wainfleet	d		17 48		18 51		19 46		20 43			
Havenhouse	d		17 51									
Skegness	a		18 00		19 05		20 00		20 57			

A not from 23 July until 30 July

For connections from London Kings Cross please refer to Table 26

Table 19

Saturdays

17 September to 24 September

Nottingham and Grantham - Skegness

		EM	EM	EM	EM	EM	EM	EM	EM	EM		EM	EM	EM	EM	EM	EM	EM	EM	EM		EM	EM	EM	EM
								◇	◇			◇		◇		◇		◇		◇			◇		◇
Nottingham 8	d	05 10		05 50	06 45	06 55	07 28	07 45	08 32	08 45		09 34	09 55	10 34	10 45	11 34	11 45	12 34	12 45	13 34		13 45	14 34	14 45	15 34
Netherfield	d									08 51															
Radcliffe (Notts)	d									08 56									12 55						
Bingham	d	05 24		06 04	06 59		07 42			09 02			10 09		10 59		11 59		13 01			13 59		14 59	
Aslockton	d	05 28					07 46			09 06					11 03							14 03			
Elton & Orston	d																								
Bottesford	d	05 35		06 13	07 08		07 53			09 12					11 10				13 09					15 08	
Grantham 7	a	05 49		06 27	07 22		08 07	08 15	09 02	09 26		10 07		11 06	11 23	12 06	12 19	13 07	13 25	14 05		14 21	15 07	15 22	16 06
	d			06 31	07 26		08 16			09 30					11 27		12 25		13 29			14 27		15 26	
Ancaster	d						08 34																		
Rauceby	d						08 40																		
Sleaford	d			06 57	07 52	08a31	08 45			09 56			10 44		11 53		12 50		13 55			14 52		15 52	
Heckington	d			07 04	07 59		08 52			10 03			10 51		12 00		12 57		14 02			14 59		15 59	
Swineshead	d				08 05																			16 05	
Hubberts Bridge	d				08 10																			16 10	
Boston	d		06 25	07 24	08 20		09 11			10 22			11 11		12 19		13 15		14 21			15 17		16 20	
Thorpe Culvert	d			07 46																					
Wainfleet	d		06 49	07 51	08 45		09 35			10 47			11 35		12 44		13 40		14 46			15 42		16 45	
Havenhouse	d			07 54																					
Skegness	a		07 03	08 05	08 59		09 48			11 00			11 50		12 58		13 54		15 00			15 56		16 59	

		EM	EM	EM	EM	EM		EM	EM	EM	EM	EM
			◇		◇			◇		◇		
Nottingham 8	d	15 45	16 34	16 45	17 34	17 45		18 34	18 45	20 34		20 51
Netherfield	d	15 51		16 51								
Radcliffe (Notts)	d	15 56		16 56		17 55						21 01
Bingham	d	16 02		17 02	17 48	18 01			18 59			21 07
Aslockton	d	16 06		17 06	17 52	18 05			19 03			21 11
Elton & Orston	d			17 10								
Bottesford	d	16 12		17 14		18 12			19 10			21 17
Grantham 7	a	16 25	17 07	17 28	18 10	18 25		19 07	19 23	21 05		21 31
	d	16 29		17 32		18 29			19 26			21 36
Ancaster	d			17 50					19 44			
Rauceby	d			17 56					19 50			
Sleaford	d	16 55		18 01		18 55			19 55		21 21	22 01
Heckington	d	17 02		18 08		19 02			20 02		21 29	22 08
Swineshead	d											
Hubberts Bridge	d										21 43	
Boston	d	17 21		18 26		19 21			20 19		21a53	22a29
Thorpe Culvert	d	17 43										
Wainfleet	d	17 48		18 51		19 46			20 43			
Havenhouse	d	17 51										
Skegness	a	18 00		19 05		20 00			20 57			

Saturdays

from 1 October

		EM	EM	EM	EM	EM	EM	EM	EM	EM		EM	EM	EM	EM	EM	EM	EM	EM	EM		EM	EM	EM	EM
								◇	◇			◇		◇		◇		◇		◇			◇		◇
Nottingham 8	d	05 10		05 50	06 45	06 53	07 28	07 45	08 32	08 45		09 34	09 55	10 34	10 45	11 34	11 45	12 34	12 45	13 34		13 45	14 34	14 45	15 34
Netherfield	d									08 51															
Radcliffe (Notts)	d									08 56									12 55						
Bingham	d	05 24		06 04	06 59		07 42			09 02			10 09		10 59		11 59		13 01			13 59		14 59	
Aslockton	d	05 28					07 46			09 06					11 03							14 03			
Elton & Orston	d																								
Bottesford	d	05 35		06 13	07 08		07 53			09 12					11 10				13 09					15 08	
Grantham 7	a	05 49		06 27	07 22		08 07	08 15	09 02	09 26		10 07		11 06	11 23	12 06	12 19	13 07	13 25	14 05		14 21	15 07	15 22	16 06
	d			06 31	07 26		08 16			09 30					11 27		12 25		13 29			14 27		15 26	
Ancaster	d						08 34																		
Rauceby	d						08 40																		
Sleaford	d			06 57	07 52	08a31	08 45			09 56			10 44		11 53		12 50		13 55			14 52		15 52	
Heckington	d			07 04	07 59		08 52			10 03			10 51		12 00		12 57		14 02			14 59		15 59	
Swineshead	d				08 05																			16 05	
Hubberts Bridge	d				08 10																			16 10	
Boston	d		06 25	07 24	08 20		09 11			10 22			11 11		12 19		13 15		14 21			15 17		16 20	
Thorpe Culvert	d			07 46																					
Wainfleet	d		06 49	07 51	08 45		09 35			10 47			11 35		12 44		13 40		14 46			15 42		16 45	
Havenhouse	d			07 54																					
Skegness	a		07 03	08 05	08 59		09 48			11 00			11 50		12 58		13 54		15 00			15 56		16 59	

For connections from London Kings Cross please refer to Table 26

Table 19

Saturdays
from 1 October

Nottingham and Grantham - Skegness

		EM	EM	EM	EM	EM		EM	EM	EM	EM	EM
			◇		◇			◇		◇		
Nottingham 8	d	15 45	16 34	16 45	17 34	17 45		18 34	18 45	20 34		20 51
Netherfield	d	15 51		16 51								
Radcliffe (Notts)	d	15 56		16 56		17 55						21 01
Bingham	d	16 02		17 02	17 48	18 01			18 59			21 07
Aslockton	d	16 06		17 06	17 52	18 05			19 03			21 11
Elton & Orston	d			17 10								
Bottesford	d	16 12		17 14		18 12			19 10			21 17
Grantham 7	a	16 25	17 07	17 28	18 10	18 25		19 07	19 23	21 05		21 31
	d	16 29		17 32		18 29			19 26			21 36
Ancaster	d			17 50					19 44			
Rauceby	d			17 56					19 50			
Sleaford	d	16 55		18 01		18 55			19 55		21 21	22 01
Heckington	d	17 02		18 08		19 02			20 02		21 29	22 08
Swineshead	d											
Hubberts Bridge	d										21 43	
Boston	d	17 21		18 26		19 21			20 19		21a53	22a29
Thorpe Culvert	d	17 43										
Wainfleet	d	17 48		18 51		19 46			20 43			
Havenhouse	d	17 51										
Skegness	a	18 00		19 05		20 00			20 57			

Sundays
29 May to 11 September

		EM	EM	EM	EM	EM	EM	EM	EM	EM		EM	EM	EM	EM	EM	EM	EM	EM	EM		EM
					◇		◇		◇	◇				◇		◇	◇		◇			◇
Nottingham 8	d		09 00	09 41	09 52	11 09	11 45	11 55	12 37	13 49		14 03	14 56	15 49	16 23	16 45	17 36	18 17	18 47	19 48		20 44
Netherfield	d														16 29		17 42					
Radcliffe (Notts)	d														16 34		17 46					
Bingham	d		09 14	09 55		11 23		12 11	12 51			14 17	15 10		16 40		17 52	18 31	19 01	20 02		20 58
Aslockton	d														16 44		17 56					
Elton & Orston	d																					
Bottesford	d														16 50		18 03					
Grantham 7	a			10 15	10 25	11 44	12 16	12 29	13 11	14 20		14 37	15 31	16 20	17 03	17 15	18 16	18 54	19 21	20 22		21 18
	d			10 20		11 49		12 33				14 41	15 36		17 07			18 59		20 27		
Ancaster	d																					
Rauceby	d																					
Sleaford	d		09 49	10 46		12 15		12 59				15 09	16 04		17 36			19 27		20 54		
Heckington	d		09 56	10 53		12 22		13 06				15 16	16 11		17 43			19 34		21 02		
Swineshead	d																					
Hubberts Bridge	d																					
Boston	d	09 31	10 16	11 11		12 41		13 24				15 39	16 31		18 02			19 52		21a21		
Thorpe Culvert	d																					
Wainfleet	d	09 55	10 40	11 36		13 06		13 49				16 03	16 55		18 27			20 16				
Havenhouse	d																					
Skegness	a	10 07	10 55	11 50		13 20		14 00				16 18	17 10		18 38			20 31				

Sundays
from 18 September

		EM	EM	EM	EM	EM	EM	EM	EM	EM		EM	EM	EM	EM
			◇		◇		◇		◇	◇			◇		◇
Nottingham 8	d	11 55	12 37		13 49	14 56	15 49	16 23	16 45	17 36		18 31	18 47	19 48	20 44
Netherfield	d							16 29		17 42					
Radcliffe (Notts)	d							16 34		17 46					
Bingham	d	12 11	12 51			15 10		16 40		17 52		18 45	19 01	20 02	20 58
Aslockton	d							16 44		17 56					
Elton & Orston	d														
Bottesford	d							16 50		18 03					
Grantham 7	a	12 29	13 11		14 20	15 31	16 20	17 03	17 15	18 16		19 08	19 21	20 22	21 18
	d	12 33		13 50		15 36		17 07				19 13		20 27	
Ancaster	d														
Rauceby	d														
Sleaford	d	12 59		14 16		16 04		17 36				19 41		20a55	
Heckington	d	13 06		14 23		16 11		17 43				19 48			
Swineshead	d														
Hubberts Bridge	d														
Boston	d	13 24		14 44		16 31		18 02				20a10			
Thorpe Culvert	d														
Wainfleet	d	13 49		15 08		16 55		18 27							
Havenhouse	d														
Skegness	a	14 00		15 23		17 10		18 38							

For connections from London Kings Cross please refer to Table 26

Network Diagram for Tables 20, 21, 22

DM-3/08
Design BAJS
© Network Rail
OPSU 2008.
All rights reserved

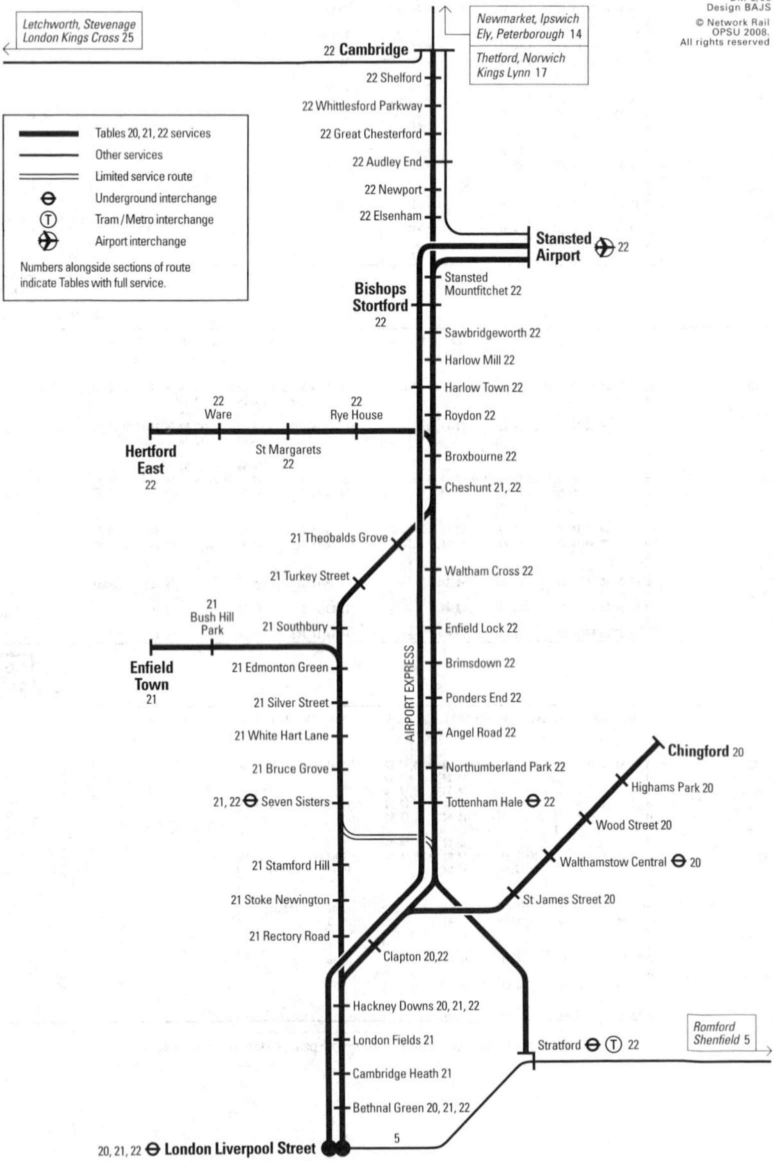

Table 20

Mondays to Fridays

London - Chingford

Miles			LE	LE	LE	LE	LE	LE	LE	LE	LE	LE	LE	LE	LE	LE	LE	LE	LE	LE	LE		LE
							MX																
0	**London Liverpool Street** 15 ⊖	d	23p48	00 03	00 18	00 33	00 48	01 03	06 03	06 33	07 03	07 30	07 48	08 00	08 18	08 33	08 48	09 03	09 18	09 33	09 48	and every 15 minutes until	15 48
1¼	Bethnal Green	d	23p51	00 06	00 21	00 36			06 06	06 36	07 06	07 33	07 51	08 03	08 21	08 36	08 51	09 06	09 21	09 36	09 51		15 51
3	Hackney Downs	d	23p55	00 10	00 25	00 40	00 55	01 10	06 10	06 40	07 10	07 37	07 55	08 07	08 25	08 40	08 55	09 10	09 25	09 40	09 55		15 55
4	Clapton	d	23p58	00 13	00 28	00 43	00 58	01 13	06 13	06 43	07 13	07 40	07 58	08 10	08 28	08 43	08 58	09 13	09 28	09 43	09 58		15 58
5¾	St James Street	d	00 01	00 16	00 32	00 47	01 02	01 17	06 16	06 46	07 16	07 44	08 01	08 14	08 31	08 46	09 01	09 16	09 31	09 46	10 01		16 01
6¼	Walthamstow Central ⊖	d	00 03	00 18	00 34	00 49	01 04	01 19	06 18	06 48	07 18	07 46	08 03	08 16	08 33	08 48	09 03	09 18	09 33	09 48	10 03		16 03
7	Wood Street	d	00 05	00 20	00 36	00 51	01 06	01 21	06 20	06 50	07 20	07 48	08 05	08 18	08 35	08 50	09 05	09 20	09 35	09 50	10 05		16 05
8½	Highams Park	d	00 08	00 23	00 39	00 54	01 09	01 24	06 23	06 53	07 23	07 51	08 08	08 21	08 38	08 53	09 08	09 23	09 38	09 53	10 08		16 08
10½	**Chingford**	a	00 14	00 29	00 44	00 59	01 14	01 29	06 29	06 59	07 29	07 56	08 14	08 26	08 44	08 59	09 15	09 30	09 44	10 00	10 14		16 14

		LE	LE	LE	LE	LE	LE	LE	LE	LE	LE	LE	LE	LE	LE	LE		LE	LE	LE
London Liverpool Street 15 ⊖	d	16 03	16 18	16 33	16 48	17 03	17 18	17 33	17 48	18 03	18 18	18 33	18 48	19 03	19 18	19 33	and every 15 minutes until	23 18	23 33	23 48
Bethnal Green	d	16 06		16 36		17 06		17 36		18 06		18 36		19 06		19 36		23 21		23 51
Hackney Downs	d	16 10	16 25	16 40	16 55	17 10	17 25	17 40	17 55	18 10	18 25	18 40	18 55	19 10	19 25	19 40		23 25		23 55
Clapton	d	16 13	16 28	16 43	16 58	17 13	17 28	17 43	17 58	18 13	18 28	18 43	18 58	19 13	19 28	19 43		23 28		23 58
St James Street	d	16 16	16 31	16 46	17 01	17 16	17 31	17 46	18 01	18 16	18 31	18 46	19 01	19 16	19 31	19 46		23 31		00 01
Walthamstow Central ⊖	d	16 19	16 34	16 49	17 04	17 19	17 34	17 49	18 04	18 19	18 34	18 49	19 04	19 18	19 33	19 48		23 33	23 44	00 03
Wood Street	d	16 21	16 36	16 51	17 06	17 21	17 36	17 51	18 06	18 21	18 36	18 51	19 06	19 20	19 35	19 50		23 35		00 05
Highams Park	d	16 24	16 39	16 54	17 09	17 24	17 39	17 54	18 09	18 24	18 39	18 54	19 09	19 23	19 38	19 53		23 38		00 08
Chingford	a	16 31	16 46	17 01	17 16	17 31	17 46	18 01	18 16	18 31	18 46	19 01	19 16	19 29	19 44	19 59		23 44	23 54	00 14

Saturdays

		LE	LE	LE	LE	LE	LE	LE	LE		LE	LE	LE
London Liverpool Street 15 ⊖	d	23p48	00 03	00 18	00 33	00 48	01 03	06 03	06 33	and every 15 minutes until	23 18	23 33	23 48
Bethnal Green	d	23p51	00 06	00 21	00 36			06 06	06 36		23 21		23 51
Hackney Downs	d	23p55	00 10	00 25	00 40	00 55	01 10	06 10	06 40		23 25		23 55
Clapton	d	23p58	00 13	00 28	00 43	00 58	01 13	06 13	06 43		23 28		23 58
St James Street	d	00 01	00 16	00 32	00 47	01 02	01 17	06 16	06 46		23 31		00 01
Walthamstow Central ⊖	d	00 03	00 18	00 34	00 49	01 04	01 19	06 18	06 48		23 33	23 44	00 03
Wood Street	d	00 05	00 20	00 36	00 51	01 06	01 21	06 20	06 50		23 35		00 05
Highams Park	d	00 08	00 23	00 39	00 54	01 09	01 24	06 23	06 53		23 38		00 08
Chingford	a	00 14	00 29	00 44	00 59	01 14	01 29	06 29	06 59		23 44	23 54	00 14

Sundays

		LE	LE	LE	LE	LE	LE	LE	LE	LE	LE	LE	LE		LE	LE
		A														
London Liverpool Street 15 ⊖	d	23p48	00 03	00 18	00 33	00 48	01 03	07 33	08 03	08 33	08 48	09 03	09 18	and every 15 minutes until	23 33	23 48
Bethnal Green	d	23p51	00 06	00 21	00 36								09 21		23 36	23 51
Hackney Downs	d	23p55	00 10	00 25	00 40	00 55	01 10	07 40	08 10	08 40	08 55	09 10	09 25		23 40	23 55
Clapton	d	23p58	00 13	00 28	00 43	00 58	01 13	07 43	08 13	08 43	08 58	09 13	09 28		23 43	23 58
St James Street	d	00 01	00 16	00 32	00 47	01 02	01 17	07 46	08 16	08 46	09 01	09 16	09 31		23 46	00 01
Walthamstow Central ⊖	d	00 03	00 18	00 34	00 49	01 04	01 19	07 48	08 18	08 48	09 03	09 18	09 33		23 48	00 03
Wood Street	d	00 05	00 20	00 36	00 51	01 06	01 21	07 50	08 20	08 50	09 05	09 20	09 35		23 50	00 05
Highams Park	d	00 08	00 23	00 39	00 54	01 09	01 24	07 53	08 23	08 53	09 08	09 23	09 38		23 53	00 08
Chingford	a	00 14	00 29	00 44	00 59	01 14	01 29	07 59	08 29	08 59	09 14	09 29	09 44		23 59	00 14

A not 22 May

Chingford - London

Mondays to Fridays

Miles			LE	LE	LE	LE	LE	LE	LE	LE	LE	LE	LE	LE	LE	LE	LE	LE	LE	LE	LE	LE
0	**Chingford**	d	05 10	05 25	05 40	05 55	06 10	06 25	06 42	06 57	07 12	07 27	07 42	07 54	08 12	08 27	08 32	08 42	08 57	09 12	09 27	09 40
2	Highams Park	d	05 14	05 29	05 44	05 59	06 14	06 29	06 46	07 01	07 16	07 31	07 46	07 58	08 16	08 31	08 36	08 46	09 01	09 16	09 31	09 44
3½	Wood Street	d	05 17	05 32	05 47	06 02	06 17	06 33	06 50	07 05	07 20	07 35	07 50	08 02	08 20	08 35	08 40	08 50	09 05	09 20	09 35	09 47
4¼	Walthamstow Central ⊖	d	05 19	05 34	05 49	06 04	06 19	06 35	06 52	07 07	07 22	07 37	07 52	08 04	08 22	08 37	08 42	08 52	09 07	09 22	09 37	09 49
4¾	St James Street	d	05 21	05 36	05 51	06 06	06 21	06 38	06 55	07 10	07 25	07 40	07 55	08 07	08 25	08 40		08 55	09 10	09 25	09 40	09 51
6½	Clapton	d	05 24	05 39	05 54	06 09	06 24	06 41	06 58	07 13	07 28	07 43	07 58	08 10	08 28	08 43		08 58	09 13	09 28	09 43	09 54
7½	Hackney Downs	d	05 28	05 43	05 58	06 13	06 28	06 45	07 02	07 17	07 32	07 47	08 02	08 14	08 32	08 47		09 02	09 17	09 32	09 47	09 58
9¼	Bethnal Green	d	05 32	05 47	06 02	06 17	06 32	06 49		07 21		07 51		08 18		08 51			09 21		09 51	10 02
10½	**London Liverpool Street** 15 ⊖	a	05 36	05 51	06 07	06 21	06 36	06 53	07 12	07 27	07 42	07 57	08 12	08 24	08 42	08 57	09 00	09 12	09 27	09 42	09 57	10 07

		LE		LE	LE	LE	LE	LE	LE	LE	LE	LE	LE	LE	LE	LE		LE
Chingford	d	09 55	and every 15 minutes until	17 25	17 40	17 55	18 10	18 25	18 40	18 55	19 10	19 25	19 40	19 55	20 10	20 25	and every 15 minutes until	23 25
Highams Park	d	09 59		17 29	17 44	17 59	18 14	18 29	18 44	18 59	19 14	19 29	19 44	19 59	20 14	20 29		23 29
Wood Street	d	10 02		17 32	17 47	18 02	18 17	18 32	18 47	19 02	19 17	19 32	19 47	20 02	20 17	20 32		23 32
Walthamstow Central ⊖	d	10 04		17 34	17 49	18 04	18 19	18 34	18 49	19 04	19 19	19 34	19 49	20 04	20 19	20 34		23 34
St James Street	d	10 06		17 36	17 51	18 06	18 21	18 36	18 51	19 06	19 21	19 36	19 51	20 06	20 21	20 36		23 36
Clapton	d	10 09		17 39	17 54	18 09	18 24	18 39	18 54	19 09	19 24	19 39	19 54	20 09	20 24	20 39		23 39
Hackney Downs	d	10 13		17 43	17 58	18 13	18 28	18 43	18 58	19 13	19 28	19 43	19 58	20 13	20 28	20 43		23 43
Bethnal Green	d	10 17		17 47	18 02	18 17	18 32	18 47	19 02	19 17	19 32	19 47	20 02	20 17	20 32	20 47		23 47
London Liverpool Street 15 ⊖	a	10 21		17 51	18 07	18 21	18 36	18 51	19 07	19 21	19 37	19 51	20 07	20 21	20 37	20 51		23 51

Saturdays

		LE		LE	LE	LE	LE
Chingford	d	05 10	and every 15 minutes until	22 40	22 55	23 10	23 25
Highams Park	d	05 14		22 44	22 59	23 14	23 29
Wood Street	d	05 17		22 47	23 02	23 17	23 32
Walthamstow Central ⊖	d	05 19		22 49	23 04	23 19	23 34
St James Street	d	05 21		22 51	23 06	23 21	23 36
Clapton	d	05 24		22 54	23 09	23 24	23 39
Hackney Downs	d	05 28		22 58	23 13	23 28	23 43
Bethnal Green	d	05 32		23 02	23 17	23 32	23 47
London Liverpool Street 15 ⊖	a	05 36		23 06	23 22	23 36	23 51

Sundays

		LE	LE	LE	LE	LE	LE	LE	LE	LE	LE		LE
Chingford	d	06 40	06 55	07 10	07 25	07 40	07 55	08 10	08 25	08 40	08 55	and every 15 minutes until	23 10
Highams Park	d	06 44	06 59	07 14	07 29	07 44	07 59	08 14	08 29	08 44	08 59		23 14
Wood Street	d	06 47	07 02	07 17	07 32	07 47	08 02	08 17	08 32	08 47	09 02		23 17
Walthamstow Central ⊖	d	06 49	07 04	07 19	07 34	07 49	08 04	08 19	08 34	08 49	09 04		23 19
St James Street	d	06 51	07 06	07 21	07 36	07 51	08 06	08 21	08 36	08 51	09 06		23 21
Clapton	d	06 54	07 09	07 24	07 39	07 54	08 09	08 24	08 39	08 54	09 09		23 24
Hackney Downs	d	06 58	07 13	07 28	07 43	07 58	08 13	08 28	08 43	08 58	09 13		23 28
Bethnal Green	d										09 17		23 32
London Liverpool Street 15 ⊖	a	07 06	07 21	07 37	07 52	08 06	08 21	08 38	08 51	09 06	09 21		23 36

London - Cheshunt (via Seven Sisters) and Enfield Town

Miles	Miles			LE	LE MX	LE MX	LE	LE	LE	LE	LE	LE	LE	LE	LE	LE	LE	LE	LE	LE	LE	LE	LE
0	0	**London Liverpool Street** 15 ⊖	d	23p30	23p45	00 01	05 45	06 00	06 14	06 21	06 30	06 44	06 51	07 00	07 18	07 21	07 33	07 44	07 51	08 03	08 14	08 21	08 30
1¼	1¼	Bethnal Green	d	23p33	23p48	00 03	05 48	06 03		06 24	06 33		06 54	07 03		07 24	07 36		07 54	08 06		08 24	08 33
1¾	1¾	Cambridge Heath	d	23p35	23p50	00 05	05 50	06 05		06 26	06 35		06 56	07 05		07 26	07 38		07 56	08 08		08 26	08 35
2½	2½	London Fields	d	23p37	23p52	00 07	05 52	06 07		06 28	06 37		06 58	07 07		07 28	07 40		07 58	08 10		08 28	08 37
3	3	Hackney Downs	d	23p39	23p54	00 09	05 54	06 09	06 22	06 30	06 39	06 52	07 00	07 09	07 25	07 30	07 42	07 52	08 00	08 12	08 22	08 30	08 39
3¾	3¾	Rectory Road	d	23p42	23p57	00 12	05 57	06 12	06 24	06 33	06 42	06 54	07 03	07 12		07 33	07 45	07 54	08 03	08 15	08 24	08 33	08 42
4¼	4¼	Stoke Newington	d	23p43	23p58	00 13	05 58	06 13	06 26	06 34	06 43	06 56	07 04	07 13		07 34	07 46	07 56	08 04	08 16	08 26	08 34	08 43
5	5	Stamford Hill	d	23p45	23p59	00 15	06 00	06 15	06 28	06 36	06 45	06 58	07 06	07 15		07 36	07 48	07 58	08 06	08 18	08 28	08 36	08 45
5½	5½	Seven Sisters ⊖	d	23p47	00 02	00 17	06 02	06 17	06 30	06 38	06 47	07 00	07 08	07 17	07 30	07 38	07 50	08 00	08 08	08 20	08 30	08 38	08 47
6¼	6¼	Bruce Grove	d	23p49	00 04	00 19	06 04	06 19	06 32	06 40	06 49	07 02	07 10	07 19	07 32	07 40	07 52	08 02	08 10	08 22	08 32	08 40	08 49
7¼	7¼	White Hart Lane	d	23p51	00 06	00 21	06 06	06 21	06 34	06 42	06 51	07 04	07 12	07 21	07 34	07 42	07 54	08 04	08 12	08 24	08 34	08 42	08 51
8	8	Silver Street	d	23p53	00 08	00 23	06 08	06 23	06 36	06 44	06 53	07 06	07 14	07 23	07 36	07 44	07 56	08 06	08 14	08 26	08 36	08 44	08 53
8½	8½	Edmonton Green	d	23p55	00 10	00 25	06 10	06 25	06 38	06 46	06 55	07 08	07 16	07 25	07 38	07 46	07 58	08 08	08 16	08 28	08 38	08 46	08 55
—	9¾	Bush Hill Park	d	23p58		00 28		06 28		06 49	06 58		07 19	07 28		07 49	08 01		08 19	08 31		08 49	08 58
—	10¾	**Enfield Town**	a	00 03		00 33		06 33		06 54	07 03		07 24	07 33		07 54	08 06		08 24	08 36		08 54	09 03
10½	—	Southbury	d		00 14		06 14		06 41			07 11			07 41			08 11			08 41		
12¼	—	Turkey Street	d		00 17		06 17		06 44			07 14			07 44			08 14			08 44		
13½	—	Theobalds Grove	d		00 19		06 19		06 47			07 17			07 47			08 17			08 47		
14½	—	**Cheshunt**	a		00 22		06 24		06 51			07 21			07 51			08 21			08 51		

		LE	LE	LE	LE	LE	LE		LE	LE	LE	LE	LE	LE	LE	LE	LE	LE	LE	LE	LE	LE
London Liverpool Street 15 ⊖	d	08 44	08 51	09 00	09 15	09 30	09 45		15 45	16 00	16 15	16 20	16 30	16 38	16 50	17 00	17 08	17 20	17 30	17 38	17 50	18 00
Bethnal Green	d		08 54	09 03	09 18	09 33	09 48		15 48	16 03	16 18	16 23	16 33		16 53	17 03		17 23	17 33		17 53	18 03
Cambridge Heath	d		08 56	09 05	09 20	09 35	09 50		15 50	16 05	16 20	16 25	16 35	16 43	16 55	17 05	17 13	17 25	17 35	17 43	17 55	18 05
London Fields	d		08 58	09 07	09 22	09 37	09 52		15 52	16 07	16 22	16 27	16 37	16 45	16 57	17 07	17 15	17 27	17 37	17 45	17 57	18 07
Hackney Downs	d	08 52	09 00	09 09	09 24	09 39	09 54		15 54	16 09	16 24	16 29	16 39	16 47	16 59	17 09	17 17	17 29	17 39	17 47	17 59	18 09
Rectory Road	d	08 54	09 03	09 12	09 27	09 42	09 57	and at	15 57	16 12	16 27	16 32	16 42	16 49	17 02	17 12	17 19	17 32	17 42	17 49	18 02	18 12
Stoke Newington	d	08 56	09 04	09 13	09 28	09 43	09 58	the same	15 58	16 13	16 28	16 33	16 43	16 51	17 03	17 13	17 21	17 33	17 43	17 51	18 03	18 13
Stamford Hill	d	08 58	09 06	09 15	09 30	09 45	10 00	minutes	16 00	16 15	16 30	16 35	16 45	16 53	17 05	17 15	17 23	17 35	17 45	17 53	18 05	18 15
Seven Sisters ⊖	d	09 00	09 08	09 17	09 32	09 47	10 02	past	16 02	16 17	16 33	16 38	16 48	16 56	17 08	17 18	17 26	17 38	17 48	17 56	18 08	18 18
Bruce Grove	d	09 02	09 10	09 19	09 34	09 49	10 04	each	16 04	16 19	16 35	16 40	16 50	16 58	17 10	17 20	17 28	17 40	17 50	17 58	18 10	18 20
White Hart Lane	d	09 04	09 12	09 21	09 36	09 51	10 06	hour until	16 06	16 21	16 37	16 42	16 52	17 00	17 12	17 22	17 30	17 42	17 52	18 00	18 12	18 22
Silver Street	d	09 06	09 14	09 23	09 38	09 53	10 08		16 08	16 23	16 39	16 44	16 54	17 02	17 14	17 24	17 32	17 44	17 54	18 02	18 14	18 24
Edmonton Green	d	09 08	09 16	09 25	09 40	09 55	10 10		16 10	16 25	16 41	16 46	16 56	17 04	17 16	17 26	17 34	17 46	17 56	18 04	18 16	18 26
Bush Hill Park	d		09 19	09 28		09 58				16 28		16 49	16 59		17 19	17 29		17 49	17 59		18 19	18 29
Enfield Town	a		09 24	09 33		10 03				16 34		16 55	17 06		17 25	17 36		17 55	18 06		18 25	18 36
Southbury	d	09 11			09 44		10 14		16 14		16 45			17 08			17 38			18 08		
Turkey Street	d	09 14			09 47		10 17		16 17		16 48			17 11			17 41			18 11		
Theobalds Grove	d	09 17			09 49		10 19		16 19		16 50			17 14			17 44			18 14		
Cheshunt	a	09 21			09 54		10 24		16 24		16 56			17 19			17 49			18 19		

		LE	LE	LE	LE	LE	LE	LE	LE	LE	LE	LE	LE		LE	LE	LE
London Liverpool Street 15 ⊖	d	18 08	18 20	18 30	18 38	18 50	19 00	19 08	19 20	19 30	19 45	20 00	20 15		23 15	23 30	23 45
Bethnal Green	d		18 23	18 33		18 53	19 03		19 23	19 33	19 48	20 03	20 18		23 18	23 33	23 48
Cambridge Heath	d	18 13	18 25	18 35	18 43	18 55	19 05	19 13	19 25	19 35	19 50	20 05	20 20		23 20	23 35	23 50
London Fields	d	18 15	18 27	18 37	18 45	18 57	19 07	19 15	19 27	19 37	19 52	20 07	20 22		23 22	23 37	23 52
Hackney Downs	d	18 17	18 29	18 39	18 47	18 59	19 09	19 17	19 29	19 39	19 54	20 09	20 24		23 24	23 39	23 54
Rectory Road	d	18 19	18 32	18 42	18 49	19 02	19 12	19 19	19 32	19 42	19 57	20 12	20 27	and at	23 27	23 42	23 57
Stoke Newington	d	18 21	18 33	18 43	18 51	19 03	19 13	19 21	19 33	19 43	19 58	20 13	20 28	the same	23 28	23 43	23 58
Stamford Hill	d	18 23	18 35	18 45	18 53	19 05	19 15	19 23	19 35	19 45	20 00	20 15	20 30	minutes	23 30	23 45	23 59
Seven Sisters ⊖	d	18 26	18 38	18 48	18 56	19 08	19 18	19 26	19 38	19 47	20 02	20 17	20 32	past	23 32	23 47	00 02
Bruce Grove	d	18 28	18 40	18 50	18 58	19 10	19 20	19 28	19 40	19 49	20 04	20 19	20 34	each	23 34	23 49	00 04
White Hart Lane	d	18 30	18 42	18 52	19 00	19 12	19 22	19 30	19 42	19 51	20 06	20 21	20 36	hour until	23 36	23 51	00 06
Silver Street	d	18 32	18 44	18 54	19 02	19 14	19 24	19 32	19 44	19 53	20 08	20 23	20 38		23 38	23 53	00 08
Edmonton Green	d	18 34	18 46	18 56	19 04	19 16	19 26	19 34	19 46	19 55	20 10	20 25	20 40		23 40	23 55	00 10
Bush Hill Park	d		18 49	18 59		19 19	19 29		19 49	19 58		20 28				23 58	
Enfield Town	a		18 55	19 06		19 25	19 35		19 54	20 03		20 33				00 03	
Southbury	d	18 38			19 08			19 38			20 14		20 44		23 44		00 14
Turkey Street	d	18 41			19 11			19 41			20 17		20 47		23 47		00 17
Theobalds Grove	d	18 44			19 14			19 44			20 19		20 49		23 49		00 19
Cheshunt	a	18 49			19 19			19 48			20 24		20 54		23 54		00 22

Saturdays

		LE	LE	LE	LE	LE	LE	LE	LE	LE		LE	LE
London Liverpool Street 15 ⊖	d	23p30	23p45	00 01	05 15	05 28	05 45	06 00	06 15	06 30		23 30	23 45
Bethnal Green	d	23p33	23p48	00 03	05 18		05 48	06 03	06 18	06 33		23 33	23 48
Cambridge Heath	d	23p35	23p50	00 05	05 20		05 50	06 05	06 20	06 35		23 35	23 50
London Fields	d	23p37	23p52	00 07	05 22		05 52	06 07	06 22	06 37		23 37	23 52
Hackney Downs	d	23p39	23p54	00 09	05 24		05 54	06 09	06 24	06 39		23 39	23 54
Rectory Road	d	23p42	23p57	00 12	05 27		05 57	06 12	06 27	06 42	and at	23 42	23 57
Stoke Newington	d	23p43	23p58	00 13	05 28		05 58	06 13	06 28	06 43	the same	23 43	23 58
Stamford Hill	d	23p45	23p59	00 15	05 30		06 00	06 15	06 30	06 45	minutes	23 45	23 59
Seven Sisters ⊖	d	23p47	00 02	00 17	05 32	05 51	06 02	06 17	06 32	06 47	past	23 47	00 02
Bruce Grove	d	23p49	00 04	00 19	05 34	05 53	06 04	06 19	06 34	06 49	each	23 49	00 04
White Hart Lane	d	23p51	00 06	00 21	05 36	05 55	06 06	06 21	06 36	06 51	hour until	23 51	00 06
Silver Street	d	23p53	00 08	00 23	05 38	05 57	06 08	06 23	06 38	06 53		23 53	00 08
Edmonton Green	d	23p55	00 10	00 25	05 40	05 59	06 10	06 25	06 40	06 55		23 55	00 10
Bush Hill Park	d	23p58		00 28		06 02		06 28		06 58		23 58	
Enfield Town	a	00 03		00 33		06 06		06 33		07 03		00 03	
Southbury	d		00 14		05 44		06 14		06 44				00 14
Turkey Street	d		00 17		05 47		06 17		06 47				00 17
Theobalds Grove	d		00 19		05 49		06 19		06 49				00 19
Cheshunt	a		00 22		05 54		06 24		06 54				00 24

Table 21

Sundays

London - Cheshunt (via Seven Sisters) and Enfield Town

		LE A	LE A	LE	LE	LE	LE	LE	LE	LE		LE	LE	LE	LE	LE		LE	LE		LE			
London Liverpool Street 15 ⊖	d	23p30	23p45	00 01	07 30	07 52	08 00	08 22	08 30	08 52		09 00	09 22	09 30	09 52	10 00		23 00	23 22		23 30			
Bethnal Green	d	23p33	23p48	00 03										09 33		10 03		23 03			23 33			
Cambridge Heath	d	23p35	23p50	00 05										09 35		10 05		23 05			23 35			
London Fields	d	23p37	23p52	00 07										09 37		10 07		23 07			23 37			
Hackney Downs	d	23p39	23p54	00 09	07 39	07 59	08 09	08 29	08 39	08 59		09 09	09 29	09 39	09 59	10 09		23 09	23 29		23 39			
Rectory Road	d	23p42	23p57	00 12	07 42		08 12		08 42			09 12		09 42		10 12	and at	23 12			23 42			
Stoke Newington	d	23p43	23p58	00 13	07 43		08 13		08 43			09 13		09 43		10 13	the same	23 13			23 43			
Stamford Hill	d	23p45	23p59	00 15	07 45		08 15		08 45			09 15		09 45		10 15	minutes	23 15			23 45			
Seven Sisters ⊖	d	23p47	00 02	00 17	07 47	08 04	08 17	08 34	08 47	09 04		09 17	09 34	09 47	10 04	10 17	past	23 17	23 34		23 47			
Bruce Grove	d	23p49	00 04	00 19	07 49		08 19		08 49			09 19		09 49		10 19	each	23 19			23 49			
White Hart Lane	d	23p51	00 06	00 21	07 51		08 21		08 51			09 21		09 51		10 21	hour until	23 21			23 51			
Silver Street	d	23p53	00 08	00 23	07 53		08 23		08 53			09 23		09 53		10 23		23 23			23 53			
Edmonton Green	d	23p55	00 10	00 25	07 55	08 08	08 25	08 38	08 55	09 08		09 25	09 38	09 55	10 08	10 25		23 25	23 38		23 55			
Bush Hill Park	d	23p58		00 28	07 58		08 28		08 58			09 28		09 58		10 28		23 28			23 58			
Enfield Town	a	00 03		00 33	08 03		08 33		09 03			09 33		10 03		10 33		23 33			00 03			
Southbury	d		00 14			08 12		08 42		09 12			09 42		10 12				23 42					
Turkey Street	d		00 17			08 15		08 45		09 15			09 45		10 15				23 45					
Theobalds Grove	d		00 19			08 17		08 47		09 17			09 47		10 17				23 47					
Cheshunt	a		00 24			08 20		08 52		09 20			09 52		10 20				23 50					

A not 22 May

Cheshunt (via Seven Sisters) and Enfield Town - London

Miles	Miles		LE MX	LE MX [1]	LE MX [1]	LE	LE	LE	LE	LE	LE	LE	LE	LE	LE	LE	LE	LE	LE	LE	LE	LE
0	—	**Cheshunt** d	23p31	23p51	23p58	05 16		06 01			06 33			07 03			07 33			08 03		
1	—	Theobalds Grove d	23p34			05 19		06 04			06 36			07 06			07 36			08 06		
2¼	—	Turkey Street d	23p36			05 21		06 06			06 38			07 08			07 38			08 08		
4	—	Southbury d	23p39			05 24		06 09			06 41			07 11			07 41			08 11		
—	0	**Enfield Town** d					05 52		06 20	06 32		06 48	07 02		07 18	07 32		07 50	08 02		08 18	08 33
—	1	Bush Hill Park d					05 55		06 23	06 35		06 51	07 05		07 21	07 35		07 53	08 05		08 21	08 36
6	2¼	Edmonton Green d	23p43			05 28	05 58	06 13	06 26	06 38	06 45	06 54	07 08	07 15	07 24	07 38	07 45	07 56	08 08	08 15	08 25	08 39
6½	2¾	Silver Street d	23p45			05 30	06 00	06 15	06 28	06 40	06 47	06 56	07 10	07 17	07 26	07 40	07 47	07 58	08 10	08 17	08 27	08 41
7¼	3½	White Hart Lane d	23p47			05 32	06 02	06 17	06 30	06 42	06 49	06 58	07 12	07 19	07 28	07 42	07 49	08 00	08 12	08 19	08 29	08 43
8¼	4½	Bruce Grove d	23p49			05 34	06 04	06 19	06 32	06 44	06 51	07 00	07 14	07 21	07 30	07 44	07 51	08 02	08 14	08 21	08 31	08 45
9	5¼	Seven Sisters ⊖ d	23p51	00 04	00 11	05 36	06 06	06 21	06 35	06 47	06 55	07 03	07 17	07 25	07 33	07 47	07 55	08 05	08 17	08 25	08 33	08 48
9½	5¾	Stamford Hill d	23p53			05 38	06 08	06 23	06 37	06 49	06 57	07 05	07 19	07 27	07 35	07 49	07 57	08 07	08 19	08 27	08 35	08 50
10¼	6½	Stoke Newington d	23p55			05 40	06 10	06 25	06 39	06 51	06 59	07 07	07 21	07 29	07 37	07 51	07 59	08 09	08 21	08 29	08 37	08 52
10¾	7	Rectory Road d	23p56			05 41	06 11	06 26	06 41	06 53	07 00	07 09	07 23	07 30	07 39	07 53	08 00	08 10	08 23	08 30	08 39	08 54
11½	7¾	Hackney Downs d	23p59		00 16	05 44	06 14	06 29	06 45	06 58	07 04	07 13	07 28	07 34	07 43	07 58	08 04	08 14	08 28	08 34	08 43	08 58
12	8¼	London Fields d	00 01			05 46	06 16	06 31	06 47	07 00	07 06	07 15	07 30	07 36	07 45	08 00	08 06	08 16	08 30	08 36	08 45	09 00
12¾	9	Cambridge Heath d	00 03			05 48	06 18	06 33	06 49	07 02	07 08	07 17	07 32	07 38	07 47	08 02	08 08	08 18	08 32	08 38	08 47	09 02
13¼	9½	Bethnal Green d	00 05			05 50	06 20	06 35	06 51		07 10	07 19		07 40	07 49		08 10	08 20		08 40	08 49	
14½	10¾	**London Liverpool Street** [15] ⊖ a	00 10	00 18	00 25	05 55	06 25	06 40	06 55	07 10	07 16	07 25	07 40	07 46	07 55	08 10	08 16	08 26	08 40	08 46	08 55	09 10

	LE	LE	LE	LE	LE	LE	LE	LE	LE	LE	and at the same minutes past each hour until	LE	LE	LE	LE	LE	LE	LE	LE	LE	LE
Cheshunt d	08 33			09 03			09 31		10 01				15 31		16 01		16 31			17 01	
Theobalds Grove d	08 36			09 06			09 34		10 04				15 34		16 04		16 34			17 04	
Turkey Street d	08 38			09 08			09 36		10 06				15 36		16 06		16 36			17 06	
Southbury d	08 41			09 11			09 39		10 09				15 39		16 09		16 39			17 09	
Enfield Town d		08 48	09 02		09 18	09 29		09 52		10 22		15 22		15 52		16 22		16 52	17 00		17 22
Bush Hill Park d		08 51	09 05		09 21	09 32		09 55		10 25		15 25		15 55		16 25		16 55	17 03		17 25
Edmonton Green d	08 45	08 54	09 08	09 15	09 24	09 35	09 43	09 58	10 13	10 28		15 28	15 43	15 58	16 13	16 28	16 43	16 58	17 06	17 13	17 28
Silver Street d	08 47	08 56	09 10	09 17	09 26	09 37	09 45	10 00	10 15	10 30		15 30	15 45	16 00	16 15	16 30	16 45	17 00	17 08	17 15	17 30
White Hart Lane d	08 49	08 58	09 12	09 19	09 28	09 39	09 47	10 02	10 17	10 32		15 32	15 47	16 02	16 17	16 32	16 47	17 02	17 10	17 17	17 32
Bruce Grove d	08 51	09 00	09 14	09 21	09 30	09 41	09 49	10 04	10 19	10 34		15 34	15 49	16 04	16 19	16 34	16 49	17 04	17 12	17 19	17 34
Seven Sisters ⊖ d	08 55	09 03	09 17	09 25	09 33	09 43	09 51	10 06	10 21	10 36		15 36	15 51	16 06	16 21	16 36	16 51	17 06	17 14	17 21	17 36
Stamford Hill d	08 57	09 05	09 19	09 27	09 35	09 45	09 53	10 08	10 23	10 38		15 38	15 53	16 08	16 23	16 38	16 53	17 08		17 23	17 38
Stoke Newington d	08 59	09 07	09 21	09 29	09 37	09 47	09 55	10 10	10 25	10 40		15 40	15 55	16 10	16 25	16 40	16 55	17 10	17 17	17 25	17 40
Rectory Road d	09 00	09 09	09 23	09 30	09 39	09 49	09 56	10 11	10 26	10 41		15 41	15 56	16 11	16 26	16 41	16 56	17 11		17 26	17 41
Hackney Downs d	09 04	09 13	09 28	09 34	09 43	09 52	09 59	10 14	10 29	10 44		15 44	15 59	16 14	16 29	16 44	16 59	17 14	17 20	17 29	17 44
London Fields d	09 06	09 15	09 30	09 36	09 45	09 54	10 01	10 16	10 31	10 46		15 46	16 01	16 16	16 31	16 46	17 01	17 16		17 31	17 46
Cambridge Heath d	09 08	09 17	09 32	09 38	09 47	09 56	10 03	10 18	10 33	10 48		15 48	16 03	16 18	16 33	16 48	17 03	17 18		17 33	17 48
Bethnal Green d	09 10	09 19		09 40	09 49		10 05	10 20	10 35	10 50		15 50	16 05	16 20	16 35	16 50	17 05	17 20		17 35	17 50
London Liverpool Street [15] ⊖ a	09 16	09 25	09 40	09 46	09 55	10 03	10 10	10 25	10 40	10 55		15 55	16 11	16 25	16 40	16 56	17 10	17 26	17 29	17 40	17 56

	LE	LE	LE	LE	LE	LE	LE	LE	LE	LE	LE	LE	LE	LE	LE	LE	LE	LE	LE	LE	LE
Cheshunt d		17 31			18 01			18 31			19 01			19 31		20 01		20 31		21 01	
Theobalds Grove d		17 34			18 04			18 34			19 04			19 34		20 04		20 34		21 04	
Turkey Street d		17 36			18 06			18 36			19 06			19 36		20 06		20 36		21 06	
Southbury d		17 39			18 09			18 39			19 09			19 39		20 09		20 39		21 09	
Enfield Town d	17 30		17 52	18 00		18 22	18 30		18 52	19 00		19 22	19 30		19 52		20 22		20 52		21 22
Bush Hill Park d	17 33		17 55	18 03		18 25	18 33		18 55	19 03		19 25	19 33		19 55		20 25		20 55		21 25
Edmonton Green d	17 36	17 43	17 58	18 06	18 13	18 28	18 36	18 43	18 58	19 06	19 13	19 28	19 36	19 43	19 58	20 13	20 28	20 43	20 58	21 13	21 28
Silver Street d	17 38	17 45	18 00	18 08	18 15	18 30	18 38	18 45	19 00	19 08	19 15	19 30	19 38	19 45	20 00	20 15	20 30	20 45	21 00	21 15	21 30
White Hart Lane d	17 40	17 47	18 02	18 10	18 17	18 32	18 40	18 47	19 02	19 10	19 17	19 32	19 40	19 47	20 02	20 17	20 32	20 47	21 02	21 17	21 32
Bruce Grove d	17 42	17 49	18 04	18 12	18 19	18 34	18 42	18 49	19 04	19 12	19 19	19 34	19 42	19 49	20 04	20 19	20 34	20 49	21 04	21 19	21 34
Seven Sisters ⊖ d	17 44	17 51	18 06	18 14	18 21	18 36	18 44	18 51	19 06	19 14	19 21	19 36	19 44	19 51	20 06	20 21	20 36	20 51	21 06	21 21	21 36
Stamford Hill d		17 53	18 08		18 23	18 38		18 53	19 08		19 23	19 38		19 53	20 08	20 23	20 38	20 53	21 08	21 23	21 38
Stoke Newington d	17 47	17 55	18 10	18 17	18 25	18 40	18 47	18 55	19 10	19 17	19 25	19 40	19 47	19 55	20 10	20 25	20 40	20 55	21 10	21 25	21 40
Rectory Road d		17 56	18 11		18 26	18 41		18 56	19 11		19 26	19 41		19 56	20 11	20 26	20 41	20 56	21 11	21 26	21 41
Hackney Downs d	17 50	17 59	18 14	18 20	18 29	18 44	18 50	18 59	19 14	19 20	19 29	19 44	19 50	19 59	20 14	20 29	20 44	20 59	21 14	21 29	21 44
London Fields d		18 01	18 16		18 31	18 46		19 01	19 16		19 31	19 46		20 01	20 16	20 31	20 46	21 01	21 16	21 31	21 46
Cambridge Heath d		18 03	18 18		18 33	18 48		19 03	19 18		19 33	19 48		20 03	20 18	20 33	20 48	21 03	21 18	21 33	21 48
Bethnal Green d		18 05	18 20		18 35	18 50		19 05	19 20		19 35	19 50		20 05	20 20	20 35	20 50	21 05	21 20	21 35	21 50
London Liverpool Street [15] ⊖ a	17 59	18 11	18 26	18 29	18 40	18 56	18 59	19 11	19 26	19 29	19 41	19 55	19 59	20 11	20 25	20 40	20 55	21 10	21 25	21 40	21 55

	LE	LE	LE	LE	LE	LE	LE	LE	LE	LE [1]	LE [1]
Cheshunt d	21 31		22 01		22 31		23 01		23 31	23 51	23 58
Theobalds Grove d	21 34		22 04		22 34		23 04		23 34		
Turkey Street d	21 36		22 06		22 36		23 06		23 36		
Southbury d	21 39		22 09		22 39		23 09		23 39		
Enfield Town d		21 52		22 22		22 52		23 22			
Bush Hill Park d		21 55		22 25		22 55		23 25			
Edmonton Green d	21 43	21 58	22 13	22 28	22 43	22 58	23 13	23 28	23 43		
Silver Street d	21 45	22 00	22 15	22 30	22 45	23 00	23 15	23 30	23 45		
White Hart Lane d	21 47	22 02	22 17	22 32	22 47	23 02	23 17	23 32	23 47		
Bruce Grove d	21 49	22 04	22 19	22 34	22 49	23 04	23 19	23 34	23 49		
Seven Sisters ⊖ d	21 51	22 06	22 21	22 36	22 51	23 06	23 21	23 36	23 51	00 04	00 11
Stamford Hill d	21 53	22 08	22 23	22 38	22 53	23 08	23 23	23 38	23 53		
Stoke Newington d	21 55	22 10	22 25	22 40	22 55	23 10	23 25	23 40	23 55		
Rectory Road d	21 56	22 11	22 26	22 41	22 56	23 11	23 26	23 41	23 56		
Hackney Downs d	21 59	22 14	22 29	22 44	22 59	23 14	23 29	23 44	23 59		00 16
London Fields d	22 01	22 16	22 31	22 46	23 01	23 16	23 31	23 46	00 01		
Cambridge Heath d	22 03	22 18	22 33	22 48	23 03	23 18	23 33	23 48	00 03		
Bethnal Green d	22 05	22 20	22 35	22 50	23 05	23 20	23 35	23 50	00 05		
London Liverpool Street [15] ⊖ a	22 10	22 25	22 40	22 55	23 10	23 25	23 40	23 55	00 10	00 18	00 25

Table 21

Saturdays

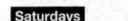

Cheshunt (via Seven Sisters) and Enfield Town - London

		LE	LE 1	LE 1	LE 1	LE	LE	LE	LE		LE		LE	LE	LE	LE
Cheshunt	d	23p31	23p51	23p58	05 16	06 01		06 31		and at the same minutes past each hour until			23 01		23 31	
Theobalds Grove	d	23p34			05 19	06 04		06 34					23 04		23 34	
Turkey Street	d	23p36			05 21	06 06		06 36					23 06		23 36	
Southbury	d	23p39			05 24	06 09		06 39					23 09		23 39	
Enfield Town	d						06 22		06 52		22 52			23 22		23 52
Bush Hill Park	d						06 25		06 55		22 55			23 25		23 55
Edmonton Green	d	23p43			05 28	06 13	06 28	06 43	06 58		22 58		23 13	23 28	23 43	23 58
Silver Street	d	23p45			05 30	06 15	06 30	06 45	07 00		23 00		23 15	23 30	23 45	23 59
White Hart Lane	d	23p47			05 32	06 17	06 32	06 47	07 02		23 02		23 17	23 32	23 47	00 02
Bruce Grove	d	23p49			05 34	06 19	06 34	06 49	07 04		23 04		23 19	23 34	23 49	00 04
Seven Sisters ⊖	d	23p51	00 04	00 11	05 36	06 21	06 36	06 51	07 06		23 06		23 21	23 36	23 51	00 06
Stamford Hill	d	23p53			05 38	06 23	06 38	06 53	07 08		23 08		23 23	23 38	23 53	00 08
Stoke Newington	d	23p55			05 40	06 25	06 40	06 55	07 10		23 10		23 25	23 40	23 55	00 10
Rectory Road	d	23p56			05 41	06 26	06 41	06 56	07 11		23 11		23 26	23 41	23 56	00 11
Hackney Downs	d	23p59		00 16	05 45	06 29	06 44	06 59	07 14		23 14		23 29	23 44	23 59	00 14
London Fields	d	00 01				06 31	06 46	07 01	07 16		23 16		23 31	23 46	00 01	00 16
Cambridge Heath	d	00 03				06 33	06 48	07 03	07 18		23 18		23 33	23 48	00 03	00 18
Bethnal Green	d	00 05			05 49	06 35	06 50	07 05	07 20		23 20		23 35	23 50	00 05	00 20
London Liverpool Street 15 ⊖	a	00 10	00 18	00 25	05 54	06 40	06 55	07 10	07 25		23 25		23 40	23 55	00 10	00 25

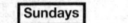

Sundays

		LE A	LE A	LE	LE	LE	LE	LE	LE	LE		LE		LE	LE	LE	LE	LE
Cheshunt	d	23p31		07 45		08 15		08 45		09 15			and at the same minutes past each hour until		22 45		23 15	
Theobalds Grove	d	23p34		07 48		08 18		08 48		09 18					22 48		23 18	
Turkey Street	d	23p36		07 51		08 21		08 51		09 21					22 51		23 21	
Southbury	d	23p39		07 54		08 24		08 54		09 24					22 54		23 24	
Enfield Town	d		23p52		07 57		08 27		08 57			09 27		22 27		22 57		23 27
Bush Hill Park	d		23p55		08 00		08 30		09 00			09 30		22 30		23 00		23 30
Edmonton Green	d	23p43	23p58	07 57	08 03	08 27	08 33	08 57	09 03	09 27		09 33		22 33	22 57	23 03	23 27	23 33
Silver Street	d	23p45	23p59		08 05		08 35		09 05			09 35		22 35		23 05		23 35
White Hart Lane	d	23p47	00 02		08 07		08 37		09 07			09 37		22 37		23 07		23 37
Bruce Grove	d	23p49	00 04		08 09		08 39		09 09			09 39		22 39		23 09		23 39
Seven Sisters ⊖	d	23p51	00 06	08 03	08 11	08 33	08 41	09 03	09 11	09 33		09 41		22 41	23 03	23 11	23 33	23 41
Stamford Hill	d	23p53	00 08		08 13		08 43		09 13			09 43		22 43		23 13		23 43
Stoke Newington	d	23p55	00 10		08 15		08 45		09 15			09 45		22 45		23 15		23 45
Rectory Road	d	23p56	00 11		08 16		08 46		09 16			09 46		22 46		23 16		23 46
Hackney Downs	d	23p59	00 14	08 09	08 19	08 39	08 49	09 09	09 19	09 39		09 49		22 49	23 09	23 19	23 39	23 49
London Fields	d	00 01	00 16						09 21			09 51		22 51		23 21		23 51
Cambridge Heath	d	00 03	00 18						09 23			09 53		22 53		23 23		23 53
Bethnal Green	d	00 05	00 20						09 25			09 55		22 55		23 25		23 55
London Liverpool Street 15 ⊖	a	00 10	00 25	08 18	08 30	08 48	09 00	09 18	09 30	09 48		10 00		23 00	23 18	23 30	23 48	23 58

A not 22 May

London - Broxbourne, Hertford East, Bishops Stortford, Stansted Airport and Cambridge

Miles	Miles			LE MO 1	LE MX 1	LE MX 1	LE MO	LE MO 1	LE MX 1	LE MX 1	LE MO	LE MO 1		LE MO	LE MX 1	LE 1	LE MO 1	LE MFO 1	LE 1 A	XC ◇1	LE TWO 1	LE 1		LE	LE 1
0	—	**London Liverpool Street 15 ⊖**	d		22p58	23p12	23p22	23p25	23p25	23p28		23p28			23p40	23p58	03 40	04 10	04 40		04 40	05 10			
1¼	—	Bethnal Green	d																						
3	—	Hackney Downs	d			23p18	23p29								23p46										
—	0	Stratford 7 ⊖	d	22p45																					
4	—	Clapton	d												23p49										
—	6¾	Seven Sisters ⊖	d				23p34																		
6	—	Tottenham Hale ⊖	d	22p55	23p10	23p25		23p37	23b37	23p40		23p40			23p53	00 10			04u52		04u59	05u22			
7	—	Northumberland Park	d												23p55										
7¾	—	Angel Road	d																						
10	—	Ponders End	d	22p59		23p29						23p44			23p59										
10¾	—	Brimsdown	d	23p02		23p32						23p47			00 02										
11¾	—	Enfield Lock	d	23p04		23p34						23p49			00 04										
12¾	—	Waltham Cross	d	23p07		23p37					←	23p52			00 07										
14	—	Cheshunt	d	23p09	23p18	23p39	23p50			23p48	23p50	23p54		←	00 09	00 18			05 00		05 07				
17¼	—	**Broxbourne 3**	a	23p14	23p22	23p44	↪			23p52	23p55	23p59		23p55	00 14	00 22			05 04		05 11				
—	0	**Broxbourne 3**	d	23p19	23p22	23p44				23p52	00 02	23p59		00 02	00 14	00 22			05 04		05 11			05 40	
—	1¾	Rye House	d			23p47					↪			00 06	00 17									05 43	
—	3	St Margarets (Herts)	d			23p50								00 09	00 20									05 46	
—	5	Ware	d			23p54								00 13	00 24									05 50	
—	7	**Hertford East**	a			00 01								00 19	00 31									05 56	
20	—	Roydon	d	23p24	23p26											00 26									
22¾	—	Harlow Town	d	23p28	23p30			23p52	23p54	23p58		00 05				00 30			05 10		05 17	05 37			
24½	—	Harlow Mill	d	23p31	23p33											00 33									
26¾	—	Sawbridgeworth	d	23p34	23p37					00 03		00 10				00 37						05 42			
30¼	—	**Bishops Stortford**	a	23p41	23p44			00 02	00 04	00 10		00 17				00 44			05 20		05 27	05 49			
—	—		d	23p42	23p44			00 03	00 04	00 11									05 20		05 27	05 50			05 55
33¾	0	Stansted Mountfitchet	d	23p46	23p48					00 15									05 24	05 27	05 31				05 59
—	—	**Stansted Airport**	a					00 12	00 13								04 30	05 00	05 39		05 39	05 59			
—	3¾	**Stansted Airport**	d																						
35½	8¼	Elsenham	d	23p50	23p52					00 19															06 03
40	—	Newport (Essex)	d	23p55	23p57					00 24															06 08
41¾	—	Audley End	d	23p58	23p59					00 27										05 37					06 11
45¾	—	Great Chesterford	d	00 03	00 05					00 32															06 16
49	—	Whittlesford Parkway	d	00 08	00 10					00 37															06 21
52½	—	Shelford	d	00 12	00 14					00 41															06 25
55¾	—	**Cambridge**	a	00 19	00 21					00 48										05 53					06 32

		XC ◇1	LE 1	LE 1	LE 1	LE	LE 1	LE 1		LE 1	LE 1	LE 1	LE 1	LE 1	XC ◇1	LE 1	LE 1	LE 1		LE	LE 1	LE 1	LE 1	LE 1	LE
London Liverpool Street 15 ⊖	d		05 25	05 28	05 40	05 42	05 52	05 55		05 58		06 10	06 12	06 25		06 28	06 40			06 42	06 55	06 58		07 10	07 12
Bethnal Green	d																								
Hackney Downs	d					05 49							06 18							06 49					07 19
Stratford 7 ⊖	d						06 03																07 02		
Clapton	d																								
Seven Sisters ⊖	d										←														
Tottenham Hale ⊖	d		05u37	05 40	05u52	05 55	06 15	06u07		06 10	06 15	06u22	06 25	06u37		06 40	06u52			06 55	07u07	07 10	07 13	07u22	07 25
Northumberland Park	d						↪				06 17												07 15		
Angel Road	d										06 19												07 17		
Ponders End	d					05 59							06 29							06 59					07 29
Brimsdown	d					06 02							06 32							07 02					07 32
Enfield Lock	d					06 04					06 24		06 34							07 04			07 22		07 34
Waltham Cross	d					06 07							06 37							07 07					07 37
Cheshunt	d		05 45	05 48		06 09				06 18	06 28		06 39			06 48				07 09		07 18	07 26		07 39
Broxbourne 3	a		05 49	05 53		06 14				06 22	06 32		06 44			06 52				07 14		07 22	07 30		07 44
Broxbourne 3	d		05 49	05 53		06 14				06 24	06 36		06 44			06 54				07 14		07 22	07 34		07 44
Rye House	d										06 39		06 47							07 17					07 47
St Margarets (Herts)	d										06 42		06 50							07 20					07 50
Ware	d										06 46		06 54							07 24					07 54
Hertford East	a					06 27					06 53		07 01							07 31					08 01
Roydon	d			05 57						06 28						06 58						07 26			
Harlow Town	d		05 55	06 01				06 25		06 32				06 55		07 08					07 24	07 30	07 40		
Harlow Mill	d			06 04						06 35						07 11						07 33			
Sawbridgeworth	d			06 07						06 38						07 14		←				07 37			
Bishops Stortford	a		06 05	06 14	06 18					06 45		06 49				07 21	07 15	07 21				07 44	07 51	07 47	
	d		06 05	06 14	06 18					06 45		06 49				07 26	07 18	07 26				07 44		07 48	
Stansted Mountfitchet	d			06 19	06 23					06 50						↪	07 23	07 30				07 48			
Stansted Airport	a		06 15		06 29			06 43				06 59		07 13			07 30				07 42			07 59	
Stansted Airport	d	06 06													07 21										
Elsenham	d			06 22						06 53								07 34				07 52			
Newport (Essex)	d			06 28						06 59								07 39				07 57			
Audley End	d	06 23		06 31						07 02					07 37			07 42				08 00			
Great Chesterford	d			06 36						07 07								07 47				08 05			
Whittlesford Parkway	d			06 40						07 11								07 52				08 10			
Shelford	d			06 45						07 16								07 56				08 14			
Cambridge	a	06 37		06 58						07 25					07 58			08 06				08 23			

A MThFO

b Previous night, stops to pick up only

London - Broxbourne, Hertford East, Bishops Stortford, Stansted Airport and Cambridge

		LE	LE	LE		XC	LE	LE	LE	LE	LE	LE	LE	LE		LE	LE	XC	LE	LE	LE	LE	LE	LE	
		1	1	1		◇1	1	1	1	1	1	1	1	1		1	1	◇1	1		1	1	1	1	
		🚲					🚲		🚲			🚲				🚲			🚲		🚲			🚲	
London Liverpool Street 15 ⊖	d	07 25	07 28				07 40	07 42	07 55	07 58		08 10	08 12			08 25	08 28		08 40	08 42	08 55	08 58		09 10	
Bethnal Green	d																								
Hackney Downs	d							07 48					08 18							08 49					
Stratford 7 ⊖	d			07 33							08 03			08 20									08 58		
Clapton	d																								
Seven Sisters ⊖	d																								
Tottenham Hale ⊖	d	07u37	07 40	07 43			07u52	07 55	08u07	08 10	08 13	08u22	08 25	08 29		08u37	08 40		08u52	08 55	09u07	09 10	09 14	09u22	
Northumberland Park	d			07 45							08 15			08 32									09 16		
Angel Road	d			07 47							08 17			08 34									09 18		
Ponders End	d							07 59					08 29							08 59					
Brimsdown	d							08 02					08 32							09 02					
Enfield Lock	d			07 52				08 04			08 22		08 34	08 39						09 04			09 23		
Waltham Cross	d							08 07					08 37							09 07					
Cheshunt	d		07 48	07 56				08 09		08 18	08 26		08 39	08 42			08 48			09 09		09 18	09 27		
Broxbourne 3	a		07 52	08 00				08 14		08 22	08 30		08 44	08 47			08 52			09 14		09 22	09 31		
Broxbourne 3	d		07 52					08 14		08 22	08 34		08 44				08 52			09 14		09 22	09 35		
Rye House	d							08 17					08 47							09 17					
St Margarets (Herts)	d							08 20					08 50							09 20					
Ware	d							08 24					08 54							09 24					
Hertford East	a							08 31					09 01							09 31					
Roydon	d		07 56							08 26												09 26			
Harlow Town	d	07 54	08 00						08 24	08 30	08 40					08 54	08 58				09 24	09 30	09 41		
Harlow Mill	d		08 03							08 33												09 33			
Sawbridgeworth	d		08 07							08 37							09 03					09 37			
Bishops Stortford	a		08 14				08 18			08 44	08 52	08 47					09 10		09 16			09 44	09 52	09 47	
	d		08 14				08 18			08 44		08 48					09 11		09 18			09 44		09 48	
Stansted Mountfitchet	d		08 18				08 23			08 48									09 23			09 48			
Stansted Airport	a	08 13					08 30		08 42			09 00				09 12			09 30		09 42			09 57	
Stansted Airport	d					08 21												09 21							
Elsenham	d		08 22							08 52												09 52			
Newport (Essex)	d		08 27							08 57												09 57			
Audley End	d		08 30			08 37				09 00							09 23	09 37				10 00			
Great Chesterford	d		08 35							09 05												10 05			
Whittlesford Parkway	d		08 40							09 10							09 30					10 10			
Shelford	d		08 44							09 14												10 14			
Cambridge	a		08 54			08 58				09 24							09 42	09 58				10 24			

		LE	LE	LE	XC	LE	LE	LE	LE	LE		LE	LE	LE	LE	LE	LE	XC	LE	LE		LE	LE	LE	LE
			1	1	◇1	1	1	1	1	1		1	1	1	1	1	1	◇1	1	1		1	1	1	1
			🚲				🚲			🚲				🚲		🚲				🚲				🚲	
London Liverpool Street 15 ⊖	d	09 12	09 25	09 28			09 40		09 42	09 55		09 58		10 10	10 12	10 25	10 28			10 40			10 42	10 55	10 58
Bethnal Green	d																								
Hackney Downs	d	09 19							09 48						10 18								10 48		
Stratford 7 ⊖	d					09 33							10 03						10 33						
Clapton	d																								
Seven Sisters ⊖	d																								
Tottenham Hale ⊖	d	09 25	09u37	09 40		09 44	09u52		09 55	10u07		10 10	10 13	10u22	10 25	10u37	10 40		10 43	10u52			10 55	11u07	11 10
Northumberland Park	d					09 46							10 15						10 45						
Angel Road	d					09 48																			
Ponders End	d	09 29							09 59						10 29								10 59		
Brimsdown	d	09 32							10 02						10 32								11 02		
Enfield Lock	d	09 34				09 53			10 04				10 21		10 34				10 51				11 04		
Waltham Cross	d	09 37							10 07						10 37								11 07		
Cheshunt	d	09 39		09 48		09 57			10 09			10 18	10 25		10 39		10 48		10 55				11 09		11 18
Broxbourne 3	a	09 44		09 52		10 01			10 14			10 22	10 29		10 44		10 52		10 59				11 14		11 22
Broxbourne 3	d	09 44		09 52		10 05			10 14			10 22	10 33		10 44		10 52		11 03				11 14		11 22
Rye House	d	09 47							10 17						10 47								11 17		
St Margarets (Herts)	d	09 50							10 20						10 50								11 20		
Ware	d	09 54							10 24						10 54								11 24		
Hertford East	a	10 01							10 31						11 01								11 31		
Roydon	d					10 09						10 26							11 08						11 26
Harlow Town	d		09 54	09 58		10 13				10 24		10 30	10 40			10 54	10 58		11 12					11 24	11 30
Harlow Mill	d					10 16						10 33							11 15						11 33
Sawbridgeworth	d			10 03		10 20		←				10 37					11 03		11 18			←			11 37
Bishops Stortford	a			10 10		10 27	10 14	10 27				10 44	10 51	10 47			11 10		11 25	11 15		11 25			11 44
	d			10 11		10 27	10 15	10 27				10 44		10 48			11 11		11 26	11 15		11 26			11 44
Stansted Mountfitchet	d					→		10 31				10 48							→			11 30			11 48
Stansted Airport	a		10 12				10 30	10 39		10 42				10 57		11 12				11 25		11 39		11 42	
Stansted Airport	d				10 21													11 25							
Elsenham	d											10 52													11 52
Newport (Essex)	d											10 57													11 57
Audley End	d			10 23	10 37							11 00					11 23	11 37							12 00
Great Chesterford	d											11 05													12 05
Whittlesford Parkway	d			10 30								11 10					11 30								12 10
Shelford	d											11 14													12 14
Cambridge	a			10 41	10 58							11 21					11 40	11 58							12 21

London - Broxbourne, Hertford East, Bishops Stortford, Stansted Airport and Cambridge

		LE	LE	LE	LE	XC		LE	LE	LE	LE	LE	LE	LE	LE	LE		LE	XC	LE	LE	LE	LE	LE	LE
		1	1	1	1	◇1		1	1	1	1	1	1	1	1	1		1	◇1	1	1	1	1	1	1
		🛒		🛒					🛒			🛒		🛒		🛒					🛒			🛒	
London Liverpool Street 15 ⊖	d	11 10	11 12	11 25	11 28				11 40		11 42	11 55	11 58	12 10	12 12	12 25		12 28			12 40		12 42	12 55	12 58
Bethnal Green	d																								
Hackney Downs	d		11 18								11 49				12 18								12 48		
Stratford 7 ⊖	d							11 33												12 33					
Clapton	d																								
Seven Sisters ⊖	d																								
Tottenham Hale ⊖	d	11u22	11 25	11u37	11 40			11 43	11u52		11 55	12u07	12 10	12u22	12 25	12u37		12 40		12 43	12u52		12 55	13u07	13 10
Northumberland Park	d							11 45												12 45					
Angel Road	d																								
Ponders End	d		11 29								11 59				12 29								12 59		
Brimsdown	d		11 32								12 02				12 32								13 02		
Enfield Lock	d		11 34					11 51			12 04				12 34					12 51			13 04		
Waltham Cross	d		11 37								12 07				12 37								13 07		
Cheshunt	d		11 39		11 48			11 55			12 09		12 18		12 39			12 48		12 55			13 09		13 18
Broxbourne 3	a		11 44		11 52			11 59			12 14		12 22		12 44			12 52		12 59			13 14		13 22
Broxbourne 3	d		11 44		11 52			12 03			12 14		12 22		12 44			12 52		13 03			13 14		13 22
Rye House	d		11 47								12 17				12 47								13 17		
St Margarets (Herts)	d		11 50								12 20				12 50								13 20		
Ware	d		11 54								12 24				12 54								13 24		
Hertford East	a		12 01								12 31				13 01								13 31		
Roydon	d							12 08					12 26							13 08					13 26
Harlow Town	d			11 54	11 58			12 12				12 24	12 30			12 54		12 58		13 12				13 24	13 30
Harlow Mill	d							12 15					12 33							13 15					13 33
Sawbridgeworth	d				12 03			12 18		←			12 37					13 03		13 18		←			13 37
Bishops Stortford	a	11 47			12 10			12 25	12 15	12 25			12 44	12 47				13 10		13 25	13 15	13 25			13 44
	d	11 48			12 11			12 26	12 15	12 26			12 44	12 48				13 11		13 26	13 15	13 26			13 44
Stansted Mountfitchet	d							↪		12 30			12 48							↪		13 30			13 48
Stansted Airport	a	11 57		12 12					12 25	12 39		12 42		12 57		13 12					13 25	13 39		13 42	
Stansted Airport	d					12 25													13 25						
Elsenham	d												12 52												13 52
Newport (Essex)	d												12 57												13 57
Audley End	d				12 23	12 37							13 00					13 23	13 37						14 00
Great Chesterford	d												13 05												14 05
Whittlesford Parkway	d				12 30								13 10					13 30							14 10
Shelford	d												13 14												14 14
Cambridge	a				12 40	12 58							13 21					13 40	13 58						14 21

		LE		LE	LE	LE	XC	LE	LE	LE	LE	LE		LE	LE	LE	LE	LE	XC	LE	LE	LE		LE	LE
		1		1	1	1	◇1	1	1	1	1	1		1	1	1	1	1	◇1	1	1	1		1	1
		🛒			🛒				🛒			🛒			🛒		🛒				🛒				🛒
London Liverpool Street 15 ⊖	d	13 10		13 12	13 25	13 28			13 40		13 42	13 55		13 58	14 10	14 12	14 25	14 28			14 40			14 42	14 55
Bethnal Green	d																								
Hackney Downs	d			13 18							13 48					14 18								14 48	
Stratford 7 ⊖	d							13 33												14 33					
Clapton	d																								
Seven Sisters ⊖	d																								
Tottenham Hale ⊖	d	13u22		13 25	13u37	13 40		13 43	13u52		13 55	14u07		14 10	14u22	14 25	14u37	14 40		14 43	14u52			14 55	15u07
Northumberland Park	d							13 45												14 45					
Angel Road	d																								
Ponders End	d			13 29							13 59					14 29								14 59	
Brimsdown	d			13 32							14 02					14 32								15 02	
Enfield Lock	d			13 34				13 51			14 04					14 34				14 51				15 04	
Waltham Cross	d			13 37							14 07					14 37								15 07	
Cheshunt	d			13 39		13 48		13 55			14 09			14 18		14 39		14 48		14 55				15 09	
Broxbourne 3	a			13 44		13 52		13 59			14 14			14 22		14 44		14 52		14 59				15 14	
Broxbourne 3	d			13 44		13 52		14 03			14 14			14 22		14 44		14 52		15 03				15 14	
Rye House	d			13 47							14 17					14 47								15 17	
St Margarets (Herts)	d			13 50							14 20					14 50								15 20	
Ware	d			13 54							14 24					14 54								15 24	
Hertford East	a			14 01							14 31					15 01								15 31	
Roydon	d							14 08						14 26						15 08					
Harlow Town	d				13 54	13 58		14 12				14 24		14 30			14 54	14 58		15 12					15 24
Harlow Mill	d							14 15						14 33						15 15					
Sawbridgeworth	d					14 03		14 18		←				14 37				15 03		15 18		←			
Bishops Stortford	a	13 47				14 10		14 25	14 15	14 25				14 44	14 47			15 10		15 25	15 15	15 25			
	d	13 48				14 11		14 26	14 15	14 26				14 44	14 48			15 11		15 26	15 15	15 26			
Stansted Mountfitchet	d							↪		14 30				14 48						↪		15 30			
Stansted Airport	a	13 57			14 12				14 25	14 39		14 42			14 57		15 12				15 25	15 39			15 42
Stansted Airport	d						14 25												15 25						
Elsenham	d													14 52											
Newport (Essex)	d													14 57											
Audley End	d					14 23	14 37							15 00				15 23	15 37						
Great Chesterford	d													15 05											
Whittlesford Parkway	d					14 30								15 10				15 30							
Shelford	d													15 14											
Cambridge	a					14 40	14 58							15 21				15 40	15 58						

London - Broxbourne, Hertford East, Bishops Stortford, Stansted Airport and Cambridge

Station		LE [1]	LE [1] 🚲	LE [1]	LE [1] 🚲	LE [1]	XC ◇[1]	LE [1]		LE [1] 🚲	LE [1]	LE [1]	LE [1] 🚲	LE [1]	LE [1] 🚲	LE	LE [1] 🚲	LE [1]		LE	XC ◇[1]	LE [1] 🚲	LE [1]	LE	LE [1] 🚲
London Liverpool Street [15] ⊖	d	14 58	15 10	15 12	15 25	15 28				15 40		15 42	15 55	15 58	16 10	16 12	16 25	16 28				16 40	16 43	16 45	16 55
Bethnal Green	d																								
Hackney Downs	d			15 18								15 48				16 18								16 51	
Stratford [7] ⊖	d							15 33												16 32					
Clapton	d																								
Seven Sisters ⊖	d																								
Tottenham Hale ⊖	d	15 10	15u22	15 25	15u37	15 40		15 43		15u52		15 55	16u07	16 10	16u22	16 25	16u37	16 40		16 43		16u52	16 55	16 58	17u07
Northumberland Park	d							15 45												16 45					
Angel Road	d							15 47												16 47					
Ponders End	d			15 29								15 59				16 29								17 02	
Brimsdown	d			15 32								16 02				16 32								17 05	
Enfield Lock	d			15 34				15 52				16 04				16 34				16 52				17 07	
Waltham Cross	d			15 37								16 07				16 37				16 55				17 10	
Cheshunt	d	15 18		15 39		15 48		15 56				16 09		16 18		16 39				16 57			17 04	17 12	
Broxbourne [3]	a	15 22		15 44		15 52		16 00				16 14		16 22		16 44		16 51		17 04			17 08	17 17	
Broxbourne [3]	d	15 22		15 44		15 52		16 04				16 14		16 22		16 44		16 52					17 09	17 17	
Rye House	d			15 47								16 17				16 48								17 21	
St Margarets (Herts)	d			15 50								16 20				16 51								17 24	
Ware	d			15 54								16 24				16 55								17 28	
Hertford East	a			16 01								16 31				17 03								17 36	
Roydon	d	15 26						16 08						16 26									17 13		
Harlow Town	d	15 30			15 54	15 58		16 12					16 24	16 30			16 54	16 59					17 18		17 27
Harlow Mill	d	15 33						16 15						16 33									17 21		
Sawbridgeworth	d	15 37				16 03		16 19			←			16 37				17 04					17 24		
Bishops Stortford	a	15 44	15 47			16 10		16 26		16 15	16 26			16 44	16 47			17 11				17 17	17 31		
	d	15 44	15 48			16 11		16 26		16 15	16 26			16 44	16 48			17 11				17 18	17 32		
Stansted Mountfitchet	d	15 48				16 15		→			16 30			16 48				17 15					17 36		
Stansted Airport	a		15 59		16 12					16 25	16 39		16 42		17 01		17 14					17 32			17 47
Stansted Airport	d						16 25														17 18				
Elsenham	d	15 52				16 19								16 52									17 40		
Newport (Essex)	d	15 58				16 24								16 57									17 45		
Audley End	d	16 02				16 27	16 37							17 00				17 25			17 33		17 49		
Great Chesterford	d	16 07				16 32								17 05									17 54		
Whittlesford Parkway	d	16 12				16 37								17 10				17 33					17 58		
Shelford	d	16 16				16 41								17 14									18 03		
Cambridge	a	16 28				16 49	16 58							17 20				17 44			17 49		18 11		

Station		LE [1]	LE	LE [1] 🚲		LE [1]	LE	LE [1] 🚲	LE [1]	LE	XC ◇[1]	LE [1] 🚲	LE [1]	LE		LE [1] 🚲	LE [1]	LE	LE [1] 🚲	LE [1]	LE	LE [1] 🚲	LE [1]	XC ◇[1]	
London Liverpool Street [15] ⊖	d	16 58		17 10		17 13	17 15	17 25	17 28			17 40	17 43	17 45		17 55	17 58		18 10	18 13	18 15	18 25	18 28		
Bethnal Green	d																								
Hackney Downs	d						17 21							17 51							18 21				
Stratford [7] ⊖	d		17 02							17 32								18 02							
Clapton	d																								
Seven Sisters ⊖	d																								
Tottenham Hale ⊖	d	17 10	17 13	17u22		17 25	17 28	17u37	17 40	17 43		17u52	17 55	17 58		18u07	18 10	18 13	18u22	18 25	18 28	18u37	18 40		
Northumberland Park	d		17 15							17 45								18 15							
Angel Road	d		17 17							17 47								18 17							
Ponders End	d						17 32							18 02							18 32				
Brimsdown	d						17 35							18 05							18 35				
Enfield Lock	d		17 22				17 37			17 52				18 07				18 22			18 37				
Waltham Cross	d		17 25				17 40			17 55				18 10				18 25			18 40				
Cheshunt	d		17 27			17 34	17 42			17 57			18 04	18 12				18 27		18 34	18 42				
Broxbourne [3]	a	17 24	17 32			17 39	17 47		17 54	18 04			18 08	18 17			18 24	18 32		18 39	18 47		18 54		
Broxbourne [3]	d	17 25	17 35			17 39	17 50		17 54				18 09	18 17			18 25	18 35		18 39	18 47		18 55		
Rye House	d		17 39				17 54							18 21				18 39			18 51				
St Margarets (Herts)	d		17 42				17 57							18 24				18 42			18 54				
Ware	d		17 48				18 01							18 28				18 48			18 58				
Hertford East	a		17 56				18 09							18 36				18 56			19 06				
Roydon	d					17 43							18 13							18 43					
Harlow Town	d	17 32				17 48		17 54				18 10	18 18			18 27				18 48		18 57	19 02		
Harlow Mill	d					17 51							18 21							18 51					
Sawbridgeworth	d					17 54			18 04				18 24				18 35			18 54			19 07		
Bishops Stortford	a	17 42		17 47		18 01		18 05	18 11			18 20	18 31			18 35	18 42		18 47	19 01			19 14		
	d	17 42		17 48		18 02		18 06	18 11			18 20	18 32			18 36	18 42		18 48	19 02			19 14		
Stansted Mountfitchet	d			17 52		18 06							18 36						18 52	19 06					
Stansted Airport	a			18 01				18 17				18 32				18 56			19 01			19 17			
Stansted Airport	d										18 21													19 21	
Elsenham	d					18 10							18 40							19 10					
Newport (Essex)	d					18 15							18 45							19 15					
Audley End	d	17 55				18 19			18 24		18 37		18 49				18 55			19 19			19 27	19 37	
Great Chesterford	d					18 24							18 54							19 24					
Whittlesford Parkway	d	18 03				18 28			18 32				18 58				19 03			19 28			19 35		
Shelford	d					18 33							19 03							19 33					
Cambridge	a	18 13				18 42			18 46		18 58		19 12				19 16			19 42			19 46	19 58	

London - Broxbourne, Hertford East, Bishops Stortford, Stansted Airport and Cambridge

		LE	LE 1 (trolley)	LE	LE 1	LE	LE 1 (trolley)	LE 1	LE	LE 1 (trolley)		LE 1	LE 1	LE 1 (trolley)	LE 1	XC ◇1	LE 1	LE 1 (trolley)	LE 1	LE 1		LE 1 (trolley)	LE 1	LE 1 (trolley)	LE 1
London Liverpool Street 15 ⊖	d		18 40		18 43	18 45	18 55	18 58		19 10		19 13	19 15	19 25	19 28			19 40		19 42		19 55	19 58	20 10	20 12
Bethnal Green	d																								
Hackney Downs	d					18 51							19 21							19 48					20 18
Stratford 7 ⊖	d	18 32							19 02								19 33								
Clapton	d																								
Seven Sisters ⊖	d																								
Tottenham Hale ⊖	d	18 43	18u52		18 55	18 58	19u07	19 10	19 13	19u22		19 25	19 28	19u37	19 40		19 43	19u52		19 55		20u07	20 10	20u22	20 25
Northumberland Park	d	18 45							19 15								19 45								
Angel Road	d	18 47							19 17																
Ponders End	d					19 02							19 32							19 59					20 29
Brimsdown	d					19 05							19 35							20 02					20 32
Enfield Lock	d	18 52				19 07			19 22				19 37				19 51			20 04					20 34
Waltham Cross	d	18 55				19 10			19 25				19 40							20 07					20 37
Cheshunt	d	18 57			19 04	19 12			19 27			19 34	19 42		19 49		19 55			20 09			20 18		20 39
Broxbourne 3	a	19 02			19 09	19 17		19 24	19 32			19 39	19 47		19 54		19 59			20 14			20 22		20 44
Broxbourne 3	d	19 05			19 09	19 17		19 25	19 35			19 39	19 47		19 54		20 03			20 14			20 22		20 44
Rye House	d					19 21							19 50							20 17					20 47
St Margarets (Herts)	d					19 24							19 53							20 20					20 50
Ware	d					19 28							19 57							20 24					20 54
Hertford East	a					19 36							20 04							20 31					21 01
Roydon	d	19 10			19 13							19 43			19 59		20 08						20 26		
Harlow Town	d	19 14			19 18		19 27	19 32	19 42			19 48		19 57	20 03		20 12					20 24	20 30		
Harlow Mill	d	19 17			19 21							19 51			20 06		20 15						20 33		
Sawbridgeworth	d	19 20		←	19 24				19 47			19 54			20 09		20 18		←				20 37		
Bishops Stortford	a	19 27	19 18	19 27	19 31			19 42	19 56	19 47		20 01			20 16		20 25	20 20	20 25				20 44	20 48	
	d	19 28	19 18	19 28	19 32			19 42		19 47		20 02			20 17		20 26	20 21	20 26				20 44	20 48	
Stansted Mountfitchet	d	→	19 23	19 32	19 36							20 06			20 21		→		20 30				20 48		
Stansted Airport	a		19 32	19 41			19 47			19 57				20 15				20 30	20 39			20 42		20 58	
Stansted Airport	d															20 21									
Elsenham	d				19 40							20 10			20 25								20 52		
Newport (Essex)	d				19 45							20 15			20 30								20 57		
Audley End	d				19 49			19 55				20 19			20 33	20 37							21 00		
Great Chesterford	d				19 54							20 24			20 38								21 05		
Whittlesford Parkway	d				19 58			20 03				20 28			20 43								21 10		
Shelford	d				20 03							20 33			20 47								21 14		
Cambridge	a				20 13			20 14				20 40			20 56	20 59							21 22		

		LE 1 (trolley)	LE 1	XC 1	LE 1	LE 1 (trolley)		LE 1	LE 1	LE 1 (trolley)	LE 1	LE 1 (trolley)	LE 1	LE 1 (trolley)	LE 1	XC 1		LE 1	LE 1 (trolley)	LE 1	LE 1	LE 1 (trolley)	LE 1	LE 1 (trolley)	LE 1
London Liverpool Street 15 ⊖	d	20 25	20 28			20 40			20 42	20 55	20 58	21 10	21 12	21 25	21 28				21 40		21 42	21 55	21 58	22 10	22 12
Bethnal Green	d																								
Hackney Downs	d								20 48				21 18								21 48				22 18
Stratford 7 ⊖	d				20 33													21 33							
Clapton	d																								
Seven Sisters ⊖	d																								
Tottenham Hale ⊖	d	20u37	20 40		20 43	20u52			20 55	21u07	21 10	21u22	21 25	21u37	21 40			21 43	21u52		21 55	22u07	22 10	22u22	22 25
Northumberland Park	d				20 45													21 45							
Angel Road	d																								
Ponders End	d								20 59				21 29								21 59				22 29
Brimsdown	d								21 02				21 32								22 02				22 32
Enfield Lock	d				20 51				21 04				21 34					21 51			22 04				22 34
Waltham Cross	d								21 07				21 37								22 07				22 37
Cheshunt	d		20 48		20 55				21 09		21 18		21 39		21 48			21 55			22 09		22 18		22 39
Broxbourne 3	a		20 52		20 59				21 14		21 22		21 44		21 52			21 59			22 14		22 22		22 44
Broxbourne 3	d		20 52		21 03				21 14		21 22		21 44		21 52			22 03			22 14		22 22		22 44
Rye House	d								21 17				21 47								22 17				22 47
St Margarets (Herts)	d								21 20				21 50								22 20				22 50
Ware	d								21 24				21 54								22 24				22 54
Hertford East	a								21 31				22 01								22 31				23 01
Roydon	d				21 08						21 26							22 08					22 26		
Harlow Town	d	20 54	20 58		21 12					21 24	21 30			21 54	21 58			22 12				22 24	22 30		
Harlow Mill	d				21 15						21 33							22 15					22 33		
Sawbridgeworth	d		21 03		21 18			←			21 37				22 03			22 18		←			22 37		
Bishops Stortford	a		21 10		21 25	21 15		21 25			21 44	21 47			22 10			22 25	22 15	22 25			22 44	22 47	
	d		21 11		21 26	21 15		21 26			21 44	21 48			22 11			22 26	22 15	22 26			22 44	22 48	
Stansted Mountfitchet	d	21 05			→			21 30			21 48			22 05				→		22 30			22 48		
Stansted Airport	a	21 13				21 25		21 39		21 42		21 57		22 13					22 25	22 39		22 42		22 57	
Stansted Airport	d			21 25												22 25									
Elsenham	d										21 52												22 52		
Newport (Essex)	d										21 57												22 57		
Audley End	d		21 23	21 37							22 00				22 23	22 37							23 00		
Great Chesterford	d										22 05												23 05		
Whittlesford Parkway	d		21 30								22 10				22 30								23 10		
Shelford	d										22 14												23 14		
Cambridge	a		21 40	21 58							22 21				22 40	22 56							23 22		

London - Broxbourne, Hertford East, Bishops Stortford, Stansted Airport and Cambridge

Mondays to Fridays

		XC	LE	LE	LE	LE	LE	LE	LE	LE	LE	LE	LE	LE FX	LE FO
		1	1 🛒	1	1	1 🛒	1	1 🛒	1	1	1	1	1	1	1
London Liverpool Street 15 ⊖	d		22 25	22 28		22 40	22 42	22 55	22 58	23 12	23 25	23 28	23 40	23 58	23 58
Bethnal Green	d														
Hackney Downs	d						22 48			23 18			23 46		
Stratford 7 ⊖	d				22 33										
Clapton	d												23 49		
Seven Sisters ⊖	d														
Tottenham Hale ⊖	d		22u37	22 40	22 43	22u52	22 55	23u07	23 10	23 25	23u37	23 40	23 53	00 10	00 10
Northumberland Park	d				22 45								23 55		
Angel Road	d														
Ponders End	d						22 59			23 29			23 59		
Brimsdown	d						23 02			23 32			00 02		
Enfield Lock	d				22 51		23 04			23 34			00 04		
Waltham Cross	d						23 07			23 37			00 07		
Cheshunt	d			22 48	22 55		23 09		23 18	23 39		23 48	00 09	00 18	00 18
Broxbourne 3	a			22 52	22 59		23 14		23 22	23 44		23 52	00 14	00 22	00 22
Broxbourne 3	d			22 52	23 03		23 14		23 22	23 44		23 52	00 14	00 22	00 22
Rye House	d						23 17			23 47			00 17		
St Margarets (Herts)	d						23 20			23 50			00 20		
Ware	d						23 24			23 54			00 24		
Hertford East	a						23 31			00 01			00 31		
Roydon	d				23 08				23 26					00 26	00 26
Harlow Town	d		22 54	22 58	23 12			23 24	23 30		23 54	23 58		00 30	00 30
Harlow Mill	d				23 15				23 33					00 33	00 33
Sawbridgeworth	d			23 03	23 18				23 37			00 03		00 37	00 37
Bishops Stortford	a			23 10	23 26	23 15			23 44		00 04	00 10		00 44	00 44
	d			23 11		23 15			23 44		00 04	00 11			00 44
Stansted Mountfitchet	d		23 05					23 35	23 48			00 15			00 48
Stansted Airport	a		23 13			23 25		23 43			00 13				
Stansted Airport	d	22 57													
Elsenham	d								23 52			00 19			00 52
Newport (Essex)	d								23 57			00 24			00 57
Audley End	d	23 10		23 23					23 59			00 27			01 00
Great Chesterford	d								00 05			00 32			01 05
Whittlesford Parkway	d			23 30					00 10			00 37			01 10
Shelford	d								00 14			00 41			
Cambridge	a	23 32		23 40					00 21			00 48			01 19

Saturdays

		LE	LE	LE	LE	LE	LE	LE	XC	LE	LE	LE	LE	LE	LE	LE	LE	XC	LE	LE	LE	LE	LE
		1	1	1	1	1	1	1	◇1	1	1	1	1	1	1	1	1	◇1	1	1	1	1	1
London Liverpool Street 15 ⊖	d	22p58	23p12	23p25	23p28	23p40	23p58	04 10		04 40		05 10	05 23	05 25		05 40	05 42			05 55	05 58	06 10	06 12
Bethnal Green	d																						
Hackney Downs	d		23p18			23p46											05 48						06 18
Stratford 7 ⊖	d												05 33										
Clapton	d					23p49																	
Seven Sisters ⊖	d														←								
Tottenham Hale ⊖	d	23p10	23p25	23b37	23p40	23p53	00 10			04u52		05u22	05 43	05u37	05 43	05u52	05 55			06u07	06 10	06u22	06 25
Northumberland Park	d					23p55							→		05 45								
Angel Road	d																						
Ponders End	d		23p29			23p59											05 59						06 29
Brimsdown	d		23p32			00 02											06 02						06 32
Enfield Lock	d		23p34			00 04									05 51		06 04						06 34
Waltham Cross	d		23p37			00 07											06 07						06 37
Cheshunt	d	23p18	23p39		23p48	00 09	00 18			05 00				05 45	05 55		06 09				06 18		06 39
Broxbourne 3	a	23p22	23p44		23p52	00 14	00 22			05 04				05 49	05 59		06 14				06 22		06 44
Broxbourne 3	d	23p22	23p44		23p52	00 14	00 22			05 04				05 49	06 03		06 14				06 22		06 44
Rye House	d		23p47			00 17											06 17						06 47
St Margarets (Herts)	d		23p50			00 20											06 20						06 50
Ware	d		23p54			00 24											06 24						06 54
Hertford East	a		00 01			00 31											06 31						07 01
Roydon	d	23p26					00 26								06 08						06 26		
Harlow Town	d	23p30		23p54	23p58		00 30			05 10		05 37		05 55	06 12					06 24	06 30		
Harlow Mill	d	23p33					00 33								06 15						06 33		
Sawbridgeworth	d	23p37			00 03		00 37					05 42			06 18				←		06 37		
Bishops Stortford	a	23p44		00 04	00 10		00 44			05 20		05 49		06 05	06 25	06 15			06 25		06 44	06 47	
	d	23p44		00 04	00 11		00 44			05 20	05 42	05 50		06 06	06 26	06 15			06 26		06 44	06 48	
Stansted Mountfitchet	d	23p48			00 15		00 48			05 24	05 46				→				06 30		06 48		
Stansted Airport	a			00 13				05 00		05 39	05 53	05 59		06 15		06 25			06 39	06 42		06 57	
Stansted Airport	d								05 25									06 25					
Elsenham	d	23p52			00 19		00 52														06 52		
Newport (Essex)	d	23p57			00 24		00 57														06 57		
Audley End	d	23p59			00 27		01 00		05 37									06 37			07 00		
Great Chesterford	d	00 05			00 32		01 05														07 05		
Whittlesford Parkway	d	00 10			00 37		01 10														07 10		
Shelford	d	00 14			00 41																07 14		
Cambridge	a	00 21			00 48		01 19		05 54									06 55			07 21		

b Previous night, stops to pick up only

Table 22

Saturdays

London - Broxbourne, Hertford East, Bishops Stortford, Stansted Airport and Cambridge

		LE 1	LE 1	LE 1	LE 1	LE 1		LE 1	XC ◇1	LE 1	LE 1	LE 1	LE 1 🛒	LE 1	LE 1 🛒	LE 1		XC ◇1	LE 1	LE 1 🛒	LE 1	LE 1	LE 1 🛒	LE 1	LE 1 🛒
London Liverpool Street 15 ⊖	d	06 23	06 25	06 28		06 40		06 42			06 55	06 58	07 10	07 12	07 25	07 28				07 40		07 42	07 55	07 58	08 10
Bethnal Green	d																								
Hackney Downs	d							06 48						07 18								07 48			
Stratford 7 ⊖	d	06 33																	07 33						
Clapton	d																								
Seven Sisters ⊖	d				←																				
Tottenham Hale ⊖	d	06 43	06u37	06 40	06 43	06u52		06 55			07u07	07 10	07u22	07 25	07u37	07 40			07 43	07u52		07 55	08u07	08 10	08u22
Northumberland Park	d	↦			06 45														07 45						
Angel Road	d																								
Ponders End	d							06 59						07 29								07 59			
Brimsdown	d							07 02						07 32								08 02			
Enfield Lock	d				06 51			07 04						07 34					07 51			08 04			
Waltham Cross	d							07 07						07 37								08 07			
Cheshunt	d			06 48	06 55			07 09				07 18		07 39		07 48			07 55			08 09		08 18	
Broxbourne 3	a			06 52	06 59			07 14				07 22		07 44		07 52			07 59			08 14		08 22	
Broxbourne 3	d			06 52	07 03			07 14				07 22		07 44		07 52			08 03			08 14		08 22	
Rye House	d							07 17						07 47								08 17			
St Margarets (Herts)	d							07 20						07 50								08 20			
Ware	d							07 24						07 54								08 24			
Hertford East	a							07 31						08 01								08 31			
Roydon	d				07 08							07 26							08 08					08 26	
Harlow Town	d		06 54	06 58	07 12						07 24	07 30			07 54	07 58			08 12				08 24	08 30	
Harlow Mill	d				07 15							07 33							08 15					08 33	
Sawbridgeworth	d			07 03	07 18					←		07 37				08 03			08 18		←			08 37	
Bishops Stortford	a			07 10	07 25	07 15				07 25		07 44	07 47			08 10			08 25	08 15	08 25			08 44	08 47
	d			07 11	07 26	07 15				07 26		07 44	07 48			08 11			08 26	08 15	08 26			08 44	08 48
Stansted Mountfitchet	d		07 05		↦					07 30		07 48			08 05				↦		08 30			08 48	
Stansted Airport	a		07 13			07 25				07 39	07 42		07 57		08 13					08 25	08 39		08 42		08 57
Stansted Airport	d								07 25									08 25							
Elsenham	d											07 52												08 52	
Newport (Essex)	d											07 57												08 57	
Audley End	d			07 23					07 37			08 00				08 23		08 37						09 00	
Great Chesterford	d											08 05												09 05	
Whittlesford Parkway	d			07 30								08 10				08 30								09 10	
Shelford	d			07 35												08 35									
Cambridge	a			07 42					07 55			08 19				08 42		08 58						09 19	

		LE 1		LE 1 🛒	LE 1	XC ◇1	LE 1	LE 1 🛒	LE 1	LE 1	LE 1 🛒	LE 1		LE 1 🛒	LE 1	LE 1 🛒	LE 1	XC ◇1	LE 1	LE 1 🛒	LE 1	LE 1		LE 1 🛒	LE 1
London Liverpool Street 15 ⊖	d	08 12		08 25	08 28			08 40		08 42	08 55	08 58		09 10	09 12	09 25	09 28			09 40		09 42		09 55	09 58
Bethnal Green	d																								
Hackney Downs	d	08 18								08 48					09 18							09 48			
Stratford 7 ⊖	d						08 33												09 33						
Clapton	d																								
Seven Sisters ⊖	d																								
Tottenham Hale ⊖	d	08 25		08u37	08 40		08 43	08u52		08 55	09u07	09 10		09u22	09 25	09u37	09 40		09 43	09u52		09 55		10u07	10 10
Northumberland Park	d						08 45												09 45						
Angel Road	d																								
Ponders End	d	08 29								08 59					09 29							09 59			
Brimsdown	d	08 32								09 02					09 32							10 02			
Enfield Lock	d	08 34					08 51			09 04					09 34				09 51			10 04			
Waltham Cross	d	08 37								09 07					09 37							10 07			
Cheshunt	d	08 39			08 48		08 55			09 09		09 18			09 39		09 48		09 55			10 09			10 18
Broxbourne 3	a	08 44			08 52		08 59			09 14		09 22			09 44		09 52		09 59			10 14			10 22
Broxbourne 3	d	08 44			08 52		09 03			09 14		09 22			09 44		09 52		10 03			10 14			10 22
Rye House	d	08 47								09 17					09 47							10 17			
St Margarets (Herts)	d	08 50								09 20					09 50							10 20			
Ware	d	08 54								09 24					09 54							10 24			
Hertford East	a	09 01								09 31					10 01							10 31			
Roydon	d						09 08					09 26							10 08						10 26
Harlow Town	d			08 54	08 58		09 12				09 24	09 30				09 54	09 58		10 12					10 24	10 30
Harlow Mill	d						09 15					09 33							10 15						10 33
Sawbridgeworth	d				09 03		09 18		←			09 37					10 03		10 18		←				10 37
Bishops Stortford	a				09 10		09 25	09 15	09 25			09 44		09 47			10 10		10 25	10 15	10 25				10 44
	d				09 11		09 26	09 15	09 26			09 44		09 48			10 11		10 26	10 15	10 26				10 44
Stansted Mountfitchet	d			09 05			↦		09 30			09 48				10 05			↦		10 30				10 48
Stansted Airport	a			09 13				09 25	09 39		09 42			09 57		10 13				10 25	10 39			10 42	
Stansted Airport	d					09 25												10 25							
Elsenham	d											09 52													10 52
Newport (Essex)	d											09 57													10 57
Audley End	d				09 23	09 37						10 00					10 23	10 37							11 00
Great Chesterford	d											10 05													11 05
Whittlesford Parkway	d				09 30							10 10					10 30								11 10
Shelford	d				09 35							10 14													11 14
Cambridge	a				09 42	09 58						10 21					10 40	10 58							11 21

Table 22

London - Broxbourne, Hertford East, Bishops Stortford, Stansted Airport and Cambridge

		LE	LE	LE	LE	XC	LE	LE		LE	LE	LE	LE	LE	LE	LE	LE	XC		LE	LE	LE	LE	LE	LE
		1	1	1	1	◇1	1	1		1	1	1	1	1	1	1	1	◇1		1	1	1	1	1	1
		🛒		🛒				🛒				🛒		🛒		🛒					🛒			🛒	
London Liverpool Street 15 ⊖	d	10 10	10 12	10 25	10 28			10 40			10 42	10 55	10 58	11 10	11 12	11 25	11 28				11 40		11 42	11 55	11 58
Bethnal Green	d																								
Hackney Downs	d		10 18								10 48				11 18								11 48		
Stratford 7 ⊖	d						10 33													11 33					
Clapton	d																								
Seven Sisters ⊖	d																								
Tottenham Hale ⊖	d	10u22	10 25	10u37	10 40		10 43	10u52			10 55	11u07	11 10	11u22	11 25	11u37	11 40			11 43	11u52		11 55	12u07	12 10
Northumberland Park	d						10 45													11 45					
Angel Road	d																								
Ponders End	d		10 29								10 59				11 29								11 59		
Brimsdown	d		10 32								11 02				11 32								12 02		
Enfield Lock	d		10 34				10 51				11 04				11 34					11 51			12 04		
Waltham Cross	d		10 37								11 07				11 37								12 07		
Cheshunt	d		10 39		10 48		10 55				11 09		11 18		11 39		11 48			11 55			12 09		12 18
Broxbourne 3	a		10 44		10 52		10 59				11 14		11 22		11 44		11 52			11 59			12 14		12 22
Broxbourne 3	d		10 44		10 52		11 03				11 14		11 22		11 44		11 52			12 03			12 14		12 22
Rye House	d		10 47								11 17				11 47								12 17		
St Margarets (Herts)	d		10 50								11 20				11 50								12 20		
Ware	d		10 54								11 24				11 54								12 24		
Hertford East	a		11 01								11 31				12 01								12 31		
Roydon	d						11 08						11 26							12 08					12 26
Harlow Town	d			10 54	10 58		11 12					11 24	11 30			11 54	11 58			12 12				12 24	12 30
Harlow Mill	d						11 15						11 33							12 15					12 33
Sawbridgeworth	d				11 03		11 18			←			11 37				12 03			12 18		←			12 37
Bishops Stortford	a	10 47			11 10		11 25	11 15		11 25			11 44	11 47			12 10			12 25	12 15	12 25			12 44
	d	10 48			11 11		11 26	11 15		11 26			11 44	11 48			12 11			12 26	12 15	12 26			12 44
Stansted Mountfitchet	d			11 05			→			11 30			11 48			12 05				→		12 30			12 48
Stansted Airport	a	10 57		11 13				11 25		11 39		11 42		11 57		12 13					12 25	12 39		12 42	
Stansted Airport	d					11 25												12 25							
Elsenham	d												11 52												12 52
Newport (Essex)	d												11 57												12 57
Audley End	d				11 23	11 37							12 00				12 23	12 37							13 00
Great Chesterford	d												12 05												13 05
Whittlesford Parkway	d				11 30								12 10				12 30								13 10
Shelford	d												12 14												13 14
Cambridge	a				11 40	11 58							12 21				12 40	12 58							13 21

		LE	LE	LE		LE	XC	LE	LE	LE	LE	LE	LE	LE		LE	LE	LE	XC	LE	LE	LE	LE	LE	
		1	1	1		1	◇1	1	1	1	1	1	1	1		1	1	1	◇1	1	1	1	1	1	
		🛒		🛒					🛒			🛒		🛒			🛒				🛒			🛒	
London Liverpool Street 15 ⊖	d	12 10	12 12	12 25		12 28			12 40		12 42	12 55	12 58	13 10		13 12	13 25	13 28			13 40		13 42	13 55	
Bethnal Green	d																								
Hackney Downs	d		12 18								12 48					13 18							13 48		
Stratford 7 ⊖	d							12 33												13 33					
Clapton	d																								
Seven Sisters ⊖	d																								
Tottenham Hale ⊖	d	12u22	12 25	12u37		12 40		12 43	12u52		12 55	13u07	13 10	13u22		13 25	13u37	13 40		13 43	13u52		13 55	14u07	
Northumberland Park	d							12 45												13 45					
Angel Road	d																								
Ponders End	d		12 29								12 59					13 29							13 59		
Brimsdown	d		12 32								13 02					13 32							14 02		
Enfield Lock	d		12 34					12 51			13 04					13 34				13 51			14 04		
Waltham Cross	d		12 37								13 07					13 37							14 07		
Cheshunt	d		12 39			12 48		12 55			13 09		13 18			13 39		13 48		13 55			14 09		
Broxbourne 3	a		12 44			12 52		12 59			13 14		13 22			13 44		13 52		13 59			14 14		
Broxbourne 3	d		12 44			12 52		13 03			13 14		13 22			13 44		13 52		14 03			14 14		
Rye House	d		12 47								13 17					13 47							14 17		
St Margarets (Herts)	d		12 50								13 20					13 50							14 20		
Ware	d		12 54								13 24					13 54							14 24		
Hertford East	a		13 01								13 31					14 01							14 31		
Roydon	d							13 08					13 26							14 08					
Harlow Town	d			12 54		12 58		13 12				13 24	13 30				13 54	13 58		14 12				14 24	
Harlow Mill	d							13 15					13 33							14 15					
Sawbridgeworth	d					13 03		13 18		←			13 37					14 03		14 18		←			
Bishops Stortford	a	12 47				13 10		13 25	13 15	13 25			13 44	13 47				14 10		14 25	14 15	14 25			
	d	12 48				13 11		13 26	13 15	13 26			13 44	13 48				14 11		14 26	14 15	14 26			
Stansted Mountfitchet	d			13 05				→		13 30			13 48				14 05			→		14 30			
Stansted Airport	a	12 57		13 13					13 25	13 39		13 42		13 57			14 13				14 25	14 39		14 42	
Stansted Airport	d						13 25												14 25						
Elsenham	d												13 52												
Newport (Essex)	d												13 57												
Audley End	d					13 23	13 37						14 00					14 23	14 37						
Great Chesterford	d												14 05												
Whittlesford Parkway	d					13 30							14 10					14 30							
Shelford	d												14 14												
Cambridge	a					13 40	13 58						14 21					14 40	14 58						

Table 22

Saturdays

London - Broxbourne, Hertford East, Bishops Stortford, Stansted Airport and Cambridge

		LE 1	LE 1 🚲	LE 1	LE 1 🚲	LE 1	XC ◇1	LE 1	LE 1 🚲	LE 1		LE 1	LE 1 🚲	LE 1	LE 1 🚲	LE 1	LE 1 🚲	LE 1	XC ◇1	LE 1		LE 1 🚲	LE 1	LE 1	LE 1 🚲
London Liverpool Street 15 ⊖	d	13 58	14 10	14 12	14 25	14 28			14 40			14 42	14 55	14 58	15 10	15 12	15 25	15 28				15 40		15 42	15 55
Bethnal Green	d																								
Hackney Downs	d			14 18								14 48				15 18								15 48	
Stratford 7 ⊖	d							14 33												15 33					
Clapton	d																								
Seven Sisters ⊖	d																								
Tottenham Hale ⊖	d	14 10	14u22	14 25	14u37	14 40		14 43	14u52			14 55	15u07	15 10	15u22	15 25	15u37	15 40		15 43		15u52		15 55	16u07
Northumberland Park	d							14 45												15 45					
Angel Road	d																								
Ponders End	d			14 29								14 59				15 29								15 59	
Brimsdown	d			14 32								15 02				15 32								16 02	
Enfield Lock	d			14 34				14 51				15 04				15 34				15 51				16 04	
Waltham Cross	d			14 37								15 07				15 37								16 07	
Cheshunt	d	14 18		14 39		14 48		14 55				15 09		15 18		15 39		15 48		15 55				16 09	
Broxbourne 3	a	14 22		14 44		14 52		14 59				15 14		15 22		15 44		15 52		15 59				16 14	
Broxbourne 3	d	14 22		14 44		14 52		15 03				15 14		15 22		15 44		15 52		16 03				16 14	
Rye House	d			14 47								15 17				15 47								16 17	
St Margarets (Herts)	d			14 50								15 20				15 50								16 20	
Ware	d			14 54								15 24				15 54								16 24	
Hertford East	a			15 01								15 31				16 01								16 31	
Roydon	d	14 26						15 08						15 26						16 08					
Harlow Town	d	14 30			14 54	14 58		15 12					15 24	15 30			15 54	15 58		16 12					16 24
Harlow Mill	d	14 33						15 15						15 33						16 15					
Sawbridgeworth	d	14 37				15 03		15 18		←				15 37				16 03		16 18			←		
Bishops Stortford	a	14 44	14 47			15 10		15 25	15 15	15 25				15 44	15 47			16 10		16 25		16 15	16 25		
	d	14 44	14 48			15 11		15 26	15 15	15 26				15 44	15 48			16 11		16 26		16 15	16 26		
Stansted Mountfitchet	d	14 48			15 05			↪		15 30				15 48			16 05			↪			16 30		
Stansted Airport	a		14 57		15 13				15 25	15 39			15 42		15 57		16 13					16 25	16 39		16 42
Stansted Airport	d						15 25												16 25						
Elsenham	d	14 52												15 52											
Newport (Essex)	d	14 57												15 57											
Audley End	d	15 00				15 23	15 37							16 00				16 23	16 37						
Great Chesterford	d	15 05												16 05											
Whittlesford Parkway	d	15 10				15 30								16 10				16 30							
Shelford	d	15 14												16 14											
Cambridge	a	15 21				15 40	15 58							16 21				16 40	16 58						

		LE 1	LE 1 🚲	LE 1	LE 1 🚲	LE 1		XC ◇1	LE 1	LE 1 🚲	LE 1	LE 1	LE 1 🚲	LE 1	LE 1 🚲	LE 1		LE 1 🚲	LE 1	XC ◇1	LE 1	LE 1 🚲	LE 1	LE 1	LE 1 🚲
London Liverpool Street 15 ⊖	d	15 58	16 10	16 12	16 25	16 28				16 40		16 42	16 55	16 58	17 10	17 12		17 25	17 28			17 40		17 42	17 55
Bethnal Green	d																								
Hackney Downs	d			16 18								16 48				17 18								17 48	
Stratford 7 ⊖	d								16 33												17 33				
Clapton	d																								
Seven Sisters ⊖	d																								
Tottenham Hale ⊖	d	16 10	16u22	16 25	16u37	16 40			16 43	16u52		16 55	17u07	17 10	17u22	17 25		17u37	17 40		17 43	17u52		17 55	18u07
Northumberland Park	d								16 45												17 45				
Angel Road	d																								
Ponders End	d			16 29								16 59				17 29								17 59	
Brimsdown	d			16 32								17 02				17 32								18 02	
Enfield Lock	d			16 34					16 51			17 04				17 34					17 51			18 04	
Waltham Cross	d			16 37								17 07				17 37								18 07	
Cheshunt	d	16 18		16 39		16 48			16 55			17 09		17 18		17 39			17 48		17 55			18 09	
Broxbourne 3	a	16 22		16 44		16 52			16 59			17 14		17 22		17 44			17 52		17 59			18 14	
Broxbourne 3	d	16 22		16 44		16 52			17 03			17 14		17 22		17 44			17 52		18 03			18 14	
Rye House	d			16 47								17 17				17 47								18 17	
St Margarets (Herts)	d			16 50								17 20				17 50								18 20	
Ware	d			16 54								17 24				17 54								18 24	
Hertford East	a			17 01								17 31				18 01								18 31	
Roydon	d	16 26							17 08					17 26							18 08				
Harlow Town	d	16 30			16 54	16 58			17 12				17 24	17 30				17 54	17 58		18 12				18 24
Harlow Mill	d	16 33							17 15					17 33							18 15				
Sawbridgeworth	d	16 37				17 03			17 18		←			17 37					18 03		18 18		←		
Bishops Stortford	a	16 44	16 47			17 10			17 25	17 15	17 25			17 44	17 47				18 10		18 25	18 15	18 25		
	d	16 44	16 48			17 11			17 26	17 15	17 26			17 44	17 48				18 11		18 26	18 15	18 26		
Stansted Mountfitchet	d	16 48			17 05				↪		17 30			17 48				18 05			↪		18 30		
Stansted Airport	a		16 57		17 13					17 25	17 39		17 42		17 57			18 13				18 25	18 39		18 42
Stansted Airport	d							17 25												18 25					
Elsenham	d	16 52												17 52											
Newport (Essex)	d	16 57												17 57											
Audley End	d	17 00				17 23		17 37						18 00					18 23	18 37					
Great Chesterford	d	17 05												18 05											
Whittlesford Parkway	d	17 10				17 30								18 10					18 30						
Shelford	d	17 14												18 14											
Cambridge	a	17 21				17 40		17 58						18 21					18 40	18 58					

Table 22

Saturdays

London - Broxbourne, Hertford East, Bishops Stortford, Stansted Airport and Cambridge

		LE 1		LE 1 🛒	LE 1	LE 1 🛒	LE 1	XC ◇1	LE 1	LE 1 🛒	LE 1	LE 1		LE 1 🛒	LE 1	LE 1 🛒	LE 1	LE 1 🛒	LE 1	XC 1	LE 1	LE 1 🛒		LE 1	LE 1
London Liverpool Street 15 ⊖	d	17 58		18 10	18 12	18 25	18 28			18 40		18 42		18 55	18 58	19 10	19 12	19 25	19 28			19 40			19 42
Bethnal Green	d																								
Hackney Downs	d				18 18							18 48					19 18								19 48
Stratford 7 ⊖	d								18 33												19 33				
Clapton	d																								
Seven Sisters ⊖	d																								
Tottenham Hale ⊖	d	18 10		18u22	18 25	18u37	18 40		18 43	18u52		18 55		19u07	19 10	19u22	19 25	19u37	19 40		19 43	19u52			19 55
Northumberland Park	d								18 45												19 45				
Angel Road	d																								
Ponders End	d				18 29							18 59					19 29								19 59
Brimsdown	d				18 32							19 02					19 32								20 02
Enfield Lock	d				18 34				18 51			19 04					19 34				19 51				20 04
Waltham Cross	d				18 37							19 07					19 37								20 07
Cheshunt	d	18 18			18 39		18 48		18 55			19 09			19 18		19 39		19 48		19 55				20 09
Broxbourne 3	a	18 22			18 44		18 52		18 59			19 14			19 22		19 44		19 52		19 59				20 14
Broxbourne 3	d	18 22			18 44		18 52		19 03			19 14			19 22		19 44		19 52		20 03				20 14
Rye House	d				18 47							19 17					19 47								20 17
St Margarets (Herts)	d				18 50							19 20					19 50								20 20
Ware	d				18 54							19 24					19 54								20 24
Hertford East	a				19 01							19 31					20 01								20 31
Roydon	d	18 26							19 08						19 26						20 08				
Harlow Town	d	18 30				18 54	18 58		19 12					19 24	19 30			19 54	19 58		20 12				
Harlow Mill	d	18 33							19 15						19 33						20 15				
Sawbridgeworth	d	18 37					19 03		19 18		←				19 37				20 03		20 18			←	
Bishops Stortford	a	18 44		18 47			19 10		19 25	19 15	19 25				19 44	19 47			20 10		20 25	20 15		20 25	
	d	18 44		18 48			19 11		19 26	19 15	19 26				19 44	19 48			20 11		20 26	20 15		20 26	
Stansted Mountfitchet	d	18 48				19 05			→		19 30				19 48			20 05			→			20 30	
Stansted Airport	a			18 57		19 13				19 25	19 39			19 42		19 57		20 13				20 25		20 39	
Stansted Airport	d							19 25												20 25					
Elsenham	d	18 52													19 52										
Newport (Essex)	d	18 57													19 57										
Audley End	d	19 00					19 23	19 37							20 00				20 23	20 38					
Great Chesterford	d	19 05													20 05										
Whittlesford Parkway	d	19 10					19 30								20 10				20 30						
Shelford	d	19 14													20 14										
Cambridge	a	19 21					19 40	19 58							20 21				20 40	20 57					

		LE 1 🛒	LE 1	LE 1 🛒	LE 1	LE 1 🛒	LE 1	XC 1		LE 1	LE 1 🛒	LE 1	LE 1	LE 1 🛒	LE 1	LE 1 🛒	LE 1	LE 1 🛒		LE 1	XC 1	LE 1	LE 1 🛒	LE 1	LE 1
London Liverpool Street 15 ⊖	d	19 55	19 58	20 10	20 12	20 25	20 28				20 40		20 42	20 55	20 58	21 10	21 12	21 25		21 28			21 40		21 42
Bethnal Green	d																								
Hackney Downs	d				20 18								20 48				21 18								21 48
Stratford 7 ⊖	d									20 33												21 33			
Clapton	d																								
Seven Sisters ⊖	d																								
Tottenham Hale ⊖	d	20u07	20 10	20u22	20 25	20u37	20 40			20 43	20u52		20 55	21u07	21 10	21u22	21 25	21u37		21 40		21 43	21u52		21 55
Northumberland Park	d									20 45												21 45			
Angel Road	d																								
Ponders End	d				20 29								20 59				21 29								21 59
Brimsdown	d				20 32								21 02				21 32								22 02
Enfield Lock	d				20 34					20 51			21 04				21 34					21 51			22 04
Waltham Cross	d				20 37								21 07				21 37								22 07
Cheshunt	d		20 18		20 39		20 48			20 55			21 09		21 18		21 39			21 48		21 55			22 09
Broxbourne 3	a		20 22		20 44		20 52			20 59			21 14		21 22		21 44			21 52		21 59			22 14
Broxbourne 3	d		20 22		20 44		20 52			21 03			21 14		21 22		21 44			21 52		22 03			22 14
Rye House	d				20 47								21 17				21 47								22 17
St Margarets (Herts)	d				20 50								21 20				21 50								22 20
Ware	d				20 54								21 24				21 54								22 24
Hertford East	a				21 01								21 31				22 01								22 31
Roydon	d		20 26							21 08					21 26							22 08			
Harlow Town	d	20 24	20 30			20 54	20 58			21 12				21 24	21 30			21 54		21 58		22 12			
Harlow Mill	d		20 33							21 15					21 33							22 15			
Sawbridgeworth	d		20 37				21 03			21 18		←			21 37					22 03		22 18		←	
Bishops Stortford	a		20 44	20 47			21 10			21 25	21 15	21 25			21 44	21 47				22 10		22 25	22 15	22 25	
	d		20 44	20 48			21 11			21 26	21 15	21 26			21 44	21 48				22 11		22 26	22 15	22 26	
Stansted Mountfitchet	d		20 48			21 05				→		21 30			21 48			22 05				→		22 30	
Stansted Airport	a	20 42		20 57		21 13					21 25	21 39		21 42		21 57		22 13					22 25	22 39	
Stansted Airport	d							21 25													22 25				
Elsenham	d		20 52												21 52										
Newport (Essex)	d		20 57												21 57										
Audley End	d		21 00				21 23	21 38							22 00					22 23	22 38				
Great Chesterford	d		21 05												22 05										
Whittlesford Parkway	d		21 10				21 30								22 10					22 30					
Shelford	d		21 14												22 14										
Cambridge	a		21 21				21 40	22 01							22 21					22 40	23 01				

Table 22

Saturdays

London - Broxbourne, Hertford East, Bishops Stortford, Stansted Airport and Cambridge

		LE	LE	LE		LE	LE	LE	LE	LE	LE	XC	LE	LE		LE	LE	LE	LE	LE
		1	1	1		1	1	1	1	1	1	1	1	1		1	1	1	1	1
		bike		bike			bike			bike			bike							
London Liverpool Street 15 ⊖	d	21 55	21 58	22 10		22 12	22 25	22 28		22 40	22 42		22 55	22 58		23 10	23 25	23 28	23 40	23 58
Bethnal Green	d																			
Hackney Downs	d					22 18					22 48					23 16			23 46	
Stratford 7 ⊖	d								22 33											
Clapton	d																		23 49	
Seven Sisters ⊖	d																			
Tottenham Hale ⊖	d	22u07	22 10	22u22		22 25	22u37	22 40	22 43	22u52	22 55		23u07	23 10		23 23	23u37	23 40	23 53	00 10
Northumberland Park	d								22 45							23 25			23 55	
Angel Road	d																			
Ponders End	d					22 29					22 59					23 29			23 59	
Brimsdown	d					22 32					23 02					23 32			00 02	
Enfield Lock	d					22 34			22 51		23 04					23 34			00 04	
Waltham Cross	d					22 37					23 07					23 37			00 07	
Cheshunt	d		22 18			22 39		22 48	22 55		23 09			23 18		23 39		23 48	00 09	00 18
Broxbourne 3	a		22 22			22 44		22 52	22 59		23 14			23 22		23 44		23 52	00 14	00 22
Broxbourne 3	d		22 22			22 44		22 52	23 03		23 14			23 22		23 44		23 52	00 14	00 22
Rye House	d					22 47					23 17					23 47			00 17	
St Margarets (Herts)	d					22 50					23 20					23 50			00 20	
Ware	d					22 54					23 24					23 54			00 24	
Hertford East	a					23 01					23 31					00 01			00 31	
Roydon	d		22 26						23 08					23 26						00 26
Harlow Town	d	22 24	22 30				22 54	22 58	23 12				23 24	23 30			23 54	23 58		00 30
Harlow Mill	d		22 33						23 15					23 33						00 33
Sawbridgeworth	d		22 37					23 03	23 18					23 37				00 03		00 37
Bishops Stortford	a		22 44	22 47				23 10	23 26	23 15				23 44			00 04	00 10		00 44
	d		22 44	22 48				23 11		23 15				23 44			00 04	00 11		00 44
Stansted Mountfitchet	d		22 48				23 05							23 48						00 48
Stansted Airport	a	22 42		22 57			23 13			23 25			23 42				00 13			
Stansted Airport	d											23 25								
Elsenham	d		22 52											23 52						00 52
Newport (Essex)	d		22 57											23 57						00 57
Audley End	d		23 00					23 23				23 38		23 59				00 23		01 00
Great Chesterford	d		23 05											00 05						01 05
Whittlesford Parkway	d		23 10					23 30						00 10				00 30		01 10
Shelford	d		23 14											00 14						
Cambridge	a		23 21					23 40				23 53		00 21				00 40		01 19

Sundays

		LE	LE	LE	LE	LE	LE	LE	LE	LE		LE	LE	LE	LE	LE	LE	LE	LE	LE		LE	LE	LE	LE
		1	1	1	1	1	1	1	1	1		1	1	1	1	1	1	1	1			1		1	1
		A	A	A	A	A	A																		
																	bike	bike	bike					bike	
London Liverpool Street 15 ⊖	d	22p58	23p10	23p25	23p28	23p40	23p58	04 10	04 40	05 10		05 40	06 10	06 25	06 40	06 55	07 10	07 25	07 40			07 43	07 52	07 55	
Bethnal Green	d																								
Hackney Downs	d		23p16			23p46																	07 59		
Stratford 7 ⊖	d																								
Clapton	d					23p49																			
Seven Sisters ⊖	d																						08 04		
Tottenham Hale ⊖	d	23p10	23p23	23b37	23p40	23p53	00 10		04u52	05u22		05u52	06u22	06u37	06u52	07 07	07 22	07 37	07 52			07 55		08 07	
Northumberland Park	d		23p25			23p55																			
Angel Road	d																								
Ponders End	d		23p29			23p59																07 59			
Brimsdown	d		23p32			00 02																08 02			
Enfield Lock	d		23p34			00 04																08 04			
Waltham Cross	d		23p37			00 07																08 07			
Cheshunt	d	23p18	23p39		23p48	00 09	00 18					06 00										08 09	08 20		
Broxbourne 3	a	23p22	23p44		23p52	00 14	00 22					06 04										08 14	08 25		
Broxbourne 3	d	23p22	23p44		23p52	00 14	00 22					06 04								07 57		08 19	08 25		
Rye House	d		23p47			00 17														08 00			08 28		
St Margarets (Herts)	d		23p50			00 20														08 03			08 31		
Ware	d		23p54			00 24														08 07			08 35		
Hertford East	a		00 01			00 31														08 14			08 42		
Roydon	d	23p26					00 26															08 24			←
Harlow Town	d	23p30		23p54	23p58		00 30		05 07	05 37		06 10		06 52		07 22		07 52				08 28		08 22	08 28
Harlow Mill	d	23p33					00 33															→			08 31
Sawbridgeworth	d	23p37			00 03		00 37																		08 34
Bishops Stortford	a	23p44		00 04	00 10		00 44		05 17	05 47		06 20	06 45		07 15		07 45		08 15						08 41
	d	23p44		00 04	00 11		00 44		05 18	05 48		06 21	06 46		07 16		07 46		08 16						08 42
Stansted Mountfitchet	d	23p48					00 48		05 22					07 03				08 03							08 46
Stansted Airport	a			00 13				04 58	05 29	05 57		06 30	06 55	07 12	07 25	07 40	07 55	08 13	08 25					08 40	
Stansted Airport	d																								
Elsenham	d	23p52					00 52																		08 50
Newport (Essex)	d	23p57					00 57																		08 55
Audley End	d	23p59			00 23		01 00																		08 58
Great Chesterford	d	00 05					01 05																		09 03
Whittlesford Parkway	d	00 10			00 30		01 10																		09 08
Shelford	d	00 14																							09 12
Cambridge	a	00 21			00 40		01 19																		09 19

A not 22 May

b Previous night, stops to pick up only

Table 22

Sundays

London - Broxbourne, Hertford East, Bishops Stortford, Stansted Airport and Cambridge

		LE 1 🚲	LE	LE 1 🚲	LE 1	LE		LE 1 🚲	LE 1	LE	LE 1 🚲	LE 1	LE 1 🚲	LE	LE 1 🚲	LE 1		LE	LE 1 🚲	XC ◇1	LE 1	LE	LE 1 🚲	LE 1	LE 1 🚲
London Liverpool Street 15 ⊖	d	08 10	08 22	08 25	08 28			08 40		08 52	08 55		09 10	09 22	09 25	09 28			09 40			09 52	09 55		10 10
Bethnal Green	d																								
Hackney Downs	d		08 29							08 59				09 29								09 59			
Stratford 7 ⊖	d								08 45												09 45				
Clapton	d																								
Seven Sisters ⊖	d		08 34							09 04				09 34								10 04			
Tottenham Hale ⊖	d	08 22		08 37	08 40			08 52	08 55		09 07		09 22		09 37	09 40			09 52		09 55		10 07		10 22
Northumberland Park	d																								
Angel Road	d																								
Ponders End	d								08 59												09 59				
Brimsdown	d								09 02												10 02				
Enfield Lock	d								09 04												10 04				
Waltham Cross	d					←			09 07									←			10 07				
Cheshunt	d		08 52		08 49	08 52			09 09	09 20				09 52		09 49		09 52			10 09	10 20			
Broxbourne 3	a		→		08 53	08 57			09 14	09 25				→		09 53		09 57			10 14	10 25			
Broxbourne 3	d				08 53	08 57			09 19	09 25						09 53		09 57			10 19	10 25			
Rye House	d					09 00				09 28								10 00				10 28			
St Margarets (Herts)	d					09 03				09 31								10 03				10 31			
Ware	d					09 07				09 35								10 07				10 35			
Hertford East	a					09 14				09 42								10 14				10 42			
Roydon	d								09 24			←									10 24			←	
Harlow Town	d			08 52	08 59				09 28		09 22	09 28			09 52	09 59					10 28		10 22	10 28	
Harlow Mill	d								→			09 31									→			10 31	
Sawbridgeworth	d				09 04							09 34				10 04								10 34	
Bishops Stortford	a	08 45			09 11			09 15				09 41	09 45			10 11			10 15					10 41	10 45
	d	08 46			09 12			09 16				09 42	09 46			10 12			10 16					10 42	10 46
Stansted Mountfitchet	d			09 03								09 46			10 03									10 46	
Stansted Airport	a	08 55		09 12				09 25			09 40		09 55		10 12				10 25				10 40		10 55
Stansted Airport	d																			10 25					
Elsenham	d											09 50												10 50	
Newport (Essex)	d											09 55												10 55	
Audley End	d				09 24							09 58				10 24				10 39				10 58	
Great Chesterford	d											10 03												11 03	
Whittlesford Parkway	d				09 31							10 08				10 31								11 08	
Shelford	d											10 12												11 12	
Cambridge	a				09 41							10 19				10 41				10 58				11 19	

		LE		LE 1 🚲	LE 1	LE	LE 1 🚲	XC ◇1	LE 1	LE	LE 1 🚲	LE 1		LE 1 🚲	LE	LE 1 🚲	LE 1	LE	LE 1 🚲	XC ◇1	LE 1	LE		LE 1 🚲	LE 1
London Liverpool Street 15 ⊖	d	10 22		10 25	10 28		10 40			10 52	10 55			11 10	11 22	11 25	11 28		11 40			11 52		11 55	
Bethnal Green	d																								
Hackney Downs	d	10 29								10 59					11 29							11 59			
Stratford 7 ⊖	d								10 45												11 45				
Clapton	d																								
Seven Sisters ⊖	d	10 34								11 04					11 34							12 04			
Tottenham Hale ⊖	d			10 37	10 40		10 52		10 55		11 07			11 22		11 37	11 40		11 52		11 55			12 07	
Northumberland Park	d																								
Angel Road	d																								
Ponders End	d								10 59												11 59				
Brimsdown	d								11 02												12 02				
Enfield Lock	d								11 04												12 04				
Waltham Cross	d					←			11 07									←			12 07				
Cheshunt	d	10 52			10 49	10 52			11 09	11 20					11 52		11 49	11 52			12 09	12 20			
Broxbourne 3	a	→			10 53	10 57			11 14	11 25					→		11 53	11 57			12 14	12 25			
Broxbourne 3	d				10 53	10 57			11 19	11 25							11 53	11 57			12 19	12 25			
Rye House	d					11 00				11 28								12 00				12 28			
St Margarets (Herts)	d					11 03				11 31								12 03				12 31			
Ware	d					11 07				11 35								12 07				12 35			
Hertford East	a					11 14				11 42								12 14				12 42			
Roydon	d								11 24			←									12 24				←
Harlow Town	d			10 52	10 59				11 28		11 22	11 28				11 52	11 59				12 28			12 22	12 28
Harlow Mill	d								→			11 31									→				12 31
Sawbridgeworth	d				11 04							11 34					12 04								12 34
Bishops Stortford	a				11 11		11 15					11 41		11 45			12 11		12 15						12 41
	d				11 12		11 16					11 42		11 46			12 12		12 16						12 42
Stansted Mountfitchet	d			11 03								11 46				12 03									12 46
Stansted Airport	a			11 12			11 25				11 40			11 55		12 12			12 25					12 40	
Stansted Airport	d							11 25												12 25					
Elsenham	d											11 50													12 50
Newport (Essex)	d											11 55													12 55
Audley End	d				11 24			11 39				11 58					12 24			12 39					12 58
Great Chesterford	d											12 03													13 03
Whittlesford Parkway	d				11 31							12 08					12 31								13 08
Shelford	d											12 12													13 12
Cambridge	a				11 41			11 57				12 19					12 41			12 58					13 19

Table 22

Sundays

London - Broxbourne, Hertford East, Bishops Stortford, Stansted Airport and Cambridge

		LE 1 ⚲	LE	LE 1 ⚲	LE 1	LE	LE 1 ⚲	XC ◇1		LE 1	LE	LE 1 ⚲	LE 1	LE 1 ⚲	LE	LE 1 ⚲	LE 1	LE		LE 1 ⚲	XC ◇1	LE 1	LE	LE 1 ⚲	LE 1
London Liverpool Street 15 ⊖	d	12 10	12 22	12 25	12 28		12 40				12 52	12 55		13 10	13 22	13 25	13 28			13 40			13 52	13 55	
Bethnal Green	d																								
Hackney Downs	d		12 29								12 59				13 29								13 59		
Stratford 7 ⊖	d									12 45												13 45			
Clapton	d																								
Seven Sisters ⊖	d		12 34								13 04				13 34								14 04		
Tottenham Hale ⊖	d	12 22		12 37	12 40		12 52			12 55		13 07		13 22		13 37	13 40			13 52		13 55		14 07	
Northumberland Park	d																								
Angel Road	d																								
Ponders End	d									12 59												13 59			
Brimsdown	d									13 02												14 02			
Enfield Lock	d									13 04												14 04			
Waltham Cross	d					←				13 07								←				14 07			
Cheshunt	d		12 52		12 49	12 52				13 09	13 20				13 52		13 49	13 52				14 09	14 20		
Broxbourne 3	a		↪		12 53	12 57				13 14	13 25				↪		13 53	13 57				14 14	14 25		
Broxbourne 3	d				12 53	12 57				13 19	13 25						13 53	13 57				14 19	14 25		
Rye House	d					13 00					13 28							14 00					14 28		
St Margarets (Herts)	d					13 03					13 31							14 03					14 31		
Ware	d					13 07					13 35							14 07					14 35		
Hertford East	a					13 14					13 42							14 14					14 42		
Roydon	d									13 24			←									14 24			←
Harlow Town	d			12 52	12 59					13 28		13 22	13 28			13 52	13 59					14 28		14 22	14 28
Harlow Mill	d									↪			13 31									↪			14 31
Sawbridgeworth	d				13 04								13 34				14 04								14 34
Bishops Stortford	a	12 45			13 11		13 15						13 41	13 45			14 11			14 15					14 41
	d	12 46			13 12		13 16						13 42	13 46			14 12			14 16					14 42
Stansted Mountfitchet	d			13 03									13 46			14 03									14 46
Stansted Airport	a	12 55		13 12			13 25					13 40		13 55		14 12				14 25				14 40	
Stansted Airport	d							13 25													14 25				
Elsenham	d												13 50												14 50
Newport (Essex)	d												13 55												14 55
Audley End	d				13 24			13 39					13 58				14 24				14 39				14 58
Great Chesterford	d												14 03												15 03
Whittlesford Parkway	d				13 31								14 08				14 31								15 08
Shelford	d												14 12												15 12
Cambridge	a				13 41			13 58					14 19				14 41				14 57				15 19

		LE 1 ⚲	LE	LE 1 ⚲		LE 1	LE	LE 1 ⚲	XC ◇1	LE 1	LE	LE 1 ⚲	LE 1	LE 1 ⚲		LE	LE 1 ⚲	LE 1	LE	LE 1 ⚲	XC ◇1	LE 1	LE	LE 1 ⚲	
London Liverpool Street 15 ⊖	d	14 10	14 22	14 25		14 28		14 40			14 52	14 55		15 10		15 22	15 25	15 28		15 40			15 52	15 55	
Bethnal Green	d																								
Hackney Downs	d		14 29								14 59					15 29							15 59		
Stratford 7 ⊖	d									14 45												15 45			
Clapton	d																								
Seven Sisters ⊖	d		14 34								15 04					15 34							16 04		
Tottenham Hale ⊖	d	14 22		14 37		14 40		14 52		14 55		15 07		15 22			15 37	15 40		15 52		15 55		16 07	
Northumberland Park	d																								
Angel Road	d																								
Ponders End	d									14 59												15 59			
Brimsdown	d									15 02												16 02			
Enfield Lock	d									15 04												16 04			
Waltham Cross	d						←			15 07									←			16 07			
Cheshunt	d		14 52			14 49	14 52			15 09	15 20					15 52		15 49	15 52			16 09	16 20		
Broxbourne 3	a		↪			14 53	14 57			15 14	15 25					↪		15 53	15 57			16 14	16 25		
Broxbourne 3	d					14 53	14 57			15 19	15 25							15 53	15 57			16 19	16 25		
Rye House	d						15 00				15 28								16 00				16 28		
St Margarets (Herts)	d						15 03				15 31								16 03				16 31		
Ware	d						15 07				15 35								16 07				16 35		
Hertford East	a						15 14				15 42								16 14				16 42		
Roydon	d									15 24			←									16 24			
Harlow Town	d			14 52		14 59				15 28		15 22	15 28				15 52	15 59				16 28		16 22	
Harlow Mill	d									↪			15 31									↪			
Sawbridgeworth	d					15 04							15 34					16 04							
Bishops Stortford	a	14 45				15 11		15 15					15 41	15 45				16 11		16 15					
	d	14 46				15 12		15 16					15 42	15 46				16 12		16 16					
Stansted Mountfitchet	d			15 03									15 46				16 03								
Stansted Airport	a	14 55		15 12				15 25				15 40		15 55			16 12			16 25				16 40	
Stansted Airport	d								15 25												16 25				
Elsenham	d												15 50												
Newport (Essex)	d												15 55												
Audley End	d					15 24			15 39				15 58					16 24			16 39				
Great Chesterford	d												16 03												
Whittlesford Parkway	d					15 31							16 08					16 31							
Shelford	d												16 12												
Cambridge	a					15 41			15 58				16 19					16 41			16 58				

Table 22

Sundays

London - Broxbourne, Hertford East, Bishops Stortford, Stansted Airport and Cambridge

		LE ■1	LE ■1 🛒	LE	LE ■1 🛒	LE ■1	LE	LE ■1 🛒	XC ◇■1	LE ■1		LE	LE ■1 🛒	LE ■1	LE ■1 🛒	LE	LE ■1 🛒	LE ■1	LE	LE ■1 🛒		XC ◇■1	LE ■1	LE	LE ■1 🛒
London Liverpool Street ■15 ⊖	d		16 10	16 22	16 25	16 28		16 40				16 52	16 55		17 10	17 22	17 25	17 28		17 40				17 52	17 55
Bethnal Green	d																								
Hackney Downs	d			16 29								16 59				17 29								17 59	
Stratford ■7 ⊖	d									16 45													17 45		
Clapton	d																								
Seven Sisters ⊖	d			16 34								17 04				17 34								18 04	
Tottenham Hale ⊖	d		16 22		16 37	16 40		16 52		16 55			17 07		17 22		17 37	17 40		17 52			17 55		18 07
Northumberland Park	d																								
Angel Road	d																								
Ponders End	d									16 59													17 59		
Brimsdown	d									17 02													18 02		
Enfield Lock	d									17 04													18 04		
Waltham Cross	d						←			17 07									←				18 07		
Cheshunt	d			16 52		16 49	16 52			17 09		17 20				17 52		17 49	17 52				18 09	18 20	
Broxbourne ■3	a			→		16 53	16 57			17 14		17 25				→		17 53	17 57				18 14	18 25	
Broxbourne ■3	d					16 53	16 57			17 19		17 25						17 53	17 57				18 19	18 25	
Rye House	d						17 00					17 28							18 00					18 28	
St Margarets (Herts)	d						17 03					17 31							18 03					18 31	
Ware	d						17 07					17 35							18 07					18 35	
Hertford East	a						17 14					17 42							18 14					18 42	
Roydon	d	←								17 24				←									18 24		
Harlow Town	d	16 28			16 52	16 59				17 28			17 22	17 28			17 52	17 59					18 28		18 22
Harlow Mill	d	16 31								→				17 31									→		
Sawbridgeworth	d	16 34				17 04								17 34				18 04							
Bishops Stortford	a	16 41	16 45			17 11		17 15						17 41	17 45			18 11		18 15					
	d	16 42	16 46			17 12		17 16						17 42	17 46			18 12		18 16					
Stansted Mountfitchet	d	16 46			17 03									17 46			18 03								
Stansted Airport	a		16 55		17 12			17 25					17 40		17 55		18 12			18 25					18 40
Stansted Airport	d								17 25													18 25			
Elsenham	d	16 50												17 50											
Newport (Essex)	d	16 55												17 55											
Audley End	d	16 58				17 24			17 39					17 58				18 24				18 39			
Great Chesterford	d	17 03												18 03											
Whittlesford Parkway	d	17 08				17 31								18 08				18 31							
Shelford	d	17 12												18 12											
Cambridge	a	17 19				17 41			17 58					18 19				18 41				18 58			

		LE ■1	LE ■1 🛒	LE	LE ■1 🛒	LE ■1		LE	LE ■1 🛒	XC ◇■1	LE ■1	LE	LE ■1 🛒	LE ■1	LE ■1 🛒	LE		LE ■1 🛒	LE ■1	LE	LE ■1 🛒	XC ■1	LE ■1	LE	LE ■1 🛒
London Liverpool Street ■15 ⊖	d		18 10	18 22	18 25	18 28			18 40			18 52	18 55		19 10	19 22		19 25	19 28		19 40			19 52	19 55
Bethnal Green	d																								
Hackney Downs	d			18 29								18 59				19 29								19 59	
Stratford ■7 ⊖	d										18 45												19 45		
Clapton	d																								
Seven Sisters ⊖	d			18 34								19 04				19 34								20 04	
Tottenham Hale ⊖	d		18 22		18 37	18 40			18 52		18 55		19 07		19 22			19 37	19 40		19 52		19 55		20 07
Northumberland Park	d																								
Angel Road	d																								
Ponders End	d										18 59												19 59		
Brimsdown	d										19 02												20 02		
Enfield Lock	d										19 04												20 04		
Waltham Cross	d							←			19 07									←			20 07		
Cheshunt	d			18 52		18 49		18 52			19 09	19 20				19 52			19 49	19 52			20 09	20 20	
Broxbourne ■3	a			→		18 53		18 57			19 14	19 25				→			19 53	19 57			20 14	20 25	
Broxbourne ■3	d					18 53		18 57			19 19	19 25							19 53	19 57			20 19	20 25	
Rye House	d							19 00				19 28								20 00				20 28	
St Margarets (Herts)	d							19 03				19 31								20 03				20 31	
Ware	d							19 07				19 35								20 07				20 35	
Hertford East	a							19 14				19 42								20 14				20 42	
Roydon	d	←									19 24			←									20 24		
Harlow Town	d	18 28			18 52	18 59					19 28		19 22	19 28				19 52	19 59				20 28		20 22
Harlow Mill	d	18 31									→			19 31									→		
Sawbridgeworth	d	18 34				19 04								19 34					20 04						
Bishops Stortford	a	18 41	18 45			19 11			19 15					19 41	19 45				20 11		20 15				
	d	18 42	18 46			19 12			19 16					19 42	19 46				20 12		20 16				
Stansted Mountfitchet	d	18 46			19 03									19 46				20 03							
Stansted Airport	a		18 55		19 12				19 25				19 40		19 55			20 12			20 25				20 40
Stansted Airport	d									19 25												20 25			
Elsenham	d	18 50												19 50											
Newport (Essex)	d	18 55												19 55											
Audley End	d	18 58				19 24				19 39				19 58					20 24			20 39			
Great Chesterford	d	19 03												20 03											
Whittlesford Parkway	d	19 08				19 31								20 08					20 31						
Shelford	d	19 12												20 12											
Cambridge	a	19 19				19 41				19 58				20 19					20 41			20 57			

London - Broxbourne, Hertford East, Bishops Stortford, Stansted Airport and Cambridge

		LE 1		LE 1 🛒	LE	LE 1 🛒	LE 1	LE	XC 1	LE 1 🛒	LE 1	LE		LE 1 🛒	LE 1	LE 1 🛒	LE	LE 1 🛒	LE 1	LE	LE 1 🛒	XC 1		LE 1	LE
London Liverpool Street 15 ⊖	d			20 10	20 22	20 25	20 28			20 40		20 52		20 55		21 10	21 22	21 25	21 28		21 40				21 52
Bethnal Green	d																								
Hackney Downs	d				20 29							20 59					21 29								21 59
Stratford 7 ⊖	d										20 45													21 45	
Clapton	d																								
Seven Sisters ⊖	d				20 34							21 04					21 34								22 04
Tottenham Hale ⊖	d			20 22		20 37	20 40			20 52	20 55			21 07		21 22		21 37	21 40		21 52			21 55	
Northumberland Park	d																								
Angel Road	d																								
Ponders End	d										20 59													21 59	
Brimsdown	d										21 02													22 02	
Enfield Lock	d										21 04													22 04	
Waltham Cross	d							←			21 07									←				22 07	
Cheshunt	d				20 52		20 49	20 52			21 09	21 20					21 52		21 49	21 52				22 09	22 20
Broxbourne 3	a				→		20 53	20 57			21 14	21 25					→		21 53	21 57				22 14	22 25
Broxbourne 3	d						20 53	20 57			21 19	21 25							21 53	21 57				22 19	22 25
Rye House	d							21 00				21 28								22 00					22 28
St Margarets (Herts)	d							21 03				21 31								22 03					22 31
Ware	d							21 07				21 35								22 07					22 35
Hertford East	a							21 14				21 42								22 14					22 42
Roydon	d	←									21 24				←									22 24	
Harlow Town	d	20 28				20 52	20 59				21 28			21 22	21 28			21 52	21 59					22 28	
Harlow Mill	d	20 31									→				21 31									→	
Sawbridgeworth	d	20 34					21 04								21 34				22 04						
Bishops Stortford	a	20 41		20 45			21 11			21 15					21 41	21 45			22 11		22 15				
	d	20 42		20 46			21 12			21 16					21 42	21 46			22 12		22 16				
Stansted Mountfitchet	d	20 46				21 03									21 46			22 03							
Stansted Airport	a			20 55		21 12				21 27				21 40		21 55		22 12			22 25				
Stansted Airport	d								21 18													22 25			
Elsenham	d	20 50													21 50										
Newport (Essex)	d	20 55													21 55										
Audley End	d	20 58					21 24		21 33						21 58				22 24			22 40			
Great Chesterford	d	21 03													22 03										
Whittlesford Parkway	d	21 08					21 31								22 08				22 31						
Shelford	d	21 12													22 12										
Cambridge	a	21 19					21 41		21 47						22 19				22 41			22 57			

		LE 1 🛒	LE 1	LE 1 🛒	XC 1	LE	LE 1 🛒	LE 1		LE	LE 1 🛒	LE 1	LE	LE 1 🛒	LE 1	LE	LE	LE 1		LE 1	LE	LE 1			
London Liverpool Street 15 ⊖	d	21 55		22 10		22 22	22 25	22 28			22 40		22 52	22 55			23 22	23 25		23 28		23 58			
Bethnal Green	d																								
Hackney Downs	d					22 29							22 59				23 29								
Stratford 7 ⊖	d											22 45													
Clapton	d																								
Seven Sisters ⊖	d					22 34							23 04				23 34								
Tottenham Hale ⊖	d	22 07		22 22			22 37	22 40			22 52	22 55		23 07				23 37		23 40		00 10			
Northumberland Park	d																								
Angel Road	d																								
Ponders End	d											22 59								23 44					
Brimsdown	d											23 02								23 47					
Enfield Lock	d											23 04								23 49					
Waltham Cross	d									←		23 07								23 52					
Cheshunt	d					22 52		22 49		22 52		23 09	23 20				23 50			23 54	←	00 18			
Broxbourne 3	a					→		22 53		22 57		23 14	23 25				23 55			23 59	23 55	00 22			
Broxbourne 3	d							22 53		22 57		23 19	23 25				00 02			23 59	00 02	00 22			
Rye House	d									23 00							→				00 06				
St Margarets (Herts)	d									23 03											00 09				
Ware	d									23 07											00 13				
Hertford East	a									23 14											00 19				
Roydon	d		←									23 24			←	←						00 26			
Harlow Town	d	22 22	22 28				22 52	22 59				23 28	23 32	23 22	23 28	23 32		23 52		00 05		00 30			
Harlow Mill	d		22 31									→	→		23 31							00 33			
Sawbridgeworth	d		22 34					23 04							23 34					00 10		00 37			
Bishops Stortford	a		22 41	22 45				23 11			23 15				23 41	23 45		00 02		00 17		00 44			
	d		22 42	22 46				23 12			23 16				23 42			00 03							
Stansted Mountfitchet	d		22 46				23 03								23 46										
Stansted Airport	a	22 40		22 55			23 12				23 25			23 40				00 12							
Stansted Airport	d				23 03																				
Elsenham	d		22 50												23 50										
Newport (Essex)	d		22 55												23 55										
Audley End	d		22 58		23 17			23 24							23 58										
Great Chesterford	d		23 03												00 03										
Whittlesford Parkway	d		23 08					23 31							00 08										
Shelford	d		23 12												00 12										
Cambridge	a		23 19		23 34			23 41							00 19										

Cambridge, Stansted Airport, Bishops Stortford, Hertford East and Broxbourne - London

Miles	Miles			LE MO 1	LE MX 1	LE MX 1	LE MX 1	LE MO 1	LE MX 1	LE MO 1	LE MX 1	LE MX 1	LE 1	LE 1	LE MFO 1	LE MFO 1	XC 1	LE 1	LE 1	LE MFO 1	XC 1	LE 1 A	LE 1
0	—	**Cambridge**	d			22p51											04 44	04 48			05 17		
3¼	—	Shelford	d			22p56																	
6¾	—	Whittlesford Parkway	d			23p00												04 55					
10	—	Great Chesterford	d			23p04																	
14	—	Audley End	d			23p10											04 58	05 03			05 35		
15¾	—	Newport (Essex)	d			23p13																	
20¼	0	Elsenham	d			23p19																	
—	—	**Stansted Airport**	a														05 11				05 50		
—	4½	**Stansted Airport**	d	23p15	23p15		23p30	23p30		23p45	23p45		23p59	00 30	01 00	01 30				05 30			
22½	8¼	Stansted Mountfitchet	d			23p22																	
25½	—	**Bishops Stortford**	a			23p28	23p39	23p39					00 08	00 39				05 16		05 39			
—	—		d			23p28	23p39	23p39					00 08	00 39				05 16		05 39		05 39	05 45
29	—	Sawbridgeworth	d			23p32												05 21					05 49
31¼	—	Harlow Mill	d			23p36												05 24					05 53
33	—	Harlow Town	d	23p30	23p30	23p39		23p47		23p59	23p59		00 16	00 47				05 27		05 47		05 47	05 56
35¾	—	Roydon	d			23p43												05 31					06 00
—	0	**Hertford East**	d						23p39			00 07							05 25				
—	2	Ware	d						23p43										05 29				
—	4	St Margarets (Herts)	d						23p47										05 33				
—	5¼	Rye House	d						23p50										05 36				
38½	—	**Broxbourne 3**	a			23p47			23p54			00 19						05 36	05 40	05 53		05 53	06 04
—	7	**Broxbourne 3**	d			23p47			23p54			00 19						05 36	05 40	05 53		05 53	06 04
41¾	—	Cheshunt	d			23p51			23p58									05 41	05 44	05 57		05 57	06 08
43	—	Waltham Cross	d																05 47				06 10
44	—	Enfield Lock	d																05 49				06 13
45	—	Brimsdown	d																05 52				06 15
45¾	—	Ponders End	d																05 54				06 17
48	—	Angel Road	d																05 57				06 21
48¾	—	Northumberland Park	d																05 59				06 23
49¾	—	Tottenham Hale ⊖	d	23p46	23p47													05 49	06 03	06 07		06 07	06 26
—	0	Seven Sisters ⊖	d			00 04	00 07	00 08	00 11	00 21	00 21												
51¾	—	Clapton	d																				
—	6¾	Stratford 7 ⊖	a																				06 39
52¾	—	Hackney Downs	d						00 16			00 41							06 08				
54½	—	Bethnal Green	d																				
55¾	—	**London Liverpool Street 15** ⊖	a	00 01	00 01	00 18	00 22	00 22	00 25	00 35	00 36	00 49	00 51	01 21	01 50	02 20		06 03	06 17	06 23		06 23	

		LE 1	LE 1 🚲	LE	LE 1	LE 1	LE 1 🚲	LE 1	LE 1	LE 1 🚲	LE	LE 1	LE 1	LE 1 🚲	LE 1	LE 1	LE 1 🚲	XC 1	LE	LE 1	LE 1 🚲	LE	LE 1
Cambridge	d	05 21				05 41			05 51				06 18			06 21		06 32		06 48			06 51
Shelford	d	05 26				05 46			05 56							06 26							06 56
Whittlesford Parkway	d	05 30				05 50			06 00				06 25			06 30				06 55			07 00
Great Chesterford	d	05 34				05 54			06 04							06 34							07 04
Audley End	d	05 40				06 00			06 10				06 34			06 40		06 46		07 04			07 10
Newport (Essex)	d	05 43				06 03			06 13							06 43							07 13
Elsenham	d	05 49				06 09			06 19							06 49							07 19
Stansted Airport	a																	07 09					
Stansted Airport	d		06 00				06 15			06 30				06 43			07 00				07 15		
Stansted Mountfitchet	d	05 52	06 06			06 12			06 22					06 49		06 52							07 22
Bishops Stortford	a	05 58	06 10			06 18	06 24		06 28	06 39			06 47	06 53		06 58	07 09			07 17	07 24		07 28
	d	05 58	06 10		06 14	06 18	06 24		06 28	06 39		06 42	06 48	06 54		06 58	07 09			07 17	07 24		07 28
Sawbridgeworth	d	06 03			06 18				06 33			06 46				07 03				07 22			07 33
Harlow Mill	d	06 06							06 36			06 50				07 06							07 36
Harlow Town	d	06 10	06 18		06 23	06 27			06 40	06 47		06 53	06 57	07 02		07 10				07 27	07 32		07 40
Roydon	d	06 14							06 44			06 57				07 14							07 44
Hertford East	d			06 05							06 35								07 09			07 15	
Ware	d			06 09							06 39								07 13			07 19	
St Margarets (Herts)	d			06 13							06 43								07 17			07 23	
Rye House	d			06 16				←			06 46				←				07 20			07 26	
Broxbourne 3	a	06 18		06 21	06 30	06 33		06 30	06 48		06 51	07 02	07 04		07 02	07 18	07 22		07 25	07 33		07 30	07 48
Broxbourne 3	d	06 18		06 25	06 39	06 34		06 39	06 48		06 55	07 11	07 05		07 11	07 18	07 22		07 25	07 34		07 40	07 48
Cheshunt	d	06 23		06 30	→			06 43	06 53		07 00	→		07 12	07 15		07 27		07 30			07 44	07 53
Waltham Cross	d			06 32				06 46			07 02				07 18				07 32			07 47	
Enfield Lock	d			06 35				06 48			07 05				07 20				07 35			07 49	
Brimsdown	d			06 37							07 07						07 31		07 37			07 52	
Ponders End	d			06 39							07 09						07 33		07 39				
Angel Road	d							06 53							07 25								
Northumberland Park	d							06 55							07 27							07 57	
Tottenham Hale ⊖	d	06 31	06 34	06 45		06 48	06 51	06 58	07 01	07 04	07 15		07 18	07 21	07 30	07 33	07 38		07 45	07 48	07 51	08 00	08 03
Seven Sisters ⊖	d																						
Clapton	d																						
Stratford 7 ⊖	a							07 12							07 44							08 13	
Hackney Downs	d			06 51							07 21								07 51				
Bethnal Green	d																						
London Liverpool Street 15 ⊖	a	06 47	06 49	07 02		07 04	07 07		07 18	07 21	07 32		07 34	07 37		07 49	07 59		08 02	08 04	08 07		08 19

A TWThO

Cambridge, Stansted Airport, Bishops Stortford, Hertford East and Broxbourne - London

		LE ■1 (trolley)	LE	LE ■1	LE ■1 (trolley)	LE	LE ■1	LE ■1 (trolley)	XC ■1	LE	LE	LE ■1	LE ■1 (trolley)	LE	LE ■1	LE ■1 (trolley)	XC ◇■1	LE	LE ■1	LE ■1 (trolley)	LE	LE ■1
Cambridge	d			07 18			07 21		07 29			07 48			07 51		08 10		08 18			08 21
Shelford	d						07 26								07 56							08 26
Whittlesford Parkway	d			07 25			07 30					07 55			08 00				08 26			08 30
Great Chesterford	d						07 34								08 04							08 34
Audley End	d			07 34			07 40		07 44			08 04			08 10		08 25		08 34			08 40
Newport (Essex)	d						07 43								08 13							08 43
Elsenham	d						07 49								08 19							08 49
Stansted Airport	a								08 09								08 39					
Stansted Airport	d	07 30			07 43			08 00					08 15			08 30				08 45		
Stansted Mountfitchet	d				07 49		07 52								08 22					08 51		08 52
Bishops Stortford	a	07 39		07 47	07 54		07 58	08 09				08 17			08 28	08 39			08 48			08 58
	d	07 39		07 48	07 54		07 58	08 09			08 12	08 17			08 28	08 39			08 48			08 58
Sawbridgeworth	d						08 03				08 16	08 22			08 33							09 03
Harlow Mill	d						08 06				08 20				08 36							09 06
Harlow Town	d			07 57	08 02		08 10				08 23	08 27	08 31		08 40				08 57	09 02		09 10
Roydon	d						08 14				08 27				08 44							09 14
Hertford East	d		07 39							08 09								08 39				
Ware	d		07 43							08 13								08 43				
St Margarets (Herts)	d		07 47							08 17								08 47				
Rye House	d		07 50							08 20				←				08 50				
Broxbourne ■3	a	07 52	07 55	08 03			08 18			08 25	08 32	08 34		08 32	08 48			08 55	09 03			09 18
Broxbourne ■3	d	07 52	07 55	08 04		08 10	08 18			08 25	08 40	08 35		08 40	08 48			08 55	09 04		09 10	09 18
Cheshunt	d		08 00			08 14	08 23			08 30	→			08 44	08 53			09 00			09 14	09 23
Waltham Cross	d	07 58	08 02			08 17				08 32				08 47				09 02			09 17	
Enfield Lock	d		08 05			08 19				08 35				08 49				09 05			09 19	
Brimsdown	d	08 02	08 07							08 37								09 07				
Ponders End	d	08 04	08 09							08 39								09 09				
Angel Road	d					08 24								08 54							09 24	
Northumberland Park	d					08 26								08 56							09 26	
Tottenham Hale ⊖	d	08 10	08 15	08 18	08 21	08 29	08 32	08 35		08 45		08 48	08 51	08 59	09 02	09 05		09 15	09 18	09 21	09 29	09 32
Seven Sisters ⊖	d																					
Clapton	d																					
Stratford ■7 ⊖	a					08 43								09 13							09 43	
Hackney Downs	d		08 21							08 51								09 21				
Bethnal Green	d																					
London Liverpool Street ■15 ⊖	a	08 28	08 32	08 34	08 37		08 49	08 52		09 02		09 04	09 07		09 19	09 22		09 32	09 34	09 37		09 49

		LE ■1 (trolley)	LE ■1	LE ■1 (trolley)	LE ■1	LE ■1	LE ■1 (trolley)	XC ◇■1	LE	LE ■1 (trolley)	LE ■1	LE ■1 (trolley)	LE	LE ■1 (trolley)	LE ■1	LE ■1	LE ■1 (trolley)	XC ◇■1	LE ■1	LE ■1 (trolley)	LE ■1	LE ■1 (trolley)	LE ■1
Cambridge	d					08 51		09 10			09 32					09 48		10 10			10 32		
Shelford	d					08 56										09 53							
Whittlesford Parkway	d					09 00					09 39					10 00					10 39		
Great Chesterford	d					09 04										10 04							
Audley End	d					09 10		09 24			09 47					10 10		10 24			10 47		
Newport (Essex)	d					09 13										10 13							
Elsenham	d					09 19										10 19							
Stansted Airport	a							09 38										10 45					
Stansted Airport	d	09 00		09 15			09 30			09 45		10 00		10 15			10 30			10 45		11 00	
Stansted Mountfitchet	d					09 23				09 51						10 22							
Bishops Stortford	a	09 09				09 28	09 39				10 00	10 09				10 28	10 39				11 00	11 09	
	d	09 09			09 14	09 28	09 39				10 00	10 09			10 14	10 28	10 39				11 00	11 09	
Sawbridgeworth	d				09 18	09 32					10 05				10 18	10 32					11 05		
Harlow Mill	d				09 22	09 36									10 22	10 36							
Harlow Town	d			09 30	09 25	09 39				10 02	10 10			10 30	10 25	10 39				11 00	11 10		
Roydon	d				09 29	09 43									10 29	10 43							
Hertford East	d		09 09						09 39				10 09						10 39				11 09
Ware	d		09 13						09 43				10 13						10 43				11 13
St Margarets (Herts)	d		09 17						09 47				10 17						10 47				11 17
Rye House	d		09 20						09 50				10 20						10 50				11 20
Broxbourne ■3	a		09 25		09 34	09 47			09 54		10 16		10 24		10 34	10 47			10 54		11 16		11 24
Broxbourne ■3	d		09 25		09 37	09 47			09 54		10 16		10 24		10 37	10 47			10 54		11 16		11 24
Cheshunt	d		09 30		09 42	09 51			09 58		10 20		10 28		10 42	10 51			10 58		11 20		11 28
Waltham Cross	d		09 32						10 01				10 31						11 01				11 31
Enfield Lock	d		09 35		09 45				10 03				10 33		10 45				11 03				11 33
Brimsdown	d		09 37						10 06				10 36						11 06				11 36
Ponders End	d		09 39						10 08				10 38						11 08				11 38
Angel Road	d				09 50																		
Northumberland Park	d				09 52										10 51								
Tottenham Hale ⊖	d	09 35	09 45	09 48	09 56	10 00	10 03		10 14	10 17	10 29	10 32	10 44	10 47	10 55	11 00	11 03		11 14	11 17	11 29	11 32	11 44
Seven Sisters ⊖	d																						
Clapton	d																						
Stratford ■7 ⊖	a				10 06										11 05								
Hackney Downs	d		09 51						10 20				10 50						11 20				11 50
Bethnal Green	d																						
London Liverpool Street ■15 ⊖	a	09 52	10 00	10 05		10 13	10 18		10 28	10 31	10 43	10 46	10 58	11 01		11 13	11 17		11 28	11 31	11 43	11 46	11 58

Table 22

Cambridge, Stansted Airport, Bishops Stortford, Hertford East and Broxbourne - London

		LE	LE	LE	LE	LE		XC	LE	LE	LE	LE	LE	LE	LE	LE		LE	LE	XC	LE	LE	LE	LE	LE
		1	1	1	1	1		◇1	1	1	1	1	1	1	1	1		1	1	◇1	1	1	1	1	1
			🚲			🚲				🚲		🚲			🚲				🚲			🚲		🚲	
Cambridge	d				10 48			11 10			11 32							11 51		12 10			12 32		
Shelford	d				10 53													11 56							
Whittlesford Parkway	d				11 00						11 39							12 00					12 39		
Great Chesterford	d				11 04													12 04							
Audley End	d				11 10			11 24			11 47							12 10		12 24			12 47		
Newport (Essex)	d				11 13													12 13							
Elsenham	d				11 19													12 19							
Stansted Airport	a							11 45												12 45					
Stansted Airport	d	11 03	11 15			11 30				11 45		12 00		12 03	12 15				12 30			12 45		13 00	
Stansted Mountfitchet	d	11 09			11 22									12 09				12 22							
Bishops Stortford	a	11 13			11 28	11 39					12 00	12 09		12 13				12 28	12 39				13 00	13 09	
	d	11 14			11 28	11 39					12 00	12 09		12 14				12 28	12 39				13 00	13 09	
Sawbridgeworth	d	11 18			11 32						12 05			12 18				12 32					13 05		
Harlow Mill	d	11 22			11 36									12 22				12 36							
Harlow Town	d	11 25	11 30		11 39					12 00	12 10			12 25	12 30			12 39				13 00	13 10		
Roydon	d	11 29			11 43									12 29				12 43							
Hertford East	d								11 39				12 09								12 39				13 09
Ware	d								11 43				12 13								12 43				13 13
St Margarets (Herts)	d								11 47				12 17								12 47				13 17
Rye House	d								11 50				12 20								12 50				13 20
Broxbourne 3	a	11 34			11 47				11 54		12 16		12 24	12 34				12 47			12 54		13 16		13 24
Broxbourne 3	d	11 37			11 47				11 54		12 16		12 24	12 37				12 47			12 54		13 16		13 24
Cheshunt	d	11 42			11 51				11 58		12 20		12 28	12 42				12 51			12 58		13 20		13 28
Waltham Cross	d								12 01				12 31								13 01				13 31
Enfield Lock	d	11 45							12 03				12 33	12 45							13 03				13 33
Brimsdown	d								12 06				12 36								13 06				13 36
Ponders End	d								12 08				12 38								13 08				13 38
Angel Road	d																								
Northumberland Park	d	11 51		←										12 51		←									
Tottenham Hale ⊖	d	11 55	11 47	11 55	12 00	12 03			12 14	12 17	12 29	12 32	12 44	12 55	12 47	12 55		13 00	13 03		13 14	13 17	13 29	13 32	13 44
Seven Sisters ⊖	d	↪												↪											
Clapton	d																								
Stratford 7 ⊖	a			12 05												13 05									
Hackney Downs	d								12 20				12 50								13 20				13 50
Bethnal Green	d																								
London Liverpool Street 15 ⊖	a		12 01		12 13	12 17			12 28	12 31	12 43	12 46	12 58		13 01			13 13	13 17		13 28	13 31	13 43	13 46	13 58

		LE		LE	LE	LE	LE	XC	LE	LE	LE	LE		LE	LE	LE	LE	LE	LE	XC	LE	LE		LE	LE
		1		1	1	1	1	◇1	1	1	1	1		1	1	1	1	1	1	◇1	1	1		1	1
				🚲			🚲			🚲		🚲				🚲			🚲			🚲			🚲
Cambridge	d					12 51		13 10			13 32							13 51		14 10				14 32	
Shelford	d					12 56												13 56							
Whittlesford Parkway	d					13 00					13 39							14 00						14 39	
Great Chesterford	d					13 04												14 04							
Audley End	d					13 10		13 24			13 47							14 10		14 24				14 47	
Newport (Essex)	d					13 13												14 13							
Elsenham	d					13 19												14 19							
Stansted Airport	a							13 45												14 45					
Stansted Airport	d	13 03		13 15			13 30			13 45		14 00			14 03	14 15			14 30			14 45			15 00
Stansted Mountfitchet	d	13 09				13 22									14 09			14 22							
Bishops Stortford	a	13 13				13 28	13 39				14 00	14 09			14 13			14 28	14 39					15 00	15 09
	d	13 14				13 28	13 39				14 00	14 09			14 14			14 28	14 39					15 00	15 09
Sawbridgeworth	d	13 18				13 32					14 05				14 18			14 32						15 05	
Harlow Mill	d	13 22				13 36									14 22			14 36							
Harlow Town	d	13 25		13 30		13 39				14 00	14 10				14 25	14 30		14 39				15 00		15 10	
Roydon	d	13 29				13 43									14 29			14 43							
Hertford East	d								13 39					14 09							14 39				
Ware	d								13 43					14 13							14 43				
St Margarets (Herts)	d								13 47					14 17							14 47				
Rye House	d								13 50					14 20							14 50				
Broxbourne 3	a	13 34				13 47			13 54		14 16			14 24	14 34			14 47			14 54			15 16	
Broxbourne 3	d	13 37				13 47			13 54		14 16			14 24	14 37			14 47			14 54			15 16	
Cheshunt	d	13 42				13 51			13 58		14 20			14 28	14 42			14 51			14 58			15 20	
Waltham Cross	d								14 01					14 31							15 01				
Enfield Lock	d	13 45							14 03					14 33	14 45						15 03				
Brimsdown	d								14 06					14 36							15 06				
Ponders End	d								14 08					14 38							15 08				
Angel Road	d																								
Northumberland Park	d	13 51			←										14 51		←								
Tottenham Hale ⊖	d	13 55		13 47	13 55	14 00	14 03		14 14	14 17	14 29	14 32		14 44	14 55	14 47	14 55	15 00	15 03		15 14	15 17		15 29	15 32
Seven Sisters ⊖	d	↪													↪										
Clapton	d																								
Stratford 7 ⊖	a				14 05												15 05								
Hackney Downs	d								14 20					14 50							15 20				
Bethnal Green	d																								
London Liverpool Street 15 ⊖	a			14 01		14 13	14 17		14 28	14 31	14 43	14 48		14 58		15 01		15 15	15 17		15 28	15 31		15 45	15 47

Cambridge, Stansted Airport, Bishops Stortford, Hertford East and Broxbourne - London

Station		LE 1	LE 1	LE 1 trolley	LE 1	LE 1	LE 1 trolley	XC ◇1		LE 1	LE 1 trolley	LE 1	LE 1	LE 1 trolley	LE 1	LE 1	LE 1 trolley	LE 1		LE 1	LE 1 trolley	XC ◇1	LE 1	LE 1 trolley	LE 1
Cambridge	d					14 51		15 10					15 21							15 51		16 10			
Shelford	d					14 56							15 26							15 56					
Whittlesford Parkway	d					15 00							15 30							16 00					
Great Chesterford	d					15 04							15 34							16 04					
Audley End	d					15 10		15 24					15 40							16 10		16 24			
Newport (Essex)	d					15 13							15 43							16 13					
Elsenham	d					15 19							15 49							16 19					
Stansted Airport	a							15 45														16 45			
Stansted Airport	d		15 03	15 15			15 30				15 45			16 00		16 03	16 15				16 30			16 45	
Stansted Mountfitchet	d		15 09			15 22							15 52			16 09				16 22					
Bishops Stortford	a		15 13			15 28	15 39						15 58	16 09		16 13				16 28	16 39				
	d		15 14			15 28	15 39					15 48	15 58	16 09		16 14				16 28	16 39				
Sawbridgeworth	d		15 18			15 32							16 02			16 18				16 32					
Harlow Mill	d		15 22			15 36							16 06			16 22				16 36					
Harlow Town	d		15 25	15 30		15 39					16 00	15 56	16 09			16 25	16 30			16 39				17 00	
Roydon	d		15 29			15 43							16 13			16 29				16 43					
Hertford East	d	15 09								15 39					16 09								16 39		
Ware	d	15 13								15 43					16 13								16 43		
St Margarets (Herts)	d	15 17								15 47					16 17								16 47		
Rye House	d	15 20								15 50					16 20								16 50		
Broxbourne 3	a	15 24	15 34			15 47				15 54		16 03	16 17		16 24	16 34				16 47			16 54		
Broxbourne 3	d	15 24	15 37			15 47				15 54		16 07	16 17		16 24	16 37				16 47			16 54		17 09
Cheshunt	d	15 28	15 42			15 51				15 58		16 12	16 21		16 28	16 42				16 51			16 58		17 13
Waltham Cross	d	15 31								16 01					16 31								17 01		
Enfield Lock	d	15 33	15 45							16 03		16 15			16 33	16 45							17 03		17 17
Brimsdown	d	15 36								16 06					16 36								17 06		
Ponders End	d	15 38								16 08					16 38								17 08		
Angel Road	d		15 50									16 20				16 50									17 22
Northumberland Park	d		15 52		←							16 22				16 52		←							17 24
Tottenham Hale ⊖	d	15 44	15 56	15 47	15 56	16 00	16 03			16 14	16 17	16 26	16 30	16 33	16 44	16 56	16 47	16 56		17 00	17 03		17 14	17 17	17 27
Seven Sisters ⊖	d		↦													↦									
Clapton	d																								
Stratford 7 ⊖	a				16 06							16 39						17 10							17 40
Hackney Downs	d	15 50								16 20					16 50								17 20		
Bethnal Green	d																								
London Liverpool Street 15 ⊖	a	15 58		16 01		16 13	16 17			16 30	16 32		16 43	16 48	16 58		17 03			17 13	17 17		17 31	17 33	

Station		LE 1	LE 1 trolley	LE 1		LE 1	LE 1 trolley	LE 1	LE 1	LE 1 trolley	XC ◇1	LE 1	LE 1 trolley	LE 1		LE 1	LE 1 trolley	LE 1	LE 1 trolley	LE 1	LE 1	LE 1 trolley	XC ◇1	LE 1	
Cambridge	d	16 21							16 51		17 10					17 21					17 51		18 18		
Shelford	d	16 26							16 56							17 26					17 56				
Whittlesford Parkway	d	16 30							17 00							17 30					18 00				
Great Chesterford	d	16 34							17 04							17 34					18 04				
Audley End	d	16 40							17 10		17 24					17 40					18 10		18 32		
Newport (Essex)	d	16 43							17 13							17 43					18 13				
Elsenham	d	16 49							17 19							17 49					18 19				
Stansted Airport	a										17 39												18 45		
Stansted Airport	d		17 00			17 03	17 15			17 30			17 45				18 00		18 15			18 30			
Stansted Mountfitchet	d	16 52				17 09			17 22							17 52	18 06				18 22				
Bishops Stortford	a	16 58	17 09			17 13			17 28	17 39						17 58	18 10				18 28	18 39			
	d	16 58	17 09			17 14			17 28	17 39						17 58	18 11				18 28	18 39			
Sawbridgeworth	d	17 02				17 18			17 32							18 02					18 32				
Harlow Mill	d	17 06				17 22			17 36							18 06					18 36				
Harlow Town	d	17 09				17 25	17 30		17 39				18 00			18 09			18 30		18 39				
Roydon	d	17 13				17 29			17 43							18 13					18 43				
Hertford East	d			17 12								17 40						18 13		18 18				18 40	
Ware	d			17 16								17 44								18 22				18 44	
St Margarets (Herts)	d			17 20								17 48								18 26				18 48	
Rye House	d			17 23								17 51								18 29				18 51	
Broxbourne 3	a	17 17		17 27		17 34			17 47			17 55				18 17		18 27		18 33	18 47			18 57	
Broxbourne 3	d	17 17		17 27		17 37			17 47			17 55		18 09		18 17		18 27		18 37	18 47			18 57	
Cheshunt	d	17 21		17 31		17 42			17 51			17 59		18 13		18 21		18 31		18 42	18 51			19 01	
Waltham Cross	d			17 34								18 02						18 34						19 04	
Enfield Lock	d			17 36		17 45						18 04		18 17				18 36		18 45				19 06	
Brimsdown	d			17 39								18 07						18 39						19 09	
Ponders End	d			17 41								18 09						18 41						19 11	
Angel Road	d					17 50								18 22						18 50					
Northumberland Park	d					17 52		←						18 24						18 52					
Tottenham Hale ⊖	d	17 30	17 33	17 46		17 56	17 49	17 56	18 00	18 03		18 14	18 18	18 27		18 30	18 33	18 46	18 49	18 56	19 00	19 03		19 16	
Seven Sisters ⊖	d					↦																			
Clapton	d																								
Stratford 7 ⊖	a							18 10						18 40						19 10					
Hackney Downs	d			17 52								18 20						18 52						19 22	
Bethnal Green	d																								
London Liverpool Street 15 ⊖	a	17 44	17 48	18 01			18 03		18 13	18 18		18 31	18 33			18 44	18 48	19 01	19 03		19 13	19 18		19 31	

Cambridge, Stansted Airport, Bishops Stortford, Hertford East and Broxbourne - London

		LE	LE	LE	LE	LE	LE	LE	LE	XC		LE	LE	LE	LE	LE	LE	LE	LE	LE		LE	XC	LE	LE
		1	1	1	1	1	1	1	1	◇1		1	1	1	1	1	1	1	1	1		1	◇1	1	1
		🚲		🚲		🚲			🚲				🚲		🚲			🚲				🚲			🚲
Cambridge	d		18 21					18 51		19 10				19 21						19 51			20 10		
Shelford	d		18 26					18 56						19 26						19 56					
Whittlesford Parkway	d		18 30					19 00						19 30						20 00					
Great Chesterford	d		18 34					19 04						19 34						20 04					
Audley End	d		18 40					19 10		19 24				19 40						20 10			20 24		
Newport (Essex)	d		18 43					19 13						19 43						20 13					
Elsenham	d		18 49					19 19						19 49						20 19					
Stansted Airport	a									19 42													20 45		
Stansted Airport	d	18 45		19 00		19 15			19 30				19 45		20 00		20 03	20 15				20 30			20 45
Stansted Mountfitchet	d		18 52	19 06				19 22						19 53			20 09			20 22					
Bishops Stortford	a		18 58	19 10				19 28	19 39					20 00	20 09		20 13			20 28		20 39			
	d		19 00	19 11				19 28	19 39					20 00	20 09		20 14			20 28		20 39			
Sawbridgeworth	d		19 05					19 32						20 05			20 18			20 32					
Harlow Mill	d							19 36									20 22			20 36					
Harlow Town	d	19 00	19 10			19 30		19 39					20 00	20 10			20 25	20 30		20 39					21 00
Roydon	d							19 43									20 29			20 43					
Hertford East	d				19 12		19 18					19 40				20 10								20 39	
Ware	d				19 16		19 22					19 44				20 14								20 43	
St Margarets (Herts)	d				19 20		19 26					19 48				20 18								20 47	
Rye House	d				19 23		19 29					19 51				20 21								20 50	
Broxbourne 3	a		19 16		19 27		19 33	19 47				19 57		20 16		20 25	20 34			20 47				20 54	
Broxbourne 3	d		19 16		19 27		19 37	19 47				19 57		20 16		20 25	20 40			20 47				20 54	
Cheshunt	d		19 20		19 31		19 42	19 51				20 01		20 20		20 29	20 45			20 51				20 58	
Waltham Cross	d				19 34							20 03				20 32								21 01	
Enfield Lock	d				19 36		19 45					20 06				20 34	20 48							21 03	
Brimsdown	d				19 39							20 08				20 37								21 06	
Ponders End	d				19 41							20 10				20 39								21 08	
Angel Road	d						19 50																		
Northumberland Park	d						19 52										20 54		←						
Tottenham Hale ⊖	d	19 19	19 29	19 32	19 46	19 49	19 56	20 00	20 03			20 15	20 18	20 29	20 32	20 45	20 57	20 48	20 57	21 00		21 03		21 14	21 17
Seven Sisters ⊖	d																→								
Clapton	d																								
Stratford 7 ⊖	a						20 06												21 08						
Hackney Downs	d				19 52							20 22				20 50								21 20	
Bethnal Green	d																								
London Liverpool Street 15 ⊖	a	19 33	19 43	19 46	20 01	20 03		20 13	20 17			20 31	20 33	20 45	20 47	21 01		21 03		21 14		21 17		21 28	21 31

		LE	LE	LE	LE	LE		LE	LE	LE	XC	LE	LE	LE	LE	LE		LE	LE	LE	LE	XC	LE	LE	LE
		1	1	1	1	1		1	1	1	◇1	1	1	1	1	1		1	1	1	1	◇1	1	1	1
			🚲			🚲				🚲			🚲												
Cambridge	d	20 32							20 51		21 10			21 32							21 51	22 11			
Shelford	d								20 56												21 56				
Whittlesford Parkway	d	20 39							21 00					21 39							22 00				
Great Chesterford	d								21 04												22 04				
Audley End	d	20 47							21 10		21 24			21 47							22 10	22 25			
Newport (Essex)	d								21 13												22 13				
Elsenham	d								21 19												22 19				
Stansted Airport	a										21 45														
Stansted Airport	d		21 00		21 03	21 15				21 30			21 45		22 00			22 03	22 15				22 30		22 45
Stansted Mountfitchet	d				21 09				21 22									22 09			22 22	22a41			
Bishops Stortford	a	21 00	21 09		21 13				21 28	21 39				22 00	22 09			22 13			22 28		22 39		
	d	21 00	21 09		21 14				21 28	21 39				22 00	22 09			22 14			22 28		22 39		
Sawbridgeworth	d	21 05			21 18				21 32					22 05				22 18			22 32				
Harlow Mill	d				21 22				21 36									22 22			22 36				
Harlow Town	d	21 10			21 25	21 30			21 39				22 00	22 10				22 25	22 30		22 39				23 00
Roydon	d				21 29				21 43									22 29			22 43				
Hertford East	d			21 09								21 39				22 09								22 39	
Ware	d			21 13								21 43				22 13								22 43	
St Margarets (Herts)	d			21 17								21 47				22 17								22 47	
Rye House	d			21 20								21 50				22 20								22 50	
Broxbourne 3	a	21 16		21 24	21 34				21 47			21 54		22 16		22 24		22 34			22 47			22 54	
Broxbourne 3	d	21 16		21 24	21 37				21 47			21 54		22 16		22 24		22 37			22 47			22 54	
Cheshunt	d	21 20		21 28	21 42				21 51			21 58		22 20		22 28		22 42			22 51			22 58	
Waltham Cross	d			21 31								22 01				22 31								23 01	
Enfield Lock	d			21 33	21 45							22 03				22 33		22 45						23 03	
Brimsdown	d			21 36								22 06				22 36								23 06	
Ponders End	d			21 38								22 08				22 38								23 08	
Angel Road	d																								
Northumberland Park	d				21 51			←										22 51		←					
Tottenham Hale ⊖	d	21 29	21 32	21 44	21 55	21 47		21 55	22 00	22 03		22 14	22 17	22 29	22 32	22 44		22 55	22 47	22 55	23 00		23 03	23 14	23 17
Seven Sisters ⊖	d				→													→							
Clapton	d																								
Stratford 7 ⊖	a							22 05												23 04					
Hackney Downs	d			21 50								22 20				22 50								23 20	
Bethnal Green	d																								
London Liverpool Street 15 ⊖	a	21 43	21 46	21 58		22 01			22 13	22 17		22 28	22 31	22 43	22 46	22 58			23 01	23 14	23 13		23 17	23 28	23 31

Cambridge, Stansted Airport, Bishops Stortford, Hertford East and Broxbourne - London

		LE [1]		LE [1]	LE [1]	LE [1]	LE [1]	LE [1]	LE [1]	LE [1]	LE [1]	LE [1]
Cambridge	d	22 32						22 51				
Shelford	d							22 56				
Whittlesford Parkway	d	22 39						23 00				
Great Chesterford	d							23 04				
Audley End	d	22 47						23 10				
Newport (Essex)	d							23 13				
Elsenham	d							23 19				
Stansted Airport	a											
Stansted Airport	d			23 00	23 03		23 15		23 30		23 45	23 59
Stansted Mountfitchet	d				23 09			23 22				
Bishops Stortford	a	23 00		23 09	23 13			23 28	23 39			00 08
	d	23 00		23 09				23 28	23 39			00 08
Sawbridgeworth	d	23 05						23 32				
Harlow Mill	d							23 36				
Harlow Town	d	23 10					23 30	23 39			23 59	00 16
Roydon	d							23 43				
Hertford East	d					23 09				23 39		
Ware	d					23 13				23 43		
St Margarets (Herts)	d					23 17				23 47		
Rye House	d					23 20				23 50		
Broxbourne [3]	a	23 16				23 24		23 47		23 54		
Broxbourne [3]	d	23 16				23 24		23 47		23 54		
Cheshunt	d	23 20				23 28		23 51		23 58		
Waltham Cross	d					23 31						
Enfield Lock	d					23 33						
Brimsdown	d					23 36						
Ponders End	d					23 38						
Angel Road	d											
Northumberland Park	d											
Tottenham Hale ⊖	d	23 29		23 32		23 44	23 47					
Seven Sisters ⊖	d							00 04	00 07	00 11	00 21	
Clapton	d											
Stratford [7] ⊖	a											
Hackney Downs	d					23 50				00 16		
Bethnal Green	d											
London Liverpool Street [15] ⊖	a	23 43		23 46		23 58	00 01	00 18	00 22	00 25	00 36	00 51

Saturdays

		LE [1]	LE [1]	LE [1]	LE [1]	LE [1]	LE [1]	LE [1]	LE [1]	LE [1]		LE [1]	LE [1]	XC [1]	LE [1]	LE [1]	LE [1]	LE [1]	LE [1] 🚲	LE [1]		LE [1]	XC [1]	LE [1] 🚲	LE [1]
Cambridge	d		22p51										04 25	04 56				05 21					05 42		
Shelford	d		22p56															05 26							
Whittlesford Parkway	d		23p00										04 32					05 30							
Great Chesterford	d		23p04															05 34							
Audley End	d		23p10										04 40					05 40					05 56		
Newport (Essex)	d		23p13															05 43							
Elsenham	d		23p19															05 49							
Stansted Airport	a													05 20									06 11		
Stansted Airport	d	23p15		23p30		23p45		23p59	00 30	01 00		01 30				05 30			06 00			06 03		06 15	
Stansted Mountfitchet	d		23p22															05 52				06 09			
Bishops Stortford	a		23p28	23p39				00 08	00 39				04 53			05 39		05 58	06 09			06 13			
	d		23p28	23p39				00 08	00 39				04 53		05 15	05 39		05 58	06 09			06 14			
Sawbridgeworth	d		23p32										04 58		05 19			06 02				06 18			
Harlow Mill	d		23p36										05 01		05 23			06 06				06 22			
Harlow Town	d	23p30	23p39			23p59		00 16	00 47				05 04		05 26			06 09				06 25		06 30	
Roydon	d		23p43										05 08		05 30			06 13				06 29			
Hertford East	d				23p39		00 07													06 09					
Ware	d				23p43															06 13					
St Margarets (Herts)	d				23p47															06 17					
Rye House	d				23p50															06 20					
Broxbourne [3]	a		23p47		23p54		00 19						05 12		05 34			06 17		06 24		06 34			
Broxbourne [3]	d		23p47		23p54		00 19						05 12		05 34		05 54	06 17		06 24		06 37			
Cheshunt	d		23p51		23p58								05 16		05 38		05 58	06 21		06 28		06 42			
Waltham Cross	d														05 40		06 01			06 31					
Enfield Lock	d														05 43		06 03			06 33		06 45			
Brimsdown	d														05 45		06 06			06 36					
Ponders End	d														05 47		06 08			06 38					
Angel Road	d																								
Northumberland Park	d														05 51							06 51			←
Tottenham Hale ⊖	d	23p47													05 55	06 01	06 14	06 30	06 33	06 44		06 55		06 47	06 55
Seven Sisters ⊖	d		00 04	00 07	00 11	00 21							05 36									↦			
Clapton	d																								
Stratford [7] ⊖	a														06 04										07 05
Hackney Downs	d				00 16		00 41						05 45				06 20			06 50					
Bethnal Green	d												05 49												
London Liverpool Street [15] ⊖	a	00 01	00 18	00 22	00 25	00 36	00 49	00 51	01 21	01 50		02 20	05 54		06 14	06 15	06 28	06 43	06 47	06 58				07 01	

Table 22

Saturdays

Cambridge, Stansted Airport, Bishops Stortford, Hertford East and Broxbourne - London

		LE	LE	LE	LE	XC		LE	LE	LE	LE	LE	LE	LE	LE	LE		LE	XC	LE	LE	LE	LE	LE	LE
		1	1	1	1	1		1	1	1	1	1	1	1	1	1		1	1	1	1	1	1	1	1
			🚲		🚲				🚲			🚲			🚲			🚲			🚲			🚲	
Cambridge	d	05 51				06 25		06 32						06 51					07 25	07 32					
Shelford	d	05 56												06 56											
Whittlesford Parkway	d	06 00						06 39						07 00						07 39					
Great Chesterford	d	06 04												07 04											
Audley End	d	06 10				06 39		06 47						07 10					07 39	07 47					
Newport (Essex)	d	06 13												07 13											
Elsenham	d	06 19												07 19											
Stansted Airport	a					06 54													07 54						
Stansted Airport	d		06 30		06 45				07 00		07 03	07 15			07 30			07 45			08 00		08 03	08 15	
Stansted Mountfitchet	d	06 22			06 51						07 09			07 22				07 51					08 09		
Bishops Stortford	a	06 28	06 39					07 00	07 09		07 13			07 28	07 39					08 00	08 09		08 13		
	d	06 28	06 39					07 00	07 09		07 14			07 28	07 39					08 00	08 09		08 14		
Sawbridgeworth	d	06 32						07 05			07 18			07 32						08 05			08 18		
Harlow Mill	d	06 36									07 22			07 36									08 22		
Harlow Town	d	06 39			07 02			07 10			07 25	07 30		07 39				08 02		08 10			08 25	08 30	
Roydon	d	06 43									07 29			07 43									08 29		
Hertford East	d			06 39						07 09						07 39						08 09			
Ware	d			06 43						07 13						07 43						08 13			
St Margarets (Herts)	d			06 47						07 17						07 47						08 17			
Rye House	d			06 50						07 20						07 50						08 20			
Broxbourne 3	a	06 47		06 54				07 16		07 24	07 34			07 47		07 54				08 16		08 24	08 34		
Broxbourne 3	d	06 47		06 54				07 16		07 24	07 37			07 47		07 54				08 16		08 24	08 37		
Cheshunt	d	06 51		06 58				07 20		07 28	07 42			07 51		07 58				08 20		08 28	08 42		
Waltham Cross	d			07 01						07 31						08 01						08 31			
Enfield Lock	d			07 03						07 33	07 45					08 03						08 33	08 45		
Brimsdown	d			07 06						07 36						08 06						08 36			
Ponders End	d			07 08						07 38						08 08						08 38			
Angel Road	d																								
Northumberland Park	d										07 51		←										08 51		←
Tottenham Hale ⊖	d	07 00	07 03	07 14	07 17			07 29	07 32	07 44	07 55	07 47	07 55	08 00	08 03	08 14		08 17		08 29	08 32	08 44	08 55	08 47	08 55
Seven Sisters ⊖	d										→												→		
Clapton	d																								
Stratford 7 ⊖	a												08 05												09 05
Hackney Downs	d			07 20						07 50						08 20						08 50			
Bethnal Green	d																								
London Liverpool Street 15 ⊖	a	07 13	07 17	07 28	07 31			07 43	07 46	07 58		08 01		08 13	08 17	08 28		08 31		08 43	08 46	08 58		09 01	

		LE		LE	XC	LE	LE	LE	LE	LE	LE	LE		LE	LE	LE	XC	LE	LE	LE	LE	LE		LE	LE
		1		1	◇1	1	1	1	1	1	1	1		1	1	1	◇1	1	1	1	1	1		1	1
				🚲			🚲		🚲			🚲				🚲			🚲		🚲				🚲
Cambridge	d	07 51			08 10			08 32							08 51		09 10			09 32					
Shelford	d	07 56													08 56										
Whittlesford Parkway	d	08 00						08 39							09 00					09 39					
Great Chesterford	d	08 04													09 04										
Audley End	d	08 10			08 24			08 47							09 10		09 24			09 47					
Newport (Essex)	d	08 13													09 13										
Elsenham	d	08 19													09 19										
Stansted Airport	a				08 45												09 45								
Stansted Airport	d			08 30			08 45		09 00		09 03	09 15				09 30			09 45		10 00			10 03	10 15
Stansted Mountfitchet	d	08 22					08 51				09 09				09 22				09 51					10 09	
Bishops Stortford	a	08 28		08 39				09 00	09 09		09 13				09 28	09 39				10 00	10 09			10 13	
	d	08 28		08 39				09 00	09 09		09 14				09 28	09 39				10 00	10 09			10 14	
Sawbridgeworth	d	08 32						09 05			09 18				09 32					10 05				10 18	
Harlow Mill	d	08 36									09 22				09 36									10 22	
Harlow Town	d	08 39					09 02	09 10			09 25	09 30			09 39				10 02	10 10				10 25	10 30
Roydon	d	08 43									09 29				09 43									10 29	
Hertford East	d					08 39				09 09								09 39				10 09			
Ware	d					08 43				09 13								09 43				10 13			
St Margarets (Herts)	d					08 47				09 17								09 47				10 17			
Rye House	d					08 50				09 20								09 50				10 20			
Broxbourne 3	a	08 47				08 54		09 16		09 24	09 34				09 47			09 54		10 16		10 24		10 34	
Broxbourne 3	d	08 47				08 54		09 16		09 24	09 37				09 47			09 54		10 16		10 24		10 37	
Cheshunt	d	08 51				08 58		09 20		09 28	09 42				09 51			09 58		10 20		10 28		10 42	
Waltham Cross	d					09 01				09 31								10 01				10 31			
Enfield Lock	d					09 03				09 33	09 45							10 03				10 33		10 45	
Brimsdown	d					09 06				09 36								10 06				10 36			
Ponders End	d					09 08				09 38								10 08				10 38			
Angel Road	d																								
Northumberland Park	d										09 51			←										10 51	
Tottenham Hale ⊖	d	09 00		09 03		09 14	09 17	09 29	09 32	09 44	09 55	09 47		09 55	10 00	10 03		10 14	10 17	10 29	10 32	10 44		10 55	10 47
Seven Sisters ⊖	d										→													→	
Clapton	d																								
Stratford 7 ⊖	a													10 05											
Hackney Downs	d					09 20				09 50								10 20				10 50			
Bethnal Green	d																								
London Liverpool Street 15 ⊖	a	09 13		09 17		09 28	09 31	09 43	09 46	09 58		10 01			10 13	10 17		10 28	10 31	10 43	10 46	10 58			11 01

Table 22

Saturdays

Cambridge, Stansted Airport, Bishops Stortford, Hertford East and Broxbourne - London

		LE 1	LE 1	LE 1 🛒	XC ◇1	LE 1	LE 1 🛒	LE 1	LE 1 🛒	LE 1	LE 1	LE 1 🛒	LE 1	LE 1	LE 1 🛒	XC ◇1	LE 1	LE 1 🛒	LE 1	LE 1 🛒	LE 1	LE 1	LE 1 🛒
Cambridge	d		09 51		10 10			10 32						10 51		11 10			11 32				
Shelford	d		09 56											10 56									
Whittlesford Parkway	d		10 00					10 39						11 00					11 39				
Great Chesterford	d		10 04											11 04									
Audley End	d		10 10		10 24			10 47						11 10		11 24			11 47				
Newport (Essex)	d		10 13											11 13									
Elsenham	d		10 19											11 19									
Stansted Airport	a				10 45											11 45							
Stansted Airport	d			10 30			10 45		11 00		11 03	11 15			11 30			11 45		12 00		12 03	12 15
Stansted Mountfitchet	d		10 22				10 51				11 09			11 22				11 51				12 09	
Bishops Stortford	a		10 28	10 39				11 00	11 09		11 13			11 28	11 39				12 00	12 09		12 13	
	d		10 28	10 39				11 00	11 09		11 14			11 28	11 39				12 00	12 09		12 14	
Sawbridgeworth	d		10 32					11 05			11 18			11 32					12 05			12 18	
Harlow Mill	d		10 36								11 22			11 36								12 22	
Harlow Town	d		10 39				11 02	11 10			11 25	11 30		11 39				12 02	12 10			12 25	12 30
Roydon	d		10 43								11 29			11 43								12 29	
Hertford East	d					10 39				11 09							11 39				12 09		
Ware	d					10 43				11 13							11 43				12 13		
St Margarets (Herts)	d					10 47				11 17							11 47				12 17		
Rye House	d					10 50				11 20							11 50				12 20		
Broxbourne 3	a		10 47			10 54		11 16		11 24	11 34			11 47			11 54		12 16		12 24	12 34	
Broxbourne 3	d		10 47			10 54		11 16		11 24	11 37			11 47			11 54		12 16		12 24	12 37	
Cheshunt	d		10 51			10 58		11 20		11 28	11 42			11 51			11 58		12 20		12 28	12 42	
Waltham Cross	d					11 01				11 31							12 01				12 31		
Enfield Lock	d					11 03				11 33	11 45						12 03				12 33	12 45	
Brimsdown	d					11 06				11 36							12 06				12 36		
Ponders End	d					11 08				11 38							12 08				12 38		
Angel Road	d																						
Northumberland Park	d	←									11 51		←									12 51	
Tottenham Hale ⊖	d	10 55	11 00	11 03		11 14	11 17	11 29	11 32	11 44	11 55	11 47	11 55	12 00	12 03		12 14	12 17	12 29	12 32	12 44	12 55	12 47
Seven Sisters ⊖	d										→											→	
Clapton	d																						
Stratford 7 ⊖	a	11 05											12 05										
Hackney Downs	d					11 20				11 50							12 20				12 50		
Bethnal Green	d																						
London Liverpool Street 15 ⊖	a		11 13	11 17		11 28	11 31	11 43	11 46	11 58		12 01		12 13	12 17		12 28	12 31	12 43	12 46	12 58		13 01

		LE 1	LE 1	LE 1 🛒	XC ◇1	LE 1	LE 1 🛒	LE 1	LE 1 🛒	LE 1	LE 1	LE 1 🛒	LE 1	LE 1	LE 1 🛒	XC ◇1	LE 1	LE 1 🛒	LE 1	LE 1 🛒	LE 1	LE 1
Cambridge	d		11 51		12 10			12 32						12 51		13 10			13 32			
Shelford	d		11 56											12 56								
Whittlesford Parkway	d		12 00					12 39						13 00					13 39			
Great Chesterford	d		12 04											13 04								
Audley End	d		12 10		12 24			12 47						13 10		13 24			13 47			
Newport (Essex)	d		12 13											13 13								
Elsenham	d		12 19											13 19								
Stansted Airport	a				12 45											13 45						
Stansted Airport	d			12 30			12 45		13 00		13 03	13 15			13 30			13 45		14 00		14 03
Stansted Mountfitchet	d		12 22				12 51				13 09			13 22				13 51				14 09
Bishops Stortford	a		12 28	12 39				13 00	13 09		13 13			13 28	13 39				14 00	14 09		14 13
	d		12 28	12 39				13 00	13 09		13 14			13 28	13 39				14 00	14 09		14 14
Sawbridgeworth	d		12 32					13 05			13 18			13 32					14 05			14 18
Harlow Mill	d		12 36								13 22			13 36								14 22
Harlow Town	d		12 39				13 02	13 10			13 25	13 30		13 39				14 02	14 10			14 25
Roydon	d		12 43								13 29			13 43								14 29
Hertford East	d					12 39				13 09							13 39				14 09	
Ware	d					12 43				13 13							13 43				14 13	
St Margarets (Herts)	d					12 47				13 17							13 47				14 17	
Rye House	d					12 50				13 20							13 50				14 20	
Broxbourne 3	a		12 47			12 54		13 16		13 24	13 34			13 47			13 54		14 16		14 24	14 34
Broxbourne 3	d		12 47			12 54		13 16		13 24	13 37			13 47			13 54		14 16		14 24	14 37
Cheshunt	d		12 51			12 58		13 20		13 28	13 42			13 51			13 58		14 20		14 28	14 42
Waltham Cross	d					13 01				13 31							14 01				14 31	
Enfield Lock	d					13 03				13 33	13 45						14 03				14 33	14 45
Brimsdown	d					13 06				13 36							14 06				14 36	
Ponders End	d					13 08				13 38							14 08				14 38	
Angel Road	d																					
Northumberland Park	d	←									13 51		←									14 51
Tottenham Hale ⊖	d	12 55	13 00	13 03		13 14	13 17	13 29	13 32	13 44	13 55	13 47	13 55	14 00	14 03		14 14	14 17	14 29	14 32	14 44	14 55
Seven Sisters ⊖	d										→											→
Clapton	d																					
Stratford 7 ⊖	a	13 05											14 05									
Hackney Downs	d					13 20				13 50							14 20				14 50	
Bethnal Green	d																					
London Liverpool Street 15 ⊖	a		13 13	13 17		13 28	13 31	13 43	13 46	13 58		14 01		14 13	14 17		14 28	14 31	14 43	14 46	14 58	

Table 22

Saturdays

Cambridge, Stansted Airport, Bishops Stortford, Hertford East and Broxbourne - London

Station		LE 1 🛒	LE 1	LE 1	LE 1 🛒	XC ◇1	LE 1	LE 1 🛒	LE 1	LE 1 🛒		LE 1	LE 1	LE 1 🛒	LE 1	LE 1	LE 1 🛒	XC ◇1	LE 1	LE 1 🛒		LE 1	LE 1 🛒	LE 1	LE 1
Cambridge	d			13 51		14 10			14 32							14 51		15 10				15 32			
Shelford	d			13 56												14 56									
Whittlesford Parkway	d			14 00					14 39							15 00						15 39			
Great Chesterford	d			14 04												15 04									
Audley End	d			14 10		14 24			14 47							15 10		15 24				15 47			
Newport (Essex)	d			14 13												15 13									
Elsenham	d			14 19												15 19									
Stansted Airport	a					14 45												15 45							
Stansted Airport	d	14 15			14 30			14 45		15 00			15 03	15 15			15 30			15 45			16 00		16 03
Stansted Mountfitchet	d			14 22				14 51					15 09			15 22				15 51					16 09
Bishops Stortford	a			14 28	14 39				15 00	15 09			15 13			15 28	15 39					16 00	16 09		16 13
	d			14 28	14 39				15 00	15 09			15 14			15 28	15 39					16 00	16 09		16 14
Sawbridgeworth	d			14 32					15 05				15 18			15 32						16 05			16 18
Harlow Mill	d			14 36									15 22			15 36									16 22
Harlow Town	d	14 30		14 39				15 02	15 10				15 25	15 30		15 39				16 02		16 10			16 25
Roydon	d			14 43									15 29			15 43									16 29
Hertford East	d						14 39					15 09							15 39					16 09	
Ware	d						14 43					15 13							15 43					16 13	
St Margarets (Herts)	d						14 47					15 17							15 47					16 17	
Rye House	d						14 50					15 20							15 50					16 20	
Broxbourne 3	a			14 47			14 54		15 16			15 24	15 34			15 47			15 54			16 16		16 24	16 34
Broxbourne 3	d			14 47			14 54		15 16			15 24	15 37			15 47			15 54			16 16		16 24	16 37
Cheshunt	d			14 51			14 58		15 20			15 28	15 42			15 51			15 58			16 20		16 28	16 42
Waltham Cross	d						15 01					15 31							16 01					16 31	
Enfield Lock	d						15 03					15 33	15 45						16 03					16 33	16 45
Brimsdown	d						15 06					15 36							16 06					16 36	
Ponders End	d						15 08					15 38							16 08					16 38	
Angel Road	d																								
Northumberland Park	d		←										15 51		←										16 51
Tottenham Hale ⊖	d	14 47	14 55	15 00	15 03		15 14	15 17	15 29	15 32		15 44	15 55	15 47	15 55	16 00	16 03		16 14	16 17		16 29	16 32	16 44	16 55
Seven Sisters ⊖	d												↦												↦
Clapton	d																								
Stratford 7 ⊖	a		15 05												16 05										
Hackney Downs	d						15 20					15 50							16 20					16 50	
Bethnal Green	d																								
London Liverpool Street 15 ⊖	a	15 01		15 13	15 17		15 28	15 31	15 43	15 46		15 58		16 01		16 13	16 17		16 28	16 31		16 43	16 46	16 58	

Station		LE 1 🛒	LE 1	LE 1	LE 1 🛒	XC ◇1		LE 1	LE 1 🛒	LE 1	LE 1 🛒	LE 1	LE 1	LE 1 🛒	LE 1	LE 1		LE 1 🛒	XC ◇1	LE 1	LE 1 🛒	LE 1	LE 1 🛒	LE 1	LE 1
Cambridge	d			15 51		16 10				16 32						16 51			17 10			17 32			
Shelford	d			15 56												16 56									
Whittlesford Parkway	d			16 00						16 39						17 00						17 39			
Great Chesterford	d			16 04												17 04									
Audley End	d			16 10		16 24				16 47						17 10			17 24			17 47			
Newport (Essex)	d			16 13												17 13									
Elsenham	d			16 19												17 19									
Stansted Airport	a					16 45													17 45						
Stansted Airport	d	16 15			16 30				16 45		17 00		17 03	17 15				17 30			17 45		18 00		18 03
Stansted Mountfitchet	d			16 22					16 51				17 09			17 22					17 51				18 09
Bishops Stortford	a			16 28	16 39					17 00	17 09		17 13			17 28		17 39				18 00	18 09		18 13
	d			16 28	16 39					17 00	17 09		17 14			17 28		17 39				18 00	18 09		18 14
Sawbridgeworth	d			16 32						17 05			17 18			17 32						18 05			18 18
Harlow Mill	d			16 36									17 22			17 36									18 22
Harlow Town	d	16 30		16 39					17 02	17 10			17 25	17 30		17 39					18 02	18 10			18 25
Roydon	d			16 43									17 29			17 43									18 29
Hertford East	d							16 39				17 09								17 39				18 09	
Ware	d							16 43				17 13								17 43				18 13	
St Margarets (Herts)	d							16 47				17 17								17 47				18 17	
Rye House	d							16 50				17 20								17 50				18 20	
Broxbourne 3	a			16 47				16 54		17 16		17 24	17 34			17 47				17 54		18 16		18 24	18 34
Broxbourne 3	d			16 47				16 54		17 16		17 24	17 37			17 47				17 54		18 16		18 24	18 37
Cheshunt	d			16 51				16 58		17 20		17 28	17 42			17 51				17 58		18 20		18 28	18 42
Waltham Cross	d							17 01				17 31								18 01				18 31	
Enfield Lock	d							17 03				17 33	17 45							18 03				18 33	18 45
Brimsdown	d							17 06				17 36								18 06				18 36	
Ponders End	d							17 08				17 38								18 08				18 38	
Angel Road	d																								
Northumberland Park	d		←										17 51		←										18 51
Tottenham Hale ⊖	d	16 47	16 55	17 00	17 03			17 14	17 17	17 29	17 32	17 44	17 55	17 47	17 55	18 00		18 03		18 14	18 17	18 29	18 32	18 44	18 55
Seven Sisters ⊖	d												↦												↦
Clapton	d																								
Stratford 7 ⊖	a		17 05												18 05										
Hackney Downs	d							17 20				17 50								18 20				18 50	
Bethnal Green	d																								
London Liverpool Street 15 ⊖	a	17 01		17 13	17 17			17 28	17 31	17 43	17 46	17 58		18 01		18 13		18 17		18 28	18 31	18 43	18 46	18 58	

Table 22

Saturdays

Cambridge, Stansted Airport, Bishops Stortford, Hertford East and Broxbourne - London

		LE 1 🚲		LE 1	LE 1	LE 1 🚲	LE 1	LE 1 🚲	XC ◇1	LE 1	LE 1 🚲	LE 1		LE 1	LE 1 🚲	LE 1	LE 1	LE 1 🚲	XC ◇1	LE 1	LE 1 🚲	LE 1		LE 1 🚲	LE 1
Cambridge	d				17 51				18 20	18 32							18 51		19 10			19 32			
Shelford	d				17 56												18 56								
Whittlesford Parkway	d				18 00					18 39							19 00					19 39			
Great Chesterford	d				18 04												19 04								
Audley End	d				18 10				18 34	18 47							19 10		19 24			19 47			
Newport (Essex)	d				18 13												19 13								
Elsenham	d				18 19												19 19								
Stansted Airport	a								18 53										19 45						
Stansted Airport	d	18 15				18 30		18 45			19 00			19 03	19 15			19 30			19 45			20 00	
Stansted Mountfitchet	d				18 22			18 51						19 09			19 22				19 51				
Bishops Stortford	a				18 28	18 39				19 00	19 09			19 13			19 28	19 39				20 00		20 09	
	d				18 28	18 39				19 00	19 09			19 14			19 28	19 39				20 00		20 09	
Sawbridgeworth	d				18 32					19 05				19 18			19 32					20 05			
Harlow Mill	d				18 36									19 22			19 36								
Harlow Town	d	18 30			18 39			19 02		19 10				19 25	19 30		19 39				20 02	20 10			
Roydon	d				18 43									19 29			19 43								
Hertford East	d						18 39					19 09								19 39					20 09
Ware	d						18 43					19 13								19 43					20 13
St Margarets (Herts)	d						18 47					19 17								19 47					20 17
Rye House	d						18 50					19 20								19 50					20 20
Broxbourne 3	a				18 47		18 54			19 16		19 24		19 34			19 47			19 54		20 16			20 24
Broxbourne 3	d				18 47		18 54			19 16		19 24		19 37			19 47			19 54		20 16			20 24
Cheshunt	d				18 51		18 58			19 20		19 28		19 42			19 51			19 58		20 20			20 28
Waltham Cross	d						19 01					19 31								20 01					20 31
Enfield Lock	d						19 03					19 33		19 45						20 03					20 33
Brimsdown	d						19 06					19 36								20 06					20 36
Ponders End	d						19 08					19 38								20 08					20 38
Angel Road	d																								
Northumberland Park	d			←										19 51		←									
Tottenham Hale ⊖	d	18 47		18 55	19 00	19 03	19 14	19 17		19 29	19 32	19 44		19 55	19 47	19 55	20 00	20 03		20 14	20 17	20 29		20 32	20 44
Seven Sisters ⊖	d													↪											
Clapton	d																								
Stratford 7 ⊖	a			19 05												20 05									
Hackney Downs	d						19 20					19 50								20 20					20 50
Bethnal Green	d																								
London Liverpool Street 15 ⊖	a	19 01			19 13	19 17	19 28	19 31		19 43	19 46	19 58			20 01		20 13	20 17		20 28	20 31	20 43		20 46	20 58

		LE 1	LE 1 🚲	LE 1	LE 1	LE 1 🚲	XC ◇1	LE 1		LE 1 🚲	LE 1	LE 1 🚲	LE 1	LE 1	LE 1 🚲	LE 1	LE 1	LE 1 🚲		XC ◇1	LE 1	LE 1 🚲	LE 1	LE 1	LE 1
Cambridge	d				19 51		20 10				20 32						20 51			21 10			21 32		
Shelford	d				19 56												20 56								
Whittlesford Parkway	d				20 00						20 39						21 00						21 39		
Great Chesterford	d				20 04												21 04								
Audley End	d				20 10		20 24				20 47						21 10			21 24			21 47		
Newport (Essex)	d				20 13												21 13								
Elsenham	d				20 19												21 19								
Stansted Airport	a						20 45													21 45					
Stansted Airport	d	20 03	20 15			20 30				20 45		21 00		21 03	21 15			21 30				21 45		22 00	
Stansted Mountfitchet	d	20 09			20 22					20 51				21 09			21 22					21 51			
Bishops Stortford	a	20 13			20 28	20 39					21 00	21 09		21 13			21 28	21 39					22 00	22 09	
	d	20 14			20 28	20 39					21 00	21 09		21 14			21 28	21 39					22 00	22 09	
Sawbridgeworth	d	20 18			20 32						21 05			21 18			21 32						22 05		
Harlow Mill	d	20 22			20 36									21 22			21 36								
Harlow Town	d	20 25	20 30		20 39					21 02	21 10			21 25	21 30		21 39					22 02	22 10		
Roydon	d	20 29			20 43									21 29			21 43								
Hertford East	d							20 39					21 09								21 39				22 09
Ware	d							20 43					21 13								21 43				22 13
St Margarets (Herts)	d							20 47					21 17								21 47				22 17
Rye House	d							20 50					21 20								21 50				22 20
Broxbourne 3	a	20 34			20 47			20 54			21 16		21 24	21 34			21 47				21 54		22 16		22 24
Broxbourne 3	d	20 37			20 47			20 54			21 16		21 24	21 37			21 47				21 54		22 16		22 24
Cheshunt	d	20 42			20 51			20 58			21 20		21 28	21 42			21 51				21 58		22 20		22 28
Waltham Cross	d							21 01					21 31								22 01				22 31
Enfield Lock	d	20 45						21 03					21 33	21 45							22 03				22 33
Brimsdown	d							21 06					21 36								22 06				22 36
Ponders End	d							21 08					21 38								22 08				22 38
Angel Road	d																								
Northumberland Park	d	20 51		←										21 51		←									
Tottenham Hale ⊖	d	20 55	20 47	20 55	21 00	21 03		21 14		21 17	21 29	21 32	21 44	21 55	21 47	21 55	22 00	22 03			22 14	22 17	22 29	22 32	22 44
Seven Sisters ⊖	d	↪												↪											
Clapton	d																								
Stratford 7 ⊖	a			21 05												22 05									
Hackney Downs	d							21 20					21 50								22 20				22 50
Bethnal Green	d																								
London Liverpool Street 15 ⊖	a		21 01		21 13	21 17		21 28		21 31	21 43	21 46	21 58		22 01		22 13	22 17			22 28	22 31	22 43	22 46	22 58

Table 22

Saturdays

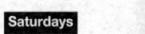

Cambridge, Stansted Airport, Bishops Stortford, Hertford East and Broxbourne - London

		LE 1	LE 1	LE 1		LE 1	LE 1	XC ◇1	LE 1	LE 1	LE 1	LE 1	LE 1	LE 1		LE 1	LE 1	LE 1	LE 1	LE 1	LE 1			
Cambridge	d					21 51		22 10			22 32						22 51							
Shelford	d					21 56											22 56							
Whittlesford Parkway	d					22 00					22 39						23 00							
Great Chesterford	d					22 04											23 04							
Audley End	d					22 10		22 24			22 47						23 10							
Newport (Essex)	d					22 13											23 13							
Elsenham	d					22 19											23 19							
Stansted Airport	a							22 45																
Stansted Airport	d	22 03	22 15				22 30			22 45		23 00	23 03			23 15		23 30		23 45	23 59			
Stansted Mountfitchet	d	22 09				22 22				22 51			23 09				23 22							
Bishops Stortford	a	22 13				22 28	22 39				23 00	23 09	23 13				23 28	23 39			00 08			
	d	22 14				22 28	22 39				23 00	23 09					23 28	23 39			00 08			
Sawbridgeworth	d	22 18				22 32					23 05						23 32							
Harlow Mill	d	22 22				22 36											23 36							
Harlow Town	d	22 25	22 30			22 39				23 02	23 10					23 30	23 39			23 59	00 16			
Roydon	d	22 29				22 43											23 43							
Hertford East	d								22 39					23 09					23 39					
Ware	d								22 43					23 13					23 43					
St Margarets (Herts)	d								22 47					23 17					23 47					
Rye House	d								22 50					23 20					23 50					
Broxbourne 3	a	22 34				22 47			22 54		23 16			23 24			23 47		23 54					
Broxbourne 3	d	22 37				22 47			22 54		23 16			23 24			23 47		23 54					
Cheshunt	d	22 42				22 51			22 58		23 20			23 28			23 51		23 58					
Waltham Cross	d								23 01					23 31					00 01					
Enfield Lock	d	22 45							23 03					23 33					00 03					
Brimsdown	d								23 06					23 36					00 06					
Ponders End	d								23 08					23 38					00 08					
Angel Road	d																							
Northumberland Park	d	22 51		←		22 58																		
Tottenham Hale ⊖	d	22 55	22 47	22 55		23 01	23 03		23 14	23 17	23 29	23 32		23 44		23 47	23 59	00 03	00 14	00 17				
Seven Sisters ⊖	d	→																						
Clapton	d																							
Stratford 7 ⊖	a			23 04																				
Hackney Downs	d								23 20					23 50					00 20					
Bethnal Green	d																							
London Liverpool Street 15 ⊖	a		23 01	23 17		23 15	23 18		23 28	23 31	23 43	23 46		23 58		00 01	00 13	00 17	00 28	00 31	00 51			

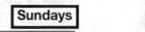

Sundays

		LE 1 A	LE 1 A	LE 1 A	LE 1 A	LE 1 A	LE 1 A	LE 1	LE 1	LE 1		LE 1 🚲	LE 1 🚲	LE 1	LE 1 🚲	LE 1 🚲	LE	LE 1	LE 1 🚲	LE 1		LE 1 🚲	LE	LE 1	LE 1 🚲
Cambridge	d		22p51																					07 32	
Shelford	d		22p56																						
Whittlesford Parkway	d		23p00																					07 39	
Great Chesterford	d		23p04																						
Audley End	d		23p10																					07 47	
Newport (Essex)	d		23p13																						
Elsenham	d		23p19																						
Stansted Airport	a																								
Stansted Airport	d	23p15		23p30		23p45	23p59		00 30	05 30		06 00	06 30		07 00	07 15			07 30			07 45			08 00
Stansted Mountfitchet	d		23p22																			07 51			
Bishops Stortford	a		23p28	23p39			00 08		00 39	05 39		06 09	06 39		07 09				07 39					08 00	08 09
	d		23p28	23p39			00 08		00 39	05 39		06 09	06 39	06 42	07 09			07 28	07 39					08 00	08 09
Sawbridgeworth	d		23p32											06 46				07 32						08 05	
Harlow Mill	d		23p36															07 36							
Harlow Town	d	23p30	23p39			23p59	00 16		00 47	05 47		06 17	06 47	06 51	07 17	07 30		07 39				08 02		08 10	
Roydon	d		23p43															07 43							
Hertford East	d				23p39			00 07															07 55		
Ware	d				23p43																		07 59		
St Margarets (Herts)	d				23p47																		08 03		
Rye House	d				23p50																		08 06		
Broxbourne 3	a		23p47		23p54			00 19		05 53				06 57				07 48					08 11	08 16	
Broxbourne 3	d		23p47		23p54					05 53				06 57			07 41	07 52					08 11	08 16	
Cheshunt	d		23p51		23p58									07 01			07 45	07 57					08 15	08 20	
Waltham Cross	d				00 01									07 04				07 59							
Enfield Lock	d				00 03									07 06				08 02							
Brimsdown	d				00 06									07 09				08 04							
Ponders End	d				00 08									07 11				08 06							
Angel Road	d																								
Northumberland Park	d																			←					
Tottenham Hale ⊖	d	23p47	23p59	00 03	00 14	00 17				06 04		06 33	07 03	07 17	07 33	07 46		08 12	08 01	08 12		08 17		08 29	08 32
Seven Sisters ⊖	d																08 03	→					08 33		
Clapton	d																								
Stratford 7 ⊖	a																			08 23					
Hackney Downs	d				00 20												08 09						08 39		
Bethnal Green	d																								
London Liverpool Street 15 ⊖	a	00 01	00 13	00 17	00 28	00 31	00 51		01 21	06 18		06 46	07 16	07 30	07 46	08 01	08 18		08 15			08 31	08 48	08 43	08 46

A not 22 May

Table 22

Sundays

Cambridge, Stansted Airport, Bishops Stortford, Hertford East and Broxbourne - London

		LE	LE	LE	LE	LE	LE	LE	LE	LE	LE	LE	LE	LE	LE	XC	LE	LE	LE	LE	LE	LE	LE
		1		1	1	1	1		1	1	1		1	1	1	1	1		1	1	1		1
		🚲			🚲		🚲			🚲	🚲			🚲			🚲			🚲	🚲		
Cambridge	d			07 51					08 32				08 51			09 15			09 32				09 51
Shelford	d			07 56									08 56										09 56
Whittlesford Parkway	d			08 00					08 39				09 00						09 39				10 00
Great Chesterford	d			08 04									09 04										10 04
Audley End	d			08 10					08 47				09 10			09 28			09 47				10 10
Newport (Essex)	d			08 13									09 13										10 13
Elsenham	d			08 19									09 19										10 19
Stansted Airport	a															09 43							
Stansted Airport	d	08 15			08 30		08 45			09 00	09 15			09 30			09 45			10 00	10 15		
Stansted Mountfitchet	d			08 22			08 51						09 22				09 51						10 22
Bishops Stortford	a			08 28	08 39				09 00	09 09			09 28	09 39					10 00	10 09			10 28
	d			08 28	08 39				09 00	09 09			09 28	09 39					10 00	10 09			10 28
Sawbridgeworth	d			08 32					09 05				09 32						10 05				10 32
Harlow Mill	d			08 36									09 36										10 36
Harlow Town	d	08 30		08 39			09 02		09 10		09 30		09 39				10 02		10 10		10 30		10 39
Roydon	d			08 43									09 43										10 43
Hertford East	d		08 25					08 55				09 25						09 55				10 25	
Ware	d		08 29					08 59				09 29						09 59				10 29	
St Margarets (Herts)	d		08 33					09 03				09 33						10 03				10 33	
Rye House	d		08 36					09 06				09 36						10 06				10 36	
Broxbourne 3	a		08 41	08 48				09 11	09 16			09 41	09 48					10 11	10 16			10 41	10 48
Broxbourne 3	d		08 41	08 52				09 11	09 16			09 41	09 52					10 11	10 16			10 41	10 52
Cheshunt	d		08 45	08 57				09 15	09 20			09 45	09 57					10 15	10 20			10 45	10 57
Waltham Cross	d			08 59									09 59										10 59
Enfield Lock	d			09 02									10 02										11 02
Brimsdown	d			09 04									10 04										11 04
Ponders End	d			09 06									10 06										11 06
Angel Road	d																						
Northumberland Park	d					←									←								
Tottenham Hale ⊖	d	08 46		09 12	09 01	09 12	09 17		09 29	09 32	09 46		10 12	10 01	10 12		10 17		10 29	10 32	10 46		11 12
Seven Sisters ⊖	d		09 03	→				09 33				10 03	→					10 33				11 03	→
Clapton	d																						
Stratford 7 ⊖	a					09 23									10 23								
Hackney Downs	d		09 09					09 39				10 09						10 39				11 09	
Bethnal Green	d																						
London Liverpool Street 15 ⊖	a	09 03	09 18		09 15		09 31	09 48	09 43	09 46	10 01	10 18		10 15			10 31	10 48	10 43	10 46	11 01	11 18	

		LE	LE	XC	LE	LE	LE	LE	LE	LE	LE	LE	LE	XC	LE	LE	LE	LE	LE	LE	LE	LE
		1	1	1	1		1	1	1		1	1	1	1	1		1	1	1		1	1
		🚲			🚲			🚲	🚲			🚲			🚲			🚲	🚲			🚲
Cambridge	d			10 15			10 32				10 51			11 15			11 32				11 51	
Shelford	d										10 56										11 56	
Whittlesford Parkway	d						10 39				11 00						11 39				12 00	
Great Chesterford	d										11 04										12 04	
Audley End	d			10 28			10 47				11 10			11 28			11 47				12 10	
Newport (Essex)	d										11 13										12 13	
Elsenham	d										11 19										12 19	
Stansted Airport	a			10 43										11 43								
Stansted Airport	d	10 30			10 45			11 00	11 15			11 30			11 45			12 00	12 15			12 30
Stansted Mountfitchet	d				10 51						11 22				11 51						12 22	
Bishops Stortford	a	10 39					11 00	11 09			11 28	11 39					12 00	12 09			12 28	12 39
	d	10 39					11 00	11 09			11 28	11 39					12 00	12 09			12 28	12 39
Sawbridgeworth	d						11 05				11 32						12 05				12 32	
Harlow Mill	d										11 36										12 36	
Harlow Town	d				11 02		11 10		11 30		11 39				12 02		12 10		12 30		12 39	
Roydon	d										11 43										12 43	
Hertford East	d					10 55				11 25						11 55				12 25		
Ware	d					10 59				11 29						11 59				12 29		
St Margarets (Herts)	d					11 03				11 33						12 03				12 33		
Rye House	d					11 06				11 36						12 06				12 36		
Broxbourne 3	a					11 11	11 16			11 41	11 48					12 11	12 16			12 41	12 48	
Broxbourne 3	d					11 11	11 16			11 41	11 52					12 11	12 16			12 41	12 52	
Cheshunt	d					11 15	11 20			11 45	11 57					12 15	12 20			12 45	12 57	
Waltham Cross	d										11 59										12 59	
Enfield Lock	d										12 02										13 02	
Brimsdown	d										12 04										13 04	
Ponders End	d										12 06										13 06	
Angel Road	d																					
Northumberland Park	d		←										←									
Tottenham Hale ⊖	d	11 01	11 12		11 17		11 29	11 32	11 46		12 12	12 01	12 12		12 17		12 29	12 32	12 46		13 12	13 01
Seven Sisters ⊖	d					11 33				12 03	→					12 33				13 03	→	
Clapton	d																					
Stratford 7 ⊖	a		11 23										12 23									
Hackney Downs	d					11 39				12 09						12 39				13 09		
Bethnal Green	d																					
London Liverpool Street 15 ⊖	a	11 15			11 31	11 48	11 43	11 46	12 01	12 18		12 15			12 31	12 48	12 43	12 46	13 01	13 18		13 15

Table 22

Sundays

Cambridge, Stansted Airport, Bishops Stortford, Hertford East and Broxbourne - London

		LE	XC	LE	LE	LE	LE	LE	LE	LE	LE	LE	XC	LE	LE	LE	LE	LE	LE	LE	LE	LE	XC
		1	1	1		1	1	1		1	1	1	1	1		1	1	1		1	1	1	◇1
				trolley			trolley	trolley			trolley			trolley			trolley	trolley			trolley		
Cambridge	d		12 15			12 32				12 51			13 15			13 32				13 51			14 10
Shelford	d									12 56										13 56			
Whittlesford Parkway	d					12 39				13 00						13 39				14 00			
Great Chesterford	d									13 04										14 04			
Audley End	d		12 28			12 47				13 10			13 28			13 47				14 10			14 24
Newport (Essex)	d									13 13										14 13			
Elsenham	d									13 19										14 19			
Stansted Airport	a		12 43										13 43										14 43
Stansted Airport	d			12 45			13 00	13 15			13 30			13 45			14 00	14 15			14 30		
Stansted Mountfitchet	d			12 51						13 22				13 51						14 22			
Bishops Stortford	a					13 00	13 09			13 28	13 39					14 00	14 09			14 28	14 39		
	d					13 00	13 09			13 28	13 39					14 00	14 09			14 28	14 39		
Sawbridgeworth	d					13 05				13 32						14 05				14 32			
Harlow Mill	d									13 36										14 36			
Harlow Town	d			13 02		13 10		13 30		13 39				14 02		14 10		14 30		14 39			
Roydon	d									13 43										14 43			
Hertford East	d				12 55				13 25						13 55				14 25				
Ware	d				12 59				13 29						13 59				14 29				
St Margarets (Herts)	d				13 03				13 33						14 03				14 33				
Rye House	d				13 06				13 36						14 06				14 36				
Broxbourne 3	a				13 11	13 16			13 41	13 48					14 11	14 16			14 41	14 48			
Broxbourne 3	d				13 11	13 16			13 41	13 52					14 11	14 16			14 41	14 52			
Cheshunt	d				13 15	13 20			13 45	13 57					14 15	14 20			14 45	14 57			
Waltham Cross	d									13 59										14 59			
Enfield Lock	d									14 02										15 02			
Brimsdown	d									14 04										15 04			
Ponders End	d									14 06										15 06			
Angel Road	d																						
Northumberland Park	d	←										←										←	
Tottenham Hale ⊖	d	13 12		13 17		13 29	13 32	13 46		14 12	14 01	14 12		14 17		14 29	14 32	14 46		15 12	15 01	15 12	
Seven Sisters ⊖	d				13 33				14 03	→					14 33				15 03	→			
Clapton	d																						
Stratford 7 ⊖	a	13 23										14 23										15 23	
Hackney Downs	d				13 39				14 09						14 39				15 09				
Bethnal Green	d																						
London Liverpool Street 15 ⊖	a			13 31	13 48	13 43	13 46	14 01	14 18		14 15			14 31	14 48	14 43	14 46	15 01	15 18		15 15		

		LE	LE	LE	LE	LE	LE	LE	LE	LE	XC	LE	LE	LE	LE	LE	LE	LE	LE	LE	XC	LE
		1		1	1	1		1	1	1	◇1	1		1	1	1		1	1	1	◇1	1
		trolley			trolley	trolley			trolley			trolley			trolley	trolley			trolley			trolley
Cambridge	d			14 32				14 51			15 10			15 32				15 51			16 10	
Shelford	d							14 56										15 56				
Whittlesford Parkway	d			14 39				15 00						15 39				16 00				
Great Chesterford	d							15 04										16 04				
Audley End	d			14 47				15 10			15 24			15 47				16 10			16 23	
Newport (Essex)	d							15 13										16 13				
Elsenham	d							15 19										16 19				
Stansted Airport	a										15 43										16 43	
Stansted Airport	d	14 45			15 00	15 15			15 30			15 45			16 00	16 15			16 30			16 45
Stansted Mountfitchet	d	14 51						15 22				15 51						16 22				16 51
Bishops Stortford	a			15 00	15 09			15 28	15 39					16 00	16 09			16 28	16 39			
	d			15 00	15 09			15 28	15 39					16 00	16 09			16 28	16 39			
Sawbridgeworth	d			15 05				15 32						16 05				16 32				
Harlow Mill	d							15 36										16 36				
Harlow Town	d	15 02		15 10		15 30		15 39				16 02		16 10		16 30		16 39				17 02
Roydon	d							15 43										16 43				
Hertford East	d		14 55				15 25						15 55				16 25					
Ware	d		14 59				15 29						15 59				16 29					
St Margarets (Herts)	d		15 03				15 33						16 03				16 33					
Rye House	d		15 06				15 36						16 06				16 36					
Broxbourne 3	a		15 11	15 16			15 41	15 48					16 11	16 16			16 41	16 48				
Broxbourne 3	d		15 11	15 16			15 41	15 52					16 11	16 16			16 41	16 52				
Cheshunt	d		15 15	15 20			15 45	15 57					16 15	16 20			16 45	16 57				
Waltham Cross	d							15 59										16 59				
Enfield Lock	d							16 02										17 02				
Brimsdown	d							16 04										17 04				
Ponders End	d							16 06										17 06				
Angel Road	d																					
Northumberland Park	d									←										←		
Tottenham Hale ⊖	d	15 17		15 29	15 32	15 46		16 12	16 01	16 12		16 17		16 29	16 32	16 46		17 12	17 01	17 12		17 17
Seven Sisters ⊖	d		15 33				16 03	→					16 33				17 03	→				
Clapton	d																					
Stratford 7 ⊖	a									16 23										17 23		
Hackney Downs	d		15 39				16 09						16 39				17 09					
Bethnal Green	d																					
London Liverpool Street 15 ⊖	a	15 31	15 48	15 43	15 46	16 01	16 18		16 15			16 31	16 48	16 43	16 46	17 01	17 18		17 15			17 31

Table 22

Sundays

Cambridge, Stansted Airport, Bishops Stortford, Hertford East and Broxbourne - London

		LE	LE [1]	LE [1] 🛒	LE [1] 🛒	LE	LE [1]	LE [1] 🛒	LE [1]	XC ◇[1]		LE [1] 🛒	LE	LE [1]	LE [1] 🛒	LE [1] 🛒	LE	LE [1]	LE [1] 🛒	LE [1]		XC ◇[1]	LE [1] 🛒	LE	LE [1]
Cambridge	d		16 32				16 51			17 10				17 32				17 51				18 10			18 32
Shelford	d						16 56											17 56							
Whittlesford Parkway	d		16 39				17 00							17 39				18 00							18 39
Great Chesterford	d						17 04											18 04							
Audley End	d		16 47				17 10			17 24				17 47				18 10				18 24			18 47
Newport (Essex)	d						17 13											18 13							
Elsenham	d						17 19											18 19							
Stansted Airport	a									17 43												18 43			
Stansted Airport	d			17 00	17 15			17 30				17 45			18 00	18 15			18 30				18 45		
Stansted Mountfitchet	d						17 22					17 51						18 22					18 51		
Bishops Stortford	a		17 00	17 09			17 28	17 39						18 00	18 09			18 28	18 39						19 00
	d		17 00	17 09			17 28	17 39						18 00	18 09			18 28	18 39						19 00
Sawbridgeworth	d		17 05				17 32							18 05				18 32							19 05
Harlow Mill	d						17 36											18 36							
Harlow Town	d		17 10		17 30		17 39					18 02		18 10		18 30		18 39					19 02		19 10
Roydon	d						17 43											18 43							
Hertford East	d	16 55				17 25							17 55				18 25							18 55	
Ware	d	16 59				17 29							17 59				18 29							18 59	
St Margarets (Herts)	d	17 03				17 33							18 03				18 33							19 03	
Rye House	d	17 06				17 36							18 06				18 36							19 06	
Broxbourne [3]	a	17 11	17 16			17 41	17 48						18 11	18 16			18 41	18 48						19 11	19 16
Broxbourne [3]	d	17 11	17 16			17 41	17 52						18 11	18 16			18 41	18 52						19 11	19 16
Cheshunt	d	17 15	17 20			17 45	17 57						18 15	18 20			18 45	18 57						19 15	19 20
Waltham Cross	d						17 59											18 59							
Enfield Lock	d						18 02											19 02							
Brimsdown	d						18 04											19 04							
Ponders End	d						18 06											19 06							
Angel Road	d																								
Northumberland Park	d								←											←					
Tottenham Hale ⊖	d		17 29	17 32	17 46		18 12	18 01	18 12			18 17		18 29	18 32	18 46		19 12	19 01	19 12			19 17		19 29
Seven Sisters ⊖	d	17 33				18 03	→						18 33				19 03	→						19 33	
Clapton	d																								
Stratford [7] ⊖	a								18 23											19 23					
Hackney Downs	d	17 39				18 09							18 39				19 09							19 39	
Bethnal Green	d																								
London Liverpool Street [15] ⊖	a	17 48	17 43	17 46	18 01	18 18		18 15				18 31	18 48	18 43	18 46	19 01	19 18		19 15				19 31	19 48	19 43

		LE [1] 🛒	LE [1] 🛒	LE	LE [1]	LE [1] 🛒		LE [1]	XC ◇[1]	LE [1] 🛒	LE	LE [1]	LE [1] 🛒	LE [1] 🛒	LE	LE [1]		LE [1] 🛒	LE [1]	XC ◇[1]	LE [1] 🛒	LE	LE [1]	LE [1] 🛒	LE [1] 🛒
Cambridge	d				18 51				19 10			19 32				19 51				20 10			20 32		
Shelford	d				18 56											19 56									
Whittlesford Parkway	d				19 00							19 39				20 00							20 39		
Great Chesterford	d				19 04											20 04									
Audley End	d				19 10				19 24			19 47				20 10				20 24			20 47		
Newport (Essex)	d				19 13											20 13									
Elsenham	d				19 19											20 19									
Stansted Airport	a								19 43											20 43					
Stansted Airport	d	19 00	19 15			19 30				19 45			20 00	20 15				20 30			20 45			21 00	21 15
Stansted Mountfitchet	d				19 22					19 51						20 22					20 51				
Bishops Stortford	a	19 09			19 28	19 39						20 00	20 09			20 28		20 39					21 00	21 09	
	d	19 09			19 28	19 39						20 00	20 09			20 28		20 39					21 00	21 09	
Sawbridgeworth	d				19 32							20 05				20 32							21 05		
Harlow Mill	d				19 36											20 36									
Harlow Town	d		19 30		19 39					20 02		20 10		20 30		20 39					21 02		21 10		21 30
Roydon	d				19 43											20 43									
Hertford East	d			19 25							19 55				20 25							20 55			
Ware	d			19 29							19 59				20 29							20 59			
St Margarets (Herts)	d			19 33							20 03				20 33							21 03			
Rye House	d			19 36							20 06				20 36							21 06			
Broxbourne [3]	a			19 41	19 48						20 11	20 16			20 41	20 48						21 11	21 16		
Broxbourne [3]	d			19 41	19 52						20 11	20 16			20 41	20 52						21 11	21 16		
Cheshunt	d			19 45	19 57						20 15	20 20			20 45	20 57						21 15	21 20		
Waltham Cross	d				19 59											20 59									
Enfield Lock	d				20 02											21 02									
Brimsdown	d				20 04											21 04									
Ponders End	d				20 06											21 06									
Angel Road	d																								
Northumberland Park	d							←											←						
Tottenham Hale ⊖	d	19 32	19 46		20 12	20 01		20 12		20 17		20 29	20 32	20 46		21 12		21 01	21 12		21 17		21 29	21 32	21 46
Seven Sisters ⊖	d			20 03	→						20 33				21 03	→						21 33			
Clapton	d																								
Stratford [7] ⊖	a							20 23											21 23						
Hackney Downs	d			20 09							20 39				21 09							21 39			
Bethnal Green	d																								
London Liverpool Street [15] ⊖	a	19 46	20 01	20 18		20 15				20 31	20 48	20 43	20 46	21 01	21 18			21 15			21 31	21 48	21 43	21 46	22 01

Table 22

Sundays

Cambridge, Stansted Airport, Bishops Stortford, Hertford East and Broxbourne - London

		LE		LE	LE	LE	XC	LE	LE	LE	LE	LE		LE	LE	LE	LE	XC	LE	LE	LE	LE		LE	LE
				1	1	1	◇1	1		1	1	1			1	1	1	◇1	1		1	1		1	1
					🚲			🚲																	
Cambridge	d			20 51			21 10			21 32					21 51			22 10			22 32	22 51			
Shelford	d			20 56											21 56							22 56			
Whittlesford Parkway	d			21 00						21 39					22 00						22 39	23 00			
Great Chesterford	d			21 04											22 04							23 04			
Audley End	d			21 10			21 24			21 47					22 10			22 24			22 47	23 10			
Newport (Essex)	d			21 13											22 13							23 13			
Elsenham	d			21 19											22 19							23 19			
Stansted Airport	a						21 43											22 43							
Stansted Airport	d				21 30			21 45			22 00	22 15				22 30			22 45					23 00	23 15
Stansted Mountfitchet	d			21 22				21 51							22 22				22 51			23 22			
Bishops Stortford	a			21 28	21 39					22 00	22 09				22 28	22 39					23 00	23 28		23 09	
	d			21 28	21 39					22 00	22 09				22 28	22 39					23 00			23 09	
Sawbridgeworth	d			21 32						22 05					22 32						23 05				
Harlow Mill	d			21 36											22 36										
Harlow Town	d			21 39				22 02		22 10		22 30			22 39				23 02		23 10				23 30
Roydon	d			21 43											22 43										
Hertford East	d	21 25							21 55					22 25						22 55					
Ware	d	21 29							21 59					22 29						22 59					
St Margarets (Herts)	d	21 33							22 03					22 33						23 03					
Rye House	d	21 36							22 06					22 36						23 06					
Broxbourne 3	a	21 41		21 48					22 11	22 16				22 41	22 48					23 11	23 16				
Broxbourne 3	d	21 41		21 52					22 11	22 16				22 41	22 52					23 11	23 16				
Cheshunt	d	21 45		21 57					22 15	22 20				22 45	22 57					23 15	23 20				
Waltham Cross	d			21 59											22 59										
Enfield Lock	d			22 02											23 02										
Brimsdown	d			22 04											23 04										
Ponders End	d			22 06											23 06										
Angel Road	d																								
Northumberland Park	d					←											←								
Tottenham Hale ⊖	d			22 12	22 01	22 12		22 17		22 29	22 32	22 46			23 12	23 01	23 12		23 17		23 29			23 32	23 46
Seven Sisters ⊖	d	22 03		↪					22 33					23 03	↪					23 33					
Clapton	d																								
Stratford 7 ⊖	a					22 23											23 22								
Hackney Downs	d	22 09							22 39					23 09						23 39					
Bethnal Green	d																								
London Liverpool Street 15 ⊖	a	22 18			22 15			22 31	22 48	22 43	22 46	23 01		23 18		23 15	23 36		23 31	23 48	23 43			23 46	00 01

		LE	LE	LE
		1	1	1
Cambridge	d			
Shelford	d			
Whittlesford Parkway	d			
Great Chesterford	d			
Audley End	d			
Newport (Essex)	d			
Elsenham	d			
Stansted Airport	a			
Stansted Airport	d	23 30	23 45	23 59
Stansted Mountfitchet	d			
Bishops Stortford	a	23 39		00 08
	d	23 39		00 08
Sawbridgeworth	d			
Harlow Mill	d			
Harlow Town	d	23 47	23 59	00 16
Roydon	d			
Hertford East	d			
Ware	d			
St Margarets (Herts)	d			
Rye House	d			
Broxbourne 3	a			
Broxbourne 3	d			
Cheshunt	d			
Waltham Cross	d			
Enfield Lock	d			
Brimsdown	d			
Ponders End	d			
Angel Road	d			
Northumberland Park	d			
Tottenham Hale ⊖	d			
Seven Sisters ⊖	d	00 08	00 21	
Clapton	d			
Stratford 7 ⊖	a			
Hackney Downs	d			
Bethnal Green	d			
London Liverpool Street 15 ⊖	a	00 22	00 35	00 51

Network Diagram for Tables 24, 25

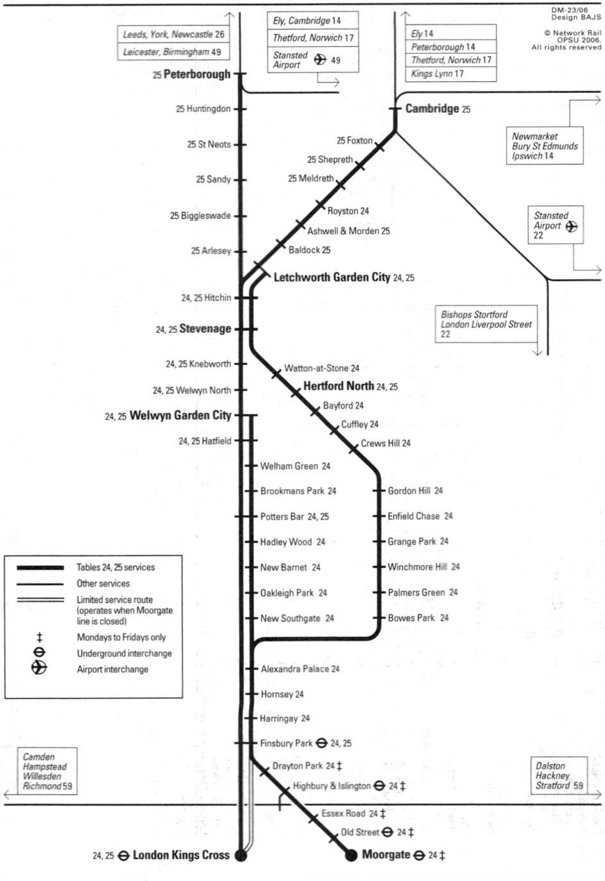

London - Welwyn Garden City, Hertford North and Letchworth Garden City

Miles	Miles				FC MO	FC MX	FC MX [1]	FC MX	FC MO	FC MX	FC MO [1] A	FC MX	FC		FC [1]
0	—	London Kings Cross [15]	⊖	d	23p26	23p26	23p36		23p41	23p41	00 07	00 06	00 11		00 36
—	0	**Moorgate**	⊖	d											
—	0½	Old Street	⊖	d											
—	1¾	Essex Road		d											
—	2¼	Highbury & Islington	⊖	d											
—	2¾	Drayton Park		d											
2½	3½	Finsbury Park	⊖	d	23p32	23p32	23p41		23p47	23p47	00 12	00 12	00 17		00 41
3½	4½	Harringay		d	23p34	23p34			23p49	23p49		00 14	00 19		
4	5	Hornsey		d	23p36	23p36			23p51	23p51		00 16	00 21		
5	6	Alexandra Palace		d	23p38	23p38			23p53	23p53	00 17	00 18	00 23		
6½	—	New Southgate		d					23p56	23p56			00 26		
8½	—	Oakleigh Park		d					23p59	23p59			00 29		
9¼	—	New Barnet		d					00 01	00 01			00 31		
10½	—	Hadley Wood		d					00 04	00 04			00 34		
12¾	—	Potters Bar		d			23p51		00 08	00 08			00 38		00 51
14½	—	Brookmans Park		d					00 11	00 11			00 41		
15½	—	Welham Green		d					00 13	00 13			00 43		
17¾	—	Hatfield		d			23p57		00 16	00 16			00 46		00 57
20¼	—	**Welwyn Garden City** [4]		d			00 01		00 20	00a24			00a54		01 01
22	—	Welwyn North		d			00 04		00 23						01s04
25	—	Knebworth		d			00 08		00 28						01s08
—	6¾	Bowes Park		d	23p41	23p41						00 21			
—	7¾	Palmers Green		d	23p43	23p43					00 20	00 23			
—	8¾	Winchmore Hill		d	23p45	23p45					00 22	00 25			
—	9½	Grange Park		d	23p47	23p47						00 27			
—	10¼	Enfield Chase		d	23p49	23p49					00 25	00 29			
—	11	Gordon Hill		d	23p51	23p51					00 27	00 31			
—	12½	Crews Hill		d	23p54	23p54						00 34			
—	14¼	Cuffley		d	23p57	23p57					00 31	00 37			
—	17¾	Bayford		d	00 02	00 02						00 42			
—	20¾	**Hertford North**		d	00 07	00 07					00 39	00 47			
—	25	Watton-at-Stone		d	00 13	00 13		←				00 53			
27½	30	**Stevenage** [4]		d	00a20	00 20	00 12	00 20	00 31		00 48	01 00			01 12
31¾	34¼	Hitchin [4]		d		→	00 20	00 26	00 37		00 56	01 06			01a17
34¾	37¼	**Letchworth Garden City**		a			00 29	00 36	00 52		01 00	01 15			

	FC MX [1]	FC MO [1]	FC [1]	FC [1]	FC	FC	FC	FC [1]		FC	FC
London Kings Cross [15] ⊖ d	01 06	01 06	01 36	05 23		05 26	05 56	06 06		06 11	06 26
Moorgate ⊖ d											
Old Street ⊖ d											
Essex Road d											
Highbury & Islington ⊖ d											
Drayton Park d											
Finsbury Park ⊖ d	01 11	01 11	01 41	05 28		05 32	06 02	06 11		06 17	06 32
Harringay d						05 34	06 04			06 19	06 34
Hornsey d						05 36	06 06			06 21	06 36
Alexandra Palace d	01 16	01 16	01 45			05 38	06 08			06 23	06 38
New Southgate d			01 48							06 26	
Oakleigh Park d			01 51							06 29	
New Barnet d			01 53							06 31	
Hadley Wood d			01 56							06 34	
Potters Bar d			01 59	05 38				06 21		06 38	
Brookmans Park d										06 41	
Welham Green d										06 43	
Hatfield d			02 05	05 44				06 27		06 46	
Welwyn Garden City [4] d			02 09	05 48				06 31		06a53	
Welwyn North d			02s12	05 51				06 34			
Knebworth d			02s16	05 55				06 38			
Bowes Park d						05 41	06 11				06 41
Palmers Green d	01 19	01 19				05 43	06 13				06 43
Winchmore Hill d	01 21	01 22				05 45	06 15				06 45
Grange Park d						05 47	06 17				06 47
Enfield Chase d	01 24	01 25				05 49	06 19				06 49
Gordon Hill d	01 26	01 27				05 51	06 21				06 51
Crews Hill d						05 54	06 24				06 54
Cuffley d	01 30	01 31				05 57	06 27				06 57
Bayford d						06 02	06 32				07 02
Hertford North d	01 38	01 40			05 50	06a10	06 40				07 10
Watton-at-Stone d					05 55		06 45				07 15
Stevenage [4] d	01 47	01 50	02 20	05 59	06a05		06a55	06 42			07a25
Hitchin [4] d	01 52	01 56	02a25	06a07				06 47			
Letchworth Garden City a	02 06	02 10						06 51			

			FC [1]	FC	FC	FC [1]	FC	FC	FC [1]		FC
London Kings Cross [15]	⊖	d	06 36			07 06			07 36		
Moorgate	⊖	d		06 35	06 50		07 05	07 20			07 33
Old Street	⊖	d		06 37	06 52		07 07	07 22			07 35
Essex Road		d		06 40	06 55		07 10	07 25			07 38
Highbury & Islington	⊖	d		06 42	06 57		07 12	07 27			07 40
Drayton Park		d		06 44	06 59		07 14	07 29			07 42
Finsbury Park	⊖	d	06 41	06 47	07 02	07 11	07 17	07 32	07 41		07 45
Harringay		d		06 49	07 04		07 19	07 34			
Hornsey		d		06 51	07 06		07 21	07 36			
Alexandra Palace		d		06 53	07 08		07 23	07 38			07 51
New Southgate		d		06 56			07 26				
Oakleigh Park		d		06 59			07 29				
New Barnet		d		07 01			07 31				
Hadley Wood		d		07 04			07 34				
Potters Bar		d	06 51	07 08		07 21	07 38		07 51		
Brookmans Park		d		07 11			07 41				
Welham Green		d		07 13			07 43				
Hatfield		d	06 57	07 16		07 27	07 46		07 57		
Welwyn Garden City [4]		d	07 01	07a21		07 31	07a51		08 01		
Welwyn North		d	07 04			07 34			08 04		
Knebworth		d	07 08			07 38			08 08		
Bowes Park		d			07 11			07 41			
Palmers Green		d			07 13			07 43			07 55
Winchmore Hill		d			07 15			07 45			07 57
Grange Park		d			07 17			07 47			
Enfield Chase		d			07 19			07 49			08 01
Gordon Hill		d			07 21			07 51			08 03
Crews Hill		d			07 24			07 54			
Cuffley		d			07 27			07 57			08 08
Bayford		d			07 32			08 02			
Hertford North		d			07 40			08 10			08a16
Watton-at-Stone		d			07 45			08 15			
Stevenage [4]		d	07 12		07a55	07 42		08a25	08 12		
Hitchin [4]		d	07a17			07 47			08a17		
Letchworth Garden City		a				07 51					

	FC	FC	FC [1]	FC	FC	FC	FC	FC		FC [1]	FC	FC	FC	FC	FC [1]
London Kings Cross [15] ⊖ d			08 03							08 36					09 06
Moorgate ⊖ d	07 38	07 48			08 03	08 08	08 18	08 23				08 33	08 38	08 43	
Old Street ⊖ d	07 40	07 50			08 05	08 10	08 20	08 25				08 35	08 40	08 45	
Essex Road d	07 43	07 53			08 08	08 13	08 23	08 28				08 38	08 43	08 48	
Highbury & Islington ⊖ d	07 45	07 55			08 10	08 15	08 25	08 30				08 40	08 45	08 50	
Drayton Park d	07 47	07 57			08 12	08 17	08 27	08 32				08 42	08 47	08 52	
Finsbury Park ⊖ d	07 50	08 00	08 08		08 15	08 20	08 30	08 35		08 41		08 45	08 50	08 55	09 11
Harringay d	07 52	08 02				08 22	08 32	08 37				08 47	08 52	08 57	
Hornsey d	07 54	08 04				08 24	08 34	08 39				08 49	08 54	08 59	
Alexandra Palace d	07 56	08 06			08 21	08 26	08 36	08 41				08 51	08 56	09 01	
New Southgate d	07 59					08 29		08 44					08 59		
Oakleigh Park d	08 02					08 32		08 47					09 02		
New Barnet d	08 04					08 34		08 49					09 04		
Hadley Wood d	08 07					08 37		08 52			←		09 07		
Potters Bar d	08 11		08 18			08 41		08 56		08 51	08 56		09 11		09 21
Brookmans Park d	08 14					08 44		→			08 59		09 14		
Welham Green d	08 16					08 46					09 01		09 16		
Hatfield d	08 19		08 25			08 49				08 57	09 04		09 19		09 27
Welwyn Garden City [4] d	08a24		08 30			08a54				09 01	09a09		09a26		09 31
Welwyn North d			08 33							09 04					09 34
Knebworth d			08 37							09 08					09 38
Bowes Park d		08 09					08 39					08 54		09 04	
Palmers Green d		08 11			08 25		08 41					08 56		09 06	
Winchmore Hill d		08 13			08 27		08 43					08 58		09 08	
Grange Park d		08 15					08 45					09 00		09 10	
Enfield Chase d		08 17			08 31		08 47					09 02		09 12	
Gordon Hill d		08 19			08 33		08 49					09 04		09a16	
Crews Hill d		08 22					08 52					09 07			
Cuffley d		08 25			08 38		08 55					09 10			
Bayford d		08 30					09 00					09 15			
Hertford North d		08 37			08a46		09 07					09a21			
Watton-at-Stone d		08 43		←			09 13								
Stevenage [4] d		08 51	08 41	08 51			09a22			09 12					09 42
Hitchin [4] d		→	08 46	08 57						09a17					09 47
Letchworth Garden City a			08 50	09 04											09 51

A Until 1 August, MO from 19 September

London - Welwyn Garden City, Hertford North and Letchworth Garden City

Station		FC	FC	FC	FC 1	FC	FC	FC	FC	FC	FC 1	FC	FC	FC	FC	FC 1	FC	FC	FC	FC	FC 1	FC
London Kings Cross 15	⊖ d				09 36						10 06					10 36					11 06	
Moorgate	⊖ d	09 02	09 12	09 22				09 32	09 42	09 52			10 02	10 12	10 22			10 32	10 42	10 52		
Old Street	⊖ d	09 04	09 14	09 24				09 34	09 44	09 54			10 04	10 14	10 24			10 34	10 44	10 54		
Essex Road	d	09 07	09 17	09 27				09 37	09 47	09 57			10 07	10 17	10 27			10 37	10 47	10 57		
Highbury & Islington	⊖ d	09 09	09 19	09 29				09 39	09 49	09 59			10 09	10 19	10 29			10 39	10 49	10 59		
Drayton Park	d	09 11	09 21	09 31				09 41	09 51	10 01			10 11	10 21	10 31			10 41	10 51	11 01		
Finsbury Park	⊖ d	09 14	09 24	09 34	09 41			09 44	09 54	10 04	10 11		10 14	10 24	10 34	10 41		10 44	10 54	11 04	11 11	
Harringay	d	09 16	09 26	09 36				09 46	09 56	10 06			10 16	10 26	10 36			10 46	10 56	11 06		
Hornsey	d	09 18	09 28	09 38				09 48	09 58	10 08			10 18	10 28	10 38			10 48	10 58	11 08		
Alexandra Palace	d	09 20	09 30	09 40				09 50	10 00	10 10			10 20	10 30	10 40			10 50	11 00	11 10		
New Southgate	d	09 23		09 43					10 03				10 23		10 43				11 03			
Oakleigh Park	d	09 26		09 46					10 06				10 26		10 46				11 06			
New Barnet	d	09 28		09 48					10 08				10 28		10 48				11 08			
Hadley Wood	d	09 31		09 51			←		10 11				10 31		10 51		←		11 11			
Potters Bar	d	09 35		09 55	09 51		09 55		10 15		10 21		10 35		10 55	10 51	10 55		11 15		11 21	
Brookmans Park	d	09 38		→			09 58		10 18				10 38		→		10 58		11 18			
Welham Green	d	09 40					10 00		10 20				10 40				11 00		11 20			
Hatfield	d	09 43			09 57		10 03		10 23		10 27		10 43			10 57	11 03		11 23		11 27	
Welwyn Garden City 4	d	09a49			10 01		10a09		10a29		10 31		10a49			11 01	11a09		11a29		11 31	
Welwyn North	d				10 04						10 34					11 04					11 34	
Knebworth	d				10 08						10 38					11 08					11 38	
Bowes Park	d		09 33					09 53		10 13				10 33				10 53		11 13		
Palmers Green	d		09 35					09 55		10 15				10 35				10 55		11 15		
Winchmore Hill	d		09 37					09 57		10 17				10 37				10 57		11 17		
Grange Park	d		09 39					09 59		10 19				10 39				10 59		11 19		
Enfield Chase	d		09 41					10 01		10 21				10 41				11 01		11 21		
Gordon Hill	d		09 43					10 03		10 23				10 43				11 03		11 23		
Crews Hill	d		09 46					10 06		10 26				10 46				11 06		11 26		
Cuffley	d		09 49					10 09		10 29				10 49				11 09		11 29		
Bayford	d		09 54					10 14		10 34				10 54				11 14		11 34		
Hertford North	d		10 09					10a20		10 39				11a00				11a20		11 39		
Watton-at-Stone	d		10 15			←				10 45		←								11 45		←
Stevenage 4	d		10 21		10 12	10 21				10 51	10 42	10 51				11 12				11 51	11 42	11 51
Hitchin 4	d		→		10a17	10 27				→	10 47	10 57				11a17				→	11 47	11 57
Letchworth Garden City	a					10 33					10 51	11 03									11 51	12 03

Station		FC	FC	FC	FC 1	FC	FC	FC	FC	FC 1	FC	FC	FC	FC	FC 1	FC	FC	FC	FC	FC 1	FC	FC	FC
London Kings Cross 15	⊖ d				11 36					12 06					12 36					13 06			
Moorgate	⊖ d	11 02	11 12	11 22			11 32	11 42	11 52			12 02	12 12	12 22			12 32	12 42	12 52			13 02	13 12
Old Street	⊖ d	11 04	11 14	11 24			11 34	11 44	11 54			12 04	12 14	12 24			12 34	12 44	12 54			13 04	13 14
Essex Road	d	11 07	11 17	11 27			11 37	11 47	11 57			12 07	12 17	12 27			12 37	12 47	12 57			13 07	13 17
Highbury & Islington	⊖ d	11 09	11 19	11 29			11 39	11 49	11 59			12 09	12 19	12 29			12 39	12 49	12 59			13 09	13 19
Drayton Park	d	11 11	11 21	11 31			11 41	11 51	12 01			12 11	12 21	12 31			12 41	12 51	13 01			13 11	13 21
Finsbury Park	⊖ d	11 14	11 24	11 34	11 41		11 44	11 54	12 04	12 11		12 14	12 24	12 34	12 41		12 44	12 54	13 04	13 11		13 14	13 24
Harringay	d	11 16	11 26	11 36			11 46	11 56	12 06			12 16	12 26	12 36			12 46	12 56	13 06			13 16	13 26
Hornsey	d	11 18	11 28	11 38			11 48	11 58	12 08			12 18	12 28	12 38			12 48	12 58	13 08			13 18	13 28
Alexandra Palace	d	11 20	11 30	11 40			11 50	12 00	12 10			12 20	12 30	12 40			12 50	13 00	13 10			13 20	13 30
New Southgate	d	11 23		11 43				12 03				12 23		12 43				13 03				13 23	
Oakleigh Park	d	11 26		11 46				12 06				12 26		12 46				13 06				13 26	
New Barnet	d	11 28		11 48				12 08				12 28		12 48				13 08				13 28	
Hadley Wood	d	11 31		11 51		←		12 11				12 31		12 51		←		13 11				13 31	
Potters Bar	d	11 35		11 55	11 51	11 55		12 15		12 21		12 35		12 55	12 51	12 55		13 15		13 21		13 35	
Brookmans Park	d	11 38		→		11 58		12 18				12 38		→		12 58		13 18				13 38	
Welham Green	d	11 40				12 00		12 20				12 40				13 00		13 20				13 40	
Hatfield	d	11 43			11 57	12 03		12 23		12 27		12 43			12 57	13 03		13 23		13 27		13 43	
Welwyn Garden City 4	d	11a49			12 01	12a09		12a29		12 31		12a49			13 01	13a09		13a29		13 31		13a49	
Welwyn North	d				12 04					12 34					13 04					13 34			
Knebworth	d				12 08					12 38					13 08					13 38			
Bowes Park	d		11 33				11 53		12 13				12 33				12 53		13 13				13 33
Palmers Green	d		11 35				11 55		12 15				12 35				12 55		13 15				13 35
Winchmore Hill	d		11 37				11 57		12 17				12 37				12 57		13 17				13 37
Grange Park	d		11 39				11 59		12 19				12 39				12 59		13 19				13 39
Enfield Chase	d		11 41				12 01		12 21				12 41				13 01		13 21				13 41
Gordon Hill	d		11 43				12 03		12 23				12 43				13 03		13 23				13 43
Crews Hill	d		11 46				12 06		12 26				12 46				13 06		13 26				13 46
Cuffley	d		11 49				12 09		12 29				12 49				13 09		13 29				13 49
Bayford	d		11 54				12 14		12 34				12 54				13 14		13 34				13 54
Hertford North	d		12a00				12a20		12 39				13a00				13a20		13 39				14a00
Watton-at-Stone	d								12 45		←								13 45		←		
Stevenage 4	d				12 12				12 51	12 42	12 51				13 12				13 51	13 42	13 51		
Hitchin 4	d				12a17				→	12 47	12 58				13a17				→	13 47	13 57		
Letchworth Garden City	a									12 51	13 03									13 51	14 03		

Table 24

Mondays to Fridays

London - Welwyn Garden City, Hertford North and Letchworth Garden City

Station		FC	FC 1	FC	FC	FC	FC	FC 1	FC	FC	FC	FC	FC 1	FC	FC	FC	FC	FC 1	FC	FC	FC	FC	FC 1
London Kings Cross 15	⊖ d		13 36					14 06					14 36					15 06					15 36
Moorgate	⊖ d	13 22			13 32	13 42	13 52			14 02	14 12	14 22			14 32	14 42	14 52			15 02	15 12	15 22	
Old Street	⊖ d	13 24			13 34	13 44	13 54			14 04	14 14	14 24			14 34	14 44	14 54			15 04	15 14	15 24	
Essex Road	d	13 27			13 37	13 47	13 57			14 07	14 17	14 27			14 37	14 47	14 57			15 07	15 17	15 27	
Highbury & Islington	⊖ d	13 29			13 39	13 49	13 59			14 09	14 19	14 29			14 39	14 49	14 59			15 09	15 19	15 29	
Drayton Park	d	13 31			13 41	13 51	14 01			14 11	14 21	14 31			14 41	14 51	15 01			15 11	15 21	15 31	
Finsbury Park	⊖ d	13 34	13 41		13 44	13 54	14 04	14 11		14 14	14 24	14 34	14 41		14 44	14 54	15 04	15 11		15 14	15 24	15 34	15 41
Harringay	d	13 36			13 46	13 56	14 06			14 16	14 26	14 36			14 46	14 56	15 06			15 16	15 26	15 36	
Hornsey	d	13 38			13 48	13 58	14 08			14 18	14 28	14 38			14 48	14 58	15 08			15 18	15 28	15 38	
Alexandra Palace	d	13 40			13 50	14 00	14 10			14 20	14 30	14 40			14 50	15 00	15 10			15 20	15 30	15 40	
New Southgate	d	13 43				14 03				14 23		14 43				15 03				15 23		15 43	
Oakleigh Park	d	13 46				14 06				14 26		14 46				15 06				15 26		15 46	
New Barnet	d	13 48				14 08				14 28		14 48				15 08				15 28		15 48	
Hadley Wood	d	13 51		←		14 11				14 31		14 51		←		15 11				15 31		15 51	
Potters Bar	d	13 55	13 51	13 55		14 15		14 21		14 35		14 55	14 51	14 55		15 15		15 21		15 35		15 55	15 51
Brookmans Park	d	→		13 58		14 18				14 38		→		14 58		15 18				15 38		→	
Welham Green	d			14 00		14 20				14 40				15 00		15 20				15 40			
Hatfield	d		13 57	14 03		14 23		14 27		14 43			14 57	15 03		15 23		15 27		15 43			15 57
Welwyn Garden City 4	d		14 01	14a10		14a29		14 31		14a49			15 01	15a09		15a29		15 31		15a49			16 01
Welwyn North	d		14 04					14 34					15 04					15 34					16 04
Knebworth	d		14 08					14 38					15 08					15 38					16 08
Bowes Park	d				13 53		14 13				14 33				14 53		15 13				15 33		
Palmers Green	d				13 55		14 15				14 35				14 55		15 15				15 35		
Winchmore Hill	d				13 57		14 17				14 37				14 57		15 17				15 37		
Grange Park	d				13 59		14 19				14 39				14 59		15 19				15 39		
Enfield Chase	d				14 01		14 21				14 41				15 01		15 21				15 41		
Gordon Hill	d				14 03		14 23				14 43				15 03		15 23				15 43		
Crews Hill	d				14 06		14 26				14 46				15 06		15 26				15 46		
Cuffley	d				14 09		14 29				14 49				15 09		15 29				15 49		
Bayford	d				14 14		14 34				14 54				15 14		15 34				15 54		
Hertford North	d				14a20		14 39				15a00				15a20		15 39				16 09		
Watton-at-Stone	d						14 45		←								15 45		←		16 15		
Stevenage 4	d		14 12				14 51	14 42	14 51				15 12				15 51	15 42	15 51		16a23		16 12
Hitchin 4	d		14a17				→	14 47	14 57				15a17				→	15 47	15 57				16a17
Letchworth Garden City	a							14 51	15 03									15 51	16 03				

Station		FC	FC	FC	FC	FC	FC 1	FC	FC	FC	FC	FC 1	FC	FC	FC	FC 1	FC	FC	FC	FC	FC	FC
London Kings Cross 15	⊖ d			15 44			16 06					16 32				16 54		16 57				
Moorgate	⊖ d		15 32		15 42	15 52		16 02	16 08	16 18	16 23		16 28	16 33	16 38		16 48		16 53	16 58	17 03	17 08
Old Street	⊖ d		15 34		15 44	15 54		16 04	16 10	16 20	16 25		16 30	16 35	16 40		16 50		16 55	17 00	17 05	17 10
Essex Road	d		15 37		15 47	15 57		16 07	16 13	16 23	16 28		16 33	16 38	16 43		16 53		16 58	17 03	17 08	17 13
Highbury & Islington	⊖ d		15 39		15 49	15 59		16 09	16 16	16 26	16 31		16 36	16 41	16 46		16 56		17 01	17 06	17 11	17 16
Drayton Park	d		15 41		15 51	16 01		16 11	16 17	16 27	16 32		16 37	16 42	16 47		16 57		17 02	17 07	17 12	17 17
Finsbury Park	⊖ d		15 44	15 50	15 54	16 04	16 11	16 14	16 20	16 30	16 35	16 37	16 40	16 45	16 50	16 59	17 00	17 03	17 05	17 10	17 15	17 20
Harringay	d		15 46		15 56	16 06		16 16	16 23	16 33			16 43		16 53				17 08		17 18	17 23
Hornsey	d		15 48		15 58	16 08		16 18	16 25	16 35			16 45		16 55				17 10		17 20	17 25
Alexandra Palace	d		15 50		16 00	16 10		16 20	16 28	16 38	16 41		16 47	16 51	16 58				17 12	17 16	17 23	17 27
New Southgate	d			15 55	16 03			16 23					16 50					17 08	17 15			17 30
Oakleigh Park	d			15 58	16 06			16 26					16 54					17 11	17 19			17 34
New Barnet	d			16 00	16 08			16 28					16 56					17 13	17 21			17 36
Hadley Wood	d	←			16 11			16 31					16 59						17 24			17 39
Potters Bar	d	15 55		16 05	16 15		16 21	16 35				16 47	17 03					17 19	17 28			17 43
Brookmans Park	d	15 58			16 18			16 38					17 06						17 31			17 46
Welham Green	d	16 00			16 20			16 40					17 08						17 33			17 48
Hatfield	d	16 03		16 11	16 23		16 27	16 43				16 54	17 11			17 15		17 25	17 36			17 51
Welwyn Garden City 4	d	16a09		16a16	16a29		16 32	16a49				16 58	17a16			17 19		17a30	17a41			17a56
Welwyn North	d						16 35					17 02				17 23						
Knebworth	d						16 39					17 06				17 27						
Bowes Park	d		15 53			16 13			16 30		16 44				17 00		17 07				17 25	
Palmers Green	d		15 55			16 15			16 32	16 41	16 46			16 54	17 02		17 09			17 19	17 27	
Winchmore Hill	d		15 57			16 17			16 35	16 44	16 49			16 57	17 05		17 12			17 22	17 30	
Grange Park	d		15 59			16 19			16 37		16 51				17 07		17 14				17 32	
Enfield Chase	d		16 01			16 21			16 39	16 47	16 53			17 01	17 09		17 16			17 26	17 34	
Gordon Hill	d		16 03			16 23			16 41	16a51	16 55			17 03	17a12		17 18			17a31	17 37	
Crews Hill	d		16 06			16 26			16 44					17 06							17 40	
Cuffley	d		16 09			16 29			16 47		17 00			17 09			17 23				17 43	
Bayford	d		16 14			16 34			16 52					17 14							17 48	
Hertford North	d		16a20			16 39			16a58		17 09			17a20			17 33				17a53	
Watton-at-Stone	d					16 45					17 15						17 38					
Stevenage 4	d					16a53	16 43				17a23	17 10				17 36	17a46					
Hitchin 4	d						16 50					17 17				17 42						
Letchworth Garden City	a						16 55					17 21				17 47						

Table 24

Mondays to Fridays

London - Welwyn Garden City, Hertford North and Letchworth Garden City

Station		FC	FC	FC	FC	FC	FC	FC		FC 1	FC	FC	FC
London Kings Cross 15	⊖ d		17 27							17 52			17 57
Moorgate	⊖ d	17 18		17 23	17 28	17 33	17 38	17 43				17 48	
Old Street	⊖ d	17 20		17 25	17 30	17 35	17 40	17 45				17 50	
Essex Road	d	17 23		17 28	17 33	17 38	17 43	17 48				17 53	
Highbury & Islington	⊖ d	17 26		17 31	17 36	17 41	17 46	17 51				17 56	
Drayton Park	d	17 27		17 32	17 37	17 42	17 47	17 52				17 57	
Finsbury Park	⊖ d	17 30	17 33	17 35	17 40	17 45	17 50	17 55		17 58		18 00	18 03
Harringay	d			17 38		17 48	17 53						
Hornsey	d			17 40		17 50	17 55						
Alexandra Palace	d			17 42	17 46	17 53	17 57	18 01					
New Southgate	d		17 38	17 45			18 00						18 08
Oakleigh Park	d		17 41	17 49			18 04						18 11
New Barnet	d		17 43	17 51			18 06						
Hadley Wood	d			17 54			18 09						18 15
Potters Bar	d		17 49	17 58			18 13						18 19
Brookmans Park	d			18 01			18 16						
Welham Green	d			18 03			18 18				←		
Hatfield	d		17 55	18 06			18 21			18 14	18 21		18 25
Welwyn Garden City 4	d		18a00	18a11			→			18 18	18a26		18a30
Welwyn North	d									18 22			
Knebworth	d									18 26			
Bowes Park	d	17 37				17 55						18 07	
Palmers Green	d	17 39			17 49	17 57		18 04				18 09	
Winchmore Hill	d	17 42			17 52	18 00		18 07				18 12	
Grange Park	d	17 44				18 02						18 14	
Enfield Chase	d	17 46			17 56	18 04		18 11				18 16	
Gordon Hill	d	17 49			17 58	18 07		18a14				18 19	
Crews Hill	d					18 10							
Cuffley	d	17 53			18 03	18 13						18 23	
Bayford	d					18 18							
Hertford North	d	18 03			18a12	18a23						18 33	
Watton-at-Stone	d	18 08										18 38	
Stevenage 4	d	18a16								18 34		18a46	
Hitchin 4	d									18 40			
Letchworth Garden City	a									18 46			

Station		FC	FC	FC	FC	FC		FC 1	FC	FC	FC	FC	FC
London Kings Cross 15	⊖ d							18 22			18 27		
Moorgate	⊖ d	17 53	17 58	18 03	18 08	18 13				18 18		18 23	18 28
Old Street	⊖ d	17 55	18 00	18 05	18 10	18 15				18 20		18 25	18 30
Essex Road	d	17 58	18 03	18 08	18 13	18 18				18 23		18 28	18 33
Highbury & Islington	⊖ d	18 01	18 06	18 11	18 16	18 21				18 26		18 31	18 36
Drayton Park	d	18 02	18 07	18 12	18 17	18 22				18 27		18 32	18 37
Finsbury Park	⊖ d	18 05	18 10	18 15	18 20	18 25		18 29		18 30	18 33	18 35	18 40
Harringay	d	18 08		18 18	18 23							18 38	
Hornsey	d	18 10		18 20	18 25							18 40	
Alexandra Palace	d	18 12	18 16	18 23	18 27	18 31						18 42	18 46
New Southgate	d	18 15			18 30						18 38	18 45	
Oakleigh Park	d	18 19			18 34						18 41	18 49	
New Barnet	d	18 21			18 36						18 43	18 51	
Hadley Wood	d	18 24			18 39							18 54	
Potters Bar	d	18 28			18 43						18 49	18 58	
Brookmans Park	d	18 31			18 46							19 01	
Welham Green	d	18 33			18 48				←			19 03	
Hatfield	d	18 36			18 51			18 45	18 51		18 55	19 06	
Welwyn Garden City 4	d	18a41			→			18 49	18a56		19a00	19a11	
Welwyn North	d							18 51					
Knebworth	d							18 55					
Bowes Park	d			18 25						18 37			
Palmers Green	d		18 19	18 27		18 34				18 39			18 49
Winchmore Hill	d		18 22	18 30		18 37				18 42			18 52
Grange Park	d			18 32						18 44			
Enfield Chase	d		18 26	18 34		18 41				18 46			18 56
Gordon Hill	d		18 28	18 37		18a44				18 49			18 58
Crews Hill	d			18 40									
Cuffley	d		18 33	18 43						18 53			19 03
Bayford	d			18 48									
Hertford North	d		18a42	18a53						19 03			19a12
Watton-at-Stone	d									19 08			
Stevenage 4	d							19 04		19 16			
Hitchin 4	d							19 10		19 22			
Letchworth Garden City	a							19 16		19 27			

Station		FC	FC	FC 1		FC	FC	FC	FC	FC	FC 1	FC	FC
London Kings Cross 15	⊖ d			18 52			18 57				19 18		
Moorgate	⊖ d	18 37	18 42					18 52	18 57	19 02		19 12	19 22
Old Street	⊖ d	18 39	18 44					18 54	18 59	19 04		19 14	19 24
Essex Road	d	18 42	18 47					18 57	19 02	19 07		19 17	19 27
Highbury & Islington	⊖ d	18 45	18 50					19 00	19 05	19 10		19 20	19 30
Drayton Park	d	18 46	18 51					19 01	19 06	19 11		19 21	19 31
Finsbury Park	⊖ d	18 49	18 54	18 58			19 03	19 04	19 09	19 14	19 23	19 24	19 34
Harringay	d	18 52	18 57						19 12	19 17		19 27	19 37
Hornsey	d	18 54	18 59						19 14	19 19		19 29	19 39
Alexandra Palace	d	18 57	19 01						19 16	19 22		19 31	19 42
New Southgate	d		19 04				19 08		19 19			19 34	
Oakleigh Park	d		19 08				19 11		19 23			19 38	
New Barnet	d		19 10				19 13		19 25			19 40	
Hadley Wood	d		19 13				19 16		19 28			19 43	
Potters Bar	d		19 17				19 21		19 32		19 37	19 47	
Brookmans Park	d		19 20						19 35			19 50	
Welham Green	d		19 22			←			19 37			19 52	
Hatfield	d		19 25	19 14		19 25	19 28		19 40		19 44	19 55	
Welwyn Garden City 4	d		→	19 19		19a30	19a33		19a45		19 49	→	
Welwyn North	d			19 24							19 53		
Knebworth	d			19 28							19 57		
Bowes Park	d	18 59						19 11		19 24			19 44
Palmers Green	d	19 01						19 13		19 26			19 46
Winchmore Hill	d	19 04						19 16		19 29			19 49
Grange Park	d	19 06						19 18		19 31			19 51
Enfield Chase	d	19 08						19 20		19 33			19 53
Gordon Hill	d	19 11						19 23		19 36			19 56
Crews Hill	d	19 14								19 39			
Cuffley	d	19 17						19 27		19 42			20 00
Bayford	d	19 22								19 47			
Hertford North	d	19a27						19 37		19a52			20 09
Watton-at-Stone	d							19 42					20 15
Stevenage 4	d			19 34				19a52			20 04		20 21
Hitchin 4	d			19 42							20 13		→
Letchworth Garden City	a			19 46							20 17		

Station		FC 1		FC	FC	FC	FC	FC	FC	FC	FC 1	FC	
London Kings Cross 15	⊖ d	19 34					19 40				20 06		
Moorgate	⊖ d					19 32		19 37	19 42	19 52		20 07	
Old Street	⊖ d					19 34		19 39	19 44	19 54		20 09	
Essex Road	d					19 37		19 42	19 47	19 57		20 12	
Highbury & Islington	⊖ d					19 40		19 45	19 50	19 59		20 14	
Drayton Park	d					19 41		19 46	19 51	20 01		20 16	
Finsbury Park	⊖ d	19 39				19 44	19 46	19 49	19 54	20 04	20 11	20 19	
Harringay	d							19 52	19 57	20 06		20 21	
Hornsey	d							19 54	19 59	20 08		20 23	
Alexandra Palace	d							19 56	20 02	20 10		20 25	
New Southgate	d						19 51	19 59				20 28	
Oakleigh Park	d						19 54	20 03				20 31	
New Barnet	d						19 56	20 05				20 33	
Hadley Wood	d							20 08				20 36	
Potters Bar	d						20 02	20 12			20 21	20 40	
Brookmans Park	d							20 15				20 43	
Welham Green	d			←				20 17				20 45	
Hatfield	d	19 53		19 55			20 08	20 20			20 27	20 48	
Welwyn Garden City 4	d	20 00		20a00			20a13	20a25			20 31	20a54	
Welwyn North	d	20 03									20 34		
Knebworth	d	20 07									20 38		
Bowes Park	d					19 51			20 04	20 13			
Palmers Green	d					19 53			20 06	20 15			
Winchmore Hill	d					19 56			20 09	20 17			
Grange Park	d					19 58			20 11	20 19			
Enfield Chase	d					20 00			20 13	20 21			
Gordon Hill	d					20 03			20 16	20 23			
Crews Hill	d					20 06				20 26			
Cuffley	d					20 09			20 20	20 29			
Bayford	d					20 14				20 34			
Hertford North	d					20a19			20a30	20 40			
Watton-at-Stone	d				←					20 45			
Stevenage 4	d	20 12			20 21					20a53	20 42		
Hitchin 4	d	20 17			20 27						20 47		
Letchworth Garden City	a	20 23			20 32						20 51		

Table 24

Mondays to Fridays

London - Welwyn Garden City, Hertford North and Letchworth Garden City

Station		FC	FC 1	FC	FC	FC	FC	FC 1	FC	FC		FC 1	FC
London Kings Cross 15	⊖ d		20 36					21 06				21 36	
Moorgate	⊖ d	20 12			20 32	20 37	20 52		21 07	21 12			
Old Street	⊖ d	20 14			20 34	20 39	20 54		21 09	21 14			
Essex Road	d	20 17			20 37	20 42	20 57		21 12	21 17			
Highbury & Islington	⊖ d	20 19			20 39	20 44	20 59		21 14	21 19			
Drayton Park	d	20 21			20 41	20 46	21 01		21 16	21 21			
Finsbury Park	⊖ d	20 24	20 41		20 44	20 49	21 04	21 11	21 19	21 24		21 41	
Harringay	d	20 26			20 46	20 51	21 06		21 21	21 26			
Hornsey	d	20 28			20 48	20 53	21 08		21 23	21 28			
Alexandra Palace	d	20 30			20 50	20 55	21 10		21 25	21 30			
New Southgate	d					20 58			21 28				
Oakleigh Park	d					21 01			21 31				
New Barnet	d					21 03			21 33				
Hadley Wood	d					21 06			21 36				
Potters Bar	d		20 51			21 10		21 21	21 40			21 51	
Brookmans Park	d					21 13			21 43				
Welham Green	d					21 15			21 45				
Hatfield	d		20 57			21 18		21 27	21 48			21 57	
Welwyn Garden City 4	d		21 01			21a24		21 31	21a54			22 01	
Welwyn North	d		21 04					21 34				22 04	
Knebworth	d		21 08					21 38				22 08	
Bowes Park	d	20 33			20 53		21 13			21 33			
Palmers Green	d	20 35			20 55		21 15			21 35			
Winchmore Hill	d	20 37			20 57		21 17			21 37			
Grange Park	d	20 39			20 59		21 19			21 39			
Enfield Chase	d	20 41			21 01		21 21			21 41			
Gordon Hill	d	20 43			21 03		21 23			21 43			
Crews Hill	d	20 46			21 06		21 26			21 46			
Cuffley	d	20 49			21 09		21 29			21 49			
Bayford	d	20 54			21 14		21 34			21 54			
Hertford North	d	21 10			21a20		21a40			22 10			
Watton-at-Stone	d	21 15		←						22 15			←
Stevenage 4	d	21 23	21 12	21 23				21 42		22 23		22 12	22 23
Hitchin 4	d	→	21 17	21 28				21 47		→		22 17	22 28
Letchworth Garden City	a		21 23	21 34				21 51				22 23	22 34

Station		FC	FC	FC	FC 1	FC	FC	FC 1		FC	FC	FC	FC 1
London Kings Cross 15	⊖ d				22 06	22 11	22 26	22 36			22 41	22 56	23 06
Moorgate	⊖ d	21 32	21 37	21 52									
Old Street	⊖ d	21 34	21 39	21 54									
Essex Road	d	21 37	21 42	21 57									
Highbury & Islington	⊖ d	21 39	21 44	21 59									
Drayton Park	d	21 41	21 46	22 01									
Finsbury Park	⊖ d	21 44	21 49	22 04	22 11	22 17	22 32	22 41			22 47	23 02	23 11
Harringay	d	21 46	21 51	22 06		22 19	22 34				22 49	23 04	
Hornsey	d	21 48	21 53	22 08		22 21	22 36				22 51	23 06	
Alexandra Palace	d	21 50	21 55	22 10		22 23	22 38				22 53	23 08	
New Southgate	d		21 58			22 26					22 56		
Oakleigh Park	d		22 01			22 29					22 59		
New Barnet	d		22 03			22 31					23 01		
Hadley Wood	d		22 06			22 34					23 04		
Potters Bar	d		22 10		22 21	22 38		22 51			23 08		23 21
Brookmans Park	d		22 13			22 41					23 11		
Welham Green	d		22 15			22 43					23 13		
Hatfield	d		22 18		22 27	22 46		22 57			23 16		23 27
Welwyn Garden City 4	d		22a24		22 31	22a51		23 01			23a24		23 31
Welwyn North	d				22 34			23 04					23 34
Knebworth	d				22 38			23 08					23 38
Bowes Park	d	21 53		22 13			22 41					23 11	
Palmers Green	d	21 55		22 15			22 43					23 13	
Winchmore Hill	d	21 57		22 17			22 45					23 15	
Grange Park	d	21 59		22 19			22 47					23 17	
Enfield Chase	d	22 01		22 21			22 49					23 19	
Gordon Hill	d	22 03		22 23			22 51					23 21	
Crews Hill	d	22 06		22 26			22 54					23 24	
Cuffley	d	22 09		22 29			22 57					23 27	
Bayford	d	22 14		22 34			23 02					23 32	
Hertford North	d	22a20		22a40			23 07					23a38	
Watton-at-Stone	d						23 13			←			
Stevenage 4	d				22 42		23 21	23 12		23 21			23 42
Hitchin 4	d				22 47		→	23 17		23 30			23 50
Letchworth Garden City	a				22 51			23 26		23 36			23 54

Station		FC	FC	FC 1	FC	FC
London Kings Cross 15	⊖ d	23 11	23 26	23 36		23 41
Moorgate	⊖ d					
Old Street	⊖ d					
Essex Road	d					
Highbury & Islington	⊖ d					
Drayton Park	d					
Finsbury Park	⊖ d	23 17	23 32	23 41		23 47
Harringay	d	23 19	23 34			23 49
Hornsey	d	23 21	23 36			23 51
Alexandra Palace	d	23 23	23 38			23 53
New Southgate	d	23 26				23 56
Oakleigh Park	d	23 29				23 59
New Barnet	d	23 31				00 01
Hadley Wood	d	23 34				00 04
Potters Bar	d	23 38		23 51		00 08
Brookmans Park	d	23 41				00 11
Welham Green	d	23 43				00 13
Hatfield	d	23 46		23 57		00 16
Welwyn Garden City 4	d	23a54		00 01		00a24
Welwyn North	d			00 04		
Knebworth	d			00 08		
Bowes Park	d		23 41			
Palmers Green	d		23 43			
Winchmore Hill	d		23 45			
Grange Park	d		23 47			
Enfield Chase	d		23 49			
Gordon Hill	d		23 51			
Crews Hill	d		23 54			
Cuffley	d		23 57			
Bayford	d		00 02			
Hertford North	d		00 07			
Watton-at-Stone	d		00 13		←	
Stevenage 4	d		00 20	00 12	00 20	
Hitchin 4	d		→	00 20	00 26	
Letchworth Garden City	a			00 29	00 36	

Table 24

Saturdays
until 18 June

London - Welwyn Garden City, Hertford North and Letchworth Garden City

		FC	FC 1	FC	FC	FC	FC	FC 1	FC 1	FC		FC 1	FC 1	FC	FC	FC 1	FC	FC	FC 1	FC		FC	FC 1	FC	FC
London Kings Cross 15 ⊖	d	23p26	23p36		23p41	00 06	00 11	00 36	01 06	01 11		01 36	05 23	05 26	05 56	06 06	06 11	06 26	06 36	06 41		06 56	07 06	07 11	07 26
Moorgate ⊖	d																								
Old Street ⊖	d																								
Essex Road	d																								
Highbury & Islington ⊖	d																								
Drayton Park	d																								
Finsbury Park ⊖	d	23p32	23p41		23p47	00 12	00 17	00 41	01 11	01 17		01 41	05 28	05 32	06 02	06 11	06 17	06 32	06 41	06 47		07 02	07 11	07 17	07 32
Harringay	d	23p34			23p49	00 14	00 19			01 19				05 34	06 04		06 19	06 34		06 49		07 04		07 19	07 34
Hornsey	d	23p36			23p51	00 16	00 21			01 21				05 36	06 06		06 21	06 36		06 51		07 06		07 21	07 36
Alexandra Palace	d	23p38			23p53	00 18	00 23		01 16	01 23		01 45		05 38	06 08		06 23	06 38		06 53		07 08		07 23	07 38
New Southgate	d				23p56		00 26			01 26		01 48					06 26			06 56				07 26	
Oakleigh Park	d				23p59		00 29			01 29		01 51					06 29			06 59				07 29	
New Barnet	d				00 01		00 31			01 31		01 53					06 31			07 01				07 31	
Hadley Wood	d				00 04		00 34			01 34		01 56					06 34			07 04				07 34	
Potters Bar	d		23p51		00 08		00 38	00 51		01 38		01 59	05 38			06 20	06 38		06 51	07 08			07 21	07 38	
Brookmans Park	d				00 11		00 41			01 41							06 41			07 11				07 41	
Welham Green	d				00 13		00 43			01 43							06 43			07 13				07 43	
Hatfield	d		23p57		00 16		00 46	00 57		01 46		02 05	05 44			06 25	06 46		06 57	07 16			07 27	07 46	
Welwyn Garden City 4	d		00 01		00a24		00a54	01 01		01a54		02 09	05 48			06 29	06a51		07 01	07a21			07 31	07a51	
Welwyn North	d		00 04					01s04				02s12	05 51			06 32			07 04				07 34		
Knebworth	d		00 08					01s08				02s16	05 55			06 36			07 08				07 38		
Bowes Park	d	23p41				00 21								05 41	06 11			06 41				07 11			07 41
Palmers Green	d	23p43				00 23			01 19					05 43	06 13			06 43				07 13			07 43
Winchmore Hill	d	23p45				00 25			01 21					05 45	06 15			06 45				07 15			07 45
Grange Park	d	23p47				00 27								05 47	06 17			06 47				07 17			07 47
Enfield Chase	d	23p49				00 29			01 24					05 49	06 19			06 49				07 19			07 49
Gordon Hill	d	23p51				00 31			01 26					05 51	06 21			06 51				07 21			07 51
Crews Hill	d	23p54				00 34								05 54	06 24			06 54				07 24			07 54
Cuffley	d	23p57				00 37			01 30					05 57	06 27			06 57				07 27			07 57
Bayford	d	00 02				00 42								06 02	06 32			07 02				07 32			08 02
Hertford North	d	00 07				00 47			01 38					06a08	06a38			07 07				07a38			08 07
Watton-at-Stone	d	00 13		←		00 53												07 13							08 13
Stevenage 4	d	00 20	00 12	00 20		01 00		01 12	01 47			02 20	05 59			06 40		07a20	07 12				07 42		08a20
Hitchin 4	d	→	00 20	00 26		01 06		01a17	01 52			02a25	06a07			06 47			07a17				07 47		
Letchworth Garden City	a		00 29	00 36		01 15			02 06							06 51							07 51		

		FC 1	FC	FC	FC 1	FC		FC	FC 1	FC	FC	FC 1	FC	FC	FC 1	FC		FC	FC 1	FC	FC	FC 1	FC	FC	FC 1
London Kings Cross 15 ⊖	d	07 36	07 41	07 56	08 06	08 11		08 26	08 36	08 41	08 56	09 06	09 11	09 26	09 36	09 41		09 56	10 06	10 11	10 26	10 36	10 41	10 56	11 06
Moorgate ⊖	d																								
Old Street ⊖	d																								
Essex Road	d																								
Highbury & Islington ⊖	d																								
Drayton Park	d																								
Finsbury Park ⊖	d	07 41	07 47	08 02	08 11	08 17		08 32	08 41	08 47	09 02	09 11	09 17	09 32	09 41	09 47		10 02	10 11	10 17	10 32	10 41	10 47	11 02	11 11
Harringay	d		07 49	08 04		08 19		08 34		08 49	09 04		09 19	09 34		09 49		10 04		10 19	10 34		10 49	11 04	
Hornsey	d		07 51	08 06		08 21		08 36		08 51	09 06		09 21	09 36		09 51		10 06		10 21	10 36		10 51	11 06	
Alexandra Palace	d		07 53	08 08		08 23		08 38		08 53	09 08		09 23	09 38		09 53		10 08		10 23	10 38		10 53	11 08	
New Southgate	d		07 56			08 26				08 56			09 26			09 56				10 26			10 56		
Oakleigh Park	d		07 59			08 29				08 59			09 29			09 59				10 29			10 59		
New Barnet	d		08 01			08 31				09 01			09 31			10 01				10 31			11 01		
Hadley Wood	d		08 04			08 34				09 04			09 34			10 04				10 34			11 04		
Potters Bar	d	07 51	08 08		08 21	08 38			08 51	09 08		09 21	09 38		09 51	10 08			10 21	10 38		10 51	11 08		11 21
Brookmans Park	d		08 11			08 41				09 11			09 41			10 11				10 41			11 11		
Welham Green	d		08 13			08 43				09 13			09 43			10 13				10 43			11 13		
Hatfield	d	07 57	08 16		08 27	08 46			08 57	09 16		09 27	09 46		09 57	10 16			10 27	10 46		10 57	11 16		11 27
Welwyn Garden City 4	d	08 01	08a21		08 31	08a51			09 01	09a21		09 31	09a51		10 01	10a21			10 31	10a51		11 01	11a21		11 31
Welwyn North	d	08 04			08 34				09 04			09 34			10 04				10 34			11 04			11 34
Knebworth	d	08 08			08 38				09 08			09 38			10 08				10 38			11 08			11 38
Bowes Park	d			08 11				08 41			09 11			09 41				10 11			10 41			11 11	
Palmers Green	d			08 13				08 43			09 13			09 43				10 13			10 43			11 13	
Winchmore Hill	d			08 15				08 45			09 15			09 45				10 15			10 45			11 15	
Grange Park	d			08 17				08 47			09 17			09 47				10 17			10 47			11 17	
Enfield Chase	d			08 19				08 49			09 19			09 49				10 19			10 49			11 19	
Gordon Hill	d			08 21				08 51			09 21			09 51				10 21			10 51			11 21	
Crews Hill	d			08 24				08 54			09 24			09 54				10 24			10 54			11 24	
Cuffley	d			08 27				08 57			09 27			09 57				10 27			10 57			11 27	
Bayford	d			08 32				09 02			09 32			10 02				10 32			11 02			11 32	
Hertford North	d			08a38				09 07			09a38			10 07				10a38			11 07			11a38	
Watton-at-Stone	d							09 13						10 13							11 13				
Stevenage 4	d	08 12			08 42			09a20	09 12			09 42		10a20	10 12				10 42		11a20	11 12			11 42
Hitchin 4	d	08a17			08 47				09a17			09 47			10a17				10 47			11a17			11 47
Letchworth Garden City	a				08 51							09 51							10 51						11 51

Table 24

Saturdays
until 18 June

London - Welwyn Garden City, Hertford North and Letchworth Garden City

		FC		FC	FC 1	FC	FC	FC 1	FC	FC	FC 1	FC		FC	FC 1	FC	FC	FC 1	FC	FC	FC 1	FC		FC	FC 1
London Kings Cross 15 ⊖	d	11 11		11 26	11 36	11 41	11 56	12 06	12 11	12 26	12 36	12 41		12 56	13 06	13 11	13 26	13 36	13 41	13 56	14 06	14 11		14 26	14 36
Moorgate ⊖	d																								
Old Street ⊖	d																								
Essex Road	d																								
Highbury & Islington ⊖	d																								
Drayton Park	d																								
Finsbury Park ⊖	d	11 17		11 32	11 41	11 47	12 02	12 11	12 17	12 32	12 41	12 47		13 02	13 11	13 17	13 32	13 41	13 47	14 02	14 11	14 17		14 32	14 41
Harringay	d	11 19		11 34		11 49	12 04		12 19	12 34		12 49		13 04		13 19	13 34		13 49	14 04		14 19		14 34	
Hornsey	d	11 21		11 36		11 51	12 06		12 21	12 36		12 51		13 06		13 21	13 36		13 51	14 06		14 21		14 36	
Alexandra Palace	d	11 23		11 38		11 53	12 08		12 23	12 38		12 53		13 08		13 23	13 38		13 53	14 08		14 23		14 38	
New Southgate	d	11 26				11 56			12 26			12 56				13 26			13 56			14 26			
Oakleigh Park	d	11 29				11 59			12 29			12 59				13 29			13 59			14 29			
New Barnet	d	11 31				12 01			12 31			13 01				13 31			14 01			14 31			
Hadley Wood	d	11 34				12 04			12 34			13 04				13 34			14 04			14 34			
Potters Bar	d	11 38			11 51	12 08		12 21	12 38		12 51	13 08			13 21	13 38		13 51	14 08		14 21	14 38			14 51
Brookmans Park	d	11 41				12 11			12 41			13 11				13 41			14 11			14 41			
Welham Green	d	11 43				12 13			12 43			13 13				13 43			14 13			14 43			
Hatfield	d	11 46			11 57	12 16		12 27	12 46		12 57	13 16			13 27	13 46		13 57	14 16		14 27	14 46			14 57
Welwyn Garden City 4	d	11a51			12 01	12a21		12 31	12a51		13 01	13a21			13 31	13a51		14 01	14a21		14 31	14a51			15 01
Welwyn North	d				12 04			12 34			13 04				13 34			14 04			14 34				15 04
Knebworth	d				12 08			12 38			13 08				13 38			14 08			14 38				15 08
Bowes Park	d			11 41			12 11			12 41				13 11			13 41			14 11				14 41	
Palmers Green	d			11 43			12 13			12 43				13 13			13 43			14 13				14 43	
Winchmore Hill	d			11 45			12 15			12 45				13 15			13 45			14 15				14 45	
Grange Park	d			11 47			12 17			12 47				13 17			13 47			14 17				14 47	
Enfield Chase	d			11 49			12 19			12 49				13 19			13 49			14 19				14 49	
Gordon Hill	d			11 51			12 21			12 51				13 21			13 51			14 21				14 51	
Crews Hill	d			11 54			12 24			12 54				13 24			13 54			14 24				14 54	
Cuffley	d			11 57			12 27			12 57				13 27			13 57			14 27				14 57	
Bayford	d			12 02			12 32			13 02				13 32			14 02			14 32				15 02	
Hertford North	d			12 07			12a38			13 07				13a38			14 07			14a38				15 07	
Watton-at-Stone	d			12 13						13 13							14 13							15 13	
Stevenage 4	d			12a20	12 12			12 42		13a20	13 12				13 42		14a20	14 12			14 42			15a20	15 12
Hitchin 4	d				12a17			12 47			13a17				13 47			14a17			14 47				15a17
Letchworth Garden City	a							12 51							13 51						14 51				

		FC	FC	FC 1	FC	FC	FC 1	FC		FC	FC 1	FC	FC	FC 1	FC	FC	FC 1	FC		FC	FC 1	FC	FC	FC 1	FC
London Kings Cross 15 ⊖	d	14 41	14 56	15 06	15 11	15 26	15 36	15 41		15 56	16 06	16 11	16 26	16 36	16 41	16 56	17 06	17 11		17 26	17 36	17 41	17 56	18 06	18 11
Moorgate ⊖	d																								
Old Street ⊖	d																								
Essex Road	d																								
Highbury & Islington ⊖	d																								
Drayton Park	d																								
Finsbury Park ⊖	d	14 47	15 02	15 11	15 17	15 32	15 41	15 47		16 02	16 11	16 17	16 32	16 41	16 47	17 02	17 11	17 17		17 32	17 41	17 47	18 02	18 11	18 17
Harringay	d	14 49	15 04		15 19	15 34		15 49		16 04		16 19	16 34		16 49	17 04		17 19		17 34		17 49	18 04		18 19
Hornsey	d	14 51	15 06		15 21	15 36		15 51		16 06		16 21	16 36		16 51	17 06		17 21		17 36		17 51	18 06		18 21
Alexandra Palace	d	14 53	15 08		15 23	15 38		15 53		16 08		16 23	16 38		16 53	17 08		17 23		17 38		17 53	18 08		18 23
New Southgate	d	14 56			15 26			15 56				16 26			16 56			17 26				17 56			18 26
Oakleigh Park	d	14 59			15 29			15 59				16 29			16 59			17 29				17 59			18 29
New Barnet	d	15 01			15 31			16 01				16 31			17 01			17 31				18 01			18 31
Hadley Wood	d	15 04			15 34			16 04				16 34			17 04			17 34				18 04			18 34
Potters Bar	d	15 08		15 21	15 38		15 51	16 08			16 21	16 38		16 51	17 08		17 21	17 38			17 51	18 08		18 21	18 38
Brookmans Park	d	15 11			15 41			16 11				16 41			17 11			17 41				18 11			18 41
Welham Green	d	15 13			15 43			16 13				16 43			17 13			17 43				18 13			18 43
Hatfield	d	15 16		15 27	15 46		15 57	16 16			16 27	16 46		16 57	17 16		17 27	17 46			17 57	18 16		18 27	18 46
Welwyn Garden City 4	d	15a21		15 31	15a51		16 01	16a21			16 31	16a51		17 01	17a21		17 31	17a51			18 01	18a21		18 31	18a51
Welwyn North	d			15 34			16 04				16 34			17 04			17 34				18 04			18 34	
Knebworth	d			15 38			16 08				16 38			17 08			17 38				18 08			18 38	
Bowes Park	d		15 11			15 41				16 11			16 41			17 11				17 41			18 11		
Palmers Green	d		15 13			15 43				16 13			16 43			17 13				17 43			18 13		
Winchmore Hill	d		15 15			15 45				16 15			16 45			17 15				17 45			18 15		
Grange Park	d		15 17			15 47				16 17			16 47			17 17				17 47			18 17		
Enfield Chase	d		15 19			15 49				16 19			16 49			17 19				17 49			18 19		
Gordon Hill	d		15 21			15 51				16 21			16 51			17 21				17 51			18 21		
Crews Hill	d		15 24			15 54				16 24			16 54			17 24				17 54			18 24		
Cuffley	d		15 27			15 57				16 27			16 57			17 27				17 57			18 27		
Bayford	d		15 32			16 02				16 32			17 02			17 32				18 02			18 32		
Hertford North	d		15a38			16 07				16a38			17 07			17a38				18 07			18a38		
Watton-at-Stone	d					16 13							17 13							18 13					
Stevenage 4	d			15 42		16a20	16 12				16 42		17a20	17 12			17 42			18a20	18 12			18 42	
Hitchin 4	d			15 47			16a17				16 47			17a17			17 47				18a17			18 47	
Letchworth Garden City	a			15 51							16 51						17 51							18 51	

Table 24

Saturdays
until 18 June

London - Welwyn Garden City, Hertford North and Letchworth Garden City

		FC	FC ■	FC	FC	FC ■	FC	FC	FC ■	FC	FC	FC ■	FC	FC	FC ■	FC	FC	FC ■	FC	FC	FC ■	FC
London Kings Cross ■	⊖ d	18 26	18 36	18 41	18 56	19 06	19 11	19 26	19 36	19 41	19 56	20 06	20 11	20 26	20 36	20 41	20 56	21 06	21 11	21 26	21 36	21 41
Moorgate	⊖ d																					
Old Street	⊖ d																					
Essex Road	d																					
Highbury & Islington	⊖ d																					
Drayton Park	d																					
Finsbury Park	⊖ d	18 32	18 41	18 47	19 02	19 11	19 17	19 32	19 41	19 47	20 02	20 11	20 17	20 33	20 41	20 47	21 03	21 11	21 17	21 32	21 41	21 47
Harringay	d	18 34		18 49	19 04		19 19	19 34		19 49	20 04		20 19	20 36		20 49	21 06		21 19	21 34		21 49
Hornsey	d	18 36		18 51	19 06		19 21	19 36		19 51	20 06		20 21	20 39		20 51	21 09		21 21	21 36		21 51
Alexandra Palace	d	18 38		18 53	19 08		19 23	19 38		19 53	20 08		20 23	20 41		20 53	21 11		21 23	21 38		21 53
New Southgate	d			18 56			19 26			19 56			20 26			20 56			21 26			21 56
Oakleigh Park	d			18 59			19 29			19 59			20 29			20 59			21 29			21 59
New Barnet	d			19 01			19 31			20 01			20 31			21 01			21 31			22 01
Hadley Wood	d			19 04			19 34			20 04			20 34			21 04			21 34			22 04
Potters Bar	d		18 51	19 08		19 21	19 38		19 51	20 08		20 21	20 38		20 51	21 08		21 21	21 38		21 51	22 08
Brookmans Park	d			19 11			19 41			20 11			20 41			21 11			21 41			22 11
Welham Green	d			19 13			19 43			20 13			20 43			21 13			21 43			22 13
Hatfield	d		18 57	19 16		19 27	19 46		19 57	20 16		20 27	20 46		20 57	21 16		21 27	21 46		21 57	22 16
Welwyn Garden City ■	d		19 01	19a21		19 31	19a51		20 01	20a21		20 31	20a51		21 01	21a21		21 31	21a51		22 01	22a21
Welwyn North	d		19 04			19 34			20 04			20 34			21 04			21 34			22 04	
Knebworth	d		19 08			19 38			20 08			20 38			21 08			21 38			22 08	
Bowes Park	d	18 41			19 11			19 41			20 11			20 44			21 14			21 41		
Palmers Green	d	18 43			19 13			19 43			20 13			20 46			21 16			21 43		
Winchmore Hill	d	18 45			19 15			19 45			20 15			20 48			21 18			21 45		
Grange Park	d	18 47			19 17			19 47			20 17			20 50			21 20			21 47		
Enfield Chase	d	18 49			19 19			19 49			20 19			20 52			21 22			21 49		
Gordon Hill	d	18 51			19 21			19 51			20 21			20 54			21 24			21 51		
Crews Hill	d	18 54			19 24			19 54			20 24			20 57			21 27			21 54		
Cuffley	d	18 57			19 27			19 57			20 27			21 00			21 30			21 57		
Bayford	d	19 02			19 32			20 02			20 32			21 05			21 35			22 02		
Hertford North	d	19 07			19a38			20 07			20a38			21a09			21a41			22a06		
Watton-at-Stone	d	19 13						20 13														
Stevenage ■	d	19a20	19 12			19 42		20a20	20 12			20 42			21 12			21 42			22 12	
Hitchin ■	d		19a17			19 47			20a17			20 47			21a17			21 47			22a17	
Letchworth Garden City	a					19 51						20 51						21 51				

		FC	FC ■	FC	FC	FC ■	FC	FC	FC ■	FC	FC	FC ■	FC	FC	FC
London Kings Cross ■	⊖ d	21 56	22 06	22 11	22 26	22 36	22 41	22 56	23 06	23 11	23 26	23 36		23 41	23 56
Moorgate	⊖ d														
Old Street	⊖ d														
Essex Road	d														
Highbury & Islington	⊖ d														
Drayton Park	d														
Finsbury Park	⊖ d	22 03	22 11	22 17	22 32	22 41	22 47	23 02	23 11	23 17	23 32	23 41		23 47	00 02
Harringay	d	22 06		22 19	22 34		22 49	23 04		23 19	23 34			23 49	00 04
Hornsey	d	22 09		22 21	22 36		22 51	23 06		23 21	23 36			23 51	00 06
Alexandra Palace	d	22 11		22 23	22 38		22 53	23 08		23 23	23 38			23 53	00 08
New Southgate	d			22 26			22 56			23 26				23 56	
Oakleigh Park	d			22 29			22 59			23 29				23 59	
New Barnet	d			22 31			23 01			23 31				00 01	
Hadley Wood	d			22 34			23 04			23 34				00 04	
Potters Bar	d		22 21	22 38		22 51	23 08		23 21	23 38		23 53		00 08	
Brookmans Park	d			22 41			23 11			23 41				00 11	
Welham Green	d			22 43			23 13			23 43				00 13	
Hatfield	d		22 27	22 46		22 57	23 16		23 27	23 46		23 59		00 16	
Welwyn Garden City ■	d		22 31	22a51		23 01	23a21		23 31	23a53		00 06		00a25	
Welwyn North	d		22 34			23 04			23 34			00 09			
Knebworth	d		22 38			23 08			23 38			00 13			
Bowes Park	d	22 14			22 41			23 11			23 41				00 11
Palmers Green	d	22 16			22 43			23 13			23 43				00 13
Winchmore Hill	d	22 18			22 45			23 15			23 45				00 15
Grange Park	d	22 20			22 47			23 17			23 47				00 17
Enfield Chase	d	22 22			22 49			23 19			23 49				00 19
Gordon Hill	d	22 24			22 51			23 21			23 51				00 21
Crews Hill	d	22 27			22 54			23 24			23 54				00 24
Cuffley	d	22 30			22 57			23 27			23 57				00 27
Bayford	d	22 35			23 02			23 32			00 02				00 32
Hertford North	d	22a41			23a06			23a38			00 07				00a40
Watton-at-Stone	d										00 13		←		
Stevenage ■	d		22 42			23 12			23 42		00 22	00 18	00 22		
Hitchin ■	d		22 47			23 20			23 50		→	00 25	00 29		
Letchworth Garden City	a		22 51			23 26			23 54			00 30	00 37		

Table 24

Saturdays
25 June to 30 July

London - Welwyn Garden City, Hertford North and Letchworth Garden City

		FC	FC ■	FC	FC	FC	FC	FC ■	FC ■	FC	FC ■	FC ■	FC	FC	FC ■	FC	FC	FC ■	FC	FC	FC ■	FC	FC
London Kings Cross ■	⊖ d	23p26	23p36		23p41	00 06	00 11	00 36	01 06	01 11	01 36	05 23	05 26	05 56	06 06	06 11	06 26	06 36	06 41	06 56	07 06	07 11	07 26
Moorgate	⊖ d																						
Old Street	⊖ d																						
Essex Road	d																						
Highbury & Islington	⊖ d																						
Drayton Park	d																						
Finsbury Park	⊖ d	23p32	23p41		23p47	00 12	00 17	00 41	01 11	01 17	01 41	05 28	05 32	06 02	06 11	06 17	06 32	06 41	06 47	07 02	07 11	07 17	07 32
Harringay	d	23p34			23p49	00 14	00 19			01 19			05 34	06 04		06 19	06 34		06 49	07 04		07 19	07 34
Hornsey	d	23p36			23p51	00 16	00 21			01 21			05 36	06 06		06 21	06 36		06 51	07 06		07 21	07 36
Alexandra Palace	d	23p38			23p53	00 18	00 23		01 16	01 23	01 45		05 38	06 08		06 23	06 38		06 53	07 08		07 23	07 38
New Southgate	d				23p56		00 26			01 26	01 48					06 26			06 56			07 26	
Oakleigh Park	d				23p59		00 29			01 29	01 51					06 29			06 59			07 29	
New Barnet	d				00 01		00 31			01 31	01 53					06 31			07 01			07 31	
Hadley Wood	d				00 04		00 34			01 34	01 56					06 34			07 04			07 34	
Potters Bar	d		23p51		00 08		00 38	00 51		01 38	01 59	05 38			06 20	06 38		06 51	07 08		07 21	07 38	
Brookmans Park	d				00 11		00 41			01 41						06 41			07 11			07 41	
Welham Green	d				00 13		00 43			01 43						06 43			07 13			07 43	
Hatfield	d		23p57		00 16		00 46	00 57		01 46	02 05	05 44			06 25	06 46		06 57	07 16		07 27	07 46	
Welwyn Garden City ■	d		00 01		00a24		00a54	01 01		01a54	02 09	05 48			06 29	06a51		07 01	07a21		07 31	07a51	
Welwyn North	d		00 04					01s04			02s12	05 51			06 32			07 04			07 34		
Knebworth	d		00 08					01s08			02s16	05 55			06 36			07 08			07 38		
Bowes Park	d	23p41				00 21							05 41	06 11			06 41			07 11			07 41
Palmers Green	d	23p43				00 23			01 19				05 43	06 13			06 43			07 13			07 43
Winchmore Hill	d	23p45				00 25			01 21				05 45	06 15			06 45			07 15			07 45
Grange Park	d	23p47				00 27							05 47	06 17			06 47			07 17			07 47
Enfield Chase	d	23p49				00 29			01 24				05 49	06 19			06 49			07 19			07 49
Gordon Hill	d	23p51				00 31			01 26				05 51	06 21			06 51			07 21			07 51
Crews Hill	d	23p54				00 34							05 54	06 24			06 54			07 24			07 54
Cuffley	d	23p57				00 37			01 30				05 57	06 27			06 57			07 27			07 57
Bayford	d	00 02				00 42							06 02	06 32			07 02			07 32			08 02
Hertford North	d	00 07				00 47			01 38				06a08	06a38			07 07			07a38			08 07
Watton-at-Stone	d	00 13		←		00 53											07 13						08 13
Stevenage ■	d	00 20	00 12	00 20		01 00		01 12	01 47		02 20	05 59			06 40		07a20	07 12			07 42		08a20
Hitchin ■	d	→	00 20	00 26		01 06		01a17	01 52		02a25	06a07			06 47			07a17			07 47		
Letchworth Garden City	a		00 29	00 36		01 15			02 06						06 51						07 51		

		FC ■	FC	FC	FC ■	FC	FC	FC ■	FC	FC	FC ■	FC	FC	FC ■	FC	FC	FC ■	FC	FC	FC ■	FC	FC	FC ■
London Kings Cross ■	⊖ d	07 36	07 41	07 56	08 06	08 11	08 26	08 36	08 41	08 56	09 06	09 11	09 26	09 36	09 41	09 56	10 06	10 11	10 26	10 36	10 41	10 56	11 06
Moorgate	⊖ d																						
Old Street	⊖ d																						
Essex Road	d																						
Highbury & Islington	⊖ d																						
Drayton Park	d																						
Finsbury Park	⊖ d	07 41	07 47	08 02	08 11	08 17	08 32	08 41	08 47	09 02	09 11	09 17	09 32	09 41	09 47	10 02	10 11	10 17	10 32	10 41	10 47	11 02	11 11
Harringay	d		07 49	08 04		08 19	08 34		08 49	09 04		09 19	09 34		09 49	10 04		10 19	10 34		10 49	11 04	
Hornsey	d		07 51	08 06		08 21	08 36		08 51	09 06		09 21	09 36		09 51	10 06		10 21	10 36		10 51	11 06	
Alexandra Palace	d		07 53	08 08		08 23	08 38		08 53	09 08		09 23	09 38		09 53	10 08		10 23	10 38		10 53	11 08	
New Southgate	d		07 56			08 26			08 56			09 26			09 56			10 26			10 56		
Oakleigh Park	d		07 59			08 29			08 59			09 29			09 59			10 29			10 59		
New Barnet	d		08 01			08 31			09 01			09 31			10 01			10 31			11 01		
Hadley Wood	d		08 04			08 34			09 04			09 34			10 04			10 34			11 04		
Potters Bar	d	07 51	08 08		08 21	08 38		08 51	09 08		09 21	09 38		09 51	10 08		10 21	10 38		10 51	11 08		11 21
Brookmans Park	d		08 11			08 41			09 11			09 41			10 11			10 41			11 11		
Welham Green	d		08 13			08 43			09 13			09 43			10 13			10 43			11 13		
Hatfield	d	07 57	08 16		08 27	08 46		08 57	09 16		09 27	09 46		09 57	10 16		10 27	10 46		10 57	11 16		11 27
Welwyn Garden City ■	d	08 01	08a21		08 31	08a51		09 01	09a21		09 31	09a51		10 01	10a21		10 31	10a51		11 01	11a21		11 31
Welwyn North	d	08 04			08 34			09 04			09 34			10 04			10 34			11 04			11 34
Knebworth	d	08 08			08 38			09 08			09 38			10 08			10 38			11 08			11 38
Bowes Park	d			08 11			08 41			09 11			09 41			10 11			10 41			11 11	
Palmers Green	d			08 13			08 43			09 13			09 43			10 13			10 43			11 13	
Winchmore Hill	d			08 15			08 45			09 15			09 45			10 15			10 45			11 15	
Grange Park	d			08 17			08 47			09 17			09 47			10 17			10 47			11 17	
Enfield Chase	d			08 19			08 49			09 19			09 49			10 19			10 49			11 19	
Gordon Hill	d			08 21			08 51			09 21			09 51			10 21			10 51			11 21	
Crews Hill	d			08 24			08 54			09 24			09 54			10 24			10 54			11 24	
Cuffley	d			08 27			08 57			09 27			09 57			10 27			10 57			11 27	
Bayford	d			08 32			09 02			09 32			10 02			10 32			11 02			11 32	
Hertford North	d			08a38			09 07			09a38			10 07			10a38			11 07			11a38	
Watton-at-Stone	d						09 13						10 13						11 13				
Stevenage ■	d	08 12			08 42		09a20	09 12			09 42		10a20	10 12			10 42		11a20	11 12			11 42
Hitchin ■	d	08a17			08 47			09a17			09 47			10a17			10 47			11a17			11 47
Letchworth Garden City	a				08 51						09 51						10 51						11 51

London - Welwyn Garden City, Hertford North and Letchworth Garden City

		FC		FC	FC 1	FC	FC	FC 1	FC	FC	FC 1	FC		FC	FC 1	FC	FC	FC 1	FC	FC	FC 1	FC		FC	FC 1
London Kings Cross 15 ⊖	d	11 11		11 26	11 36	11 41	11 56	12 06	12 11	12 26	12 36	12 41		12 56	13 06	13 11	13 26	13 36	13 41	13 56	14 06	14 11		14 26	14 36
Moorgate ⊖	d																								
Old Street ⊖	d																								
Essex Road	d																								
Highbury & Islington ⊖	d																								
Drayton Park	d																								
Finsbury Park ⊖	d	11 17		11 32	11 41	11 47	12 02	12 11	12 17	12 32	12 41	12 47		13 02	13 11	13 17	13 32	13 41	13 47	14 02	14 11	14 17		14 32	14 41
Harringay	d	11 19		11 34		11 49	12 04		12 19	12 34		12 49		13 04		13 19	13 34		13 49	14 04		14 19		14 34	
Hornsey	d	11 21		11 36		11 51	12 06		12 21	12 36		12 51		13 06		13 21	13 36		13 51	14 06		14 21		14 36	
Alexandra Palace	d	11 23		11 38		11 53	12 08		12 23	12 38		12 53		13 08		13 23	13 38		13 53	14 08		14 23		14 38	
New Southgate	d	11 26				11 56			12 26			12 56				13 26			13 56			14 26			
Oakleigh Park	d	11 29				11 59			12 29			12 59				13 29			13 59			14 29			
New Barnet	d	11 31				12 01			12 31			13 01				13 31			14 01			14 31			
Hadley Wood	d	11 34				12 04			12 34			13 04				13 34			14 04			14 34			
Potters Bar	d	11 38			11 51	12 08		12 21	12 38		12 51	13 08			13 21	13 38		13 51	14 08		14 21	14 38			14 51
Brookmans Park	d	11 41				12 11			12 41			13 11				13 41			14 11			14 41			
Welham Green	d	11 43				12 13			12 43			13 13				13 43			14 13			14 43			
Hatfield	d	11 46			11 57	12 16		12 27	12 46		12 57	13 16			13 27	13 46		13 57	14 16		14 27	14 46			14 57
Welwyn Garden City 4	d	11a51			12 01	12a21		12 31	12a51		13 01	13a21			13 31	13a51		14 01	14a21		14 31	14a51			15 01
Welwyn North	d				12 04			12 34			13 04				13 34			14 04			14 34				15 04
Knebworth	d				12 08			12 38			13 08				13 38			14 08			14 38				15 08
Bowes Park	d			11 41			12 11			12 41				13 11			13 41			14 11				14 41	
Palmers Green	d			11 43			12 13			12 43				13 13			13 43			14 13				14 43	
Winchmore Hill	d			11 45			12 15			12 45				13 15			13 45			14 15				14 45	
Grange Park	d			11 47			12 17			12 47				13 17			13 47			14 17				14 47	
Enfield Chase	d			11 49			12 19			12 49				13 19			13 49			14 19				14 49	
Gordon Hill	d			11 51			12 21			12 51				13 21			13 51			14 21				14 51	
Crews Hill	d			11 54			12 24			12 54				13 24			13 54			14 24				14 54	
Cuffley	d			11 57			12 27			12 57				13 27			13 57			14 27				14 57	
Bayford	d			12 02			12 32			13 02				13 32			14 02			14 32				15 02	
Hertford North	d			12 07			12a38			13 07				13a38			14 07			14a38				15 07	
Watton-at-Stone	d			12 13						13 13							14 13							15 13	
Stevenage 4	d			12a20	12 12			12 42		13a20	13 12				13 42		14a20	14 12			14 42			15a20	15 12
Hitchin 4	d				12a17			12 47			13a17				13 47			14a17			14 47				15a17
Letchworth Garden City	a							12 51							13 51						14 51				

		FC	FC	FC 1	FC	FC	FC 1	FC		FC	FC 1	FC	FC	FC 1	FC	FC	FC 1	FC		FC	FC 1	FC	FC	FC 1	FC
London Kings Cross 15 ⊖	d	14 41	14 56	15 06	15 11	15 26	15 36	15 41		15 56	16 06	16 11	16 26	16 36	16 41	16 56	17 06	17 11		17 26	17 36	17 41	17 56	18 06	18 11
Moorgate ⊖	d																								
Old Street ⊖	d																								
Essex Road	d																								
Highbury & Islington ⊖	d																								
Drayton Park	d																								
Finsbury Park ⊖	d	14 47	15 02	15 11	15 17	15 32	15 41	15 47		16 02	16 11	16 17	16 32	16 41	16 47	17 02	17 11	17 17		17 32	17 41	17 47	18 02	18 11	18 17
Harringay	d	14 49	15 04		15 19	15 34		15 49		16 04		16 19	16 34		16 49	17 04		17 19		17 34		17 49	18 04		18 19
Hornsey	d	14 51	15 06		15 21	15 36		15 51		16 06		16 21	16 36		16 51	17 06		17 21		17 36		17 51	18 06		18 21
Alexandra Palace	d	14 53	15 08		15 23	15 38		15 53		16 08		16 23	16 38		16 53	17 08		17 23		17 38		17 53	18 08		18 23
New Southgate	d	14 56			15 26			15 56				16 26			16 56			17 26				17 56			18 26
Oakleigh Park	d	14 59			15 29			15 59				16 29			16 59			17 29				17 59			18 29
New Barnet	d	15 01			15 31			16 01				16 31			17 01			17 31				18 01			18 31
Hadley Wood	d	15 04			15 34			16 04				16 34			17 04			17 34				18 04			18 34
Potters Bar	d	15 08		15 21	15 38		15 51	16 08			16 21	16 38		16 51	17 08		17 21	17 38			17 51	18 08		18 21	18 38
Brookmans Park	d	15 11			15 41			16 11				16 41			17 11			17 41				18 11			18 41
Welham Green	d	15 13			15 43			16 13				16 43			17 13			17 43				18 13			18 43
Hatfield	d	15 16		15 27	15 46		15 57	16 16			16 27	16 46		16 57	17 16		17 27	17 46			17 57	18 16		18 27	18 46
Welwyn Garden City 4	d	15a21		15 31	15a51		16 01	16a21			16 31	16a51		17 01	17a21		17 31	17a51			18 01	18a21		18 31	18a51
Welwyn North	d			15 34			16 04				16 34			17 04			17 34				18 04			18 34	
Knebworth	d			15 38			16 08				16 38			17 08			17 38				18 08			18 38	
Bowes Park	d		15 11			15 41				16 11			16 41			17 11				17 41			18 11		
Palmers Green	d		15 13			15 43				16 13			16 43			17 13				17 43			18 13		
Winchmore Hill	d		15 15			15 45				16 15			16 45			17 15				17 45			18 15		
Grange Park	d		15 17			15 47				16 17			16 47			17 17				17 47			18 17		
Enfield Chase	d		15 19			15 49				16 19			16 49			17 19				17 49			18 19		
Gordon Hill	d		15 21			15 51				16 21			16 51			17 21				17 51			18 21		
Crews Hill	d		15 24			15 54				16 24			16 54			17 24				17 54			18 24		
Cuffley	d		15 27			15 57				16 27			16 57			17 27				17 57			18 27		
Bayford	d		15 32			16 02				16 32			17 02			17 32				18 02			18 32		
Hertford North	d		15a38			16 07				16a38			17 07			17a38				18 07			18a38		
Watton-at-Stone	d					16 13							17 13							18 13					
Stevenage 4	d			15 42		16a20	16 12				16 42		17a20	17 12			17 42			18a20	18 12			18 42	
Hitchin 4	d			15 47			16a17				16 47			17a17			17 47				18a17			18 47	
Letchworth Garden City	a			15 51							16 51						17 51							18 51	

London - Welwyn Garden City, Hertford North and Letchworth Garden City

		FC	FC 1	FC		FC	FC 1	FC	FC	FC 1	FC	FC	FC	FC		FC 1	FC	FC	FC	FC	FC 1	FC	FC	FC	
London Kings Cross 15 ⊖	d	18 26	18 36	18 41		18 56	19 06	19 11	19 26	19 36	19 41	19 56	20 11	20 26		20 36	20 41	20 56	21 11	21 26	21 36	21 41	21 56	22 11	
Moorgate ⊖	d																								
Old Street ⊖	d																								
Essex Road	d																								
Highbury & Islington ⊖	d																								
Drayton Park	d																								
Finsbury Park ⊖	d	18 32	18 41	18 47		19 02	19 11	19 17	19 32	19 41	19 47	20 02	20 17	20 33		20 41	20 47	21 03	21 17	21 32	21 41	21 47	22 03	22 17	
Harringay	d	18 34		18 49		19 04		19 19	19 34		19 49	20 04	20 19	20 36			20 49	21 06	21 19	21 34		21 49	22 06	22 19	
Hornsey	d	18 36		18 51		19 06		19 21	19 36		19 51	20 06	20 21	20 39			20 51	21 09	21 21	21 36		21 51	22 09	22 21	
Alexandra Palace	d	18 38		18 53		19 08		19 23	19 38		19 53	20 08	20 23	20 41			20 53	21 11	21 23	21 38		21 53	22 11	22 23	
New Southgate	d			18 56				19 26			19 56		20 26				20 56		21 26			21 56		22 26	
Oakleigh Park	d			18 59				19 29			19 59		20 29				20 59		21 29			21 59		22 29	
New Barnet	d			19 01				19 31			20 01		20 31				21 01		21 31			22 01		22 31	
Hadley Wood	d			19 04				19 34			20 04		20 34				21 04		21 34			22 04		22 34	
Potters Bar	d		18 51	19 08			19 21	19 38		19 51	20 08		20 38			20 51	21 08		21 38		21 51	22 08		22 38	
Brookmans Park	d			19 11				19 41			20 11		20 41				21 11		21 41			22 11		22 41	
Welham Green	d			19 13				19 43			20 13		20 43				21 13		21 43			22 13		22 43	
Hatfield	d		18 57	19 16			19 27	19 46		19 57	20 16		20 46			20 57	21 16		21 46		21 57	22 16		22 46	
Welwyn Garden City 4	d		19 01	19a21			19 31	19a51		20 01	20a21		20a51			21 01	21a21		21a51		22 01	22a21		22a51	
Welwyn North	d		19 04				19 34			20 05						21 04					22 04				
Knebworth	d		19 08				19 38			20 09						21 08					22 08				
Bowes Park	d	18 41				19 11			19 41			20 11		20 44				21 14		21 41			22 14		
Palmers Green	d	18 43				19 13			19 43			20 13		20 46				21 16		21 43			22 16		
Winchmore Hill	d	18 45				19 15			19 45			20 15		20 48				21 18		21 45			22 18		
Grange Park	d	18 47				19 17			19 47			20 17		20 50				21 20		21 47			22 20		
Enfield Chase	d	18 49				19 19			19 49			20 19		20 52				21 22		21 49			22 22		
Gordon Hill	d	18 51				19 21			19 51			20 21		20 54				21 24		21 51			22 24		
Crews Hill	d	18 54				19 24			19 54			20 24		20 57				21 27		21 54			22 27		
Cuffley	d	18 57				19 27			19 57			20 27		21 00				21 30		21 57			22 30		
Bayford	d	19 02				19 32			20 02			20 32		21 05				21 35		22 02			22 35		
Hertford North	d	19 07				19a38			20 07			20a38		21a09				21a41		22a06			22a41		
Watton-at-Stone	d	19 13							20 13																
Stevenage 4	d	19a20	19 12				19 42		20a20	20 13						21 12					22 12				
Hitchin 4	d		19a17				19 47			20a18						21a17					22a17				
Letchworth Garden City	a						19 51																		

		FC	FC	FC	FC 1	FC	FC	FC	FC
London Kings Cross 15 ⊖	d	22 26	22 41	22 56	23 06	23 11	23 26	23 41	23 56
Moorgate ⊖	d								
Old Street ⊖	d								
Essex Road	d								
Highbury & Islington ⊖	d								
Drayton Park	d								
Finsbury Park ⊖	d	22 32	22 47	23 02	23 11	23 17	23 32	23 47	00 02
Harringay	d	22 34	22 49	23 04		23 19	23 34	23 49	00 04
Hornsey	d	22 36	22 51	23 06		23 21	23 36	23 51	00 06
Alexandra Palace	d	22 38	22 53	23 08		23 23	23 38	23 53	00 08
New Southgate	d		22 56			23 26		23 56	
Oakleigh Park	d		22 59			23 29		23 59	
New Barnet	d		23 01			23 31		00 01	
Hadley Wood	d		23 04			23 34		00 04	
Potters Bar	d		23 08		23 21	23 38		00 08	
Brookmans Park	d		23 11			23 41		00 11	
Welham Green	d		23 13			23 43		00 13	
Hatfield	d		23 16		23 27	23 46		00 16	
Welwyn Garden City 4	d		23a21		23 31	23a53		00a25	
Welwyn North	d				23 34				
Knebworth	d				23 38				
Bowes Park	d	22 41		23 11			23 41		00 11
Palmers Green	d	22 43		23 13			23 43		00 13
Winchmore Hill	d	22 45		23 15			23 45		00 15
Grange Park	d	22 47		23 17			23 47		00 17
Enfield Chase	d	22 49		23 19			23 49		00 19
Gordon Hill	d	22 51		23 21			23 51		00 21
Crews Hill	d	22 54		23 24			23 54		00 24
Cuffley	d	22 57		23 27			23 57		00 27
Bayford	d	23 02		23 32			00 02		00 32
Hertford North	d	23a06		23a38			00 07		00a40
Watton-at-Stone	d						00 13		
Stevenage 4	d				23 42		00 22		
Hitchin 4	d				23 50		00 29		
Letchworth Garden City	a				23 54		00 37		

London - Welwyn Garden City, Hertford North and Letchworth Garden City

Station		FC	FC 1	FC	FC	FC	FC	FC 1	FC 1	FC	FC 1	FC 1	FC	FC	FC 1	FC	FC	FC 1	FC	FC	FC 1	FC	FC
London Kings Cross 15 ⊖	d	23p26	23p36		23p41	00 06	00 11	00 36	01 06	01 11	01 36	05 23	05 26	05 56	06 06	06 11	06 26	06 36	06 41	06 56	07 06	07 11	07 26
Moorgate ⊖	d																						
Old Street ⊖	d																						
Essex Road	d																						
Highbury & Islington ⊖	d																						
Drayton Park	d																						
Finsbury Park ⊖	d	23p32	23p41		23p47	00 12	00 17	00 41	01 11	01 17	01 41	05 28	05 32	06 02	06 11	06 17	06 32	06 41	06 47	07 02	07 11	07 17	07 32
Harringay	d	23p34			23p49	00 14	00 19			01 19			05 34	06 04		06 19	06 34		06 49	07 04		07 19	07 34
Hornsey	d	23p36			23p51	00 16	00 21			01 21			05 36	06 06		06 21	06 36		06 51	07 06		07 21	07 36
Alexandra Palace	d	23p38			23p53	00 18	00 23		01 16	01 23	01 45		05 38	06 08		06 23	06 38		06 53	07 08		07 23	07 38
New Southgate	d				23p56		00 26			01 26	01 48					06 26			06 56			07 26	
Oakleigh Park	d				23p59		00 29			01 29	01 51					06 29			06 59			07 29	
New Barnet	d				00 01		00 31			01 31	01 53					06 31			07 01			07 31	
Hadley Wood	d				00 04		00 34			01 34	01 56					06 34			07 04			07 34	
Potters Bar	d		23p51		00 08		00 38	00 51		01 38	01 59	05 38			06 20	06 38		06 51	07 08		07 21	07 38	
Brookmans Park	d				00 11		00 41			01 41						06 41			07 11			07 41	
Welham Green	d				00 13		00 43			01 43						06 43			07 13			07 43	
Hatfield	d		23p57		00 16		00 46	00 57		01 46	02 05	05 44			06 25	06 46		06 57	07 16		07 27	07 46	
Welwyn Garden City 4	d		00 01		00a24		00a54	01 01		01a54	02 09	05 48			06 29	06a51		07 01	07a21		07 31	07a51	
Welwyn North	d		00 04					01s04			02s12	05 51			06 32			07 04			07 34		
Knebworth	d		00 08					01s08			02s16	05 55			06 36			07 08			07 38		
Bowes Park	d	23p41				00 21							05 41	06 11			06 41			07 11			07 41
Palmers Green	d	23p43				00 23			01 19				05 43	06 13			06 43			07 13			07 43
Winchmore Hill	d	23p45				00 25			01 21				05 45	06 15			06 45			07 15			07 45
Grange Park	d	23p47				00 27							05 47	06 17			06 47			07 17			07 47
Enfield Chase	d	23p49				00 29			01 24				05 49	06 19			06 49			07 19			07 49
Gordon Hill	d	23p51				00 31			01 26				05 51	06 21			06 51			07 21			07 51
Crews Hill	d	23p54				00 34							05 54	06 24			06 54			07 24			07 54
Cuffley	d	23p57				00 37			01 30				05 57	06 27			06 57			07 27			07 57
Bayford	d	00 02				00 42							06 02	06 32			07 02			07 32			08 02
Hertford North	d	00 07				00 47			01 38				06a08	06a38			07 07			07a38			08 07
Watton-at-Stone	d	00 13		←		00 53											07 13						08 13
Stevenage 4	d	00 20	00 12	00 20		01 00		01 12	01 47		02 20	05 59			06 40		07a20	07 12			07 42		08a20
Hitchin 4	d	→	00 20	00 26		01 06		01a17	01 52		02a25	06a07			06 47			07a17			07 47		
Letchworth Garden City	a		00 29	00 36		01 15			02 06						06 51						07 51		

Station		FC 1	FC	FC	FC 1	FC	FC	FC 1	FC	FC	FC 1	FC	FC	FC 1	FC	FC	FC 1	FC	FC	FC 1	FC	FC	FC 1
London Kings Cross 15 ⊖	d	07 36	07 41	07 56	08 06	08 11	08 26	08 36	08 41	08 56	09 06	09 11	09 26	09 36	09 41	09 56	10 06	10 11	10 26	10 36	10 41	10 56	11 06
Moorgate ⊖	d																						
Old Street ⊖	d																						
Essex Road	d																						
Highbury & Islington ⊖	d																						
Drayton Park	d																						
Finsbury Park ⊖	d	07 41	07 47	08 02	08 11	08 17	08 32	08 41	08 47	09 02	09 11	09 17	09 32	09 41	09 47	10 02	10 11	10 17	10 32	10 41	10 47	11 02	11 11
Harringay	d		07 49	08 04		08 19	08 34		08 49	09 04		09 19	09 34		09 49	10 04		10 19	10 34		10 49	11 04	
Hornsey	d		07 51	08 06		08 21	08 36		08 51	09 06		09 21	09 36		09 51	10 06		10 21	10 36		10 51	11 06	
Alexandra Palace	d		07 53	08 08		08 23	08 38		08 53	09 08		09 23	09 38		09 53	10 08		10 23	10 38		10 53	11 08	
New Southgate	d		07 56			08 26			08 56			09 26			09 56			10 26			10 56		
Oakleigh Park	d		07 59			08 29			08 59			09 29			09 59			10 29			10 59		
New Barnet	d		08 01			08 31			09 01			09 31			10 01			10 31			11 01		
Hadley Wood	d		08 04			08 34			09 04			09 34			10 04			10 34			11 04		
Potters Bar	d	07 51	08 08		08 21	08 38		08 51	09 08		09 21	09 38		09 51	10 08		10 21	10 38		10 51	11 08		11 21
Brookmans Park	d		08 11			08 41			09 11			09 41			10 11			10 41			11 11		
Welham Green	d		08 13			08 43			09 13			09 43			10 13			10 43			11 13		
Hatfield	d	07 57	08 16		08 27	08 46		08 57	09 16		09 27	09 46		09 57	10 16		10 27	10 46		10 57	11 16		11 27
Welwyn Garden City 4	d	08 01	08a21		08 31	08a51		09 01	09a21		09 31	09a51		10 01	10a21		10 31	10a51		11 01	11a21		11 31
Welwyn North	d	08 04			08 34			09 04			09 34			10 04			10 34			11 04			11 34
Knebworth	d	08 08			08 38			09 08			09 38			10 08			10 38			11 08			11 38
Bowes Park	d			08 11			08 41			09 11			09 41			10 11			10 41			11 11	
Palmers Green	d			08 13			08 43			09 13			09 43			10 13			10 43			11 13	
Winchmore Hill	d			08 15			08 45			09 15			09 45			10 15			10 45			11 15	
Grange Park	d			08 17			08 47			09 17			09 47			10 17			10 47			11 17	
Enfield Chase	d			08 19			08 49			09 19			09 49			10 19			10 49			11 19	
Gordon Hill	d			08 21			08 51			09 21			09 51			10 21			10 51			11 21	
Crews Hill	d			08 24			08 54			09 24			09 54			10 24			10 54			11 24	
Cuffley	d			08 27			08 57			09 27			09 57			10 27			10 57			11 27	
Bayford	d			08 32			09 02			09 32			10 02			10 32			11 02			11 32	
Hertford North	d			08a38			09 07			09a38			10 07			10a38			11 07			11a38	
Watton-at-Stone	d						09 13						10 13						11 13				
Stevenage 4	d	08 12			08 42		09a20	09 12			09 42		10a20	10 12			10 42		11a20	11 12			11 42
Hitchin 4	d	08a17			08 47			09a17			09 47			10a17			10 47			11a17			11 47
Letchworth Garden City	a				08 51						09 51						10 51						11 51

Table 24

Saturdays

6 August to 10 September

London - Welwyn Garden City, Hertford North and Letchworth Garden City

Station		FC	FC	FC 1	FC	FC	FC 1	FC	FC	FC 1	FC	FC	FC 1	FC	FC	FC 1	FC	FC	FC 1	FC	FC	FC 1
London Kings Cross 15 ⊖	d	11 11	11 26	11 36	11 41	11 56	12 06	12 11	12 26	12 36	12 41	12 56	13 06	13 11	13 26	13 36	13 41	13 56	14 06	14 11	14 26	14 36
Moorgate ⊖	d																					
Old Street ⊖	d																					
Essex Road	d																					
Highbury & Islington ⊖	d																					
Drayton Park	d																					
Finsbury Park ⊖	d	11 17	11 32	11 41	11 47	12 02	12 11	12 17	12 32	12 41	12 47	13 02	13 11	13 17	13 32	13 41	13 47	14 02	14 11	14 17	14 32	14 41
Harringay	d	11 19	11 34		11 49	12 04		12 19	12 34		12 49	13 04		13 19	13 34		13 49	14 04		14 19	14 34	
Hornsey	d	11 21	11 36		11 51	12 06		12 21	12 36		12 51	13 06		13 21	13 36		13 51	14 06		14 21	14 36	
Alexandra Palace	d	11 23	11 38		11 53	12 08		12 23	12 38		12 53	13 08		13 23	13 38		13 53	14 08		14 23	14 38	
New Southgate	d	11 26			11 56			12 26			12 56			13 26			13 56			14 26		
Oakleigh Park	d	11 29			11 59			12 29			12 59			13 29			13 59			14 29		
New Barnet	d	11 31			12 01			12 31			13 01			13 31			14 01			14 31		
Hadley Wood	d	11 34			12 04			12 34			13 04			13 34			14 04			14 34		
Potters Bar	d	11 38		11 51	12 08		12 21	12 38		12 51	13 08		13 21	13 38		13 51	14 08		14 21	14 38		14 51
Brookmans Park	d	11 41			12 11			12 41			13 11			13 41			14 11			14 41		
Welham Green	d	11 43			12 13			12 43			13 13			13 43			14 13			14 43		
Hatfield	d	11 46		11 57	12 16		12 27	12 46		12 57	13 16		13 27	13 46		13 57	14 16		14 27	14 46		14 57
Welwyn Garden City 4	d	11a51		12 01	12a21		12 31	12a51		13 01	13a21		13 31	13a51		14 01	14a21		14 31	14a51		15 01
Welwyn North	d			12 04			12 34			13 04			13 34			14 04			14 34			15 04
Knebworth	d			12 08			12 38			13 08			13 38			14 08			14 38			15 08
Bowes Park	d		11 41			12 11			12 41			13 11			13 41			14 11			14 41	
Palmers Green	d		11 43			12 13			12 43			13 13			13 43			14 13			14 43	
Winchmore Hill	d		11 45			12 15			12 45			13 15			13 45			14 15			14 45	
Grange Park	d		11 47			12 17			12 47			13 17			13 47			14 17			14 47	
Enfield Chase	d		11 49			12 19			12 49			13 19			13 49			14 19			14 49	
Gordon Hill	d		11 51			12 21			12 51			13 21			13 51			14 21			14 51	
Crews Hill	d		11 54			12 24			12 54			13 24			13 54			14 24			14 54	
Cuffley	d		11 57			12 27			12 57			13 27			13 57			14 27			14 57	
Bayford	d		12 02			12 32			13 02			13 32			14 02			14 32			15 02	
Hertford North	d		12 07			12a38			13 07			13a38			14 07			14a38			15 07	
Watton-at-Stone	d		12 13						13 13						14 13						15 13	
Stevenage 4	d		12a20	12 12			12 42		13a20	13 12			13 42		14a20	14 12			14 42		15a20	15 12
Hitchin 4	d			12a17			12 47			13a17			13 47			14a17			14 47			15a17
Letchworth Garden City	a						12 51						13 51						14 51			

Station		FC	FC	FC 1	FC	FC	FC 1	FC	FC	FC 1	FC	FC	FC 1	FC	FC	FC 1	FC	FC	FC 1	FC	FC	FC 1	FC
London Kings Cross 15 ⊖	d	14 41	14 56	15 06	15 11	15 26	15 36	15 41	15 56	16 06	16 11	16 26	16 36	16 41	16 56	17 06	17 11	17 26	17 36	17 41	17 56	18 06	18 11
Moorgate ⊖	d																						
Old Street ⊖	d																						
Essex Road	d																						
Highbury & Islington ⊖	d																						
Drayton Park	d																						
Finsbury Park ⊖	d	14 47	15 02	15 11	15 17	15 32	15 41	15 47	16 02	16 11	16 17	16 32	16 41	16 47	17 02	17 11	17 17	17 32	17 41	17 47	18 02	18 11	18 17
Harringay	d	14 49	15 04		15 19	15 34		15 49	16 04		16 19	16 34		16 49	17 04		17 19	17 34		17 49	18 04		18 19
Hornsey	d	14 51	15 06		15 21	15 36		15 51	16 06		16 21	16 36		16 51	17 06		17 21	17 36		17 51	18 06		18 21
Alexandra Palace	d	14 53	15 08		15 23	15 38		15 53	16 08		16 23	16 38		16 53	17 08		17 23	17 38		17 53	18 08		18 23
New Southgate	d	14 56			15 26			15 56			16 26			16 56			17 26			17 56			18 26
Oakleigh Park	d	14 59			15 29			15 59			16 29			16 59			17 29			17 59			18 29
New Barnet	d	15 01			15 31			16 01			16 31			17 01			17 31			18 01			18 31
Hadley Wood	d	15 04			15 34			16 04			16 34			17 04			17 34			18 04			18 34
Potters Bar	d	15 08		15 21	15 38		15 51	16 08		16 21	16 38		16 51	17 08		17 21	17 38		17 51	18 08		18 21	18 38
Brookmans Park	d	15 11			15 41			16 11			16 41			17 11			17 41			18 11			18 41
Welham Green	d	15 13			15 43			16 13			16 43			17 13			17 43			18 13			18 43
Hatfield	d	15 16		15 27	15 46		15 57	16 16		16 27	16 46		16 57	17 16		17 27	17 46		17 57	18 16		18 27	18 46
Welwyn Garden City 4	d	15a21		15 31	15a51		16 01	16a21		16 31	16a51		17 01	17a21		17 31	17a51		18 01	18a21		18 31	18a51
Welwyn North	d			15 34			16 04			16 34			17 04			17 34			18 04			18 34	
Knebworth	d			15 38			16 08			16 38			17 08			17 38			18 08			18 38	
Bowes Park	d		15 11			15 41			16 11			16 41			17 11			17 41			18 11		
Palmers Green	d		15 13			15 43			16 13			16 43			17 13			17 43			18 13		
Winchmore Hill	d		15 15			15 45			16 15			16 45			17 15			17 45			18 15		
Grange Park	d		15 17			15 47			16 17			16 47			17 17			17 47			18 17		
Enfield Chase	d		15 19			15 49			16 19			16 49			17 19			17 49			18 19		
Gordon Hill	d		15 21			15 51			16 21			16 51			17 21			17 51			18 21		
Crews Hill	d		15 24			15 54			16 24			16 54			17 24			17 54			18 24		
Cuffley	d		15 27			15 57			16 27			16 57			17 27			17 57			18 27		
Bayford	d		15 32			16 02			16 32			17 02			17 32			18 02			18 32		
Hertford North	d		15a38			16 07			16a38			17 07			17a38			18 07			18a38		
Watton-at-Stone	d					16 13						17 13						18 13					
Stevenage 4	d			15 42		16a20	16 12			16 42		17a20	17 12			17 42		18a20	18 12			18 42	
Hitchin 4	d			15 47			16a17			16 47			17a17			17 47			18a17			18 47	
Letchworth Garden City	a			15 51						16 51						17 51						18 51	

Table 24

London - Welwyn Garden City, Hertford North and Letchworth Garden City

Saturdays

6 August to 10 September

		FC	FC ■	FC	FC	FC ■	FC	FC	FC ■	FC	FC	FC ■	FC	FC	FC ■	FC	FC	FC ■	FC	FC	FC ■	FC
London Kings Cross ■ ⊖	d	18 26	18 36	18 41	18 56	19 06	19 11	19 26	19 36	19 41	19 56	20 06	20 11	20 26	20 36	20 41	20 56	21 06	21 11	21 26	21 36	21 41
Moorgate ⊖	d																					
Old Street ⊖	d																					
Essex Road	d																					
Highbury & Islington ⊖	d																					
Drayton Park	d																					
Finsbury Park ⊖	d	18 32	18 41	18 47	19 02	19 11	19 17	19 32	19 41	19 47	20 02	20 11	20 17	20 33	20 41	20 47	21 03	21 11	21 17	21 32	21 41	21 47
Harringay	d	18 34		18 49	19 04		19 19	19 34		19 49	20 04		20 19	20 36		20 49	21 06		21 19	21 34		21 49
Hornsey	d	18 36		18 51	19 06		19 21	19 36		19 51	20 06		20 21	20 39		20 51	21 09		21 21	21 36		21 51
Alexandra Palace	d	18 38		18 53	19 08		19 23	19 38		19 53	20 08		20 23	20 41		20 53	21 11		21 23	21 38		21 53
New Southgate	d			18 56			19 26			19 56			20 26			20 56			21 26			21 56
Oakleigh Park	d			18 59			19 29			19 59			20 29			20 59			21 29			21 59
New Barnet	d			19 01			19 31			20 01			20 31			21 01			21 31			22 01
Hadley Wood	d			19 04			19 34			20 04			20 34			21 04			21 34			22 04
Potters Bar	d		18 51	19 08		19 21	19 38		19 51	20 08		20 21	20 38		20 51	21 08		21 21	21 38		21 51	22 08
Brookmans Park	d			19 11			19 41			20 11			20 41			21 11			21 41			22 11
Welham Green	d			19 13			19 43			20 13			20 43			21 13			21 43			22 13
Hatfield	d		18 57	19 16		19 27	19 46		19 57	20 16		20 27	20 46		20 57	21 16		21 27	21 46		21 57	22 16
Welwyn Garden City ■	d		19 01	19a21		19 31	19a51		20 01	20a21		20 31	20a51		21 01	21a21		21 31	21a51		22 01	22a21
Welwyn North	d		19 04			19 34			20 04			20 34			21 04			21 34			22 04	
Knebworth	d		19 08			19 38			20 08			20 38			21 08			21 38			22 08	
Bowes Park	d	18 41			19 11			19 41			20 11			20 44			21 14			21 41		
Palmers Green	d	18 43			19 13			19 43			20 13			20 46			21 16			21 43		
Winchmore Hill	d	18 45			19 15			19 45			20 15			20 48			21 18			21 45		
Grange Park	d	18 47			19 17			19 47			20 17			20 50			21 20			21 47		
Enfield Chase	d	18 49			19 19			19 49			20 19			20 52			21 22			21 49		
Gordon Hill	d	18 51			19 21			19 51			20 21			20 54			21 24			21 51		
Crews Hill	d	18 54			19 24			19 54			20 24			20 57			21 27			21 54		
Cuffley	d	18 57			19 27			19 57			20 27			21 00			21 30			21 57		
Bayford	d	19 02			19 32			20 02			20 32			21 05			21 35			22 02		
Hertford North	d	19 07			19a38			20 07			20a38			21a09			21a41			22a06		
Watton-at-Stone	d	19 13						20 13														
Stevenage ■	d	19a20	19 12			19 42		20a20	20 12			20 42			21 12			21 42			22 12	
Hitchin ■	d		19a17			19 47			20a17			20 47			21a17			21 47			22a17	
Letchworth Garden City	a					19 51						20 51						21 51				

		FC	FC ■	FC	FC	FC ■	FC	FC	FC ■	FC	FC	FC ■	FC	FC	FC
London Kings Cross ■ ⊖	d	21 56	22 06	22 11	22 26	22 36	22 41	22 56	23 06	23 11	23 26	23 36		23 41	23 56
Moorgate ⊖	d														
Old Street ⊖	d														
Essex Road	d														
Highbury & Islington ⊖	d														
Drayton Park	d														
Finsbury Park ⊖	d	22 03	22 11	22 17	22 32	22 41	22 47	23 02	23 11	23 17	23 32	23 41		23 47	00 02
Harringay	d	22 06		22 19	22 34		22 49	23 04		23 19	23 34			23 49	00 04
Hornsey	d	22 09		22 21	22 36		22 51	23 06		23 21	23 36			23 51	00 06
Alexandra Palace	d	22 11		22 23	22 38		22 53	23 08		23 23	23 38			23 53	00 08
New Southgate	d			22 26			22 56			23 26				23 56	
Oakleigh Park	d			22 29			22 59			23 29				23 59	
New Barnet	d			22 31			23 01			23 31				00 01	
Hadley Wood	d			22 34			23 04			23 34				00 04	
Potters Bar	d		22 21	22 38		22 51	23 08		23 21	23 38		23 53		00 08	
Brookmans Park	d			22 41			23 11			23 41				00 11	
Welham Green	d			22 43			23 13			23 43				00 13	
Hatfield	d		22 27	22 46		22 57	23 16		23 27	23 46		23 59		00 16	
Welwyn Garden City ■	d		22 31	22a51		23 01	23a21		23 31	23a53		00 06		00a25	
Welwyn North	d		22 34			23 04			23 34			00 09			
Knebworth	d		22 38			23 08			23 38			00 13			
Bowes Park	d	22 14			22 41			23 11			23 41				00 11
Palmers Green	d	22 16			22 43			23 13			23 43				00 13
Winchmore Hill	d	22 18			22 45			23 15			23 45				00 15
Grange Park	d	22 20			22 47			23 17			23 47				00 17
Enfield Chase	d	22 22			22 49			23 19			23 49				00 19
Gordon Hill	d	22 24			22 51			23 21			23 51				00 21
Crews Hill	d	22 27			22 54			23 24			23 54				00 24
Cuffley	d	22 30			22 57			23 27			23 57				00 27
Bayford	d	22 35			23 02			23 32			00 02				00 32
Hertford North	d	22a41			23a06			23a38			00 07				00a40
Watton-at-Stone	d										00 13		←		
Stevenage ■	d		22 42			23 12			23 42		00 22	00 18	00 22		
Hitchin ■	d		22 47			23 20			23 50		→	00 25	00 29		
Letchworth Garden City	a		22 51			23 26			23 54			00 30	00 37		

Table 24

London - Welwyn Garden City, Hertford North and Letchworth Garden City

Saturdays

from 24 September

		FC	FC ■	FC	FC	FC	FC	FC ■	FC ■	FC	FC ■	FC ■	FC	FC	FC ■	FC	FC	FC ■	FC	FC	FC ■	FC	FC
London Kings Cross ■ ⊖	d	23p26	23p36		23p41	00 06	00 11	00 36	01 06	01 11	01 36	05 23	05 26	05 56	06 06	06 11	06 26	06 36	06 41	06 56	07 06	07 11	07 26
Moorgate ⊖	d																						
Old Street ⊖	d																						
Essex Road	d																						
Highbury & Islington ⊖	d																						
Drayton Park	d																						
Finsbury Park ⊖	d	23p32	23p41		23p47	00 12	00 17	00 41	01 11	01 17	01 41	05 28	05 32	06 02	06 11	06 17	06 32	06 41	06 47	07 02	07 11	07 17	07 32
Harringay	d	23p34			23p49	00 14	00 19			01 19			05 34	06 04		06 19	06 34		06 49	07 04		07 19	07 34
Hornsey	d	23p36			23p51	00 16	00 21			01 21			05 36	06 06		06 21	06 36		06 51	07 06		07 21	07 36
Alexandra Palace	d	23p38			23p53	00 18	00 23		01 16	01 23	01 45		05 38	06 08		06 23	06 38		06 53	07 08		07 23	07 38
New Southgate	d				23p56		00 26			01 26	01 48					06 26			06 56			07 26	
Oakleigh Park	d				23p59		00 29			01 29	01 51					06 29			06 59			07 29	
New Barnet	d				00 01		00 31			01 31	01 53					06 31			07 01			07 31	
Hadley Wood	d				00 04		00 34			01 34	01 56					06 34			07 04			07 34	
Potters Bar	d		23p51		00 08		00 38	00 51		01 38	01 59	05 38			06 20	06 38		06 51	07 08		07 21	07 38	
Brookmans Park	d				00 11		00 41			01 41						06 41			07 11			07 41	
Welham Green	d				00 13		00 43			01 43						06 43			07 13			07 43	
Hatfield	d		23p57		00 16		00 46	00 57		01 46	02 05	05 44			06 25	06 46		06 57	07 16		07 27	07 46	
Welwyn Garden City ■	d		00 01		00a24		00a54	01 01		01a54	02 09	05 48			06 29	06a51		07 01	07a21		07 31	07a51	
Welwyn North	d		00 04					01s04			02s12	05 51			06 32			07 04			07 34		
Knebworth	d		00 08					01s08			02s16	05 55			06 36			07 08			07 38		
Bowes Park	d	23p41				00 21							05 41	06 11			06 41			07 11			07 41
Palmers Green	d	23p43				00 23			01 19				05 43	06 13			06 43			07 13			07 43
Winchmore Hill	d	23p45				00 25			01 21				05 45	06 15			06 45			07 15			07 45
Grange Park	d	23p47				00 27							05 47	06 17			06 47			07 17			07 47
Enfield Chase	d	23p49				00 29			01 24				05 49	06 19			06 49			07 19			07 49
Gordon Hill	d	23p51				00 31			01 26				05 51	06 21			06 51			07 21			07 51
Crews Hill	d	23p54				00 34							05 54	06 24			06 54			07 24			07 54
Cuffley	d	23p57				00 37			01 30				05 57	06 27			06 57			07 27			07 57
Bayford	d	00 02				00 42							06 02	06 32			07 02			07 32			08 02
Hertford North	d	00 07				00 47			01 38				06a08	06a38			07 07			07a38			08 07
Watton-at-Stone	d	00 13		←		00 53											07 13						08 13
Stevenage ■	d	00 20	00 12	00 20		01 00		01 12	01 47		02 20	05 59			06 40		07a20	07 12			07 42		08a20
Hitchin ■	d	→	00 20	00 26		01 06		01a17	01 52		02a25	06a07			06 47			07a17			07 47		
Letchworth Garden City	a		00 29	00 36		01 15			02 06						06 51						07 51		

		FC ■	FC	FC	FC ■	FC	FC	FC ■	FC	FC	FC ■	FC	FC	FC ■	FC	FC	FC ■	FC	FC	FC ■	FC	FC	FC ■
London Kings Cross ■ ⊖	d	07 36	07 41	07 56	08 06	08 11	08 26	08 36	08 41	08 56	09 06	09 11	09 26	09 36	09 41	09 56	10 06	10 11	10 26	10 36	10 41	10 56	11 06
Moorgate ⊖	d																						
Old Street ⊖	d																						
Essex Road	d																						
Highbury & Islington ⊖	d																						
Drayton Park	d																						
Finsbury Park ⊖	d	07 41	07 47	08 02	08 11	08 17	08 32	08 41	08 47	09 02	09 11	09 17	09 32	09 41	09 47	10 02	10 11	10 17	10 32	10 41	10 47	11 02	11 11
Harringay	d		07 49	08 04		08 19	08 34		08 49	09 04		09 19	09 34		09 49	10 04		10 19	10 34		10 49	11 04	
Hornsey	d		07 51	08 06		08 21	08 36		08 51	09 06		09 21	09 36		09 51	10 06		10 21	10 36		10 51	11 06	
Alexandra Palace	d		07 53	08 08		08 23	08 38		08 53	09 08		09 23	09 38		09 53	10 08		10 23	10 38		10 53	11 08	
New Southgate	d		07 56			08 26			08 56			09 26			09 56			10 26			10 56		
Oakleigh Park	d		07 59			08 29			08 59			09 29			09 59			10 29			10 59		
New Barnet	d		08 01			08 31			09 01			09 31			10 01			10 31			11 01		
Hadley Wood	d		08 04			08 34			09 04			09 34			10 04			10 34			11 04		
Potters Bar	d	07 51	08 08		08 21	08 38		08 51	09 08		09 21	09 38		09 51	10 08		10 21	10 38		10 51	11 08		11 21
Brookmans Park	d		08 11			08 41			09 11			09 41			10 11			10 41			11 11		
Welham Green	d		08 13			08 43			09 13			09 43			10 13			10 43			11 13		
Hatfield	d	07 57	08 16		08 27	08 46		08 57	09 16		09 27	09 46		09 57	10 16		10 27	10 46		10 57	11 16		11 27
Welwyn Garden City ■	d	08 01	08a21		08 31	08a51		09 01	09a21		09 31	09a51		10 01	10a21		10 31	10a51		11 01	11a21		11 31
Welwyn North	d	08 04			08 34			09 04			09 34			10 04			10 34			11 04			11 34
Knebworth	d	08 08			08 38			09 08			09 38			10 08			10 38			11 08			11 38
Bowes Park	d			08 11			08 41			09 11			09 41			10 11			10 41			11 11	
Palmers Green	d			08 13			08 43			09 13			09 43			10 13			10 43			11 13	
Winchmore Hill	d			08 15			08 45			09 15			09 45			10 15			10 45			11 15	
Grange Park	d			08 17			08 47			09 17			09 47			10 17			10 47			11 17	
Enfield Chase	d			08 19			08 49			09 19			09 49			10 19			10 49			11 19	
Gordon Hill	d			08 21			08 51			09 21			09 51			10 21			10 51			11 21	
Crews Hill	d			08 24			08 54			09 24			09 54			10 24			10 54			11 24	
Cuffley	d			08 27			08 57			09 27			09 57			10 27			10 57			11 27	
Bayford	d			08 32			09 02			09 32			10 02			10 32			11 02			11 32	
Hertford North	d			08a38			09 07			09a38			10 07			10a38			11 07			11a38	
Watton-at-Stone	d						09 13						10 13						11 13				
Stevenage ■	d	08 12			08 42		09a20	09 12			09 42		10a20	10 12			10 42		11a20	11 12			11 42
Hitchin ■	d	08a17			08 47			09a17			09 47			10a17			10 47			11a17			11 47
Letchworth Garden City	a				08 51						09 51						10 51						11 51

Table 24

Saturdays
from 24 September

London - Welwyn Garden City, Hertford North and Letchworth Garden City

		FC	FC	FC 1	FC	FC	FC 1	FC	FC	FC 1	FC	FC	FC 1	FC	FC	FC 1	FC	FC	FC 1	FC	FC	FC 1
London Kings Cross 15 ⊖	d	11 11	11 26	11 36	11 41	11 56	12 06	12 11	12 26	12 36	12 41	12 56	13 06	13 11	13 26	13 36	13 41	13 56	14 06	14 11	14 26	14 36
Moorgate ⊖	d																					
Old Street ⊖	d																					
Essex Road	d																					
Highbury & Islington ⊖	d																					
Drayton Park	d																					
Finsbury Park ⊖	d	11 17	11 32	11 41	11 47	12 02	12 11	12 17	12 32	12 41	12 47	13 02	13 11	13 17	13 32	13 41	13 47	14 02	14 11	14 17	14 32	14 41
Harringay	d	11 19	11 34		11 49	12 04		12 19	12 34		12 49	13 04		13 19	13 34		13 49	14 04		14 19	14 34	
Hornsey	d	11 21	11 36		11 51	12 06		12 21	12 36		12 51	13 06		13 21	13 36		13 51	14 06		14 21	14 36	
Alexandra Palace	d	11 23	11 38		11 53	12 08		12 23	12 38		12 53	13 08		13 23	13 38		13 53	14 08		14 23	14 38	
New Southgate	d	11 26			11 56			12 26			12 56			13 26			13 56			14 26		
Oakleigh Park	d	11 29			11 59			12 29			12 59			13 29			13 59			14 29		
New Barnet	d	11 31			12 01			12 31			13 01			13 31			14 01			14 31		
Hadley Wood	d	11 34			12 04			12 34			13 04			13 34			14 04			14 34		
Potters Bar	d	11 38		11 51	12 08		12 21	12 38		12 51	13 08		13 21	13 38		13 51	14 08		14 21	14 38		14 51
Brookmans Park	d	11 41			12 11			12 41			13 11			13 41			14 11			14 41		
Welham Green	d	11 43			12 13			12 43			13 13			13 43			14 13			14 43		
Hatfield	d	11 46		11 57	12 16		12 27	12 46		12 57	13 16		13 27	13 46		13 57	14 16		14 27	14 46		14 57
Welwyn Garden City 4	d	11a51		12 01	12a21		12 31	12a51		13 01	13a21		13 31	13a51		14 01	14a21		14 31	14a51		15 01
Welwyn North	d			12 04			12 34			13 04			13 34			14 04			14 34			15 04
Knebworth	d			12 08			12 38			13 08			13 38			14 08			14 38			15 08
Bowes Park	d		11 41			12 11			12 41			13 11			13 41			14 11			14 41	
Palmers Green	d		11 43			12 13			12 43			13 13			13 43			14 13			14 43	
Winchmore Hill	d		11 45			12 15			12 45			13 15			13 45			14 15			14 45	
Grange Park	d		11 47			12 17			12 47			13 17			13 47			14 17			14 47	
Enfield Chase	d		11 49			12 19			12 49			13 19			13 49			14 19			14 49	
Gordon Hill	d		11 51			12 21			12 51			13 21			13 51			14 21			14 51	
Crews Hill	d		11 54			12 24			12 54			13 24			13 54			14 24			14 54	
Cuffley	d		11 57			12 27			12 57			13 27			13 57			14 27			14 57	
Bayford	d		12 02			12 32			13 02			13 32			14 02			14 32			15 02	
Hertford North	d		12 07			12a38			13 07			13a38			14 07			14a38			15 07	
Watton-at-Stone	d		12 13						13 13						14 13						15 13	
Stevenage 4	d		12a20	12 12			12 42		13a20	13 12			13 42		14a20	14 12			14 42		15a20	15 12
Hitchin 4	d			12a17			12 47			13a17			13 47			14a17			14 47			15a17
Letchworth Garden City	a						12 51						13 51						14 51			

		FC	FC	FC 1	FC	FC	FC 1	FC	FC	FC 1	FC	FC	FC 1	FC	FC	FC 1	FC	FC	FC 1	FC	FC	FC 1	FC
London Kings Cross 15 ⊖	d	14 41	14 56	15 06	15 11	15 26	15 36	15 41	15 56	16 06	16 11	16 26	16 36	16 41	16 56	17 06	17 11	17 26	17 36	17 41	17 56	18 06	18 11
Moorgate ⊖	d																						
Old Street ⊖	d																						
Essex Road	d																						
Highbury & Islington ⊖	d																						
Drayton Park	d																						
Finsbury Park ⊖	d	14 47	15 02	15 11	15 17	15 32	15 41	15 47	16 02	16 11	16 17	16 32	16 41	16 47	17 02	17 11	17 17	17 32	17 41	17 47	18 02	18 11	18 17
Harringay	d	14 49	15 04		15 19	15 34		15 49	16 04		16 19	16 34		16 49	17 04		17 19	17 34		17 49	18 04		18 19
Hornsey	d	14 51	15 06		15 21	15 36		15 51	16 06		16 21	16 36		16 51	17 06		17 21	17 36		17 51	18 06		18 21
Alexandra Palace	d	14 53	15 08		15 23	15 38		15 53	16 08		16 23	16 38		16 53	17 08		17 23	17 38		17 53	18 08		18 23
New Southgate	d	14 56			15 26			15 56			16 26			16 56			17 26			17 56			18 26
Oakleigh Park	d	14 59			15 29			15 59			16 29			16 59			17 29			17 59			18 29
New Barnet	d	15 01			15 31			16 01			16 31			17 01			17 31			18 01			18 31
Hadley Wood	d	15 04			15 34			16 04			16 34			17 04			17 34			18 04			18 34
Potters Bar	d	15 08		15 21	15 38		15 51	16 08		16 21	16 38		16 51	17 08		17 21	17 38		17 51	18 08		18 21	18 38
Brookmans Park	d	15 11			15 41			16 11			16 41			17 11			17 41			18 11			18 41
Welham Green	d	15 13			15 43			16 13			16 43			17 13			17 43			18 13			18 43
Hatfield	d	15 16		15 27	15 46		15 57	16 16		16 27	16 46		16 57	17 16		17 27	17 46		17 57	18 16		18 27	18 46
Welwyn Garden City 4	d	15a21		15 31	15a51		16 01	16a21		16 31	16a51		17 01	17a21		17 31	17a51		18 01	18a21		18 31	18a51
Welwyn North	d			15 34			16 04			16 34			17 04			17 34			18 04			18 34	
Knebworth	d			15 38			16 08			16 38			17 08			17 38			18 08			18 38	
Bowes Park	d		15 11			15 41			16 11			16 41			17 11			17 41			18 11		
Palmers Green	d		15 13			15 43			16 13			16 43			17 13			17 43			18 13		
Winchmore Hill	d		15 15			15 45			16 15			16 45			17 15			17 45			18 15		
Grange Park	d		15 17			15 47			16 17			16 47			17 17			17 47			18 17		
Enfield Chase	d		15 19			15 49			16 19			16 49			17 19			17 49			18 19		
Gordon Hill	d		15 21			15 51			16 21			16 51			17 21			17 51			18 21		
Crews Hill	d		15 24			15 54			16 24			16 54			17 24			17 54			18 24		
Cuffley	d		15 27			15 57			16 27			16 57			17 27			17 57			18 27		
Bayford	d		15 32			16 02			16 32			17 02			17 32			18 02			18 32		
Hertford North	d		15a38			16 07			16a38			17 07			17a38			18 07			18a38		
Watton-at-Stone	d					16 13						17 13						18 13					
Stevenage 4	d			15 42		16a20	16 12			16 42		17a20	17 12			17 42		18a20	18 12			18 42	
Hitchin 4	d			15 47			16a17			16 47			17a17			17 47			18a17			18 47	
Letchworth Garden City	a			15 51						16 51						17 51						18 51	

Table 24

Saturdays
from 24 September

London - Welwyn Garden City, Hertford North and Letchworth Garden City

		FC	FC 1	FC	FC	FC 1	FC	FC	FC 1	FC	FC	FC 1	FC	FC	FC 1	FC	FC	FC 1	FC	FC	FC 1	FC
London Kings Cross 15 ⊖	d	18 26	18 36	18 41	18 56	19 06	19 11	19 26	19 36	19 41	19 56	20 06	20 11	20 26	20 36	20 41	20 56	21 06	21 11	21 26	21 36	21 41
Moorgate ⊖	d																					
Old Street ⊖	d																					
Essex Road	d																					
Highbury & Islington ⊖	d																					
Drayton Park	d																					
Finsbury Park ⊖	d	18 32	18 41	18 47	19 02	19 11	19 17	19 32	19 41	19 47	20 02	20 11	20 17	20 33	20 41	20 47	21 03	21 11	21 17	21 32	21 41	21 47
Harringay	d	18 34		18 49	19 04		19 19	19 34		19 49	20 04		20 19	20 36		20 49	21 06		21 19	21 34		21 49
Hornsey	d	18 36		18 51	19 06		19 21	19 36		19 51	20 06		20 21	20 39		20 51	21 09		21 21	21 36		21 51
Alexandra Palace	d	18 38		18 53	19 08		19 23	19 38		19 53	20 08		20 23	20 41		20 53	21 11		21 23	21 38		21 53
New Southgate	d			18 56			19 26			19 56			20 26			20 56			21 26			21 56
Oakleigh Park	d			18 59			19 29			19 59			20 29			20 59			21 29			21 59
New Barnet	d			19 01			19 31			20 01			20 31			21 01			21 31			22 01
Hadley Wood	d			19 04			19 34			20 04			20 34			21 04			21 34			22 04
Potters Bar	d		18 51	19 08		19 21	19 38		19 51	20 08		20 21	20 38		20 51	21 08		21 21	21 38		21 51	22 08
Brookmans Park	d			19 11			19 41			20 11			20 41			21 11			21 41			22 11
Welham Green	d			19 13			19 43			20 13			20 43			21 13			21 43			22 13
Hatfield	d		18 57	19 16		19 27	19 46		19 57	20 16		20 27	20 46		20 57	21 16		21 27	21 46		21 57	22 16
Welwyn Garden City 4	d		19 01	19a21		19 31	19a51		20 01	20a21		20 31	20a51		21 01	21a21		21 31	21a51		22 01	22a21
Welwyn North	d		19 04			19 34			20 04			20 34			21 04			21 34			22 04	
Knebworth	d		19 08			19 38			20 08			20 38			21 08			21 38			22 08	
Bowes Park	d	18 41			19 11			19 41			20 11			20 44			21 14			21 41		
Palmers Green	d	18 43			19 13			19 43			20 13			20 46			21 16			21 43		
Winchmore Hill	d	18 45			19 15			19 45			20 15			20 48			21 18			21 45		
Grange Park	d	18 47			19 17			19 47			20 17			20 50			21 20			21 47		
Enfield Chase	d	18 49			19 19			19 49			20 19			20 52			21 22			21 49		
Gordon Hill	d	18 51			19 21			19 51			20 21			20 54			21 24			21 51		
Crews Hill	d	18 54			19 24			19 54			20 24			20 57			21 27			21 54		
Cuffley	d	18 57			19 27			19 57			20 27			21 00			21 30			21 57		
Bayford	d	19 02			19 32			20 02			20 32			21 05			21 35			22 02		
Hertford North	d	19 07			19a38			20 07			20a38			21a09			21a41			22a06		
Watton-at-Stone	d	19 13						20 13														
Stevenage 4	d	19a20	19 12			19 42		20a20	20 12			20 42			21 12			21 42			22 12	
Hitchin 4	d		19a17			19 47			20a17			20 47			21a17			21 47			22a17	
Letchworth Garden City	a					19 51						20 51						21 51				

		FC	FC 1	FC	FC	FC 1	FC	FC	FC 1	FC	FC	FC 1	FC	FC	FC
London Kings Cross 15 ⊖	d	21 56	22 06	22 11	22 26	22 36	22 41	22 56	23 06	23 11	23 26	23 36		23 41	23 56
Moorgate ⊖	d														
Old Street ⊖	d														
Essex Road	d														
Highbury & Islington ⊖	d														
Drayton Park	d														
Finsbury Park ⊖	d	22 03	22 11	22 17	22 32	22 41	22 47	23 02	23 11	23 17	23 32	23 41		23 47	00 02
Harringay	d	22 06		22 19	22 34		22 49	23 04		23 19	23 34			23 49	00 04
Hornsey	d	22 09		22 21	22 36		22 51	23 06		23 21	23 36			23 51	00 06
Alexandra Palace	d	22 11		22 23	22 38		22 53	23 08		23 23	23 38			23 53	00 08
New Southgate	d			22 26			22 56			23 26				23 56	
Oakleigh Park	d			22 29			22 59			23 29				23 59	
New Barnet	d			22 31			23 01			23 31				00 01	
Hadley Wood	d			22 34			23 04			23 34				00 04	
Potters Bar	d		22 21	22 38		22 51	23 08		23 21	23 38		23 53		00 08	
Brookmans Park	d			22 41			23 11			23 41				00 11	
Welham Green	d			22 43			23 13			23 43				00 13	
Hatfield	d		22 27	22 46		22 57	23 16		23 27	23 46		23 59		00 16	
Welwyn Garden City 4	d		22 31	22a51		23 01	23a21		23 31	23a53		00 06		00a25	
Welwyn North	d		22 34			23 04			23 34			00 09			
Knebworth	d		22 38			23 08			23 38			00 13			
Bowes Park	d	22 14			22 41			23 11			23 41				00 11
Palmers Green	d	22 16			22 43			23 13			23 43				00 13
Winchmore Hill	d	22 18			22 45			23 15			23 45				00 15
Grange Park	d	22 20			22 47			23 17			23 47				00 17
Enfield Chase	d	22 22			22 49			23 19			23 49				00 19
Gordon Hill	d	22 24			22 51			23 21			23 51				00 21
Crews Hill	d	22 27			22 54			23 24			23 54				00 24
Cuffley	d	22 30			22 57			23 27			23 57				00 27
Bayford	d	22 35			23 02			23 32			00 02				00 32
Hertford North	d	22a41			23a06			23a38			00 07				00a40
Watton-at-Stone	d										00 13		←		
Stevenage 4	d		22 42			23 12			23 42		00 22	00 18	00 22		
Hitchin 4	d		22 47			23 20			23 50		→	00 25	00 29		
Letchworth Garden City	a		22 51			23 26			23 54			00 30	00 37		

London - Welwyn Garden City, Hertford North and Letchworth Garden City

		FC	FC	FC	FC	FC	FC	FC	FC	FC	FC	FC	FC	FC	FC	FC	FC	FC	FC	FC	FC	FC	FC
			1				1									1					1		
		A	A	A	A	A																	
London Kings Cross 15 ⊖	d	23p26	23p36		23p41	23p56	00 06	00 26	00 41	01 11	05 56	06 11	06 26	06 41	06 56	07 06	07 11	07 26	07 41	07 56	08 06	08 11	08 26
Moorgate ⊖	d																						
Old Street ⊖	d																						
Essex Road	d																						
Highbury & Islington ⊖	d																						
Drayton Park	d																						
Finsbury Park ⊖	d	23p32	23p41		23p47	00 02	00 11	00 32	00 47	01 17	06 02	06 17	06 32	06 47	07 02	07 11	07 17	07 32	07 47	08 02	08 11	08 17	08 32
Harringay	d	23p34			23p49	00 04		00 34	00 49	01 19	06 04	06 19	06 34	06 49	07 04		07 19	07 34	07 49	08 04		08 19	08 34
Hornsey	d	23p36			23p51	00 06		00 36	00 51	01 21	06 06	06 21	06 36	06 51	07 06		07 21	07 36	07 51	08 06		08 21	08 36
Alexandra Palace	d	23p38			23p53	00 08		00 38	00 53	01 23	06 08	06 23	06 38	06 53	07 08		07 23	07 38	07 53	08 08		08 23	08 38
New Southgate	d				23p56			00 41		01 26		06 26		06 56			07 26		07 56			08 26	
Oakleigh Park	d				23p59			00 44		01 29		06 29		06 59			07 29		07 59			08 29	
New Barnet	d				00 01			00 46		01 31		06 31		07 01			07 31		08 01			08 31	
Hadley Wood	d				00 04			00 49		01 34		06 34		07 04			07 34		08 04			08 34	
Potters Bar	d		23p53		00 08		00 23	00 53		01 38		06 38		07 08		07 21	07 38		08 08		08 21	08 38	
Brookmans Park	d				00 11			00 56		01 41		06 41		07 11			07 41		08 11			08 41	
Welham Green	d				00 13			00 58		01 43		06 43		07 13			07 43		08 13			08 43	
Hatfield	d		23p59		00 16		00 29	01 01		01 46		06 46		07 16		07 27	07 46		08 16		08 27	08 46	
Welwyn Garden City 4	d		00 06		00a25		00 41	01a10		01a55		06a55		07a25		07 33	07a55		08a25		08 31	08a55	
Welwyn North	d		00 09				00 44									07 36					08 34		
Knebworth	d		00 13				00 48									07 40					08 38		
Bowes Park	d	23p41				00 11			00 56		06 11		06 41		07 11			07 41		08 11			08 41
Palmers Green	d	23p43				00 13			00 58		06 13		06 43		07 13			07 43		08 13			08 43
Winchmore Hill	d	23p45				00 15			01 00		06 15		06 45		07 15			07 45		08 15			08 45
Grange Park	d	23p47				00 17			01 02		06 17		06 47		07 17			07 47		08 17			08 47
Enfield Chase	d	23p49				00 19			01 04		06 19		06 49		07 19			07 49		08 19			08 49
Gordon Hill	d	23p51				00 21			01 06		06 21		06 51		07 21			07 51		08 21			08 51
Crews Hill	d	23p54				00 24			01 09		06 24		06 54		07 24			07 54		08 24			08 54
Cuffley	d	23p57				00 27			01 12		06 27		06 57		07 27			07 57		08 27			08 57
Bayford	d	00 02				00 32			01 17		06 32		07 02		07 32			08 02		08 32			09 02
Hertford North	d	00 07				00a40			01 22		06a40		07 07		07a40			08 07		08a40			09 07
Watton-at-Stone	d	00 13		←					01 28				07 13					08 13					09 13
Stevenage 4	d	00 22	00 18	00 22			00 53		01 36				07a22			07 45		08a23			08 42		09a20
Hitchin 4	d	→	00 25	00 29			01 00		01 44							07 52					08 47		
Letchworth Garden City	a		00 30	00 37			01 04		01 50							07 56					08 51		

		FC	FC	FC	FC	FC	FC	FC	FC	FC	FC	FC	FC	FC	FC	FC	FC	FC	FC	FC	FC	FC	FC
				1					1					1					1				
London Kings Cross 15 ⊖	d	08 41	08 56	09 06	09 20	09 26	09 41	09 56	10 06	10 11	10 26	10 41	10 56	11 06	11 11	11 26	11 41	11 56	12 06	12 11	12 26	12 41	12 56
Moorgate ⊖	d																						
Old Street ⊖	d																						
Essex Road	d																						
Highbury & Islington ⊖	d																						
Drayton Park	d																						
Finsbury Park ⊖	d	08 47	09 02	09 11	09 26	09 32	09 47	10 02	10 11	10 17	10 32	10 47	11 02	11 11	11 17	11 32	11 47	12 02	12 11	12 17	12 32	12 47	13 02
Harringay	d	08 49	09 04		09 28	09 34	09 49	10 04		10 19	10 34	10 49	11 04		11 19	11 34	11 49	12 04		12 19	12 34	12 49	13 04
Hornsey	d	08 51	09 06		09 30	09 36	09 51	10 06		10 21	10 36	10 51	11 06		11 21	11 36	11 51	12 06		12 21	12 36	12 51	13 06
Alexandra Palace	d	08 53	09 08		09 32	09 38	09 53	10 08		10 23	10 38	10 53	11 08		11 23	11 38	11 53	12 08		12 23	12 38	12 53	13 08
New Southgate	d	08 56			09 35		09 56			10 26		10 56			11 26		11 56			12 26		12 56	
Oakleigh Park	d	08 59			09 38		09 59			10 29		10 59			11 29		11 59			12 29		12 59	
New Barnet	d	09 01			09 40		10 01			10 31		11 01			11 31		12 01			12 31		13 01	
Hadley Wood	d	09 04			09 43		10 04			10 34		11 04			11 34		12 04			12 34		13 04	
Potters Bar	d	09 08		09 21	09 47		10 08		10 21	10 38		11 08		11 21	11 38		12 08		12 21	12 38		13 08	
Brookmans Park	d	09 11			09 50		10 11			10 41		11 11			11 41		12 11			12 41		13 11	
Welham Green	d	09 13			09 52		10 13			10 43		11 13			11 43		12 13			12 43		13 13	
Hatfield	d	09 16		09 27	09 55		10 16		10 27	10 46		11 16		11 27	11 46		12 16		12 27	12 46		13 16	
Welwyn Garden City 4	d	09a21		09 31	10a00		10a21		10 31	10a51		11a21		11 31	11a51		12a21		12 31	12a51		13a21	
Welwyn North	d			09 34					10 34					11 34					12 34				
Knebworth	d			09 38					10 38					11 38					12 38				
Bowes Park	d		09 11			09 41		10 11			10 41		11 11			11 41		12 11			12 41		13 11
Palmers Green	d		09 13			09 43		10 13			10 43		11 13			11 43		12 13			12 43		13 13
Winchmore Hill	d		09 15			09 45		10 15			10 45		11 15			11 45		12 15			12 45		13 15
Grange Park	d		09 17			09 47		10 17			10 47		11 17			11 47		12 17			12 47		13 17
Enfield Chase	d		09 19			09 49		10 19			10 49		11 19			11 49		12 19			12 49		13 19
Gordon Hill	d		09 21			09 51		10 21			10 51		11 21			11 51		12 21			12 51		13 21
Crews Hill	d		09 24			09 54		10 24			10 54		11 24			11 54		12 24			12 54		13 24
Cuffley	d		09 27			09 57		10 27			10 57		11 27			11 57		12 27			12 57		13 27
Bayford	d		09 32			10 02		10 32			11 02		11 32			12 02		12 32			13 02		13 32
Hertford North	d		09a38			10 07		10a38			11 07		11a38			12 07		12a38			13 07		13a38
Watton-at-Stone	d					10 13					11 13					12 13					13 13		
Stevenage 4	d			09 42		10a20			10 42		11a20			11 42		12a20			12 42		13a20		
Hitchin 4	d			09 47					10 47					11 47					12 47				
Letchworth Garden City	a			09 51					10 51					11 51					12 51				

A not 22 May

		FC	FC	FC	FC	FC	FC	FC	FC	FC	FC	FC	FC	FC	FC	FC	FC	FC	FC	FC	FC	FC
		1					1					1					1			1		
London Kings Cross 15 ⊖	d	13 06	13 11	13 26	13 41	13 56	14 06	14 11	14 26	14 41	14 56	15 06	15 11	15 26	15 41	15 56	16 06	16 11	16 26	16 36	16 41	16 56
Moorgate ⊖	d																					
Old Street ⊖	d																					
Essex Road	d																					
Highbury & Islington ⊖	d																					
Drayton Park	d																					
Finsbury Park ⊖	d	13 11	13 17	13 32	13 47	14 02	14 11	14 17	14 32	14 47	15 02	15 11	15 17	15 32	15 47	16 02	16 11	16 17	16 32	16 41	16 47	17 02
Harringay	d		13 19	13 34	13 49	14 04		14 19	14 34	14 49	15 04		15 19	15 34	15 49	16 04		16 19	16 34		16 49	17 04
Hornsey	d		13 21	13 36	13 51	14 06		14 21	14 36	14 51	15 06		15 21	15 36	15 51	16 06		16 21	16 36		16 51	17 06
Alexandra Palace	d		13 23	13 38	13 53	14 08		14 23	14 38	14 53	15 08		15 23	15 38	15 53	16 08		16 23	16 38		16 53	17 08
New Southgate	d		13 26		13 56			14 26		14 56			15 26		15 56			16 26			16 56	
Oakleigh Park	d		13 29		13 59			14 29		14 59			15 29		15 59			16 29			16 59	
New Barnet	d		13 31		14 01			14 31		15 01			15 31		16 01			16 31			17 01	
Hadley Wood	d		13 34		14 04			14 34		15 04			15 34		16 04			16 34			17 04	
Potters Bar	d	13 21	13 38		14 08		14 21	14 38		15 08		15 21	15 38		16 08		16 21	16 38		16 51	17 08	
Brookmans Park	d		13 41		14 11			14 41		15 11			15 41		16 11			16 41			17 11	
Welham Green	d		13 43		14 13			14 43		15 13			15 43		16 13			16 43			17 13	
Hatfield	d	13 27	13 46		14 16		14 27	14 46		15 16		15 27	15 46		16 16		16 27	16 46		16 57	17 16	
Welwyn Garden City 4	d	13 31	13a51		14a21		14 31	14a51		15a21		15 31	15a51		16a21		16 31	16a51		17 01	17a21	
Welwyn North	d	13 34					14 34					15 34					16 34			17 04		
Knebworth	d	13 38					14 38					15 38					16 38			17 08		
Bowes Park	d			13 41		14 11			14 41		15 11			15 41		16 11			16 41			17 11
Palmers Green	d			13 43		14 13			14 43		15 13			15 43		16 13			16 43			17 13
Winchmore Hill	d			13 45		14 15			14 45		15 15			15 45		16 15			16 45			17 15
Grange Park	d			13 47		14 17			14 47		15 17			15 47		16 17			16 47			17 17
Enfield Chase	d			13 49		14 19			14 49		15 19			15 49		16 19			16 49			17 19
Gordon Hill	d			13 51		14 21			14 51		15 21			15 51		16 21			16 51			17 21
Crews Hill	d			13 54		14 24			14 54		15 24			15 54		16 24			16 54			17 24
Cuffley	d			13 57		14 27			14 57		15 27			15 57		16 27			16 57			17 27
Bayford	d			14 02		14 32			15 02		15 32			16 02		16 32			17 02			17 32
Hertford North	d			14 07		14a38			15 07		15a38			16 07		16a38			17 07			17a38
Watton-at-Stone	d			14 13					15 13					16 13					17 13			
Stevenage 4	d	13 42		14a20			14 42		15a20			15 42		16a20			16 42		17a20	17 12		
Hitchin 4	d	13 47					14 47					15 47					16 47			17a17		
Letchworth Garden City	a	13 51					14 51					15 51					16 51					

		FC	FC	FC	FC	FC	FC	FC	FC	FC	FC	FC	FC	FC	FC	FC	FC	FC	FC	FC	FC	FC	FC
		1			1			1					1					1					1
London Kings Cross 15 ⊖	d	17 06	17 11	17 26	17 36	17 41	17 56	18 06	18 11	18 26	18 41	18 56	19 06	19 11	19 26	19 41	19 56	20 06	20 11	20 26	20 41	20 56	21 06
Moorgate ⊖	d																						
Old Street ⊖	d																						
Essex Road	d																						
Highbury & Islington ⊖	d																						
Drayton Park	d																						
Finsbury Park ⊖	d	17 11	17 17	17 32	17 41	17 47	18 02	18 11	18 17	18 32	18 47	19 02	19 11	19 17	19 32	19 47	20 02	20 11	20 17	20 32	20 47	21 02	21 11
Harringay	d		17 19	17 34		17 49	18 04		18 19	18 34	18 49	19 04		19 19	19 34	19 49	20 04		20 19	20 34	20 49	21 04	
Hornsey	d		17 21	17 36		17 51	18 06		18 21	18 36	18 51	19 06		19 21	19 36	19 51	20 06		20 21	20 36	20 51	21 06	
Alexandra Palace	d		17 23	17 38		17 53	18 08		18 23	18 38	18 53	19 08		19 23	19 38	19 53	20 08		20 23	20 38	20 53	21 08	
New Southgate	d		17 26			17 56			18 26		18 56			19 26		19 56			20 26		20 56		
Oakleigh Park	d		17 29			17 59			18 29		18 59			19 29		19 59			20 29		20 59		
New Barnet	d		17 31			18 01			18 31		19 01			19 31		20 01			20 31		21 01		
Hadley Wood	d		17 34			18 04			18 34		19 04			19 34		20 04			20 34		21 04		
Potters Bar	d	17 21	17 38		17 51	18 08		18 21	18 38		19 08		19 21	19 38		20 08		20 21	20 38		21 08		21 21
Brookmans Park	d		17 41			18 11			18 41		19 11			19 41		20 11			20 41		21 11		
Welham Green	d		17 43			18 13			18 43		19 13			19 43		20 13			20 43		21 13		
Hatfield	d	17 27	17 46		17 57	18 16		18 27	18 46		19 16		19 27	19 46		20 16		20 27	20 46		21 16		21 27
Welwyn Garden City 4	d	17 31	17a51		18 01	18a21		18 31	18a51		19a21		19 31	19a51		20a21		20 31	20a51		21a21		21 31
Welwyn North	d	17 34			18 04			18 34					19 34					20 34					21 34
Knebworth	d	17 38			18 08			18 38					19 38					20 38					21 38
Bowes Park	d			17 41			18 11			18 41		19 11			19 41		20 11			20 41		21 11	
Palmers Green	d			17 43			18 13			18 43		19 13			19 43		20 13			20 43		21 13	
Winchmore Hill	d			17 45			18 15			18 45		19 15			19 45		20 15			20 45		21 15	
Grange Park	d			17 47			18 17			18 47		19 17			19 47		20 17			20 47		21 17	
Enfield Chase	d			17 49			18 19			18 49		19 19			19 49		20 19			20 49		21 19	
Gordon Hill	d			17 51			18 21			18 51		19 21			19 51		20 21			20 51		21 21	
Crews Hill	d			17 54			18 24			18 54		19 24			19 54		20 24			20 54		21 24	
Cuffley	d			17 57			18 27			18 57		19 27			19 57		20 27			20 57		21 27	
Bayford	d			18 02			18 32			19 02		19 32			20 02		20 32			21 02		21 32	
Hertford North	d			18 07			18a38			19 07		19a38			20 07		20a38			21 07		21a38	
Watton-at-Stone	d			18 13						19 13					20 13					21 13			
Stevenage 4	d	17 42		18a20	18 12			18 42		19a20			19 42		20a20			20 42		21a20			21 42
Hitchin 4	d	17 47			18a17			18 47					19 47					20 47					21 47
Letchworth Garden City	a	17 51						18 52					19 51					20 51					21 51

Table 24

Sundays
until 19 June

London - Welwyn Garden City, Hertford North and Letchworth Garden City

		FC	FC	FC	FC	FC ■	FC	FC	FC	FC	FC ■	FC	FC	FC
London Kings Cross 15 ⊖	d	21 11	21 26	21 41	21 56	22 06	22 11	22 26	22 41	22 56	23 06	23 11	23 26	23 41
Moorgate ⊖	d													
Old Street ⊖	d													
Essex Road	d													
Highbury & Islington ⊖	d													
Drayton Park	d													
Finsbury Park ⊖	d	21 17	21 32	21 47	22 02	22 11	22 17	22 32	22 47	23 02	23 11	23 17	23 32	23 47
Harringay	d	21 19	21 34	21 49	22 04		22 19	22 34	22 49	23 04		23 19	23 34	23 49
Hornsey	d	21 21	21 36	21 51	22 06		22 21	22 36	22 51	23 06		23 21	23 36	23 51
Alexandra Palace	d	21 23	21 38	21 53	22 08		22 23	22 38	22 53	23 08		23 23	23 38	23 53
New Southgate	d	21 26		21 56			22 26		22 56			23 26		23 56
Oakleigh Park	d	21 29		21 59			22 29		22 59			23 29		23 59
New Barnet	d	21 31		22 01			22 31		23 01			23 31		00 01
Hadley Wood	d	21 34		22 04			22 34		23 04			23 34		00 04
Potters Bar	d	21 38		22 08		22 21	22 38		23 08		23 21	23 38		00 08
Brookmans Park	d	21 41		22 11			22 41		23 11			23 41		00 11
Welham Green	d	21 43		22 13			22 43		23 13			23 43		00 13
Hatfield	d	21 46		22 16		22 27	22 46		23 16		23 27	23 46		00 16
Welwyn Garden City 4	d	21a51		22a21		22 31	22a51		23a21		23 31	23a51		00 20
Welwyn North	d					22 34					23 34			00 23
Knebworth	d					22 38					23 38			00 28
Bowes Park	d		21 41		22 11			22 41		23 11			23 41	
Palmers Green	d		21 43		22 13			22 43		23 13			23 43	
Winchmore Hill	d		21 45		22 15			22 45		23 15			23 45	
Grange Park	d		21 47		22 17			22 47		23 17			23 47	
Enfield Chase	d		21 49		22 19			22 49		23 19			23 49	
Gordon Hill	d		21 51		22 21			22 51		23 21			23 51	
Crews Hill	d		21 54		22 24			22 54		23 24			23 54	
Cuffley	d		21 57		22 27			22 57		23 27			23 57	
Bayford	d		22 02		22 32			23 02		23 32			00 02	
Hertford North	d		22 07		22a38			23 07		23a38			00 07	
Watton-at-Stone	d		22 13					23 13					00 13	
Stevenage 4	d		22a20			22 42		23a20			23 42		00a20	00 31
Hitchin 4	d					22 47					23 47			00 37
Letchworth Garden City	a					22 51					23 51			00 52

Sundays
26 June to 31 July

		FC	FC	FC	FC ■	FC	FC ■	FC	FC	FC	FC	FC	FC	FC	FC	FC	FC	FC	FC	FC	FC	FC	FC
London Kings Cross 15 ⊖	d	23p26	23p41	23p56	00 06	00 26	00 36		00 41	01 11	05 56	06 11	06 41	06 53	07 11	07 22	07 41	07 52	08 11	08 17	08 41	08 52	09 20
Moorgate ⊖	d																						
Old Street ⊖	d																						
Essex Road	d																						
Highbury & Islington ⊖	d																						
Drayton Park	d																						
Finsbury Park ⊖	d	23p32	23p47	00 02	00 11	00 32	00 41		00 47	01 17	06 02	06 17	06 47	06 59	07 17	07 28	07 47	07 58	08 17	08 23	08 47	08 58	09 26
Harringay	d	23p34	23p49	00 04		00 34			00 49	01 19	06 04	06 19	06 49	07 01	07 19	07 30	07 49	08 00	08 19	08 25	08 49	09 00	09 28
Hornsey	d	23p36	23p51	00 06		00 36			00 51	01 21	06 06	06 21	06 51	07 03	07 21	07 32	07 51	08 02	08 21	08 27	08 51	09 02	09 30
Alexandra Palace	d	23p38	23p53	00 08		00 38			00 53	01 23	06 08	06 23	06 53	07 05	07 23	07 34	07 53	08 04	08 23	08 29	08 53	09 04	09 32
New Southgate	d		23p56			00 41				01 26		06 26	06 56		07 26		07 56		08 26		08 56		09 35
Oakleigh Park	d		23p59			00 44				01 29		06 29	06 59		07 29		07 59		08 29		08 59		09 38
New Barnet	d		00 01			00 46				01 31		06 31	07 01		07 31		08 01		08 31		09 01		09 40
Hadley Wood	d		00 04			00 49				01 34		06 34	07 04		07 34		08 04		08 34		09 04		09 43
Potters Bar	d		00 08		00 23	00 53	00 53			01 38		06 38	07 08		07 38		08 08		08 38		09 08		09 47
Brookmans Park	d		00 11			00 56				01 41		06 41	07 11		07 41		08 11		08 41		09 11		09 50
Welham Green	d		00 13			00 58		←		01 43		06 43	07 13		07 43		08 13		08 43		09 13		09 52
Hatfield	d		00 16		00 29	01 01	00 59	01 01		01 46		06 46	07 16		07 46		08 16		08 46		09 16		09 55
Welwyn Garden City 4	d		00a25		00 41	→	01 05	01a10		01a55		06a55	07a25		07a55		08a25		08a55		09a21		10a00
Welwyn North	d				00 44		01s08																
Knebworth	d				00 48		01s12																
Bowes Park	d	23p41		00 11					00 56		06 11			07 08		07 37		08 07		08 32			
Palmers Green	d	23p43		00 13					00 58		06 13			07 10		07 39		08 09		08 34			
Winchmore Hill	d	23p45		00 15					01 00		06 15			07 12		07 41		08 11		08 36			
Grange Park	d	23p47		00 17					01 02		06 17			07 14		07 43		08 13		08 38			
Enfield Chase	d	23p49		00 19					01 04		06 19			07 16		07 45		08 15		08 40			
Gordon Hill	d	23p51		00 21					01 06		06 21			07 18		07 47		08 17		08 42		09 11	
Crews Hill	d	23p54		00 24					01 09		06 24			07 21		07 50		08 20		08 45		09 14	
Cuffley	d	23p57		00 27					01 12		06 27			07 24		07 53		08 23		08 48		09 17	
Bayford	d	00 02		00 32					01 17		06 32			07 29		07 58		08 28		08 53		09 22	
Hertford North	d	00 07		00a40					01 22		06a40			07a37		08a05		08a36		09a00		09a27	
Watton-at-Stone	d	00 13							01 28														
Stevenage 4	d	00 22			00 53		01 18		01a40														
Hitchin 4	d	00 29			01 00		01a25																
Letchworth Garden City	a	00 37			01 04																		

Table 24

Sundays
26 June to 31 July

London - Welwyn Garden City, Hertford North and Letchworth Garden City

		FC	FC	FC	FC	FC	FC	FC	FC	FC	FC	FC	FC	FC	FC	FC	FC ■	FC	FC	FC	FC	FC ■	FC
London Kings Cross 15 ⊖	d	09 22	09 41	09 56	10 11	10 26	10 41	10 56	11 11	11 26	11 41	11 56	12 11	12 26	12 41	12 56	13 06	13 11	13 26	13 41	13 56	14 06	14 11
Moorgate ⊖	d																						
Old Street ⊖	d																						
Essex Road	d																						
Highbury & Islington ⊖	d																						
Drayton Park	d																						
Finsbury Park ⊖	d	09 28	09 47	10 02	10 17	10 32	10 47	11 02	11 17	11 32	11 47	12 02	12 17	12 32	12 47	13 02	13 11	13 17	13 32	13 47	14 02	14 11	14 17
Harringay	d	09 30	09 49	10 04	10 19	10 34	10 49	11 04	11 19	11 34	11 49	12 04	12 19	12 34	12 49	13 04		13 19	13 34	13 49	14 04		14 19
Hornsey	d	09 32	09 51	10 06	10 21	10 36	10 51	11 06	11 21	11 36	11 51	12 06	12 21	12 36	12 51	13 06		13 21	13 36	13 51	14 06		14 21
Alexandra Palace	d	09 35	09 53	10 08	10 23	10 38	10 53	11 08	11 23	11 38	11 53	12 08	12 23	12 38	12 53	13 08		13 23	13 38	13 53	14 08		14 23
New Southgate	d		09 56		10 26		10 56		11 26		11 56		12 26		12 56			13 26		13 56			14 26
Oakleigh Park	d		09 59		10 29		10 59		11 29		11 59		12 29		12 59			13 29		13 59			14 29
New Barnet	d		10 01		10 31		11 01		11 31		12 01		12 31		13 01			13 31		14 01			14 31
Hadley Wood	d		10 04		10 34		11 04		11 34		12 04		12 34		13 04			13 34		14 04			14 34
Potters Bar	d		10 08		10 38		11 08		11 38		12 08		12 38		13 08		13 21	13 38		14 08		14 21	14 38
Brookmans Park	d		10 11		10 41		11 11		11 41		12 11		12 41		13 11			13 41		14 11			14 41
Welham Green	d		10 13		10 43		11 13		11 43		12 13		12 43		13 13			13 43		14 13			14 43
Hatfield	d		10 16		10 46		11 16		11 46		12 16		12 46		13 16		13 27	13 46		14 16		14 27	14 46
Welwyn Garden City 4	d		10a21		10a51		11a21		11a51		12a21		12a51		13a21		13 31	13a51		14a21		14 31	14a51
Welwyn North	d																13 34					14 34	
Knebworth	d																13 38					14 38	
Bowes Park	d	09 37		10 11		10 41		11 11		11 41		12 11		12 41		13 11			13 41		14 11		
Palmers Green	d	09 39		10 13		10 43		11 13		11 43		12 13		12 43		13 13			13 43		14 13		
Winchmore Hill	d	09 42		10 15		10 45		11 15		11 45		12 15		12 45		13 15			13 45		14 15		
Grange Park	d	09 44		10 17		10 47		11 17		11 47		12 17		12 47		13 17			13 47		14 17		
Enfield Chase	d	09 46		10 19		10 49		11 19		11 49		12 19		12 49		13 19			13 49		14 19		
Gordon Hill	d	09 48		10 21		10 51		11 21		11 51		12 21		12 51		13 21			13 51		14 21		
Crews Hill	d			10 24		10 54		11 24		11 54		12 24		12 54		13 24			13 54		14 24		
Cuffley	d			10 27		10 57		11 27		11 57		12 27		12 57		13 27			13 57		14 27		
Bayford	d			10 32		11 02		11 32		12 02		12 32		13 02		13 32			14 02		14 32		
Hertford North	d	09a58		10a38		11 07		11a38		12a06		12a38		13 07		13a38			14 07		14a38		
Watton-at-Stone	d					11 13								13 13					14 13				
Stevenage 4	d					11a20								13a20			13 42		14a20			14 42	
Hitchin 4	d																13 47					14 47	
Letchworth Garden City	a																13 51					14 51	

		FC	FC	FC	FC ■	FC	FC	FC	FC	FC ■	FC	FC	FC ■	FC	FC	FC ■	FC	FC	FC ■	FC	FC	FC ■
London Kings Cross 15 ⊖	d	14 26	14 41	14 56	15 06	15 11	15 26	15 41	15 56	16 06	16 11	16 26	16 36	16 41	16 56	17 06	17 11	17 26	17 36	17 41	17 56	18 06
Moorgate ⊖	d																					
Old Street ⊖	d																					
Essex Road	d																					
Highbury & Islington ⊖	d																					
Drayton Park	d																					
Finsbury Park ⊖	d	14 32	14 47	15 02	15 11	15 17	15 32	15 47	16 02	16 11	16 17	16 32	16 41	16 47	17 02	17 11	17 17	17 32	17 41	17 47	18 02	18 11
Harringay	d	14 34	14 49	15 04		15 19	15 34	15 49	16 04		16 19	16 34		16 49	17 04		17 19	17 34		17 49	18 04	
Hornsey	d	14 36	14 51	15 06		15 21	15 36	15 51	16 06		16 21	16 36		16 51	17 06		17 21	17 36		17 51	18 06	
Alexandra Palace	d	14 38	14 53	15 08		15 23	15 38	15 53	16 08		16 23	16 38		16 53	17 08		17 23	17 38		17 53	18 08	
New Southgate	d		14 56			15 26		15 56			16 26			16 56			17 26			17 56		
Oakleigh Park	d		14 59			15 29		15 59			16 29			16 59			17 29			17 59		
New Barnet	d		15 01			15 31		16 01			16 31			17 01			17 31			18 01		
Hadley Wood	d		15 04			15 34		16 04			16 34			17 04			17 34			18 04		
Potters Bar	d		15 08		15 21	15 38		16 08		16 21	16 38		16 51	17 08		17 21	17 38		17 51	18 08		18 21
Brookmans Park	d		15 11			15 41		16 11			16 41			17 11			17 41			18 11		
Welham Green	d		15 13			15 43		16 13			16 43			17 13			17 43			18 13		
Hatfield	d		15 16		15 27	15 46		16 16		16 27	16 46		16 57	17 16		17 27	17 46		17 57	18 16		18 27
Welwyn Garden City 4	d		15a21		15 31	15a51		16a21		16 31	16a51		17 01	17a21		17 31	17a51		18 01	18a21		18 31
Welwyn North	d				15 34					16 34			17 04			17 34			18 04			18 34
Knebworth	d				15 38					16 38			17 08			17 38			18 08			18 38
Bowes Park	d	14 41		15 11			15 41		16 11			16 41			17 11			17 41			18 11	
Palmers Green	d	14 43		15 13			15 43		16 13			16 43			17 13			17 43			18 13	
Winchmore Hill	d	14 45		15 15			15 45		16 15			16 45			17 15			17 45			18 15	
Grange Park	d	14 47		15 17			15 47		16 17			16 47			17 17			17 47			18 17	
Enfield Chase	d	14 49		15 19			15 49		16 19			16 49			17 19			17 49			18 19	
Gordon Hill	d	14 51		15 21			15 51		16 21			16 51			17 21			17 51			18 21	
Crews Hill	d	14 54		15 24			15 54		16 24			16 54			17 24			17 54			18 24	
Cuffley	d	14 57		15 27			15 57		16 27			16 57			17 27			17 57			18 27	
Bayford	d	15 02		15 32			16 02		16 32			17 02			17 32			18 02			18 32	
Hertford North	d	15 07		15a38			16 07		16a38			17 07			17a38			18 07			18a38	
Watton-at-Stone	d	15 13					16 13					17 13						18 13				
Stevenage 4	d	15a20			15 42		16a20			16 42		17a20	17 12			17 42		18a20	18 12			18 42
Hitchin 4	d				15 47					16 47			17a17			17 47			18a17			18 47
Letchworth Garden City	a				15 51					16 51						17 51						18 52

Sundays

26 June to 31 July

London - Welwyn Garden City, Hertford North and Letchworth Garden City

Station		FC	FC	FC	FC	FC [1]	FC	FC
London Kings Cross [15] ⊖	d	18 11	18 26	18 41	18 56	19 06	19 11	19 26
Moorgate ⊖	d							
Old Street ⊖	d							
Essex Road	d							
Highbury & Islington ⊖	d							
Drayton Park	d							
Finsbury Park ⊖	d	18 17	18 32	18 47	19 02	19 11	19 17	19 32
Harringay	d	18 19	18 34	18 49	19 04		19 19	19 34
Hornsey	d	18 21	18 36	18 51	19 06		19 21	19 36
Alexandra Palace	d	18 23	18 38	18 53	19 08		19 23	19 38
New Southgate	d	18 26		18 56			19 26	
Oakleigh Park	d	18 29		18 59			19 29	
New Barnet	d	18 31		19 01			19 31	
Hadley Wood	d	18 34		19 04			19 34	
Potters Bar	d	18 38		19 08		19 21	19 38	
Brookmans Park	d	18 41		19 11			19 41	
Welham Green	d	18 43		19 13			19 43	
Hatfield	d	18 46		19 16		19 27	19 46	
Welwyn Garden City [4]	d	18a51		19a21		19 31	19a51	
Welwyn North	d					19 34		
Knebworth	d					19 38		
Bowes Park	d		18 41		19 11			19 41
Palmers Green	d		18 43		19 13			19 43
Winchmore Hill	d		18 45		19 15			19 45
Grange Park	d		18 47		19 17			19 47
Enfield Chase	d		18 49		19 19			19 49
Gordon Hill	d		18 51		19 21			19 51
Crews Hill	d		18 54		19 24			19 54
Cuffley	d		18 57		19 27			19 57
Bayford	d		19 02		19 32			20 02
Hertford North	d		19 07		19a38			20 07
Watton-at-Stone	d		19 13					20 13
Stevenage [4]	d		19a20			19 42		20a20
Hitchin [4]	d					19 47		
Letchworth Garden City	a					19 51		

Station		FC	FC	FC [1]	FC	FC	FC	FC	FC [1]	FC
London Kings Cross [15] ⊖	d	19 41	19 56	20 06	20 11	20 26	20 41	20 56	21 06	21 11
Moorgate ⊖	d									
Old Street ⊖	d									
Essex Road	d									
Highbury & Islington ⊖	d									
Drayton Park	d									
Finsbury Park ⊖	d	19 47	20 02	20 11	20 17	20 32	20 47	21 02	21 11	21 17
Harringay	d	19 49	20 04		20 19	20 34	20 49	21 04		21 19
Hornsey	d	19 51	20 06		20 21	20 36	20 51	21 06		21 21
Alexandra Palace	d	19 53	20 08		20 23	20 38	20 53	21 08		21 23
New Southgate	d	19 56			20 26		20 56			21 26
Oakleigh Park	d	19 59			20 29		20 59			21 29
New Barnet	d	20 01			20 31		21 01			21 31
Hadley Wood	d	20 04			20 34		21 04			21 34
Potters Bar	d	20 08		20 21	20 38		21 08		21 21	21 38
Brookmans Park	d	20 11			20 41		21 11			21 41
Welham Green	d	20 13			20 43		21 13			21 43
Hatfield	d	20 16		20 27	20 46		21 16		21 27	21 46
Welwyn Garden City [4]	d	20a21		20 31	20a51		21a21		21 31	21a51
Welwyn North	d			20 34					21 34	
Knebworth	d			20 38					21 38	
Bowes Park	d		20 11			20 41		21 11		
Palmers Green	d		20 13			20 43		21 13		
Winchmore Hill	d		20 15			20 45		21 15		
Grange Park	d		20 17			20 47		21 17		
Enfield Chase	d		20 19			20 49		21 19		
Gordon Hill	d		20 21			20 51		21 21		
Crews Hill	d		20 24			20 54		21 24		
Cuffley	d		20 27			20 57		21 27		
Bayford	d		20 32			21 02		21 32		
Hertford North	d		20a38			21 07		21a38		
Watton-at-Stone	d					21 13				
Stevenage [4]	d			20 42		21a20			21 42	
Hitchin [4]	d			20 47					21 47	
Letchworth Garden City	a			20 51					21 51	

Station		FC	FC	FC	FC [1]	FC	FC
London Kings Cross [15] ⊖	d	21 26	21 41	21 56	22 06	22 11	22 26
Moorgate ⊖	d						
Old Street ⊖	d						
Essex Road	d						
Highbury & Islington ⊖	d						
Drayton Park	d						
Finsbury Park ⊖	d	21 32	21 47	22 02	22 11	22 17	22 32
Harringay	d	21 34	21 49	22 04		22 19	22 34
Hornsey	d	21 36	21 51	22 06		22 21	22 36
Alexandra Palace	d	21 38	21 53	22 08		22 23	22 38
New Southgate	d		21 56			22 26	
Oakleigh Park	d		21 59			22 29	
New Barnet	d		22 01			22 31	
Hadley Wood	d		22 04			22 34	
Potters Bar	d		22 08		22 21	22 38	
Brookmans Park	d		22 11			22 41	
Welham Green	d		22 13			22 43	
Hatfield	d		22 16		22 27	22 46	
Welwyn Garden City [4]	d		22a21		22 31	22a51	
Welwyn North	d				22 34		
Knebworth	d				22 38		
Bowes Park	d	21 41		22 11			22 41
Palmers Green	d	21 43		22 13			22 43
Winchmore Hill	d	21 45		22 15			22 45
Grange Park	d	21 47		22 17			22 47
Enfield Chase	d	21 49		22 19			22 49
Gordon Hill	d	21 51		22 21			22 51
Crews Hill	d	21 54		22 24			22 54
Cuffley	d	21 57		22 27			22 57
Bayford	d	22 02		22 32			23 02
Hertford North	d	22 07		22a38			23 07
Watton-at-Stone	d	22 13					23 13
Stevenage [4]	d	22a20			22 42		23a20
Hitchin [4]	d				22 47		
Letchworth Garden City	a				22 51		

Station		FC	FC	FC [1]	FC	FC	FC
London Kings Cross [15] ⊖	d	22 41	22 56	23 06	23 11	23 26	23 41
Moorgate ⊖	d						
Old Street ⊖	d						
Essex Road	d						
Highbury & Islington ⊖	d						
Drayton Park	d						
Finsbury Park ⊖	d	22 47	23 02	23 11	23 17	23 32	23 47
Harringay	d	22 49	23 04		23 19	23 34	23 49
Hornsey	d	22 51	23 06		23 21	23 36	23 51
Alexandra Palace	d	22 53	23 08		23 23	23 38	23 53
New Southgate	d	22 56			23 26		23 56
Oakleigh Park	d	22 59			23 29		23 59
New Barnet	d	23 01			23 31		00 01
Hadley Wood	d	23 04			23 34		00 04
Potters Bar	d	23 08		23 21	23 38		00 08
Brookmans Park	d	23 11			23 41		00 11
Welham Green	d	23 13			23 43		00 13
Hatfield	d	23 16		23 27	23 46		00 16
Welwyn Garden City [4]	d	23a21		23 31	23a51		00 20
Welwyn North	d			23 34			00 23
Knebworth	d			23 38			00 28
Bowes Park	d		23 11			23 41	
Palmers Green	d		23 13			23 43	
Winchmore Hill	d		23 15			23 45	
Grange Park	d		23 17			23 47	
Enfield Chase	d		23 19			23 49	
Gordon Hill	d		23 21			23 51	
Crews Hill	d		23 24			23 54	
Cuffley	d		23 27			23 57	
Bayford	d		23 32			00 02	
Hertford North	d		23a38			00 07	
Watton-at-Stone	d					00 13	
Stevenage [4]	d			23 42		00a20	00 31
Hitchin [4]	d			23 47			00 37
Letchworth Garden City	a			23 51			00 52

Sundays

7 August to 11 September

London - Welwyn Garden City, Hertford North and Letchworth Garden City

Station		FC	FC [1]	FC	FC	FC	FC [1]	FC	FC	FC
London Kings Cross [15] ⊖	d	23p26	23p36		23p41	23p56	00 06	00 26	00 41	01 11
Moorgate ⊖	d									
Old Street ⊖	d									
Essex Road	d									
Highbury & Islington ⊖	d									
Drayton Park	d									
Finsbury Park ⊖	d	23p32	23p41		23p47	00 02	00 11	00 32	00 47	01 17
Harringay	d	23p34			23p49	00 04		00 34	00 49	01 19
Hornsey	d	23p36			23p51	00 06		00 36	00 51	01 21
Alexandra Palace	d	23p38			23p53	00 08		00 38	00 53	01 23
New Southgate	d				23p56			00 41		01 26
Oakleigh Park	d				23p59			00 44		01 29
New Barnet	d				00 01			00 46		01 31
Hadley Wood	d				00 04			00 49		01 34
Potters Bar	d		23p53		00 08		00 23	00 53		01 38
Brookmans Park	d				00 11			00 56		01 41
Welham Green	d				00 13			00 58		01 43
Hatfield	d		23p59		00 16		00 29	01 01		01 46
Welwyn Garden City [4]	d		00 06		00a25		00 41	01a10		01a55
Welwyn North	d		00 09				00 44			
Knebworth	d		00 13				00 48			
Bowes Park	d	23p41				00 11			00 56	
Palmers Green	d	23p43				00 13			00 58	
Winchmore Hill	d	23p45				00 15			01 00	
Grange Park	d	23p47				00 17			01 02	
Enfield Chase	d	23p49				00 19			01 04	
Gordon Hill	d	23p51				00 21			01 06	
Crews Hill	d	23p54				00 24			01 09	
Cuffley	d	23p57				00 27			01 12	
Bayford	d	00 02				00 32			01 17	
Hertford North	d	00 07				00a40			01 22	
Watton-at-Stone	d	00 13		←					01 28	
Stevenage [4]	d	00 22	00 18	00 22			00 53		01 36	
Hitchin [4]	d	→	00 25	00 29			01 00		01 44	
Letchworth Garden City	a		00 30	00 37			01 04		01 50	

Station		FC	FC	FC	FC	FC	FC [1]	FC	FC	FC
London Kings Cross [15] ⊖	d	06 11		06 26	06 41	06 56	07 06	07 11	07 41	
Moorgate ⊖	d									
Old Street ⊖	d									
Essex Road	d									
Highbury & Islington ⊖	d									
Drayton Park	d									
Finsbury Park ⊖	d	06 17		06 32	06 47	07 02	07 11	07 17	07 47	
Harringay	d	06 19		06 34	06 49	07 04		07 19	07 49	
Hornsey	d	06 21		06 36	06 51	07 06		07 21	07 51	
Alexandra Palace	d	06 23		06 38	06 53	07 08		07 23	07 53	
New Southgate	d	06 26			06 56			07 26	07 56	
Oakleigh Park	d	06 29			06 59			07 29	07 59	
New Barnet	d	06 31			07 01			07 31	08 01	
Hadley Wood	d	06 34			07 04			07 34	08 04	
Potters Bar	d	06 38			07 08		07 21	07 38	08 08	
Brookmans Park	d	06 41			07 11			07 41	08 11	
Welham Green	d	06 43			07 13			07 43	08 13	
Hatfield	d	06 46			07 16		07 27	07 46	08 16	
Welwyn Garden City [4]	d	06a55			07a25		07 33	07a55	08a25	
Welwyn North	d						07 36			
Knebworth	d						07 40			
Bowes Park	d			06 41		07 11				
Palmers Green	d			06 43		07 13				
Winchmore Hill	d			06 45		07 15				
Grange Park	d			06 47		07 17				
Enfield Chase	d			06 49		07 19				
Gordon Hill	d			06 51		07 21				
Crews Hill	d			06 54		07 24				
Cuffley	d		06 27	06 57		07 27				08 01
Bayford	d		06 32	07 02		07 32				08 06
Hertford North	d		06a40	07 07		07a40				08 10
Watton-at-Stone	d			07 13						08 16
Stevenage [4]	d			07a22			07 45			08a25
Hitchin [4]	d						07 52			
Letchworth Garden City	a						07 56			

Station		FC	FC [1]	FC	FC
London Kings Cross [15] ⊖	d	07 56	08 06	08 11	08 41
Moorgate ⊖	d				
Old Street ⊖	d				
Essex Road	d				
Highbury & Islington ⊖	d				
Drayton Park	d				
Finsbury Park ⊖	d	08 02	08 11	08 17	08 47
Harringay	d	08 04		08 19	08 49
Hornsey	d	08 06		08 21	08 51
Alexandra Palace	d	08 08		08 23	08 53
New Southgate	d			08 26	08 56
Oakleigh Park	d			08 29	08 59
New Barnet	d			08 31	09 01
Hadley Wood	d			08 34	09 04
Potters Bar	d		08 21	08 38	09 08
Brookmans Park	d			08 41	09 11
Welham Green	d			08 43	09 13
Hatfield	d		08 27	08 46	09 16
Welwyn Garden City [4]	d		08 31	08a55	09a21
Welwyn North	d		08 34		
Knebworth	d		08 38		
Bowes Park	d	08 11			
Palmers Green	d	08 13			
Winchmore Hill	d	08 15			
Grange Park	d	08 17			
Enfield Chase	d	08 19			
Gordon Hill	d	08 21			
Crews Hill	d	08 24			
Cuffley	d	08 27			
Bayford	d	08 32			
Hertford North	d	08a40			
Watton-at-Stone	d				
Stevenage [4]	d		08 42		
Hitchin [4]	d		08 47		
Letchworth Garden City	a		08 51		

Station		FC	FC [1]	FC	FC	FC	FC [1]	FC	FC	FC	FC	FC	FC [1]	FC	FC
London Kings Cross [15] ⊖	d		09 06		09 41		10 06	10 11		10 41		10 56	11 06	11 11	11 26
Moorgate ⊖	d														
Old Street ⊖	d														
Essex Road	d														
Highbury & Islington ⊖	d														
Drayton Park	d														
Finsbury Park ⊖	d		09 11		09 47		10 11	10 17		10 47		11 02	11 11	11 17	11 32
Harringay	d				09 49			10 19		10 49		11 04		11 19	11 34
Hornsey	d				09 51			10 21		10 51		11 06		11 21	11 36
Alexandra Palace	d				09 53			10 23		10 53		11 08		11 23	11 38
New Southgate	d				09 56			10 26		10 56				11 26	
Oakleigh Park	d				09 59			10 29		10 59				11 29	
New Barnet	d				10 01			10 31		11 01				11 31	
Hadley Wood	d				10 04			10 34		11 04				11 34	
Potters Bar	d		09 21		10 08		10 21	10 38		11 08			11 21	11 38	
Brookmans Park	d				10 11			10 41		11 11				11 41	
Welham Green	d				10 13			10 43		11 13				11 43	
Hatfield	d		09 27		10 16		10 27	10 46		11 16			11 27	11 46	
Welwyn Garden City [4]	d		09 31		10a21		10 31	10a51		11a21			11 31	11a51	
Welwyn North	d		09 34				10 34						11 34		
Knebworth	d		09 38				10 38						11 38		
Bowes Park	d											11 11			11 41
Palmers Green	d											11 13			11 43
Winchmore Hill	d											11 15			11 45
Grange Park	d											11 17			11 47
Enfield Chase	d											11 19			11 49
Gordon Hill	d											11 21			11 51
Crews Hill	d											11 24			11 54
Cuffley	d	09 03		09 33		10 03			10 33		11 03	11 27			11 57
Bayford	d	09 08		09 38		10 08			10 38		11 08	11 32			12 02
Hertford North	d	09 12		09a44		10 12			10a44		11 12	11a38			12 07
Watton-at-Stone	d	09 18				10 18					11 18				12 13
Stevenage [4]	d	09a25	09 42			10a25	10 42				11a25		11 42		12a20
Hitchin [4]	d		09 47				10 47						11 47		
Letchworth Garden City	a		09 51				10 51						11 51		

Station		FC	FC	FC [1]	FC	FC	FC	FC	FC [1]
London Kings Cross [15] ⊖	d	11 41	11 56	12 06	12 11	12 26	12 41	12 56	13 06
Moorgate ⊖	d								
Old Street ⊖	d								
Essex Road	d								
Highbury & Islington ⊖	d								
Drayton Park	d								
Finsbury Park ⊖	d	11 47	12 02	12 11	12 17	12 32	12 47	13 02	13 11
Harringay	d	11 49	12 04		12 19	12 34	12 49	13 04	
Hornsey	d	11 51	12 06		12 21	12 36	12 51	13 06	
Alexandra Palace	d	11 53	12 08		12 23	12 38	12 53	13 08	
New Southgate	d	11 56			12 26		12 56		
Oakleigh Park	d	11 59			12 29		12 59		
New Barnet	d	12 01			12 31		13 01		
Hadley Wood	d	12 04			12 34		13 04		
Potters Bar	d	12 08		12 21	12 38		13 08		13 21
Brookmans Park	d	12 11			12 41		13 11		
Welham Green	d	12 13			12 43		13 13		
Hatfield	d	12 16		12 27	12 46		13 16		13 27
Welwyn Garden City [4]	d	12a21		12 31	12a51		13a21		13 31
Welwyn North	d			12 34					13 34
Knebworth	d			12 38					13 38
Bowes Park	d		12 11			12 41		13 11	
Palmers Green	d		12 13			12 43		13 13	
Winchmore Hill	d		12 15			12 45		13 15	
Grange Park	d		12 17			12 47		13 17	
Enfield Chase	d		12 19			12 49		13 19	
Gordon Hill	d		12 21			12 51		13 21	
Crews Hill	d		12 24			12 54		13 24	
Cuffley	d		12 27			12 57		13 27	
Bayford	d		12 32			13 02		13 32	
Hertford North	d		12a38			13 07		13a38	
Watton-at-Stone	d					13 13			
Stevenage [4]	d			12 42		13a20			13 42
Hitchin [4]	d			12 47					13 47
Letchworth Garden City	a			12 51					13 51

Table 24

London - Welwyn Garden City, Hertford North and Letchworth Garden City

Sundays
7 August to 11 September

		FC	FC	FC	FC	FC 1	FC	FC	FC	FC	FC 1	FC	FC	FC	FC	FC 1	FC	FC	FC 1	FC	FC	FC 1
London Kings Cross 15	⊖ d	13 11	13 26	13 41	13 56	14 06	14 11	14 26	14 41	14 56	15 06	15 11	15 26	15 41	15 56	16 06	16 11	16 26	16 36	16 41	16 56	17 06
Moorgate	⊖ d																					
Old Street	⊖ d																					
Essex Road	d																					
Highbury & Islington	⊖ d																					
Drayton Park	d																					
Finsbury Park	⊖ d	13 17	13 32	13 47	14 02	14 11	14 17	14 32	14 47	15 02	15 11	15 17	15 32	15 47	16 02	16 11	16 17	16 32	16 41	16 47	17 02	17 11
Harringay	d	13 19	13 34	13 49	14 04		14 19	14 34	14 49	15 04		15 19	15 34	15 49	16 04		16 19	16 34		16 49	17 04	
Hornsey	d	13 21	13 36	13 51	14 06		14 21	14 36	14 51	15 06		15 21	15 36	15 51	16 06		16 21	16 36		16 51	17 06	
Alexandra Palace	d	13 23	13 38	13 53	14 08		14 23	14 38	14 53	15 08		15 23	15 38	15 53	16 08		16 23	16 38		16 53	17 08	
New Southgate	d	13 26		13 56			14 26		14 56			15 26		15 56			16 26			16 56		
Oakleigh Park	d	13 29		13 59			14 29		14 59			15 29		15 59			16 29			16 59		
New Barnet	d	13 31		14 01			14 31		15 01			15 31		16 01			16 31			17 01		
Hadley Wood	d	13 34		14 04			14 34		15 04			15 34		16 04			16 34			17 04		
Potters Bar	d	13 38		14 08		14 21	14 38		15 08		15 21	15 38		16 08		16 21	16 38		16 51	17 08		17 21
Brookmans Park	d	13 41		14 11			14 41		15 11			15 41		16 11			16 41			17 11		
Welham Green	d	13 43		14 13			14 43		15 13			15 43		16 13			16 43			17 13		
Hatfield	d	13 46		14 16		14 27	14 46		15 16		15 27	15 46		16 16		16 27	16 46		16 57	17 16		17 27
Welwyn Garden City 4	d	13a51		14a21		14 31	14a51		15a21		15 31	15a51		16a21		16 31	16a51		17 01	17a21		17 31
Welwyn North	d					14 34					15 34					16 34			17 04			17 34
Knebworth	d					14 38					15 38					16 38			17 08			17 38
Bowes Park	d		13 41		14 11			14 41		15 11			15 41		16 11			16 41			17 11	
Palmers Green	d		13 43		14 13			14 43		15 13			15 43		16 13			16 43			17 13	
Winchmore Hill	d		13 45		14 15			14 45		15 15			15 45		16 15			16 45			17 15	
Grange Park	d		13 47		14 17			14 47		15 17			15 47		16 17			16 47			17 17	
Enfield Chase	d		13 49		14 19			14 49		15 19			15 49		16 19			16 49			17 19	
Gordon Hill	d		13 51		14 21			14 51		15 21			15 51		16 21			16 51			17 21	
Crews Hill	d		13 54		14 24			14 54		15 24			15 54		16 24			16 54			17 24	
Cuffley	d		13 57		14 27			14 57		15 27			15 57		16 27			16 57			17 27	
Bayford	d		14 02		14 32			15 02		15 32			16 02		16 32			17 02			17 32	
Hertford North	d		14 07		14a38			15 07		15a38			16 07		16a38			17 07			17a38	
Watton-at-Stone	d		14 13					15 13					16 13					17 13				
Stevenage 4	d		14a20			14 42		15a20			15 42		16a20			16 42		17a20	17 12			17 42
Hitchin 4	d					14 47					15 47					16 47			17a17			17 47
Letchworth Garden City	a					14 51					15 51					16 51						17 51

		FC	FC	FC 1	FC	FC	FC 1	FC	FC	FC	FC	FC 1	FC	FC	FC	FC	FC 1	FC	FC	FC	FC	FC 1	FC
London Kings Cross 15	⊖ d	17 11	17 26	17 36	17 41	17 56	18 06	18 11	18 26	18 41	18 56	19 06	19 11	19 26	19 41	19 56	20 06	20 11	20 26	20 41	20 56	21 06	21 11
Moorgate	⊖ d																						
Old Street	⊖ d																						
Essex Road	d																						
Highbury & Islington	⊖ d																						
Drayton Park	d																						
Finsbury Park	⊖ d	17 17	17 32	17 41	17 47	18 02	18 11	18 17	18 32	18 47	19 02	19 11	19 17	19 32	19 47	20 02	20 11	20 17	20 32	20 47	21 02	21 11	21 17
Harringay	d	17 19	17 34		17 49	18 04		18 19	18 34	18 49	19 04		19 19	19 34	19 49	20 04		20 19	20 34	20 49	21 04		21 19
Hornsey	d	17 21	17 36		17 51	18 06		18 21	18 36	18 51	19 06		19 21	19 36	19 51	20 06		20 21	20 36	20 51	21 06		21 21
Alexandra Palace	d	17 23	17 38		17 53	18 08		18 23	18 38	18 53	19 08		19 23	19 38	19 53	20 08		20 23	20 38	20 53	21 08		21 23
New Southgate	d	17 26			17 56			18 26		18 56			19 26		19 56			20 26		20 56			21 26
Oakleigh Park	d	17 29			17 59			18 29		18 59			19 29		19 59			20 29		20 59			21 29
New Barnet	d	17 31			18 01			18 31		19 01			19 31		20 01			20 31		21 01			21 31
Hadley Wood	d	17 34			18 04			18 34		19 04			19 34		20 04			20 34		21 04			21 34
Potters Bar	d	17 38		17 51	18 08		18 21	18 38		19 08		19 21	19 38		20 08		20 21	20 38		21 08		21 21	21 38
Brookmans Park	d	17 41			18 11			18 41		19 11			19 41		20 11			20 41		21 11			21 41
Welham Green	d	17 43			18 13			18 43		19 13			19 43		20 13			20 43		21 13			21 43
Hatfield	d	17 46		17 57	18 16		18 27	18 46		19 16		19 27	19 46		20 16		20 27	20 46		21 16		21 27	21 46
Welwyn Garden City 4	d	17a51		18 01	18a21		18 31	18a51		19a21		19 31	19a51		20a21		20 31	20a51		21a21		21 31	21a51
Welwyn North	d			18 04			18 34					19 34					20 34					21 34	
Knebworth	d			18 08			18 38					19 38					20 38					21 38	
Bowes Park	d		17 41			18 11			18 41		19 11			19 41		20 11			20 41		21 11		
Palmers Green	d		17 43			18 13			18 43		19 13			19 43		20 13			20 43		21 13		
Winchmore Hill	d		17 45			18 15			18 45		19 15			19 45		20 15			20 45		21 15		
Grange Park	d		17 47			18 17			18 47		19 17			19 47		20 17			20 47		21 17		
Enfield Chase	d		17 49			18 19			18 49		19 19			19 49		20 19			20 49		21 19		
Gordon Hill	d		17 51			18 21			18 51		19 21			19 51		20 21			20 51		21 21		
Crews Hill	d		17 54			18 24			18 54		19 24			19 54		20 24			20 54		21 24		
Cuffley	d		17 57			18 27			18 57		19 27			19 57		20 27			20 57		21 27		
Bayford	d		18 02			18 32			19 02		19 32			20 02		20 32			21 02		21 32		
Hertford North	d		18 07			18a38			19 07		19a38			20 07		20a38			21 07		21a38		
Watton-at-Stone	d		18 13						19 13					20 13					21 13				
Stevenage 4	d		18a20	18 12			18 42		19a20			19 42		20a20			20 42		21a20			21 42	
Hitchin 4	d			18a17			18 47					19 47					20 47					21 47	
Letchworth Garden City	a						18 52					19 51					20 51					21 51	

Table 24

London - Welwyn Garden City, Hertford North and Letchworth Garden City

Sundays
7 August to 11 September

		FC	FC	FC	FC 1	FC	FC	FC	FC	FC 1	FC	FC	FC
London Kings Cross 15	⊖ d	21 26	21 41	21 56	22 06	22 11	22 26	22 41	22 56	23 06	23 11	23 26	23 41
Moorgate	⊖ d												
Old Street	⊖ d												
Essex Road	d												
Highbury & Islington	⊖ d												
Drayton Park	d												
Finsbury Park	⊖ d	21 32	21 47	22 02	22 11	22 17	22 32	22 47	23 02	23 11	23 17	23 32	23 47
Harringay	d	21 34	21 49	22 04		22 19	22 34	22 49	23 04		23 19	23 34	23 49
Hornsey	d	21 36	21 51	22 06		22 21	22 36	22 51	23 06		23 21	23 36	23 51
Alexandra Palace	d	21 38	21 53	22 08		22 23	22 38	22 53	23 08		23 23	23 38	23 53
New Southgate	d		21 56			22 26		22 56			23 26		23 56
Oakleigh Park	d		21 59			22 29		22 59			23 29		23 59
New Barnet	d		22 01			22 31		23 01			23 31		00 01
Hadley Wood	d		22 04			22 34		23 04			23 34		00 04
Potters Bar	d		22 08		22 21	22 38		23 08		23 21	23 38		00 08
Brookmans Park	d		22 11			22 41		23 11			23 41		00 11
Welham Green	d		22 13			22 43		23 13			23 43		00 13
Hatfield	d		22 16		22 27	22 46		23 16		23 27	23 46		00 16
Welwyn Garden City 4	d		22a21		22 31	22a51		23a21		23 31	23a51		00 20
Welwyn North	d				22 34					23 34			00 23
Knebworth	d				22 38					23 38			00 28
Bowes Park	d	21 41		22 11			22 41		23 11			23 41	
Palmers Green	d	21 43		22 13			22 43		23 13			23 43	
Winchmore Hill	d	21 45		22 15			22 45		23 15			23 45	
Grange Park	d	21 47		22 17			22 47		23 17			23 47	
Enfield Chase	d	21 49		22 19			22 49		23 19			23 49	
Gordon Hill	d	21 51		22 21			22 51		23 21			23 51	
Crews Hill	d	21 54		22 24			22 54		23 24			23 54	
Cuffley	d	21 57		22 27			22 57		23 27			23 57	
Bayford	d	22 02		22 32			23 02		23 32			00 02	
Hertford North	d	22 07		22a38			23 07		23a38			00 07	
Watton-at-Stone	d	22 13					23 13					00 13	
Stevenage 4	d	22a20			22 42		23a20			23 42		00a20	00 31
Hitchin 4	d				22 47					23 47			00 37
Letchworth Garden City	a				22 51					23 51			00 52

Sundays
18 September to 23 October

		FC	FC 1	FC	FC	FC	FC 1	FC	FC	FC	FC	FC	FC	FC 1	FC	FC	FC	FC 1	FC 1	FC	FC 1	FC	FC
London Kings Cross 15	⊖ d	23p26	23p36		23p41	23p56	00 06	00 26	00 41	01 11	06 26	06 41	06 56	07 06	07 11	07 41	07 56	08 06	09 06	09 41	10 06	10 11	10 41
Moorgate	⊖ d																						
Old Street	⊖ d																						
Essex Road	d																						
Highbury & Islington	⊖ d																						
Drayton Park	d																						
Finsbury Park	⊖ d	23p32	23p41		23p47	00 02	00 11	00 32	00 47	01 17	06 32	06 47	07 02	07 11	07 17	07 47	08 02	08 11	09 11	09 47	10 11	10 17	10 47
Harringay	d	23p34			23p49	00 04		00 34	00 49	01 19	06 34	06 49	07 04		07 19	07 49	08 04			09 49		10 19	10 49
Hornsey	d	23p36			23p51	00 06		00 36	00 51	01 21	06 36	06 51	07 06		07 21	07 51	08 06			09 51		10 21	10 51
Alexandra Palace	d	23p38			23p53	00 08		00 38	00 53	01 23	06 38	06 53	07 08		07 23	07 53	08 08			09 53		10 23	10 53
New Southgate	d				23p56			00 41		01 26		06 56			07 26	07 56				09 56		10 26	10 56
Oakleigh Park	d				23p59			00 44		01 29		06 59			07 29	07 59				09 59		10 29	10 59
New Barnet	d				00 01			00 46		01 31		07 01			07 31	08 01				10 01		10 31	11 01
Hadley Wood	d				00 04			00 49		01 34		07 04			07 34	08 04				10 04		10 34	11 04
Potters Bar	d		23p53		00 08		00 23	00 53		01 38		07 08		07 21	07 38	08 08		08 20	09 21	10 08	10 21	10 38	11 08
Brookmans Park	d				00 11			00 56		01 41		07 11			07 41	08 11				10 11		10 41	11 11
Welham Green	d				00 13			00 58		01 43		07 13			07 43	08 13				10 13		10 43	11 13
Hatfield	d		23p59		00 16		00 29	01 01		01 46		07 16		07 27	07 46	08 16		08 26	09 27	10 16	10 27	10 46	11 16
Welwyn Garden City 4	d		00 06		00a25		00 41	01a10		01a55		07a25		07 33	07a55	08a25		08 30	09 31	10a21	10 31	10a51	11a21
Welwyn North	d		00 09				00 44							07 36				08 33	09 34		10 34		
Knebworth	d		00 13				00 48							07 40				08 37	09 38		10 38		
Bowes Park	d	23p41				00 11			00 56		06 41		07 11				08 11						
Palmers Green	d	23p43				00 13			00 58		06 43		07 13				08 13						
Winchmore Hill	d	23p45				00 15			01 00		06 45		07 15				08 15						
Grange Park	d	23p47				00 17			01 02		06 47		07 17				08 17						
Enfield Chase	d	23p49				00 19			01 04		06 49		07 19				08 19						
Gordon Hill	d	23p51				00 21			01 06		06 51		07 21				08 21						
Crews Hill	d	23p54				00 24			01 09		06 54		07 24				08 24						
Cuffley	d	23p57				00 27			01 12		06 57		07 27				08 27						
Bayford	d	00 02				00 32			01 17		07 02		07 32				08 32						
Hertford North	d	00 07				00a40			01 22		07 07		07a40				08a40						
Watton-at-Stone	d	00 13		←					01 28		07 13												
Stevenage 4	d	00 22	00 18	00 22			00 53		01 36		07a22			07 45				08 40	09 42		10 42		
Hitchin 4	d	→	00 25	00 29			01 00		01 44					07 52				08 45	09 47		10 47		
Letchworth Garden City	a		00 30	00 37			01 04		01 50					07 56				08 49	09 51		10 51		

London - Welwyn Garden City, Hertford North and Letchworth Garden City

		FC	FC 1	FC	FC	FC	FC	FC 1	FC	FC	FC	FC	FC 1	FC	FC	FC	FC	FC 1	FC	FC	FC	FC	FC 1
London Kings Cross 15 ⊖	d	10 56	11 06	11 11	11 26	11 41	11 56	12 06	12 11	12 26	12 41	12 56	13 06	13 11	13 26	13 41	13 56	14 06	14 11	14 26	14 41	14 56	15 06
Moorgate ⊖	d																						
Old Street ⊖	d																						
Essex Road	d																						
Highbury & Islington ⊖	d																						
Drayton Park	d																						
Finsbury Park ⊖	d	11 02	11 11	11 17	11 32	11 47	12 02	12 11	12 17	12 32	12 47	13 02	13 11	13 17	13 32	13 47	14 02	14 11	14 17	14 32	14 47	15 02	15 12
Harringay	d	11 04		11 19	11 34	11 49	12 04		12 19	12 34	12 49	13 04		13 19	13 34	13 49	14 04		14 19	14 34	14 49	15 04	
Hornsey	d	11 06		11 21	11 36	11 51	12 06		12 21	12 36	12 51	13 06		13 21	13 36	13 51	14 06		14 21	14 36	14 51	15 06	
Alexandra Palace	d	11 08		11 23	11 38	11 53	12 08		12 23	12 38	12 53	13 08		13 23	13 38	13 53	14 08		14 23	14 38	14 53	15 08	
New Southgate	d			11 26		11 56			12 26		12 56			13 26		13 56			14 26		14 56		
Oakleigh Park	d			11 29		11 59			12 29		12 59			13 29		13 59			14 29		14 59		
New Barnet	d			11 31		12 01			12 31		13 01			13 31		14 01			14 31		15 01		
Hadley Wood	d			11 34		12 04			12 34		13 04			13 34		14 04			14 34		15 04		
Potters Bar	d		11 21	11 38		12 08		12 21	12 38		13 08		13 21	13 38		14 08		14 21	14 38		15 08		15 21
Brookmans Park	d			11 41		12 11			12 41		13 11			13 41		14 11			14 41		15 11		
Welham Green	d			11 43		12 13			12 43		13 13			13 43		14 13			14 43		15 13		
Hatfield	d		11 27	11 46		12 16		12 27	12 46		13 16		13 27	13 46		14 16		14 27	14 46		15 16		15 27
Welwyn Garden City 4	d		11 31	11a51		12a21		12 31	12a51		13a21		13 31	13a51		14a21		14 31	14a51		15a21		15 31
Welwyn North	d		11 34					12 34					13 34					14 34					15 34
Knebworth	d		11 38					12 38					13 38					14 38					15 38
Bowes Park	d	11 11			11 41		12 11			12 41		13 11			13 41		14 11			14 41		15 11	
Palmers Green	d	11 13			11 43		12 13			12 43		13 13			13 43		14 13			14 43		15 13	
Winchmore Hill	d	11 15			11 45		12 15			12 45		13 15			13 45		14 15			14 45		15 15	
Grange Park	d	11 17			11 47		12 17			12 47		13 17			13 47		14 17			14 47		15 17	
Enfield Chase	d	11 19			11 49		12 19			12 49		13 19			13 49		14 19			14 49		15 19	
Gordon Hill	d	11 21			11 51		12 21			12 51		13 21			13 51		14 21			14 51		15 21	
Crews Hill	d	11 24			11 54		12 24			12 54		13 24			13 54		14 24			14 54		15 24	
Cuffley	d	11 27			11 57		12 27			12 57		13 27			13 57		14 27			14 57		15 27	
Bayford	d	11 32			12 02		12 32			13 02		13 32			14 02		14 32			15 02		15 32	
Hertford North	d	11a38			12 07		12a38			13 07		13a38			14 07		14a38			15 07		15a38	
Watton-at-Stone	d				12 13					13 13					14 13					15 13			
Stevenage 4	d		11 42		12a20			12 42		13a20			13 42		14a20			14 42		15a20			15 42
Hitchin 4	d		11 47					12 47					13 47					14 47					15 47
Letchworth Garden City	a		11 51					12 51					13 51					14 51					15 51

		FC	FC	FC	FC	FC 1	FC	FC	FC 1	FC	FC	FC 1	FC	FC	FC 1	FC	FC	FC 1	FC	FC	FC	FC
London Kings Cross 15 ⊖	d	15 11	15 26	15 41	15 56	16 06	16 11	16 26	16 36	16 41	16 56	17 06	17 11	17 26	17 36	17 41	17 56	18 06	18 11	18 26	18 41	18 56
Moorgate ⊖	d																					
Old Street ⊖	d																					
Essex Road	d																					
Highbury & Islington ⊖	d																					
Drayton Park	d																					
Finsbury Park ⊖	d	15 17	15 32	15 47	16 02	16 12	16 17	16 32	16 41	16 47	17 02	17 12	17 17	17 32	17 41	17 47	18 02	18 12	18 17	18 32	18 47	19 02
Harringay	d	15 19	15 34	15 49	16 04		16 19	16 34		16 49	17 04		17 19	17 34		17 49	18 04		18 19	18 34	18 49	19 04
Hornsey	d	15 21	15 36	15 51	16 06		16 21	16 36		16 51	17 06		17 21	17 36		17 51	18 06		18 21	18 36	18 51	19 06
Alexandra Palace	d	15 23	15 38	15 53	16 08		16 23	16 38		16 53	17 08		17 23	17 38		17 53	18 08		18 23	18 38	18 53	19 08
New Southgate	d	15 26		15 56			16 26			16 56			17 26			17 56			18 26		18 56	
Oakleigh Park	d	15 29		15 59			16 29			16 59			17 29			17 59			18 29		18 59	
New Barnet	d	15 31		16 01			16 31			17 01			17 31			18 01			18 31		19 01	
Hadley Wood	d	15 34		16 04			16 34			17 04			17 34			18 04			18 34		19 04	
Potters Bar	d	15 38		16 08		16 21	16 38		16 51	17 08		17 21	17 38		17 51	18 08		18 21	18 38		19 08	
Brookmans Park	d	15 41		16 11			16 41			17 11			17 41			18 11			18 41		19 11	
Welham Green	d	15 43		16 13			16 43			17 13			17 43			18 13			18 43		19 13	
Hatfield	d	15 46		16 16		16 27	16 46		16 57	17 16		17 27	17 46		17 57	18 16		18 27	18 46		19 16	
Welwyn Garden City 4	d	15a51		16a21		16 31	16a51		17 01	17a21		17 31	17a51		18 01	18a21		18 31	18a51		19a21	
Welwyn North	d					16 34			17 04			17 34			18 04			18 34				
Knebworth	d					16 38			17 08			17 38			18 08			18 38				
Bowes Park	d		15 41		16 11			16 41			17 11			17 41			18 11			18 41		19 11
Palmers Green	d		15 43		16 13			16 43			17 13			17 43			18 13			18 43		19 13
Winchmore Hill	d		15 45		16 15			16 45			17 15			17 45			18 15			18 45		19 15
Grange Park	d		15 47		16 17			16 47			17 17			17 47			18 17			18 47		19 17
Enfield Chase	d		15 49		16 19			16 49			17 19			17 49			18 19			18 49		19 19
Gordon Hill	d		15 51		16 21			16 51			17 21			17 51			18 21			18 51		19 21
Crews Hill	d		15 54		16 24			16 54			17 24			17 54			18 24			18 54		19 24
Cuffley	d		15 57		16 27			16 57			17 27			17 57			18 27			18 57		19 27
Bayford	d		16 02		16 32			17 02			17 32			18 02			18 32			19 02		19 32
Hertford North	d		16 07		16a38			17 07			17a38			18 07			18a38			19 07		19a38
Watton-at-Stone	d		16 13					17 13						18 13						19 13		
Stevenage 4	d		16a20			16 42		17a20	17 12			17 42		18a20	18 12			18 42		19a20		
Hitchin 4	d					16 47			17a17			17 47			18a17			18 47				
Letchworth Garden City	a					16 51						17 51						18 52				

Table 24

Sundays

18 September to 23 October

London - Welwyn Garden City, Hertford North and Letchworth Garden City

		FC 1	FC	FC	FC	FC	FC 1	FC	FC	FC	FC	FC 1	FC	FC	FC	FC	FC 1	FC	FC	FC	FC	FC 1	FC
London Kings Cross 15 ⊖	d	19 03	19 11	19 26	19 41	19 56	20 06	20 11	20 26	20 41	20 56	21 06	21 11	21 26	21 41	21 56	22 06	22 11	22 26	22 41	22 56	23 06	23 11
Moorgate ⊖	d																						
Old Street ⊖	d																						
Essex Road	d																						
Highbury & Islington ⊖	d																						
Drayton Park	d																						
Finsbury Park ⊖	d	19 11	19 17	19 32	19 47	20 02	20 12	20 17	20 32	20 47	21 02	21 11	21 17	21 32	21 47	22 02	22 12	22 17	22 32	22 47	23 02	23 12	23 17
Harringay	d		19 19	19 34	19 49	20 04		20 19	20 34	20 49	21 04		21 19	21 34	21 49	22 04		22 19	22 34	22 49	23 04		23 19
Hornsey	d		19 21	19 36	19 51	20 06		20 21	20 36	20 51	21 06		21 21	21 36	21 51	22 06		22 21	22 36	22 51	23 06		23 21
Alexandra Palace	d		19 23	19 38	19 53	20 08		20 23	20 38	20 53	21 08		21 23	21 38	21 53	22 08		22 23	22 38	22 53	23 08		23 23
New Southgate	d		19 26		19 56			20 26		20 56			21 26		21 56			22 26		22 56			23 26
Oakleigh Park	d		19 29		19 59			20 29		20 59			21 29		21 59			22 29		22 59			23 29
New Barnet	d		19 31		20 01			20 31		21 01			21 31		22 01			22 31		23 01			23 31
Hadley Wood	d		19 34		20 04			20 34		21 04			21 34		22 04			22 34		23 04			23 34
Potters Bar	d	19 21	19 38		20 08		20 21	20 38		21 08		21 21	21 38		22 08		22 21	22 38		23 08		23 21	23 38
Brookmans Park	d		19 41		20 11			20 41		21 11			21 41		22 11			22 41		23 11			23 41
Welham Green	d		19 43		20 13			20 43		21 13			21 43		22 13			22 43		23 13			23 43
Hatfield	d	19 27	19 46		20 16		20 27	20 46		21 16		21 27	21 46		22 16		22 27	22 46		23 16		23 27	23 46
Welwyn Garden City 4	d	19 31	19a51		20a21		20 31	20a51		21a21		21 31	21a51		22a21		22 31	22a51		23a21		23 31	23a51
Welwyn North	d	19 34					20 34					21 34					22 34					23 34	
Knebworth	d	19 38					20 38					21 38					22 38					23 38	
Bowes Park	d			19 41		20 11			20 41		21 11			21 41		22 11			22 41		23 11		
Palmers Green	d			19 43		20 13			20 43		21 13			21 43		22 13			22 43		23 13		
Winchmore Hill	d			19 45		20 15			20 45		21 15			21 45		22 15			22 45		23 15		
Grange Park	d			19 47		20 17			20 47		21 17			21 47		22 17			22 47		23 17		
Enfield Chase	d			19 49		20 19			20 49		21 19			21 49		22 19			22 49		23 19		
Gordon Hill	d			19 51		20 21			20 51		21 21			21 51		22 21			22 51		23 21		
Crews Hill	d			19 54		20 24			20 54		21 24			21 54		22 24			22 54		23 24		
Cuffley	d			19 57		20 27			20 57		21 27			21 57		22 27			22 57		23 27		
Bayford	d			20 02		20 32			21 02		21 32			22 02		22 32			23 02		23 32		
Hertford North	d			20 07		20a38			21 07		21a38			22 07		22a38			23 07		23a38		
Watton-at-Stone	d			20 13					21 13					22 13					23 13				
Stevenage 4	d	19 42		20a20			20 42		21a20			21 42		22a20			22 42		23a20			23 42	
Hitchin 4	d	19 47					20 47					21 47					22 47					23 47	
Letchworth Garden City	a	19 51					20 51					21 51					22 51					23 51	

		FC	FC
London Kings Cross 15 ⊖	d	23 26	23 41
Moorgate ⊖	d		
Old Street ⊖	d		
Essex Road	d		
Highbury & Islington ⊖	d		
Drayton Park	d		
Finsbury Park ⊖	d	23 32	23 47
Harringay	d	23 34	23 49
Hornsey	d	23 36	23 51
Alexandra Palace	d	23 38	23 53
New Southgate	d		23 56
Oakleigh Park	d		23 59
New Barnet	d		00 01
Hadley Wood	d		00 04
Potters Bar	d		00 08
Brookmans Park	d		00 11
Welham Green	d		00 13
Hatfield	d		00 16
Welwyn Garden City 4	d		00 20
Welwyn North	d		00 23
Knebworth	d		00 28
Bowes Park	d	23 41	
Palmers Green	d	23 43	
Winchmore Hill	d	23 45	
Grange Park	d	23 47	
Enfield Chase	d	23 49	
Gordon Hill	d	23 51	
Crews Hill	d	23 54	
Cuffley	d	23 57	
Bayford	d	00 02	
Hertford North	d	00 07	
Watton-at-Stone	d	00 13	
Stevenage 4	d	00a20	00 31
Hitchin 4	d		00 37
Letchworth Garden City	a		00 52

Table 24

Sundays from 30 October

London - Welwyn Garden City, Hertford North and Letchworth Garden City

		FC	FC ■	FC	FC	FC	FC ■	FC	FC	FC	FC	FC	FC	FC	FC	FC ■	FC	FC	FC	FC	FC ■	FC	FC
London Kings Cross [15] ⊖	d	23p26	23p36		23p41	23p56	00 06	00 26	00 41	01 11	05 56	06 11	06 26	06 41	06 56	07 06	07 11	07 26	07 41	07 56	08 06	08 11	08 26
Moorgate ⊖	d																						
Old Street ⊖	d																						
Essex Road	d																						
Highbury & Islington ⊖	d																						
Drayton Park	d																						
Finsbury Park ⊖	d	23p32	23p41		23p47	00 02	00 11	00 32	00 47	01 17	06 02	06 17	06 32	06 47	07 02	07 11	07 17	07 32	07 47	08 02	08 11	08 17	08 32
Harringay	d	23p34			23p49	00 04		00 34	00 49	01 19	06 04	06 19	06 34	06 49	07 04		07 19	07 34	07 49	08 04		08 19	08 34
Hornsey	d	23p36			23p51	00 06		00 36	00 51	01 21	06 06	06 21	06 36	06 51	07 06		07 21	07 36	07 51	08 06		08 21	08 36
Alexandra Palace	d	23p38			23p53	00 08		00 38	00 53	01 23	06 08	06 23	06 38	06 53	07 08		07 23	07 38	07 53	08 08		08 23	08 38
New Southgate	d				23p56			00 41		01 26		06 26		06 56			07 26		07 56			08 26	
Oakleigh Park	d				23p59			00 44		01 29		06 29		06 59			07 29		07 59			08 29	
New Barnet	d				00 01			00 46		01 31		06 31		07 01			07 31		08 01			08 31	
Hadley Wood	d				00 04			00 49		01 34		06 34		07 04			07 34		08 04			08 34	
Potters Bar	d		23p53		00 08		00 23	00 53		01 38		06 38		07 08		07 21	07 38		08 08		08 21	08 38	
Brookmans Park	d				00 11			00 56		01 41		06 41		07 11			07 41		08 11			08 41	
Welham Green	d				00 13			00 58		01 43		06 43		07 13			07 43		08 13			08 43	
Hatfield	d		23p59		00 16		00 29	01 01		01 46		06 46		07 16		07 27	07 46		08 16		08 27	08 46	
Welwyn Garden City [4]	d		00 06		00a25		00 41	01a10		01a55		06a55		07a25		07 33	07a55		08a25		08 31	08a55	
Welwyn North	d		00 09				00 44									07 36					08 34		
Knebworth	d		00 13				00 48									07 40					08 38		
Bowes Park	d	23p41				00 11			00 56		06 11		06 41		07 11			07 41		08 11			08 41
Palmers Green	d	23p43				00 13			00 58		06 13		06 43		07 13			07 43		08 13			08 43
Winchmore Hill	d	23p45				00 15			01 00		06 15		06 45		07 15			07 45		08 15			08 45
Grange Park	d	23p47				00 17			01 02		06 17		06 47		07 17			07 47		08 17			08 47
Enfield Chase	d	23p49				00 19			01 04		06 19		06 49		07 19			07 49		08 19			08 49
Gordon Hill	d	23p51				00 21			01 06		06 21		06 51		07 21			07 51		08 21			08 51
Crews Hill	d	23p54				00 24			01 09		06 24		06 54		07 24			07 54		08 24			08 54
Cuffley	d	23p57				00 27			01 12		06 27		06 57		07 27			07 57		08 27			08 57
Bayford	d	00 02				00 32			01 17		06 32		07 02		07 32			08 02		08 32			09 02
Hertford North	d	00 07				00a40			01 22		06a40		07 07		07a40			08 07		08a40			09 07
Watton-at-Stone	d	00 13		←					01 28				07 13					08 13					09 13
Stevenage [4]	d	00 22	00 18	00 22			00 53		01 36				07a22			07 45		08a23			08 42		09a20
Hitchin [4]	d	→	00 25	00 29			01 00		01 44							07 52					08 47		
Letchworth Garden City	a		00 30	00 37			01 04		01 50							07 56					08 51		

		FC	FC ■	FC	FC	FC	FC ■	FC	FC	FC	FC	FC ■	FC	FC	FC	FC	FC ■	FC	FC	FC	FC	FC ■	FC
London Kings Cross [15] ⊖	d	08 41	09 06	09 20	09 26	09 41	10 06	10 11	10 26	10 41	10 56	11 06	11 11	11 26	11 41	11 56	12 06	12 11	12 26	12 41	12 56	13 06	13 11
Moorgate ⊖	d																						
Old Street ⊖	d																						
Essex Road	d																						
Highbury & Islington ⊖	d																						
Drayton Park	d																						
Finsbury Park ⊖	d	08 47	09 11	09 26	09 32	09 47	10 11	10 17	10 32	10 47	11 02	11 11	11 17	11 32	11 47	12 02	12 11	12 17	12 32	12 47	13 02	13 11	13 17
Harringay	d	08 49		09 28	09 34	09 49		10 19	10 34	10 49	11 04		11 19	11 34	11 49	12 04		12 19	12 34	12 49	13 04		13 19
Hornsey	d	08 51		09 30	09 36	09 51		10 21	10 36	10 51	11 06		11 21	11 36	11 51	12 06		12 21	12 36	12 51	13 06		13 21
Alexandra Palace	d	08 53		09 32	09 38	09 53		10 23	10 38	10 53	11 08		11 23	11 38	11 53	12 08		12 23	12 38	12 53	13 08		13 23
New Southgate	d	08 56		09 35		09 56		10 26		10 56			11 26		11 56			12 26		12 56			13 26
Oakleigh Park	d	08 59		09 38		09 59		10 29		10 59			11 29		11 59			12 29		12 59			13 29
New Barnet	d	09 01		09 40		10 01		10 31		11 01			11 31		12 01			12 31		13 01			13 31
Hadley Wood	d	09 04		09 43		10 04		10 34		11 04			11 34		12 04			12 34		13 04			13 34
Potters Bar	d	09 08	09 21	09 47		10 08	10 21	10 38		11 08		11 21	11 38		12 08		12 21	12 38		13 08		13 21	13 38
Brookmans Park	d	09 11		09 50		10 11		10 41		11 11			11 41		12 11			12 41		13 11			13 41
Welham Green	d	09 13		09 52		10 13		10 43		11 13			11 43		12 13			12 43		13 13			13 43
Hatfield	d	09 16	09 27	09 55		10 16	10 27	10 46		11 16		11 27	11 46		12 16		12 27	12 46		13 16		13 27	13 46
Welwyn Garden City [4]	d	09a21	09 31	10a00		10a21	10 31	10a51		11a21		11 31	11a51		12a21		12 31	12a51		13a21		13 31	13a51
Welwyn North	d		09 34				10 34					11 34					12 34					13 34	
Knebworth	d		09 38				10 38					11 38					12 38					13 38	
Bowes Park	d				09 41				10 41		11 11			11 41		12 11			12 41		13 11		
Palmers Green	d				09 43				10 43		11 13			11 43		12 13			12 43		13 13		
Winchmore Hill	d				09 45				10 45		11 15			11 45		12 15			12 45		13 15		
Grange Park	d				09 47				10 47		11 17			11 47		12 17			12 47		13 17		
Enfield Chase	d				09 49				10 49		11 19			11 49		12 19			12 49		13 19		
Gordon Hill	d				09 51				10 51		11 21			11 51		12 21			12 51		13 21		
Crews Hill	d				09 54				10 54		11 24			11 54		12 24			12 54		13 24		
Cuffley	d				09 57				10 57		11 27			11 57		12 27			12 57		13 27		
Bayford	d				10 02				11 02		11 32			12 02		12 32			13 02		13 32		
Hertford North	d				10 07				11 07		11a38			12 07		12a38			13 07		13a38		
Watton-at-Stone	d				10 13				11 13					12 13					13 13				
Stevenage [4]	d		09 42		10a20		10 42		11a20			11 42		12a20			12 42		13a20			13 42	
Hitchin [4]	d		09 47				10 47					11 47					12 47					13 47	
Letchworth Garden City	a		09 51				10 51					11 51					12 51					13 51	

Table 24

Sundays from 30 October

London - Welwyn Garden City, Hertford North and Letchworth Garden City

		FC	FC	FC	FC ■	FC	FC	FC	FC	FC ■	FC	FC	FC	FC	FC ■	FC	FC	FC ■	FC	FC	FC ■	FC
London Kings Cross [15] ⊖	d	13 26	13 41	13 56	14 06	14 11	14 26	14 41	14 56	15 06	15 11	15 26	15 41	15 56	16 06	16 11	16 26	16 36	16 41	16 56	17 06	17 11
Moorgate ⊖	d																					
Old Street ⊖	d																					
Essex Road	d																					
Highbury & Islington ⊖	d																					
Drayton Park	d																					
Finsbury Park ⊖	d	13 32	13 47	14 02	14 11	14 17	14 32	14 47	15 02	15 11	15 17	15 32	15 47	16 02	16 11	16 17	16 32	16 41	16 47	17 02	17 11	17 17
Harringay	d	13 34	13 49	14 04		14 19	14 34	14 49	15 04		15 19	15 34	15 49	16 04		16 19	16 34		16 49	17 04		17 19
Hornsey	d	13 36	13 51	14 06		14 21	14 36	14 51	15 06		15 21	15 36	15 51	16 06		16 21	16 36		16 51	17 06		17 21
Alexandra Palace	d	13 38	13 53	14 08		14 23	14 38	14 53	15 08		15 23	15 38	15 53	16 08		16 23	16 38		16 53	17 08		17 23
New Southgate	d		13 56			14 26		14 56			15 26		15 56			16 26			16 56			17 26
Oakleigh Park	d		13 59			14 29		14 59			15 29		15 59			16 29			16 59			17 29
New Barnet	d		14 01			14 31		15 01			15 31		16 01			16 31			17 01			17 31
Hadley Wood	d		14 04			14 34		15 04			15 34		16 04			16 34			17 04			17 34
Potters Bar	d		14 08		14 21	14 38		15 08		15 21	15 38		16 08		16 21	16 38		16 51	17 08		17 21	17 38
Brookmans Park	d		14 11			14 41		15 11			15 41		16 11			16 41			17 11			17 41
Welham Green	d		14 13			14 43		15 13			15 43		16 13			16 43			17 13			17 43
Hatfield	d		14 16		14 27	14 46		15 16		15 27	15 46		16 16		16 27	16 46		16 57	17 16		17 27	17 46
Welwyn Garden City [4]	d		14a21		14 31	14a51		15a21		15 31	15a51		16a21		16 31	16a51		17 01	17a21		17 31	17a51
Welwyn North	d				14 34					15 34					16 34			17 04			17 34	
Knebworth	d				14 38					15 38					16 38			17 08			17 38	
Bowes Park	d	13 41		14 11			14 41		15 11			15 41		16 11			16 41			17 11		
Palmers Green	d	13 43		14 13			14 43		15 13			15 43		16 13			16 43			17 13		
Winchmore Hill	d	13 45		14 15			14 45		15 15			15 45		16 15			16 45			17 15		
Grange Park	d	13 47		14 17			14 47		15 17			15 47		16 17			16 47			17 17		
Enfield Chase	d	13 49		14 19			14 49		15 19			15 49		16 19			16 49			17 19		
Gordon Hill	d	13 51		14 21			14 51		15 21			15 51		16 21			16 51			17 21		
Crews Hill	d	13 54		14 24			14 54		15 24			15 54		16 24			16 54			17 24		
Cuffley	d	13 57		14 27			14 57		15 27			15 57		16 27			16 57			17 27		
Bayford	d	14 02		14 32			15 02		15 32			16 02		16 32			17 02			17 32		
Hertford North	d	14 07		14a38			15 07		15a38			16 07		16a38			17 07			17a38		
Watton-at-Stone	d	14 13					15 13					16 13					17 13					
Stevenage [4]	d	14a20			14 42		15a20			15 42		16a20			16 42		17a20	17 12			17 42	
Hitchin [4]	d				14 47					15 47					16 47			17a17			17 47	
Letchworth Garden City	a				14 51					15 51					16 51						17 51	

		FC	FC ■	FC	FC	FC ■	FC	FC	FC	FC	FC ■	FC	FC	FC	FC	FC ■	FC	FC	FC	FC	FC ■	FC	FC
London Kings Cross [15] ⊖	d	17 26	17 36	17 41	17 56	18 06	18 11	18 26	18 41	18 56	19 06	19 11	19 26	19 41	19 56	20 06	20 11	20 26	20 41	20 56	21 06	21 11	21 26
Moorgate ⊖	d																						
Old Street ⊖	d																						
Essex Road	d																						
Highbury & Islington ⊖	d																						
Drayton Park	d																						
Finsbury Park ⊖	d	17 32	17 41	17 47	18 02	18 11	18 17	18 32	18 47	19 02	19 11	19 17	19 32	19 47	20 02	20 11	20 17	20 32	20 47	21 02	21 11	21 17	21 32
Harringay	d	17 34		17 49	18 04		18 19	18 34	18 49	19 04		19 19	19 34	19 49	20 04		20 19	20 34	20 49	21 04		21 19	21 34
Hornsey	d	17 36		17 51	18 06		18 21	18 36	18 51	19 06		19 21	19 36	19 51	20 06		20 21	20 36	20 51	21 06		21 21	21 36
Alexandra Palace	d	17 38		17 53	18 08		18 23	18 38	18 53	19 08		19 23	19 38	19 53	20 08		20 23	20 38	20 53	21 08		21 23	21 38
New Southgate	d			17 56			18 26		18 56			19 26		19 56			20 26		20 56			21 26	
Oakleigh Park	d			17 59			18 29		18 59			19 29		19 59			20 29		20 59			21 29	
New Barnet	d			18 01			18 31		19 01			19 31		20 01			20 31		21 01			21 31	
Hadley Wood	d			18 04			18 34		19 04			19 34		20 04			20 34		21 04			21 34	
Potters Bar	d		17 51	18 08		18 21	18 38		19 08		19 21	19 38		20 08		20 21	20 38		21 08		21 21	21 38	
Brookmans Park	d			18 11			18 41		19 11			19 41		20 11			20 41		21 11			21 41	
Welham Green	d			18 13			18 43		19 13			19 43		20 13			20 43		21 13			21 43	
Hatfield	d		17 57	18 16		18 27	18 46		19 16		19 27	19 46		20 16		20 27	20 46		21 16		21 27	21 46	
Welwyn Garden City [4]	d		18 01	18a21		18 31	18a51		19a21		19 31	19a51		20a21		20 31	20a51		21a21		21 31	21a51	
Welwyn North	d		18 04			18 34					19 34					20 34					21 34		
Knebworth	d		18 08			18 38					19 38					20 38					21 38		
Bowes Park	d	17 41			18 11			18 41		19 11			19 41		20 11			20 41		21 11			21 41
Palmers Green	d	17 43			18 13			18 43		19 13			19 43		20 13			20 43		21 13			21 43
Winchmore Hill	d	17 45			18 15			18 45		19 15			19 45		20 15			20 45		21 15			21 45
Grange Park	d	17 47			18 17			18 47		19 17			19 47		20 17			20 47		21 17			21 47
Enfield Chase	d	17 49			18 19			18 49		19 19			19 49		20 19			20 49		21 19			21 49
Gordon Hill	d	17 51			18 21			18 51		19 21			19 51		20 21			20 51		21 21			21 51
Crews Hill	d	17 54			18 24			18 54		19 24			19 54		20 24			20 54		21 24			21 54
Cuffley	d	17 57			18 27			18 57		19 27			19 57		20 27			20 57		21 27			21 57
Bayford	d	18 02			18 32			19 02		19 32			20 02		20 32			21 02		21 32			22 02
Hertford North	d	18 07			18a38			19 07		19a38			20 07		20a38			21 07		21a38			22 07
Watton-at-Stone	d	18 13						19 13					20 13					21 13					22 13
Stevenage [4]	d	18a20	18 12			18 42		19a20			19 42		20a20			20 42		21a20			21 42		22a20
Hitchin [4]	d		18a17			18 47					19 47					20 47					21 47		
Letchworth Garden City	a					18 52					19 51					20 51					21 51		

Table 24

Sundays from 30 October

London - Welwyn Garden City, Hertford North and Letchworth Garden City

		FC	FC	FC 1	FC	FC	FC	FC	FC 1	FC	FC	FC
London Kings Cross 15 ⊖	d	21 41	21 56	22 06	22 11	22 26	22 41	22 56	23 06	23 11	23 26	23 41
Moorgate ⊖	d											
Old Street ⊖	d											
Essex Road	d											
Highbury & Islington ⊖	d											
Drayton Park	d											
Finsbury Park ⊖	d	21 47	22 02	22 11	22 17	22 32	22 47	23 02	23 11	23 17	23 32	23 47
Harringay	d	21 49	22 04		22 19	22 34	22 49	23 04		23 19	23 34	23 49
Hornsey	d	21 51	22 06		22 21	22 36	22 51	23 06		23 21	23 36	23 51
Alexandra Palace	d	21 53	22 08		22 23	22 38	22 53	23 08		23 23	23 38	23 53
New Southgate	d	21 56			22 26		22 56			23 26		23 56
Oakleigh Park	d	21 59			22 29		22 59			23 29		23 59
New Barnet	d	22 01			22 31		23 01			23 31		00 01
Hadley Wood	d	22 04			22 34		23 04			23 34		00 04
Potters Bar	d	22 08		22 21	22 38		23 08		23 21	23 38		00 08
Brookmans Park	d	22 11			22 41		23 11			23 41		00 11
Welham Green	d	22 13			22 43		23 13			23 43		00 13
Hatfield	d	22 16		22 27	22 46		23 16		23 27	23 46		00 16
Welwyn Garden City 4	d	22a21		22 31	22a51		23a21		23 31	23a51		00 20
Welwyn North	d			22 34					23 34			00 23
Knebworth	d			22 38					23 38			00 28
Bowes Park	d		22 11			22 41		23 11			23 41	
Palmers Green	d		22 13			22 43		23 13			23 43	
Winchmore Hill	d		22 15			22 45		23 15			23 45	
Grange Park	d		22 17			22 47		23 17			23 47	
Enfield Chase	d		22 19			22 49		23 19			23 49	
Gordon Hill	d		22 21			22 51		23 21			23 51	
Crews Hill	d		22 24			22 54		23 24			23 54	
Cuffley	d		22 27			22 57		23 27			23 57	
Bayford	d		22 32			23 02		23 32			00 02	
Hertford North	d		22a38			23 07		23a38			00 07	
Watton-at-Stone	d					23 13					00 13	
Stevenage 4	d			22 42		23a20			23 42		00a20	00 31
Hitchin 4	d			22 47					23 47			00 37
Letchworth Garden City	a			22 51					23 51			00 52

Table 24

Mondays to Fridays

Letchworth Garden City, Hertford North and Welwyn Garden City - London

Miles	Miles			FC MX 1	FC MX	FC MO	FC MO 1	FC MX 1	FC	FC 1	FC	FC 1
0	0	**Letchworth Garden City**	d		23p18		23p40	23p47			04 50	
3	3	Hitchin 4	d	23p16	23p22		23p44	23p54		04 08	04 54	04 58
7¼	7¼	**Stevenage** 4	d	23p22	23p27	23p29	23p49	23p59		04 13	04 59	05 04
—	12¼	Watton-at-Stone	d		23p34	23p36					05 06	
—	16½	**Hertford North**	d		23p40	23p42				04 23	05 12	
—	19½	Bayford	d		23p44	23p46					05 16	
—	23	Cuffley	d		23p49	23p51				04 30	05 21	
—	24¾	Crews Hill	d		23p52	23p54					05 24	
—	26¼	Gordon Hill	d		23p55	23p57				04 34	05 27	
—	27	Enfield Chase	d		23p57	23p59				04 36	05 29	
—	27¾	Grange Park	d		23p59	00 01					05 31	
—	28½	Winchmore Hill	d		00 01	00 03					05 33	
—	29½	Palmers Green	d		00 03	00 05					05 35	
—	30½	Bowes Park	d		00 06	00 08					05 38	
9¾	—	Knebworth	d	23p25			23p52	00 02				05 07
12¾	—	Welwyn North	d	23p29			23p56	00 06				05 11
14½	—	**Welwyn Garden City** 4	d	23p32			23p59	00 09	04 10			05 15
17	—	Hatfield	d	23p35			00 02	00 12	04 14			05 19
19¼	—	Welham Green	d									
20¼	—	Brookmans Park	d						04 19			
22	—	Potters Bar	d	23p41			00 08	00 18	04 22			05 25
24¼	—	Hadley Wood	d						04 25			
25½	—	New Barnet	d						04 28			05 29
26¼	—	Oakleigh Park	d						04 30			05 31
28¼	—	New Southgate	d						04 33			05 34
29¾	31¼	Alexandra Palace	d		00 08	00 10			04 36		05 40	05 37
30¾	32¼	Hornsey	d		00 10	00 12			04 38	04 43	05 42	
31¼	32¾	Harringay	d		00 12	00 14			04 40		05 44	
32¼	33¾	Finsbury Park ⊖	d	23b51	00 15	00 17	00 21	00 29	04 42	04s45	05 47	05 41
—	34½	Drayton Park	d								→	
—	35	Highbury & Islington ⊖	d									
—	35½	Essex Road	d									
—	36¾	Old Street ⊖	d									
—	37¼	**Moorgate** ⊖	a									
34¾	—	London Kings Cross 15 ⊖	a	00 01	00 26	00 26	00 33	00 42	04 51	04 59		05 50

		FC	FC	FC	FC 1	FC	FC	FC	FC 1	FC	FC	FC 1
Letchworth Garden City	d			05 20	05 30			05 48	05 59			06 19
Hitchin 4	d			05 24	05 34			05 52	06 04			06 23
Stevenage 4	d			05 29	05 40			05 57	06 09		06 10	06 29
Watton-at-Stone	d			05 36				06 04			06 17	
Hertford North	d			05 42				06 12			06 26	
Bayford	d			05 46				06 16				
Cuffley	d			05 51				06 21			06 34	
Crews Hill	d			05 54				06 24				
Gordon Hill	d			05 57				06 27			06 38	
Enfield Chase	d			05 59				06 29			06 41	
Grange Park	d			06 01				06 31				
Winchmore Hill	d			06 03				06 33			06 44	
Palmers Green	d			06 05				06 35			06 46	
Bowes Park	d			06 08				06 38				
Knebworth	d				05 44				06 13			06 33
Welwyn North	d				05 48				06 17			06 37
Welwyn Garden City 4	d		05 33		05 51		05 58		06 20			06 40
Hatfield	d		05 37		05 55		06 02		06 24			06 44
Welham Green	d		05 41				06 06					
Brookmans Park	d		05 43				06 08					
Potters Bar	d		05 46		06 01		06 11		06 30			06 49
Hadley Wood	d		05 50				06 15					
New Barnet	d		05 52				06 17					
Oakleigh Park	d		05 54				06 19					
New Southgate	d		05 57				06 22					
Alexandra Palace	d		06 00	06 10			06 25	06 40				
Hornsey	d		06 02	06 12			06 27	06 42				
Harringay	d	←	06 04	06 14		←	06 29	06 44		←		
Finsbury Park ⊖	d	05 47	06 07	06 17	06 10	06 17	06 32	06 47	06 39	06 47	06 54	06 58
Drayton Park	d			→		06 19	06 34	→		06 49	06 56	
Highbury & Islington ⊖	d					06 20	06 35			06 50	06 58	
Essex Road	d					06 22	06 37			06 52	07 00	
Old Street ⊖	d					06 25	06 40			06 55	07 03	
Moorgate ⊖	a					06 30	06 45			07 01	07 08	
London Kings Cross 15 ⊖	a	05 58	06 15		06 19				06 48			07 07

		FC	FC	FC	FC	FC	FC	FC	FC	FC	FC	FC 1
Letchworth Garden City	d				06 23				06 47			07 04
Hitchin 4	d				06 27				06 51			07 08
Stevenage 4	d				06 33				06 57		07 03	07 14
Watton-at-Stone	d				06 40						07 10	
Hertford North	d			06 34	06 46					07 04	07 16	
Bayford	d			06 38						07 08		
Cuffley	d			06 43	06 54					07 13	07 24	
Crews Hill	d			06 46						07 16		
Gordon Hill	d			06 49	06 58		07 06			07 19	07 28	
Enfield Chase	d			06 52	07 01		07 08			07 22	07 31	
Grange Park	d			06 54			07 10			07 24		
Winchmore Hill	d			06 56	07 04		07 12			07 26	07 34	
Palmers Green	d			06 58	07 06		07 15			07 28	07 36	
Bowes Park	d			07 01			07 17			07 31		
Knebworth	d											07 18
Welwyn North	d											07 24
Welwyn Garden City 4	d	06 25	06 35			06 45		06 57	07 08			07 27
Hatfield	d	06 29	06 39			06 49		07 01	07 12			07 31
Welham Green	d	06 33				06 53		07 05				
Brookmans Park	d	06 35				06 55		07 07				
Potters Bar	d	06 38	06 46			06 58		07 10	07 18			
Hadley Wood	d	06 42	06 49			07 02		07 14				
New Barnet	d	06 45	06 52			07 05		07 17	07 23			
Oakleigh Park	d	06 47	06 54			07 07		07 19	07 25			
New Southgate	d	06 50	06 57			07 10		07 22	07 28			
Alexandra Palace	d	06 53		07 03		07 13	07 20	07 25		07 33		
Hornsey	d	06 55		07 05		07 15	07 22	07 27		07 35		
Harringay	d	06 57		07 07		07 17	07 24	07 29		07 37		
Finsbury Park ⊖	d	07 00	07 03	07 10	07 14	07 20	07 27	07 32	07 35	07 40	07 44	07 46
Drayton Park	d	07 02		07 12	07 16	07 22	07 29	07 34		07 42	07 46	
Highbury & Islington ⊖	d	07 04		07 14	07 18	07 24	07 31	07 36		07 44	07 48	
Essex Road	d	07 06		07 16	07 20	07 26	07 33	07 38		07 46	07 50	
Old Street ⊖	d	07 09		07 19	07 23	07 29	07 36	07 41		07 49	07 53	
Moorgate ⊖	a	07 14		07 24	07 28	07 34	07 41	07 46		07 54	07 58	
London Kings Cross 15 ⊖	a		07 10						07 43			07 57

		FC	FC	FC	FC	FC	FC	FC	FC	FC	FC	FC
Letchworth Garden City	d						07 20					
Hitchin 4	d						07 24					
Stevenage 4	d						07 30		07 35			
Watton-at-Stone	d								07 42			
Hertford North	d			07 24	07 33			07 38	07 50		07 55	
Bayford	d			07 28				07 42				
Cuffley	d			07 33	07 41			07 47	07 57		08 02	
Crews Hill	d			07 36				07 50				
Gordon Hill	d		07 33	07 39	07 45			07 53	08 02		08 07	
Enfield Chase	d		07 35	07 42	07 48			07 55	08 04		08 09	
Grange Park	d		07 37	07 44				07 57			08 11	
Winchmore Hill	d		07 39	07 46	07 51			07 59			08 13	
Palmers Green	d		07 42	07 48	07 53			08 02			08 16	
Bowes Park	d		07 44	07 51				08 04	08 08		08 18	
Knebworth	d											
Welwyn North	d											
Welwyn Garden City 4	d	07 17				07 32	07 42			07 47		07 58
Hatfield	d	07 21				07 36	07 46			07 51		08 02
Welham Green	d	07 25				07 40				07 55		08 06
Brookmans Park	d	07 27				07 42				07 57		08 08
Potters Bar	d	07 30				07 45	07 52			08 00		08 11
Hadley Wood	d	07 34				07 49				08 04		08 15
New Barnet	d	07 37				07 52	07 57			08 07		08 18
Oakleigh Park	d	07 39				07 54	07 59			08 09		08 20
New Southgate	d	07 42				07 57	08 02			08 12		08 23
Alexandra Palace	d		07 47	07 53		08 00		08 07	08 11	08 15	08 21	
Hornsey	d		07 49			08 02		08 09	08 13	08 17	08 23	08 27
Harringay	d		07 51			08 04		08 11	08 15	08 19	08 25	08 29
Finsbury Park ⊖	d	07 49	07 54	07 58	08 02	08 07	08 10	08 14	08 18	08 22	08 28	08 32
Drayton Park	d	07 51	07 56	08 00	08 04	08 09		08 16	08 20	08 24	08 30	08 34
Highbury & Islington ⊖	d	07 53	07 58	08 02	08 06	08 11		08 18	08 22	08 26	08 32	08 36
Essex Road	d	07 55	08 00	08 04	08 08	08 13		08 20	08 24	08 28	08 34	08 38
Old Street ⊖	d	07 58	08 03	08 07	08 11	08 16		08 23	08 27	08 31	08 37	08 41
Moorgate ⊖	a	08 03	08 08	08 12	08 17	08 22		08 28	08 32	08 37	08 42	08 46
London Kings Cross 15 ⊖	a						08 17					

b Previous night, stops to set down only

Letchworth Garden City, Hertford North and Welwyn Garden City - London

Station		FC	FC	FC		FC	FC	FC	FC	FC	FC	FC	FC	FC		FC	FC	FC	FC	FC	FC 1	FC	FC	FC
Letchworth Garden City	d																				08 59			
Hitchin 4	d													08 39							09 03			
Stevenage 4	d					08 05							08 34	08 45						09 04	09 09			
Watton-at-Stone	d					08 12							08 41							09 11				
Hertford North	d		08 05			08 20			08 30				08 50							09 17				
Bayford	d		08 09						08 34				08 54							09 21				
Cuffley	d		08 14			08 27			08 39				08 59							09 26				
Crews Hill	d		08 17						08 42				09 02							09 29				
Gordon Hill	d	08 15	08 20			08 32		08 37	08 45			08 55	09 05				09 12		09 27	09 32				
Enfield Chase	d	08 17	08 22			08 34		08 39	08 47			08 57	09 07				09 14		09 29	09 34				
Grange Park	d	08 19	08 24					08 41				08 59	09 09				09 16		09 31	09 36				
Winchmore Hill	d	08 21	08 26					08 43				09 01	09 11				09 18		09 33	09 38				
Palmers Green	d	08 24	08 29					08 46				09 04	09 14				09 21		09 36	09 41				
Bowes Park	d	08 26	08 31			08 38		08 48	08 52			09 06	09 16				09 23		09 38	09 43				
Knebworth	d													08 49							09 13			
Welwyn North	d													08 53							09 17			
Welwyn Garden City 4	d			08 14			08 18			08 32	08 42			08 58				09 04			09 21			09 24
Hatfield	d			08 18			08 22			08 36	08 46			09 02				09 08			09 24			09 28
Welham Green	d						08 26			08 40								09 12						09 32
Brookmans Park	d						08 28			08 42								09 14						09 34
Potters Bar	d			08 25			08 31			08 46	08 53							09 17			09 31			09 37
Hadley Wood	d						08 35			08 49								09 21						09 41
New Barnet	d			08 30			08 38			08 52	08 57							09 23						09 43
Oakleigh Park	d			08 32			08 40			08 54	08 59							09 25						09 45
New Southgate	d			08 35			08 43			08 57	09 02							09 28						09 48
Alexandra Palace	d	08 29	08 34	08 38		08 41	08 46	08 51	08 55	09 00	09 05	09 09	09 19				09 26	09 31	09 42	09 46				09 51
Hornsey	d	08 31				08 43	08 48		08 57	09 02		09 11	09 21				09 28	09 33		09 48				09 53
Harringay	d	08 33				08 45	08 50		08 59	09 04		09 13	09 23			←	09 30	09 35		09 50		←	←	09 55
Finsbury Park	⊖ d	08 36	08 40	08 43		08 48	08 53	08 57	09 02	09 07	09 10	09 16	09 26	09 19		09 26	09 33	09 38	09 46	09 53	09 40	09 46	09 53	09 58
Drayton Park	d	08 38	08 42			08 50	08 55	08 59	09 04	09 09		09 18	→			09 28	09 35	09 40	→	→		09 48	09 55	10 00
Highbury & Islington	⊖ d	08 40	08 44			08 52	08 57	09 01	09 06	09 11		09 20				09 30	09 36	09 41				09 49	09 56	10 01
Essex Road	d	08 42	08 46			08 54	08 59	09 03	09 08	09 13		09 22				09 32	09 38	09 43				09 51	09 58	10 03
Old Street	⊖ d	08 45	08 49			08 57	09 02	09 06	09 11	09 16		09 25				09 35	09 41	09 46				09 54	10 01	10 06
Moorgate	⊖ a	08 50	08 55			09 02	09 07	09 11	09 16	09 21		09 30				09 40	09 46	09 51				09 59	10 06	10 11
London Kings Cross 15	⊖ a			08 51							09 20			09 26							09 49			

Station		FC	FC	FC	FC	FC 1	FC	FC	FC	FC		FC 1	FC	FC	FC	FC 1	FC	FC	FC	FC		FC 1	FC	FC	FC
Letchworth Garden City	d					09 29				09 50		09 59				10 29				10 50					
Hitchin 4	d					09 33				09 54		10 03				10 33				10 54		11 03			
Stevenage 4	d				09 34	09 39				10 00		10 09				10 39				11 00		11 09			
Watton-at-Stone	d				09 41					10 06										11 06					
Hertford North	d		09 33		09 53					10 13					10 33			10 53		11 13					11 33
Bayford	d		09 37		09 57					10 17					10 37			10 57		11 17					11 37
Cuffley	d		09 42		10 02					10 22					10 42			11 02		11 22					11 42
Crews Hill	d		09 45		10 05					10 25					10 45			11 05		11 25					11 45
Gordon Hill	d		09 48		10 08					10 28					10 48			11 08		11 28					11 48
Enfield Chase	d		09 50		10 10					10 30					10 50			11 10		11 30					11 50
Grange Park	d		09 52		10 12					10 32					10 52			11 12		11 32					11 52
Winchmore Hill	d		09 54		10 14					10 34					10 54			11 14		11 34					11 54
Palmers Green	d		09 56		10 16					10 36					10 56			11 16		11 36					11 56
Bowes Park	d		09 59		10 19					10 39					10 59			11 19		11 39					11 59
Knebworth	d					09 43						10 13				10 43						11 13			
Welwyn North	d					09 47						10 17				10 47						11 17			
Welwyn Garden City 4	d	09 40		09 44		09 51			10 04			10 21		10 24		10 51	10 44		11 04			11 21		11 24	
Hatfield	d	09 43		09 48		09 55			10 08			10 23		10 28		10 55	10 48		11 08			11 25		11 28	
Welham Green	d			09 52					10 12					10 32			10 52		11 12					11 32	
Brookmans Park	d			09 54					10 14					10 34			10 54		11 14					11 34	
Potters Bar	d	09 49		09 57		10 01			10 17			10 29		10 37		11 01	10 57		11 17			11 31		11 37	
Hadley Wood	d			10 01					10 21					10 41			11 01		11 21					11 41	
New Barnet	d			10 03					10 23					10 43			11 03		11 23					11 43	
Oakleigh Park	d			10 05					10 25					10 45			11 05		11 25					11 45	
New Southgate	d			10 08					10 28					10 48			11 08		11 28					11 48	
Alexandra Palace	d		10 01	10 11	10 21				10 31	10 41				10 51	11 01		11 11	11 21	11 31	11 41				11 51	12 01
Hornsey	d		10 03	10 13	10 23				10 33	10 43				10 53	11 03		11 13	11 23	11 33	11 43				11 53	12 03
Harringay	d		10 05	10 15	10 25		←	←	10 35	10 45			←	10 55	11 05		11 15	11 25	11 35	11 45			←	11 55	12 05
Finsbury Park	⊖ d	10 03	10 08	10 18	10 28	10 11	10 18	10 28	10 38	10 48		10 40	10 48	10 58	11 08	11 10	11 18	11 28	11 38	11 48		11 40	11 48	11 58	12 08
Drayton Park	d		10 10	→	→		10 20	10 30	10 40	→			10 50	11 00	11 10		11 20	11 30	11 40	→			11 50	12 00	12 10
Highbury & Islington	⊖ d		10 11				10 21	10 31	10 41				10 51	11 01	11 11		11 21	11 31	11 41				11 51	12 01	12 11
Essex Road	d		10 13				10 23	10 33	10 43				10 53	11 03	11 13		11 23	11 33	11 43				11 53	12 03	12 13
Old Street	⊖ d		10 16				10 26	10 36	10 46				10 56	11 06	11 16		11 26	11 36	11 46				11 56	12 06	12 16
Moorgate	⊖ a		10 21				10 31	10 41	10 51				11 01	11 11	11 21		11 31	11 41	11 51				12 01	12 11	12 21
London Kings Cross 15	⊖ a	10 10				10 18						10 50				11 19						11 49			

Letchworth Garden City, Hertford North and Welwyn Garden City - London

Station		FC 1	FC	FC	FC	FC		FC 1	FC	FC	FC	FC 1	FC	FC	FC	FC		FC 1	FC	FC	FC	FC 1	FC	FC	FC
Letchworth Garden City	d	11 29				11 50						12 29				12 50						13 29			
Hitchin 4	d	11 33				11 54		12 03				12 33				12 54		13 03				13 33			
Stevenage 4	d	11 39				12 00		12 09				12 39				13 00		13 09				13 39			
Watton-at-Stone	d					12 06										13 06									
Hertford North	d			11 53		12 13					12 33			12 53		13 13					13 33			13 53	
Bayford	d			11 57		12 17					12 37			12 57		13 17					13 37			13 57	
Cuffley	d			12 02		12 22					12 42			13 02		13 22					13 42			14 02	
Crews Hill	d			12 05		12 25					12 45			13 05		13 25					13 45			14 05	
Gordon Hill	d			12 08		12 28					12 48			13 08		13 28					13 48			14 08	
Enfield Chase	d			12 10		12 30					12 50			13 10		13 30					13 50			14 10	
Grange Park	d			12 12		12 32					12 52			13 12		13 32					13 52			14 12	
Winchmore Hill	d			12 14		12 34					12 54			13 14		13 34					13 54			14 14	
Palmers Green	d			12 16		12 36					12 56			13 16		13 36					13 56			14 16	
Bowes Park	d			12 19		12 39					12 59			13 19		13 39					13 59			14 19	
Knebworth	d	11 43						12 13				12 43						13 13				13 43			
Welwyn North	d	11 47						12 17				12 47						13 17				13 47			
Welwyn Garden City 4	d	11 51	11 44		12 04			12 21		12 24		12 51	12 44		13 04			13 21		13 24		13 51	13 44		14 04
Hatfield	d	11 55	11 48		12 08			12 25		12 28		12 55	12 48		13 08			13 25		13 28		13 55	13 48		14 08
Welham Green	d		11 52		12 12					12 32			12 52		13 12					13 32			13 52		14 12
Brookmans Park	d		11 54		12 14					12 34			12 54		13 14					13 34			13 54		14 14
Potters Bar	d	12 01	11 57		12 17			12 31		12 37		13 01	12 57		13 17			13 31		13 37		14 01	13 57		14 17
Hadley Wood	d		12 01		12 21					12 41			13 01		13 21					13 41			14 01		14 21
New Barnet	d		12 03		12 23					12 43			13 03		13 23					13 43			14 03		14 23
Oakleigh Park	d		12 05		12 25					12 45			13 05		13 25					13 45			14 05		14 25
New Southgate	d		12 08		12 28					12 48			13 08		13 28					13 48			14 08		14 28
Alexandra Palace	d		12 11	12 21	12 31	12 41				12 51	13 01		13 11	13 21	13 31	13 41				13 51	14 01		14 11	14 21	14 31
Hornsey	d		12 13	12 23	12 33	12 43				12 53	13 03		13 13	13 23	13 33	13 43				13 53	14 03		14 13	14 23	14 33
Harringay	d		12 15	12 25	12 35	12 45			←	12 55	13 05		13 15	13 25	13 35	13 45			←	13 55	14 05		14 15	14 25	14 35
Finsbury Park	⊖ d	12 10	12 18	12 28	12 38	12 48		12 40	12 48	12 58	13 08	13 10	13 18	13 28	13 38	13 48		13 40	13 48	13 58	14 08	14 10	14 18	14 28	14 38
Drayton Park	d		12 20	12 30	12 40	→			12 50	13 00	13 10		13 20	13 30	13 40	→			13 50	14 00	14 10		14 20	14 30	14 40
Highbury & Islington	⊖ d		12 21	12 31	12 41				12 51	13 01	13 11		13 21	13 31	13 41				13 51	14 01	14 11		14 21	14 31	14 41
Essex Road	d		12 23	12 33	12 43				12 53	13 03	13 13		13 23	13 33	13 43				13 53	14 03	14 13		14 23	14 33	14 43
Old Street	⊖ d		12 26	12 36	12 46				12 56	13 06	13 16		13 26	13 36	13 46				13 56	14 06	14 16		14 26	14 36	14 46
Moorgate	⊖ a		12 31	12 41	12 51				13 01	13 11	13 21		13 31	13 40	13 51				14 01	14 11	14 21		14 31	14 41	14 51
London Kings Cross 15	⊖ a	12 19						12 49				13 19						13 49				14 19			

Station		FC		FC 1	FC	FC	FC	FC 1	FC	FC	FC	FC		FC 1	FC	FC	FC	FC	FC	FC 1	FC	FC		FC	FC
Letchworth Garden City	d	13 50						14 29				14 50							15 20	15 29					15 50
Hitchin 4	d	13 54		14 03				14 34				14 54		15 03					15 24	15 33					15 54
Stevenage 4	d	14 00		14 09				14 39				15 00		15 09					15 30	15 39					16 00
Watton-at-Stone	d	14 06										15 06							15 36						16 06
Hertford North	d	14 13					14 33			14 53		15 13					15 33		15 53						16 13
Bayford	d	14 17					14 37			14 57		15 17					15 37		15 57						16 17
Cuffley	d	14 22					14 42			15 02		15 22					15 42		16 02						16 22
Crews Hill	d	14 25					14 45			15 05		15 25					15 45		16 05						16 25
Gordon Hill	d	14 28					14 48			15 08		15 28					15 48		16 08						16 28
Enfield Chase	d	14 30					14 50			15 10		15 30					15 50		16 10						16 30
Grange Park	d	14 32					14 52			15 12		15 32					15 52		16 12						16 32
Winchmore Hill	d	14 34					14 54			15 14		15 34					15 54		16 14						16 34
Palmers Green	d	14 36					14 56			15 16		15 36					15 56		16 16						16 36
Bowes Park	d	14 39					14 59			15 19		15 39					15 59		16 19						16 39
Knebworth	d			14 13				14 43						15 13						15 43					
Welwyn North	d			14 17				14 47						15 17						15 47					
Welwyn Garden City 4	d			14 21		14 24		14 51	14 44		15 04			15 21		15 24		15 44		15 51				16 04	
Hatfield	d			14 25		14 28		14 55	14 48		15 08			15 25		15 28		15 48		15 55				16 08	
Welham Green	d					14 32			14 52		15 12					15 32		15 52						16 12	
Brookmans Park	d					14 34			14 54		15 14					15 34		15 54						16 14	
Potters Bar	d			14 31		14 37		15 01	14 57		15 17			15 31		15 37		15 57		16 01				16 17	
Hadley Wood	d					14 41			15 01		15 21					15 41		16 01						16 21	
New Barnet	d					14 43			15 03		15 23					15 43		16 03						16 23	
Oakleigh Park	d					14 45			15 05		15 25					15 45		16 05						16 25	
New Southgate	d					14 48			15 08		15 28					15 48		16 08						16 28	
Alexandra Palace	d	14 41				14 51	15 01		15 11	15 21	15 31	15 41				15 51	16 01	16 11	16 21					16 31	16 41
Hornsey	d	14 43				14 53	15 03		15 13	15 23	15 33	15 43				15 53	16 03	16 13	16 23					16 33	16 43
Harringay	d	14 45			←	14 55	15 05		15 15	15 25	15 35	15 45			←	15 55	16 05	16 15	16 25		←	←		16 35	16 45
Finsbury Park	⊖ d	14 48		14 40	14 48	14 58	15 08	15 10	15 18	15 28	15 38	15 48		15 40	15 48	15 58	16 08	16 18	16 28	16 10	16 18	16 28		16 38	16 48
Drayton Park	d	→			14 50	15 00	15 10		15 20	15 30	15 40	→			15 50	16 00	16 10	→	→		16 20	16 30		16 40	→
Highbury & Islington	⊖ d				14 51	15 01	15 11		15 21	15 31	15 41				15 51	16 01	16 11				16 21	16 31		16 41	
Essex Road	d				14 53	15 03	15 13		15 23	15 33	15 43				15 53	16 03	16 13				16 23	16 33		16 43	
Old Street	⊖ d				14 56	15 06	15 16		15 26	15 36	15 46				15 56	16 06	16 16				16 26	16 36		16 46	
Moorgate	⊖ a				15 01	15 11	15 21		15 31	15 41	15 51				16 01	16 12	16 21				16 31	16 41		16 51	
London Kings Cross 15	⊖ a			14 49				15 19						15 49						16 19					

Letchworth Garden City, Hertford North and Welwyn Garden City - London

		FC 1	FC	FC	FC	FC	FC	FC 1		FC	FC	FC	FC	FC	FC	FC 1	FC	FC		FC	FC	FC	FC	FC 1	FC
Letchworth Garden City	d						16 20	16 29																17 29	
Hitchin 4	d	16 03					16 24	16 33								17 04								17 33	
Stevenage 4	d	16 09					16 30	16 39							16 59	17 10							17 29	17 39	
Watton-at-Stone	d						16 36								17 06								17 36		
Hertford North	d					16 33	16 43					16 53			17 13					17 36			17 43		
Bayford	d					16 37	16 47					16 57			17 17								17 47		
Cuffley	d					16 42	16 52					17 02			17 22					17 43			17 52		
Crews Hill	d					16 45	16 55					17 05			17 25								17 55		
Gordon Hill	d					16 48	16 58					17 08	17 18		17 28			17 38		17 48			17 58		
Enfield Chase	d					16 50	17 00					17 10	17 20		17 30			17 40		17 50			18 00		
Grange Park	d					16 52						17 12			17 32			17 42					18 02		
Winchmore Hill	d					16 54	17 02					17 14	17 22		17 34			17 44		17 52			18 04		
Palmers Green	d					16 56	17 05					17 16	17 25		17 36			17 46		17 55			18 06		
Bowes Park	d					16 59						17 19			17 39			17 49					18 09		
Knebworth	d	16 13						16 43								17 13								17 43	
Welwyn North	d	16 17						16 47								17 17								17 47	
Welwyn Garden City 4	d	16 21		16 24	16 40			16 51			16 44			17 04		17 21					17 34	17 46		17 51	
Hatfield	d	16 25		16 28	16 44			16 55			16 48			17 08		17 25					17 38	17 50		17 55	
Welham Green	d			16 32							16 52			17 12							17 42				
Brookmans Park	d			16 34							16 54			17 14							17 44				
Potters Bar	d	16 31		16 37	16 50			17 01			16 57			17 17		17 31					17 47	17 56		18 01	
Hadley Wood	d			16 41							17 01			17 21							17 51				
New Barnet	d			16 43							17 03			17 23							17 53				
Oakleigh Park	d			16 45							17 05			17 25							17 55				
New Southgate	d			16 48							17 08			17 28							17 58				
Alexandra Palace	d			16 51		17 01					17 11	17 21		17 31	17 41			17 51			18 01		18 11		
Hornsey	d			16 53		17 03					17 13	17 23		17 33	17 43			17 53			18 03		18 13		
Harringay	d		←	16 55		17 05				←	17 15	17 25		17 35	17 45		←	17 55			18 05		18 15		←
Finsbury Park	⊖ d	16 40	16 48	16 58	17 01	17 08	17 12	17 10		17 12	17 18	17 28	17 32	17 38	17 48	17 40	17 48	17 58		18 02	18 08	18 08	18 18	18 10	18 18
Drayton Park	d		16 50	17 00		17 10	→			17 14	17 20	17 30	17 34	17 40	→		17 50	18 00		18 04	18 10		→		18 20
Highbury & Islington	⊖ d		16 51	17 01		17 11				17 15	17 21	17 31	17 35	17 41			17 51	18 01		18 05	18 11				18 21
Essex Road	d		16 53	17 03		17 13				17 17	17 23	17 33	17 37	17 43			17 53	18 03		18 07	18 13				18 23
Old Street	⊖ d		16 56	17 06		17 16				17 20	17 26	17 36	17 40	17 46			17 56	18 06		18 10	18 16				18 26
Moorgate	⊖ a		17 01	17 11		17 21				17 26	17 31	17 41	17 46	17 51			18 01	18 11		18 16	18 22				18 31
London Kings Cross 15	⊖ a	16 49			17 08			17 18								17 49						18 17		18 21	

		FC	FC	FC		FC 1	FC	FC	FC	FC 1	FC	FC	FC	FC		FC 1	FC	FC	FC	FC 1	FC	FC	FC	FC 1	
Letchworth Garden City	d									18 29										19 29					
Hitchin 4	d					18 11				18 33						19 11				19 33				20 04	
Stevenage 4	d	17 53				18 17		18 23		18 39			18 53			19 17				19 39			19 59	20 10	
Watton-at-Stone	d	18 00						18 30					19 00										20 06		
Hertford North	d	18 06					18 18	18 36				18 48	19 06				19 18	19 36			19 48		20 12		
Bayford	d						18 22					18 52					19 22				19 52		20 16		
Cuffley	d	18 13					18 27	18 43				18 57	19 13				19 27	19 43			19 57		20 21		
Crews Hill	d						18 30					19 00					19 30				20 00		20 24		
Gordon Hill	d	18 18		18 23			18 33	18 48			18 53	19 03	19 18				19 33	19 48			20 03		20 27		
Enfield Chase	d	18 20		18 25			18 35	18 50			18 55	19 05	19 20				19 35	19 50			20 05		20 29		
Grange Park	d			18 27			18 37				18 57	19 07					19 37				20 07		20 31		
Winchmore Hill	d	18 22		18 29			18 39	18 52			18 59	19 09	19 22				19 39	19 52			20 09		20 33		
Palmers Green	d	18 25		18 31			18 41	18 55			19 01	19 11	19 25				19 41	19 55			20 11		20 35		
Bowes Park	d			18 34			18 44				19 04	19 14					19 44				20 14		20 38		
Knebworth	d					18 20				18 43						19 20				19 43				20 14	
Welwyn North	d					18 24				18 47						19 24				19 47				20 18	
Welwyn Garden City 4	d		18 04			18 29			18 34	18 51				19 04		19 28			19 34	19 51		19 58		20 21	
Hatfield	d		18 08			18 32			18 38	18 55				19 08		19 32			19 38	19 55		20 02		20 25	
Welham Green	d		18 12						18 42					19 12					19 42			20 06			
Brookmans Park	d		18 14						18 44					19 14					19 44			20 08			
Potters Bar	d		18 17			18 39			18 47	19 01				19 17		19 38			19 47	20 01		20 11		20 31	
Hadley Wood	d		18 21						18 51					19 21					19 51			20 15			
New Barnet	d		18 23						18 53					19 23					19 53			20 17			
Oakleigh Park	d		18 25						18 55					19 25					19 55			20 19			
New Southgate	d		18 28						18 58					19 28					19 58			20 22			
Alexandra Palace	d		18 31	18 36			18 46		19 01		19 06	19 16		19 31			19 46		20 01		20 16	20 25	20 40		
Hornsey	d		18 33	18 38			18 48		19 03		19 08	19 18		19 33			19 48		20 03		20 18	20 27	20 42		
Harringay	d		18 35	18 40			18 50		19 05		19 10	19 20		19 35			19 50		20 05		20 20	20 29	20 44		
Finsbury Park	⊖ d	18 32	18 38	18 43		18 47	18 53	19 02	19 08	19 10	19 13	19 23	19 32	19 38		19 47	19 53	20 02	20 08	20 10	20 23	20 32	20 47	20 40	
Drayton Park	d	18 34	18 40	18 45			18 55	19 04	19 10		19 15	19 25	19 34	19 40			19 55	20 04	20 10		20 25	20 34	→		
Highbury & Islington	⊖ d	18 35	18 41	18 46			18 56	19 05	19 11		19 16	19 26	19 35	19 41			19 56	20 05	20 11		20 26	20 35			
Essex Road	d	18 37	18 43	18 48			18 58	19 07	19 13		19 18	19 28	19 37	19 43			19 58	20 07	20 13		20 28	20 37			
Old Street	⊖ d	18 40	18 46	18 51			19 01	19 10	19 16		19 21	19 31	19 40	19 46			20 01	20 10	20 16		20 31	20 40			
Moorgate	⊖ a	18 45	18 51	18 56			19 06	19 15	19 21		19 26	19 36	19 45	19 51			20 06	20 15	20 21		20 36	20 45			
London Kings Cross 15	⊖ a					18 56				19 22						19 56				20 19				20 51	

Table 24

Mondays to Fridays

Letchworth Garden City, Hertford North and Welwyn Garden City - London

		FC	FC	FC	FC 1	FC	FC	FC	FC 1	FC		FC	FC	FC 1	FC	FC	FC 1	FC	FC	FC		FC 1	FC	FC	FC
Letchworth Garden City	d			20 20	20 29								21 20	21 29						22 20		22 29			
Hitchin 4	d			20 24	20 33				21 04				21 24	21 33			22 13			22 24		22 33			
Stevenage 4	d			20 29	20 39			20 59	21 10				21 29	21 39			22 18			22 29		22 39			
Watton-at-Stone	d			20 36				21 06					21 36							22 36					
Hertford North	d			20 42				21 12					21 42					22 12		22 42					23 10
Bayford	d			20 46				21 16					21 46					22 16		22 46					23 14
Cuffley	d			20 51				21 21					21 51					22 21		22 51					23 19
Crews Hill	d			20 54				21 24					21 54					22 24		22 54					23 22
Gordon Hill	d			20 57				21 27					21 57					22 27		22 57					23 25
Enfield Chase	d			20 59				21 29					21 59					22 29		22 59					23 27
Grange Park	d			21 01				21 31					22 01					22 31		23 01					23 29
Winchmore Hill	d			21 03				21 33					22 03					22 33		23 03					23 31
Palmers Green	d			21 05				21 35					22 05					22 35		23 05					23 33
Bowes Park	d			21 08				21 38					22 08					22 38		23 08					23 36
Knebworth	d				20 43				21 14					21 43			22 22					22 43			
Welwyn North	d				20 47				21 18					21 47			22 25					22 47			
Welwyn Garden City 4	d		20 28		20 51		20 58		21 21			21 28		21 51		21 58	22 28		22 30			22 51		23 00	
Hatfield	d		20 32		20 55		21 02		21 25			21 32		21 55		22 02	22 32		22 34			22 55		23 04	
Welham Green	d		20 36				21 06					21 36				22 06			22 38					23 08	
Brookmans Park	d		20 38				21 08					21 38				22 08			22 40					23 10	
Potters Bar	d		20 41		21 01		21 11		21 32			21 41		22 01		22 11	22 37		22 43			23 01		23 13	
Hadley Wood	d		20 45				21 15					21 45				22 15			22 47					23 17	
New Barnet	d		20 47				21 17					21 47				22 17			22 49					23 19	
Oakleigh Park	d		20 49				21 19					21 49				22 19			22 51					23 21	
New Southgate	d		20 52				21 22					21 52				22 22			22 54					23 24	
Alexandra Palace	d		20 55	21 10			21 25	21 40				21 55	22 10			22 25		22 40	22 57	23 10				23 27	23 38
Hornsey	d		20 57	21 12			21 27	21 42				21 57	22 12			22 27		22 42	22 59	23 12				23 29	23 40
Harringay	d	←	20 59	21 14		←	21 29	21 44		←		21 59	22 14		←	22 29		22 44	23 01	23 14			←	23 31	23 42
Finsbury Park	⊖ d	20 47	21 02	21 17	21 10	21 17	21 32	21 47	21 41	21 47		22 02	22 17	22 10	22 17	22 32	22 46	22 47	23 04	23 17		23 10	23 17	23 34	23 45
Drayton Park	d	20 49	21 04	→		21 19	21 34	→		21 49			→							→					
Highbury & Islington	⊖ d	20 50	21 05			21 20	21 35			21 50															
Essex Road	d	20 52	21 07			21 22	21 37			21 52															
Old Street	⊖ d	20 55	21 10			21 25	21 40			21 55															
Moorgate	⊖ a	21 00	21 15			21 30	21 45			22 00															
London Kings Cross 15	⊖ a				21 19				21 50			22 10		22 19	22 25	22 40	22 57	22 55	23 12			23 20	23 25	23 42	23 53

		FC 1	FC	FC 1
Letchworth Garden City	d		23 18	23 47
Hitchin 4	d	23 16	23 22	23 54
Stevenage 4	d	23 22	23 27	23 59
Watton-at-Stone	d		23 34	
Hertford North	d		23 40	
Bayford	d		23 44	
Cuffley	d		23 49	
Crews Hill	d		23 52	
Gordon Hill	d		23 55	
Enfield Chase	d		23 57	
Grange Park	d		23 59	
Winchmore Hill	d		00 01	
Palmers Green	d		00 03	
Bowes Park	d		00 06	
Knebworth	d	23 25		00 02
Welwyn North	d	23 29		00 06
Welwyn Garden City 4	d	23 32		00 09
Hatfield	d	23 35		00 12
Welham Green	d			
Brookmans Park	d			
Potters Bar	d	23 41		00 18
Hadley Wood	d			
New Barnet	d			
Oakleigh Park	d			
New Southgate	d			
Alexandra Palace	d		00 08	
Hornsey	d		00 10	
Harringay	d		00 12	
Finsbury Park	⊖ d	23s51	00 15	00 29
Drayton Park	d			
Highbury & Islington	⊖ d			
Essex Road	d			
Old Street	⊖ d			
Moorgate	⊖ a			
London Kings Cross 15	⊖ a	00 01	00 26	00 42

Letchworth Garden City, Hertford North and Welwyn Garden City - London

		FC ■	FC	FC ■	FC	FC ■	FC	FC ■	FC	FC		FC ■	FC	FC	FC ■	FC	FC	FC	FC ■	FC		FC	FC ■	FC	FC
Letchworth Garden City	d		23p18	23p47			04 50			05 20		05 29						06 20	06 29						
Hitchin ■	d	23p16	23p22	23p54		04 08	04 54	04 59		05 24		05 33			06 03			06 24	06 33				07 03		
Stevenage ■	d	23p22	23p27	23p59		04 14	04 59	05 05		05 29		05 39			06 09			06 29	06 39				07 09		
Watton-at-Stone	d		23p34				05 06			05 36								06 36							
Hertford North	d		23p40			04 24	05 12			05 42						06 12		06 42						07 12	
Bayford	d		23p44				05 16			05 46						06 16		06 46						07 16	
Cuffley	d		23p49			04 31	05 21			05 51						06 21		06 51						07 21	
Crews Hill	d		23p52				05 24			05 54						06 24		06 54						07 24	
Gordon Hill	d		23p55			04 36	05 27			05 57						06 27		06 57						07 27	
Enfield Chase	d		23p57			04 38	05 29			05 59						06 29		06 59						07 29	
Grange Park	d		23p59				05 31			06 01						06 31		07 01						07 31	
Winchmore Hill	d		00 01				05 33			06 03						06 33		07 03						07 33	
Palmers Green	d		00 03				05 35			06 05						06 35		07 05						07 35	
Bowes Park	d		00 06				05 38			06 08						06 38		07 08						07 38	
Knebworth	d	23p25		00 02				05 08				05 43			06 13				06 43				07 13		
Welwyn North	d	23p29		00 06				05 12				05 47			06 17				06 47				07 17		
Welwyn Garden City ■	d	23p32		00 09	04 10			05 15				05 51		05 58	06 21		06 28		06 51			06 58	07 21		07 28
Hatfield	d	23p35		00 12	04 14			05 19				05 55		06 02	06 25		06 32		06 55			07 02	07 25		07 32
Welham Green	d													06 06			06 36					07 06			07 36
Brookmans Park	d				04 19									06 08			06 38					07 08			07 38
Potters Bar	d	23p41		00 18	04 22			05 25				06 01		06 11	06 31		06 41		07 01			07 11	07 31		07 41
Hadley Wood	d				04 25									06 15			06 45					07 15			07 45
New Barnet	d				04 28			05 29						06 17			06 47					07 17			07 47
Oakleigh Park	d				04 30			05 31						06 19			06 49					07 19			07 49
New Southgate	d				04 33			05 34						06 22			06 52					07 22			07 52
Alexandra Palace	d		00 08		04 36		05 40	05 37		06 10				06 25		06 40	06 55	07 10				07 25		07 40	07 55
Hornsey	d		00 10		04 38	04 46	05 42			06 12				06 27		06 42	06 57	07 12				07 27		07 42	07 57
Harringay	d		00 12		04 40		05 44		←	06 14			←	06 29		06 44	06 59	07 14		←		07 29		07 44	07 59
Finsbury Park	⊖ d	23b51	00 15	00 29	04 42	04s49	05 47	05 42	05 47	06 17		06 10	06 17	06 32	06 40	06 47	07 02	07 17	07 10	07 17		07 32	07 40	07 47	08 02
Drayton Park	d						→			→								→							
Highbury & Islington	⊖ d																								
Essex Road	d																								
Old Street	⊖ d																								
Moorgate	⊖ a																								
London Kings Cross ■	⊖ a	00 01	00 26	00 42	04 51	05 02		05 56	05 55			06 20	06 25	06 40	06 47	06 55	07 10		07 19	07 25		07 40	07 47	07 55	08 10

		FC	FC ■	FC	FC	FC ■		FC	FC	FC	FC ■	FC	FC	FC ■	FC	FC		FC	FC ■	FC	FC	FC ■	FC	FC	FC
Letchworth Garden City	d		07 29								08 29								09 29						
Hitchin ■	d		07 33			08 03					08 33			09 03					09 34			10 03			
Stevenage ■	d	07 29	07 39			08 09				08 29	08 39			09 09				09 29	09 40			10 09			10 29
Watton-at-Stone	d	07 36								08 36								09 36							10 36
Hertford North	d	07 42						08 12		08 42					09 12			09 42					10 12		10 42
Bayford	d	07 46						08 16		08 46					09 16			09 46					10 16		10 46
Cuffley	d	07 51						08 21		08 51					09 21			09 51					10 21		10 51
Crews Hill	d	07 54						08 24		08 54					09 24			09 54					10 24		10 54
Gordon Hill	d	07 57						08 27		08 57					09 27			09 57					10 27		10 57
Enfield Chase	d	07 59						08 29		08 59					09 29			09 59					10 29		10 59
Grange Park	d	08 01						08 31		09 01					09 31			10 01					10 31		11 01
Winchmore Hill	d	08 03						08 33		09 03					09 33			10 03					10 33		11 03
Palmers Green	d	08 05						08 35		09 05					09 35			10 05					10 35		11 05
Bowes Park	d	08 08						08 38		09 08					09 38			10 08					10 38		11 08
Knebworth	d		07 43			08 13					08 43			09 13					09 43			10 13			
Welwyn North	d		07 47			08 17					08 47			09 17					09 47			10 17			
Welwyn Garden City ■	d		07 51		07 58	08 21			08 28		08 51		08 58	09 21		09 28			09 51		09 58	10 21		10 28	
Hatfield	d		07 55		08 02	08 25			08 32		08 55		09 02	09 25		09 32			09 55		10 02	10 25		10 32	
Welham Green	d				08 06				08 36				09 06			09 36					10 06			10 36	
Brookmans Park	d				08 08				08 38				09 08			09 38					10 08			10 38	
Potters Bar	d		08 01		08 11	08 31			08 41		09 01		09 11	09 31		09 41			10 01		10 11	10 31		10 41	
Hadley Wood	d				08 15				08 45				09 15			09 45					10 15			10 45	
New Barnet	d				08 17				08 47				09 17			09 47					10 17			10 47	
Oakleigh Park	d				08 19				08 49				09 19			09 49					10 19			10 49	
New Southgate	d				08 22				08 52				09 22			09 52					10 22			10 52	
Alexandra Palace	d	08 10			08 25			08 40	08 55	09 10			09 25		09 40	09 55		10 10			10 25		10 40	10 55	11 10
Hornsey	d	08 12			08 27			08 42	08 57	09 12			09 27		09 42	09 57		10 12			10 27		10 42	10 57	11 12
Harringay	d	08 14		←	08 29			08 44	08 59	09 14		←	09 29		09 44	09 59		10 14		←	10 29		10 44	10 59	11 14
Finsbury Park	⊖ d	08 17	08 10	08 17	08 32	08 40		08 47	09 02	09 17	09 10	09 17	09 32	09 40	09 47	10 02		10 17	10 10	10 17	10 32	10 40	10 47	11 02	11 17
Drayton Park	d	→								→								→							→
Highbury & Islington	⊖ d																								
Essex Road	d																								
Old Street	⊖ d																								
Moorgate	⊖ a																								
London Kings Cross ■	⊖ a		08 19	08 25	08 40	08 49		08 55	09 10		09 20	09 25	09 40	09 49	09 55	10 10			10 20	10 25	10 40	10 49	10 55	11 10	

b Previous night, stops to set down only

Letchworth Garden City, Hertford North and Welwyn Garden City - London

		FC ■		FC	FC	FC ■	FC	FC	FC	FC ■	FC	FC		FC ■	FC	FC	FC	FC ■	FC	FC	FC ■	FC		FC	FC
Letchworth Garden City	d	10 29								11 29								12 29							
Hitchin ■	d	10 33				11 03				11 33				12 03				12 33			13 03				
Stevenage ■	d	10 39				11 09			11 29	11 39				12 09			12 29	12 39			13 09				13 29
Watton-at-Stone	d								11 36								12 36								13 36
Hertford North	d						11 12		11 42						12 12		12 42					13 12			13 42
Bayford	d						11 16		11 46						12 16		12 46					13 16			13 46
Cuffley	d						11 21		11 51						12 21		12 51					13 21			13 51
Crews Hill	d						11 24		11 54						12 24		12 54					13 24			13 54
Gordon Hill	d						11 27		11 57						12 27		12 57					13 27			13 57
Enfield Chase	d						11 29		11 59						12 29		12 59					13 29			13 59
Grange Park	d						11 31		12 01						12 31		13 01					13 31			14 01
Winchmore Hill	d						11 33		12 03						12 33		13 03					13 33			14 03
Palmers Green	d						11 35		12 05						12 35		13 05					13 35			14 05
Bowes Park	d						11 38		12 08						12 38		13 08					13 38			14 08
Knebworth	d	10 43				11 13				11 43				12 13				12 43			13 13				
Welwyn North	d	10 47				11 17				11 47				12 17				12 47			13 17				
Welwyn Garden City ■	d	10 51			10 58	11 21		11 28		11 51		11 58		12 21		12 28		12 51		12 58	13 21			13 28	
Hatfield	d	10 55			11 02	11 25		11 32		11 55		12 02		12 25		12 32		12 55		13 02	13 25			13 32	
Welham Green	d				11 06			11 36				12 06				12 36				13 06				13 36	
Brookmans Park	d				11 08			11 38				12 08				12 38				13 08				13 38	
Potters Bar	d	11 01			11 11	11 31		11 41		12 01		12 11		12 31		12 41		13 01		13 11	13 31			13 41	
Hadley Wood	d				11 15			11 45				12 15				12 45				13 15				13 45	
New Barnet	d				11 17			11 47				12 17				12 47				13 17				13 47	
Oakleigh Park	d				11 19			11 49				12 19				12 49				13 19				13 49	
New Southgate	d				11 22			11 52				12 22				12 52				13 22				13 52	
Alexandra Palace	d				11 25		11 40	11 55	12 10			12 25			12 40	12 55	13 10			13 25		13 40		13 55	14 10
Hornsey	d				11 27		11 42	11 57	12 12			12 27			12 42	12 57	13 12			13 27		13 42		13 57	14 12
Harringay	d			←	11 29		11 44	11 59	12 14		←	12 29			12 44	12 59	13 14		←	13 29		13 44		13 59	14 14
Finsbury Park	⊖ d	11 10		11 17	11 32	11 40	11 47	12 02	12 17	12 10	12 17	12 32		12 40	12 47	13 02	13 17	13 10	13 17	13 32	13 40	13 47		14 02	14 17
Drayton Park	d								→								→								→
Highbury & Islington	⊖ d																								
Essex Road	d																								
Old Street	⊖ d																								
Moorgate	⊖ a																								
London Kings Cross ■	⊖ a	11 20		11 25	11 40	11 49	11 55	12 10		12 19	12 25	12 40		12 49	12 55	13 10		13 19	13 25	13 40	13 49	13 55		14 10	

		FC ■	FC	FC	FC ■	FC	FC	FC		FC ■	FC	FC	FC ■	FC	FC	FC	FC ■	FC		FC	FC ■	FC	FC	FC	FC ■
Letchworth Garden City	d	13 29								14 29							15 29								16 29
Hitchin ■	d	13 33			14 03					14 33			15 03				15 33				16 03				16 33
Stevenage ■	d	13 39			14 09			14 29		14 39			15 09			15 29	15 39				16 09			16 29	16 39
Watton-at-Stone	d							14 36								15 36								16 36	
Hertford North	d					14 12		14 42						15 12		15 42						16 12		16 42	
Bayford	d					14 16		14 46						15 16		15 46						16 16		16 46	
Cuffley	d					14 21		14 51						15 21		15 51						16 21		16 51	
Crews Hill	d					14 24		14 54						15 24		15 54						16 24		16 54	
Gordon Hill	d					14 27		14 57						15 27		15 57						16 27		16 57	
Enfield Chase	d					14 29		14 59						15 29		15 59						16 29		16 59	
Grange Park	d					14 31		15 01						15 31		16 01						16 31		17 01	
Winchmore Hill	d					14 33		15 03						15 33		16 03						16 33		17 03	
Palmers Green	d					14 35		15 05						15 35		16 05						16 35		17 05	
Bowes Park	d					14 38		15 08						15 38		16 08						16 38		17 08	
Knebworth	d	13 43			14 13					14 43			15 13				15 43				16 13				16 43
Welwyn North	d	13 47			14 17					14 47			15 17				15 47				16 17				16 47
Welwyn Garden City ■	d	13 51		13 58	14 21		14 28			14 51		14 58	15 21		15 28		15 51			15 58	16 21		16 28		16 51
Hatfield	d	13 55		14 02	14 25		14 32			14 55		15 02	15 25		15 32		15 55			16 02	16 25		16 32		16 55
Welham Green	d			14 06			14 36					15 06			15 36					16 06			16 36		
Brookmans Park	d			14 08			14 38					15 08			15 38					16 08			16 38		
Potters Bar	d	14 01		14 11	14 31		14 41			15 01		15 11	15 31		15 41		16 01			16 11	16 31		16 41		17 01
Hadley Wood	d			14 15			14 45					15 15			15 45					16 15			16 45		
New Barnet	d			14 17			14 47					15 17			15 47					16 17			16 47		
Oakleigh Park	d			14 19			14 49					15 19			15 49					16 19			16 49		
New Southgate	d			14 22			14 52					15 22			15 52					16 22			16 52		
Alexandra Palace	d			14 25		14 40	14 55	15 10				15 25		15 40	15 55	16 10				16 25		16 40	16 55	17 10	
Hornsey	d			14 27		14 42	14 57	15 12				15 27		15 42	15 57	16 12				16 27		16 42	16 57	17 12	
Harringay	d		←	14 29		14 44	14 59	15 14			←	15 29		15 44	15 59	16 14		←		16 29		16 44	16 59	17 14	
Finsbury Park	⊖ d	14 10	14 17	14 33	14 40	14 47	15 02	15 17		15 10	15 17	15 32	15 40	15 47	16 02	16 17	16 10	16 17		16 32	16 40	16 47	17 04	17 17	17 10
Drayton Park	d							→								→								→	
Highbury & Islington	⊖ d																								
Essex Road	d																								
Old Street	⊖ d																								
Moorgate	⊖ a																								
London Kings Cross ■	⊖ a	14 19	14 25	14 40	14 49	14 55	15 10			15 19	15 25	15 40	15 49	15 55	16 10		16 19	16 25		16 40	16 49	16 55	17 10		17 19

Letchworth Garden City, Hertford North and Welwyn Garden City - London

Saturdays
until 18 June

		FC	FC	FC 1	FC	FC	FC	FC 1	FC	FC	FC 1	FC	FC	FC	FC 1	FC	FC	FC 1	FC	FC	FC	FC 1
Letchworth Garden City	d							17 29							18 29							19 29
Hitchin 4	d			17 03				17 34			18 03				18 33			19 03				19 33
Stevenage 4	d			17 09			17 29	17 40			18 09			18 29	18 39			19 09			19 29	19 39
Watton-at-Stone	d						17 36							18 36							19 36	
Hertford North	d				17 12		17 42					18 12		18 42					19 12		19 42	
Bayford	d				17 16		17 46					18 16		18 46					19 16		19 46	
Cuffley	d				17 21		17 51					18 21		18 51					19 21		19 51	
Crews Hill	d				17 24		17 54					18 24		18 54					19 24		19 54	
Gordon Hill	d				17 27		17 57					18 27		18 57					19 27		19 57	
Enfield Chase	d				17 29		17 59					18 29		18 59					19 29		19 59	
Grange Park	d				17 31		18 01					18 31		19 01					19 31		20 01	
Winchmore Hill	d				17 33		18 03					18 33		19 03					19 33		20 03	
Palmers Green	d				17 35		18 05					18 35		19 05					19 35		20 05	
Bowes Park	d				17 38		18 08					18 38		19 08					19 38		20 08	
Knebworth	d			17 13				17 43			18 13				18 43			19 13				19 43
Welwyn North	d			17 17				17 47			18 17				18 47			19 17				19 47
Welwyn Garden City 4	d		16 58	17 21		17 28		17 51		17 58	18 21		18 28		18 51		18 58	19 21		19 28		19 51
Hatfield	d		17 02	17 25		17 32		17 55		18 02	18 25		18 32		18 55		19 02	19 25		19 32		19 55
Welham Green	d		17 06			17 36				18 06			18 36				19 06			19 36		
Brookmans Park	d		17 08			17 38				18 08			18 38				19 08			19 38		
Potters Bar	d		17 11	17 31		17 41		18 01		18 11	18 31		18 41		19 01		19 11	19 31		19 41		20 01
Hadley Wood	d		17 15			17 45				18 15			18 45				19 15			19 45		
New Barnet	d		17 17			17 47				18 17			18 47				19 17			19 47		
Oakleigh Park	d		17 19			17 49				18 19			18 49				19 19			19 49		
New Southgate	d		17 22			17 52				18 22			18 52				19 22			19 52		
Alexandra Palace	d		17 25		17 40	17 55	18 10			18 25		18 40	18 55	19 10			19 25		19 40	19 55	20 10	
Hornsey	d		17 27		17 42	17 57	18 12			18 27		18 42	18 57	19 12			19 27		19 42	19 57	20 12	
Harringay	d	←	17 29		17 44	17 59	18 14		←	18 29		18 44	18 59	19 14		←	19 29		19 44	19 59	20 14	
Finsbury Park ⊖	d	17 17	17 32	17 40	17 47	18 02	18 17	18 10	18 17	18 32	18 40	18 47	19 02	19 17	19 10	19 17	19 32	19 40	19 47	20 02	20 17	20 10
Drayton Park	d						→							→							→	
Highbury & Islington ⊖	d																					
Essex Road	d																					
Old Street ⊖	d																					
Moorgate ⊖	a																					
London Kings Cross 15 ⊖	a	17 25	17 40	17 49	17 55	18 10		18 19	18 25	18 40	18 49	18 55	19 10		19 19	19 25	19 40	19 49	19 55	20 10		20 19

		FC	FC	FC 1	FC	FC	FC	FC 1	FC	FC	FC 1	FC	FC	FC 1	FC	FC	FC 1	FC	FC	FC 1	FC	FC	FC 1
Letchworth Garden City	d							20 29						21 29						22 29			
Hitchin 4	d			20 03				20 34			21 03			21 34			22 03			22 34			23 03
Stevenage 4	d			20 09			20 29	20 40			21 09			21 40			22 09			22 40			23 09
Watton-at-Stone	d						20 36																
Hertford North	d				20 12		20 42					21 12			21 42			22 12			22 42		
Bayford	d				20 16		20 46					21 16			21 46			22 16			22 46		
Cuffley	d				20 21		20 51					21 21			21 51			22 21			22 51		
Crews Hill	d				20 24		20 54					21 24			21 54			22 24			22 54		
Gordon Hill	d				20 27		20 57					21 27			21 57			22 27			22 57		
Enfield Chase	d				20 29		20 59					21 29			21 59			22 29			22 59		
Grange Park	d				20 31		21 01					21 31			22 01			22 31			23 01		
Winchmore Hill	d				20 33		21 03					21 33			22 03			22 33			23 03		
Palmers Green	d				20 35		21 05					21 35			22 05			22 35			23 05		
Bowes Park	d				20 38		21 08					21 38			22 08			22 38			23 08		
Knebworth	d			20 13				20 46			21 13			21 43			22 13			22 43			23 13
Welwyn North	d			20 17				20 50			21 17			21 47			22 17			22 47			23 17
Welwyn Garden City 4	d		19 58	20 21		20 28		20 53		20 58	21 21		21 28	21 51		21 58	22 21		22 28	22 51		22 58	23 21
Hatfield	d		20 02	20 25		20 32		20 57		21 02	21 25		21 32	21 55		22 02	22 25		22 32	22 55		23 02	23 25
Welham Green	d		20 06			20 36				21 06			21 36			22 06			22 36			23 06	
Brookmans Park	d		20 08			20 38				21 08			21 38			22 08			22 38			23 08	
Potters Bar	d		20 11	20 31		20 41		21 03		21 11	21 31		21 41	22 01		22 11	22 31		22 41	23 01		23 11	23 31
Hadley Wood	d		20 15			20 45				21 15			21 45			22 15			22 45			23 15	
New Barnet	d		20 17			20 47				21 17			21 47			22 17			22 47			23 17	
Oakleigh Park	d		20 19			20 49				21 19			21 49			22 19			22 49			23 19	
New Southgate	d		20 22			20 52				21 22			21 52			22 22			22 52			23 22	
Alexandra Palace	d		20 25		20 40	20 55	21 10			21 25		21 40	21 55		22 10	22 25		22 40	22 55		23 10	23 25	
Hornsey	d		20 27		20 42	20 57	21 12			21 27		21 42	21 57		22 12	22 27		22 42	22 57		23 12	23 27	
Harringay	d	←	20 29		20 44	20 59	21 14		←	21 29		21 44	21 59		22 14	22 29		22 44	22 59		23 14	23 29	
Finsbury Park ⊖	d	20 17	20 32	20 40	20 47	21 02	21 17	21 12	21 17	21 32	21 40	21 47	22 02	22 10	22 17	22 32	22 40	22 47	23 02	23 10	23 17	23 32	23 40
Drayton Park	d						→																
Highbury & Islington ⊖	d																						
Essex Road	d																						
Old Street ⊖	d																						
Moorgate ⊖	a																						
London Kings Cross 15 ⊖	a	20 25	20 40	20 48	20 55	21 10		21 21	21 25	21 40	21 49	21 55	22 10	22 19	22 25	22 40	22 49	22 55	23 10	23 19	23 25	23 40	23 50

Letchworth Garden City, Hertford North and Welwyn Garden City - London

Saturdays
until 18 June

		FC	FC	FC 1
Letchworth Garden City	d			23 46
Hitchin 4	d			23 50
Stevenage 4	d			23 55
Watton-at-Stone	d			
Hertford North	d	23 12	23 42	
Bayford	d	23 16	23 46	
Cuffley	d	23 21	23 51	
Crews Hill	d	23 24	23 54	
Gordon Hill	d	23 27	23 57	
Enfield Chase	d	23 29	23 59	
Grange Park	d	23 31	00 01	
Winchmore Hill	d	23 33	00 03	
Palmers Green	d	23 35	00 05	
Bowes Park	d	23 38	00 08	
Knebworth	d			23 59
Welwyn North	d			00 06
Welwyn Garden City 4	d			00 09
Hatfield	d			00 13
Welham Green	d			
Brookmans Park	d			
Potters Bar	d			00 18
Hadley Wood	d			
New Barnet	d			
Oakleigh Park	d			
New Southgate	d			
Alexandra Palace	d	23 40	00 10	
Hornsey	d	23 42	00 12	
Harringay	d	23 44	00 14	
Finsbury Park ⊖	d	23 47	00 17	00s32
Drayton Park	d			
Highbury & Islington ⊖	d			
Essex Road	d			
Old Street ⊖	d			
Moorgate ⊖	a			
London Kings Cross 15 ⊖	a	23 55	00 25	00 40

Saturdays
25 June to 30 July

		FC 1	FC	FC 1	FC	FC 1	FC	FC 1	FC	FC	FC 1	FC	FC	FC 1	FC	FC	FC	FC 1	FC	FC	FC 1	FC	FC
Letchworth Garden City	d		23p18	23p47			04 50			05 20	05 29						06 20	06 29					
Hitchin 4	d	23p16	23p22	23p54		04 08	04 54	04 59		05 24	05 33			06 03			06 24	06 33			07 03		
Stevenage 4	d	23p22	23p27	23p59		04 14	04 59	05 05		05 29	05 39			06 09			06 29	06 39			07 09		
Watton-at-Stone	d		23p34				05 06			05 36							06 36						
Hertford North	d		23p40			04 24	05 12			05 42					06 12		06 42					07 12	
Bayford	d		23p44				05 16			05 46					06 16		06 46					07 16	
Cuffley	d		23p49			04 31	05 21			05 51					06 21		06 51					07 21	
Crews Hill	d		23p52				05 24			05 54					06 24		06 54					07 24	
Gordon Hill	d		23p55			04 36	05 27			05 57					06 27		06 57					07 27	
Enfield Chase	d		23p57			04 38	05 29			05 59					06 29		06 59					07 29	
Grange Park	d		23p59				05 31			06 01					06 31		07 01					07 31	
Winchmore Hill	d		00 01				05 33			06 03					06 33		07 03					07 33	
Palmers Green	d		00 03				05 35			06 05					06 35		07 05					07 35	
Bowes Park	d		00 06				05 38			06 08					06 38		07 08					07 38	
Knebworth	d	23p25		00 02				05 08			05 43			06 13				06 43			07 13		
Welwyn North	d	23p29		00 06				05 12			05 47			06 17				06 47			07 17		
Welwyn Garden City 4	d	23p32		00 09	04 10			05 15			05 51		05 58	06 21		06 28		06 51		06 58	07 21		07 28
Hatfield	d	23p35		00 12	04 14			05 19			05 55		06 02	06 25		06 32		06 55		07 02	07 25		07 32
Welham Green	d												06 06			06 36				07 06			07 36
Brookmans Park	d				04 19								06 08			06 38				07 08			07 38
Potters Bar	d	23p41		00 18	04 22			05 25			06 01		06 11	06 31		06 41		07 01		07 11	07 31		07 41
Hadley Wood	d				04 25								06 15			06 45				07 15			07 45
New Barnet	d				04 28			05 29					06 17			06 47				07 17			07 47
Oakleigh Park	d				04 30			05 31					06 19			06 49				07 19			07 49
New Southgate	d				04 33			05 34					06 22			06 52				07 22			07 52
Alexandra Palace	d		00 08		04 36		05 40	05 37		06 10			06 25		06 40	06 55	07 10			07 25		07 40	07 55
Hornsey	d		00 10		04 38	04 46	05 42			06 12			06 27		06 42	06 57	07 12			07 27		07 42	07 57
Harringay	d		00 12		04 40		05 44		←	06 14		←	06 29		06 44	06 59	07 14		←	07 29		07 44	07 59
Finsbury Park ⊖	d	23b51	00 15	00 29	04 42	04s49	05 47	05 42	05 47	06 17	06 10	06 17	06 32	06 40	06 47	07 02	07 17	07 10	07 17	07 32	07 40	07 47	08 02
Drayton Park	d						→			→							→						
Highbury & Islington ⊖	d																						
Essex Road	d																						
Old Street ⊖	d																						
Moorgate ⊖	a																						
London Kings Cross 15 ⊖	a	00 01	00 26	00 42	04 51	05 02		05 56	05 55		06 20	06 25	06 40	06 47	06 55	07 10		07 19	07 25	07 40	07 47	07 55	08 10

b Previous night, stops to set down only

Letchworth Garden City, Hertford North and Welwyn Garden City - London

	FC	FC 1	FC	FC	FC 1		FC	FC	FC	FC 1	FC	FC	FC 1	FC	FC		FC	FC 1	FC	FC	FC 1	FC	FC	FC
Letchworth Garden City d		07 29								08 29								09 29						
Hitchin 4 d		07 33			08 03					08 33			09 03					09 34			10 03			
Stevenage 4 d	07 29	07 39			08 09				08 29	08 39			09 09				09 29	09 40			10 09			10 29
Watton-at-Stone d	07 36								08 36								09 36							10 36
Hertford North d	07 42						08 12		08 42					09 12			09 42					10 12		10 42
Bayford d	07 46						08 16		08 46					09 16			09 46					10 16		10 46
Cuffley d	07 51						08 21		08 51					09 21			09 51					10 21		10 51
Crews Hill d	07 54						08 24		08 54					09 24			09 54					10 24		10 54
Gordon Hill d	07 57						08 27		08 57					09 27			09 57					10 27		10 57
Enfield Chase d	07 59						08 29		08 59					09 29			09 59					10 29		10 59
Grange Park d	08 01						08 31		09 01					09 31			10 01					10 31		11 01
Winchmore Hill d	08 03						08 33		09 03					09 33			10 03					10 33		11 03
Palmers Green d	08 05						08 35		09 05					09 35			10 05					10 35		11 05
Bowes Park d	08 08						08 38		09 08					09 38			10 08					10 38		11 08
Knebworth d		07 43			08 13					08 43			09 13					09 43			10 13			
Welwyn North d		07 47			08 17					08 47			09 17					09 47			10 17			
Welwyn Garden City 4 d		07 51		07 58	08 21			08 28		08 51		08 58	09 21		09 28			09 51		09 58	10 21		10 28	
Hatfield d		07 55		08 02	08 25			08 32		08 55		09 02	09 25		09 32			09 55		10 02	10 25		10 32	
Welham Green d				08 06				08 36				09 06			09 36					10 06			10 36	
Brookmans Park d				08 08				08 38				09 08			09 38					10 08			10 38	
Potters Bar d		08 01		08 11	08 31			08 41		09 01		09 11	09 31		09 41			10 01		10 11	10 31		10 41	
Hadley Wood d				08 15				08 45				09 15			09 45					10 15			10 45	
New Barnet d				08 17				08 47				09 17			09 47					10 17			10 47	
Oakleigh Park d				08 19				08 49				09 19			09 49					10 19			10 49	
New Southgate d				08 22				08 52				09 22			09 52					10 22			10 52	
Alexandra Palace d	08 10			08 25			08 40	08 55	09 10			09 25		09 40	09 55		10 10			10 25		10 40	10 55	11 10
Hornsey d	08 12			08 27			08 42	08 57	09 12			09 27		09 42	09 57		10 12			10 27		10 42	10 57	11 12
Harringay d	08 14		←	08 29			08 44	08 59	09 14		←	09 29		09 44	09 59		10 14		←	10 29		10 44	10 59	11 14
Finsbury Park ⊖ d	08 17	08 10	08 17	08 32	08 40		08 47	09 02	09 17	09 10	09 17	09 32	09 40	09 47	10 02		10 17	10 10	10 17	10 32	10 40	10 47	11 02	11 17
Drayton Park d	→								→								→							→
Highbury & Islington ⊖ d																								
Essex Road d																								
Old Street ⊖ d																								
Moorgate ⊖ a																								
London Kings Cross 15 ⊖ a		08 19	08 25	08 40	08 49		08 55	09 10		09 20	09 25	09 40	09 49	09 55	10 10			10 20	10 25	10 40	10 49	10 55	11 10	

	FC 1		FC	FC	FC 1	FC	FC	FC	FC 1	FC	FC		FC 1	FC	FC	FC	FC 1	FC	FC	FC 1	FC		FC	FC
Letchworth Garden City d	10 29								11 29								12 29							
Hitchin 4 d	10 33				11 03				11 33				12 03				12 33			13 03				
Stevenage 4 d	10 39				11 09			11 29	11 39				12 09			12 29	12 39			13 09				13 29
Watton-at-Stone d								11 36								12 36								13 36
Hertford North d						11 12		11 42						12 12		12 42					13 12			13 42
Bayford d						11 16		11 46						12 16		12 46					13 16			13 46
Cuffley d						11 21		11 51						12 21		12 51					13 21			13 51
Crews Hill d						11 24		11 54						12 24		12 54					13 24			13 54
Gordon Hill d						11 27		11 57						12 27		12 57					13 27			13 57
Enfield Chase d						11 29		11 59						12 29		12 59					13 29			13 59
Grange Park d						11 31		12 01						12 31		13 01					13 31			14 01
Winchmore Hill d						11 33		12 03						12 33		13 03					13 33			14 03
Palmers Green d						11 35		12 05						12 35		13 05					13 35			14 05
Bowes Park d						11 38		12 08						12 38		13 08					13 38			14 08
Knebworth d	10 43				11 13				11 43				12 13				12 43			13 13				
Welwyn North d	10 47				11 17				11 47				12 17				12 47			13 17				
Welwyn Garden City 4 d	10 51			10 58	11 21		11 28		11 51		11 58		12 21		12 28		12 51		12 58	13 21			13 28	
Hatfield d	10 55			11 02	11 25		11 32		11 55		12 02		12 25		12 32		12 55		13 02	13 25			13 32	
Welham Green d				11 06			11 36				12 06				12 36				13 06				13 36	
Brookmans Park d				11 08			11 38				12 08				12 38				13 08				13 38	
Potters Bar d	11 01			11 11	11 31		11 41		12 01		12 11		12 31		12 41		13 01		13 11	13 31			13 41	
Hadley Wood d				11 15			11 45				12 15				12 45				13 15				13 45	
New Barnet d				11 17			11 47				12 17				12 47				13 17				13 47	
Oakleigh Park d				11 19			11 49				12 19				12 49				13 19				13 49	
New Southgate d				11 22			11 52				12 22				12 52				13 22				13 52	
Alexandra Palace d				11 25		11 40	11 55	12 10			12 25			12 40	12 55	13 10			13 25		13 40		13 55	14 10
Hornsey d				11 27		11 42	11 57	12 12			12 27			12 42	12 57	13 12			13 27		13 42		13 57	14 12
Harringay d			←	11 29		11 44	11 59	12 14		←	12 29			12 44	12 59	13 14		←	13 29		13 44		13 59	14 14
Finsbury Park ⊖ d	11 10		11 17	11 32	11 40	11 47	12 02	12 17	12 10	12 17	12 32		12 40	12 47	13 02	13 17	13 10	13 17	13 32	13 40	13 47		14 02	14 17
Drayton Park d								→								→								→
Highbury & Islington ⊖ d																								
Essex Road d																								
Old Street ⊖ d																								
Moorgate ⊖ a																								
London Kings Cross 15 ⊖ a	11 20		11 25	11 40	11 49	11 55	12 10		12 19	12 25	12 40		12 49	12 55	13 10		13 19	13 25	13 40	13 49	13 55		14 10	

Letchworth Garden City, Hertford North and Welwyn Garden City - London

	FC 1	FC	FC	FC 1	FC	FC	FC		FC 1	FC	FC	FC 1	FC	FC	FC	FC 1	FC		FC	FC 1	FC	FC	FC	FC 1
Letchworth Garden City d	13 29								14 29							15 29								16 29
Hitchin 4 d	13 33			14 03					14 33			15 03				15 33				16 03				16 33
Stevenage 4 d	13 39			14 09			14 29		14 39			15 09			15 29	15 39				16 09			16 29	16 39
Watton-at-Stone d							14 36								15 36								16 36	
Hertford North d					14 12		14 42						15 12		15 42						16 12		16 42	
Bayford d					14 16		14 46						15 16		15 46						16 16		16 46	
Cuffley d					14 21		14 51						15 21		15 51						16 21		16 51	
Crews Hill d					14 24		14 54						15 24		15 54						16 24		16 54	
Gordon Hill d					14 27		14 57						15 27		15 57						16 27		16 57	
Enfield Chase d					14 29		14 59						15 29		15 59						16 29		16 59	
Grange Park d					14 31		15 01						15 31		16 01						16 31		17 01	
Winchmore Hill d					14 33		15 03						15 33		16 03						16 33		17 03	
Palmers Green d					14 35		15 05						15 35		16 05						16 35		17 05	
Bowes Park d					14 38		15 08						15 38		16 08						16 38		17 08	
Knebworth d	13 43			14 13					14 43			15 13				15 43				16 13				16 43
Welwyn North d	13 47			14 17					14 47			15 17				15 47				16 17				16 47
Welwyn Garden City 4 d	13 51		13 58	14 21		14 28			14 51		14 58	15 21		15 28		15 51			15 58	16 21		16 28		16 51
Hatfield d	13 55		14 02	14 25		14 32			14 55		15 02	15 25		15 32		15 55			16 02	16 25		16 32		16 55
Welham Green d			14 06			14 36					15 06			15 36					16 06			16 36		
Brookmans Park d			14 08			14 38					15 08			15 38					16 08			16 38		
Potters Bar d	14 01		14 11	14 31		14 41			15 01		15 11	15 31		15 41		16 01			16 11	16 31		16 41		17 01
Hadley Wood d			14 15			14 45					15 15			15 45					16 15			16 45		
New Barnet d			14 17			14 47					15 17			15 47					16 17			16 47		
Oakleigh Park d			14 19			14 49					15 19			15 49					16 19			16 49		
New Southgate d			14 22			14 52					15 22			15 52					16 22			16 52		
Alexandra Palace d			14 25		14 40	14 55	15 10				15 25		15 40	15 55	16 10				16 25		16 40	16 55	17 10	
Hornsey d			14 27		14 42	14 57	15 12				15 27		15 42	15 57	16 12				16 27		16 42	16 57	17 12	
Harringay d		←	14 29		14 44	14 59	15 14			←	15 29		15 44	15 59	16 14		←		16 29		16 44	16 59	17 14	
Finsbury Park ⊖ d	14 10	14 17	14 33	14 40	14 47	15 02	15 17		15 10	15 17	15 32	15 40	15 47	16 02	16 17	16 10	16 17		16 32	16 40	16 47	17 04	17 17	17 10
Drayton Park d							→								→								→	
Highbury & Islington ⊖ d																								
Essex Road d																								
Old Street ⊖ d																								
Moorgate ⊖ a																								
London Kings Cross 15 ⊖ a	14 19	14 25	14 40	14 49	14 55	15 10			15 19	15 25	15 40	15 49	15 55	16 10		16 19	16 25		16 40	16 49	16 55	17 10		17 19

	FC	FC	FC 1		FC	FC	FC	FC 1	FC	FC	FC 1	FC	FC		FC	FC 1	FC	FC	FC 1	FC	FC	FC	FC 1	
Letchworth Garden City d								17 29								18 29							19 29	
Hitchin 4 d			17 03					17 34			18 03					18 33			19 03				19 33	
Stevenage 4 d			17 09				17 29	17 40			18 09				18 29	18 39			19 09			19 29	19 39	
Watton-at-Stone d							17 36								18 36							19 36		
Hertford North d					17 12		17 42					18 12			18 42					19 12		19 42		
Bayford d					17 16		17 46					18 16			18 46					19 16		19 46		
Cuffley d					17 21		17 51					18 21			18 51					19 21		19 51		
Crews Hill d					17 24		17 54					18 24			18 54					19 24		19 54		
Gordon Hill d					17 27		17 57					18 27			18 57					19 27		19 57		
Enfield Chase d					17 29		17 59					18 29			18 59					19 29		19 59		
Grange Park d					17 31		18 01					18 31			19 01					19 31		20 01		
Winchmore Hill d					17 33		18 03					18 33			19 03					19 33		20 03		
Palmers Green d					17 35		18 05					18 35			19 05					19 35		20 05		
Bowes Park d					17 38		18 08					18 38			19 08					19 38		20 08		
Knebworth d			17 13					17 43			18 13					18 43			19 13				19 43	
Welwyn North d			17 17					17 47			18 17					18 47			19 17				19 47	
Welwyn Garden City 4 d		16 58	17 21			17 28		17 51		17 58	18 21		18 28			18 51		18 58	19 21		19 28		19 51	
Hatfield d		17 02	17 25			17 32		17 55		18 02	18 25		18 32			18 55		19 02	19 25		19 32		19 55	
Welham Green d		17 06				17 36				18 06			18 36					19 06			19 36			
Brookmans Park d		17 08				17 38				18 08			18 38					19 08			19 38			
Potters Bar d		17 11	17 31			17 41		18 01		18 11	18 31		18 41			19 01		19 11	19 31		19 41		20 01	
Hadley Wood d		17 15				17 45				18 15			18 45					19 15			19 45			
New Barnet d		17 17				17 47				18 17			18 47					19 17			19 47			
Oakleigh Park d		17 19				17 49				18 19			18 49					19 19			19 49			
New Southgate d		17 22				17 52				18 22			18 52					19 22			19 52			
Alexandra Palace d		17 25			17 40	17 55	18 10			18 25		18 40	18 55		19 10			19 25		19 40	19 55	20 10		
Hornsey d		17 27			17 42	17 57	18 12			18 27		18 42	18 57		19 12			19 27		19 42	19 57	20 12		
Harringay d	←	17 29			17 44	17 59	18 14		←	18 29		18 44	18 59		19 14		←	19 29		19 44	19 59	20 14		
Finsbury Park ⊖ d	17 17	17 32	17 40		17 47	18 02	18 17	18 10	18 17	18 32	18 40	18 47	19 02		19 17	19 10	19 17	19 32	19 40	19 47	20 02	20 17	20 10	
Drayton Park d							→								→							→		
Highbury & Islington ⊖ d																								
Essex Road d																								
Old Street ⊖ d																								
Moorgate ⊖ a																								
London Kings Cross 15 ⊖ a	17 25	17 40	17 49		17 55	18 10		18 19	18 25	18 40	18 49	18 55	19 10			19 19	19 25	19 40	19 49	19 55	20 10		20 19	

Letchworth Garden City, Hertford North and Welwyn Garden City - London

Saturdays
25 June to 30 July

Station		FC	FC	FC ■	FC	FC	FC	FC	FC ■	FC		FC	FC	FC	FC ■	FC	FC	FC	FC	FC		FC
Letchworth Garden City	d																					
Hitchin ■	d			20 04					21 04						22 04							
Stevenage ■	d			20 10			20 29		21 10						22 10							
Watton-at-Stone	d						20 36															
Hertford North	d				20 12		20 42			21 12			21 42			22 12		22 42		23 12		23 42
Bayford	d				20 16		20 46			21 16			21 46			22 16		22 46		23 16		23 46
Cuffley	d				20 21		20 51			21 21			21 51			22 21		22 51		23 21		23 51
Crews Hill	d				20 24		20 54			21 24			21 54			22 24		22 54		23 24		23 54
Gordon Hill	d				20 27		20 57			21 27			21 57			22 27		22 57		23 27		23 57
Enfield Chase	d				20 29		20 59			21 29			21 59			22 29		22 59		23 29		23 59
Grange Park	d				20 31		21 01			21 31			22 01			22 31		23 01		23 31		00 01
Winchmore Hill	d				20 33		21 03			21 33			22 03			22 33		23 03		23 33		00 03
Palmers Green	d				20 35		21 05			21 35			22 05			22 35		23 05		23 35		00 05
Bowes Park	d				20 38		21 08			21 38			22 08			22 38		23 08		23 38		00 08
Knebworth	d			20 14					21 14						22 14							
Welwyn North	d			20 18					21 18						22 18							
Welwyn Garden City ■	d		19 58	20 21		20 28		20 58	21 21			21 28		21 58	22 21		22 28		22 58			
Hatfield	d		20 02	20 25		20 32		21 02	21 25			21 32		22 02	22 25		22 32		23 02			
Welham Green	d		20 06			20 36		21 06				21 36		22 06			22 36		23 06			
Brookmans Park	d		20 08			20 38		21 08				21 38		22 08			22 38		23 08			
Potters Bar	d		20 11	20 31		20 41		21 11	21 31			21 41		22 11	22 31		22 41		23 11			
Hadley Wood	d		20 15			20 45		21 15				21 45		22 15			22 45		23 15			
New Barnet	d		20 17			20 47		21 17				21 47		22 17			22 47		23 17			
Oakleigh Park	d		20 19			20 49		21 19				21 49		22 19			22 49		23 19			
New Southgate	d		20 22			20 52		21 22				21 52		22 22			22 52		23 22			
Alexandra Palace	d		20 25		20 40	20 55	21 10	21 25		21 40		21 55	22 10	22 25		22 40	22 55	23 10	23 25	23 40		00 10
Hornsey	d		20 27		20 42	20 57	21 12	21 27		21 42		21 57	22 12	22 27		22 42	22 57	23 12	23 27	23 42		00 12
Harringay	d	←	20 29		20 44	20 59	21 14	21 29		21 44		21 59	22 14	22 29		22 44	22 59	23 14	23 29	23 44		00 14
Finsbury Park	⊖ d	20 17	20 32	20 40	20 47	21 02	21 17	21 32	21 40	21 47		22 02	22 17	22 32	22 40	22 47	23 02	23 17	23 32	23 47		00 17
Drayton Park	d																					
Highbury & Islington	⊖ d																					
Essex Road	d																					
Old Street	⊖ d																					
Moorgate	⊖ a																					
London Kings Cross ■	⊖ a	20 25	20 40	20 47	20 55	21 10	21 25	21 40	21 47	21 55		22 10	22 25	22 40	22 47	22 55	23 10	23 25	23 40	23 55		00 25

Saturdays
6 August to 10 September

Station		FC ■	FC	FC ■	FC	FC ■	FC	FC ■	FC	FC		FC ■	FC	FC	FC ■	FC	FC	FC	FC ■	FC		FC	FC ■	FC	FC
Letchworth Garden City	d		23p18	23p47			04 50			05 20		05 29						06 20	06 29						
Hitchin ■	d	23p16	23p22	23p54		04 08	04 54	04 59		05 24		05 33			06 03			06 24	06 33				07 03		
Stevenage ■	d	23p22	23p27	23p59		04 14	04 59	05 05		05 29		05 39			06 09			06 29	06 39				07 09		
Watton-at-Stone	d		23p34				05 06			05 36								06 36							
Hertford North	d		23p40			04 24	05 12			05 42						06 12		06 42						07 12	
Bayford	d		23p44				05 16			05 46						06 16		06 46						07 16	
Cuffley	d		23p49			04 31	05 21			05 51						06 21		06 51						07 21	
Crews Hill	d		23p52				05 24			05 54						06 24		06 54						07 24	
Gordon Hill	d		23p55			04 36	05 27			05 57						06 27		06 57						07 27	
Enfield Chase	d		23p57			04 38	05 29			05 59						06 29		06 59						07 29	
Grange Park	d		23p59				05 31			06 01						06 31		07 01						07 31	
Winchmore Hill	d		00 01				05 33			06 03						06 33		07 03						07 33	
Palmers Green	d		00 03				05 35			06 05						06 35		07 05						07 35	
Bowes Park	d		00 06				05 38			06 08						06 38		07 08						07 38	
Knebworth	d	23p25		00 02				05 08				05 43			06 13				06 43				07 13		
Welwyn North	d	23p29		00 06				05 12				05 47			06 17				06 47				07 17		
Welwyn Garden City ■	d	23p32		00 09	04 10			05 15				05 51		05 58	06 21		06 28		06 51			06 58	07 21		07 28
Hatfield	d	23p35		00 12	04 14			05 19				05 55		06 02	06 25		06 32		06 55			07 02	07 25		07 32
Welham Green	d													06 06			06 36					07 06			07 36
Brookmans Park	d				04 19									06 08			06 38					07 08			07 38
Potters Bar	d	23p41		00 18	04 22			05 25				06 01		06 11	06 31		06 41		07 01			07 11	07 31		07 41
Hadley Wood	d				04 25									06 15			06 45					07 15			07 45
New Barnet	d				04 28			05 29						06 17			06 47					07 17			07 47
Oakleigh Park	d				04 30			05 31						06 19			06 49					07 19			07 49
New Southgate	d				04 33			05 34						06 22			06 52					07 22			07 52
Alexandra Palace	d		00 08		04 36		05 40	05 37		06 10				06 25		06 40	06 55	07 10				07 25		07 40	07 55
Hornsey	d		00 10		04 38	04 46	05 42			06 12				06 27		06 42	06 57	07 12				07 27		07 42	07 57
Harringay	d		00 12		04 40		05 44		←	06 14			←	06 29		06 44	06 59	07 14		←		07 29		07 44	07 59
Finsbury Park	⊖ d	23b51	00 15	00 29	04 42	04s49	05 47	05 42	05 47	06 17		06 10	06 17	06 32	06 40	06 47	07 02	07 17	07 10	07 17		07 32	07 40	07 47	08 02
Drayton Park	d						→			→								→							
Highbury & Islington	⊖ d																								
Essex Road	d																								
Old Street	⊖ d																								
Moorgate	⊖ a																								
London Kings Cross ■	⊖ a	00 01	00 26	00 42	04 51	05 02		05 56	05 55			06 20	06 25	06 40	06 47	06 55	07 10		07 19	07 25		07 40	07 47	07 55	08 10

b Previous night, stops to set down only

Saturdays
6 August to 10 September

Letchworth Garden City, Hertford North and Welwyn Garden City - London

Station		FC	FC ■	FC	FC	FC ■		FC	FC	FC	FC ■	FC	FC	FC ■	FC	FC		FC	FC ■	FC	FC	FC ■	FC	FC	FC
Letchworth Garden City	d		07 29								08 29								09 29						
Hitchin ■	d		07 33			08 03					08 33			09 03					09 34			10 03			
Stevenage ■	d	07 29	07 39			08 09				08 29	08 39			09 09				09 29	09 40			10 09			10 29
Watton-at-Stone	d	07 36								08 36								09 36							10 36
Hertford North	d	07 42						08 12		08 42					09 12			09 42				10 12		10 42
Bayford	d	07 46						08 16		08 46					09 16			09 46					10 16		10 46
Cuffley	d	07 51						08 21		08 51					09 21			09 51					10 21		10 51
Crews Hill	d	07 54						08 24		08 54					09 24			09 54					10 24		10 54
Gordon Hill	d	07 57						08 27		08 57					09 27			09 57					10 27		10 57
Enfield Chase	d	07 59						08 29		08 59					09 29			09 59					10 29		10 59
Grange Park	d	08 01						08 31		09 01					09 31			10 01					10 31		11 01
Winchmore Hill	d	08 03						08 33		09 03					09 33			10 03					10 33		11 03
Palmers Green	d	08 05						08 35		09 05					09 35			10 05					10 35		11 05
Bowes Park	d	08 08						08 38		09 08					09 38			10 08					10 38		11 08
Knebworth	d		07 43			08 13					08 43			09 13					09 43			10 13			
Welwyn North	d		07 47			08 17					08 47			09 17					09 47			10 17			
Welwyn Garden City ■	d		07 51		07 58	08 21			08 28		08 51		08 58	09 21		09 28			09 51		09 58	10 21		10 28	
Hatfield	d		07 55		08 02	08 25			08 32		08 55		09 02	09 25		09 32			09 55		10 02	10 25		10 32	
Welham Green	d				08 06				08 36				09 06			09 36					10 06			10 36	
Brookmans Park	d				08 08				08 38				09 08			09 38					10 08			10 38	
Potters Bar	d		08 01		08 11	08 31			08 41		09 01		09 11	09 31		09 41			10 01		10 11	10 31		10 41	
Hadley Wood	d				08 15				08 45				09 15			09 45					10 15			10 45	
New Barnet	d				08 17				08 47				09 17			09 47					10 17			10 47	
Oakleigh Park	d				08 19				08 49				09 19			09 49					10 19			10 49	
New Southgate	d				08 22				08 52				09 22			09 52					10 22			10 52	
Alexandra Palace	d	08 10			08 25			08 40	08 55	09 10			09 25		09 40	09 55		10 10			10 25		10 40	10 55	11 10
Hornsey	d	08 12			08 27			08 42	08 57	09 12			09 27		09 42	09 57		10 12			10 27		10 42	10 57	11 12
Harringay	d	08 14		←	08 29			08 44	08 59	09 14		←	09 29		09 44	09 59		10 14		←	10 29		10 44	10 59	11 14
Finsbury Park	⊖ d	08 17	08 10	08 17	08 32	08 40		08 47	09 02	09 17	09 10	09 17	09 32	09 40	09 47	10 02		10 17	10 10	10 17	10 32	10 40	10 47	11 02	11 17
Drayton Park	d	→								→								→							→
Highbury & Islington	⊖ d																								
Essex Road	d																								
Old Street	⊖ d																								
Moorgate	⊖ a																								
London Kings Cross ■	⊖ a		08 19	08 25	08 40	08 49		08 55	09 10		09 20	09 25	09 40	09 49	09 55	10 10			10 20	10 25	10 40	10 49	10 55	11 10	

Station		FC ■		FC	FC	FC ■	FC	FC	FC	FC ■	FC	FC		FC ■	FC	FC	FC	FC ■	FC	FC	FC ■	FC		FC	FC
Letchworth Garden City	d	10 29								11 29								12 29							
Hitchin ■	d	10 33				11 03				11 33				12 03				12 33			13 03				
Stevenage ■	d	10 39				11 09			11 29	11 39				12 09			12 29	12 39			13 09				13 29
Watton-at-Stone	d								11 36								12 36								13 36
Hertford North	d						11 12		11 42						12 12		12 42					13 12			13 42
Bayford	d						11 16		11 46						12 16		12 46					13 16			13 46
Cuffley	d						11 21		11 51						12 21		12 51					13 21			13 51
Crews Hill	d						11 24		11 54						12 24		12 54					13 24			13 54
Gordon Hill	d						11 27		11 57						12 27		12 57					13 27			13 57
Enfield Chase	d						11 29		11 59						12 29		12 59					13 29			13 59
Grange Park	d						11 31		12 01						12 31		13 01					13 31			14 01
Winchmore Hill	d						11 33		12 03						12 33		13 03					13 33			14 03
Palmers Green	d						11 35		12 05						12 35		13 05					13 35			14 05
Bowes Park	d						11 38		12 08						12 38		13 08					13 38			14 08
Knebworth	d	10 43				11 13				11 43				12 13				12 43			13 13				
Welwyn North	d	10 47				11 17				11 47				12 17				12 47			13 17				
Welwyn Garden City ■	d	10 51			10 58	11 21		11 28		11 51		11 58		12 21		12 28		12 51		12 58	13 21			13 28	
Hatfield	d	10 55			11 02	11 25		11 32		11 55		12 02		12 25		12 32		12 55		13 02	13 25			13 32	
Welham Green	d				11 06			11 36				12 06				12 36				13 06				13 36	
Brookmans Park	d				11 08			11 38				12 08				12 38				13 08				13 38	
Potters Bar	d	11 01			11 11	11 31		11 41		12 01		12 11		12 31		12 41		13 01		13 11	13 31			13 41	
Hadley Wood	d				11 15			11 45				12 15				12 45				13 15				13 45	
New Barnet	d				11 17			11 47				12 17				12 47				13 17				13 47	
Oakleigh Park	d				11 19			11 49				12 19				12 49				13 19				13 49	
New Southgate	d				11 22			11 52				12 22				12 52				13 22				13 52	
Alexandra Palace	d				11 25		11 40	11 55	12 10			12 25			12 40	12 55	13 10			13 25		13 40		13 55	14 10
Hornsey	d				11 27		11 42	11 57	12 12			12 27			12 42	12 57	13 12			13 27		13 42		13 57	14 12
Harringay	d			←	11 29		11 44	11 59	12 14		←	12 29			12 44	12 59	13 14		←	13 29		13 44		13 59	14 14
Finsbury Park	⊖ d	11 10		11 17	11 32	11 40	11 47	12 02	12 17	12 10	12 17	12 32		12 40	12 47	13 02	13 17	13 10	13 17	13 32	13 40	13 47		14 02	14 17
Drayton Park	d								→								→								→
Highbury & Islington	⊖ d																								
Essex Road	d																								
Old Street	⊖ d																								
Moorgate	⊖ a																								
London Kings Cross ■	⊖ a	11 20		11 25	11 40	11 49	11 55	12 10		12 19	12 25	12 40		12 49	12 55	13 10		13 19	13 25	13 40	13 49	13 55		14 10	

Letchworth Garden City, Hertford North and Welwyn Garden City - London

		FC [1]	FC	FC	FC [1]	FC	FC	FC		FC [1]	FC	FC	FC [1]	FC	FC	FC	FC [1]	FC		FC	FC [1]	FC	FC	FC	FC [1]
Letchworth Garden City	d	13 29								14 29							15 29								16 29
Hitchin [4]	d	13 33			14 03					14 33			15 03				15 33				16 03				16 33
Stevenage [4]	d	13 39			14 09			14 29		14 39			15 09			15 29	15 39				16 09			16 29	16 39
Watton-at-Stone	d							14 36								15 36								16 36	
Hertford North	d					14 12		14 42						15 12		15 42						16 12		16 42	
Bayford	d					14 16		14 46						15 16		15 46						16 16		16 46	
Cuffley	d					14 21		14 51						15 21		15 51						16 21		16 51	
Crews Hill	d					14 24		14 54						15 24		15 54						16 24		16 54	
Gordon Hill	d					14 27		14 57						15 27		15 57						16 27		16 57	
Enfield Chase	d					14 29		14 59						15 29		15 59						16 29		16 59	
Grange Park	d					14 31		15 01						15 31		16 01						16 31		17 01	
Winchmore Hill	d					14 33		15 03						15 33		16 03						16 33		17 03	
Palmers Green	d					14 35		15 05						15 35		16 05						16 35		17 05	
Bowes Park	d					14 38		15 08						15 38		16 08						16 38		17 08	
Knebworth	d	13 43			14 13					14 43			15 13				15 43				16 13				16 43
Welwyn North	d	13 47			14 17					14 47			15 17				15 47				16 17				16 47
Welwyn Garden City [4]	d	13 51		13 58	14 21		14 28			14 51		14 58	15 21		15 28		15 51			15 58	16 21		16 28		16 51
Hatfield	d	13 55		14 02	14 25		14 32			14 55		15 02	15 25		15 32		15 55			16 02	16 25		16 32		16 55
Welham Green	d			14 06			14 36					15 06			15 36					16 06			16 36		
Brookmans Park	d			14 08			14 38					15 08			15 38					16 08			16 38		
Potters Bar	d	14 01		14 11	14 31		14 41			15 01		15 11	15 31		15 41		16 01			16 11	16 31		16 41		17 01
Hadley Wood	d			14 15			14 45					15 15			15 45					16 15			16 45		
New Barnet	d			14 17			14 47					15 17			15 47					16 17			16 47		
Oakleigh Park	d			14 19			14 49					15 19			15 49					16 19			16 49		
New Southgate	d			14 22			14 52					15 22			15 52					16 22			16 52		
Alexandra Palace	d			14 25		14 40	14 55	15 10				15 25		15 40	15 55	16 10				16 25		16 40	16 55	17 10	
Hornsey	d			14 27		14 42	14 57	15 12				15 27		15 42	15 57	16 12				16 27		16 42	16 57	17 12	
Harringay	d		←	14 29		14 44	14 59	15 14			←	15 29		15 44	15 59	16 14		←		16 29		16 44	16 59	17 14	
Finsbury Park ⊖	d	14 10	14 17	14 33	14 40	14 47	15 02	15 17		15 10	15 17	15 32	15 40	15 47	16 02	16 17	16 10	16 17		16 32	16 40	16 47	17 04	17 17	17 10
Drayton Park	d							→								→								→	
Highbury & Islington ⊖	d																								
Essex Road	d																								
Old Street ⊖	d																								
Moorgate ⊖	a																								
London Kings Cross [15] ⊖	a	14 19	14 25	14 40	14 49	14 55	15 10			15 19	15 25	15 40	15 49	15 55	16 10		16 19	16 25		16 40	16 49	16 55	17 10		17 19

		FC	FC	FC [1]		FC	FC	FC	FC [1]	FC	FC	FC [1]	FC	FC		FC	FC [1]	FC	FC	FC [1]	FC	FC	FC	FC [1]	
Letchworth Garden City	d								17 29								18 29							19 29	
Hitchin [4]	d			17 03					17 34			18 03					18 33			19 03				19 33	
Stevenage [4]	d			17 09				17 29	17 40			18 09				18 29	18 39			19 09			19 29	19 39	
Watton-at-Stone	d							17 36								18 36							19 36		
Hertford North	d					17 12		17 42					18 12			18 42					19 12		19 42		
Bayford	d					17 16		17 46					18 16			18 46					19 16		19 46		
Cuffley	d					17 21		17 51					18 21			18 51					19 21		19 51		
Crews Hill	d					17 24		17 54					18 24			18 54					19 24		19 54		
Gordon Hill	d					17 27		17 57					18 27			18 57					19 27		19 57		
Enfield Chase	d					17 29		17 59					18 29			18 59					19 29		19 59		
Grange Park	d					17 31		18 01					18 31			19 01					19 31		20 01		
Winchmore Hill	d					17 33		18 03					18 33			19 03					19 33		20 03		
Palmers Green	d					17 35		18 05					18 35			19 05					19 35		20 05		
Bowes Park	d					17 38		18 08					18 38			19 08					19 38		20 08		
Knebworth	d			17 13					17 43			18 13					18 43			19 13				19 43	
Welwyn North	d			17 17					17 47			18 17					18 47			19 17				19 47	
Welwyn Garden City [4]	d		16 58	17 21			17 28		17 51		17 58	18 21		18 28			18 51		18 58	19 21		19 28		19 51	
Hatfield	d		17 02	17 25			17 32		17 55		18 02	18 25		18 32			18 55		19 02	19 25		19 32		19 55	
Welham Green	d		17 06				17 36				18 06			18 36					19 06			19 36			
Brookmans Park	d		17 08				17 38				18 08			18 38					19 08			19 38			
Potters Bar	d		17 11	17 31			17 41		18 01		18 11	18 31		18 41			19 01		19 11	19 31		19 41		20 01	
Hadley Wood	d		17 15				17 45				18 15			18 45					19 15			19 45			
New Barnet	d		17 17				17 47				18 17			18 47					19 17			19 47			
Oakleigh Park	d		17 19				17 49				18 19			18 49					19 19			19 49			
New Southgate	d		17 22				17 52				18 22			18 52					19 22			19 52			
Alexandra Palace	d		17 25			17 40	17 55	18 10			18 25		18 40	18 55		19 10			19 25		19 40	19 55	20 10		
Hornsey	d		17 27			17 42	17 57	18 12			18 27		18 42	18 57		19 12			19 27		19 42	19 57	20 12		
Harringay	d	←	17 29			17 44	17 59	18 14		←	18 29		18 44	18 59		19 14		←	19 29		19 44	19 59	20 14		
Finsbury Park ⊖	d	17 17	17 32	17 40		17 47	18 02	18 17	18 10	18 17	18 32	18 40	18 47	19 02		19 17	19 10	19 17	19 32	19 40	19 47	20 02	20 17	20 10	
Drayton Park	d							→								→							→		
Highbury & Islington ⊖	d																								
Essex Road	d																								
Old Street ⊖	d																								
Moorgate ⊖	a																								
London Kings Cross [15] ⊖	a	17 25	17 40	17 49		17 55	18 10		18 19	18 25	18 40	18 49	18 55	19 10			19 19	19 25	19 40	19 49	19 55	20 10		20 19	

Table 24

Saturdays

6 August to 10 September

Letchworth Garden City, Hertford North and Welwyn Garden City - London

		FC	FC	FC [1]	FC	FC	FC	FC [1]	FC	FC		FC [1]	FC	FC	FC [1]	FC	FC	FC [1]	FC	FC		FC [1]	FC	FC	FC [1]
Letchworth Garden City	d							20 29							21 29							22 29			
Hitchin [4]	d			20 03				20 34				21 03			21 34			22 03				22 34			23 03
Stevenage [4]	d			20 09			20 29	20 40				21 09			21 40			22 09				22 40			23 09
Watton-at-Stone	d						20 36																		
Hertford North	d				20 12		20 42						21 12			21 42			22 12				22 42		
Bayford	d				20 16		20 46						21 16			21 46			22 16				22 46		
Cuffley	d				20 21		20 51						21 21			21 51			22 21				22 51		
Crews Hill	d				20 24		20 54						21 24			21 54			22 24				22 54		
Gordon Hill	d				20 27		20 57						21 27			21 57			22 27				22 57		
Enfield Chase	d				20 29		20 59						21 29			21 59			22 29				22 59		
Grange Park	d				20 31		21 01						21 31			22 01			22 31				23 01		
Winchmore Hill	d				20 33		21 03						21 33			22 03			22 33				23 03		
Palmers Green	d				20 35		21 05						21 35			22 05			22 35				23 05		
Bowes Park	d				20 38		21 08						21 38			22 08			22 38				23 08		
Knebworth	d			20 13				20 46				21 13			21 43			22 13				22 43			23 13
Welwyn North	d			20 17				20 50				21 17			21 47			22 17				22 47			23 17
Welwyn Garden City [4]	d		19 58	20 21		20 28		20 53		20 58		21 21		21 28	21 51		21 58	22 21		22 28		22 51		22 58	23 21
Hatfield	d		20 02	20 25		20 32		20 57		21 02		21 25		21 32	21 55		22 02	22 25		22 32		22 55		23 02	23 25
Welham Green	d		20 06			20 36				21 06				21 36			22 06			22 36				23 06	
Brookmans Park	d		20 08			20 38				21 08				21 38			22 08			22 38				23 08	
Potters Bar	d		20 11	20 31		20 41		21 03		21 11		21 31		21 41	22 01		22 11	22 31		22 41		23 01		23 11	23 31
Hadley Wood	d		20 15			20 45				21 15				21 45			22 15			22 45				23 15	
New Barnet	d		20 17			20 47				21 17				21 47			22 17			22 47				23 17	
Oakleigh Park	d		20 19			20 49				21 19				21 49			22 19			22 49				23 19	
New Southgate	d		20 22			20 52				21 22				21 52			22 22			22 52				23 22	
Alexandra Palace	d		20 25		20 40	20 55	21 10			21 25			21 40	21 55		22 10	22 25		22 40	22 55			23 10	23 25	
Hornsey	d		20 27		20 42	20 57	21 12			21 27			21 42	21 57		22 12	22 27		22 42	22 57			23 12	23 27	
Harringay	d	←	20 29		20 44	20 59	21 14		←	21 29			21 44	21 59		22 14	22 29		22 44	22 59			23 14	23 29	
Finsbury Park ⊖	d	20 17	20 32	20 40	20 47	21 02	21 17	21 12	21 17	21 32		21 40	21 47	22 02	22 10	22 17	22 32	22 40	22 47	23 02		23 10	23 17	23 32	23 40
Drayton Park	d						→																		
Highbury & Islington ⊖	d																								
Essex Road	d																								
Old Street ⊖	d																								
Moorgate ⊖	a																								
London Kings Cross [15] ⊖	a	20 25	20 40	20 48	20 55	21 10		21 21	21 25	21 40		21 49	21 55	22 10	22 19	22 25	22 40	22 49	22 55	23 10		23 19	23 25	23 40	23 50

		FC	FC	FC [1]
Letchworth Garden City	d			23 46
Hitchin [4]	d			23 50
Stevenage [4]	d			23 55
Watton-at-Stone	d			
Hertford North	d	23 12	23 42	
Bayford	d	23 16	23 46	
Cuffley	d	23 21	23 51	
Crews Hill	d	23 24	23 54	
Gordon Hill	d	23 27	23 57	
Enfield Chase	d	23 29	23 59	
Grange Park	d	23 31	00 01	
Winchmore Hill	d	23 33	00 03	
Palmers Green	d	23 35	00 05	
Bowes Park	d	23 38	00 08	
Knebworth	d			23 59
Welwyn North	d			00 06
Welwyn Garden City [4]	d			00 09
Hatfield	d			00 13
Welham Green	d			
Brookmans Park	d			
Potters Bar	d			00 18
Hadley Wood	d			
New Barnet	d			
Oakleigh Park	d			
New Southgate	d			
Alexandra Palace	d	23 40	00 10	
Hornsey	d	23 42	00 12	
Harringay	d	23 44	00 14	
Finsbury Park ⊖	d	23 47	00 17	00s32
Drayton Park	d			
Highbury & Islington ⊖	d			
Essex Road	d			
Old Street ⊖	d			
Moorgate ⊖	a			
London Kings Cross [15] ⊖	a	23 55	00 25	00 40

Letchworth Garden City, Hertford North and Welwyn Garden City - London

		FC [1]	FC	FC [1]	FC	FC [1]	FC	FC [1]	FC	FC	FC [1]	FC	FC	FC [1]	FC	FC	FC	FC [1]	FC	FC	FC [1]	FC	FC
Letchworth Garden City	d		23p18	23p47			04 50			05 20	05 29						06 20	06 29					
Hitchin [4]	d	23p16	23p22	23p54		04 08	04 54	04 59		05 24	05 33			06 03			06 24	06 33			07 03		
Stevenage [4]	d	23p22	23p27	23p59		04 14	04 59	05 05		05 29	05 39			06 09			06 29	06 39			07 09		
Watton-at-Stone	d		23p34				05 06			05 36							06 36						
Hertford North	d		23p40			04 24	05 12			05 42					06 12		06 42					07 12	
Bayford	d		23p44				05 16			05 46					06 16		06 46					07 16	
Cuffley	d		23p49			04 31	05 21			05 51					06 21		06 51					07 21	
Crews Hill	d		23p52				05 24			05 54					06 24		06 54					07 24	
Gordon Hill	d		23p55			04 36	05 27			05 57					06 27		06 57					07 27	
Enfield Chase	d		23p57			04 38	05 29			05 59					06 29		06 59					07 29	
Grange Park	d		23p59				05 31			06 01					06 31		07 01					07 31	
Winchmore Hill	d		00 01				05 33			06 03					06 33		07 03					07 33	
Palmers Green	d		00 03				05 35			06 05					06 35		07 05					07 35	
Bowes Park	d		00 06				05 38			06 08					06 38		07 08					07 38	
Knebworth	d	23p25		00 02				05 08			05 43			06 13				06 43			07 13		
Welwyn North	d	23p29		00 06				05 12			05 47			06 17				06 47			07 17		
Welwyn Garden City [4]	d	23p32		00 09	04 10			05 15			05 51		05 58	06 21		06 28		06 51		06 58	07 21		07 28
Hatfield	d	23p35		00 12	04 14			05 19			05 55		06 02	06 25		06 32		06 55		07 02	07 25		07 32
Welham Green	d												06 06			06 36				07 06			07 36
Brookmans Park	d				04 19								06 08			06 38				07 08			07 38
Potters Bar	d	23p41		00 18	04 22			05 25			06 01		06 11	06 31		06 41		07 01		07 11	07 31		07 41
Hadley Wood	d				04 25								06 15			06 45				07 15			07 45
New Barnet	d				04 28			05 29					06 17			06 47				07 17			07 47
Oakleigh Park	d				04 30			05 31					06 19			06 49				07 19			07 49
New Southgate	d				04 33			05 34					06 22			06 52				07 22			07 52
Alexandra Palace	d		00 08		04 36		05 40	05 37		06 10			06 25		06 40	06 55	07 10			07 25		07 40	07 55
Hornsey	d		00 10		04 38	04 46	05 42			06 12			06 27		06 42	06 57	07 12			07 27		07 42	07 57
Harringay	d		00 12		04 40		05 44		←	06 14		←	06 29		06 44	06 59	07 14		←	07 29		07 44	07 59
Finsbury Park ⊖	d	23b51	00 15	00 29	04 42	04s49	05 47	05 42	05 47	06 17	06 10	06 17	06 32	06 40	06 47	07 02	07 17	07 10	07 17	07 32	07 40	07 47	08 02
Drayton Park	d						→			→							→						
Highbury & Islington ⊖	d																						
Essex Road	d																						
Old Street ⊖	d																						
Moorgate ⊖	a																						
London Kings Cross [15] ⊖	a	00 01	00 26	00 42	04 51	05 02		05 56	05 55		06 20	06 25	06 40	06 47	06 55	07 10		07 19	07 25	07 40	07 47	07 55	08 10

		FC	FC [1]	FC	FC	FC [1]	FC	FC	FC	FC [1]	FC	FC	FC [1]	FC	FC	FC	FC [1]	FC	FC	FC [1]	FC	FC	FC
Letchworth Garden City	d		07 29							08 29							09 29						
Hitchin [4]	d		07 33			08 03				08 33			09 03				09 34			10 03			
Stevenage [4]	d	07 29	07 39			08 09			08 29	08 39			09 09			09 29	09 40			10 09			10 29
Watton-at-Stone	d	07 36							08 36							09 36							10 36
Hertford North	d	07 42					08 12		08 42					09 12		09 42					10 12		10 42
Bayford	d	07 46					08 16		08 46					09 16		09 46					10 16		10 46
Cuffley	d	07 51					08 21		08 51					09 21		09 51					10 21		10 51
Crews Hill	d	07 54					08 24		08 54					09 24		09 54					10 24		10 54
Gordon Hill	d	07 57					08 27		08 57					09 27		09 57					10 27		10 57
Enfield Chase	d	07 59					08 29		08 59					09 29		09 59					10 29		10 59
Grange Park	d	08 01					08 31		09 01					09 31		10 01					10 31		11 01
Winchmore Hill	d	08 03					08 33		09 03					09 33		10 03					10 33		11 03
Palmers Green	d	08 05					08 35		09 05					09 35		10 05					10 35		11 05
Bowes Park	d	08 08					08 38		09 08					09 38		10 08					10 38		11 08
Knebworth	d		07 43			08 13				08 43			09 13				09 43			10 13			
Welwyn North	d		07 47			08 17				08 47			09 17				09 47			10 17			
Welwyn Garden City [4]	d		07 51		07 58	08 21		08 28		08 51		08 58	09 21		09 28		09 51		09 58	10 21		10 28	
Hatfield	d		07 55		08 02	08 25		08 32		08 55		09 02	09 25		09 32		09 55		10 02	10 25		10 32	
Welham Green	d				08 06			08 36				09 06			09 36				10 06			10 36	
Brookmans Park	d				08 08			08 38				09 08			09 38				10 08			10 38	
Potters Bar	d		08 01		08 11	08 31		08 41		09 01		09 11	09 31		09 41		10 01		10 11	10 31		10 41	
Hadley Wood	d				08 15			08 45				09 15			09 45				10 15			10 45	
New Barnet	d				08 17			08 47				09 17			09 47				10 17			10 47	
Oakleigh Park	d				08 19			08 49				09 19			09 49				10 19			10 49	
New Southgate	d				08 22			08 52				09 22			09 52				10 22			10 52	
Alexandra Palace	d	08 10			08 25		08 40	08 55	09 10			09 25		09 40	09 55	10 10			10 25		10 40	10 55	11 10
Hornsey	d	08 12			08 27		08 42	08 57	09 12			09 27		09 42	09 57	10 12			10 27		10 42	10 57	11 12
Harringay	d	08 14		←	08 29		08 44	08 59	09 14		←	09 29		09 44	09 59	10 14		←	10 29		10 44	10 59	11 14
Finsbury Park ⊖	d	08 17	08 10	08 17	08 32	08 40	08 47	09 02	09 17	09 10	09 17	09 32	09 40	09 47	10 02	10 17	10 10	10 17	10 32	10 40	10 47	11 02	11 17
Drayton Park	d	→							→							→							→
Highbury & Islington ⊖	d																						
Essex Road	d																						
Old Street ⊖	d																						
Moorgate ⊖	a																						
London Kings Cross [15] ⊖	a		08 19	08 25	08 40	08 49	08 55	09 10		09 20	09 25	09 40	09 49	09 55	10 10		10 20	10 25	10 40	10 49	10 55	11 10	

b Previous night, stops to set down only

Table 24

Saturdays
from 24 September

Letchworth Garden City, Hertford North and Welwyn Garden City - London

		FC [1]	FC	FC	FC [1]	FC	FC	FC	FC [1]	FC	FC	FC [1]	FC	FC	FC	FC [1]	FC	FC	FC [1]	FC	FC	FC
Letchworth Garden City	d	10 29							11 29							12 29						
Hitchin [4]	d	10 33			11 03				11 33			12 03				12 33			13 03			
Stevenage [4]	d	10 39			11 09			11 29	11 39			12 09			12 29	12 39			13 09			13 29
Watton-at-Stone	d							11 36							12 36							13 36
Hertford North	d					11 12		11 42					12 12		12 42					13 12		13 42
Bayford	d					11 16		11 46					12 16		12 46					13 16		13 46
Cuffley	d					11 21		11 51					12 21		12 51					13 21		13 51
Crews Hill	d					11 24		11 54					12 24		12 54					13 24		13 54
Gordon Hill	d					11 27		11 57					12 27		12 57					13 27		13 57
Enfield Chase	d					11 29		11 59					12 29		12 59					13 29		13 59
Grange Park	d					11 31		12 01					12 31		13 01					13 31		14 01
Winchmore Hill	d					11 33		12 03					12 33		13 03					13 33		14 03
Palmers Green	d					11 35		12 05					12 35		13 05					13 35		14 05
Bowes Park	d					11 38		12 08					12 38		13 08					13 38		14 08
Knebworth	d	10 43			11 13				11 43			12 13				12 43			13 13			
Welwyn North	d	10 47			11 17				11 47			12 17				12 47			13 17			
Welwyn Garden City [4]	d	10 51		10 58	11 21		11 28		11 51		11 58	12 21		12 28		12 51		12 58	13 21		13 28	
Hatfield	d	10 55		11 02	11 25		11 32		11 55		12 02	12 25		12 32		12 55		13 02	13 25		13 32	
Welham Green	d			11 06			11 36				12 06			12 36				13 06			13 36	
Brookmans Park	d			11 08			11 38				12 08			12 38				13 08			13 38	
Potters Bar	d	11 01		11 11	11 31		11 41		12 01		12 11	12 31		12 41		13 01		13 11	13 31		13 41	
Hadley Wood	d			11 15			11 45				12 15			12 45				13 15			13 45	
New Barnet	d			11 17			11 47				12 17			12 47				13 17			13 47	
Oakleigh Park	d			11 19			11 49				12 19			12 49				13 19			13 49	
New Southgate	d			11 22			11 52				12 22			12 52				13 22			13 52	
Alexandra Palace	d			11 25		11 40	11 55	12 10			12 25		12 40	12 55	13 10			13 25		13 40	13 55	14 10
Hornsey	d			11 27		11 42	11 57	12 12			12 27		12 42	12 57	13 12			13 27		13 42	13 57	14 12
Harringay	d		←	11 29		11 44	11 59	12 14		←	12 29		12 44	12 59	13 14		←	13 29		13 44	13 59	14 14
Finsbury Park ⊖	d	11 10	11 17	11 32	11 40	11 47	12 02	12 17	12 10	12 17	12 32	12 40	12 47	13 02	13 17	13 10	13 17	13 32	13 40	13 47	14 02	14 17
Drayton Park	d							→							→							→
Highbury & Islington ⊖	d																					
Essex Road	d																					
Old Street ⊖	d																					
Moorgate ⊖	a																					
London Kings Cross [15] ⊖	a	11 20	11 25	11 40	11 49	11 55	12 10		12 19	12 25	12 40	12 49	12 55	13 10		13 19	13 25	13 40	13 49	13 55	14 10	

		FC [1]	FC	FC	FC [1]	FC	FC	FC	FC [1]	FC	FC	FC [1]	FC	FC	FC	FC [1]	FC	FC	FC [1]	FC	FC	FC	FC [1]
Letchworth Garden City	d	13 29							14 29							15 29							16 29
Hitchin [4]	d	13 33			14 03				14 33			15 03				15 33			16 03				16 33
Stevenage [4]	d	13 39			14 09			14 29	14 39			15 09			15 29	15 39			16 09			16 29	16 39
Watton-at-Stone	d							14 36							15 36							16 36	
Hertford North	d					14 12		14 42					15 12		15 42					16 12		16 42	
Bayford	d					14 16		14 46					15 16		15 46					16 16		16 46	
Cuffley	d					14 21		14 51					15 21		15 51					16 21		16 51	
Crews Hill	d					14 24		14 54					15 24		15 54					16 24		16 54	
Gordon Hill	d					14 27		14 57					15 27		15 57					16 27		16 57	
Enfield Chase	d					14 29		14 59					15 29		15 59					16 29		16 59	
Grange Park	d					14 31		15 01					15 31		16 01					16 31		17 01	
Winchmore Hill	d					14 33		15 03					15 33		16 03					16 33		17 03	
Palmers Green	d					14 35		15 05					15 35		16 05					16 35		17 05	
Bowes Park	d					14 38		15 08					15 38		16 08					16 38		17 08	
Knebworth	d	13 43			14 13				14 43			15 13				15 43			16 13				16 43
Welwyn North	d	13 47			14 17				14 47			15 17				15 47			16 17				16 47
Welwyn Garden City [4]	d	13 51		13 58	14 21		14 28		14 51		14 58	15 21		15 28		15 51		15 58	16 21		16 28		16 51
Hatfield	d	13 55		14 02	14 25		14 32		14 55		15 02	15 25		15 32		15 55		16 02	16 25		16 32		16 55
Welham Green	d			14 06			14 36				15 06			15 36				16 06			16 36		
Brookmans Park	d			14 08			14 38				15 08			15 38				16 08			16 38		
Potters Bar	d	14 01		14 11	14 31		14 41		15 01		15 11	15 31		15 41		16 01		16 11	16 31		16 41		17 01
Hadley Wood	d			14 15			14 45				15 15			15 45				16 15			16 45		
New Barnet	d			14 17			14 47				15 17			15 47				16 17			16 47		
Oakleigh Park	d			14 19			14 49				15 19			15 49				16 19			16 49		
New Southgate	d			14 22			14 52				15 22			15 52				16 22			16 52		
Alexandra Palace	d			14 25		14 40	14 55	15 10			15 25		15 40	15 55	16 10			16 25		16 40	16 55	17 10	
Hornsey	d			14 27		14 42	14 57	15 12			15 27		15 42	15 57	16 12			16 27		16 42	16 57	17 12	
Harringay	d		←	14 29		14 44	14 59	15 14		←	15 29		15 44	15 59	16 14		←	16 29		16 44	16 59	17 14	
Finsbury Park ⊖	d	14 10	14 17	14 33	14 40	14 47	15 02	15 17	15 10	15 17	15 32	15 40	15 47	16 02	16 17	16 10	16 17	16 32	16 40	16 47	17 04	17 17	17 10
Drayton Park	d							→							→							→	
Highbury & Islington ⊖	d																						
Essex Road	d																						
Old Street ⊖	d																						
Moorgate ⊖	a																						
London Kings Cross [15] ⊖	a	14 19	14 25	14 40	14 49	14 55	15 10		15 19	15 25	15 40	15 49	15 55	16 10		16 19	16 25		16 40	16 49	16 55	17 10	17 19

Table 24

Saturdays from 24 September

Letchworth Garden City, Hertford North and Welwyn Garden City - London

		FC	FC	FC 1	FC	FC	FC	FC 1	FC	FC	FC 1	FC	FC	FC	FC 1	FC	FC	FC 1	FC	FC	FC	FC 1
Letchworth Garden City	d							17 29							18 29							19 29
Hitchin [4]	d			17 03				17 34			18 03				18 33			19 03				19 33
Stevenage [4]	d			17 09			17 29	17 40			18 09			18 29	18 39			19 09			19 29	19 39
Watton-at-Stone	d						17 36							18 36							19 36	
Hertford North	d				17 12		17 42					18 12		18 42					19 12		19 42	
Bayford	d				17 16		17 46					18 16		18 46					19 16		19 46	
Cuffley	d				17 21		17 51					18 21		18 51					19 21		19 51	
Crews Hill	d				17 24		17 54					18 24		18 54					19 24		19 54	
Gordon Hill	d				17 27		17 57					18 27		18 57					19 27		19 57	
Enfield Chase	d				17 29		17 59					18 29		18 59					19 29		19 59	
Grange Park	d				17 31		18 01					18 31		19 01					19 31		20 01	
Winchmore Hill	d				17 33		18 03					18 33		19 03					19 33		20 03	
Palmers Green	d				17 35		18 05					18 35		19 05					19 35		20 05	
Bowes Park	d				17 38		18 08					18 38		19 08					19 38		20 08	
Knebworth	d			17 13				17 43			18 13				18 43			19 13				19 43
Welwyn North	d			17 17				17 47			18 17				18 47			19 17				19 47
Welwyn Garden City [4]	d		16 58	17 21		17 28		17 51		17 58	18 21		18 28		18 51		18 58	19 21		19 28		19 51
Hatfield	d		17 02	17 25		17 32		17 55		18 02	18 25		18 32		18 55		19 02	19 25		19 32		19 55
Welham Green	d		17 06			17 36				18 06			18 36				19 06			19 36		
Brookmans Park	d		17 08			17 38				18 08			18 38				19 08			19 38		
Potters Bar	d		17 11	17 31		17 41		18 01		18 11	18 31		18 41		19 01		19 11	19 31		19 41		20 01
Hadley Wood	d		17 15			17 45				18 15			18 45				19 15			19 45		
New Barnet	d		17 17			17 47				18 17			18 47				19 17			19 47		
Oakleigh Park	d		17 19			17 49				18 19			18 49				19 19			19 49		
New Southgate	d		17 22			17 52				18 22			18 52				19 22			19 52		
Alexandra Palace	d		17 25		17 40	17 55	18 10			18 25		18 40	18 55	19 10			19 25		19 40	19 55	20 10	
Hornsey	d		17 27		17 42	17 57	18 12			18 27		18 42	18 57	19 12			19 27		19 42	19 57	20 12	
Harringay	d	←	17 29		17 44	17 59	18 14		←	18 29		18 44	18 59	19 14		←	19 29		19 44	19 59	20 14	
Finsbury Park ⊖	d	17 17	17 32	17 40	17 47	18 02	18 17	18 10	18 17	18 32	18 40	18 47	19 02	19 17	19 10	19 17	19 32	19 40	19 47	20 02	20 17	20 10
Drayton Park	d						→							→							→	
Highbury & Islington ⊖	d																					
Essex Road	d																					
Old Street ⊖	d																					
Moorgate ⊖	a																					
London Kings Cross [15] ⊖	a	17 25	17 40	17 49	17 55	18 10		18 19	18 25	18 40	18 49	18 55	19 10		19 19	19 25	19 40	19 49	19 55	20 10		20 19

		FC	FC	FC 1	FC	FC	FC	FC 1	FC	FC	FC 1	FC	FC	FC 1	FC	FC	FC 1	FC	FC	FC 1	FC	FC	FC 1
Letchworth Garden City	d							20 29						21 29						22 29			
Hitchin [4]	d			20 03				20 34			21 03			21 34			22 03			22 34			23 03
Stevenage [4]	d			20 09			20 29	20 40			21 09			21 40			22 09			22 40			23 09
Watton-at-Stone	d						20 36																
Hertford North	d				20 12		20 42					21 12			21 42			22 12			22 42		
Bayford	d				20 16		20 46					21 16			21 46			22 16			22 46		
Cuffley	d				20 21		20 51					21 21			21 51			22 21			22 51		
Crews Hill	d				20 24		20 54					21 24			21 54			22 24			22 54		
Gordon Hill	d				20 27		20 57					21 27			21 57			22 27			22 57		
Enfield Chase	d				20 29		20 59					21 29			21 59			22 29			22 59		
Grange Park	d				20 31		21 01					21 31			22 01			22 31			23 01		
Winchmore Hill	d				20 33		21 03					21 33			22 03			22 33			23 03		
Palmers Green	d				20 35		21 05					21 35			22 05			22 35			23 05		
Bowes Park	d				20 38		21 08					21 38			22 08			22 38			23 08		
Knebworth	d			20 13				20 46			21 13			21 43			22 13			22 43			23 13
Welwyn North	d			20 17				20 50			21 17			21 47			22 17			22 47			23 17
Welwyn Garden City [4]	d		19 58	20 21		20 28		20 53		20 58	21 21		21 28	21 51		21 58	22 21		22 28	22 51		22 58	23 21
Hatfield	d		20 02	20 25		20 32		20 57		21 02	21 25		21 32	21 55		22 02	22 25		22 32	22 55		23 02	23 25
Welham Green	d		20 06			20 36				21 06			21 36			22 06			22 36			23 06	
Brookmans Park	d		20 08			20 38				21 08			21 38			22 08			22 38			23 08	
Potters Bar	d		20 11	20 31		20 41		21 03		21 11	21 31		21 41	22 01		22 11	22 31		22 41	23 01		23 11	23 31
Hadley Wood	d		20 15			20 45				21 15			21 45			22 15			22 45			23 15	
New Barnet	d		20 17			20 47				21 17			21 47			22 17			22 47			23 17	
Oakleigh Park	d		20 19			20 49				21 19			21 49			22 19			22 49			23 19	
New Southgate	d		20 22			20 52				21 22			21 52			22 22			22 52			23 22	
Alexandra Palace	d		20 25		20 40	20 55	21 10			21 25		21 40	21 55		22 10	22 25		22 40	22 55		23 10	23 25	
Hornsey	d		20 27		20 42	20 57	21 12			21 27		21 42	21 57		22 12	22 27		22 42	22 57		23 12	23 27	
Harringay	d	←	20 29		20 44	20 59	21 14		←	21 29		21 44	21 59		22 14	22 29		22 44	22 59		23 14	23 29	
Finsbury Park ⊖	d	20 17	20 32	20 40	20 47	21 02	21 17	21 12	21 17	21 32	21 40	21 47	22 02	22 10	22 17	22 32	22 40	22 47	23 02	23 10	23 17	23 32	23 40
Drayton Park	d						→																
Highbury & Islington ⊖	d																						
Essex Road	d																						
Old Street ⊖	d																						
Moorgate ⊖	a																						
London Kings Cross [15] ⊖	a	20 25	20 40	20 48	20 55	21 10		21 21	21 25	21 40	21 49	21 55	22 10	22 19	22 25	22 40	22 49	22 55	23 10	23 19	23 25	23 40	23 50

Table 24

Saturdays from 24 September

Letchworth Garden City, Hertford North and Welwyn Garden City - London

		FC	FC	FC 1
Letchworth Garden City	d			23 46
Hitchin [4]	d			23 50
Stevenage [4]	d			23 55
Watton-at-Stone	d			
Hertford North	d	23 12	23 42	
Bayford	d	23 16	23 46	
Cuffley	d	23 21	23 51	
Crews Hill	d	23 24	23 54	
Gordon Hill	d	23 27	23 57	
Enfield Chase	d	23 29	23 59	
Grange Park	d	23 31	00 01	
Winchmore Hill	d	23 33	00 03	
Palmers Green	d	23 35	00 05	
Bowes Park	d	23 38	00 08	
Knebworth	d			23 59
Welwyn North	d			00 06
Welwyn Garden City [4]	d			00 09
Hatfield	d			00 13
Welham Green	d			
Brookmans Park	d			
Potters Bar	d			00 18
Hadley Wood	d			
New Barnet	d			
Oakleigh Park	d			
New Southgate	d			
Alexandra Palace	d	23 40	00 10	
Hornsey	d	23 42	00 12	
Harringay	d	23 44	00 14	
Finsbury Park ⊖	d	23 47	00 17	00s32
Drayton Park	d			
Highbury & Islington ⊖	d			
Essex Road	d			
Old Street ⊖	d			
Moorgate ⊖	a			
London Kings Cross [15] ⊖	a	23 55	00 25	00 40

Sundays until 19 June

		FC A	FC 1 A	FC	FC	FC 1	FC	FC	FC	FC	FC	FC 1	FC	FC	FC	FC	FC	FC 1	FC	FC	FC	FC	FC
Letchworth Garden City	d		23p46															08 29					
Hitchin [4]	d		23p50			06 34						07 34						08 33					
Stevenage [4]	d		23p55			06 40					07 29	07 40					08 29	08 39					09 29
Watton-at-Stone	d										07 36						08 36						09 36
Hertford North	d	23p42		06 12			06 42		07 12		07 42				08 12		08 42				09 12		09 42
Bayford	d	23p46		06 16			06 46		07 16		07 46				08 16		08 46				09 16		09 46
Cuffley	d	23p51		06 21			06 51		07 21		07 51				08 21		08 51				09 21		09 51
Crews Hill	d	23p54		06 24			06 54		07 24		07 54				08 24		08 54				09 24		09 54
Gordon Hill	d	23p57		06 27			06 57		07 27		07 57				08 27		08 57				09 27		09 57
Enfield Chase	d	23p59		06 29			06 59		07 29		07 59				08 29		08 59				09 29		09 59
Grange Park	d	00 01		06 31			07 01		07 31		08 01				08 31		09 01				09 31		10 01
Winchmore Hill	d	00 03		06 33			07 03		07 33		08 03				08 33		09 03				09 33		10 03
Palmers Green	d	00 05		06 35			07 05		07 35		08 05				08 35		09 05				09 35		10 05
Bowes Park	d	00 08		06 38			07 08		07 38		08 08				08 38		09 08				09 38		10 08
Knebworth	d		23p59			06 43						07 43						08 43					
Welwyn North	d		00 06			06 47						07 47						08 47					
Welwyn Garden City [4]	d		00 09		06 28	06 51		06 58		07 28		07 51		07 58		08 28		08 51		08 58		09 28	
Hatfield	d		00 13		06 32	06 54		07 02		07 32		07 54		08 02		08 32		08 54		09 02		09 32	
Welham Green	d				06 36			07 06		07 36				08 06		08 36				09 06		09 36	
Brookmans Park	d				06 38			07 08		07 38				08 08		08 38				09 08		09 38	
Potters Bar	d		00 18		06 41	07 00		07 11		07 41		08 00		08 11		08 41		09 00		09 11		09 41	
Hadley Wood	d				06 45			07 15		07 45				08 15		08 45				09 15		09 45	
New Barnet	d				06 47			07 17		07 47				08 17		08 47				09 17		09 47	
Oakleigh Park	d				06 49			07 19		07 49				08 19		08 49				09 19		09 49	
New Southgate	d				06 52			07 22		07 52				08 22		08 52				09 22		09 52	
Alexandra Palace	d	00 10		06 40	06 55		07 10	07 25	07 40	07 55	08 11			08 25	08 40	08 55	09 10			09 25	09 40	09 55	10 11
Hornsey	d	00 12		06 42	06 57		07 12	07 27	07 42	07 57	08 13			08 27	08 42	08 57	09 12			09 27	09 42	09 57	10 13
Harringay	d	00 14		06 44	06 59		07 14	07 29	07 44	07 59	08 15		←	08 29	08 44	08 59	09 14		←	09 29	09 44	09 59	10 15
Finsbury Park ⊖	d	00 17	00s32	06 47	07 02	07 10	07 17	07 32	07 47	08 02	08 17	08 10	08 17	08 32	08 47	09 02	09 17	09 10	09 17	09 32	09 47	10 02	10 17
Drayton Park	d										→						→						→
Highbury & Islington ⊖	d																						
Essex Road	d																						
Old Street ⊖	d																						
Moorgate ⊖	a																						
London Kings Cross [15] ⊖	a	00 25	00 40	06 57	07 13	07 20	07 29	07 45	07 56	08 15		08 20	08 26	08 40	08 55	09 10		09 19	09 25	09 40	09 55	10 10	

A not 22 May

Table 24

Letchworth Garden City, Hertford North and Welwyn Garden City - London

		FC [1]	FC	FC	FC [1]	FC		FC	FC	FC [1]	FC	FC	FC	FC	FC	FC [1]		FC	FC	FC	FC	FC [1]	FC	FC	FC
Letchworth Garden City	d	09 29			10 00					10 29						11 29						12 29			
Hitchin [4]	d	09 33			10 04					10 33						11 33						12 33			
Stevenage [4]	d	09 39			10 10				10 29	10 39					11 29	11 39						12 39			
Watton-at-Stone	d								10 36						11 36										
Hertford North	d					10 12			10 42				11 12		11 42					12 12			12 42		13 12
Bayford	d					10 16			10 46				11 16		11 46					12 16			12 46		13 16
Cuffley	d					10 21			10 51				11 21		11 51					12 21			12 51		13 21
Crews Hill	d					10 24			10 54				11 24		11 54					12 24			12 54		13 24
Gordon Hill	d					10 27			10 57				11 27		11 57					12 27			12 57		13 27
Enfield Chase	d					10 29			10 59				11 29		11 59					12 29			12 59		13 29
Grange Park	d					10 31			11 01				11 31		12 01					12 31			13 01		13 31
Winchmore Hill	d					10 33			11 03				11 33		12 03					12 33			13 03		13 33
Palmers Green	d					10 35			11 05				11 35		12 05					12 35			13 05		13 35
Bowes Park	d					10 38			11 08				11 38		12 08					12 38			13 08		13 38
Knebworth	d	09 43			10 13					10 43						11 43						12 43			
Welwyn North	d	09 47			10 17					10 47						11 47						12 47			
Welwyn Garden City [4]	d	09 51		09 58	10 21			10 28		10 50		10 58		11 28		11 51			11 58		12 28	12 50		12 58	
Hatfield	d	09 54		10 02	10 24			10 32		10 54		11 02		11 32		11 54			12 02		12 32	12 54		13 02	
Welham Green	d			10 06				10 36				11 06		11 36					12 06		12 36			13 06	
Brookmans Park	d			10 08				10 38				11 08		11 38					12 08		12 38			13 08	
Potters Bar	d	10 00		10 11	10 30			10 41		10 59		11 11		11 41		12 00			12 11		12 41	13 00		13 11	
Hadley Wood	d			10 15				10 45				11 15		11 45					12 15		12 45			13 15	
New Barnet	d			10 17				10 47				11 17		11 47					12 17		12 47			13 17	
Oakleigh Park	d			10 19				10 49				11 19		11 49					12 19		12 49			13 19	
New Southgate	d			10 22				10 52				11 22		11 52					12 22		12 52			13 22	
Alexandra Palace	d			10 25		10 41		10 55	11 10			11 25	11 40	11 55	12 10				12 25	12 40	12 55		13 10	13 25	13 40
Hornsey	d			10 27		10 43		10 57	11 12			11 27	11 42	11 57	12 12				12 27	12 42	12 57		13 12	13 27	13 42
Harringay	d		←	10 29		10 45		10 59	11 14		←	11 29	11 44	11 59	12 14			←	12 29	12 44	12 59		13 14	13 29	13 44
Finsbury Park ⊖	d	10 10	10 17	10 32	10 40	10 47		11 02	11 17	11 11	11 17	11 32	11 47	12 02	12 17	12 10		12 17	12 32	12 47	13 02	13 11	13 17	13 32	13 47
Drayton Park	d								→						→										
Highbury & Islington ⊖	d																								
Essex Road	d																								
Old Street ⊖	d																								
Moorgate ⊖	a																								
London Kings Cross [15] ⊖	a	10 19	10 25	10 40	10 49	10 55		11 10		11 20	11 25	11 40	11 55	12 10		12 19		12 25	12 40	12 55	13 10	13 19	13 25	13 40	13 55

		FC		FC	FC [1]	FC	FC	FC	FC	FC	FC [1]	FC		FC	FC	FC	FC	FC [1]	FC	FC	FC	FC		FC	FC [1]
Letchworth Garden City	d				13 29						14 29							15 29							16 29
Hitchin [4]	d				13 34						14 34							15 34							16 34
Stevenage [4]	d			13 29	13 40					14 29	14 40						15 29	15 40						16 29	16 40
Watton-at-Stone	d			13 36						14 36							15 36							16 36	
Hertford North	d			13 42				14 12		14 42					15 12		15 42				16 12			16 42	
Bayford	d			13 46				14 16		14 46					15 16		15 46				16 16			16 46	
Cuffley	d			13 51				14 21		14 51					15 21		15 51				16 21			16 51	
Crews Hill	d			13 54				14 24		14 54					15 24		15 54				16 24			16 54	
Gordon Hill	d			13 57				14 27		14 57					15 27		15 57				16 27			16 57	
Enfield Chase	d			13 59				14 29		14 59					15 29		15 59				16 29			16 59	
Grange Park	d			14 01				14 31		15 01					15 31		16 01				16 31			17 01	
Winchmore Hill	d			14 03				14 33		15 03					15 33		16 03				16 33			17 03	
Palmers Green	d			14 05				14 35		15 05					15 35		16 05				16 35			17 05	
Bowes Park	d			14 08				14 38		15 08					15 38		16 08				16 38			17 08	
Knebworth	d				13 43						14 43							15 43							16 43
Welwyn North	d				13 47						14 47							15 47							16 47
Welwyn Garden City [4]	d	13 28			13 51		13 58		14 28		14 51			14 58		15 28		15 51		15 58		16 28			16 51
Hatfield	d	13 32			13 54		14 02		14 32		14 54			15 02		15 32		15 54		16 02		16 32			16 54
Welham Green	d	13 36					14 06		14 36					15 06		15 36				16 06		16 36			
Brookmans Park	d	13 38					14 08		14 38					15 08		15 38				16 08		16 38			
Potters Bar	d	13 41			14 00		14 11		14 41		15 00			15 11		15 41		16 00		16 11		16 41			17 00
Hadley Wood	d	13 45					14 15		14 45					15 15		15 45				16 15		16 45			
New Barnet	d	13 47					14 17		14 47					15 17		15 47				16 17		16 47			
Oakleigh Park	d	13 49					14 19		14 49					15 19		15 49				16 19		16 49			
New Southgate	d	13 52					14 22		14 52					15 22		15 52				16 22		16 52			
Alexandra Palace	d	13 55		14 10			14 25	14 40	14 55	15 10				15 25	15 40	15 55	16 10			16 25	16 40	16 55		17 10	
Hornsey	d	13 57		14 12			14 27	14 42	14 57	15 12				15 27	15 42	15 57	16 12			16 27	16 42	16 57		17 12	
Harringay	d	13 59		14 14		←	14 29	14 44	14 59	15 14		←		15 29	15 44	15 59	16 14		←	16 29	16 44	16 59		17 14	
Finsbury Park ⊖	d	14 02		14 17	14 11	14 17	14 32	14 47	15 02	15 17	15 10	15 17		15 32	15 47	16 02	16 17	16 10	16 17	16 32	16 47	17 02		17 17	17 10
Drayton Park	d			→						→							→							→	
Highbury & Islington ⊖	d																								
Essex Road	d																								
Old Street ⊖	d																								
Moorgate ⊖	a																								
London Kings Cross [15] ⊖	a	14 10			14 19	14 25	14 40	14 55	15 10		15 19	15 25		15 40	15 55	16 10		16 19	16 25	16 40	16 55	17 10			17 19

Table 24

Letchworth Garden City, Hertford North and Welwyn Garden City - London

		FC	FC	FC	FC	FC	FC [1]	FC		FC	FC	FC	FC	FC [1]	FC	FC	FC	FC		FC	FC [1]	FC	FC	FC	FC
Letchworth Garden City	d						17 29							18 29							19 29				
Hitchin [4]	d						17 34							18 34							19 34				
Stevenage [4]	d					17 29	17 40						18 29	18 40						19 29	19 40				
Watton-at-Stone	d					17 36							18 36							19 36					
Hertford North	d			17 12		17 42					18 12		18 42				19 12			19 42				20 12	
Bayford	d			17 16		17 46					18 16		18 46				19 16			19 46				20 16	
Cuffley	d			17 21		17 51					18 21		18 51				19 21			19 51				20 21	
Crews Hill	d			17 24		17 54					18 24		18 54				19 24			19 54				20 24	
Gordon Hill	d			17 27		17 57					18 27		18 57				19 27			19 57				20 27	
Enfield Chase	d			17 29		17 59					18 29		18 59				19 29			19 59				20 29	
Grange Park	d			17 31		18 01					18 31		19 01				19 31			20 01				20 31	
Winchmore Hill	d			17 33		18 03					18 33		19 03				19 33			20 03				20 33	
Palmers Green	d			17 35		18 05					18 35		19 05				19 35			20 05				20 35	
Bowes Park	d			17 38		18 08					18 38		19 08				19 38			20 08				20 38	
Knebworth	d						17 43							18 43							19 43				
Welwyn North	d						17 47							18 47							19 47				
Welwyn Garden City [4]	d		16 58		17 28		17 51			17 58		18 28		18 51		18 58		19 28			19 51		19 58		20 28
Hatfield	d		17 02		17 32		17 54			18 02		18 32		18 54		19 02		19 32			19 54		20 02		20 32
Welham Green	d		17 06		17 36					18 06		18 36				19 06		19 36					20 06		20 36
Brookmans Park	d		17 08		17 38					18 08		18 38				19 08		19 38					20 08		20 38
Potters Bar	d		17 11		17 41		18 00			18 11		18 41		19 00		19 11		19 41			20 00		20 11		20 41
Hadley Wood	d		17 15		17 45					18 15		18 45				19 15		19 45					20 15		20 45
New Barnet	d		17 17		17 47					18 17		18 47				19 17		19 47					20 17		20 47
Oakleigh Park	d		17 19		17 49					18 19		18 49				19 19		19 49					20 19		20 49
New Southgate	d		17 22		17 52					18 22		18 52				19 22		19 52					20 22		20 52
Alexandra Palace	d		17 25	17 40	17 55	18 10				18 25	18 40	18 55	19 10			19 25	19 40	19 55		20 10			20 25	20 40	20 55
Hornsey	d		17 27	17 42	17 57	18 12				18 27	18 42	18 57	19 12			19 27	19 42	19 57		20 12			20 27	20 42	20 57
Harringay	d	←	17 29	17 44	17 59	18 14		←		18 29	18 44	18 59	19 14		←	19 29	19 44	19 59		20 14		←	20 29	20 44	20 59
Finsbury Park ⊖	d	17 17	17 32	17 47	18 02	18 17	18 10	18 17		18 32	18 47	19 02	19 17	19 10	19 17	19 32	19 47	20 02		20 17	20 10	20 17	20 32	20 47	21 02
Drayton Park	d					→							→							→					
Highbury & Islington ⊖	d																								
Essex Road	d																								
Old Street ⊖	d																								
Moorgate ⊖	a																								
London Kings Cross [15] ⊖	a	17 25	17 40	17 55	18 10		18 19	18 25		18 40	18 55	19 10		19 19	19 25	19 40	19 55	20 10			20 19	20 25	20 40	20 55	21 10

		FC	FC [1]	FC		FC	FC	FC	FC	FC [1]	FC	FC	FC	FC		FC	FC [1]	FC	FC	FC	FC	FC [1]
Letchworth Garden City	d		20 29							21 29							22 29					23 40
Hitchin [4]	d		20 34							21 34							22 33					23 44
Stevenage [4]	d	20 29	20 40						21 29	21 40						22 29	22 39				23 29	23 49
Watton-at-Stone	d	20 36							21 36							22 36					23 36	
Hertford North	d	20 42					21 12		21 42				22 12			22 42				23 12	23 42	
Bayford	d	20 46					21 16		21 46				22 16			22 46				23 16	23 46	
Cuffley	d	20 51					21 21		21 51				22 21			22 51				23 21	23 51	
Crews Hill	d	20 54					21 24		21 54				22 24			22 54				23 24	23 54	
Gordon Hill	d	20 57					21 27		21 57				22 27			22 57				23 27	23 57	
Enfield Chase	d	20 59					21 29		21 59				22 29			22 59				23 29	23 59	
Grange Park	d	21 01					21 31		22 01				22 31			23 01				23 31	00 01	
Winchmore Hill	d	21 03					21 33		22 03				22 33			23 03				23 33	00 03	
Palmers Green	d	21 05					21 35		22 05				22 35			23 05				23 35	00 05	
Bowes Park	d	21 08					21 38		22 08				22 38			23 08				23 38	00 08	
Knebworth	d		20 43							21 43							22 43					23 52
Welwyn North	d		20 47							21 47							22 47					23 56
Welwyn Garden City [4]	d		20 51			20 58		21 28		21 51		21 58		22 28			22 51		22 58			23 59
Hatfield	d		20 54			21 02		21 32		21 54		22 02		22 32			22 54		23 02			00 02
Welham Green	d					21 06		21 36				22 06		22 36					23 06			
Brookmans Park	d					21 08		21 38				22 08		22 38					23 08			
Potters Bar	d		21 00			21 11		21 41		22 00		22 11		22 41			23 00		23 11			00 08
Hadley Wood	d					21 15		21 45				22 15		22 45					23 15			
New Barnet	d					21 17		21 47				22 17		22 47					23 17			
Oakleigh Park	d					21 19		21 49				22 19		22 49					23 19			
New Southgate	d					21 22		21 52				22 22		22 52					23 22			
Alexandra Palace	d	21 10				21 25	21 40	21 55	22 10			22 25	22 40	22 55		23 10			23 25	23 40	00 10	
Hornsey	d	21 12				21 27	21 42	21 57	22 12			22 27	22 42	22 57		23 12			23 27	23 42	00 12	
Harringay	d	21 14		←		21 29	21 44	21 59	22 14		←	22 29	22 44	22 59		23 14		←	23 29	23 44	00 14	
Finsbury Park ⊖	d	21 17	21 10	21 17		21 32	21 47	22 02	22 17	22 10	22 17	22 32	22 47	23 02		23 17	23 10	23 17	23 32	23 47	00 17	00 21
Drayton Park	d	→							→							→						
Highbury & Islington ⊖	d																					
Essex Road	d																					
Old Street ⊖	d																					
Moorgate ⊖	a																					
London Kings Cross [15] ⊖	a		21 19	21 25		21 40	21 55	22 10		22 19	22 25	22 40	22 55	23 12			23 19	23 26	23 44	23 56	00 26	00 33

Table 24

Letchworth Garden City, Hertford North and Welwyn Garden City - London

		FC	FC	FC	FC ■1	FC	FC	FC	FC	FC ■1	FC	FC	FC	FC	FC	FC	FC	FC	FC	FC	FC	FC	FC
Letchworth Garden City	d																						
Hitchin ■4	d				06 37					07 36													
Stevenage ■4	d				06 45					07 52												10 29	
Watton-at-Stone	d																					10 36	
Hertford North	d	23p42	06 12			06 42		07 12				08 12		08 42		09 12		09 42		10 12		10 42	
Bayford	d	23p46	06 16			06 46		07 16				08 16		08 46		09 16		09 46		10 16		10 46	
Cuffley	d	23p51	06 21			06 51		07 21				08 21		08 51		09 21		09 51		10 21		10 51	
Crews Hill	d	23p54	06 24			06 54		07 24				08 24		08 54		09 24		09 54		10 24		10 54	
Gordon Hill	d	23p57	06 27			06 57		07 27				08 27		08 57		09 27		09 57		10 27		10 57	
Enfield Chase	d	23p59	06 29			06 59		07 29				08 29		08 59		09 29		09 59		10 29		10 59	
Grange Park	d	00 01	06 31			07 01		07 31				08 31		09 01		09 31		10 01		10 31		11 01	
Winchmore Hill	d	00 03	06 33			07 03		07 33				08 33		09 03		09 33		10 03		10 33		11 03	
Palmers Green	d	00 05	06 35			07 05		07 35				08 35		09 05		09 35		10 05		10 35		11 05	
Bowes Park	d	00 08	06 38			07 08		07 38				08 38		09 08		09 38		10 08		10 38		11 08	
Knebworth	d				06 49																		
Welwyn North	d				06 53					08 08													
Welwyn Garden City ■4	d			06 28	06 56		06 58		07 28	08 12	07 58		08 28		08 58		09 28		09 58		10 28		10 58
Hatfield	d			06 32	06 59		07 02		07 32	08 15	08 02		08 32		09 02		09 32		10 02		10 32		11 02
Welham Green	d			06 36			07 06		07 36		08 06		08 36		09 06		09 36		10 06		10 36		11 06
Brookmans Park	d			06 38			07 08		07 38		08 08		08 38		09 08		09 38		10 08		10 38		11 08
Potters Bar	d			06 41	07 05		07 11		07 41	08 21	08 11		08 41		09 11		09 41		10 11		10 41		11 11
Hadley Wood	d			06 45			07 15		07 45		08 15		08 45		09 15		09 45		10 15		10 45		11 15
New Barnet	d			06 47			07 17		07 47		08 17		08 47		09 17		09 47		10 17		10 47		11 17
Oakleigh Park	d			06 49			07 19		07 49		08 19		08 49		09 19		09 49		10 19		10 49		11 19
New Southgate	d			06 52			07 22		07 52		08 22		08 52		09 22		09 52		10 22		10 52		11 22
Alexandra Palace	d	00 10	06 40	06 55		07 10	07 25	07 40	07 55		08 25	08 40	08 55	09 10	09 25	09 40	09 55	10 11	10 25	10 41	10 55	11 10	11 25
Hornsey	d	00 12	06 42	06 57		07 12	07 27	07 42	07 57		08 27	08 42	08 57	09 12	09 27	09 42	09 57	10 13	10 27	10 43	10 57	11 12	11 27
Harringay	d	00 14	06 44	06 59		07 14	07 29	07 44	07 59		08 29	08 44	08 59	09 14	09 29	09 44	09 59	10 15	10 29	10 45	10 59	11 14	11 29
Finsbury Park ⊖	d	00 17	06 47	07 02	07 17	07 17	07 32	07 47	08 02	08 31	08 32	08 47	09 02	09 17	09 32	09 47	10 02	10 17	10 32	10 47	11 02	11 17	11 32
Drayton Park	d																						
Highbury & Islington ⊖	d																						
Essex Road	d																						
Old Street ⊖	d																						
Moorgate ⊖	a																						
London Kings Cross ■15 ⊖	a	00 25	06 57	07 13	07 25	07 29	07 45	07 56	08 15	08 38	08 40	08 55	09 10	09 25	09 40	09 55	10 10	10 25	10 40	10 55	11 10	11 25	11 40

		FC	FC	FC	FC	FC	FC	FC	FC	FC	FC	FC	FC ■1	FC	FC	FC	FC	FC	FC ■1	FC	FC	FC	FC
Letchworth Garden City	d												13 29						14 29				
Hitchin ■4	d												13 34						14 34				
Stevenage ■4	d			11 29								13 29	13 40					14 29	14 40				
Watton-at-Stone	d			11 36								13 36						14 36					
Hertford North	d	11 12		11 42		12 12		12 42		13 12		13 42				14 12		14 42				15 12	
Bayford	d	11 16		11 46		12 16		12 46		13 16		13 46				14 16		14 46				15 16	
Cuffley	d	11 21		11 51		12 21		12 51		13 21		13 51				14 21		14 51				15 21	
Crews Hill	d	11 24		11 54		12 24		12 54		13 24		13 54				14 24		14 54				15 24	
Gordon Hill	d	11 27		11 57		12 27		12 57		13 27		13 57				14 27		14 57				15 27	
Enfield Chase	d	11 29		11 59		12 29		12 59		13 29		13 59				14 29		14 59				15 29	
Grange Park	d	11 31		12 01		12 31		13 01		13 31		14 01				14 31		15 01				15 31	
Winchmore Hill	d	11 33		12 03		12 33		13 03		13 33		14 03				14 33		15 03				15 33	
Palmers Green	d	11 35		12 05		12 35		13 05		13 35		14 05				14 35		15 05				15 35	
Bowes Park	d	11 38		12 08		12 38		13 08		13 38		14 08				14 38		15 08				15 38	
Knebworth	d												13 43						14 43				
Welwyn North	d												13 47						14 47				
Welwyn Garden City ■4	d		11 28		11 58		12 28		12 58		13 28		13 51		13 58		14 28		14 51		14 58		15 28
Hatfield	d		11 32		12 02		12 32		13 02		13 32		13 54		14 02		14 32		14 54		15 02		15 32
Welham Green	d		11 36		12 06		12 36		13 06		13 36				14 06		14 36				15 06		15 36
Brookmans Park	d		11 38		12 08		12 38		13 08		13 38				14 08		14 38				15 08		15 38
Potters Bar	d		11 41		12 11		12 41		13 11		13 41		14 00		14 11		14 41		15 00		15 11		15 41
Hadley Wood	d		11 45		12 15		12 45		13 15		13 45				14 15		14 45				15 15		15 45
New Barnet	d		11 47		12 17		12 47		13 17		13 47				14 17		14 47				15 17		15 47
Oakleigh Park	d		11 49		12 19		12 49		13 19		13 49				14 19		14 49				15 19		15 49
New Southgate	d		11 52		12 22		12 52		13 22		13 52				14 22		14 52				15 22		15 52
Alexandra Palace	d	11 40	11 55	12 10	12 25	12 40	12 55	13 10	13 25	13 40	13 55	14 10			14 25	14 40	14 55	15 10			15 25	15 40	15 55
Hornsey	d	11 42	11 57	12 12	12 27	12 42	12 57	13 12	13 27	13 42	13 57	14 12			14 27	14 42	14 57	15 12			15 27	15 42	15 57
Harringay	d	11 44	11 59	12 14	12 29	12 44	12 59	13 14	13 29	13 44	13 59	14 14		←	14 29	14 44	14 59	15 14		←	15 29	15 44	15 59
Finsbury Park ⊖	d	11 47	12 02	12 17	12 32	12 47	13 02	13 17	13 32	13 47	14 02	14 17	14 11	14 17	14 32	14 47	15 02	15 17	15 10	15 17	15 32	15 47	16 02
Drayton Park	d											→						→					
Highbury & Islington ⊖	d																						
Essex Road	d																						
Old Street ⊖	d																						
Moorgate ⊖	a																						
London Kings Cross ■15 ⊖	a	11 55	12 10	12 25	12 40	12 55	13 10	13 25	13 40	13 55	14 10		14 19	14 25	14 40	14 55	15 10		15 19	15 25	15 40	15 55	16 10

Table 24

Sundays
26 June to 31 July

Letchworth Garden City, Hertford North and Welwyn Garden City - London

		FC	FC ■1	FC	FC	FC	FC	FC	FC ■1	FC	FC	FC	FC	FC	FC ■1	FC	FC	FC	FC	FC	FC ■1	FC
Letchworth Garden City	d		15 29						16 29						17 29						18 29	
Hitchin ■4	d		15 34						16 34						17 34						18 34	
Stevenage ■4	d	15 29	15 40					16 29	16 40					17 29	17 40					18 29	18 40	
Watton-at-Stone	d	15 36						16 36						17 36						18 36		
Hertford North	d	15 42				16 12		16 42				17 12		17 42				18 12		18 42		
Bayford	d	15 46				16 16		16 46				17 16		17 46				18 16		18 46		
Cuffley	d	15 51				16 21		16 51				17 21		17 51				18 21		18 51		
Crews Hill	d	15 54				16 24		16 54				17 24		17 54				18 24		18 54		
Gordon Hill	d	15 57				16 27		16 57				17 27		17 57				18 27		18 57		
Enfield Chase	d	15 59				16 29		16 59				17 29		17 59				18 29		18 59		
Grange Park	d	16 01				16 31		17 01				17 31		18 01				18 31		19 01		
Winchmore Hill	d	16 03				16 33		17 03				17 33		18 03				18 33		19 03		
Palmers Green	d	16 05				16 35		17 05				17 35		18 05				18 35		19 05		
Bowes Park	d	16 08				16 38		17 08				17 38		18 08				18 38		19 08		
Knebworth	d		15 43						16 43						17 43						18 43	
Welwyn North	d		15 47						16 47						17 47						18 47	
Welwyn Garden City ■4	d		15 51		15 58		16 28		16 51		16 58		17 28		17 51		17 58		18 28		18 51	
Hatfield	d		15 54		16 02		16 32		16 54		17 02		17 32		17 54		18 02		18 32		18 54	
Welham Green	d				16 06		16 36				17 06		17 36				18 06		18 36			
Brookmans Park	d				16 08		16 38				17 08		17 38				18 08		18 38			
Potters Bar	d		16 00		16 11		16 41		17 00		17 11		17 41		18 00		18 11		18 41		19 00	
Hadley Wood	d				16 15		16 45				17 15		17 45				18 15		18 45			
New Barnet	d				16 17		16 47				17 17		17 47				18 17		18 47			
Oakleigh Park	d				16 19		16 49				17 19		17 49				18 19		18 49			
New Southgate	d				16 22		16 52				17 22		17 52				18 22		18 52			
Alexandra Palace	d	16 10			16 25	16 40	16 55	17 10			17 25	17 40	17 55	18 10			18 25	18 40	18 55	19 10		
Hornsey	d	16 12			16 27	16 42	16 57	17 12			17 27	17 42	17 57	18 12			18 27	18 42	18 57	19 12		
Harringay	d	16 14		←	16 29	16 44	16 59	17 14		←	17 29	17 44	17 59	18 14		←	18 29	18 44	18 59	19 14		←
Finsbury Park ⊖	d	16 17	16 10	16 17	16 32	16 47	17 02	17 17	17 10	17 17	17 32	17 47	18 02	18 17	18 10	18 17	18 32	18 47	19 02	19 17	19 10	19 17
Drayton Park	d	→						→						→						→		
Highbury & Islington ⊖	d																					
Essex Road	d																					
Old Street ⊖	d																					
Moorgate ⊖	a																					
London Kings Cross ■15 ⊖	a		16 19	16 25	16 40	16 55	17 10		17 19	17 25	17 40	17 55	18 10		18 19	18 25	18 40	18 55	19 10		19 19	19 25

		FC	FC	FC	FC	FC ■1	FC	FC	FC	FC	FC	FC ■1	FC	FC	FC	FC	FC	FC ■1	FC	FC	FC	FC	FC
Letchworth Garden City	d					19 29						20 29						21 29					
Hitchin ■4	d					19 34						20 34						21 34					
Stevenage ■4	d				19 29	19 40					20 29	20 40					21 29	21 40					22 29
Watton-at-Stone	d				19 36						20 36						21 36						22 36
Hertford North	d		19 12		19 42				20 12		20 42				21 12		21 42				22 12		22 42
Bayford	d		19 16		19 46				20 16		20 46				21 16		21 46				22 16		22 46
Cuffley	d		19 21		19 51				20 21		20 51				21 21		21 51				22 21		22 51
Crews Hill	d		19 24		19 54				20 24		20 54				21 24		21 54				22 24		22 54
Gordon Hill	d		19 27		19 57				20 27		20 57				21 27		21 57				22 27		22 57
Enfield Chase	d		19 29		19 59				20 29		20 59				21 29		21 59				22 29		22 59
Grange Park	d		19 31		20 01				20 31		21 01				21 31		22 01				22 31		23 01
Winchmore Hill	d		19 33		20 03				20 33		21 03				21 33		22 03				22 33		23 03
Palmers Green	d		19 35		20 05				20 35		21 05				21 35		22 05				22 35		23 05
Bowes Park	d		19 38		20 08				20 38		21 08				21 38		22 08				22 38		23 08
Knebworth	d					19 43						20 43						21 43					
Welwyn North	d					19 47						20 47						21 47					
Welwyn Garden City ■4	d	18 58		19 28		19 51		19 58		20 28		20 51		20 58		21 28		21 51		21 58		22 28	
Hatfield	d	19 02		19 32		19 54		20 02		20 32		20 54		21 02		21 32		21 54		22 02		22 32	
Welham Green	d	19 06		19 36				20 06		20 36				21 06		21 36				22 06		22 36	
Brookmans Park	d	19 08		19 38				20 08		20 38				21 08		21 38				22 08		22 38	
Potters Bar	d	19 11		19 41		20 00		20 11		20 41		21 00		21 11		21 41		22 00		22 11		22 41	
Hadley Wood	d	19 15		19 45				20 15		20 45				21 15		21 45				22 15		22 45	
New Barnet	d	19 17		19 47				20 17		20 47				21 17		21 47				22 17		22 47	
Oakleigh Park	d	19 19		19 49				20 19		20 49				21 19		21 49				22 19		22 49	
New Southgate	d	19 22		19 52				20 22		20 52				21 22		21 52				22 22		22 52	
Alexandra Palace	d	19 25	19 40	19 55	20 10			20 25	20 40	20 55	21 10			21 25	21 40	21 55	22 10			22 25	22 40	22 55	23 10
Hornsey	d	19 27	19 42	19 57	20 12			20 27	20 42	20 57	21 12			21 27	21 42	21 57	22 12			22 27	22 42	22 57	23 12
Harringay	d	19 29	19 44	19 59	20 14		←	20 29	20 44	20 59	21 14		←	21 29	21 44	21 59	22 14		←	22 29	22 44	22 59	23 14
Finsbury Park ⊖	d	19 32	19 47	20 02	20 17	20 10	20 17	20 32	20 47	21 02	21 17	21 10	21 17	21 32	21 47	22 02	22 17	22 10	22 17	22 32	22 47	23 02	23 17
Drayton Park	d				→						→						→						→
Highbury & Islington ⊖	d																						
Essex Road	d																						
Old Street ⊖	d																						
Moorgate ⊖	a																						
London Kings Cross ■15 ⊖	a	19 40	19 55	20 10		20 19	20 25	20 40	20 55	21 10		21 19	21 25	21 40	21 55	22 10		22 19	22 25	22 40	22 55	23 12	

Table 24

Sundays

26 June to 31 July

Letchworth Garden City, Hertford North and Welwyn Garden City - London

		FC [1]	FC	FC	FC	FC	FC [1]
Letchworth Garden City	d	22 29					23 40
Hitchin [4]	d	22 33					23 44
Stevenage [4]	d	22 39				23 29	23 49
Watton-at-Stone	d					23 36	
Hertford North	d				23 12	23 42	
Bayford	d				23 16	23 46	
Cuffley	d				23 21	23 51	
Crews Hill	d				23 24	23 54	
Gordon Hill	d				23 27	23 57	
Enfield Chase	d				23 29	23 59	
Grange Park	d				23 31	00 01	
Winchmore Hill	d				23 33	00 03	
Palmers Green	d				23 35	00 05	
Bowes Park	d				23 38	00 08	
Knebworth	d	22 43					23 52
Welwyn North	d	22 47					23 56
Welwyn Garden City [4]	d	22 51		22 58			23 59
Hatfield	d	22 54		23 02			00 02
Welham Green	d			23 06			
Brookmans Park	d			23 08			
Potters Bar	d	23 00		23 11			00 08
Hadley Wood	d			23 15			
New Barnet	d			23 17			
Oakleigh Park	d			23 19			
New Southgate	d			23 22			
Alexandra Palace	d			23 25	23 40	00 10	
Hornsey	d			23 27	23 42	00 12	
Harringay	d		←	23 29	23 44	00 14	
Finsbury Park ⊖	d	23 10	23 17	23 32	23 47	00 17	00 21
Drayton Park	d						
Highbury & Islington ⊖	d						
Essex Road	d						
Old Street ⊖	d						
Moorgate ⊖	a						
London Kings Cross [15] ⊖	a	23 19	23 26	23 44	23 56	00 26	00 33

Sundays

7 August to 11 September

		FC	FC [1]	FC	FC	FC [1]	FC	FC	FC	FC	FC	FC [1]
Letchworth Garden City	d		23p46									
Hitchin [4]	d		23p50			06 34						07 34
Stevenage [4]	d		23p55			06 40					07 29	07 40
Watton-at-Stone	d										07 36	
Hertford North	d	23p42		06 12			06 42		07 12		07 42	
Bayford	d	23p46		06 16			06 46		07 16		07 46	
Cuffley	d	23p51		06 21			06 51		07 21		07 51	
Crews Hill	d	23p54		06 24			06 54		07 24		07 54	
Gordon Hill	d	23p57		06 27			06 57		07 27		07 57	
Enfield Chase	d	23p59		06 29			06 59		07 29		07 59	
Grange Park	d	00 01		06 31			07 01		07 31		08 01	
Winchmore Hill	d	00 03		06 33			07 03		07 33		08 03	
Palmers Green	d	00 05		06 35			07 05		07 35		08 05	
Bowes Park	d	00 08		06 38			07 08		07 38		08 08	
Knebworth	d		23p59			06 43						07 43
Welwyn North	d		00 06			06 47						07 47
Welwyn Garden City [4]	d		00 09		06 28	06 51		06 58		07 28		07 51
Hatfield	d		00 13		06 32	06 54		07 02		07 32		07 54
Welham Green	d				06 36			07 06		07 36		
Brookmans Park	d				06 38			07 08		07 38		
Potters Bar	d		00 18		06 41	07 00		07 11		07 41		08 00
Hadley Wood	d				06 45			07 15		07 45		
New Barnet	d				06 47			07 17		07 47		
Oakleigh Park	d				06 49			07 19		07 49		
New Southgate	d				06 52			07 22		07 52		
Alexandra Palace	d	00 10		06 40	06 55		07 10	07 25	07 40	07 55	08 11	
Hornsey	d	00 12		06 42	06 57		07 12	07 27	07 42	07 57	08 13	
Harringay	d	00 14		06 44	06 59		07 14	07 29	07 44	07 59	08 15	
Finsbury Park ⊖	d	00 17	00s32	06 47	07 02	07 10	07 17	07 32	07 47	08 02	08 17	08 10
Drayton Park	d										→	
Highbury & Islington ⊖	d											
Essex Road	d											
Old Street ⊖	d											
Moorgate ⊖	a											
London Kings Cross [15] ⊖	a	00 25	00 40	06 57	07 13	07 20	07 29	07 45	07 56	08 15		08 20

		FC	FC	FC	FC	FC [1]	FC	FC	FC	FC [1]	FC	FC [1]
Letchworth Garden City	d					08 29				09 29		10 00
Hitchin [4]	d					08 33				09 33		10 04
Stevenage [4]	d					08 39				09 39		10 10
Watton-at-Stone	d											
Hertford North	d			08 12				09 12				
Bayford	d			08 16				09 16				
Cuffley	d			08 21				09 21				
Crews Hill	d			08 24				09 24				
Gordon Hill	d			08 27				09 27				
Enfield Chase	d			08 29				09 29				
Grange Park	d			08 31				09 31				
Winchmore Hill	d			08 33				09 33				
Palmers Green	d			08 35				09 35				
Bowes Park	d			08 38				09 38				
Knebworth	d					08 43				09 43		10 13
Welwyn North	d					08 47				09 47		10 17
Welwyn Garden City [4]	d		07 58		08 28	08 51	08 58		09 28	09 51	09 58	10 21
Hatfield	d		08 02		08 32	08 54	09 02		09 32	09 54	10 02	10 24
Welham Green	d		08 06		08 36		09 06		09 36		10 06	
Brookmans Park	d		08 08		08 38		09 08		09 38		10 08	
Potters Bar	d		08 11		08 41	09 00	09 11		09 41	10 00	10 11	10 30
Hadley Wood	d		08 15		08 45		09 15		09 45		10 15	
New Barnet	d		08 17		08 47		09 17		09 47		10 17	
Oakleigh Park	d		08 19		08 49		09 19		09 49		10 19	
New Southgate	d		08 22		08 52		09 22		09 52		10 22	
Alexandra Palace	d		08 25	08 40	08 55		09 25	09 40	09 55		10 25	
Hornsey	d		08 27	08 42	08 57		09 27	09 42	09 57		10 27	
Harringay	d	←	08 29	08 44	08 59		09 29	09 44	09 59		10 29	
Finsbury Park ⊖	d	08 17	08 32	08 47	09 02	09 10	09 32	09 47	10 02	10 10	10 32	10 40
Drayton Park	d											
Highbury & Islington ⊖	d											
Essex Road	d											
Old Street ⊖	d											
Moorgate ⊖	a											
London Kings Cross [15] ⊖	a	08 26	08 40	08 55	09 10	09 19	09 40	09 55	10 10	10 19	10 40	10 49

Table 24

Sundays

7 August to 11 September

Letchworth Garden City, Hertford North and Welwyn Garden City - London

		FC	FC	FC	FC [1]	FC	FC	FC	FC	FC [1]	FC	FC
Letchworth Garden City	d				10 29					11 29		
Hitchin [4]	d				10 33					11 33		
Stevenage [4]	d			10 29	10 39					11 39		
Watton-at-Stone	d			10 36								
Hertford North	d	10 12		10 42				11 12				12 12
Bayford	d	10 16		10 46				11 16				12 16
Cuffley	d	10 21		10 51				11 21				12 21
Crews Hill	d	10 24		10 54				11 24				12 24
Gordon Hill	d	10 27		10 57				11 27				12 27
Enfield Chase	d	10 29		10 59				11 29				12 29
Grange Park	d	10 31		11 01				11 31				12 31
Winchmore Hill	d	10 33		11 03				11 33				12 33
Palmers Green	d	10 35		11 05				11 35				12 35
Bowes Park	d	10 38		11 08				11 38				12 38
Knebworth	d				10 43					11 43		
Welwyn North	d				10 47					11 47		
Welwyn Garden City [4]	d		10 28		10 50		10 58		11 28	11 51	11 58	
Hatfield	d		10 32		10 54		11 02		11 32	11 54	12 02	
Welham Green	d		10 36				11 06		11 36		12 06	
Brookmans Park	d		10 38				11 08		11 38		12 08	
Potters Bar	d		10 41		10 59		11 11		11 41	12 00	12 11	
Hadley Wood	d		10 45				11 15		11 45		12 15	
New Barnet	d		10 47				11 17		11 47		12 17	
Oakleigh Park	d		10 49				11 19		11 49		12 19	
New Southgate	d		10 52				11 22		11 52		12 22	
Alexandra Palace	d	10 41	10 55	11 10			11 25	11 40	11 55		12 25	12 40
Hornsey	d	10 43	10 57	11 12			11 27	11 42	11 57		12 27	12 42
Harringay	d	10 45	10 59	11 14		←	11 29	11 44	11 59		12 29	12 44
Finsbury Park ⊖	d	10 47	11 02	11 17	11 11	11 17	11 32	11 47	12 02	12 10	12 32	12 47
Drayton Park	d			→								
Highbury & Islington ⊖	d											
Essex Road	d											
Old Street ⊖	d											
Moorgate ⊖	a											
London Kings Cross [15] ⊖	a	10 55	11 10		11 20	11 25	11 40	11 55	12 10	12 19	12 40	12 55

		FC	FC [1]	FC	FC	FC	FC	FC	FC [1]	FC	FC	FC
Letchworth Garden City	d		12 29						13 29			
Hitchin [4]	d		12 33						13 34			
Stevenage [4]	d		12 39					13 29	13 40			
Watton-at-Stone	d							13 36				
Hertford North	d			12 42		13 12		13 42				14 12
Bayford	d			12 46		13 16		13 46				14 16
Cuffley	d			12 51		13 21		13 51				14 21
Crews Hill	d			12 54		13 24		13 54				14 24
Gordon Hill	d			12 57		13 27		13 57				14 27
Enfield Chase	d			12 59		13 29		13 59				14 29
Grange Park	d			13 01		13 31		14 01				14 31
Winchmore Hill	d			13 03		13 33		14 03				14 33
Palmers Green	d			13 05		13 35		14 05				14 35
Bowes Park	d			13 08		13 38		14 08				14 38
Knebworth	d		12 43						13 43			
Welwyn North	d		12 47						13 47			
Welwyn Garden City [4]	d	12 28	12 50		12 58		13 28		13 51		13 58	
Hatfield	d	12 32	12 54		13 02		13 32		13 54		14 02	
Welham Green	d	12 36			13 06		13 36				14 06	
Brookmans Park	d	12 38			13 08		13 38				14 08	
Potters Bar	d	12 41	13 00		13 11		13 41		14 00		14 11	
Hadley Wood	d	12 45			13 15		13 45				14 15	
New Barnet	d	12 47			13 17		13 47				14 17	
Oakleigh Park	d	12 49			13 19		13 49				14 19	
New Southgate	d	12 52			13 22		13 52				14 22	
Alexandra Palace	d	12 55		13 10	13 25	13 40	13 55	14 10			14 25	14 40
Hornsey	d	12 57		13 12	13 27	13 42	13 57	14 12			14 27	14 42
Harringay	d	12 59		13 14	13 29	13 44	13 59	14 14		←	14 29	14 44
Finsbury Park ⊖	d	13 02	13 11	13 17	13 32	13 47	14 02	14 17	14 11	14 17	14 32	14 47
Drayton Park	d							→				
Highbury & Islington ⊖	d											
Essex Road	d											
Old Street ⊖	d											
Moorgate ⊖	a											
London Kings Cross [15] ⊖	a	13 10	13 19	13 25	13 40	13 55	14 10		14 19	14 25	14 40	14 55

		FC	FC	FC [1]	FC	FC	FC	FC	FC	FC [1]	FC
Letchworth Garden City	d			14 29						15 29	
Hitchin [4]	d			14 34						15 34	
Stevenage [4]	d		14 29	14 40					15 29	15 40	
Watton-at-Stone	d		14 36						15 36		
Hertford North	d		14 42				15 12		15 42		
Bayford	d		14 46				15 16		15 46		
Cuffley	d		14 51				15 21		15 51		
Crews Hill	d		14 54				15 24		15 54		
Gordon Hill	d		14 57				15 27		15 57		
Enfield Chase	d		14 59				15 29		15 59		
Grange Park	d		15 01				15 31		16 01		
Winchmore Hill	d		15 03				15 33		16 03		
Palmers Green	d		15 05				15 35		16 05		
Bowes Park	d		15 08				15 38		16 08		
Knebworth	d			14 43						15 43	
Welwyn North	d			14 47						15 47	
Welwyn Garden City [4]	d	14 28		14 51		14 58		15 28		15 51	
Hatfield	d	14 32		14 54		15 02		15 32		15 54	
Welham Green	d	14 36				15 06		15 36			
Brookmans Park	d	14 38				15 08		15 38			
Potters Bar	d	14 41		15 00		15 11		15 41		16 00	
Hadley Wood	d	14 45				15 15		15 45			
New Barnet	d	14 47				15 17		15 47			
Oakleigh Park	d	14 49				15 19		15 49			
New Southgate	d	14 52				15 22		15 52			
Alexandra Palace	d	14 55	15 10			15 25	15 40	15 55	16 10		
Hornsey	d	14 57	15 12			15 27	15 42	15 57	16 12		
Harringay	d	14 59	15 14		←	15 29	15 44	15 59	16 14		←
Finsbury Park ⊖	d	15 02	15 17	15 10	15 17	15 32	15 47	16 02	16 17	16 10	16 17
Drayton Park	d		→						→		
Highbury & Islington ⊖	d										
Essex Road	d										
Old Street ⊖	d										
Moorgate ⊖	a										
London Kings Cross [15] ⊖	a	15 10		15 19	15 25	15 40	15 55	16 10		16 19	16 25

		FC	FC	FC	FC	FC [1]	FC	FC	FC	FC	FC	FC [1]
Letchworth Garden City	d					16 29						17 29
Hitchin [4]	d					16 34						17 34
Stevenage [4]	d				16 29	16 40					17 29	17 40
Watton-at-Stone	d				16 36						17 36	
Hertford North	d		16 12		16 42				17 12		17 42	
Bayford	d		16 16		16 46				17 16		17 46	
Cuffley	d		16 21		16 51				17 21		17 51	
Crews Hill	d		16 24		16 54				17 24		17 54	
Gordon Hill	d		16 27		16 57				17 27		17 57	
Enfield Chase	d		16 29		16 59				17 29		17 59	
Grange Park	d		16 31		17 01				17 31		18 01	
Winchmore Hill	d		16 33		17 03				17 33		18 03	
Palmers Green	d		16 35		17 05				17 35		18 05	
Bowes Park	d		16 38		17 08				17 38		18 08	
Knebworth	d					16 43						17 43
Welwyn North	d					16 47						17 47
Welwyn Garden City [4]	d	15 58		16 28		16 51		16 58		17 28		17 51
Hatfield	d	16 02		16 32		16 54		17 02		17 32		17 54
Welham Green	d	16 06		16 36				17 06		17 36		
Brookmans Park	d	16 08		16 38				17 08		17 38		
Potters Bar	d	16 11		16 41		17 00		17 11		17 41		18 00
Hadley Wood	d	16 15		16 45				17 15		17 45		
New Barnet	d	16 17		16 47				17 17		17 47		
Oakleigh Park	d	16 19		16 49				17 19		17 49		
New Southgate	d	16 22		16 52				17 22		17 52		
Alexandra Palace	d	16 25	16 40	16 55	17 10			17 25	17 40	17 55	18 10	
Hornsey	d	16 27	16 42	16 57	17 12			17 27	17 42	17 57	18 12	
Harringay	d	16 29	16 44	16 59	17 14		←	17 29	17 44	17 59	18 14	
Finsbury Park ⊖	d	16 32	16 47	17 02	17 17	17 10	17 17	17 32	17 47	18 02	18 17	18 10
Drayton Park	d				→						→	
Highbury & Islington ⊖	d											
Essex Road	d											
Old Street ⊖	d											
Moorgate ⊖	a											
London Kings Cross [15] ⊖	a	16 40	16 55	17 10		17 19	17 25	17 40	17 55	18 10		18 19

Table 24

Sundays

7 August to 11 September

Letchworth Garden City, Hertford North and Welwyn Garden City - London

		FC	FC	FC	FC	FC	FC	FC	FC	FC	FC	FC	FC	FC	FC	FC	FC	FC	FC	FC	FC	FC	FC
							1						1						1				
Letchworth Garden City	d						18 29						19 29						20 29				
Hitchin 4	d						18 34						19 34						20 34				
Stevenage 4	d					18 29	18 40					19 29	19 40					20 29	20 40				
Watton-at-Stone	d					18 36						19 36						20 36					
Hertford North	d			18 12		18 42				19 12		19 42				20 12		20 42				21 12	
Bayford	d			18 16		18 46				19 16		19 46				20 16		20 46				21 16	
Cuffley	d			18 21		18 51				19 21		19 51				20 21		20 51				21 21	
Crews Hill	d			18 24		18 54				19 24		19 54				20 24		20 54				21 24	
Gordon Hill	d			18 27		18 57				19 27		19 57				20 27		20 57				21 27	
Enfield Chase	d			18 29		18 59				19 29		19 59				20 29		20 59				21 29	
Grange Park	d			18 31		19 01				19 31		20 01				20 31		21 01				21 31	
Winchmore Hill	d			18 33		19 03				19 33		20 03				20 33		21 03				21 33	
Palmers Green	d			18 35		19 05				19 35		20 05				20 35		21 05				21 35	
Bowes Park	d			18 38		19 08				19 38		20 08				20 38		21 08				21 38	
Knebworth	d						18 43						19 43						20 43				
Welwyn North	d						18 47						19 47						20 47				
Welwyn Garden City 4	d		17 58		18 28		18 51		18 58		19 28		19 51		19 58		20 28		20 51		20 58		21 28
Hatfield	d		18 02		18 32		18 54		19 02		19 32		19 54		20 02		20 32		20 54		21 02		21 32
Welham Green	d		18 06		18 36				19 06		19 36				20 06		20 36				21 06		21 36
Brookmans Park	d		18 08		18 38				19 08		19 38				20 08		20 38				21 08		21 38
Potters Bar	d		18 11		18 41		19 00		19 11		19 41		20 00		20 11		20 41		21 00		21 11		21 41
Hadley Wood	d		18 15		18 45				19 15		19 45				20 15		20 45				21 15		21 45
New Barnet	d		18 17		18 47				19 17		19 47				20 17		20 47				21 17		21 47
Oakleigh Park	d		18 19		18 49				19 19		19 49				20 19		20 49				21 19		21 49
New Southgate	d		18 22		18 52				19 22		19 52				20 22		20 52				21 22		21 52
Alexandra Palace	d		18 25	18 40	18 55	19 10			19 25	19 40	19 55	20 10			20 25	20 40	20 55	21 10			21 25	21 40	21 55
Hornsey	d		18 27	18 42	18 57	19 12			19 27	19 42	19 57	20 12			20 27	20 42	20 57	21 12			21 27	21 42	21 57
Harringay	d	←	18 29	18 44	18 59	19 14		←	19 29	19 44	19 59	20 14		←	20 29	20 44	20 59	21 14		←	21 29	21 44	21 59
Finsbury Park ⊖	d	18 17	18 32	18 47	19 02	19 17	19 10	19 17	19 32	19 47	20 02	20 17	20 10	20 17	20 32	20 47	21 02	21 17	21 10	21 17	21 32	21 47	22 02
Drayton Park	d					↳						↳						↳					
Highbury & Islington ⊖	d																						
Essex Road	d																						
Old Street ⊖	d																						
Moorgate ⊖	a																						
London Kings Cross 15 ⊖	a	18 25	18 40	18 55	19 10		19 19	19 25	19 40	19 55	20 10		20 19	20 25	20 40	20 55	21 10		21 19	21 25	21 40	21 55	22 10

		FC	FC	FC	FC	FC	FC	FC	FC	FC	FC	FC	FC	FC
			1						1					1
Letchworth Garden City	d		21 29						22 29					23 40
Hitchin 4	d		21 34						22 33					23 44
Stevenage 4	d	21 29	21 40					22 29	22 39				23 29	23 49
Watton-at-Stone	d	21 36						22 36					23 36	
Hertford North	d	21 42				22 12		22 42				23 12	23 42	
Bayford	d	21 46				22 16		22 46				23 16	23 46	
Cuffley	d	21 51				22 21		22 51				23 21	23 51	
Crews Hill	d	21 54				22 24		22 54				23 24	23 54	
Gordon Hill	d	21 57				22 27		22 57				23 27	23 57	
Enfield Chase	d	21 59				22 29		22 59				23 29	23 59	
Grange Park	d	22 01				22 31		23 01				23 31	00 01	
Winchmore Hill	d	22 03				22 33		23 03				23 33	00 03	
Palmers Green	d	22 05				22 35		23 05				23 35	00 05	
Bowes Park	d	22 08				22 38		23 08				23 38	00 08	
Knebworth	d		21 43						22 43					23 52
Welwyn North	d		21 47						22 47					23 56
Welwyn Garden City 4	d		21 51		21 58		22 28		22 51		22 58			23 59
Hatfield	d		21 54		22 02		22 32		22 54		23 02			00 02
Welham Green	d				22 06		22 36				23 06			
Brookmans Park	d				22 08		22 38				23 08			
Potters Bar	d		22 00		22 11		22 41		23 00		23 11			00 08
Hadley Wood	d				22 15		22 45				23 15			
New Barnet	d				22 17		22 47				23 17			
Oakleigh Park	d				22 19		22 49				23 19			
New Southgate	d				22 22		22 52				23 22			
Alexandra Palace	d	22 10			22 25	22 40	22 55	23 10			23 25	23 40	00 10	
Hornsey	d	22 12			22 27	22 42	22 57	23 12			23 27	23 42	00 12	
Harringay	d	22 14		←	22 29	22 44	22 59	23 14		←	23 29	23 44	00 14	
Finsbury Park ⊖	d	22 17	22 10	22 17	22 32	22 47	23 02	23 17	23 10	23 17	23 32	23 47	00 17	00 21
Drayton Park	d	↳						↳						
Highbury & Islington ⊖	d													
Essex Road	d													
Old Street ⊖	d													
Moorgate ⊖	a													
London Kings Cross 15 ⊖	a		22 19	22 25	22 40	22 55	23 12		23 19	23 26	23 44	23 56	00 26	00 33

Table 24

Sundays

18 September to 23 October

Letchworth Garden City, Hertford North and Welwyn Garden City - London

		FC	FC	FC	FC	FC	FC	FC	FC	FC	FC	FC	FC	FC	FC	FC	FC	FC	FC	FC	FC	FC	FC
			1	1		1		1		1				1					1				1
Letchworth Garden City	d		23p46	06 29		08 29		09 29		10 00				10 29					11 29				12 29
Hitchin 4	d		23p50	06 34		08 33		09 33		10 04				10 33					11 33				12 33
Stevenage 4	d		23p55	06 40		08 39		09 39		10 10			10 29	10 39					11 39				12 39
Watton-at-Stone	d												10 36										
Hertford North	d	23p42			07 12						10 12		10 42				11 12				12 12		
Bayford	d	23p46			07 16						10 16		10 46				11 16				12 16		
Cuffley	d	23p51			07 21						10 21		10 51				11 21				12 21		
Crews Hill	d	23p54			07 24						10 24		10 54				11 24				12 24		
Gordon Hill	d	23p57			07 27						10 27		10 57				11 27				12 27		
Enfield Chase	d	23p59			07 29						10 29		10 59				11 29				12 29		
Grange Park	d	00 01			07 31						10 31		11 01				11 31				12 31		
Winchmore Hill	d	00 03			07 33						10 33		11 03				11 33				12 33		
Palmers Green	d	00 05			07 35						10 35		11 05				11 35				12 35		
Bowes Park	d	00 08			07 38						10 38		11 08				11 38				12 38		
Knebworth	d		23p59	06 43		08 43		09 43		10 13				10 43					11 43				12 43
Welwyn North	d		00 06	06 47		08 47		09 47		10 17				10 47					11 47				12 47
Welwyn Garden City 4	d		00 09	06 51		08 51	08 58	09 51	09 58	10 21		10 28		10 50		10 58		11 28	11 51	11 58		12 28	12 50
Hatfield	d		00 13	06 54		08 54	09 02	09 54	10 02	10 24		10 32		10 54		11 02		11 32	11 54	12 02		12 32	12 54
Welham Green	d						09 06		10 06			10 36				11 06		11 36		12 06		12 36	
Brookmans Park	d						09 08		10 08			10 38				11 08		11 38		12 08		12 38	
Potters Bar	d		00 18	07 00		09 00	09 11	10 00	10 11	10 30		10 41		10 59		11 11		11 41	12 00	12 11		12 41	13 00
Hadley Wood	d						09 15		10 15			10 45				11 15		11 45		12 15		12 45	
New Barnet	d						09 17		10 17			10 47				11 17		11 47		12 17		12 47	
Oakleigh Park	d						09 19		10 19			10 49				11 19		11 49		12 19		12 49	
New Southgate	d						09 22		10 22			10 52				11 22		11 52		12 22		12 52	
Alexandra Palace	d	00 10			07 40		09 25		10 25		10 41	10 55	11 10			11 25	11 40	11 55		12 25	12 40	12 55	
Hornsey	d	00 12			07 42		09 27		10 27		10 43	10 57	11 12			11 27	11 42	11 57		12 27	12 42	12 57	
Harringay	d	00 14			07 44		09 29		10 29		10 45	10 59	11 14		←	11 29	11 44	11 59		12 29	12 44	12 59	
Finsbury Park ⊖	d	00 17	00s32	07 10	07 47	09 10	09 32	10 10	10 32	10 40	10 47	11 02	11 17	11 11	11 17	11 32	11 47	12 02	12 10	12 32	12 47	13 02	13 11
Drayton Park	d												↳										
Highbury & Islington ⊖	d																						
Essex Road	d																						
Old Street ⊖	d																						
Moorgate ⊖	a																						
London Kings Cross 15 ⊖	a	00 25	00 40	07 20	07 56	09 19	09 40	10 19	10 40	10 49	10 55	11 10		11 20	11 25	11 40	11 55	12 10	12 19	12 40	12 55	13 10	13 19

		FC	FC	FC	FC	FC	FC	FC	FC	FC	FC	FC	FC	FC	FC	FC	FC	FC	FC	FC	FC	FC	FC
							1						1						1				
Letchworth Garden City	d						13 29						14 29						15 29				
Hitchin 4	d						13 34						14 34						15 34				
Stevenage 4	d					13 29	13 40					14 29	14 40					15 29	15 40				
Watton-at-Stone	d					13 36						14 36						15 36					
Hertford North	d	12 42		13 12		13 42				14 12		14 42				15 12		15 42				16 12	
Bayford	d	12 46		13 16		13 46				14 16		14 46				15 16		15 46				16 16	
Cuffley	d	12 51		13 21		13 51				14 21		14 51				15 21		15 51				16 21	
Crews Hill	d	12 54		13 24		13 54				14 24		14 54				15 24		15 54				16 24	
Gordon Hill	d	12 57		13 27		13 57				14 27		14 57				15 27		15 57				16 27	
Enfield Chase	d	12 59		13 29		13 59				14 29		14 59				15 29		15 59				16 29	
Grange Park	d	13 01		13 31		14 01				14 31		15 01				15 31		16 01				16 31	
Winchmore Hill	d	13 03		13 33		14 03				14 33		15 03				15 33		16 03				16 33	
Palmers Green	d	13 05		13 35		14 05				14 35		15 05				15 35		16 05				16 35	
Bowes Park	d	13 08		13 38		14 08				14 38		15 08				15 38		16 08				16 38	
Knebworth	d						13 43						14 43						15 43				
Welwyn North	d						13 47						14 47						15 47				
Welwyn Garden City 4	d		12 58		13 28		13 51		13 58		14 28		14 51		14 58		15 28		15 51		15 58		16 28
Hatfield	d		13 02		13 32		13 54		14 02		14 32		14 54		15 02		15 32		15 54		16 02		16 32
Welham Green	d		13 06		13 36				14 06		14 36				15 06		15 36				16 06		16 36
Brookmans Park	d		13 08		13 38				14 08		14 38				15 08		15 38				16 08		16 38
Potters Bar	d		13 11		13 41		14 00		14 11		14 41		15 00		15 11		15 41		16 00		16 11		16 41
Hadley Wood	d		13 15		13 45				14 15		14 45				15 15		15 45				16 15		16 45
New Barnet	d		13 17		13 47				14 17		14 47				15 17		15 47				16 17		16 47
Oakleigh Park	d		13 19		13 49				14 19		14 49				15 19		15 49				16 19		16 49
New Southgate	d		13 22		13 52				14 22		14 52				15 22		15 52				16 22		16 52
Alexandra Palace	d	13 10	13 25	13 40	13 55	14 10			14 25	14 40	14 55	15 10			15 25	15 40	15 55	16 10			16 25	16 40	16 55
Hornsey	d	13 12	13 27	13 42	13 57	14 12			14 27	14 42	14 57	15 12			15 27	15 42	15 57	16 12			16 27	16 42	16 57
Harringay	d	13 14	13 29	13 44	13 59	14 14		←	14 29	14 44	14 59	15 14		←	15 29	15 44	15 59	16 14		←	16 29	16 44	16 59
Finsbury Park ⊖	d	13 17	13 32	13 47	14 02	14 17	14 11	14 17	14 32	14 47	15 02	15 17	15 10	15 17	15 32	15 47	16 02	16 17	16 10	16 17	16 32	16 47	17 02
Drayton Park	d					↳						↳						↳					
Highbury & Islington ⊖	d																						
Essex Road	d																						
Old Street ⊖	d																						
Moorgate ⊖	a																						
London Kings Cross 15 ⊖	a	13 25	13 40	13 55	14 10		14 19	14 25	14 40	14 55	15 10		15 19	15 25	15 40	15 55	16 10		16 19	16 25	16 40	16 55	17 10

Table 24

Sundays
18 September to 23 October

Letchworth Garden City, Hertford North and Welwyn Garden City - London

		FC		FC 1	FC	FC	FC	FC	FC	FC 1	FC	FC		FC	FC	FC	FC 1	FC	FC	FC	FC	FC		FC 1	FC
Letchworth Garden City	d			16 29						17 29							18 29							19 29	
Hitchin 4	d			16 34						17 34							18 34							19 34	
Stevenage 4	d	16 29		16 40					17 29	17 40						18 29	18 40					19 29		19 40	
Watton-at-Stone	d	16 36							17 36							18 36						19 36			
Hertford North	d	16 42					17 12		17 42					18 12		18 42				19 12		19 42			
Bayford	d	16 46					17 16		17 46					18 16		18 46				19 16		19 46			
Cuffley	d	16 51					17 21		17 51					18 21		18 51				19 21		19 51			
Crews Hill	d	16 54					17 24		17 54					18 24		18 54				19 24		19 54			
Gordon Hill	d	16 57					17 27		17 57					18 27		18 57				19 27		19 57			
Enfield Chase	d	16 59					17 29		17 59					18 29		18 59				19 29		19 59			
Grange Park	d	17 01					17 31		18 01					18 31		19 01				19 31		20 01			
Winchmore Hill	d	17 03					17 33		18 03					18 33		19 03				19 33		20 03			
Palmers Green	d	17 05					17 35		18 05					18 35		19 05				19 35		20 05			
Bowes Park	d	17 08					17 38		18 08					18 38		19 08				19 38		20 08			
Knebworth	d			16 43						17 43							18 43							19 43	
Welwyn North	d			16 47						17 47							18 47							19 47	
Welwyn Garden City 4	d			16 51		16 58		17 28		17 51		17 58			18 28		18 51		18 58		19 28			19 51	
Hatfield	d			16 54		17 02		17 32		17 54		18 02			18 32		18 54		19 02		19 32			19 54	
Welham Green	d					17 06		17 36				18 06			18 36				19 06		19 36				
Brookmans Park	d					17 08		17 38				18 08			18 38				19 08		19 38				
Potters Bar	d			17 00		17 11		17 41		18 00		18 11			18 41		19 00		19 11		19 41			20 00	
Hadley Wood	d					17 15		17 45				18 15			18 45				19 15		19 45				
New Barnet	d					17 17		17 47				18 17			18 47				19 17		19 47				
Oakleigh Park	d					17 19		17 49				18 19			18 49				19 19		19 49				
New Southgate	d					17 22		17 52				18 22			18 52				19 22		19 52				
Alexandra Palace	d	17 10				17 25	17 40	17 55	18 10			18 25		18 40	18 55	19 10			19 25	19 40	19 55	20 10			
Hornsey	d	17 12				17 27	17 42	17 57	18 12			18 27		18 42	18 57	19 12			19 27	19 42	19 57	20 12			
Harringay	d	17 14			←	17 29	17 44	17 59	18 14		←	18 29		18 44	18 59	19 14		←	19 29	19 44	19 59	20 14			←
Finsbury Park	⊖ d	17 17		17 10	17 17	17 32	17 47	18 02	18 17	18 10	18 17	18 32		18 47	19 02	19 17	19 10	19 17	19 32	19 47	20 02	20 17		20 10	20 17
Drayton Park	d	→							→							→						→			
Highbury & Islington	⊖ d																								
Essex Road	d																								
Old Street	⊖ d																								
Moorgate	⊖ a																								
London Kings Cross 15	⊖ a			17 19	17 25	17 40	17 55	18 10		18 19	18 25	18 40		18 55	19 10		19 19	19 25	19 40	19 55	20 10			20 19	20 25

		FC	FC	FC	FC	FC 1	FC	FC		FC	FC	FC	FC 1	FC	FC	FC	FC	FC		FC 1	FC	FC	FC	FC	FC 1
Letchworth Garden City	d					20 29							21 29							22 29					23 40
Hitchin 4	d					20 34							21 34							22 33					23 44
Stevenage 4	d				20 29	20 40						21 29	21 40					22 29		22 39				23 29	23 49
Watton-at-Stone	d				20 36							21 36						22 36						23 36	
Hertford North	d		20 12		20 42					21 12		21 42				22 12		22 42					23 12	23 42	
Bayford	d		20 16		20 46					21 16		21 46				22 16		22 46					23 16	23 46	
Cuffley	d		20 21		20 51					21 21		21 51				22 21		22 51					23 21	23 51	
Crews Hill	d		20 24		20 54					21 24		21 54				22 24		22 54					23 24	23 54	
Gordon Hill	d		20 27		20 57					21 27		21 57				22 27		22 57					23 27	23 57	
Enfield Chase	d		20 29		20 59					21 29		21 59				22 29		22 59					23 29	23 59	
Grange Park	d		20 31		21 01					21 31		22 01				22 31		23 01					23 31	00 01	
Winchmore Hill	d		20 33		21 03					21 33		22 03				22 33		23 03					23 33	00 03	
Palmers Green	d		20 35		21 05					21 35		22 05				22 35		23 05					23 35	00 05	
Bowes Park	d		20 38		21 08					21 38		22 08				22 38		23 08					23 38	00 08	
Knebworth	d					20 43							21 43							22 43					23 52
Welwyn North	d					20 47							21 47							22 47					23 56
Welwyn Garden City 4	d	19 58		20 28		20 51		20 58			21 28		21 51		21 58		22 28			22 51		22 58			23 59
Hatfield	d	20 02		20 32		20 54		21 02			21 32		21 54		22 02		22 32			22 54		23 02			00 02
Welham Green	d	20 06		20 36				21 06			21 36				22 06		22 36					23 06			
Brookmans Park	d	20 08		20 38				21 08			21 38				22 08		22 38					23 08			
Potters Bar	d	20 11		20 41		21 00		21 11			21 41		22 00		22 11		22 41			23 00		23 11			00 08
Hadley Wood	d	20 15		20 45				21 15			21 45				22 15		22 45					23 15			
New Barnet	d	20 17		20 47				21 17			21 47				22 17		22 47					23 17			
Oakleigh Park	d	20 19		20 49				21 19			21 49				22 19		22 49					23 19			
New Southgate	d	20 22		20 52				21 22			21 52				22 22		22 52					23 22			
Alexandra Palace	d	20 25	20 40	20 55	21 10			21 25		21 40	21 55	22 10			22 25	22 40	22 55	23 10				23 25	23 40	00 10	
Hornsey	d	20 27	20 42	20 57	21 12			21 27		21 42	21 57	22 12			22 27	22 42	22 57	23 12				23 27	23 42	00 12	
Harringay	d	20 29	20 44	20 59	21 14		←	21 29		21 44	21 59	22 14		←	22 29	22 44	22 59	23 14			←	23 29	23 44	00 14	
Finsbury Park	⊖ d	20 32	20 47	21 02	21 17	21 10	21 17	21 32		21 47	22 02	22 17	22 10	22 17	22 32	22 47	23 02	23 17		23 10	23 17	23 32	23 47	00 17	00 21
Drayton Park	d				→							→						→							
Highbury & Islington	⊖ d																								
Essex Road	d																								
Old Street	⊖ d																								
Moorgate	⊖ a																								
London Kings Cross 15	⊖ a	20 40	20 55	21 10		21 19	21 25	21 40		21 55	22 10		22 19	22 25	22 40	22 55	23 12			23 19	23 26	23 44	23 56	00 26	00 33

Table 24

Sundays
from 30 October

Letchworth Garden City, Hertford North and Welwyn Garden City - London

		FC	FC 1	FC	FC	FC 1	FC	FC	FC	FC		FC	FC 1	FC	FC	FC	FC	FC	FC 1	FC		FC	FC	FC	FC
Letchworth Garden City	d		23p46			06 29							07 29						08 29						
Hitchin 4	d		23p50			06 34							07 34						08 33						
Stevenage 4	d		23p55			06 40						07 29	07 40					08 29	08 39						09 29
Watton-at-Stone	d											07 36						08 36							09 36
Hertford North	d	23p42		06 12			06 42		07 12			07 42				08 12		08 42					09 12		09 42
Bayford	d	23p46		06 16			06 46		07 16			07 46				08 16		08 46					09 16		09 46
Cuffley	d	23p51		06 21			06 51		07 21			07 51				08 21		08 51					09 21		09 51
Crews Hill	d	23p54		06 24			06 54		07 24			07 54				08 24		08 54					09 24		09 54
Gordon Hill	d	23p57		06 27			06 57		07 27			07 57				08 27		08 57					09 27		09 57
Enfield Chase	d	23p59		06 29			06 59		07 29			07 59				08 29		08 59					09 29		09 59
Grange Park	d	00 01		06 31			07 01		07 31			08 01				08 31		09 01					09 31		10 01
Winchmore Hill	d	00 03		06 33			07 03		07 33			08 03				08 33		09 03					09 33		10 03
Palmers Green	d	00 05		06 35			07 05		07 35			08 05				08 35		09 05					09 35		10 05
Bowes Park	d	00 08		06 38			07 08		07 38			08 08				08 38		09 08					09 38		10 08
Knebworth	d		23p59			06 43							07 43						08 43						
Welwyn North	d		00 06			06 47							07 47						08 47						
Welwyn Garden City 4	d		00 09		06 28	06 51		06 58		07 28			07 51		07 58		08 28		08 51			08 58		09 28	
Hatfield	d		00 13		06 32	06 54		07 02		07 32			07 54		08 02		08 32		08 54			09 02		09 32	
Welham Green	d				06 36			07 06		07 36					08 06		08 36					09 06		09 36	
Brookmans Park	d				06 38			07 08		07 38					08 08		08 38					09 08		09 38	
Potters Bar	d		00 18		06 41	07 00		07 11		07 41			08 00		08 11		08 41		09 00			09 11		09 41	
Hadley Wood	d				06 45			07 15		07 45					08 15		08 45					09 15		09 45	
New Barnet	d				06 47			07 17		07 47					08 17		08 47					09 17		09 47	
Oakleigh Park	d				06 49			07 19		07 49					08 19		08 49					09 19		09 49	
New Southgate	d				06 52			07 22		07 52					08 22		08 52					09 22		09 52	
Alexandra Palace	d	00 10		06 40	06 55		07 10	07 25	07 40	07 55		08 11			08 25	08 40	08 55	09 10				09 25	09 40	09 55	10 11
Hornsey	d	00 12		06 42	06 57		07 12	07 27	07 42	07 57		08 13			08 27	08 42	08 57	09 12				09 27	09 42	09 57	10 13
Harringay	d	00 14		06 44	06 59		07 14	07 29	07 44	07 59		08 15		←	08 29	08 44	08 59	09 14		←		09 29	09 44	09 59	10 15
Finsbury Park	⊖ d	00 17	00s32	06 47	07 02	07 10	07 17	07 32	07 47	08 02		08 17	08 09	08 17	08 32	08 47	09 02	09 17	09 10	09 17		09 32	09 47	10 02	10 17
Drayton Park	d											→						→							→
Highbury & Islington	⊖ d																								
Essex Road	d																								
Old Street	⊖ d																								
Moorgate	⊖ a																								
London Kings Cross 15	⊖ a	00 25	00 40	06 57	07 13	07 20	07 29	07 45	07 56	08 15			08 20	08 26	08 40	08 55	09 10		09 19	09 25		09 40	09 55	10 10	

		FC 1	FC	FC	FC 1	FC		FC	FC	FC 1	FC	FC	FC	FC	FC	FC 1		FC	FC	FC	FC	FC 1	FC	FC	FC
Letchworth Garden City	d	09 29			10 00					10 29						11 29						12 29			
Hitchin 4	d	09 33			10 04					10 33						11 33						12 33			
Stevenage 4	d	09 39			10 10				10 29	10 39					11 29	11 39						12 39			
Watton-at-Stone	d								10 36						11 36										
Hertford North	d					10 12			10 42				11 12		11 42					12 12			12 42		13 12
Bayford	d					10 16			10 46				11 16		11 46					12 16			12 46		13 16
Cuffley	d					10 21			10 51				11 21		11 51					12 21			12 51		13 21
Crews Hill	d					10 24			10 54				11 24		11 54					12 24			12 54		13 24
Gordon Hill	d					10 27			10 57				11 27		11 57					12 27			12 57		13 27
Enfield Chase	d					10 29			10 59				11 29		11 59					12 29			12 59		13 29
Grange Park	d					10 31			11 01				11 31		12 01					12 31			13 01		13 31
Winchmore Hill	d					10 33			11 03				11 33		12 03					12 33			13 03		13 33
Palmers Green	d					10 35			11 05				11 35		12 05					12 35			13 05		13 35
Bowes Park	d					10 38			11 08				11 38		12 08					12 38			13 08		13 38
Knebworth	d	09 43			10 13					10 43						11 43						12 43			
Welwyn North	d	09 47			10 17					10 47						11 47						12 47			
Welwyn Garden City 4	d	09 51		09 58	10 21			10 28		10 50		10 58		11 28		11 51			11 58		12 28	12 50		12 58	
Hatfield	d	09 54		10 02	10 24			10 32		10 54		11 02		11 32		11 54			12 02		12 32	12 54		13 02	
Welham Green	d			10 06				10 36				11 06		11 36					12 06		12 36			13 06	
Brookmans Park	d			10 08				10 38				11 08		11 38					12 08		12 38			13 08	
Potters Bar	d	10 00		10 11	10 30			10 41		10 59		11 11		11 41		12 00			12 11		12 41	13 00		13 11	
Hadley Wood	d			10 15				10 45				11 15		11 45					12 15		12 45			13 15	
New Barnet	d			10 17				10 47				11 17		11 47					12 17		12 47			13 17	
Oakleigh Park	d			10 19				10 49				11 19		11 49					12 19		12 49			13 19	
New Southgate	d			10 22				10 52				11 22		11 52					12 22		12 52			13 22	
Alexandra Palace	d			10 25		10 41		10 55	11 10			11 25	11 40	11 55	12 10				12 25	12 40	12 55		13 10	13 25	13 40
Hornsey	d			10 27		10 43		10 57	11 12			11 27	11 42	11 57	12 12				12 27	12 42	12 57		13 12	13 27	13 42
Harringay	d		←	10 29		10 45		10 59	11 14		←	11 29	11 44	11 59	12 14			←	12 29	12 44	12 59		13 14	13 29	13 44
Finsbury Park	⊖ d	10 10	10 17	10 32	10 40	10 47		11 02	11 17	11 11	11 17	11 32	11 47	12 02	12 17	12 10		12 17	12 32	12 47	13 02	13 11	13 17	13 32	13 47
Drayton Park	d								→						→										
Highbury & Islington	⊖ d																								
Essex Road	d																								
Old Street	⊖ d																								
Moorgate	⊖ a																								
London Kings Cross 15	⊖ a	10 19	10 25	10 40	10 49	10 55		11 10		11 20	11 25	11 40	11 55	12 10		12 19		12 25	12 40	12 55	13 10	13 19	13 25	13 40	13 55

Table 24

Sundays
from 30 October

Letchworth Garden City, Hertford North and Welwyn Garden City - London

		FC		FC	FC 1	FC	FC	FC	FC	FC	FC 1	FC		FC	FC	FC	FC	FC 1	FC	FC	FC	FC		FC	FC 1
Letchworth Garden City	d				13 29						14 29							15 29							16 29
Hitchin 4	d				13 34						14 34							15 34							16 34
Stevenage 4	d			13 29	13 40					14 29	14 40						15 29	15 40						16 29	16 40
Watton-at-Stone	d			13 36						14 36							15 36							16 36	
Hertford North	d			13 42				14 12		14 42					15 12		15 42				16 12			16 42	
Bayford	d			13 46				14 16		14 46					15 16		15 46				16 16			16 46	
Cuffley	d			13 51				14 21		14 51					15 21		15 51				16 21			16 51	
Crews Hill	d			13 54				14 24		14 54					15 24		15 54				16 24			16 54	
Gordon Hill	d			13 57				14 27		14 57					15 27		15 57				16 27			16 57	
Enfield Chase	d			13 59				14 29		14 59					15 29		15 59				16 29			16 59	
Grange Park	d			14 01				14 31		15 01					15 31		16 01				16 31			17 01	
Winchmore Hill	d			14 03				14 33		15 03					15 33		16 03				16 33			17 03	
Palmers Green	d			14 05				14 35		15 05					15 35		16 05				16 35			17 05	
Bowes Park	d			14 08				14 38		15 08					15 38		16 08				16 38			17 08	
Knebworth	d				13 43						14 43							15 43							16 43
Welwyn North	d				13 47						14 47							15 47							16 47
Welwyn Garden City 4	d	13 28			13 51		13 58		14 28		14 51			14 58		15 28		15 51		15 58		16 28			16 51
Hatfield	d	13 32			13 54		14 02		14 32		14 54			15 02		15 32		15 54		16 02		16 32			16 54
Welham Green	d	13 36					14 06		14 36					15 06		15 36				16 06		16 36			
Brookmans Park	d	13 38					14 08		14 38					15 08		15 38				16 08		16 38			
Potters Bar	d	13 41			14 00		14 11		14 41		15 00			15 11		15 41		16 00		16 11		16 41			17 00
Hadley Wood	d	13 45					14 15		14 45					15 15		15 45				16 15		16 45			
New Barnet	d	13 47					14 17		14 47					15 17		15 47				16 17		16 47			
Oakleigh Park	d	13 49					14 19		14 49					15 19		15 49				16 19		16 49			
New Southgate	d	13 52					14 22		14 52					15 22		15 52				16 22		16 52			
Alexandra Palace	d	13 55		14 10			14 25	14 40	14 55	15 10				15 25	15 40	15 55	16 10			16 25	16 40	16 55		17 10	
Hornsey	d	13 57		14 12			14 27	14 42	14 57	15 12				15 27	15 42	15 57	16 12			16 27	16 42	16 57		17 12	
Harringay	d	13 59		14 14		←	14 29	14 44	14 59	15 14		←		15 29	15 44	15 59	16 14		←	16 29	16 44	16 59		17 14	
Finsbury Park ⊖	d	14 02		14 17	14 11	14 17	14 32	14 47	15 02	15 17	15 10	15 17		15 32	15 47	16 02	16 17	16 10	16 17	16 32	16 47	17 02		17 17	17 10
Drayton Park	d			→						→							→							→	
Highbury & Islington ⊖	d																								
Essex Road	d																								
Old Street ⊖	d																								
Moorgate ⊖	a																								
London Kings Cross 15 ⊖	a	14 10			14 19	14 25	14 40	14 55	15 10		15 19	15 25		15 40	15 55	16 10		16 19	16 25	16 40	16 55	17 10			17 19

		FC	FC	FC	FC	FC	FC 1	FC		FC	FC	FC	FC	FC 1	FC	FC	FC	FC		FC	FC 1	FC	FC	FC	FC
Letchworth Garden City	d						17 29							18 29							19 29				
Hitchin 4	d						17 34							18 34							19 34				
Stevenage 4	d					17 29	17 40						18 29	18 40						19 29	19 40				
Watton-at-Stone	d					17 36							18 36							19 36					
Hertford North	d			17 12		17 42					18 12		18 42				19 12			19 42				20 12	
Bayford	d			17 16		17 46					18 16		18 46				19 16			19 46				20 16	
Cuffley	d			17 21		17 51					18 21		18 51				19 21			19 51				20 21	
Crews Hill	d			17 24		17 54					18 24		18 54				19 24			19 54				20 24	
Gordon Hill	d			17 27		17 57					18 27		18 57				19 27			19 57				20 27	
Enfield Chase	d			17 29		17 59					18 29		18 59				19 29			19 59				20 29	
Grange Park	d			17 31		18 01					18 31		19 01				19 31			20 01				20 31	
Winchmore Hill	d			17 33		18 03					18 33		19 03				19 33			20 03				20 33	
Palmers Green	d			17 35		18 05					18 35		19 05				19 35			20 05				20 35	
Bowes Park	d			17 38		18 08					18 38		19 08				19 38			20 08				20 38	
Knebworth	d						17 43							18 43							19 43				
Welwyn North	d						17 47							18 47							19 47				
Welwyn Garden City 4	d		16 58		17 28		17 51			17 58		18 28		18 51		18 58		19 28			19 51		19 58		20 28
Hatfield	d		17 02		17 32		17 54			18 02		18 32		18 54		19 02		19 32			19 54		20 02		20 32
Welham Green	d		17 06		17 36					18 06		18 36				19 06		19 36					20 06		20 36
Brookmans Park	d		17 08		17 38					18 08		18 38				19 08		19 38					20 08		20 38
Potters Bar	d		17 11		17 41		18 00			18 11		18 41		19 00		19 11		19 41			20 00		20 11		20 41
Hadley Wood	d		17 15		17 45					18 15		18 45				19 15		19 45					20 15		20 45
New Barnet	d		17 17		17 47					18 17		18 47				19 17		19 47					20 17		20 47
Oakleigh Park	d		17 19		17 49					18 19		18 49				19 19		19 49					20 19		20 49
New Southgate	d		17 22		17 52					18 22		18 52				19 22		19 52					20 22		20 52
Alexandra Palace	d		17 25	17 40	17 55	18 10				18 25	18 40	18 55	19 10			19 25	19 40	19 55		20 10			20 25	20 40	20 55
Hornsey	d		17 27	17 42	17 57	18 12				18 27	18 42	18 57	19 12			19 27	19 42	19 57		20 12			20 27	20 42	20 57
Harringay	d	←	17 29	17 44	17 59	18 14		←		18 29	18 44	18 59	19 14		←	19 29	19 44	19 59		20 14		←	20 29	20 44	20 59
Finsbury Park ⊖	d	17 17	17 32	17 47	18 02	18 17	18 10	18 17		18 32	18 47	19 02	19 17	19 10	19 17	19 32	19 47	20 02		20 17	20 10	20 17	20 32	20 47	21 02
Drayton Park	d					→							→							→					
Highbury & Islington ⊖	d																								
Essex Road	d																								
Old Street ⊖	d																								
Moorgate ⊖	a																								
London Kings Cross 15 ⊖	a	17 25	17 40	17 55	18 10		18 19	18 25		18 40	18 55	19 10		19 19	19 25	19 40	19 55	20 10			20 19	20 25	20 40	20 55	21 10

Table 24

Sundays
from 30 October

Letchworth Garden City, Hertford North and Welwyn Garden City - London

		FC	FC 1	FC		FC	FC	FC	FC	FC 1	FC	FC	FC	FC		FC	FC 1	FC	FC	FC	FC	FC 1			
Letchworth Garden City	d		20 29							21 29							22 29					23 40			
Hitchin 4	d		20 34							21 34							22 33					23 44			
Stevenage 4	d	20 29	20 40						21 29	21 40						22 29	22 39				23 29	23 49			
Watton-at-Stone	d	20 36							21 36							22 36					23 36				
Hertford North	d	20 42					21 12		21 42				22 12			22 42				23 12	23 42				
Bayford	d	20 46					21 16		21 46				22 16			22 46				23 16	23 46				
Cuffley	d	20 51					21 21		21 51				22 21			22 51				23 21	23 51				
Crews Hill	d	20 54					21 24		21 54				22 24			22 54				23 24	23 54				
Gordon Hill	d	20 57					21 27		21 57				22 27			22 57				23 27	23 57				
Enfield Chase	d	20 59					21 29		21 59				22 29			22 59				23 29	23 59				
Grange Park	d	21 01					21 31		22 01				22 31			23 01				23 31	00 01				
Winchmore Hill	d	21 03					21 33		22 03				22 33			23 03				23 33	00 03				
Palmers Green	d	21 05					21 35		22 05				22 35			23 05				23 35	00 05				
Bowes Park	d	21 08					21 38		22 08				22 38			23 08				23 38	00 08				
Knebworth	d		20 43							21 43							22 43					23 52			
Welwyn North	d		20 47							21 47							22 47					23 56			
Welwyn Garden City 4	d		20 51			20 58		21 28		21 51		21 58		22 28			22 51		22 58			23 59			
Hatfield	d		20 54			21 02		21 32		21 54		22 02		22 32			22 54		23 02			00 02			
Welham Green	d					21 06		21 36				22 06		22 36					23 06						
Brookmans Park	d					21 08		21 38				22 08		22 38					23 08						
Potters Bar	d		21 00			21 11		21 41		22 00		22 11		22 41			23 00		23 11			00 08			
Hadley Wood	d					21 15		21 45				22 15		22 45					23 15						
New Barnet	d					21 17		21 47				22 17		22 47					23 17						
Oakleigh Park	d					21 19		21 49				22 19		22 49					23 19						
New Southgate	d					21 22		21 52				22 22		22 52					23 22						
Alexandra Palace	d	21 10				21 25	21 40	21 55	22 10			22 25	22 40	22 55		23 10			23 25	23 40	00 10				
Hornsey	d	21 12				21 27	21 42	21 57	22 12			22 27	22 42	22 57		23 12			23 27	23 42	00 12				
Harringay	d	21 14		←		21 29	21 44	21 59	22 14		←	22 29	22 44	22 59		23 14		←	23 29	23 44	00 14				
Finsbury Park ⊖	d	21 17	21 10	21 17		21 32	21 47	22 02	22 17	22 10	22 17	22 32	22 47	23 02		23 17	23 10	23 17	23 32	23 47	00 17	00 21			
Drayton Park	d	→							→							→									
Highbury & Islington ⊖	d																								
Essex Road	d																								
Old Street ⊖	d																								
Moorgate ⊖	a																								
London Kings Cross 15 ⊖	a		21 19	21 25		21 40	21 55	22 10		22 19	22 25	22 40	22 55	23 12			23 19	23 26	23 44	23 56	00 26	00 33			

Table 25

Mondays to Fridays

London - Stevenage, Cambridge and Peterborough

Miles	Miles			FC	FC	FC	FC	FC	FC	FC	FC	FC	FC	FC	FC	FC	FC	FC	FC	FC	FC	FC	FC
				MX			MX					MX	MO	MX	MO	MX	MX	MX	MO	MX	MX		
				1	1	1	1	1	1	1	1	1	1	1			1			1		1	1
					A	B		C	D	A	B											C	E
0	0	**London Kings Cross** 15 ⊖	d	23p01	23p06	23p06	23p06	23p10	23p15				23p23	23p23	23p26	23p26	23p36		23p41	00 04	00 06	00 07	00 07
2½	2½	Finsbury Park ⊖	d		23p11	23p12	23p11						23p28	23p28	23p32	23p32	23p41		23p47	00 09	00 12	00 12	00 12
12¾	12¾	Potters Bar	d		23p21	23p21	23p21										23p51		00 08				
17¾	17¾	Hatfield	d		23p27	23p27	23p27										23p57		00 16				
20¼	20¼	Welwyn Garden City 4	d		23p31	23p31	23p31										00 01		00 20				
22	22	Welwyn North	d		23p34	23p34	23p34										00 04		00 23				
25	25	Knebworth	d		23p38	23p38	23p38										00 08		00 28				
—	—	Hertford North	d												00 07	00 07		←			00 47		00 39
27½	27½	**Stevenage** 4	d		23p42	23p42	23p42						23p47	23p47	00a20	00 20	00 12	00 20	00 31	00 31	01 00	00 48	00 48
31¾	31¾	Hitchin 4	d		23p47	23p47	23p50			←	←	←	23p52	23p53		→	00 20	00 26	00 37	00 39	→	00 56	00 56
34¾	—	Letchworth Garden City	d		23p51	23p51	23p54	23p44	23p44	23p51	23p51	23p54					00a29	00a36	00a52	00 43		01 00	01 00
36¾	—	Baldock	d		→	→	→			23p54	23p54	23p57								00 46		01 04	01 04
41	—	Ashwell & Morden	d							23p59	23p59	00 02								00 51		01 09	01 09
45	—	Royston	d					23p54	23p54	00 04	00 04	00 07								00 56		01 13	01 13
48	—	Meldreth	d							00 08	00 08	00 11								00 59		01 17	01 17
50	—	Shepreth	d							00 11	00 11	00 14								01 02		01 20	01 20
51	—	Foxton	d							00 14	00 14	00 17								01 05		01 23	01 23
58	—	**Cambridge**	a					00 10	00 10	00 29	00 29	00 29								01 22		01 39	01 39
—	37	Arlesey	d										23p57	23p59									
—	41	Biggleswade	d	23p29									00 02	00 04									
—	44	Sandy	d										00 06	00 08									
—	51½	St Neots	d	23p38									00 13	00 15									
—	58¾	Huntingdon	d	23p45									00 21	00 23									
—	76¼	**Peterborough** 8	a	00 12									00 43	00 42									

		FC	FC	FC	FC	FC	FC	FC	FC	FC	GR	FC	FC	GR	FC	FC	FC	GR	FC	FC	FC	FC	GR
		MX	MO	MX	MX	MO																	
			1	1	1	1	1	1		1	1		1	1	1	1		1	1	1	1	1	1
London Kings Cross 15 ⊖	d		00 36	00 36	01 06	01 06	01 36	05 23		05 45	05 50	05 56	06 06	06 15		06 23	06 26	06 30	06 36	06 45	06 53	07 06	07 08
Finsbury Park ⊖	d		00 41	00 41	01 11	01 11	01 41	05 28		05 50		06 02	06 11			06 28	06 32		06 41		06 58	07 11	
Potters Bar	d		00 51	00 51			01 59	05 38					06 21						06 51			07 21	
Hatfield	d		00 57	00 57			02 05	05 44					06 27						06 57			07 27	
Welwyn Garden City 4	d		01 01	01 01			02 09	05 48					06 31						07 01			07 31	
Welwyn North	d		01s04	01s04			02s12	05 51					06 34						07 04			07 34	
Knebworth	d		01s08	01s08			02s16	05 55					06 38						07 08			07 38	
Hertford North	d	←			01 38	01 40			05 50			06 40			←		07 10						
Stevenage 4	d	01 00	01 12	01 12	01 47	01 50	02 20	05 59	06a05	06 08	06 11	06a55	06 42	06 34	06 42	06 47	07a25	06 49	07 12		07 17	07 42	07 27
Hitchin 4	d	01 06	01 17	01 17	01 52	01 56	02 25	06 07		06 13			→		06 47	06 52			07 17		07 22	→	
Letchworth Garden City	d	01a15			02a06	02a10				06 18					06 51						07 26		
Baldock	d									06 21					06 55						07 29		
Ashwell & Morden	d									06 26					07 00						07 35		
Royston	d									06 31					07 06						07 39		
Meldreth	d									06 35					07 10						07 43		
Shepreth	d									06 38					07 13						07 46		
Foxton	d									06 40					07 16						07 49		
Cambridge	a									06 55					07 29					07 32	08 02		
Arlesey	d		01s25	01s25				06 13								06 57			07 23				
Biggleswade	d		01s30	01s30			02s37	06 18								07 02			07 28				
Sandy	d		01s34	01s34				06 22								07 06			07 32				
St Neots	d		01s42	01s42			02s47	06 29								07 13			07 39				
Huntingdon	d		01s52	01s52			02s57	06 37								07 21			07 47				
Peterborough 8	a		02 11	02 13			03 16	06 54			06 41			07 04		07 38		07 19	08 06				07 57

		FC	FC	FC	GR	FC	FC	FC	FC	FC	FC	GR	FC	FC	FC	FC	GR	FC	FC	FC	GR
		1	1	1	1	1	1	1	1	1	1	1	1	1	1	1	1	1	1	1	1
London Kings Cross 15 ⊖	d	07 15		07 22	07 35	07 36	07 45	07 53	08 03	08 15	08 23	08 35	08 36	08 45	08 53	09 06	09 08	09 15		09 23	09 35
Finsbury Park ⊖	d			07 28		07 41		07 58	08 08		08 28		08 41		08 58	09 11				09 28	
Potters Bar	d					07 51			08 18				08 51			09 21					
Hatfield	d					07 57			08 25				08 57			09 27					
Welwyn Garden City 4	d					08 01			08 30				09 01			09 31					
Welwyn North	d					08 04			08 33				09 04			09 34					
Knebworth	d					08 08			08 37				09 08			09 38					
Hertford North	d		←																←		
Stevenage 4	d		07 42	07 47	07a54	08 12		08 17	08 41		08 47	08a54	09 12		09 17	09 42	09 29		09 42	09 47	09a54
Hitchin 4	d		07 47	07 52		08 17		08 22	08 46		08 52		09 17		09 22	→			09 47	09 52	
Letchworth Garden City	d		07 51					08 26	08 54						09 26				09 51		
Baldock	d		07 55					08 29	08 58						09 29				09 55		
Ashwell & Morden	d		08 00					08 35	09 03						09 35				10 00		
Royston	d		08 06					08 39	09 07						09 39				10 04		
Meldreth	d		08 10					08 43	09 11						09 43				10 08		
Shepreth	d		08 13					08 46	09 14						09 46				10 11		
Foxton	d		08 16					08 49	09 17						09 49				10 14		
Cambridge	a	08 02	08 28				08 32	09 00	09 29	09 03				09 31	10 02			10 03	10 29		
Arlesey	d			07 57		08 23					08 57		09 23							09 57	
Biggleswade	d			08 02		08 28					09 02		09 28							10 02	
Sandy	d			08 06		08 32					09 06		09 32							10 06	
St Neots	d			08 13		08 39					09 13		09 39							10 13	
Huntingdon	d			08 21		08 47					09 21		09 47							10 21	
Peterborough 8	a			08 38		09 05					09 38		10 06				10 00			10 38	

A MO until 12 September, MO from 31 October
B MO from 19 September until 24 October
C MO from 8 August until 12 September
D until 5 August, MX from 9 August until 9 September, from 13 September
E MO until 1 August, MO from 19 September

London - Stevenage, Cambridge and Peterborough

		FC	FC	FC	FC	GR	FC	FC	FC	GR		FC	FC	FC	FC	GR	FC	FC	FC	GR		FC	FC	FC	FC
						[R]				[R]						[R]				[R]					
		[1]	[1]	[1]	[1]	[1]	[1]	[1]	[1]	[1]		[1]	[1]	[1]	[1]	[1]	[1]	[1]	[1]	[1]		[1]	[1]	[1]	[1]
						[trolley]				[restaurant] [trolley]						[trolley] [Ø]				[restaurant] [trolley]					
London Kings Cross [15] ⊖	d	09 36	09 45	09 53	10 06	10 08	10 15		10 23	10 35		10 36	10 45	10 53	11 06	11 08	11 15		11 23	11 35		11 36	11 45	11 53	12 06
Finsbury Park ⊖	d	09 41		09 58	10 11				10 28			10 41		10 58	11 11				11 28			11 41		11 58	12 11
Potters Bar	d	09 51			10 21							10 51			11 21							11 51			12 21
Hatfield	d	09 57			10 27							10 57			11 27							11 57			12 27
Welwyn Garden City [4]	d	10 01			10 31							11 01			11 31							12 01			12 31
Welwyn North	d	10 04			10 34							11 04			11 34							12 04			12 34
Knebworth	d	10 08			10 38							11 08			11 38							12 08			12 38
Hertford North	d							←										←							
Stevenage [4]	d	10 12		10 17	10 42	10 28		10 42	10 47	10a54		11 12		11 17	11 42	11 27		11 42	11 47	11a54		12 12		12 17	12 42
Hitchin [4]	d	10 17		10 22	→			10 47	10 52			11 17		11 22	→			11 47	11 52			12 17		12 22	→
Letchworth Garden City	d			10 26				10 51						11 26				11 51						12 26	
Baldock	d			10 29				10 55						11 29				11 55						12 29	
Ashwell & Morden	d							11 00										12 00							
Royston	d			10 37				11 04						11 37				12 04						12 37	
Meldreth	d							11 08										12 08							
Shepreth	d							11 11										12 11							
Foxton	d							11 14										12 14							
Cambridge	a		10 31	10 54			11 01	11 29					11 31	11 54			12 01	12 27					12 31	12 54	
Arlesey	d	10 23							10 57			11 23							11 57			12 23			
Biggleswade	d	10 28							11 02			11 28							12 02			12 28			
Sandy	d	10 32							11 06			11 32							12 06			12 32			
St Neots	d	10 39							11 13			11 39							12 13			12 39			
Huntingdon	d	10 47							11 21			11 47							12 21			12 47			
Peterborough [8]	a	11 06				10 58			11 38			12 06				11 57			12 38			13 06			

		GR	FC	FC	FC	GR		FC	FC	FC	FC	GR	FC	FC	FC	GR		FC	FC	FC	FC	GR	FC	FC	FC
		[R]				[R]						[R]				[R]						[R]			
		[1]	[1]	[1]	[1]	[1]		[1]	[1]	[1]	[1]	[1]	[1]	[1]	[1]	[1]		[1]	[1]	[1]	[1]	[1]	[1]	[1]	[1]
		[restaurant]				[restaurant] [trolley]						[trolley] [Ø]				[restaurant] [trolley]						[restaurant]			
London Kings Cross [15] ⊖	d	12 08	12 15		12 23	12 35		12 36	12 45	12 53	13 06	13 08	13 15		13 23	13 35		13 36	13 45	13 53	14 06	14 08	14 15		14 23
Finsbury Park ⊖	d				12 28			12 41		12 58	13 11				13 28			13 41		13 58	14 11				14 28
Potters Bar	d							12 51			13 21							13 51			14 21				
Hatfield	d							12 57			13 27							13 57			14 27				
Welwyn Garden City [4]	d							13 01			13 31							14 01			14 31				
Welwyn North	d							13 04			13 34							14 04			14 34				
Knebworth	d							13 08			13 38							14 08			14 38				
Hertford North	d			←										←										←	
Stevenage [4]	d	12 28		12 42	12 47	12a54		13 12		13 17	13 42	13 29		13 42	13 47	13a54		14 12		14 17	14 42	14 28		14 42	14 47
Hitchin [4]	d			12 47	12 52			13 17		13 22	→			13 47	13 52			14 17		14 22	→			14 47	14 52
Letchworth Garden City	d			12 51						13 26				13 51						14 26				14 51	
Baldock	d			12 55						13 29				13 55						14 29				14 55	
Ashwell & Morden	d			13 00										14 00										15 00	
Royston	d			13 04						13 37				14 04						14 37				15 04	
Meldreth	d			13 08										14 08										15 08	
Shepreth	d			13 11										14 11										15 11	
Foxton	d			13 14										14 14										15 14	
Cambridge	a		13 01	13 27					13 31	13 54			14 01	14 27					14 31	14 54			15 01	15 29	
Arlesey	d				12 57			13 23							13 57			14 23							14 57
Biggleswade	d				13 02			13 28							14 02			14 28							15 02
Sandy	d				13 06			13 32							14 06			14 32							15 06
St Neots	d				13 13			13 39							14 13			14 39							15 13
Huntingdon	d				13 21			13 47							14 21			14 47							15 21
Peterborough [8]	a	12 58			13 38			14 06				13 59			14 38			15 06				14 58			15 38

		GR		FC	FC	FC	FC	GR	FC	FC	FC	GR		FC	FC	FC	FC	GR	FC	FC	FC	FC		FC	GR
		[R]						[R]				[R]						[R]							[R]
		[1]		[1]	[1]	[1]	[1]	[1]	[1]	[1]	[1]	[1]		[1]	[1]	[1]	[1]	[1]	[1]	[1]	[1]	[1]		[1]	[1]
		[restaurant] [trolley]						[trolley] [Ø]				[restaurant] [trolley]						[restaurant]							[restaurant] [trolley]
London Kings Cross [15] ⊖	d	14 35		14 36	14 45	14 53	15 06	15 08	15 15		15 23	15 35		15 36	15 44	15 53	16 06	16 08	16 14	16 17		16 22		16 32	16 33
Finsbury Park ⊖	d			14 41		14 58	15 11				15 28			15 41		15 58	16 11					16 27		16 37	
Potters Bar	d			14 51			15 21							15 51			16 21							16 47	
Hatfield	d			14 57			15 27							15 57			16 27							16 54	
Welwyn Garden City [4]	d			15 01			15 31							16 01			16 32							16 58	
Welwyn North	d			15 04			15 34							16 04			16 35							17 02	
Knebworth	d			15 08			15 38							16 08			16 39							17 06	
Hertford North	d									←											←				
Stevenage [4]	d	14a54		15 12		15 17	15 42	15 28		15 42	15 47	15a54		16 12		16 17	16 43	16 29		16 37	16 43	16 47		17 10	16a52
Hitchin [4]	d			15 17		15 22	→			15 47	15 52			16 17		16 22	→				16 50	16 54		17 17	
Letchworth Garden City	d					15 26				15 51					16 09	16 26				16 46	16 55			17 25	
Baldock	d					15 29				15 55						16 29				16 49	16 59			→	
Ashwell & Morden	d									16 00						16 34				16 54	17 04				
Royston	d					15 37				16 04					16 19	16 38				17a01	17 08				
Meldreth	d									16 08											17 12				
Shepreth	d									16 11											17 15				
Foxton	d									16 14											17 18				
Cambridge	a				15 31	15 54			16 02	16 29					16 34	16 54			17 01		17 30				
Arlesey	d			15 23							15 57			16 23								16 59			
Biggleswade	d			15 28							16 02			16 28								17 04			
Sandy	d			15 32							16 06			16 32								17 12			
St Neots	d			15 39							16 13			16 39								17 23			
Huntingdon	d			15 47							16 21			16 47								17a33			
Peterborough [8]	a			16 06				15 58			16 38			17 06				16 59							

London - Stevenage, Cambridge and Peterborough

		FC	FC	FC	FC	FC	FC	FC		FC	FC	FC	FC	GR	FC	FC	FC	FC		FC	FC	FC	FC	FC	FC
														R											
		1	1	1	1	1	1	1		1	1	1	1	1	1	1	1	1		1	1	1	1	1	1
London Kings Cross 15 ⊖	d	16 40	16 44		16 52	16 54	17 10	17 14			17 14	17 22	17 23	17 33	17 40	17 44		17 44		17 52	17 53	18 10	18 14		
Finsbury Park ⊖	d				16 57	16 59					17 19	17 28						17 49		17 58					
Potters Bar	d																								
Hatfield	d					17 15														18 14					
Welwyn Garden City 4	d					17 19						17 47								18 18					
Welwyn North	d				17 12	17 23						17 51								18 22					
Knebworth	d					17 27					17 35	17 55								18 26					
Hertford North	d																←								←
Stevenage 4	d				17 17	17 36				←	17 40	18 04	17 43	17a53			18 04	18 09		18 34	18 13				18 34
Hitchin 4	d			←	17 24	17 42	17 34			17 42	17 46	→			18 04		18 10	18 16		→		18 34			18 40
Letchworth Garden City	d		17 10	17 25		→				17 47			17 52				18 16				18 22				18 47
Baldock	d			17 29						17 51			17 55								18 25				18 51
Ashwell & Morden	d			17 34						17 56			18 00								18 30				18 56
Royston	d		17 20	17 38				17 48		18 01			18a07			18 18	18 30				18a37		18 51	18 55	19 01
Meldreth	d			17 42						18 05							18 34							18 58	
Shepreth	d			17 45						18 08							18 37							19 01	
Foxton	d			17 48						18 10							18 39							19 04	
Cambridge	a		17 35	18 02				18 03		18 24						18 33	18 54						19 07	19 18	19 24
Arlesey	d				17 29						17 51							18 21							
Biggleswade	d	17 07			17 34						17 56							18 26							
Sandy	d				17 38						18 00							18 30							
St Neots	d	17 17			17 46		17 51				18 08				18 21			18 38				18 51			
Huntingdon	d	17 26			17 54		17 59				18 16				18 29			18 46				18 59			
Peterborough 8	a	17 42			18 12		18 22				18 32				18 50			19 04				19 21			

		FC	FC	FC		GR	FC	FC	FC	FC	FC	FC	GR	FC		FC	FC	FC	FC	GR	FC	FC	FC	FC	
						R							R							R					
		1	1	1		1	1	1	1	1	1	1	1	1		1	1	1	1	1	1	1	1	1	
London Kings Cross 15 ⊖	d	18 14	18 22	18 23		18 33	18 40	18 44		18 44	18 52	18 53	19 06	19 10		19 15		19 18	19 23	19 33		19 34	19 45		
Finsbury Park ⊖	d	18 19	18 29							18 49	18 58							19 23	19 28			19 39			
Potters Bar	d																	19 37							
Hatfield	d		18 45								19 14							19 44				19 53			
Welwyn Garden City 4	d		18 49								19 19							19 49				20 00			
Welwyn North	d		18 51	18 41							19 24							19 53				20 03			
Knebworth	d		18 55							19 05	19 28							19 57				20 07			
Hertford North	d																←				←				
Stevenage 4	d	18 39	19 04			18a52			←	19 10	19 34	19 13	19 26				19 34	20 04	19 47	19a52	20 04	20 12			
Hitchin 4	d	18 46	19 10	18 52					19 10	19 16	→			19 36			19 42	→	19 53		20 13	20 17		←	
Letchworth Garden City	d		→	18 56					19 16			19 22				19 40	19 50				20 17	20a23	20 10	20 17	
Baldock	d			19 00								19 26					19 54				→			20 21	
Ashwell & Morden	d			19 05								19 31					19 59							20 26	
Royston	d			19a12				19 18	19 30			19a37				19 50	20 04						20 20	20 31	
Meldreth	d								19 34								20 08							20 35	
Shepreth	d								19 37								20 11							20 38	
Foxton	d								19 40								20 14							20 40	
Cambridge	a							19 33	19 56							20 08	20 27						20 35	20 54	
Arlesey	d	18 51								19 21									19 59						
Biggleswade	d	18 56					19 07			19 26									20 04						
Sandy	d	19 00								19 30									20 08						
St Neots	d	19 08					19 17			19 38				19 54					20 15						
Huntingdon	d	19 16					19 26			19 46				20 02					20 23						
Peterborough 8	a	19 40					19 44			20 03			19 56	20 22					20 41						

		FC	FC	FC	FC	FC	FC	GR	FC	FC		FC	GR	FC	FC	FC	FC	FC	FC	FC		FC	FC	FC	FC
								R					R												
		1	1	1	1	1	1	1	1	1		1	1	1	1	1	1	1	1	1		1	1	1	1
London Kings Cross 15 ⊖	d	19 53	20 06	20 10	20 15		20 23	20 35	20 36	20 45		20 53	21 00	21 06	21 07	21 15		21 23	21 36	21 53		22 06	22 07	22 15	
Finsbury Park ⊖	d	19 58	20 11				20 28		20 41			20 58		21 11				21 28	21 41	21 58		22 11			
Potters Bar	d		20 21						20 51					21 21					21 51			22 21			
Hatfield	d		20 27						20 57					21 27					21 57			22 27			
Welwyn Garden City 4	d		20 31						21 01					21 31					22 01			22 31			
Welwyn North	d		20 34						21 04					21 34					22 04			22 34			
Knebworth	d		20 38						21 08					21 38					22 08			22 38			
Hertford North	d																								
Stevenage 4	d	20 17	20 42				20 47	20 54	21 12			21 17	21 20	21 42				21 48	22 12	22 17		22 42			
Hitchin 4	d	20 23	20 47			←	20 53		21 17			21 22		21 47			←	21 53	22 17	22 22		22 47			←
Letchworth Garden City	d		20 51		20 40	20 51			21a23			21 29		21 51		21 40	21 51		22a23	22 29		22 51		22 40	22 51
Baldock	d		→			20 55						21 32		→			21 55			22 32		→			22 55
Ashwell & Morden	d					21 00						21 37					22 00			22 37					23 00
Royston	d				20 50	21 04						21 42				21 50	22 04			22 41				22 50	23 04
Meldreth	d					21 08						21 45					22 08								23 08
Shepreth	d					21 11						21 48					22 11								23 11
Foxton	d					21 14						21 51					22 14								23 14
Cambridge	a				21 04	21 27				21 31		22 03				22 06	22 27			22 58				23 05	23 27
Arlesey	d	20 29					20 59											21 59							
Biggleswade	d	20 34					21 04								21 35			22 04					22 35		
Sandy	d	20 38					21 08											22 08							
St Neots	d	20 45		20 45			21 15								21 44			22 15					22 44		
Huntingdon	d	20 58		20 53			21 23								21 51			22 23					22 51		
Peterborough 8	a	21 21		21 12			21 41	21 24					21 50		22 07			22 41					23 07		

London - Stevenage, Cambridge and Peterborough

		FC 1	FC	FC 1	FC 1	FC		FC 1	FC 1	FC 1	FC 1	FC 1	FC	FC 1	FC
London Kings Cross 15 ⊖	d	22 23	22 26	22 36	22 53			23 01	23 06	23 15		23 23	23 26	23 36	
Finsbury Park ⊖	d	22 28	22 32	22 41	22 58				23 11			23 28	23 32	23 41	
Potters Bar	d			22 51					23 21					23 51	
Hatfield	d			22 57					23 27					23 57	
Welwyn Garden City 4	d			23 01					23 31					00 01	
Welwyn North	d			23 04					23 34					00 04	
Knebworth	d			23 08					23 38					00 08	
Hertford North	d		23 07			←							00 07		←
Stevenage 4	d	22 47	23 21	23 12	23 17	23 21			23 42			23 47	00 20	00 12	00 20
Hitchin 4	d	22 53	→	23 17	23 25	23 30			23 50		←	23 53	→	00 20	00 26
Letchworth Garden City	d			23a26	23 31	23a36			23 54	23 44	23 54			00a29	00a36
Baldock	d				23 34				→		23 57				
Ashwell & Morden	d				23 39						00 02				
Royston	d				23 44					23 54	00 07				
Meldreth	d										00 11				
Shepreth	d										00 14				
Foxton	d										00 17				
Cambridge	a				23 59					00 10	00 29				
Arlesey	d	22 59										23 59			
Biggleswade	d	23 04						23 29				00 04			
Sandy	d	23 08										00 08			
St Neots	d	23 15						23 38				00 15			
Huntingdon	d	23 23						23 45				00 23			
Peterborough 8	a	23 43						00 12				00 42			

Saturdays
until 18 June

		FC 1	FC 1	FC 1	FC 1	FC 1	FC	FC 1	FC	FC 1		FC 1	FC	FC 1	FC	FC 1	FC 1	FC 1	FC 1	FC 1		FC 1	GR R 1	FC 1	FC
London Kings Cross 15 ⊖	d	23p01	23p06	23p15		23p23	23p26	23p36		00 01		00 04	00 06	00 31		00 36	01 06	01 36	05 23	05 45		06 06	06 20	06 23	06 26
Finsbury Park ⊖	d		23p11			23p28	23p32	23p41				00 09	00 12			00 41	01 11	01 41	05 28	05 50		06 11		06 28	06 32
Potters Bar	d		23p21					23p51								00 51		01 59	05 38			06 20			
Hatfield	d		23p27					23p57								00 57		02 05	05 44			06 25			
Welwyn Garden City 4	d		23p31					00 01								01 01		02 09	05 48			06 29			
Welwyn North	d		23p34					00 04								01s04		02s12	05 51			06 32			
Knebworth	d		23p38					00 08								01s08		02s16	05 55			06 36			
Hertford North	d						00 07		←				00 47		←		01 38								07 07
Stevenage 4	d		23p42			23p47	00 20	00 12	00 20	00s20		00 31	01 00	00s50	01 00	01 12	01 47	02 20	05 59	06 08		06 40	06 40	06 47	07a20
Hitchin 4	d		23p50		←	23p53	→	00 20	00 26	00s35		00 39	→	01s05	01 06	01 17	01 52	02 25	06 07	06 13		06 47		06 52	
Letchworth Garden City	d		23p54	23p44	23p54			00a29	00a36			00 43		01s08	01a15		02a06			06 16		06 51			
Baldock	d		→		23p57							00 46		01s11						06 19		06 54			
Ashwell & Morden	d				00 02							00 51								06 24		06 59			
Royston	d			23p54	00 07							00 56		01s19						06 29		07 04			
Meldreth	d				00 11							00 59								06 32		07 08			
Shepreth	d				00 14							01 02								06 35		07 11			
Foxton	d				00 17							01 05								06 38		07 13			
Cambridge	a			00 10	00 29							01 22		01 35						06 50		07 27			
Arlesey	d					23p59										01s25			06 13					06 57	
Biggleswade	d	23p29				00 04				00s44						01s30		02s37	06 18					07 02	
Sandy	d					00 08										01s34			06 22					07 06	
St Neots	d	23p38				00 15				00s53						01s42		02s47	06 29					07 13	
Huntingdon	d	23p45				00 23				01s04						01s52		02s57	06 37					07 21	
Peterborough 8	a	00 12				00 42				01 24						02 13		03 16	06 54				07 11	07 37	

		FC 1	FC 1	FC 1	GR R 1	FC 1		FC 1	FC	FC 1	FC 1	FC 1	FC 1	FC 1	FC 1	FC		FC 1	FC 1	FC 1	GR R 1	FC 1	FC 1	FC 1	FC
London Kings Cross 15 ⊖	d	06 36	06 44	06 53	07 03	07 06		07 23	07 26	07 36	07 44	07 53	08 06	08 15	08 23	08 26		08 36	08 44	08 53	09 03	09 06	09 15	09 23	09 26
Finsbury Park ⊖	d	06 41		06 58		07 11		07 28	07 32	07 41		07 58	08 11		08 28	08 32		08 41		08 58		09 11		09 28	09 32
Potters Bar	d	06 51				07 21				07 51			08 21					08 51				09 21			
Hatfield	d	06 57				07 27				07 57			08 27					08 57				09 27			
Welwyn Garden City 4	d	07 01				07 31				08 01			08 31					09 01				09 31			
Welwyn North	d	07 04				07 34				08 04			08 34					09 04				09 34			
Knebworth	d	07 08				07 38				08 08			08 38					09 08				09 38			
Hertford North	d								08 07							09 07									10 07
Stevenage 4	d	07 12		07 17	07 22	07 42		07 47	08a20	08 12		08 17	08 42		08 46	09a20		09 12		09 17	09 22	09 42		09 47	10a20
Hitchin 4	d	07 17		07 22		07 47		07 52		08 17		08 22	08 47		08 51			09 17		09 22		09 47		09 52	
Letchworth Garden City	d			07 26		07 51						08 26	08 51							09 26		09 52			
Baldock	d			07 29		07 55						08 29	08 55							09 29		09 55			
Ashwell & Morden	d			07 34		08 00							09 00									10 00			
Royston	d			07 38		08 04						08 37	09 04							09 37		10 04			
Meldreth	d			07 42		08 08							09 08									10 09			
Shepreth	d			07 45		08 11							09 11									10 12			
Foxton	d			07 47		08 14							09 14									10 14			
Cambridge	a		07 31	07 59		08 29					08 29	08 54	09 29	09 01					09 29	09 54		10 29	10 01		
Arlesey	d	07 23						07 57		08 23					08 57			09 23						09 57	
Biggleswade	d	07 28						08 02		08 28					09 02			09 28						10 02	
Sandy	d	07 32						08 06		08 32					09 05			09 32						10 06	
St Neots	d	07 39						08 13		08 39					09 13			09 39						10 13	
Huntingdon	d	07 47						08 21		08 47					09 20			09 47						10 21	
Peterborough 8	a	08 06			07 52			08 38		09 08					09 36			10 06			09 52			10 38	

Table 25

Saturdays
until 18 June

London - Stevenage, Cambridge and Peterborough

		FC		FC	FC	FC	FC	FC	FC	FC	FC	FC		GR	FC	FC	FC	FC	FC	FC	FC	FC		FC	FC
		1		1	1	1	1	1		1	1	1		R 1 🍴	1	1	1		1	1	1	1		1	1
London Kings Cross 15 ⊖	d	09 36		09 44	09 53	10 06	10 15	10 22	10 26	10 36	10 44	10 53		11 03	11 06	11 15	11 23	11 26	11 36	11 44	11 53	12 06		12 15	12 23
Finsbury Park ⊖	d	09 41			09 58	10 11		10 28	10 32	10 41		10 58			11 11		11 28	11 32	11 41		11 58	12 11			12 28
Potters Bar	d	09 51				10 21				10 51					11 21				11 51			12 21			
Hatfield	d	09 57				10 27				10 57					11 27				11 57			12 27			
Welwyn Garden City 4	d	10 01				10 31				11 01					11 31				12 01			12 31			
Welwyn North	d	10 04				10 34				11 04					11 34				12 04			12 34			
Knebworth	d	10 08				10 38				11 08					11 38				12 08			12 38			
Hertford North	d								11 07									12 07							
Stevenage 4	d	10 12			10 17	10 42		10 47	11a20	11 12		11 17		11 22	11 42		11 47	12a20	12 12		12 17	12 42			12 47
Hitchin 4	d	10 17			10 22	10 47		10 52		11 17		11 22			11 47		11 52		12 17		12 22	12 47			12 52
Letchworth Garden City	d				10 26	10 51						11 26			11 51						12 26	12 51			
Baldock	d				10 29	10 55						11 29			11 55						12 29	12 55			
Ashwell & Morden	d					11 00									12 00							13 00			
Royston	d				10 37	11 04						11 37			12 04						12 37	13 04			
Meldreth	d					11 08									12 08							13 08			
Shepreth	d					11 11									12 11							13 11			
Foxton	d					11 14									12 14							13 14			
Cambridge	a			10 29	10 54	11 29	11 01				11 29	11 54			12 29	12 01				12 29	12 54	13 29		13 01	
Arlesey	d	10 23						10 57		11 23							11 57		12 23						12 57
Biggleswade	d	10 28						11 02		11 28							12 02		12 28						13 02
Sandy	d	10 32						11 06		11 32							12 06		12 32						13 06
St Neots	d	10 39						11 13		11 39							12 13		12 39						13 13
Huntingdon	d	10 47						11 21		11 47							12 21		12 47						13 21
Peterborough 8	a	11 06						11 38		12 06				11 52			12 38		13 06						13 37

		FC	FC	FC	FC	GR	FC	FC		FC	FC	FC	FC	FC	FC	FC	FC	FC		FC	FC	FC	GR	FC	FC
			1	1	1	R 1 🍴	1	1		1		1	1	1	1	1	1			1	1	1	R 1 🍴	1	1
London Kings Cross 15 ⊖	d	12 26	12 36	12 44	12 53	13 03	13 06	13 15		13 23	13 26	13 36	13 44	13 53	14 06	14 15	14 23	14 26		14 36	14 44	14 53	15 03	15 06	15 15
Finsbury Park ⊖	d	12 32	12 41		12 58		13 11			13 28	13 32	13 41		13 58	14 11		14 28	14 32		14 41		14 58		15 11	
Potters Bar	d		12 51				13 21					13 51			14 21					14 51				15 21	
Hatfield	d		12 57				13 27					13 57			14 27					14 57				15 27	
Welwyn Garden City 4	d		13 01				13 31					14 01			14 31					15 01				15 31	
Welwyn North	d		13 04				13 34					14 04			14 34					15 04				15 34	
Knebworth	d		13 08				13 38					14 08			14 38					15 08				15 38	
Hertford North	d	13 07									14 07							15 07							
Stevenage 4	d	13a20	13 12		13 17	13 22	13 42			13 47	14a20	14 12		14 17	14 42		14 47	15a20		15 12		15 17	15 22	15 42	
Hitchin 4	d		13 17		13 22		13 47			13 52		14 17		14 22	14 47		14 52			15 18		15 22		15 47	
Letchworth Garden City	d				13 26		13 51							14 26	14 51							15 26		15 51	
Baldock	d				13 29		13 55							14 29	14 55							15 29		15 55	
Ashwell & Morden	d						14 00								15 00									16 00	
Royston	d				13 37		14 04							14 37	15 04							15 37		16 04	
Meldreth	d						14 08								15 08									16 08	
Shepreth	d						14 11								15 11									16 11	
Foxton	d						14 14								15 14									16 14	
Cambridge	a			13 29	13 54		14 29	14 01					14 29	14 54	15 30	15 01					15 29	15 54		16 29	16 01
Arlesey	d		13 23							13 57		14 23					14 57			15 23					
Biggleswade	d		13 28							14 02		14 28					15 02			15 28					
Sandy	d		13 32							14 06		14 32					15 06			15 32					
St Neots	d		13 39							14 13		14 39					15 13			15 39					
Huntingdon	d		13 47							14 21		14 47					15 21			15 47					
Peterborough 8	a		14 06			13 52				14 38		15 06					15 38			16 06			15 52		

		FC	FC	FC		FC	FC	FC	FC	FC	FC	FC	FC	FC		FC	GR	FC	FC	FC	FC	FC	FC	FC	
		1		1		1	1	1	1	1		1	1	1		1	R 1 🍴	1	1	1		1	1	1	
London Kings Cross 15 ⊖	d	15 23	15 26	15 36		15 44	15 53	16 06	16 15	16 23	16 26	16 36	16 40	16 44		16 53	17 03	17 06	17 15	17 23	17 26	17 36	17 40	17 44	
Finsbury Park ⊖	d	15 28	15 32	15 41			15 58	16 11		16 28	16 32	16 41				16 58		17 11		17 28	17 32	17 41			
Potters Bar	d			15 51				16 21				16 51						17 21				17 51			
Hatfield	d			15 57				16 27				16 57						17 27				17 57			
Welwyn Garden City 4	d			16 01				16 31				17 01						17 31				18 01			
Welwyn North	d			16 04				16 34				17 04						17 34				18 04			
Knebworth	d			16 08				16 38				17 08						17 38				18 08			
Hertford North	d		16 07								17 07										18 07				
Stevenage 4	d	15 47	16a20	16 12			16 17	16 42		16 47	17a20	17 12				17 17	17 22	17 42		17 47	18a20	18 12			
Hitchin 4	d	15 52		16 17			16 22	16 47		16 52		17 17				17 22		17 47		17 52		18 17			
Letchworth Garden City	d						16 26	16 51								17 26		17 51							
Baldock	d						16 29	16 55								17 29		17 55							
Ashwell & Morden	d							17 00										18 00							
Royston	d						16 37	17 04								17 37		18 04							
Meldreth	d							17 08										18 08							
Shepreth	d							17 11										18 11							
Foxton	d							17 14										18 14							
Cambridge	a					16 29	16 54	17 29	17 01					17 29		17 54		18 29	18 01					18 29	
Arlesey	d	15 57		16 23						16 57		17 23								17 57		18 23			
Biggleswade	d	16 02		16 28						17 02		17 28	17 08							18 02		18 28	18 08		
Sandy	d	16 06		16 32						17 06		17 32								18 06		18 32			
St Neots	d	16 13		16 39						17 13		17 39	17 18							18 13		18 39	18 18		
Huntingdon	d	16 21		16 47						17 21		17 47	17 26							18 21		18 47	18 26		
Peterborough 8	a	16 38		17 06						17 38		18 06	17 45				17 52			18 38		19 06	18 42		

Table 25

Saturdays

until 18 June

London - Stevenage, Cambridge and Peterborough

		FC [1]	FC [1]	GR (R) [1] (icon)	FC [1]	FC [1]	FC [1]	FC	FC [1]	FC [1]		FC [1]	FC [1]	FC [1]	FC [1]	FC [1]	FC	GR (R) [1] (icon)	FC [1]	FC [1]		FC [1]	FC [1]	FC [1]	FC [1]
London Kings Cross [15] ⊖	d	17 53	18 06	18 08	18 15		18 23	18 26	18 36	18 40		18 45	18 53	19 06	19 15	19 23	19 26	19 30	19 36	19 40		19 45	19 53	20 06	20 23
Finsbury Park ⊖	d	17 58	18 11				18 28	18 32	18 41				18 58	19 11		19 28	19 32		19 41				19 58	20 11	20 28
Potters Bar	d		18 21						18 51					19 21					19 51					20 21	
Hatfield	d		18 27						18 57					19 27					19 57					20 27	
Welwyn Garden City [4]	d		18 31						19 01					19 31					20 01					20 31	
Welwyn North	d		18 34						19 04					19 34					20 04					20 34	
Knebworth	d		18 38						19 08					19 38					20 08					20 38	
Hertford North	d					←		19 07									20 07								
Stevenage [4]	d	18 17	18 42	18 28		18 42	18 47	19a20	19 12				19 17	19 42		19 47	20a20	19 49	20 12				20 17	20 42	20 47
Hitchin [4]	d	18 22	→			18 47	18 52		19 17				19 22	19 47		19 52			20 17				20 22	20 47	20 52
Letchworth Garden City	d	18 26				18 51							19 26	19 51									20 26	20 51	
Baldock	d	18 29				18 55							19 29	19 55									20 29	20 55	
Ashwell & Morden	d					19 00								20 00										21 00	
Royston	d	18 37				19 04						19 18	19 37	20 04								20 17	20 37	21 04	
Meldreth	d					19 08								20 08										21 08	
Shepreth	d					19 11								20 11										21 11	
Foxton	d					19 14								20 14										21 14	
Cambridge	a	18 54			19 01	19 27						19 35	19 54	20 27	20 01							20 35	20 54	21 27	
Arlesey	d						18 57		19 23							19 57			20 23						20 57
Biggleswade	d						19 02		19 28	19 08						20 02			20 28	20 08					21 02
Sandy	d						19 06		19 32							20 06			20 32						21 06
St Neots	d						19 13		19 39	19 18						20 13			20 39	20 18					21 13
Huntingdon	d						19 21		19 47	19 26						20 21			20 47	20 26					21 21
Peterborough [8]	a			18 58			19 38		20 06	19 42						20 39		20 19	21 06	20 43					21 37

		FC [1]	FC [1]	FC [1]	FC [1]	FC [1]		FC [1]	FC [1]	FC [1]	FC [1]	FC [1]	FC [1]	FC [1]	FC [1]	FC [1]	FC [1]	FC [1]	FC [1]	FC [1]	FC [1]	FC	FC [1]	FC	FC [1]
London Kings Cross [15] ⊖	d	20 36	20 40	20 45	20 53	21 06		21 23	21 36	21 40	21 53	22 06	22 15		22 23	22 36	22 53	23 06	23 15		23 23	23 26	23 36		23 53
Finsbury Park ⊖	d	20 41			20 58	21 11		21 28	21 41		21 58	22 11			22 28	22 41	22 58	23 11			23 28	23 32	23 41		23 58
Potters Bar	d	20 51				21 21			21 51			22 21				22 51		23 21					23 53		
Hatfield	d	20 57				21 27			21 57			22 27				22 57		23 27					23 59		
Welwyn Garden City [4]	d	21 01				21 31			22 01			22 31				23 01		23 31					00 06		
Welwyn North	d	21 04				21 34			22 04			22 34				23 04		23 34					00 09		
Knebworth	d	21 08				21 38			22 08			22 38				23 08		23 38					00 13		
Hertford North	d																					00 07		←	
Stevenage [4]	d	21 12			21 17	21 42		21 47	22 12		22 17	22 42			22 47	23 12	23 17	23 42			23 47	00 22	00 18	00 22	00 30
Hitchin [4]	d	21 17			21 22	21 47		21 52	22 17		22 22	22 47		←	22 54	23 20	23 24	23 50		←	23 54	→	00 25	00 29	00 37
Letchworth Garden City	d				21 26	21 51					22 26	22 51	22 40	22 51		23a26		23 54	23 45	23 54			00a30	00a37	
Baldock	d				21 29	21 55					22 29	→		22 55				→		23 57					
Ashwell & Morden	d					22 00								23 00						00 02					
Royston	d			21 18	21 37	22 04					22 37		22 50	23 04					23 54	00 07					
Meldreth	d					22 08								23 08						00 11					
Shepreth	d					22 11								23 11						00 14					
Foxton	d					22 14								23 14						00 16					
Cambridge	a			21 35	21 54	22 27					22 54		23 05	23 27					00 09	00 29					
Arlesey	d	21 23						21 57	22 23						22 59		23 29				23 59				00s43
Biggleswade	d	21 28	21 08					22 02	22 28	22 08					23 04		23 34				00 04				00s48
Sandy	d	21 32						22 06	22 32						23 08		23 38				00 08				00s51
St Neots	d	21 39	21 18					22 13	22 39	22 18					23 15		23 45				00 15				00s59
Huntingdon	d	21 47	21 26					22 21	22 47	22 26					23 23		23 53				00 23				01s06
Peterborough [8]	a	22 06	21 42					22 37	23 06	22 42					23 43		00 13				00 43				01 25

Table 25

Saturdays

25 June to 30 July

London - Stevenage, Cambridge and Peterborough

		FC	FC	FC	FC	FC	FC	FC	FC	FC		FC	FC	FC	FC	FC	FC	FC	FC	FC		FC	GR	FC	FC
		1	1	1	1	1		1		1		1		1		1	1	1	1	1		1	R 1	1	
London Kings Cross 15 ⊖	d	23p01	23p06	23p15		23p23	23p26	23p36		00 01		00 04	00 06	00 31		00 36	01 06	01 36	05 23	05 45		06 06	06 20	06 23	06 26
Finsbury Park ⊖	d		23p11			23p28	23p32	23p41				00 09	00 12			00 41	01 11	01 41	05 28	05 50		06 11		06 28	06 32
Potters Bar	d		23p21					23p51								00 51		01 59	05 38			06 20			
Hatfield	d		23p27					23p57								00 57		02 05	05 44			06 25			
Welwyn Garden City 4	d		23p31					00 01								01 01		02 09	05 48			06 29			
Welwyn North	d		23p34					00 04								01s04		02s12	05 51			06 32			
Knebworth	d		23p38					00 08								01s08		02s16	05 55			06 36			
Hertford North	d						00 07		←				00 47		←		01 38								07 07
Stevenage 4	d		23p42			23p47	00 20	00 12	00 20	00s20		00 31	01 00	00s50	01 00	01 12	01 47	02 20	05 59	06 08		06 40	06 40	06 47	07a20
Hitchin 4	d		23p50		←	23p53	→	00 20	00 26	00s35		00 39	→	01s05	01 06	01 17	01 52	02 25	06 07	06 13		06 47		06 52	
Letchworth Garden City	d		23p54	23p44	23p54			00a29	00a36			00 43		01s08	01a15		02a06			06 16		06 51			
Baldock	d		→		23p57							00 46		01s11						06 19		06 54			
Ashwell & Morden	d				00 02							00 51								06 24		06 59			
Royston	d			23p54	00 07							00 56		01s19						06 29		07 04			
Meldreth	d				00 11							00 59								06 32		07 08			
Shepreth	d				00 14							01 02								06 35		07 11			
Foxton	d				00 17							01 05								06 38		07 13			
Cambridge	a			00 10	00 29							01 22		01 35						06 50		07 27			
Arlesey	d					23p59										01s25			06 13					06 57	
Biggleswade	d	23p29				00 04				00s44						01s30		02s37	06 18					07 02	
Sandy	d					00 08										01s34			06 22					07 06	
St Neots	d	23p38				00 15				00s53						01s42		02s47	06 29					07 13	
Huntingdon	d	23p45				00 23				01s04						01s52		02s57	06 37					07 21	
Peterborough 8	a	00 12				00 42				01 24						02 13		03 16	06 54				07 11	07 37	

		FC	FC	FC	GR	FC		FC	FC	FC	FC	FC	FC	FC	FC	FC		FC	FC	FC	GR	FC	FC	FC	FC
		1	1	1	R 1	1		1		1	1	1	1	1	1			1	1	1	R 1	1	1	1	
London Kings Cross 15 ⊖	d	06 36	06 44	06 53	07 03	07 06		07 23	07 26	07 36	07 44	07 53	08 06	08 15	08 23	08 26		08 36	08 44	08 53	09 03	09 06	09 15	09 23	09 26
Finsbury Park ⊖	d	06 41		06 58		07 11		07 28	07 32	07 41		07 58	08 11		08 28	08 32		08 41		08 58		09 11		09 28	09 32
Potters Bar	d	06 51				07 21				07 51			08 21					08 51				09 21			
Hatfield	d	06 57				07 27				07 57			08 27					08 57				09 27			
Welwyn Garden City 4	d	07 01				07 31				08 01			08 31					09 01				09 31			
Welwyn North	d	07 04				07 34				08 04			08 34					09 04				09 34			
Knebworth	d	07 08				07 38				08 08			08 38					09 08				09 38			
Hertford North	d								08 07							09 07									10 07
Stevenage 4	d	07 12		07 17	07 22	07 42		07 47	08a20	08 12		08 17	08 42		08 46	09a20		09 12		09 17	09 22	09 42		09 47	10a20
Hitchin 4	d	07 17		07 22		07 47		07 52		08 17		08 22	08 47		08 51			09 17		09 22		09 47		09 52	
Letchworth Garden City	d			07 26		07 51						08 26	08 51							09 26		09 52			
Baldock	d			07 29		07 55						08 29	08 55							09 29		09 55			
Ashwell & Morden	d			07 34		08 00							09 00									10 00			
Royston	d			07 38		08 04						08 37	09 04							09 37		10 04			
Meldreth	d			07 42		08 08							09 08									10 09			
Shepreth	d			07 45		08 11							09 11									10 12			
Foxton	d			07 47		08 14							09 14									10 14			
Cambridge	a		07 31	07 59		08 29					08 29	08 54	09 29	09 01					09 29	09 54		10 29	10 01		
Arlesey	d	07 23						07 57		08 23					08 57			09 23						09 57	
Biggleswade	d	07 28						08 02		08 28					09 02			09 28						10 02	
Sandy	d	07 32						08 06		08 32					09 05			09 32						10 06	
St Neots	d	07 39						08 13		08 39					09 13			09 39						10 13	
Huntingdon	d	07 47						08 21		08 47					09 20			09 47						10 21	
Peterborough 8	a	08 06			07 52			08 38		09 08					09 36			10 06			09 52			10 38	

		FC		FC	FC	FC	FC	FC	FC	FC	FC	FC		GR	FC	FC	FC	FC	FC	FC	FC	FC		FC	FC
		1		1	1	1	1	1		1	1	1		R 1	1	1	1		1	1	1	1		1	1
London Kings Cross 15 ⊖	d	09 36		09 44	09 53	10 06	10 15	10 22	10 26	10 36	10 44	10 53		11 03	11 06	11 15	11 23	11 26	11 36	11 44	11 53	12 06		12 15	12 23
Finsbury Park ⊖	d	09 41			09 58	10 11		10 28	10 32	10 41		10 58			11 11		11 28	11 32	11 41		11 58	12 11			12 28
Potters Bar	d	09 51				10 21				10 51					11 21				11 51			12 21			
Hatfield	d	09 57				10 27				10 57					11 27				11 57			12 27			
Welwyn Garden City 4	d	10 01				10 31				11 01					11 31				12 01			12 31			
Welwyn North	d	10 04				10 34				11 04					11 34				12 04			12 34			
Knebworth	d	10 08				10 38				11 08					11 38				12 08			12 38			
Hertford North	d								11 07									12 07							
Stevenage 4	d	10 12			10 17	10 42		10 47	11a20	11 12		11 17		11 22	11 42		11 47	12a20	12 12		12 17	12 42			12 47
Hitchin 4	d	10 17			10 22	10 47		10 52		11 17		11 22			11 47		11 52		12 17		12 22	12 47			12 52
Letchworth Garden City	d				10 26	10 51						11 26			11 51						12 26	12 51			
Baldock	d				10 29	10 55						11 29			11 55						12 29	12 55			
Ashwell & Morden	d					11 00									12 00							13 00			
Royston	d				10 37	11 04						11 37			12 04						12 37	13 04			
Meldreth	d					11 08									12 08							13 08			
Shepreth	d					11 11									12 11							13 11			
Foxton	d					11 14									12 14							13 14			
Cambridge	a			10 29	10 54	11 29	11 01				11 29	11 54			12 29	12 01				12 29	12 54	13 29		13 01	
Arlesey	d	10 23						10 57		11 23							11 57		12 23						12 57
Biggleswade	d	10 28						11 02		11 28							12 02		12 28						13 02
Sandy	d	10 32						11 06		11 32							12 06		12 32						13 06
St Neots	d	10 39						11 13		11 39							12 13		12 39						13 13
Huntingdon	d	10 47						11 21		11 47							12 21		12 47						13 21
Peterborough 8	a	11 06						11 38		12 06				11 52			12 38		13 06						13 37

Table 25

London - Stevenage, Cambridge and Peterborough

		FC	FC	FC	FC	GR	FC	FC		FC	FC	FC	FC	FC	FC	FC	FC	FC		FC	FC	FC	GR	FC	FC
						R																	R		
			1	1	1	1	1	1		1		1	1	1	1	1	1			1	1	1	1	1	1
						[trolley]																	[trolley]		
London Kings Cross 15 ⊖	d	12 26	12 36	12 44	12 53	13 03	13 06	13 15		13 23	13 26	13 36	13 44	13 53	14 06	14 15	14 23	14 26		14 36	14 44	14 53	15 03	15 06	15 15
Finsbury Park ⊖	d	12 32	12 41		12 58		13 11			13 28	13 32	13 41		13 58	14 11		14 28	14 32		14 41		14 58		15 11	
Potters Bar	d		12 51				13 21					13 51			14 21					14 51				15 21	
Hatfield	d		12 57				13 27					13 57			14 27					14 57				15 27	
Welwyn Garden City 4	d		13 01				13 31					14 01			14 31					15 01				15 31	
Welwyn North	d		13 04				13 34					14 04			14 34					15 04				15 34	
Knebworth	d		13 08				13 38					14 08			14 38					15 08				15 38	
Hertford North	d	13 07									14 07							15 07							
Stevenage 4	d	13a20	13 12		13 17	13 22	13 42			13 47	14a20	14 12		14 17	14 42		14 47	15a20		15 12		15 17	15 22	15 42	
Hitchin 4	d		13 17		13 22		13 47			13 52		14 17		14 22	14 47		14 52			15 18		15 22		15 47	
Letchworth Garden City	d				13 26		13 51							14 26	14 51							15 26		15 51	
Baldock	d				13 29		13 55							14 29	14 55							15 29		15 55	
Ashwell & Morden	d						14 00								15 00									16 00	
Royston	d				13 37		14 04							14 37	15 04							15 37		16 04	
Meldreth	d						14 08								15 08									16 08	
Shepreth	d						14 11								15 11									16 11	
Foxton	d						14 14								15 14									16 14	
Cambridge	a			13 29	13 54		14 29	14 01					14 29	14 54	15 30	15 01					15 29	15 54		16 29	16 01
Arlesey	d		13 23							13 57		14 23					14 57			15 23					
Biggleswade	d		13 28							14 02		14 28					15 02			15 28					
Sandy	d		13 32							14 06		14 32					15 06			15 32					
St Neots	d		13 39							14 13		14 39					15 13			15 39					
Huntingdon	d		13 47							14 21		14 47					15 21			15 47					
Peterborough 8	a		14 06			13 52				14 38		15 06					15 38			16 06			15 52		

		FC	FC	FC		FC	FC	FC	FC	FC	FC	FC	FC	FC		FC	GR	FC	FC	FC	FC	FC	FC	FC	
																	R								
		1		1		1	1	1	1	1		1	1	1		1	1	1	1	1		1	1	1	
																	[trolley]								
London Kings Cross 15 ⊖	d	15 23	15 26	15 36		15 44	15 53	16 06	16 15	16 23	16 26	16 36	16 40	16 44		16 53	17 03	17 06	17 15	17 23	17 26	17 36	17 40	17 44	
Finsbury Park ⊖	d	15 28	15 32	15 41			15 58	16 11		16 28	16 32	16 41				16 58		17 11		17 28	17 32	17 41			
Potters Bar	d			15 51				16 21				16 51						17 21				17 51			
Hatfield	d			15 57				16 27				16 57						17 27				17 57			
Welwyn Garden City 4	d			16 01				16 31				17 01						17 31				18 01			
Welwyn North	d			16 04				16 34				17 04						17 34				18 04			
Knebworth	d			16 08				16 38				17 08						17 38				18 08			
Hertford North	d		16 07								17 07										18 07				
Stevenage 4	d	15 47	16a20	16 12			16 17	16 42		16 47	17a20	17 12				17 17	17 22	17 42		17 47	18a20	18 12			
Hitchin 4	d	15 52		16 17			16 22	16 47		16 52		17 17				17 22		17 47		17 52		18 17			
Letchworth Garden City	d						16 26	16 51								17 26		17 51							
Baldock	d						16 29	16 55								17 29		17 55							
Ashwell & Morden	d							17 00										18 00							
Royston	d						16 37	17 04								17 37		18 04							
Meldreth	d							17 08										18 08							
Shepreth	d							17 11										18 11							
Foxton	d							17 14										18 14							
Cambridge	a					16 29	16 54	17 29	17 01					17 29		17 54		18 29	18 01					18 29	
Arlesey	d	15 57		16 23						16 57		17 23								17 57		18 23			
Biggleswade	d	16 02		16 28						17 02		17 28	17 08							18 02		18 28	18 08		
Sandy	d	16 06		16 32						17 06		17 32								18 06		18 32			
St Neots	d	16 13		16 39						17 13		17 39	17 18							18 13		18 39	18 18		
Huntingdon	d	16 21		16 47						17 21		17 47	17 26							18 21		18 47	18 26		
Peterborough 8	a	16 38		17 06						17 38		18 06	17 45				17 52			18 38		19 06	18 42		

		FC	FC	GR	FC	FC	FC	FC	FC	FC		FC	FC	FC	FC	FC	FC	GR	FC	FC		FC	FC	FC	FC
				R														R							
		1	1	1	1	1	1		1	1		1	1	1	1	1		1	1	1		1	1	1	1
				[trolley]														[trolley]							
London Kings Cross 15 ⊖	d	17 53	18 06	18 08	18 15		18 23	18 26	18 36	18 40		18 45	18 53	19 06	19 15	19 23	19 26	19 30	19 36	19 40		19 45	19 53		20 23
Finsbury Park ⊖	d	17 58	18 11				18 28	18 32	18 41				18 58	19 11		19 28	19 32		19 41				19 58		20 28
Potters Bar	d		18 21						18 51					19 21					19 51						
Hatfield	d		18 27						18 57					19 27					19 57						
Welwyn Garden City 4	d		18 31						19 01					19 31					20 01						
Welwyn North	d		18 34						19 04					19 34					20 05						
Knebworth	d		18 38						19 08					19 38					20 09						
Hertford North	d					←		19 07									20 07								
Stevenage 4	d	18 17	18 42	18 28		18 42	18 47	19a20	19 12				19 17	19 42		19 47	20a20	19 49	20 13				20 17		20 53
Hitchin 4	d	18 22	→			18 47	18 52		19 17				19 22	19 47		19 52			20 18				20 22	20 42	20 58
Letchworth Garden City	d	18 26				18 51							19 26	19 51									20 26	20 51	
Baldock	d	18 29				18 55							19 29	19 55									20 29	20 55	
Ashwell & Morden	d					19 00								20 00										21 00	
Royston	d	18 37				19 04						19 18	19 37	20 04								20 17	20 37	21 04	
Meldreth	d					19 08								20 08										21 08	
Shepreth	d					19 11								20 11										21 11	
Foxton	d					19 14								20 14										21 14	
Cambridge	a	18 54			19 01	19 27						19 35	19 54	20 27	20 01							20 35	20 54	21 27	
Arlesey	d						18 57		19 23							19 57			20 24						21 04
Biggleswade	d						19 02		19 28	19 08						20 02			20 29	20 08					21 09
Sandy	d						19 06		19 32							20 06			20 33						21 12
St Neots	d						19 13		19 39	19 18						20 13			20 40	20 18					21 20
Huntingdon	d						19 21		19 47	19 26						20 21			20 48	20 26					21 27
Peterborough 8	a			18 58			19 38		20 06	19 42						20 39		20 19	21 06	20 43					21 43

London - Stevenage, Cambridge and Peterborough

Saturdays
25 June to 30 July

		FC	FC	FC	FC	FC		FC	FC	FC	FC	FC	FC	FC	FC	FC		FC	FC	FC	FC				
		1	1	1	1	1		1	1	1	1	1	1	1	1	1		1	1		1				
London Kings Cross 15 ⊖	d		20 36	20 40				21 23		21 36	21 40			22 23	22 53	23 06		23 15		23 26	23 53				
Finsbury Park ⊖	d		20 41					21 28		21 41				22 28	22 58	23 11				23 32	23 58				
Potters Bar	d		20 51							21 51						23 21									
Hatfield	d		20 57							21 57						23 27									
Welwyn Garden City 4	d		21 01							22 01						23 31									
Welwyn North	d		21 04							22 04						23 34									
Knebworth	d		21 08							22 08						23 38									
Hertford North	d																			00 07					
Stevenage 4	d		21 12					21 54		22 12				22 53	23 23	23 42				00 22	00 30				
Hitchin 4	d	21 05	21 17		21 18	21 42		21 59	22 08	22 17		22 28	22 42	23 01	23 31	23 50			←	00 29	00 37				
Letchworth Garden City	d				21 25	21 51			22 16			22 40	22 51			23 54		23 45	23 54	00a37					
Baldock	d				21 28	21 55			22 19				22 55			↪			23 57						
Ashwell & Morden	d					22 00							23 00						00 02						
Royston	d	21 20			21 37	22 04			22 27			22 50	23 04					23 54	00 07						
Meldreth	d					22 08							23 08						00 11						
Shepreth	d					22 11							23 11						00 14						
Foxton	d					22 14							23 14						00 16						
Cambridge	a	21 35			21 54	22 27			22 44			23 05	23 27					00 09	00 29						
Arlesey	d		21 23					22 05		22 23				23 06	23 36						00s43				
Biggleswade	d		21 28	21 08				22 10		22 28	22 08			23 11	23 41						00s48				
Sandy	d		21 32					22 13		22 32				23 15	23 45						00s51				
St Neots	d		21 39	21 18				22 21		22 39	22 18			23 22	23 52						00s59				
Huntingdon	d		21 47	21 26				22 28		22 47	22 26			23 30	00 01						01s06				
Peterborough 8	a		22 06	21 42				22 44		23 06	22 42			23 50	00 20						01 25				

Saturdays
from 6 August

		FC	FC	FC	FC	FC	FC	FC	FC	FC		FC	FC	FC	FC	FC	FC	FC	FC	FC		FC	GR	FC	FC
																							R		
		1	1	1	1	1		1		1		1		1		1	1	1	1	1		1	1	1	
																							(trolley)		
London Kings Cross 15 ⊖	d	23p01	23p06	23p15		23p23	23p26	23p36		00 01		00 04	00 06	00 31		00 36	01 06	01 36	05 23	05 45		06 06	06 20	06 23	06 26
Finsbury Park ⊖	d		23p11			23p28	23p32	23p41				00 09	00 12			00 41	01 11	01 41	05 28	05 50		06 11		06 28	06 32
Potters Bar	d		23p21					23p51								00 51		01 59	05 38			06 20			
Hatfield	d		23p27					23p57								00 57		02 05	05 44			06 25			
Welwyn Garden City 4	d		23p31					00 01								01 01		02 09	05 48			06 29			
Welwyn North	d		23p34					00 04								01s04		02s12	05 51			06 32			
Knebworth	d		23p38					00 08								01s08		02s16	05 55			06 36			
Hertford North	d						00 07		←				00 47		←		01 38								07 07
Stevenage 4	d		23p42			23p47	00 20	00 12	00 20	00s20		00 31	01 00	00s50	01 00	01 12	01 47	02 20	05 59	06 08		06 40	06 40	06 47	07a20
Hitchin 4	d		23p50		←	23p53	→	00 20	00 26	00s35		00 39	→	01s05	01 06	01 17	01 52	02 25	06 07	06 13		06 47		06 52	
Letchworth Garden City	d		23p54	23p44	23p54			00a29	00a36			00 43		01s08	01a15		02a06			06 16		06 51			
Baldock	d		→		23p57							00 46		01s11						06 19		06 54			
Ashwell & Morden	d				00 02							00 51								06 24		06 59			
Royston	d			23p54	00 07							00 56		01s19						06 29		07 04			
Meldreth	d				00 11							00 59								06 32		07 08			
Shepreth	d				00 14							01 02								06 35		07 11			
Foxton	d				00 17							01 05								06 38		07 13			
Cambridge	a			00 10	00 29							01 22		01 35						06 50		07 27			
Arlesey	d					23p59										01s25			06 13					06 57	
Biggleswade	d	23p29				00 04				00s44						01s30		02s37	06 18					07 02	
Sandy	d					00 08										01s34			06 22					07 06	
St Neots	d	23p38				00 15				00s53						01s42		02s47	06 29					07 13	
Huntingdon	d	23p45				00 23				01s04						01s52		02s57	06 37					07 21	
Peterborough 8	a	00 12				00 42				01 24						02 13		03 16	06 54				07 11	07 37	

		FC	FC	FC	GR	FC		FC	FC	FC	FC	FC	FC	FC	FC	FC		FC	FC	FC	GR	FC	FC	FC	FC
					R																R				
		1	1	1	1	1		1		1	1	1	1	1	1			1	1	1	1	1	1	1	
					(trolley)																(trolley)				
London Kings Cross 15 ⊖	d	06 36	06 44	06 53	07 03	07 06		07 23	07 26	07 36	07 44	07 53	08 06	08 15	08 23	08 26		08 36	08 44	08 53	09 03	09 06	09 15	09 23	09 26
Finsbury Park ⊖	d	06 41		06 58		07 11		07 28	07 32	07 41		07 58	08 11		08 28	08 32		08 41		08 58		09 11		09 28	09 32
Potters Bar	d	06 51				07 21				07 51			08 21					08 51				09 21			
Hatfield	d	06 57				07 27				07 57			08 27					08 57				09 27			
Welwyn Garden City 4	d	07 01				07 31				08 01			08 31					09 01				09 31			
Welwyn North	d	07 04				07 34				08 04			08 34					09 04				09 34			
Knebworth	d	07 08				07 38				08 08			08 38					09 08				09 38			
Hertford North	d								08 07							09 07									10 07
Stevenage 4	d	07 12		07 17	07 22	07 42		07 47	08a20	08 12		08 17	08 42		08 46	09a20		09 12		09 17	09 22	09 42		09 47	10a20
Hitchin 4	d	07 17		07 22		07 47		07 52		08 17		08 22	08 47		08 51			09 17		09 22		09 47		09 52	
Letchworth Garden City	d			07 26		07 51						08 26	08 51							09 26		09 52			
Baldock	d			07 29		07 55						08 29	08 55							09 29		09 55			
Ashwell & Morden	d			07 34		08 00							09 00									10 00			
Royston	d			07 38		08 04						08 37	09 04							09 37		10 04			
Meldreth	d			07 42		08 08							09 08									10 09			
Shepreth	d			07 45		08 11							09 11									10 12			
Foxton	d			07 47		08 14							09 14									10 14			
Cambridge	a		07 31	07 59		08 29					08 29	08 54	09 29	09 01					09 29	09 54		10 29	10 01		
Arlesey	d	07 23						07 57		08 23					08 57			09 23						09 57	
Biggleswade	d	07 28						08 02		08 28					09 02			09 28						10 02	
Sandy	d	07 32						08 06		08 32					09 05			09 32						10 06	
St Neots	d	07 39						08 13		08 39					09 13			09 39						10 13	
Huntingdon	d	07 47						08 21		08 47					09 20			09 47						10 21	
Peterborough 8	a	08 06			07 52			08 38		09 08					09 36			10 06			09 52			10 38	

Table 25

Saturdays

from 6 August

London - Stevenage, Cambridge and Peterborough

		FC		FC	FC	FC	FC	FC	FC	FC	FC	FC		GR	FC	FC	FC	FC	FC	FC	FC	FC		FC	FC
		1		1	1	1	1	1		1	1	1		R 1	1	1	1		1	1	1	1		1	1
London Kings Cross 15 ⊖	d	09 36		09 44	09 53	10 06	10 15	10 22	10 26	10 36	10 44	10 53		11 03	11 06	11 15	11 23	11 26	11 36	11 44	11 53	12 06		12 15	12 23
Finsbury Park ⊖	d	09 41			09 58	10 11		10 28	10 32	10 41		10 58			11 11		11 28	11 32	11 41		11 58	12 11			12 28
Potters Bar	d	09 51				10 21				10 51					11 21				11 51			12 21			
Hatfield	d	09 57				10 27				10 57					11 27				11 57			12 27			
Welwyn Garden City 4	d	10 01				10 31				11 01					11 31				12 01			12 31			
Welwyn North	d	10 04				10 34				11 04					11 34				12 04			12 34			
Knebworth	d	10 08				10 38				11 08					11 38				12 08			12 38			
Hertford North	d								11 07									12 07							
Stevenage 4	d	10 12			10 17	10 42		10 47	11a20	11 12		11 17		11 22	11 42		11 47	12a20	12 12		12 17	12 42			12 47
Hitchin 4	d	10 17			10 22	10 47		10 52		11 17		11 22			11 47		11 52		12 17		12 22	12 47			12 52
Letchworth Garden City	d				10 26	10 51						11 26			11 51						12 26	12 51			
Baldock	d				10 29	10 55						11 29			11 55						12 29	12 55			
Ashwell & Morden	d					11 00									12 00							13 00			
Royston	d				10 37	11 04						11 37			12 04						12 37	13 04			
Meldreth	d					11 08									12 08							13 08			
Shepreth	d					11 11									12 11							13 11			
Foxton	d					11 14									12 14							13 14			
Cambridge	a			10 29	10 54	11 29	11 01				11 29	11 54			12 29	12 01				12 29	12 54	13 29		13 01	
Arlesey	d	10 23						10 57		11 23							11 57		12 23						12 57
Biggleswade	d	10 28						11 02		11 28							12 02		12 28						13 02
Sandy	d	10 32						11 06		11 32							12 06		12 32						13 06
St Neots	d	10 39						11 13		11 39							12 13		12 39						13 13
Huntingdon	d	10 47						11 21		11 47							12 21		12 47						13 21
Peterborough 8	a	11 06						11 38		12 06				11 52			12 38		13 06						13 37

		FC	FC	FC	FC	GR	FC	FC		FC	FC	FC	FC	FC	FC	FC	FC	FC		FC	FC	FC	GR	FC	FC
			1	1	1	R 1	1	1		1		1	1	1	1	1	1			1	1	1	R 1	1	1
London Kings Cross 15 ⊖	d	12 26	12 36	12 44	12 53	13 03	13 06	13 15		13 23	13 26	13 36	13 44	13 53	14 06	14 15	14 23	14 26		14 36	14 44	14 53	15 03	15 06	15 15
Finsbury Park ⊖	d	12 32	12 41		12 58		13 11			13 28	13 32	13 41		13 58	14 11		14 28	14 32		14 41		14 58		15 11	
Potters Bar	d		12 51				13 21					13 51			14 21					14 51				15 21	
Hatfield	d		12 57				13 27					13 57			14 27					14 57				15 27	
Welwyn Garden City 4	d		13 01				13 31					14 01			14 31					15 01				15 31	
Welwyn North	d		13 04				13 34					14 04			14 34					15 04				15 34	
Knebworth	d		13 08				13 38					14 08			14 38					15 08				15 38	
Hertford North	d	13 07									14 07							15 07							
Stevenage 4	d	13a20	13 12		13 17	13 22	13 42			13 47	14a20	14 12		14 17	14 42		14 47	15a20		15 12		15 17	15 22	15 42	
Hitchin 4	d		13 17		13 22		13 47			13 52		14 17		14 22	14 47		14 52			15 18		15 22		15 47	
Letchworth Garden City	d				13 26		13 51							14 26	14 51							15 26		15 51	
Baldock	d				13 29		13 55							14 29	14 55							15 29		15 55	
Ashwell & Morden	d						14 00								15 00									16 00	
Royston	d				13 37		14 04							14 37	15 04							15 37		16 04	
Meldreth	d						14 08								15 08									16 08	
Shepreth	d						14 11								15 11									16 11	
Foxton	d						14 14								15 14									16 14	
Cambridge	a			13 29	13 54		14 29	14 01					14 29	14 54	15 30	15 01					15 29	15 54		16 29	16 01
Arlesey	d		13 23							13 57		14 23					14 57			15 23					
Biggleswade	d		13 28							14 02		14 28					15 02			15 28					
Sandy	d		13 32							14 06		14 32					15 06			15 32					
St Neots	d		13 39							14 13		14 39					15 13			15 39					
Huntingdon	d		13 47							14 21		14 47					15 21			15 47					
Peterborough 8	a		14 06			13 52				14 38		15 06					15 38			16 06			15 52		

		FC	FC	FC		FC	FC	FC	FC	FC	FC	FC	FC	FC		FC	GR	FC	FC	FC	FC	FC	FC	FC	
		1		1		1	1	1	1	1		1	1	1		1	R 1	1	1	1		1	1	1	
London Kings Cross 15 ⊖	d	15 23	15 26	15 36		15 44	15 53	16 06	16 15	16 23	16 26	16 36	16 40	16 44		16 53	17 03	17 06	17 15	17 23	17 26	17 36	17 40	17 44	
Finsbury Park ⊖	d	15 28	15 32	15 41			15 58	16 11		16 28	16 32	16 41				16 58		17 11		17 28	17 32	17 41			
Potters Bar	d			15 51				16 21				16 51						17 21				17 51			
Hatfield	d			15 57				16 27				16 57						17 27				17 57			
Welwyn Garden City 4	d			16 01				16 31				17 01						17 31				18 01			
Welwyn North	d			16 04				16 34				17 04						17 34				18 04			
Knebworth	d			16 08				16 38				17 08						17 38				18 08			
Hertford North	d		16 07								17 07										18 07				
Stevenage 4	d	15 47	16a20	16 12			16 17	16 42		16 47	17a20	17 12				17 17	17 22	17 42		17 47	18a20	18 12			
Hitchin 4	d	15 52		16 17			16 22	16 47		16 52		17 17				17 22		17 47		17 52		18 17			
Letchworth Garden City	d						16 26	16 51								17 26		17 51							
Baldock	d						16 29	16 55								17 29		17 55							
Ashwell & Morden	d							17 00										18 00							
Royston	d						16 37	17 04								17 37		18 04							
Meldreth	d							17 08										18 08							
Shepreth	d							17 11										18 11							
Foxton	d							17 14										18 14							
Cambridge	a					16 29	16 54	17 29	17 01					17 29		17 54		18 29	18 01					18 29	
Arlesey	d	15 57		16 23						16 57		17 23								17 57		18 23			
Biggleswade	d	16 02		16 28						17 02		17 28	17 08							18 02		18 28	18 08		
Sandy	d	16 06		16 32						17 06		17 32								18 06		18 32			
St Neots	d	16 13		16 39						17 13		17 39	17 18							18 13		18 39	18 18		
Huntingdon	d	16 21		16 47						17 21		17 47	17 26							18 21		18 47	18 26		
Peterborough 8	a	16 38		17 06						17 38		18 06	17 45				17 52			18 38		19 06	18 42		

Table 25

Saturdays
from 6 August

London - Stevenage, Cambridge and Peterborough

		FC	FC	GR	FC	FC	FC	FC	FC	FC		FC	FC	FC	FC	FC	FC	GR	FC	FC		FC	FC	FC	FC
				[R]														[R]							
		[1]	[1]	[1]	[1]	[1]	[1]		[1]	[1]		[1]	[1]	[1]	[1]	[1]		[1]	[1]	[1]		[1]	[1]	[1]	[1]
				[trolley]														[trolley]							
London Kings Cross [15] ⊖	d	17 53	18 06	18 08	18 15		18 23	18 26	18 36	18 40		18 45	18 53	19 06	19 15	19 23	19 26	19 30	19 36	19 40		19 45	19 53	20 06	20 23
Finsbury Park ⊖	d	17 58	18 11				18 28	18 32	18 41				18 58	19 11		19 28	19 32		19 41				19 58	20 11	20 28
Potters Bar	d		18 21						18 51					19 21					19 51					20 21	
Hatfield	d		18 27						18 57					19 27					19 57					20 27	
Welwyn Garden City [4]	d		18 31						19 01					19 31					20 01					20 31	
Welwyn North	d		18 34						19 04					19 34					20 04					20 34	
Knebworth	d		18 38						19 08					19 38					20 08					20 38	
Hertford North	d					←		19 07									20 07								
Stevenage [4]	d	18 17	18 42	18 28		18 42	18 47	19a20	19 12				19 17	19 42		19 47	20a20	19 49	20 12				20 17	20 42	20 47
Hitchin [4]	d	18 22	→			18 47	18 52		19 17				19 22	19 47		19 52			20 17				20 22	20 47	20 52
Letchworth Garden City	d	18 26				18 51							19 26	19 51									20 26	20 51	
Baldock	d	18 29				18 55							19 29	19 55									20 29	20 55	
Ashwell & Morden	d					19 00								20 00										21 00	
Royston	d	18 37				19 04						19 18	19 37	20 04								20 17	20 37	21 04	
Meldreth	d					19 08								20 08										21 08	
Shepreth	d					19 11								20 11										21 11	
Foxton	d					19 14								20 14										21 14	
Cambridge	a	18 54			19 01	19 27						19 35	19 54	20 27	20 01							20 35	20 54	21 27	
Arlesey	d						18 57		19 23							19 57			20 23						20 57
Biggleswade	d						19 02		19 28	19 08						20 02			20 28	20 08					21 02
Sandy	d						19 06		19 32							20 06			20 32						21 06
St Neots	d						19 13		19 39	19 18						20 13			20 39	20 18					21 13
Huntingdon	d						19 21		19 47	19 26						20 21			20 47	20 26					21 21
Peterborough [8]	a			18 58			19 38		20 06	19 42						20 39		20 19	21 06	20 43					21 37

		FC	FC	FC	FC	FC		FC	FC	FC	FC	FC	FC	FC	FC	FC		FC	FC	FC	FC	FC	FC	FC	FC
		[1]	[1]	[1]	[1]	[1]		[1]	[1]	[1]	[1]	[1]	[1]	[1]	[1]	[1]		[1]	[1]	[1]	[1]	[1]		[1]	
																				A					
London Kings Cross [15] ⊖	d	20 36	20 40	20 45	20 53	21 06		21 23	21 36	21 40	21 53	22 06	22 15		22 23	22 36		22 53	23 06	23 15		23 23	23 26	23 36	
Finsbury Park ⊖	d	20 41			20 58	21 11		21 28	21 41		21 58	22 11			22 28	22 41		22 58	23 11			23 28	23 32	23 41	
Potters Bar	d	20 51				21 21			21 51			22 21				22 51			23 21					23 53	
Hatfield	d	20 57				21 27			21 57			22 27				22 57			23 27					23 59	
Welwyn Garden City [4]	d	21 01				21 31			22 01			22 31				23 01			23 31					00 06	
Welwyn North	d	21 04				21 34			22 04			22 34				23 04			23 34					00 09	
Knebworth	d	21 08				21 38			22 08			22 38				23 08			23 38					00 13	
Hertford North	d																						00 07		←
Stevenage [4]	d	21 12			21 17	21 42		21 47	22 12		22 17	22 42			22 47	23 12		23 17	23 42			23 47	00 22	00 18	00 22
Hitchin [4]	d	21 17			21 22	21 47		21 52	22 17		22 22	22 47		←	22 54	23 20		23 24	23 50		←	23 54	→	00 25	00 29
Letchworth Garden City	d				21 26	21 51					22 26	22 51	22 40	22 51		23a26			23 54	23 45	23 54			00a30	00a37
Baldock	d				21 29	21 55					22 29	→		22 55					→		23 57				
Ashwell & Morden	d					22 00								23 00							00 02				
Royston	d			21 18	21 37	22 04					22 37		22 50	23 04						23 54	00 07				
Meldreth	d					22 08								23 08							00 11				
Shepreth	d					22 11								23 11							00 14				
Foxton	d					22 14								23 14							00 16				
Cambridge	a			21 35	21 54	22 27					22 54		23 05	23 27						00 09	00 29				
Arlesey	d	21 23						21 57	22 23						22 59			23 29				23 59			
Biggleswade	d	21 28	21 08					22 02	22 28	22 08					23 04			23 34				00 04			
Sandy	d	21 32						22 06	22 32						23 08			23 38				00 08			
St Neots	d	21 39	21 18					22 13	22 39	22 18					23 15			23 45				00 15			
Huntingdon	d	21 47	21 26					22 21	22 47	22 26					23 23			23 53				00 23			
Peterborough [8]	a	22 06	21 42					22 37	23 06	22 42					23 43			00 13				00 43			

		FC
		[1]
London Kings Cross [15] ⊖	d	23 53
Finsbury Park ⊖	d	23 58
Potters Bar	d	
Hatfield	d	
Welwyn Garden City [4]	d	
Welwyn North	d	
Knebworth	d	
Hertford North	d	
Stevenage [4]	d	00 30
Hitchin [4]	d	00 37
Letchworth Garden City	d	
Baldock	d	
Ashwell & Morden	d	
Royston	d	
Meldreth	d	
Shepreth	d	
Foxton	d	
Cambridge	a	
Arlesey	d	00s43
Biggleswade	d	00s48
Sandy	d	00s51
St Neots	d	00s59
Huntingdon	d	01s06
Peterborough [8]	a	01 25

A from 17 September

Table 25

Sundays
until 19 June

London - Stevenage, Cambridge and Peterborough

		FC 1 A	FC 1 A	FC 1 A	FC 1 A	FC 1 A	FC A	FC 1 A	FC A	FC 1 A		FC 1	FC 1	FC 1	FC 1	FC	FC 1	FC	FC	FC 1		FC 1	FC 1	FC	FC 1
London Kings Cross 15 ⊖	d	22p53	23p06	23p15		23p23	23p26	23p36		23p53		00 06	00 15		00 23	00 41	00 53		06 26	06 53		07 06	07 23	07 26	07 53
Finsbury Park ⊖	d	22p58	23p11			23p28	23p32	23p41		23p58		00 11			00 28	00 47	00 58		06 32	06 58		07 11	07 28	07 32	07 58
Potters Bar	d		23p21					23p53				00 23										07 21			
Hatfield	d		23p27					23p59				00 29										07 27			
Welwyn Garden City 4	d		23p31					00⌇06				00 41					01 17					07 33			
Welwyn North	d		23p34					00⌇09				00 44					01s22					07 36			
Knebworth	d		23p38					00⌇13				00 48					01s25					07 40			
Hertford North	d						00⌇07		←					←		01 22		←	07 07					08 07	
Stevenage 4	d	23p17	23p42			23p47	00⌇22	00⌇18	00⌇22	00⌇30		00 53	00 47	00 53	00 58	01 36	01 29	01 36	07a22	07 17		07 45	07 51	08a23	08 17
Hitchin 4	d	23p24	23p50		←	23p54	→	00⌇25	00⌇29	00⌇37		→	00 54	01 00	01 05	→	01 36	01 44		07 26		07 52	08 01		08 22
Letchworth Garden City	d		23p54	23p45	23p54			00a30	00a37				00 58	01 04				01a50		07 35		07 56			08 26
Baldock	d		→		23p57								01 01	01 08						07 38		07 59			08 29
Ashwell & Morden	d				00⌇02									01 13								08 04			
Royston	d			23p54	00⌇07								01 09	01 17						07 46		08 09			08 37
Meldreth	d				00⌇11									01 21								08 13			
Shepreth	d				00⌇14									01 24								08 16			
Foxton	d				00⌇16									01 27								08 18			
Cambridge	a			00⌇09	00⌇29								01 25	01 40						08 04		08 34			08 54
Arlesey	d	23p29				23p59				00s43					01s10		01s43						08 06		
Biggleswade	d	23p34				00⌇04				00s48					01s15		01s48						08 11		
Sandy	d	23p38				00⌇08				00s51					01s19		01s52						08 15		
St Neots	d	23p45				00⌇15				00s59					01s26		01s59						08 22		
Huntingdon	d	23p53				00⌇23				01s06					01s34		02s07						08 30		
Peterborough 8	a	00⌇13				00⌇43				01⌇25					01 54		02 27						08 51		

		FC 1	FC 1	FC	FC 1	GR R 1		FC 1	FC 1	FC 1	FC	FC 1	FC 1	FC 1	FC 1	FC		FC 1	GR R 1	FC 1	FC 1	FC 1	FC	FC 1	FC 1
London Kings Cross 15 ⊖	d	08 06	08 23	08 26	08 53	09 03		09 06	09 15	09 23	09 26	09 53	10 06	10 15	10 23	10 26		10 53	11 03	11 06	11 15	11 23	11 26	11 53	12 06
Finsbury Park ⊖	d	08 11	08 28	08 32	08 58			09 11		09 28	09 32	09 58	10 11		10 28	10 32		10 58		11 11		11 28	11 32	11 58	12 11
Potters Bar	d	08 21						09 21					10 21							11 21					12 21
Hatfield	d	08 27						09 27					10 27							11 27					12 27
Welwyn Garden City 4	d	08 31						09 31					10 31							11 31					12 31
Welwyn North	d	08 34						09 34					10 34							11 34					12 34
Knebworth	d	08 38						09 38					10 38							11 38					12 38
Hertford North	d			09 07							10 07					11 07							12 07		
Stevenage 4	d	08 42	08 47	09a20	09 17	09 22		09 42		09 47	10a20	10 17	10 42		10 47	11a20		11 17	11 22	11 42		11 47	12a20	12 17	12 42
Hitchin 4	d	08 47	08 52		09 22			09 47		09 52		10 22	10 47		10 52			11 22		11 47		11 52		12 22	12 47
Letchworth Garden City	d	08 51			09 26			09 51				10 26	10 51					11 26		11 51				12 26	12 51
Baldock	d	08 54			09 29			09 55				10 29	10 55					11 29		11 55				12 29	12 55
Ashwell & Morden	d	08 59						10 00					11 00							12 00					13 00
Royston	d	09 04			09 37			10 04				10 37	11 04					11 37		12 04				12 37	13 04
Meldreth	d	09 08						10 08					11 08							12 08					13 08
Shepreth	d	09 11						10 11					11 11							12 11					13 11
Foxton	d	09 13						10 14					11 14							12 14					13 14
Cambridge	a	09 28			09 55			10 27	10 00			10 54	11 27	11 00				11 54		12 27	12 00			12 54	13 27
Arlesey	d		08 57							09 57					10 57							11 57			
Biggleswade	d		09 02							10 02					11 02							12 02			
Sandy	d		09 06							10 06					11 06							12 06			
St Neots	d		09 13							10 13					11 13							12 13			
Huntingdon	d		09 21							10 21					11 21							12 21			
Peterborough 8	a		09 40			09 51				10 38					11 38				11 51			12 39			

		FC 1		FC 1	FC	FC 1	GR R 1	FC 1	FC 1	FC 1	FC	FC 1		FC 1	FC 1	FC 1	FC	FC 1	GR R 1	FC 1	FC 1	FC 1		FC	FC 1
London Kings Cross 15 ⊖	d	12 15		12 23	12 26	12 53	13 03	13 06	13 15	13 23	13 26	13 53		14 06	14 15	14 23	14 26	14 53	15 03	15 06	15 15	15 23		15 26	15 53
Finsbury Park ⊖	d			12 28	12 32	12 58		13 11		13 28	13 32	13 58		14 11		14 28	14 32	14 58		15 11		15 28		15 32	15 58
Potters Bar	d							13 21						14 21						15 21					
Hatfield	d							13 27						14 27						15 27					
Welwyn Garden City 4	d							13 31						14 31						15 31					
Welwyn North	d							13 34						14 34						15 34					
Knebworth	d							13 38						14 38						15 38					
Hertford North	d				13 07						14 07						15 07							16 07	
Stevenage 4	d			12 47	13a20	13 17	13 22	13 42		13 47	14a20	14 17		14 42		14 47	15a20	15 17	15 22	15 42		15 47		16a20	16 17
Hitchin 4	d			12 52		13 22		13 47		13 52		14 22		14 47		14 52		15 22		15 47		15 52			16 22
Letchworth Garden City	d					13 26		13 51				14 26		14 51				15 26		15 51					16 26
Baldock	d					13 29		13 55				14 29		14 55				15 29		15 55					16 29
Ashwell & Morden	d							14 00						15 00						16 00					
Royston	d					13 37		14 04				14 37		15 04				15 37		16 04					16 37
Meldreth	d							14 08						15 08						16 08					
Shepreth	d							14 11						15 11						16 11					
Foxton	d							14 14						15 14						16 14					
Cambridge	a	13 00				13 54		14 27	14 00			14 54		15 27	15 00			15 54		16 27	16 00				16 54
Arlesey	d			12 57						13 57						14 57						15 57			
Biggleswade	d			13 02						14 02						15 02						16 02			
Sandy	d			13 06						14 06						15 06						16 06			
St Neots	d			13 13						14 13						15 13						16 13			
Huntingdon	d			13 21						14 21						15 21						16 21			
Peterborough 8	a			13 38			13 51			14 38						15 38			15 51			16 38			

A not 22 May

Table 25

Sundays

until 19 June

London - Stevenage, Cambridge and Peterborough

		FC	FC	FC	FC	GR	FC	FC		FC	FC	FC	FC	GR	FC	FC	FC	FC		FC	FC	GR	FC	FC	GR
		1	1	1		R 1	1	1		1	1	1		R 1	1	1	1	1		1		R 1	1	1	R 1
						trolley								trolley								trolley			trolley
London Kings Cross 15 ⊖	d	16 06	16 15	16 23	16 26	16 35	16 36	16 53		17 06	17 15	17 23	17 26	17 35	17 36	17 53	18 06	18 15		18 22	18 26	18 35	18 53	19 06	19 08
Finsbury Park ⊖	d	16 11		16 28	16 32		16 41	16 58		17 11		17 28	17 32		17 41	17 58	18 11			18 27	18 32		18 58	19 11	
Potters Bar	d	16 21					16 51			17 21					17 51		18 21							19 21	
Hatfield	d	16 27					16 57			17 27					17 57		18 27							19 27	
Welwyn Garden City 4	d	16 31					17 01			17 31					18 01		18 31							19 31	
Welwyn North	d	16 34					17 04			17 34					18 04		18 34							19 34	
Knebworth	d	16 38					17 08			17 38					18 08		18 38							19 38	
Hertford North	d				17 07								18 07								19 07				
Stevenage 4	d	16 42		16 47	17a20	16a54	17 12	17 17		17 42		17 47	18a20	17a54	18 12	18 17	18 42			18 47	19a20	18a54	19 17	19 42	19 28
Hitchin 4	d	16 47		16 52			17 17	17 22		17 47		17 52			18 17	18 22	18 47			18 52			19 22	→	
Letchworth Garden City	d	16 51						17 26		17 51						18 26	18 52						19 26		
Baldock	d	16 55						17 29		17 55						18 29	18 55						19 29		
Ashwell & Morden	d	17 00								18 00							19 00								
Royston	d	17 04						17 37		18 04						18 37	19 05						19 37		
Meldreth	d	17 08								18 08							19 09								
Shepreth	d	17 11								18 11							19 12								
Foxton	d	17 14								18 14							19 14								
Cambridge	a	17 27	17 00					17 54		18 27	18 00					18 54	19 27	19 01					19 54		
Arlesey	d			16 57			17 23					17 57			18 23					18 58					
Biggleswade	d			17 02			17 28					18 02			18 28					19 03					
Sandy	d			17 06			17 32					18 06			18 32					19 06					
St Neots	d			17 13			17 39					18 13			18 39					19 14					
Huntingdon	d			17 21			17 47					18 21			18 47					19 21					
Peterborough 8	a			17 39			18 06					18 38			19 05					19 39					19 59

		FC	FC	FC		FC	GR		FC	FC	FC	FC	FC	GR		FC	FC	FC	FC	FC	GR	FC	FC	FC	
		1	1	1			R 1		1	1	1	1		R 1		1	1	1	1		R 1	1	1	1	
							trolley							trolley							trolley				
London Kings Cross 15 ⊖	d	19 15		19 22		19 26	19 35		19 53	20 06	20 15	20 23	20 26	20 35		20 53	21 06	21 15	21 23	21 26	21 35	21 53	22 06	22 15	
Finsbury Park ⊖	d			19 27		19 32			19 58	20 11		20 28	20 32			20 58	21 11		21 28	21 32		21 58	22 11		
Potters Bar	d									20 21							21 21						22 21		
Hatfield	d									20 27							21 27						22 27		
Welwyn Garden City 4	d									20 31							21 31						22 31		
Welwyn North	d									20 34							21 34						22 34		
Knebworth	d									20 38							21 38						22 38		
Hertford North	d		←			20 07							21 07							22 07					
Stevenage 4	d		19 42	19 47		20a20	19 54		20 17	20 42		20 47	21a20	20 54		21 16	21 42		21 47	22a20	21 55	22 17	22 42		
Hitchin 4	d		19 47	19 52					20 22	20 47		20 52				21 21	21 47		21 52			22 22	22 47		
Letchworth Garden City	d		19 51						20 26	20 51						21 25	21 51					22 26	22 51		
Baldock	d		19 55						20 29	20 55						21 29	21 55					22 29	22 55		
Ashwell & Morden	d		20 00							21 00							22 00						23 00		
Royston	d		20 04						20 37	21 04						21 37	22 04					22 37	23 04		
Meldreth	d		20 08							21 08							22 08						23 08		
Shepreth	d		20 11							21 11							22 11						23 11		
Foxton	d		20 14							21 14							22 14						23 14		
Cambridge	a	20 00	20 27						20 54	21 27	21 00					21 54	22 27	22 00				22 54	23 27	23 00	
Arlesey	d			19 57								20 57							21 57						
Biggleswade	d			20 02								21 02							22 02						
Sandy	d			20 06								21 06							22 06						
St Neots	d			20 13								21 13							22 13						
Huntingdon	d			20 21								21 21							22 21						
Peterborough 8	a			20 38			20 23					21 37		21 23					22 37		22 24				

		FC	FC	FC	FC	FC	FC	FC	FC	FC
		1		1	1	1	1	1		
London Kings Cross 15 ⊖	d	22 23	22 26	22 53	23 06	23 15		23 23	23 26	23 41
Finsbury Park ⊖	d	22 28	22 32	22 58	23 11			23 28	23 32	23 47
Potters Bar	d				23 21					00 08
Hatfield	d				23 27					00 16
Welwyn Garden City 4	d				23 31					00 20
Welwyn North	d				23 34					00 23
Knebworth	d				23 38					00 28
Hertford North	d		23 07						00 07	
Stevenage 4	d	22 47	23a20	23 17	23 42			23 47	00a20	00 31
Hitchin 4	d	22 52		23 22	23 47		←	23 52		00 37
Letchworth Garden City	d			23 26	23 51	23 44	23 51			00a52
Baldock	d			23 29	→		23 54			
Ashwell & Morden	d						23 59			
Royston	d			23 37		23 54	00 04			
Meldreth	d						00 08			
Shepreth	d						00 11			
Foxton	d						00 14			
Cambridge	a			23 55		00 10	00 29			
Arlesey	d	22 57						23 57		
Biggleswade	d	23 02						00 02		
Sandy	d	23 06						00 06		
St Neots	d	23 13						00 13		
Huntingdon	d	23 21						00 21		
Peterborough 8	a	23 41						00 43		

Table 25

Sundays

26 June to 31 July

London - Stevenage, Cambridge and Peterborough

		FC	FC	FC	FC	FC	FC	FC	FC	FC		FC	FC	FC	FC	FC	FC	FC	FC	GR		FC	FC	FC	FC
		1	1	1	1		1	1	1	1		1	1		1	1	1	1	1	R 1		1	1	1	1
London Kings Cross 15 ⊖	d	22p53	23p06	23p15		23p26	23p53	00 06	00 15			00 23	00 36	00 41	07 20			08 15		08 47			09 15		
Finsbury Park ⊖	d	22p58	23p11			23p32	23p58	00 11				00 28	00 41	00 47	07 25			08 20					09 20		
Potters Bar	d		23p21					00 23					00 53												
Hatfield	d		23p27					00 29					00 59												
Welwyn Garden City 4	d		23p31					00 41					01 05												
Welwyn North	d		23p34					00 44					01s08												
Knebworth	d		23p38					00 48					01s12												
Hertford North	d					00 07				←				01 22											
Stevenage 4	d	23p23	23p42			00 22	00 30	00 53	00 47	00 53		00 58	01 18	01a40	07 51			08 48		09 17			09 47		
Hitchin 4	d	23p31	23p50		←	00 29	00 37	→	00 54	01 00		01 05	01 25		08 01			08 53					09 52		
Letchworth Garden City	d		23p54	23p45	23p54	00a37			00 58	01 04															
Baldock	d		→		23p57				01 01	01 08						07 38	07 59		08 35			08 55		09 29	09 55
Ashwell & Morden	d				00 02					01 13							08 04					09 00			10 00
Royston	d			23p54	00 07				01 09	01 17						07 46	08 09		08 43			09 04		09 37	10 04
Meldreth	d				00 11					01 21							08 13					09 08			10 08
Shepreth	d				00 14					01 24							08 16					09 11			10 11
Foxton	d				00 16					01 27							08 18					09 14			10 14
Cambridge	a			00 09	00 29				01 25	01 40						08 04	08 34		09 00			09 26		09 54	10 27
Arlesey	d	23p36					00s43					01s10	01s30		08 06			08 58					09 57		
Biggleswade	d	23p41					00s48					01s15	01s35		08 11			09 03					10 02		
Sandy	d	23p45					00s51					01s19	01s39		08 15			09 07					10 06		
St Neots	d	23p52					00s59					01s26	01s47		08 22			09 14					10 13		
Huntingdon	d	00 01					01s06					01s34	01s54		08 30			09 22					10 21		
Peterborough 8	a	00 20					01 25					01 54	02 16		08 51			09 39		09 51			10 38		

		FC	FC	FC	FC	GR		FC	FC	FC	FC	FC	FC	FC	GR	FC		FC	FC	FC	FC	FC	FC	FC	FC
		1		1	1	R 1		1	1	1	1		1	1	R 1	1		1	1	1		1	1	1	1
London Kings Cross 15 ⊖	d	10 23	10 26			11 03		11 23			12 23	12 26			13 03			13 06	13 15	13 23	13 26	13 53	14 06	14 15	14 23
Finsbury Park ⊖	d	10 28	10 32					11 28			12 28	12 32						13 11		13 28	13 32	13 58	14 11		14 28
Potters Bar	d																	13 21					14 21		
Hatfield	d																	13 27					14 27		
Welwyn Garden City 4	d																	13 31					14 31		
Welwyn North	d																	13 34					14 34		
Knebworth	d																	13 38					14 38		
Hertford North	d		11 07									13 07									14 07				
Stevenage 4	d	10 47	11a20			11 22		11 47			12 47	13a20			13 22			13 42		13 47	14a20	14 17	14 42		14 47
Hitchin 4	d	10 52						11 52			12 52							13 47		13 52		14 22	14 47		14 52
Letchworth Garden City	d																	13 51				14 26	14 51		
Baldock	d			10 29	10 55				11 29	11 55			12 29	12 55		13 29		13 55				14 29	14 55		
Ashwell & Morden	d				11 00					12 00				13 00				14 00					15 00		
Royston	d			10 37	11 04				11 37	12 04			12 37	13 04		13 37		14 04				14 37	15 04		
Meldreth	d				11 08					12 08				13 08				14 08					15 08		
Shepreth	d				11 11					12 11				13 11				14 11					15 11		
Foxton	d				11 14					12 14				13 14				14 14					15 14		
Cambridge	a			10 54	11 27				11 54	12 27			12 54	13 27		13 54		14 27	14 00			14 54	15 27	15 00	
Arlesey	d	10 57						11 57			12 57									13 57					14 57
Biggleswade	d	11 02						12 02			13 02									14 02					15 02
Sandy	d	11 06						12 06			13 06									14 06					15 06
St Neots	d	11 13						12 13			13 13									14 13					15 13
Huntingdon	d	11 21						12 21			13 21									14 21					15 21
Peterborough 8	a	11 38				11 51		12 39			13 38				13 51					14 38					15 38

		FC		FC	GR	FC	FC	FC	FC	FC	FC	FC		FC	FC	GR	FC	FC	FC	FC	FC	FC		GR	FC
				1	R 1	1	1	1		1	1	1		1		R 1	1	1	1	1	1			R 1	1
London Kings Cross 15 ⊖	d	14 26		14 53	15 03	15 06	15 15	15 23	15 26	15 53	16 06	16 15		16 23	16 26	16 35	16 36	16 53	17 06	17 15	17 23	17 26		17 35	17 36
Finsbury Park ⊖	d	14 32		14 58		15 11		15 28	15 32	15 58	16 11			16 28	16 32		16 41	16 58	17 11		17 28	17 32			17 41
Potters Bar	d					15 21					16 21						16 51		17 21						17 51
Hatfield	d					15 27					16 27						16 57		17 27						17 57
Welwyn Garden City 4	d					15 31					16 31						17 01		17 31						18 01
Welwyn North	d					15 34					16 34						17 04		17 34						18 04
Knebworth	d					15 38					16 38						17 08		17 38						18 08
Hertford North	d	15 07							16 07						17 07							18 07			
Stevenage 4	d	15a20		15 17	15 22	15 42		15 47	16a20	16 17	16 42			16 47	17a20	16a54	17 12	17 17	17 42		17 47	18a20		17a54	18 12
Hitchin 4	d			15 22		15 47		15 52		16 22	16 47			16 52			17 17	17 22	17 47		17 52				18 17
Letchworth Garden City	d			15 26		15 51				16 26	16 51							17 26	17 51						
Baldock	d			15 29		15 55				16 29	16 55							17 29	17 55						
Ashwell & Morden	d					16 00					17 00								18 00						
Royston	d			15 37		16 04				16 37	17 04							17 37	18 04						
Meldreth	d					16 08					17 08								18 08						
Shepreth	d					16 11					17 11								18 11						
Foxton	d					16 14					17 14								18 14						
Cambridge	a			15 54		16 27	16 00			16 54	17 27	17 00						17 54	18 27	18 00					
Arlesey	d							15 57						16 57			17 23				17 57				18 23
Biggleswade	d							16 02						17 02			17 28				18 02				18 28
Sandy	d							16 06						17 06			17 32				18 06				18 32
St Neots	d							16 13						17 13			17 39				18 13				18 39
Huntingdon	d							16 21						17 21			17 47				18 21				18 47
Peterborough 8	a				15 51			16 38						17 39			18 06				18 38				19 05

Table 25

Sundays

26 June to 31 July

London - Stevenage, Cambridge and Peterborough

		FC	FC	FC	FC	FC	GR	FC		FC	GR	FC	FC	FC	FC	GR		FC		FC	FC	FC	FC	GR	FC
							R				R					R								R	
		1	1	1	1		1	1		1	1	1	1	1		1		1		1	1	1		1	1
London Kings Cross 15 ⊖	d	17 53	18 06	18 15	18 22	18 26	18 35	18 53		19 06	19 08	19 15		19 22	19 26	19 35		19 53		20 06	20 15	20 23	20 26	20 35	20 53
Finsbury Park ⊖	d	17 58	18 11		18 27	18 32		18 58		19 11				19 27	19 32			19 58		20 11		20 28	20 32		20 58
Potters Bar	d		18 21							19 21										20 21					
Hatfield	d		18 27							19 27										20 27					
Welwyn Garden City 4	d		18 31							19 31										20 31					
Welwyn North	d		18 34							19 34										20 34					
Knebworth	d		18 38							19 38										20 38					
Hertford North	d					19 07							←		20 07								21 07		
Stevenage 4	d	18 17	18 42		18 47	19a20	18a54	19 17		19 42	19 28		19 42	19 47	20a20	19 54		20 17		20 42		20 47	21a20	20 54	21 16
Hitchin 4	d	18 22	18 47		18 52			19 22		→			19 47	19 52				20 22		20 47		20 52			21 21
Letchworth Garden City	d	18 26	18 52					19 26					19 51					20 26		20 51					21 25
Baldock	d	18 29	18 55					19 29					19 55					20 29		20 55					21 29
Ashwell & Morden	d		19 00										20 00							21 00					
Royston	d	18 37	19 05					19 37					20 04					20 37		21 04					21 37
Meldreth	d		19 09										20 08							21 08					
Shepreth	d		19 12										20 11							21 11					
Foxton	d		19 14										20 14							21 14					
Cambridge	a	18 54	19 27	19 01				19 54				20 00	20 27					20 54		21 27	21 00				21 54
Arlesey	d				18 58									19 57								20 57			
Biggleswade	d				19 03									20 02								21 02			
Sandy	d				19 06									20 06								21 06			
St Neots	d				19 14									20 13								21 13			
Huntingdon	d				19 21									20 21								21 21			
Peterborough 8	a				19 39						19 59			20 38		20 23						21 37		21 23	

		FC	FC	FC		FC	GR	FC	FC	FC	FC	FC	FC	FC		FC	FC	FC	FC	FC					
							R																		
		1	1	1			1	1	1	1	1		1	1		1	1	1							
London Kings Cross 15 ⊖	d	21 06	21 15	21 23		21 26	21 35	21 53	22 06	22 15	22 23	22 26	22 53	23 06		23 15		23 23	23 26	23 41					
Finsbury Park ⊖	d	21 11		21 28		21 32		21 58	22 11		22 28	22 32	22 58	23 11				23 28	23 32	23 47					
Potters Bar	d	21 21							22 21					23 21						00 08					
Hatfield	d	21 27							22 27					23 27						00 16					
Welwyn Garden City 4	d	21 31							22 31					23 31						00 20					
Welwyn North	d	21 34							22 34					23 34						00 23					
Knebworth	d	21 38							22 38					23 38						00 28					
Hertford North	d					22 07						23 07							00 07						
Stevenage 4	d	21 42		21 47		22a20	21 55	22 17	22 42		22 47	23a20	23 17	23 42				23 47	00a20	00 31					
Hitchin 4	d	21 47		21 52				22 22	22 47		22 52		23 22	23 47			←	23 52		00 37					
Letchworth Garden City	d	21 51						22 26	22 51				23 26	23 51		23 44	23 51			00a52					
Baldock	d	21 55						22 29	22 55				23 29	→			23 54								
Ashwell & Morden	d	22 00							23 00								23 59								
Royston	d	22 04						22 37	23 04				23 37			23 54	00 04								
Meldreth	d	22 08							23 08								00 08								
Shepreth	d	22 11							23 11								00 11								
Foxton	d	22 14							23 14								00 14								
Cambridge	a	22 27	22 00					22 54	23 27	23 00			23 55			00 10	00 29								
Arlesey	d			21 57							22 57							23 57							
Biggleswade	d			22 02							23 02							00 02							
Sandy	d			22 06							23 06							00 06							
St Neots	d			22 13							23 13							00 13							
Huntingdon	d			22 21							23 21							00 21							
Peterborough 8	a			22 37			22 24				23 41							00 43							

Sundays

7 August to 11 September

		FC	FC	FC	FC	FC	FC	FC	FC	FC		FC	FC	FC	FC	FC	FC	FC	FC	FC		FC	FC	FC	FC
		1	1	1		1		1	1	1		1	1		1			1	1	1		1		1	1
London Kings Cross 15 ⊖	d	22p53	23p06	23p23	23p26	23p36		23p53	00 06	00 15			00 23	00 41	00 53		06 26	06 50	07 06	07 23		07 50		08 06	08 23
Finsbury Park ⊖	d	22p58	23p11	23p28	23p32	23p41		23p58	00 11				00 28	00 47	00 58		06 32	06 56	07 11	07 28		07 56		08 11	08 28
Potters Bar	d		23p21			23p53			00 23										07 21					08 21	
Hatfield	d		23p27			23p59			00 29										07 27					08 27	
Welwyn Garden City 4	d		23p31			00 06			00 41						01 17				07 33					08 31	
Welwyn North	d		23p34			00 09			00 44						01s22				07 36					08 34	
Knebworth	d		23p38			00 13			00 48						01s25				07 40					08 38	
Hertford North	d				00 07		←					←		01 22		←	07 07						08 10		
Stevenage 4	d	23p17	23p42	23p47	00 22	00 18	00 22	00 30	00 53	00 47		00 53	00 58	01 36	01 29	01 36	07a22	07 17	07 45	07 51		08 17	08a25	08 42	08 47
Hitchin 4	d	23p24	23p50	23p54	→	00 25	00 29	00 37	→	00 54		01 00	01 05	→	01 36	01 44		07 26	07 52	08 01		08 22		08 47	08 52
Letchworth Garden City	d		23p54			00a30	00a37			00 58		01 04				01a50		07 35	07 56			08 26		08 51	
Baldock	d		23p57							01 01		01 08						07 38	07 59			08 29		08 54	
Ashwell & Morden	d		00 02									01 13							08 04					08 59	
Royston	d		00 07							01 09		01 17						07 46	08 09			08 37		09 04	
Meldreth	d		00 11									01 21							08 13					09 08	
Shepreth	d		00 14									01 24							08 16					09 11	
Foxton	d		00 16									01 27							08 18					09 13	
Cambridge	a		00 29							01 25		01 40						08 04	08 34			08 54		09 28	
Arlesey	d	23p29		23p59				00s43					01s10		01s43					08 06					08 57
Biggleswade	d	23p34		00 04				00s48					01s15		01s48					08 11					09 02
Sandy	d	23p38		00 08				00s51					01s19		01s52					08 15					09 06
St Neots	d	23p45		00 15				00s59					01s26		01s59					08 22					09 13
Huntingdon	d	23p53		00 23				01s06					01s34		02s07					08 30					09 21
Peterborough 8	a	00 13		00 43				01 25					01 54		02 27					08 51					09 40

Table 25

Sundays

7 August to 11 September

London - Stevenage, Cambridge and Peterborough

		FC	GR	FC	FC	FC		FC	FC	FC	FC	FC	FC	GR	FC	FC		FC	FC	FC	FC	FC	FC	FC	FC
		■1	■R ■1 trolley		■1	■1		■1	■1		■1	■1	■1	■R ■1 trolley		■1		■1	■1		■1	■1	■1 A	■1 B	■1
London Kings Cross ■15 ⊖	d	08 50	08 59		09 06	09 10		09 23	09 50		10 06	10 10	10 50	10 59		11 06		11 10	11 23	11 26	11 50	12 06	12 10	12 15	12 23
Finsbury Park ⊖	d	08 56			09 11			09 28	09 56		10 11		10 56			11 11			11 28	11 32	11 56	12 11			12 28
Potters Bar	d				09 21						10 21					11 21						12 21			
Hatfield	d				09 27						10 27					11 27						12 27			
Welwyn Garden City ■4	d				09 31						10 31					11 31						12 31			
Welwyn North	d				09 34						10 34					11 34						12 34			
Knebworth	d				09 38						10 38					11 38						12 38			
Hertford North	d			09 12						10 12					11 12					12 07					
Stevenage ■4	d	09 17	09 22	09a25	09 42			09 47	10 17	10a25	10 42		11 17	11 22	11a25	11 42			11 47	12a20	12 17	12 42			12 47
Hitchin ■4	d	09 22			09 47			09 52	10 22		10 47		11 22			11 47			11 52		12 22	12 47			12 52
Letchworth Garden City	d	09 26			09 51				10 26		10 51		11 26			11 51					12 26	12 51			
Baldock	d	09 29			09 55				10 29		10 55		11 29			11 55					12 29	12 55			
Ashwell & Morden	d				10 00						11 00					12 00						13 00			
Royston	d	09 37			10 04				10 37		11 04		11 37			12 04					12 37	13 04			
Meldreth	d				10 08						11 08					12 08						13 08			
Shepreth	d				10 11						11 11					12 11						13 11			
Foxton	d				10 14						11 14					12 14						13 14			
Cambridge	a	09 55			10 27	10 00			10 54		11 27	11 02	11 54			12 27		12 00			12 54	13 27	13 00	13 00	
Arlesey	d							09 57											11 57						12 57
Biggleswade	d							10 02											12 02						13 02
Sandy	d							10 06											12 06						13 06
St Neots	d							10 13											12 13						13 13
Huntingdon	d							10 21											12 21						13 21
Peterborough ■8	a		09 51					10 38						11 51					12 39						13 38

		FC		FC	GR	FC	FC	FC	FC	FC	FC	FC		FC	FC	GR	FC	FC	FC	FC	FC	FC		FC	FC
				■1	■R ■1 trolley	■1	■1		■1	■1	■1	■1			■1	■R ■1 trolley	■1	■1	■1		■1	■1		■1	■1
London Kings Cross ■15 ⊖	d	12 26		12 50	12 59	13 06	13 10	13 26	13 50	14 06	14 10	14 23		14 26	14 50	14 59	15 06	15 15	15 23	15 26	15 53	16 06		16 10	16 23
Finsbury Park ⊖	d	12 32		12 56		13 11		13 32	13 56	14 11		14 28		14 32	14 56		15 11		15 28	15 32	15 58	16 11			16 28
Potters Bar	d					13 21				14 21							15 21					16 21			
Hatfield	d					13 27				14 27							15 27					16 27			
Welwyn Garden City ■4	d					13 31				14 31							15 31					16 31			
Welwyn North	d					13 34				14 34							15 34					16 34			
Knebworth	d					13 38				14 38							15 38					16 38			
Hertford North	d	13 07						14 07						15 07						16 07					
Stevenage ■4	d	13a20		13 17	13 22	13 42		14a20	14 17	14 42		14 47		15a20	15 17	15 22	15 42		15 47	16a20	16 17	16 42			16 47
Hitchin ■4	d			13 22		13 47			14 22	14 47		14 52			15 22		15 47		15 52		16 22	16 47			16 52
Letchworth Garden City	d			13 26		13 51			14 26	14 51					15 26		15 51				16 26	16 51			
Baldock	d			13 29		13 55			14 29	14 55					15 29		15 55				16 29	16 55			
Ashwell & Morden	d					14 00				15 00							16 00					17 00			
Royston	d			13 37		14 04			14 37	15 04					15 37		16 04				16 37	17 04			
Meldreth	d					14 08				15 08							16 08					17 08			
Shepreth	d					14 11				15 11							16 11					17 11			
Foxton	d					14 14				15 14							16 14					17 14			
Cambridge	a			13 54		14 27	14 00		14 54	15 27	15 00				15 54		16 27	16 00			16 54	17 27		17 00	
Arlesey	d											14 57							15 57						16 57
Biggleswade	d											15 02							16 02						17 02
Sandy	d											15 06							16 06						17 06
St Neots	d											15 13							16 13						17 13
Huntingdon	d											15 21							16 21						17 21
Peterborough ■8	a				13 51							15 38				15 51			16 38						17 39

		FC	GR	FC	FC	FC	FC	FC		FC	GR	FC	FC	FC	FC	FC	FC	GR		FC	GR	FC	GR	FC	FC
			■R ■1 trolley	■1	■1	■1	■1	■1			■R ■1 trolley	■1	■1	■1	■1	■1		■R ■1 trolley		■1	■R ■1 A trolley	■1	■R ■1 B trolley	■1	■1
London Kings Cross ■15 ⊖	d	16 26	16 31	16 36	16 50	17 06	17 10	17 23		17 26	17 31	17 36	17 50	18 06	18 10	18 22	18 26	18 31		18 50	19 03	19 06	19 08	19 10	
Finsbury Park ⊖	d	16 32		16 41	16 56	17 11		17 28		17 32		17 41	17 56	18 11		18 27	18 32			18 56		19 11			
Potters Bar	d			16 51		17 21						17 51		18 21								19 21			
Hatfield	d			16 57		17 27						17 57		18 27								19 27			
Welwyn Garden City ■4	d			17 01		17 31						18 01		18 31								19 31			
Welwyn North	d			17 04		17 34						18 04		18 34								19 34			
Knebworth	d			17 08		17 38						18 08		18 38								19 38			
Hertford North	d	17 07								18 07							19 07								←
Stevenage ■4	d	17a20	16a54	17 12	17 17	17 42		17 47		18a20	17a54	18 12	18 17	18 42		18 47	19a20	18a54		19 17	19 28	19 42	19 28		19 42
Hitchin ■4	d			17 17	17 22	17 47		17 52				18 17	18 22	18 47		18 52				19 22		→			19 47
Letchworth Garden City	d				17 26	17 51							18 26	18 52						19 26					19 51
Baldock	d				17 29	17 55							18 29	18 55						19 29					19 55
Ashwell & Morden	d					18 00								19 00											20 00
Royston	d				17 37	18 04							18 37	19 05						19 37					20 04
Meldreth	d					18 08								19 09											20 08
Shepreth	d					18 11								19 12											20 11
Foxton	d					18 14								19 14											20 14
Cambridge	a				17 54	18 27	18 00						18 54	19 27	19 01					19 54				20 00	20 27
Arlesey	d			17 23				17 57				18 23				18 58									
Biggleswade	d			17 28				18 02				18 28				19 03									
Sandy	d			17 32				18 06				18 32				19 06									
St Neots	d			17 39				18 13				18 39				19 14									
Huntingdon	d			17 47				18 21				18 47				19 21									
Peterborough ■8	a			18 06				18 38				19 05				19 39					19 59		19 59		

A not 28 August

B 28 August

Table 25

Sundays

7 August to 11 September

London - Stevenage, Cambridge and Peterborough

		FC 1	FC	GR R 1			FC 1	FC 1	FC 1	FC 1	FC	GR R 1	FC 1	FC 1		FC 1	FC 1	FC	GR R 1	FC 1	FC 1	FC 1	FC 1	FC
London Kings Cross 15 ⊖	d	19 22	19 26	19 31			19 50	20 06	20 10	20 23	20 26	20 31	20 50	21 06		21 10	21 23	21 26	21 32	21 50	22 06	22 10	22 23	22 26
Finsbury Park ⊖	d	19 27	19 32				19 56	20 11		20 28	20 32		20 56	21 11			21 28	21 32		21 56	22 11		22 28	22 32
Potters Bar	d							20 21						21 21							22 21			
Hatfield	d							20 27						21 27							22 27			
Welwyn Garden City 4	d							20 31						21 31							22 31			
Welwyn North	d							20 34						21 34							22 34			
Knebworth	d							20 38						21 38							22 38			
Hertford North	d		20 07								21 07							22 07						23 07
Stevenage 4	d	19 47	20a20	19 54			20 17	20 42		20 47	21a20	20 54	21 16	21 42			21 47	22a20	21 55	22 17	22 42		22 47	23a20
Hitchin 4	d	19 52					20 22	20 47		20 52			21 21	21 47			21 52			22 22	22 47		22 52	
Letchworth Garden City	d						20 26	20 51					21 25	21 51						22 26	22 51			
Baldock	d						20 29	20 55					21 29	21 55						22 29	22 55			
Ashwell & Morden	d							21 00						22 00							23 00			
Royston	d						20 37	21 04					21 37	22 04						22 37	23 04			
Meldreth	d							21 08						22 08							23 08			
Shepreth	d							21 11						22 11							23 11			
Foxton	d							21 14						22 14							23 14			
Cambridge	a						20 54	21 27	21 00				21 54	22 27		22 00				22 54	23 27	23 00		
Arlesey	d	19 57								20 57							21 57						22 57	
Biggleswade	d	20 02								21 02							22 02						23 02	
Sandy	d	20 06								21 06							22 06						23 06	
St Neots	d	20 13								21 13							22 13						23 13	
Huntingdon	d	20 21								21 21							22 21						23 21	
Peterborough 8	a	20 38		20 23						21 37		21 23					22 37		22 24				23 41	

		FC 1 A	FC 1 B	FC 1	FC 1	FC 1	FC 1	FC	FC
London Kings Cross 15 ⊖	d	22 50	22 53	23 06	23 10		23 23	23 26	23 41
Finsbury Park ⊖	d	22 56	22 58	23 11			23 28	23 32	23 47
Potters Bar	d			23 21					00 08
Hatfield	d			23 27					00 16
Welwyn Garden City 4	d			23 31					00 20
Welwyn North	d			23 34					00 23
Knebworth	d			23 38					00 28
Hertford North	d							00 07	
Stevenage 4	d	23 17	23 17	23 42			23 47	00a20	00 31
Hitchin 4	d	23 22	23 22	23 47		←	23 52		00 37
Letchworth Garden City	d	23 26	23 26	23 51	23 44	23 51			00a52
Baldock	d	23 29	23 29	→		23 54			
Ashwell & Morden	d					23 59			
Royston	d	23 37	23 37		23 54	00 04			
Meldreth	d					00 08			
Shepreth	d					00 11			
Foxton	d					00 14			
Cambridge	a	23 55	23 55		00 10	00 29			
Arlesey	d						23 57		
Biggleswade	d						00 02		
Sandy	d						00 06		
St Neots	d						00 13		
Huntingdon	d						00 21		
Peterborough 8	a						00 43		

Sundays

18 September to 23 October

		FC 1	FC 1	FC 1	FC 1	FC 1	FC	FC 1	FC	FC 1		FC 1	FC 1	FC 1	FC 1	FC	FC 1	FC	FC	FC 1		FC 1	FC 1	FC 1	FC 1
London Kings Cross 15 ⊖	d	22p53	23p06	23p15		23p23	23p26	23p36		23p53		00 06	00 15		00 23	00 41	00 53		06 26	06 53		07 06	07 23	07 53	08 06
Finsbury Park ⊖	d	22p58	23p11			23p28	23p32	23p41		23p58		00 11			00 28	00 47	00 58		06 32	06 58		07 11	07 28	07 58	08 11
Potters Bar	d		23p21					23p53				00 23										07 21			08 20
Hatfield	d		23p27					23p59				00 29										07 27			08 26
Welwyn Garden City 4	d		23p31					00 06				00 41					01 17					07 33			08 30
Welwyn North	d		23p34					00 09				00 44					01s22					07 36			08 33
Knebworth	d		23p38					00 13				00 48					01s25					07 40			08 37
Hertford North	d						00 07		←					←		01 22		←	07 07						
Stevenage 4	d	23p17	23p42			23p47	00 22	00 18	00 22	00 30		00 53	00 47	00 53	00 58	01 36	01 29	01 36	07a22	07 17		07 45	07 51	08 17	08 40
Hitchin 4	d	23p24	23p50		←	23p54	→	00 25	00 29	00 37		→	00 54	01 00	01 05	→	01 36	01 44		07 26		07 52	08 01	08 22	08 45
Letchworth Garden City	d		23p54	23p45	23p54			00a30	00a37				00 58	01 04	01a11		01a44	01a50		07 35		07 56		08 26	08 49
Baldock	d		→		23p57								01 01	01 08						07 38		07 59		08 29	08 53
Ashwell & Morden	d				00 02									01 13								08 04			08 58
Royston	d			23p54	00 07								01 09	01 17						07 46		08 09		08 37	09 02
Meldreth	d				00 11									01 21								08 13			09 06
Shepreth	d				00 14									01 24								08 16			09 09
Foxton	d				00 16									01 27								08 18			09 12
Cambridge	a			00 09	00 29								01 25	01 40						08 04		08 34		08 54	09 27
Arlesey	d	23p29				23p59				00s43													08 06		
Biggleswade	d	23p34				00 04				00s48													08 11		
Sandy	d	23p38				00 08				00s51													08 15		
St Neots	d	23p45				00 15				00s59													08 22		
Huntingdon	d	23p53				00 23				01s06													08 30		
Peterborough 8	a	00 13				00 43				01 25													08 51		

A not 28 August

B 28 August

Table 25

Sundays

18 September to 23 October

London - Stevenage, Cambridge and Peterborough

		FC 1	FC 1	GR R 1	FC 1	FC 1	FC 1	FC 1	FC 1	FC 1	FC 1	FC 1	GR R 1	FC 1	FC 1	FC 1	FC	FC 1	FC 1	FC 1	FC 1	FC	FC 1
London Kings Cross 15 ⊖	d	08 23	08 53	09 03	09 06	09 15	09 23	09 53	10 06	10 15	10 23	10 53	11 03	11 06	11 15	11 23	11 26	11 53	12 06	12 15	12 23	12 26	12 53
Finsbury Park ⊖	d	08 28	08 58		09 11		09 28	09 58	10 11		10 28	10 58		11 11		11 28	11 32	11 58	12 11		12 28	12 32	12 58
Potters Bar	d				09 21				10 21					11 21					12 21				
Hatfield	d				09 27				10 27					11 27					12 27				
Welwyn Garden City 4	d				09 31				10 31					11 31					12 31				
Welwyn North	d				09 34				10 34					11 34					12 34				
Knebworth	d				09 38				10 38					11 38					12 38				
Hertford North	d																12 07					13 07	
Stevenage 4	d	08 47	09 17	09 22	09 42		09 47	10 17	10 42		10 47	11 17	11 22	11 42		11 47	12a20	12 17	12 42		12 47	13a20	13 17
Hitchin 4	d	08 52	09 22		09 47		09 52	10 22	10 47		10 52	11 22		11 47		11 52		12 22	12 47		12 52		13 22
Letchworth Garden City	d		09 26		09 51			10 26	10 51			11 26		11 51				12 26	12 51				13 26
Baldock	d		09 29		09 55			10 29	10 55			11 29		11 55				12 29	12 55				13 29
Ashwell & Morden	d				10 00				11 00					12 00					13 00				
Royston	d		09 37		10 04			10 37	11 04			11 37		12 04				12 37	13 04				13 37
Meldreth	d				10 08				11 08					12 08					13 08				
Shepreth	d				10 11				11 11					12 11					13 11				
Foxton	d				10 14				11 14					12 14					13 14				
Cambridge	a		09 55		10 27	10 00		10 54	11 27	11 00		11 54		12 27	12 00			12 54	13 27	13 00			13 54
Arlesey	d	08 57					09 57				10 57					11 57					12 57		
Biggleswade	d	09 02					10 02				11 02					12 02					13 02		
Sandy	d	09 06					10 06				11 06					12 06					13 06		
St Neots	d	09 13					10 13				11 13					12 13					13 13		
Huntingdon	d	09 21					10 21				11 21					12 21					13 21		
Peterborough 8	a	09 40		09 51			10 38				11 38		11 51			12 39					13 38		

		GR R 1	FC 1	FC 1	FC 1	FC	FC 1	FC 1	FC 1	FC 1	FC	FC 1	GR R 1	FC 1	FC 1	FC 1	FC	FC 1	FC 1	FC 1	FC 1	FC
London Kings Cross 15 ⊖	d	13 03	13 06	13 15	13 23	13 26	13 53	14 06	14 15	14 23	14 26	14 53	15 03	15 06	15 15	15 23	15 26	15 53	16 06	16 15	16 23	16 26
Finsbury Park ⊖	d		13 11		13 28	13 32	13 58	14 11		14 28	14 32	14 58		15 12		15 28	15 32	15 58	16 12		16 28	16 32
Potters Bar	d		13 21					14 21						15 21					16 21			
Hatfield	d		13 27					14 27						15 27					16 27			
Welwyn Garden City 4	d		13 31					14 31						15 31					16 31			
Welwyn North	d		13 34					14 34						15 34					16 34			
Knebworth	d		13 38					14 38						15 38					16 38			
Hertford North	d					14 07					15 07						16 07					17 07
Stevenage 4	d	13 22	13 42		13 47	14a20	14 17	14 42		14 47	15a20	15 17	15 22	15 42		15 47	16a20	16 17	16 42		16 47	17a20
Hitchin 4	d		13 47		13 52		14 22	14 47		14 52		15 22		15 47		15 52		16 22	16 47		16 52	
Letchworth Garden City	d		13 51				14 26	14 51				15 26		15 51				16 26	16 51			
Baldock	d		13 55				14 29	14 55				15 29		15 55				16 29	16 55			
Ashwell & Morden	d		14 00					15 00						16 00					17 00			
Royston	d		14 04				14 37	15 04				15 37		16 04				16 37	17 04			
Meldreth	d		14 08					15 08						16 08					17 08			
Shepreth	d		14 11					15 11						16 11					17 11			
Foxton	d		14 14					15 14						16 14					17 14			
Cambridge	a		14 27	14 00			14 54	15 27	15 00			15 54		16 27	16 00			16 54	17 27	17 00		
Arlesey	d				13 57					14 57						15 57					16 57	
Biggleswade	d				14 02					15 02						16 02					17 02	
Sandy	d				14 06					15 06						16 06					17 06	
St Neots	d				14 13					15 13						16 13					17 13	
Huntingdon	d				14 21					15 21						16 21					17 21	
Peterborough 8	a	13 51			14 38					15 38			15 51			16 38					17 39	

		GR R 1	FC 1	FC 1	FC 1	FC 1	FC 1	FC	GR R 1	FC 1	FC 1	FC 1	FC 1	FC 1	FC	GR R 1	FC 1	FC 1	GR R 1	FC 1	FC 1	FC 1	FC
London Kings Cross 15 ⊖	d	16 35	16 36	16 53	17 06	17 15	17 23	17 26	17 35	17 36	17 53	18 06	18 15	18 22	18 26	18 35	18 53	19 03	19 08	19 15		19 22	19 26
Finsbury Park ⊖	d		16 41	16 58	17 12		17 28	17 32		17 41	17 58	18 12		18 27	18 32		18 58	19 11				19 27	19 32
Potters Bar	d		16 51		17 21					17 51		18 21						19 21					
Hatfield	d		16 57		17 27					17 57		18 27						19 27					
Welwyn Garden City 4	d		17 01		17 31					18 01		18 31						19 31					
Welwyn North	d		17 04		17 34					18 04		18 34						19 34					
Knebworth	d		17 08		17 38					18 08		18 38						19 38					
Hertford North	d							18 07							19 07						←		20 07
Stevenage 4	d	16a54	17 12	17 17	17 42		17 47	18a20	17a54	18 12	18 17	18 42		18 47	19a20	18a54	19 17	19 42	19 28		19 42	19 47	20a20
Hitchin 4	d		17 17	17 22	17 47		17 52			18 17	18 22	18 47		18 52			19 22	→			19 47	19 52	
Letchworth Garden City	d			17 26	17 51						18 26	18 52					19 26				19 51		
Baldock	d			17 29	17 55						18 29	18 55					19 29				19 55		
Ashwell & Morden	d				18 00							19 00									20 00		
Royston	d			17 37	18 04						18 37	19 05					19 37				20 04		
Meldreth	d				18 08							19 09									20 08		
Shepreth	d				18 11							19 12									20 11		
Foxton	d				18 14							19 14									20 14		
Cambridge	a			17 54	18 27	18 00					18 54	19 27	19 01				19 54			20 00	20 27		
Arlesey	d		17 23				17 57			18 23				18 58								19 57	
Biggleswade	d		17 28				18 02			18 28				19 03								20 02	
Sandy	d		17 32				18 06			18 32				19 06								20 06	
St Neots	d		17 39				18 13			18 39				19 14								20 13	
Huntingdon	d		17 47				18 21			18 47				19 21								20 21	
Peterborough 8	a		18 06				18 38			19 05				19 39					19 59			20 38	

Table 25

London - Stevenage, Cambridge and Peterborough

Sundays

18 September to 23 October

		GR	FC	FC	FC	FC	FC	GR	FC	FC	FC	FC	FC	GR	FC	FC	FC	FC	FC	FC	FC
		1	1	1	1	1		1	1	1	1	1		1	1	1	1	1		1	1
London Kings Cross 15 ⊖	d	19 35	19 53	20 06	20 15	20 23	20 26	20 35	20 53	21 06	21 15	21 23	21 26	21 35	21 53	22 06	22 15	22 23	22 26	22 53	23 06
Finsbury Park ⊖	d		19 58	20 12		20 28	20 32		20 58	21 11		21 28	21 32		21 58	22 12		22 28	22 32	22 58	23 12
Potters Bar	d			20 21						21 21						22 21					23 21
Hatfield	d			20 27						21 27						22 27					23 27
Welwyn Garden City 4	d			20 31						21 31						22 31					23 31
Welwyn North	d			20 34						21 34						22 34					23 34
Knebworth	d			20 38						21 38						22 38					23 38
Hertford North	d						21 07						22 07						23 07		
Stevenage 4	d	19 54	20 17	20 42		20 47	21a20	20 54	21 16	21 42		21 47	22a20	21 55	22 17	22 42		22 47	23a20	23 17	23 42
Hitchin 4	d		20 22	20 47		20 52			21 21	21 47		21 52			22 22	22 47		22 52		23 22	23 47
Letchworth Garden City	d		20 26	20 51					21 25	21 51					22 26	22 51				23 26	23 51
Baldock	d		20 29	20 55					21 29	21 55					22 29	22 55				23 29	→
Ashwell & Morden	d			21 00						22 00						23 00					
Royston	d		20 37	21 04					21 37	22 04					22 37	23 04				23 37	
Meldreth	d			21 08						22 08						23 08					
Shepreth	d			21 11						22 11						23 11					
Foxton	d			21 14						22 14						23 14					
Cambridge	a		20 54	21 27	21 00				21 54	22 27	22 00				22 54	23 27	23 00			23 55	
Arlesey	d					20 57						21 57						22 57			
Biggleswade	d					21 02						22 02						23 02			
Sandy	d					21 06						22 06						23 06			
St Neots	d					21 13						22 13						23 13			
Huntingdon	d					21 21						22 21						23 21			
Peterborough 8	a	20 23				21 37		21 23				22 37		22 24				23 41			

		FC	FC	FC	FC	FC
		1	1	1		
London Kings Cross 15 ⊖	d	23 15		23 23	23 26	23 41
Finsbury Park ⊖	d			23 28	23 32	23 47
Potters Bar	d					00 08
Hatfield	d					00 16
Welwyn Garden City 4	d					00 20
Welwyn North	d					00 23
Knebworth	d					00 28
Hertford North	d				00 07	
Stevenage 4	d			23 47	00a20	00 31
Hitchin 4	d		←	23 52		00 37
Letchworth Garden City	d	23 44	23 51			00a52
Baldock	d		23 54			
Ashwell & Morden	d		23 59			
Royston	d	23 54	00 04			
Meldreth	d		00 08			
Shepreth	d		00 11			
Foxton	d		00 14			
Cambridge	a	00 10	00 29			
Arlesey	d			23 57		
Biggleswade	d			00 02		
Sandy	d			00 06		
St Neots	d			00 13		
Huntingdon	d			00 21		
Peterborough 8	a			00 43		

Sundays

from 30 October

		FC	FC	FC	FC	FC	FC	FC	FC	FC	FC	FC	FC	FC	FC	FC	FC	FC	FC	FC	FC	FC	FC
		1	1	1	1	1		1		1	1	1	1	1		1			1	1	1		1
London Kings Cross 15 ⊖	d	22p53	23p06	23p15		23p23	23p26	23p36		23p53	00 06	00 15		00 23	00 41	00 53		06 26	06 53	07 06	07 23	07 26	07 53
Finsbury Park ⊖	d	22p58	23p11			23p28	23p32	23p41		23p58	00 11			00 28	00 47	00 58		06 32	06 58	07 11	07 28	07 32	07 58
Potters Bar	d		23p21					23p53			00 23									07 21			
Hatfield	d		23p27					23p59			00 29									07 27			
Welwyn Garden City 4	d		23p31					00 06			00 41					01 17				07 33			
Welwyn North	d		23p34					00 09			00 44					01s22				07 36			
Knebworth	d		23p38					00 13			00 48					01s25				07 40			
Hertford North	d						00 07		←				←		01 22		←	07 07				08 07	
Stevenage 4	d	23p17	23p42			23p47	00 22	00 18	00 22	00 30	00 53	00 47	00 53	00 58	01 36	01 29	01 36	07a22	07 17	07 45	07 51	08a23	08 17
Hitchin 4	d	23p24	23p50		←	23p54	→	00 25	00 29	00 37	→	00 54	01 00	01 05	→	01 36	01 44		07 26	07 52	08 01		08 22
Letchworth Garden City	d		23p54	23p45	23p54			00a30	00a37			00 58	01 04	01a11		01a44	01a50		07 35	07 56			08 26
Baldock	d		→		23p57							01 01	01 08						07 38	07 59			08 29
Ashwell & Morden	d				00 02								01 13							08 04			
Royston	d			23p54	00 07							01 09	01 17						07 46	08 09			08 37
Meldreth	d				00 11								01 21							08 13			
Shepreth	d				00 14								01 24							08 16			
Foxton	d				00 16								01 27							08 18			
Cambridge	a			00 09	00 29							01 25	01 40						08 04	08 34			08 54
Arlesey	d	23p29				23p59				00s43											08 06		
Biggleswade	d	23p34				00 04				00s48											08 11		
Sandy	d	23p38				00 08				00s51											08 15		
St Neots	d	23p45				00 15				00s59											08 22		
Huntingdon	d	23p53				00 23				01s06											08 30		
Peterborough 8	a	00 13				00 43				01 25											08 51		

Table 25

Sundays
from 30 October

London - Stevenage, Cambridge and Peterborough

		FC	FC	FC	FC	GR		FC	FC	FC	FC	FC	FC	FC	FC	FC		FC	GR	FC	FC	FC	FC	FC	FC
		1	1		1	R 1 🛒		1	1	1		1	1	1	1			1	R 1 🛒	1	1	1		1	1
London Kings Cross 15 ⊖	d	08 06	08 23	08 26	08 53	09 03		09 06	09 15	09 23	09 26	09 53	10 06	10 15	10 23	10 26		10 53	11 03	11 06	11 15	11 23	11 26	11 53	12 06
Finsbury Park ⊖	d	08 11	08 28	08 32	08 58			09 11		09 28	09 32	09 58	10 11		10 28	10 32		10 58		11 11		11 28	11 32	11 58	12 11
Potters Bar	d	08 21						09 21					10 21							11 21					12 21
Hatfield	d	08 27						09 27					10 27							11 27					12 27
Welwyn Garden City 4	d	08 31						09 31					10 31							11 31					12 31
Welwyn North	d	08 34						09 34					10 34							11 34					12 34
Knebworth	d	08 38						09 38					10 38							11 38					12 38
Hertford North	d			09 07							10 07					11 07							12 07		
Stevenage 4	d	08 42	08 47	09a20	09 17	09 22		09 42		09 47	10a20	10 17	10 42		10 47	11a20		11 17	11 22	11 42		11 47	12a20	12 17	12 42
Hitchin 4	d	08 47	08 52		09 22			09 47		09 52		10 22	10 47		10 52			11 22		11 47		11 52		12 22	12 47
Letchworth Garden City	d	08 51			09 26			09 51				10 26	10 51					11 26		11 51				12 26	12 51
Baldock	d	08 54			09 29			09 55				10 29	10 55					11 29		11 55				12 29	12 55
Ashwell & Morden	d	08 59						10 00					11 00							12 00					13 00
Royston	d	09 04			09 37			10 04				10 37	11 04					11 37		12 04				12 37	13 04
Meldreth	d	09 08						10 08					11 08							12 08					13 08
Shepreth	d	09 11						10 11					11 11							12 11					13 11
Foxton	d	09 13						10 14					11 14							12 14					13 14
Cambridge	a	09 28			09 55			10 27	10 00			10 54	11 27	11 00				11 54		12 27	12 00			12 54	13 27
Arlesey	d		08 57							09 57					10 57							11 57			
Biggleswade	d		09 02							10 02					11 02							12 02			
Sandy	d		09 06							10 06					11 06							12 06			
St Neots	d		09 13							10 13					11 13							12 13			
Huntingdon	d		09 21							10 21					11 21							12 21			
Peterborough 8	a		09 40			09 51				10 38					11 38				11 51			12 39			

		FC		FC	FC	FC	GR	FC	FC	FC	FC	FC		FC	FC	FC	FC	FC	GR	FC	FC	FC		FC	FC
		1		1		1	R 1 🛒	1	1	1		1		1	1	1		1	R 1 🛒	1	1	1			1
London Kings Cross 15 ⊖	d	12 15		12 23	12 26	12 53	13 03	13 06	13 15	13 23	13 26	13 53		14 06	14 15	14 23	14 26	14 53	15 03	15 06	15 15	15 23		15 26	15 53
Finsbury Park ⊖	d			12 28	12 32	12 58		13 11		13 28	13 32	13 58		14 11		14 28	14 32	14 58		15 11		15 28		15 32	15 58
Potters Bar	d							13 21						14 21						15 21					
Hatfield	d							13 27						14 27						15 27					
Welwyn Garden City 4	d							13 31						14 31						15 31					
Welwyn North	d							13 34						14 34						15 34					
Knebworth	d							13 38						14 38						15 38					
Hertford North	d				13 07						14 07						15 07							16 07	
Stevenage 4	d			12 47	13a20	13 17	13 22	13 42		13 47	14a20	14 17		14 42		14 47	15a20	15 17	15 22	15 42		15 47		16a20	16 17
Hitchin 4	d			12 52		13 22		13 47		13 52		14 22		14 47		14 52		15 22		15 47		15 52			16 22
Letchworth Garden City	d					13 26		13 51				14 26		14 51				15 26		15 51					16 26
Baldock	d					13 29		13 55				14 29		14 55				15 29		15 55					16 29
Ashwell & Morden	d							14 00						15 00						16 00					
Royston	d					13 37		14 04				14 37		15 04				15 37		16 04					16 37
Meldreth	d							14 08						15 08						16 08					
Shepreth	d							14 11						15 11						16 11					
Foxton	d							14 14						15 14						16 14					
Cambridge	a	13 00				13 54		14 27	14 00			14 54		15 27	15 00			15 54		16 27	16 00				16 54
Arlesey	d			12 57						13 57						14 57						15 57			
Biggleswade	d			13 02						14 02						15 02						16 02			
Sandy	d			13 06						14 06						15 06						16 06			
St Neots	d			13 13						14 13						15 13						16 13			
Huntingdon	d			13 21						14 21						15 21						16 21			
Peterborough 8	a			13 38			13 51			14 38						15 38			15 51			16 38			

		FC	FC	FC	FC	GR	FC	FC		FC	FC	FC	FC	GR	FC	FC	FC	FC		FC	FC	GR	FC	FC	GR
		1	1	1		R 1 🛒	1	1		1	1	1		R 1 🛒	1	1	1	1		1		R 1 🛒	1	1	R 1 🛒
London Kings Cross 15 ⊖	d	16 06	16 15	16 23	16 26	16 35	16 36	16 53		17 06	17 15	17 23	17 26	17 35	17 36	17 53	18 06	18 15		18 22	18 26	18 35	18 53	19 06	19 08
Finsbury Park ⊖	d	16 11		16 28	16 32		16 41	16 58		17 11		17 28	17 32		17 41	17 58	18 11			18 27	18 32		18 58	19 11	
Potters Bar	d	16 21					16 51			17 21					17 51		18 21							19 21	
Hatfield	d	16 27					16 57			17 27					17 57		18 27							19 27	
Welwyn Garden City 4	d	16 31					17 01			17 31					18 01		18 31							19 31	
Welwyn North	d	16 34					17 04			17 34					18 04		18 34							19 34	
Knebworth	d	16 38					17 08			17 38					18 08		18 38							19 38	
Hertford North	d				17 07								18 07								19 07				
Stevenage 4	d	16 42		16 47	17a20	16a54	17 12	17 17		17 42		17 47	18a20	17a54	18 12	18 17	18 42			18 47	19a20	18a54	19 17	19 42	19 28
Hitchin 4	d	16 47		16 52			17 17	17 22		17 47		17 52			18 17	18 22	18 47			18 52			19 22	→	
Letchworth Garden City	d	16 51						17 26		17 51						18 26	18 52						19 26		
Baldock	d	16 55						17 29		17 55						18 29	18 55						19 29		
Ashwell & Morden	d	17 00								18 00							19 00								
Royston	d	17 04						17 37		18 04						18 37	19 05						19 37		
Meldreth	d	17 08								18 08							19 09								
Shepreth	d	17 11								18 11							19 12								
Foxton	d	17 14								18 14							19 14								
Cambridge	a	17 27	17 00					17 54		18 27	18 00					18 54	19 27	19 01					19 54		
Arlesey	d			16 57			17 23					17 57			18 23					18 58					
Biggleswade	d			17 02			17 28					18 02			18 28					19 03					
Sandy	d			17 06			17 32					18 06			18 32					19 06					
St Neots	d			17 13			17 39					18 13			18 39					19 14					
Huntingdon	d			17 21			17 47					18 21			18 47					19 21					
Peterborough 8	a			17 39			18 06					18 38			19 05					19 39					19 59

Table 25

Sundays

from 30 October

London - Stevenage, Cambridge and Peterborough

		FC	FC	FC	FC	GR	FC	FC	FC	FC	FC	GR	FC	FC	FC	FC	FC	GR	FC	FC	FC
						R						R						R			
		[1]	[1]	[1]		[1]	[1]	[1]	[1]	[1]		[1]	[1]	[1]	[1]	[1]		[1]	[1]	[1]	[1]
						(trolley)						(trolley)						(trolley)			
London Kings Cross [15] ⊖	d	19 15		19 22	19 26	19 35	19 53	20 06	20 15	20 23	20 26	20 35	20 53	21 06	21 15	21 23	21 26	21 35	21 53	22 06	22 15
Finsbury Park ⊖	d			19 27	19 32		19 58	20 11		20 28	20 32		20 58	21 11		21 28	21 32		21 58	22 11	
Potters Bar	d							20 21						21 21						22 21	
Hatfield	d							20 27						21 27						22 27	
Welwyn Garden City [4]	d							20 31						21 31						22 31	
Welwyn North	d							20 34						21 34						22 34	
Knebworth	d							20 38						21 38						22 38	
Hertford North	d		←		20 07						21 07						22 07				
Stevenage [4]	d		19 42	19 47	20a20	19 54	20 17	20 42		20 47	21a20	20 54	21 16	21 42		21 47	22a20	21 55	22 17	22 42	
Hitchin [4]	d		19 47	19 52			20 22	20 47		20 52			21 21	21 47		21 52			22 22	22 47	
Letchworth Garden City	d		19 51				20 26	20 51					21 25	21 51					22 26	22 51	
Baldock	d		19 55				20 29	20 55					21 29	21 55					22 29	22 55	
Ashwell & Morden	d		20 00					21 00						22 00						23 00	
Royston	d		20 04				20 37	21 04					21 37	22 04					22 37	23 04	
Meldreth	d		20 08					21 08						22 08						23 08	
Shepreth	d		20 11					21 11						22 11						23 11	
Foxton	d		20 14					21 14						22 14						23 14	
Cambridge	a	20 00	20 27				20 54	21 27	21 00				21 54	22 27	22 00				22 54	23 27	23 00
Arlesey	d			19 57						20 57						21 57					
Biggleswade	d			20 02						21 02						22 02					
Sandy	d			20 06						21 06						22 06					
St Neots	d			20 13						21 13						22 13					
Huntingdon	d			20 21						21 21						22 21					
Peterborough [8]	a			20 38		20 23				21 37		21 23				22 37		22 24			

		FC	FC	FC	FC	FC	FC	FC	FC	FC
		[1]		[1]	[1]	[1]	[1]	[1]		
London Kings Cross [15] ⊖	d	22 23	22 26	22 53	23 06	23 15		23 23	23 26	23 41
Finsbury Park ⊖	d	22 28	22 32	22 58	23 11			23 28	23 32	23 47
Potters Bar	d				23 21					00 08
Hatfield	d				23 27					00 16
Welwyn Garden City [4]	d				23 31					00 20
Welwyn North	d				23 34					00 23
Knebworth	d				23 38					00 28
Hertford North	d		23 07						00 07	
Stevenage [4]	d	22 47	23a20	23 17	23 42			23 47	00a20	00 31
Hitchin [4]	d	22 52		23 22	23 47		←	23 52		00 37
Letchworth Garden City	d			23 26	23 51	23 44	23 51			00a52
Baldock	d			23 29	→		23 54			
Ashwell & Morden	d						23 59			
Royston	d			23 37		23 54	00 04			
Meldreth	d						00 08			
Shepreth	d						00 11			
Foxton	d						00 14			
Cambridge	a			23 55		00 10	00 29			
Arlesey	d	22 57						23 57		
Biggleswade	d	23 02						00 02		
Sandy	d	23 06						00 06		
St Neots	d	23 13						00 13		
Huntingdon	d	23 21						00 21		
Peterborough [8]	a	23 41						00 43		

Peterborough, Cambridge and Stevenage - London

Miles	Miles			FC MX [1]	FC MX	FC MO	FC MO [1]	GR MO [R] [1]	FC MO [1]	FC MO [1]	FC MX [1]	GR MX [R] [1]	FC [1]	FC	FC [1]	FC [1]	FC [1]	FC [1]	FC [1]	FC [1]	FC [1]	FC [1]	FC [1]
0	—	**Peterborough [8]**	d	22p30			22p57	23p00				23p39	03 25		04 12		05 12		05 40			05 50	
17½	—	Huntingdon	d	22p44			23p11						03 39		04 26		05 27		05 55			06 05	
24¾	—	St Neots	d	22p51			23p18						03 46		04 34		05 34		06 02			06 13	
32¼	—	Sandy	d	22p59			23p26								04 41		05 42					06 21	
35¼	—	Biggleswade	d	23p02			23p29						03 56		04 45		05 46					06 25	
39¼	—	Arlesey	d	23p07			23p34								04 50		05 51					06 30	
—	0	**Cambridge**	d							23p14	23p15									05 35	05 45		06 15
—	7	Foxton	d								23p25									05 44			
—	8	Shepreth	d								23p27									05 46			
—	10	Meldreth	d								23p30									05 49			
—	13	Royston	d							23p29	23p35					05 16		05 46		06 05	05 59		06 29
—	17	Ashwell & Morden	d								23p39					05 21		05 51		06 10			
—	21¼	Baldock	d							23p37	23p44					05 26		05 56		06 15			
—	23¼	Letchworth Garden City	d		23p18					23p40	23p47			04 50		05 30		05 59		06 19	06 09		06 39
44½	26	Hitchin [4]	d	23p16	23p22		23p40		←	23p44	23p54		04 08	04 54	04 58	05 34	05 59	06 04	06 18	06 23		06 36	06 43
48¾	30¼	**Stevenage [4]**	d	23p22	23p27	23p29	23p45	23b34	23p45	23p49	23p59	00s20	04 13	04 59	05 04	05 40	06 04	06 09	06 24	06 29		06 42	06 48
—	—	Hertford North	a		23p40	23p42	→						04 23	05 12									
51¼	33	Knebworth	d	23p25						23p52	00 02				05 07	05 44		06 13		06 33		06 46	
54¼	36	Welwyn North	d	23p29						23p56	00 06				05 11	05 48		06 17		06 37		06 50	
56	37¾	Welwyn Garden City [4]	d	23p32						23p59	00 09				05 15	05 51		06 20		06 40		06 54	
58½	40¼	Hatfield	d	23p35						00 02	00 12				05 19	05 55		06 24		06 44			
63½	45¼	Potters Bar	d	23p41						00 08	00 18				05 25	06 01		06 30		06 49			
73¾	55½	Finsbury Park ⊖	d	23b51	00 15	00 17			00 11	00 21	00 29		04s45	05 47	05 41	06 10	06 24	06 39	06 42	06 58		07 11	07 06
76¼	58	**London Kings Cross [15]** ⊖	a	00 01	00 26	00 26		00 02	00 20	00 33	00 42	00 59	04 59	05 58	05 50	06 19	06 30	06 48	06 50	07 07	06 38	07 19	07 15

		FC	FC [1]	FC [1]	FC [1]	FC [1]	FC [1]	FC [1]	FC	FC [1]	FC [1]	FC [1]	FC [1]	FC [1]	FC [1]	FC [1]	FC [1]	FC [1]	FC [1]	FC [1]	FC [1]	FC [1]
Peterborough [8]	d		06 19					06 32		06 53					07 04	07 14		07 25				07 33
Huntingdon	d		06 34		06 40			06 47		07 09					07 24	07 32		07 40				07 51
St Neots	d		06 42		06 48			06 55		07 17					07 33	07 40		07 47				07 59
Sandy	d				06 55			07 03							07 41							08 06
Biggleswade	d				06 59			07 07							07 45			07 55				08 10
Arlesey	d				07 04			07 12							07 50							08 15
Cambridge	d					06 27	06 45					06 57	07 15							07 26	07 45	
Foxton	d					06 37						07 07								07 36		
Shepreth	d					06 40						07 10								07 39		
Meldreth	d					06 43						07 13								07 43		
Royston	d			06 43		06 50	06 59				07 13	07 21	07 29	07 34					07 43	07 51	07 59	
Ashwell & Morden	d			06 48		06 55					07 18			07 38					07 48			
Baldock	d			06 53		07 00					07 23			07 43					07 53			
Letchworth Garden City	d	06 47		06 57		07 04	07 09		07 20		07 27	07 32		07 47					07 57	08 02		
Hitchin [4]	d	06 51		07 01		07 08		07 18	07 24		07 31	07 36		07 51	07 56		←		08 01	08 06		08 21
Stevenage [4]	d	06 57	07 01	07 07		07 14		07 23	07 30	07 36	07 37	07 42			08 01	07 59	08 01		08 07	08 12		08 27
Hertford North	a														→							
Knebworth	d			07 11		07 18						07 46							08 11	08 16		
Welwyn North	d					07 24						07 50		07 59						08 20		
Welwyn Garden City [4]	d	07 08				07 27			07 42			07 54								08 24		
Hatfield	d	07 12				07 31			07 46													
Potters Bar	d	07 18							07 52													
Finsbury Park ⊖	d	07 35		07 27		07 46		07 41	08 10		07 57	08 09					08 19			08 36		08 47
London Kings Cross [15] ⊖	a	07 43	07 26	07 36	07 40	07 57	07 42	07 49	08 17	08 00	08 04	08 18	08 06	08 20		08 23	08 28	08 30	08 36	08 47	08 39	08 55

		FC [1]	FC [1]	FC [1]	FC	FC [1]	FC [1]	GR [R] [1]	GR [R] [1]	FC [1]	FC [1]	FC [1]	FC [1]	FC [1]	FC [1]	FC [1]	FC [1]	GR [R] [1]	FC [1]	FC [1]
Peterborough [8]	d	07 46					08 16	08 26					08 46			09 16				
Huntingdon	d	08 06					08 30						09 00			09 30				
St Neots	d	08 14					08 38						09 08			09 38				
Sandy	d						08 45						09 15							
Biggleswade	d						08 49						09 19			09 47				
Arlesey	d						08 54						09 24							
Cambridge	d		07 55	08 16							08 25	08 45		08 55	09 21		09 26		09 51	
Foxton	d		08 05								08 35			09 05						
Shepreth	d		08 07								08 37			09 07						
Meldreth	d		08 10								08 40			09 10						
Royston	d		08 15	08 29		08 34					08 45	09 01		09 15	09 35		09 44		10 05	
Ashwell & Morden	d		08 19			08 38					08 50			09 20						
Baldock	d		08 24			08 43					08 55			09 25			09 52			
Letchworth Garden City	d		08 28	08 39		08 47					08 59	09 11		09 29	09 44		09 55		10 14	09 59
Hitchin [4]	d		08 32		08 39	08 51	08 59			←	09 03		09 29	09 33			09 59			10 03
Stevenage [4]	d	08 33			08 45	08 56	09 05	08 58	09 03	09 05	09 09		09 35	09 39		09 58	10 05	10 09		10 09
Hertford North	a						→													
Knebworth	d				08 49						09 13			09 43						10 13
Welwyn North	d				08 53						09 17			09 47						10 17
Welwyn Garden City [4]	d				08 58						09 21			09 51						10 21
Hatfield	d				09 02						09 24			09 55						10 23
Potters Bar	d										09 31			10 01						10 29
Finsbury Park ⊖	d				09 19	09 14				09 26	09 40		09 56	10 11			10 24			10 40
London Kings Cross [15] ⊖	a	08 58	09 02	09 10	09 26	09 20		09 28	09 30	09 34	09 49	09 43	10 04	10 18	10 15	10 22	10 32	10 38	10 47	10 50

b Previous night, stops to set down only

Table 25

Mondays to Fridays

Peterborough, Cambridge and Stevenage - London

		FC	FC	FC	FC	GR	FC	FC	FC			FC	FC	FC	FC		GR	GR	FC	FC		FC	FC	FC	FC
						R											R	R							
		1	1	1	1	1	1	1	1			1	1	1	1		1	1	1	1		1	1	1	1
						☕											🍴	☕							
Peterborough 8	d	09 26	09 46						10 16			10 46			11 16		11 26						11 46		
Huntingdon	d	09 41	10 00						10 33			11 00			11 33								12 00		
St Neots	d	09 49	10 08						10 41			11 08			11 41								12 08		
Sandy	d	09 57	10 15						10 48			11 15			11 48								12 15		
Biggleswade	d	10 01	10 19						10 52			11 19			11 52								12 19		
Arlesey	d	10 06	10 24						10 57			11 24			11 57								12 24		
Cambridge	d			09 55	10 15		10 26	10 50					10 55	11 15					11 26	11 45				11 55	12 15
Foxton	d			10 05									11 05											12 05	
Shepreth	d			10 07									11 07											12 07	
Meldreth	d			10 10									11 10											12 10	
Royston	d			10 15			10 44	11 05					11 15						11 44					12 15	
Ashwell & Morden	d			10 20									11 20											12 20	
Baldock	d			10 25			10 52						11 25						11 52					12 25	
Letchworth Garden City	d			10 29			10 55	11 14					11 29						11 55					12 29	
Hitchin 4	d	10 12	10 29	10 33			10 59		11 03			11 29	11 33		12 03				11 59			←	12 29	12 33	
Stevenage 4	d	10 18	10 35	10 39		11 00	11 05		11 09			11 35	11 39		12 09		11 55	12 00	12 05			12 09	12 35	12 39	
Hertford North	a														→										
Knebworth	d			10 43					11 13				11 43									12 13		12 43	
Welwyn North	d			10 47					11 17				11 47									12 17		12 47	
Welwyn Garden City 4	d			10 51					11 21				11 51									12 21		12 51	
Hatfield	d			10 55					11 25				11 55									12 25		12 55	
Potters Bar	d			11 01					11 31				12 01									12 31		13 01	
Finsbury Park ⊖	d		10 54	11 10			11 24		11 40			11 54	12 10						12 24			12 40	12 54	13 10	
London Kings Cross 15 ⊖	a	10 47	11 02	11 19	11 05	11 29	11 31	11 44	11 49			12 02	12 19	12 04			12 25	12 29	12 32	12 35		12 49	13 03	13 19	13 04

		FC		GR	GR	FC		FC	FC	FC	FC	FC	FC		GR	GR		FC	FC	FC	FC	FC	FC	FC	
				R	R										R	R									
		1		1	1	1		1	1	1	1	1	1		1	1		1	1	1	1	1	1	1	
				🍴	☕										🍴	☕									
Peterborough 8	d	12 16		12 26						12 46			13 16		13 27						13 46			14 16	
Huntingdon	d	12 33								13 00			13 33								14 00			14 33	
St Neots	d	12 41								13 08			13 41								14 08			14 41	
Sandy	d	12 48								13 15			13 48								14 15			14 48	
Biggleswade	d	12 52								13 19			13 52								14 19			14 52	
Arlesey	d	12 57								13 24			13 57								14 24			14 57	
Cambridge	d					12 26		12 45			12 55	13 15						13 26	13 45			13 55	14 15		
Foxton	d										13 05											14 05			
Shepreth	d										13 07											14 07			
Meldreth	d										13 10											14 10			
Royston	d					12 44					13 15							13 44				14 15			
Ashwell & Morden	d										13 20											14 20			
Baldock	d					12 52					13 25							13 52				14 25			
Letchworth Garden City	d					12 55					13 29							13 55				14 29			
Hitchin 4	d	13 03				12 59			←	13 29	13 33		14 03					13 59		←	14 29	14 34		15 03	
Stevenage 4	d	13 09		12 56	13 00	13 05			13 09	13 35	13 39		14 09		13 57	14 02		14 05		14 09	14 35	14 39		15 09	
Hertford North	a	→											→											→	
Knebworth	d								13 13		13 43									14 13		14 43			
Welwyn North	d								13 17		13 47									14 17		14 47			
Welwyn Garden City 4	d								13 21		13 51									14 21		14 51			
Hatfield	d								13 25		13 55									14 25		14 55			
Potters Bar	d								13 31		14 01									14 31		15 01			
Finsbury Park ⊖	d					13 24			13 40	13 54	14 10							14 24		14 40	14 54	15 10			
London Kings Cross 15 ⊖	a			13 25	13 29	13 32		13 34	13 49	14 02	14 19	14 05			14 26	14 29		14 32	14 34	14 49	15 03	15 19	15 05		

		GR		GR	FC	FC	FC	FC	FC	FC	FC			GR	GR	FC	FC	FC	FC	FC	FC	FC			GR
		R		R										R	R										R
		1		1	1	1	1	1	1	1	1			1	1	1	1	1	1	1	1	1			1
		🍴		☕										🍴	☕										🍴
Peterborough 8	d	14 26						14 46			15 16			15 26					15 46			16 16			16 24
Huntingdon	d							15 00			15 33								16 00			16 33			
St Neots	d							15 08			15 41								16 08			16 41			
Sandy	d							15 15			15 48								16 15			16 48			
Biggleswade	d							15 19			15 52								16 19			16 52			
Arlesey	d							15 24			15 57								16 24			16 57			
Cambridge	d				14 26	14 45			14 55	15 15						15 26	15 45			15 55	16 15				
Foxton	d								15 05											16 05					
Shepreth	d								15 07											16 07					
Meldreth	d								15 10											16 10					
Royston	d				14 44				15 15							15 44				16 15					
Ashwell & Morden	d								15 20											16 20					
Baldock	d				14 52				15 25							15 52				16 25					
Letchworth Garden City	d				14 55				15 29							15 55				16 29					
Hitchin 4	d				14 59		←	15 29	15 33		16 03					15 59		←	16 29	16 33		17 04			
Stevenage 4	d	14 56		15 00	15 05		15 09	15 35	15 39		16 09			15 55	16 00	16 05		16 09	16 35	16 39		17 10			16 54
Hertford North	a										→											→			
Knebworth	d						15 13		15 43									16 13		16 43					
Welwyn North	d						15 17		15 47									16 17		16 47					
Welwyn Garden City 4	d						15 21		15 51									16 21		16 51					
Hatfield	d						15 25		15 55									16 25		16 55					
Potters Bar	d						15 31		16 01									16 31		17 01					
Finsbury Park ⊖	d				15 24		15 40	15 54	16 10							16 24		16 40	16 54	17 10					
London Kings Cross 15 ⊖	a	15 27		15 29	15 32	15 34	15 49	16 03	16 19	16 05				16 26	16 29	16 31	16 34	16 49	17 03	17 18	17 08				17 25

Table 25

Mondays to Fridays

Peterborough, Cambridge and Stevenage - London

		GR	FC	FC	FC	FC	FC	FC			FC	GR	GR	FC	FC	FC	FC	FC		FC	FC		FC	GR	FC
		R										R	R											R	
		1	1	1	1	1	1	1			1	1	1	1	1	1	1	1		1	1		1	1	1
		🍴										🍴	🍴											🍴	
Peterborough 8	d					16 46					17 21	17 27									17 54		18 21	18 26	
Huntingdon	d					17 00					17 41						18 04				18 14		18 41		
St Neots	d					17 08					17 48						18 11				18 21		18 48		
Sandy	d					17 15					17 56										18 29		18 56		
Biggleswade	d					17 19					18 00										18 32		19 00		
Arlesey	d					17 24					18 05										18 37		19 05		
Cambridge	d		16 24	16 45			16 55	17 15						17 24	17 45			17 55		18 15					18 26
Foxton	d		16 33				17 05							17 33				18 05							18 35
Shepreth	d		16 35				17 07							17 35				18 07							18 37
Meldreth	d		16 38				17 10							17 38				18 10							18 40
Royston	d		16 43				17 15							17 43				18 15							18 46
Ashwell & Morden	d		16 48				17 20							17 48				18 20							18 51
Baldock	d		16 53				17 25							17 53				18 25							18 56
Letchworth Garden City	d		16 56				17 29							17 56				18 29							18 59
Hitchin 4	d		16 59		←	17 29	17 33				18 11			17 59		←	18 29	18 33			18 44		19 11		19 03
Stevenage 4	d	17 00	17 06		17 10	17 35	17 39				18 17	17 57	18 02	18 06		18 17	18 35	18 39			18 49		19 17	18 56	19 09
Hertford North	a										↳												↳		
Knebworth	d				17 13		17 43									18 20		18 43							
Welwyn North	d				17 17		17 47									18 24		18 47							
Welwyn Garden City 4	d				17 21		17 51									18 29		18 51							
Hatfield	d				17 25		17 55									18 32		18 55							
Potters Bar	d				17 31		18 01									18 39		19 01							
Finsbury Park ⊖	d		17 24		17 40	17 54	18 10							18 24		18 47	18 54	19 10			19 08				19 29
London Kings Cross 15 ⊖	a	17 29	17 32	17 35	17 49	18 02	18 21	18 05				18 28	18 30	18 32	18 35	18 56	19 02	19 22		19 08	19 14			19 27	19 35

		GR	FC	FC		FC	FC	FC	FC		GR	GR	FC	FC		FC	FC	GR	GR	FC	FC	GR	FC	FC	
		R									R	R						R	R			R			
		1	1	1		1	1	1	1		1	1	1	1		1	1	1	1	1	1	1	1	1	
		🍴									🍴	🍴						🍴	🍴			🍴			
Peterborough 8	d					18 45			19 16		19 27						19 46	19 49							
Huntingdon	d					19 00			19 33								20 00								
St Neots	d					19 08			19 41								20 08								
Sandy	d					19 15			19 48								20 15								
Biggleswade	d					19 19			19 52								20 19								
Arlesey	d					19 24			19 57								20 24								
Cambridge	d		18 45				18 55	19 15					19 24	19 45							19 55		20 28	20 45	
Foxton	d						19 05						19 33								20 05				
Shepreth	d						19 07						19 35								20 07				
Meldreth	d						19 10						19 38								20 10				
Royston	d						19 15						19 43								20 15		20 44		
Ashwell & Morden	d						19 20						19 48								20 20				
Baldock	d						19 25						19 53								20 25		20 52		
Letchworth Garden City	d						19 29						19 56								20 29		20 55		
Hitchin 4	d			←		19 29	19 33		20 04				20 00			←	20 29			←	20 33		20 59		
Stevenage 4	d	19 08		19 17		19 35	19 39		20 10		19 57	20 01	20 05			20 10	20 35	20 20	20 26	20 35	20 39	21 00	21 05		
Hertford North	a								↳								↳								
Knebworth	d			19 20			19 43									20 14					20 43				
Welwyn North	d			19 24			19 47									20 18					20 47				
Welwyn Garden City 4	d			19 28			19 51									20 21					20 51				
Hatfield	d			19 32			19 55									20 25					20 55				
Potters Bar	d			19 38			20 01									20 31					21 01				
Finsbury Park ⊖	d			19 47		19 54	20 10						20 24			20 40				20 54	21 10		21 24		
London Kings Cross 15 ⊖	a	19 36	19 38	19 56		20 00	20 19	20 11			20 28	20 30	20 32	20 40		20 51		20 49	20 55	21 03	21 19	21 29	21 32	21 34	

		FC		GR	FC	FC	FC	GR		FC		FC	FC	FC	FC	GR	FC	FC	GR	FC		FC	FC	GR	
				R				R								R			R					R	
		1		1		1	1	1		1		1	1		1	1	1	1	1	1			1	1	
				🍴				🍴								🍴			🍴					🍴	
Peterborough 8	d	20 16		20 45			20 57	21 16					21 30			22 16		22 30	22 36					23 39	
Huntingdon	d	20 33					21 12						21 44					22 44							
St Neots	d	20 41					21 19						21 51					22 51							
Sandy	d	20 48					21 27						21 59					22 59							
Biggleswade	d	20 52					21 30						22 02					23 02							
Arlesey	d	20 57					21 35						22 07					23 07							
Cambridge	d					20 55				21 28		21 45			21 55		22 28						23 15		
Foxton	d					21 05									22 05								23 25		
Shepreth	d					21 07									22 07								23 27		
Meldreth	d					21 10									22 10								23 30		
Royston	d					21 15				21 44					22 15		22 43						23 35		
Ashwell & Morden	d					21 20									22 20								23 39		
Baldock	d					21 25				21 52					22 25		22 51						23 44		
Letchworth Garden City	d				21 20	21 29				21 55				22 20	22 29		22 54					23 18	23 47		
Hitchin 4	d	21 04			21 24	21 33	21 41			21 59			22 13	22 24	22 33		22 58	23 16		←		23 22	23 54		
Stevenage 4	d	21 10		21 16	21 29	21 39	21 47	21 50		22 05			22 18	22 29	22 39	22 47	23 04	23 22	23 07	23 22		23 27	23 59	00s20	
Hertford North	a				21 42									22 42				↳				23 40			
Knebworth	d	21 14				21 43							22 22		22 43					23 25			00 02		
Welwyn North	d	21 18				21 47							22 25		22 47					23 29			00 06		
Welwyn Garden City 4	d	21 21				21 51							22 28		22 51					23 32			00 09		
Hatfield	d	21 25				21 55							22 32		22 55					23 35			00 12		
Potters Bar	d	21 32				22 01							22 37		23 01					23 41			00 18		
Finsbury Park ⊖	d	21 41			22 17	22 10	22 05			22 24			22 46	23 17	23 10		23 22			23s51		00 15	00 29		
London Kings Cross 15 ⊖	a	21 50		21 44	22 25	22 19	22 14	22 20		22 32		22 34	22 57	23 25	23 20	23 14	23 31		23 36	00 01		00 26	00 42	00 59	

Table 25

Saturdays
until 18 June

Peterborough, Cambridge and Stevenage - London

		FC	FC	FC	GR	FC	FC	FC	FC	FC		FC	FC	FC	FC	FC	FC	FC	FC	GR		FC	FC	FC	FC
					■															■					
		1		1	1	1		1		1		1	1		1	1	1	1	1	1		1		1	1
					🍴															🍴					
Peterborough 8	d	22p30			23p39	03 25		04 12					05 16		05 46				06 16	06 38				06 46	
Huntingdon	d	22p44				03 39		04 26					05 33		06 00				06 33					07 00	
St Neots	d	22p51				03 47		04 34					05 41		06 08				06 41					07 08	
Sandy	d	22p59						04 41					05 48		06 15				06 48					07 15	
Biggleswade	d	23p02				03 57		04 45					05 52		06 19				06 52					07 19	
Arlesey	d	23p07						04 50					05 57		06 24				06 57					07 24	
Cambridge	d			23p15								05 45				05 55	06 28	06 45							06 55
Foxton	d			23p25												06 05									07 05
Shepreth	d			23p27												06 07									07 07
Meldreth	d			23p30												06 10									07 10
Royston	d			23p35						05 15		06 00				06 15	06 43								07 15
Ashwell & Morden	d			23p39						05 20						06 20									07 20
Baldock	d			23p44						05 25						06 25	06 51								07 25
Letchworth Garden City	d		23p18	23p47			04 50		05 20	05 29		06 09		06 20		06 29	06 54								07 29
Hitchin 4	d	23p16	23p22	23p54		04 08	04 54	04 59	05 24	05 33			06 03	06 24	06 29	06 33	06 59		07 03			←		07 29	07 33
Stevenage 4	d	23p22	23p27	23p59	00s20	04 14	04 59	05 05	05 29	05 39			06 09	06 29	06 35	06 39	07 04		07 09	07 06		07 09	07 29	07 35	07 39
Hertford North	a		23p40			04 24	05 12		05 42					06 42					→				07 42		
Knebworth	d	23p25		00 02				05 08		05 43			06 13			06 43						07 13			07 43
Welwyn North	d	23p29		00 06				05 12		05 47			06 17			06 47						07 17			07 47
Welwyn Garden City 4	d	23p32		00 09				05 15		05 51			06 21			06 51						07 21			07 51
Hatfield	d	23p35		00 12				05 19		05 55			06 25			06 55						07 25			07 55
Potters Bar	d	23p41		00 18				05 25		06 01			06 31			07 01						07 31			08 01
Finsbury Park ⊖	d	23b51	00 15	00 29		04s49	05 47	05 42	06 17	06 10			06 40	07 17	06 54	07 10	07 22					07 40	08 17	07 54	08 10
London Kings Cross 15 ⊖	a	00 01	00 26	00 42	00 59	05 02	05 55	05 56	06 25	06 20		06 39	06 47	07 25	07 01	07 19	07 30	07 36		07 37		07 47	08 25	08 01	08 19

			FC	FC	FC	GR		FC	FC	FC	FC	FC	FC	FC		GR		FC	FC	FC	FC	FC	FC	FC	FC
						■										■									
			1	1	1	1		1		1	1	1	1	1		1		1	1	1		1	1	1	1
						🍴										🍴									
Peterborough 8	d				07 16	07 37				07 46			08 08	08 16		08 31						08 46			09 07
Huntingdon	d				07 33					08 00			08 23	08 33								09 00			09 22
St Neots	d				07 41					08 08			08 31	08 41								09 08			09 30
Sandy	d				07 48					08 15				08 48								09 15			
Biggleswade	d				07 52					08 19			08 42	08 52								09 19			09 39
Arlesey	d				07 57					08 24				08 57								09 24			
Cambridge	d		07 28	07 45							07 55	08 15						08 26	08 45				08 55	09 15	
Foxton	d										08 05												09 05		
Shepreth	d										08 07												09 07		
Meldreth	d										08 10												09 10		
Royston	d		07 43								08 15							08 44					09 15		
Ashwell & Morden	d										08 20												09 20		
Baldock	d		07 51								08 25							08 52					09 25		
Letchworth Garden City	d		07 54								08 29							08 55					09 29		
Hitchin 4	d		07 59		08 03			←		08 29	08 33			09 03				08 59		←		09 29	09 34		
Stevenage 4	d		08 04		08 09	08 06		08 09	08 29	08 35	08 39			09 09		09 00		09 05		09 09	09 29	09 35	09 40		
Hertford North	a				→				08 42					→							09 42				
Knebworth	d							08 13			08 43									09 13			09 43		
Welwyn North	d							08 17			08 47									09 17			09 47		
Welwyn Garden City 4	d							08 21			08 51									09 21			09 51		
Hatfield	d							08 25			08 55									09 25			09 55		
Potters Bar	d							08 31			09 01									09 31			10 01		
Finsbury Park ⊖	d		08 22					08 40	09 17	08 54	09 10							09 24		09 40	10 17	09 54	10 10		
London Kings Cross 15 ⊖	a		08 30	08 36		08 36		08 49	09 25	09 01	09 20	09 04	09 12			09 30		09 31	09 38	09 49	10 25	10 01	10 20	10 04	10 10

		FC		FC	FC		FC	FC	FC	FC	FC			FC	GR	GR	FC	FC	FC	FC	FC	FC		FC	FC
															■	■									
		1		1	1			1	1	1	1			1	1	1	1	1	1		1	1		1	1
															🍴	🍴									
Peterborough 8	d				09 16			09 46			10 08			10 18	10 23	10 33					10 46				11 08
Huntingdon	d				09 33			10 00			10 24			10 33							11 00				11 22
St Neots	d				09 41			10 08			10 32			10 41							11 08				11 30
Sandy	d				09 48			10 15						10 48							11 15				
Biggleswade	d				09 52			10 19			10 40			10 52							11 19				11 39
Arlesey	d				09 57			10 24						10 57							11 24				
Cambridge	d	09 26		09 45					09 55	10 15							10 26	10 45				10 55		11 15	
Foxton	d								10 05													11 05			
Shepreth	d								10 07													11 07			
Meldreth	d								10 10													11 10			
Royston	d	09 44							10 15								10 44					11 15			
Ashwell & Morden	d								10 20													11 20			
Baldock	d	09 52							10 25								10 52					11 25			
Letchworth Garden City	d	09 55							10 29								10 55					11 29			
Hitchin 4	d	09 59			10 03			10 29	10 33					11 03			10 59		←		11 29	11 33			
Stevenage 4	d	10 05			10 09		10 29	10 35	10 39					11 09	10 55	11 03	11 05		11 09	11 29	11 35	11 39			
Hertford North	a						10 42							→						11 42					
Knebworth	d				10 13				10 43										11 13			11 43			
Welwyn North	d				10 17				10 47										11 17			11 47			
Welwyn Garden City 4	d				10 21				10 51										11 21			11 51			
Hatfield	d				10 25				10 55										11 25			11 55			
Potters Bar	d				10 31				11 01										11 31			12 01			
Finsbury Park ⊖	d	10 24			10 40		11 17	10 54	11 10								11 25		11 40	12 17	11 54	12 10			
London Kings Cross 15 ⊖	a	10 31		10 34	10 49		11 25	11 01	11 20	11 03	11 11				11 26	11 33	11 33	11 34	11 49	12 25	12 01	12 19		12 04	12 11

b Previous night, stops to set down only

Table 25

Peterborough, Cambridge and Stevenage - London

	FC	FC	FC	FC	FC	FC	FC	FC	FC	GR	FC	FC	FC	FC	FC	FC	FC	FC	FC	FC
	1	1	1		1	1	1	1	1	R 1 [catering]	1	1	1		1	1	1	1	1	1
Peterborough 8 d			11 18		11 46			12 06	12 10	12 32					12 46			13 08		
Huntingdon d			11 33		12 00			12 21	12 33						13 00			13 22		
St Neots d			11 41		12 08			12 32	12 41						13 08			13 30		
Sandy d			11 48		12 15				12 48						13 15					
Biggleswade d			11 52		12 19			12 40	12 52						13 19			13 38		
Arlesey d			11 57		12 24				12 57						13 24					
Cambridge d	11 26	11 45				11 55	12 15				12 26	12 45				12 55	13 15		13 26	13 45
Foxton d						12 05										13 05				
Shepreth d						12 07										13 07				
Meldreth d						12 10										13 10				
Royston d	11 44					12 15					12 44					13 15			13 44	
Ashwell & Morden d						12 20										13 20				
Baldock d	11 52					12 25					12 52					13 25			13 52	
Letchworth Garden City d	11 55					12 29					12 55					13 29			13 55	
Hitchin 4 d	11 59		12 03		12 29	12 33			13 03		12 59		←		13 29	13 33			13 59	
Stevenage 4 d	12 05		12 09	12 29	12 35	12 39			13 09	13 01	13 05		13 09	13 29	13 35	13 39			14 05	
Hertford North a				12 42					↪					13 42						
Knebworth d			12 13			12 43							13 13			13 43				
Welwyn North d			12 17			12 47							13 17			13 47				
Welwyn Garden City 4 d			12 21			12 51							13 21			13 51				
Hatfield d			12 25			12 55							13 25			13 55				
Potters Bar d			12 31			13 01							13 31			14 01				
Finsbury Park ⊖ d	12 24		12 40	13 17	12 54	13 10					13 24		13 40	14 17	13 54	14 10			14 24	
London Kings Cross 15 ⊖ a	12 31	12 34	12 49	13 25	13 01	13 19	13 04	13 11		13 30	13 31	13 34	13 49	14 25	14 01	14 19	14 04	14 10	14 31	14 34

	FC	FC	FC	FC	FC	FC	GR	FC	FC	FC	FC	FC	FC	FC	FC	FC	FC	FC
	1		1	1	1	1	R 1 [catering]	1	1	1		1	1	1	1	1	1	
Peterborough 8 d	13 16		13 46			14 16	14 32					14 46					15 10	
Huntingdon d	13 33		14 00			14 33						15 00					15 33	
St Neots d	13 41		14 08			14 41						15 08					15 41	
Sandy d	13 48		14 15			14 48						15 15					15 48	
Biggleswade d	13 52		14 19			14 52						15 19					15 52	
Arlesey d	13 57		14 24			14 57						15 24					15 57	
Cambridge d				13 55	14 15			14 26	14 45				14 55	15 15	15 26	15 45		
Foxton d				14 05									15 05					
Shepreth d				14 07									15 07					
Meldreth d				14 10									15 10					
Royston d				14 15				14 44					15 15		15 44			
Ashwell & Morden d				14 20									15 20					
Baldock d				14 25				14 52					15 25		15 52			
Letchworth Garden City d				14 29				14 55					15 29		15 55			
Hitchin 4 d	14 03		14 29	14 33		15 03		14 59		←		15 29	15 33		15 59		16 03	
Stevenage 4 d	14 09	14 29	14 35	14 39		15 09	15 01	15 05		15 09	15 29	15 35	15 39		16 05		16 09	16 29
Hertford North a		14 42				↪					15 42							16 42
Knebworth d	14 13			14 43						15 13			15 43				16 13	
Welwyn North d	14 17			14 47						15 17			15 47				16 17	
Welwyn Garden City 4 d	14 21			14 51						15 21			15 51				16 21	
Hatfield d	14 25			14 55						15 25			15 55				16 25	
Potters Bar d	14 31			15 01						15 31			16 01				16 31	
Finsbury Park ⊖ d	14 40	15 17	14 54	15 10				15 24		15 40	16 17	15 54	16 10		16 24		16 40	17 17
London Kings Cross 15 ⊖ a	14 49	15 25	15 01	15 19	15 05		15 30	15 31	15 34	15 49	16 25	16 01	16 19	16 04	16 31	16 34	16 49	17 25

	FC	FC	FC	FC	GR	FC	FC	FC	FC	FC	FC	FC	FC	FC	FC	FC	FC	FC	FC	FC
	1	1	1	1	R 1 [catering]	1	1	1		1	1	1	1	1	1		1	1	1	1
Peterborough 8 d	15 46			16 16	16 32					16 46					17 18		17 46			18 16
Huntingdon d	16 00			16 33						17 00					17 33		18 00			18 33
St Neots d	16 08			16 41						17 08					17 41		18 08			18 41
Sandy d	16 15			16 48						17 15					17 48		18 15			18 48
Biggleswade d	16 19			16 52						17 19					17 52		18 19			18 52
Arlesey d	16 24			16 57						17 24					17 57		18 24			18 57
Cambridge d		15 55	16 15			16 26	16 45				16 55	17 15	17 26	17 45				17 55	18 15	
Foxton d		16 05									17 05							18 05		
Shepreth d		16 07									17 07							18 07		
Meldreth d		16 10									17 10							18 10		
Royston d		16 15				16 44					17 15		17 44					18 15		
Ashwell & Morden d		16 20									17 20							18 20		
Baldock d		16 25				16 52					17 25		17 52					18 25		
Letchworth Garden City d		16 29				16 55					17 29		17 55					18 29		
Hitchin 4 d	16 29	16 33		17 03		16 59		←		17 29	17 34		17 59		18 03		18 29	18 33		19 03
Stevenage 4 d	16 35	16 39		17 09	17 02	17 05		17 09	17 29	17 35	17 40		18 05		18 09	18 29	18 35	18 39		19 09
Hertford North a				↪					17 42							18 42				↪
Knebworth d		16 43						17 13			17 43				18 13			18 43		
Welwyn North d		16 47						17 17			17 47				18 17			18 47		
Welwyn Garden City 4 d		16 51						17 21			17 51				18 21			18 51		
Hatfield d		16 55						17 25			17 55				18 25			18 55		
Potters Bar d		17 01						17 31			18 01				18 31			19 01		
Finsbury Park ⊖ d	16 54	17 10				17 24		17 40	18 17	17 54	18 10		18 24		18 40	19 17	18 54	19 10		
London Kings Cross 15 ⊖ a	17 01	17 19	17 05		17 32	17 31	17 34	17 49	18 25	18 01	18 19	18 04	18 31	18 35	18 49	19 25	19 01	19 19	19 05	

Table 25

Saturdays
until 18 June

Peterborough, Cambridge and Stevenage - London

			GR	FC	FC	FC		FC	FC	FC	FC	FC	FC	FC		FC		FC	FC	FC	FC		GR	FC	FC
			R 1	1	1	1			1	1	1	1	1	1				1	1	1	1		R 1	1	1
Peterborough 8	d		18 32						18 46					19 16				19 46			20 16		20 33		
Huntingdon	d								19 00					19 33				20 00			20 33				
St Neots	d								19 08					19 41				20 08			20 41				
Sandy	d								19 15					19 48				20 15			20 48				
Biggleswade	d								19 19					19 52				20 19			20 52				
Arlesey	d								19 24					19 57				20 24			20 57				
Cambridge	d			18 26	18 45					18 55	19 15	19 28	19 45						19 55	20 15				20 28	20 45
Foxton	d									19 05									20 05						
Shepreth	d									19 07									20 07						
Meldreth	d									19 10									20 10						
Royston	d			18 44						19 15		19 44							20 15					20 44	
Ashwell & Morden	d									19 20									20 20						
Baldock	d			18 52						19 25		19 52							20 25					20 52	
Letchworth Garden City	d			18 55						19 29		19 55							20 29					20 55	
Hitchin 4	d			18 59		←			19 29	19 33		19 59		20 03				20 29	20 34		21 03			20 59	
Stevenage 4	d		19 01	19 05		19 09		19 29	19 35	19 39		20 05		20 09		20 29		20 35	20 40		21 09		21 02	21 05	
Hertford North	a							19 42								20 42					↪				
Knebworth	d					19 13				19 43				20 13					20 46						
Welwyn North	d					19 17				19 47				20 17					20 50						
Welwyn Garden City 4	d					19 21				19 51				20 21					20 53						
Hatfield	d					19 25				19 55				20 25					20 57						
Potters Bar	d					19 31				20 01				20 31					21 03						
Finsbury Park ⊖	d			19 24		19 40		20 17	19 54	20 10		20 24		20 40		21 17		20 54	21 12					21 24	
London Kings Cross 15 ⊖	a		19 30	19 31	19 34	19 49		20 25	20 01	20 19	20 05	20 31	20 32	20 48		21 25		21 01	21 21	21 03			21 31	21 31	21 34

		FC		FC	FC	FC		GR	FC	FC	FC	FC		FC	FC	FC	FC	FC
		1		1	1	1		R 1	1	1	1	1		1	1	1	1	1
Peterborough 8	d			20 46		21 16		21 21				21 46				22 16	22 46	
Huntingdon	d			21 00		21 33						22 00				22 33	23 00	
St Neots	d			21 08		21 41						22 08				22 41	23 08	
Sandy	d			21 15		21 48						22 15				22 48	23 15	
Biggleswade	d			21 19		21 52						22 19				22 52	23 19	
Arlesey	d			21 24		21 57						22 24				22 57	23 24	
Cambridge	d				20 55				21 28	21 45				21 55	22 28			23 15
Foxton	d				21 05									22 05				23 24
Shepreth	d				21 07									22 07				23 27
Meldreth	d				21 10									22 10				23 30
Royston	d				21 15				21 44					22 15	22 44			23 34
Ashwell & Morden	d				21 20									22 20				23 39
Baldock	d				21 25				21 52					22 25	22 52			23 43
Letchworth Garden City	d				21 29				21 55					22 29	22 55			23 46
Hitchin 4	d	←		21 29	21 34	22 03			21 59		←	22 29		22 34	22 59	23 03	23 29	23 50
Stevenage 4	d	21 09		21 35	21 40	22 09		21 55	22 05		22 09	22 35		22 40	23 05	23 09	23 35	23 55
Hertford North	a					↪												
Knebworth	d	21 13			21 43						22 13			22 43		23 13		23 59
Welwyn North	d	21 17			21 47						22 17			22 47		23 17		00 06
Welwyn Garden City 4	d	21 21			21 51						22 21			22 51		23 21		00 09
Hatfield	d	21 25			21 55						22 25			22 55		23 25		00 13
Potters Bar	d	21 31			22 01						22 31			23 01		23 31		00 18
Finsbury Park ⊖	d	21 40		21 54	22 10				22 24		22 40	22 54		23 10	23 24	23 40	00 04	00s32
London Kings Cross 15 ⊖	a	21 49		22 01	22 19			22 24	22 31	22 34	22 49	23 01		23 19	23 31	23 50	00 12	00 40

Saturdays
25 June to 30 July

		FC	FC	FC	GR	FC	FC	FC	FC	FC		FC	FC	FC	FC	FC	FC	FC	FC	GR		FC	FC	FC	FC
		1		1	R 1	1		1		1		1	1		1	1	1	1	1	R 1		1		1	1
Peterborough 8	d	22p30			23p39	03 25		04 12					05 16		05 46				06 16	06 38				06 46	
Huntingdon	d	22p44				03 39		04 26					05 33		06 00				06 33					07 00	
St Neots	d	22p51				03 47		04 34					05 41		06 08				06 41					07 08	
Sandy	d	22p59						04 41					05 48		06 15				06 48					07 15	
Biggleswade	d	23p02				03 57		04 45					05 52		06 19				06 52					07 19	
Arlesey	d	23p07						04 50					05 57		06 24				06 57					07 24	
Cambridge	d			23p15								05 45				05 55	06 28	06 45							06 55
Foxton	d			23p25												06 05									07 05
Shepreth	d			23p27												06 07									07 07
Meldreth	d			23p30												06 10									07 10
Royston	d			23p35						05 15		06 00				06 15	06 43								07 15
Ashwell & Morden	d			23p39						05 20						06 20									07 20
Baldock	d			23p44						05 25						06 25	06 51								07 25
Letchworth Garden City	d		23p18	23p47			04 50		05 20	05 29		06 09		06 20		06 29	06 54								07 29
Hitchin 4	d	23p16	23p22	23p54		04 08	04 54	04 59	05 24	05 33			06 03	06 24	06 29	06 33	06 59		07 03			←		07 29	07 33
Stevenage 4	d	23p22	23p27	23p59	00s20	04 14	04 59	05 05	05 29	05 39			06 09	06 29	06 35	06 39	07 04		07 09	07 06		07 09	07 29	07 35	07 39
Hertford North	a		23p40			04 24	05 12		05 42					06 42					↪				07 42		
Knebworth	d	23p25		00 02				05 08		05 43			06 13			06 43						07 13			07 43
Welwyn North	d	23p29		00 06				05 12		05 47			06 17			06 47						07 17			07 47
Welwyn Garden City 4	d	23p32		00 09				05 15		05 51			06 21			06 51						07 21			07 51
Hatfield	d	23p35		00 12				05 19		05 55			06 25			06 55						07 25			07 55
Potters Bar	d	23p41		00 18				05 25		06 01			06 31			07 01						07 31			08 01
Finsbury Park ⊖	d	23b51	00 15	00 29		04s49	05 47	05 42	06 17	06 10			06 40	07 17	06 54	07 10	07 22					07 40	08 17	07 54	08 10
London Kings Cross 15 ⊖	a	00 01	00 26	00 42	00 59	05 02	05 55	05 56	06 25	06 20		06 39	06 47	07 25	07 01	07 19	07 30	07 36		07 37		07 47	08 25	08 01	08 19

b Previous night, stops to set down only

Table 25

Saturdays

25 June to 30 July

Peterborough, Cambridge and Stevenage - London

			FC	FC	FC	GR		FC	FC	FC	FC	FC	FC	FC		GR		FC	FC	FC	FC	FC	FC	FC	FC
			1	1	1	R 1		1		1	1	1	1	1		R 1		1	1	1		1	1	1	1
Peterborough 8	d				07 16	07 37				07 46			08 08	08 16		08 31						08 46			09 07
Huntingdon	d				07 33					08 00			08 23	08 33								09 00			09 22
St Neots	d				07 41					08 08			08 31	08 41								09 08			09 30
Sandy	d				07 48					08 15				08 48								09 15			
Biggleswade	d				07 52					08 19			08 42	08 52								09 19			09 39
Arlesey	d				07 57					08 24				08 57								09 24			
Cambridge	d		07 28	07 45							07 55	08 15						08 26	08 45				08 55	09 15	
Foxton	d										08 05												09 05		
Shepreth	d										08 07												09 07		
Meldreth	d										08 10												09 10		
Royston	d		07 43								08 15							08 44					09 15		
Ashwell & Morden	d										08 20												09 20		
Baldock	d		07 51								08 25							08 52					09 25		
Letchworth Garden City	d		07 54								08 29							08 55					09 29		
Hitchin 4	d		07 59		08 03			←		08 29	08 33			09 03				08 59		←		09 29	09 34		
Stevenage 4	d		08 04		08 09	08 06		08 09	08 29	08 35	08 39			09 09		09 00		09 05		09 09	09 29	09 35	09 40		
Hertford North	a				→				08 42					→							09 42				
Knebworth	d							08 13			08 43									09 13			09 43		
Welwyn North	d							08 17			08 47									09 17			09 47		
Welwyn Garden City 4	d							08 21			08 51									09 21			09 51		
Hatfield	d							08 25			08 55									09 25			09 55		
Potters Bar	d							08 31			09 01									09 31			10 01		
Finsbury Park ⊖	d		08 22					08 40	09 17	08 54	09 10							09 24		09 40	10 17	09 54	10 10		
London Kings Cross 15 ⊖	a		08 30	08 36		08 36		08 49	09 25	09 01	09 20	09 04	09 12			09 30		09 31	09 38	09 49	10 25	10 01	10 20	10 04	10 10

		FC		FC	FC		FC	FC	FC	FC	FC			FC	GR	GR	FC	FC	FC	FC	FC	FC		FC	FC
		1		1	1			1	1	1	1			1	R 1	R 1	1	1	1		1	1		1	1
Peterborough 8	d				09 16			09 46			10 08			10 18	10 23	10 33					10 46				11 08
Huntingdon	d				09 33			10 00			10 24			10 33							11 00				11 22
St Neots	d				09 41			10 08			10 32			10 41							11 08				11 30
Sandy	d				09 48			10 15						10 48							11 15				
Biggleswade	d				09 52			10 19			10 40			10 52							11 19				11 39
Arlesey	d				09 57			10 24						10 57							11 24				
Cambridge	d	09 26		09 45					09 55	10 15							10 26	10 45				10 55		11 15	
Foxton	d								10 05													11 05			
Shepreth	d								10 07													11 07			
Meldreth	d								10 10													11 10			
Royston	d	09 44							10 15								10 44					11 15			
Ashwell & Morden	d								10 20													11 20			
Baldock	d	09 52							10 25								10 52					11 25			
Letchworth Garden City	d	09 55							10 29								10 55					11 29			
Hitchin 4	d	09 59			10 03			10 29	10 33					11 03			10 59		←		11 29	11 33			
Stevenage 4	d	10 05			10 09		10 29	10 35	10 39					11 09	10 55	11 03	11 05		11 09	11 29	11 35	11 39			
Hertford North	a						10 42							→						11 42					
Knebworth	d				10 13				10 43										11 13			11 43			
Welwyn North	d				10 17				10 47										11 17			11 47			
Welwyn Garden City 4	d				10 21				10 51										11 21			11 51			
Hatfield	d				10 25				10 55										11 25			11 55			
Potters Bar	d				10 31				11 01										11 31			12 01			
Finsbury Park ⊖	d	10 24			10 40		11 17	10 54	11 10								11 25		11 40	12 17	11 54	12 10			
London Kings Cross 15 ⊖	a	10 31		10 34	10 49		11 25	11 01	11 20	11 03	11 11				11 26	11 33	11 33	11 34	11 49	12 25	12 01	12 19		12 04	12 11

			FC	FC	FC	FC	FC	FC		FC	FC	FC		GR	FC	FC	FC	FC		FC	FC	FC	FC	FC	FC
			1	1	1		1	1		1	1	1		R 1	1	1	1			1	1	1	1	1	1
Peterborough 8	d				11 18		11 46				12 06	12 10		12 32						12 46			13 08		
Huntingdon	d				11 33		12 00				12 21	12 33								13 00			13 22		
St Neots	d				11 41		12 08				12 32	12 41								13 08			13 30		
Sandy	d				11 48		12 15					12 48								13 15					
Biggleswade	d				11 52		12 19				12 40	12 52								13 19			13 38		
Arlesey	d				11 57		12 24					12 57								13 24					
Cambridge	d		11 26	11 45				11 55		12 15					12 26	12 45					12 55	13 15		13 26	13 45
Foxton	d							12 05													13 05				
Shepreth	d							12 07													13 07				
Meldreth	d							12 10													13 10				
Royston	d		11 44					12 15							12 44						13 15			13 44	
Ashwell & Morden	d							12 20													13 20				
Baldock	d		11 52					12 25							12 52						13 25			13 52	
Letchworth Garden City	d		11 55					12 29							12 55						13 29			13 55	
Hitchin 4	d		11 59		12 03		12 29	12 33				13 03			12 59		←			13 29	13 33			13 59	
Stevenage 4	d		12 05		12 09	12 29	12 35	12 39				13 09		13 01	13 05		13 09	13 29		13 35	13 39			14 05	
Hertford North	a					12 42						→						13 42							
Knebworth	d				12 13			12 43									13 13				13 43				
Welwyn North	d				12 17			12 47									13 17				13 47				
Welwyn Garden City 4	d				12 21			12 51									13 21				13 51				
Hatfield	d				12 25			12 55									13 25				13 55				
Potters Bar	d				12 31			13 01									13 31				14 01				
Finsbury Park ⊖	d		12 24		12 40	13 17	12 54	13 10							13 24		13 40	14 17		13 54	14 10			14 24	
London Kings Cross 15 ⊖	a		12 31	12 34	12 49	13 25	13 01	13 19		13 04	13 11			13 30	13 31	13 34	13 49	14 25		14 01	14 19	14 04	14 10	14 31	14 34

Table 25

Saturdays

25 June to 30 July

Peterborough, Cambridge and Stevenage - London

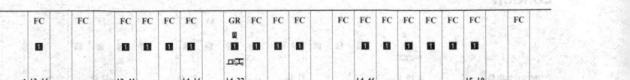

		FC		FC		FC	FC	FC	FC		GR	FC	FC	FC		FC	FC	FC	FC	FC	FC	FC		FC	
		1				1	1	1	1		R 1	1	1	1			1	1	1	1	1	1			
Peterborough 8	d	13 16				13 46			14 16		14 32						14 46					15 10			
Huntingdon	d	13 33				14 00			14 33								15 00					15 33			
St Neots	d	13 41				14 08			14 41								15 08					15 41			
Sandy	d	13 48				14 15			14 48								15 15					15 48			
Biggleswade	d	13 52				14 19			14 52								15 19					15 52			
Arlesey	d	13 57				14 24			14 57								15 24					15 57			
Cambridge	d						13 55	14 15				14 26	14 45					14 55	15 15	15 26	15 45				
Foxton	d						14 05											15 05							
Shepreth	d						14 07											15 07							
Meldreth	d						14 10											15 10							
Royston	d						14 15					14 44						15 15		15 44					
Ashwell & Morden	d						14 20											15 20							
Baldock	d						14 25					14 52						15 25		15 52					
Letchworth Garden City	d						14 29					14 55						15 29		15 55					
Hitchin 4	d	14 03				14 29	14 33		15 03			14 59		←			15 29	15 33		15 59		16 03			
Stevenage 4	d	14 09		14 29		14 35	14 39		15 09		15 01	15 05		15 09		15 29	15 35	15 39		16 05		16 09		16 29	
Hertford North	a			14 42					↪							15 42								16 42	
Knebworth	d	14 13					14 43							15 13				15 43				16 13			
Welwyn North	d	14 17					14 47							15 17				15 47				16 17			
Welwyn Garden City 4	d	14 21					14 51							15 21				15 51				16 21			
Hatfield	d	14 25					14 55							15 25				15 55				16 25			
Potters Bar	d	14 31					15 01							15 31				16 01				16 31			
Finsbury Park ⊖	d	14 40		15 17		14 54	15 10					15 24		15 40		16 17	15 54	16 10		16 24		16 40		17 17	
London Kings Cross 15 ⊖	a	14 49		15 25		15 01	15 19	15 05			15 30	15 31	15 34	15 49		16 25	16 01	16 19	16 04	16 31	16 34	16 49		17 25	

		FC	FC	FC	FC		GR	FC	FC	FC		FC	FC	FC	FC		FC	FC	FC	FC		FC	FC	FC	FC
		1	1	1	1		R 1	1	1	1			1	1	1		1	1	1			1	1	1	1
Peterborough 8	d	15 46			16 16		16 32						16 46						17 18			17 46			18 16
Huntingdon	d	16 00			16 33								17 00						17 33			18 00			18 33
St Neots	d	16 08			16 41								17 08						17 41			18 08			18 41
Sandy	d	16 15			16 48								17 15						17 48			18 15			18 48
Biggleswade	d	16 19			16 52								17 19						17 52			18 19			18 52
Arlesey	d	16 24			16 57								17 24						17 57			18 24			18 57
Cambridge	d		15 55	16 15				16 26	16 45					16 55	17 15		17 26	17 45					17 55	18 15	
Foxton	d		16 05											17 05									18 05		
Shepreth	d		16 07											17 07									18 07		
Meldreth	d		16 10											17 10									18 10		
Royston	d		16 15					16 44						17 15			17 44						18 15		
Ashwell & Morden	d		16 20											17 20									18 20		
Baldock	d		16 25					16 52						17 25			17 52						18 25		
Letchworth Garden City	d		16 29					16 55						17 29			17 55						18 29		
Hitchin 4	d	16 29	16 33		17 03			16 59		←			17 29	17 34			17 59		18 03			18 29	18 33		19 03
Stevenage 4	d	16 35	16 39		17 09		17 02	17 05		17 09		17 29	17 35	17 40			18 05		18 09	18 29		18 35	18 39		19 09
Hertford North	a				↪							17 42								18 42					↪
Knebworth	d		16 43							17 13				17 43					18 13				18 43		
Welwyn North	d		16 47							17 17				17 47					18 17				18 47		
Welwyn Garden City 4	d		16 51							17 21				17 51					18 21				18 51		
Hatfield	d		16 55							17 25				17 55					18 25				18 55		
Potters Bar	d		17 01							17 31				18 01					18 31				19 01		
Finsbury Park ⊖	d	16 54	17 10					17 24		17 40		18 17	17 54	18 10			18 24		18 40	19 17		18 54	19 10		
London Kings Cross 15 ⊖	a	17 01	17 19	17 05			17 32	17 31	17 34	17 49		18 25	18 01	18 19	18 04		18 31	18 35	18 49	19 25		19 01	19 19	19 05	

			GR	FC	FC	FC		FC	FC	FC	FC	FC	FC	FC		FC		FC	FC	FC	FC		GR	FC	FC
			R 1	1	1	1			1	1	1	1	1	1		1			1	1	1		R 1	1	1
Peterborough 8	d		18 32						18 46					19 16					19 46		20 14		20 33		20 46
Huntingdon	d								19 00					19 34					20 00		20 34				21 00
St Neots	d								19 08					19 41					20 08		20 41				21 08
Sandy	d								19 15					19 49					20 15		20 49				21 15
Biggleswade	d								19 19					19 53					20 19		20 53				21 19
Arlesey	d								19 24					19 58					20 24		20 58				21 29
Cambridge	d			18 26	18 45					18 55	19 15	19 28	19 45			19 55				20 28				20 45	
Foxton	d									19 05						20 05									
Shepreth	d									19 07						20 07									
Meldreth	d									19 10						20 10									
Royston	d			18 44						19 15		19 44				20 15				20 44					
Ashwell & Morden	d									19 20						20 20									
Baldock	d			18 52						19 25		19 52				20 25				20 52					
Letchworth Garden City	d			18 55						19 29		19 55				20 29				20 55					
Hitchin 4	d			18 59		←			19 29	19 33		19 59		20 04		20a34			20 35	20a59	21 04		21 11	21a10	
Stevenage 4	d		19 01	19 05		19 09		19 29	19 35	19 39		20 05		20 10				20 29	20 51		21 10		21 26		21 47
Hertford North	a							19 42										20 42							↪
Knebworth	d					19 13				19 43				20 14							21 14				
Welwyn North	d					19 17				19 47				20 18							21 18				
Welwyn Garden City 4	d					19 21				19 51				20 21							21 21				
Hatfield	d					19 25				19 55				20 25							21 25				
Potters Bar	d					19 31				20 01				20 31							21 31				
Finsbury Park ⊖	d			19 24		19 40		20 17	19 54	20 10		20 24		20 40				21 17	21 22		21 40				
London Kings Cross 15 ⊖	a		19 30	19 31	19 34	19 49		20 25	20 01	20 19	20 05	20 31	20 32	20 47				21 25	21 29		21 47		22 09		

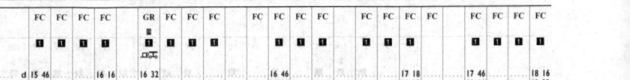

Table 25

Saturdays
25 June to 30 July

Peterborough, Cambridge and Stevenage - London

		GR		FC	FC	FC	FC		GR	FC	FC	FC		FC	FC	FC	FC
		R 1		1	1	1	1		R 1	1	1	1		1	1	1	1
Peterborough 8	d	20 49					21 16		21 21			21 46				22 46	
Huntingdon	d						21 34					22 00				23 00	
St Neots	d						21 41					22 08				23 08	
Sandy	d						21 49					22 15				23 15	
Biggleswade	d						21 53					22 19				23 19	
Arlesey	d						21 58					22 24				23 24	
Cambridge	d				20 54	21 28					21 45			21 55	22 28		23 15
Foxton	d				21 05									22 05			23 24
Shepreth	d				21 07									22 07			23 27
Meldreth	d				21 10									22 10			23 30
Royston	d				21 15	21 44								22 15	22 44		23 34
Ashwell & Morden	d				21 20									22 21			23 38
Baldock	d				21 25	21 52								22 26	22 52		23 43
Letchworth Garden City	d				21 29	21 55								22 29	22 55		23 46
Hitchin 4	d	21 30		←	21a34	21a59	22 04		22 00	←	22a14	22 30		22a34	22a59	23a32	23a51
Stevenage 4	d	21 45		21 47			22 10		22 08	22 10		22 35					
Hertford North	a						↪										
Knebworth	d									22 14							
Welwyn North	d									22 18							
Welwyn Garden City 4	d									22 21							
Hatfield	d									22 25							
Potters Bar	d									22 31							
Finsbury Park ⊖	d			22 12						22 40		22 54					
London Kings Cross 15 ⊖	a	22 26		22 18					22 44	22 47		23 01					

Saturdays
from 6 August

		FC	FC	FC	GR	FC	FC	FC	FC	FC		FC	FC	FC	FC	FC	FC	FC	FC	GR		FC	FC	FC	FC
		1		1	R 1	1		1		1		1	1		1	1	1	1	1	R 1		1		1	1
Peterborough 8	d	22p30			23p39	03 25		04 12					05 16		05 46				06 16	06 38				06 46	
Huntingdon	d	22p44				03 39		04 26					05 33		06 00				06 33					07 00	
St Neots	d	22p51				03 47		04 34					05 41		06 08				06 41					07 08	
Sandy	d	22p59						04 41					05 48		06 15				06 48					07 15	
Biggleswade	d	23p02				03 57		04 45					05 52		06 19				06 52					07 19	
Arlesey	d	23p07						04 50					05 57		06 24				06 57					07 24	
Cambridge	d			23p15								05 45				05 55	06 28	06 45							06 55
Foxton	d			23p25												06 05									07 05
Shepreth	d			23p27												06 07									07 07
Meldreth	d			23p30												06 10									07 10
Royston	d			23p35						05 15		06 00				06 15	06 43								07 15
Ashwell & Morden	d			23p39						05 20						06 20									07 20
Baldock	d			23p44						05 25						06 25	06 51								07 25
Letchworth Garden City	d		23p18	23p47			04 50		05 20	05 29		06 09		06 20		06 29	06 54								07 29
Hitchin 4	d	23p16	23p22	23p54		04 08	04 54	04 59	05 24	05 33			06 03	06 24	06 29	06 33	06 59		07 03			←		07 29	07 33
Stevenage 4	d	23p22	23p27	23p59	00s20	04 14	04 59	05 05	05 29	05 39			06 09	06 29	06 35	06 39	07 04		07 09	07 06		07 09	07 29	07 35	07 39
Hertford North	a		23p40			04 24	05 12		05 42					06 42					↪				07 42		
Knebworth	d	23p25		00 02				05 08		05 43			06 13			06 43						07 13			07 43
Welwyn North	d	23p29		00 06				05 12		05 47			06 17			06 47						07 17			07 47
Welwyn Garden City 4	d	23p32		00 09				05 15		05 51			06 21			06 51						07 21			07 51
Hatfield	d	23p35		00 12				05 19		05 55			06 25			06 55						07 25			07 55
Potters Bar	d	23p41		00 18				05 25		06 01			06 31			07 01						07 31			08 01
Finsbury Park ⊖	d	23c51	00 15	00 29		04s49	05 47	05 42	06 17	06 10			06 40	07 17	06 54	07 10	07 22					07 40	08 17	07 54	08 10
London Kings Cross 15 ⊖	a	00 01	00 26	00 42	00 59	05 02	05 55	05 56	06 25	06 20		06 39	06 47	07 25	07 01	07 19	07 30	07 36		07 37		07 47	08 25	08 01	08 19

			FC	FC	FC	GR		FC	FC	FC	FC	FC	FC	FC		GR		FC	FC	FC	FC	FC	FC	FC	FC
			1	1	1	R 1		1		1	1	1	1	1		R 1		1	1	1		1	1	1	1
Peterborough 8	d				07 16	07 37				07 46			08 08	08 16		08 31						08 46			09 07
Huntingdon	d				07 33					08 00			08 23	08 33								09 00			09 22
St Neots	d				07 41					08 08			08 31	08 41								09 08			09 30
Sandy	d				07 48					08 15				08 48								09 15			
Biggleswade	d				07 52					08 19			08 42	08 52								09 19			09 39
Arlesey	d				07 57					08 24				08 57								09 24			
Cambridge	d		07 28	07 45							07 55	08 15						08 26	08 45				08 55	09 15	
Foxton	d										08 05												09 05		
Shepreth	d										08 07												09 07		
Meldreth	d										08 10												09 10		
Royston	d		07 43								08 15							08 44					09 15		
Ashwell & Morden	d										08 20												09 20		
Baldock	d		07 51								08 25							08 52					09 25		
Letchworth Garden City	d		07 54								08 29							08 55					09 29		
Hitchin 4	d		07 59		08 03			←		08 29	08 33			09 03				08 59		←		09 29	09 34		
Stevenage 4	d		08 04		08 09	08 06		08 09	08 29	08 35	08 39			09 09		09 00		09 05		09 09	09 29	09 35	09 40		
Hertford North	a				↪				08 42					↪							09 42				
Knebworth	d							08 13			08 43									09 13			09 43		
Welwyn North	d							08 17			08 47									09 17			09 47		
Welwyn Garden City 4	d							08 21			08 51									09 21			09 51		
Hatfield	d							08 25			08 55									09 25			09 55		
Potters Bar	d							08 31			09 01									09 31			10 01		
Finsbury Park ⊖	d		08 22					08 40	09 17	08 54	09 10							09 24		09 40	10 17	09 54	10 10		
London Kings Cross 15 ⊖	a		08 30	08 36		08 36		08 49	09 25	09 01	09 20	09 04	09 12			09 30		09 31	09 38	09 49	10 25	10 01	10 20	10 04	10 10

c Previous night, stops to set down only

Table 25

Saturdays

from 6 August

Peterborough, Cambridge and Stevenage - London

		FC		FC	FC		FC	FC	FC	FC	FC			FC	GR	GR	FC	FC	FC	FC	FC	FC		FC	FC
															R	R									
		1		1	1			1	1	1	1			1	1	1	1	1	1		1	1		1	1
															🛒	🛒									
Peterborough 8	d				09 16			09 46			10 08			10 18	10 23	10 33					10 46				11 08
Huntingdon	d				09 33			10 00			10 24			10 33							11 00				11 22
St Neots	d				09 41			10 08			10 32			10 41							11 08				11 30
Sandy	d				09 48			10 15						10 48							11 15				
Biggleswade	d				09 52			10 19			10 40			10 52							11 19				11 39
Arlesey	d				09 57			10 24						10 57							11 24				
Cambridge	d	09 26		09 45					09 55	10 15							10 26	10 45				10 55		11 15	
Foxton	d								10 05													11 05			
Shepreth	d								10 07													11 07			
Meldreth	d								10 10													11 10			
Royston	d	09 44							10 15								10 44					11 15			
Ashwell & Morden	d								10 20													11 20			
Baldock	d	09 52							10 25								10 52					11 25			
Letchworth Garden City	d	09 55							10 29								10 55					11 29			
Hitchin 4	d	09 59			10 03			10 29	10 33					11 03			10 59		←		11 29	11 33			
Stevenage 4	d	10 05			10 09		10 29	10 35	10 39					11 09	10 55	11 03	11 05		11 09	11 29	11 35	11 39			
Hertford North	a						10 42							↪						11 42					
Knebworth	d				10 13				10 43										11 13			11 43			
Welwyn North	d				10 17				10 47										11 17			11 47			
Welwyn Garden City 4	d				10 21				10 51										11 21			11 51			
Hatfield	d				10 25				10 55										11 25			11 55			
Potters Bar	d				10 31				11 01										11 31			12 01			
Finsbury Park ⊖	d	10 24			10 40		11 17	10 54	11 10								11 25		11 40	12 17	11 54	12 10			
London Kings Cross 15 ⊖	a	10 31		10 34	10 49		11 25	11 01	11 20	11 03	11 11				11 26	11 33	11 33	11 34	11 49	12 25	12 01	12 19		12 04	12 11

			FC	FC	FC	FC	FC	FC		FC	FC	FC		GR	FC	FC	FC	FC		FC	FC	FC	FC	FC	FC
														R											
			1	1	1		1	1		1	1	1		1	1	1	1			1	1	1	1	1	1
														🛒											
Peterborough 8	d				11 18		11 46				12 06	12 10		12 32						12 46			13 08		
Huntingdon	d				11 33		12 00				12 21	12 33								13 00			13 22		
St Neots	d				11 41		12 08				12 32	12 41								13 08			13 30		
Sandy	d				11 48		12 15					12 48								13 15					
Biggleswade	d				11 52		12 19				12 40	12 52								13 19			13 38		
Arlesey	d				11 57		12 24					12 57								13 24					
Cambridge	d		11 26	11 45				11 55		12 15					12 26	12 45					12 55	13 15		13 26	13 45
Foxton	d							12 05													13 05				
Shepreth	d							12 07													13 07				
Meldreth	d							12 10													13 10				
Royston	d		11 44					12 15							12 44						13 15			13 44	
Ashwell & Morden	d							12 20													13 20				
Baldock	d		11 52					12 25							12 52						13 25			13 52	
Letchworth Garden City	d		11 55					12 29							12 55						13 29			13 55	
Hitchin 4	d		11 59		12 03		12 29	12 33				13 03			12 59		←			13 29	13 33			13 59	
Stevenage 4	d		12 05		12 09	12 29	12 35	12 39				13 09		13 01	13 05		13 09	13 29		13 35	13 39			14 05	
Hertford North	a					12 42						↪						13 42							
Knebworth	d				12 13			12 43									13 13				13 43				
Welwyn North	d				12 17			12 47									13 17				13 47				
Welwyn Garden City 4	d				12 21			12 51									13 21				13 51				
Hatfield	d				12 25			12 55									13 25				13 55				
Potters Bar	d				12 31			13 01									13 31				14 01				
Finsbury Park ⊖	d		12 24		12 40	13 17	12 54	13 10							13 24		13 40	14 17		13 54	14 10			14 24	
London Kings Cross 15 ⊖	a		12 31	12 34	12 49	13 25	13 01	13 19		13 04	13 11			13 30	13 31	13 34	13 49	14 25		14 01	14 19	14 04	14 10	14 31	14 34

		FC		FC		FC	FC	FC	FC		GR	FC	FC	FC		FC	FC	FC	FC	FC	FC	FC		FC	
											R														
		1				1	1	1	1		1	1	1	1			1	1	1	1	1	1			
											🛒														
Peterborough 8	d	13 16				13 46			14 16		14 32						14 46					15 10			
Huntingdon	d	13 33				14 00			14 33								15 00					15 33			
St Neots	d	13 41				14 08			14 41								15 08					15 41			
Sandy	d	13 48				14 15			14 48								15 15					15 48			
Biggleswade	d	13 52				14 19			14 52								15 19					15 52			
Arlesey	d	13 57				14 24			14 57								15 24					15 57			
Cambridge	d						13 55	14 15				14 26	14 45					14 55	15 15	15 26	15 45				
Foxton	d						14 05											15 05							
Shepreth	d						14 07											15 07							
Meldreth	d						14 10											15 10							
Royston	d						14 15					14 44						15 15		15 44					
Ashwell & Morden	d						14 20											15 20							
Baldock	d						14 25					14 52						15 25		15 52					
Letchworth Garden City	d						14 29					14 55						15 29		15 55					
Hitchin 4	d	14 03				14 29	14 33		15 03			14 59		←			15 29	15 33		15 59		16 03			
Stevenage 4	d	14 09		14 29		14 35	14 39		15 09		15 01	15 05		15 09		15 29	15 35	15 39		16 05		16 09		16 29	
Hertford North	a			14 42					↪							15 42								16 42	
Knebworth	d	14 13					14 43							15 13				15 43				16 13			
Welwyn North	d	14 17					14 47							15 17				15 47				16 17			
Welwyn Garden City 4	d	14 21					14 51							15 21				15 51				16 21			
Hatfield	d	14 25					14 55							15 25				15 55				16 25			
Potters Bar	d	14 31					15 01							15 31				16 01				16 31			
Finsbury Park ⊖	d	14 40		15 17		14 54	15 10					15 24		15 40		16 17	15 54	16 10		16 24		16 40		17 17	
London Kings Cross 15 ⊖	a	14 49		15 25		15 01	15 19	15 05			15 30	15 31	15 34	15 49		16 25	16 01	16 19	16 04	16 31	16 34	16 49		17 25	

Table 25

Saturdays
from 6 August

Peterborough, Cambridge and Stevenage - London

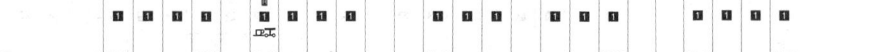

		FC	FC	FC	FC		GR	FC	FC	FC		FC	FC	FC	FC		FC	FC	FC	FC		FC	FC	FC	FC
		1	1	1	1		R 1	1	1	1			1	1	1		1	1	1			1	1	1	1
Peterborough 8	d	15 46			16 16		16 32						16 46						17 18			17 46			18 16
Huntingdon	d	16 00			16 33								17 00						17 33			18 00			18 33
St Neots	d	16 08			16 41								17 08						17 41			18 08			18 41
Sandy	d	16 15			16 48								17 15						17 48			18 15			18 48
Biggleswade	d	16 19			16 52								17 19						17 52			18 19			18 52
Arlesey	d	16 24			16 57								17 24						17 57			18 24			18 57
Cambridge	d		15 55	16 15				16 26	16 45					16 55	17 15		17 26	17 45					17 55	18 15	
Foxton	d		16 05											17 05									18 05		
Shepreth	d		16 07											17 07									18 07		
Meldreth	d		16 10											17 10									18 10		
Royston	d		16 15					16 44						17 15			17 44						18 15		
Ashwell & Morden	d		16 20											17 20									18 20		
Baldock	d		16 25					16 52						17 25			17 52						18 25		
Letchworth Garden City	d		16 29					16 55						17 29			17 55						18 29		
Hitchin 4	d	16 29	16 33		17 03			16 59		↩			17 29	17 34			17 59		18 03			18 29	18 33		19 03
Stevenage 4	d	16 35	16 39		17 09		17 02	17 05		17 09		17 29	17 35	17 40			18 05		18 09	18 29		18 35	18 39		19 09
Hertford North	a				↪							17 42								18 42					↪
Knebworth	d		16 43							17 13				17 43					18 13				18 43		
Welwyn North	d		16 47							17 17				17 47					18 17				18 47		
Welwyn Garden City 4	d		16 51							17 21				17 51					18 21				18 51		
Hatfield	d		16 55							17 25				17 55					18 25				18 55		
Potters Bar	d		17 01							17 31				18 01					18 31				19 01		
Finsbury Park ⊖	d	16 54	17 10					17 24		17 40		18 17	17 54	18 10			18 24		18 40	19 17		18 54	19 10		
London Kings Cross 15 ⊖	a	17 01	17 19	17 05			17 32	17 31	17 34	17 49		18 25	18 01	18 19	18 04		18 31	18 35	18 49	19 25		19 01	19 19	19 05	

			GR	FC	FC	FC		FC	FC	FC	FC	FC	FC	FC		FC		FC	FC	FC	FC		GR	FC	FC
			R 1	1	1	1			1	1	1	1	1	1				1	1	1	1		R 1	1	1
Peterborough 8	d		18 32						18 46					19 16				19 46			20 16		20 33		
Huntingdon	d								19 00					19 33				20 00			20 33				
St Neots	d								19 08					19 41				20 08			20 41				
Sandy	d								19 15					19 48				20 15			20 48				
Biggleswade	d								19 19					19 52				20 19			20 52				
Arlesey	d								19 24					19 57				20 24			20 57				
Cambridge	d			18 26	18 45					18 55	19 15	19 28	19 45						19 55	20 15				20 28	20 45
Foxton	d									19 05									20 05						
Shepreth	d									19 07									20 07						
Meldreth	d									19 10									20 10						
Royston	d			18 44						19 15		19 44							20 15					20 44	
Ashwell & Morden	d									19 20									20 20						
Baldock	d			18 52						19 25		19 52							20 25					20 52	
Letchworth Garden City	d			18 55						19 29		19 55							20 29					20 55	
Hitchin 4	d			18 59		↩			19 29	19 33		19 59		20 03				20 29	20 34		21 03			20 59	
Stevenage 4	d		19 01	19 05		19 09		19 29	19 35	19 39		20 05		20 09		20 29		20 35	20 40		21 09		21 02	21 05	
Hertford North	a							19 42								20 42					↪				
Knebworth	d					19 13				19 43				20 13					20 46						
Welwyn North	d					19 17				19 47				20 17					20 50						
Welwyn Garden City 4	d					19 21				19 51				20 21					20 53						
Hatfield	d					19 25				19 55				20 25					20 57						
Potters Bar	d					19 31				20 01				20 31					21 03						
Finsbury Park ⊖	d			19 24		19 40		20 17	19 54	20 10		20 24		20 40		21 17		20 54	21 12					21 24	
London Kings Cross 15 ⊖	a		19 30	19 31	19 34	19 49		20 25	20 01	20 19	20 05	20 31	20 32	20 48		21 25		21 01	21 21	21 03			21 31	21 31	21 34

		FC		FC	FC	FC		GR	FC	FC	FC	FC		FC	FC	FC	FC	FC
		1		1	1	1		R 1	1	1	1	1		1	1	1	1	1
Peterborough 8	d			20 46		21 16		21 21				21 46				22 16	22 46	
Huntingdon	d			21 00		21 33						22 00				22 33	23 00	
St Neots	d			21 08		21 41						22 08				22 41	23 08	
Sandy	d			21 15		21 48						22 15				22 48	23 15	
Biggleswade	d			21 19		21 52						22 19				22 52	23 19	
Arlesey	d			21 24		21 57						22 24				22 57	23 24	
Cambridge	d				20 55				21 28	21 45				21 55	22 28			23 15
Foxton	d				21 05									22 05				23 24
Shepreth	d				21 07									22 07				23 27
Meldreth	d				21 10									22 10				23 30
Royston	d				21 15				21 44					22 15	22 44			23 34
Ashwell & Morden	d				21 20									22 20				23 39
Baldock	d				21 25				21 52					22 25	22 52			23 43
Letchworth Garden City	d				21 29				21 55					22 29	22 55			23 46
Hitchin 4	d	↩		21 29	21 34	22 03			21 59		↩	22 29		22 34	22 59	23 03	23 29	23 50
Stevenage 4	d	21 09		21 35	21 40	22 09		21 55	22 05		22 09	22 35		22 40	23 05	23 09	23 35	23 55
Hertford North	a					↪												
Knebworth	d	21 13			21 43						22 13			22 43		23 13		23 59
Welwyn North	d	21 17			21 47						22 17			22 47		23 17		00 06
Welwyn Garden City 4	d	21 21			21 51						22 21			22 51		23 21		00 09
Hatfield	d	21 25			21 55						22 25			22 55		23 25		00 13
Potters Bar	d	21 31			22 01						22 31			23 01		23 31		00 18
Finsbury Park ⊖	d	21 40		21 54	22 10				22 24		22 40	22 54		23 10	23 24	23 40	00 04	00s32
London Kings Cross 15 ⊖	a	21 49		22 01	22 19			22 24	22 31	22 34	22 49	23 01		23 19	23 31	23 50	00 12	00 40

Table 25

Sundays
until 19 June

Peterborough, Cambridge and Stevenage - London

		FC 1 A	FC 1 A	FC 1	FC 1	FC	FC 1	FC 1	FC	FC 1		FC 1	FC 1	FC	FC 1	FC 1	FC 1	FC 1	FC 1	FC 1		FC	FC 1	FC 1	FC 1
Peterborough 8	d	22p46		05 46			06 46			07 46					08 46			09 15					09 46		
Huntingdon	d	23p00		06 00			07 00			08 00					09 00			09 30					10 00		
St Neots	d	23p08		06 08			07 08			08 08					09 08			09 37					10 08		
Sandy	d	23p15		06 15			07 15			08 15					09 15								10 15		
Biggleswade	d	23p19		06 19			07 19			08 19					09 19			09 45					10 19		
Arlesey	d	23p24		06 24			07 24			08 24					09 24								10 24		
Cambridge	d		23p15		06 28			07 28				07 55	08 28			08 55	09 20		09 28					09 55	10 20
Foxton	d		23p24									08 05				09 05								10 05	
Shepreth	d		23p27									08 07				09 07								10 07	
Meldreth	d		23p30									08 10				09 10								10 10	
Royston	d		23p34		06 43			07 43				08 15	08 42			09 15			09 42					10 15	
Ashwell & Morden	d		23p39									08 20				09 20								10 20	
Baldock	d		23p43		06 51			07 51				08 25	08 50			09 25			09 50					10 25	
Letchworth Garden City	d		23p46		06 54			07 54				08 29	08 53			09 29			09 53	10 00				10 29	
Hitchin 4	d	23p29	23p50	06 34	06 58		07 34	07 59		08 29		08 33	08 57		09 29	09 33			09 57	10 04			10 29	10 33	
Stevenage 4	d	23p35	23p55	06 40	07 04	07 29	07 40	08 05	08 29	08 35		08 39	09 03	09 29	09 35	09 39			10 03	10 10		10 29	10 35	10 39	
Hertford North	a					07 42			08 42					09 42								10 42			
Knebworth	d		23p59	06 43			07 43					08 43				09 43				10 13				10 43	
Welwyn North	d		00 06	06 47			07 47					08 47				09 47				10 17				10 47	
Welwyn Garden City 4	d		00 09	06 51			07 51					08 51				09 51				10 21				10 50	
Hatfield	d		00 13	06 54			07 54					08 54				09 54				10 24				10 54	
Potters Bar	d		00 18	07 00			08 00					09 00				10 00				10 30				10 59	
Finsbury Park ⊖	d	00 04	00s32	07 10	07 32	08 17	08 10	08 22	09 17	08 54		09 10	09 21	10 17	09 54	10 10			10 21	10 40		11 17	10 54	11 11	
London Kings Cross 15 ⊖	a	00 12	00 40	07 20	07 39	08 26	08 20	08 30	09 25	09 01		09 19	09 28	10 25	10 01	10 19	10 08	10 15	10 28	10 49		11 25	11 01	11 20	11 08

		FC 1	FC 1	GR R 1	FC	FC 1		FC 1	FC 1		FC 1	FC 1	FC 1	FC 1	FC 1	GR R 1		FC	FC 1	FC 1		FC 1		FC 1	FC
Peterborough 8	d	10 15		10 32		10 46						11 46				12 34			12 46						
Huntingdon	d	10 30				11 00						12 00							13 00						
St Neots	d	10 37				11 08						12 08							13 08						
Sandy	d					11 15						12 15							13 15						
Biggleswade	d	10 45				11 19						12 19							13 19						
Arlesey	d					11 24						12 24							13 24						
Cambridge	d		10 28					10 55	11 20		11 28		11 55	12 20	12 28					12 55		13 20		13 28	
Foxton	d							11 05					12 05							13 05					
Shepreth	d							11 07					12 07							13 07					
Meldreth	d							11 10					12 10							13 10					
Royston	d		10 42					11 15			11 42		12 15		12 42					13 15				13 42	
Ashwell & Morden	d							11 20					12 20							13 20					
Baldock	d		10 50					11 25			11 50		12 25		12 50					13 25				13 50	
Letchworth Garden City	d		10 53					11 29			11 53		12 29		12 53					13 29				13 53	
Hitchin 4	d		10 57			11 29		11 33			11 57	12 29	12 33		12 57				13 29	13 34				13 57	
Stevenage 4	d		11 03	11 04	11 29	11 35		11 39			12 03	12 35	12 39		13 03	13 07		13 29	13 35	13 40				14 03	14 29
Hertford North	a				11 42													13 42							14 42
Knebworth	d							11 43					12 43							13 43					
Welwyn North	d							11 47					12 47							13 47					
Welwyn Garden City 4	d							11 51					12 50							13 51					
Hatfield	d							11 54					12 54							13 54					
Potters Bar	d							12 00					13 00							14 00					
Finsbury Park ⊖	d		11 21		12 17	11 54		12 10			12 21	12 54	13 11		13 21			14 17	13 54	14 11				14 21	15 17
London Kings Cross 15 ⊖	a	11 15	11 28	11 35	12 25	12 01		12 19	12 08		12 28	13 01	13 19	13 08	13 28	13 35		14 25	14 01	14 19		14 08		14 28	15 25

		FC 1		FC 1		FC 1	FC 1	GR R 1	FC	FC 1	FC 1			FC 1	FC 1	FC	FC 1	FC 1		FC 1		FC 1		GR R 1	FC
Peterborough 8	d	13 46						14 32		14 46							15 46							16 32	
Huntingdon	d	14 00								15 00							16 00								
St Neots	d	14 08								15 08							16 08								
Sandy	d	14 15								15 15							16 15								
Biggleswade	d	14 19								15 19							16 19								
Arlesey	d	14 24								15 24							16 24								
Cambridge	d			13 55		14 20	14 28				14 55			15 20	15 28			15 55		16 20		16 28			
Foxton	d			14 05							15 05							16 05							
Shepreth	d			14 07							15 07							16 07							
Meldreth	d			14 10							15 10							16 10							
Royston	d			14 15			14 42				15 15				15 42			16 15				16 42			
Ashwell & Morden	d			14 20							15 20							16 20							
Baldock	d			14 25			14 50				15 25				15 50			16 25				16 50			
Letchworth Garden City	d			14 29			14 53				15 29				15 53			16 29				16 53			
Hitchin 4	d	14 29		14 34			14 57			15 29	15 34				15 57		16 29	16 34				16 57			
Stevenage 4	d	14 35		14 40			15 03	15 05	15 29	15 35	15 40				16 03	16 29	16 35	16 40				17 03		17 04	17 29
Hertford North	a								15 42							16 42									17 42
Knebworth	d			14 43							15 43							16 43							
Welwyn North	d			14 47							15 47							16 47							
Welwyn Garden City 4	d			14 51							15 51							16 51							
Hatfield	d			14 54							15 54							16 54							
Potters Bar	d			15 00							16 00							17 00							
Finsbury Park ⊖	d	14 54		15 10			15 21		16 17	15 54	16 10				16 21	17 17	16 54	17 10				17 21			18 17
London Kings Cross 15 ⊖	a	15 01		15 19		15 08	15 28	15 35	16 25	16 01	16 19			16 08	16 29	17 25	17 01	17 19		17 08		17 28		17 35	18 25

A not 22 May

Table 25

Sundays

until 19 June

Peterborough, Cambridge and Stevenage - London

		FC 1	FC 1		FC 1	FC 1	GR R 1	FC		FC 1	FC 1		FC 1		FC 1	FC 1	GR R 1	FC		FC 1	FC 1		FC 1	FC 1	GR R 1
Peterborough 8	d	16 46								17 46										18 46					
Huntingdon	d	17 00								18 00										19 00					
St Neots	d	17 08								18 08										19 08					
Sandy	d	17 15								18 15										19 15					
Biggleswade	d	17 19								18 19										19 19					
Arlesey	d	17 24								18 24										19 24					
Cambridge	d		16 55		17 20	17 28					17 55		18 21		18 28	18 45					18 55		19 21	19 28	
Foxton	d		17 05								18 05										19 05				
Shepreth	d		17 07								18 07										19 07				
Meldreth	d		17 10								18 10										19 10				
Royston	d		17 15			17 42					18 15				18 42						19 15			19 42	
Ashwell & Morden	d		17 20								18 20										19 20				
Baldock	d		17 25			17 50					18 25				18 50						19 25			19 50	
Letchworth Garden City	d		17 29			17 53					18 29				18 53						19 29			19 53	
Hitchin 4	d	17 29	17 34			17 57				18 29	18 34				18 57					19 29	19 34			19 57	
Stevenage 4	d	17 35	17 40			18 03	18 04	18 29		18 35	18 40				19 03		19 11	19 29		19 35	19 40			20 03	20 08
Hertford North	a							18 42										19 42							
Knebworth	d		17 43								18 43										19 43				
Welwyn North	d		17 47								18 47										19 47				
Welwyn Garden City 4	d		17 51								18 51										19 51				
Hatfield	d		17 54								18 54										19 54				
Potters Bar	d		18 00								19 00										20 00				
Finsbury Park ⊖	d	17 54	18 10			18 21		19 17		18 54	19 10				19 21			20 17		19 54	20 10			20 21	
London Kings Cross 15 ⊖	a	18 01	18 19		18 08	18 28	18 36	19 25		19 01	19 19		19 10		19 28	19 38	19 38	20 25		20 01	20 19		20 11	20 28	20 36

		FC	FC 1	FC 1			FC 1		FC 1	GR R 1	FC	FC 1	FC 1			FC 1	FC 1	FC	FC 1	FC 1	FC 1	GR R 1	GR R 1	FC 1	
Peterborough 8	d		19 46									20 46							21 46			22 13	22 23		
Huntingdon	d		20 00									21 00							22 00						
St Neots	d		20 08									21 08							22 08						
Sandy	d		20 15									21 15							22 15						
Biggleswade	d		20 19									21 19							22 19						
Arlesey	d		20 24									21 24							22 24						
Cambridge	d			19 55			20 21		20 28				20 55			21 21	21 28			21 55	22 21			22 28	
Foxton	d			20 05									21 05							22 05					
Shepreth	d			20 07									21 07							22 07					
Meldreth	d			20 10									21 10							22 10					
Royston	d			20 15					20 42				21 15				21 42			22 15				22 42	
Ashwell & Morden	d			20 20									21 20							22 20					
Baldock	d			20 25					20 50				21 25				21 50			22 25				22 50	
Letchworth Garden City	d			20 29					20 53				21 29				21 53			22 29				22 53	
Hitchin 4	d		20 29	20 34					20 57			21 29	21 34				21 57		22 29	22 33				22 57	
Stevenage 4	d	20 29	20 35	20 40					21 03	21 09	21 29	21 35	21 40				22 03	22 29	22 35	22 39		22 45	22 55	23 03	
Hertford North	a	20 42									21 42							22 42							
Knebworth	d			20 43									21 43							22 43					
Welwyn North	d			20 47									21 47							22 47					
Welwyn Garden City 4	d			20 51									21 51							22 51					
Hatfield	d			20 54									21 54							22 54					
Potters Bar	d			21 00									22 00							23 00					
Finsbury Park ⊖	d	21 17	20 54	21 10					21 21		22 17	21 54	22 10				22 21	23 17	22 54	23 10				23 21	
London Kings Cross 15 ⊖	a	21 25	21 01	21 19			21 10		21 28	21 37	22 25	22 03	22 19			22 10	22 28	23 26	23 01	23 19	23 08	23 16	23 22	23 29	

		FC	FC 1	GR R 1	FC 1	FC 1
Peterborough 8	d		22 57	23 00		
Huntingdon	d		23 11			
St Neots	d		23 18			
Sandy	d		23 26			
Biggleswade	d		23 29			
Arlesey	d		23 34			
Cambridge	d					23 14
Foxton	d					
Shepreth	d					
Meldreth	d					
Royston	d					23 29
Ashwell & Morden	d					
Baldock	d					23 37
Letchworth Garden City	d					23 40
Hitchin 4	d		23 40		←	23 44
Stevenage 4	d	23 29	23 45	23s34	23 45	23 49
Hertford North	a	23 42	→			
Knebworth	d					23 52
Welwyn North	d					23 56
Welwyn Garden City 4	d					23 59
Hatfield	d					00 02
Potters Bar	d					00 08
Finsbury Park ⊖	d	00 17			00 11	00 21
London Kings Cross 15 ⊖	a	00 26		00 02	00 20	00 33

Table 25

Sundays

26 June to 31 July

Peterborough, Cambridge and Stevenage - London

		FC	FC	FC	FC	FC	FC	FC	FC	FC		FC	FC	FC	FC	FC	FC	FC	FC	FC		FC	GR	FC	FC
																							R		
		1	1	1	1	1	1	1	1	1		1	1	1	1		1	1	1	1		1	1	1	1
																							🍴		
Peterborough 8	d	05 46		06 46		07 46			08 46			09 15										09 46	10 00		10 15
Huntingdon	d	06 00		07 00		08 00			09 01			09 30										10 00			10 30
St Neots	d	06 08		07 08		08 08			09 09			09 37										10 08			10 37
Sandy	d	06 15		07 15		08 15			09 16													10 15			
Biggleswade	d	06 19		07 19		08 19			09 20			09 45										10 19			10 45
Arlesey	d	06 24		07 24		08 24			09 25													10 24			
Cambridge	d		06 28		07 28		07 55	08 28		08 55			09 28	09 55	10 28		10 55	11 28	11 55	12 28					
Foxton	d						08 05			09 05				10 05			11 05		12 05						
Shepreth	d						08 07			09 07				10 07			11 07		12 07						
Meldreth	d						08 10			09 10				10 10			11 10		12 10						
Royston	d		06 43		07 43		08 15	08 43		09 15			09 43	10 15	10 43		11 15	11 43	12 15	12 43					
Ashwell & Morden	d						08 20			09 20				10 20			11 20		12 20						
Baldock	d		06a51		07a51		08a26	08a51		09a25			09a51	10a25	10a51		11a25	11a51	12a25	12a51					
Letchworth Garden City	d																								
Hitchin 4	d	06 37		07 36		08 35			09 44			10 07											10 31	←	
Stevenage 4	d	06 45		07 52		08 52			10 01							10 29						10 44	10 36	10 44	
Hertford North	a															10 42						↪			
Knebworth	d	06 49																							
Welwyn North	d	06 53		08 08																					
Welwyn Garden City 4	d	06 56		08 12																					
Hatfield	d	06 59		08 15																					
Potters Bar	d	07 05		08 21																					
Finsbury Park ⊖	d	07 17		08 31		09 20			10 30							11 17								11 02	
London Kings Cross 15 ⊖	a	07 25		08 38		09 27			10 37			10 58				11 25							11 07	11 09	11 20

		GR	FC	FC		FC		GR	FC	FC	FC		FC		FC	FC		FC	FC		FC	FC	GR	FC	FC
		R						R															R		
		1		1		1		1		1	1		1		1			1	1		1	1	1		1
		🍴						🍴															🍴		
Peterborough 8	d	10 32		10 46		11 46		12 34		12 46								13 46					14 32		14 46
Huntingdon	d			11 00		12 00				13 00								14 00							15 00
St Neots	d			11 08		12 08				13 08								14 08							15 08
Sandy	d			11 15		12 15				13 15								14 15							15 15
Biggleswade	d			11 19		12 19				13 19								14 19							15 19
Arlesey	d			11 24		12 24				13 24								14 24							15 24
Cambridge	d										12 55		13 20		13 28				13 55		14 20	14 28			
Foxton	d										13 05								14 05						
Shepreth	d										13 07								14 07						
Meldreth	d										13 10								14 10						
Royston	d										13 15				13 42				14 15			14 42			
Ashwell & Morden	d										13 20								14 20						
Baldock	d										13 25				13 50				14 25			14 50			
Letchworth Garden City	d										13 29				13 53				14 29			14 53			
Hitchin 4	d			11 29		12 30				13 29	13 34				13 57			14 29	14 34			14 57			15 29
Stevenage 4	d	11 01	11 29	11 35		12 36		13 07	13 29	13 35	13 40				14 03	14 29		14 35	14 40			15 03	15 05	15 29	15 35
Hertford North	a		11 42						13 42							14 42								15 42	
Knebworth	d										13 43								14 43						
Welwyn North	d										13 47								14 47						
Welwyn Garden City 4	d										13 51								14 51						
Hatfield	d										13 54								14 54						
Potters Bar	d										14 00								15 00						
Finsbury Park ⊖	d		12 17	11 58		12 58			14 17	13 54	14 11				14 21	15 17		14 54	15 10			15 21		16 17	15 54
London Kings Cross 15 ⊖	a	11 37	12 25	12 05		13 05		13 35	14 25	14 01	14 19		14 08		14 28	15 25		15 01	15 19		15 08	15 28	15 35	16 25	16 01

		FC			FC	FC	FC	FC	FC		FC			FC	GR	FC	FC	FC		FC	FC	GR		FC	FC
															R							R			
		1			1	1		1	1		1			1	1		1	1		1	1	1			1
															🍴							🍴			
Peterborough 8	d							15 46							16 32		16 46								17 46
Huntingdon	d							16 00									17 00								18 00
St Neots	d							16 08									17 08								18 08
Sandy	d							16 15									17 15								18 15
Biggleswade	d							16 19									17 19								18 19
Arlesey	d							16 24									17 24								18 24
Cambridge	d	14 55			15 20	15 28			15 55		16 20			16 28				16 55		17 20	17 28				
Foxton	d	15 05							16 05									17 05							
Shepreth	d	15 07							16 07									17 07							
Meldreth	d	15 10							16 10									17 10							
Royston	d	15 15				15 42			16 15					16 42				17 15			17 42				
Ashwell & Morden	d	15 20							16 20									17 20							
Baldock	d	15 25				15 50			16 25					16 50				17 25			17 50				
Letchworth Garden City	d	15 29				15 53			16 29					16 53				17 29			17 53				
Hitchin 4	d	15 34				15 57		16 29	16 34					16 57			17 29	17 34			17 57				18 29
Stevenage 4	d	15 40				16 03	16 29	16 35	16 40					17 03	17 04	17 29	17 35	17 40			18 03	18 04		18 29	18 35
Hertford North	a						16 42									17 42								18 42	
Knebworth	d	15 43							16 43									17 43							
Welwyn North	d	15 47							16 47									17 47							
Welwyn Garden City 4	d	15 51							16 51									17 51							
Hatfield	d	15 54							16 54									17 54							
Potters Bar	d	16 00							17 00									18 00							
Finsbury Park ⊖	d	16 10				16 21	17 17	16 54	17 10					17 21		18 17	17 54	18 10			18 21			19 17	18 54
London Kings Cross 15 ⊖	a	16 19			16 08	16 29	17 25	17 01	17 19		17 08			17 28	17 35	18 25	18 01	18 19		18 08	18 28	18 36		19 25	19 01

Table 25

Sundays
26 June to 31 July

Peterborough, Cambridge and Stevenage - London

		FC		FC		FC	FC	GR		FC	FC	FC		FC	FC	GR	FC	FC		FC		FC		FC	GR
		1		1		1	1	R 1			1	1		1	1	R 1		1		1		1		1	R 1
Peterborough 8	d										18 46							19 46							
Huntingdon	d										19 00							20 00							
St Neots	d										19 08							20 08							
Sandy	d										19 15							20 15							
Biggleswade	d										19 19							20 19							
Arlesey	d										19 24							20 24							
Cambridge	d	17 55		18 21		18 28	18 45					18 55		19 21	19 28					19 55		20 21		20 28	
Foxton	d	18 05										19 05								20 05					
Shepreth	d	18 07										19 07								20 07					
Meldreth	d	18 10										19 10								20 10					
Royston	d	18 15				18 42						19 15			19 42					20 15				20 42	
Ashwell & Morden	d	18 20										19 20								20 20					
Baldock	d	18 25				18 50						19 25			19 50					20 25				20 50	
Letchworth Garden City	d	18 29				18 53						19 29			19 53					20 29				20 53	
Hitchin 4	d	18 34				18 57					19 29	19 34			19 57			20 29		20 34				20 57	
Stevenage 4	d	18 40				19 03		19 11		19 29	19 35	19 40			20 03	20 08	20 29	20 35		20 40				21 03	21 09
Hertford North	a									19 42							20 42								
Knebworth	d	18 43										19 43								20 43					
Welwyn North	d	18 47										19 47								20 47					
Welwyn Garden City 4	d	18 51										19 51								20 51					
Hatfield	d	18 54										19 54								20 54					
Potters Bar	d	19 00										20 00								21 00					
Finsbury Park ⊖	d	19 10				19 21				20 17	19 54	20 10			20 21		21 17	20 54		21 10				21 21	
London Kings Cross 15 ⊖	a	19 19		19 10		19 28	19 38	19 38		20 25	20 01	20 19		20 11	20 28	20 36	21 25	21 01		21 19		21 10		21 28	21 37

		FC	FC	FC			FC	FC	FC	FC	FC	FC	GR	GR		FC	FC	FC	GR	FC	FC				
			1	1			1	1		1	1	1	R 1	R 1		1		1	R 1	1	1				
Peterborough 8	d		20 46							21 46			22 13	22 23				22 57	23 00						
Huntingdon	d		21 00							22 00								23 11							
St Neots	d		21 08							22 08								23 18							
Sandy	d		21 15							22 15								23 26							
Biggleswade	d		21 19							22 19								23 29							
Arlesey	d		21 24							22 24								23 34							
Cambridge	d			20 55			21 21	21 28			21 55	22 21				22 28					23 14				
Foxton	d			21 05							22 05														
Shepreth	d			21 07							22 07														
Meldreth	d			21 10							22 10														
Royston	d			21 15				21 42			22 15					22 42					23 29				
Ashwell & Morden	d			21 20							22 20														
Baldock	d			21 25				21 50			22 25					22 50					23 37				
Letchworth Garden City	d			21 29				21 53			22 29					22 53					23 40				
Hitchin 4	d		21 29	21 34				21 57		22 29	22 33					22 57		23 40		←	23 44				
Stevenage 4	d	21 29	21 35	21 40				22 03	22 29	22 35	22 39		22 45	22 55		23 03	23 29	23 45	23s34	23 45	23 49				
Hertford North	a	21 42							22 42								23 42	↪							
Knebworth	d			21 43							22 43										23 52				
Welwyn North	d			21 47							22 47										23 56				
Welwyn Garden City 4	d			21 51							22 51										23 59				
Hatfield	d			21 54							22 54										00 02				
Potters Bar	d			22 00							23 00										00 08				
Finsbury Park ⊖	d	22 17	21 54	22 10				22 21	23 17	22 54	23 10					23 21	00 17			00 11	00 21				
London Kings Cross 15 ⊖	a	22 25	22 03	22 19			22 10	22 28	23 26	23 01	23 19	23 08	23 16	23 22		23 29	00 26		00 02	00 20	00 33				

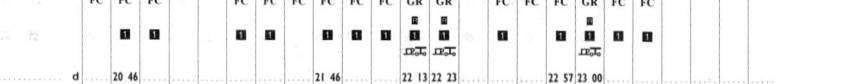

Sundays
7 August to 11 September

		FC	FC	FC	FC	FC	FC	FC	FC	FC		FC	FC	FC	FC	FC	FC	FC	FC	FC		FC	FC	FC	FC
		1	1	1	1		1	1	1	1		1	1	1	1	1	1	1		1		1	1	1	1
Peterborough 8	d	22p46		05 46			06 46		07 46				08 46			09 15				09 46				10 15	
Huntingdon	d	23p00		06 00			07 00		08 00				09 00			09 30				10 00				10 30	
St Neots	d	23p08		06 08			07 08		08 08				09 08			09 37				10 08				10 37	
Sandy	d	23p15		06 15			07 15		08 15				09 15							10 15					
Biggleswade	d	23p19		06 19			07 19		08 19				09 19			09 45				10 19				10 45	
Arlesey	d	23p24		06 24			07 24		08 24				09 24							10 24					
Cambridge	d		23p15		06 28			07 28		07 55		08 28		08 55	09 20		09 28					09 55	10 20		10 28
Foxton	d		23p24							08 05				09 05								10 05			
Shepreth	d		23p27							08 07				09 07								10 07			
Meldreth	d		23p30							08 10				09 10								10 10			
Royston	d		23p34		06 43			07 43		08 15		08 42		09 15			09 42					10 15			10 42
Ashwell & Morden	d		23p39							08 20				09 20								10 20			
Baldock	d		23p43		06 51			07 51		08 25		08 50		09 25			09 50					10 25			10 50
Letchworth Garden City	d		23p46		06 54			07 54		08 29		08 53		09 29			09 53	10 00				10 29			10 53
Hitchin 4	d	23p29	23p50	06 34	06 58		07 34	07 59	08 29	08 33		08 57	09 29	09 33			09 57	10 04		10 29		10 33			10 57
Stevenage 4	d	23p35	23p55	06 40	07 04	07 29	07 40	08 05	08 35	08 39		09 03	09 35	09 39			10 03	10 10	10 29	10 35		10 39			11 03
Hertford North	a					07 42													10 42						
Knebworth	d		23p59	06 43			07 43			08 43				09 43				10 13				10 43			
Welwyn North	d		00 06	06 47			07 47			08 47				09 47				10 17				10 47			
Welwyn Garden City 4	d		00 09	06 51			07 51			08 51				09 51				10 21				10 50			
Hatfield	d		00 13	06 54			07 54			08 54				09 54				10 24				10 54			
Potters Bar	d		00 18	07 00			08 00			09 00				10 00				10 30				10 59			
Finsbury Park ⊖	d	00 04	00s32	07 10	07 32	08 17	08 10	08 22	08 54	09 10		09 21	09 54	10 10			10 21	10 40	11 17	10 54		11 11			11 21
London Kings Cross 15 ⊖	a	00 12	00 40	07 20	07 39	08 26	08 20	08 30	09 01	09 19		09 28	10 01	10 19	10 08	10 15	10 28	10 49	11 25	11 01		11 20	11 08	11 15	11 28

Table 25

Sundays

7 August to 11 September

Peterborough, Cambridge and Stevenage - London

		GR	FC	FC	FC			FC	FC	FC	FC	GR	FC	FC	FC			FC		FC	FC	FC	FC		FC
		R										R													
		1	1	1	1			1	1	1	1	1		1	1			1		1		1	1		1
		(trolley)										(trolley)													
Peterborough 8	d	10 32	10 46						11 46			12 34		12 46								13 46			
Huntingdon	d		11 00						12 00					13 00								14 00			
St Neots	d		11 08						12 08					13 08								14 08			
Sandy	d		11 15						12 15					13 15								14 15			
Biggleswade	d		11 19						12 19					13 19								14 19			
Arlesey	d		11 24						12 24					13 24								14 24			
Cambridge	d			10 55	11 20			11 28		11 55	12 28				12 55			13 20		13 28			13 55		14 20
Foxton	d			11 05						12 05					13 05								14 05		
Shepreth	d			11 07						12 07					13 07								14 07		
Meldreth	d			11 10						12 10					13 10								14 10		
Royston	d			11 15				11 42		12 15	12 42				13 15					13 42			14 15		
Ashwell & Morden	d			11 20						12 20					13 20								14 20		
Baldock	d			11 25				11 50		12 25	12 50				13 25					13 50			14 25		
Letchworth Garden City	d			11 29				11 53		12 29	12 53				13 29					13 53			14 29		
Hitchin 4	d		11 29	11 33				11 57	12 29	12 33	12 57			13 29	13 34					13 57		14 29	14 34		
Stevenage 4	d	11 04	11 35	11 39				12 03	12 35	12 39	13 03	13 07	13 29	13 35	13 40					14 03	14 29	14 35	14 40		
Hertford North	a												13 42								14 42				
Knebworth	d			11 43						12 43					13 43								14 43		
Welwyn North	d			11 47						12 47					13 47								14 47		
Welwyn Garden City 4	d			11 51						12 50					13 51								14 51		
Hatfield	d			11 54						12 54					13 54								14 54		
Potters Bar	d			12 00						13 00					14 00								15 00		
Finsbury Park ⊖	d		11 54	12 10				12 21	12 54	13 11	13 21		14 17	13 54	14 11					14 21	15 17	14 54	15 10		
London Kings Cross 15 ⊖	a	11 35	12 01	12 19	12 08			12 28	13 01	13 19	13 28	13 35	14 25	14 01	14 19			14 08		14 28	15 25	15 01	15 19		15 08

		FC		GR	FC	FC	FC		FC	FC	FC	FC		FC		FC		FC	GR	FC	FC	FC			FC
				R															R						
		1		1		1	1		1	1		1		1		1		1	1		1	1			1
				(trolley)															(trolley)						
Peterborough 8	d			14 32		14 46						15 46							16 32		16 46				
Huntingdon	d					15 00						16 00									17 00				
St Neots	d					15 08						16 08									17 08				
Sandy	d					15 15						16 15									17 15				
Biggleswade	d					15 19						16 19									17 19				
Arlesey	d					15 24						16 24									17 24				
Cambridge	d	14 28					14 55		15 20	15 28				15 55		16 20		16 28				16 55			17 20
Foxton	d						15 05							16 05								17 05			
Shepreth	d						15 07							16 07								17 07			
Meldreth	d						15 10							16 10								17 10			
Royston	d	14 42					15 15			15 42				16 15				16 42				17 15			
Ashwell & Morden	d						15 20							16 20								17 20			
Baldock	d	14 50					15 25			15 50				16 25				16 50				17 25			
Letchworth Garden City	d	14 53					15 29			15 53				16 29				16 53				17 29			
Hitchin 4	d	14 57				15 29	15 34			15 57		16 29		16 34				16 57			17 29	17 34			
Stevenage 4	d	15 03		15 05	15 29	15 35	15 40			16 03	16 29	16 35		16 40				17 03	17 04	17 29	17 35	17 40			
Hertford North	a				15 42						16 42									17 42					
Knebworth	d						15 43							16 43								17 43			
Welwyn North	d						15 47							16 47								17 47			
Welwyn Garden City 4	d						15 51							16 51								17 51			
Hatfield	d						15 54							16 54								17 54			
Potters Bar	d						16 00							17 00								18 00			
Finsbury Park ⊖	d	15 21			16 17	15 54	16 10			16 21	17 17	16 54		17 10				17 21		18 17	17 54	18 10			
London Kings Cross 15 ⊖	a	15 28		15 35	16 25	16 01	16 19		16 08	16 29	17 25	17 01		17 19		17 08		17 28	17 35	18 25	18 01	18 19			18 08

		FC	GR	FC	FC	FC		FC			FC	FC	GR	FC	FC	FC		FC		FC	GR	FC	FC	FC	
			R										R								R				
		1	1		1	1		1			1	1	1		1	1		1		1	1		1	1	
			(trolley)										(trolley)								(trolley)				
Peterborough 8	d				17 46										18 46								19 46		
Huntingdon	d				18 00										19 00								20 00		
St Neots	d				18 08										19 08								20 08		
Sandy	d				18 15										19 15								20 15		
Biggleswade	d				18 19										19 19								20 19		
Arlesey	d				18 24										19 24								20 24		
Cambridge	d	17 28				17 55		18 21			18 28	18 45				18 55		19 21		19 28				19 55	
Foxton	d					18 05										19 05								20 05	
Shepreth	d					18 07										19 07								20 07	
Meldreth	d					18 10										19 10								20 10	
Royston	d	17 42				18 15					18 42					19 15				19 42				20 15	
Ashwell & Morden	d					18 20										19 20								20 20	
Baldock	d	17 50				18 25					18 50					19 25				19 50				20 25	
Letchworth Garden City	d	17 53				18 29					18 53					19 29				19 53				20 29	
Hitchin 4	d	17 57			18 29	18 34					18 57				19 29	19 34				19 57			20 29	20 34	
Stevenage 4	d	18 03	18 04	18 29	18 35	18 40					19 03		19 11	19 29	19 35	19 40				20 03	20 08	20 29	20 35	20 40	
Hertford North	a			18 42										19 42								20 42			
Knebworth	d					18 43										19 43								20 43	
Welwyn North	d					18 47										19 47								20 47	
Welwyn Garden City 4	d					18 51										19 51								20 51	
Hatfield	d					18 54										19 54								20 54	
Potters Bar	d					19 00										20 00								21 00	
Finsbury Park ⊖	d	18 21		19 17	18 54	19 10					19 21			20 17	19 54	20 10				20 21		21 17	20 54	21 10	
London Kings Cross 15 ⊖	a	18 28	18 36	19 25	19 01	19 19		19 10			19 28	19 38	19 38	20 25	20 01	20 19		20 11		20 28	20 36	21 25	21 01	21 19	

Table 25

Sundays

7 August to 11 September

Peterborough, Cambridge and Stevenage - London

		FC		FC		GR	FC	FC	FC		FC	FC	FC	FC		FC	FC	GR	GR	FC	FC	FC	GR	FC	FC
						R												R	R				R		1
		1		1		1		1	1		1	1		1		1	1	1	1	1		1	1	1	
						[trolley]												[trolley]	[trolley]				[trolley]		
Peterborough 8	d							20 46						21 46				22 13	22 23			22 57	23 00		
Huntingdon	d							21 00						22 00								23 11			
St Neots	d							21 08						22 08								23 18			
Sandy	d							21 15						22 15								23 26			
Biggleswade	d							21 19						22 19								23 29			23 14
Arlesey	d							21 24						22 24								23 34			
Cambridge	d	20 21		20 28					20 55		21 21	21 28				21 55	22 21			22 28					
Foxton	d								21 05							22 05									
Shepreth	d								21 07							22 07									23 29
Meldreth	d								21 10							22 10									
Royston	d			20 42					21 15			21 42				22 15				22 42					23 37
Ashwell & Morden	d								21 20							22 20									23 40
Baldock	d			20 50					21 25			21 50				22 25				22 50					23 44
Letchworth Garden City	d			20 53					21 29			21 53				22 29				22 53					23 49
Hitchin 4	d			20 57				21 29	21 34			21 57		22 29		22 33				22 57		23 40		←	
Stevenage 4	d			21 03		21 09	21 29	21 35	21 40			22 03	22 29	22 35		22 39		22 45	22 55	23 03	23 29	23 45	23s34	23 45	23 52
Hertford North	a						21 42						22 42								23 42	→			23 56
Knebworth	d								21 43							22 43									23 59
Welwyn North	d								21 47							22 47									00 02
Welwyn Garden City 4	d								21 51							22 51									00 08
Hatfield	d								21 54							22 54									00 21
Potters Bar	d								22 00							23 00									00 33
Finsbury Park ⊖	d			21 21			22 17	21 54	22 10			22 21	23 17	22 54		23 10				23 21	00 17			00 11	FC
London Kings Cross 15 ⊖	a	21 10		21 28		21 37	22 25	22 03	22 19		22 10	22 28	23 26	23 01		23 19	23 08	23 16	23 22	23 29	00 26		00 02	00 20	1

Sundays

18 September to 23 October

		FC	FC	FC	FC	FC	FC	FC	FC	FC		FC	FC	FC	FC	FC	FC	FC	FC	FC		GR	FC	FC	FC
																						R			
		1	1	1	1	1	1	1	1	1		1	1	1		1	1	1	1	1		1	1	1	1
																						[trolley]			
Peterborough 8	d	22p46					07 46									09 46			10 15			10 32	10 46		
Huntingdon	d	23p00					08 00									10 00			10 30				11 00		
St Neots	d	23p08					08 08									10 08			10 37				11 08		
Sandy	d	23p15					08 15									10 15							11 15		
Biggleswade	d	23p19					08 19									10 19			10 45				11 19		
Arlesey	d	23p24					08 24									10 24							11 24		
Cambridge	d		23p15		06 28	07 28		07 55	08 28	08 55		09 20	09 28				09 55	10 20		10 28				10 55	11 20
Foxton	d		23p24					08 05		09 05							10 05							11 05	
Shepreth	d		23p27					08 07		09 07							10 07							11 07	
Meldreth	d		23p30					08 10		09 10							10 10							11 10	
Royston	d		23p34		06 43	07 43		08 15	08 42	09 15			09 42				10 15			10 42				11 15	
Ashwell & Morden	d		23p39					08 20		09 20							10 20							11 20	
Baldock	d		23p43		06 51	07 51		08 25	08 50	09 25			09 50				10 25			10 50				11 25	
Letchworth Garden City	d		23p46	06 29	06 54	07 54		08 29	08 53	09 29			09 53	10 00			10 29			10 53				11 29	
Hitchin 4	d	23p29	23p50	06 34	06 58	07 59	08 29	08 33	08 57	09 33			09 57	10 04		10 29	10 33			10 57			11 29	11 33	
Stevenage 4	d	23p35	23p55	06 40	07 04	08 05	08 35	08 39	09 03	09 39			10 03	10 10	10 29	10 35	10 39			11 03		11 04	11 35	11 39	
Hertford North	a														10 42										
Knebworth	d		23p59	06 43				08 43		09 43				10 13			10 43							11 43	
Welwyn North	d		00 06	06 47				08 47		09 47				10 17			10 47							11 47	
Welwyn Garden City 4	d		00 09	06 51				08 51		09 51				10 21			10 50							11 51	
Hatfield	d		00 13	06 54				08 54		09 54				10 24			10 54							11 54	
Potters Bar	d		00 18	07 00				09 00		10 00				10 30			10 59							12 00	
Finsbury Park ⊖	d	00 04	00s32	07 10	07 32	08 22	08 54	09 10	09 21	10 10			10 21	10 40	11 17	10 54	11 11			11 21			11 54	12 10	
London Kings Cross 15 ⊖	a	00 12	00 40	07 20	07 39	08 30	09 01	09 19	09 28	10 19		10 08	10 28	10 49	11 25	11 01	11 20	11 08	11 15	11 28		11 35	12 01	12 19	12 08

			FC	FC	FC	FC		GR	FC	FC	FC		FC		FC	FC		FC	FC		FC	FC	GR	FC	FC
								R															R		
			1	1	1	1		1		1	1		1		1			1	1		1	1	1		1
								[trolley]															[trolley]		
Peterborough 8	d			11 46				12 34		12 46								13 46					14 32		14 46
Huntingdon	d			12 00						13 00								14 00							15 00
St Neots	d			12 08						13 08								14 08							15 08
Sandy	d			12 15						13 15								14 15							15 15
Biggleswade	d			12 19						13 19								14 19							15 19
Arlesey	d			12 24						13 24								14 24							15 24
Cambridge	d		11 28		11 55	12 28					12 55		13 20		13 28				13 55		14 20	14 28			
Foxton	d				12 05						13 05								14 05						
Shepreth	d				12 07						13 07								14 07						
Meldreth	d				12 10						13 10								14 10						
Royston	d		11 42		12 15	12 42					13 15				13 42				14 15			14 42			
Ashwell & Morden	d				12 20						13 20								14 20						
Baldock	d		11 50		12 25	12 50					13 25				13 50				14 25			14 50			
Letchworth Garden City	d		11 53		12 29	12 53					13 29				13 53				14 29			14 53			
Hitchin 4	d		11 57	12 29	12 33	12 57				13 29	13 34				13 57			14 29	14 34			14 57			15 29
Stevenage 4	d		12 03	12 35	12 39	13 03		13 07	13 29	13 35	13 40				14 03	14 29		14 35	14 40			15 03	15 05	15 29	15 35
Hertford North	a								13 42							14 42								15 42	
Knebworth	d				12 43						13 43								14 43						
Welwyn North	d				12 47						13 47								14 47						
Welwyn Garden City 4	d				12 50						13 51								14 51						
Hatfield	d				12 54						13 54								14 54						
Potters Bar	d				13 00						14 00								15 00						
Finsbury Park ⊖	d		12 21	12 54	13 11	13 21			14 17	13 54	14 11				14 21	15 17		14 54	15 10			15 21		16 17	15 54
London Kings Cross 15 ⊖	a		12 28	13 01	13 19	13 28		13 35	14 25	14 01	14 19		14 08		14 28	15 25		15 01	15 19		15 08	15 28	15 35	16 25	16 01

Table 25

Sundays

18 September to 23 October

Peterborough, Cambridge and Stevenage - London

		FC			FC	FC	FC	FC	FC		FC			FC	GR	FC	FC	FC		FC	FC	GR		FC	FC
															R							R			
		1			1	1		1	1		1			1	1		1	1		1	1	1			1
															Trolley							Trolley			
Peterborough 8	d							15 46							16 32		16 46								17 46
Huntingdon	d							16 00									17 00								18 00
St Neots	d							16 08									17 08								18 08
Sandy	d							16 15									17 15								18 15
Biggleswade	d							16 19									17 19								18 19
Arlesey	d							16 24									17 24								18 24
Cambridge	d	14 55			15 20	15 28			15 55		16 20			16 28				16 55		17 20	17 28				
Foxton	d	15 05							16 05									17 05							
Shepreth	d	15 07							16 07									17 07							
Meldreth	d	15 10							16 10									17 10							
Royston	d	15 15				15 42			16 15					16 42				17 15			17 42				
Ashwell & Morden	d	15 20							16 20									17 20							
Baldock	d	15 25				15 50			16 25					16 50				17 25			17 50				
Letchworth Garden City	d	15 29				15 53			16 29					16 53				17 29			17 53				
Hitchin 4	d	15 34				15 57		16 29	16 34					16 57			17 29	17 34			17 57				18 29
Stevenage 4	d	15 40				16 03	16 29	16 35	16 40					17 03	17 04	17 29	17 35	17 40			18 03	18 04		18 29	18 35
Hertford North	a						16 42									17 42								18 42	
Knebworth	d	15 43							16 43									17 43							
Welwyn North	d	15 47							16 47									17 47							
Welwyn Garden City 4	d	15 51							16 51									17 51							
Hatfield	d	15 54							16 54									17 54							
Potters Bar	d	16 00							17 00									18 00							
Finsbury Park	⊖ d	16 10				16 21	17 17	16 54	17 10					17 21		18 17	17 54	18 10			18 21			19 17	18 54
London Kings Cross 15	⊖ a	16 19			16 08	16 29	17 25	17 01	17 19		17 08			17 28	17 35	18 25	18 01	18 19		18 08	18 28	18 36		19 25	19 01

		FC		FC		FC	FC	GR		FC	FC	FC		FC	FC	GR	FC	FC		FC		FC		FC	GR
								R								R									R
		1		1		1	1	1			1	1		1	1	1		1		1		1		1	1
								Trolley								Trolley									Trolley
Peterborough 8	d										18 46							19 46							
Huntingdon	d										19 00							20 00							
St Neots	d										19 08							20 08							
Sandy	d										19 15							20 15							
Biggleswade	d										19 19							20 19							
Arlesey	d										19 24							20 24							
Cambridge	d	17 55		18 21		18 28	18 45					18 55		19 21	19 28					19 55		20 21		20 28	
Foxton	d	18 05										19 05								20 05					
Shepreth	d	18 07										19 07								20 07					
Meldreth	d	18 10										19 10								20 10					
Royston	d	18 15				18 42						19 15			19 42					20 15				20 42	
Ashwell & Morden	d	18 20										19 20								20 20					
Baldock	d	18 25				18 50						19 25			19 50					20 25				20 50	
Letchworth Garden City	d	18 29				18 53						19 29			19 53					20 29				20 53	
Hitchin 4	d	18 34				18 57					19 29	19 34			19 57			20 29		20 34				20 57	
Stevenage 4	d	18 40				19 03		19 11		19 29	19 35	19 40			20 03	20 08	20 29	20 35		20 40				21 03	21 09
Hertford North	a									19 42							20 42								
Knebworth	d	18 43										19 43								20 43					
Welwyn North	d	18 47										19 47								20 47					
Welwyn Garden City 4	d	18 51										19 51								20 51					
Hatfield	d	18 54										19 54								20 54					
Potters Bar	d	19 00										20 00								21 00					
Finsbury Park	⊖ d	19 10				19 21				20 17	19 54	20 10			20 21		21 17	20 54		21 10				21 21	
London Kings Cross 15	⊖ a	19 19		19 10		19 28	19 38	19 38		20 25	20 01	20 19		20 11	20 28	20 36	21 25	21 01		21 19		21 10		21 28	21 37

		FC	FC	FC			FC	FC	FC	FC	FC	FC	GR	GR		FC	FC	FC	GR	FC	FC				
													R	R					R						
			1	1			1	1		1	1	1	1	1		1		1	1	1	1				
													Trolley	Trolley					Trolley						
Peterborough 8	d		20 46							21 46			22 13	22 23				22 57	23 00						
Huntingdon	d		21 00							22 00								23 11							
St Neots	d		21 08							22 08								23 18							
Sandy	d		21 15							22 15								23 26							
Biggleswade	d		21 19							22 19								23 29							
Arlesey	d		21 24							22 24								23 34							
Cambridge	d			20 55			21 21	21 28			21 55	22 21				22 28					23 14				
Foxton	d			21 05							22 05														
Shepreth	d			21 07							22 07														
Meldreth	d			21 10							22 10														
Royston	d			21 15				21 42			22 15					22 42					23 29				
Ashwell & Morden	d			21 20							22 20														
Baldock	d			21 25				21 50			22 25					22 50					23 37				
Letchworth Garden City	d			21 29				21 53			22 29					22 53					23 40				
Hitchin 4	d		21 29	21 34				21 57		22 29	22 33					22 57		23 40		←	23 44				
Stevenage 4	d	21 29	21 35	21 40				22 03	22 29	22 35	22 39		22 45	22 55		23 03	23 29	23 45	23s34	23 45	23 49				
Hertford North	a	21 42							22 42								23 42	→							
Knebworth	d			21 43							22 43										23 52				
Welwyn North	d			21 47							22 47										23 56				
Welwyn Garden City 4	d			21 51							22 51										23 59				
Hatfield	d			21 54							22 54										00 02				
Potters Bar	d			22 00							23 00										00 08				
Finsbury Park	⊖ d	22 17	21 54	22 10				22 21	23 17	22 54	23 10					23 21	00 17			00 11	00 21				
London Kings Cross 15	⊖ a	22 25	22 03	22 19			22 10	22 28	23 26	23 01	23 19	23 08	23 16	23 22		23 29	00 26		00 02	00 20	00 33				

Table 25

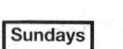

Sundays
from 30 October

Peterborough, Cambridge and Stevenage - London

		FC 1	FC 1	FC 1	FC 1	FC	FC 1	FC 1	FC	FC 1		FC 1	FC 1	FC	FC 1	FC 1	FC 1	FC 1	FC 1	FC 1		FC	FC 1	FC 1	FC 1
Peterborough 8	d	22p46								07 46					08 46			09 15					09 46		
Huntingdon	d	23p00								08 00					09 00			09 30					10 00		
St Neots	d	23p08								08 08					09 08			09 37					10 08		
Sandy	d	23p15								08 15					09 15								10 15		
Biggleswade	d	23p19								08 19					09 19			09 45					10 19		
Arlesey	d	23p24								08 24					09 24								10 24		
Cambridge	d		23p15		06 28			07 28				07 55	08 28			08 55	09 20		09 28					09 55	10 20
Foxton	d		23p24									08 05				09 05								10 05	
Shepreth	d		23p27									08 07				09 07								10 07	
Meldreth	d		23p30									08 10				09 10								10 10	
Royston	d		23p34		06 43			07 43				08 15	08 42			09 15			09 42					10 15	
Ashwell & Morden	d		23p39									08 20				09 20								10 20	
Baldock	d		23p43		06 51			07 51				08 25	08 50			09 25			09 50					10 25	
Letchworth Garden City	d		23p46	06 29	06 54		07 29	07 54				08 29	08 53			09 29			09 53	10 00				10 29	
Hitchin 4	d	23p29	23p50	06 34	06 58		07 34	07 59		08 29		08 33	08 57		09 29	09 33			09 57	10 04			10 29	10 33	
Stevenage 4	d	23p35	23p55	06 40	07 04	07 29	07 40	08 05	08 29	08 35		08 39	09 03	09 29	09 35	09 39			10 03	10 10		10 29	10 35	10 39	
Hertford North	a					07 42			08 42					09 42								10 42			
Knebworth	d		23p59	06 43			07 43					08 43				09 43				10 13				10 43	
Welwyn North	d		00 06	06 47			07 47					08 47				09 47				10 17				10 47	
Welwyn Garden City 4	d		00 09	06 51			07 51					08 51				09 51				10 21				10 50	
Hatfield	d		00 13	06 54			07 54					08 54				09 54				10 24				10 54	
Potters Bar	d		00 18	07 00			08 00					09 00				10 00				10 30				10 59	
Finsbury Park ⊖	d	00 04	00s32	07 10	07 32	08 17	08 09	08 22	09 17	08 54		09 10	09 21	10 17	09 54	10 10			10 21	10 40		11 17	10 54	11 11	
London Kings Cross 15 ⊖	a	00 12	00 40	07 20	07 39	08 26	08 20	08 30	09 25	09 01		09 19	09 28	10 25	10 01	10 19	10 08	10 15	10 28	10 49		11 25	11 01	11 20	11 08

		FC 1	FC 1	GR R 1	FC	FC 1		FC 1	FC 1		FC 1	FC 1	FC 1	FC 1	GR R 1	FC		FC 1	FC 1		FC 1		FC 1	FC	FC 1
Peterborough 8	d	10 15		10 32		10 46						11 46			12 34			12 46							13 46
Huntingdon	d	10 30				11 00						12 00						13 00							14 00
St Neots	d	10 37				11 08						12 08						13 08							14 08
Sandy	d					11 15						12 15						13 15							14 15
Biggleswade	d	10 45				11 19						12 19						13 19							14 19
Arlesey	d					11 24						12 24						13 24							14 24
Cambridge	d		10 28					10 55	11 20		11 28		11 55	12 28					12 55		13 20		13 28		
Foxton	d							11 05					12 05						13 05						
Shepreth	d							11 07					12 07						13 07						
Meldreth	d							11 10					12 10						13 10						
Royston	d		10 42					11 15			11 42		12 15	12 42					13 15				13 42		
Ashwell & Morden	d							11 20					12 20						13 20						
Baldock	d		10 50					11 25			11 50		12 25	12 50					13 25				13 50		
Letchworth Garden City	d		10 53					11 29			11 53		12 29	12 53					13 29				13 53		
Hitchin 4	d		10 57			11 29		11 33			11 57	12 29	12 33	12 57				13 29	13 34				13 57		14 29
Stevenage 4	d		11 03	11 04	11 29	11 35		11 39			12 03	12 35	12 39	13 03	13 07	13 29		13 35	13 40				14 03	14 29	14 35
Hertford North	a				11 42											13 42								14 42	
Knebworth	d							11 43					12 43						13 43						
Welwyn North	d							11 47					12 47						13 47						
Welwyn Garden City 4	d							11 51					12 50						13 51						
Hatfield	d							11 54					12 54						13 54						
Potters Bar	d							12 00					13 00						14 00						
Finsbury Park ⊖	d		11 21		12 17	11 54		12 10			12 21	12 54	13 11	13 21		14 17		13 54	14 11				14 21	15 17	14 54
London Kings Cross 15 ⊖	a	11 15	11 28	11 35	12 25	12 01		12 19	12 08		12 28	13 01	13 19	13 28	13 35	14 25		14 01	14 19		14 08		14 28	15 25	15 01

		FC 1			FC 1	FC 1	GR R 1	FC	FC 1	FC 1		FC 1		FC 1	FC	FC 1	FC 1		FC 1		FC 1	GR R 1		FC	FC 1
Peterborough 8	d						14 32		14 46							15 46						16 32			16 46
Huntingdon	d								15 00							16 00									17 00
St Neots	d								15 08							16 08									17 08
Sandy	d								15 15							16 15									17 15
Biggleswade	d								15 19							16 19									17 19
Arlesey	d								15 24							16 24									17 24
Cambridge	d	13 55			14 20	14 28				14 55		15 20		15 28			15 55		16 20		16 28				
Foxton	d	14 05								15 05							16 05								
Shepreth	d	14 07								15 07							16 07								
Meldreth	d	14 10								15 10							16 10								
Royston	d	14 15				14 42				15 15				15 42			16 15				16 42				
Ashwell & Morden	d	14 20								15 20							16 20								
Baldock	d	14 25				14 50				15 25				15 50			16 25				16 50				
Letchworth Garden City	d	14 29				14 53				15 29				15 53			16 29				16 53				
Hitchin 4	d	14 34				14 57			15 29	15 34				15 57		16 29	16 34				16 57				17 29
Stevenage 4	d	14 40				15 03	15 05	15 29	15 35	15 40				16 03	16 29	16 35	16 40				17 03	17 04		17 29	17 35
Hertford North	a							15 42							16 42									17 42	
Knebworth	d	14 43								15 43							16 43								
Welwyn North	d	14 47								15 47							16 47								
Welwyn Garden City 4	d	14 51								15 51							16 51								
Hatfield	d	14 54								15 54							16 54								
Potters Bar	d	15 00								16 00							17 00								
Finsbury Park ⊖	d	15 10				15 21		16 17	15 54	16 10				16 21	17 17	16 54	17 10				17 21			18 17	17 54
London Kings Cross 15 ⊖	a	15 19			15 08	15 28	15 35	16 25	16 01	16 19		16 08		16 29	17 25	17 01	17 19		17 08		17 28	17 35		18 25	18 01

Table 25

Sundays
from 30 October

Peterborough, Cambridge and Stevenage - London

		FC		FC	FC	GR	FC	FC		FC		FC		FC	FC	GR	FC	FC		FC		FC	FC	GR	FC
						R										R								R	
		1		1	1	1		1		1		1		1	1	1		1		1		1	1	1	
Peterborough 8	d							17 46										18 46							
Huntingdon	d							18 00										19 00							
St Neots	d							18 08										19 08							
Sandy	d							18 15										19 15							
Biggleswade	d							18 19										19 19							
Arlesey	d							18 24										19 24							
Cambridge	d	16 55		17 20	17 28					17 55		18 21		18 28	18 45					18 55		19 21	19 28		
Foxton	d	17 05								18 05										19 05					
Shepreth	d	17 07								18 07										19 07					
Meldreth	d	17 10								18 10										19 10					
Royston	d	17 15			17 42					18 15				18 42						19 15			19 42		
Ashwell & Morden	d	17 20								18 20										19 20					
Baldock	d	17 25			17 50					18 25				18 50						19 25			19 50		
Letchworth Garden City	d	17 29			17 53					18 29				18 53						19 29			19 53		
Hitchin 4	d	17 34			17 57			18 29		18 34				18 57				19 29		19 34			19 57		
Stevenage 4	d	17 40			18 03	18 04	18 29	18 35		18 40				19 03		19 11	19 29	19 35		19 40			20 03	20 08	20 29
Hertford North	a						18 42										19 42								20 42
Knebworth	d	17 43								18 43										19 43					
Welwyn North	d	17 47								18 47										19 47					
Welwyn Garden City 4	d	17 51								18 51										19 51					
Hatfield	d	17 54								18 54										19 54					
Potters Bar	d	18 00								19 00										20 00					
Finsbury Park ⊖	d	18 10			18 21		19 17	18 54		19 10				19 21			20 17	19 54		20 10			20 21		21 17
London Kings Cross 15 ⊖	a	18 19		18 08	18 28	18 36	19 25	19 01		19 19		19 10		19 28	19 38	19 38	20 25	20 01		20 19		20 11	20 28	20 36	21 25

		FC	FC			FC		FC	GR	FC	FC	FC		FC		FC	FC	FC	FC	FC	GR	GR	FC	FC	
									R												R	R			
		1	1			1		1	1		1	1		1		1		1	1	1	1	1	1		
Peterborough 8	d	19 46									20 46							21 46			22 13	22 23			
Huntingdon	d	20 00									21 00							22 00							
St Neots	d	20 08									21 08							22 08							
Sandy	d	20 15									21 15							22 15							
Biggleswade	d	20 19									21 19							22 19							
Arlesey	d	20 24									21 24							22 24							
Cambridge	d		19 55			20 21		20 28				20 55		21 21		21 28			21 55	22 21			22 28		
Foxton	d		20 05									21 05							22 05						
Shepreth	d		20 07									21 07							22 07						
Meldreth	d		20 10									21 10							22 10						
Royston	d		20 15					20 42				21 15				21 42			22 15				22 42		
Ashwell & Morden	d		20 20									21 20							22 20						
Baldock	d		20 25					20 50				21 25				21 50			22 25				22 50		
Letchworth Garden City	d		20 29					20 53				21 29				21 53			22 29				22 53		
Hitchin 4	d	20 29	20 34					20 57			21 29	21 34				21 57		22 29	22 33				22 57		
Stevenage 4	d	20 35	20 40					21 03	21 09	21 29	21 35	21 40				22 03	22 29	22 35	22 39		22 45	22 55	23 03	23 29	
Hertford North	a									21 42							22 42							23 42	
Knebworth	d		20 43									21 43							22 43						
Welwyn North	d		20 47									21 47							22 47						
Welwyn Garden City 4	d		20 51									21 51							22 51						
Hatfield	d		20 54									21 54							22 54						
Potters Bar	d		21 00									22 00							23 00						
Finsbury Park ⊖	d	20 54	21 10					21 21		22 17	21 54	22 10				22 21	23 17	22 54	23 10				23 21	00 17	
London Kings Cross 15 ⊖	a	21 01	21 19			21 10		21 28	21 37	22 25	22 03	22 19		22 10		22 28	23 26	23 01	23 19	23 08	23 16	23 22	23 29	00 26	

		FC	GR	FC	FC
			R		
		1	1	1	1
Peterborough 8	d	22 57	23 00		
Huntingdon	d	23 11			
St Neots	d	23 18			
Sandy	d	23 26			
Biggleswade	d	23 29			
Arlesey	d	23 34			
Cambridge	d				23 14
Foxton	d				
Shepreth	d				
Meldreth	d				
Royston	d				23 29
Ashwell & Morden	d				
Baldock	d				23 37
Letchworth Garden City	d				23 40
Hitchin 4	d	23 40		←	23 44
Stevenage 4	d	23 45	23s34	23 45	23 49
Hertford North	a	↦			
Knebworth	d				23 52
Welwyn North	d				23 56
Welwyn Garden City 4	d				23 59
Hatfield	d				00 02
Potters Bar	d				00 08
Finsbury Park ⊖	d			00 11	00 21
London Kings Cross 15 ⊖	a		00 02	00 20	00 33

Route Diagram for Table 26

DM-4/10
Design BAJS

© 2010 Network Rail.
All rights reserved

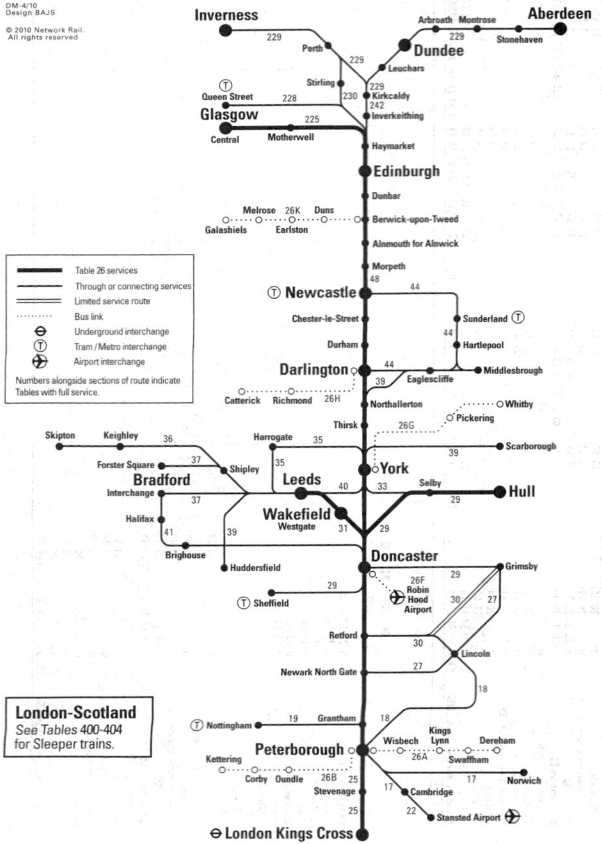

London - Humberside, Yorkshire, North East England and Scotland

Miles	Miles	Miles	Station		TP MO A	TP MO B	GR MO C	GR MO D	GR MX	GR C	GR MX	GR D	TP MX	NT	GR	XC F	GR C	GR MO G	GR C	GR MO H	GR MX I	GR C	GR D
0	—	—	London Kings Cross ⊖	d			20p56	21p00	21p00	21p32	21p35	21p35					21p57	22p00		22p00	22p00	22p32	22p35
27½	—	—	Stevenage	d					21p20	21p55		21p55											
76¼	—	—	Peterborough	a			21p44	21p44	21p50	22p24	22p20	22p24					22p44	22p44		22p44	22p45	23e24	23e24
—	—	—	Norwich	d																			
—	—	—	Peterborough	d			21p44	21p44	21p50	22p24	22p21	22p24					22p45	22p45		22p45	22p46		
105¼	—	—	Grantham	a						22p48	22p43	22p48									23p08	23e49	23e49
—	—	—		d						22p48	22p43	22p48									23p08		
120	—	—	Newark North Gate	a					22p20	23p00	22p54	23p00									23p19	23e59	23e59
—	—	—		d					22p20	23p00	22p54	23p00									23p19		
—	—	—	Lincoln	a																			
138½	—	—	Retford	d						23p15	23p10	23p15											
156	0	—	Doncaster	a					22p45	23p31	23p25	23p31					23p42	23p42		23p42	23p49	00s30	00s30
—	—	—	Selby	a																			
—	—	—	Hull	a																			
—	—	—	Pontefract Monkhill	a																			
—	—	—	Wakefield Kirkgate	a																			
—	19¾	—	Wakefield Westgate	a						23p49	23p44	23p49											
—	29¾	—	Leeds	a						00 27	00 03	00 27										01 37	01 37
—	—	—	Brighouse	a																			
—	—	—	Halifax	a																			
—	—	—	Shipley	a																			
—	—	—	Bradford Forster Square	a																			
—	—	—	Bradford Interchange	a																			
—	—	—	Keighley	a																			
—	—	—	Skipton	a																			
—	—	—	Sheffield	d																			
—	—	—	Doncaster	d					22p46								23p43	23p43		23p43	23p49		
188½	—	—	York	a			22p59	22p59	23p10								00 33	00 10		00 33	00 39		
—	—	—	Scarborough	a																			
—	—	—	Harrogate	a																			
—	—	—	Leeds	d	22p12	22p12							22p42										
—	—	—	York	d	22b44	22p42	23p04	23p04	23p12				23c18				00 35	00 12	00 35	00 35	00 41		
210¾	—	—	Thirsk	d	23p06	23p06							23p31										
218½	—	—	Northallerton	d	23p16	23p16	23p39	23p39	23p40				23p49					00s47	01s07	01s07	01s11		
232½	—	—	Darlington	a	23p28	23p28	23p51	23p51	23p53				00 01					01s01	01s21	01s21	01s25		
—	—	—	Eaglescliffe	a																			
—	—	—	Middlesbrough	a																			
—	—	—	Darlington	d	23p28	23p28	23p52	23p52	23p53				00 02										
254½	—	—	Durham	d	23p45	23p45	00 09	00 09	00 11				00 18					01s19	01s39	01s39	01s43		
260¼	—	—	Chester-le-Street	d																			
—	—	—	Newcastle	a	00 15	00 15	00 45	00 45	00 47				00 52					01 54	02 14	02 14	02 20		
—	—	—	Hartlepool	a																			
—	—	—	Sunderland	a																			
268½	—	—	Newcastle	d										05 55	06 25	07 35							
285	—	—	Morpeth	d										06 15	06 38	07 48							
303¼	—	—	Alnmouth for Alnwick	d										06a32	06 52								
335½	—	—	Berwick-upon-Tweed	d											07 16	08 19							
363¾	—	—	Dunbar	d											07 40								
393	—	—	Edinburgh	a											08 10	09 04							
—	—	0	Edinburgh	d												09 11							
394¾	—	1¼	Haymarket	d												09 16							
437¼	—	—	Motherwell	a												10 02							
450¼	—	—	Glasgow Central	a												10 26							
—	—	—	Stirling	a																			
—	—	—	Perth	a																			
—	—	—	Inverness	a																			
—	—	13¼	Inverkeithing	a																			
—	—	26	Kirkcaldy	a																			
—	—	51	Leuchars	a																			
—	—	59¼	Dundee	a																			
—	—	76¼	Arbroath	a																			
—	—	90	Montrose	a																			
—	—	114¼	Stonehaven	a																			
—	—	130½	Aberdeen	a																			

A until 12 September, MO from 31 October
B from 19 September until 24 October
C from 8 August until 12 September
D until 1 August, MO from 19 September
F to Berwick-upon-Tweed
G until 20 June
H from 27 June until 1 August, MO from 19 September
I from Doncaster
b Previous night, arr. 2238
c Previous night, arr. 2309
e Previous night, stops to set down only

London - Humberside, Yorkshire, North East England and Scotland

		GR	GR	TP	NT	GR	NT	TP	XC	TP	NT	GR	TP	NT	NT	XC	GR	GR	TP	XC	EM	GR	GR
		MX														A			B				
		1	1	◇1		1		◇1	◇1	◇1		1	◇1			◇1	1	1	◇1	◇1	◇	1	1
London Kings Cross ⊖	d	23p30	05 50														06 15	06 30				07 00	07 05
Stevenage	d		06 11														06 34	06 49					
Peterborough	a	00s24	06 41														07 04	07 19				07 45	07 51
Norwich	d																				05 50		
Peterborough	d		06 42														07 05	07 21			07 27	07 45	07 51
Grantham	a	00s48	07 02														07 25	07 39			07 58		
	d		07 02														07 25	07 39			07 58		
Newark North Gate	a	01s01	07 14														07 37						
	d		07 14														07 37						
Lincoln	a																						
Retford	d		07 29														07 53						
Doncaster	a	01s33	07 43														08 08	08 12					08 41
Selby	a																						
Hull	a																						
Pontefract Monkhill	a																						
Wakefield Kirkgate	a																						
Wakefield Westgate	a		08 01															08 30					09 00
Leeds	a	02 46	08 21															08 50					09 19
Brighouse	a																						
Halifax	a																						
Shipley	a																						
Bradford Forster Square	a																						
Bradford Interchange	a																						
Keighley	a																						
Skipton	a																						
Sheffield	d								06 33							07 12				07 54	09a38		
Doncaster	d					06 15			06 59								08 09			08 25			
York	a					06 35			07 28								08 32			08 46		08 52	
Scarborough	a																						
Harrogate	a																						
Leeds	d							06 35				07 10	07 50			07 57			08 12				
York	d			05 54		06 37		07 06	07 30	07 32		07 37	08 23			08 28	08 34		08 42	08 49		08 53	
Thirsk	d			06 10				07 22		07 52			08 39										
Northallerton	d			06 18				07 30		08 00			08 49										
Darlington	a			06 29		07 04		07 41	07 56			08 05				08 55	09 03		09 11	09 16		09 21	
Eaglescliffe	a																						
Middlesbrough	a			07 03						08 32			09 21										
Darlington	d				06 14	07 05	07 20	07 42	07 57			08 05		08 22		08 57	09 04		09 12	09 17		09 21	
Durham	d				06 35	07 22	07 41	07 59	08 16			08 23		08 43		09 12	09 21		09 29	09 34			
Chester-le-Street	d				06 42		07 48	08 05						08 50									
Newcastle	a				06 57	07 39	08 05	08 17	08 36			08 40		09 06		09 30	09 42		09 45	09 48		09 51	
Hartlepool	a																						
Sunderland	a																						
Newcastle	d					07 41					07 58	08 41			09 15	09 35						09 52	
Morpeth	d										08a19	08 56			09a36								
Alnmouth for Alnwick	d					08 07										09 59							
Berwick-upon-Tweed	d					08 31						09 31				10 20						10 37	
Dunbar	d					08 54						09 55											
Edinburgh	a					09 24						10 20				11 05						11 25	
Edinburgh	d											10 27				11 11							
Haymarket	d											10 32				11 16							
Motherwell	a															11 52							
Glasgow Central	a															12 14							
Stirling	a																						
Perth	a																						
Inverness	a																						
Inverkeithing	a											10 47											
Kirkcaldy	a											11 04											
Leuchars	a											11 28											
Dundee	a											11 43											
Arbroath	a											12 00											
Montrose	a											12 16											
Stonehaven	a											12 39											
Aberdeen	a											13 05											

A to Berwick-upon-Tweed

B to York

London - Humberside, Yorkshire, North East England and Scotland

		GR	HT	TP	TP	NT	XC	GR	GR	EM	XC	GC	GR	GR	TP	GC	TP	NT	XC	GR	GR	XC	EM
																			C				
		1	◇1	◇1	◇1		◇1	1	1		◇1	1	1	1	◇1	1	◇1		◇1	1	1	◇1	◇
London Kings Cross ⊖	d	07 08	07 20					07 30	07 35			07 49	08 00	08 03						08 30	08 35		
Stevenage	d	07 27	07 44						07 54												08 54		
Peterborough	a	07 57						08 16						08 50						09 15			
Norwich	d																						07 57
Peterborough	d	07 58						08 16		08 33				08 50						09 15			09 27
Grantham	a	08 18	08 26						08 39												09 39		09 57
	d	08 18	08 27						08 39												09 39		09 58
Newark North Gate	a	08 30						08 43												09 43			
	d	08 30						08 43												09 43			
Lincoln	a									09 59													
Retford	d	08 44	08 50																				
Doncaster	a	08 59	09 04					09 08	09 12					09 39						10 08	10 12		
Selby	a		09 22																				
Hull	a		10 04																				
Pontefract Monkhill	a																						
Wakefield Kirkgate	a																						
Wakefield Westgate	a								09 30					10 00							10 30		
Leeds	a								09 50					10 19							10 50		
Brighouse	a																						
Halifax	a																						
Shipley	a																						
Bradford Forster Square	a																						
Bradford Interchange	a																						
Keighley	a																						
Skipton	a																						
Sheffield	d						08 21				08 48								09 21			09 47	11a38
Doncaster	d	09 00						09 09			09 20									10 09		10 19	
York	a	09 31						09 33			09 45	09 48	09 51							10 33		10 45	
Scarborough	a																						
Harrogate	a																						
Leeds	d			08 28	08 57		09 05								09 28	←	09 57		10 05				
York	d			08 58	09 26		09 32	09 35			09 48	10 01	09 53		09 58	10 01	10 26		10 32	10 35		10 48	
Thirsk	d				09 46							→				10 18	10 46						
Northallerton	d			09 19	09 59										10 19	10 29	10 59			10 54			
Darlington	a			09 30			09 58	10 03			10 13		10 20		10 30				11 00	11 07		11 14	
Eaglescliffe	a															10 47							
Middlesbrough	a				10 30												11 30						
Darlington	d			09 31			10 00	10 04			10 15		10 21		10 31				11 02	11 07		11 15	
Durham	d			09 47			10 17	10 21			10 32				10 47				11 20	11 25		11 32	
Chester-le-Street	d			09 55																			
Newcastle	a			10 07			10 31	10 39			10 46		10 50		11 05				11 35	11 46		11 47	
Hartlepool	a															11 14							
Sunderland	a															11 40							
Newcastle	d					10 15	10 35	10 41					10 52					11 15	11 38				
Morpeth	d					10a36												11a36					
Alnmouth for Alnwick	d							11 07															
Berwick-upon-Tweed	d												11 37						12 22				
Dunbar	d						11 37																
Edinburgh	a						12 03	12 15					12 25						13 06				
Edinburgh	d																		13 11				
Haymarket	d																		13 16				
Motherwell	a																		13 52				
Glasgow Central	a																		14 12				
Stirling	a																						
Perth	a																						
Inverness	a																						
Inverkeithing	a																						
Kirkcaldy	a																						
Leuchars	a																						
Dundee	a																						
Arbroath	a																						
Montrose	a																						
Stonehaven	a																						
Aberdeen	a																						

C to Berwick-upon-Tweed

London - Humberside, Yorkshire, North East England and Scotland

Station		EM	GR	GR	GR	TP	TP	NT	XC	GR	GR	HT	XC	GR	TP	TP	NT	XC	EM	EM	GR	GR
																		A				
London Kings Cross ⊖	d		09 00	09 03	09 08					09 30	09 35	09 48		10 00							10 03	10 08
Stevenage	d				09 29						09 54											10 28
Peterborough	a		09 45	09 51	10 00					10 15											10 49	10 58
Norwich	d																		08 57			
Peterborough	d	09 35	09 45	09 51	10 00					10 15									10 28	10 38	10 50	10 59
Grantham	a				10 21						10 40	10 49							10 58			11 20
	d				10 21						10 40	10 50							11 00			11 21
Newark North Gate	a				10 33					10 43												11 37
	d				10 33					10 43												
Lincoln	a	10 59																		12 04		
Retford	d				10 48							11 11										
Doncaster	a			10 40	11 03					11 08	11 12	11 23									11 40	
Selby	a											11 39										
Hull	a											12 18										
Pontefract Monkhill	a																					
Wakefield Kirkgate	a																					
Wakefield Westgate	a			11 00							11 31										12 00	
Leeds	a			11 19							11 51										12 19	
Brighouse	a																					
Halifax	a																					
Shipley	a																					
Bradford Forster Square	a																					
Bradford Interchange	a																					
Keighley	a																					
Skipton	a																					
Sheffield ⇌	d								10 21				10 47					11 21	12a38			
Doncaster	d				11 04					11 10			11 19									
York	a		10 52		11 33					11 34			11 47	11 52								
Scarborough	a																					
Harrogate	a																					
Leeds	d					10 28	10 57		11 05						11 28	11 57		12 05				
York	d		10 53			10 58	11 26		11 32	11 35			11 48	11 53	11 58	12 26		12 32				
Thirsk	d						11 46									12 46						
Northallerton	d					11 19	11 59								12 19	12 59						
Darlington	a		11 21			11 30			11 57	12 04			12 14	12 21	12 30			12 58				
Eaglescliffe	a																					
Middlesbrough	a						12 30									13 30						
Darlington	d		11 21			11 31			12 00	12 05			12 15	12 22	12 31			13 00				
Durham	d					11 47			12 23	12 27			12 32		12 47			13 16				
Chester-le-Street	d					11 53																
Newcastle ⇌	a		11 51			12 06			12 35	12 42			12 47	12 51	13 03			13 30				
Hartlepool	a																					
Sunderland ⇌	a																					
Newcastle ⇌	d		11 52					12 15	12 38	12 44				12 53			13 15	13 38				
Morpeth	d							12a36									13a36					
Alnmouth for Alnwick	d									13 10								14 02				
Berwick-upon-Tweed	d		12 37											13 39				14 23				
Dunbar	d								13 41													
Edinburgh	a		13 25						14 10	14 18				14 22				15 06				
Edinburgh	d													14 27				15 11				
Haymarket	d													14 32				15 16				
Motherwell	a																	15 51				
Glasgow Central	a																	16 23				
Stirling	a																					
Perth	a																					
Inverness	a																					
Inverkeithing	a													14 46								
Kirkcaldy	a													15 03								
Leuchars	a													15 28								
Dundee	a													15 46								
Arbroath	a													16 04								
Montrose	a													16 20								
Stonehaven	a													16 43								
Aberdeen	a													17 09								

A to Berwick-upon-Tweed

London - Humberside, Yorkshire, North East England and Scotland

Station		GR	GR	GC	XC	EM	GR	EM	GR	GR	TP	GC	TP	NT	XC	GR	GR	HT	XC	GR	TP	TP	NT
																				A			
London Kings Cross ⊖	d	10 30	10 35	10 48			11 00		11 05	11 08		11 23				11 30	11 35	11 48		12 00			
Stevenage	d		10 54							11 27							11 54						
Peterborough	a	11 15							11 50	11 57						12 15							
Norwich	d					09 57																	
Peterborough	d	11 15				11 26		11 48	11 51	11 58						12 15							
Grantham	a		11 40			11 57				12 18							12 40	12 48					
	d		11 40			11 58				12 18							12 40	12 49					
Newark North Gate	a	11 43								12 30						12 43							
	d	11 44								12 30						12 43							
Lincoln	a							13 14															
Retford	d									12 45								13 11					
Doncaster	a	12 08	12 12	12 24				14 06	12 41	13 03						13 08	13 12	13 23					
Selby	a																	13 39					
Hull	a																	14 19					
Pontefract Monkhill	a			12 49																			
Wakefield Kirkgate	a			13 09																			
Wakefield Westgate	a		12 30						13 00								13 30						
Leeds	a		12 50						13 19								13 50						
Brighouse	a			13 31																			
Halifax	a			13 42																			
Shipley	a																						
Bradford Forster Square	a																						
Bradford Interchange	a			13 55																			
Keighley	a																						
Skipton	a																						
Sheffield ⇌	d				11 47	13a38									12 21				12 47				
Doncaster	d	12 09			12 19					13 04						13 10			13 19				
York	a	12 32			12 48		12 51			13 33		13 21				13 34			13 45	13 52			
Scarborough	a																						
Harrogate	a																						
Leeds	d										12 28		12 57		13 05						13 28	13 57	
York	d	12 35			12 48		12 52				12 58	13 24	13c29		13 32	13 35			13 48	13 53	13 58	14 26	
Thirsk	d												13 46									14 46	
Northallerton	d	12 54									13 19	13 45	13 59								14 19	14 59	
Darlington	a	13 07			13 15		13 21				13 30				13 59	14 04			14 13	14 21	14 30		
Eaglescliffe	a											14 04											
Middlesbrough	a												14 30									15 30	
Darlington	d	13 07			13 16		13 21				13 31				14 00	14 05			14 15	14 22	14 31		
Durham	d	13 25			13 34						13 47				14 17	14 22			14 31		14 47		
Chester-le-Street	d										13 53												
Newcastle ⇌	a	13 45			13 46		13 50				14 06				14 31	14 39			14 46	14 51	15 05		
Hartlepool	a											14 23											
Sunderland ⇌	a											14 50											
Newcastle ⇌	d						13 51							14 15	14 36	14 43				14 53			15 15
Morpeth	d													14a36	14 50								15a36
Alnmouth for Alnwick	d															15 09							
Berwick-upon-Tweed	d						14 36													15 39			
Dunbar	d														15 41								
Edinburgh	a						15 25								16 05	16 17				16 22			
Edinburgh	d																			16 33			
Haymarket	d																			16 38			
Motherwell	a																						
Glasgow Central	a																						
Stirling	a																			17 19			
Perth	a																			17 59			
Inverness	a																			20 11			
Inverkeithing	a																						
Kirkcaldy	a																						
Leuchars	a																						
Dundee	a																						
Arbroath	a																						
Montrose	a																						
Stonehaven	a																						
Aberdeen	a																						

A The Northern Lights

London - Humberside, Yorkshire, North East England and Scotland

		XC	EM	EM	GR	GR	GR	GR	XC	EM	EM	GR	GR	GR	TP	TP	NT	XC	GR	GR	HT	XC
		A																D				
London Kings Cross ⊖	d				12 05	12 08	12 30	12 35				13 00	13 05	13 08					13 30	13 35	13 48	
Stevenage	d					12 28		12 54						13 29						13 54		
Peterborough	a				12 50	12 58	13 15					13 45	13 51	13 59					14 15			
Norwich	d		10 57							11 57												
Peterborough	d		12 25	12 41	12 50	12 59	13 15			13 26	13 40	13 45	13 51	13 59					14 15			
Grantham	a		12 58			13 20		13 40		13 56				14 21						14 40	14 48	
	d		12 58			13 21		13 40		13 58				14 21						14 40	14 49	
Newark North Gate	a					13 37	13 43							14 33					14 43			
	d						13 44							14 33					14 43			
Lincoln	a			14 05							15 05											
Retford	d													14 49							15 11	
Doncaster	a				13 40		14 08	14 12					14 39	15 04					15 08	15 12	15 23	
Selby	a																				15 39	
Hull	a																				16 18	
Pontefract Monkhill	a																					
Wakefield Kirkgate	a																					
Wakefield Westgate	a				14 00			14 30					15 00							15 30		
Leeds	a				14 19			14 50					15 19							15 50		
Brighouse	a																					
Halifax	a																					
Shipley	a																					
Bradford Forster Square	a																					
Bradford Interchange	a																					
Keighley	a																					
Skipton	a																					
Sheffield	d	13 21	14a38						13 47	15a38								14 21				14 47
Doncaster	d						14 09		14 19					15 04					15 10			15 19
York	a						14 33		14 46			14 51		15 33					15 34			15 45
Scarborough	a																					
Harrogate	a																					
Leeds	d	14 05													14 28	14 57		15 05				
York	d	14 32					14 35		14 48			14 52			14 58	15 26		15 32	15 35			15 48
Thirsk	d															15 46						
Northallerton	d						14 54								15 19	15 59			15 54			
Darlington	a	14 58					15 07		15 14			15 20			15 30			15 58	16 07			16 14
Eaglescliffe	a																					
Middlesbrough	a															16 30						
Darlington	d	15 00					15 07		15 15			15 20			15 31			16 00	16 07			16 15
Durham	d	15 16					15 25		15 32						15 47			16 17	16 25			16 32
Chester-le-Street	d														15 53							
Newcastle	a	15 33					15 45		15 46			15 50			16 09			16 31	16 46			16 47
Hartlepool	a																					
Sunderland	a																					
Newcastle	d	15 37										15 51					16 15	16 37				
Morpeth	d																16a36					
Alnmouth for Alnwick	d	16 01																17 02				
Berwick-upon-Tweed	d	16 22										16 36										
Dunbar	d																	17 43				
Edinburgh	a	17 06										17 25						18 07				
Edinburgh	d	17 11																18 11				
Haymarket	d	17 16																18 15				
Motherwell	a	17 51																				
Glasgow Central	a	18 16																				
Stirling	a																					
Perth	a																					
Inverness	a																					
Inverkeithing	a																	18 28				
Kirkcaldy	a																	18 46				
Leuchars	a																	19 17				
Dundee	a																	19 32				
Arbroath	a																	19 49				
Montrose	a																	20 03				
Stonehaven	a																	20 23				
Aberdeen	a																	20 43				

A Buffet to Berwick-upon-Tweed

D Buffet to Dunbar

Table 26

Mondays to Fridays

London - Humberside, Yorkshire, North East England and Scotland

		GR	TP	NT	XC	EM	GR	GR	EM	GR	GR	GC	XC	NT	GR	TP	NT	XC	EM	GR	GR	GR	GR
					B													C					
London Kings Cross ⊖	d	14 00					14 05	14 08		14 30	14 35	14 48			15 00					15 05	15 08	15 30	15 35
Stevenage	d							14 28			14 54										15 28		15 54
Peterborough	a						14 50	14 58		15 16										15 50	15 58	16 15	
Norwich	d					12 57													13 57				
Peterborough	d					14 26	14 50	14 58	15 10	15 16									15 27	15 50	15 59	16 15	
Grantham	a					14 56		15 19			15 40								15 59		16 21		16 40
	d					14 58		15 19			15 40								16 01		16 21		16 40
Newark North Gate	a							15 37		15 43											16 32	16 43	
	d									15 44											16 32	16 44	
Lincoln	a								16 47														
Retford	d																				16 49		
Doncaster	a						15 39			16 08	16 12	16 24								16 39	17 04	17 10	17 13
Selby	a																						
Hull	a																						
Pontefract Monkhill	a											16 48											
Wakefield Kirkgate	a											17 08											
Wakefield Westgate	a						15 59				16 30									17 00			17 31
Leeds	a						16 19				16 50									17 19			17 51
Brighouse	a											17 28											
Halifax	a											17 39											
Shipley	a																						
Bradford Forster Square	a																						
Bradford Interchange	a											17 55											
Keighley	a																						
Skipton	a																						
Sheffield	d				15 21	16a38							15 47					16 21	17a34				
Doncaster	d									16 09			16 19								17 04	17 11	
York	a	15 52								16 33			16 46		16 50						17 35	17 36	
Scarborough	a																						
Harrogate	a																						
Leeds	d		15 56		16 05											16 28		17 07					
York	d	15 53	16 26		16 32					16 35			16 48		16 51	16 55		17 32				17 37	
Thirsk	d		16 46													17 13							
Northallerton	d		16 59							16 54						17 21						17 55	
Darlington	a	16 21			16 57					17 07			17 14		17 19	17 32		17 58				18 08	
Eaglescliffe	a																						
Middlesbrough	a		17 30																				
Darlington	d	16 22			16 59					17 07			17 15		17 19	17 33		18 00				18 08	
Durham	d				17 15					17 25			17 32			17 50		18 16				18 26	
Chester-le-Street	d															17 56							
Newcastle	a	16 51			17 31					17 45			17 46		17 49	18 10		18 34				18 42	
Hartlepool	a																						
Sunderland	a																						
Newcastle	d	16 53		17 15	17 37									17 38	17 51		18 25	18 39				18 43	
Morpeth	d			17 36										18a00			18a48						
Alnmouth for Alnwick	d			18a18	18 02																	19 11	
Berwick-upon-Tweed	d	17 39			18 23										18 34			19 21					
Dunbar	d																	19 44					
Edinburgh	a	18 23			19 06										19 19			20 09				20 19	
Edinburgh	d	18 30			19 11										19 24			20 13					
Haymarket	d	18 34			19 16													20 17					
Motherwell	a				19 55										20 03								
Glasgow Central	a				20 15										20 37								
Stirling	a																						
Perth	a																						
Inverness	a																						
Inverkeithing	a	18 54																20 30					
Kirkcaldy	a	19 11																					
Leuchars	a	19 40																21 26					
Dundee	a	19 55																21 42					
Arbroath	a	20 12																					
Montrose	a	20 28																					
Stonehaven	a	20 51																					
Aberdeen	a	21 17																					

B Buffet to Berwick-upon-Tweed

C Buffet to Dunbar

London - Humberside, Yorkshire, North East England and Scotland

		HT	EM	TP	XC	GR	TP	XC	EM	GR	GR	GR	GR	GC	GR	TP	XC	EM	GR	GR	TP	GR	GR
								A												C			
London Kings Cross 15 ⊖	d	15 48				16 00				16 05	16 08	16 30	16 33	16 48	17 00				17 03	17 19		17 30	17 33
Stevenage 4	d										16 29		16 52										17 53
Peterborough 8	a									16 50	16 59	17 15							17 49	18 05		18 15	
Norwich	d								14 57									15 52					
Peterborough 8	d		16 25						16 28	16 51	16 59	17 15						17 27	17 50	18 06		18 16	
Grantham 7	a	16 48							16 59		17 20		17 39					17 58		18 28			18 41
	d	16 49							17 00		17 21		17 39					17 58		18 28			18 42
Newark North Gate 7	a										17 38	17 43								18 39		18 44	
	d											17 44								18 39		18 44	
Lincoln	a		17 51																				
Retford 10	d	17 11											18 02										
Doncaster 7	a	17 23								17 41		18 09							18 40	19 05			19 15
Selby	a	17 39																		19 22			
Hull	a	18 21																		20 08			
Pontefract Monkhill	a																						
Wakefield Kirkgate 4	a																						
Wakefield Westgate 7	a									18 00			18 31						18 58				19 35
Leeds 10	a									18 19			18 51						19 19				19 52
Brighouse	a																						
Halifax	a																						
Shipley	a																						
Bradford Forster Square	a																						
Bradford Interchange	a																						
Keighley	a																						
Skipton	a																						
Sheffield 7	d				16 47			17 22	18a39								17 47	19a39					
Doncaster 7	d				17 19							18 09											
York 8	a				17 43	17 52						18 33		18 40	18 50							19 27	
Scarborough	a																						
Harrogate	a																						20 29
Leeds 10	d			17 12			17 57	18 06								18 28	18 35				18 57		
York 8	d			17 40	17 47	17 53	18 26	18 33				18 36		18 44	18 51	18 58	19 05				19 26	19 29	
Thirsk	d			18 01			18 46							19 00							19 46		
Northallerton	d			18 09			18 59					18 56		19 15		19 19					19 57		
Darlington 7	a				18 13	18 22		19 00				19 08			19 19	19 30	19 37					19 56	
Eaglescliffe	a													19 34									
Middlesbrough	a			18 40			19 32														20 30		
Darlington 7	d				18 15	18 22		19 01				19 09			19 20	19 31	19 38					19 57	
Durham	d				18 32			19 19				19 26				19 47	19 55					20 14	
Chester-le-Street	d															19 53							
Newcastle 8	a				18 46	18 52		19 34				19 42			19 49	20 08	20 09					20 35	
Hartlepool	a													19 53									
Sunderland	a													20 21									
Newcastle 8	d					18 53		19 38				19 44			19 52		20 12						
Morpeth	d											20 00											
Alnmouth for Alnwick	d							20 06															
Berwick-upon-Tweed	d					19 39		20 27							20 39								
Dunbar	d																						
Edinburgh 10	a					20 22		21 11				21 20			21 27		21 35						
Edinburgh	d					20 29		21 14															
Haymarket	d					20 34		21 19															
Motherwell	a							22 01															
Glasgow Central 15	a							22 27															
Stirling	a																						
Perth	a																						
Inverness	a																						
Inverkeithing	a					20 51																	
Kirkcaldy	a					21 08																	
Leuchars 3	a					21 37																	
Dundee	a					21 51																	
Arbroath	a					22 09																	
Montrose	a					22 25																	
Stonehaven	a					22 48																	
Aberdeen	a					23 14																	

A to Berwick-upon-Tweed

C The Hull Executive

London - Humberside, Yorkshire, North East England and Scotland

		XC	XC	EM	GR	GR	GR	GR	TP	XC	GR	GR	HT	EM	XC	GR	GR	GR	TP	GC	GR	XC
		A																C			FX	
London Kings Cross 15 ⊖	d				17 49	18 00	18 03	18 19			18 30	18 33	18 50			19 00	19 03	19 06		19 18	19 30	
Stevenage 4	d											18 52						19 26				
Peterborough 8	a				18 37		18 53				19 17						19 50	19 56			20 15	
Norwich	d			16 57										17 54								
Peterborough 8	d			18 26	18 39		18 54				19 18			19 26			19 51	19 57			20 16	
Grantham 7	a			18 57	19 04			19 22				19 42	19 51	19 58				20 19				
	d			18 58	19 04			19 22				19 43	19 53					20 19				
Newark North Gate 7	a						19 23				19 46							20 31			20 44	
	d						19 23				19 46							20 32			20 44	
Lincoln	a																	21 01				
Retford 10	d				19 26							20 06	20 14									
Doncaster 7	a				19 41		19 48				20 10	20 20	20 27				20 40				21 09	
Selby	a												20 48									
Hull	a												21 28									
Pontefract Monkhill	a																					
Wakefield Kirkgate 4	a																					
Wakefield Westgate 7	a				20 01		20 06					20 38					20 59					
Leeds 10	a				20 22		20 24					20 54					21 20					
Brighouse	a																					
Halifax	a																					
Shipley	a											21s12										
Bradford Forster Square	a											21 24										
Bradford Interchange	a																					
Keighley	a						20s55															
Skipton	a						21 16															
Sheffield 7	d	18 21	18 47	20a28						19 26					19 54							20 21
Doncaster 7	d		19 16								20 11				20 17						21 09	
York 8	a		19 39			19 49		20 12			20 34				20 46	20 51				21 17	21 32	
Scarborough	a																					
Harrogate	a																					
Leeds 10	d	19 05							19 57	20 08									20 45			21a05
York 8	d	19 35	19 45			19 50		20 14	20 30	20 34	20 36				20 48	20 52			21 14	21 19	21 33	
Thirsk	d								20 50										21 31	21 36		
Northallerton	d							20 33	20 58										21 39	21 47	21 53	
Darlington 7	a	20 02	20 10			20 19		20 46		20 59	21 04				21 14	21 20			21 51		22 05	
Eaglescliffe	a																			22 05		
Middlesbrough	a								21 32													
Darlington 7	d	20 04	20 12			20 19		20 46		21 01	21 04				21 15	21 20			21 52		22 06	
Durham	d	20 21	20 28					21 04		21 18	21 22				21 32				22 08		22 23	
Chester-le-Street	d																		22 14			
Newcastle 8	a	20 36	20 43			20 51		21 25		21 32	21 38				21 46	21 50			22 30		22 41	
Hartlepool	a																			22 25		
Sunderland	a																			22 51		
Newcastle 8	d	20 39				20 52				21 36	21 39					21 55						
Morpeth	d	20 55									21 55											
Alnmouth for Alnwick	d									22 02	22 11											
Berwick-upon-Tweed	d	21 26				21 39										22 38						
Dunbar	d	21 51				22 04																
Edinburgh 10	a	22 16				22 35				23 04	23 22					23 33						
Edinburgh	d																					
Haymarket	d																					
Motherwell	a																					
Glasgow Central 15	a																					
Stirling	a																					
Perth	a																					
Inverness	a																					
Inverkeithing	a																					
Kirkcaldy	a																					
Leuchars 3	a																					
Dundee	a																					
Arbroath	a																					
Montrose	a																					
Stonehaven	a																					
Aberdeen	a																					

A to Durham

C until 2 December

Table 26

Mondays to Fridays

London - Humberside, Yorkshire, North East England and Scotland

Station		NT	GR FO	GR	EM	GC	XC	GR	GR	HT	GR	XC	EM	XC	GR	GR	TP	GR	EM	XC	EM	GR
			1	1	◇	◇1 A ⊠	◇1	1	1	◇1 ⊠	1	◇1	◇1	◇1	1 B	1	◇1	1	◇1	◇1	◇1	1
London Kings Cross 15 ⊖	d		19 30	19 33		19 48		20 00	20 05	20 30	20 35				21 00	21 35		22 00				23 30
Stevenage 4	d			19 52							20 54				21 20							
Peterborough 8	a		20 15						20 50		21 24				21 50	22 20		22 45				00s24
Norwich	d				18 57																	
Peterborough 8	d		20 16		20 28				20 50		21 25				21 50	22 21		22 46				
Grantham 7	a			20 40	20 58					21 31	21 46					22 43		23 08				00s48
	d			20 40						21 32	21 46					22 43		23 08				
Newark North Gate 7	a		20 44						21 18		21 58				22 20	22 54		23 19				01s01
	d		20 44						21 18		21 58				22 20	22 54		23 19				
Lincoln	a																					
Retford 10	d									21 52						23 10						
Doncaster 7	a		21 09	21 13		21 25			21 42	22 06	22 22				22 45	23 25		23 49				01s33
Selby	a									22 21												
Hull	a									23 06												
Pontefract Monkhill	a					21 49																
Wakefield Kirkgate 4	a					22 18																
Wakefield Westgate 7	a			21 31					22 05		22 39					23 44						
Leeds 10	a			21 51					22 25		23 00					00 03						02 46
Brighouse	a					22 43																
Halifax	a					22 54																
Shipley	a																					
Bradford Forster Square	a																					
Bradford Interchange	a					23 07																
Keighley	a																					
Skipton	a																					
Sheffield 7	d						20 53					21 21	21 25	21 54					22 19	22 30	22 50	
Doncaster 7	d		21 09				21 20							22 31	22 46			23 49				
York 8	a		21 32				21 46	21 51						22 54	23 10			00 39				
Scarborough	a																					
Harrogate	a																					
Leeds 10	d											22a02	22a19				22 42		23a05	23a15	23a40	
York 8	d		21 33				21 49	21 53							23 12		23 18	00 41				
Thirsk	d																23 31					
Northallerton	d		21 53												23 40		23 49	01s11				
Darlington 7	a		22 05				22 15	22 20							23 53		00 01	01s25				
Eaglescliffe	a																					
Middlesbrough	a																					
Darlington 7	d		22 06				22 17	22 21							23 53		00 02					
Durham	d		22 23				22 33								00 11		00 18	01s43				
Chester-le-Street	d																					
Newcastle 8	a		22 41				22 51	22 55							00 47		00 52	02 20				
Hartlepool	a																					
Sunderland	a																					
Newcastle 8	d	22 00	22 42																			
Morpeth	d	22a21	22 56																			
Alnmouth for Alnwick	d		23 12																			
Berwick-upon-Tweed	d		23 38																			
Dunbar	d																					
Edinburgh 10	a		00 31																			
Edinburgh	d																					
Haymarket	d																					
Motherwell	a																					
Glasgow Central 15	a																					
Stirling	a																					
Perth	a																					
Inverness	a																					
Inverkeithing	a																					
Kirkcaldy	a																					
Leuchars 3	a																					
Dundee	a																					
Arbroath	a																					
Montrose	a																					
Stonehaven	a																					
Aberdeen	a																					

A ⊠ from Doncaster ◇ from Doncaster

Table 26

Saturdays
until 18 June

London - Humberside, Yorkshire, North East England and Scotland

Station		GR	GR	GR	TP	GR	GR	TP	NT	GR	XC	GR	NT	TP	TP	NT	GR	XC	TP	NT	NT	XC	GR
		1	1	1	◇1	1	1	◇1		1	◇1 C	1		◇1	◇1		1	◇1	◇1			◇1 C	1
London Kings Cross 15 ⊖	d	19p30	21p00	21p35		22p00	23p30																06 20
Stevenage 4	d		21p20																				06 40
Peterborough 8	a	20p15	21p50	22p20		22p45	00s24																07 11
Norwich	d																						
Peterborough 8	d	20p16	21p50	22p21		22p46																	07 12
Grantham 7	a			22p43		23p08	00s48																07 32
	d			22p43		23p08																	07 32
Newark North Gate 7	a	20p44	22p20	22p54		23p19	01s01																07 44
	d	20p44	22p20	22p54		23p19																	07 44
Lincoln	a																						
Retford 10	d			23p10																			
Doncaster 7	a	21p09	22p45	23p25		23p49	01s33																08 09
Selby	a																						
Hull	a																						
Pontefract Monkhill	a																						
Wakefield Kirkgate 4	a																						
Wakefield Westgate 7	a			23p44																			
Leeds 10	a			00 03			02 46																
Brighouse	a																						
Halifax	a																						
Shipley	a																						
Bradford Forster Square	a																						
Bradford Interchange	a																						
Keighley	a																						
Skipton	a																						
Sheffield 7	d																	06 49				07 12	
Doncaster 7	d	21p09	22p46			23p49						06 10						07 17					08 10
York 8	a	21p32	23p10			00 39						06 30						07 43					08 32
Scarborough	a																						
Harrogate	a																						
Leeds 10	d				22p42									06 35			07 10		07 50			07 57	
York 8	d	21p33	23p12		23b18	00 41		05 54				06 32		07 06	07 32		07 35	07 48	08 23			08 27	08 35
Thirsk	d				23p31			06 10						07 22	07 52				08 39				
Northallerton	d	21p53	23p40		23p49	01s11		06 18				06 51		07 30	08 00				08 49				08 54
Darlington 7	a	22p05	23p53		00 01	01s25		06 29				07 05		07 41			08 04	08 13				08 56	09 07
Eaglescliffe	a																						
Middlesbrough	a							07 03							08 32				09 21				
Darlington 7	d	22p06	23p53		00 02							07 05	07 21	07 42			08 05	08 15		08 22		08 57	09 07
Durham	d	22p23	00 11		00 18	01s43						07 23	07 42	07 59			08 23	08 31		08 43		09 14	09 25
Chester-le-Street	d												07 49	08 05						08 50			
Newcastle 8	a	22p41	00 47		00 52	02 20						07 39	08 05	08 17			08 39	08 46		09 01		09 28	09 41
Hartlepool	a																						
Sunderland	a																						
Newcastle 8	d	22p42							05 55	06 30	07 38	07 42				07 58	08 41				09 15	09 35	09 44
Morpeth	d	22p56							06 15	06 43	07 51					08a19	08 56				09a36		
Alnmouth for Alnwick	d	23p12							06a34	06 57		08 08										09 59	
Berwick-upon-Tweed	d	23p38								07 21	08 24	08 32					09 31					10 20	
Dunbar	d									07 48		08 55					09 55						
Edinburgh 10	a	00 31								08 17	09 07	09 24					10 24					11 07	11 15
Edinburgh	d										09 11						10 27					11 11	
Haymarket	d										09 16						10 32					11 16	
Motherwell	a										10 00											11 52	
Glasgow Central 15	a										10 23											12 13	
Stirling	a																						
Perth	a																						
Inverness	a																						
Inverkeithing	a																10 47						
Kirkcaldy	a																11 04						
Leuchars 3	a																11 28						
Dundee	a																11 43						
Arbroath	a																12 00						
Montrose	a																12 16						
Stonehaven	a																12 39						
Aberdeen	a																13 05						

C to Berwick-upon-Tweed

b Previous night, arr. 2309

Table 26

Saturdays
until 18 June

London - Humberside, Yorkshire, North East England and Scotland

		TP	XC	GR	TP	TP	NT	XC	EM	GR	GR	GC	EM	XC	GR	GR	EM	TP	TP	NT	XC	GR	XC
																					A		
London Kings Cross 15 ⊖	d			07 00						07 03	07 30	07 47			08 00	08 03						08 30	
Stevenage 4	d									07 22													
Peterborough 8	a									07 52	08 15					08 50						09 15	
Norwich	d								05 52														
Peterborough 8	d								07 27	07 53	08 15		08 33			08 50						09 15	
Grantham 7	a								07 56	08 13						09 10							
	d								07 58	08 13						09 10							
Newark North Gate 7	a									08 25						09 22						09 43	
	d									08 25						09 22						09 43	
Lincoln	a												09 59										
Retford 10	d										08 54												
Doncaster 7	a									08 49	09 09					09 49						10 08	
Selby	a																						
Hull	a																						
Pontefract Monkhill	a																						
Wakefield Kirkgate 4	a																						
Wakefield Westgate 7	a									09 07						10 07							
Leeds 10	a									09 27						10 27							
Brighouse	a																						
Halifax	a																						
Shipley	a																						
Bradford Forster Square	a																						
Bradford Interchange	a																						
Keighley	a																						
Skipton	a																						
Sheffield 7	d		07 54					08 21	09a38					08 48			09 21				09 21		09 47
Doncaster 7	d		08 25								09 11			09 20			09 55					10 09	10 19
York 8	a		08 47	08 52							09 33	09 39		09 45	09 49		10 14					10 33	10 45
Scarborough	a																11 06						
Harrogate	a																						
Leeds 10	d				08 28	08 57		09 05										09 28	09 57		10 05		
York 8	d	08 42	08 50	08 53	08 58	09 26		09 33			09 36	09 44		09 49	09 53			09 58	10 26		10 32	10 35	10 48
Thirsk	d					09 46						10 00							10 46				
Northallerton	d				09 19	09 59						10 16						10 19	10 59			10 54	
Darlington 7	a	09 11	09 16	09 22	09 30			09 58			10 03			10 15	10 20			10 30			10 58	11 07	11 13
Eaglescliffe	a											10 38											
Middlesbrough	a					10 30													11 30				
Darlington 7	d	09 12	09 18	09 23	09 31			10 00			10 04			10 16	10 22			10 31			11 00	11 07	11 15
Durham	d	09 29	09 35		09 47			10 16			10 21			10 33				10 47			11 16	11 25	11 31
Chester-le-Street	d				09 55																		
Newcastle 8	a	09 45	09 48	09 51	10 07			10 31			10 37			10 47	10 51			11 05			11 31	11 41	11 47
Hartlepool	a											11 14											
Sunderland	a											11 40											
Newcastle 8	d			09 54			10 14	10 36			10 39				10 54					11 15	11 36	11 44	
Morpeth	d						10a35													11a36			
Alnmouth for Alnwick	d										11 05												
Berwick-upon-Tweed	d			10 39											11 39						12 20		
Dunbar	d							11 38															
Edinburgh 10	a			11 31				12 07			12 15				12 31						13 04	13 13	
Edinburgh	d																				13 11		
Haymarket	d																				13 15		
Motherwell	a																				13 52		
Glasgow Central 15	a																				14 13		
Stirling	a																						
Perth	a																						
Inverness	a																						
Inverkeithing	a																						
Kirkcaldy	a																						
Leuchars 8	a																						
Dundee	a																						
Arbroath	a																						
Montrose	a																						
Stonehaven	a																						
Aberdeen	a																						

A ⊼ to Berwick-upon-Tweed

Table 26

Saturdays
until 18 June

London - Humberside, Yorkshire, North East England and Scotland

		GR	TP	TP	NT	XC	EM	EM	GR	GR	HT	XC	GR	TP	TP	NT	XC	EM	GR	GR	GC	XC
													A				B					
London Kings Cross 15 ⊖	d	09 00							09 03	09 30	09 48		10 00						10 03	10 30	10 48	
Stevenage 4	d								09 22													
Peterborough 8	a								09 52	10 15									10 50	11 15		
Norwich	d						07 57											08 57				
Peterborough 8	d						09 30	09 33	09 53	10 15								10 26	10 51	11 15		
Grantham 7	a						09 58		10 13		10 48							10 57	11 10			
	d						09 58		10 13		10 49							10 58	11 10			
Newark North Gate 7	a								10 25										11 23	11 43		
	d								10 25										11 23	11 43		
Lincoln	a							10 59														
Retford 10	d									10 53	11 10											
Doncaster 7	a								10 50	11 08	11 24								11 50	12 08	12 20	
Selby	a										11 40											
Hull	a										12 20											
Pontefract Monkhill	a																				12 45	
Wakefield Kirkgate 4	a																				13 10	
Wakefield Westgate 7	a								11 07										12 07			
Leeds 10	a								11 28										12 28			
Brighouse	a																				13 31	
Halifax	a																				13 42	
Shipley	a																					
Bradford Forster Square	a																					
Bradford Interchange	a																				13 55	
Keighley	a																					
Skipton	a																					
Sheffield 7	d					10 21	11a38					10 47					11 21	12a38				11 47
Doncaster 7	d									11 09		11 19								12 09		12 17
York 8	a	10 52								11 33		11 45	11 52							12 33		12 45
Scarborough	a																					
Harrogate	a																					
Leeds 10	d		10 28	10 57		11 05								11 28	11 57		12 05					
York 8	d	10 53	10 58	11 26		11 32				11 35		11 48	11 53	11 58	12 26		12 32			12 35		12 48
Thirsk	d			11 46											12 46							
Northallerton	d		11 19	11 59										12 19	12 59					12 54		
Darlington 7	a	11 21	11 30			11 58				12 04		12 13	12 21	12 30			12 58			13 07		13 13
Eaglescliffe	a																					
Middlesbrough	a			12 30											13 30							
Darlington 7	d	11 22	11 31			12 00				12 04		12 15	12 22	12 31			13 00			13 07		13 15
Durham	d		11 47			12 16				12 22		12 31		12 47			13 18			13 25		13 31
Chester-le-Street	d		11 53																			
Newcastle 8	a	11 51	12 06			12 31				12 38		12 46	12 51	13 03			13 34			13 41		13 46
Hartlepool	a																					
Sunderland	a																					
Newcastle 8	d	11 54			12 15	12 36				12 40			12 54			13 15	13 35			13 44		
Morpeth	d				12a35											13a37						
Alnmouth for Alnwick	d									13 06							14 00					
Berwick-upon-Tweed	d	12 39											13 40				14 20					
Dunbar	d					13 38																
Edinburgh 10	a	13 31				14 07				14 15			14 24				15 07			15 15		
Edinburgh	d												14 27				15 11					
Haymarket	d												14 32				15 16					
Motherwell	a																15 52					
Glasgow Central 15	a																16 20					
Stirling	a																					
Perth	a																					
Inverness	a																					
Inverkeithing	a												14 46									
Kirkcaldy	a												15 03									
Leuchars 8	a												15 28									
Dundee	a												15 46									
Arbroath	a												16 04									
Montrose	a												16 20									
Stonehaven	a												16 43									
Aberdeen	a												17 09									

A The Northern Lights

B ⊼ to Berwick-upon-Tweed

Table 26

Saturdays until 18 June

London - Humberside, Yorkshire, North East England and Scotland

Station		EM	GR	EM	GR	TP	GC	TP	NT	XC	GR	GR	HT	XC	GR	TP	TP	NT	XC	EM	EM	GR	GR
															B				A				
London Kings Cross ⊖	d		11 00		11 03		11 20				11 30	11 35	11 48		12 00							12 03	12 30
Stevenage	d				11 22																		
Peterborough	a				11 52						12 15	12 21										12 51	13 15
Norwich	d	09 57																		10 57			
Peterborough	d	11 25		11 48	11 53						12 15	12 21								12 25	12 41	12 51	13 15
Grantham	a	11 57			12 13								12 48							12 58		13 16	
	d	11 58			12 13								12 49							12 58		13 16	
Newark North Gate	a				12 25																	13 27	13 43
	d				12 25																	13 27	13 43
Lincoln	a			13 14																	14 07		
Retford	d										12 53		13 10										
Doncaster	a				12 50						13 08	13 12	13 24									13 52	14 09
Selby	a												13 40										
Hull	a												14 20										
Pontefract Monkhill	a																						
Wakefield Kirkgate	a																						
Wakefield Westgate	a				13 07							13 30										14 11	
Leeds	a				13 28							13 50										14 31	
Brighouse	a																						
Halifax	a																						
Shipley	a																						
Bradford Forster Square	a																						
Bradford Interchange	a																						
Keighley	a																						
Skipton	a																						
Sheffield	d	13a38								12 21				12 47					13 21	14a38			
Doncaster	d										13 09			13 19									14 10
York	a		12 52				13 14				13 33			13 45	13 53								14 33
Scarborough	a																						
Harrogate	a																						
Leeds	d					12 28		12 57		13 05						13 28	13 57		14 05				
York	d		12 53			12 58	13 16	13 26		13 32	13 35			13 48	13 54	13 58	14 26		14 32				14 35
Thirsk	d						13 33	13 46									14 46						
Northallerton	d					13 19	13 42	13 59								14 19	14 59						14 54
Darlington	a		13 21			13 30				13 58	14 04			14 13	14 22	14 30			14 58				15 07
Eaglescliffe	a						14 00																
Middlesbrough	a							14 30									15 30						
Darlington	d		13 22			13 31				14 00	14 04			14 15	14 23	14 31			15 00				15 07
Durham	d					13 47				14 16	14 22			14 31		14 47			15 16				15 25
Chester-le-Street	d					13 53																	
Newcastle	a		13 51			14 06				14 32	14 38			14 46	14 52	15 05			15 31				15 41
Hartlepool	a						14 22																
Sunderland	a						14 50																
Newcastle	d		13 54						14 15	14 35	14 40				14 54			15 15	15 34				15 44
Morpeth	d								14a37	14 48								15a35					
Alnmouth for Alnwick	d										15 06								15 59				
Berwick-upon-Tweed	d		14 39												15 40				16 19				
Dunbar	d									15 40													
Edinburgh	a		15 31							16 04	16 15				16 26				17 07				17 15
Edinburgh	d														16 32				17 11				
Haymarket	d														16 38				17 16				
Motherwell	a																		17 52				
Glasgow Central	a																		18 11				
Stirling	a														17 19								
Perth	a														18 00								
Inverness	a														20 11								
Inverkeithing	a																						
Kirkcaldy	a																						
Leuchars	a																						
Dundee	a																						
Arbroath	a																						
Montrose	a																						
Stonehaven	a																						
Aberdeen	a																						

A to Berwick-upon-Tweed

B The Northern Lights

Table 26

Saturdays until 18 June

London - Humberside, Yorkshire, North East England and Scotland

Station		XC	EM	GR	GR	TP	TP	NT	XC	GR	XC	GR	TP	NT	NT	XC	EM	GR	EM	GR	HT	XC
									A							B						
London Kings Cross ⊖	d			13 00	13 03					13 30		14 00						14 03		14 30	14 48	
Stevenage	d				13 22																	
Peterborough	a				13 52					14 15								14 50		15 15		
Norwich	d		11 57														12 57					
Peterborough	d		13 28		13 53					14 15							14 26	14 50	15 11	15 15		
Grantham	a		13 56	14 00	14 13												14 57	15 09			15 48	
	d		13 58	14 00	14 13												14 58	15 09			15 49	
Newark North Gate	a				14 25													15 22		15 43		
	d				14 25													15 22		15 43		
Lincoln	a																		16 48			
Retford	d									14 53											16 10	
Doncaster	a				14 50					15 08								15 47		16 08	16 24	
Selby	a																				16 41	
Hull	a																				17 28	
Pontefract Monkhill	a																					
Wakefield Kirkgate	a																					
Wakefield Westgate	a				15 07													16 07				
Leeds	a				15 28													16 28				
Brighouse	a																					
Halifax	a																					
Shipley	a																					
Bradford Forster Square	a																					
Bradford Interchange	a																					
Keighley	a																					
Skipton	a																					
Sheffield	d	13 47	15a38						14 21		14 47					15 21	16a38					15 47
Doncaster	d	14 19								15 10	15 19									16 09		16 19
York	a	14 45		14 51						15 33	15 45	15 51								16 33		16 46
Scarborough	a																					
Harrogate	a																					
Leeds	d					14 28	14 57		15 05				15 56			16 05						
York	d	14 48		14 53		14b58	15 26		15 32	15 35	15 48	15 53	16 25			16 32				16 35		16 48
Thirsk	d						15 46						16 45									
Northallerton	d					15 19	15 59						16 58							16 54		
Darlington	a	15 13		15 20		15 30			15 58	16 03	16 13	16 21				16 58				17 07		17 13
Eaglescliffe	a																					
Middlesbrough	a						16 30						17 30									
Darlington	d	15 15		15 21		15 31			16 00	16 04	16 15	16 21				17 00				17 07		17 15
Durham	d	15 31				15 47			16 16	16 21	16 31					17 16				17 25		17 31
Chester-le-Street	d					15 53																
Newcastle	a	15 46		15 51		16 09			16 31	16 39	16 46	16 51				17 31				17 41		17 46
Hartlepool	a																					
Sunderland	a																					
Newcastle	d			15 54				16 15	16 35	16 44		16 52		17 00	17 22	17 37				17 44		
Morpeth	d							16a36						17 22	17a42							
Alnmouth for Alnwick	d								17 00					17a45		18 01						
Berwick-upon-Tweed	d			16 39								17 40				18 21						
Dunbar	d								17 39													
Edinburgh	a			17 31					18 05	18 17		18 27				19 08				19 15		
Edinburgh	d								18 11			18 30				19 11						
Haymarket	d								18 15			18 35				19 16						
Motherwell	a															19 52						
Glasgow Central	a															20 11						
Stirling	a																					
Perth	a																					
Inverness	a																					
Inverkeithing	a								18 28			18 54										
Kirkcaldy	a								18 46			19 11										
Leuchars	a								19 17			19 38										
Dundee	a								19 32			19 52										
Arbroath	a								19 49			20 10										
Montrose	a								20 03			20 26										
Stonehaven	a								20 23			20 49										
Aberdeen	a								20 43			21 15										

A to Dunbar

B to Berwick-upon-Tweed

Table 26

Saturdays until 18 June

London - Humberside, Yorkshire, North East England and Scotland

		GR	TP	TP	NT	XC	EM	GR	GR	GC	EM	XC	GR	TP	XC	EM	GR	GR	GC	GR	TP	XC	TP
						A	◇								B	◇						C	
London Kings Cross ⊖	d	15 00						15 03	15 30	15 48			16 00				16 03	16 30	16 48	17 00			
Stevenage	d							15 22															
Peterborough	a							15 52	16 15								16 50	17 15					
Norwich	d						13 57									14 57							
Peterborough	d						15 25	15 53	16 15		16 25					16 27	16 51	17 15					
Grantham	a						15 57	16 13								16 57	17 10						
	d						15 58	16 13								16 58	17 10						
Newark North Gate	a							16 25									17 23	17 43					
	d							16 25									17 23	17 43					
Lincoln	a										17 51												
Retford	d								16 53														
Doncaster	a							16 50	17 08	17 22							17 49	18 08					
Selby	a																						
Hull	a																						
Pontefract Monkhill	a									17 47													
Wakefield Kirkgate	a									18 10													
Wakefield Westgate	a							17 07									18 07						
Leeds	a							17 28									18 27						
Brighouse	a									18 30													
Halifax	a									18 42													
Shipley	a																						
Bradford Forster Square	a																						
Bradford Interchange	a									18 55													
Keighley	a																						
Skipton	a																						
Sheffield	d					16 21	17a34					16 47			17 21	18a39						17 47	
Doncaster	d								17 10			17 19						18 09					
York	a	16 52							17 33			17 38	17 50					18 33	18 39	18 52			
Scarborough	a																						
Harrogate	a																						
Leeds	d		16 28	16 57		17 05								17 57	18 06						18 28	18 35	18 57
York	d	16 53	16 58	17 26		17 32			17 35			17 48	17 53	18 26	18 33			18 36	18 43	18 53	18 58	19 05	19 26
Thirsk	d		17 14	17 46										18 46					18 59				19 46
Northallerton	d		17 22	17 58										18 59				18 56	19 10		19 19		19 57
Darlington	a	17 21	17 32			17 58			18 05			18 13	18 21		19 00			19 08		19 25	19 30	19 37	
Eaglescliffe	a																		19 29				
Middlesbrough	a			18 32										19 32									20 30
Darlington	d	17 22	17 34			18 00			18 05			18 15	18 22		19 01			19 09		19 26	19 31	19 39	
Durham	d		17 50			18 16			18 23			18 31			19 19			19 26			19 47	19 55	
Chester-le-Street	d		17 56																		19 53		
Newcastle	a	17 51	18 10			18 31			18 40			18 46	18 51		19 34			19 42		19 55	20 08	20 10	
Hartlepool	a																		19 49				
Sunderland	a																		20 21				
Newcastle	d	17 54			18 19	18 37			18 42				18 53		19 37			19 45		19 57		20 12	
Morpeth	d				18a40													20 00					
Alnmouth for Alnwick	d								19 08						20 04								
Berwick-upon-Tweed	d	18 40				19 19							19 39		20 25					20 43			
Dunbar	d					19 42																	
Edinburgh	a	19 31				20 07			20 16				20 27		21 09			21 20		21 33		21 35	
Edinburgh	d					20 15									21 13								
Haymarket	d					20 20									21 17								
Motherwell	a														21 58								
Glasgow Central	a														22 17								
Stirling	a																						
Perth	a																						
Inverness	a																						
Inverkeithing	a					20 34																	
Kirkcaldy	a					20 51																	
Leuchars	a					21 27																	
Dundee	a					21 44																	
Arbroath	a																						
Montrose	a																						
Stonehaven	a																						
Aberdeen	a																						

A to Dunbar
B to Berwick-upon-Tweed
C to Durham

Table 26

Saturdays until 18 June

London - Humberside, Yorkshire, North East England and Scotland

		NT	XC	EM	GR	GR	GR	GR	HT	XC	GR	TP	XC	EM	GR	GR	GR	GR	EM	XC	GR	GC	GC
				◇										◇		B			◇				
London Kings Cross ⊖	d				17 03	17 10	17 30	17 35	17 48		18 00				18 03	18 08	18 30	18 35			19 00	19 20	19 20
Stevenage	d				17 22											18 28							
Peterborough	a				17 52	17 57	18 15	18 21							18 50	18 58	19 15	19 21					
Norwich	d			15 52										16 57					17 54				
Peterborough	d			17 27	17 53	17 58	18 16	18 22						18 26	18 51	18 58	19 15	19 21	19 27				
Grantham	a			17 58	18 13	18 20			18 48					18 55		19 19			19 57				
	d			18 03	18 13	18 21			18 49					18 58		19 20							
Newark North Gate	a				18 25		18 45								19 19	19 33	19 43						
	d				18 25		18 46								19 19	19 33	19 43						
Lincoln	a															20 03							
Retford	d								19 12						19 35								
Doncaster	a				18 49	18 53	19 09	19 14	19 26						19 50		20 08	20 12					20 53
Selby	a					19 09			19 42														
Hull	a					19 57			20 22														
Pontefract Monkhill	a																						21 16
Wakefield Kirkgate	a																						21 39
Wakefield Westgate	a				19 07			19 32							20 07			20 31					
Leeds	a				19 27			19 48							20 28			20 47					
Brighouse	a																						21 58
Halifax	a																						22 09
Shipley	a																						
Bradford Forster Square	a																						
Bradford Interchange	a																						22 40
Keighley	a																	21s13					
Skipton	a																	21 30					
Sheffield	d		18 21	19a39						18 47			19 22	20a27						19 54			
Doncaster	d						19 10			19 18							20 09			20 19			
York	a						19 34			19 40	19 53						20 35			20 46	20 52	20 17	
Scarborough	a																						
Harrogate	a							20 29															
Leeds	d		19 05									19 57	20 08										
York	d		19 32				19 36			19 44	19 55	20 26	20 34				20 37			20 48	20 53	20 17	
Thirsk	d											20 46										21 36	
Northallerton	d											21 01					20 56					21 45	
Darlington	a		19 58				20 04			20 11	20 22		21 00				21 09			21 14	21 21		
Eaglescliffe	a																					22 03	
Middlesbrough	a											21 32											
Darlington	d		19 59				20 04			20 13	20 23		21 01				21 09			21 16	21 22		
Durham	d		20 17				20 22			20 30			21 18				21 27			21 33			
Chester-le-Street	d																						
Newcastle	a		20 28				20 43			20 44	20 52		21 32				21 48			21 47	21 56		
Hartlepool	a																					22 23	
Sunderland	a																					22 51	
Newcastle	d	20 20	20 38								20 54		21 38										
Morpeth	d	20a41	20 54								21 09												
Alnmouth for Alnwick	d										21 25		22 02										
Berwick-upon-Tweed	d		21 25								21 49												
Dunbar	d		21 50								22 13												
Edinburgh	a		22 14								22 41		23 10										
Edinburgh	d																						
Haymarket	d																						
Motherwell	a																						
Glasgow Central	a																						
Stirling	a																						
Perth	a																						
Inverness	a																						
Inverkeithing	a																						
Kirkcaldy	a																						
Leuchars	a																						
Dundee	a																						
Arbroath	a																						
Montrose	a																						
Stonehaven	a																						
Aberdeen	a																						

B 1 to Grantham

Table 26

Saturdays
until 18 June

London - Humberside, Yorkshire, North East England and Scotland

		GR	HT	EM	TP	XC	XC	GR	GR	XC	EM	EM	GR	GR	XC	EM	XC	XC
		■ 1	◇1	◇	◇1	◇1	◇1	■ 1	■ 1	◇1	◇1		■ 1	■ 1	◇1	◇1	◇1	◇1
		⊡⌶	☒				⌶	⊡⌶	⊡⌶		⊡		⊡⌶	⊡⌶		⊡	⌶	
London Kings Cross 15 ⊖	d	19 30	19 48					20 00	20 30				21 00	22 00				
Stevenage 4	d	19 49																
Peterborough 8	a	20 19						20 46	21 15				21 45	22 46				
Norwich	d			18 57														
Peterborough 8	d	20 20		20 27				20 47	21 15			21 27	21 46	22 47				
Grantham 7	a	20 40	20 49	20 58					21 35			22 00		23 06				
	d	20 40	20 50						21 35					23 06				
Newark North Gate 7	a	20 52						21 15	21 47					23 18				
	d	20 52						21 15	21 47					23 18				
Lincoln	a																	
Retford 10	d		21 14						22 02					23 33				
Doncaster 7	a	21 16	21 28					21 40	22 17					23 48				
Selby	a		21 44															
Hull	a		22 24															
Pontefract Monkhill	a																	
Wakefield Kirkgate 4	a																	
Wakefield Westgate 7	a	21 34							22 35					00 05				
Leeds 10	a	21 54							22 55					00 26				
Brighouse	a																	
Halifax	a																	
Shipley	a	22s11																
Bradford Forster Square	a	22 24																
Bradford Interchange	a																	
Keighley	a																	
Skipton	a																	
Sheffield 7	d					20 53	20 24			21 21	21 24				22 09	22 19	22 27	23 12
Doncaster 7	d					21 23		21 40							22 32		22 53	
York 8	a					21 45		22 04					22 51		22 55			
Scarborough	a																	
Harrogate	a																	
Leeds 10	d				20 45		21b15			22a02	22a21					23a04	23a27	23a51
York 8	d				21 14	21 48	21a57	22 05					22 53					
Thirsk	d				21 31													
Northallerton	d				21 39								23 14					
Darlington 7	a				21 51	22 13		22 33					23 26					
Eaglescliffe	a																	
Middlesbrough	a																	
Darlington 7	d				21 52	22 15		22 33					23 27					
Durham	d				22 08	22 32		22 52					23 44					
Chester-le-Street	d				22 14													
Newcastle 8	a				22 27	22 49		23 13					00 06					
Hartlepool	a																	
Sunderland	a																	
Newcastle 8	d																	
Morpeth	d																	
Alnmouth for Alnwick	d																	
Berwick-upon-Tweed	d																	
Dunbar	d																	
Edinburgh 10	a																	
Edinburgh	d																	
Haymarket	d																	
Motherwell	a																	
Glasgow Central 15	a																	
Stirling	a																	
Perth	a																	
Inverness	a																	
Inverkeithing	a																	
Kirkcaldy	a																	
Leuchars 3	a																	
Dundee	a																	
Arbroath	a																	
Montrose	a																	
Stonehaven	a																	
Aberdeen	a																	

Table 26

Saturdays
25 June to 30 July

London - Humberside, Yorkshire, North East England and Scotland

		GR	GR	GR	TP	GR	GR	TP	NT	GR	XC	GR	NT	TP	TP	NT	GR	XC	TP	NT	NT	XC	GR
		■ 1	■ 1	■ 1	◇1	■ 1	■ 1	◇1		■ 1	◇1	■ 1		◇1	◇1		■ 1	◇1	◇1			◇1	■ 1
											C											C	
		⌶⊘	⊡⌶	⊡		⊡	⊡			⊡⌶	⌶	⊡⌶					⊡⌶	⌶	⌶			⌶	⊡⌶
London Kings Cross 15 ⊖	d	19p30	21p00	21p35		22p00	23p30																06 20
Stevenage 4	d		21p20																				06 40
Peterborough 8	a	20p15	21p50	22p20		22p45	00s24																07 11
Norwich	d																						
Peterborough 8	d	20p16	21p50	22p21		22p46																	07 12
Grantham 7	a			22p43		23p08	00s48																07 32
	d			22p43		23p08																	07 32
Newark North Gate 7	a	20p44	22p20	22p54		23p19	01s01																07 44
	d	20p44	22p20	22p54		23p19																	07 44
Lincoln	a																						
Retford 10	d			23p10																			
Doncaster 7	a	21p09	22p45	23p25		23p49	01s33																08 09
Selby	a																						
Hull	a																						
Pontefract Monkhill	a																						
Wakefield Kirkgate 4	a																						
Wakefield Westgate 7	a			23p44																			
Leeds 10	a			00 03			02 46																
Brighouse	a																						
Halifax	a																						
Shipley	a																						
Bradford Forster Square	a																						
Bradford Interchange	a																						
Keighley	a																						
Skipton	a																						
Sheffield 7	d																	06 49				07 12	
Doncaster 7	d	21p09	22p46			23p49						06 10						07 17					08 10
York 8	a	21p32	23p10			00 39						06 30						07 43					08 32
Scarborough	a																						
Harrogate	a																						
Leeds 10	d				22p42									06 35			07 10		07 50			07 57	
York 8	d	21p33	23p12		23b18	00 41		05 54				06 32		07 06	07 32		07 35	07 48	08 23			08 27	08 35
Thirsk	d				23p31			06 10						07 22	07 52				08 39				
Northallerton	d	21p53	23p40		23p49	01s11		06 18				06 51		07 30	08 00				08 49				08 54
Darlington 7	a	22p05	23p53		00 01	01s25		06 29				07 05		07 41			08 04	08 13				08 56	09 07
Eaglescliffe	a																						
Middlesbrough	a							07 03							08 32				09 21				
Darlington 7	d	22p06	23p53		00 02							07 05	07 21	07 42			08 05	08 15		08 22		08 57	09 07
Durham	d	22p23	00 11		00 18	01s43						07 23	07 42	07 59			08 23	08 31		08 43		09 14	09 25
Chester-le-Street	d												07 49	08 05						08 50			
Newcastle 8	a	22p41	00 47		00 52	02 20						07 39	08 05	08 17			08 39	08 46		09 01		09 28	09 41
Hartlepool	a																						
Sunderland	a																						
Newcastle 8	d	22p42							05 55	06 30	07 38	07 42				07 58	08 41				09 15	09 35	09 44
Morpeth	d	22p56							06 15	06 43	07 51					08a19	08 56				09a36		
Alnmouth for Alnwick	d	23p12							06a34	06 57		08 08										09 59	
Berwick-upon-Tweed	d	23p38								07 21	08 24	08 32					09 31					10 20	
Dunbar	d									07 48		08 55					09 55						
Edinburgh 10	a	00 31								08 17	09 07	09 24					10 24					11 07	11 15
Edinburgh	d										09 11						10 27					11 11	
Haymarket	d										09 16						10 32					11 16	
Motherwell	a										10 00											11 52	
Glasgow Central 15	a										10 23											12 13	
Stirling	a																						
Perth	a																						
Inverness	a																						
Inverkeithing	a																10 47						
Kirkcaldy	a																11 04						
Leuchars 3	a																11 28						
Dundee	a																11 43						
Arbroath	a																12 00						
Montrose	a																12 16						
Stonehaven	a																12 39						
Aberdeen	a																13 05						

C ⌶ to Berwick-upon-Tweed

b Previous night, arr. 2309

Table 26

Saturdays
25 June to 30 July

London - Humberside, Yorkshire, North East England and Scotland

		TP	XC	GR	TP	TP	NT	XC	EM	GR	GR	GC	EM	XC	GR	GR	EM	TP	TP	NT	XC	GR	XC
		◇1	◇1	1	◇1	◇1		◇1	◇	1	1	1		◇1	1	1	◇1	◇1	◇1		◇1 A	1	◇1
London Kings Cross 15 ⊖	d			07 00						07 03	07 30	07 47			08 00	08 03						08 30	
Stevenage 4	d									07 22													
Peterborough 8	a									07 52	08 15					08 50						09 15	
Norwich	d								05 52														
Peterborough 8	d								07 27	07 53	08 15		08 33			08 50						09 15	
Grantham 7	a								07 56	08 13						09 10							
	d								07 58	08 13						09 10							
Newark North Gate 7	a									08 25						09 22						09 43	
	d									08 25						09 22						09 43	
Lincoln	a												09 59										
Retford 10	d										08 54												
Doncaster 7	a									08 49	09 09					09 49						10 08	
Selby	a																						
Hull	a																						
Pontefract Monkhill	a																						
Wakefield Kirkgate 4	a																						
Wakefield Westgate 7	a									09 07						10 07							
Leeds 10	a									09 27						10 27							
Brighouse	a																						
Halifax	a																						
Shipley	a																						
Bradford Forster Square	a																						
Bradford Interchange	a																						
Keighley	a																						
Skipton	a																						
Sheffield 7	d		07 54					08 21	09a38					08 48			09 21				09 21		09 47
Doncaster 7	d		08 25								09 11			09 20			09 55					10 09	10 19
York 8	a		08 47	08 52							09 33	09 39		09 45	09 49		10 14					10 33	10 45
Scarborough	a																11 06						
Harrogate	a																						
Leeds 10	d				08 28	08 57		09 05										09 28	09 57		10 05		
York 8	d	08 42	08 50	08 53	08 58	09 26		09 33			09 36	09 44		09 49	09 53			09 58	10 26		10 32	10 35	10 48
Thirsk	d					09 46						10 00							10 46				
Northallerton	d				09 19	09 59						10 16						10 19	10 59			10 54	
Darlington 7	a	09 11	09 16	09 22	09 30			09 58			10 03			10 15	10 20			10 30			10 58	11 07	11 13
Eaglescliffe	a											10 37											
Middlesbrough	a					10 30													11 30				
Darlington 7	d	09 12	09 18	09 23	09 31			10 00			10 04			10 16	10 22			10 31			11 00	11 07	11 15
Durham	d	09 29	09 35		09 47			10 16			10 21			10 33				10 47			11 16	11 25	11 31
Chester-le-Street	d				09 55																		
Newcastle 8 ⛴	a	09 45	09 48	09 51	10 07			10 31			10 37			10 47	10 51			11 05			11 31	11 41	11 47
Hartlepool	a											11 07											
Sunderland ⛴	a											11 40											
Newcastle 8 ⛴	d			09 54			10 14	10 36			10 39				10 54					11 15	11 36	11 44	
Morpeth	d						10a35													11a36			
Alnmouth for Alnwick	d										11 05												
Berwick-upon-Tweed	d			10 39											11 39						12 20		
Dunbar	d							11 38															
Edinburgh 10	a			11 31				12 07			12 15				12 31						13 04	13 13	
Edinburgh	d																				13 11		
Haymarket	d																				13 15		
Motherwell	a																				13 52		
Glasgow Central 15	a																				14 13		
Stirling	a																						
Perth	a																						
Inverness	a																						
Inverkeithing	a																						
Kirkcaldy	a																						
Leuchars 3	a																						
Dundee	a																						
Arbroath	a																						
Montrose	a																						
Stonehaven	a																						
Aberdeen	a																						

A ⚹ to Berwick-upon-Tweed

Table 26

Saturdays
25 June to 30 July

London - Humberside, Yorkshire, North East England and Scotland

		GR	TP	TP	NT	XC	EM	EM	GR	GR	HT	XC	GR	TP	TP	NT	XC	EM	GR	GR	GC	XC
		1	◇1	◇1		◇1	◇		1	1	◇1	◇1	1 A	◇1	◇1		◇1 B	◇	1	1		◇1
London Kings Cross 15 ⊖	d	09 00							09 03	09 30	09 48		10 00						10 03	10 30	10 48	
Stevenage 4	d								09 22													
Peterborough 8	a								09 52	10 15									10 50	11 15		
Norwich	d						07 57											08 57				
Peterborough 8	d						09 30	09 33	09 53	10 15								10 26	10 51	11 15		
Grantham 7	a						09 58		10 13		10 48							10 57	11 10			
	d						09 58		10 13		10 49							10 58	11 10			
Newark North Gate 7	a								10 25										11 23	11 43		
	d								10 25										11 23	11 43		
Lincoln	a							10 59														
Retford 10	d									10 53	11 10											
Doncaster 7	a								10 50	11 08	11 24								11 50	12 08	12 18	
Selby	a										11 40											
Hull	a										12 20											
Pontefract Monkhill	a																				12 44	
Wakefield Kirkgate 4	a																				13 04	
Wakefield Westgate 7	a								11 07										12 07			
Leeds 10	a								11 28										12 28			
Brighouse	a																				13 29	
Halifax	a																				13 40	
Shipley	a																					
Bradford Forster Square	a																					
Bradford Interchange	a																				13 55	
Keighley	a																					
Skipton	a																					
Sheffield 7	d					10 21	11a38					10 47					11 21	12a38				11 47
Doncaster 7	d									11 09		11 19								12 09		12 17
York 8	a	10 52								11 33		11 45	11 52							12 33		12 45
Scarborough	a																					
Harrogate	a																					
Leeds 10	d		10 28	10 57		11 05								11 28	11 57		12 05					
York 8	d	10 53	10 58	11 26		11 32				11 35		11 48	11 53	11 58	12 26		12 32			12 35		12 48
Thirsk	d			11 46											12 46							
Northallerton	d		11 19	11 59										12 19	12 59					12 54		
Darlington 7	a	11 21	11 30			11 58				12 04		12 13	12 21	12 30			12 58			13 07		13 13
Eaglescliffe	a																					
Middlesbrough	a			12 30											13 30							
Darlington 7	d	11 22	11 31			12 00				12 04		12 15	12 22	12 31			13 00			13 07		13 15
Durham	d		11 47			12 16				12 22		12 31		12 47			13 18			13 25		13 31
Chester-le-Street	d		11 53																			
Newcastle 8 ⛴	a	11 51	12 06			12 31				12 38		12 46	12 51	13 03			13 34			13 41		13 46
Hartlepool	a																					
Sunderland ⛴	a																					
Newcastle 8 ⛴	d	11 54			12 15	12 36				12 40			12 54			13 15	13 35			13 44		
Morpeth	d				12a35											13a37						
Alnmouth for Alnwick	d									13 06							14 00					
Berwick-upon-Tweed	d	12 39											13 40				14 20					
Dunbar	d					13 38																
Edinburgh 10	a	13 31				14 07				14 15			14 24				15 07			15 15		
Edinburgh	d												14 27				15 11					
Haymarket	d												14 32				15 16					
Motherwell	a																15 52					
Glasgow Central 15	a																16 20					
Stirling	a																					
Perth	a																					
Inverness	a																					
Inverkeithing	a												14 46									
Kirkcaldy	a												15 03									
Leuchars 3	a												15 28									
Dundee	a												15 46									
Arbroath	a												16 04									
Montrose	a												16 20									
Stonehaven	a												16 43									
Aberdeen	a												17 09									

A The Northern Lights

B ⚹ to Berwick-upon-Tweed

Table 26

London - Humberside, Yorkshire, North East England and Scotland

		EM	GR	EM	GR	TP	GC	TP	NT	XC	GR	GR	HT	XC	GR	TP	TP	NT	XC	EM	EM	GR	GR
		◇				◇		◇		◇			◇	◇	B	◇	◇		◇ A	◇			
London Kings Cross ⊖	d		11 00		11 03		11 20				11 30	11 35	11 48		12 00							12 03	12 30
Stevenage	d				11 22																		
Peterborough	a				11 52						12 15	12 21										12 51	13 15
Norwich	d	09 57																		10 57			
Peterborough	d	11 25		11 48	11 53						12 15	12 21								12 25	12 41	12 51	13 15
Grantham	a	11 57			12 13								12 48							12 58		13 16	
	d	11 58			12 13								12 49							12 58		13 16	
Newark North Gate	a				12 25																	13 27	13 43
	d				12 25																	13 27	13 43
Lincoln	a			13 14																	14 07		
Retford	d										12 53		13 10										
Doncaster	a				12 50						13 08	13 12	13 24									13 52	14 09
Selby	a												13 40										
Hull	a												14 20										
Pontefract Monkhill	a																						
Wakefield Kirkgate	a																						
Wakefield Westgate	a				13 07							13 30										14 11	
Leeds	a				13 28							13 50										14 31	
Brighouse	a																						
Halifax	a																						
Shipley	a																						
Bradford Forster Square	a																						
Bradford Interchange	a																						
Keighley	a																						
Skipton	a																						
Sheffield	d	13a38								12 21				12 47					13 21	14a38			
Doncaster	d										13 09			13 19									14 10
York	a		12 52				13 14				13 33			13 45	13 53								14 33
Scarborough	a																						
Harrogate	a																						
Leeds	d					12 28		12 57		13 05						13 28	13 57		14 05				
York	d		12 53			12 58	13 16	13 26		13 32	13 35			13 48	13 54	13 58	14 26		14 32				14 35
Thirsk	d						13 33	13 46									14 46						
Northallerton	d					13 19	13 42	13 59								14 19	14 59						14 54
Darlington	a		13 21			13 30				13 58	14 04			14 13	14 22	14 30			14 58				15 07
Eaglescliffe	a						13 59																
Middlesbrough	a							14 30									15 30						
Darlington	d		13 22			13 31				14 00	14 04			14 15	14 23	14 31			15 00				15 07
Durham	d					13 47				14 16	14 22			14 31		14 47			15 16				15 25
Chester-le-Street	d					13 53																	
Newcastle	a		13 51			14 06				14 32	14 38			14 46	14 52	15 05			15 31				15 41
Hartlepool	a						14 20																
Sunderland	a						14 50																
Newcastle	d		13 54						14 15	14 35	14 40				14 54			15 15	15 34				15 44
Morpeth	d								14a37	14 48								15a35					
Alnmouth for Alnwick	d										15 06								15 59				
Berwick-upon-Tweed	d		14 39												15 40				16 19				
Dunbar	d									15 40													
Edinburgh	a		15 31							16 04	16 15				16 26				17 07				17 15
Edinburgh	d														16 32				17 11				
Haymarket	d														16 38				17 16				
Motherwell	a																		17 52				
Glasgow Central	a																		18 11				
Stirling	a														17 19								
Perth	a														18 00								
Inverness	a														20 11								
Inverkeithing	a																						
Kirkcaldy	a																						
Leuchars	a																						
Dundee	a																						
Arbroath	a																						
Montrose	a																						
Stonehaven	a																						
Aberdeen	a																						

A to Berwick-upon-Tweed

B The Highland Chieftain

Table 26

London - Humberside, Yorkshire, North East England and Scotland

		XC	EM	GR	GR	TP	TP	NT	XC	GR	XC	GR	TP	NT	NT	XC	EM	GR	EM	GR	HT	XC
		◇	◇			◇	◇		◇ A		◇		◇			◇ B	◇				◇	◇
London Kings Cross ⊖	d			13 00	13 03					13 30		14 00						14 03		14 30	14 48	
Stevenage	d				13 22																	
Peterborough	a				13 52					14 15								14 50		15 15		
Norwich	d		11 57														12 57					
Peterborough	d		13 28		13 53					14 15							14 26	14 50	15 11	15 15		
Grantham	a		13 56	14 00	14 13												14 57	15 09			15 48	
	d		13 58	14 00	14 13												14 58	15 09			15 49	
Newark North Gate	a				14 25													15 22		15 43		
	d				14 25													15 22		15 43		
Lincoln	a																		16 48			
Retford	d									14 53											16 10	
Doncaster	a				14 50					15 08								15 47		16 08	16 24	
Selby	a																				16 41	
Hull	a																				17 28	
Pontefract Monkhill	a																					
Wakefield Kirkgate	a																					
Wakefield Westgate	a				15 07													16 07				
Leeds	a				15 28													16 28				
Brighouse	a																					
Halifax	a																					
Shipley	a																					
Bradford Forster Square	a																					
Bradford Interchange	a																					
Keighley	a																					
Skipton	a																					
Sheffield	d	13 47	15a38						14 21		14 47					15 21	16a38					15 47
Doncaster	d	14 19								15 10	15 19									16 09		16 19
York	a	14 45		14 51						15 33	15 45	15 51								16 33		16 46
Scarborough	a																					
Harrogate	a																					
Leeds	d					14 28	14 57		15 05				15 56			16 05						
York	d	14 48		14 53		14 58	15 26		15 32	15 35	15 48	15 53	16 25			16 32				16 35		16 48
Thirsk	d						15 46						16 45									
Northallerton	d					15 19	15 59						16 58							16 54		
Darlington	a	15 13		15 20		15 30			15 58	16 03	16 13	16 21				16 58				17 07		17 13
Eaglescliffe	a																					
Middlesbrough	a						16 30						17 30									
Darlington	d	15 15		15 21		15 31			16 00	16 04	16 15	16 21				17 00				17 07		17 15
Durham	d	15 31				15 47			16 16	16 21	16 31					17 16				17 25		17 31
Chester-le-Street	d					15 53																
Newcastle	a	15 46		15 51		16 09			16 31	16 39	16 46	16 51				17 31				17 41		17 46
Hartlepool	a																					
Sunderland	a																					
Newcastle	d			15 54				16 15	16 35	16 44		16 52		17 00	17 22	17 37				17 44		
Morpeth	d							16a36						17 22	17a42							
Alnmouth for Alnwick	d								17 00					17a45		18 01						
Berwick-upon-Tweed	d			16 39								17 40				18 21						
Dunbar	d								17 39													
Edinburgh	a			17 31					18 05	18 17		18 27				19 08				19 15		
Edinburgh	d								18 11			18 30				19 11						
Haymarket	d								18 15			18 35				19 16						
Motherwell	a															19 52						
Glasgow Central	a															20 11						
Stirling	a																					
Perth	a																					
Inverness	a																					
Inverkeithing	a								18 28			18 54										
Kirkcaldy	a								18 46			19 11										
Leuchars	a								19 17			19 38										
Dundee	a								19 32			19 52										
Arbroath	a								19 49			20 10										
Montrose	a								20 03			20 26										
Stonehaven	a								20 23			20 49										
Aberdeen	a								20 43			21 15										

A to Dunbar

B to Berwick-upon-Tweed

Table 26

Saturdays
25 June to 30 July

London - Humberside, Yorkshire, North East England and Scotland

		GR	TP	TP	NT	XC	EM	GR	GR	GC	EM	XC	GR	TP	XC	EM	GR	GR	GC	GR	TP	XC	TP
		■ 1	◇1	◇1		◇1	◇	■ 1	■ 1			◇1	■ 1	◇1	◇1	◇	■ 1	■ 1	■ 1	■ 1	◇1	◇1	◇1
						A									B							C	
		✕	⌶	⌶		⌶		✕	✕			⌶	✕		⌶		✕	✕	☐	✕		⌶	
London Kings Cross 15 ⊖	d	15 00						15 03	15 30	15 48			16 00				16 03	16 30	16 48	17 00			
Stevenage 4	d							15 22															
Peterborough 8	a							15 52	16 15								16 50	17 15					
Norwich	d						13 57									14 57							
Peterborough 8	d						15 25	15 53	16 15		16 25					16 27	16 51	17 15					
Grantham 7	a						15 57	16 13								16 57	17 10						
	d						15 58	16 13								16 58	17 10						
Newark North Gate 7	a							16 25									17 23	17 43					
	d							16 25									17 23	17 43					
Lincoln	a										17 51												
Retford 10	d								16 53														
Doncaster 7	a							16 50	17 08	17 20							17 49	18 08					
Selby	a																						
Hull	a																						
Pontefract Monkhill	a									17 45													
Wakefield Kirkgate 4	a									18 03													
Wakefield Westgate 7	a							17 07									18 07						
Leeds 10	a							17 28									18 27						
Brighouse	a									18 28													
Halifax	a									18 40													
Shipley	a																						
Bradford Forster Square	a																						
Bradford Interchange	a									18 55													
Keighley	a																						
Skipton	a																						
Sheffield 7	d					16 21	17a34					16 47			17 21	18a39						17 47	
Doncaster 7	d								17 10			17 19						18 09					
York 8	a	16 52							17 33			17 38	17 50					18 33	18 39	18 52			
Scarborough	a																						
Harrogate	a																						
Leeds 10	d		16 28	16 57		17 05								17 57	18 06						18 28	18 35	18 57
York 8	d	16 53	16 58	17 26		17 32			17 35			17 48	17 53	18 26	18 33			18 36	18 43	18 53	18 58	19 05	19 26
Thirsk	d		17 14	17 46										18 46					18 59				19 46
Northallerton	d		17 22	17 58										18 59				18 56	19 10		19 19		19 57
Darlington 7	a	17 21	17 32			17 58			18 05			18 13	18 21		19 00			19 08		19 25	19 30	19 37	
Eaglescliffe	a																		19 28				
Middlesbrough	a			18 32										19 32									20 30
Darlington 7	d	17 22	17 34			18 00			18 05			18 15	18 22		19 01			19 09		19 26	19 31	19 39	
Durham	d		17 50			18 16			18 23			18 31			19 19			19 26			19 47	19 55	
Chester-le-Street	d		17 56																		19 53		
Newcastle 8	a	17 51	18 10			18 31			18 40			18 46	18 51		19 34			19 42		19 55	20 08	20 10	
Hartlepool	a																		19 47				
Sunderland	a																		20 21				
Newcastle 8	d	17 54			18 19	18 37			18 42				18 53		19 37			19 45		19 57		20 12	
Morpeth	d				18a40													20 00					
Alnmouth for Alnwick	d								19 08						20 04								
Berwick-upon-Tweed	d	18 40				19 19							19 39		20 25					20 43			
Dunbar	d					19 42																	
Edinburgh 10	a	19 31				20 07			20 16				20 27		21 09			21 20		21 33		21 35	
Edinburgh	d					20 15									21 13								
Haymarket	d					20 20									21 17								
Motherwell	a														21 58								
Glasgow Central 15	a														22 17								
Stirling	a																						
Perth	a																						
Inverness	a																						
Inverkeithing	a					20 34																	
Kirkcaldy	a					20 51																	
Leuchars 3	a					21 27																	
Dundee	a					21 44																	
Arbroath	a																						
Montrose	a																						
Stonehaven	a																						
Aberdeen	a																						

A ⌶ to Dunbar
B ⌶ to Berwick-upon-Tweed
C ⌶ to Durham

Table 26

Saturdays
25 June to 30 July

London - Humberside, Yorkshire, North East England and Scotland

		NT	XC	EM	GR	GR	GR	GR	HT	XC	GR	TP	XC	EM	GR	GR	GR	GR	EM	XC	GR	GC	GC
			◇1	◇	■ 1	■ 1	■ 1	■ 1	◇1	◇1	■ 1	◇1	◇1	◇	■ 1	■ 1	■ 1	■ 1	◇	◇1	■ 1	■ 1	
			⌶		✕	✕	✕	✕	☒	⌶	✕		⌶		✕	✕	✕	✕		⌶	✕	☐	
London Kings Cross 15 ⊖	d				17 03	17 10	17 30	17 35	17 48		18 00				18 03	18 08	18 30	18 35			19 00	19 07	19 20
Stevenage 4	d				17 22											18 28							
Peterborough 8	a				17 52	17 57	18 15	18 21							18 50	18 58	19 15	19 21					
Norwich	d			15 52										16 57					17 54				
Peterborough 8	d			17 27	17 53	17 58	18 16	18 22						18 26	18 51	18 58	19 15	19 21	19 27				
Grantham 7	a			17 58	18 13	18 20			18 48					18 55		19 19			19 57				
	d			18 03	18 13	18 21			18 49					18 58		19 20							
Newark North Gate 7	a				18 25		18 45								19 19	19 33	19 43						
	d				18 25		18 46								19 19	19 33	19 43						
Lincoln	a															20 03							
Retford 10	d								19 12						19 35								
Doncaster 7	a				18 49	18 53	19 09	19 14	19 26						19 50		20 08	20 12					20 53
Selby	a					19 09			19 42														
Hull	a					19 57			20 22														
Pontefract Monkhill	a																						21 16
Wakefield Kirkgate 4	a																						21 39
Wakefield Westgate 7	a				19 07			19 32							20 07			20 31					
Leeds 10	a				19 27			19 48							20 28			20 47					
Brighouse	a																						21 58
Halifax	a																						22 09
Shipley	a																						
Bradford Forster Square	a																						
Bradford Interchange	a																						22 40
Keighley	a																	21s13					
Skipton	a																	21 30					
Sheffield 7	d		18 21	19a39						18 47			19 22	20a27						19 54			
Doncaster 7	d						19 10			19 18							20 09			20 19			
York 8	a						19 34			19 40	19 53						20 35			20 46	20 52	20 55	
Scarborough	a																						
Harrogate	a							20 29															
Leeds 10	d		19 05									19 57	20 08										
York 8	d		19 32				19 36			19 44	19 55	20 26	20 34				20 37			20 48	20 53	20 58	
Thirsk	d											20 46										21 17	
Northallerton	d											21 01					20 56					21 26	
Darlington 7	a		19 58				20 04			20 11	20 22		21 00				21 09			21 14	21 21		
Eaglescliffe	a																					21 46	
Middlesbrough	a											21 32											
Darlington 7	d		19 59				20 04			20 13	20 23		21 01				21 09			21 16	21 22		
Durham	d		20 17				20 22			20 30			21 18				21 27			21 33			
Chester-le-Street	d																						
Newcastle 8	a		20 28				20 43			20 44	20 52		21 32				21 48			21 47	21 56		
Hartlepool	a																					22 04	
Sunderland	a																					22 36	
Newcastle 8	d	20 20	20 38								20 54		21 38										
Morpeth	d	20a41	20 54								21 09												
Alnmouth for Alnwick	d										21 25		22 02										
Berwick-upon-Tweed	d		21 25								21 49												
Dunbar	d		21 50								22 13												
Edinburgh 10	a		22 14								22 41		23 10										
Edinburgh	d																						
Haymarket	d																						
Motherwell	a																						
Glasgow Central 15	a																						
Stirling	a																						
Perth	a																						
Inverness	a																						
Inverkeithing	a																						
Kirkcaldy	a																						
Leuchars 3	a																						
Dundee	a																						
Arbroath	a																						
Montrose	a																						
Stonehaven	a																						
Aberdeen	a																						

Table 26

Saturdays
25 June to 30 July

London - Humberside, Yorkshire, North East England and Scotland

		GR		HT	EM	TP	XC	XC	GR	XC	EM	EM		GR	XC	GR	GR	EM	XC	XC
		1		◇1	◇	◇1	◇1	◇1	1	◇1	◇1			1	◇1	1	1	◇1	◇1	◇1
London Kings Cross 15 ⊖	d	19 30		19 48					20 00					20 30		21 00	22 00			
Stevenage 4	d	19 49																		
Peterborough 8	a	20 19							20 46					21 36		22 02	23 03			
Norwich	d				18 57															
Peterborough 8	d	20 20			20 27				20 47			21 27		21 37		22 03	23 04			
Grantham 7	a	20 40		20 49	20 58							22 00		22 06			23 23			
	d	20 40		20 50										22 06			23 23			
Newark North Gate 7	a	20 52							21 15					22 18			23 35			
	d	20 52							21 15					22 18			23 35			
Lincoln	a																			
Retford 10	d			21 14										22 33			23 50			
Doncaster 7	a	21 16		21 28					21 40					22 47			00 05			
Selby	a			21 44																
Hull	a			22 24																
Pontefract Monkhill	a																			
Wakefield Kirkgate 4	a																			
Wakefield Westgate 7	a	21 34												23 24			00 20			
Leeds 10	a	21 54												23 46			00 40			
Brighouse	a																			
Halifax	a																			
Shipley	a	22s11																		
Bradford Forster Square	a	22 24																		
Bradford Interchange	a																			
Keighley	a																			
Skipton	a																			
Sheffield 7 ⇌	d						20 53	20 24		21 21	21 24				22 09			22 19	22 27	23 12
Doncaster 7	d						21 23		21 40						22 32				22 53	
York 8	a						21 45		22 04						22 55	23 12				
Scarborough	a																			
Harrogate	a																			
Leeds 10	d					20 45		21 15		22a02	22a21							23a04	23a27	23a51
York 8	d					21 14	21 48	21a57	22 05							23 14				
Thirsk	d					21 31														
Northallerton	d					21 39										23 34				
Darlington 7	a					21 51	22 13		22 33							23 46				
Eaglescliffe	a																			
Middlesbrough	a																			
Darlington 7	d					21 52	22 15		22 33							23 47				
Durham	d					22 08	22 32		22 52							00 04				
Chester-le-Street	d					22 14														
Newcastle 8 ⇌	a					22 27	22 49		23 13							00 25				
Hartlepool	a																			
Sunderland ⇌	a																			
Newcastle 8 ⇌	d																			
Morpeth	d																			
Alnmouth for Alnwick	d																			
Berwick-upon-Tweed	d																			
Dunbar	d																			
Edinburgh 10	a																			
Edinburgh	d																			
Haymarket	d																			
Motherwell	a																			
Glasgow Central 15	a																			
Stirling	a																			
Perth	a																			
Inverness	a																			
Inverkeithing	a																			
Kirkcaldy	a																			
Leuchars 3	a																			
Dundee	a																			
Arbroath	a																			
Montrose	a																			
Stonehaven	a																			
Aberdeen	a																			

Table 26

Saturdays
6 August to 10 September

London - Humberside, Yorkshire, North East England and Scotland

		GR	GR	GR	TP	GR	GR	TP	NT	GR		XC	GR	NT	TP	TP	NT	GR	XC	TP		NT	NT	XC	GR
		1	1	1	◇1	1	1	◇1		1		◇1	1		◇1	◇1		1	◇1	◇1				◇1	1
			A									C												C	
London Kings Cross 15 ⊖	d	19p30	21p00	21p35		22p00	23p30																		06 20
Stevenage 4	d		21p20																						06 40
Peterborough 8	a	20p15	21p50	22p20		22p45	00s24																		07 11
Norwich	d																								
Peterborough 8	d	20p16	21p50	22p21		22p46																			07 12
Grantham 7	a			22p43		23p08	00s48																		07 32
	d			22p43		23p08																			07 32
Newark North Gate 7	a	20p44	22p20	22p54		23p19	01s01																		07 44
	d	20p44	22p20	22p54		23p19																			07 44
Lincoln	a																								
Retford 10	d			23p10																					
Doncaster 7	a	21p09	22p45	23p25		23p49	01s33																		08 09
Selby	a																								
Hull	a																								
Pontefract Monkhill	a																								
Wakefield Kirkgate 4	a																								
Wakefield Westgate 7	a			23p44																					
Leeds 10	a			00 03			02 46																		
Brighouse	a																								
Halifax	a																								
Shipley	a																								
Bradford Forster Square	a																								
Bradford Interchange	a																								
Keighley	a																								
Skipton	a																								
Sheffield 7 ⇌	d																		06 49					07 12	
Doncaster 7	d	21p09	22p46			23p49							06 10						07 17						08 10
York 8	a	21p32	23p10			00 39							06 30						07 43						08 32
Scarborough	a																								
Harrogate	a																								
Leeds 10	d				22p42										06 35			07 10		07 50				07 57	
York 8	d	21p33	23p12		23b18	00 41		05 54					06 32		07 06	07 32		07 35	07 48	08 23				08 27	08 35
Thirsk	d				23p31			06 10							07 22	07 52				08 39					
Northallerton	d	21p53	23p40		23p49	01s11		06 18					06 51		07 30	08 00				08 49					08 54
Darlington 7	a	22p05	23p53		00 01	01s25		06 29					07 05		07 41			08 04	08 13					08 56	09 07
Eaglescliffe	a																								
Middlesbrough	a							07 03								08 32				09 21					
Darlington 7	d	22p06	23p53		00 02								07 05	07 21	07 42			08 05	08 15			08 22		08 57	09 07
Durham	d	22p23	00 11		00 18	01s43							07 23	07 42	07 59			08 23	08 31			08 43		09 14	09 25
Chester-le-Street	d													07 49	08 05							08 50			
Newcastle 8 ⇌	a	22p41	00 47		00 52	02 20							07 39	08 05	08 17			08 39	08 46			09 01		09 28	09 41
Hartlepool	a																								
Sunderland ⇌	a																								
Newcastle 8 ⇌	d	22p42							05 55	06 30		07 38	07 42				07 58	08 41					09 15	09 35	09 44
Morpeth	d	22p56							06 15	06 43		07 51					08a19	08 56					09a36		
Alnmouth for Alnwick	d	23p12							06a34	06 57			08 08											09 59	
Berwick-upon-Tweed	d	23p38								07 21		08 24	08 32					09 31						10 20	
Dunbar	d									07 48			08 55					09 55							
Edinburgh 10	a	00 31								08 17		09 07	09 24					10 24						11 07	11 15
Edinburgh	d											09 11						10 27						11 11	
Haymarket	d											09 16						10 32						11 16	
Motherwell	a											10 00												11 52	
Glasgow Central 15	a											10 23												12 13	
Stirling	a																								
Perth	a																								
Inverness	a																								
Inverkeithing	a																	10 47							
Kirkcaldy	a																	11 04							
Leuchars 3	a																	11 28							
Dundee	a																	11 43							
Arbroath	a																	12 00							
Montrose	a																	12 16							
Stonehaven	a																	12 39							
Aberdeen	a																	13 05							

A The Northern Lights

C to Berwick-upon-Tweed

b Previous night, arr. 2309

Table 26

6 August to 10 September

London - Humberside, Yorkshire, North East England and Scotland

		TP	XC	GR	TP	TP	NT	XC	EM	GR	GR	GC	EM	XC	GR	GR	EM	TP	TP	NT	XC	GR	XC
		◇1	◇1	1	◇1	◇1		◇1	◇	1	1	1		◇1	1	1	◇1	◇1	◇1		◇1 A	1	◇1
London Kings Cross 15 ⊖	d			07 00						07 03	07 30	07 47			08 00	08 03						08 30	
Stevenage 4	d									07 22													
Peterborough 8	a									07 52	08 15					08 50						09 15	
Norwich	d								05 52														
Peterborough 8	d								07 27	07 53	08 15		08 33			08 50						09 15	
Grantham 7	a								07 56	08 13						09 10							
	d								07 58	08 13						09 10							
Newark North Gate 7	a									08 25						09 22						09 43	
	d									08 25						09 22						09 43	
Lincoln	a												09 59										
Retford 10	d										08 54												
Doncaster 7	a									08 49	09 09					09 49						10 08	
Selby	a																						
Hull	a																						
Pontefract Monkhill	a																						
Wakefield Kirkgate 4	a																						
Wakefield Westgate 7	a									09 07						10 07							
Leeds 10	a									09 27						10 27							
Brighouse	a																						
Halifax	a																						
Shipley	a																						
Bradford Forster Square	a																						
Bradford Interchange	a																						
Keighley	a																						
Skipton	a																						
Sheffield 7	d		07 54					08 21	09a38					08 48			09 21				09 21		09 47
Doncaster 7	d		08 25								09 11			09 20			09 55					10 09	10 19
York 8	a		08 47	08 52							09 33	09 39		09 45	09 49		10 14					10 33	10 45
Scarborough	a																11 06						
Harrogate	a																						
Leeds 10	d				08 28	08 57		09 05										09 28	09 57		10 05		
York 8	d	08 42	08 50	08 53	08 58	09 26		09 33			09 36	09 44		09 49	09 53			09 58	10 26		10 32	10 35	10 48
Thirsk	d					09 46						10 00							10 46				
Northallerton	d				09 19	09 59						10 16						10 19	10 59			10 54	
Darlington 7	a	09 11	09 16	09 22	09 30			09 58			10 03			10 15	10 20			10 30			10 58	11 07	11 13
Eaglescliffe	a											10 37											
Middlesbrough	a					10 30													11 30				
Darlington 7	d	09 12	09 18	09 23	09 31			10 00			10 04			10 16	10 22			10 31			11 00	11 07	11 15
Durham	d	09 29	09 35		09 47			10 16			10 21			10 33				10 47			11 16	11 25	11 31
Chester-le-Street	d				09 55																		
Newcastle 8	a	09 45	09 48	09 51	10 07			10 31			10 37			10 47	10 51			11 05			11 31	11 41	11 47
Hartlepool	a											11 07											
Sunderland	a											11 40											
Newcastle 8	d			09 54			10 14	10 36			10 39				10 54					11 15	11 36	11 44	
Morpeth	d						10a35													11a36			
Alnmouth for Alnwick	d										11 05												
Berwick-upon-Tweed	d			10 39											11 39						12 20		
Dunbar	d							11 38															
Edinburgh 10	a			11 31				12 07			12 15				12 31						13 04	13 13	
Edinburgh	d																				13 11		
Haymarket	d																				13 15		
Motherwell	a																				13 52		
Glasgow Central 15	a																				14 13		
Stirling	a																						
Perth	a																						
Inverness	a																						
Inverkeithing	a																						
Kirkcaldy	a																						
Leuchars 3	a																						
Dundee	a																						
Arbroath	a																						
Montrose	a																						
Stonehaven	a																						
Aberdeen	a																						

A ✕ to Berwick-upon-Tweed

Table 26

6 August to 10 September

London - Humberside, Yorkshire, North East England and Scotland

		GR	TP	TP	NT	XC	EM	EM	GR	GR	HT	XC	GR	TP	TP	NT	XC	EM	GR	GR	GC	XC
		1	◇1	◇1		◇1	◇		1	1	◇1	◇1	1 A	◇1	◇1		◇1 B	◇	1	1		◇1
London Kings Cross 15 ⊖	d	09 00							09 03	09 30	09 48		10 00						10 03	10 30	10 48	
Stevenage 4	d								09 22													
Peterborough 8	a								09 52	10 15									10 50	11 15		
Norwich	d						07 57											08 57				
Peterborough 8	d						09 30	09 33	09 53	10 15								10 26	10 51	11 15		
Grantham 7	a						09 58		10 13		10 48							10 57	11 10			
	d						09 58		10 13		10 49							10 58	11 10			
Newark North Gate 7	a								10 25										11 23	11 43		
	d								10 25										11 23	11 43		
Lincoln	a							10 59														
Retford 10	d									10 53	11 10											
Doncaster 7	a								10 50	11 08	11 24								11 50	12 08	12 18	
Selby	a										11 40											
Hull	a										12 20											
Pontefract Monkhill	a																				12 44	
Wakefield Kirkgate 4	a																				13 04	
Wakefield Westgate 7	a								11 07										12 07			
Leeds 10	a								11 28										12 28			
Brighouse	a																				13 29	
Halifax	a																				13 40	
Shipley	a																					
Bradford Forster Square	a																					
Bradford Interchange	a																				13 55	
Keighley	a																					
Skipton	a																					
Sheffield 7	d					10 21	11a38					10 47					11 21	12a38				11 47
Doncaster 7	d									11 09		11 19								12 09		12 17
York 8	a	10 52								11 33		11 45	11 52							12 33		12 45
Scarborough	a																					
Harrogate	a																					
Leeds 10	d		10 28	10 57		11 05								11 28	11 57		12 05					
York 8	d	10 53	10 58	11 26		11 32				11 35		11 48	11 53	11 58	12 26		12 32			12 35		12 48
Thirsk	d			11 46											12 46							
Northallerton	d		11 19	11 59										12 19	12 59					12 54		
Darlington 7	a	11 21	11 30			11 58				12 04		12 13	12 21	12 30			12 58			13 07		13 13
Eaglescliffe	a																					
Middlesbrough	a			12 30											13 30							
Darlington 7	d	11 22	11 31			12 00				12 04		12 15	12 22	12 31			13 00			13 07		13 15
Durham	d		11 47			12 16				12 22		12 31		12 47			13 18			13 25		13 31
Chester-le-Street	d		11 53																			
Newcastle 8	a	11 51	12 06			12 31				12 38		12 46	12 51	13 03			13 34			13 41		13 46
Hartlepool	a																					
Sunderland	a																					
Newcastle 8	d	11 54			12 15	12 36				12 40			12 54			13 15	13 35			13 44		
Morpeth	d				12a35											13a37						
Alnmouth for Alnwick	d									13 06							14 00					
Berwick-upon-Tweed	d	12 39											13 40				14 20					
Dunbar	d					13 38																
Edinburgh 10	a	13 31				14 07				14 15			14 24				15 07			15 15		
Edinburgh	d												14 27				15 11					
Haymarket	d												14 32				15 16					
Motherwell	a																15 52					
Glasgow Central 15	a																16 20					
Stirling	a																					
Perth	a																					
Inverness	a																					
Inverkeithing	a												14 46									
Kirkcaldy	a												15 03									
Leuchars 3	a												15 28									
Dundee	a												15 46									
Arbroath	a												16 04									
Montrose	a												16 20									
Stonehaven	a												16 43									
Aberdeen	a												17 09									

A The Flying Scotsman

B ✕ to Berwick-upon-Tweed

Table 26

Saturdays
6 August to 10 September

London - Humberside, Yorkshire, North East England and Scotland

		EM	GR	EM	GR	TP	GC	TP	NT	XC	GR	GR	HT	XC	GR	TP	TP	NT	XC	EM	EM	GR	GR
		◇	■ 1		■ 1	◇1	■ 1	◇1		◇1	■ 1	■ 1	◇1	◇1	■ 1 B	◇1	◇1		◇1 A	◇		■ 1	■ 1
London Kings Cross 15 ⊖	d		11 00		11 03		11 20				11 30	11 35	11 48		12 00							12 03	12 30
Stevenage 4	d				11 22																		
Peterborough 8	a				11 52						12 15	12 21										12 51	13 15
Norwich	d	09 57																		10 57			
Peterborough 8	d	11 25		11 48	11 53						12 15	12 21								12 25	12 41	12 51	13 15
Grantham 7	a	11 57			12 13								12 48							12 58		13 16	
	d	11 58			12 13								12 49							12 58		13 16	
Newark North Gate 7	a				12 25																	13 27	13 43
	d				12 25																	13 27	13 43
Lincoln	a			13 14																	14 07		
Retford 10	d										12 53		13 10										
Doncaster 7	a				12 50						13 08	13 12	13 24									13 52	14 09
Selby	a												13 40										
Hull	a												14 20										
Pontefract Monkhill	a																						
Wakefield Kirkgate 4	a																						
Wakefield Westgate 7	a				13 07							13 30										14 11	
Leeds 10	a				13 28							13 50										14 31	
Brighouse	a																						
Halifax	a																						
Shipley	a																						
Bradford Forster Square	a																						
Bradford Interchange	a																						
Keighley	a																						
Skipton	a																						
Sheffield 7	d	13a38								12 21				12 47					13 21	14a38			
Doncaster 7	d										13 09			13 19									14 10
York 8	a		12 52				13 14				13 33			13 45	13 53								14 33
Scarborough	a																						
Harrogate	a																						
Leeds 10	d					12 28		12 57		13 05						13 28	13 57		14 05				
York 8	d		12 53			12 58	13 16	13 26		13 32	13 35			13 48	13 54	13 58	14 26		14 32				14 35
Thirsk	d						13 33	13 46									14 46						
Northallerton	d					13 19	13 42	13 59								14 19	14 59						14 54
Darlington 7	a		13 21			13 30				13 58	14 04			14 13	14 22	14 30			14 58				15 07
Eaglescliffe	a						13 59																
Middlesbrough	a							14 30									15 30						
Darlington 7	d		13 22			13 31				14 00	14 04			14 15	14 23	14 31			15 00				15 07
Durham	d					13 47				14 16	14 22			14 31		14 47			15 16				15 25
Chester-le-Street	d					13 53																	
Newcastle 8	a		13 51			14 06				14 32	14 38			14 46	14 52	15 05			15 31				15 41
Hartlepool	a						14 20																
Sunderland	a						14 50																
Newcastle 8	d		13 54						14 15	14 35	14 40				14 54			15 15	15 34				15 44
Morpeth	d								14a37	14 48								15a35					
Alnmouth for Alnwick	d										15 06								15 59				
Berwick-upon-Tweed	d		14 39												15 40				16 19				
Dunbar	d									15 40													
Edinburgh 10	a		15 31							16 04	16 15				16 26				17 07				17 15
Edinburgh	d														16 32				17 11				
Haymarket	d														16 38				17 16				
Motherwell	a																		17 52				
Glasgow Central 15	a																		18 11				
Stirling	a														17 19								
Perth	a														18 00								
Inverness	a														20 11								
Inverkeithing	a																						
Kirkcaldy	a																						
Leuchars 3	a																						
Dundee	a																						
Arbroath	a																						
Montrose	a																						
Stonehaven	a																						
Aberdeen	a																						

A to Berwick-upon-Tweed

B The Highland Chieftan

Table 26

Saturdays
6 August to 10 September

London - Humberside, Yorkshire, North East England and Scotland

		XC	EM	GR	GR	TP	TP	NT	XC	GR	XC	GR	TP	NT	NT	XC	EM	GR	EM	GR	HT	XC
		◇1	◇	■ 1	■ 1	◇1	◇1		◇1 A	■ 1	◇1	■ 1	◇1			◇1 B	◇	■ 1		■ 1	◇1	◇1
London Kings Cross 15 ⊖	d			13 00	13 03					13 30		14 00						14 03		14 30	14 48	
Stevenage 4	d				13 22																	
Peterborough 8	a				13 52					14 15								14 50		15 15		
Norwich	d		11 57														12 57					
Peterborough 8	d		13 28		13 53					14 15							14 26	14 50	15 11	15 15		
Grantham 7	a		13 56	14 00	14 13												14 57	15 09			15 48	
	d		13 58	14 00	14 13												14 58	15 09			15 49	
Newark North Gate 7	a				14 25													15 22		15 43		
	d				14 25													15 22		15 43		
Lincoln	a																		16 48			
Retford 10	d									14 53											16 10	
Doncaster 7	a				14 50					15 08								15 47		16 08	16 24	
Selby	a																				16 41	
Hull	a																				17 28	
Pontefract Monkhill	a																					
Wakefield Kirkgate 4	a																					
Wakefield Westgate 7	a				15 07													16 07				
Leeds 10	a				15 28													16 28				
Brighouse	a																					
Halifax	a																					
Shipley	a																					
Bradford Forster Square	a																					
Bradford Interchange	a																					
Keighley	a																					
Skipton	a																					
Sheffield 7	d	13 47	15a38						14 21		14 47					15 21	16a38					15 47
Doncaster 7	d	14 19								15 10	15 19									16 09		16 19
York 8	a	14 45		14 51						15 33	15 45	15 51								16 33		16 46
Scarborough	a																					
Harrogate	a																					
Leeds 10	d					14 28	14 57		15 05				15 56			16 05						
York 8	d	14 48		14 53		14 58	15 26		15 32	15 35	15 48	15 53	16 25			16 32				16 35		16 48
Thirsk	d						15 46						16 45									
Northallerton	d					15 19	15 59						16 58							16 54		
Darlington 7	a	15 13		15 20		15 30			15 58	16 03	16 13	16 21				16 58				17 07		17 13
Eaglescliffe	a																					
Middlesbrough	a						16 30						17 30									
Darlington 7	d	15 15		15 21		15 31			16 00	16 04	16 15	16 21				17 00				17 07		17 15
Durham	d	15 31				15 47			16 16	16 21	16 31					17 16				17 25		17 31
Chester-le-Street	d					15 53																
Newcastle 8	a	15 46		15 51		16 09			16 31	16 39	16 46	16 51				17 31				17 41		17 46
Hartlepool	a																					
Sunderland	a																					
Newcastle 8	d			15 54				16 15	16 35	16 44		16 52		17 00	17 22	17 37				17 44		
Morpeth	d							16a36						17 22	17a42							
Alnmouth for Alnwick	d								17 00					17a45		18 01						
Berwick-upon-Tweed	d			16 39								17 40				18 21						
Dunbar	d								17 39													
Edinburgh 10	a			17 31					18 05	18 17		18 27				19 08				19 15		
Edinburgh	d								18 11			18 30				19 11						
Haymarket	d								18 15			18 35				19 16						
Motherwell	a															19 52						
Glasgow Central 15	a															20 11						
Stirling	a																					
Perth	a																					
Inverness	a																					
Inverkeithing	a								18 28			18 54										
Kirkcaldy	a								18 46			19 11										
Leuchars 3	a								19 17			19 38										
Dundee	a								19 32			19 52										
Arbroath	a								19 49			20 10										
Montrose	a								20 03			20 26										
Stonehaven	a								20 23			20 49										
Aberdeen	a								20 43			21 15										

A to Dunbar

B to Berwick-upon-Tweed

6 August to 10 September

London - Humberside, Yorkshire, North East England and Scotland

		GR	TP	TP	NT	XC	EM	GR	GR	GC		EM	XC	GR	TP	XC	EM	GR	GR	GC		GR	TP	XC	TP
						A										B								C	
London Kings Cross	d	15 00						15 03	15 30	15 48				16 00				16 03	16 30	16 48		17 00			
Stevenage	d							15 22																	
Peterborough	a							15 52	16 15									16 50	17 15						
Norwich	d						13 57										14 57								
Peterborough	d						15 25	15 53	16 15			16 25					16 27	16 51	17 15						
Grantham	a						15 57	16 13									16 57	17 10							
	d						15 58	16 13									16 58	17 10							
Newark North Gate	a							16 25										17 23	17 43						
	d							16 25										17 23	17 43						
Lincoln	a											17 51													
Retford	d								16 53																
Doncaster	a							16 50	17 08	17 20								17 49	18 08						
Selby	a																								
Hull	a																								
Pontefract Monkhill	a									17 45															
Wakefield Kirkgate	a									18 03															
Wakefield Westgate	a							17 07										18 07							
Leeds	a							17 28										18 27							
Brighouse	a									18 28															
Halifax	a									18 40															
Shipley	a																								
Bradford Forster Square	a																								
Bradford Interchange	a									18 55															
Keighley	a																								
Skipton	a																								
Sheffield	d					16 21	17a34						16 47			17 21	18a39							17 47	
Doncaster	d								17 10				17 19						18 09						
York	a	16 52							17 33				17 38	17 50					18 33	18 39		18 52			
Scarborough	a																								
Harrogate	a																								
Leeds	d		16 28	16 57		17 05									17 57	18 06							18 28	18 35	18 57
York	d	16 53	16 58	17 26		17 32			17 35				17 48	17 53	18 26	18 33			18 36	18 43		18 53	18 58	19 05	19 26
Thirsk	d		17 14	17 46											18 46					18 59					19 46
Northallerton	d		17 22	17 58											18 59				18 56	19 10			19 19		19 57
Darlington	a	17 21	17 32			17 58			18 05				18 13	18 21		19 00			19 08			19 25	19 30	19 37	
Eaglescliffe	a																			19 28					
Middlesbrough	a			18 32											19 32										20 30
Darlington	d	17 22	17 34			18 00			18 05				18 15	18 22		19 01			19 09			19 26	19 31	19 39	
Durham	d		17 50			18 16			18 23				18 31			19 19			19 26				19 47	19 55	
Chester-le-Street	d		17 56																				19 53		
Newcastle	a	17 51	18 10			18 31			18 40				18 46	18 51		19 34			19 42			19 55	20 08	20 10	
Hartlepool	a																			19 47					
Sunderland	a																			20 21					
Newcastle	d	17 54			18 19	18 37			18 42					18 53		19 37			19 45			19 57		20 12	
Morpeth	d				18a40														20 00						
Alnmouth for Alnwick	d								19 08							20 04									
Berwick-upon-Tweed	d	18 40				19 19								19 39		20 25						20 43			
Dunbar	d					19 42																			
Edinburgh	a	19 31				20 07			20 16					20 27		21 09			21 20			21 33		21 35	
Edinburgh	d					20 15										21 13									
Haymarket	d					20 20										21 17									
Motherwell	a															21 58									
Glasgow Central	a															22 17									
Stirling	a																								
Perth	a																								
Inverness	a																								
Inverkeithing	a					20 34																			
Kirkcaldy	a					20 51																			
Leuchars	a					21 27																			
Dundee	a					21 44																			
Arbroath	a																								
Montrose	a																								
Stonehaven	a																								
Aberdeen	a																								

A to Dunbar
B to Berwick-upon-Tweed
C to Durham

Table 26

Saturdays

6 August to 10 September

London - Humberside, Yorkshire, North East England and Scotland

		NT	XC	EM	GR	GR		GR	GR	HT	XC	GR	TP	XC	EM	GR		GR	GR	GR	EM	XC	GR	GC	GC
London Kings Cross	d				17 03	17 10		17 30	17 35	17 48		18 00				18 03		18 08	18 30	18 35			19 00	19 07	19 20
Stevenage	d				17 22													18 28							
Peterborough	a				17 52	17 57		18 15	18 21							18 50		18 58	19 15	19 21					
Norwich	d			15 52											16 57						17 54				
Peterborough	d			17 27	17 53	17 58		18 16	18 22						18 26	18 51		18 58	19 15	19 21	19 27				
Grantham	a			17 58	18 13	18 20				18 48					18 55			19 19			19 57				
	d			18 03	18 13	18 21				18 49					18 58			19 20							
Newark North Gate	a				18 25			18 45								19 19		19 33	19 43						
	d				18 25			18 46								19 19		19 33	19 43						
Lincoln	a																	20 03							
Retford	d									19 12						19 35									
Doncaster	a				18 49	18 53		19 09	19 14	19 26						19 50			20 08	20 12					20 53
Selby	a					19 09				19 42															
Hull	a					19 57				20 22															
Pontefract Monkhill	a																								21 16
Wakefield Kirkgate	a																								21 39
Wakefield Westgate	a				19 07				19 32							20 07				20 31					
Leeds	a				19 27				19 48							20 28				20 47					
Brighouse	a																								21 58
Halifax	a																								22 09
Shipley	a																								
Bradford Forster Square	a																								
Bradford Interchange	a																								22 40
Keighley	a																			21s13					
Skipton	a																			21 30					
Sheffield	d		18 21	19a39							18 47			19 22	20a27							19 54			
Doncaster	d							19 10			19 18								20 09			20 19			
York	a							19 34			19 40	19 53							20 35			20 46	20 52	20 55	
Scarborough	a																								
Harrogate	a								20 29																
Leeds	d		19 05										19 57	20 08											
York	d		19 32					19 36			19 44	19 55	20 26	20 34					20 37			20 48	20 53	20 58	
Thirsk	d												20 46											21 17	
Northallerton	d												21 01						20 56					21 26	
Darlington	a		19 58					20 04			20 11	20 22		21 00					21 09			21 14	21 21		
Eaglescliffe	a																							21 46	
Middlesbrough	a												21 32												
Darlington	d		19 59					20 04			20 13	20 23		21 01					21 09			21 16	21 22		
Durham	d		20 17					20 22			20 30			21 18					21 27			21 33			
Chester-le-Street	d																								
Newcastle	a		20 28					20 43			20 44	20 52		21 32					21 48			21 47	21 56		
Hartlepool	a																							22 04	
Sunderland	a																							22 36	
Newcastle	d	20 20	20 38									20 54		21 38											
Morpeth	d	20a41	20 54									21 09													
Alnmouth for Alnwick	d											21 25		22 02											
Berwick-upon-Tweed	d		21 25									21 49													
Dunbar	d		21 50									22 13													
Edinburgh	a		22 14									22 41		23 10											
Edinburgh	d																								
Haymarket	d																								
Motherwell	a																								
Glasgow Central	a																								
Stirling	a																								
Perth	a																								
Inverness	a																								
Inverkeithing	a																								
Kirkcaldy	a																								
Leuchars	a																								
Dundee	a																								
Arbroath	a																								
Montrose	a																								
Stonehaven	a																								
Aberdeen	a																								

Table 26

Saturdays
6 August to 10 September

London - Humberside, Yorkshire, North East England and Scotland

		GR		HT	EM	TP	XC	XC	GR	GR	XC	EM		EM	GR	GR	XC	EM	XC	XC
London Kings Cross ⊖	d	19 30		19 48					20 00	20 30					21 00	22 00				
Stevenage	d	19 49																		
Peterborough	a	20 19							20 46	21 15					21 45	22 46				
Norwich	d				18 57															
Peterborough	d	20 20			20 27				20 47	21 15				21 27	21 46	22 47				
Grantham	a	20 40		20 49	20 58					21 35				22 00		23 06				
	d	20 40		20 50						21 35						23 06				
Newark North Gate	a	20 52							21 15	21 47						23 18				
	d	20 52							21 15	21 47						23 18				
Lincoln	a																			
Retford	d			21 14						22 02						23 33				
Doncaster	a	21 16		21 28					21 40	22 17						23 48				
Selby	a			21 44																
Hull	a			22 24																
Pontefract Monkhill	a																			
Wakefield Kirkgate	a																			
Wakefield Westgate	a	21 34								22 35						00 05				
Leeds	a	21 54								22 55						00 26				
Brighouse	a																			
Halifax	a																			
Shipley	a	22s11																		
Bradford Forster Square	a	22 24																		
Bradford Interchange	a																			
Keighley	a																			
Skipton	a																			
Sheffield	d						20 53	20 24			21 21	21 24					22 09	22 19	22 27	23 11
Doncaster	d						21 23		21 40								22 32		22 53	
York	a						21 45		22 04						22 51		22 55			
Scarborough	a																			
Harrogate	a																			
Leeds	d					20 45		21 15			22a02	22a21						23a04	23a27	23a51
York	d					21 14	21 48	21a57	22 05						22 53					
Thirsk	d					21 31														
Northallerton	d					21 39									23 14					
Darlington	a					21 51	22 13		22 33						23 26					
Eaglescliffe	a																			
Middlesbrough	a																			
Darlington	d					21 52	22 15		22 33						23 27					
Durham	d					22 08	22 32		22 52						23 44					
Chester-le-Street	d					22 14														
Newcastle	a					22 27	22 49		23 13						00 06					
Hartlepool	a																			
Sunderland	a																			
Newcastle	d																			
Morpeth	d																			
Alnmouth for Alnwick	d																			
Berwick-upon-Tweed	d																			
Dunbar	d																			
Edinburgh	a																			
Edinburgh	d																			
Haymarket	d																			
Motherwell	a																			
Glasgow Central	a																			
Stirling	a																			
Perth	a																			
Inverness	a																			
Inverkeithing	a																			
Kirkcaldy	a																			
Leuchars	a																			
Dundee	a																			
Arbroath	a																			
Montrose	a																			
Stonehaven	a																			
Aberdeen	a																			

Table 26

Saturdays
from 17 September

London - Humberside, Yorkshire, North East England and Scotland

		GR	GR	GR	TP	GR	GR	TP	NT	GR		XC	GR	NT	TP	TP	NT	GR	XC	TP		NT	NT	XC	GR
												C												C	
London Kings Cross ⊖	d	19p30	21p00	21p35		22p00	23p30																		06 20
Stevenage	d		21p20																						06 40
Peterborough	a	20p15	21p50	22p20		22p45	00s24																		07 11
Norwich	d																								
Peterborough	d	20p16	21p50	22p21		22p46																			07 12
Grantham	a			22p43		23p08	00s48																		07 32
	d			22p43		23p08																			07 32
Newark North Gate	a	20p44	22p20	22p54		23p19	01s01																		07 44
	d	20p44	22p20	22p54		23p19																			07 44
Lincoln	a																								
Retford	d			23p10																					
Doncaster	a	21p09	22p45	23p25		23p49	01s33																		08 09
Selby	a																								
Hull	a																								
Pontefract Monkhill	a																								
Wakefield Kirkgate	a																								
Wakefield Westgate	a			23p44																					
Leeds	a			00 03			02 46																		
Brighouse	a																								
Halifax	a																								
Shipley	a																								
Bradford Forster Square	a																								
Bradford Interchange	a																								
Keighley	a																								
Skipton	a																								
Sheffield	d																		06 49					07 12	
Doncaster	d	21p09	22p46			23p49							06 10						07 17						08 10
York	a	21p32	23p10			00 39							06 30						07 43						08 32
Scarborough	a																								
Harrogate	a																								
Leeds	d				22p42										06 35			07 10		07 50				07 57	
York	d	21p33	23p12		23b18	00 41		05 54					06 32		07 06	07 32		07 35	07 48	08 23				08 27	08 35
Thirsk	d				23p31			06 10							07 22	07 52				08 39					
Northallerton	d	21p53	23p40		23p49	01s11		06 18					06 51		07 30	08 00				08 49					08 54
Darlington	a	22p05	23p53		00 01	01s25		06 29					07 05		07 41			08 04	08 13					08 56	09 07
Eaglescliffe	a																								
Middlesbrough	a							07 03								08 32				09 21					
Darlington	d	22p06	23p53		00 02								07 05	07 21	07 42			08 05	08 15			08 22		08 57	09 07
Durham	d	22p23	00 11		00 18	01s43							07 23	07 42	07 59			08 23	08 31			08 43		09 14	09 25
Chester-le-Street	d													07 49	08 05							08 50			
Newcastle	a	22p41	00 47		00 52	02 20							07 39	08 05	08 17			08 39	08 46			09 01		09 28	09 41
Hartlepool	a																								
Sunderland	a																								
Newcastle	d	22p42							05 55	06 30		07 38	07 42				07 58	08 41					09 15	09 35	09 44
Morpeth	d	22p56							06 15	06 43		07 51					08a19	08 56					09a36		
Alnmouth for Alnwick	d	23p12							06a34	06 57			08 08											09 59	
Berwick-upon-Tweed	d	23p38								07 21		08 24	08 32					09 31						10 20	
Dunbar	d									07 48			08 55					09 55							
Edinburgh	a	00 31								08 17		09 07	09 24					10 24						11 07	11 15
Edinburgh	d											09 11						10 27						11 11	
Haymarket	d											09 16						10 32						11 16	
Motherwell	a											10 00												11 52	
Glasgow Central	a											10 23												12 13	
Stirling	a																								
Perth	a																								
Inverness	a																								
Inverkeithing	a																	10 47							
Kirkcaldy	a																	11 04							
Leuchars	a																	11 28							
Dundee	a																	11 43							
Arbroath	a																	12 00							
Montrose	a																	12 16							
Stonehaven	a																	12 39							
Aberdeen	a																	13 05							

C to Berwick-upon-Tweed

b Previous night, arr. 2309

Table 26

Saturdays

from 17 September

London - Humberside, Yorkshire, North East England and Scotland

		TP	XC	GR	TP	TP	NT	XC	EM	GR	GR	GC	EM	XC	GR	GR	EM	TP	TP	NT	XC	GR	XC
		◇1	◇1	■ 1	◇1	◇1		◇1	◇	■ 1	■ 1	■ 1		◇1	■ 1	■ 1	◇1	◇1	◇1		◇1 A	■ 1	◇1
			✕	▭✕	✕	✕		✕		▭✕	▭✕	▭		✕	▭✕	▭✕	▭	✕	✕		✕	▭✕	✕
London Kings Cross 15 ⊖	d			07 00						07 03	07 30	07 47			08 00	08 03						08 30	
Stevenage 4	d									07 22													
Peterborough 8	a									07 52	08 15					08 50						09 15	
Norwich	d								05 52														
Peterborough 8	d								07 27	07 53	08 15		08 33			08 50						09 15	
Grantham 7	a								07 56	08 13						09 10							
	d								07 58	08 13						09 10							
Newark North Gate 7	a									08 25						09 22						09 43	
	d									08 25						09 22						09 43	
Lincoln	a												09 59										
Retford 10	d										08 54												
Doncaster 7	a									08 49	09 09					09 49						10 08	
Selby	a																						
Hull	a																						
Pontefract Monkhill	a																						
Wakefield Kirkgate 4	a																						
Wakefield Westgate 7	a									09 07						10 07							
Leeds 10	a									09 27						10 27							
Brighouse	a																						
Halifax	a																						
Shipley	a																						
Bradford Forster Square	a																						
Bradford Interchange	a																						
Keighley	a																						
Skipton	a																						
Sheffield 7 ⇌	d		07 54					08 21	09a38					08 48			09 21				09 21		09 47
Doncaster 7	d		08 25								09 11			09 20			09 55					10 09	10 19
York 8	a		08 47	08 52							09 33	09 39		09 45	09 49		10 16					10 33	10 45
Scarborough	a																						
Harrogate	a																						
Leeds 10	d				08 28	08 57		09 05										09 28	09 57		10 05		
York 8	d	08 42	08 50	08 53	08 58	09 26		09 33			09 36	09 44		09 49	09 53			09 58	10 26		10 32	10 35	10 48
Thirsk	d					09 46						10 00							10 46				
Northallerton	d				09 19	09 59						10 16						10 19	10 59			10 54	
Darlington 7	a	09 11	09 16	09 22	09 30			09 58			10 03			10 15	10 20			10 30			10 58	11 07	11 13
Eaglescliffe	a											10 37											
Middlesbrough	a					10 30													11 30				
Darlington 7	d	09 12	09 18	09 23	09 31			10 00			10 04			10 16	10 22			10 31			11 00	11 07	11 15
Durham	d	09 29	09 35		09 47			10 16			10 21			10 33				10 47			11 16	11 25	11 31
Chester-le-Street	d				09 55																		
Newcastle 8 ⇌	a	09 45	09 48	09 51	10 07			10 31			10 37			10 47	10 51			11 05			11 31	11 41	11 47
Hartlepool	a											11 07											
Sunderland ⇌	a											11 40											
Newcastle 8 ⇌	d			09 54			10 14	10 36			10 39				10 54					11 15	11 36	11 44	
Morpeth	d						10a35													11a36			
Alnmouth for Alnwick	d										11 05												
Berwick-upon-Tweed	d			10 39											11 39						12 20		
Dunbar	d							11 38															
Edinburgh 10	a			11 31				12 07			12 15				12 31						13 04	13 13	
Edinburgh	d																				13 11		
Haymarket	d																				13 15		
Motherwell	a																				13 52		
Glasgow Central 15	a																				14 13		
Stirling	a																						
Perth	a																						
Inverness	a																						
Inverkeithing	a																						
Kirkcaldy	a																						
Leuchars 3	a																						
Dundee	a																						
Arbroath	a																						
Montrose	a																						
Stonehaven	a																						
Aberdeen	a																						

A ✕ to Berwick-upon-Tweed

Table 26

Saturdays

from 17 September

London - Humberside, Yorkshire, North East England and Scotland

		GR	TP	TP	NT	XC	EM	EM	GR	GR	HT	XC	GR	TP	TP	NT	XC	EM	GR	GR	GC	XC
		■ 1	◇1	◇1		◇1	◇		■ 1	■ 1	◇1	◇1	■ 1 A	◇1	◇1		◇1 B	◇	■ 1	■ 1		◇1
		▭✕	✕	✕		✕			▭✕	▭✕	⊠	✕	▭✕		✕		✕		▭✕	▭✕		✕
London Kings Cross 15 ⊖	d	09 00							09 03	09 30	09 48		10 00						10 03	10 30	10 48	
Stevenage 4	d								09 22													
Peterborough 8	a								09 52	10 15									10 50	11 15		
Norwich	d						07 57											08 57				
Peterborough 8	d						09 30	09 33	09 53	10 15								10 26	10 51	11 15		
Grantham 7	a						09 58		10 13		10 48							10 57	11 10			
	d						09 58		10 13		10 49							10 58	11 10			
Newark North Gate 7	a								10 25										11 23	11 43		
	d								10 25										11 23	11 43		
Lincoln	a							10 59														
Retford 10	d									10 53	11 10											
Doncaster 7	a								10 50	11 08	11 24								11 50	12 08	12 18	
Selby	a										11 40											
Hull	a										12 20											
Pontefract Monkhill	a																				12 44	
Wakefield Kirkgate 4	a																				13 04	
Wakefield Westgate 7	a								11 07										12 07			
Leeds 10	a								11 28										12 28			
Brighouse	a																				13 29	
Halifax	a																				13 40	
Shipley	a																					
Bradford Forster Square	a																					
Bradford Interchange	a																				13 55	
Keighley	a																					
Skipton	a																					
Sheffield 7 ⇌	d					10 21	11a38					10 47					11 21	12a38				11 47
Doncaster 7	d									11 09		11 19								12 09		12 17
York 8	a	10 52								11 33		11 45	11 52							12 33		12 45
Scarborough	a																					
Harrogate	a																					
Leeds 10	d		10 28	10 57		11 05								11 28	11 57		12 05					
York 8	d	10 53	10 58	11 26		11 32				11 35		11 48	11 53	11 58	12 26		12 32			12 35		12 48
Thirsk	d			11 46											12 46							
Northallerton	d		11 19	11 59										12 19	12 59					12 54		
Darlington 7	a	11 21	11 30			11 58				12 04		12 13	12 21	12 30			12 58			13 07		13 13
Eaglescliffe	a																					
Middlesbrough	a			12 30											13 30							
Darlington 7	d	11 22	11 31			12 00				12 04		12 15	12 22	12 31			13 00			13 07		13 15
Durham	d		11 47			12 16				12 22		12 31		12 47			13 18			13 25		13 31
Chester-le-Street	d		11 53																			
Newcastle 8 ⇌	a	11 51	12 06			12 31				12 38		12 46	12 51	13 03			13 34			13 41		13 46
Hartlepool	a																					
Sunderland ⇌	a																					
Newcastle 8 ⇌	d	11 54			12 15	12 36				12 40			12 54			13 15	13 35			13 44		
Morpeth	d				12a35											13a37						
Alnmouth for Alnwick	d									13 06							14 00					
Berwick-upon-Tweed	d	12 39											13 40				14 20					
Dunbar	d					13 38																
Edinburgh 10	a	13 31				14 07				14 15			14 24				15 07			15 15		
Edinburgh	d												14 27				15 11					
Haymarket	d												14 32				15 16					
Motherwell	a																15 52					
Glasgow Central 15	a																16 20					
Stirling	a																					
Perth	a																					
Inverness	a																					
Inverkeithing	a												14 46									
Kirkcaldy	a												15 03									
Leuchars 3	a												15 28									
Dundee	a												15 46									
Arbroath	a												16 04									
Montrose	a												16 20									
Stonehaven	a												16 43									
Aberdeen	a												17 09									

A The Highland Chieftan

B ✕ to Berwick-upon-Tweed

Table 26

Saturdays from 17 September

London - Humberside, Yorkshire, North East England and Scotland

Station		EM	GR	EM	GR	TP	GC	TP	NT	XC	GR	GR	HT	XC	GR	TP	TP	NT	XC	EM	EM	GR	GR
															B				A				
London Kings Cross ⊖	d		11 00		11 03		11 20				11 30	11 35	11 48		12 00							12 03	12 30
Stevenage	d				11 22																		
Peterborough	a				11 52						12 15	12 21										12 51	13 15
Norwich	d	09 57																		10 57			
Peterborough	d	11 25		11 48	11 53						12 15	12 21								12 25	12 41	12 51	13 15
Grantham	a	11 57			12 13								12 48							12 58		13 16	
	d	11 58			12 13								12 49							12 58		13 16	
Newark North Gate	a				12 25																	13 27	13 43
	d				12 25																	13 27	13 43
Lincoln	a			13 14																	14 07		
Retford	d										12 53		13 10										
Doncaster	a				12 50						13 08	13 12	13 24									13 52	14 09
Selby	a												13 40										
Hull	a												14 20										
Pontefract Monkhill	a																						
Wakefield Kirkgate	a																						
Wakefield Westgate	a				13 07							13 30										14 11	
Leeds	a				13 28							13 50										14 31	
Brighouse	a																						
Halifax	a																						
Shipley	a																						
Bradford Forster Square	a																						
Bradford Interchange	a																						
Keighley	a																						
Skipton	a																						
Sheffield	d	13a38								12 21				12 47					13 21	14a38			
Doncaster	d										13 09			13 19									14 10
York	a		12 52				13 14				13 33			13 45	13 53								14 33
Scarborough	a																						
Harrogate	a																						
Leeds	d					12 28		12 57		13 05						13 28	13 57		14 05				
York	d		12 53			12b58	13 16	13 26		13 32	13 35			13 48	13 54	13 58	14 26		14 32				14 35
Thirsk	d						13 33	13 46									14 46						
Northallerton	d					13 19	13 42	13 59								14 19	14 59						14 54
Darlington	a		13 21			13 30				13 58	14 04			14 13	14 22	14 30			14 58				15 07
Eaglescliffe	a						13 59																
Middlesbrough	a							14 30									15 30						
Darlington	d		13 22			13 31				14 00	14 04			14 15	14 23	14 31			15 00				15 07
Durham	d					13 47				14 16	14 22			14 31		14 47			15 16				15 25
Chester-le-Street	d					13 53																	
Newcastle	a		13 51			14 06				14 32	14 38			14 46	14 52	15 05			15 31				15 41
Hartlepool	a						14 20																
Sunderland	a						14 50																
Newcastle	d		13 54						14 15	14 35	14 40				14 54			15 15	15 34				15 44
Morpeth	d								14a37	14 48								15a35					
Alnmouth for Alnwick	d										15 06								15 59				
Berwick-upon-Tweed	d		14 39												15 40				16 19				
Dunbar	d									15 40													
Edinburgh	a		15 31							16 04	16 15				16 26				17 07				17 15
Edinburgh	d														16 32				17 11				
Haymarket	d														16 38				17 16				
Motherwell	a																		17 52				
Glasgow Central	a																		18 11				
Stirling	a														17 19								
Perth	a														18 00								
Inverness	a														20 11								
Inverkeithing	a																						
Kirkcaldy	a																						
Leuchars	a																						
Dundee	a																						
Arbroath	a																						
Montrose	a																						
Stonehaven	a																						
Aberdeen	a																						

A ⚲ to Berwick-upon-Tweed

B The Highland Chieftan

Table 26

Saturdays from 17 September

London - Humberside, Yorkshire, North East England and Scotland

Station		XC	EM	GR	GR	TP	TP	NT	XC	GR	XC	GR	TP	NT	NT	XC	EM	GR	EM	GR	HT	XC
									A							B						
London Kings Cross ⊖	d			13 00	13 03					13 30		14 00						14 03		14 30	14 48	
Stevenage	d				13 22																	
Peterborough	a				13 52					14 15								14 50		15 15		
Norwich	d		11 57														12 57					
Peterborough	d		13 28		13 53					14 15							14 26	14 50	15 11	15 15		
Grantham	a		13 56	14 00	14 13												14 57	15 09			15 48	
	d		13 58	14 00	14 13												14 58	15 09			15 49	
Newark North Gate	a				14 25													15 22		15 43		
	d				14 25													15 22		15 43		
Lincoln	a																		16 48			
Retford	d									14 53											16 10	
Doncaster	a				14 50					15 08								15 47		16 08	16 24	
Selby	a																				16 41	
Hull	a																				17 28	
Pontefract Monkhill	a																					
Wakefield Kirkgate	a																					
Wakefield Westgate	a				15 07													16 07				
Leeds	a				15 28													16 28				
Brighouse	a																					
Halifax	a																					
Shipley	a																					
Bradford Forster Square	a																					
Bradford Interchange	a																					
Keighley	a																					
Skipton	a																					
Sheffield	d	13 47	15a38						14 21		14 47					15 21	16a38					15 47
Doncaster	d	14 19								15 10	15 19									16 09		16 19
York	a	14 45		14 51						15 33	15 45	15 51								16 33		16 46
Scarborough	a																					
Harrogate	a																					
Leeds	d					14 28	14 57		15 05				15 56			16 05						
York	d	14 48		14 53		14 58	15 26		15 32	15 35	15 48	15 53	16 25			16 32				16 35		16 48
Thirsk	d						15 46						16 45									
Northallerton	d					15 19	15 59						16 58							16 54		
Darlington	a	15 13		15 20		15 30			15 58	16 03	16 13	16 21				16 58				17 07		17 13
Eaglescliffe	a																					
Middlesbrough	a						16 30						17 30									
Darlington	d	15 15		15 21		15 31			16 00	16 04	16 15	16 21				17 00				17 07		17 15
Durham	d	15 31				15 47			16 16	16 21	16 31					17 16				17 25		17 31
Chester-le-Street	d					15 53																
Newcastle	a	15 46		15 51		16 09			16 31	16 39	16 46	16 51				17 31				17 41		17 46
Hartlepool	a																					
Sunderland	a																					
Newcastle	d			15 54				16 15	16 35	16 44		16 52		17 00	17 22	17 37				17 44		
Morpeth	d							16a36						17 22	17a42							
Alnmouth for Alnwick	d								17 00					17a45		18 01						
Berwick-upon-Tweed	d			16 39								17 40				18 21						
Dunbar	d								17 39													
Edinburgh	a			17 31					18 05	18 17		18 27				19 08				19 15		
Edinburgh	d								18 11			18 30				19 11						
Haymarket	d								18 15			18 35				19 16						
Motherwell	a															19 52						
Glasgow Central	a															20 11						
Stirling	a																					
Perth	a																					
Inverness	a																					
Inverkeithing	a								18 28			18 54										
Kirkcaldy	a								18 46			19 11										
Leuchars	a								19 17			19 38										
Dundee	a								19 32			19 52										
Arbroath	a								19 49			20 10										
Montrose	a								20 03			20 26										
Stonehaven	a								20 23			20 49										
Aberdeen	a								20 43			21 15										

A ⚲ to Dunbar

B ⚲ to Berwick-upon-Tweed

London - Humberside, Yorkshire, North East England and Scotland

		GR	TP	TP	NT	XC	EM	GR	GR	GC	EM	XC	GR	TP	XC	EM	GR	GR	GC	GR	TP	XC	TP
			◇	◇		◇ A	◇					◇		◇	◇ B	◇					◇	◇	◇
London Kings Cross ⊖	d	15 00						15 03	15 30	15 48			16 00				16 03	16 30	16 48	17 00			
Stevenage	d							15 22															
Peterborough	a							15 52	16 15								16 50	17 15					
Norwich	d						13 57									14 57							
Peterborough	d						15 25	15 53	16 15		16 25					16 27	16 51	17 15					
Grantham	a						15 57	16 13								16 57	17 10						
	d						15 58	16 13								16 58	17 10						
Newark North Gate	a							16 25									17 23	17 43					
	d							16 25									17 23	17 43					
Lincoln	a										17 51												
Retford	d								16 53														
Doncaster	a							16 50	17 08	17 20							17 49	18 08					
Selby	a																						
Hull	a																						
Pontefract Monkhill	a									17 45													
Wakefield Kirkgate	a									18 03													
Wakefield Westgate	a							17 07									18 07						
Leeds	a							17 28									18 27						
Brighouse	a									18 28													
Halifax	a									18 40													
Shipley	a																						
Bradford Forster Square	a																						
Bradford Interchange	a									18 55													
Keighley	a																						
Skipton	a																						
Sheffield	d					16 21	17a34					16 47			17 21	18a39						17 47	
Doncaster	d								17 10			17 19						18 09					
York	a	16 52							17 33			17 38	17 50					18 33	18 39	18 52			
Scarborough	a																						
Harrogate	a																						
Leeds	d		16 28	16 57		17 05								17 57	18 06						18 28	18 35	18 57
York	d	16 53	16 58	17 26		17 32			17 35			17 48	17 53	18 26	18 33			18 36	18 43	18 53	18 58	19 05	19 26
Thirsk	d		17 14	17 46										18 46					18 59				19 46
Northallerton	d		17 22	17 58										18 59				18 56	19 10		19 19		19 57
Darlington	a	17 21	17 32			17 58			18 05			18 13	18 21		19 00			19 08		19 25	19 30	19 37	
Eaglescliffe	a																		19 28				
Middlesbrough	a			18 32										19 32									20 30
Darlington	d	17 22	17 34			18 00			18 05			18 15	18 22		19 01			19 09		19 26	19 31	19 39	
Durham	d		17 50			18 16			18 23			18 31			19 19			19 26			19 47	19 55	
Chester-le-Street	d		17 56																		19 53		
Newcastle	a	17 51	18 10			18 31			18 40			18 46	18 51		19 34			19 42		19 55	20 08	20 10	
Hartlepool	a																		19 47				
Sunderland	a																		20 21				
Newcastle	d	17 54			18 19	18 37			18 42				18 53		19 37			19 45		19 57			
Morpeth	d				18a40													20 00					
Alnmouth for Alnwick	d								19 08						20 04								
Berwick-upon-Tweed	d	18 40				19 19							19 39		20 25					20 43			
Dunbar	d					19 42																	
Edinburgh	a	19 31				20 07			20 16				20 27		21 09			21 20		21 33			
Edinburgh	d					20 15									21 13								
Haymarket	d					20 20									21 17								
Motherwell	a														21 58								
Glasgow Central	a														22 17								
Stirling	a																						
Perth	a																						
Inverness	a																						
Inverkeithing	a					20 34																	
Kirkcaldy	a					20 51																	
Leuchars	a					21 26																	
Dundee	a					21 44																	
Arbroath	a																						
Montrose	a																						
Stonehaven	a																						
Aberdeen	a																						

A ⌶ to Dunbar

B ⌶ to Berwick-upon-Tweed

Table 26

Saturdays
from 17 September

London - Humberside, Yorkshire, North East England and Scotland

		NT	XC	EM	GR	GR	GR	GR	HT	XC	GR	TP	XC	EM	GR	GR	GR	GR	EM	XC	GR	GC	GC
			◇	◇					◇	◇		◇	◇	◇					◇	◇			
London Kings Cross ⊖	d				17 03	17 10	17 30	17 35	17 48		18 00				18 03	18 08	18 30	18 35			19 00	19 07	19 20
Stevenage	d				17 22											18 28							
Peterborough	a				17 52	17 57	18 15	18 21							18 50	18 58	19 15	19 21					
Norwich	d			15 52										16 57					17 54				
Peterborough	d			17 27	17 53	17 58	18 16	18 22						18 26	18 51	18 58	19 15	19 21	19 27				
Grantham	a			17 58	18 13	18 20			18 48					18 55		19 19			19 57				
	d			18 03	18 13	18 21			18 49					18 58		19 20							
Newark North Gate	a				18 25		18 45								19 19	19 33	19 43						
	d				18 25		18 46								19 19	19 33	19 43						
Lincoln	a															20 03							
Retford	d								19 12						19 35								
Doncaster	a				18 49	18 53	19 09	19 14	19 26						19 50		20 08	20 12					20 53
Selby	a					19 09			19 42														
Hull	a					19 57			20 22														
Pontefract Monkhill	a																						21 16
Wakefield Kirkgate	a																						21 39
Wakefield Westgate	a				19 07			19 32							20 07			20 31					
Leeds	a				19 27			19 48							20 28			20 47					
Brighouse	a																						21 58
Halifax	a																						22 09
Shipley	a																						
Bradford Forster Square	a																						
Bradford Interchange	a																						22 40
Keighley	a																	21s13					
Skipton	a																	21 30					
Sheffield	d		18 21	19a39						18 47			19 22	20a27						19 54			
Doncaster	d						19 10			19 18							20 09			20 19			
York	a						19 34			19 40	19 53						20 35			20 46	20 52	20 55	
Scarborough	a																						
Harrogate	a							20 29															
Leeds	d		19 05									19 57	20 08										
York	d		19 32				19 36			19 44	19 55	20 26	20 34				20 37			20 48	20 53	20 58	
Thirsk	d											20 46										21 17	
Northallerton	d											21 01					20 56					21 26	
Darlington	a		19 58				20 04			20 11	20 22		21 00				21 09			21 14	21 21		
Eaglescliffe	a																					21 46	
Middlesbrough	a											21 32											
Darlington	d		19 59				20 04			20 13	20 23		21 01				21 09			21 16	21 22		
Durham	d		20 17				20 22			20 30			21 18				21 27			21 33			
Chester-le-Street	d																						
Newcastle	a		20 28				20 43			20 44	20 52		21 32				21 48			21 47	21 56		
Hartlepool	a																					22 04	
Sunderland	a																					22 36	
Newcastle	d	20 20	20 38								20 54		21 38										
Morpeth	d	20a41	20 54								21 09												
Alnmouth for Alnwick	d										21 25		22 02										
Berwick-upon-Tweed	d		21 25								21 49												
Dunbar	d		21 50								22 13												
Edinburgh	a		22 14								22 41		23 10										
Edinburgh	d																						
Haymarket	d																						
Motherwell	a																						
Glasgow Central	a																						
Stirling	a																						
Perth	a																						
Inverness	a																						
Inverkeithing	a																						
Kirkcaldy	a																						
Leuchars	a																						
Dundee	a																						
Arbroath	a																						
Montrose	a																						
Stonehaven	a																						
Aberdeen	a																						

Table 26

Saturdays from 17 September

London - Humberside, Yorkshire, North East England and Scotland

		GR	HT	EM	TP	XC	XC	GR	GR	XC	EM	EM	GR	GR	XC	EM	XC
		■ 1	◇1	◇	◇1	◇1	◇1	■ 1	■ 1	◇1	◇1		■ 1	■ 1	◇1	◇1	◇1
		☕⊼	⊠				⊼	☕⊼	☕⊼		☕		☕⊼	☕⊼		☕	
London Kings Cross 15 ⊖	d	19 30	19 48					20 00	20 30				21 00	22 00			
Stevenage 4	d	19 49															
Peterborough 8	a	20 19						20 46	21 15				21 45	22 46			
Norwich	d			18 57													
Peterborough 8	d	20 20		20 27				20 47	21 15			21 27	21 46	22 47			
Grantham 7	a	20 40	20 49	20 58					21 35			22 00		23 06			
	d	20 40	20 50						21 35					23 06			
Newark North Gate 7	a	20 52						21 15	21 47					23 18			
	d	20 52						21 15	21 47					23 18			
Lincoln	a																
Retford 10	d		21 14						22 02					23 33			
Doncaster 7	a	21 16	21 28					21 40	22 17					23 48			
Selby	a		21 44														
Hull	a		22 24														
Pontefract Monkhill	a																
Wakefield Kirkgate 4	a																
Wakefield Westgate 7	a	21 34							22 35					00 05			
Leeds 10	a	21 54							22 55					00 26			
Brighouse	a																
Halifax	a																
Shipley	a	22s11															
Bradford Forster Square	a	22 24															
Bradford Interchange	a																
Keighley	a																
Skipton	a																
Sheffield 7	d					20 53	20 24			21 21	21 24				22 09	22 19	22 27
Doncaster 7	d					21 23		21 40							22 32		22 53
York 8	a					21 45		22 04					22 51		22 55		
Scarborough	a																
Harrogate	a																
Leeds 10	d				20 45		21 15			22a02	22a21					23a04	23a27
York 8	d				21 14	21 48	21a57	22 05					22 53				
Thirsk	d				21 31												
Northallerton	d				21 39								23 14				
Darlington 7	a				21 51	22 13		22 33					23 26				
Eaglescliffe	a																
Middlesbrough	a																
Darlington 7	d				21 52	22 15		22 33					23 27				
Durham	d				22 08	22 32		22 52					23 44				
Chester-le-Street	d				22 14												
Newcastle 8	a				22 27	22 49		23 13					00 06				
Hartlepool	a																
Sunderland	a																
Newcastle 8	d																
Morpeth	d																
Alnmouth for Alnwick	d																
Berwick-upon-Tweed	d																
Dunbar	d																
Edinburgh 10	a																
Edinburgh	d																
Haymarket	d																
Motherwell	a																
Glasgow Central 15	a																
Stirling	a																
Perth	a																
Inverness	a																
Inverkeithing	a																
Kirkcaldy	a																
Leuchars 3	a																
Dundee	a																
Arbroath	a																
Montrose	a																
Stonehaven	a																
Aberdeen	a																

Table 26

Sundays until 19 June

London - Humberside, Yorkshire, North East England and Scotland

		GR	GR	TP	XC	GR	TP	XC	GR	TP	XC	TP	GR	GR	TP	GR	GC	GR	GR	TP	XC	EM	EM
		■ 1	■ 1	◇1	◇1	■ 1	◇1	◇1	■ 1	◇1	◇1	◇1	■ 1	■ 1	◇1	■ 1	■ 1	■ 1	■ 1	◇1	◇1	◇1	◇
		A	A					B			B							C			B		
		☕⊼	☕⊼		⊼	☕⊼		⊼	☕⊼		⊼		☕⊼	☕⊼		☕⊼	☕	☕⊼	☕⊼		⊼	☕	
London Kings Cross 15 ⊖	d	21p00	22p00										09 00	09 03		09 30	09 48	10 00	10 03				
Stevenage 4	d													09 22									
Peterborough 8	a	21p45	22p46											09 51		10 14			10 49				
Norwich	d																						09 33
Peterborough 8	d	21p46	22p47											09 52		10 14			10 49				11 11
Grantham 7	a		23p06											10 14					11 11				11 54
	d		23p06											10 14					11 11				11 56
Newark North Gate 7	a		23p18											10 26					11 23				
	d		23p18											10 26					11 23				
Lincoln	a																						
Retford 10	d		23p33													10 54							
Doncaster 7	a		23p48											10 51		11 10			11 48				
Selby	a																						
Hull	a																						
Pontefract Monkhill	a																						
Wakefield Kirkgate 4	a																						
Wakefield Westgate 7	a		00 05											11 09					12 06				
Leeds 10	a		00 26											11 30					12 29				
Brighouse	a																						
Halifax	a																						
Shipley	a																						
Bradford Forster Square	a																						
Bradford Interchange	a																						
Keighley	a																						
Skipton	a																						
Sheffield 7	d										09 21										11 21	11 31	13a33
Doncaster 7	d								09 37							11 11						11 58	
York 8	a	22p51							09 59				1C 51			11 36	11 42	11 52				12 20	
Scarborough	a																						
Harrogate	a																						
Leeds 10	d			07 40			08 40	09 08		09 40	10 08				10 40					11 40	12 08		
York 8	d	22p53		08 21		09 00	09 10	09 37	10 01	10 13	10 36	10 42	1C 53		11 10	11 39	11 45	11 53		12 08	12 34		
Thirsk	d			08 37								10 59					12 01						
Northallerton	d	23p14		08 45		09 18	09 31			10 36		11 07			11 31		12 10			12 29			
Darlington 7	a	23p26		08 56		09 31	09 42	10 03	10 28	10 47	11 02		11 20		11 42	12 08		12 23		12 40	13 00		
Eaglescliffe	a																12 29						
Middlesbrough	a			09 27								11 39											
Darlington 7	d	23p27				09 31	09 43	10 04	10 29	10 48	11 04		11 21		11 43	12 08		12 24		12 41	13 02		
Durham	d	23p44				09 49	09 59	10 21	10 46	11 08	11 20				11 59	12 26				12 57	13 18		
Chester-le-Street	d																						
Newcastle 8	a	00 06				10 05	10 18	10 35	11 02	11 24	11 35		11 50		12 15	12 42		12 53		13 12	13 33		
Hartlepool	a																12 52						
Sunderland	a																13 21						
Newcastle 8	d				09 45	10 13		10 38	11 04		11 38		11 54			12 44		12 55			13 35		
Morpeth	d				09 58	10 29																	
Alnmouth for Alnwick	d				10 12	10 45										13 10					14 00		
Berwick-upon-Tweed	d					11 07		11 20	11 47		12 20		12 37					13 39			14 20		
Dunbar	d					11 31										13 53							
Edinburgh 10	a				11 13	12 01		12 03	12 36		13 03		13 26			14 23		14 24			15 06		
Edinburgh	d							12 12			13 10							14 38			15 11		
Haymarket	d							12 16			13 15							14 43			15 15		
Motherwell	a							12 53			13 50										15 51		
Glasgow Central 15	a							13 12			14 14										16 14		
Stirling	a																						
Perth	a																						
Inverness	a																						
Inverkeithing	a																	15 01					
Kirkcaldy	a																	15 18					
Leuchars 3	a																	15 42					
Dundee	a																	15 57					
Arbroath	a																	16 14					
Montrose	a																	16 30					
Stonehaven	a																	16 53					
Aberdeen	a																	17 19					

A not 22 May
B ⊼ to Berwick-upon-Tweed
C The Northern Lights

Table 26

Sundays until 19 June

London - Humberside, Yorkshire, North East England and Scotland

		GR	HT	TP	GR	GR	TP	XC	GR	EM	GC	GR	GR	TP	GR	XC	GR	HT	TP	GR	GR	TP	XC
												A				B							C
London Kings Cross ⊖	d	10 30	10 45		11 00	11 03			11 30		11 48	12 00	12 03		12 20		12 30	12 45		13 00	13 03		
Stevenage	d		11u05			11 22												13u05			13 22		
Peterborough	a	11 14				11 51			12 14				12 49		13 07		13 14				13 51		
Norwich	d									10 47													
Peterborough	d	11 14				11 52			12 14	12 18			12 49		13 07		13 14				13 52		
Grantham	a		11 49			12 14				12 53			13 11					13 49			14 14		
	d		11 50			12 14				12 54			13 11					13 50			14 14		
Newark North Gate	a	11 44				12 26							13 23				13 44				14 26		
	d	11 44				12 26							13 23				13 44				14 26		
Lincoln	a																						
Retford	d		12 11						12 54									14 11					
Doncaster	a	12 10	12 28			12 51			13 10		13 17		13 48		13 58		14 09	14 25			14 51		
Selby	a		12 45															14 41					
Hull	a		13 25															15 21					
Pontefract Monkhill	a										13 42												
Wakefield Kirkgate	a										13 59												
Wakefield Westgate	a					13 09							14 06								15 09		
Leeds	a					13 30							14 29								15 30		
Brighouse	a										14 24												
Halifax	a										14 37												
Shipley	a																						
Bradford Forster Square	a																						
Bradford Interchange	a										14 50												
Keighley	a																						
Skipton	a																						
Sheffield	d							12 21		14a36						13 21							14 21
Doncaster	d	12 10							13 11						13 58		14 10						
York	a	12 34			12 50				13 34			13 52			14 22		14 36			14 53			
Scarborough	a																						
Harrogate	a																						
Leeds	d			12 12			12 40	13 08						13 40		14 08			14 12			14 40	15 08
York	d	12 37		12 42	12 53		13 10	13 34	13 37			13 53		14 10	14 23	14 34	14 37		14 50	14 54		15 10	15 34
Thirsk	d			13 00															15 13				
Northallerton	d	12 57		13 08			13 31							14 31			14 57		15 21			15 31	
Darlington	a	13 09			13 21		13 42	14 00	14 05			14 21		14 42	14 51	15 00	15 09			15 22		15 42	15 59
Eaglescliffe	a																						
Middlesbrough	a			13 40															15 52				
Darlington	d	13 10			13 22		13 43	14 01	14 06			14 22		14 43	14 51	15 02	15 10			15 22		15 44	16 01
Durham	d	13 27					13 59	14 18	14 23					14 59	15 09	15 20	15 27					16 00	16 18
Chester-le-Street	d						14 05															16 06	
Newcastle	a	13 43			13 51		14 17	14 32	14 39			14 51		15 15	15 30	15 35	15 43			15 52		16 18	16 32
Hartlepool	a																						
Sunderland	a																						
Newcastle	d	13 45			13 54			14 36	14 42			14 53				15 37	15 45			15 54			16 34
Morpeth	d							14 49															
Alnmouth for Alnwick	d								15 08							16 02							16 59
Berwick-upon-Tweed	d				14 37							15 37				16 22				16 37			
Dunbar	d							15 41															17 40
Edinburgh	a	15 18			15 26			16 06	16 16			16 22				17 06	17 17			17 27			18 07
Edinburgh	d											16 30				17 11							18 11
Haymarket	d											16 35				17 15							18 16
Motherwell	a															17 52							
Glasgow Central	a															18 12							
Stirling	a											17 17											
Perth	a											17 53											
Inverness	a											20 19											
Inverkeithing	a																						18 28
Kirkcaldy	a																						18 44
Leuchars	a																						19 14
Dundee	a																						19 29
Arbroath	a																						19 46
Montrose	a																						20 00
Stonehaven	a																						20 23
Aberdeen	a																						20 43

A The Highland Chieftain
B to Berwick-upon-Tweed
C to Dunbar

Table 26

Sundays until 19 June

London - Humberside, Yorkshire, North East England and Scotland

		GR	GC	GR	GR	TP	XC	GR	HT	TP	GR	TP	XC	EM	GR	GR	GC	GR	TP	XC	EM	EM
							A													A		
London Kings Cross ⊖	d	13 30	13 48	14 00	14 03			14 30	14 45		15 00				15 03	15 30	15 48	16 00				
Stevenage	d								15u05						15 22							
Peterborough	a	14 14			14 49			15 14							15 51	16 14						
Norwich	d													13 49								14 49
Peterborough	d	14 14			14 50			15 15						15 26	15 52	16 16						16 24
Grantham	a				15 12				15 49					15 56	16 14	16 39						16 54
	d				15 12				15 50					15 59	16 14	16 40						16 56
Newark North Gate	a				15 24			15 46							16 26							
	d				15 24			15 46							16 26							
Lincoln	a																					
Retford	d	14 54							16 11						16 42							
Doncaster	a	15 10			15 49			16 11	16 28						16 57	17 11	17 20					
Selby	a								16 45													
Hull	a								17 25													
Pontefract Monkhill	a																17 45					
Wakefield Kirkgate	a																18 02					
Wakefield Westgate	a				16 07										17 16							
Leeds	a				16 29										17 39							
Brighouse	a																18 24					
Halifax	a																18 37					
Shipley	a																					
Bradford Forster Square	a																					
Bradford Interchange	a																18 50					
Keighley	a																					
Skipton	a																					
Sheffield	d						15 21						16 21	17a40						17 21	17 34	18a34
Doncaster	d	15 11						16 12								17 13						
York	a	15 35	15 41	15 52				16 36			16 52					17 37		17 48				
Scarborough	a																					
Harrogate	a																					
Leeds	d					15 40	16 08			16 12		16 40	17 08						17 40	18 08	18a24	
York	d	15 37	15 50	15 53		16 08	16 35	16 38		16 42	16 53	17 10	17 34			17 39		17 52	18 10	18 34		
Thirsk	d		16 07							17 04												
Northallerton	d		16 18			16 29		16 58		17 16		17 31							18 31			
Darlington	a	16 05		16 22		16 40	17 00	17 10			17 21	17 42	18 00			18 07		18 19	18 42	19 00		
Eaglescliffe	a		16 36																			
Middlesbrough	a									17 50												
Darlington	d	16 06		16 23		16 41	17 02	17 11			17 22	17 43	18 01			18 07		18 20	18 43	19 01		
Durham	d	16 23				16 57	17 18	17 29				17 59	18 18			18 26			18 59	19 18		
Chester-le-Street	d											18 05										
Newcastle	a	16 39		16 52		17 12	17 33	17 45			17 52	18 18	18 32			18 42		18 49	19 16	19 35		
Hartlepool	a		16 55																			
Sunderland	a		17 22																			
Newcastle	d	16 42		16 54			17 38	17 47			17 54		18 36			18 43		18 51		19 40		
Morpeth	d																					
Alnmouth for Alnwick	d	17 08					18 02									19 11				20 05		
Berwick-upon-Tweed	d			17 38			18 23				18 37		19 18					19 39		20 25		
Dunbar	d												19 41									
Edinburgh	a	18 18		18 23			19 06	19 19			19 26		20 05			20 18		20 28		21 08		
Edinburgh	d			18 42			19 18													21 12		
Haymarket	d			18 47			19 23													21 16		
Motherwell	a						20 00													21 53		
Glasgow Central	a						20 20													22 14		
Stirling	a																					
Perth	a																					
Inverness	a																					
Inverkeithing	a			19 01																		
Kirkcaldy	a			19 18																		
Leuchars	a			19 43																		
Dundee	a			19 57																		
Arbroath	a			20 15																		
Montrose	a			20 31																		
Stonehaven	a			20 54																		
Aberdeen	a			21 20																		

A to Berwick-upon-Tweed

Table 26

Sundays until 19 June

London - Humberside, Yorkshire, North East England and Scotland

		GR	EM	GR	GR	TP	GR	GR	GR	TP	XC	GR	GR	HT	EM	GR	GR	TP	GC	XC	GR	GR	EM
London Kings Cross 15 ⊖	d	16 05		16 30	16 35		17 00	17 05	17 20			17 30	17 35	17 45		18 00	18 05		18 27		18 30	18 35	
Stevenage 4	d				16 54								17 54	18u05								18 54	
Peterborough 8	a	16 49		17 14				17 50				18 14					18 52				19 15		
Norwich	d		15 53												16 53								17 53
Peterborough 8	d	16 49	17 11	17 14				17 50				18 15			18 26		18 53				19 16		19 26
Grantham 7	a	17 11	17 45		17 40				18 25			18 36	18 41	18 49	18 56							19 42	19 56
	d	17 11	17 55		17 40				18 25			18 37	18 41	18 50	18 58							19 42	
Newark North Gate 7	a	17 23		17 44				18 21	18 37								19 24				19 46		
	d	17 23		17 44				18 21	18 37								19 24				19 46		
Lincoln	a																						
Retford 10	d				18 02									19 11								20 04	
Doncaster 7	a	17 48		18 10	18 18			18 48	19 03			19 09	19 14	19 28			19 50				20 11	20 20	
Selby	a								19 24					19 45									
Hull	a								20 06					20 25									
Pontefract Monkhill	a																						
Wakefield Kirkgate 4	a																						
Wakefield Westgate 7	a	18 11			18 38			19 07					19 31				20 08					20 37	
Leeds 10	a	18 31			18 58			19 28					19 53				20 25					20 55	
Brighouse	a																						
Halifax	a																						
Shipley	a																						
Bradford Forster Square	a																						
Bradford Interchange	a																						
Keighley	a																					21s22	
Skipton	a																					21 43	
Sheffield 7 ⇌	d		19a31								18 21				20a31					19 21			
Doncaster 7	d			18 10								19 12									20 12		
York 8	a			18 35			18 50					19 38				19 50			20 17		20 36		
Scarborough	a																						
Harrogate	a																21 07						
Leeds 10	d					18 12				18 40	19 08							19 40		20 08			
York 8	d			18 37		18 42	18 52			19 10	19 35	19 40				19 52		20 10	20 21	20 35	20 38		
Thirsk	d					18 59												20 26	20 37				
Northallerton	d			18 56		19 08				19 31								20 36	20 49		20 57		
Darlington 7	a			19 09			19 20			19 42	20 01	20 07				20 19				21 02	21 10		
Eaglescliffe	a																		21 07				
Middlesbrough	a					19 40												21 08					
Darlington 7	d			19 09			19 21			19 44	20 01	20 08				20 20				21 03	21 10		
Durham	d			19 27						20 00	20 19	20 25								21 21	21 28		
Chester-le-Street	d									20 06													
Newcastle 8 ⇌	a			19 43			19 50			20 17	20 33	20 41				20 51				21 36	21 49		
Hartlepool	a																		21 26				
Sunderland ⇌	a																		21 53				
Newcastle 8 ⇌	d			19 44			19 52				20 38	20 43				20 53				21 38			
Morpeth	d			19 58							20 53					21 10							
Alnmouth for Alnwick	d															21 25				22 06			
Berwick-upon-Tweed	d						20 37				21 27					21 47							
Dunbar	d						21 02				21 51												
Edinburgh 10	a			21 18			21 27				22 16	22 22				22 36				23 09			
Edinburgh	d						21 33																
Haymarket	d						21 37																
Motherwell	a						22 14																
Glasgow Central 15	a						22 39																
Stirling	a																						
Perth	a																						
Inverness	a																						
Inverkeithing	a																						
Kirkcaldy	a																						
Leuchars 3	a																						
Dundee	a																						
Arbroath	a																						
Montrose	a																						
Stonehaven	a																						
Aberdeen	a																						

Table 26

Sundays until 19 June

London - Humberside, Yorkshire, North East England and Scotland

		GR	GR	GR	GC	TP	GR	GR	HT	EM	XC	GR	GR	GR	EM	XC	TP	GR	EM	GR	GR	XC
London Kings Cross 15 ⊖	d	19 00	19 05	19 08	19 27		19 30	19 35	19 45			20 00	20 05	20 35				21 00		21 35	22 00	
Stevenage 4	d			19 28				19 54	20 05					20 54						21 55		
Peterborough 8	a		19 50	19 59			20 15	20 23				20 44	20 50	21 23				21 44		22 24	22 44	
Norwich	d									18 56									20 52			
Peterborough 8	d		19 51	20 00			20 16	20 24		20 31		20 44	20 50	21 24				21 44	22 22	22 24	22 45	
Grantham 7	a			20 21				20 46	20 53	21 01				21 46					22 54	22 48		
	d			20 21				20 46	20 54					21 46						22 48		
Newark North Gate 7	a		20 21	20 33			20 47							21 58						23 00		
	d		20 21	20 34			20 48							21 58						23 00		
Lincoln	a			21 03																		
Retford 10	d								21 15					22 13						23 15		
Doncaster 7	a		20 47		21 01		21 13	21 18	21 29				21 41	22 29						23 31	23 42	
Selby	a								21 45													
Hull	a								22 25													
Pontefract Monkhill	a				21 25																	
Wakefield Kirkgate 4	a				21 42																	
Wakefield Westgate 7	a		21 05					21 36					21 59	22 49						23 49		
Leeds 10	a		21 29					21 57					22 20	23 10						00 27		
Brighouse	a				22 06																	
Halifax	a				22 19																	
Shipley	a																					
Bradford Forster Square	a																					
Bradford Interchange	a				22 32																	
Keighley	a																					
Skipton	a																					
Sheffield 7 ⇌	d										20 21				21 03	21 21						22 21
Doncaster 7	d						21 14														23 43	
York 8	a	20 52					21 38					21 57						22 59			00 10	
Scarborough	a																					
Harrogate	a																					
Leeds 10	d					20 40					21 08				21a45	22a04	22 12					23a03
York 8	d	20 53				21 08	21 40				21 47	21 59					22 44	23 04			00 12	
Thirsk	d					21 26											23 06					
Northallerton	d					21 34											23 16	23 39			00s47	
Darlington 7	a	21 21				21 45	22 17				22 23	22 39					23 28	23 51			01s01	
Eaglescliffe	a																					
Middlesbrough	a																					
Darlington 7	d	21 22				21 46	22 18				22 25	22 40					23 28	23 52				
Durham	d					22 03	22 35				22 43	22 57					23 45	00 09			01s19	
Chester-le-Street	d																					
Newcastle 8 ⇌	a	21 54				22 17	23 09				23 15	23 33					00 15	00 45			01 54	
Hartlepool	a																					
Sunderland ⇌	a																					
Newcastle 8 ⇌	d	21 56																				
Morpeth	d	22 12																				
Alnmouth for Alnwick	d	22 28																				
Berwick-upon-Tweed	d	22 50																				
Dunbar	d	23 15																				
Edinburgh 10	a	23 46																				
Edinburgh	d																					
Haymarket	d																					
Motherwell	a																					
Glasgow Central 15	a																					
Stirling	a																					
Perth	a																					
Inverness	a																					
Inverkeithing	a																					
Kirkcaldy	a																					
Leuchars 3	a																					
Dundee	a																					
Arbroath	a																					
Montrose	a																					
Stonehaven	a																					
Aberdeen	a																					

Table 26

Sundays
until 19 June

London - Humberside, Yorkshire, North East England and Scotland

		GR	XC	EM
		■ 1 ✕	◇1	◇1 🛒
London Kings Cross 15 ⊖	d	22 35		
Stevenage 4	d			
Peterborough 8	a	23s24		
Norwich	d			
Peterborough 8	d			
Grantham 7	a	23s49		
	d			
Newark North Gate 7	a	23s59		
	d			
Lincoln	a			
Retford 10	d			
Doncaster 7	a	00s30		
Selby	a			
Hull	a			
Pontefract Monkhill	a			
Wakefield Kirkgate 4	a			
Wakefield Westgate 7	a			
Leeds 10	a	01 37		
Brighouse	a			
Halifax	a			
Shipley	a			
Bradford Forster Square	a			
Bradford Interchange	a			
Keighley	a			
Skipton	a			
Sheffield 7 ⇌	d		23 24	23 30
Doncaster 7	d			
York 8	a			
Scarborough	a			
Harrogate	a			
Leeds 10	d		00a34	00a28
York 8	d			
Thirsk	d			
Northallerton	d			
Darlington 7	a			
Eaglescliffe	a			
Middlesbrough	a			
Darlington 7	d			
Durham	d			
Chester-le-Street	d			
Newcastle 8 ⇌	a			
Hartlepool	a			
Sunderland ⇌	a			
Newcastle 8 ⇌	d			
Morpeth	d			
Alnmouth for Alnwick	d			
Berwick-upon-Tweed	d			
Dunbar	d			
Edinburgh 10	a			
Edinburgh	d			
Haymarket	d			
Motherwell	a			
Glasgow Central 15	a			
Stirling	a			
Perth	a			
Inverness	a			
Inverkeithing	a			
Kirkcaldy	a			
Leuchars 3	a			
Dundee	a			
Arbroath	a			
Montrose	a			
Stonehaven	a			
Aberdeen	a			

Table 26

Sundays
26 June to 31 July

London - Humberside, Yorkshire, North East England and Scotland

		GR	GR	TP	XC	GR	TP	XC	NT	GR	TP	XC	TP	GR	GR	TP	GR	GC	GR	GR	TP	XC	EM
		■ 1	■ 1	◇1	◇1	■ 1	◇1	◇1		■ 1	◇1	◇1	◇1	■ 1	■ 1	◇1	■ 1	■ 1	■ 1	■ 1	◇1	◇1	◇1
								A				A							B			A	
		✕	✕		✕	✕		✕		✕		✕		✕	✕		✕	🛒	✕	✕		✕	🛒
London Kings Cross 15 ⊖	d	21p00	22p00											08 40	08 47		09 10	09 27	09 40	09 47			
Stevenage 4	d														09 17								
Peterborough 8	a	22p02	23p03												09 51		10 14			10 49			
Norwich	d																						
Peterborough 8	d	22p03	23p04												09 52		10 14			10 49			
Grantham 7	a		23p23												10 14					11 11			
	d		23p23												10 14					11 11			
Newark North Gate 7	a		23p35												10 26					11 23			
	d		23p35												10 26					11 23			
Lincoln	a																						
Retford 10	d		23p50														10 54						
Doncaster 7	a		00 05												10 51		11 10			11 48			
Selby	a																						
Hull	a																						
Pontefract Monkhill	a																						
Wakefield Kirkgate 4	a																						
Wakefield Westgate 7	a		00 20												11 09					12 06			
Leeds 10	a		00 40												11 30					12 29			
Brighouse	a																						
Halifax	a																						
Shipley	a																						
Bradford Forster Square	a																						
Bradford Interchange	a																						
Keighley	a																						
Skipton	a																						
Sheffield 7 ⇌	d											09 21										11 21	11 31
Doncaster 7	d									09 37							11 11						11 58
York 8	a	23p12								09 59				10 51			11 36	11 42	11 52				12 20
Scarborough	a																						
Harrogate	a																						
Leeds 10	d			07 40			08 40	09 08			09 40	10 08				10 40					11 40	12 08	
York 8	d	23p14		08 21		09 00	09 10	09 37		10 01	10 13	10 36	10 42	10 53		11 10	11 39	11 45	11 53		12 08	12 34	
Thirsk	d			08 37									10 59					12 01					
Northallerton	d	23p34		08 45		09 18	09 31				10 36		11 07			11 31		12 10			12 29		
Darlington 7	a	23p46		08 56		09 31	09 42	10 03		10 28	10 47	11 02		11 20		11 42	12 08		12 23		12 40	13 00	
Eaglescliffe	a																	12 28					
Middlesbrough	a			09 27									11 39										
Darlington 7	d	23p47				09 31	09 43	10 04	10 20	10 29	10 48	11 04		11 21		11 43	12 08		12 24		12 41	13 02	
Durham	d	00 04				09 49	09 59	10 21		10 46	11 08	11 20				11 59	12 26				12 57	13 18	
Chester-le-Street	d																						
Newcastle 8 ⇌	a	00 25				10 05	10 18	10 35		11 02	11 24	11 35		11 50		12 15	12 42		12 53		13 12	13 33	
Hartlepool	a								10 59									12 51					
Sunderland ⇌	a								11 26									13 21					
Newcastle 8 ⇌	d				09 45	10 13		10 38	11a48	11 04		11 38		11 54			12 44		12 55			13 35	
Morpeth	d				09 58	10 29																	
Alnmouth for Alnwick	d				10 12	10 45											13 10					14 00	
Berwick-upon-Tweed	d					11 07		11 20		11 47		12 20		12 37					13 39			14 20	
Dunbar	d					11 31											13 53						
Edinburgh 10	a				11 13	12 01		12 03		12 36		13 03		13 26			14 23		14 24			15 06	
Edinburgh	d							12 12				13 10							14 38			15 11	
Haymarket	d							12 16				13 15							14 43			15 15	
Motherwell	a							12 53				13 50										15 51	
Glasgow Central 15	a							13 12				14 14										16 14	
Stirling	a																						
Perth	a																						
Inverness	a																						
Inverkeithing	a																		15 01				
Kirkcaldy	a																		15 18				
Leuchars 3	a																		15 42				
Dundee	a																		15 57				
Arbroath	a																		16 14				
Montrose	a																		16 30				
Stonehaven	a																		16 53				
Aberdeen	a																		17 19				

A ✕ to Berwick-upon-Tweed

B The Northern Lights

26 June to 31 July

London - Humberside, Yorkshire, North East England and Scotland

		EM	GR	HT	TP	GR	GR	TP	XC	GR	EM	GC	GR	GR	TP	GR	XC	GR	HT	XC	TP	GR	GR
													A				B						
London Kings Cross ⊖	d		10 30	10 45		11 00	11 03			11 30		11 48	12 00	12 03		12 20		12 30	12 45			13 00	13 03
Stevenage	d			11u05			11 22												13u05				13 22
Peterborough	a		11 14				11 51			12 14				12 49		13 07		13 14					13 51
Norwich	d	09 33									10 47												
Peterborough	d	11 11	11 14				11 52			12 14	12 18			12 49		13 07		13 14					13 52
Grantham	a	11 54		11 49			12 14				12 53			13 11					13 49				14 14
	d	11 56		11 50			12 14				12 54			13 11					13 50				14 14
Newark North Gate	a		11 44				12 26							13 23				13 44					14 26
	d		11 44				12 26							13 23				13 44					14 26
Lincoln	a																						
Retford	d			12 11						12 54									14 11				
Doncaster	a		12 10	12 28			12 51			13 10		13 16		13 48		13 58		14 09	14 25				14 51
Selby	a			12 45															14 41				
Hull	a			13 25															15 21				
Pontefract Monkhill	a											13 41											
Wakefield Kirkgate	a											13 58											
Wakefield Westgate	a						13 09							14 06									15 09
Leeds	a						13 30							14 29									15 30
Brighouse	a											14 20											
Halifax	a											14 35											
Shipley	a																						
Bradford Forster Square	a																						
Bradford Interchange	a											14 50											
Keighley	a																						
Skipton	a																						
Sheffield	d	13a33							12 21		14a36						13 21			13 51			
Doncaster	d		12 10							13 11						13 58		14 10		14 15			
York	a		12 34			12 50				13 34			13 52			14 22		14 36		14 41		14 53	
Scarborough	a																						
Harrogate	a																						
Leeds	d				12 12			12 40	13 08						13 40		14 08				14 12		
York	d		12 37		12 42	12 53		13 10	13 34	13 37			13 53		14 10	14 23	14 34	14 37		14 46	14 50	14 54	
Thirsk	d				13 00																15 13		
Northallerton	d		12 57		13 08			13 31							14 31			14 57			15 21		
Darlington	a		13 09			13 21		13 42	14 00	14 05			14 21		14 42	14 51	15 00	15 09		15 15		15 22	
Eaglescliffe	a																						
Middlesbrough	a				13 40																15 52		
Darlington	d		13 10			13 22		13 43	14 01	14 06			14 22		14 43	14 51	15 02	15 10		15 17		15 22	
Durham	d		13 27					13 59	14 18	14 23					14 59	15 09	15 20	15 27		15 33			
Chester-le-Street	d							14 05															
Newcastle	a		13 43			13 51		14 17	14 32	14 39			14 51		15 15	15 30	15 35	15 43		15 47		15 52	
Hartlepool	a																						
Sunderland	a																						
Newcastle	d		13 45			13 54			14 36	14 42			14 53				15 37	15 45				15 54	
Morpeth	d								14 49														
Alnmouth for Alnwick	d									15 08							16 02						
Berwick-upon-Tweed	d					14 37							15 37				16 22					16 37	
Dunbar	d								15 41														
Edinburgh	a		15 18			15 26			16 06	16 16			16 22				17 06	17 17				17 27	
Edinburgh	d												16 30				17 11						
Haymarket	d												16 35				17 15						
Motherwell	a																17 52						
Glasgow Central	a																18 12						
Stirling	a												17 17										
Perth	a												17 53										
Inverness	a												20 19										
Inverkeithing	a																						
Kirkcaldy	a																						
Leuchars	a																						
Dundee	a																						
Arbroath	a																						
Montrose	a																						
Stonehaven	a																						
Aberdeen	a																						

A The Highland Chieftain

B ⚲ to Berwick-upon-Tweed

26 June to 31 July

London - Humberside, Yorkshire, North East England and Scotland

		TP	XC	GR	NT	GC	XC	GC	GR	GR	TP	XC	GR	HT	TP	XC	GR	TP	XC	EM	GR	GR
			A									B										
London Kings Cross ⊖	d			13 30		13 48			14 00	14 03			14 30	14 45			15 00				15 03	15 30
Stevenage	d													15u05							15 22	
Peterborough	a			14 14						14 49			15 14								15 51	16 14
Norwich	d																			13 49		
Peterborough	d			14 14						14 50			15 15							15 26	15 52	16 16
Grantham	a									15 12				15 49						15 56	16 14	16 39
	d									15 12				15 50						15 59	16 14	16 40
Newark North Gate	a									15 24			15 46								16 26	
	d									15 24			15 46								16 26	
Lincoln	a																					
Retford	d			14 54										16 11							16 42	
Doncaster	a			15 10						15 49			16 11	16 28							16 57	17 11
Selby	a													16 45								
Hull	a													17 25								
Pontefract Monkhill	a																					
Wakefield Kirkgate	a																					
Wakefield Westgate	a									16 07											17 16	
Leeds	a									16 29											17 39	
Brighouse	a																					
Halifax	a																					
Shipley	a																					
Bradford Forster Square	a																					
Bradford Interchange	a																					
Keighley	a																					
Skipton	a																					
Sheffield	d		14 21				14 51					15 21				15 51			16 21	17a40		
Doncaster	d			15 11			15 19						16 12			16 17						17 13
York	a			15 35		15 41	15 44		15 52				16 36			16 44	16 52					17 37
Scarborough	a																					
Harrogate	a																					
Leeds	d	14 40	15 08					←			15 40	16 08			16 12			16 40	17 08			
York	d	15 10	15 34	15 37		15 50	15 47	15 50	15 53		16 08	16 35	16 38		16 42	16 47	16 53	17 10	17 34			17 39
Thirsk	d					→		16 07							17 04							
Northallerton	d	15 31						16 18			16 29		16 58		17 16			17 31				
Darlington	a	15 42	15 59	16 05			16 12		16 22		16 40	17 00	17 10			17 16	17 21	17 42	18 00			18 07
Eaglescliffe	a							16 35														
Middlesbrough	a														17 50							
Darlington	d	15 44	16 01	16 06	16 11		16 14		16 23		16 41	17 02	17 11			17 18	17 22	17 43	18 01			18 07
Durham	d	16 00	16 18	16 23			16 31				16 57	17 18	17 29			17 35		17 59	18 18			18 26
Chester-le-Street	d	16 06																18 05				
Newcastle	a	16 18	16 32	16 39			16 45		16 52		17 12	17 33	17 45			17 48	17 52	18 18	18 32			18 42
Hartlepool	a				16 50			16 58														
Sunderland	a				17 22			17 27														
Newcastle	d		16 34	16 42	17a48				16 54			17 38	17 47				17 54		18 36			18 43
Morpeth	d																					
Alnmouth for Alnwick	d		16 59	17 08								18 02										19 11
Berwick-upon-Tweed	d								17 38			18 23					18 37		19 18			
Dunbar	d		17 40																19 41			
Edinburgh	a		18 07	18 18					18 23			19 06	19 19				19 26		20 05			20 18
Edinburgh	d		18 11						18 42			19 18										
Haymarket	d		18 16						18 47			19 23										
Motherwell	a											20 00										
Glasgow Central	a											20 20										
Stirling	a																					
Perth	a																					
Inverness	a																					
Inverkeithing	a		18 28						19 01													
Kirkcaldy	a		18 44						19 18													
Leuchars	a		19 14						19 43													
Dundee	a		19 29						19 57													
Arbroath	a		19 46						20 15													
Montrose	a		20 00						20 31													
Stonehaven	a		20 23						20 54													
Aberdeen	a		20 43						21 20													

A ⚲ to Dunbar

B ⚲ to Berwick-upon-Tweed

Sundays
26 June to 31 July

London - Humberside, Yorkshire, North East England and Scotland

		GC	XC	GR	TP	XC	EM	EM	GR	EM	GR	GR	TP	GR	GR	GR	TP	XC	XC	GR	GR	HT	XC
						A													B				
London Kings Cross 15 ⊖	d	15 48		16 00					16 05		16 30	16 35		17 00	17 05	17 20				17 30	17 35	17 45	
Stevenage 4	d											16 54									17 54	18u05	
Peterborough 8	a								16 49		17 14				17 50					18 14			
Norwich	d							14 49		15 53													
Peterborough 8	d							16 24	16 49	17 11	17 14				17 50					18 15			
Grantham 7	a							16 54	17 11	17 45		17 40				18 25				18 36	18 41	18 49	
	d							16 56	17 11	17 55		17 40				18 25				18 37	18 41	18 50	
Newark North Gate 7	a								17 23		17 44				18 21	18 37							
	d								17 23		17 44				18 21	18 37							
Lincoln	a																						
Retford 10	d											18 02										19 11	
Doncaster 7	a	17 19							17 48		18 10	18 18			18 48	19 03				19 09	19 14	19 28	
Selby	a															19 24						19 45	
Hull	a															20 06						20 25	
Pontefract Monkhill	a	17 43																					
Wakefield Kirkgate 4	a	18 00																					
Wakefield Westgate 7	a								18 11			18 38			19 07						19 31		
Leeds 10	a								18 31			18 58			19 28						19 53		
Brighouse	a	18 21																					
Halifax	a	18 35																					
Shipley	a																						
Bradford Forster Square	a																						
Bradford Interchange	a	18 50																					
Keighley	a																						
Skipton	a																						
Sheffield 7 ⇌	d		16 51			17 21	17 34	18a34		19a31								17 51	18 21				18 51
Doncaster 7	d		17 17								18 10							18 15		19 12			19 18
York 8	a		17 42	17 48							18 35			18 50						19 38			19 44
Scarborough	a																						
Harrogate	a																						
Leeds 10	d				17 40	18 08	18a24						18 12				18 40	18 57	19 08				
York 8	d		17 45	17 52	18 10	18 34					18 37		18 42	18 52			19 10	19 24	19 35	19 40			19 47
Thirsk	d												18 59										
Northallerton	d				18 31						18 56		19 08				19 31						
Darlington 7	a		18 12	18 19	18 42	19 00					19 09			19 20			19 42	19 51	20 02	20 07			20 12
Eaglescliffe	a																						
Middlesbrough	a												19 40										
Darlington 7	d		18 14	18 20	18 43	19 01					19 09			19 21			19 44	19 53	20 03	20 08			20 14
Durham	d		18 31		18 59	19 18					19 27						20 00	20 09	20 21	20 25			20 31
Chester-le-Street	d																20 06						
Newcastle 8 ⇌	a		18 46	18 49	19 16	19 35					19 43			19 50			20 17	20 24	20 36	20 41			20 45
Hartlepool	a																						
Sunderland ⇌	a																						
Newcastle 8 ⇌	d			18 51		19 40					19 44			19 52					20 38	20 43			20 51
Morpeth	d										19 58								20 53				
Alnmouth for Alnwick	d					20 05																	
Berwick-upon-Tweed	d			19 39		20 25								20 37					21 26				
Dunbar	d													21 02					21 51				
Edinburgh 10	a			20 28		21 08					21 18			21 27					22 16	22 22			22 23
Edinburgh	d					21 12								21 33									
Haymarket	d					21 16								21 37									
Motherwell	a					21 53								22 14									
Glasgow Central 15	a					22 14								22 39									
Stirling	a																						
Perth	a																						
Inverness	a																						
Inverkeithing	a																						
Kirkcaldy	a																						
Leuchars 3	a																						
Dundee	a																						
Arbroath	a																						
Montrose	a																						
Stonehaven	a																						
Aberdeen	a																						

A ✕ to Berwick-upon-Tweed

B ✕ to Durham

Sundays
26 June to 31 July

London - Humberside, Yorkshire, North East England and Scotland

		EM	GR	GR	TP	GC	XC	GR	GR	EM	XC	GR	GR	GR	GC	TP	XC	GR	GR	HT	EM	XC
London Kings Cross 15 ⊖	d		18 00	18 05		18 27		18 30	18 35			19 00	19 05	19 08	19 27			19 30	19 35	19 45		
Stevenage 4	d								18 54					19 28					19 54	20 05		
Peterborough 8	a			18 52				19 15					19 50	19 59				20 15	20 23			
Norwich	d	16 53								17 53											18 56	
Peterborough 8	d	18 26		18 53				19 16		19 26			19 51	20 00				20 16	20 24		20 31	
Grantham 7	a	18 56							19 42	19 56				20 21					20 46	20 53	21 01	
	d	18 58							19 42					20 21					20 46	20 54		
Newark North Gate 7	a			19 24				19 46					20 21	20 33				20 47				
	d			19 24				19 46					20 21	20 34				20 48				
Lincoln	a													21 03								
Retford 10	d								20 04											21 15		
Doncaster 7	a			19 50				20 11	20 20				20 47		21 00			21 13	21 18	21 29		
Selby	a																			21 45		
Hull	a																			22 25		
Pontefract Monkhill	a														21 24							
Wakefield Kirkgate 4	a														21 41							
Wakefield Westgate 7	a			20 08					20 37				21 05						21 36			
Leeds 10	a			20 25					20 55				21 29						21 57			
Brighouse	a														22 04							
Halifax	a														22 17							
Shipley	a																					
Bradford Forster Square	a																					
Bradford Interchange	a														22 32							
Keighley	a								21s22													
Skipton	a								21 43													
Sheffield 7 ⇌	d	20a31					19 21				19 51						20 21					20 51
Doncaster 7	d							20 12			20 18							21 14				21 23
York 8	a		19 50			20 17		20 36			20 45	20 52						21 38				21 44
Scarborough	a																					
Harrogate	a			21 07																		
Leeds 10	d				19 40		20 08									20 40	21 08					
York 8	d		19 52		20 10	20 21	20 35	20 38			20 48	20 53				21 08	21a32	21 40				21 47
Thirsk	d				20 26	20 37										21 26						
Northallerton	d				20 36	20 49		20 57								21 34						
Darlington 7	a		20 19				21 02	21 10			21 15	21 21				21 45		22 17				22 22
Eaglescliffe	a					21 06																
Middlesbrough	a				21 08																	
Darlington 7	d		20 20				21 03	21 10			21 16	21 22				21 46		22 18				22 24
Durham	d						21 21	21 28			21 34					22 03		22 35				22 41
Chester-le-Street	d																					
Newcastle 8 ⇌	a		20 51				21 36	21 49			21 51	21 54				22 17		23 09				23 10
Hartlepool	a					21 26																
Sunderland ⇌	a					21 53																
Newcastle 8 ⇌	d		20 53				21 38					21 56										
Morpeth	d		21 10									22 12										
Alnmouth for Alnwick	d		21 25				22 06					22 28										
Berwick-upon-Tweed	d		21 47									22 50										
Dunbar	d											23 15										
Edinburgh 10	a		22 36				23 09					23 46										
Edinburgh	d																					
Haymarket	d																					
Motherwell	a																					
Glasgow Central 15	a																					
Stirling	a																					
Perth	a																					
Inverness	a																					
Inverkeithing	a																					
Kirkcaldy	a																					
Leuchars 3	a																					
Dundee	a																					
Arbroath	a																					
Montrose	a																					
Stonehaven	a																					
Aberdeen	a																					

Table 26

Sundays

26 June to 31 July

London - Humberside, Yorkshire, North East England and Scotland

		GR	GR	GR	EM	XC	TP	GR	EM	GR	GR	XC	GR	XC	EM
		1	1	1	◇1	◇1	◇1	1	◇	1	1	◇1	1	◇1	◇1
London Kings Cross 15 ⊖	d	20 00	20 05	20 35				21 00		21 35	22 00		22 35		
Stevenage 4	d			20 54						21 55					
Peterborough 8	a	20 44	20 50	21 23				21 44		22 24	22 44		23s24		
Norwich	d								20 52						
Peterborough 8	d	20 44	20 50	21 24				21 44	22 22	22 24	22 45				
Grantham 7	a			21 46					22 54	22 48			23s49		
	d			21 46						22 48					
Newark North Gate 7	a			21 58						23 00			23s59		
	d			21 58						23 00					
Lincoln	a														
Retford 10	d			22 13						23 15					
Doncaster 7	a		21 41	22 29						23 31	23 42		00s30		
Selby	a														
Hull	a														
Pontefract Monkhill	a														
Wakefield Kirkgate 4	a														
Wakefield Westgate 7	a		21 59	22 49						23 49					
Leeds 10	a		22 20	23 10						00 27			01 37		
Brighouse	a														
Halifax	a														
Shipley	a														
Bradford Forster Square	a														
Bradford Interchange	a														
Keighley	a														
Skipton	a														
Sheffield 7	d				21 03	21 21						22 21		23 24	23 30
Doncaster 7	d										23 43				
York 8	a	21 57						22 59			00 33				
Scarborough	a														
Harrogate	a														
Leeds 10	d				21a45	22a04	22 12					23a03		00a34	00a28
York 8	d	21 59					22 44	23 04			00 35				
Thirsk	d						23 06								
Northallerton	d						23 16	23 39			01s07				
Darlington 7	a	22 39					23 28	23 51			01s21				
Eaglescliffe	a														
Middlesbrough	a														
Darlington 7	d	22 40					23 28	23 52							
Durham	d	22 57					23 45	00 09			01s39				
Chester-le-Street	d														
Newcastle 8	a	23 33					00 15	00 45			02 14				
Hartlepool	a														
Sunderland	a														
Newcastle 8	d														
Morpeth	d														
Alnmouth for Alnwick	d														
Berwick-upon-Tweed	d														
Dunbar	d														
Edinburgh 10	a														
Edinburgh	d														
Haymarket	d														
Motherwell	a														
Glasgow Central 15	a														
Stirling	a														
Perth	a														
Inverness	a														
Inverkeithing	a														
Kirkcaldy	a														
Leuchars 3	a														
Dundee	a														
Arbroath	a														
Montrose	a														
Stonehaven	a														
Aberdeen	a														

Table 26

Sundays

7 August to 23 October

London - Humberside, Yorkshire, North East England and Scotland

		GR	GR	TP	TP	GR	XC	GR	TP	XC	NT	GR	TP	TP	XC	TP	TP	GR	GR	TP	XC	GR	GR
		1	1	◇1	◇1	1	◇1	1	◇1	◇1		1	◇1	◇1	◇1	◇1	◇1	1	1	◇1	◇1	1	1
				A	B	A				C			A	B	C	B	A	D	B			A	B
London Kings Cross 15 ⊖	d	21p00	22p00			08 59												09 00	09 03			09 26	09 30
Stevenage 4	d					09 22													09 22				
Peterborough 8	a	21p45	22p46			09 51													09 51			10 14	10 14
Norwich	d																						
Peterborough 8	d	21p46	22p47			09 52													09 52			10 14	10 14
Grantham 7	a		23p06			10 14													10 14				
	d		23p06			10 14													10 14				
Newark North Gate 7	a		23p18			10 26													10 26				
	d		23p18			10 26													10 26				
Lincoln	a																						
Retford 10	d		23p33																			10 54	10 54
Doncaster 7	a		23p48			10 51													10 51			11 10	11 10
Selby	a																						
Hull	a																						
Pontefract Monkhill	a																						
Wakefield Kirkgate 4	a																						
Wakefield Westgate 7	a		00 05			11 09													11 09				
Leeds 10	a		00 26			11 30													11 30				
Brighouse	a																						
Halifax	a																						
Shipley	a																						
Bradford Forster Square	a																						
Bradford Interchange	a																						
Keighley	a																						
Skipton	a																						
Sheffield 7	d														09 21						10 21		
Doncaster 7	d											09 37										11 11	11 11
York 8	a	22p51										09 59						10 51				11 36	11 36
Scarborough	a																						
Harrogate	a																						
Leeds 10	d			07 40					08 40	09 08			09 40	09 45	10 08	10 17				10 40	11 08		
York 8	d	22p53		08 21	08 21			09 00	09 10	09 37		10 01	10 13	10 13	10 36	10 42	10 42	10 53		11 10	11 36	11 39	11 39
Thirsk	d			08 37	08 37											10 59	10 59						
Northallerton	d	23p14		08 45	08 45			09 18	09 31				10 36	10 36		11 07	11 07			11 31			
Darlington 7	a	23p26		08 56	08 56			09 31	09 42	10 03		10 28	10 47	10 47	11 02			11 20		11 42	12 02	12 08	12 08
Eaglescliffe	a																						
Middlesbrough	a			09 27	09 27											11 39	11 39						
Darlington 7	d	23p27						09 31	09 43	10 04	10 20	10 29	10 48	10 48	11 04			11 21		11 43	12 03	12 08	12 08
Durham	d	23p44						09 49	09 59	10 21		10 46	11 08	11 08	11 20					11 59	12 20	12 26	12 26
Chester-le-Street	d																						
Newcastle 8	a	00 06						10 05	10 18	10 35		11 02	11 24	11 24	11 35			11 50		12 15	12 35	12 42	12 42
Hartlepool	a										10 59												
Sunderland	a										11 26												
Newcastle 8	d						09 45	10 13		10 38	11a48	11 04			11 38			11 54			12 38	12 44	12 44
Morpeth	d						09 58	10 29															
Alnmouth for Alnwick	d						10 12	10 45														13 10	13 10
Berwick-upon-Tweed	d							11 07		11 20		11 47			12 20			12 37					
Dunbar	d							11 31													13 40	13 53	13 53
Edinburgh 10	a						11 13	12 01		12 03		12 36			13 03			13 26			14 07	14 23	14 23
Edinburgh	d									12 12					13 10								
Haymarket	d									12 16					13 15								
Motherwell	a									12 53					13 50								
Glasgow Central 15	a									13 12					14 14								
Stirling	a																						
Perth	a																						
Inverness	a																						
Inverkeithing	a																						
Kirkcaldy	a																						
Leuchars 3	a																						
Dundee	a																						
Arbroath	a																						
Montrose	a																						
Stonehaven	a																						
Aberdeen	a																						

A from 7 August until 11 September
B from 18 September until 23 October
C to Berwick-upon-Tweed
D not 23 October

Table 26

Sundays

7 August to 23 October

London - Humberside, Yorkshire, North East England and Scotland

Station		GC	GR	GR	GR	GR	TP	XC	EM	EM	GR	GR	HT	TP	GR	GR	GR	GR	TP	XC	GR	GR	EM
			A	B	C	D		E		B	B	D			B	B	D	D		B	B	D	
London Kings Cross	d	09 48	09 56	09 59	10 00	10 03					10 26	10 30	10 45		10 55	10 59	11 00	11 03			11 26	11 30	
Stevenage	d												11u05			11 22		11 22					
Peterborough	a			10 49		10 49					11 14	11 14				11 51		11 51			12 14	12 14	
Norwich	d									09 33													10 47
Peterborough	d			10 49		10 49				11 11	11 14	11 14				11 52		11 52			12 14	12 14	12 18
Grantham	a			11 11		11 11				11 54			11 49			12 14		12 14					12 53
	d			11 11		11 11				11 56			11 50			12 14		12 14					12 54
Newark North Gate	a			11 23		11 23					11 44	11 44				12 26		12 26					
	d			11 23		11 23					11 44	11 44				12 26		12 26					
Lincoln	a																						
Retford	d												12 11								12 54	12 54	
Doncaster	a			11 48		11 48					12 10	12 10	12 28			12 51		12 51			13 10	13 10	
Selby	a												12 45										
Hull	a												13 25										
Pontefract Monkhill	a																						
Wakefield Kirkgate	a																						
Wakefield Westgate	a			12 06		12 06										13 09		13 09					
Leeds	a			12 29		12 29										13 30		13 30					
Brighouse	a																						
Halifax	a																						
Shipley	a																						
Bradford Forster Square	a																						
Bradford Interchange	a																						
Keighley	a																						
Skipton	a																						
Sheffield	d							11 21	11 45	13a33										12 21			14a36
Doncaster	d								12 07		12 10	12 10									13 11	13 11	
York	a	11 42	11 52		11 52				12 29		12 34	12 34			12 50		12 50				13 34	13 34	
Scarborough	a																						
Harrogate	a																						
Leeds	d						11 40	12 08						12 12					12 40	13 08			
York	d	11 45	11 53		11 53		12 08	12 34			12 37	12 37		12 42	12 53		12 53		13 10	13 34	13 37	13 37	
Thirsk	d	12 01												13 00									
Northallerton	d	12 10					12 29				12 57	12 57		13 08					13 31				
Darlington	a		12 23		12 23		12 40	13 00			13 09	13 09			13 21		13 21		13 42	14 00	14 05	14 05	
Eaglescliffe	a	12 28																					
Middlesbrough	a													13 40									
Darlington	d		12 24		12 24		12 41	13 02			13 10	13 10			13 22		13 22		13 43	14 01	14 06	14 06	
Durham	d						12 57	13 18			13 27	13 27							13 59	14 18	14 23	14 23	
Chester-le-Street	d																		14 05				
Newcastle	a		12 53		12 53		13 12	13 33			13 43	13 43			13 51		13 51		14 17	14 32	14 39	14 39	
Hartlepool	a	12 51																					
Sunderland	a	13 21																					
Newcastle	d		12 55		12 55			13 35			13 45	13 45			13 54		13 54			14 36	14 42	14 42	
Morpeth	d																			14 49			
Alnmouth for Alnwick	d							14 00													15 08	15 08	
Berwick-upon-Tweed	d		13 39		13 39			14 20							14 37		14 37						
Dunbar	d																			15 41			
Edinburgh	a		14 24		14 24			15 06			15 18	15 18			15 26		15 26			16 06	16 16	16 16	
Edinburgh	d		14 38		14 38			15 11															
Haymarket	d		14 43		14 43			15 15															
Motherwell	a							15 51															
Glasgow Central	a							16 14															
Stirling	a																						
Perth	a																						
Inverness	a																						
Inverkeithing	a		15 01		15 01																		
Kirkcaldy	a		15 18		15 18																		
Leuchars	a		15 42		15 42																		
Dundee	a		15 57		15 57																		
Arbroath	a		16 14		16 14																		
Montrose	a		16 30		16 30																		
Stonehaven	a		16 53		16 53																		
Aberdeen	a		17 19		17 19																		

A from 7 August until 11 September. The Flying Scotsman
B from 7 August until 11 September
C from 18 September until 23 October. The Northern Lights
D from 18 September until 23 October
E to Berwick-upon-Tweed

Table 26

Sundays

7 August to 23 October

London - Humberside, Yorkshire, North East England and Scotland

Station		GC	GC	GR	GR	GR	GR	TP	GR	GR	XC	GR	GR	HT	XC	TP	GR	GR	GR	GR	TP	XC
		A	B	C	D	E	A		D	A	F	D	A				D	D	A	A		G
London Kings Cross	d	11 48	11 48	11 56	11 59	12 00	12 03		12 16	12 20		12 26	12 30	12 45			12 55	12 59	13 00	13 03		
Stevenage	d													13u05				13 22		13 22		
Peterborough	a				12 49		12 49		13 07	13 07		13 15	13 14					13 51		13 51		
Norwich	d																					
Peterborough	d				12 49		12 49		13 07	13 07		13 15	13 14					13 52		13 52		
Grantham	a				13 11		13 11							13 49				14 14		14 14		
	d				13 11		13 11							13 50				14 14		14 14		
Newark North Gate	a				13 23		13 23					13 44	13 44					14 26		14 26		
	d				13 23		13 23					13 44	13 44					14 26		14 26		
Lincoln	a																					
Retford	d													14 11								
Doncaster	a	13 16	13 16		13 48		13 48		13 58	13 58		14 09	14 09	14 25				14 51		14 51		
Selby	a													14 41								
Hull	a													15 21								
Pontefract Monkhill	a	13 41	13 41																			
Wakefield Kirkgate	a	13 58	13 58																			
Wakefield Westgate	a				14 06		14 06											15 09		15 09		
Leeds	a				14 29		14 29											15 30		15 30		
Brighouse	a	14 22	14 20																			
Halifax	a	14 35	14 35																			
Shipley	a																					
Bradford Forster Square	a																					
Bradford Interchange	a	14 50	14 50																			
Keighley	a																					
Skipton	a																					
Sheffield	d										13 21				13 51							14 21
Doncaster	d								13 58	13 58		14 10	14 10		14 15							
York	a			13 52		13 52			14 22	14 22		14 36	14 36		14 41		14 53		14 53			
Scarborough	a																					
Harrogate	a																					
Leeds	d							13 40			14 08					14 12					14 40	15 08
York	d			13 53		13 53		14 10	14 23	14 23	14 34	14 37	14 37		14 46	14 50	14 54		14 54		15 10	15 34
Thirsk	d															15 13						
Northallerton	d							14 31				14 57	14 57			15 21					15 31	
Darlington	a			14 21		14 21		14 42	14 51	14 51	15 00	15 09	15 09		15 15		15 22		15 22		15 42	15 59
Eaglescliffe	a																					
Middlesbrough	a															15 52						
Darlington	d			14 22		14 22		14 43	14 51	14 51	15 02	15 10	15 10		15 17		15 22		15 22		15 44	16 01
Durham	d							14 59	15 09	15 09	15 20	15 27	15 27		15 33						16 00	16 18
Chester-le-Street	d																				16 06	
Newcastle	a			14 51		14 51		15 15	15 30	15 30	15 35	15 43	15 43		15 47		15 52		15 52		16 18	16 32
Hartlepool	a																					
Sunderland	a																					
Newcastle	d			14 53		14 53					15 37	15 45	15 45				15 54		15 54			16 34
Morpeth	d																					
Alnmouth for Alnwick	d										16 02											16 59
Berwick-upon-Tweed	d			15 37		15 37					16 22						16 37		16 37			
Dunbar	d																					17 40
Edinburgh	a			16 22		16 22					17 06	17 17	17 17				17 27		17 27			18 07
Edinburgh	d			16 30		16 30					17 11											18 11
Haymarket	d			16 35		16 35					17 15											18 16
Motherwell	a										17 52											
Glasgow Central	a										18 12											
Stirling	a			17 17		17 17																
Perth	a			17 53		17 53																
Inverness	a			20 19		20 19																
Inverkeithing	a																					18 28
Kirkcaldy	a																					18 44
Leuchars	a																					19 14
Dundee	a																					19 29
Arbroath	a																					19 46
Montrose	a																					20 00
Stonehaven	a																					20 23
Aberdeen	a																					20 43

A from 18 September until 23 October
B 7 August, 14 August, 21 August, 4 September, 11 September
C from 7 August until 11 September. The Highland Chieftain
D from 7 August until 11 September
E from 18 September until 23 October. The Highland Chieftain
F to Berwick-upon-Tweed
G to Dunbar

7 August to 23 October

London - Humberside, Yorkshire, North East England and Scotland

		GR	GR	NT	GC	XC	GC	GR	GR	GR	GR	TP	XC	GR	GR	HT	HT	TP	XC	EM	GR	GR	GR
		A	B					A	A	B	B		C	A	B	D	E				A	A	B
London Kings Cross 15 ⊖	d	13 26	13 30		13 48			13 56	13 59	14 00	14 03			14 26	14 30	14 43	14 45				14 55	14 59	15 00
Stevenage 4	d															15u05	15u05					15 22	
Peterborough 8	a	14 14	14 14						14 49		14 49			15 14	15 14							15 51	
Norwich	d																			13 49			
Peterborough 8	d	14 14	14 14						14 50		14 50			15 15	15 15					15 26		15 52	
Grantham 7	a								15 12		15 12					15 49	15 49			15 56		16 14	
	d								15 12		15 12					15 50	15 50			15 59		16 14	
Newark North Gate 7	a								15 24		15 24			15 46	15 46							16 26	
	d								15 24		15 24			15 46	15 46							16 26	
Lincoln	a																						
Retford 10	d	14 54	14 54													16 11	16 11					16 42	
Doncaster 7	a	15 10	15 10						15 49		15 49			16 11	16 11	16 28	16 28					16 57	
Selby	a															16 45	16 45						
Hull	a															17 25	17 25						
Pontefract Monkhill	a																						
Wakefield Kirkgate 4	a																						
Wakefield Westgate 7	a								16 07		16 07											17 16	
Leeds 10	a								16 29		16 29											17 39	
Brighouse	a																						
Halifax	a																						
Shipley	a																						
Bradford Forster Square	a																						
Bradford Interchange	a																						
Keighley	a																						
Skipton	a																						
Sheffield 7	d					14 51							15 21						15 51	17a40			
Doncaster 7	d	15 11	15 11			15 19								16 12	16 12				16 17				
York 8	a	15 35	15 35		15 41	15 44		15 52		15 52				16 36	16 36				16 44		16 52		16 52
Scarborough	a																						
Harrogate	a																						
Leeds 10	d						←					15 40	16 08					16 12					
York 8	d	15 37	15 37		15 50	15 47	15 50	15 53		15 53		16 08	16 35	16 38	16 38			16 42	16 47		16 53		16 53
Thirsk	d				→		16 07											17 04					
Northallerton	d						16 18					16 29		16 58	16 58			17 16					
Darlington 7	a	16 05	16 05			16 12		16 22		16 22		16 40	17 00	17 10	17 10				17 16		17 21		17 21
Eaglescliffe	a						16 35																
Middlesbrough	a																	17 50					
Darlington 7	d	16 06	16 06	16 11		16 14		16 23		16 23		16 41	17 02	17 11	17 11				17 18		17 22		17 22
Durham	d	16 23	16 23			16 31						16 57	17 18	17 29	17 29				17 35				
Chester-le-Street	d																						
Newcastle 8	a	16 39	16 39			16 45		16 52		16 52		17 12	17 33	17 45	17 45				17 48		17 52		17 52
Hartlepool	a			16 50			16 58																
Sunderland	a			17 22			17 27																
Newcastle 8	d	16 42	16 42	17a48				16 54		16 54			17 38	17 47	17 47						17 54		17 54
Morpeth	d																						
Alnmouth for Alnwick	d	17 08	17 08										18 02										
Berwick-upon-Tweed	d							17 38		17 38			18 23								18 37		18 37
Dunbar	d																						
Edinburgh 10	a	18 18	18 18					18 23		18 23			19 06	19 19	19 19						19 26		19 26
Edinburgh	d							18 42		18 42			19 18										
Haymarket	d							18 47		18 47			19 23										
Motherwell	a												20 00										
Glasgow Central 15	a												20 20										
Stirling	a																						
Perth	a																						
Inverness	a																						
Inverkeithing	a							19 01		19 01													
Kirkcaldy	a							19 18		19 18													
Leuchars 3	a							19 43		19 43													
Dundee	a							19 57		19 57													
Arbroath	a							20 15		20 15													
Montrose	a							20 31		20 31													
Stonehaven	a							20 54		20 54													
Aberdeen	a							21 20		21 20													

A from 7 August until 11 September
B from 18 September until 23 October
C ⚒ to Berwick-upon-Tweed
D 7 August, 14 August, 21 August, 4 September, 11 September
E from 28 August until 23 October, not 4 September, 11 September

7 August to 23 October

London - Humberside, Yorkshire, North East England and Scotland

		GR	TP	XC	XC	GR	GR	GC	GC	XC	GR	GR	TP	XC	EM	EM	GR	GR	EM	GR	GR	GR
		A		B	A	B	A	B	A	B	B	A		C			B	A		B	A	B
London Kings Cross 15 ⊖	d	15 03				15 26	15 30	15 40	15 48		15 56	16 00					16 01	16 05		16 26	16 30	16 31
Stevenage 4	d	15 22																				16 54
Peterborough 8	a	15 51				16 14	16 14										16 49	16 49		17 14	17 14	
Norwich	d															14 49			15 53			
Peterborough 8	d	15 52				16 16	16 16									16 24	16 49	16 49	17 11	17 14	17 14	
Grantham 7	a	16 14				16 39	16 39									16 54	17 11	17 11	17 45			17 40
	d	16 14				16 40	16 40									16 56	17 11	17 11	17 55			17 40
Newark North Gate 7	a	16 26															17 23	17 23		17 44	17 44	
	d	16 26															17 23	17 23		17 44	17 44	
Lincoln	a																					
Retford 10	d	16 42																				18 02
Doncaster 7	a	16 57				17 11	17 11	17 19	17 19								17 48	17 48		18 10	18 10	18 18
Selby	a																					
Hull	a																					
Pontefract Monkhill	a							17 43	17 43													
Wakefield Kirkgate 4	a							18 00	18 00													
Wakefield Westgate 7	a	17 16															18 11	18 11				18 38
Leeds 10	a	17 39															18 31	18 31				18 58
Brighouse	a							18 21	18 22													
Halifax	a							18 35	18 35													
Shipley	a																					
Bradford Forster Square	a																					
Bradford Interchange	a							18 50	18 50													
Keighley	a																					
Skipton	a																					
Sheffield 7	d			16 21	16 21					16 51				17 21	17 34	18a34			19a31			
Doncaster 7	d					17 13	17 13			17 17										18 10	18 10	
York 8	a					17 37	17 37			17 42	17 48	17 48								18 35	18 35	
Scarborough	a																					
Harrogate	a																					
Leeds 10	d		16 40	17b08	17 08								17 40	18 08	18a24							
York 8	d		17 10	17 34	17 34	17 39	17 39			17 45	17 52	17 52	18 10	18 34						18 37	18 37	
Thirsk	d																					
Northallerton	d		17 31										18 31							18 56	18 56	
Darlington 7	a		17 42	17 59	18 00	18 07	18 07			18 12	18 19	18 19	18 42	19 00						19 09	19 09	
Eaglescliffe	a																					
Middlesbrough	a																					
Darlington 7	d		17 43	18 01	18 01	18 07	18 07			18 14	18 20	18 20	18 43	19 01						19 09	19 09	
Durham	d		17 59	18 17	18 18	18 26	18 26			18 31			18 59	19 18						19 27	19 27	
Chester-le-Street	d		18 05																			
Newcastle 8	a		18 18	18 32	18 32	18 42	18 42			18 46	18 49	18 49	19 16	19 35						19 43	19 43	
Hartlepool	a																					
Sunderland	a																					
Newcastle 8	d			18 36	18 36	18 43	18 43				18 51	18 51		19 40						19 44	19 44	
Morpeth	d																			19 58	19 58	
Alnmouth for Alnwick	d					19 11	19 11							20 05								
Berwick-upon-Tweed	d			19 18	19 18						19 39	19 39		20 25								
Dunbar	d			19 41	19 41																	
Edinburgh 10	a			20 05	20 05	20 18	20 18				20 28	20 28		21 08						21 18	21 18	
Edinburgh	d													21 12								
Haymarket	d													21 16								
Motherwell	a													21 53								
Glasgow Central 15	a													22 14								
Stirling	a																					
Perth	a																					
Inverness	a																					
Inverkeithing	a																					
Kirkcaldy	a																					
Leuchars 3	a																					
Dundee	a																					
Arbroath	a																					
Montrose	a																					
Stonehaven	a																					
Aberdeen	a																					

A from 18 September until 23 October
B from 7 August until 11 September
C ⚒ to Berwick-upon-Tweed

Table 26

London - Humberside, Yorkshire, North East England and Scotland

Sundays
7 August to 23 October

		GR	TP	GR	GR	GR	GR	GR	GR	TP	XC	XC	GR	GR	GR	GR	HT	XC	EM	GR	GR	GR	GR
		A		B	A	B	A	B	A				B	A	B	A				B	A	B	A
London Kings Cross 15 ⊖	d	16 35		16 56	17 00	17 01	17 05	17 17	17 20				17 26	17 30	17 31	17 35	17 45			17 56	18 00	18 02	18 05
Stevenage 4	d	16 54													17 54	17 54	18u05						
Peterborough 8	a					17 50	17 50						18 15	18 14								18 52	18 52
Norwich	d																		16 53				
Peterborough 8	d					17 50	17 50						18 16	18 15					18 26			18 53	18 53
Grantham 7	a	17 40						18 25	18 25				18 36	18 36	18 41	18 41	18 49		18 56				
	d	17 40						18 26	18 25				18 37	18 37	18 41	18 41	18 50		18 58				
Newark North Gate 7	a					18 21	18 21	18 37	18 37													19 24	19 24
	d					18 21	18 21	18 38	18 37													19 24	19 24
Lincoln	a																						
Retford 10	d	18 02															19 11						
Doncaster 7	a	18 18				18 48	18 48	19 03	19 03				19 09	19 09	19 14	19 14	19 28					19 50	19 50
Selby	a							19 24	19 24								19 45						
Hull	a							20 06	20 06								20 25						
Pontefract Monkhill	a																						
Wakefield Kirkgate 4	a																						
Wakefield Westgate 7	a	18 38				19 07	19 07								19 31	19 31						20 08	20 08
Leeds 10	a	18 58				19 28	19 28								19 53	19 53						20 25	20 25
Brighouse	a																						
Halifax	a																						
Shipley	a																						
Bradford Forster Square	a																						
Bradford Interchange	a																						
Keighley	a																						
Skipton	a																						
Sheffield 7	d										17 51	18 21						18 51	20a31				
Doncaster 7	d										18 15		19 12	19 12				19 18					
York 8	a			18 50	18 50								19 38	19 38				19 44		19 50	19 50		
Scarborough	a																						
Harrogate	a																					21 07	21 07
Leeds 10	d		18 12							18 40	18 57	19 08											
York 8	d		18 42	18 52	18 52					19 10	19 24	19 35	19 40	19 40				19 47		19 52	19 52		
Thirsk	d		18 59																				
Northallerton	d		19 08							19 31													
Darlington 7	a			19 20	19 20					19 42	19 51	20 02	20 07	20 07				20 12		20 19	20 19		
Eaglescliffe	a																						
Middlesbrough	a		19 40																				
Darlington 7	d			19 21	19 21					19 44	19 53	20 03	20 08	20 08				20 14		20 20	20 20		
Durham	d									20 00	20 09	20 21	20 25	20 25				20 31					
Chester-le-Street	d									20 06													
Newcastle 8	a			19 50	19 50					20 17	20 24	20 36	20 41	20 41				20 45		20 51	20 51		
Hartlepool	a																						
Sunderland	a																						
Newcastle 8	d			19 52	19 52							20 38	20 43	20 43				20 51		20 53	20 53		
Morpeth	d											20 53								21 10	21 10		
Alnmouth for Alnwick	d																			21 25	21 25		
Berwick-upon-Tweed	d			20 37	20 37							21 26								21 47	21 47		
Dunbar	d			21 02	21 02							21 51											
Edinburgh 10	a			21 27	21 27							22 16	22 22	22 22				22 23		22 36	22 36		
Edinburgh	d			21 33	21 33																		
Haymarket	d			21 37	21 37																		
Motherwell	a			22 14	22 14																		
Glasgow Central 15	a			22 39	22 39																		
Stirling	a																						
Perth	a																						
Inverness	a																						
Inverkeithing	a																						
Kirkcaldy	a																						
Leuchars 3	a																						
Dundee	a																						
Arbroath	a																						
Montrose	a																						
Stonehaven	a																						
Aberdeen	a																						

A from 18 September until 23 October
B from 7 August until 11 September

Table 26

London - Humberside, Yorkshire, North East England and Scotland

Sundays
7 August to 23 October

		TP	GC	GC	XC	GR	GR	GR	GR	EM	XC	GR	GR	GR	GR	GR	GR	GC	GC	TP	XC	GR	GR
			A	B		A	B	A	B			A	A	B	C	B	D	A	B			A	B
London Kings Cross 15 ⊖	d		18 24	18 27		18 27	18 30	18 31	18 35			18 55	18 58	19 00	19 03	19 05	19 08	19 24	19 27			19 27	19 30
Stevenage 4	d							18 54	18 54						19 28		19 28						
Peterborough 8	a					19 15	19 15						19 50		19 59	19 50	19 59					20 16	20 15
Norwich	d									17 53													
Peterborough 8	d					19 16	19 16			19 26			19 51		20 00	19 51	20 00					20 17	20 16
Grantham 7	a							19 42	19 42	19 56					20 21		20 21						
	d							19 42	19 42						20 21		20 21						
Newark North Gate 7	a					19 46	19 46						20 21		20 33	20 21	20 33					20 47	20 47
	d					19 46	19 46						20 21		20 34	20 21	20 34					20 48	20 48
Lincoln	a														21 03		21 03						
Retford 10	d							20 04	20 04														
Doncaster 7	a					20 11	20 11	20 20	20 20				20 47			20 47		21 00	21 00			21 13	21 13
Selby	a																						
Hull	a																						
Pontefract Monkhill	a																	21 24	21 24				
Wakefield Kirkgate 4	a																	21 41	21 41				
Wakefield Westgate 7	a							20 37	20 37				21 05			21 05							
Leeds 10	a							20 55	20 55				21 29			21 29							
Brighouse	a																	22 04	22 04				
Halifax	a																	22 17	22 17				
Shipley	a																						
Bradford Forster Square	a																						
Bradford Interchange	a																	22 32	22 32				
Keighley	a							21s22	21s22														
Skipton	a							21 43	21 43														
Sheffield 7	d				19 21						19 51										20 21		
Doncaster 7	d					20 12	20 12				20 18											21 14	21 14
York 8	a		20 17	20 17		20 36	20 36				20 45	20 52		20 52								21 38	21 38
Scarborough	a																						
Harrogate	a																						
Leeds 10	d	19 40			20 08															20 40	21 08		
York 8	d	20 10	20 21	20 21	20 35	20 38	20 38				20 48	20 53		20 53						21 08	21a32	21 40	21 40
Thirsk	d	20 26	20 37	20 37																21 26			
Northallerton	d	20 36	20 49	20 49		20 57	20 57													21 34			
Darlington 7	a				21 02	21 10	21 10				21 15	21 21		21 21						21 45		22 17	22 17
Eaglescliffe	a		21 06	21 06																			
Middlesbrough	a	21 08																					
Darlington 7	d				21 03	21 10	21 10				21 16	21 22		21 22						21 46		22 18	22 18
Durham	d				21 21	21 28	21 28				21 34									22 03		22 35	22 35
Chester-le-Street	d																						
Newcastle 8	a				21 36	21 49	21 49				21 51	21 54		21 54						22 17		23 09	23 09
Hartlepool	a		21 26	21 26																			
Sunderland	a		21 53	21 53																			
Newcastle 8	d				21 38							21 56		21 56									
Morpeth	d											22 12		22 12									
Alnmouth for Alnwick	d				22 06							22 28		22 28									
Berwick-upon-Tweed	d											22 50		22 50									
Dunbar	d											23 15		23 15									
Edinburgh 10	a				23 09							23 46		23 46									
Edinburgh	d																						
Haymarket	d																						
Motherwell	a																						
Glasgow Central 15	a																						
Stirling	a																						
Perth	a																						
Inverness	a																						
Inverkeithing	a																						
Kirkcaldy	a																						
Leuchars 3	a																						
Dundee	a																						
Arbroath	a																						
Montrose	a																						
Stonehaven	a																						
Aberdeen	a																						

A from 7 August until 11 September
B from 18 September until 23 October
C 7 August, 14 August, 21 August, 4 September, 11 September
D from 28 August until 23 October, not 4 September, 11 September

Table 26

Sundays
7 August to 23 October

London - Humberside, Yorkshire, North East England and Scotland

		GR	GR	HT	EM	XC	GR	GR	GR	GR	GR	GR	EM	XC	XC	TP	TP	GR	GR	EM	GR	GR
		A	B				A	B	A	B	A	B		B	A	A	B	A	B		A	B
London Kings Cross ⊖	d	19 31	19 35	19 45			19 56	20 00	20 01	20 05	20 31	20 35						20 56	21 00		21 32	21 35
Stevenage	d	19 54	19 54	20 05							20 54	20 54									21 55	21 55
Peterborough	a	20 23	20 23				20 44	20 44	20 50	20 50	21 23	21 23						21 44	21 44		22 24	22 24
Norwich	d				18 56															20 52		
Peterborough	d	20 24	20 24		20 31		20 44	20 44	20 50	20 50	21 24	21 24						21 44	21 44	22 22	22 24	22 24
Grantham	a	20 46	20 46	20 53	21 01						21 46	21 46								22 54	22 48	22 48
	d	20 46	20 46	20 54							21 46	21 46									22 48	22 48
Newark North Gate	a										21 58	21 58									23 00	23 00
	d										21 58	21 58									23 00	23 00
Lincoln	a																					
Retford	d			21 15							22 13	22 13									23 15	23 15
Doncaster	a	21 18	21 18	21 29					21 41	21 41	22 29	22 29									23 31	23 31
Selby	a			21 45																		
Hull	a			22 25																		
Pontefract Monkhill	a																					
Wakefield Kirkgate	a																					
Wakefield Westgate	a	21 36	21 36						21 59	21 59	22 49	22 49									23 49	23 49
Leeds	a	21 57	21 57						22 20	22 20	23 10	23 10									00 27	00 27
Brighouse	a																					
Halifax	a																					
Shipley	a																					
Bradford Forster Square	a																					
Bradford Interchange	a																					
Keighley	a																					
Skipton	a																					
Sheffield	d					20 51							21 03	21 20	21 21							
Doncaster	d					21 23																
York	a					21 44	21 57	21 57										22 59	22 59			
Scarborough	a																					
Harrogate	a																					
Leeds	d												21a45	22a04	22a04	22 12	22 12					
York	d					21 47	21 59	21 59								22 44	22 42	23 04	23 04			
Thirsk	d															23 06	23 06					
Northallerton	d															23 16	23 16	23 39	23 39			
Darlington	a					22 22	22 39	22 39								23 28	23 28	23 51	23 51			
Eaglescliffe	a																					
Middlesbrough	a																					
Darlington	d					22 24	22 40	22 40								23 28	23 28	23 52	23 52			
Durham	d					22 41	22 57	22 57								23 45	23 45	00 09	00 09			
Chester-le-Street	d																					
Newcastle	a					23 10	23 33	23 33								00 15	00 15	00 45	00 45			
Hartlepool	a																					
Sunderland	a																					
Newcastle	d																					
Morpeth	d																					
Alnmouth for Alnwick	d																					
Berwick-upon-Tweed	d																					
Dunbar	d																					
Edinburgh	a																					
Edinburgh	d																					
Haymarket	d																					
Motherwell	a																					
Glasgow Central	a																					
Stirling	a																					
Perth	a																					
Inverness	a																					
Inverkeithing	a																					
Kirkcaldy	a																					
Leuchars	a																					
Dundee	a																					
Arbroath	a																					
Montrose	a																					
Stonehaven	a																					
Aberdeen	a																					

A from 7 August until 11 September
B from 18 September until 23 October

Table 26

Sundays
7 August to 23 October

London - Humberside, Yorkshire, North East England and Scotland

		GR	GR	XC	GR	GR	XC	EM
		A	B		A	B		
London Kings Cross ⊖	d	21 57	22 00		22 32	22 35		
Stevenage	d							
Peterborough	a	22 44	22 44		23s24	23s24		
Norwich	d							
Peterborough	d	22 45	22 45					
Grantham	a				23s49	23s49		
	d							
Newark North Gate	a				23s59	23s59		
	d							
Lincoln	a							
Retford	d							
Doncaster	a	23 42	23 42		00s30	00s30		
Selby	a							
Hull	a							
Pontefract Monkhill	a							
Wakefield Kirkgate	a							
Wakefield Westgate	a							
Leeds	a				01 37	01 37		
Brighouse	a							
Halifax	a							
Shipley	a							
Bradford Forster Square	a							
Bradford Interchange	a							
Keighley	a							
Skipton	a							
Sheffield	d			22 21			23 24	23 30
Doncaster	d	23 43	23 43					
York	a	00 33	00 33					
Scarborough	a							
Harrogate	a							
Leeds	d			23a01			00a34	00a28
York	d	00 35	00 35					
Thirsk	d							
Northallerton	d	01s07	01s07					
Darlington	a	01s21	01s21					
Eaglescliffe	a							
Middlesbrough	a							
Darlington	d							
Durham	d	01s39	01s39					
Chester-le-Street	d							
Newcastle	a	02 14	02 14					
Hartlepool	a							
Sunderland	a							
Newcastle	d							
Morpeth	d							
Alnmouth for Alnwick	d							
Berwick-upon-Tweed	d							
Dunbar	d							
Edinburgh	a							
Edinburgh	d							
Haymarket	d							
Motherwell	a							
Glasgow Central	a							
Stirling	a							
Perth	a							
Inverness	a							
Inverkeithing	a							
Kirkcaldy	a							
Leuchars	a							
Dundee	a							
Arbroath	a							
Montrose	a							
Stonehaven	a							
Aberdeen	a							

A from 7 August until 11 September
B from 18 September until 23 October

Sundays
from 30 October

London - Humberside, Yorkshire, North East England and Scotland

		GR	GR	TP	GR	XC	GR	TP	XC	NT	GR	TP	XC	TP	TP	XC	GR	GC	GR	GR	TP	XC	EM
		1	1	◇1	1	◇1	1	◇1	◇1		1	◇1	◇1	◇1	◇1	◇1	1	1	1	1	◇1	◇1	◇1
									A				A						B			A	
London Kings Cross 15 ⊖	d	21p00	22p00		09 03												09 30	09 48	10 00	10 03			
Stevenage 4	d				09 22																		
Peterborough 8	a	21p45	22p46		09 51												10 14			10 49			
Norwich	d																						
Peterborough 8	d	21p46	22p47		09 52												10 14			10 49			
Grantham 7	a		23p06		10 14															11 11			
	d		23p06		10 14															11 11			
Newark North Gate 7	a		23p18		10 26															11 23			
	d		23p18		10 26															11 23			
Lincoln	a																						
Retford 10	d		23p33														10 54						
Doncaster 7	a		23p48		10 51												11 10			11 48			
Selby	a																						
Hull	a																						
Pontefract Monkhill	a																						
Wakefield Kirkgate 4	a																						
Wakefield Westgate 7	a		00 05		11 09															12 06			
Leeds 10	a		00 26		11 30															12 29			
Brighouse	a																						
Halifax	a																						
Shipley	a																						
Bradford Forster Square	a																						
Bradford Interchange	a																						
Keighley	a																						
Skipton	a																						
Sheffield 7 ⇌	d												09 21			10 21						11 21	11 31
Doncaster 7	d										09 37						11 11						11 58
York 8	a	22p51									09 59						11 36	11 42	11 52				12 20
Scarborough	a																						
Harrogate	a																						
Leeds 10	d							08 40	09 08			09 45	10 08		10 39	11 08					11 40	12 08	
York 8	d	22p53		08 21			09 00	09 10	09 37		10 01	10 13	10 36	10 42	11 10	11 36	11 39	11 45	11 53		12 08	12 34	
Thirsk	d			08 37										10 59				12 01					
Northallerton	d	23p14		08 45			09 18	09 31				10 36		11 07	11 31			12 10			12 29		
Darlington 7	a	23p26		08 56			09 31	09 42	10 03		10 28	10 47	11 02		11 42	12 02	12 08		12 23		12 40	13 00	
Eaglescliffe	a																	12 28					
Middlesbrough	a			09 27										11 39									
Darlington 7	d	23p27					09 31	09 43	10 04	10 20	10 29	10 48	11 04		11 43	12 03	12 08		12 24		12 41	13 02	
Durham	d	23p44					09 49	09 59	10 21		10 46	11 08	11 20		11 59	12 20	12 26				12 57	13 18	
Chester-le-Street	d																						
Newcastle 8 ⇌	a	00 06					10 05	10 18	10 35		11 02	11 24	11 35		12 15	12 35	12 42		12 53		13 12	13 33	
Hartlepool	a									10 59								12 51					
Sunderland ⇌	a									11 26								13 21					
Newcastle 8 ⇌	d					09 45	10 13		10 38	11a48	11 04		11 38			12 38	12 44		12 55			13 35	
Morpeth	d					09 58	10 29																
Alnmouth for Alnwick	d					10 12	10 45										13 10					14 00	
Berwick-upon-Tweed	d						11 07		11 20		11 47		12 20						13 39			14 20	
Dunbar	d						11 31									13 40	13 53						
Edinburgh 10	a					11 13	12 01		12 03		12 36		13 03			14 07	14 23		14 24			15 06	
Edinburgh	d								12 12				13 10						14 38			15 11	
Haymarket	d								12 16				13 15						14 43			15 15	
Motherwell	a								12 53				13 50									15 51	
Glasgow Central 15	a								13 12				14 14									16 14	
Stirling	a																						
Perth	a																						
Inverness	a																						
Inverkeithing	a																		15 01				
Kirkcaldy	a																		15 18				
Leuchars 3	a																		15 42				
Dundee	a																		15 57				
Arbroath	a																		16 14				
Montrose	a																		16 30				
Stonehaven	a																		16 53				
Aberdeen	a																		17 19				

A ⊼ to Berwick-upon-Tweed   B The Northern Lights

Table 26

Sundays
from 30 October

London - Humberside, Yorkshire, North East England and Scotland

		GR	HT	TP	GR	GR	TP	XC	GR	EM	GC	GR	GR	TP	GR	XC	GR	HT	XC	TP	GR	GR	TP
		1	◇1	◇1	1	1	◇1	◇1	1	◇	■	1	1	◇1	1	◇1	1	◇1	◇1	◇1	1	1	◇1
												A				B							
London Kings Cross 15 ⊖	d	10 30	10 45		11 00	11 03			11 30		11 48	12 00	12 03		12 20		12 30	12 45			13 00	13 03	
Stevenage 4	d		11u05			11 22												13u05				13 22	
Peterborough 8	a	11 14				11 51			12 14				12 49		13 07		13 14					13 51	
Norwich	d									10 47													
Peterborough 8	d	11 14				11 52			12 14	12 18			12 49		13 07		13 14					13 52	
Grantham 7	a		11 49			12 14				12 53			13 11					13 49				14 14	
	d		11 50			12 14				12 54			13 11					13 50				14 14	
Newark North Gate 7	a	11 44				12 26							13 23				13 44					14 26	
	d	11 44				12 26							13 23				13 44					14 26	
Lincoln	a																						
Retford 10	d		12 11						12 54									14 11					
Doncaster 7	a	12 10	12 28			12 51			13 10		13 16		13 48		13 58		14 09	14 25				14 51	
Selby	a		12 45															14 41					
Hull	a		13 25															15 21					
Pontefract Monkhill	a										13 41												
Wakefield Kirkgate 4	a										13 58												
Wakefield Westgate 7	a					13 09							14 06									15 09	
Leeds 10	a					13 30							14 29									15 30	
Brighouse	a										14 20												
Halifax	a										14 35												
Shipley	a																						
Bradford Forster Square	a																						
Bradford Interchange	a										14 50												
Keighley	a																						
Skipton	a																						
Sheffield 7 ⇌	d							12 21		14a36						13 21			13 51				
Doncaster 7	d	12 10							13 11						13 58		14 10		14 15				
York 8	a	12 34			12 50				13 34			13 52			14 22		14 36		14 41		14 53		
Scarborough	a																						
Harrogate	a																						
Leeds 10	d			12 12			12 40	13 08						13 40		14 08				14 12			14 40
York 8	d	12 37		12 42	12 53		13 10	13 34	13 37			13 53		14 10	14 23	14 34	14 37		14 46	14 50	14 54		15 10
Thirsk	d			13 00																15 13			
Northallerton	d	12 57		13 08			13 31							14 31			14 57			15 21			15 31
Darlington 7	a	13 09			13 21		13 42	14 00	14 05			14 21		14 42	14 51	15 00	15 09		15 15		15 22		15 42
Eaglescliffe	a																						
Middlesbrough	a			13 40																15 52			
Darlington 7	d	13 10			13 22		13 43	14 01	14 06			14 22		14 43	14 51	15 02	15 10		15 17		15 22		15 44
Durham	d	13 27					13 59	14 18	14 23					14 59	15 09	15 20	15 27		15 33				16 00
Chester-le-Street	d						14 05																16 06
Newcastle 8 ⇌	a	13 43			13 51		14 17	14 32	14 39			14 51		15 15	15 30	15 35	15 43		15 47		15 52		16 18
Hartlepool	a																						
Sunderland ⇌	a																						
Newcastle 8 ⇌	d	13 45			13 54			14 36	14 42			14 53				15 37	15 45				15 54		
Morpeth	d							14 49															
Alnmouth for Alnwick	d								15 08							16 02							
Berwick-upon-Tweed	d				14 37							15 37				16 22					16 37		
Dunbar	d							15 41															
Edinburgh 10	a	15 18			15 26			16 06	16 16			16 22				17 06	17 17				17 27		
Edinburgh	d											16 30				17 11							
Haymarket	d											16 35				17 15							
Motherwell	a															17 52							
Glasgow Central 15	a															18 12							
Stirling	a											17 17											
Perth	a											17 53											
Inverness	a											20 19											
Inverkeithing	a																						
Kirkcaldy	a																						
Leuchars 3	a																						
Dundee	a																						
Arbroath	a																						
Montrose	a																						
Stonehaven	a																						
Aberdeen	a																						

A The Highland Chieftain   B ⊼ to Berwick-upon-Tweed

Table 26

Sundays
from 30 October

London - Humberside, Yorkshire, North East England and Scotland

		XC	GR	NT	GC	XC	GC	GR	GR	TP	XC	GR	HT	TP	XC	GR	TP	XC	EM	GR	GR	GC
		◇1	■ 1		■ 1	◇1	■ 1	■ 1	■ 1	◇1	◇1	■ 1	◇1	◇1	◇1	■ 1	◇1	◇1	◇	■ 1	■ 1	■
		A									B											
London Kings Cross 15 ⊖	d		13 30		13 48			14 00	14 03			14 30	14 45			15 00				15 03	15 30	15 48
Stevenage 4	d												15u05							15 22		
Peterborough 8	a		14 14						14 49			15 14								15 51	16 14	
Norwich	d																		13 49			
Peterborough 8	d		14 14						14 50			15 15							15 26	15 52	16 16	
Grantham 7	a								15 12				15 49						15 56	16 14	16 39	
	d								15 12				15 50						15 59	16 14	16 40	
Newark North Gate 7	a								15 24			15 46								16 26		
	d								15 24			15 46								16 26		
Lincoln	a																					
Retford 10	d		14 54										16 11							16 42		
Doncaster 7	a		15 10						15 49			16 11	16 28							16 57	17 11	17 19
Selby	a												16 45									
Hull	a												17 25									
Pontefract Monkhill	a																					17 43
Wakefield Kirkgate 4	a																					18 00
Wakefield Westgate 7	a								16 07											17 16		
Leeds 10	a								16 29											17 39		
Brighouse	a																					18 21
Halifax	a																					18 35
Shipley	a																					
Bradford Forster Square	a																					
Bradford Interchange	a																					18 50
Keighley	a																					
Skipton	a																					
Sheffield 7 ⇌	d	14 21				14 51					15 21				15 51			16 21	17a40			
Doncaster 7	d		15 11			15 19						16 12			16 17						17 13	
York 8	a		15 35		15 41	15 44		15 52				16 36			16 44	16 52					17 37	
Scarborough	a																					
Harrogate	a																					
Leeds 10	d	15 08					←			15 40	16 08			16 12			16 40	17 08				
York 8	d	15 34	15 37		15 50	15 47	15 50	15 53		16 08	16 35	16 38		16 42	16 47	16 53	17 10	17 34			17 39	
Thirsk	d				→		16 07							17 04								
Northallerton	d						16 18			16 29		16 58		17 16			17 31					
Darlington 7	a	15 59	16 05			16 12		16 22		16 40	17 00	17 10			17 16	17 21	17 42	17 59			18 07	
Eaglescliffe	a						16 35															
Middlesbrough	a													17 50								
Darlington 7	d	16 01	16 06	16 11		16 14		16 23		16 41	17 02	17 11			17 18	17 22	17 43	18 01			18 07	
Durham	d	16 18	16 23			16 31				16 57	17 18	17 29			17 35		17 59	18 17			18 26	
Chester-le-Street	d																18 05					
Newcastle 8 ⇌	a	16 32	16 39			16 45		16 52		17 12	17 33	17 45			17 48	17 52	18 18	18 32			18 42	
Hartlepool	a			16 50			16 58															
Sunderland ⇌	a			17 22			17 27															
Newcastle 8 ⇌	d	16 34	16 42	17a48				16 54			17 38	17 47				17 54		18 36			18 43	
Morpeth	d																					
Alnmouth for Alnwick	d	16 59	17 08								18 02										19 11	
Berwick-upon-Tweed	d							17 38			18 23					18 37		19 18				
Dunbar	d	17 40																19 41				
Edinburgh 10	a	18 07	18 18					18 23			19 06	19 19				19 26		20 05			20 18	
Edinburgh	d	18 11						18 42			19 18											
Haymarket	d	18 16						18 47			19 23											
Motherwell	a										20 00											
Glasgow Central 15	a										20 20											
Stirling	a																					
Perth	a																					
Inverness	a																					
Inverkeithing	a	18 28						19 01														
Kirkcaldy	a	18 44						19 18														
Leuchars 3	a	19 14						19 43														
Dundee	a	19 29						19 57														
Arbroath	a	19 46						20 15														
Montrose	a	20 00						20 31														
Stonehaven	a	20 23						20 54														
Aberdeen	a	20 43						21 20														

A ✠ to Dunbar

B ✠ to Berwick-upon-Tweed

Table 26

Sundays
from 30 October

London - Humberside, Yorkshire, North East England and Scotland

		GR	TP	XC	EM	EM	GR	EM	GR	GR	TP	GR	GR	GR	TP	XC	XC	GR	GR	HT	XC	EM	GR
		■ 1	◇1	◇1	◇1	◇	■ 1	◇	■ 1	■ 1	◇1	■ 1	■ 1	■ 1	◇1	◇1	◇1	■ 1	■ 1	◇1	◇1	◇	■ 1
				A																			
London Kings Cross 15 ⊖	d	16 00					16 05		16 30	16 35		17 00	17 05	17 20				17 30	17 35	17 45			18 00
Stevenage 4	d									16 54									17 54	18u05			
Peterborough 8	a						16 49		17 14				17 50					18 14					
Norwich	d					14 49		15 53														16 53	
Peterborough 8	d					16 24	16 49	17 11	17 14				17 50					18 15				18 26	
Grantham 7	a					16 54	17 11	17 45		17 40				18 25				18 36	18 41	18 49		18 56	
	d					16 56	17 11	17 55		17 40				18 25				18 37	18 41	18 50		18 58	
Newark North Gate 7	a						17 23		17 44				18 21	18 37									
	d						17 23		17 44				18 21	18 37									
Lincoln	a																						
Retford 10	d									18 02										19 11			
Doncaster 7	a						17 48		18 10	18 18			18 48	19 03				19 09	19 14	19 28			
Selby	a													19 24						19 45			
Hull	a													20 06						20 25			
Pontefract Monkhill	a																						
Wakefield Kirkgate 4	a																						
Wakefield Westgate 7	a						18 11			18 38			19 07						19 31				
Leeds 10	a						18 31			18 58			19 28						19 53				
Brighouse	a																						
Halifax	a																						
Shipley	a																						
Bradford Forster Square	a																						
Bradford Interchange	a																						
Keighley	a																						
Skipton	a																						
Sheffield 7 ⇌	d			17 21	17 34	18a34		19a31								17 51	18 21				18 51	20a31	
Doncaster 7	d								18 10							18 15		19 12			19 18		
York 8	a	17 48							18 35			18 50						19 38			19 44		19 50
Scarborough	a																						
Harrogate	a																						
Leeds 10	d		17 40	18 08	18a24						18 12				18 40	18 57	19 08						
York 8	d	17 52	18 10	18 34					18 37		18 42	18 52			19 10	19 24	19 35	19 40			19 47		19 52
Thirsk	d										18 59												
Northallerton	d		18 31						18 56		19 08				19 31								
Darlington 7	a	18 19	18 42	19 00					19 09			19 20			19 42	19 51	20 02	20 07			20 12		20 19
Eaglescliffe	a																						
Middlesbrough	a										19 40												
Darlington 7	d	18 20	18 43	19 01					19 09			19 21			19 44	19 53	20 03	20 08			20 14		20 20
Durham	d		18 59	19 18					19 27						20 00	20 09	20 21	20 25			20 31		
Chester-le-Street	d														20 06								
Newcastle 8 ⇌	a	18 49	19 16	19 35					19 43			19 50			20 17	20 24	20 36	20 41			20 45		20 51
Hartlepool	a																						
Sunderland ⇌	a																						
Newcastle 8 ⇌	d	18 51		19 40					19 44			19 52					20 38	20 43			20 51		20 53
Morpeth	d								19 58								20 53						21 10
Alnmouth for Alnwick	d			20 05																			21 25
Berwick-upon-Tweed	d	19 39		20 25								20 37					21 26						21 47
Dunbar	d											21 02					21 51						
Edinburgh 10	a	20 28		21 08					21 18			21 27					22 16	22 22			22 23		22 36
Edinburgh	d			21 12								21 33											
Haymarket	d			21 16								21 37											
Motherwell	a			21 53								22 14											
Glasgow Central 15	a			22 14								22 39											
Stirling	a																						
Perth	a																						
Inverness	a																						
Inverkeithing	a																						
Kirkcaldy	a																						
Leuchars 3	a																						
Dundee	a																						
Arbroath	a																						
Montrose	a																						
Stonehaven	a																						
Aberdeen	a																						

A ✠ to Berwick-upon-Tweed

Table 26

Sundays
from 30 October

London - Humberside, Yorkshire, North East England and Scotland

		GR	TP	GC	XC	GR	GR	EM	XC	GR	GR	GR	GC	TP	XC	GR	GR	HT	EM	XC	GR	GR
London Kings Cross ⊖	d	18 05		18 27		18 30	18 35			19 00	19 05	19 08	19 27			19 30	19 35	19 45			20 00	20 05
Stevenage	d						18 54					19 28					19 54	20 05				
Peterborough	a	18 52				19 15					19 50	19 59				20 15	20 23				20 44	20 50
Norwich	d							17 53											18 56			
Peterborough	d	18 53				19 16		19 26			19 51	20 00				20 16	20 24		20 31		20 44	20 50
Grantham	a						19 42	19 56				20 21					20 46	20 53	21 01			
	d						19 42					20 21					20 46	20 54				
Newark North Gate	a	19 24				19 46					20 21	20 33				20 47						
	d	19 24				19 46					20 21	20 34				20 48						
Lincoln	a											21 03										
Retford	d						20 04											21 15				
Doncaster	a	19 50				20 11	20 20				20 47		21 00			21 13	21 18	21 29				21 41
Selby	a																	21 45				
Hull	a																	22 25				
Pontefract Monkhill	a												21 24									
Wakefield Kirkgate	a												21 41									
Wakefield Westgate	a	20 08					20 37				21 05						21 36					21 59
Leeds	a	20 25					20 55				21 29						21 57					22 20
Brighouse	a												22 04									
Halifax	a												22 17									
Shipley	a																					
Bradford Forster Square	a																					
Bradford Interchange	a												22 32									
Keighley	a						21s22															
Skipton	a						21 43															
Sheffield	d				19 21				19 51						20 21					20 51		
Doncaster	d					20 12			20 18							21 14				21 23		
York	a			20 17		20 36			20 45	20 52						21 38				21 44	21 57	
Scarborough	a																					
Harrogate	a	21 07																				
Leeds	d		19 40		20 08									20 40	21 08							
York	d		20 10	20 21	20 35	20 38			20 48	20 53				21 08	21a32	21 40				21 47	21 59	
Thirsk	d		20 26	20 37										21 26								
Northallerton	d		20 36	20 49		20 57								21 34								
Darlington	a				21 02	21 10			21 15	21 21				21 45		22 17				22 22	22 39	
Eaglescliffe	a			21 06																		
Middlesbrough	a		21 08																			
Darlington	d				21 03	21 10			21 16	21 22				21 46		22 18				22 24	22 40	
Durham	d				21 21	21 28			21 34					22 03		22 35				22 41	22 57	
Chester-le-Street	d																					
Newcastle	a				21 36	21 49			21 51	21 54				22 17		23 09				23 10	23 33	
Hartlepool	a			21 26																		
Sunderland	a			21 53																		
Newcastle	d				21 38					21 56												
Morpeth	d									22 12												
Alnmouth for Alnwick	d				22 06					22 28												
Berwick-upon-Tweed	d									22 50												
Dunbar	d									23 15												
Edinburgh	a				23 09					23 46												
Edinburgh	d																					
Haymarket	d																					
Motherwell	a																					
Glasgow Central	a																					
Stirling	a																					
Perth	a																					
Inverness	a																					
Inverkeithing	a																					
Kirkcaldy	a																					
Leuchars	a																					
Dundee	a																					
Arbroath	a																					
Montrose	a																					
Stonehaven	a																					
Aberdeen	a																					

Table 26

Sundays
from 30 October

London - Humberside, Yorkshire, North East England and Scotland

		GR	EM	XC	TP	GR	EM	GR	GR	XC	GR	XC	EM
London Kings Cross ⊖	d	20 35				21 00		21 35	22 00		22 35		
Stevenage	d	20 54						21 55					
Peterborough	a	21 23				21 44		22 24	22 44		23s24		
Norwich	d						20 52						
Peterborough	d	21 24				21 44	22 22	22 24	22 45				
Grantham	a	21 46					22 54	22 48			23s49		
	d	21 46						22 48					
Newark North Gate	a	21 58						23 00			23s59		
	d	21 58						23 00					
Lincoln	a												
Retford	d	22 13						23 15					
Doncaster	a	22 29						23 31	23 42		00s30		
Selby	a												
Hull	a												
Pontefract Monkhill	a												
Wakefield Kirkgate	a												
Wakefield Westgate	a	22 49						23 49					
Leeds	a	23 10						00 27			01 37		
Brighouse	a												
Halifax	a												
Shipley	a												
Bradford Forster Square	a												
Bradford Interchange	a												
Keighley	a												
Skipton	a												
Sheffield	d		21 03	21 21						22 21		23 24	23 30
Doncaster	d								23 43				
York	a					22 59			00 33				
Scarborough	a												
Harrogate	a												
Leeds	d		21a45	22a04	22 12					23a01		00a34	00a28
York	d				22 44	23 04			00 35				
Thirsk	d				23 06								
Northallerton	d				23 16	23 39			01s07				
Darlington	a				23 28	23 51			01s21				
Eaglescliffe	a												
Middlesbrough	a												
Darlington	d				23 28	23 52							
Durham	d				23 45	00 09			01s39				
Chester-le-Street	d												
Newcastle	a				00 15	00 45			02 14				
Hartlepool	a												
Sunderland	a												
Newcastle	d												
Morpeth	d												
Alnmouth for Alnwick	d												
Berwick-upon-Tweed	d												
Dunbar	d												
Edinburgh	a												
Edinburgh	d												
Haymarket	d												
Motherwell	a												
Glasgow Central	a												
Stirling	a												
Perth	a												
Inverness	a												
Inverkeithing	a												
Kirkcaldy	a												
Leuchars	a												
Dundee	a												
Arbroath	a												
Montrose	a												
Stonehaven	a												
Aberdeen	a												

Table 26

Scotland, North East England, Yorkshire and Humberside - London

Miles	Miles	Miles	Station		GR MO	SR MO	SR MX	GR MX	GR MX	SR	EM	GR	FC	GR	EM	GR	XC	NT	FC	GR	FC	FC	GR
										A													
—	—	0	**Aberdeen**	d					18p16	21p40													
—	—	16¼	Stonehaven	d					18p33	22c00													
—	—	40½	Montrose	d					18p56	22c25													
—	—	54¼	Arbroath	d					19p12	22c43													
—	—	71¼	**Dundee**	d					19p30	23c06													
—	—	79½	Leuchars	d					19p44	23c25													
—	—	104½	Kirkcaldy	d					20p08	23c53													
—	—	117¼	Inverkeithing	d					20p24	00u12													
—	—	—	**Inverness**	d		20p25	20p46																
—	—	—	Perth	d		23c00	23c21																
—	—	—	Stirling	d		23c45	00u06																
0	—	—	**Glasgow Central**	d																			
12¾	—	—	Motherwell	d																			
56	—	129¼	Haymarket	d					20p43														
57¼	—	130½	**Edinburgh**	a		00 47	01 00		20p48	00u41													
—	—	—	**Edinburgh**	d	19p00				21p00														
86½	—	—	Dunbar	d	19p21				21p21														
114¾	—	—	**Berwick-upon-Tweed**	d	19p44				21p47														
147	—	—	Alnmouth for Alnwick	d					22p10														
165¼	—	—	Morpeth	d					22p26														
181¾	—	—	**Newcastle**	a	20p30				22p43														
—	—	—	Sunderland	d																			
—	—	—	Hartlepool	d														06 20					
—	—	—	**Newcastle**	d	20p32			21p15	22p44									06a46		04 40			
190	—	—	Chester-le-Street	d																			
195¾	—	—	**Durham**	d	20p46			21p27	23p00											04 54			
217¾	—	—	**Darlington**	a	21p02			21p45	23p19											05 11			
—	—	—	Middlesbrough	d																			
—	—	—	Eaglescliffe	d																			
—	—	—	**Darlington**	d	21p03			21p46	23p19											05 12			
231¼	—	—	Northallerton	d				21p57	23b46											05 31			
239½	—	—	Thirsk	d																			
261¾	—	—	**York**	a	21p31			22p17	00 13											05 57			
—	—	—	Leeds	a					00 50														
—	—	—	Harrogate	d																			
—	—	—	Scarborough	d																			
—	—	—	**York**	d	21p33			22p19												06 00			
294¼	—	—	**Doncaster**	a	21p56			22p42												06 21			
—	—	—	Skipton	d																			
—	—	—	Keighley	d																			
—	—	—	**Bradford Interchange**	d																			
—	—	—	Bradford Forster Square	d																			
—	—	—	Shipley	d																			
—	—	—	Halifax	d																			
—	—	—	Brighouse	d																			
—	0	—	**Leeds**	d										05 05	05 25	05 30	06 00						06 05
—	10	—	**Wakefield Westgate**	d										05 17	05 37	05 42	06 12						06 17
—	—	—	Wakefield Kirkgate	d																			
—	—	—	Pontefract Monkhill	d																			
—	—	—	Sheffield	a													06 41						
—	—	—	Hull	d																			
—	—	—	Selby	d																			
—	29¾	—	**Doncaster**	d	21p57			22p42						05 35	05a55	06 01				06 22			06 35
311¾	—	—	**Retford**	d										05 49									06 50
—	—	—	Lincoln	d																			
330¼	—	—	**Newark North Gate**	a	22p19			23p06						06 04		06 26				06 46			07 05
—	—	—		d	22p20			23p06						06 04		06 26				06 46			07 06
344¾	—	—	**Grantham**	a	22p32			23p18						06 17		06 39				06 59			07 18
—	—	—		d	22p33			23p18			05 51			06 17		06 39				06 59			07 19
374	—	—	**Peterborough**	a	22p53			23p39			06 25			06 36		06 59				07 19			07 39
—	—	—	Norwich	a																			
—	—	—	**Peterborough**	d	23p00			23p39				06 10	06 19	06 40		07 00			06 53	07 20	07 14	07 25	07 40
422¾	—	—	**Stevenage**	a	23b34			00s20					07 00						07 35		07 58		
450¼	—	—	**London Kings Cross** ⊖	a	00 02			00 59				07 03	07 26	07 33		07 54			08 00	08 16	08 23	08 30	08 36

A TWThO until 16 June, TWThO from 25 October

b Previous night, stops to set down only

c Previous night, stops to pick up only

Table 26

Mondays to Fridays

Scotland, North East England, Yorkshire and Humberside - London

Station		NT	XC	GR	TP	NT	EM	GR	FC	GR	XC
Aberdeen	d										
Stonehaven	d										
Montrose	d										
Arbroath	d										
Dundee	d										
Leuchars	d										
Kirkcaldy	d										
Inverkeithing	d										
Inverness	d										
Perth	d										
Stirling	d										
Glasgow Central	d										
Motherwell	d										
Haymarket	d										
Edinburgh	a										
Edinburgh	d										
Dunbar	d										
Berwick-upon-Tweed	d										
Alnmouth for Alnwick	d										
Morpeth	d										
Newcastle	a										
Sunderland	d										
Hartlepool	d										
Newcastle	d		05 25								
Chester-le-Street	d										
Durham	d		05 38								
Darlington	a		05 56								
Middlesbrough	d			05 55							
Eaglescliffe	d										
Darlington	d		05 57	06 23							
Northallerton	d		06 08	06 31							
Thirsk	d										
York	a		06 28	06 49							
Leeds	a			07 20							
Harrogate	d										
Scarborough	d										
York	d		06 30								
Doncaster	a		06 52								
Skipton	d										
Keighley	d										
Bradford Interchange	d										
Bradford Forster Square	d										
Shipley	d										
Halifax	d										
Brighouse	d										
Leeds	d	06 24									
Wakefield Westgate	d	06 29									
Wakefield Kirkgate	d	06a46									
Pontefract Monkhill	d										
Sheffield	a										
Hull	d										
Selby	d										
Doncaster	d	[illegible]	[illegible]								
Retford	d										
Lincoln	d										
Newark North Gate	a										
	d										
Grantham	a										
	d										
Peterborough	a										
Norwich	a										
Peterborough	d										
Stevenage	a										
London Kings Cross ⊖	a										

D The [illegible] Executive

Table 26

Mondays to Fridays

Scotland, North East England, Yorkshire and Humberside - London

	GR	GR	GC	TP		EM	FC	GC	XC	GR	GR	GR	TP	XC		TP	SR	GR	SR	NT	HT	EM	GR	GR
	■1	■1	■1	◇1		◇	1	■1	◇1	■1	■1	■1	◇1	◇1		◇1		■1			◇1	◇	■1	■1
											D								F					D
Aberdeen d																								
Stonehaven d																								
Montrose d																								
Arbroath d																								
Dundee d																								
Leuchars d																								
Kirkcaldy d																								
Inverkeithing d																								
Inverness d																								
Perth d																								
Stirling d																								
Glasgow Central 15 d																								
Motherwell d																								
Haymarket d																	06 14		06 33					
Edinburgh 10 a																	06 18		06 39					
Edinburgh d		05 40									05 45			06 06			06 20	06 25	06 41					06 55
Dunbar d											06 06													
Berwick-upon-Tweed d	06 00										06 31			06 46				07 06						
Alnmouth for Alnwick d	06 19										06 52			07 08										
Morpeth d	06 35										07 07													
Newcastle 8 a	06 52	07 02									07 24			07 38				07 53		07 19				08 22
Sunderland d								06 45												07 54				
Hartlepool d								07 09												08 19				
Newcastle 8 d	06 55	07 03							07 25		07 28		07 33	07 41				[illegible]						08 25
Chester-le-Street d													07 42											
Durham d	07 07								07 37		07 41		07 49	07 55										08 37
Darlington 7 a	07 25								07 53		07 58		08 05	08 10				08 23						08 55
Middlesbrough d				07 12																				
Eaglescliffe d								07 30																
Darlington 7 d	07 31								07 54		07 59		08 06	08 12				08 24						08 56
Northallerton d				07 45				07 50					08 17											09 07
Thirsk d				07 53				07 59					08 25			←								
York 8 a	07 59			08 12				08 16	08 21		08 27		08 47	08 41		08 47		08 53						09 27
Leeds 10 a				08 52									→	09 08		09 22								
Harrogate d										07 28														
Scarborough d																								
York 8 d	08 00							08 20	08 24		08 29							08 55						09 29
Doncaster 7 a									08 48		08 52													09 52
Skipton d																								
Keighley d																								
Bradford Interchange d			06 51																					
Bradford Forster Square d																								
Shipley d																								
Halifax d			07 07																					
Brighouse d			07 18																					
Leeds 10 d										08 15		08 45		09 11									09 15	
Wakefield Westgate 7 d										08 27		08 57		09 24									09 27	
Wakefield Kirkgate 4 d			07 42																					
Pontefract Monkhill d			08 01																					
Sheffield 7 a									09 17					09 51										
Hull d																					08 25			
Selby d																					08 58			
Doncaster 7 d			08 31							08 45	08 53	09 16									09 24		09 45	09 53
Retford 10 d	08 33																				09 39			
Lincoln d																								
Newark North Gate 7 a											09 16													10 16
Newark North Gate d											09 16													10 16
Grantham 7 a										09 19											[illegible]		10 16	
Grantham d						09 10				09 19											[illegible]	10 11	10 16	
Peterborough 8 a						09 39					09 47	10 07										10 40		10 47
Norwich a						11 14																[illegible]		
Peterborough 8 d							09 16				09 48	[illegible]												10 48
Stevenage 4 a							09 58			10 08													11 00	
London Kings Cross 15 ⊖ a	10 06	09 40	10 13				10 22	10 25		10 38	10 45	[illegible]						10 54			11 10		11 29	11 46

D ⊘ to Peterborough

F from 30 May

Table 26

Mondays to Fridays

Scotland, North East England, Yorkshire and Humberside - London

	XC	GR	XC	GR	NT	TP	GR	GC	TP	EM	EM	GR	GR	XC	GR	XC	GR	SR	NT	TP	TP
	◇1	■1	◇1	■1		◇1	■1	■1	◇1	◇		■1	■1	◇1	■1	◇1	■1			◇1	◇1
			A	B			C						D			A	B				
Aberdeen d																					
Stonehaven d																					
Montrose d																					
Arbroath d																					
Dundee d																					
Leuchars d																					
Kirkcaldy d																					
Inverkeithing d																					
Inverness d																					
Perth d																					
Stirling d																					
Glasgow Central d																					
Motherwell d																					
Haymarket d																					
Edinburgh a																					
Edinburgh d																					
Dunbar d																					
Berwick-upon-Tweed d																					
Alnmouth for Alnwick d																					
Morpeth d																					
Newcastle a																					
Sunderland d																					
Hartlepool d																					
Newcastle d																					
Chester-le-Street d																					
Durham d																					
Darlington a																					
Middlesbrough d																					
Eaglescliffe d																					
Northallerton d																					
Thirsk d																					
York a																					
Leeds a																					
Harrogate d																					
Scarborough d																					
York d																					
Doncaster a																					
Skipton d																					
Keighley d																					
Bradford Interchange d																					
Bradford Forster Square d																					
Shipley d																					
Halifax d																					
Brighouse d																					
Leeds d																					
Wakefield Westgate d																					
Wakefield Kirkgate d																					
Pontefract Monkhill d																					
Sheffield a																					
Hull d																					
Selby d																					
Doncaster d																					
Retford d																					
Lincoln d																					
Newark North Gate a																					
Newark North Gate d																					
Grantham a																					
Grantham d																					
Peterborough a																					
Norwich a																					
Peterborough d																					
Stevenage a																					
London Kings Cross ⊖ a																					

A from Edinburgh

B ⊘ to York

C ⊘ to [illegible]

D ⊘ to [illegible]

Scotland, North East England, Yorkshire and Humberside - London

Miles	Miles	Miles			GR	SR	SR	GR	GR	SR	EM	GR	FC		GR	EM	GR	XC	NT	FC	GR	FC	FC		GR
					MO	MO	MX	MX	MX																
										A															
—	—	0	**Aberdeen**	d					18p16	21p40															
—	—	16¼	Stonehaven	d					18p33	22c00															
—	—	40½	Montrose	d					18p56	22c25															
—	—	54¼	Arbroath	d					19p12	22c43															
—	—	71¼	**Dundee**	d					19p30	23c06															
—	—	79½	Leuchars [3]	d					19p44	23c25															
—	—	104½	Kirkcaldy	d					20p08	23c53															
—	—	117¼	Inverkeithing	d					20p24	00u12															
—	—	—	**Inverness**	d		20p25	20p46																		
—	—	—	Perth	d		23c00	23c21																		
—	—	—	Stirling	d		23c45	00u06																		
0	—	—	**Glasgow Central** [15]	d																					
12¾	—	—	Motherwell	d																					
56	—	129¼	Haymarket	d					20p43																
57¼	—	130½	**Edinburgh** [10]	a		00 47	01 00		20p48	00 41															
—	—	—	**Edinburgh**	d	19p00				21p00																
86½	—	—	Dunbar	d	19p21				21p21																
114¾	—	—	**Berwick-upon-Tweed**	d	19p44				21p47																
147	—	—	Alnmouth for Alnwick	d					22p10																
165¼	—	—	Morpeth	d					22p26																
181¾	—	—	**Newcastle** [8]	a	20p30				22p43																
—	—	—	Sunderland	d															06 20						
—	—	—	Hartlepool	d															06a46						
—	—	—	**Newcastle** [8]	d	20p32			21p15	22p44												04 40				
190	—	—	Chester-le-Street	d																					
195¾	—	—	**Durham**	d	20p46			21p27	23p00												04 54				
217¾	—	—	**Darlington** [7]	a	21p02			21p45	23p19												05 11				
—	—	—	Middlesbrough	d																					
—	—	—	Eaglescliffe	d																					
—	—	—	**Darlington** [7]	d	21p03			21p46	23p19												05 12				
231¾	—	—	Northallerton	d				21p57	23b46												05 31				
239½	—	—	Thirsk	d																					
261¾	—	—	**York** [8]	a	21p31			22p17	00 13												05 57				
—	—	—	Leeds [10]	a					00 50																
—	—	—	Harrogate	d																					
—	—	—	Scarborough	d																					
—	—	—	**York** [8]	d	21p33			22p19													06 00				
294¼	—	—	**Doncaster** [7]	a	21p56			22p42													06 21				
—	—	—	Skipton	d																					
—	—	—	Keighley	d																					
—	—	—	**Bradford Interchange**	d																					
—	—	—	Bradford Forster Square	d																					
—	—	—	Shipley	d																					
—	—	—	Halifax	d																					
—	—	—	Brighouse	d																					
—	0	—	**Leeds** [10]	d											05 05	05 25	05 30	06 00							06 05
—	10	—	**Wakefield Westgate** [7]	d											05 17	05 37	05 42	06 12							06 17
—	—	—	Wakefield Kirkgate [4]	d																					
—	—	—	Pontefract Monkhill	d																					
—	—	—	Sheffield [7]	a														06 41							
—	—	—	Hull	d																					
—	—	—	Selby	d																					
—	29¾	—	**Doncaster** [7]	d	21p57			22p42							05 35	05a55	06 01				06 22				06 35
311¾	—	—	**Retford** [10]	d											05 49										06 50
—	—	—	Lincoln	d																					
330¼	—	—	**Newark North Gate** [7]	a	22p19			23p06							06 04		06 26				06 46				07 05
—	—	—		d	22p20			23p06							06 04		06 26				06 46				07 06
344¾	—	—	**Grantham** [7]	a	22p32			23p18							06 17		06 39				06 59				07 18
—	—	—		d	22p33			23p18			05 51				06 17		06 39				06 59				07 19
374	—	—	**Peterborough** [8]	a	22p53			23p39			06 25				06 36		06 59				07 19				07 39
—	—	—	Norwich	a																					
—	—	—	**Peterborough** [8]	d	23p00			23p39				06 10	06 19		06 40		07 00			06 53	07 20	07 14	07 25		07 40
422¾	—	—	**Stevenage** [4]	a	23b34			00s20					07 00							07 35		07 58			
450¼	—	—	**London Kings Cross** [15] ⊖	a	00 02			00 59				07 03	07 26		07 33		07 54			08 00	08 16	08 23	08 30		08 36

A TWThO until 16 June, TWThO from 25 October

b Previous night, stops to set down only

c Previous night, stops to pick up only

Scotland, North East England, Yorkshire and Humberside - London

		NT	XC	GR	TP	NT	EM	GR	FC		GR	XC	GR	HT	GR	GR	TP	XC	TP		GR	EM	GR	GR	XC
																							D		
Aberdeen	d																								
Stonehaven	d																								
Montrose	d																								
Arbroath	d																								
Dundee	d																								
Leuchars [3]	d																								
Kirkcaldy	d																								
Inverkeithing	d																								
Inverness	d																								
Perth	d																								
Stirling	d																								
Glasgow Central [15]	d																								
Motherwell	d																								
Haymarket	d																								
Edinburgh [10]	a																								
Edinburgh	d																								
Dunbar	d																								
Berwick-upon-Tweed	d																								
Alnmouth for Alnwick	d																								
Morpeth	d																								
Newcastle [8]	a																								
Sunderland	d																								
Hartlepool	d																								
Newcastle [8]	d			05 25									05 56				06 11	06 22			06 30				06 44
Chester-le-Street	d																06 21								
Durham	d			05 38									06 09				06 28	06 37			06 42				06 56
Darlington [7]	a			05 56									06 27				06 44	06 53			07 00				07 12
Middlesbrough	d				05 55																				
Eaglescliffe	d																								
Darlington [7]	d			05 57									06 28				06 45	06 54			07 00				07 14
Northallerton	d			06 08	06 23												06 56				07 13				
Thirsk	d				06 31												07 04		←						
York [8]	a			06 28	06 49								06 56				07 30	07 20	07 30		07 33				07 40
Leeds [10]	a				07 20												→		08 04						08 08
Harrogate	d																								
Scarborough	d																								
York [8]	d			06 30								06 32	06 58					07 23			07 35				
Doncaster [7]	a			06 52														07 48							
Skipton	d																							06 55	
Keighley	d																							07u06	
Bradford Interchange	d																								
Bradford Forster Square	d										06 30														
Shipley	d										06u35													07u14	
Halifax	d																								
Brighouse	d																								
Leeds [10]	d		06 15				06 34	06 40			07 00	07 05				07 15								07 40	08 11
Wakefield Westgate [7]	d	06 24	06 27			06 41	06 46	06 52			07 12	07 18				07 27								07 52	08 23
Wakefield Kirkgate [4]	d	06 29				06a44																			
Pontefract Monkhill	d	06a46																							
Sheffield [7]	a						07 25					07 50						08 18							08 51
Hull	d													06 25									07 00		
Selby	d													07 00									07 34		
Doncaster [7]	d		06a43	06 53				07 11						07 18		07 45							07 55	08 10	
Retford [10]	d													07 40											
Lincoln	d														07 20										
Newark North Gate [7]	a							07 35							07 46								08 21	08 37	
	d							07 35							07 55								08 21	08 37	
Grantham [7]	a			07 25										08 01		08 16							08 34		
	d			07 25										08 02		08 16						08 27	08 34		
Peterborough [8]	a			07 46									08 09		08 25						08 41	08 57	09 00	09 06	
Norwich	a																					10 44			
Peterborough [8]	d			07 50					07 46				08 11		08 26						08 41		09 01	09 06	
Stevenage [4]	a								08 33						08 58	09 03									
London Kings Cross [15] ⊖	a			08 46				08 52	08 58		08 59		09 10	09 18	09 28	09 30					09 39		09 58	10 02	

D The Hull Executive

Scotland, North East England, Yorkshire and Humberside - London

Station		GR	GR	GC	TP	EM	FC	GC	XC	GR	GR	GR	TP	XC	TP	SR	GR	SR	NT	HT	EM	GR	GR
											D							F					D
Aberdeen	d																						
Stonehaven	d																						
Montrose	d																						
Arbroath	d																						
Dundee	d																						
Leuchars 3	d																						
Kirkcaldy	d																						
Inverkeithing	d																						
Inverness	d																						
Perth	d																						
Stirling	d																						
Glasgow Central 15	d																						
Motherwell	d																						
Haymarket	d															06 14		06 33					
Edinburgh 10	a															06 18		06 39					
Edinburgh	d		05 40								05 45			06 06		06 20	06 25	06 41					06 55
Dunbar	d										06 06												
Berwick-upon-Tweed	d	06 00									06 31			06 46			07 06						
Alnmouth for Alnwick	d	06 19									06 52			07 08					07 19				
Morpeth	d	06 35									07 07								07 54				
Newcastle 8	a	06 52	07 02								07 24			07 38			07 53		08 19				08 22
Sunderland	d							06 45															
Hartlepool	d							07 09															
Newcastle 8	d	06 55	07 03						07 25		07 28		07 33	07 41			07 55						08 25
Chester-le-Street	d												07 42										
Durham	d	07 07							07 37		07 41		07 49	07 55									08 37
Darlington 7	a	07 25							07 53		07 58		08 05	08 10			08 23						08 55
Middlesbrough	d				07 12																		
Eaglescliffe	d							07 30															
Darlington 7	d	07 31							07 54		07 59		08 06	08 12			08 24						08 56
Northallerton	d				07 45			07 50					08 17										09 07
Thirsk	d				07 53			07 59					08 25		←								
York 8	a	07 59			08 12			08 16	08 21		08 27		08 47	08 41	08 47		08 53						09 27
Leeds 10	a				08 52								→	09 08	09 22								
Harrogate	d									07 28													
Scarborough	d																						
York 8	d	08 00						08 20	08 24		08 29						08 55						09 29
Doncaster 7	a								08 48		08 52												09 52
Skipton	d																						
Keighley	d																						
Bradford Interchange	d			06 51																			
Bradford Forster Square	d																						
Shipley	d																						
Halifax	d			07 07																			
Brighouse	d			07 18																			
Leeds 10	d									08 15		08 45		09 11								09 15	
Wakefield Westgate 7	d									08 27		08 57		09 24								09 27	
Wakefield Kirkgate 4	d			07 42																			
Pontefract Monkhill	d			08 01																			
Sheffield 7	a								09 17					09 51									
Hull	d																			08 25			
Selby	d																			08 58			
Doncaster 7	d			08 31						08 45	08 53	09 16								09 24		09 45	09 53
Retford 10	d	08 33																		09 39			
Lincoln	d																						
Newark North Gate 7	a										09 16												10 16
	d										09 16												10 16
Grantham 7	a									09 19										10 00		10 16	
	d					09 10				09 19										10 01	10 11	10 16	
Peterborough 8	a					09 39					09 47	10 07									10 40		10 47
Norwich	a					11 14															12 13		
Peterborough 8	d						09 16				09 48	10 07											10 48
Stevenage 4	a						09 58			10 08												11 00	
London Kings Cross 15 ⊖	a	10 06	09 40	10 13			10 22	10 25		10 38	10 45	11 01					10 54			11 10		11 29	11 46

D ⊘ to Peterborough

F from 30 May

Table 26

Mondays to Fridays

Scotland, North East England, Yorkshire and Humberside - London

Station		XC	GR	XC	GR	NT	TP	GR	GC	TP	EM	EM	GR	GR	XC	GR	XC	GR	SR	NT	TP	TP
				A	B			C						D			A	B				
Aberdeen	d																					
Stonehaven	d																					
Montrose	d																					
Arbroath	d																					
Dundee	d																06 32					
Leuchars 3	d																06 46					
Kirkcaldy	d																07 21					
Inverkeithing	d																07 42					
Inverness	d																					
Perth	d																					
Stirling	d																					
Glasgow Central 15	d			06 01										06 50					07 03			
Motherwell	d			06 16										07 04					07 27			
Haymarket	d			06 57										07 45			08 01		08 26			
Edinburgh 10	a			07 02										07 52			08 05		08 33			
Edinburgh	d	07 00		07 07	07 30									08 00			08 10	08 30	08 45			
Dunbar	d			07 27																		
Berwick-upon-Tweed	d	07 39			08 11												08 50					
Alnmouth for Alnwick	d	07 59												08 58								
Morpeth	d	08 13				08 49														09 49		
Newcastle 8	a	08 30		08 38	08 56	09 14								09 27			09 39	09 55		10 13		
Sunderland	d								08 42													
Hartlepool	d								09 07													
Newcastle 8	d	08 34		08 43	08 58					09 15				09 28	09 35		09 41	09 56				10 17
Chester-le-Street	d									09 24												
Durham	d	08 46		08 56						09 31				09 41	09 47		09 55					10 31
Darlington 7	a	09 02		09 11	09 25					09 47				09 59	10 04		10 10	10 25				10 46
Middlesbrough	d						08 50														09 50	
Eaglescliffe	d								09 27													
Darlington 7	d	09 04		09 13	09 26					09 48				09 59	10 05		10 12	10 25				10 48
Northallerton	d						09 18		09 46	09 59											10 18	10 59
Thirsk	d						09 28		09 57												10 28	
York 8	a	09 32		09 41	09 53		09 47		10 16	10 21				10 28	10 32		10 41	10 53			10 47	11 23
Leeds 10	a			10 08			10 22			10 52							11 07				11 22	11 52
Harrogate	d																					
Scarborough	d																					
York 8	d	09 35			09 55			10 01	10 25					10 29	10 34			10 55				
Doncaster 7	a	09 57						10 24						10 53	10 57							
Skipton	d																					
Keighley	d																					
Bradford Interchange	d																					
Bradford Forster Square	d																					
Shipley	d																					
Halifax	d																					
Brighouse	d																					
Leeds 10	d		09 45	10 11									10 15			10 45	11 11					
Wakefield Westgate 7	d		09 57	10 23									10 27			10 57	11 24					
Wakefield Kirkgate 4	d																					
Pontefract Monkhill	d																					
Sheffield 7	a	10 20		10 51											11 20		11 51					
Hull	d																					
Selby	d																					
Doncaster 7	d		10 16					10 24			10 24		10 45	10 53		11 16						
Retford 10	d							10 39														
Lincoln	d										11a17											
Newark North Gate 7	a							10 54						11 17								
	d							10 54						11 17								
Grantham 7	a							11 06					11 16									
	d							11 06				11 10	11 16									
Peterborough 8	a		11 05					11 26				11 40		11 47		12 07						
Norwich	a											13 13										
Peterborough 8	d		11 05					11 26						11 49		12 08						
Stevenage 4	a							11 55					12 00									
London Kings Cross 15 ⊖	a		11 59		11 55			12 25	12 29				12 29	12 46		13 02		12 55				

A from Edinburgh

B ⊘ to York

C ⊘ to Stevenage

D ⊘ to Peterborough

Scotland, North East England, Yorkshire and Humberside - London

		HT ◇1 ⊠	GR ■ 1 ⊼⊘	EM ◇	GR ■ 1 ▭⊼	GR ■ 1 ⊼⊘	GC ■ 1 ✕	XC ◇1 ⊼	GR ■ 1 ▭⊼	XC ◇1 ⊼	GR ■ 1 ⊼⊘	NT	TP ◇1 ⊼	TP ◇1 ⊼	GR ■ 1 ⊼⊘	EM ◇	GR ■ 1 ▭⊼	GR ■ 1 ⊼⊘	XC ◇1 ⊼	EM	GR ■ 1 ▭⊼	XC ◇1 ⊼	SR
Aberdeen	d																						
Stonehaven	d																						
Montrose	d																						
Arbroath	d																						
Dundee	d																						
Leuchars 3	d																						
Kirkcaldy	d																						
Inverkeithing	d																						
Inverness	d																						
Perth	d																						
Stirling	d																						
Glasgow Central 15	d									07 50												09 00	
Motherwell	d									08 05												09 15	
Haymarket	d									08 50												09 58	
Edinburgh 10	a									08 55												10 02	
Edinburgh	d									09 08	09 30							10 00				10 10	10 13
Dunbar	d									09 28													10a38
Berwick-upon-Tweed	d									09 51	10 11											10 49	
Alnmouth for Alnwick	d																	10 58					
Morpeth	d											10 49										11 21	
Newcastle 8	a									10 38	10 56	11 14						11 27				11 39	
Sunderland	d																						
Hartlepool	d																						
Newcastle 8	d					10 25		10 35		10 43	10 58			11 15				11 28	11 35			11 44	
Chester-le-Street	d													11 24									
Durham	d					10 37		10 47		10 55				11 31				11 41	11 47			11 56	
Darlington 7	a					10 55		11 03		11 11	11 25			11 46				11 59	12 04			12 12	
Middlesbrough	d												10 50										
Eaglescliffe	d																						
Darlington 7	d					10 56		11 04		11 12	11 26			11 48				11 59	12 05			12 13	
Northallerton	d					11 07							11 18	11 59									
Thirsk	d												11 28										
York 8	a					11 27		11 31		11 41	11 53		11 47	12 21				12 28	12 31			12 41	
Leeds 10	a									12 08			12 22	12 52								13 10	
Harrogate	d																						
Scarborough	d																						
York 8	d					11 29		11 34			11 55				12 01			12 29	12 34				
Doncaster 7	a					11 52		11 57							12 24			12 53	12 57				
Skipton	d																						
Keighley	d																						
Bradford Interchange	d						10 22																
Bradford Forster Square	d																						
Shipley	d																						
Halifax	d						10 38																
Brighouse	d						10 50																
Leeds 10	d				11 15				11 45	12 12							12 15				12 45	13 11	
Wakefield Westgate 7	d				11 27				11 57	12 24							12 27				12 57	13 23	
Wakefield Kirkgate 4	d						11 11																
Pontefract Monkhill	d						11 34																
Sheffield 7	a							12 20		12 51									13 20			13 51	
Hull	d	10 30																					
Selby	d	11 03																					
Doncaster 7	d	11 24			11 45	11 53	12 08		12 16						12 24		12 45	12 53		13 05	13 16		
Retford 10	d	11 39													12 39								
Lincoln	d																			13a55			
Newark North Gate 7	a					12 16									12 54			13 17					
	d		11 54			12 16									12 55			13 17					
Grantham 7	a	12 00	12 05		12 16										13 07		13 16						
	d	12 01	12 05	12 11	12 16										13 07	13 09	13 16						
Peterborough 8	a		12 25	12 41		12 49			13 05						13 27	13 39		13 47			14 07		
Norwich	a			14 09												15 13							
Peterborough 8	d		12 26			12 49			13 07						13 27			13 49			14 07		
Stevenage 4	a		12 56		13 00										13 57		14 02						
London Kings Cross 15 ⊖	a	13 10	13 25		13 29	13 44	13 45		14 02		13 55				14 26		14 29	14 46			15 03		

Scotland, North East England, Yorkshire and Humberside - London

		GR ■ 1 ⊼⊘	NT	TP ◇1 ⊼	TP ◇1 ⊼	HT ◇1 ⊠	GR ■ 1 ⊼⊘	EM ◇	GR ■ 1 ▭⊼	GR ■ 1 ⊼⊘	XC ◇1 ⊼	GR ■ 1 ▭⊼	XC ◇1 ⊼	GR ■ 1 E ⊼⊘	NT	TP ◇1 ⊼	GR ■ 1 ⊼⊘	GC ■ 1 ▭	TP ◇1 ⊼	EM	EM ◇	GR ■ 1 ▭⊼
Aberdeen	d	07 52											08 20									
Stonehaven	d	08 09											08 38									
Montrose	d	08 32											08 59									
Arbroath	d	08 48											09 15									
Dundee	d	09 06											09 32									
Leuchars 3	d	09 20											09 47									
Kirkcaldy	d	09 44											10 17									
Inverkeithing	d	10 01											10 32									
Inverness	d													07 55								
Perth	d													09 56								
Stirling	d													10 30								
Glasgow Central 15	d																					
Motherwell	d																					
Haymarket	d	10 19											10 54	11 11								
Edinburgh 10	a	10 25											10 58	11 17								
Edinburgh	d	10 30											11 05	11 30								
Dunbar	d												11 25									
Berwick-upon-Tweed	d												11 48									
Alnmouth for Alnwick	d												12 08									
Morpeth	d		11 49												12 49							
Newcastle 8	a	11 55	12 13										12 38	12 55	13 13							
Sunderland	d																	12 28				
Hartlepool	d																	12 52				
Newcastle 8	d	11 56			12 17					12 25	12 35		12 41	12 56					13 15			
Chester-le-Street	d																		13 24			
Durham	d				12 29					12 37	12 47		12 53						13 31			
Darlington 7	a	12 25			12 45					12 55	13 03		13 10	13 25					13 46			
Middlesbrough	d			11 50												12 50						
Eaglescliffe	d																	13 12				
Darlington 7	d	12 25			12 46					12 56	13 04		13 11	13 25					13 48			
Northallerton	d			12 18	12 58					13 07						13 18		13 31	13 59			
Thirsk	d			12 28												13 28		13 42				
York 8	a	12 53		12 47	13 21					13 27	13 31		13 41	13 53		13 47		14 00	14 24			
Leeds 10	a			13 22	13 52								14 07			14 22			14 52			
Harrogate	d																					
Scarborough	d																					
York 8	d	12 55								13 29	13 34			13 55			14 01	14 05				
Doncaster 7	a									13 52	13 57						14 22					
Skipton	d																					
Keighley	d																					
Bradford Interchange	d																					
Bradford Forster Square	d																					
Shipley	d																					
Halifax	d																					
Brighouse	d																					
Leeds 10	d								13 15			13 45	14 11									14 15
Wakefield Westgate 7	d								13 27			13 57	14 23									14 27
Wakefield Kirkgate 4	d																					
Pontefract Monkhill	d																					
Sheffield 7	a										14 20		14 51									
Hull	d					12 30																
Selby	d					13 03																
Doncaster 7	d					13 24			13 45	13 53		14 16					14 23			14 27		14 45
Retford 10	d					13 39											14 40					
Lincoln	d																			15a18		
Newark North Gate 7	a									14 16							14 54					
	d						13 54			14 16							14 54					
Grantham 7	a					14 00	14 05		14 16								15 06					15 16
	d					14 01	14 05	14 10	14 16								15 06				15 11	15 16
Peterborough 8	a						14 25	14 39		14 47		15 08					15 26				15 38	
Norwich	a							16 14													17 13	
Peterborough 8	d						14 26			14 49		15 08					15 26					
Stevenage 4	a						14 56		15 00								15 55					16 00
London Kings Cross 15 ⊖	a	14 55				15 10	15 27		15 29	15 46		16 04		15 55			16 26	16 09				16 29

E The Highland Chieftain

Scotland, North East England, Yorkshire and Humberside - London

		GR	XC	GR	XC	SR	GR	NT	TP	TP	GR	EM	GR	GR	XC	HT	GR	XC FO	XC FX	TP FO	GR	NT	TP FX
							C											E	F				
Aberdeen	d						09 52																
Stonehaven	d						10 09																
Montrose	d						10 32																
Arbroath	d						10 49																
Dundee	d						11 06																
Leuchars 3	d						11 20																
Kirkcaldy	d						11 44																
Inverkeithing	d						12 01																
Inverness	d																						
Perth	d																						
Stirling	d																						
Glasgow Central 15	d				10 59																		
Motherwell	d				11 14																		
Haymarket	d				11 57		12 19																
Edinburgh 10	a				12 02		12 25																
Edinburgh	d	12 00			12 08	12 11	12 30											13 06	13 06		13 30		
Dunbar	d					12a36												13 28	13 28				
Berwick-upon-Tweed	d	12 41			12 47																14 11		
Alnmouth for Alnwick	d																	14 08	14 08				
Morpeth	d							13 49														14 49	
Newcastle 8	a	13 26			13 34		13 56	14 13										14 40	14 40		14 56	15 13	
Sunderland	d																						
Hartlepool	d																						
Newcastle 8	d	13 28	13 35		13 41		13 57			14 18				14 25	14 33			14 42	14 42		14 58		
Chester-le-Street	d																						
Durham	d	13 41	13 47		13 53					14 31				14 38	14 48			14 51	14 52				
Darlington 7	a	13 59	14 04		14 10		14 26			14 46				14 55	15 03			15 10	15 10		15 24		
Middlesbrough	d								13 50											14 50			14 50
Eaglescliffe	d																						
Darlington 7	d	13 59	14 05		14 11		14 26			14 48				14 56	15 05			15 11	15 12		15 25		
Northallerton	d								14 18	14 59				15 07						15 18			15 18
Thirsk	d								14 28											15 28			15 28
York 8	a	14 28	14 31		14 41		14 54		14 47	15 22				15 27	15 31			15 41	15 41	15 47	15 53		15 47
Leeds 10	a				15 07				15 22	15 52								16 08	16 07				16 22
Harrogate	d																						
Scarborough	d																						
York 8	d	14 29	14 34				14 56							15 29	15 34						15 55		
Doncaster 7	a	14 53	14 57											15 52	15 57								
Skipton	d																						
Keighley	d																						
Bradford Interchange	d																						
Bradford Forster Square	d																						
Shipley	d																						
Halifax	d																						
Brighouse	d																						
Leeds 10	d			14 45	15 11								15 15				15 45	16 11	16 11				
Wakefield Westgate 7	d			14 57	15 23								15 27				15 57	16 22	16 23				
Wakefield Kirkgate 4	d																						
Pontefract Monkhill	d																						
Sheffield 7	a		15 20		15 51										16 20			16 51	16 51				
Hull	d															15 10							
Selby	d															15 45							
Doncaster 7	d	14 53		15 16									15 45	15 53		16 04	16 16						
Retford 10	d															16 19							
Lincoln	d																						
Newark North Gate 7	a	15 17												16 18									
	d	15 18									15 52			16 18									
Grantham 7	a										16 03		16 16			16 39							
	d										16 03	16 10	16 16			16 40							
Peterborough 8	a	15 47		16 08							16 23	16 39		16 48			17 06						
Norwich	a											18 13											
Peterborough 8	d	15 49		16 08							16 24			16 49			17 06						
Stevenage 4	a										16 54		17 00										
London Kings Cross 15 ⊖	a	16 46		17 02			16 56				17 25		17 29	17 44		17 45	18 01				17 56		

C The Northern Lights

E until 9 September

F until 8 September, from 12 September

Table 26 Mondays to Fridays

Scotland, North East England, Yorkshire and Humberside - London

		GR	EM	GR	XC	TP	GR	GR	XC	SR	GR	GC	NT	TP	TP	GR	EM	GR	GR	XC	HT	GR	XC
			B																				
Aberdeen	d																						
Stonehaven	d																						
Montrose	d																						
Arbroath	d																						
Dundee	d																						
Leuchars 3	d																						
Kirkcaldy	d																						
Inverkeithing	d																						
Inverness	d																						
Perth	d																						
Stirling	d																						
Glasgow Central 15	d								12 51														
Motherwell	d								13 06														
Haymarket	d																						
Edinburgh 10	a								13 54														
Edinburgh	d						14 00		14 08	14 11	14 30												15 08
Dunbar	d									14a36													15 28
Berwick-upon-Tweed	d								14 49		15 11												
Alnmouth for Alnwick	d						14 58																
Morpeth	d												15 49										
Newcastle 8	a						15 27		15 34		15 56		16 13										16 38
Sunderland	d																						
Hartlepool	d																						
Newcastle 8	d				15 03	15 15	15 28		15 41		15 58				16 15				16 25	16 35			16 42
Chester-le-Street	d					15 24									16 24								
Durham	d				15 16	15 31	15 41		15 53						16 31				16 37	16 47			16 52
Darlington 7	a				15 32	15 46	16 00		16 09		16 25				16 46				16 55	17 03			17 10
Middlesbrough	d													15 50									
Eaglescliffe	d																						
Darlington 7	d				15 33	15 48	16 00		16 10		16 26				16 48				16 56	17 04			17 10
Northallerton	d					15 59								16 18	16 59				17 07				
Thirsk	d													16 28									
York 8	a				16 01	16 21	16 28		16 41		16 53			16 47	17 23				17 28	17 31			17 41
Leeds 10	a				16 32	16 52			17 06					17 22	17 52								18 07
Harrogate	d																						
Scarborough	d																						
York 8	d	16 01					16 29				16 55								17 30	17 34			
Doncaster 7	a	16 24					16 52												17 52	17 57			
Skipton	d																						
Keighley	d																						
Bradford Interchange	d											15 37											
Bradford Forster Square	d																						
Shipley	d																						
Halifax	d											15 51											
Brighouse	d											16 09											
Leeds 10	d			16 15	16 38			16 45	17 11									17 15				17 45	18 11
Wakefield Westgate 7	d			16 27	16 50			16 57	17 23									17 27				17 57	18 23
Wakefield Kirkgate 4	d											16 40											
Pontefract Monkhill	d											16 56											
Sheffield 7	a				17 20				17 51											18 20			18 51
Hull	d																				17 10		
Selby	d																				17 43		
Doncaster 7	d	16 24		16 45			16 52	17 17				17 25						17 45	17 54		18 02	18 16	
Retford 10	d	16 39																17 59			18 17		
Lincoln	d																						
Newark North Gate 7	a	16 54					17 19												18 17				
	d	16 54					17 19									17 54			18 17				
Grantham 7	a	17 07		17 16												18 05		18 22			18 38		
	d	17 07	17 11	17 16												18 05	18 11	18 22			18 39		
Peterborough 8	a	17 27	17 40				17 49	18 05								18 25	18 39		18 48			19 04	
Norwich	a		19 15														20 22						
Peterborough 8	d	17 27					17 49	18 06								18 26			18 49			19 05	
Stevenage 4	a	17 57		18 02												18 56		19 07					
London Kings Cross 15 ⊖	a	18 28		18 30			18 45	19 02			18 54	19 05				19 27		19 36	19 46		19 47	19 59	

B from 1 August

Scotland, North East England, Yorkshire and Humberside - London

		GR	NT	TP	TP	GR	EM	GR	NT	NT	GR	XC	NT	GR	XC	GR	SR	SR	TP	GC	EM	GR
				◇	◇		◇		C	D		◇			◇				◇			
Aberdeen	d																					
Stonehaven	d																					
Montrose	d																					
Arbroath	d																					
Dundee	d																					
Leuchars 3	d																					
Kirkcaldy	d																					
Inverkeithing	d																					
Inverness	d																					
Perth	d																					
Stirling	d																					
Glasgow Central 15	d														15 00			15 14				
Motherwell	d														15 14			15 36				
Haymarket	d														15 56			16 34				
Edinburgh 10	a														16 01			16 39				
Edinburgh	d	15 30													16 05	16 30	16 33	16 41				
Dunbar	d																16a58					
Berwick-upon-Tweed	d	16 11														17 11						
Alnmouth for Alnwick	d														17 03							
Morpeth	d		16 49												17 18							
Newcastle 8	a	16 56	17 14												17 36	17 57						
Sunderland	d																			17 31		
Hartlepool	d																			17 55		
Newcastle 8	d	16 58			17 02						17 25	17 32			17 41	17 59						
Chester-le-Street	d				17 11							17 41										
Durham	d				17 18						17 37	17 48			17 53							
Darlington 7	a	17 25			17 34						17 55	18 03			18 09	18 25						
Middlesbrough	d			16 50															17 50			
Eaglescliffe	d																			18 20		
Darlington 7	d	17 26			17 35						17 56	18 05			18 10	18 26						
Northallerton	d			17 18	17 46						18 07								18 18	18 40		
Thirsk	d			17 28															18 28	18 49		
York 8	a	17 53		17 48	18 09						18 27	18 31			18 41	18 54			18 47	19 07		
Leeds 10	a			18 22	18 37										19 08				19 35			
Harrogate	d																					
Scarborough	d								16 21	16 23												
York 8	d	17 55				18 01					18 29	18 34				18 56				19 10		
Doncaster 7	a					18 23					18 52	18 57										
Skipton	d																					
Keighley	d																					
Bradford Interchange	d																					
Bradford Forster Square	d																					
Shipley	d																					
Halifax	d																					
Brighouse	d																					
Leeds 10	d							18 15						18 45	19 11							19 15
Wakefield Westgate 7	d							18 27					18 39	18 57	19 23							19 27
Wakefield Kirkgate 4	d												18a42									
Pontefract Monkhill	d																					
Sheffield 7	a											19 20			19 51							
Hull	d								17 52	17 52												
Selby	d								18 26	18 26												
Doncaster 7	d					18 24		18 45	18a47	18a47	18 53			19 16							19 34	19 45
Retford 10	d					18 39																
Lincoln	d																				20a25	
Newark North Gate 7	a					18 54					19 17											
	d					18 54					19 17											
Grantham 7	a					19 06		19 16														20 16
	d					19 06	19 07	19 16														20 16
Peterborough 8	a					19 26	19 38				19 48			20 07								
Norwich	a						21 14															
Peterborough 8	d					19 27					19 49			20 07								
Stevenage 4	a					19 57		20 01			20 20					20 26						21 00
London Kings Cross 15 ⊖	a	19 55				20 28		20 30			20 49			21 03		20 55				21 04		21 29

C from 3 October
D until 30 September

Table 26 Mondays to Fridays

Scotland, North East England, Yorkshire and Humberside - London

		GR	XC	HT	NT	GR	XC	SR	NT	TP	SR	NT	TP	GR	TP	SR	NT	XC	EM	EM	GR	XC	NT
			◇	◇			◇			◇			◇		◇			◇		◇		◇	
Aberdeen	d													14 50									
Stonehaven	d													15 07									
Montrose	d													15 30									
Arbroath	d													15 46									
Dundee	d													16 04									
Leuchars 3	d													16 18									
Kirkcaldy	d													16 45									
Inverkeithing	d													17 03									
Inverness	d										20 46												
Perth	d										23u21												
Stirling	d										00u06												
Glasgow Central 15	d																					16 52	
Motherwell	d																					17 14	
Haymarket	d							17 05						17 21		17 42						17 54	
Edinburgh 10	a							17 10			01 00			17 27		17 46						17 59	
Edinburgh	d	17 00					17 08	17 13						17 30		17 48						18 04	
Dunbar	d						17 28							17 51								18 25	
Berwick-upon-Tweed	d						17 51							18 16								18 48	
Alnmouth for Alnwick	d	17 58																				19 08	19 20
Morpeth	d								18 26								19 01						19 45
Newcastle 8	a	18 27					18 38		18 49					19 03			19 25					19 38	20 08
Sunderland	d																						
Hartlepool	d																						
Newcastle 8	d	18 28	18 35				18 41						18 52	19 04				19 33				19 40	
Chester-le-Street	d												19 01										
Durham	d	18 41	18 47				18 53						19 08					19 48				19 53	
Darlington 7	a	19 00	19 04				19 09						19 23	19 33				20 03				20 08	
Middlesbrough	d									18 50													
Eaglescliffe	d																						
Darlington 7	d	19 00	19 05				19 10						19 25	19 33				20 05				20 10	
Northallerton	d									19 18			19 36										
Thirsk	d									19 26					←								
York 8	a	19 28	19 31				19 39			19 52			20 07	20 01	20 07			20 31				20 41	
Leeds 10	a						20 09						→		20 35							21 08	
Harrogate	d																						
Scarborough	d																						
York 8	d	19 29	19 34											20 03				20 34					
Doncaster 7	a	19 53	19 57											20 26				21 00					
Skipton	d																						
Keighley	d																						
Bradford Interchange	d																						
Bradford Forster Square	d																						
Shipley	d																						
Halifax	d																						
Brighouse	d																						
Leeds 10	d					19 45	20 11														20 45	21 11	
Wakefield Westgate 7	d				19 42	19 57	20 23					20 50									20 57	21 23	
Wakefield Kirkgate 4	d				19a44							20a52											
Pontefract Monkhill	d																						
Sheffield 7	a		20 20				20 51											21 26				21 51	
Hull	d			19 10																			
Selby	d			19 43																			
Doncaster 7	d	19 54		20 02		20 16								20 27					20 33		21 16		
Retford 10	d			20 17																	21 33		
Lincoln	d																		21a26				
Newark North Gate 7	a	20 17																					
	d	20 17																					
Grantham 7	a			20 37																	21 56		
	d			20 38																21 10	21 56		
Peterborough 8	a	20 45				21 02								21 16						21 37	22 15		
Norwich	a																			23 18			
Peterborough 8	d	20 45				21 03								21 16							22 16		
Stevenage 4	a	21 16												21 49							22 47		
London Kings Cross 15 ⊖	a	21 44		21 45		21 57								22 20							23 14		

Table 26

Mondays to Fridays

Scotland, North East England, Yorkshire and Humberside - London

		TP FO	TP FX	GR	SR	SR	XC	GR	NT	TP	TP	NT	NT	GR	SR B	SR FX	NT	NT	SR FO	NT
Aberdeen	d													18 16	21 40					
Stonehaven	d													18 33	22u00					
Montrose	d													18 56	22u25					
Arbroath	d													19 12	22u43					
Dundee	d													19 30	23u06					
Leuchars 3	d													19 44	23u25					
Kirkcaldy	d					18 44								20 08	23u53					
Inverkeithing	d					19 00								20 24	00u12					
Inverness	d																			
Perth	d																			
Stirling	d																			
Glasgow Central 15	d						18 58													
Motherwell	d						19 14													
Haymarket	d				18 40	19 15								20 43						
Edinburgh 10	a				18 44	19 21	19 56							20 48	00 41					
Edinburgh	d			18 30	18 45	19 22	20 05							21 00		22 06			23 01	
Dunbar	d			18 51			20 25							21 21		22a41			23a33	
Berwick-upon-Tweed	d			19 14			20 48							21 47						
Alnmouth for Alnwick	d			19 36			21 08							22 10						
Morpeth	d			19 53										22 26			22 45			
Newcastle 8	a			20 12			21 38							22 43			23 09			
Sunderland	d																			
Hartlepool	d																			
Newcastle 8	d			20 14				21 15			21 55		22 21	22 44						
Chester-le-Street	d												22 30							
Durham	d			20 27				21 27			22 08		22 39	23 00						
Darlington 7	a			20 45				21 45			22 24		22 59	23 19						
Middlesbrough	d	19 50	19 50							21 50										
Eaglescliffe	d																			
Darlington 7	d	20 26	20b26	20 46				21 46		22 19	22 25			23 19						
Northallerton	d	20 39	20 39					21 57		22 30	22 36			23s46						
Thirsk	d	20 47	20 47							22 38										
York 8	a	21 06	21 06	21 14				22 17		22 57	23 00			00 13						
Leeds 10	a		21 37								23 33			00 50						
Harrogate	d																			
Scarborough	d																			
York 8	d			21 16				22 19												
Doncaster 7	a			21 38				22 42												
Skipton	d																			
Keighley	d																			
Bradford Interchange	d																			
Bradford Forster Square	d																			
Shipley	d																			
Halifax	d																			
Brighouse	d																			
Leeds 10	d																			
Wakefield Westgate 7	d								21 41			21 57						22 48		23 04
Wakefield Kirkgate 4	d								21a44			22 00						22a51		23 07
Pontefract Monkhill	d											22a18								23a25
Sheffield 7	a																			
Hull	d																			
Selby	d																			
Doncaster 7	d			21 39				22 42												
Retford 10	d																			
Lincoln	d																			
Newark North Gate 7	a			22 02				23 06												
	d			22 02				23 06												
Grantham 7	a			22 15				23 18												
	d			22 15				23 18												
Peterborough 8	a			22 35				23 39												
Norwich	a																			
Peterborough 8	d			22 36				23 39												
Stevenage 4	a			23 07				00s20												
London Kings Cross 15 ⊖	a			23 36				00 59												

B MTWO until 15 June, MTWO from 24 October

Table 26

Saturdays
until 18 June

Scotland, North East England, Yorkshire and Humberside - London

		SR	GR	GR	EM	GR	GR	TP	XC	GR	NT	XC	NT	EM	FC	GR	XC	GR	GR	GR	TP	XC	TP
Aberdeen	d			18p16																			
Stonehaven	d			18p33																			
Montrose	d			18p56																			
Arbroath	d			19p12																			
Dundee	d			19p30																			
Leuchars 3	d			19p44																			
Kirkcaldy	d			20p08																			
Inverkeithing	d			20p24																			
Inverness	d	20p46																					
Perth	d	23b21																					
Stirling	d	00u06																					
Glasgow Central 15	d																						
Motherwell	d																						
Haymarket	d			20p43																			
Edinburgh 10	a	01 00		20p48																			
Edinburgh	d			21p00																			
Dunbar	d			21p21																			
Berwick-upon-Tweed	d			21p47																			
Alnmouth for Alnwick	d			22p10																			
Morpeth	d			22p26																			
Newcastle 8	a			22p43																			
Sunderland	d												06 28										
Hartlepool	d												06a54										
Newcastle 8	d		21p15	22p44			04 40											06 00			06 11	06 22	
Chester-le-Street	d																				06 21		
Durham	d		21p27	23p00			04 54											06 12			06 28	06 37	
Darlington 7	a		21p45	23p19			05 11											06 30			06 44	06 52	
Middlesbrough	d							05 55															
Eaglescliffe	d																						
Darlington 7	d		21p46	23p19			05 12											06 30			06 45	06 54	
Northallerton	d		21p57	23c46			05 31	06 23													06 56		
Thirsk	d							06 31													07 04		←
York 8	a		22p17	00 13			05 57	06 49										06 58			07 30	07 21	07 30
Leeds 10	a			00 50				07 20													→		08 04
Harrogate	d																						
Scarborough	d																						
York 8	d		22p19				06 00										06 40	07 00				07 24	
Doncaster 7	a		22p42				06 22											07 23				07 49	
Skipton	d																						
Keighley	d																						
Bradford Interchange	d																						
Bradford Forster Square	d																						
Shipley	d																						
Halifax	d																						
Brighouse	d																						
Leeds 10	d					05 05			06 00	06 05		06 15		06 34		07 05	07 10						
Wakefield Westgate 7	d					05 17			06 12	06 17	06 24	06 29		06 46		07 17	07 23						
Wakefield Kirkgate 4	d										06 29												
Pontefract Monkhill	d										06a46												
Sheffield 7	a								06 45					07 22			07 51					08 18	
Hull	d																			06 50			
Selby	d																		←	07 24			
Doncaster 7	d		22p42			05 35	06 23			06 35		06a46				07 35		07 24	07 35	07 43			
Retford 10	d					05 49				06 49						→							
Lincoln	d																						
Newark North Gate 7	a		23p06			06 04				07 04									07 59				
	d		23p06			06 04				07 04									07 59				
Grantham 7	a		23p18			06 17				07 17									08 11	08 16			
	d		23p18		05 51	06 17				07 17									08 11	08 17			
Peterborough 8	a		23p39		06 25	06 36	07 10			07 36								08 13	08 31	08 38			
Norwich	a																						
Peterborough 8	d		23p39			06 38	07 12			07 37					08 08			08 14	08 31	08 39			
Stevenage 4	a		00s20			07 06				08 06									09 00				
London Kings Cross 15 ⊖	a		00 59			07 37	08 10			08 36					09 12			09 12	09 30	09 38			

b Previous night, stops to pick up only

c Previous night, stops to set down only

Table 26

Saturdays until 18 June

Scotland, North East England, Yorkshire and Humberside - London

		GR	EM	EM	GR	GR	XC	GR	GC	TP	FC	GC	GR	EM	GR	XC	GR	HT	EM	GR	TP	XC	TP
Aberdeen	d																						
Stonehaven	d																						
Montrose	d																						
Arbroath	d																						
Dundee	d																						
Leuchars 3	d																						
Kirkcaldy	d																						
Inverkeithing	d																						
Inverness	d																						
Perth	d																						
Stirling	d																						
Glasgow Central 15	d																						
Motherwell	d																						
Haymarket	d																						
Edinburgh 10	a																						
Edinburgh	d																					06 06	
Dunbar	d																						
Berwick-upon-Tweed	d																					06 48	
Alnmouth for Alnwick	d																					07 08	
Morpeth	d																						
Newcastle 8	a																					07 38	
Sunderland	d											06 43											
Hartlepool	d											07 09											
Newcastle 8	d	06 30						06 55							07 24	07 30					07 33	07 44	
Chester-le-Street	d																				07 42		
Durham	d	06 42						07 07							07 36	07 43					07 49	07 56	
Darlington 7	a	07 00						07 25							07 54	08 00					08 05	08 12	
Middlesbrough	d									07 12													
Eaglescliffe	d											07 30											
Darlington 7	d	07 01						07 26							07 54	08 02					08 06	08 13	
Northallerton	d	07 12								07 42		07 48			08 06						08 17		
Thirsk	d									07 50		07 57									08 25		←
York 8	a	07 32						07 53		08 08		08 14			08 27	08 31					08 47	08 41	08 47
Leeds 10	a									08 52											→	09 07	09 22
Harrogate	d																			08 13			
Scarborough	d																						
York 8	d	07 34					07 44	07 55				08 16			08 28	08 34							
Doncaster 7	a	07 56						08 17							08 53	08 57							
Skipton	d				06 55																		
Keighley	d				07u08																		
Bradford Interchange	d								06 51														
Bradford Forster Square	d					07 33																	
Shipley	d				07u18	07u39																	
Halifax	d								07 04														
Brighouse	d								07 17														
Leeds 10	d		07 34		07 35	08 05	08 12										08 40			09 05		09 11	
Wakefield Westgate 7	d		07 46			08 17	08 24										08 52			09 17		09 24	
Wakefield Kirkgate 4	d								07 38														
Pontefract Monkhill	d								07 58														
Sheffield 7	a		08 21				08 51									09 20						09 52	
Hull	d																	08 25					
Selby	d												←					09 00					
Doncaster 7	d	07 57			08 09	08 35		08 18	08 31				08 35		08 53		09 13	09 23		09 35			
Retford 10	d					→							08 52					09 38					
Lincoln	d																						
Newark North Gate 7	a	08 21											09 08		09 18					09 59			
	d	08 21											09 08		09 18					10 00			
Grantham 7	a				08 42										09 30			09 59		10 12			
	d			08 20	08 42									09 03	09 30			09 59	10 08	10 13			
Peterborough 8	a	08 50		08 58									09 35	09 41			09 58		10 37	10 33			
Norwich	a			10 43										11 15					12 18				
Peterborough 8	d	08 50									09 07		09 36				09 59			10 33			
Stevenage 4	a																			11 03			
London Kings Cross 15 ⊖	a	09 48			09 53			09 57	10 09		10 10	10 15	10 30		10 46		10 54	11 09		11 33			

Table 26

Saturdays until 18 June

Scotland, North East England, Yorkshire and Humberside - London

		SR	GR	SR	NT	FC	GR	GR	XC	EM	EM	GR	XC	GR	NT	TP	GC	TP	FC	GR	XC	HT
Aberdeen	d																					
Stonehaven	d																					
Montrose	d																					
Arbroath	d																					
Dundee	d																					
Leuchars 3	d																					
Kirkcaldy	d																					
Inverkeithing	d																					
Inverness	d																					
Perth	d																					
Stirling	d																					
Glasgow Central 15	d												06 01							06 50		
Motherwell	d												06 16							07 05		
Haymarket	d	06 14		06 33									06 57							07 46		
Edinburgh 10	a	06 18		06 39									07 02							07 52		
Edinburgh	d	06 20	06 20	06 41				06 55	07 00				07 07	07 30						08 00		
Dunbar	d		06 40										07 28									
Berwick-upon-Tweed	d		07 05						07 40					08 12								
Alnmouth for Alnwick	d		07 25		07 22				08 00											08 58		
Morpeth	d		07 41		07 55				08 14						08 49							
Newcastle 8	a		07 58		08 20			08 22	08 32				08 37	08 57	09 14					09 27		
Sunderland	d																08 30					
Hartlepool	d																08 54					
Newcastle 8	d		07 59					08 25	08 36				08 44	08 59				09 15		09 28	09 35	
Chester-le-Street	d																	09 24				
Durham	d							08 37	08 48				08 57					09 31		09 41	09 47	
Darlington 7	a		08 27					08 55	09 04				09 12	09 25				09 47		09 59	10 04	
Middlesbrough	d															08 50						
Eaglescliffe	d																09 17					
Darlington 7	d		08 27					08 56	09 05				09 14	09 26				09 48		09 59	10 05	
Northallerton	d							09 07								09 18	09 40	09 59				
Thirsk	d															09 28	09 49					
York 8	a		08 55					09 27	09 32				09 43	09 54		09 47	10 06	10 21		10 28	10 31	
Leeds 10	a												10 09			10 22		10 52				
Harrogate	d																					
Scarborough	d																					
York 8	d		08 56					09 29	09 35					09 56			10 09			10 29	10 34	
Doncaster 7	a							09 52	09 57											10 52	10 57	
Skipton	d																					
Keighley	d																					
Bradford Interchange	d																					
Bradford Forster Square	d																					
Shipley	d																					
Halifax	d																					
Brighouse	d																					
Leeds 10	d											10 05	10 12									
Wakefield Westgate 7	d											10 17	10 24									
Wakefield Kirkgate 4	d																					
Pontefract Monkhill	d																					
Sheffield 7	a								10 20				10 51								11 20	
Hull	d																					10 30
Selby	d																					11 05
Doncaster 7	d							09 52		10 24		10 35								10 52		11 25
Retford 10	d							10 07														11 40
Lincoln	d						09 30			11a16												
Newark North Gate 7	a						09 52					10 59								11 18		
	d						09 53					10 59								11 18		
Grantham 7	a							10 29				11 11										12 00
	d							10 29			11 10	11 13										12 00
Peterborough 8	a		10 04				10 23	10 50			11 39	11 35								11 47		
Norwich	a										13 13											
Peterborough 8	d		10 06			10 08	10 23	10 50				11 35							11 08	11 49		
Stevenage 4	a						10 54															
London Kings Cross 15 ⊖	a		11 00			11 11	11 26	11 46				12 30		11 56			12 07		12 11	12 46		13 07

Scotland, North East England, Yorkshire and Humberside - London

Station		EM	GR	XC	GR	SR	NT	TP	TP	FC	GR	GC	XC	EM	GR	XC	GR	NT	TP	TP	FC	GR	XC
				A												A							
Aberdeen	d																						
Stonehaven	d																						
Montrose	d																						
Arbroath	d																						
Dundee	d			06 32																			
Leuchars	d			06 46																			
Kirkcaldy	d			07 21																			
Inverkeithing	d			07 38																			
Inverness	d																						
Perth	d																						
Stirling	d																						
Glasgow Central	d					07 03										07 50							
Motherwell	d					07 27										08 05							
Haymarket	d			07 56		08 26										08 50							
Edinburgh	a			08 01		08 33										08 54							
Edinburgh	d			08 05	08 30	08 40					09 00					09 06	09 30					10 00	
Dunbar	d															09 26							
Berwick-upon-Tweed	d			08 46												09 49	10 11						
Alnmouth for Alnwick	d																					10 58	
Morpeth	d						09 49											10 49					
Newcastle	a			09 35	09 55		10 13				10 23					10 38	10 57	11 13				11 27	
Sunderland	d																						
Hartlepool	d																						
Newcastle	d			09 41	09 58				10 17		10 25		10 35			10 44	10 59			11 15		11 28	11 35
Chester-le-Street	d																			11 24			
Durham	d			09 55					10 31		10 38		10 47			10 56				11 31		11 41	11 47
Darlington	a			10 10	10 26				10 46		10 55		11 03			11 12	11 27			11 46		11 59	12 04
Middlesbrough	d							09 50											10 50				
Eaglescliffe	d																						
Darlington	d			10 12	10 27				10 48		10 56		11 04			11 13	11 28			11 48		11 59	12 05
Northallerton	d							10 18	10 59		11 07								11 18	11 59			
Thirsk	d							10 28											11 28				
York	a			10 41	10 55			10 47	11 23		11 27		11 31			11 41	11 56		11 47	12 21		12 28	12 31
Leeds	a			11 08				11 22	11 52							12 08			12 22	12 52			
Harrogate	d																						
Scarborough	d																						
York	d				10 56						11 29		11 34				11 57					12 29	12 34
Doncaster	a										11 52		11 57									12 52	12 57
Skipton	d																						
Keighley	d																						
Bradford Interchange	d											10 22											
Bradford Forster Square	d																						
Shipley	d																						
Halifax	d											10 38											
Brighouse	d											10 49											
Leeds	d		11 05	11 11											12 05	12 11							
Wakefield Westgate	d		11 17	11 23											12 17	12 24							
Wakefield Kirkgate	d											11 11											
Pontefract Monkhill	d											11 35											
Sheffield	a			11 51									12 20			12 51							13 20
Hull	d																						
Selby	d																						
Doncaster	d		11 35								11 54	12 05			12 35							12 52	
Retford	d										12 08												
Lincoln	d																						
Newark North Gate	a		11 59												13 02							13 17	
	d		11 59												13 02							13 17	
Grantham	a		12 11												13 14								
	d	12 07	12 11											13 10	13 14								
Peterborough	a	12 38	12 31								12 47			13 39	13 35							13 45	
Norwich	a	14 13												15 13									
Peterborough	d		12 32							12 06	12 50				13 36						13 08	13 49	
Stevenage	a		13 01																				
London Kings Cross	a		13 30		12 55					13 11	13 45	13 46			14 30		13 55				14 10	14 46	

A from Edinburgh

Scotland, North East England, Yorkshire and Humberside - London

Station		EM	EM	GR	XC	GR	NT	TP	TP	GR	XC	HT	EM	GR	XC	GR	NT	TP	GC	TP	GR	XC
					A										A	B						
Aberdeen	d					07 52									08 20							
Stonehaven	d					08 09									08 38							
Montrose	d					08 32									08 59							
Arbroath	d					08 48									09 15							
Dundee	d					09 06									09 32							
Leuchars	d					09 20									09 47							
Kirkcaldy	d					09 44									10 17							
Inverkeithing	d					10 01									10 32							
Inverness	d															07 55						
Perth	d															09 56						
Stirling	d															10 30						
Glasgow Central	d				09 00																	
Motherwell	d				09 15																	
Haymarket	d				09 57	10 21									10 52	11 11						
Edinburgh	a				10 02	10 26									10 58	11 17						
Edinburgh	d				10 05	10 30				11 00					11 05	11 30					12 00	
Dunbar	d														11 25							
Berwick-upon-Tweed	d				10 48										11 48						12 41	
Alnmouth for Alnwick	d														12 08							
Morpeth	d				11 19		11 49										12 49					
Newcastle	a				11 38	11 55	12 13			12 23					12 38	12 55	13 13				13 26	
Sunderland	d																		12 18			
Hartlepool	d																		12 43			
Newcastle	d				11 42	11 56			12 17	12 25	12 35				12 44	12 56				13 15	13 28	13 35
Chester-le-Street	d																			13 24		
Durham	d				11 55				12 29	12 38	12 47				12 56					13 31	13 41	13 47
Darlington	a				12 11	12 25			12 45	12 55	13 03				13 12	13 24				13 46	13 59	14 04
Middlesbrough	d							11 50										12 50				
Eaglescliffe	d																		13 05			
Darlington	d				12 12	12 25			12 46	12 56	13 04				13 13	13 24				13 48	13 59	14 05
Northallerton	d							12 18	12 58	13 07								13 18	13 27	13 59		
Thirsk	d							12 28										13 28	13 41			
York	a				12 42	12 53		12 47	13 21	13 27	13 31				13 41	13 53		13 47	13 57	14 24	14 28	14 31
Leeds	a				13 08			13 22	13 52						14 09			14 22		14 52		
Harrogate	d																					
Scarborough	d																					
York	d					12 55				13 29	13 34					13 55			14 00		14 29	14 34
Doncaster	a									13 52	13 57										14 53	14 57
Skipton	d																					
Keighley	d																					
Bradford Interchange	d																					
Bradford Forster Square	d																					
Shipley	d																					
Halifax	d																					
Brighouse	d																					
Leeds	d			13 05	13 11									14 05	14 11							
Wakefield Westgate	d			13 17	13 23									14 17	14 24							
Wakefield Kirkgate	d																					
Pontefract Monkhill	d																					
Sheffield	a				13 51						14 20				14 51							15 20
Hull	d											13 30										
Selby	d											14 06										
Doncaster	d	13 05		13 35						13 53		14 25		14 35							14 53	
Retford	d									14 07		14 40										
Lincoln	d	13a55																				
Newark North Gate	a			13 59										15 03							15 17	
	d			13 59										15 03							15 18	
Grantham	a			14 12								15 01		15 16								
	d		14 07	14 12								15 01	15 10	15 16								
Peterborough	a		14 41	14 31						14 47			15 39	15 35							15 47	
Norwich	a		16 15										17 13									
Peterborough	d			14 32						14 49				15 36							15 49	
Stevenage	a			15 01																		
London Kings Cross	a			15 30		14 55				15 46		16 08		16 31		15 52			15 55		16 46	

A from Edinburgh

B The Highland Chieftain

Table 26

Scotland, North East England, Yorkshire and Humberside - London

		EM	GR	EM	GR	XC	GR	NT	TP	TP	GR	XC	HT	EM	GR	XC	GR	NT	TP	XC	TP	GR	GC
							B																
Aberdeen	d						09 52																
Stonehaven	d						10 09																
Montrose	d						10 32																
Arbroath	d						10 49																
Dundee	d						11 06																
Leuchars 3	d						11 20																
Kirkcaldy	d						11 44																
Inverkeithing	d						12 01																
Inverness	d																						
Perth	d																						
Stirling	d																						
Glasgow Central 15	d					10 59																	
Motherwell	d					11 14																	
Haymarket	d					11 56	12 19																
Edinburgh 10	a					12 02	12 25																
Edinburgh	d					12 09	12 30				13 00					13 08	13 30					14 00	
Dunbar	d															13 29							
Berwick-upon-Tweed	d					12 48											14 11						
Alnmouth for Alnwick	d															14 09						14 58	
Morpeth	d							13 49										14 49					
Newcastle 8	a					13 35	13 55	14 13			14 23					14 39	14 56	15 13				15 27	
Sunderland	d																						
Hartlepool	d																						
Newcastle 8	d					13 44	13 56			14 18	14 25	14 35				14 44	14 58			15 03	15 15	15 28	
Chester-le-Street	d																				15 24		
Durham	d					13 56				14 31	14 38	14 47				14 56				15 16	15 31	15 41	
Darlington 7	a					14 12	14 25			14 46	14 55	15 03				15 12	15 25			15 31	15 46	15 59	
Middlesbrough	d								13 50										14 50				
Eaglescliffe	d																						
Darlington 7	d					14 13	14 25			14 48	14 56	15 04				15 13	15 26			15 33	15 48	15 59	
Northallerton	d								14 18	14 59	15 07								15 18		15 59		
Thirsk	d								14 28										15 28				
York 8	a					14 41	14 53		14 47	15 22	15 28	15 31				15 41	15 53		15 47	16 03	16 21	16 28	
Leeds 10	a					15 08			15 22	15 52						16 08			16 22	16 32	16 52		
Harrogate	d																						
Scarborough	d																						
York 8	d						14 55				15 30	15 34					15 55					16 29	
Doncaster 7	a										15 52	15 57										16 55	
Skipton	d																						
Keighley	d																						
Bradford Interchange	d																						15 22
Bradford Forster Square	d																						
Shipley	d																						
Halifax	d																						15 35
Brighouse	d																						15 46
Leeds 10	d		14 35		15 05	15 12									16 05	16 12				16 40			
Wakefield Westgate 7	d		14 47		15 17	15 24									16 17	16 24				16 52			
Wakefield Kirkgate 4	d																						16 11
Pontefract Monkhill	d																						16 29
Sheffield 7	a					15 51						16 20				16 51				17 20			
Hull	d												15 30										
Selby	d												16 05										
Doncaster 7	d	15 07	15 11		15 35						15 53		16 23	16 27	16 35							16 56	17 03
Retford 10	d										16 07		16 38										
Lincoln	d	15a57												17a20									
Newark North Gate 7	a				15 59										16 59							17 19	
	d				15 59										16 59							17 19	
Grantham 7	a				16 12								16 59		17 11								
	d			16 07	16 12								16 59		17 13								
Peterborough 8	a		15 59	16 40	16 32						16 47				17 35							17 48	
Norwich	a			18 18																			
Peterborough 8	d		16 00		16 32						16 49				17 35							17 49	
Stevenage 4	a				17 02																		
London Kings Cross 15 ⊖	a		16 55		17 32		17 00				17 46		18 07		18 30		17 55					18 44	18 45

B The Northern Lights

Table 26

Scotland, North East England, Yorkshire and Humberside - London

		GR	XC	GR	NT	TP	TP	EM	GR	XC	EM	GR	NT	EM	XC	GR	NT	TP	TP	GR	XC	NT	HT
Aberdeen	d																						
Stonehaven	d																						
Montrose	d																						
Arbroath	d																						
Dundee	d																						
Leuchars 3	d																						
Kirkcaldy	d																						
Inverkeithing	d																						
Inverness	d																						
Perth	d																						
Stirling	d																						
Glasgow Central 15	d		12 51																				
Motherwell	d		13 12																				
Haymarket	d																						
Edinburgh 10	a		13 55																				
Edinburgh	d		14 08	14 30					15 00						15 08	15 30				16 00			
Dunbar	d														15 28								
Berwick-upon-Tweed	d		14 49	15 11												16 11							
Alnmouth for Alnwick	d																						
Morpeth	d				15 49												16 49						
Newcastle 8	a		15 35	15 56	16 13				16 23						16 35	16 56	17 14			17 23			
Sunderland	d																						
Hartlepool	d																						
Newcastle 8	d		15 41	15 58			16 15		16 25	16 35					16 41	16 58			17 02	17 25	17 32		
Chester-le-Street	d						16 24												17 11		17 41		
Durham	d		15 53				16 31		16 38	16 47					16 52				17 18	17 38	17 48		
Darlington 7	a		16 10	16 25			16 46		16 55	17 03					17 09	17 25			17 34	17 55	18 03		
Middlesbrough	d					15 50												16 50					
Eaglescliffe	d																						
Darlington 7	d		16 11	16 26			16 48		16 56	17 04					17 10	17 26			17 35	17 56	18 05		
Northallerton	d					16 18	16 59		17 07									17 18	17 46	18 07			
Thirsk	d					16 28												17 28					
York 8	a		16 41	16 53		16 47	17 23		17 27	17 31					17 41	17 53		17 47	18 09	18 27	18 31		
Leeds 10	a		17 08			17 22	17 52								18 08			18 22	18 37				
Harrogate	d																						
Scarborough	d												16 23	17 03									
York 8	d			16 55					17 29	17 34				17 50		17 55				18 29	18 34		
Doncaster 7	a								17 52	17 57				18 11						18 52	18 57		
Skipton	d																						
Keighley	d																						
Bradford Interchange	d																						
Bradford Forster Square	d																						
Shipley	d																						
Halifax	d																						
Brighouse	d																						
Leeds 10	d	17 05	17 11									18 05			18 11								
Wakefield Westgate 7	d	17 17	17 23									18 17			18 23							18 29	
Wakefield Kirkgate 4	d																					18a33	
Pontefract Monkhill	d																						
Sheffield 7	a		17 51							18 20				18 44	18 51						19 21		
Hull	d												17 52										18 30
Selby	d												18 26										19 05
Doncaster 7	d	17 35							17 53			18 35	18a47							18 53			19 27
Retford 10	d								18 07														
Lincoln	d																						
Newark North Gate 7	a	17 59										19 02								19 17			
	d	17 59										19 02								19 17			
Grantham 7	a	18 11										19 15											19 57
	d	18 11						18 15			19 08	19 15											19 57
Peterborough 8	a	18 31						18 45	18 49		19 39	19 35								19 47			
Norwich	a							20 21			21 14												
Peterborough 8	d	18 32							18 50			19 35								19 49			
Stevenage 4	a	19 01																					
London Kings Cross 15 ⊖	a	19 30		18 55					19 46			20 30				19 55				20 46			21 05

Scotland, North East England, Yorkshire and Humberside - London

		GR		XC	GR	SR	TP	GC	NT	GR	XC	NT		GR	XC	TP	NT	TP	GR	TP	NT	NT		XC	XC
		1		◇1	1		◇1	1		1	◇1			1	◇1	◇1		◇1	1	◇1				◇1	◇1
Aberdeen	d																		14 50						
Stonehaven	d																		15 07						
Montrose	d																		15 30						
Arbroath	d																		15 46						
Dundee	d																		16 04						
Leuchars 3	d																		16 18						
Kirkcaldy	d																		16 45						
Inverkeithing	d																		17 01						
Inverness	d																								
Perth	d																								
Stirling	d																								
Glasgow Central 15	d			15 00		15 14																			16 52
Motherwell	d			15 14		15 36																			17 14
Haymarket	d			15 56		16 34													17 20						17 56
Edinburgh 10	a			16 01		16 39													17 26						18 01
Edinburgh	d			16 05	16 30	16 41				17 00					17 08				17 30						18 05
Dunbar	d														17 28				17 50						18 25
Berwick-upon-Tweed	d				17 11										17 51				18 15						18 48
Alnmouth for Alnwick	d			17 01						17 58												18 48			19 08
Morpeth	d			17 16					17 52												18 50	19 13			
Newcastle 8	a			17 34	17 56				18 15	18 27					18 40				19 01		19 13	19 36			19 41
Sunderland	d							17 29																	
Hartlepool	d							17 53																	
Newcastle 8	d			17 43	17 58					18 28	18 35				18 44			18 52	19 03					19 17	19 44
Chester-le-Street	d																	19 01							
Durham	d			17 55						18 41	18 48				18 56			19 08						19 29	19 56
Darlington 7	a			18 12	18 25					18 59	19 04				19 12			19 23	19 31					19 45	20 12
Middlesbrough	d						17 50									18 50									
Eaglescliffe	d							18 12																	
Darlington 7	d			18 13	18 26					18 59	19 05				19 13			19 25	19 32					19 46	20 13
Northallerton	d						18 18	18 31								19 18		19 36							
Thirsk	d						18 28	18 41								19 26				←					
York 8	a			18 41	18 53		18 47	18 58		19 28	19 31				19 41	19 52		20 07	20 00	20 07				20 13	20 42
Leeds 10	a			19 08			19 35								20 08			↦		20 35					21 08
Harrogate	d																								
Scarborough	d																								
York 8	d				18 55			19 01		19 29	19 34								20 01					20 23	
Doncaster 7	a									19 53	19 57								20 25						
Skipton	d																								
Keighley	d																								
Bradford Interchange	d																								
Bradford Forster Square	d																								
Shipley	d																								
Halifax	d																								
Brighouse	d																								
Leeds 10	d	19 05		19 11										20 05	20 11										21 11
Wakefield Westgate 7	d	19 17		19 24								19 41		20 17	20 23		20 50								21 23
Wakefield Kirkgate 4	d											19a43					20a52								
Pontefract Monkhill	d																								
Sheffield 7	a			19 51							20 20				20 52									21 20	21 51
Hull	d																								
Selby	d																								
Doncaster 7	d	19 36								19 54				20 35					20 25						
Retford 10	d													↦											
Lincoln	d																								
Newark North Gate 7	a	20 00																							
	d	20 00																							
Grantham 7	a	20 12								20 26									20 58						
	d	20 12								20 26									20 58						
Peterborough 8	a	20 32								20 48									21 19						
Norwich	a																								
Peterborough 8	d	20 33								20 49									21 21						
Stevenage 4	a	21 02																	21 54						
London Kings Cross 15 ⊖	a	21 31			20 55			20 56		21 46									22 24						

Scotland, North East England, Yorkshire and Humberside - London

		GR	TP	GR	SR	EM	GR	EM		NT	NT	TP	NT	NT	NT	NT
		1	◇1	1			1	◇				◇1				
Aberdeen	d															
Stonehaven	d															
Montrose	d															
Arbroath	d															
Dundee	d															
Leuchars 3	d															
Kirkcaldy	d				18 44											
Inverkeithing	d				19 00											
Inverness	d															
Perth	d															
Stirling	d															
Glasgow Central 15	d															
Motherwell	d															
Haymarket	d				19 15											
Edinburgh 10	a				19 21											
Edinburgh	d	18 30		19 00	19 22											
Dunbar	d			19 20												
Berwick-upon-Tweed	d	19 11		19 45												
Alnmouth for Alnwick	d			20 07												
Morpeth	d			20 24						21 15						
Newcastle 8	a	20 01		20 41						21 39						
Sunderland	d															
Hartlepool	d															
Newcastle 8	d			20 42									21 50			
Chester-le-Street	d												21 59			
Durham	d			20 55									22 08			
Darlington 7	a			21 14									22 29			
Middlesbrough	d		20 10									21 50				
Eaglescliffe	d												22a43			
Darlington 7	d			21 14								22 19				
Northallerton	d		20 39	21 26								22 30				
Thirsk	d		20 47									22 38				
York 8	a		21 06	21 46								22 57				
Leeds 10	a		21 37									23 33				
Harrogate	d															
Scarborough	d															
York 8	d			21 47												
Doncaster 7	a			22 16												
Skipton	d															
Keighley	d															
Bradford Interchange	d															
Bradford Forster Square	d															
Shipley	d															
Halifax	d															
Brighouse	d															
Leeds 10	d															
Wakefield Westgate 7	d										21 41			21 57	22 42	23 04
Wakefield Kirkgate 4	d										21a44			22 00	22a45	23 07
Pontefract Monkhill	d													22a18		23a29
Sheffield 7	a															
Hull	d															
Selby	d						←									
Doncaster 7	d					20 33	20 35									
Retford 10	d						20 50									
Lincoln	d					21a26										
Newark North Gate 7	a						21 05									
	d						21 05									
Grantham 7	a															
	d							21 07								
Peterborough 8	a						21 33	21 36								
Norwich	a							23 20								
Peterborough 8	d						21 35									
Stevenage 4	a															
London Kings Cross 15 ⊖	a						22 30									

Table 26

Scotland, North East England, Yorkshire and Humberside - London

		SR	GR	GR	EM	GR	GR	TP	XC	GR		NT	XC	NT	EM	FC	GR	XC	GR	GR		GR	TP	XC	TP
Aberdeen	d			18p16																					
Stonehaven	d			18p33																					
Montrose	d			18p56																					
Arbroath	d			19p12																					
Dundee	d			19p30																					
Leuchars	d			19p44																					
Kirkcaldy	d			20p08																					
Inverkeithing	d			20p24																					
Inverness	d	20p46																							
Perth	d	23b21																							
Stirling	d	00u06																							
Glasgow Central	d																								
Motherwell	d																								
Haymarket	d			20p43																					
Edinburgh	a	01 00		20p48																					
Edinburgh	d			21p00																					
Dunbar	d			21p21																					
Berwick-upon-Tweed	d			21p47																					
Alnmouth for Alnwick	d			22p10																					
Morpeth	d			22p26																					
Newcastle	a			22p43																					
Sunderland	d													06 28											
Hartlepool	d													06a54											
Newcastle	d		21p15	22p44			04 40												06 00				06 11	06 22	
Chester-le-Street	d																						06 21		
Durham	d		21p27	23p00			04 54												06 12				06 28	06 37	
Darlington	a		21p45	23p19			05 11												06 30				06 44	06 52	
Middlesbrough	d							05 55																	
Eaglescliffe	d																								
Darlington	d		21p46	23p19			05 12												06 30				06 45	06 54	
Northallerton	d		21p57	23c46			05 31	06 23															06 56		
Thirsk	d							06 31															07 04		←
York	a		22p17	00 13			05 57	06 49											06 58				07 30	07 21	07 30
Leeds	a			00 50				07 20															→		08 04
Harrogate	d																								
Scarborough	d																								
York	d		22p19				06 00											06 40	07 00					07 24	
Doncaster	a		22p42				06 22												07 23					07 49	
Skipton	d																								
Keighley	d																								
Bradford Interchange	d																								
Bradford Forster Square	d																								
Shipley	d																								
Halifax	d																								
Brighouse	d																								
Leeds	d					05 05			06 00	06 05			06 15		06 34		07 05	07 10							
Wakefield Westgate	d					05 17			06 12	06 17		06 24	06 29		06 46		07 17	07 23							
Wakefield Kirkgate	d											06 29													
Pontefract Monkhill	d											06a46													
Sheffield	a								06 45						07 22			07 51						08 18	
Hull	d																					06 50			
Selby	d																			←		07 24			
Doncaster	d		22p42			05 35	06 23			06 35			06a46				07 35		07 24	07 35		07 43			
Retford	d					05 49				06 49							→								
Lincoln	d																								
Newark North Gate	a		23p06			06 04				07 04										07 59					
	d		23p06			06 04				07 04										07 59					
Grantham	a		23p18			06 17				07 17										08 11		08 16			
	d		23p18		05 51	06 17				07 17										08 11		08 17			
Peterborough	a		23p39		06 25	06 36	07 10			07 36									08 13	08 31		08 38			
Norwich	a																								
Peterborough	d		23p39			06 38	07 12			07 37						08 08			08 14	08 31		08 39			
Stevenage	a		00s20			07 06				08 06										09 00					
London Kings Cross	a		00 59			07 37	08 10			08 36						09 12			09 12	09 30		09 38			

b Previous night, stops to pick up only

c Previous night, stops to set down only

Table 26

Scotland, North East England, Yorkshire and Humberside - London

		GR	EM	EM	GR	GR		XC	GR	GC	TP	FC	GC	GR	EM	GR		XC	GR	HT	EM	GR	TP	XC	TP
Aberdeen	d																								
Stonehaven	d																								
Montrose	d																								
Arbroath	d																								
Dundee	d																								
Leuchars	d																								
Kirkcaldy	d																								
Inverkeithing	d																								
Inverness	d																								
Perth	d																								
Stirling	d																								
Glasgow Central	d																								
Motherwell	d																								
Haymarket	d																								
Edinburgh	a																								
Edinburgh	d																							06 06	
Dunbar	d																								
Berwick-upon-Tweed	d																							06 48	
Alnmouth for Alnwick	d																							07 08	
Morpeth	d																								
Newcastle	a																							07 38	
Sunderland	d												06 43												
Hartlepool	d												07 09												
Newcastle	d	06 30							06 55							07 24		07 30					07 33	07 44	
Chester-le-Street	d																						07 42		
Durham	d	06 42							07 07							07 36		07 43					07 49	07 56	
Darlington	a	07 00							07 25							07 54		08 00					08 05	08 12	
Middlesbrough	d										07 12														
Eaglescliffe	d												07 30												
Darlington	d	07 01							07 26							07 54		08 02					08 06	08 13	
Northallerton	d	07 12									07 42		07 48			08 06							08 17		
Thirsk	d										07 50		07 57										08 25		←
York	a	07 32							07 53		08 08		08 14			08 27		08 31					08 47	08 41	08 47
Leeds	a										08 52												→	09 07	09 22
Harrogate	d																					08 13			
Scarborough	d																								
York	d	07 34						07 44	07 55				08 16			08 28		08 34							
Doncaster	a	07 56							08 17							08 53		08 57							
Skipton	d				06 55																				
Keighley	d				07u08																				
Bradford Interchange	d									06 51															
Bradford Forster Square	d					07 33																			
Shipley	d				07u18	07u39																			
Halifax	d									07 04															
Brighouse	d									07 17															
Leeds	d		07 34		07 35	08 05		08 12											08 40			09 05		09 11	
Wakefield Westgate	d		07 46			08 17		08 24											08 52			09 17		09 24	
Wakefield Kirkgate	d									07 38															
Pontefract Monkhill	d									07 58															
Sheffield	a		08 21					08 51										09 20						09 52	
Hull	d																			08 25					
Selby	d													←						09 00					
Doncaster	d	07 57			08 09	08 35			08 18	08 31				08 35		08 53			09 13	09 23		09 35			
Retford	d					→								08 52						09 38					
Lincoln	d																								
Newark North Gate	a	08 21												09 08		09 18						09 59			
	d	08 21												09 08		09 18						10 00			
Grantham	a				08 42											09 30				09 59		10 12			
	d			08 20	08 42										09 03	09 30				09 59	10 08	10 13			
Peterborough	a	08 50		08 58										09 35	09 41				09 58		10 37	10 33			
Norwich	a			10 43											11 15						12 18				
Peterborough	d	08 50										09 07		09 36					09 59			10 33			
Stevenage	a																					11 03			
London Kings Cross	a	09 48			09 53				09 57	10 09		10 10	10 15	10 30		10 46			10 54	11 09		11 33			

Table 26

Saturdays
25 June to 30 July

Scotland, North East England, Yorkshire and Humberside - London

		SR	GR	SR	NT	FC	GR	GR	XC	EM	EM	GR	XC	GR	NT	TP	GC	TP	FC	GR	XC	HT
			■ 1			1	■ 1	■ 1	◇1		◇	■ 1	◇1	■ 1		◇1	■ 1	◇1	1	■ 1	◇1	◇1
													A									
Aberdeen	d																					
Stonehaven	d																					
Montrose	d																					
Arbroath	d																					
Dundee	d																					
Leuchars 3	d																					
Kirkcaldy	d																					
Inverkeithing	d																					
Inverness	d																					
Perth	d																					
Stirling	d																					
Glasgow Central 15	d												06 01							06 50		
Motherwell	d												06 16							07 05		
Haymarket	d	06 14		06 33									06 57							07 46		
Edinburgh 10	a	06 18		06 39									07 02							07 52		
Edinburgh	d	06 20	06 20	06 41				06 55	07 00				07 07	07 30						08 00		
Dunbar	d		06 40										07 28									
Berwick-upon-Tweed	d		07 05						07 40					08 12								
Alnmouth for Alnwick	d		07 25		07 22				08 00											08 58		
Morpeth	d		07 41		07 55				08 14						08 49							
Newcastle 8 ⇌	a		07 58		08 20			08 22	08 32				08 37	08 57	09 14					09 27		
Sunderland ⇌	d																08 30					
Hartlepool	d																08 54					
Newcastle 8 ⇌	d		07 59					08 25	08 36				08 44	08 59				09 15		09 28	09 35	
Chester-le-Street	d																	09 24				
Durham	d							08 37	08 48				08 57					09 31		09 41	09 47	
Darlington 7	a		08 27					08 55	09 04				09 12	09 25				09 47		09 59	10 04	
Middlesbrough	d															08 50						
Eaglescliffe	d																09 17					
Darlington 7	d		08 27					08 56	09 05				09 14	09 26				09 48		09 59	10 05	
Northallerton	d							09 07								09 18	09 40	09 59				
Thirsk	d															09 28	09 49					
York 8	a		08 55					09 27	09 32				09 43	09 54		09 47	10 06	10 21		10 28	10 31	
Leeds 10	a												10 09			10 22		10 52				
Harrogate	d																					
Scarborough	d																					
York 8	d		08 56					09 29	09 35					09 56			10 09			10 29	10 34	
Doncaster 7	a							09 52	09 57											10 52	10 57	
Skipton	d																					
Keighley	d																					
Bradford Interchange	d																					
Bradford Forster Square	d																					
Shipley	d																					
Halifax	d																					
Brighouse	d																					
Leeds 10	d											10 05	10 12									
Wakefield Westgate 7	d											10 17	10 24									
Wakefield Kirkgate 4	d																					
Pontefract Monkhill	d																					
Sheffield 7 ⇌	a								10 20				10 51								11 20	
Hull	d																					10 30
Selby	d																					11 05
Doncaster 7	d							09 52		10 24		10 35								10 52		11 25
Retford 10	d							10 07														11 40
Lincoln	d						09 30			11a16												
Newark North Gate 7	a						09 52					10 59								11 18		
	d						09 53					10 59								11 18		
Grantham 7	a							10 29				11 11										12 00
	d							10 29			11 10	11 13										12 00
Peterborough 8	a		10 04				10 23	10 50			11 39	11 35								11 47		
Norwich	a										13 13											
Peterborough 8	d		10 06			10 08	10 23	10 50				11 35							11 08	11 49		
Stevenage 4	a						10 54															
London Kings Cross 15 ⊖	a		11 00			11 11	11 26	11 46				12 30		11 56			12 07		12 11	12 46		13 07

Table 26

Saturdays
25 June to 30 July

Scotland, North East England, Yorkshire and Humberside - London

		EM	GR	XC	GR	SR	NT	TP	TP	FC	GR	GC	XC	EM	GR	XC	GR	NT	TP	TP	FC	GR	XC
		◇	■ 1	◇1	■ 1			◇1	◇1	1	■ 1	■ 1	◇1	◇	■ 1	◇1	■ 1		◇1	◇1	1	■ 1	◇1
				A												A							
Aberdeen	d																						
Stonehaven	d																						
Montrose	d																						
Arbroath	d																						
Dundee	d			06 32																			
Leuchars 3	d			06 46																			
Kirkcaldy	d			07 21																			
Inverkeithing	d			07 38																			
Inverness	d																						
Perth	d																						
Stirling	d																						
Glasgow Central 15	d					07 03										07 50							
Motherwell	d					07 27										08 05							
Haymarket	d			07 56		08 26										08 50							
Edinburgh 10	a			08 01		08 33										08 54							
Edinburgh	d			08 05	08 30	08 40					09 00					09 06	09 30					10 00	
Dunbar	d															09 26							
Berwick-upon-Tweed	d			08 46												09 49	10 11						
Alnmouth for Alnwick	d																					10 58	
Morpeth	d						09 49											10 49					
Newcastle 8 ⇌	a			09 35	09 55		10 13				10 23					10 38	10 57	11 13				11 27	
Sunderland ⇌	d																						
Hartlepool	d																						
Newcastle 8 ⇌	d			09 41	09 58				10 17		10 25		10 35			10 44	10 59			11 15		11 28	11 35
Chester-le-Street	d																			11 24			
Durham	d			09 55					10 31		10 38		10 47			10 56				11 31		11 41	11 47
Darlington 7	a			10 10	10 26				10 46		10 55		11 03			11 12	11 27			11 46		11 59	12 04
Middlesbrough	d							09 50											10 50				
Eaglescliffe	d																						
Darlington 7	d			10 12	10 27				10 48		10 56		11 04			11 13	11 28			11 48		11 59	12 05
Northallerton	d							10 18	10 59		11 07								11 18	11 59			
Thirsk	d							10 28											11 28				
York 8	a			10 41	10 55			10 47	11 23		11 27		11 31			11 41	11 56		11 47	12 21		12 28	12 31
Leeds 10	a			11 08				11 22	11 52							12 08			12 22	12 52			
Harrogate	d																						
Scarborough	d																						
York 8	d				10 56						11 29		11 34				11 57					12 29	12 34
Doncaster 7	a										11 52		11 57									12 52	12 57
Skipton	d																						
Keighley	d																						
Bradford Interchange	d											10 22											
Bradford Forster Square	d																						
Shipley	d																						
Halifax	d											10 38											
Brighouse	d											10 49											
Leeds 10	d		11 05	11 11											12 05	12 11							
Wakefield Westgate 7	d		11 17	11 23											12 17	12 24							
Wakefield Kirkgate 4	d											11 11											
Pontefract Monkhill	d											11 35											
Sheffield 7 ⇌	a			11 51									12 20			12 51							13 20
Hull	d																						
Selby	d																						
Doncaster 7	d		11 35								11 54	12 05			12 35							12 52	
Retford 10	d										12 08												
Lincoln	d																						
Newark North Gate 7	a		11 59												13 02							13 17	
	d		11 59												13 02							13 17	
Grantham 7	a		12 11												13 14								
	d	12 07	12 11											13 10	13 14								
Peterborough 8	a	12 38	12 31								12 47			13 39	13 35							13 45	
Norwich	a	14 13												15 13									
Peterborough 8	d		12 32							12 06	12 50				13 36						13 08	13 49	
Stevenage 4	a		13 01																				
London Kings Cross 15 ⊖	a		13 30		12 55					13 11	13 45	13 46			14 30		13 55				14 10	14 46	

Table 26

Saturdays
25 June to 30 July

Scotland, North East England, Yorkshire and Humberside - London

		EM	EM	GR	XC	GR	NT	TP	TP	GR	XC	HT	EM	GR	XC	GR	NT	TP	GC	TP	GR	XC
			◇	■ 1	◇1	■ 1		◇1	◇1	■ 1	◇1	◇1	◇	■ 1	◇1	■ 1		◇1	■ 1	◇1	■ 1	◇1
																B						
Aberdeen	d					07 52									08 20							
Stonehaven	d					08 09									08 38							
Montrose	d					08 32									08 59							
Arbroath	d					08 48									09 15							
Dundee	d					09 06									09 32							
Leuchars 8	d					09 20									09 47							
Kirkcaldy	d					09 44									10 17							
Inverkeithing	d					10 01									10 32							
Inverness	d															07 55						
Perth	d															09 56						
Stirling	d															10 30						
Glasgow Central 15	d				09 00																	
Motherwell	d				09 15																	
Haymarket	d				09 57	10 21									10 52	11 11						
Edinburgh 10	a				10 02	10 26									10 58	11 17						
Edinburgh	d				10 05	10 30				11 00					11 05	11 30					12 00	
Dunbar	d														11 25							
Berwick-upon-Tweed	d				10 48										11 48						12 41	
Alnmouth for Alnwick	d														12 08							
Morpeth	d				11 19		11 49										12 49					
Newcastle 8	a				11 38	11 55	12 13			12 23					12 38	12 55	13 13				13 26	
Sunderland	d																		12 18			
Hartlepool	d																		12 43			
Newcastle 8	d				11 42	11 56			12 17	12 25	12 35				12 44	12 56				13 15	13 28	13 35
Chester-le-Street	d																			13 24		
Durham	d				11 55				12 29	12 38	12 47				12 56					13 31	13 41	13 47
Darlington 7	a				12 11	12 25			12 45	12 55	13 03				13 12	13 24				13 46	13 59	14 04
Middlesbrough	d							11 50										12 50				
Eaglescliffe	d																		13 05			
Darlington 7	d				12 12	12 25			12 46	12 56	13 04				13 13	13 24				13 48	13 59	14 05
Northallerton	d							12 18	12 58	13 07								13 18	13 27	13 59		
Thirsk	d							12 28										13 28	13 41			
York 8	a				12 42	12 53		12 47	13 21	13 27	13 31				13 41	13 53		13 47	13 57	14 24	14 28	14 31
Leeds 10	a				13 08			13 22	13 52						14 09			14 22		14 52		
Harrogate	d																					
Scarborough	d																					
York 8	d					12 55				13 29	13 34					13 55			14 00		14 29	14 34
Doncaster 7	a									13 52	13 57										14 53	14 57
Skipton	d																					
Keighley	d																					
Bradford Interchange	d																					
Bradford Forster Square	d																					
Shipley	d																					
Halifax	d																					
Brighouse	d																					
Leeds 10	d			13 05	13 11									14 05	14 11							
Wakefield Westgate 7	d			13 17	13 23									14 17	14 24							
Wakefield Kirkgate 4	d																					
Pontefract Monkhill	d																					
Sheffield 7	a				13 51						14 20				14 51							15 20
Hull	d											13 30										
Selby	d											14 06										
Doncaster 7	d	13 05		13 35						13 53		14 25		14 35							14 53	
Retford 10	d									14 07		14 40										
Lincoln	d	13a55																				
Newark North Gate 7	a			13 59										15 03							15 17	
	d			13 59										15 03							15 18	
Grantham 7	a			14 12								15 01		15 16								
	d		14 07	14 12								15 01	15 10	15 16								
Peterborough 8	a		14 41	14 31						14 47			15 39	15 35							15 47	
Norwich	a		16 15										17 13									
Peterborough 8	d			14 32						14 49				15 36							15 49	
Stevenage 4	a			15 01																		
London Kings Cross 15 ⊖	a			15 30		14 55				15 46		16 08		16 31		15 52			15 55		16 46	

B The Highland Chieftain

Table 26

Saturdays
25 June to 30 July

Scotland, North East England, Yorkshire and Humberside - London

		EM	GR	EM	GR	XC	GR	NT	TP	TP	GR	XC	HT	EM	GR	XC	GR	NT	TP	XC	TP	GR	GC
			■ 1	◇	■ 1	◇1	■ 1		◇1	◇1	■ 1	◇1	◇1		■ 1	◇1	■ 1		◇1	◇1	◇1	■ 1	■ 1
							B																
Aberdeen	d						09 52																
Stonehaven	d						10 09																
Montrose	d						10 32																
Arbroath	d						10 49																
Dundee	d						11 06																
Leuchars 8	d						11 20																
Kirkcaldy	d						11 44																
Inverkeithing	d						12 01																
Inverness	d																						
Perth	d																						
Stirling	d																						
Glasgow Central 15	d					10 59																	
Motherwell	d					11 14																	
Haymarket	d					11 56	12 19																
Edinburgh 10	a					12 02	12 25																
Edinburgh	d					12 09	12 30				13 00					13 08	13 30					14 00	
Dunbar	d															13 29							
Berwick-upon-Tweed	d					12 48											14 11						
Alnmouth for Alnwick	d															14 09						14 58	
Morpeth	d							13 49										14 49					
Newcastle 8	a					13 35	13 55	14 13			14 23					14 39	14 56	15 13				15 27	
Sunderland	d																						
Hartlepool	d																						
Newcastle 8	d					13 44	13 56			14 18	14 25	14 35				14 44	14 58			15 03	15 15	15 28	
Chester-le-Street	d																				15 24		
Durham	d					13 56				14 31	14 38	14 47				14 56				15 16	15 31	15 41	
Darlington 7	a					14 12	14 25			14 46	14 55	15 03				15 12	15 25			15 31	15 46	15 59	
Middlesbrough	d								13 50										14 50				
Eaglescliffe	d																						
Darlington 7	d					14 13	14 25			14 48	14 56	15 04				15 13	15 26			15 33	15 48	15 59	
Northallerton	d								14 18	14 59	15 07								15 18		15 59		
Thirsk	d								14 28										15 28				
York 8	a					14 41	14 53		14 47	15 22	15 28	15 31				15 41	15 53		15 47	16 03	16 21	16 28	
Leeds 10	a					15 08			15 22	15 52						16 08			16 22	16 32	16 52		
Harrogate	d																						
Scarborough	d																						
York 8	d						14 55				15 30	15 34					15 55					16 29	
Doncaster 7	a										15 52	15 57										16 55	
Skipton	d																						
Keighley	d																						
Bradford Interchange	d																						15 22
Bradford Forster Square	d																						
Shipley	d																						
Halifax	d																						15 35
Brighouse	d																						15 46
Leeds 10	d		14 35		15 05	15 12									16 05	16 12				16 40			
Wakefield Westgate 7	d		14 47		15 17	15 24									16 17	16 24				16 52			
Wakefield Kirkgate 4	d																						16 11
Pontefract Monkhill	d																						16 29
Sheffield 7	a					15 51						16 20				16 51				17 20			
Hull	d												15 30										
Selby	d												16 05										
Doncaster 7	d	15 07	15 11		15 35						15 53		16 23	16 27	16 35							16 56	17 03
Retford 10	d										16 07		16 38										
Lincoln	d	15a57												17a20									
Newark North Gate 7	a				15 59										16 59							17 19	
	d				15 59										16 59							17 19	
Grantham 7	a				16 12								16 59		17 11								
	d			16 07	16 12								16 59		17 13								
Peterborough 8	a		15 59	16 40	16 32						16 47				17 35							17 48	
Norwich	a			18 18																			
Peterborough 8	d		16 00		16 32						16 49				17 35							17 49	
Stevenage 4	a				17 02																		
London Kings Cross 15 ⊖	a		16 55		17 32		17 00				17 46		18 07		18 30		17 55					18 44	18 45

B The Northern Lights

Table 26

Saturdays
25 June to 30 July

Scotland, North East England, Yorkshire and Humberside - London

		GR	XC	GR	NT	TP	TP	EM	GR	XC	EM	GR	NT	EM	XC	GR	NT	TP	TP	GR	XC	NT	HT
		■		■					■			■				■				■			
		1	◇1	1		◇1	◇1	◇	1	◇1	◇	1		◇1	◇1	1		◇1	◇1	1	◇1		◇1
		🍴	⌶	🍴		⌶	⌶		🍴	⌶		🍴		☕	⌶	🍴				🍴	⌶		☒
Aberdeen	d																						
Stonehaven	d																						
Montrose	d																						
Arbroath	d																						
Dundee	d																						
Leuchars 3	d																						
Kirkcaldy	d																						
Inverkeithing	d																						
Inverness	d																						
Perth	d																						
Stirling	d																						
Glasgow Central 15	d		12 51																				
Motherwell	d		13 12																				
Haymarket	d																						
Edinburgh 10	a		13 55																				
Edinburgh	d		14 08	14 30					15 00						15 08	15 30				16 00			
Dunbar	d														15 28								
Berwick-upon-Tweed	d		14 49	15 11												16 11							
Alnmouth for Alnwick	d																						
Morpeth	d				15 49												16 49						
Newcastle 8	a		15 35	15 56	16 13				16 23						16 35	16 56	17 14			17 23			
Sunderland	d																						
Hartlepool	d																						
Newcastle 8	d		15 41	15 58			16 15		16 25	16 35					16 41	16 58			17 02	17 25	17 32		
Chester-le-Street	d						16 24												17 11		17 41		
Durham	d		15 53				16 31		16 38	16 47					16 52				17 18	17 38	17 48		
Darlington 7	a		16 10	16 25			16 46		16 55	17 03					17 09	17 25			17 34	17 55	18 03		
Middlesbrough	d					15 50												16 50					
Eaglescliffe	d																						
Darlington 7	d		16 11	16 26			16 48		16 56	17 04					17 10	17 26			17 35	17 56	18 05		
Northallerton	d					16 18	16 59		17 07									17 18	17 46	18 07			
Thirsk	d					16 28												17 28					
York 8	a		16 41	16 53		16 47	17 23		17 27	17 31					17 41	17 53		17 47	18 09	18 27	18 31		
Leeds 10	a		17 08			17 22	17 52								18 08			18 22	18 37				
Harrogate	d																						
Scarborough	d												16 23	17 03									
York 8	d			16 55					17 29	17 34				17 50		17 55				18 29	18 34		
Doncaster 7	a								17 52	17 57				18 11						18 52	18 57		
Skipton	d																						
Keighley	d																						
Bradford Interchange	d																						
Bradford Forster Square	d																						
Shipley	d																						
Halifax	d																						
Brighouse	d																						
Leeds 10	d	17 05	17 11									18 05			18 11								
Wakefield Westgate 7	d	17 17	17 23									18 17			18 23							18 29	
Wakefield Kirkgate 4	d																					18a33	
Pontefract Monkhill	d																						
Sheffield 7	a		17 51							18 20				18 44	18 51						19 21		
Hull	d												17 52										18 30
Selby	d												18 26										19 05
Doncaster 7	d	17 35							17 53			18 35	18a47							18 53			19 27
Retford 10	d								18 07														
Lincoln	d																						
Newark North Gate 7	a	17 59										19 02								19 17			
	d	17 59										19 02								19 17			
Grantham 7	a	18 11										19 15											19 57
	d	18 11						18 15			19 08	19 15											19 57
Peterborough 8	a	18 31						18 45	18 49		19 39	19 35								19 47			
Norwich	a							20 21			21 14												
Peterborough 8	d	18 32							18 50			19 35								19 49			
Stevenage 4	a	19 01																					
London Kings Cross 15 ⊖	a	19 30		18 55					19 46			20 30				19 55				20 46			21 39

Table 26

Saturdays
25 June to 30 July

Scotland, North East England, Yorkshire and Humberside - London

		GR	XC	GR	SR	TP	GC	NT	GR	XC	NT	GR	XC	TP	NT	TP	GR	TP	NT	NT	XC	XC
		■		■			■		■			■					■					
		1	◇1	1		◇1	1		1	◇1		1	◇1	◇1		◇1	1	◇1			◇1	◇1
		🍴	⌶	🍴			✕		🍴	⌶		🍴	⌶				🍴				⌶	⌶
Aberdeen	d																14 50					
Stonehaven	d																15 07					
Montrose	d																15 30					
Arbroath	d																15 46					
Dundee	d																16 04					
Leuchars 3	d																16 18					
Kirkcaldy	d																16 45					
Inverkeithing	d																17 01					
Inverness	d																					
Perth	d																					
Stirling	d																					
Glasgow Central 15	d		15 00		15 14																	16 52
Motherwell	d		15 14		15 36																	17 14
Haymarket	d		15 56		16 34												17 20					17 56
Edinburgh 10	a		16 01		16 39												17 26					18 01
Edinburgh	d		16 05	16 30	16 41				17 00				17 08				17 30					18 05
Dunbar	d												17 28				17 50					18 25
Berwick-upon-Tweed	d			17 11									17 51				18 15					18 48
Alnmouth for Alnwick	d		17 01						17 58											18 48		19 08
Morpeth	d		17 16					17 52											18 50	19 13		
Newcastle 8	a		17 34	17 56				18 15	18 27				18 40				19 01		19 13	19 36		19 41
Sunderland	d						17 29															
Hartlepool	d						17 53															
Newcastle 8	d		17 43	17 58					18 28	18 35			18 44			18 52	19 03				19 17	19 44
Chester-le-Street	d															19 01						
Durham	d		17 55						18 41	18 48			18 56			19 08					19 29	19 56
Darlington 7	a		18 12	18 25					18 59	19 04			19 12			19 23	19 31				19 45	20 12
Middlesbrough	d					17 50								18 50								
Eaglescliffe	d						18 12															
Darlington 7	d		18 13	18 26					18 59	19 05			19 13			19 25	19 32				19 46	20 13
Northallerton	d					18 18	18 31							19 18		19 36						
Thirsk	d					18 28	18 41							19 26				←				
York 8	a		18 41	18 53		18 47	18 58		19 28	19 31			19 41	19 52		20 07	20 00	20 07			20 13	20 42
Leeds 10	a		19 08			19 35							20 08			→		20 35				21 08
Harrogate	d																					
Scarborough	d																					
York 8	d			18 55			19 01		19 29	19 34							20 01				20 23	
Doncaster 7	a								19 53	19 57							20 25					
Skipton	d																					
Keighley	d																					
Bradford Interchange	d																					
Bradford Forster Square	d																					
Shipley	d																					
Halifax	d																					
Brighouse	d																					
Leeds 10	d	19 05	19 11									20 05	20 11									21 11
Wakefield Westgate 7	d	19 17	19 24								19 41	20 17	20 23		20 50							21 23
Wakefield Kirkgate 4	d										19a43				20a52							
Pontefract Monkhill	d																					
Sheffield 7	a		19 51							20 20			20 52								21 20	21 51
Hull	d																					
Selby	d																					
Doncaster 7	d	19 36							19 54			20 35					20 25					
Retford 10	d											↪										
Lincoln	d																					
Newark North Gate 7	a	20 00																				
	d	20 00																				
Grantham 7	a	20 12							20 26								20 58					
	d	20 12							20 26								20 58					
Peterborough 8	a	20 32							20 48								21 19					
Norwich	a																					
Peterborough 8	d	20 33							20 49								21 21					
Stevenage 4	a	21 26							21 45								22 08					
London Kings Cross 15 ⊖	a	22 09		20 55			21 24		22 26								22 44					

Table 26

Saturdays

25 June to 30 July

Scotland, North East England, Yorkshire and Humberside - London

		GR	TP	GR	SR	EM	GR	EM	NT	NT	TP	NT	NT	NT	NT
Aberdeen	d														
Stonehaven	d														
Montrose	d														
Arbroath	d														
Dundee	d														
Leuchars	d														
Kirkcaldy	d				18 44										
Inverkeithing	d				19 00										
Inverness	d														
Perth	d														
Stirling	d														
Glasgow Central	d														
Motherwell	d														
Haymarket	d				19 15										
Edinburgh	a				19 21										
Edinburgh	d	18 30		19 00	19 22										
Dunbar	d			19 20											
Berwick-upon-Tweed	d	19 11		19 45											
Alnmouth for Alnwick	d			20 07											
Morpeth	d			20 24					21 15						
Newcastle	a	20 01		20 41					21 39						
Sunderland	d														
Hartlepool	d														
Newcastle	d			20 42								21 50			
Chester-le-Street	d											21 59			
Durham	d			20 55								22 08			
Darlington	a			21 14								22 29			
Middlesbrough	d		20 10								21 50				
Eaglescliffe	d											22a43			
Darlington	d			21 14							22 19				
Northallerton	d		20 39	21 26							22 30				
Thirsk	d		20 47								22 38				
York	a		21 06	21 46							22 57				
Leeds	a		21 37								23 33				
Harrogate	d														
Scarborough	d														
York	d			21 47											
Doncaster	a			22 16											
Skipton	d														
Keighley	d														
Bradford Interchange	d														
Bradford Forster Square	d														
Shipley	d														
Halifax	d														
Brighouse	d														
Leeds	d														
Wakefield Westgate	d									21 41			21 57	22 42	23 04
Wakefield Kirkgate	d									21a44			22 00	22a45	23 07
Pontefract Monkhill	d												22a18		23a29
Sheffield	a														
Hull	d														
Selby	d						←								
Doncaster	d					20 33	20 35								
Retford	d						20 50								
Lincoln	d					21a26									
Newark North Gate	a						21 05								
	d						21 05								
Grantham	a														
	d							21 07							
Peterborough	a						21 33	21 36							
Norwich	a							23 20							
Peterborough	d						21 35								
Stevenage	a														
London Kings Cross	a						22 48								

Table 26

Saturdays

6 August to 10 September

Scotland, North East England, Yorkshire and Humberside - London

		SR	GR	GR	EM	GR	GR	TP	XC	GR	NT	XC	NT	EM	FC	GR	XC	GR	GR	GR	TP	XC	TP
Aberdeen	d			18p16																			
Stonehaven	d			18p33																			
Montrose	d			18p56																			
Arbroath	d			19p12																			
Dundee	d			19p30																			
Leuchars	d			19p44																			
Kirkcaldy	d			20p08																			
Inverkeithing	d			20p24																			
Inverness	d	20p46																					
Perth	d	23b21																					
Stirling	d	00u06																					
Glasgow Central	d																						
Motherwell	d																						
Haymarket	d			20p43																			
Edinburgh	a	01 00		20p48																			
Edinburgh	d			21p00																			
Dunbar	d			21p21																			
Berwick-upon-Tweed	d			21p47																			
Alnmouth for Alnwick	d			22p10																			
Morpeth	d			22p26																			
Newcastle	a			22p43																			
Sunderland	d												06 28										
Hartlepool	d												06a54										
Newcastle	d		21p15	22p44			04 40											06 00			06 11	06 22	
Chester-le-Street	d																				06 21		
Durham	d		21p27	23p00			04 54											06 12			06 28	06 37	
Darlington	a		21p45	23p19			05 11											06 30			06 44	06 52	
Middlesbrough	d							05 55															
Eaglescliffe	d																						
Darlington	d		21p46	23p19			05 12											06 30			06 45	06 54	
Northallerton	d		21p57	23c46			05 31	06 23													06 56		
Thirsk	d							06 31													07 04		←
York	a		22p17	00 13			05 57	06 49										06 58			07 30	07 21	07 30
Leeds	a			00 50				07 20													→		08 04
Harrogate	d																						
Scarborough	d																						
York	d		22p19				06 00										06 40	07 00				07 24	
Doncaster	a		22p42				06 22											07 23				07 49	
Skipton	d																						
Keighley	d																						
Bradford Interchange	d																						
Bradford Forster Square	d																						
Shipley	d																						
Halifax	d																						
Brighouse	d																						
Leeds	d					05 05			06 00	06 05		06 15		06 34		07 05	07 10						
Wakefield Westgate	d					05 17			06 12	06 17	06 24	06 29		06 46		07 17	07 23						
Wakefield Kirkgate	d										06 29												
Pontefract Monkhill	d										06a46												
Sheffield	a								06 45					07 22			07 51					08 18	
Hull	d																			06 50			
Selby	d																		←	07 24			
Doncaster	d		22p42			05 35	06 23			06 35		06a46				07 35		07 24	07 35	07 43			
Retford	d					05 49				06 49						→							
Lincoln	d																						
Newark North Gate	a		23p06			06 04				07 04									07 59				
	d		23p06			06 04				07 04									07 59				
Grantham	a		23p18			06 17				07 17									08 11	08 16			
	d		23p18		05 51	06 17				07 17									08 11	08 17			
Peterborough	a		23p39		06 25	06 36	07 10			07 36								08 13	08 31	08 38			
Norwich	a																						
Peterborough	d		23p39			06 38	07 12			07 37					08 08			08 14	08 31	08 39			
Stevenage	a		00s20			07 06				08 06									09 00				
London Kings Cross	a		00 59			07 37	08 10			08 36					09 12			09 12	09 30	09 38			

b Previous night, stops to pick up only

c Previous night, stops to set down only

Table 26

Saturdays

6 August to 10 September

Scotland, North East England, Yorkshire and Humberside - London

Station		GR	EM	EM	GR	GR	XC	GR	GC	TP	FC	GC	GR	EM	GR	XC	GR	HT	EM	GR	TP	XC	TP
Aberdeen	d																						
Stonehaven	d																						
Montrose	d																						
Arbroath	d																						
Dundee	d																						
Leuchars	d																						
Kirkcaldy	d																						
Inverkeithing	d																						
Inverness	d																						
Perth	d																						
Stirling	d																						
Glasgow Central	d																						
Motherwell	d																						
Haymarket	d																						
Edinburgh	a																						
Edinburgh	d																					06 06	
Dunbar	d																						
Berwick-upon-Tweed	d																					06 48	
Alnmouth for Alnwick	d																					07 08	
Morpeth	d																						
Newcastle	a																					07 38	
Sunderland	d											06 43											
Hartlepool	d											07 09											
Newcastle	d	06 30						06 55							07 24	07 30					07 33	07 44	
Chester-le-Street	d																				07 42		
Durham	d	06 42						07 07							07 36	07 43					07 49	07 56	
Darlington	a	07 00						07 25							07 54	08 00					08 05	08 12	
Middlesbrough	d									07 12													
Eaglescliffe	d											07 30											
Darlington	d	07 01						07 26							07 54	08 02					08 06	08 13	
Northallerton	d	07 12								07 42		07 48			08 06						08 17		
Thirsk	d									07 50		07 57									08 25		←
York	a	07 32						07 53		08 08		08 14			08 27	08 31					08 47	08 41	08 47
Leeds	a									08 52											→	09 07	09 22
Harrogate	d																			08 13			
Scarborough	d																						
York	d	07 34					07 44	07 55				08 16			08 28	08 34							
Doncaster	a	07 56						08 17							08 53	08 57							
Skipton	d				06 55																		
Keighley	d				07u08																		
Bradford Interchange	d								06 51														
Bradford Forster Square	d					07 33																	
Shipley	d				07u18	07u39																	
Halifax	d								07 04														
Brighouse	d								07 17														
Leeds	d		07 34		07 35	08 05	08 12										08 40			09 05		09 11	
Wakefield Westgate	d		07 46			08 17	08 24										08 52			09 17		09 24	
Wakefield Kirkgate	d								07 38														
Pontefract Monkhill	d								07 58														
Sheffield	a		08 21				08 51									09 20						09 52	
Hull	d																	08 25					
Selby	d												←					09 00					
Doncaster	d	07 57			08 09	08 35		08 18	08 31				08 35		08 53		09 13	09 23		09 35			
Retford	d					→							08 52					09 38					
Lincoln	d																						
Newark North Gate	a	08 21											09 08		09 18					09 59			
	d	08 21											09 08		09 18					10 00			
Grantham	a				08 42										09 30			09 59		10 12			
	d			08 20	08 42									09 03	09 30			09 59	10 08	10 13			
Peterborough	a	08 50		08 58									09 35	09 41			09 58		10 37	10 33			
Norwich	a			10 43										11 15					12 18				
Peterborough	d	08 50									09 07		09 36				09 59			10 33			
Stevenage	a																			11 03			
London Kings Cross ⊖	a	09 48			09 53			09 57	10 09		10 10	10 15	10 30		10 46		10 54	11 09		11 33			

Table 26

Saturdays

6 August to 10 September

Scotland, North East England, Yorkshire and Humberside - London

Station		SR	GR	SR	NT	FC	GR	GR	XC	EM	EM	GR	XC	GR	NT	TP	GC	TP	FC	GR	XC	HT
Aberdeen	d																					
Stonehaven	d																					
Montrose	d																					
Arbroath	d																					
Dundee	d																					
Leuchars	d																					
Kirkcaldy	d																					
Inverkeithing	d																					
Inverness	d																					
Perth	d																					
Stirling	d																					
Glasgow Central	d											06 01							06 50		
Motherwell	d											06 16							07 05		
Haymarket	d	06 14		06 33									06 57							07 46		
Edinburgh	a	06 18		06 39									07 02							07 52		
Edinburgh	d	06 20	06 20	06 41				06 55	07 00				07 07	07 30						08 00		
Dunbar	d		06 40										07 28									
Berwick-upon-Tweed	d		07 05						07 40					08 12								
Alnmouth for Alnwick	d		07 25		07 22				08 00											08 58		
Morpeth	d		07 41		07 55				08 14						08 49							
Newcastle	a		07 58		08 20			08 22	08 32				08 37	08 57	09 14					09 27		
Sunderland	d																08 30					
Hartlepool	d																08 54					
Newcastle	d		07 59					08 25	08 36				08 44	08 59				09 15		09 28	09 35	
Chester-le-Street	d																	09 24				
Durham	d							08 37	08 48				08 57					09 31		09 41	09 47	
Darlington	a		08 27					08 55	09 04				09 12	09 25				09 47		09 59	10 04	
Middlesbrough	d															08 50						
Eaglescliffe	d																09 17					
Darlington	d		08 27					08 56	09 05				09 14	09 26				09 48		09 59	10 05	
Northallerton	d							09 07								09 18	09 40	09 59				
Thirsk	d															09 28	09 49					
York	a		08 55					09 27	09 32				09 43	09 54		09 47	10 06	10 21		10 28	10 31	
Leeds	a												10 09			10 22		10 52				
Harrogate	d																					
Scarborough	d																					
York	d		08 56					09 29	09 35					09 56			10 09			10 29	10 34	
Doncaster	a							09 52	09 57											10 52	10 57	
Skipton	d																					
Keighley	d																					
Bradford Interchange	d																					
Bradford Forster Square	d																					
Shipley	d																					
Halifax	d																					
Brighouse	d																					
Leeds	d											10 05	10 12									
Wakefield Westgate	d											10 17	10 24									
Wakefield Kirkgate	d																					
Pontefract Monkhill	d																					
Sheffield	a								10 20				10 51								11 20	
Hull	d																					10 30
Selby	d																					11 05
Doncaster	d							09 52		10 24		10 35								10 52		11 25
Retford	d							10 07														11 40
Lincoln	d						09 30			11a16												
Newark North Gate	a						09 52					10 59								11 18		
	d						09 53					10 59								11 18		
Grantham	a							10 29				11 11										12 00
	d							10 29			11 10	11 13										12 00
Peterborough	a		10 04				10 23	10 50			11 39	11 35								11 47		
Norwich	a										13 13											
Peterborough	d		10 06			10 08	10 23	10 50				11 35							11 08	11 49		
Stevenage	a						10 54															
London Kings Cross ⊖	a		11 00			11 11	11 26	11 46				12 30		11 56			12 07		12 11	12 46		13 07

Scotland, North East England, Yorkshire and Humberside - London

		EM	GR	XC	GR	SR	NT	TP	TP	FC	GR	GC	XC	EM	GR	XC	GR	NT	TP	TP	FC	GR	XC
		◇	■ 1	◇1	■ 1			◇1	◇1	1	■ 1	■ 1	◇1	◇	■ 1	◇1	■ 1		◇1	◇1	1	■ 1	◇1
Aberdeen	d																						
Stonehaven	d																						
Montrose	d																						
Arbroath	d																						
Dundee	d			06 32																			
Leuchars 3	d			06 46																			
Kirkcaldy	d			07 21																			
Inverkeithing	d			07 38																			
Inverness	d																						
Perth	d																						
Stirling	d																						
Glasgow Central 15	d					07 03										07 50							
Motherwell	d					07 27										08 05							
Haymarket	d			07 56		08 26										08 50							
Edinburgh 10	a			08 01		08 33										08 54							
Edinburgh	d			08 05	08 30	08 40					09 00					09 06	09 30					10 00	
Dunbar	d															09 26							
Berwick-upon-Tweed	d			08 46												09 49	10 11						
Alnmouth for Alnwick	d																					10 58	
Morpeth	d						09 49											10 49					
Newcastle 8	a			09 35	09 55		10 13				10 23					10 38	10 57	11 13				11 27	
Sunderland	d																						
Hartlepool	d																						
Newcastle 8	d			09 41	09 58				10 17		10 25		10 35			10 44	10 59			11 15		11 28	11 35
Chester-le-Street	d																			11 24			
Durham	d			09 55					10 31		10 38		10 47			10 56				11 31		11 41	11 47
Darlington 7	a			10 10	10 26				10 46		10 55		11 03			11 12	11 27			11 46		11 59	12 04
Middlesbrough	d							09 50											10 50				
Eaglescliffe	d																						
Darlington 7	d			10 12	10 27				10 48		10 56		11 04			11 13	11 28			11 48		11 59	12 05
Northallerton	d							10 18	10 59		11 07								11 18	11 59			
Thirsk	d							10 28											11 28				
York 8	a			10 41	10 55			10 47	11 23		11 27		11 31			11 41	11 56		11 47	12 21		12 28	12 31
Leeds 10	a			11 08				11 22	11 52							12 08			12 22	12 52			
Harrogate	d																						
Scarborough	d																						
York 8	d				10 56						11 29		11 34				11 57					12 29	12 34
Doncaster 7	a										11 52		11 57									12 52	12 57
Skipton	d																						
Keighley	d																						
Bradford Interchange	d											10 22											
Bradford Forster Square	d																						
Shipley	d																						
Halifax	d											10 38											
Brighouse	d											10 49											
Leeds 10	d		11 05	11 11											12 05	12 11							
Wakefield Westgate 7	d		11 17	11 23											12 17	12 24							
Wakefield Kirkgate 4	d											11 11											
Pontefract Monkhill	d											11 35											
Sheffield 7	a			11 51									12 20			12 51							13 20
Hull	d																						
Selby	d																						
Doncaster 7	d		11 35								11 54	12 05			12 35							12 52	
Retford 10	d										12 08												
Lincoln	d																						
Newark North Gate 7	a		11 59												13 02							13 17	
	d		11 59												13 02							13 17	
Grantham 7	a		12 11												13 14								
	d	12 07	12 11											13 10	13 14								
Peterborough 8	a	12 38	12 31								12 47			13 39	13 35							13 45	
Norwich	a	14 13												15 13									
Peterborough 8	d		12 32							12 06	12 50				13 36						13 08	13 49	
Stevenage 4	a		13 01																				
London Kings Cross 15 ⊖	a		13 30		12 55					13 11	13 45	13 46			14 30		13 55				14 10	14 46	

Table 26

Saturdays
6 August to 10 September

Scotland, North East England, Yorkshire and Humberside - London

		EM	EM	GR	XC	GR	NT	TP	TP	GR	XC	HT	EM	GR	XC	GR	NT	TP	GC	TP	GR	XC
			◇	■ 4	◇1	■ 1		◇1	◇1	■ 1	◇1	◇1	◇	■ 1	◇1	■ 1		◇1	■ 1	◇1	■ 1	◇1
																B						
Aberdeen	d					07 52									08 20							
Stonehaven	d					08 09									08 38							
Montrose	d					08 32									08 59							
Arbroath	d					08 48									09 15							
Dundee	d					09 06									09 32							
Leuchars 3	d					09 20									09 47							
Kirkcaldy	d					09 44									10 17							
Inverkeithing	d					10 01									10 32							
Inverness	d															07 55						
Perth	d															09 56						
Stirling	d															10 30						
Glasgow Central 15	d				09 00																	
Motherwell	d				09 15																	
Haymarket	d				09 57	10 21									10 52	11 11						
Edinburgh 10	a				10 02	10 26									10 58	11 17						
Edinburgh	d				10 05	10 30				11 00					11 05	11 30					12 00	
Dunbar	d														11 25							
Berwick-upon-Tweed	d				10 48										11 48						12 41	
Alnmouth for Alnwick	d														12 08							
Morpeth	d				11 19		11 49										12 49					
Newcastle 8	a				11 38	11 55	12 13			12 23					12 38	12 55	13 13				13 26	
Sunderland	d																		12 18			
Hartlepool	d																		12 43			
Newcastle 8	d				11 42	11 56			12 17	12 25	12 35				12 44	12 56				13 15	13 28	13 35
Chester-le-Street	d																			13 24		
Durham	d				11 55				12 29	12 38	12 47				12 56					13 31	13 41	13 47
Darlington 7	a				12 11	12 25			12 45	12 55	13 03				13 12	13 24				13 46	13 59	14 04
Middlesbrough	d							11 50										12 50				
Eaglescliffe	d																		13 05			
Darlington 7	d				12 12	12 25			12 46	12 56	13 04				13 13	13 24				13 48	13 59	14 05
Northallerton	d							12 18	12 58	13 07								13 18	13 27	13 59		
Thirsk	d							12 28										13 28	13 41			
York 8	a				12 42	12 53		12 47	13 21	13 27	13 31				13 41	13 53		13 47	13 57	14 24	14 28	14 31
Leeds 10	a				13 08			13 22	13 52						14 09			14 22		14 52		
Harrogate	d																					
Scarborough	d																					
York 8	d					12 55				13 29	13 34					13 55			14 00		14 29	14 34
Doncaster 7	a									13 52	13 57										14 53	14 57
Skipton	d																					
Keighley	d																					
Bradford Interchange	d																					
Bradford Forster Square	d																					
Shipley	d																					
Halifax	d																					
Brighouse	d																					
Leeds 10	d			13 05	13 11									14 05	14 11							
Wakefield Westgate 7	d			13 17	13 23									14 17	14 24							
Wakefield Kirkgate 4	d																					
Pontefract Monkhill	d																					
Sheffield 7	a				13 51						14 20				14 51							15 20
Hull	d											13 30										
Selby	d											14 06										
Doncaster 7	d	13 05		13 35						13 53		14 25		14 35							14 53	
Retford 10	d									14 07		14 40										
Lincoln	d	13a55																				
Newark North Gate 7	a			13 59										15 03							15 17	
	d			13 59										15 03							15 18	
Grantham 7	a			14 12								15 01		15 16								
	d		14 07	14 12								15 01	15 10	15 16								
Peterborough 8	a		14 41	14 31						14 47			15 39	15 35							15 47	
Norwich	a		16 15										17 13									
Peterborough 8	d			14 32						14 49				15 36							15 49	
Stevenage 4	a			15 01																		
London Kings Cross 15 ⊖	a			15 30		14 55				15 46		16 08		16 31		15 52			15 55		16 46	

B The Highland Chieftain

Scotland, North East England, Yorkshire and Humberside - London

		EM	GR	EM	GR	XC	GR	NT	TP	TP	GR	XC	HT	EM	EM	GR	XC	GR	NT	TP	XC	TP	GR
							B																
Aberdeen	d						09 52																
Stonehaven	d						10 09																
Montrose	d						10 32																
Arbroath	d						10 49																
Dundee	d						11 06																
Leuchars	d						11 20																
Kirkcaldy	d						11 44																
Inverkeithing	d						12 01																
Inverness	d																						
Perth	d																						
Stirling	d																						
Glasgow Central	d					10 59																	
Motherwell	d					11 14																	
Haymarket	d					11 56	12 19																
Edinburgh	a					12 02	12 25																
Edinburgh	d					12 09	12 30				13 00						13 08	13 30					14 00
Dunbar	d																13 29						
Berwick-upon-Tweed	d					12 48												14 11					
Alnmouth for Alnwick	d																14 09						14 58
Morpeth	d							13 49											14 49				
Newcastle	a					13 35	13 55	14 13			14 23						14 39	14 56	15 13				15 27
Sunderland	d																						
Hartlepool	d																						
Newcastle	d					13 44	13 56			14 18	14 25	14 35					14 44	14 58			15 03	15 15	15 28
Chester-le-Street	d																					15 24	
Durham	d					13 56				14 31	14 38	14 47					14 56				15 16	15 31	15 41
Darlington	a					14 12	14 25			14 46	14 55	15 03					15 12	15 25			15 31	15 46	15 59
Middlesbrough	d								13 50											14 50			
Eaglescliffe	d																						
Darlington	d					14 13	14 25			14 48	14 56	15 04					15 13	15 26			15 33	15 48	15 59
Northallerton	d								14 18	14 59	15 07									15 18		15 59	
Thirsk	d								14 28											15 28			
York	a					14 41	14 53		14 47	15 22	15 28	15 31					15 41	15 53		15 47	16 03	16 21	16 28
Leeds	a					15 08			15 22	15 52							16 08			16 22	16 32	16 52	
Harrogate	d																						
Scarborough	d																						
York	d						14 55				15 30	15 34						15 55					16 29
Doncaster	a										15 52	15 57											16 55
Skipton	d																						
Keighley	d																						
Bradford Interchange	d																						
Bradford Forster Square	d																						
Shipley	d																						
Halifax	d																						
Brighouse	d																						
Leeds	d		14 35		15 05	15 12										16 05	16 12				16 40		
Wakefield Westgate	d		14 47		15 17	15 24										16 17	16 24				16 52		
Wakefield Kirkgate	d																						
Pontefract Monkhill	d																						
Sheffield	a					15 51						16 20					16 51				17 20		
Hull	d												15 30										
Selby	d												16 05										
Doncaster	d	15 07	15 11		15 35						15 53		16 23	16 27		16 35							16 56
Retford	d										16 07		16 38										
Lincoln	d	15a57												17a20									
Newark North Gate	a				15 59											16 59							17 19
	d				15 59											16 59							17 19
Grantham	a				16 12								16 59			17 11							
	d			16 07	16 12								16 59		17 10	17 13							
Peterborough	a		15 59	16 40	16 32						16 47				17 39	17 35							17 48
Norwich	a			18 18											19 21								
Peterborough	d		16 00		16 32						16 49					17 35							17 49
Stevenage	a				17 02																		
London Kings Cross ⊖	a		16 55		17 32		17 00				17 46		18 07			18 30		17 55					18 44

B The Northern Lights

Table 26

Saturdays
6 August to 10 September

Scotland, North East England, Yorkshire and Humberside - London

		GC	GR	XC	GR	NT	TP	TP	EM	GR	XC	EM	GR	NT	EM	XC	GR	NT	TP	TP	GR	XC	NT
Aberdeen	d																						
Stonehaven	d																						
Montrose	d																						
Arbroath	d																						
Dundee	d																						
Leuchars	d																						
Kirkcaldy	d																						
Inverkeithing	d																						
Inverness	d																						
Perth	d																						
Stirling	d																						
Glasgow Central	d			12 51																			
Motherwell	d			13 12																			
Haymarket	d																						
Edinburgh	a			13 55																			
Edinburgh	d			14 08	14 30					15 00						15 08	15 30				16 00		
Dunbar	d															15 28							
Berwick-upon-Tweed	d			14 49	15 11												16 11						
Alnmouth for Alnwick	d																						
Morpeth	d					15 49												16 49					
Newcastle	a			15 35	15 56	16 13				16 23						16 35	16 56	17 14			17 23		
Sunderland	d																						
Hartlepool	d																						
Newcastle	d			15 41	15 58			16 15		16 25	16 35					16 41	16 58			17 02	17 25	17 32	
Chester-le-Street	d							16 24												17 11		17 41	
Durham	d			15 53				16 31		16 38	16 47					16 52				17 18	17 38	17 48	
Darlington	a			16 10	16 25			16 46		16 55	17 03					17 09	17 25			17 34	17 55	18 03	
Middlesbrough	d						15 50												16 50				
Eaglescliffe	d																						
Darlington	d			16 11	16 26			16 48		16 56	17 04					17 10	17 26			17 35	17 56	18 05	
Northallerton	d						16 18	16 59		17 07									17 18	17 46	18 07		
Thirsk	d						16 28												17 28				
York	a			16 41	16 53		16 47	17 23		17 27	17 31					17 41	17 53		17 47	18 09	18 27	18 31	
Leeds	a			17 08			17 22	17 52								18 08			18 22	18 37			
Harrogate	d																						
Scarborough	d													16 23	17 03								
York	d				16 55					17 29	17 34				17 50		17 55				18 29	18 34	
Doncaster	a									17 52	17 57				18 11						18 52	18 57	
Skipton	d																						
Keighley	d																						
Bradford Interchange	d	15 22																					
Bradford Forster Square	d																						
Shipley	d																						
Halifax	d	15 35																					
Brighouse	d	15 46																					
Leeds	d		17 05	17 11									18 05			18 11							
Wakefield Westgate	d		17 17	17 23									18 17			18 23							18 29
Wakefield Kirkgate	d	16 11																					18a33
Pontefract Monkhill	d	16 29																					
Sheffield	a			17 51							18 20				18 44	18 51						19 21	
Hull	d													17 52									
Selby	d													18 26									
Doncaster	d	17 03	17 35							17 53			18 35	18a47							18 53		
Retford	d									18 07													
Lincoln	d																						
Newark North Gate	a		17 59										19 02								19 17		
	d		17 59										19 02								19 17		
Grantham	a		18 11										19 15										
	d		18 11						18 15			19 08	19 15										
Peterborough	a		18 31						18 45	18 49		19 39	19 35								19 47		
Norwich	a								20 21			21 14											
Peterborough	d		18 32							18 50			19 35								19 49		
Stevenage	a		19 01																				
London Kings Cross ⊖	a	18 45	19 30		18 55					19 46			20 30				19 55				20 46		

Table 26

Saturdays
6 August to 10 September

Scotland, North East England, Yorkshire and Humberside - London

		HT	GR	XC	GR	SR	TP	GC	NT	GR	XC	NT	GR	XC	TP	NT	TP	GR	TP	NT	NT	XC
		◇1	1	◇1	1		◇1	1		1	◇1		1	◇1	◇1		◇1	1	◇1			◇1
				A										B								
Aberdeen	d																	14 50				
Stonehaven	d																	15 07				
Montrose	d																	15 30				
Arbroath	d																	15 46				
Dundee	d																	16 04				
Leuchars 3	d																	16 18				
Kirkcaldy	d																	16 45				
Inverkeithing	d																	17 01				
Inverness	d																					
Perth	d																					
Stirling	d																					
Glasgow Central 15	d			15 00		15 14																
Motherwell	d			15 14		15 36																
Haymarket	d			15 56		16 34												17 20				
Edinburgh 10	a			16 01		16 39												17 26				
Edinburgh	d			16 05	16 30	16 41				17 00				17 08				17 30				
Dunbar	d													17 28				17 50				
Berwick-upon-Tweed	d				17 11									17 51				18 15				
Alnmouth for Alnwick	d			17 01						17 58											18 48	
Morpeth	d			17 16					17 52											18 50	19 13	
Newcastle 8	a			17 34	17 56				18 15	18 27				18 40				19 01		19 13	19 36	
Sunderland	d							17 29														
Hartlepool	d							17 53														
Newcastle 8	d			17 43	17 58					18 28	18 35			18 44			18 52	19 03				19 17
Chester-le-Street	d																19 01					
Durham	d			17 55						18 41	18 48			18 56			19 08					19 29
Darlington 7	a			18 12	18 25					18 59	19 04			19 12			19 23	19 31				19 45
Middlesbrough	d						17 50								18 50							
Eaglescliffe	d							18 12														
Darlington 7	d			18 13	18 26					18 59	19 05			19 13			19 25	19 32				19 46
Northallerton	d						18 18	18 31							19 18		19 36					
Thirsk	d						18 28	18 41							19 26				←			
York 8	a			18 41	18 53		18 47	18 58		19 28	19 31			19 41	19 52		20 07	20 00	20 07			20 13
Leeds 10	a			19 08			19 35							20 08			→		20 35			
Harrogate	d																					
Scarborough	d																					
York 8	d				18 55			19 01		19 29	19 34							20 01				20 23
Doncaster 7	a									19 53	19 57							20 25				
Skipton	d																					
Keighley	d																					
Bradford Interchange	d																					
Bradford Forster Square	d																					
Shipley	d																					
Halifax	d																					
Brighouse	d																					
Leeds 10	d		19 05	19 11									20 05	20 11								
Wakefield Westgate 7	d		19 17	19 24								19 41	20 17	20 23		20 50						
Wakefield Kirkgate 4	d											19a43				20a52						
Pontefract Monkhill	d																					
Sheffield 7	a			19 51							20 20			20 52								21 20
Hull	d	18 30																				
Selby	d	19 05																				
Doncaster 7	d	19 27	19 36							19 54			20 35					20 25				
Retford 10	d												→									
Lincoln	d																					
Newark North Gate 7	a		20 00																			
	d		20 00																			
Grantham 7	a	19 57	20 12							20 26								20 58				
	d	19 57	20 12							20 26								20 58				
Peterborough 8	a		20 32							20 48								21 19				
Norwich	a																					
Peterborough 8	d		20 33							20 49								21 21				
Stevenage 4	a		21 02															21 54				
London Kings Cross 15 ⊖	a	21 05	21 31		20 55			20 56		21 46								22 24				

A from Edinburgh
B to York

Table 26

Saturdays
6 August to 10 September

Scotland, North East England, Yorkshire and Humberside - London

		XC	GR	TP	GR	SR	EM	GR	EM	NT	NT	TP	NT	NT	NT	NT
		◇1	1	◇1	1			1	◇			◇1				
		A														
Aberdeen	d															
Stonehaven	d															
Montrose	d															
Arbroath	d															
Dundee	d															
Leuchars 3	d															
Kirkcaldy	d					18 44										
Inverkeithing	d					19 00										
Inverness	d															
Perth	d															
Stirling	d															
Glasgow Central 15	d	16 52														
Motherwell	d	17 14														
Haymarket	d	17 56				19 15										
Edinburgh 10	a	18 01				19 21										
Edinburgh	d	18 05	18 30		19 00	19 22										
Dunbar	d	18 25			19 20											
Berwick-upon-Tweed	d	18 48	19 11		19 45											
Alnmouth for Alnwick	d	19 08			20 07											
Morpeth	d				20 24					21 15						
Newcastle 8	a	19 41	20 01		20 41					21 39						
Sunderland	d															
Hartlepool	d															
Newcastle 8	d	19 44			20 42								21 50			
Chester-le-Street	d												21 59			
Durham	d	19 56			20 55								22 08			
Darlington 7	a	20 12			21 14								22 29			
Middlesbrough	d			20 10								21 50				
Eaglescliffe	d												22a43			
Darlington 7	d	20 13			21 14							22 19				
Northallerton	d			20 39	21 26							22 30				
Thirsk	d			20 47								22 38				
York 8	a	20 42		21 06	21 46							22 57				
Leeds 10	a	21 08		21 37								23 33				
Harrogate	d															
Scarborough	d															
York 8	d				21 47											
Doncaster 7	a				22 16											
Skipton	d															
Keighley	d															
Bradford Interchange	d															
Bradford Forster Square	d															
Shipley	d															
Halifax	d															
Brighouse	d															
Leeds 10	d	21 11														
Wakefield Westgate 7	d	21 23									21 41			21 57	22 42	23 04
Wakefield Kirkgate 4	d										21a44			22 00	22a45	23 07
Pontefract Monkhill	d													22a18		23a29
Sheffield 7	a	21 51														
Hull	d															
Selby	d							←								
Doncaster 7	d						20 33	20 35								
Retford 10	d							20 50								
Lincoln	d						21a26									
Newark North Gate 7	a							21 05								
	d							21 05								
Grantham 7	a															
	d								21 07							
Peterborough 8	a							21 33	21 36							
Norwich	a								23 20							
Peterborough 8	d							21 35								
Stevenage 4	a															
London Kings Cross 15 ⊖	a							22 30								

A from Edinburgh to York

Table 26

Saturdays
from 17 September

Scotland, North East England, Yorkshire and Humberside - London

		SR	GR	GR	EM	GR	GR	TP	XC	GR	NT	XC	NT	EM	FC	GR	XC	GR	GR	GR	TP	XC	TP
Aberdeen	d			18p16																			
Stonehaven	d			18p33																			
Montrose	d			18p56																			
Arbroath	d			19p12																			
Dundee	d			19p30																			
Leuchars 3	d			19p44																			
Kirkcaldy	d			20p08																			
Inverkeithing	d			20p24																			
Inverness	d	20p46																					
Perth	d	23b21																					
Stirling	d	00u06																					
Glasgow Central 15	d																						
Motherwell	d																						
Haymarket	d			20p43																			
Edinburgh 10	a	01 00		20p48																			
Edinburgh	d			21p00																			
Dunbar	d			21p21																			
Berwick-upon-Tweed	d			21p47																			
Alnmouth for Alnwick	d			22p10																			
Morpeth	d			22p26																			
Newcastle 8	a			22p43																			
Sunderland	d												06 28										
Hartlepool	d												06a54										
Newcastle 8	d		21p15	22p44			04 40											06 00			06 11	06 22	
Chester-le-Street	d																				06 21		
Durham	d		21p27	23p00			04 54											06 12			06 28	06 37	
Darlington 7	a		21p45	23p19			05 11											06 30			06 44	06 52	
Middlesbrough	d							05 55															
Eaglescliffe	d																						
Darlington 7	d		21p46	23p19			05 12											06 30			06 45	06 54	
Northallerton	d		21p57	23c46			05 31	06 23													06 56		
Thirsk	d							06 31													07 04		←
York 8	a		22p17	00 13			05 57	06 49										06 58			07 30	07 21	07 30
Leeds 10	a			00 50				07 20													→		08 04
Harrogate	d																						
Scarborough	d																						
York 8	d		22p19				06 00										06 40	07 00				07 24	
Doncaster 7	a		22p42				06 22											07 23				07 49	
Skipton	d																						
Keighley	d																						
Bradford Interchange	d																						
Bradford Forster Square	d																						
Shipley	d																						
Halifax	d																						
Brighouse	d																						
Leeds 10	d					05 05			06 00	06 05		06 15		06 34		07 05	07 10						
Wakefield Westgate 7	d					05 17			06 12	06 17	06 24	06 29		06 46		07 17	07 23						
Wakefield Kirkgate 4	d										06 29												
Pontefract Monkhill	d										06a46												
Sheffield 7	a								06 45					07 22			07 51					08 18	
Hull	d																			06 50			
Selby	d																		←	07 24			
Doncaster 7	d		22p42			05 35	06 23			06 35		06a46				07 35		07 24	07 35	07 43			
Retford 10	d					05 49				06 49						→							
Lincoln	d																						
Newark North Gate 7	a		23p06			06 04				07 04									07 59				
	d		23p06			06 04				07 04									07 59				
Grantham 7	a		23p18			06 17				07 17									08 11	08 16			
	d		23p18		05 51	06 17				07 17									08 11	08 17			
Peterborough 8	a		23p39		06 25	06 36	07 10			07 36								08 13	08 31	08 38			
Norwich	a																						
Peterborough 8	d		23p39			06 38	07 12			07 37					08 08			08 14	08 31	08 39			
Stevenage 4	a		00s20			07 06				08 06									09 00				
London Kings Cross 15 ⊖	a		00 59			07 37	08 10			08 36					09 12			09 12	09 30	09 38			

b Previous night, stops to pick up only
c Previous night, stops to set down only

Table 26

Saturdays
from 17 September

Scotland, North East England, Yorkshire and Humberside - London

		GR	EM	EM	GR	GR	XC	GR	GC	TP	FC	GC	GR	EM	GR	XC	GR	HT	EM	GR	TP	XC	TP
Aberdeen	d																						
Stonehaven	d																						
Montrose	d																						
Arbroath	d																						
Dundee	d																						
Leuchars 3	d																						
Kirkcaldy	d																						
Inverkeithing	d																						
Inverness	d																						
Perth	d																						
Stirling	d																						
Glasgow Central 15	d																						
Motherwell	d																						
Haymarket	d																						
Edinburgh 10	a																						
Edinburgh	d																					06 06	
Dunbar	d																						
Berwick-upon-Tweed	d																					06 48	
Alnmouth for Alnwick	d																					07 08	
Morpeth	d																						
Newcastle 8	a																					07 38	
Sunderland	d											06 43											
Hartlepool	d											07 09											
Newcastle 8	d	06 30					06 45	06 55							07 24	07 30					07 33	07 44	
Chester-le-Street	d																				07 42		
Durham	d	06 42					06 57	07 07							07 36	07 43					07 49	07 56	
Darlington 7	a	07 00					07 13	07 25							07 54	08 00					08 05	08 12	
Middlesbrough	d									07 12													
Eaglescliffe	d											07 30											
Darlington 7	d	07 01					07 14	07 26							07 54	08 02					08 06	08 13	
Northallerton	d	07 12								07 42		07 48			08 06						08 17		
Thirsk	d									07 50		07 57									08 25		←
York 8	a	07 32					07 40	07 53		08 08		08 14			08 27	08 31					08 47	08 41	08 47
Leeds 10	a						08 08			08 52											→	09 07	09 22
Harrogate	d																			08 13			
Scarborough	d																						
York 8	d	07 34						07 55				08 16			08 28	08 34							
Doncaster 7	a	07 56						08 17							08 53	08 57							
Skipton	d				06 55																		
Keighley	d				07u08																		
Bradford Interchange	d								06 51														
Bradford Forster Square	d					07 33																	
Shipley	d				07u18	07u39																	
Halifax	d								07 04														
Brighouse	d								07 17														
Leeds 10	d		07 34		07 35	08 05	08 12										08 40			09 05		09 11	
Wakefield Westgate 7	d		07 46			08 17	08 24										08 52			09 17		09 24	
Wakefield Kirkgate 4	d								07 38														
Pontefract Monkhill	d								07 58														
Sheffield 7	a		08 21				08 51									09 20						09 52	
Hull	d																	08 25					
Selby	d												←					09 00					
Doncaster 7	d	07 57			08 09	08 35		08 18	08 31				08 35		08 53		09 13	09 23		09 35			
Retford 10	d					→							08 52					09 38					
Lincoln	d																						
Newark North Gate 7	a	08 21											09 08		09 18					09 59			
	d	08 21											09 08		09 18					10 00			
Grantham 7	a				08 42										09 30			09 59		10 12			
	d			08 20	08 42									09 03	09 30			09 59	10 08	10 13			
Peterborough 8	a	08 50		08 58									09 35	09 41			09 58		10 37	10 33			
Norwich	a			10 43										11 15					12 18				
Peterborough 8	d	08 50									09 07		09 36				09 59			10 33			
Stevenage 4	a																			11 03			
London Kings Cross 15 ⊖	a	09 48			09 53			09 57	10 09		10 10	10 15	10 30		10 46		10 54	11 09		11 33			

Table 26

Saturdays from 17 September

Scotland, North East England, Yorkshire and Humberside - London

		SR	GR	SR	NT	FC	GR	GR	XC	EM	EM	GR	XC	GR	NT	TP	GC	TP	FC	GR	XC	HT
			■ 1 ⊡✕			1	■ 1 ⊡✕	■ 1 ⊡✕	◇1 ✕		◇	■ 1 ⊡✕	◇1 A ✕	■ 1 ⊡✕		◇1 ✕	■ 1 ⊡	◇1 ✕	1	■ 1 ⊡✕	◇1 ✕	◇1 ⊠
Aberdeen	d																					
Stonehaven	d																					
Montrose	d																					
Arbroath	d																					
Dundee	d																					
Leuchars 3	d																					
Kirkcaldy	d																					
Inverkeithing	d																					
Inverness	d																					
Perth	d																					
Stirling	d																					
Glasgow Central 15	d												06 01							06 50		
Motherwell	d												06 16							07 05		
Haymarket	d	06 14		06 33									06 54							07 46		
Edinburgh 10	a	06 18		06 39									07 01							07 52		
Edinburgh	d	06 20	06 20	06 41				06 55	07 00				07 07	07 30						08 00		
Dunbar	d		06 40										07 27									
Berwick-upon-Tweed	d		07 05						07 40					08 12								
Alnmouth for Alnwick	d		07 25		07 22				08 00											08 58		
Morpeth	d		07 41		07 55				08 14						08 49							
Newcastle 8	a		07 58		08 20			08 22	08 32				08 37	08 57	09 14					09 27		
Sunderland	d																08 30					
Hartlepool	d																08 54					
Newcastle 8	d		07 59					08 25	08 36				08 45	08 59				09 15		09 28	09 35	
Chester-le-Street	d																	09 24				
Durham	d							08 37	08 48				08 57					09 31		09 41	09 47	
Darlington 7	a		08 27					08 55	09 04				09 13	09 25				09 47		09 59	10 04	
Middlesbrough	d															08 50						
Eaglescliffe	d																09 17					
Darlington 7	d		08 27					08 56	09 05				09 14	09 26				09 48		09 59	10 05	
Northallerton	d							09 07								09 18	09 40	09 59				
Thirsk	d															09 28	09 49					
York 8	a		08 55					09 27	09 32				09 43	09 54		09 47	10 06	10 21		10 28	10 31	
Leeds 10	a												10 09			10 22		10 52				
Harrogate	d																					
Scarborough	d																					
York 8	d		08 56					09 29	09 35					09 56			10 09			10 29	10 34	
Doncaster 7	a							09 52	09 57											10 52	10 57	
Skipton	d																					
Keighley	d																					
Bradford Interchange	d																					
Bradford Forster Square	d																					
Shipley	d																					
Halifax	d																					
Brighouse	d																					
Leeds 10	d											10 05	10 12									
Wakefield Westgate 7	d											10 17	10 24									
Wakefield Kirkgate 4	d																					
Pontefract Monkhill	d																					
Sheffield 7	a								10 20				10 51								11 20	
Hull	d																					10 30
Selby	d																					11 05
Doncaster 7	d							09 52		10 24		10 35								10 52		11 25
Retford 10	d							10 07														11 40
Lincoln	d						09 30			11a16												
Newark North Gate 7	a						09 52					10 59								11 18		
	d						09 53					10 59								11 18		
Grantham 7	a							10 29				11 11										12 00
	d							10 29			11 10	11 13										12 00
Peterborough 8	a		10 04				10 23	10 50			11 39	11 35								11 47		
Norwich	a										13 13											
Peterborough 8	d		10 06			10 08	10 23	10 50				11 35							11 08	11 49		
Stevenage 4	a						10 54															
London Kings Cross 15 ⊖	a		11 00			11 11	11 26	11 46				12 30		11 56			12 07		12 11	12 46		13 07

A ✕ from Edinburgh

Table 26

Saturdays from 17 September

Scotland, North East England, Yorkshire and Humberside - London

		EM	GR	XC	GR	SR	NT	TP	TP	FC	GR	GC	XC	EM	GR	XC	GR	NT	TP	TP	FC	GR	XC
		◇	■ 1 ⊡✕	◇1 A ✕	■ 1 ⊡✕			◇1 ✕	◇1 ✕	1	■ 1 ⊡✕	■ 1 ⊡	◇1 ✕	◇	■ 1 ⊡✕	◇1 A ✕	■ 1 ⊡✕		◇1 ✕	◇1 ✕	1	■ 1 ⊡✕	◇1 ✕
Aberdeen	d																						
Stonehaven	d																						
Montrose	d																						
Arbroath	d																						
Dundee	d			06 32																			
Leuchars 3	d			06 46																			
Kirkcaldy	d			07 21																			
Inverkeithing	d			07 38																			
Inverness	d																						
Perth	d																						
Stirling	d																						
Glasgow Central 15	d					07 03										07 50							
Motherwell	d					07 27										08 05							
Haymarket	d			07 56		08 26										08 50							
Edinburgh 10	a			08 01		08 33										08 54							
Edinburgh	d			08 05	08 30	08 40					09 00					09 06	09 30					10 00	
Dunbar	d															09 26							
Berwick-upon-Tweed	d			08 46												09 49	10 11						
Alnmouth for Alnwick	d																					10 58	
Morpeth	d						09 49											10 49					
Newcastle 8	a			09 35	09 55		10 13				10 23					10 38	10 57	11 13				11 27	
Sunderland	d																						
Hartlepool	d																						
Newcastle 8	d			09 41	09 58				10 17		10 25		10 35			10 44	10 59			11 15		11 28	11 35
Chester-le-Street	d																			11 24			
Durham	d			09 55					10 31		10 38		10 47			10 56				11 31		11 41	11 47
Darlington 7	a			10 10	10 26				10 46		10 55		11 03			11 12	11 27			11 46		11 59	12 04
Middlesbrough	d							09 50											10 50				
Eaglescliffe	d																						
Darlington 7	d			10 12	10 27				10 48		10 56		11 04			11 13	11 28			11 48		11 59	12 05
Northallerton	d							10 18	10 59		11 07								11 18	11 59			
Thirsk	d							10 28											11 28				
York 8	a			10 41	10 55			10 47	11 23		11 27		11 31			11 41	11 56		11 47	12 21		12 28	12 31
Leeds 10	a			11 08				11 22	11 52							12 08			12 22	12 52			
Harrogate	d																						
Scarborough	d																						
York 8	d				10 56						11 29		11 34				11 57					12 29	12 34
Doncaster 7	a										11 52		11 57									12 52	12 57
Skipton	d																						
Keighley	d																						
Bradford Interchange	d											10 22											
Bradford Forster Square	d																						
Shipley	d																						
Halifax	d											10 38											
Brighouse	d											10 49											
Leeds 10	d		11 05	11 11											12 05	12 11							
Wakefield Westgate 7	d		11 17	11 23											12 17	12 24							
Wakefield Kirkgate 4	d											11 11											
Pontefract Monkhill	d											11 35											
Sheffield 7	a			11 51									12 20			12 51							13 20
Hull	d																						
Selby	d																						
Doncaster 7	d		11 35								11 54	12 05			12 35							12 52	
Retford 10	d										12 08												
Lincoln	d																						
Newark North Gate 7	a		11 59												13 02							13 17	
	d		11 59												13 02							13 17	
Grantham 7	a		12 11												13 14								
	d	12 07	12 11											13 10	13 14								
Peterborough 8	a	12 38	12 31								12 47			13 39	13 35							13 45	
Norwich	a	14 13												15 13									
Peterborough 8	d		12 32							12 06	12 50				13 36						13 08	13 49	
Stevenage 4	a		13 01																				
London Kings Cross 15 ⊖	a		13 30		12 55					13 11	13 45	13 46			14 30		13 55				14 10	14 46	

A ✕ from Edinburgh

Table 26

Saturdays
from 17 September

Scotland, North East England, Yorkshire and Humberside - London

		EM	EM	GR	XC	GR	NT	TP	TP	GR	XC	HT	EM	GR	XC	GR	NT	TP	GC	TP	GR	XC
			◇	■ 1	◇1	■ 1		◇1	◇1	■ 1	◇1	◇1	◇	■ 1	◇1	■ 1		◇1	■ 1	◇1	■ 1	◇1
					A										A	B						
				⌶	⌶	⌶		⌶	⌶	⌶	⌶	⊠		⌶	⌶	⌶		⌶	⌶	⌶	⌶	⌶
Aberdeen	d					07 52									08 20							
Stonehaven	d					08 09									08 38							
Montrose	d					08 32									08 59							
Arbroath	d					08 48									09 15							
Dundee	d					09 06									09 32							
Leuchars 3	d					09 20									09 47							
Kirkcaldy	d					09 44									10 17							
Inverkeithing	d					10 01									10 32							
Inverness	d															07 55						
Perth	d															09 56						
Stirling	d															10 30						
Glasgow Central 15	d				09 00																	
Motherwell	d				09 15																	
Haymarket	d				09 57	10 21									10 52	11 11						
Edinburgh 10	a				10 02	10 26									10 58	11 17						
Edinburgh	d				10 05	10 30				11 00					11 05	11 30					12 00	
Dunbar	d														11 25							
Berwick-upon-Tweed	d				10 48										11 48						12 41	
Alnmouth for Alnwick	d														12 08							
Morpeth	d				11 19		11 49										12 49					
Newcastle 8 ⇌	a				11 38	11 55	12 13			12 23					12 38	12 55	13 13				13 26	
Sunderland ⇌	d																		12 18			
Hartlepool	d																		12 43			
Newcastle 8 ⇌	d				11 42	11 56			12 17	12 25	12 35				12 44	12 56				13 15	13 28	13 35
Chester-le-Street	d																			13 24		
Durham	d				11 55				12 29	12 38	12 47				12 56					13 31	13 41	13 47
Darlington 7	a				12 11	12 25			12 45	12 55	13 03				13 12	13 24				13 46	13 59	14 04
Middlesbrough	d							11 50										12 50				
Eaglescliffe	d																		13 05			
Darlington 7	d				12 12	12 25			12 46	12 56	13 04				13 13	13 24				13 48	13 59	14 05
Northallerton	d							12 18	12 58	13 07								13 18	13 27	13 59		
Thirsk	d							12 28										13 28	13 41			
York 8	a				12 42	12 53		12 47	13 21	13 27	13 31				13 41	13 53		13 47	13 57	14 24	14 28	14 31
Leeds 10	a				13 08			13 22	13 52						14 09			14 22		14 52		
Harrogate	d																					
Scarborough	d																					
York 8	d					12 55				13 29	13 34					13 55			14 00		14 29	14 34
Doncaster 7	a									13 52	13 57										14 53	14 57
Skipton	d																					
Keighley	d																					
Bradford Interchange	d																					
Bradford Forster Square	d																					
Shipley	d																					
Halifax	d																					
Brighouse	d																					
Leeds 10	d			13 05	13 11									14 05	14 11							
Wakefield Westgate 7	d			13 17	13 23									14 17	14 24							
Wakefield Kirkgate 4	d																					
Pontefract Monkhill	d																					
Sheffield 7 ⇌	a				13 51						14 20				14 51							15 20
Hull	d											13 30										
Selby	d											14 06										
Doncaster 7	d	13 05		13 35						13 53		14 25		14 35							14 53	
Retford 10	d									14 07		14 40										
Lincoln	d	13a55																				
Newark North Gate 7	a			13 59										15 03							15 17	
	d			13 59										15 03							15 18	
Grantham 7	a			14 12								15 01		15 16								
	d		14 07	14 12								15 01	15 10	15 16								
Peterborough 8	a		14 41	14 31						14 47			15 39	15 35							15 47	
Norwich	a		16 15										17 13									
Peterborough 8	d			14 32						14 49				15 36							15 49	
Stevenage 4	a			15 01																		
London Kings Cross 15 ⊖	a			15 30		14 55				15 46		16 08		16 31		15 52			15 55		16 46	

A ⌶ from Edinburgh
B The Highland Chieftain

Table 26

Saturdays
from 17 September

Scotland, North East England, Yorkshire and Humberside - London

		EM	GR	EM	GR	XC	GR	NT	TP	TP	GR	XC	HT	EM	EM	GR	XC	GR	NT	TP	XC	TP	GR
			■ 1	◇	■ 1	◇1	■ 1		◇1	◇1	■ 1	◇1	◇1		◇	■ 1	◇1	■ 1		◇1	◇1	◇1	■ 1
						A	B																
			⌶		⌶	⌶	⌶		⌶	⌶	⌶	⌶	⊠			⌶	⌶	⌶		⌶	⌶	⌶	⌶
Aberdeen	d						09 52																
Stonehaven	d						10 09																
Montrose	d						10 32																
Arbroath	d						10 49																
Dundee	d						11 06																
Leuchars 3	d						11 20																
Kirkcaldy	d						11 44																
Inverkeithing	d						12 01																
Inverness	d																						
Perth	d																						
Stirling	d																						
Glasgow Central 15	d					10 59																	
Motherwell	d					11 14																	
Haymarket	d					11 56	12 19																
Edinburgh 10	a					12 02	12 25																
Edinburgh	d					12 09	12 30				13 00						13 08	13 30					14 00
Dunbar	d																13 29						
Berwick-upon-Tweed	d					12 48												14 11					
Alnmouth for Alnwick	d																14 09						14 58
Morpeth	d							13 49											14 49				
Newcastle 8 ⇌	a					13 35	13 55	14 13			14 23						14 39	14 56	15 13				15 27
Sunderland ⇌	d																						
Hartlepool	d																						
Newcastle 8 ⇌	d					13 44	13 56			14 18	14 25	14 35					14 44	14 58			15 03	15 15	15 28
Chester-le-Street	d																					15 24	
Durham	d					13 56				14 31	14 38	14 47					14 56				15 16	15 31	15 41
Darlington 7	a					14 12	14 25			14 46	14 55	15 03					15 12	15 25			15 31	15 46	15 59
Middlesbrough	d								13 50											14 50			
Eaglescliffe	d																						
Darlington 7	d					14 13	14 25			14 48	14 56	15 04					15 13	15 26			15 33	15 48	15 59
Northallerton	d								14 18	14 59	15 07									15 18		15 59	
Thirsk	d								14 28											15 28			
York 8	a					14 41	14 53		14 47	15 22	15 28	15 31					15 41	15 53		15 47	16 03	16 21	16 28
Leeds 10	a					15 08			15 22	15 52							16 08			16 22	16 32	16 52	
Harrogate	d																						
Scarborough	d																						
York 8	d						14 55				15 30	15 34						15 55					16 29
Doncaster 7	a										15 52	15 57											16 55
Skipton	d																						
Keighley	d																						
Bradford Interchange	d																						
Bradford Forster Square	d																						
Shipley	d																						
Halifax	d																						
Brighouse	d																						
Leeds 10	d		14 35		15 05	15 12										16 05	16 12				16 40		
Wakefield Westgate 7	d		14 47		15 17	15 24										16 17	16 24				16 52		
Wakefield Kirkgate 4	d																						
Pontefract Monkhill	d																						
Sheffield 7 ⇌	a					15 51						16 20					16 51				17 20		
Hull	d												15 30										
Selby	d												16 05										
Doncaster 7	d	15 07	15 11		15 35						15 53		16 23	16 27		16 35							16 56
Retford 10	d										16 07		16 38										
Lincoln	d	15a57												17a20									
Newark North Gate 7	a				15 59											16 59							17 19
	d				15 59											16 59							17 19
Grantham 7	a				16 12								16 59			17 11							
	d			16 07	16 12								16 59		17 10	17 13							
Peterborough 8	a		15 59	16 40	16 32						16 47				17 39	17 35							17 48
Norwich	a			18 18											19 21								
Peterborough 8	d		16 00		16 32						16 49					17 35							17 49
Stevenage 4	a				17 02																		
London Kings Cross 15 ⊖	a		16 55		17 32		17 00				17 46		18 07			18 30		17 55					18 44

A ⌶ from Edinburgh
B The Northern Lights

Scotland, North East England, Yorkshire and Humberside - London

		GC	GR	XC	GR	NT		TP	TP	EM	GR	XC	EM	EM	GR	XC		GR	NT	NT	NT	TP	TP	GR	XC
		■1	■1	◇1	■1			◇1	◇1	◇	■1	◇1	◇1	◇	■1	◇1		■1				◇1	◇1	■1	◇1
				A															B	C					
Aberdeen	d																								
Stonehaven	d																								
Montrose	d																								
Arbroath	d																								
Dundee	d																								
Leuchars 3	d																								
Kirkcaldy	d																								
Inverkeithing	d																								
Inverness	d																								
Perth	d																								
Stirling	d																								
Glasgow Central 15	d			12 51																					
Motherwell	d			13 12																					
Haymarket	d																								
Edinburgh 10	a			13 55																					
Edinburgh	d			14 08	14 30						15 00					15 08		15 30						16 00	
Dunbar	d															15 28									
Berwick-upon-Tweed	d			14 49	15 11													16 11							
Alnmouth for Alnwick	d																								
Morpeth	d					15 49															16 49				
Newcastle 8	a			15 35	15 56	16 13					16 23					16 35		16 56			17 14			17 23	
Sunderland	d																								
Hartlepool	d																								
Newcastle 8	d			15 41	15 58				16 15		16 25	16 35				16 41		16 58					17 02	17 25	17 32
Chester-le-Street	d								16 24														17 11		17 41
Durham	d			15 53					16 31		16 38	16 47				16 52							17 18	17 38	17 48
Darlington 7	a			16 10	16 25				16 46		16 55	17 03				17 09		17 25					17 34	17 55	18 03
Middlesbrough	d							15 50														16 50			
Eaglescliffe	d																								
Darlington 7	d			16 11	16 26				16 48		16 56	17 04				17 10		17 26					17 35	17 56	18 05
Northallerton	d							16 18	16 59		17 07											17 18	17 46	18 07	
Thirsk	d							16 28														17 28			
York 8	a			16 41	16 53			16 47	17 23		17 27	17 31				17 41		17 53				17 47	18 09	18 27	18 31
Leeds 10	a			17 08				17 22	17 52							18 08						18 22	18 37		
Harrogate	d																								
Scarborough	d																		16 21	16 23					
York 8	d				16 55						17 29	17 34	17 50					17 55						18 29	18 34
Doncaster 7	a										17 52	17 57	18 11											18 52	18 57
Skipton	d																								
Keighley	d																								
Bradford Interchange	d	15 22																							
Bradford Forster Square	d																								
Shipley	d																								
Halifax	d	15 35																							
Brighouse	d	15 46																							
Leeds 10	d		17 05	17 11											18 05	18 11									
Wakefield Westgate 7	d		17 17	17 23											18 17	18 23									
Wakefield Kirkgate 4	d	16 11																							
Pontefract Monkhill	d	16 29																							
Sheffield 7	a			17 51								18 20	18 44			18 51									19 21
Hull	d																		17 52	17 52					
Selby	d																		18 26	18 26					
Doncaster 7	d	17 03	17 35								17 53				18 35				18a47	18a47				18 53	
Retford 10	d										18 07														
Lincoln	d																								
Newark North Gate 7	a		17 59												19 02									19 17	
	d		17 59												19 02									19 17	
Grantham 7	a		18 11												19 15										
	d		18 11							18 15				19 08	19 15										
Peterborough 8	a		18 31							18 45	18 49			19 39	19 35									19 47	
Norwich	a									20 21				21 14											
Peterborough 8	d		18 32								18 50				19 35									19 49	
Stevenage 4	a		19 01																						
London Kings Cross 15 ⊖	a	18 45	19 30		18 55						19 46				20 30			19 55						20 46	

A from Edinburgh
B from 8 October
C 17 September, 24 September, 1 October

Table 26

Saturdays
from 17 September

Scotland, North East England, Yorkshire and Humberside - London

		NT		HT	GR	XC	GR	SR	TP	GC	NT	GR		XC	NT	GR	XC	TP	NT	TP	GR	TP		NT	NT
				◇1	■1	◇1	■1		◇1	■1		■1		◇1		■1	◇1	◇1		◇1	■1	◇1			
						A											B								
Aberdeen	d																				14 50				
Stonehaven	d																				15 07				
Montrose	d																				15 30				
Arbroath	d																				15 46				
Dundee	d																				16 04				
Leuchars 3	d																				16 18				
Kirkcaldy	d																				16 45				
Inverkeithing	d																				17 01				
Inverness	d																								
Perth	d																								
Stirling	d																								
Glasgow Central 15	d					15 00		15 14																	
Motherwell	d					15 14		15 36																	
Haymarket	d					15 56		16 34													17 20				
Edinburgh 10	a					16 01		16 39													17 26				
Edinburgh	d					16 05	16 30	16 41				17 00					17 08				17 30				
Dunbar	d																17 28				17 50				
Berwick-upon-Tweed	d						17 11										17 51				18 15				
Alnmouth for Alnwick	d					17 01						17 58													18 48
Morpeth	d					17 16					17 52													18 50	19 13
Newcastle 8	a					17 34	17 56				18 15	18 27					18 40				19 01			19 13	19 36
Sunderland	d									17 29															
Hartlepool	d									17 53															
Newcastle 8	d					17 43	17 58					18 28		18 35			18 44			18 52	19 03				
Chester-le-Street	d																			19 01					
Durham	d					17 55						18 41		18 48			18 56			19 08					
Darlington 7	a					18 12	18 25					18 59		19 04			19 12			19 23	19 31				
Middlesbrough	d								17 50									18 50							
Eaglescliffe	d									18 12															
Darlington 7	d					18 13	18 26					18 59		19 05			19 13			19 25	19 32				
Northallerton	d								18 18	18 31								19 18		19 36					
Thirsk	d								18 28	18 41								19 26				←			
York 8	a					18 41	18 53		18 47	18 58		19 28		19 31			19 41	19 52		20 07	20 00	20 07			
Leeds 10	a					19 08			19 35								20 08			→		20 35			
Harrogate	d																								
Scarborough	d																								
York 8	d						18 55			19 01		19 29		19 34							20 01				
Doncaster 7	a											19 53		19 57							20 25				
Skipton	d																								
Keighley	d																								
Bradford Interchange	d																								
Bradford Forster Square	d																								
Shipley	d																								
Halifax	d																								
Brighouse	d																								
Leeds 10	d				19 05	19 11										20 05	20 11								
Wakefield Westgate 7	d	18 29			19 17	19 24									19 41	20 17	20 23		20 50						
Wakefield Kirkgate 4	d	18a33													19a43				20a52						
Pontefract Monkhill	d																								
Sheffield 7	a					19 51								20 20			20 52								
Hull	d			18 30																					
Selby	d			19 05																					
Doncaster 7	d			19 27	19 36							19 54				20 35					20 25				
Retford 10	d															→									
Lincoln	d																								
Newark North Gate 7	a				20 00																				
	d				20 00																				
Grantham 7	a			19 57	20 12							20 26									20 58				
	d			19 57	20 12							20 26									20 58				
Peterborough 8	a				20 32							20 48									21 19				
Norwich	a																								
Peterborough 8	d				20 33							20 49									21 21				
Stevenage 4	a				21 02																21 54				
London Kings Cross 15 ⊖	a			21 05	21 31		20 55			20 56		21 46									22 24				

A from Edinburgh
B to York

Table 26

Saturdays
from 17 September

Scotland, North East England, Yorkshire and Humberside - London

		XC	XC	GR	TP	GR	SR	EM		GR	EM	NT	NT	NT	TP	NT	NT	NT
				■		■				■								
		◇1	◇1	1	◇1	1				1	◇				◇1			
			A															
		⌶	⌶	⊡⌶		⊡⌶				⊡⌶								
Aberdeen	d																	
Stonehaven	d																	
Montrose	d																	
Arbroath	d																	
Dundee	d																	
Leuchars 3	d																	
Kirkcaldy	d						18 44											
Inverkeithing	d						19 00											
Inverness	d																	
Perth	d																	
Stirling	d																	
Glasgow Central 15	d		16 52															
Motherwell	d		17 14															
Haymarket	d		17 56				19 15											
Edinburgh 10	a		18 01				19 21											
Edinburgh	d		18 05	18 30		19 00	19 22											
Dunbar	d		18 25			19 20												
Berwick-upon-Tweed	d		18 48	19 11		19 45												
Alnmouth for Alnwick	d		19 08			20 07												
Morpeth	d					20 24						21 15						
Newcastle 8 ⇌	a		19 41	20 01		20 41						21 39						
Sunderland ⇌	d																	
Hartlepool	d																	
Newcastle 8 ⇌	d	19 17	19 44			20 42								21 50				
Chester-le-Street	d													21 59				
Durham	d	19 29	19 56			20 55								22 08				
Darlington 7	a	19 45	20 12			21 14								22 29				
Middlesbrough	d				20 10										21 50			
Eaglescliffe	d													22a43				
Darlington 7	d	19 46	20 13			21 14									22 19			
Northallerton	d				20 39	21 26									22 30			
Thirsk	d				20 47										22 38			
York 8	a	20 13	20 42		21 06	21 46									22 57			
Leeds 10	a		21 08		21 37										23 33			
Harrogate	d																	
Scarborough	d																	
York 8	d	20 23				21 47												
Doncaster 7	a					22 16												
Skipton	d																	
Keighley	d																	
Bradford Interchange	d																	
Bradford Forster Square	d																	
Shipley	d																	
Halifax	d																	
Brighouse	d																	
Leeds 10	d		21 11															
Wakefield Westgate 7	d		21 23										21 41			21 57	22 42	23 04
Wakefield Kirkgate 4	d												21a44			22 00	22a45	23 07
Pontefract Monkhill	d															22a18		23a29
Sheffield 7 ⇌	a	21 20	21 51															
Hull	d																	
Selby	d									⟵								
Doncaster 7	d							20 33		20 35								
Retford 10	d									20 50								
Lincoln	d							21a26										
Newark North Gate 7	a									21 05								
	d									21 05								
Grantham 7	a																	
	d										21 07							
Peterborough 8	a									21 33	21 36							
Norwich	a										23 20							
Peterborough 8	d									21 35								
Stevenage 4	a																	
London Kings Cross 15 ⊖	a									22 30								

A ⌶ from Edinburgh to York

Table 26

Sundays
until 19 June

Scotland, North East England, Yorkshire and Humberside - London

		NT	FC	GR	GR	GC	XC	XC	FC	GR		TP	GR	EM	EM	HT	XC	GR	GR	EM		XC	GR	TP	GC
				■	■	■				■			■					■	■				■		■
			1	1	1	◇1	◇1	◇1	1	1		◇1	1	◇1	◇	◇1	◇1	1	1	◇1		◇1	1	◇1	1
						A																			
		═		⊡⌶	⊡⌶	⊡	⌶	⌶		⊡⌶			⊡⌶	⊡		⊠	⌶	⊡⌶	⊡⌶	⊡		⌶	⊡⌶		⊡
Aberdeen	d																								
Stonehaven	d																								
Montrose	d																								
Arbroath	d																								
Dundee	d																								
Leuchars 3	d																								
Kirkcaldy	d																								
Inverkeithing	d																								
Inverness	d																								
Perth	d																								
Stirling	d																								
Glasgow Central 15	d																								
Motherwell	d																								
Haymarket	d																								
Edinburgh 10	a																								
Edinburgh	d																								
Dunbar	d																								
Berwick-upon-Tweed	d																								
Alnmouth for Alnwick	d																								
Morpeth	d																								
Newcastle 8 ⇌	a																								
Sunderland ⇌	d	09 12																							09 12
Hartlepool	d																								09 36
Newcastle 8 ⇌	d	09a50								07 55		08 00						08 55				09 20	09 25	09 31	
Chester-le-Street	d																							09 40	
Durham	d									08 07		08 13						09 07				09 33	09 37	09 47	
Darlington 7	a									08 25		08 30						09 24				09 48	09 54	10 03	
Middlesbrough	d																								
Eaglescliffe	d																								09 59
Darlington 7	d									08 25		08 30						09 25				09 50	09 55	10 04	
Northallerton	d											08 42											10 06	10 15	10 20
Thirsk	d											08 50													10 29
York 8	a									08 53		09 11						09 54				10 18	10 26	10 41	10 45
Leeds 10	a											09 38										10 51		11 08	
Harrogate	d																								
Scarborough	d																								
York 8	d			08 00						08 55							09 28	09 56					10 28		10 50
Doncaster 7	a			08 22																			10 51		
Skipton	d																								
Keighley	d																								
Bradford Interchange	d					07 55																			
Bradford Forster Square	d																								
Shipley	d																								
Halifax	d					08 09																			
Brighouse	d					08 20																			
Leeds 10	d				08 05		08 10	09 00					09 05	09 44			10 00		10 05	10 15		11 00			
Wakefield Westgate 7	d				08 17		08 23	09 11					09 17	09 57			10 12		10 17	10 28		11 12			
Wakefield Kirkgate 4	d					08 43																			
Pontefract Monkhill	d																								
Sheffield 7 ⇌	a						08 51							10 25						10 57					
Hull	d															09 30									
Selby	d															10 05									
Doncaster 7	d			08 23	08 35	09 06		09a31					09 35			10 24	10a28		10 35			11a28	10 52		
Retford 10	d			08 38												10 38			10 51						
Lincoln	d																								
Newark North Gate 7	a				08 57								09 58						11 05				11 14		
	d				08 58								09 58						11 05				11 14		
Grantham 7	a				09 10								10 10			10 58			11 18						
	d				09 11								10 10		10 29	10 58			11 18						
Peterborough 8	a			09 23	09 39					10 11			10 32		11 06			11 01	11 40				11 46		
Norwich	a														13 06										
Peterborough 8	d		09 15	09 24	09 40				10 15	10 17			10 32					11 01	11 41				11 49		
Stevenage 4	a												11 04			11s49									
London Kings Cross 15 ⊖	a		10 15	10 25	10 36	10 43			11 15	11 17			11 35			12 12		12 00	12 37				12 45		12 44

A ◇ from Doncaster ■ to Wakefield Kirkgate

Table 26

Sundays until 19 June

Scotland, North East England, Yorkshire and Humberside - London

		GR	TP	NT	NT	GR	XC	NT	EM	GR	GR	TP	HT	NT	EM	GR	XC	GR	GC	GR	TP	GR	GR
Aberdeen	d																						
Stonehaven	d																						
Montrose	d																						
Arbroath	d																						
Dundee	d																						
Leuchars 3	d																						
Kirkcaldy	d																						
Inverkeithing	d																						
Inverness	d																						
Perth	d																						
Stirling	d																						
Glasgow Central 15	d																						
Motherwell	d																						
Haymarket	d																						
Edinburgh 10	a																						
Edinburgh	d						08 50			09 00	09 30						09 50	10 00		10 30			10 55
Dunbar	d																						
Berwick-upon-Tweed	d						09 31				10 10									11 09			
Alnmouth for Alnwick	d																10 47	10 56					
Morpeth	d																11 02						12 05
Newcastle 8	a						10 19			10 25	10 57						11 19	11 27		11 56			12 23
Sunderland	d				10 30			11 50						12 50									
Hartlepool	d																						
Newcastle 8	d	10 00		10 04	11a10		10 24	12a30		10 28	10 59	11 08		13a30			11 25	11 28		11 58	12 10		12 25
Chester-le-Street	d																						
Durham	d						10 37			10 42		11 20					11 37	11 41			12 22		12 38
Darlington 7	a	10 25		10 37			10 53			10 59	11 25	11 36					11 54	11 59		12 24	12 38		12 55
Middlesbrough	d		10 13	11a03																			
Eaglescliffe	d																						
Darlington 7	d	10 26					10 54			11 00	11 26	11 37					11 55	11 59		12 25	12 39		12 56
Northallerton	d		10 41							11 12		11 49											13 07
Thirsk	d		10 49																				
York 8	a	10 53	11 10				11 24			11 33	11 54	12 12					12 23	12 28		12 53	13 11		13 28
Leeds 10	a		11 38				11 51					12 38					12 51				13 38		
Harrogate	d																						
Scarborough	d																						
York 8	d	10 55								11 35	11 56							12 30		12 55			13 30
Doncaster 7	a									11 59								12 53					13 53
Skipton	d																						
Keighley	d																						
Bradford Interchange	d																		11 42				
Bradford Forster Square	d																						
Shipley	d																						
Halifax	d																		11 55				
Brighouse	d																		12 06				
Leeds 10	d					11 05	12 00									12 05	13 00					13 05	
Wakefield Westgate 7	d					11 17	12 12									12 17	13 12					13 18	
Wakefield Kirkgate 4	d																		12 29				
Pontefract Monkhill	d																		12 46				
Sheffield 7	a																						
Hull	d												11 30										
Selby	d												12 05										
Doncaster 7	d					11 35	12a28			12 00			12 25			12 37	13a28	12 54	13 11			13 35	13 54
Retford 10	d									12 15			12 39										14 08
Lincoln	d																						
Newark North Gate 7	a					11 59										12 59		13 16				13 58	
	d					11 59										12 59		13 16				13 58	
Grantham 7	a					12 11							12 59			13 12						14 10	
	d					12 11			12 18				12 59		13 12	13 15						14 10	
Peterborough 8	a	12 00				12 33			12 50	12 55					13 41	13 38		13 46				14 32	14 48
Norwich	a								14 35						15 30								
Peterborough 8	d	12 00				12 34				12 56						13 38		13 49				14 32	14 49
Stevenage 4	a					13 07							13s47									15 05	
London Kings Cross 15 ⊖	a	12 56				13 35				13 53	13 56		14 12			14 34		14 46	14 48	14 57		15 35	15 45

Table 26

Sundays until 19 June

Scotland, North East England, Yorkshire and Humberside - London

		NT	EM	EM	GR	XC	TP	GR	TP	GR	GR	HT	GR	XC	GR	TP	GR	GR	XC	TP	GC	GR
															A				B			C
Aberdeen	d														09 48							
Stonehaven	d														10 05							
Montrose	d														10 28							
Arbroath	d														10 44							
Dundee	d														11 02							
Leuchars 3	d														11 16							
Kirkcaldy	d														11 40							
Inverkeithing	d														11 56							
Inverness	d																					09 40
Perth	d																					11 58
Stirling	d																					12 34
Glasgow Central 15	d																		11 52			
Motherwell	d																		12 07			
Haymarket	d														12 18				12 47			13 14
Edinburgh 10	a														12 25				12 52			13 19
Edinburgh	d					11 05		11 30			12 00			12 08	12 30			13 00	13 06			13 30
Dunbar	d					11 25													13 25			
Berwick-upon-Tweed	d					11 48		12 09						12 47								14 10
Alnmouth for Alnwick	d					12 08					12 56								14 06			
Morpeth	d																					
Newcastle 8	a					12 35		12 56			13 27			13 34	13 55			14 23	14 35			14 58
Sunderland	d	13 20																			14 12	
Hartlepool	d																				14 36	
Newcastle 8	d	14a00				12 38		12 58	13 04	13 12	13 28			13 40	13 56	14 08	14 12	14 25	14 40			15 00
Chester-le-Street	d								13 13													
Durham	d					12 50			13 20	13 24	13 41			13 52		14 20	14 24	14 38	14 52			
Darlington 7	a					13 06		13 25	13 36	13 41	13 59			14 09	14 24	14 36	14 42	14 55	15 08			15 27
Middlesbrough	d						12 45													14 42		
Eaglescliffe	d																				14 59	
Darlington 7	d					13 07		13 26	13 37	13 42	13 59			14 10	14 24	14 37	14 42	14 56	15 09			15 28
Northallerton	d						13 13			13 54						14 49	14 56			15 10	15 22	
Thirsk	d						13 21													15 18	15 31	
York 8	a					13 35	13 42	13 55	14 10	14 14	14 29			14 38	14 53	15 12	15 16	15 24	15 35	15 42	15 46	15 57
Leeds 10	a					14 03	14 08		14 38					15 05		15 38			16 03	16 08		
Harrogate	d																					
Scarborough	d																					
York 8	d							13 56		14 16	14 30				14 55		15 18	15 29			15 48	15 58
Doncaster 7	a									14 44	14 54						15 42	15 52				
Skipton	d																					
Keighley	d																					
Bradford Interchange	d																					
Bradford Forster Square	d																					
Shipley	d																					
Halifax	d																					
Brighouse	d																					
Leeds 10	d		13 59		14 05	14 10							15 05	15 10					16 10			
Wakefield Westgate 7	d		14 12		14 17	14 23							15 17	15 23					16 22			
Wakefield Kirkgate 4	d																					
Pontefract Monkhill	d																					
Sheffield 7	a		14 40			14 52								15 51					16 51			
Hull	d											14 30										
Selby	d											15 05										
Doncaster 7	d				14 35					14 44	14 54	15 24	15 35				15 43	15 54				
Retford 10	d											15 38						16 08				
Lincoln	d																					
Newark North Gate 7	a				14 58						15 17		15 58				16 07					
	d				14 58						15 17		15 58				16 07					
Grantham 7	a				15 10							15 58	16 10									
	d			14 22	15 10							15 58	16 10									
Peterborough 8	a			14 51	15 32					15 37	15 46		16 32				16 38	16 48				
Norwich	a			16 35																		
Peterborough 8	d				15 32					15 38	15 49		16 32				16 38	16 49				
Stevenage 4	a											16s46	17 04									
London Kings Cross 15 ⊖	a				16 27			15 57		16 35	16 46	17 12	17 35		16 55		17 39	17 45			17 46	17 59

A The Northern Lights

B from Edinburgh

C The Highland Chieftain

Table 26

Sundays until 19 June

Scotland, North East England, Yorkshire and Humberside - London

Station		NT	TP	NT	EM	GR	GR	GC	NT	EM	GR	XC	GR	TP	HT	GR	NT	EM	GR	GR	GR	EM	XC
												A											A
Aberdeen	d											11 12	11 47										
Stonehaven	d											11 29	12 04										
Montrose	d											11 50	12 27										
Arbroath	d											12 06	12 43										
Dundee	d											12 25	13 01										
Leuchars	d											12 38	13 15										
Kirkcaldy	d											13 03	13 39										
Inverkeithing	d											13 18	13 55										
Inverness	d																						
Perth	d																						
Stirling	d																						
Glasgow Central	d																						13 49
Motherwell	d																						14 04
Haymarket	d											13 37	14 19										14 43
Edinburgh	a											13 42	14 25										14 47
Edinburgh	d						14 00					14 08	14 30							15 00			15 07
Dunbar	d																						15 27
Berwick-upon-Tweed	d											14 47	15 09										
Alnmouth for Alnwick	d						14 56																
Morpeth	d																						
Newcastle	a						15 27					15 34	15 57							16 23			16 34
Sunderland	d	14 50		15 20					16 50								17 49						
Hartlepool	d																						
Newcastle	d	15a30	15 07	16a00			15 28		17a30			15 39	15 59	16 08		16 12	18a29			16 25			16 40
Chester-le-Street	d		15 16																				
Durham	d		15 23				15 41					15 51		16 20		16 24				16 38			16 52
Darlington	a		15 39				15 59					16 07	16 26	16 36		16 41				16 55			17 08
Middlesbrough	d																						
Eaglescliffe	d																						
Darlington	d		15 40				15 59					16 08	16 27	16 37		16 42				16 56			17 09
Northallerton	d													16 49		16 53							
Thirsk	d																						
York	a		16 13				16 28					16 35	16 56	17 12		17 16				17 24			17 38
Leeds	a		16 38									17 01		17 38									18 04
Harrogate	d																				17 05		
Scarborough	d																						
York	d						16 29						16 57			17 17				17 29		17 40	
Doncaster	a						16 54													17 52		18 05	
Skipton	d																						
Keighley	d																						
Bradford Interchange	d							15 42															
Bradford Forster Square	d																						
Shipley	d																						
Halifax	d							15 56															
Brighouse	d							16 06															
Leeds	d					16 15					16 45	17 10							17 15		17 45		18 10
Wakefield Westgate	d					16 28					16 57	17 22							17 28		17 58		18 22
Wakefield Kirkgate	d							16 29															
Pontefract Monkhill	d							16 46															
Sheffield	a											17 51										18 28	18 51
Hull	d														16 30								
Selby	d														17 05								
Doncaster	d					16 46	16 54	17 10			17 17				17 26				17 46	17 54	18 17		
Retford	d														17 40				18 00				
Lincoln	d																						
Newark North Gate	a						17 17				17 43					17 58					18 42		
	d						17 17				17 43					17 58					18 42		
Grantham	a					17 16									18 00				18 22	18 27			
	d				16 22	17 16				17 19					18 00			18 17	18 22	18 27			
Peterborough	a				16 55		17 46			17 50	18 14					18 27		18 46		18 51	19 13		
Norwich	a				18 31					19 29								20 29					
Peterborough	d						17 49				18 15					18 28				18 51	19 13		
Stevenage	a					18 04									18s51				19 10				
London Kings Cross ⊖	a					18 36	18 46	18 51			19 10		18 58		19 15	19 24			19 38	19 48	20 12		

A ⌶ from Edinburgh

Table 26

Sundays until 19 June

Scotland, North East England, Yorkshire and Humberside - London

Station		TP	GR	TP	GR	GR	EM	GR	XC	SR	TP	GR	TP	HT	GR	GR	GR	XC	TP	GC	GR	NT
									A									B				
Aberdeen	d											13 50										
Stonehaven	d											14 07										
Montrose	d											14 30										
Arbroath	d											14 46										
Dundee	d											15 04										
Leuchars	d											15 18										
Kirkcaldy	d											15 42										
Inverkeithing	d											15 58										
Inverness	d									20 25												
Perth	d									23u00												
Stirling	d									23u45												
Glasgow Central	d								14 55													
Motherwell	d								15 11													
Haymarket	d								15 51			16 20										
Edinburgh	a								15 56	00 47		16 25										
Edinburgh	d		15 30			16 00			16 05			16 30				17 00		17 07			17 30	
Dunbar	d								16 25									17 27			17 50	
Berwick-upon-Tweed	d		16 09									17 09						17 50			18 13	
Alnmouth for Alnwick	d					16 56			17 05													
Morpeth	d								17 20													
Newcastle	a		16 56			17 27			17 37			17 57				18 23		18 36			19 00	
Sunderland	d																			18 12		19 00
Hartlepool	d																			18 36		
Newcastle	d		16 58	17 05		17 28			17 40		17 52	17 59				18 25		18 38			19 02	19a40
Chester-le-Street	d			17 14																		
Durham	d			17 21		17 41			17 52		18 04					18 38		18 51				
Darlington	a		17 24	17 37		17 59			18 08		18 20	18 26				18 55		19 06			19 28	
Middlesbrough	d	16 42																	18 45			
Eaglescliffe	d																			18 59		
Darlington	d		17 25	17 38		17 59			18 09		18 21	18 27				18 56		19 08			19 29	
Northallerton	d	17 10		17 49							18 33					19 07			19 13	19 20		
Thirsk	d	17 18											←						19 21	19 29		
York	a	17 42	17 53	18 12		18 28			18 37		19 04	18 56	19 04			19 28		19 35	19 42	19 46	19 57	
Leeds	a	18 08		18 38					19 04		→		19 38					20 05	20 08			
Harrogate	d																					
Scarborough	d																					
York	d		17 55			18 29						18 57				19 30				19 48	19 59	
Doncaster	a					18 53										19 53						
Skipton	d																					
Keighley	d																					
Bradford Interchange	d																					
Bradford Forster Square	d																					
Shipley	d																					
Halifax	d																					
Brighouse	d																					
Leeds	d				18 15			18 45	19 10						19 15		19 45	20 10				
Wakefield Westgate	d				18 28			18 57	19 22						19 27		19 57	20 22				
Wakefield Kirkgate	d																					
Pontefract Monkhill	d																					
Sheffield	a								19 50									20 51				
Hull	d													18 30								
Selby	d													19 05								
Doncaster	d				18 46	18 53		19 17						19 26	19 45	19 54	20 20					
Retford	d													19 40	19 59							
Lincoln	d																					
Newark North Gate	a					19 16		19 43								20 17	20 43					
	d					19 16		19 44								20 17	20 43					
Grantham	a				19 16									20 00	20 21						20 47	
	d				19 16		19 27							20 00	20 21						20 48	
Peterborough	a					19 46	19 56	20 14								20 47	21 13				21 08	
Norwich	a						21 35															
Peterborough	d					19 49		20 15								20 49	21 13				21 09	
Stevenage	a				20 08									20s51	21 09							
London Kings Cross ⊖	a		19 54		20 36	20 46		21 11				20 58		21 14	21 37	21 46	22 12			21 48	22 05	

A ⌶ from Edinburgh

B ⌶ to York

Table 26

Sundays until 19 June

Scotland, North East England, Yorkshire and Humberside - London

		TP	GR	NT	EM	GR	XC	GR	TP	TP	NT	GR	NT	GR	XC	GR	TP
							A										
Aberdeen	d																
Stonehaven	d																
Montrose	d																
Arbroath	d																
Dundee	d																
Leuchars	d																
Kirkcaldy	d																
Inverkeithing	d																
Inverness	d																
Perth	d																
Stirling	d																
Glasgow Central	d						16 55								18 57		
Motherwell	d						17 11								19 11		
Haymarket	d						17 55								19 51		
Edinburgh	a						17 59								19 56		
Edinburgh	d		18 00				18 07	18 30				19 00		20 00	20 05	21 00	
Dunbar	d						18 26					19 21		20 21	20 29	21 21	
Berwick-upon-Tweed	d						18 50	19 09				19 44		20 44	20 53	21 44	
Alnmouth for Alnwick	d		18 56											21 07		22 06	
Morpeth	d													21 24			
Newcastle	a		19 27				19 34	19 56				20 30		21 42	21 48	22 37	
Sunderland	d			21 00													
Hartlepool	d																
Newcastle	d	19 10	19 28	21a40			19 40	19 58		20 08	20 11	20 32	21 06	21 44			
Chester-le-Street	d												21 15				
Durham	d	19 22	19 41				19 52			20 20		20 46	21 24	21 57			
Darlington	a	19 38	19 59				20 08	20 24		20 36		21 02	21 44	22 15			
Middlesbrough	d								20 06		21a16						22 06
Eaglescliffe	d												22a00				
Darlington	d	19 39	19 59				20 09	20 25		20 37		21 03		22 15			
Northallerton	d								20 38	20 49				22 29			22 34
Thirsk	d								20 46								22 42
York	a	20 11	20 28				20 36	20 53	21 06	21 12		21 31		23 02			23 09
Leeds	a	20 38					21 02			21 38				23 34			23 38
Harrogate	d																
Scarborough	d																
York	d		20 29					20 55				21 33					
Doncaster	a		20 53					21 18				21 56					
Skipton	d																
Keighley	d																
Bradford Interchange	d																
Bradford Forster Square	d																
Shipley	d																
Halifax	d																
Brighouse	d																
Leeds	d					20 45	21 10										
Wakefield Westgate	d					20 57	21 22										
Wakefield Kirkgate	d																
Pontefract Monkhill	d																
Sheffield	a						21 50										
Hull	d																
Selby	d																
Doncaster	d		20 53			21 15		21 19				21 57					
Retford	d					21 29											
Lincoln	d																
Newark North Gate	a		21 16					21 47				22 19					
	d		21 16					21 47				22 20					
Grantham	a					21 51		22 00				22 32					
	d				21 19	21 51		22 00				22 33					
Peterborough	a		21 45		21 49	22 12		22 21				22 53					
Norwich	a				23 28												
Peterborough	d		21 49			22 13		22 23				23 00					
Stevenage	a					22 45		22 54				23s34					
London Kings Cross	a		22 46			23 16		23 22				00 02					

A from Edinburgh to York

Table 26

Sundays 26 June to 31 July

Scotland, North East England, Yorkshire and Humberside - London

		GR	XC	FC	GR	GC	XC	FC	GR	TP	GR	EM	EM	HT	XC	GR	GR	EM	XC	GR	TP	GC	GR
						A																	
Aberdeen	d																						
Stonehaven	d																						
Montrose	d																						
Arbroath	d																						
Dundee	d																						
Leuchars	d																						
Kirkcaldy	d																						
Inverkeithing	d																						
Inverness	d																						
Perth	d																						
Stirling	d																						
Glasgow Central	d																						
Motherwell	d																						
Haymarket	d																						
Edinburgh	a																						
Edinburgh	d																						
Dunbar	d																						
Berwick-upon-Tweed	d																						
Alnmouth for Alnwick	d																						
Morpeth	d																						
Newcastle	a																						
Sunderland	d																					09 12	
Hartlepool	d																					09 36	
Newcastle	d								07 55	08 00						08 55			09 20	09 25	09 31		10 00
Chester-le-Street	d																				09 40		
Durham	d								08 07	08 13						09 07			09 33	09 37	09 47		
Darlington	a								08 25	08 30						09 24			09 48	09 54	10 03		10 25
Middlesbrough	d																						
Eaglescliffe	d																					09 59	
Darlington	d								08 25	08 30						09 25			09 50	09 55	10 04		10 26
Northallerton	d									08 42										10 06	10 15	10 20	
Thirsk	d									08 50												10 29	
York	a								08 53	09 11						09 54			10 18	10 26	10 41	10 45	10 53
Leeds	a									09 38									10 51		11 08		
Harrogate	d																						
Scarborough	d																						
York	d	08 00							08 55						09 28	09 56				10 28		10 50	10 55
Doncaster	a	08 22																		10 51			
Skipton	d																						
Keighley	d																						
Bradford Interchange	d					07 55																	
Bradford Forster Square	d																						
Shipley	d																						
Halifax	d					08 09																	
Brighouse	d					08 20																	
Leeds	d		08 10		08 25		09 00				09 05	09 44			10 00		10 05	10 15	11 00				
Wakefield Westgate	d		08 23		08 37		09 11				09 17	09 57			10 12		10 17	10 28	11 12				
Wakefield Kirkgate	d					08 43																	
Pontefract Monkhill	d																						
Sheffield	a		08 51									10 25						10 57					
Hull	d													09 30									
Selby	d													10 05									
Doncaster	d	08 23			08 55	09 06	09a31				09 35			10 24	10a28		10 35		11a28	10 52			
Retford	d	08 38												10 38			10 51						
Lincoln	d																						
Newark North Gate	a				09 17						09 58						11 05			11 14			
	d				09 17						09 58						11 05			11 14			
Grantham	a				09 30						10 10			10 58			11 18						
	d				09 31						10 10		10 29	10 58			11 18						
Peterborough	a	09 24			09 59				10 11		10 32		11 06			11 01	11 40			11 46			12 00
Norwich	a												13 06										
Peterborough	d	09 24		09 15	10 00			10 15	10 17		10 32					11 01	11 41			11 49			12 00
Stevenage	a				10 36						11 01			11s49									
London Kings Cross	a	10 25		10 58	11 07	11 11		11 20	11 20		11 37			12 12		12 00	12 39			12 45		12 46	12 56

A ◇ from Doncaster to Wakefield Kirkgate

Table 26

Sundays
26 June to 31 July

Scotland, North East England, Yorkshire and Humberside - London

		TP	GR	XC	EM	GR	GR	TP	HT	EM	GR	XC	GR	GC	GR	TP	GR	GR	EM	EM	GR	XC	TP
Aberdeen	d																						
Stonehaven	d																						
Montrose	d																						
Arbroath	d																						
Dundee	d																						
Leuchars 8	d																						
Kirkcaldy	d																						
Inverkeithing	d																						
Inverness	d																						
Perth	d																						
Stirling	d																						
Glasgow Central 15	d																						
Motherwell	d																						
Haymarket	d																						
Edinburgh 10	a																						
Edinburgh	d			08 50		09 00	09 30					09 50	10 00		10 30			10 55				11 05	
Dunbar	d																					11 25	
Berwick-upon-Tweed	d			09 31			10 10								11 09							11 48	
Alnmouth for Alnwick	d											10 47	10 56									12 08	
Morpeth	d											11 02						12 05					
Newcastle 8	a			10 19		10 25	10 57					11 19	11 27		11 56			12 23				12 35	
Sunderland	d																						
Hartlepool	d																						
Newcastle 8	d			10 24		10 28	10 59	11 08				11 25	11 28		11 58	12 10		12 25				12 38	
Chester-le-Street	d																						
Durham	d			10 37		10 42		11 20				11 37	11 41			12 22		12 38				12 50	
Darlington 7	a			10 53		10 59	11 25	11 36				11 54	11 59		12 24	12 38		12 55				13 06	
Middlesbrough	d	10 13																					12 45
Eaglescliffe	d																						
Darlington 7	d			10 54		11 00	11 26	11 37				11 55	11 59		12 25	12 39		12 56				13 07	
Northallerton	d	10 41				11 12		11 49										13 07					13 13
Thirsk	d	10 49																					13 21
York 8	a	11 11		11 24		11 33	11 54	12 12				12 23	12 28		12 53	13 11		13 28				13 35	13 42
Leeds 10	a	11 38		11 51				12 38				12 51				13 38						14 03	14 08
Harrogate	d																						
Scarborough	d																						
York 8	d					11 35	11 56						12 30		12 55			13 30					
Doncaster 7	a					11 59							12 53					13 53					
Skipton	d																						
Keighley	d																						
Bradford Interchange	d													11 42									
Bradford Forster Square	d																						
Shipley	d																						
Halifax	d													11 55									
Brighouse	d													12 06									
Leeds 10	d		11 05	12 00							12 05	13 00					13 05		13 59		14 05	14 10	
Wakefield Westgate 7	d		11 17	12 12							12 17	13 12					13 18		14 12		14 17	14 23	
Wakefield Kirkgate 4	d													12 29									
Pontefract Monkhill	d													12 46									
Sheffield 7	a																		14 40			14 52	
Hull	d								11 30														
Selby	d								12 05														
Doncaster 7	d		11 35	12a28		12 00			12 25		12 37	13a28	12 54	13 11			13 35	13 54			14 35		
Retford 10	d					12 15			12 39									14 08					
Lincoln	d																						
Newark North Gate 7	a		11 59								12 59		13 16				13 58				14 58		
	d		11 59								12 59		13 16				13 58				14 58		
Grantham 7	a		12 11						12 59		13 12						14 10				15 10		
	d		12 11		12 18				12 59	13 12	13 15						14 10			14 22	15 10		
Peterborough 8	a		12 33		12 50	12 55				13 41	13 38		13 46				14 32	14 48		14 51	15 32		
Norwich	a				14 35					15 30										16 35			
Peterborough 8	d		12 34			12 56					13 38		13 49				14 32	14 49			15 32		
Stevenage 4	a		13 07						13s47								15 05						
London Kings Cross 15 ⊖	a		13 35			13 53	13 56		14 12		14 34		14 46	14 48	14 57		15 35	15 45			16 27		

Table 26

Sundays
26 June to 31 July

Scotland, North East England, Yorkshire and Humberside - London

		GR	TP	GR	GR	XC	HT	GR	XC	GR	TP	GR	GR	XC	XC	TP	GC	GR	TP	XC	EM	GR
									A	B					A			C				
Aberdeen	d									09 48												
Stonehaven	d									10 05												
Montrose	d									10 28												
Arbroath	d									10 44												
Dundee	d									11 02												
Leuchars 8	d									11 16												
Kirkcaldy	d									11 40												
Inverkeithing	d									11 56												
Inverness	d																	09 40				
Perth	d																	11 58				
Stirling	d																	12 34				
Glasgow Central 15	d								10 55						11 52							
Motherwell	d								11 10						12 07							
Haymarket	d								11 51	12 18					12 47			13 14				
Edinburgh 10	a								11 55	12 25					12 52			13 19				
Edinburgh	d	11 30			12 00				12 08	12 30			13 00		13 06			13 30		13 50		
Dunbar	d														13 25							
Berwick-upon-Tweed	d	12 09							12 47									14 10		14 31		
Alnmouth for Alnwick	d				12 56										14 06							
Morpeth	d																					
Newcastle 8	a	12 56			13 27				13 34	13 55			14 23		14 35			14 58		15 18		
Sunderland	d																14 12					
Hartlepool	d																14 36					
Newcastle 8	d	12 58	13 04	13 12	13 28	13 35			13 40	13 56	14 08	14 12	14 25	14 35	14 40			15 00	15 07	15 23		
Chester-le-Street	d		13 13																15 16			
Durham	d		13 20	13 24	13 41	13 47			13 52		14 20	14 24	14 38	14 47	14 52				15 23	15 36		
Darlington 7	a	13 25	13 36	13 41	13 59	14 04			14 09	14 24	14 36	14 42	14 55	15 03	15 08			15 27	15 39	15 52		
Middlesbrough	d															14 42						
Eaglescliffe	d																14 59					
Darlington 7	d	13 26	13 37	13 42	13 59	14 05			14 10	14 24	14 37	14 42	14 56	15 04	15 09			15 28	15 40	15 53		
Northallerton	d			13 54							14 49	14 56				15 10	15 22					
Thirsk	d															15 18	15 31					
York 8	a	13 55	14 10	14 14	14 29	14 32			14 38	14 53	15 12	15 16	15 24	15 31	15 36	15 42	15 46	15 57	16 13	16 19		
Leeds 10	a		14 38						15 05		15 38				16 03	16 08			16 38			
Harrogate	d																					
Scarborough	d																					
York 8	d	13 56		14 16	14 30	14 34				14 55		15 18	15 29	15 34			15 48	15 58		16 23		
Doncaster 7	a			14 44	14 54	14 57						15 42	15 52	15 57						16 48		
Skipton	d																					
Keighley	d																					
Bradford Interchange	d																					
Bradford Forster Square	d																					
Shipley	d																					
Halifax	d																					
Brighouse	d																					
Leeds 10	d							15 05	15 10						16 10							16 15
Wakefield Westgate 7	d							15 17	15 23						16 22							16 28
Wakefield Kirkgate 4	d																					
Pontefract Monkhill	d																					
Sheffield 7	a					15 21			15 51					16 21	16 51					17 19		
Hull	d						14 30															
Selby	d						15 05															
Doncaster 7	d			14 44	14 54		15 24	15 35				15 43	15 54									16 46
Retford 10	d						15 38						16 08									
Lincoln	d																					
Newark North Gate 7	a				15 17			15 58				16 07										
	d				15 17			15 58				16 07										
Grantham 7	a						15 58	16 10														17 16
	d						15 58	16 10													16 22	17 16
Peterborough 8	a			15 37	15 46			16 32				16 38	16 48								16 55	
Norwich	a																				18 31	
Peterborough 8	d			15 38	15 49			16 32				16 38	16 49									
Stevenage 4	a						16s46	17 04														18 04
London Kings Cross 15 ⊖	a	15 57		16 35	16 46		17 12	17 35		16 55		17 39	17 45				17 46	17 59				18 36

A from Edinburgh
B The Northern Lights
C The Highland Chieftain

Table 26

Sundays
26 June to 31 July

Scotland, North East England, Yorkshire and Humberside - London

Station		GR	GC	EM	GR	XC	GR	TP	HT	GR	EM	GR	GR	XC	GR	EM	XC	TP	GR	TP	GR	GR	XC
				◇		◇ A		◇	◇		◇			◇		◇	◇ A	◇		◇			◇
Aberdeen	d					11 12	11 47																
Stonehaven	d					11 29	12 04																
Montrose	d					11 50	12 27																
Arbroath	d					12 06	12 43																
Dundee	d					12 25	13 01																
Leuchars 3	d					12 38	13 15																
Kirkcaldy	d					13 03	13 39																
Inverkeithing	d					13 18	13 55																
Inverness	d																						
Perth	d																						
Stirling	d																						
Glasgow Central 15	d																13 49						
Motherwell	d																14 04						
Haymarket	d					13 37	14 19										14 43						
Edinburgh 10	a					13 42	14 25										14 47						
Edinburgh	d	14 00				14 08	14 30						15 00				15 07		15 30			16 00	
Dunbar	d																15 27						
Berwick-upon-Tweed	d					14 47	15 09																
Alnmouth for Alnwick	d	14 56																	16 09				
Morpeth	d																					16 56	
Newcastle 8	a	15 27				15 34	15 57						16 23				16 34		16 56			17 27	
Sunderland	d																						
Hartlepool	d																						
Newcastle 8	d	15 28				15 39	15 59	16 08		16 12			16 25	16 35			16 40		16 58	17 05		17 28	17 35
Chester-le-Street	d																			17 14			
Durham	d	15 41				15 51		16 20		16 24			16 38	16 47			16 52			17 21		17 41	17 47
Darlington 7	a	15 59				16 07	16 26	16 36		16 41			16 55	17 04			17 08		17 24	17 37		17 59	18 04
Middlesbrough	d																	16 42					
Eaglescliffe	d																						
Darlington 7	d	15 59				16 08	16 27	16 37		16 42			16 56	17 05			17 09		17 25	17 38		17 59	18 05
Northallerton	d							16 49		16 53								17 10		17 49			
Thirsk	d																	17 18					
York 8	a	16 28				16 35	16 56	17 12		17 16			17 24	17 31			17 38	17 42	17 53	18 12		18 28	18 31
Leeds 10	a					17 01		17 38									18 04	18 08		18 38			
Harrogate	d														17 05								
Scarborough	d																						
York 8	d	16 29					16 57			17 17			17 29	17 34		17 40			17 55			18 29	18 34
Doncaster 7	a	16 54											17 52	17 57		18 05						18 53	18 57
Skipton	d																						
Keighley	d																						
Bradford Interchange	d		15 42																				
Bradford Forster Square	d																						
Shipley	d																						
Halifax	d		15 56																				
Brighouse	d		16 06																				
Leeds 10	d				16 45	17 10						17 15			17 45		18 10				18 15		
Wakefield Westgate 7	d				16 57	17 22						17 28			17 58		18 22				18 28		
Wakefield Kirkgate 4	d		16 29																				
Pontefract Monkhill	d		16 46																				
Sheffield 7	a					17 51								18 23		18 28	18 51						19 21
Hull	d								16 30														
Selby	d								17 05														
Doncaster 7	d	16 54	17 10		17 17				17 26			17 46	17 54		18 17						18 46	18 53	
Retford 10	d								17 40			18 00											
Lincoln	d																						
Newark North Gate 7	a	17 17			17 43					17 58					18 42							19 16	
	d	17 17			17 43					17 58					18 42							19 16	
Grantham 7	a								18 00			18 22	18 27								19 16		
	d			17 19					18 00		18 17	18 22	18 27								19 16		
Peterborough 8	a	17 46		17 50	18 14					18 27	18 46		18 51		19 13							19 46	
Norwich	a			19 29							20 29												
Peterborough 8	d	17 49			18 15					18 28			18 51		19 13							19 49	
Stevenage 4	a								18s51			19 10									20 08		
London Kings Cross 15 ⊖	a	18 46	18 51		19 10		18 58		19 15	19 24		19 38	19 48		20 12				19 54		20 36	20 46	

A ⚲ from Edinburgh

Table 26

Sundays
26 June to 31 July

Scotland, North East England, Yorkshire and Humberside - London

Station		EM	GR	XC	SR	TP	GR	TP	XC	HT	GR	GR	GR	XC	TP	GC	GR	TP	XC	GR	NT	EM
		◇		◇ A		◇		◇	◇	◇				◇ B	◇			◇	◇			◇
Aberdeen	d						13 50															
Stonehaven	d						14 07															
Montrose	d						14 30															
Arbroath	d						14 46															
Dundee	d						15 04															
Leuchars 3	d						15 18															
Kirkcaldy	d						15 42															
Inverkeithing	d						15 58															
Inverness	d				20 25																	
Perth	d				23u00																	
Stirling	d				23u45																	
Glasgow Central 15	d			14 55																		
Motherwell	d			15 11																		
Haymarket	d			15 51			16 20															
Edinburgh 10	a			15 56	00 47		16 25															
Edinburgh	d			16 05			16 30					17 00		17 07			17 30			18 00		
Dunbar	d			16 25										17 27			17 50					
Berwick-upon-Tweed	d						17 09							17 50			18 13					
Alnmouth for Alnwick	d			17 05																18 56		
Morpeth	d			17 20																		
Newcastle 8	a			17 37			17 57					18 23		18 36			19 00			19 27		
Sunderland	d															18 12					19 28	
Hartlepool	d															18 36						
Newcastle 8	d			17 40		17 52	17 59		18 20			18 25		18 38			19 02	19 10	19 25	19 28	19a52	
Chester-le-Street	d																					
Durham	d			17 52		18 04			18 32			18 38		18 51				19 22	19 37	19 41		
Darlington 7	a			18 08		18 20	18 26		18 49			18 55		19 06			19 28	19 38	19 53	19 59		
Middlesbrough	d														18 45							
Eaglescliffe	d															18 59						
Darlington 7	d			18 09		18 21	18 27		18 50			18 56		19 08			19 29	19 39	19 54	19 59		
Northallerton	d					18 33						19 07			19 13	19 20						
Thirsk	d							←							19 21	19 29						
York 8	a			18 37		19 04	18 56	19 04	19 21			19 28		19 35	19 42	19 46	19 57	20 11	20 21	20 28		
Leeds 10	a			19 04		→		19 38						20 05	20 08			20 38				
Harrogate	d																					
Scarborough	d																					
York 8	d						18 57		19 24			19 30				19 48	19 59		20 24	20 29		
Doncaster 7	a								19 48			19 53							20 47	20 53		
Skipton	d																					
Keighley	d																					
Bradford Interchange	d																					
Bradford Forster Square	d																					
Shipley	d																					
Halifax	d																					
Brighouse	d																					
Leeds 10	d		18 45	19 10							19 15		19 45	20 10								
Wakefield Westgate 7	d		18 57	19 22							19 27		19 57	20 22								
Wakefield Kirkgate 4	d																					
Pontefract Monkhill	d																					
Sheffield 7	a			19 50					20 16					20 51					21 17			
Hull	d									18 30												
Selby	d									19 05												
Doncaster 7	d		19 17							19 26	19 45	19 54	20 20							20 53		
Retford 10	d									19 40	19 59											
Lincoln	d																					
Newark North Gate 7	a		19 43									20 17	20 43							21 16		
	d		19 44									20 17	20 43							21 16		
Grantham 7	a									20 00	20 21						20 47					
	d	19 27								20 00	20 21						20 48					21 19
Peterborough 8	a	19 56	20 14									20 47	21 13				21 08			21 45		21 49
Norwich	a	21 35																				23 28
Peterborough 8	d		20 15									20 49	21 13				21 09			21 49		
Stevenage 4	a									20s51	21 09											
London Kings Cross 15 ⊖	a		21 11				20 58			21 14	21 37	21 46	22 12			21 48	22 05			22 46		

A ⚲ from Edinburgh

B ⚲ to York

Table 26

Sundays
26 June to 31 July

Scotland, North East England, Yorkshire and Humberside - London

		GR	XC	GR	TP	TP	GR	NT	GR	XC	GR	TP
			A									
Aberdeen	d											
Stonehaven	d											
Montrose	d											
Arbroath	d											
Dundee	d											
Leuchars 3	d											
Kirkcaldy	d											
Inverkeithing	d											
Inverness	d											
Perth	d											
Stirling	d											
Glasgow Central 15	d		16 55							18 57		
Motherwell	d		17 11							19 11		
Haymarket	d		17 55							19 51		
Edinburgh 10	a		17 59							19 56		
Edinburgh	d		18 07	18 30			19 00		20 00	20 05	21 00	
Dunbar	d		18 26				19 21		20 21	20 29	21 21	
Berwick-upon-Tweed	d		18 50	19 09			19 44		20 44	20 53	21 44	
Alnmouth for Alnwick	d								21 07		22 06	
Morpeth	d								21 24			
Newcastle 8	a		19 34	19 56			20 30		21 42	21 48	22 37	
Sunderland	d											
Hartlepool	d											
Newcastle 8	d		19 40	19 58		20 08	20 32	21 06	21 44			
Chester-le-Street	d							21 15				
Durham	d		19 52			20 20	20 46	21 24	21 57			
Darlington 7	a		20 08	20 24		20 36	21 02	21 44	22 15			
Middlesbrough	d				20 06							22 06
Eaglescliffe	d							22a00				
Darlington 7	d		20 09	20 25		20 37	21 03		22 15			
Northallerton	d				20 38	20 49			22 29			22 34
Thirsk	d				20 46							22 42
York 8	a		20 36	20 53	21 06	21 12	21 31		23 02			23 09
Leeds 10	a		21 02			21 38			23 34			23 38
Harrogate	d											
Scarborough	d											
York 8	d			20 55			21 33					
Doncaster 7	a			21 18			21 56					
Skipton	d											
Keighley	d											
Bradford Interchange	d											
Bradford Forster Square	d											
Shipley	d											
Halifax	d											
Brighouse	d											
Leeds 10	d	20 45	21 10									
Wakefield Westgate 7	d	20 57	21 22									
Wakefield Kirkgate 4	d											
Pontefract Monkhill	d											
Sheffield 7	a		21 50									
Hull	d											
Selby	d											
Doncaster 7	d	21 15		21 19			21 57					
Retford 10	d	21 29										
Lincoln	d											
Newark North Gate 7	a			21 47			22 19					
	d			21 47			22 20					
Grantham 7	a	21 51		22 00			22 32					
	d	21 51		22 00			22 33					
Peterborough 8	a	22 12		22 21			22 53					
Norwich	a											
Peterborough 8	d	22 13		22 23			23 00					
Stevenage 4	a	22 45		22 54			23s34					
London Kings Cross 15 ⊖	a	23 16		23 22			00 02					

A from Edinburgh to York

Table 26

Sundays
7 August to 23 October

Scotland, North East England, Yorkshire and Humberside - London

		FC	GR	GR	GC	GC	XC	XC	FC	GR	TP	GR	EM	EM	HT	XC	GR	GR	EM	XC	GR	TP	GC
		A			B	C								A									
Aberdeen	d																						
Stonehaven	d																						
Montrose	d																						
Arbroath	d																						
Dundee	d																						
Leuchars 3	d																						
Kirkcaldy	d																						
Inverkeithing	d																						
Inverness	d																						
Perth	d																						
Stirling	d																						
Glasgow Central 15	d																						
Motherwell	d																						
Haymarket	d																						
Edinburgh 10	a																						
Edinburgh	d																						
Dunbar	d																						
Berwick-upon-Tweed	d																						
Alnmouth for Alnwick	d																						
Morpeth	d																						
Newcastle 8	a																						
Sunderland	d																						09 12
Hartlepool	d																						09 36
Newcastle 8	d									07 55	08 00						08 55			09 20	09 25	09 31	
Chester-le-Street	d																					09 40	
Durham	d									08 07	08 13						09 07			09 33	09 37	09 47	
Darlington 7	a									08 25	08 30						09 24			09 48	09 54	10 03	
Middlesbrough	d																						
Eaglescliffe	d																						09 59
Darlington 7	d									08 25	08 30						09 25			09 50	09 55	10 04	
Northallerton	d										08 42										10 06	10 15	10 20
Thirsk	d										08 50												10 29
York 8	a									08 53	09 11						09 54			10 18	10 26	10 41	10 45
Leeds 10	a										09 38									10 51		11 08	
Harrogate	d																						
Scarborough	d																						
York 8	d		08 00							08 55						09 28	09 56				10 28		10 50
Doncaster 7	a		08 22																		10 51		
Skipton	d																						
Keighley	d																						
Bradford Interchange	d				07 55	08 05																	
Bradford Forster Square	d																						
Shipley	d																						
Halifax	d				08 09																		
Brighouse	d				08 20																		
Leeds 10	d			08 05			08 10	09 00				09 05	09 44			10 00		10 05	10 15	11 00			
Wakefield Westgate 7	d			08 17			08 23	09 11				09 17	09 57			10 12		10 17	10 28	11 12			
Wakefield Kirkgate 4	d				08 43	08 43																	
Pontefract Monkhill	d																						
Sheffield 7	a						08 51						10 25						10 57				
Hull	d														09 30								
Selby	d														10 05								
Doncaster 7	d		08 23	08 35	09 06	09 06		09a31				09 35			10 24	10a28		10 35		11a28	10 52		
Retford 10	d		08 38												10 38			10 51					
Lincoln	d																						
Newark North Gate 7	a			08 57								09 58						11 05			11 14		
	d			08 58								09 58						11 05			11 14		
Grantham 7	a			09 10								10 10			10 58			11 18					
	d			09 11								10 10		10 29	10 58			11 18					
Peterborough 8	a		09 23	09 39						10 11		10 32		11 06			11 01	11 40			11 46		
Norwich	a													13 06									
Peterborough 8	d	09 15	09 24	09 40					10 15	10 17		10 32					11 01	11 41			11 49		
Stevenage 4	a											11 04			11s49								
London Kings Cross 15 ⊖	a	10 15	10 25	10 36	10 42	10 42			11 15	11 17		11 35			12 12		12 00	12 37			12 45		12 44

A from 7 August until 11 September

B from 7 August until 11 September.

◇ from Doncaster to Wakefield Kirkgate

C from 18 September until 23 October.

◇ from Doncaster to Wakefield Kirkgate

Table 26

Scotland, North East England, Yorkshire and Humberside - London

Sundays

7 August to 23 October

Station		GR	TP	GR	XC	EM	GR	GR	TP	HT	EM	GR	XC	GR	GC	GR	TP	TP	GR	GR	EM	EM	GR
						A											B	A					
Aberdeen	d																						
Stonehaven	d																						
Montrose	d																						
Arbroath	d																						
Dundee	d																						
Leuchars	d																						
Kirkcaldy	d																						
Inverkeithing	d																						
Inverness	d																						
Perth	d																						
Stirling	d																						
Glasgow Central	d																						
Motherwell	d																						
Haymarket	d																						
Edinburgh	a																						
Edinburgh	d				08 50		09 00	09 30					09 50	10 00		10 30				10 55			
Dunbar	d																						
Berwick-upon-Tweed	d				09 31			10 10								11 09							
Alnmouth for Alnwick	d												10 47	10 56									
Morpeth	d												11 02							12 05			
Newcastle	a				10 19		10 25	10 57					11 19	11 27		11 56				12 23			
Sunderland	d																						
Hartlepool	d																						
Newcastle	d	10 00			10 24		10 28	10 59	11 08				11 25	11 28		11 58	12 10	12 10		12 25			
Chester-le-Street	d																						
Durham	d				10 37		10 42		11 20				11 37	11 41			12 22	12 22		12 38			
Darlington	a	10 25			10 53		10 59	11 25	11 36				11 54	11 59		12 24	12 38	12 38		12 55			
Middlesbrough	d		10 13																				
Eaglescliffe	d																						
Darlington	d	10 26			10 54		11 00	11 26	11 37				11 55	11 59		12 25	12 39	12 39		12 56			
Northallerton	d		10 41				11 12		11 49											13 07			
Thirsk	d		10 49																				
York	a	10 53	11 11		11 24		11 33	11 54	12 12				12 23	12 28		12 53	13 11	13 11		13 28			
Leeds	a		11 38		11 51				12 38				12 51				13 37	13 38					
Harrogate	d																						
Scarborough	d																						
York	d	10 55					11 35	11 56						12 30		12 55				13 30			
Doncaster	a						11 59							12 53						13 53			
Skipton	d																						
Keighley	d																						
Bradford Interchange	d														11 42								
Bradford Forster Square	d																						
Shipley	d																						
Halifax	d														11 55								
Brighouse	d														12 06								
Leeds	d			11 05	12 00							12 05	13 00						13 05		13 59		14 05
Wakefield Westgate	d			11 17	12 12							12 17	13 12						13 18		14 12		14 17
Wakefield Kirkgate	d														12 29								
Pontefract Monkhill	d														12 46								
Sheffield	a																				14 40		
Hull	d									11 30													
Selby	d									12 05													
Doncaster	d			11 35	12a28		12 00			12 25		12 37	13a28	12 54	13 11				13 35	13 54			14 35
Retford	d						12 15			12 39										14 08			
Lincoln	d																						
Newark North Gate	a			11 59								12 59		13 16					13 58				14 58
	d			11 59								12 59		13 16					13 58				14 58
Grantham	a			12 11						12 59		13 12							14 10				15 10
	d			12 11		12 18				12 59	13 12	13 15							14 10			14 22	15 10
Peterborough	a	12 00		12 33		12 50	12 55				13 41	13 38		13 46					14 32	14 48		14 51	15 32
Norwich	a					14 35					15 30											16 35	
Peterborough	d	12 00		12 34			12 56					13 38		13 49					14 32	14 49			15 32
Stevenage	a			13 07						13s47									15 05				
London Kings Cross	a	12 56		13 35			13 53	13 56		14 12		14 34		14 46	14 48	14 57			15 35	15 45			16 27

A from 7 August until 11 September

B from 18 September until 23 October

Table 26

Scotland, North East England, Yorkshire and Humberside - London

Sundays

7 August to 23 October

Station		XC	XC	TP	GR	TP	GR	GR	XC	HT	GR	XC	XC	GR	TP	GR	GR	XC	XC	TP	GC	GR
		A	B									C	D	E					F			G
Aberdeen	d													09 48								
Stonehaven	d													10 05								
Montrose	d													10 28								
Arbroath	d													10 44								
Dundee	d													11 02								
Leuchars	d													11 16								
Kirkcaldy	d													11 40								
Inverkeithing	d													11 56								
Inverness	d																					09 40
Perth	d																					11 58
Stirling	d																					12 34
Glasgow Central	d											10 55	10 55						11 52			
Motherwell	d											11 10	11 10						12 07			
Haymarket	d												11 51	12 18					12 47			13 14
Edinburgh	a											11 56	11 55	12 25					12 52			13 19
Edinburgh	d	11 05	11 05		11 30			12 00				12 08	12 08	12 30			13 00		13 06			13 30
Dunbar	d	11 25	11 26																13 25			
Berwick-upon-Tweed	d	11 48			12 09							12 47	12 47									14 10
Alnmouth for Alnwick	d	12 08	12 08					12 56											14 06			
Morpeth	d																					
Newcastle	a	12 35	12 35		12 56			13 27				13 34	13 34	13 55			14 23		14 35			14 58
Sunderland	d																				14 12	
Hartlepool	d																				14 36	
Newcastle	d	12 38	12 38		12 58	13 04	13 12	13 28	13 35			13 40	13 40	13 56	14 08	14 12	14 25	14 35	14 40			15 00
Chester-le-Street	d					13 13																
Durham	d	12 50	12 50			13 20	13 24	13 41	13 47			13 52	13 52		14 20	14 24	14 38	14 47	14 52			
Darlington	a	13 06	13 06		13 25	13 36	13 41	13 59	14 04			14 09	14 09	14 24	14 36	14 42	14 55	15 03	15 08			15 27
Middlesbrough	d			12 45																14 42		
Eaglescliffe	d																				14 59	
Darlington	d	13 07	13 07		13 26	13 37	13 42	13 59	14 05			14 10	14 10	14 24	14 37	14 42	14 56	15 04	15 09			15 28
Northallerton	d			13 13			13 54								14 49	14 56				15 10	15 22	
Thirsk	d			13 21																15 18	15 31	
York	a	13 35	13 36	13 42	13 55	14 10	14 14	14 29	14 32			14 38	14 38	14 53	15 12	15 16	15 24	15 31	15 36	15 42	15 46	15 57
Leeds	a	14 03	14 03	14 08		14 38						15 05	15 05		15 38				16 03	16 08		
Harrogate	d																					
Scarborough	d																					
York	d				13 56		14 16	14 30	14 34					14 55		15 18	15 29	15 34			15 48	15 58
Doncaster	a						14 44	14 54	14 57							15 42	15 52	15 57				
Skipton	d																					
Keighley	d																					
Bradford Interchange	d																					
Bradford Forster Square	d																					
Shipley	d																					
Halifax	d																					
Brighouse	d																					
Leeds	d	14 10	14 10								15 05	15 10	15 10						16 10			
Wakefield Westgate	d	14 23	14 23								15 17	15 23	15 23						16 22			
Wakefield Kirkgate	d																					
Pontefract Monkhill	d																					
Sheffield	a	14 52	14 52						15 21			15 51	15 51					16 21	16 51			
Hull	d									14 30												
Selby	d									15 05												
Doncaster	d						14 44	14 54		15 24	15 35					15 43	15 54					
Retford	d									15 38							16 08					
Lincoln	d																					
Newark North Gate	a							15 17			15 58					16 07						
	d							15 17			15 58					16 07						
Grantham	a									15 58	16 10											
	d									15 58	16 10											
Peterborough	a						15 37	15 46			16 32					16 38	16 48					
Norwich	a																					
Peterborough	d						15 38	15 49			16 32					16 38	16 49					
Stevenage	a									16s46	17 04											
London Kings Cross	a				15 57		16 35	16 46		17 12	17 35			16 55		17 39	17 45				17 46	17 59

A from 7 August until 11 September

B from 18 September until 23 October

C from 18 September until 23 October. ⚐ from Edinburgh

D from 7 August until 11 September. ⚐ from Edinburgh

E The Northern Lights

F ⚐ from Edinburgh

G The Highland Chieftain

Table 26

Sundays

7 August to 23 October

Scotland, North East England, Yorkshire and Humberside - London

		TP	XC	EM	GR	GR	GC	GC	EM	GR	XC	GR	TP	HT	GR	EM	GR	GR	XC	GR	EM	XC	TP
							A	B			C											C	
Aberdeen	d										11 12	11 47											
Stonehaven	d										11 29	12 04											
Montrose	d										11 50	12 27											
Arbroath	d										12 06	12 43											
Dundee	d										12 25	13 01											
Leuchars	d										12 38	13 15											
Kirkcaldy	d										13 03	13 39											
Inverkeithing	d										13 18	13 55											
Inverness	d																						
Perth	d																						
Stirling	d																						
Glasgow Central	d																					13 49	
Motherwell	d																					14 04	
Haymarket	d										13 37	14 19										14 43	
Edinburgh	a										13 42	14 25										14 47	
Edinburgh	d		13 50			14 00					14 08	14 30						15 00				15 07	
Dunbar	d																					15 27	
Berwick-upon-Tweed	d		14 31								14 47	15 09											
Alnmouth for Alnwick	d					14 56																	
Morpeth	d																						
Newcastle	a		15 18			15 27					15 34	15 57						16 23				16 34	
Sunderland	d																						
Hartlepool	d																						
Newcastle	d	15 07	15 23			15 28					15 39	15 59	16 08		16 12			16 25	16 35			16 40	
Chester-le-Street	d	15 16																					
Durham	d	15 23	15 36			15 41					15 51		16 20		16 24			16 38	16 47			16 52	
Darlington	a	15 39	15 52			15 59					16 07	16 26	16 36		16 41			16 55	17 04			17 08	
Middlesbrough	d																						16 42
Eaglescliffe	d																						
Darlington	d	15 40	15 53			15 59					16 08	16 27	16 37		16 42			16 56	17 05			17 09	
Northallerton	d												16 49		16 53								17 10
Thirsk	d																						17 18
York	a	16 13	16 19			16 28					16 35	16 56	17 12		17 16			17 24	17 31			17 38	17 42
Leeds	a	16 38									17 01		17 38									18 04	18 08
Harrogate	d																			17 05			
Scarborough	d																						
York	d		16 23			16 29						16 57			17 17			17 29	17 34		17 40		
Doncaster	a		16 48			16 54												17 52	17 57		18 05		
Skipton	d																						
Keighley	d																						
Bradford Interchange	d						15 42	15 42															
Bradford Forster Square	d																						
Shipley	d																						
Halifax	d						15 55	15 56															
Brighouse	d						16 06	16 06															
Leeds	d				16 15					16 45	17 10						17 15			17 45		18 10	
Wakefield Westgate	d				16 28					16 57	17 22						17 28			17 58		18 22	
Wakefield Kirkgate	d						16 29	16 29															
Pontefract Monkhill	d						16 46	16 46															
Sheffield	a		17 19								17 51								18 23		18 28	18 51	
Hull	d													16 30									
Selby	d													17 05									
Doncaster	d				16 46	16 54	17 10	17 10		17 17				17 26			17 46	17 54		18 17			
Retford	d													17 40			18 00						
Lincoln	d																						
Newark North Gate	a					17 17				17 43					17 58					18 42			
	d					17 17				17 43					17 58					18 42			
Grantham	a				17 16									18 00			18 22	18 27					
	d			16 22	17 16				17 19					18 00		18 17	18 22	18 27					
Peterborough	a			16 55		17 46			17 50	18 14					18 27	18 46		18 51		19 13			
Norwich	a			18 31					19 29							20 29							
Peterborough	d					17 49				18 15					18 28			18 51		19 13			
Stevenage	a				18 04									18s51			19 10						
London Kings Cross	a				18 36	18 46	18 51	18 51		19 10		18 58		19 15	19 24		19 38	19 48		20 12			

A from 18 September until 23 October
B from 7 August until 11 September
C from Edinburgh

Table 26

Sundays

7 August to 23 October

Scotland, North East England, Yorkshire and Humberside - London

		GR	TP	GR	GR	XC	EM	GR	XC	SR	TP	GR	TP	XC	HT	GR	GR	GR	XC	TP	GC	GR
									A										B			
Aberdeen	d											13 50										
Stonehaven	d											14 07										
Montrose	d											14 30										
Arbroath	d											14 46										
Dundee	d											15 04										
Leuchars	d											15 18										
Kirkcaldy	d											15 42										
Inverkeithing	d											15 58										
Inverness	d									20 25												
Perth	d									23u00												
Stirling	d									23u45												
Glasgow Central	d								14 55													
Motherwell	d								15 11													
Haymarket	d								15 51			16 20										
Edinburgh	a								15 56	00 47		16 25										
Edinburgh	d	15 30			16 00				16 05			16 30					17 00		17 07			17 30
Dunbar	d								16 25										17 27			17 50
Berwick-upon-Tweed	d	16 09										17 09							17 50			18 13
Alnmouth for Alnwick	d				16 56				17 05													
Morpeth	d								17 20													
Newcastle	a	16 56			17 27				17 37			17 57					18 23		18 36			19 00
Sunderland	d																				18 12	
Hartlepool	d																				18 36	
Newcastle	d	16 58	17 05		17 28	17 35			17 40		17 52	17 59		18 20			18 25		18 38			19 02
Chester-le-Street	d		17 14																			
Durham	d		17 21		17 41	17 47			17 52		18 04			18 32			18 38		18 51			
Darlington	a	17 24	17 37		17 59	18 04			18 08		18 20	18 26		18 49			18 55		19 06			19 28
Middlesbrough	d																			18 45		
Eaglescliffe	d																				18 59	
Darlington	d	17 25	17 38		17 59	18 05			18 09		18 21	18 27		18 50			18 56		19 08			19 29
Northallerton	d		17 49								18 33						19 07			19 13	19 20	
Thirsk	d												←							19 21	19 29	
York	a	17 53	18 12		18 28	18 31			18 37		19 04	18 56	19 04	19 21			19 28		19 35	19 42	19 46	19 57
Leeds	a		18 38						19 04		→		19 38						20 05	20 08		
Harrogate	d																					
Scarborough	d																					
York	d	17 55			18 29	18 34						18 57		19 24			19 30				19 48	19 59
Doncaster	a				18 53	18 57								19 48			19 53					
Skipton	d																					
Keighley	d																					
Bradford Interchange	d																					
Bradford Forster Square	d																					
Shipley	d																					
Halifax	d																					
Brighouse	d																					
Leeds	d			18 15				18 45	19 10							19 15		19 45	20 10			
Wakefield Westgate	d			18 28				18 57	19 22							19 27		19 57	20 22			
Wakefield Kirkgate	d																					
Pontefract Monkhill	d																					
Sheffield	a					19 21			19 50					20 16					20 51			
Hull	d														18 30							
Selby	d														19 05							
Doncaster	d			18 46	18 53			19 17							19 26	19 45	19 54	20 20				
Retford	d														19 40	19 59						
Lincoln	d																					
Newark North Gate	a				19 16			19 43									20 17	20 43				
	d				19 16			19 44									20 17	20 43				
Grantham	a			19 16											20 00	20 21						20 47
	d			19 16			19 27								20 00	20 21						20 48
Peterborough	a				19 46		19 56	20 14									20 47	21 13				21 08
Norwich	a						21 35															
Peterborough	d				19 49			20 15									20 49	21 13				21 09
Stevenage	a			20 08											20s51	21 09						
London Kings Cross	a	19 54		20 36	20 46			21 11				20 58			21 14	21 37	21 46	22 12			21 48	22 05

A from Edinburgh
B to York

Table 26

Sundays
7 August to 23 October

Scotland, North East England, Yorkshire and Humberside - London

		TP	XC	GR	NT	EM	GR	XC	GR	TP	TP	GR	NT	GR	XC	GR	TP
		◇1	◇1	1		◇	1	◇1 A	1	◇1	◇1	1		1	◇1	1	◇1
Aberdeen	d																
Stonehaven	d																
Montrose	d																
Arbroath	d																
Dundee	d																
Leuchars 3	d																
Kirkcaldy	d																
Inverkeithing	d																
Inverness	d																
Perth	d																
Stirling	d																
Glasgow Central 15	d							16 55							18 57		
Motherwell	d							17 11							19 11		
Haymarket	d							17 55							19 51		
Edinburgh 10	a							17 59							19 56		
Edinburgh	d			18 00				18 07	18 30			19 00		20 00	20 05	21 00	
Dunbar	d							18 26				19 21		20 21	20 29	21 21	
Berwick-upon-Tweed	d							18 50	19 09			19 44		20 44	20 53	21 44	
Alnmouth for Alnwick	d			18 56										21 07		22 06	
Morpeth	d													21 24			
Newcastle 8	a			19 27				19 34	19 56			20 30		21 42	21 48	22 37	
Sunderland	d				19 28												
Hartlepool	d																
Newcastle 8	d	19 10	19 25	19 28	19a52			19 40	19 58		20 08	20 32	21 06	21 44			
Chester-le-Street	d												21 15				
Durham	d	19 22	19 37	19 41				19 52			20 20	20 46	21 24	21 57			
Darlington 7	a	19 38	19 53	19 59				20 08	20 24		20 36	21 02	21 44	22 15			
Middlesbrough	d									20 06							22 06
Eaglescliffe	d												22a00				
Darlington 7	d	19 39	19 54	19 59				20 09	20 25		20 37	21 03		22 15			
Northallerton	d									20 38	20 49			22 29			22 34
Thirsk	d									20 46							22 42
York 8	a	20 11	20 21	20 28				20 36	20 53	21 06	21 12	21 31		23 02			23 09
Leeds 10	a	20 38						21 02			21 38			23 34			23 38
Harrogate	d																
Scarborough	d																
York 8	d		20 24	20 29					20 55			21 33					
Doncaster 7	a		20 47	20 53					21 18			21 56					
Skipton	d																
Keighley	d																
Bradford Interchange	d																
Bradford Forster Square	d																
Shipley	d																
Halifax	d																
Brighouse	d																
Leeds 10	d						20 45	21 10									
Wakefield Westgate 7	d						20 57	21 22									
Wakefield Kirkgate 4	d																
Pontefract Monkhill	d																
Sheffield 7	a		21 17					21 50									
Hull	d																
Selby	d																
Doncaster 7	d			20 53			21 15		21 19			21 57					
Retford 10	d						21 29										
Lincoln	d																
Newark North Gate 7	a			21 16					21 47			22 19					
	d			21 16					21 47			22 20					
Grantham 7	a						21 51		22 00			22 32					
	d					21 19	21 51		22 00			22 33					
Peterborough 8	a			21 45		21 49	22 12		22 21			22 53					
Norwich	a					23 28											
Peterborough 8	d			21 49			22 13		22 23			23 00					
Stevenage 4	a						22 45		22 54			23s34					
London Kings Cross 15 ⊖	a			22 46			23 16		23 22			00 02					

A from Edinburgh to York

Table 26

Sundays
from 30 October

Scotland, North East England, Yorkshire and Humberside - London

		FC	GR	GR	GC	XC	XC	FC	GR	TP	GR	HT	EM	XC	GR	GR	EM	XC	GR	TP	GC	GR	TP
		1	1	1	◇1 A	◇1	◇1	1	1	◇1	1	◇1	◇1	◇1	1	1	◇1	◇1	1	◇1	1	1	◇1
Aberdeen	d																						
Stonehaven	d																						
Montrose	d																						
Arbroath	d																						
Dundee	d																						
Leuchars 3	d																						
Kirkcaldy	d																						
Inverkeithing	d																						
Inverness	d																						
Perth	d																						
Stirling	d																						
Glasgow Central 15	d																						
Motherwell	d																						
Haymarket	d																						
Edinburgh 10	a																						
Edinburgh	d																						
Dunbar	d																						
Berwick-upon-Tweed	d																						
Alnmouth for Alnwick	d																						
Morpeth	d																						
Newcastle 8	a																						
Sunderland	d																				09 12		
Hartlepool	d																				09 36		
Newcastle 8	d								07 55	08 00					08 55			09 20	09 25	09 31		10 00	
Chester-le-Street	d																			09 40			
Durham	d								08 07	08 13					09 07			09 33	09 37	09 47			
Darlington 7	a								08 25	08 30					09 24			09 48	09 54	10 03		10 25	
Middlesbrough	d																						10 13
Eaglescliffe	d																				09 59		
Darlington 7	d								08 25	08 30					09 25			09 50	09 55	10 04		10 26	
Northallerton	d									08 42									10 06	10 15	10 20		10 41
Thirsk	d									08 50											10 29		10 49
York 8	a								08 53	09 11					09 54			10 18	10 26	10 41	10 45	10 53	11 11
Leeds 10	a									09 38								10 51		11 08			11 38
Harrogate	d																						
Scarborough	d																						
York 8	d		08 00						08 55					09 28	09 56				10 28		10 50	10 55	
Doncaster 7	a		08 22																10 51				
Skipton	d																						
Keighley	d																						
Bradford Interchange	d				08 05																		
Bradford Forster Square	d																						
Shipley	d																						
Halifax	d																						
Brighouse	d																						
Leeds 10	d			08 05		08 10	09 00				09 05		09 44	10 00		10 05	10 15	11 00					
Wakefield Westgate 7	d			08 17		08 23	09 11				09 17		09 57	10 12		10 17	10 28	11 12					
Wakefield Kirkgate 4	d				08 43																		
Pontefract Monkhill	d																						
Sheffield 7	a					08 51							10 25				10 57						
Hull	d											09 30											
Selby	d											10 05											
Doncaster 7	d		08 23	08 35	09 06		09a31				09 35	10 24		10a28		10 35		11a28	10 52				
Retford 10	d		08 38									10 38				10 51							
Lincoln	d																						
Newark North Gate 7	a			08 57							09 58					11 05			11 14				
	d			08 58							09 58					11 05			11 14				
Grantham 7	a			09 10							10 10	10 58				11 18							
	d			09 11							10 10	10 58				11 18							
Peterborough 8	a		09 23	09 39					10 11		10 32				11 01	11 40			11 46			12 00	
Norwich	a																						
Peterborough 8	d	09 15	09 24	09 40				10 15	10 17		10 32				11 01	11 41			11 49			12 00	
Stevenage 4	a										11 04	11s49											
London Kings Cross 15 ⊖	a	10 15	10 25	10 36	10 42			11 15	11 17		11 35	12 12			12 00	12 37			12 45		12 44	12 56	

A ◇ from Doncaster ■ to Wakefield Kirkgate

Scotland, North East England, Yorkshire and Humberside - London

		GR	XC	GR	GR	TP	HT	EM	GR	XC	GR	GC	GR	TP	GR	GR	EM	EM	GR	XC	TP	GR	TP
		1	◇1	1	1	◇1	◇1	◇	1	◇1	1	1	1	◇1	1	1	◇1	◇	1	◇1	◇1	1	◇1
Aberdeen	d																						
Stonehaven	d																						
Montrose	d																						
Arbroath	d																						
Dundee	d																						
Leuchars 3	d																						
Kirkcaldy	d																						
Inverkeithing	d																						
Inverness	d																						
Perth	d																						
Stirling	d																						
Glasgow Central 15	d																						
Motherwell	d																						
Haymarket	d																						
Edinburgh 10	a																						
Edinburgh	d		08 50	09 00	09 30					09 50	10 00		10 30			10 55				11 05		11 30	
Dunbar	d																			11 25			
Berwick-upon-Tweed	d		09 31		10 10								11 09							11 48		12 09	
Alnmouth for Alnwick	d									10 47	10 56									12 08			
Morpeth	d									11 02						12 05							
Newcastle 8	a		10 19	10 25	10 57					11 19	11 27		11 56			12 23				12 35		12 56	
Sunderland	d																						
Hartlepool	d																						
Newcastle 8	d		10 24	10 28	10 59	11 08				11 25	11 28		11 58	12 10		12 25				12 38		12 58	13 04
Chester-le-Street	d																						13 13
Durham	d		10 37	10 42		11 20				11 37	11 41			12 22		12 38				12 50			13 20
Darlington 7	a		10 53	10 59	11 25	11 36				11 54	11 59		12 24	12 38		12 55				13 06		13 25	13 36
Middlesbrough	d																				12 45		
Eaglescliffe	d																						
Darlington 7	d		10 54	11 00	11 26	11 37				11 55	11 59		12 25	12 39		12 56				13 07		13 26	13 37
Northallerton	d			11 12		11 49										13 07					13 13		
Thirsk	d																				13 21		
York 8	a		11 24	11 33	11 54	12 12				12 23	12 28		12 53	13 11		13 28				13 35	13 42	13 55	14 10
Leeds 10	a		11 51			12 38				12 51				13 38						14 03	14 08		14 38
Harrogate	d																						
Scarborough	d																						
York 8	d			11 35	11 56						12 30		12 55			13 30						13 56	
Doncaster 7	a			11 59							12 53					13 53							
Skipton	d																						
Keighley	d																						
Bradford Interchange	d											11 42											
Bradford Forster Square	d																						
Shipley	d																						
Halifax	d											11 55											
Brighouse	d											12 06											
Leeds 10	d	11 05	12 00						12 05	13 00					13 05		13 59		14 05	14 10			
Wakefield Westgate 7	d	11 17	12 12						12 17	13 12					13 18		14 12		14 17	14 23			
Wakefield Kirkgate 4	d											12 29											
Pontefract Monkhill	d											12 46											
Sheffield 7	a																14 40			14 52			
Hull	d						11 30																
Selby	d						12 05																
Doncaster 7	d	11 35	12a28	12 00			12 25		12 37	13a28	12 54	13 11			13 35	13 54			14 35				
Retford 10	d			12 15			12 39									14 08							
Lincoln	d																						
Newark North Gate 7	a	11 59							12 59		13 16				13 58				14 58				
	d	11 59							12 59		13 16				13 58				14 58				
Grantham 7	a	12 11					12 59		13 12						14 10				15 10				
	d	12 11					12 59	13 12	13 15						14 10			14 22	15 10				
Peterborough 8	a	12 33		12 55				13 41	13 38		13 46				14 32	14 48		14 51	15 32				
Norwich	a							15 30										16 35					
Peterborough 8	d	12 34		12 56					13 38		13 49				14 32	14 49			15 32				
Stevenage 4	a	13 07					13s47								15 05								
London Kings Cross 15 ⊖	a	13 35		13 53	13 56		14 12		14 34		14 46	14 48	14 57		15 35	15 45			16 27			15 57	

Table 26

Sundays
from 30 October

Scotland, North East England, Yorkshire and Humberside - London

		GR	GR	XC	HT	GR	XC	GR	TP	GR	GR	XC	TP	GC	GR	TP	XC	EM	GR	GR	GC	EM
		1	1	◇1	◇1	1	◇1	1	◇1	1	1	◇1	◇1	1	1	◇1	◇1	◇	1	1	1	◇
							A	B				A			C							
Aberdeen	d							09 48														
Stonehaven	d							10 05														
Montrose	d							10 28														
Arbroath	d							10 44														
Dundee	d							11 02														
Leuchars 3	d							11 16														
Kirkcaldy	d							11 40														
Inverkeithing	d							11 56														
Inverness	d														09 40							
Perth	d														11 58							
Stirling	d														12 34							
Glasgow Central 15	d						10 55					11 52										
Motherwell	d						11 10					12 07										
Haymarket	d						11 51	12 18				12 47			13 14							
Edinburgh 10	a						11 55	12 25				12 52			13 19							
Edinburgh	d		12 00				12 08	12 30			13 00	13 06			13 30		13 50			14 00		
Dunbar	d											13 25										
Berwick-upon-Tweed	d						12 47								14 10		14 31					
Alnmouth for Alnwick	d		12 56									14 06								14 56		
Morpeth	d																					
Newcastle 8	a		13 27				13 34	13 55			14 23	14 35			14 58		15 18			15 27		
Sunderland	d													14 12								
Hartlepool	d													14 36								
Newcastle 8	d	13 12	13 28	13 35			13 40	13 56	14 08	14 12	14 25	14 40			15 00	15 07	15 23			15 28		
Chester-le-Street	d															15 16						
Durham	d	13 24	13 41	13 47			13 52		14 20	14 24	14 38	14 52				15 23	15 36			15 41		
Darlington 7	a	13 41	13 59	14 04			14 09	14 24	14 36	14 42	14 55	15 08			15 27	15 39	15 52			15 59		
Middlesbrough	d												14 42									
Eaglescliffe	d													14 59								
Darlington 7	d	13 42	13 59	14 05			14 10	14 24	14 37	14 42	14 56	15 09			15 28	15 40	15 53			15 59		
Northallerton	d	13 54							14 49	14 56			15 10	15 22								
Thirsk	d												15 18	15 31								
York 8	a	14 14	14 29	14 32			14 38	14 53	15 12	15 16	15 24	15 36	15 42	15 46	15 57	16 13	16 19			16 28		
Leeds 10	a						15 05		15 38			16 03	16 08			16 38						
Harrogate	d																					
Scarborough	d																					
York 8	d	14 16	14 30	14 34				14 55		15 18	15 29			15 48	15 58		16 23			16 29		
Doncaster 7	a	14 44	14 54	14 57						15 42	15 52						16 48			16 54		
Skipton	d																					
Keighley	d																					
Bradford Interchange	d																				15 42	
Bradford Forster Square	d																					
Shipley	d																					
Halifax	d																				15 56	
Brighouse	d																				16 06	
Leeds 10	d					15 05	15 10					16 10							16 15			
Wakefield Westgate 7	d					15 17	15 23					16 22							16 28			
Wakefield Kirkgate 4	d																				16 29	
Pontefract Monkhill	d																				16 46	
Sheffield 7	a			15 21			15 51					16 51					17 19					
Hull	d				14 30																	
Selby	d				15 05																	
Doncaster 7	d	14 44	14 54		15 24	15 35				15 43	15 54								16 46	16 54	17 10	
Retford 10	d				15 38						16 08											
Lincoln	d																					
Newark North Gate 7	a		15 17			15 58				16 07										17 17		
	d		15 17			15 58				16 07										17 17		
Grantham 7	a				15 58	16 10													17 16			
	d				15 58	16 10												16 22	17 16			17 19
Peterborough 8	a	15 37	15 46			16 32				16 38	16 48							16 55		17 46		17 50
Norwich	a																	18 31				19 29
Peterborough 8	d	15 38	15 49			16 32				16 38	16 49									17 49		
Stevenage 4	a				16s46	17 04													18 04			
London Kings Cross 15 ⊖	a	16 35	16 46		17 12	17 35		16 55		17 39	17 45			17 46	17 59				18 36	18 46	18 51	

A from Edinburgh   B The Northern Lights   C The Highland Chieftain

Sundays from 30 October

Scotland, North East England, Yorkshire and Humberside - London

		GR	XC	GR	TP	HT	GR	EM	GR	GR	XC	GR	EM	XC	TP	GR	TP	GR	GR	XC	EM	GR	XC
			A											A									A
Aberdeen	d		11 12	11 47																			
Stonehaven	d		11 29	12 04																			
Montrose	d		11 50	12 27																			
Arbroath	d		12 06	12 43																			
Dundee	d		12 25	13 01																			
Leuchars 3	d		12 38	13 15																			
Kirkcaldy	d		13 03	13 39																			
Inverkeithing	d		13 18	13 55																			
Inverness	d																						
Perth	d																						
Stirling	d																						
Glasgow Central 15	d													13 49									14 55
Motherwell	d													14 04									15 11
Haymarket	d		13 37	14 19										14 43									15 51
Edinburgh 10	a		13 42	14 25										14 47									15 56
Edinburgh	d		14 08	14 30						15 00				15 07		15 30			16 00				16 05
Dunbar	d													15 27									16 25
Berwick-upon-Tweed	d		14 47	15 09												16 09							
Alnmouth for Alnwick	d																		16 56				17 05
Morpeth	d																						17 20
Newcastle 8	a		15 34	15 57						16 23				16 34		16 56			17 27				17 37
Sunderland	d																						
Hartlepool	d																						
Newcastle 8	d		15 39	15 59	16 08		16 12			16 25	16 35			16 40		16 58	17 05		17 28	17 35			17 40
Chester-le-Street	d																17 14						
Durham	d		15 51		16 20		16 24			16 38	16 47			16 52			17 21		17 41	17 47			17 52
Darlington 7	a		16 07	16 26	16 36		16 41			16 55	17 04			17 08		17 24	17 37		17 59	18 04			18 08
Middlesbrough	d														16 42								
Eaglescliffe	d																						
Darlington 7	d		16 08	16 27	16 37		16 42			16 56	17 05			17 09		17 25	17 38		17 59	18 05			18 09
Northallerton	d				16 49		16 53								17 10		17 49						
Thirsk	d														17 18								
York 8	a		16 35	16 56	17 12		17 16			17 24	17 31			17 38	17 42	17 53	18 12		18 28	18 31			18 37
Leeds 10	a		17 01		17 38									18 04	18 08		18 38						19 04
Harrogate	d											17 05											
Scarborough	d																						
York 8	d			16 57			17 17			17 29	17 34		17 40			17 55			18 29	18 34			
Doncaster 7	a									17 52	17 57		18 05						18 53	18 57			
Skipton	d																						
Keighley	d																						
Bradford Interchange	d																						
Bradford Forster Square	d																						
Shipley	d																						
Halifax	d																						
Brighouse	d																						
Leeds 10	d	16 45	17 10						17 15			17 45		18 10				18 15				18 45	19 10
Wakefield Westgate 7	d	16 57	17 22						17 28			17 58		18 22				18 28				18 57	19 22
Wakefield Kirkgate 4	d																						
Pontefract Monkhill	d																						
Sheffield 7	a		17 51								18 23		18 28	18 51						19 21			19 50
Hull	d					16 30																	
Selby	d					17 05																	
Doncaster 7	d	17 17				17 26			17 46	17 54		18 17						18 46	18 53			19 17	
Retford 10	d					17 40			18 00														
Lincoln	d																						
Newark North Gate 7	a	17 43					17 58					18 42							19 16			19 43	
	d	17 43					17 58					18 42							19 16			19 44	
Grantham 7	a					18 00			18 22	18 27								19 16					
	d					18 00		18 17	18 22	18 27								19 16			19 27		
Peterborough 8	a	18 14					18 27	18 46		18 51		19 13							19 46		19 56	20 14	
Norwich	a							20 29													21 35		
Peterborough 8	d	18 15					18 28			18 51		19 13							19 49			20 15	
Stevenage 4	a					18s51			19 10									20 08					
London Kings Cross 15 ⊖	a	19 10		18 58		19 15	19 24		19 38	19 48		20 12				19 54		20 36	20 46			21 11	

A from Edinburgh

Sundays from 30 October

Scotland, North East England, Yorkshire and Humberside - London

		SR	TP	GR	TP	XC	HT	GR	GR	GR	XC	TP	GC	GR	TP	XC	GR	NT	EM	GR	XC	GR
											A										B	
Aberdeen	d			13 50																		
Stonehaven	d			14 07																		
Montrose	d			14 30																		
Arbroath	d			14 46																		
Dundee	d			15 04																		
Leuchars 3	d			15 18																		
Kirkcaldy	d			15 42																		
Inverkeithing	d			15 58																		
Inverness	d	20 25																				
Perth	d	23u00																				
Stirling	d	23u45																				
Glasgow Central 15	d																				16 55	
Motherwell	d																				17 11	
Haymarket	d			16 20																	17 55	
Edinburgh 10	a	00 47		16 25																	17 59	
Edinburgh	d			16 30					17 00		17 07			17 30			18 00				18 07	18 30
Dunbar	d										17 27			17 50							18 26	
Berwick-upon-Tweed	d			17 09							17 50			18 13							18 50	19 09
Alnmouth for Alnwick	d																18 56					
Morpeth	d																					
Newcastle 8	a			17 57					18 23		18 36			19 00			19 27				19 34	19 56
Sunderland	d												18 12					19 28				
Hartlepool	d												18 36									
Newcastle 8	d		17 52	17 59		18 20			18 25		18 38			19 02	19 10	19 25	19 28	19a52			19 40	19 58
Chester-le-Street	d																					
Durham	d		18 04			18 32			18 38		18 51				19 22	19 37	19 41				19 52	
Darlington 7	a		18 20	18 26		18 49			18 55		19 06			19 28	19 38	19 53	19 59				20 08	20 24
Middlesbrough	d											18 45										
Eaglescliffe	d												18 59									
Darlington 7	d		18 21	18 27		18 50			18 56		19 08			19 29	19 39	19 54	19 59				20 09	20 25
Northallerton	d		18 33						19 07			19 13	19 20									
Thirsk	d				←							19 21	19 29									
York 8	a		19 04	18 56	19 04	19 21			19 28		19 35	19 42	19 46	19 57	20 11	20 21	20 28				20 36	20 53
Leeds 10	a		→		19 38						20 05	20 08			20 38						21 02	
Harrogate	d																					
Scarborough	d																					
York 8	d			18 57		19 24			19 30				19 48	19 59		20 24	20 29					20 55
Doncaster 7	a					19 48			19 53							20 47	20 53					21 18
Skipton	d																					
Keighley	d																					
Bradford Interchange	d																					
Bradford Forster Square	d																					
Shipley	d																					
Halifax	d																					
Brighouse	d																					
Leeds 10	d							19 15		19 45	20 10									20 45	21 10	
Wakefield Westgate 7	d							19 27		19 57	20 22									20 57	21 22	
Wakefield Kirkgate 4	d																					
Pontefract Monkhill	d																					
Sheffield 7	a					20 16					20 51					21 17					21 50	
Hull	d						18 30															
Selby	d						19 05															
Doncaster 7	d						19 26	19 45	19 54	20 20							20 53			21 15		21 19
Retford 10	d						19 40	19 59												21 29		
Lincoln	d																					
Newark North Gate 7	a								20 17	20 43							21 16					21 47
	d								20 17	20 43							21 16					21 47
Grantham 7	a						20 00	20 21						20 47						21 51		22 00
	d						20 00	20 21						20 48					21 19	21 51		22 00
Peterborough 8	a								20 47	21 13				21 08			21 45		21 49	22 12		22 21
Norwich	a																		23 28			
Peterborough 8	d								20 49	21 13				21 09			21 49			22 13		22 23
Stevenage 4	a						20s51	21 09												22 45		22 54
London Kings Cross 15 ⊖	a			20 58			21 14	21 37	21 46	22 12			21 48	22 05			22 46			23 16		23 22

A to York

B from Edinburgh to York

Table 26

Sundays
from 30 October

Scotland, North East England, Yorkshire and Humberside - London

		TP	TP	GR	NT	GR	XC	GR	TP
		◇1	◇1	1		1	◇1	1	◇1
Aberdeen	d								
Stonehaven	d								
Montrose	d								
Arbroath	d								
Dundee	d								
Leuchars 3	d								
Kirkcaldy	d								
Inverkeithing	d								
Inverness	d								
Perth	d								
Stirling	d								
Glasgow Central 15	d						18 57		
Motherwell	d						19 11		
Haymarket	d						19 51		
Edinburgh 10	a						19 56		
Edinburgh	d			19 00		20 00	20 05	21 00	
Dunbar	d			19 21		20 21	20 29	21 21	
Berwick-upon-Tweed	d			19 44		20 44	20 53	21 44	
Alnmouth for Alnwick	d					21 07		22 06	
Morpeth	d					21 24			
Newcastle 8 ⛴	a			20 30		21 42	21 48	22 37	
Sunderland ⛴	d								
Hartlepool	d								
Newcastle 8 ⛴	d		20 08	20 32	21 06	21 44			
Chester-le-Street	d				21 15				
Durham	d		20 20	20 46	21 24	21 57			
Darlington 7	a		20 36	21 02	21 44	22 15			
Middlesbrough	d	20 06							22 06
Eaglescliffe	d				22a00				
Darlington 7	d		20 37	21 03		22 15			
Northallerton	d	20 38	20 49			22 29			22 34
Thirsk	d	20 46							22 42
York 8	a	21 06	21 12	21 31		23 02			23 09
Leeds 10	a		21 38			23 34			23 38
Harrogate	d								
Scarborough	d								
York 8	d			21 33					
Doncaster 7	a			21 56					
Skipton	d								
Keighley	d								
Bradford Interchange	d								
Bradford Forster Square	d								
Shipley	d								
Halifax	d								
Brighouse	d								
Leeds 10	d								
Wakefield Westgate 7	d								
Wakefield Kirkgate 4	d								
Pontefract Monkhill	d								
Sheffield 7 ⛴	a								
Hull	d								
Selby	d								
Doncaster 7	d			21 57					
Retford 10	d								
Lincoln	d								
Newark North Gate 7	a			22 19					
	d			22 20					
Grantham 7	a			22 32					
	d			22 33					
Peterborough 8	a			22 53					
Norwich	a								
Peterborough 8	d			23 00					
Stevenage 4	a			23s34					
London Kings Cross 15 ⊖	a			00 02					

Table 26A

Mondays to Saturdays

Peterborough - Wisbech, Kings Lynn, Swaffham and Dereham

Bus Service

		GR SX	GR SX	GR SO	GR	GR	GR	GR	GR	GR	GR	GR	GR	GR	GR	GR	GR	GR	GR	GR	GR	GR	GR
Peterborough	d	07 00	07 30	07 35	08 05	08 35	09 05	09 35	10 05	10 35	11 05	11 35	12 05	12 35	13 05	13 35	14 05	14 35	15 05	15 35	16 05	16 35	17 10
Wisbech Bus Station	d	07 51	08 21	08 26	08 56	09 26	09 56	10 26	10 56	11 26	11 56	12 26	12 56	13 26	13 56	14 26	14 56	15 26	15 56	16 26	16 56	17 26	18 00
Kings Lynn Bus Station	d	08 32	09 02	09 02	09 32	10 02	10 32	11 02	11 32	12 02	12 32	13 02	13 32	14 02	14 32	15 02	15 32	16 02	16 32	17 02	17 32	18 02	18 35
Swaffham Market Place	d	09 04	09 34	09 34	10 04	10 34	11 04	11 34	12 04	12 34	13 04	13 34	14 04	14 34	15 04	15 34	16 04	16 34	17 04	17 34	18 04	18 34	19 06
Dereham Market Place	a	09 37	10 07	10 07	10 37	11 07	11 37	12 07	12 37	13 07	13 37	14 07	14 37	15 07	15 37	16 07	16 37	17 07	17 37	18 07	18 37	19 07	19 37

		GR	GR	GR	GR	GR		GR	GR
Peterborough	d	17 40	18 10	18 40	19 10	20 10		21 10	22 10
Wisbech Bus Station	d	18 30	19 00	19 30	20 00	21 00		22 00	23 00
Kings Lynn Bus Station	d	18a58	19 35	19a58	20 35	21 35		22a28	23a28
Swaffham Market Place	d		20 06		21 06	22 06			
Dereham Market Place	a		20 37		21 37	22 37			

Sundays

		GR	GR	GR	GR	GR	GR	GR	GR	GR	GR	GR	GR	GR	GR	GR
Peterborough	d	08 10	09 10	10 10	11 10	12 10	13 10	14 10	15 10	16 10	17 10	18 10	19 10	20 10	21 10	22 10
Wisbech Bus Station	d	09 00	10 00	11 00	12 00	13 00	14 00	15 00	16 00	17 00	18 00	19 00	20 00	21 00	22 00	23 00
Kings Lynn Bus Station	d	09 35	10 35	11 35	12 35	13 35	14 35	15 35	16 35	17 35	18 35	19 35	20 35	21 35	22a28	23a28
Swaffham Market Place	d	10 06	11 06	12 06	13 06	14 06	15 06	16 06	17 06	18 06	19 06	20 06	21 06	22 06		
Dereham Market Place	a	10 37	11 37	12 37	13 37	14 37	15 37	16 37	17 37	18 37	19 37	20 37	21 37	22 37		

Table 26A

Mondays to Saturdays

Dereham, Swaffham, Kings Lynn and Wisbech - Peterborough

Bus Service

		GR SX	GR SX	GR	GR	GR	GR SX	GR SO	GR SX	GR SO	GR SX	GR SO	GR SX	GR SO	GR	GR	GR	GR	GR	GR	GR	GR	GR
Dereham Market Place	d						07 05	07 09	07 30	07 39	08 00	08 09	08 35	08 36	09 05	09 35	10 05	10 35	11 05	11 35	12 05	12 35	13 05
Swaffham Market Place	d						07 35	07 39	08 02	08 09	08 32	08 39	09 07	09 07	09 37	10 07	10 37	11 07	11 35	12 07	12 37	13 07	13 37
Kings Lynn Bus Station	d	05 40	06 10	06 45	07 15	07 45	08 15	08 15	08 45	08 45	09 15	09 15	09 45	09 45	10 15	10 45	11 15	11 45	12 15	12 45	13 15	13 45	14 15
Wisbech Bus Station	d	06 13	06 43	07 18	07 48	08 18	08 48	08 48	09 18	09 18	09 48	09 48	10 18	10 18	10 48	11 18	11 48	12 18	12 48	13 18	13 48	14 18	14 48
Peterborough	a	06 54	07 24	07 59	08 29	08 59	09 29	09 29	09 59	09 59	10 29	10 29	10 59	10 59	11 29	11 59	12 29	12 59	13 29	13 59	14 29	14 59	15 29

		GR	GR	GR	GR	GR		GR	GR	GR SO	GR SX	GR SO	GR SX	GR	GR
Dereham Market Place	d	13 35	14 05	14 35	15 05	15 35		16 05	16 35	17 40	17 44	18 40	18 44	19 44	20 44
Swaffham Market Place	d	14 07	14 37	15 07	15 37	16 07		16 37	17 07	18 12	18 14	19 12	19 14	20 14	21 14
Kings Lynn Bus Station	d	14 45	15 15	15 45	16 15	16 45		17 15	17 45	18 50	18 50	19 50	19 50	20 50	21 50
Wisbech Bus Station	d	15 18	15 48	16 18	16 48	17 18		17 48	18 18	19 22	19 22	20 22	20 22	21 22	22 22
Peterborough	a	15 59	16 29	16 59	17 29	17 59		18 29	18 59	20 01	20 01	21 01	21 01	22 01	23 01

Sundays

		GR	GR	GR	GR	GR	GR	GR	GR	GR	GR	GR	GR	GR	GR	GR	GR
Dereham Market Place	d				08 44	09 44	10 44	11 44	12 44	13 44	14 44	15 44	16 44	17 44	18 44	19 44	20 44
Swaffham Market Place	d				09 14	10 14	11 14	12 14	13 14	14 14	15 14	16 14	17 14	18 14	19 14	20 14	21 14
Kings Lynn Bus Station	d	06 50	07 50	08 50	09 50	10 50	11 50	12 50	13 50	14 50	15 50	16 50	17 50	18 50	19 50	20 50	21 50
Wisbech Bus Station	d	07 22	08 22	09 22	10 22	11 22	12 22	13 22	14 22	15 22	16 22	17 22	18 22	19 22	20 22	21 22	22 22
Peterborough	a	08 01	09 01	10 01	11 01	12 01	13 01	14 01	15 01	16 01	17 01	18 01	19 01	20 01	21 01	22 01	23 01

Table 26B

Mondays to Saturdays

Peterborough - Oundle, Corby and Kettering

Bus Service

		GR	GR	GR	GR	GR	GR	GR	GR	GR	GR	GR	GR	GR	GR
Peterborough Queensgate	d	07 05	07 40	09 10	10 10	11 10	12 10	13 10	14 10	15 10	16 10	17 10	18 30	19 30	20 30
Oundle Market Place	a	07 27	08 22	09 32	10 32	11 32	12 32	13 32	14 32	15 32	16 32	17 32	18 57	19 57	20 57
Corby George Street	a	08 05	09 05	10 05	11 05	12 05	13 05	14 05	15 05	16 05	17 05	18 05	19 25	20 25	21 25
Kettering Library	a	08 35	09 35	10 35	11 35	12 35	13 35	14 35	15 35	16 35	17 35	18 35	19 55	20 55	21 55

Sundays

		GR	GR	GR	GR	GR	GR
Peterborough Queensgate	d	10 10	12 10	14 10	16 10	18 10	20 10
Oundle Market Place	a	10 37	12 37	14 37	16 37	18 37	20 37
Corby George Street	a	11 05	13 05	15 05	17 05	19 05	21 05
Kettering Library	a	11 35	13 35	15 35	17 35	19 35	21 33

Table 26B

Mondays to Saturdays

Kettering and Corby, Oundle - Peterborough

Bus Service

		GR	GR	GR	GR	GR	GR	GR	GR	GR	GR	GR	GR	GR	GR	GR
Kettering Library	d	05 30	06 00	07 05		08 45	09 45	10 45	11 45	12 45	13 45	14 45	15 45	16 50	17 55	18 55
Corby George Street	d	05 55	06 25	07 30		09 10	10 10	11 10	12 10	13 10	14 10	15 10	16 10	17 15	18 20	19 20
Oundle Market Place	d	06 23	06 53	07 58	08 38	09 38	10 38	11 38	12 38	13 38	14 38	15 38	16 38	17 43	18 48	19 48
Peterborough Queensgate	a	06 40	07 25	08 30	09 00	10 00	11 00	12 00	13 00	14 00	15 00	16 00	17 00	18 05	19 10	20 20

Sundays

		GR	GR	GR	GR	GR	GR
Kettering Library	d	08 15	10 15	12 15	14 15	16 15	18 15
Corby George Street	d	08 40	10 40	12 40	14 40	16 40	18 40
Oundle Market Place	d	09 08	11 08	13 08	15 08	17 08	19 08
Peterborough Queensgate	a	09 40	11 40	13 40	15 40	17 40	19 40

Table 26F

Mondays to Saturdays

Doncaster - Robin Hood Airport

Bus Service

		GR	GR	GR	GR	GR	GR	GR	GR	GR	GR	GR	GR	GR	GR	GR	GR	GR	GR
Doncaster Interchange	d	05 35	06 35	07 35	08 35	09 35	10 35	11 35	12 35	13 35	14 35	15 35	16 35	17 35	18 35	19 35	20 35	21 35	22 35
Robin Hood Airport	a	05 59	06 59	07 59	08 59	09 59	10 59	11 59	12 59	13 59	14 59	15 59	16 59	17 59	18 59	19 59	20 59	21 59	22 59

Sundays

		GR	GR	GR	GR	GR	GR	GR	GR	GR
Doncaster Interchange	d	08 35	09 35	10 35	11 35	12 35	13 35	15 35	16 35	17 35
Robin Hood Airport	a	08 59	09 59	10 59	11 59	12 59	13 59	15 59	16 59	17 59

Table 26F

Mondays to Saturdays

Robin Hood Airport - Doncaster

Bus Service

		GR	GR	GR	GR	GR	GR	GR	GR	GR	GR	GR	GR	GR	GR	GR	GR	GR	GR
Robin Hood Airport	d	06 05	07 05	08 05	09 05	10 05	11 05	12 05	13 05	14 05	15 05	16 05	17 05	18 05	19 05	20 05	21 05	22 05	23 05
Doncaster Interchange	a	06 30	07 30	08 30	09 30	10 30	11 30	12 30	13 30	14 30	15 30	16 30	17 30	18 30	19 30	20 30	21 30	22 30	23 30

Sundays

		GR	GR	GR	GR	GR	GR	GR	GR	GR	GR
Robin Hood Airport	d	09 05	10 05	11 05	12 05	13 05	14 05	15 05	16 05	17 05	18 05
Doncaster Interchange	a	09 30	10 30	11 30	12 30	13 30	14 30	15 30	16 30	17 30	18 30

Table 26G

Mondays to Fridays

York - Pickering and Whitby

Bus Service

		GR	GR	GR	GR	GR	GR	GR	GR	GR	GR	GR	GR	GR
York	d	06 46	08 18	09 20	10 01	10 22	11 22	12 22	13 22	14 22	15 22	16 24	17 34	18 31
Eden Camp	a	08 02	09 22	10 22	10 57	11 22	12 22	13 22	14 22	15 22	16 22	17 27	18 32	19 27
Flamingo Land	a			10 35		11 35								
Pickering Eastgate	a	08 16	09 36	10 43	11 09	11 43	12 36	13 36	14 36	15 36	16 36	17 41	18 46	19 41
Whitby Bus Station	a		10 37		11 51	12 44		14 37		16 37	17 37		19 41	

Saturdays

		GR	GR	GR	GR	GR	GR	GR	GR	GR	GR	GR	GR
York	d	08 22	09 22	09 56	10 22	11 22	12 22	13 22	14 22	15 22	16 22	17 34	18 27
Eden Camp	a	09 22	10 22	10 52	11 22	12 22	13 22	14 22	15 22	16 22	17 22	18 27	19 27
Flamingo Land	a		10 35		11 35								
Pickering Eastgate	a	09 36	10 43	11 04	11 43	12 36	13 36	14 36	15 36	16 36	17 36	18 41	19 41
Whitby Bus Station	a	10 37		11 46	12 44		14 37		16 37	17 37		19 42	

Sundays

		GR	GR	GR	GR	GR	GR
York	d	09 22	09 52	09 56	12 52	14 52	16 12
Eden Camp	a	10 22	10 52	10 52	13 52	15 52	17 12
Flamingo Land	a	10 35	11 05				
Pickering Eastgate	a	10 48		11 06	14 06	16 06	17 26
Whitby Bus Station	a			12 07	15 07	17 07	18 27

Table 26G

Mondays to Fridays

Whitby and Pickering - York

Bus Service

		GR	GR	GR	GR	GR	GR	GR	GR	GR	GR	GR	GR	GR	GR	GR
Whitby Bus Station	d					11 06	12 31	13 06		15 06		17 31		18 16		20 16
Pickering Eastgate	d	06 47	08 37	09 07	11 07	12 07	13 13	14 07	15 07	16 07		18 13	17 57	19 17	19 57	21 17
Flamingo Land	d										17 12		18 15			
Eden Camp	d	07 03	08 53	09 23	11 23	12 23	13 23	14 23	15 23	16 23	17 23	18 23	18 26	19 33	20 13	21 33
York	a	08 06	09 56	10 26	12 26	13 26	14 26	15 26	16 26	17 27	18 27	19 23	19 23	20 30	21 30	22 30

Saturdays

		GR	GR	GR	GR	GR	GR	GR	GR	GR	GR	GR	GR	GR	GR	GR
Whitby Bus Station	d					11 06	12 31	13 06		15 06		17 31		18 16		20 16
Pickering Eastgate	d	07 07	08 37	09 07	11 07	12 07	13 13	14 07	15 07	16 07		18 13	17 57	19 17	19 57	21 17
Flamingo Land	d										17 12		18 15			
Eden Camp	d	07 23	08 53	09 23	11 23	12 23	13 23	14 23	15 23	16 23	17 23	18 23	18 26	19 33	20 13	21 33
York	a	08 26	09 56	10 26	12 26	13 26	14 26	15 26	16 26	17 26	18 25	19 23	19 23	20 30	21 30	22 30

Sundays

		GR	GR	GR	GR	GR	GR	GR
Whitby Bus Station	d			12 26	15 46		17 46	18 46
Pickering Eastgate	d	08 57	10 57	13 27	16 47		18 47	19 47
Flamingo Land	d					17 52		
Eden Camp	d	09 13	11 13	13 43	17 03	18 03	19 03	20 03
York	a	10 26	12 26	14 46	18 06	19 03	20 03	21 00

Table 26H

Mondays to Saturdays

Darlington - Richmond and Catterick

Bus Service

		GR SX	GR SX	GR	GR	GR	GR	GR	GR	GR	GR	GR	GR	GR	GR	GR	GR	GR	GR	GR	GR	GR	GR
Darlington	d	06 23	06 53	07 33	08 03	08 33	09 03	09 33	10 03	10 33	11 03	11 33	12 03	12 33	13 03	13 33	14 03	14 33	15 03	15 33	16 03	16 33	17 03
Richmond (Market)	a	06 54	07 24	08 04	08 34	09 04	09 34	10 04	10 34	11 04	11 34	12 04	12 34	13 04	13 34	14 04	14 34	15 04	15 34	16 04	16 34	17 04	17 34
Catterick Garrison Tesco	a	07 05	07 35	08 15	08 45	09 15	09 45	10 15	10 45	11 15	11 45	12 15	12 45	13 15	13 45	14 15	14 45	15 15	15 45	16 15	16 45	17 15	17 45
Catterick Camp Centre	a	07 07	07 37	08 17	08 47	09 17	09 47	10 17	10 47	11 17	11 47	12 17	12 47	13 17	13 47	14 17	14 47	15 17	15 47	16 17	16 47	17 17	17 47
Catterick Garrison Kemmel	a	07 15	07 45	08 25	08 55	09 25	09 55	10 25	10 55	11 25	11 55	12 25	12 55	13 25	13 55	14 25	14 55	15 25	15 55	16 25	16 55	17 25	17 55

		GR	GR	GR	GR	GR	GR
Darlington	d	17 33	18 03	19 03	20 03	21 03	23 03
Richmond (Market)	a	18 04	18 36	19 36	20 36	21 36	23 36
Catterick Garrison Tesco	a	18 15	18 47	19 47	20 47	21 47	23 47
Catterick Camp Centre	a	18 17	18 49	19 49	20 49	21 49	23 49
Catterick Garrison Kemmel	a	18 25	18 57	19 57	20 57	21 57	23 57

Sundays

		GR	GR	GR	GR	GR	GR	GR	GR	GR	GR	GR	GR	GR	GR	GR	GR	GR
Darlington	d	09 03	10 03	11 03	12 03	13 03	14 03	15 03	16 03	17 03	18 03	18 33	19 03	19 33	20 03	21 03	22 03	23 03
Richmond (Market)	a	09 34	10 34	11 34	12 34	13 34	14 34	15 34	16 34	17 34	18 36	19 06	19 36	20 06	20 36	21 36	22 36	23 36
Catterick Garrison Tesco	a	09 45	10 45	11 45	12 45	13 45	14 45	15 45	16 45	17 45	18 47	19 17	19 47	20 17	20 47	21 47	22 47	23 47
Catterick Camp Centre	a	09 47	10 47	11 47	12 47	13 47	14 47	15 47	16 47	17 47	18 49	19 19	19 49	20 19	20 49	21 49	22 49	23 49
Catterick Garrison Kemmel	a	09 55	10 55	11 55	12 55	13 55	14 55	15 55	16 55	17 55	18 57	19 27	19 57	20 27	20 57	21 57	22 57	23 57

Table 26H

Mondays to Saturdays

Catterick and Richmond - Darlington

Bus Service

		GR SX	GR SX	GR SX	GR SO	GR SX	GR SO	GR	GR	GR	GR	GR	GR	GR	GR	GR	GR	GR	GR	GR	GR	GR	GR
Catterick Garrison Kemmel	d	06 22	06 52	07 22	07 27	07 52	07 57	08 32	09 02	09 32	10 02	10 32	11 02	11 32	12 02	12 32	13 02	13 32	14 02	14 32	15 02	15 32	16 02
Catterick Camp Centre	d	06 30	07 00	07 30	07 35	08 00	08 05	08 40	09 10	09 40	10 10	10 40	11 10	11 40	12 10	12 40	13 10	13 40	14 10	14 40	15 10	15 40	16 10
Catterick Garrison Tesco	d	06 32	07 02	07 32	07 37	08 02	08 07	08 42	09 12	09 42	10 12	10 42	11 12	11 42	12 12	12 42	13 12	13 42	14 12	14 42	15 12	15 42	16 12
Richmond (Market)	d	06 44	07 14	07 44	07 49	08 14	08 19	08 54	09 24	09 54	10 24	10 54	11 24	11 54	12 24	12 54	13 24	13 54	14 24	14 54	15 24	15 54	16 24
Darlington	a	07 15	07 45	08 20	08 20	08 45	08 50	09 25	09 55	10 25	10 55	11 25	11 55	12 25	12 55	13 25	13 55	14 25	14 55	15 25	15 55	16 25	16 55

		GR	GR	GR	GR	GR	GR	GR	GR	GR
Catterick Garrison Kemmel	d	16 32	17 02	17 32	18 02	18 32	19 02	20 02	21 02	22 02
Catterick Camp Centre	d	16 40	17 10	17 40	18 10	18 40	19 10	20 10	21 10	22 10
Catterick Garrison Tesco	d	16 42	17 12	17 42	18 12	18 42	19 12	20 12	21 12	22 12
Richmond (Market)	d	16 54	17 24	17 54	18 24	18 54	19 24	20 24	21 24	22 24
Darlington	a	17 25	17 55	18 25	18 55	19 25	19 57	20 57	21 57	22 57

Sundays

		GR	GR	GR	GR	GR	GR	GR	GR	GR	GR	GR	GR	GR	GR
Catterick Garrison Kemmel	d	09 02	10 02	11 02	12 02	13 02	14 02	15 02	16 02	17 02	18 02	19 02	20 02	21 02	22 02
Catterick Camp Centre	d	09 10	10 10	11 10	12 10	13 10	14 10	15 10	16 10	17 10	18 10	19 10	20 10	21 10	22 10
Catterick Garrison Tesco	d	09 12	10 12	11 12	12 12	13 12	14 12	15 12	16 12	17 12	18 12	19 12	20 12	21 12	22 12
Richmond (Market)	d	09 24	10 24	11 24	12 24	13 24	14 24	15 24	16 24	17 24	18 24	19 24	20 24	21 24	22 24
Darlington	a	09 55	10 55	11 55	12 55	13 55	14 55	15 55	16 55	17 55	18 55	19 57	20 57	21 57	22 57

Table 26K

Mondays to Fridays

Berwick-upon-Tweed - Scottish Border Towns

Bus Service

This service is operated by First Lowland under contract to Scottish Borders Council. Telephone 01835 824000

		XC 🚌	XC 🚌	XC 🚌	XC 🚌	XC 🚌	XC 🚌	XC 🚌	XC 🚌	XC 🚌
Berwick-upon-Tweed	d	06 57	08 12	09 52	10 52	12 52	15 07	17 47	18 47	20 22
Duns	a	07 30	08 45	10 25	11 25	13 25	15 40	18 20	19 20	20 55
Earlston	a	08 08	09 33	11 03	12 03	14 03	16 28	18 58	19 58	21 33
Melrose	a	08 22	09 47	11 15	12 15	14 15	16 40	19 10	20 10	21 45
Galashiels Bus Station	a	08 40	10 02	11 30	12 30	14 30	16 55	19 25	20 25	22 00

Saturdays

		XC 🚌	XC 🚌	XC 🚌	XC 🚌	XC 🚌	XC 🚌
Berwick-upon-Tweed	d	08 22	10 52	12 52	15 17	17 17	19 17
Duns	a	08 55	11 25	13 25	15 50	17 50	19 50
Earlston	a	09 33	12 03	14 03	16 28	18 28	20 28
Melrose	a	09 47	12 15	14 15	16 40	18 40	20 40
Galashiels Bus Station	a	10 02	12 30	14 30	16 55	18 55	20 55

Sundays

		XC 🚌	XC 🚌	XC 🚌	XC 🚌	XC 🚌	XC 🚌
Berwick-upon-Tweed	d	10 52	12 52	15 17	17 42	19 07	20 37
Duns	a	11 25	13 40	15 50	18 30	19 55	21 10
Earlston	a	12 03	14 18	16 28	19 08	20 33	21 48
Melrose	a	12 15	14 30	16 40	19 20	20 45	22 00
Galashiels Bus Station	a	12 30	14 45	16 55	19 35	21 00	22 15

Table 26K

Mondays to Fridays

Scottish Border Towns - Berwick-upon-Tweed

Bus Service

This service is operated by First Lowland under contract to Scottish Borders Council. Telephone 01835 824000

		XC 🚌	XC 🚌	XC 🚌	XC 🚌	XC 🚌	XC 🚌	XC 🚌	XC 🚌
Galashiels Bus Station	d	06 25	07 40	08 10	10 50	12 50	14 40	16 32	17 20
Melrose	d	06 40	07 55	08 28	11 05	13 05	14 55	16 50	17 35
Earlston	d	06 52	08 07	08 40	11 17	13 17	15 07	17 02	17 47
Duns	d	07 30	08 50	09 20	11 55	13 55	15 55	17 40	18 30
Berwick-upon-Tweed	a	08 01	09 26	09 56	12 26	14 26	16 26	18 11	19 01

Saturdays

		XC 🚌	XC 🚌	XC 🚌	XC 🚌	XC 🚌	XC 🚌
Galashiels Bus Station	d	06 35	08 20	10 50	12 50	14 50	17 20
Melrose	d	06 50	08 35	11 05	13 05	15 05	17 35
Earlston	d	07 02	08 47	11 17	13 17	15 17	17 52
Duns	d	07 40	09 25	11 55	13 55	15 55	18 30
Berwick-upon-Tweed	a	08 11	09 56	12 26	14 26	16 26	19 01

Sundays

		XC 🚌	XC 🚌	XC 🚌	XC 🚌	XC 🚌	XC 🚌
Galashiels Bus Station	d	08 50	10 50	12 35	14 50	16 35	18 35
Melrose	d	09 05	11 05	12 50	15 05	16 50	18 50
Earlston	d	09 17	11 17	13 02	15 17	17 02	19 02
Duns	d	09 55	11 55	13 40	15 55	17 40	19 40
Berwick-upon-Tweed	a	10 26	12 26	14 26	16 26	18 26	20 26

Table 27

Cleethorpes - Lincoln - Newark - Nottingham

Mondays to Fridays

until 23 September

Miles	Miles			EM	EM	EM	GR	EM	EM	EM	EM	EM		EM	EM	EM	EM	EM	EM	EM	EM	EM		EM	EM
						◇1 A	R 1 B	C		D		D			D		D		D	D	D			D	D
0	—	**Cleethorpes**	d		05 49																				
3¼	—	**Grimsby Town**	d		05 56				07 03					09 20				11 28				13 49			
11¼	—	Habrough	d		06 06				07 13					09 30				11 38				13 59			
17¾	—	Barnetby	d		06 15				07 22					09 39				11 47				14 08			
32¼	—	Market Rasen	d		06 32				07 39					09 55				12 03				14 24			
47	—	**Lincoln**	a		06 51				07 57					10 14				12 22				14 44			
—	—		d	05 26	06 53	07 08	07 20	07 26	07 59	08 35	09 11	09 32		10 15	10 36	11 35	11 42	12 23	12 30	13 40	14 35	14 46		15 30	16 34
51	—	Hykeham	d	05 34	07 01			07 34		08 43					10 44				12 38					15 37	16 42
55¾	—	Swinderby	d	05 40	07 07			07 40		08 49					10 50				12 44					15 43	16 48
58½	0	Collingham	d	05 45	07 12	07 23		07 45	08 15	08 54	09 26			10 32	10 55			12 39	12 48			15 02		15 48	16 53
—	5	**Newark North Gate 7**	a	05 56	07 22		07 46		08 25		09 36			10 44		12 01		12 50				15 11			
—	—		d	05 59																					
63½	—	**Newark Castle**	d	06 10		07 33		07 56		09 03		09 56			11 05		12 05		12 57	14 05	15 00			15 58	17 04
67	—	Rolleston	d	06 16				08 02				10 02							13 04					16 04	
68	—	Fiskerton	d	06 18				08 04				10 04							13 06					16 06	
69¾	—	Bleasby	d	06 22				08 08				10 08							13 09					16 10	
70¾	—	Thurgarton	d	06 25				08 10				10 11							13 12					16 12	
71½	—	Lowdham	d	06 29				08 14		09 18		10 15			11 18		12 18		13 17	14 17	15 13			16 16	17 16
75¾	—	Burton Joyce	d	06 34				08 18				10 19									15 17				
77¾	—	Carlton	d	06 38				08 22				10 23							13 23		15 21			16 23	17 22
80¾	—	**Nottingham 8**	a	06 47		07 57		08 30		09 30		10 30			11 30		12 30		13 30	14 30	15 29			16 30	17 30

		EM	EM	EM	EM	EM	EM	EM		EM	EM
			D		D						
Cleethorpes	d									21 15	
Grimsby Town	d	15 45				18 29				21 22	
Habrough	d	15 55				18 39				21 33	
Barnetby	d	16 04				18 48				21 42	
Market Rasen	d	16 19				19 03				21 57	
Lincoln	a	16 38				19 22				22 18	
	d	16 44	17 28	18 18	18 35	19 25	20 45	21 42			22 27
Hykeham	d		17 36			19 33					22 35
Swinderby	d		17 42			19 39					22 41
Collingham	d	16 59	17 47	18 34		19 44	21 00				22 46
Newark North Gate 7	a	17 12		18 44		19 54					
	d										
Newark Castle	d		17 58		19 03		21 13	22 09			22 57
Rolleston	d		18 04								
Fiskerton	d		18 06								23 04
Bleasby	d		18 10								23 07
Thurgarton	d		18 13								
Lowdham	d		18 17		19 16		21 26	22 22			23 12
Burton Joyce	d		18 21								23 16
Carlton	d		18 24								23 20
Nottingham 8	a		18 32		19 29		21 42	22 34			23 32

Mondays to Fridays

from 26 September

		EM	EM	EM	GR	EM	EM	EM	EM	EM		EM	EM	EM	EM	EM	EM	EM	EM	EM		EM	EM	EM	EM
				◇1 A	R 1 B	C		D		D			D		D		D	D	D			D	D		D
Cleethorpes	d		05 49																						
Grimsby Town	d		05 56				07 03					09 20				11 28				13 49				15 45	
Habrough	d		06 06				07 13					09 30				11 38				13 59				15 55	
Barnetby	d		06 15				07 22					09 39				11 47				14 08				16 04	
Market Rasen	d		06 32				07 39					09 55				12 03				14 24				16 19	
Lincoln	a		06 51				07 57					10 14				12 22				14 44				16 38	
	d	05 26	06 53	07 08	07 20	07 26	07 59	08 35	09 11	09 32		10 15	10 36	11 35	11 42	12 23	12 30	13 40	14 35	14 46		15 30	16 34	16 44	17 28
Hykeham	d	05 34	07 01			07 34		08 43					10 44				12 38					15 37	16 42		17 36
Swinderby	d	05 40	07 07			07 40		08 49					10 50				12 44					15 43	16 48		17 42
Collingham	d	05 45	07 12	07 23		07 45	08 15	08 54	09 26			10 32	10 55			12 39	12 48			15 02		15 48	16 53	16 59	17 47
Newark North Gate 7	a	05 56	07 22		07 46		08 25		09 36			10 44		12 01		12 50				15 11				17 12	
	d	05 59																							
Newark Castle	d	06 10		07 33		07 56		09 03		09 56			11 05		12 05		12 57	14 05	15 00			15 58	17 04		17 58
Rolleston	d	06 16				08 02				10 02							13 04					16 04			18 04
Fiskerton	d	06 18				08 04				10 04							13 06					16 06			18 06
Bleasby	d	06 22				08 08				10 08							13 09					16 10			18 10
Thurgarton	d	06 25				08 10				10 11							13 12					16 12			18 13
Lowdham	d	06 29				08 14		09 18		10 15			11 18		12 18		13 17	14 17	15 13			16 16	17 16		18 17
Burton Joyce	d	06 34				08 18				10 19									15 17						18 21
Carlton	d	06 38				08 22				10 23							13 23		15 21			16 23	17 22		18 24
Nottingham 8	a	06 48		07 57		08 32		09 32		10 32			11 32		12 32		13 32	14 32	15 31			16 32	17 32		18 33

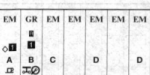

A To St Pancras International
B To London Kings Cross
C From Sleaford to Leicester
D To Leicester

For connections to London Kings Cross please refer to Table 26

Mondays to Fridays

from 26 September

Cleethorpes - Lincoln - Newark - Nottingham

		EM	EM A	EM	EM	EM	EM	EM
Cleethorpes	d						21 15	
Grimsby Town	d			18 29			21 22	
Habrough	d			18 39			21 33	
Barnetby	d			18 48			21 42	
Market Rasen	d			19 03			21 57	
Lincoln	a			19 22			22 18	
	d	18 18	18 35	19 25	20 45	21 42		22 27
Hykeham	d			19 33				22 35
Swinderby	d			19 39				22 41
Collingham	d	18 34		19 44	21 00			22 46
Newark North Gate 7	a	18 44		19 54				
	d							
Newark Castle	d		19 03		21 13	22 09		22 57
Rolleston	d							
Fiskerton	d							23 04
Bleasby	d							23 07
Thurgarton	d							
Lowdham	d		19 16		21 26	22 22		23 12
Burton Joyce	d							23 16
Carlton	d							23 20
Nottingham 8	a		19 31		21 42	22 34		23 32

Saturdays

until 24 September

		EM	EM ◇1 B 🍴	EM C	EM	EM A	EM	EM A	GR R 1 D 🍴	EM
Cleethorpes	d									
Grimsby Town	d				06 50					09 20
Habrough	d				07 00					09 30
Barnetby	d				07 09					09 39
Market Rasen	d				07 26					09 55
Lincoln	a				07 44					10 14
	d	05 26	07 08	07 26	07 46	08 35	09 01	09 19	09 30	10 15
Hykeham	d	05 34		07 34		08 43				
Swinderby	d	05 40		07 40		08 49				
Collingham	d	05 45	07 23	07 45	08 02	08 54	09 16	09 34		10 32
Newark North Gate 7	a	05 56			08 12		09 26		09 52	10 44
	d	05 59								
Newark Castle	d	06 10	07 35	07 55		09 04		09 50		
Rolleston	d	06 16		08 02				09 56		
Fiskerton	d	06 18		08 04				09 58		
Bleasby	d	06 22		08 07				10 02		
Thurgarton	d	06 25		08 10				10 05		
Lowdham	d	06 29		08 14		09 18		10 09		
Burton Joyce	d	06 34		08 18				10 14		
Carlton	d	06 38		08 22				10 18		
Nottingham 8	a	06 47	07 58	08 30		09 30		10 25		

		EM A	EM	EM A	EM	EM A	EM A	EM A	EM	EM A	EM A	EM	EM A	EM A
Cleethorpes	d													
Grimsby Town	d				11 28				13 49			16 00		
Habrough	d				11 38				13 59			16 09		
Barnetby	d				11 47				14 08			16 18		
Market Rasen	d				12 03				14 24			16 33		
Lincoln	a				12 22				14 44			16 52		
	d	10 36	11 35	11 42	12 23	12 30	13 40	14 35	14 45	15 27	16 34	16 54	17 26	18 34
Hykeham	d	10 44				12 38				15 34	16 42		17 34	
Swinderby	d	10 50				12 44				15 40	16 48		17 40	
Collingham	d	10 55			12 39	12 48			15 01	15 45	16 53	17 09	17 45	
Newark North Gate 7	a		12 01		12 50				15 11			17 22		
	d													
Newark Castle	d	11 04		12 05		12 57	14 05	15 01		15 58	17 03		17 57	19 02
Rolleston	d					13 04				16 04			18 03	
Fiskerton	d					13 06				16 06			18 05	
Bleasby	d					13 09				16 10			18 09	
Thurgarton	d					13 12				16 12			18 12	
Lowdham	d	11 17		12 18		13 17	14 17	15 14		16 16	17 16		18 16	19 16
Burton Joyce	d							15 19					18 20	
Carlton	d					13 23		15 23		16 23	17 22		18 23	
Nottingham 8	a	11 29		12 30		13 30	14 30	15 30		16 30	17 30		18 31	19 29

		EM	EM	EM	EM
Cleethorpes	d				
Grimsby Town	d	18 26		19 45	
Habrough	d	18 36		19 54	
Barnetby	d	18 47		20 03	
Market Rasen	d	19 02		20 18	
Lincoln	a	19 21		20 37	
	d	19 23	19 35		20 45
Hykeham	d	19 31			
Swinderby	d	19 37			
Collingham	d	19 42			21 00
Newark North Gate 7	a	19 52			
	d				
Newark Castle	d		20 03		21 10
Rolleston	d				
Fiskerton	d				
Bleasby	d				
Thurgarton	d				
Lowdham	d		20 16		21 23
Burton Joyce	d				
Carlton	d				
Nottingham 8	a		20 30		21 39

A To Leicester
B To St Pancras International
C From Sleaford to Leicester
D To London Kings Cross

For connections to London Kings Cross please refer to Table 26

Table 27

Cleethorpes - Lincoln - Newark - Nottingham

Saturdays
from 1 October

		EM	EM	EM	EM	EM	EM	GR	EM	EM	EM	EM	EM	EM	EM	EM	EM	EM	EM	EM	EM	EM	EM
			◇1					R 1															
			A	B		C		D	C		C		C		C	C	C		C	C		C	C
Cleethorpes	d																						
Grimsby Town	d				06 50					09 20				11 28				13 49			16 00		
Habrough	d				07 00					09 30				11 38				13 59			16 09		
Barnetby	d				07 09					09 39				11 47				14 08			16 18		
Market Rasen	d				07 26					09 55				12 03				14 24			16 33		
Lincoln	a				07 44					10 14				12 22				14 44			16 52		
	d	05 26	07 08	07 26	07 46	08 35	09 01	09 30	09 31	10 15	10 36	11 35	11 42	12 23	12 30	13 40	14 35	14 45	15 27	16 34	16 54	17 26	18 34
Hykeham	d	05 34		07 34		08 43					10 44				12 38				15 34	16 42		17 34	
Swinderby	d	05 40		07 40		08 49					10 50				12 44				15 40	16 48		17 40	
Collingham	d	05 45	07 23	07 45	08 02	08 54	09 16			10 32	10 55			12 39	12 48			15 01	15 45	16 53	17 09	17 45	
Newark North Gate 7	a	05 56			08 12		09 26	09 52		10 44		12 01		12 50				15 11			17 22		
	d	05 59																					
Newark Castle	d	06 10	07 35	07 55		09 04			09 55		11 04		12 05		12 57	14 05	15 01		15 58	17 03		17 57	19 02
Rolleston	d	06 16		08 02					10 01						13 04				16 04			18 03	
Fiskerton	d	06 18		08 04					10 03						13 06				16 06			18 05	
Bleasby	d	06 22		08 07					10 07						13 09				16 10			18 09	
Thurgarton	d	06 25		08 10					10 10						13 12				16 12			18 12	
Lowdham	d	06 29		08 14		09 18			10 14		11 17		12 18		13 17	14 17	15 14		16 16	17 16		18 16	19 16
Burton Joyce	d	06 34		08 18					10 19								15 19					18 20	
Carlton	d	06 38		08 22					10 23						13 23		15 23		16 23	17 22		18 23	
Nottingham 8	a	06 48	07 58	08 32		09 32			10 32		11 31		12 30		13 32	14 32	15 32		16 32	17 30		18 32	19 31

		EM	EM	EM	EM
Cleethorpes	d				
Grimsby Town	d	18 26		19 45	
Habrough	d	18 36		19 54	
Barnetby	d	18 47		20 03	
Market Rasen	d	19 02		20 18	
Lincoln	a	19 21		20 37	
	d	19 23	19 35		20 45
Hykeham	d	19 31			
Swinderby	d	19 37			
Collingham	d	19 42			21 00
Newark North Gate 7	a	19 52			
	d				
Newark Castle	d		20 03		21 10
Rolleston	d				
Fiskerton	d				
Bleasby	d				
Thurgarton	d				
Lowdham	d		20 16		21 23
Burton Joyce	d				
Carlton	d				
Nottingham 8	a		20 30		21 39

Sundays
until 11 September

		EM	EM	EM	EM	EM	EM	EM	EM	EM	EM	EM	EM	EM
Cleethorpes	d			13 56						18 18			20 15	
Grimsby Town	d			14 03						18 25			20 22	
Habrough	d			14 13						18 35			20 33	
Barnetby	d			14 22						18 44			20 42	
Market Rasen	d			14 37						18 59			20 57	
Lincoln	a			14 56						19 18			21 15	
	d	11 05	13 00	15 00	15 45	17 08	17 25	18 05	19 03	19 22	20 05	21 00	21 26	22 10
Hykeham	d			15 08		17 16		18 13	19 11		20 13	21 08	21 34	22 18
Swinderby	d			15 14		17 22		18 19	19 17		20 19	21 14	21 40	22 24
Collingham	d	11 20	13 15	15 18		17 26		18 23	19 22		20 23	21 18	21 45	22 28
Newark North Gate 7	a	11 30	13 25	15 28	16 09		17 49			19 46		21 27	21 55	
	d			15 32								21 31		
Newark Castle	d			15 42		17 36		18 34	19 33		20 35	21 40		22 39
Rolleston	d							18 40						22 45
Fiskerton	d							18 42						22 47
Bleasby	d							18 46						22 50
Thurgarton	d							18 49						22 53
Lowdham	d			15 55		17 49		18 53	19 45		20 47	21 53		22 58
Burton Joyce	d							18 57						23 02
Carlton	d							19 01						23 05
Nottingham 8	a			16 11		18 06		19 12	20 03		21 03	22 09		23 17

A To St Pancras International
B From Sleaford to Leicester
C To Leicester
D To London Kings Cross

For connections to London Kings Cross please refer to Table 26

Table 27

Sundays

from 18 September

Cleethorpes - Lincoln - Newark - Nottingham

		EM	EM	EM	EM	EM	EM	EM	EM	EM
Cleethorpes	d									
Grimsby Town	d									
Habrough	d									
Barnetby	d									
Market Rasen	d									
Lincoln	a									
	d	11 05	13 00	15 00	18 05	19 03	20 05	21 00	21 26	22 10
Hykeham	d			15 08	18 13	19 11	20 13	21 08	21 34	22 18
Swinderby	d			15 14	18 19	19 17	20 19	21 14	21 40	22 24
Collingham	d	11 20	13 15	15 18	18 23	19 22	20 23	21 18	21 45	22 28
Newark North Gate 7	a	11 30	13 25	15 28				21 27	21 55	
	d			15 32				21 31		
Newark Castle	d			15 42	18 34	19 33	20 35	21 40		22 39
Rolleston	d				18 40					22 45
Fiskerton	d				18 42					22 47
Bleasby	d				18 46					22 50
Thurgarton	d				18 49					22 53
Lowdham	d			15 55	18 53	19 45	20 47	21 53		22 58
Burton Joyce	d				18 57					23 02
Carlton	d				19 01					23 05
Nottingham 8	a			16 11	19 12	20 03	21 03	22 09		23 17

For connections to London Kings Cross please refer to Table 26

Table 27

Mondays to Fridays

until 23 September

Nottingham - Newark - Lincoln - Cleethorpes

Miles	Miles			EM	EM	EM A	EM	EM	EM B	EM C	EM	EM	EM C	EM C	EM	EM C	EM A	EM C	EM	EM C	EM A	EM C	EM D
0	—	**Nottingham** 8	d		05 55	06 53			08 05	09 21			10 29	11 17		12 27		13 17		14 29		15 27	16 14
3	—	Carlton	d		06 01	06 59			08 12	09 28				11 23				13 23				15 33	16 20
5	—	Burton Joyce	d		06 05	07 03			08 16					11 27				13 27					16 24
9¼	—	Lowdham	d		06 10	07 08			08 20	09 34			10 40	11 32		12 38		13 32		14 40		15 40	16 29
10	—	Thurgarton	d		06 14	07 12			08 24					11 36				13 36					16 33
11	—	Bleasby	d		06 17	07 15			08 27					11 39				13 39					16 36
12¾	—	Fiskerton	d		06 20	07 18			08 30					11 42				13 42					16 39
13¾	—	Rolleston	d		06 22	07 20			08 33					11 45				13 44					16 42
17¼	—	**Newark Castle**	d		06 30	07 28			08 40	09 51			10 59	11 52		12 54		13 53		14 53		15 54	16 54
—	0	**Newark North Gate** 7	a																				
—	—		d				07 40	08 31			09 57	10 50			12 06		13 02				15 28		
22¼	5	Collingham	d		06 40	07 36	07 49	08 40			10 05		11 09	12 01	12 15		13 11	14 01			15 37	16 03	17 03
25	—	Swinderby	d		06 44		07 54	08 45					11 13		12 19			14 05				16 07	
29¾	—	Hykeham	d		06 50		08 00	08 51					11 19		12 26			14 11				16 13	
33¾	—	**Lincoln**	a		07 04	07 56	08 10	09 02	09 07	10 18	10 23	11 14	11 31	12 21	12 36	13 20	13 30	14 23		15 22	15 55	16 25	17 18
—	—		d	05 57			08 14				10 25				12 37				14 37				
48½	—	Market Rasen	d	06 13			08 31				10 42				12 54				14 53				
63½	—	Barnetby	a	06 30			08 48				10 59				13 10				15 10				
69½	—	Habrough	a	06 41			09 01				11 08				13 19				15 19				
77½	—	**Grimsby Town**	a	06 56			09 15				11 23				13 35				15 34				
80¾	—	**Cleethorpes**	a																				

		EM	EM	EM C	EM	EM C	EM	EM	GR R 1 E	EM ◇1 F	EM
Nottingham 8	d			17 17	17 50	18 15				20 29	22 25
Carlton	d			17 23		18 21					22 31
Burton Joyce	d			17 27		18 25					22 35
Lowdham	d			17 32	18 01	18 30				20 40	22 40
Thurgarton	d			17 36		18 34					
Bleasby	d			17 39		18 37					22 45
Fiskerton	d			17 42		18 40					22 48
Rolleston	d			17 45		18 43					
Newark Castle	d			17 53	18 18	18 53				20 57	22 57
Newark North Gate 7	a										23 06
	d		17 28				19 24	20 03	20 32		23 09
Collingham	d		17 36	18 02	18 27	19 02	19 33	20 12		21 05	23 18
Swinderby	d			18 07	18 31	19 06					23 23
Hykeham	d			18 13	18 37	19 12					23 29
Lincoln	a		18 00	18 26	18 50	19 25	19 51	20 27	21 01	21 22	23 41
	d	17 23					19 55				
Market Rasen	d	17 39					20 12				
Barnetby	a	17 54					20 33				
Habrough	a	18 03					20 43				
Grimsby Town	a	18 18					20 55				
Cleethorpes	a						21 06				

Mondays to Fridays

from 26 September

		EM	EM	EM A	EM	EM	EM B	EM C	EM	EM	EM C	EM C	EM	EM C	EM A	EM C	EM	EM C	EM A	EM C	EM D	EM	EM
Nottingham 8	d		05 55	06 53			08 05	09 19			10 29	11 17		12 27		13 17		14 29		15 27	16 14		
Carlton	d		06 01	06 59			08 12	09 26				11 23				13 23				15 33	16 20		
Burton Joyce	d		06 05	07 03			08 16					11 27				13 27					16 24		
Lowdham	d		06 10	07 08			08 20	09 32			10 40	11 32		12 38		13 32		14 40		15 40	16 29		
Thurgarton	d		06 14	07 12			08 24					11 36				13 36					16 33		
Bleasby	d		06 17	07 15			08 27					11 39				13 39					16 36		
Fiskerton	d		06 20	07 18			08 30					11 42				13 42					16 39		
Rolleston	d		06 22	07 20			08 33					11 45				13 44					16 42		
Newark Castle	d		06 30	07 28			08 40	09 52			10 59	11 52		12 54		13 53		14 53		15 54	16 54		
Newark North Gate 7	a																						
	d				07 40	08 31			09 57	10 50			12 06		13 02				15 28				17 28
Collingham	d		06 40	07 36	07 49	08 40			10 05		11 09	12 01	12 15		13 11	14 01			15 37	16 03	17 03		17 36
Swinderby	d		06 44		07 54	08 45					11 13		12 19			14 05				16 07			
Hykeham	d		06 50		08 00	08 51					11 19		12 26			14 11				16 13			
Lincoln	a		07 06	07 58	08 10	09 02	09 09	10 19	10 23	11 14	11 33	12 23	12 36	13 22	13 30	14 26		15 24	15 55	16 27	17 19		18 00
	d	05 57			08 14				10 25				12 37				14 37					17 23	
Market Rasen	d	06 13			08 31				10 42				12 54				14 53					17 39	
Barnetby	a	06 30			08 48				10 59				13 10				15 10					17 54	
Habrough	a	06 41			09 01				11 08				13 19				15 19					18 03	
Grimsby Town	a	06 56			09 15				11 23				13 35				15 34					18 18	
Cleethorpes	a																						

A To Peterborough
B From Worksop
C From Leicester
D From Leicester to Sleaford
E From London Kings Cross
F From St Pancras International

For connections from London Kings Cross please refer to Table 26

Table 27

Mondays to Fridays

from 26 September

Nottingham - Newark - Lincoln - Cleethorpes

		EM	EM	EM	EM	EM	EM	EM
							◇1	
		A		A			C	
							☕	
Nottingham 8	d	17 17	17 50	18 15			20 29	22 25
Carlton	d	17 23		18 21				22 31
Burton Joyce	d	17 27		18 25				22 35
Lowdham	d	17 32	18 01	18 30			20 40	22 40
Thurgarton	d	17 36		18 34				
Bleasby	d	17 39		18 37				22 45
Fiskerton	d	17 42		18 40				22 48
Rolleston	d	17 45		18 43				
Newark Castle	d	17 53	18 18	18 53			20 57	22 57
Newark North Gate 7	a							23 06
	d				19 24	20 03		23 09
Collingham	d	18 02	18 27	19 02	19 33	20 12	21 05	23 18
Swinderby	d	18 07	18 31	19 06				23 23
Hykeham	d	18 13	18 37	19 12				23 29
Lincoln	a	18 28	18 52	19 27	19 51	20 27	21 22	23 41
	d				19 55			
Market Rasen	d				20 12			
Barnetby	a				20 33			
Habrough	a				20 43			
Grimsby Town	a				20 55			
Cleethorpes	a				21 06			

Saturdays

until 24 September

		EM	EM	EM	EM	EM	EM	EM	EM	EM	EM	EM	EM	EM	EM	EM	EM	EM	EM	EM	EM	EM	EM
				D					A		A	A		A	D	A		A	D	A	A		A
Nottingham 8	d		05 55	06 55			08 01		09 23		10 29	11 17		12 27		13 17		14 29		15 23	16 14		17 13
Carlton	d		06 01	07 01			08 08		09 29			11 23				13 23				15 29	16 20		17 19
Burton Joyce	d		06 05	07 05			08 12					11 27				13 27					16 24		17 23
Lowdham	d		06 10	07 10			08 17		09 36		10 40	11 32		12 38		13 32		14 40		15 36	16 29		17 28
Thurgarton	d		06 14	07 14			08 21					11 36				13 36					16 33		17 32
Bleasby	d		06 17	07 17			08 24					11 39				13 39					16 36		17 35
Fiskerton	d		06 20	07 20			08 27					11 42				13 42					16 39		17 38
Rolleston	d		06 22	07 22			08 30					11 45				13 44					16 42		17 41
Newark Castle	d		06 30	07 29			08 37		09 50		10 58	11 55		12 51		13 51		14 55		15 50	16 51		17 49
Newark North Gate 7	a																						
	d					08 20		09 35		10 52			12 06		13 02				15 28				
Collingham	d		06 40	07 39		08 29		09 43			11 08	12 08	12 15		13 11	14 00			15 37	15 59	17 00		17 58
Swinderby	d		06 44			08 34					11 12		12 19			14 05				16 03			18 03
Hykeham	d		06 50			08 41					11 18		12 26			14 11				16 09			18 09
Lincoln	a		07 04	07 58		08 55	09 09	09 59	10 17	11 20	11 30	12 27	12 36	13 18	13 30	14 23		15 22	15 55	16 21	17 16		18 22
	d	05 38			08 12			10 07					12 37				14 52					17 20	
Market Rasen	d	05 54			08 30			10 24					12 54				15 07					17 36	
Barnetby	a	06 11			08 47			10 40					13 10				15 23					17 52	
Habrough	a	06 22			09 01			10 50					13 20				15 33					18 01	
Grimsby Town	a	06 37			09 15			11 08					13 37				15 48					18 16	
Cleethorpes	a																						

		EM	EM	GR	EM	EM	EM	EM
				[R]	◇1			
			A	E	C		A	A
				☕🍴	☕			
Nottingham 8	d		18 15		19 29		20 29	21 25
Carlton	d		18 21					
Burton Joyce	d		18 25					21 33
Lowdham	d		18 30		19 40		20 40	21 37
Thurgarton	d		18 34					
Bleasby	d		18 37					21 42
Fiskerton	d		18 40					21 46
Rolleston	d		18 43					
Newark Castle	d		18 53		19 58		20 56	21 57
Newark North Gate 7	a							22 06
	d	18 07		19 33		20 32		22 09
Collingham	d	18 16	19 02		20 07	20 41	21 04	22 18
Swinderby	d		19 07					22 22
Hykeham	d		19 13					22 28
Lincoln	a	18 35	19 25	20 03	20 25	20 56	21 23	22 40
	d	18 35				20 58		
Market Rasen	d	18 51				21a15		
Barnetby	a	19 07						
Habrough	a	19 16						
Grimsby Town	a	19 31						
Cleethorpes	a							

A From Leicester
C From St Pancras International
D To Peterborough
E From London Kings Cross

For connections from London Kings Cross please refer to Table 26

Table 27

Saturdays
from 1 October

Nottingham - Newark - Lincoln - Cleethorpes

		EM	EM	EM A	EM	EM	EM	EM	EM B	EM		EM B	EM B	EM	EM B	EM A	EM B	EM	EM B	EM A		EM B	EM B	EM	EM B
Nottingham 8	d		05 55	06 53			08 01		09 23			10 29	11 17		12 27		13 17		14 29			15 23	16 14		17 13
Carlton	d		06 01	06 59			08 08		09 29				11 23				13 23					15 29	16 20		17 19
Burton Joyce	d		06 05	07 03			08 12						11 27				13 27						16 24		17 23
Lowdham	d		06 10	07 09			08 17		09 36			10 40	11 32		12 38		13 32		14 40			15 36	16 29		17 28
Thurgarton	d		06 14	07 13			08 21						11 36				13 36						16 33		17 32
Bleasby	d		06 17	07 16			08 24						11 39				13 39						16 36		17 35
Fiskerton	d		06 20	07 19			08 27						11 42				13 42						16 39		17 38
Rolleston	d		06 22	07 21			08 30						11 45				13 44						16 42		17 41
Newark Castle	d		06 30	07 29			08 37		09 50			10 58	11 55		12 51		13 51		14 55			15 50	16 51		17 49
Newark North Gate 7	a																								
	d					08 20		09 35		10 52				12 06		13 02				15 28					
Collingham	d		06 40	07 39		08 29		09 43				11 08	12 08	12 15		13 11	14 00			15 37		15 59	17 00		17 58
Swinderby	d		06 44			08 34						11 12		12 19			14 05					16 03			18 03
Hykeham	d		06 50			08 41						11 18		12 26			14 11					16 09			18 09
Lincoln	a		07 06	07 58		08 55	09 11	09 59	10 18	11 20		11 32	12 29	12 36	13 20	13 30	14 26		15 24	15 55		16 23	17 17		18 24
	d	05 38			08 12			10 07						12 37				14 52						17 20	
Market Rasen	d	05 54			08 30			10 24						12 54				15 07						17 36	
Barnetby	a	06 11			08 47			10 40						13 10				15 23						17 52	
Habrough	a	06 22			09 01			10 50						13 20				15 33						18 01	
Grimsby Town	a	06 37			09 15			11 08						13 37				15 48						18 16	
Cleethorpes	a																								

		EM	EM B	GR R C	EM ◇1 D	EM		EM B	EM B
Nottingham 8	d		18 15		19 29			20 29	21 25
Carlton	d		18 21						
Burton Joyce	d		18 25						21 33
Lowdham	d		18 30		19 40			20 40	21 37
Thurgarton	d		18 34						
Bleasby	d		18 37						21 42
Fiskerton	d		18 40						21 46
Rolleston	d		18 43						
Newark Castle	d		18 53		19 58			20 56	21 57
Newark North Gate 7	a								22 06
	d	18 07		19 33		20 32			22 09
Collingham	d	18 16	19 02		20 07	20 41		21 04	22 18
Swinderby	d		19 07						22 22
Hykeham	d		19 13						22 28
Lincoln	a	18 35	19 27	20 03	20 25	20 56		21 23	22 40
	d	18 35				20 58			
Market Rasen	d	18 51				21a15			
Barnetby	a	19 07							
Habrough	a	19 16							
Grimsby Town	a	19 31							
Cleethorpes	a								

Sundays
until 11 September

		EM	EM	EM	EM	EM	EM	EM	EM	EM		EM	GR C	EM	EM	EM
Nottingham 8	d			15 29		16 33		17 25	18 42			19 33		20 37		22 26
Carlton	d							17 31								22 32
Burton Joyce	d							17 34								22 35
Lowdham	d			15 39		16 44		17 38	18 52			19 43		20 47		22 40
Thurgarton	d							17 42								22 44
Bleasby	d							17 45								22 47
Fiskerton	d							17 49								22 50
Rolleston	d							17 51								22 52
Newark Castle	d			15 59		16 59		18 00	19 07			19 58		21 03		23 01
Newark North Gate 7	a								19 17							23 11
	d	11 35	13 35		16 37		17 56		19 22	19 53			20 34		22 10	23 15
Collingham	d	11 43	13 43	16 08	16 45	17 08		18 09	19 30			20 07		21 12	22 19	23 23
Swinderby	d				16 50	17 12		18 14	19 35			20 12		21 17		23 28
Hykeham	d				16 56	17 18		18 20	19 41			20 18		21 23		23 34
Lincoln	a	12 02	14 02	16 26	17 08	17 31	18 20	18 33	19 53	20 19		20 30	21 03	21 35	22 37	23 46
	d	12 02		16 27			18 22									
Market Rasen	d	12 18		16 43			18 38									
Barnetby	a	12 33		16 58			18 53									
Habrough	a	12 41		17 06			19 01									
Grimsby Town	a	12 53		17 18			19 13									
Cleethorpes	a	13 15		17 28			19 24									

A To Peterborough
B From Leicester
C From London Kings Cross
D From St Pancras International

For connections from London Kings Cross please refer to Table 26

Table 27

Sundays

from 18 September

Nottingham - Newark - Lincoln - Cleethorpes

		EM	EM	EM	EM	EM	EM	GR A 🚂	EM	EM		EM
Nottingham 8 🚌	d			16 33	17 25	18 42	19 33		20 37			22 26
Carlton	d				17 31							22 32
Burton Joyce	d				17 34							22 35
Lowdham	d			16 44	17 38	18 52	19 43		20 47			22 40
Thurgarton	d				17 42							22 44
Bleasby	d				17 45							22 47
Fiskerton	d				17 49							22 50
Rolleston	d				17 51							22 52
Newark Castle	d			16 59	18 00	19 07	19 58		21 03			23 01
Newark North Gate 7	a					19 17						23 11
	d	11 35	13 35			19 22		20 34		22 10		23 15
Collingham	d	11 43	13 43	17 08	18 09	19 30	20 07		21 12	22 19		23 23
Swinderby	d			17 12	18 14	19 35	20 12		21 17			23 28
Hykeham	d			17 18	18 20	19 41	20 18		21 23			23 34
Lincoln	a	12 02	14 02	17 31	18 33	19 53	20 30	21 03	21 35	22 37		23 46
	d											
Market Rasen	d											
Barnetby	a											
Habrough	a											
Grimsby Town	a											
Cleethorpes	a											

A From London Kings Cross

For connections from London Kings Cross please refer to Table 26

Table 29

Hull and Cleethorpes - Doncaster - Meadowhall, Sheffield, Manchester and Manchester Airport, Cleethorpes - Barton-on-Humber

Miles	Miles	Miles	Miles	Miles			NT	NT	TP	TP	TP	TP	EM	TP	NT	NT	NT	NT	TP	TP	EM	TP	NT	NT
							MX	MX	MX	MO														
									◇1	◇1	◇1	◇1	◇1	◇1					◇1	◇1		◇1		
								A					B			A					C	D		
													⊠						🛒	🛒		🛒		
0	0	—	—	—	**Hull**	d	22p20										05 20					06 00		06 06
4¾	4¾	—	—	—	Hessle	d	22p27																	06 13
7½	7½	—	—	—	Ferriby	d	22p32																	06 18
10½	10½	—	—	—	Brough	d	22p37										05 32					06 12		06 23
14½	14½	—	—	—	Broomfleet	d																		
17	17	—	—	—	Gilberdyke	d																06 19		06 30
—	19¼	—	—	—	Eastrington	d																		
—	22¼	—	—	—	Howden	d																06 26		
—	25	—	—	—	Wressle	d																		
—	31	—	—	—	**Selby**	a																06 36		
—	—	—	—	—		d												06 18				06 36		
—	—	—	—	—	York 8 33	a																		
20¾	—	—	—	—	Saltmarshe	d																		06 36
23¾	—	—	—	—	Goole	d	22p51										05 47							06 41
31	—	—	—	—	Thorne North	d	23p00										05 56							06 50
—	—	0	0	—	**Cleethorpes**	d														05 18	05 49		06 00	
—	—	1½	1½	—	New Clee	d																		
—	—	2¼	2¼	—	Grimsby Docks	d																		
—	—	3¼	3¼	—	**Grimsby Town**	a														05 25	05 55		06 08	
—	—	—	—	—		d														05 26	05 56		06 08	
—	—	5¼	5¼	—	Great Coates	d																		
—	—	6¼	6¼	—	Healing	d																	06 15	
—	—	7½	7½	—	Stallingborough	d																	06 18	
—	—	11¼	11¼	—	Habrough	d														05 36	06 06		06 24	
—	—	—	13	—	Ulceby	d																	06 28	
—	—	—	15¾	—	Thornton Abbey	d																		
—	—	—	17¼	—	Goxhill	d																	06 35	
—	—	—	19¼	—	New Holland	d																	06 40	
—	—	—	20¾	—	Barrow Haven	d																	06 43	
—	—	—	22¾	—	**Barton-on-Humber**	a																	06 48	
—	—	—	—	—	Barton-on-Humber	d																		
—	—	—	—	—	Hull Paragon Interchange	a																		
—	—	17¾	—	—	Barnetby	d														05 45	06a15			
—	—	29	—	—	**Scunthorpe**	a														06 00				
—	—	—	—	—		d														06 00				
—	—	32½	—	—	Althorpe	d														06 05				
—	—	36¼	—	—	Crowle	d														06 11				
—	—	42¼	—	—	Thorne South	d														06 20				
34¼	—	45¼	—	—	Hatfield & Stainforth	d	23p06										06 03			06 25				06 56
37	—	48	—	—	Kirk Sandall	d	23p10										06 10							07 00
—	—	—	—	0	Adwick 31	d																		
—	—	—	—	2¼	Bentley (S.Yorks) 31	d																		
41	49¼	52	—	4	**Doncaster 7** 31	a	23p21										06 16	06 38		06 38				07 11
—	—	—	—	—	London Kings Cross 15 ⊖26	a																		
—	—	—	—	—	York 8 26	d			04 00	04 23	05 26			05 57					06 28					
—	—	—	—	—	**Doncaster 7**	d	23p22					05 40	05 57		06 00		06 25			06 40				
45¾	—	—	—	—	Conisbrough	d	23p29								06 07		06 32							
48	—	—	—	—	Mexborough	d	23p33								06 11		06 36							
49¼	—	—	—	—	Swinton (S.Yorks)	d	23p36	23p56							06 14	06 23	06 39							
53¾	—	—	—	—	Rotherham Central	d	23p45	00 03							06 22	06 31	06 46							
56½	—	—	—	—	**Meadowhall**	d	23p54	00 09				05 58			06 27	06 38	06 52			06 58				
60	—	—	—	—	**Sheffield 7**	a	00 04	00 23				06 08	06 18		06 38	06 47	07 07			07 06				
—	—	—	—	—		d						06 11								07 09				
96¾	—	—	—	—	Stockport 78	a						06 53								07 53				
102¾	—	—	—	—	**Manchester Piccadilly 10**	a			06 02	06 02	06 50	07 02		07 19					07 51	08 02		08 05		
112½	—	—	—	—	**Manchester Airport** 85	a			06 24	06 24	07 12	07 29		07 42					08 12	08 26				

A From Leeds
B From Leeds to St Pancras International
C To Newark North Gate
D To Liverpool Lime Street

Table 29

Hull and Cleethorpes - Doncaster - Meadowhall, Sheffield, Manchester and Manchester Airport, Cleethorpes - Barton-on-Humber

		HT	TP	XC	NT	NT	XC	NT	TP	EM	NT	NT	XC	NT	GR	NT	NT	TP	XC	NT	NT	NT
					BHX															BHX		
		◇1	◇1	◇1			◇1		◇1				◇1		1			◇1	◇1			
				A		B	C	D		E			F		G	H	I		J		D	
					🚌															🚌		
		⊠	🛒	🛒			🛒		🛒				🛒		🛒			🛒	🛒			
Hull	d	06 25	06 37											06 40	07 00	07 07		07 37				
Hessle	d													06 47								
Ferriby	d													06 52								
Brough	d	06 37	06 49											06 57	07 12	07 19		07 49				
Broomfleet	d																					
Gilberdyke	d													07 04		07 26						
Eastrington	d															07 31						
Howden	d	06 49														07 35		08 01				
Wressle	d															07 40						
Selby	a	06 59	07 07												07 33	07 48		08 10				
	d	07 00	07 07												07 34	07 48		08 11				
York 8 33	a															08 21						
Saltmarshe	d													07 10								
Goole	d													07 15								
Thorne North	d													07 24								
Cleethorpes	d								06 18		07 00											
New Clee	d																					
Grimsby Docks	d										07 05											
Grimsby Town	a								06 25		07 08											
	d								06 26	07 03	07 08											
Great Coates	d										07 12											
Healing	d										07 15											
Stallingborough	d										07 18											
Habrough	d								06 36	07 13	07 24											
Ulceby	d										07 28											
Thornton Abbey	d										07 32											
Goxhill	d										07 35											
New Holland	d										07 40											
Barrow Haven	d										07 43											
Barton-on-Humber	a										07 48											
Barton-on-Humber	d				06 53															08 20		
Hull Paragon Interchange	a				07 20															08 52		
Barnetby	d								06 45	07a22												
Scunthorpe	a								07 00													
	d								07 00								07 30					
Althorpe	d																07 35					
Crowle	d																07 41					
Thorne South	d																07 49					
Hatfield & Stainforth	d													07 30			07 56					
Kirk Sandall	d													07 34			08 00					
Adwick 31	d											07 29										08 15
Bentley (S.Yorks) 31	d											07 33										08 18
Doncaster 7 31	a	07 17							07 33			07 37		07 46	07 52		08 13					08 23
London Kings Cross 15 ⊖26	a	09 18													09 58							
York 8 26	d						06 32						07 23						07 44			
Doncaster 7	d			06 45		07 02			07 35			07 39	07 55	07 48								08 25
Conisbrough	d					07 09						07 46		07 55								08 32
Mexborough	d					07 13						07 50		07 59								08 36
Swinton (S.Yorks)	d					07 16		07 30				07 53		08 02							08 34	08 42
Rotherham Central	d					07 27		07 39				08 00		08 12							08 43	08 50
Meadowhall	d					07 33		07 45	07 53			08 06		08 23							08 51	08 57
Sheffield 7	a			07 11		07 40	07 50	07 56	08 00			08 18	08 18	08 33					08 51		08 59	09 05
	d								08 05													
Stockport 78	a								08 53													
Manchester Piccadilly 10	a		08 36						09 02									09 36				
Manchester Airport 85	a								09 33													

A From Leeds to Southampton Central
B To Worksop
C To Plymouth
D From Leeds
E To Newark North Gate
F From Newcastle to Reading
G The Hull Executive
H From Beverley
I To Adwick
J From Newcastle to Plymouth

Table 29

Hull and Cleethorpes - Doncaster - Meadowhall, Sheffield, Manchester and Manchester Airport, Cleethorpes - Barton-on-Humber

Mondays to Fridays

Station		TP	XC	NT	NT	NT	NT	HT	XC	NT	NT	NT	TP	TP	TP	NT	NT	NT	EM	XC	NT	XC	NT
		◇1 🍴	◇1 A 🍴		B	B	C	◇1 ⊠	◇1 D 🍴	E		F	◇1 🍴	◇1 🍴	◇1 🍴		B		G	◇1 H 🍴	C	◇1 I 🍴	BHX 🚌
Hull	d				07 40	08 03		08 25				08 28	08 40				08 56	09 02					
Hessle	d				07 47							08 35											
Ferriby	d				07 52							08 40											
Brough	d				07 57	08 15		08 37				08 45	08 52				09 08	09 14					
Broomfleet	d				08 02																		
Gilberdyke	d				08 07							08 52						09 21					
Eastrington	d																						
Howden	d							08 49										09 28					
Wressle	d																						
Selby	a							08 58					09 11					09 38					
	d							08 58					09 11					09 38					
York 8 33	a																	10 10					
Saltmarshe	d				08 12																		
Goole	d				08 17	08 29						09 01					09 23						
Thorne North	d				08 26							09 09											
Cleethorpes	d	07 26													08 26	08 55							
New Clee	d															08x58							
Grimsby Docks	d															09 00							
Grimsby Town	a	07 33													08 33	09 03							
	d	07 34													08 34	09 03			09 20				
Great Coates	d															09 07							
Healing	d															09 10							
Stallingborough	d															09 13							
Habrough	d	07 44													08 44	09 19			09 30				
Ulceby	d															09 23							
Thornton Abbey	d															09 27							
Goxhill	d															09 30							
New Holland	d															09 35							
Barrow Haven	d															09 38							
Barton-on-Humber	a															09 43							
Barton-on-Humber	d																						10 00
Hull Paragon Interchange	a																						10 27
Barnetby	d	07 53													08 53				09a39				
Scunthorpe	a	08 08													09 08								
	d	08 08					08 19								09 08						09 19		
Althorpe	d						08 24														09 24		
Crowle	d						08 30														09 30		
Thorne South	d						08 39														09 39		
Hatfield & Stainforth	d				08 33		08 45					09 16									09 44		
Kirk Sandall	d				08 36		08 50					09 20									09 49		
Adwick 31	d			08 33							09 15												
Bentley (S.Yorks) 31	d			08 37							09 19												
Doncaster 7 31	a	08 38		08 42	08 46	08 53	09 01	09 24			09 24	09 31			09 38		09 49				10 01		
London Kings Cross 15 ⊖26	a							11 10															
York 8 26	d		08 24						08 44					09 28						09 35		09 44	
Doncaster 7	d	08 41	08 50			08 56	09 01				09 26				09 42		09 50			09 58	10 04		
Conisbrough	d						09 08				09 33										10 11		
Mexborough	d						09 12				09 35										10 15		
Swinton (S.Yorks)	d						09 16			09 35	09 42										10 18		
Rotherham Central	d						09 27			09 44	09 50										10 27		
Meadowhall 🚊	d	09 01				09 16	09 33			09 50	09 55				10 01		10 08				10 33		
Sheffield 7 🚊	a	09 08	09 17			09 26	09 41		09 51	10 00	10 05				10 08		10 19			10 20	10 41	10 51	
	d	09 11													10 11								
Stockport 78	a	09 53													10 53								
Manchester Piccadilly 10 🚊	a	10 02											10 36	10 49	11 02								
Manchester Airport 85 ✈	a	10 26												11 12	11 26								

A From Newcastle to Southampton Central
B From Bridlington
C To Lincoln
D From Edinburgh to Plymouth
E From Leeds
F From Scarborough
G To Newark North Gate
H From Edinburgh to Reading
I From Glasgow Central to Plymouth

Table 29

Hull and Cleethorpes - Doncaster - Meadowhall, Sheffield, Manchester and Manchester Airport, Cleethorpes - Barton-on-Humber

Mondays to Fridays

Station		NT	NT	NT	TP	TP	NT	NT	XC	NT	XC	NT	NT	NT	HT	TP	TP	NT	NT	EM	XC	NT
		A		B	◇1 🍴	◇1 🍴	C		◇1 D 🍴	E	◇1 F 🍴	A			◇1 ⊠	◇1 🍴	◇1 🍴		C	G	◇1 H 🍴	
Hull	d			09 25	09 40		09 56	10 08						10 18	10 30	10 40			10 57			
Hessle	d			09 32										10 25								
Ferriby	d			09 37										10 30								
Brough	d			09 42	09 52		10 08	10 20						10 35	10 42	10 52			11 09			
Broomfleet	d																					
Gilberdyke	d			09 49				10 26						10 42								
Eastrington	d																					
Howden	d							10 34							10 54							
Wressle	d																					
Selby	a				10 11			10 47							11 03	11 11						
	d				10 11			10 47							11 03	11 11						
York 8 33	a							11 18														
Saltmarshe	d																					
Goole	d			10 01			10 22							11 01					11 23			
Thorne North	d			10 09										11 08								
Cleethorpes	d					09 26											10 26	10 55				
New Clee	d																	10x58				
Grimsby Docks	d																	11 00				
Grimsby Town	a					09 33											10 33	11 03				
	d					09 34											10 34	11 03		11 28		
Great Coates	d																	11 07				
Healing	d																	11 10				
Stallingborough	d																	11 13				
Habrough	d																10 44	11 19		11 38		
Ulceby	d																	11 23				
Thornton Abbey	d																	11 27				
Goxhill	d																	11 30				
New Holland	d																	11 35				
Barrow Haven	d																	11 38				
Barton-on-Humber	a																	11 43				
Barton-on-Humber	d																					
Hull Paragon Interchange	a																					
Barnetby	d					09 53											10 53			11a47		
Scunthorpe	a					10 08											11 08					
	d					10 08				10 19							11 08					
Althorpe	d									10 24												
Crowle	d									10 30												
Thorne South	d									10 39												
Hatfield & Stainforth	d			10 15						10 44				11 14								
Kirk Sandall	d			10 20						10 49				11 19								
Adwick 31	d		10 15										11 15									
Bentley (S.Yorks) 31	d		10 19										11 19									
Doncaster 7 31	a		10 24	10 30		10 38	10 47			11 00			11 24	11 29	11 24		11 38		11 47			
London Kings Cross 15 ⊖26	a														13 10							
York 8 26	d								10 34		10 44										11 34	11 05
Doncaster 7	d		10 26			10 42	10 49		10 58	11 04			11 26				11 42		11 48		11 58	
Conisbrough	d		10 33							11 11			11 33									
Mexborough	d		10 37							11 15			11 37									
Swinton (S.Yorks)	d	10 35	10 43							11 18		11 35	11 43									12 10
Rotherham Central	d	10 44	10 52							11 27		11 44	11 52									12 19
Meadowhall 🚊	d	10 50	10 58			11 01	11 08			11 33		11 51	11 56				12 01		12 08			12 24
Sheffield 7 🚊	a	11 01	11 05			11 08	11 20		11 20	11 41	11 51	12 01	12 05				12 08		12 19		12 20	12 36
	d					11 11											12 11					
Stockport 78	a					11 53											12 53					
Manchester Piccadilly 10 🚊	a				11 36	12 02										12 36	13 02					
Manchester Airport 85 ✈	a					12 26											13 26					

A From Leeds
B From Beverley
C From Bridlington
D From Newcastle to Southampton Central
E To Lincoln
F From Dundee to Plymouth
G To Newark North Gate
H From Newcastle to Reading

Table 29

Hull and Cleethorpes - Doncaster - Meadowhall, Sheffield, Manchester and Manchester Airport, Cleethorpes - Barton-on-Humber

		NT A	XC ◇1 B ⌶	NT BHX	NT C	NT	NT	TP ◇1 ⌶	TP ◇1 ⌶	NT D	NT	XC ◇1 E ⌶	NT A	NT	HT ◇1 ☒	TP ◇1 ⌶	XC ◇1 F ⌶	NT C	NT	TP ◇1 ⌶	NT	NT G	NT
Hull	d						11 23	11 40		11 55	12 03			12 18	12 30	12 40						12 57	13 12
Hessle	d						11 30							12 25									
Ferriby	d						11 35							12 30									
Brough	d						11 40	11 52		12 07	12 15			12 35	12 42	12 52						13 09	13 24
Broomfleet	d						11 45																
Gilberdyke	d						11 50							12 43									13 32
Eastrington	d																						13 36
Howden	d										12 27				12 55								13 41
Wressle	d																						13 47
Selby	a							12 11			12 37				13 03	13 11							13 54
	d							12 11			12 38				13 03	13 11							13 55
York 8 33	a										13 04												14 27
Saltmarshe	d													12 49									
Goole	d						12 01			12 22				13 01								13 23	
Thorne North	d						12 09							13 09									
Cleethorpes	d								11 26											12 26	12 55		
New Clee	d																				12x58		
Grimsby Docks	d																				13 00		
Grimsby Town	a								11 33											12 33	13 03		
	d								11 34											12 34	13 03		
Great Coates	d																				13 07		
Healing	d																				13 10		
Stallingborough	d																				13 13		
Habrough	d																				13 19		
Ulceby	d																				13 23		
Thornton Abbey	d																				13 27		
Goxhill	d																				13 30		
New Holland	d																				13 35		
Barrow Haven	d																				13 38		
Barton-on-Humber	a																				13 43		
Barton-on-Humber	d			12 00																			
Hull Paragon Interchange	a			12 27																			
Barnetby	d								11 53											12 53			
Scunthorpe	a								12 08											13 08			
	d	11 19							12 08				12 19							13 08			
Althorpe	d	11 24											12 24										
Crowle	d	11 30											12 30										
Thorne South	d	11 39											12 39										
Hatfield & Stainforth	d	11 44					12 15						12 44	13 13									
Kirk Sandall	d	11 49					12 20						12 49	13 18									
Adwick 31	d					12 15													13 14				
Bentley (S.Yorks) 31	d					12 19													13 18				
Doncaster 7 31	a	12 00				12 25	12 30		12 38	12 47			13 01	13 30	13 24				13 26	13 38		13 47	
London Kings Cross 15 ⊖26	a														15 10								
York 8 26	d		11 44									12 34					12 44						
Doncaster 7	d	12 03				12 26			12 42	12 48		12 59	13 02						13 26	13 42		13 48	
Conisbrough	d	12 11				12 33							13 11						13 33				
Mexborough	d	12 15				12 37							13 15						13 37				
Swinton (S.Yorks)	d	12 18			12 35	12 43							13 18					13 35	13 42				
Rotherham Central	d	12 27			12 44	12 52							13 27					13 44	13 52				
Meadowhall ⇌	d	12 33			12 51	12 56			13 01	13 07			13 33					13 51	13 56	14 01		14 05	
Sheffield 7 ⇌	a	12 41	12 51		13 01	13 05			13 08	13 20		13 20	13 41				13 51	14 01	14 05	14 08		14 20	
	d								13 11											14 11			
Stockport 78	a								13 53											14 53			
Manchester Piccadilly 10 ⇌	a							13 36	14 02							14 36				15 02			
Manchester Airport 85 ✈	a								14 26											15 26			

A To Lincoln
B From Glasgow Central to Plymouth
C From Leeds
D From Bridlington
E From Newcastle to Southampton Central
F From Glasgow Central to Penzance
G From Scarborough

Table 29

Hull and Cleethorpes - Doncaster - Meadowhall, Sheffield, Manchester and Manchester Airport, Cleethorpes - Barton-on-Humber

		XC ◇1 A ⌶	NT B	XC ◇1 C ⌶	NT BHX	NT D	NT	NT	TP ◇1 ⌶	TP ◇1 ⌶	EM E	NT F	NT	XC ◇1 G ⌶	NT B	XC ◇1 H ⌶	NT D	NT	NT	TP ◇1 ⌶	TP ◇1 ⌶	NT	NT I
Hull	d							13 25	13 40			13 57	14 18						14 25	14 40			14 57
Hessle	d							13 32											14 32				
Ferriby	d							13 37											14 37				
Brough	d							13 42	13 52			14 09	14 30						14 42	14 52			15 09
Broomfleet	d																						
Gilberdyke	d							13 49											14 49				
Eastrington	d																						
Howden	d												14 42										
Wressle	d																						
Selby	a								14 11				14 53							15 11			
	d								14 11				14 53							15 11			
York 8 33	a												15 25										
Saltmarshe	d																						
Goole	d							14 01				14 23							15 01				15 23
Thorne North	d							14 09											15 09				
Cleethorpes	d									13 26											14 26	14 55	
New Clee	d																					14x58	
Grimsby Docks	d																					15 00	
Grimsby Town	a									13 33											14 33	15 03	
	d									13 34	13 49										14 34	15 03	
Great Coates	d																					15 07	
Healing	d																					15 10	
Stallingborough	d																					15 13	
Habrough	d										13 59										14 44	15 19	
Ulceby	d																					15 23	
Thornton Abbey	d																					15 27	
Goxhill	d																					15 30	
New Holland	d																					15 35	
Barrow Haven	d																					15 38	
Barton-on-Humber	a																					15 43	
Barton-on-Humber	d				14 00																		
Hull Paragon Interchange	a				14 27																		
Barnetby	d									13 53	14a08										14 53		
Scunthorpe	a									14 08											15 08		
	d		13 19							14 08					14 19						15 08		
Althorpe	d		13 24												14 24								
Crowle	d		13 30												14 30								
Thorne South	d		13 39												14 39								
Hatfield & Stainforth	d		13 44					14 15							14 44				15 15				
Kirk Sandall	d		13 49					14 20							14 49				15 20				
Adwick 31	d						14 15											15 15					
Bentley (S.Yorks) 31	d						14 19											15 19					
Doncaster 7 31	a		13 59				14 24	14 31		14 38		14 46			14 59			15 24	15 30		15 38		15 47
London Kings Cross 15 ⊖26	a																						
York 8 26	d	13 34		13 44										14 34		14 44							
Doncaster 7	d	13 58	14 03				14 26			14 42		14 48		14 58	15 04			15 25			15 42		15 48
Conisbrough	d		14 12				14 31								15 11			15 32					
Mexborough	d		14 16				14 35								15 15			15 37					
Swinton (S.Yorks)	d		14 18			14 35	14 42								15 18		15 35	15 42					
Rotherham Central	d		14 29			14 44	14 52								15 27		15 44	15 50					
Meadowhall ⇌	d		14 34			14 50	14 56			15 01		15 07			15 33		15 50	15 57			16 01		16 07
Sheffield 7 ⇌	a	14 20	14 43	14 51		15 01	15 05			15 08		15 19		15 20	15 41	15 51	16 01	16 05			16 08		16 20
	d									15 11											16 10		
Stockport 78	a									15 53											16 53		
Manchester Piccadilly 10 ⇌	a								15 36	16 02										16 36	17 02		
Manchester Airport 85 ✈	a									16 26											17 32		

A From Newcastle to Reading
B To Lincoln
C From Aberdeen to Penzance
D From Leeds
E To Newark North Gate
F From Bridlington
G From Newcastle to Southampton Central
H From Glasgow Central to Penzance
I From Scarborough

Table 29

Hull and Cleethorpes - Doncaster - Meadowhall, Sheffield, Manchester and Manchester Airport, Cleethorpes - Barton-on-Humber

		NT	XC	NT	NT	HT	XC	NT BHX	NT	NT	NT	TP	TP	EM	NT	XC	NT	NT	NT	TP	NT
			◇1			◇1	◇1					◇1	◇1			◇1				◇1	
			A		B		C		D	E				F	G	A		B	H		D
			⊼			⊠	⊼	🚌				⊼	⊼			⊼				⊼	
Hull	d	15 02				15 10					15 24	15 39			15 57		16 10		16 26	16 40	
Hessle	d										15 31								16 33		
Ferriby	d										15 36								16 38		
Brough	d	15 14				15 22					15 41	15 51			16 09		16 22		16 43	16 52	
Broomfleet	d																		16 49		
Gilberdyke	d										15 49						16 29		16 53		
Eastrington	d																				
Howden	d	15 26				15 36											16 36				
Wressle	d																				
Selby	a	15 36				15 45						16 10					16 46			17 11	
	d	15 38				15 45						16 10					16 47			17 11	
York ■8 33	a	16 06															17 13				
Saltmarshe	d																		16 59		
Goole	d										16 00				16 23				17 04		
Thorne North	d										16 09								17 12		
Cleethorpes	d												15 26								
New Clee	d																				
Grimsby Docks	d																				
Grimsby Town	a												15 33								
	d												15 34	15 45							
Great Coates	d																				
Healing	d																				
Stallingborough	d																				
Habrough	d													15 55							
Ulceby	d																				
Thornton Abbey	d																				
Goxhill	d																				
New Holland	d																				
Barrow Haven	d																				
Barton-on-Humber	a																				
Barton-on-Humber	d							16 00													
Hull Paragon Interchange	a							16 27													
Barnetby	d												15 53	16a03							
Scunthorpe	a												16 08								
	d				15 19								16 08					16 19			
Althorpe	d				15 24													16 24			
Crowle	d				15 30													16 30			
Thorne South	d				15 39													16 39			
Hatfield & Stainforth	d				15 44						16 14							16 44	17 18		
Kirk Sandall	d				15 49						16 19							16 49	17 22		
Adwick 31	d									16 15											
Bentley (S.Yorks) 31	d									16 19											
Doncaster ■7 31	a				15 59	16 03				16 24	16 30		16 38		16 47			16 59	17 34		
London Kings Cross ■15 ⊖26	a					17 45															
York ■8 26	d		15 34	15 01			15 44									16 04					
Doncaster ■7	d		15 58		16 03					16 26			16 42		16 48			17 01			
Conisbrough	d				16 11					16 33								17 08			
Mexborough	d				16 15					16 37								17 12			
Swinton (S.Yorks)	d			16 01	16 16				16 35	16 42								17 16			17 35
Rotherham Central	d			16 11	16 27				16 44	16 50								17 27			17 44
Meadowhall ⇌	d			16 18	16 33				16 50	16 55			17 01		17 09			17 33			17 50
Sheffield ■7 ⇌	a		16 20	16 25	16 41		16 51		17 00	17 05			17 08		17 20	17 20		17 41			18 01
	d												17 11								
Stockport 78	a												17 53								
Manchester Piccadilly ■10 ⇌	a											17 37	18 02							18 37	
Manchester Airport 85 ✈	a												18 26								

A From Newcastle to Reading
B To Lincoln
C From Edinburgh to Plymouth
D From Leeds
E To Retford Low Level
F To Newark North Gate
G From Bridlington
H From Scarborough

Table 29

Hull and Cleethorpes - Doncaster - Meadowhall, Sheffield, Manchester and Manchester Airport, Cleethorpes - Barton-on-Humber

		NT	TP	TP	NT	NT	TP	XC	NT	HT	NT	XC	NT BHX	NT	NT	TP	EM	NT BHX	NT	NT	NT	TP	XC
			◇1	◇1			◇1	◇1		◇1		◇1				◇1						◇1	◇1
			A	B	C		D	E				F		G			H			I	J		K
			⊼	⊼				⊼		⊠		⊼	🚌			⊼		🚌	🚌			⊼	⊼
Hull	d				16 54		17 01			17 10	17 18									17 42	17 52	17 58	
Hessle	d										17 25									17 49			
Ferriby	d										17 30									17 54			
Brough	d				17 06		17 13			17 22	17 35									17 59	18 04	18 10	
Broomfleet	d										17 40												
Gilberdyke	d				17 13						17 45									18 06			
Eastrington	d										17 49												
Howden	d									17 34	17 54												
Wressle	d										17 58												
Selby	a						17 31			17 42	18 06										18 25	18 29	
	d									17 43	18 06										18 26	18 29	
York ■8 33	a										18 33												
Saltmarshe	d																			18 12			
Goole	d				17 22															18 19			
Thorne North	d																			18 28			
Cleethorpes	d		16 26	16 26		16 55										17 26							
New Clee	d																						
Grimsby Docks	d					17 00																	
Grimsby Town	a		16 33	16 33		17 03										17 33							
	d		16 34	16 34		17 04										17 34	18 29						
Great Coates	d					17 08																	
Healing	d					17 11																	
Stallingborough	d					17 14																	
Habrough	d		16 44	16 44		17 20										17 44	18 39						
Ulceby	d					17 23																	
Thornton Abbey	d					17 28																	
Goxhill	d					17 31																	
New Holland	d					17 35																	
Barrow Haven	d					17 38																	
Barton-on-Humber	a					17 44																	
Barton-on-Humber	d												18 00					19 53	21 53				
Hull Paragon Interchange	a												18 27					20 20	22 20				
Barnetby	d		16 53	16 53												17 53	18a47						
Scunthorpe	a		17 08	17 08												18 08							
	d		17 08	17 08					17 19							18 08							
Althorpe	d								17 24														
Crowle	d								17 30														
Thorne South	d								17 39														
Hatfield & Stainforth	d								17 44											18 34			
Kirk Sandall	d								17 49											18 39			
Adwick 31	d																						
Bentley (S.Yorks) 31	d																						
Doncaster ■7 31	a		17 38	17 38	17 46				17 58	18 02						18 38				18 51	18 47		
London Kings Cross ■15 ⊖26	a									19 47										→			
York ■8 26	d							17 34				17 44											18 34
Doncaster ■7	d	17 24	17 42	17 42	17 47			17 59	18 02						18 26	18 42					18 49		18 58
Conisbrough	d	17 31							18 09						18 33								
Mexborough	d	17 35							18 13						18 37								
Swinton (S.Yorks)	d	17 42							18 16					18 35	18 42								
Rotherham Central	d	17 50							18 27					18 45	18 49								
Meadowhall ⇌	d	17 57	18 01	18 01	18 07				18 32					18 50	18 57	19 01					19 06		
Sheffield ■7 ⇌	a	18 04	18 08	18 08	18 19			18 20	18 42			18 51		19 00	19 06	19 08					19 17		19 20
	d		18 10	18 10												19 11							
Stockport 78	a		18 53	18 53												19 53							
Manchester Piccadilly ■10 ⇌	a		19 02	19 02												20 02						19 57	
Manchester Airport 85 ✈	a		19 28	19 33												20 38							

A from 18 July
B until 15 July
C From Bridlington
D To Huddersfield
E From Newcastle to Reading
F From Edinburgh to Plymouth
G From Leeds
H To Newark North Gate
I To Sheffield
J From Scarborough
K From Newcastle to Guildford

Table 29

Mondays to Fridays

Hull and Cleethorpes - Doncaster - Meadowhall, Sheffield, Manchester and Manchester Airport, Cleethorpes - Barton-on-Humber

		NT	NT	NT	XC	NT	NT	TP	NT	TP	NT	NT	HT	NT	NT	XC	NT	XC	NT	TP	NT	XC
					◇1			◇1		◇1			◇1			◇1		◇1		◇1		◇1
		A		B	C	D				E						F	G	H	D			F
					✕								⊠			✕						
Hull	d			18 23					18 53	18 59			19 10	19 15	19 25							
Hessle	d			18 30											19 32							
Ferriby	d			18 35											19 37							
Brough	d			18 40					19 05	19 11			19 22	19 28	19 42							
Broomfleet	d																					
Gilberdyke	d			18 47										19 36	19 49							
Eastrington	d																					
Howden	d												19 34	19 43								
Wressle	d																					
Selby	a									19 29			19 42	19 53								
	d												19 43	19 53								
York 8	33 a													20 21								
Saltmarshe	d																					
Goole	d			18 59					19 19						20 01							
Thorne North	d			19 08											20 09							
Cleethorpes	d							18 26			19 00									19 26		
New Clee	d																					
Grimsby Docks	d										19 05											
Grimsby Town	a							18 33			19 08									19 33		
	d							18 34			19 09									19 34		
Great Coates	d										19 13											
Healing	d										19 16											
Stallingborough	d										19 19											
Habrough	d										19 25									19 44		
Ulceby	d										19 28											
Thornton Abbey	d										19 33											
Goxhill	d										19 36											
New Holland	d										19 40											
Barrow Haven	d										19 43											
Barton-on-Humber	a										19 49											
Barton-on-Humber	d																					
Hull Paragon Interchange	a																					
Barnetby	d							18 53												19 53		
Scunthorpe	a							19 08												20 08		
	d		18 19					19 08				19 15								20 08	20 21	
Althorpe	d		18 24									19 20									20 26	
Crowle	d		18 30									19 26									20 32	
Thorne South	d		18 39									19 35									20 41	
Hatfield & Stainforth	d		18 46	19 15								19 40			20 15						20 46	
Kirk Sandall	d		18 50	19 19								19 45			20 20						20 51	
Adwick	31 d																					
Bentley (S.Yorks)	31 d	←																				
Doncaster 7	31 a	18 51	19 01	19 31				19 38	19 48			19 57	20 01		20 33					20 38	21 01	
London Kings Cross 15	⊖26 a												21 45									
York 8	26 d				18 45											19 34		19 44				20 34
Doncaster 7	d	19 01					19 28	19 42	19 49							19 58	20 03			20 42		21 02
Conisbrough	d	19 08					19 35										20 10			20 50		
Mexborough	d	19 12					19 39										20 14			20 54		
Swinton (S.Yorks)	d	19 15				19 35	19 43										20 17		20 35	20 57		
Rotherham Central	d	19 23				19 45	19 50										20 28		20 45	21 03		
Meadowhall	⇌ d	19 28				19 51	19 57	20 01	20 08								20 33		20 51	21 09		
Sheffield 7	⇌ a	19 37			19 51	19 58	20 05	20 08	20 18							20 20	20 41	20 51	21 02	21 19		21 26
	d							20 11														
Stockport	78 a							20 53														
Manchester Piccadilly 10	⇌ a							21 02														
Manchester Airport	85 ✈ a							21 36														

A From Hull
B From Bridlington
C From Glasgow Central to Bristol Temple Meads
D From Leeds
E To Leeds
F From Newcastle to Birmingham New Street
G To Worksop
H From Edinburgh to Bristol Temple Meads

Table 29

Mondays to Fridays

Hull and Cleethorpes - Doncaster - Meadowhall, Sheffield, Manchester and Manchester Airport, Cleethorpes - Barton-on-Humber

		NT	TP FO	XC	TP FX	NT	NT	TP	NT	NT	EM	TP	NT	NT	NT	NT	NT	NT
			◇1	◇1	◇1			◇1				◇1						
		A		B	C	D					E					D		D
Hull	d	20 03	20 35		20 45				20 56			21 33					22 20	
Hessle	d	20 10															22 27	
Ferriby	d	20 15															22 32	
Brough	d	20 20	20 47		20 57				21 08			21 45					22 37	
Broomfleet	d																	
Gilberdyke	d	20 27										21 52						
Eastrington	d																	
Howden	d																	
Wressle	d																	
Selby	a		21 06		21 16							22 07						
	d		21 06									22 07						
York 8	33 a																	
Saltmarshe	d																	
Goole	d	20 36							21 22				21 35				22 51	
Thorne North	d	20 44											21 44				23 00	
Cleethorpes	d							20 26		21 03	21 15							
New Clee	d																	
Grimsby Docks	d									21 08								
Grimsby Town	a							20 33		21 11	21 21							
	d							20 34		21 11	21 22							
Great Coates	d									21 15								
Healing	d									21 18								
Stallingborough	d									21 21								
Habrough	d									21 27	21 33							
Ulceby	d									21 31								
Thornton Abbey	d									21 35								
Goxhill	d									21 38								
New Holland	d									21 43								
Barrow Haven	d									21 46								
Barton-on-Humber	a									21 51								
Barton-on-Humber	d																	
Hull Paragon Interchange	a																	
Barnetby	d							20 53			21a42							
Scunthorpe	a							21 08										
	d							21 08						21 31	22 21			
Althorpe	d													21 36	22 26			
Crowle	d													21 42	22 32			
Thorne South	d													21 51	22 41			
Hatfield & Stainforth	d	20 51											21 50	21 56	22 46		23 06	
Kirk Sandall	d	20 56											21 54	22 01	22 51		23 10	
Adwick	31 d																	
Bentley (S.Yorks)	31 d																	
Doncaster 7	31 a	21 05						21 40	21 47				22 08	22 11	23 03		23 21	
London Kings Cross 15	⊖26 a																	
York 8	26 d			20 44														
Doncaster 7	d	21 07					21 30	21 42	21 48					22 13			23 22	
Conisbrough	d	21 14					21 37							22 20			23 29	
Mexborough	d	21 17					21 41							22 24			23 33	
Swinton (S.Yorks)	d	21 20				21 35	21 44							22 29		22 35	23 36	23 56
Rotherham Central	d	21 28				21 44	21 55							22 38		22 46	23 45	00 03
Meadowhall	⇌ d	21 34				21 52	22 03	21 59	22 07					22 44		22 53	23 54	00 09
Sheffield 7	⇌ a	21 46		21 51		22 04	22 11	22 08	22 21					22 54		23 02	00 04	00 23
	d							22 11										
Stockport	78 a							22 53										
Manchester Piccadilly 10	⇌ a		22 33					23 02				23 37						
Manchester Airport	85 ✈ a		22 57					23 26										

A From Bridlington
B From Glasgow Central to Birmingham New Street
C To Leeds
D From Leeds
E To Lincoln

Table 29

Hull and Cleethorpes - Doncaster - Meadowhall, Sheffield, Manchester and Manchester Airport, Cleethorpes - Barton-on-Humber

		NT	NT	TP	TP	TP	TP	NT	NT	TP	TP	NT	NT	TP	NT	TP	XC	NT	XC	NT	NT BHX	NT BHX	NT BHX
				◇1	◇1	◇1	◇1			◇1	◇1			◇1		◇1	◇1		◇1				
			A											B			C		D	A			
											🍴			🍴			🍴		🍴		🚌	🚌	🚌
Hull	d	22p20							05 20					06 00	06 06	06 37							
Hessle	d	22p27													06 13								
Ferriby	d	22p32													06 18								
Brough	d	22p37							05 32					06 12	06 23	06 49							
Broomfleet	d																						
Gilberdyke	d													06 19	06 31								
Eastrington	d																						
Howden	d													06 26									
Wressle	d																						
Selby	a													06 36		07 07							
	d												06 18	06 36		07 07							
York 8 33	a																						
Saltmarshe	d														06 37								
Goole	d	22p51							05 46						06 42								
Thorne North	d	23p00							05 55						06 50								
Cleethorpes	d										05 18	06 00											
New Clee	d																						
Grimsby Docks	d																						
Grimsby Town	a										05 25	06 08											
	d										05 26	06 08											
Great Coates	d																						
Healing	d											06 15											
Stallingborough	d											06 18											
Habrough	d										05 36	06 24											
Ulceby	d											06 28											
Thornton Abbey	d																						
Goxhill	d											06 35											
New Holland	d											06 40											
Barrow Haven	d											06 43											
Barton-on-Humber	a											06 48											
Barton-on-Humber	d																				08 20	10 00	12 00
Hull Paragon Interchange	a																				08 52	10 27	12 27
Barnetby	d										05 45												
Scunthorpe	a										06 00												
	d										06 00												
Althorpe	d										06 05												
Crowle	d										06 11												
Thorne South	d										06 20												
Hatfield & Stainforth	d	23p06							06 01		06 25				06 56								
Kirk Sandall	d	23p10							06 06						07 01								
Adwick 31	d																						
Bentley (S.Yorks) 31	d																						
Doncaster 7 31	a	23p21							06 15		06 38		06 39		07 11								
London Kings Cross 15 ⊖26	a																						
York 8 26	d			03 52	05 26		05 57			06 28									06 40				
Doncaster 7	d	23p22				05 40		06 00	06 23		06 40						06 47	07 02					
Conisbrough	d	23p29						06 07	06 30									07 09					
Mexborough	d	23p33						06 11	06 34									07 13					
Swinton (S.Yorks)	d	23p36	23p56					06 14	06 37									07 16		07 30			
Rotherham Central	d	23p45	00 03					06 25	06 49									07 26		07 38			
Meadowhall ⇌	d	23p54	00 09			05 58		06 30	06 52		06 58							07 32		07 47			
Sheffield 7 ⇌	a	00 04	00 23			06 08		06 38	07 07		07 06						07 15	07 40	07 51	07 54			
	d					06 11					07 09												
Stockport 78	a					06 53					07 53												
Manchester Piccadilly 10 ⇌	a			06 02	06 50	07 02	07 19			07 51	08 02			08 05		08 36							
Manchester Airport 85 ✈	a			06 24	07 12	07 29	07 42			08 12	08 26												

A From Leeds
B To Liverpool Lime Street
C From Leeds to Southampton Central
D To Plymouth

Table 29

Hull and Cleethorpes - Doncaster - Meadowhall, Sheffield, Manchester and Manchester Airport, Cleethorpes - Barton-on-Humber

		NT BHX	NT BHX	NT BHX	NT BHX	NT	NT	NT	TP	NT	EM	GR	NT	NT	NT	XC	NT	TP	XC	NT	NT	TP	NT
									◇1			1				◇1		◇1	◇1			◇1	
							A	A		B	C		D		E	F	G		H	I			
		🚌	🚌	🚌	🚌	🚌			🍴			🍴				🍴		🍴	🍴			🍴	
Hull	d						06 40					06 50			07 07			07 37					
Hessle	d						06 47																
Ferriby	d						06 52																
Brough	d						06 57					07 02			07 19			07 49					
Broomfleet	d																						
Gilberdyke	d						07 04								07 26								
Eastrington	d														07 31								
Howden	d														07 35			08 01					
Wressle	d														07 40								
Selby	a											07 23			07 48			08 10					
	d											07 24			07 48			08 11					
York 8 33	a														08 21								
Saltmarshe	d						07 10																
Goole	d						07 15																
Thorne North	d						07 24																
Cleethorpes	d								06 18					07 00								07 26	
New Clee	d																						
Grimsby Docks	d													07 05									
Grimsby Town	a								06 25					07 08								07 33	
	d								06 26		06 50			07 08								07 34	
Great Coates	d													07 12									
Healing	d													07 15									
Stallingborough	d													07 18									
Habrough	d								06 36		07 00			07 24								07 44	
Ulceby	d													07 28									
Thornton Abbey	d													07 32									
Goxhill	d													07 35									
New Holland	d													07 40									
Barrow Haven	d													07 43									
Barton-on-Humber	a													07 48									
Barton-on-Humber	d	14 00	16 00	18 00	19 53	21 53																	
Hull Paragon Interchange	a	14 27	16 27	18 27	20 20	22 20																	
Barnetby	d								06 45		07a09											07 53	
Scunthorpe	a								07 00													08 08	
	d								07 00								07 30					08 08	
Althorpe	d																07 35						
Crowle	d																07 42						
Thorne South	d																07 51						
Hatfield & Stainforth	d						07 30										07 56						
Kirk Sandall	d						07 34										08 01						
Adwick 31	d							07 23													08 15		08 33
Bentley (S.Yorks) 31	d							07 27					←								08 19		08 37
Doncaster 7 31	a						07 46	07 31	07 33			07 43	07 46				08 12				08 23	08 38	08 42
London Kings Cross 15 ⊖26	a						↪					09 38											
York 8 26	d									←						07 24			07 44				
Doncaster 7	d							07 39	07 35	07 39			07 48			07 52					08 26	08 41	
Conisbrough	d							→		07 46			07 55								08 33		
Mexborough	d									07 50			07 59								08 37		
Swinton (S.Yorks)	d									07 53			08 02							08 35	08 43		
Rotherham Central	d									08 01			08 14							08 44	08 50		
Meadowhall ⇌	d								07 53	08 07			08 25							08 51	08 56	09 01	
Sheffield 7 ⇌	a								08 00	08 18			08 32			08 18			08 51	08 59	09 05	09 08	
	d								08 05													09 11	
Stockport 78	a								08 53													09 53	
Manchester Piccadilly 10 ⇌	a								09 02									09 36				10 02	
Manchester Airport 85 ✈	a								09 26													10 26	

A To Sheffield
B From Adwick
C To Newark North Gate
D From Hull
E From Beverley
F From Newcastle to Reading
G To Adwick
H From Newcastle to Plymouth
I From Leeds

Hull and Cleethorpes - Doncaster - Meadowhall, Sheffield, Manchester and Manchester Airport, Cleethorpes - Barton-on-Humber

		NT	XC	NT	NT	HT	XC	NT	NT	NT	TP	TP	TP	NT	NT	NT	EM	XC	NT	XC	NT	NT
			◇1			◇1	◇1				◇1	◇1	◇1					◇1		◇1		
			A	B	C		D	E		F				B			G	H	C	I	E	
			⌶			⊠	⌶				⌶	⌶	⌶					⌶		⌶		
Hull	d	07 40		08 03		08 25				08 29	08 40			08 56		09 02						
Hessle	d	07 47								08 36												
Ferriby	d	07 52								08 41												
Brough	d	07 57		08 15		08 37				08 46	08 52			09 08		09 14						
Broomfleet	d	08 02																				
Gilberdyke	d	08 07								08 53						09 21						
Eastrington	d																					
Howden	d					08 49										09 28						
Wressle	d																					
Selby	a					08 59					09 11					09 38						
	d					09 00					09 11					09 38						
York [8] 33	a															10 14						
Saltmarshe	d	08 12																				
Goole	d	08 17		08 29						09 02				09 23								
Thorne North	d	08 26								09 10												
Cleethorpes	d												08 26		09 00							
New Clee	d														09x03							
Grimsby Docks	d														09 05							
Grimsby Town	a												08 33		09 08							
	d												08 34		09 08		09 20					
Great Coates	d														09 12							
Healing	d														09 15							
Stallingborough	d														09 18							
Habrough	d												08 44		09 24		09 30					
Ulceby	d														09 28							
Thornton Abbey	d														09 32							
Goxhill	d														09 35							
New Holland	d														09 40							
Barrow Haven	d														09 43							
Barton-on-Humber	a														09 48							
Barton-on-Humber	d																					
Hull Paragon Interchange	a																					
Barnetby	d												08 53				09a39					
Scunthorpe	a												09 08									
	d				08 19								09 08						09 19			
Althorpe	d				08 24														09 24			
Crowle	d				08 30														09 30			
Thorne South	d				08 39														09 39			
Hatfield & Stainforth	d	08 33			08 46					09 17									09 44			
Kirk Sandall	d	08 37			08 50					09 21									09 49			
Adwick 31	d								09 15													10 15
Bentley (S.Yorks) 31	d								09 19													10 19
Doncaster [7] 31	a	08 50		08 59	09 02	09 23			09 24	09 32			09 38	09 48					10 01			10 24
London Kings Cross [15] ⊖26	a					11 07																
York [8] 26	d		08 34				08 44					09 25						09 35		09 46		
Doncaster [7]	d		08 58	09 01	09 03				09 26				09 42	09 49				09 58	10 04			10 26
Conisbrough	d				09 11				09 33										10 11			10 33
Mexborough	d				09 15				09 37										10 15			10 37
Swinton (S.Yorks)	d				09 18			09 35	09 42										10 18		10 35	10 43
Rotherham Central	d				09 27			09 46	09 51										10 27		10 44	10 52
Meadowhall ⇌	d			09 24	09 33			09 50	09 55				10 01	10 08					10 33		10 50	10 58
Sheffield [7] ⇌	a		09 20	09 33	09 41		09 52	10 00	10 05				10 08	10 19				10 20	10 41	10 51	11 00	11 06
	d												10 11									
Stockport 78	a												10 53									
Manchester Piccadilly [10] ⇌	a										10 36	10 49	11 02									
Manchester Airport 85 ✈	a											11 12	11 26									

A From Newcastle to Southampton Central
B From Bridlington
C To Lincoln
D From Edinburgh to Plymouth
E From Leeds
F From Scarborough
G To Newark North Gate
H From Edinburgh to Reading
I From Glasgow Central to Paignton

Hull and Cleethorpes - Doncaster - Meadowhall, Sheffield, Manchester and Manchester Airport, Cleethorpes - Barton-on-Humber

		NT	TP	TP	NT	NT	XC	NT	XC	NT	NT	NT	HT	TP	TP	NT	NT	NT	XC	NT	NT	XC	NT
			◇1	◇1			◇1		◇1				◇1	◇1	◇1				◇1			◇1	
		A			B		C	D	E	F							B		G		D	H	F
				⌶			⌶		⌶				⊠		⌶				⌶			⌶	
Hull	d	09 25	09 40		09 56	10 08						10 18	10 30	10 40			10 57	11 05					
Hessle	d	09 32										10 25											
Ferriby	d	09 37										10 30											
Brough	d	09 42	09 52		10 08	10 20						10 35	10 42	10 52			11 09	11 17					
Broomfleet	d																						
Gilberdyke	d	09 49				10 26						10 43											
Eastrington	d																						
Howden	d					10 34							10 54					11 29					
Wressle	d																						
Selby	a		10 11			10 47							11 04	11 11				11 40					
	d		10 11			10 47							11 05	11 11				11 41					
York [8] 33	a					11 18												12 08					
Saltmarshe	d																						
Goole	d	09 58			10 22							10 58					11 23						
Thorne North	d	10 06										11 06											
Cleethorpes	d			09 26											10 26	10 55							
New Clee	d															10x58							
Grimsby Docks	d															11 00							
Grimsby Town	a			09 34											10 33	11 03							
	d			09 34											10 34	11 03							
Great Coates	d															11 07							
Healing	d															11 10							
Stallingborough	d															11 13							
Habrough	d														10 44	11 19							
Ulceby	d															11 23							
Thornton Abbey	d															11 27							
Goxhill	d															11 30							
New Holland	d															11 35							
Barrow Haven	d															11 38							
Barton-on-Humber	a															11 43							
Barton-on-Humber	d																						
Hull Paragon Interchange	a																						
Barnetby	d			09 53											10 53								
Scunthorpe	a			10 08											11 08								
	d			10 08				10 19							11 08						11 18		
Althorpe	d							10 24													11 23		
Crowle	d							10 30													11 29		
Thorne South	d							10 39													11 38		
Hatfield & Stainforth	d	10 12						10 44				11 11									11 43		
Kirk Sandall	d	10 17						10 49				11 17									11 48		
Adwick 31	d										11 15												
Bentley (S.Yorks) 31	d										11 19												
Doncaster [7] 31	a	10 27		10 38	10 47			11 00			11 24	11 27	11 24		11 38		11 47				11 58		
London Kings Cross [15] ⊖26	a												13 07										
York [8] 26	d						10 34		10 45										11 34	11 05		11 45	
Doncaster [7]	d			10 42	10 49		10 58	11 04			11 26				11 42		11 49		11 58		12 03		
Conisbrough	d							11 11			11 33										12 11		
Mexborough	d							11 15			11 37										12 15		
Swinton (S.Yorks)	d							11 18		11 35	11 43									12 10	12 18		12 35
Rotherham Central	d							11 27		11 44	11 52									12 19	12 27		12 44
Meadowhall ⇌	d			11 01	11 08			11 33		11 50	11 58				12 01		12 08			12 24	12 33		12 50
Sheffield [7] ⇌	a			11 08	11 20		11 20	11 41	11 51	12 00	12 05				12 08		12 20		12 20	12 36	12 41	12 51	13 00
	d			11 11											12 11								
Stockport 78	a			11 53											12 53								
Manchester Piccadilly [10] ⇌	a		11 36	12 02										12 36	13 02								
Manchester Airport 85 ✈	a			12 26											13 26								

A From Beverley
B From Bridlington
C From Newcastle to Southampton Central
D To Lincoln
E From Dundee to Plymouth
F From Leeds
G From Newcastle to Reading
H From Glasgow Central to Plymouth

Table 29

Saturdays

Hull and Cleethorpes - Doncaster - Meadowhall, Sheffield, Manchester and Manchester Airport, Cleethorpes - Barton-on-Humber

		NT	NT	NT	EM	TP	TP	NT	NT	XC	NT	XC	NT	NT	NT	TP	TP	NT	NT	NT	XC	NT
					A	◇1 ✠	◇1 ✠	B		◇1 C ✠	D	◇1 E ✠	F			◇1 ✠	◇1 ✠		G		◇1 H ✠	D
Hull	d			11 23		11 40		11 55	12 03						12 18	12 40			12 57	13 12		
Hessle	d			11 30											12 25							
Ferriby	d			11 35											12 30							
Brough	d			11 40		11 52		12 07	12 15						12 35	12 52			13 09	13 24		
Broomfleet	d			11 45																		
Gilberdyke	d			11 50											12 42					13 32		
Eastrington	d																			13 36		
Howden	d								12 27											13 42		
Wressle	d																			13 47		
Selby	a					12 11			12 37							13 11				13 54		
	d					12 11			12 38							13 11				13 55		
York 8 33	a								13 04											14 27		
Saltmarshe	d														12 48							
Goole	d			11 58				12 22							12 58				13 23			
Thorne North	d			12 07											13 06							
Cleethorpes	d		11 10				11 26										12 26	12 55				
New Clee	d																	12x58				
Grimsby Docks	d																	13 00				
Grimsby Town	a		11 16				11 33										12 33	13 03				
	d		11 17		11 28		11 34										12 34	13 03				
Great Coates	d																	13 07				
Healing	d																	13 10				
Stallingborough	d																	13 13				
Habrough	d		11 28		11 38													13 19				
Ulceby	d																	13 23				
Thornton Abbey	d																	13 27				
Goxhill	d																	13 30				
New Holland	d																	13 35				
Barrow Haven	d																	13 38				
Barton-on-Humber	a																	13 43				
Barton-on-Humber	d																					
Hull Paragon Interchange	a																					
Barnetby	d		11 38		11a47		11 53										12 53					
Scunthorpe	a						12 08										13 08					
	d						12 08				12 18						13 08					13 19
Althorpe	d										12 23											13 24
Crowle	d										12 29											13 30
Thorne South	d										12 38											13 39
Hatfield & Stainforth	d			12 13							12 43				13 12							13 44
Kirk Sandall	d			12 17							12 48				13 17							13 49
Adwick 31	d	12 14												13 15								
Bentley (S.Yorks) 31	d	12 18												13 19								
Doncaster 7 31	a	12 24		12 28			12 38	12 48			12 59			13 24	13 27		13 38		13 46			13 57
London Kings Cross 15 ⊖26	a																					
York 8 26	d									12 34		12 45									13 34	
Doncaster 7	d	12 26					12 42	12 49		12 58	13 04			13 24			13 42		13 48		13 58	14 01
Conisbrough	d	12 33									13 11			13 32								14 11
Mexborough	d	12 37									13 15			13 36								14 15
Swinton (S.Yorks)	d	12 43									13 18		13 35	13 42								14 19
Rotherham Central	d	12 52									13 27		13 44	13 52								14 29
Meadowhall ⇌	d	12 58					13 01	13 08			13 33		13 50	13 58			14 01		14 08			14 34
Sheffield 7 ⇌	a	13 05	13 23				13 08	13 20		13 20	13 41	13 51	14 00	14 05			14 08		14 20		14 20	14 43
	d						13 11										14 11					
Stockport 78	a						13 53										14 53					
Manchester Piccadilly 10 ⇌	a					13 36	14 02									14 36	15 02					
Manchester Airport 85 ✈	a						14 26										15 26					

A To Newark North Gate
B From Bridlington
C From Newcastle to Southampton Central
D To Lincoln
E From Glasgow Central to Penzance
F From Leeds
G From Scarborough
H From Newcastle to Reading

Table 29

Saturdays

Hull and Cleethorpes - Doncaster - Meadowhall, Sheffield, Manchester and Manchester Airport, Cleethorpes - Barton-on-Humber

		XC	NT	NT	NT	HT	TP	TP	EM	NT	NT	XC	NT	XC	NT	NT	NT	TP	TP	NT	NT	NT	XC
		◇1 A ✠	B			◇1 ⊠	◇1	◇1 ✠	C	D		◇1 E ✠	F	◇1 G ✠	B			◇1	◇1 ✠	H			◇1 I ✠
Hull	d				13 18	13 30	13 40			13 57	14 18						14 25	14 40		14 56		15 02	
Hessle	d				13 25												14 32						
Ferriby	d				13 30												14 37						
Brough	d				13 35	13 42	13 52			14 09	14 30						14 42	14 52		15 08		15 14	
Broomfleet	d																						
Gilberdyke	d				13 43												14 49						
Eastrington	d																						
Howden	d					13 56					14 42											15 26	
Wressle	d																						
Selby	a					14 05	14 11				14 53							15 11				15 36	
	d					14 06	14 11				14 53							15 11				15 38	
York 8 33	a										15 25											16 06	
Saltmarshe	d																						
Goole	d				13 58					14 23							14 58			15 23			
Thorne North	d				14 07												15 06						
Cleethorpes	d							13 26											14 26		15 00		
New Clee	d																				15x03		
Grimsby Docks	d																				15 05		
Grimsby Town	a							13 33											14 33		15 08		
	d							13 34	13 49										14 34		15 08		
Great Coates	d																				15 12		
Healing	d																				15 15		
Stallingborough	d																				15 18		
Habrough	d								13 59										14 44		15 24		
Ulceby	d																				15 28		
Thornton Abbey	d																				15 32		
Goxhill	d																				15 35		
New Holland	d																				15 40		
Barrow Haven	d																				15 43		
Barton-on-Humber	a																				15 48		
Barton-on-Humber	d																						
Hull Paragon Interchange	a																						
Barnetby	d							13 53	14a08										14 53				
Scunthorpe	a							14 08											15 08				
	d							14 08					14 19						15 08				
Althorpe	d												14 24										
Crowle	d												14 30										
Thorne South	d												14 39										
Hatfield & Stainforth	d				14 13								14 44				15 12						
Kirk Sandall	d				14 17								14 49				15 17						
Adwick 31	d			14 15												15 15							
Bentley (S.Yorks) 31	d			14 19												15 19							
Doncaster 7 31	a			14 24	14 30	14 25		14 38		14 47			14 59			15 24	15 27		15 38	15 47			
London Kings Cross 15 ⊖26	a					16 08																	
York 8 26	d	13 44										14 34		14 44									15 34
Doncaster 7	d			14 26				14 42		14 48		14 58	15 04			15 26			15 42	15 49			15 58
Conisbrough	d			14 33									15 11			15 33							
Mexborough	d			14 37									15 15			15 37							
Swinton (S.Yorks)	d		14 35	14 43									15 18		15 35	15 42							
Rotherham Central	d		14 44	14 52									15 27		15 44	15 50							
Meadowhall ⇌	d		14 50	14 58				15 01		15 07			15 33		15 50	15 57			16 01	16 07			
Sheffield 7 ⇌	a	14 51	15 00	15 05				15 08		15 20		15 20	15 41	15 51	16 00	16 05			16 08	16 22			16 20
	d							15 11											16 10				
Stockport 78	a							15 53											16 53				
Manchester Piccadilly 10 ⇌	a						15 36	16 02										16 36	17 02				
Manchester Airport 85 ✈	a							16 26											17 32				

A From Aberdeen to Penzance
B From Leeds
C To Newark North Gate
D From Bridlington
E From Newcastle to Southampton Central
F To Lincoln
G From Glasgow Central to Plymouth
H From Scarborough
I From Newcastle to Reading

Hull and Cleethorpes - Doncaster - Meadowhall, Sheffield, Manchester and Manchester Airport, Cleethorpes - Barton-on-Humber

		NT	NT	NT	HT	TP	XC	NT	NT	NT	TP	NT	EM	XC	NT	NT	NT	TP	XC	NT	NT	TP	NT
					◇1	◇1	◇1				◇1			◇1				◇1	◇1			◇1	
			A				B	C	D			E	F	G		A			H	C			E
Hull	d			15 18	15 30	15 40						15 57			16 10		16 27	16 40					16 54
Hessle	d			15 25													16 34						
Ferriby	d			15 30													16 39						
Brough	d			15 35	15 42	15 52						16 09			16 22		16 44	16 52					17 06
Broomfleet	d																16 49						
Gilberdyke	d			15 42											16 29		16 54						17 13
Eastrington	d																						
Howden	d				15 54										16 36								
Wressle	d																						
Selby	a				16 04	16 11									16 46			17 11					
	d				16 05	16 11									16 47			17 11					
York 8 33	a														17 13								
Saltmarshe	d																16 59						
Goole	d			15 58								16 23					17 04						17 22
Thorne North	d			16 06													17 13						
Cleethorpes	d									15 20	15 26											16 26	
New Clee	d																						
Grimsby Docks	d																						
Grimsby Town	a									15 26	15 33											16 33	
	d									15 27	15 34		16 00									16 34	
Great Coates	d																						
Healing	d																						
Stallingborough	d																						
Habrough	d									15 37			16 09										
Ulceby	d																						
Thornton Abbey	d																						
Goxhill	d																						
New Holland	d																						
Barrow Haven	d																						
Barton-on-Humber	a																						
Barton-on-Humber	d																						
Hull Paragon Interchange	a																						
Barnetby	d									15 48	15 53		16a18									16 53	
Scunthorpe	a										16 08											17 08	
	d		15 18								16 08					16 19						17 08	
Althorpe	d		15 23													16 24							
Crowle	d		15 29													16 30							
Thorne South	d		15 38													16 39							
Hatfield & Stainforth	d		15 43	16 12												16 44	17 19						
Kirk Sandall	d		15 48	16 17												16 49	17 23						
Adwick 31	d								16 15														
Bentley (S.Yorks) 31	d								16 18														
Doncaster 7 31	a		15 58	16 27	16 23				16 25		16 38	16 47				16 57	17 35					17 38	17 49
London Kings Cross 15 ⊖26	a				18 07																		
York 8 26	d	15 01					15 45							16 06					16 44				
Doncaster 7	d		16 01						16 26		16 42	16 48				17 00					17 24	17 42	17 49
Conisbrough	d		16 11						16 33							17 08					17 31		
Mexborough	d		16 15						16 37							17 12					17 35		
Swinton (S.Yorks)	d	16 01	16 18					16 35	16 41							17 16				17 35	17 42		
Rotherham Central	d	16 09	16 27					16 44	16 50							17 27				17 44	17 50		
Meadowhall	d	16 18	16 33					16 50	16 55		17 01	17 08				17 33				17 50	17 57	18 01	18 08
Sheffield 7	a	16 27	16 41				16 51	17 00	17 05	17 23	17 08	17 19		17 20		17 41			17 51	18 00	18 05	18 08	18 21
	d										17 11											18 10	
Stockport 78	a										17 53											18 53	
Manchester Piccadilly 10	a					17 37					18 02							18 37				19 02	
Manchester Airport 85 ✈	a										18 26											19 28	

A To Lincoln
B From Edinburgh to Plymouth
C From Leeds
D To Retford Low Level
E From Bridlington
F To Newark North Gate
G From Newcastle to Reading
H From Glasgow Central to Taunton

Table 29

Saturdays

Hull and Cleethorpes - Doncaster - Meadowhall, Sheffield, Manchester and Manchester Airport, Cleethorpes - Barton-on-Humber

		NT	TP	NT	XC	NT	EM	XC	NT	NT	TP	EM	NT	NT	TP	XC	NT	NT	HT	HT	NT	XC
			◇1		◇1		◇1	◇1			◇1				◇1	◇1			◇1	◇1		◇1
			A		B	C	D	E	F			G	H	I		J	K		L	M	N	O
Hull	d		17 01	17 18									17 42	17 52	17 58				18 30	18 30	18 32	
Hessle	d			17 25									17 49								18 39	
Ferriby	d			17 30									17 54								18 44	
Brough	d		17 13	17 35									17 59	18 03	18 10				18 43	18 43	18 49	
Broomfleet	d			17 40																		
Gilberdyke	d			17 45									18 06								18 56	
Eastrington	d			17 49																		
Howden	d			17 54															18 55	18 55		
Wressle	d			17 59																		
Selby	a		17 32	18 06										18 26	18 29				19 04	19 04		
	d			18 07										18 26	18 29				19 05	19 05		
York 8 33	a			18 33																		
Saltmarshe	d												18 12									
Goole	d												18 19								19 05	
Thorne North	d												18 28								19 14	
Cleethorpes	d	17 00									17 26											
New Clee	d																					
Grimsby Docks	d	17 05																				
Grimsby Town	a	17 08									17 33											
	d	17 09									17 34	18 26										
Great Coates	d	17 13																				
Healing	d	17 16																				
Stallingborough	d	17 19																				
Habrough	d	17 25									17 44	18 36										
Ulceby	d	17 28																				
Thornton Abbey	d	17 33																				
Goxhill	d	17 36																				
New Holland	d	17 40																				
Barrow Haven	d	17 43																				
Barton-on-Humber	a	17 49																				
Barton-on-Humber	d																					
Hull Paragon Interchange	a																					
Barnetby	d										17 53	18a44										
Scunthorpe	a										18 10											
	d					17 18					18 10							18 19				
Althorpe	d					17 23												18 24				
Crowle	d					17 29												18 30				
Thorne South	d					17 38												18 39				
Hatfield & Stainforth	d					17 43							18 34					18 46			19 21	
Kirk Sandall	d					17 48							18 39					18 50			19 25	
Adwick 31	d																					
Bentley (S.Yorks) 31	d																←					
Doncaster 7 31	a					17 58					18 40		18 50	18 47			18 50	19 01	19 26	19 26	19 36	
London Kings Cross 15 ⊖26	a												→						21 05	21 39		
York 8 26	d				17 34		17 50	17 44								18 34						18 44
Doncaster 7	d				17 58	18 02	18 18			18 26	18 42			18 48		18 58	19 01					
Conisbrough	d					18 09				18 33							19 08					
Mexborough	d					18 13				18 37							19 12					
Swinton (S.Yorks)	d					18 16			18 35	18 42							19 15					
Rotherham Central	d					18 27			18 44	18 49							19 23					
Meadowhall	d					18 33			18 50	18 56	19 01			19 08			19 28					
Sheffield 7	a				18 20	18 41	18 44	18 51	19 00	19 06	19 08			19 19		19 21	19 37					19 51
	d										19 11											
Stockport 78	a										19 53											
Manchester Piccadilly 10	a										20 02				19 57							
Manchester Airport 85 ✈	a										20 36											

A To Leeds
B From Newcastle to Reading
C To Lincoln
D From Scarborough to St Pancras International
E From Edinburgh to Plymouth
F From Leeds
G To Newark North Gate
H To Sheffield
I From Scarborough
J From Newcastle to Birmingham New Street
K From Hull
L until 18 June, from 6 August
M from 25 June until 30 July
N From Bridlington
O From Glasgow Central to Bristol Temple Meads

Hull and Cleethorpes - Doncaster - Meadowhall, Sheffield, Manchester and Manchester Airport, Cleethorpes - Barton-on-Humber

		NT	NT	TP	NT	TP	NT	XC	NT	NT	NT	NT	XC	TP	NT	TP	EM	NT	XC	NT	XC	NT	NT
				◇1		◇1		◇1					◇1	◇1		◇1			◇1		◇1		
		A				B		C ✠			D		E	B	A		F		C ✠	G	H	A	
Hull	d				18 53	18 59	19 15					19 25		19 56						20 03			
Hessle	d											19 32								20 10			
Ferriby	d											19 37								20 15			
Brough	d				19 05	19 11	19 28					19 42		20 08						20 20			
Broomfleet	d																						
Gilberdyke	d						19 36					19 50								20 27			
Eastrington	d																						
Howden	d						19 43																
Wressle	d																						
Selby	a					19 29	19 52							20 26									
	d						19 53																
York 8 33	a						20 21																
Saltmarshe	d																						
Goole	d				19 19							19 58								20 36			
Thorne North	d											20 07								20 44			
Cleethorpes	d			18 26					18 36	19 00						19 26							
New Clee	d																						
Grimsby Docks	d									19 05													
Grimsby Town	a			18 33					18 42	19 08						19 33							
	d			18 34					18 43	19 09						19 34	19 45						
Great Coates	d									19 13													
Healing	d									19 16													
Stallingborough	d									19 19													
Habrough	d								18 53	19 25						19 44	19 54						
Ulceby	d									19 29													
Thornton Abbey	d									19 34													
Goxhill	d									19 37													
New Holland	d									19 41													
Barrow Haven	d									19 44													
Barton-on-Humber	a									19 50													
Barton-on-Humber	d																						
Hull Paragon Interchange	a																						
Barnetby	d			18 53					19 02							19 53	20a03						
Scunthorpe	a			19 08												20 07							
	d			19 08							19 19					20 07		20 21					
Althorpe	d										19 24							20 26					
Crowle	d										19 30							20 32					
Thorne South	d										19 39							20 41					
Hatfield & Stainforth	d										19 44	20 16						20 46		20 51			
Kirk Sandall	d										19 49	20 20						20 51		20 56			
Adwick 31	d																						
Bentley (S.Yorks) 31	d																						
Doncaster 7 31	a			19 38	19 47						19 59	20 31				20 38		21 03		21 05			
London Kings Cross 15 ⊖26	a																						
York 8 26	d							19 34					19 44						20 23		20 45		
Doncaster 7	d		19 28	19 42	19 49			19 58			20 03					20 42				21 07			21 30
Conisbrough	d		19 35								20 10					20 50				21 14			21 37
Mexborough	d		19 39								20 14					20 54				21 18			21 41
Swinton (S.Yorks)	d	19 35	19 43								20 17				20 35	20 57				21 21		21 34	21 44
Rotherham Central	d	19 44	19 51								20 28				20 45	21 04				21 28		21 42	21 55
Meadowhall ⇌	d	19 51	19 57	20 01	20 08						20 33				20 51	21 09				21 35		21 50	22 03
Sheffield 7 ⇌	a	20 00	20 06	20 08	20 18			20 20	20 34		20 41		20 52		21 00	21 19			21 20	21 46	21 51	22 02	22 13
	d			20 11																			
Stockport 78	a			20 53																			
Manchester Piccadilly 10 ⇌	a			21 02																			
Manchester Airport 85 ✈	a			21 36																			

A From Leeds
B To Leeds
C From Newcastle to Birmingham New Street
D To Worksop
E From Edinburgh to Birmingham New Street
F To Lincoln
G From Bridlington
H From Glasgow Central to Birmingham New Street

Hull and Cleethorpes - Doncaster - Meadowhall, Sheffield, Manchester and Manchester Airport, Cleethorpes - Barton-on-Humber

		TP	NT	NT		NT	NT	TP	NT	NT	NT	NT
		◇1						◇1				
										A	A	B
Hull	d		20 55	21 01				21 33				22 17
Hessle	d											22 24
Ferriby	d											22 29
Brough	d		21 07	21 13				21 45				22 34
Broomfleet	d											
Gilberdyke	d							21 52				
Eastrington	d											
Howden	d			21 25								
Wressle	d											
Selby	a			21 35				22 07				
	d			21 35				22 07				
York 8 33	a			21 57								
Saltmarshe	d											
Goole	d		21 21		21 35							22 48
Thorne North	d				21 44							22 57
Cleethorpes	d	20 26				21 03						
New Clee	d											
Grimsby Docks	d					21 08						
Grimsby Town	a	20 33				21 11						
	d	20 34				21 11						
Great Coates	d					21 15						
Healing	d					21 18						
Stallingborough	d					21 21						
Habrough	d					21 27						
Ulceby	d					21 31						
Thornton Abbey	d					21 35						
Goxhill	d					21 38						
New Holland	d					21 43						
Barrow Haven	d					21 46						
Barton-on-Humber	a					21 51						
Barton-on-Humber	d											
Hull Paragon Interchange	a											
Barnetby	d	20 53										
Scunthorpe	a	21 08										
	d	21 08					21 31		22 21			
Althorpe	d						21 36		22 26			
Crowle	d						21 42		22 32			
Thorne South	d						21 51		22 41			
Hatfield & Stainforth	d				21 50		21 56		22 46			23 03
Kirk Sandall	d				21 54		22 01		22 51			23 07
Adwick 31	d											
Bentley (S.Yorks) 31	d											
Doncaster 7 31	a	21 38	21 45		22 12		22 11		23 02			23 18
London Kings Cross 15 ⊖26	a											
York 8 26	d											
Doncaster 7	d	21 42	21 47				22 13					23 19
Conisbrough	d						22 20					23 26
Mexborough	d						22 24					23 30
Swinton (S.Yorks)	d						22 29			22 37	23 30	23 33
Rotherham Central	d						22 37			22 46	23 38	23 43
Meadowhall ⇌	d	21 59	22 12				22 43			22 53	23 44	23 49
Sheffield 7 ⇌	a	22 10	22 22				22 54			23 03	23 58	23 59
	d											
Stockport 78	a											
Manchester Piccadilly 10 ⇌	a							23 37				
Manchester Airport 85 ✈	a											

A From Leeds
B From Bridlington

Table 29

Hull and Cleethorpes - Doncaster - Meadowhall, Sheffield, Manchester and Manchester Airport, Cleethorpes - Barton-on-Humber

		TP	TP	TP	TP	TP	NT	TP	NT	XC	NT	NT	NT	TP	NT	XC	HT	NT	TP	NT	NT BHX	NT
		◇1	◇1	◇1	◇1	◇1		◇1		◇1 B 🍴	C			◇1		◇1 D 🍴	◇1 ⊠		◇1		🚌	
Hull	d											08 40	08 54	09 00			09 30	09 33				
Hessle	d																	09 40				
Ferriby	d																	09 45				
Brough	d											08 52	09 06	09 12			09 42	09 50				
Broomfleet	d																					
Gilberdyke	d											08 59						09 57				
Eastrington	d																					
Howden	d												09 18				09 54					
Wressle	d																					
Selby	a												09 27	09 32			10 04					
	d												09 28	09 33			10 05					
York 8 33	a												09 52									
Saltmarshe	d																					
Goole	d											09 09			09 43			10 06				
Thorne North	d														09 51							
Cleethorpes	d																		09 26	09 58		
New Clee	d																			10 01		
Grimsby Docks	d																			10 04		
Grimsby Town	a																		09 33	10 06		
	d																		09 34	10 07		
Great Coates	d																			10 11		
Healing	d																			10 14		
Stallingborough	d																			10 15		
Habrough	d																		09 44	10 21		
Ulceby	d																			10 25		
Thornton Abbey	d																			10 30		
Goxhill	d																			10 33		
New Holland	d																			10 38		
Barrow Haven	d																			10 41		
Barton-on-Humber	a																			10 48		
Barton-on-Humber	d																				10 55	
Hull Paragon Interchange	a																				11 19	
Barnetby	d																		09 53			
Scunthorpe	a																		10 08			
	d																		10 08			
Althorpe	d																					
Crowle	d																					
Thorne South	d																					
Hatfield & Stainforth	d														09 57			10 20				
Kirk Sandall	d														10 02			10 25				
Adwick 31	d																					
Bentley (S.Yorks) 31	d																					
Doncaster 7 31	a											09 29			10 11		10 23	10 35	10 40			
London Kings Cross 15 ⊖26	a																12 12					
York 8 26	d	02 44	03 59	05 12	06 12	07 12		08 10								09 28						
Doncaster 7	d						08 03		09 13	09 32		09 39			10 13	10 30			10 42			11 13
Conisbrough	d						08 10		09 20						10 20							11 20
Mexborough	d						08 14		09 24						10 24							11 24
Swinton (S.Yorks)	d						08 17		09 28		09 35				10 27							11 27
Rotherham Central	d						08 25		09 35		09 48				10 35							11 35
Meadowhall ⇌	d						08 30		09 41		09 54	10 00			10 40				11 00			11 40
Sheffield 7 ⇌	a						08 41		09 51	09 55	10 03	10 08			10 52	10 54			11 07			11 51
	d																		11 10			
Stockport 78	a																		11 53			
Manchester Piccadilly 10 ⇌	a	04 02	05 17	06 34	07 34	08 34		09 34						11 03					12 06			
Manchester Airport 85 ✈	a	04 23	05 38	06 55	07 55	08 55		09 55											12 29			

A To Liverpool Lime Street
B From Leeds to Plymouth
C From Leeds
D To Bristol Temple Meads

Table 29

Hull and Cleethorpes - Doncaster - Meadowhall, Sheffield, Manchester and Manchester Airport, Cleethorpes - Barton-on-Humber

		XC	TP	NT	TP	NT	NT	XC	HT	TP	NT	NT	TP	NT	NT	XC	NT	TP	TP	NT	TP	NT BHX	NT
		◇1 A 🍴	◇1	B	◇1	C		◇1 D 🍴	◇1 ⊠	◇1			◇1			◇1 E 🍴	F	◇1 G	◇1		◇1	🚌	C
Hull	d			10 50	10 58				11 30		11 46	11 53	12 00				12 46		12 58	13 29			
Hessle	d																						
Ferriby	d																						
Brough	d			11 02	11 10				11 42		11 58	12 05	12 12				12 58		13 10	13 41			
Broomfleet	d																						
Gilberdyke	d			11 09								12 12					13 05						
Eastrington	d																						
Howden	d								11 54		12 10									13 53			
Wressle	d																						
Selby	a				11 28				12 04		12 19		12 32						13 28	14 02			
	d				11 29				12 05		12 20		12 32						13 29	14 03			
York 8 33	a										12 44									14 30			
Saltmarshe	d																						
Goole	d			11 18			11 43					12 21					13 14						
Thorne North	d			11 26			11 51					12 29											
Cleethorpes	d		10 26							11 26				12 58									
New Clee	d													13 01									
Grimsby Docks	d													13 04									
Grimsby Town	a		10 33							11 33				13 06									
	d		10 34							11 34				13 07									
Great Coates	d													13 11									
Healing	d													13 14									
Stallingborough	d													13 15									
Habrough	d		10 44											13 21									
Ulceby	d													13 25									
Thornton Abbey	d													13 30									
Goxhill	d													13 33									
New Holland	d													13 35									
Barrow Haven	d													13 41									
Barton-on-Humber	a													13 48									
Barton-on-Humber	d																					13 55	
Hull Paragon Interchange	a																					14 19	
Barnetby	d		10 53							11 53													
Scunthorpe	a		11 08							12 08													
	d		11 08							12 08													
Althorpe	d																						
Crowle	d																						
Thorne South	d																						
Hatfield & Stainforth	d						11 57																
Kirk Sandall	d						12 02																
Adwick 31	d																						
Bentley (S.Yorks) 31	d																						
Doncaster 7 31	a		11 38	11 46			12 11		12 24	12 40		12 47					13 37						
London Kings Cross 15 ⊖26	a								14 12														
York 8 26	d	10 28						11 28								12 28		13 15					
Doncaster 7	d	11 30	11 42	11 48			12 13	12 30		12 42					13 13	13 30	13 38				13 42		
Conisbrough	d						12 20								13 20								
Mexborough	d						12 24								13 24								
Swinton (S.Yorks)	d					12 05	12 27								13 27								14 05
Rotherham Central	d					12 13	12 38								13 36								14 13
Meadowhall ⇌	d		12 00	12 08		12 21	12 43			13 00					13 44		13 56				14 00		14 21
Sheffield 7 ⇌	a	11 53	12 07	12 18		12 32	12 55	12 54		13 07					13 52	13 54	14 06				14 07		14 32
	d		12 10							13 10											14 11		
Stockport 78	a		12 53							13 53											14 53		
Manchester Piccadilly 10 ⇌	a		13 06		12 54					14 06			13 54					14 34	14 54		15 06		
Manchester Airport 85 ✈	a		13 29							14 29								14 55			15 29		

A From Newcastle to Plymouth
B From Bridlington
C From Leeds
D From Edinburgh to Penzance
E From Edinburgh to Plymouth
F From Scarborough
G From Newcastle

Table 29

Sundays
until 19 June

Hull and Cleethorpes - Doncaster - Meadowhall, Sheffield, Manchester and Manchester Airport, Cleethorpes - Barton-on-Humber

		XC	NT	NT	TP	NT	TP	EM	HT	XC	NT	NT	TP	TP	NT BHX	NT	NT	XC	NT	NT	NT	TP
		◇1			◇1		◇1		◇1	◇1			◇1	◇1				◇1				◇1
		A		B	C			D		E		F					G	H		B		C
		✠							⊠	✠					🚌			✠				
Hull	d			13 35		14 23			14 30			14 41	14 58							15 41	16 00	
Hessle	d			13 42																		
Ferriby	d			13 47																		
Brough	d			13 52		14 35			14 42			14 53	15 10							15 53	16 12	
Broomfleet	d																					
Gilberdyke	d			14 00								15 00								16 00		
Eastrington	d																					
Howden	d					14 47			14 54												16 24	
Wressle	d																					
Selby	a					14 56			15 04				15 28								16 33	
	d					14 57			15 05				15 29								16 34	
York 8 33	a					15 25															16 59	
Saltmarshe	d																					
Goole	d		13 43	14 08								15 09							15 43	16 09		
Thorne North	d		13 51																15 51			
Cleethorpes	d						13 26	13 56						14 26		14 58						
New Clee	d															15 01						
Grimsby Docks	d															15 04						
Grimsby Town	a						13 33	14 02						14 33		15 06						
	d						13 34	14 03						14 34		15 07						
Great Coates	d															15 11						
Healing	d															15 14						
Stallingborough	d															15 15						
Habrough	d							14 13						14 44		15 21						
Ulceby	d															15 25						
Thornton Abbey	d															15 30						
Goxhill	d															15 36						
New Holland	d															15 38						
Barrow Haven	d															15 41						
Barton-on-Humber	a															15 49						
Barton-on-Humber	d														15 55							
Hull Paragon Interchange	a														16 20							
Barnetby	d						13 53	14a21						14 53								
Scunthorpe	a						14 08							15 08								
	d						14 08							15 08								
Althorpe	d																					
Crowle	d																					
Thorne South	d																					
Hatfield & Stainforth	d		13 57																15 57			
Kirk Sandall	d		14 02																16 02			
Adwick 31	d																					
Bentley (S.Yorks) 31	d																					
Doncaster 7 31	a		14 11	14 31			14 37		15 23			15 32		15 39					16 11	16 32		
London Kings Cross 15 ⊖26	a								17 12													
York 8 26	d	13 40			14 15					14 41								15 39				16 15
Doncaster 7	d		14 13	14 33			14 42				15 13	15 33		15 42					16 13	16 33		
Conisbrough	d		14 20								15 20								16 20			
Mexborough	d		14 24								15 24								16 24			
Swinton (S.Yorks)	d		14 30								15 30						16 05		16 29			
Rotherham Central	d		14 42								15 41						16 13		16 41			
Meadowhall ⇌	d		14 48	14 52			15 00				15 48	15 52		16 00			16 21		16 47	16 53		
Sheffield 7 ⇌	a	14 52	14 55	15 03			15 07			15 51	15 55	16 01		16 07			16 31	16 51	16 55	17 04		
	d						15 11							16 11								
Stockport 78	a						15 53							16 53								
Manchester Piccadilly 10 ⇌	a				15 34		16 06						16 54	17 06								17 34
Manchester Airport 85 ✈	a				15 55		16 34							17 29								17 55

A From Edinburgh to Penzance
B From Scarborough
C From Newcastle
D To Nottingham
E From Edinburgh to Plymouth
F From Bridlington
G From Leeds
H From Glasgow Central to Plymouth

Table 29

Sundays
until 19 June

Hull and Cleethorpes - Doncaster - Meadowhall, Sheffield, Manchester and Manchester Airport, Cleethorpes - Barton-on-Humber

		TP	TP	HT	NT	NT	TP	TP	NT	EM	NT	NT	XC	NT	NT	TP	NT	EM	HT	NT	NT BHX
		◇1	◇1	◇1			◇1	◇1		◇1			◇1			◇1			◇1		
						B				C		D	E		F			G			
				⊠						🍴			✠						⊠	🚌	🚌
Hull	d			16 30		16 41	16 58		17 23						17 41				18 30		
Hessle	d																				
Ferriby	d																				
Brough	d			16 42		16 53	17 10		17 35						17 53				18 42		
Broomfleet	d																				
Gilberdyke	d					17 00									18 00						
Eastrington	d																				
Howden	d			16 54					17 47										18 54		
Wressle	d																				
Selby	a			17 04			17 28		17 56										19 04		
	d			17 05			17 29		17 57										19 05		
York 8 33	a								18 25												
Saltmarshe	d																				
Goole	d					17 09					17 42				18 09						
Thorne North	d										17 50										
Cleethorpes	d		15 26					16 26								17 26	17 58	18 18			
New Clee	d																18 01				
Grimsby Docks	d																18 04				
Grimsby Town	a		15 33					16 33								17 33	18 06	18 24			
	d		15 34					16 34								17 34	18 07	18 25			
Great Coates	d																18 11				
Healing	d																18 14				
Stallingborough	d																18 15				
Habrough	d															17 44	18 21	18 35			
Ulceby	d																18 25				
Thornton Abbey	d																18 30				
Goxhill	d																18 33				
New Holland	d																18 38				
Barrow Haven	d																18 41				
Barton-on-Humber	a																18 51				
Barton-on-Humber	d																				18 55
Hull Paragon Interchange	a																				19 20
Barnetby	d		15 53					16 53								17 53		18a43			
Scunthorpe	a		16 08					17 08								18 08					
	d		16 08					17 08								18 08					
Althorpe	d																				
Crowle	d																				
Thorne South	d																				
Hatfield & Stainforth	d										17 56										
Kirk Sandall	d										18 01										
Adwick 31	d																				
Bentley (S.Yorks) 31	d																				
Doncaster 7 31	a		16 38	17 25		17 31		17 38			18 09				18 33	18 38			19 25		
London Kings Cross 15 ⊖26	a			19 15															21 14		
York 8 26	d	16 33								17 40			17 41							18 40	
Doncaster 7	d		16 42		17 13	17 32		17 42		18 06				18 19	18 34	18 42					
Conisbrough	d				17 21									18 26							
Mexborough	d				17 25									18 30							
Swinton (S.Yorks)	d				17 30							18 10		18 33						20a22	
Rotherham Central	d				17 41							18 19		18 42							
Meadowhall ⇌	d		17 01		17 48	17 53		18 00				18 25		18 47	18 53	19 00					
Sheffield 7 ⇌	a		17 07		17 55	18 01		18 07		18 28		18 36	18 51	18 57	19 03	19 07					
	d		17 11					18 11								19 11					
Stockport 78	a		17 53					18 53								19 55					
Manchester Piccadilly 10 ⇌	a	17 54	18 06				18 54	19 06								20 09					
Manchester Airport 85 ✈	a		18 29					19 29								20 32					

A From Aberdeen to Plymouth
B From Bridlington
C To St Pancras International
D From Leeds
E From Glasgow Central to Bristol Temple Meads
F From Scarborough
G To Newark North Gate

Table 29

Sundays
until 19 June

Hull and Cleethorpes - Doncaster - Meadowhall, Sheffield, Manchester and Manchester Airport, Cleethorpes - Barton-on-Humber

		NT	XC	NT	NT	TP	TP	NT	NT	XC	NT	NT	TP	NT	EM	NT	TP	NT	TP	NT	NT
			◇■			◇■	◇■			◇■			◇■				◇■		◇■		
		A	B ✠		C				D	E				G	H		J	A		D	
Hull	d				18 38	18 58		19 24				20 29		20 01		20 29	21 00				21 35
Hessle	d													20 08							
Ferriby	d													20 13							
Brough	d				18 50	19 10		19 36				20 41		20 18		20 41	21 12				21 47
Broomfleet	d																				
Gilberdyke	d				18 57									20 25							21 54
Eastrington	d																				
Howden	d							19 48				20 53				20 53					
Wressle	d																				
Selby	a					19 28		19 57				21 02				21 02	21 30				
	d					19 29		19 58				21 03				21 03					
York 8 33	a							20 25				21 30				21 30					
Saltmarshe	d																				
Goole	d				19 06									20 34							22 03
Thorne North	d				19 14									20 42							22 11
Cleethorpes	d						18 26						19 26		20 15				20 26		
New Clee	d																				
Grimsby Docks	d																				
Grimsby Town	a						18 33						19 33		20 21				20 33		
	d						18 34						19 34		20 22				20 34		
Great Coates	d																				
Healing	d																				
Stallingborough	d																				
Habrough	d														20 33				20 44		
Ulceby	d																				
Thornton Abbey	d																				
Goxhill	d																				
New Holland	d																				
Barrow Haven	d																				
Barton-on-Humber	a																				
Barton-on-Humber	d																				
Hull Paragon Interchange	a																				
Barnetby	d						18 53						19 53		20a42				20 53		
Scunthorpe	a						19 08						20 08						21 08		
	d						19 08						20 08						21 08		
Althorpe	d																				
Crowle	d																				
Thorne South	d																				
Hatfield & Stainforth	d				19 20																22 15
Kirk Sandall	d				19 25																22 20
Adwick 31	d																				
Bentley (S.Yorks) 31	d																				
Doncaster 7 31	a				19 35		19 38						20 40	20 59					21 40		22 32
London Kings Cross 15 ⊖26	a																				
York 8 26	d		18 40							19 39											
Doncaster 7	d			19 18	19 37		19 42				20 14		20 42	21 01					21 42		22 40
Conisbrough	d			19 25							20 21			21 08							22 47
Mexborough	d			19 29							20 25			21 12							22 51
Swinton (S.Yorks)	d	19 01		19 33					20 07		20 29			21 15				21 45	21 52	22 32	22 53
Rotherham Central	d	19 13		19 41					20 15		20 41			21 22				21 52	21 58	22 40	22 58
Meadowhall 🚋	d	19 18		19 47	19 57		20 00		20 21		20 47		21 00	21 28				21 58	22 04	22 45	23 04
Sheffield 7 🚋	a	19 27	19 50	19 55	20 06		20 07		20 34	20 51	20 55		21 07	21 38				22 09	22 15	22 54	23 15
	d						20 11						21 11								
Stockport 78	a						20 53						21 53								
Manchester Piccadilly 10 🚋	a					20 54	21 06						22 06								
Manchester Airport 85 ✈	a						21 29						22 29								

A From Moorthorpe
B From Glasgow Central to Bristol Temple Meads
C From Bridlington
D From Leeds
E From Edinburgh to Birmingham New Street
F From Newcastle
G From Scarborough
H To Newark North Gate
I From Glasgow Central to Birmingham New Street
J To Leeds

Table 29

Sundays
until 19 June

Hull and Cleethorpes - Doncaster - Meadowhall, Sheffield, Manchester and Manchester Airport, Cleethorpes - Barton-on-Humber

		NT
		🚌
Hull	d	
Hessle	d	
Ferriby	d	
Brough	d	
Broomfleet	d	
Gilberdyke	d	
Eastrington	d	
Howden	d	
Wressle	d	
Selby	a	
	d	
York 8 33	a	
Saltmarshe	d	
Goole	d	
Thorne North	d	
Cleethorpes	d	
New Clee	d	
Grimsby Docks	d	
Grimsby Town	a	
	d	
Great Coates	d	
Healing	d	
Stallingborough	d	
Habrough	d	
Ulceby	d	
Thornton Abbey	d	
Goxhill	d	
New Holland	d	
Barrow Haven	d	
Barton-on-Humber	a	
Barton-on-Humber	d	
Hull Paragon Interchange	a	
Barnetby	d	
Scunthorpe	a	
	d	
Althorpe	d	
Crowle	d	
Thorne South	d	
Hatfield & Stainforth	d	
Kirk Sandall	d	
Adwick 31	d	
Bentley (S.Yorks) 31	d	
Doncaster 7 31	a	
London Kings Cross 15 ⊖26	a	
York 8 26	d	21 15
Doncaster 7	d	
Conisbrough	d	
Mexborough	d	
Swinton (S.Yorks)	d	22s57
Rotherham Central	d	23s17
Meadowhall 🚋	d	23s27
Sheffield 7 🚋	a	23 47
	d	
Stockport 78	a	
Manchester Piccadilly 10 🚋	a	
Manchester Airport 85 ✈	a	

Table 29

Sundays
26 June to 11 September

Hull and Cleethorpes - Doncaster - Meadowhall, Sheffield, Manchester and Manchester Airport, Cleethorpes - Barton-on-Humber

		TP	TP	TP	TP	TP	NT	TP	NT	NT	NT	NT	TP	NT	XC	HT	NT	TP	NT	NT BHX	NT
		◇1	◇1	◇1	◇1	◇1		◇1		C			◇1		◇1 D	◇1		◇1		🚌	
															⊼	⊠					
Hull	d										08 40	08 54	09 00			09 30	09 33				
Hessle	d																09 40				
Ferriby	d																09 45				
Brough	d										08 52	09 06	09 12			09 42	09 50				
Broomfleet	d																				
Gilberdyke	d										08 59						09 57				
Eastrington	d																				
Howden	d											09 18				09 54					
Wressle	d																				
Selby	a											09 27	09 32			10 04					
	d											09 28	09 33			10 05					
York 8	33 a											09 52									
Saltmarshe	d																				
Goole	d										09 09			09 43			10 06				
Thorne North	d													09 51							
Cleethorpes	d																	09 26	10 05		
New Clee	d																		10 08		
Grimsby Docks	d																		10 11		
Grimsby Town	a																	09 33	10 13		
	d																	09 34	10 14		
Great Coates	d																		10 18		
Healing	d																		10 21		
Stallingborough	d																		10 22		
Habrough	d																	09 44	10 29		
Ulceby	d																		10 33		
Thornton Abbey	d																		10 38		
Goxhill	d																		10 41		
New Holland	d																		10 46		
Barrow Haven	d																		10 49		
Barton-on-Humber	a																		10 56		
Barton-on-Humber	d																			10 55	
Hull Paragon Interchange	a																			11 19	
Barnetby	d																	09 53			
Scunthorpe	a																	10 08			
	d																	10 08			
Althorpe	d																				
Crowle	d																				
Thorne South	d																				
Hatfield & Stainforth	d													09 57			10 20				
Kirk Sandall	d													10 02			10 25				
Adwick	31 d																				
Bentley (S.Yorks)	31 d																				
Doncaster 7	31 a										09 29			10 11		10 23	10 35	10 40			
London Kings Cross 15	⊖26 a															12 12					
York 8	26 d	02 44	03 59	05 12	06 12	07 12		08 10							09 28						
Doncaster 7	d						08 03		09 13		09 39			10 13	10 30			10 42			11 13
Conisbrough	d						08 10		09 20					10 20							11 20
Mexborough	d						08 14		09 24					10 24							11 24
Swinton (S.Yorks)	d						08 17		09 28	09 35				10 27							11 27
Rotherham Central	d						08 25		09 35	09 48				10 35							11 35
Meadowhall	⇌ d						08 30		09 41	09 54	10 00			10 40				11 00			11 40
Sheffield 7	⇌ a						08 41		09 51	10 03	10 08			10 52	10 54			11 07			11 51
	d																	11 10			
Stockport	78 a																	11 53			
Manchester Piccadilly 10	⇌ a	04 02	05 17	06 34	07 34	08 34		09 34					11 03					12 06			
Manchester Airport	85 ✈ a	04 23	05 38	06 55	07 55	08 55		09 55										12 29			

C From Leeds
D To Plymouth

Table 29

Sundays
26 June to 11 September

Hull and Cleethorpes - Doncaster - Meadowhall, Sheffield, Manchester and Manchester Airport, Cleethorpes - Barton-on-Humber

		XC	TP	NT	TP	NT	NT	XC	HT	TP	NT	NT	TP	NT	NT	XC	NT	TP	TP	NT	TP	NT BHX	NT
		◇1 A	◇1	B	◇1	C		◇1 D	◇1	◇1			◇1			◇1 D	E	◇1 F	◇1		◇1	🚌	C
		⊼						⊼	⊠							⊼							
Hull	d			10 50	10 58				11 30		11 46	11 53	12 00				12 46		12 58	13 29			
Hessle	d																						
Ferriby	d																						
Brough	d			11 02	11 10				11 42		11 58	12 05	12 12				12 58		13 10	13 41			
Broomfleet	d																						
Gilberdyke	d			11 09								12 12					13 05						
Eastrington	d																						
Howden	d								11 54		12 10									13 53			
Wressle	d																						
Selby	a				11 28				12 04		12 19		12 32						13 28	14 02			
	d				11 29				12 05		12 20		12 32						13 29	14 03			
York 8	33 a										12 44									14 30			
Saltmarshe	d																						
Goole	d			11 18			11 43					12 21					13 14						
Thorne North	d			11 26			11 51					12 29											
Cleethorpes	d		10 26							11 26				12 58									
New Clee	d													13 01									
Grimsby Docks	d													13 04									
Grimsby Town	a		10 33							11 33				13 06									
	d		10 34							11 34				13 07									
Great Coates	d													13 11									
Healing	d													13 14									
Stallingborough	d													13 15									
Habrough	d		10 44											13 21									
Ulceby	d													13 25									
Thornton Abbey	d													13 30									
Goxhill	d													13 33									
New Holland	d													13 35									
Barrow Haven	d													13 41									
Barton-on-Humber	a													13 48									
Barton-on-Humber	d																					13 55	
Hull Paragon Interchange	a																					14 20	
Barnetby	d		10 53							11 53													
Scunthorpe	a		11 08							12 08													
	d		11 08							12 08													
Althorpe	d																						
Crowle	d																						
Thorne South	d																						
Hatfield & Stainforth	d						11 57																
Kirk Sandall	d						12 02																
Adwick	31 d																						
Bentley (S.Yorks)	31 d																						
Doncaster 7	31 a		11 38	11 46			12 11		12 24	12 40		12 47					13 37						
London Kings Cross 15	⊖26 a								14 12														
York 8	26 d	10 28						11 28								12 28		13 15					
Doncaster 7	d	11 30	11 42	11 48			12 13	12 30		12 42					13 13	13 30	13 38				13 42		
Conisbrough	d						12 20								13 20								
Mexborough	d						12 24								13 24								
Swinton (S.Yorks)	d					12 05	12 27								13 27								14 05
Rotherham Central	d					12 13	12 38								13 36								14 13
Meadowhall	⇌ d		12 00	12 08		12 21	12 43			13 00					13 44		13 56				14 00		14 21
Sheffield 7	⇌ a	11 53	12 07	12 18		12 32	12 55	12 54		13 07					13 52	13 54	14 06				14 07		14 32
	d		12 10							13 10											14 11		
Stockport	78 a		12 53							13 53											14 53		
Manchester Piccadilly 10	⇌ a		13 06		12 54					14 06			13 54					14 34	14 54		15 06		
Manchester Airport	85 ✈ a		13 29							14 29								14 55			15 29		

A From Newcastle to Birmingham New Street
B From Bridlington
C From Leeds
D From Edinburgh to Plymouth
E From Scarborough
F From Newcastle

Table 29

Sundays
26 June to 11 September

Hull and Cleethorpes - Doncaster - Meadowhall, Sheffield, Manchester and Manchester Airport, Cleethorpes - Barton-on-Humber

		NT	NT	TP	NT	TP	EM	HT	XC	NT	NT	TP	TP	NT	XC	NT	NT	NT
				◇1		◇1		◇1	◇1			◇1	◇1		◇1			
			B	C			D	⊠	E		G				E	H		B
Hull	d		13 35		14 23			14 30			14 41	14 58						15 41
Hessle	d		13 42															
Ferriby	d		13 47															
Brough	d		13 52		14 35			14 42			14 53	15 10						15 53
Broomfleet	d																	
Gilberdyke	d		14 00								15 00							16 00
Eastrington	d																	
Howden	d				14 47			14 54										
Wressle	d																	
Selby	a				14 56			15 04				15 28						
	d				14 57			15 05				15 29						
York 8 33	a				15 25													
Saltmarshe	d																	
Goole	d	13 43	14 08								15 09						15 43	16 09
Thorne North	d	13 51															15 51	
Cleethorpes	d					13 26	13 56						14 26	14 58				
New Clee	d													15 01				
Grimsby Docks	d													15 04				
Grimsby Town	a					13 33	14 02						14 33	15 06				
	d					13 34	14 03						14 34	15 07				
Great Coates	d													15 11				
Healing	d													15 14				
Stallingborough	d													15 15				
Habrough	d						14 13						14 44	15 21				
Ulceby	d													15 25				
Thornton Abbey	d													15 30				
Goxhill	d													15 36				
New Holland	d													15 38				
Barrow Haven	d													15 41				
Barton-on-Humber	a													15 49				
Barton-on-Humber	d																	
Hull Paragon Interchange	a																	
Barnetby	d					13 53	14a21						14 53					
Scunthorpe	a					14 08							15 08					
	d					14 08							15 08					
Althorpe	d																	
Crowle	d																	
Thorne South	d																	
Hatfield & Stainforth	d	13 57															15 57	
Kirk Sandall	d	14 02															16 02	
Adwick 31	d																	
Bentley (S.Yorks) 31	d																	
Doncaster 7 31	a	14 11	14 31			14 37		15 23			15 32		15 39				16 11	16 32
London Kings Cross 15 ⊖26	a							17 12										
York 8 26	d			14 15					14 34						15 34			
Doncaster 7	d	14 13	14 33			14 42			14 59	15 13	15 33		15 42		15 59		16 13	16 33
Conisbrough	d	14 20								15 20							16 20	
Mexborough	d	14 24								15 24							16 24	
Swinton (S.Yorks)	d	14 30								15 30						16 05	16 29	
Rotherham Central	d	14 42								15 41						16 13	16 41	
Meadowhall	d	14 48	14 52			15 00				15 48	15 52		16 00			16 21	16 47	16 53
Sheffield 7	a	14 55	15 03			15 07			15 21	15 55	16 01		16 07		16 21	16 31	16 55	17 04
	d					15 11							16 11					
Stockport 78	a					15 53							16 53					
Manchester Piccadilly 10	a			15 34		16 06						16 54	17 06					
Manchester Airport 85	a			15 55		16 34							17 29					

B From Scarborough
C From Newcastle
D To Nottingham
E From Newcastle to Reading
F From Glasgow Central to Plymouth
G From Bridlington
H From Leeds

Table 29

Sundays
26 June to 11 September

Hull and Cleethorpes - Doncaster - Meadowhall, Sheffield, Manchester and Manchester Airport, Cleethorpes - Barton-on-Humber

		NT	TP	TP	XC	HT	TP	NT	NT	TP	TP	NT	XC	EM	NT	NT	NT	NT	TP	NT	EM
			◇1	◇1	◇1	◇1	◇1			◇1	◇1		◇1	◇1					◇1		
			A		B	⊠			D				E	F		G		I			J
Hull	d	16 00				16 30			16 41	16 58		17 23						17 41			
Hessle	d																				
Ferriby	d																				
Brough	d	16 12				16 42			16 53	17 10		17 35						17 53			
Broomfleet	d																				
Gilberdyke	d								17 00									18 00			
Eastrington	d																				
Howden	d	16 24				16 54						17 47									
Wressle	d																				
Selby	a	16 33				17 04				17 28		17 56									
	d	16 34				17 05				17 29		17 57									
York 8 33	a	16 59										18 25									
Saltmarshe	d																				
Goole	d								17 09						17 42			18 09			
Thorne North	d														17 50						
Cleethorpes	d			15 26							16 26								17 26	17 58	18 18
New Clee	d																			18 01	
Grimsby Docks	d																			18 04	
Grimsby Town	a			15 33							16 33								17 33	18 06	18 24
	d			15 34							16 34								17 34	18 07	18 25
Great Coates	d																			18 11	
Healing	d																			18 14	
Stallingborough	d																			18 15	
Habrough	d																		17 44	18 21	18 35
Ulceby	d																			18 25	
Thornton Abbey	d																			18 30	
Goxhill	d																			18 33	
New Holland	d																			18 38	
Barrow Haven	d																			18 41	
Barton-on-Humber	a																			18 51	
Barton-on-Humber	d																				
Hull Paragon Interchange	a																				
Barnetby	d			15 53							16 53								17 53		18a43
Scunthorpe	a			16 08							17 08								18 08		
	d			16 08							17 08								18 08		
Althorpe	d																				
Crowle	d																				
Thorne South	d																				
Hatfield & Stainforth	d														17 56						
Kirk Sandall	d														18 01						
Adwick 31	d																				
Bentley (S.Yorks) 31	d																				
Doncaster 7 31	a			16 38		17 25			17 31		17 38				18 09			18 33	18 38		
London Kings Cross 15 ⊖26	a					19 15															
York 8 26	d		16 15		16 23		16 33						17 34	17 40							
Doncaster 7	d			16 42	16 51			17 13	17 32		17 42		17 59	18 06			18 19	18 34	18 42		
Conisbrough	d							17 21									18 26				
Mexborough	d							17 25									18 30				
Swinton (S.Yorks)	d							17 30								18 10	18 33				
Rotherham Central	d							17 41								18 19	18 42				
Meadowhall	d			17 01				17 48	17 53		18 00					18 25	18 47	18 53	19 00		
Sheffield 7	a			17 07	17 19			17 55	18 01		18 07		18 23	18 28		18 36	18 57	19 03	19 07		
	d			17 11							18 11								19 11		
Stockport 78	a			17 53							18 53								19 55		
Manchester Piccadilly 10	a		17 34	18 06			17 54			18 54	19 06								20 09		
Manchester Airport 85	a		17 55	18 29							19 29								20 32		

A From Newcastle
B From Edinburgh to Reading
D From Bridlington
E From Newcastle to Reading
F To St Pancras International
G From Leeds
H From Glasgow Central to Bristol Temple Meads
I From Scarborough
J To Newark North Gate

Table 29

Sundays
26 June to 11 September

Hull and Cleethorpes - Doncaster - Meadowhall, Sheffield, Manchester and Manchester Airport, Cleethorpes - Barton-on-Humber

		HT	XC	NT	TP	NT BHX	NT	NT	TP	TP	XC	NT	NT	NT	TP	TP	EM	XC	NT	NT
		◇1	◇1		◇1				◇1	◇1	◇1				◇1	◇1		◇1		
			A					C			D		E		G		H	D	I	
		⊠	⌶			🚌					⌶							⌶		
Hull	d	18 30						18 38	18 58			19 24							20 01	20 29
Hessle	d																		20 08	
Ferriby	d																		20 13	
Brough	d	18 42						18 50	19 10			19 36							20 18	20 41
Broomfleet	d																			
Gilberdyke	d							18 57											20 25	
Eastrington	d																			
Howden	d	18 54										19 48								20 53
Wressle	d																			
Selby	a	19 04							19 28			19 57								21 02
	d	19 05							19 29			19 58								21 03
York 8 33	a											20 25								21 30
Saltmarshe	d																			
Goole	d							19 06											20 34	
Thorne North	d							19 14											20 42	
Cleethorpes	d									18 26						19 26	20 15			
New Clee	d																			
Grimsby Docks	d																			
Grimsby Town	a									18 33						19 33	20 21			
	d									18 34						19 34	20 22			
Great Coates	d																			
Healing	d																			
Stallingborough	d																			
Habrough	d																20 33			
Ulceby	d																			
Thornton Abbey	d																			
Goxhill	d																			
New Holland	d																			
Barrow Haven	d																			
Barton-on-Humber	a																			
Barton-on-Humber	d					18 55														
Hull Paragon Interchange	a					19 20														
Barnetby	d									18 53						19 53	20a42			
Scunthorpe	a									19 08						20 08				
	d									19 08						20 08				
Althorpe	d																			
Crowle	d																			
Thorne South	d																			
Hatfield & Stainforth	d							19 20												
Kirk Sandall	d							19 25												
Adwick 31	d																			
Bentley (S.Yorks) 31	d																			
Doncaster 7 31	a	19 25						19 35		19 38						20 40			20 59	
London Kings Cross 15 ⊖26	a	21 14																		
York 8 26	d		18 34	18 10	18 33						19 24				20 15			20 24		
Doncaster 7	d		18 59				19 18	19 37		19 42	19 50			20 14		20 42		20 50	21 01	
Conisbrough	d						19 25							20 21					21 08	
Mexborough	d						19 29							20 25					21 12	
Swinton (S.Yorks)	d			19 01			19 33						20 07	20 29					21 15	
Rotherham Central	d			19 13			19 41						20 15	20 41					21 22	
Meadowhall ⇌	d			19 18			19 47	19 57		20 00			20 21	20 47		21 00			21 28	
Sheffield 7 ⇌	a		19 21	19 27			19 55	20 06		20 07	20 16		20 34	20 55		21 07		21 17	21 38	
	d									20 11						21 11				
Stockport 78	a									20 53						21 53				
Manchester Piccadilly 10 ⇌	a				19 54				20 54	21 06					21 36	22 06				
Manchester Airport 85 ✈	a									21 29						22 29				

A From Newcastle to Reading
B From Glasgow Central to Bristol Temple Meads
C From Bridlington
D From Newcastle to Birmingham New Street
E From Leeds
G From Newcastle
H To Newark North Gate
I From Scarborough

Table 29

Sundays
26 June to 11 September

Hull and Cleethorpes - Doncaster - Meadowhall, Sheffield, Manchester and Manchester Airport, Cleethorpes - Barton-on-Humber

		NT	TP	TP	NT	NT
			◇1	◇1		
				B	C	
Hull	d			21 00		21 35
Hessle	d					
Ferriby	d					
Brough	d			21 12		21 47
Broomfleet	d					
Gilberdyke	d					21 54
Eastrington	d					
Howden	d					
Wressle	d					
Selby	a			21 30		
	d					
York 8 33	a					
Saltmarshe	d					
Goole	d					22 03
Thorne North	d					22 11
Cleethorpes	d		20 26			
New Clee	d					
Grimsby Docks	d					
Grimsby Town	a		20 33			
	d		20 34			
Great Coates	d					
Healing	d					
Stallingborough	d					
Habrough	d		20 44			
Ulceby	d					
Thornton Abbey	d					
Goxhill	d					
New Holland	d					
Barrow Haven	d					
Barton-on-Humber	a					
Barton-on-Humber	d					
Hull Paragon Interchange	a					
Barnetby	d		20 53			
Scunthorpe	a		21 08			
	d		21 08			
Althorpe	d					
Crowle	d					
Thorne South	d					
Hatfield & Stainforth	d					22 15
Kirk Sandall	d					22 20
Adwick 31	d					
Bentley (S.Yorks) 31	d					
Doncaster 7 31	a		21 40			22 32
London Kings Cross 15 ⊖26	a					
York 8 26	d	20 50				
Doncaster 7	d		21 42			22 40
Conisbrough	d					22 47
Mexborough	d					22 51
Swinton (S.Yorks)	d	21 45	21 52		22 32	22 53
Rotherham Central	d	21 52	21 58		22 40	22 58
Meadowhall ⇌	d	21 58	22 04		22 45	23 04
Sheffield 7 ⇌	a	22 09	22 15		22 54	23 15
	d					
Stockport 78	a					
Manchester Piccadilly 10 ⇌	a					
Manchester Airport 85 ✈	a					

B To Leeds
C From Leeds

Table 29

Sundays

18 September to 23 October

Hull and Cleethorpes - Doncaster - Meadowhall, Sheffield, Manchester and Manchester Airport, Cleethorpes - Barton-on-Humber

		NT	NT	NT B	NT	NT	TP ◇1 C	NT	XC ◇1 D	HT ◇1 ⊠	NT	TP ◇1	NT	XC ◇1 E	TP ◇1	NT F	TP ◇1 G	NT B	NT	XC ◇1 H	HT ◇1 ⊠	TP ◇1
Hull	d				08 40	08 54	09 00			09 30	09 33					10 50	10 58				11 30	
Hessle	d										09 40											
Ferriby	d										09 45											
Brough	d				08 52	09 06	09 12			09 42	09 50					11 02	11 10				11 42	
Broomfleet	d																					
Gilberdyke	d				08 59						09 57					11 09						
Eastrington	d																					
Howden	d					09 18				09 54											11 54	
Wressle	d																					
Selby	a					09 27	09 32			10 04							11 28				12 04	
	d					09 28				10 05											12 05	
York 8	33 a					09 52																
Saltmarshe	d																					
Goole	d				09 09			09 43			10 06					11 18			11 43			
Thorne North	d							09 51								11 26			11 51			
Cleethorpes	d											09 26			10 26							11 26
New Clee	d																					
Grimsby Docks	d																					
Grimsby Town	a											09 33			10 33							11 33
	d											09 34			10 34							11 34
Great Coates	d																					
Healing	d																					
Stallingborough	d																					
Habrough	d											09 44			10 44							
Ulceby	d																					
Thornton Abbey	d																					
Goxhill	d																					
New Holland	d																					
Barrow Haven	d																					
Barton-on-Humber	a																					
Barton-on-Humber	d																					
Hull Paragon Interchange	a																					
Barnetby	d											09 53			10 53							11 53
Scunthorpe	a											10 08			11 08							12 08
	d											10 08			11 08							12 08
Althorpe	d																					
Crowle	d																					
Thorne South	d																					
Hatfield & Stainforth	d							09 57			10 20								11 57			
Kirk Sandall	d							10 02			10 25								12 02			
Adwick	31 d																					
Bentley (S.Yorks)	31 d																					
Doncaster 7	31 a				09 29			10 11		10 23	10 35	10 40			11 38	11 46			12 11		12 24	12 40
London Kings Cross 15 ⊖	26 a									12 12											14 12	
York 8	26 d								09 28					10 28						11 28		
Doncaster 7	d	08 03	09 13		09 39			10 13	10 30			10 42	11 13	11 30	11 42	11 48			12 13	12 30		12 42
Conisbrough	d	08 10	09 20					10 20					11 20						12 20			
Mexborough	d	08 14	09 24					10 24					11 24						12 24			
Swinton (S.Yorks)	d	08 17	09 28	09 35				10 27					11 27					12 05	12 27			
Rotherham Central	d	08 25	09 35	09 48				10 35					11 35					12 13	12 38			
Meadowhall	d	08 30	09 41	09 54	10 00			10 40				11 00	11 40		12 00	12 08		12 21	12 43			13 00
Sheffield 7	a	08 41	09 51	10 03	10 08			10 52	10 54			11 07	11 51	11 53	12 07	12 18		12 32	12 55	12 54		13 07
	d											11 10			12 10							13 10
Stockport	78 a											11 53			12 53							13 53
Manchester Piccadilly 10	a											12 06			13 06							14 06
Manchester Airport	85 a											12 34			13 29							14 34

B From Leeds
C To Leeds
D To Bristol Parkway
E From Newcastle to Bristol Parkway
F From Bridlington
G To Huddersfield
H From Edinburgh to Bristol Parkway

Table 29

Sundays

18 September to 23 October

Hull and Cleethorpes - Doncaster - Meadowhall, Sheffield, Manchester and Manchester Airport, Cleethorpes - Barton-on-Humber

		NT	NT	TP ◇1 A	NT	XC ◇1 B	NT C	TP ◇1 A	TP ◇1	NT D	NT	NT C	TP ◇1	NT	HT ◇1 ⊠	XC ◇1 E	NT	NT G	TP ◇1	TP ◇1 A	XC ◇1 E
Hull	d	11 46	11 53	12 00			12 46	12 58				13 35		14 23	14 30			14 41		14 58	
Hessle	d											13 42									
Ferriby	d											13 47									
Brough	d	11 58	12 05	12 12			12 58	13 10				13 52		14 35	14 42			14 53		15 10	
Broomfleet	d																				
Gilberdyke	d		12 12				13 05					14 00						15 00			
Eastrington	d																				
Howden	d	12 10												14 47	14 54						
Wressle	d																				
Selby	a	12 19		12 32				13 28						14 56	15 04					15 28	
	d	12 20												14 57	15 05						
York 8	33 a	12 44												15 25							
Saltmarshe	d																				
Goole	d		12 21				13 14				13 43	14 08						15 09			
Thorne North	d		12 29								13 51										
Cleethorpes	d												13 26						14 26		
New Clee	d																				
Grimsby Docks	d																				
Grimsby Town	a												13 33						14 33		
	d												13 34						14 34		
Great Coates	d																				
Healing	d																				
Stallingborough	d																				
Habrough	d																		14 44		
Ulceby	d																				
Thornton Abbey	d																				
Goxhill	d																				
New Holland	d																				
Barrow Haven	d																				
Barton-on-Humber	a																				
Barton-on-Humber	d																				
Hull Paragon Interchange	a																				
Barnetby	d												13 53						14 53		
Scunthorpe	a												14 08						15 08		
	d												14 08						15 08		
Althorpe	d																				
Crowle	d																				
Thorne South	d																				
Hatfield & Stainforth	d										13 57										
Kirk Sandall	d										14 02										
Adwick	31 d																				
Bentley (S.Yorks)	31 d																				
Doncaster 7	31 a		12 47				13 37				14 11	14 31	14 37		15 23			15 32	15 39		
London Kings Cross 15 ⊖	26 a														17 12						
York 8	26 d					12 28										14 34					15 34
Doncaster 7	d				13 13	13 30	13 38		13 42		14 13	14 33	14 42			14 59	15 13	15 33	15 42		15 59
Conisbrough	d				13 20						14 20						15 20				
Mexborough	d				13 24						14 24						15 24				
Swinton (S.Yorks)	d				13 27					14 05	14 30						15 30				
Rotherham Central	d				13 36					14 13	14 42						15 41				
Meadowhall	d				13 44		13 56		14 00	14 21	14 48	14 52	15 00				15 48	15 52	16 00		
Sheffield 7	a				13 52	13 54	14 06		14 07	14 32	14 55	15 03	15 07			15 21	15 55	16 01	16 07		16 21
	d								14 11				15 11						16 11		
Stockport	78 a								14 53				15 53						16 53		
Manchester Piccadilly 10	a								15 06				16 06						17 06		
Manchester Airport	85 a								15 34				16 34						17 29		

A To Huddersfield
C From Scarborough
D From Leeds
E From Newcastle to Reading
G From Bridlington

Table 29

Sundays
18 September to 23 October

Hull and Cleethorpes - Doncaster - Meadowhall, Sheffield, Manchester and Manchester Airport, Cleethorpes - Barton-on-Humber

		NT	NT	NT	TP	XC	HT	NT	NT	TP	TP	NT	XC	EM	NT	NT	NT	NT	NT
					◇■	◇■	◇■			◇■	◇■		◇■	◇■					
		A		C		D			F		G		H	I		A		J	K
						⌶	⊠						⌶	⊡					
Hull	d			15 41			16 30		16 41		16 58	17 23						17 39	17 41
Hessle	d																		
Ferriby	d																		
Brough	d			15 53			16 42		16 53		17 10	17 35						17 51	17 53
Broomfleet	d																		
Gilberdyke	d			16 00					17 00									17 58	18 00
Eastrington	d																		
Howden	d						16 54					17 47							
Wressle	d																		
Selby	a						17 04				17 28	17 56							
	d						17 05					17 57							
York [8] 33	a											18 25							
Saltmarshe	d																		
Goole	d		15 43	16 09					17 09						17 42			18 07	18 09
Thorne North	d		15 51												17 50				
Cleethorpes	d				15 26					16 26									
New Clee	d																		
Grimsby Docks	d																		
Grimsby Town	a				15 33					16 33									
	d				15 34					16 34									
Great Coates	d																		
Healing	d																		
Stallingborough	d																		
Habrough	d																		
Ulceby	d																		
Thornton Abbey	d																		
Goxhill	d																		
New Holland	d																		
Barrow Haven	d																		
Barton-on-Humber	a																		
Barton-on-Humber	d																		
Hull Paragon Interchange	a																		
Barnetby	d				15 53					16 53									
Scunthorpe	a				16 08					17 08									
	d				16 08					17 08									
Althorpe	d																		
Crowle	d																		
Thorne South	d																		
Hatfield & Stainforth	d		15 57												17 56				
Kirk Sandall	d		16 02												18 01				
Adwick 31	d																		
Bentley (S.Yorks) 31	d																		
Doncaster [7] 31	a		16 11	16 32	16 38		17 25		17 31	17 38					18 09			18 33	18 33
London Kings Cross [15] ⊖26	a						19 15												
York [8] 26	d					16 23							17 34	17 40					
Doncaster [7]	d		16 13	16 33	16 42	16 51		17 13	17 32	17 42			17 59	18 06			18 19	18 34	18 34
Conisbrough	d		16 20					17 21									18 26		
Mexborough	d		16 24					17 25									18 30		
Swinton (S.Yorks)	d	16 05	16 29					17 30								18 10	18 33		
Rotherham Central	d	16 13	16 41					17 41								18 19	18 42		
Meadowhall ⇌	d	16 21	16 47	16 53	17 01			17 48	17 53	18 00						18 25	18 47	18 53	18 53
Sheffield [7] ⇌	a	16 31	16 55	17 04	17 07	17 19		17 55	18 01	18 07			18 23	18 28		18 36	18 57	19 03	19 03
	d				17 11					18 11									
Stockport 78	a				17 53					18 53									
Manchester Piccadilly [10] ⇌	a				18 06					19 06									
Manchester Airport 85 ✈	a				18 29					19 29									

A From Leeds
C From Scarborough
D From Edinburgh to Reading
F From Bridlington
G To Huddersfield
H From Newcastle to Reading
I To St Pancras International
J 9 October, 16 October, 23 October. From Scarborough
K 18 September, 25 September, 2 October. From Scarborough

Table 29

Sundays
18 September to 23 October

Hull and Cleethorpes - Doncaster - Meadowhall, Sheffield, Manchester and Manchester Airport, Cleethorpes - Barton-on-Humber

		TP	HT	XC	NT	NT	NT	TP	TP	XC	NT	NT	TP	XC	NT	NT	NT	TP	TP	NT
		◇■	◇■	◇■				◇■	◇■	◇■			◇■	◇■				◇■	◇■	
				A			C		D	E	F			E	H				J	F
			⊠	⌶						⌶				⌶						
Hull	d		18 30				18 38		18 58						20 01	20 29			21 00	
Hessle	d														20 08					
Ferriby	d														20 13					
Brough	d		18 42				18 50		19 10						20 18	20 41			21 12	
Broomfleet	d																			
Gilberdyke	d						18 57								20 25					
Eastrington	d																			
Howden	d		18 54													20 53				
Wressle	d																			
Selby	a		19 04						19 28							21 02			21 30	
	d		19 05													21 03				
York [8] 33	a															21 30				
Saltmarshe	d																			
Goole	d						19 06								20 34					
Thorne North	d						19 14								20 42					
Cleethorpes	d	17 26						18 26					19 26					20 26		
New Clee	d																			
Grimsby Docks	d																			
Grimsby Town	a	17 33						18 33					19 33					20 33		
	d	17 34						18 34					19 34					20 34		
Great Coates	d																			
Healing	d																			
Stallingborough	d																			
Habrough	d	17 44																20 44		
Ulceby	d																			
Thornton Abbey	d																			
Goxhill	d																			
New Holland	d																			
Barrow Haven	d																			
Barton-on-Humber	a																			
Barton-on-Humber	d																			
Hull Paragon Interchange	a																			
Barnetby	d	17 53						18 53					19 53					20 53		
Scunthorpe	a	18 08						19 08					20 08					21 08		
	d	18 08						19 08					20 08					21 08		
Althorpe	d																			
Crowle	d																			
Thorne South	d																			
Hatfield & Stainforth	d						19 20													
Kirk Sandall	d						19 25													
Adwick 31	d																			
Bentley (S.Yorks) 31	d																			
Doncaster [7] 31	a	18 38	19 25				19 35	19 38					20 40		20 59			21 40		
London Kings Cross [15] ⊖26	a		21 14																	
York [8] 26	d			18 34	18 10					19 24				20 24			20 50			
Doncaster [7]	d	18 42		18 59		19 18	19 37	19 42		19 50		20 14	20 42	20 50	21 01			21 42		
Conisbrough	d					19 25						20 21			21 08					
Mexborough	d					19 29						20 25			21 12					
Swinton (S.Yorks)	d				19 01	19 33					20 07	20 29			21 15		21 45	21 52		22 32
Rotherham Central	d				19 13	19 41					20 15	20 41			21 22		21 52	21 58		22 40
Meadowhall ⇌	d	19 00			19 18	19 47	19 57	20 00			20 21	20 47	21 00		21 28		21 58	22 04		22 45
Sheffield [7] ⇌	a	19 07		19 21	19 27	19 55	20 06	20 07		20 16	20 34	20 55	21 07	21 17	21 38		22 09	22 15		22 54
	d	19 11						20 11					21 11							
Stockport 78	a	19 55						20 53					21 53							
Manchester Piccadilly [10] ⇌	a	20 09						21 06					22 06							
Manchester Airport 85 ✈	a	20 32						21 29					22 29							

A From Newcastle to Guildford
C From Bridlington
D To Huddersfield
E From Newcastle to Birmingham New Street
F From Leeds
H From Scarborough
J To Leeds

Table 29

Sundays
18 September to 23 October

Hull and Cleethorpes - Doncaster - Meadowhall, Sheffield, Manchester and Manchester Airport, Cleethorpes - Barton-on-Humber

		NT
Hull	d	21 35
Hessle	d	
Ferriby	d	
Brough	d	21 47
Broomfleet	d	
Gilberdyke	d	21 54
Eastrington	d	
Howden	d	
Wressle	d	
Selby	a	
	d	
York 8 33	a	
Saltmarshe	d	
Goole	d	22 03
Thorne North	d	22 11
Cleethorpes	d	
New Clee	d	
Grimsby Docks	d	
Grimsby Town	a	
	d	
Great Coates	d	
Healing	d	
Stallingborough	d	
Habrough	d	
Ulceby	d	
Thornton Abbey	d	
Goxhill	d	
New Holland	d	
Barrow Haven	d	
Barton-on-Humber	a	
Barton-on-Humber	d	
Hull Paragon Interchange	a	
Barnetby	d	
Scunthorpe	a	
	d	
Althorpe	d	
Crowle	d	
Thorne South	d	
Hatfield & Stainforth	d	22 15
Kirk Sandall	d	22 20
Adwick 31	d	
Bentley (S.Yorks) 31	d	
Doncaster 7 31	a	22 32
London Kings Cross 15 ⊖26	a	
York 8 26	d	
Doncaster 7	d	22 40
Conisbrough	d	22 47
Mexborough	d	22 51
Swinton (S.Yorks)	d	22 53
Rotherham Central	d	22 58
Meadowhall ⇌	d	23 04
Sheffield 7 ⇌	a	23 15
	d	
Stockport 78	a	
Manchester Piccadilly 10 ⇌	a	
Manchester Airport 85 ✈	a	

Table 29

Sundays
from 30 October

Hull and Cleethorpes - Doncaster - Meadowhall, Sheffield, Manchester and Manchester Airport, Cleethorpes - Barton-on-Humber

		NT	NT	XC	NT	NT	NT	TP	NT	XC	HT	NT	TP	NT	XC	TP	NT	TP	NT	NT	XC	HT
				◇1				◇1		◇1	◇1		◇1		◇1	◇1		◇1			◇1	◇1
				B	C					D					E		F		C		G	
				🛒						🛒	⊠				🛒						🛒	⊠
Hull	d					08 40	08 54	09 00			09 30	09 33					10 50	10 58				11 30
Hessle	d											09 40										
Ferriby	d											09 45										
Brough	d					08 52	09 06	09 12			09 42	09 50					11 02	11 10				11 42
Broomfleet	d																					
Gilberdyke	d					08 59						09 57					11 09					
Eastrington	d																					
Howden	d						09 18				09 54											11 54
Wressle	d																					
Selby	a						09 27	09 32			10 04							11 28				12 04
	d						09 28	09 33			10 05							11 29				12 05
York 8 33	a						09 52															
Saltmarshe	d																					
Goole	d					09 09			09 43			10 06					11 18			11 43		
Thorne North	d								09 51								11 26			11 51		
Cleethorpes	d												09 26			10 26						
New Clee	d																					
Grimsby Docks	d																					
Grimsby Town	a												09 33			10 33						
	d												09 34			10 34						
Great Coates	d																					
Healing	d																					
Stallingborough	d																					
Habrough	d												09 44			10 44						
Ulceby	d																					
Thornton Abbey	d																					
Goxhill	d																					
New Holland	d																					
Barrow Haven	d																					
Barton-on-Humber	a																					
Barton-on-Humber	d																					
Hull Paragon Interchange	a																					
Barnetby	d												09 53			10 53						
Scunthorpe	a												10 08			11 08						
	d												10 08			11 08						
Althorpe	d																					
Crowle	d																					
Thorne South	d																					
Hatfield & Stainforth	d								09 57			10 20								11 57		
Kirk Sandall	d								10 02			10 25								12 02		
Adwick 31	d																					
Bentley (S.Yorks) 31	d																					
Doncaster 7 31	a					09 29			10 11		10 23	10 35	10 40			11 38	11 46			12 11		12 24
London Kings Cross 15 ⊖26	a										12 12											14 12
York 8 26	d									09 28					10 28						11 28	
Doncaster 7	d	08 03	09 13	09 32		09 39			10 13	10 30			10 42	11 13	11 30	11 42	11 48			12 13	12 30	
Conisbrough	d	08 10	09 20						10 20					11 20						12 20		
Mexborough	d	08 14	09 24						10 24					11 24						12 24		
Swinton (S.Yorks)	d	08 17	09 28		09 35				10 27					11 27					12 05	12 27		
Rotherham Central	d	08 25	09 35		09 48				10 35					11 35					12 13	12 38		
Meadowhall ⇌	d	08 30	09 41		09 54	10 00			10 40				11 00	11 40		12 00	12 08		12 21	12 43		
Sheffield 7 ⇌	a	08 41	09 51	09 55	10 03	10 08			10 52	10 54			11 07	11 51	11 53	12 07	12 18		12 32	12 55	12 54	
	d												11 10			12 10						
Stockport 78	a												11 53			12 53						
Manchester Piccadilly 10 ⇌	a							11 03					12 06			13 06		12 58				
Manchester Airport 85 ✈	a												12 34			13 29						

B From Leeds to Plymouth
C From Leeds
D To Plymouth
E From Newcastle to Plymouth
F From Bridlington
G From Edinburgh to Plymouth

Table 29

Sundays from 30 October

Hull and Cleethorpes - Doncaster - Meadowhall, Sheffield, Manchester and Manchester Airport, Cleethorpes - Barton-on-Humber

		TP	NT	NT	TP	NT	XC	NT	TP	TP	TP	NT	XC	NT	NT	TP	NT	TP	TP	HT	XC	NT
		◇■			◇■		◇■ A 🍴	B	◇■ C	◇■	◇■	D	◇■ E 🍴		B	◇■ C		◇■	◇■	◇■ ⊠	◇■ F 🍴	
Hull	d		11 46	11 53	12 00			12 46		12 58					13 35		14 23			14 30		
Hessle	d														13 42							
Ferriby	d														13 47							
Brough	d		11 58	12 05	12 12			12 58		13 10					13 52		14 35			14 42		
Broomfleet	d																					
Gilberdyke	d			12 12				13 05							14 00							
Eastrington	d																					
Howden	d		12 10														14 47			14 54		
Wressle	d																					
Selby	a		12 19		12 32					13 28							14 56			15 04		
	d		12 20		12 32					13 29							14 57			15 05		
York ■8	33 a		12 44														15 25					
Saltmarshe	d																					
Goole	d			12 21				13 14						13 43	14 08							
Thorne North	d			12 29										13 51								
Cleethorpes	d	11 26																	13 26			
New Clee	d																					
Grimsby Docks	d																					
Grimsby Town	a	11 33																	13 33			
	d	11 34																	13 34			
Great Coates	d																					
Healing	d																					
Stallingborough	d																					
Habrough	d																					
Ulceby	d																					
Thornton Abbey	d																					
Goxhill	d																					
New Holland	d																					
Barrow Haven	d																					
Barton-on-Humber	a																					
Barton-on-Humber	d																					
Hull Paragon Interchange	a																					
Barnetby	d	11 53																	13 53			
Scunthorpe	a	12 08																	14 08			
	d	12 08																	14 08			
Althorpe	d																					
Crowle	d																					
Thorne South	d																					
Hatfield & Stainforth	d													13 57								
Kirk Sandall	d													14 02								
Adwick	31 d																					
Bentley (S.Yorks)	31 d																					
Doncaster ■7	31 a	12 40		12 47				13 37						14 11	14 31				14 37	15 23		
London Kings Cross ■15 ⊖	26 a																			17 12		
York ■8	26 d						12 28		13 15				13 40			14 15		14 33			14 34	
Doncaster ■7	d	12 42				13 13	13 30	13 38			13 42			14 13	14 33				14 42		14 59	15 13
Conisbrough	d					13 20								14 20								15 20
Mexborough	d					13 24								14 24								15 24
Swinton (S.Yorks)	d					13 27						14 05		14 30								15 30
Rotherham Central	d					13 36						14 13		14 42								15 41
Meadowhall 🚋	d	13 00				13 44		13 56			14 00	14 21		14 48	14 52				15 00			15 48
Sheffield ■7 🚋	a	13 07				13 52	13 54	14 06			14 07	14 32	14 52	14 55	15 03				15 07		15 21	15 55
	d	13 10									14 11								15 11			
Stockport	78 a	13 53									14 53								15 53			
Manchester Piccadilly ■10 🚋	a	14 06			13 54				14 34	14 54	15 06					15 34		15 54	16 06			
Manchester Airport ✈	85 a	14 29							14 55		15 29					15 55			16 34			

A From Edinburgh to Penzance
B From Scarborough
C From Newcastle
D From Leeds
E From Edinburgh to Plymouth
F From Newcastle to Reading

Table 29

Sundays from 30 October

Hull and Cleethorpes - Doncaster - Meadowhall, Sheffield, Manchester and Manchester Airport, Cleethorpes - Barton-on-Humber

		NT	TP	TP	XC	NT	NT	NT	TP	TP	XC	HT	TP	NT	NT	TP	TP	NT	XC	EM
		A	◇■	◇■	◇■ B 🍴	C		E	◇■ F	◇■	◇■ G 🍴	◇■ ⊠	◇■		A	◇■	◇■		◇■ B 🍴	◇■ I ☕
Hull	d	14 41	14 58					15 41				16 30			16 41	16 58		17 23		
Hessle	d																			
Ferriby	d																			
Brough	d	14 53	15 10					15 53				16 42			16 53	17 10		17 35		
Broomfleet	d																			
Gilberdyke	d	15 00						16 00							17 00					
Eastrington	d																			
Howden	d											16 54						17 47		
Wressle	d																			
Selby	a		15 28									17 04				17 28		17 56		
	d		15 29									17 05				17 29		17 57		
York ■8	33 a																	18 25		
Saltmarshe	d																			
Goole	d	15 09					15 43	16 09							17 09					
Thorne North	d						15 51													
Cleethorpes	d			14 26						15 26							16 26			
New Clee	d																			
Grimsby Docks	d																			
Grimsby Town	a			14 33						15 33							16 33			
	d			14 34						15 34							16 34			
Great Coates	d																			
Healing	d																			
Stallingborough	d																			
Habrough	d			14 44																
Ulceby	d																			
Thornton Abbey	d																			
Goxhill	d																			
New Holland	d																			
Barrow Haven	d																			
Barton-on-Humber	a																			
Barton-on-Humber	d																			
Hull Paragon Interchange	a																			
Barnetby	d			14 53						15 53							16 53			
Scunthorpe	a			15 08						16 08							17 08			
	d			15 08						16 08							17 08			
Althorpe	d																			
Crowle	d																			
Thorne South	d																			
Hatfield & Stainforth	d						15 57													
Kirk Sandall	d						16 02													
Adwick	31 d																			
Bentley (S.Yorks)	31 d																			
Doncaster ■7	31 a	15 32		15 39			16 11	16 32		16 38		17 25			17 31		17 38			
London Kings Cross ■15 ⊖	26 a											19 15								
York ■8	26 d				15 34				16 15		16 23		16 33						17 34	17 40
Doncaster ■7	d	15 33		15 42	15 59		16 13	16 33		16 42	16 51			17 13	17 32		17 42		17 59	18 06
Conisbrough	d						16 20							17 21						
Mexborough	d						16 24							17 25						
Swinton (S.Yorks)	d					16 05	16 29							17 30						
Rotherham Central	d					16 13	16 41							17 41						
Meadowhall 🚋	d	15 52		16 00		16 21	16 47	16 53		17 01				17 48	17 53		18 00			
Sheffield ■7 🚋	a	16 01		16 07	16 21	16 31	16 55	17 04		17 07	17 19			17 55	18 01		18 07		18 23	18 28
	d			16 11						17 11							18 11			
Stockport	78 a			16 53						17 53							18 53			
Manchester Piccadilly ■10 🚋	a		16 54	17 06					17 34	18 06			17 54			18 54	19 06			
Manchester Airport ✈	85 a			17 29					17 55	18 29							19 29			

A From Bridlington
B From Newcastle to Reading
C From Leeds
E From Scarborough
F From Newcastle
G From Edinburgh to Reading
I To St Pancras International

Hull and Cleethorpes - Doncaster - Meadowhall, Sheffield, Manchester and Manchester Airport, Cleethorpes - Barton-on-Humber

		NT	NT	NT	NT	TP	HT	XC	NT	TP	NT	NT	TP	TP	XC	NT	NT	TP	XC
						◇1	◇1	◇1		◇1			◇1	◇1	◇1			◇1	◇1
			A		C		⊠	D				F			G	A			G
Hull	d				17 39		18 30					18 38	18 58						
Hessle	d																		
Ferriby	d																		
Brough	d				17 51		18 42					18 50	19 10						
Broomfleet	d																		
Gilberdyke	d				17 58							18 57							
Eastrington	d																		
Howden	d						18 54												
Wressle	d																		
Selby	a						19 04						19 28						
	d						19 05						19 29						
York 8 33	a																		
Saltmarshe	d																		
Goole	d	17 42			18 07							19 06							
Thorne North	d	17 50										19 14							
Cleethorpes	d					17 26								18 26				19 26	
New Clee	d																		
Grimsby Docks	d																		
Grimsby Town	a					17 33								18 33				19 33	
	d					17 34								18 34				19 34	
Great Coates	d																		
Healing	d																		
Stallingborough	d																		
Habrough	d					17 44													
Ulceby	d																		
Thornton Abbey	d																		
Goxhill	d																		
New Holland	d																		
Barrow Haven	d																		
Barton-on-Humber	a																		
Barton-on-Humber	d																		
Hull Paragon Interchange	a																		
Barnetby	d					17 53								18 53				19 53	
Scunthorpe	a					18 08								19 08				20 08	
	d					18 08								19 08				20 08	
Althorpe	d																		
Crowle	d																		
Thorne South	d																		
Hatfield & Stainforth	d	17 56										19 20							
Kirk Sandall	d	18 01										19 25							
Adwick 31	d																		
Bentley (S.Yorks) 31	d																		
Doncaster 7 31	a	18 09			18 33	18 38	19 25					19 35		19 38				20 40	
London Kings Cross 15 ⊖26	a						21 14												
York 8 26	d							18 34	18 10	18 33					19 24				20 24
Doncaster 7	d			18 19	18 34	18 42		18 59			19 18	19 37		19 42	19 50		20 14	20 42	20 50
Conisbrough	d			18 26							19 25						20 21		
Mexborough	d			18 30							19 29						20 25		
Swinton (S.Yorks)	d		18 10	18 33					19 01		19 33					20 07	20 29		
Rotherham Central	d		18 19	18 42					19 13		19 41					20 15	20 41		
Meadowhall ⇌	d		18 25	18 47	18 53	19 00			19 18		19 47	19 57		20 00		20 21	20 47	21 00	
Sheffield 7 ⇌	a		18 36	18 57	19 03	19 07		19 21	19 27		19 55	20 06		20 07	20 16	20 34	20 55	21 07	21 17
	d					19 11								20 11				21 11	
Stockport 78	a					19 55								20 53				21 53	
Manchester Piccadilly 10 ⇌	a					20 09				19 54			20 54	21 06				22 06	
Manchester Airport 85 ✈	a					20 32								21 29				22 29	

A From Leeds
C From Scarborough
D From Newcastle to Guildford
F From Bridlington
G From Newcastle to Birmingham New Street
I From Newcastle

Table 29

Sundays
from 30 October

Hull and Cleethorpes - Doncaster - Meadowhall, Sheffield, Manchester and Manchester Airport, Cleethorpes - Barton-on-Humber

		NT	NT	NT	TP	TP	NT	NT
					◇1	◇1		
		A				C	D	
Hull	d	20 01	20 29			21 00		21 35
Hessle	d	20 08						
Ferriby	d	20 13						
Brough	d	20 18	20 41			21 12		21 47
Broomfleet	d							
Gilberdyke	d	20 25						21 54
Eastrington	d							
Howden	d		20 53					
Wressle	d							
Selby	a		21 02			21 30		
	d		21 03					
York 8 33	a		21 30					
Saltmarshe	d							
Goole	d	20 34						22 03
Thorne North	d	20 42						22 11
Cleethorpes	d				20 26			
New Clee	d							
Grimsby Docks	d							
Grimsby Town	a				20 33			
	d				20 34			
Great Coates	d							
Healing	d							
Stallingborough	d							
Habrough	d				20 44			
Ulceby	d							
Thornton Abbey	d							
Goxhill	d							
New Holland	d							
Barrow Haven	d							
Barton-on-Humber	a							
Barton-on-Humber	d							
Hull Paragon Interchange	a							
Barnetby	d				20 53			
Scunthorpe	a				21 08			
	d				21 08			
Althorpe	d							
Crowle	d							
Thorne South	d							
Hatfield & Stainforth	d							22 15
Kirk Sandall	d							22 20
Adwick 31	d							
Bentley (S.Yorks) 31	d							
Doncaster 7 31	a	20 59			21 40			22 32
London Kings Cross 15 ⊖26	a							
York 8 26	d			20 50				
Doncaster 7	d	21 01			21 42			22 40
Conisbrough	d	21 08						22 47
Mexborough	d	21 12						22 51
Swinton (S.Yorks)	d	21 15		21 45	21 52		22 32	22 53
Rotherham Central	d	21 22		21 52	21 58		22 40	22 58
Meadowhall ⇌	d	21 28		21 58	22 04		22 45	23 04
Sheffield 7 ⇌	a	21 38		22 09	22 15		22 54	23 15
	d							
Stockport 78	a							
Manchester Piccadilly 10 ⇌	a							
Manchester Airport 85 ✈	a							

A From Scarborough
C To Leeds
D From Leeds

Manchester Airport, Manchester, Sheffield and Meadowhall - Doncaster - Cleethorpes and Hull
Barton-on-Humber - Cleethorpes

Miles	Miles	Miles	Miles	Miles	Station		TP MX	TP MO	GR A	GR B	GR MX C	NT MX	NT MO	NT D	NT	NT E	GR F	NT BHX	NT D	EM G	NT	NT	NT D	XC H
0	—	—	—	—	**Manchester Airport** 85	d	20p47																	
9¾	—	—	—	—	**Manchester Piccadilly**	d	21 20																	
15¾	—	—	—	—	Stockport 78	d	21p28																	
52½	—	—	—	—	**Sheffield**	a	22p08																	
—	—	—	—	—		d	22p11	22p30				23p27	23p34	05 22		05 29						06 18	06 28	06 33
56	—	—	—	—	**Meadowhall**	d	22p16	22p35				23p33	23p40	05 28		05 35						06 24	06 34	
58¾	—	—	—	—	Rotherham Central	d						23p39	23p47	05 34		05 41						06 30	06 40	
63¼	—	—	—	—	Swinton (S.Yorks)	d						23p48	23p55	05a42		05 49						06 38	06a51	
64½	—	—	—	—	Mexborough	d						23p51	23p58			05 52						06 41		
66¾	—	—	—	—	Conisbrough	d						23p55	00 02			05 56						06 45		
—	—	—	—	—	London Kings Cross	d			22p00	22p00	22p00													
71½	—	—	—	—	**Doncaster**	a	22p42	22p56	23p42	23p42	23p49	00 07	00 13			06 06						06 56		06 57
—	—	—	—	—	York 26	a			00s10	00s33	00 39													07 28
—	0	0	—	0	**Doncaster** 31	d	22p44	22p58							05 52	06 12	06 15		06 26		06 47	06 59		
—	—	—	—	1¾	Bentley (S.Yorks) 31	a													06 29			07 02		
—	—	—	—	4	Adwick 31	a													06 33			07 08		
75½	—	4	—	—	Kirk Sandall	d	22p49									06 18					06 53			
78¼	—	6¾	—	—	Hatfield & Stainforth	d	22p54									06 23					06 58			
—	—	9¾	—	—	Thorne South	d	22p58														07 03			
—	—	15¾	—	—	Crowle	d	23p07														07 11			
—	—	19½	—	—	Althorpe	d	23p12														07 17			
—	—	23	—	—	**Scunthorpe**	a	23p17	23p23													07 26			
—	—	—	—	—		d	23p18	23p24																
—	—	34½	—	—	Barnetby	d	23p35	23p38												06 31				
—	—	—	—	—	Hull Paragon Interchange	d												06 20						
—	—	—	—	—	Barton-on-Humber	a												06 52						
—	—	—	0	—	**Barton-on-Humber**	d																		
—	—	—	2	—	Barrow Haven	d																		
—	—	—	3½	—	New Holland	d																		
—	—	—	5½	—	Goxhill	d																		
—	—	—	7	—	Thornton Abbey	d																		
—	—	—	9¾	—	Ulceby	d																		
—	—	40¾	11½	—	Habrough	d	23p44													06 41				
—	—	44½	15¼	—	Stallingborough	d																		
—	—	45½	16¼	—	Healing	d																		
—	—	46½	17¼	—	Great Coates	d																		
—	—	48¾	19½	—	**Grimsby Town**	a	23p57	23p57												06 56				
—	—	—	—	—		d	23p58	23p58																
—	—	49¾	20½	—	Grimsby Docks	d																		
—	—	50½	21¼	—	New Clee	d																		
—	—	52	22¾	—	**Cleethorpes**	a	00 09	00 09																
81¼	—	—	—	—	Thorne North	d										06 28								
88¾	—	—	—	—	Goole	d										06 37								
92¼	—	—	—	—	Saltmarshe	d										06 42								
—	—	—	—	—	York 33	d											06a35							
—	18¼	—	—	—	**Selby**	a									06 14									
—	24½	—	—	—	Wressle	d																		
—	27	—	—	—	Howden	d																		
—	30	—	—	—	Eastrington	d																		
95½	32¼	—	—	—	Gilberdyke	d										06 51								
98	34¾	—	—	—	Broomfleet	d										06 55								
102	38¾	—	—	—	Brough	d										07 01								
105	41¾	—	—	—	Ferriby	d										07 05								
107¾	44½	—	—	—	Hessle	d										07 10								
112	49¾	—	—	—	**Hull**	a										07 21								

A MO until 20 June. To Newcastle
B MO from 27 June. To Newcastle
C To Newcastle. from Doncaster
D To Leeds
E To Beverley
F To Edinburgh
G From Lincoln
H From Derby to Newcastle

Manchester Airport, Manchester, Sheffield and Meadowhall - Doncaster - Cleethorpes and Hull
Barton-on-Humber - Cleethorpes

Station		NT	NT	TP	NT BHX	XC A	NT B	NT B	NT C	TP	NT D	NT	NT B	NT	GR E	NT F	XC G	NT	NT B	EM H	TP	GR
Manchester Airport 85	d			05 15																	06 55	
Manchester Piccadilly	d			05 44						06 21											07 20	
Stockport 78	d			05 52																	07 28	
Sheffield	a			06 49																	08 10	
	d	06 52		06 55		07 12	07 14							07 24		07 41	07 54				08 11	
Meadowhall	d	06 58		07 01			07 21							07 30		07 47					08 18	
Rotherham Central	d	07 04					07 27							07 36		07 55						
Swinton (S.Yorks)	d	07 14					07a35							07 44		08 03						
Mexborough	d	07 17												07 47		08 06						
Conisbrough	d	07 21												07 51		08 10						
London Kings Cross	d														06 15							07 08
Doncaster	a	07 32		07 22										08 01	08 08	08 20	08 24				08 38	08 59
York 26	a					08 23									08 32		08 46					09 31
Doncaster 31	d	07 34		07 24				07 26			07 28		07 56	08 03		08 22			08 26		08 41	
Bentley (S.Yorks) 31	a	07 37						07 29					07 59						08 29			
Adwick 31	a	07 43						07 33					08 03						08 33			
Kirk Sandall	d										07 34			08 09								
Hatfield & Stainforth	d										07 39			08 14								
Thorne South	d													08 18								
Crowle	d													08 27								
Althorpe	d													08 33								
Scunthorpe	a			07 49										08 44							09 06	
	d			07 50																	09 07	
Barnetby	d			08 04																08 49	09 21	
Hull Paragon Interchange	d				06 55																	
Barton-on-Humber	a				07 30																	
Barton-on-Humber	d		06 58															07 58				
Barrow Haven	d		07 03															08 03				
New Holland	d		07 07															08 06				
Goxhill	d		07 11															08 11				
Thornton Abbey	d																	08 14				
Ulceby	d		07 19															08 18				
Habrough	d		07 23	08 12														08 23		09 01	09 29	
Stallingborough	d		07 28															08 28				
Healing	d		07 31															08 31				
Great Coates	d																	08 34				
Grimsby Town	a		07 38	08 26														08 39		09 15	09 43	
	d		07 39	08 33														08 39			09 44	
Grimsby Docks	d																	08 42				
New Clee	d																	08x44				
Cleethorpes	a		07 51	08 44														08 49			09 55	
Thorne North	d										07 44											
Goole	d										07 53					08 43						
Saltmarshe	d										07 58											
York 33	d											07 29										
Selby	a									07 43		07 50										
Wressle	d											07 58										
Howden	d									07 52		08 03										
Eastrington	d											08 08										
Gilberdyke	d								07 39		08 04	08 12										
Broomfleet	d								07 43			08 16										
Brough	d								07 49	08 04	08 12	08 22				08 57						
Ferriby	d								07 53		08 16	08 27										
Hessle	d								07 58		08 21	08 31										
Hull	a								08 11	08 20	08 34	08 46				09 13						

A From Birmingham New Street to Glasgow Central
B To Leeds
C To Scarborough
D To Beverley
E To Newcastle
F To Bridlington
G From Birmingham New Street to Newcastle
H From Newark North Gate

Table 29

Manchester Airport, Manchester, Sheffield and Meadowhall - Doncaster - Cleethorpes and Hull
Barton-on-Humber - Cleethorpes

		TP	NT	XC	NT	NT	NT	HT	NT	GR	NT	XC	NT BHX	NT	NT	NT	TP	TP	NT	XC	NT	NT	GR
		◇1	A	◇1 B				◇1		1 C	D	◇1 E		A	F		◇1	◇1	A	◇1 G			1 H
Manchester Airport 85	d																07 53						
Manchester Piccadilly 10	d	07 36															08 20	08 42					
Stockport 78	d																08 28						
Sheffield 7	a																09 08						
	d		08 14	08 21					08 24		08 41	08 48			08 53		09 11		09 14	09 21		09 24	
Meadowhall	d		08 21						08 31		08 47				09 00		09 16		09 21			09 30	
Rotherham Central	d		08 28						08 37						09 06				09 27			09 37	
Swinton (S.Yorks)	d		08a37						08 48						09 16				09a36			09 48	
Mexborough	d								08 51						09 19							09 51	
Conisbrough	d								08 55						09 23							09 55	
London Kings Cross	d							07 20		07 30													08 30
Doncaster 7	a							09 04	09 06	09 08	09 15	09 18			09 31		09 35					10 05	10 08
York 8 26	a			09 32						09 33		09 45								10 28			10 33
Doncaster 31	d					08 49	08 54	09 04	09 06		09 18			09 26	09 34		09 37				09 51	10 07	
Bentley (S.Yorks) 31	a					08 52								09 29	09 37								
Adwick 31	a					08 58								09 33	09 43								
Kirk Sandall	d						09 00		09 14												09 57	10 13	
Hatfield & Stainforth	d						09 05		09 19												10 02	10 18	
Thorne South	d								09 24													10 23	
Crowle	d								09 32													10 32	
Althorpe	d								09 38													10 38	
Scunthorpe	a								09 46								10 02					10 46	
	d																10 03						
Barnetby	d																10 17						
Hull Paragon Interchange	d												09 05										
Barton-on-Humber	a												09 40										
Barton-on-Humber	d															09 52							
Barrow Haven	d															09 57							
New Holland	d															10 00							
Goxhill	d															10 05							
Thornton Abbey	d															10 08							
Ulceby	d															10 12							
Habrough	d															10 17							
Stallingborough	d															10 22							
Healing	d															10 25							
Great Coates	d															10 28							
Grimsby Town	a															10 33	10 40						
	d															10 33	10 40						
Grimsby Docks	d															10 36							
New Clee	d															10x38							
Cleethorpes	a															10 43	10 51						
Thorne North	d						09 10														10 07		
Goole	d						09 19				09 35										10 16		
Saltmarshe	d																						
York 8 33	d				08 43																		
Selby	a	08 57			09 05			09 22										09 57					
Wressle	d																						
Howden	d				09 15			09 33															
Eastrington	d																						
Gilberdyke	d						09 27														10 24		
Broomfleet	d																						
Brough	d				09 27		09 35	09 45			09 52							10 16			10 32		
Ferriby	d						09 40														10 37		
Hessle	d						09 44														10 41		
Hull	a	09 31			09 47		09 57	10 02			10 09							10 34			10 54		

A To Leeds
B From Birmingham New Street to Edinburgh
C To Edinburgh
D To Bridlington
E From Birmingham New Street to Newcastle
F From Worksop
G From Bath Spa to Glasgow Central
H To Newcastle

Table 29

Manchester Airport, Manchester, Sheffield and Meadowhall - Doncaster - Cleethorpes and Hull
Barton-on-Humber - Cleethorpes

		NT	NT	XC	NT	NT	NT	EM	TP	TP	NT	XC	GR	NT	NT	GR	NT	XC	HT	NT BHX	NT	NT
			A	◇1 B		C	D	E	◇1	◇1	C	◇1 F	G			1 H	I	◇1 J	◇1		C	D
Manchester Airport 85	d								08 55													
Manchester Piccadilly 10	d								09 20	09 42												
Stockport 78	d								09 28													
Sheffield 7	a								10 08													
	d	09 29	09 41	09 47			09 53		10 11		10 14	10 21			10 24		10 41	10 47				10 53
Meadowhall	d	09 35	09 47				09 59		10 16		10 21				10 30		10 47					10 59
Rotherham Central	d	09 42					10 06				10 27				10 36							11 05
Swinton (S.Yorks)	d	09 51					10 15				10a36				10 44							11 16
Mexborough	d						10 18								10 47							11 19
Conisbrough	d						10 22								10 51							11 23
London Kings Cross	d												09 08			09 30			09 48			
Doncaster 7	a		10 15	10 18			10 32		10 35				11 03		11 04	11 08	11 14	11 18	11 23			11 32
York 8 26	a	10 56		10 45								11 27	11 33			11 34		11 47				
Doncaster 31	d		10 19			10 26	10 34		10 37					10 51	11 08		11 19		11 24		11 26	11 34
Bentley (S.Yorks) 31	a					10 29	10 37														11 29	11 37
Adwick 31	a					10 33	10 43														11 33	11 43
Kirk Sandall	d													10 57	11 14							
Hatfield & Stainforth	d													11 02	11 19							
Thorne South	d														11 24							
Crowle	d														11 32							
Althorpe	d														11 38							
Scunthorpe	a								11 02						11 46							
	d								11 03													
Barnetby	d							10 59	11 17													
Hull Paragon Interchange	d																			11 05		
Barton-on-Humber	a																			11 40		
Barton-on-Humber	d																					
Barrow Haven	d																					
New Holland	d																					
Goxhill	d																					
Thornton Abbey	d																					
Ulceby	d																					
Habrough	d							11 08														
Stallingborough	d																					
Healing	d																					
Great Coates	d																					
Grimsby Town	a							11 23	11 37													
	d								11 38													
Grimsby Docks	d																					
New Clee	d																					
Cleethorpes	a								11 50													
Thorne North	d													11 07								
Goole	d		10 38											11 16			11 37					
Saltmarshe	d																					
York 8 33	d				10 20																	
Selby	a				10 40					10 57									11 39			
Wressle	d																					
Howden	d				10 50														11 50			
Eastrington	d																					
Gilberdyke	d				10 57									11 25								
Broomfleet	d													11 30								
Brough	d		10 51		11 05					11 16				11 36			11 51		12 02			
Ferriby	d													11 40								
Hessle	d													11 45								
Hull	a		11 09		11 23					11 34				12 01			12 09		12 19			

A To Scarborough
B From Guildford to Newcastle
C To Leeds
D From Lincoln
E From Newark North Gate
F From Plymouth to Edinburgh
G from Doncaster
H To Edinburgh
I To Bridlington
J From Reading to Newcastle

Table 29

Manchester Airport, Manchester, Sheffield and Meadowhall - Doncaster - Cleethorpes and Hull
Barton-on-Humber - Cleethorpes

		NT	TP	TP	NT	XC	NT	NT	NT	GR	NT	XC	NT	NT	NT BHX	EM	TP	TP	NT	XC	GR	NT	NT
			◇■	◇■		◇■				■ ■		◇■					◇■	◇■		◇■			
					A	B				C	D	E	A	F	🚌	G			A	H			
			✕	✕		✕				✕		✕					✕	✕		✕	✕		
Manchester Airport 85 ✈	d		09 55														10 55						
Manchester Piccadilly ■	d		10 20	10 42													11 20	11 42					
Stockport 78	d		10 28														11 28						
Sheffield ■	a		11 08														12 08						
	d		11 11		11 14	11 21			11 24		11 41	11 47		11 53			12 11		12 14	12 21			
Meadowhall	d		11 16		11 21				11 30		11 47			11 59			12 16		12 21				
Rotherham Central	d				11 27				11 37					12 05					12 27				
Swinton (S.Yorks)	d				11a36				11 48					12 16					12a36				
Mexborough	d								11 51					12 19									
Conisbrough	d								11 55					12 23									
London Kings Cross	d									10 30											11 08		
Doncaster ■	a		11 35						12 04	12 08	12 15	12 18		12 32			12 35				13 03		
York ■ 26	a					12 27				12 32		12 48								13 27	13 33		
Doncaster 31	d		11 37					11 51	12 08		12 19		12 26	12 34			12 37						12 51
Bentley (S.Yorks) 31	a												12 29	12 38									
Adwick 31	a												12 33	12 43									
Kirk Sandall	d							11 57	12 14														12 57
Hatfield & Stainforth	d							12 02	12 19														13 02
Thorne South	d								12 24														
Crowle	d								12 32														
Althorpe	d								12 38														
Scunthorpe	a		12 02						12 46								13 02						
	d		12 03														13 03						
Barnetby	d		12 17													13 10	13 17						
Hull Paragon Interchange	d														13 05								
Barton-on-Humber	a														13 40								
Barton-on-Humber	d	11 52																					
Barrow Haven	d	11 57																					
New Holland	d	12 00																					
Goxhill	d	12 05																					
Thornton Abbey	d	12 08																					
Ulceby	d	12 12																					
Habrough	d	12 17	12 26													13 19							
Stallingborough	d	12 22																					
Healing	d	12 25																					
Great Coates	d	12 28																					
Grimsby Town	a	12 33	12 40													13 35	13 39						
	d	12 33	12 40														13 40						
Grimsby Docks	d	12 36																					
New Clee	d	12x38																					
Cleethorpes	a	12 43	12 52														13 52						
Thorne North	d							12 07															13 07
Goole	d							12 16			12 35												13 16
Saltmarshe	d																						
York ■ 33	d						11 45															12 47	
Selby	a			11 57			12 04											12 57				13 06	
Wressle	d																						
Howden	d						12 14															13 16	
Eastrington	d																						
Gilberdyke	d						12 21	12 27															13 27
Broomfleet	d																						
Brough	d			12 16			12 29	12 35			12 49							13 16				13 28	13 35
Ferriby	d							12 40															13 40
Hessle	d							12 44															13 44
Hull	a			12 36			12 49	12 58			13 09							13 34				13 48	14 00

A To Leeds
B From Plymouth to Glasgow Central
C To Newcastle
D To Scarborough
E From Winchester to Newcastle
F From Lincoln
G From Newark North Gate
H From Plymouth to Edinburgh

Table 29

Manchester Airport, Manchester, Sheffield and Meadowhall - Doncaster - Cleethorpes and Hull
Barton-on-Humber - Cleethorpes

		NT	GR	NT	XC	HT	NT	NT	NT	TP	TP	NT	XC	NT	NT	NT	GR	NT	NT	XC	NT	NT	NT BHX
			■ ■		◇■	◇■				◇■	◇■		◇■				■ ■			◇■			
			A	B	C		D	E				D	F				G		B	H	D	E	🚌
			✕		✕	⊠				✕	✕		✕				✕			✕			
Manchester Airport 85 ✈	d									11 55													
Manchester Piccadilly ■	d									12 20	12 42												
Stockport 78	d									12 28													
Sheffield ■	a									13 08													
	d	12 24		12 41	12 47			12 53		13 11		13 14	13 21			13 24		13 28	13 41	13 47		13 53	
Meadowhall	d	12 30		12 47				12 59		13 16		13 21				13 30		13 35	13 46			13 59	
Rotherham Central	d	12 37						13 05				13 27				13 37		13 41				14 05	
Swinton (S.Yorks)	d	12 48						13 16				13a36				13 47		13 50				14 17	
Mexborough	d	12 51						13 19								13 50						14 20	
Conisbrough	d	12 55						13 23								13 54						14 24	
London Kings Cross	d		11 30			11 48											12 30						
Doncaster ■	a	13 04	13 08	13 15	13 18	13 23		13 33		13 35						14 04	14 08		14 15	14 18		14 32	
York ■ 26	a		13 34		13 45								14 27				14 33	14 55		14 46			
Doncaster 31	d	13 08		13 19		13 24	13 26	13 34		13 37					13 50	14 08			14 18		14 26	14 34	
Bentley (S.Yorks) 31	a						13 29	13 37													14 29	14 37	
Adwick 31	a						13 33	13 43													14 33	14 43	
Kirk Sandall	d	13 14													13 56	14 14							
Hatfield & Stainforth	d	13 19													14 01	14 19							
Thorne South	d	13 24														14 26							
Crowle	d	13 33														14 34							
Althorpe	d	13 39														14 40							
Scunthorpe	a	13 46								14 02						14 48							
	d									14 03													
Barnetby	d									14 17													
Hull Paragon Interchange	d																						15 05
Barton-on-Humber	a																						15 40
Barton-on-Humber	d								13 52														
Barrow Haven	d								13 57														
New Holland	d								14 00														
Goxhill	d								14 05														
Thornton Abbey	d								14 08														
Ulceby	d								14 12														
Habrough	d								14 17	14 26													
Stallingborough	d								14 22														
Healing	d								14 25														
Great Coates	d								14 28														
Grimsby Town	a								14 33	14 39													
	d								14 33	14 40													
Grimsby Docks	d								14 36														
New Clee	d								14x38														
Cleethorpes	a								14 43	14 52													
Thorne North	d														14 06								
Goole	d			13 38											14 16				14 37				
Saltmarshe	d														14 21								
York ■ 33	d													13 44									
Selby	a					13 39					13 57			14 07									
Wressle	d																						
Howden	d					13 50								14 17									
Eastrington	d																						
Gilberdyke	d														14 27								
Broomfleet	d																						
Brough	d			13 52		14 02					14 16			14 30	14 36				14 54				
Ferriby	d														14 40								
Hessle	d														14 45								
Hull	a			14 09		14 19					14 34			14 52	14 56				15 12				

A To Edinburgh
B To Bridlington
C From Reading to Newcastle
D To Leeds
E From Lincoln
F From Penzance to Glasgow Central
G To Newcastle
H From Southampton Central to Newcastle

Manchester Airport, Manchester, Sheffield and Meadowhall - Doncaster - Cleethorpes and Hull
Barton-on-Humber - Cleethorpes

		EM	TP	TP	NT	XC	GR	NT	NT	NT	GR	NT	XC	HT	NT	NT	NT	TP	TP	NT	XC	NT
			◇1	◇1		◇1					1		◇1	◇1				◇1	◇1		◇1	
		A			B	C			D		E	F	G		B	A				B	H	
Manchester Airport 85 ✈	d		12 55															13 55				
Manchester Piccadilly 10	d		13 20	13 42														14 20	14 42			
Stockport 78	d		13 28															14 28				
Sheffield 7	a		14 08															15 08				
	d		14 11		14 14	14 21				14 24		14 41	14 47			14 53		15 11		15 14	15 21	
Meadowhall	d		14 16		14 21					14 30		14 47				14 59		15 16		15 20		
Rotherham Central	d				14 27					14 37						15 05				15 26		
Swinton (S.Yorks)	d				14a35					14 48						15 16				15a34		
Mexborough	d									14 51						15 19						
Conisbrough	d									14 55						15 23						
London Kings Cross	d						13 08				13 30			13 48								
Doncaster 7	a		14 35				15 03			15 04	15 08	15 17	15 18	15 23		15 33		15 35				
York 8 26	a					15 27	15 33				15 34		15 45								16 29	
Doncaster 31	d		14 37						14 50	15 08		15 19		15 24	15 26	15 34		15 37				15 51
Bentley (S.Yorks) 31	a														15 29	15 37						
Adwick 31	a														15 33	15 42						
Kirk Sandall	d								14 57	15 14												15 57
Hatfield & Stainforth	d								15 02	15 19												16 02
Thorne South	d									15 24												
Crowle	d									15 32												
Althorpe	d									15 38												
Scunthorpe	a		15 02							15 47								16 02				
	d		15 03															16 03				
Barnetby	d	15 11	15 17															16 17				
Hull Paragon Interchange	d																					
Barton-on-Humber	a																					
Barton-on-Humber	d																15 52					
Barrow Haven	d																15 57					
New Holland	d																16 00					
Goxhill	d																16 05					
Thornton Abbey	d																16 08					
Ulceby	d																16 12					
Habrough	d	15 19															16 17	16 26				
Stallingborough	d																16 22					
Healing	d																16 25					
Great Coates	d																16 28					
Grimsby Town	a	15 34	15 37														16 33	16 39				
	d		15 38														16 33	16 40				
Grimsby Docks	d																16 36					
New Clee	d																					
Cleethorpes	a		15 52														16 42	16 52				
Thorne North	d								15 07													16 07
Goole	d								15 16			15 37										16 16
Saltmarshe	d																					16 21
York 8 33	d							14 47														
Selby	a			14 57				15 06						15 39					15 57			
Wressle	d																					
Howden	d							15 16						15 50								
Eastrington	d																					
Gilberdyke	d								15 27													16 27
Broomfleet	d																					
Brough	d			15 16				15 28	15 35			15 51		16 02					16 16			16 35
Ferriby	d								15 40													16 39
Hessle	d								15 44													16 44
Hull	a			15 34				15 48	15 55			16 08		16 19					16 34			16 57

A From Lincoln
B To Leeds
C From Plymouth to Aberdeen
D To Beverley
E To Newcastle
F To Scarborough
G From Reading to Newcastle
H From Penzance to Glasgow Central

Manchester Airport, Manchester, Sheffield and Meadowhall - Doncaster - Cleethorpes and Hull
Barton-on-Humber - Cleethorpes

		NT	GR	NT	NT	XC	NT	TP	NT	TP	NT	XC	GR	NT	GR	NT	NT	XC	NT BHX	NT	HT	NT	NT
			1			◇1		◇1		◇1		◇1			1			◇1			◇1		
			A	B	C	D	E				B	F			G	H	C	I					B
Manchester Airport 85 ✈	d							14 55															
Manchester Piccadilly 10	d							15 20		15 42													
Stockport 78	d							15 28															
Sheffield 7	a							16 08															
	d	15 24			15 41	15 47	15 53	16 11			16 14	16 21		16 23			16 41	16 47					
Meadowhall	d	15 30			15 47		15 59	16 16			16 20			16 29			16 47						
Rotherham Central	d	15 37					16 05				16 26			16 37									
Swinton (S.Yorks)	d	15 48					16 16				16a36			16 47									
Mexborough	d	15 51					16 19							16 50									
Conisbrough	d	15 55					16 23							16 54									
London Kings Cross	d		14 30										15 08		15 30						15 48		
Doncaster 7	a	16 04	16 08		16 15	16 18	16 32	16 35					17 04	17 07	17 10		17 16	17 18			17 23		
York 8 26	a		16 33			16 46						17 29	17 35		17 36			17 43					
Doncaster 31	d	16 08		16 16	16 19		16 34	16 37								16 51	17 19			17 22	17 24		17 26
Bentley (S.Yorks) 31	a			16 19			16 37																17 29
Adwick 31	a			16 23			16 43																17 33
Kirk Sandall	d	16 14														16 57				17 28			
Hatfield & Stainforth	d	16 19														17 02				17 33			
Thorne South	d	16 24																		17 39			
Crowle	d	16 33																		17 48			
Althorpe	d	16 39																		17 54			
Scunthorpe	a	16 46						17 02												18 01			
	d							17 03															
Barnetby	d							17 20															
Hull Paragon Interchange	d																		17 10				
Barton-on-Humber	a																		17 45				
Barton-on-Humber	d																						
Barrow Haven	d																						
New Holland	d																						
Goxhill	d																						
Thornton Abbey	d																						
Ulceby	d																						
Habrough	d																						
Stallingborough	d																						
Healing	d																						
Great Coates	d																						
Grimsby Town	a							17 40															
	d							17 40															
Grimsby Docks	d																						
New Clee	d																						
Cleethorpes	a							17 53															
Thorne North	d															17 07	17 33						
Goole	d				16 38											17 16	17 42						
Saltmarshe	d																						
York 8 33	d								16 12													17 19	
Selby	a								16 36	17 00											17 39	17 45	
Wressle	d								16 44														
Howden	d								16 49												17 50	17 56	
Eastrington	d																						
Gilberdyke	d								16 55							17 24						18 03	
Broomfleet	d																						
Brough	d				16 52				17 03	17 18						17 32	17 55				18 02	18 11	
Ferriby	d								17 08							17 37							
Hessle	d								17 12							17 41							
Hull	a				17 06				17 27	17 37						17 54	18 13				18 19	18 30	

A To Newcastle
B To Leeds
C To Bridlington
D From Southampton Central to Newcastle
E From Lincoln
F From Plymouth to Dundee
G To Edinburgh
H To Beverley
I From Reading to Newcastle

Table 29

Manchester Airport, Manchester, Sheffield and Meadowhall - Doncaster - Cleethorpes and Hull
Barton-on-Humber - Cleethorpes

		NT	EM	NT	TP	TP	NT	XC	NT	GR	NT	NT	XC	NT	TP	NT	NT	NT	NT	XC	TP	GR
					◇1	◇1		◇1		1			◇1		◇1					◇1	◇1	1
		A	A				B	C		D		E	F			B	G	A	B	H		I
					✠	✠		✠		✠			✠		✠					✠	✠	✠
Manchester Airport	85 ✈ d				15 55																16 55	
Manchester Piccadilly 10	⇌ d				16 20	16 42									17 42						17 20	
Stockport	78 d				16 28																17 28	
Sheffield 7	⇌ a				17 08																18 15	
	d	16 53			17 11		17 13	17 22	17 27			17 41	17 47					17 53	18 13	18 21	18 24	
Meadowhall	⇌ d	16 59			17 16		17 20		17 33			17 47						17 59	18 20		18 29	
Rotherham Central	d	17 05					17 26		17 39									18 05	18 26			
Swinton (S.Yorks)	d	17 16					17a36		17 48									18 16	18a36			
Mexborough	d	17 19							17 51									18 20				
Conisbrough	d	17 23							17 55									18 24				
London Kings Cross	d									16 30												17 19
Doncaster 7	a	17 32			17 35				18 07	18 09		18 12						18 35			18 53	19 05
York 8	26 a							18 30		18 33			19 02							19 30		
Doncaster	31 d	17 34			17 47						17 56	18 16				18 26	18 29	18 39			18 55	19 07
Bentley (S.Yorks)	31 a	17 37														18 29						
Adwick	31 a	17 43														18 33						
Kirk Sandall	d										18 02						18 37	18 45				
Hatfield & Stainforth	d										18 07						18 42	18 50				
Thorne South	d																18 47					
Crowle	d																18 55					
Althorpe	d																19 01					
Scunthorpe	a				18 12												19 10				19 23	
	d				18 13																19 23	
Barnetby	d		17 55		18 28																19 37	
Hull Paragon Interchange	d																					
Barton-on-Humber	a																					
Barton-on-Humber	d			17 55																		
Barrow Haven	d			18 00																		
New Holland	d			18 03																		
Goxhill	d			18 08																		
Thornton Abbey	d			18 11																		
Ulceby	d			18 15																		
Habrough	d		18 03	18 20	18 36																	
Stallingborough	d			18 25																		
Healing	d			18 28																		
Great Coates	d			18 31																		
Grimsby Town	a		18 18	18 36	18 49																19 57	
	d			18 36	18 50																19 58	
Grimsby Docks	d			18 39																		
New Clee	d																					
Cleethorpes	a			18 45	19 02																20 10	
Thorne North	d										18 12							18 55				
Goole	d										18 21	18 36						19 12				
Saltmarshe	d										18 26											
York 8	33 d													18 18								
Selby	a					17 59								18 42	19 00							19 22
Wressle	d													18 50								
Howden	d					18 08								18 54								
Eastrington	d													18 59								
Gilberdyke	d										18 37			19 03				19 21				
Broomfleet	d										18 41											
Brough	d					18 20					18 47	18 53		19 10	19 19			19 29				19 45
Ferriby	d										18 51							19 34				
Hessle	d										18 56							19 38				
Hull	a					18 40					19 06	19 09		19 29	19 37			19 50				20 08

A From Lincoln
B To Leeds
C From Plymouth to Glasgow Central
D To Edinburgh
E To Scarborough
F From Southampton Central to Edinburgh
G From Adwick
H From Plymouth to Edinburgh
I The Hull Executive

Table 29 Mondays to Fridays

Manchester Airport, Manchester, Sheffield and Meadowhall - Doncaster - Cleethorpes and Hull
Barton-on-Humber - Cleethorpes

		NT	NT	XC	NT	NT	NT	NT BHX	NT	TP	TP	NT	XC	NT	GR	NT	NT	XC	NT	NT	HT	NT	EM
				◇1						◇1	◇1		◇1		1			◇1			◇1		
			A	B	C	D						D	E		F		G	H		D		A	I
				✠				bus		✠	✠				✠						⊠		
Manchester Airport	85 ✈ d									17 55													
Manchester Piccadilly 10	⇌ d									18 20	18 42												
Stockport	78 d									18 28													
Sheffield 7	⇌ a									19 09													
	d	18 29	18 41	18 47	19 00					19 11		19 18	19 26	19 30			19 44	19 54				19 58	
Meadowhall	⇌ d	18 35	18 47		19 06					19 16		19 25		19 36			19 50					20 04	
Rotherham Central	d	18 42			19 12							19 31		19 42								20 11	
Swinton (S.Yorks)	d	18 50			19 20							19a40		19 51								20 22	
Mexborough	d	18 53			19 23									19 55								20 25	
Conisbrough	d	18 57			19 27									19 59								20 29	
London Kings Cross	d														18 30						18 50		
Doncaster 7	a	19 09	19 12	19 14	19 36					19 41				20 08	20 10		20 12	20 15			20 27	20 37	
York 8	26 a			19 39									20 30		20 34			20 46					
Doncaster	31 d		19 16			19 20	19 21			19 48						19 53	20 17		20 25	20 26	20 33	20 44	
Bentley (S.Yorks)	31 a					19 23														20 29			
Adwick	31 a					19 27														20 33			
Kirk Sandall	d						19 27									19 59			20 31				
Hatfield & Stainforth	d						19 32									20 04			20 36				
Thorne South	d						19 36												20 41				
Crowle	d						19 45												20 50				
Althorpe	d						19 51												20 56				
Scunthorpe	a						19 59			20 14									21 04				
	d									20 14													
Barnetby	d									20 28													20 34
Hull Paragon Interchange	d							19 25															
Barton-on-Humber	a							19 52															
Barton-on-Humber	d								19 58														
Barrow Haven	d								20 03														
New Holland	d								20 06														
Goxhill	d								20 11														
Thornton Abbey	d								20 14														
Ulceby	d								20 18														
Habrough	d								20 23														20 43
Stallingborough	d								20 28														
Healing	d								20 31														
Great Coates	d								20 34														
Grimsby Town	a								20 39	20 47													20 55
	d								20 39	20 48													20 56
Grimsby Docks	d								20 42														
New Clee	d																						
Cleethorpes	a								20 48	21 00													21 06
Thorne North	d															20 09							
Goole	d		19 37													20 18	20 36						
Saltmarshe	d																						
York 8	33 d																						
Selby	a										20 00										20 48	21 01	
Wressle	d																						
Howden	d										20 10										20 59		
Eastrington	d																						
Gilberdyke	d															20 26						21 15	
Broomfleet	d																						
Brough	d		19 54								20 22					20 34	20 50				21 11	21 23	
Ferriby	d															20 39						21 28	
Hessle	d															20 43						21 32	
Hull	a		20 10								20 41					20 56	21 07				21 28	21 45	

A To Bridlington
B From Reading to Newcastle
C From Retford Low Level
D To Leeds
E From Plymouth to Edinburgh
F To Edinburgh
G To Beverley
H From Southampton Central to Newcastle
I From Newark North Gate

Manchester Airport, Manchester, Sheffield and Meadowhall - Doncaster - Cleethorpes and Hull
Barton-on-Humber - Cleethorpes

			TP	TP FX	TP FO	NT	GR	NT	NT	XC	NT	NT	NT	TP FO	NT	NT	TP FX	HT	XC	NT	TP	HT	NT	TP
			◇1	◇1 A	◇1 A		1 B	C		◇1 D	C	(bus)		◇1	E	C	◇1	◇1 ⊠	◇1 G		◇1 H	◇1 F ⊠	C	◇1
Manchester Airport	85	d	18 55											19 55										20 47
Manchester Piccadilly 10		d	19 18	20 11	20 11									20b20										21 20
Stockport	78	d	19 26											20 28										21 28
Sheffield 7		a	20 08											21 09										22 08
		d	20 11			20 15		20 27	20 38	20 53				21 11	21 15	21 30	21 34		21 54					22 11
Meadowhall		d	20 16			20 21		20 35	20 45					21 16	21 21	21 36	21 40							22 16
Rotherham Central		d				20 27		20 41	20 52						21 27	21 42								
Swinton (S.Yorks)		d				20 36		20 50	21 00						21 36	21a50								
Mexborough		d				20 39			21 03						21 39									
Conisbrough		d				20 43			21 07						21 43									
London Kings Cross		d					19 30											20 30						
Doncaster 7		a	20 45			20 55	21 09		21 18	21 19				21 40	21 54		22 02	22 06	22 29					22 42
York 8	26	a					21 32			21 46									22 54					
Doncaster	31	d	20 46			20 56			21 18		21 22			21 42	21 56		22 05	22 06				22 20	22 26	22 44
Bentley (S.Yorks)	31	a									21 25												22 29	
Adwick	31	a									21 29												22 33	
Kirk Sandall		d				21 03			21 26						22 02									22 49
Hatfield & Stainforth		d				21 08			21 31						22 07									22 54
Thorne South		d							21 38															22 58
Crowle		d							21 46															23 07
Althorpe		d							21 52															23 12
Scunthorpe		a	21 12						22 01					22 07			22 30							23 17
		d	21 12											22 08			22 31							23 18
Barnetby		d	21 26											22 22			22 46							23 35
Hull Paragon Interchange		d										21 25												
Barton-on-Humber		a										21 52												
Barton-on-Humber		d											21 58											
Barrow Haven		d											22 03											
New Holland		d											22 06											
Goxhill		d											22 11											
Thornton Abbey		d											22 14											
Ulceby		d											22 18											
Habrough		d	21 35										22 23	22 31			22 55							23 44
Stallingborough		d											22 28											
Healing		d											22 31											
Great Coates		d											22 34											
Grimsby Town		a	21 48										22 39	22 44			23 10							23 57
		d	21 49										22 39	22 45			23 11							23 58
Grimsby Docks		d											22 42											
New Clee		d																						
Cleethorpes		a	22 00										22 48	22 57			23 20							00 09
Thorne North		d				21 14									22 13									
Goole		d				21a23									22 22									
Saltmarshe		d													22 26									
York 8	33	d																		22 13				
Selby		a		21 33	21 34													22 21		22 32		22 50		
Wressle		d																						
Howden		d		21 43	21 43													22 32		22 41		23 03		
Eastrington		d																						
Gilberdyke		d													22 32					22 48				
Broomfleet		d																						
Brough		d		21 55	21 55										22 39			22 47		22 55	23 06	23 15		
Ferriby		d																		23 00				
Hessle		d																		23 05				
Hull		a		22 12	22 12										22 58			23 04		23 18	23 23	23 32		

A From Liverpool Lime Street
B To Edinburgh
C To Leeds
D From Reading to Newcastle
E To Beverley
G From Southampton Central
H From Leeds

Manchester Airport, Manchester, Sheffield and Meadowhall - Doncaster - Cleethorpes and Hull
Barton-on-Humber - Cleethorpes

			GR	NT	NT	GR	NT	NT
			1 A	B		1 C	B	
Manchester Airport	85	d						
Manchester Piccadilly 10		d						
Stockport	78	d						
Sheffield 7		a						
		d		22 24	22 34		23 15	23 27
Meadowhall		d		22 30	22 40		23 21	23 33
Rotherham Central		d		22 36	22 46		23 27	23 39
Swinton (S.Yorks)		d		22a45	22 54		23a36	23 48
Mexborough		d			22 57			23 51
Conisbrough		d			23 01			23 55
London Kings Cross		d	21 00			22 00		
Doncaster 7		a	22 45		23 12	23 49		00 07
York 8	26	a	23 10			00 39		
Doncaster	31	d			23 15			
Bentley (S.Yorks)	31	a						
Adwick	31	a						
Kirk Sandall		d			23 21			
Hatfield & Stainforth		d			23 26			
Thorne South		d						
Crowle		d						
Althorpe		d						
Scunthorpe		a						
		d						
Barnetby		d						
Hull Paragon Interchange		d						
Barton-on-Humber		a						
Barton-on-Humber		d						
Barrow Haven		d						
New Holland		d						
Goxhill		d						
Thornton Abbey		d						
Ulceby		d						
Habrough		d						
Stallingborough		d						
Healing		d						
Great Coates		d						
Grimsby Town		a						
		d						
Grimsby Docks		d						
New Clee		d						
Cleethorpes		a						
Thorne North		d			23 32			
Goole		d			23a43			
Saltmarshe		d						
York 8	33	d						
Selby		a						
Wressle		d						
Howden		d						
Eastrington		d						
Gilberdyke		d						
Broomfleet		d						
Brough		d						
Ferriby		d						
Hessle		d						
Hull		a						

A To Newcastle. The Flying Scotsman
B To Leeds
C To Newcastle. from Doncaster

Table 29

Saturdays

Manchester Airport, Manchester, Sheffield and Meadowhall - Doncaster - Cleethorpes and Hull
Barton-on-Humber - Cleethorpes

	TP	GR	NT	NT	GR	NT	EM	NT	NT	NT	NT	XC	NT	NT	TP	NT BHX	XC	NT	NT	NT	TP	NT
	◇1	1			1							◇1			◇1	bus	◇1				◇1	
		A			B	C	D	E			E	F					G	E	E	H		C
		⊡			⊡⊼							⊼					⊼					
Manchester Airport 85 ✈ d	20p47														05 20							
Manchester Piccadilly 10 ⇌ d	21 20														05 44						06 21	
Stockport 78 d	21p28														05 52							
Sheffield 7 ⇌ a	22p08														06 49							
d	22p11		23p27			05 29				06 12	06 28	06 49	06 52		06 55		07 12	07 14				
Meadowhall ⇌ d	22p16		23p33			05 35				06 18	06 34		06 58		07 01			07 21				
Rotherham Central d			23p39			05 41				06 24	06 40		07 04					07 27				
Swinton (S.Yorks) d			23p48			05 49				06 35	06a51		07 15					07a33				
Mexborough d			23p51			05 52				06 38			07 18									
Conisbrough d			23p55			05 56				06 42			07 22									
London Kings Cross d		22p00																				
Doncaster 7 a	22p42	23p49	00 07			06 06				06 53		07 16	07 33		07 22							
York 8 26 a		00 39										07 43					08 24					
Doncaster 31 d	22p44			05 52	06 10	06 12		06 26	06 47	06 55			07 34		07 24				07 26			07 28
Bentley (S.Yorks) 31 a								06 29		06 58			07 37						07 29			
Adwick 31 a								06 33		07 05			07 43						07 33			
Kirk Sandall d	22p49					06 18			06 53													07 34
Hatfield & Stainforth d	22p54					06 23			06 58													07 39
Thorne South d	22p58								07 03													
Crowle d	23p07								07 11													
Althorpe d	23p12								07 17													
Scunthorpe a	23p17								07 27						07 49							
d	23p18														07 50							
Barnetby d	23p35						06 12								08 04							
Hull Paragon Interchange d																06 55						
Barton-on-Humber a																07 30						
Barton-on-Humber d														06 58								
Barrow Haven d														07 03								
New Holland d														07 07								
Goxhill d														07 11								
Thornton Abbey d																						
Ulceby d														07 19								
Habrough d	23p44						06 22							07 23								
Stallingborough d														07 28								
Healing d														07 31								
Great Coates d																						
Grimsby Town a	23p57						06 37							07 38	08 24							
d	23p58													07 39	08 33							
Grimsby Docks d																						
New Clee d																						
Cleethorpes a	00 09													07 51	08 44							
Thorne North d						06 28																07 44
Goole d						06 37																07 53
Saltmarshe d						06 42																07 58
York 8 33 d					06a30																	
Selby a				06 11																	07 43	
Wressle d																						
Howden d																					07 52	
Eastrington d																						
Gilberdyke d						06 51														07 39		08 04
Broomfleet d						06 55														07 43		
Brough d						07 01														07 49	08 04	08 12
Ferriby d						07 05														07 53		08 16
Hessle d						07 10														07 58		08 21
Hull a						07 22														08 11	08 20	08 37

A To Newcastle. ⊡ from Doncaster
B To Edinburgh
C To Beverley
D From Lincoln
E To Leeds
F From Derby to Newcastle
G From Birmingham New Street to Glasgow Central
H To Scarborough

Table 29

Saturdays

Manchester Airport, Manchester, Sheffield and Meadowhall - Doncaster - Cleethorpes and Hull
Barton-on-Humber - Cleethorpes

	NT	GR	NT	NT	XC	NT	NT	EM	NT	TP	TP	NT	XC	NT	NT	NT	NT	GR	NT	XC	NT BHX	NT
		1			◇1					◇1	◇1		◇1					1		◇1	bus	
		A		B	C		D	E				D	F					A	B	C		D
		⊡⊼			⊼					⊼	⊼		⊼					⊡⊼		⊼		
Manchester Airport 85 ✈ d										06 55												
Manchester Piccadilly 10 ⇌ d										07 20	07 36											
Stockport 78 d										07 28												
Sheffield 7 ⇌ a										08 10												
d	07 24			07 41	07 54				08 03	08 11		08 14	08 21				08 25		08 41	08 48		
Meadowhall ⇌ d	07 30			07 47						08 18		08 22					08 31		08 47			
Rotherham Central d	07 36			07 55								08 28					08 35					
Swinton (S.Yorks) d	07 46			08 03								08a37					08 47					
Mexborough d	07 49			08 06													08 51					
Conisbrough d	07 53			08 10													08 55					
London Kings Cross d		06 20																07 30				
Doncaster 7 a	08 01	08 09		08 22	08 23					08 38							09 05	09 09	09 14	09 18		
York 8 26 a		08 32			08 47								09 30					09 33		09 45		
Doncaster 31 d	08 03			08 22			08 26			08 41					08 53	08 54	09 07		09 18			09 26
Bentley (S.Yorks) 31 a							08 29									08 57						09 29
Adwick 31 a							08 33									09 04						09 33
Kirk Sandall d	08 09														09 00		09 14					
Hatfield & Stainforth d	08 14														09 05		09 19					
Thorne South d	08 18																09 24					
Crowle d	08 27																09 32					
Althorpe d	08 33																09 38					
Scunthorpe a	08 44									09 06							09 47					
d										09 07												
Barnetby d								08 52	09 39	09 21												
Hull Paragon Interchange d																					09 05	
Barton-on-Humber a																					09 40	
Barton-on-Humber d						08 00																
Barrow Haven d						08 05																
New Holland d						08 08																
Goxhill d						08 13																
Thornton Abbey d						08 16																
Ulceby d						08 20																
Habrough d						08 25		09 01	09 48	09 29												
Stallingborough d						08 30																
Healing d						08 33																
Great Coates d						08 36																
Grimsby Town a						08 41		09 15	10 00	09 43												
d						08 43			10 01	09 44												
Grimsby Docks d						08 45																
New Clee d						08x48																
Cleethorpes a						08 52			10 13	09 55												
Thorne North d															09 10							
Goole d				08 43											09 19				09 38			
Saltmarshe d																						
York 8 33 d			07 38											08 43								
Selby a			07 57								08 57			09 05								
Wressle d			08 05																			
Howden d			08 10											09 15								
Eastrington d			08 15																			
Gilberdyke d			08 17												09 24							
Broomfleet d			08 21																			
Brough d			08 27	08 57										09 27	09 31				09 55			
Ferriby d			08 32												09 36							
Hessle d			08 36												09 40							
Hull a			08 50	09 13							09 31			09 47	09 57				10 12			

A To Edinburgh
B To Bridlington
C From Birmingham New Street to Newcastle
D To Leeds
E From Lincoln
F From Birmingham New Street to Edinburgh

Table 29

Saturdays

Manchester Airport, Manchester, Sheffield and Meadowhall - Doncaster - Cleethorpes and Hull
Barton-on-Humber - Cleethorpes

		NT	NT	TP ◇1	TP ◇1	NT A	EM ◇1 B	EM ◇1 C	XC ◇1 D	NT	NT	GR 1 E	NT	NT	NT F	XC ◇1 G	NT A	NT H	EM I	TP ◇1	TP ◇1	NT A
Manchester Airport 85 ✈	d			07 53																08 55		
Manchester Piccadilly 10	d			08 20	08 42															09 20	09 42	
Stockport 78	d			08 28																09 28		
Sheffield 7	a			09 08																10 08		
	d	08 53		09 11		09 14	09 21	09 21	09 21		09 25		09 31		09 41	09 47		09 53		10 11		10 14
Meadowhall	d	09 00		09 16		09 21					09 34		09 38		09 47			09 59		10 16		10 21
Rotherham Central	d	09 06				09 27					09 41		09 45					10 05				10 27
Swinton (S.Yorks)	d	09 16				09a36					09 49		09 53					10 15				10a36
Mexborough	d	09 19									09 52							10 18				
Conisbrough	d	09 23									09 56							10 22				
London Kings Cross	d											08 30										
Doncaster 7	a	09 33		09 35			09 53	09 53			10 07	10 08			10 14	10 17		10 32		10 35		
York 8 26	a						10 14	10 16	10 27			10 33	10 56			10 45						
Doncaster 31	d	09 34		09 37						09 41	10 08				10 19		10 26	10 34		10 37		
Bentley (S.Yorks) 31	a	09 37															10 29	10 37				
Adwick 31	a	09 43															10 33	10 43				
Kirk Sandall	d									09 48	10 15											
Hatfield & Stainforth	d									09 53	10 20											
Thorne South	d										10 25											
Crowle	d										10 33											
Althorpe	d										10 39											
Scunthorpe	a			10 02							10 48									11 02		
	d			10 03																11 03		
Barnetby	d			10 17															10 41	11 17		
Hull Paragon Interchange	d																					
Barton-on-Humber	a																					
Barton-on-Humber	d		09 52																			
Barrow Haven	d		09 57																			
New Holland	d		10 00																			
Goxhill	d		10 05																			
Thornton Abbey	d		10 08																			
Ulceby	d		10 12																			
Habrough	d		10 17																10 50			
Stallingborough	d		10 22																			
Healing	d		10 25																			
Great Coates	d		10 28																			
Grimsby Town	a		10 33	10 40															11 08	11 37		
	d		10 33	10 40																11 38		
Grimsby Docks	d		10 36																			
New Clee	d		10x38																			
Cleethorpes	a		10 43	10 51																11 50		
Thorne North	d									09 58												
Goole	d									10 07					10 38							
Saltmarshe	d																					
York 8 33	d													09 50								
Selby	a				09 57									10 09							10 57	
Wressle	d																					
Howden	d													10 19								
Eastrington	d																					
Gilberdyke	d									10 15				10 26								
Broomfleet	d																					
Brough	d				10 16					10 23				10 34	10 51						11 16	
Ferriby	d									10 28												
Hessle	d									10 32												
Hull	a				10 34					10 45				10 53	11 09						11 34	

A To Leeds
B until 10 September. From St Pancras International to Scarborough
C from 17 September. From St Pancras International
D From Bristol Temple Meads to Glasgow Central
E To Edinburgh
F To Scarborough
G From Guildford to Newcastle
H From Lincoln
I From Newark North Gate

Table 29

Saturdays

Manchester Airport, Manchester, Sheffield and Meadowhall - Doncaster - Cleethorpes and Hull
Barton-on-Humber - Cleethorpes

		XC ◇1 A	NT	NT	GR 1 B	NT	NT C	XC ◇1 D	HT ◇1	NT BHX	NT E	NT F	NT	TP ◇1	TP ◇1	NT E	XC ◇1 G	NT	NT	GR 1 B	NT	NT H	XC ◇1 I
Manchester Airport 85 ✈	d													09 55									
Manchester Piccadilly 10	d													10 20	10 42								
Stockport 78	d													10 28									
Sheffield 7	a													11 08									
	d	10 21		10 24			10 41	10 47				10 53		11 11		11 14	11 21		11 24			11 41	11 47
Meadowhall	d			10 30			10 47					10 59		11 16		11 21			11 30			11 47	
Rotherham Central	d			10 36								11 05				11 27			11 37				
Swinton (S.Yorks)	d			10 44								11 16				11a36			11 47				
Mexborough	d			10 50								11 19							11 50				
Conisbrough	d			10 54								11 23							11 54				
London Kings Cross	d				09 30				09 48											10 30			
Doncaster 7	a			11 04	11 08		11 13	11 15	11 24			11 32		11 35					12 04	12 08		12 15	12 15
York 8 26	a	11 27			11 33			11 45									12 29			12 33			12 45
Doncaster 31	d		10 41	11 08			11 18		11 26		11 26	11 34		11 37				11 41	12 08			12 17	
Bentley (S.Yorks) 31	a										11 29	11 37											
Adwick 31	a										11 33	11 43											
Kirk Sandall	d		10 47	11 14														11 47	12 14				
Hatfield & Stainforth	d		10 52	11 19														11 52	12 19				
Thorne South	d			11 24															12 24				
Crowle	d			11 32															12 32				
Althorpe	d			11 38															12 38				
Scunthorpe	a			11 46										12 02					12 46				
	d													12 03									
Barnetby	d													12 17									
Hull Paragon Interchange	d									11 05													
Barton-on-Humber	a									11 40													
Barton-on-Humber	d												11 52										
Barrow Haven	d												11 57										
New Holland	d												12 00										
Goxhill	d												12 05										
Thornton Abbey	d												12 08										
Ulceby	d												12 12										
Habrough	d												12 17	12 26									
Stallingborough	d												12 22										
Healing	d												12 25										
Great Coates	d												12 28										
Grimsby Town	a												12 33	12 40									
	d												12 33	12 40									
Grimsby Docks	d												12 36										
New Clee	d												12x38										
Cleethorpes	a												12 43	12 52									
Thorne North	d		10 57															11 57					
Goole	d		11 07				11 38											12 07				12 38	
Saltmarshe	d																						
York 8 33	d					10 43															11 45		
Selby	a					11 03			11 40						11 57						12 04		
Wressle	d																						
Howden	d					11 15			11 51												12 14		
Eastrington	d																						
Gilberdyke	d		11 17			11 21												12 16			12 21		
Broomfleet	d		11 21																				
Brough	d		11 27			11 31	11 52		12 03						12 16			12 24			12 29	12 51	
Ferriby	d		11 32															12 29					
Hessle	d		11 36															12 33					
Hull	a		11 51			11 51	12 10		12 20						12 36			12 45			12 49	13 11	

A From Plymouth to Edinburgh
B To Edinburgh
C To Bridlington
D From Bournemouth to Newcastle
E To Leeds
F From Lincoln
G From Plymouth to Glasgow Central
H To Scarborough
I From Southampton Central to Newcastle

Manchester Airport, Manchester, Sheffield and Meadowhall - Doncaster - Cleethorpes and Hull
Barton-on-Humber - Cleethorpes

		NT A	NT B	NT BHX	EM C	NT	TP ◇1	TP ◇1	NT A	XC ◇1 D	NT	NT	GR 1 E	NT	NT F	XC ◇1 G	HT ◇1	NT A	NT B	NT	TP ◇1	TP ◇1
Manchester Airport 85 ✈	d						10 55														11 55	
Manchester Piccadilly 10	d						11 20	11 42													12 20	12 42
Stockport 78	d						11 28														12 28	
Sheffield 7	a						12 08														13 08	
	d		11 53			12 00	12 11		12 14	12 21		12 24			12 41	12 47			12 53		13 11	
Meadowhall	d		11 59				12 16		12 21			12 30			12 47				12 59		13 16	
Rotherham Central	d		12 05						12 27			12 37							13 05			
Swinton (S.Yorks)	d		12 16						12a36			12 47							13 16			
Mexborough	d		12 19									12 50							13 19			
Conisbrough	d		12 23									12 54							13 23			
London Kings Cross	d												11 30				11 48					
Doncaster 7	a		12 33				12 35					13 04	13 08		13 15	13 17	13 24		13 32		13 35	
York 8 26	a									13 29			13 33			13 45						
Doncaster 31	d	12 26	12 34				12 37				12 42	13 08			13 17		13 26	13 26	13 34		13 37	
Bentley (S.Yorks) 31	a	12 29	12 37															13 29	13 37			
Adwick 31	a	12 33	12 43															13 33	13 43			
Kirk Sandall	d										12 48	13 14										
Hatfield & Stainforth	d										12 53	13 19										
Thorne South	d											13 24										
Crowle	d											13 33										
Althorpe	d											13 39										
Scunthorpe	a						13 02					13 46									14 02	
	d						13 03														14 03	
Barnetby	d				13 11	13 38	13 17														14 18	
Hull Paragon Interchange	d			13 05																		
Barton-on-Humber	a			13 40																		
Barton-on-Humber	d																			13 52		
Barrow Haven	d																			13 57		
New Holland	d																			14 00		
Goxhill	d																			14 05		
Thornton Abbey	d																			14 08		
Ulceby	d																			14 12		
Habrough	d				13 20	13 47														14 17	14 26	
Stallingborough	d																			14 22		
Healing	d																			14 25		
Great Coates	d																			14 28		
Grimsby Town	a				13 37	14 00	13 39													14 33	14 39	
	d					14 00	13 40													14 33	14 40	
Grimsby Docks	d																			14 36		
New Clee	d																			14x38		
Cleethorpes	a					14 11	13 52													14 43	14 52	
Thorne North	d										12 58											
Goole	d										13 07				13 37							
Saltmarshe	d																					
York 8 33	d													12 47								
Selby	a							12 57						13 06			13 40					13 57
Wressle	d																					
Howden	d													13 16			13 51					
Eastrington	d																					
Gilberdyke	d										13 15											
Broomfleet	d																					
Brough	d							13 16			13 23			13 28	13 51		14 03					14 16
Ferriby	d										13 28											
Hessle	d										13 32											
Hull	a							13 34			13 45			13 48	14 08		14 20					14 34

A To Leeds
B From Lincoln
C From Newark North Gate
D From Plymouth to Edinburgh
E To Edinburgh
F To Bridlington
G From Reading to Newcastle

Table 29

Saturdays

Manchester Airport, Manchester, Sheffield and Meadowhall - Doncaster - Cleethorpes and Hull
Barton-on-Humber - Cleethorpes

		NT A	XC ◇1 B	NT	NT	GR 1 C	NT	NT	NT D	XC ◇1 E	NT A	NT F	TP ◇1	TP ◇1	NT A	XC ◇1 G	NT	NT	GR 1 C	NT	NT H	XC ◇1 I	NT BHX
Manchester Airport 85 ✈	d												12 55										
Manchester Piccadilly 10	d												13 20	13 42									
Stockport 78	d												13 28										
Sheffield 7	a												14 08										
	d	13 14	13 21		13 24		13 28		13 41	13 47		13 53	14 11		14 14	14 21		14 24			14 41	14 47	
Meadowhall	d	13 21			13 30		13 35		13 47			13 59	14 16		14 21			14 30			14 47		
Rotherham Central	d	13 27			13 37		13 42					14 05			14 27			14 37					
Swinton (S.Yorks)	d	13a36			13 47		13 51					14 17			14a36			14 48					
Mexborough	d				13 50							14 20						14 51					
Conisbrough	d				13 54							14 24						14 55					
London Kings Cross	d					12 30													13 30				
Doncaster 7	a				14 03	14 09			14 16	14 18		14 32	14 35					15 04	15 08		15 17	15 18	
York 8 26	a		14 27			14 33	14 56			14 45						15 29			15 33			15 45	
Doncaster 31	d			13 41	14 07				14 17		14 26	14 34	14 37				14 40	15 07			15 17		
Bentley (S.Yorks) 31	a										14 29	14 37											
Adwick 31	a										14 33	14 43											
Kirk Sandall	d			13 47	14 13												14 46	15 13					
Hatfield & Stainforth	d			13 52	14 18												14 51	15 18					
Thorne South	d				14 25													15 23					
Crowle	d				14 33													15 31					
Althorpe	d				14 39													15 37					
Scunthorpe	a				14 48								15 02					15 46					
	d												15 03										
Barnetby	d												15 17										
Hull Paragon Interchange	d																						15 05
Barton-on-Humber	a																						15 40
Barton-on-Humber	d																						
Barrow Haven	d																						
New Holland	d																						
Goxhill	d																						
Thornton Abbey	d																						
Ulceby	d																						
Habrough	d																						
Stallingborough	d																						
Healing	d																						
Great Coates	d																						
Grimsby Town	a												15 37										
	d												15 38										
Grimsby Docks	d																						
New Clee	d																						
Cleethorpes	a												15 52										
Thorne North	d			13 57													14 56						
Goole	d			14 07					14 38								15 07				15 37		
Saltmarshe	d			14 12																			
York 8 33	d							13 44												14 47			
Selby	a							14 07						14 57						15 06			
Wressle	d																						
Howden	d							14 17												15 16			
Eastrington	d																						
Gilberdyke	d			14 14													15 15						
Broomfleet	d																						
Brough	d			14 22				14 30	14 52					15 16			15 23			15 28	15 51		
Ferriby	d			14 27													15 28						
Hessle	d			14 31													15 32						
Hull	a			14 48				14 52	15 09					15 34			15 45			15 48	16 08		

A To Leeds
B From Penzance to Glasgow Central
C To Edinburgh
D To Bridlington
E From Southampton Central to Newcastle
F From Lincoln
G From Plymouth to Aberdeen
H To Scarborough
I From Reading to Newcastle

Manchester Airport, Manchester, Sheffield and Meadowhall - Doncaster - Cleethorpes and Hull
Barton-on-Humber - Cleethorpes

Station		EM	NT	NT	NT	TP	TP	NT	XC	NT	NT	GR	NT	XC	NT	HT	NT	NT	TP	NT	TP	NT	XC
		A	B	A				B	C			D	E	F	B		A					B	G
Manchester Airport 85	d					13 55													14 55				
Manchester Piccadilly 10	d					14 20	14 42												15 20		15 42		
Stockport 78	d					14 28													15 28				
Sheffield 7	a					15 08													16 08				
	d			14 53		15 11		15 14	15 21		15 24		15 41	15 47			15 53	16 00	16 11			16 14	16 21
Meadowhall	d			14 59		15 16		15 21			15 30		15 47				15 59		16 16			16 21	
Rotherham Central	d			15 05				15 27			15 36						16 05					16 27	
Swinton (S.Yorks)	d			15 17				15a36			15 47						16 16					16a36	
Mexborough	d			15 20							15 50						16 19						
Conisbrough	d			15 24							15 54						16 23						
London Kings Cross	d											14 30				14 48							
Doncaster 7	a			15 34		15 35					16 04	16 08	16 14	16 18		16 24	16 32		16 35				
York 8 26	a								16 27			16 33		16 46									17 27
Doncaster 31	d		15 26	15 34		15 37				15 41	16 08		16 19		16 25	16 26	16 34		16 37				
Bentley (S.Yorks) 31	a		15 29	15 37											16 28		16 37						
Adwick 31	a		15 33	15 43											16 32		16 43						
Kirk Sandall	d									15 47	16 14												
Hatfield & Stainforth	d									15 52	16 19												
Thorne South	d										16 24												
Crowle	d										16 33												
Althorpe	d										16 39												
Scunthorpe	a					16 02					16 46								17 02				
	d					16 03													17 03				
Barnetby	d	15 25				16 17												17 38	17 20				
Hull Paragon Interchange	d																						
Barton-on-Humber	a																						
Barton-on-Humber	d				15 54																		
Barrow Haven	d				15 59																		
New Holland	d				16 02																		
Goxhill	d				16 07																		
Thornton Abbey	d				16 10																		
Ulceby	d				16 14																		
Habrough	d	15 33			16 19	16 26												17 47					
Stallingborough	d				16 24																		
Healing	d				16 27																		
Great Coates	d				16 30																		
Grimsby Town	a	15 48			16 35	16 39												18 01	17 40				
	d				16 35	16 40												18 02	17 40				
Grimsby Docks	d				16 38																		
New Clee	d																						
Cleethorpes	a				16 44	16 52												18 11	17 53				
Thorne North	d									15 57													
Goole	d									16 07			16 38										
Saltmarshe	d																						
York 8 33	d																			16 12			
Selby	a						15 57									16 41				16 36	17 00		
Wressle	d																			16 44			
Howden	d															16 54				16 49			
Eastrington	d																						
Gilberdyke	d									16 18										16 55			
Broomfleet	d																						
Brough	d						16 16			16 26			16 52			17 10				17 03	17 18		
Ferriby	d									16 30										17 08			
Hessle	d									16 35										17 12			
Hull	a						16 34			16 48			17 06			17 28				17 29	17 37		

A From Lincoln
B To Leeds
C From Penzance to Glasgow Central
D To Edinburgh
E To Bridlington
F From Southampton Central to Newcastle
G From Newquay to Dundee

Manchester Airport, Manchester, Sheffield and Meadowhall - Doncaster - Cleethorpes and Hull
Barton-on-Humber - Cleethorpes

Station		NT	GR	NT	NT	XC	NT BHX	NT	NT	NT	NT	EM	NT	TP	TP	NT	XC	NT	GR	NT	NT	XC
			A	B	C	D				E	F	F				E	G		A		H	I
Manchester Airport 85	d													15 55								
Manchester Piccadilly 10	d													16 20	16 42							
Stockport 78	d													16 28								
Sheffield 7	a													17 08								
	d	16 24			16 41	16 47					16 53			17 11		17 14	17 21	17 25			17 41	17 47
Meadowhall	d	16 30			16 47						16 59			17 16		17 21		17 31			17 47	
Rotherham Central	d	16 37									17 05					17 27		17 37				
Swinton (S.Yorks)	d	16 46									17 16					17a37		17 45				
Mexborough	d	16 49									17 19							17 48				
Conisbrough	d	16 53									17 23							17 52				
London Kings Cross	d		15 30																16 30			
Doncaster 7	a	17 06	17 08		17 12	17 16					17 32			17 35				18 07	18 08		18 11	
York 8 26	a		17 33			17 38											18 30		18 33			18 59
Doncaster 31	d			16 42	17 19				17 22	17 26	17 34			17 43						17 47	18 16	
Bentley (S.Yorks) 31	a									17 29	17 37											
Adwick 31	a									17 33	17 43											
Kirk Sandall	d			16 48					17 29											17 53		
Hatfield & Stainforth	d			16 53					17 34											17 58		
Thorne South	d								17 39													
Crowle	d								17 48													
Althorpe	d								17 54													
Scunthorpe	a								18 02					18 08								
	d													18 09								
Barnetby	d											17 53		18 23								
Hull Paragon Interchange	d						17 10															
Barton-on-Humber	a						17 45															
Barton-on-Humber	d												17 55									
Barrow Haven	d												18 00									
New Holland	d												18 03									
Goxhill	d												18 08									
Thornton Abbey	d												18 11									
Ulceby	d												18 15									
Habrough	d											18 01	18 20	18 32								
Stallingborough	d												18 25									
Healing	d												18 28									
Great Coates	d												18 31									
Grimsby Town	a											18 16	18 36	18 45								
	d												18 36	18 46								
Grimsby Docks	d												18 43									
New Clee	d																					
Cleethorpes	a												18 50	18 58								
Thorne North	d			16 58	17 31															18 03		
Goole	d			17 07	17 40															18 12	18 36	
Saltmarshe	d																			18 17		
York 8 33	d							17 19														
Selby	a							17 45							17 59							
Wressle	d																					
Howden	d							17 56							18 08							
Eastrington	d																					
Gilberdyke	d			17 14				18 03												18 23		
Broomfleet	d																			18 27		
Brough	d			17 22	17 52			18 11							18 20					18 33	18 53	
Ferriby	d			17 27																18 38		
Hessle	d			17 31																18 42		
Hull	a			17 47	18 13			18 30							18 40					18 55	19 09	

A To Edinburgh
B To Beverley
C To Bridlington
D From Reading to Newcastle
E To Leeds
F From Lincoln
G From Plymouth to Glasgow Central
H To Scarborough
I From Southampton Central to Edinburgh

Table 29

Saturdays

Manchester Airport, Manchester, Sheffield and Meadowhall - Doncaster - Cleethorpes and Hull
Barton-on-Humber - Cleethorpes

		NT	TP	NT	NT	NT	GR	NT	XC	EM	TP	GR	NT	NT	XC	NT	NT	HT	NT	NT BHX	NT	TP	TP
			◇1	A	B	C	1	A	◇1 D	E	◇1	1 F		G	◇1 H		A	◇1	I			◇1	◇1
Manchester Airport 85	d										16 55											17 55	
Manchester Piccadilly 10	d		17 42								17 20											18 20	18 42
Stockport 78	d										17 28											18 28	
Sheffield 7	a										18 15											19 09	
	d					17 53		18 13	18 21		18 24		18 29	18 41	18 47				19 00			19 11	
Meadowhall	d					17 58		18 21			18 30		18 35	18 47					19 06			19 17	
Rotherham Central	d					18 05		18 27					18 42						19 12				
Swinton (S.Yorks)	d					18 16		18a37					18 50						19 18				
Mexborough	d					18 20							18 53						19 23				
Conisbrough	d					18 24							18 57						19 25				
London Kings Cross	d						17 10					17 30						17 48					
Doncaster 7	a					18 38	18 53				18 58	19 09	19 09	19 13	19 15			19 26	19 39			19 41	
York 8 26	a								19 29			19 34			19 40								
Doncaster 31	d			18 26	18 29	18 40	18 54				19 00			19 16		19 20	19 22	19 28				19 46	
Bentley (S.Yorks) 31	a			18 29													19 25						
Adwick 31	a			18 33													19 29						
Kirk Sandall	d				18 36	18 47										19 27							
Hatfield & Stainforth	d				18 41	18 52										19 32							
Thorne South	d				18 46											19 37							
Crowle	d				18 54											19 46							
Althorpe	d				19 00											19 52							
Scunthorpe	a				19 10						19 25					20 01						20 14	
	d										19 26											20 14	
Barnetby	d									19 08	19 40											20 28	
Hull Paragon Interchange	d																			19 25			
Barton-on-Humber	a																			19 52			
Barton-on-Humber	d																				19 58		
Barrow Haven	d																				20 03		
New Holland	d																				20 06		
Goxhill	d																				20 11		
Thornton Abbey	d																				20 14		
Ulceby	d																				20 18		
Habrough	d									19 16											20 23		
Stallingborough	d																				20 28		
Healing	d																				20 31		
Great Coates	d																				20 34		
Grimsby Town	a									19 31	20 00										20 39	20 47	
	d										20 01										20 39	20 48	
Grimsby Docks	d																				20 42		
New Clee	d																						
Cleethorpes	a										20 12										20 48	21 00	
Thorne North	d					18 57																	
Goole	d					19 12								19 37									
Saltmarshe	d																						
York 8 33	d	18 18																					
Selby	a	18 42	19 00				19 09											19 42					20 00
Wressle	d	18 50																					
Howden	d	18 54																19 53					20 10
Eastrington	d	18 59																					
Gilberdyke	d	19 03				19 21																	
Broomfleet	d																						
Brough	d	19 10	19 19			19 29	19 36							19 54				20 05					20 22
Ferriby	d					19 34																	
Hessle	d					19 38																	
Hull	a	19 29	19 37			19 50	19 57							20 10				20 22					20 41

A To Leeds
B From Adwick
C From Lincoln
D From Plymouth to Edinburgh
E From Newark North Gate
F To Newcastle. The Flying Scotsman
G To Bridlington
H From Reading to Newcastle
I From Retford Low Level

Table 29

Saturdays

Manchester Airport, Manchester, Sheffield and Meadowhall - Doncaster - Cleethorpes and Hull
Barton-on-Humber - Cleethorpes

		NT	XC	NT	NT	NT	GR	NT	XC	NT	NT	TP	NT	XC	NT	NT	XC	NT	NT	TP	HT	GR
		A	◇1 B				1 C	D	◇1 E	A	F	◇1		◇1 G	A		◇1 H	A		◇1 I	◇1	1 J
Manchester Airport 85	d											18 55										
Manchester Piccadilly 10	d											19 18										
Stockport 78	d											19 26										
Sheffield 7	a											20 08										
	d	19 18	19 22			19 25		19 44	19 54		19 58	20 11	20 15	20 24	20 27	20 38	20 53					
Meadowhall	d	19 25				19 31		19 50			20 04	20 16	20 21		20 35	20 45						
Rotherham Central	d	19 31				19 37					20 11		20 27		20 41	20 53						
Swinton (S.Yorks)	d	19a40				19 47					20 21		20 40		20a50	21 01						
Mexborough	d					19 50					20 24		20 43			21 04						
Conisbrough	d					19 54					20 28		20 47			21 08						
London Kings Cross	d						18 30														19 48	20 00
Doncaster 7	a					20 02	20 08	20 14	20 17		20 36	20 43	20 55			21 18	21 21				21 28	21 40
York 8 26	a		20 32				20 35		20 46					21 57			21 45					22 04
Doncaster 31	d				19 55	20 07		20 16		20 26	20 43	20 46	20 56			21 19		21 22			21 30	
Bentley (S.Yorks) 31	a									20 29								21 25				
Adwick 31	a									20 33								21 29				
Kirk Sandall	d				20 01	20 13							21 03			21 26						
Hatfield & Stainforth	d				20 06	20 18							21 08			21 31						
Thorne South	d					20 22										21 38						
Crowle	d					20 31										21 46						
Althorpe	d					20 37										21 52						
Scunthorpe	a					20 45						21 12				22 01						
	d											21 12										
Barnetby	d											21 26										
Hull Paragon Interchange	d																		21 25			
Barton-on-Humber	a																		21 52			
Barton-on-Humber	d																					
Barrow Haven	d																					
New Holland	d																					
Goxhill	d																					
Thornton Abbey	d																					
Ulceby	d																					
Habrough	d											21 35										
Stallingborough	d																					
Healing	d																					
Great Coates	d																					
Grimsby Town	a											21 48										
	d											21 49										
Grimsby Docks	d																					
New Clee	d																					
Cleethorpes	a											22 00										
Thorne North	d				20 11								21 14									
Goole	d				20 20			20 36					21a23									
Saltmarshe	d																					
York 8 33	d			19 47																		
Selby	a			20 06							21 01										21 44	
Wressle	d																					
Howden	d			20 16																21 39	21 55	
Eastrington	d																					
Gilberdyke	d				20 28						21 15											
Broomfleet	d																					
Brough	d			20 30	20 36			20 49			21 23									21 51	22 07	
Ferriby	d				20 41						21 28											
Hessle	d				20 45						21 32											
Hull	a			20 48	21 00			21 07			21 47									22 08	22 24	

A To Leeds
B From Plymouth to Edinburgh
C To Newcastle
D To Beverley
E From Southampton Central to Newcastle
F To Bridlington
G From Plymouth
H From Reading to Newcastle
I From Leeds
J To Newcastle. The Flying Scotsman

Table 29

Saturdays

Manchester Airport, Manchester, Sheffield and Meadowhall - Doncaster - Cleethorpes and Hull
Barton-on-Humber - Cleethorpes

		NT	NT	NT	TP	XC	NT	NT	TP	NT	XC	XC	NT	TP	NT
					◇1	◇1			◇1		◇1	◇1		◇1	
		A	B			C		B		B	D	E		F	
Manchester Airport 85 ✈	d								20 47						
Manchester Piccadilly 10	d								21 20						
Stockport 78	d								21 28						
Sheffield 7	a								22 08						
	d	21 14	21 30		21 34	22 09			22 11	22 24	22 27	22 27	22 30		23 27
Meadowhall	d	21 21	21 36		21 40				22 16	22 30			22 36		23 33
Rotherham Central	d	21 27	21 42							22 36			22 45		23 39
Swinton (S.Yorks)	d	21 32	21a50							22a45			22 53		23 48
Mexborough	d	21 35											22 56		23 51
Conisbrough	d	21 39											23 00		23 55
London Kings Cross	d														
Doncaster 7	a	21 54			22 03	22 30			22 36		22 51	22 51	23 09		00 08
York 8 26	a					22 55									
Doncaster 31	d	21 56			22 05			22 26	22 38				23 10		
Bentley (S.Yorks) 31	a							22 29							
Adwick 31	a							22 33							
Kirk Sandall	d	22 02							22 44				23 17		
Hatfield & Stainforth	d	22 07							22 48				23 22		
Thorne South	d								22 53						
Crowle	d								23 02						
Althorpe	d								23 08						
Scunthorpe	a				22 30				23 13						
	d				22 31				23 13						
Barnetby	d				22 45				23 28						
Hull Paragon Interchange	d														
Barton-on-Humber	a														
Barton-on-Humber	d			21 58											
Barrow Haven	d			22 03											
New Holland	d			22 06											
Goxhill	d			22 11											
Thornton Abbey	d			22 14											
Ulceby	d			22 18											
Habrough	d			22 23	22 54				23 36						
Stallingborough	d			22 28											
Healing	d			22 31											
Great Coates	d			22 34											
Grimsby Town	a			22 39	23 09				23 49						
	d			22 39	23 10				23 50						
Grimsby Docks	d			22 42											
New Clee	d														
Cleethorpes	a			22 48	23 19				00 01						
Thorne North	d	22 13											23 27		
Goole	d	22 22											23a38		
Saltmarshe	d	22 26													
York 8 33	d						22 11								
Selby	a						22 29								
Wressle	d														
Howden	d						22 39								
Eastrington	d														
Gilberdyke	d	22 32					22 45								
Broomfleet	d														
Brough	d	22 40					22 53							23 06	
Ferriby	d						22 58								
Hessle	d						23 02								
Hull	a	22 58					23 14							23 23	

A To Beverley
B To Leeds
C From Southampton Central
D from 17 September. From Plymouth to Leeds
E until 10 September. From Bournemouth to Leeds
F From Leeds

Table 29

Sundays
until 19 June

Manchester Airport, Manchester, Sheffield and Meadowhall - Doncaster - Cleethorpes and Hull
Barton-on-Humber - Cleethorpes

		TP	NT	NT	NT	NT	NT	XC	NT	GR	NT	TP	TP	NT	NT	NT	GR	NT	NT	NT	NT	XC	EM
														BHX									
		◇1						◇1		1		◇1	◇1				1					◇1	◇1
		A	A			B	C	D	B	E	F	G				C	E				B	H	I
Manchester Airport 85 ✈	d	20p47																					
Manchester Piccadilly 10	d	21 20										09 11											
Stockport 78	d	21p28																					
Sheffield 7	a	22p08																					
	d	22p11	23p27	08 00			08 45	09 21	09 36				09 52			10 26			11 05			11 21	11 31
Meadowhall	d	22p16	23p33	08 06			08 51		09 42				09 57			10 32			11 11				
Rotherham Central	d		23p39	08 12			08 57		09 48				10 03						11 17				
Swinton (S.Yorks)	d		23p48	08 20			09 05		09a58				10 09						11 25				
Mexborough	d		23p51	08 23			09 08						10 13						11 28				
Conisbrough	d		23p55	08 27			09 12						10 17						11 32				
London Kings Cross	d																09 30						
Doncaster 7	a	22p36	00 08	08 38			09 22						10 26			10 51	11 10		11 43				11 56
York 8 26	a							10 33									11 36					12 32	12 20
Doncaster 31	d	22p38			09 07	09 12	09 26			09 37	10 19		10 28			10 55				11 07	11 12		
Bentley (S.Yorks) 31	a					09 15															11 15		
Adwick 31	a					09 19															11 19		
Kirk Sandall	d	22p44			09 13															11 13			
Hatfield & Stainforth	d	22p48			09 18															11 18			
Thorne South	d	22p53																					
Crowle	d	23p02																					
Althorpe	d	23p08																					
Scunthorpe	a	23p13											10 54										
	d	23p13											10 55										
Barnetby	d	23p28											11 09										
Hull Paragon Interchange	d													10 25									
Barton-on-Humber	a													10 50									
Barton-on-Humber	d																	11 00					
Barrow Haven	d																	11 05					
New Holland	d																	11 08					
Goxhill	d																	11 13					
Thornton Abbey	d																	11 16					
Ulceby	d																	11 20					
Habrough	d	23p36																11 25					
Stallingborough	d																	11 30					
Healing	d																	11 33					
Great Coates	d																	11 36					
Grimsby Town	a	23p49											11 29					11 41					
	d	23p50											11 33					11 41					
Grimsby Docks	d																	11 44					
New Clee	d																	11 47					
Cleethorpes	a	00 01											11 42					11 55					
Thorne North	d				09 24		09 38				10 31									11 25			
Goole	d				09a35		09 47				10 40					11 14				11a36			
Saltmarshe	d																						
York 8 33	d									09a59					10 40								
Selby	a											10 44			10 58								
Wressle	d																						
Howden	d														11 08								
Eastrington	d																						
Gilberdyke	d						09 55				10 48					11 24							
Broomfleet	d																						
Brough	d						10 03				10 56	11 04			11 19	11 32							
Ferriby	d										11 00												
Hessle	d										11 05												
Hull	a						10 21				11 17	11 18			11 41	11 47							

A not 22 May
B To Leeds
C To Scarborough
D To Glasgow Central
E To Edinburgh
F To Bridlington
G From Liverpool Lime Street
H From Birmingham New Street to Glasgow Central
I From Leicester

Table 29

Sundays
until 19 June

Manchester Airport, Manchester, Sheffield and Meadowhall - Doncaster - Cleethorpes and Hull
Barton-on-Humber - Cleethorpes

Station			GR	NT	NT	HT	EM	TP	XC	NT	NT	GR	TP	TP	GR	EM	NT	XC	NT BHX	NT	NT	GR	HT	NT
			A	B			C		D		E	A			F	G	B	H			I	A		B
Manchester Airport	85	d						10 44																
Manchester Piccadilly		d						11 18					12 02	12 18		12 44								
Stockport	78	d						11 27						12 28		12 55								
Sheffield		a						12 08						13 08		13 37								
		d		11 36				12 11	12 21	12 24	12 28			13 11				13 21			13 24			13 36
Meadowhall		d		11 42				12 16		12 30	12 34			13 16							13 30			13 42
Rotherham Central		d		11 49						12 36											13 36			13 49
Swinton (S.Yorks)		d		12a00						12 49											13 47			13a57
Mexborough		d								12 52											13 50			
Conisbrough		d								12 56											13 54			
London Kings Cross		d	10 30			10 45						11 30			12 20							12 30	12 45	
Doncaster		a	12 10			12 28		12 35		13 04	12 56	13 10		13 35	13 58						14 02	14 09	14 25	
York	26	a	12 34						13 32			13 34			14 22			14 31				14 36		
Doncaster	31	d				12 31		12 37		13 05	12 58						13 12				14 05		14 27	
Bentley (S.Yorks)	31	a															13 15							
Adwick	31	a															13 19							
Kirk Sandall		d								13 11														
Hatfield & Stainforth		d								13 16														
Thorne South		d																						
Crowle		d																						
Althorpe		d																						
Scunthorpe		a						13 06																
		d						13 06																
Barnetby		d					12 33	13 21																
Hull Paragon Interchange		d																	13 25					
Barton-on-Humber		a																	13 50					
Barton-on-Humber		d																						
Barrow Haven		d																						
New Holland		d																						
Goxhill		d																						
Thornton Abbey		d																						
Ulceby		d																						
Habrough		d					12 41	13 29																
Stallingborough		d																						
Healing		d																						
Great Coates		d																						
Grimsby Town		a					12 53	13 42																
		d					13 06	13 43																
Grimsby Docks		d																						
New Clee		d																						
Cleethorpes		a					13 15	13 56																
Thorne North		d								13 22														
Goole		d								13a32	13 17										14 25			
Saltmarshe		d																						
York	33	d			12 05															13 40				
Selby		a			12 24	12 45							13 23							13 59			14 41	
Wressle		d																						
Howden		d			12 34	12 56														14 09			14 52	
Eastrington		d																						
Gilberdyke		d									13 25										14 33			
Broomfleet		d																						
Brough		d			12 46	13 08					13 33		13 41							14 21	14 41		15 04	
Ferriby		d									13 38													
Hessle		d									13 42													
Hull		a			13 06	13 25					13 57		13 59							14 40	15 01		15 21	

A To Edinburgh
B To Leeds
C From Newark North Gate
D From Birmingham New Street to Edinburgh
E To Scarborough
F To Newcastle
G To Norwich
H From Birmingham New Street to Glasgow Central
I To Bridlington

Table 29

Sundays
until 19 June

Manchester Airport, Manchester, Sheffield and Meadowhall - Doncaster - Cleethorpes and Hull
Barton-on-Humber - Cleethorpes

Station			NT	TP	XC	NT	NT	NT	GR	TP	NT	TP	XC	NT	NT	GR	NT BHX	NT	NT	HT	NT	EM	TP
					A			B	C		D		E		F	C		D				G	
Manchester Airport	85	d		12 55								13 55											14 55
Manchester Piccadilly		d		13 20						14 02		14c20											15 20
Stockport	78	d		13 28								14 28											15 28
Sheffield		a		14 08								15 08											16 08
		d		14 11	14 21	14 22		14 28				15 11	15 21	15 24	15 28			15 36					16 11
Meadowhall		d		14 16		14 28		14 34				15 16		15 30	15 34			15 42					16 16
Rotherham Central		d				14 35								15 37				15 50					
Swinton (S.Yorks)		d				14 46								15 47				15a58					
Mexborough		d				14 49								15 50									
Conisbrough		d				14 53								15 54									
London Kings Cross		d							13 30							14 30				14 45			
Doncaster		a		14 35		15 03		14 56	15 10			15 35		16 04	15 56	16 11				16 28			16 35
York	26	a			15 31				15 35				16 32			16 36							
Doncaster	31	d		14 37		15 05		14 59			15 12	15 37			15 56					16 31			16 37
Bentley (S.Yorks)	31	a									15 15												
Adwick	31	a									15 19												
Kirk Sandall		d				15 11																	
Hatfield & Stainforth		d				15 16																	
Thorne South		d																					
Crowle		d																					
Althorpe		d																					
Scunthorpe		a		15 02								16 02											17 02
		d		15 03								16 03											17 03
Barnetby		d		15 17								16 17										16 58	17 17
Hull Paragon Interchange		d															15 30						
Barton-on-Humber		a															15 55						
Barton-on-Humber		d	14 00																		16 15		
Barrow Haven		d	14 05																		16 20		
New Holland		d	14 08																		16 23		
Goxhill		d	14 13																		16 28		
Thornton Abbey		d	14 16																		16 31		
Ulceby		d	14 20																		16 35		
Habrough		d	14 25									16 26									16 40	17 06	
Stallingborough		d	14 30																		16 45		
Healing		d	14 33																		16 48		
Great Coates		d	14 36																		16 51		
Grimsby Town		a	14 41	15 37								16 39									16 56	17 18	17 37
		d	14 41	15 38								16 40									16 56	17 19	17 38
Grimsby Docks		d	14 44																		16 59		
New Clee		d	14 47																		17 02		
Cleethorpes		a	14 55	15 51								16 52									17 10	17 28	17 50
Thorne North		d				15 24									16 10								
Goole		d				15a33		15 19							16 19								
Saltmarshe		d																					
York	33	d					14 49												16 06				
Selby		a					15 08			15 22									16 24	16 45			
Wressle		d																					
Howden		d					15 18												16 34	16 56			
Eastrington		d																					
Gilberdyke		d						15 29							16 27								
Broomfleet		d																					
Brough		d					15 30	15 37		15 40					16 35				16 46	17 08			
Ferriby		d																					
Hessle		d																					
Hull		a					15 49	15 56		15 59					16 53				17 07	17 25			

A From Bristol Temple Meads to Aberdeen
B To Scarborough
C To Edinburgh
D To Leeds
E From Bristol Temple Meads to Glasgow Central
F To Bridlington
G From Nottingham

Table 29

Sundays until 19 June

Manchester Airport, Manchester, Sheffield and Meadowhall - Doncaster - Cleethorpes and Hull

Barton-on-Humber - Cleethorpes

	XC	NT	NT	GR	TP	NT	NT	NT	TP	XC	NT	NT	GR	NT	NT BHX	EM	TP	XC	NT	NT	GR	GR
	◇1			■1	◇1				◇1	◇1			■1				◇1	◇1			■1	■1
	A		B	C		D		E		F		G	C	E		H		I		J		C
	✕			✕✕						✕			✕✕		🚌			✕			✕✕	✕✕
Manchester Airport 85 ✈ d									15 55								16 55					
Manchester Piccadilly 10 ⇌ d					16 02				16 20								17 20					
Stockport 78 d									16 28								17 28					
Sheffield 7 ⇌ a									17 08								18 08					
d	16 21	16 24	16 28			16 36			17 11	17 21	17 25	17 28		17 36			18 11	18 21	18 25	18 28		
Meadowhall ⇌ d		16 30	16 34			16 42			17 16		17 31	17 34		17 44			18 16		18 31	18 35		
Rotherham Central d		16 37				16 49					17 37			17 50					18 37			
Swinton (S.Yorks) d		16 47				16a58					17 47			17a58					18 48			
Mexborough d		16 50									17 50								18 51			
Conisbrough d		16 54									17 54								18 55			
London Kings Cross d				15 30									16 30								17 20	17 30
Doncaster 7 a		17 03	16 56	17 11					17 35		18 05	17 55	18 10				18 35		19 06	18 54	19 03	19 09
York 8 26 a	17 32			17 37						18 32			18 35					19 32				19 38
Doncaster 31 d		17 04	16 58					17 14	17 37			17 57					18 37			18 55	19 05	
Bentley (S.Yorks) 31 a								17 17														
Adwick 31 a								17 21														
Kirk Sandall d		17 10																		19 01		
Hatfield & Stainforth d		17 15																		19 06		
Thorne South d																						
Crowle d																						
Althorpe d																						
Scunthorpe a									18 02								19 02					
d									18 03								19 03					
Barnetby d									18 17							18 53	19 17					
Hull Paragon Interchange d															18 30							
Barton-on-Humber a															18 55							
Barton-on-Humber d																						
Barrow Haven d																						
New Holland d																						
Goxhill d																						
Thornton Abbey d																						
Ulceby d																						
Habrough d																19 01	19 26					
Stallingborough d																						
Healing d																						
Great Coates d																						
Grimsby Town a									18 37							19 13	19 39					
d									18 38							19 13	19 40					
Grimsby Docks d																						
New Clee d																						
Cleethorpes a									18 50							19 24	19 52					
Thorne North d		17 24																		19 12		
Goole d		17a33	17 17									18 16								19 21		
Saltmarshe d																						
York 8 33 d							17 11															
Selby a					17 23		17 30														19 24	
Wressle d																						
Howden d							17 41															
Eastrington d																						
Gilberdyke d			17 25									18 24								19 29		
Broomfleet d																						
Brough d			17 33		17 41		17 53					18 32								19 37	19 46	
Ferriby d																						
Hessle d																						
Hull a			17 51		17 59		18 12					18 48								19 55	20 06	

A From Plymouth to Edinburgh
B To Scarborough
C To Edinburgh
D To Moorthorpe
E To Leeds
F From Plymouth to Glasgow Central
G To Bridlington
H From Newark North Gate
I From Penzance to Edinburgh
J To Beverley

Table 29

Sundays until 19 June

Manchester Airport, Manchester, Sheffield and Meadowhall - Doncaster - Cleethorpes and Hull

Barton-on-Humber - Cleethorpes

	TP	NT	NT	NT	NT	HT	TP	TP	XC	NT	GR	NT	NT	TP	TP	XC	NT	GR	HT	TP	NT
	◇1					◇1	◇1	◇1	◇1		■1			◇1	◇1	◇1		■1	◇1	◇1	
		A			B				C		D	B				E		D			
						⊠					✕✕					✕		✕✕	⊠		
Manchester Airport 85 ✈ d							17 55							18 55						19 55	
Manchester Piccadilly 10 ⇌ d	18 02						18 20	19 02						19 20	20 06					20 18	
Stockport 78 d							18 28							19 28						20 27	
Sheffield 7 ⇌ a							19 08							20 08						21 08	
d		18 57					19 11		19 21	19 29		19 36	20 02	20 11		20 21	20 28			21 11	
Meadowhall ⇌ d		19 05					19 16			19 35		19 42	20 09	20 16			20 34			21 16	
Rotherham Central d		19 11								19 41		19 49					20 40				
Swinton (S.Yorks) d		19a19								19 49		19a57					20 48				
Mexborough d										19 52							20 51				
Conisbrough d										19 56							20 55				
London Kings Cross d						17 45					18 30							19 30	19 45		
Doncaster 7 a						19 28	19 35			20 07	20 11		20 30	20 35			21 05	21 13	21 29	21 35	
York 8 26 a									20 32		20 36					21 32		21 38			
Doncaster 31 d					19 27	19 31	19 37						20 30	20 37			21 07		21 31	21 37	
Bentley (S.Yorks) 31 a					19 30																
Adwick 31 a					19 34																
Kirk Sandall d																	21 13				
Hatfield & Stainforth d																	21 18				
Thorne South d																					
Crowle d																					
Althorpe d																					
Scunthorpe a							20 02							21 02						22 02	
d							20 03							21 03						22 03	
Barnetby d							20 17							21 17						22 17	
Hull Paragon Interchange d																					
Barton-on-Humber a																					
Barton-on-Humber d				19 15																	
Barrow Haven d				19 20																	
New Holland d				19 23																	
Goxhill d				19 28																	
Thornton Abbey d				19 31																	
Ulceby d				19 35																	
Habrough d				19 40										21 26						22 26	
Stallingborough d				19 45																	
Healing d				19 48																	
Great Coates d				19 51																	
Grimsby Town a				19 56			20 37							21 39						22 39	
d				19 56			20 38							21 40						22 40	
Grimsby Docks d				19 59																	
New Clee d				20 02																	
Cleethorpes a				20 10			20 50							21 52						22 52	
Thorne North d																	21 24				
Goole d													20 49				21a34				
Saltmarshe d																					
York 8 33 d			19 10																		21 41
Selby a	19 29		19 35			19 45		20 17							21 38				21 45		22 00
Wressle d																					
Howden d			19 46			19 56													21 56		22 10
Eastrington d																					
Gilberdyke d													20 57								
Broomfleet d																					
Brough d	19 48		19 58			20 08		20 36					21 05		21 58				22 08		22 22
Ferriby d																					
Hessle d																					
Hull a	20 06		20 17			20 25		20 54					21 23		22 15				22 25		22 36

A To Moorthorpe
B To Leeds
C From Newquay to Edinburgh
D To Newcastle
E From Plymouth to Newcastle

Table 29

Sundays
until 19 June

Manchester Airport, Manchester, Sheffield and Meadowhall - Doncaster - Cleethorpes and Hull
Barton-on-Humber - Cleethorpes

Station		NT	NT	NT	TP	NT	NT	TP	GR	NT
		A		A	◇1 B			◇1	1 C	
Manchester Airport 85	d									
Manchester Piccadilly 10	d									
Stockport 78	d									
Sheffield 7	a									
	d		21 24	21 36		22 13	22 26	22 30		23 34
Meadowhall	d		21 30	21 42		22 19	22 32	22 35		23 40
Rotherham Central	d		21 37	21 48			22 38			23 47
Swinton (S.Yorks)	d		21 47	21a56			22 48			23 55
Mexborough	d		21 50				22 51			23 58
Conisbrough	d		21 54				22 55			00 02
London Kings Cross	d								22 00	
Doncaster 7	a		22 03			22 38	23 05	22 56	23 42	00 13
York 8 26	a								00 10	
Doncaster 31	d	21 49	22 04			22 41		22 58		
Bentley (S.Yorks) 31	a	21 52								
Adwick 31	a	21 56								
Kirk Sandall	d									
Hatfield & Stainforth	d									
Thorne South	d									
Crowle	d									
Althorpe	d									
Scunthorpe	a							23 23		
	d							23 24		
Barnetby	d							23 38		
Hull Paragon Interchange	d									
Barton-on-Humber	a									
Barton-on-Humber	d									
Barrow Haven	d									
New Holland	d									
Goxhill	d									
Thornton Abbey	d									
Ulceby	d									
Habrough	d									
Stallingborough	d									
Healing	d									
Great Coates	d									
Grimsby Town	a							23 57		
	d							23 58		
Grimsby Docks	d									
New Clee	d									
Cleethorpes	a							00 09		
Thorne North	d					22 53				
Goole	d		22 23			23 02				
Saltmarshe	d									
York 8 33	d									
Selby	a									
Wressle	d									
Howden	d									
Eastrington	d									
Gilberdyke	d		22 31			23 10				
Broomfleet	d									
Brough	d		22 39		23 02	23 18				
Ferriby	d									
Hessle	d									
Hull	a		22 56		23 19	23 39				

A To Leeds
B From Leeds
C To Newcastle

Table 29

Sundays
26 June to 11 September

Manchester Airport, Manchester, Sheffield and Meadowhall - Doncaster - Cleethorpes and Hull
Barton-on-Humber - Cleethorpes

Station		TP	NT	NT	NT	NT	NT	XC	NT	GR	NT	TP	TP	XC	NT BHX	NT	NT	GR	GR	NT	NT	NT	NT
		◇1				A	B	◇1 C	A	1 D	E	◇1 F	◇1	◇1 G			B	1 H	1 I				A
Manchester Airport 85	d	20p47																					
Manchester Piccadilly 10	d	21 20										09 11											
Stockport 78	d	21p28																					
Sheffield 7	a	22p08																					
	d	22p11	23p27	08 00			08 45	09 21	09 36				09 52	10 21			10 26				11 05		
Meadowhall	d	22p16	23p33	08 06			08 51		09 42				09 57				10 32				11 11		
Rotherham Central	d		23p39	08 12			08 57		09 48				10 03								11 17		
Swinton (S.Yorks)	d		23p48	08 20			09 05		09a58				10 09								11 25		
Mexborough	d		23p51	08 23			09 08						10 13								11 28		
Conisbrough	d		23p55	08 27			09 12						10 17								11 32		
London Kings Cross	d																	09 10	09 30				
Doncaster 7	a	22p36	00 08	08 38			09 22						10 26				10 51	11 10	11 10		11 43		
York 8 26	a							10 33						11 35				11 36	11 36				
Doncaster 31	d	22p38			09 07	09 12	09 26			09 37	10 19		10 28				10 55					11 07	11 12
Bentley (S.Yorks) 31	a					09 15																	11 15
Adwick 31	a					09 19																	11 19
Kirk Sandall	d	22p44			09 13																	11 13	
Hatfield & Stainforth	d	22p48			09 18																	11 18	
Thorne South	d	22p53																					
Crowle	d	23p02																					
Althorpe	d	23p08																					
Scunthorpe	a	23p13											10 54										
	d	23p13											10 55										
Barnetby	d	23p28											11 09										
Hull Paragon Interchange	d														10 25								
Barton-on-Humber	a														10 50								
Barton-on-Humber	d																			11 00			
Barrow Haven	d																			11 05			
New Holland	d																			11 08			
Goxhill	d																			11 13			
Thornton Abbey	d																			11 16			
Ulceby	d																			11 20			
Habrough	d	23p36																		11 25			
Stallingborough	d																			11 30			
Healing	d																			11 33			
Great Coates	d																			11 36			
Grimsby Town	a	23p49											11 29							11 41			
	d	23p50											11 33							11 41			
Grimsby Docks	d																			11 44			
New Clee	d																			11 47			
Cleethorpes	a	00 01											11 42							11 55			
Thorne North	d				09 24		09 38				10 31											11 25	
Goole	d				09a35		09 47				10 40						11 14					11a36	
Saltmarshe	d																						
York 8 33	d									09a59						10 40							
Selby	a											10 44				10 58							
Wressle	d																						
Howden	d															11 08							
Eastrington	d																						
Gilberdyke	d						09 55				10 48						11 24						
Broomfleet	d																						
Brough	d						10 03				10 56	11 04				11 19	11 32						
Ferriby	d										11 00												
Hessle	d										11 05												
Hull	a						10 21				11 17	11 18				11 41	11 47						

A To Leeds
B To Scarborough
C To Glasgow Central
D To Edinburgh
E To Bridlington
F From Liverpool Lime Street
G from 7 August until 11 September. From Birmingham New Street to Edinburgh
H from 26 June until 31 July. To Edinburgh
I from 7 August until 11 September. To Edinburgh

Table 29

Sundays 26 June to 11 September

Manchester Airport, Manchester, Sheffield and Meadowhall - Doncaster - Cleethorpes and Hull
Barton-on-Humber - Cleethorpes

	XC	EM	NT	EM	GR	GR	NT	HT	EM	TP	XC	NT	NT	GR	TP	TP	GR	EM	NT	XC	NT	NT
	◇1 A	◇1 B	C	◇1 D	1 E	1 F		◇1	G	◇1	◇1 H		I	1 J	◇1	◇1	1 K	◇ L	C	◇1 M	BHX	
Manchester Airport 85 d										10 44												
Manchester Piccadilly d										11 18					12 02	12 18		12 44				
Stockport 78 d										11 27						12 28		12 55				
Sheffield a										12 08						13 08		13 37				
d	11 21	11 31	11 36	11 45						12 11	12 21	12 24	12 28			13 11				13 21		
Meadowhall d			11 42							12 16		12 30	12 34			13 16						
Rotherham Central d			11 49									12 36										
Swinton (S.Yorks) d			12a00									12 49										
Mexborough d												12 52										
Conisbrough d												12 56										
London Kings Cross d					10 11	10 30		10 45						11 30			12 20					
Doncaster a		11 56		12 06	12 10	12 10		12 28		12 35		13 04	12 56	13 10		13 35	13 58					
York 26 a	12 32	12 20		12 29	12 34	12 34					13 32			13 34			14 22			14 31		
Doncaster 31 d								12 31		12 37		13 05	12 58						13 12			
Bentley (S.Yorks) 31 a																			13 15			
Adwick 31 a																			13 19			
Kirk Sandall d												13 11										
Hatfield & Stainforth d												13 16										
Thorne South d																						
Crowle d																						
Althorpe d																						
Scunthorpe a										13 06												
d										13 06												
Barnetby d									12 33	13 21												
Hull Paragon Interchange d																					13 25	
Barton-on-Humber a																					13 50	
Barton-on-Humber d																						
Barrow Haven d																						
New Holland d																						
Goxhill d																						
Thornton Abbey d																						
Ulceby d																						
Habrough d									12 41	13 29												
Stallingborough d																						
Healing d																						
Great Coates d																						
Grimsby Town a									12 53	13 42												
d									13 06	13 43												
Grimsby Docks d																						
New Clee d																						
Cleethorpes a									13 15	13 56												
Thorne North d												13 22										
Goole d												13a32	13 17									
Saltmarshe d																						
York 33 d							12 05															13 40
Selby a							12 24	12 45							13 23							13 59
Wressle d																						
Howden d							12 34	12 56														14 09
Eastrington d																						
Gilberdyke d													13 25									
Broomfleet d																						
Brough d							12 46	13 08					13 33		13 41							14 21
Ferriby d													13 38									
Hessle d													13 42									
Hull a							13 06	13 25					13 57		13 59							14 40

A From Birmingham New Street to Glasgow Central
B from 26 June until 31 July. From Leicester
C To Leeds
D from 7 August until 11 September. From Leicester
E from 26 June until 31 July. To Edinburgh
F from 7 August until 11 September. To Edinburgh
G From Newark North Gate
H From Bristol Temple Meads to Edinburgh
I To Scarborough
J To Edinburgh
K To Newcastle
L To Norwich
M From Bristol Temple Meads to Glasgow Central

Table 29

Sundays 26 June to 11 September

Manchester Airport, Manchester, Sheffield and Meadowhall - Doncaster - Cleethorpes and Hull
Barton-on-Humber - Cleethorpes

	NT	GR	NT	XC	HT	NT	TP	XC	NT	NT	NT	GR	TP	XC	NT	TP	XC	NT	NT	GR	NT
	A	1 B	C	◇1 D	◇1		◇1	◇1 E			F	1 B	◇1	◇1 D	C	◇1	◇1 G		A	1 B	BHX
Manchester Airport 85 d							12 55									13 55					
Manchester Piccadilly d							13 20						14 02			14 20					
Stockport 78 d							13 28									14 28					
Sheffield a							14 08									15 08					
d	13 24		13 36	13 51			14 11	14 21	14 22		14 28			14 51		15 11	15 21	15 24	15 28		
Meadowhall d	13 30		13 42				14 16		14 28		14 34					15 16		15 30	15 34		
Rotherham Central d	13 36		13 49						14 35									15 37			
Swinton (S.Yorks) d	13 47		13a57						14 46									15 47			
Mexborough d	13 50								14 49									15 50			
Conisbrough d	13 54								14 53									15 54			
London Kings Cross d		12 30			12 45							13 30								14 30	
Doncaster a	14 02	14 09		14 13	14 25		14 35		15 03		14 56	15 10		15 13		15 35		16 04	15 56	16 11	
York 26 a		14 36		14 41				15 31				15 35		15 44			16 32			16 36	
Doncaster 31 d	14 05				14 27		14 37		15 05		14 59				15 12	15 37			15 56		
Bentley (S.Yorks) 31 a															15 15						
Adwick 31 a															15 19						
Kirk Sandall d									15 11												
Hatfield & Stainforth d									15 16												
Thorne South d																					
Crowle d																					
Althorpe d																					
Scunthorpe a							15 02									16 02					
d							15 03									16 03					
Barnetby d							15 17									16 17					
Hull Paragon Interchange d																					15 30
Barton-on-Humber a																					15 55
Barton-on-Humber d						14 00															
Barrow Haven d						14 05															
New Holland d						14 08															
Goxhill d						14 13															
Thornton Abbey d						14 16															
Ulceby d						14 20															
Habrough d						14 25										16 26					
Stallingborough d						14 30															
Healing d						14 33															
Great Coates d						14 36															
Grimsby Town a						14 41	15 37									16 39					
d						14 41	15 38									16 40					
Grimsby Docks d						14 44															
New Clee d						14 47															
Cleethorpes a						14 55	15 51									16 52					
Thorne North d									15 24										16 10		
Goole d	14 25								15a33		15 19								16 19		
Saltmarshe d																					
York 33 d										14 49											
Selby a					14 41					15 08			15 22								
Wressle d																					
Howden d					14 52					15 18											
Eastrington d																					
Gilberdyke d	14 33										15 29								16 27		
Broomfleet d																					
Brough d	14 41				15 04					15 30	15 37		15 40						16 35		
Ferriby d																					
Hessle d																					
Hull a	15 01				15 21					15 49	15 56		15 59						16 53		

A To Bridlington
B To Edinburgh
C To Leeds
D From Birmingham New Street to Newcastle
E From Plymouth to Aberdeen
F To Scarborough
G From Plymouth to Glasgow Central

Table 29

Sundays
26 June to 11 September

Manchester Airport, Manchester, Sheffield and Meadowhall - Doncaster - Cleethorpes and Hull
Barton-on-Humber - Cleethorpes

	NT	XC	NT	HT	NT	EM	TP	XC	XC	NT	NT	GR	TP	NT	XC	NT	NT	TP	XC	NT	NT	GR
		◇1		◇1			◇1	◇1	◇1			1	◇1		◇1			◇1	◇1			1
	A	B		⊠		C		D	E		F	G			B		A		H		I	G
Manchester Airport 85 d							14 55											15 55				
Manchester Piccadilly 10 d							15 20						16 02					16 20				
Stockport 78 d							15 28											16 28				
Sheffield 7 a							16 08											17 08				
d	15 36	15 51					16 11	16 21	16 21	16 24	16 28			16 36	16 51			17 11	17 21	17 25	17 28	
Meadowhall d	15 42						16 16			16 30	16 34			16 42				17 16		17 31	17 34	
Rotherham Central d	15 50									16 37				16 49						17 37		
Swinton (S.Yorks) d	15a58									16 47				16 58						17 47		
Mexborough d										16 50										17 50		
Conisbrough d										16 54										17 54		
London Kings Cross d				14 45								15 30										16 30
Doncaster 7 a		16 15		16 28			16 35			17 03	16 56	17 11			17 13			17 35		18 05	17 55	18 10
York 8 26 a		16 44						17 31	17 32			17 37		17 59	17 42				18 32			18 35
Doncaster 31 d				16 31			16 37			17 04	16 58						17 14	17 37			17 57	
Bentley (S.Yorks) 31 a																	17 17					
Adwick 31 a																	17 21					
Kirk Sandall d										17 10												
Hatfield & Stainforth d										17 15												
Thorne South d																						
Crowle d																						
Althorpe d																						
Scunthorpe a							17 02											18 02				
d							17 03											18 03				
Barnetby d						16 58	17 17											18 17				
Hull Paragon Interchange d																						
Barton-on-Humber a																						
Barton-on-Humber d					16 15																	
Barrow Haven d					16 20																	
New Holland d					16 23																	
Goxhill d					16 28																	
Thornton Abbey d					16 31																	
Ulceby d					16 35																	
Habrough d					16 40	17 06																
Stallingborough d					16 45																	
Healing d					16 48																	
Great Coates d					16 51																	
Grimsby Town a					16 56	17 18	17 37											18 37				
d					16 56	17 19	17 38											18 38				
Grimsby Docks d					16 59																	
New Clee d					17 02																	
Cleethorpes a					17 10	17 28	17 50											18 50				
Thorne North d										17 24												
Goole d										17a33	17 17										18 16	
Saltmarshe d																						
York 8 33 d			16 06													17 11						
Selby a			16 24	16 45									17 23			17 30						
Wressle d																						
Howden d			16 34	16 56												17 41						
Eastrington d																						
Gilberdyke d											17 25										18 24	
Broomfleet d																						
Brough d			16 46	17 08							17 33		17 41			17 53					18 32	
Ferriby d																						
Hessle d																						
Hull a			17 07	17 25							17 51		17 59			18 12					18 48	

A To Leeds
B From Reading to Newcastle
C From Nottingham
D from 7 August until 11 September. From Penzance to Edinburgh
E from 26 June until 31 July. From Plymouth to Edinburgh
F To Scarborough
G To Edinburgh
H From Penzance to Glasgow Central
I To Bridlington

Table 29

Sundays
26 June to 11 September

Manchester Airport, Manchester, Sheffield and Meadowhall - Doncaster - Cleethorpes and Hull
Barton-on-Humber - Cleethorpes

	NT	XC	NT BHX	EM	TP	XC	NT	NT	GR	GR	TP	XC	NT	NT	NT	NT	HT	TP	TP	XC	NT
		◇1			◇1	◇1			1	1	◇1	◇1					◇1	◇1	◇1	◇1	
	A	B		C		D		E		F		G				A	⊠			D	
Manchester Airport 85 d					16 55													17 55			
Manchester Piccadilly 10 d					17 20						18 02							18 20	19 02		
Stockport 78 d					17 28													18 28			
Sheffield 7 a					18 08													19 08			
d	17 36	17 51			18 11	18 21	18 25	18 28				18 51	18 57					19 11		19 21	19 29
Meadowhall d	17 44				18 16		18 31	18 35					19 05					19 16			19 35
Rotherham Central d	17 50						18 37						19 11								19 41
Swinton (S.Yorks) d	17a58						18 48						19 19								19 49
Mexborough d							18 51														19 52
Conisbrough d							18 55														19 56
London Kings Cross d									17 20	17 30							17 45				
Doncaster 7 a		18 13			18 35		19 06	18 54	19 03	19 09		19 15					19 28	19 35			20 07
York 8 26 a		19 21				19 32				19 38		19 44	20 18							20 32	
Doncaster 31 d					18 37			18 55	19 05							19 27	19 31	19 37			
Bentley (S.Yorks) 31 a																19 30					
Adwick 31 a																19 34					
Kirk Sandall d								19 01													
Hatfield & Stainforth d								19 06													
Thorne South d																					
Crowle d																					
Althorpe d																					
Scunthorpe a					19 02													20 02			
d					19 03													20 03			
Barnetby d				18 53	19 17													20 17			
Hull Paragon Interchange d			18 30																		
Barton-on-Humber a			18 55																		
Barton-on-Humber d															19 15						
Barrow Haven d															19 20						
New Holland d															19 23						
Goxhill d															19 28						
Thornton Abbey d															19 31						
Ulceby d															19 35						
Habrough d				19 01	19 26										19 40						
Stallingborough d															19 45						
Healing d															19 48						
Great Coates d															19 51						
Grimsby Town a				19 13	19 39										19 56			20 37			
d				19 13	19 40										19 56			20 38			
Grimsby Docks d															19 59						
New Clee d															20 02						
Cleethorpes a				19 24	19 52										20 10			20 50			
Thorne North d								19 12													
Goole d								19 21													
Saltmarshe d																					
York 8 33 d														19 10							
Selby a									19 24		19 29			19 35			19 45		20 17		
Wressle d																					
Howden d														19 46			19 56				
Eastrington d																					
Gilberdyke d								19 29													
Broomfleet d																					
Brough d								19 37	19 46		19 48			19 58			20 08		20 36		
Ferriby d																					
Hessle d																					
Hull a								19 55	20 06		20 06			20 17			20 25		20 54		

A To Leeds
B From Reading to Newcastle
C From Newark North Gate
D From Newquay to Edinburgh
E To Beverley
F To Edinburgh
G From Reading to Edinburgh

Table 29

Sundays 26 June to 11 September

Manchester Airport, Manchester, Sheffield and Meadowhall - Doncaster - Cleethorpes and Hull
Barton-on-Humber - Cleethorpes

	GR	NT	XC	NT	TP	TP	XC	NT	GR	XC	HT	TP	NT	NT	NT	NT	TP	NT	NT	TP	GR	NT
	1 A	B	◇1 C		◇1	◇1	◇1 D		1 A	◇1 C	◇1	◇1		B		B	◇1 E			◇1	1 A	
Manchester Airport 85 ✈ d					18 55							19 55										
Manchester Piccadilly 10 d					19 20	20 06						20 18										
Stockport 78 d					19 28							20 27										
Sheffield 7 a					20 08							21 08										
d		19 36	19 51	20 02	20 11		20 21	20 28		20 51		21 11			21 24	21 36		22 13	22 26	22 30		23 34
Meadowhall d		19 42		20 09	20 16			20 34				21 16			21 30	21 42		22 19	22 32	22 35		23 40
Rotherham Central d		19 49						20 40							21 37	21 48			22 38			23 47
Swinton (S.Yorks) d		19a57						20 48							21 47	21a56			22 48			23 55
Mexborough d								20 51							21 50				22 51			23 58
Conisbrough d								20 55							21 54				22 55			00 02
London Kings Cross d	18 30								19 30		19 45										22 00	
Doncaster 7 a	20 11		20 16	20 30	20 35			21 05	21 13	21 19	21 29	21 35			22 03			22 38	23 05	22 56	23 42	00 13
York 8 26 a	20 36		20 45				21 32		21 38	21 44											00 33	
Doncaster 31 d				20 30	20 37			21 07			21 31	21 37		21 49	22 04			22 41		22 58		
Bentley (S.Yorks) 31 a														21 52								
Adwick 31 a														21 56								
Kirk Sandall d								21 13														
Hatfield & Stainforth d								21 18														
Thorne South d																						
Crowle d																						
Althorpe d																						
Scunthorpe a					21 02							22 02								23 23		
d					21 03							22 03								23 24		
Barnetby d					21 17							22 17								23 38		
Hull Paragon Interchange d																						
Barton-on-Humber a																						
Barton-on-Humber d																						
Barrow Haven d																						
New Holland d																						
Goxhill d																						
Thornton Abbey d																						
Ulceby d																						
Habrough d					21 26							22 26										
Stallingborough d																						
Healing d																						
Great Coates d																						
Grimsby Town a					21 39							22 39								23 57		
d					21 40							22 40								23 58		
Grimsby Docks d																						
New Clee d																						
Cleethorpes a					21 52							22 52								00 09		
Thorne North d								21 24										22 53				
Goole d				20 49				21a34							22 23			23 02				
Saltmarshe d																						
York 8 33 d													21 41									
Selby a						21 38					21 45		22 00									
Wressle d																						
Howden d											21 56		22 10									
Eastrington d																						
Gilberdyke d				20 57											22 31			23 10				
Broomfleet d																						
Brough d				21 05		21 58					22 08		22 22		22 39		23 02	23 18				
Ferriby d																						
Hessle d																						
Hull a				21 23		22 15					22 25		22 36		22 56		23 19	23 39				

A To Newcastle
B To Leeds
C From Reading to Newcastle
D From Plymouth
E From Leeds

Table 29

Sundays 18 September to 23 October

Manchester Airport, Manchester, Sheffield and Meadowhall - Doncaster - Cleethorpes and Hull
Barton-on-Humber - Cleethorpes

	TP	NT	NT	NT	NT	NT	XC	NT	GR	NT	TP	XC	TP	NT	NT	GR	NT	NT	NT	XC	NT	EM
	◇1				A	B	◇1 C	A	1 D	E	◇1	◇1 F	◇1 G		B	1 D			A	◇1 H	A	◇1 I
Manchester Airport 85 ✈ d	20p47																					
Manchester Piccadilly 10 d	21 20																					
Stockport 78 d	21p28																					
Sheffield 7 a	22p08																					
d	22p11	23p27	08 00			08 45	09 21	09 36			09 52	10 21			10 26		11 05			11 21	11 36	11 45
Meadowhall d	22p16	23p33	08 06			08 51		09 42			09 57				10 32		11 11				11 42	
Rotherham Central d		23p39	08 12			08 57		09 48			10 03						11 17				11 49	
Swinton (S.Yorks) d		23p48	08 20			09 05		09a58			10 09						11 25				12a00	
Mexborough d		23p51	08 23			09 08					10 13						11 28					
Conisbrough d		23p55	08 27			09 12					10 17						11 32					
London Kings Cross d																09 30						
Doncaster 7 a	22p36	00 08	08 38			09 22					10 26				10 51	11 10	11 43					12 06
York 8 26 a							10 33					11 35				11 36				12 32		12 29
Doncaster 31 d	22p38			09 07	09 12	09 26			09 37	10 19	10 28				10 55			11 07	11 12			
Bentley (S.Yorks) 31 a					09 15														11 15			
Adwick 31 a					09 19														11 19			
Kirk Sandall d	22p44			09 13														11 13				
Hatfield & Stainforth d	22p48			09 18														11 18				
Thorne South d	22p53																					
Crowle d	23p02																					
Althorpe d	23p08																					
Scunthorpe a	23p13										10 54											
d	23p13										10 55											
Barnetby d	23p28										11 09											
Hull Paragon Interchange d																						
Barton-on-Humber a																						
Barton-on-Humber d																						
Barrow Haven d																						
New Holland d																						
Goxhill d																						
Thornton Abbey d																						
Ulceby d																						
Habrough d	23p36																					
Stallingborough d																						
Healing d																						
Great Coates d																						
Grimsby Town a	23p49										11 29											
d	23p50										11 33											
Grimsby Docks d																						
New Clee d																						
Cleethorpes a	00 01										11 42											
Thorne North d				09 24		09 38				10 31								11 25				
Goole d				09a35		09 47				10 40					11 14			11a36				
Saltmarshe d																						
York 8 33 d									09a59					10 40								
Selby a														10 58								
Wressle d																						
Howden d														11 08								
Eastrington d																						
Gilberdyke d						09 55				10 48					11 24							
Broomfleet d																						
Brough d						10 03				10 56			11 04	11 19	11 32							
Ferriby d										11 00												
Hessle d										11 05												
Hull a						10 21				11 17			11 21	11 41	11 47							

A To Leeds
B To Scarborough
C To Glasgow Central
D To Edinburgh
E To Bridlington
F From Birmingham New Street to Edinburgh
G From Leeds
H From Birmingham New Street to Glasgow Central
I From Leicester

Table 29

Sundays
18 September to 23 October

Manchester Airport, Manchester, Sheffield and Meadowhall - Doncaster - Cleethorpes and Hull
Barton-on-Humber - Cleethorpes

	GR	HT	TP	NT	NT	GR	TP	GR	EM	NT	XC	TP	NT	NT	GR	NT	XC	HT	TP	XC	NT	NT
	A	◇1	◇1		B	A	◇1	C	◇ D	E	◇1 F	◇1 G		H	A	E	◇1 I	◇1	◇1	◇1 J		B
Manchester Airport 85 ✈ d			10 44																12 55			
Manchester Piccadilly 10 ⇌ d			11 18				12 18		12 44										13 20			
Stockport 78 d			11 27				12 28		12 55										13 28			
Sheffield 7 ⇌ a			12 08				13 08		13 37										14 08			
d			12 11	12 24	12 28		13 11				13 21			13 24		13 36	13 51		14 11	14 21	14 22	14 28
Meadowhall ⇌ d			12 16	12 30	12 34		13 16							13 30		13 42			14 16		14 28	14 34
Rotherham Central d				12 36										13 36		13 49					14 35	
Swinton (S.Yorks) d				12 49										13 47		13a57					14 46	
Mexborough d				12 52										13 50							14 49	
Conisbrough d				12 56										13 54							14 53	
London Kings Cross d	10 30	10 45				11 30		12 20							12 30			12 45				
Doncaster 7 a	12 10	12 28	12 35	13 04	12 56	13 10	13 35	13 58						14 02	14 09		14 13	14 25	14 35		15 03	14 56
York 8 26 a	12 34					13 34		14 22			14 31				14 36		14 41			15 31		
Doncaster 31 d		12 31	12 37	13 05	12 58					13 12				14 05				14 27	14 37		15 05	14 59
Bentley (S.Yorks) 31 a										13 15												
Adwick 31 a										13 19												
Kirk Sandall d				13 11																	15 11	
Hatfield & Stainforth d				13 16																	15 16	
Thorne South d																						
Crowle d																						
Althorpe d																						
Scunthorpe a			13 06																15 02			
d			13 06																15 03			
Barnetby d			13 21																15 17			
Hull Paragon Interchange d																						
Barton-on-Humber a																						
Barton-on-Humber d																						
Barrow Haven d																						
New Holland d																						
Goxhill d																						
Thornton Abbey d																						
Ulceby d																						
Habrough d			13 29																			
Stallingborough d																						
Healing d																						
Great Coates d																						
Grimsby Town a			13 42																15 37			
d			13 43																15 38			
Grimsby Docks d																						
New Clee d																						
Cleethorpes a			13 56																15 51			
Thorne North d				13 22																	15 24	
Goole d				13a32	13 17									14 25							15a33	15 19
Saltmarshe d																						
York 8 33 d													13 40									
Selby a		12 45											13 59					14 41				
Wressle d																						
Howden d		12 56											14 09					14 52				
Eastrington d																						
Gilberdyke d					13 25									14 33								15 29
Broomfleet d																						
Brough d		13 08			13 33							13 41	14 21	14 41				15 04				15 37
Ferriby d					13 38																	
Hessle d					13 42																	
Hull a		13 25			13 57							13 59	14 40	15 01				15 21				15 56

A To Edinburgh
B To Scarborough
C To Newcastle
D To Norwich
E To Leeds
F From Bristol Parkway to Glasgow Central
G From Huddersfield
H To Bridlington
I From Birmingham New Street to Newcastle
J From Bristol Parkway to Aberdeen

Table 29

Sundays
18 September to 23 October

Manchester Airport, Manchester, Sheffield and Meadowhall - Doncaster - Cleethorpes and Hull
Barton-on-Humber - Cleethorpes

	GR	XC	NT	TP	XC	NT	TP	NT	GR	NT	XC	NT	HT	TP	XC	NT	NT	GR	NT	NT	TP
	A	◇1 B	C	◇1	◇1 D		◇1 E	F	A	C	◇1 B		◇1	◇1	◇1 G		H	A		C	◇1
Manchester Airport 85 ✈ d				13 55										14 55							15 55
Manchester Piccadilly 10 ⇌ d				14 20										15 20							16 20
Stockport 78 d				14 28										15 28							16 28
Sheffield 7 ⇌ a				15 08										16 08							17 08
d		14 51		15 11	15 21	15 24		15 28		15 36	15 51			16 11	16 21	16 24	16 28		16 36		17 11
Meadowhall ⇌ d				15 16		15 30		15 34		15 42				16 16		16 30	16 34		16 42		17 16
Rotherham Central d						15 37				15 50						16 37			16 49		
Swinton (S.Yorks) d						15 47				15a58						16 47			16 58		
Mexborough d						15 50										16 50					
Conisbrough d						15 54										16 54					
London Kings Cross d	13 30								14 30				14 45					15 30			
Doncaster 7 a	15 10	15 13		15 35		16 04		15 56	16 11		16 15		16 28	16 35		17 03	16 56	17 11			17 35
York 8 26 a	15 35	15 44			16 32				16 36		16 44				17 32			17 37	17 59		
Doncaster 31 d			15 12	15 37				15 56					16 31	16 37		17 04	16 58			17 14	17 37
Bentley (S.Yorks) 31 a			15 15																	17 17	
Adwick 31 a			15 19																	17 21	
Kirk Sandall d																17 10					
Hatfield & Stainforth d																17 15					
Thorne South d																					
Crowle d																					
Althorpe d																					
Scunthorpe a				16 02										17 02							18 02
d				16 03										17 03							18 03
Barnetby d				16 17										17 17							18 17
Hull Paragon Interchange d																					
Barton-on-Humber a																					
Barton-on-Humber d																					
Barrow Haven d																					
New Holland d																					
Goxhill d																					
Thornton Abbey d																					
Ulceby d																					
Habrough d				16 26																	
Stallingborough d																					
Healing d																					
Great Coates d																					
Grimsby Town a				16 39										17 37							18 37
d				16 40										17 38							18 38
Grimsby Docks d																					
New Clee d																					
Cleethorpes a				16 52										17 50							18 50
Thorne North d								16 10								17 24					
Goole d								16 19								17a33	17 17				
Saltmarshe d																					
York 8 33 d												16 06									
Selby a												16 24	16 45								
Wressle d																					
Howden d												16 34	16 56								
Eastrington d																					
Gilberdyke d								16 27									17 25				
Broomfleet d																					
Brough d							15 41	16 35				16 46	17 08				17 33				
Ferriby d																					
Hessle d																					
Hull a							15 59	16 53				17 07	17 25				17 51				

A To Edinburgh
B From Birmingham New Street to Newcastle
C To Leeds
D From Bristol Parkway to Glasgow Central
E From Huddersfield
F To Bridlington
G From Bristol Parkway to Edinburgh
H To Scarborough

Table 29

Sundays
18 September to 23 October

Manchester Airport, Manchester, Sheffield and Meadowhall - Doncaster - Cleethorpes and Hull
Barton-on-Humber - Cleethorpes

		XC	NT	TP	NT	GR	NT	XC	TP	XC	NT	NT	GR	GR	XC	NT	NT	TP	NT	HT	TP	XC	NT
		◇1 A		◇1 B	C	1 D	E	◇1 F	◇1	◇1 G		H	1	1 D	◇1 I		E	◇1 B		◇1	◇1	◇1 G	
Manchester Airport 85	d								16 55												17 55		
Manchester Piccadilly 10	d								17 20												18 20		
Stockport 78	d								17 28												18 28		
Sheffield 7	a								18 08												19 08		
	d	17 21	17 25		17 28		17 36	17 51	18 11	18 21	18 25	18 28			18 51	18 57					19 11	19 21	19 29
Meadowhall	d		17 31		17 34		17 44		18 16		18 31	18 35				19 05					19 16		19 35
Rotherham Central	d		17 37				17 50				18 37					19 11							19 41
Swinton (S.Yorks)	d		17 47				17a58				18 48					19 19							19 49
Mexborough	d		17 50								18 51												19 52
Conisbrough	d		17 54								18 55												19 56
London Kings Cross	d					16 30							17 20	17 30						17 45			
Doncaster 7	a		18 05		17 55	18 10		18 13	18 35		19 06	18 54	19 03	19 09	19 15					19 28	19 35		20 07
York 8 26	a	18 32				18 35		19 21		19 32				19 38	19 44	20 18						20 32	
Doncaster 31	d				17 57				18 37			18 55	19 05				19 27			19 31	19 37		
Bentley (S.Yorks) 31	a																19 30						
Adwick 31	a																19 34						
Kirk Sandall	d											19 01											
Hatfield & Stainforth	d											19 06											
Thorne South	d																						
Crowle	d																						
Althorpe	d																						
Scunthorpe	a								19 02												20 02		
	d								19 03												20 03		
Barnetby	d								19 17												20 17		
Hull Paragon Interchange	d																						
Barton-on-Humber	a																						
Barton-on-Humber	d																						
Barrow Haven	d																						
New Holland	d																						
Goxhill	d																						
Thornton Abbey	d																						
Ulceby	d																						
Habrough	d								19 26														
Stallingborough	d																						
Healing	d																						
Great Coates	d																						
Grimsby Town	a								19 39												20 37		
	d								19 40												20 38		
Grimsby Docks	d																						
New Clee	d																						
Cleethorpes	a								19 52												20 50		
Thorne North	d											19 12											
Goole	d				18 16							19 21											
Saltmarshe	d																						
York 8 33	d																		19 10				
Selby	a												19 24						19 35	19 45			
Wressle	d																						
Howden	d																		19 46	19 56			
Eastrington	d																						
Gilberdyke	d				18 24							19 29											
Broomfleet	d																						
Brough	d			17 41	18 32							19 37	19 46					19 51	19 58	20 08			
Ferriby	d																						
Hessle	d																						
Hull	a			17 59	18 48							19 55	20 06					20 06	20 17	20 25			

A From Bristol Parkway to Glasgow Central
B From Huddersfield
C To Bridlington
D To Edinburgh
E To Leeds
F From Reading to Newcastle
G From Bristol Parkway to Edinburgh
H To Beverley
I From Reading to Edinburgh

Table 29

Sundays
18 September to 23 October

Manchester Airport, Manchester, Sheffield and Meadowhall - Doncaster - Cleethorpes and Hull
Barton-on-Humber - Cleethorpes

		GR	NT	XC	TP	NT	TP	XC	NT	GR	XC	TP	HT	TP	NT	NT	NT	NT	TP	NT	NT	TP
		1 A	B	◇1 C	◇1 D		◇1	◇1 E		1 A	◇1 C	◇1 D	◇1	◇1		B		B	◇1 F			◇1
Manchester Airport 85	d						18 55							19 55								
Manchester Piccadilly 10	d						19 20							20 18								
Stockport 78	d						19 28							20 27								
Sheffield 7	a						20 08							21 08								
	d		19 36	19 51		20 02	20 11	20 21	20 28		20 51			21 11			21 24	21 36		22 13	22 26	22 30
Meadowhall	d		19 42			20 09	20 16		20 34					21 16			21 30	21 42		22 19	22 32	22 35
Rotherham Central	d		19 49						20 40								21 37	21 48			22 38	
Swinton (S.Yorks)	d		19a57						20 48								21 47	21a56			22 48	
Mexborough	d								20 51								21 50				22 51	
Conisbrough	d								20 55								21 54				22 55	
London Kings Cross	d	18 30								19 30			19 45									
Doncaster 7	a	20 11		20 16		20 30	20 35		21 05	21 13	21 19		21 29	21 35			22 03			22 38	23 05	22 56
York 8 26	a	20 36		20 45				21 32		21 38	21 44											
Doncaster 31	d					20 30	20 37		21 07				21 31	21 37		21 49	22 04			22 41		22 58
Bentley (S.Yorks) 31	a															21 52						
Adwick 31	a															21 56						
Kirk Sandall	d								21 13													
Hatfield & Stainforth	d								21 18													
Thorne South	d																					
Crowle	d																					
Althorpe	d																					
Scunthorpe	a						21 02							22 02								23 23
	d						21 03							22 03								23 24
Barnetby	d						21 17							22 17								23 38
Hull Paragon Interchange	d																					
Barton-on-Humber	a																					
Barton-on-Humber	d																					
Barrow Haven	d																					
New Holland	d																					
Goxhill	d																					
Thornton Abbey	d																					
Ulceby	d																					
Habrough	d						21 26							22 26								
Stallingborough	d																					
Healing	d																					
Great Coates	d																					
Grimsby Town	a						21 39							22 39								23 57
	d						21 40							22 40								23 58
Grimsby Docks	d																					
New Clee	d																					
Cleethorpes	a						21 52							22 52								00 09
Thorne North	d								21 24											22 53		
Goole	d					20 49			21a34								22 23			23 02		
Saltmarshe	d																					
York 8 33	d														21 41							
Selby	a												21 45		22 00							
Wressle	d																					
Howden	d												21 56		22 10							
Eastrington	d																					
Gilberdyke	d					20 57											22 31			23 10		
Broomfleet	d																					
Brough	d				20 36	21 05						21 58	22 08		22 22		22 39		23 02	23 18		
Ferriby	d																					
Hessle	d																					
Hull	a				20 54	21 23						22 15	22 25		22 36		22 56		23 19	23 39		

A To Newcastle
B To Leeds
C From Reading to Newcastle
D From Huddersfield
E From Bristol Parkway
F From Leeds

Table 29

Sundays
18 September to 23 October

Manchester Airport, Manchester, Sheffield and Meadowhall - Doncaster - Cleethorpes and Hull
Barton-on-Humber - Cleethorpes

Station			GR	NT
			1	
			A	
Manchester Airport	85 ✈	d		
Manchester Piccadilly 10		d		
Stockport	78	d		
Sheffield 7		a		
		d		23 34
Meadowhall		d		23 40
Rotherham Central		d		23 47
Swinton (S.Yorks)		d		23 55
Mexborough		d		23 58
Conisbrough		d		00 02
London Kings Cross		d	22 00	
Doncaster 7		a	23 42	00 13
York 8	26	a	00 33	
Doncaster	31	d		
Bentley (S.Yorks)	31	a		
Adwick	31	a		
Kirk Sandall		d		
Hatfield & Stainforth		d		
Thorne South		d		
Crowle		d		
Althorpe		d		
Scunthorpe		a		
		d		
Barnetby		d		
Hull Paragon Interchange		d		
Barton-on-Humber		a		
Barton-on-Humber		d		
Barrow Haven		d		
New Holland		d		
Goxhill		d		
Thornton Abbey		d		
Ulceby		d		
Habrough		d		
Stallingborough		d		
Healing		d		
Great Coates		d		
Grimsby Town		a		
		d		
Grimsby Docks		d		
New Clee		d		
Cleethorpes		a		
Thorne North		d		
Goole		d		
Saltmarshe		d		
York 8	33	d		
Selby		a		
Wressle		d		
Howden		d		
Eastrington		d		
Gilberdyke		d		
Broomfleet		d		
Brough		d		
Ferriby		d		
Hessle		d		
Hull		a		

A To Newcastle

Table 29

Sundays
from 30 October

Manchester Airport, Manchester, Sheffield and Meadowhall - Doncaster - Cleethorpes and Hull
Barton-on-Humber - Cleethorpes

Station			TP	NT	NT	NT	NT	NT	XC	NT	GR	NT	TP	TP	XC	NT	NT	GR	NT	NT	NT	XC	EM	GR
			◇1						◇1		1		◇1	◇1	◇1			1				◇1	◇1	1
							A	B	C	A	D	E	F		G		B	D			A	H	I	D
Manchester Airport	85 ✈	d	20p47																					
Manchester Piccadilly 10		d	21 20										09 11											
Stockport	78	d	21p28																					
Sheffield 7		a	22p08																					
		d	22p11	23p27	08 00			08 45	09 21	09 36				09 52	10 21		10 26		11 05			11 21	11 31	
Meadowhall		d	22p16	23p33	08 06			08 51		09 42				09 57			10 32		11 11					
Rotherham Central		d		23p39	08 12			08 57		09 48				10 03					11 17					
Swinton (S.Yorks)		d		23p48	08 20			09 05		09a58				10 09					11 25					
Mexborough		d		23p51	08 23			09 08						10 13					11 28					
Conisbrough		d		23p55	08 27			09 12						10 17					11 32					
London Kings Cross		d																09 30						10 30
Doncaster 7		a	22p36	00 08	08 38			09 22						10 26			10 51	11 10	11 43				11 56	12 10
York 8	26	a							10 33						11 35			11 36				12 32	12 20	12 34
Doncaster	31	d	22p38			09 07	09 12	09 26			09 37	10 19		10 28			10 55			11 07	11 12			
Bentley (S.Yorks)	31	a					09 15														11 15			
Adwick	31	a					09 19														11 19			
Kirk Sandall		d	22p44			09 13														11 13				
Hatfield & Stainforth		d	22p48			09 18														11 18				
Thorne South		d	22p53																					
Crowle		d	23p02																					
Althorpe		d	23p08																					
Scunthorpe		a	23p13											10 54										
		d	23p13											10 55										
Barnetby		d	23p28											11 09										
Hull Paragon Interchange		d																						
Barton-on-Humber		a																						
Barton-on-Humber		d																						
Barrow Haven		d																						
New Holland		d																						
Goxhill		d																						
Thornton Abbey		d																						
Ulceby		d																						
Habrough		d	23p36																					
Stallingborough		d																						
Healing		d																						
Great Coates		d																						
Grimsby Town		a	23p49											11 29										
		d	23p50											11 33										
Grimsby Docks		d																						
New Clee		d																						
Cleethorpes		a	00 01											11 42										
Thorne North		d				09 24		09 38				10 31								11 25				
Goole		d				09a35		09 47				10 40					11 14			11a36				
Saltmarshe		d																						
York 8	33	d									09a59					10 40								
Selby		a											10 44			10 58								
Wressle		d																						
Howden		d														11 08								
Eastrington		d																						
Gilberdyke		d						09 55				10 48					11 24							
Broomfleet		d																						
Brough		d						10 03				10 56	11 04			11 19	11 32							
Ferriby		d										11 00												
Hessle		d										11 05												
Hull		a						10 21				11 17	11 18			11 41	11 47							

A To Leeds
B To Scarborough
C To Glasgow Central
D To Edinburgh
E To Bridlington
F From Liverpool Lime Street
G From Birmingham New Street to Edinburgh
H From Birmingham New Street to Glasgow Central
I From Leicester

Table 29

Sundays from 30 October

Manchester Airport, Manchester, Sheffield and Meadowhall - Doncaster - Cleethorpes and Hull
Barton-on-Humber - Cleethorpes

	HT	NT	TP	XC	NT	NT	GR	TP	TP	GR	EM	NT	XC	NT	NT	GR	NT	XC	HT	TP	XC	NT
	◇1	A	◇1	◇1 B		C	1 D	◇1	◇1	1 E	◇ F	A	◇1 G		H	1 D	A	◇1 I	◇1	◇1	◇1 J	
Manchester Airport 85 ✈ d			10 44																	12 55		
Manchester Piccadilly 10 d			11 18					11 58	12 18		12 44									13 20		
Stockport 78 d			11 27						12 28		12 55									13 28		
Sheffield 7 a			12 08						13 08		13 37									14 08		
d		11 36	12 11	12 21	12 24	12 28			13 11				13 21		13 24		13 36	13 51		14 11	14 21	14 22
Meadowhall d		11 42	12 16		12 30	12 34			13 16						13 30		13 42			14 16		14 28
Rotherham Central d		11 49			12 36										13 36		13 49					14 35
Swinton (S.Yorks) d		12a00			12 49										13 47		13a57					14 46
Mexborough d					12 52										13 50							14 49
Conisbrough d					12 56										13 54							14 53
London Kings Cross d	10 45						11 30			12 20						12 30			12 45			
Doncaster 7 a	12 28		12 35		13 04	12 56	13 10		13 35	13 58					14 02	14 09		14 13	14 25	14 35		15 03
York 8 26 a				13 32			13 34			14 22			14 31			14 36		14 41			15 31	
Doncaster 31 d	12 31		12 37		13 05	12 58						13 12			14 05				14 27	14 37		15 05
Bentley (S.Yorks) 31 a												13 15										
Adwick 31 a												13 19										
Kirk Sandall d					13 11																	15 11
Hatfield & Stainforth d					13 16																	15 16
Thorne South d																						
Crowle d																						
Althorpe d																						
Scunthorpe a			13 06																	15 02		
d			13 06																	15 03		
Barnetby d			13 21																	15 17		
Hull Paragon Interchange d																						
Barton-on-Humber a																						
Barton-on-Humber d																						
Barrow Haven d																						
New Holland d																						
Goxhill d																						
Thornton Abbey d																						
Ulceby d																						
Habrough d			13 29																			
Stallingborough d																						
Healing d																						
Great Coates d																						
Grimsby Town a			13 42																	15 37		
d			13 43																	15 38		
Grimsby Docks d																						
New Clee d																						
Cleethorpes a			13 56																	15 51		
Thorne North d					13 22																	15 24
Goole d					13a32	13 17									14 25							15a33
Saltmarshe d																						
York 8 33 d														13 40								
Selby a	12 45							13 23						13 59					14 41			
Wressle d																						
Howden d	12 56													14 09					14 52			
Eastrington d																						
Gilberdyke d						13 25									14 33							
Broomfleet d																						
Brough d	13 08					13 33		13 41						14 21	14 41				15 04			
Ferriby d						13 38																
Hessle d						13 42																
Hull a	13 25					13 57		13 59						14 40	15 01				15 21			

A To Leeds
B From Bristol Temple Meads to Edinburgh
C To Scarborough
D To Edinburgh
E To Newcastle
F To Norwich
G From Bristol Temple Meads to Glasgow Central
H To Bridlington
I From Birmingham New Street to Newcastle
J From Plymouth to Aberdeen

Table 29

Sundays from 30 October

Manchester Airport, Manchester, Sheffield and Meadowhall - Doncaster - Cleethorpes and Hull
Barton-on-Humber - Cleethorpes

	NT	GR	TP	XC	NT	TP	XC	NT	NT	GR	NT	XC	NT	HT	TP	XC	NT	NT	GR	TP	NT
	A	1 B	◇1	◇1 C	D	◇1	◇1 E		F	1 B	D	◇1 C		◇1	◇1	◇1 G		A	1 B	◇1	
Manchester Airport 85 ✈ d						13 55									14 55						
Manchester Piccadilly 10 d			14 02			14 20									15 20					16 02	
Stockport 78 d						14 28									15 28						
Sheffield 7 a						15 08									16 08						
d	14 28			14 51		15 11	15 21	15 24	15 28		15 36	15 51			16 11	16 21	16 24	16 28			16 36
Meadowhall d	14 34					15 16		15 30	15 34		15 42				16 16		16 30	16 34			16 42
Rotherham Central d								15 37			15 50						16 37				16 49
Swinton (S.Yorks) d								15 47			15a58						16 47				16 58
Mexborough d								15 50									16 50				
Conisbrough d								15 54									16 54				
London Kings Cross d		13 30								14 30				14 45					15 30		
Doncaster 7 a	14 56	15 10		15 13		15 35		16 04	15 56	16 11		16 15		16 28	16 35		17 03	16 56	17 11		
York 8 26 a		15 35		15 44			16 32			16 36		16 44				17 31			17 37		17 59
Doncaster 31 d	14 59				15 12	15 37			15 56					16 31	16 37		17 04	16 58			
Bentley (S.Yorks) 31 a					15 15																
Adwick 31 a					15 19																
Kirk Sandall d																	17 10				
Hatfield & Stainforth d																	17 15				
Thorne South d																					
Crowle d																					
Althorpe d																					
Scunthorpe a						16 02									17 02						
d						16 03									17 03						
Barnetby d						16 17									17 17						
Hull Paragon Interchange d																					
Barton-on-Humber a																					
Barton-on-Humber d																					
Barrow Haven d																					
New Holland d																					
Goxhill d																					
Thornton Abbey d																					
Ulceby d																					
Habrough d						16 26															
Stallingborough d																					
Healing d																					
Great Coates d																					
Grimsby Town a						16 39									17 37						
d						16 40									17 38						
Grimsby Docks d																					
New Clee d																					
Cleethorpes a						16 52									17 50						
Thorne North d									16 10								17 24				
Goole d	15 19								16 19								17a33	17 17			
Saltmarshe d																					
York 8 33 d													16 06								
Selby a			15 22										16 24	16 45						17 23	
Wressle d																					
Howden d													16 34	16 56							
Eastrington d																					
Gilberdyke d	15 29								16 27									17 25			
Broomfleet d																					
Brough d	15 37		15 40						16 35				16 46	17 08				17 33		17 41	
Ferriby d																					
Hessle d																					
Hull a	15 56		15 59						16 53				17 07	17 25				17 51		17 59	

A To Scarborough
B To Edinburgh
C From Birmingham New Street to Newcastle
D To Leeds
E From Plymouth to Glasgow Central
F To Bridlington
G From Penzance to Edinburgh

Sundays
from 30 October

Manchester Airport, Manchester, Sheffield and Meadowhall - Doncaster - Cleethorpes and Hull
Barton-on-Humber - Cleethorpes

		NT	TP	XC	NT	NT	GR	NT	XC	TP	XC	NT	NT	GR	GR	TP	XC	NT	NT	NT	HT	TP	TP
			◇1	◇1			1		◇1	◇1	◇1			1	1	◇1	◇1				◇1	◇1	◇1
		A		B		C	D	A	E		F		G		D		H			A	⊠		
Manchester Airport 85	d		15 55							16 55												17 55	
Manchester Piccadilly 10	d		16 20							17 20						18 02						18 20	19 02
Stockport 78	d		16 28							17 28												18 28	
Sheffield 7	a		17 08							18 08												19 08	
	d		17 11	17 21	17 25	17 28		17 36	17 51	18 11	18 21	18 25	18 28				18 51	18 57				19 11	
Meadowhall	d		17 16		17 31	17 34		17 44		18 16		18 31	18 35					19 05				19 16	
Rotherham Central	d				17 37			17 50				18 37						19 11					
Swinton (S.Yorks)	d				17 47			17a58				18 48						19 19					
Mexborough	d				17 50							18 51											
Conisbrough	d				17 54							18 55											
London Kings Cross	d						16 30							17 20	17 30						17 45		
Doncaster 7	a		17 35		18 05	17 55	18 10		18 13	18 35		19 06	18 54	19 03	19 09		19 15				19 28	19 35	
York 8 26	a			18 32			18 35		19 21		19 32				19 38		19 44	20 18					
Doncaster 31	d	17 14	17 37			17 57				18 37			18 55	19 05						19 27	19 31	19 37	
Bentley (S.Yorks) 31	a	17 17																		19 30			
Adwick 31	a	17 21																		19 34			
Kirk Sandall	d												19 01										
Hatfield & Stainforth	d												19 06										
Thorne South	d																						
Crowle	d																						
Althorpe	d																						
Scunthorpe	a		18 02							19 02												20 02	
	d		18 03							19 03												20 03	
Barnetby	d		18 17							19 17												20 17	
Hull Paragon Interchange	d																						
Barton-on-Humber	a																						
Barton-on-Humber	d																						
Barrow Haven	d																						
New Holland	d																						
Goxhill	d																						
Thornton Abbey	d																						
Ulceby	d																						
Habrough	d									19 26													
Stallingborough	d																						
Healing	d																						
Great Coates	d																						
Grimsby Town	a		18 37							19 39												20 37	
	d		18 38							19 40												20 38	
Grimsby Docks	d																						
New Clee	d																						
Cleethorpes	a		18 50							19 52												20 50	
Thorne North	d												19 12										
Goole	d					18 16							19 21										
Saltmarshe	d																						
York 8 33	d																		19 10				
Selby	a													19 24		19 29			19 35		19 45		20 17
Wressle	d																						
Howden	d																		19 46		19 56		
Eastrington	d																						
Gilberdyke	d					18 24							19 29										
Broomfleet	d																						
Brough	d					18 32							19 37	19 46		19 48			19 58		20 08		20 36
Ferriby	d																						
Hessle	d																						
Hull	a					18 48							19 55	20 06		20 06			20 17		20 25		20 54

A To Leeds
B From Plymouth to Glasgow Central
C To Bridlington
D To Edinburgh
E From Reading to Newcastle
F From Penzance to Edinburgh
G To Beverley
H From Reading to Edinburgh

Table 29

Sundays
from 30 October

Manchester Airport, Manchester, Sheffield and Meadowhall - Doncaster - Cleethorpes and Hull
Barton-on-Humber - Cleethorpes

		XC	NT	GR	NT	XC	NT	TP	TP	XC	NT	GR	XC	HT	TP	NT	NT	NT	NT	TP	NT	NT
		◇1		1		◇1		◇1	◇1	◇1		1	◇1	◇1	◇1					◇1		
		A		B	C	D				E		B	D	⊠			C		C	F		
Manchester Airport 85	d							18 55							19 55							
Manchester Piccadilly 10	d							19 20	20 06						20 18							
Stockport 78	d							19 28							20 27							
Sheffield 7	a							20 08							21 08							
	d	19 21	19 29		19 36	19 51	20 02	20 11		20 21	20 28		20 51		21 11			21 24	21 36		22 13	22 26
Meadowhall	d		19 35		19 42		20 09	20 16			20 34				21 16			21 30	21 42		22 19	22 32
Rotherham Central	d		19 41		19 49						20 40							21 37	21 48			22 38
Swinton (S.Yorks)	d		19 49		19a57						20 48							21 47	21a56			22 48
Mexborough	d		19 52								20 51							21 50				22 51
Conisbrough	d		19 56								20 55							21 54				22 55
London Kings Cross	d			18 30								19 30		19 45								
Doncaster 7	a		20 07	20 11		20 16	20 30	20 35			21 05	21 13	21 19	21 29	21 35			22 03			22 38	23 05
York 8 26	a	20 32		20 36		20 45				21 32		21 38	21 44									
Doncaster 31	d						20 30	20 37			21 07			21 31	21 37		21 49	22 04			22 41	
Bentley (S.Yorks) 31	a																21 52					
Adwick 31	a																21 56					
Kirk Sandall	d										21 13											
Hatfield & Stainforth	d										21 18											
Thorne South	d																					
Crowle	d																					
Althorpe	d																					
Scunthorpe	a							21 02							22 02							
	d							21 03							22 03							
Barnetby	d							21 17							22 17							
Hull Paragon Interchange	d																					
Barton-on-Humber	a																					
Barton-on-Humber	d																					
Barrow Haven	d																					
New Holland	d																					
Goxhill	d																					
Thornton Abbey	d																					
Ulceby	d																					
Habrough	d							21 26							22 26							
Stallingborough	d																					
Healing	d																					
Great Coates	d																					
Grimsby Town	a							21 39							22 39							
	d							21 40							22 40							
Grimsby Docks	d																					
New Clee	d																					
Cleethorpes	a							21 52							22 52							
Thorne North	d										21 24										22 53	
Goole	d						20 49				21a34							22 23			23 02	
Saltmarshe	d																					
York 8 33	d															21 41						
Selby	a								21 38					21 45		22 00						
Wressle	d																					
Howden	d													21 56		22 10						
Eastrington	d																					
Gilberdyke	d						20 57											22 31			23 10	
Broomfleet	d																					
Brough	d						21 05		21 58					22 08		22 22		22 39		23 02	23 18	
Ferriby	d																					
Hessle	d																					
Hull	a						21 23		22 15					22 25		22 36		22 56		23 19	23 39	

A From Plymouth to Edinburgh
B To Newcastle
C To Leeds
D From Reading to Newcastle
E From Plymouth
F From Leeds

Sundays
from 30 October

Manchester Airport, Manchester, Sheffield and Meadowhall - Doncaster - Cleethorpes and Hull
Barton-on-Humber - Cleethorpes

			TP	GR	NT
			◇1	1 A	
Manchester Airport	85	d			
Manchester Piccadilly 10		d			
Stockport	78	d			
Sheffield 7		a			
		d	22 30		23 34
Meadowhall		d	22 35		23 40
Rotherham Central		d			23 47
Swinton (S.Yorks)		d			23 55
Mexborough		d			23 58
Conisbrough		d			00 02
London Kings Cross		d		22 00	
Doncaster 7		a	22 56	23 42	00 13
York 8	26	a		00 33	
Doncaster	31	d	22 58		
Bentley (S.Yorks)	31	a			
Adwick	31	a			
Kirk Sandall		d			
Hatfield & Stainforth		d			
Thorne South		d			
Crowle		d			
Althorpe		d			
Scunthorpe		a	23 23		
		d	23 24		
Barnetby		d	23 38		
Hull Paragon Interchange		d			
Barton-on-Humber		a			
Barton-on-Humber		d			
Barrow Haven		d			
New Holland		d			
Goxhill		d			
Thornton Abbey		d			
Ulceby		d			
Habrough		d			
Stallingborough		d			
Healing		d			
Great Coates		d			
Grimsby Town		a	23 57		
		d	23 58		
Grimsby Docks		d			
New Clee		d			
Cleethorpes		a	00 09		
Thorne North		d			
Goole		d			
Saltmarshe		d			
York 8	33	d			
Selby		a			
Wressle		d			
Howden		d			
Eastrington		d			
Gilberdyke		d			
Broomfleet		d			
Brough		d			
Ferriby		d			
Hessle		d			
Hull		a			

A To Newcastle

Table 30

Mondays to Fridays

Sheffield - Retford and Lincoln

Miles			NT	TP ◇[1] A	NT	NT	NT B	NT	NT C	NT C
—	Huddersfield	34 d								
—	Barnsley	34 d								
—	Meadowhall	34 d		05 58			07 33		09 33	10 33
0	**Sheffield** [7]	d	05 39	06a08	06 43	07 30	07 44	08 44	09 44	10 44
2¼	Darnall	d			06 48	07 35		08 49	09 49	10 49
5¼	Woodhouse	d			06 53	07 40		08 54	09 54	10 54
9½	Kiveton Bridge	d			07 00	07 47		09 01	10 01	11 01
10¾	Kiveton Park	d	05 54		07 03	07 50	07 59	09 04	10 04	11 04
13¾	Shireoaks	d			07 08	07 55		09 09	10 09	11 09
15¾	Worksop	d	06 01		07 14	07 59	08a10	09 13	10 13	11 13
23½	**Retford** [10]	a	06 10		07 23	08 09		09 23	10 23	11 23
—		d	06 10		07 24	08 09		09 23	10 24	11 23
33	Gainsborough Lea Road	18 d	06 25		07 38	08 24		09 38	10 38	11 38
42½	Saxilby	18 d	06 37		07 51	08 37		09 51	10 51	11 51
48½	**Lincoln**	18 a	06 53		08 06	08 52		10 06	11 06	12 06

Miles			NT C	NT C	NT C	NT C	NT C	NT C	NT D	NT C	NT	NT	NT B	NT
—	Huddersfield	34 d												20 18
—	Barnsley	34 d												21 12
—	Meadowhall	34 d	11 33	12 33	13 33	14 34	15 33	16 33	16 55	17 33			20 33	21 29
0	**Sheffield** [7]	d	11 44	12 44	13 44	14 44	15 44	16 44	17 24	17 44	18 45	19 48	20 44	21 44
2¼	Darnall	d	11 49	12 49	13 49	14 50	15 49	16 49	17 29	17 49	18 50	19 53	20 49	21 49
5¼	Woodhouse	d	11 54	12 54	13 54	14 55	15 54	16 54	17 34	17 54	18 55	19 58	20 54	21 54
9½	Kiveton Bridge	d	12 01	13 01	14 01	15 02	16 01	17 01	17 41	18 01	19 02	20 05	21 01	22 01
10¾	Kiveton Park	d	12 04	13 04	14 04	15 05	16 04	17 04	17 44	18 04	19 05	20 08	21 04	22 04
13¾	Shireoaks	d	12 09	13 09	14 09	15 09	16 09	17 09	17 48	18 09	19 10	20 13	21 09	22 07
15¾	Worksop	d	12 13	13 13	14 13	15 14	16 13	17 13	17 52	18 13	19 14	20 17	21a21	22 14
23½	**Retford** [10]	a	12 23	13 23	14 23	15 23	16 23	17 23	18 06	18 23	19 24	20 27		22 28
—		d	12 23	13 23	14 23	15 24	16 23	17 23		18 23	19 24	20 27		
33	Gainsborough Lea Road	18 d	12 38	13 39	14 38	15 38	16 38	17 38		18 38	19 39	20 42		
42½	Saxilby	18 d	12 51	13 52	14 51	15 51	16 51	17 51		18 51	19 52	20 55		
48½	**Lincoln**	18 a	13 06	14 06	15 06	16 10	17 06	18 06		19 07	20 06	21 10		

		NT
Huddersfield	34 d	
Barnsley	34 d	
Meadowhall	34 d	
Sheffield [7]	d	22 44
Darnall	d	22 49
Woodhouse	d	22 54
Kiveton Bridge	d	23 01
Kiveton Park	d	23 04
Shireoaks	d	23 09
Worksop	d	23a22
Retford [10]	a	
	d	
Gainsborough Lea Road	18 d	
Saxilby	18 d	
Lincoln	18 a	

Sundays

		NT	NT	NT	NT	NT	NT
Huddersfield	34 d						
Barnsley	34 d						
Meadowhall	34 d						
Sheffield [7]	d	13 42	13 57	15 43	17 43	19 32	21 06
Darnall	d		14 03	15 48	17 48	19 37	21 11
Woodhouse	d		14 08	15 53	17 53	19 42	21 16
Kiveton Bridge	d		14 14	16 00	18 00	19 49	21 23
Kiveton Park	d		14 17	16 03	18 03	19 52	21 26
Shireoaks	d		14 22	16 07	18 07	19 56	21 30
Worksop	d	14 02	14 26	16 11	18 11	20 00	21 39
Retford [10]	a	14 11	14 39	16 20	18 20	20 09	21 48
	d	14 12		16 21	18 21	20 10	
Gainsborough Lea Road	18 d	14 26		16 35	18 35	20 24	
Saxilby	18 d	14 39		16 48	18 48	20 37	
Lincoln	18 a	14 54		17 02	19 03	20 51	

A From Doncaster to Manchester Airport
B From Doncaster
C From Scunthorpe
D From Adwick
E To Manchester Piccadilly

For connections to London Kings Cross please refer to Table 26

Table 30

Saturdays

Sheffield - Retford and Lincoln

		NT	NT	NT A	NT	NT	NT	NT	NT B	NT B	NT B	NT	NT B	NT B	NT B	NT B	NT	NT B	NT C	NT B	NT B	NT	NT B
Huddersfield	34 d																						
Barnsley	34 d			06 21																			
Meadowhall	34 d			06 42					09 33	10 33	11 33		12 33	13 33	14 34	15 33		16 33	16 55	17 33	18 33		20 33
Sheffield 7	d	05 39	05 46	06a55	06 43	07 30	08 03	08 44	09 44	10 44	11 44	12 00	12 44	13 44	14 44	15 44	16 00	16 44	17 23	17 44	18 45	19 48	20 44
Darnall	d		05 51		06 48	07 35	08 08	08 49	09 49	10 49	11 49	12 05	12 49	13 49	14 50	15 49	16 05	16 49	17 29	17 49	18 50	19 53	20 48
Woodhouse	d		05 56		06 53	07 40	08 13	08 54	09 54	10 54	11 54	12 10	12 54	13 54	14 55	15 54	16 10	16 54	17 34	17 54	18 55	19 58	20 54
Kiveton Bridge	d		06 03		07 00	07 47	08 20	09 01	10 01	11 01	12 01	12 17	13 01	14 01	15 02	16 01	16 17	17 01	17 40	18 01	19 02	20 05	21 00
Kiveton Park	d	05 54	06 06		07 03	07 50	08 23	09 04	10 04	11 04	12 04	12 20	13 04	14 04	15 05	16 04	16 20	17 04	17 43	18 04	19 05	20 08	21 04
Shireoaks	d		06 11		07 08	07 55	08 28	09 09	10 09	11 09	12 09	12 25	13 09	14 09	15 09	16 09	16 25	17 09	17 48	18 09	19 10	20 13	21 09
Worksop	d	06 01	06 23		07 14	07 59	08 32	09 13	10 13	11 13	12 13	12 35	13 13	14 13	15 14	16 13	16 36	17 13	17 52	18 13	19 14	20 17	21a21
Retford 10	a	06 10	06 38		07 23	08 09	08 42	09 23	10 23	11 23	12 23	12 44	13 23	14 23	15 23	16 23	16 46	17 23	18 06	18 23	19 24	20 27	
	d	06 10			07 24	08 09	08 42	09 23	10 23	11 23	12 23	12 45	13 23	14 23	15 24	16 23	16 46	17 23		18 24	19 24	20 27	
Gainsborough Lea Road	18 d	06 25			07 38	08 24		09 38	10 38	11 38	12 38		13 37	14 36	15 40	16 38		17 38		18 38	19 39	20 42	
Saxilby	18 d	06 37			07 51	08 37		09 51	10 51	11 51	12 51		13 50	14 49	15 53	16 51		17 51		18 51	19 52	20 55	
Lincoln	18 a	06 53			08 06	08 52		10 06	11 06	12 06	13 06		14 07	15 06	16 10	17 06		18 06		19 07	20 06	21 10	
Gainsborough Central	d						08 57					13 00					17 01						
Kirton Lindsey	d						09 11					13 13					17 15						
Brigg	d						09 24					13 22					17 27						
Barnetby	29 a						09 38					13 37					17 37						
Habrough	29 a						09 48					13 47					17 47						
Grimsby Town	29 a						10 00					14 00					18 01						
Cleethorpes	29 a						10 13					14 11					18 11						

		NT	NT
Huddersfield	34 d	20 18	
Barnsley	34 d	21 12	
Meadowhall	34 d	21 29	
Sheffield 7	d	21 44	22 44
Darnall	d	21 49	22 49
Woodhouse	d	21 54	22 54
Kiveton Bridge	d	22 01	23 01
Kiveton Park	d	22 04	23 04
Shireoaks	d	22 08	23 09
Worksop	d	22 14	23a22
Retford 10	a	22 28	
	d		
Gainsborough Lea Road	18 d		
Saxilby	18 d		
Lincoln	18 a		
Gainsborough Central	d		
Kirton Lindsey	d		
Brigg	d		
Barnetby	29 a		
Habrough	29 a		
Grimsby Town	29 a		
Cleethorpes	29 a		

A To Nottingham
B From Scunthorpe
C From Adwick

For connections to London Kings Cross please refer to Table 26

Table 30

Mondays to Fridays

Lincoln and Retford - Sheffield

Miles			NT MX	NT	NT A	NT A	NT A	NT A	NT A	NT A	NT A	NT A	NT A	NT B	NT	NT C	NT	NT	NT	NT	NT	NT	NT
0	**Lincoln**	18 d		07 04		08 25	09 25	10 25	11 25	12 27	13 26	14 25	15 24	16 25	17 22		18 24	19 43	20 27		21 27		
6	Saxilby	18 d		07 14		08 34	09 34	10 34	11 34	12 36	13 35	14 34	15 33	16 35	17 31		18 33	19 52	20 36		21 36		
15½	Gainsborough Lea Road	18 d		07 26		08 48	09 48	10 48	11 48	12 49	13 48	14 48	15 48	16 48	17 44		18 46	20 05	20 49		21 49		
25	**Retford** 10	a		07 40		09 02	10 02	11 02	12 02	13 03	14 02	15 02	16 02	17 02	17 58		19 04	20 18	21 03		22 03		
—		d		07 40		09 02	10 02	11 02	12 02	13 03	14 02	15 02	16 02	17 02	17 58	18 14	19 04	20 19	21 03		22 03	22 45	
32¾	Worksop	d	23p28	07 52	08 14	09 14	10 14	11 14	12 14	13 15	14 14	15 14	16 14	17 14	18 10	18 25	19 16	20 31	21 15	21 26	22 15	22 58	23 28
34¾	Shireoaks	d	23p32	07 55	08 19	09 18	10 18	11 18	12 18	13 19	14 18	15 18	16 18	17 18		18 29	19 20	20 35		21 30	22 19	23 02	23 32
37¾	Kiveton Park	d	23p38	08 01	08 25	09 24	10 24	11 24	12 24	13 25	14 24	15 24	16 24	17 24		18 34	19 26	20 41	21 23	21 36	22 25	23 08	23 38
39	Kiveton Bridge	d	23p41	08 04	08 28	09 27	10 27	11 27	12 27	13 28	14 27	15 27	16 27	17 27		18 37	19 29	20 44		21 39	22 28	23 11	23 41
43¼	Woodhouse	d	23p52	08 10	08 34	09 33	10 33	11 33	12 33	13 34	14 33	15 33	16 33	17 33		18 43	19 35	20 50		21 46	22 34	23 17	23 52
46¼	Darnall	d	23p57	08 15	08 39	09 38	10 38	11 38	12 38	13 39	14 38	15 38	16 38	17 38		18 48	19 40	20 55		21 51	22 39	23 22	23 57
48½	**Sheffield** 7	a	00 04	08 26	08 48	09 47	10 47	11 47	12 48	13 48	14 48	15 48	16 48	17 49	18 35	18 57	19 53	21 05	21 44	22 02	22 50	23 33	00 04
—	Meadowhall	34 a			08 59	09 58	10 58	11 58	12 58	13 58	14 58	15 58	16 58	17 58		19 06							
—	Barnsley	34 a																					
—	Huddersfield	34 a																					

Sundays

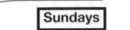

		NT D	NT E	NT F	NT	NT	NT	NT
Lincoln	18 d				17 15	19 15	21 10	
Saxilby	18 d				17 25	19 25	21 20	
Gainsborough Lea Road	18 d				17 37	19 37	21 32	
Retford 10	a				17 51	19 51	21 46	
	d		14 50	14 50	17 51	19 51	21 46	22 24
Worksop	d	23p28	15 01	15 01	18 03	20 03	21 58	22 35
Shireoaks	d	23p32	15 05	15 05	18 06	20 06	22 01	22 39
Kiveton Park	d	23p38	15 10	15 10	18 12	20 12	22 07	22 44
Kiveton Bridge	d	23p41	15 13	15 13	18 15	20 15	22 10	22 47
Woodhouse	d	23p47	15 19	15 19	18 21	20 21	22 16	22 53
Darnall	d	23p52	15 24	15 24	18 26	20 26	22 21	22 58
Sheffield 7	a	00 01	15 33	15 33	18 35	20 35	22 29	23 07
Meadowhall	34 a		15 42	15 42				
Barnsley	34 a		16 03	16 03				
Huddersfield	34 a		16 53	16 57				

A To Adwick
B To Hull
C To Doncaster
D not 22 May
E until 2 October
F from 9 October

For connections from London Kings Cross please refer to Table 26

Lincoln and Retford - Sheffield

Miles			NT MX	NT	NT A	NT A	NT A	NT A	NT A	NT A	NT A		NT A	NT A	NT B	NT	NT C	NT	NT	NT	NT		NT	NT	NT
0	**Lincoln**	18 d		07 04		08 25	09 25	10 25	11 25	12 27	13 26		14 25	15 24	16 25	17 22		18 24	19 43	20 27			21 27		
6	Saxilby	18 d		07 14		08 34	09 34	10 34	11 34	12 36	13 35		14 34	15 33	16 35	17 31		18 33	19 52	20 36			21 36		
15½	Gainsborough Lea Road	18 d		07 26		08 48	09 48	10 48	11 48	12 49	13 48		14 48	15 48	16 48	17 44		18 46	20 05	20 49			21 49		
25	**Retford** 10	a		07 40		09 02	10 02	11 02	12 02	13 03	14 02		15 02	16 02	17 02	17 58		19 04	20 18	21 03			22 03		
—		d		07 40		09 02	10 02	11 02	12 02	13 03	14 02		15 02	16 02	17 02	17 58	18 14	19 04	20 19	21 03			22 03	22 45	
32¾	Worksop	d	23p28	07 52	08 14	09 14	10 14	11 14	12 14	13 15	14 14		15 14	16 14	17 14	18 10	18 25	19 16	20 31	21 15	21 26		22 15	22 58	23 28
34¾	Shireoaks	d	23p32	07 55	08 19	09 18	10 18	11 18	12 18	13 19	14 18		15 18	16 18	17 18		18 29	19 20	20 35		21 30		22 19	23 02	23 32
37¾	Kiveton Park	d	23p38	08 01	08 25	09 24	10 24	11 24	12 24	13 25	14 24		15 24	16 24	17 24		18 34	19 26	20 41	21 23	21 36		22 25	23 08	23 38
39	Kiveton Bridge	d	23p41	08 04	08 28	09 27	10 27	11 27	12 27	13 28	14 27		15 27	16 27	17 27		18 37	19 29	20 44		21 39		22 28	23 11	23 41
43¼	Woodhouse	d	23p52	08 10	08 34	09 33	10 33	11 33	12 33	13 34	14 33		15 33	16 33	17 33		18 43	19 35	20 50		21 46		22 34	23 17	23 52
46¼	Darnall	d	23p57	08 15	08 39	09 38	10 38	11 38	12 38	13 39	14 38		15 38	16 38	17 38		18 48	19 40	20 55		21 51		22 39	23 22	23 57
48½	**Sheffield** 7	a	00 04	08 26	08 48	09 47	10 47	11 47	12 48	13 48	14 48		15 48	16 48	17 49	18 35	18 57	19 53	21 05	21 44	22 02		22 50	23 33	00 04
—	Meadowhall	34 a			08 59	09 58	10 58	11 58	12 58	13 58	14 58		15 58	16 58	17 58		19 06								
—	Barnsley	34 a																							
—	Huddersfield	34 a																							

Sundays

		NT D	NT E	NT F	NT	NT	NT	NT
Lincoln	18 d				17 15	19 15	21 10	
Saxilby	18 d				17 25	19 25	21 20	
Gainsborough Lea Road	18 d				17 37	19 37	21 32	
Retford 10	a				17 51	19 51	21 46	
	d		14 50	14 50	17 51	19 51	21 46	22 24
Worksop	d	23p28	15 01	15 01	18 03	20 03	21 58	22 35
Shireoaks	d	23p32	15 05	15 05	18 06	20 06	22 01	22 39
Kiveton Park	d	23p38	15 10	15 10	18 12	20 12	22 07	22 44
Kiveton Bridge	d	23p41	15 13	15 13	18 15	20 15	22 10	22 47
Woodhouse	d	23p47	15 19	15 19	18 21	20 21	22 16	22 53
Darnall	d	23p52	15 24	15 24	18 26	20 26	22 21	22 58
Sheffield 7	a	00 01	15 33	15 33	18 35	20 35	22 29	23 07
Meadowhall	34 a		15 42	15 42				
Barnsley	34 a		16 03	16 03				
Huddersfield	34 a		16 53	16 57				

A To Adwick
B To Hull
C To Doncaster
D not 22 May
E until 2 October
F from 9 October

For connections from London Kings Cross please refer to Table 26

Network Diagram for Tables 31, 32, 33, 34

DM-5/10
Design BAJS

© 2010 Network Rail.
All rights reserved

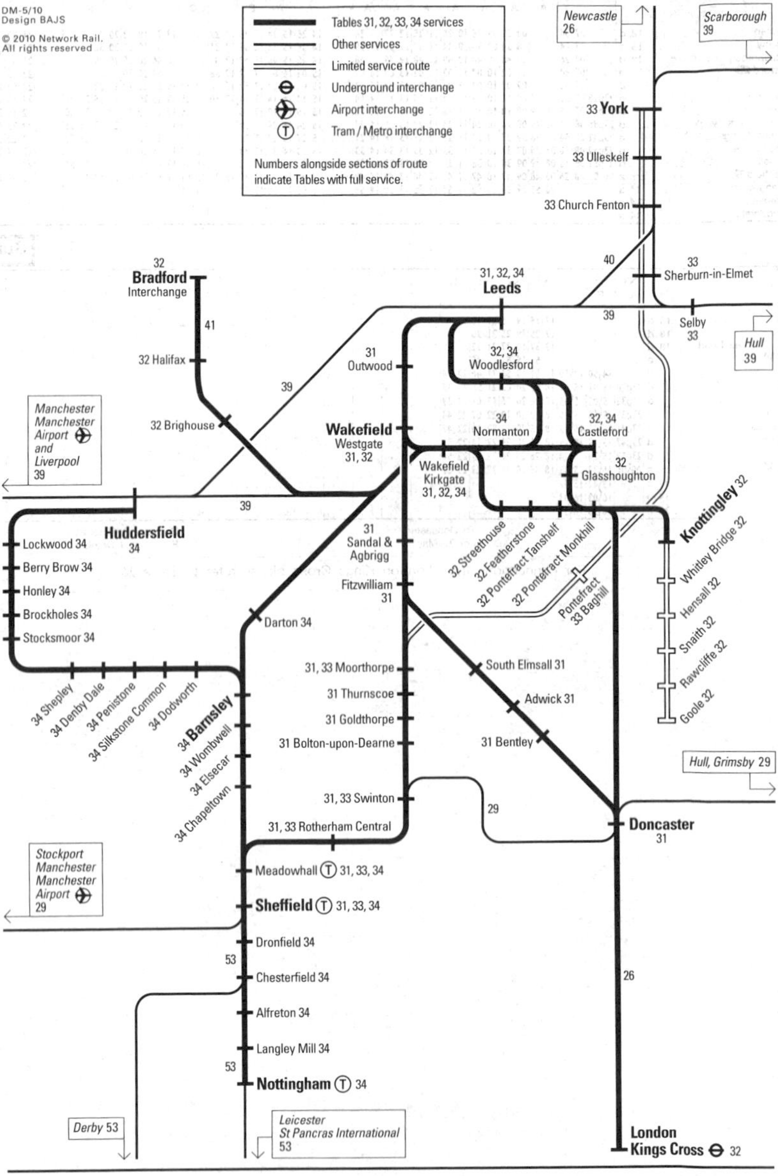

Sheffield, Doncaster and Wakefield - Leeds

Miles	Miles				GR	NT	GR	NT	NT	EM	NT	NT	NT		NT	NT	NT	NT	NT	NT	NT	NT	NT		XC	NT
					MX	MO	MO	MX	MX	MO	MX															
					R 1 🍴		R 1 🍴🛒			◇1 🍴															◇1 🛒	
—	0	**Sheffield** 7	29 🚋	d		22p39		23p15	23p24	23p30		05 22	05 50				06 06	06 18	06 28	06 49		06 52	07 06		07 12	
—	3½	Meadowhall	29 🚋	d		22p45		23p21	23p30			05 28	05 56				06 12	06 24	06 34	06 55		06 58	07 12			
—	6¼	Rotherham Central	29	d				23p27				05 34						06 30	06 40			07 04				
—	10¾	Swinton (S.Yorks)	29	d				23p36				05 42						06 38	06 51			07 14				
—	13	Bolton-upon-Dearne		d				23p41				05 46							06 56							
—	14¼	Goldthorpe		d				23p44				05 49							06 58							
—	15	Thurnscoe		d				23p47				05 52							07 01							
—	18½	Moorthorpe		d				23p52				05 57							07 06							
0	—	**Doncaster** 7		d	23p26		23p32									06 26		06 59			07 26	07 34				
1¾	—	Bentley (S.Yorks)		d												06 29		07 02			07 29	07 37				
4	—	Adwick		a												06 33		07 08			07 33	07 43				
—	—			d												06 33					07 33					
8¾	—	South Elmsall		d												06 39					07 39					
13¼	22¼	Fitzwilliam		d								06 02				06 44			07 12		07 44					
18	27	Sandal & Agbrigg		d							←	06 08				06 50			07 18		07 50					←
19¾	28¾	**Wakefield Westgate** 7	32,39	a	23p44		23p49	00 09		23p55	00 09	06 12				06 54			07 22		07 54				07 36	07 54
—	—			d	23p44		23p49	00 10		23p56	00 10	06 13			06 24	06 54			07 23		07 54				07 37	07 54
—	—	Pontefract Monkhill	32	d				→													→					
—	—	Wakefield Kirkgate 4	32,34,39	a		23p26			00s10				06 27		06 29		06 49			07 27			07 49			
—	—			d		23p27							06 28				06 50			07 28			07 50			
22¼	31¼	Outwood		d								06 18				06 59			07 28							07 59
29¾	38¾	**Leeds** 10	32,34	a	00 03	00 05	00 27			00 28	00 30	06 33	06 50			07 14	07 28		07 44	07 51			08 25		07 52	08 13

			GR	NT	NT	NT	NT	GR	NT		NT	NT	NT	XC	NT	GR	NT	NT	NT		GR	NT	NT	NT	NT	NT
			R 1 🍴					R 1 🍴						◇1 🛒		R 1 🍴🛒					R 1 🍴🛒					
Sheffield 7	29 🚋	d		07 14	07 20		07 51		08 06			08 14	08 18	08 21					08 51				08 53	09 06	09 14	09 18
Meadowhall	29 🚋	d		07 21	07 26		07 57		08 12			08 21	08 25						08 57				09 00	09 12	09 21	09 24
Rotherham Central	29	d		07 27								08 28											09 06		09 27	
Swinton (S.Yorks)	29	d		07 35								08 37											09 16		09 36	
Bolton-upon-Dearne		d		07 39								08 41													09 41	
Goldthorpe		d		07 42								08 44													09 43	
Thurnscoe		d		07 45								08 47													09 46	
Moorthorpe		d		07 54								08 52													09 51	
Doncaster 7		d	07 44			07 56		08 12			08 16				08 26	08 41		08 49			09 12	09 26	09 34			
Bentley (S.Yorks)		d				07 59					08 19				08 29			08 52				09 29	09 37			
Adwick		a				08 03					08 25				08 33			08 58				09 33	09 43			
		d				08 03									08 33							09 33				
South Elmsall		d				08 09									08 39							09 39				
Fitzwilliam		d		08 00		08 14						08 59			08 45							09 44			09 56	
Sandal & Agbrigg		d		08 06		08 20						09 05			08 50		←					09 50			10 02	
Wakefield Westgate 7	32,39	a	08 01	08 10		08 24		08 30				09 06		08 46	08 54	09 00	09 06				09 30	09 54			10 06	
		d	08 01	08 11		08 25		08 30				09 06		08 47	08 55	09 00	09 06				09 30	09 54			10 06	
Pontefract Monkhill	32	d										→										→			→	
Wakefield Kirkgate 4	32,34,39	a			07 57		08 27		08 49				08 57						09 27					09 49		09 57
		d			07 58		08 28		08 50				08 58						09 28					09 50		09 58
Outwood		d		08 16		08 29									08 59		09 11									
Leeds 10	32,34	a	08 21	08 36	08 21	08 42	08 49	08 50	09 25				09 20	09 03	09 14	09 19	09 31		09 49		09 50			10 25		10 18

			XC	NT	NT		GR	NT	NT	GR	NT	NT	NT	NT	NT		XC	NT	GR	NT	NT	GR	NT	NT	NT	
			◇1 🛒				R 1 🍴🛒			R 1 🍴🛒							◇1 🛒		R 1 🍴🛒			R 1 🍴🛒				
Sheffield 7	29 🚋	d	09 21		09 29				09 50			09 53	10 06	10 14	10 18		10 21				10 50			10 53	11 06	
Meadowhall	29 🚋	d			09 35				09 56			09 59	10 12	10 21	10 24						10 56			10 59	11 12	
Rotherham Central	29	d			09 42							10 06		10 27										11 05		
Swinton (S.Yorks)	29	d			09 51							10 15		10 36										11 16		
Bolton-upon-Dearne		d												10 41												
Goldthorpe		d												10 43												
Thurnscoe		d												10 46												
Moorthorpe		d			10a01									10 53												
Doncaster 7		d					09 42			10 12	10 26	10 34							10 42			11 13	11 26	11 34		
Bentley (S.Yorks)		d									10 29	10 37											11 29	11 37		
Adwick		a									10 33	10 43											11 33	11 43		
		d									10 33												11 33			
South Elmsall		d									10 39												11 39			
Fitzwilliam		d									10 44			10 59									11 45			
Sandal & Agbrigg		d		←				←			10 50			11 05				←		←			11 50			
Wakefield Westgate 7	32,39	a	09 46	09 54			10 00	10 06		10 30	10 54			11 09			10 46	10 54	11 00	11 09		11 31	11 54			
		d	09 47	09 54			10 00	10 06		10 30	10 54			11 09			10 47	10 54	11 00	11 09		11 31	11 55			
Pontefract Monkhill	32	d									→			→									→			
Wakefield Kirkgate 4	32,34,39	a							10 27				10 49		10 57						11 27				11 49	
		d							10 28				10 50		10 58						11 28				11 50	
Outwood		d		09 59				10 11										10 59		11 14						
Leeds 10	32,34	a	10 02	10 14			10 19	10 31	10 48	10 50			11 25		11 18		11 02	11 15	11 19	11 31	11 48	11 51			12 25	

Sheffield, Doncaster and Wakefield - Leeds

Station			NT	NT	XC	NT	GR	NT	NT	GR	GC		NT	NT	NT	NT	NT	XC	NT	GR	NT		NT	GR	NT	NT
					◇1		R 1			R 1	R 1 ⊠							◇1		R 1				R 1		
Sheffield 7	29	d	11 14	11 18	11 21				11 50					11 53	12 06	12 14	12 18	12 21					12 50			12 53
Meadowhall	29	d	11 21	11 24					11 56					11 59	12 12	12 21	12 24						12 56			12 59
Rotherham Central	29	d	11 27											12 05		12 27										13 05
Swinton (S.Yorks)	29	d	11 36											12 16		12 36										13 16
Bolton-upon-Dearne		d	11 41													12 41										
Goldthorpe		d	11 43													12 43										
Thurnscoe		d	11 46													12 46										
Moorthorpe		d	11 53													12 53										
Doncaster 7		d					11 42			12 12	12 24		12 26	12 34						12 42				13 12	13 26	13 34
Bentley (S.Yorks)		d											12 29	12 38											13 29	13 37
Adwick		a											12 33	12 43											13 33	13 43
		d											12 33												13 33	
South Elmsall		d											12 39												13 39	
Fitzwilliam		d	11 59										12 44			12 59									13 45	
Sandal & Agbrigg		d	12 05			←		←					12 49			13 05			←		←				13 50	
Wakefield Westgate 7	32,39	a	12 09		11 46	11 54	12 00	12 09		12 30			12 51			13 09		12 46	12 51	13 00	13 09			13 30	13 54	
		d	12 09		11 47	11 55	12 00	12 09		12 30			12 52			13 09		12 47	12 52	13 00	13 09			13 30	13 55	
Pontefract Monkhill	32	d	↦								12 49		↦			↦									↦	
Wakefield Kirkgate 4	32,34,39	a		11 57					12 27		13 07				12 49		12 57						13 27			
		d		11 58					12 28						12 50		12 58						13 28			
Outwood		d				11 59		12 14											12 56		13 14					
Leeds 10	32,34	a		12 18	12 01	12 15	12 19	12 31	12 48	12 50					13 25		13 18	13 03	13 13	13 19	13 29		13 49	13 50		

Station			NT	NT	NT	XC	NT		NT	GR	NT	NT	GR	NT	NT	NT	NT		NT	XC	NT	GR	NT	NT	GR	NT
						◇1				R 1			R 1							◇1		R 1			R 1	
Sheffield 7	29	d	13 06	13 14	13 18	13 21			13 28			13 50			13 53	14 06	14 14		14 18	14 21				14 50		
Meadowhall	29	d	13 12	13 21	13 24				13 35			13 56			13 59	14 12	14 21		14 24					14 56		
Rotherham Central	29	d		13 27					13 41						14 05		14 27									
Swinton (S.Yorks)	29	d		13 36					13 50						14 17		14 35									
Bolton-upon-Dearne		d		13 41													14 40									
Goldthorpe		d		13 43													14 42									
Thurnscoe		d		13 46													14 45									
Moorthorpe		d		13 53					14a01								14 52									
Doncaster 7		d								13 42			14 12	14 26	14 34							14 42			15 12	15 26
Bentley (S.Yorks)		d												14 29	14 37											15 29
Adwick		a												14 33	14 43											15 33
		d												14 33												15 33
South Elmsall		d												14 39												15 39
Fitzwilliam		d		13 59										14 45			14 58									15 44
Sandal & Agbrigg		d		14 05			←				←			14 50			15 04				←		←			15 50
Wakefield Westgate 7	32,39	a		14 09		13 46	13 54			14 00	14 09		14 30	14 54			15 08			14 46	14 54	15 00	15 08		15 30	15 54
		d		14 09		13 47	13 55			14 00	14 09		14 30	14 55			15 08			14 47	14 55	15 00	15 08		15 30	15 54
Pontefract Monkhill	32	d		↦										↦			↦									↦
Wakefield Kirkgate 4	32,34,39	a	13 50		13 57							14 27				14 49			14 57					15 27		
		d	13 50		13 58							14 28				14 50			14 58					15 28		
Outwood		d					13 59				14 14										14 59		15 13			
Leeds 10	32,34	a	14 25		14 18	14 02	14 14			14 19	14 31	14 48	14 50			15 25			15 18	15 01	15 13	15 19	15 31	15 49	15 50	

Station			NT		NT	NT	NT	XC	NT	GR	NT	NT	GR		NT	GC	NT	NT	NT	NT	XC	GR	NT		NT	GR
								◇1		R 1			R 1			R 1 ⊠					◇1	R 1				R 1
Sheffield 7	29	d	14 53		15 06	15 14	15 18	15 21				15 50					15 53	16 06	16 14	16 18	16 21				16 50	
Meadowhall	29	d	14 59		15 12	15 20	15 24					15 56					15 59	16 12	16 20	16 24					16 56	
Rotherham Central	29	d	15 05			15 26											16 05		16 26							
Swinton (S.Yorks)	29	d	15 16			15 34											16 16		16 36							
Bolton-upon-Dearne		d				15 39													16 40							
Goldthorpe		d				15 41													16 43							
Thurnscoe		d				15 44													16 46							
Moorthorpe		d				15 51													16 53							
Doncaster 7		d	15 34							15 41			16 12		16 16	16 24	16 34					16 42				17 13
Bentley (S.Yorks)		d	15 37												16 19		16 37									
Adwick		a	15 42												16 23		16 43									
		d													16 23											
South Elmsall		d													16 29											
Fitzwilliam		d				15 57									16 33				16 59							
Sandal & Agbrigg		d				16 03			←		←				16 39				17 05				←			
Wakefield Westgate 7	32,39	a				16 08		15 46	15 54	15 59	16 08		16 30		16 43				17 09		16 49	17 00	17 09			17 31
		d				16 08		15 47	15 54	15 59	16 08		16 30		16 43				17 09		16 50	17 00	17 09			17 31
Pontefract Monkhill	32	d				↦										16 48			↦							
Wakefield Kirkgate 4	32,34,39	a			15 49		15 57					16 27				17 04		16 49		16 57					17 28	
		d			15 50		15 58					16 28						16 50		16 58					17 28	
Outwood		d							15 59		16 13				16 49								17 14			
Leeds 10	32,34	a			16 25		16 18	16 02	16 14	16 19	16 31	16 48	16 50		17 04			17 25		17 18	17 04	17 19	17 31		17 48	17 51

Sheffield, Doncaster and Wakefield - Leeds

		NT	NT	NT	NT	NT	XC	NT		GR	NT	XC	NT	GR	NT	NT	NT	XC		NT	GR	NT	GR	NT	NT
							◇1 🛒			R 1 ☕🛒		◇1 🛒		R 1 ☕🛒				◇1 🛒			R 1 ☕🛒		R 1 ☕🛒		
Sheffield 7	29 🚊 d		16 53	17 06	17 13	17 18	17 22					17 47	17 50		18 06	18 13	18 18	18 21						18 50	19 06
Meadowhall	29 🚊 d		16 59	17 12	17 20	17 24							17 56		18 12	18 20	18 24							18 56	19 12
Rotherham Central	29 d		17 05		17 26											18 26									
Swinton (S.Yorks)	29 d		17 16		17 36											18 36									
Bolton-upon-Dearne	d				17 40											18 41									
Goldthorpe	d				17 43											18 43									
Thurnscoe	d				17 46											18 46									
Moorthorpe	d				17 52											18 53									
Doncaster 7	d	17 26	17 34							17 42										18 26	18 40		19 18		
Bentley (S.Yorks)	d	17 29	17 37																	18 29					
Adwick	a	17 33	17 43																	18 33					
	d	17 33																		18 33					
South Elmsall	d	17 39																		18 39					
Fitzwilliam	d	17 45			17 58											18 59				18 45					
Sandal & Agbrigg	d	17 51			18 05			←			←					19 05				18 50		←			
Wakefield Westgate 7	32,39 a	17 55			18 09		17 47	17 55		18 00	18 09	18 13				19 10		18 47		18 54	18 58	19 10	19 35		
	d	17 55			18 09		17 48	17 55		18 00	18 09	18 14		18 31		19 10		18 48		18 55	18 58	19 10	19 36		
Pontefract Monkhill	32 d	↪			↪											↪									
Wakefield Kirkgate 4	32,34,39 a			17 49		17 57							18 28		18 50		18 58							19 29	19 50
	d			17 50		17 58							18 32		18 50		18 59							19 32	19 50
Outwood	d							18 00			18 14									18 59		19 15			
Leeds 10	32,34 a			18 25		18 18	18 03	18 14		18 19	18 32	18 31	18 51	18 51	19 27		19 23	19 02		19 14	19 19	19 31	19 52	19 55	20 26

		NT FX	NT FO	NT		XC	NT	GR	GR	NT FX	NT FO	NT	GR	NT		NT	XC	NT	GR	NT	GR	NT	XC	NT FX	
						◇1 A 🛒		R 1 ☕🛒	R 1 ☕🛒				R 1 ☕🛒				◇1 🛒		R 1 ☕🛒		R 1 ☕🛒		◇1		
Sheffield 7	29 🚊 d	19 18	19 18	19 22		19 26						19 51		20 06		20 18	20 21			20 27		21 09	21 21		
Meadowhall	29 🚊 d	19 25	19 25	19 28								19 57		20 12		20 24				20 35		21 15			
Rotherham Central	29 d	19 31	19 31																	20 41					
Swinton (S.Yorks)	29 d	19 40	19 40																	20 50					
Bolton-upon-Dearne	d	19 44	19 44																	20 55					
Goldthorpe	d	19 47	19 47																	20 57					
Thurnscoe	d	19 50	19 50																	21 00					
Moorthorpe	d	20 00	20 00																	21 05					
Doncaster 7	d						19 20	19 42	19 49				20 20					20 26	20 40		21 13			21 22	
Bentley (S.Yorks)	d						19 23											20 29						21 25	
Adwick	a						19 27											20 33						21 29	
	d						19 27											20 33						21 29	
South Elmsall	d						19 33											20 39						21 35	
Fitzwilliam	d	20 05	20 05				19 46											20 45		21 11				21 46	
Sandal & Agbrigg	d	20 11	20 11				19 51			←	←							20 51		21 17				21 52	
Wakefield Westgate 7	32,39 a	20 15	20 15			19 50	19 55	20 01	20 06	20 16	20 21		20 38				20 46	20 55	20 59	21 22	21 31		21 46	21 56	
	d	20 16	20 16			19 51	19 56	20 01	20 06	20 16	20 21		20 38				20 47	20 55	20 59	21 22	21 31		21 47	21 56	
Pontefract Monkhill	32 d	↪	↪																						
Wakefield Kirkgate 4	32,34,39 a			19 58								20 28		20 49		20 57						21 52			
	d			19 58								20 28		20 50		20 58						21 52			
Outwood	d						20 00			20 21	20 21							21 00		21 27				22 01	
Leeds 10	32,34 a			20 19		20 05	20 16	20 22	20 24	20 36	20 34	20 48	20 54	21 26		21 19	21 05	21 14	21 20	21 47	21 51	22 29	22 02	22 15	

		NT FO	NT	EM	GC	GR	NT	GR	NT FX	EM		NT	NT	XC	NT FO	NT	NT	EM	GR	NT FO		NT FX	NT FX		
				◇1 ☕	◇1 ⊠	R 1 ☕🛒		R 1 ☕		◇1 ☕				◇1				◇1 ☕	R 1 ☕						
Sheffield 7	29 🚊 d			21 25			21 30		22 06	22 19			22 24	22 30				22 50		23 15		23 15	23 24		
Meadowhall	29 🚊 d						21 36		22 12				22 30							23 21		23 21	23 30		
Rotherham Central	29 d						21 42						22 36							23 27		23 27			
Swinton (S.Yorks)	29 d						21 50						22 45							23 36		23 36			
Bolton-upon-Dearne	d						21 55						22 49							23 41		23 41			
Goldthorpe	d						21 57						22 52							23 44		23 44			
Thurnscoe	d						22 00						22 55							23 47		23 47			
Moorthorpe	d						22 05						23 00							23 52		23 52			
Doncaster 7	d	21 22			21 25	21 43		22 22				22 26							23 26						
Bentley (S.Yorks)	d	21 25										22 29													
Adwick	a	21 29										22 33													
	d	21 29										22 33													
South Elmsall	d	21 35										22 39													
Fitzwilliam	d	21 46					22 11					22 45	23 07												
Sandal & Agbrigg	d	21 52					22 17					22 51	23 13				←								
Wakefield Westgate 7	32,39 a	21 56		21 59		22 05	22 21	22 39		22 46		22 55	23 17	22 59			23 17	23 21	23 44			00 09			
	d	21 57	21 57	22 00		22 05	22 21	22 39		22 47		22 55	23 18	23 00		23 04	23 18	23 22	23 44			00 10			
Pontefract Monkhill	32 d				21 49								↪												
Wakefield Kirkgate 4	32,34,39 a		22 00		22 09				22 51							23 07							00s10		
	d								22 51						22 51										
Outwood	d	22 02					22 26					23 00					23 23								
Leeds 10	32,34 a	22 15		22 19		22 25	22 46	23 00	23 30	23 05		23 14		23 15	23 29		23 41	23 40	00 03	00 30		00 30			

A 🛒 to Wakefield Westgate

Table 31

Saturdays
until 18 June

Sheffield, Doncaster and Wakefield - Leeds

			GR	NT	NT	NT	NT	NT	NT	NT	NT		NT	XC	NT	NT	NT	NT	NT	NT	NT		XC	NT	GR	NT
			B 1 ☕											◇1 🍴									◇1 🍴		B 1 ☕🍴	
Sheffield 7	29 ⇌	d		23p15			06 06	06 12	06 28		06 52		07 06	07 12		07 14	07 51	08 06		08 14	08 18		08 21			
Meadowhall	29 ⇌	d		23p21			06 12	06 18	06 34		06 58		07 12			07 21	07 57	08 12		08 22	08 25					
Rotherham Central	29	d		23p27				06 24	06 40		07 04					07 27				08 28						
Swinton (S.Yorks)	29	d		23p36				06 35	06 51		07 15					07 33				08 37						
Bolton-upon-Dearne		d		23p41					06 56							07 38				08 42						
Goldthorpe		d		23p44					06 58							07 40				08 44						
Thurnscoe		d		23p47					07 01							07 43				08 47						
Moorthorpe		d		23p52					07 06							07 52				08 53						
Doncaster 7		d	23p26			06 26		06 55		07 26	07 34								08 17					08 26	08 50	
Bentley (S.Yorks)		d				06 29		06 58		07 29	07 37								08 20					08 29		
Adwick		a				06 33		07 05		07 33	07 43								08 25					08 33		
		d				06 33				07 33														08 33		
South Elmsall		d				06 39				07 39														08 39		
Fitzwilliam		d				06 44			07 12	07 44						07 58				09 09				08 45		
Sandal & Agbrigg		d				06 50			07 18	07 50					←	08 04				09 15				08 49		←
Wakefield Westgate 7	32,39	a	23p44			06 54			07 22	07 54				07 36	07 54	08 10				09 19			08 45	08 54	09 07	09 19
		d	23p44		06 24	06 54			07 23	07 54				07 37	07 54	08 11				09 19			08 46	08 55	09 07	09 19
Pontefract Monkhill	32	d								↦										↦						
Wakefield Kirkgate 4	32,34,39	a			06 29		06 49						07 49				08 27	08 49			08 57					
		d					06 50						07 50				08 28	08 50			08 58					
Outwood		d				06 59			07 28						07 59	08 16								08 58		09 24
Leeds 10	32,34	a	00 03	00 30		07 13	07 28		07 44				08 25	07 52	08 13	08 32	08 49	09 25			09 20		09 03	09 14	09 27	09 40

			NT	NT	NT	NT	NT		NT	NT	XC	NT	NT	GR	NT	NT	NT		NT	NT	NT	NT	XC	NT	GR	NT
											◇1 🍴			B 1 ☕🍴									◇1 🍴		B 1 ☕🍴	
Sheffield 7	29 ⇌	d	08 51			08 53	09 06		09 14	09 18	09 21		09 31			09 50			09 53	10 06	10 14	10 18	10 21			
Meadowhall	29 ⇌	d	08 57			09 00	09 12		09 21	09 24			09 38			09 56			09 59	10 12	10 21	10 24				
Rotherham Central	29	d				09 06			09 27				09 45						10 05		10 27					
Swinton (S.Yorks)	29	d				09 16			09 36				09 53						10 15		10 36					
Bolton-upon-Dearne		d							09 41												10 41					
Goldthorpe		d							09 43												10 43					
Thurnscoe		d							09 46												10 46					
Moorthorpe		d							09 53				10a03								10 53					
Doncaster 7		d		08 54	09 26	09 34								09 50			10 26		10 34						10 50	
Bentley (S.Yorks)		d		08 57	09 29	09 37											10 29		10 37							
Adwick		a		09 04	09 33	09 43											10 33		10 43							
		d			09 33												10 33									
South Elmsall		d			09 39												10 39									
Fitzwilliam		d			09 45				10 09								10 45				11 09					
Sandal & Agbrigg		d			09 49				10 15			←			←		10 49				11 15			←		←
Wakefield Westgate 7	32,39	a			09 54				10 19		09 46	09 54		10 07	10 19		10 54				11 19		10 46	10 54	11 07	11 19
		d			09 55				10 19		09 47	09 55		10 07	10 19		10 55				11 19		10 47	10 55	11 07	11 19
Pontefract Monkhill	32	d			↦				↦								↦				↦					
Wakefield Kirkgate 4	32,34,39	a	09 27				09 49			09 57						10 27				10 49		10 57				
		d	09 28				09 50			09 58						10 28				10 50		10 58				
Outwood		d										09 58			10 24									10 58		11 24
Leeds 10	32,34	a	09 49				10 25			10 18	10 02	10 14		10 27	10 40	10 48				11 25		11 18	11 02	11 14	11 28	11 40

			NT		NT	NT	NT	NT	NT	XC	NT	GR	NT		NT	GC	NT	NT	NT	NT	NT	XC	NT		GR	NT
										◇1 🍴		B 1 ☕🍴				B 1 ☕						◇1 🍴			B 1 ☕🍴	
Sheffield 7	29 ⇌	d	10 50			10 53	11 06	11 14	11 18	11 21					11 50			11 53	12 06	12 14	12 18	12 21				
Meadowhall	29 ⇌	d	10 56			10 59	11 12	11 21	11 24						11 56			11 59	12 12	12 21	12 24					
Rotherham Central	29	d				11 05		11 27										12 05		12 27						
Swinton (S.Yorks)	29	d				11 16		11 36										12 16		12 36						
Bolton-upon-Dearne		d						11 41												12 41						
Goldthorpe		d						11 43												12 43						
Thurnscoe		d						11 46												12 46						
Moorthorpe		d						11 53												12 53						
Doncaster 7		d			11 26	11 34						11 50				12 20	12 26	12 34							12 50	
Bentley (S.Yorks)		d			11 29	11 37											12 29	12 37								
Adwick		a			11 33	11 43											12 33	12 43								
		d			11 33												12 33									
South Elmsall		d			11 39												12 39									
Fitzwilliam		d			11 45			12 09									12 45			13 09						
Sandal & Agbrigg		d			11 49			12 15			←		←				12 49			13 15			←			←
Wakefield Westgate 7	32,39	a			11 54			12 19		11 46	11 54	12 07	12 19				12 54			13 19		12 46	12 54		13 07	13 19
		d			11 55			12 19		11 47	11 55	12 07	12 19				12 55			13 19		12 47	12 55		13 07	13 19
Pontefract Monkhill	32	d			↦			↦								12 45	↦			↦						
Wakefield Kirkgate 4	32,34,39	a	11 27				11 49		11 57						12 27	13 04			12 49		12 57					
		d	11 28				11 50		11 58						12 28				12 50		12 58					
Outwood		d									11 58		12 24										12 58			13 24
Leeds 10	32,34	a	11 48				12 25		12 18	12 02	12 14	12 28	12 40		12 48				13 25		13 18	13 02	13 13		13 28	13 43

Table 31

Saturdays until 18 June

Sheffield, Doncaster and Wakefield - Leeds

Station			NT	GR	NT	NT	NT	NT	NT		XC	NT	NT	GR	NT	NT	NT	NT	NT		NT	NT	XC	NT	GR	NT
				R 1							◇1			R 1									◇1		R 1	
Sheffield 7	29	d	12 50			12 53	13 06	13 14	13 18		13 21		13 28			13 50		13 53	14 06		14 14	14 18	14 21			
Meadowhall	29	d	12 56			12 59	13 12	13 21	13 24				13 35			13 56		13 59	14 12		14 21	14 24				
Rotherham Central	29	d				13 05		13 27					13 42					14 05			14 27					
Swinton (S.Yorks)	29	d				13 16		13 36					13 51					14 17			14 36					
Bolton-upon-Dearne		d						13 41													14 41					
Goldthorpe		d						13 43													14 43					
Thurnscoe		d						13 46													14 46					
Moorthorpe		d						13 53					14a01								14 53					
Doncaster 7		d		13 12	13 26	13 34								13 52			14 26	14 34							14 50	
Bentley (S.Yorks)		d			13 29	13 37											14 29	14 37								
Adwick		a			13 33	13 43											14 33	14 43								
		d			13 33												14 33									
South Elmsall		d			13 39												14 39									
Fitzwilliam		d			13 45			14 09									14 45				15 09					
Sandal & Agbrigg		d			13 49			14 15				←			←		14 49				15 15			←		←
Wakefield Westgate 7	32,39	a		13 30	13 54			14 19			13 46	13 54		14 11	14 19		14 54				15 19		14 46	14 54	15 07	15 19
		d		13 30	13 55			14 19			13 47	13 55		14 11	14 19		14 55				15 19		14 47	14 55	15 07	15 19
Pontefract Monkhill	32	d			→			→									→				→					
Wakefield Kirkgate 4	32,34,39	a	13 27				13 50		13 57							14 27			14 49			14 57				
		d	13 28				13 50		13 58							14 28			14 50			14 58				
Outwood		d										13 58			14 24									14 58		15 24
Leeds 10	32,34	a	13 49	13 50			14 25		14 18		14 02	14 14		14 31	14 40	14 48			15 25			15 18	15 02	15 14	15 28	15 40

Station			NT	NT	NT		NT	NT	NT	XC	NT	GR	NT	NT	NT		NT	NT	NT	NT	XC	NT	GR	NT	NT	
										◇1		R 1									◇1		R 1			
Sheffield 7	29	d	14 50		14 53		15 06	15 14	15 18	15 21				15 50			15 53	16 06	16 14	16 18	16 21				16 50	
Meadowhall	29	d	14 56		14 59		15 12	15 21	15 24					15 56			15 59	16 12	16 21	16 24					16 56	
Rotherham Central	29	d			15 05			15 27									16 05		16 27							
Swinton (S.Yorks)	29	d			15 17			15 36									16 16		16 36							
Bolton-upon-Dearne		d						15 41											16 41							
Goldthorpe		d						15 43											16 43							
Thurnscoe		d						15 46											16 46							
Moorthorpe		d						15 53											16 53							
Doncaster 7		d		15 26	15 34							15 50			16 25		16 34						16 50			
Bentley (S.Yorks)		d		15 29	15 37										16 28		16 37									
Adwick		a		15 33	15 43										16 32		16 43									
		d		15 33											16 32											
South Elmsall		d		15 39											16 38											
Fitzwilliam		d		15 45				16 09							16 42				17 09							
Sandal & Agbrigg		d		15 49				16 15			←		←		16 48				17 15			←		←		
Wakefield Westgate 7	32,39	a		15 54				16 19		15 46	15 54	16 07	16 19		16 52				17 19		16 46	16 52	17 07	17 19		
		d		15 55				16 19		15 47	15 55	16 07	16 19		16 52				17 19		16 47	16 52	17 07	17 19		
Pontefract Monkhill	32	d		→				→							→				→							
Wakefield Kirkgate 4	32,34,39	a	15 27				15 49		15 57					16 27				16 49		16 57					17 28	
		d	15 28				15 50		15 58					16 28				16 50		16 58					17 28	
Outwood		d									15 58		16 24									16 59		17 24		
Leeds 10	32,34	a	15 49				16 25		16 18	16 02	16 13	16 28	16 40	16 48				17 25		17 18	17 02	17 13	17 28	17 41	17 48	

Station			GC	NT	NT	NT	NT	NT	XC	NT	GR		XC	NT	NT	NT	NT	NT	XC	NT	GR		NT	GR	NT	NT
			R 1						◇1		R 1		◇1						◇1		R 1			R 1		
Sheffield 7	29	d			16 53	17 06	17 14	17 18	17 21				17 47		17 50	18 06	18 13	18 18	18 21						18 50	19 06
Meadowhall	29	d			16 59	17 12	17 21	17 24							17 56	18 12	18 21	18 24							18 56	19 12
Rotherham Central	29	d			17 05		17 27										18 27									
Swinton (S.Yorks)	29	d			17 16		17 37										18 37									
Bolton-upon-Dearne		d					17 41										18 41									
Goldthorpe		d					17 44										18 44									
Thurnscoe		d					17 47										18 47									
Moorthorpe		d					17 52										18 53									
Doncaster 7		d	17 22	17 26	17 34						17 50									18 26	18 50			19 15		
Bentley (S.Yorks)		d		17 29	17 37															18 29						
Adwick		a		17 33	17 43															18 33						
		d		17 33																18 33						
South Elmsall		d		17 39																18 39						
Fitzwilliam		d		17 45			18 13										19 09			18 44						
Sandal & Agbrigg		d		17 51			18 19			←				←			19 15			18 50			←			
Wakefield Westgate 7	32,39	a		17 55			18 23		17 47	17 55	18 07		18 12	18 23			19 19		18 46	18 53	19 07		19 19	19 32		
		d		17 55			18 23		17 47	17 55	18 07		18 13	18 23			19 19		18 47	18 54	19 07		19 19	19 32		
Pontefract Monkhill	32	d	17 47	→			→										→									
Wakefield Kirkgate 4	32,34,39	a	18 03			17 49		17 57							18 28	18 50		18 59							19 29	19 50
		d				17 50		17 58							18 32	18 50		18 59							19 32	19 50
Outwood		d								18 00				18 28						18 57			19 24			
Leeds 10	32,34	a				18 25		18 18	18 02	18 14	18 27		18 31	18 44	18 51	19 27		19 23	19 01	19 14	19 27		19 43	19 48	19 55	20 26

Table 31

Saturdays

until 18 June

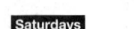

Sheffield, Doncaster and Wakefield - Leeds

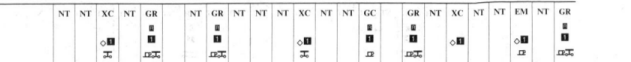

		NT	NT	XC	NT	GR		NT	GR	NT	NT	NT	XC	NT	NT	GC		GR	NT	XC	NT	NT	EM	NT	GR
				◇1		R 1			R 1				◇1			R 1		R 1		◇1			◇1		R 1
Sheffield 7	29 d	19 16	19 18	19 22						19 51	20 06	20 18	20 24		20 27				21 06	21 21			21 24	21 30	
Meadowhall	29 d	19 22	19 25							19 57	20 12	20 24			20 35				21 12					21 36	
Rotherham Central	29 d		19 31												20 41									21 42	
Swinton (S.Yorks)	29 d		19 40												20 50									21 50	
Bolton-upon-Dearne	d		19 44												20 55									21 54	
Goldthorpe	d		19 47												20 57									21 57	
Thurnscoe	d		19 50												21 00									22 00	
Moorthorpe	d		20 01												21 05									22 05	
Doncaster 7	d				19 22	19 50			20 13					20 26		20 37		21 17			21 22				22 18
Bentley (S.Yorks)	d				19 25									20 29							21 25				
Adwick	a				19 29									20 33							21 29				
	d				19 29									20 33							21 29				
South Elmsall	d				19 35									20 39							21 35				
Fitzwilliam	d		20 07		19 48									20 44	21 11						21 42			22 11	
Sandal & Agbrigg	d		20 13		19 53			←						20 50	21 17						21 48			22 17	
Wakefield Westgate 7	32,39 a		20 17	19 49	19 57	20 07		20 17	20 31				20 48	20 54	21 22			21 34		21 49	21 52		21 59	22 21	22 35
	d		20 17	19 50	19 58	20 07		20 17	20 32				20 49	20 54	21 22			21 34		21 50	21 53	21 57	22 00	22 21	22 35
Pontefract Monkhill	32 d		→													21 00									
Wakefield Kirkgate 4	32,34,39 a	19 58								20 28	20 49	20 57				21 17			21 52			22 00			
	d	19 58								20 28	20 50	20 58							21 52						
Outwood	d				20 02			20 22						20 59	21 27						21 58			22 26	
Leeds 10	32,34 a	20 20		20 05	20 16	20 28		20 38	20 47	20 48	21 26	21 19	21 03	21 18	21 47			21 54	22 29	22 03	22 16		22 21	22 45	22 55

		EM		NT	NT	NT	XC	NT	NT	GR
		◇1					◇1			R 1
Sheffield 7	29 d	22 19				22 24	22 27			
Meadowhall	29 d					22 30				
Rotherham Central	29 d					22 36				
Swinton (S.Yorks)	29 d					22 45				
Bolton-upon-Dearne	d					22 49				
Goldthorpe	d					22 52				
Thurnscoe	d					22 55				
Moorthorpe	d					23 00				
Doncaster 7	d			22 26			22 53			23 48
Bentley (S.Yorks)	d			22 29						
Adwick	a			22 33						
	d			22 33						
South Elmsall	d			22 39						
Fitzwilliam	d			22 44		23 07				
Sandal & Agbrigg	d			22 50		23 13			←	
Wakefield Westgate 7	32,39 a	22 44		22 54		23 18	23 10		23 18	00 05
	d	22 45		22 54	23 04	23 18	23 11		23 18	00 05
Pontefract Monkhill	32 d					→				
Wakefield Kirkgate 4	32,34,39 a				23 07					
	d							22 51		
Outwood	d			22 59					23 23	
Leeds 10	32,34 a	23 04		23 14			23 27	23 29	23 40	00 26

Saturdays

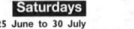

25 June to 30 July

		GR	NT	NT	NT	NT	NT	NT	NT	NT		NT	XC	NT	NT	NT	NT	NT	NT	NT		XC	NT	GR	NT
		R 1											◇1									◇1		R 1	
Sheffield 7	29 d		23p15			06 06	06 12	06 28		06 52		07 06	07 12		07 14	07 51	08 06		08 14	08 18		08 21			
Meadowhall	29 d		23p21			06 12	06 18	06 34		06 58		07 12			07 21	07 57	08 12		08 22	08 25					
Rotherham Central	29 d		23p27				06 24	06 40		07 04					07 27				08 28						
Swinton (S.Yorks)	29 d		23p36				06 35	06 51		07 15					07 33				08 37						
Bolton-upon-Dearne	d		23p41					06 56							07 38				08 42						
Goldthorpe	d		23p44					06 58							07 40				08 44						
Thurnscoe	d		23p47					07 01							07 43				08 47						
Moorthorpe	d		23p52					07 06							07 52				08 53						
Doncaster 7	d	23p26			06 26		06 55		07 26	07 34								08 17					08 26	08 50	
Bentley (S.Yorks)	d				06 29		06 58		07 29	07 37								08 20					08 29		
Adwick	a				06 33		07 05		07 33	07 43								08 25					08 33		
	d				06 33				07 33														08 33		
South Elmsall	d				06 39				07 39														08 39		
Fitzwilliam	d				06 44			07 12	07 44						07 58				09 09				08 45		
Sandal & Agbrigg	d				06 50			07 18	07 50					←	08 04				09 15				08 49		←
Wakefield Westgate 7	32,39 a	23p44			06 54			07 22	07 54				07 36	07 54	08 10				09 19			08 45	08 54	09 07	09 19
	d	23p44		06 24	06 54			07 23	07 54				07 37	07 54	08 11				09 19			08 46	08 55	09 07	09 19
Pontefract Monkhill	32 d								→										→						
Wakefield Kirkgate 4	32,34,39 a			06 29		06 49						07 49				08 27	08 49			08 57					
	d					06 50						07 50				08 28	08 50			08 58					
Outwood	d				06 59			07 28						07 59	08 16								08 58		09 24
Leeds 10	32,34 a	00 03	00 30		07 13	07 28		07 44				08 25	07 52	08 13	08 32	08 49	09 25			09 20		09 03	09 14	09 27	09 40

Table 31

Saturdays

25 June to 30 July

Sheffield, Doncaster and Wakefield - Leeds

			NT	NT	NT	NT	NT		NT	NT	XC	NT	NT	GR	NT	NT	NT		NT	NT	NT	NT	XC	NT	GR	NT
											◇1			R 1									◇1		R 1	
Sheffield 7	29	d	08 51			08 53	09 06		09 14	09 18	09 21		09 31			09 50			09 53	10 06	10 14	10 18	10 21			
Meadowhall	29	d	08 57			09 00	09 12		09 21	09 24			09 38			09 56			09 59	10 12	10 21	10 24				
Rotherham Central	29	d				09 06			09 27				09 45						10 05		10 27					
Swinton (S.Yorks)	29	d				09 16			09 36				09 53						10 15		10 36					
Bolton-upon-Dearne		d							09 41												10 41					
Goldthorpe		d							09 43												10 43					
Thurnscoe		d							09 46												10 46					
Moorthorpe		d							09 53				10a03								10 53					
Doncaster 7		d		08 54	09 26	09 34								09 50			10 26		10 34						10 50	
Bentley (S.Yorks)		d		08 57	09 29	09 37											10 29		10 37							
Adwick		a		09 04	09 33	09 43											10 33		10 43							
		d			09 33												10 33									
South Elmsall		d			09 39												10 39									
Fitzwilliam		d			09 45				10 09								10 45				11 09					
Sandal & Agbrigg		d			09 49				10 15			←			←		10 49				11 15			←		←
Wakefield Westgate 7	32,39	a			09 54				10 19		09 46	09 54		10 07	10 19		10 54				11 19		10 46	10 54	11 07	11 19
		d			09 55				10 19		09 47	09 55		10 07	10 19		10 55				11 19		10 47	10 55	11 07	11 19
Pontefract Monkhill	32	d			→				→								→				→					
Wakefield Kirkgate 4	32,34,39	a	09 27				09 49			09 57						10 27				10 49		10 57				
		d	09 28				09 50			09 58						10 28				10 50		10 58				
Outwood		d										09 58			10 24									10 58		11 24
Leeds 10	32,34	a	09 49				10 25			10 18	10 02	10 14		10 27	10 40	10 48				11 25		11 18	11 02	11 14	11 28	11 40

			NT		NT	NT	NT	NT	NT	XC	NT	GR	NT		NT	GC	NT	NT	NT	NT	NT	XC	NT		GR	NT
										◇1		R 1				R 1						◇1			R 1	
Sheffield 7	29	d	10 50			10 53	11 06	11 14	11 18	11 21					11 50			11 53	12 06	12 14	12 18	12 21				
Meadowhall	29	d	10 56			10 59	11 12	11 21	11 24						11 56			11 59	12 12	12 21	12 24					
Rotherham Central	29	d				11 05		11 27										12 05		12 27						
Swinton (S.Yorks)	29	d				11 16		11 36										12 16		12 36						
Bolton-upon-Dearne		d						11 41												12 41						
Goldthorpe		d						11 43												12 43						
Thurnscoe		d						11 46												12 46						
Moorthorpe		d						11 53												12 53						
Doncaster 7		d			11 26	11 34						11 50				12 20	12 26	12 34							12 50	
Bentley (S.Yorks)		d			11 29	11 37											12 29	12 37								
Adwick		a			11 33	11 43											12 33	12 43								
		d			11 33												12 33									
South Elmsall		d			11 39												12 39									
Fitzwilliam		d			11 45			12 09									12 45			13 09						
Sandal & Agbrigg		d			11 49			12 15			←		←				12 49			13 15			←			←
Wakefield Westgate 7	32,39	a			11 54			12 19		11 46	11 54	12 07	12 19				12 54			13 19		12 46	12 54		13 07	13 19
		d			11 55			12 19		11 47	11 55	12 07	12 19				12 55			13 19		12 47	12 55		13 07	13 19
Pontefract Monkhill	32	d			→			→								12 45	→			→						
Wakefield Kirkgate 4	32,34,39	a	11 27				11 49		11 57						12 27	13 04			12 49		12 57					
		d	11 28				11 50		11 58						12 28				12 50		12 58					
Outwood		d									11 58		12 24										12 58			13 24
Leeds 10	32,34	a	11 48				12 25		12 18	12 02	12 14	12 28	12 40		12 48				13 25		13 18	13 02	13 13		13 28	13 43

			NT	GR	NT	NT	NT	NT	NT		XC	NT	NT	GR	NT	NT	NT	NT	NT		NT	NT	XC	NT	GR	NT
				R 1							◇1			R 1									◇1		R 1	
Sheffield 7	29	d	12 50			12 53	13 06	13 14	13 18		13 21		13 28			13 50		13 53	14 06		14 14	14 18	14 21			
Meadowhall	29	d	12 56			12 59	13 12	13 21	13 24				13 35			13 56		13 59	14 12		14 21	14 24				
Rotherham Central	29	d				13 05		13 27					13 42					14 05			14 27					
Swinton (S.Yorks)	29	d				13 16		13 36					13 51					14 17			14 36					
Bolton-upon-Dearne		d						13 41													14 41					
Goldthorpe		d						13 43													14 43					
Thurnscoe		d						13 46													14 46					
Moorthorpe		d						13 53					14a01								14 53					
Doncaster 7		d		13 12	13 26	13 34								13 52			14 26	14 34							14 50	
Bentley (S.Yorks)		d			13 29	13 37											14 29	14 37								
Adwick		a			13 33	13 43											14 33	14 43								
		d			13 33												14 33									
South Elmsall		d			13 39												14 39									
Fitzwilliam		d			13 45			14 09									14 45				15 09					
Sandal & Agbrigg		d			13 49			14 15				←			←		14 49				15 15			←		←
Wakefield Westgate 7	32,39	a		13 30	13 54			14 19			13 46	13 54		14 11	14 19		14 54				15 19		14 46	14 54	15 07	15 19
		d		13 30	13 55			14 19			13 47	13 55		14 11	14 19		14 55				15 19		14 47	14 55	15 07	15 19
Pontefract Monkhill	32	d			→			→									→				→					
Wakefield Kirkgate 4	32,34,39	a	13 27				13 50		13 57							14 27			14 49			14 57				
		d	13 28				13 50		13 58							14 28			14 50			14 58				
Outwood		d										13 58			14 24									14 58		15 24
Leeds 10	32,34	a	13 49	13 50			14 25		14 18		14 02	14 14		14 31	14 40	14 48			15 25			15 18	15 02	15 14	15 28	15 40

Table 31

Saturdays

25 June to 30 July

Sheffield, Doncaster and Wakefield - Leeds

Station		NT	NT	NT		NT	NT	NT	XC	NT	GR	NT	NT	NT		NT	NT	NT	NT	XC	NT	GR	NT	NT	
									◇1		R 1									◇1		R 1			
Sheffield 7 29	d	14 50		14 53		15 06	15 14	15 18	15 21				15 50			15 53	16 06	16 14	16 18	16 21				16 50	
Meadowhall 29	d	14 56		14 59		15 12	15 21	15 24					15 56			15 59	16 12	16 21	16 24					16 56	
Rotherham Central 29	d			15 05			15 27									16 05		16 27							
Swinton (S.Yorks) 29	d			15 17			15 36									16 16		16 36							
Bolton-upon-Dearne	d						15 41											16 41							
Goldthorpe	d						15 43											16 43							
Thurnscoe	d						15 46											16 46							
Moorthorpe	d						15 53											16 53							
Doncaster 7	d		15 26	15 34							15 50			16 25		16 34						16 50			
Bentley (S.Yorks)	d		15 29	15 37										16 28		16 37									
Adwick	a		15 33	15 43										16 32		16 43									
	d		15 33											16 32											
South Elmsall	d		15 39											16 38											
Fitzwilliam	d		15 45				16 09							16 42				17 09							
Sandal & Agbrigg	d		15 49				16 15			←		←		16 48				17 15			←		←		
Wakefield Westgate 7 32,39	a		15 54				16 19		15 46	15 54	16 07	16 19		16 52				17 19		16 46	16 52	17 07	17 19		
	d		15 55				16 19		15 47	15 55	16 07	16 19		16 52				17 19		16 47	16 52	17 07	17 19		
Pontefract Monkhill 32	d		↦				↦							↦				↦							
Wakefield Kirkgate 4 32,34,39	a	15 27				15 49		15 57					16 27				16 49		16 57					17 28	
	d	15 28				15 50		15 58					16 28				16 50		16 58					17 28	
Outwood	d									15 58		16 24									16 59		17 24		
Leeds 10 32,34	a	15 49				16 25		16 18	16 02	16 13	16 28	16 40	16 48				17 25		17 18	17 02	17 13	17 28	17 41	17 48	

Station		GC	NT	NT	NT	NT	NT	XC	NT	GR		XC	NT	NT	NT	NT	NT	XC	NT	GR		NT	GR	NT	NT
		R 1						◇1		R 1		◇1						◇1		R 1			R 1		
Sheffield 7 29	d			16 53	17 06	17 14	17 18	17 21				17 47		17 50	18 06	18 13	18 18	18 21						18 50	19 06
Meadowhall 29	d			16 59	17 12	17 21	17 24							17 56	18 12	18 21	18 24							18 56	19 12
Rotherham Central 29	d			17 05		17 27										18 27									
Swinton (S.Yorks) 29	d			17 16		17 37										18 37									
Bolton-upon-Dearne	d					17 41										18 41									
Goldthorpe	d					17 44										18 44									
Thurnscoe	d					17 47										18 47									
Moorthorpe	d					17 52										18 53									
Doncaster 7	d	17 22	17 26	17 34						17 50									18 26	18 50			19 15		
Bentley (S.Yorks)	d		17 29	17 37															18 29						
Adwick	a		17 33	17 43															18 33						
	d		17 33																18 33						
South Elmsall	d		17 39																18 39						
Fitzwilliam	d		17 45			18 13										19 09			18 44						
Sandal & Agbrigg	d		17 51			18 19			←				←			19 15			18 50			←			
Wakefield Westgate 7 32,39	a		17 55			18 23		17 47	17 55	18 07		18 12	18 23			19 19		18 46	18 53	19 07		19 19	19 32		
	d		17 55			18 23		17 47	17 55	18 07		18 13	18 23			19 19		18 47	18 54	19 07		19 19	19 32		
Pontefract Monkhill 32	d	17 47	↦			↦										↦									
Wakefield Kirkgate 4 32,34,39	a	18 03			17 49		17 57							18 28	18 50		18 59							19 29	19 50
	d				17 50		17 58							18 32	18 50		18 59							19 32	19 50
Outwood	d								18 00				18 28						18 57			19 24			
Leeds 10 32,34	a				18 25		18 18	18 02	18 14	18 27		18 31	18 44	18 51	19 27		19 23	19 01	19 14	19 27		19 43	19 48	19 55	20 26

Station		NT	NT	XC	NT	GR		NT	GR	NT	NT	NT	XC	NT	NT	GC		GR	NT	XC	NT	NT	EM	NT	EM
				◇1		R 1			R 1				◇1			R 1		R 1		◇1			◇1		◇1
Sheffield 7 29	d	19 16	19 18	19 22						19 51	20 06	20 18	20 24		20 27				21 06	21 21			21 24	21 30	22 19
Meadowhall 29	d	19 22	19 25							19 57	20 12	20 24			20 35				21 12					21 36	
Rotherham Central 29	d		19 31												20 41									21 42	
Swinton (S.Yorks) 29	d		19 40												20 50									21 50	
Bolton-upon-Dearne	d		19 44												20 55									21 54	
Goldthorpe	d		19 47												20 57									21 57	
Thurnscoe	d		19 50												21 00									22 00	
Moorthorpe	d		20b01												21 05									22 05	
Doncaster 7	d				19 22	19 50			20 13					20 26		20 37		21 17			21 22				
Bentley (S.Yorks)	d				19 25									20 29							21 25				
Adwick	a				19 29									20 33							21 29				
	d				19 29									20 33							21 29				
South Elmsall	d				19 35									20 39							21 35				
Fitzwilliam	d		20 07		19 48									20 44	21 11						21 42			22 11	
Sandal & Agbrigg	d		20 13		19 53			←						20 50	21 17						21 48			22 17	
Wakefield Westgate 7 32,39	a		20 17	19 49	19 57	20 07		20 17	20 31				20 48	20 54	21 22			21 34		21 49	21 52		21 59	22 21	22 44
	d		20 17	19 50	19 58	20 07		20 17	20 32				20 49	20 54	21 22			21 34		21 50	21 53	21 57	22 00	22 21	22 45
Pontefract Monkhill 32	d		↦													21 00									
Wakefield Kirkgate 4 32,34,39	a	19 58								20 28	20 49	20 57				21 17			21 52			22 00			
	d	19 58								20 28	20 50	20 58							21 52						
Outwood	d				20 02			20 22						20 59	21 27						21 58			22 26	
Leeds 10 32,34	a	20 20		20 05	20 16	20 28		20 38	20 47	20 48	21 26	21 19	21 03	21 18	21 47			21 54	22 29	22 03	22 16		22 21	22 45	23 04

Table 31

Sheffield, Doncaster and Wakefield - Leeds

Saturdays
25 June to 30 July

			NT		NT	NT	XC	NT	NT	GR
							◇1			R 1
Sheffield 7	29	d				22 24	22 27			
Meadowhall	29	d				22 30				
Rotherham Central	29	d				22 36				
Swinton (S.Yorks)	29	d				22 45				
Bolton-upon-Dearne		d				22 49				
Goldthorpe		d				22 52				
Thurnscoe		d				22 55				
Moorthorpe		d				23 00				
Doncaster 7		d	22 26				22 53			23 09
Bentley (S.Yorks)		d	22 29							
Adwick		a	22 33							
		d	22 33							
South Elmsall		d	22 39							
Fitzwilliam		d	22 44			23 07				
Sandal & Agbrigg		d	22 50			23 13			←	
Wakefield Westgate 7	32,39	a	22 54			23 18	23 10		23 18	23 26
		d	22 54		23 04	23 18	23 11		23 18	23 26
Pontefract Monkhill	32	d				↪				
Wakefield Kirkgate 4	32,34,39	a			23 07					
		d						22 51		
Outwood		d	22 59						23 23	
Leeds 10	32,34	a	23 14				23 27	23 29	23 40	23 46

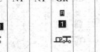

Saturdays
6 August to 10 September

			GR	NT	NT	NT	NT	NT	NT	NT	NT		NT	XC	NT	NT	NT	NT	NT	NT	NT		XC	NT	GR	NT
			R 1											◇1									◇1		R 1	
Sheffield 7	29	d		23p15			06 06	06 12	06 28		06 52		07 06	07 12		07 14	07 51	08 06		08 14	08 18		08 21			
Meadowhall	29	d		23p21			06 12	06 18	06 34		06 58		07 12			07 21	07 57	08 12		08 22	08 25					
Rotherham Central	29	d		23p27				06 24	06 40		07 04					07 27				08 28						
Swinton (S.Yorks)	29	d		23p36				06 35	06 51		07 15					07 33				08 37						
Bolton-upon-Dearne		d		23p41					06 56							07 38				08 42						
Goldthorpe		d		23p44					06 58							07 40				08 44						
Thurnscoe		d		23p47					07 01							07 43				08 47						
Moorthorpe		d		23p52					07 06							07 52				08 53						
Doncaster 7		d	23p26			06 26		06 55		07 26	07 34								08 17					08 26	08 50	
Bentley (S.Yorks)		d				06 29		06 58		07 29	07 37								08 20					08 29		
Adwick		a				06 33		07 05		07 33	07 43								08 25					08 33		
		d				06 33				07 33														08 33		
South Elmsall		d				06 39				07 39														08 39		
Fitzwilliam		d				06 44			07 12	07 44						07 58				09 09				08 45		
Sandal & Agbrigg		d				06 50			07 18	07 50					←	08 04				09 15				08 49		←
Wakefield Westgate 7	32,39	a	23p44			06 54			07 22	07 54				07 36	07 54	08 10				09 19			08 45	08 54	09 07	09 19
		d	23p44		06 24	06 54			07 23	07 54				07 37	07 54	08 11				09 19			08 46	08 55	09 07	09 19
Pontefract Monkhill	32	d								↪										↪						
Wakefield Kirkgate 4	32,34,39	a			06 29		06 49						07 49				08 27	08 49			08 57					
		d					06 50						07 50				08 28	08 50			08 58					
Outwood		d				06 59			07 28						07 59	08 16								08 58		09 24
Leeds 10	32,34	a	00 03	00 30		07 13	07 28		07 44				08 25	07 52	08 13	08 32	08 49	09 25			09 20		09 03	09 14	09 27	09 40

			NT	NT	NT	NT	NT		NT	NT	XC	NT	NT	GR	NT	NT	NT		NT	NT	NT	NT	XC	NT	GR	NT
											◇1			R 1									◇1		R 1	
Sheffield 7	29	d	08 51			08 53	09 06		09 14	09 18	09 21		09 31			09 50			09 53	10 06	10 14	10 18	10 21			
Meadowhall	29	d	08 57			09 00	09 12		09 21	09 24			09 38			09 56			09 59	10 12	10 21	10 24				
Rotherham Central	29	d				09 06			09 27				09 45						10 05		10 27					
Swinton (S.Yorks)	29	d				09 16			09 36				09 53						10 15		10 36					
Bolton-upon-Dearne		d							09 41												10 41					
Goldthorpe		d							09 43												10 43					
Thurnscoe		d							09 46												10 46					
Moorthorpe		d							09 53				10a03								10 53					
Doncaster 7		d		08 54	09 26	09 34								09 50			10 26		10 34						10 50	
Bentley (S.Yorks)		d		08 57	09 29	09 37											10 29		10 37							
Adwick		a		09 04	09 33	09 43											10 33		10 43							
		d			09 33												10 33									
South Elmsall		d			09 39												10 39									
Fitzwilliam		d			09 45				10 09								10 45				11 09					
Sandal & Agbrigg		d			09 49				10 15			←			←		10 49				11 15			←		←
Wakefield Westgate 7	32,39	a			09 54				10 19		09 46	09 54		10 07	10 19		10 54				11 19		10 46	10 54	11 07	11 19
		d			09 55				10 19		09 47	09 55		10 07	10 19		10 55				11 19		10 47	10 55	11 07	11 19
Pontefract Monkhill	32	d			↪				↪								↪				↪					
Wakefield Kirkgate 4	32,34,39	a	09 27				09 49			09 57						10 27				10 49		10 57				
		d	09 28				09 50			09 58						10 28				10 50		10 58				
Outwood		d										09 58			10 24									10 58		11 24
Leeds 10	32,34	a	09 49				10 25			10 18	10 02	10 14		10 27	10 40	10 48				11 25		11 18	11 02	11 14	11 28	11 40

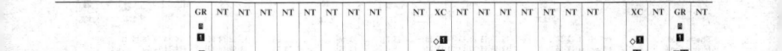

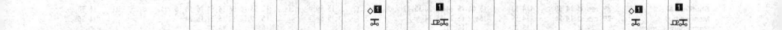

Table 31

Sheffield, Doncaster and Wakefield - Leeds

Saturdays

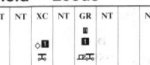

6 August to 10 September

	NT		NT	NT	NT	NT	NT	XC	NT	GR	NT		NT	GC	NT	NT	NT	NT	NT	XC	NT		GR	NT
								◇1		R 1				R 1						◇1			R 1	
Sheffield 7 29 🚊 d	10 50			10 53	11 06	11 14	11 18	11 21					11 50			11 53	12 06	12 14	12 18	12 21				
Meadowhall 29 🚊 d	10 56			10 59	11 12	11 21	11 24						11 56			11 59	12 12	12 21	12 24					
Rotherham Central 29 d				11 05		11 27										12 05		12 27						
Swinton (S.Yorks) 29 d				11 16		11 36										12 16		12 36						
Bolton-upon-Dearne d						11 41												12 41						
Goldthorpe d						11 43												12 43						
Thurnscoe d						11 46												12 46						
Moorthorpe d						11 53												12 53						
Doncaster 7 d			11 26	11 34						11 50				12 20	12 26	12 34							12 50	
Bentley (S.Yorks) d			11 29	11 37											12 29	12 37								
Adwick a			11 33	11 43											12 33	12 43								
d			11 33												12 33									
South Elmsall d			11 39												12 39									
Fitzwilliam d			11 45			12 09									12 45			13 09						
Sandal & Agbrigg d			11 49			12 15			←		←				12 49			13 15			←			←
Wakefield Westgate 7 32,39 a			11 54			12 19		11 46	11 54	12 07	12 19				12 54			13 19		12 46	12 54		13 07	13 19
d			11 55			12 19		11 47	11 55	12 07	12 19				12 55			13 19		12 47	12 55		13 07	13 19
Pontefract Monkhill 32 d			↪			↪								12 45	↪			↪						
Wakefield Kirkgate 4 32,34,39 a	11 27				11 49		11 57						12 27	13 04			12 49		12 57					
d	11 28				11 50		11 58						12 28				12 50		12 58					
Outwood d									11 58		12 24										12 58			13 24
Leeds 10 32,34 a	11 48				12 25		12 18	12 02	12 14	12 28	12 40		12 48				13 25		13 18	13 02	13 13		13 28	13 43

	NT	GR	NT	NT	NT	NT	NT		XC	NT	NT	GR	NT	NT	NT	NT	NT		NT	NT	XC	NT	GR	NT
		R 1							◇1			R 1									◇1		R 1	
Sheffield 7 29 🚊 d	12 50			12 53	13 06	13 14	13 18		13 21		13 28			13 50		13 53	14 06		14 14	14 18	14 21			
Meadowhall 29 🚊 d	12 56			12 59	13 12	13 21	13 24				13 35			13 56		13 59	14 12		14 21	14 24				
Rotherham Central 29 d				13 05		13 27					13 42					14 05			14 27					
Swinton (S.Yorks) 29 d				13 16		13 36					13 51					14 17			14 36					
Bolton-upon-Dearne d						13 41													14 41					
Goldthorpe d						13 43													14 43					
Thurnscoe d						13 46													14 46					
Moorthorpe d						13 53					14a01								14 53					
Doncaster 7 d		13 12	13 26	13 34								13 52			14 26	14 34							14 50	
Bentley (S.Yorks) d			13 29	13 37											14 29	14 37								
Adwick a			13 33	13 43											14 33	14 43								
d			13 33												14 33									
South Elmsall d			13 39												14 39									
Fitzwilliam d			13 45			14 09									14 45				15 09					
Sandal & Agbrigg d			13 49			14 15				←			←		14 49				15 15			←		←
Wakefield Westgate 7 32,39 a		13 30	13 54			14 19			13 46	13 54		14 11	14 19		14 54				15 19		14 46	14 54	15 07	15 19
d		13 30	13 55			14 19			13 47	13 55		14 11	14 19		14 55				15 19		14 47	14 55	15 07	15 19
Pontefract Monkhill 32 d			↪			↪									↪				↪					
Wakefield Kirkgate 4 32,34,39 a	13 27				13 50		13 57							14 27			14 49			14 57				
d	13 28				13 50		13 58							14 28			14 50			14 58				
Outwood d										13 58			14 24									14 58		15 24
Leeds 10 32,34 a	13 49	13 50			14 25		14 18		14 02	14 14		14 31	14 40	14 48			15 25			15 18	15 02	15 14	15 28	15 40

	NT	NT	NT		NT	NT	NT	XC	NT	GR	NT	NT	NT		NT	NT	NT	NT	XC	NT	GR	NT	NT	
								◇1		R 1									◇1		R 1			
Sheffield 7 29 🚊 d	14 50		14 53		15 06	15 14	15 18	15 21				15 50			15 53	16 06	16 14	16 18	16 21				16 50	
Meadowhall 29 🚊 d	14 56		14 59		15 12	15 21	15 24					15 56			15 59	16 12	16 21	16 24					16 56	
Rotherham Central 29 d			15 05			15 27									16 05		16 27							
Swinton (S.Yorks) 29 d			15 17			15 36									16 16		16 36							
Bolton-upon-Dearne d						15 41											16 41							
Goldthorpe d						15 43											16 43							
Thurnscoe d						15 46											16 46							
Moorthorpe d						15 53											16 53							
Doncaster 7 d		15 26	15 34							15 50			16 25		16 34						16 50			
Bentley (S.Yorks) d		15 29	15 37										16 28		16 37									
Adwick a		15 33	15 43										16 32		16 43									
d		15 33											16 32											
South Elmsall d		15 39											16 38											
Fitzwilliam d		15 45				16 09							16 42				17 09							
Sandal & Agbrigg d		15 49				16 15			←		←		16 48				17 15			←		←		
Wakefield Westgate 7 32,39 a		15 54				16 19		15 46	15 54	16 07	16 19		16 52				17 19		16 46	16 52	17 07	17 19		
d		15 55				16 19		15 47	15 55	16 07	16 19		16 52				17 19		16 47	16 52	17 07	17 19		
Pontefract Monkhill 32 d		↪				↪							↪				↪							
Wakefield Kirkgate 4 32,34,39 a	15 27				15 49		15 57					16 27				16 49		16 57					17 28	
d	15 28				15 50		15 58					16 28				16 50		16 58					17 28	
Outwood d									15 58		16 24									16 59		17 24		
Leeds 10 32,34 a	15 49				16 25		16 18	16 02	16 13	16 28	16 40	16 48				17 25		17 18	17 02	17 13	17 28	17 41	17 48	

Table 31

Saturdays

6 August to 10 September

Sheffield, Doncaster and Wakefield - Leeds

			GC	NT	NT	NT	NT	NT	XC	NT	GR		XC	NT	NT	NT	NT	NT	XC	NT	GR		NT	GR	NT	NT
			R 1 ☕						◇1 🛒		R 1 ☕🛒		◇1 🛒						◇1 🛒		R 1 ☕🛒			R 1 ☕🛒		
Sheffield 7	29 🚊	d			16 53	17 06	17 14	17 18	17 21				17 47		17 50	18 06	18 13	18 18	18 21						18 50	19 06
Meadowhall	29 🚊	d			16 59	17 12	17 21	17 24							17 56	18 12	18 21	18 24							18 56	19 12
Rotherham Central	29	d			17 05		17 27										18 27									
Swinton (S.Yorks)	29	d			17 16		17 37										18 37									
Bolton-upon-Dearne		d					17 41										18 41									
Goldthorpe		d					17 44										18 44									
Thurnscoe		d					17 47										18 47									
Moorthorpe		d					17 52										18 53									
Doncaster 7		d	17 22	17 26	17 34						17 50									18 26	18 50			19 15		
Bentley (S.Yorks)		d		17 29	17 37															18 29						
Adwick		a		17 33	17 43															18 33						
		d		17 33																18 33						
South Elmsall		d		17 39																18 39						
Fitzwilliam		d		17 45			18 13										19 09			18 44						
Sandal & Agbrigg		d		17 51			18 19			←				←			19 15			18 50			←			
Wakefield Westgate 7	32,39	a		17 55			18 23		17 47	17 55	18 07		18 12	18 23			19 19		18 46	18 53	19 07		19 19	19 32		
		d		17 55			18 23		17 47	17 55	18 07		18 13	18 23			19 19		18 47	18 54	19 07		19 19	19 32		
Pontefract Monkhill	32	d	17 47	→			→										→									
Wakefield Kirkgate 4	32,34,39	a	18 03			17 49		17 57							18 28	18 50		18 59							19 29	19 50
		d				17 50		17 58							18 32	18 50		18 59							19 32	19 50
Outwood		d								18 00				18 28						18 57			19 24			
Leeds 10	32,34	a				18 25		18 18	18 02	18 14	18 27		18 31	18 44	18 51	19 27		19 23	19 01	19 14	19 27		19 43	19 48	19 55	20 26

			NT	NT	XC	NT	GR		NT	GR	NT	NT	NT	XC	NT	NT	GC		GR	NT	XC	NT	NT	EM	NT	GR
					◇1 🛒		R 1 ☕🛒			R 1 ☕🛒				◇1 🛒			R 1 ☕		R 1 ☕🛒		◇1			◇1 ☕		R 1 ☕🛒
Sheffield 7	29 🚊	d	19 16	19 18	19 22						19 51	20 06	20 18	20 24		20 27				21 06	21 21			21 24	21 30	
Meadowhall	29 🚊	d	19 22	19 25							19 57	20 12	20 24			20 35				21 12					21 36	
Rotherham Central	29	d		19 31												20 41									21 42	
Swinton (S.Yorks)	29	d		19 40												20 50									21 50	
Bolton-upon-Dearne		d		19 44												20 55									21 54	
Goldthorpe		d		19 47												20 57									21 57	
Thurnscoe		d		19 50												21 00									22 00	
Moorthorpe		d		20 01												21 05									22 05	
Doncaster 7		d				19 22	19 50			20 13					20 26		20 37		21 17			21 22				22 18
Bentley (S.Yorks)		d				19 25									20 29							21 25				
Adwick		a				19 29									20 33							21 29				
		d				19 29									20 33							21 29				
South Elmsall		d				19 35									20 39							21 35				
Fitzwilliam		d		20 07		19 48									20 44	21 11						21 42			22 11	
Sandal & Agbrigg		d		20 13		19 53			←						20 50	21 17						21 48			22 17	
Wakefield Westgate 7	32,39	a		20 17	19 49	19 57	20 07		20 17	20 31				20 48	20 54	21 22			21 34		21 49	21 52		21 59	22 21	22 35
		d		20 17	19 50	19 58	20 07		20 17	20 32				20 49	20 54	21 22			21 34		21 50	21 53	21 57	22 00	22 21	22 35
Pontefract Monkhill	32	d		→													21 00									
Wakefield Kirkgate 4	32,34,39	a	19 58								20 28	20 49	20 57				21 17			21 52			22 00			
		d	19 58								20 28	20 50	20 58							21 52						
Outwood		d				20 02			20 22						20 59	21 27						21 58			22 26	
Leeds 10	32,34	a	20 20		20 05	20 16	20 28		20 38	20 47	20 48	21 26	21 19	21 03	21 18	21 47			21 54	22 29	22 03	22 16		22 21	22 45	22 55

			EM		NT	NT	NT	XC	NT	NT	GR
			◇1 ☕					◇1 🛒			R 1 ☕🛒
Sheffield 7	29 🚊	d	22 19				22 24	22 27			
Meadowhall	29 🚊	d					22 30				
Rotherham Central	29	d					22 36				
Swinton (S.Yorks)	29	d					22 45				
Bolton-upon-Dearne		d					22 49				
Goldthorpe		d					22 52				
Thurnscoe		d					22 55				
Moorthorpe		d					23 00				
Doncaster 7		d			22 26			22 53			23 48
Bentley (S.Yorks)		d			22 29						
Adwick		a			22 33						
		d			22 33						
South Elmsall		d			22 39						
Fitzwilliam		d			22 44		23 07				
Sandal & Agbrigg		d			22 50		23 13			←	
Wakefield Westgate 7	32,39	a	22 44		22 54		23 18	23 10		23 18	00 05
		d	22 45		22 54	23 04	23 18	23 11		23 18	00 05
Pontefract Monkhill	32	d					→				
Wakefield Kirkgate 4	32,34,39	a				23 07					
		d							22 51		
Outwood		d			22 59					23 23	
Leeds 10	32,34	a	23 04		23 14			23 27	23 29	23 40	00 26

Table 31

Saturdays

from 17 September

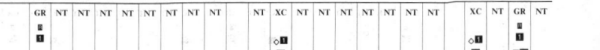

Sheffield, Doncaster and Wakefield - Leeds

			GR	NT	NT	NT	NT	NT	NT	NT	NT		NT	XC	NT	NT	NT	NT	NT	NT	NT		XC	NT	GR	NT
			R 1 ⊐P											◇1 ⊼									◇1 ⊼		R 1 ⊐P⊼	
Sheffield 7	29 ⇌	d		23p15			06 06	06 12	06 28		06 52		07 06	07 12		07 14	07 51	08 06		08 14	08 18		08 21			
Meadowhall	29 ⇌	d		23p21			06 12	06 18	06 34		06 58		07 12			07 21	07 57	08 12		08 22	08 25					
Rotherham Central	29	d		23p27				06 24	06 40		07 04					07 27				08 28						
Swinton (S.Yorks)	29	d		23p36				06 35	06 51		07 15					07 33				08 37						
Bolton-upon-Dearne		d		23p41					06 56							07 38				08 42						
Goldthorpe		d		23p44					06 58							07 40				08 44						
Thurnscoe		d		23p47					07 01							07 43				08 47						
Moorthorpe		d		23p52					07 06							07 52				08 53						
Doncaster 7		d	23p26			06 26		06 55		07 26	07 34								08 17					08 26	08 50	
Bentley (S.Yorks)		d				06 29		06 58		07 29	07 37								08 20					08 29		
Adwick		a				06 33		07 05		07 33	07 43								08 25					08 33		
		d				06 33				07 33														08 33		
South Elmsall		d				06 39				07 39														08 39		
Fitzwilliam		d				06 44			07 12	07 44						07 58				09 09				08 45		
Sandal & Agbrigg		d				06 50			07 18	07 50					←	08 04				09 15				08 49		←
Wakefield Westgate 7	32,39	a	23p44			06 54			07 22	07 54				07 36	07 54	08 10				09 19			08 45	08 54	09 07	09 19
		d	23p44		06 24	06 54			07 23	07 54				07 37	07 54	08 11				09 19			08 46	08 55	09 07	09 19
Pontefract Monkhill	32	d								↦										↦						
Wakefield Kirkgate 4	32,34,39	a			06 29		06 49						07 49				08 27	08 49			08 57					
		d					06 50						07 50				08 28	08 50			08 58					
Outwood		d				06 59			07 28						07 59	08 16								08 58		09 24
Leeds 10	32,34	a	00 03	00 30		07 13	07 28		07 44				08 25	07 52	08 13	08 32	08 49	09 25			09 20		09 03	09 14	09 27	09 40

			NT	NT	NT	NT	NT		NT	NT	XC	NT	NT	GR	NT	NT	NT		NT	NT	NT	NT	XC	NT	GR	NT
											◇1 ⊼			R 1 ⊐P⊼									◇1 ⊼		R 1 ⊐P⊼	
Sheffield 7	29 ⇌	d	08 51			08 53	09 06		09 14	09 18	09 21		09 31			09 50			09 53	10 06	10 14	10 18	10 21			
Meadowhall	29 ⇌	d	08 57			09 00	09 12		09 21	09 24			09 38			09 56			09 59	10 12	10 21	10 24				
Rotherham Central	29	d				09 06			09 27				09 45						10 05		10 27					
Swinton (S.Yorks)	29	d				09 16			09 36				09 53						10 15		10 36					
Bolton-upon-Dearne		d							09 41												10 41					
Goldthorpe		d							09 43												10 43					
Thurnscoe		d							09 46												10 46					
Moorthorpe		d							09 53				10a03								10 53					
Doncaster 7		d		08 54	09 26	09 34								09 50			10 26		10 34						10 50	
Bentley (S.Yorks)		d		08 57	09 29	09 37											10 29		10 37							
Adwick		a		09 04	09 33	09 43											10 33		10 43							
		d			09 33												10 33									
South Elmsall		d			09 39												10 39									
Fitzwilliam		d			09 45				10 09								10 45				11 09					
Sandal & Agbrigg		d			09 49				10 15			←			←		10 49				11 15			←		←
Wakefield Westgate 7	32,39	a			09 54				10 19		09 46	09 54		10 07	10 19		10 54				11 19		10 46	10 54	11 07	11 19
		d			09 55				10 19		09 47	09 55		10 07	10 19		10 55				11 19		10 47	10 55	11 07	11 19
Pontefract Monkhill	32	d			↦				↦								↦				↦					
Wakefield Kirkgate 4	32,34,39	a	09 27				09 49			09 57						10 27				10 49		10 57				
		d	09 28				09 50			09 58						10 28				10 50		10 58				
Outwood		d										09 58			10 24									10 58		11 24
Leeds 10	32,34	a	09 49				10 25			10 18	10 02	10 14		10 27	10 40	10 48				11 25		11 18	11 02	11 14	11 28	11 40

			NT		NT	NT	NT	NT	NT	XC	NT	GR	NT		NT	GC	NT	NT	NT	NT	NT	XC	NT		GR	NT
										◇1 ⊼		R 1 ⊐P⊼				R 1 ⊐P						◇1 ⊼			R 1 ⊐P⊼	
Sheffield 7	29 ⇌	d	10 50			10 53	11 06	11 14	11 18	11 21					11 50			11 53	12 06	12 14	12 18	12 21				
Meadowhall	29 ⇌	d	10 56			10 59	11 12	11 21	11 24						11 56			11 59	12 12	12 21	12 24					
Rotherham Central	29	d				11 05		11 27										12 05		12 27						
Swinton (S.Yorks)	29	d				11 16		11 36										12 16		12 36						
Bolton-upon-Dearne		d						11 41												12 41						
Goldthorpe		d						11 43												12 43						
Thurnscoe		d						11 46												12 46						
Moorthorpe		d						11 53												12 53						
Doncaster 7		d			11 26	11 34						11 50				12 20	12 26	12 34							12 50	
Bentley (S.Yorks)		d			11 29	11 37											12 29	12 37								
Adwick		a			11 33	11 43											12 33	12 43								
		d			11 33												12 33									
South Elmsall		d			11 39												12 39									
Fitzwilliam		d			11 45			12 09									12 45			13 09						
Sandal & Agbrigg		d			11 49			12 15			←		←				12 49			13 15			←			←
Wakefield Westgate 7	32,39	a			11 54			12 19		11 46	11 54	12 07	12 19				12 54			13 19		12 46	12 54		13 07	13 19
		d			11 55			12 19		11 47	11 55	12 07	12 19				12 55			13 19		12 47	12 55		13 07	13 19
Pontefract Monkhill	32	d			↦			↦								12 45	↦			↦						
Wakefield Kirkgate 4	32,34,39	a	11 27				11 49		11 57						12 27	13 04			12 49		12 57					
		d	11 28				11 50		11 58						12 28				12 50		12 58					
Outwood		d									11 58		12 24										12 58			13 24
Leeds 10	32,34	a	11 48				12 25		12 18	12 02	12 14	12 28	12 40		12 48				13 25		13 18	13 02	13 13		13 28	13 43

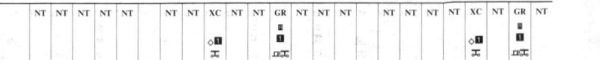

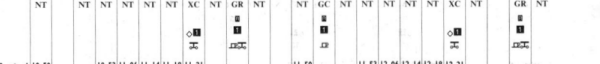

Table 31

Saturdays

from 17 September

Sheffield, Doncaster and Wakefield - Leeds

			NT	GR	NT	NT	NT	NT	NT		XC	NT	NT	GR	NT	NT	NT	NT	NT		NT	NT	XC	NT	GR	NT
				R 1 🍴							◇1 🛒			R 1 🍴									◇1 🛒		R 1 🍴	
Sheffield [7]	29 🚊	d	12 50			12 53	13 06	13 14	13 18		13 21		13 28			13 50		13 53	14 06		14 14	14 18	14 21			
Meadowhall	29 🚊	d	12 56			12 59	13 12	13 21	13 24				13 35			13 56		13 59	14 12		14 21	14 24				
Rotherham Central	29	d				13 05		13 27					13 42					14 05			14 27					
Swinton (S.Yorks)	29	d				13 16		13 36					13 51					14 17			14 36					
Bolton-upon-Dearne		d						13 41													14 41					
Goldthorpe		d						13 43													14 43					
Thurnscoe		d						13 46													14 46					
Moorthorpe		d						13 53					14a01								14 53					
Doncaster [7]		d		13 12	13 26	13 34								13 52			14 26	14 34							14 50	
Bentley (S.Yorks)		d			13 29	13 37											14 29	14 37								
Adwick		a			13 33	13 43											14 33	14 43								
		d			13 33												14 33									
South Elmsall		d			13 39												14 39									
Fitzwilliam		d			13 45			14 09									14 45				15 09					
Sandal & Agbrigg		d			13 49			14 15				←			←		14 49				15 15			←		←
Wakefield Westgate [7]	32,39	a		13 30	13 54			14 19			13 46	13 54		14 11	14 19		14 54				15 19		14 46	14 54	15 07	15 19
		d		13 30	13 55			14 19			13 47	13 55		14 11	14 19		14 55				15 19		14 47	14 55	15 07	15 19
Pontefract Monkhill	32	d			→			→									→				→					
Wakefield Kirkgate [4]	32,34,39	a	13 27				13 50		13 57							14 27			14 49			14 57				
		d	13 28				13 50		13 58							14 28			14 50			14 58				
Outwood		d										13 58			14 24									14 58		15 24
Leeds [10]	32,34	a	13 49	13 50			14 25		14 18		14 02	14 14		14 31	14 40	14 48			15 25			15 18	15 02	15 14	15 28	15 40

			NT	NT	NT		NT	NT	NT	XC	NT	GR	NT	NT	NT		NT	NT	NT	NT	XC	NT	GR	NT	NT	
										◇1 🛒		R 1 🍴									◇1 🛒		R 1 🍴			
Sheffield [7]	29 🚊	d	14 50		14 53		15 06	15 14	15 18	15 21				15 50			15 53	16 06	16 14	16 18	16 21				16 50	
Meadowhall	29 🚊	d	14 56		14 59		15 12	15 21	15 24					15 56			15 59	16 12	16 21	16 24					16 56	
Rotherham Central	29	d			15 05			15 27									16 05		16 27							
Swinton (S.Yorks)	29	d			15 17			15 36									16 16		16 36							
Bolton-upon-Dearne		d						15 41											16 41							
Goldthorpe		d						15 43											16 43							
Thurnscoe		d						15 46											16 46							
Moorthorpe		d						15 53											16 53							
Doncaster [7]		d		15 26	15 34							15 50			16 25		16 34						16 50			
Bentley (S.Yorks)		d		15 29	15 37										16 28		16 37									
Adwick		a		15 33	15 43										16 32		16 43									
		d		15 33											16 32											
South Elmsall		d		15 39											16 38											
Fitzwilliam		d		15 45				16 09							16 42				17 09							
Sandal & Agbrigg		d		15 49				16 15			←		←		16 48				17 15			←		←		
Wakefield Westgate [7]	32,39	a		15 54				16 19		15 46	15 54	16 07	16 19		16 52				17 19		16 46	16 52	17 07	17 19		
		d		15 55				16 19		15 47	15 55	16 07	16 19		16 52				17 19		16 47	16 52	17 07	17 19		
Pontefract Monkhill	32	d		→				→							→				→							
Wakefield Kirkgate [4]	32,34,39	a	15 27				15 49		15 57					16 27				16 49		16 57					17 28	
		d	15 28				15 50		15 58					16 28				16 50		16 58					17 28	
Outwood		d									15 58		16 24									16 59		17 24		
Leeds [10]	32,34	a	15 49				16 25		16 18	16 02	16 13	16 28	16 40	16 48				17 25		17 18	17 02	17 13	17 28	17 41	17 48	

			GC	NT	NT	NT	NT	NT	XC	NT	GR		XC	NT	NT	NT	NT	NT	XC	NT	GR		NT	GR	NT	NT
			R 1 ⊡						◇1 🛒		R 1 🍴		◇1 🛒						◇1 🛒		R 1 🍴			R 1 🍴		
Sheffield [7]	29 🚊	d			16 53	17 06	17 14	17 18	17 21				17 47		17 50	18 06	18 13	18 18	18 21						18 50	19 06
Meadowhall	29 🚊	d			16 59	17 12	17 21	17 24							17 56	18 12	18 21	18 24							18 56	19 12
Rotherham Central	29	d			17 05		17 27										18 27									
Swinton (S.Yorks)	29	d			17 16		17 37										18 37									
Bolton-upon-Dearne		d					17 41										18 41									
Goldthorpe		d					17 44										18 44									
Thurnscoe		d					17 47										18 47									
Moorthorpe		d					17 52										18 53									
Doncaster [7]		d	17 22	17 26	17 34						17 50									18 26	18 50			19 15		
Bentley (S.Yorks)		d		17 29	17 37															18 29						
Adwick		a		17 33	17 43															18 33						
		d		17 33																18 33						
South Elmsall		d		17 39																18 39						
Fitzwilliam		d		17 45			18 13										19 09			18 44						
Sandal & Agbrigg		d		17 51			18 19			←				←			19 15			18 50			←			
Wakefield Westgate [7]	32,39	a		17 55			18 23		17 47	17 55	18 07		18 12	18 23			19 19		18 46	18 53	19 07		19 19	19 32		
		d		17 55			18 23		17 47	17 55	18 07		18 13	18 23			19 19		18 47	18 54	19 07		19 19	19 32		
Pontefract Monkhill	32	d	17 47	→			→										→									
Wakefield Kirkgate [4]	32,34,39	a	18 03			17 49		17 57							18 28	18 50		18 59							19 29	19 50
		d				17 50		17 58							18 32	18 50		18 59							19 32	19 50
Outwood		d								18 00				18 28						18 57			19 24			
Leeds [10]	32,34	a				18 25		18 18	18 02	18 14	18 27		18 31	18 44	18 51	19 27		19 23	19 01	19 14	19 27		19 43	19 48	19 55	20 26

Table 31

Saturdays
from 17 September

Sheffield, Doncaster and Wakefield - Leeds

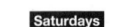

	NT	NT	XC	NT	GR		NT	GR	NT	NT	NT	XC	NT	NT	GC		GR	NT	XC	NT	NT	EM	NT	GR
					R			R							R		R							R
			◇1		1			1				◇1			1		1		◇1			◇1		1
			⊥		Ꮲ⊥			Ꮲ⊥				⊥			Ꮲ		Ꮲ⊥					Ꮲ		Ꮲ⊥
Sheffield 7 29 d	19 16	19 18	19 22						19 51	20 06	20 18	20 24		20 27				21 06	21 21			21 24	21 30	
Meadowhall 29 d	19 22	19 25							19 57	20 12	20 24			20 35				21 12					21 36	
Rotherham Central 29 d		19 31												20 41									21 42	
Swinton (S.Yorks) 29 d		19 40												20 50									21 50	
Bolton-upon-Dearne d		19 44												20 55									21 54	
Goldthorpe d		19 47												20 57									21 57	
Thurnscoe d		19 50												21 00									22 00	
Moorthorpe d		20 01												21 05									22 05	
Doncaster 7 d				19 22	19 50			20 13					20 26		20 37		21 17			21 22				22 18
Bentley (S.Yorks) d				19 25									20 29							21 25				
Adwick a				19 29									20 33							21 29				
d				19 29									20 33							21 29				
South Elmsall d				19 35									20 39							21 35				
Fitzwilliam d		20 07		19 48									20 44	21 11						21 42			22 11	
Sandal & Agbrigg d		20 13		19 53			←						20 50	21 17						21 48			22 17	
Wakefield Westgate 7 32,39 a		20 17	19 49	19 57	20 07		20 17	20 31				20 48	20 54	21 22			21 34		21 49	21 52		21 59	22 21	22 35
d		20 17	19 50	19 58	20 07		20 17	20 32				20 49	20 54	21 22			21 34		21 50	21 53	21 57	22 00	22 21	22 35
Pontefract Monkhill 32 d		↪													21 00									
Wakefield Kirkgate 4 32,34,39 a	19 58								20 28	20 49	20 57				21 17			21 52			22 00			
d	19 58								20 28	20 50	20 58							21 52						
Outwood d				20 02			20 22						20 59	21 27						21 58			22 26	
Leeds 10 32,34 a	20 20		20 05	20 16	20 28		20 38	20 47	20 48	21 26	21 19	21 03	21 18	21 47			21 54	22 29	22 03	22 16		22 21	22 45	22 55

	EM		NT	NT	NT	XC	NT	NT	GR
									R
	◇1					◇1			1
	Ꮲ								Ꮲ⊥
Sheffield 7 29 d	22 19				22 24	22 27			
Meadowhall 29 d					22 30				
Rotherham Central 29 d					22 36				
Swinton (S.Yorks) 29 d					22 45				
Bolton-upon-Dearne d					22 49				
Goldthorpe d					22 52				
Thurnscoe d					22 55				
Moorthorpe d					23 00				
Doncaster 7 d			22 26			22 53			23 48
Bentley (S.Yorks) d			22 29						
Adwick a			22 33						
d			22 33						
South Elmsall d			22 39						
Fitzwilliam d			22 44		23 07				
Sandal & Agbrigg d			22 50		23 13			←	
Wakefield Westgate 7 32,39 a	22 44		22 54		23 18	23 10		23 18	00 05
d	22 45		22 54	23 04	23 18	23 11		23 18	00 05
Pontefract Monkhill 32 d					↪				
Wakefield Kirkgate 4 32,34,39 a				23 07					
d							22 51		
Outwood d			22 59					23 23	
Leeds 10 32,34 a	23 04		23 14			23 27	23 29	23 40	00 26

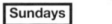

Sundays
29 May to 19 June

	GR	NT	NT	NT	XC	NT	GR	NT	NT		NT	XC	GR	NT	NT	XC	GR	NT	NT		NT	GC	XC	GR
	R						R						R				R					R		R
	1			◇	◇1		1					◇1	1			◇1	1						◇1	1
	Ꮲ⊥				⊥		Ꮲ⊥					⊥	Ꮲ⊥			⊥	Ꮲ⊥					Ꮲ	⊥	Ꮲ⊥
Sheffield 7 29 d			08 39	09 17	09 21	09 36			10 39		11 17	11 21		11 36	12 16	12 21			12 39		13 17		13 21	
Meadowhall 29 d			08 45	09 23		09 42			10 45		11 23			11 42	12 23				12 45		13 23			
Rotherham Central 29 d						09 48								11 49										
Swinton (S.Yorks) 29 d						09 58								12 00										
Bolton-upon-Dearne d						10 03								12 04										
Goldthorpe d						10 05								12 07										
Thurnscoe d						10 08								12 10										
Moorthorpe d						10 13								12 15										
Doncaster 7 d	23p48	09 12					10 52	11 12					11 49				12 52	13 12				13 17		13 49
Bentley (S.Yorks) d		09 15						11 15										13 15						
Adwick a		09 19						11 19										13 19						
d		09 19						11 19										13 19						
South Elmsall d		09 25						11 25										13 25						
Fitzwilliam d		09 30				10 19		11 30						12 21				13 30						
Sandal & Agbrigg d		09 36				10 25		11 36						12 27				13 36						
Wakefield Westgate 7 32,39 a	00 05	09 40			09 44	10 29	11 09	11 40				11 44	12 06	12 31		12 44	13 09	13 40					13 44	14 06
d	00 05	09 40			09 45	10 30	11 09	11 40				11 45	12 06	12 31		12 45	13 09	13 40					13 45	14 06
Pontefract Monkhill 32 d																						13 42		
Wakefield Kirkgate 4 32,34,39 a			09 29	09 55					11 29		11 52				12 52				13 29		13 52	13 58		
d			09 30	09 55					11 30		11 53				12 53				13 30		13 53			
Outwood d		09 45				10 35		11 45						12 36				13 45						
Leeds 10 32,34 a	00 26	09 59	10 04	10 15	10 02	10 52	11 30	11 59	12 05		12 18	12 02	12 29	12 53	13 18	13 02	13 30	13 59	14 04		14 18		14 02	14 29

Table 31

Sundays

29 May to 19 June

Sheffield, Doncaster and Wakefield - Leeds

Station		NT	NT	XC	GR	NT		NT	NT	XC	GR	NT	NT	XC	GR	NT		NT	NT	GC	XC	EM	GR	NT	GR
					[R]						[R]				[R]					[R]			[R]		[R]
				◇[1]	[1]					◇[1]	[1]			◇[1]	[1]					[1]	◇[1]	◇[1]	[1]		[1]
				trolley	rest.+trolley					trolley	rest.+trolley			trolley	rest.+trolley					rest.	trolley	rest.	rest.+trolley		rest.+trolley
Sheffield [7]	29 tram d	13 36	14 17	14 21				14 39	15 17	15 21		15 36	16 17	16 21				16 39	17 17		17 21	17 34		17 36	
Meadowhall	29 tram d	13 42	14 23					14 45	15 23			15 42	16 23					16 45	17 23					17 44	
Rotherham Central	29 d	13 49										15 50												17 50	
Swinton (S.Yorks)	29 d	13 57										15 58												17 58	
Bolton-upon-Dearne	d	14 01										16 02												18 03	
Goldthorpe	d	14 04										16 05												18 05	
Thurnscoe	d	14 07										16 08												18 08	
Moorthorpe	d	14 12										16 13												18 13	
Doncaster [7]	d				14 52	15 12					15 50				16 59	17 14				17 20			17 49		18 19
Bentley (S.Yorks)	d					15 15										17 17									
Adwick	a					15 19										17 21									
	d					15 19										17 21									
South Elmsall	d					15 25										17 27									
Fitzwilliam	d	14 17				15 30						16 19				17 32								18 19	
Sandal & Agbrigg	d	14 23				15 36						16 25				17 38								18 25	
Wakefield Westgate [7]	32,39 a	14 27		14 44	15 09	15 40				15 44	16 07	16 29		16 44	17 16	17 42					17 46	18 06	18 11	18 29	18 38
	d	14 28		14 45	15 09	15 40				15 45	16 07	16 29		16 45	17 16	17 42					17 46	18 07	18 11	18 30	18 38
Pontefract Monkhill	32 d																			17 45					
Wakefield Kirkgate [4]	32,34,39 a		14 52					15 29	15 52				16 52					17 29	17 52	18 00					
	d		14 53					15 30	15 53				16 53					17 30	17 53						
Outwood	d	14 33				15 45						16 34				17 47								18 35	
Leeds [10]	32,34 a	14 47	15 18	15 02	15 30	15 59		16 04	16 18	16 02	16 29	16 54	17 18	17 02	17 39	18 01		18 05	18 18		18 02	18 24	18 31	18 49	18 58

Station		NT		XC	GR	GR	NT	NT	XC	NT	NT	GR		NT	GR	NT	XC	GR	NT	GC	EM	GR		XC	GR
					[R]	[R]						[R]			[R]			[R]		[R]		[R]			[R]
				◇[1]	[1]	[1]			◇[1]			[1]			[1]		◇[1]	[1]			◇[1]	[1]		◇[1]	[1]
									A																
											bus														
				trolley	rest.+trolley	rest.+trolley			trolley			rest.+trolley			rest.+trolley		trolley	rest.+trolley		rest.	rest.	rest.+trolley			rest.+trolley
Sheffield [7]	29 tram d	18 17		18 21			18 39	19 16	19 21					19 36		20 17	20 21		20 39		21 03			21 21	
Meadowhall	29 tram d	18 23					18 45	19 23						19 42		20 23			20 45						
Rotherham Central	29 d													19 49											
Swinton (S.Yorks)	29 d										19 30			19 57											
Bolton-upon-Dearne	d													20 02											
Goldthorpe	d													20 04											
Thurnscoe	d													20 07											
Moorthorpe	d										20a00			20 12											
Doncaster [7]	d				18 49	19 14				19 27		19 50			20 20			20 48		21 01		21 19			21 41
Bentley (S.Yorks)	d									19 30															
Adwick	a									19 34															
	d									19 34															
South Elmsall	d									19 41															
Fitzwilliam	d									19 47				20 18											
Sandal & Agbrigg	d									19 53				20 24											
Wakefield Westgate [7]	32,39 a			18 47	19 07	19 31			19 48	19 57		20 08		20 28	20 37		20 46	21 05			21 27	21 36		21 47	21 59
	d			18 47	19 07	19 31			19 49	19 57		20 08		20 28	20 37		20 47	21 05			21 28	21 36		21 48	21 59
Pontefract Monkhill	32 d																			21 25					
Wakefield Kirkgate [4]	32,34,39 a	18 52					19 29	19 52								20 52			21 29	21 41					
	d	18 53					19 30	19 53								20 53			21 30						
Outwood	d									20 02				20 33											
Leeds [10]	32,34 a	19 18		19 04	19 28	19 53	20 05	20 18	20 05	20 16		20 25		20 52	20 55	21 16	21 03	21 29	22 04		21 45	21 57		22 04	22 20

Station		NT	NT	XC	GR	NT	GR	EM
					[R]		[R]	
				◇[1]	[1]		[1]	◇[1]
					rest.+trolley		rest.+trolley	rest.
Sheffield [7]	29 tram d		21 36	22 21		22 39		23 30
Meadowhall	29 tram d		21 42			22 45		
Rotherham Central	29 d		21 48					
Swinton (S.Yorks)	29 d		21 56					
Bolton-upon-Dearne	d		22 00					
Goldthorpe	d		22 03					
Thurnscoe	d		22 06					
Moorthorpe	d		22 11					
Doncaster [7]	d	21 49			22 29		23 32	
Bentley (S.Yorks)	d	21 52						
Adwick	a	21 56						
	d	21 56						
South Elmsall	d	22 02						
Fitzwilliam	d	22 09	22 16					
Sandal & Agbrigg	d	22 15	22 22					
Wakefield Westgate [7]	32,39 a	22 19	22 26	22 45	22 49		23 49	23 55
	d	22 20	22 27	22 45	22 49		23 49	23 56
Pontefract Monkhill	32 d							
Wakefield Kirkgate [4]	32,34,39 a					23 26		
	d					23 27		
Outwood	d	22 25	22 32					
Leeds [10]	32,34 a	22 39	22 52	23 03	23 10	00 05	00 27	00 28

A trolley to Wakefield Westgate

Table 31

Sheffield, Doncaster and Wakefield - Leeds

Sundays

26 June to 31 July

Station			GR	NT	NT	NT	XC	NT	GR	NT	NT	NT	XC	GR	NT	NT	XC	GR	NT	NT	NT	GC	XC	GR
			R 1			◇	◇1		R 1				◇1	R 1			◇1	R 1				R 1	◇1	R 1
			□✕				✕		□✕				✕	□✕			✕	□✕				□	✕	□✕
Sheffield 7	29 🚊	d			08 39	09 17	09 21	09 36			10 39	11 17	11 21		11 36	12 16	12 21			12 39	13 17		13 21	
Meadowhall	29 🚊	d			08 45	09 23		09 42			10 45	11 23			11 42	12 23				12 45	13 23			
Rotherham Central	29	d						09 48							11 49									
Swinton (S.Yorks)	29	d						09 58							12 00									
Bolton-upon-Dearne		d						10 03							12 04									
Goldthorpe		d						10 05							12 07									
Thurnscoe		d						10 08							12 10									
Moorthorpe		d						10 13							12 15									
Doncaster 7		d	00 05	09 12					10 52	11 12				11 49				12 52	13 12			13 17		13 49
Bentley (S.Yorks)		d		09 15						11 15									13 15					
Adwick		a		09 19						11 19									13 19					
		d		09 19						11 19									13 19					
South Elmsall		d		09 25						11 25									13 25					
Fitzwilliam		d		09 30				10 19		11 30					12 21				13 30					
Sandal & Agbrigg		d		09 36				10 25		11 36					12 27				13 36					
Wakefield Westgate 7	32,39	a	00 20	09 40			09 44	10 29	11 09	11 40			11 44	12 06	12 31		12 44	13 09	13 40				13 44	14 06
		d	00 20	09 40			09 45	10 30	11 09	11 40			11 45	12 06	12 31		12 45	13 09	13 40				13 45	14 06
Pontefract Monkhill	32	d																				13 42		
Wakefield Kirkgate 4	32,34,39	a			09 29	09 55					11 29	11 52				12 52				13 29	13 52	13 58		
		d			09 30	09 55					11 30	11 53				12 53				13 30	13 53			
Outwood		d		09 45				10 35		11 45					12 36				13 45					
Leeds 10	32,34	a	00 40	09 59	10 04	10 15	10 02	10 52	11 30	11 59	12 05	12 18	12 02	12 29	12 53	13 18	13 02	13 30	13 59	14 04	14 18		14 02	14 29

Station			NT	NT	XC	GR	NT	NT	NT	XC	GR	NT	NT	XC	NT	GR	NT	NT	NT	GC	XC	EM	GR	NT
					◇1	R 1				◇1	R 1			◇1		R 1				R 1	◇1	◇1	R 1	
					✕	□✕				✕	□✕			✕		□✕				□	✕	□	□✕	
Sheffield 7	29 🚊	d	13 36	14 17	14 21			14 39	15 17	15 21		15 36	16 17	16 21	16 36			16 39	17 17		17 21	17 34		17 36
Meadowhall	29 🚊	d	13 42	14 23				14 45	15 23			15 42	16 23		16 42			16 45	17 23					17 44
Rotherham Central	29	d	13 49									15 50			16 49									17 50
Swinton (S.Yorks)	29	d	13 57									15 58			16 58									17 58
Bolton-upon-Dearne		d	14 01									16 02			17 02									18 03
Goldthorpe		d	14 04									16 05			17 05									18 05
Thurnscoe		d	14 07									16 08			17 08									18 08
Moorthorpe		d	14 12									16 13			17a13									18 13
Doncaster 7		d				14 52	15 12				15 50					16 59	17 14			17 20			17 49	
Bentley (S.Yorks)		d					15 15										17 17							
Adwick		a					15 19										17 21							
		d					15 19										17 21							
South Elmsall		d					15 25										17 27							
Fitzwilliam		d	14 17				15 30					16 19					17 32							18 19
Sandal & Agbrigg		d	14 23				15 36					16 25					17 38							18 25
Wakefield Westgate 7	32,39	a	14 27		14 44	15 09	15 40			15 44	16 07	16 29		16 44		17 16	17 42				17 46	18 06	18 11	18 29
		d	14 28		14 45	15 09	15 40			15 45	16 07	16 29		16 45		17 16	17 42				17 46	18 07	18 11	18 30
Pontefract Monkhill	32	d																		17 45				
Wakefield Kirkgate 4	32,34,39	a		14 52				15 29	15 52				16 52					17 29	17 52	18 00				
		d		14 53				15 30	15 53				16 53					17 30	17 53					
Outwood		d	14 33				15 45					16 34					17 47							18 35
Leeds 10	32,34	a	14 47	15 18	15 02	15 30	15 59	16 04	16 18	16 02	16 29	16 54	17 18	17 02		17 39	18 01	18 05	18 18		18 02	18 24	18 31	18 49

Station			XC	GR	NT	XC	GR	GR	NT	NT	NT	XC	NT	GR	NT	GR	NT	XC	GR	NT	GC	EM	GR
			◇1	R 1		◇1	R 1	R 1				◇1 A		R 1		R 1		◇1	R 1		R 1	◇1	R 1
			✕	□✕		✕	□✕	□✕				✕		□✕		□✕		✕	□✕		□	□	□✕
Sheffield 7	29 🚊	d	17 51		18 17	18 21			18 39	18 57	19 16	19 21			19 36		20 17	20 21		20 39		21 03	
Meadowhall	29 🚊	d			18 23				18 45	19 05	19 23				19 42		20 23			20 45			
Rotherham Central	29	d								19 11					19 49								
Swinton (S.Yorks)	29	d								19 19					19 57								
Bolton-upon-Dearne		d													20 02								
Goldthorpe		d													20 04								
Thurnscoe		d													20 07								
Moorthorpe		d								19a29					20 12								
Doncaster 7		d	18 15	18 19			18 49	19 14					19 27	19 50		20 20			20 48		21 01		21 19
Bentley (S.Yorks)		d											19 30										
Adwick		a											19 34										
		d											19 34										
South Elmsall		d											19 41										
Fitzwilliam		d											19 47		20 18								
Sandal & Agbrigg		d											19 53		20 24								
Wakefield Westgate 7	32,39	a	18 33	18 38		18 47	19 07	19 31				19 48	19 57	20 08	20 28	20 37		20 46	21 05			21 27	21 36
		d	18 34	18 38		18 48	19 07	19 31				19 49	19 57	20 08	20 28	20 37		20 47	21 05			21 28	21 36
Pontefract Monkhill	32	d																			21 25		
Wakefield Kirkgate 4	32,34,39	a			18 52				19 29		19 52						20 52			21 29	21 41		
		d			18 53				19 30		19 53						20 53			21 30			
Outwood		d											20 02		20 33								
Leeds 10	32,34	a	18 51	18 58	19 18	19 04	19 28	19 53	20 05		20 18	20 05	20 16	20 25	20 52	20 55	21 16	21 03	21 29	22 04		21 45	21 57

A ✕ to Wakefield Westgate

Table 31

Sundays

26 June to 31 July

Sheffield, Doncaster and Wakefield - Leeds

			XC	GR	NT	NT	XC	GR	NT		GR	EM
			◇1	R 1 ⊡⊥			◇1	R 1 ⊡⊥			R 1 ⊡⊥	◇1 ⊡
Sheffield 7	29	d	21 21			21 36	22 21		22 39			23 30
Meadowhall	29	d				21 42			22 45			
Rotherham Central	29	d				21 48						
Swinton (S.Yorks)	29	d				21 56						
Bolton-upon-Dearne		d				22 00						
Goldthorpe		d				22 03						
Thurnscoe		d				22 06						
Moorthorpe		d				22 11						
Doncaster 7		d		21 41	21 49			22 29			23 32	
Bentley (S.Yorks)		d			21 52							
Adwick		a			21 56							
		d			21 56							
South Elmsall		d			22 02							
Fitzwilliam		d			22 09	22 16						
Sandal & Agbrigg		d			22 15	22 22						
Wakefield Westgate 7	32,39	a	21 47	21 59	22 19	22 26	22 46	22 49			23 49	23 55
		d	21 48	21 59	22 20	22 27	22 46	22 49			23 49	23 56
Pontefract Monkhill	32	d										
Wakefield Kirkgate 4	32,34,39	a							23 26			
		d							23 27			
Outwood		d			22 25	22 32						
Leeds 10	32,34	a	22 04	22 20	22 39	22 52	23 03	23 10	00 05		00 27	00 28

Sundays

7 August to 11 September

			GR	NT	NT	NT	XC	NT	XC	GR	NT		NT	NT	XC	GR	NT	NT	XC	GR	NT		NT	NT	GC	XC
			R 1 ⊡⊥			◇	◇1 ⊥		◇1 ⊥	R 1 ⊡⊥					◇1 ⊥	R 1 ⊡⊥			◇1 ⊥	R 1 ⊡⊥					R 1 ⊡	◇1 ⊥
Sheffield 7	29	d			08 39	09 17	09 21	09 36	10 21				10 39	11 17	11 21		11 36	12 16	12 21				12 39	13 17		13 21
Meadowhall	29	d			08 45	09 23		09 42					10 45	11 23			11 42	12 23					12 45	13 23		
Rotherham Central	29	d						09 48									11 49									
Swinton (S.Yorks)	29	d						09 58									12 00									
Bolton-upon-Dearne		d						10 03									12 04									
Goldthorpe		d						10 05									12 07									
Thurnscoe		d						10 08									12 10									
Moorthorpe		d						10 13									12 15									
Doncaster 7		d	23p48	09 12						10 52	11 12					11 49				12 52	13 12				13 17	
Bentley (S.Yorks)		d		09 15							11 15										13 15					
Adwick		a		09 19							11 19										13 19					
		d		09 19							11 19										13 19					
South Elmsall		d		09 25							11 25										13 25					
Fitzwilliam		d		09 30				10 19			11 30						12 21				13 30					
Sandal & Agbrigg		d		09 36				10 25			11 36						12 27				13 36					
Wakefield Westgate 7	32,39	a	00 05	09 40			09 44	10 29	10 44	11 09	11 40				11 44	12 06	12 31		12 44	13 09	13 40					13 44
		d	00 05	09 40			09 45	10 30	10 45	11 09	11 40				11 45	12 06	12 31		12 45	13 09	13 40					13 45
Pontefract Monkhill	32	d																							13 42	
Wakefield Kirkgate 4	32,34,39	a			09 29	09 55							11 29	11 52				12 52					13 29	13 52	13 58	
		d			09 30	09 55							11 30	11 53				12 53					13 30	13 53		
Outwood		d		09 45				10 35			11 45						12 36				13 45					
Leeds 10	32,34	a	00 26	09 59	10 04	10 15	10 02	10 52	11 02	11 30	11 59		12 05	12 18	12 01	12 29	12 53	13 18	13 02	13 30	13 59		14 04	14 18		14 02

			GR	NT	NT	XC	GR		NT	NT	NT	XC	GR	NT	NT	XC	NT		GR	NT	NT	NT	GC	XC	EM	GR
			R 1 ⊡⊥			◇1 ⊥	R 1 ⊡⊥					◇1 ⊥	R 1 ⊡⊥			◇1 ⊥			R 1 ⊡⊥				R 1 ⊡	◇1 ⊥	◇1 ⊡	R 1 ⊡⊥
Sheffield 7	29	d		13 36	14 17	14 21				14 39	15 17	15 21		15 36	16 17	16 21	16 36				16 39	17 17		17 21	17 34	
Meadowhall	29	d		13 42	14 23					14 45	15 23			15 42	16 23		16 42				16 45	17 23				
Rotherham Central	29	d		13 49										15 50			16 49									
Swinton (S.Yorks)	29	d		13 57										15 58			16 58									
Bolton-upon-Dearne		d		14 01										16 02			17 02									
Goldthorpe		d		14 04										16 05			17 05									
Thurnscoe		d		14 07										16 08			17 08									
Moorthorpe		d		14 12										16 13			17a13									
Doncaster 7		d	13 49				14 52		15 12				15 50						16 59	17 14			17 20			17 49
Bentley (S.Yorks)		d							15 15											17 17						
Adwick		a							15 19											17 21						
		d							15 19											17 21						
South Elmsall		d							15 25											17 27						
Fitzwilliam		d		14 17					15 30					16 19						17 32						
Sandal & Agbrigg		d		14 23					15 36					16 25						17 38						
Wakefield Westgate 7	32,39	a	14 06	14 27		14 44	15 09		15 40			15 44	16 07	16 29		16 44			17 16	17 42				17 46	18 06	18 11
		d	14 06	14 28		14 45	15 09		15 40			15 45	16 07	16 29		16 45			17 16	17 42				17 46	18 07	18 11
Pontefract Monkhill	32	d																					17 45			
Wakefield Kirkgate 4	32,34,39	a			14 52					15 29	15 52				16 52						17 29	17 52	18 00			
		d			14 53					15 30	15 53				16 53						17 30	17 53				
Outwood		d		14 33					15 45					16 34						17 47						
Leeds 10	32,34	a	14 29	14 47	15 18	15 02	15 30		15 59	16 04	16 18	16 02	16 29	16 54	17 18	17 02			17 39	18 01	18 05	18 18		18 02	18 24	18 31

Table 31

Sundays

7 August to 11 September

Sheffield, Doncaster and Wakefield - Leeds

		NT		XC	GR	NT	XC	GR	GR	NT	NT	NT		XC	NT	GR	NT	GR	NT	XC	GR	NT		GC	EM
				◇1	R 1		◇1	R 1	R 1					◇1 A		R 1		R 1		◇1	R 1			R 1	◇1
Sheffield 7 ... 29	d	17 36		17 51		18 17	18 21			18 39	18 57	19 16		19 21			19 36		20 17	20 21		20 39			21 03
Meadowhall ... 29	d	17 44				18 23				18 45	19 05	19 23					19 42		20 23			20 45			
Rotherham Central ... 29	d	17 50									19 11						19 49								
Swinton (S.Yorks) ... 29	d	17 58									19 19						19 57								
Bolton-upon-Dearne	d	18 03															20 02								
Goldthorpe	d	18 05															20 04								
Thurnscoe	d	18 08															20 07								
Moorthorpe	d	18 13									19a29						20 12								
Doncaster 7	d			18 15	18 19			18 49	19 14						19 27	19 50		20 20			20 48			21 01	
Bentley (S.Yorks)	d														19 30										
Adwick	a														19 34										
	d														19 34										
South Elmsall	d														19 41										
Fitzwilliam	d	18 19													19 47		20 18								
Sandal & Agbrigg	d	18 25													19 53		20 24								
Wakefield Westgate 7 ... 32,39	a	18 29		18 33	18 38		18 47	19 07	19 31					19 48	19 57	20 08	20 28	20 37		20 46	21 05				21 27
	d	18 30		18 34	18 38		18 48	19 07	19 31					19 49	19 57	20 08	20 28	20 37		20 47	21 05				21 28
Pontefract Monkhill ... 32	d																							21 25	
Wakefield Kirkgate 4 ... 32,34,39	a					18 52				19 29		19 52							20 52			21 29		21 41	
	d					18 53				19 30		19 53							20 53			21 30			
Outwood	d	18 35													20 02		20 33								
Leeds 10 ... 32,34	a	18 49		18 51	18 58	19 18	19 04	19 28	19 53	20 05		20 18		20 05	20 16	20 25	20 52	20 55	21 16	21 03	21 29	22 04			21 45

		GR	XC	GR	NT	NT	XC	GR		NT	GR	EM
		R 1	◇1	R 1			◇1	R 1			R 1	◇1
Sheffield 7 ... 29	d		21 21			21 36	22 21			22 39		23 30
Meadowhall ... 29	d					21 42				22 45		
Rotherham Central ... 29	d					21 48						
Swinton (S.Yorks) ... 29	d					21 56						
Bolton-upon-Dearne	d					22 00						
Goldthorpe	d					22 03						
Thurnscoe	d					22 06						
Moorthorpe	d					22 11						
Doncaster 7	d	21 19		21 41	21 49			22 29			23 32	
Bentley (S.Yorks)	d				21 52							
Adwick	a				21 56							
	d				21 56							
South Elmsall	d				22 02							
Fitzwilliam	d				22 09	22 16						
Sandal & Agbrigg	d				22 15	22 22						
Wakefield Westgate 7 ... 32,39	a	21 36	21 47	21 59	22 19	22 26	22 43	22 49			23 49	23 55
	d	21 36	21 48	21 59	22 20	22 27	22 43	22 49			23 49	23 56
Pontefract Monkhill ... 32	d											
Wakefield Kirkgate 4 ... 32,34,39	a									23 26		
	d									23 27		
Outwood	d				22 25	22 32						
Leeds 10 ... 32,34	a	21 57	22 04	22 20	22 39	22 52	23 01	23 10		00 05	00 27	00 28

Sundays

11 September to 23 October

		GR	NT	NT	NT	XC	NT	XC	GR	NT		NT	NT	XC	GR	NT	NT	XC	GR	NT		NT	NT	GC	GC
		R 1			◇	◇1		◇1	R 1					◇1	R 1			◇1 B	R 1					R 1 C	R 1 B
Sheffield 7 ... 29	d			08 39	09 17	09 21	09 36	10 21				10 39	11 17	11 21		11 36	12 16	12 21				12 39	13 17		
Meadowhall ... 29	d			08 45	09 23		09 42					10 45	11 23			11 42	12 23					12 45	13 23		
Rotherham Central ... 29	d						09 48									11 49									
Swinton (S.Yorks) ... 29	d						09 58									12 00									
Bolton-upon-Dearne	d						10 03									12 04									
Goldthorpe	d						10 05									12 07									
Thurnscoe	d						10 08									12 10									
Moorthorpe	d						10 13									12 15									
Doncaster 7	d	23p48	09 12						10 52	11 12					11 49				12 52	13 12				13 17	13 17
Bentley (S.Yorks)	d		09 15							11 15										13 15					
Adwick	a		09 19							11 19										13 19					
	d		09 19							11 19										13 19					
South Elmsall	d		09 25							11 25										13 25					
Fitzwilliam	d		09 30				10 19			11 30						12 21				13 30					
Sandal & Agbrigg	d		09 36				10 25			11 36						12 27				13 36					
Wakefield Westgate 7 ... 32,39	a	00 05	09 40			09 44	10 29	10 44	11 09	11 40				11 44	12 06	12 31		12 44	13 09	13 40					
	d	00 05	09 40			09 45	10 30	10 45	11 09	11 40				11 45	12 06	12 31		12 45	13 09	13 40					
Pontefract Monkhill ... 32	d																							13 42	13 42
Wakefield Kirkgate 4 ... 32,34,39	a			09 29	09 55							11 29	11 52				12 52					13 29	13 52	13 58	13 58
	d			09 30	09 55							11 30	11 53				12 53					13 30	13 53		
Outwood	d		09 45				10 35			11 45						12 36				13 45					
Leeds 10 ... 32,34	a	00 26	09 59	10 04	10 15	10 02	10 52	11 02	11 30	11 59		12 05	12 18	12 01	12 29	12 53	13 18	13 02	13 30	13 59		14 04	14 18		

A to Wakefield Westgate

B 11 September

C not 11 September

Table 31

Sundays

11 September to 23 October

Sheffield, Doncaster and Wakefield - Leeds

		XC	GR	NT	NT	XC		GR	NT	NT	NT	XC	GR	NT	NT	XC		NT	GR	NT	NT	NT	GC	GC	XC
			R					R					R						R					R	
		◇1	1			◇1		1				◇1	1			◇1			1					1	◇1
																							A	[restaurant] B	
		[trolley]	[restaurant][trolley]			[trolley]		[restaurant][trolley]				[trolley]	[restaurant][trolley]			[trolley]			[restaurant][trolley]						[trolley]
Sheffield 7	29 [tram] d	13 21		13 36	14 17	14 21				14 39	15 17	15 21		15 36	16 17	16 21		16 36			16 39	17 17			17 21
Meadowhall	29 [tram] d			13 42	14 23					14 45	15 23			15 42	16 23			16 42			16 45	17 23			
Rotherham Central	29 d			13 49										15 50				16 49							
Swinton (S.Yorks)	29 d			13 57										15 58				16 58							
Bolton-upon-Dearne	d			14 01										16 02				17 02							
Goldthorpe	d			14 04										16 05				17 05							
Thurnscoe	d			14 07										16 08				17 08							
Moorthorpe	d			14 12										16 13				17a13							
Doncaster 7	d		13 49					14 52	15 12				15 50						16 59	17 14			17 20	17 20	
Bentley (S.Yorks)	d								15 15											17 17					
Adwick	a								15 19											17 21					
	d								15 19											17 21					
South Elmsall	d								15 25											17 27					
Fitzwilliam	d			14 17					15 30					16 19						17 32					
Sandal & Agbrigg	d			14 23					15 36					16 25						17 38					
Wakefield Westgate 7	32,39 a	13 44	14 06	14 27		14 44		15 09	15 40			15 44	16 07	16 29		16 44			17 16	17 42					17 46
	d	13 45	14 06	14 28		14 45		15 09	15 40			15 45	16 07	16 29		16 45			17 16	17 42					17 46
Pontefract Monkhill	32 d																						17 45	17 45	
Wakefield Kirkgate 4	32,34,39 a				14 52					15 29	15 52				16 52						17 29	17 52	18 00	18 00	
	d				14 53					15 30	15 53				16 53						17 30	17 53			
Outwood	d			14 33					15 45					16 34						17 47					
Leeds 10	32,34 a	14 02	14 29	14 47	15 18	15 02		15 30	15 59	16 04	16 18	16 02	16 29	16 54	17 18	17 02			17 39	18 01	18 05	18 18			18 02

		EM		GR	NT	XC	GR	NT	XC	GR	GR	NT		NT	NT	XC	NT	GR	NT	GR	NT	XC		GR	NT
				R			R			R	R							R		R				R	
		◇1		1		◇1	1		◇1	1	1					◇1		1		1		◇1		1	
																C									
		[restaurant]		[restaurant][trolley]		[trolley]	[restaurant][trolley]		[trolley]	[restaurant][trolley]	[restaurant][trolley]					[trolley]		[restaurant][trolley]		[restaurant][trolley]		[trolley]		[restaurant][trolley]	
Sheffield 7	29 [tram] d	17 34			17 36	17 51		18 17	18 21			18 39		18 57	19 16	19 21			19 36		20 17	20 21			20 39
Meadowhall	29 [tram] d				17 44			18 23				18 45		19 05	19 23				19 42		20 23				20 45
Rotherham Central	29 d				17 50									19 11					19 49						
Swinton (S.Yorks)	29 d				17 58									19 19					19 57						
Bolton-upon-Dearne	d				18 03														20 02						
Goldthorpe	d				18 05														20 04						
Thurnscoe	d				18 08														20 07						
Moorthorpe	d				18 13									19a29					20 12						
Doncaster 7	d			17 49		18 15	18 19			18 49	19 14						19 27	19 50		20 20				20 48	
Bentley (S.Yorks)	d																19 30								
Adwick	a																19 34								
	d																19 34								
South Elmsall	d																19 41								
Fitzwilliam	d				18 19												19 47		20 18						
Sandal & Agbrigg	d				18 25												19 53		20 24						
Wakefield Westgate 7	32,39 a	18 06		18 11	18 29	18 33	18 38		18 47	19 07	19 31					19 48	19 57	20 08	20 28	20 37		20 46		21 05	
	d	18 07		18 11	18 30	18 34	18 38		18 48	19 07	19 31					19 49	19 57	20 08	20 28	20 37		20 47		21 05	
Pontefract Monkhill	32 d																								
Wakefield Kirkgate 4	32,34,39 a							18 52				19 29			19 52						20 52				21 29
	d							18 53				19 30			19 53						20 53				21 30
Outwood	d				18 35												20 02		20 33						
Leeds 10	32,34 a	18 24		18 31	18 49	18 51	18 58	19 18	19 04	19 28	19 53	20 05			20 18	20 05	20 16	20 25	20 52	20 55	21 16	21 03		21 29	22 04

		GC	EM	GR	XC	GR	NT	NT		XC	GR	NT	GR	EM
		R		R		R					R		R	
		1	◇1	1	◇1	1				◇1	1		1	◇1
		[restaurant]	[restaurant]	[restaurant][trolley]		[restaurant][trolley]					[restaurant][trolley]		[restaurant][trolley]	[restaurant]
Sheffield 7	29 [tram] d		21 03		21 21			21 36		22 21		22 39		23 30
Meadowhall	29 [tram] d							21 42				22 45		
Rotherham Central	29 d							21 48						
Swinton (S.Yorks)	29 d							21 56						
Bolton-upon-Dearne	d							22 00						
Goldthorpe	d							22 03						
Thurnscoe	d							22 06						
Moorthorpe	d							22 11						
Doncaster 7	d	21 01		21 19		21 41	21 49				22 29		23 32	
Bentley (S.Yorks)	d						21 52							
Adwick	a						21 56							
	d						21 56							
South Elmsall	d						22 02							
Fitzwilliam	d						22 09	22 16						
Sandal & Agbrigg	d						22 15	22 22						
Wakefield Westgate 7	32,39 a		21 27	21 36	21 47	21 59	22 19	22 26		22 43	22 49		23 49	23 55
	d		21 28	21 36	21 48	21 59	22 20	22 27		22 43	22 49		23 49	23 56
Pontefract Monkhill	32 d	21 25												
Wakefield Kirkgate 4	32,34,39 a	21 41										23 26		
	d											23 27		
Outwood	d						22 25	22 32						
Leeds 10	32,34 a		21 45	21 57	22 04	22 20	22 39	22 52		23 01	23 10	00 05	00 27	00 28

A not 11 September

B 11 September

C [trolley] to Wakefield Westgate

Table 31

Sundays

18 September to 30 October

Sheffield, Doncaster and Wakefield - Leeds

	GR	NT	NT	NT	XC	NT	XC	GR	NT		NT	NT	XC	GR	NT	NT	XC	GR	NT		NT	NT	GC	GC
	R 1 ⊡⊥			◇	◇1 ⊥		◇1 ⊥	R 1 ⊡⊥					◇1 ⊥	R 1 ⊡⊥			◇1 A ⊥	R 1 ⊡⊥					R 1 B ⊡	R 1 A ⊡
Sheffield 7 29 🚊 d			08 39	09 17	09 21	09 36	10 21				10 39	11 17	11 21		11 36	12 16	12 21				12 39	13 17		
Meadowhall 29 🚊 d			08 45	09 23		09 42					10 45	11 23			11 42	12 23					12 45	13 23		
Rotherham Central 29 d						09 48									11 49									
Swinton (S.Yorks) 29 d						09 58									12 00									
Bolton-upon-Dearne d						10 03									12 04									
Goldthorpe d						10 05									12 07									
Thurnscoe d						10 08									12 10									
Moorthorpe d						10 13									12 15									
Doncaster 7 d	23p48	09 12						10 52	11 12					11 49				12 52	13 12				13 17	13 17
Bentley (S.Yorks) d		09 15							11 15										13 15					
Adwick a		09 19							11 19										13 19					
d		09 19							11 19										13 19					
South Elmsall d		09 25							11 25										13 25					
Fitzwilliam d		09 30				10 19			11 30						12 21				13 30					
Sandal & Agbrigg d		09 36				10 25			11 36						12 27				13 36					
Wakefield Westgate 7 32,39 a	00 05	09 40			09 44	10 29	10 44	11 09	11 40				11 44	12 06	12 31		12 44	13 09	13 40					
d	00 05	09 40			09 45	10 30	10 45	11 09	11 40				11 45	12 06	12 31		12 45	13 09	13 40					
Pontefract Monkhill 32 d																							13 42	13 42
Wakefield Kirkgate 4 32,34,39 a			09 29	09 55							11 29	11 52				12 52					13 29	13 52	13 58	13 58
d			09 30	09 55							11 30	11 53				12 53					13 30	13 53		
Outwood d		09 45				10 35			11 45						12 36				13 45					
Leeds 10 32,34 a	00 26	09 59	10 04	10 15	10 02	10 52	11 02	11 30	11 59		12 05	12 18	12 01	12 29	12 53	13 18	13 02	13 30	13 59		14 04	14 18		

	XC	GR	NT	NT	XC		GR	NT	NT	NT	XC	GR	NT	NT	XC		NT	GR	NT	NT	NT	GC	GC	XC
	◇1 ⊥	R 1 ⊡⊥			◇1 ⊥		R 1 ⊡⊥				◇1 ⊥	R 1 ⊡⊥			◇1 ⊥			R 1 ⊡⊥				R 1 B ⊡	R A ⊡	◇1 ⊥
Sheffield 7 29 🚊 d	13 21		13 36	14 17	14 21				14 39	15 17	15 21		15 36	16 17	16 21		16 36			16 39	17 17			17 21
Meadowhall 29 🚊 d			13 42	14 23					14 45	15 23			15 42	16 23			16 42			16 45	17 23			
Rotherham Central 29 d			13 49										15 50				16 49							
Swinton (S.Yorks) 29 d			13 57										15 58				16 58							
Bolton-upon-Dearne d			14 01										16 02				17 02							
Goldthorpe d			14 04										16 05				17 05							
Thurnscoe d			14 07										16 08				17 08							
Moorthorpe d			14 12										16 13				17a13							
Doncaster 7 d		13 49					14 52	15 12				15 50						16 59	17 14			17 20	17 20	
Bentley (S.Yorks) d								15 15											17 17					
Adwick a								15 19											17 21					
d								15 19											17 21					
South Elmsall d								15 25											17 27					
Fitzwilliam d			14 17					15 30					16 19						17 32					
Sandal & Agbrigg d			14 23					15 36					16 25						17 38					
Wakefield Westgate 7 32,39 a	13 44	14 06	14 27		14 44		15 09	15 40			15 44	16 07	16 29		16 44			17 16	17 42					17 46
d	13 45	14 06	14 28		14 45		15 09	15 40			15 45	16 07	16 29		16 45			17 16	17 42					17 46
Pontefract Monkhill 32 d																						17 45	17 45	
Wakefield Kirkgate 4 32,34,39 a				14 52					15 29	15 52				16 52						17 29	17 52	18 00	18 00	
d				14 53					15 30	15 53				16 53						17 30	17 53			
Outwood d			14 33					15 45					16 34						17 47					
Leeds 10 32,34 a	14 02	14 29	14 47	15 18	15 02		15 30	15 59	16 04	16 18	16 02	16 29	16 54	17 18	17 02			17 39	18 01	18 05	18 18			18 02

	EM		GR	NT	XC	GR	NT	XC	GR	GR	NT		NT	NT	XC	NT	GR	NT	GR	NT	XC		GR	NT
	◇1 ⊡		R 1 ⊡⊥		◇1 ⊥	R 1 ⊡⊥		◇1 ⊥	R 1 ⊡⊥	R 1 ⊡⊥					◇1 C ⊥		R 1 ⊡⊥		R 1 ⊡⊥		◇1 ⊥		R 1 ⊡⊥	
Sheffield 7 29 🚊 d	17 34			17 36	17 51		18 17	18 21			18 39		18 57	19 16	19 21			19 36		20 17	20 21			20 39
Meadowhall 29 🚊 d				17 44			18 23				18 45		19 05	19 23				19 42		20 23				20 45
Rotherham Central 29 d				17 50									19 11					19 49						
Swinton (S.Yorks) 29 d				17 58									19 19					19 57						
Bolton-upon-Dearne d				18 03														20 02						
Goldthorpe d				18 05														20 04						
Thurnscoe d				18 08														20 07						
Moorthorpe d				18 13									19a29					20 12						
Doncaster 7 d			17 49		18 15	18 19			18 49	19 14						19 27	19 50		20 20				20 48	
Bentley (S.Yorks) d																19 30								
Adwick a																19 34								
d																19 34								
South Elmsall d																19 41								
Fitzwilliam d				18 19												19 47		20 18						
Sandal & Agbrigg d				18 25												19 53		20 24						
Wakefield Westgate 7 32,39 a	18 06		18 11	18 29	18 33	18 38		18 47	19 07	19 31					19 48	19 57	20 08	20 28	20 37		20 46		21 05	
d	18 07		18 11	18 30	18 34	18 38		18 48	19 07	19 31					19 49	19 57	20 08	20 28	20 37		20 47		21 05	
Pontefract Monkhill 32 d																								
Wakefield Kirkgate 4 32,34,39 a							18 52				19 29			19 52						20 52				21 29
d							18 53				19 30			19 53						20 53				21 30
Outwood d				18 35												20 02		20 33						
Leeds 10 32,34 a	18 24		18 31	18 49	18 51	18 58	19 18	19 04	19 28	19 53	20 05			20 18	20 05	20 16	20 25	20 52	20 55	21 16	21 03		21 29	22 04

A 30 October

B not 30 October

C ⊥ to Wakefield Westgate

Table 31

Sheffield, Doncaster and Wakefield - Leeds

Sundays

18 September to 30 October

		GC	EM	GR	XC	GR	NT	NT		XC	GR	NT	GR	EM
		R ⊏P	◇1 ⊏P	R 1 ⊏P⊤	◇1	R 1 ⊏P⊤				◇1	R 1 ⊏P⊤		R 1 ⊏P⊤	◇1 ⊏P
Sheffield 7	29 ⇌ d		21 03		21 21			21 36		22 21		22 39		23 30
Meadowhall	29 ⇌ d							21 42				22 45		
Rotherham Central	29 d							21 48						
Swinton (S.Yorks)	29 d							21 56						
Bolton-upon-Dearne	d							22 00						
Goldthorpe	d							22 03						
Thurnscoe	d							22 06						
Moorthorpe	d							22 11						
Doncaster 7	d	21 01		21 19		21 41	21 49				22 29		23 32	
Bentley (S.Yorks)	d						21 52							
Adwick	a						21 56							
	d						21 56							
South Elmsall	d						22 02							
Fitzwilliam	d						22 09	22 16						
Sandal & Agbrigg	d						22 15	22 22						
Wakefield Westgate 7	32,39 a		21 27	21 36	21 47	21 59	22 19	22 26		22 43	22 49		23 49	23 55
	d		21 28	21 36	21 48	21 59	22 20	22 27		22 43	22 49		23 49	23 56
Pontefract Monkhill	32 d	21 25												
Wakefield Kirkgate 4	32,34,39 a	21 41										23 26		
	d											23 27		
Outwood	d						22 25	22 32						
Leeds 10	32,34 a		21 45	21 57	22 04	22 20	22 39	22 52		23 01	23 10	00 05	00 27	00 28

Sundays

from 30 October

		GR	NT	NT	NT	XC	NT	XC	GR	NT		NT	NT	XC	GR	NT	NT	XC	GR	NT		NT	NT	GC	XC
		R 1 ⊏P⊤			◇	◇1 ⊤		◇1 ⊤	R 1 ⊏P⊤					◇1 ⊤	R 1 ⊏P⊤			◇1 ⊤	R 1 ⊏P⊤					R 1 ⊏P	◇1 ⊤
Sheffield 7	29 ⇌ d			08 39	09 17	09 21	09 36	10 21				10 39	11 17	11 21		11 36	12 16	12 21				12 39	13 17		13 21
Meadowhall	29 ⇌ d			08 45	09 23		09 42					10 45	11 23			11 42	12 23					12 45	13 23		
Rotherham Central	29 d						09 48									11 49									
Swinton (S.Yorks)	29 d						09 58									12 00									
Bolton-upon-Dearne	d						10 03									12 04									
Goldthorpe	d						10 05									12 07									
Thurnscoe	d						10 08									12 10									
Moorthorpe	d						10 13									12 15									
Doncaster 7	d	23p48	09 12						10 52	11 12					11 49				12 52	13 12				13 17	
Bentley (S.Yorks)	d		09 15							11 15										13 15					
Adwick	a		09 19							11 19										13 19					
	d		09 19							11 19										13 19					
South Elmsall	d		09 25							11 25										13 25					
Fitzwilliam	d		09 30				10 19			11 30						12 21				13 30					
Sandal & Agbrigg	d		09 36				10 25			11 36						12 27				13 36					
Wakefield Westgate 7	32,39 a	00 05	09 40			09 44	10 29	10 44	11 09	11 40				11 44	12 06	12 31		12 44	13 09	13 40					13 44
	d	00 05	09 40			09 45	10 30	10 45	11 09	11 40				11 45	12 06	12 31		12 45	13 09	13 40					13 45
Pontefract Monkhill	32 d																							13 42	
Wakefield Kirkgate 4	32,34,39 a			09 29	09 55							11 29	11 52				12 52					13 29	13 52	13 58	
	d			09 30	09 55							11 30	11 53				12 53					13 30	13 53		
Outwood	d		09 45				10 35			11 45						12 36				13 45					
Leeds 10	32,34 a	00 26	09 59	10 04	10 15	10 02	10 52	11 02	11 30	11 59		12 05	12 18	12 01	12 29	12 53	13 18	13 02	13 30	13 59		14 04	14 18		14 02

		GR	NT	NT	XC	GR		NT	NT	NT	XC	GR	NT	NT	XC	NT		GR	NT	NT	NT	GC	XC	EM	GR
		R 1 ⊏P⊤			◇1 ⊤	R 1 ⊏P⊤					◇1 ⊤	R 1 ⊏P⊤			◇1 ⊤			R 1 ⊏P⊤				R 1 ⊏P	◇1 ⊤	◇1 ⊏P	R 1 ⊏P⊤
Sheffield 7	29 ⇌ d		13 36	14 17	14 21				14 39	15 17	15 21		15 36	16 17	16 21	16 36				16 39	17 17		17 21	17 34	
Meadowhall	29 ⇌ d		13 42	14 23					14 45	15 23			15 42	16 23		16 42				16 45	17 23				
Rotherham Central	29 d		13 49										15 50			16 49									
Swinton (S.Yorks)	29 d		13 57										15 58			16 58									
Bolton-upon-Dearne	d		14 01										16 02			17 02									
Goldthorpe	d		14 04										16 05			17 05									
Thurnscoe	d		14 07										16 08			17 08									
Moorthorpe	d		14 12										16 13			17a13									
Doncaster 7	d	13 49				14 52		15 12				15 50						16 59	17 14			17 20			17 49
Bentley (S.Yorks)	d							15 15											17 17						
Adwick	a							15 19											17 21						
	d							15 19											17 21						
South Elmsall	d							15 25											17 27						
Fitzwilliam	d		14 17					15 30					16 19						17 32						
Sandal & Agbrigg	d		14 23					15 36					16 25						17 38						
Wakefield Westgate 7	32,39 a	14 06	14 27		14 44	15 09		15 40			15 44	16 07	16 29		16 44			17 16	17 42				17 46	18 06	18 11
	d	14 06	14 28		14 45	15 09		15 40			15 45	16 07	16 29		16 45			17 16	17 42				17 46	18 07	18 11
Pontefract Monkhill	32 d																					17 45			
Wakefield Kirkgate 4	32,34,39 a			14 52					15 29	15 52				16 52						17 29	17 52	18 00			
	d			14 53					15 30	15 53				16 53						17 30	17 53				
Outwood	d		14 33					15 45					16 34						17 47						
Leeds 10	32,34 a	14 29	14 47	15 18	15 02	15 30		15 59	16 04	16 18	16 02	16 29	16 54	17 18	17 02			17 39	18 01	18 05	18 18		18 02	18 24	18 31

Table 31

Sundays
from 30 October

Sheffield, Doncaster and Wakefield - Leeds

		NT		XC	GR	NT	XC	GR	GR	NT	NT	NT		XC	NT	GR	NT	GR	NT	XC	GR	NT		GC	EM
					R			R	R							R		R			R			R	
				◇1	1		◇1	1	1					◇1		1		1		◇1	1			1	◇1
														A										🍴	
				🛒	🍴🛒		🛒	🍴🛒	🍴🛒					🛒		🍴🛒		🍴🛒		🛒	🍴🛒				🍴
Sheffield 7 29 ⇌	d	17 36		17 51		18 17	18 21			18 39	18 57	19 16		19 21			19 36		20 17	20 21		20 39			21 03
Meadowhall 29 ⇌	d	17 44				18 23				18 45	19 05	19 23					19 42		20 23			20 45			
Rotherham Central 29	d	17 50									19 11						19 49								
Swinton (S.Yorks) 29	d	17 58									19 19						19 57								
Bolton-upon-Dearne	d	18 03															20 02								
Goldthorpe	d	18 05															20 04								
Thurnscoe	d	18 08															20 07								
Moorthorpe	d	18 13									19a29						20 12								
Doncaster 7	d			18 15	18 19			18 49	19 14						19 27	19 50		20 20			20 48			21 01	
Bentley (S.Yorks)	d														19 30										
Adwick	a														19 34										
	d														19 34										
South Elmsall	d														19 41										
Fitzwilliam	d	18 19													19 47		20 18								
Sandal & Agbrigg	d	18 25													19 53		20 24								
Wakefield Westgate 7 32,39	a	18 29		18 33	18 38		18 47	19 07	19 31					19 48	19 57	20 08	20 28	20 37		20 46	21 05				21 27
	d	18 30		18 34	18 38		18 48	19 07	19 31					19 49	19 57	20 08	20 28	20 37		20 47	21 05				21 28
Pontefract Monkhill 32	d																							21 25	
Wakefield Kirkgate 4 32,34,39	a					18 52				19 29		19 52							20 52			21 29		21 41	
	d					18 53				19 30		19 53							20 53			21 30			
Outwood	d	18 35													20 02		20 33								
Leeds 10 32,34	a	18 49		18 51	18 58	19 18	19 04	19 28	19 53	20 05		20 18		20 05	20 16	20 25	20 52	20 55	21 16	21 03	21 29	22 04			21 45

		GR	XC	GR	NT	NT	XC	GR		NT	GR	EM
		R		R				R			R	
		1	◇1	1			◇1	1			1	◇1
		🍴🛒		🍴🛒				🍴🛒			🍴🛒	🍴
Sheffield 7 29 ⇌	d		21 21			21 36	22 21			22 39		23 30
Meadowhall 29 ⇌	d					21 42				22 45		
Rotherham Central 29	d					21 48						
Swinton (S.Yorks) 29	d					21 56						
Bolton-upon-Dearne	d					22 00						
Goldthorpe	d					22 03						
Thurnscoe	d					22 06						
Moorthorpe	d					22 11						
Doncaster 7	d	21 19		21 41	21 49			22 29			23 32	
Bentley (S.Yorks)	d				21 52							
Adwick	a				21 56							
	d				21 56							
South Elmsall	d				22 02							
Fitzwilliam	d				22 09	22 16						
Sandal & Agbrigg	d				22 15	22 22						
Wakefield Westgate 7 32,39	a	21 36	21 47	21 59	22 19	22 26	22 43	22 49			23 49	23 55
	d	21 36	21 48	21 59	22 20	22 27	22 43	22 49			23 49	23 56
Pontefract Monkhill 32	d											
Wakefield Kirkgate 4 32,34,39	a									23 26		
	d									23 27		
Outwood	d				22 25	22 32						
Leeds 10 32,34	a	21 57	22 04	22 20	22 39	22 52	23 01	23 10		00 05	00 27	00 28

A 🛒 to Wakefield Westgate

Table 31

Mondays to Fridays

23 May to 5 December

Leeds - Wakefield, Doncaster and Sheffield

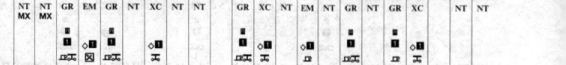

Miles	Miles	Station			NT MX	NT MX	GR	EM	GR	NT	XC	NT	NT		GR	XC	NT	EM	NT	GR	NT	GR	XC		NT	NT
							R 1	◇1 ⊠	R 1		◇1				R 1	◇1		◇1		R 1		R 1	◇1			
0	0	**Leeds** 10	32,34	d	22p37	23p09	05 05	05 25	05 30	05 33	06 00		06 05		06 05	06 15	06 20	06 34	06 38	06 40	06 43	07 00	07 05			07 05
7½	7½	Outwood		d		23p20				05 44							06 29				06 54					
—	—	Wakefield Kirkgate 4	32,34,39	a	23p10								06 21						07 07							07 25
—	—			d	23p10							06 04	06 21						07 08							07 25
—	—	Pontefract Monkhill		d																						
10	10	**Wakefield Westgate** 7	32,39	a		23p24	05 17	05 36	05 42	05 49	06 11				06 17	06 26	06 33	06 45		06 52	06 58	07 12	07 17			
—	—			d		23p24	05 17	05 37	05 42	05 49	06 12				06 17	06 27	06 33	06 46		06 52	06 58		07 18			
11¾	11¾	Sandal & Agbrigg		d		23p28				05 53							06 36				07 02					
16½	16½	Fitzwilliam		d		23p35				06 00							06 43				07 09					
21	—	South Elmsall		d													06 48									
25¾	—	Adwick		a													06 53									
—	—			d													06 54									
28	—	Bentley (S.Yorks)		d													06 58									
29¾	—	**Doncaster** 7		a			05 34	05 55	06 01						06 34	06 43	07 08			07 10						
—	20¼	Moorthorpe		d		23p41				06 06											07 15					
—	23¾	Thurnscoe		d		23p47				06 12											07 21					
—	24½	Goldthorpe		d		23p49				06 15											07 23					
—	25¾	Bolton-upon-Dearne		d		23p52				06 18											07 26					
—	28	Swinton (S.Yorks)	29	a		23p56				06 23											07 30					
—	32½	Rotherham Central	29	a		00 03				06 31											07 37				←	
—	35¼	Meadowhall	29 ⇌	a	23p51	00 08				06 37		06 41	06 49						07 48		07 44				07 48	07 53
—	38¾	**Sheffield** 7	29 ⇌	a	00 02	00 23		06 18		06 47	06 41	06 55	07 00			07 11		07 25	→		07 56		07 50		07 59	08 05

Station			NT	GR	NT	GC	NT	NT	NT		GR	NT	NT	XC	NT	NT	GR	NT	NT		NT	NT	GR	NT	NT	XC
				R 1		R 1 ✕					R 1			◇1			R 1						R 1			◇1
Leeds 10	32,34	d		07 15	07 18		07 29	07 35			07 40	07 48	08 02	08 11			08 15	08 19	08 32		08 37		08 45	08 48	09 05	09 11
Outwood		d			07 28				←			07 59						08 28				←		08 59		
Wakefield Kirkgate 4	32,34,39	a					08 00	07 54	08 00				08 23						09 03		08 54	09 03			09 23	
		d				07 42	08 04	07 55	08 04				08 23						09 05		08 55	09 05			09 23	
Pontefract Monkhill		d				08 01	→												→							
Wakefield Westgate 7	32,39	a		07 27	07 34						07 52	08 03		08 22			08 27	08 31					08 57	09 03		09 23
		d		07 27	07 34						07 52	08 03		08 23			08 27	08 32					08 57	09 03		09 24
Sandal & Agbrigg		d			07 36							08 07						08 36						09 07		
Fitzwilliam		d			07 43							08 14						08 41						09 14		
South Elmsall		d			07 49													08 46								
Adwick		a			07 52													08 52								
		d	07 29		07 52										08 15	08 33		08 52								
Bentley (S.Yorks)		d	07 33		07 56										08 18	08 37		08 56								
Doncaster 7		a	07 37	07 44	08 07	08 29					08 09				08 23	08 42	08 45	09 06					09 15			
Moorthorpe		d										08 20												09 20		
Thurnscoe		d										08 26												09 26		
Goldthorpe		d										08 28												09 28		
Bolton-upon-Dearne		d										08 31												09 31		
Swinton (S.Yorks)	29	a	07 53									08 34			08 42									09 35		
Rotherham Central	29	a	08 00									08 43			08 50									09 44		
Meadowhall	29 ⇌	a	08 05					08 31	08 45			08 50	08 52		08 56						09 27	09 46		09 50	09 52	
Sheffield 7	29 ⇌	a	08 18					08 39	08 56			08 59	09 02	08 51	09 05						09 37	09 56		10 00	10 02	09 51

Station			NT	GR	NT		NT	NT	NT	GR	NT	NT	XC	NT	GR		NT	NT	NT	NT	GR	NT	GC	NT	XC	
				R 1						R 1			◇1		R 1						R 1		R 1 ✕		◇1	
Leeds 10	32,34	d		09 15	09 20		09 32	09 37		09 45	09 48	10 05	10 11		10 15		10 20	10 32	10 37		10 45	10 48		11 05	11 11	
Outwood		d			09 29				←		09 59						10 29			←		10 59				
Wakefield Kirkgate 4	32,34,39	a					10 01	09 55	10 01			10 23						11 01	10 54	11 01				11 23		
		d					10 04	09 56	10 04			10 23						11 04	10 55	11 04			11 11	11 23		
Pontefract Monkhill		d					→											→					11 34			
Wakefield Westgate 7	32,39	a		09 27	09 33					09 57	10 03		10 22		10 27		10 33				10 57	11 03			11 23	
		d		09 27	09 33					09 57	10 03		10 23		10 27		10 33				10 57	11 03			11 24	
Sandal & Agbrigg		d			09 35						10 07						10 36					11 07				
Fitzwilliam		d			09 44						10 14						10 44					11 14				
South Elmsall		d			09 47												10 49									
Adwick		a			09 52												10 54									
		d	09 15		09 53									10 15			10 55									
Bentley (S.Yorks)		d	09 19		09 57									10 19			10 59									
Doncaster 7		a	09 24	09 44	10 08					10 15				10 24	10 44		11 09				11 15		12 06			
Moorthorpe		d									10 20											11 20				
Thurnscoe		d									10 26											11 26				
Goldthorpe		d									10 28											11 28				
Bolton-upon-Dearne		d									10 31											11 31				
Swinton (S.Yorks)	29	a	09 42								10 35			10 42								11 35				
Rotherham Central	29	a	09 50								10 44			10 52								11 44				
Meadowhall	29 ⇌	a	09 55					10 27	10 46		10 50	10 52		10 57					11 27	11 46		11 51		11 52		
Sheffield 7	29 ⇌	a	10 05					10 37	10 56		11 01	11 02	10 51	11 05					11 37	11 57		12 01		12 02	11 51	

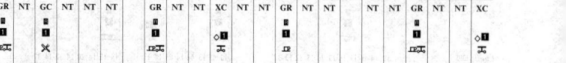

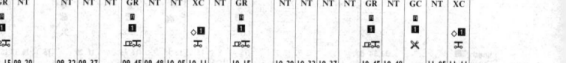

Table 31

Mondays to Fridays

23 May to 5 December

Leeds - Wakefield, Doncaster and Sheffield

			NT	GR	NT	NT	NT	NT	NT	GR	NT		NT	XC	NT	GR	NT	NT	NT	NT	GR		NT	NT	XC	NT
				R 1						R 1				◇1		R 1					R 1				R 1	
Leeds 10	32,34	d		11 15	11 20		11 32	11 37		11 45	11 48		12 05	12 12		12 15	12 20	12 32	12 37		12 45		12 48	13 05	13 11	
Outwood		d			11 29				←		11 59						12 29			←			12 59			
Wakefield Kirkgate 4	32,34,39	a					12 01	11 54	12 01				12 23					13 02	12 54	13 02				13 23		
		d					12 04	11 55	12 04				12 23					13 04	12 55	13 04				13 23		
Pontefract Monkhill		d					↦											↦								
Wakefield Westgate 7	32,39	a		11 27	11 33					11 57	12 03			12 23		12 27	12 33				12 57		13 03		13 22	
		d		11 27	11 33					11 57	12 03			12 24		12 27	12 33				12 57		13 03		13 23	
Sandal & Agbrigg		d			11 36						12 07						12 36						13 07			
Fitzwilliam		d			11 44						12 14						12 44						13 14			
South Elmsall		d			11 49												12 49									
Adwick		a			11 54												12 52									
		d	11 15		11 55										12 15		12 53									13 14
Bentley (S.Yorks)		d	11 19		11 59										12 19		12 57									13 18
Doncaster 7		a	11 24	11 44	12 08					12 15					12 25	12 44	13 07				13 15					13 26
Moorthorpe		d				11 59					12 20												13 20			
Thurnscoe		d									12 26												13 26			
Goldthorpe		d									12 28												13 28			
Bolton-upon-Dearne		d									12 31												13 31			
Swinton (S.Yorks)	29	a	11 43			12 08					12 35				12 42								13 35			13 42
Rotherham Central	29	a	11 52			12 18					12 44				12 52								13 44			13 51
Meadowhall	29	a	11 55			12 24		12 27	12 46		12 51		12 52		12 55				13 27	13 46			13 51	13 52		13 55
Sheffield 7	29	a	12 05			12 36		12 37	12 56		13 01		13 02	12 51	13 05				13 37	13 56			14 01	14 02	13 51	14 05

			GR	NT	NT	NT	NT		GR	NT	NT	XC	NT	GR	NT	NT	NT		NT	GR	NT	NT	XC	NT	GR	NT
			R 1						R 1			◇1		R 1						R 1			◇1		R 1	
Leeds 10	32,34	d	13 15	13 20	13 32	13 37			13 45	13 48	14 05	14 11		14 15	14 20	14 32	14 37			14 45	14 48	15 05	15 11		15 15	15 20
Outwood		d		13 29			←			13 59					14 29				←		14 59					15 29
Wakefield Kirkgate 4	32,34,39	a			14 01	13 54	14 01				14 23					15 01	14 54		15 01			15 23				
		d			14 04	13 55	14 04				14 23					15 04	14 55		15 04			15 23				
Pontefract Monkhill		d			↦											↦										
Wakefield Westgate 7	32,39	a	13 27	13 33					13 57	14 03		14 22		14 27	14 33					14 57	15 03		15 22		15 27	15 33
		d	13 27	13 33					13 57	14 03		14 23		14 27	14 33					14 57	15 03		15 23		15 27	15 33
Sandal & Agbrigg		d		13 36						14 07					14 36						15 07					15 36
Fitzwilliam		d		13 44						14 14					14 44						15 14					15 44
South Elmsall		d		13 49											14 49											15 49
Adwick		a		13 54											14 52											15 54
		d		13 55									14 15		14 53									15 15		15 55
Bentley (S.Yorks)		d		13 59									14 19		14 57									15 19		15 59
Doncaster 7		a	13 44	14 08					14 15				14 24	14 44	15 08					15 15				15 24	15 44	16 08
Moorthorpe		d								14 20											15 20					
Thurnscoe		d								14 26											15 26					
Goldthorpe		d								14 28											15 28					
Bolton-upon-Dearne		d								14 31											15 31					
Swinton (S.Yorks)	29	a								14 35			14 41								15 35			15 42		
Rotherham Central	29	a								14 44			14 52								15 44			15 50		
Meadowhall	29	a				14 27	14 46			14 50	14 52		14 55				15 27		15 46		15 50	15 51		15 55		
Sheffield 7	29	a				14 37	14 57			15 01	15 02	14 51	15 05				15 37		15 57		16 01	16 03	15 51	16 05		

			NT		NT	NT	NT	GR	NT	NT	XC	NT	GR		NT	GC	NT	NT	XC	NT	GR	NT	NT		GR	NT
								R 1			◇1		R 1			R 1 ✕			◇1		R 1				R 1	
Leeds 10	32,34	d			15 32	15 37		15 45	15 48	16 05	16 11		16 15		16 20		16 32	16 37	16 40		16 45	16 48	17 05		17 15	17 20
Outwood		d					←		15 59						16 29					←		16 59				17 29
Wakefield Kirkgate 4	32,34,39	a			16 01	15 54	16 01			16 23							17 01	16 54		17 01			17 22			
		d			16 04	15 55	16 04			16 23						16 40	17 04	16 55		17 04			17 23			
Pontefract Monkhill		d			↦											16 56	↦									
Wakefield Westgate 7	32,39	a						15 57	16 03		16 22		16 27		16 32				16 51		16 57	17 03			17 27	17 33
		d						15 57	16 03		16 22		16 27		16 32				16 52		16 57	17 03			17 27	17 33
Sandal & Agbrigg		d							16 07						16 35							17 07				17 36
Fitzwilliam		d							16 14						16 43							17 14				17 44
South Elmsall		d													16 48											17 49
Adwick		a													16 53											17 54
		d										16 15			16 54											17 55
Bentley (S.Yorks)		d										16 19			16 58											17 59
Doncaster 7		a						16 15				16 24	16 44		17 07	17 24					17 16				17 44	18 08
Moorthorpe		d	15 50						16 20													17 20				
Thurnscoe		d							16 26													17 26				
Goldthorpe		d							16 28													17 28				
Bolton-upon-Dearne		d							16 31													17 31				
Swinton (S.Yorks)	29	a	16 00						16 35			16 42										17 35				
Rotherham Central	29	a	16 11						16 44			16 50										17 44				
Meadowhall	29	a	16 17			16 27	16 46		16 50	16 52		16 55						17 27		17 46		17 50	17 51			
Sheffield 7	29	a	16 25			16 37	16 57		17 00	17 02	16 51	17 05						17 37	17 20	17 57		18 01	18 03			

Leeds - Wakefield, Doncaster and Sheffield

	NT	NT	NT	GR	NT	NT	XC		NT	GR	NT	NT	NT	NT	GR	NT	NT		XC	GR	NT	NT	NT	NT
				R						R					R					R				
				1			◇1			1					1				◇1	1				
				🍴			🛒			🍴					🍴🛒				🛒	🍴🛒				
Leeds [10] 32,34 d	17 32	17 37		17 45	17 46	18 05	18 11			18 15	18 20	18 32	18 43		18 45	18 48	19 05		19 11	19 15	19 19	19 37	19 43	
Outwood d			←		17 57						18 29			←		18 59					19 28			←
Wakefield Kirkgate [4] 32,34,39 a	18 01	17 54	18 01			18 23						19 04	18 59	19 04			19 24					20 06	19 59	20 06
d	18 04	17 55	18 04			18 23						19 05	18 59	19 05			19 24					20 07	20 00	20 07
Pontefract Monkhill d	↦											↦										↦		
Wakefield Westgate [7] 32,39 a				17 57	18 01		18 22			18 27	18 33				18 57	19 03			19 22	19 27	19 32			
d				17 57	18 01		18 23			18 27	18 33				18 57	19 03			19 23	19 27	19 32			
Sandal & Agbrigg d					18 07						18 36					19 07					19 35			
Fitzwilliam d					18 14						18 44					19 14					19 42			
South Elmsall d											18 50										19 47			
Adwick a											18 55										19 52			
d									18 14		18 56										19 53			
Bentley (S.Yorks) d									18 18		19 00										19 59			
Doncaster [7] a				18 15					18 25	18 44	19 08				19 15					19 44	20 07			
Moorthorpe d					18 20											19 20								
Thurnscoe d					18 26											19 26								
Goldthorpe d					18 28											19 28								
Bolton-upon-Dearne d					18 31											19 31								
Swinton (S.Yorks) 29 a					18 35											19 35								
Rotherham Central 29 a					18 44											19 45								
Meadowhall 29 🚊 a		18 27	18 46		18 50	18 52							19 33	19 47		19 50	19 52						20 32	20 45
Sheffield [7] 29 🚊 a		18 37	18 56		19 00	19 04	18 51						19 43	19 57		19 58	20 03		19 51				20 44	20 58

	GR	NT	XC		NT	NT	NT	GR	NT	XC	NT	NT	NT		NT	NT	NT	NT	NT					
	R							R																
	1		◇1					1		◇1														
	🍴🛒							🍴🛒																
Leeds [10] 32,34 d	19 45	19 48	20 11		20 20	20 30	20 37	20 45	20 48	21 11	21 20		21 37		21 48		22 37	22 40	23 09					
Outwood d		19 59			20 29				20 59		21 29				21 59			22 49	23 20					
Wakefield Kirkgate [4] 32,34,39 a						20 46	21 06						22 06				23 10							
d						20 46	21 07					21 47	22 07			22 55	23 10							
Pontefract Monkhill d																								
Wakefield Westgate [7] 32,39 a	19 57	20 03	20 22		20 33			20 57	21 03	21 22	21 33	21 53			22 03	23 01		22 53	23 24					
d	19 57	20 03	20 23		20 33			20 57	21 03	21 23	21 33				22 03			22 53	23 24					
Sandal & Agbrigg d		20 07			20 36				21 07		21 36				22 07			22 56	23 28					
Fitzwilliam d		20 14			20 44				21 13		21 44				22 14			23 03	23 35					
South Elmsall d					20 49						21 49							23 08						
Adwick a					20 54						21 54							23 13						
d					20 55						21 55							23 14						
Bentley (S.Yorks) d					20 59						21 59							23 18						
Doncaster [7] a	20 16				21 08			21 15			22 08							23 28						
Moorthorpe d		20 20							21 20						22 20				23 41					
Thurnscoe d		20 26							21 27						22 26				23 47					
Goldthorpe d		20 28							21 29						22 28				23 49					
Bolton-upon-Dearne d		20 31							21 32						22 31				23 52					
Swinton (S.Yorks) 29 a		20 35							21 35						22 35				23 56					
Rotherham Central 29 a		20 44							21 44						22 46				00 03					
Meadowhall 29 🚊 a		20 51				21 18	21 45		21 51				22 47		22 52		23 51		00 08					
Sheffield [7] 29 🚊 a		21 02	20 51			21 30	21 57		22 04	21 51			22 58		23 02		00 02		00 23					

Saturdays

	NT	NT	GR	XC	GR	XC	NT	EM	NT		NT	NT	NT	GR	XC	NT	NT	GC	NT		EM	NT	NT	NT
			R		R									R				R						
			1	◇1	1	◇1		◇1						1	◇1			1			◇1			
			🍴🛒	🛒	🍴🛒	🛒		🍴						🍴🛒	🛒			🍴			🍴			
Leeds [10] 32,34 d	22p37	23p09	05 05	06 00	06 05	06 15	06 20	06 34	06 38		06 43		07 05	07 05	07 10		07 20		07 29		07 34	07 35		07 48
Outwood d		23p20					06 29				06 54						07 29						←	07 59
Wakefield Kirkgate [4] 32,34,39 a	23p10								07 06				07 25						08 00			07 54	08 00	
d	23p10								07 07				07 25					07 38	08 04			07 55	08 04	
Pontefract Monkhill d																		07 58	↦					
Wakefield Westgate [7] 32,39 a		23p24	05 17	06 11	06 17	06 28	06 33	06 45			06 58			07 17	07 22		07 34				07 45			08 03
d		23p24	05 17	06 12	06 17	06 29	06 33	06 46			06 58			07 17	07 23		07 34				07 46			08 03
Sandal & Agbrigg d		23p28					06 36				07 02						07 37							08 07
Fitzwilliam d		23p35					06 44				07 09						07 44							08 14
South Elmsall d							06 49										07 49							
Adwick a							06 54										07 54							
d							06 55									07 23	07 55							
Bentley (S.Yorks) d							06 59									07 27	07 59							
Doncaster [7] a			05 34		06 34	06 46	07 07							07 35		07 31	08 07	08 27						
Moorthorpe d		23p41									07 15													08 20
Thurnscoe d		23p47									07 21													08 26
Goldthorpe d		23p49									07 23													08 28
Bolton-upon-Dearne d		23p52									07 26													08 31
Swinton (S.Yorks) 29 a		23p56									07 30					07 53								08 35
Rotherham Central 29 a		00 03									07 37	←				08 01								08 44
Meadowhall 29 🚊 a	23p51	00 08							07 47		07 46	07 47	07 53			08 06						08 31	08 45	08 49
Sheffield [7] 29 🚊 a	00 02	00 23		06 45		07 15		07 22	↦		07 54	07 57	08 05		07 51	08 18					08 21	08 39	08 56	08 59

Leeds - Wakefield, Doncaster and Sheffield

Station			GR	NT	XC	NT	NT		NT	NT	NT	NT	GR	NT	GR	NT	XC		NT	NT	NT	NT	NT	NT	GR	XC
			R 1		◇1								R 1		R 1		◇1								R 1	◇1
Leeds 10	32,34	d	08 05	08 05	08 12				08 20	08 32	08 37		08 40	08 48	09 05	09 05	09 11			09 32	09 37		09 48	10 05	10 05	10 12
Outwood		d							08 29			←		08 59								←	09 59			
Wakefield Kirkgate 4	32,34,39	a		08 23						09 03	08 54	09 03				09 23				10 01	09 55	10 01		10 23		
		d		08 23						09 05	08 55	09 05				09 23				10 04	09 56	10 04		10 23		
Pontefract Monkhill		d								↪										↪						
Wakefield Westgate 7	32,39	a	08 17		08 23				08 33				08 52	09 03	09 17		09 23						10 03		10 17	10 23
		d	08 17		08 24				08 33				08 52	09 03	09 17		09 24						10 03		10 17	10 24
Sandal & Agbrigg		d							08 36					09 07									10 07			
Fitzwilliam		d							08 44					09 14									10 14			
South Elmsall		d							08 49																	
Adwick		a							08 54																	
		d				08 15	08 33		08 55										09 15							
Bentley (S.Yorks)		d				08 19	08 37		08 59										09 19							
Doncaster 7		a	08 34			08 23	08 42		09 07				09 12		09 34				09 24						10 35	
Moorthorpe		d												09 20									10 20			
Thurnscoe		d												09 26									10 26			
Goldthorpe		d												09 28									10 28			
Bolton-upon-Dearne		d												09 31									10 31			
Swinton (S.Yorks)	29	a				08 43								09 35					09 42				10 35			
Rotherham Central	29	a				08 50								09 45					09 50				10 44			
Meadowhall	29 ⇌	a		08 52		08 56					09 27	09 46		09 50		09 52			09 54		10 27	10 46	10 50	10 52		
Sheffield 7	29 ⇌	a		09 02	08 51	09 05					09 37	09 56		10 00		10 02	09 52		10 05		10 37	10 57	11 00	11 02		10 51

Station			NT		NT	NT	NT	NT	NT	GR	GC	NT	XC		NT	NT	NT	NT	NT	NT	NT	NT	GR		XC	NT
										R 1	R 1		◇1										R 1		◇1	
Leeds 10	32,34	d			10 20	10 32	10 37		10 48	11 05		11 05	11 11			11 20		11 32	11 37		11 48	12 05	12 05		12 11	
Outwood		d			10 29			←	10 59							11 29				←	11 59					
Wakefield Kirkgate 4	32,34,39	a				11 01	10 54	11 01				11 23						12 01	11 54	12 01		12 23				
		d				11 04	10 55	11 04			11 11	11 23						12 04	11 55	12 04		12 23				
Pontefract Monkhill		d				↪					11 35							↪								
Wakefield Westgate 7	32,39	a			10 33				11 03	11 17			11 22			11 33					12 03		12 17		12 23	
		d			10 33				11 03	11 17			11 23			11 33					12 03		12 17		12 24	
Sandal & Agbrigg		d			10 36				11 07							11 36					12 07					
Fitzwilliam		d			10 44				11 14							11 44					12 14					
South Elmsall		d			10 49											11 49										
Adwick		a			10 54											11 54										
		d	10 15		10 55										11 15	11 55										12 14
Bentley (S.Yorks)		d	10 19		10 59										11 19	11 59										12 18
Doncaster 7		a	10 24		11 07					11 35	12 03				11 24	12 07							12 35			12 24
Moorthorpe		d							11 20								11 59				12 20					
Thurnscoe		d							11 26												12 26					
Goldthorpe		d							11 28												12 28					
Bolton-upon-Dearne		d							11 31												12 31					
Swinton (S.Yorks)	29	a	10 42						11 35						11 42		12 08				12 35					12 42
Rotherham Central	29	a	10 52						11 44						11 52		12 18				12 43					12 52
Meadowhall	29 ⇌	a	10 57				11 27	11 46	11 50			11 52			11 57		12 24		12 27	12 46	12 49	12 52				12 57
Sheffield 7	29 ⇌	a	11 06				11 37	11 57	12 00			12 02	11 51		12 05		12 36		12 37	12 57	13 00	13 02			12 51	13 05

Station			NT	NT	NT	NT	NT	NT	GR		XC	NT	NT	NT	NT	NT	NT	NT	GR		XC	NT	NT	NT	GR	NT
									R 1		◇1								R 1		◇1				R 1	
Leeds 10	32,34	d	12 20	12 32	12 37		12 48	13 05	13 05		13 11		13 20	13 32	13 37		13 48	14 05	14 05		14 11		14 20	14 32	14 35	14 37
Outwood		d	12 29			←	12 59						13 29			←	13 59						14 29			
Wakefield Kirkgate 4	32,34,39	a		13 02	12 54	13 02		13 23						14 01	13 54	14 01		14 23						15 01		14 54
		d		13 04	12 55	13 04		13 23						14 04	13 55	14 04		14 23						15 04		14 55
Pontefract Monkhill		d		↪										↪										↪		
Wakefield Westgate 7	32,39	a	12 33				13 03		13 17		13 22		13 33				14 03		14 17		14 23		14 33		14 47	
		d	12 33				13 03		13 17		13 23		13 33				14 03		14 17		14 24		14 33		14 47	
Sandal & Agbrigg		d	12 36				13 07						13 36				14 07						14 36			
Fitzwilliam		d	12 44				13 14						13 44				14 14						14 44			
South Elmsall		d	12 49										13 49										14 49			
Adwick		a	12 54										13 54										14 54			
		d	12 55									13 15	13 55									14 15	14 55			
Bentley (S.Yorks)		d	12 59									13 19	13 59									14 19	14 59			
Doncaster 7		a	13 07						13 35			13 24	14 07						14 35			14 24	15 07		15 10	
Moorthorpe		d					13 20										14 20									
Thurnscoe		d					13 26										14 26									
Goldthorpe		d					13 28										14 28									
Bolton-upon-Dearne		d					13 31										14 31									
Swinton (S.Yorks)	29	a					13 35					13 42					14 35					14 43				
Rotherham Central	29	a					13 43					13 52					14 43					14 52				
Meadowhall	29 ⇌	a			13 27	13 46	13 49	13 52				13 57			14 27	14 46	14 49	14 52				14 57				15 27
Sheffield 7	29 ⇌	a			13 37	13 57	14 00	14 02			13 51	14 05			14 37	14 57	15 00	15 02			14 51	15 05				15 37

Leeds - Wakefield, Doncaster and Sheffield

Station			NT	NT	NT		GR	XC	NT	NT	NT	NT	NT	NT	NT		GR	GC	NT	XC	NT	NT	NT	NT	XC
							■R ■1	◇■1									■R ■1	■R ■1		◇■1					◇■1
Leeds ■10	32,34	d		14 48	15 05		15 05	15 12		15 20		15 32	15 37		15 48		16 05		16 05	16 12		16 20	16 32	16 37	16 40
Outwood		d	←	14 59						15 29				←	15 59							16 29			
Wakefield Kirkgate ■4	32,34,39	a	15 01		15 23							16 01	15 54	16 01					16 23				17 01	16 54	
		d	15 04		15 23							16 04	15 55	16 04				16 11	16 23				17 04	16 55	
Pontefract Monkhill		d										→						16 29					→		
Wakefield Westgate ■7	32,39	a		15 03			15 17	15 23		15 33					16 03		16 17			16 23		16 33			16 51
		d		15 03			15 17	15 24		15 33					16 03		16 17			16 24		16 33			16 52
Sandal & Agbrigg		d		15 07						15 36					16 07							16 36			
Fitzwilliam		d		15 14						15 44					16 14							16 44			
South Elmsall		d								15 49												16 49			
Adwick		a								15 54												16 54			
		d							15 15	15 55											16 15	16 55			
Bentley (S.Yorks)		d							15 19	15 59											16 18	16 59			
Doncaster ■7		a					15 34		15 24	16 07							16 35	17 02			16 25	17 07			
Moorthorpe		d		15 20							15 50				16 20										
Thurnscoe		d		15 26											16 26										
Goldthorpe		d		15 28											16 28										
Bolton-upon-Dearne		d		15 31											16 31										
Swinton (S.Yorks)	29	a		15 35					15 42		16 01				16 35						16 41				
Rotherham Central	29	a		15 43					15 50		16 08				16 43						16 50				
Meadowhall	29 🚊	a	15 46	15 49	15 51				15 56		16 17		16 27	16 46	16 49				16 52		16 55			17 27	
Sheffield ■7	29 🚊	a	15 57	16 00	16 03			15 51	16 05		16 27		16 37	16 57	17 00				17 02	16 51	17 05			17 37	17 20

Station			NT	NT	NT	GR	XC	NT	NT	NT	NT		NT	NT	NT	GR	XC	NT	NT	NT	NT		NT	NT	GR	XC
						■R ■1	◇■1									■R ■1	◇■1								■R ■1	◇■1
Leeds ■10	32,34	d		16 48	17 05	17 05	17 11	17 20		17 32	17 37			17 48	18 05	18 05	18 11	18 20	18 32	18 37			18 48	19 05	19 05	19 11
Outwood		d	←	16 59				17 29					←	17 59				18 29			←		18 59			
Wakefield Kirkgate ■4	32,34,39	a	17 01		17 22					18 01	17 54		18 01		18 23				19 04	18 54	19 04			19 24		
		d	17 04		17 23					18 04	17 55		18 04		18 23				19 05	18 55	19 05			19 24		
Pontefract Monkhill		d								→									→							
Wakefield Westgate ■7	32,39	a		17 03		17 17	17 22	17 33						18 03		18 17	18 22	18 33					19 03		19 17	19 23
		d		17 03		17 17	17 23	17 33						18 03		18 17	18 23	18 33					19 03		19 17	19 24
Sandal & Agbrigg		d		17 07				17 36						18 07				18 36					19 07			
Fitzwilliam		d		17 14				17 44						18 14				18 44					19 14			
South Elmsall		d						17 49										18 49								
Adwick		a						17 54										18 54								
		d						17 55	18 16									18 55								
Bentley (S.Yorks)		d						17 59	18 20									18 59								
Doncaster ■7		a				17 35		18 07	18 27							18 35		19 07							19 36	
Moorthorpe		d		17 20										18 20									19 20			
Thurnscoe		d		17 26										18 26									19 26			
Goldthorpe		d		17 28										18 28									19 28			
Bolton-upon-Dearne		d		17 31										18 31									19 31			
Swinton (S.Yorks)	29	a		17 35										18 35									19 35			
Rotherham Central	29	a		17 43										18 44									19 44			
Meadowhall	29 🚊	a	17 46	17 49	17 51						18 27		18 46	18 50	18 52					19 28	19 47		19 50	19 52		
Sheffield ■7	29 🚊	a	17 57	18 00	18 03		17 51				18 38		18 56	19 00	19 04		18 51			19 39	19 57		20 00	20 03		19 51

Station			NT	NT	NT	NT	NT		GR	XC	NT	NT	NT	NT	XC	NT	NT		NT	NT	NT	NT	NT	NT	NT
									■R ■1	◇■1					◇■1										
Leeds ■10	32,34	d	19 20	19 37	19 43		19 48		20 05	20 11	20 20	20 30	20 37	20 48	21 11	21 20			21 37	21 48	22 19			22 37	22 44
Outwood		d	19 29			←	19 59				20 29			20 59		21 29				21 59	22 28				22 55
Wakefield Kirkgate ■4	32,34,39	a		20 06	19 59	20 06						20 46	21 06						22 06					23 10	
		d		20 07	20 00	20 07						20 47	21 07				21 48		22 07			22 55	23 07		
Pontefract Monkhill		d		→																			23a29		
Wakefield Westgate ■7	32,39	a	19 33				20 03		20 17	20 22	20 33			21 03	21 22	21 33	21 53			22 03	22 32	23 01			22 59
		d	19 33				20 03		20 17	20 23	20 33			21 03	21 23	21 33				22 03	22 32				22 59
Sandal & Agbrigg		d	19 36				20 07				20 36			21 07		21 36				22 07	22 35				23 03
Fitzwilliam		d	19 44				20 14				20 44			21 13		21 44				22 14	22 42				23 10
South Elmsall		d	19 49								20 49					21 49					22 47				
Adwick		a	19 54								20 54					21 54					22 52				
		d	19 55								20 55					21 55					22 53				
Bentley (S.Yorks)		d	19 59								20 59					21 59					22 57				
Doncaster ■7		a	20 07						20 35		21 07					22 07					23 08				
Moorthorpe		d					20 20							21 19						22 20					23 15
Thurnscoe		d					20 26							21 25						22 26					23 21
Goldthorpe		d					20 28							21 27						22 28					23 23
Bolton-upon-Dearne		d					20 31							21 30						22 31					23 26
Swinton (S.Yorks)	29	a					20 35							21 34						22 37					23 30
Rotherham Central	29	a					20 45							21 41						22 44					23 37
Meadowhall	29 🚊	a			20 36	20 45	20 50					21 17	21 45	21 49					22 47	22 52					23 43
Sheffield ■7	29 🚊	a			20 44	20 58	21 00			20 52		21 30	21 59	22 02	21 51				22 58	23 03					23 58

Table 31

Sundays

Leeds - Wakefield, Doncaster and Sheffield

		GR	XC	GC	NT	NT	XC	NT	GR	EM	XC	NT	GR	EM	NT	NT	NT	XC	GR	NT	NT	NT	XC
		R 1	◇1	R 1			◇1		R 1	◇1	◇1		R 1	◇1				◇1	R 1				◇1
Leeds 10 32,34	d	08 05	08 10		08 34	08 48	09 00	09 05	09 05	09 44	10 00	10 02	10 05	10 15	10 17	10 18	10 57	11 00	11 05	11 18	11 29		12 00
Outwood	d					08 59										10 27				11 29			
Wakefield Kirkgate 4 32,34,39	a				09 03			09 21				10 18			10 46		11 13				11 46		
	d			08 43	09 03			09 21				10 18			10 46		11 13				11 46		
Pontefract Monkhill	d																						
Wakefield Westgate 7 32,39	a	08 17	08 22			09 03	09 11		09 17	09 56	10 11		10 17	10 27		10 32		11 11	11 17	11 33			12 11
	d	08 17	08 23			09 03	09 11		09 17	09 57	10 12		10 17	10 28		10 32		11 12	11 17	11 33			12 12
Sandal & Agbrigg	d					09 07										10 35				11 37			
Fitzwilliam	d					09 14										10 42				11 44			
South Elmsall	d															10 47							
Adwick	a															10 52							
	d															10 53							
Bentley (S.Yorks)	d															10 57							
Doncaster 7	a	08 34		09 04			09 31		09 35		10 28		10 35			11 05		11 28	11 35				12 28
Moorthorpe	d					09 20														11 50			
Thurnscoe	d					09 26														11 56			
Goldthorpe	d					09 28														11 58			
Bolton-upon-Dearne	d					09 31														12 01			
Swinton (S.Yorks) 29	a					09 35														12 05			
Rotherham Central 29	a					09 44														12 12		←	
Meadowhall 29	a				09 44	09 53		09 57				10 51			11 32		11 46			12 20	12 17	12 20	
Sheffield 7 29	a		08 51		09 55	10 03	09 55	10 04		10 25	10 54	11 02		10 57	11 44		11 56	11 53		→	12 29	12 32	12 54

		GR	NT	GC	NT	NT	XC	GR	NT	EM	NT	GR	XC	NT	NT	GR	NT	XC	NT	NT	XC	GR	GC
		R 1		R 1			◇1	R 1		◇1		R 1	◇1			R 1		◇1			◇1	R 1	R 1
Leeds 10 32,34	d	12 05	12 18		12 29	12 34	13 00	13 05	13 18	13 59	14 05	14 05	14 10	14 17	14 18	15 05	15 05	15 10	15 18	16 04	16 10	16 15	
Outwood	d		12 27						13 29						14 27				15 29				
Wakefield Kirkgate 4 32,34,39	a				12 46	13 04					14 21			14 46			15 22			16 21			
	d			12 29	12 46	13 04					14 21			14 46			15 22			16 22			16 29
Pontefract Monkhill	d			12 46																			16 46
Wakefield Westgate 7 32,39	a	12 17	12 31				13 11	13 18	13 33	14 11		14 17	14 22		14 31	15 17		15 22	15 33		16 21	16 28	
	d	12 17	12 32				13 12	13 18	13 33	14 12		14 17	14 23		14 32	15 17		15 23	15 33		16 22	16 28	
Sandal & Agbrigg	d		12 35						13 37						14 35				15 37				
Fitzwilliam	d		12 41						13 44						14 41				15 44				
South Elmsall	d		12 46												14 46								
Adwick	a		12 52												14 52								
	d		12 52												14 52								
Bentley (S.Yorks)	d		12 56												14 56								
Doncaster 7	a	12 36	13 04	13 09			13 28	13 35				14 35			15 05	15 35						16 45	17 09
Moorthorpe	d								13 50										15 50				
Thurnscoe	d								13 56										15 56				
Goldthorpe	d								13 58										15 58				
Bolton-upon-Dearne	d								14 01										16 01				
Swinton (S.Yorks) 29	a								14 05										16 05				
Rotherham Central 29	a								14 12										16 12				
Meadowhall 29	a				13 18	13 48			14 20		14 54			15 35			15 55		16 20	16 56			
Sheffield 7 29	a				13 29	13 58	13 54		14 32	14 40	15 06		14 52	15 44			16 05	15 51	16 31	17 05	16 51		

		NT	NT	GR	NT	XC	GR	NT	GR	NT	XC	GR	NT	NT	NT	GR	NT	XC	GR	NT	GR	NT
				R 1		◇1	R 1		R 1		◇1	R 1				R 1		◇1	R 1		R 1	A
Leeds 10 32,34	d	16 17	16 18	16 45	17 05	17 10	17 15	17 18	17 45	18 05	18 10	18 15		18 17	18 18	18 45	19 04	19 10	19 15	19 18	19 45	
Outwood	d		16 27					17 29							18 27					19 29		
Wakefield Kirkgate 4 32,34,39	a	16 46			17 21					18 21				18 45			19 21					
	d	16 46			17 21					18 22				18 45			19 21					
Pontefract Monkhill	d																					
Wakefield Westgate 7 32,39	a		16 32	16 57		17 21	17 28	17 33	17 57		18 21	18 28			18 32	18 57		19 21	19 27	19 33	19 57	
	d		16 32	16 57		17 22	17 28	17 33	17 58		18 22	18 28			18 32	18 57		19 22	19 27	19 33	19 57	
Sandal & Agbrigg	d		16 35					17 37							18 35					19 37		
Fitzwilliam	d		16 42					17 44							18 42					19 44		
South Elmsall	d		16 47												18 47							
Adwick	a		16 52												18 52							
	d		16 53												18 53							
Bentley (S.Yorks)	d		16 57												18 57							
Doncaster 7	a		17 06	17 17			17 45		18 16			18 45			19 06	19 17			19 44		20 17	
Moorthorpe	d							17 54					18 52							19 50		19 52
Thurnscoe	d							18 00												19 56		
Goldthorpe	d							18 02												19 58		
Bolton-upon-Dearne	d							18 05												20 01		
Swinton (S.Yorks) 29	a							18 10					19 01							20 07		20 22
Rotherham Central 29	a							18 17					19 12							20 14		
Meadowhall 29	a	17 34			17 55			18 25		18 56			19 18	19 32			19 54			20 20		
Sheffield 7 29	a	17 44			18 05	17 51		18 36		19 05	18 51		19 27	19 43			20 04	19 50		20 34		

A until 19 June

Table 31

Sundays

Leeds - Wakefield, Doncaster and Sheffield

			XC	NT	NT	GR	XC	NT	NT		NT	NT	NT
			◇1			1 (🍴)	◇1					A (bus)	
Leeds 10	32,34	d	20 10	20 17	20 18	20 45	21 10	21 18			21 40		22 17
Outwood		d			20 27			21 27			21 51		
Wakefield Kirkgate 4	32,34,39	a		20 46									22 46
		d		20 46									22 46
Pontefract Monkhill		d											
Wakefield Westgate 7	32,39	a	20 21		20 31	20 57	21 21	21 31			21 55		
		d	20 22		20 32	20 57	21 22	21 31			21 55		
Sandal & Agbrigg		d			20 35			21 34			21 59		
Fitzwilliam		d			20 41			21 41			22 06		
South Elmsall		d			20 46			21 46					
Adwick		a			20 52			21 51					
		d			20 52			21 52					
Bentley (S.Yorks)		d			20 56			21 56					
Doncaster 7		a			21 05	21 14		22 05					
Moorthorpe		d							21 36		22 12		
Thurnscoe		d									22 18		
Goldthorpe		d									22 20		
Bolton-upon-Dearne		d									22 23		
Swinton (S.Yorks)	29	a							21 45		22 32	22s57	
Rotherham Central	29	a							21 52		22 39	23s17	
Meadowhall	29 (tram)	a		21 33					21 57		22 45	23s27	23 30
Sheffield 7	29 (tram)	a	20 51	21 42			21 50		22 09		22 54	23s47	23 43

A until 19 June

Bradford, Leeds and Wakefield - Pontefract, Knottingley and Goole

Miles	Miles				NT SX	NT	NT SO	NT SX	NT SO	NT SX	NT SX	NT SO	GC SO R 1 ☕		GC SX R 1 ☕	NT	NT SO	NT SX	NT	NT	NT	NT	NT		NT SX	NT SO
—	—	Bradford Interchange	41	d									06 51		06 51											
—	—	Halifax	41	d									07 04		07 07											
—	—	Brighouse	41	d									07 17		07 18											
0	—	**Leeds** 10	31,34	d	05 46		06 38	06 38	07 00	07 00						07 29	08 00	08 05		08 32	09 00		09 32		10 00	10 00
6	—	Woodlesford	34	d	05 54		06 46	06 46	07 08	07 08						07 37	08 08	08 15		08 40	09 08		09 40		10 08	10 08
10¾	—	Castleford	34	a	06 03		06 54	06 54	07 19	07 17						07 45	08 17	08 24		08 48	09 17		09 48		10 17	10 17
—	—			d	06 05		06 57	06 57	07 19	07 19						07 48	08 19	08 26		08 51	09 19		09 51		10 19	10 18
12¼	—	Glasshoughton		d	06 09				07 24	07 24							08 24	08 31			09 24				10 24	10 23
—	0	**Wakefield Westgate** 7	31,39	d		06 24																				
—	1	Wakefield Kirkgate 4	31,34,39	a		06 29	07 06	07 07					07 36		07 40	08 00				09 03			10 01			
—	—			d		06 29					07 31	07 31	07 38		07 42				08 31			09 31				
—	5¼	Streethouse		d		06 36					07 39	07 39							08 39			09 39				
—	7	Featherstone		d		06 40					07 43	07 43							08 43			09 43				
—	9	Pontefract Tanshelf		d		06 44					07 46	07 46							08 46			09 46				
14	9¾	Pontefract Monkhill		a	06 14	06 46			07 27	07 28	07 47	07 50	07 56		07 58		08 28	08 35	08 49		09 28	09 49			10 28	10 27
—	—			d	06 14	06 47			07 27	07 28	07 47	07 50	07 58		08 01		08 28	08 35	08 49		09 28	09 49			10 28	10 27
—	—	London Kings Cross 15 ⊖	26	a									10 09		10 13											
16	—	**Knottingley**		a	06 20	06 55			07 36	07 36	07 56	07 56					08 36	08 44	08 56		09 37	09 56			10 35	10 36
—	—			d																						
20¼	—	Whitley Bridge		d																						
22	—	Hensall		d																						
25¾	—	Snaith		d																						
28½	—	Rawcliffe		d																						
32½	—	**Goole**		a																						

			NT	NT	NT	GC SX R 1 ☕	GC SO R 1 ☕	NT	NT		NT	NT	NT	NT	NT	NT	NT	NT	NT		NT SO	NT SX	NT	NT	GC SO R 1 ☕	NT
Bradford Interchange	41	d				10 22	10 22																		15 22	
Halifax	41	d				10 38	10 38																		15 35	
Brighouse	41	d				10 50	10 49																		15 46	
Leeds 10	31,34	d		10 32	11 00				11 32		12 00		12 32	13 00		13 32	14 00		14 32		15 00	15 00		15 32		16 00
Woodlesford	34	d		10 40	11 08				11 40		12 08		12 40	13 08		13 40	14 08		14 40		15 08	15 08		15 40		16 08
Castleford	34	a		10 48	11 17				11 48		12 17		12 48	13 17		13 48	14 17		14 48		15 17	15 17		15 48		16 17
		d		10 51	11 19				11 51		12 19		12 51	13 19		13 51	14 19		14 51		15 19	15 19		15 51		16 19
Glasshoughton		d			11 24						12 24			13 24			14 24				15 24	15 24				16 24
Wakefield Westgate 7	31,39	d																								
Wakefield Kirkgate 4	31,34,39	a		11 01		11 10	11 09		12 01				13 02			14 01			15 01					16 01	16 09	
		d	10 31			11 11	11 11	11 31				12 31			13 31			14 31					15 31		16 11	
Streethouse		d	10 39					11 39				12 39			13 39			14 39					15 39			
Featherstone		d	10 43					11 43				12 43			13 43			14 43					15 43			
Pontefract Tanshelf		d	10 46					11 46				12 46			13 46			14 46					15 46			
Pontefract Monkhill		a	10 49		11 29	11 33	11 34	11 49			12 28	12 49		13 28	13 49		14 28	14 49			15 28	15 28	15 49		16 27	16 28
		d	10 49		11 29	11 34	11 35	11 49			12 28	12 49		13 28	13 49		14 28	14 49			15 28	15 28	15 49		16 29	16 28
London Kings Cross 15 ⊖	26	a				13 45	13 46																		18 45	
Knottingley		a	10 56		11 35			11 56			12 35	12 56		13 35	13 56		14 35	14 56			15 34	15 35	15 56			16 36
		d																								
Whitley Bridge		d																								
Hensall		d																								
Snaith		d																								
Rawcliffe		d																								
Goole		a																								

			NT	GC SX R 1 ☕	NT		NT SO	NT SX	NT	NT	NT	NT	NT	NT SO	NT SX		NT	NT	NT	NT	NT	NT	NT	NT	NT FX	
Bradford Interchange	41	d		15 37																						
Halifax	41	d		15 51																						
Brighouse	41	d		16 09																						
Leeds 10	31,34	d			16 32		17 16	17 16		17 32	18 00		18 32	18 59	18 59			19 37	20 05		20 37	21 05		21 37	22 08	
Woodlesford	34	d			16 40		17 24	17 24		17 40	18 08		18 40	19 08	19 08			19 45	20 13		20 45	21 13		21 45	22 16	
Castleford	34	a			16 48		17 33	17 34		17 48	18 17		18 48	19 17	19 18			19 53	20 22		20 53	21 22		21 53	22 25	
		d			16 51		17 36	17 36		17 51	18 19		18 51	19 19	19 19			19 56	20 24		20 56	21 24		21 56	22 27	
Glasshoughton		d					17 40	17 40			18 24			19 24	19 24				20 29			21 29			22 32	
Wakefield Westgate 7	31,39	d																					21 57			
Wakefield Kirkgate 4	31,34,39	a		16 36	17 01					18 01			19 04					20 06			21 06		22 00	22 06		
		d	16 31	16 40					17 31			18 33					19 33			20 54			22 00			
Streethouse		d	16 39						17 39			18 41					19 41			21 02			22 08			
Featherstone		d	16 43						17 43			18 45					19 45			21 06			22 12			
Pontefract Tanshelf		d	16 46						17 46			18 48					19 48			21 09			22 16			
Pontefract Monkhill		a	16 49	16 55			17 44	17 44	17 49		18 28	18 51		19 28	19 28		19 51		20 33	21 12		21 33	22 18		22 36	
		d	16 49	16 56			17 44	17 44	17 49		18 28	18 51		19 28	19 28		19 51		20 33	21 12		21 33	22 19		22 36	
London Kings Cross 15 ⊖	26	a		19 05																						
Knottingley		a	16 56				17 51	17 51	17 57		18 35	18 58		19 35	19 35		19 58		20 40	21 19		21 40	22 25		22 42	
		d					17 53	17 53																		
Whitley Bridge		d					17 59	17 59																		
Hensall		d					18 03	18 03																		
Snaith		d					18 10	18 10																		
Rawcliffe		d					18 15	18 15																		
Goole		a					18 30	18 30																		

Table 32

Mondays to Saturdays

Bradford, Leeds and Wakefield - Pontefract, Knottingley and Goole

		NT FO	NT SX	NT SO	NT
Bradford Interchange 41	d				
Halifax 41	d				
Brighouse 41	d				
Leeds 10 31,34	d	22 08			22 37
Woodlesford 34	d	22 16			22 45
Castleford 34	a	22 27			22 53
	d	22 27			22 56
Glasshoughton	d	22 32			
Wakefield Westgate 7 31,39	d		23 04	23 04	
Wakefield Kirkgate 4 31,34,39	a		23 07	23 07	23 10
	d		23 07	23 07	
Streethouse	d		23 15	23 15	
Featherstone	d		23 19	23 19	
Pontefract Tanshelf	d		23 23	23 23	
Pontefract Monkhill	a	22 36	23 25	23 29	
	d	22 36	23 26		
London Kings Cross 15 ⊖26	a				
Knottingley	a	22 42	23 32		
	d				
Whitley Bridge	d				
Hensall	d				
Snaith	d				
Rawcliffe	d				
Goole	a				

Sundays

until 11 September

		NT	NT	NT	NT	GC R 1	NT	NT	NT	NT	GC R 1	NT	NT	NT	NT	NT	NT	NT
Bradford Interchange 41	d					11 42					15 42							
Halifax 41	d					11 55					15 56							
Brighouse 41	d					12 06					16 06							
Leeds 10 31,34	d	08 34	09 34	10 17	11 17		12 34	13 17	14 17	15 17		16 17	17 17	18 17	19 17	20 17	21 17	22 17
Woodlesford 34	d	08 42	09 42	10 25	11 25		12 42	13 25	14 25	15 25		16 25	17 25	18 25	19 25	20 25	21 25	22 25
Castleford 34	a	08 50	09 50	10 33	11 33		12 50	13 33	14 33	15 33		16 33	17 33	18 33	19 35	20 33	21 33	22 33
	d	08 53	09 53	10 36	11 36		12 53	13 36	14 36	15 36		16 36	17 36	18 36	19 36	20 36	21 36	22 36
Glasshoughton	d		09 57		11 40			13 40		15 40			17 40		19 40		21 40	
Wakefield Westgate 7 31,39	d																	
Wakefield Kirkgate 4 31,34,39	a	09 03		10 46		12 26	13 04		14 46		16 28	16 46		18 45		20 46		22 46
	d					12 29					16 29							
Streethouse	d																	
Featherstone	d																	
Pontefract Tanshelf	d																	
Pontefract Monkhill	a		10 02		11 45	12 45		13 45		15 45	16 45		17 45		19 45		21 45	
	d		10 02		11 45	12 46		13 45		15 45	16 46		17 45		19 45		21 45	
London Kings Cross 15 ⊖26	a					14 48					18 51							
Knottingley	a		10 08		11 52			13 52		15 52			17 52		19 52		21 52	
	d																	
Whitley Bridge	d																	
Hensall	d																	
Snaith	d																	
Rawcliffe	d																	
Goole	a																	

Sundays

18 September to 23 October

		NT	NT	NT	NT	GC R 1	NT	NT	NT	NT	GC R 1	NT	NT	NT	NT	NT	NT	NT
Bradford Interchange 41	d					11 42					15 42							
Halifax 41	d					11 55					15 55							
Brighouse 41	d					12 06					16 06							
Leeds 10 31,34	d	08 34	09 34	10 17	11 17		12 34	13 17	14 17	15 17		16 17	17 17	18 17	19 17	20 17	21 17	22 17
Woodlesford 34	d	08 42	09 42	10 25	11 25		12 42	13 25	14 25	15 25		16 25	17 25	18 25	19 25	20 25	21 25	22 25
Castleford 34	a	08 50	09 50	10 33	11 33		12 50	13 33	14 33	15 33		16 33	17 33	18 33	19 35	20 33	21 33	22 33
	d	08 53	09 53	10 36	11 36		12 53	13 36	14 36	15 36		16 36	17 36	18 36	19 36	20 36	21 36	22 36
Glasshoughton	d		09 57		11 40			13 40		15 40			17 40		19 40		21 40	
Wakefield Westgate 7 31,39	d																	
Wakefield Kirkgate 4 31,34,39	a	09 03		10 46		12 26	13 04		14 46		16 26	16 46		18 45		20 46		22 46
	d					12 29					16 29							
Streethouse	d																	
Featherstone	d																	
Pontefract Tanshelf	d																	
Pontefract Monkhill	a		10 02		11 45	12 45		13 45		15 45	16 45		17 45		19 45		21 45	
	d		10 02		11 45	12 46		13 45		15 45	16 46		17 45		19 45		21 45	
London Kings Cross 15 ⊖26	a					14 48					18 51							
Knottingley	a		10 08		11 52			13 52		15 52			17 52		19 52		21 52	
	d																	
Whitley Bridge	d																	
Hensall	d																	
Snaith	d																	
Rawcliffe	d																	
Goole	a																	

Table 32

Sundays
from 30 October

Bradford, Leeds and Wakefield - Pontefract, Knottingley and Goole

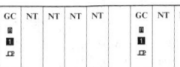

			NT	NT	NT	NT	GC	NT	NT	NT	NT		GC	NT	NT	NT	NT	NT	NT	NT
							R 1						R 1							
Bradford Interchange	41	d					11 42						15 42							
Halifax	41	d					11 55						15 56							
Brighouse	41	d					12 06						16 06							
Leeds 10	31,34	d	08 34	09 34	10 17	11 17		12 34	13 17	14 17	15 17			16 17	17 17	18 17	19 17	20 17	21 17	22 17
Woodlesford	34	d	08 42	09 42	10 25	11 25		12 42	13 25	14 25	15 25			16 25	17 25	18 25	19 25	20 25	21 25	22 25
Castleford	34	a	08 50	09 50	10 33	11 33		12 50	13 33	14 33	15 33			16 33	17 33	18 33	19 35	20 33	21 33	22 33
		d	08 53	09 53	10 36	11 36		12 53	13 36	14 36	15 36			16 36	17 36	18 36	19 36	20 36	21 36	22 36
Glasshoughton		d		09 57		11 40			13 40		15 40				17 40		19 40		21 40	
Wakefield Westgate 7	31,39	d																		
Wakefield Kirkgate 4	31,34,39	a	09 03		10 46		12 26	13 04		14 46			16 28	16 46		18 45		20 46		22 46
		d					12 29						16 29							
Streethouse		d																		
Featherstone		d																		
Pontefract Tanshelf		d																		
Pontefract Monkhill		a		10 02		11 45	12 45		13 45		15 45		16 45		17 45		19 45		21 45	
		d		10 02		11 45	12 46		13 45		15 45		16 46		17 45		19 45		21 45	
London Kings Cross 15 ⊖	26	a					14 48						18 51							
Knottingley		a		10 08		11 52			13 52		15 52				17 52		19 52		21 52	
		d																		
Whitley Bridge		d																		
Hensall		d																		
Snaith		d																		
Rawcliffe		d																		
Goole		a																		

Goole, Knottingley and Pontefract - Wakefield and Leeds, Bradford

Miles	Miles			NT SX	NT SO	NT SX	NT	NT SX	NT SO	NT SX	NT	NT		NT	NT	NT	NT	NT	NT	NT SX	NT SO	NT		NT	NT
0	—	**Goole**	d						07 04	07 04															
4	—	Rawcliffe	d						07 11	07 11															
6¾	—	Snaith	d						07 16	07 16															
10½	—	Hensall	d						07 23	07 23															
12¼	—	Whitley Bridge	d						07 30	07 30															
16½	—	**Knottingley**	a						07 37	07 38															
—	—		d	06 25			06 56		07 38	07 38		07 53		08 16		08 53	09 16		09 53	10 16	10 17			10 53	11 16
—	—	London Kings Cross 15 ⊖26	d																						
18½	0	Pontefract Monkhill	a	06 29			07 00		07 42	07 42		07 57		08 20		08 57	09 20		09 57	10 20	10 20			10 57	11 20
—	—		d	06 29			07 00		07 42	07 42		07 57		08 20		08 57	09 20		09 57	10 20	10 20			10 57	11 20
—	0¾	Pontefract Tanshelf	d				07 03					08 00				09 00			10 00					11 00	
—	2¾	Featherstone	d				07 06					08 03				09 03			10 03					11 03	
—	4½	Streethouse	d				07 10					08 07				09 07			10 07					11 07	
—	8¾	Wakefield Kirkgate 4 31,34,39	a				07 21					08 18				09 18			10 20					11 18	
—	—		d		06 50	06 50					07 50				08 50			09 50				10 50			
—	9¾	**Wakefield Westgate** 7 31,39	a																						
20	—	Glasshoughton 34	d	06 34					07 48	07 48				08 25			09 25			10 25	10 25				11 25
21½	—	Castleford	a	06 38	07 00	06 59			07 52	07 52	07 59			08 30	09 00		09 29	10 00		10 29	10 29	11 00			11 29
—	—		d	06 41	07 02	07 02		07 38	07 55	07 55	08 01			08 32	09 02		09 32	10 02		10 32	10 32	11 02			11 32
26½	—	Woodlesford 34	d	06 50	07 12	07 12		07 47	08 04	08 04	08 11			08 41	09 12		09 41	10 12		10 41	10 41	11 12			11 41
32½	—	**Leeds** 10 31,34	a	07 04	07 28	07 28		08 01	08 18	08 19	08 25			08 54	09 25		09 53	10 25		10 55	10 54	11 25			11 54
—	—	Brighouse 41	a																						
—	—	Halifax 41	a																						
—	—	Bradford Interchange 41	a																						

		NT	NT	NT	NT	GC SO	GC SX	NT		NT	NT	NT	NT SO	NT SX	NT	NT	NT	NT		NT	NT	NT	GC SX	NT	NT SO
Goole	d																								
Rawcliffe	d																								
Snaith	d																								
Hensall	d																								
Whitley Bridge	d																								
Knottingley	a																								
	d		11 53	12 16				12 53		13 16		13 53	14 16	14 16		14 53	15 16			15 53	16 16			16 53	17 15
London Kings Cross 15 ⊖26	d					10 48	10 48																14 48		
Pontefract Monkhill	a		11 57	12 20		12 44	12 47	12 57		13 20		13 57	14 20	14 20		14 57	15 20			15 57	16 20		16 47	16 57	17 18
	d		11 57	12 20		12 45	12 49	12 57		13 20		13 57	14 20	14 20		14 57	15 20			15 57	16 20		16 48	16 57	17 18
Pontefract Tanshelf	d		12 00					13 00				14 00				15 00				16 00				17 00	
Featherstone	d		12 03					13 03				14 03				15 03				16 03				17 03	
Streethouse	d		12 07					13 07				14 07				15 07				16 07				17 07	
Wakefield Kirkgate 4 31,34,39	a		12 18			13 04	13 07	13 18				14 18				15 18				16 19			17 04	17 18	
	d	11 50			12 50	13 10	13 09				13 50				14 50			15 50				16 50	17 08		
Wakefield Westgate 7 31,39	a																								
Glasshoughton 34	d			12 25						13 25			14 25	14 25			15 25				16 25				17 23
Castleford	a	12 00		12 29	13 00					13 29	14 00		14 28	14 29	15 00		15 29	16 00			16 29	17 00			17 27
	d	12 02		12 32	13 02					13 32	14 02		14 32	14 32	15 02		15 32	16 02			16 32	17 02			17 30
Woodlesford 34	d	12 12		12 41	13 12					13 41	14 12		14 41	14 41	15 12		15 41	16 12			16 41	17 12			17 41
Leeds 10 31,34	a	12 25		12 54	13 25					13 53	14 25		14 53	14 53	15 25		15 54	16 25			16 54	17 25			17 53
Brighouse 41	a					13 29	13 30																17 27		
Halifax 41	a					13 40	13 40																17 38		
Bradford Interchange 41	a					13 55	13 55																17 55		

		NT SX	NT	GC SO		NT	NT	NT	NT	NT SO	NT SX	NT	NT	NT		NT	GC SO	NT	NT SX	NT SO	NT	GC SX	NT	NT SO
Goole	d									18 49	18 49													
Rawcliffe	d									18 56	18 56													
Snaith	d									19 01	19 01													
Hensall	d									19 08	19 08													
Whitley Bridge	d									19 12	19 12													
Knottingley	a									19 20	19 20													
	d	17 15				18 02	18 39		19 02	19 21	19 21		19 55	20 16				21 16	21 23	21 23			22 16	
London Kings Cross 15 ⊖26	d			15 48													19 07					19 48		
Pontefract Monkhill	a	17 19		17 45		18 06	18 43		19 06	19 25	19 25		19 59	20 20			20 59	21 20	21 27	21 27		21 48	22 22	
	d	17 19		17 47		18 06	18 43		19 06	19 25	19 25		19 59	20 20			21 00	21 20	21 27	21 27		21 49	22 22	
Pontefract Tanshelf	d					18 09			19 09				20 02						21 30	21 30				
Featherstone	d					18 12			19 12				20 05						21 33	21 33				
Streethouse	d					18 16			19 16				20 09						21 37	21 37				
Wakefield Kirkgate 4 31,34,39	a			18 03		18 27			19 28				20 20				21 17		21 47	21 47		22 09		
	d		17 50	18 10				18 50				19 50				20 50	21 18		21 47	21 48	21 52	22 18		22 51
Wakefield Westgate 7 31,39	a																		21 53	21 53				
Glasshoughton 34	d	17 24					18 48			19 30	19 30			20 25				21 25					22 27	
Castleford	a	17 28	18 00				18 54	19 00		19 34	19 34	20 00		20 29		21 00		21 29			22 04		22 31	23 02
	d	17 31	18 02				18 57	19 03		19 37	19 37	20 02		20 32		21 02		21 32			22 05		22 34	23 04
Woodlesford 34	d	17 41	18 12				19 06	19 13		19 46	19 46	20 12		20 44		21 12		21 41			22 15		22 43	23 14
Leeds 10 31,34	a	17 53	18 25				19 20	19 27		19 58	20 00	20 26		20 57		21 26		21 53			22 29		22 57	23 29
Brighouse 41	a			18 28													21 42					22 42		
Halifax 41	a			18 40													21 53					22 53		
Bradford Interchange 41	a			18 55													22 09					23 07		

Goole, Knottingley and Pontefract - Wakefield and Leeds, Bradford

		NT FO	NT FSX	NT	NT
Goole	d				
Rawcliffe	d				
Snaith	d				
Hensall	d				
Whitley Bridge	d				
Knottingley	a				
	d			22 30	23 05
London Kings Cross 15 ⊖26	d				
Pontefract Monkhill	a			22 34	23 09
	d			22 34	23 09
Pontefract Tanshelf	d			22 37	
Featherstone	d			22 40	
Streethouse	d			22 44	
Wakefield Kirkgate 4 31,34,39	a			22 55	
	d	22 51	22 51	22 55	
Wakefield Westgate 7 31,39	a			23 01	
Glasshoughton 34	d				23 14
Castleford	a	23 01	23 01		23 18
	d	23 04	23 04		23 21
Woodlesford 34	d	23 14	23 14		23 30
Leeds 10 31,34	a	23 29	23 30		23 44
Brighouse 41	a				
Halifax 41	a				
Bradford Interchange 41	a				

Sundays
until 11 September

		NT	NT	NT	NT	NT	GC R 1 ☕	NT	NT	NT	NT	GC R 1 ☕	NT	NT	NT	NT	GC R 1 ☕	NT
Goole	d																	
Rawcliffe	d																	
Snaith	d																	
Hensall	d																	
Whitley Bridge	d																	
Knottingley	a																	
	d		10 26		12 26			14 26		16 26			18 26		20 26			22 26
London Kings Cross 15 ⊖26	d						11 48					15 48					19 27	
Pontefract Monkhill	a		10 30		12 30		13 41	14 30		16 30		17 43	18 30		20 30		21 24	22 30
	d		10 30		12 30		13 42	14 30		16 30		17 45	18 30		20 30		21 25	22 30
Pontefract Tanshelf	d																	
Featherstone	d																	
Streethouse	d																	
Wakefield Kirkgate 4 31,34,39	a						13 58					18 00					21 41	
	d	09 30		11 30		13 30	13 59		15 30		17 30	18 02		19 30		21 30	21 42	
Wakefield Westgate 7 31,39	a																	
Glasshoughton 34	d		10 35		12 35			14 35		16 35			18 35		20 35			22 35
Castleford	a	09 40	10 39	11 40	12 39	13 40		14 39	15 40	16 39	17 40		18 39	19 41	20 39	21 40		22 39
	d	09 42	10 42	11 41	12 42	13 42		14 42	15 41	16 42	17 42		18 42	19 44	20 42	21 42		22 42
Woodlesford 34	d	09 52	10 51	11 51	12 52	13 51		14 51	15 51	16 51	17 51		18 51	19 53	20 51	21 51		22 51
Leeds 10 31,34	a	10 04	11 04	12 05	13 05	14 04		15 04	16 04	17 04	18 05		19 04	20 05	21 03	22 04		23 04
Brighouse 41	a						14 20					18 21					22 04	
Halifax 41	a						14 35					18 35					22 17	
Bradford Interchange 41	a						14 50					18 50					22 32	

Sundays
18 September to 23 October

		NT	NT	NT	NT	NT	GC R 1 ☕	NT	NT	NT	NT	GC R 1 ☕	NT	NT	NT	NT	GC R 1 ☕	NT
Goole	d																	
Rawcliffe	d																	
Snaith	d																	
Hensall	d																	
Whitley Bridge	d																	
Knottingley	a																	
	d		10 26		12 26			14 26		16 26			18 26		20 26			22 26
London Kings Cross 15 ⊖26	d						11 48					15 48					19 27	
Pontefract Monkhill	a		10 30		12 30		13 41	14 30		16 30		17 43	18 30		20 30		21 24	22 30
	d		10 30		12 30		13 42	14 30		16 30		17 45	18 30		20 30		21 25	22 30
Pontefract Tanshelf	d																	
Featherstone	d																	
Streethouse	d																	
Wakefield Kirkgate 4 31,34,39	a						13 58					18 00					21 41	
	d	09 30		11 30		13 30	13 59		15 30		17 30	18 02		19 30		21 30	21 42	
Wakefield Westgate 7 31,39	a																	
Glasshoughton 34	d		10 35		12 35			14 35		16 35			18 35		20 35			22 35
Castleford	a	09 40	10 39	11 40	12 39	13 40		14 39	15 40	16 39	17 40		18 39	19 41	20 39	21 40		22 39
	d	09 42	10 42	11 41	12 42	13 42		14 42	15 41	16 42	17 42		18 42	19 44	20 42	21 42		22 42
Woodlesford 34	d	09 52	10 51	11 51	12 52	13 51		14 51	15 51	16 51	17 51		18 51	19 53	20 51	21 51		22 51
Leeds 10 31,34	a	10 04	11 04	12 05	13 05	14 04		15 04	16 04	17 04	18 05		19 04	20 05	21 03	22 04		23 04
Brighouse 41	a						14 22					18 22					22 04	
Halifax 41	a						14 35					18 35					22 17	
Bradford Interchange 41	a						14 50					18 50					22 32	

Table 32

Sundays
from 30 October

Goole, Knottingley and Pontefract - Wakefield and Leeds, Bradford

		NT	NT	NT	NT	NT	GC	NT	NT	NT		NT	GC	NT	NT	NT	NT	GC	NT
							R 1						R 1					R 1	
Goole	d																		
Rawcliffe	d																		
Snaith	d																		
Hensall	d																		
Whitley Bridge	d																		
Knottingley	a																		
	d		10 26		12 26			14 26		16 26				18 26		20 26			22 26
London Kings Cross 15 ⊖26	d						11 48						15 48					19 27	
Pontefract Monkhill	a		10 30		12 30		13 41	14 30		16 30			17 43	18 30		20 30		21 24	22 30
	d		10 30		12 30		13 42	14 30		16 30			17 45	18 30		20 30		21 25	22 30
Pontefract Tanshelf	d																		
Featherstone	d																		
Streethouse	d																		
Wakefield Kirkgate 4 31,34,39	a						13 58						18 00					21 41	
	d	09 30		11 30		13 30	13 59		15 30			17 30	18 02		19 30		21 30	21 42	
Wakefield Westgate 7 31,39	a																		
Glasshoughton 34	d		10 35		12 35			14 35		16 35				18 35		20 35			22 35
Castleford	a	09 40	10 39	11 40	12 39	13 40		14 39	15 40	16 39		17 40		18 39	19 41	20 39	21 40		22 39
	d	09 42	10 42	11 41	12 42	13 42		14 42	15 41	16 42		17 42		18 42	19 44	20 42	21 42		22 42
Woodlesford 34	d	09 52	10 51	11 51	12 52	13 51		14 51	15 51	16 51		17 51		18 51	19 53	20 51	21 51		22 51
Leeds 10 31,34	a	10 04	11 04	12 05	13 05	14 04		15 04	16 04	17 04		18 05		19 04	20 05	21 03	22 04		23 04
Brighouse 41	a						14 20						18 21					22 04	
Halifax 41	a						14 35						18 35					22 17	
Bradford Interchange 41	a						14 50						18 50					22 32	

Table 33

Sheffield and Selby - York

Local services only

Miles	Miles		NT	NT	NT	NT	NT	NT	NT	NT	NT		NT	NT	NT	NT	NT	NT	NT	NT	NT		NT	NT
				A	B	A		A					A		A					A			C	
0	—	**Sheffield 7** 29,31 🚌 d							09 29								13 28							
3½	—	Meadowhall 29,31 🚌 d							09 35								13 35							
6¼	—	Rotherham Central 29,31 d							09 42								13 41							
10¾	—	Swinton (S.Yorks) 29,31 d							09 51								13 50							
18½	—	Moorthorpe 31 d							10 01								14 01							
25½	—	Pontefract Baghill d							10 10								14 10							
—	—	Hull 29 d			07 07		09 02			10 08				12 03		13 12		14 18	15 02		16 10			17 18
—	0	**Selby** d	06 48		07 48		09 38			10 47	11 41			12 38		13 55		14 53	15 38		16 47			18 06
33¾	8¼	Sherburn-in-Elmet d	07 00		08 03		09 53		10 25							14 09	14 28							
36	10½	Church Fenton d	07 04	08 00		09 05		10 05	10 30				12 05		14 06		14 32			16 05			17 53	
38	12½	Ulleskelf d			08 09				10 34								14 36						17 58	
46¾	21	**York 8** 29 a	07 20	08 16	08 21	09 21	10 10	10 24	10 56	11 18	12 08		12 21	13 04	14 22	14 27	14 55	15 25	16 06	16 21	17 13		18 10	18 33

	NT	NT	NT	NT	NT
	A		A		A
Sheffield 7 29,31 🚌 d					
Meadowhall 29,31 🚌 d					
Rotherham Central 29,31 d					
Swinton (S.Yorks) 29,31 d					
Moorthorpe 31 d					
Pontefract Baghill d					
Hull 29 d		19 15			
Selby d		19 53		21 21	
Sherburn-in-Elmet d					
Church Fenton d	19 05		21 11		23 27
Ulleskelf d			21 15		
York 8 29 a	19 21	20 21	21 30	21 43	23 44

Saturdays

	NT	NT	NT	NT	NT	NT	NT	NT	NT		NT	NT	NT	NT	NT	NT	NT	NT	NT			NT		NT
		A	B	A		A					A		A					A						A
Sheffield 7 29,31 🚌 d							09 31								13 28									
Meadowhall 29,31 🚌 d							09 38								13 35									
Rotherham Central 29,31 d							09 45								13 42									
Swinton (S.Yorks) 29,31 d							09 53								13 51									
Moorthorpe 31 d							10 03								14 01									
Pontefract Baghill d							10 12								14 10									
Hull 29 d			07 07		09 02			10 08	11 05			12 03		13 12		14 18	15 02		16 10			17 18		
Selby d	06 48		07 48		09 38			10 47	11 41			12 38		13 55		14 53	15 38		16 47			18 07		
Sherburn-in-Elmet d	07 00		08 03		09 53		10 30							14 09	14 28									
Church Fenton d	07 04	08 05		09 05		10 05	10 34				12 05		14 06		14 32			16 05						19 05
Ulleskelf d			08 09				10 41								14 36									
York 8 29 a	07 20	08 19	08 21	09 22	10 14	10 22	10 56	11 18	12 08		12 21	13 04	14 22	14 27	14 56	15 25	16 06	16 24	17 13			18 33		19 19

	NT	NT	NT	NT
		A		A
Sheffield 7 29,31 🚌 d				
Meadowhall 29,31 🚌 d				
Rotherham Central 29,31 d				
Swinton (S.Yorks) 29,31 d				
Moorthorpe 31 d				
Pontefract Baghill d				
Hull 29 d	19 15		21 01	
Selby d	19 53		21 35	
Sherburn-in-Elmet d				
Church Fenton d		21 13		23 21
Ulleskelf d		21 17		
York 8 29 a	20 21	21 31	21 57	23 38

Sundays

until 19 June

	NT	NT	NT	NT	NT	NT	NT	NT	NT		NT	NT	NT	NT	NT	NT	NT	NT	NT
	E		F		A		A				A		🚌	A		🚌	A		C
Sheffield 7 29,31 🚌 d																			
Meadowhall 29,31 🚌 d																			
Rotherham Central 29,31 d																			
Swinton (S.Yorks) 29,31 d																19 30			
Moorthorpe 31 d													17 25			20 00			
Pontefract Baghill d													17 40			20 15			
Hull 29 d		08 54		11 46		13 29		14 23	16 00			17 23			19 24			20 29	
Selby d		09 28		12 20		14 03		14 57	16 34			17 57			19 58			21 03	
Sherburn-in-Elmet d													18 00			20 35			
Church Fenton d	09 18		10 51		12 49		14 49				16 49		18 07	18 47		20 42	20 49		23 07
Ulleskelf d																			
York 8 29 a	09 34	09 52	11 05	12 44	13 02	14 30	15 02	15 25	16 59		17 03	18 25	18 37	19 03	20 25	21 12	21 03	21 30	23 23

A From Blackpool North
B From Beverley
C From Leeds
D To Leeds
E From Bradford Interchange
F From Huddersfield

Table 33

Sheffield and Selby - York

Local services only

Sundays

26 June to 11 September

		NT A	NT	NT B	NT	NT C	NT	NT C	NT	NT		NT C	NT	NT	NT C	NT	NT	NT C	NT	NT D
Sheffield 7	29,31 🚌 d												16 36			18 57				
Meadowhall	29,31 🚌 d												16 42			19 05				
Rotherham Central	29,31 d												16 49			19 11				
Swinton (S.Yorks)	29,31 d												16 58			19 19				
Moorthorpe	31 d												17 13			19 29				
Pontefract Baghill	d												17 21			19 38				
Hull	29 d		08 54		11 46		13 29		14 23	16 00				17 23			19 24		20 29	
Selby	d		09 28		12 20		14 03		14 57	16 34				17 57			19 58		21 03	
Sherburn-in-Elmet	d												17 38			19 56				
Church Fenton	d	09 18		10 51		12 49		14 49				16 49	17 43		18 47	20 00		20 49		23 07
Ulleskelf	d																			
York 8	29 a	09 34	09 52	11 05	12 44	13 02	14 30	15 02	15 25	16 59		17 03	17 59	18 25	19 03	20 18	20 25	21 03	21 30	23 23

Sundays

18 September to 23 October

		NT A	NT	NT B	NT	NT C	NT C	NT	NT C	NT		NT	NT C	NT	NT C	NT	NT D
Sheffield 7	29,31 🚌 d									16 36				18 57			
Meadowhall	29,31 🚌 d									16 42				19 05			
Rotherham Central	29,31 d									16 49				19 11			
Swinton (S.Yorks)	29,31 d									16 58				19 19			
Moorthorpe	31 d									17 13				19 29			
Pontefract Baghill	d									17 21				19 38			
Hull	29 d		08 54		11 46			14 23				17 23				20 29	
Selby	d		09 28		12 20			14 57				17 57				21 03	
Sherburn-in-Elmet	d									17 38				19 56			
Church Fenton	d	09 18		10 52		12 49	14 49		16 49	17 43			18 47	20 00	20 49		23 07
Ulleskelf	d																
York 8	29 a	09 34	09 52	11 08	12 44	13 02	15 02	15 25	17 03	17 59		18 25	19 03	20 18	21 03	21 30	23 23

Sundays

from 30 October

		NT A	NT	NT B	NT	NT E	NT E	NT	NT E	NT		NT	NT E	NT	NT E	NT	NT D
Sheffield 7	29,31 🚌 d									16 36				18 57			
Meadowhall	29,31 🚌 d									16 42				19 05			
Rotherham Central	29,31 d									16 49				19 11			
Swinton (S.Yorks)	29,31 d									16 58				19 19			
Moorthorpe	31 d									17 13				19 29			
Pontefract Baghill	d									17 21				19 38			
Hull	29 d		08 54		11 46			14 23				17 23				20 29	
Selby	d		09 28		12 20			14 57				17 57				21 03	
Sherburn-in-Elmet	d									17 38				19 56			
Church Fenton	d	09 18		10 51		12 49	14 49		16 49	17 43			18 47	20 00	20 49		23 07
Ulleskelf	d																
York 8	29 a	09 34	09 52	11 05	12 44	13 02	15 02	15 25	17 02	17 59		18 25	19 01	20 18	21 03	21 30	23 23

A From Bradford Interchange
B From Huddersfield
C From Blackpool North
D From Leeds
E From Hebden Bridge

York - Selby and Sheffield

Local services only

Mondays to Fridays

Miles	Miles		NT	NT A	NT	NT B	NT	NT A	NT	NT	NT	NT A
0	0	York [8] 29 d	06 09	07 06	07 29	07 48	08 43	09 11	10 20	11 00	11 05	11 09
8¾	8¾	Ulleskelf d		07 15							11 15	
10¾	10¾	Church Fenton a		07 20		08 00		09 22			11 19	11 20
—	—	d									11 19	
12¾	12¾	Sherburn-in-Elmet d									11 23	
—	21	**Selby** a	06 30		07 50		09 05		10 40	11 21		
—	—	Hull 29 a			08 46		09 47		11 23			
21¼	—	Pontefract Baghill d									11 43	
28¼	—	Moorthorpe 31 a									11 59	
36	—	Swinton (S.Yorks) 29,31 a									12 08	
40½	—	Rotherham Central 29,31 a									12 18	
43¼	—	Meadowhall 29,31 🚊 a									12 24	
46¾	—	**Sheffield [7]** 29,31 🚊 a									12 36	

	NT	NT	NT A	NT	NT	NT	NT A	NT A	NT	NT
York [8] 29 d	11 45	12 47	13 09	13 44	14 47	15 01	15 08	16 09	16 12	17 19
Ulleskelf d						15 11				
Church Fenton a			13 20			15 15	15 20	16 20		17 30
d						15 15				17 30
Sherburn-in-Elmet d				13 56		15 19			16 25	17 34
Selby a	12 04	13 06		14 07	15 06				16 36	17 45
Hull 29 a	12 49	13 48		14 52	15 48				17 27	18 30
Pontefract Baghill d						15 38				
Moorthorpe 31 a						15 50				
Swinton (S.Yorks) 29,31 a						16 00				
Rotherham Central 29,31 a						16 11				
Meadowhall 29,31 🚊 a						16 17				
Sheffield [7] 29,31 🚊 a						16 25				

	NT A	NT	NT B	NT	NT B	NT	NT B
York [8] 29 d	18 05	18 18	19 04	20 21	21 22	22 13	23 13
Ulleskelf d	18 15				21 31		
Church Fenton a	18 18		19 15		21 34		23 28
d							
Sherburn-in-Elmet d		18 31					
Selby a		18 42		20 42		22 32	
Hull 29 a		19 29				23 18	
Pontefract Baghill d							
Moorthorpe 31 a							
Swinton (S.Yorks) 29,31 a							
Rotherham Central 29,31 a							
Meadowhall 29,31 🚊 a							
Sheffield [7] 29,31 🚊 a							

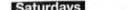

Saturdays

	NT	NT A	NT	NT	NT A	NT	NT	NT	NT A	NT	NT
York [8] 29 d	06 09	07 06	07 38	08 43	09 11	09 50	10 43	11 05	11 09	11 45	12 47
Ulleskelf d		07 15						11 15			
Church Fenton a		07 20			09 22			11 19	11 20		
d								11 19			
Sherburn-in-Elmet d								11 23			
Selby a	06 30		07 57	09 05		10 09	11 03			12 04	13 06
Hull 29 a			08 50	09 47		10 53	11 51			12 49	13 48
Pontefract Baghill d								11 43			
Moorthorpe 31 a								11 59			
Swinton (S.Yorks) 29,31 a								12 08			
Rotherham Central 29,31 a								12 18			
Meadowhall 29,31 🚊 a								12 24			
Sheffield [7] 29,31 🚊 a								12 36			

	NT A	NT	NT	NT	NT A	NT A	NT	NT	NT A	NT	NT B
York [8] 29 d	13 09	13 44	14 47	15 01	15 09	16 09	16 12	17 19	18 05	18 18	19 04
Ulleskelf d				15 11					18 16		
Church Fenton a	13 20			15 15	15 21	16 20		17 30	18 19		19 15
d				15 15				17 30			
Sherburn-in-Elmet d		13 56		15 19			16 25	17 34		18 31	
Selby a		14 07	15 06				16 36	17 45		18 42	
Hull 29 a		14 52	15 48				17 29	18 30		19 29	
Pontefract Baghill d				15 39							
Moorthorpe 31 a				15 50							
Swinton (S.Yorks) 29,31 a				16 01							
Rotherham Central 29,31 a				16 08							
Meadowhall 29,31 🚊 a				16 17							
Sheffield [7] 29,31 🚊 a				16 27							

	NT	NT B	NT	NT B
York [8] 29 d	19 47	21 18	22 11	23 13
Ulleskelf d		21 27		
Church Fenton a		21 33		23 28
d				
Sherburn-in-Elmet d				
Selby a	20 06		22 29	
Hull 29 a	20 48		23 14	
Pontefract Baghill d				
Moorthorpe 31 a				
Swinton (S.Yorks) 29,31 a				
Rotherham Central 29,31 a				
Meadowhall 29,31 🚊 a				
Sheffield [7] 29,31 🚊 a				

Sundays

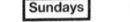

until 19 June

	NT A	NT A	NT	NT A	NT	NT	NT A	NT	NT A
York [8] 29 d	08 50	09 52	10 40	11 52	12 05	13 40	13 52	14 49	15 52
Ulleskelf d									
Church Fenton a	09 01	10 03		12 03			14 03		16 03
d									
Sherburn-in-Elmet d									
Selby a			10 58		12 24	13 59		15 08	
Hull 29 a			11 41		13 06	14 40		15 49	
Pontefract Baghill d									
Moorthorpe 31 a									
Swinton (S.Yorks) 29,31 a									
Rotherham Central 29,31 a									
Meadowhall 29,31 🚊 a									
Sheffield [7] 29,31 🚊 a									

	NT	NT	NT A	NT 🚌	NT	NT A	NT 🚌	NT	NT B
York [8] 29 d	16 06	17 11	17 52	18 40	19 10	19 52	21 15	21 41	21 52
Ulleskelf d									
Church Fenton a			18 03	19 10		20 03	21 45		22 04
d				19 10			21 45		
Sherburn-in-Elmet d				19 17			21 52		
Selby a	16 24	17 30			19 35			22 00	
Hull 29 a	17 07	18 12			20 17			22 36	
Pontefract Baghill d				19 37			22 12		
Moorthorpe 31 a				19 52			22s27		
Swinton (S.Yorks) 29,31 a				20 22			22s57		
Rotherham Central 29,31 a							23s17		
Meadowhall 29,31 🚊 a							23s27		
Sheffield [7] 29,31 🚊 a							23 47		

A To Blackpool North

B To Leeds

Table 33

York - Selby and Sheffield

Local services only

Sundays

26 June to 11 September

		NT A	NT A	NT	NT A	NT	NT	NT A	NT	NT A	NT	NT	NT A	NT	NT	NT A	NT	NT	NT B
York 8 29	d	08 50	09 52	10 40	11 52	12 05	13 40	13 52	14 49	15 52	16 06	17 11	17 52	18 10	19 10	19 52	20 50	21 41	21 52
Ulleskelf	d																		
Church Fenton	a	09 01	10 03		12 03			14 03		16 03			18 03	18 21		20 03	21 01		22 04
	d													18 21			21 01		
Sherburn-in-Elmet	d													18 25			21 05		
Selby	a			10 58		12 24	13 59		15 08		16 24	17 30			19 35			22 00	
Hull 29	a			11 41		13 06	14 40		15 49		17 07	18 12			20 17			22 36	
Pontefract Baghill	d													18 40			21 20		
Moorthorpe 31	a													18 51			21 35		
Swinton (S.Yorks) 29,31	a													19 01			21 45		
Rotherham Central 29,31	a													19 12			21 52		
Meadowhall 29,31 ⇌	a													19 18			21 57		
Sheffield 7 29,31 ⇌	a													19 27			22 09		

Sundays

from 18 September

		NT A	NT C	NT	NT C	NT	NT C	NT C	NT	NT C	NT	NT	NT C	NT	NT	NT B
York 8 29	d	08 50	09 52	10 40	11 52	13 40	13 52	15 52	16 06	17 52	18 10	19 10	19 52	20 50	21 41	21 52
Ulleskelf	d															
Church Fenton	a	09 01	10 03		12 03		14 03	16 03		18 03	18 21		20 03	21 01		22 04
	d										18 21			21 01		
Sherburn-in-Elmet	d										18 25			21 05		
Selby	a			10 58		13 59			16 24			19 35			22 00	
Hull 29	a			11 41		14 40			17 07			20 17			22 36	
Pontefract Baghill	d										18 40			21 20		
Moorthorpe 31	a										18 51			21 35		
Swinton (S.Yorks) 29,31	a										19 01			21 45		
Rotherham Central 29,31	a										19 12			21 52		
Meadowhall 29,31 ⇌	a										19 18			21 57		
Sheffield 7 29,31 ⇌	a										19 27			22 09		

A To Blackpool North   B To Leeds   C To Hebden Bridge

Table 34

Mondays to Fridays

until 30 September

Nottingham, Sheffield - Barnsley - Huddersfield and Leeds

Miles	Miles				NT	NT	NT	NT	NT	NT	NT	NT	NT		NT	NT	NT	NT	NT	TP	NT	NT	NT		NT	EM
					MO	MX	MX																			
																				◇1						◇
							A			B					C				C	D	E				F	G
0	—	**Nottingham 8**		d	21p20																		06 23			06 40
12	—	Langley Mill		d	21p41																		06 38			
18¼	—	Alfreton		d	21p49																		06 46			07 02
28¼	—	Chesterfield		d	22p08													06 26					06 58			07 13
33½	—	Dronfield		d	22p15													06 33					07 05			07 20
40½	—	**Sheffield 7**	29,31	a	22p32													06 46					07 18			07 31
—	—			d	22p39	23p15	23p24	05 16	05 22	05 29	05 36	05 50	06 06		06 18	06 28	06 36	06 49	06 52	06 55	07 06	07 14	07 20		07 24	
44	3½	**Meadowhall 4**	29,31	a	22p44	23p20	23p29	05 22	05 27	05 34	05 41	05 55	06 11		06 23	06 33	06 41	06 54	06 57	07 00	07 11	07 20	07 25		07 30	
—	—			d	22p45	23p21	23p30	05 22	05 28		05 42	05 56	06 12			06 34	06 42	06 55			07 12	07 21	07 26			
47¾	7¼	Chapeltown		d	22p51		23p36	05 28			05 48		06 18				06 48				07 18					
51	10½	Elsecar		d	22p56		23p41	05 33					06 23								07 23					
52½	12	Wombwell		d	23p00		23p45	05 37			05 55		06 27				06 55				07 27					
56½	16	**Barnsley**		a	23p05		23p50	05 44			06 00	06 10	06 32				07 00	07 09			07 32		07 41			
—	—			d	23p10		23p51				06 01	06 10	06 33				07 01	07 12			07 33		07 42			
—	19	Dodworth		d							06 07						07 07									
—	20¼	Silkstone Common		d							06 11						07 11									
—	23½	Penistone		d							06 18						07 18									
—	27½	Denby Dale		d							06 24						07 24									
—	29¾	Shepley		d							06 29						07 29									
—	30¾	Stocksmoor		d							06 32						07 32									
—	32¾	Brockholes		d							06 36						07 36									
—	33¾	Honley		d							06 38						07 38									
—	34¾	Berry Brow		d							06 41						07 41									
—	35¾	Lockwood		d							06 44						07 44									
—	37	**Huddersfield**		a							06 49						07 49									
60	—	Darton		d	23p15		23p56						06 38								07 38					
67½	—	**Wakefield Kirkgate 4**	31	a	23p26		00s10					06 27	06 49					07 27			07 49		07 57			
—	—			d	23p27							06 28	06 50					07 28			07 50		07 58			
70½	—	Normanton		d	23p34							06 33	06 54					07 33			07 54					
74	—	Castleford		a	23p40								06 59								07 59					
78¾	—	Woodlesford		a	23p53								07 12								08 11					
84¾	—	**Leeds 10**	31	a	00 05	00 30			06 33			06 50	07 28			07 44		07 51			08 25	08 36	08 21			

			NT	NT	NT	EM	NT	TP	NT		NT	NT	NT	EM	NT	NT	NT	NT	TP		NT	NT	NT	NT	NT	NT
						◇1		◇1						◇					◇1							
				H		J		D				F		G	H		K		D				F	L		M
Nottingham 8		d									07 13			07 45								08 11				
Langley Mill		d									07 29											08 31				
Alfreton		d									07 37			08 07								08 39				
Chesterfield		d				07 42					07 50			08 18								08 51				
Dronfield		d				07 49								08 25								08 58				
Sheffield 7	29,31	a				08 00					08 08			08 38								09 16				
		d	07 36	07 41	07 51		08 06	08 11	08 14		08 18	08 24	08 36		08 41	08 51	08 53	09 06	09 11		09 14	09 18	09 24	09 29	09 36	09 41
Meadowhall 4	29,31	a	07 41	07 46	07 57		08 11	08 17	08 21		08 24	08 30	08 41		08 46	08 56	08 59	09 11	09 16		09 20	09 23	09 29	09 34	09 41	09 46
		d	07 42		07 57		08 12		08 21		08 25		08 42			08 57		09 12			09 21	09 24			09 42	
Chapeltown		d	07 48				08 18						08 48					09 18							09 48	
Elsecar		d					08 23											09 23								
Wombwell		d	07 55				08 27						08 55					09 27							09 55	
Barnsley		a	08 00		08 11		08 32				08 40		09 00			09 11		09 32				09 40			10 00	
		d	08 01		08 12		08 33				08 42		09 01			09 12		09 33				09 42			10 01	
Dodworth		d	08 07										09 07												10 07	
Silkstone Common		d	08 11										09 11												10 11	
Penistone		d	08 18										09 18												10 18	
Denby Dale		d	08 24										09 24												10 24	
Shepley		d	08 29										09 29												10 29	
Stocksmoor		d	08 32										09 32												10 32	
Brockholes		d	08 36										09 36												10 36	
Honley		d	08 38										09 38												10 38	
Berry Brow		d	08 41										09 41												10 41	
Lockwood		d	08 44										09 44												10 44	
Huddersfield		a	08 49										09 49												10 49	
Darton		d					08 38											09 38								
Wakefield Kirkgate 4	31	a			08 27		08 49				08 57					09 27		09 49				09 57				
		d			08 28		08 50				08 58					09 28		09 50				09 58				
Normanton		d					08 54											09 54								
Castleford		a					09 00											10 00								
Woodlesford		a					09 12											10 12								
Leeds 10	31	a			08 49		09 25		09 31		09 20					09 49		10 25			10 31	10 18				

A To Wakefield Westgate
B To Beverley
C To Adwick
D From Manchester Airport to Cleethorpes
E From Worksop
F To Scunthorpe
G To Liverpool Lime Street
H To Bridlington
J From Derby
K From Worksop to Adwick
L To York
M To Scarborough

Nottingham, Sheffield - Barnsley - Huddersfield and Leeds

	NT	NT	NT		TP	NT	NT	NT	NT	NT	NT	NT	NT		TP	NT	NT	NT	NT	NT	NT	NT	NT	
					◇1										◇1									
		A			B			C		D		A			B			C		E		A		
Nottingham 8 d							09 15										10 15							
Langley Mill d							09 32										10 32							
Alfreton d							09 40										10 40							
Chesterfield d							09 52										10 52							
Dronfield d							09 59										10 59							
Sheffield 7 29,31 a							10 16										11 16							
d	09 50	09 53	10 06		10 11	10 14	10 18	10 24	10 36	10 41	10 50	10 53	11 06		11 11	11 14	11 18	11 24	11 36	11 41	11 50	11 53	12 06	
Meadowhall 4 29,31 a	09 55	09 58	10 11		10 16	10 20	10 23	10 29	10 41	10 46	10 55	10 58	11 11		11 16	11 20	11 23	11 29	11 41	11 46	11 55	11 58	12 11	
d	09 56		10 12			10 21	10 24		10 42		10 56		11 12			11 21	11 24		11 42		11 56		12 12	
Chapeltown d			10 18						10 48				11 18						11 48				12 18	
Elsecar d			10 23										11 23										12 23	
Wombwell d			10 27						10 55				11 27						11 55				12 27	
Barnsley a	10 11		10 32				10 40		11 00		11 11		11 32				11 40		12 00		12 10		12 32	
d	10 12		10 33				10 42		11 01		11 12		11 33				11 41		12 01		12 11		12 33	
Dodworth d									11 07										12 07					
Silkstone Common d									11 11										12 11					
Penistone d									11 18										12 18					
Denby Dale d									11 24										12 24					
Shepley d									11 29										12 29					
Stocksmoor d									11 32										12 32					
Brockholes d									11 36										12 36					
Honley d									11 38										12 38					
Berry Brow d									11 41										12 41					
Lockwood d									11 44										12 44					
Huddersfield a									11 49										12 49					
Darton d			10 38										11 38										12 38	
Wakefield Kirkgate 4 31 a	10 27		10 49				10 57				11 27		11 49				11 57				12 27		12 49	
d	10 28		10 50				10 58				11 28		11 50				11 58				12 28		12 50	
Normanton d			10 54										11 54										12 54	
Castleford a			11 00										12 00										13 00	
Woodlesford a			11 12										12 12										13 12	
Leeds 10 31 a	10 48		11 25			11 31	11 18				11 48		12 25			12 31	12 18				12 48		13 25	

	TP	NT	NT	NT	NT	NT	NT	NT	NT		TP	NT	NT	NT	NT	NT	NT	NT	NT		NT	TP	NT	NT
	◇1										◇1											◇1		
	B			C		D		A			B			C	F		D		A			B		
Nottingham 8 d			11 15										12 15											13 15
Langley Mill d			11 31										12 32											13 32
Alfreton d			11 39										12 40											13 40
Chesterfield d			11 52										12 52											13 52
Dronfield d			11 59										12 59											13 59
Sheffield 7 29,31 a			12 16										13 16											14 16
d	12 11	12 14	12 18	12 24	12 36	12 41	12 50	12 53	13 06		13 11	13 14	13 18	13 24	13 28	13 36	13 41	13 50	13 53		14 06	14 11	14 14	14 18
Meadowhall 4 29,31 a	12 16	12 20	12 23	12 29	12 41	12 46	12 55	12 58	13 11		13 16	13 20	13 23	13 29	13 34	13 41	13 46	13 55	13 58		14 11	14 16	14 20	14 23
d		12 21	12 24		12 42		12 56		13 12			13 21	13 24			13 42		13 56			14 12		14 21	14 24
Chapeltown d					12 48				13 18							13 48					14 18			
Elsecar d									13 23												14 23			
Wombwell d					12 55				13 27							13 55					14 27			
Barnsley a			12 40		13 00		13 11		13 32				13 40			14 00		14 11			14 32			14 40
d			12 42		13 01		13 12		13 33				13 42			14 01		14 12			14 33			14 42
Dodworth d					13 07											14 07								
Silkstone Common d					13 11											14 11								
Penistone d					13 18											14 18								
Denby Dale d					13 24											14 24								
Shepley d					13 29											14 29								
Stocksmoor d					13 32											14 32								
Brockholes d					13 36											14 36								
Honley d					13 38											14 38								
Berry Brow d					13 41											14 41								
Lockwood d					13 44											14 44								
Huddersfield a					13 49											14 49								
Darton d									13 38												14 38			
Wakefield Kirkgate 4 31 a			12 57				13 27		13 50				13 57					14 27			14 49			14 57
d			12 58				13 28		13 50				13 58					14 28			14 50			14 58
Normanton d									13 54												14 54			
Castleford a									14 00												15 00			
Woodlesford a									14 12												15 12			
Leeds 10 31 a		13 29	13 18				13 49		14 25			14 31	14 18					14 48			15 25		15 31	15 18

A From Lincoln to Adwick
B From Manchester Airport to Cleethorpes
C To Scunthorpe
D To Bridlington
E To Scarborough
F To York

Table 34

Mondays to Fridays

until 30 September

Nottingham, Sheffield - Barnsley - Huddersfield and Leeds

		NT A	NT	NT B	NT	NT C	NT	TP ◇1 D	NT	NT	NT A	NT	NT E	NT	NT C	NT	TP ◇1 D	NT	NT	NT F	NT	NT E	NT
Nottingham 8	d									14 15									15 15				
Langley Mill	d									14 30									15 32				
Alfreton	d									14 38									15 40				
Chesterfield	d									14 52									15 53				
Dronfield	d									14 59									16 00				
Sheffield 7 29,31	a									15 16									16 16				
	d	14 24	14 36	14 41	14 50	14 53	15 06	15 11	15 14	15 18	15 24	15 36	15 41	15 50	15 53	16 06	16 11	16 14	16 18	16 23	16 36	16 41	16 50
Meadowhall 4 29,31	a	14 29	14 41	14 46	14 55	14 58	15 11	15 16	15 20	15 23	15 29	15 41	15 46	15 55	15 58	16 11	16 16	16 20	16 23	16 29	16 41	16 46	16 55
	d		14 42		14 56		15 12		15 20	15 24		15 42		15 56		16 12		16 20	16 24		16 42		16 56
Chapeltown	d		14 48				15 18					15 48				16 18					16 48		
Elsecar	d						15 23									16 23					16 53		
Wombwell	d		14 55				15 27					15 55				16 27					16 57		
Barnsley	a		15 00		15 11		15 32			15 40		16 00		16 11		16 32			16 40		17 02		17 11
	d		15 01		15 12		15 33			15 42		16 01		16 12		16 33			16 42		17 03		17 12
Dodworth	d		15 07									16 07									17 09		
Silkstone Common	d		15 11									16 11									17 13		
Penistone	d		15 18									16 18									17 20		
Denby Dale	d		15 24									16 24									17 26		
Shepley	d		15 29									16 29									17 31		
Stocksmoor	d		15 32									16 32									17 34		
Brockholes	d		15 36									16 36									17 38		
Honley	d		15 38									16 38									17 40		
Berry Brow	d		15 41									16 41									17 43		
Lockwood	d		15 44									16 44									17 46		
Huddersfield	a		15 49									16 49									17 50		
Darton	d						15 38									16 38							
Wakefield Kirkgate 4 31	a				15 27		15 49			15 57				16 27		16 49			16 57				17 28
	d				15 28		15 50			15 58				16 28		16 50			16 58				17 28
Normanton	d						15 54									16 54							
Castleford	a						16 00									17 00							
Woodlesford	a						16 12									17 12							
Leeds 10 31	a				15 49		16 25		16 31	16 18				16 48		17 25		17 31	17 18				17 48

		NT C	NT	TP ◇1 D	NT	NT	NT F	NT	NT B	NT	NT G	NT	NT	NT	TP ◇1 D	NT F	NT	NT E	NT	NT H	NT	TP ◇1 D
Nottingham 8	d					16 15								17 15								
Langley Mill	d					16 32								17 31								
Alfreton	d					16 40								17 39								
Chesterfield	d					16 55								17 52								
Dronfield	d					17 02								17 59								
Sheffield 7 29,31	a					17 17								18 15								
	d	16 53	17 06	17 11	17 13	17 18	17 27	17 36	17 41	17 50	17 53	18 06	18 13	18 18	18 24	18 29	18 36	18 41	18 50	19 00	19 06	19 11
Meadowhall 4 29,31	a	16 58	17 11	17 16	17 20	17 23	17 32	17 41	17 46	17 55	17 58	18 12	18 20	18 23	18 29	18 34	18 41	18 46	18 55	19 06	19 12	19 16
	d		17 12		17 20	17 24		17 42		17 56		18 12	18 20	18 24			18 42		18 56		19 12	
Chapeltown	d		17 18					17 48				18 18					18 48				19 18	
Elsecar	d		17 23					17 53				18 23					18 53				19 23	
Wombwell	d		17 27					17 57				18 27					18 57				19 27	
Barnsley	a		17 32			17 40		18 02		18 11		18 33		18 42			19 02		19 14		19 33	
	d		17 33			17 42		18 03		18 12		18 33		18 42			19 08		19 14		19 33	
Dodworth	d							18 09									19 14					
Silkstone Common	d							18 13									19 18					
Penistone	d							18 27									19 25					
Denby Dale	d							18 33									19 31					
Shepley	d							18 38									19 36					
Stocksmoor	d							18 41									19 39					
Brockholes	d							18 45									19 43					
Honley	d							18 47									19 45					
Berry Brow	d							18 50									19 48					
Lockwood	d							18 53									19 51					
Huddersfield	a							18 57									19 56					
Darton	d		17 38									18 38									19 38	
Wakefield Kirkgate 4 31	a		17 49			17 57				18 28		18 50		18 58					19 29		19 50	
	d		17 50			17 58				18 32		18 50		18 59					19 32		19 50	
Normanton	d		17 54									18 54									19 54	
Castleford	a		18 00									19 00									20 00	
Woodlesford	a		18 12									19 13									20 12	
Leeds 10 31	a		18 25		18 32	18 18				18 51		19 27	19 31	19 23					19 55		20 26	

A To Scunthorpe
B To Scarborough
C From Lincoln to Adwick
D From Manchester Airport to Cleethorpes
E To Bridlington
F To Doncaster
G From Lincoln to Hull
H From Retford to Doncaster

until 30 September

Nottingham, Sheffield - Barnsley - Huddersfield and Leeds

Station			NT FX	NT FO	NT	NT A	NT	NT B	NT		NT C	NT	TP ◇1 D	NT E	NT	NT	NT F	NT	NT		TP FO ◇1 D	NT B	NT	TP FX ◇1 G	NT	NT FO
Nottingham 8		d			18 15										19 15											
Langley Mill		d			18 32										19 32											
Alfreton		d			18 40										19 40											
Chesterfield		d			18 52										19 52											
Dronfield		d			18 59										19 59											
Sheffield 7	29,31	a			19 17										20 15											
		d	19 18	19 18	19 22	19 30	19 36	19 44	19 51		19 58	20 06	20 11	20 15	20 18	20 27	20 38	20 41	21 09		21 11	21 15	21 30	21 34	21 41	22 06
Meadowhall 4	29,31	a	19 24	19 24	19 27	19 35	19 41	19 49	19 56		20 03	20 11	20 16	20 20	20 24	20 34	20 44	20 47	21 14		21 16	21 21	21 35	21 39	21 46	22 11
		d	19 25	19 25	19 28		19 42		19 57			20 12			20 24	20 35		20 47	21 15				21 36		21 47	22 12
Chapeltown		d					19 48					20 18						20 53	21 21						21 53	22 18
Elsecar		d					19 53					20 23							21 26							22 23
Wombwell		d					19 57					20 27						21 00	21 30						22 00	22 27
Barnsley		a			19 42		20 02		20 12			20 32			20 40			21 07	21 35						22 05	22 32
		d			19 42		20 08		20 12			20 33			20 42			21 08	21 36						22 08	
Dodworth		d					20 14											21 14							22 14	
Silkstone Common		d					20 18											21 18							22 18	
Penistone		d					20 25											21 25							22 25	
Denby Dale		d					20 31											21 31							22 31	
Shepley		d					20 36											21 36							22 36	
Stocksmoor		d					20 39											21 39							22 39	
Brockholes		d					20 43											21 43							22 43	
Honley		d					20 45											21 45							22 45	
Berry Brow		d					20 48											21 48							22 48	
Lockwood		d					20 51											21 51							22 51	
Huddersfield		a					20 55											22 00							22 57	
Darton		d										20 38							21 41							
Wakefield Kirkgate 4	31	a			19 58				20 28			20 49			20 57				21 52							
		d			19 58				20 28			20 50			20 58				21 52							
Normanton		d										20 54							21 57							
Castleford		a										21 00							22 04							
Woodlesford		a										21 12							22 14							
Leeds 10	31	a	20 37	20 42	20 19				20 48			21 26			21 19	21 47			22 29				22 46			

Station			NT FO	NT FX	TP ◇1 D		NT	NT	NT E	NT	NT	NT FX H	NT A
Nottingham 8		d					21 11						
Langley Mill		d					21 31						
Alfreton		d					21 39						
Chesterfield		d					22 00						
Dronfield		d					22 07						
Sheffield 7	29,31	a					22 19						
		d		22 06	22 11			22 24	22 34	22 41	23 15	23 24	23 27
Meadowhall 4	29,31	a		22 11	22 16			22 30	22 39	22 46	23 20	23 29	23 32
		d		22 12				22 30		22 47	23 21	23 30	
Chapeltown		d		22 18						22 53		23 36	
Elsecar		d		22 23						22 58		23 41	
Wombwell		d		22 27						23 02		23 45	
Barnsley		a		22 32						23 07		23 50	
		d		22 33						23 08		23 51	
Dodworth		d								23 14			
Silkstone Common		d								23 18			
Penistone		d								23 25			
Denby Dale		d								23 31			
Shepley		d								23 36			
Stocksmoor		d								23 39			
Brockholes		d								23 43			
Honley		d								23 45			
Berry Brow		d								23 48			
Lockwood		d								23 51			
Huddersfield		a								23 55			
Darton		d		22 38								23 56	
Wakefield Kirkgate 4	31	a		22 51								00s10	
		d	22 51	22 51									
Normanton		d	22 56	22 56									
Castleford		a	23 01	23 01									
Woodlesford		a	23 14	23 14									
Leeds 10	31	a	23 29	23 30				23 41			00 30		

A To Doncaster
B To Beverley
C To Bridlington
D From Manchester Airport to Cleethorpes
E To Goole
F To Scunthorpe
G To Cleethorpes
H To Wakefield Westgate

Nottingham, Sheffield - Barnsley - Huddersfield and Leeds

Station			NT MO	NT MX	NT MX	NT	NT	NT	NT	NT	NT	NT	NT	NT	NT	NT	TP	NT	NT	NT	NT	EM	NT	NT
					A			B				C				C	◇1 D	E			F	◇ G		H
Nottingham 8		d	21p20																	06 23		06 40		
Langley Mill		d	21p41																	06 38				
Alfreton		d	21p49																	06 46		07 02		
Chesterfield		d	22p08												06 26					06 58		07 13		
Dronfield		d	22p15												06 33					07 05		07 20		
Sheffield 7	29,31	a	22p32												06 46					07 18		07 31		
		d	22p39	23p15	23p24	05 15	05 22	05 29	05 36	05 50	06 06	06 18	06 28	06 36	06 49	06 52	06 55	07 06	07 14	07 20	07 24		07 36	07 41
Meadowhall 4	29,31	a	22p44	23p20	23p29	05 21	05 27	05 34	05 41	05 55	06 11	06 23	06 33	06 41	06 54	06 57	07 00	07 11	07 20	07 25	07 30		07 41	07 46
		d	22p45	23p21	23p30	05 21	05 28		05 42	05 56	06 12		06 34	06 42	06 55			07 12	07 21	07 26			07 42	
Chapeltown		d	22p51		23p36	05 27			05 48		06 18			06 48				07 18					07 48	
Elsecar		d	22p56		23p41	05 32					06 23							07 23						
Wombwell		d	23p00		23p45	05 36			05 55		06 27			06 55				07 27					07 55	
Barnsley		a	23p05		23p50	05 43			06 00	06 10	06 32			07 00	07 09			07 32		07 41			08 00	
		d	23p10		23p51				06 01	06 10	06 33			07 01	07 12			07 33		07 42			08 01	
Dodworth		d							06 07					07 07									08 07	
Silkstone Common		d							06 11					07 11									08 11	
Penistone		d							06 18					07 18									08 18	
Denby Dale		d							06 24					07 24									08 24	
Shepley		d							06 29					07 29									08 29	
Stocksmoor		d							06 32					07 32									08 32	
Brockholes		d							06 36					07 36									08 36	
Honley		d							06 38					07 38									08 38	
Berry Brow		d							06 41					07 41									08 41	
Lockwood		d							06 44					07 44									08 44	
Huddersfield		a							06 55					07 54									08 53	
Darton		d	23p15		23p56						06 38							07 38						
Wakefield Kirkgate 4	31	a	23p26		00s10					06 27	06 49				07 27			07 49		07 57				
		d	23p27							06 28	06 50				07 28			07 50		07 58				
Normanton		d	23p34							06 33	06 54				07 33			07 54						
Castleford		a	23p40								06 59							07 59						
Woodlesford		a	23p53								07 12							08 11						
Leeds 10	31	a	00 05	00 30			06 33			06 50	07 28		07 44		07 51			08 25	08 36	08 21				

Station			NT	EM	NT	TP	NT	NT	NT	NT	EM	NT	NT	NT	NT	TP	NT	NT	NT	NT	NT	NT	NT	NT
			I	◇1 J		◇1 D			F		◇ G	H		K		◇1 D			F	L		M		N
Nottingham 8		d						07 13			07 45							08 11						
Langley Mill		d						07 29										08 31						
Alfreton		d						07 37			08 07							08 39						
Chesterfield		d		07 42				07 50			08 18							08 51						
Dronfield		d		07 49							08 25							08 58						
Sheffield 7	29,31	a		08 00				08 08			08 38							09 16						
		d	07 51		08 06	08 11	08 14	08 18	08 24	08 36		08 41	08 51	08 53	09 06	09 11	09 14	09 18	09 24	09 29	09 36	09 41	09 50	09 53
Meadowhall 4	29,31	a	07 57		08 11	08 17	08 21	08 24	08 30	08 41		08 46	08 56	08 59	09 11	09 16	09 20	09 23	09 29	09 34	09 41	09 46	09 55	09 58
		d	07 57		08 12		08 21	08 25		08 42			08 57		09 12		09 21	09 24			09 42		09 56	
Chapeltown		d			08 18					08 48					09 18						09 48			
Elsecar		d			08 23										09 23									
Wombwell		d			08 27					08 55					09 27						09 55			
Barnsley		a	08 11		08 32			08 40		09 00			09 11		09 32			09 40			10 00		10 11	
		d	08 12		08 33			08 42		09 01			09 12		09 33			09 42			10 01		10 12	
Dodworth		d								09 07											10 07			
Silkstone Common		d								09 11											10 11			
Penistone		d								09 18											10 18			
Denby Dale		d								09 24											10 24			
Shepley		d								09 29											10 29			
Stocksmoor		d								09 32											10 32			
Brockholes		d								09 36											10 36			
Honley		d								09 38											10 38			
Berry Brow		d								09 41											10 41			
Lockwood		d								09 44											10 44			
Huddersfield		a								09 50											10 53			
Darton		d			08 38										09 38									
Wakefield Kirkgate 4	31	a	08 27		08 49			08 57					09 27		09 49			09 57					10 27	
		d	08 28		08 50			08 58					09 28		09 50			09 58					10 28	
Normanton		d			08 54										09 54									
Castleford		a			09 00										10 00									
Woodlesford		a			09 12										10 12									
Leeds 10	31	a	08 49		09 25		09 31	09 20					09 49		10 25		10 31	10 18					10 48	

A To Wakefield Westgate
B To Beverley
C To Adwick
D From Manchester Airport to Cleethorpes
E From Worksop
F To Scunthorpe
G To Liverpool Lime Street
H To Bridlington
I From Retford
J From Derby
K From Worksop to Adwick
L To York
M To Scarborough
N From Lincoln to Adwick

Table 34

Mondays to Fridays

from 3 October

Nottingham, Sheffield - Barnsley - Huddersfield and Leeds

		NT	TP ◇1 A	NT	NT	NT B	NT	NT C	NT	NT D	NT	TP ◇1 A	NT	NT	NT B	NT	NT E	NT	NT D	NT	TP ◇1 A	NT
Nottingham 8	d				09 15									10 15								
Langley Mill	d				09 32									10 32								
Alfreton	d				09 40									10 40								
Chesterfield	d				09 52									10 52								
Dronfield	d				09 59									10 59								
Sheffield 7 29,31	a				10 16									11 16								
	d	10 06	10 11	10 14	10 18	10 24	10 36	10 41	10 50	10 53	11 06	11 11	11 14	11 18	11 24	11 36	11 41	11 50	11 53	12 06	12 11	12 14
Meadowhall 4 29,31	a	10 11	10 16	10 20	10 23	10 29	10 41	10 46	10 55	10 58	11 11	11 16	11 20	11 23	11 29	11 41	11 46	11 55	11 58	12 11	12 16	12 20
	d	10 12		10 21	10 24		10 42		10 56		11 12		11 21	11 24		11 42		11 56		12 12		12 21
Chapeltown	d	10 18					10 48				11 18					11 48				12 18		
Elsecar	d	10 23									11 23									12 23		
Wombwell	d	10 27					10 55				11 27					11 55				12 27		
Barnsley	a	10 32			10 40		11 00		11 11		11 32			11 40		12 00		12 10		12 32		
	d	10 33			10 42		11 01		11 12		11 33			11 41		12 01		12 11		12 33		
Dodworth	d						11 07									12 07						
Silkstone Common	d						11 11									12 11						
Penistone	d						11 18									12 18						
Denby Dale	d						11 24									12 24						
Shepley	d						11 29									12 29						
Stocksmoor	d						11 32									12 32						
Brockholes	d						11 36									12 36						
Honley	d						11 38									12 38						
Berry Brow	d						11 41									12 41						
Lockwood	d						11 44									12 44						
Huddersfield	a						11 53									12 52						
Darton	d	10 38									11 38									12 38		
Wakefield Kirkgate 4 31	a	10 49			10 57				11 27		11 49			11 57				12 27		12 49		
	d	10 50			10 58				11 28		11 50			11 58				12 28		12 50		
Normanton	d	10 54									11 54									12 54		
Castleford	a	11 00									12 00									13 00		
Woodlesford	a	11 12									12 12									13 12		
Leeds 10 31	a	11 25		11 31	11 18				11 48		12 25		12 31	12 18				12 48		13 25		13 29

		NT	NT B	NT	NT C	NT	NT D	NT	TP ◇1 A	NT	NT	NT B	NT F	NT	NT C	NT	NT D	NT	TP ◇1 A	NT	NT	NT B	NT
Nottingham 8	d	11 15									12 15										13 15		
Langley Mill	d	11 31									12 32										13 32		
Alfreton	d	11 39									12 40										13 40		
Chesterfield	d	11 52									12 52										13 52		
Dronfield	d	11 59									12 59										13 59		
Sheffield 7 29,31	a	12 16									13 16										14 16		
	d	12 18	12 24	12 36	12 41	12 50	12 53	13 06	13 11	13 14	13 18	13 24	13 28	13 36	13 41	13 50	13 53	14 06	14 11	14 14	14 18	14 24	14 36
Meadowhall 4 29,31	a	12 23	12 29	12 41	12 46	12 55	12 58	13 11	13 16	13 20	13 23	13 29	13 34	13 41	13 46	13 55	13 58	14 11	14 16	14 20	14 23	14 29	14 41
	d	12 24		12 42		12 56		13 12		13 21	13 24			13 42		13 56		14 12		14 21	14 24		14 42
Chapeltown	d			12 48				13 18						13 48				14 18					14 48
Elsecar	d							13 23										14 23					
Wombwell	d			12 55				13 27						13 55				14 27					14 55
Barnsley	a	12 40		13 00		13 11		13 32			13 40			14 00		14 11		14 32			14 40		15 00
	d	12 42		13 01		13 12		13 33			13 42			14 01		14 12		14 33			14 42		15 01
Dodworth	d			13 07										14 07									15 07
Silkstone Common	d			13 11										14 11									15 11
Penistone	d			13 18										14 18									15 18
Denby Dale	d			13 24										14 24									15 24
Shepley	d			13 29										14 29									15 29
Stocksmoor	d			13 32										14 32									15 32
Brockholes	d			13 36										14 36									15 36
Honley	d			13 38										14 38									15 38
Berry Brow	d			13 41										14 41									15 41
Lockwood	d			13 44										14 44									15 44
Huddersfield	a			13 53										14 53									15 53
Darton	d							13 38										14 38					
Wakefield Kirkgate 4 31	a	12 57				13 27		13 50			13 57					14 27		14 49			14 57		
	d	12 58				13 28		13 50			13 58					14 28		14 50			14 58		
Normanton	d							13 54										14 54					
Castleford	a							14 00										15 00					
Woodlesford	a							14 12										15 12					
Leeds 10 31	a	13 18				13 49		14 25		14 31	14 18					14 48		15 25		15 31	15 18		

A From Manchester Airport to Cleethorpes
B To Scunthorpe
C To Bridlington
D From Lincoln to Adwick
E To Scarborough
F To York

Table 34

Mondays to Fridays

from 3 October

Nottingham, Sheffield - Barnsley - Huddersfield and Leeds

			NT	NT	NT	NT	TP	NT	NT	NT	NT	NT	NT	NT	NT	TP	NT	NT	NT	NT	NT	NT	NT
							◇1									◇1							
			A		B		C			D		E		B		C			F		E		B
							🍴									🍴							
Nottingham 8		d							14 15									15 15					
Langley Mill		d							14 30									15 32					
Alfreton		d							14 38									15 40					
Chesterfield		d							14 52									15 53					
Dronfield		d							14 59									16 00					
Sheffield 7	29,31	a							15 16									16 16					
		d	14 41	14 50	14 53	15 06	15 11	15 14	15 18	15 24	15 36	15 41	15 50	15 53	16 06	16 11	16 14	16 18	16 23	16 36	16 41	16 50	16 53
Meadowhall 4	29,31	a	14 46	14 55	14 58	15 11	15 16	15 20	15 23	15 29	15 41	15 46	15 55	15 58	16 11	16 16	16 20	16 23	16 29	16 41	16 46	16 55	16 58
		d		14 56		15 12		15 20	15 24		15 42		15 56		16 12		16 20	16 24		16 42		16 56	
Chapeltown		d				15 18					15 48				16 18					16 48			
Elsecar		d				15 23									16 23					16 53			
Wombwell		d				15 27					15 55				16 27					16 57			
Barnsley		a		15 11		15 32			15 40		16 00		16 11		16 32			16 40		17 02		17 11	
		d		15 12		15 33			15 42		16 01		16 12		16 33			16 42		17 03		17 12	
Dodworth		d									16 07									17 09			
Silkstone Common		d									16 11									17 13			
Penistone		d									16 18									17 20			
Denby Dale		d									16 24									17 26			
Shepley		d									16 29									17 31			
Stocksmoor		d									16 32									17 34			
Brockholes		d									16 36									17 38			
Honley		d									16 38									17 40			
Berry Brow		d									16 41									17 43			
Lockwood		d									16 44									17 46			
Huddersfield		a									16 52									17 51			
Darton		d				15 38									16 38								
Wakefield Kirkgate 4	31	a		15 27		15 49			15 57				16 27		16 49			16 57				17 28	
		d		15 28		15 50			15 58				16 28		16 50			16 58				17 28	
Normanton		d				15 54									16 54								
Castleford		a				16 00									17 00								
Woodlesford		a				16 12									17 12								
Leeds 10	31	a		15 49		16 25		16 31	16 18				16 48		17 25		17 31	17 18				17 48	

			NT	TP	NT	NT	NT	NT	NT	NT	NT	NT	NT	NT	TP	NT	NT	NT	NT	NT	NT	TP	NT	NT
																							FX	FO
				◇1											◇1							◇1		
				C			F		A		G				C	F		E		H		C		
				🍴											🍴							🍴		
Nottingham 8		d				16 15								17 15										
Langley Mill		d				16 32								17 31										
Alfreton		d				16 40								17 39										
Chesterfield		d				16 55								17 52										
Dronfield		d				17 02								17 59										
Sheffield 7	29,31	a				17 17								18 15										
		d	17 06	17 11	17 13	17 18	17 27	17 36	17 41	17 50	17 53	18 06	18 13	18 18	18 24	18 29	18 36	18 41	18 50	19 00	19 06	19 11	19 18	19 18
Meadowhall 4	29,31	a	17 11	17 16	17 20	17 23	17 32	17 41	17 46	17 55	17 58	18 12	18 20	18 23	18 29	18 34	18 41	18 46	18 55	19 06	19 12	19 16	19 24	19 24
		d	17 12		17 20	17 24		17 42		17 56		18 12	18 20	18 24			18 42		18 56		19 12		19 25	19 25
Chapeltown		d	17 18					17 48				18 18					18 48				19 18			
Elsecar		d	17 23					17 53				18 23					18 53				19 23			
Wombwell		d	17 27					17 57				18 27					18 57				19 27			
Barnsley		a	17 32			17 40		18 02		18 11		18 33		18 42			19 02		19 14		19 33			
		d	17 33			17 42		18 03		18 12		18 33		18 42			19 08		19 14		19 33			
Dodworth		d						18 09									19 14							
Silkstone Common		d						18 13									19 18							
Penistone		d						18 27									19 25							
Denby Dale		d						18 33									19 31							
Shepley		d						18 38									19 36							
Stocksmoor		d						18 41									19 39							
Brockholes		d						18 45									19 43							
Honley		d						18 47									19 45							
Berry Brow		d						18 50									19 48							
Lockwood		d						18 53									19 51							
Huddersfield		a						19 02									20 01							
Darton		d	17 38									18 38									19 38			
Wakefield Kirkgate 4	31	a	17 49			17 57				18 28		18 50		18 58					19 29		19 50			
		d	17 50			17 58				18 32		18 50		18 59					19 32		19 50			
Normanton		d	17 54									18 54									19 54			
Castleford		a	18 00									19 00									20 00			
Woodlesford		a	18 12									19 13									20 12			
Leeds 10	31	a	18 25		18 32	18 18				18 51		19 27	19 31	19 23					19 55		20 26		20 37	20 42

A To Scarborough
B From Lincoln to Adwick
C From Manchester Airport to Cleethorpes
D To Scunthorpe
E To Bridlington
F To Doncaster
G From Lincoln to Hull
H From Retford to Doncaster

Table 34

Mondays to Fridays

from 3 October

Nottingham, Sheffield - Barnsley - Huddersfield and Leeds

			NT	NT	NT	NT	NT		NT	NT	TP	NT	NT	NT	NT	NT	NT		TP FO	NT	NT	TP FX	NT	NT FO	NT FO	NT FX
											◇1								◇1			◇1				
				A		B			C		D	E			F				D	B		G				
Nottingham 8		d	18 15										19 15													
Langley Mill		d	18 32										19 32													
Alfreton		d	18 40										19 40													
Chesterfield		d	18 52										19 52													
Dronfield		d	18 59										19 59													
Sheffield 7	29,31	a	19 17										20 15													
		d	19 22	19 30	19 36	19 44	19 51		19 58	20 06	20 11	20 15	20 18	20 27	20 38	20 41	21 09		21 11	21 15	21 30	21 34	21 41	22 06		22 06
Meadowhall 4	29,31	a	19 27	19 35	19 41	19 49	19 56		20 03	20 11	20 16	20 20	20 24	20 34	20 44	20 47	21 14		21 16	21 21	21 35	21 39	21 46	22 11		22 11
		d	19 28		19 42		19 57			20 12			20 24	20 35		20 47	21 15				21 36		21 47	22 12		22 12
Chapeltown		d			19 48					20 18						20 53	21 21						21 53	22 18		22 18
Elsecar		d			19 53					20 23							21 26							22 23		22 23
Wombwell		d			19 57					20 27						21 00	21 30						22 00	22 27		22 27
Barnsley		a	19 42		20 02		20 12			20 32			20 40			21 07	21 35						22 05	22 32		22 32
		d	19 42		20 08		20 12			20 33			20 42			21 08	21 36						22 08			22 33
Dodworth		d			20 14											21 14							22 14			
Silkstone Common		d			20 18											21 18							22 18			
Penistone		d			20 25											21 25							22 25			
Denby Dale		d			20 31											21 31							22 31			
Shepley		d			20 36											21 36							22 36			
Stocksmoor		d			20 39											21 39							22 39			
Brockholes		d			20 43											21 43							22 43			
Honley		d			20 45											21 45							22 45			
Berry Brow		d			20 48											21 48							22 48			
Lockwood		d			20 51											21 51							22 51			
Huddersfield		a			21 00											21 56							23 00			
Darton		d								20 38							21 41									22 38
Wakefield Kirkgate 4	31	a	19 58				20 28			20 49			20 57				21 52									22 51
		d	19 58				20 28			20 50			20 58				21 52								22 51	22 51
Normanton		d								20 54							21 57								22 56	22 56
Castleford		a								21 00							22 04								23 01	23 01
Woodlesford		a								21 12							22 14								23 14	23 14
Leeds 10	31	a	20 19				20 48			21 26			21 19	21 47			22 29				22 46				23 29	23 30

			TP		NT	NT	NT	NT	NT	NT FX	NT
			◇1								
			D				E			H	A
Nottingham 8		d			21 11						
Langley Mill		d			21 31						
Alfreton		d			21 39						
Chesterfield		d			22 00						
Dronfield		d			22 07						
Sheffield 7	29,31	a			22 19						
		d	22 11			22 24	22 34	22 41	23 15	23 24	23 27
Meadowhall 4	29,31	a	22 16			22 30	22 39	22 46	23 20	23 29	23 32
		d				22 30		22 47	23 21	23 30	
Chapeltown		d						22 53		23 36	
Elsecar		d						22 58		23 41	
Wombwell		d						23 02		23 45	
Barnsley		a						23 07		23 50	
		d						23 08		23 51	
Dodworth		d						23 14			
Silkstone Common		d						23 18			
Penistone		d						23 25			
Denby Dale		d						23 31			
Shepley		d						23 36			
Stocksmoor		d						23 39			
Brockholes		d						23 43			
Honley		d						23 45			
Berry Brow		d						23 48			
Lockwood		d						23 51			
Huddersfield		a						23 55			
Darton		d								23 56	
Wakefield Kirkgate 4	31	a								00s10	
		d									
Normanton		d									
Castleford		a									
Woodlesford		a									
Leeds 10	31	a				23 41			00 30		

A To Doncaster
B To Beverley
C To Bridlington
D From Manchester Airport to Cleethorpes
E To Goole
F To Scunthorpe
G To Cleethorpes
H To Wakefield Westgate

Table 34

Saturdays
until 1 October

Nottingham, Sheffield - Barnsley - Huddersfield and Leeds

		NT	NT	NT A	NT	NT	NT B	NT	NT	NT B		TP ◇1 C	NT	NT	NT D	EM ◇ E	NT	NT F	NT G	EM ◇1 H		NT	TP ◇1 C	NT	NT
Nottingham 8	d															06 40									07 15
Langley Mill	d																								07 30
Alfreton	d															07 02									07 38
Chesterfield	d															07 13				07 42					07 50
Dronfield	d															07 20				07 49					
Sheffield 7 29,31	a															07 31				07 59					08 08
	d	23p15	05 15	05 29	05 43	06 06	06 12	06 28	06 36	06 52		06 55	07 06	07 14	07 24		07 36	07 41	07 51			08 06	08 11	08 14	08 18
Meadowhall 4 29,31	a	23p20	05 20	05 34	05 48	06 11	06 17	06 33	06 41	06 57		07 00	07 11	07 20	07 29		07 41	07 46	07 57			08 11	08 17	08 21	08 25
	d	23p21	05 21		05 49	06 12		06 34	06 42				07 12	07 21			07 42		07 57			08 12		08 22	08 25
Chapeltown	d		05 27		05 55	06 18			06 48				07 18				07 48					08 18			
Elsecar	d		05 32		06 01	06 23							07 23									08 23			
Wombwell	d		05 36		06 05	06 27			06 55				07 27				07 55					08 27			
Barnsley	a		05 43		06 11	06 32			07 00				07 32				08 00		08 11			08 32			08 40
	d					06 33			07 01				07 33				08 01		08 12			08 33			08 42
Dodworth	d								07 07								08 07								
Silkstone Common	d								07 11								08 11								
Penistone	d								07 18								08 18								
Denby Dale	d								07 24								08 24								
Shepley	d								07 29								08 29								
Stocksmoor	d								07 32								08 32								
Brockholes	d								07 36								08 36								
Honley	d								07 38								08 38								
Berry Brow	d								07 41								08 41								
Lockwood	d								07 44								08 44								
Huddersfield	a								07 49								08 49								
Darton	d					06 38							07 38									08 38			
Wakefield Kirkgate 4 31	a					06 49							07 49						08 27			08 49			08 57
	d					06 50							07 50						08 28			08 50			08 58
Normanton	d					06 54							07 54									08 54			
Castleford	a					07 00							07 59									09 00			
Woodlesford	a					07 12							08 11									09 12			
Leeds 10 31	a	00 30				07 28		07 44					08 25	08 32					08 49			09 25		09 40	09 20

		NT D	NT	EM ◇ E	NT F	NT		NT B	NT	TP ◇1 C	NT	NT	NT D	NT I	NT	NT J		NT	NT K	NT	TP ◇1 C	NT	NT	NT D	NT
Nottingham 8	d			07 45								08 11											09 15		
Langley Mill	d											08 31											09 32		
Alfreton	d			08 07								08 39											09 40		
Chesterfield	d			08 18								08 51											09 52		
Dronfield	d			08 25								08 58											09 59		
Sheffield 7 29,31	a			08 38								09 15											10 15		
	d	08 25	08 36		08 41	08 51		08 53	09 06	09 11	09 14	09 18	09 25	09 31	09 36	09 41		09 50	09 53	10 06	10 11	10 14	10 18	10 24	10 36
Meadowhall 4 29,31	a	08 30	08 41		08 46	08 56		08 59	09 11	09 15	09 20	09 23	09 33	09 38	09 41	09 46		09 55	09 58	10 11	10 16	10 20	10 23	10 29	10 41
	d		08 42			08 57			09 12		09 21	09 24			09 42			09 56		10 12		10 21	10 24		10 42
Chapeltown	d		08 48						09 18						09 48					10 18					10 48
Elsecar	d								09 23											10 23					
Wombwell	d		08 55						09 27						09 55					10 27					10 55
Barnsley	a		09 00			09 11			09 32			09 40			10 00			10 11		10 32			10 40		11 00
	d		09 01			09 12			09 33			09 42			10 01			10 12		10 33			10 42		11 01
Dodworth	d		09 07												10 07										11 07
Silkstone Common	d		09 11												10 11										11 11
Penistone	d		09 18												10 18										11 18
Denby Dale	d		09 24												10 24										11 24
Shepley	d		09 29												10 29										11 29
Stocksmoor	d		09 32												10 32										11 32
Brockholes	d		09 36												10 36										11 36
Honley	d		09 38												10 38										11 38
Berry Brow	d		09 41												10 41										11 41
Lockwood	d		09 44												10 44										11 44
Huddersfield	a		09 49												10 49										11 49
Darton	d								09 38											10 38					
Wakefield Kirkgate 4 31	a					09 27			09 49			09 57						10 27		10 49			10 57		
	d					09 28			09 50			09 58						10 28		10 50			10 58		
Normanton	d								09 54											10 54					
Castleford	a								10 00											11 00					
Woodlesford	a								10 12											11 12					
Leeds 10 31	a					09 49			10 25		10 40	10 18						10 48		11 25		11 40	11 18		

A To Beverley
B To Adwick
C From Manchester Airport to Cleethorpes
D To Scunthorpe
E To Liverpool Lime Street
F To Bridlington
G From Retford
H From Derby
I To York
J To Scarborough
K From Lincoln to Adwick

Table 34

Saturdays
until 1 October

Nottingham, Sheffield - Barnsley - Huddersfield and Leeds

		NT		NT	NT	NT	TP	NT	NT	NT	NT	NT		NT	NT	NT	TP	NT	NT	NT	NT	NT		NT	NT
							◇1										◇1								
		A			B		C			D		E			B		C			D		A			B
							🍴										🍴								
Nottingham 8	d								10 15										11 15						
Langley Mill	d								10 32										11 31						
Alfreton	d								10 40										11 39						
Chesterfield	d								10 52										11 52						
Dronfield	d								10 59																
Sheffield 7 29,31	a								11 15										12 16						
	d	10 41		10 50	10 53	11 06	11 11	11 14	11 18	11 24	11 36	11 41		11 50	11 53	12 06	12 11	12 14	12 18	12 24	12 36	12 41		12 50	12 53
Meadowhall 4 29,31	a	10 46		10 55	10 58	11 11	11 16	11 20	11 23	11 29	11 41	11 46		11 55	11 58	12 11	12 16	12 20	12 23	12 29	12 41	12 46		12 55	12 58
	d			10 56		11 12		11 21	11 24		11 42			11 56		12 12		12 21	12 24		12 42			12 56	
Chapeltown	d					11 18					11 48					12 18					12 48				
Elsecar	d					11 23										12 23									
Wombwell	d					11 27					11 55					12 27					12 55				
Barnsley	a			11 11		11 32			11 40		12 00			12 10		12 32			12 40		13 00			13 11	
	d			11 12		11 33			11 41		12 01			12 11		12 33			12 42		13 01			13 12	
Dodworth	d										12 07										13 07				
Silkstone Common	d										12 11										13 11				
Penistone	d										12 18										13 18				
Denby Dale	d										12 24										13 24				
Shepley	d										12 29										13 29				
Stocksmoor	d										12 32										13 32				
Brockholes	d										12 36										13 36				
Honley	d										12 38										13 38				
Berry Brow	d										12 41										13 41				
Lockwood	d										12 44										13 44				
Huddersfield	a										12 49										13 49				
Darton	d					11 38										12 38									
Wakefield Kirkgate 4 31	a			11 27		11 49			11 57					12 27		12 49			12 57					13 27	
	d			11 28		11 50			11 58					12 28		12 50			12 58					13 28	
Normanton	d					11 54										12 54									
Castleford	a					12 00										13 00									
Woodlesford	a					12 12										13 12									
Leeds 10 31	a			11 48		12 25		12 40	12 18					12 48		13 25		13 43	13 18					13 49	

		NT	TP	NT	NT	NT	NT	NT		NT	NT	NT	NT	TP	NT	NT	NT	NT		NT	NT	NT	NT	TP	NT
			◇1											◇1										◇1	
			C			D	F			A		B		C			D			E		B		C	
			🍴											🍴										🍴	
Nottingham 8	d				12 15											13 15									
Langley Mill	d				12 32											13 32									
Alfreton	d				12 40											13 40									
Chesterfield	d				12 52											13 52									
Dronfield	d				12 59											13 59									
Sheffield 7 29,31	a				13 15											14 15									
	d	13 06	13 11	13 14	13 18	13 24	13 28	13 36		13 41	13 50	13 53	14 06	14 11	14 14	14 18	14 24	14 36		14 41	14 50	14 53	15 06	15 11	15 14
Meadowhall 4 29,31	a	13 11	13 16	13 20	13 23	13 29	13 34	13 41		13 46	13 55	13 58	14 11	14 16	14 20	14 23	14 29	14 41		14 46	14 55	14 58	15 11	15 16	15 20
	d	13 12		13 21	13 24			13 42			13 56		14 12		14 21	14 24		14 42			14 56		15 12		15 21
Chapeltown	d	13 18						13 48					14 18					14 48					15 18		
Elsecar	d	13 23											14 23										15 23		
Wombwell	d	13 27						13 55					14 27					14 55					15 27		
Barnsley	a	13 32			13 40			14 00			14 11		14 32			14 40		15 00			15 11		15 32		
	d	13 33			13 42			14 01			14 12		14 33			14 42		15 01			15 12		15 33		
Dodworth	d							14 07										15 07							
Silkstone Common	d							14 11										15 11							
Penistone	d							14 18										15 18							
Denby Dale	d							14 24										15 24							
Shepley	d							14 29										15 29							
Stocksmoor	d							14 32										15 32							
Brockholes	d							14 36										15 36							
Honley	d							14 38										15 38							
Berry Brow	d							14 41										15 41							
Lockwood	d							14 44										15 44							
Huddersfield	a							14 49										15 49							
Darton	d	13 38											14 38										15 38		
Wakefield Kirkgate 4 31	a	13 50			13 57						14 27		14 49			14 57					15 27		15 49		
	d	13 50			13 58						14 28		14 50			14 58					15 28		15 50		
Normanton	d	13 54											14 54										15 54		
Castleford	a	14 00											15 00										16 00		
Woodlesford	a	14 12											15 12										16 12		
Leeds 10 31	a	14 25		14 40	14 18						14 48		15 25		15 40	15 18					15 49		16 25		16 40

A To Bridlington
B From Lincoln to Adwick
C From Manchester Airport to Cleethorpes
D To Scunthorpe
E To Scarborough
F To York

Table 34

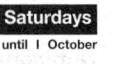

Nottingham, Sheffield - Barnsley - Huddersfield and Leeds

			NT	NT	NT	NT	NT	NT	NT	TP	NT	NT	NT	NT	NT	NT	NT	NT	TP	NT	NT	NT	NT
				A		B		C		◇1 D			E		B		C		◇1 D			E	
Nottingham 8		d	14 15									15 15									16 15		
Langley Mill		d	14 30									15 32									16 32		
Alfreton		d	14 38									15 40									16 40		
Chesterfield		d	14 52									15 53									16 54		
Dronfield		d	14 59									16 00									17 01		
Sheffield 7	29,31	a	15 15									16 14									17 17		
		d	15 18	15 24	15 36	15 41	15 50	15 53	16 06	16 11	16 14	16 18	16 24	16 36	16 41	16 50	16 53	17 06	17 11	17 14	17 18	17 25	17 36
Meadowhall 4	29,31	a	15 23	15 29	15 41	15 46	15 55	15 58	16 11	16 16	16 20	16 23	16 29	16 41	16 46	16 55	16 58	17 11	17 16	17 21	17 23	17 30	17 41
		d	15 24		15 42		15 56		16 12		16 21	16 24		16 42		16 56		17 12		17 21	17 24		17 42
Chapeltown		d			15 48				16 18					16 48				17 18					17 48
Elsecar		d							16 23					16 53				17 23					17 53
Wombwell		d			15 55				16 27					16 57				17 27					17 57
Barnsley		a	15 40		16 00		16 11		16 32			16 40		17 02		17 11		17 32			17 40		18 02
		d	15 42		16 01		16 12		16 33			16 42		17 03		17 12		17 33			17 42		18 03
Dodworth		d			16 07									17 09									18 09
Silkstone Common		d			16 11									17 13									18 13
Penistone		d			16 18									17 20									18 20
Denby Dale		d			16 24									17 26									18 26
Shepley		d			16 29									17 31									18 31
Stocksmoor		d			16 32									17 34									18 34
Brockholes		d			16 36									17 38									18 38
Honley		d			16 38									17 40									18 40
Berry Brow		d			16 41									17 43									18 43
Lockwood		d			16 44									17 46									18 46
Huddersfield		a			16 49									17 50									18 51
Darton		d							16 38									17 38					
Wakefield Kirkgate 4	31	a	15 57				16 27		16 49			16 57				17 28		17 49			17 57		
		d	15 58				16 28		16 50			16 58				17 28		17 50			17 58		
Normanton		d							16 54									17 54					
Castleford		a							17 00									18 00					
Woodlesford		a							17 12									18 12					
Leeds 10	31	a	16 18				16 48		17 25		17 41	17 18				17 48		18 25		18 44	18 18		

			NT	NT	NT	NT	NT	NT	TP	NT	NT	NT	NT	NT	NT	TP	NT	NT	NT	NT	NT	NT	NT	NT
			F		G				◇1 D	E		B		H		◇1 D			A		I		B	
Nottingham 8		d						17 15									18 15							
Langley Mill		d						17 32									18 32							
Alfreton		d						17 40									18 40							
Chesterfield		d						17 52									18 55							
Dronfield		d						17 59									19 02							
Sheffield 7	29,31	a						18 16									19 15							
		d	17 41	17 50	17 53	18 06	18 13	18 18	18 24	18 29	18 36	18 41	18 50	19 00	19 06	19 11	19 16	19 18	19 25	19 36	19 44	19 51	19 58	20 06
Meadowhall 4	29,31	a	17 46	17 55	17 57	18 12	18 20	18 23	18 29	18 34	18 41	18 46	18 55	19 06	19 11	19 16	19 22	19 24	19 30	19 41	19 49	19 56	20 03	20 11
		d		17 56		18 12	18 21	18 24			18 42		18 56		19 12		19 22	19 25		19 42		19 57		20 12
Chapeltown		d				18 18					18 48				19 18					19 48				20 18
Elsecar		d				18 23					18 53				19 23					19 53				20 23
Wombwell		d				18 27					18 57				19 27					19 57				20 27
Barnsley		a		18 11		18 33		18 42			19 02		19 14		19 33		19 40			20 02		20 12		20 32
		d		18 12		18 33		18 42			19 03		19 14		19 33		19 42			20 08		20 12		20 33
Dodworth		d									19 09									20 14				
Silkstone Common		d									19 13									20 18				
Penistone		d									19 20									20 25				
Denby Dale		d									19 26									20 31				
Shepley		d									19 31									20 36				
Stocksmoor		d									19 34									20 39				
Brockholes		d									19 38									20 43				
Honley		d									19 41									20 45				
Berry Brow		d									19 44									20 48				
Lockwood		d									19 46									20 51				
Huddersfield		a									19 51									20 55				
Darton		d				18 38									19 38									20 38
Wakefield Kirkgate 4	31	a		18 28		18 50		18 59					19 29		19 50		19 58					20 28		20 49
		d		18 32		18 50		18 59					19 32		19 50		19 58					20 28		20 50
Normanton		d				18 54									19 54									20 54
Castleford		a				19 00									20 00									21 00
Woodlesford		a				19 13									20 12									21 12
Leeds 10	31	a		18 51		19 27	19 43	19 23					19 55		20 26		20 20	20 38				20 48		21 26

A To Scunthorpe
B To Bridlington
C From Lincoln to Adwick
D From Manchester Airport to Cleethorpes
E To Doncaster
F To Scarborough
G From Lincoln to Hull
H From Retford to Doncaster
I To Beverley

Table 34

Saturdays
until 1 October

Nottingham, Sheffield - Barnsley - Huddersfield and Leeds

		TP	NT	NT	NT	NT		NT	NT	NT	NT	TP	NT	NT	TP	NT		NT	NT	NT	NT	NT			
		◇1										◇1			◇1										
		A	B			C				D		E			A					B		F			
Nottingham 8	d			19 15												21 15									
Langley Mill	d			19 32												21 31									
Alfreton	d			19 40												21 39									
Chesterfield	d			19 52												21 50									
Dronfield	d			19 59												21 57									
Sheffield 7 29,31	a			20 15												22 13									
	d	20 11	20 15	20 18	20 27	20 38		20 41	21 06	21 14	21 30	21 34	21 41	22 06	22 11				22 24	22 30	22 41	23 27			
Meadowhall 4 29,31	a	20 16	20 20	20 24	20 34	20 44		20 47	21 11	21 21	21 36	21 39	21 46	22 11	22 16				22 30	22 35	22 46	23 32			
	d			20 24	20 35			20 47	21 12		21 36		21 47	22 12					22 30		22 47				
Chapeltown	d							20 53	21 18				21 53	22 18							22 53				
Elsecar	d								21 23					22 23							22 58				
Wombwell	d							21 00	21 27				22 00	22 27							23 02				
Barnsley	a			20 40				21 07	21 33				22 05	22 32							23 07				
	d			20 42				21 08	21 33				22 08								23 08				
Dodworth	d							21 14					22 14								23 14				
Silkstone Common	d							21 18					22 18								23 18				
Penistone	d							21 25					22 25								23 25				
Denby Dale	d							21 31					22 31								23 31				
Shepley	d							21 36					22 36								23 36				
Stocksmoor	d							21 39					22 39								23 39				
Brockholes	d							21 43					22 43								23 43				
Honley	d							21 45					22 45								23 45				
Berry Brow	d							21 48					22 48								23 48				
Lockwood	d							21 51					22 51								23 51				
Huddersfield	a							21 56					22 56								23 59				
Darton	d								21 38																
Wakefield Kirkgate 4 31	a			20 57					21 52																
	d			20 58					21 52									22 51							
Normanton	d								21 57									22 56							
Castleford	a								22 04									23 02							
Woodlesford	a								22 14									23 14							
Leeds 10 31	a			21 19	21 47				22 29		22 45							23 29	23 40						

Saturdays
from 8 October

		NT	NT	NT	NT	NT	NT	NT	NT	NT		TP	NT	NT	NT	EM	NT	NT	NT	EM		NT	TP	NT	NT
												◇1				◇				◇1			◇1		
				D			G			G		A			C	H		I	J	K			A		
Nottingham 8	d															06 40									07 15
Langley Mill	d																								07 30
Alfreton	d															07 02									07 38
Chesterfield	d															07 13				07 42					07 50
Dronfield	d															07 20				07 49					
Sheffield 7 29,31	a															07 31				07 59					08 08
	d	23p15	05 15	05 29	05 43	06 06	06 12	06 28	06 36	06 52		06 55	07 06	07 14	07 24		07 36	07 41	07 51			08 06	08 11	08 14	08 18
Meadowhall 4 29,31	a	23p20	05 20	05 34	05 48	06 11	06 17	06 33	06 41	06 57		07 00	07 11	07 20	07 29		07 41	07 46	07 57			08 11	08 17	08 21	08 25
	d	23p21	05 21		05 49	06 12		06 34	06 42				07 12	07 21			07 42		07 57			08 12		08 22	08 25
Chapeltown	d		05 27		05 55	06 18			06 48				07 18				07 48					08 18			
Elsecar	d		05 32		06 01	06 23							07 23									08 23			
Wombwell	d		05 36		06 05	06 27			06 55				07 27				07 55					08 27			
Barnsley	a		05 43		06 11	06 32			07 00				07 32				08 00		08 11			08 32			08 40
	d					06 33			07 01				07 33				08 01		08 12			08 33			08 42
Dodworth	d								07 07								08 07								
Silkstone Common	d								07 11								08 11								
Penistone	d								07 18								08 18								
Denby Dale	d								07 24								08 24								
Shepley	d								07 29								08 29								
Stocksmoor	d								07 32								08 32								
Brockholes	d								07 36								08 36								
Honley	d								07 38								08 38								
Berry Brow	d								07 41								08 41								
Lockwood	d								07 44								08 44								
Huddersfield	a								07 54								08 53								
Darton	d					06 38							07 38									08 38			
Wakefield Kirkgate 4 31	a					06 49							07 49						08 27			08 49			08 57
	d					06 50							07 50						08 28			08 50			08 58
Normanton	d					06 54							07 54									08 54			
Castleford	a					07 00							07 59									09 00			
Woodlesford	a					07 12							08 11									09 12			
Leeds 10 31	a	00 30				07 28		07 44					08 25	08 32					08 49			09 25		09 40	09 20

A From Manchester Airport to Cleethorpes
B To Goole
C To Scunthorpe
D To Beverley
E To Cleethorpes
F To Doncaster
G To Adwick
H To Liverpool Lime Street
I To Bridlington
J From Retford
K From Derby

Table 34

Saturdays from 8 October

Nottingham, Sheffield - Barnsley - Huddersfield and Leeds

			NT A	NT	EM ◇ B	NT C	NT		NT D	NT	TP ◇1 E	NT	NT	NT A	NT F	NT	NT G		NT	NT H	NT	TP ◇1 E	NT	NT	NT A	NT
Nottingham 8		d			07 45								08 11											09 15		
Langley Mill		d											08 31											09 32		
Alfreton		d			08 07								08 39											09 40		
Chesterfield		d			08 18								08 51											09 52		
Dronfield		d			08 25								08 58											09 59		
Sheffield 7	29,31	a			08 38								09 15											10 15		
		d	08 25	08 36		08 41	08 51		08 53	09 06	09 11	09 14	09 18	09 25	09 31	09 36	09 41		09 50	09 53	10 06	10 11	10 14	10 18	10 24	10 36
Meadowhall 4	29,31	a	08 30	08 41		08 46	08 56		08 59	09 11	09 15	09 20	09 23	09 33	09 38	09 41	09 46		09 55	09 58	10 11	10 16	10 20	10 23	10 29	10 41
		d		08 42			08 57			09 12		09 21	09 24			09 42			09 56		10 12		10 21	10 24		10 42
Chapeltown		d		08 48						09 18						09 48					10 18					10 48
Elsecar		d								09 23											10 23					
Wombwell		d		08 55						09 27						09 55					10 27					10 55
Barnsley		a		09 00			09 11			09 32			09 40			10 00			10 11		10 32			10 40		11 00
		d		09 01			09 12			09 33			09 42			10 01			10 12		10 33			10 42		11 01
Dodworth		d		09 07												10 07										11 07
Silkstone Common		d		09 11												10 11										11 11
Penistone		d		09 18												10 18										11 18
Denby Dale		d		09 24												10 24										11 24
Shepley		d		09 29												10 29										11 29
Stocksmoor		d		09 32												10 32										11 32
Brockholes		d		09 36												10 36										11 36
Honley		d		09 38												10 38										11 38
Berry Brow		d		09 41												10 41										11 41
Lockwood		d		09 44												10 44										11 44
Huddersfield		a		09 50												10 53										11 53
Darton		d								09 38											10 38					
Wakefield Kirkgate 4	31	a					09 27			09 49			09 57						10 27		10 49			10 57		
		d					09 28			09 50			09 58						10 28		10 50			10 58		
Normanton		d								09 54											10 54					
Castleford		a								10 00											11 00					
Woodlesford		a								10 12											11 12					
Leeds 10	31	a					09 49			10 25		10 40	10 18						10 48		11 25		11 40	11 18		

			NT C		NT	NT H	NT	TP ◇1 E	NT	NT	NT A	NT	NT G		NT	NT H	NT	TP ◇1 E	NT	NT	NT A	NT	NT C		NT	NT H
Nottingham 8		d								10 15										11 15						
Langley Mill		d								10 32										11 31						
Alfreton		d								10 40										11 39						
Chesterfield		d								10 52										11 52						
Dronfield		d								10 59																
Sheffield 7	29,31	a								11 15										12 16						
		d	10 41		10 50	10 53	11 06	11 11	11 14	11 18	11 24	11 36	11 41		11 50	11 53	12 06	12 11	12 14	12 18	12 24	12 36	12 41		12 50	12 53
Meadowhall 4	29,31	a	10 46		10 55	10 58	11 11	11 16	11 20	11 23	11 29	11 41	11 46		11 55	11 58	12 11	12 16	12 20	12 23	12 29	12 41	12 46		12 55	12 58
		d			10 56		11 12		11 21	11 24		11 42			11 56		12 12		12 21	12 24		12 42			12 56	
Chapeltown		d					11 18					11 48					12 18					12 48				
Elsecar		d					11 23										12 23									
Wombwell		d					11 27					11 55					12 27					12 55				
Barnsley		a			11 11		11 32			11 40		12 00			12 10		12 32			12 40		13 00			13 11	
		d			11 12		11 33			11 41		12 01			12 11		12 33			12 42		13 01			13 12	
Dodworth		d										12 07										13 07				
Silkstone Common		d										12 11										13 11				
Penistone		d										12 18										13 18				
Denby Dale		d										12 24										13 24				
Shepley		d										12 29										13 29				
Stocksmoor		d										12 32										13 32				
Brockholes		d										12 36										13 36				
Honley		d										12 38										13 38				
Berry Brow		d										12 41										13 41				
Lockwood		d										12 44										13 44				
Huddersfield		a										12 52										13 53				
Darton		d					11 38										12 38									
Wakefield Kirkgate 4	31	a			11 27		11 49			11 57					12 27		12 49			12 57					13 27	
		d			11 28		11 50			11 58					12 28		12 50			12 58					13 28	
Normanton		d					11 54										12 54									
Castleford		a					12 00										13 00									
Woodlesford		a					12 12										13 12									
Leeds 10	31	a			11 48		12 25		12 40	12 18					12 48		13 25		13 43	13 18					13 49	

A To Scunthorpe
B To Liverpool Lime Street
C To Bridlington
D To Adwick
E From Manchester Airport to Cleethorpes
F To York
G To Scarborough
H From Lincoln to Adwick

Table 34

Saturdays
from 8 October

Nottingham, Sheffield - Barnsley - Huddersfield and Leeds

		NT	TP	NT	NT	NT	NT	NT		NT	NT	NT	NT	TP	NT	NT	NT	NT		NT	NT	NT	NT	TP	NT
			◇1											◇1										◇1	
			A			B	C			D		E		A			B			F		E		A	
Nottingham 8	d				12 15											13 15									
Langley Mill	d				12 32											13 32									
Alfreton	d				12 40											13 40									
Chesterfield	d				12 52											13 52									
Dronfield	d				12 59											13 59									
Sheffield 7 29,31	a				13 15											14 15									
	d	13 06	13 11	13 14	13 18	13 24	13 28	13 36		13 41	13 50	13 53	14 06	14 11	14 14	14 18	14 24	14 36		14 41	14 50	14 53	15 06	15 11	15 14
Meadowhall 4 29,31	a	13 11	13 16	13 20	13 23	13 29	13 34	13 41		13 46	13 55	13 58	14 11	14 16	14 20	14 23	14 29	14 41		14 46	14 55	14 58	15 11	15 16	15 20
	d	13 12		13 21	13 24			13 42			13 56		14 12		14 21	14 24		14 42			14 56		15 12		15 21
Chapeltown	d	13 18						13 48					14 18					14 48					15 18		
Elsecar	d	13 23											14 23										15 23		
Wombwell	d	13 27						13 55					14 27					14 55					15 27		
Barnsley	a	13 32			13 40			14 00			14 11		14 32			14 40		15 00			15 11		15 32		
	d	13 33			13 42			14 01			14 12		14 33			14 42		15 01			15 12		15 33		
Dodworth	d							14 07										15 07							
Silkstone Common	d							14 11										15 11							
Penistone	d							14 18										15 18							
Denby Dale	d							14 24										15 24							
Shepley	d							14 29										15 29							
Stocksmoor	d							14 32										15 32							
Brockholes	d							14 36										15 36							
Honley	d							14 38										15 38							
Berry Brow	d							14 41										15 41							
Lockwood	d							14 44										15 44							
Huddersfield	a							14 53										15 53							
Darton	d	13 38											14 38										15 38		
Wakefield Kirkgate 4 31	a	13 50			13 57						14 27		14 49			14 57					15 27		15 49		
	d	13 50			13 58						14 28		14 50			14 58					15 28		15 50		
Normanton	d	13 54											14 54										15 54		
Castleford	a	14 00											15 00										16 00		
Woodlesford	a	14 12											15 12										16 12		
Leeds 10 31	a	14 25		14 40	14 18						14 48		15 25		15 40	15 18					15 49		16 25		16 40

		NT	NT	NT		NT	NT	NT	NT	TP	NT	NT	NT	NT		NT	NT	NT	NT	TP	NT	NT	NT	NT	
										◇1										◇1					
			B			D		E		A			G			D		E		A			G		
Nottingham 8	d	14 15										15 15										16 15			
Langley Mill	d	14 30										15 32										16 32			
Alfreton	d	14 38										15 40										16 40			
Chesterfield	d	14 52										15 53										16 54			
Dronfield	d	14 59										16 00										17 01			
Sheffield 7 29,31	a	15 15										16 14										17 17			
	d	15 18	15 24	15 36		15 41	15 50	15 53	16 06	16 11	16 14	16 18	16 24	16 36		16 41	16 50	16 53	17 06	17 11	17 14	17 18	17 25	17 36	
Meadowhall 4 29,31	a	15 23	15 29	15 41		15 46	15 55	15 58	16 11	16 16	16 20	16 23	16 29	16 41		16 46	16 55	16 58	17 11	17 16	17 21	17 23	17 30	17 41	
	d	15 24		15 42			15 56		16 12		16 21	16 24		16 42			16 56		17 12		17 21	17 24		17 42	
Chapeltown	d			15 48					16 18					16 48					17 18					17 48	
Elsecar	d								16 23					16 53					17 23					17 53	
Wombwell	d			15 55					16 27					16 57					17 27					17 57	
Barnsley	a	15 40		16 00			16 11		16 32			16 40		17 02			17 11		17 32			17 40		18 02	
	d	15 42		16 01			16 12		16 33			16 42		17 03			17 12		17 33			17 42		18 03	
Dodworth	d			16 07										17 09										18 09	
Silkstone Common	d			16 11										17 13										18 13	
Penistone	d			16 18										17 20										18 20	
Denby Dale	d			16 24										17 26										18 26	
Shepley	d			16 29										17 31										18 31	
Stocksmoor	d			16 32										17 34										18 34	
Brockholes	d			16 36										17 38										18 38	
Honley	d			16 38										17 40										18 40	
Berry Brow	d			16 41										17 43										18 43	
Lockwood	d			16 44										17 46										18 46	
Huddersfield	a			16 52										17 54										18 53	
Darton	d								16 38										17 38						
Wakefield Kirkgate 4 31	a	15 57					16 27		16 49			16 57					17 28		17 49			17 57			
	d	15 58					16 28		16 50			16 58					17 28		17 50			17 58			
Normanton	d								16 54										17 54						
Castleford	a								17 00										18 00						
Woodlesford	a								17 12										18 12						
Leeds 10 31	a	16 18					16 48		17 25		17 41	17 18					17 48		18 25		18 44	18 18			

A From Manchester Airport to Cleethorpes
B To Scunthorpe
C To York
D To Bridlington
E From Lincoln to Adwick
F To Scarborough
G To Doncaster

Table 34

Saturdays
from 8 October

Nottingham, Sheffield - Barnsley - Huddersfield and Leeds

		NT	NT	NT	NT	NT	NT	TP	NT	NT		NT	NT	NT	NT	TP	NT	NT	NT	NT		NT	NT	NT	NT
								◇1								◇1									
		A		B				C 🛒	D			E		F		C 🛒			G			H		E	
Nottingham 8 🚌	d						17 15										18 15								
Langley Mill	d						17 32										18 32								
Alfreton	d						17 40										18 40								
Chesterfield	d						17 52										18 55								
Dronfield	d						17 59										19 02								
Sheffield 7 29,31 🚌	a						18 16										19 15								
	d	17 41	17 50	17 53	18 06	18 13	18 18	18 24	18 29	18 36		18 41	18 50	19 00	19 06	19 11	19 16	19 18	19 25	19 36		19 44	19 51	19 58	20 06
Meadowhall 4 29,31 🚌	a	17 46	17 55	17 57	18 12	18 20	18 23	18 29	18 34	18 41		18 46	18 55	19 06	19 11	19 16	19 22	19 24	19 30	19 41		19 49	19 56	20 03	20 11
	d		17 56		18 12	18 21	18 24			18 42			18 56		19 12		19 22	19 25		19 42			19 57		20 12
Chapeltown	d				18 18					18 48					19 18					19 48					20 18
Elsecar	d				18 23					18 53					19 23					19 53					20 23
Wombwell	d				18 27					18 57					19 27					19 57					20 27
Barnsley	a		18 11		18 33		18 42			19 02			19 14		19 33		19 40			20 02			20 12		20 32
	d		18 12		18 33		18 42			19 03			19 14		19 33		19 42			20 08			20 12		20 33
Dodworth	d									19 09										20 14					
Silkstone Common	d									19 13										20 18					
Penistone	d									19 20										20 25					
Denby Dale	d									19 26										20 31					
Shepley	d									19 31										20 36					
Stocksmoor	d									19 34										20 39					
Brockholes	d									19 38										20 43					
Honley	d									19 41										20 45					
Berry Brow	d									19 44										20 48					
Lockwood	d									19 46										20 51					
Huddersfield	a									19 54										21 00					
Darton	d				18 38										19 38										20 38
Wakefield Kirkgate 4 31	a		18 28		18 50		18 59						19 29		19 50		19 58						20 28		20 49
	d		18 32		18 50		18 59						19 32		19 50		19 58						20 28		20 50
Normanton	d				18 54										19 54										20 54
Castleford	a				19 00										20 00										21 00
Woodlesford	a				19 13										20 12										21 12
Leeds 10 31	a		18 51		19 27	19 43	19 23						19 55		20 26		20 20	20 38					20 48		21 26

		TP	NT	NT	NT	NT		NT	NT	NT	NT	TP	NT	NT	TP	NT		NT	NT	NT	NT	NT
		◇1										◇1			◇1							
		C	I			G				H		J			C					I		D
Nottingham 8 🚌	d			19 15												21 15						
Langley Mill	d			19 32												21 31						
Alfreton	d			19 40												21 39						
Chesterfield	d			19 52												21 50						
Dronfield	d			19 59												21 57						
Sheffield 7 29,31 🚌	a			20 15												22 13						
	d	20 11	20 15	20 18	20 27	20 38		20 41	21 06	21 14	21 30	21 34	21 41	22 06	22 11				22 24	22 30	22 41	23 27
Meadowhall 4 29,31 🚌	a	20 16	20 20	20 24	20 34	20 44		20 47	21 11	21 21	21 36	21 39	21 46	22 11	22 16				22 30	22 35	22 46	23 32
	d			20 24	20 35			20 47	21 12		21 36		21 47	22 12					22 30		22 47	
Chapeltown	d							20 53	21 18				21 53	22 18							22 53	
Elsecar	d								21 23					22 23							22 58	
Wombwell	d							21 00	21 27				22 00	22 27							23 02	
Barnsley	a			20 40				21 07	21 33				22 05	22 32							23 07	
	d			20 42				21 08	21 33				22 08								23 08	
Dodworth	d							21 14					22 14								23 14	
Silkstone Common	d							21 18					22 18								23 18	
Penistone	d							21 25					22 25								23 25	
Denby Dale	d							21 31					22 31								23 31	
Shepley	d							21 36					22 36								23 36	
Stocksmoor	d							21 39					22 39								23 39	
Brockholes	d							21 43					22 43								23 43	
Honley	d							21 45					22 45								23 45	
Berry Brow	d							21 48					22 48								23 48	
Lockwood	d							21 51					22 51								23 51	
Huddersfield	a							22 01					23 01								00 03	
Darton	d								21 38													
Wakefield Kirkgate 4 31	a			20 57					21 52													
	d			20 58					21 52									22 51				
Normanton	d								21 57									22 56				
Castleford	a								22 04									23 02				
Woodlesford	a								22 14									23 14				
Leeds 10 31	a			21 19	21 47				22 29		22 45							23 29	23 40			

A To Scarborough
B From Lincoln to Hull
C From Manchester Airport to Cleethorpes
D To Doncaster
E To Bridlington
F From Retford to Doncaster
G To Scunthorpe
H To Beverley
I To Goole
J To Cleethorpes

Table 34

Sundays

until 2 October

Nottingham, Sheffield - Barnsley - Huddersfield and Leeds

		NT A	NT	NT B	NT ◇	NT	NT	TP ◇1 C	NT B	NT		NT A	NT	NT	NT	TP ◇1 D	NT	NT E	NT B	NT		NT	TP ◇1 F	NT	NT G
Nottingham 8 🚊	d												10 06				11 15							12 19	
Langley Mill	d												10 27				11 31							12 35	
Alfreton	d												10 35				11 39							12 43	
Chesterfield	d												10 54				11 51							12 54	
Dronfield	d												11 01				11 58							13 01	
Sheffield 7 29,31 🚊	a												11 15				12 15							13 16	
	d	08 00	08 39	08 45	09 17	09 36	09 39	09 52	10 26	10 39		11 05	11 17	11 36	11 49	12 11	12 16	12 24	12 28	12 35		12 39	13 11	13 17	13 24
Meadowhall 4 29,31 🚊	a	08 05	08 44	08 50	09 22	09 41	09 44	09 57	10 31	10 44		11 10	11 22	11 41	11 54	12 16	12 22	12 29	12 33	12 40		12 44	13 16	13 22	13 29
	d		08 45		09 23	09 42	09 45			10 45			11 23	11 42	11 55		12 23			12 41		12 45		13 23	
Chapeltown	d		08 51				09 51			10 51					12 01							12 55			
Elsecar	d		08 56				09 56			10 56					12 06							13 00			
Wombwell	d		09 00				10 00			11 00					12 10							13 04			
Barnsley	a		09 05		09 37		10 05			11 05			11 37		12 15		12 37			12 55		13 09		13 37	
	d		09 10		09 37		10 06			11 10			11 37		12 16		12 37			13 06		13 10		13 37	
Dodworth	d						10 12								12 22					13 12					
Silkstone Common	d						10 16								12 26					13 16					
Penistone	d						10 23								12 33					13 23					
Denby Dale	d						10 29								12 39					13 29					
Shepley	d						10 34								12 44					13 34					
Stocksmoor	d						10 37								12 47					13 37					
Brockholes	d						10 41								12 51					13 41					
Honley	d						10 43								12 53					13 43					
Berry Brow	d						10 46								12 56					13 46					
Lockwood	d						10 49								12 59					13 49					
Huddersfield	a						10 53								13 08					13 53					
Darton	d		09 15							11 15												13 15			
Wakefield Kirkgate 4 31	a		09 29		09 55					11 29			11 52				12 52					13 29		13 52	
	d		09 30		09 55					11 30			11 53				12 53					13 30		13 53	
Normanton	d		09 34							11 34												13 34			
Castleford	a		09 40							11 40												13 40			
Woodlesford	a		09 52							11 51												13 51			
Leeds 10 31	a		10 04		10 15	10 52				12 05			12 18	12 53			13 18					14 04		14 18	

		NT	NT	TP ◇1 D	NT	NT E		NT B	NT	TP ◇1 D	NT	NT A	NT G	NT	NT H	TP ◇1 D		NT	NT E	NT B	NT I	NT J	NT	TP ◇1 D	NT
Nottingham 8 🚊	d				13 09						14 19							15 12							16 14
Langley Mill	d				13 27						14 35							15 34							16 30
Alfreton	d				13 35						14 43							15 44							16 38
Chesterfield	d				13 46						14 54							15 53							16 50
Dronfield	d				13 53						15 01							16 00							16 57
Sheffield 7 29,31 🚊	a				14 07						15 15							16 15							17 15
	d	13 36	13 39	14 11	14 17	14 22		14 28	14 39	15 11	15 17	15 24	15 28	15 36	15 39	16 11		16 17	16 24	16 28	16 36	16 39	16 54	17 11	17 17
Meadowhall 4 29,31 🚊	a	13 41	13 44	14 16	14 22	14 27		14 33	14 44	15 16	15 22	15 29	15 33	15 41	15 42	16 16		16 22	16 29	16 33	16 41	16 44	16 59	17 16	17 22
	d	13 42	13 45		14 23				14 45		15 23			15 42	15 43			16 23				16 45	17 00		17 23
Chapeltown	d		13 51						14 51						15 49							16 51			
Elsecar	d		13 56						14 56						15 54							16 56			
Wombwell	d		14 00						15 00						15 58							17 00			
Barnsley	a		14 05		14 37				15 05		15 37				16 03			16 37				17 05	17 14		17 37
	d		14 06		14 37				15 10		15 37				16 04			16 37				17 10	17 15		17 37
Dodworth	d		14 12												16 10								17 21		
Silkstone Common	d		14 16												16 14								17 25		
Penistone	d		14 23												16 21								17 32		
Denby Dale	d		14 29												16 27								17 38		
Shepley	d		14 34												16 32								17 43		
Stocksmoor	d		14 37												16 35								17 46		
Brockholes	d		14 41												16 39								17 50		
Honley	d		14 43												16 41								17 52		
Berry Brow	d		14 46												16 44								17 55		
Lockwood	d		14 49												16 47								17 58		
Huddersfield	a		14 53												16 53								18 05		
Darton	d								15 15													17 15			
Wakefield Kirkgate 4 31	a				14 52				15 29		15 52							16 52				17 29			17 52
	d				14 53				15 30		15 53							16 53				17 30			17 53
Normanton	d								15 34													17 34			
Castleford	a								15 40													17 40			
Woodlesford	a								15 51													17 51			
Leeds 10 31	a	14 47			15 18				16 04		16 18			16 54				17 18				18 05			18 18

A To Doncaster
B To Scarborough
C To Cleethorpes
D From Manchester Airport to Cleethorpes
E To Goole
F From Manchester Piccadilly to Doncaster
G To Bridlington
H From Retford
I To Moorthorpe
J From Lincoln

Table 34

Sundays

until 2 October

Nottingham, Sheffield - Barnsley - Huddersfield and Leeds

		NT		NT	NT	NT	TP	NT	NT	NT	NT	NT		TP	NT	NT	NT	NT	NT	TP	NT	NT		NT	TP
							◇1							◇1						◇1					◇1
		A		B			C		A	D		E		C		A			F	C		G			C
Nottingham 8 ⇌	d							17 14							18 14						19 19				
Langley Mill	d							17 30							18 30						19 35				
Alfreton	d							17 38							18 38						19 43				
Chesterfield	d							17 51							18 50						19 54				
Dronfield	d							17 58							18 56						20 01				
Sheffield 7 29,31 ⇌	a							18 15							19 16						20 15				
	d	17 25		17 28	17 36	17 39	18 11	18 17	18 25	18 28	18 39	18 57		19 11	19 16	19 29	19 36	19 39	20 02	20 11	20 17	20 28		20 39	21 11
Meadowhall 4 29,31 ⇌	a	17 30		17 33	17 44	17 46	18 16	18 22	18 30	18 34	18 44	19 04		19 16	19 22	19 34	19 41	19 44	20 08	20 16	20 22	20 33		20 44	21 16
	d				17 44	17 46		18 23			18 45				19 23		19 42	19 45			20 23			20 45	
Chapeltown	d					17 52					18 51							19 51						20 51	
Elsecar	d					17 58					18 56							19 56						20 56	
Wombwell	d					18 01					19 00							20 00						21 00	
Barnsley	a					18 08		18 37			19 05				19 37			20 05			20 37			21 06	
	d					18 10		18 37			19 10				19 37			20 06			20 37			21 10	
Dodworth	d					18 16												20 12							
Silkstone Common	d					18 20												20 16							
Penistone	d					18 27												20 23							
Denby Dale	d					18 34												20 29							
Shepley	d					18 39												20 34							
Stocksmoor	d					18 41												20 37							
Brockholes	d					18 45												20 41							
Honley	d					18 48												20 43							
Berry Brow	d					18 51												20 46							
Lockwood	d					18 53												20 49							
Huddersfield	a					18 58												20 53							
Darton	d										19 15													21 15	
Wakefield Kirkgate 4 31	a							18 52			19 29				19 52						20 52			21 29	
	d							18 53			19 30				19 53						20 53			21 30	
Normanton	d										19 34													21 34	
Castleford	a										19 41													21 40	
Woodlesford	a										19 53													21 51	
Leeds 10 31	a				18 49			19 18			20 05				20 18		20 52				21 16			22 04	

		NT	NT	NT	NT	NT	NT	TP	NT		NT
								◇1			
			F			F	A	H			A
Nottingham 8 ⇌	d	20 13							21 20		
Langley Mill	d	20 29							21 41		
Alfreton	d	20 37							21 49		
Chesterfield	d	20 48							22 08		
Dronfield	d								22 15		
Sheffield 7 29,31 ⇌	a	21 14							22 32		
	d		21 24	21 36	21 43	22 13	22 26	22 30	22 39		23 34
Meadowhall 4 29,31 ⇌	a		21 29	21 41	21 48	22 18	22 31	22 35	22 44		23 39
	d			21 42	21 49				22 45		
Chapeltown	d				21 55				22 51		
Elsecar	d				22 00				22 56		
Wombwell	d				22 04				23 00		
Barnsley	a				22 09				23 05		
	d								23 10		
Dodworth	d										
Silkstone Common	d										
Penistone	d										
Denby Dale	d										
Shepley	d										
Stocksmoor	d										
Brockholes	d										
Honley	d										
Berry Brow	d										
Lockwood	d										
Huddersfield	a										
Darton	d								23 15		
Wakefield Kirkgate 4 31	a								23 26		
	d								23 27		
Normanton	d								23 34		
Castleford	a								23 40		
Woodlesford	a								23 53		
Leeds 10 31	a			22 52					00 05		

A To Doncaster
B To Bridlington
C From Manchester Airport to Cleethorpes
D To Beverley
E To Moorthorpe
F To Hull
G To Goole
H To Cleethorpes

Table 34

Sundays
from 9 October

Nottingham, Sheffield - Barnsley - Huddersfield and Leeds

			NT	NT	NT	NT	NT	NT	NT	TP	NT	NT	NT	NT	NT	NT	TP	NT	NT	NT	NT	NT	TP	NT
							◇			◇1							◇1						◇1	
				A		B				C	B		A				D		E	B			F	
Nottingham 8	⇌	d												10 06				11 15						12 19
Langley Mill		d												10 27				11 31						12 35
Alfreton		d												10 35				11 39						12 43
Chesterfield		d												10 54				11 51						12 54
Dronfield		d												11 01				11 58						13 01
Sheffield 7	29,31 ⇌	a												11 15				12 15						13 16
		d	22p41	08 00	08 39	08 45	09 17	09 36	09 39	09 52	10 26	10 39	11 05	11 17	11 36	11 49	12 11	12 16	12 24	12 28	12 35	12 39	13 11	13 17
Meadowhall 4	29,31 ⇌	a	22p46	08 05	08 44	08 50	09 22	09 41	09 44	09 57	10 31	10 44	11 10	11 22	11 41	11 54	12 16	12 22	12 29	12 33	12 40	12 44	13 16	13 22
		d	22p47		08 45		09 23	09 42	09 45			10 45		11 23	11 42	11 55		12 23			12 41	12 45		13 23
Chapeltown		d	22p53		08 51				09 51			10 51				12 01						12 55		
Elsecar		d	22p58		08 56				09 56			10 56				12 06						13 00		
Wombwell		d	23p02		09 00				10 00			11 00				12 10						13 04		
Barnsley		a	23p07		09 05		09 37		10 05			11 05		11 37		12 15		12 37			12 55	13 09		13 37
		d	23p08		09 10		09 37		10 06			11 10		11 37		12 16		12 37			13 06	13 10		13 37
Dodworth		d	23p14						10 12							12 22					13 12			
Silkstone Common		d	23p18						10 16							12 26					13 16			
Penistone		d	23p25						10 23							12 33					13 23			
Denby Dale		d	23p31						10 29							12 39					13 29			
Shepley		d	23p36						10 34							12 44					13 34			
Stocksmoor		d	23p39						10 37							12 47					13 37			
Brockholes		d	23p43						10 41							12 51					13 41			
Honley		d	23p45						10 43							12 53					13 43			
Berry Brow		d	23p48						10 46							12 56					13 46			
Lockwood		d	23p51						10 49							12 59					13 49			
Huddersfield		a	00 03						10 58							13 08					13 58			
Darton		d			09 15							11 15										13 15		
Wakefield Kirkgate 4	31	a			09 29		09 55					11 29		11 52				12 52				13 29		13 52
		d			09 30		09 55					11 30		11 53				12 53				13 30		13 53
Normanton		d			09 34							11 34										13 34		
Castleford		a			09 40							11 40										13 40		
Woodlesford		a			09 52							11 51										13 51		
Leeds 10	31	a			10 04		10 15	10 52				12 05		12 18	12 53			13 18				14 04		14 18

			NT	NT	NT	TP	NT	NT	NT	NT	TP	NT	NT	NT	NT	NT	TP	NT	NT	NT	NT	NT	NT	TP
						◇1					◇1						◇1							◇1
			G			D		E	B		D		A	G		H	D		E	B	I	J		D
Nottingham 8	⇌	d					13 09					14 19						15 12						
Langley Mill		d					13 27					14 35						15 34						
Alfreton		d					13 35					14 43						15 44						
Chesterfield		d					13 46					14 54						15 53						
Dronfield		d					13 53					15 01						16 00						
Sheffield 7	29,31 ⇌	a					14 07					15 15						16 15						
		d	13 24	13 36	13 39	14 11	14 17	14 22	14 28	14 39	15 11	15 17	15 24	15 28	15 36	15 39	16 11	16 17	16 24	16 28	16 36	16 39	16 54	17 11
Meadowhall 4	29,31 ⇌	a	13 29	13 41	13 44	14 16	14 22	14 27	14 33	14 44	15 16	15 22	15 29	15 33	15 41	15 42	16 16	16 22	16 29	16 33	16 41	16 44	16 59	17 16
		d		13 42	13 45		14 23			14 45		15 23			15 42	15 43		16 23				16 45	17 00	
Chapeltown		d			13 51					14 51						15 49						16 51		
Elsecar		d			13 56					14 56						15 54						16 56		
Wombwell		d			14 00					15 00						15 58						17 00		
Barnsley		a			14 05		14 37			15 05		15 37				16 03		16 37				17 05	17 14	
		d			14 06		14 37			15 10		15 37				16 04		16 37				17 10	17 15	
Dodworth		d			14 12											16 10							17 21	
Silkstone Common		d			14 16											16 14							17 25	
Penistone		d			14 23											16 21							17 32	
Denby Dale		d			14 29											16 27							17 38	
Shepley		d			14 34											16 32							17 43	
Stocksmoor		d			14 37											16 35							17 46	
Brockholes		d			14 41											16 39							17 50	
Honley		d			14 43											16 41							17 52	
Berry Brow		d			14 46											16 44							17 55	
Lockwood		d			14 49											16 47							17 58	
Huddersfield		a			14 58											16 57							18 07	
Darton		d								15 15												17 15		
Wakefield Kirkgate 4	31	a					14 52			15 29		15 52						16 52				17 29		
		d					14 53			15 30		15 53						16 53				17 30		
Normanton		d								15 34												17 34		
Castleford		a								15 40												17 40		
Woodlesford		a								15 51												17 51		
Leeds 10	31	a		14 47			15 18			16 04		16 18			16 54			17 18				18 05		

A To Doncaster
B To Scarborough
C To Cleethorpes
D From Manchester Airport to Cleethorpes
E To Goole
F From Manchester Piccadilly to Doncaster
G To Bridlington
H From Retford
I To York
J From Lincoln

Table 34

Sundays
from 9 October

Nottingham, Sheffield - Barnsley - Huddersfield and Leeds

		NT		NT	NT	NT	NT	TP	NT	NT	NT	NT		NT	TP	NT	NT	NT	NT	NT	TP	NT		NT	NT
								◇1							◇1						◇1				
				A	B			C		A	D			E	C		A			F	C			G	
Nottingham 8	d	16 14							17 14							18 14						19 19			
Langley Mill	d	16 30							17 30							18 30						19 35			
Alfreton	d	16 38							17 38							18 38						19 43			
Chesterfield	d	16 50							17 51							18 50						19 54			
Dronfield	d	16 57							17 58							18 56						20 01			
Sheffield 7 29,31	a	17 15							18 15							19 16						20 15			
	d	17 17		17 25	17 28	17 36	17 39	18 11	18 17	18 25	18 28	18 39		18 57	19 11	19 16	19 29	19 36	19 39	20 02	20 11	20 17		20 28	20 39
Meadowhall 4 29,31	a	17 22		17 30	17 33	17 44	17 46	18 16	18 22	18 30	18 34	18 44		19 04	19 16	19 22	19 34	19 41	19 44	20 08	20 16	20 22		20 33	20 44
	d	17 23				17 44	17 46		18 23			18 45				19 23		19 42	19 45			20 23			20 45
Chapeltown	d						17 52					18 51							19 51						20 51
Elsecar	d						17 58					18 56							19 56						20 56
Wombwell	d						18 01					19 00							20 00						21 00
Barnsley	a	17 37					18 08		18 37			19 05				19 37			20 05			20 37			21 06
	d	17 37					18 10		18 37			19 10				19 37			20 06			20 37			21 10
Dodworth	d						18 16												20 12						
Silkstone Common	d						18 20												20 16						
Penistone	d						18 27												20 23						
Denby Dale	d						18 34												20 29						
Shepley	d						18 39												20 34						
Stocksmoor	d						18 41												20 37						
Brockholes	d						18 45												20 41						
Honley	d						18 48												20 44						
Berry Brow	d						18 51												20 47						
Lockwood	d						18 53												20 49						
Huddersfield	a						19 02												20 57						
Darton	d											19 15													21 15
Wakefield Kirkgate 4 31	a	17 52							18 52			19 29				19 52						20 52			21 29
	d	17 53							18 53			19 30				19 53						20 53			21 30
Normanton	d											19 34													21 34
Castleford	a											19 41													21 40
Woodlesford	a											19 53													21 51
Leeds 10 31	a	18 18				18 49			19 18			20 05				20 18		20 52				21 16			22 04

		TP	NT	NT	NT	NT	NT	NT	TP		NT	NT
		◇1							◇1			
		C		F			F	A	H			A
Nottingham 8	d		20 13								21 20	
Langley Mill	d		20 29								21 41	
Alfreton	d		20 37								21 49	
Chesterfield	d		20 48								22 08	
Dronfield	d										22 15	
Sheffield 7 29,31	a		21 14								22 32	
	d	21 11		21 24	21 36	21 43	22 13	22 26	22 30		22 39	23 34
Meadowhall 4 29,31	a	21 16		21 29	21 41	21 48	22 18	22 31	22 35		22 44	23 39
	d				21 42	21 49					22 45	
Chapeltown	d					21 55					22 51	
Elsecar	d					22 00					22 56	
Wombwell	d					22 04					23 00	
Barnsley	a					22 09					23 05	
	d										23 10	
Dodworth	d											
Silkstone Common	d											
Penistone	d											
Denby Dale	d											
Shepley	d											
Stocksmoor	d											
Brockholes	d											
Honley	d											
Berry Brow	d											
Lockwood	d											
Huddersfield	a											
Darton	d										23 15	
Wakefield Kirkgate 4 31	a										23 26	
	d										23 27	
Normanton	d										23 34	
Castleford	a										23 40	
Woodlesford	a										23 53	
Leeds 10 31	a				22 52						00 05	

A To Doncaster
B To Bridlington
C From Manchester Airport to Cleethorpes
D To Beverley
E To York
F To Hull
G To Goole
H To Cleethorpes

Leeds and Huddersfield - Barnsley - Sheffield, Nottingham

Miles	Miles				NT MX	NT MX A	NT MX	NT	NT	TP ◇1 B	NT	NT C	NT	NT	NT	NT A	TP ◇1 D ⚲	NT	NT E	NT	NT	TP ◇1 D ⚲	NT	NT F
0	—	**Leeds** 10	31	d	22p37		23p09						05 33		06 05					06 38	06 43		07 05	
6	—	Woodlesford		d	22p45															06 46				
10¾	—	Castleford		d	22p56															06 57				
14¼	—	Normanton		d	23p01															07 03				
17¼	—	Wakefield Kirkgate 4	31	a	23p10										06 21					07 07			07 25	
—	—			d	23p10									06 04	06 21					07 08			07 25	
24¾	—	Darton		d	23p24									06 15						07 19				
—	0	**Huddersfield**		d														06 10						
—	1¼	Lockwood		d														06 13						
—	2¼	Berry Brow		d														06 16						
—	3¼	Honley		d														06 19						
—	4¼	Brockholes		d														06 22						
—	6¼	Stocksmoor		d														06 26						
—	7¼	Shepley		d														06 28						
—	9½	Denby Dale		d														06 34						
—	13½	Penistone		d														06 42						
—	16¾	Silkstone Common		d														06 47						
—	18	Dodworth		d														06 51						
28¼	21	**Barnsley**		a	23p31									06 20	06 37			06 57		07 25			07 40	
—	—			d	23p31			05 23			05 50			06 21	06 38			06 58		07 25			07 40	
32¼	25	Wombwell		d	23p36			05 28			05 55			06 26				07 03		07 30				
33¾	26½	Elsecar		d	23p40			05 32			05 59			06 30				07 07		07 34				
37	29¾	Chapeltown		d	23p45			05 37			06 04			06 35				07 12		07 39				
40¾	33½	**Meadowhall**	29,31 ⇌	a	23p51		00 08	05 43			06 15		06 37	06 41	06 49			07 20		07 48	07 44		07 53	
—	—			d	23p51	23p54	00 09	05 43		05 58	06 18	06 27	06 38	06 42	06 49	06 52	06 58	07 20	07 33	07 48	07 45	07 53	07 54	08 06
44¼	37	**Sheffield** 7	29,31 ⇌	a	00 02	00 04	00 23	05 54		06 08	06 25	06 38	06 47	06 55	07 00	07 07	07 06	07 29	07 40	07 59	07 56	08 00	08 05	08 18
—	—			d					06 00						07 03								08 05	
51¼	—	Dronfield		d					06 10						07 13								08 15	
56½	—	Chesterfield		d					06 16						07 20								08 24	
66½	—	Alfreton		d					06 30						07 33								08 35	
72¾	—	Langley Mill		d					06 37						07 40								08 42	
84¾	—	**Nottingham**		a					07 08						08 02								09 02	

			NT	NT A	NT G	NT	NT H	NT	NT	NT F	TP ◇1 D ⚲	NT I	NT	NT G	NT	NT J	NT H	NT	NT	NT F	TP ◇1 D ⚲	NT I	NT	NT G
Leeds 10	31	d			07 29	07 35		07 48	08 02					08 32	08 37			08 48	09 05					09 32
Woodlesford		d			07 37									08 40										09 40
Castleford		d			07 48									08 51										09 51
Normanton		d			07 54		←							08 57			←							09 57
Wakefield Kirkgate 4	31	a			08 00	07 54	08 00		08 23					09 03	08 54		09 03		09 23					10 01
		d			08 04	07 55	08 04		08 23					09 05	08 55		09 05		09 23					10 04
Darton		d			→		08 15							→			09 17							→
Huddersfield		d	07 10										08 10										09 13	
Lockwood		d	07 13										08 13										09 16	
Berry Brow		d	07 16										08 16										09 19	
Honley		d	07 19										08 19										09 22	
Brockholes		d	07 22										08 22										09 25	
Stocksmoor		d	07 26										08 26										09 29	
Shepley		d	07 28										08 28										09 31	
Denby Dale		d	07 34										08 34										09 36	
Penistone		d	07 42										08 42										09 44	
Silkstone Common		d	07 47										08 47										09 49	
Dodworth		d	07 51										08 51										09 53	
Barnsley		a	07 57			08 11	08 21		08 39				08 57		09 11		09 23		09 39				10 00	
		d	07 58			08 14	08 24		08 40				08 58		09 14		09 24		09 40				10 01	
Wombwell		d	08 03				08 29						09 03				09 29						10 06	
Elsecar		d	08 07				08 33						09 07				09 33							
Chapeltown		d	08 12				08 38						09 12				09 38						10 13	
Meadowhall	29,31 ⇌	a	08 20			08 31	08 45	08 50	08 52				09 19		09 27		09 46	09 50	09 52				10 20	
		d	08 21	08 23		08 31	08 45	08 51	08 52	08 57	09 01	09 16	09 21		09 28	09 33	09 46	09 50	09 52	09 55	10 01	10 08	10 21	
Sheffield 7	29,31 ⇌	a	08 30	08 33		08 39	08 56	08 59	09 02	09 05	09 08	09 26	09 30		09 37	09 41	09 56	10 00	10 02	10 05	10 08	10 19	10 31	
		d							09 05										10 05					
Dronfield		d							09 15										10 15					
Chesterfield		d							09 22										10 22					
Alfreton		d							09 33										10 33					
Langley Mill		d							09 40										10 40					
Nottingham		a							10 01										11 00					

A From Hull
B From Doncaster to Manchester Airport
C From Doncaster
D From Cleethorpes to Manchester Airport
E From Doncaster to Worksop
F From Adwick
G To Sheffield
H From Leeds
I From Bridlington
J From Scunthorpe to Lincoln

Table 34

Mondays to Fridays

until 30 September

Leeds and Huddersfield - Barnsley - Sheffield, Nottingham

		NT	NT	NT		NT	NT	NT	TP	NT	NT	NT	NT	NT		NT	NT	NT	NT	TP	NT	NT	NT	NT
									◇1											◇1				
			A	B				C	D	E		F		A		B			C	D	E		G	F
Leeds 10	31 d	09 37				09 48	10 05					10 32	10 37				10 48	11 05						11 32
Woodlesford	d											10 40												11 40
Castleford	d											10 51												11 51
Normanton	d			←								10 57				←								11 57
Wakefield Kirkgate 4	31 a	09 55		10 01			10 23					11 01	10 54			11 01		11 23						12 01
	d	09 56		10 04			10 23					11 04	10 55			11 04		11 23						12 04
Darton	d			10 15								↪				11 15								↪
Huddersfield	d										10 13											11 13		
Lockwood	d										10 16											11 16		
Berry Brow	d										10 19											11 19		
Honley	d										10 22											11 22		
Brockholes	d										10 25											11 25		
Stocksmoor	d										10 29											11 29		
Shepley	d										10 31											11 31		
Denby Dale	d										10 36											11 36		
Penistone	d										10 44											11 44		
Silkstone Common	d										10 49											11 49		
Dodworth	d										10 53											11 53		
Barnsley	a	10 12		10 21			10 39				11 00		11 11			11 21		11 39				12 00		
	d	10 14		10 24			10 40				11 01		11 14			11 24		11 40				12 01		
Wombwell	d			10 29							11 06					11 29						12 06		
Elsecar	d			10 33												11 33								
Chapeltown	d			10 38							11 13					11 38						12 13		
Meadowhall	29,31 a	10 27		10 46		10 50	10 52				11 19		11 27			11 46	11 51	11 52				12 20		
	d	10 28	10 33	10 47		10 50	10 52	10 58	11 01	11 08	11 19		11 28	11 33		11 46	11 51	11 52	11 56	12 01	12 08	12 21	12 24	
Sheffield 7	29,31 a	10 37	10 41	10 56		11 01	11 02	11 05	11 08	11 20	11 30		11 37	11 41		11 57	12 01	12 02	12 05	12 08	12 19	12 30	12 36	
	d						11 05											12 05						
Dronfield	d						11 15											12 15						
Chesterfield	d						11 22											12 22						
Alfreton	d						11 33											12 33						
Langley Mill	d						11 40											12 40						
Nottingham	a						12 02											13 00						

		NT	NT	NT	NT	NT	NT	TP	NT	NT		NT	NT	NT	NT	NT	NT	NT	TP	NT		NT	NT	NT	NT
								◇1											◇1						
			A	B			C	D	E			F		A	B			C	D	H			F		A
Leeds 10	31 d	11 37			11 48	12 05						12 32	12 37			12 48	13 05						13 32	13 37	
Woodlesford	d											12 40											13 40		
Castleford	d											12 51											13 51		
Normanton	d			←								12 57			←								13 57		
Wakefield Kirkgate 4	31 a	11 54		12 01		12 23						13 02	12 54		13 02		13 23						14 01	13 54	
	d	11 55		12 04		12 23						13 04	12 55		13 04		13 23						14 04	13 55	
Darton	d			12 15								↪			13 17								↪		
Huddersfield	d									12 13												13 13			
Lockwood	d									12 16												13 16			
Berry Brow	d									12 19												13 19			
Honley	d									12 22												13 22			
Brockholes	d									12 25												13 25			
Stocksmoor	d									12 29												13 29			
Shepley	d									12 31												13 31			
Denby Dale	d									12 36												13 36			
Penistone	d									12 44												13 44			
Silkstone Common	d									12 49												13 49			
Dodworth	d									12 53												13 53			
Barnsley	a	12 11		12 21		12 39				13 00			13 11		13 22		13 39					14 00		14 11	
	d	12 14		12 24		12 40				13 01			13 14		13 24		13 40					14 01		14 14	
Wombwell	d			12 29						13 06					13 29							14 06			
Elsecar	d			12 33											13 33										
Chapeltown	d			12 38						13 13					13 38							14 13			
Meadowhall	29,31 a	12 27		12 46	12 51	12 52				13 20			13 27		13 46	13 51	13 52					14 20		14 27	
	d	12 28	12 33	12 46	12 51	12 52	12 56	13 01	13 07	13 20			13 28	13 33	13 46	13 51	13 52	13 56	14 01	14 05		14 20		14 28	14 34
Sheffield 7	29,31 a	12 37	12 41	12 56	13 01	13 02	13 05	13 08	13 20	13 30			13 37	13 41	13 56	14 01	14 02	14 05	14 08	14 20		14 30		14 37	14 43
	d					13 05											14 05								
Dronfield	d					13 15											14 15								
Chesterfield	d					13 22											14 22								
Alfreton	d					13 33											14 33								
Langley Mill	d					13 40											14 40								
Nottingham	a					14 00											15 00								

A From Scunthorpe to Lincoln
B From Leeds
C From Adwick
D From Cleethorpes to Manchester Airport
E From Bridlington
F To Sheffield
G From York
H From Scarborough

Table 34

Mondays to Fridays

until 30 September

Leeds and Huddersfield - Barnsley - Sheffield, Nottingham

		NT	NT	NT	NT	TP		NT	NT	NT	NT	NT	NT	NT	NT	NT		TP	NT	NT	NT	NT	NT	EM	NT
						◇1												◇1						◇	
		A			B	C		D		E		F	A			B		C	G	H		E		I	F
Leeds 10	31 d		13 48	14 05						14 32	14 37			14 48	15 05							15 32	15 37		
Woodlesford	d									14 40												15 40			
Castleford	d									14 51												15 51			
Normanton	d	←								14 57			←									15 57			
Wakefield Kirkgate 4	31 a	14 01		14 23						15 01	14 54		15 01		15 23							16 01	15 54		
	d	14 04		14 23						15 04	14 55		15 04		15 23							16 04	15 55		
Darton	d	14 15								→			15 15									→			
Huddersfield	d								14 13												15 13				
Lockwood	d								14 16												15 16				
Berry Brow	d								14 19												15 19				
Honley	d								14 22												15 22				
Brockholes	d								14 25												15 25				
Stocksmoor	d								14 29												15 29				
Shepley	d								14 31												15 31				
Denby Dale	d								14 36												15 36				
Penistone	d								14 44												15 44				
Silkstone Common	d								14 49												15 49				
Dodworth	d								14 53												15 53				
Barnsley	a	14 21		14 39					15 00		15 13		15 21		15 39						16 00		16 11		
	d	14 24		14 40					15 01		15 14		15 24		15 40						16 01		16 14		
Wombwell	d	14 29							15 06				15 29								16 06				
Elsecar	d	14 33											15 33												
Chapeltown	d	14 38							15 13				15 38								16 13				
Meadowhall	29,31 a	14 46	14 50	14 52					15 20		15 27		15 46	15 50	15 51						16 20		16 27		
	d	14 46	14 50	14 52	14 56	15 01		15 07	15 20		15 28	15 33	15 46	15 50	15 52	15 57		16 01	16 07	16 18	16 20		16 28		16 33
Sheffield 7	29,31 a	14 57	15 01	15 02	15 05	15 08		15 19	15 30		15 37	15 41	15 57	16 01	16 03	16 05		16 08	16 20	16 25	16 30		16 37		16 41
	d			15 05											16 05									16 38	
Dronfield	d			15 15											16 15									16 48	
Chesterfield	d			15 22											16 22									16 56	
Alfreton	d			15 33											16 33									17 07	
Langley Mill	d			15 40											16 40										
Nottingham	a			16 00											17 00									17 31	

		NT		NT	NT	NT	TP	NT	NT	NT	NT	NT		EM	NT	NT	NT	NT	TP	NT	NT	NT		NT	NT
							◇1							◇					◇1						
		A				J	C	D		E		F		I	A			K	C	D		E			L
Leeds 10	31 d			15 48	16 05					16 32	16 37					16 48	17 05					17 32		17 37	
Woodlesford	d									16 40												17 40			
Castleford	d									16 51												17 51			
Normanton	d	←								16 57					←		17 18					17 57			
Wakefield Kirkgate 4	31 a	16 01			16 23					17 01	16 54				17 01		17 22					18 01		17 54	
	d	16 04			16 23					17 04	16 55				17 04		17 23					18 04		17 55	
Darton	d	16 15								→					17 15							→			
Huddersfield	d								16 13												17 13				
Lockwood	d								16 16												17 16				
Berry Brow	d								16 19												17 19				
Honley	d								16 22												17 22				
Brockholes	d								16 25												17 25				
Stocksmoor	d								16 29												17 29				
Shepley	d								16 31												17 31				
Denby Dale	d								16 36												17 36				
Penistone	d								16 44												17 44				
Silkstone Common	d								16 49												17 49				
Dodworth	d								16 53												17 53				
Barnsley	a	16 21			16 39				17 00		17 11				17 21		17 39				18 00			18 11	
	d	16 24			16 40				17 01		17 14				17 24		17 40				18 01			18 14	
Wombwell	d	16 29							17 06						17 29						18 06				
Elsecar	d	16 33													17 33										
Chapeltown	d	16 38							17 13						17 38						18 13				
Meadowhall	29,31 a	16 46		16 50	16 52				17 20		17 27				17 46	17 50	17 51				18 20			18 27	
	d	16 46		16 50	16 52	16 55	17 01	17 09	17 21		17 28	17 33			17 46	17 50	17 52	17 57	18 01	18 07	18 20			18 28	18 32
Sheffield 7	29,31 a	16 57		17 00	17 02	17 05	17 08	17 20	17 32		17 37	17 41			17 57	18 01	18 03	18 04	18 08	18 19	18 30			18 37	18 42
	d				17 05									17 44			18 05								
Dronfield	d				17 15									17 56			18 15								
Chesterfield	d				17 22									18 02			18 22								
Alfreton	d				17 33									18 12			18 33								
Langley Mill	d				17 40												18 40								
Nottingham	a				18 00									18 34			18 57								

A From Leeds
B From Adwick
C From Cleethorpes to Manchester Airport
D From Bridlington
E To Sheffield
F From Scunthorpe to Lincoln
G From Scarborough
H From York
I From Liverpool Lime Street to Norwich
J From Adwick to Retford
K From Doncaster
L From Scunthorpe

Leeds and Huddersfield - Barnsley - Sheffield, Nottingham

	NT A	NT B	NT B	NT	NT	NT C	TP ◇1 D 🍴	NT E	NT F	NT G	NT A	NT B	NT	NT A	NT	NT	NT C	TP ◇1 D	NT G	NT	NT B	NT
Leeds [10] 31 d			17 43	17 46	18 05							18 32	18 43		18 48	19 05					19 37	19 43
Woodlesford d												18 40									19 45	
Castleford d												18 51									19 56	
Normanton d	←											19 00		←							20 02	
Wakefield Kirkgate [4] 31 a	18 01				18 23							19 04	18 59	19 04		19 24					20 06	19 59
d	18 04				18 23							19 05	18 59	19 05		19 24					20 07	20 00
Darton d	18 15											→		19 19							→	
Huddersfield d		17 56	18 22																	19 18		
Lockwood d		17 59	18 25																	19 21		
Berry Brow d		18 02	18 28																	19 24		
Honley d		18 05	18 31																	19 27		
Brockholes d		18 08	18 34																	19 30		
Stocksmoor d		18 12	18 38																	19 34		
Shepley d		18 14	18 40																	19 36		
Denby Dale d		18 19	18 45																	19 43		
Penistone d		18 31	18 53																	19 49		
Silkstone Common d		18 36	18 58																	19 54		
Dodworth d		18 40	19 02						←		←									19 58		
Barnsley a	18 21	18 47	19 08		18 39				18 47		19 08		19 15	19 26		19 40				20 05		20 16
d	18 24	18 55	19 10		18 40				18 55		19 10		19 18	19 26		19 40				20 06		20 16
Wombwell d	18 29	→	→						19 00		19 15			19 31						20 11		
Elsecar d	18 33								19 04					19 35								
Chapeltown d	18 38								19 09		19 22			19 38						20 18		
Meadowhall 29,31 🚋 a	18 46			18 50	18 52				19 17		19 27		19 33	19 47	19 50	19 52				20 24		20 32
d	18 46			18 50	18 52	18 57	19 01	19 06	19 17	19 28	19 30		19 34	19 47	19 51	19 52	19 57	20 01	20 08	20 26		20 32
Sheffield [7] 29,31 🚋 a	18 56			19 00	19 04	19 06	19 08	19 17	19 27	19 37	19 42		19 43	19 57	19 58	20 03	20 05	20 08	20 18	20 36		20 44
d					19 05											20 04						
Dronfield d					19 15											20 15						
Chesterfield d					19 22											20 22						
Alfreton d					19 33											20 33						
Langley Mill d					19 40											20 40						
Nottingham a					20 00											21 01						

	NT H	NT A	NT	TP ◇1 I	NT	EM ◇ J	NT K	NT L	NT	NT	TP ◇1 D	NT C	NT G	NT	NT M	NT	NT	NT	NT	NT G	NT
Leeds [10] 31 d			19 48		20 30				20 37	20 48						21 37	21 48		22 37		23 09
Woodlesford d									20 45							21 45			22 45		
Castleford d									20 56							21 56			22 56		
Normanton d		←							21 02							22 02			23 01		
Wakefield Kirkgate [4] 31 a		20 06			20 46				21 06							22 06			23 10		
d		20 07			20 46				21 07							22 07			23 10		
Darton d		20 19							21 18							22 21			23 24		
Huddersfield d							20 18							21 18				22 18			
Lockwood d							20 21							21 21				22 21			
Berry Brow d							20 24							21 24				22 24			
Honley d							20 27							21 27				22 27			
Brockholes d							20 30							21 30				22 30			
Stocksmoor d							20 34							21 34				22 34			
Shepley d							20 36							21 36				22 36			
Denby Dale d							20 41							21 41				22 41			
Penistone d							20 49							21 49				22 49			
Silkstone Common d							20 54							21 54				22 54			
Dodworth d							20 58							21 58				22 58			
Barnsley a		20 24			21 02		21 08		21 24					22 05		22 27		23 05	23 31		
d		20 24			21 03		21 12		21 24					22 06		22 28		23 06	23 31		
Wombwell d		20 29					21 16		21 29					22 11		22 33		23 11	23 36		
Elsecar d		20 33							21 33							22 37		23 15	23 40		
Chapeltown d		20 38					21 23		21 38					22 18		22 42		23 20	23 45		
Meadowhall 29,31 🚋 a		20 45	20 51		21 18		21 28		21 45	21 51				22 24		22 47	22 52	23 25	23 51		00 08
d	20 33	20 46	20 51	21 09	21 20		21 29	21 34	21 46	21 52	21 59	22 03	22 07	22 25	22 44	22 47	22 53	23 26	23 51	23 54	00 09
Sheffield [7] 29,31 🚋 a	20 41	20 58	21 02	21 19	21 30		21 40	21 46	21 57	22 04	22 08	22 11	22 21	22 36	22 54	22 58	23 02	23 36	00 02	00 04	00 23
d						21 39															
Dronfield d						21 49															
Chesterfield d						21 55															
Alfreton d						22 05															
Langley Mill d						22 12															
Nottingham a						22 38															

A From Leeds
B To Sheffield
C From Doncaster
D From Cleethorpes to Manchester Airport
E From Scarborough
F From Huddersfield
G From Hull
H From Doncaster to Worksop
I From Cleethorpes
J From Liverpool Lime Street
K To Retford
L From Bridlington
M From Scunthorpe

Table 34

Mondays to Fridays

from 3 October

Leeds and Huddersfield - Barnsley - Sheffield, Nottingham

Station			NT MX	NT MX	NT MX	NT	NT	TP	NT	NT	NT		NT	NT	NT	TP	NT	NT	NT	NT	TP		NT	NT	NT	NT
								◇1								◇1					◇1					
				A				B		C					A	D		E			D			F		A
Leeds 10	31	d	22p37		23p09						05 33			06 05					06 38	06 43			07 05			
Woodlesford		d	22p45																06 46							
Castleford		d	22p56																06 57							
Normanton		d	23p01																07 03							
Wakefield Kirkgate 4	31	a	23p10											06 21					07 07				07 25			
		d	23p10										06 04	06 21					07 08				07 25			
Darton		d	23p24										06 15						07 19							
Huddersfield		d															06 05								07 08	
Lockwood		d															06 08								07 11	
Berry Brow		d															06 11								07 14	
Honley		d															06 14								07 17	
Brockholes		d															06 17								07 20	
Stocksmoor		d															06 21								07 24	
Shepley		d															06 23								07 26	
Denby Dale		d															06 34								07 34	
Penistone		d															06 42								07 42	
Silkstone Common		d															06 47								07 47	
Dodworth		d															06 51								07 51	
Barnsley		a	23p31										06 20	06 37			06 57		07 25				07 40		07 57	
		d	23p31			05 23			05 50				06 21	06 38			06 58		07 25				07 40		07 58	
Wombwell		d	23p36			05 28			05 55				06 26				07 03		07 30						08 03	
Elsecar		d	23p40			05 32			05 59				06 30				07 07		07 34						08 07	
Chapeltown		d	23p45			05 37			06 04				06 35				07 12		07 39						08 12	
Meadowhall	29,31	a	23p51		00 08	05 43			06 15		06 37		06 41	06 49			07 21		07 48	07 44			07 53		08 20	
		d	23p51	23p54	00 09	05 43		05 58	06 18	06 27	06 38		06 42	06 49	06 52	06 58	07 21	07 33	07 48	07 45	07 53		07 54	08 06	08 21	08 23
Sheffield 7	29,31	a	00 02	00 04	00 23	05 54		06 08	06 25	06 38	06 47		06 55	07 00	07 07	07 06	07 29	07 40	07 59	07 56	08 00		08 05	08 18	08 30	08 33
		d					06 00							07 03									08 05			
Dronfield		d					06 10							07 13									08 15			
Chesterfield		d					06 16							07 20									08 24			
Alfreton		d					06 30							07 33									08 35			
Langley Mill		d					06 37							07 40									08 42			
Nottingham		a					07 08							08 02									09 02			

Station			NT	NT	NT	NT	NT		NT	TP	NT	NT	NT	NT	NT	NT	NT		NT	NT	TP	NT	NT	NT	NT	NT
										◇1											◇1					
			G		H				F	D	I		G		J	H				F	D	I		G		J
Leeds 10	31	d	07 29	07 35		07 48	08 02						08 32	08 37			08 48		09 05					09 32	09 37	
Woodlesford		d	07 37										08 40											09 40		
Castleford		d	07 48										08 51											09 51		
Normanton		d	07 54		←								08 57			←								09 57		
Wakefield Kirkgate 4	31	a	08 00	07 54	08 00		08 23						09 03	08 54		09 03			09 23					10 01	09 55	
		d	08 04	07 55	08 04		08 23						09 05	08 55		09 05			09 23					10 04	09 56	
Darton		d	→		08 15								→			09 17								→		
Huddersfield		d										08 07											09 08			
Lockwood		d										08 10											09 11			
Berry Brow		d										08 13											09 14			
Honley		d										08 16											09 17			
Brockholes		d										08 19											09 20			
Stocksmoor		d										08 23											09 24			
Shepley		d										08 25											09 26			
Denby Dale		d										08 34											09 36			
Penistone		d										08 42											09 44			
Silkstone Common		d										08 47											09 49			
Dodworth		d										08 51											09 53			
Barnsley		a		08 11	08 21		08 39					08 57		09 11		09 23			09 39				10 00		10 12	
		d		08 14	08 24		08 40					08 58		09 14		09 24			09 40				10 01		10 14	
Wombwell		d			08 29							09 03				09 29							10 06			
Elsecar		d			08 33							09 07				09 33										
Chapeltown		d			08 38							09 12				09 38							10 13			
Meadowhall	29,31	a		08 31	08 45	08 50	08 52					09 20		09 27		09 46	09 50		09 52				10 20		10 27	
		d		08 31	08 45	08 51	08 52		08 57	09 01	09 16	09 21		09 28	09 33	09 46	09 50		09 52	09 55	10 01	10 08	10 21		10 28	10 33
Sheffield 7	29,31	a		08 39	08 56	08 59	09 02		09 05	09 08	09 26	09 30		09 37	09 41	09 56	10 00		10 02	10 05	10 08	10 19	10 31		10 37	10 41
		d					09 05												10 05							
Dronfield		d					09 15												10 15							
Chesterfield		d					09 22												10 22							
Alfreton		d					09 33												10 33							
Langley Mill		d					09 40												10 40							
Nottingham		a					10 01												11 00							

A From Hull
B From Doncaster to Manchester Airport
C From Doncaster
D From Cleethorpes to Manchester Airport
E From Doncaster to Worksop
F From Adwick
G To Sheffield
H From Leeds
I From Bridlington
J From Scunthorpe to Lincoln

Table 34

Mondays to Fridays

from 3 October

Leeds and Huddersfield - Barnsley - Sheffield, Nottingham

			NT A		NT	NT	NT B	TP ◇1 C 🚲	NT D	NT	NT E	NT	NT F		NT A	NT	NT	NT B	TP ◇1 C 🚲	NT D	NT	NT G	NT E		NT	NT F
Leeds 10	31	d			09 48	10 05					10 32	10 37				10 48	11 05						11 32		11 37	
Woodlesford		d									10 40												11 40			
Castleford		d									10 51												11 51			
Normanton		d	←								10 57				←								11 57			
Wakefield Kirkgate 4	31	a	10 01			10 23					11 01	10 54			11 01		11 23						12 01		11 54	
		d	10 04			10 23					11 04	10 55			11 04		11 23						12 04		11 55	
Darton		d	10 15								→				11 15								→			
Huddersfield		d								10 08											11 08					
Lockwood		d								10 11											11 11					
Berry Brow		d								10 14											11 14					
Honley		d								10 17											11 17					
Brockholes		d								10 20											11 20					
Stocksmoor		d								10 24											11 24					
Shepley		d								10 26											11 26					
Denby Dale		d								10 36											11 36					
Penistone		d								10 44											11 44					
Silkstone Common		d								10 49											11 49					
Dodworth		d								10 53											11 53					
Barnsley		a	10 21			10 39				11 00		11 11			11 21		11 39				12 00				12 11	
		d	10 24			10 40				11 01		11 14			11 24		11 40				12 01				12 14	
Wombwell		d	10 29							11 06					11 29						12 06					
Elsecar		d	10 33												11 33											
Chapeltown		d	10 38							11 13					11 38						12 13					
Meadowhall	29,31 ⇌	a	10 46		10 50	10 52				11 18		11 27			11 46	11 51	11 52				12 20				12 27	
		d	10 47		10 50	10 52	10 58	11 01	11 08	11 19		11 28	11 33		11 46	11 51	11 52	11 56	12 01	12 08	12 21	12 24			12 28	12 33
Sheffield 7	29,31 ⇌	a	10 56		11 01	11 02	11 05	11 08	11 20	11 30		11 37	11 41		11 57	12 01	12 02	12 05	12 08	12 19	12 30	12 36			12 37	12 41
		d				11 05											12 05									
Dronfield		d				11 15											12 15									
Chesterfield		d				11 22											12 22									
Alfreton		d				11 33											12 33									
Langley Mill		d				11 40											12 40									
Nottingham		a				12 02											13 00									

			NT A	NT	NT	NT B	TP ◇1 C 🚲	NT D	NT		NT E	NT	NT F	NT A	NT	NT	NT B	TP ◇1 C 🚲	NT H		NT	NT E	NT	NT F	NT A	NT
Leeds 10	31	d		11 48	12 05						12 32	12 37			12 48	13 05						13 32	13 37			13 48
Woodlesford		d									12 40											13 40				
Castleford		d									12 51											13 51				
Normanton		d	←								12 57			←								13 57			←	
Wakefield Kirkgate 4	31	a	12 01		12 23						13 02	12 54		13 02		13 23						14 01	13 54		14 01	
		d	12 04		12 23						13 04	12 55		13 04		13 23						14 04	13 55		14 04	
Darton		d	12 15								→			13 17								→			14 15	
Huddersfield		d							12 08												13 08					
Lockwood		d							12 11												13 11					
Berry Brow		d							12 14												13 14					
Honley		d							12 17												13 17					
Brockholes		d							12 20												13 20					
Stocksmoor		d							12 24												13 24					
Shepley		d							12 26												13 26					
Denby Dale		d							12 36												13 36					
Penistone		d							12 44												13 44					
Silkstone Common		d							12 49												13 49					
Dodworth		d							12 53												13 53					
Barnsley		a	12 21		12 39				13 00			13 11		13 22		13 39					14 00		14 11		14 21	
		d	12 24		12 40				13 01			13 14		13 24		13 40					14 01		14 14		14 24	
Wombwell		d	12 29						13 06					13 29							14 06				14 29	
Elsecar		d	12 33											13 33											14 33	
Chapeltown		d	12 38						13 13					13 38							14 13				14 38	
Meadowhall	29,31 ⇌	a	12 46	12 51	12 52				13 20			13 27		13 46	13 51	13 52					14 20		14 27		14 46	14 50
		d	12 46	12 51	12 52	12 56	13 01	13 07	13 20			13 28	13 33	13 46	13 51	13 52	13 56	14 01	14 05		14 20		14 28	14 34	14 46	14 50
Sheffield 7	29,31 ⇌	a	12 56	13 01	13 02	13 05	13 08	13 20	13 30			13 37	13 41	13 56	14 01	14 02	14 05	14 08	14 20		14 30		14 37	14 43	14 57	15 01
		d			13 05											14 05										
Dronfield		d			13 15											14 15										
Chesterfield		d			13 22											14 22										
Alfreton		d			13 33											14 33										
Langley Mill		d			13 40											14 40										
Nottingham		a			14 00											15 00										

A From Leeds
B From Adwick
C From Cleethorpes to Manchester Airport
D From Bridlington
E To Sheffield
F From Scunthorpe to Lincoln
G From York
H From Scarborough

Table 34

Mondays to Fridays

from 3 October

Leeds and Huddersfield - Barnsley - Sheffield, Nottingham

			NT	NT	TP		NT	NT	NT	NT	NT	NT	NT	NT	NT		TP	NT	NT	NT	NT	NT	EM	NT	NT
				A	◇■1 B		C		D		E	F			A		◇■1 B	G	H		D		◇ I	E	F
Leeds ■10	31	d	14 05						14 32	14 37			14 48	15 05							15 32	15 37			
Woodlesford		d							14 40												15 40				
Castleford		d							14 51												15 51				
Normanton		d							14 57			←									15 57				←
Wakefield Kirkgate ■4	31	a	14 23						15 01	14 54		15 01		15 23							16 01	15 54			16 01
		d	14 23						15 04	14 55		15 04		15 23							16 04	15 55			16 04
Darton		d							→			15 15									→				16 15
Huddersfield		d						14 08												15 08					
Lockwood		d						14 11												15 11					
Berry Brow		d						14 14												15 14					
Honley		d						14 17												15 17					
Brockholes		d						14 20												15 20					
Stocksmoor		d						14 24												15 24					
Shepley		d						14 26												15 26					
Denby Dale		d						14 36												15 36					
Penistone		d						14 44												15 44					
Silkstone Common		d						14 49												15 49					
Dodworth		d						14 53												15 53					
Barnsley		a	14 39					15 00		15 13		15 21		15 39						16 00		16 11			16 21
		d	14 40					15 01		15 14		15 24		15 40						16 01		16 14			16 24
Wombwell		d						15 06				15 29								16 06					16 29
Elsecar		d										15 33													16 33
Chapeltown		d						15 13				15 38								16 13					16 38
Meadowhall	29,31	a	14 52					15 20		15 27		15 46	15 50	15 51						16 20		16 27			16 46
		d	14 52	14 56	15 01		15 07	15 20		15 28	15 33	15 46	15 50	15 52	15 57		16 01	16 07	16 18	16 20		16 28		16 33	16 46
Sheffield ■7	29,31	a	15 02	15 05	15 08		15 19	15 30		15 37	15 41	15 57	16 01	16 03	16 05		16 08	16 20	16 25	16 30		16 37		16 41	16 57
		d	15 05											16 05									16 38		
Dronfield		d	15 15											16 15									16 48		
Chesterfield		d	15 22											16 22									16 56		
Alfreton		d	15 33											16 33									17 07		
Langley Mill		d	15 40											16 40											
Nottingham		a	16 00											17 00									17 31		

			NT	NT	NT	TP	NT	NT	NT	NT	NT		EM	NT	NT	NT	NT	TP	NT	NT	NT		NT	NT	NT	NT
					J	◇■1 B	C		D		E		◇ I	F			K	◇■1 B	C		D			L	F	D
Leeds ■10	31	d	15 48	16 05					16 32	16 37					16 48	17 05					17 32		17 37			
Woodlesford		d							16 40												17 40					
Castleford		d							16 51												17 51					
Normanton		d							16 57					←		17 18					17 57				←	
Wakefield Kirkgate ■4	31	a		16 23					17 01	16 54				17 01		17 22					18 01		17 54		18 01	
		d		16 23					17 04	16 55				17 04		17 23					18 04		17 55		18 04	
Darton		d							→					17 15							→				18 15	
Huddersfield		d						16 08												17 08						17 56
Lockwood		d						16 11												17 11						17 59
Berry Brow		d						16 14												17 14						18 02
Honley		d						16 17												17 17						18 05
Brockholes		d						16 20												17 20						18 08
Stocksmoor		d						16 24												17 24						18 12
Shepley		d						16 26												17 26						18 14
Denby Dale		d						16 36												17 36						18 19
Penistone		d						16 44												17 44						18 31
Silkstone Common		d						16 49												17 49						18 36
Dodworth		d						16 53												17 53						18 40
Barnsley		a		16 39				17 00		17 11				17 21		17 39				18 00			18 11		18 21	18 47
		d		16 40				17 01		17 14				17 24		17 40				18 01			18 14		18 24	18 55
Wombwell		d						17 06						17 29						18 06					18 29	→
Elsecar		d												17 33											18 33	
Chapeltown		d						17 13						17 38						18 13					18 38	
Meadowhall	29,31	a	16 50	16 52				17 20		17 27				17 46	17 50	17 51				18 20			18 27		18 46	
		d	16 50	16 52	16 55	17 01	17 09	17 21		17 28	17 33			17 46	17 50	17 52	17 57	18 01	18 07	18 20			18 28	18 32	18 46	
Sheffield ■7	29,31	a	17 00	17 02	17 05	17 08	17 20	17 32		17 37	17 41			17 57	18 01	18 03	18 04	18 08	18 19	18 30			18 37	18 42	18 56	
		d		17 05									17 44			18 05										
Dronfield		d		17 15									17 56			18 15										
Chesterfield		d		17 22									18 02			18 22										
Alfreton		d		17 33									18 12			18 33										
Langley Mill		d		17 40												18 40										
Nottingham		a		18 00									18 34			18 57										

A From Adwick
B From Cleethorpes to Manchester Airport
C From Bridlington
D To Sheffield
E From Scunthorpe to Lincoln
F From Leeds
G From Scarborough
H From York
I From Liverpool Lime Street to Norwich
J From Adwick to Retford
K From Doncaster
L From Scunthorpe

from 3 October

Leeds and Huddersfield - Barnsley - Sheffield, Nottingham

		NT	NT	NT	NT	TP		NT	NT	NT	NT	NT	NT	NT	NT	NT		NT	TP	NT	NT	NT	NT	NT	NT
						◇1													◇1						
		A			B	C		D	E	F	G	A		G				B	C	F		A		H	G
						⚲																			
Leeds 10 31	d	17 43	17 46	18 05								18 32	18 43		18 48	19 05						19 37	19 43		
Woodlesford	d											18 40										19 45			
Castleford	d											18 51										19 56			
Normanton	d											19 00		←								20 02			←
Wakefield Kirkgate 4 31	a			18 23								19 04	18 59	19 04		19 24						20 06	19 59		20 06
	d			18 23								19 05	18 59	19 05		19 24						20 07	20 00		20 07
Darton	d											↦		19 19								↦			20 19
Huddersfield	d	18 22																			19 15				
Lockwood	d	18 25																			19 18				
Berry Brow	d	18 28																			19 21				
Honley	d	18 31																			19 24				
Brockholes	d	18 34																			19 27				
Stocksmoor	d	18 38																			19 31				
Shepley	d	18 40																			19 33				
Denby Dale	d	18 45																			19 43				
Penistone	d	18 53																			19 49				
Silkstone Common	d	18 58																			19 54				
Dodworth	d	19 02							←		←										19 58				
Barnsley	a	19 08		18 39					18 47		19 08		19 15	19 26		19 40					20 05		20 16		20 24
	d	19 10		18 40					18 55		19 10		19 18	19 26		19 40					20 06		20 16		20 24
Wombwell	d	↦							19 00		19 15			19 31							20 11				20 29
Elsecar	d								19 04					19 35											20 33
Chapeltown	d								19 09		19 22			19 38							20 18				20 38
Meadowhall 29,31 🚋	a		18 50	18 52					19 17		19 27		19 33	19 47	19 50	19 52					20 24		20 32		20 45
	d		18 50	18 52	18 57	19 01		19 06	19 17	19 28	19 30		19 34	19 47	19 51	19 52		19 57	20 01	20 08	20 26		20 32	20 33	20 46
Sheffield 7 29,31 🚋	a		19 00	19 04	19 06	19 08		19 17	19 27	19 37	19 42		19 43	19 57	19 58	20 03		20 05	20 08	20 18	20 36		20 44	20 41	20 58
	d			19 05												20 04									
Dronfield	d			19 15												20 15									
Chesterfield	d			19 22												20 22									
Alfreton	d			19 33												20 33									
Langley Mill	d			19 40												20 40									
Nottingham	a			20 00												21 01									

		NT		TP	NT	EM	NT	NT	NT	NT	TP	NT		NT	NT	NT	NT	NT	NT	NT	NT	NT
				◇1		◇					◇1											
				I		J	K	L			C	B		F		M					F	
Leeds 10 31	d	19 48			20 30				20 37	20 48							21 37	21 48		22 37		23 09
Woodlesford	d								20 45								21 45			22 45		
Castleford	d								20 56								21 56			22 56		
Normanton	d								21 02								22 02			23 01		
Wakefield Kirkgate 4 31	a				20 46				21 06								22 06			23 10		
	d				20 46				21 07								22 07			23 10		
Darton	d								21 18								22 21			23 24		
Huddersfield	d						20 18								21 18				22 15			
Lockwood	d						20 21								21 21				22 18			
Berry Brow	d						20 24								21 24				22 21			
Honley	d						20 27								21 27				22 24			
Brockholes	d						20 30								21 30				22 27			
Stocksmoor	d						20 34								21 34				22 31			
Shepley	d						20 36								21 36				22 36			
Denby Dale	d						20 41								21 41				22 41			
Penistone	d						20 49								21 49				22 49			
Silkstone Common	d						20 54								21 54				22 54			
Dodworth	d						20 58								21 58				22 58			
Barnsley	a				21 02		21 08		21 24						22 05		22 27		23 05	23 31		
	d				21 03		21 12		21 24						22 06		22 28		23 06	23 31		
Wombwell	d						21 16		21 29						22 11		22 33		23 11	23 36		
Elsecar	d								21 33								22 37		23 15	23 40		
Chapeltown	d						21 23		21 38						22 18		22 42		23 20	23 45		
Meadowhall 29,31 🚋	a	20 51			21 18		21 28		21 45	21 51					22 24		22 47	22 52	23 25	23 51		00 08
	d	20 51		21 09	21 20		21 29	21 34	21 46	21 52	21 59	22 03		22 07	22 25	22 44	22 47	22 53	23 26	23 51	23 54	00 09
Sheffield 7 29,31 🚋	a	21 02		21 19	21 30		21 40	21 46	21 57	22 04	22 08	22 11		22 21	22 36	22 54	22 58	23 02	23 36	00 02	00 04	00 23
	d					21 39																
Dronfield	d					21 49																
Chesterfield	d					21 55																
Alfreton	d					22 05																
Langley Mill	d					22 12																
Nottingham	a					22 38																

A To Sheffield
B From Doncaster
C From Cleethorpes to Manchester Airport
D From Scarborough
E From Huddersfield
F From Hull
G From Leeds
H From Doncaster to Worksop
I From Cleethorpes
J From Liverpool Lime Street
K To Retford
L From Bridlington
M From Scunthorpe

Table 34

Saturdays

until 1 October

Leeds and Huddersfield - Barnsley - Sheffield, Nottingham

		NT	NT	NT	NT	TP	NT	NT	NT	NT		TP	NT	NT	NT	NT	TP	NT	NT	NT		NT	NT	NT	NT
						◇1						◇1					◇1								
			A			B		C		A		D ⊥		C			D ⊥		E			A	F		G
Leeds 10	31 d	22p37		23p09											06 38	06 43		07 05					07 29	07 35	
Woodlesford	d	22p45													06 46								07 37		
Castleford	d	22p56													06 57								07 48		
Normanton	d	23p01													07 03								07 54		←
Wakefield Kirkgate 4	31 a	23p10													07 06			07 25					08 00	07 54	08 00
	d	23p10													07 07			07 25					08 04	07 55	08 04
Darton	d	23p24													07 18								→		08 15
Huddersfield	d												06 10							07 10					
Lockwood	d												06 13							07 13					
Berry Brow	d												06 16							07 16					
Honley	d												06 19							07 19					
Brockholes	d												06 22							07 22					
Stocksmoor	d												06 26							07 26					
Shepley	d												06 28							07 28					
Denby Dale	d												06 34							07 34					
Penistone	d												06 42							07 42					
Silkstone Common	d												06 47							07 47					
Dodworth	d												06 51							07 51					
Barnsley	a	23p31											06 57		07 24			07 40		07 57				08 11	08 21
	d	23p31			05 23		05 50		06 21				06 58		07 24			07 40		07 58				08 14	08 24
Wombwell	d	23p36			05 28		05 55		06 26				07 03		07 29					08 03					08 29
Elsecar	d	23p40			05 32		05 59		06 30				07 07		07 33					08 07					08 33
Chapeltown	d	23p45			05 37		06 04		06 35				07 12		07 38					08 12					08 38
Meadowhall	29,31 ⇌ a	23p51		00 08	05 43		06 10		06 41				07 20		07 47	07 46		07 53		08 20				08 31	08 45
	d	23p51	23p54	00 09	05 43	05 58	06 10	06 30	06 42	06 52		06 58	07 21	07 32	07 49	07 47	07 53	07 54	08 07	08 22		08 25		08 31	08 46
Sheffield 7	29,31 ⇌ a	00 02	00 04	00 23	05 54	06 08	06 25	06 38	06 55	07 07		07 06	07 29	07 40	07 57	07 54	08 00	08 05	08 18	08 30		08 32		08 39	08 56
	d								07 03									08 05							
Dronfield	d								07 13									08 15							
Chesterfield	d								07 20									08 24							
Alfreton	d								07 33									08 35							
Langley Mill	d								07 40									08 42							
Nottingham	a								08 02									09 02							

		NT	NT	NT	TP	NT		NT	NT	NT	NT	NT	NT	NT	NT	TP		NT	NT	NT	NT	NT	NT	NT	NT
					◇1											◇1									
				E	D ⊥			H	F		I	G			E	D ⊥		H		F		I	G		
Leeds 10	31 d	07 48	08 05						08 32	08 37			08 48	09 05						09 32	09 37			09 48	10 05
Woodlesford	d								08 40											09 40					
Castleford	d								08 51											09 51					
Normanton	d								08 57			←								09 57			←		
Wakefield Kirkgate 4	31 a		08 23						09 03	08 54		09 03		09 23						10 01	09 55		10 01		10 23
	d		08 23						09 05	08 55		09 05		09 23						10 04	09 56		10 04		10 23
Darton	d								→			09 17								→			10 15		
Huddersfield	d					08 10													09 13						
Lockwood	d					08 13													09 16						
Berry Brow	d					08 16													09 19						
Honley	d					08 19													09 22						
Brockholes	d					08 22													09 25						
Stocksmoor	d					08 26													09 29						
Shepley	d					08 28													09 31						
Denby Dale	d					08 34													09 36						
Penistone	d					08 42													09 44						
Silkstone Common	d					08 47													09 49						
Dodworth	d					08 51													09 53						
Barnsley	a		08 39			08 57				09 11		09 23		09 39					10 00		10 12		10 21		10 39
	d		08 40			08 58				09 14		09 24		09 40					10 01		10 14		10 24		10 40
Wombwell	d					09 03						09 29							10 06				10 29		
Elsecar	d					09 07						09 33											10 33		
Chapeltown	d					09 12						09 38							10 13				10 38		
Meadowhall	29,31 ⇌ a	08 49	08 52			09 19				09 27		09 46	09 50	09 52					10 20		10 27		10 46	10 50	10 52
	d	08 51	08 52	08 56	09 01	09 20		09 24		09 29	09 33	09 46	09 50	09 52	09 55	10 01		10 08	10 21		10 28	10 33	10 47	10 50	10 52
Sheffield 7	29,31 ⇌ a	08 59	09 02	09 05	09 08	09 30		09 33		09 37	09 41	09 56	10 00	10 02	10 05	10 08		10 19	10 31		10 37	10 41	10 57	11 00	11 02
	d		09 05											10 04											11 05
Dronfield	d		09 16											10 14											11 15
Chesterfield	d		09 23											10 21											11 22
Alfreton	d		09 33											10 32											11 33
Langley Mill	d		09 41											10 40											11 40
Nottingham	a		10 02											11 00											12 02

A From Hull
B From Doncaster to Manchester Airport
C From Doncaster
D From Cleethorpes to Manchester Airport
E From Adwick
F To Sheffield
G From Leeds
H From Bridlington
I From Scunthorpe to Lincoln

Table 34

Saturdays
until 1 October

Leeds and Huddersfield - Barnsley - Sheffield, Nottingham

Station		NT A		TP ◇1 B	NT C	NT	NT D	NT	NT E	NT F	NT	NT		NT A	TP ◇1 B	NT C	NT	NT G	NT D	NT	NT E	NT F		NT	NT
Leeds 10	31 d						10 32	10 37			10 48	11 05							11 32	11 37				11 48	12 05
Woodlesford	d						10 40												11 40						
Castleford	d						10 51												11 51						
Normanton	d						10 57			←									11 57			←			
Wakefield Kirkgate 4	31 a						11 01	10 54		11 01		11 23							12 01	11 54		12 01			12 23
	d						11 04	10 55		11 04		11 23							12 04	11 55		12 04			12 23
Darton	d						→			11 15									→			12 15			
Huddersfield	d					10 13											11 13								
Lockwood	d					10 16											11 16								
Berry Brow	d					10 19											11 19								
Honley	d					10 22											11 22								
Brockholes	d					10 25											11 25								
Stocksmoor	d					10 29											11 29								
Shepley	d					10 31											11 31								
Denby Dale	d					10 36											11 36								
Penistone	d					10 44											11 44								
Silkstone Common	d					10 49											11 49								
Dodworth	d					10 53											11 53								
Barnsley	a					11 00		11 11		11 21		11 39					12 00			12 11		12 21			12 39
	d					11 01		11 14		11 24		11 40					12 01			12 14		12 24			12 40
Wombwell	d					11 06				11 29							12 06					12 29			
Elsecar	d									11 33												12 33			
Chapeltown	d					11 13				11 38							12 13					12 38			
Meadowhall	29,31 a					11 18		11 27		11 46	11 50	11 52					12 20			12 27		12 46		12 49	12 52
	d	10 58		11 01	11 08	11 19		11 28	11 33	11 46	11 50	11 52		11 58	12 01	12 08	12 21	12 24		12 28	12 33	12 46		12 50	12 52
Sheffield 7	29,31 a	11 06		11 08	11 20	11 30		11 37	11 41	11 57	12 00	12 02		12 05	12 08	12 20	12 30	12 36		12 37	12 41	12 57		13 00	13 02
	d											12 06													13 05
Dronfield	d											12 17													13 15
Chesterfield	d											12 23													13 22
Alfreton	d											12 34													13 34
Langley Mill	d											12 41													13 41
Nottingham	a											13 01													14 00

Station		NT A	TP ◇1 B	NT C	NT	NT D	NT	NT E		NT F	NT	NT	NT A	TP ◇1 B	NT H	NT	NT D	NT		NT E	NT F	NT	NT	NT A	TP ◇1 B
Leeds 10	31 d					12 32	12 37				12 48	13 05					13 32	13 37				13 48	14 05		
Woodlesford	d					12 40											13 40								
Castleford	d					12 51											13 51								
Normanton	d					12 57				←							13 57				←				
Wakefield Kirkgate 4	31 a					13 02	12 54			13 02		13 23					14 01	13 54			14 01		14 23		
	d					13 04	12 55			13 04		13 23					14 04	13 55			14 04		14 23		
Darton	d					→				13 17							→				14 15				
Huddersfield	d				12 13											13 13									
Lockwood	d				12 16											13 16									
Berry Brow	d				12 19											13 19									
Honley	d				12 22											13 22									
Brockholes	d				12 25											13 25									
Stocksmoor	d				12 29											13 29									
Shepley	d				12 31											13 31									
Denby Dale	d				12 36											13 36									
Penistone	d				12 44											13 44									
Silkstone Common	d				12 49											13 49									
Dodworth	d				12 53											13 53									
Barnsley	a				13 00		13 11			13 22		13 38				14 00		14 11			14 21		14 39		
	d				13 01		13 14			13 24		13 40				14 01		14 14			14 24		14 40		
Wombwell	d				13 06					13 29						14 06					14 29				
Elsecar	d									13 33											14 33				
Chapeltown	d				13 13					13 38						14 13					14 38				
Meadowhall	29,31 a				13 20		13 27			13 46	13 49	13 52				14 20		14 27			14 46	14 49	14 52		
	d	12 58	13 01	13 08	13 20		13 28	13 33		13 46	13 50	13 52	13 58	14 01	14 08	14 20		14 28		14 34	14 46	14 50	14 52	14 58	15 01
Sheffield 7	29,31 a	13 05	13 08	13 20	13 30		13 37	13 41		13 57	14 00	14 02	14 05	14 08	14 20	14 30		14 37		14 43	14 57	15 00	15 02	15 05	15 08
	d											14 05											15 05		
Dronfield	d											14 15											15 15		
Chesterfield	d											14 22											15 22		
Alfreton	d											14 33											15 33		
Langley Mill	d											14 40											15 40		
Nottingham	a											15 00											16 02		

A From Adwick
B From Cleethorpes to Manchester Airport
C From Bridlington
D To Sheffield
E From Scunthorpe to Lincoln
F From Leeds
G From York
H From Scarborough

Table 34

Saturdays

until 1 October

Leeds and Huddersfield - Barnsley - Sheffield, Nottingham

		NT	NT	NT		NT	NT	NT	NT	NT	NT	TP	NT
												◇1	
		A		B			C	D			E	F	G
Leeds 10	31 d			14 32		14 37			14 48	15 05			
Woodlesford	d			14 40									
Castleford	d			14 51									
Normanton	d			14 57				←					
Wakefield Kirkgate 4	31 a			15 01		14 54		15 01		15 23			
	d			15 04		14 55		15 04		15 23			
Darton	d			→				15 15					
Huddersfield	d		14 13										
Lockwood	d		14 16										
Berry Brow	d		14 19										
Honley	d		14 22										
Brockholes	d		14 25										
Stocksmoor	d		14 29										
Shepley	d		14 31										
Denby Dale	d		14 36										
Penistone	d		14 44										
Silkstone Common	d		14 49										
Dodworth	d		14 53										
Barnsley	a		15 00			15 13		15 21		15 39			
	d		15 01			15 14		15 24		15 40			
Wombwell	d		15 06					15 29					
Elsecar	d							15 33					
Chapeltown	d		15 13					15 38					
Meadowhall 29,31	a		15 20			15 27		15 46	15 49	15 51			
	d	15 07	15 20			15 28	15 33	15 46	15 50	15 52	15 57	16 01	16 07
Sheffield 7 29,31	a	15 20	15 30			15 37	15 41	15 57	16 00	16 03	16 05	16 08	16 22
	d									16 04			
Dronfield	d									16 14			
Chesterfield	d									16 21			
Alfreton	d									16 32			
Langley Mill	d									16 40			
Nottingham	a									17 00			

		NT		NT	NT	NT	EM	NT	NT	NT	NT	NT	
							◇						
		H			B		I	C	D			J	
Leeds 10	31 d				15 32	15 37				15 48	16 05		
Woodlesford	d				15 40								
Castleford	d				15 51								
Normanton	d				15 57				←				
Wakefield Kirkgate 4	31 a				16 01	15 54			16 01		16 23		
	d				16 04	15 55			16 04		16 23		
Darton	d				→				16 15				
Huddersfield	d			15 13									
Lockwood	d			15 16									
Berry Brow	d			15 19									
Honley	d			15 22									
Brockholes	d			15 25									
Stocksmoor	d			15 29									
Shepley	d			15 31									
Denby Dale	d			15 36									
Penistone	d			15 44									
Silkstone Common	d			15 49									
Dodworth	d			15 53									
Barnsley	a			16 00		16 11			16 21		16 39		
	d			16 01		16 14			16 24		16 40		
Wombwell	d			16 06					16 29				
Elsecar	d								16 33				
Chapeltown	d			16 13					16 38				
Meadowhall 29,31	a			16 20		16 27			16 46	16 49	16 52		
	d	16 18		16 20		16 28		16 33	16 46	16 50	16 52	16 55	
Sheffield 7 29,31	a	16 27		16 30		16 37		16 41	16 57	17 00	17 02	17 05	
	d						16 38				17 05		
Dronfield	d						16 48				17 15		
Chesterfield	d						16 53				17 22		
Alfreton	d						17 04				17 33		
Langley Mill	d										17 40		
Nottingham	a						17 29				18 00		

		TP	NT	NT	NT	NT	NT	EM	NT	NT		NT	NT
		◇1						◇					
		F	A		B		C	I	D				K
Leeds 10	31 d				16 32	16 37				16 48		17 05	
Woodlesford	d				16 40								
Castleford	d				16 51								
Normanton	d				16 57				←			17 18	
Wakefield Kirkgate 4	31 a				17 01	16 54			17 01			17 22	
	d				17 04	16 55			17 04			17 23	
Darton	d				→				17 15				
Huddersfield	d			16 13									
Lockwood	d			16 16									
Berry Brow	d			16 19									
Honley	d			16 22									
Brockholes	d			16 25									
Stocksmoor	d			16 29									
Shepley	d			16 31									
Denby Dale	d			16 36									
Penistone	d			16 44									
Silkstone Common	d			16 49									
Dodworth	d			16 53									
Barnsley	a			17 00		17 11			17 21			17 39	
	d			17 01		17 14			17 24			17 40	
Wombwell	d			17 06					17 29				
Elsecar	d								17 33				
Chapeltown	d			17 13					17 38				
Meadowhall 29,31	a			17 20		17 27			17 46	17 49		17 51	
	d	17 01	17 08	17 21		17 28	17 33		17 46	17 50		17 52	17 57
Sheffield 7 29,31	a	17 08	17 19	17 32		17 37	17 41		17 57	18 00		18 03	18 05
	d							17 44				18 06	
Dronfield	d							17 55				18 16	
Chesterfield	d							18 01				18 23	
Alfreton	d							18 11				18 34	
Langley Mill	d											18 41	
Nottingham	a							18 33				18 58	

		TP	NT	NT	NT	NT	NT	NT		NT	NT	NT	TP
		◇1											◇1
		F	A		B		C	D				K	F
Leeds 10	31 d				17 32	17 37				17 48	18 05		
Woodlesford	d				17 40								
Castleford	d				17 51								
Normanton	d				17 57			←					
Wakefield Kirkgate 4	31 a				18 01	17 54		18 01			18 23		
	d				18 04	17 55		18 04			18 23		
Darton	d				→			18 15					
Huddersfield	d			17 13									
Lockwood	d			17 16									
Berry Brow	d			17 19									
Honley	d			17 22									
Brockholes	d			17 25									
Stocksmoor	d			17 29									
Shepley	d			17 31									
Denby Dale	d			17 36									
Penistone	d			17 44									
Silkstone Common	d			17 49									
Dodworth	d			17 53									
Barnsley	a			18 00		18 11		18 21			18 39		
	d			18 01		18 14		18 24			18 40		
Wombwell	d			18 06				18 29					
Elsecar	d							18 33					
Chapeltown	d			18 13				18 38					
Meadowhall 29,31	a			18 20		18 27		18 46		18 50	18 52		
	d	18 01	18 08	18 20		18 28	18 33	18 46		18 50	18 52	18 56	19 01
Sheffield 7 29,31	a	18 08	18 21	18 30		18 38	18 41	18 56		19 00	19 04	19 06	19 08
	d										19 07		
Dronfield	d										19 17		
Chesterfield	d										19 23		
Alfreton	d										19 33		
Langley Mill	d										19 41		
Nottingham	a										20 01		

A From Bridlington
B To Sheffield
C From Scunthorpe to Lincoln
D From Leeds
E From Adwick
F From Cleethorpes to Manchester Airport
G From Scarborough
H From York
I From Liverpool Lime Street to Norwich
J From Adwick to Retford
K From Doncaster

Table 34

Saturdays
until 1 October

Leeds and Huddersfield - Barnsley - Sheffield, Nottingham

		NT	NT	NT	NT	NT		NT	NT	NT	NT	TP	NT	NT	NT	NT		NT	NT	NT	TP	NT	EM	NT	NT
												◇1									◇1		◇		
		A		B	C			D			E	F	B		G	C			D		H		I	J	K
Leeds 10 31	d				18 32	18 37			18 48	19 05						19 37		19 43		19 48		20 30			
Woodlesford	d				18 40											19 45									
Castleford	d				18 51											19 56									
Normanton	d				19 00			←								20 02			←						
Wakefield Kirkgate 4 31	a				19 04	18 54		19 04		19 24						20 06		19 59	20 06			20 46			
	d				19 05	18 55		19 05		19 24						20 07		20 00	20 07			20 47			
Darton	d				↪			19 19								↪			20 19						
Huddersfield	d		18 13											19 18										20 18	
Lockwood	d		18 16											19 21										20 21	
Berry Brow	d		18 19											19 24										20 24	
Honley	d		18 22											19 27										20 27	
Brockholes	d		18 25											19 30										20 30	
Stocksmoor	d		18 29											19 34										20 34	
Shepley	d		18 31											19 36										20 36	
Denby Dale	d		18 36											19 41										20 41	
Penistone	d		18 44											19 49										20 52	
Silkstone Common	d		18 49											19 54										20 57	
Dodworth	d		18 53											19 58										21 01	
Barnsley	a		19 01			19 11		19 26		19 40				20 05				20 16	20 24			21 02		21 09	
	d		19 01			19 14		19 26		19 40				20 06				20 16	20 24			21 03		21 12	
Wombwell	d		19 06					19 31						20 11					20 29					21 17	
Elsecar	d							19 35											20 33						
Chapeltown	d		19 13					19 40						20 18					20 38					21 24	
Meadowhall 29,31 ⛴	a		19 20			19 28		19 47	19 50	19 52				20 24				20 36	20 45	20 50		21 17		21 28	
	d	19 08	19 20	19 28		19 30		19 47	19 51	19 52	19 57	20 01	20 08	20 24	20 33			20 37	20 46	20 51	21 09	21 18		21 29	21 35
Sheffield 7 29,31 ⛴	a	19 19	19 30	19 37		19 39		19 57	20 00	20 03	20 06	20 08	20 18	20 36	20 41			20 44	20 58	21 00	21 19	21 30		21 41	21 46
	d									20 05													21 38		
Dronfield	d									20 15													21 48		
Chesterfield	d									20 22													21 54		
Alfreton	d									20 33													22 05		
Langley Mill	d									20 40													22 12		
Nottingham	a									21 00													22 33		

		NT		NT	TP	NT	NT	NT	NT	NT	NT	NT		NT	NT
					◇1										
					H	E	B		L						K
Leeds 10 31	d	20 37		20 48						21 37	21 48			22 44	
Woodlesford	d	20 45								21 45					
Castleford	d	20 56								21 56					
Normanton	d	21 02								22 02					
Wakefield Kirkgate 4 31	a	21 06								22 06					
	d	21 07								22 07					
Darton	d	21 18								22 21					
Huddersfield	d							21 18				22 18			
Lockwood	d							21 21				22 21			
Berry Brow	d							21 24				22 24			
Honley	d							21 27				22 27			
Brockholes	d							21 30				22 30			
Stocksmoor	d							21 34				22 34			
Shepley	d							21 36				22 36			
Denby Dale	d							21 41				22 41			
Penistone	d							21 49				22 49			
Silkstone Common	d							21 54				22 54			
Dodworth	d							21 58				22 58			
Barnsley	a	21 24						22 05		22 27		23 05			
	d	21 24						22 06		22 28		23 06			
Wombwell	d	21 29						22 11		22 33		23 11			
Elsecar	d	21 33								22 37		23 15			
Chapeltown	d	21 38						22 18		22 42		23 20			
Meadowhall 29,31 ⛴	a	21 45		21 49				22 24		22 47	22 52	23 25		23 43	
	d	21 46		21 50	21 59	22 03	22 12	22 25	22 43	22 48	22 53	23 26		23 44	23 49
Sheffield 7 29,31 ⛴	a	21 59		22 02	22 10	22 13	22 22	22 36	22 54	22 58	23 03	23 36		23 58	23 59
	d														
Dronfield	d														
Chesterfield	d														
Alfreton	d														
Langley Mill	d														
Nottingham	a														

A From Scarborough
B From Hull
C To Sheffield
D From Leeds
E From Doncaster
F From Cleethorpes to Manchester Airport
G From Scunthorpe to Worksop
H From Cleethorpes
I From Liverpool Lime Street
J To Retford
K From Bridlington
L From Scunthorpe

Table 34

Saturdays
from 8 October

Leeds and Huddersfield - Barnsley - Sheffield, Nottingham

Station			NT	NT A	NT	NT	TP ◇1 B	NT	NT C	NT	NT A		TP ◇1 D	NT	NT C	NT	NT	TP ◇1 D	NT	NT E	NT		NT A	NT F	NT	NT G
Leeds 10	31	d	22p37		23p09											06 38	06 43		07 05					07 29	07 35	
Woodlesford		d	22p45													06 46								07 37		
Castleford		d	22p56													06 57								07 48		
Normanton		d	23p01													07 03								07 54		←
Wakefield Kirkgate 4	31	a	23p10													07 06			07 25					08 00	07 54	08 00
		d	23p10													07 07			07 25					08 04	07 55	08 04
Darton		d	23p24													07 18								→		08 15
Huddersfield		d												06 05							07 05					
Lockwood		d												06 08							07 08					
Berry Brow		d												06 11							07 11					
Honley		d												06 14							07 14					
Brockholes		d												06 17							07 17					
Stocksmoor		d												06 21							07 21					
Shepley		d												06 23							07 23					
Denby Dale		d												06 34							07 34					
Penistone		d												06 42							07 42					
Silkstone Common		d												06 47							07 47					
Dodworth		d												06 51							07 51					
Barnsley		a	23p31											06 57		07 24			07 40		07 57				08 11	08 21
		d	23p31			05 23		05 50		06 21				06 58		07 24			07 40		07 58				08 14	08 24
Wombwell		d	23p36			05 28		05 55		06 26				07 03		07 29					08 03					08 29
Elsecar		d	23p40			05 32		05 59		06 30				07 07		07 33					08 07					08 33
Chapeltown		d	23p45			05 37		06 04		06 35				07 12		07 38					08 12					08 38
Meadowhall	29,31 ⇌	a	23p51		00 08	05 43		06 10		06 41				07 21		07 47	07 46		07 53		08 20				08 31	08 45
		d	23p51	23p54	00 09	05 43	05 58	06 10	06 30	06 42	06 52		06 58	07 21	07 32	07 49	07 47	07 53	07 54	08 07	08 21		08 25		08 31	08 46
Sheffield 7	29,31 ⇌	a	00 02	00 04	00 23	05 54	06 08	06 25	06 38	06 55	07 07		07 06	07 29	07 40	07 57	07 54	08 00	08 05	08 18	08 29		08 32		08 39	08 56
		d								07 03									08 05							
Dronfield		d								07 13									08 15							
Chesterfield		d								07 20									08 24							
Alfreton		d								07 33									08 35							
Langley Mill		d								07 40									08 42							
Nottingham		a								08 02									09 02							

Station			NT	NT	NT E	TP ◇1 D	NT		NT H	NT F	NT	NT I	NT G	NT	NT	NT E	TP ◇1 D		NT H	NT	NT F	NT	NT I	NT G	NT	NT
Leeds 10	31	d	07 48	08 05						08 32	08 37			08 48	09 05						09 32	09 37			09 48	10 05
Woodlesford		d								08 40											09 40					
Castleford		d								08 51											09 51					
Normanton		d								08 57			←								09 57			←		
Wakefield Kirkgate 4	31	a		08 23						09 03	08 54		09 03		09 23						10 01	09 55		10 01		10 23
		d		08 23						09 05	08 55		09 05		09 23						10 04	09 56		10 04		10 23
Darton		d								→			09 17								→			10 15		
Huddersfield		d					08 07													09 08						
Lockwood		d					08 10													09 11						
Berry Brow		d					08 13													09 14						
Honley		d					08 16													09 17						
Brockholes		d					08 19													09 20						
Stocksmoor		d					08 23													09 24						
Shepley		d					08 25													09 26						
Denby Dale		d					08 34													09 36						
Penistone		d					08 42													09 44						
Silkstone Common		d					08 47													09 49						
Dodworth		d					08 51													09 53						
Barnsley		a		08 39			08 57				09 11		09 23		09 39					10 00		10 12		10 21		10 39
		d		08 40			08 58				09 14		09 24		09 40					10 01		10 14		10 24		10 40
Wombwell		d					09 03						09 29							10 06				10 29		
Elsecar		d					09 07						09 33											10 33		
Chapeltown		d					09 12						09 38							10 13				10 38		
Meadowhall	29,31 ⇌	a	08 49	08 52			09 19				09 27		09 46	09 50	09 52					10 20		10 27		10 46	10 50	10 52
		d	08 51	08 52	08 56	09 01	09 20		09 24		09 29	09 33	09 46	09 50	09 52	09 55	10 01		10 08	10 21		10 28	10 33	10 47	10 50	10 52
Sheffield 7	29,31 ⇌	a	08 59	09 02	09 05	09 08	09 28		09 33		09 37	09 41	09 56	10 00	10 02	10 05	10 08		10 19	10 30		10 37	10 41	10 57	11 00	11 02
		d		09 05											10 04											11 05
Dronfield		d		09 16											10 14											11 15
Chesterfield		d		09 23											10 21											11 22
Alfreton		d		09 33											10 32											11 33
Langley Mill		d		09 41											10 40											11 40
Nottingham		a		10 02											11 00											12 02

A From Hull
B From Doncaster to Manchester Airport
C From Doncaster
D From Cleethorpes to Manchester Airport
E From Adwick
F To Sheffield
G From Leeds
H From Bridlington
I From Scunthorpe to Lincoln

Table 34

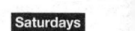

Saturdays
from 8 October

Leeds and Huddersfield - Barnsley - Sheffield, Nottingham

Station			NT A		TP ◇1 B	NT C	NT	NT D	NT	NT E	NT F	NT	NT		NT A	TP ◇1 B	NT C	NT	NT G	NT D	NT	NT E	NT F		NT	NT
Leeds 10	31	d						10 32	10 37			10 48	11 05							11 32	11 37				11 48	12 05
Woodlesford		d						10 40												11 40						
Castleford		d						10 51												11 51						
Normanton		d						10 57			←									11 57			←			
Wakefield Kirkgate 4	31	a						11 01	10 54		11 01		11 23							12 01	11 54		12 01			12 23
		d						11 04	10 55		11 04		11 23							12 04	11 55		12 04			12 23
Darton		d						→			11 15									→			12 15			
Huddersfield		d					10 08											11 08								
Lockwood		d					10 11											11 11								
Berry Brow		d					10 14											11 14								
Honley		d					10 17											11 17								
Brockholes		d					10 20											11 20								
Stocksmoor		d					10 24											11 24								
Shepley		d					10 26											11 26								
Denby Dale		d					10 36											11 36								
Penistone		d					10 44											11 44								
Silkstone Common		d					10 49											11 49								
Dodworth		d					10 53											11 53								
Barnsley		a					11 00		11 11		11 21		11 39					12 00			12 11		12 21			12 39
		d					11 01		11 14		11 24		11 40					12 01			12 14		12 24			12 40
Wombwell		d					11 06				11 29							12 06					12 29			
Elsecar		d									11 33												12 33			
Chapeltown		d					11 13				11 38							12 13					12 38			
Meadowhall	29,31	a					11 18		11 27		11 46	11 50	11 52					12 20			12 27		12 46		12 49	12 52
		d	10 58		11 01	11 08	11 19		11 28	11 33	11 46	11 50	11 52		11 58	12 01	12 08	12 21	12 24		12 28	12 33	12 46		12 50	12 52
Sheffield 7	29,31	a	11 06		11 08	11 20	11 30		11 37	11 41	11 57	12 00	12 02		12 05	12 08	12 20	12 30	12 36		12 37	12 41	12 57		13 00	13 02
		d											12 06													13 05
Dronfield		d											12 17													13 15
Chesterfield		d											12 23													13 22
Alfreton		d											12 34													13 34
Langley Mill		d											12 41													13 41
Nottingham		a											13 01													14 00

Station			NT A	TP ◇1 B	NT C	NT	NT D	NT	NT E		NT F	NT	NT	NT A	TP ◇1 B	NT H	NT	NT D	NT		NT E	NT F	NT	NT	NT A	TP ◇1 B
Leeds 10	31	d					12 32	12 37				12 48	13 05					13 32	13 37				13 48	14 05		
Woodlesford		d					12 40											13 40								
Castleford		d					12 51											13 51								
Normanton		d					12 57				←							13 57				←				
Wakefield Kirkgate 4	31	a					13 02	12 54			13 02		13 23					14 01	13 54			14 01		14 23		
		d					13 04	12 55			13 04		13 23					14 04	13 55			14 04		14 23		
Darton		d					→				13 17							→				14 15				
Huddersfield		d				12 08											13 08									
Lockwood		d				12 11											13 11									
Berry Brow		d				12 14											13 14									
Honley		d				12 17											13 17									
Brockholes		d				12 20											13 20									
Stocksmoor		d				12 24											13 24									
Shepley		d				12 26											13 26									
Denby Dale		d				12 36											13 36									
Penistone		d				12 44											13 44									
Silkstone Common		d				12 49											13 49									
Dodworth		d				12 53											13 53									
Barnsley		a				13 00		13 11			13 22		13 38				14 00		14 11			14 21		14 39		
		d				13 01		13 14			13 24		13 40				14 01		14 14			14 24		14 40		
Wombwell		d				13 06					13 29						14 06					14 29				
Elsecar		d									13 33											14 33				
Chapeltown		d				13 13					13 38						14 13					14 38				
Meadowhall	29,31	a				13 20		13 27			13 46	13 49	13 52				14 20		14 27			14 46	14 49	14 52		
		d	12 58	13 01	13 08	13 20		13 28	13 33		13 46	13 50	13 52	13 58	14 01	14 08	14 20		14 28		14 34	14 46	14 50	14 52	14 58	15 01
Sheffield 7	29,31	a	13 05	13 08	13 20	13 30		13 37	13 41		13 57	14 00	14 02	14 05	14 08	14 20	14 30		14 37		14 43	14 57	15 00	15 02	15 05	15 08
		d											14 05											15 05		
Dronfield		d											14 15											15 15		
Chesterfield		d											14 22											15 22		
Alfreton		d											14 33											15 33		
Langley Mill		d											14 40											15 40		
Nottingham		a											15 00											16 02		

A From Adwick
B From Cleethorpes to Manchester Airport
C From Bridlington
D To Sheffield
E From Scunthorpe to Lincoln
F From Leeds
G From York
H From Scarborough

Table 34

Saturdays
from 8 October

Leeds and Huddersfield - Barnsley - Sheffield, Nottingham

			NT	NT	NT		NT	NT	NT	NT	NT	NT	TP	NT	NT		NT	NT	NT	EM	NT	NT	NT	NT	NT	
													◇1							◇						
			A		B			C	D			E	F	G	H			B		I	C	D			J	
													⚲													
Leeds 10	31	d			14 32		14 37			14 48	15 05							15 32	15 37				15 48	16 05		
Woodlesford		d			14 40													15 40								
Castleford		d			14 51													15 51								
Normanton		d			14 57				←									15 57				←				
Wakefield Kirkgate 4	31	a			15 01		14 54		15 01		15 23							16 01	15 54			16 01		16 23		
		d			15 04		14 55		15 04		15 23							16 04	15 55			16 04		16 23		
Darton		d			→				15 15									→				16 15				
Huddersfield		d		14 08													15 08									
Lockwood		d		14 11													15 11									
Berry Brow		d		14 14													15 14									
Honley		d		14 17													15 17									
Brockholes		d		14 20													15 20									
Stocksmoor		d		14 24													15 24									
Shepley		d		14 26													15 26									
Denby Dale		d		14 36													15 36									
Penistone		d		14 44													15 44									
Silkstone Common		d		14 49													15 49									
Dodworth		d		14 53													15 53									
Barnsley		a		15 00			15 13		15 21		15 39						16 00		16 11			16 21		16 39		
		d		15 01			15 14		15 24		15 40						16 01		16 14			16 24		16 40		
Wombwell		d		15 06					15 29								16 06					16 29				
Elsecar		d							15 33													16 33				
Chapeltown		d		15 13					15 38								16 13					16 38				
Meadowhall	29,31 ⛴	a		15 20			15 27		15 46	15 49	15 51						16 20		16 27			16 46	16 49	16 52		
		d	15 07	15 20			15 28	15 33	15 46	15 50	15 52	15 57	16 01	16 07	16 18		16 20		16 28		16 33	16 46	16 50	16 52	16 55	
Sheffield 7	29,31 ⛴	a	15 20	15 30			15 37	15 41	15 57	16 00	16 03	16 05	16 08	16 22	16 27		16 30		16 37		16 41	16 57	17 00	17 02	17 05	
		d									16 04									16 38				17 05		
Dronfield		d									16 14									16 48				17 15		
Chesterfield		d									16 21									16 53				17 22		
Alfreton		d									16 32									17 04				17 33		
Langley Mill		d									16 40													17 40		
Nottingham		a									17 00									17 29				18 00		

			TP	NT	NT	NT	NT	NT	EM	NT	NT		NT	NT	TP	NT	NT	NT	NT	NT	NT		NT	NT	NT	TP
			◇1						◇						◇1											◇1
			F	A		B		C	I	D				K	F	A		B		C	D				K	F
			⚲												⚲											⚲
Leeds 10	31	d				16 32	16 37				16 48		17 05					17 32	17 37				17 48	18 05		
Woodlesford		d				16 40												17 40								
Castleford		d				16 51												17 51								
Normanton		d				16 57				←			17 18					17 57			←					
Wakefield Kirkgate 4	31	a				17 01	16 54			17 01			17 22					18 01	17 54		18 01			18 23		
		d				17 04	16 55			17 04			17 23					18 04	17 55		18 04			18 23		
Darton		d				→				17 15								→			18 15					
Huddersfield		d			16 08												17 08									
Lockwood		d			16 11												17 11									
Berry Brow		d			16 14												17 14									
Honley		d			16 17												17 17									
Brockholes		d			16 20												17 20									
Stocksmoor		d			16 24												17 24									
Shepley		d			16 26												17 26									
Denby Dale		d			16 36												17 36									
Penistone		d			16 44												17 44									
Silkstone Common		d			16 49												17 49									
Dodworth		d			16 53												17 53									
Barnsley		a			17 00		17 11			17 21			17 39				18 00		18 11		18 21			18 39		
		d			17 01		17 14			17 24			17 40				18 01		18 14		18 24			18 40		
Wombwell		d			17 06					17 29							18 06				18 29					
Elsecar		d								17 33											18 33					
Chapeltown		d			17 13					17 38							18 13				18 38					
Meadowhall	29,31 ⛴	a			17 20		17 27			17 46	17 49		17 51				18 20		18 27		18 46		18 50	18 52		
		d	17 01	17 08	17 21		17 28	17 33		17 46	17 50		17 52	17 57	18 01	18 08	18 20		18 28	18 33	18 46		18 50	18 52	18 56	19 01
Sheffield 7	29,31 ⛴	a	17 08	17 19	17 32		17 37	17 41		17 57	18 00		18 03	18 05	18 08	18 21	18 30		18 38	18 41	18 56		19 00	19 04	19 06	19 08
		d							17 44				18 06											19 07		
Dronfield		d							17 55				18 16											19 17		
Chesterfield		d							18 01				18 23											19 23		
Alfreton		d							18 11				18 34											19 33		
Langley Mill		d											18 41											19 41		
Nottingham		a							18 33				18 58											20 01		

A From Bridlington
B To Sheffield
C From Scunthorpe to Lincoln
D From Leeds
E From Adwick
F From Cleethorpes to Manchester Airport
G From Scarborough
H From York
I From Liverpool Lime Street to Norwich
J From Adwick to Retford
K From Doncaster

Table 34

Saturdays
from 8 October

Leeds and Huddersfield - Barnsley - Sheffield, Nottingham

Station			NT	NT	NT	NT	NT		NT	NT	NT	NT	TP	NT	NT	NT	NT		NT	NT	NT	TP	NT	EM	NT	NT
													◇1									◇1		◇		
			A		B	C			D			E	F	B		G	C			D		H		I	J	K
Leeds 10	31	d				18 32	18 37			18 48	19 05						19 37		19 43		19 48		20 30			
Woodlesford		d				18 40											19 45									
Castleford		d				18 51											19 56									
Normanton		d				19 00			←								20 02			←						
Wakefield Kirkgate 4	31	a				19 04	18 54		19 04		19 24						20 06		19 59	20 06			20 46			
		d				19 05	18 55		19 05		19 24						20 07		20 00	20 07			20 47			
Darton		d				→			19 19								→			20 19						
Huddersfield		d		18 08											19 18										20 18	
Lockwood		d		18 11											19 21										20 21	
Berry Brow		d		18 14											19 24										20 24	
Honley		d		18 17											19 27										20 27	
Brockholes		d		18 20											19 30										20 30	
Stocksmoor		d		18 24											19 34										20 34	
Shepley		d		18 26											19 36										20 36	
Denby Dale		d		18 36											19 41										20 41	
Penistone		d		18 44											19 49										20 52	
Silkstone Common		d		18 49											19 54										20 57	
Dodworth		d		18 53											19 58										21 01	
Barnsley		a		19 01			19 11		19 26		19 40				20 05				20 16	20 24			21 02		21 09	
		d		19 01			19 14		19 26		19 40				20 06				20 16	20 24			21 03		21 12	
Wombwell		d		19 06					19 31						20 11					20 29					21 17	
Elsecar		d							19 35											20 33						
Chapeltown		d		19 13					19 40						20 18					20 38					21 24	
Meadowhall	29,31 🚋	a		19 20			19 28		19 47	19 50	19 52				20 24				20 36	20 45	20 50		21 17		21 28	
		d	19 08	19 20	19 28		19 30		19 47	19 51	19 52	19 57	20 01	20 08	20 24	20 33			20 37	20 46	20 51	21 09	21 18		21 29	21 35
Sheffield 7	29,31 🚋	a	19 19	19 30	19 37		19 39		19 57	20 00	20 03	20 06	20 08	20 18	20 37	20 41			20 44	20 58	21 00	21 19	21 30		21 41	21 46
		d									20 05													21 38		
Dronfield		d									20 15													21 48		
Chesterfield		d									20 22													21 54		
Alfreton		d									20 33													22 05		
Langley Mill		d									20 40													22 12		
Nottingham		a									21 00													22 33		

Station			NT		NT	TP	NT	NT	NT	NT	NT	NT	NT		NT	NT
						◇1										
						H	E	B		L						K
Leeds 10	31	d	20 37		20 48						21 37	21 48			22 44	
Woodlesford		d	20 45								21 45					
Castleford		d	20 56								21 56					
Normanton		d	21 02								22 02					
Wakefield Kirkgate 4	31	a	21 06								22 06					
		d	21 07								22 07					
Darton		d	21 18								22 21					
Huddersfield		d							21 15				22 15			
Lockwood		d							21 18				22 18			
Berry Brow		d							21 21				22 21			
Honley		d							21 24				22 24			
Brockholes		d							21 27				22 27			
Stocksmoor		d							21 31				22 31			
Shepley		d							21 33				22 33			
Denby Dale		d							21 41				22 41			
Penistone		d							21 49				22 49			
Silkstone Common		d							21 54				22 54			
Dodworth		d							21 58				22 58			
Barnsley		a	21 24						22 05		22 27		23 05			
		d	21 24						22 06		22 28		23 06			
Wombwell		d	21 29						22 11		22 33		23 11			
Elsecar		d	21 33								22 37		23 15			
Chapeltown		d	21 38						22 18		22 42		23 20			
Meadowhall	29,31 🚋	a	21 45		21 49				22 24		22 47	22 52	23 25		23 43	
		d	21 46		21 50	21 59	22 03	22 12	22 25	22 43	22 48	22 53	23 26		23 44	23 49
Sheffield 7	29,31 🚋	a	21 59		22 02	22 10	22 13	22 22	22 36	22 54	22 58	23 03	23 36		23 58	23 59
		d														
Dronfield		d														
Chesterfield		d														
Alfreton		d														
Langley Mill		d														
Nottingham		a														

- **A** From Scarborough
- **B** From Hull
- **C** To Sheffield
- **D** From Leeds
- **E** From Doncaster
- **F** From Cleethorpes to Manchester Airport
- **G** From Scunthorpe to Worksop
- **H** From Cleethorpes
- **I** From Liverpool Lime Street
- **J** To Retford
- **K** From Bridlington
- **L** From Scunthorpe

Table 34

Sundays
until 2 October

Leeds and Huddersfield - Barnsley - Sheffield, Nottingham

			NT A	NT	TP ◇1 B	NT A	NT	NT	NT	NT C	NT		NT D	NT	TP ◇1 E	NT	NT	NT A	NT	TP ◇1 E	NT F		NT	NT	NT	NT D
Leeds 10	31	d					08 34	08 48	09 05					10 02			10 17		10 57				11 18	11 29		
Woodlesford		d					08 42										10 25									
Castleford		d					08 53										10 36									
Normanton		d					08 58										10 41									
Wakefield Kirkgate 4	31	a					09 03		09 21					10 18			10 46		11 13					11 46		
		d					09 03		09 21					10 18			10 46		11 13					11 46		
Darton		d					09 17										11 00									
Huddersfield		d									09 19					10 15									11 29	
Lockwood		d									09 22					10 18									11 32	
Berry Brow		d									09 25					10 21									11 35	
Honley		d									09 28					10 24									11 38	
Brockholes		d									09 31					10 27									11 41	
Stocksmoor		d									09 35					10 31									11 45	
Shepley		d									09 37					10 33									11 47	
Denby Dale		d									09 42					10 39									11 52	
Penistone		d									09 50					10 46									12 00	
Silkstone Common		d									09 55					10 52									12 05	
Dodworth		d									09 59					10 55									12 09	
Barnsley		a					09 24		09 40		10 06			10 37		11 03	11 08		11 32					12 05	12 16	
		d					09 24		09 41		10 12			10 38		11 03	11 12		11 33					12 06	12 17	
Wombwell		d					09 29				10 17						11 17								12 22	
Elsecar		d					09 33				10 21						11 21								12 26	
Chapeltown		d					09 38				10 26						11 26								12 31	
Meadowhall	29,31	a					09 44	09 53	09 57		10 32			10 51		11 20	11 32		11 46				12 20	12 17	12 34	
		d	08 30		09 00	09 41	09 44	09 54	09 57	10 00	10 33		10 40	10 51	11 00	11 20	11 35	11 40	11 46	12 00	12 08		12 21	12 17	12 35	12 43
Sheffield 7	29,31	a	08 41		09 07	09 51	09 55	10 03	10 04	10 08	10 43		10 52	11 02	11 07	11 28	11 44	11 51	11 56	12 07	12 18		12 32	12 29	12 47	12 55
		d		09 00					10 07					11 03					12 00					12 31		
Dronfield		d		09 10					10 17					11 13					12 10					12 42		
Chesterfield		d		09 17					10 23					11 20					12 18					12 49		
Alfreton		d		09 28					10 33					11 30					12 28					12 59		
Langley Mill		d		09 35					10 41					11 38					12 36					13 07		
Nottingham		a		09 53					10 59					11 54					12 53					13 25		

			TP ◇1 E	NT	NT A	NT	NT G		TP ◇1 H	NT	NT	NT D	NT G	NT	TP ◇1 E	NT	NT		NT A	NT F	NT	TP ◇1 E	NT	NT	NT D	NT G
Leeds 10	31	d		12 29		12 34				13 18				14 05			14 17				15 05		15 18			
Woodlesford		d				12 42											14 25									
Castleford		d				12 53											14 36									
Normanton		d				12 58											14 41									
Wakefield Kirkgate 4	31	a		12 46		13 04								14 21			14 46				15 22					
		d		12 46		13 04								14 21			14 46				15 22					
Darton		d				13 18											15 00									
Huddersfield		d									13 19					14 15								15 19		
Lockwood		d									13 22					14 18								15 22		
Berry Brow		d									13 25					14 21								15 25		
Honley		d									13 28					14 24								15 28		
Brockholes		d									13 31					14 27								15 31		
Stocksmoor		d									13 35					14 31								15 35		
Shepley		d									13 37					14 33								15 37		
Denby Dale		d									13 42					14 39								15 42		
Penistone		d									13 50					14 46								15 50		
Silkstone Common		d									13 55					14 52								15 55		
Dodworth		d									13 59					14 55								15 59		
Barnsley		a		13 05		13 24					14 06			14 40		15 03	15 07				15 41			16 06		
		d		13 06		13 24					14 12			14 41		15 03	15 12				15 42			16 12		
Wombwell		d				13 29					14 17						15 17							16 17		
Elsecar		d				13 33					14 21						15 21							16 21		
Chapeltown		d				13 38					14 26						15 26							16 26		
Meadowhall	29,31	a		13 18		13 48				14 20	14 32			14 54		15 20	15 35				15 55		16 20	16 32		
		d	13 00	13 18	13 44	13 51	13 56		14 00	14 21	14 33	14 48	14 52	14 56	15 00	15 21	15 35		15 48	15 52	15 56	16 00	16 21	16 34	16 47	16 53
Sheffield 7	29,31	a	13 07	13 29	13 52	13 58	14 06		14 07	14 32	14 48	14 55	15 03	15 06	15 07	15 28	15 44		15 55	16 01	16 05	16 07	16 31	16 44	16 55	17 04
		d		13 31										15 07							16 07					
Dronfield		d		13 42										15 17							16 17					
Chesterfield		d		13 48										15 24							16 23					
Alfreton		d		13 59										15 34							16 33					
Langley Mill		d		14 06										15 42							16 41					
Nottingham		a		14 22										16 00							16 59					

A From Doncaster
B To Manchester Piccadilly
C From Hull
D From Goole
E From Cleethorpes to Manchester Airport
F From Bridlington
G From Scarborough
H From Doncaster to Manchester Airport

Table 34

Sundays
until 2 October

Leeds and Huddersfield - Barnsley - Sheffield, Nottingham

			NT		TP	NT	NT	NT	NT	TP	NT	NT	NT		NT	NT	TP	NT	NT	NT	NT	NT	TP		NT	NT
					◇1					◇1							◇1						◇1			
					A		B	C		A			B		D		A	E		B		C	A			
Leeds 10	31	d	16 04			16 17			17 05		17 18					18 05			18 17		19 04				19 18	
Woodlesford		d				16 25													18 25							
Castleford		d				16 36													18 36							
Normanton		d				16 41													18 40							
Wakefield Kirkgate 4	31	a	16 21			16 46			17 21							18 21			18 45		19 21					
		d	16 22			16 46			17 21							18 22			18 45		19 21					
Darton		d				17 00													18 59							
Huddersfield		d										17 19														19 19
Lockwood		d										17 22														19 22
Berry Brow		d										17 25														19 25
Honley		d										17 28														19 28
Brockholes		d										17 31														19 31
Stocksmoor		d										17 35														19 35
Shepley		d										17 37														19 37
Denby Dale		d										17 47														19 42
Penistone		d										17 54														19 50
Silkstone Common		d										18 00														19 55
Dodworth		d										18 03														19 59
Barnsley		a	16 41			17 07			17 40			18 11				18 41			19 05		19 40					20 06
		d	16 42			17 12			17 41			18 12				18 42			19 11		19 40					20 12
Wombwell		d				17 17						18 17							19 17							20 17
Elsecar		d				17 21						18 21							19 21							20 21
Chapeltown		d				17 26						18 26							19 26							20 26
Meadowhall	29,31 ⇌	a	16 56			17 34			17 55		18 25	18 32				18 56			19 32		19 54				20 20	20 34
		d	16 56		17 01	17 35	17 48	17 53	17 56	18 00	18 25	18 33	18 47		18 53	18 56	19 00	19 18	19 33	19 47	19 54	19 57	20 00		20 21	20 34
Sheffield 7	29,31 ⇌	a	17 05		17 07	17 44	17 55	18 01	18 05	18 07	18 36	18 44	18 57		19 03	19 05	19 07	19 27	19 43	19 55	20 04	20 06	20 07		20 34	20 43
		d	17 07						18 07							19 07					20 06					
Dronfield		d	17 17						18 17							19 17					20 16					
Chesterfield		d	17 23						18 25							19 25					20 23					
Alfreton		d	17 33						18 36							19 36					20 34					
Langley Mill		d	17 41						18 43							19 43					20 41					
Nottingham		a	17 59						19 00							19 59					20 57					

			NT	TP	NT	EM	NT	NT	TP		NT	NT	NT	NT
				◇1		◇			◇1					
			B	A	D	F		E	G				H	
Leeds 10	31	d					20 17					21 40		22 17
Woodlesford		d					20 25							22 25
Castleford		d					20 36							22 36
Normanton		d					20 41							22 41
Wakefield Kirkgate 4	31	a					20 46							22 46
		d					20 46							22 46
Darton		d					21 00							23 00
Huddersfield		d												
Lockwood		d												
Berry Brow		d												
Honley		d												
Brockholes		d												
Stocksmoor		d												
Shepley		d												
Denby Dale		d												
Penistone		d												
Silkstone Common		d												
Dodworth		d												
Barnsley		a					21 07							23 07
		d					21 12				22 21			23 12
Wombwell		d					21 17				22 26			23 17
Elsecar		d					21 21				22 30			23 21
Chapeltown		d					21 26				22 35			23 26
Meadowhall	29,31 ⇌	a					21 33				22 40	22 45		23 30
		d	20 47	21 00	21 28		21 33	21 58	22 04		22 41	22 45	23 04	23 32
Sheffield 7	29,31 ⇌	a	20 55	21 07	21 38		21 42	22 09	22 15		22 51	22 54	23 15	23 43
		d				21 40								
Dronfield		d				21 50								
Chesterfield		d				21 56								
Alfreton		d				22 07								
Langley Mill		d				22 14								
Nottingham		a				22 36								

A From Cleethorpes to Manchester Airport
B From Doncaster
C From Bridlington
D From Scarborough
E From York
F From Liverpool Lime Street
G From Cleethorpes
H From Hull
I until 19 June. From York

Table 34

Sundays

from 9 October

Leeds and Huddersfield - Barnsley - Sheffield, Nottingham

			NT	NT	TP	NT	NT	NT	NT	NT	NT		NT	NT	TP	NT	NT	NT	NT	TP	NT		NT	NT	NT	NT
					◇1										◇1					◇1						
			A		B	A				C			D		E			A		E	F					D
Leeds 10	31	d					08 34	08 48	09 05					10 02			10 17		10 57				11 18	11 29		
Woodlesford		d					08 42										10 25									
Castleford		d					08 53										10 36									
Normanton		d					08 58										10 41									
Wakefield Kirkgate 4	31	a					09 03		09 21					10 18			10 46		11 13					11 46		
		d					09 03		09 21					10 18			10 46		11 13					11 46		
Darton		d					09 17										11 00									
Huddersfield		d									09 16					10 11									11 24	
Lockwood		d									09 19					10 14									11 27	
Berry Brow		d									09 22					10 17									11 30	
Honley		d									09 25					10 20									11 33	
Brockholes		d									09 28					10 23									11 36	
Stocksmoor		d									09 32					10 27									11 40	
Shepley		d									09 34					10 29									11 42	
Denby Dale		d									09 42					10 39									11 52	
Penistone		d									09 50					10 46									12 00	
Silkstone Common		d									09 55					10 52									12 05	
Dodworth		d									09 59					10 55									12 09	
Barnsley		a					09 24		09 40		10 06			10 37		11 03	11 08		11 32					12 05	12 16	
		d					09 24		09 41		10 12			10 38		11 03	11 12		11 33					12 06	12 17	
Wombwell		d					09 29				10 17						11 17								12 22	
Elsecar		d					09 33				10 21						11 21								12 26	
Chapeltown		d					09 38				10 26						11 26								12 31	
Meadowhall	29,31 ⇌	a					09 44	09 53	09 57		10 32			10 51		11 20	11 32		11 46				12 20	12 17	12 34	
		d	08 30		09 00	09 41	09 44	09 54	09 57	10 00	10 33		10 40	10 51	11 00	11 20	11 35	11 40	11 46	12 00	12 08		12 21	12 17	12 35	12 43
Sheffield 7	29,31 ⇌	a	08 41		09 07	09 51	09 55	10 03	10 04	10 08	10 43		10 52	11 02	11 07	11 28	11 44	11 51	11 56	12 07	12 18		12 32	12 29	12 47	12 55
		d		09 00					10 07					11 03					12 00					12 31		
Dronfield		d		09 10					10 17					11 13					12 10					12 42		
Chesterfield		d		09 17					10 23					11 20					12 18					12 49		
Alfreton		d		09 28					10 33					11 30					12 28					12 59		
Langley Mill		d		09 35					10 41					11 38					12 36					13 07		
Nottingham		a		09 53					10 59					11 54					12 53					13 25		

			TP	NT	NT	NT	NT		TP	NT	NT	NT	NT	NT	TP	NT	NT		NT	NT	NT	TP	NT	NT	NT	NT
			◇1						◇1						◇1							◇1				
			E		A		G		H			D	G		E				A	F		E			D	G
Leeds 10	31	d		12 29		12 34				13 18				14 05			14 17				15 05		15 18			
Woodlesford		d				12 42											14 25									
Castleford		d				12 53											14 36									
Normanton		d				12 58											14 41									
Wakefield Kirkgate 4	31	a		12 46		13 04								14 21			14 46				15 22					
		d		12 46		13 04								14 21			14 46				15 22					
Darton		d				13 18											15 00									
Huddersfield		d									13 14					14 11								15 14		
Lockwood		d									13 17					14 14								15 17		
Berry Brow		d									13 20					14 17								15 20		
Honley		d									13 23					14 20								15 23		
Brockholes		d									13 26					14 23								15 26		
Stocksmoor		d									13 30					14 27								15 30		
Shepley		d									13 32					14 29								15 32		
Denby Dale		d									13 42					14 39								15 42		
Penistone		d									13 50					14 46								15 50		
Silkstone Common		d									13 55					14 52								15 55		
Dodworth		d									13 59					14 55								15 59		
Barnsley		a		13 05		13 24					14 06			14 40		15 03	15 07				15 41			16 06		
		d		13 06		13 24					14 12			14 41		15 03	15 12				15 42			16 12		
Wombwell		d				13 29					14 17						15 17							16 17		
Elsecar		d				13 33					14 21						15 21							16 21		
Chapeltown		d				13 38					14 26						15 26							16 26		
Meadowhall	29,31 ⇌	a		13 18		13 48				14 20	14 32			14 54		15 20	15 35				15 55		16 20	16 32		
		d	13 00	13 18	13 44	13 51	13 56		14 00	14 21	14 33	14 48	14 52	14 56	15 00	15 21	15 35		15 48	15 52	15 56	16 00	16 21	16 34	16 47	16 53
Sheffield 7	29,31 ⇌	a	13 07	13 29	13 52	13 58	14 06		14 07	14 32	14 48	14 55	15 03	15 06	15 07	15 28	15 44		15 55	16 01	16 05	16 07	16 31	16 44	16 55	17 04
		d		13 31										15 07							16 07					
Dronfield		d		13 42										15 17							16 17					
Chesterfield		d		13 48										15 24							16 23					
Alfreton		d		13 59										15 34							16 33					
Langley Mill		d		14 06										15 42							16 41					
Nottingham		a		14 22										16 00							16 59					

A From Doncaster
B To Manchester Piccadilly
C From Hull
D From Goole
E From Cleethorpes to Manchester Airport
F From Bridlington
G From Scarborough
H From Doncaster to Manchester Airport

Table 34

Sundays
from 9 October

Leeds and Huddersfield - Barnsley - Sheffield, Nottingham

		NT		TP	NT	NT	NT	NT	TP	NT	NT	NT		NT	NT	TP	NT	NT	NT	NT	NT	TP		NT	NT
				◇1					◇1							◇1						◇1			
				A		B	C		A			B		D		A	E		B		C	A			
Leeds 10 31	d	16 04			16 17			17 05		17 18					18 05			18 17		19 04				19 18	
Woodlesford	d				16 25													18 25							
Castleford	d				16 36													18 36							
Normanton	d				16 41													18 40							
Wakefield Kirkgate 4 31	a	16 21			16 46			17 21							18 21			18 45		19 21					
	d	16 22			16 46			17 21							18 22			18 45		19 21					
Darton	d				17 00													18 59							
Huddersfield	d										17 19														19 14
Lockwood	d										17 22														19 17
Berry Brow	d										17 25														19 20
Honley	d										17 28														19 23
Brockholes	d										17 31														19 26
Stocksmoor	d										17 35														19 30
Shepley	d										17 37														19 32
Denby Dale	d										17 47														19 42
Penistone	d										17 54														19 50
Silkstone Common	d										18 00														19 55
Dodworth	d										18 03														19 59
Barnsley	a	16 41			17 07			17 40			18 11				18 41			19 05		19 40					20 06
	d	16 42			17 12			17 41			18 12				18 42			19 11		19 40					20 12
Wombwell	d				17 17						18 17							19 17							20 17
Elsecar	d				17 21						18 21							19 21							20 21
Chapeltown	d				17 26						18 26							19 26							20 26
Meadowhall 29,31 🚋	a	16 56			17 34			17 55		18 25	18 32				18 56			19 32		19 54				20 20	20 34
	d	16 56		17 01	17 35	17 48	17 53	17 56	18 00	18 25	18 33	18 47		18 53	18 56	19 00	19 18	19 33	19 47	19 54	19 57	20 00		20 21	20 34
Sheffield 7 29,31 🚋	a	17 05		17 07	17 44	17 55	18 01	18 05	18 07	18 36	18 44	18 57		19 03	19 05	19 07	19 27	19 43	19 55	20 04	20 06	20 07		20 34	20 43
	d	17 07						18 07							19 07					20 06					
Dronfield	d	17 17						18 17							19 17					20 16					
Chesterfield	d	17 23						18 25							19 25					20 23					
Alfreton	d	17 33						18 36							19 36					20 34					
Langley Mill	d	17 41						18 43							19 43					20 41					
Nottingham	a	17 59						19 00							19 59					20 57					

		NT	TP	NT	EM	NT	NT	TP		NT	NT	NT	NT
			◇1		◇			◇1					
		B	A	D	F		E	G				H	
Leeds 10 31	d					20 17					21 40		22 17
Woodlesford	d					20 25							22 25
Castleford	d					20 36							22 36
Normanton	d					20 41							22 41
Wakefield Kirkgate 4 31	a					20 46							22 46
	d					20 46							22 46
Darton	d					21 00							23 00
Huddersfield	d												
Lockwood	d												
Berry Brow	d												
Honley	d												
Brockholes	d												
Stocksmoor	d												
Shepley	d												
Denby Dale	d												
Penistone	d												
Silkstone Common	d												
Dodworth	d												
Barnsley	a					21 07							23 07
	d					21 12				22 21			23 12
Wombwell	d					21 17				22 26			23 17
Elsecar	d					21 21				22 30			23 21
Chapeltown	d					21 26				22 35			23 26
Meadowhall 29,31 🚋	a					21 33				22 40	22 45		23 30
	d	20 47	21 00	21 28		21 33	21 58	22 04		22 41	22 45	23 04	23 32
Sheffield 7 29,31 🚋	a	20 55	21 07	21 38		21 42	22 09	22 15		22 51	22 54	23 15	23 43
	d				21 40								
Dronfield	d				21 50								
Chesterfield	d				21 56								
Alfreton	d				22 07								
Langley Mill	d				22 14								
Nottingham	a				22 36								

A From Cleethorpes to Manchester Airport
B From Doncaster
C From Bridlington
D From Scarborough
E From York
F From Liverpool Lime Street
G From Cleethorpes
H From Hull

Network Diagram for Tables 35, 36, 37, 38

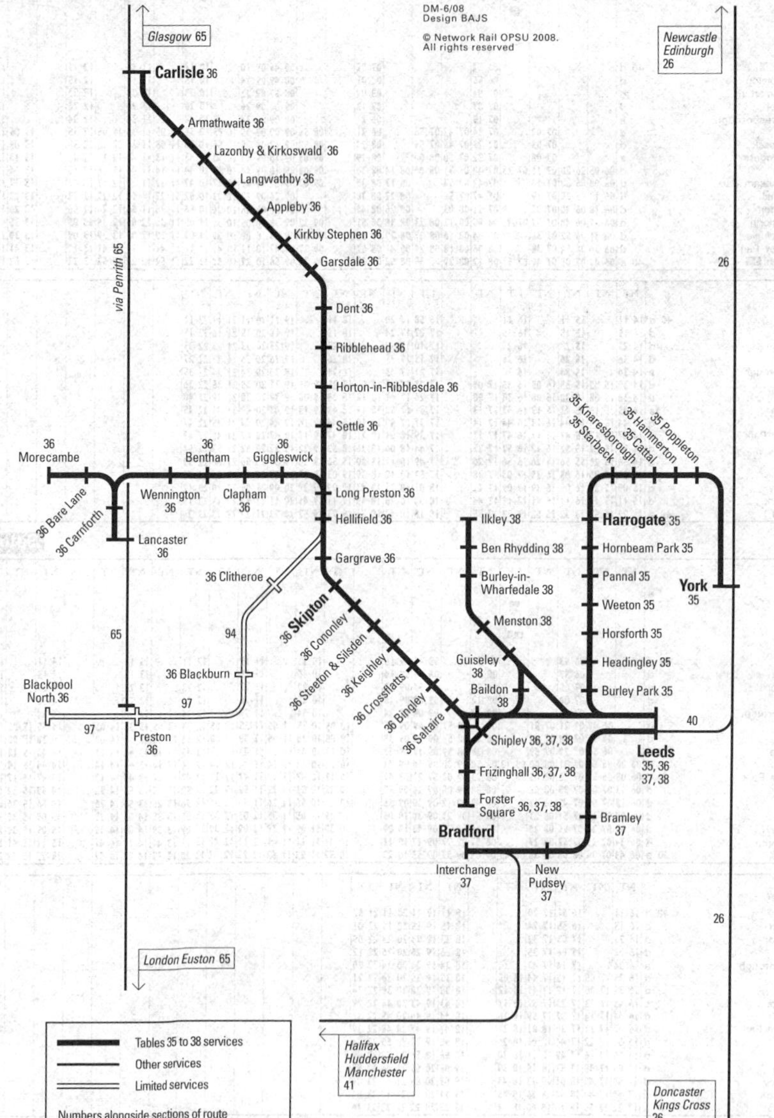

© Network Rail OPSU 2008.
All rights reserved

York - Harrogate - Leeds

Mondays to Fridays

Miles			NT	NT	NT	GR 8 1 A	NT	NT	NT	NT	NT	NT	NT	NT	NT	NT	NT	NT	NT	NT	NT	NT	NT
0	York 8	40 d					06 52				07 57		08 45	09 10		10 11		11 11		12 11		13 11	
3	Poppleton	d					06 56				08 01		08 49	09 14		10 15		11 15		12 15		13 15	
8¾	Hammerton	d					07 04				08 09		08 57	09 22		10 23		11 23		12 23		13 23	
10¼	Cattal	d					07 07				08 12		09 00	09 26		10 26		11 26		12 26		13 26	
16¾	**Knaresborough**	a					07 15				08 21		09 09	09 34		10 34		11 34		12 34		13 34	
—		d			07 00		07 24	07 42	07 56		08 21	08 55	09 09	09 35	10 05	10 35	11 05	11 35	12 05	12 35	13 05	13 35	14 05
18¼	Starbeck	d			07 03		07 27	07 45	07 59		08 24	08 58	09 12	09 38	10 08	10 38	11 08	11 38	12 08	12 38	13 08	13 38	14 08
20½	**Harrogate**	a			07 08		07 32	07 50	08 04		08 29	09 03	09 18	09 43	10 13	10 43	11 13	11 43	12 13	12 43	13 13	13 43	14 13
—		d	06 05	06 28	07 11	07 28	07 40	07 51	08 06	08 14	08 30	09 04	09 18	09 44	10 14	10 44	11 14	11 44	12 14	12 44	13 14	13 44	14 14
21½	Hornbeam Park	d	06 08	06 30	07 14		07 42	07 54		08 17	08 33	09 07	09 21	09 47	10 17	10 47	11 17	11 47	12 17	12 47	13 17	13 47	14 17
23¾	Pannal	d	06 13	06 35	07 19		07 47	07 59		08 22	08 38		09 26	09 52	10 22	10 52	11 22	11 52	12 22	12 52	13 22	13 52	14 22
27	Weeton	d	06 18	06 40	07 23		07 51	08 03		08 26	08 42		09 30	09 56	10 26	10 56	11 26	11 56	12 26	12 56	13 26	13 56	14 26
33	Horsforth	d	06 27	06 48	07 32	07u45	08 00	08 12	08 23	08 35	08 51	09 22	09 39	10 05	10 35	11 05	11 35	12 05	12 35	13 05	13 35	14 05	14 35
35¾	Headingley	d	06 31	06 52	07 36		08 04	08 16	08 27	08 39	08 55	09 26	09 43	10 09	10 39	11 09	11 39	12 09	12 39	13 09	13 39	14 09	14 39
36½	Burley Park	d	06 34	06 54	07 38		08 06	08 18	08 29	08 41	08 57	09 27	09 47	10 11	10 41	11 11	11 41	12 11	12 41	13 11	13 41	14 11	14 41
38¾	**Leeds 10**	40 a	06 44	07 05	07 49	07 57	08 17	08 29	08 59	08 52	09 08	09 38	09 56	10 22	10 52	11 22	11 52	12 22	12 52	13 22	13 52	14 22	14 52

		NT	NT	NT	NT	NT	NT	NT	NT	NT	NT	NT	NT	NT	NT	NT
York 8	40 d	14 11		15 11		16 11		16 58	17 20		18 11		19 11	20 11	21 11	22 11
Poppleton	d	14 15		15 15		16 15		17 02	17 24		18 15		19 15	20 15	21 16	22 15
Hammerton	d	14 23		15 23		16 23		17 10	17 32		18 23		19 23	20 23	21 23	22 23
Cattal	d	14 26		15 26		16 26		17 13	17 35		18 26		19 26	20 26	21 27	22 27
Knaresborough	a	14 34		15 34		16 34		17 21	17 43		18 34		19 34	20 34	21 34	22 35
	d	14 35	15 05	15 35	16 05	16 35	17 05	17 23	17 44	18 05	18 35	19 05	19 35	20 35	21 35	22 36
Starbeck	d	14 38	15 08	15 38	16 08	16 38	17 08	17 26	17 47	18 12	18 38	19 08	19 38	20 38	21 39	22 40
Harrogate	a	14 43	15 13	15 43	16 13	16 43	17 13	17 31	17 52	18 17	18 43	19 13	19 43	20 43	21 43	22 45
	d	14 44	15 14	15 44	16 14	16 44	17 14	17 37	17 59	18 18	18 44	19 14	19 44	20 44	21 45	22 47
Hornbeam Park	d	14 47	15 17	15 47	16 17	16 47	17 17	17 39	18 01	18 21	18 47	19 17	19 47	20 47	21 48	22 49
Pannal	d	14 52	15 22	15 52	16 22	16 52	17 22	17 44	18 06	18 26	18 52	19 22	19 52	20 52	21 53	22 54
Weeton	d	14 56	15 26	15 56	16 26	16 56	17 26	17 49	18 11	18 30	18 56	19 26	19 56	20 56	21 58	22 59
Horsforth	d	15 05	15 35	16 05	16 35	17 05	17 38	17 57	18 19	18 39	19 05	19 35	20 05	21 05	22 06	23 08
Headingley	d	15 09	15 39	16 09	16 39	17 09	17 42	18 01	18 23	18 43	19 09	19 39	20 09	21 09	22 10	23 12
Burley Park	d	15 11	15 41	16 11	16 41	17 11	17 44	18 04	18 26	18 45	19 11	19 41	20 11	21 11	22 13	23 15
Leeds 10	40 a	15 22	15 52	16 22	16 52	17 22	17 55	18 16	18 40	18 56	19 23	19 52	20 22	21 22	22 23	23 25

Saturdays

		NT	NT	NT	NT	GR 8 1	NT	NT	NT	NT	NT	NT	NT	NT	NT	NT	NT	NT	NT	NT	NT	NT	NT
York 8	40 d			06 53			07 57		08 45	09 10		10 11		11 11		12 11		13 11		14 11		15 11	
Poppleton	d			06 57			08 01		08 49	09 14		10 15		11 15		12 15		13 15		14 15		15 15	
Hammerton	d			07 05			08 09		08 57	09 22		10 23		11 23		12 23		13 23		14 23		15 23	
Cattal	d			07 08			08 12		09 00	09 26		10 26		11 26		12 26		13 26		14 26		15 26	
Knaresborough	a			07 16			08 20		09 08	09 34		10 34		11 34		12 34		13 34		14 34		15 34	
	d		06 47	07 21	07 51		08 21	08 51	09 09	09 35	10 05	10 35	11 05	11 35	12 05	12 35	13 05	13 35	14 05	14 35	15 05	15 35	16 05
Starbeck	d		06 50	07 24	07 54		08 24	08 54	09 12	09 38	10 08	10 38	11 08	11 38	12 08	12 38	13 08	13 38	14 08	14 38	15 08	15 38	16 08
Harrogate	a		06 55	07 29	07 59		08 29	08 59	09 17	09 43	10 13	10 43	11 13	11 43	12 13	12 43	13 13	13 43	14 13	14 43	15 13	15 43	16 13
	d	06 06	06 56	07 31	08 00	08 13	08 30	09 00	09 18	09 44	10 14	10 44	11 14	11 44	12 14	12 44	13 14	13 44	14 14	14 44	15 14	15 44	16 14
Hornbeam Park	d	06 08	06 59	07 33	08 03		08 33	09 03	09 21	09 47	10 17	10 47	11 17	11 47	12 17	12 47	13 17	13 47	14 17	14 47	15 17	15 47	16 17
Pannal	d	06 13	07 04	07 38	08 08		08 38	09 08	09 26	09 52	10 22	10 52	11 22	11 52	12 22	12 52	13 22	13 52	14 22	14 52	15 22	15 52	16 22
Weeton	d	06 18	07 08	07 42	08 12		08 42	09 12	09 30	09 56	10 26	10 56	11 26	11 56	12 26	12 56	13 26	13 56	14 26	14 56	15 26	15 56	16 26
Horsforth	d	06 28	07 17	07 51	08 21		08 51	09 21	09 39	10 05	10 35	11 05	11 35	12 05	12 35	13 05	13 35	14 05	14 35	15 05	15 35	16 05	16 35
Headingley	d	06 32	07 21	07 55	08 25		08 55	09 25	09 43	10 09	10 39	11 09	11 39	12 09	12 39	13 09	13 39	14 09	14 39	15 09	15 39	16 09	16 39
Burley Park	d	06 34	07 23	07 57	08 27		08 57	09 27	09 47	10 11	10 41	11 11	11 41	12 11	12 41	13 11	13 41	14 11	14 41	15 11	15 41	16 11	16 41
Leeds 10	40 a	06 44	07 34	08 08	08 38	08 45	09 08	09 37	09 55	10 22	10 52	11 22	11 52	12 22	12 52	13 20	13 52	14 22	14 52	15 22	15 52	16 22	16 52

		NT	NT	NT	NT	NT	NT	NT	NT	NT
York 8	40 d	16 11		16 51	17 20		18 11	19 11	20 11	21 57
Poppleton	d	16 15		16 55	17 24		18 15	19 15	20 15	22 01
Hammerton	d	16 23		17 03	17 32		18 23	19 23	20 23	22 09
Cattal	d	16 26		17 06	17 35		18 26	19 26	20 26	22 12
Knaresborough	a	16 34		17 14	17 43		18 34	19 34	20 34	22 20
	d	16 35	17 05	17 15	17 44	18 05	18 35	19 35	20 36	22 21
Starbeck	d	16 38	17 08	17 18	17 47	18 12	18 38	19 38	20 39	22 24
Harrogate	a	16 43	17 13	17 23	17 52	18 17	18 43	19 43	20 44	22 29
	d	16 44	17 14	17 37	17 59	18 18	18 44	19 44	20 45	22 37
Hornbeam Park	d	16 47	17 17	17 39	18 01	18 21	18 47	19 47	20 48	22 39
Pannal	d	16 52	17 22	17 44	18 06	18 26	18 52	19 52	20 53	22 44
Weeton	d	16 56	17 26	17 49	18 11	18 30	18 56	19 56	20 57	22 49
Horsforth	d	17 05	17 38	17 57	18 19	18 39	19 05	20 05	21 06	22 57
Headingley	d	17 09	17 42	18 01	18 23	18 43	19 09	20 09	21 10	23 01
Burley Park	d	17 11	17 44	18 04	18 26	18 45	19 11	20 11	21 12	23 04
Leeds 10	40 a	17 22	17 55	18 16	18 40	18 56	19 23	20 22	21 23	23 14

A To London Kings Cross

Table 35

Sundays

York - Harrogate - Leeds

			NT	NT	NT	NT	NT	NT	GR	NT	NT	NT	NT	NT	NT
									R 1 A						
York	40	d				12 18	14 20	16 18		17 17	18 17	19 17	20 18	21 26	
Poppleton		d				12 22	14 24	16 22		17 21	18 21	19 21	20 22	21 30	
Hammerton		d				12 30	14 32	16 30		17 29	18 29	19 29	20 30	21 38	
Cattal		d				12 33	14 35	16 33		17 32	18 32	19 32	20 33	21 41	
Knaresborough		a				12 41	14 43	16 41		17 40	18 40	19 40	20 41	21 49	
		d			11 42	12 42	14 44	16 42		17 42	18 42	19 42	20 42	21 50	
Starbeck		d			11 45	12 45	14 47	16 45		17 45	18 45	19 45	20 45	21 53	
Harrogate		a			11 50	12 50	14 52	16 50		17 50	18 50	19 50	20 50	21 58	
		d	09 53	10 53	11 53	12 53	14 53	16 53	17 05	17 53	18 53	19 53	20 53	22 02	23 12
Hornbeam Park		d	09 56	10 56	11 56	12 56	14 56	16 56		17 56	18 56	19 56	20 56	22 04	23 15
Pannal		d	10 01	11 01	12 01	13 01	15 01	17 01		18 01	19 01	20 01	21 01	22 09	23 20
Weeton		d	10 05	11 05	12 05	13 05	15 05	17 05		18 05	19 05	20 05	21 05	22 14	23 24
Horsforth		d	10 14	11 14	12 14	13 14	15 14	17 14		18 14	19 14	20 14	21 14	22 23	23 33
Headingley		d	10 18	11 18	12 18	13 18	15 18	17 18		18 18	19 18	20 18	21 18	22 27	23 37
Burley Park		d	10 20	11 20	12 20	13 20	15 20	17 20		18 20	19 20	20 20	21 20	22 30	23 39
Leeds	40	a	10 30	11 30	12 30	13 30	15 30	17 30	17 32	18 30	19 30	20 30	21 30	22 40	23 50

A To London Kings Cross

Table 35

Mondays to Fridays

Leeds - Harrogate - York

Miles				NT MX	NT	NT	NT	NT	NT	NT	NT	NT	NT	NT	NT	NT	NT	NT	NT	NT	NT	NT	NT	NT
0	**Leeds** 10	40	d	23p29	06 09	06 29	07 13	07 43	07 59	08 29	08 59	09 29	09 59	10 29	10 59	11 29	11 59	12 29	12 59	13 29	13 59	14 29	14 59	15 29
2¼	Burley Park		d	23p33	06 13	06 33	07 17	07 47	08 03	08 33	09 03	09 33	10 03	10 33	11 03	11 33	12 03	12 33	13 03	13 33	14 03	14 33	15 03	15 33
3	Headingley		d	23p36	06 16	06 36	07 20	07 50	08 06	08 36	09 06	09 36	10 06	10 36	11 06	11 36	12 06	12 36	13 06	13 36	14 06	14 36	15 06	15 36
5¾	Horsforth		d	23p41	06 21	06 41	07 25	07 55	08 11	08 41	09 11	09 41	10 11	10 41	11 11	11 41	12 11	12 41	13 11	13 41	14 11	14 41	15 11	15 41
11¾	Weeton		d	23p49	06 29	06 49	07 33		08 19	08 49	09 19	09 49	10 19	10 49	11 19	11 49	12 19	12 49	13 19	13 49	14 19	14 49	15 19	15 49
15	Pannal		d	23p55	06 35	06 55	07 39		08 25	08 55	09 25	09 55	10 25	10 55	11 25	11 55	12 25	12 55	13 25	13 55	14 25	14 55	15 25	15 55
17¼	Hornbeam Park		d	23p58	06 40	07 00	07 44	08 10	08 30	09 00	09 30	10 00	10 30	11 00	11 30	12 00	12 30	13 00	13 30	14 00	14 30	15 00	15 30	16 00
18¼	**Harrogate**		a	00 06	06 43	07 04	07 49	08 13	08 33	09 03	09 33	10 03	10 33	11 03	11 33	12 03	12 33	13 05	13 33	14 03	14 33	15 03	15 33	16 03
—			d		06 45	07 05	07 49	08 16	08 34	09 05	09 35	10 05	10 35	11 05	11 35	12 05	12 35	13 07	13 35	14 05	14 35	15 05	15 35	16 05
20½	Starbeck		d		06 49	07 08	07 52	08 19	08 38	09 08	09 38	10 08	10 38	11 08	11 38	12 08	12 38	13 10	13 38	14 08	14 38	15 08	15 38	16 08
22	**Knaresborough**		a		06 54	07 15	07 59	08 25	08 45	09 14	09 45	10 14	10 45	11 14	11 45	12 14	12 45	13 16	13 45	14 14	14 45	15 14	15 45	16 14
—			d		06 55	07 19	07 59	08 28		09 15		10 14		11 14		12 14		13 16		14 14		15 14		16 14
28½	Cattal		d		07 03	07 27	08 07	08 36		09 23		10 22		11 22		12 22		13 24		14 22		15 22		16 22
30	Hammerton		d		07 06	07 30	08 11	08 39		09 27		10 26		11 26		12 26		13 28		14 26		15 26		16 26
35¾	Poppleton		d		07 13	07 37	08 18	08 46		09 34		10 33		11 33		12 33		13 35		14 33		15 33		16 33
38¾	**York** 8	40	a		07 21	07 48	08 32	08 58		09 45		10 45		11 45		12 45		13 45		14 45		15 45		16 45

			NT	NT	NT	NT	NT	NT	NT	NT	NT	NT	NT	GR R 1 A (catering)	NT	NT	NT	NT
Leeds 10	40	d	15 59	16 29	16 42	16 59	17 13	17 29	17 44	17 59	18 29	18 59	19 29	19 59	20 29	21 29	22 31	23 29
Burley Park		d	16 03	16 33	16 46	17 03	17 17	17 33	17 48	18 03	18 33	19 03	19 33		20 33	21 33	22 35	23 33
Headingley		d	16 06	16 36	16 49	17 06	17 20	17 36	17 51	18 06	18 36	19 06	19 36		20 36	21 36	22 38	23 36
Horsforth		d	16 11	16 41	16a55	17 11	17 25	17 41	17 56	18 11	18 41	19 11	19 41		20 41	21 41	22 43	23 41
Weeton		d	16 19	16 49		17 19	17 33	17 49		18 19	18 49	19 19	19 49		20 49	21 49	22 52	23 49
Pannal		d	16 25	16 55		17 25	17 39	17 55		18 25	18 55	19 25	19 55		20 55	21 55	22 57	23 55
Hornbeam Park		d	16 30	17 00		17 30	17 44	18 00		18 30	19 00	19 30	20 00		21 00	22 00	23 03	23 58
Harrogate		a	16 33	17 03		17 33	17 47	18 03	18 15	18 33	19 03	19 33	20 03	20 29	21 03	22 03	23 09	00 06
		d	16 35	17 08		17 35	17 49	18 05	18 16	18 35	19 05	19 35	20 05		21 05	22 05		
Starbeck		d	16 38	17 11		17 38	17 52	18 08	18 20	18 39	19 08	19 38	20 08		21 08	22 08		
Knaresborough		a	16 45	17 17		17 45	18 01	18 14	18 26	18 45	19 14	19 45	20 14		21 14	22 16		
		d		17 24				18 14			19 14		20 14		21 14			
Cattal		d		17 32				18 22			19 22		20 22		21 22			
Hammerton		d		17 35				18 26			19 26		20 26		21 26			
Poppleton		d		17 42				18 33			19 33		20 33		21 33			
York 8	40	a		17 52				18 46			19 45		20 45		21 47			

Saturdays

			NT	NT	NT	NT	NT	NT	NT	NT	NT	NT	NT	NT	NT	NT	NT	NT	NT	NT	NT	NT	NT	NT
Leeds 10	40	d	23p29	06 09	06 36	07 13	07 39	07 54	08 29	08 59	09 29	09 59	10 29	10 59	11 29	11 59	12 29	12 59	13 29	13 59	14 29	14 59	15 29	15 59
Burley Park		d	23p33	06 13	06 40	07 17	07 43	07 58	08 33	09 03	09 33	10 03	10 33	11 03	11 33	12 03	12 33	13 03	13 33	14 03	14 33	15 03	15 33	16 03
Headingley		d	23p36	06 16	06 43	07 20	07 46	08 01	08 36	09 06	09 36	10 06	10 36	11 06	11 36	12 06	12 36	13 06	13 36	14 06	14 36	15 06	15 36	16 06
Horsforth		d	23p41	06 21	06 48	07 25	07 51	08 06	08 41	09 11	09 41	10 11	10 41	11 11	11 41	12 11	12 41	13 11	13 41	14 11	14 41	15 11	15 41	16 11
Weeton		d	23p49	06 29	06 56	07 33	07 59	08 14	08 49	09 19	09 49	10 19	10 49	11 19	11 49	12 19	12 49	13 19	13 49	14 19	14 49	15 19	15 49	16 19
Pannal		d	23p55	06 35	07 02	07 39	08 09	08 22	08 55	09 25	09 55	10 25	10 55	11 25	11 55	12 25	12 55	13 25	13 55	14 25	14 55	15 25	15 55	16 25
Hornbeam Park		d	23p58	06 40	07 07	07 44	08 14	08 28	09 00	09 30	10 00	10 30	11 00	11 30	12 00	12 30	13 00	13 30	14 00	14 30	15 00	15 30	16 00	16 30
Harrogate		a	00 06	06 43	07 10	07 47	08 17	08 31	09 03	09 33	10 03	10 33	11 03	11 33	12 03	12 33	13 03	13 33	14 03	14 33	15 03	15 33	16 03	16 33
		d		06 45	07 12	07 49	08 19	08 31	09 05	09 35	10 05	10 35	11 05	11 35	12 05	12 35	13 05	13 35	14 05	14 35	15 05	15 35	16 05	16 35
Starbeck		d		06 49	07 15	07 52	08 22	08 36	09 08	09 38	10 08	10 38	11 08	11 38	12 08	12 38	13 08	13 38	14 08	14 38	15 08	15 38	16 08	16 38
Knaresborough		a		06 54	07 21	07 59	08 28	08 42	09 14	09 45	10 14	10 45	11 14	11 45	12 14	12 45	13 14	13 45	14 14	14 45	15 14	15 45	16 14	16 45
		d		06 55	07 21	07 59	08 28		09 15		10 14		11 14		12 14		13 14		14 14		15 14		16 14	
Cattal		d		07 03	07 29	08 07	08 36		09 23		10 22		11 22		12 22		13 22		14 22		15 22		16 22	
Hammerton		d		07 06	07 33	08 11	08 40		09 27		10 26		11 26		12 26		13 26		14 26		15 26		16 26	
Poppleton		d		07 13	07 40	08 19	08 47		09 34		10 33		11 33		12 33		13 33		14 33		15 33		16 33	
York 8	40	a		07 21	07 46	08 26	08 59		09 45		10 45		11 45		12 45		13 45		14 45		15 45		16 44	

			NT	NT	NT	NT	NT	NT	NT	GR R 1 A (catering)	NT	NT	NT	NT
Leeds 10	40	d	16 29	16 59	17 13	17 29	17 59	18 29	19 29	19 59	20 33	21 20	22 33	23 21
Burley Park		d	16 33	17 03	17 17	17 33	18 03	18 33	19 33		20 37	21 24	22 37	23 25
Headingley		d	16 36	17 06	17 20	17 36	18 06	18 36	19 36		20 40	21 27	22 40	23 28
Horsforth		d	16 41	17 11	17 25	17 41	18 11	18 41	19 41		20 45	21 32	22 45	23 33
Weeton		d	16 49	17 19	17 33	17 49	18 19	18 49	19 49		20 53	21 40	22 53	23 41
Pannal		d	16 55	17 25	17 39	17 55	18 25	18 55	19 55		20 59	21 46	22 59	23 47
Hornbeam Park		d	17 00	17 30	17 44	18 00	18 30	19 00	20 00		21 04	21 51	23 04	23 52
Harrogate		a	17 03	17 33	17 47	18 03	18 33	19 03	20 04	20 29	21 07	21 54	23 10	23 58
		d	17 08	17 35	17 49	18 05	18 35	19 05	20 04		21 09	21 56		
Starbeck		d	17 11	17 38	17 52	18 08	18 38	19 08	20 08		21 12	21 59		
Knaresborough		a	17 17	17 45	18 00	18 14	18 45	19 14	20 14		21 18	22 06		
		d	17 21			18 14		19 14	20 14		21 18			
Cattal		d	17 29			18 22		19 22	20 22		21 26			
Hammerton		d	17 34			18 26		19 26	20 26		21 31			
Poppleton		d	17 41			18 33		19 33	20 33		21 38			
York 8	40	a	17 52			18 45		19 45	20 45		21 48			

A From London Kings Cross

Table 35

Sundays

Leeds - Harrogate - York

			NT	NT	NT	NT	NT	NT	NT	NT	NT		GR	NT	NT	NT
													R 1			
								B					C	B		
													(restaurant car symbol)			
Leeds 10	40	d	09 54	10 54	12 54	14 54	15 54	16 54	17 54	18 54	19 54		20 37	21 15	22 26	23 23
Burley Park		d	09 59	10 59	12 59	14 59	15 59	16 59	17 59	18 59	19 59			21 20	22 31	23 28
Headingley		d	10 01	11 01	13 01	15 01	16 01	17 01	18 01	19 01	20 01			21 22	22 33	23 30
Horsforth		d	10 07	11 07	13 07	15 07	16 07	17 07	18 07	19 07	20 07			21 28	22 39	23 36
Weeton		d	10 14	11 14	13 14	15 14	16 14	17 14	18 14	19 14	20 14			21 36	22 46	23 43
Pannal		d	10 20	11 20	13 20	15 20	16 20	17 20	18 20	19 20	20 20			21 42	22 52	23 49
Hornbeam Park		d	10 25	11 25	13 25	15 25	16 25	17 25	18 25	19 25	20 25			21 47	22 57	23 54
Harrogate		a	10 31	11 28	13 28	15 28	16 28	17 28	18 28	19 28	20 28		21 07	21 50	23 03	23 59
		d		11 30	13 30	15 30	16 30	17 30	18 30	19 30	20 30			21 52		
Starbeck		d		11 34	13 34	15 34	16 34	17 34	18 34	19 34	20 34			21 56		
Knaresborough		a		11 39	13 39	15 39	16 39	17 39	18 39	19 39	20 39			22 02		
		d		11 40	13 40	15 40	16 45	17 44	18 44	19 44	20 45					
Cattal		d		11 48	13 48	15 48	16 53	17 52	18 52	19 52	20 53					
Hammerton		d		11 51	13 51	15 51	16 56	17 55	18 55	19 55	20 56					
Poppleton		d		11 58	13 58	15 58	17 03	18 02	19 02	20 02	21 03					
York 8	40	a		12 07	14 08	16 06	17 10	18 10	19 12	20 11	21 15					

B until 11 September, from 30 October

C From London Kings Cross

Table 36

Mondays to Fridays

until 15 July

Leeds and Bradford - Skipton, Lancaster, Morecambe and Carlisle

Miles	Miles	Miles		NT MX	NT	NT	NT	NT	NT	NT	NT	NT		NT	NT	NT	NT	NT	NT	NT	NT	NT		NT
—	—	—	London Kings Cross 15 ⊖26 d																					
0	0	—	**Leeds 10** 37 d	23p18		05 55		06 21		06 56		07 25			07 51		08 19	08 25		08 49	08 56			09 26
—	—	0	**Bradford Forster Square** 37 d				06 10		06 40		07 15			07 42		08 11			08 41			09 11		
—	—	1¾	Frizinghall 37 d				06 13		06 43		07 18			07 45		08 14			08 44			09 14		
10¾	10¾	2¾	Shipley 37 a	23p31		06 07	06 17	06 32	06 47	07 08	07 22	07 36		07 49	08 02	08 18	08 31	08 37	08 48	09 01	09 07	09 18		09 37
—	—	—	d	23p32		06 08	06 19	06 33	06 48	07 08	07 23	07 37		07 50	08 03	08 19	08 32	08 37	08 49	09 02	09 09	09 19		09 38
11½	11½	—	Saltaire d	23p34		06 10	06 22	06 35	06 50	07 10	07 25	07 39		07 52	08 05	08 22		08 40	08 52		09 11	09 22		09 40
13¾	13¾	—	Bingley d	23p38		06 15	06 26	06 39	06 54	07 14	07 29	07 43		07 56	08 09	08 26	08 37	08 44	08 56	09 06	09 14	09 26		09 44
14½	14½	—	Crossflatts d	23p40		06 17	06 28	06 41	06 56	07 17	07 31	07 46		07 58	08 11	08 28		08 46	08 58		09 17	09 28		09 47
17	17	—	Keighley d	23p44		06 22	06 33	06 45	07 01	07 21	07 36	07 50		08 03	08 15	08 33	08 43	08 50	09 03	09 12	09 21	09 33		09 51
20	20	—	Steeton & Silsden d	23p48		06 26	06 37	06 49	07 05	07 26	07 40	07 55		08 07	08 19	08 37		08 54	09 07		09 26	09 37		09 56
23¼	23¼	—	Cononley d	23p52		06 31	06 42	06 53	07 09	07 30	07 44	07 59		08 11	08 23	08 42		08 59	09 12		09 30	09 42		10 00
26¼	26¼	—	**Skipton** a	00 02		06 38	06 49	07 03	07 18	07 39	07 52	08 08		08 20	08 32	08 50	08 55	09 09	09 20	09 24	09 40	09 50		10 11
—	—	—	d		05 40	06 42											09 00			09 26				
30	30	—	Gargrave d		05 45												09 05			09 32				
—	—	—	Blackpool North 94 d																					
—	—	—	Preston d																					
—	—	—	Blackburn 97 d																					
—	—	—	Clitheroe 94 d																					
36¼	36¼	—	Hellifield d		05 54	06 53											09 14			09 40				
37½	37½	—	Long Preston d		05 57												09 17			09 43				
—	41¼	—	Giggleswick d		06 07												09 24							
—	48	—	Clapham (Nth Yorkshire) d		06 15												09 33							
—	51¼	—	Bentham d		06 21												09 39							
—	54½	—	Wennington d		06 26												09 44							
—	64	—	Carnforth 82 a		06 42												10 00							
—	70¼	—	**Lancaster 6** 65,82,98 a		06 52												10 12							
—	72¾	—	Bare Lane 98 a														10 26							
—	75½	—	**Morecambe** 98 a														10 33							
41¼	—	—	Settle d			07 01														09 50				
47½	—	—	Horton-in-Ribblesdale d																	09 58				
52¼	—	—	Ribblehead d																	10 06				
58¼	—	—	Dent d																	10 16				
61¾	—	—	Garsdale d																	10 21				
71½	—	—	Kirkby Stephen d			07 43														10 34				
82¼	—	—	Appleby d			07 55														10 47				
93¼	—	—	Langwathby d			08 09														11 01				
97½	—	—	Lazonby & Kirkoswald d			08 15														11 07				
103	—	—	Armathwaite d			08 23														11 15				
113	—	—	**Carlisle 8** 65 a			08 41														11 34				

	NT	NT	NT	NT	NT A	NT	NT	NT		NT	NT	NT	NT	NT	NT	NT	NT	NT		NT	NT	NT	NT	NT
London Kings Cross 15 ⊖26 d																								
Leeds 10 37 d		09 47	09 56		10 19	10 26		10 49		10 56		11 26		11 56		12 26		12 49		12 56		13 26		13 49
Bradford Forster Square 37 d	09 41			10 11			10 41				11 11		11 41		12 11		12 41				13 11		13 41	
Frizinghall 37 d	09 44			10 14			10 44				11 14		11 44		12 14		12 44				13 14		13 44	
Shipley 37 a	09 48	10 01	10 07	10 18	10 31	10 37	10 48	11 01		11 07	11 18	11 39	11 48	12 07	12 18	12 37	12 48	13 01		13 07	13 18	13 37	13 48	14 03
d	09 49	10 02	10 08	10 19	10 32	10 38	10 49	11 02		11 08	11 19	11 39	11 49	12 08	12 19	12 38	12 49	13 02		13 08	13 19	13 38	13 49	14 03
Saltaire d	09 52		10 10	10 22		10 40	10 52			11 10	11 21	11 40	11 52	12 10	12 22	12 40	12 52			13 10	13 22	13 40	13 52	
Bingley d	09 56	10 06	10 14	10 26	10 37	10 44	10 56	11 06		11 14	11 25	11 44	11 56	12 14	12 26	12 44	12 56	13 06		13 14	13 26	13 44	13 56	14 08
Crossflatts d	09 58		10 17	10 28		10 47	10 58			11 17	11 27	11 47	11 58	12 17	12 28	12 47	12 58			13 17	13 28	13 47	13 58	
Keighley d	10 03	10 12	10 21	10 33	10 42	10 51	11 03	11 12		11 21	11 32	11 51	12 03	12 21	12 33	12 51	13 03	13 12		13 21	13 33	13 51	14 03	14 14
Steeton & Silsden d	10 07		10 26	10 37		10 56	11 07			11 26	11 36	11 56	12 07	12 26	12 37	12 56	13 07			13 26	13 37	13 56	14 07	
Cononley d	10 12		10 30	10 42		11 00	11 12			11 30	11 40	12 00	12 12	12 30	12 42	13 00	13 11			13 30	13 42	14 00	14 11	
Skipton a	10 20	10 24	10 39	10 50	10 55	11 09	11 20	11 24		11 40	11 47	12 11	12 20	12 40	12 50	13 10	13 20	13 24		13 38	13 50	14 10	14 20	14 26
d		10 26			11 00			11 26										13 26						14 34
Gargrave d					11 05													13 31						14 39
Blackpool North 94 d																								
Preston d																								
Blackburn 97 d																								
Clitheroe 94 d																								
Hellifield d					11 14			11 37										13 40						14 48
Long Preston d					11 17													13 42						14 51
Giggleswick d					11 24																			14 58
Clapham (Nth Yorkshire) d					11 33																			15 07
Bentham d					11 39																			15 13
Wennington d					11 44																			15 18
Carnforth 82 a					12 00																			15 34
Lancaster 6 65,82,98 a					12 11																			15 47
Bare Lane 98 a					12 34																			16 09
Morecambe 98 a					12 39																			16 13
Settle d		10 44						11 46										13 48						
Horton-in-Ribblesdale d								11 54										13 57						
Ribblehead d								12 02										14 05						
Dent d								12 12										14 14						
Garsdale d								12 17										14 20						
Kirkby Stephen d		11 22						12 30										14 32						
Appleby d		11 36						12 43										14 45						
Langwathby d								12 57										14 59						
Lazonby & Kirkoswald d								13 03										15 04						
Armathwaite d								13 11										15 12						
Carlisle 8 65 a		12 17						13 29										15 32						

A To Heysham Port

until 15 July

Leeds and Bradford - Skipton, Lancaster, Morecambe and Carlisle

	NT	NT	NT	NT		NT	NT	NT	NT	NT	NT	NT	NT	NT		NT	NT	NT	NT	NT	NT	NT	NT	NT
London Kings Cross ■15 ⊖26 d																								
Leeds ■10 37 d	13 56		14 26			14 49	14 56		15 26		15 56		16 26			16 39	16 56		17 26		17 50	17 56		18 23
Bradford Forster Square 37 d		14 11		14 41				15 11		15 41		16 11		16 40				17 11		17 38			18 11	
Frizinghall 37 d		14 14		14 44				15 14		15 44		16 14		16 43				17 14		17 41			18 14	
Shipley 37 a	14 07	14 18	14 37	14 48		15 01	15 07	15 18	15 37	15 48	16 07	16 18	16 37	16 48		16 53	17 07	17 18	17 37	17 45	18 02	18 08	18 18	18 38
d	14 08	14 19	14 38	14 49		15 02	15 08	15 19	15 38	15 49	16 08	16 19	16 38	16 49		16 55	17 08	17 19	17 38	17 46	18 03	18 08	18 19	18 38
Saltaire d	14 10	14 22	14 40	14 52			15 10	15 22	15 40	15 52	16 10	16 22	16 40	16 52			17 10	17 22	17 40	17 49	18 05		18 22	18 40
Bingley d	14 14	14 26	14 44	14 56		15 06	15 14	15 26	15 44	15 56	16 14	16 26	16 44	16 56		17 03	17 14	17 26	17 44	17 53	18 09	18 17	18 26	18 44
Crossflatts d	14 17	14 28	14 47	14 58			15 17	15 28	15 47	15 58	16 17	16 28	16 47	16 58			17 17	17 28	17 47	17 55	18 12		18 28	18 47
Keighley d	14 21	14 33	14 51	15 03		15 12	15 21	15 33	15 51	16 03	16 21	16 33	16 51	17 03		17 10	17 21	17 33	17 51	18 00	18 16	18 24	18 33	18 51
Steeton & Silsden d	14 26	14 37	14 56	15 07			15 26	15 37	15 56	16 07	16 26	16 37	16 56	17 07			17 26	17 37	17 56	18 04	18 21	18 29	18 37	18 56
Cononley d	14 30	14 41	15 00	15 12			15 30	15 42	16 00	16 11	16 30	16 41	17 00	17 11			17 30	17 42	18 00	18 09	18 25		18 42	19 00
Skipton a	14 40	14 50	15 10	15 20		15 24	15 40	15 50	16 10	16 17	16 40	16 49	17 10	17 19		17 24	17 40	17 50	18 10	18 17	18 34	18 40	18 50	19 10
d						15 26										17 24						18 41		
Gargrave d																17 30						18 46		
Blackpool North 94 d																								
Preston d																								
Blackburn 97 d																								
Clitheroe 94 d																								
Hellifield d						15 37										17 39						18 55		
Long Preston d																17 42						18 57		
Giggleswick d																17 49								
Clapham (Nth Yorkshire) d																17 57								
Bentham d																18 03								
Wennington d																18 09								
Carnforth 82 a																18 29								
Lancaster ■6 65,82,98 a																18 42								
Bare Lane 98 a																18 55								
Morecambe 98 a																19 01								
Settle d						15 45																19 03		
Horton-in-Ribblesdale d						15 53																19 12		
Ribblehead d						16 01																19 20		
Dent d						16 11																19 29		
Garsdale d						16 16																19 35		
Kirkby Stephen d						16 29																19 47		
Appleby d						16 41																20 00		
Langwathby d						16 55																20 14		
Lazonby & Kirkoswald d						17 01																20 19		
Armathwaite d						17 09																20 27		
Carlisle ■8 65 a						17 28																20 48		

		NT	NT	NT	NT	NT	NT	NT	NT	NT		GR R ■1 (trolley)	NT	NT	NT	NT	NT	NT	NT	NT		NT		
London Kings Cross ■15 ⊖26 d												18 03												
Leeds ■10 37 d			18 54		19 19	19 26		19 56		20 26		20 33	20 55		21 26	21 56		22 28	22 51			23 18		
Bradford Forster Square 37 d		18 41		19 07			19 36		20 07					21 05			22 05			23 09				
Frizinghall 37 d		18 44		19 10			19 39		20 10					21 08			22 08			23 12				
Shipley 37 a		18 48	19 05	19 14	19 31	19 38	19 43	20 07	20 15	20 37			21 07	21 12	21 38	22 07	22 12	22 37	23 05	23 16		23 31		
d		18 49	19 06	19 15	19 32	19 39	19 44	20 08	20 15	20 38			21 08	21 14	21 38	22 08	22 14	22 38	23 06	23 17		23 32		
Saltaire d		18 51	19 08	19 18		19 40	19 47	20 10	20 17	20 40			21 10	21 17	21 40	22 10	22 16	22 40	23 08	23 20		23 34		
Bingley d		18 55	19 12	19 22	19 36	19 44	19 51	20 14	20 21	20 44			21 14	21 21	21 44	22 14	22 20	22 44	23 13	23 24		23 38		
Crossflatts d		18 57	19 15	19 24		19 47	19 53	20 17	20 23	20 47			21 17	21 23	21 47	22 17	22 22	22 47	23 15	23 26		23 40		
Keighley d		19 02	19 19	19 29	19 42	19 51	19 58	20 21	20 28	20 51		20s55	21 21	21 28	21 51	22 21	22 27	22 51	23 20	23 31		23 44		
Steeton & Silsden d		19 06	19 24	19 33		19 56	20 02	20 26	20 32	20 56			21 26	21 32	21 56	22 26	22 31	22 56	23 24	23 35		23 48		
Cononley d		19 10	19 28	19 38		20 00	20 07	20 30	20 36	21 00			21 30	21 36	22 00	22 30	22 35	23 00	23 29	23 40		23 52		
Skipton a		19 19	19 35	19 46	19 54	20 10	20 15	20 37	20 47	21 09		21 16	21 40	21 44	22 10	22 40	22 42	23 11	23 35	23 48		00 02		
d					20 00																			
Gargrave d					20 06																			
Blackpool North 94 d																								
Preston d																								
Blackburn 97 d																								
Clitheroe 94 d																								
Hellifield d					20 15																			
Long Preston d					20 18																			
Giggleswick d																								
Clapham (Nth Yorkshire) d																								
Bentham d																								
Wennington d																								
Carnforth 82 a																								
Lancaster ■6 65,82,98 a																								
Bare Lane 98 a																								
Morecambe 98 a																								
Settle d					20 24																			
Horton-in-Ribblesdale d					20 32																			
Ribblehead d					20a42																			
Dent d																								
Garsdale d																								
Kirkby Stephen d																								
Appleby d																								
Langwathby d																								
Lazonby & Kirkoswald d																								
Armathwaite d																								
Carlisle ■8 65 a																								

Leeds and Bradford - Skipton, Lancaster, Morecambe and Carlisle

	NT MX	NT	NT		NT	NT	NT	NT	NT		NT	NT	NT	NT	NT	NT	NT	NT	NT		NT	NT	NT	NT
London Kings Cross 15 ⊖26 d																								
Leeds 10 37 d	23p18		05 57			06 21		06 56			07 25		07 51		08 19	08 25		08 49	08 56			09 26		09 47
Bradford Forster Square 37 d					06 10		06 40		07 15			07 42		08 11			08 41				09 11		09 41	
Frizinghall 37 d					06 13		06 43		07 18			07 45		08 14			08 44				09 14		09 44	
Shipley 37 a	23p31		06 10		06 17	06 32	06 47	07 08	07 22		07 36	07 49	08 02	08 18	08 31	08 37	08 48	09 01	09 07		09 18	09 37	09 48	10 01
d	23p32		06 10		06 19	06 33	06 48	07 08	07 23		07 37	07 50	08 03	08 19	08 32	08 37	08 49	09 02	09 09		09 19	09 38	09 49	10 02
Saltaire d	23p34		06 13		06 22	06 35	06 50	07 10	07 25		07 39	07 52	08 05	08 22		08 40	08 52		09 11		09 22	09 40	09 52	
Bingley d	23p38		06 17		06 26	06 39	06 54	07 14	07 29		07 43	07 56	08 09	08 26	08 37	08 44	08 56	09 06	09 14		09 26	09 44	09 56	10 06
Crossflatts d	23p40		06 19		06 28	06 41	06 56	07 17	07 31		07 46	07 58	08 11	08 28		08 46	08 58		09 17		09 28	09 47	09 58	
Keighley d	23p44		06 24		06 33	06 45	07 01	07 21	07 36		07 50	08 03	08 15	08 33	08 43	08 50	09 03	09 12	09 21		09 33	09 51	10 03	10 12
Steeton & Silsden d	23p48		06 29		06 37	06 49	07 05	07 26	07 40		07 55	08 07	08 19	08 37		08 54	09 07		09 26		09 37	09 56	10 07	
Cononley d	23p52		06 34		06 42	06 53	07 09	07 30	07 44		07 59	08 11	08 23	08 42		08 59	09 12		09 30		09 42	10 00	10 12	
Skipton a	00 02		06 40		06 49	07 03	07 18	07 39	07 52		08 08	08 20	08 32	08 50	08 55	09 09	09 20	09 24	09 40		09 50	10 11	10 20	10 24
d		05 40	06 42												09 00			09 26						10 26
Gargrave d		05 45													09 05			09 32						
Blackpool North 94 d																								
Preston d																								
Blackburn 97 d																								
Clitheroe 94 d																								
Hellifield d		05 54	06 53												09 14			09 40						
Long Preston d		05 57													09 17			09 43						
Giggleswick d		06 07													09 24									
Clapham (Nth Yorkshire) d		06 15													09 33									
Bentham d		06 21													09 39									
Wennington d		06 26													09 44									
Carnforth 82 a		06 42													10 00									
Lancaster 6 65,82,98 a		06 52													10 12									
Bare Lane 98 a															10 26									
Morecambe 98 a															10 33									
Settle d			07 01															09 50						10 44
Horton-in-Ribblesdale d																		09 58						
Ribblehead d																		10 06						
Dent d																		10 16						
Garsdale d																		10 21						
Kirkby Stephen d			07 43															10 34						11 22
Appleby d			07 55															10 47						11 36
Langwathby d			08 09															11 01						
Lazonby & Kirkoswald d			08 15															11 07						
Armathwaite d			08 23															11 15						
Carlisle 8 65 a			08 41															11 34						12 17

		NT	NT	NT A	NT		NT	NT	NT	NT	NT	NT	NT	NT	NT		NT	NT	NT	NT	NT	NT	NT	NT
London Kings Cross 15 ⊖26 d																								
Leeds 10 37 d		09 56		10 19	10 26			10 49	10 56		11 26		11 56		12 26			12 49	12 56		13 26		13 49	13 56
Bradford Forster Square 37 d			10 11				10 41			11 11		11 41		12 11			12 41			13 11		13 41		
Frizinghall 37 d			10 14				10 44			11 14		11 44		12 14			12 44			13 14		13 44		
Shipley 37 a		10 07	10 18	10 31	10 37		10 48	11 01	11 07	11 18	11 39	11 48	12 07	12 18	12 37		12 48	13 01	13 07	13 18	13 37	13 48	14 03	14 07
d		10 08	10 19	10 32	10 38		10 49	11 02	11 08	11 19	11 39	11 49	12 08	12 19	12 38		12 49	13 02	13 08	13 19	13 38	13 49	14 03	14 08
Saltaire d		10 10	10 22		10 40		10 52		11 10	11 21	11 40	11 52	12 10	12 22	12 40		12 52		13 10	13 22	13 40	13 52		14 10
Bingley d		10 14	10 26	10 37	10 44		10 56	11 06	11 14	11 25	11 44	11 56	12 14	12 26	12 44		12 56	13 06	13 14	13 26	13 44	13 56	14 08	14 14
Crossflatts d		10 17	10 28		10 47		10 58		11 17	11 27	11 47	11 58	12 17	12 28	12 47		12 58		13 17	13 28	13 47	13 58		14 17
Keighley d		10 21	10 33	10 42	10 51		11 03	11 12	11 21	11 32	11 51	12 03	12 21	12 33	12 51		13 03	13 12	13 21	13 33	13 51	14 03	14 14	14 21
Steeton & Silsden d		10 26	10 37		10 56		11 07		11 26	11 36	11 56	12 07	12 26	12 37	12 56		13 07		13 26	13 37	13 56	14 07		14 26
Cononley d		10 30	10 42		11 00		11 12		11 30	11 40	12 00	12 12	12 30	12 42	13 00		13 11		13 30	13 42	14 00	14 11		14 30
Skipton a		10 39	10 50	10 55	11 09		11 20	11 24	11 40	11 47	12 11	12 20	12 40	12 50	13 10		13 20	13 24	13 38	13 50	14 10	14 20	14 26	14 40
d				11 00				11 26										13 26					14 34	
Gargrave d				11 05														13 31					14 39	
Blackpool North 94 d																								
Preston d																								
Blackburn 97 d																								
Clitheroe 94 d																								
Hellifield d				11 14				11 37										13 40					14 48	
Long Preston d				11 17														13 42					14 51	
Giggleswick d				11 24																			14 58	
Clapham (Nth Yorkshire) d				11 33																			15 07	
Bentham d				11 39																			15 13	
Wennington d				11 44																			15 18	
Carnforth 82 a				12 00																			15 34	
Lancaster 6 65,82,98 a				12 11																			15 47	
Bare Lane 98 a				12 34																			16 09	
Morecambe 98 a				12 39																			16 13	
Settle d								11 46										13 48						
Horton-in-Ribblesdale d								11 54										13 57						
Ribblehead d								12 02										14 05						
Dent d								12 12										14 14						
Garsdale d								12 17										14 20						
Kirkby Stephen d								12 30										14 32						
Appleby d								12 43										14 45						
Langwathby d								12 57										14 59						
Lazonby & Kirkoswald d								13 03										15 04						
Armathwaite d								13 11										15 12						
Carlisle 8 65 a								13 29										15 32						

A To Heysham Port

Table 36

Mondays to Fridays

from 18 July

Leeds and Bradford - Skipton, Lancaster, Morecambe and Carlisle

	NT		NT	NT	NT	NT	NT	NT	NT	NT	NT		NT	NT	NT	NT	NT	NT	NT	NT	NT		NT	NT
London Kings Cross 15 ⊖26 d																								
Leeds 10 37 d			14 26		14 49	14 56		15 26		15 56			16 26		16 39	16 56		17 26		17 50	17 56			18 23
Bradford Forster Square 37 d	14 11			14 41			15 11		15 41		16 11			16 40			17 11		17 38				18 11	
Frizinghall 37 d	14 14			14 44			15 14		15 44		16 14			16 43			17 14		17 41				18 14	
Shipley 37 a	14 18		14 37	14 48	15 01	15 07	15 18	15 37	15 48	16 07	16 18		16 37	16 48	16 53	17 07	17 18	17 37	17 45	18 02	18 08		18 18	18 38
d	14 19		14 38	14 49	15 02	15 08	15 19	15 38	15 49	16 08	16 19		16 38	16 49	16 55	17 08	17 19	17 38	17 46	18 03	18 08		18 19	18 38
Saltaire d	14 22		14 40	14 52		15 10	15 22	15 40	15 52	16 10	16 22		16 40	16 52		17 10	17 22	17 40	17 49	18 05			18 22	18 40
Bingley d	14 26		14 44	14 56	15 06	15 14	15 26	15 44	15 56	16 14	16 26		16 44	16 56	17 03	17 14	17 26	17 44	17 53	18 09	18 17		18 26	18 44
Crossflatts d	14 28		14 47	14 58		15 17	15 28	15 47	15 58	16 17	16 28		16 47	16 58		17 17	17 28	17 47	17 55	18 12			18 28	18 47
Keighley d	14 33		14 51	15 03	15 12	15 21	15 33	15 51	16 03	16 21	16 33		16 51	17 03	17 10	17 21	17 33	17 51	18 00	18 16	18 24		18 33	18 51
Steeton & Silsden d	14 37		14 56	15 07		15 26	15 37	15 56	16 07	16 26	16 37		16 56	17 07		17 26	17 37	17 56	18 04	18 21	18 29		18 37	18 56
Cononley d	14 41		15 00	15 12		15 30	15 42	16 00	16 11	16 30	16 41		17 00	17 11		17 30	17 42	18 00	18 09	18 25			18 42	19 00
Skipton a	14 50		15 10	15 20	15 24	15 40	15 50	16 10	16 17	16 40	16 49		17 10	17 19	17 24	17 40	17 50	18 10	18 17	18 34	18 40		18 50	19 10
d					15 26										17 24						18 41			
Gargrave d															17 30						18 46			
Blackpool North 94 d																								
Preston d																								
Blackburn 97 d																								
Clitheroe 94 d																								
Hellifield d					15 37										17 39						18 55			
Long Preston d															17 42						18 57			
Giggleswick d															17 49									
Clapham (Nth Yorkshire) d															17 57									
Bentham d															18 03									
Wennington d															18 09									
Carnforth 82 a															18 29									
Lancaster 6 65,82,98 a															18 42									
Bare Lane 98 a															18 55									
Morecambe 98 a															19 01									
Settle d					15 45																19 03			
Horton-in-Ribblesdale d					15 53																19 12			
Ribblehead d					16 01																19 20			
Dent d					16 11																19 29			
Garsdale d					16 16																19 35			
Kirkby Stephen d					16 29																19 47			
Appleby d					16 41																20 00			
Langwathby d					16 55																20 14			
Lazonby & Kirkoswald d					17 01																20 19			
Armathwaite d					17 09																20 27			
Carlisle 8 65 a					17 28																20 48			

	NT	NT	NT	NT	NT	NT	NT		NT	NT	GR 1	NT	NT	NT	NT	NT	NT		NT	NT	NT			
London Kings Cross 15 ⊖26 d											18 03													
Leeds 10 37 d		18 54		19 19	19 26		19 56			20 26	20 33	20 55		21 26	21 56		22 28		22 51		23 18			
Bradford Forster Square 37 d	18 41		19 07			19 36			20 07				21 05			22 05				23 09				
Frizinghall 37 d	18 44		19 10			19 39			20 10				21 08			22 08				23 12				
Shipley 37 a	18 48	19 05	19 14	19 31	19 38	19 43	20 07		20 15	20 37		21 07	21 12	21 38	22 07	22 12	22 37		23 05	23 16	23 31			
d	18 49	19 06	19 15	19 32	19 39	19 44	20 08		20 15	20 38		21 08	21 14	21 38	22 08	22 14	22 38		23 06	23 17	23 32			
Saltaire d	18 51	19 08	19 18		19 40	19 47	20 10		20 17	20 40		21 10	21 17	21 40	22 10	22 16	22 40		23 08	23 20	23 34			
Bingley d	18 55	19 12	19 22	19 36	19 44	19 51	20 14		20 21	20 44		21 14	21 21	21 44	22 14	22 20	22 44		23 13	23 24	23 38			
Crossflatts d	18 57	19 15	19 24		19 47	19 53	20 17		20 23	20 47		21 17	21 23	21 47	22 17	22 22	22 47		23 15	23 26	23 40			
Keighley d	19 02	19 19	19 29	19 42	19 51	19 58	20 21		20 28	20 51	20s55	21 21	21 28	21 51	22 21	22 27	22 51		23 20	23 31	23 44			
Steeton & Silsden d	19 06	19 24	19 33		19 56	20 02	20 26		20 32	20 56		21 26	21 32	21 56	22 26	22 31	22 56		23 24	23 35	23 48			
Cononley d	19 10	19 28	19 38		20 00	20 07	20 30		20 36	21 00		21 30	21 36	22 00	22 30	22 35	23 00		23 29	23 40	23 52			
Skipton a	19 19	19 35	19 46	19 54	20 10	20 15	20 37		20 47	21 09	21 16	21 40	21 44	22 10	22 40	22 42	23 11		23 35	23 48	00 02			
d				20 00																				
Gargrave d				20 06																				
Blackpool North 94 d																								
Preston d																								
Blackburn 97 d																								
Clitheroe 94 d																								
Hellifield d				20 15																				
Long Preston d				20 18																				
Giggleswick d																								
Clapham (Nth Yorkshire) d																								
Bentham d																								
Wennington d																								
Carnforth 82 a																								
Lancaster 6 65,82,98 a																								
Bare Lane 98 a																								
Morecambe 98 a																								
Settle d				20 24																				
Horton-in-Ribblesdale d				20 32																				
Ribblehead d				20a42																				
Dent d																								
Garsdale d																								
Kirkby Stephen d																								
Appleby d																								
Langwathby d																								
Lazonby & Kirkoswald d																								
Armathwaite d																								
Carlisle 8 65 a																								

Table 36

Saturdays

Leeds and Bradford - Skipton, Lancaster, Morecambe and Carlisle

		NT	NT	NT	NT	NT	NT	NT	NT	NT		NT	NT	NT	NT	NT	NT	NT	NT			NT	NT	NT C	NT
London Kings Cross 15	⊖26 d																								
Leeds 10	37 d	23p18	05 55		06 19	06 56		07 56		08 19		08 25		08 49	08 56		09 26		09 47			09 56		10 19	10 26
Bradford Forster Square	37 d			06 10			07 11		08 11				08 41			09 11		09 41					10 11		
Frizinghall	37 d			06 13			07 14		08 14				08 44			09 14		09 44					10 14		
Shipley	37 a	23p31	06 07	06 17	06 31	07 08	07 18	08 08	08 18	08 31		08 37	08 48	09 01	09 07	09 18	09 37	09 48	10 01			10 07	10 18	10 31	10 37
	d	23p32	06 08	06 19	06 32	07 08	07 19	08 08	08 19	08 32		08 37	08 49	09 02	09 08	09 19	09 38	09 49	10 02			10 08	10 19	10 32	10 38
Saltaire	d	23p34	06 10	06 22		07 10	07 22	08 10	08 22			08 40	08 52		09 10	09 22	09 40	09 52				10 10	10 22		10 40
Bingley	d	23p38	06 15	06 26	06 36	07 14	07 26	08 14	08 26	08 37		08 44	08 56	09 06	09 14	09 26	09 44	09 56	10 06			10 14	10 26	10 37	10 44
Crossflatts	d	23p40	06 17	06 28		07 17	07 28	08 16	08 28			08 46	08 58		09 17	09 28	09 47	09 58				10 17	10 28		10 47
Keighley	d	23p44	06 22	06 33	06 42	07 21	07 33	08 20	08 33	08 43		08 50	09 03	09 12	09 21	09 33	09 51	10 03	10 12			10 21	10 33	10 42	10 51
Steeton & Silsden	d	23p48	06 26	06 37		07 26	07 37	08 24	08 37			08 54	09 07		09 26	09 37	09 56	10 07				10 26	10 37		10 56
Cononley	d	23p52	06 31	06 42		07 30	07 42	08 28	08 42			08 59	09 12		09 30	09 42	10 00	10 12				10 30	10 42		11 00
Skipton	a	00 02	06 40	06 49	06 55	07 39	07 50	08 39	08 50	08 55		09 09	09 20	09 24	09 40	09 50	10 11	10 20	10 24			10 39	10 50	10 55	11 11
	d		06 40		06 56					09 00				09 26					10 26					11 00	
Gargrave	d		06 45							09 05				09 32										11 05	
Blackpool North	94 d																								
Preston	d																								
Blackburn	97 d																								
Clitheroe	94 d																								
Hellifield	d		06 54		07 08					09 14				09 40										11 14	
Long Preston	d		06 57							09 17				09 43										11 17	
Giggleswick	d		07 07							09 24														11 25	
Clapham (Nth Yorkshire)	d		07 15							09 33														11 33	
Bentham	d		07 21							09 39														11 39	
Wennington	d		07 26							09 44														11 44	
Carnforth	82 a		07 42							10 00														12 00	
Lancaster 6	65,82,98 a		07 52							10 12														12 11	
Bare Lane	98 a									10 25														12 31	
Morecambe	98 a									10 32														12 36	
Settle	d				07 15									09 50					10 44						
Horton-in-Ribblesdale	d				07 24									09 58											
Ribblehead	d				07 32									10 06											
Dent	d				07 41									10 16											
Garsdale	d				07 47									10 21											
Kirkby Stephen	d				07 59									10 34					11 22						
Appleby	d				08 12									10 47					11 36						
Langwathby	d				08 26									11 01											
Lazonby & Kirkoswald	d				08 31									11 07											
Armathwaite	d				08 39									11 15											
Carlisle 8	65 a				08 58									11 34					12 17						

		NT	NT	NT	NT	NT		NT	NT	NT	NT	NT	NT	NT	NT	NT		NT	NT	NT	NT	NT	NT	NT	NT
London Kings Cross 15	⊖26 d																								
Leeds 10	37 d		10 49	10 56		11 26			11 56		12 26		12 49	12 56		13 26			13 49	13 56		14 26		14 49	14 56
Bradford Forster Square	37 d	10 41			11 11			11 41		12 11		12 41			13 11			13 41			14 11		14 41		
Frizinghall	37 d	10 44			11 14			11 44		12 14		12 44			13 14			13 44			14 14		14 44		
Shipley	37 a	10 48	11 01	11 07	11 18	11 37		11 48	12 07	12 18	12 37	12 48	13 01	13 07	13 18	13 37		13 48	14 03	14 07	14 18	14 37	14 48	15 01	15 07
	d	10 49	11 02	11 08	11 19	11 38		11 49	12 08	12 19	12 38	12 49	13 02	13 08	13 19	13 38		13 49	14 03	14 08	14 19	14 38	14 49	15 02	15 08
Saltaire	d	10 52		11 10	11 21	11 40		11 52	12 10	12 22	12 40	12 52		13 10	13 22	13 40		13 52		14 10	14 22	14 40	14 52		15 10
Bingley	d	10 56	11 06	11 14	11 25	11 44		11 56	12 14	12 26	12 44	12 56	13 06	13 14	13 26	13 44		13 56	14 08	14 14	14 26	14 44	14 56	15 06	15 14
Crossflatts	d	10 58		11 17	11 27	11 47		11 58	12 17	12 28	12 47	12 58		13 17	13 28	13 47		13 58		14 17	14 28	14 47	14 58		15 17
Keighley	d	11 03	11 12	11 21	11 32	11 51		12 03	12 21	12 33	12 51	13 03	13 12	13 21	13 33	13 51		14 03	14 14	14 21	14 33	14 51	15 03	15 12	15 21
Steeton & Silsden	d	11 07		11 26	11 36	11 56		12 07	12 26	12 37	12 56	13 07		13 26	13 37	13 56		14 07		14 26	14 37	14 56	15 07		15 26
Cononley	d	11 12		11 30	11 40	12 00		12 12	12 30	12 42	13 00	13 12		13 30	13 42	14 00		14 11		14 30	14 41	15 00	15 12		15 30
Skipton	a	11 20	11 24	11 40	11 50	12 11		12 20	12 40	12 50	13 10	13 20	13 24	13 38	13 50	14 10		14 20	14 26	14 40	14 50	15 10	15 20	15 24	15 40
	d		11 26										13 26						14 34					15 26	
Gargrave	d												13 31						14 39						
Blackpool North	94 d																								
Preston	d																								
Blackburn	97 d																								
Clitheroe	94 d																								
Hellifield	d		11 37										13 40						14 48					15 37	
Long Preston	d												13 42						14 51						
Giggleswick	d																		14 59						
Clapham (Nth Yorkshire)	d																		15 07						
Bentham	d																		15 13						
Wennington	d																		15 18						
Carnforth	82 a																		15 34						
Lancaster 6	65,82,98 a																		15 45						
Bare Lane	98 a																		15 55						
Morecambe	98 a																		16 02						
Settle	d		11 46										13 48											15 45	
Horton-in-Ribblesdale	d		11 54										13 57											15 53	
Ribblehead	d		12 02										14 05											16 01	
Dent	d		12 12										14 14											16 11	
Garsdale	d		12 17										14 20											16 16	
Kirkby Stephen	d		12 30										14 32											16 29	
Appleby	d		12 43										14 45											16 41	
Langwathby	d		12 57										14 59											16 55	
Lazonby & Kirkoswald	d		13 03										15 04											17 01	
Armathwaite	d		13 11										15 12											17 09	
Carlisle 8	65 a		13 29										15 27											17 28	

C To Heysham Port

Table 36

Saturdays

Leeds and Bradford - Skipton, Lancaster, Morecambe and Carlisle

Station		NT		NT	NT	NT	NT	NT	NT	NT	NT	NT		NT	NT	NT	NT	NT	NT	NT	NT	NT		NT	NT
London Kings Cross 15 ⊖26	d																								
Leeds 10 37	d			15 26		15 56		16 26		16 39	16 56			17 26		17 50	17 56		18 26		18 56			19 19	19 26
Bradford Forster Square 37	d	15 11			15 41		16 11		16 40			17 11			17 41			18 11		18 41		19 07			
Frizinghall 37	d	15 14			15 44		16 14		16 43			17 14			17 44			18 14		18 44		19 10			
Shipley 37	a	15 18		15 37	15 48	16 07	16 18	16 37	16 48	16 53	17 07	17 18		17 37	17 48	18 02	18 08	18 18	18 38	18 48	19 07	19 14		19 31	19 37
	d	15 19		15 38	15 49	16 08	16 19	16 38	16 49	16 55	17 08	17 19		17 38	17 49	18 03	18 08	18 19	18 38	18 49	19 08	19 15		19 32	19 38
Saltaire	d	15 22		15 40	15 52	16 10	16 22	16 40	16 52		17 10	17 22		17 40	17 51		18 10	18 22	18 40	18 51	19 10	19 18			19 40
Bingley	d	15 26		15 44	15 56	16 14	16 26	16 44	16 56	17 03	17 14	17 26		17 44	17 55	18 08	18 14	18 26	18 44	18 55	19 14	19 22		19 36	19 44
Crossflatts	d	15 28		15 47	15 58	16 17	16 28	16 47	16 58		17 17	17 28		17 47	17 57		18 17	18 28	18 47	18 57	19 17	19 24			19 47
Keighley	d	15 33		15 51	16 03	16 21	16 33	16 51	17 03	17 10	17 21	17 33		17 51	18 02	18 14	18 21	18 33	18 51	19 02	19 21	19 29		19 42	19 51
Steeton & Silsden	d	15 37		15 56	16 07	16 26	16 37	16 56	17 07		17 26	17 37		17 56	18 06	18 19	18 26	18 37	18 56	19 06	19 26	19 33			19 56
Cononley	d	15 42		16 00	16 11	16 30	16 41	17 00	17 11		17 30	17 42		18 00	18 10		18 30	18 42	19 00	19 10	19 30	19 38			20 00
Skipton	a	15 50		16 10	16 20	16 40	16 50	17 10	17 19	17 24	17 40	17 50		18 10	18 17	18 29	18 40	18 50	19 10	19 19	19 40	19 46		19 54	20 10
	d									17 24						18 35								20 00	
Gargrave	d									17 30						18 40								20 06	
Blackpool North 94	d																								
Preston	d																								
Blackburn 97	d																								
Clitheroe 94	d																								
Hellifield	d									17 39						18 49								20 15	
Long Preston	d									17 42						18 51								20 18	
Giggleswick	d									17 49															
Clapham (Nth Yorkshire)	d									17 57															
Bentham	d									18 04															
Wennington	d									18 09															
Carnforth 82	a									18 26															
Lancaster 6 65,82,98	a									18 38															
Bare Lane 98	a									18 53															
Morecambe 98	a									18 59															
Settle	d															18 57								20 24	
Horton-in-Ribblesdale	d															19 06								20 32	
Ribblehead	d															19 14								20a42	
Dent	d															19 23									
Garsdale	d															19 29									
Kirkby Stephen	d															19 41									
Appleby	d															19 54									
Langwathby	d															20 08									
Lazonby & Kirkoswald	d															20 13									
Armathwaite	d															20 21									
Carlisle 8 65	a															20 41									

Station		NT	NT	NT	NT	GR	NT	NT		NT	NT	NT	NT	NT	NT	NT
						8 1 🍴										
London Kings Cross 15 ⊖26	d					18 35										
Leeds 10 37	d		19 55		20 26	20 54	20 58			21 26		22 03	22 26	22 56		23 18
Bradford Forster Square 37	d	19 36		20 07				21 05			22 01				23 05	
Frizinghall 37	d	19 39		20 10				21 08			22 04				23 08	
Shipley 37	a	19 43	20 07	20 15	20 37		21 07	21 12		21 38	22 08	22 15	22 37	23 07	23 12	23 31
	d	19 44	20 08	20 15	20 38		21 09	21 17		21 38	22 09	22 16	22 38	23 09	23 14	23 32
Saltaire	d	19 47	20 10	20 17	20 40		21 10	21 20		21 40	22 12	22 18	22 40	23 11	23 17	23 34
Bingley	d	19 51	20 14	20 21	20 44		21 14	21 24		21 44	22 16	22 22	22 44	23 15	23 21	23 38
Crossflatts	d	19 53	20 17	20 23	20 47		21 17	21 26		21 47	22 18	22 25	22 47	23 18	23 23	23 40
Keighley	d	19 58	20 21	20 28	20 51	21s13	21 21	21 31		21 51	22 23	22 29	22 51	23 22	23 28	23 44
Steeton & Silsden	d	20 02	20 26	20 32	20 56		21 26	21 35		21 56	22 27	22 34	22 56	23 27	23 32	23 48
Cononley	d	20 07	20 30	20 36	20 59		21 30	21 39		22 00	22 31	22 38	23 00	23 31	23 37	23 52
Skipton	a	20 15	20 37	20 47	21 10	21 30	21 40	21 47		22 10	22 39	22 47	23 11	23 40	23 44	00 02
	d															
Gargrave	d															
Blackpool North 94	d															
Preston	d															
Blackburn 97	d															
Clitheroe 94	d															
Hellifield	d															
Long Preston	d															
Giggleswick	d															
Clapham (Nth Yorkshire)	d															
Bentham	d															
Wennington	d															
Carnforth 82	a															
Lancaster 6 65,82,98	a															
Bare Lane 98	a															
Morecambe 98	a															
Settle	d															
Horton-in-Ribblesdale	d															
Ribblehead	d															
Dent	d															
Garsdale	d															
Kirkby Stephen	d															
Appleby	d															
Langwathby	d															
Lazonby & Kirkoswald	d															
Armathwaite	d															
Carlisle 8 65	a															

Table 36

Sundays until 11 September

Leeds and Bradford - Skipton, Lancaster, Morecambe and Carlisle

	NT A	NT	NT	NT 🚲	NT 🚲	NT	NT	NT	NT	NT	NT	NT	NT	NT	NT	NT	NT	NT	NT	NT	NT	NT
London Kings Cross 15 ⊖26 d																						
Leeds 10 37 d	23p18	08 40	09 00			10 08		10 51	11 08	12 08		13 08	13 15	14 08		14 57	15 08	16 08		17 08	17 21	17 33
Bradford Forster Square 37 d							10 48				12 48				14 48				16 48			
Frizinghall 37 d							10 51				12 51				14 51				16 51			
Shipley 37 a	23p31	08 52	09 15			10 19	10 54	11 03	11 19	12 19	12 54	13 19	13 28	14 19	14 54	15 09	15 19	16 19	16 54	17 19	17 33	17 45
d	23p32	08 53	09 16			10 20	10 55	11 04	11 20	12 20	12 55	13 20	13 29	14 20	14 55	15 10	15 20	16 20	16 55	17 20	17 34	17 46
Saltaire d	23p34	08 55	09 18			10 22	10 57		11 22	12 22	12 57	13 22		14 22	14 57		15 22	16 22	16 57	17 22		
Bingley d	23p38	09 00	09 23			10 26	11 01	11 09	11 26	12 26	13 01	13 26	13 34	14 26	15 01	15 15	15 26	16 26	17 01	17 26	17 39	17 50
Crossflatts d	23p40	09 02	09 25			10 28	11 03		11 28	12 28	13 03	13 28		14 28	15 03		15 28	16 28	17 03	17 28		
Keighley d	23p44	09 07	09 30			10 32	11 08	11 15	11 32	12 32	13 08	13 32	13 39	14 32	15 08	15 20	15 32	16 32	17 08	17 32	17 44	17 56
Steeton & Silsden d	23p48	09 11	09 34			10 36	11 12		11 36	12 36	13 12	13 36		14 36	15 12		15 36	16 36	17 12	17 36		
Cononley d	23p52	09 16	09 39			10 40	11 16		11 40	12 40	13 16	13 40		14 40	15 16		15 40	16 40	17 16	17 40		
Skipton a	00 02	09 23	09 46			10 48	11 23	11 28	11 48	12 48	13 23	13 48	13 53	14 48	15 23	15 33	15 48	16 48	17 23	17 48	17 57	18 08
d		09 26	09 48					11 30					13 54			15 36					18 00	18 11
Gargrave d		09 31	09 53					11 35					14 00			15 41					18 05	
Blackpool North 94 d				08 36																		
Preston d				09 05	10 00																	
Blackburn 97 d				09 27	10 22																	
Clitheroe 94 d				09 51	10 45																	
Hellifield d		09 40	10 02	10 15	11 08			11 44					14 08			15 50					18 14	18 22
Long Preston d		09 43						11 46					14 11			15 53					18 18	
Giggleswick d		09 52						11 54								16 00					18 25	
Clapham (Nth Yorkshire) d		10 00						12 02								16 08					18 33	
Bentham d		10 06						12 08								16 15					18 39	
Wennington d		10 11						12 13								16 20					18 44	
Carnforth 82 a		10 28						12 30								16 36					19 00	
Lancaster 6 65,82,98 a		10 40						12 44								16 46					19 13	
Bare Lane 98 a		10 51						13 07								16 56					19 29	
Morecambe 98 a		10 57						13 13								17 03					19 35	
Settle d			10 10	10 35	11 17								14 17									18 30
Horton-in-Ribblesdale d			10 19	10 44	11 26								14 26									18 39
Ribblehead d			10 27	10 52	11 34								14 34									18 47
Dent d			10 37	11 02	11 44								14 44									18 57
Garsdale d			10 43	11 07	11 49								14 50									19 02
Kirkby Stephen d			10 56	11 20	12 02								15 03									19 15
Appleby d			11 09	11 34	12 16								15 15									19 28
Langwathby d			11 23	11 48	12 30								15 29									19 42
Lazonby & Kirkoswald d			11 29	11 54	12 36								15 35									19 48
Armathwaite d			11 37	12 02	12 44								15 43									19 56
Carlisle 8 65 a			11 56	12 17	13 05								16 00									20 13

	NT	NT	NT	NT	NT	GR R 1 🚲	NT	NT	NT	NT
London Kings Cross 15 ⊖26 d						18 35				
Leeds 10 37 d	18 08		19 08	20 08		21 03	21 08	22 08		23 20
Bradford Forster Square 37 d		18 48			20 48				22 48	
Frizinghall 37 d		18 51			20 51				22 51	
Shipley 37 a	18 19	18 54	19 19	20 19	20 54		21 19	22 19	22 54	23 31
d	18 20	18 55	19 20	20 20	20 55		21 20	22 20	22 55	23 32
Saltaire d	18 22	18 57	19 22	20 22	20 57		21 22	22 22	22 57	23 34
Bingley d	18 26	19 01	19 26	20 26	21 01		21 26	22 26	23 01	23 38
Crossflatts d	18 28	19 03	19 28	20 28	21 03		21 28	22 28	23 03	23 40
Keighley d	18 32	19 08	19 32	20 32	21 08	21s22	21 32	22 32	23 08	23 44
Steeton & Silsden d	18 36	19 12	19 36	20 36	21 12		21 36	22 36	23 12	23 48
Cononley d	18 40	19 16	19 40	20 40	21 16		21 40	22 40	23 16	23 52
Skipton a	18 48	19 23	19 48	20 48	21 23	21 43	21 48	22 48	23 23	23 59
d										
Gargrave d										
Blackpool North 94 d										
Preston d										
Blackburn 97 d										
Clitheroe 94 d										
Hellifield d										
Long Preston d										
Giggleswick d										
Clapham (Nth Yorkshire) d										
Bentham d										
Wennington d										
Carnforth 82 a										
Lancaster 6 65,82,98 a										
Bare Lane 98 a										
Morecambe 98 a										
Settle d										
Horton-in-Ribblesdale d										
Ribblehead d										
Dent d										
Garsdale d										
Kirkby Stephen d										
Appleby d										
Langwathby d										
Lazonby & Kirkoswald d										
Armathwaite d										
Carlisle 8 65 a										

A not 22 May

Table 36

Sundays

18 September to 23 October

Leeds and Bradford - Skipton, Lancaster, Morecambe and Carlisle

Station		NT	NT	NT	NT 🚌	NT	NT	NT	NT	NT	NT	NT	NT	NT	NT	NT	NT	NT	NT	NT	NT	NT	NT
London Kings Cross 15 ⊖26	d																						
Leeds 10 37	d	23p18	08 40	09 00		10 08		10 51	11 08	12 08		13 08	13 15	14 08		14 57	15 08	16 08		17 08	17 21	17 33	18 08
Bradford Forster Square 37	d						10 48				12 48				14 48				16 48				
Frizinghall 37	d						10 51				12 51				14 51				16 51				
Shipley 37	a	23p31	08 52	09 15		10 19	10 54	11 03	11 19	12 19	12 54	13 19	13 28	14 19	14 54	15 09	15 19	16 19	16 54	17 19	17 33	17 45	18 19
	d	23p32	08 53	09 16		10 20	10 55	11 04	11 20	12 20	12 55	13 20	13 29	14 20	14 55	15 10	15 20	16 20	16 55	17 20	17 34	17 46	18 20
Saltaire	d	23p34	08 55	09 18		10 22	10 57		11 22	12 22	12 57	13 22		14 22	14 57		15 22	16 22	16 57	17 22			18 22
Bingley	d	23p38	09 00	09 23		10 26	11 01	11 09	11 26	12 26	13 01	13 26	13 34	14 26	15 01	15 15	15 26	16 26	17 01	17 26	17 39	17 50	18 26
Crossflatts	d	23p40	09 02	09 25		10 28	11 03		11 28	12 28	13 03	13 28		14 28	15 03		15 28	16 28	17 03	17 28			18 28
Keighley	d	23p44	09 07	09 30		10 32	11 08	11 15	11 32	12 32	13 08	13 32	13 39	14 32	15 08	15 20	15 32	16 32	17 08	17 32	17 44	17 56	18 32
Steeton & Silsden	d	23p48	09 11	09 34		10 36	11 12		11 36	12 36	13 12	13 36		14 36	15 12		15 36	16 36	17 12	17 36			18 36
Cononley	d	23p52	09 16	09 39		10 40	11 16		11 40	12 40	13 16	13 40		14 40	15 16		15 40	16 40	17 16	17 40			18 40
Skipton	a	00 02	09 23	09 46		10 48	11 23	11 28	11 48	12 48	13 23	13 48	13 53	14 48	15 23	15 33	15 48	16 48	17 23	17 48	17 57	18 08	18 48
	d		09 26	09 48				11 30					13 54			15 36					18 00	18 11	
Gargrave	d		09 31	09 53				11 35					14 00			15 41					18 05		
Blackpool North 94	d				08 36																		
Preston	d				09 05																		
Blackburn 97	d				09 27																		
Clitheroe 94	d				09 51																		
Hellifield	d		09 40	10 02	10 15			11 44					14 08			15 50					18 14	18 22	
Long Preston	d		09 43					11 46					14 11			15 53					18 18		
Giggleswick	d		09 52					11 54								16 00					18 25		
Clapham (Nth Yorkshire)	d		10 00					12 02								16 08					18 33		
Bentham	d		10 06					12 08								16 15					18 39		
Wennington	d		10 11					12 13								16 20					18 44		
Carnforth 82	a		10 28					12 30								16 36					19 00		
Lancaster 6 65,82,98	a		10 40					12 44								16 46					19 13		
Bare Lane 98	a		10 51					13 07								16 56					19 29		
Morecambe 98	a		10 57					13 13								17 03					19 35		
Settle	d			10 10	10 35								14 17									18 30	
Horton-in-Ribblesdale	d			10 19	10 44								14 26									18 39	
Ribblehead	d			10 27	10 52								14 34									18 47	
Dent	d			10 37	11 02								14 44									18 57	
Garsdale	d			10 43	11 07								14 50									19 02	
Kirkby Stephen	d			10 56	11 20								15 03									19 15	
Appleby	d			11 09	11 34								15 15									19 28	
Langwathby	d			11 23	11 48								15 29									19 42	
Lazonby & Kirkoswald	d			11 29	11 54								15 35									19 48	
Armathwaite	d			11 37	12 02								15 43									19 56	
Carlisle 8 65	a			11 56	12 17								16 00									20 13	

Station		NT	NT	NT	NT	GR R 1	NT	NT	NT	NT
London Kings Cross 15 ⊖26	d					18 35				
Leeds 10 37	d		19 08	20 08		21 03	21 08	22 08		23 20
Bradford Forster Square 37	d	18 48			20 48				22 48	
Frizinghall 37	d	18 51			20 51				22 51	
Shipley 37	a	18 54	19 19	20 19	20 54		21 19	22 19	22 54	23 31
	d	18 55	19 20	20 20	20 55		21 20	22 20	22 55	23 32
Saltaire	d	18 57	19 22	20 22	20 57		21 22	22 22	22 57	23 34
Bingley	d	19 01	19 26	20 26	21 01		21 26	22 26	23 01	23 38
Crossflatts	d	19 03	19 28	20 28	21 03		21 28	22 28	23 03	23 40
Keighley	d	19 08	19 32	20 32	21 08	21s22	21 32	22 32	23 08	23 44
Steeton & Silsden	d	19 12	19 36	20 36	21 12		21 36	22 36	23 12	23 48
Cononley	d	19 16	19 40	20 40	21 16		21 40	22 40	23 16	23 52
Skipton	a	19 23	19 48	20 48	21 23	21 43	21 48	22 48	23 23	23 59
	d									
Gargrave	d									
Blackpool North 94	d									
Preston	d									
Blackburn 97	d									
Clitheroe 94	d									
Hellifield	d									
Long Preston	d									
Giggleswick	d									
Clapham (Nth Yorkshire)	d									
Bentham	d									
Wennington	d									
Carnforth 82	a									
Lancaster 6 65,82,98	a									
Bare Lane 98	a									
Morecambe 98	a									
Settle	d									
Horton-in-Ribblesdale	d									
Ribblehead	d									
Dent	d									
Garsdale	d									
Kirkby Stephen	d									
Appleby	d									
Langwathby	d									
Lazonby & Kirkoswald	d									
Armathwaite	d									
Carlisle 8 65	a									

Table 36

Sundays
from 30 October

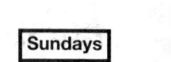

Leeds and Bradford - Skipton, Lancaster, Morecambe and Carlisle

	NT	NT	NT	NT	NT	NT	NT	NT	NT	NT	NT	NT	NT	NT	NT	NT	NT	NT	NT	NT	NT	NT
London Kings Cross 15 ⊖26 d																						
Leeds 10 37 d	23p18	08 40	09 00	10 08		10 51	11 08	12 08		13 08	13 15	14 08		14 57	15 08	16 08		17 08	17 21	17 33	18 08	
Bradford Forster Square 37 d					10 48				12 48				14 48				16 48					18 48
Frizinghall 37 d					10 51				12 51				14 51				16 51					18 51
Shipley 37 a	23p31	08 52	09 15	10 19	10 54	11 03	11 19	12 19	12 54	13 19	13 28	14 19	14 54	15 09	15 19	16 19	16 54	17 19	17 33	17 45	18 19	18 54
d	23p32	08 53	09 16	10 20	10 55	11 04	11 20	12 20	12 55	13 20	13 29	14 20	14 55	15 10	15 20	16 20	16 55	17 20	17 34	17 46	18 20	18 55
Saltaire d	23p34	08 55	09 18	10 22	10 57		11 22	12 22	12 57	13 22		14 22	14 57		15 22	16 22	16 57	17 22			18 22	18 57
Bingley d	23p38	09 00	09 23	10 26	11 01	11 09	11 26	12 26	13 01	13 26	13 34	14 26	15 01	15 15	15 26	16 26	17 01	17 26	17 39	17 50	18 26	19 01
Crossflatts d	23p40	09 02	09 25	10 28	11 03		11 28	12 28	13 03	13 28		14 28	15 03		15 28	16 28	17 03	17 28			18 28	19 03
Keighley d	23p44	09 07	09 30	10 32	11 08	11 15	11 32	12 32	13 08	13 32	13 39	14 32	15 08	15 20	15 32	16 32	17 08	17 32	17 44	17 56	18 32	19 08
Steeton & Silsden d	23p48	09 11	09 34	10 36	11 12		11 36	12 36	13 12	13 36		14 36	15 12		15 36	16 36	17 12	17 36			18 36	19 12
Cononley d	23p52	09 16	09 39	10 40	11 16		11 40	12 40	13 16	13 40		14 40	15 16		15 40	16 40	17 16	17 40			18 40	19 16
Skipton a	00 02	09 23	09 46	10 48	11 23	11 28	11 48	12 48	13 23	13 48	13 53	14 48	15 23	15 33	15 48	16 48	17 23	17 48	17 57	18 08	18 48	19 23
d		09 26	09 48			11 30					13 54			15 36					18 00	18 11		
Gargrave d		09 31	09 53			11 35					14 00			15 41					18 05			
Blackpool North 94 d																						
Preston d																						
Blackburn 97 d																						
Clitheroe 94 d																						
Hellifield d		09 40	10 02			11 44					14 08			15 50					18 14	18 22		
Long Preston d		09 43				11 46					14 11			15 53					18 18			
Giggleswick d		09 52				11 54								16 00					18 25			
Clapham (Nth Yorkshire) d		10 00				12 02								16 08					18 33			
Bentham d		10 06				12 08								16 15					18 39			
Wennington d		10 11				12 13								16 20					18 44			
Carnforth 82 a		10 28				12 30								16 36					19 00			
Lancaster 6 65,82,98 a		10 40				12 44								16 46					19 13			
Bare Lane 98 a		10 51				13 07								16 56					19 29			
Morecambe 98 a		10 57				13 13								17 03					19 35			
Settle d			10 10								14 17									18 30		
Horton-in-Ribblesdale d			10 19								14 26									18 39		
Ribblehead d			10 27								14 34									18 47		
Dent d			10 37								14 44									18 57		
Garsdale d			10 43								14 50									19 02		
Kirkby Stephen d			10 56								15 03									19 15		
Appleby d			11 09								15 15									19 28		
Langwathby d			11 23								15 29									19 42		
Lazonby & Kirkoswald d			11 29								15 35									19 48		
Armathwaite d			11 37								15 43									19 56		
Carlisle 8 65 a			11 56								16 00									20 13		

	NT	NT	NT	GR 1	NT	NT	NT	NT
London Kings Cross 15 ⊖26 d				18 35				
Leeds 10 37 d	19 08	20 08		21 03	21 08	22 08		23 20
Bradford Forster Square 37 d			20 48				22 48	
Frizinghall 37 d			20 51				22 51	
Shipley 37 a	19 19	20 19	20 54		21 19	22 19	22 54	23 31
d	19 20	20 20	20 55		21 20	22 20	22 55	23 32
Saltaire d	19 22	20 22	20 57		21 22	22 22	22 57	23 34
Bingley d	19 26	20 26	21 01		21 26	22 26	23 01	23 38
Crossflatts d	19 28	20 28	21 03		21 28	22 28	23 03	23 40
Keighley d	19 32	20 32	21 08	21s22	21 32	22 32	23 08	23 44
Steeton & Silsden d	19 36	20 36	21 12		21 36	22 36	23 12	23 48
Cononley d	19 40	20 40	21 16		21 40	22 40	23 16	23 52
Skipton a	19 48	20 48	21 23	21 43	21 48	22 48	23 23	23 59
d								
Gargrave d								
Blackpool North 94 d								
Preston d								
Blackburn 97 d								
Clitheroe 94 d								
Hellifield d								
Long Preston d								
Giggleswick d								
Clapham (Nth Yorkshire) d								
Bentham d								
Wennington d								
Carnforth 82 a								
Lancaster 6 65,82,98 a								
Bare Lane 98 a								
Morecambe 98 a								
Settle d								
Horton-in-Ribblesdale d								
Ribblehead d								
Dent d								
Garsdale d								
Kirkby Stephen d								
Appleby d								
Langwathby d								
Lazonby & Kirkoswald d								
Armathwaite d								
Carlisle 8 65 a								

Carlisle, Morecambe, Lancaster and Skipton - Bradford and Leeds

Miles	Miles	Miles			NT	NT	NT	NT	NT	GR	NT	NT	NT		NT	NT	NT	NT	NT	NT	NT	NT	NT		NT
										R 1 ⊘															
0	—	—	**Carlisle** 8	65 d													05 58								
10	—	—	Armathwaite	d													06 12								
15½	—	—	Lazonby & Kirkoswald	d													06 19								
19¾	—	—	Langwathby	d																					
30¾	—	—	Appleby	d													06 38								
41½	—	—	Kirkby Stephen	d													06 51								
51¼	—	—	Garsdale	d																					
54¾	—	—	Dent	d																					
60¾	—	—	Ribblehead	d													07 16								
65½	—	—	Horton-in-Ribblesdale	d													07 22								
71¾	—	—	Settle	d													07 30								
—	0	—	**Morecambe**	98 d																					
—	1¾	—	Bare Lane	98 d																					
—	4¼	—	**Lancaster** 6	65,82,98 d																07 10					
—	11½	—	Carnforth	82 d																07 20					
—	21	—	Wennington	d																07 33					
—	24¼	—	Bentham	d																07 39					
—	27½	—	Clapham (Nth Yorkshire)	d																07 45					
—	34¼	—	Giggleswick	d																07 54					
75½	38	—	Long Preston	d													07 36			08 02					
76¾	39¼	—	Hellifield	d													07 39			08 06					
—	—	—	Clitheroe	94 a																					
—	—	—	Blackburn	94,97 a																					
—	—	—	Preston 8	97 a																					
—	—	—	Blackpool North	97 a																					
83	45½	—	Gargrave	d													07 47			08 14					
86¾	49¼	—	**Skipton**	a													07 55			08 23					
—	—	—		d	05 48	06 02	06 18	06 27	06 42	06 55	07 01	07 08	07 24		07 32	07 47	07 57	08 01	08 15	08 27	08 32	08 43	09 02		09 18
89¾	52¼	—	Cononley	d	05 52	06 06	06 22	06 31	06 46		07 05	07 12	07 28		07 36	07 51		08 05	08 19		08 36	08 47	09 06		09 22
93	55½	—	Steeton & Silsden	d	05 56	06 10	06 26	06 35	06 51		07 10	07 17	07 33		07 41	07 56	08 04	08 10	08 24		08 40	08 51	09 10		09 26
96	58½	—	Keighley	d	06 01	06 15	06 31	06 40	06 56	07u06	07 15	07 21	07 37		07 45	08 00	08 09	08 14	08 28	08 37	08 45	08 56	09 15		09 31
98½	61	—	Crossflatts	d	06 04	06 18	06 34	06 43	07 00		07 19	07 26	07 41		07 49	08 04		08 18	08 32		08 48	08 59	09 18		09 34
99¾	61¾	—	Bingley	d	06 07	06 21	06 37	06 46	07 02		07 22	07 28	07 44		07 52	08 07	08 14	08 21	08 35	08 42	08 51	09 02	09 21		09 37
101½	64	—	Saltaire	d	06 10	06 24	06 40	06 49	07 06		07 25	07 32	07 48		07 56	08 11		08 25	08 39		08 54	09 05	09 24		09 40
102¼	64¾	0	Shipley	a	06 12	06 27	06 42	06 53	07 08		07 27	07 34	07 50		07 58	08 13	08 18	08 27	08 41	08 46	08 58	09 07	09 27		09 42
—	—	—		d	06 13	06 28	06 44	06 53	07 09	07u14	07 28	07 35	07 50		08 00	08 13	08 19	08 28	08 41	08 47	08 58	09 08	09 28		09 44
—	—	1	Frizinghall	37 a		06 32		06 57			07 32				08 03			08 31			09 02		09 32		
—	—	2¾	**Bradford Forster Square**	37 a		06 38		07 03			07 39				08 09			08 38			09 09		09 38		
113	75½	—	**Leeds** 10	37 a	06 27		06 58		07 23	07 29		07 49	08 05			08 27	08 37		08 56	09 04		09 23			09 59
—	—	—	London Kings Cross 15	⊖26 a						10 02															

		NT	NT	NT	NT	NT	NT	NT	NT		NT	NT	NT	NT	NT	NT	NT	NT	NT		NT	NT	NT	NT	NT
Carlisle 8	65 d							08 53																11 55	
Armathwaite	d							09 07																12 09	
Lazonby & Kirkoswald	d							09 14																12 16	
Langwathby	d							09 20																12 22	
Appleby	d							09 35																12 37	
Kirkby Stephen	d							09 48																12 50	
Garsdale	d							10 02																13 03	
Dent	d							10 07																13 08	
Ribblehead	d							10 17																13 18	
Horton-in-Ribblesdale	d							10 24																13 24	
Settle	d							10 32																13 32	
Morecambe	98 d														10 34										
Bare Lane	98 d														10 38										
Lancaster 6	65,82,98 d														10 49										
Carnforth	82 d														11 09										
Wennington	d														11 23										
Bentham	d														11 29										
Clapham (Nth Yorkshire)	d														11 35										
Giggleswick	d														11 44										
Long Preston	d														11 52									13 38	
Hellifield	d							10 39							11 56									13 41	
Clitheroe	94 a																								
Blackburn	94,97 a																								
Preston 8	97 a																								
Blackpool North	97 a																								
Gargrave	d														12 04									13 49	
Skipton	a							10 54							12 13									13 57	
	d	09 32	09 48	10 02	10 18	10 32	10 48	10 59	11 02		11 18	11 33	11 48	12 02	12 13	12 18	12 32	12 48	13 02		13 18	13 32	13 48	13 58	14 02
Cononley	d	09 36	09 52	10 06	10 22	10 36	10 52		11 06		11 22	11 37	11 52	12 06		12 22	12 36	12 52	13 06		13 22	13 36	13 52		14 06
Steeton & Silsden	d	09 40	09 56	10 10	10 26	10 40	10 56		11 10		11 26	11 41	11 56	12 10		12 26	12 40	12 56	13 10		13 26	13 40	13 56		14 10
Keighley	d	09 45	10 01	10 15	10 31	10 45	11 01	11 09	11 15		11 31	11 46	12 01	12 15	12 23	12 31	12 45	13 01	13 15		13 31	13 45	14 01	14 09	14 15
Crossflatts	d	09 48	10 04	10 18	10 34	10 48	11 04		11 18		11 34	11 49	12 04	12 18		12 34	12 48	13 04	13 18		13 34	13 48	14 04		14 18
Bingley	d	09 51	10 07	10 21	10 37	10 51	11 07	11 13	11 21		11 37	11 52	12 07	12 21		12 37	12 51	13 07	13 21		13 37	13 51	14 07	14 13	14 21
Saltaire	d	09 54	10 10	10 24	10 40	10 54	11 10		11 24		11 40	11 55	12 10	12 24		12 40	12 54	13 10	13 24		13 40	13 54	14 10		14 24
Shipley	a	09 58	10 12	10 27	10 42	10 57	11 12	11 18	11 28		11 42	11 58	12 14	12 27	12 33	12 42	12 57	13 12	13 27		13 42	13 57	14 12	14 18	14 28
	d	09 58	10 14	10 28	10 44	10 58	11 14	11 18	11 28		11 44	11 58	12 14	12 28	12 33	12 44	12 58	13 14	13 28		13 44	13 58	14 14	14 18	14 28
Frizinghall	37 a	10 02		10 32		11 02			11 32			12 02		12 32			13 02		13 32			14 02			14 32
Bradford Forster Square	37 a	10 08		10 38		11 08			11 38			12 10		12 38			13 08		13 38			14 08			14 38
Leeds 10	37 a		10 28		10 58		11 28	11 36			11 58		12 29		12 55	12 58		13 28			13 58		14 28	14 37	
London Kings Cross 15	⊖26 a																								

Table 36

Mondays to Fridays

until 15 July

Carlisle, Morecambe, Lancaster and Skipton - Bradford and Leeds

		NT	NT	NT	NT	NT A	NT	NT	NT	NT	NT	NT	NT	NT	NT	NT	NT	NT	NT	NT	NT	NT	NT
Carlisle 8	65 d										14 04				15 05								16 18
Armathwaite	d										14 18												16 32
Lazonby & Kirkoswald	d										14 25												16 39
Langwathby	d										14 31												16 45
Appleby	d										14 47				15 42								17 01
Kirkby Stephen	d										15 00				15 55								17 14
Garsdale	d										15 13												17 27
Dent	d										15 18												17 32
Ribblehead	d										15 27												17 42
Horton-in-Ribblesdale	d										15 34												17 48
Settle	d										15 43				16 35								17 57
Morecambe	98 d					13 29													16 19				
Bare Lane	98 d					13 36													16 23				
Lancaster 6	65,82,98 d					13 48																	
Carnforth	82 d					13 58													16 32				
Wennington	d					14 12													16 46				
Bentham	d					14 18													16 52				
Clapham (Nth Yorkshire)	d					14 24													16 59				
Giggleswick	d					14 33													17 10				
Long Preston	d					14 40													17 18				18 03
Hellifield	d					14 44					15 50								17 22				18 06
Clitheroe	94 a																						
Blackburn	94,97 a																						
Preston 8	97 a																						
Blackpool North	97 a																						
Gargrave	d					14 52													17 30				18 14
Skipton	a					15 03					16 05				16 52				17 39				18 23
	d	14 18	14 32	14 48	15 00	15 10	15 18	15 32	15 48	16 02	16 10	16 18	16 36	16 49	16 59	17 02	17 19	17 28	17 40	17 49	18 02	18 16	18 28
Cononley	d	14 22	14 36	14 52	15 04		15 22	15 36	15 52	16 06		16 22	16 40	16 53		17 06	17 23	17 32		17 53	18 06	18 20	
Steeton & Silsden	d	14 27	14 40	14 56	15 08		15 26	15 40	15 56	16 10		16 26	16 44	16 57		17 10	17 27	17 36		17 57	18 10	18 25	
Keighley	d	14 31	14 45	15 01	15 13	15 20	15 31	15 45	16 01	16 15	16 21	16 31	16 49	17 02	17 09lee	17 15	17 32	17 41	17 50	18 02	18 15	18 29	18 38
Crossflatts	d	14 35	14 48	15 04	15 16		15 34	15 48	16 04	16 18		16 34	16 52	17 05		17 18	17 35	17 44		18 05	18 18	18 33	
Bingley	d	14 38	14 51	15 07	15 19	15 25	15 37	15 51	16 07	16 21	16 26	16 37	16 55	17 08	17 15	17 21	17 38	17 47		18 08	18 21	18 35	18 42
Saltaire	d	14 42	14 54	15 10	15 22		15 40	15 54	16 10	16 24		16 40	16 58	17 11		17 24	17 41	17 50		18 11	18 24	18 39	
Shipley	a	14 44	14 57	15 12	15 25	15 30	15 42	15 57	16 12	16 27	16 31	16 42	17 02	17 13	17 20	17 28	17 43	17 55	17 58	18 13	18 28	18 42	18 48
	d	14 45	14 58	15 14	15 28	15 30	15 44	15 58	16 14	16 28	16 31	16 44	17 02	17 15	17 20	17 28	17 45	17 56	17 58	18 14	18 28	18 44	18 48
Frizinghall	37 a		15 02		15 32			16 02		16 31			17 06			17 32		17 59			18 32		
Bradford Forster Square	37 a		15 08		15 38			16 08		16 38			17 12			17 38		18 05			18 38		
Leeds 10	37 a	15 01		15 28		15 47	15 58		16 28		16 51	16 58		17 29	17 40		18 00		18 15	18 29		18 59	19 07
London Kings Cross 15	⊖26 a																						

		NT	NT	NT	NT	NT	NT	NT	NT	NT	NT	NT	NT	NT	NT	NT	NT
Carlisle 8	65 d								18 18								
Armathwaite	d								18 32								
Lazonby & Kirkoswald	d								18 39								
Langwathby	d								18 45								
Appleby	d								19 00								
Kirkby Stephen	d								19 13								
Garsdale	d								19 26								
Dent	d								19 31								
Ribblehead	d								19 41						21 00		
Horton-in-Ribblesdale	d								19 47						21 06		
Settle	d								19 55						21 14		
Morecambe	98 d										19 08						
Bare Lane	98 d										19 12						
Lancaster 6	65,82,98 d										19 24						
Carnforth	82 d										19 34						
Wennington	d										19 48						
Bentham	d										19 54						
Clapham (Nth Yorkshire)	d										20 00						
Giggleswick	d										20 09						
Long Preston	d										20 17				21 20		
Hellifield	d								20 03		20 21				21 23		
Clitheroe	94 a																
Blackburn	94,97 a																
Preston 8	97 a																
Blackpool North	97 a																
Gargrave	d										20 29				21 31		
Skipton	a								20 18		20 38				21 38		
	d	18 32	18 48	19 00	19 18	19 32	19 48	19 54	20 20	20 23	20 42	20 48	20 54	21 18	21 48	21 54	22 18
Cononley	d	18 36	18 52	19 04	19 22	19 36	19 52	19 58		20 29		20 52	20 58	21 22	21 52	21 58	22 22
Steeton & Silsden	d	18 40	18 56	19 08	19 26	19 40	19 56	20 02		20 33		20 56	21 02	21 26	21 56	22 02	22 26
Keighley	d	18 45	19 01	19 13	19 31	19 45	20 01	20 07	20 30	20 38	20 52	21 01	21 07	21 31	22 01	22 07	22 31
Crossflatts	d	18 48	19 04	19 16	19 34	19 48	20 04	20 10		20 41		21 04	21 10	21 34	22 04	22 10	22 34
Bingley	d	18 51	19 07	19 19	19 37	19 51	20 07	20 13	20 34	20 44		21 07	21 13	21 37	22 07	22 13	22 37
Saltaire	d	18 54	19 10	19 22	19 40	19 54	20 10	20 16		20 47		21 10	21 16	21 40	22 10	22 16	22 40
Shipley	a	18 58	19 12	19 25	19 42	19 58	20 12	20 19	20 39	20 49	20 59	21 12	21 19	21 42	22 15	22 19	22 42
	d	18 58	19 14	19 26	19 44	19 58	20 14	20 20	20 41	20 50	20 59	21 14	21 19	21 43	22 15	22 19	22 43
Frizinghall	37 a	19 02		19 29		20 01		20 24					21 23			22 23	
Bradford Forster Square	37 a	19 08		19 35		20 08		20 32					21 29			22 31	
Leeds 10	37 a		19 31		19 59		20 28		21 01	21 04	21 17	21 30		21 59	22 33		23 01
London Kings Cross 15	⊖26 a																

A From Heysham Port

Table 36

Mondays to Fridays

from 18 July

Carlisle, Morecambe, Lancaster and Skipton - Bradford and Leeds

Station		NT	NT	NT	NT	NT	GR ■ 1 A	NT	NT	NT		NT	NT	NT	NT	NT	NT	NT	NT	NT		NT B	NT	NT	NT
Carlisle [8] 65	d													05 58											
Armathwaite	d																								
Lazonby & Kirkoswald	d																								
Langwathby	d																								
Appleby	d													06 34											
Kirkby Stephen	d													06 47											
Garsdale	d													07 00											
Dent	d													07 05											
Ribblehead	d													07 15											
Horton-in-Ribblesdale	d													07 21											
Settle	d													07 29											
Morecambe 98	d																								
Bare Lane 98	d																								
Lancaster [6] 65,82,98	d																07 10								
Carnforth 82	d																07 20								
Wennington	d																07 33								
Bentham	d																07 39								
Clapham (Nth Yorkshire)	d																07 45								
Giggleswick	d																07 54								
Long Preston	d													07 35			08 02								
Hellifield	d													07 38			08 06								
Clitheroe 94	a																								
Blackburn 94,97	a																								
Preston [8] 97	a																								
Blackpool North 97	a																								
Gargrave	d													07 46			08 14								
Skipton	a													07 55			08 23								
	d	05 48	06 02	06 18	06 27	06 42	06 55	07 01	07 08	07 24		07 32	07 47	07 56	08 01	08 15	08 27	08 32	08 43	09 02		09 18	09 32	09 48	10 02
Cononley	d	05 52	06 06	06 22	06 31	06 46		07 05	07 12	07 28		07 36	07 51		08 05	08 19		08 36	08 47	09 06		09 22	09 36	09 52	10 06
Steeton & Silsden	d	05 56	06 10	06 26	06 35	06 51		07 10	07 17	07 33		07 41	07 56	08 04	08 10	08 24		08 40	08 51	09 10		09 26	09 40	09 56	10 10
Keighley	d	06 01	06 15	06 31	06 40	06 56	07u06	07 15	07 21	07 37		07 45	08 00	08 09	08 14	08 28	08 37	08 45	08 56	09 15		09 31	09 45	10 01	10 15
Crossflatts	d	06 04	06 18	06 34	06 43	07 00		07 19	07 26	07 41		07 49	08 04		08 18	08 32		08 48	08 59	09 18		09 34	09 48	10 04	10 18
Bingley	d	06 07	06 21	06 37	06 46	07 02		07 22	07 28	07 44		07 52	08 07	08 14	08 21	08 35	08 42	08 51	09 02	09 21		09 37	09 51	10 07	10 21
Saltaire	d	06 10	06 24	06 40	06 49	07 06		07 25	07 32	07 48		07 56	08 11		08 25	08 39		08 54	09 05	09 24		09 40	09 54	10 10	10 24
Shipley	a	06 12	06 27	06 42	06 53	07 08		07 27	07 34	07 50		07 58	08 13	08 18	08 27	08 41	08 46	08 58	09 07	09 27		09 42	09 58	10 12	10 27
	d	06 13	06 28	06 44	06 53	07 09	07u14	07 28	07 35	07 50		08 00	08 13	08 19	08 28	08 41	08 47	08 58	09 08	09 28		09 44	09 58	10 14	10 28
Frizinghall 37	a		06 32		06 57			07 32				08 03			08 31			09 02		09 32			10 02		10 32
Bradford Forster Square 37	a		06 38		07 03			07 39				08 09			08 38			09 09		09 38			10 08		10 38
Leeds [10] 37	a	06 27		06 58		07 23	07 29		07 49	08 05			08 27	08 37		08 56	09 04		09 23			09 59		10 28	
London Kings Cross [15] ⊖26	a						10 02																		

Station		NT	NT	NT	NT	NT		NT	NT	NT	NT	NT		NT	NT	NT		NT	NT	NT	NT	NT	NT	NT	NT
Carlisle [8] 65	d				08 53																	11 55			
Armathwaite	d				09 07																	12 09			
Lazonby & Kirkoswald	d				09 14																	12 16			
Langwathby	d				09 20																	12 22			
Appleby	d				09 35																	12 37			
Kirkby Stephen	d				09 48																	12 50			
Garsdale	d				10 02																	13 03			
Dent	d				10 07																	13 08			
Ribblehead	d				10 17																	13 18			
Horton-in-Ribblesdale	d				10 24																	13 24			
Settle	d				10 32																	13 32			
Morecambe 98	d											10 34													
Bare Lane 98	d											10 38													
Lancaster [6] 65,82,98	d											10 49													
Carnforth 82	d											11 09													
Wennington	d											11 23													
Bentham	d											11 29													
Clapham (Nth Yorkshire)	d											11 35													
Giggleswick	d											11 44													
Long Preston	d											11 52										13 38			
Hellifield	d				10 39							11 56										13 41			
Clitheroe 94	a																								
Blackburn 94,97	a																								
Preston [8] 97	a																								
Blackpool North 97	a																								
Gargrave	d											12 04										13 49			
Skipton	a				10 54							12 13										13 57			
	d	10 18	10 32	10 48	10 59	11 02		11 18	11 33	11 48	12 02	12 13		12 18	12 32	12 48		13 02	13 18	13 32	13 48	13 58	14 02	14 18	14 32
Cononley	d	10 22	10 36	10 52		11 06		11 22	11 37	11 52	12 06			12 22	12 36	12 52		13 06	13 22	13 36	13 52		14 06	14 22	14 36
Steeton & Silsden	d	10 26	10 40	10 56		11 10		11 26	11 41	11 56	12 10			12 26	12 40	12 56		13 10	13 26	13 40	13 56		14 10	14 27	14 40
Keighley	d	10 31	10 45	11 01	11 09	11 15		11 31	11 46	12 01	12 15	12 23		12 31	12 45	13 01		13 15	13 31	13 45	14 01	14 09	14 15	14 31	14 45
Crossflatts	d	10 34	10 48	11 04		11 18		11 34	11 49	12 04	12 18			12 34	12 48	13 04		13 18	13 34	13 48	14 04		14 18	14 35	14 48
Bingley	d	10 37	10 51	11 07	11 13	11 21		11 37	11 52	12 07	12 21			12 37	12 51	13 07		13 21	13 37	13 51	14 07	14 13	14 21	14 38	14 51
Saltaire	d	10 40	10 54	11 10		11 24		11 40	11 55	12 10	12 24			12 40	12 54	13 10		13 24	13 40	13 54	14 10		14 24	14 42	14 54
Shipley	a	10 42	10 57	11 12	11 18	11 28		11 42	11 58	12 14	12 27	12 33		12 42	12 57	13 12		13 27	13 42	13 57	14 12	14 18	14 28	14 44	14 57
	d	10 44	10 58	11 14	11 18	11 28		11 44	11 58	12 14	12 28	12 33		12 44	12 58	13 14		13 28	13 44	13 58	14 14	14 18	14 28	14 45	14 58
Frizinghall 37	a		11 02			11 32			12 02		12 32				13 02			13 32		14 02			14 32		15 02
Bradford Forster Square 37	a		11 08			11 38			12 10		12 38				13 08			13 38		14 08			14 38		15 08
Leeds [10] 37	a	10 58		11 28	11 36			11 58		12 29		12 55		12 58		13 28			13 58		14 28	14 37		15 01	
London Kings Cross [15] ⊖26	a																								

A — from Leeds ⊘ to Shipley

B — From Leeds

Carlisle, Morecambe, Lancaster and Skipton - Bradford and Leeds

		NT		NT	NT A	NT	NT	NT	NT	NT	NT	NT		NT	NT		NT	NT	NT	NT	NT	NT		NT	NT
Carlisle [8]	65 d									14 04					15 05										16 18
Armathwaite	d									14 18															16 32
Lazonby & Kirkoswald	d									14 25															16 39
Langwathby	d									14 31															16 45
Appleby	d									14 47					15 42										17 01
Kirkby Stephen	d									15 00					15 55										17 14
Garsdale	d									15 13															17 27
Dent	d									15 18															17 32
Ribblehead	d									15 27															17 42
Horton-in-Ribblesdale	d									15 34															17 48
Settle	d									15 43					16 35										17 57
Morecambe	98 d				13 29															16 19					
Bare Lane	98 d				13 36															16 23					
Lancaster [6]	65,82,98 d				13 48																				
Carnforth	82 d				13 58															16 32					
Wennington	d				14 12															16 46					
Bentham	d				14 18															16 52					
Clapham (Nth Yorkshire)	d				14 24															16 59					
Giggleswick	d				14 33															17 10					
Long Preston	d				14 40															17 18					18 03
Hellifield	d				14 44					15 50										17 22					18 06
Clitheroe	94 a																								
Blackburn	94,97 a																								
Preston [8]	97 a																								
Blackpool North	97 a																								
Gargrave	d				14 52															17 30					18 14
Skipton	a				15 03					16 05					16 55					17 39					18 23
	d	14 48		15 00	15 10	15 18	15 32	15 48	16 02	16 10	16 18	16 36		16 49	16 58		17 02	17 19	17 28	17 40	17 49	18 02		18 16	18 28
Cononley	d	14 52		15 04		15 22	15 36	15 52	16 06		16 22	16 40		16 53			17 06	17 23	17 32		17 53	18 06		18 20	
Steeton & Silsden	d	14 56		15 08		15 26	15 40	15 56	16 10		16 26	16 44		16 57			17 10	17 27	17 36		17 57	18 10		18 25	
Keighley	d	15 01		15 13	15 20	15 31	15 45	16 01	16 15	16 21	16 31	16 49		17 02	17 08		17 15	17 32	17 41	17 50	18 02	18 15		18 29	18 38
Crossflatts	d	15 04		15 16		15 34	15 48	16 04	16 18		16 34	16 52		17 05			17 18	17 35	17 44		18 05	18 18		18 33	
Bingley	d	15 07		15 19	15 25	15 37	15 51	16 07	16 21	16 26	16 37	16 55		17 08	17 15		17 21	17 38	17 47		18 08	18 21		18 35	18 42
Saltaire	d	15 10		15 22		15 40	15 54	16 10	16 24		16 40	16 58		17 11			17 24	17 41	17 50		18 11	18 24		18 39	
Shipley	a	15 12		15 25	15 30	15 42	15 57	16 12	16 27	16 31	16 42	17 02		17 13	17 20		17 28	17 43	17 55	17 58	18 13	18 28		18 42	18 48
	d	15 14		15 28	15 30	15 44	15 58	16 14	16 28	16 31	16 44	17 02		17 15	17 20		17 28	17 45	17 56	17 58	18 14	18 28		18 44	18 48
Frizinghall	37 a			15 32			16 02		16 31			17 06					17 32		17 59			18 32			
Bradford Forster Square	37 a			15 38			16 08		16 38			17 12					17 38		18 05			18 38			
Leeds [10]	37 a	15 28			15 47	15 58		16 28		16 51	16 58			17 29	17 40			18 00		18 15	18 29			18 59	19 07
London Kings Cross [15]	⊖26 a																								

		NT	NT	NT	NT	NT	NT	NT		NT	NT	NT	NT	NT	NT	NT	NT	NT
Carlisle [8]	65 d									18 18								
Armathwaite	d									18 32								
Lazonby & Kirkoswald	d									18 39								
Langwathby	d									18 45								
Appleby	d									19 00								
Kirkby Stephen	d									19 13								
Garsdale	d									19 26								
Dent	d									19 31								
Ribblehead	d									19 41						21 00		
Horton-in-Ribblesdale	d									19 47						21 06		
Settle	d									19 55						21 14		
Morecambe	98 d											19 08						
Bare Lane	98 d											19 12						
Lancaster [6]	65,82,98 d											19 24						
Carnforth	82 d											19 34						
Wennington	d											19 48						
Bentham	d											19 54						
Clapham (Nth Yorkshire)	d											20 00						
Giggleswick	d											20 09						
Long Preston	d											20 17				21 20		
Hellifield	d									20 03		20 21				21 23		
Clitheroe	94 a																	
Blackburn	94,97 a																	
Preston [8]	97 a																	
Blackpool North	97 a																	
Gargrave	d											20 29				21 31		
Skipton	a									20 18		20 38				21 38		
	d	18 32	18 48	19 00	19 18	19 32	19 48	19 54		20 20	20 23	20 42	20 48	20 54	21 18	21 48	21 54	22 18
Cononley	d	18 36	18 52	19 04	19 22	19 36	19 52	19 58			20 29		20 52	20 58	21 22	21 52	21 58	22 22
Steeton & Silsden	d	18 40	18 56	19 08	19 26	19 40	19 56	20 02			20 33		20 56	21 02	21 26	21 56	22 02	22 26
Keighley	d	18 45	19 01	19 13	19 31	19 45	20 01	20 07		20 30	20 38	20 52	21 01	21 07	21 31	22 01	22 07	22 31
Crossflatts	d	18 48	19 04	19 16	19 34	19 48	20 04	20 10			20 41		21 04	21 10	21 34	22 04	22 10	22 34
Bingley	d	18 51	19 07	19 19	19 37	19 51	20 07	20 13		20 34	20 44		21 07	21 13	21 37	22 07	22 13	22 37
Saltaire	d	18 54	19 10	19 22	19 40	19 54	20 10	20 16			20 47		21 10	21 16	21 40	22 10	22 16	22 40
Shipley	a	18 58	19 12	19 25	19 42	19 58	20 12	20 19		20 39	20 49	20 59	21 12	21 19	21 42	22 15	22 19	22 42
	d	18 58	19 14	19 26	19 44	19 58	20 14	20 20		20 41	20 50	20 59	21 14	21 19	21 43	22 15	22 19	22 43
Frizinghall	37 a	19 02		19 29		20 01		20 24						21 23			22 23	
Bradford Forster Square	37 a	19 08		19 35		20 08		20 32						21 29			22 31	
Leeds [10]	37 a		19 31		19 59		20 28			21 01	21 04	21 17	21 30		21 59	22 33		23 01
London Kings Cross [15]	⊖26 a																	

A From Heysham Port

Table 36

Saturdays

Carlisle, Morecambe, Lancaster and Skipton - Bradford and Leeds

		NT	NT	NT	GR	NT	NT	NT	NT	NT		NT	NT	NT	NT	NT	NT	NT	NT	NT		NT	NT	NT	NT
					R 1																				
Carlisle 8	65 d																			07 52					
Armathwaite	d																			08 06					
Lazonby & Kirkoswald	d																			08 13					
Langwathby	d																			08 19					
Appleby	d																			08 34					
Kirkby Stephen	d																			08 47					
Garsdale	d																			09 00					
Dent	d																			09 05					
Ribblehead	d								07 14											09 15					
Horton-in-Ribblesdale	d								07 21											09 21					
Settle	d								07 29											09 29					
Morecambe	98 d																								
Bare Lane	98 d																								
Lancaster 6	65,82,98 d																	08 24							
Carnforth	82 d																	08 34							
Wennington	d																	08 48							
Bentham	d																	08 53							
Clapham (Nth Yorkshire)	d																	09 00							
Giggleswick	d																	09 08							
Long Preston	d								07 34									09 16							
Hellifield	d								07 37									09 20		09 37					
Clitheroe	94 a																								
Blackburn	94,97 a																								
Preston 8	97 a																								
Blackpool North	97 a																								
Gargrave	d								07 46									09 28							
Skipton	a								07 54									09 37		09 53					
	d	05 48	06 02	06 47	06 55	07 01	07 32	07 47	07 56	08 01		08 18	08 32	08 48	09 02	09 18	09 32	09 42	09 48	09 57		10 02	10 18	10 32	10 48
Cononley	d	05 52	06 06	06 51		07 05	07 36	07 51		08 05		08 22	08 36	08 52	09 06	09 22	09 36		09 52			10 06	10 22	10 36	10 52
Steeton & Silsden	d	05 56	06 10	06 56		07 10	07 41	07 56	08 04	08 10		08 27	08 40	08 56	09 10	09 26	09 40		09 56			10 10	10 26	10 40	10 56
Keighley	d	06 01	06 15	07 00	07u08	07 15	07 45	08 00	08 09	08 14		08 31	08 45	09 01	09 15	09 31	09 45	09 52	10 01	10 08		10 15	10 31	10 45	11 01
Crossflatts	d	06 04	06 18	07 04		07 19	07 49	08 04		08 18		08 35	08 48	09 04	09 18	09 34	09 48		10 04			10 18	10 34	10 48	11 04
Bingley	d	06 07	06 21	07 07		07 22	07 52	08 07	08 14	08 21		08 38	08 51	09 07	09 21	09 37	09 51	09 58	10 07	10 12		10 21	10 37	10 51	11 07
Saltaire	d	06 10	06 24	07 11		07 25	07 56	08 11		08 25		08 42	08 54	09 10	09 24	09 40	09 54		10 10			10 24	10 40	10 54	11 10
Shipley	a	06 12	06 27	07 13		07 28	07 58	08 13	08 18	08 27		08 44	08 57	09 12	09 27	09 43	09 58	10 02	10 12	10 19		10 27	10 42	10 57	11 12
	d	06 13	06 28	07 13	07u18	07 28	08 00	08 13	08 19	08 28		08 44	08 58	09 14	09 28	09 44	09 58	10 02	10 14	10 19		10 28	10 44	10 58	11 14
Frizinghall	37 a		06 32			07 32	08 03			08 31			09 02		09 32		10 02					10 32		11 02	
Bradford Forster Square	37 a		06 38			07 39	08 09			08 38			09 09		09 38		10 08					10 38		11 08	
Leeds 10	37 a	06 27		07 27	07 33			08 27	08 37			08 58		09 28		09 59		10 20	10 28	10 34			10 58		11 28
London Kings Cross 15	⊖26 a				09 53																				

		NT	NT	NT	NT	NT		NT	NT		NT	NT	NT	NT	NT	NT		NT	NT	NT	NT	NT	NT	NT	NT B
Carlisle 8	65 d			09 26															11 51						
Armathwaite	d			09 40															12 05						
Lazonby & Kirkoswald	d			09 47															12 12						
Langwathby	d			09 53															12 18						
Appleby	d			10 08															12 33						
Kirkby Stephen	d			10 21															12 46						
Garsdale	d			10 35															12 59						
Dent	d			10 40															13 04						
Ribblehead	d			10 49															13 14						
Horton-in-Ribblesdale	d			10 56															13 20						
Settle	d			11 04															13 28						
Morecambe	98 d								10 34																13 29
Bare Lane	98 d								10 38																13 36
Lancaster 6	65,82,98 d								10 49																13 48
Carnforth	82 d								11 09																13 58
Wennington	d								11 23																14 12
Bentham	d								11 29																14 18
Clapham (Nth Yorkshire)	d								11 36																14 25
Giggleswick	d								11 44																14 33
Long Preston	d								11 52										13 34						14 40
Hellifield	d			11 11					11 56										13 37						14 44
Clitheroe	94 a																								
Blackburn	94,97 a																								
Preston 8	97 a																								
Blackpool North	97 a																								
Gargrave	d								12 04										13 45						14 52
Skipton	a			11 26					12 13										13 55						15 03
	d	11 02	11 18	11 28	11 33	11 48		12 02	12 13		12 18	12 32	12 48	13 02	13 18	13 32		13 48	13 58	14 02	14 18	14 32	14 48	15 00	15 10
Cononley	d	11 06	11 22		11 37	11 52		12 06			12 22	12 36	12 52	13 06	13 22	13 36		13 52		14 06	14 22	14 36	14 52	15 04	
Steeton & Silsden	d	11 10	11 26		11 41	11 56		12 10			12 26	12 40	12 56	13 10	13 26	13 40		13 56		14 10	14 27	14 40	14 56	15 08	
Keighley	d	11 15	11 31	11 38	11 46	12 01		12 15	12 23		12 31	12 45	13 01	13 15	13 31	13 45		14 01	14 09	14 15	14 31	14 45	15 01	15 13	15 20
Crossflatts	d	11 18	11 34		11 49	12 04		12 18			12 34	12 48	13 04	13 18	13 34	13 48		14 04		14 18	14 35	14 48	15 04	15 16	
Bingley	d	11 21	11 37	11 42	11 52	12 07		12 21			12 37	12 51	13 07	13 21	13 37	13 51		14 07	14 13	14 21	14 38	14 51	15 07	15 19	15 25
Saltaire	d	11 24	11 40		11 55	12 10		12 24			12 40	12 54	13 10	13 24	13 40	13 54		14 10		14 24	14 42	14 54	15 10	15 22	
Shipley	a	11 27	11 43	11 49	11 58	12 14		12 27	12 33		12 42	12 57	13 12	13 27	13 42	13 57		14 12	14 18	14 28	14 44	14 58	15 12	15 26	15 30
	d	11 28	11 44	11 49	11 58	12 14		12 28	12 33		12 44	12 58	13 14	13 28	13 44	13 58		14 14	14 18	14 28	14 45	14 58	15 14	15 28	15 30
Frizinghall	37 a	11 32			12 02			12 32				13 02		13 32		14 02				14 32		15 02		15 32	
Bradford Forster Square	37 a	11 38			12 10			12 38				13 08		13 38		14 08				14 38		15 08		15 38	
Leeds 10	37 a		11 58	12 06		12 29			12 55		12 58		13 28		13 58			14 28	14 37		15 00		15 28		15 47
London Kings Cross 15	⊖26 a																								

B From Heysham Port

Table 36

Saturdays

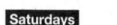

Carlisle, Morecambe, Lancaster and Skipton - Bradford and Leeds

			NT	NT	NT	NT	NT	NT		NT	NT		NT	NT	NT	NT	NT	NT	NT	NT	NT		NT	NT
Carlisle [8] 65 d								14 26								15 49					16 18			
Armathwaite d								14 40													16 32			
Lazonby & Kirkoswald d								14 47													16 39			
Langwathby d								14 53													16 45			
Appleby d								15 09								16 26					17 01			
Kirkby Stephen d								15 22								16 39					17 14			
Garsdale d								15 35													17 27			
Dent d								15 40													17 32			
Ribblehead d								15 49													17 42			
Horton-in-Ribblesdale d								15 56													17 48			
Settle d								16 04								17 16					17 57			
Morecambe 98 d																		16 19						
Bare Lane 98 d																		16 24						
Lancaster [6] 65,82,98 d																		16 40						
Carnforth 82 d																		16 50						
Wennington d																		17 04						
Bentham d																		17 09						
Clapham (Nth Yorkshire) d																		17 16						
Giggleswick d																		17 25						
Long Preston d																		17 33			18 03			
Hellifield d								16 11										17 36			18 06			
Clitheroe 94 a																								
Blackburn 94,97 a																								
Preston [8] 97 a																								
Blackpool North 97 a																								
Gargrave d																		17 44			18 14			
Skipton a								16 26								17 38		17 54			18 23			
d			15 18	15 32	15 48	16 02	16 18	16 28		16 33	16 49		17 02	17 19	17 28	17 41	17 49	17 58	18 02	18 16	18 28		18 32	18 48
Cononley d			15 22	15 36	15 52	16 06	16 22			16 37	16 53		17 06	17 23	17 32		17 53		18 06	18 20			18 36	18 52
Steeton & Silsden d			15 26	15 40	15 56	16 10	16 26			16 41	16 57		17 10	17 27	17 36		17 57		18 10	18 25			18 40	18 56
Keighley d			15 31	15 45	16 01	16 15	16 31	16 38		16 46	17 02		17 15	17 32	17 41	17 51	18 02	18 08	18 15	18 29	18 38		18 45	19 01
Crossflatts d			15 34	15 48	16 04	16 18	16 34			16 49	17 05		17 18	17 35	17 44		18 05		18 18	18 33			18 48	19 04
Bingley d			15 37	15 51	16 07	16 21	16 37	16 42		16 52	17 08		17 21	17 38	17 47	17 55	18 08	18 14	18 21	18 35	18 42		18 51	19 07
Saltaire d			15 40	15 54	16 10	16 24	16 40			16 55	17 11		17 24	17 41	17 50		18 11		18 24	18 39			18 54	19 10
Shipley a			15 43	15 57	16 12	16 27	16 42	16 49		16 59	17 13		17 27	17 43	17 55	18 00	18 13	18 19	18 28	18 42	18 48		18 58	19 12
d			15 44	15 58	16 14	16 28	16 44	16 49		16 59	17 15		17 28	17 45	17 56	18 00	18 14	18 19	18 28	18 44	18 48		18 58	19 14
Frizinghall 37 a				16 02		16 31				17 03			17 32		17 59				18 32				19 02	
Bradford Forster Square 37 a				16 08		16 38				17 08			17 38		18 05				18 38				19 08	
Leeds [10] 37 a			15 58		16 28		16 58	17 07			17 29			18 00		18 17	18 29	18 42		18 59	19 07			19 29
London Kings Cross [15] ⊖26 a																								

	NT	NT	NT	NT	NT	NT	NT		NT	NT	NT	NT	NT	NT	NT	NT
Carlisle [8] 65 d						18 07										
Armathwaite d						18 21										
Lazonby & Kirkoswald d						18 28										
Langwathby d						18 34										
Appleby d						18 49										
Kirkby Stephen d						19 02										
Garsdale d						19 15										
Dent d						19 20										
Ribblehead d						19 30							21 00			
Horton-in-Ribblesdale d						19 36							21 06			
Settle d						19 44							21 14			
Morecambe 98 d									19 09							
Bare Lane 98 d									19 13							
Lancaster [6] 65,82,98 d									19 24							
Carnforth 82 d									19 35							
Wennington d									19 49							
Bentham d									19 54							
Clapham (Nth Yorkshire) d									20 01							
Giggleswick d									20 10							
Long Preston d									20 18				21 20			
Hellifield d						19 52			20 21				21 23			
Clitheroe 94 a																
Blackburn 94,97 a																
Preston [8] 97 a																
Blackpool North 97 a																
Gargrave d									20 29				21 31			
Skipton a						20 07			20 38				21 40			
d	19 00	19 18	19 32	19 48	19 54	20 07	20 18		20 38	20 48	20 54	21 18		21 48	21 54	22 18
Cononley d	19 04	19 22	19 36	19 52	19 58		20 22			20 52	20 58	21 22		21 52	21 58	22 22
Steeton & Silsden d	19 08	19 26	19 40	19 56	20 02		20 26			20 56	21 02	21 26		21 56	22 02	22 26
Keighley d	19 13	19 31	19 45	20 01	20 07	20 17	20 31		20 48	21 01	21 07	21 31		22 01	22 07	22 31
Crossflatts d	19 16	19 34	19 48	20 04	20 10		20 33			21 04	21 10	21 34		22 04	22 10	22 34
Bingley d	19 19	19 37	19 51	20 07	20 13	20 22	20 37		20 53	21 07	21 13	21 37		22 07	22 13	22 37
Saltaire d	19 22	19 40	19 54	20 10	20 16		20 39			21 10	21 16	21 40		22 10	22 16	22 40
Shipley a	19 25	19 42	19 57	20 12	20 20	20 27	20 42		20 57	21 12	21 22	21 42		22 13	22 20	22 42
d	19 26	19 44	19 58	20 14	20 20	20 28	20 43		20 57	21 14	21 22	21 43		22 14	22 21	22 43
Frizinghall 37 a	19 29		20 01		20 24						21 26				22 24	
Bradford Forster Square 37 a	19 35		20 08		20 32						21 32				22 31	
Leeds [10] 37 a		19 59		20 28		20 46	21 00		21 16	21 30		21 59		22 32		23 01
London Kings Cross [15] ⊖26 a																

Table 36

Sundays
until 11 September

Carlisle, Morecambe, Lancaster and Skipton - Bradford and Leeds

		NT	NT	NT	NT	NT	NT	NT	NT	NT		NT	NT	NT	NT	NT	NT	NT A	NT	NT		NT	NT	NT	NT
Carlisle 8	65 d						09 25										13 51		15 35						16 37
Armathwaite	d						09 39										14 05		15 51						16 51
Lazonby & Kirkoswald	d						09 46										14 12		15 58						16 58
Langwathby	d						09 53										14 19		16 05						17 05
Appleby	d						10 07										14 33		16 20						17 20
Kirkby Stephen	d						10 21										14 47		16 34						17 34
Garsdale	d						10 34										15 00		16 47						17 47
Dent	d						10 40										15 06		16 53						17 53
Ribblehead	d						10 49										15 15		17 02						18 02
Horton-in-Ribblesdale	d						10 56										15 22		17 09						18 09
Settle	d						11 04										15 30		17 21						18 19
Morecambe	98 d												12 20					14 46							
Bare Lane	98 d												12 24					14 50							
Lancaster 6	65,82,98 d												12 48												
Carnforth	82 d												12 58					15 00							
Wennington	d												13 12					15 14							
Bentham	d												13 17					15 20							
Clapham (Nth Yorkshire)	d												13 24					15 26							
Giggleswick	d												13 32					15 35							
Long Preston	d						11 10						13 40				15 36	15 45							
Hellifield	d						11 13						13 44				15 39	15 49	17 34						18 26
Clitheroe	94 a																								
Blackburn	94,97 a																								
Preston 8	97 a																		18 29						
Blackpool North	97 a																								
Gargrave	d						11 21						13 52				15 47	15 57							
Skipton	a						11 30						14 01				15 54	16 06							18 41
	d	08 35	09 15	09 36	10 15	11 15	11 30	11 37	12 15	13 15		13 37	14 02	14 15	15 15	15 37	15 57	16 08		16 15		17 15	17 37	18 15	18 43
Cononley	d	08 39	09 19	09 40	10 19	11 19		11 41	12 19	13 19		13 41		14 19	15 19	15 41				16 19		17 19	17 41	18 19	
Steeton & Silsden	d	08 44	09 23	09 44	10 23	11 23		11 45	12 23	13 23		13 45		14 23	15 23	15 45				16 23		17 23	17 45	18 23	
Keighley	d	08 48	09 28	09 49	10 28	11 28	11 40	11 50	12 28	13 28		13 50	14 12	14 28	15 28	15 50	16 07	16 18		16 28		17 28	17 50	18 28	18 53
Crossflatts	d	08 52	09 31	09 52	10 31	11 31		11 53	12 31	13 31		13 53		14 31	15 31	15 53				16 31		17 31	17 53	18 31	
Bingley	d	08 54	09 34	09 55	10 34	11 34	11 44	11 56	12 34	13 34		13 56	14 16	14 34	15 34	15 56	16 11	16 23		16 34		17 34	17 56	18 34	18 57
Saltaire	d	08 58	09 37	09 58	10 37	11 37		11 59	12 37	13 37		13 59		14 37	15 37	15 59				16 37		17 37	17 59	18 37	
Shipley	a	09 00	09 39	10 01	10 39	11 39	11 49	12 02	12 39	13 39		14 02	14 21	14 39	15 39	16 02	16 16	16 27		16 39		17 39	18 02	18 39	19 02
	d	09 00	09 40	10 01	10 40	11 40	11 49	12 02	12 40	13 40		14 02	14 21	14 40	15 40	16 02	16 16	16 29		16 40		17 40	18 02	18 40	19 03
Frizinghall	37 a			10 05				12 06				14 06				16 06							18 06		
Bradford Forster Square	37 a			10 12				12 12				14 12				16 12							18 12		
Leeds 10	37 a	09 14	09 54		10 54	11 54	12 06		12 54	13 54			14 39	14 54	15 54		16 34	16 47		16 54		17 54		18 54	19 21
London Kings Cross 15	⊖26 a																								

		NT	NT ⊼	NT	NT	NT		NT	NT	NT	NT	NT
Carlisle 8	65 d		17 41									
Armathwaite	d		17 55									
Lazonby & Kirkoswald	d		18 03									
Langwathby	d		18 09									
Appleby	d		18 25									
Kirkby Stephen	d		18 38									
Garsdale	d		18 52									
Dent	d		18 57									
Ribblehead	d		19 07									
Horton-in-Ribblesdale	d		19 14									
Settle	d		19 22									
Morecambe	98 d	17 45							20 00			
Bare Lane	98 d	17 49							20 04			
Lancaster 6	65,82,98 d	18 04							20 20			
Carnforth	82 d	18 14							20 30			
Wennington	d	18 28							20 44			
Bentham	d	18 33							20 49			
Clapham (Nth Yorkshire)	d	18 40							20 56			
Giggleswick	d	18 49							21 05			
Long Preston	d	18 57							21 13			
Hellifield	d	19 00	19 32						21 16			
Clitheroe	94 a		19 56									
Blackburn	94,97 a		20 22									
Preston 8	97 a		20 47									
Blackpool North	97 a		21 16									
Gargrave	d	19 09							21 24			
Skipton	a	19 17							21 33			
	d	19 18		19 24	19 37	20 15		21 15	21 33	21 39	22 15	23 15
Cononley	d			19 28	19 41	20 19		21 19		21 43	22 19	23 19
Steeton & Silsden	d			19 32	19 45	20 23		21 23		21 47	22 23	23 23
Keighley	d	19 28		19 37	19 50	20 28		21 28	21 43	21 52	22 28	23 29
Crossflatts	d			19 40	19 53	20 31		21 31		21 55	22 31	23 31
Bingley	d	19 32		19 43	19 56	20 34		21 34	21 48	21 58	22 34	23 34
Saltaire	d			19 46	19 59	20 37		21 37		22 01	22 37	23 37
Shipley	a	19 37		19 48	20 02	20 39		21 39	21 53	22 04	22 39	23 41
	d	19 38		19 49	20 02	20 40		21 40	21 54	22 04	22 40	23 41
Frizinghall	37 a				20 06					22 08		
Bradford Forster Square	37 a				20 12					22 14		
Leeds 10	37 a	19 56		20 03		20 54		21 54	22 10		22 54	23 58
London Kings Cross 15	⊖26 a											

A From Lancaster

Table 36 **Sundays**

18 September to 23 October

Carlisle, Morecambe, Lancaster and Skipton - Bradford and Leeds

		NT	NT	NT	NT	NT	NT	NT	NT	NT		NT	NT	NT	NT	NT	NT	NT A	NT	NT		NT	NT	NT	NT
Carlisle [8] 65	d						09 25										13 51							16 37	
Armathwaite	d						09 39										14 05							16 51	
Lazonby & Kirkoswald	d						09 46										14 12							16 58	
Langwathby	d						09 53										14 19							17 05	
Appleby	d						10 07										14 33							17 20	
Kirkby Stephen	d						10 21										14 47							17 34	
Garsdale	d						10 34										15 00							17 47	
Dent	d						10 40										15 06							17 53	
Ribblehead	d						10 49										15 15							18 02	
Horton-in-Ribblesdale	d						10 56										15 22							18 09	
Settle	d						11 04										15 30							18 19	
Morecambe 98	d												12 20					14 46							17 45
Bare Lane 98	d												12 24					14 50							17 49
Lancaster [6] 65,82,98	d												12 48												18 04
Carnforth 82	d												12 58					15 00							18 14
Wennington	d												13 12					15 14							18 28
Bentham	d												13 17					15 20							18 33
Clapham (Nth Yorkshire)	d												13 24					15 26							18 40
Giggleswick	d												13 32					15 35							18 49
Long Preston	d						11 10						13 40				15 36	15 45							18 57
Hellifield	d						11 13						13 44				15 39	15 49						18 26	19 00
Clitheroe 94	a																								
Blackburn 94,97	a																								
Preston [8] 97	a																								
Blackpool North 97	a																								
Gargrave	d						11 21						13 52				15 47	15 57							19 09
Skipton	a						11 30						14 01				15 54	16 06						18 41	19 17
	d	08 35	09 15	09 36	10 15	11 15	11 30	11 37	12 15	13 15		13 37	14 02	14 15	15 15	15 37	15 57	16 08	16 15	17 15		17 37	18 15	18 43	19 18
Cononley	d	08 39	09 19	09 40	10 19	11 19		11 41	12 19	13 19		13 41		14 19	15 19	15 41			16 19	17 19		17 41	18 19		
Steeton & Silsden	d	08 44	09 23	09 44	10 23	11 23		11 45	12 23	13 23		13 45		14 23	15 23	15 45			16 23	17 23		17 45	18 23		
Keighley	d	08 48	09 28	09 49	10 28	11 28	11 40	11 50	12 28	13 28		13 50	14 12	14 28	15 28	15 50	16 07	16 18	16 28	17 28		17 50	18 28	18 53	19 28
Crossflatts	d	08 52	09 31	09 52	10 31	11 31		11 53	12 31	13 31		13 53		14 31	15 31	15 53			16 31	17 31		17 53	18 31		
Bingley	d	08 54	09 34	09 55	10 34	11 34	11 44	11 56	12 34	13 34		13 56	14 16	14 34	15 34	15 56	16 11	16 23	16 34	17 34		17 56	18 34	18 57	19 32
Saltaire	d	08 58	09 37	09 58	10 37	11 37		11 59	12 37	13 37		13 59		14 37	15 37	15 59			16 37	17 37		17 59	18 37		
Shipley	a	09 00	09 39	10 01	10 39	11 39	11 49	12 02	12 39	13 39		14 02	14 21	14 39	15 39	16 02	16 16	16 27	16 39	17 39		18 02	18 39	19 02	19 37
	d	09 00	09 40	10 01	10 40	11 40	11 49	12 02	12 40	13 40		14 02	14 21	14 40	15 40	16 02	16 16	16 29	16 40	17 40		18 02	18 40	19 03	19 38
Frizinghall 37	a			10 05				12 06				14 06				16 06						18 06			
Bradford Forster Square 37	a			10 12				12 12				14 12				16 12						18 12			
Leeds [10] 37	a	09 14	09 54		10 54	11 54	12 06		12 54	13 54			14 39	14 54	15 54		16 34	16 47	16 54	17 54			18 54	19 21	19 56
London Kings Cross [15] ⊖26	a																								

		NT 🚌	NT	NT	NT	NT		NT	NT	NT	NT
Carlisle [8] 65	d	17 41									
Armathwaite	d	17 55									
Lazonby & Kirkoswald	d	18 03									
Langwathby	d	18 09									
Appleby	d	18 25									
Kirkby Stephen	d	18 38									
Garsdale	d	18 52									
Dent	d	18 57									
Ribblehead	d	19 07									
Horton-in-Ribblesdale	d	19 14									
Settle	d	19 22									
Morecambe 98	d							20 00			
Bare Lane 98	d							20 04			
Lancaster [6] 65,82,98	d							20 20			
Carnforth 82	d							20 30			
Wennington	d							20 44			
Bentham	d							20 49			
Clapham (Nth Yorkshire)	d							20 56			
Giggleswick	d							21 05			
Long Preston	d							21 13			
Hellifield	d	19 32						21 16			
Clitheroe 94	a	19 56									
Blackburn 94,97	a	20 22									
Preston [8] 97	a	20 47									
Blackpool North 97	a	21 16									
Gargrave	d							21 24			
Skipton	a							21 33			
	d		19 24	19 37	20 15	21 15		21 33	21 39	22 15	23 15
Cononley	d		19 28	19 41	20 19	21 19			21 43	22 19	23 19
Steeton & Silsden	d		19 32	19 45	20 23	21 23			21 47	22 23	23 23
Keighley	d		19 37	19 50	20 28	21 28		21 43	21 52	22 28	23 29
Crossflatts	d		19 40	19 53	20 31	21 31			21 55	22 31	23 31
Bingley	d		19 43	19 56	20 34	21 34		21 48	21 58	22 34	23 34
Saltaire	d		19 46	19 59	20 37	21 37			22 01	22 37	23 37
Shipley	a		19 48	20 02	20 39	21 39		21 53	22 04	22 39	23 41
	d		19 49	20 02	20 40	21 40		21 54	22 04	22 40	23 41
Frizinghall 37	a			20 06					22 08		
Bradford Forster Square 37	a			20 12					22 14		
Leeds [10] 37	a		20 03		20 54	21 54		22 10		22 54	23 58
London Kings Cross [15] ⊖26	a										

A From Lancaster

Table 36

Sundays
from 30 October

Carlisle, Morecambe, Lancaster and Skipton - Bradford and Leeds

			NT	NT	NT	NT	NT	NT	NT	NT	NT		NT	NT	NT	NT	NT	NT	NT A	NT	NT		NT	NT	NT	NT
Carlisle 8	65	d						09 25										13 51							16 37	
Armathwaite		d						09 39										14 05							16 51	
Lazonby & Kirkoswald		d						09 46										14 12							16 58	
Langwathby		d						09 53										14 19							17 05	
Appleby		d						10 07										14 33							17 20	
Kirkby Stephen		d						10 21										14 47							17 34	
Garsdale		d						10 34										15 00							17 47	
Dent		d						10 40										15 06							17 53	
Ribblehead		d						10 49										15 15							18 02	
Horton-in-Ribblesdale		d						10 56										15 22							18 09	
Settle		d						11 04										15 30							18 19	
Morecambe	98	d												12 20					14 46							17 45
Bare Lane	98	d												12 24					14 50							17 49
Lancaster 6	65,82,98	d												12 48												18 04
Carnforth	82	d												12 58					15 00							18 14
Wennington		d												13 12					15 14							18 28
Bentham		d												13 17					15 20							18 33
Clapham (Nth Yorkshire)		d												13 24					15 26							18 40
Giggleswick		d												13 32					15 35							18 49
Long Preston		d						11 10						13 40				15 36	15 45							18 57
Hellifield		d						11 13						13 44				15 39	15 49						18 26	19 00
Clitheroe	94	a																								
Blackburn	94,97	a																								
Preston 8	97	a																								
Blackpool North	97	a																								
Gargrave		d						11 21						13 52				15 47	15 57							19 09
Skipton		a						11 30						14 01				15 54	16 06						18 41	19 17
		d	08 35	09 15	09 36	10 15	11 15	11 30	11 37	12 15	13 15		13 37	14 02	14 15	15 15	15 37	15 57	16 08	16 15	17 15		17 37	18 15	18 43	19 18
Cononley		d	08 39	09 19	09 40	10 19	11 19		11 41	12 19	13 19		13 41		14 19	15 19	15 41			16 19	17 19		17 41	18 19		
Steeton & Silsden		d	08 44	09 23	09 44	10 23	11 23		11 45	12 23	13 23		13 45		14 23	15 23	15 45			16 23	17 23		17 45	18 23		
Keighley		d	08 48	09 28	09 49	10 28	11 28	11 40	11 50	12 28	13 28		13 50	14 12	14 28	15 28	15 50	16 07	16 18	16 28	17 28		17 50	18 28	18 53	19 28
Crossflatts		d	08 52	09 31	09 52	10 31	11 31		11 53	12 31	13 31		13 53		14 31	15 31	15 53			16 31	17 31		17 53	18 31		
Bingley		d	08 54	09 34	09 55	10 34	11 34	11 44	11 56	12 34	13 34		13 56	14 16	14 34	15 34	15 56	16 11	16 23	16 34	17 34		17 56	18 34	18 57	19 32
Saltaire		d	08 58	09 37	09 58	10 37	11 37		11 59	12 37	13 37		13 59		14 37	15 37	15 59			16 37	17 37		17 59	18 37		
Shipley		a	09 00	09 39	10 01	10 39	11 39	11 49	12 02	12 39	13 39		14 02	14 21	14 39	15 39	16 02	16 16	16 27	16 39	17 39		18 02	18 39	19 02	19 37
		d	09 00	09 40	10 01	10 40	11 40	11 49	12 02	12 40	13 40		14 02	14 21	14 40	15 40	16 02	16 16	16 29	16 40	17 40		18 02	18 40	19 03	19 38
Frizinghall	37	a			10 05				12 06				14 06				16 06						18 06			
Bradford Forster Square	37	a			10 12				12 12				14 12				16 12						18 12			
Leeds 10	37	a	09 14	09 54		10 54	11 54	12 06		12 54	13 54			14 39	14 54	15 54		16 34	16 47	16 54	17 54			18 54	19 21	19 56
London Kings Cross 15	⊖26	a																								

			NT	NT	NT	NT	NT		NT	NT	NT
Carlisle 8	65	d									
Armathwaite		d									
Lazonby & Kirkoswald		d									
Langwathby		d									
Appleby		d									
Kirkby Stephen		d									
Garsdale		d									
Dent		d									
Ribblehead		d									
Horton-in-Ribblesdale		d									
Settle		d									
Morecambe	98	d					20 00				
Bare Lane	98	d					20 04				
Lancaster 6	65,82,98	d					20 20				
Carnforth	82	d					20 30				
Wennington		d					20 44				
Bentham		d					20 49				
Clapham (Nth Yorkshire)		d					20 56				
Giggleswick		d					21 05				
Long Preston		d					21 13				
Hellifield		d					21 16				
Clitheroe	94	a									
Blackburn	94,97	a									
Preston 8	97	a									
Blackpool North	97	a									
Gargrave		d					21 24				
Skipton		a					21 33				
		d	19 24	19 37	20 15	21 15	21 33		21 39	22 15	23 15
Cononley		d	19 28	19 41	20 19	21 19			21 43	22 19	23 19
Steeton & Silsden		d	19 32	19 45	20 23	21 23			21 47	22 23	23 23
Keighley		d	19 37	19 50	20 28	21 28	21 43		21 52	22 28	23 29
Crossflatts		d	19 40	19 53	20 31	21 31			21 55	22 31	23 31
Bingley		d	19 43	19 56	20 34	21 34	21 48		21 58	22 34	23 34
Saltaire		d	19 46	19 59	20 37	21 37			22 01	22 37	23 37
Shipley		a	19 48	20 02	20 39	21 39	21 53		22 04	22 39	23 41
		d	19 49	20 02	20 40	21 40	21 54		22 04	22 40	23 41
Frizinghall	37	a		20 06					22 08		
Bradford Forster Square	37	a		20 12					22 14		
Leeds 10	37	a	20 03		20 54	21 54	22 10			22 54	23 58
London Kings Cross 15	⊖26	a									

A From Lancaster

Table 37

Leeds - Shipley and Bradford

Miles	Miles			NT	NT	NT MO	NT	NT	NT	NT	NT	NT		NT	NT	NT	NT	NT	NT	NT	NT	NT		NT	NT
0	0	**Leeds 10**	d	05 08	05 51	05 57	06 03		06 21	06 22	06 37				06 49	06 51	06 56	07 08		07 22		07 25		07 37	
10¾	—	**Shipley**	a			06 10			06 32						07 01		07 08					07 36			
—	—		d					06 28				06 41		06 53	07 02				07 15		07 28				07 47
11¾	—	Frizinghall	d					06 32				06 44		06 57	07 04				07 17		07 32				07 49
—	4	Bramley	d	05 15	05 58					06 29	06 44							07 15		07 29				07 44	
—	5¾	New Pudsey	d	05 20	06 02		06 13			06 34	06 49					07 01		07 20		07 34				07 49	
—	9½	**Bradford Interchange**	a	05 28	06 13		06 21			06 42	06 57					07 11		07 28		07 43				07 57	
13½	—	**Bradford Forster Square**	a					06 38				06 50		07 03	07 10				07 22		07 39				07 56

		NT	NT	NT	NT	NT	NT	NT		NT	NT	NT	NT	NT	NT	NT	NT	NT		NT	NT	NT	NT	NT	NT
Leeds 10	d	07 39	07 51		07 51	08 08		08 10			08 19	08 23	08 25	08 37		08 40		08 49		08 51	08 56	09 07		09 10	09 23
Shipley	a	07 50			08 02			08 22			08 31		08 37			08 51		09 01			09 07			09 21	
	d	07 51		08 00			08 13	08 23		08 28					08 48	08 52	08 58						09 18	09 22	
Frizinghall	d	07 53		08 03			08 16	08 25		08 31					08 50	08 54	09 02						09 21	09 24	
Bramley	d					08 15						08 30		08 44								09 14			09 30
New Pudsey	d		08 01			08 20						08 35		08 49						09 00		09 19			09 35
Bradford Interchange	a		08 09			08 28						08 43		08 57						09 12		09 28			09 43
Bradford Forster Square	a	07 59		08 09			08 22	08 31		08 38					08 56	09 00	09 09						09 27	09 31	

		NT	NT	NT		NT	NT	NT	NT	NT	NT	NT	NT	NT		NT	NT	NT	NT	NT	NT	NT	NT	NT	
Leeds 10	d		09 26	09 37			09 40		09 47	09 53	09 56	10 07		10 10			10 19	10 23	10 26	10 37		10 40		10 49	
Shipley	a		09 37				09 52		10 01		10 07			10 21			10 31		10 37			10 51		11 01	
	d	09 28				09 44	09 52	09 58					10 14	10 22		10 28					10 44	10 52	10 58		
Frizinghall	d	09 32				09 47	09 54	10 02					10 17	10 24		10 32					10 47	10 54	11 02		
Bramley	d			09 44								10 14						10 30		10 44					
New Pudsey	d			09 49						10 02		10 20						10 35		10 49					
Bradford Interchange	a			09 57						10 12		10 28						10 43		10 57					
Bradford Forster Square	a	09 38				09 53	10 02	10 08					10 23	10 30		10 38					10 53	11 00	11 08		

		NT	NT	NT	NT	NT	NT	NT	NT	NT		NT	NT	NT	NT	NT	NT	NT	NT	NT		NT	NT	NT	NT
Leeds 10	d	10 53	10 56	11 07		11 10		11 26	11 37			11 40	11 53		11 56	12 07		12 10	12 23			12 26	12 37		12 40
Shipley	a		11 07			11 21		11 39				11 51			12 07			12 21				12 37			12 51
	d				11 14	11 22	11 28			11 44		11 52		11 58			12 14	12 22		12 28				12 44	12 52
Frizinghall	d				11 17	11 24	11 32			11 47		11 54		12 02			12 17	12 24		12 32				12 47	12 54
Bramley	d			11 14					11 44							12 14			12 30				12 44		
New Pudsey	d	11 02		11 19					11 49				12 02			12 19			12 35				12 49		
Bradford Interchange	a	11 11		11 28					11 57				12 11			12 28			12 43				12 57		
Bradford Forster Square	a				11 23	11 30	11 38			11 53		12 00		12 10			12 24	12 31		12 38				12 53	13 00

		NT	NT	NT	NT	NT		NT	NT	NT	NT	NT	NT	NT	NT	NT		NT	NT	NT	NT	NT	NT	NT	NT
Leeds 10	d		12 49	12 53	12 56	13 07			13 10	13 23		13 26	13 37		13 40			13 49	13 53	13 56	14 07		14 10	14 23	
Shipley	a		13 01		13 07				13 21			13 37			13 51			14 03		14 07			14 21		
	d	12 58						13 14	13 22		13 28			13 44	13 52	13 58						14 14	14 22		14 28
Frizinghall	d	13 02						13 17	13 24		13 32			13 47	13 54	14 02						14 17	14 24		14 32
Bramley	d					13 14				13 30			13 44								14 14			14 30	
New Pudsey	d			13 02		13 19				13 35			13 49						14 02		14 19			14 35	
Bradford Interchange	a			13 12		13 28				13 43			13 58						14 12		14 28			14 43	
Bradford Forster Square	a	13 08						13 23	13 30		13 38			13 53	14 00	14 08						14 23	14 30		14 38

		NT		NT	NT	NT	NT	NT	NT	NT	NT	NT		NT	NT	NT	NT	NT	NT	NT	NT	NT		NT	NT
Leeds 10	d	14 26		14 37		14 40		14 49	14 53	14 56	15 07			15 10	15 23		15 26	15 37		15 40	15 52			15 56	16 07
Shipley	a	14 37				14 51		15 01		15 07				15 21			15 37			15 52				16 07	
	d				14 44	14 52	14 58					15 14		15 22		15 28			15 44	15 52		15 58			
Frizinghall	d				14 47	14 54	15 02					15 17		15 24		15 32			15 47	15 55		16 02			
Bramley	d			14 44							15 14				15 30			15 44							16 14
New Pudsey	d			14 49					15 02		15 19				15 35			15 49			16 01				16 19
Bradford Interchange	a			14 57					15 12		15 28				15 43			15 57			16 10				16 28
Bradford Forster Square	a				14 53	15 00	15 08					15 23		15 30		15 38			15 53	16 01		16 08			

		NT	NT	NT	NT	NT	NT	NT		NT	NT	NT	NT	NT	NT	NT	NT	NT		NT	NT	NT	NT	NT	NT
Leeds 10	d		16 10	16 22		16 26		16 35		16 37	16 39	16 51		16 56	17 07		17 10	17 23			17 26		17 36	17 37	
Shipley	a		16 21			16 37		16 49			16 53			17 07			17 21				17 37		17 49		
	d	16 14	16 22		16 28		16 44	16 49					17 02			17 15	17 22			17 28		17 44	17 50		17 56
Frizinghall	d	16 17	16 24		16 31		16 47	16 52					17 06			17 17	17 24			17 32		17 46	17 52		17 59
Bramley	d			16 30						16 44					17 14			17 30						17 44	
New Pudsey	d			16 35						16 49		17 01			17 19			17 35						17 49	
Bradford Interchange	a			16 43						16 57		17 10			17 28			17 43						17 57	
Bradford Forster Square	a	16 23	16 30		16 38		16 53	16 58					17 12			17 23	17 30			17 38		17 53	17 58		18 05

		NT	NT	NT		NT	NT	NT	NT	NT	NT	NT	NT	NT		NT	NT	NT	NT	NT	NT	NT	NT	NT	
Leeds 10	d	17 50	17 51	17 56		18 08		18 10	18 22		18 23	18 37		18 40		18 51		18 54	19 08		19 10		19 19	19 22	
Shipley	a	18 02		18 08				18 21			18 38			18 52				19 05			19 21		19 31		
	d						18 14	18 22		18 28			18 44	18 52			18 58			19 14	19 22	19 26			
Frizinghall	d						18 17	18 24		18 32			18 46	18 55			19 02			19 17	19 24	19 29			
Bramley	d					18 15			18 30			18 44							19 15					19 30	
New Pudsey	d		18 01			18 20			18 35			18 49				19 01			19 20					19 35	
Bradford Interchange	a		18 10			18 28			18 43			18 58				19 09			19 28					19 44	
Bradford Forster Square	a						18 23	18 31		18 38			18 52	19 01			19 08			19 23	19 30	19 35			

Leeds - Shipley and Bradford

		NT	NT	NT	NT	NT	NT	NT	NT	NT		NT	NT	NT	NT	NT	GR	NT	NT	NT		NT	NT	NT	NT
Leeds 10	d	19 26	19 37			19 56	20 08			20 26		20 37		20 51		20 55	21 00	21 08		21 26		21 37			21 56
Shipley	a	19 38				20 07				20 37						21 07	21s12			21 38					22 07
	d			19 44	19 58			20 20	20 28				20 48		21 03				21 19				21 48	22 03	
Frizinghall	d			19 47	20 01			20 24	20 30				20 51		21 05				21 23				21 51	22 05	
Bramley	d		19 44				20 15					20 44						21 15				21 44			
New Pudsey	d		19 49				20 20					20 49		21 01				21 20				21 49			
Bradford Interchange	a		19 57				20 28					20 57		21 10				21 28				21 57			
Bradford Forster Square	a			19 53	20 08			20 32	20 36				20 57		21 12		21 24		21 29				21 57	22 11	

		NT	NT	NT	NT	NT		NT	NT	NT	NT														
Leeds 10	d	22 08		22 28	22 37				22 51	23 08	23 18														
Shipley	a			22 37					23 05		23 31														
	d		22 19			22 48		23 03																	
Frizinghall	d		22 23			22 51		23 05																	
Bramley	d	22 15			22 44					23 15															
New Pudsey	d	22 20			22 49					23 20															
Bradford Interchange	a	22 28			22 57					23 29															
Bradford Forster Square	a		22 31			22 57		23 13																	

Saturdays

		NT	NT	NT	NT	NT	NT	NT	NT	NT		NT	NT	NT	NT	NT	NT	NT	NT	NT		NT	NT	NT	NT
Leeds 10	d	05 37	05 51	05 55	06 16		06 19	06 37		06 51		06 56	07 08	07 10	07 22		07 37		07 51			07 56	08 08	08 10	
Shipley	a			06 07			06 31					07 08		07 21								08 08		08 22	
	d					06 28			06 44					07 22		07 28		07 47		08 00				08 23	08 28
Frizinghall	d					06 32			06 47					07 24		07 32		07 49		08 03				08 25	08 31
Bramley	d	05 44	05 58		06 23			06 44					07 15		07 29		07 44						08 15		
New Pudsey	d	05 49	06 02		06 28			06 49		07 01			07 20		07 34		07 49		08 01				08 20		
Bradford Interchange	a	05 57	06 13		06 36			06 57		07 11			07 28		07 43		07 57		08 09				08 28		
Bradford Forster Square	a					06 38			06 55					07 30		07 39		07 56		08 09				08 31	08 38

		NT	NT	NT	NT	NT		NT	NT	NT	NT	NT	NT	NT	NT	NT		NT	NT	NT	NT	NT	NT	NT	NT
Leeds 10	d	08 19	08 23	08 25	08 37			08 40		08 49	08 51	08 56	09 07		09 10	09 23			09 26	09 37		09 40		09 47	09 53
Shipley	a	08 31		08 37				08 51		09 01		09 07			09 21				09 37			09 52		10 01	
	d					08 44		08 52	08 58					09 14	09 22			09 28			09 44	09 52	09 58		
Frizinghall	d					08 46		08 54	09 02					09 17	09 24			09 32			09 47	09 54	10 02		
Bramley	d		08 30		08 44								09 14			09 30				09 44					
New Pudsey	d		08 35		08 49						09 00		09 19			09 35				09 49					10 02
Bradford Interchange	a		08 43		08 57						09 12		09 28			09 43				09 57					10 11
Bradford Forster Square	a					08 53		09 00	09 09					09 24	09 31			09 38			09 53	10 02	10 08		

		NT		NT	NT	NT	NT	NT	NT	NT	NT	NT		NT	NT	NT	NT	NT	NT	NT	NT	NT		NT	NT
Leeds 10	d	09 56		10 07		10 10		10 19	10 23	10 26	10 37			10 40		10 49	10 53	10 56	11 07		11 10	11 23			11 26
Shipley	a	10 07				10 21		10 31		10 37				10 51		11 01		11 07			11 21				11 37
	d				10 14	10 22	10 28					10 44		10 52	10 58					11 14	11 22			11 28	
Frizinghall	d				10 17	10 24	10 32					10 47		10 54	11 02					11 17	11 24			11 32	
Bramley	d			10 14					10 30		10 44								11 14			11 30			
New Pudsey	d			10 19					10 35		10 49						11 02		11 19			11 35			
Bradford Interchange	a			10 28					10 43		10 57						11 12		11 28			11 43			
Bradford Forster Square	a				10 23	10 30	10 38					10 53		11 00	11 08					11 23	11 30			11 38	

		NT	NT	NT	NT	NT	NT	NT		NT	NT	NT	NT	NT	NT	NT	NT	NT		NT	NT	NT	NT	NT	NT
Leeds 10	d	11 37		11 40	11 53		11 56	12 07			12 10	12 23		12 26	12 37		12 40			12 49	12 53	12 56	13 07		13 10
Shipley	a			11 51			12 07				12 21			12 37			12 51			13 01		13 07			13 21
	d		11 44	11 52		11 58				12 14	12 22		12 28			12 44	12 52	12 58						13 14	13 22
Frizinghall	d		11 47	11 54		12 02				12 17	12 24		12 32			12 47	12 54	13 02						13 17	13 24
Bramley	d	11 44						12 14				12 30			12 44								13 14		
New Pudsey	d	11 49			12 02			12 19				12 35			12 49						13 02		13 19		
Bradford Interchange	a	11 57			12 12			12 28				12 43			12 57						13 12		13 28		
Bradford Forster Square	a		11 53	12 00		12 10				12 24	12 31		12 38			12 53	13 00	13 08						13 23	13 30

		NT	NT	NT		NT	NT	NT	NT	NT	NT	NT	NT	NT		NT	NT	NT	NT	NT	NT	NT	NT	NT	
Leeds 10	d	13 23		13 26		13 37		13 40		13 49	13 53	13 56	14 07			14 10	14 23		14 26	14 37		14 40		14 49	
Shipley	a			13 37				13 51		14 03		14 07				14 21			14 37			14 51		15 01	
	d		13 28				13 44	13 52	13 58					14 14		14 22		14 28			14 44	14 52	14 58		
Frizinghall	d		13 32				13 47	13 54	14 02					14 17		14 24		14 32			14 47	14 54	15 02		
Bramley	d	13 30				13 44							14 14				14 30			14 44					
New Pudsey	d	13 35				13 49					14 02		14 19				14 35			14 49					
Bradford Interchange	a	13 43				13 58					14 12		14 28				14 43			14 58					
Bradford Forster Square	a		13 38				13 53	14 00	14 08					14 23		14 30		14 38			14 53	15 00	15 08		

		NT	NT	NT	NT	NT	NT	NT	NT	NT		NT	NT	NT	NT	NT	NT	NT	NT	NT		NT	NT	NT	NT
Leeds 10	d	14 53	14 56	15 07		15 10	15 23		15 26	15 37			15 40	15 52		15 56	16 07		16 10	16 23			16 26		16 35
Shipley	a		15 07			15 21			15 37				15 52			16 07			16 21				16 37		16 49
	d				15 14	15 22		15 28				15 44	15 52		15 58			16 14	16 22			16 28		16 44	16 49
Frizinghall	d				15 17	15 24		15 32				15 47	15 55		16 02			16 17	16 24			16 31		16 47	16 52
Bramley	d			15 14			15 30			15 44							16 14			16 30					
New Pudsey	d	15 02		15 19			15 35			15 49				16 01			16 19			16 35					
Bradford Interchange	a	15 12		15 28			15 43			15 57				16 10			16 28			16 43					
Bradford Forster Square	a				15 23	15 30		15 38				15 53	16 01		16 08			16 23	16 30			16 38		16 53	16 58

Table 37

Saturdays

Leeds - Shipley and Bradford

		NT	NT	NT	NT	NT		NT	NT	NT	NT	NT	NT	NT	NT	NT		NT	NT	NT	NT	NT	NT	NT	NT
Leeds 10	d	16 37	16 39	16 51		16 56		17 07		17 10	17 23		17 26	17 37		17 40			17 50	17 51	17 56	18 08		18 10	18 22
Shipley	a		16 53			17 07				17 21			17 37			17 51			18 02		18 08			18 21	
	d				16 59				17 15	17 22		17 28			17 44	17 52		17 56					18 14	18 22	
Frizinghall	d				17 03				17 17	17 24		17 32			17 46	17 54		17 59					18 17	18 24	
Bramley	d	16 44						17 14			17 30			17 44								18 15			18 30
New Pudsey	d	16 49		17 01				17 19			17 35			17 49						18 01		18 20			18 35
Bradford Interchange	a	16 57		17 10				17 28			17 43			17 57						18 09		18 28			18 43
Bradford Forster Square	a				17 08				17 23	17 30		17 38			17 53	18 00		18 05					18 23	18 31	

		NT		NT	NT	NT	NT	NT	NT	NT	NT	NT		NT	NT	NT	NT	NT	NT	NT	NT	NT		NT	NT
Leeds 10	d			18 26	18 37		18 40	18 51		18 56	19 08			19 10		19 19	19 23	19 26	19 37			19 55		20 08	
Shipley	a			18 38			18 52			19 07				19 21		19 31		19 37				20 07			
	d	18 28				18 44	18 52		18 58			19 14		19 22	19 26					19 44	19 58				20 20
Frizinghall	d	18 32				18 46	18 55		19 02			19 17		19 24	19 29					19 47	20 01				20 24
Bramley	d				18 44						19 15						19 31		19 44					20 15	
New Pudsey	d				18 49			19 01			19 20						19 35		19 49					20 20	
Bradford Interchange	a				18 58			19 10			19 28						19 44		19 57					20 28	
Bradford Forster Square	a	18 38				18 52	19 01		19 08			19 23		19 30	19 35					19 53	20 08				20 32

		NT	NT	NT	NT	NT	NT	NT		NT	NT	NT	NT	NT	NT	GR R 1 (restaurant symbol)	NT	NT		NT	NT	NT	NT	NT	NT
Leeds 10	d		20 26	20 37		20 51		20 58		21 08		21 26	21 37			21 59	22 03	22 08			22 26	22 37			22 56
Shipley	a		20 37					21 07				21 38				22s11	22 15				22 37				23 07
	d	20 28			20 48		21 03				21 22			21 48	22 03					22 21			22 48	23 03	
Frizinghall	d	20 30			20 51		21 05				21 26			21 51	22 05					22 24			22 51	23 05	
Bramley	d			20 44						21 15			21 44					22 15				22 44			
New Pudsey	d			20 49		21 01				21 20			21 49					22 20				22 49			
Bradford Interchange	a			20 57		21 10				21 28			21 57					22 28				22 57			
Bradford Forster Square	a	20 36			20 57		21 12				21 32			21 57	22 11	22 24				22 31			22 57	23 13	

		NT	NT
Leeds 10	d	23 00	23 18
Shipley	a		23 31
	d		
Frizinghall	d		
Bramley	d	23 07	
New Pudsey	d	23 12	
Bradford Interchange	a	23 21	
Bradford Forster Square	a		

Sundays

until 11 September

		NT	NT	NT	NT	NT	NT	NT	NT	NT		NT	NT	NT	NT	NT	NT	NT	NT	NT		NT	NT	NT	NT
Leeds 10	d	08 02	08 21	08 34	08 40	08 45	09 00	09 02	09 18	09 34		09 35	09 54			10 08	10 12	10 34	10 35	10 51		10 54	11 08	11 12	11 34
Shipley	a			08 45	08 52		09 15			09 45						10 19		10 45		11 03			11 19		11 45
	d			08 46						09 46				10 01	10 15			10 46							11 46
Frizinghall	d			08 48						09 48				10 05	10 18			10 48							11 48
Bramley	d	08 09	08 28					09 09	09 25				10 01				10 19					11 01		11 19	
New Pudsey	d	08 14	08 33			08 54		09 14	09 30			09 44	10 06				10 24		10 44			11 06		11 24	
Bradford Interchange	a	08 22	08 41			09 03		09 22	09 38			09 53	10 14				10 32		10 53			11 14		11 32	
Bradford Forster Square	a			08 54						09 54				10 12	10 24			10 54							11 54

		NT	NT	NT	NT	NT		NT	NT	NT	NT	NT	NT	NT	NT	NT		NT	NT	NT	NT	NT	NT	NT	NT
Leeds 10	d	11 35	11 54			12 08		12 12	12 34	12 35	12 54	13 08	13 12	13 15	13 34	13 35		13 54			14 08	14 12	14 34	14 35	14 54
Shipley	a					12 19			12 45			13 19		13 28	13 45						14 19		14 45		
	d			12 02	12 15				12 46						13 46				14 02	14 15			14 46		
Frizinghall	d			12 06	12 18				12 48						13 48				14 06	14 18			14 48		
Bramley	d		12 01					12 19			13 01		13 19					14 01				14 19			15 01
New Pudsey	d	11 44	12 06					12 24		12 44	13 06		13 24			13 44		14 06				14 24		14 44	15 06
Bradford Interchange	a	11 53	12 14					12 32		12 53	13 14		13 32			13 53		14 14				14 32		14 53	15 14
Bradford Forster Square	a			12 12	12 24				12 54						13 54				14 12	14 24			14 54		

		NT		NT	NT	NT	NT	NT	NT	NT	NT	NT		NT	NT	NT	NT	NT	NT	NT	NT	NT		NT	NT
Leeds 10	d	14 57		15 08	15 12	15 34	15 35	15 54			16 08	16 13		16 35	16 35	16 54	17 08	17 12	17 21	17 33	17 35	17 37		17 54	
Shipley	a	15 09		15 19		15 45					16 19				16 46		17 19		17 33	17 45		17 48			
	d					15 46			16 02	16 15					16 46							17 49			18 02
Frizinghall	d					15 48			16 06	16 18					16 48							17 51			18 06
Bramley	d				15 19			16 01				16 20				17 01		17 19						18 01	
New Pudsey	d				15 24		15 44	16 06				16 25		16 44		17 06		17 24			17 44			18 06	
Bradford Interchange	a				15 32		15 53	16 14				16 33		16 53		17 14		17 32			17 53			18 14	
Bradford Forster Square	a					15 54			16 12	16 24					16 55							17 58			18 12

		NT	NT	NT	NT	NT	NT	NT		NT	NT	NT	NT	NT	NT	NT	NT	NT		NT	NT	NT	NT	NT	NT
Leeds 10	d		18 08	18 13	18 34	18 35	19 03	19 08		19 34	19 35	19 54			20 08	20 12	20 34	20 35		21 04	21 08	21 34	21 35		22 05
Shipley	a		18 19		18 45			19 19		19 45					20 19		20 45				21 19	21 45			
	d	18 15			18 46					19 46			20 02	20 15			20 46					21 46		22 04	
Frizinghall	d	18 18			18 48					19 48			20 06	20 18			20 48					21 48		22 08	
Bramley	d			18 20			19 10					20 01				20 20				21 12			21 43		22 12
New Pudsey	d			18 25		18 44	19 15				19 44	20 06				20 25		20 44		21 17			21 47		22 17
Bradford Interchange	a			18 33		18 53	19 23				19 53	20 14				20 34		20 53		21 25			21 56		22 27
Bradford Forster Square	a	18 24			18 54					19 54			20 12	20 24			20 54					21 54		22 14	

Table 37

Leeds - Shipley and Bradford

Sundays

until 11 September

		NT	NT	NT		NT	NT	NT																	
Leeds 10	d		22 08	22 34		22 35	23 20	23 22																	
Shipley	a		22 19	22 45			23 31																		
	d	22 15		22 46																					
Frizinghall	d	22 18		22 48																					
Bramley	d					22 43		23 29																	
New Pudsey	d					22 47		23 34																	
Bradford Interchange	a					22 56		23 43																	
Bradford Forster Square	a	22 24		22 54																					

Sundays

18 September to 23 October

		NT	NT	NT	NT	NT	NT	NT	NT	NT		NT	NT	NT	NT	NT	NT	NT	NT	NT		NT	NT	NT	NT
Leeds 10	d	08 02	08 21	08 34	08 40	08 45	09 00	09 02	09 18	09 34		09 35	09 54			10 08	10 12	10 34	10 35	10 51		10 54	11 08	11 12	11 34
Shipley	a			08 45	08 52		09 15			09 45						10 19		10 45		11 03			11 19		11 45
	d			08 46						09 46				10 01	10 15			10 46							11 46
Frizinghall	d			08 48						09 48				10 05	10 18			10 48							11 48
Bramley	d	08 09	08 28					09 09	09 25				10 01				10 19					11 01		11 19	
New Pudsey	d	08 14	08 33			08 54		09 14	09 30			09 44	10 06				10 24		10 44			11 06		11 24	
Bradford Interchange	a	08 22	08 41			09 03		09 22	09 38			09 53	10 14				10 32		10 53			11 14		11 32	
Bradford Forster Square	a			08 54						09 54				10 12	10 24			10 54							11 54

		NT	NT	NT	NT	NT		NT	NT	NT	NT	NT	NT	NT	NT	NT		NT	NT	NT	NT	NT	NT	NT	NT
Leeds 10	d	11 35	11 54			12 08		12 12	12 34	12 35	12 54	13 08	13 12	13 15	13 34	13 35		13 54			14 08	14 12	14 34	14 35	14 54
Shipley	a					12 19			12 45			13 19		13 28	13 45						14 19		14 45		
	d			12 02	12 15				12 46						13 46				14 02	14 15			14 46		
Frizinghall	d			12 06	12 18				12 48						13 48				14 06	14 18			14 48		
Bramley	d		12 01					12 19			13 01		13 19					14 01				14 19			15 01
New Pudsey	d	11 44	12 06					12 24		12 44	13 06		13 24			13 44		14 06				14 24		14 44	15 06
Bradford Interchange	a	11 53	12 14					12 32		12 53	13 14		13 32			13 53		14 14				14 32		14 53	15 14
Bradford Forster Square	a			12 12	12 24				12 54						13 54				14 12	14 24			14 54		

		NT		NT	NT	NT	NT	NT	NT	NT	NT	NT		NT	NT	NT	NT	NT	NT	NT	NT	NT		NT	NT
Leeds 10	d	14 57		15 08	15 12	15 34	15 35	15 54			16 08	16 13		16 35	16 35	16 54	17 08	17 12	17 21	17 33	17 35	17 37		17 54	
Shipley	a	15 09		15 19		15 45					16 19				16 46		17 19		17 33	17 45		17 48			
	d					15 46			16 02	16 15					16 46							17 49			18 02
Frizinghall	d					15 48			16 06	16 18					16 48							17 51			18 06
Bramley	d				15 19			16 01				16 20				17 01		17 19						18 01	
New Pudsey	d				15 24		15 44	16 06				16 25		16 44		17 06		17 24			17 44			18 06	
Bradford Interchange	a				15 32		15 53	16 14				16 33		16 53		17 14		17 32			17 53			18 14	
Bradford Forster Square	a					15 54			16 12	16 24					16 55							17 58			18 12

		NT	NT	NT	NT	NT	NT	NT		NT	NT	NT	NT	NT	NT	NT	NT	NT		NT	NT	NT	NT	NT	NT
Leeds 10	d		18 08	18 13	18 34	18 35	19 03	19 08		19 34	19 35	19 54			20 08	20 12	20 34	20 35		21 04	21 08	21 34	21 35		22 05
Shipley	a		18 19		18 45			19 19		19 45					20 19		20 45				21 19	21 45			
	d	18 15			18 46					19 46			20 02	20 15			20 46					21 46		22 04	
Frizinghall	d	18 18			18 48					19 48			20 06	20 18			20 48					21 48		22 08	
Bramley	d			18 20			19 10					20 01				20 19				21 12			21 43		22 12
New Pudsey	d			18 25		18 44	19 15				19 44	20 06				20 24		20 44		21 17			21 47		22 17
Bradford Interchange	a			18 33		18 53	19 23				19 53	20 14				20 34		20 53		21 25			21 56		22 27
Bradford Forster Square	a	18 24			18 54					19 54			20 12	20 24			20 54					21 54		22 14	

		NT	NT	NT		NT	NT	NT																	
Leeds 10	d		22 08	22 34		22 35	23 20	23 22																	
Shipley	a		22 19	22 45			23 31																		
	d	22 15		22 46																					
Frizinghall	d	22 18		22 48																					
Bramley	d					22 43		23 29																	
New Pudsey	d					22 47		23 34																	
Bradford Interchange	a					22 56		23 43																	
Bradford Forster Square	a	22 24		22 54																					

Sundays

from 30 October

		NT	NT	NT	NT	NT	NT	NT	NT	NT		NT	NT	NT	NT	NT	NT	NT	NT	NT		NT	NT	NT	NT
Leeds 10	d	08 02	08 21	08 34	08 40	08 45	09 00	09 02	09 18	09 34		09 35	09 54			10 08	10 12	10 34	10 35	10 51		10 54	11 08	11 12	11 34
Shipley	a			08 45	08 52		09 15			09 45						10 19		10 45		11 03			11 19		11 45
	d			08 46						09 46				10 01	10 15			10 46							11 46
Frizinghall	d			08 48						09 48				10 05	10 18			10 48							11 48
Bramley	d	08 09	08 28					09 09	09 25				10 01				10 19					11 01		11 19	
New Pudsey	d	08 14	08 33			08 54		09 14	09 30			09 44	10 06				10 24		10 44			11 06		11 24	
Bradford Interchange	a	08 22	08 41			09 03		09 22	09 38			09 53	10 14				10 32		10 53			11 14		11 32	
Bradford Forster Square	a			08 54						09 54				10 12	10 24			10 54							11 54

		NT	NT	NT	NT	NT		NT	NT	NT	NT	NT	NT	NT	NT	NT		NT	NT	NT	NT	NT	NT	NT	NT
Leeds 10	d	11 35	11 54			12 08		12 12	12 34	12 35	12 54	13 08	13 12	13 15	13 34	13 35		13 54			14 08	14 12	14 34	14 35	14 54
Shipley	a					12 19			12 45			13 19		13 28	13 45						14 19		14 45		
	d			12 02	12 15				12 46						13 46				14 02	14 15			14 46		
Frizinghall	d			12 06	12 18				12 48						13 48				14 06	14 18			14 48		
Bramley	d		12 01					12 19			13 01		13 19					14 01				14 19			15 01
New Pudsey	d	11 44	12 06					12 24		12 44	13 06		13 24			13 44		14 06				14 24		14 44	15 06
Bradford Interchange	a	11 53	12 14					12 32		12 53	13 14		13 32			13 53		14 14				14 32		14 53	15 14
Bradford Forster Square	a			12 12	12 24				12 54						13 54				14 12	14 24			14 54		

Table 37

Sundays

from 30 October

Leeds - Shipley and Bradford

		NT		NT	NT	NT	NT	NT	NT	NT	NT	NT		NT	NT	NT	NT	NT	NT	NT	NT	NT		NT	NT
Leeds 10	d	14 57		15 08	15 12	15 34	15 35	15 54			16 08	16 13		16 35	16 35	16 54	17 08	17 12	17 21	17 33	17 35	17 37		17 54	
Shipley	a	15 09		15 19		15 45					16 19				16 46		17 19		17 33	17 45		17 48			
	d					15 46			16 02	16 15					16 46							17 49			18 02
Frizinghall	d					15 48			16 06	16 18					16 48							17 51			18 06
Bramley	d				15 19			16 01				16 20				17 01		17 19						18 01	
New Pudsey	d				15 24		15 44	16 06				16 25		16 44		17 06		17 24			17 44			18 06	
Bradford Interchange	a				15 32		15 53	16 14				16 33		16 53		17 14		17 32			17 53			18 14	
Bradford Forster Square	a					15 54			16 12	16 24					16 55							17 58			18 12

		NT	NT	NT	NT	NT	NT	NT		NT	NT	NT	NT	NT	NT	NT	NT	NT		NT	NT	NT	NT	NT	NT
Leeds 10	d		18 08	18 13	18 34	18 35	19 03	19 08		19 34	19 35	19 54			20 08	20 12	20 34	20 35		21 04	21 08	21 34	21 35		22 05
Shipley	a		18 19		18 45			19 19		19 45					20 19		20 45				21 19	21 45			
	d	18 15			18 46					19 46			20 02	20 15			20 46					21 46		22 04	
Frizinghall	d	18 18			18 48					19 48			20 06	20 18			20 48					21 48		22 08	
Bramley	d			18 20			19 10					20 01				20 20				21 12			21 43		22 12
New Pudsey	d			18 25		18 44	19 15				19 44	20 06				20 25		20 44		21 17			21 47		22 17
Bradford Interchange	a			18 33		18 53	19 23				19 53	20 14				20 34		20 53		21 25			21 56		22 27
Bradford Forster Square	a	18 24			18 54					19 54			20 12	20 24			20 54					21 54		22 14	

		NT	NT	NT		NT	NT	NT
Leeds 10	d		22 08	22 34		22 35	23 20	23 22
Shipley	a		22 19	22 45			23 31	
	d	22 15		22 46				
Frizinghall	d	22 18		22 48				
Bramley	d					22 43		23 29
New Pudsey	d					22 47		23 34
Bradford Interchange	a					22 56		23 43
Bradford Forster Square	a	22 24		22 54				

Bradford and Shipley - Leeds

Miles	Miles			NT MX	NT MO	NT A	NT MX	NT	NT	NT	NT	NT		GR	NT	NT	NT	NT	NT	NT	NT	NT		GR	NT
0	—	**Bradford Forster Square**	d					06 01	06 10		06 15			06 30	06 40		06 44		06 55			07 11			07 15
—	0	**Bradford Interchange**	d	23p46	23p47	00 23	00 37					06 18						06 48			07 02				
—	3½	New Pudsey	d	23p54	23p55	00 33						06 27						06 57			07 11				
—	5½	Bramley	d	23p58	23p59	00 43						06 31						07 01			07 15				
1¾	—	Frizinghall	d					06 04	06 13		06 18				06 43		06 47		06 58			07 14			07 18
2¾	—	**Shipley**	a					06 08	06 17		06 22				06 47		06 51		07 02			07 18			07 22
—	—		d					06 08		06 13				06u35		06 44			07 02	07 09				07u14	
13½	9½	**Leeds** 10	a	00 09	00 08	01 03	00 55	06 22		06 27		06 41		06 52		06 58		07 09	07 16	07 23	07 27			07 29	

		NT	NT	NT	NT	NT	NT	NT		NT	NT	NT	NT	NT	NT	NT	NT	NT		NT	NT	NT	NT	NT	NT
Bradford Forster Square	d				07 42	07 46				07 59	08 11			08 16			08 26				08 41	08 46			
Bradford Interchange	d	07 20		07 34				07 50					08 05			08 20				08 34				08 50	
New Pudsey	d	07 28		07 42				07 58					08 13			08 28				08 42				08 58	
Bramley	d			07 46				08 02					08 18							08 46				09 02	
Frizinghall	d				07 45	07 49				08 02	08 14			08 19			08 29				08 44	08 49			
Shipley	a				07 49	07 53				08 06	08 18			08 23			08 33				08 48	08 53			
	d		07 35				07 50			08 07		08 13			08 19		08 33	08 41					08 47		09 08
Leeds 10	a	07 39	07 49	07 57			08 05	08 12		08 24		08 27	08 29		08 37	08 39	08 49	08 56		08 57			09 04	09 12	09 23

		NT	NT	NT		NT	NT	NT	NT	NT	NT	NT	NT	NT		NT	NT	NT	NT	NT	NT	NT	NT	NT	
Bradford Forster Square	d	09 01		09 11		09 16		09 31	09 41			09 46		10 01		10 11			10 16		10 31	10 41			
Bradford Interchange	d		09 04				09 20				09 34		09 50					10 05		10 18				10 34	
New Pudsey	d		09 12				09 27				09 42		09 58					10 14		10 28				10 42	
Bramley	d		09 16								09 46		10 02					10 18						10 46	
Frizinghall	d	09 04		09 14		09 19		09 34	09 44			09 49		10 04		10 14			10 19		10 34	10 44			
Shipley	a	09 08		09 18		09 23		09 38	09 48			09 53		10 08		10 18			10 23		10 38	10 48			
	d	09 09						09 39		09 44				10 09			10 14				10 39		10 44		
Leeds 10	a	09 25	09 27				09 39	09 53		09 59	10 00		10 12	10 25			10 28	10 29		10 38	10 53		10 58	11 00	

		NT	NT	NT	NT	NT	NT	NT	NT	NT		NT	NT	NT	NT	NT	NT	NT	NT	NT		NT	NT	NT	NT
Bradford Forster Square	d	10 46		11 01		11 11		11 16				11 31	11 41			11 46		12 01		12 11			12 16		
Bradford Interchange	d		10 50		11 05					11 20					11 34		11 50		12 05					12 19	
New Pudsey	d		10 58		11 13					11 28					11 42		11 58		12 13					12 28	
Bramley	d		11 02		11 17										11 46		12 02		12 17						
Frizinghall	d	10 49		11 04		11 14		11 19				11 34	11 44			11 49		12 04		12 14			12 19		
Shipley	a	10 53		11 08		11 18		11 23				11 38	11 48			11 53		12 08		12 18			12 23		
	d			11 09			11 14		11 18			11 39		11 44				12 09				12 14			12 33
Leeds 10	a		11 13	11 24	11 27		11 28		11 36	11 39		11 55		11 58	12 00		12 12	12 24	12 27			12 29		12 39	12 55

		NT	NT	NT	NT	NT		NT	NT	NT	NT	NT	NT	NT	NT	NT		NT	NT	NT	NT	NT	NT	NT	NT
Bradford Forster Square	d	12 31	12 41			12 46			13 01		13 11		13 16		13 31	13 41				13 46		14 01		14 11	
Bradford Interchange	d				12 34			12 50		13 05				13 19					13 34		13 50		14 05		
New Pudsey	d				12 42			12 58		13 13				13 28					13 42		13 58		14 13		
Bramley	d				12 46			13 02		13 17									13 46		14 02		14 17		
Frizinghall	d	12 34	12 44			12 49			13 04		13 14		13 19		13 34	13 44				13 49		14 04		14 14	
Shipley	a	12 38	12 48			12 53			13 08		13 18		13 23		13 38	13 48				13 53		14 08		14 18	
	d	12 39		12 44					13 09			13 14			13 39			13 44				14 09			14 14
Leeds 10	a	12 55		12 58	12 59			13 12	13 24	13 27		13 28		13 40	13 54			13 58	14 00		14 13	14 24	14 26		14 28

		NT		NT	NT	NT	NT	NT	NT	NT	NT	NT		NT	NT	NT	NT	NT	NT	NT	NT	NT		NT	NT
Bradford Forster Square	d	14 16				14 31		14 41		14 46		15 01			15 11		15 16			15 31	15 41				15 46
Bradford Interchange	d				14 19		14 34				14 50			15 05				15 19						15 34	
New Pudsey	d				14 28		14 42				14 58			15 13				15 28						15 42	
Bramley	d						14 46				15 02			15 17										15 46	
Frizinghall	d	14 19				14 34		14 44		14 49		15 04			15 14		15 19			15 34	15 44				15 49
Shipley	a	14 23				14 38		14 48		14 53		15 08			15 18		15 23			15 38	15 48				15 53
	d			14 18		14 39			14 45			15 09				15 14			15 30	15 39		15 44			
Leeds 10	a			14 37	14 39	14 53	15 00		15 01		15 12	15 24		15 27		15 28		15 39	15 47	15 54		15 58		16 00	

		NT	NT	NT	NT	NT	NT	NT		NT	NT	NT	NT	NT	NT	NT	NT	NT		NT	NT	NT	NT	NT	NT
Bradford Forster Square	d		16 01		16 11		16 16				16 31	16 40			16 44		17 01			17 11		17 16			17 31
Bradford Interchange	d	15 50		16 05				16 19						16 34		16 50		17 04					17 19		
New Pudsey	d	15 58		16 13				16 28						16 42		16 58		17 13					17 28		
Bramley	d	16 02		16 17										16 46		17 02		17 17							
Frizinghall	d		16 04		16 14		16 19				16 34	16 43			16 48		17 04			17 14		17 19			17 34
Shipley	a		16 08		16 18		16 23				16 38	16 48			16 52		17 08			17 18		17 23			17 38
	d		16 09			16 14				16 31	16 39		16 44				17 09				17 15			17 20	17 39
Leeds 10	a	16 12	16 24	16 27		16 28		16 39		16 51	16 53		16 58	16 59		17 12	17 24	17 27			17 29		17 39	17 40	17 55

		NT	NT	NT		NT	NT	NT	NT	NT	NT	NT	NT	NT		NT	NT	NT	NT	NT	NT	NT	NT	NT	
Bradford Forster Square	d		17 38			17 46			18 01	18 11			18 16			18 27		18 41		18 46			19 01		
Bradford Interchange	d	17 34					17 50					18 04		18 19			18 34					18 52		19 05	
New Pudsey	d	17 42					17 58					18 12		18 28			18 40					19 00		19 13	
Bramley	d	17 46					18 02					18 16					18 45					19 04		19 17	
Frizinghall	d		17 41			17 49			18 04	18 14			18 19			18 30		18 44		18 49			19 04		
Shipley	a		17 45			17 53			18 08	18 18			18 23			18 34		18 48		18 53			19 08		
	d			17 45				17 58	18 09		18 14					18 34			18 44		18 48		19 09		
Leeds 10	a	17 57		18 00			18 12	18 15	18 24		18 29	18 31		18 39		18 48	18 56		18 59		19 07	19 13	19 26	19 28	

A MO from 31 October

Table 37

Mondays to Fridays

Bradford and Shipley - Leeds

		NT	NT	NT	NT	NT	NT	NT	NT	NT		NT	NT	NT	NT	NT	NT	NT	NT	NT		NT	NT	NT	NT
Bradford Forster Square	d	19 07			19 31		19 36	19 41				20 07				20 25		20 38						21 05	
Bradford Interchange	d			19 19		19 34				19 50				20 04	20 19		20 37						21 04		
New Pudsey	d			19 27		19 42				19 59				20 13	20 28		20 46						21 13		
Bramley	d					19 46				20 03				20 17			20 50						21 17		
Frizinghall	d	19 10			19 34		19 39	19 44				20 10				20 28		20 41						21 08	
Shipley	a	19 14			19 38		19 43	19 48				20 15				20 32		20 45						21 12	
	d		19 14		19 39				19 44				20 14						20 41	20 50		20 59			21 14
Leeds 10	a		19 31	19 39	19 55	19 56			19 59	20 13			20 28	20 29	20 41		20 59		21 01	21 04		21 17	21 25		21 30

		NT	NT	NT	NT	NT		NT	NT	NT	NT	NT	NT	NT	NT FX	NT FO		NT	NT	NT					
Bradford Forster Square	d	21 25	21 38					22 05			22 25		22 38					23 09	23 20						
Bradford Interchange	d				21 37	22 04				22 19		22 37			23 04	23 04				23 46					
New Pudsey	d				21 46	22 13				22 28		22 46			23 13	23 13				23 54					
Bramley	d				21 50	22 17						22 50			23 17	23 17				23 58					
Frizinghall	d	21 28	21 41					22 08			22 28		22 41					23 12	23 23						
Shipley	a	21 32	21 45					22 12			22 32		22 45					23 16	23 27						
	d			21 43					22 15					22 43											
Leeds 10	a			21 59	22 01	22 25			22 33	22 37		23 01		23 01	23 26	23 27				00 09					

Saturdays

		NT	NT	NT	NT	NT	NT	NT	NT	NT		NT	NT	NT	GR R 1	NT	GR R 1	NT	NT	NT		NT	NT	NT	NT
Bradford Forster Square	d			06 01	06 10		06 15		07 01			07 11		07 15			07 33			07 59		08 11			08 16
Bradford Interchange	d	23p46	00 37					06 26		07 05						07 20		07 34	07 50					08 05	
New Pudsey	d	23p54						06 35		07 14						07 28		07 42	07 58					08 14	
Bramley	d	23p58						06 39		07 18								07 46	08 02					08 18	
Frizinghall	d			06 04	06 13		06 18		07 04			07 14		07 18						08 02		08 14			08 19
Shipley	a			06 08	06 17		06 22		07 08			07 18		07 23						08 06		08 18			08 23
	d			06 08		06 13			07 09				07 13		07u18		07u39			08 07			08 13		
Leeds 10	a	00 09	00 55	06 22		06 27		06 49	07 23	07 27			07 27		07 33	07 39	07 54	07 57	08 11	08 24			08 27	08 30	

		NT	NT	NT	NT	NT		NT	NT	NT	NT	NT	NT	NT	NT	NT		NT	NT	NT	NT	NT	NT	NT	NT
Bradford Forster Square	d			08 31		08 41			08 46		09 01		09 11		09 16			09 31		09 41		09 46			10 01
Bradford Interchange	d		08 20		08 34					08 50		09 04				09 20			09 34				09 50		
New Pudsey	d		08 28		08 42					08 58		09 12				09 27			09 42				09 58		
Bramley	d				08 46					09 02		09 16							09 46				10 02		
Frizinghall	d			08 34		08 44			08 49		09 04		09 14		09 19			09 34		09 44		09 49			10 04
Shipley	a			08 38		08 48			08 53		09 08		09 18		09 23			09 38		09 48		09 53			10 08
	d	08 19		08 38				08 44			09 09			09 14				09 39			09 44			10 02	10 09
Leeds 10	a	08 37	08 39	08 54	08 56			08 58		09 12	09 25	09 27		09 28		09 39		09 53	09 58		09 59		10 12	10 20	10 25

		NT		NT	NT	NT	NT	NT	NT	NT	NT	NT		NT	NT	NT	NT	NT	NT	NT	NT	NT		NT	NT
Bradford Forster Square	d			10 11		10 16			10 31	10 41				10 46		11 01		11 11		11 16		11 31		11 41	
Bradford Interchange	d	10 04						10 18				10 34			10 50		11 05				11 20				
New Pudsey	d	10 12						10 28				10 42			10 58		11 13				11 28				
Bramley	d	10 16										10 46			11 02		11 17								
Frizinghall	d			10 14		10 19			10 34	10 44				10 49		11 04		11 14		11 19		11 34		11 44	
Shipley	a			10 18		10 23			10 38	10 48				10 53		11 08		11 18		11 23		11 38		11 48	
	d				10 14		10 19		10 39		10 44					11 09			11 14			11 39			11 44
Leeds 10	a	10 27			10 28		10 34	10 38	10 53		10 58	11 00			11 13	11 24	11 27		11 28		11 39	11 55			11 58

		NT	NT	NT	NT	NT	NT	NT		NT	NT	NT	NT	NT	NT	NT	NT	NT		NT	NT	NT	NT	NT	NT
Bradford Forster Square	d		11 46			12 01		12 11			12 16			12 31		12 41		12 46			13 01		13 11		13 16
Bradford Interchange	d	11 34			11 50		12 05					12 19			12 34					12 50		13 05			
New Pudsey	d	11 42			11 58		12 13					12 28			12 42					12 58		13 13			
Bramley	d	11 46			12 02		12 17								12 46					13 02		13 17			
Frizinghall	d		11 49			12 04		12 14			12 19			12 34		12 44		12 49			13 04		13 14		13 19
Shipley	a		11 53			12 08		12 18			12 23			12 38		12 48		12 53			13 08		13 18		13 23
	d			11 49		12 09				12 14			12 33	12 39			12 44				13 09			13 14	
Leeds 10	a	12 00		12 06	12 12	12 24	12 27			12 29		12 39	12 55	12 55	12 58		12 58			13 12	13 24	13 27		13 28	

		NT	NT	NT		NT	NT	NT	NT	NT	NT	NT	NT	NT		NT	NT	NT	NT	NT	NT	NT	NT	NT	
Bradford Forster Square	d		13 31			13 41		13 46		14 01		14 11		14 16				14 31		14 41		14 46		15 01	
Bradford Interchange	d	13 19		13 34					13 50		14 05						14 19		14 34				14 50		
New Pudsey	d	13 28		13 42					13 58		14 13						14 28		14 42				14 58		
Bramley	d			13 46					14 02		14 17								14 46				15 02		
Frizinghall	d		13 34			13 44		13 49		14 04		14 14		14 19				14 34		14 44		14 49		15 04	
Shipley	a		13 38			13 48		13 53		14 08		14 18		14 23				14 38		14 48		14 53		15 08	
	d		13 39				13 44			14 09			14 14			14 18		14 39			14 45			15 09	
Leeds 10	a	13 39	13 54	13 58			13 58		14 14	14 24	14 26		14 28			14 37	14 39	14 53	14 58		15 00		15 10	15 24	

		NT	NT	NT	NT	NT	NT	NT	NT	NT		NT	NT	NT	NT	NT	NT	NT	NT	NT		NT	NT	NT	NT
Bradford Forster Square	d		15 11		15 16			15 31	15 41				15 46		16 01		16 11		16 16			16 31	16 40		
Bradford Interchange	d	15 05				15 19						15 34		15 50		16 05				16 19					16 34
New Pudsey	d	15 13				15 28						15 42		15 58		16 13				16 28					16 42
Bramley	d	15 17										15 46		16 02		16 17									16 46
Frizinghall	d		15 14		15 19			15 34	15 44				15 49		16 04		16 14		16 19			16 34	16 43		
Shipley	a		15 18		15 23			15 38	15 48				15 53		16 08		16 18		16 23			16 38	16 48		
	d			15 14			15 30	15 39		15 44					16 09			16 14				16 39		16 44	
Leeds 10	a	15 27		15 28		15 39	15 47	15 54		15 58		16 00		16 12	16 24	16 27		16 28		16 39		16 53		16 58	16 59

Table 37

Saturdays

Bradford and Shipley - Leeds

		NT	NT	NT	NT	NT		NT	NT	NT	NT	NT	NT	NT	NT	NT		NT	NT	NT	NT	NT	NT	NT	NT
Bradford Forster Square	d	16 44			17 01			17 11		17 16		17 31		17 41		17 46				18 01		18 11		18 16	
Bradford Interchange	d			16 50		17 04					17 19		17 34					17 50			18 04				18 19
New Pudsey	d			16 58		17 13					17 28		17 42					17 58			18 13				18 28
Bramley	d			17 02		17 17							17 46					18 02			18 17				
Frizinghall	d	16 48			17 04			17 14		17 19		17 34		17 44		17 49				18 04		18 14		18 19	
Shipley	a	16 52			17 08			17 18		17 23		17 38		17 48		17 53				18 08		18 18		18 23	
	d		16 49		17 09				17 15			17 39			17 45				18 00	18 09			18 14		
Leeds 10	a		17 07	17 12	17 24	17 27			17 29		17 39	17 55	17 57		18 00			18 12	18 17	18 24	18 28		18 29		18 39

		NT		NT	NT	NT	NT	NT	NT	NT	NT	NT		NT	NT	NT	NT	NT	NT	NT	NT	NT		NT	NT
Bradford Forster Square	d			18 31		18 41		18 46			19 01			19 07			19 31		19 36	19 41				20 07	
Bradford Interchange	d				18 34					18 52		19 05				19 18		19 34				19 50			
New Pudsey	d				18 43					19 00		19 13				19 28		19 42				19 58			
Bramley	d				18 47					19 04		19 17						19 46				20 02			
Frizinghall	d			18 34		18 44		18 49			19 04			19 10			19 34		19 39	19 44				20 10	
Shipley	a			18 38		18 48		18 53			19 08			19 14			19 38		19 43	19 48				20 15	
	d	18 19		18 38			18 44		18 48		19 09				19 14		19 39				19 44				20 14
Leeds 10	a	18 42		18 52	18 56		18 59		19 07	19 13	19 26	19 28			19 29	19 39	19 55	19 58			19 59	20 12			20 28

		NT	NT	NT	NT	NT	NT	NT		NT	NT	NT	NT	NT	NT	NT	NT	NT		NT	NT	NT	NT	NT	NT
Bradford Forster Square	d			20 25			20 38					21 05		21 25		21 38		22 01					22 25		22 38
Bradford Interchange	d	20 04	20 20			20 37					21 04				21 37					22 04		22 19		22 37	
New Pudsey	d	20 13	20 28			20 46					21 13				21 46					22 13		22 28		22 46	
Bramley	d	20 17				20 50					21 17				21 50					22 17				22 50	
Frizinghall	d			20 28			20 41					21 08		21 28		21 41		22 04					22 28		22 41
Shipley	a			20 32			20 45					21 12		21 32		21 45		22 08					22 32		22 45
	d				20 28			20 43		20 57			21 14				21 43				22 14				
Leeds 10	a	20 30	20 39		20 46	20 59		21 00		21 16	21 25		21 30		21 59		21 59			22 24	22 32	22 37		23 01	

		NT	NT	NT		NT																			
Bradford Forster Square	d			23 05		23 20																			
Bradford Interchange	d		23 04																						
New Pudsey	d		23 13																						
Bramley	d		23 17																						
Frizinghall	d			23 08		23 23																			
Shipley	a			23 12		23 27																			
	d	22 43																							
Leeds 10	a	23 01	23 26																						

Sundays

until 11 September

		NT A	NT	NT	NT	NT	NT	NT	NT	NT		NT	NT	NT	NT	NT	NT	NT	NT	NT		NT	NT	NT	NT
Bradford Forster Square	d				09 02			10 02				10 38		10 48		11 02							12 02		12 38
Bradford Interchange	d	00 04	08 31			09 20			10 02	10 25					11 02		11 25		11 44			12 02		12 25	
New Pudsey	d	00 12	08 39			09 29			10 10	10 33					11 10		11 33		11 53			12 10		12 33	
Bramley	d	00 16	08 43			09 33			10 14	10 37							11 37		11 57					12 37	
Frizinghall	d				09 05			10 05				10 41		10 51		11 05							12 05		12 41
Shipley	a				09 08			10 08				10 44		10 54		11 09							12 08		12 44
	d			09 00	09 10		09 40	10 08					10 40			11 10		11 40		11 49			12 08		
Leeds 10	a	00 27	08 51	09 14	09 24	09 42	09 54	10 22	10 24	10 46			10 54		11 21	11 24	11 48	11 54	12 05	12 06		12 22	12 22	12 46	

		NT	NT	NT	NT	NT		NT	NT	NT	NT	NT	NT	NT	NT	NT		NT	NT	NT	NT	NT	NT	NT	NT
Bradford Forster Square	d			12 48		13 02						14 02			14 38				14 48		15 02				16 02
Bradford Interchange	d		12 44		13 02			13 25		13 44	14 02			14 25				14 44		15 02		15 25		15 44	
New Pudsey	d		12 53		13 10			13 33		13 53	14 11			14 33				14 53		15 10		15 33		15 53	
Bramley	d		12 57					13 37		13 57				14 37				14 57				15 37		15 57	
Frizinghall	d			12 51		13 05						14 05			14 41				14 51		15 05				16 05
Shipley	a			12 54		13 08						14 08			14 44				14 54		15 08				16 08
	d	12 40				13 08			13 40			14 08	14 21			14 40					15 08		15 40		16 08
Leeds 10	a	12 54	13 06		13 22	13 22		13 46	13 54	14 06	14 22	14 22	14 39	14 48		14 54		15 06		15 22	15 24	15 46	15 54	16 06	16 22

		NT		NT	NT	NT	NT	NT	NT	NT	NT	NT		NT	NT	NT	NT	NT	NT	NT	NT	NT		NT	NT
Bradford Forster Square	d						16 38			16 48		17 02						18 02		18 38				18 48	
Bradford Interchange	d	16 03				16 26			16 44		17 02			17 25		17 44	18 02		18 25			18 44			19 02
New Pudsey	d	16 11				16 34			16 53		17 10			17 33		17 53	18 10		18 33			18 53			19 10
Bramley	d					16 38			16 57					17 37		17 57			18 37			18 57			
Frizinghall	d						16 41			16 51		17 05						18 05		18 41				18 51	
Shipley	a						16 44			16 54		17 08						18 08		18 44				18 54	
	d			16 16	16 29			16 40				17 09			17 40			18 08			18 40				
Leeds 10	a	16 22		16 34	16 47	16 48		16 54	17 05		17 21	17 23		17 46	17 54	18 05	18 21	18 23	18 46		18 54	19 07			19 21

		NT	NT	NT	NT	NT	NT	NT		NT	NT	NT	NT	NT	NT	NT	NT	NT		NT	NT	NT	NT	NT	NT
Bradford Forster Square	d		19 02							20 02		20 38		20 48		21 02							22 02		22 38
Bradford Interchange	d			19 25			19 44	20 02			20 25				21 02		21 26			21 44		22 02		22 26	
New Pudsey	d			19 33			19 53	20 10			20 33				21 10		21 34			21 53		22 10		22 35	
Bramley	d			19 37			19 57				20 37						21 38			21 57				22 39	
Frizinghall	d		19 05							20 05		20 41		20 51		21 05							22 05		22 41
Shipley	a		19 08							20 08		20 44		20 54		21 08							22 09		22 44
	d	19 03	19 08		19 38	19 49				20 08			20 40			21 08		21 40			21 54		22 09		
Leeds 10	a	19 21	19 22	19 47	19 56	20 03	20 08	20 22		20 22	20 47		20 54		21 22	21 24	21 48	21 54		22 05	22 10	22 22	22 23	22 47	

A not 22 May

Table 37

Bradford and Shipley - Leeds

Sundays
until 11 September

		NT	NT	NT		NT	NT	NT	NT
Bradford Forster Square	d		22 48			23 05			
Bradford Interchange	d			23 04			23 25		23 47
New Pudsey	d			23 12			23 33		23 55
Bramley	d						23 37		23 59
Frizinghall	d		22 51			23 08			
Shipley	a		22 54			23 11			
	d	22 40				23 11		23 41	
Leeds 10	a	22 54		23 23		23 27	23 46	23 58	00 08

Sundays
18 September to 23 October

		NT	NT	NT	NT	NT	NT	NT	NT	NT		NT	NT	NT	NT	NT	NT	NT	NT	NT		NT	NT	NT	NT
Bradford Forster Square	d				09 02			10 02				10 38		10 48		11 02							12 02		12 38
Bradford Interchange	d	00 04	08 31			09 20			10 04	10 25					11 02		11 25		11 44			12 02		12 25	
New Pudsey	d	00 12	08 39			09 29			10 12	10 33					11 10		11 33		11 53			12 10		12 33	
Bramley	d	00 16	08 43			09 33			10 16	10 37							11 37		11 57					12 37	
Frizinghall	d				09 05			10 05				10 41		10 51		11 05							12 05		12 41
Shipley	a				09 08			10 08				10 44		10 54		11 09							12 08		12 44
	d			09 00	09 10		09 40	10 08					10 40			11 10		11 40		11 49			12 08		
Leeds 10	a	00 27	08 51	09 14	09 24	09 42	09 54	10 22	10 25	10 46			10 54		11 21	11 24	11 48	11 54	12 05	12 06		12 22	12 22	12 46	

		NT	NT	NT	NT	NT		NT	NT	NT	NT	NT	NT	NT	NT	NT		NT	NT	NT	NT	NT	NT	NT	NT
Bradford Forster Square	d			12 48		13 02						14 02			14 38				14 48		15 02				16 02
Bradford Interchange	d		12 44		13 02			13 25		13 44	14 02			14 25				14 44		15 02		15 25		15 44	
New Pudsey	d		12 53		13 10			13 33		13 53	14 11			14 33				14 53		15 10		15 33		15 53	
Bramley	d		12 57					13 37		13 57				14 37				14 57				15 37		15 57	
Frizinghall	d			12 51		13 05						14 05			14 41				14 51		15 05				16 05
Shipley	a			12 54		13 08						14 08			14 44				14 54		15 08				16 08
	d	12 40				13 08			13 40			14 08	14 21			14 40					15 08		15 40		16 08
Leeds 10	a	12 54	13 06		13 22	13 22		13 46	13 54	14 06	14 22	14 22	14 39	14 48		14 54		15 06		15 22	15 24	15 46	15 54	16 06	16 22

		NT		NT	NT	NT	NT	NT	NT	NT	NT	NT		NT	NT	NT	NT	NT	NT	NT	NT	NT		NT	NT
Bradford Forster Square	d						16 38			16 48		17 02						18 02		18 38				18 48	
Bradford Interchange	d	16 03				16 26			16 44		17 02			17 25		17 44	18 02		18 25			18 44			19 02
New Pudsey	d	16 11				16 34			16 53		17 10			17 33		17 53	18 10		18 33			18 53			19 10
Bramley	d					16 38			16 57					17 37		17 57			18 37			18 57			
Frizinghall	d						16 41			16 51		17 05						18 05		18 41				18 51	
Shipley	a						16 44			16 54		17 08						18 08		18 44				18 54	
	d			16 16	16 29			16 40				17 09			17 40			18 08			18 40				
Leeds 10	a	16 22		16 34	16 47	16 48		16 54	17 05		17 21	17 23		17 46	17 54	18 05	18 21	18 23	18 46		18 54	19 07			19 21

		NT	NT	NT	NT	NT	NT	NT		NT	NT	NT	NT	NT	NT	NT	NT	NT		NT	NT	NT	NT	NT	NT
Bradford Forster Square	d		19 02							20 02		20 38		20 48		21 02							22 02		22 38
Bradford Interchange	d			19 25			19 44	20 02			20 25				21 02		21 26			21 44		22 02		22 26	
New Pudsey	d			19 33			19 53	20 10			20 33				21 10		21 34			21 53		22 10		22 35	
Bramley	d			19 37			19 57				20 37						21 38			21 57				22 39	
Frizinghall	d		19 05							20 05		20 41		20 51		21 05							22 05		22 41
Shipley	a		19 08							20 08		20 44		20 54		21 08							22 09		22 44
	d	19 03	19 08		19 38	19 49				20 08			20 40			21 08		21 40			21 54		22 09		
Leeds 10	a	19 21	19 22	19 47	19 56	20 03	20 08	20 22		20 22	20 47		20 54		21 22	21 24	21 48	21 54		22 05	22 10	22 22	22 23	22 47	

		NT	NT	NT		NT	NT	NT	NT
Bradford Forster Square	d		22 48			23 05			
Bradford Interchange	d			23 04			23 25		23 47
New Pudsey	d			23 12			23 33		23 55
Bramley	d						23 37		23 59
Frizinghall	d		22 51			23 08			
Shipley	a		22 54			23 11			
	d	22 40				23 11		23 41	
Leeds 10	a	22 54		23 23		23 27	23 46	23 58	00 08

Sundays
from 30 October

		NT	NT	NT	NT	NT	NT	NT	NT	NT		NT	NT	NT	NT	NT	NT	NT	NT	NT		NT	NT	NT	NT
Bradford Forster Square	d				09 02			10 02				10 38		10 48		11 02							12 02		12 38
Bradford Interchange	d	00 04	08 31			09 20			10 02	10 25					11 02		11 25		11 44			12 02		12 25	
New Pudsey	d	00 12	08 39			09 29			10 10	10 33					11 10		11 33		11 53			12 10		12 33	
Bramley	d	00 16	08 43			09 33			10 14	10 37							11 37		11 57					12 37	
Frizinghall	d				09 05			10 05				10 41		10 51		11 05							12 05		12 41
Shipley	a				09 08			10 08				10 44		10 54		11 09							12 08		12 44
	d			09 00	09 10		09 40	10 08					10 40			11 10		11 40		11 49			12 08		
Leeds 10	a	00 27	08 51	09 14	09 24	09 42	09 54	10 22	10 24	10 46			10 54		11 21	11 24	11 48	11 54	12 05	12 06		12 22	12 22	12 46	

		NT	NT	NT	NT	NT		NT	NT	NT	NT	NT	NT	NT	NT	NT		NT	NT	NT	NT	NT	NT	NT	NT
Bradford Forster Square	d			12 48		13 02						14 02			14 38				14 48		15 02				16 02
Bradford Interchange	d		12 44		13 02			13 25		13 44	14 02			14 25				14 44		15 02		15 25		15 44	
New Pudsey	d		12 53		13 10			13 33		13 53	14 11			14 33				14 53		15 10		15 33		15 53	
Bramley	d		12 57					13 37		13 57				14 37				14 57				15 37		15 57	
Frizinghall	d			12 51		13 05						14 05			14 41				14 51		15 05				16 05
Shipley	a			12 54		13 08						14 08			14 44				14 54		15 08				16 08
	d	12 40				13 08			13 40			14 08	14 21			14 40					15 08		15 40		16 08
Leeds 10	a	12 54	13 06		13 22	13 22		13 46	13 54	14 06	14 22	14 22	14 39	14 48		14 54		15 06		15 22	15 24	15 46	15 54	16 06	16 22

Table 37

Sundays

from 30 October

Bradford and Shipley - Leeds

		NT		NT	NT	NT	NT	NT	NT	NT	NT	NT		NT	NT	NT	NT	NT	NT	NT	NT	NT		NT	NT
Bradford Forster Square	d						16 38			16 48		17 02						18 02		18 38				18 48	
Bradford Interchange	d	16 03				16 26			16 44		17 02			17 25		17 44	18 02		18 25			18 44			19 02
New Pudsey	d	16 11				16 34			16 53		17 10			17 33		17 53	18 10		18 33			18 53			19 10
Bramley	d					16 38			16 57					17 37		17 57			18 37			18 57			
Frizinghall	d						16 41			16 51		17 05						18 05		18 41				18 51	
Shipley	a						16 44			16 54		17 08						18 08		18 44				18 54	
	d			16 16	16 29			16 40				17 09			17 40			18 08			18 40				
Leeds 10	a	16 22		16 34	16 47	16 48		16 54	17 05		17 21	17 23		17 46	17 54	18 05	18 21	18 23	18 46		18 54	19 07			19 21

		NT	NT	NT	NT	NT	NT	NT		NT	NT	NT	NT	NT	NT	NT	NT	NT		NT	NT	NT	NT	NT	NT
Bradford Forster Square	d		19 02							20 02		20 38		20 48		21 02							22 02		22 38
Bradford Interchange	d			19 25			19 44	20 02			20 25				21 02		21 26			21 44		22 02		22 26	
New Pudsey	d			19 33			19 53	20 10			20 33				21 10		21 34			21 53		22 10		22 35	
Bramley	d			19 37			19 57				20 37						21 38			21 57				22 39	
Frizinghall	d		19 05							20 05		20 41		20 51		21 05							22 05		22 41
Shipley	a		19 08							20 08		20 44		20 54		21 08							22 09		22 44
	d	19 03	19 08		19 38	19 49				20 08			20 40			21 08		21 40			21 54		22 09		
Leeds 10	a	19 21	19 22	19 47	19 56	20 03	20 08	20 22		20 22	20 47		20 54		21 22	21 24	21 48	21 54		22 05	22 10	22 22	22 23	22 47	

		NT	NT	NT		NT	NT	NT	NT
Bradford Forster Square	d		22 48			23 05			
Bradford Interchange	d			23 04			23 25		23 47
New Pudsey	d			23 12			23 33		23 55
Bramley	d						23 37		23 59
Frizinghall	d		22 51			23 08			
Shipley	a		22 54			23 11			
	d	22 40				23 11		23 41	
Leeds 10	a	22 54		23 23		23 27	23 46	23 58	00 08

Table 38

Mondays to Saturdays

Leeds and Bradford - Ilkley

Miles	Miles			NT	NT	NT SX	NT SX	NT SO	NT SX	NT SX	NT SO	NT SX		NT SX	NT SX	NT	NT	NT	NT	NT	NT	NT		NT	NT
0	—	**Leeds** 10	d	06 02		06 34		07 02	07 09			07 29		07 35		08 02		08 32		09 02		09 32			10 02
—	0	**Bradford Forster Square** 37	d		06 15		06 44			07 11	07 15				07 46		08 16		08 46		09 16			09 46	
—	1¾	Frizinghall 37	d		06 18		06 47			07 14	07 18				07 49		08 19		08 49		09 19			09 49	
—	2¾	Shipley 37	d		06 22		06 51			07 18	07 23				07 53		08 23		08 53		09 23			09 53	
—	4¼	Baildon	d		06 25		06 54			07 21	07 26				07 56		08 26		08 56		09 26			09 56	
10¼	7½	Guiseley	d	06 14	06 31	06 48	07 00	07 14	07 21	07 28	07 32	07 42		07 50	08 02	08 14	08 32	08 44	09 02	09 14	09 32	09 45		10 02	10 14
11½	8¾	Menston	d	06 17	06 34	06 51	07 03	07 17	07 24	07 31	07 35	07 45		07 53	08 05	08 17	08 35	08 47	09 05	09 17	09 35	09 48		10 05	10 17
13	10¼	Burley-in-Wharfedale	d	06 20	06 37	06 54	07 06	07 20	07 27	07 35	07 38	07 48		07 56	08 09	08 20	08 38	08 50	09 08	09 20	09 38	09 52		10 08	10 20
15¼	12½	Ben Rhydding	d	06 23	06 40	06 57	07 09	07 24	07 30	07 39	07 41	07 52		07 59	08 12	08 23	08 41	08 53	09 11	09 24	09 41	09 55		10 11	10 23
16¼	13½	**Ilkley**	a	06 29	06 46	07 03	07 15	07 29	07 36	07 44	07 47	07 57		08 05	08 18	08 29	08 49	09 02	09 17	09 33	09 47	10 01		10 17	10 30

		NT	NT	NT	NT	NT	NT	NT		NT	NT	NT	NT	NT	NT	NT	NT	NT		NT	NT	NT	NT	NT	NT
Leeds 10	d		10 32		11 02		11 32			12 02		12 32		13 02		13 32		14 02			14 32		15 02		15 32
Bradford Forster Square 37	d	10 16		10 46		11 16		11 46			12 16		12 46		13 16		13 46			14 16		14 46		15 16	
Frizinghall 37	d	10 19		10 49		11 19		11 49			12 19		12 49		13 19		13 49			14 19		14 49		15 19	
Shipley 37	d	10 23		10 53		11 23		11 53			12 23		12 53		13 23		13 53			14 23		14 53		15 23	
Baildon	d	10 26		10 56		11 26		11 56			12 26		12 56		13 26		13 56			14 26		14 56		15 26	
Guiseley	d	10 32	10 44	11 02	11 14	11 32	11 44	12 02		12 14	12 32	12 44	13 02	13 14	13 32	13 44	14 02	14 14		14 32	14 44	15 02	15 14	15 32	15 44
Menston	d	10 35	10 47	11 05	11 17	11 35	11 47	12 05		12 17	12 35	12 47	13 05	13 17	13 35	13 47	14 05	14 17		14 35	14 47	15 05	15 17	15 35	15 47
Burley-in-Wharfedale	d	10 38	10 50	11 08	11 20	11 38	11 50	12 08		12 20	12 38	12 50	13 08	13 20	13 38	13 50	14 08	14 20		14 38	14 50	15 08	15 20	15 38	15 50
Ben Rhydding	d	10 41	10 53	11 11	11 23	11 41	11 53	12 11		12 23	12 41	12 53	13 11	13 23	13 41	13 53	14 11	14 23		14 41	14 53	15 11	15 23	15 41	15 53
Ilkley	a	10 47	10 59	11 17	11 29	11 47	12 00	12 17		12 29	12 47	13 01	13 17	13 29	13 47	13 59	14 17	14 29		14 47	14 59	15 17	15 31	15 47	15 59

		NT	NT	NT		NT	NT	NT	NT SX	NT SO	NT SX	NT	NT	NT		NT	NT	NT	NT	NT	NT	NT	NT	NT	
Leeds 10	d		16 02			16 32		17 02	17 15			17 32		18 02			18 32		19 02	19 32		20 02		21 06	
Bradford Forster Square 37	d	15 46		16 16			16 44			17 16	17 16		17 46			18 16		18 46			19 41		20 38		
Frizinghall 37	d	15 49		16 19			16 48			17 19	17 19		17 49			18 19		18 49			19 44		20 41		
Shipley 37	d	15 53		16 23			16 52			17 23	17 25		17 53			18 23		18 53			19 48		20 46		
Baildon	d	15 56		16 26			16 55			17 26	17 28		17 57			18 26		18 56			19 51		20 49		
Guiseley	d	16 02	16 14	16 32		16 44	17 01	17 14	17 28	17 32	17 35	17 44	18 02	18 14		18 32	18 44	19 02	19 14	19 44	19 56	20 14	20 54	21 18	
Menston	d	16 05	16 17	16 35		16 47	17 04	17 17	17 31	17 35	17 38	17 47	18 05	18 17		18 35	18 47	19 05	19 17	19 47	19 59	20 17	20 57	21 21	
Burley-in-Wharfedale	d	16 08	16 20	16 38		16 50	17 07	17 20	17 34	17 38	17 42	17 51	18 08	18 20		18 38	18 50	19 08	19 20	19 50	20 02	20 20	21 00	21 24	
Ben Rhydding	d	16 11	16 23	16 41		16 53	17 10	17 23	17 37	17 41	17 46	17 54	18 12	18 23		18 41	18 53	19 11	19 24	19 53	20 06	20 23	21 04	21 27	
Ilkley	a	16 17	16 29	16 47		17 00	17 17	17 29	17 43	17 47	17 51	18 00	18 17	18 30		18 47	19 01	19 17	19 29	20 00	20 12	20 30	21 10	21 33	

		NT	NT	NT	NT	NT
Leeds 10	d		22 06		23 15	
Bradford Forster Square 37	d	21 38		22 38		23 20
Frizinghall 37	d	21 41		22 41		23 23
Shipley 37	d	21 45		22 45		23 27
Baildon	d	21 48		22 48		23 30
Guiseley	d	21 54	22 18	22 54	23 27	23 36
Menston	d	21 57	22 21	22 57	23 30	23 39
Burley-in-Wharfedale	d	22 00	22 24	23 00	23 33	23 42
Ben Rhydding	d	22 03	22 27	23 03	23 36	23 45
Ilkley	a	22 09	22 34	23 09	23 42	23 51

Sundays

		NT	NT	NT	NT	NT	NT	NT	NT	NT		NT	NT	NT	NT	NT	NT	NT	NT	NT		NT	NT	NT	NT
Leeds 10	d	09 12	10 12		11 12	12 12		13 12	14 12			15 12	16 12		17 12	18 12		19 12	20 12			21 12	22 12		23 16
Bradford Forster Square 37	d			10 38			12 38			14 38				16 38			18 38			20 38				22 38	
Frizinghall 37	d			10 41			12 41			14 41				16 41			18 41			20 41				22 41	
Shipley 37	d			10 44			12 44			14 44				16 44			18 44			20 44				22 44	
Baildon	d			10 47			12 47			14 47				16 47			18 47			20 47				22 47	
Guiseley	d	09 23	10 23	10 52	11 23	12 23	12 52	13 23	14 23	14 52		15 23	16 23	16 52	17 23	18 23	18 52	19 23	20 23	20 52		21 23	22 23	22 52	23 27
Menston	d	09 26	10 26	10 55	11 26	12 26	12 55	13 26	14 26	14 55		15 26	16 26	16 55	17 26	18 26	18 55	19 26	20 26	20 55		21 26	22 26	22 55	23 30
Burley-in-Wharfedale	d	09 29	10 29	10 58	11 29	12 29	12 58	13 29	14 29	14 58		15 29	16 29	16 58	17 29	18 29	18 58	19 29	20 29	20 58		21 29	22 29	22 58	23 33
Ben Rhydding	d	09 33	10 33	11 02	11 33	12 33	13 02	13 33	14 33	15 02		15 33	16 33	17 02	17 33	18 33	19 02	19 33	20 33	21 02		21 33	22 33	23 02	23 37
Ilkley	a	09 38	10 38	11 07	11 38	12 38	13 07	13 38	14 38	15 07		15 38	16 38	17 07	17 38	18 38	19 07	19 38	20 38	21 07		21 38	22 38	23 07	23 42

Ilkley - Bradford and Leeds

Miles	Miles			NT SX	NT SO	NT SX	NT SO	NT SX	NT SX	NT	NT	NT SX		NT SX	NT SX	NT SO	NT SX	NT SO	NT SX	NT	NT SO	NT SX		NT	NT
0	0	**Ilkley**	d	06 04	06 09	06 17	06 19	06 34	06 50	07 10	07 22	07 39		07 50	08 05	08 10	08 17	08 21	08 24	08 40	08 51	08 54		09 10	09 21
1	1	Ben Rhydding	d	06 06	06 11	06 19	06 21	06 36	06 52	07 12	07 24	07 42		07 52	08 07	08 12	08 19	08 23	08 26	08 42	08 53	08 56		09 12	09 23
3¼	3¼	Burley-in-Wharfedale	d	06 12	06 17	06 25	06 27	06 42	06 58	07 18	07 30	07 48		07 58	08 13	08 18	08 25	08 29	08 32	08 48	08 59	09 02		09 18	09 29
4¾	4¾	Menston	d	06 15	06 20	06 28	06 30	06 45	07 01	07 21	07 33	07 51		08 01	08 16	08 21	08 28	08 32	08 35	08 51	09 02	09 05		09 21	09 32
6	6	Guiseley	d	06 18	06 23	06 31	06 34	06 48	07 04	07 24	07 36	07 54		08 04	08 19	08 24	08 31	08 35	08 39	08 54	09 05	09 08		09 24	09 35
—	9¼	Baildon	d			06 36	06 39		07 09		07 41			08 09				08 40	08 44		09 10	09 13			09 40
—	10¾	Shipley	37 a			06 41	06 43		07 14		07 47			08 12				08 43	08 47		09 14	09 18			09 44
—	11¾	Frizinghall	37 a			06 44	06 47		07 17		07 49			08 16				08 46	08 50		09 17	09 21			09 47
—	13½	**Bradford Forster Square**	37 a			06 50	06 55		07 22		07 56			08 22				08 53	08 56		09 24	09 27			09 53
16¼	—	**Leeds** 10	a	06 32	06 39			07 02		07 38		08 09			08 34	08 39	08 46			09 11				09 39	

		NT	NT	NT	NT	NT	NT	NT		NT	NT	NT	NT	NT	NT	NT	NT	NT		NT	NT	NT	NT	NT	NT
Ilkley	d	09 40	09 51	10 10	10 21	10 40	10 51	11 10		11 21	11 40	11 51	12 10	12 21	12 40	12 51	13 10	13 21		13 40	13 51	14 10	14 21	14 40	14 51
Ben Rhydding	d	09 42	09 53	10 12	10 23	10 42	10 53	11 12		11 23	11 42	11 53	12 12	12 23	12 42	12 53	13 12	13 23		13 42	13 53	14 12	14 23	14 42	14 53
Burley-in-Wharfedale	d	09 48	09 59	10 18	10 29	10 48	10 59	11 18		11 29	11 48	11 59	12 18	12 29	12 48	12 59	13 18	13 29		13 48	13 59	14 18	14 29	14 48	14 59
Menston	d	09 51	10 02	10 21	10 32	10 51	11 02	11 21		11 32	11 51	12 02	12 21	12 32	12 51	13 02	13 21	13 32		13 51	14 02	14 21	14 32	14 51	15 02
Guiseley	d	09 54	10 05	10 25	10 35	10 54	11 05	11 24		11 35	11 54	12 05	12 24	12 35	12 54	13 05	13 24	13 35		13 54	14 05	14 24	14 35	14 54	15 05
Baildon	d		10 10		10 40		11 10			11 40		12 10		12 40		13 10		13 40			14 10		14 40		15 10
Shipley	37 a		10 14		10 44		11 14			11 44		12 14		12 44		13 14		13 44			14 14		14 44		15 14
Frizinghall	37 a		10 17		10 47		11 17			11 47		12 17		12 47		13 17		13 47			14 17		14 47		15 17
Bradford Forster Square	37 a		10 23		10 53		11 23			11 53		12 24		12 53		13 23		13 53			14 23		14 53		15 23
Leeds 10	a	10 11		10 41		11 08		11 39			12 08		12 39		13 08		13 38			14 09		14 39		15 10	

		NT	NT	NT SO		NT SX	NT	NT SO	NT SX	NT	NT	NT	NT SO	NT SX		NT	NT SO	NT SX	NT	NT SX	NT SO	NT SX	NT	NT	
Ilkley	d	15 10	15 21	15 40		15 40	15 51	16 10	16 12	16 21	16 40	16 51	17 10	17 14		17 21	17 40	17 42	17 51	18 04	18 10	18 10	18 21	18 40	
Ben Rhydding	d	15 12	15 23	15 42		15 42	15 53	16 12	16 14	16 23	16 42	16 53	17 12	17 16		17 23	17 42	17 44	17 53	18 06	18 12	18 12	18 23	18 42	
Burley-in-Wharfedale	d	15 18	15 29	15 48		15 48	15 59	16 18	16 20	16 29	16 48	16 59	17 18	17 22		17 29	17 48	17 50	17 59	18 12	18 18	18 18	18 29	18 48	
Menston	d	15 21	15 32	15 51		15 51	16 02	16 21	16 23	16 32	16 51	17 02	17 21	17 25		17 32	17 51	17 53	18 02	18 15	18 21	18 21	18 32	18 51	
Guiseley	d	15 24	15 35	15 54		15 54	16 05	16 24	16 27	16 35	16 54	17 05	17 24	17 29		17 35	17 54	17 56	18 05	18 18	18 24	18 24	18 35	18 54	
Baildon	d		15 40				16 10			16 40		17 10				17 40			18 10				18 40		
Shipley	37 a		15 44				16 14			16 44		17 14				17 43			18 14				18 43		
Frizinghall	37 a		15 47				16 17			16 47		17 17				17 46			18 17				18 46		
Bradford Forster Square	37 a		15 53				16 23			16 53		17 23				17 53			18 23				18 52		
Leeds 10	a	15 40		16 08		16 10		16 38	16 46		17 09		17 38	17 44			18 09	18 16		18 35	18 40	18 45		19 09	

		NT	NT	NT	NT SO	NT SX	NT	NT	NT	NT		NT	NT	NT	NT
Ilkley	d	18 51	19 10	19 21	19 40	19 40	20 05	20 21	20 40	21 21		21 40	22 21	22 40	23 20
Ben Rhydding	d	18 53	19 12	19 23	19 42	19 42	20 07	20 23	20 42	21 23		21 42	22 23	22 42	23 23
Burley-in-Wharfedale	d	18 59	19 18	19 29	19 48	19 48	20 13	20 29	20 48	21 29		21 48	22 29	22 48	23 28
Menston	d	19 02	19 21	19 32	19 51	19 51	20 16	20 32	20 51	21 32		21 51	22 32	22 51	23 31
Guiseley	d	19 05	19 24	19 35	19 54	19 54	20 19	20 35	20 54	21 35		21 54	22 35	22 54	23 35
Baildon	d	19 10		19 40			20 24		20 59			21 59		22 59	
Shipley	37 a	19 14		19 44			20 27		21 03			22 02		23 02	
Frizinghall	37 a	19 17		19 47			20 30		21 05			22 05		23 05	
Bradford Forster Square	37 a	19 23		19 53			20 36		21 12			22 11		23 13	
Leeds 10	a		19 40		20 10	20 12		20 53		21 49			22 49		23 49

Sundays

		NT	NT	NT	NT	NT	NT	NT	NT	NT		NT	NT	NT	NT	NT	NT	NT	NT	NT		NT	NT	NT	NT
Ilkley	d	09 21	09 53	10 21	11 21	11 53	12 21	13 21	13 53	14 21		15 21	15 53	16 21	17 21	17 53	18 21	19 21	19 53	20 21		21 21	21 53	22 21	23 21
Ben Rhydding	d	09 23	09 55	10 23	11 23	11 55	12 23	13 23	13 55	14 23		15 23	15 55	16 23	17 23	17 55	18 23	19 23	19 55	20 23		21 23	21 55	22 23	23 23
Burley-in-Wharfedale	d	09 29	10 01	10 29	11 29	12 01	12 29	13 29	14 01	14 29		15 29	16 01	16 29	17 29	18 01	18 29	19 29	20 01	20 29		21 29	22 01	22 29	23 29
Menston	d	09 32	10 04	10 32	11 32	12 04	12 32	13 32	14 04	14 32		15 32	16 04	16 32	17 32	18 04	18 32	19 32	20 04	20 32		21 32	22 04	22 32	23 32
Guiseley	d	09 35	10 07	10 35	11 35	12 07	12 35	13 35	14 07	14 35		15 35	16 07	16 35	17 35	18 07	18 35	19 35	20 07	20 35		21 35	22 07	22 35	23 35
Baildon	d		10 12			12 12			14 12				16 12			18 12			20 12				22 12		
Shipley	37 a		10 15			12 15			14 15				16 15			18 15			20 15				22 15		
Frizinghall	37 a		10 18			12 18			14 18				16 18			18 18			20 18				22 18		
Bradford Forster Square	37 a		10 24			12 24			14 24				16 24			18 24			20 24				22 24		
Leeds 10	a	09 50		10 49	11 49		12 49	13 49		14 49		15 49		16 49	17 49		18 49	19 49		20 49		21 49		22 49	23 50

Network Diagram for Tables 39, 40, 41, 43

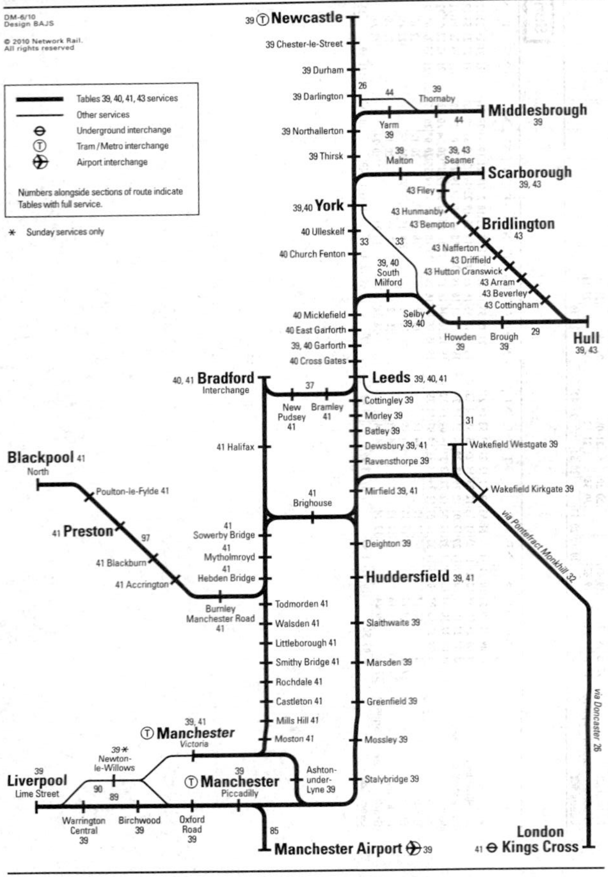

Table 39

Mondays to Fridays

Newcastle, Middlesbrough, Scarborough, York, Hull, Leeds and Wakefield - Huddersfield - Manchester, Manchester Airport and Liverpool

Miles	Miles	Miles	Miles	Miles			TP ◇■ A	TP MX ◇■	TP ◇■ B	TP ◇■ A	TP MO ◇■	TP MX ◇■	NT	TP MO ◇■	TP MX ◇■		TP MX ◇■	TP MO ◇■	TP ◇■	NT	NT	NT	TP ◇■	TP ◇■	NT
0	—	—	—	—	Newcastle ■	d		21p55																	
8¼	—	—	—	—	Chester-le-Street	d																			
14	—	—	—	—	Durham	d		22p08																	
—	—	0	—	—	**Middlesbrough**	d			22p06	22p06															
—	—	3¼	—	—	Thornaby	d			22p11	22p11															
—	—	8½	—	—	Yarm	d			22p19	22p19															
36	—	—	—	—	**Darlington** ■	d		22p25																	
50	—	20¾	—	—	Northallerton	d		22p36	22p34	22p34															
57¾	—	28½	—	—	Thirsk	d			22p42	22p42															
—	—	—	0	—	**Scarborough**	d	21p20																		
—	—	—	2¾	—	Seamer	d	21p25																		
—	—	—	21	—	Malton	d	21p43																		
80	—	50¾	42	—	**York** ■	a	22p09	23p00	23p09	23p09															
—	—	—	—	—		d	22p12	23p06	23p12	23p12	01 38	01 38		02 47	02 52		04 00	04 23	05 26					05 57	
—	—	—	—	0	**Wakefield Westgate**	d																			
—	—	—	—	1	Wakefield Kirkgate	d																			
—	0	—	—	—	**Hull**	d																			
—	10½	—	—	—	Brough	d																			
—	22¼	—	—	—	Howden	d																			
—	31	—	—	—	Selby	d																			
—	38¾	—	—	—	South Milford	d																			
98¾	44½	—	60¼	—	Garforth	d																		06 12	
105½	51¼	—	67½	—	**Leeds** ■	a	22p36	23p33	23p38	23p38	02 04	02 19		03 13	03 33		04 42	04 49	05 52					06 22	
—	—	—	—	—		d	22p40	23p35	23p40	23p40	02 05	02 20		03 15	03 35		04 50	04 50	05 55		06 13			06 25	
108½	—	—	—	—	Cottingley	d																			
110	—	—	—	—	Morley	d															06 21				
113½	—	—	—	—	Batley	d															06 26				
114¾	—	—	—	—	**Dewsbury**	a	22p50	23p45	23p51	23p51									06 06		06 29			06 36	
—	—	—	—	—		d	22p51	23p46	23p51	23p51									06 06		06 29			06 36	
116	—	—	—	—	Ravensthorpe	d																			
117¾	—	—	—	10½	Mirfield	d															06 35				
120¼	—	—	—	13½	Deighton	d																			
122¾	—	—	—	15½	**Huddersfield**	a	23p02	23p55	23p59	00 02	02 42	02 42		03 56	03 56		05 27	05 27	06 14					06 44	
—	—	—	—	—		d	23p04	23p56	00 01	00 04	02 45	02 45		03 59	03 59		05 28	05 28	06 15	06 29				06 45	06 57
127¾	—	—	—	20	Slaithwaite	d														06 36					07 04
129¾	—	—	—	22½	Marsden	d														06 42					07 12
135¾	—	—	—	28½	Greenfield	d														06 50					07 20
138	—	—	—	30¾	Mossley (Grtr Manchester)	d														06 54					07 24
140¾	—	—	—	33½	**Stalybridge**	a													06 33	06 59				07 03	07 29
—	—	—	—	—		d													06 33	07 00				07 04	07 30
—	—	—	—	34¾	Ashton-under-Lyne	d														07 04					07 34
—	—	—	—	41¼	**Manchester Victoria**	a	23b53			00s53										07 17	07 53				07 47
148¼	—	—	—	—	**Manchester Piccadilly** ■	a	00 10	00 53	00 43	01 08	03 44	03 44		04 58	04 58		06 02	06 02	06 50					07 19	
—	—	—	—	—		d		00 54	00 44	01 10	03 44	03 44	04 49	05 00	05 00		06 08	06 08	06 54			06 58	07 07	07 23	
—	—	—	—	—	**Manchester Airport**	a		01 10	01 00	01 25	04 00	04 00		05 19	05 19		06 24	06 24	07 12					07 42	
148¾	—	—	—	—	Manchester Oxford Road	a																07 00	07 09		
161¼	—	—	—	—	Birchwood	a																	07 25		
164½	—	—	—	—	Warrington Central	a																	07 30		
177½	—	—	—	—	L'pool South Parkway ■	a																			
183	—	—	—	—	**Liverpool Lime Street** ■	a							05 32									07 49	07 56		

A MO from 19 September until 24 October

B MO until 12 September, MO from 31 October

b Previous night, stops to set down only

Newcastle, Middlesbrough, Scarborough, York, Hull, Leeds and Wakefield - Huddersfield - Manchester, Manchester Airport and Liverpool

		NT	NT	TP ◇1 ⊼	NT	TP ◇1 ⊼	NT	NT	TP ◇1 ⊼	NT		TP ◇1 ⊼	NT	NT	NT	NT	NT	TP ◇1 ⊼	NT	TP ◇1 A ⊼		NT	NT	NT
Newcastle	d																			06 11				
Chester-le-Street	d																			06 21				
Durham	d																			06 28				
Middlesbrough	d								05 55															
Thornaby	d								06 00															
Yarm	d								06 08															
Darlington	d																			06 45				
Northallerton	d								06 23											06 56				
Thirsk	d								06 31											07 04				
Scarborough	d																	06 30						
Seamer	d																	06 35						
Malton	d																	06 53						
York	a								06 49									07 23		07 30				
	d			06 28					06 55									07 26		07 40				
Wakefield Westgate	d	06 41														07 41								
Wakefield Kirkgate	d	06 46														07 46								
Hull	d					06 00						06 37	07 07											
Brough	d					06 12						06 49	07 19											
Howden	d					06 26							07 35											
Selby	d					06 36						07 07	07a48											
South Milford	d																							
Garforth	d								07 10			07 24												
Leeds	a			06 52		07 00			07 20			07 35						07 52		08 04				
	d		06 43	06 55		07 08	07 13		07 23			07 38					07 43	07 55		08 08				08 13
Cottingley	d		06 48														07 48							08 18
Morley	d		06 52				07 21										07 52							08 22
Batley	d		06 57				07 26										07 57							08 27
Dewsbury	a		07 00	07 06			07 29		07 34								08 00	08 06						08 30
	d		07 01	07 06			07 29		07 34								08 01	08 06						08 31
Ravensthorpe	d		07 04														08 04							08 34
Mirfield	d	06 59	07 08				07 35									07 59	08 08							08 38
Deighton	d	07 06	07 16													08 04	08 13							
Huddersfield	a	07 12	07 20	07 15		07 25			07 43			07 56				08 11	08 20	08 15		08 25				
	d			07 16		07 26		07 33	07 44			07 57			08 02			08 16		08 26		08 30		
Slaithwaite	d							07 40							08 09							08 37		
Marsden	d							07 55							08 15							08 43		
Greenfield	d							08 03							08 23							08 51		
Mossley (Grtr Manchester)	d							08 07		←					08 27							08 55		
Stalybridge	a			07 34		07 43		08 12	08 01	08 12		08 17			08 32					08 43		09 00		
	d			07 34		07 46		08 13	08 02	08 13		08 17		08 22	08 33					08 46		09 01	09 22	
Ashton-under-Lyne	d							→		08 17				08 26	08 37							09 05	09 26	
Manchester Victoria	a						08 53			08 31				08 36	08 52							09 20	09 37	09 53
Manchester Piccadilly	a			07 51		08 05			08 19			08 36						08 51		09 05				
	d			07 54	07 59	08 07			08 24									08 54	09 01	09 07				
Manchester Airport ✈	a			08 12					08 42									09 12						
Manchester Oxford Road	a				08 01	08 09													09 03	09 09				
Birchwood	a					08 25														09 25				
Warrington Central	a					08 30														09 30				
L'pool South Parkway ✈	a					08 47														09 47				
Liverpool Lime Street	a				08 59	08 58								09 43					09 48	09 58			10 43	

A ⊼ from York

Table 39 Mondays to Fridays

Newcastle, Middlesbrough, Scarborough, York, Hull, Leeds and Wakefield - Huddersfield - Manchester, Manchester Airport and Liverpool

		TP ◇1 ⊼	TP ◇1 ⊼	NT	NT	TP ◇1 ⊼	NT		TP ◇1 ⊼	NT	NT	NT	TP ◇1 ⊼	TP ◇1 ⊼	NT	NT	NT		TP ◇1 ⊼	NT	TP ◇1 ⊼	NT	NT	NT	TP ◇1 ⊼
Newcastle	d												07 33												
Chester-le-Street	d												07 42												
Durham	d												07 49												
Middlesbrough	d					07 12																			08 50
Thornaby	d					07 17																			08 55
Yarm	d					07 27																			09 03
Darlington	d												08 06												
Northallerton	d					07 45							08 17												09 18
Thirsk	d					07 53							08 25												09 28
Scarborough	d	07 00							07 40												08 48				
Seamer	d	07 05							07 45												08 53				
Malton	d	07 23							08 03												09 11				
York	a	07 50				08 12			08 30				08 47								09 37				09 47
	d	07 55				08 25			08 40				08 57						09 28		09 40				09 57
Wakefield Westgate	d			08 39												09 39									
Wakefield Kirkgate	d			08 45												09 45									
Hull	d		07 37											08 40	09 02										
Brough	d		07 49											08 52	09 14										
Howden	d		08 01												09 28										
Selby	d		08 11											09 11	09a38										
South Milford	d																								
Garforth	d	08 12				08 40							09 12												10 12
Leeds	a	08 22	08 36			08 52			09 04				09 22	09 36					09 52		10 04				10 22
	d	08 25	08 40		08 43	08 55			09 08			09 13	09 25	09 40			09 43		09 55		10 08			10 13	10 25
Cottingley	d				08 48							09 18					09 48								
Morley	d				08 52							09 22					09 52							10 21	
Batley	d				08 57							09 27					09 57							10 26	
Dewsbury	a	08 36			09 00	09 06						09 30	09 36				10 00		10 06					10 29	10 36
	d	08 36			09 01	09 06						09 31	09 36				10 01		10 06					10 29	10 36
Ravensthorpe	d				09 04												10 04								
Mirfield	d			08 58	09 08							09 37				09 59	10 08							10 35	
Deighton	d			09 02	09 16											10 04	10 14								
Huddersfield	a	08 44	08 58	09 11	09 20	09 15			09 25				09 45	09 58		10 11	10 21		10 15		10 25				10 45
	d	08 45	08 59			09 16			09 26	09 30			09 46	09 59					10 16		10 26	10 30			10 46
Slaithwaite	d									09 37												10 37			
Marsden	d									09 43												10 43			
Greenfield	d									09 51												10 51			
Mossley (Grtr Manchester)	d									09 55												10 55			
Stalybridge	a								09 43	10 00											10 43	11 00			
	d								09 46	10 01	10 22										10 46	11 01	11 22		
Ashton-under-Lyne	d									10 05	10 26											11 05	11 26		
Manchester Victoria	a									10 20	10 36	10 53										11 20	11 35	11 53	
Manchester Piccadilly	a	09 19	09 36			09 49			10 05				10 19	10 36					10 49		11 05				11 19
	d	09 24				09 54	10 01		10 07				10 24						10 54	11 01	11 07				11 24
Manchester Airport ✈	a	09 42				10 12							10 42						11 12						11 45
Manchester Oxford Road	a						10 03		10 09											11 03	11 09				
Birchwood	a								10 25												11 25				
Warrington Central	a								10 30												11 30				
L'pool South Parkway ✈	a								10 47												11 47				
Liverpool Lime Street	a						10 48		10 58		11 43									11 48	11 58		12 43		

Newcastle, Middlesbrough, Scarborough, York, Hull, Leeds and Wakefield - Huddersfield - Manchester, Manchester Airport and Liverpool

		TP ◇1	NT	NT	NT	TP ◇1	NT	TP ◇1	NT	NT	NT	TP ◇1	TP ◇1	NT	NT	TP ◇1	NT	TP ◇1	NT	NT	NT	TP ◇1
Newcastle 8	d					09 15										10 17						
Chester-le-Street	d					09 24																
Durham	d					09 31										10 31						
Middlesbrough	d											09 50										10 50
Thornaby	d											09 55										10 55
Yarm	d											10 03										11 03
Darlington 7	d					09 48										10 48						
Northallerton	d					09 59						10 18				10 59						11 18
Thirsk	d											10 28										11 28
Scarborough	d							09 48										10 48				
Seamer	d							09 53										10 53				
Malton	d							10 11										11 11				
York 8	a					10 21		10 38				10 47				11 23		11 38				11 47
	d					10 28		10 40				10 57				11 26		11 40				11 57
Wakefield Westgate	d			10 39										11 39								
Wakefield Kirkgate	d			10 45										11 44								
Hull	d	09 40	10 08										10 40									
Brough	d	09 52	10 20										10 52									
Howden	d		10 34																			
Selby	d	10 11	10a47										11 11									
South Milford	d																					
Garforth	d											11 12										12 12
Leeds 10	a	10 36				10 52		11 04				11 22	11 36			11 52		12 04				12 22
	d	10 40			10 43	10 55		11 08			11 13	11 25	11 40		11 43	11 55		12 08			12 13	12 25
Cottingley	d				10 48										11 48							
Morley	d				10 52						11 21				11 52						12 21	
Batley	d				10 57						11 26				11 57						12 26	
Dewsbury	a				11 00	11 06					11 29	11 36			12 00	12 06					12 29	12 36
	d				11 01	11 06					11 29	11 36			12 01	12 06					12 29	12 36
Ravensthorpe	d				11 04										12 04							
Mirfield	d			10 58	11 08						11 35			11 58	12 08						12 35	
Deighton	d			11 05	11 14									12 02	12 17							
Huddersfield	a	10 58		11 11	11 22	11 15		11 25				11 45	11 58	12 11	12 21	12 15		12 25				12 45
	d	10 59				11 16		11 26	11 30			11 46	11 59			12 16		12 26	12 30			12 46
Slaithwaite	d								11 37										12 37			
Marsden	d								11 43										12 43			
Greenfield	d								11 51										12 51			
Mossley (Grtr Manchester)	d								11 55										12 55			
Stalybridge	a							11 43	12 00									12 43	13 00			
	d							11 46	12 01	12 22								12 46	13 01	13 22		
Ashton-under-Lyne	d								12 05	12 26									13 05	13 26		
Manchester Victoria	a								12 20	12 35	12 53								13 20	13 35	13 53	
Manchester Piccadilly 10	a	11 36				11 49		12 05				12 19	12 36			12 49		13 05				13 19
	d					11 54	12 01	12 07				12 24				12 54	13 01	13 07				13 24
Manchester Airport	a					12 12						12 42				13 12						13 42
Manchester Oxford Road	a						12 03	12 09									13 03	13 09				
Birchwood	a							12 25										13 25				
Warrington Central	a							12 30										13 30				
L'pool South Parkway 7	a							12 47										13 47				
Liverpool Lime Street 10	a						12 48	12 58		13 43							13 48	13 58		14 43		

Newcastle, Middlesbrough, Scarborough, York, Hull, Leeds and Wakefield - Huddersfield - Manchester, Manchester Airport and Liverpool

		TP ◇1	NT	NT	NT	TP ◇1	NT	TP ◇1	NT	NT	NT	TP ◇1	TP ◇1	NT	NT	NT	TP ◇1	NT	TP ◇1	NT	NT	NT	TP ◇1
Newcastle 8	d					11 15											12 17						
Chester-le-Street	d					11 24																	
Durham	d					11 31											12 29						
Middlesbrough	d											11 50											12 50
Thornaby	d											11 55											12 55
Yarm	d											12 03											13 03
Darlington 7	d					11 48											12 46						
Northallerton	d					11 59						12 18					12 58						13 18
Thirsk	d											12 28											13 28
Scarborough	d							11 48											12 48				
Seamer	d							11 53											12 53				
Malton	d							12 11											13 11				
York 8	a					12 21		12 38				12 47					13 21		13 38				13 47
	d					12 26		12 40				12 57					13 24		13 40				13 57
Wakefield Westgate	d			12 39											13 39								
Wakefield Kirkgate	d			12 43											13 45								
Hull	d	11 40	12 03										12 40	13 12									
Brough	d	11 52	12 15										12 52	13 24									
Howden	d		12 27											13 41									
Selby	d	12 11	12a37										13 11	13a54									
South Milford	d																						
Garforth	d											13 12											14 12
Leeds 10	a	12 36				12 52		13 04				13 22	13 36				13 52		14 04				14 22
	d	12 40			12 43	12 55		13 08			13 13	13 25	13 40			13 43	13 55		14 08			14 13	14 25
Cottingley	d				12 48											13 48							
Morley	d				12 52						13 21					13 52						14 21	
Batley	d				12 57						13 26					13 57						14 26	
Dewsbury	a				13 00	13 06					13 29	13 36				14 00	14 06					14 29	14 36
	d				13 01	13 06					13 29	13 36				14 01	14 06					14 29	14 36
Ravensthorpe	d				13 04											14 04							
Mirfield	d			12 58	13 08						13 35				13 58	14 08						14 35	
Deighton	d			13 02	13 14										14 05	14 14							
Huddersfield	a	12 58		13 10	13 21	13 15		13 25				13 45	13 58		14 23	14 21	14 15		14 25				14 45
	d	12 59				13 16		13 26	13 30			13 46	13 59				14 16		14 26	14 30			14 46
Slaithwaite	d								13 37											14 37			
Marsden	d								13 43											14 43			
Greenfield	d								13 51											14 51			
Mossley (Grtr Manchester)	d								13 55											14 55			
Stalybridge	a							13 43	14 00										14 43	15 00			
	d							13 46	14 01	14 22									14 46	15 01	15 22		
Ashton-under-Lyne	d								14 05	14 26										15 05	15 26		
Manchester Victoria	a								14 20	14 35	14 52									15 20	15 35	15 53	
Manchester Piccadilly 10	a	13 36				13 49		14 05				14 19	14 36				14 49		15 05				15 19
	d					13 54	14 01	14 07				14 24					14 54	15 01	15 07				15 24
Manchester Airport	a					14 12						14 42					15 12						15 42
Manchester Oxford Road	a						14 03	14 09										15 03	15 09				
Birchwood	a							14 25											15 25				
Warrington Central	a							14 30											15 30				
L'pool South Parkway 7	a							14 47											15 47				
Liverpool Lime Street 10	a						14 48	14 58		15 43								15 48	15 58		16 43		

Table 39

Mondays to Fridays

Newcastle, Middlesbrough, Scarborough, York, Hull, Leeds and Wakefield - Huddersfield - Manchester, Manchester Airport and Liverpool

		TP	NT	NT	NT	TP	NT	TP	NT	NT	NT	TP	TP	NT	NT	NT	TP	NT	NT	TP	TP	NT	NT
																					FO		
		◇1 ✠				◇1 ✠		◇1 ✠				◇1 ✠	◇1 ✠				◇1 ✠			◇1 ✠	◇1		
Newcastle 8	d					13 15											14 18						
Chester-le-Street	d					13 24																	
Durham	d					13 31											14 31						
Middlesbrough	d											13 50									14 50		
Thornaby	d											13 55									14 55		
Yarm	d											14 03									15 03		
Darlington 7	d					13 48											14 48						
Northallerton	d					13 59						14 18					14 59				15 18		
Thirsk	d											14 28									15 28		
Scarborough	d							13 48												14 48			
Seamer	d							13 53												14 53			
Malton	d							14 11												15 11			
York 8	a					14 24		14 38				14 47					15 22			15 38	15 47		
	d					14 26		14 40				14 57					15 26			15 40			
Wakefield Westgate	d			14 39											15 39								
Wakefield Kirkgate	d			14 45											15 45								
Hull	d	13 40	14 18										14 40	15 02									
Brough	d	13 52	14 30										14 52	15 14									
Howden	d		14 42											15 26									
Selby	d	14 11	14a53										15 11	15a36									
South Milford	d																						
Garforth	d											15 12											
Leeds 10	a	14 36				14 52		15 04				15 22	15 36				15 52			16 04			
	d	14 40			14 43	14 55		15 08			15 13	15 25	15 40			15 43	15 55			16 08			16 13
Cottingley	d				14 48											15 48							16 18
Morley	d				14 52						15 21					15 52							16 22
Batley	d				14 57						15 26					15 57							16 27
Dewsbury	a				15 00	15 06					15 29	15 36				16 00	16 06						16 30
	d				15 01	15 06					15 29	15 36				16 01	16 06						16 31
Ravensthorpe	d				15 04											16 04							16 34
Mirfield	d			14 58	15 08						15 35				15 58	16 08							16 38
Deighton	d			15 05	15 16										16 05	16 14							
Huddersfield	a	14 58		15 23	15 21	15 15		15 25				15 45	15 58		16 23	16 21	16 15			16 25			
	d	14 59				15 16		15 26	15 30			15 46	15 59				16 16			16 26		16 30	
Slaithwaite	d								15 37													16 37	
Marsden	d								15 43													16 43	
Greenfield	d								15 51													16 51	
Mossley (Grtr Manchester)	d								15 55													16 55	
Stalybridge	a							15 43	16 00											16 43		17 00	
	d							15 46	16 01	16 22								16 42		16 46		17 01	
Ashton-under-Lyne	d								16 05	16 26								16 46				17 05	
Manchester Victoria	a								16 21	16 35	16 52							16 58				17 24	17 53
Manchester Piccadilly 10	a	15 36				15 49		16 05				16 19	16 36				16 49			17 05			
	d					15 54	16 01	16 07				16 24					16 54		17 01	17 07			
Manchester Airport	a					16 12						16 42					17 12						
Manchester Oxford Road	a						16 03	16 09											17 03	17 09			
Birchwood	a							16 25												17 25			
Warrington Central	a							16 30												17 30			
L'pool South Parkway 7	a							16 47												17 47			
Liverpool Lime Street 10	a						16 48	16 58		17 43									17 48	18 00			

Table 39

Mondays to Fridays

Newcastle, Middlesbrough, Scarborough, York, Hull, Leeds and Wakefield - Huddersfield - Manchester, Manchester Airport and Liverpool

		TP	TP	TP	NT	NT	NT	TP	NT	TP	NT	NT	TP	TP	NT	NT	NT	TP	TP	NT	NT	TP
		FX	FO																			
		◇1 ✠	◇1 ✠	◇1 ✠				◇1 ✠		◇1 ✠			◇1 ✠	◇1 ✠				◇1 ✠	◇1			◇1 ✠
Newcastle 8	d							15 15										16 15				
Chester-le-Street	d							15 24										16 24				
Durham	d							15 31										16 31				
Middlesbrough	d	14 50											15 50									
Thornaby	d	14 55											15 55									
Yarm	d	15 03											16 03									
Darlington 7	d							15 48										16 48				
Northallerton	d	15 18						15 59					16 18					16 59				
Thirsk	d	15 28											16 28									
Scarborough	d									15 48												16 48
Seamer	d									15 53												16 53
Malton	d									16 11												17 11
York 8	a	15 47						16 21		16 38			16 47					17 23				17 38
	d	15 57	15 57					16 26		16 40			16 57					17 26				17 41
Wakefield Westgate	d					16 39										17 39						
Wakefield Kirkgate	d					16 45										17 42						
Hull	d			15 39	16 10									16 40					17 01	17 18		
Brough	d			15 51	16 22									16 52					17 13	17 35		
Howden	d				16 36															17 54		
Selby	d			16 10	16a46									17 11					17 32	18a06		
South Milford	d																					
Garforth	d			16 27									17 12									
Leeds 10	a	16 22	16 22	16 37				16 52		17 04			17 22	17 36				17 52	17 58			18 04
	d	16 25	16 25	16 40			16 43	16 55		17 08		17 13	17 26	17 40			17 43	17 55	18 02			18 08
Cottingley	d						16 48					17 18					17 48					
Morley	d						16 52					17 22					17 52					
Batley	d						16 57					17 27					17 57					
Dewsbury	a	16 36	16 36				17 00	17 06				17 30	17 37				18 00	18 06	18 13			
	d	16 36	16 36				17 01	17 06				17 31	17 37				18 01	18 06	18 13			
Ravensthorpe	d						17 04					17 34					18 04					
Mirfield	d					16 58	17 08					17 38				17 58	18 08					
Deighton	d					17 02	17 14									18 04	18 13					
Huddersfield	a	16 45	16 45	16 58		17 11	17 21	17 15		17 25			17 46	17 58		18 11	18 20	18 15	18 23			18 25
	d	16 46	16 46	16 59				17 16		17 26	17 30		17 46	17 59	18 04			18 16				18 26
Slaithwaite	d										17 37				18 11							
Marsden	d										17 43				18 17							
Greenfield	d										17 51											
Mossley (Grtr Manchester)	d										17 55											
Stalybridge	a			17 18						17 43	18 00			18 18	18 30							18 43
	d			17 18						17 46	18 01			18 18	18 31							18 46
Ashton-under-Lyne	d										18 05				18 35							
Manchester Victoria	a										18 20	18 54			18 48							
Manchester Piccadilly 10	a	17 25	17 25	17 37				17 49		18 05			18 19	18 37				18 49				19 05
	d							17 54	18 01	18 07			18 24					18 54			19 01	19 07
Manchester Airport	a							18 12					18 42					19 13				
Manchester Oxford Road	a								18 03	18 09											19 03	19 09
Birchwood	a									18 25												19 25
Warrington Central	a									18 30												19 30
L'pool South Parkway 7	a									18 47												19 47
Liverpool Lime Street 10	a								19 00	18 59											19 48	19 59

Newcastle, Middlesbrough, Scarborough, York, Hull, Leeds and Wakefield - Huddersfield - Manchester, Manchester Airport and Liverpool

Station		NT	NT	TP ◇1 ✠	TP ◇1 ✠	NT	NT	TP ◇1 ✠	NT	TP ◇1	NT	NT	TP ◇1	TP ◇1	NT	NT	TP ◇1	TP ◇1	NT	NT	TP ◇1	NT	NT
Newcastle 8 ⇌	d				17 02																18 52		
Chester-le-Street	d				17 11																19 01		
Durham	d				17 18																19 08		
Middlesbrough	d			16 50									17 50					18 50					
Thornaby	d			16 55									17 55					18 55					
Yarm	d			17 03									18 03					19 03					
Darlington 7	d				17 35																19 25		
Northallerton	d			17 18	17 46								18 18					19 18			19 36		
Thirsk	d			17 28									18 28					19 26					
Scarborough	d									17 48							18 48						
Seamer	d									17 53							18 53						
Malton	d									18 11							19 11						
York 8	a			17 48	18 09					18 38			18 47				19 38	19 52			20 07		
	d			17 57	18 12					18 40			19 10				19 40				20 10		
Wakefield Westgate	d					18 39										19 42						20 50	
Wakefield Kirkgate	d					18 42										19 45						20 56	
Hull	d							17 58						18 59	19 15								
Brough	d							18 10						19 11	19 28								
Howden	d														19 43								
Selby	d							18 29						19 30	19a53								
South Milford	d																						
Garforth	d			18 12									19 22										
Leeds 10	a			18 22	18 37			18 52		19 04			19 35	19 56			20 04				20 35		
	d		18 13	18 25	18 40		18 43	18 55		19 08		19 13	19 40				20 08			20 13	20 40		
Cottingley	d		18 18				18 48					19 18								20 18			
Morley	d		18 22				18 52					19 22								20 22			
Batley	d		18 27				18 57					19 27								20 27			
Dewsbury	a		18 30	18 36			19 00	19 06				19 30	19 51							20 30	20 51		
	d		18 31	18 36			19 01	19 06				19 31	19 51							20 31	20 51		
Ravensthorpe	d		18 34				19 04					19 34								20 34			
Mirfield	d		18 38			18 58	19 08					19 38				20 00				20 37		21 09	
Deighton	d					19 04	19 13					19 45				20 08				20 44		21 16	
Huddersfield	a			18 45	19 00	19 11	19 20	19 15		19 25		19 49	19 59			20 13	20 25			20 51	20 59	21 21	
	d	18 30		18 46	19 01			19 16		19 26	19 30		20 00				20 26		20 30		21 00		
Slaithwaite	d	18 37									19 37								20 37				
Marsden	d	18 43									19 43								20 43				
Greenfield	d	18 51									19 51								20 51				
Mossley (Grtr Manchester)	d	18 55									19 55								20 55				
Stalybridge	a	19 01								19 43	20 00						20 43		21 00				
	d	19 01								19 46	20 01						20 46		21 01				
Ashton-under-Lyne	d	19 05									20 05								21 05				
Manchester Victoria ⇌	a	19 20	19 54								20 20								21 20				
Manchester Piccadilly 10 ⇌	a			19 21	19 32			19 57		20 05			20 33				21 05				21 33		
	d				19 40				20 01	20 07			20 40				21 07				21 40		22 01
Manchester Airport ✈	a				19 59								20 57								21 57		
Manchester Oxford Road	a								20 03	20 09							21 09						22 03
Birchwood	a									20 25							21 25						
Warrington Central	a									20 30							21 30						
L'pool South Parkway 7 ✈	a									20 47							21 47						
Liverpool Lime Street 10	a								20 48	20 59							21 58						22 48

Newcastle, Middlesbrough, Scarborough, York, Hull, Leeds and Wakefield - Huddersfield - Manchester, Manchester Airport and Liverpool

Station		TP ◇1	TP FO ◇1	NT	NT	TP FX ◇1	TP FO ◇1	TP FX ◇1	TP ◇1	NT	TP ◇1	TP ◇1	TP ◇1	NT	NT	TP ◇1	NT	NT	NT	TP ◇1	NT	NT FX
Newcastle 8 ⇌	d																			21 55	22 21	
Chester-le-Street	d																				22 30	
Durham	d																			22 08	22 39	
Middlesbrough	d		19 50			19 50					20 50		21 50									23 09
Thornaby	d		19 55			19 55					20 55		21 55									
Yarm	d										21 03											
Darlington 7	d		20b26			20 26							22 19							22 25	22a59	23a34
Northallerton	d		20 39			20 39					21 18		22 30							22 36		
Thirsk	d		20 47			20 47							22 38									
Scarborough	d	19 48							20 48			22 03										
Seamer	d	19 53							20 53			22 08										
Malton	d	20 11							21 11			22 26										
York 8	a	20 38	21 06			21 06			21 38		21 44	22 55	22 57							23 00		
	d	20 40				21 14					21 46									23 06		
Wakefield Westgate	d									21 41								22 48				
Wakefield Kirkgate	d									21 50								22 53				
Hull	d						20 35	20 45								21 33						
Brough	d						20 47	20 57								21 45						
Howden	d																					
Selby	d						21 06	21 16								22 07						
South Milford	d						21 16	21 26								22 16						
Garforth	d																					
Leeds 10	a	21 04				21 37	21 35	21 44			22 07					22 35				23 33		
	d	21 08			21 13	21 40	21 40				22 10				22 18	22 40			23 13	23 35		
Cottingley	d				21 18										22 23				23 18			
Morley	d				21 22										22 27				23 22			
Batley	d				21 27										22 32				23 27			
Dewsbury	a				21 30	21 51	21 51								22 35	22 51			23 30	23 45		
	d				21 31	21 51	21 51								22 36	22 51			23 31	23 46		
Ravensthorpe	d				21 34										22 39				23 34			
Mirfield	d				21 38					22 03					22 44			23 06	23 38			
Deighton	d				21 45					22 10					22 49			23 14	23 45			
Huddersfield	a	21 25			21 49	21 59	21 59			22 14	22 27				22 54	22 59		23 21	23 49	23 55		
	d	21 26		21 30		22 00	22 00				22 28			22 34		23 00	23 05			23 56		
Slaithwaite	d			21 37										22 41			23 12					
Marsden	d			21 43										22 47			23 18					
Greenfield	d			21 51										22 55			23 26					
Mossley (Grtr Manchester)	d			21 55										22 59			23 30					
Stalybridge	a	21 43		22 00							22 45			23 04			23 35					
	d	21 46		22 01							22 46			23 05			23 36					
Ashton-under-Lyne	d			22 05										23 09			23 40					
Manchester Victoria ⇌	a			22 20										23 24			23 53					
Manchester Piccadilly 10 ⇌	a	22 05				22 33	22 33				23 05					23 37				00 53		
	d	22 07				22 40	22 40													00 54		
Manchester Airport ✈	a					22 57	22 57													01 10		
Manchester Oxford Road	a	22 09																				
Birchwood	a	22 25																				
Warrington Central	a	22 30																				
L'pool South Parkway 7 ✈	a	22 47																				
Liverpool Lime Street 10	a	23 00																				

Table 39

Saturdays

Newcastle, Middlesbrough, Scarborough, York, Hull, Leeds and Wakefield - Huddersfield - Manchester, Manchester Airport and Liverpool

		TP	TP	NT	TP	TP	TP	NT	TP	TP		TP	NT	TP	NT	NT	TP	NT	TP	NT		NT	NT	NT	NT
		◇1	◇1		◇1	◇1	◇1		◇1	◇1		◇1		◇1 🛒			◇1		◇1						
Newcastle [8]	d	21p55																							
Chester-le-Street	d																								
Durham	d	22p08																							
Middlesbrough	d																05 55								
Thornaby	d																06 00								
Yarm	d																06 08								
Darlington [7]	d	22p25																							
Northallerton	d	22p36															06 23								
Thirsk	d																06 31								
Scarborough	d																								
Seamer	d																								
Malton	d																								
York [8]	a	23p00															06 50								
	d	23p06	01 52		02 40	03 52	05 26			05 57		06 28					06 55								
Wakefield Westgate	d																							07 29	
Wakefield Kirkgate	d																							07 35	
Hull	d													06 00					06 37	07 07					
Brough	d													06 12					06 49	07 19					
Howden	d													06 26						07 35					
Selby	d													06 36					07 07	07a48					
South Milford	d																								
Garforth	d									06 12							07 09								
Leeds [10]	a	23p33	02 18		03 06	04 34	05 52			06 22		06 53		07 00			07 20		07 33						
	d	23p35	02 20		03 10	04 45	05 55			06 25		06 55		07 08	07 13		07 23		07 38						07 43
Cottingley	d																								07 48
Morley	d														07 21										07 52
Batley	d														07 26										07 57
Dewsbury	a	23p45					06 06			06 36		07 06			07 29		07 34								08 00
	d	23p46					06 06			06 36		07 06			07 29		07 34								08 01
Ravensthorpe	d																								08 04
Mirfield	d														07 35									07 50	08 08
Deighton	d																							07 56	08 13
Huddersfield	a	23p55	02 56		03 49	05 27	06 14			06 44		07 15		07 25			07 43		07 56					08 03	08 20
	d	23p56	02 56		03 59	05 28	06 15			06 45		07 16		07 26		07 33	07 44		07 57				08 02		
Slaithwaite	d															07 40							08 09		
Marsden	d															07 55							08 15		
Greenfield	d															08 03							08 23		
Mossley (Grtr Manchester)	d															08 07		←					08 27		
Stalybridge	a						06 33			07 03		07 34		07 43		08 12	08 01	08 12	08 17				08 32		
	d						06 33			07 04		07 34		07 46		08 13	08 02	08 13	08 17			08 22	08 33		
Ashton-under-Lyne	d															→		08 17				08 26	08 37		
Manchester Victoria	a														08 53			08 31				08 35	08 52		
Manchester Piccadilly [10]	a	00 53	03 44		04 52	06 02	06 50			07 19		07 51		08 05			08 19		08 36						
	d	00 54	03 44	04 49	04 54	06 08	06 54	06 58	07 07	07 23		07 54	07 59	08 07			08 24								
Manchester Airport ✈	a	01 10	04 00		05 10	06 24	07 12			07 42		08 12					08 42								
Manchester Oxford Road	a							07 00	07 09				08 01	08 09											
Birchwood	a								07 25					08 25											
Warrington Central	a								07 30					08 30											
L'pool South Parkway [7] ✈	a													08 47											
Liverpool Lime Street [10]	a			05 32				07 49	07 56				08 59	08 58								09 43			

Table 39

Saturdays

Newcastle, Middlesbrough, Scarborough, York, Hull, Leeds and Wakefield - Huddersfield - Manchester, Manchester Airport and Liverpool

		TP	NT	TP	NT	NT		NT	TP	TP	NT	NT	TP	NT	TP	NT		NT	NT	TP	TP	NT	NT	NT	TP
		◇1		◇1 🛒					◇1 🛒	◇1 🛒			◇1 🛒		◇1 🛒					◇1 🛒	◇1 🛒				◇1 🛒
Newcastle [8]	d			06 11																07 33					
Chester-le-Street	d			06 21																07 42					
Durham	d			06 28																07 49					
Middlesbrough	d												07 12												
Thornaby	d												07 17												
Yarm	d												07 27												
Darlington [7]	d			06 45																08 06					
Northallerton	d			06 56									07 42							08 17					
Thirsk	d			07 04									07 50							08 25					
Scarborough	d	06 30							06 58						07 47										
Seamer	d	06 35							07 03						07 52										
Malton	d	06 53							07 21						08 10										
York [8]	a	07 24		07 28					07 47				08 08		08 37					08 47					
	d	07 27		07 40					07 53				08 25		08 40					08 57					09 25
Wakefield Westgate	d										08 27												09 29		
Wakefield Kirkgate	d										08 35												09 35		
Hull	d									07 37											08 40	09 02			
Brough	d									07 49											08 52	09 14			
Howden	d									08 01												09 28			
Selby	d									08 11											09 11	09a38			
South Milford	d																								
Garforth	d								08 12											09 12					
Leeds [10]	a	07 51		08 03					08 22	08 36			08 52		09 04					09 22	09 36				09 53
	d	07 55		08 08				08 13	08 25	08 40		08 43	08 55		09 08				09 13	09 25	09 40			09 43	09 55
Cottingley	d							08 18				08 48							09 18					09 48	
Morley	d							08 22				08 52							09 22					09 52	
Batley	d							08 27				08 57							09 27					09 57	
Dewsbury	a	08 06						08 30	08 36			09 00	09 06						09 30	09 36				10 00	10 06
	d	08 06						08 31	08 36			09 01	09 06						09 31	09 36				10 01	10 06
Ravensthorpe	d							08 34				09 04												10 04	
Mirfield	d							08 38			08 51	09 08							09 37				09 51	10 08	
Deighton	d										08 58	09 17											09 58	10 14	
Huddersfield	a	08 15		08 25					08 44	08 58	09 05	09 21	09 15		09 25					09 45	09 58		10 05	10 21	10 15
	d	08 16		08 26	08 30				08 45	08 59			09 16		09 26	09 30				09 46	09 59				10 16
Slaithwaite	d				08 37											09 37									
Marsden	d				08 43											09 43									
Greenfield	d				08 51											09 51									
Mossley (Grtr Manchester)	d				08 55											09 55									
Stalybridge	a			08 43	09 00										09 43	10 00									
	d			08 46	09 01	09 22									09 46	10 01		10 22							
Ashton-under-Lyne	d				09 05	09 26										10 05		10 26							
Manchester Victoria	a				09 20	09 35		09 53								10 20		10 35	10 53						
Manchester Piccadilly [10]	a	08 51		09 05					09 19	09 36			09 49		10 05					10 19	10 36				10 49
	d	08 54	09 01	09 07					09 24				09 54	10 01	10 07					10 24					10 54
Manchester Airport ✈	a	09 12							09 42				10 12							10 42					11 12
Manchester Oxford Road	a		09 03	09 09										10 03	10 09										
Birchwood	a			09 25											10 25										
Warrington Central	a			09 30											10 30										
L'pool South Parkway [7] ✈	a			09 47											10 47										
Liverpool Lime Street [10]	a		09 48	09 58		10 43								10 48	10 58			11 43							

Table 39

Saturdays

Newcastle, Middlesbrough, Scarborough, York, Hull, Leeds and Wakefield - Huddersfield - Manchester, Manchester Airport and Liverpool

		NT		TP	NT	NT	NT	TP	TP	NT	NT	NT		TP	NT	TP	NT	NT	NT	TP	TP	TP		NT	NT
				◇1				◇1	◇1					◇1		◇1				◇1	◇1	◇1			
																					A				
								⊼						⊼		⊼				⊼					
Newcastle 8 ⇌	d													09 15											
Chester-le-Street	d													09 24											
Durham	d													09 31											
Middlesbrough	d							08 50												09 50					
Thornaby	d							08 55												09 55					
Yarm	d							09 03												10 03					
Darlington 7	d													09 48											
Northallerton	d							09 18						09 59						10 18					
Thirsk	d							09 28												10 28					
Scarborough	d			08 48												09 48					10 30				
Seamer	d			08 53												09 53									
Malton	d			09 11												10 11					10 51				
York 8	a			09 37				09 47						10 21		10 38				10 47	11 18				
	d			09 40				09 57						10 28		10 40				10 57					
Wakefield Westgate	d										10 29														11 29
Wakefield Kirkgate	d										10 35														11 35
Hull	d								09 40	10 08												10 40		11 05	
Brough	d								09 52	10 20												10 52		11 17	
Howden	d									10 34														11 30	
Selby	d								10 11	10a47												11 11		11a40	
South Milford	d																								
Garforth	d							10 12												11 12					
Leeds 10	a			10 04				10 22	10 36					10 52		11 04				11 22		11 36			
	d			10 08			10 13	10 25	10 40			10 43		10 55		11 08			11 13	11 25		11 40			
Cottingley	d											10 48													
Morley	d						10 21					10 52							11 21						
Batley	d						10 26					10 57							11 26						
Dewsbury	a						10 29	10 36				11 00		11 06					11 29	11 36					
	d						10 29	10 36				11 01		11 06					11 29	11 36					
Ravensthorpe	d											11 04													
Mirfield	d						10 35				10 51	11 08							11 35						11 49
Deighton	d										10 58	11 14													11 58
Huddersfield	a			10 25				10 45	10 58		11 05	11 21		11 15		11 25				11 45		11 58			12 05
	d			10 26	10 30			10 46	10 59					11 16		11 26	11 30			11 46		11 59			
Slaithwaite	d				10 37												11 37								
Marsden	d				10 43												11 43								
Greenfield	d				10 51												11 51								
Mossley (Grtr Manchester)	d				10 55												11 55								
Stalybridge	a			10 43	11 00											11 43	12 00								
	d			10 46	11 01	11 22										11 46	12 01	12 22							
Ashton-under-Lyne	d				11 05	11 26											12 05	12 26							
Manchester Victoria ⇌	a				11 20	11 35	11 53										12 20	12 36	12 53						
Manchester Piccadilly 10 ⇌	a			11 05				11 19	11 36					11 49		12 05				12 19		12 36			
	d	11 01		11 07				11 24						11 54	12 01	12 07				12 24					
Manchester Airport ✈	a							11 42						12 12						12 42					
Manchester Oxford Road	a	11 03		11 09											12 03	12 09									
Birchwood	a			11 25												12 25									
Warrington Central	a			11 30												12 30									
L'pool South Parkway 7 ✈	a			11 47												12 47									
Liverpool Lime Street 10	a	11 48		11 58		12 43									12 48	12 58		13 43							

A from 25 June until 10 September

Table 39

Saturdays

Newcastle, Middlesbrough, Scarborough, York, Hull, Leeds and Wakefield - Huddersfield - Manchester, Manchester Airport and Liverpool

		NT	TP	NT	TP	NT	NT	NT		TP	TP	NT	NT	NT	TP	NT	TP	NT		NT	NT	TP	TP	NT	NT
			◇1		◇1					◇1	◇1				◇1		◇1					◇1	◇1		
			⊼		⊼					⊼	⊼				⊼							⊼	⊼		
Newcastle 8 ⇌	d		10 17												11 15										
Chester-le-Street	d														11 24										
Durham	d		10 31												11 31										
Middlesbrough	d									10 50												11 50			
Thornaby	d									10 55												11 55			
Yarm	d									11 03												12 03			
Darlington 7	d		10 48												11 48										
Northallerton	d		10 59							11 18					11 59							12 18			
Thirsk	d									11 28												12 28			
Scarborough	d				10 48												11 48								
Seamer	d				10 53												11 53								
Malton	d				11 11												12 11								
York 8	a		11 23		11 38					11 47					12 21		12 38					12 47			
	d		11 26		11 40					11 57					12 26		12 40					12 57			
Wakefield Westgate	d												12 29												13 39
Wakefield Kirkgate	d												12 34												13 45
Hull	d										11 40	12 03											12 40	13 12	
Brough	d										11 52	12 15											12 52	13 24	
Howden	d											12 27												13 42	
Selby	d										12 11	12a37											13 11	13a54	
South Milford	d																								
Garforth	d									12 12												13 12			
Leeds 10	a		11 53		12 04					12 22	12 36				12 52		13 04					13 22	13 36		
	d	11 43	11 55		12 08			12 13		12 25	12 40			12 43	12 55		13 08				13 13	13 25	13 40		
Cottingley	d	11 48												12 48											
Morley	d	11 52						12 21						12 52							13 21				
Batley	d	11 57						12 26						12 57							13 26				
Dewsbury	a	12 00	12 06					12 29		12 36				13 00	13 06						13 29	13 36			
	d	12 01	12 06					12 29		12 36				13 01	13 06						13 29	13 36			
Ravensthorpe	d	12 04												13 04											
Mirfield	d	12 08						12 35					12 48	13 08							13 35				13 58
Deighton	d	12 14											12 59	13 14											14 05
Huddersfield	a	12 21	12 15		12 25					12 45	12 58		13 06	13 21	13 15		13 25					13 45	13 58		14 11
	d		12 16		12 26	12 30				12 46	12 59				13 16		13 26	13 30				13 46	13 59		
Slaithwaite	d					12 37												13 37							
Marsden	d					12 43												13 43							
Greenfield	d					12 51												13 51							
Mossley (Grtr Manchester)	d					12 55												13 55							
Stalybridge	a				12 43	13 00											13 43	14 00							
	d				12 46	13 01	13 22										13 46	14 01		14 22					
Ashton-under-Lyne	d					13 05	13 26											14 05		14 26					
Manchester Victoria ⇌	a					13 20	13 35	13 53										14 20		14 35	14 53				
Manchester Piccadilly 10 ⇌	a		12 49		13 05					13 19	13 36				13 49		14 05					14 19	14 36		
	d		12 54	13 01	13 07					13 24					13 54	14 01	14 07					14 24			
Manchester Airport ✈	a		13 12							13 42					14 12							14 42			
Manchester Oxford Road	a			13 03	13 09											14 03	14 09								
Birchwood	a				13 25												14 25								
Warrington Central	a				13 30												14 30								
L'pool South Parkway 7 ✈	a				13 47												14 47								
Liverpool Lime Street 10	a			13 48	13 58		14 43									14 48	14 58			15 43					

Table 39

Newcastle, Middlesbrough, Scarborough, York, Hull, Leeds and Wakefield - Huddersfield - Manchester, Manchester Airport and Liverpool

		NT	TP	NT	TP	NT	NT	NT	TP	TP	NT	NT	NT	TP	NT	TP	NT	NT	NT	TP	TP	NT
			◇1 🛒		◇1 🛒				◇1 🛒	◇1				◇1 🛒		◇1 🛒				◇1 🛒	◇1	
Newcastle 8 ⇌	d		12 17											13 15								
Chester-le-Street	d													13 24								
Durham	d		12 29											13 31								
Middlesbrough	d								12 50											13 50		
Thornaby	d								12 55											13 55		
Yarm	d								13 03											14 03		
Darlington 7	d		12 46											13 48								
Northallerton	d		12 58						13 18					13 59						14 18		
Thirsk	d								13 28											14 28		
Scarborough	d				12 48											13 48						
Seamer	d				12 53											13 53						
Malton	d				13 11											14 11						
York 8	a		13 21		13 38				13 47					14 24		14 38				14 47		
	d		13 24		13 40				13 57					14 26		14 40				14 57		
Wakefield Westgate	d											14 39										
Wakefield Kirkgate	d											14 45										
Hull	d									13 40	14 18										14 40	15 02
Brough	d									13 52	14 30										14 52	15 14
Howden	d										14 42											15 26
Selby	d									14 11	14a53										15 11	15a36
South Milford	d																					
Garforth	d								14 12											15 12		
Leeds 10	a		13 52		14 04				14 22	14 35				14 52		15 04				15 22	15 36	
	d	13 43	13 55		14 08			14 13	14 25	14 37			14 43	14 55		15 08			15 13	15 25	15 40	
Cottingley	d	13 48											14 48									
Morley	d	13 52						14 21					14 52						15 21			
Batley	d	13 57						14 26					14 57						15 26			
Dewsbury	a	14 00	14 06					14 29	14 36				15 00	15 06					15 29	15 36		
	d	14 01	14 06					14 29	14 36				15 01	15 06					15 29	15 36		
Ravensthorpe	d	14 04											15 04									
Mirfield	d	14 08						14 35				14 58	15 08						15 35			
Deighton	d	14 14										15 02	15 14									
Huddersfield	a	14 21	14 15		14 25				14 45	14 55		15 10	15 21	15 15		15 25				15 45	15 58	
	d		14 16		14 26	14 30			14 46	14 56				15 16		15 26	15 30			15 46	15 59	
Slaithwaite	d					14 37											15 37					
Marsden	d					14 43											15 43					
Greenfield	d					14 51											15 51					
Mossley (Grtr Manchester)	d					14 55											15 55					
Stalybridge	a				14 43	15 00										15 43	16 00					
	d				14 46	15 01	15 22									15 46	16 01	16 22				
Ashton-under-Lyne	d					15 05	15 26										16 05	16 26				
Manchester Victoria ⇌	a					15 20	15 35	15 53									16 20	16 35	16 53			
Manchester Piccadilly 10 ⇌	a		14 49		15 05				15 19	15 36				15 49		16 05				16 19	16 36	
	d		14 54	15 01	15 07				15 24					15 54	16 01	16 07				16 24		
Manchester Airport ✈	a		15 12						15 42					16 12						16 42		
Manchester Oxford Road	a			15 03	15 09										16 03	16 09						
Birchwood	a				15 25											16 25						
Warrington Central	a				15 30											16 30						
L'pool South Parkway 7 ✈	a				15 47											16 47						
Liverpool Lime Street 10	a			15 48	15 58		16 43								16 48	16 58		17 43				

Table 39

Newcastle, Middlesbrough, Scarborough, York, Hull, Leeds and Wakefield - Huddersfield - Manchester, Manchester Airport and Liverpool

		NT	NT	TP	NT	TP	NT	NT	TP	TP	NT	NT	NT	NT	TP	NT	NT	TP	NT	NT	TP	TP	NT
				◇1 🛒		◇1 🛒			◇1 🛒	◇1 🛒					◇1 🛒			◇1 🛒			◇1 🛒	◇1	
Newcastle 8 ⇌	d			14 18											15 15								
Chester-le-Street	d														15 24								
Durham	d			14 31											15 31								
Middlesbrough	d								14 50												15 50		
Thornaby	d								14 55												15 55		
Yarm	d								15 03												16 03		
Darlington 7	d			14 48											15 48								
Northallerton	d			14 59					15 18						15 59						16 18		
Thirsk	d								15 28												16 28		
Scarborough	d					14 48												15 48					
Seamer	d					14 53												15 53					
Malton	d					15 11												16 11					
York 8	a			15 22		15 38			15 47						16 21			16 38			16 47		
	d			15 26		15 40			15 57						16 26			16 40			16 57		
Wakefield Westgate	d	15 29											16 29										17 29
Wakefield Kirkgate	d	15 35											16 35										17 35
Hull	d									15 40	16 10											16 40	
Brough	d									15 52	16 22											16 52	
Howden	d										16 36												
Selby	d									16 11	16a46											17 11	
South Milford	d																						
Garforth	d								16 12												17 12		
Leeds 10	a			15 53		16 04			16 22	16 36					16 52			17 04			17 22	17 36	
	d		15 43	15 55		16 08		16 13	16 25	16 40				16 43	16 55			17 08		17 13	17 26	17 40	
Cottingley	d		15 48					16 18						16 48						17 18			
Morley	d		15 52					16 22						16 52						17 22			
Batley	d		15 57					16 27						16 57						17 27			
Dewsbury	a		16 00	16 06				16 30	16 36					17 00	17 06					17 30	17 37		
	d		16 01	16 06				16 31	16 36					17 01	17 06					17 31	17 37		
Ravensthorpe	d		16 04					16 34						17 04						17 34			
Mirfield	d	15 51	16 08					16 38					16 51	17 08						17 38			17 51
Deighton	d	15 58	16 15										16 58	17 14									17 58
Huddersfield	a	16 05	16 21	16 15		16 25			16 45	16 58			17 05	17 21	17 15			17 25			17 46	17 58	18 05
	d			16 16		16 26	16 30		16 46	16 59		17 04			17 16			17 26	17 30		17 46	17 59	
Slaithwaite	d						16 37					17 11							17 37				
Marsden	d						16 43					17a17							17 43				
Greenfield	d						16 51												17 51				
Mossley (Grtr Manchester)	d						16 55												17 55				
Stalybridge	a					16 43	17 00			17 18								17 43	18 00			18 18	
	d					16 46	17 01			17 18						17 22		17 46	18 01			18 18	
Ashton-under-Lyne	d						17 05									17 26			18 05				
Manchester Victoria ⇌	a						17 20	17 53								17 35			18 20	18 54			
Manchester Piccadilly 10 ⇌	a			16 49		17 05			17 21	17 37					17 49			18 05			18 19	18 37	
	d			16 54	17 01	17 07									17 54		18 01	18 07			18 24		
Manchester Airport ✈	a			17 12											18 12						18 42		
Manchester Oxford Road	a				17 03	17 09											18 03	18 09					
Birchwood	a					17 25												18 25					
Warrington Central	a					17 30												18 30					
L'pool South Parkway 7 ✈	a					17 47												18 47					
Liverpool Lime Street 10	a				17 48	18 00										18 43	19 00	18 59					

Table 39

Newcastle, Middlesbrough, Scarborough, York, Hull, Leeds and Wakefield - Huddersfield - Manchester, Manchester Airport and Liverpool

		NT	TP ◇1	TP ◇1	NT	NT	NT	TP ◇1	NT	NT	TP ◇1	TP ◇1	NT	NT	TP ◇1	NT	TP ◇1	NT	NT	TP ◇1	TP ◇1	NT	NT
Newcastle 8	d		16 15									17 02											
Chester-le-Street	d		16 24									17 11											
Durham	d		16 31									17 18											
Middlesbrough	d										16 50									17 50			
Thornaby	d										16 55									17 55			
Yarm	d										17 03									18 03			
Darlington 7	d		16 48									17 35											
Northallerton	d		16 59								17 18	17 46								18 18			
Thirsk	d										17 28									18 28			
Scarborough	d							16 48									17 48						
Seamer	d							16 53									17 53						
Malton	d							17 11									18 11						
York 8	a		17 23					17 38			17 47	18 09					18 38			18 45			
	d		17 26					17 40			17 57	18 12					18 40			19 10			
Wakefield Westgate	d												18 29										19 41
Wakefield Kirkgate	d												18 35										19 43
Hull	d			17 01	17 18										17 58						18 59	19 15	
Brough	d			17 13	17 35										18 10						19 11	19 28	
Howden	d				17 54																	19 43	
Selby	d			17 32	18a06										18 29						19 30	19a52	
South Milford	d																						
Garforth	d										18 12									19 22			
Leeds 10	a		17 52	17 58				18 04			18 22	18 37			18 52		19 04			19 35	19 56		
	d	17 43	17 55					18 08		18 13	18 25	18 40		18 43	18 55		19 08		19 13	19 39			
Cottingley	d	17 48								18 18				18 48					19 18				
Morley	d	17 52								18 22				18 52					19 22				
Batley	d	17 57								18 27				18 57					19 27				
Dewsbury	a	18 00	18 06							18 30	18 36			19 00	19 06				19 30	19 51			
	d	18 01	18 06							18 31	18 36			19 01	19 06				19 31	19 51			
Ravensthorpe	d	18 04								18 34				19 04					19 34				
Mirfield	d	18 08								18 38			18 51	19 08					19 38				19 59
Deighton	d	18 13											18 58	19 13					19 45				20 06
Huddersfield	a	18 21	18 15					18 25			18 45	18 58	19 05	19 20	19 15		19 25		19 49	19 59			20 13
	d		18 16					18 26	18 30		18 46	18 59			19 16		19 26	19 30		20 00			
Slaithwaite	d								18 37									19 37					
Marsden	d								18 43									19 43					
Greenfield	d								18 51									19 51					
Mossley (Grtr Manchester)	d								18 55									19 55					
Stalybridge	a							18 43	19 00								19 43	20 00					
	d					18 22		18 46	19 01								19 46	20 01					
Ashton-under-Lyne	d					18 26			19 05									20 05					
Manchester Victoria	a					18 35			19 20	19 54								20 20					
Manchester Piccadilly 10	a		18 49					19 05			19 21	19 32			19 57		20 05			20 33			
	d		18 54				19 01	19 07				19 40				20 01	20 07			20 40			
Manchester Airport	a		19 13									19 59								20 57			
Manchester Oxford Road	a						19 03	19 09								20 03	20 09						
Birchwood	a							19 25									20 25						
Warrington Central	a							19 30									20 30						
L'pool South Parkway 7	a							19 47									20 47						
Liverpool Lime Street 10	a					19 43	19 48	19 59								20 48	20 59						

Table 39

Newcastle, Middlesbrough, Scarborough, York, Hull, Leeds and Wakefield - Huddersfield - Manchester, Manchester Airport and Liverpool

		TP ◇1	TP ◇1	NT	NT	TP ◇1	TP ◇1	NT	NT	NT	TP ◇1	NT	NT	TP ◇1	NT	TP ◇1	TP ◇1	NT	NT	TP ◇1	NT A	NT B
Newcastle 8	d					18 52																
Chester-le-Street	d					19 01																
Durham	d					19 08																
Middlesbrough	d		18 50											20 10		20 50						
Thornaby	d		18 55											20 15		20 55						
Yarm	d		19 03											20 23		21 03						
Darlington 7	d					19 25																
Northallerton	d		19 18			19 36								20 39		21 18						
Thirsk	d		19 26											20 47								
Scarborough	d	18 48									19 48						22 03					
Seamer	d	18 53									19 53						22 08					
Malton	d	19 11									20 11						22 26					
York 8	a	19 38	19 52			20 07					20 38			21 06		21 44	22 55					
	d	19 40				20 10					20 40			21 14		21 46						
Wakefield Westgate	d							20 50							21 41							
Wakefield Kirkgate	d							20 53							21 50							
Hull	d						19 56		21 01											21 33		
Brough	d						20 08		21 13											21 45		
Howden	d								21 25													
Selby	d						20 27		21a35											22 07		
South Milford	d						20 36													22 16		
Garforth	d																					
Leeds 10	a	20 04				20 35	20 56				21 04			21 37		22 07				22 35		
	d	20 08			20 13	20 40					21 08		21 13	21 40		22 10			22 17	22 40		
Cottingley	d				20 18								21 18						22 22			
Morley	d				20 22								21 22						22 26			
Batley	d				20 27								21 27						22 31			
Dewsbury	a				20 30	20 51							21 30	21 51					22 34	22 51		
	d				20 31	20 51							21 31	21 51					22 35	22 51		
Ravensthorpe	d				20 34								21 34						22 38			
Mirfield	d				20 38			21 08					21 38		22 03				22 42			
Deighton	d				20 44			21 13					21 45		22 10				22 48			
Huddersfield	a	20 25			20 48	20 59		21 20			21 25		21 49	21 59	22 14	22 27			22 53	22 59		
	d	20 26		20 30	20 48	21 00					21 26	21 30		22 00		22 28		22 34		23 00		23 05
Slaithwaite	d			20 37	20 55							21 37						22 41				23 12
Marsden	d			20 43	21a02							21 43						22 47				23 18
Greenfield	d			20 51								21 51						22 55				23 26
Mossley (Grtr Manchester)	d			20 55								21 55						22 59				23 30
Stalybridge	a	20 43		21 00							21 43	22 01				22 45		23 04				23 35
	d	20 46		21 01							21 46	22 01				22 46		23 05			23 32	23 36
Ashton-under-Lyne	d			21 05								22 06						23 09			23 36	23 40
Manchester Victoria	a			21 20								22 20						23 24			23 49	23 53
Manchester Piccadilly 10	a	21 05				21 33					22 05			22 33		23 05				23 37		
	d	21 07				21 40				22 01	22 07			22 40								
Manchester Airport	a					21 57								22 57								
Manchester Oxford Road	a	21 09								22 03	22 09											
Birchwood	a	21 25									22 25											
Warrington Central	a	21 30									22 30											
L'pool South Parkway 7	a	21 47									22 47											
Liverpool Lime Street 10	a	21 58								22 48	23 00											

A from 17 September until 22 October

B until 10 September, from 29 October

Table 39

Saturdays

Newcastle, Middlesbrough, Scarborough, York, Hull, Leeds and Wakefield - Huddersfield - Manchester, Manchester Airport and Liverpool

		NT	NT	TP	TP	NT
				◇1	◇1	
				A	B	
Newcastle 8	d					21 50
Chester-le-Street	d					21 59
Durham	d					22 08
Middlesbrough	d			21 50	21 50	
Thornaby	d			21 55	21 55	
Yarm	d					
Darlington 7	d			22 19	22 19	22a29
Northallerton	d			22 30	22 30	
Thirsk	d			22 38	22 38	
Scarborough	d					
Seamer	d					
Malton	d					
York 8	a			22 57	22 57	
	d			23 07	23 07	
Wakefield Westgate	d	22 42				
Wakefield Kirkgate	d	22 47				
Hull	d					
Brough	d					
Howden	d					
Selby	d					
South Milford	d					
Garforth	d					
Leeds 10	a			23 33	23 33	
	d		23 05	23 35		
Cottingley	d		23 10			
Morley	d		23 14			
Batley	d		23 19			
Dewsbury	a		23 22	23 46		
	d		23 23	23 46		
Ravensthorpe	d		23 26			
Mirfield	d	23 00	23 30			
Deighton	d	23 08	23 37			
Huddersfield	a	23 15	23 41	23 55		
	d			23 56		
Slaithwaite	d					
Marsden	d					
Greenfield	d					
Mossley (Grtr Manchester)	d					
Stalybridge	a					
	d					
Ashton-under-Lyne	d					
Manchester Victoria	a					
Manchester Piccadilly 10	a			00 41		
	d			00 45		
Manchester Airport	a			01 00		
Manchester Oxford Road	a					
Birchwood	a					
Warrington Central	a					
L'pool South Parkway 7	a					
Liverpool Lime Street 10	a					

A until 10 September

B from 17 September

Table 39

Sundays
until 22 May

Newcastle, Middlesbrough, Scarborough, York, Hull and Leeds - Huddersfield - Manchester, Manchester Airport and Liverpool

		TP	TP	TP	TP	TP	NT	TP	TP	NT		TP	NT	NT	TP	TP	NT	TP	TP	NT		TP	NT	NT	TP
		◇1	◇1	◇1	◇1	◇1		◇1	◇1			◇1			◇1	◇1		◇1	◇1			◇1			◇1
Newcastle 8	d														08 00							09 31	10 04		
Chester-le-Street	d																					09 40			
Durham	d														08 13							09 47			
Middlesbrough	d												09 12												10 13
Thornaby	d												09a17												10 18
Yarm	d																								10 26
Darlington 7	d														08 30							10 04	10a37		
Northallerton	d														08 42							10 15			10 41
Thirsk	d														08 50										10 49
Scarborough	d																		09 20						
Seamer	d																		09 25						
Malton	d																		09 43						
York 8	a														09 11				10 09			10 41			11 10
	d	02 44	03 59	05 12	06 12	07 12			08 10			08 40			09 15				10 15			10 45			11 15
Hull	d						08 54									09 00									
Brough	d						09 06									09 12									
Howden	d						09 18																		
Selby	d						09a27									09 33									
South Milford	d															09 42									
Garforth	d																								
Leeds 10	a	03 10	04 25	05 38	06 38	07 38			08 37			09 03			09 38	10 00			10 38			11 08			11 38
	d	03 10	04 25	05 40	06 40	07 40			08 40	08 44		09 10			09 40	10 08			10 40	10 44		11 10			11 40
Cottingley	d									09 49										10 49					
Morley	d									08 53										10 53					
Batley	d									08 58										10 58					
Dewsbury	a			05 51	06 51	07 51			08 51	09 01					09 51				10 51	11 01					11 51
	d			05 51	06 51	07 51			08 51	09 02					09 51				10 51	11 02					11 51
Ravensthorpe	d									09 05										11 05					
Mirfield	d									09 09										11 09					
Deighton	d									09 16										11 15					
Huddersfield	a	03 29	04 44	06 00	07 00	08 00			09 00	09 20		09 27			10 00	10 25			11 00	11 20		11 27			12 00
	d	03 30	04 45	06 01	07 01	08 01			09 01			09 28		09 37	10 01	10 26	10 37		11 01			11 28		11 37	12 01
Slaithwaite	d													09 44			10 44							11 44	
Marsden	d													09 50			10 50							11 50	
Greenfield	d													09 58			10 58							11 58	
Mossley (Grtr Manchester)	d													10 02			11 02							12 02	
Stalybridge	a				07 18	08 18			09 18			09 45		10 07		10 45	11 07					11 45		12 07	
	d				07 19	08 19			09 19			09 46		10 08		10 46	11 08					11 46		12 08	
Ashton-under-Lyne	d													10 12			11 12							12 12	
Manchester Victoria	a													10 26			11 26							12 26	
	d																								
Manchester Piccadilly 10	a	04 02	05 17	06 34	07 34	08 34			09 34			10 05			10 34	11 03			11 34			12 05			12 34
	d	04 06	05 21	06 38	07 38	08 38		09 07	09 38			10 07			10 38			11 07	11 38			12 07			12 38
Manchester Airport	a	04 23	05 38	06 55	07 55	08 55			09 55						10 55				11 55						12 55
Manchester Oxford Road	a							09 09				10 09						11 09				12 09			
Newton-le-Willows	a																								
Birchwood	a							09 25				10 25						11 25				12 25			
Warrington Central	a							09 30				10 30						11 30				12 30			
L'pool South Parkway 7	a							09 47				10 47						11 47				12 47			
Liverpool Lime Street 10	a							10 00				10 59						11 59				12 58			

Table 39

Sundays until 22 May

Newcastle, Middlesbrough, Scarborough, York, Hull and Leeds - Huddersfield - Manchester, Manchester Airport and Liverpool

		TP ◇1	TP ◇1	NT	NT	NT	TP ◇1	NT	TP ◇1	TP ◇1	NT	TP ◇1	TP ◇1	TP ◇1	NT	NT	NT	NT	TP ◇1	NT	TP ◇1	TP ◇1	NT
Newcastle 8 ⇌	d						11 08					12 10							13 04				
Chester-le-Street	d																		13 13				
Durham	d						11 20					12 22							13 20				
Middlesbrough	d			11 31										12 45		13 31							
Thornaby	d			11a36										12 50		13a36							
Yarm	d													12 58									
Darlington 7	d						11 37					12 39							13 37				
Northallerton	d						11 49							13 13									
Thirsk	d													13 21									
Scarborough	d		10 51							11 51												13 51	
Seamer	d		10 56							11 56												13 56	
Malton	d		11 14							12 14												14 14	
York 8	a		11 40				12 12			12 40		13 11		13 42					14 10			14 40	
	d		11 45				12 15			12 45		13 15		13 45					14 15		14 33	14 45	
Hull	d	10 58			11 46				12 00				12 58		13 29		14 23						
Brough	d	11 10			11 58				12 12				13 10		13 41		14 35						
Howden	d				12 10										13 53		14 47						
Selby	d	11 29			12a19				12 32				13 29		14a02		14a56						
South Milford	d	11 38											13 38										
Garforth	d																						
Leeds 10	a	11 56	12 08				12 38		12 56	13 08		13 38	13 56	14 08					14 38		14 56	15 09	
	d	11 59	12 10				12 40	12 44	12 59	13 10		13 40	13 59	14 10					14 40	14 44	14 59	15 11	
Cottingley	d							12 49												14 49			
Morley	d							12 53												14 53			
Batley	d							12 58												14 58			
Dewsbury	a						12 51	13 01				13 51							14 51	15 01			
	d						12 51	13 02				13 51							14 51	15 02			
Ravensthorpe	d							13 05												15 05			
Mirfield	d							13 09												15 09			
Deighton	d							13 20												15 20			
Huddersfield	a	12 16	12 27				13 00	13 24	13 16	13 27		14 00	14 16	14 27					15 00	15 24	15 16	15 28	
	d	12 17	12 28			12 37	13 01		13 17	13 28	13 37	14 01	14 17	14 28				14 37	15 01		15 17	15 29	15 37
Slaithwaite	d					12 44					13 44							14 44					15 44
Marsden	d					12 50					13 50							14 50					15 50
Greenfield	d					12 58					13 58							14 58					15 58
Mossley (Grtr Manchester)	d					13 02					14 02							15 02					16 02
Stalybridge	a		12 45			13 07				13 45	14 07			14 45				15 07				15 46	16 07
	d		12 46			13 08				13 46	14 08			14 46				15 08				15 47	16 08
Ashton-under-Lyne	d					13 12					14 12							15 12					16 12
Manchester Victoria ⇌	a					13 26					14 26							15 26					16 26
	d																						
Manchester Piccadilly 10 ⇌	a	12 54	13 05				13 34		13 54	14 05		14 34	14 54	15 05					15 34		15 54	16 05	
	d		13 07				13 38			14 07		14 38		15 07					15 38			16 07	
Manchester Airport ✈	a						13 55					14 55							15 55				
Manchester Oxford Road	a		13 09							14 09				15 09								16 09	
Newton-le-Willows	a																						
Birchwood	a		13 25							14 25				15 25								16 25	
Warrington Central	a		13 30							14 30				15 30								16 30	
L'pool South Parkway 7 ✈	a		13 47							14 47				15 47								16 47	
Liverpool Lime Street 10	a		13 58							14 58				15 58								16 58	

Table 39

Sundays until 22 May

Newcastle, Middlesbrough, Scarborough, York, Hull and Leeds - Huddersfield - Manchester, Manchester Airport and Liverpool

		TP ◇1	TP ◇1	TP ◇1	NT	NT	NT	TP ◇1	NT	TP ◇1	TP ◇1	NT	TP ◇1	TP ◇1	TP ◇1	NT	NT	NT	TP ◇1	NT	TP ◇1	TP ◇1
Newcastle 8 ⇌	d	14 08						15 07					16 08						17 05			
Chester-le-Street	d							15 16											17 14			
Durham	d	14 20						15 23					16 20						17 21			
Middlesbrough	d			14 42	15 31										16 42		17 45					
Thornaby	d			14 47	15a36										16 47		17a50					
Yarm	d			14 55											16 55							
Darlington 7	d	14 37						15 40					16 37						17 38			
Northallerton	d	14 49		15 10									16 49		17 10				17 49			
Thirsk	d			15 18											17 18							
Scarborough	d										15 51											17 51
Seamer	d										15 56											17 56
Malton	d										16 14											18 14
York 8	a	15 12		15 42				16 13			16 40		17 12		17 42				18 12			18 40
	d	15 15		15 45				16 15		16 33	16 45		17 15		17 45				18 15		18 33	18 45
Hull	d		14 58			16 00								16 58		17 23						
Brough	d		15 10			16 12								17 10		17 35						
Howden	d					16 24										17 47						
Selby	d		15 29			16a33								17 29		17a56						
South Milford	d		15 38											17 38								
Garforth	d																					
Leeds 10	a	15 38	15 56	16 08				16 38		16 56	17 08		17 38	17 56	18 08				18 38		18 57	19 08
	d	15 40	15 59	16 10				16 40	16 44	16 59	17 10		17 40	17 59	18 10				18 40	18 44	18 59	19 10
Cottingley	d								16 49											18 49		
Morley	d								16 53											18 53		
Batley	d								16 58											18 58		
Dewsbury	a	15 51						16 51	17 01				17 51						18 51	19 01		
	d	15 51						16 51	17 02				17 51						18 51	19 02		
Ravensthorpe	d								17 05											19 05		
Mirfield	d								17 09											19 09		
Deighton	d								17 20											19 20		
Huddersfield	a	16 00	16 16	16 27				17 00	17 24	17 16	17 27		18 00	18 16	18 27				19 00	19 24	19 16	19 27
	d	16 01	16 17	16 28			16 37	17 01		17 17	17 28	17 37	18 01	18 17	18 28			18 37	19 01		19 17	19 28
Slaithwaite	d						16 44					17 44						18 44				
Marsden	d						16 50					17 50						18 50				
Greenfield	d						16 58					17 58						18 58				
Mossley (Grtr Manchester)	d						17 02					18 02						19 02				
Stalybridge	a			16 45			17 07				17 45	18 07			18 45			19 07				19 45
	d			16 46			17 08				17 46	18 08			18 46			19 08				19 46
Ashton-under-Lyne	d						17 12					18 12						19 12				
Manchester Victoria ⇌	a						17 26					18 26						19 26				
	d																					
Manchester Piccadilly 10 ⇌	a	16 34	16 54	17 05				17 34		17 54	18 05		18 34	18 54	19 05				19 34		19 54	20 05
	d	16 38		17 07				17 38			18 07		18 38		19 07				19 38			20 07
Manchester Airport ✈	a	16 55						17 55					18 55						19 55			
Manchester Oxford Road	a			17 09							18 09				19 09							20 09
Newton-le-Willows	a																					
Birchwood	a			17 25							18 25				19 25							20 25
Warrington Central	a			17 30							18 30				19 30							20 30
L'pool South Parkway 7 ✈	a			17 47							18 47				19 47							20 47
Liverpool Lime Street 10	a			17 58							18 58				19 58							20 58

Table 39

Sundays until 22 May

Newcastle, Middlesbrough, Scarborough, York, Hull and Leeds - Huddersfield - Manchester, Manchester Airport and Liverpool

		NT	TP	TP	TP	NT	NT	NT	TP	NT	NT	NT	TP	TP	NT	TP	NT	TP	NT	TP	NT	TP
			◇1	◇1	◇1				◇1				◇1	◇1		◇1		◇1		◇1		◇1
Newcastle 8	d		17 52						19 10							20 08	20 11		21 06			
Chester-le-Street	d																		21 15			
Durham	d		18 04						19 22							20 20			21 24			
Middlesbrough	d				18 45					19 31	19 40			20 06								22 06
Thornaby	d				18 50					19 36	19a45			20 11			21a04					22 11
Yarm	d				18 58									20 19								22 19
Darlington 7	d		18 21						19 39	19a53						20 37			21a44			
Northallerton	d		18 33		19 13									20 38		20 49						22 34
Thirsk	d				19 21									20 46								22 42
Scarborough	d												19 51							21 20		
Seamer	d												19 56							21 25		
Malton	d												20 14							21 43		
York 8	a		19 04		19 42				20 11				20 40	21 06		21 12				22 09		23 09
	d		19 15		19 45				20 15				20 45			21 15				22 12		23 12
Hull	d			18 58		19 24	20 29											21 00				
Brough	d			19 10		19 36	20 41											21 12				
Howden	d					19 48	20 53															
Selby	d			19 29		19a57	21a02											21 31				
South Milford	d			19 38														21 40				
Garforth	d																					
Leeds 10	a		19 38	19 54	20 08				20 38				21 08			21 38		21 59		22 36		23 38
	d		19 40	19 59	20 10				20 40			20 44	21 10			21 40				22 40	22 44	23 40
Cottingley	d											20 49									22 49	
Morley	d											20 53									22 53	
Batley	d											20 58									22 58	
Dewsbury	a		19 51						20 51			21 01				21 51					23 01	23 51
	d		19 51						20 51			21 02				21 51					23 02	23 51
Ravensthorpe	d											21 05									23 05	
Mirfield	d											21 09									23 09	
Deighton	d											21 15									23 16	
Huddersfield	a		20 00	20 16	20 27				21 00			21 19	21 27			22 00				22 57	23 20	23 59
	d	19 37	20 01	20 17	20 28			20 37	21 01			21 19	21 28		21 37	22 01				22 58		00 01
Slaithwaite	d	19 44						20 44				21 26			21 44							
Marsden	d	19 50						20 50				21a33			21 50							
Greenfield	d	19 58						20 58							21 58							
Mossley (Grtr Manchester)	d	20 02						21 02							22 02							
Stalybridge	a	20 07			20 45			21 07	21 18						22 07	22 18				23 18		
	d	20 08			20 46			21 08	21 19						22 08	22 19				23 19		
Ashton-under-Lyne	d	20 12						21 12							22 12							
Manchester Victoria	a	20 26						21 26							22 26							
	d																					
Manchester Piccadilly 10	a		20 34	20 54	21 05				21 36				22 05			22 36				23 36		00 43
	d		20 38		21 07								22 07			22 38						00 44
Manchester Airport	a		20 55													22 55						01 00
Manchester Oxford Road	a				21 09								22 09									
Newton-le-Willows	a																					
Birchwood	a				21 25								22 25									
Warrington Central	a				21 30								22 30									
L'pool South Parkway 7	a				21 47								22 47									
Liverpool Lime Street 10	a				21 58								23 00									

Table 39

Sundays 29 May to 11 September

Newcastle, Middlesbrough, Scarborough, York, Hull and Leeds - Huddersfield - Manchester, Manchester Airport and Liverpool

		TP	TP	TP	TP	TP	TP	NT	TP	TP	NT	TP	NT	NT	TP	TP	NT	TP	TP	NT	TP	NT	NT
		◇1	◇1	◇1	◇1	◇1	◇1		◇1	◇1		◇1			◇1	◇1		◇1	◇1		◇1		
													A									A	
Newcastle 8	d														08 00						09 31	10∫04	
Chester-le-Street	d																				09 40		
Durham	d														08 13						09 47		
Middlesbrough	d	21p50											09∫12										
Thornaby	d	21p55											09a17										
Yarm	d																						
Darlington 7	d	22p19													08 30						10 04	10a37	
Northallerton	d	22p30													08 42						10 15		
Thirsk	d	22p38													08 50								
Scarborough	d																		09 20				
Seamer	d																		09 25				
Malton	d																		09 43				
York 8	a	22p57													09 11				10 09		10 41		
	d	23p07	02 44	03 59	05 12	06 12	07 12			08 10		08 40			09 15				10 15		10 45		
Hull	d							08 54								09 00							
Brough	d							09 06								09 12							
Howden	d							09 18															
Selby	d							09a27								09 33							
South Milford	d															09 42							
Garforth	d																						
Leeds 10	a	23p33	03 10	04 25	05 38	06 38	07 38			08 37		09 03			09 38	10 00			10 38		11 08		
	d	23p35	03 10	04 25	05 40	06 40	07 40			08 40	08 44	09 10			09 40	10 08			10 40	10 44	11 10		
Cottingley	d										09 49									10 49			
Morley	d										08 53									10 53			
Batley	d										08 58									10 58			
Dewsbury	a	23p46			05 51	06 51	07 51			08 51	09 01				09 51				10 51	11 01			
	d	23p46			05 51	06 51	07 51			08 51	09 02				09 51				10 51	11 02			
Ravensthorpe	d										09 05									11 05			
Mirfield	d										09 09									11 09			
Deighton	d										09 16									11 15			
Huddersfield	a	23p55	03 29	04 44	06 00	07 00	08 00			09 00	09 20	09 27			10 00	10 25			11 00	11 20	11 27		
	d	23p56	03 30	04 45	06 01	07 01	08 01			09 01		09 28		09 37	10 01	10 26	10 37		11 01		11 28		11 37
Slaithwaite	d													09 44			10 44						11 44
Marsden	d													09 50			10 50						11 50
Greenfield	d													09 58			10 58						11 58
Mossley (Grtr Manchester)	d													10 02			11 02						12 02
Stalybridge	a					07 18	08 18			09 18		09 45		10 07		10 45	11 07				11 45		12 07
	d					07 19	08 19			09 19		09 46		10 08		10 46	11 08				11 46		12 08
Ashton-under-Lyne	d													10 12			11 12						12 12
Manchester Victoria	a													10 26			11 26						12 26
	d																						
Manchester Piccadilly 10	a	00 41	04 02	05 17	06 34	07 34	08 34			09 34		10 05			10 34	11 03			11 34		12 05		
	d	00 45	04 06	05 21	06 38	07 38	08 38		09 07	09 38		10 07			10 38			11 07	11 38		12 07		
Manchester Airport	a	01 00	04 23	05 38	06 55	07 55	08 55			09 55					10 55				11 55				
Manchester Oxford Road	a								09 09			10 09						11 09			12 09		
Newton-le-Willows	a																						
Birchwood	a								09 25			10 25						11 25			12 25		
Warrington Central	a								09 30			10 30						11 30			12 30		
L'pool South Parkway 7	a								09 47			10 47						11 47			12 47		
Liverpool Lime Street 10	a								10 00			10 59						11 59			12 58		

A from 29 May until 19 June

Table 39

Sundays

29 May to 11 September

Newcastle, Middlesbrough, Scarborough, York, Hull and Leeds - Huddersfield - Manchester, Manchester Airport and Liverpool

		TP ◇1 A	TP ◇1 B	TP ◇1	TP ◇1	NT B	NT	NT	TP ◇1	NT	TP ◇1	TP ◇1	NT	TP ◇1	TP ◇1	TP ◇1	NT	NT B	NT	NT	TP ◇1	NT	TP ◇1
Newcastle 8	d								11 08					12 10							13 04		
Chester-le-Street	d																				13 13		
Durham	d								11 20					12 22							13 20		
Middlesbrough	d	10 13	10 13			11 31										12 45		13 31					
Thornaby	d	10 18	10 18			11a36										12 50		13a36					
Yarm	d	10 26	10 26													12 58							
Darlington 7	d								11 37					12 39							13 37		
Northallerton	d	10 41	10 41						11 49							13 13							
Thirsk	d	10 49	10 49													13 21							
Scarborough	d				10 51							11 51											
Seamer	d				10 56							11 56											
Malton	d				11 14							12 14											
York 8	a	11 11	11 10		11 40				12 12			12 40		13 11		13 42					14 10		
	d	11 15	11 15		11 45				12 15			12 45		13 15		13 45					14 15		14 33
Hull	d			10 58			11 46				12 00				12 58		13 29		14 23				
Brough	d			11 10			11 58				12 12				13 10		13 41		14 35				
Howden	d						12 10										13 53		14 47				
Selby	d			11 29			12a19				12 32				13 29		14a02		14a56				
South Milford	d			11 38											13 38								
Garforth	d																						
Leeds 10	a	11 38	11 38	11 56	12 08				12 38		12 56	13 08		13 38	13 56	14 08					14 38		14 56
	d	11 40	11 40	11 59	12 10				12 40	12 44	12 59	13 10		13 40	13 59	14 10					14 40	14 44	14 59
Cottingley	d									12 49												14 49	
Morley	d									12 53												14 53	
Batley	d									12 58												14 58	
Dewsbury	a	11 51	11 51						12 51	13 01				13 51							14 51	15 01	
	d	11 51	11 51						12 51	13 02				13 51							14 51	15 02	
Ravensthorpe	d									13 05												15 05	
Mirfield	d									13 09												15 09	
Deighton	d									13 20												15 20	
Huddersfield	a	12 00	12 00	12 16	12 27				13 00	13 24	13 16	13 27		14 00	14 16	14 27					15 00	15 24	15 16
	d	12 01	12 01	12 17	12 28			12 37	13 01		13 17	13 28	13 37	14 01	14 17	14 28				14 37	15 01		15 17
Slaithwaite	d							12 44					13 44							14 44			
Marsden	d							12 50					13 50							14 50			
Greenfield	d							12 58					13 58							14 58			
Mossley (Grtr Manchester)	d							13 02					14 02							15 02			
Stalybridge	a				12 45			13 07				13 45	14 07			14 45				15 07			
	d				12 46			13 08				13 46	14 08			14 46				15 08			
Ashton-under-Lyne	d							13 12					14 12							15 12			
Manchester Victoria	a							13 26					14 26							15 26			
	d																						
Manchester Piccadilly 10	a	12 34	12 34	12 54	13 05				13 34		13 54	14 05		14 34	14 54	15 05					15 34		15 54
	d	12 38	12 38		13 07				13 38			14 07		14 38		15 07					15 38		
Manchester Airport	a	12 55	12 55						13 55					14 55							15 55		
Manchester Oxford Road	a				13 09							14 09				15 09							
Newton-le-Willows	a																						
Birchwood	a				13 25							14 25				15 25							
Warrington Central	a				13 30							14 30				15 30							
L'pool South Parkway 7	a				13 47							14 47				15 47							
Liverpool Lime Street 10	a				13 58							14 58				15 58							

A from 26 June until 11 September

B from 29 May until 19 June

Table 39

Sundays

29 May to 11 September

Newcastle, Middlesbrough, Scarborough, York, Hull and Leeds - Huddersfield - Manchester, Manchester Airport and Liverpool

		TP ◇1	NT	TP ◇1	TP ◇1	TP ◇1	NT A	NT	NT	TP ◇1	NT	TP ◇1	TP ◇1	NT	TP ◇1	TP ◇1	TP ◇1	NT	NT A	NT	TP ◇1	NT
Newcastle 8	d			14 08						15 07					16 08						17 05	
Chester-le-Street	d									15 16											17 14	
Durham	d			14 20						15 23					16 20						17 21	
Middlesbrough	d					14 42	15 31										16 42		17 45			
Thornaby	d					14 47	15a36										16 47		17a50			
Yarm	d					14 55											16 55					
Darlington 7	d			14 37						15 40					16 37						17 38	
Northallerton	d			14 49		15 10									16 49		17 10				17 49	
Thirsk	d					15 18											17 18					
Scarborough	d	13 51											15 51									
Seamer	d	13 56											15 56									
Malton	d	14 14											16 14									
York 8	a	14 40		15 12		15 42				16 13			16 40		17 12		17 42				18 12	
	d	14 45		15 15		15 45				16 15		16 33	16 45		17 15		17 45				18 15	
Hull	d				14 58			16 00								16 58		17 23				
Brough	d				15 10			16 12								17 10		17 35				
Howden	d							16 24										17 47				
Selby	d				15 29			16a33								17 29		17a56				
South Milford	d				15 38											17 38						
Garforth	d																					
Leeds 10	a	15 09		15 38	15 56	16 08				16 38		16 56	17 08		17 38	17 56	18 08				18 38	
	d	15 11		15 40	15 59	16 10				16 40	16 44	16 59	17 10		17 40	17 59	18 10				18 40	18 44
Cottingley	d										16 49											18 49
Morley	d										16 53											18 53
Batley	d										16 58											18 58
Dewsbury	a			15 51						16 51	17 01				17 51						18 51	19 01
	d			15 51						16 51	17 02				17 51						18 51	19 02
Ravensthorpe	d										17 05											19 05
Mirfield	d										17 09											19 09
Deighton	d										17 20											19 20
Huddersfield	a	15 28		16 00	16 16	16 27				17 00	17 24	17 16	17 27		18 00	18 16	18 27				19 00	19 24
	d	15 29	15 37	16 01	16 17	16 28			16 37	17 01		17 17	17 28	17 37	18 01	18 17	18 28			18 37	19 01	
Slaithwaite	d		15 44						16 44					17 44						18 44		
Marsden	d		15 50						16 50					17 50						18 50		
Greenfield	d		15 58						16 58					17 58						18 58		
Mossley (Grtr Manchester)	d		16 02						17 02					18 02						19 02		
Stalybridge	a	15 46	16 07			16 45			17 07				17 45	18 07			18 45			19 07		
	d	15 47	16 08			16 46			17 08				17 46	18 08			18 46			19 08		
Ashton-under-Lyne	d		16 12						17 12					18 12						19 12		
Manchester Victoria	a		16 26						17 26					18 26						19 26		
	d																					
Manchester Piccadilly 10	a	16 05		16 34	16 54	17 05				17 34		17 54	18 05		18 34	18 54	19 05				19 34	
	d	16 07		16 38		17 07				17 38			18 07		18 38		19 07				19 38	
Manchester Airport	a			16 55						17 55					18 55						19 55	
Manchester Oxford Road	a	16 09				17 09							18 09				19 09					
Newton-le-Willows	a																					
Birchwood	a	16 25				17 25							18 25				19 25					
Warrington Central	a	16 30				17 30							18 30				19 30					
L'pool South Parkway 7	a	16 47				17 47							18 47				19 47					
Liverpool Lime Street 10	a	16 58				17 58							18 58				19 58					

A from 29 May until 19 June

Sundays

29 May to 11 September

Newcastle, Middlesbrough, Scarborough, York, Hull and Leeds - Huddersfield - Manchester, Manchester Airport and Liverpool

		TP	TP	NT	TP	TP	TP	NT		NT	NT	TP	NT	NT	NT	TP	TP	NT		TP	NT	TP	NT	TP	NT
		◇1	◇1		◇1	◇1	◇1					◇1				◇1	◇1			◇1		◇1		◇1	
													A	A							A				
Newcastle 8	d				17 52							19 10								20 08	20 11		21 06		
Chester-le-Street	d																						21 15		
Durham	d				18 04							19 22								20 20			21 24		
Middlesbrough	d						18 45						19 31	19 40			20 06								
Thornaby	d						18 50						19 36	19a45			20 11				21a04				
Yarm	d						18 58										20 19								
Darlington 7	d				18 21							19 39	19a53							20 37			21a44		
Northallerton	d				18 33		19 13										20 38			20 49					
Thirsk	d						19 21										20 46								
Scarborough	d		17 51													19 51								21 20	
Seamer	d		17 56													19 56								21 25	
Malton	d		18 14													20 14								21 43	
York 8	a		18 40		19 04		19 42					20 11				20 40	21 06			21 12				22 09	
	d	18 33	18 45		19 15		19 45					20 15				20 45				21 15				22 12	
Hull	d					18 58		19 24		20 29												21 00			
Brough	d					19 10		19 36		20 41												21 12			
Howden	d							19 48		20 53															
Selby	d					19 29		19a57		21a02												21 31			
South Milford	d					19 38																21 40			
Garforth	d																								
Leeds 10	a	18 57	19 08		19 38	19 54	20 08					20 38				21 08				21 38		21 59		22 36	
	d	18 59	19 10		19 40	19 59	20 10					20 40			20 44	21 10				21 40				22 40	22 44
Cottingley	d														20 49										22 49
Morley	d														20 53										22 53
Batley	d														20 58										22 58
Dewsbury	a				19 51							20 51			21 01					21 51					23 01
	d				19 51							20 51			21 02					21 51					23 02
Ravensthorpe	d														21 05										23 05
Mirfield	d														21 09										23 09
Deighton	d														21 15										23 16
Huddersfield	a	19 16	19 27		20 00	20 16	20 27					21 00			21 19	21 27				22 00				22 57	23 20
	d	19 17	19 28	19 37	20 01	20 17	20 28				20 37	21 01			21 19	21 28		21 37		22 01				22 58	
Slaithwaite	d			19 44							20 44				21 26			21 44							
Marsden	d			19 50							20 50				21a33			21 50							
Greenfield	d			19 58							20 58							21 58							
Mossley (Grtr Manchester)	d			20 02							21 02							22 02							
Stalybridge	a		19 45	20 07			20 45				21 07	21 18						22 07		22 18				23 18	
	d		19 46	20 08			20 46				21 08	21 19						22 08		22 19				23 19	
Ashton-under-Lyne	d			20 12							21 12							22 12							
Manchester Victoria	a			20 26							21 26							22 26							
	d																								
Manchester Piccadilly 10	a	19 54	20 05		20 34	20 54	21 05					21 36				22 05				22 36				23 36	
	d		20 07		20 38		21 07									22 07				22 38					
Manchester Airport	a				20 55															22 55					
Manchester Oxford Road	a		20 09				21 09									22 09									
Newton-le-Willows	a																								
Birchwood	a		20 25				21 25									22 25									
Warrington Central	a		20 30				21 30									22 30									
L'pool South Parkway 7	a		20 47				21 47									22 47									
Liverpool Lime Street 10	a		20 58				21 58									23 00									

A from 29 May until 19 June

Sundays

29 May to 11 September

Newcastle, Middlesbrough, Scarborough, York, Hull and Leeds - Huddersfield - Manchester, Manchester Airport and Liverpool

		TP
		◇1
Newcastle 8	d	
Chester-le-Street	d	
Durham	d	
Middlesbrough	d	22 06
Thornaby	d	22 11
Yarm	d	22 19
Darlington 7	d	
Northallerton	d	22 34
Thirsk	d	22 42
Scarborough	d	
Seamer	d	
Malton	d	
York 8	a	23 09
	d	23 12
Hull	d	
Brough	d	
Howden	d	
Selby	d	
South Milford	d	
Garforth	d	
Leeds 10	a	23 38
	d	23 40
Cottingley	d	
Morley	d	
Batley	d	
Dewsbury	a	23 51
	d	23 51
Ravensthorpe	d	
Mirfield	d	
Deighton	d	
Huddersfield	a	23 59
	d	00 01
Slaithwaite	d	
Marsden	d	
Greenfield	d	
Mossley (Grtr Manchester)	d	
Stalybridge	a	
	d	
Ashton-under-Lyne	d	
Manchester Victoria	a	
	d	
Manchester Piccadilly 10	a	00 43
	d	00 44
Manchester Airport	a	01 00
Manchester Oxford Road	a	
Newton-le-Willows	a	
Birchwood	a	
Warrington Central	a	
L'pool South Parkway 7	a	
Liverpool Lime Street 10	a	

Table 39

Sundays
18 September to 23 October

Newcastle, Middlesbrough, Scarborough, York, Hull and Leeds - Huddersfield - Manchester, Manchester Airport and Liverpool

		NT	NT	TP	NT	TP		NT	TP	TP	TP	NT	NT	TP	NT	NT	TP	NT	TP	NT	TP	TP	NT	NT
				◇1		◇1			◇1	◇1	◇1			◇1			◇1		◇1		◇1	◇1		
			🚌		🚌							🚌			🚌					🚌				
Newcastle 8	d								08 00								09 31							
Chester-le-Street	d																09 40							
Durham	d								08 13								09 47							
Middlesbrough	d																		10 13					
Thornaby	d																		10 18					
Yarm	d																		10 26					
Darlington 7	d								08 30								10 04							
Northallerton	d								08 42								10 15		10 41					
Thirsk	d								08 50										10 49					
Scarborough	d													09 20								10 51		
Seamer	d													09 25								10 56		
Malton	d													09 43								11 14		
York 8	a								09 11					10 09			10 41		11 11			11 40		
	d					08 30			09 15		09 45			10 15			10 45		11 15			11 45		
Hull	d	08 54								09 00											10 58		11 46	
Brough	d	09 06								09 12											11 10		11 58	
Howden	d	09 18																					12 10	
Selby	d	09a27								09 33											11 29		12a19	
South Milford	d									09 42											11 38			
Garforth	d																							
Leeds 10	a					08 53			09 38	10 00	10 08			10 38			11 08		11 38		11 56	12 08		
	d				08 44	09 00			09 40		10 10			10 40		10 44	11 10		11 40		11 59	12 10		
Cottingley	d				09 00											10 49								
Morley	d				09 11											10 53								
Batley	d				09 22											10 58								
Dewsbury	a				09 30	09 10			09 51					10 51		11 01			11 51		12 10			
	d				09 31	09 11			09 51					10 51		11 02			11 51		12 10			
Ravensthorpe	d				09 39											11 05								
Mirfield	d				09 45											11 09								
Deighton	d				09 56											11 15								
Huddersfield	a				10 05	09 19			10 02					11 02		11 20			12 02		12 24			
	d		09 10			09 24			10 03			10 10		11 04	11 10				12 04	12 10				
Slaithwaite	d																							
Marsden	d																							
Greenfield	d		09 51									10 51			11 51					12 51				
Mossley (Grtr Manchester)	d		09 57									10 57			11 57					12 57				
Stalybridge	a		10 05									11 05			12 05					13 05				
	d							10 18					11 18					12 18						13 18
Ashton-under-Lyne	d							10 22					11 22					12 22						13 22
Manchester Victoria	a					10 10		10 36	10 53		11 04		11 36	11 53			12 04	12 36	12 53			13 04		13 36
	d			09 15		10 18	10 15		10 54		11 09			11 54			12 09		12 54			13 09		
Manchester Piccadilly 10	a					10 33			11 08					12 08					13 08					
	d					10 37			11 10					12 10					13 10					
Manchester Airport	a					10 55			11 25					12 25					13 25					
Manchester Oxford Road	a																							
Newton-le-Willows	a			09 33			10 33				11 26						12 26					13 26		
Birchwood	a																							
Warrington Central	a																							
L'pool South Parkway 7	a																							
Liverpool Lime Street 10	a			09 58			10 58				11 58						12 58					13 58		

Table 39

Sundays
18 September to 23 October

Newcastle, Middlesbrough, Scarborough, York, Hull and Leeds - Huddersfield - Manchester, Manchester Airport and Liverpool

		TP	NT	NT	TP	TP	NT	TP	NT	TP	TP	NT	NT	TP	NT	NT	TP	TP	NT	TP	NT	TP	TP
		◇1			◇1	◇1		◇1		◇1	◇1			◇1			◇1	◇1		◇1		◇1	◇1
			🚌						🚌						🚌						🚌		
Newcastle 8	d	11 08						12 10						13 04						14 08			
Chester-le-Street	d													13 13									
Durham	d	11 20						12 22						13 20						14 20			
Middlesbrough	d										12 45												14 42
Thornaby	d										12 50												14 47
Yarm	d										12 58												14 55
Darlington 7	d	11 37						12 39						13 37						14 37			
Northallerton	d	11 49									13 13									14 49			15 10
Thirsk	d										13 21												15 18
Scarborough	d					11 51												13 51					
Seamer	d					11 56												13 56					
Malton	d					12 14												14 14					
York 8	a	12 12				12 40		13 11			13 42			14 10				14 40		15 12			15 42
	d	12 15				12 45		13 15			13 45			14 15			14 33	14 45		15 15			15 45
Hull	d				12 00					12 58		14 23										14 58	
Brough	d				12 12					13 10		14 35										15 10	
Howden	d											14 47											
Selby	d				12 32					13 29		14a56										15 29	
South Milford	d									13 38												15 38	
Garforth	d																						
Leeds 10	a	12 38			12 56	13 08		13 37		13 56	14 08			14 38			14 56	15 08		15 38		15 56	16 08
	d	12 40		12 44	12 59	13 10		13 40		13 59	14 10			14 40		14 44	14 59	15 11		15 40		15 59	16 10
Cottingley	d			12 49												14 49							
Morley	d			12 53												14 53							
Batley	d			12 58												14 58							
Dewsbury	a	12 51		13 01	13 10			13 51		14 10				14 51		15 01	15 10			15 51		16 10	
	d	12 51		13 02	13 10			13 51		14 10				14 51		15 02	15 10			15 51		16 10	
Ravensthorpe	d			13 05												15 05							
Mirfield	d			13 09												15 09							
Deighton	d			13 20												15 20							
Huddersfield	a	13 02		13 24	13 20			14 02		14 20				15 02		15 24	15 20			16 02		16 22	
	d	13 04	13 10					14 04	14 10					15 04	15 10					16 04	16 10		
Slaithwaite	d																						
Marsden	d																						
Greenfield	d		13 51						14 51						15 51						16 51		
Mossley (Grtr Manchester)	d		13 57						14 57						15 57						16 57		
Stalybridge	a		14 05						15 05						16 05						17 05		
	d						14 18						15 18						16 18				
Ashton-under-Lyne	d						14 22						15 22						16 22				
Manchester Victoria	a	13 53				14 04	14 36	14 53			15 09		15 36	15 53				16 05	16 36	16 53			17 04
	d	13 54				14 09		14 54			15 09			15 54				16 09		16 54			17 09
Manchester Piccadilly 10	a	14 08						15 08						16 08						17 08			
	d	14 10						15 10						16 10						17 10			
Manchester Airport	a	14 25						15 25						16 25						17 25			
Manchester Oxford Road	a																						
Newton-le-Willows	a					14 26					15 26							16 26					17 26
Birchwood	a																						
Warrington Central	a																						
L'pool South Parkway 7	a																						
Liverpool Lime Street 10	a					14 58					15 58							16 58					17 58

Table 39

Sundays

18 September to 23 October

Newcastle, Middlesbrough, Scarborough, York, Hull and Leeds - Huddersfield - Manchester, Manchester Airport and Liverpool

		NT		TP	NT	NT	TP	TP	NT	TP	NT	TP		TP	NT	NT	TP	NT	NT	TP	TP	NT		TP	NT
				◇1			◇1	◇1		◇1		◇1		◇1			◇1			◇1	◇1			◇1	
Newcastle 8	d			15 07						16 08							17 05							17 52	
Chester-le-Street	d			15 16													17 14								
Durham	d			15 23						16 20							17 21							18 04	
Middlesbrough	d													16 42											
Thornaby	d													16 47											
Yarm	d													16 55											
Darlington 7	d			15 40						16 37							17 38							18 21	
Northallerton	d									16 49				17 10			17 49							18 33	
Thirsk	d													17 18											
Scarborough	d							15 51													17 51				
Seamer	d							15 56													17 56				
Malton	d							16 14													18 14				
York 8	a			16 13				16 40		17 12				17 42			18 12				18 40			19 04	
	d			16 15			16 33	16 45		17 15				17 45			18 15			18 33	18 45			19 15	
Hull	d											16 58			17 23										
Brough	d											17 10			17 35										
Howden	d														17 47										
Selby	d											17 29			17a56										
South Milford	d											17 38													
Garforth	d																								
Leeds 10	a			16 38			16 56	17 08		17 38		17 56		18 08			18 38			18 57	19 08			19 38	
	d			16 40		16 44	16 59	17 10		17 40		17 59		18 10			18 40		18 44	18 59	19 10			19 40	
Cottingley	d					16 49													18 49						
Morley	d					16 53													18 53						
Batley	d					16 58													18 58						
Dewsbury	a			16 51		17 01	17 10			17 51		18 10					18 51		19 01	19 10				19 51	
	d			16 51		17 02	17 10			17 51		18 10					18 51		19 02	19 10				19 51	
Ravensthorpe	d					17 05													19 05						
Mirfield	d					17 09													19 09						
Deighton	d					17 20													19 20						
Huddersfield	a			17 02		17 24	17 20			18 02		18 20					19 02		19 24	19 20				20 02	
	d			17 04	17 10					18 04	18 10						19 04	19 10						20 04	20 10
Slaithwaite	d																								
Marsden	d																								
Greenfield	d				17 51						18 51							19 51							20 51
Mossley (Grtr Manchester)	d				17 57						18 57							19 57							20 57
Stalybridge	a				18 05						19 05							20 05							21 05
	d	17 18							18 18							19 18						20 18			
Ashton-under-Lyne	d	17 22							18 22							19 22						20 22			
Manchester Victoria	a	17 36		17 53				18 04	18 35	18 53				19 09		19 36	19 53				20 04	20 36		20 53	
	d			17 54				18 09		18 54				19 09			19 54				20 09			20 54	
Manchester Piccadilly 10	a			18 08						19 08							20 08							21 08	
	d			18 10						19 10							20 10							21 10	
Manchester Airport	a			18 25						19 25							20 25							21 25	
Manchester Oxford Road	a																								
Newton-le-Willows	a							18 26						19 26							20 26				
Birchwood	a																								
Warrington Central	a																								
L'pool South Parkway 7	a																								
Liverpool Lime Street 10	a							18 58						19 58							20 58				

Table 39

Sundays

18 September to 23 October

Newcastle, Middlesbrough, Scarborough, York, Hull and Leeds - Huddersfield - Manchester, Manchester Airport and Liverpool

		TP	TP	NT	NT	TP	NT	TP		TP	NT	TP	TP	NT	TP	NT	TP
		◇1	◇1			◇1		◇1		◇1		◇1	◇1		◇1		◇1
Newcastle 8	d					19 10						20 08		21 06			
Chester-le-Street	d													21 15			
Durham	d					19 22						20 20		21 24			
Middlesbrough	d		18 45							20 06							22 06
Thornaby	d		18 50							20 11							22 11
Yarm	d		18 58							20 19							22 19
Darlington 7	d					19 39						20 37		21a44			
Northallerton	d		19 13							20 38		20 49					22 34
Thirsk	d		19 21							20 46							22 42
Scarborough	d							19 51							21 20		
Seamer	d							19 56							21 25		
Malton	d							20 14							21 43		
York 8	a		19 42			20 11		20 40		21 06		21 12			22 09		23 09
	d		19 45			20 15		20 45				21 15			22 12		23 12
Hull	d	18 58		20 29									21 00				
Brough	d	19 10		20 41									21 12				
Howden	d			20 53													
Selby	d	19 29		21a02									21 31				
South Milford	d	19 38											21 40				
Garforth	d																
Leeds 10	a	19 56	20 08			20 38		21 08				21 38	21 59		22 36		23 38
	d	19 59	20 10			20 40	20 44	21 10				21 40			22 40	22 44	23 40
Cottingley	d						20 49									22 49	
Morley	d						20 53									22 53	
Batley	d						20 58									22 58	
Dewsbury	a	20 10				20 51	21 01					21 51			22 50	23 01	23 51
	d	20 10				20 51	21 02					21 51			22 51	23 02	23 51
Ravensthorpe	d						21 05									23 05	
Mirfield	d						21 09									23 09	
Deighton	d						21 15									23 16	
Huddersfield	a	20 20				21 02	21 20					22 02			23 02	23 20	00 02
	d					21 04						22 04			23 04		00 04
Slaithwaite	d																
Marsden	d																
Greenfield	d																
Mossley (Grtr Manchester)	d																
Stalybridge	a																
	d				21 18						22 18						
Ashton-under-Lyne	d				21 22						22 22						
Manchester Victoria	a		21 04		21 36	21 52		22 04			22 36	22 53			23s53		00s53
	d		21 09			21 54		22 09				22 54					
Manchester Piccadilly 10	a					22 10						23 08			00 10		01 08
	d											23 10					01 10
Manchester Airport	a											23 25					01 25
Manchester Oxford Road	a																
Newton-le-Willows	a		21 26					22 26									
Birchwood	a																
Warrington Central	a																
L'pool South Parkway 7	a																
Liverpool Lime Street 10	a		21 58					22 58									

Table 39

Sundays
from 30 October

Newcastle, Middlesbrough, Scarborough, York, Hull and Leeds - Huddersfield - Manchester, Manchester Airport and Liverpool

		NT	NT	TP	TP	NT	TP	TP	NT	TP	TP	NT	TP	NT	TP	TP	TP	NT	NT	TP	NT	TP	TP	NT
		🚌		◇1	◇1		◇1	◇1		◇1	◇1		◇1		◇1	◇1	◇1			◇1		◇1	◇1	
Newcastle 8	d						08 00						09 31							11 08				
Chester-le-Street	d												09 40											
Durham	d						08 13						09 47							11 20				
Middlesbrough	d														10 13									
Thornaby	d														10 18									
Yarm	d														10 26									
Darlington 7	d						08 30						10 04							11 37				
Northallerton	d						08 42						10 15		10 41					11 49				
Thirsk	d						08 50								10 49									
Scarborough	d										09 20						10 51						11 51	
Seamer	d										09 25						10 56						11 56	
Malton	d										09 43						11 14						12 14	
York 8	a						09 11				10 09		10 41		11 11		11 40			12 12			12 40	
	d				08 40		09 15				10 15		10 45		11 15		11 45			12 15			12 45	
Hull	d		08 54					09 00								10 58		11 46				12 00		
Brough	d		09 06					09 12								11 10		11 58				12 12		
Howden	d		09 18															12 10						
Selby	d		09a27					09 33								11 29		12a19				12 32		
South Milford	d							09 42								11 38								
Garforth	d																							
Leeds 10	a				09 03		09 38	10 00			10 38		11 08		11 38	11 56	12 08			12 38		12 56	13 08	
	d	08 44			09 10		09 40	10 08			10 40	10 44	11 10		11 40	11 59	12 10			12 40	12 44	12 59	13 10	
Cottingley	d	09 00										10 49									12 49			
Morley	d	09 11										10 53									12 53			
Batley	d	09 22										10 58									12 58			
Dewsbury	a	09 30			09 20		09 51				10 51	11 01			11 51					12 51	13 01			
	d	09 31			09 21		09 51				10 51	11 02			11 51					12 51	13 02			
Ravensthorpe	d	09 39										11 05									13 05			
Mirfield	d	09 45										11 09									13 09			
Deighton	d	09 56										11 15									13 20			
Huddersfield	a	10 05			09 30		10 00	10 25			11 00	11 20	11 27		12 00	12 16	12 27			13 00	13 24	13 16	13 27	
	d				09 31	09 37	10 01	10 26	10 37		11 01		11 28	11 37	12 01	12 17	12 28		12 37	13 01		13 17	13 28	13 37
Slaithwaite	d					09 44			10 44					11 44					12 44					13 44
Marsden	d					09 50			10 50					11 50					12 50					13 50
Greenfield	d					09 58			10 58					11 58					12 58					13 58
Mossley (Grtr Manchester)	d					10 02			11 02					12 02					13 02					14 02
Stalybridge	a				09 50	10 07		10 45	11 07				11 45	12 07			12 45		13 07				13 45	14 07
	d				09 50	10 08		10 46	11 08				11 46	12 08			12 46		13 08				13 46	14 08
Ashton-under-Lyne	d					10 12			11 12					12 12					13 12					14 12
Manchester Victoria	a					10 26			11 26					12 26					13 26					14 26
	d																							
Manchester Piccadilly 10	a				10 10		10 34	11 03			11 34		12 05		12 34	12 58	13 05			13 34		13 54	14 05	
	d			09 07	10 12		10 38			11 07	11 38		12 07		12 38		13 07			13 38			14 07	
Manchester Airport	a						10 55				11 55				12 55					13 55				
Manchester Oxford Road	a			09 09	10 14					11 09			12 09				13 09						14 09	
Newton-le-Willows	a																							
Birchwood	a			09 25	10 28					11 25			12 25				13 25						14 25	
Warrington Central	a			09 30	10 33					11 30			12 30				13 30						14 30	
L'pool South Parkway 7	a			09 47	10 49					11 46			12 47				13 47						14 47	
Liverpool Lime Street 10	a			10 00	11 00					11 59			12 58				13 58						14 58	

Table 39

Sundays
from 30 October

Newcastle, Middlesbrough, Scarborough, York, Hull and Leeds - Huddersfield - Manchester, Manchester Airport and Liverpool

		TP	TP	TP	NT	NT	TP	NT	TP	TP	NT	TP	TP	TP	NT	TP	NT	TP	TP	NT	TP	TP	TP
		◇1	◇1	◇1			◇1		◇1	◇1		◇1	◇1	◇1		◇1		◇1	◇1		◇1	◇1	◇1
Newcastle 8	d	12 10					13 04					14 08				15 07					16 08		
Chester-le-Street	d						13 13									15 16							
Durham	d	12 22					13 20					14 20				15 23					16 20		
Middlesbrough	d			12 45										14 42									16 42
Thornaby	d			12 50										14 47									16 47
Yarm	d			12 58										14 55									16 55
Darlington 7	d	12 39					13 37					14 37				15 40					16 37		
Northallerton	d			13 13								14 49		15 10							16 49		17 10
Thirsk	d			13 21										15 18									17 18
Scarborough	d									13 51									15 51				
Seamer	d									13 56									15 56				
Malton	d									14 14									16 14				
York 8	a	13 11		13 42			14 10			14 40		15 12		15 42		16 13			16 40		17 12		17 42
	d	13 15		13 45			14 15		14 33	14 45		15 15		15 45		16 15		16 33	16 45		17 15		17 45
Hull	d		12 58		14 23								14 58									16 58	
Brough	d		13 10		14 35								15 10									17 10	
Howden	d				14 47																		
Selby	d		13 29		14a56								15 29									17 29	
South Milford	d		13 38										15 38									17 38	
Garforth	d																						
Leeds 10	a	13 38	13 56	14 08			14 38		14 56	15 09		15 38	15 56	16 08		16 38		16 56	17 08		17 38	17 56	18 08
	d	13 40	13 59	14 10			14 40	14 44	14 59	15 11		15 40	15 59	16 10		16 40	16 44	16 59	17 10		17 40	17 59	18 10
Cottingley	d							14 49									16 49						
Morley	d							14 53									16 53						
Batley	d							14 58									16 58						
Dewsbury	a	13 51					14 51	15 01				15 51				16 51	17 01				17 51		
	d	13 51					14 51	15 02				15 51				16 51	17 02				17 51		
Ravensthorpe	d							15 05									17 05						
Mirfield	d							15 09									17 09						
Deighton	d							15 20									17 20						
Huddersfield	a	14 00	14 16	14 27			15 00	15 24	15 16	15 28		16 00	16 16	16 27		17 00	17 24	17 16	17 27		18 00	18 16	18 27
	d	14 01	14 17	14 28		14 37	15 01		15 17	15 29	15 37	16 01	16 17	16 28	16 37	17 01		17 17	17 28	17 37	18 01	18 17	18 28
Slaithwaite	d					14 44					15 44				16 44					17 44			
Marsden	d					14 50					15 50				16 50					17 50			
Greenfield	d					14 58					15 58				16 58					17 58			
Mossley (Grtr Manchester)	d					15 02					16 02				17 02					18 02			
Stalybridge	a			14 45		15 07				15 46	16 07			16 45	17 07				17 45	18 07			18 45
	d			14 46		15 08				15 47	16 08			16 46	17 08				17 46	18 08			18 46
Ashton-under-Lyne	d					15 12					16 12				17 12					18 12			
Manchester Victoria	a					15 26					16 26				17 26					18 26			
	d																						
Manchester Piccadilly 10	a	14 34	14 54	15 05			15 34		15 54	16 05		16 34	16 54	17 05		17 34		17 54	18 05		18 34	18 54	19 05
	d	14 38		15 07			15 38			16 07		16 38		17 07		17 38			18 07		18 38		19 07
Manchester Airport	a	14 55					15 55					16 55				17 55					18 55		
Manchester Oxford Road	a			15 09						16 09				17 09					18 09				19 09
Newton-le-Willows	a																						
Birchwood	a			15 25						16 25				17 25					18 25				19 25
Warrington Central	a			15 30						16 30				17 30					18 30				19 30
L'pool South Parkway 7	a			15 47						16 47				17 47					18 47				19 47
Liverpool Lime Street 10	a			15 58						16 58				17 58					18 58				19 58

Table 39

Sundays
from 30 October

Newcastle, Middlesbrough, Scarborough, York, Hull and Leeds - Huddersfield - Manchester, Manchester Airport and Liverpool

		NT	NT	TP	NT	TP	TP	NT	TP	TP	TP	NT	NT	TP	NT	TP	TP	NT	TP	TP	NT	TP
				◇1		◇1	◇1		◇1	◇1	◇1			◇1		◇1	◇1		◇1	◇1		◇1
Newcastle 8	d			17 05					17 52					19 10					20 08		21 06	
Chester-le-Street	d			17 14																	21 15	
Durham	d			17 21					18 04					19 22					20 20		21 24	
Middlesbrough	d										18 45						20 06					
Thornaby	d										18 50						20 11					
Yarm	d										18 58						20 19					
Darlington 7	d			17 38					18 21					19 39					20 37		21a44	
Northallerton	d			17 49					18 33		19 13						20 38		20 49			
Thirsk	d										19 21						20 46					
Scarborough	d						17 51									19 51						21 20
Seamer	d						17 56									19 56						21 25
Malton	d						18 14									20 14						21 43
York 8	a			18 12			18 40		19 04		19 42			20 11		20 40	21 06		21 12			22 09
	d			18 15		18 33	18 45		19 15		19 45			20 15		20 45			21 15			22 12
Hull	d	17 23								18 58		20 29								21 00		
Brough	d	17 35								19 10		20 41								21 12		
Howden	d	17 47										20 53										
Selby	d	17a56								19 29		21a02								21 31		
South Milford	d									19 38										21 40		
Garforth	d																					
Leeds 10	a			18 38		18 57	19 08		19 38	19 54	20 08			20 38		21 08			21 38	21 59		22 36
	d			18 40	18 44	18 59	19 10		19 40	19 59	20 10			20 40	20 44	21 10			21 40			22 40
Cottingley	d				18 49										20 49							
Morley	d				18 53										20 53							
Batley	d				18 58										20 58							
Dewsbury	a			18 51	19 01				19 51					20 51	21 01				21 51			
	d			18 51	19 02				19 51					20 51	21 02				21 51			
Ravensthorpe	d				19 05										21 05							
Mirfield	d				19 09										21 09							
Deighton	d				19 20										21 15							
Huddersfield	a			19 00	19 24	19 16	19 27		20 00	20 16	20 27			21 00	21 19	21 27			22 00			22 57
	d		18 37	19 01		19 17	19 28	19 37	20 01	20 17	20 28		20 37	21 01	21 19	21 28		21 37	22 01			22 58
Slaithwaite	d		18 44					19 44					20 44		21 26			21 44				
Marsden	d		18 50					19 50					20 50		21a33			21 50				
Greenfield	d		18 58					19 58					20 58					21 58				
Mossley (Grtr Manchester)	d		19 02					20 02					21 02					22 02				
Stalybridge	a		19 07				19 45	20 07			20 45		21 07	21 18				22 07	22 18			23 18
	d		19 08				19 46	20 08			20 46		21 08	21 19				22 08	22 19			23 19
Ashton-under-Lyne	d		19 12					20 12					21 12					22 12				
Manchester Victoria	a		19 26					20 26					21 26					22 26				
	d																					
Manchester Piccadilly 10	a			19 34		19 54	20 05		20 34	20 54	21 05			21 36		22 05			22 36			23 36
	d			19 38			20 07		20 38		21 07					22 07			22 38			
Manchester Airport	a			19 55					20 55										22 55			
Manchester Oxford Road	a						20 09				21 09					22 09						
Newton-le-Willows	a																					
Birchwood	a						20 25				21 25					22 25						
Warrington Central	a						20 30				21 30					22 30						
L'pool South Parkway 7	a						20 47				21 47					22 47						
Liverpool Lime Street 10	a						20 58				21 58					23 00						

Table 39

Sundays
from 30 October

Newcastle, Middlesbrough, Scarborough, York, Hull and Leeds - Huddersfield - Manchester, Manchester Airport and Liverpool

		NT	TP
			◇1
Newcastle 8	d		
Chester-le-Street	d		
Durham	d		
Middlesbrough	d		22 06
Thornaby	d		22 11
Yarm	d		22 19
Darlington 7	d		
Northallerton	d		22 34
Thirsk	d		22 42
Scarborough	d		
Seamer	d		
Malton	d		
York 8	a		23 09
	d		23 12
Hull	d		
Brough	d		
Howden	d		
Selby	d		
South Milford	d		
Garforth	d		
Leeds 10	a		23 38
	d	22 44	23 40
Cottingley	d	22 49	
Morley	d	22 53	
Batley	d	22 58	
Dewsbury	a	23 01	23 51
	d	23 02	23 51
Ravensthorpe	d	23 05	
Mirfield	d	23 09	
Deighton	d	23 16	
Huddersfield	a	23 20	23 59
	d		00 01
Slaithwaite	d		
Marsden	d		
Greenfield	d		
Mossley (Grtr Manchester)	d		
Stalybridge	a		
	d		
Ashton-under-Lyne	d		
Manchester Victoria	a		
	d		
Manchester Piccadilly 10	a		00 43
	d		00 44
Manchester Airport	a		01 00
Manchester Oxford Road	a		
Newton-le-Willows	a		
Birchwood	a		
Warrington Central	a		
L'pool South Parkway 7	a		
Liverpool Lime Street 10	a		

Liverpool, Manchester Airport and Manchester - Huddersfield - Wakefield, Leeds, Hull, York, Scarborough, Middlesbrough and Newcastle

Miles	Miles	Miles	Miles	Miles			TP	TP	TP MX	TP	TP	TP MX	TP	TP MX	TP MX	TP	TP	TP MX	TP MO	NT	TP	TP	TP	NT
							◇1 A	◇1 B	◇1	◇1 C	◇1 D	◇1	◇1 B	◇1	◇1	◇1 B	◇1 A	◇1	◇1		◇1	◇1	◇1	
0	—	—	—	—	**Liverpool Lime Street** 10	d	20p22	20p22		21p52	21p52		21p52	22p30										
5½	—	—	—	—	L'pool South Parkway 7 ✈	d	20p32			22p02	22p02			22p40										
18½	—	—	—	—	Warrington Central	d	20p45			22p15	22p15			22p53										
21¾	—	—	—	—	Birchwood	d	20p50			22p20	22p20			22p58										
34¼	—	—	—	—	Manchester Oxford Road	d	21p07			22p37	22p37			23p17										
—	—	—	—	—	**Manchester Airport** ✈	d			21p20			22p22			23p18	23p25	23p20	00 38	00 48			04 12		
34¾	—	—	—	—	**Manchester Piccadilly** 10	a	21p09		21p36	22p39	22p39	22p36		23p19	23p34	23p38	23p37	00 51	01 01			04 27		
—	—	—	—	—		d	21p11		21p42	22p42	22p42	22p42		23p21	23p38	23p40	23p42	00 53	01 03			04 30	05 39	
—	—	—	—	0	**Manchester Victoria**	d		21p05					22b38		23p56	23p55								
—	—	—	—	6½	Ashton-under-Lyne	d																		
42¼	—	—	—	7¾	**Stalybridge**	a	21p24		21p55	22p54	22p54	22p55		23p34									05 52	
—	—	—	—	—		d	21p24		21p55	22p54	22p54	22p55		23p34									05 52	
45	—	—	—	10½	Mossley (Grtr Manchester)	d																		
47½	—	—	—	12¾	Greenfield	d																		
53¼	—	—	—	18¾	Marsden	d																		
55¾	—	—	—	21¼	Slaithwaite	d																		
60¼	—	—	—	25¾	**Huddersfield**	a	21p42		22p15	23p12	23p12	23p15	23p23	23p52	00 25	00 40	00 11					05 31	06 10	
—	—	—	—	—		d	21p43		22p16	23p12	23p12	23p16	23p26	23p53	00 26	00 43	00 12			05 32		05 38	06 11	
62¼	—	—	—	27¾	Deighton	d														05 36				
65¼	—	—	—	30¾	Mirfield	d														05 41				
66¾	—	—	—	—	Ravensthorpe	d																		
68¼	—	—	—	—	**Dewsbury**	a		21p58	22p25	23p22	23p22	23p25	23p35		00s35									
—	—	—	—	—		d		21p59	22p26	23p22	23p22	23p26	23p35											
69¾	—	—	—	—	Batley	d																		
73	—	—	—	—	Morley	d																		
74½	—	—	—	—	Cottingley	d																		
77½	0	—	0	—	**Leeds** 10	a	22p04	22p12	22p41	23p37	23p39	23p41	23p50	00 32	00 50	01 04	00 51	02 03	02 32			06 01	06 32	
—	—	—	—	—		d	22p12	22p12	22p42	23p40	23p42	23p45	23p53	00 32	00 54	01 06	00 54	02 08	02 34			06 04	06 35	06 38
84¾	7¼	—	7¼	—	Garforth	d																		06 50
—	12¾	—	—	—	South Milford	a																		
—	20¾	—	—	—	Selby	a																		
—	29½	—	—	—	Howden	a																		
—	41¼	—	—	—	Brough	a																		
—	51¾	—	—	—	**Hull**	a																		
—	—	—	—	—	Wakefield Kirkgate	a														05 57				
—	—	—	—	—	**Wakefield Westgate**	a														06 05				
103	—	0	25½	—	**York** 8	a	22p40	22p40	23p09	00 09	00 26	00 28	00 22	01 16	01 43	01 34	01 22	02 45	03 04			06 28	07 01	07 15
—	—	—	—	—		d	22p42	22p42	23p18												05 54	06 40	07 06	
—	—	—	46½	—	Malton	d																07 04		
—	—	—	64¾	—	Seamer	a																07 21		
—	—	—	67½	—	**Scarborough**	a																07 30		
125½	—	22¼	—	—	Thirsk	a	23p06	23p05	23p31												06 10		07 22	
133	—	30½	—	—	Northallerton	a	23p16	23p15	23p49												06 18		07 30	
147	—	—	—	—	**Darlington** 7	a	23p28	23p28	00 01												06 29		07 41	
—	—	42¼	—	—	Yarm	d																		
—	—	47½	—	—	Thornaby	a															06 52			
—	—	50¾	—	—	**Middlesbrough**	a															07 03			
169	—	—	—	—	Durham	a	23p45	23p45	00 18														07 58	
174¾	—	—	—	—	Chester-le-Street	a																	08 04	
183	—	—	—	—	**Newcastle** 8	a	00 15	00 15	00 52														08 17	

A MO until 12 September, MO from 31 October
B MO from 19 September until 24 October
C MO until 20 June
D MO from 27 June until 12 September, MO from 31 October
b Previous night, arr. 2229

Liverpool, Manchester Airport and Manchester - Huddersfield - Wakefield, Leeds, Hull, York, Scarborough, Middlesbrough and Newcastle

		NT	TP	NT	NT	NT	TP	NT	NT	NT	TP	TP	NT	NT	NT	NT	TP		NT	NT	TP	NT
			◇1				◇1 ⚲				◇1	◇1 ⚲					◇1 ⚲				◇1 ⚲	
Liverpool Lime Street 10	d																06 15					
L'pool South Parkway 7 ✈	d																06 25					
Warrington Central	d																06 38					
Birchwood	d																06 43					
Manchester Oxford Road	d																07 07					
Manchester Airport ✈	d		05 37									06 23									07 05	
Manchester Piccadilly 10	a		05 51									06 39					07 09				07 22	
	d		05 57				06 21					06 54					07 11				07 27	
Manchester Victoria	d							05 51						06 17	06 55				06 43			06 58
Ashton-under-Lyne	d														07 05							
Stalybridge	a											07 07			07 10		07 23					
	d									06 41		07 07			07 11		07 23					
Mossley (Grtr Manchester)	d									06 45					07 15							
Greenfield	d									06 49					07 19							
Marsden	d								06 48	06 58					07 28							
Slaithwaite	d								06 52	07 02					07 32							
Huddersfield	a		06 26				06 54		07 00	07 10		07 25			07 41		07 44				07 56	
	d		06 27		06 31	06 41	06 56		07 00			07 26				07 29	07 45			07 49	07 57	
Deighton	d				06 34	06 45			07 03											07 53		
Mirfield	d				06 39	06 50			07 08				07 20							07 58		08 06
Ravensthorpe	d				06 42				07 11				07 23									
Dewsbury	a		06 36		06 46		07 05		07 15				07 27				07 54				08 06	08 11
	d		06 37		06 46		07 06		07 15				07 35				07 55				08 07	08 12
Batley	d				06 49				07 18				07 38									08 15
Morley	d				06 55				07 24				07 44									08 21
Cottingley	d				06 59				07 28				07 47									08 24
Leeds 10	a		06 52		07 09		07 19	07 27	07 38			07 48	07 55	07 57		08 29	08 10		08 12		08 24	08 33
	d	06 48	06 55	06 58			07 23	07 29				07 50		08 00			08 12		08 15		08 28	
Garforth	d	06 58		07 10				07 41				08 00		08 12					08 27			
South Milford	a			07 20										08 22					08 38			
Selby	a	07 20		07 31			07 43							08 36					08 53			
Howden	a						07 52															
Brough	a						08 04															
Hull	a						08 20															
Wakefield Kirkgate	a					07 03														08 13		
Wakefield Westgate	a					07 10														08 20		
York 8	a		07 22					08 06				08 21					08 35				08 55	
	d		07 25								07 32	08 23					08 40	08 42			08 58	
Malton	d		07 49														09 04					
Seamer	a		08 06														09 21					
Scarborough	a		08 15														09 30					
Thirsk	a										07 52	08 39										
Northallerton	a										08 00	08 49									09 18	
Darlington 7	a																	09 11			09 30	
Yarm	d										08 14	09 03										
Thornaby	a										08 24	09 11										
Middlesbrough	a										08 32	09 21										
Durham	a																	09 28			09 47	
Chester-le-Street	a																				09 55	
Newcastle 8	a																	09 45			10 07	

Liverpool, Manchester Airport and Manchester - Huddersfield - Wakefield, Leeds, Hull, York, Scarborough, Middlesbrough and Newcastle

		TP	NT	NT	TP	NT	NT		TP	NT	TP	NT	NT	NT	NT	TP	TP		NT	NT	TP	NT	NT	TP	NT
		◇1			◇1				◇1		◇1					◇1	◇1				◇1			◇1	
Liverpool Lime Street 10	d								07 15					07 16							08 22				
L'pool South Parkway 7 ✈	d								07 25												08 32				
Warrington Central	d								07 40												08 45				
Birchwood	d								07 45												08 50				
Manchester Oxford Road	d								08 06												09 07				
Manchester Airport ✈	d				07 35						08 05						08 35							09 05	
Manchester Piccadilly 10	a				07 49				08 08		08 22						08 49				09 09			09 22	
	d	07 36			07 56				08 10		08 26					08 42	08 55				09 11			09 27	
Manchester Victoria	d		07 40							07 48		08 00	08 02	08 27								08 48	08 57		09 00
Ashton-under-Lyne	d		07 49										08 12	08 37									09 07		
Stalybridge	a	07 49	07 54		08 09				08 26				08 18	08 41							09 26		09 13		
	d	07 49	07 54		08 09				08 26					08 42							09 26				
Mossley (Grtr Manchester)	d		07 59											08 46											
Greenfield	d		08 03											08 50											
Marsden	d		08 11											08 59											
Slaithwaite	d		08 16											09 03											
Huddersfield	a	08 09	08 24		08 28				08 44		08 56			09 13		09 15	09 26				09 44			09 56	
	d	08 10		08 13	08 30	08 33	08 37		08 45		08 57					09 16	09 27		09 31	09 35	09 45			09 57	
Deighton	d			08 16		08 36	08 40												09 34	09 38					
Mirfield	d			08 21		08 41	08 45					09 07							09 39	09 43					10 07
Ravensthorpe	d			08 24		08 44													09 42						
Dewsbury	a	08 19		08 27	08 39	08 48					09 06	09 12					09 36		09 46					10 06	10 12
	d	08 20		08 27	08 39	08 53					09 07	09 12					09 37		09 46					10 07	10 12
Batley	d			08 30		08 56						09 15							09 49						10 15
Morley	d			08 36		09 02						09 21							09 55						10 21
Cottingley	d			08 39		09 06													09 59						
Leeds 10	a	08 36		08 52	08 54	09 17			09 09	09 12	09 22	09 32				09 36	09 52		10 07		10 09	10 12		10 22	10 32
	d	08 38			08 57				09 12	09 15	09 28				09 33	09 38	09 57				10 12	10 15		10 28	
Garforth	d				09 05					09 27							10 05					10 27			
South Milford	a									09 38												10 38			
Selby	a	08 57								09 53						09 57						10 53			
Howden	a																								
Brough	a															10 15									
Hull	a	09 31														10 34									
Wakefield Kirkgate	a						09 02													10 03					
Wakefield Westgate	a						09 08													10 10					
York 8	a				09 23				09 36		09 54				10 06		10 23				10 36			10 52	
	d				09 26				09 41		09 58						10 26				10 41			10 58	
Malton	d								10 04												11 04				
Seamer	a								10 21												11 21				
Scarborough	a								10 32												11 30				
Thirsk	a				09 45												10 45								
Northallerton	a				09 58						10 18						10 58							11 18	
Darlington 7	a										10 30													11 30	
Yarm	d				10 14												11 14								
Thornaby	a				10 22												11 22								
Middlesbrough	a				10 30												11 30								
Durham	a										10 47													11 47	
Chester-le-Street	a																							11 53	
Newcastle 8	a										11 05													12 06	

Liverpool, Manchester Airport and Manchester - Huddersfield - Wakefield, Leeds, Hull, York, Scarborough, Middlesbrough and Newcastle

		NT	NT		TP	NT	TP	NT	NT	TP	NT	TP	NT		NT	NT	TP	TP	NT	NT	TP	NT	TP		NT
					◇1		◇1			◇1		◇1					◇1	◇1			◇1		◇1		
Liverpool Lime Street 10	d		08 44							09 22						09 46					10 22				
L'pool South Parkway 7 ✈	d									09 32											10 32				
Warrington Central	d									09 45											10 45				
Birchwood	d									09 50											10 50				
Manchester Oxford Road	d									10 07											11 07				
Manchester Airport ✈	d						09 35					10 05						10 35					11 05		
Manchester Piccadilly 10	a						09 52			10 09		10 22						10 52			11 09		11 22		
	d				09 42		09 57			10 11		10 27					10 42	10 57			11 11		11 27		
Manchester Victoria	d	09 27	09 57								09 48		10 00		10 27	10 57						10 48			11 00
Ashton-under-Lyne	d	09 37	10 07												10 37	11 07									
Stalybridge	a	09 42	10 13							10 26					10 42	11 13					11 26				
	d	09 42								10 26					10 42						11 26				
Mossley (Grtr Manchester)	d	09 47													10 47										
Greenfield	d	09 51													10 51										
Marsden	d	09 59													10 59										
Slaithwaite	d	10 04													11 04										
Huddersfield	a	10 12			10 15		10 26			10 44		10 56			11 12		11 15	11 26			11 44		11 56		
	d				10 16		10 27	10 31	10 35	10 45		10 57					11 16	11 27	11 31	11 35	11 45		11 57		
Deighton	d							10 34	10 38										11 34	11 38					
Mirfield	d							10 39	10 43				11 07						11 39	11 43					12 07
Ravensthorpe	d							10 42											11 42						
Dewsbury	a						10 36	10 46				11 06	11 12					11 36	11 46				12 06		12 12
	d						10 37	10 46				11 07	11 12					11 37	11 46				12 07		12 12
Batley	d							10 49					11 15						11 49						12 15
Morley	d							10 55					11 21						11 55						12 21
Cottingley	d							10 59											11 59						
Leeds 10	a				10 36		10 52	11 07		11 09	11 13	11 22	11 33				11 36	11 52	12 07		12 09	12 12	12 22		12 31
	d				10 38	10 41	10 57			11 12	11 15	11 28					11 38	11 57			12 12	12 15	12 28		
Garforth	d					10 53	11 05				11 27							12 05				12 27			
South Milford	a										11 38											12 38			
Selby	a				10 57						11 54						11 57					12 50			
Howden	a																								
Brough	a				11 15												12 15								
Hull	a				11 34												12 36								
Wakefield Kirkgate	a								11 02											12 02					
Wakefield Westgate	a								11 08											12 08					
York 8	a					11 19	11 23			11 36		11 54						12 23			12 36		12 52		
	d						11 26			11 41		11 58						12 26			12 41		12 58		
Malton	d									12 04											13 04				
Seamer	a									12 21											13 21				
Scarborough	a									12 30											13 32				
Thirsk	a						11 45											12 45							
Northallerton	a						11 58					12 18						12 59					13 18		
Darlington 7	a											12 30											13 30		
Yarm	d						12 14											13 14							
Thornaby	a						12 22											13 22							
Middlesbrough	a						12 30											13 30							
Durham	a											12 47											13 47		
Chester-le-Street	a																						13 53		
Newcastle 8	a											13 03											14 06		

Liverpool, Manchester Airport and Manchester - Huddersfield - Wakefield, Leeds, Hull, York, Scarborough, Middlesbrough and Newcastle

		NT	NT	TP	NT	TP	NT	TP	NT	TP	NT	NT	NT	TP	TP	NT	NT	TP	NT	TP	NT	NT	NT
				◇1 🛒		◇1 🛒		◇1 🛒		◇1 🛒				◇1 🛒	◇1 🛒			◇1 🛒		◇1 🛒			
Liverpool Lime Street 10	d		10 46					11 22					11 46					12 22					12 46
L'pool South Parkway 7 ✈	d							11 32										12 32					
Warrington Central	d							11 45										12 45					
Birchwood	d							11 50										12 50					
Manchester Oxford Road	d							12 07										13 07					
Manchester Airport ✈	d					11 35				12 05					12 35					13 05			
Manchester Piccadilly 10	a					11 52		12 09		12 22					12 52			13 09		13 22			
	d			11 42		11 57		12 11		12 27				12 42	12 57			13 11		13 27			
Manchester Victoria	d	11 27	11 57						11 48		12 00	12 27	12 57						12 48		13 00	13 27	13 57
Ashton-under-Lyne	d	11 37	12 07									12 37	13 07									13 37	14 07
Stalybridge	a	11 42	12 13					12 26				12 42	13 13					13 26				13 42	14 13
	d	11 42						12 26				12 42						13 26				13 42	
Mossley (Grtr Manchester)	d	11 47										12 47										13 47	
Greenfield	d	11 51										12 51										13 51	
Marsden	d	11 59										12 59										13 59	
Slaithwaite	d	12 04										13 04										14 04	
Huddersfield	a	12 12		12 15		12 26		12 44		12 56		13 12		13 15	13 26			13 44		13 56		14 12	
	d			12 16		12 27	12 31	12 45		12 57				13 16	13 27	13 31	13 35	13 45		13 57			
Deighton	d						12 34									13 34	13 38						
Mirfield	d						12 39				13 07					13 39	13 43				14 07		
Ravensthorpe	d						12 42									13 42							
Dewsbury	a					12 36	12 46			13 06	13 12				13 36	13 46				14 06	14 12		
	d					12 37	12 46			13 07	13 12				13 37	13 46				14 07	14 12		
Batley	d						12 49				13 15					13 49					14 15		
Morley	d						12 55				13 21					13 55					14 21		
Cottingley	d						12 59									13 59							
Leeds 10	a			12 36		12 52	13 07	13 09	13 12	13 22	13 32			13 36	13 52	14 07		14 09	14 13	14 22	14 32		
	d			12 38	12 41	12 57		13 12	13 15	13 28				13 38	13 57			14 12	14 15	14 28			
Garforth	d				12 53	13 05			13 27						14 05				14 27				
South Milford	a								13 38										14 38				
Selby	a			12 57					13 51					13 57					14 51				
Howden	a																						
Brough	a			13 15										14 15									
Hull	a			13 34										14 34									
Wakefield Kirkgate	a																14 02						
Wakefield Westgate	a																14 08						
York 8	a				13 19	13 23		13 36		13 54					14 23			14 36		14 52			
	d					13 29		13 41		13 58					14 26			14 41		14 58			
Malton	d							14 04										15 04					
Seamer	a							14 21										15 21					
Scarborough	a							14 30										15 30					
Thirsk	a					13 45									14 45								
Northallerton	a					13 58				14 18					14 58					15 18			
Darlington 7	a									14 30										15 30			
Yarm	d					14 14									15 14								
Thornaby	a					14 22									15 22								
Middlesbrough	a					14 30									15 30								
Durham	a									14 47										15 47			
Chester-le-Street	a																			15 53			
Newcastle 8	a									15 05										16 09			

Table 39

Mondays to Fridays

Liverpool, Manchester Airport and Manchester - Huddersfield - Wakefield, Leeds, Hull, York, Scarborough, Middlesbrough and Newcastle

		TP	NT	TP	NT	NT	TP	NT	TP	TP	NT	NT	NT	TP	TP	NT	NT	TP	NT	TP	NT	NT	NT
									FO	FX													
		◇1 🛒		◇1 🛒			◇1 🛒		◇1 🛒	◇1 🛒				◇1 🛒	◇1 🛒			◇1 🛒		◇1 🛒			
Liverpool Lime Street 10	d						13 22						13 46					14 22					14 46
L'pool South Parkway 7 ✈	d						13 32											14 32					
Warrington Central	d						13 45											14 45					
Birchwood	d						13 50											14 50					
Manchester Oxford Road	d						14 07											15 07					
Manchester Airport ✈	d			13 35					14 05	14 05					14 35					15 05			
Manchester Piccadilly 10	a			13 52			14 09		14 22	14 22					14 52			15 09		15 22			
	d	13 42		13 57			14 11		14 27	14 27				14 42	14 57			15 11		15 27			
Manchester Victoria	d							13 48			14 00	14 27	14 57						14 48		15 00	15 27	15 57
Ashton-under-Lyne	d											14 37	15 07									15 37	16 07
Stalybridge	a						14 26					14 42	15 13					15 26				15 42	16 13
	d						14 26					14 42						15 26				15 42	
Mossley (Grtr Manchester)	d											14 47										15 47	
Greenfield	d											14 51										15 51	
Marsden	d											14 59										15 59	
Slaithwaite	d											15 04										16 04	
Huddersfield	a	14 15		14 26			14 44		14 56	14 56		15 12		15 15	15 26			15 44		15 56		16 12	
	d	14 16		14 27	14 31	14 35	14 45		14 57	14 57				15 16	15 27	15 31	15 35	15 45		15 57			
Deighton	d				14 34	14 38										15 34	15 38						
Mirfield	d				14 39	14 43					15 07					15 39	15 43				16 07		
Ravensthorpe	d				14 42											15 42							
Dewsbury	a			14 36	14 46				15 06	15 06	15 12				15 36	15 46				16 06	16 12		
	d			14 37	14 46				15 08	15 07	15 12				15 37	15 46				16 07	16 12		
Batley	d				14 49						15 15					15 49					16 15		
Morley	d				14 55						15 21					15 55					16 21		
Cottingley	d				14 59											15 59							
Leeds 10	a	14 36		14 52	15 07		15 09	15 12	15 22	15 22	15 32			15 36	15 52	16 07		16 09	16 12	16 22	16 32		
	d	14 38	14 41	14 57			15 12	15 15	15 28	15 28				15 38	15 56			16 12	16 15	16 28			
Garforth	d		14 53	15 05				15 27							16 05				16 27				
South Milford	a							15 38											16 39				
Selby	a	14 57						15 53						15 57					16 54				
Howden	a																						
Brough	a	15 15												16 15									
Hull	a	15 34												16 34									
Wakefield Kirkgate	a					15 02											16 02						
Wakefield Westgate	a					15 08											16 08						
York 8	a		15 18	15 23			15 36		15 53	15 53					16 23			16 36		16 52			
	d			15 26			15 41								16 25			16 41		16 55			
Malton	d						16 04											17 04					
Seamer	a						16 21											17 21					
Scarborough	a						16 30											17 30					
Thirsk	a			15 45											16 45					17 13			
Northallerton	a			15 58											16 59					17 21			
Darlington 7	a																			17 32			
Yarm	d			16 14											17 14								
Thornaby	a			16 22											17 22								
Middlesbrough	a			16 30											17 30								
Durham	a																			17 49			
Chester-le-Street	a																			17 55			
Newcastle 8	a																			18 08			

Table 39

Mondays to Fridays

Liverpool, Manchester Airport and Manchester - Huddersfield - Wakefield, Leeds, Hull, York, Scarborough, Middlesbrough and Newcastle

		TP ◇1 ⌶	NT	TP ◇1 ⌶	NT	NT	TP ◇1 ⌶	NT	TP ◇1 ⌶	NT	NT	NT	TP ◇1 ⌶	NT	NT	TP ◇1 ⌶	NT	NT	NT	TP ◇1 ⌶	NT	NT A
Liverpool Lime Street 10	d						15 22										15 46			16 22		
L'pool South Parkway 7 ✈	d						15 32													16 32		
Warrington Central	d						15 45													16 45		
Birchwood	d						15 50													16 50		
Manchester Oxford Road	d						16 07													17 07		
Manchester Airport ✈	d			15 35					16 05							16 35						
Manchester Piccadilly 10	a			15 52			16 09		16 22							16 52				17 09		
	d	15 42		15 57			16 11		16 27				16 42			16 56				17 11		
Manchester Victoria	d							15 48		16 00	16 17	16 27					16 57				16 48	17 15
Ashton-under-Lyne	d										16 27	16 37					17 07					17 24
Stalybridge	a						16 26				16 33	16 42				17 08	17 12			17 26		17 29
	d						16 26					16 42				17 08	17 12			17 26		17 29
Mossley (Grtr Manchester)	d											16 47					17 17					17 34
Greenfield	d											16 51					17 21					17 38
Marsden	d											16 59					17 29					
Slaithwaite	d											17 04					17 34					
Huddersfield	a	16 15		16 26			16 44		16 56			17 12	17 15			17 26	17 42			17 44		17 54
	d	16 16		16 27	16 31	16 35	16 45		16 57				17 16			17 27		17 31	17 35	17 45		
Deighton	d				16 34	16 38												17 34	17 38			
Mirfield	d				16 39	16 43				17 07								17 39	17 43			
Ravensthorpe	d				16 42													17 42				
Dewsbury	a			16 36	16 46				17 06	17 12						17 36		17 46				
	d			16 37	16 46				17 07	17 12						17 37		17 46				
Batley	d				16 49					17 15								17 49				
Morley	d				16 55					17 21								17 55				
Cottingley	d				16 59													17 59				
Leeds 10	a	16 36		16 52	17 07		17 09	17 12	17 22	17 31			17 36			17 52		18 06		18 09	18 12	
	d	16 38	16 41	16 57			17 12	17 15	17 24				17 38	17 41	17 46	17 57				18 12	18 15	
Garforth	d		16 53	17 05				17 28	17 34					17 53	17 58	18 05					18 27	
South Milford	a							17 39							18 09						18 38	
Selby	a	17 00						17 51					17 59		18 21						18 49	
Howden	a												18 08									
Brough	a	17 18											18 20									
Hull	a	17 37											18 40									
Wakefield Kirkgate	a					17 02													18 02			
Wakefield Westgate	a					17 08													18 08			
York 8	a		17 20	17 21			17 37		17 55					18 19		18 23				18 35		
	d			17 24			17 40		18 00							18 26				18 43		
Malton	d			17 47					18 24											19 07		
Seamer	a			18 04					18 41											19 24		
Scarborough	a			18 15					18 50											19 32		
Thirsk	a						18 00									18 45						
Northallerton	a						18 08									18 58						
Darlington 7	a																					
Yarm	d						18 24									19 14						
Thornaby	a						18 32									19 22						
Middlesbrough	a						18 40									19 32						
Durham	a																					
Chester-le-Street	a																					
Newcastle 8	a																					

A until 30 September

Table 39

Mondays to Fridays

Liverpool, Manchester Airport and Manchester - Huddersfield - Wakefield, Leeds, Hull, York, Scarborough, Middlesbrough and Newcastle

		TP ◇1 ⌶	NT	NT	TP ◇1 ⌶	TP ◇1 ⌶	NT	NT FO	NT FX	NT	TP ◇1 ⌶	NT	TP ◇1 ⌶	NT	NT	TP FO ◇1 ⌶	TP FX ◇1 ⌶	NT	NT	TP ◇1	NT	NT	TP ◇1
Liverpool Lime Street 10	d						16 46				17 22												18 22
L'pool South Parkway 7 ✈	d										17 32												18 32
Warrington Central	d										17 45												18 45
Birchwood	d										17 50												18 50
Manchester Oxford Road	d										18 07												19 07
Manchester Airport ✈	d	17 05				17 35														18 35			
Manchester Piccadilly 10	a	17 22				17 52					18 09									18 52			19 09
	d	17 26			17 42	17 56					18 11		18 27			18 42	18 42			18 57			19 11
Manchester Victoria	d		17 00	17 27			17 57					17 43		18 00	18 27								
Ashton-under-Lyne	d			17 38			18 07								18 37								
Stalybridge	a	17 38		17 43		18 08	18 12				18 26				18 42								19 26
	d	17 38		17 43		18 08	18 12				18 26				18 42								19 26
Mossley (Grtr Manchester)	d			17 48			18 17								18 47								
Greenfield	d			17 52			18 21								18 51								
Marsden	d			18 01			18 29								18 59								
Slaithwaite	d						18 34								19 04								
Huddersfield	a	17 56		18 12	18 15	18 26	18 43				18 44		18 56		19 12	19 15	19 15			19 26			19 44
	d	17 57			18 16	18 27		18 36	18 36	18 40	18 45		18 57			19 16	19 16		19 23	19 27	19 31	19 35	19 45
Deighton	d							18 39	18 39	18 43											19 34	19 38	
Mirfield	d		18 07					18 44	18 44	18 48				19 08							19 39	19 43	
Ravensthorpe	d							18 47	18 47												19 42		
Dewsbury	a	18 06	18 13			18 36		18 51	18 51				19 06	19 13						19 36	19 46		
	d	18 07	18 13			18 37		18 56	18 56				19 07	19 13						19 37	19 46		
Batley	d		18 16					18 59	18 59					19 16							19 49		
Morley	d		18 22					19 05	19 05					19 22							19 55		
Cottingley	d							19 09	19 09												19 59		
Leeds 10	a	18 22	18 34		18 36	18 52		19 18	19 19		19 09	19 13	19 23	19 33		19 36	19 36		20 29	19 52	20 07		20 09
	d	18 28			18 38	18 57					19 12	19 15	19 28			19 38	19 38	19 41		19 57			20 12
Garforth	d					19 05						19 27						19 53		20 05			
South Milford	a				18 51											19 51	19 50						
Selby	a				19 00											20 00	20 00						
Howden	a															20 09	20 09						
Brough	a				19 18											20 21	20 21						
Hull	a				19 37											20 41	20 41						
Wakefield Kirkgate	a									19 02												20 03	
Wakefield Westgate	a									19 08												20 09	
York 8	a	18 51				19 23					19 36	19 53	19 55					20 21		20 23			20 38
	d	18 58				19 26					19 42									20 30			20 43
Malton	d										20 05												21 06
Seamer	a										20 22												21 23
Scarborough	a										20 31												21 32
Thirsk	a					19 45														20 49			
Northallerton	a	19 18				19 57														20 58			
Darlington 7	a	19 30																					
Yarm	d					20 11														21 12			
Thornaby	a					20 21														21 23			
Middlesbrough	a					20 30														21 32			
Durham	a	19 47																					
Chester-le-Street	a	19 53																					
Newcastle 8	a	20 08																					

Table 39

Mondays to Fridays

Liverpool, Manchester Airport and Manchester - Huddersfield - Wakefield, Leeds, Hull, York, Scarborough, Middlesbrough and Newcastle

		NT	TP	NT	NT	NT	NT	TP FX	TP FO	TP	NT	NT
			◇1					◇1	◇1	◇1		
Liverpool Lime Street 10	d							19 22	19 22			
L'pool South Parkway 7 ✈	d							19 32	19 32			
Warrington Central	d							19 45	19 45			
Birchwood	d							19 50	19 50			
Manchester Oxford Road	d							20 07	20 07			
Manchester Airport ✈	d		19 19							20 20		
Manchester Piccadilly 10 ⇌	a		19 36					20 09	20 09	20 36		
	d		19 42					20 11	20 11	20 42		
Manchester Victoria ⇌	d	19 00		19 27							20 27	
Ashton-under-Lyne	d			19 37							20 37	
Stalybridge	a			19 42				20 26	20 26		20 42	
	d			19 42				20 26	20 26		20 42	
Mossley (Grtr Manchester)	d			19 47							20 47	
Greenfield	d			19 51							20 51	
Marsden	d			19 59							20 59	
Slaithwaite	d			20 04							21 04	
Huddersfield	a		20 15	20 12				20 44	20 44	21 15	21 12	
	d		20 16		20 25	20 31	20 35	20 45	20 45	21 16		
Deighton	d					20 34	20 38					
Mirfield	d	20 07				20 39	20 43					
Ravensthorpe	d					20 42						
Dewsbury	a	20 12	20 25			20 46				21 25		
	d	20 12	20 26			20 46				21 26		
Batley	d	20 15				20 49						
Morley	d	20 21				20 55						
Cottingley	d					20 59						
Leeds 10	a	20 34	20 41		21 25	21 07		21 09	21 09	21 41		
	d		20 45					21 12	21 12	21 42		21 55
Garforth	d											22 07
South Milford	a							21 23	21 24			
Selby	a							21 33	21 34			
Howden	a							21 42	21 43			
Brough	a							21 54	21 55			
Hull	a							22 12	22 12			
Wakefield Kirkgate	a						21 03					
Wakefield Westgate	a						21 09					
York 8	a		21 09							22 06		22 32
	d		21 14							22 09		
Malton	d									22 32		
Seamer	a									22 49		
Scarborough	a									22 58		
Thirsk	a		21 30									
Northallerton	a		21 38									
Darlington 7	a		21 51									
Yarm	d											
Thornaby	a											
Middlesbrough	a											
Durham	a		22 08									
Chester-le-Street	a		22 14									
Newcastle 8 ⇌	a		22 30									

		NT	NT	NT	TP	NT	TP	TP	NT	NT FX	NT FO
					◇1		◇1	◇1			
Liverpool Lime Street 10	d				20 22						
L'pool South Parkway 7 ✈	d				20 32						
Warrington Central	d				20 45						
Birchwood	d				20 50						
Manchester Oxford Road	d				21 07						
Manchester Airport ✈	d							21 20			
Manchester Piccadilly 10 ⇌	a				21 09			21 36			
	d				21 11			21 42			
Manchester Victoria ⇌	d					21 27			22 08		
Ashton-under-Lyne	d					21 37			22 18		
Stalybridge	a				21 26	21 42		21 55	22 22		
	d				21 26	21 42		21 55	22 23		
Mossley (Grtr Manchester)	d					21 47			22 27		
Greenfield	d					21 51			22 31		
Marsden	d					21 59			22 40		
Slaithwaite	d					22 04			22 44		
Huddersfield	a				21 44	22 12		22 15	22 53		
	d	21 27	21 31	21 35	21 45			22 16		22 25	22 25
Deighton	d		21 34	21 39							
Mirfield	d		21 39	21 44							
Ravensthorpe	d		21 42								
Dewsbury	a		21 46					22 25			
	d		21 46					22 26			
Batley	d		21 49								
Morley	d		21 55								
Cottingley	d		21 59								
Leeds 10	a	22 25	22 08		22 09			22 41		23 26	23 27
	d				22 12		22 22	22 42			
Garforth	d										
South Milford	a						22 36				
Selby	a						22 46				
Howden	a										
Brough	a						23 05				
Hull	a						23 23				
Wakefield Kirkgate	a			21 58							
Wakefield Westgate	a			22 10							
York 8	a				22 38			23 09			
	d							23 18			
Malton	d										
Seamer	a										
Scarborough	a										
Thirsk	a							23 31			
Northallerton	a							23 49			
Darlington 7	a							00 01			
Yarm	d										
Thornaby	a										
Middlesbrough	a										
Durham	a							00 18			
Chester-le-Street	a										
Newcastle 8 ⇌	a							00 52			

Table 39

Mondays to Fridays

Liverpool, Manchester Airport and Manchester - Huddersfield - Wakefield, Leeds, Hull, York, Scarborough, Middlesbrough and Newcastle

		NT	TP	NT	TP FX	TP FO	TP FO	TP FX
			◇1		◇1	◇1	◇1	◇1
Liverpool Lime Street 10	d				22 30	22 30		
L'pool South Parkway 7 ✈	d				22 40	22 40		
Warrington Central	d				22 53	22 53		
Birchwood	d				22 58	22 58		
Manchester Oxford Road	d				23 17	23 17		
Manchester Airport ✈	d		22 22				23 18	23 18
Manchester Piccadilly 10 ⇌	a		22 36		23 19	23 19	23 34	23 34
	d		22 42		23 21	23 21	23 38	23 38
Manchester Victoria ⇌	d			23 00				23 56
Ashton-under-Lyne	d			23 10				
Stalybridge	a		22 55	23 14	23 34	23 34		
	d		22 55	23 15	23 34	23 34		
Mossley (Grtr Manchester)	d			23 19				
Greenfield	d			23 23				
Marsden	d			23 32				
Slaithwaite	d			23 36				
Huddersfield	a		23 15	23 44	23 52	23 52	00 09	00 25
	d	22 31	23 16		23 53	23 53	00 09	00 26
Deighton	d	22 34						
Mirfield	d	22 39						
Ravensthorpe	d	22 42						
Dewsbury	a	22 46	23 25				00s18	00s35
	d	22 46	23 26					
Batley	d	22 49						
Morley	d	22 55						
Cottingley	d	22 59						
Leeds 10	a	23 07	23 41		00 32	00 31	00 35	00 50
	d		23 45		00 32	00 34	00 37	00 54
Garforth	d							
South Milford	a							
Selby	a							
Howden	a							
Brough	a							
Hull	a							
Wakefield Kirkgate	a							
Wakefield Westgate	a							
York 8	a		00 28		01 16	01 16	01 20	01 43
	d							
Malton	d							
Seamer	a							
Scarborough	a							
Thirsk	a							
Northallerton	a							
Darlington 7	a							
Yarm	d							
Thornaby	a							
Middlesbrough	a							
Durham	a							
Chester-le-Street	a							
Newcastle 8 ⇌	a							

Liverpool, Manchester Airport and Manchester - Huddersfield - Wakefield, Leeds, Hull, York, Scarborough, Middlesbrough and Newcastle

		TP	TP	TP	TP	TP	TP	TP	TP	TP		NT	TP	NT	NT	NT	NT	TP	TP	TP		NT	NT	NT	NT
		◇1	◇1	◇1	◇1	◇1	◇1	◇1	◇1	◇1			◇1					◇1	◇1	◇1 ✕					
Liverpool Lime Street 10	d			22p30																					
L'pool South Parkway 7 ✈	d			22p40																					
Warrington Central	d			22p53																					
Birchwood	d			22p58																					
Manchester Oxford Road	d			23p17																					
Manchester Airport ✈	d	21p20	22p22		23p18	00 38	04 15						05 37							06 23					
Manchester Piccadilly 10 ⛴	a	21p36	22p36	23p19	23p34	00 51	04 29						05 51							06 39					
	d	21p42	22p42	23p21	23p38	00 53	04 30			05 39			05 57					06 21		06 54					
Manchester Victoria ⛴	d																					06 17	06 55		
Ashton-under-Lyne	d																						07 05		
Stalybridge	a	21p55	22p55	23p34						05 52										07 07			07 10		
	d	21p55	22p55	23p34						05 52										07 07			07 11		
Mossley (Grtr Manchester)	d																						07 15		
Greenfield	d																						07 19		
Marsden	d															07 00							07 28		
Slaithwaite	d															07 04							07 32		
Huddersfield	a	22p15	23p15	23p52	00 09	01 34	05 10			06 10			06 26			07 12		06 54		07 25			07 41		
	d	22p16	23p16	23p53	00 09	01 35	05 11			06 11			06 27	06 31	06 41			06 56		07 26					07 29
Deighton	d													06 34	06 45										
Mirfield	d													06 39	06 50										
Ravensthorpe	d													06 42											
Dewsbury	a	22p25	23p25		00s18								06 36	06 46				07 05							
	d	22p26	23p26										06 37	06 46				07 06							
Batley	d													06 49											
Morley	d													06 55											
Cottingley	d													06 59											
Leeds 10	a	22p41	23p41	00 31	00 35	02 13	05 32			06 32			06 52	07 07				07 19		07 48		07 57			08 30
	d	22p42	23p45	00 34	00 37	02 16	05 34			06 35		06 38	06 55				07 14	07 23		07 50		08 00		08 12	
Garforth	d											06 50								08 00		08 12		08 24	
South Milford	a																					08 22		08 36	
Selby	a																07 37	07 43				08 36		08 54	
Howden	a																	07 52							
Brough	a																	08 04							
Hull	a																	08 20							
Wakefield Kirkgate	a														07 03										
Wakefield Westgate	a														07 10										
York 8	a	23p09	00 28	01 16	01 20	02 45	06 00			07 01		07 15	07 22							08 21					
	d	23p18						05 54	06 40	07 06			07 25						07 32	08 23					
Malton	d								07 04				07 49												
Seamer	a								07 21				08 06												
Scarborough	a								07 30				08 15												
Thirsk	a	23p31						06 10		07 22									07 52	08 39					
Northallerton	a	23p49						06 18		07 30									08 00	08 49					
Darlington 7	a	00 01						06 29		07 41															
Yarm	d																		08 14	09 03					
Thornaby	a							06 52											08 24	09 11					
Middlesbrough	a							07 03											08 32	09 21					
Durham	a	00 18								07 58															
Chester-le-Street	a									08 04															
Newcastle 8 ⛴	a	00 52								08 17															

Table 39

Saturdays

Liverpool, Manchester Airport and Manchester - Huddersfield - Wakefield, Leeds, Hull, York, Scarborough, Middlesbrough and Newcastle

		NT	TP	TP	TP	NT		TP	NT	NT	NT	TP	NT	NT	TP	TP		NT	TP	NT	NT	TP	TP	NT	NT
			◇1 ✕	◇1	◇1 ✕			◇1 ✕				◇1 ✕			◇1 A	◇1 ✕			◇1 ✕			◇1	◇1 ✕		
Liverpool Lime Street 10	d		06 15							06 46						07 15					07 16				
L'pool South Parkway 7 ✈	d		06 25													07 25									
Warrington Central	d		06 38													07 40									
Birchwood	d		06 43													07 45									
Manchester Oxford Road	d		07 07													08 06									
Manchester Airport ✈	d				07 05							07 33							08 05				08 35		
Manchester Piccadilly 10 ⛴	a		07 09		07 22							07 48				08 08			08 22				08 49		
	d		07 11		07 27			07 36				07 56				08 10			08 26			08 42	08 57		
Manchester Victoria ⛴	d					06 58			07 40	07 57								07 48		08 00	08 27				
Ashton-under-Lyne	d								07 49	08 07											08 37				
Stalybridge	a		07 23					07 49	07 54	08 13		08 09				08 26					08 41				
	d		07 23					07 49	07 54			08 09				08 26					08 42				
Mossley (Grtr Manchester)	d								07 59												08 46				
Greenfield	d								08 03												08 50				
Marsden	d								08 11												08 59				
Slaithwaite	d								08 16												09 03				
Huddersfield	a		07 44		07 56			08 09	08 24			08 28				08 44			08 56		09 12	09 15	09 26		
	d	07 32	07 45		07 57			08 10			08 14	08 30	08 33	08 37		08 45			08 57			09 16	09 27	09 31	09 35
Deighton	d	07 36									08 17		08 36	08 40										09 34	09 38
Mirfield	d	07 41				08 06					08 22		08 41	08 45						09 07				09 39	09 43
Ravensthorpe	d										08 25		08 44											09 42	
Dewsbury	a		07 54		08 06	08 11		08 19			08 29	08 39	08 48						09 06	09 12			09 36	09 46	
	d		07 55		08 07	08 12		08 20			08 29	08 39	08 53						09 07	09 12			09 37	09 46	
Batley	d					08 15					08 32		08 56							09 15				09 49	
Morley	d					08 21					08 38		09 02							09 21				09 55	
Cottingley	d					08 24					08 42		09 06											09 59	
Leeds 10	a		08 10		08 24	08 31		08 36			08 52	08 54	09 16			09 09		09 12	09 22	09 32		09 36	09 52	10 07	
	d		08 12		08 28			08 38				08 57				09 12		09 15	09 28			09 38	09 57		
Garforth	d											09 05						09 27					10 05		
South Milford	a																	09 38							
Selby	a							08 57										09 53				09 57			
Howden	a																								
Brough	a																					10 15			
Hull	a							09 31														10 34			
Wakefield Kirkgate	a	07 57												09 02											10 04
Wakefield Westgate	a	08 08												09 08											10 10
York 8	a		08 35		08 55							09 23				09 36			09 54				10 23		
	d		08 40	08 42	08 58							09 26			09 31	09 41			09 58				10 26		
Malton	d		09 04													10 04									
Seamer	a		09 21													10 21									
Scarborough	a		09 30												10 17	10 30									
Thirsk	a											09 45											10 45		
Northallerton	a				09 18							09 58							10 18				10 58		
Darlington 7	a			09 11	09 30														10 30						
Yarm	d											10 14											11 14		
Thornaby	a											10 22											11 22		
Middlesbrough	a											10 30											11 30		
Durham	a			09 28	09 47														10 47						
Chester-le-Street	a				09 55																				
Newcastle 8 ⛴	a			09 45	10 07														11 05						

A from 25 June until 10 September

Table 39

Saturdays

Liverpool, Manchester Airport and Manchester - Huddersfield - Wakefield, Leeds, Hull, York, Scarborough, Middlesbrough and Newcastle

		TP ◇1 ✠	NT	NT	TP ◇1 ✠	NT	NT	NT	TP ◇1 ✠	NT	TP ◇1 ✠	NT	NT	TP ◇1 A	TP ◇1 ✠	NT	TP ◇1	NT	NT	NT	TP ◇1 ✠	TP ◇1 ✠
Liverpool Lime Street 10	d	08 22						08 44							09 22					09 46		
L'pool South Parkway 7 ✈	d	08 32													09 32							
Warrington Central	d	08 45													09 45							
Birchwood	d	08 50													09 50							
Manchester Oxford Road	d	09 07													10 07							
Manchester Airport ✈	d				09 05						09 35						10 05					10 35
Manchester Piccadilly 10	a	09 09			09 22						09 52				10 09		10 22					10 52
	d	09 11			09 27				09 42		09 57				10 11		10 27				10 42	10 57
Manchester Victoria	d		08 48	08 57		09 00	09 27	09 57								09 48		10 00	10 27	10 57		
Ashton-under-Lyne	d			09 07			09 37	10 07											10 37	11 07		
Stalybridge	a	09 26		09 13			09 42	10 13							10 26				10 42	11 13		
	d	09 26					09 42								10 26				10 42			
Mossley (Grtr Manchester)	d						09 47												10 47			
Greenfield	d						09 51												10 51			
Marsden	d						09 59												10 59			
Slaithwaite	d						10 04												11 04			
Huddersfield	a	09 44			09 56		10 12		10 15		10 26				10 44		10 56		11 12		11 15	11 26
	d	09 45			09 57				10 16		10 27	10 31	10 35		10 45		10 57				11 16	11 27
Deighton	d											10 34	10 38									
Mirfield	d					10 07						10 39	10 43					11 07				
Ravensthorpe	d											10 42										
Dewsbury	a				10 06	10 12					10 36	10 46					11 06	11 12				11 36
	d				10 07	10 12					10 37	10 46					11 07	11 12				11 37
Batley	d					10 15						10 49						11 15				
Morley	d					10 21						10 55						11 21				
Cottingley	d											10 59										
Leeds 10	a	10 09	10 12		10 22	10 32			10 36		10 52	11 06			11 09	11 13	11 22	11 35			11 36	11 52
	d	10 12	10 15		10 28				10 38	10 41	10 57				11 12	11 15	11 28				11 38	11 57
Garforth	d		10 27							10 53	11 05					11 27						12 05
South Milford	a		10 38													11 38						
Selby	a		10 53						10 57							11 55					11 57	
Howden	a																					
Brough	a								11 15												12 15	
Hull	a								11 34												12 36	
Wakefield Kirkgate	a												11 02									
Wakefield Westgate	a												11 08									
York 8	a	10 36			10 52					11 18	11 23				11 36		11 54					12 23
	d	10 41			10 58						11 26			11 31	11 41		11 58					12 26
Malton	d	11 04													12 04							
Seamer	a	11 21													12 21							
Scarborough	a	11 30												12 17	12 30							
Thirsk	a										11 45											12 45
Northallerton	a				11 18						11 58						12 18					12 59
Darlington 7	a				11 30												12 30					
Yarm	d										12 14											13 14
Thornaby	a										12 22											13 22
Middlesbrough	a										12 30											13 30
Durham	a				11 47												12 47					
Chester-le-Street	a				11 53																	
Newcastle 8	a				12 06												13 03					

A from 25 June until 10 September

Table 39

Saturdays

Liverpool, Manchester Airport and Manchester - Huddersfield - Wakefield, Leeds, Hull, York, Scarborough, Middlesbrough and Newcastle

		NT	NT	TP ◇1 ✠	NT	TP ◇1 ✠	NT	NT	NT	TP ◇1	NT	TP ◇1 ✠	NT	NT	TP ◇1 A	TP ◇1 ✠	NT	TP ◇1 ✠	NT	NT	NT	TP ◇1	TP ◇1 ✠
Liverpool Lime Street 10	d			10 22					10 46							11 22					11 46		
L'pool South Parkway 7 ✈	d			10 32												11 32							
Warrington Central	d			10 45												11 45							
Birchwood	d			10 50												11 50							
Manchester Oxford Road	d			11 07												12 07							
Manchester Airport ✈	d					11 05						11 35						12 05					12 35
Manchester Piccadilly 10	a			11 09		11 22						11 52				12 09		12 22					12 52
	d			11 11		11 27				11 42		11 57				12 11		12 27				12 42	12 57
Manchester Victoria	d				10 48		11 00	11 27	11 57								11 48		12 00	12 27	12 57		
Ashton-under-Lyne	d							11 37	12 07											12 37	13 07		
Stalybridge	a			11 26				11 42	12 13							12 26				12 42	13 13		
	d			11 26				11 42								12 26				12 42			
Mossley (Grtr Manchester)	d							11 47												12 47			
Greenfield	d							11 51												12 51			
Marsden	d							11 59												12 59			
Slaithwaite	d							12 04												13 04			
Huddersfield	a			11 44		11 56		12 12		12 15		12 26				12 44		12 56		13 12		13 15	13 26
	d	11 31	11 35	11 45		11 57				12 16		12 27	12 31	12 35		12 45		12 57				13 16	13 27
Deighton	d	11 34	11 38										12 34	12 38									
Mirfield	d	11 39	11 43				12 07						12 39	12 43					13 07				
Ravensthorpe	d	11 42											12 42										
Dewsbury	a	11 46				12 06	12 12					12 36	12 46					13 06	13 12				13 36
	d	11 46				12 07	12 12					12 37	12 46					13 07	13 12				13 37
Batley	d	11 49					12 15						12 49						13 15				
Morley	d	11 55					12 21						12 55						13 21				
Cottingley	d	11 59											12 59										
Leeds 10	a	12 07		12 09	12 12	12 22	12 32			12 36		12 52	13 07			13 09	13 12	13 22	13 32			13 36	13 52
	d			12 12	12 15	12 28				12 38	12 41	12 57				13 12	13 15	13 28				13 38	13 57
Garforth	d				12 27						12 53	13 05					13 27						14 05
South Milford	a				12 38												13 38						
Selby	a				12 50					12 57							13 52					13 57	
Howden	a																						
Brough	a									13 15												14 15	
Hull	a									13 34												14 34	
Wakefield Kirkgate	a		12 02											13 02									
Wakefield Westgate	a		12 08											13 08									
York 8	a			12 36		12 52					13 19	13 23				13 36		13 54					14 23
	d			12 41		12 58						13 26			13 31	13 41		13 58					14 26
Malton	d			13 04												14 04							
Seamer	a			13 21												14 21							
Scarborough	a			13 30											14 17	14 30							
Thirsk	a											13 45											14 45
Northallerton	a					13 18						13 58						14 18					14 58
Darlington 7	a					13 30												14 30					
Yarm	d											14 14											15 14
Thornaby	a											14 22											15 22
Middlesbrough	a											14 30											15 30
Durham	a					13 47												14 47					
Chester-le-Street	a					13 53																	
Newcastle 8	a					14 06												15 05					

A from 25 June until 10 September

Table 39

Saturdays

Liverpool, Manchester Airport and Manchester - Huddersfield - Wakefield, Leeds, Hull, York, Scarborough, Middlesbrough and Newcastle

		NT	NT	TP	NT	TP	NT	NT	NT	TP	NT	TP	NT	NT	TP	NT	TP	NT	NT	NT	TP	TP
				◇1		◇1				◇1		◇1			◇1		◇1				◇1	◇1
				🛒		🛒				🛒		🛒			🛒		🛒					
Liverpool Lime Street 10	d			12 22					12 46						13 22					13 46		
L'pool South Parkway 7 ✈	d			12 32											13 32							
Warrington Central	d			12 45											13 45							
Birchwood	d			12 50											13 50							
Manchester Oxford Road	d			13 07											14 07							
Manchester Airport ✈	d					13 05						13 35					14 05					14 35
Manchester Piccadilly 10	a			13 09		13 22						13 52			14 09		14 22					14 52
	d			13 11		13 27				13 42		13 57			14 11		14 27				14 42	14 57
Manchester Victoria	d				12 48		13 00	13 27	13 57							13 48		14 00	14 27	14 57		
Ashton-under-Lyne	d							13 37	14 07										14 37	15 07		
Stalybridge	a			13 26				13 42	14 13						14 26				14 42	15 13		
	d			13 26				13 42							14 26				14 42			
Mossley (Grtr Manchester)	d							13 47											14 47			
Greenfield	d							13 51											14 51			
Marsden	d							13 59											14 59			
Slaithwaite	d							14 04											15 04			
Huddersfield	a			13 44		13 56		14 12		14 15		14 26			14 44		14 56		15 12		15 15	15 26
	d	13 31	13 35	13 45		13 57				14 16		14 27	14 31	14 35	14 45		14 57				15 16	15 27
Deighton	d	13 34	13 38										14 34	14 38								
Mirfield	d	13 39	13 43				14 07						14 39	14 43				15 07				
Ravensthorpe	d	13 42											14 42									
Dewsbury	a	13 46				14 06	14 12					14 36	14 46				15 06	15 12				15 36
	d	13 46				14 07	14 12					14 37	14 46				15 07	15 12				15 37
Batley	d	13 49					14 15						14 49					15 15				
Morley	d	13 55					14 21						14 55					15 21				
Cottingley	d	13 59											14 59									
Leeds 10	a	14 07		14 09	14 14	14 22	14 32			14 36		14 52	15 07		15 09	15 10	15 22	15 32			15 36	15 52
	d			14 12	14 15	14 28				14 38	14 41	14 57			15 12	15 15	15 28				15 38	15 56
Garforth	d				14 27						14 53	15 05				15 27						16 05
South Milford	a				14 38											15 38						
Selby	a				14 51					14 57						15 53					15 57	
Howden	a																					
Brough	a									15 15											16 15	
Hull	a									15 34											16 34	
Wakefield Kirkgate	a		14 02											15 02								
Wakefield Westgate	a		14 08											15 08								
York 8	a			14 36		14 52					15 17	15 23			15 36		15 53					16 23
	d			14 41		14 58						15 26			15 41							16 25
Malton	d			15 04											16 04							
Seamer	a			15 21											16 21							
Scarborough	a			15 30											16 30							
Thirsk	a											15 45										16 45
Northallerton	a					15 18						15 59										16 57
Darlington 7	a					15 30																
Yarm	d											16 14										17 14
Thornaby	a											16 22										17 22
Middlesbrough	a											16 30										17 30
Durham	a					15 47																
Chester-le-Street	a					15 53																
Newcastle 8	a					16 09																

Table 39

Saturdays

Liverpool, Manchester Airport and Manchester - Huddersfield - Wakefield, Leeds, Hull, York, Scarborough, Middlesbrough and Newcastle

		NT	NT	TP	NT	TP	NT	NT	NT	TP	NT	TP	NT	NT	TP	NT	TP	NT	NT	NT	TP	NT	NT
				◇1		◇1				◇1		◇1			◇1		◇1				◇1		
				🛒		🛒						🛒											
Liverpool Lime Street 10	d			14 22					14 46						15 22					15 46			
L'pool South Parkway 7 ✈	d			14 32											15 32								
Warrington Central	d			14 45											15 45								
Birchwood	d			14 50											15 50								
Manchester Oxford Road	d			15 07											16 07								
Manchester Airport ✈	d					15 05						15 35					16 05						
Manchester Piccadilly 10	a			15 09		15 22						15 52			16 09		16 22						
	d			15 11		15 27				15 42		15 57			16 11		16 27				16 42		
Manchester Victoria	d				14 48		15 00	15 27	15 57							15 48		16 00	16 27	16 57			
Ashton-under-Lyne	d							15 37	16 07										16 37	17 07			
Stalybridge	a			15 26				15 42	16 13						16 26				16 42	17 13			
	d			15 26				15 42							16 26				16 42				
Mossley (Grtr Manchester)	d							15 47											16 47				
Greenfield	d							15 51											16 51				
Marsden	d							15 59											16 59			17 29	
Slaithwaite	d							16 04											17 04			17 33	
Huddersfield	a			15 44		15 56		16 12		16 15		16 26			16 44		16 56		17 12		17 15	17 41	
	d	15 31	15 35	15 45		15 57				16 16		16 27	16 31	16 35	16 45		16 57				17 16		
Deighton	d	15 34	15 38										16 34	16 38									
Mirfield	d	15 39	15 43				16 07						16 39	16 43				17 07					
Ravensthorpe	d	15 42											16 42										
Dewsbury	a	15 46				16 06	16 12					16 36	16 46				17 06	17 12					
	d	15 46				16 07	16 12					16 37	16 46				17 07	17 12					
Batley	d	15 49					16 15						16 49					17 15					
Morley	d	15 55					16 21						16 55					17 21					
Cottingley	d	15 59											16 59										
Leeds 10	a	16 08		16 09	16 12	16 22	16 31			16 36		16 52	17 08		17 09	17 12	17 22	17 31			17 36		
	d			16 12	16 15	16 28				16 38	16 41	16 57			17 12	17 15	17 24				17 38		17 41
Garforth	d				16 27						16 53	17 05				17 30	17 34						17 53
South Milford	a				16 39											17 41							
Selby	a				16 54					17 00						17 55					17 59		
Howden	a																				18 08		
Brough	a									17 18											18 20		
Hull	a									17 37											18 40		
Wakefield Kirkgate	a		16 02											17 02									
Wakefield Westgate	a		16 08											17 08									
York 8	a			16 36		16 52					17 21	17 23			17 36		17 55						18 19
	d			16 41		16 58						17 26			17 41								
Malton	d			17 04											18 04								
Seamer	a			17 21											18 21								
Scarborough	a			17 30											18 30								
Thirsk	a					17 13						17 45											
Northallerton	a					17 21						17 58											
Darlington 7	a					17 32																	
Yarm	d											18 14											
Thornaby	a											18 24											
Middlesbrough	a											18 32											
Durham	a					17 50																	
Chester-le-Street	a					17 56																	
Newcastle 8	a					18 10																	

Table 39

Saturdays

Liverpool, Manchester Airport and Manchester - Huddersfield - Wakefield, Leeds, Hull, York, Scarborough, Middlesbrough and Newcastle

		TP ◇1	NT	NT	TP ◇1	NT		TP ◇1	NT	NT	NT	TP ◇1	TP ◇1	NT	NT	TP ◇1		NT	TP ◇1	NT	NT	TP ◇1	NT	NT	TP ◇1
Liverpool Lime Street 10	d				16 22						16 46					17 22									
L'pool South Parkway 7 ✈	d				16 32											17 32									
Warrington Central	d				16 45											17 45									
Birchwood	d				16 50											17 50									
Manchester Oxford Road	d				17 07											18 07									
Manchester Airport ✈	d	16 35						17 05					17 35												18 35
Manchester Piccadilly 10	a	16 52			17 09			17 22					17 52			18 09									18 52
	d	16 56			17 11			17 26				17 42	17 56			18 11						18 42			18 57
Manchester Victoria	d					16 48			17 00	17 27	17 57							17 43		18 00	18 27				
Ashton-under-Lyne	d									17 37	18 07										18 37				
Stalybridge	a	17 08			17 26			17 38		17 42	18 13		18 08			18 26					18 42				
	d	17 08			17 26			17 38		17 42			18 08			18 26					18 42				
Mossley (Grtr Manchester)	d									17 47											18 47				
Greenfield	d									17 51											18 51				
Marsden	d									17 59											18 59				
Slaithwaite	d									18 04											19 04				
Huddersfield	a	17 26			17 44			17 56		18 12		18 15	18 26			18 44					19 12	19 15			19 26
	d	17 27	17 31	17 35	17 45			17 57				18 16	18 27	18 31	18 35	18 45						19 16		19 23	19 27
Deighton	d		17 34	17 38										18 34	18 39										
Mirfield	d		17 39	17 43					18 07					18 39	18 44					19 08					
Ravensthorpe	d		17 42											18 42											
Dewsbury	a	17 36	17 46					18 06	18 12				18 36	18 46		18 55				19 13					19 36
	d	17 37	17 46					18 07	18 13				18 37	18 46		18 55				19 13					19 37
Batley	d		17 49						18 16					18 49						19 16					
Morley	d		17 55						18 22					18 55						19 22					
Cottingley	d		17 59											18 59											
Leeds 10	a	17 52	18 06		18 09	18 12		18 21	18 31			18 36	18 52	19 07		19 10		19 13		19 33		19 36		20 30	19 52
	d	17 57			18 12	18 15		18 28				18 38	18 57			19 12		19 16	19 28			19 38	19 41		19 57
Garforth	d	18 05				18 27							19 05					19 28					19 53		20 05
South Milford	a					18 38						18 51										19 51			
Selby	a					18 50						19 00										20 00			
Howden	a																					20 09			
Brough	a											19 18										20 21			
Hull	a											19 37										20 41			
Wakefield Kirkgate	a			18 02											19 02										
Wakefield Westgate	a			18 08											19 08										
York 8	a	18 23			18 35			18 52					19 23			19 36		19 54	19 56				20 18		20 23
	d	18 26			18 43			18 58					19 26			19 42									20 26
Malton	d				19 07											20 05									
Seamer	a				19 24											20 22									
Scarborough	a				19 32											20 31									
Thirsk	a	18 45											19 45												20 45
Northallerton	a	18 58						19 18					19 57												21 01
Darlington 7	a							19 30																	
Yarm	d	19 14											20 11												21 15
Thornaby	a	19 22											20 21												21 23
Middlesbrough	a	19 32											20 30												21 32
Durham	a							19 47																	
Chester-le-Street	a							19 53																	
Newcastle 8	a							20 08																	

Table 39

Saturdays

Liverpool, Manchester Airport and Manchester - Huddersfield - Wakefield, Leeds, Hull, York, Scarborough, Middlesbrough and Newcastle

		NT		NT	TP ◇1	NT	TP ◇1	NT	NT	NT	NT	TP ◇1		TP ◇1	NT	XC ◇1	TP ◇1	NT	NT	NT	NT	TP ◇1		NT	TP ◇1
Liverpool Lime Street 10	d				18 22									19 22								20 22			
L'pool South Parkway 7 ✈	d				18 32									19 32								20 32			
Warrington Central	d				18 45									19 45								20 45			
Birchwood	d				18 50									19 50								20 50			
Manchester Oxford Road	d				19 07									20 07								21 07			
Manchester Airport ✈	d						19 19										20 20								
Manchester Piccadilly 10	a				19 09		19 36							20 09			20 36					21 09			
	d				19 11		19 42							20 11			20 42					21 11			
Manchester Victoria	d					19 00		19 27							20 27									21 27	
Ashton-under-Lyne	d							19 37							20 37									21 37	
Stalybridge	a				19 26			19 42						20 26	20 42							21 26		21 41	
	d				19 26			19 42						20 26	20 42							21 26		21 42	
Mossley (Grtr Manchester)	d							19 47							20 47									21 46	
Greenfield	d							19 51							20 51									21 50	
Marsden	d							19 59							20 59					21 19				21 59	
Slaithwaite	d							20 04							21 04					21 23				22 03	
Huddersfield	a				19 44		20 15	20 12						20 44	21 12		21 15			21 30		21 44		22 12	
	d	19 31		19 35	19 45		20 16		20 25	20 31	20 35			20 45			21 16		21 27	21 31	21 35	21 45			
Deighton	d	19 34		19 38						20 34	20 38									21 34	21 39				
Mirfield	d	19 39		19 43		20 07				20 39	20 43									21 39	21 44				
Ravensthorpe	d	19 42								20 42										21 42					
Dewsbury	a	19 46				20 12	20 25			20 46							21 25			21 46					
	d	19 46				20 12	20 26			20 46							21 26			21 46					
Batley	d	19 49				20 15				20 49										21 49					
Morley	d	19 55				20 21				20 55										21 55					
Cottingley	d	19 59								20 59										21 59					
Leeds 10	a	20 07			20 10	20 33	20 41		21 25	21 07				21 09			21 41		22 24	22 07		22 11			
	d				20 12		20 45					21 08		21 12		21 15	21 42	22 00				22 12			22 22
Garforth	d																	22 12							
South Milford	a											21 20													22 36
Selby	a											21 30													22 46
Howden	a											21 39													
Brough	a											21 51													23 05
Hull	a											22 08													23 23
Wakefield Kirkgate	a			20 03							21 02										22 05				
Wakefield Westgate	a			20 09							21 08										22 10				
York 8	a				20 38		21 09							21 41		21 57	22 06	22 36				22 38			
	d				20 43		21 14										22 14								
Malton	d				21 06												22 37								
Seamer	a				21 23												22 54								
Scarborough	a				21 32												23 03								
Thirsk	a						21 30																		
Northallerton	a						21 38																		
Darlington 7	a						21 51																		
Yarm	d																								
Thornaby	a																								
Middlesbrough	a																								
Durham	a						22 08																		
Chester-le-Street	a						22 14																		
Newcastle 8	a						22 27																		

Table 39

Saturdays

Liverpool, Manchester Airport and Manchester - Huddersfield - Wakefield, Leeds, Hull, York, Scarborough, Middlesbrough and Newcastle

		NT	TP ◇1	NT	NT	NT	TP ◇1	TP ◇1 A	NT B	NT C	TP ◇1 D	TP ◇1 D
Liverpool Lime Street 10	d							22 30			22 30	
L'pool South Parkway 7 ✈	d							22 40			22 40	
Warrington Central	d							22 53			22 53	
Birchwood	d							22 58			22 58	
Manchester Oxford Road	d							23 17			23 17	
Manchester Airport ✈	d		21 20				22 22					23 24
Manchester Piccadilly 10	a		21 36				22 36	23 19			23 19	23 39
	d		21 42				22 42	23 21			23 21	23 41
Manchester Victoria	d			22 08					23 00	23 00		23 56
Ashton-under-Lyne	d			22 18					23 10	23 10		
Stalybridge	a		21 55	22 22			22 55	23 38	23 14	23 14	23 34	
	d		21 55	22 23			22 55			23 15	23 34	
Mossley (Grtr Manchester)	d			22 27						23 19		
Greenfield	d			22 31						23 23		
Marsden	d			22 40						23 32		
Slaithwaite	d			22 44						23 36		
Huddersfield	a		22 15	22 53			23 15			23 44	23 52	00 25
	d		22 16		22 20	22 25	23 16				23 53	00 26
Deighton	d				22 23							
Mirfield	d				22 28							
Ravensthorpe	d				22 31							
Dewsbury	a		22 25		22 35		23 25					00s35
	d		22 26		22 35		23 26					
Batley	d				22 38							
Morley	d				22 44							
Cottingley	d				22 48							
Leeds 10	a		22 41		22 57	23 26	23 41				00 14	00 50
	d	22 37	22 42				23 42				00 15	00 54
Garforth	d											
South Milford	a											
Selby	a											
Howden	a											
Brough	a											
Hull	a											
Wakefield Kirkgate	a	23 10										
Wakefield Westgate	a											
York 8	a		23 09				00 09				00 42	01 22
	d											
Malton	d											
Seamer	a											
Scarborough	a											
Thirsk	a											
Northallerton	a											
Darlington 7	a											
Yarm	d											
Thornaby	a											
Middlesbrough	a											
Durham	a											
Chester-le-Street	a											
Newcastle 8	a											

A from 17 September
B from 17 September until 22 October
C until 10 September, from 29 October
D until 10 September

Table 39

Sundays
until 22 May

Liverpool, Manchester Airport and Manchester - Huddersfield, Leeds, Hull, York, Scarborough, Middlesbrough and Newcastle

		TP ◇1	TP ◇1	TP ◇1	NT	TP ◇1	TP ◇1	TP ◇1	NT	TP ◇1	TP ◇1
Liverpool Lime Street 10	d										08 22
L'pool South Parkway 7 ✈	d										08 32
Warrington Central	d										08 45
Birchwood	d										08 50
Newton-le-Willows	d										
Manchester Oxford Road	d										09 07
Manchester Airport ✈	d	01 22	04 43	06 24		07 24		08 06			
Manchester Piccadilly 10	a	01 36	04 57	06 38		07 37		08 24			09 09
	d	01 42	05 02	06 42		07 42		08 28			09 11
Manchester Victoria	a										
	d								08 43		
Ashton-under-Lyne	d								08 53		
Stalybridge	a			06 53		07 54		08 41	08 57		09 24
	d			06 54		07 54		08 41	08 58		09 24
Mossley (Grtr Manchester)	d								09 02		
Greenfield	d								09 06		
Marsden	d								09 15		
Slaithwaite	d								09 19		
Huddersfield	a	02 11	05 31	07 11		08 11		08 59	09 28		09 42
	d	02 12	05 32	07 12	07 51	08 12		09 02			09 43
Deighton	d				07 54						
Mirfield	d				07 59						
Ravensthorpe	d				08 02						
Dewsbury	a			07 21	08 06	08 21		09 11			
	d			07 22	08 06	08 22		09 11			
Batley	d				08 09						
Morley	d				08 15						
Cottingley	d				08 19						
Leeds 10	a	02 33	05 53	07 37	08 27	08 37		09 27			10 07
	d	02 35	05 55	07 40		08 40	09 12	09 40		10 04	10 22
Garforth	d										
South Milford	a										10 34
Selby	a										10 44
Howden	a										
Brough	a										11 03
Hull	a										11 18
York 8	a	03 03	06 23	08 08		09 07	09 37	10 07		10 29	
	d			08 21		09 10	09 40	10 13		10 32	
Malton	d						10 04			10 56	
Seamer	a						10 20			11 13	
Scarborough	a						10 30			11 22	
Thirsk	a			08 37							
Northallerton	a			08 45		09 30		10 35			
Darlington 7	a			08 56		09 42		10 47			
Yarm	d										
Thornaby	a			09 16							
Middlesbrough	a			09 27							
Durham	a					09 59		11 08			
Chester-le-Street	a										
Newcastle 8	a					10 18		11 24			

		NT	NT	TP ◇1	TP ◇1	TP ◇1	TP ◇1	NT	TP ◇1	NT	NT	TP ◇1	TP ◇1
Liverpool Lime Street 10	d					09 22			10 22				
L'pool South Parkway 7 ✈	d					09 32			10 32				
Warrington Central	d					09 45			10 45				
Birchwood	d					09 50			10 50				
Newton-le-Willows	d												
Manchester Oxford Road	d					10 08			11 07				
Manchester Airport ✈	d				09 20		10 20						11 20
Manchester Piccadilly 10	a				09 37	10 09	10 37		11 09				11 35
	d				09 42	10 11	10 42		11 11				11 42
Manchester Victoria	a												
	d	09 43						10 43		11 43			
Ashton-under-Lyne	d	09 53						10 53		11 53			
Stalybridge	a	09 57				10 24		10 57	11 24	11 57			
	d	09 58				10 24		10 58	11 24	11 58			
Mossley (Grtr Manchester)	d	10 02						11 02		12 02			
Greenfield	d	10 06						11 06		12 06			
Marsden	d	10 15						11 15		12 15			
Slaithwaite	d	10 19						11 19		12 19			
Huddersfield	a	10 28			10 11	10 42	11 11	11 28	11 42	12 28			12 11
	d		09 51		10 12	10 43	11 12		11 43		11 58		12 12
Deighton	d		09 54								12 01		
Mirfield	d		09 59								12 06		
Ravensthorpe	d		10 02								12 09		
Dewsbury	a		10 06		10 22		11 21				12 13		12 21
	d		10 06		10 22		11 22				12 13		12 22
Batley	d		10 09								12 16		
Morley	d		10 15								12 22		
Cottingley	d		10 19								12 26		
Leeds 10	a		10 27		10 37	11 04	11 37		12 04		12 34		12 37
	d				10 40	11 12	11 40		12 12				12 40
Garforth	d												
South Milford	a												
Selby	a												
Howden	a												
Brough	a												
Hull	a												
York 8	a				11 07	11 39	12 05		12 39				13 07
	d			10 42	11 10	11 44	12 08		12 42			12 49	13 10
Malton	d					12 08							
Seamer	a					12 25							
Scarborough	a					12 34						13 36	
Thirsk	a			10 59					12 59				
Northallerton	a			11 07	11 30		12 28		13 07				13 30
Darlington 7	a				11 42		12 40						13 42
Yarm	d			11 21					13 22				
Thornaby	a			11 29					13 30				
Middlesbrough	a			11 39					13 40				
Durham	a				11 59		12 57						13 59
Chester-le-Street	a												14 05
Newcastle 8	a				12 15		13 12						14 17

Table 39

Sundays until 22 May

Liverpool, Manchester Airport and Manchester - Huddersfield, Leeds, Hull, York, Scarborough, Middlesbrough and Newcastle

		TP	TP	TP	NT	TP		TP	NT	NT	TP	TP	TP	TP	NT	TP		TP	NT	NT	TP	TP	TP	TP	NT
		◇1	◇1	◇1		◇1		◇1			◇1	◇1	◇1	◇1		◇1		◇1			◇1	◇1	◇1	◇1	
Liverpool Lime Street 10	d		11 22					12 22					13 22					14 22					15 22		
L'pool South Parkway 7	d		11 32					12 32					13 32					14 32					15 32		
Warrington Central	d		11 45					12 45					13 45					14 45					15 45		
Birchwood	d		11 50					12 50					13 50					14 50					15 50		
Newton-le-Willows	d																								
Manchester Oxford Road	d		12 07					13 07					14 07					15 07					16 07		
Manchester Airport	d			12 20							13 20			14 20							15 20			16 20	
Manchester Piccadilly 10	a		12 09	12 37				13 09			13 37		14 09	14 37				15 09			15 37		16 09	16 37	
	d	12 02	12 11	12 42		13 02		13 11			13 42	14 02	14 11	14 42		15 02		15 11			15 42	16 02	16 11	16 42	
Manchester Victoria	a																								
	d				12 43				13 43						14 43				15 43						16 43
Ashton-under-Lyne	d				12 53				13 53						14 53				15 53						16 53
Stalybridge	a		12 24		12 57			13 24	13 57				14 24		14 57			15 24	15 57				16 24		16 57
	d		12 24		12 58			13 24	13 58				14 24		14 58			15 24	15 58				16 24		16 58
Mossley (Grtr Manchester)	d				13 02				14 02						15 02				16 02						17 02
Greenfield	d				13 06				14 06						15 06				16 06						17 06
Marsden	d				13 15				14 15						15 15				16 15						17 15
Slaithwaite	d				13 19				14 19						15 19				16 19						17 19
Huddersfield	a	12 32	12 42	13 11	13 28	13 32		13 42	14 28		14 11	14 32	14 42	15 11	15 28	15 32		15 42	16 28		16 11	16 32	16 42	17 11	17 28
	d	12 33	12 43	13 12		13 33		13 43		13 58	14 12	14 33	14 43	15 12		15 33		15 43		15 58	16 12	16 33	16 43	17 12	
Deighton	d									14 01										16 01					
Mirfield	d									14 06										16 06					
Ravensthorpe	d									14 09										16 09					
Dewsbury	a			13 21						14 13	14 21			15 21						16 13	16 21			17 21	
	d			13 22						14 13	14 22			15 22						16 13	16 22			17 22	
Batley	d									14 16										16 16					
Morley	d									14 22										16 22					
Cottingley	d									14 26										16 26					
Leeds 10	a	12 54	13 04	13 37		13 54		14 04		14 34	14 37	14 52	15 04	15 37		15 54		16 04		16 34	16 37	16 54	17 04	17 37	
	d	13 01	13 12	13 40		13 57		14 12			14 40	15 00	15 12	15 40		15 57		16 12			16 40	17 01	17 12	17 40	
Garforth	d																								
South Milford	a	13 13										15 12										17 14			
Selby	a	13 23										15 22										17 23			
Howden	a																								
Brough	a	13 41										15 40										17 41			
Hull	a	13 59										15 59										17 59			
York 8	a		13 39	14 07		14 24		14 38			15 07		15 38	16 05		16 24		16 38			17 07		17 38	18 07	
	d		13 43	14 10				14 50			15 10		15 43	16 08				16 42			17 10		17 43	18 10	
Malton	d		14 07										16 07										18 07		
Seamer	a		14 24										16 24										18 24		
Scarborough	a		14 33										16 33										18 33		
Thirsk	a							15 12										17 04							
Northallerton	a			14 30				15 20			15 30			16 28				17 16			17 30			18 30	
Darlington 7	a			14 42							15 42			16 40							17 42			18 42	
Yarm	d							15 35										17 32							
Thornaby	a							15 43										17 41							
Middlesbrough	a							15 52										17 50							
Durham	a			14 59							16 00			16 57							17 59			18 59	
Chester-le-Street	a										16 06										18 05				
Newcastle 8	a			15 15							16 18			17 12							18 18			19 16	

Table 39

Sundays until 22 May

Liverpool, Manchester Airport and Manchester - Huddersfield, Leeds, Hull, York, Scarborough, Middlesbrough and Newcastle

		TP		TP	NT	NT	TP	TP	TP	TP	TP	NT		TP	TP	NT	NT	TP	TP	TP	TP	NT		TP	NT
		◇1		◇1			◇1	◇1	◇1	◇1	◇1			◇1	◇1			◇1	◇1	◇1	◇1			◇1	
Liverpool Lime Street 10	d			16 22						17 22					18 22					19 22				20 22	
L'pool South Parkway 7	d			16 32						17 32					18 32					19 32				20 32	
Warrington Central	d			16 45						17 45					18 45					19 45				20 45	
Birchwood	d			16 50						17 50					18 50					19 50				20 50	
Newton-le-Willows	d																								
Manchester Oxford Road	d			17 07						18 07					19 07					20 07				21 07	
Manchester Airport	d							17 20			18 20							19 20			20 20				
Manchester Piccadilly 10	a			17 09				17 37		18 09	18 37				19 09			19 37		20 09	20 37			21 09	
	d	17 02		17 11				17 42	18 02	18 11	18 42			19 02	19 11			19 42	20 06	20 11	20 42			21 11	
Manchester Victoria	a																								
	d				17 43							18 43				19 43						20 43			21 43
Ashton-under-Lyne	d				17 53							18 53				19 53						20 53			21 53
Stalybridge	a			17 24	17 57					18 24		18 57			19 24	19 57				20 24		20 57		21 24	21 57
	d			17 24	17 58					18 24		18 58			19 24	19 58				20 24		20 58		21 24	
Mossley (Grtr Manchester)	d				18 02							19 02				20 02						21 02			
Greenfield	d				18 06							19 06				20 06						21 06			
Marsden	d				18 15							19 15				20 15						21 15			
Slaithwaite	d				18 19							19 19				20 19						21 19			
Huddersfield	a	17 32		17 42	18 28			18 11	18 32	18 42	19 11	19 28		19 32	19 42	20 28		20 11	20 36	20 42	21 11	21 28		21 42	
	d	17 33		17 43		17 58		18 12	18 33	18 43	19 12			19 33	19 43		19 58	20 12	20 37	20 43	21 12			21 43	
Deighton	d					18 01											20 01								
Mirfield	d					18 06											20 06								
Ravensthorpe	d					18 09											20 09								
Dewsbury	a					18 13		18 21			19 21						20 13	20 21			21 21				
	d					18 13		18 22			19 22						20 13	20 22			21 22				
Batley	d					18 16											20 16								
Morley	d					18 22											20 22								
Cottingley	d					18 26											20 26								
Leeds 10	a	17 54		18 04		18 34		18 37	18 54	19 04	19 37			19 54	20 04		20 34	20 37	20 58	21 04	21 37			22 04	
	d	17 57		18 12				18 40	19 01	19 12	19 40			19 57	20 12			20 40	21 04	21 12	21 40			22 12	
Garforth	d																								
South Milford	a								19 14																
Selby	a								19 29					20 17					21 38						
Howden	a																								
Brough	a								19 48					20 36					21 58						
Hull	a								20 06					20 54					22 15						
York 8	a	18 24		18 38				19 07		19 35	20 04				20 38			21 05		21 38	22 08			22 40	
	d			18 42			18 46	19 10		19 45	20 10				20 44			21 08			22 10			22 42	
Malton	d									20 09					21 08						22 35				
Seamer	a									20 26					21 25						22 51				
Scarborough	a						19 33			20 35					21 34						22 59				
Thirsk	a			18 59							20 26							21 26						23 06	
Northallerton	a			19 07				19 30			20 34							21 34						23 16	
Darlington 7	a							19 42										21 45						23 28	
Yarm	d			19 22							20 50														
Thornaby	a			19 30							20 58														
Middlesbrough	a			19 40							21 08														
Durham	a							20 00										22 02						23 45	
Chester-le-Street	a							20 06																	
Newcastle 8	a							20 17										22 17						00 15	

Liverpool, Manchester Airport and Manchester - Huddersfield, Leeds, Hull, York, Scarborough, Middlesbrough and Newcastle

		TP	NT	TP	TP	TP
		◇1		◇1	◇1	◇1
Liverpool Lime Street 10	d				21 52	
L'pool South Parkway 7 ✈	d				22 02	
Warrington Central	d				22 15	
Birchwood	d				22 20	
Newton-le-Willows	d					
Manchester Oxford Road	d				22 37	
Manchester Airport ✈	d			21 20		23 20
Manchester Piccadilly 10 ⇌	a			21 37	22 39	23 37
	d			21 42	22 42	23 42
Manchester Victoria ⇌	a					
	d					
Ashton-under-Lyne	d					
Stalybridge	a				22 54	
	d				22 54	
Mossley (Grtr Manchester)	d					
Greenfield	d					
Marsden	d		21 47			
Slaithwaite	d		21 51			
Huddersfield	a		21 57	22 11	23 12	00 11
	d		21 57	22 12	23 12	00 12
Deighton	d		22 01			
Mirfield	d		22 06			
Ravensthorpe	d		22 09			
Dewsbury	a		22 12	22 21	23 22	
	d		22 13	22 22	23 22	
Batley	d		22 16			
Morley	d		22 22			
Cottingley	d		22 25			
Leeds 10	a		22 34	22 37	23 37	00 51
	d	22 22		22 40	23 40	00 54
Garforth	d					
South Milford	a	22 34				
Selby	a	22 44				
Howden	a					
Brough	a	23 02				
Hull	a	23 19				
York 8	a			23 11	00 09	01 22
	d					
Malton	d					
Seamer	a					
Scarborough	a					
Thirsk	a					
Northallerton	a					
Darlington 7	a					
Yarm	d					
Thornaby	a					
Middlesbrough	a					
Durham	a					
Chester-le-Street	a					
Newcastle 8 ⇌	a					

Liverpool, Manchester Airport and Manchester - Huddersfield, Leeds, Hull, York, Scarborough, Middlesbrough and Newcastle

		TP	TP	TP	TP	TP	TP	NT	TP	TP		TP	NT	TP	TP	NT	NT	TP	TP	TP		TP	NT	TP	NT
		◇1	◇1	◇1	◇1	◇1	◇1		◇1	◇1		◇1		◇1	◇1			◇1	◇1	◇1		◇1		◇1	
Liverpool Lime Street 10	d		22p30												08 22					09 22				10 22	
L'pool South Parkway 7 ✈	d		22p40												08 32					09 32				10 32	
Warrington Central	d		22p53												08 45					09 45				10 45	
Birchwood	d		22p58												08 50					09 50				10 50	
Newton-le-Willows	d																								
Manchester Oxford Road	d		23p17												09 07					10 08				11 07	
Manchester Airport ✈	d	22p22		23p24	01 22	04 43	06 24		07 24			08 06							09 20			10 20			
Manchester Piccadilly 10 ⇌	a	22p36	23p19	23p39	01 36	04 57	06 38		07 37			08 24			09 09				09 37	10 09		10 37		11 09	
	d	22p42	23p21	23p41	01 42	05 02	06 42		07 42			08 28			09 11				09 42	10 11		10 42		11 11	
Manchester Victoria ⇌	a			23p55																					
	d			23p56									08 43			09 43							10 43		11 43
Ashton-under-Lyne	d												08 53			09 53							10 53		11 53
Stalybridge	a	22p55	23p34				06 53		07 54			08 41	08 57		09 24	09 57				10 24			10 57	11 24	11 57
	d	22p55	23p34				06 54		07 54			08 41	08 58		09 24	09 58				10 24			10 58	11 24	11 58
Mossley (Grtr Manchester)	d												09 02			10 02							11 02		12 02
Greenfield	d												09 06			10 06							11 06		12 06
Marsden	d												09 15			10 15							11 15		12 15
Slaithwaite	d												09 19			10 19							11 19		12 19
Huddersfield	a	23p15	23p52	00 25	02 11	05 31	07 11		08 11			08 59	09 28		09 42	10 28			10 11	10 42		11 11	11 28	11 42	12 28
	d	23p16	23p53	00 26	02 12	05 32	07 12	07 51	08 12			09 02			09 43		09 51		10 12	10 43		11 12		11 43	
Deighton	d							07 54									09 54								
Mirfield	d							07 59									09 59								
Ravensthorpe	d							08 02									10 02								
Dewsbury	a	23p25		00s35			07 21	08 06	08 21			09 11					10 06		10 22			11 21			
	d	23p26					07 22	08 06	08 22			09 11					10 06		10 22			11 22			
Batley	d							08 09									10 09								
Morley	d							08 15									10 15								
Cottingley	d							08 19									10 19								
Leeds 10	a	23p41	00 14	00 50	02 33	05 53	07 37	08 27	08 37			09 27			10 07		10 27		10 37	11 04		11 37		12 04	
	d	23p42	00 15	00 54	02 35	05 55	07 40		08 40	09 12		09 40		10 04	10 22				10 40	11 12		11 40		12 12	
Garforth	d																								
South Milford	a														10 34										
Selby	a														10 44										
Howden	a																								
Brough	a														11 03										
Hull	a														11 18										
York 8	a	00 09	00 42	01 22	03 03	06 23	08 08		09 07	09 37		10 07		10 29					11 07	11 39		12 05		12 39	
	d						08 21		09 10	09 40		10 13		10 32				10 42	11 10	11 44		12 08		12 42	
Malton	d									10 04				10 56						12 08					
Seamer	a									10 20				11 13						12 25					
Scarborough	a									10 30				11 22						12 34					
Thirsk	a						08 37											10 59						12 59	
Northallerton	a						08 45		09 30			10 35						11 07	11 30			12 28		13 07	
Darlington 7	a						08 56		09 42			10 47							11 42			12 40			
Yarm	d																	11 21						13 22	
Thornaby	a						09 16											11 29						13 30	
Middlesbrough	a						09 27											11 39						13 40	
Durham	a								09 59			11 08							11 59			12 57			
Chester-le-Street	a																								
Newcastle 8 ⇌	a								10 18			11 24							12 15			13 12			

Table 39

Sundays

29 May to 11 September

Liverpool, Manchester Airport and Manchester - Huddersfield, Leeds, Hull, York, Scarborough, Middlesbrough and Newcastle

		NT	TP	TP	TP	TP	TP	NT	TP	TP	NT	NT	TP	TP	TP	TP	NT	TP	TP	NT	NT	TP	TP
			◇1	◇1	◇1	◇1	◇1		◇1	◇1			◇1	◇1	◇1	◇1		◇1	◇1			◇1	◇1
															A								
Liverpool Lime Street 10	d					11 22				12 22					13 22				14 22				
L'pool South Parkway 7 ✈	d					11 32				12 32					13 32				14 32				
Warrington Central	d					11 45				12 45					13 45				14 45				
Birchwood	d					11 50				12 50					13 50				14 50				
Newton-le-Willows	d																						
Manchester Oxford Road	d					12 07				13 07					14 07				15 07				
Manchester Airport ✈	d			11 20			12 20						13 20			14 20						15 20	
Manchester Piccadilly 10	a			11 35		12 09	12 37			13 09			13 37		14 09	14 37			15 09			15 37	
	d			11 42	12 02	12 11	12 42		13 02	13 11			13 42	14 02	14 11	14 42		15 02	15 11			15 42	16 02
Manchester Victoria	a																						
	d							12 43			13 43						14 43			15 43			
Ashton-under-Lyne	d							12 53			13 53						14 53			15 53			
Stalybridge	a					12 24		12 57		13 24	13 57				14 24		14 57		15 24	15 57			
	d					12 24		12 58		13 24	13 58				14 24		14 58		15 24	15 58			
Mossley (Grtr Manchester)	d							13 02			14 02						15 02			16 02			
Greenfield	d							13 06			14 06						15 06			16 06			
Marsden	d							13 15			14 15						15 15			16 15			
Slaithwaite	d							13 19			14 19						15 19			16 19			
Huddersfield	a			12 11	12 32	12 42	13 11	13 28	13 32	13 42	14 28		14 11	14 32	14 42	15 11	15 28	15 32	15 42	16 28		16 11	16 32
	d	11 58		12 12	12 33	12 43	13 12		13 33	13 43		13 58	14 12	14 33	14 43	15 12		15 33	15 43		15 58	16 12	16 33
Deighton	d	12 01										14 01									16 01		
Mirfield	d	12 06										14 06									16 06		
Ravensthorpe	d	12 09										14 09									16 09		
Dewsbury	a	12 13		12 21			13 21					14 13	14 21			15 21					16 13	16 21	
	d	12 13		12 22			13 22					14 13	14 22			15 22					16 13	16 22	
Batley	d	12 16										14 16									16 16		
Morley	d	12 22										14 22									16 22		
Cottingley	d	12 26										14 26									16 26		
Leeds 10	a	12 34		12 37	12 54	13 04	13 37		13 54	14 04		14 34	14 37	14 52	15 04	15 37		15 54	16 04		16 34	16 37	16 54
	d			12 40	13 01	13 12	13 40		13 57	14 12			14 40	15 00	15 12	15 40		15 57	16 12			16 40	17 01
Garforth	d																						
South Milford	a				13 13									15 12									17 14
Selby	a				13 23									15 22									17 23
Howden	a																						
Brough	a				13 41									15 40									17 41
Hull	a				13 59									15 59									17 59
York 8	a			13 07		13 39	14 07		14 24	14 38			15 07		15 38	16 05		16 24	16 38			17 07	
	d		12 49	13 10		13 43	14 10			14 50			15 10		15 43	16 08			16 42			17 10	
Malton	d					14 07									16 07								
Seamer	a					14 24									16 24								
Scarborough	a		13 36			14 33									16 33								
Thirsk	a									15 12									17 04				
Northallerton	a			13 30			14 30			15 20			15 30			16 28			17 16			17 30	
Darlington 7	a			13 42			14 42						15 42			16 40						17 42	
Yarm	d									15 35									17 32				
Thornaby	a									15 43									17 41				
Middlesbrough	a									15 52									17 50				
Durham	a			13 59			14 59						16 00			16 57						17 59	
Chester-le-Street	a			14 05									16 06									18 05	
Newcastle 8	a			14 17			15 15						16 18			17 12						18 18	

A from 29 May until 31 July

Table 39

Sundays

29 May to 11 September

Liverpool, Manchester Airport and Manchester - Huddersfield, Leeds, Hull, York, Scarborough, Middlesbrough and Newcastle

		TP	TP	NT	TP	TP	NT	NT	TP	TP	TP	TP	TP	NT	TP	TP	NT	NT	TP	TP	TP	TP
		◇1	◇1		◇1	◇1			◇1	◇1	◇1	◇1	◇1		◇1	◇1			◇1	◇1	◇1	◇1
Liverpool Lime Street 10	d	15 22				16 22						17 22				18 22					19 22	
L'pool South Parkway 7 ✈	d	15 32				16 32						17 32				18 32					19 32	
Warrington Central	d	15 45				16 45						17 45				18 45					19 45	
Birchwood	d	15 50				16 50						17 50				18 50					19 50	
Newton-le-Willows	d																					
Manchester Oxford Road	d	16 07				17 07						18 07				19 07					20 07	
Manchester Airport ✈	d		16 20							17 20			18 20						19 20			20 20
Manchester Piccadilly 10	a	16 09	16 37			17 09				17 37		18 09	18 37			19 09			19 37		20 09	20 37
	d	16 11	16 42		17 02	17 11				17 42	18 02	18 11	18 42		19 02	19 11			19 42	20 06	20 11	20 42
Manchester Victoria	a																					
	d			16 43			17 43							18 43			19 43					
Ashton-under-Lyne	d			16 53			17 53							18 53			19 53					
Stalybridge	a	16 24		16 57		17 24	17 57					18 24		18 57		19 24	19 57				20 24	
	d	16 24		16 58		17 24	17 58					18 24		18 58		19 24	19 58				20 24	
Mossley (Grtr Manchester)	d			17 02			18 02							19 02			20 02					
Greenfield	d			17 06			18 06							19 06			20 06					
Marsden	d			17 15			18 15							19 15			20 15					
Slaithwaite	d			17 19			18 19							19 19			20 19					
Huddersfield	a	16 42	17 11	17 28	17 32	17 42	18 28			18 11	18 32	18 42	19 11	19 28	19 32	19 42	20 28		20 11	20 36	20 42	21 11
	d	16 43	17 12		17 33	17 43		17 58		18 12	18 33	18 43	19 12		19 33	19 43		19 58	20 12	20 37	20 43	21 12
Deighton	d							18 01										20 01				
Mirfield	d							18 06										20 06				
Ravensthorpe	d							18 09										20 09				
Dewsbury	a		17 21					18 13		18 21			19 21					20 13	20 21			21 21
	d		17 22					18 13		18 22			19 22					20 13	20 22			21 22
Batley	d							18 16										20 16				
Morley	d							18 22										20 22				
Cottingley	d							18 26										20 26				
Leeds 10	a	17 04	17 37		17 54	18 04		18 34		18 37	18 54	19 04	19 37		19 54	20 04		20 34	20 37	20 58	21 04	21 37
	d	17 12	17 40		17 57	18 12				18 40	19 01	19 12	19 40		19 57	20 12			20 40	21 04	21 12	21 40
Garforth	d																					
South Milford	a										19 14											
Selby	a										19 29				20 17					21 38		
Howden	a																					
Brough	a										19 48				20 36					21 58		
Hull	a										20 06				20 54					22 15		
York 8	a	17 38	18 07		18 24	18 38				19 07		19 35	20 04			20 38			21 05		21 38	22 08
	d	17 43	18 10			18 42			18 46	19 10		19 45	20 10			20 44			21 08			22 10
Malton	d	18 07										20 09				21 08						22 35
Seamer	a	18 24										20 26				21 25						22 51
Scarborough	a	18 33							19 33			20 35				21 34						22 59
Thirsk	a					18 59							20 26						21 26			
Northallerton	a		18 30			19 07				19 30			20 34						21 34			
Darlington 7	a		18 42							19 42									21 45			
Yarm	d					19 22							20 50									
Thornaby	a					19 30							20 58									
Middlesbrough	a					19 40							21 08									
Durham	a		18 59							20 00									22 02			
Chester-le-Street	a									20 06												
Newcastle 8	a		19 16							20 17									22 17			

Table 39

Sundays

29 May to 11 September

Liverpool, Manchester Airport and Manchester - Huddersfield, Leeds, Hull, York, Scarborough, Middlesbrough and Newcastle

		NT	TP	NT	TP	NT	TP	TP	TP	TP
			◇1		◇1		◇1	◇1	◇1	◇1
								A	B	
Liverpool Lime Street 10	d		20 22					21 52	21 52	
L'pool South Parkway 7 ✈	d		20 32					22 02	22 02	
Warrington Central	d		20 45					22 15	22 15	
Birchwood	d		20 50					22 20	22 20	
Newton-le-Willows	d									
Manchester Oxford Road	d		21 07					22 37	22 37	
Manchester Airport ✈	d						21 20			23 20
Manchester Piccadilly 10	a		21 09				21 37	22 39	22 39	23 37
	d		21 11				21 42	22 42	22 42	23 42
Manchester Victoria	a									
	d	20 43		21 43						
Ashton-under-Lyne	d	20 53		21 53						
Stalybridge	a	20 57	21 24	21 57				22 54	22 54	
	d	20 58	21 24					22 54	22 54	
Mossley (Grtr Manchester)	d	21 02								
Greenfield	d	21 06								
Marsden	d	21 15				21 47				
Slaithwaite	d	21 19				21 51				
Huddersfield	a	21 28	21 42			21 57	22 11	23 12	23 12	00 11
	d		21 43			21 57	22 12	23 12	23 12	00 12
Deighton	d					22 01				
Mirfield	d					22 06				
Ravensthorpe	d					22 09				
Dewsbury	a					22 12	22 21	23 22	23 22	
	d					22 13	22 22	23 22	23 22	
Batley	d					22 16				
Morley	d					22 22				
Cottingley	d					22 25				
Leeds 10	a		22 04			22 34	22 37	23 37	23 39	00 51
	d		22 12		22 22		22 40	23 40	23 42	00 54
Garforth	d									
South Milford	a				22 34					
Selby	a				22 44					
Howden	a									
Brough	a				23 02					
Hull	a				23 19					
York 8	a		22 40				23 11	00 09	00 26	01 22
	d		22 42							
Malton	d									
Seamer	a									
Scarborough	a									
Thirsk	a		23 06							
Northallerton	a		23 16							
Darlington 7	a		23 28							
Yarm	d									
Thornaby	a									
Middlesbrough	a									
Durham	a		23 45							
Chester-le-Street	a									
Newcastle 8	a		00 15							

A from 29 May until 19 June

B from 26 June until 11 September

Table 39

Sundays

18 September to 23 October

Liverpool, Manchester Airport and Manchester - Huddersfield, Leeds, Hull, York, Scarborough, Middlesbrough and Newcastle

		TP	TP	NT	TP	TP	NT	TP	TP	NT	NT	TP	NT	TP	TP	NT	TP	TP	NT	TP	NT	NT	TP	NT
		◇1	1		◇1	◇1	🚌	◇1	◇1			◇1	🚌	◇1	◇1		◇1	◇1		◇1	🚌		◇1	
Liverpool Lime Street 10	d											08 23					09 22			10 22				
L'pool South Parkway 7 ✈	d																							
Warrington Central	d																							
Birchwood	d																							
Newton-le-Willows	d											08 41					09 40			10 41				
Manchester Oxford Road	d																							
Manchester Airport ✈	d	22p22							07 40						09 03			10 03					11 03	
Manchester Piccadilly 10	a	22p36							07 53						09 19			10 18					11 18	
	d	22p42							07 55						09 20			10 21					11 21	
Manchester Victoria	a								08 10			09 03			09 35		10 03	10 35		11 03			11 35	
	d								08 30	08 43		09 05			09 38	09 43	10 05	10 38	10 43	11 05			11 38	11 43
Ashton-under-Lyne	d									08 53						09 53			10 53					11 53
Stalybridge	a	22p55								08 58						09 59			10 59					11 59
	d	22p55					09 10						10 10								11 10			
Mossley (Grtr Manchester)	d						09 18						10 18								11 18			
Greenfield	d						09 24						10 24								11 24			
Marsden	d																							
Slaithwaite	d																							
Huddersfield	a	23p15					10 05		09 15			09 51	11 05				10 54				12 05			
	d	23p16		07 13					09 18		09 44	09 53					10 56					11 58		
Deighton	d			07 25							09 47											12 01		
Mirfield	d			07 37							09 52											12 06		
Ravensthorpe	d			07 43							09 55											12 09		
Dewsbury	a	23p25		07 51					09 27		09 59				10 21			11 21		11 58		12 13	12 21	
	d	23p26		07 52					09 27		10 03				10 23			11 22		11 59		12 13	12 22	
Batley	d			08 01							10 06											12 16		
Morley	d			08 14							10 12											12 22		
Cottingley	d			08 25							10 15											12 26		
Leeds 10	a	23p41		08 40					09 43		10 23	10 14			10 38		11 15	11 37		12 12		12 34	12 37	
	d	23p42	00 16			08 40		09 12	09 45			10 17		10 24	10 40		11 18	11 40		12 12			12 40	
Garforth	d																							
South Milford	a													10 36										
Selby	a													10 46										
Howden	a																							
Brough	a													11 04										
Hull	a													11 21										
York 8	a	00 09	00 43			09 08		09 37	10 11			10 41			11 08		11 41	12 05		12 38			13 07	
	d				08 21	09 10		09 40	10 13			10 42			11 10		11 44	12 08		12 42			13 10	
Malton	d							10 04									12 08							
Seamer	a							10 20									12 25							
Scarborough	a							10 30									12 34							
Thirsk	a				08 37							10 59								12 59				
Northallerton	a				08 45	09 30			10 35			11 07			11 30			12 28		13 07			13 30	
Darlington 7	a				08 56	09 42			10 47						11 42			12 40					13 42	
Yarm	d											11 22								13 22				
Thornaby	a				09 16							11 30								13 30				
Middlesbrough	a				09 27							11 40								13 40				
Durham	a					09 59			11 08						11 59			12 57					13 59	
Chester-le-Street	a																						14 05	
Newcastle 8	a					10 18			11 24						12 15			13 12					14 17	

Table 39

Sundays
18 September to 23 October

Liverpool, Manchester Airport and Manchester - Huddersfield, Leeds, Hull, York, Scarborough, Middlesbrough and Newcastle

		NT	TP	TP	TP	NT	NT	TP	TP	NT	TP	NT	NT	TP	TP	TP	NT	NT	TP	TP	NT	TP	NT
		🚌	◇1	◇1	◇1		🚌	◇1	◇1		◇1		🚌	◇1	◇1	◇1		🚌	◇1	◇1		◇1	
Liverpool Lime Street 10	d			11 22					12 22						13 22					14 22			
L'pool South Parkway 7 ✈	d																						
Warrington Central	d																						
Birchwood	d																						
Newton-le-Willows	d			11 40					12 41						13 40					14 41			
Manchester Oxford Road	d																						
Manchester Airport ✈	d				12 03						13 03					14 03						15 03	
Manchester Piccadilly 10	a				12 18						13 18					14 18						15 18	
	d				12 21						13 21					14 21						15 21	
Manchester Victoria	a			12 03	12 35				13 03		13 35				14 03	14 35				15 03		15 35	
	d			12 05	12 38	12 43			13 05		13 38	13 43			14 05	14 38	14 43			15 05		15 38	15 43
Ashton-under-Lyne	d					12 53						13 53					14 53						15 53
Stalybridge	a					12 59						13 59					14 59						15 59
	d	12 10					13 10						14 10					15 10					
Mossley (Grtr Manchester)	d	12 18					13 18						14 18					15 18					
Greenfield	d	12 24					13 24						14 24					15 24					
Marsden	d																						
Slaithwaite	d																						
Huddersfield	a	13 05					14 05						15 05					16 05					
	d		12 30					13 30		13 58				14 30					15 30		15 58		
Deighton	d									14 01											16 01		
Mirfield	d									14 06											16 06		
Ravensthorpe	d									14 09											16 09		
Dewsbury	a		12 39	12 58	13 21			13 39	13 58	14 13	14 21			14 39	14 58	15 21			15 39	15 58	16 13	16 21	
	d		12 40	12 59	13 22			13 40	13 59	14 13	14 22			14 40	14 59	15 22			15 40	15 59	16 13	16 22	
Batley	d									14 16											16 16		
Morley	d									14 22											16 22		
Cottingley	d									14 26											16 26		
Leeds 10	a		12 54	13 12	13 37			13 54	14 11	14 34	14 37			14 54	15 12	15 37			15 54	16 12	16 34	16 37	
	d		13 01	13 12	13 40			13 57	14 12		14 40			15 01	15 12	15 40			15 57	16 12		16 40	
Garforth	d																						
South Milford	a		13 13											15 13									
Selby	a		13 23											15 23									
Howden	a																						
Brough	a		13 41											15 41									
Hull	a		13 59											15 59									
York 8	a			13 39	14 06			14 24	14 38		15 07				15 38	16 05			16 24	16 38		17 07	
	d			13 43	14 10				14 50		15 10				15 43	16 08				16 42		17 10	
Malton	d			14 07											16 07								
Seamer	a			14 24											16 24								
Scarborough	a			14 33											16 33								
Thirsk	a								15 12											17 04			
Northallerton	a				14 30				15 20		15 30					16 28				17 16		17 30	
Darlington 7	a				14 42						15 42					16 40						17 42	
Yarm	d								15 35											17 32			
Thornaby	a								15 43											17 40			
Middlesbrough	a								15 52											17 50			
Durham	a				14 59						16 00					16 57						17 59	
Chester-le-Street	a										16 06											18 05	
Newcastle 8	a				15 15						16 18					17 12						18 18	

Table 39

Sundays
18 September to 23 October

Liverpool, Manchester Airport and Manchester - Huddersfield, Leeds, Hull, York, Scarborough, Middlesbrough and Newcastle

		NT	TP	TP	TP	NT	NT	TP	TP	NT	TP	NT	NT	TP	TP	TP	NT	NT	TP	TP	NT	TP
		🚌	◇1	◇1	◇1		🚌	◇1	◇1		◇1		🚌	◇1	◇1	◇1		🚌	◇1	◇1		◇1
Liverpool Lime Street 10	d			15 22					16 22						17 22					18 22		
L'pool South Parkway 7 ✈	d																					
Warrington Central	d																					
Birchwood	d																					
Newton-le-Willows	d			15 40					16 41						17 41					18 40		
Manchester Oxford Road	d																					
Manchester Airport ✈	d				16 03						17 03					18 03						19 03
Manchester Piccadilly 10	a				16 18						17 18					18 18						19 18
	d				16 21						17 21					18 21						19 21
Manchester Victoria	a			16 03	16 35				17 03		17 35				18 03	18 35				19 03		19 35
	d			16 05	16 38	16 43			17 05		17 38	17 43			18 05	18 38	18 43			19 05		19 38
Ashton-under-Lyne	d					16 53						17 53					18 53					
Stalybridge	a					16 59						17 59					18 59					
	d	16 10					17 10						18 10					19 10				
Mossley (Grtr Manchester)	d	16 18					17 18						18 18					19 18				
Greenfield	d	16 24					17 24						18 24					19 24				
Marsden	d																					
Slaithwaite	d																					
Huddersfield	a	17 05					18 05						19 05					20 05				
	d		16 30					17 30		17 58				18 30					19 30		19 58	
Deighton	d									18 01											20 01	
Mirfield	d									18 06											20 06	
Ravensthorpe	d									18 09											20 09	
Dewsbury	a		16 39	16 58	17 21			17 39	17 58	18 13	18 21			18 39	18 58	19 21			19 39	19 58	20 13	20 21
	d		16 40	16 59	17 22			17 40	17 59	18 13	18 22			18 40	18 59	19 22			19 40	19 59	20 13	20 22
Batley	d									18 16											20 16	
Morley	d									18 22											20 22	
Cottingley	d									18 26											20 26	
Leeds 10	a		16 54	17 12	17 37			17 54	18 12	18 34	18 37			18 54	19 12	19 37			19 55	20 12	20 34	20 37
	d		17 01	17 12	17 40			17 57	18 12		18 40			19 01	19 12	19 40			19 57	20 12		20 40
Garforth	d																					
South Milford	a		17 14											19 14								
Selby	a		17 23											19 30					20 17			
Howden	a																					
Brough	a		17 41											19 51					20 36			
Hull	a		17 59											20 06					20 54			
York 8	a			17 38	18 07			18 24	18 38		19 05				19 35	20 04				20 38		21 05
	d			17 43	18 10				18 42		19 10				19 45	20 10				20 44		21 08
Malton	d			18 07											20 09					21 08		
Seamer	a			18 24											20 26					21 25		
Scarborough	a			18 33											20 35					21 34		
Thirsk	a								18 58							20 26						21 26
Northallerton	a				18 30				19 07		19 30					20 34						21 34
Darlington 7	a				18 42						19 42											21 45
Yarm	d								19 22							20 50						
Thornaby	a								19 30							20 58						
Middlesbrough	a								19 40							21 08						
Durham	a				18 59						20 00											22 02
Chester-le-Street	a										20 06											
Newcastle 8	a				19 16						20 17											22 17

Table 39

Sundays
18 September to 23 October

Liverpool, Manchester Airport and Manchester - Huddersfield, Leeds, Hull, York, Scarborough, Middlesbrough and Newcastle

		NT	NT	TP ◇1	TP ◇1	TP ◇1	NT	TP ◇1	NT	TP ◇1	NT	TP ◇1	NT	TP ◇1	TP ◇1
Liverpool Lime Street 10	d				19 22			20 22						21 52	
L'pool South Parkway 7	d														
Warrington Central	d														
Birchwood	d														
Newton-le-Willows	d				19 40			20 40						22 09	
Manchester Oxford Road	d														
Manchester Airport	d					20 03						21 03			23 25
Manchester Piccadilly 10	a					20 18						21 18			23 38
	d					20 21						21 21			23 40
Manchester Victoria	a				20 03	20 35		21 03				21 35		22 29	23 53
	d	19 43			20 05	20 38	20 43	21 05				21 38	21 43	22 38	23 55
Ashton-under-Lyne	d	19 53					20 53						21 53		
Stalybridge	a	19 59					20 59						21 57		
	d		20 10						21 10						
Mossley (Grtr Manchester)	d		20 18						21 18						
Greenfield	d		20 24						21 24						
Marsden	d														
Slaithwaite	d														
Huddersfield	a		21 05						22 05			22 23		23 23	00 40
	d			20 33							21 57	22 26		23 26	00 43
Deighton	d										22 01				
Mirfield	d										22 06				
Ravensthorpe	d										22 09				
Dewsbury	a			20 42	20 56	21 22		21 58			22 12	22 35		23 35	
	d			20 43	20 57	21 22		21 59			22 13	22 35		23 35	
Batley	d										22 16				
Morley	d										22 22				
Cottingley	d										22 25				
Leeds 10	a			20 58	21 12	21 37		22 12			22 34	22 50		23 50	01 04
	d			21 04	21 12	21 40		22 12		22 22		22 53		23 53	01 06
Garforth	d														
South Milford	a									22 34					
Selby	a			21 38						22 44					
Howden	a														
Brough	a			21 58						23 02					
Hull	a			22 15						23 19					
York 8	a				21 38	22 08		22 40				23 28		00 22	01 34
	d					22 10		22 42							
Malton	d					22 35									
Seamer	a					22 51									
Scarborough	a					22 59									
Thirsk	a							23 05							
Northallerton	a							23 15							
Darlington 7	a							23 28							
Yarm	d														
Thornaby	a														
Middlesbrough	a														
Durham	a							23 45							
Chester-le-Street	a														
Newcastle 8	a							00 15							

Table 39

Sundays
from 30 October

Liverpool, Manchester Airport and Manchester - Huddersfield, Leeds, Hull, York, Scarborough, Middlesbrough and Newcastle

		TP ◇1	TP 1	TP ◇1	TP ◇1	TP ◇1	TP ◇1	NT	TP ◇1	NT	NT	TP ◇1	TP ◇1	TP ◇1	TP ◇1	NT	TP ◇1	NT	NT	TP ◇1	TP ◇1	TP ◇1	TP ◇1
Liverpool Lime Street 10	d								08 22					09 22			10 22					11 22	
L'pool South Parkway 7	d								08 32					09 32			10 32					11 32	
Warrington Central	d								08 45					09 45			10 45					11 45	
Birchwood	d								08 50					09 50			10 50					11 50	
Newton-le-Willows	d																						
Manchester Oxford Road	d								09 07					10 07			11 07					12 07	
Manchester Airport	d	22p22					07 40						09 03		10 20					11 20			12 20
Manchester Piccadilly 10	a	22p36					07 53		09 09				09 19	10 09	10 37		11 09			11 37		12 09	12 34
	d	22p42					07 55		09 11				09 27	10 11	10 42		11 11			11 42	11 58	12 11	12 41
Manchester Victoria	a						08 10																
	d						08 30	08 43		09 43						10 43		11 43					
Ashton-under-Lyne	d							08 53		09 53						10 53		11 53					
Stalybridge	a	22p55						08 57	09 24	09 57				10 24		10 57	11 24	11 57				12 24	
	d	22p55						08 58	09 24	09 58				10 24		10 58	11 24	11 58				12 24	
Mossley (Grtr Manchester)	d							09 02		10 02						11 02		12 02					
Greenfield	d							09 06		10 06						11 06		12 06					
Marsden	d							09 15		10 15						11 15		12 15					
Slaithwaite	d							09 19		10 19						11 19		12 19					
Huddersfield	a	23p15					09 15	09 28	09 42	10 28			09 55	10 42	11 11	11 28	11 42	12 28		12 11	12 32	12 42	13 11
	d	23p16					09 18		09 43		09 51		10 12	10 43	11 12		11 43		11 58	12 12	12 33	12 43	13 12
Deighton	d										09 54								12 01				
Mirfield	d										09 59								12 06				
Ravensthorpe	d										10 02								12 09				
Dewsbury	a	23p25					09 27				10 06		10 21		11 21				12 13	12 21			13 21
	d	23p26					09 27				10 06		10 22		11 22				12 13	12 22			13 22
Batley	d										10 09								12 16				
Morley	d										10 15								12 22				
Cottingley	d										10 19								12 26				
Leeds 10	a	23p41					09 43		10 07		10 27		10 37	11 04	11 37		12 04		12 34	12 37	12 54	13 04	13 37
	d	23p42	00 16		08 40	09 12	09 45		10 22				10 39	11 12	11 40		12 12			12 40	13 01	13 12	13 40
Garforth	d																						
South Milford	a								10 34												13 13		
Selby	a								10 44												13 23		
Howden	a																						
Brough	a								11 03												13 41		
Hull	a								11 18												13 59		
York 8	a	00 09	00 43		09 08	09 37	10 11						11 07	11 39	12 05		12 39			13 07		13 39	14 07
	d			08 21	09 10	09 40	10 13					10 42	11 10	11 44	12 08		12 42			13 10		13 43	14 10
Malton	d					10 04								12 08								14 07	
Seamer	a					10 20								12 25								14 24	
Scarborough	a					10 30								12 34								14 33	
Thirsk	a			08 37								10 59					12 59						
Northallerton	a			08 45	09 30		10 35					11 07	11 30		12 28		13 07			13 30			14 30
Darlington 7	a			08 56	09 42		10 47						11 42		12 40					13 42			14 42
Yarm	d											11 21					13 22						
Thornaby	a			09 16								11 29					13 30						
Middlesbrough	a			09 27								11 39					13 40						
Durham	a				09 59		11 08						11 59		12 57					13 59			14 59
Chester-le-Street	a																			14 05			
Newcastle 8	a				10 18		11 24						12 15		13 12					14 17			15 15

Table 39

Sundays
from 30 October

Liverpool, Manchester Airport and Manchester - Huddersfield, Leeds, Hull, York, Scarborough, Middlesbrough and Newcastle

		NT	TP	TP	NT	NT	TP	TP	TP	NT	TP	TP	NT	NT	TP	TP	TP	TP	NT	TP	TP	NT	NT
			◇1	◇1			◇1	◇1	◇1		◇1	◇1			◇1	◇1	◇1	◇1		◇1	◇1		
Liverpool Lime Street 10	d			12 22								14 22					15 22				16 22		
L'pool South Parkway 7 ✈	d			12 32								14 32					15 32				16 32		
Warrington Central	d			12 45								14 45					15 45				16 45		
Birchwood	d			12 50								14 50					15 50				16 50		
Newton-le-Willows	d																						
Manchester Oxford Road	d			13 07								15 07					16 07				17 07		
Manchester Airport ✈	d						13 20		14 20						15 20			16 20					
Manchester Piccadilly 10 ⇌	a			13 09			13 37		14 37			15 09			15 37		16 09	16 37			17 09		
	d		13 02	13 11			13 42	14 02	14 42		15 02	15 11			15 42	16 02	16 11	16 42		17 02	17 11		
Manchester Victoria ⇌	a																						
	d	12 43			13 43					14 43			15 43						16 43			17 43	
Ashton-under-Lyne	d	12 53			13 53					14 53			15 53						16 53			17 53	
Stalybridge	a	12 57		13 24	13 57					14 57		15 24	15 57				16 24		16 57		17 24	17 57	
	d	12 58		13 24	13 58					14 58		15 24	15 58				16 24		16 58		17 24	17 58	
Mossley (Grtr Manchester)	d	13 02			14 02					15 02			16 02						17 02			18 02	
Greenfield	d	13 06			14 06					15 06			16 06						17 06			18 06	
Marsden	d	13 15			14 15					15 15			16 15						17 15			18 15	
Slaithwaite	d	13 19			14 19					15 19			16 19						17 19			18 19	
Huddersfield	a	13 28	13 32	13 42	14 28		14 11	14 32	15 11	15 28	15 32	15 42	16 28		16 11	16 32	16 42	17 11	17 28	17 32	17 42	18 28	
	d		13 33	13 43		13 58	14 12	14 33	15 12		15 33	15 43		15 58	16 12	16 33	16 43	17 12		17 33	17 43		17 58
Deighton	d					14 01								16 01									18 01
Mirfield	d					14 06								16 06									18 06
Ravensthorpe	d					14 09								16 09									18 09
Dewsbury	a					14 13	14 21		15 21					16 13	16 21			17 21					18 13
	d					14 13	14 22		15 22					16 13	16 22			17 22					18 13
Batley	d					14 16								16 16									18 16
Morley	d					14 22								16 22									18 22
Cottingley	d					14 26								16 26									18 26
Leeds 10	a		13 54	14 04		14 34	14 37	14 52	15 37		15 54	16 04		16 34	16 37	16 54	17 04	17 37		17 54	18 04		18 34
	d		13 57	14 12			14 40	15 00	15 40		15 57	16 12			16 40	17 01	17 12	17 40		17 57	18 12		
Garforth	d																						
South Milford	a							15 12								17 14							
Selby	a							15 22								17 23							
Howden	a																						
Brough	a							15 40								17 41							
Hull	a							15 59								17 59							
York 8	a		14 24	14 38			15 07		16 05		16 24	16 38			17 07		17 38	18 07		18 24	18 38		
	d			14 50			15 10		16 08			16 42			17 10		17 43	18 10			18 42		
Malton	d																18 07						
Seamer	a																18 24						
Scarborough	a																18 33						
Thirsk	a			15 12								17 04									18 58		
Northallerton	a			15 20			15 30		16 28			17 16			17 30			18 30			19 07		
Darlington 7	a						15 42		16 40						17 42			18 42					
Yarm	d			15 35								17 32									19 22		
Thornaby	a			15 43								17 41									19 30		
Middlesbrough	a			15 52								17 50									19 40		
Durham	a						16 00		16 57						17 59			18 59					
Chester-le-Street	a						16 06								18 05								
Newcastle 8 ⇌	a						16 18		17 12						18 18			19 16					

Table 39

Sundays
from 30 October

Liverpool, Manchester Airport and Manchester - Huddersfield, Leeds, Hull, York, Scarborough, Middlesbrough and Newcastle

		TP	TP	TP	TP	NT	TP	TP	NT	NT	TP	TP	TP	TP	NT	TP	NT	TP	NT	TP	TP	TP
		◇1	◇1	◇1	◇1		◇1	◇1			◇1	◇1	◇1	◇1		◇1		◇1		◇1	◇1	◇1
Liverpool Lime Street 10	d			17 22				18 22					19 22			20 22					21 52	
L'pool South Parkway 7 ✈	d			17 32				18 32					19 32			20 32					22 02	
Warrington Central	d			17 45				18 45					19 45			20 45					22 15	
Birchwood	d			17 50				18 50					19 50			20 50					22 20	
Newton-le-Willows	d																					
Manchester Oxford Road	d			18 07				19 07					20 07			21 07					22 37	
Manchester Airport ✈	d	17 20			18 20						19 20			20 20						21 20		23 20
Manchester Piccadilly 10 ⇌	a	17 37		18 09	18 37			19 09			19 37		20 09	20 37		21 09				21 37	22 39	23 37
	d	17 42	18 02	18 11	18 42		19 02	19 11			19 42	20 06	20 11	20 42		21 11				21 42	22 42	23 42
Manchester Victoria ⇌	a																					
	d					18 43			19 43						20 43		21 43					
Ashton-under-Lyne	d					18 53			19 53						20 53		21 53					
Stalybridge	a			18 24		18 57		19 24	19 57				20 24		20 57	21 24	21 57				22 54	
	d			18 24		18 58		19 24	19 58				20 24		20 58	21 24					22 54	
Mossley (Grtr Manchester)	d					19 02			20 02						21 02							
Greenfield	d					19 06			20 06						21 06							
Marsden	d					19 15			20 15						21 15				21 47			
Slaithwaite	d					19 19			20 19						21 19				21 51			
Huddersfield	a	18 11	18 32	18 42	19 11	19 28	19 32	19 42	20 28		20 11	20 36	20 42	21 11	21 28	21 42			21 57	22 11	23 12	00 11
	d	18 12	18 33	18 43	19 12		19 33	19 43		19 58	20 12	20 37	20 43	21 12		21 43			21 57	22 12	23 12	00 12
Deighton	d									20 01									22 01			
Mirfield	d									20 06									22 06			
Ravensthorpe	d									20 09									22 09			
Dewsbury	a	18 21			19 21					20 13	20 21			21 21					22 12	22 21	23 22	
	d	18 22			19 22					20 13	20 22			21 22					22 13	22 22	23 22	
Batley	d									20 16									22 16			
Morley	d									20 22									22 22			
Cottingley	d									20 26									22 25			
Leeds 10	a	18 37	18 54	19 04	19 37		19 54	20 04		20 34	20 37	20 58	21 04	21 37		22 04			22 34	22 37	23 39	00 51
	d	18 40	19 01	19 12	19 40		19 57	20 12			20 40	21 04	21 12	21 40		22 12		22 22		22 40	23 42	00 54
Garforth	d																					
South Milford	a		19 14															22 34				
Selby	a		19 29				20 17					21 38						22 44				
Howden	a																					
Brough	a		19 48				20 36					21 58						23 02				
Hull	a		20 06				20 54					22 15						23 19				
York 8	a	19 07		19 35	20 04			20 38			21 05		21 38	22 08		22 40				23 11	00 26	01 22
	d	19 10		19 45	20 10			20 44			21 08			22 10		22 42						
Malton	d			20 09				21 08						22 35								
Seamer	a			20 26				21 25						22 51								
Scarborough	a			20 35				21 34						22 59								
Thirsk	a				20 26						21 26					23 06						
Northallerton	a	19 30			20 34						21 34					23 16						
Darlington 7	a	19 42									21 45					23 28						
Yarm	d				20 50																	
Thornaby	a				20 58																	
Middlesbrough	a				21 08																	
Durham	a	20 00									22 02					23 45						
Chester-le-Street	a	20 06																				
Newcastle 8 ⇌	a	20 17									22 17					00 15						

York and Selby - Leeds

Miles	Miles				GR MX	TP MO	TP MX	TP MO	TP MX	TP MX	TP MO	TP	NT		TP	NT	NT	TP	XC	TP	NT	TP	TP		NT	TP
					R 1	◇1	◇1	◇1	◇1	◇1	◇1	◇1			◇1			◇1 trolley	◇1 trolley	◇1 trolley		◇1 trolley	◇1 trolley			◇1 trolley
0	—	**York 8**	33	d	00 17	01 38	01 38	02 47	02 52	04 00	04 23	05 26	05 40		05 57	06 09	06 13	06 28	06 32			06 55			07 06	07 26
8¾	—	Ulleskelf	33	d																					07 15	
10¾	—	Church Fenton	33	d																					07 21	
—	0	**Selby**		d												06a30				06 36	06 42		07 07			
—	7¾	South Milford		d																	06 51					
15¾	11	Micklefield		d									05 58				06 28				06 58				07 28	
17½	12¾	East Garforth		d									06 02				06 32				07 02				07 32	
18	13¼	Garforth		d									06 05		06 12		06 35				07 04	07 10	07 24		07 35	
21	16¼	Cross Gates		d									06 10				06 40				07 09				07 40	07 44
25½	20¾	**Leeds 10**		a	00 50	02 04	02 19	03 13	03 33	04 42	04 49	05 52	06 21		06 22		06 49	06 52	06 55	07 00	07 19	07 20	07 35		07 49	07 52
—	—	Bradford Interchange	37	a													07 11				07 43				08 09	

			NT	NT	TP	XC	NT	NT	TP		TP	NT	TP	NT	TP	NT	XC	NT	TP		TP	NT	TP	TP	XC	NT
					◇1 trolley	◇1 trolley			◇1 trolley		◇1 trolley		◇1 trolley		◇1 trolley		◇1 trolley		◇1 trolley		◇1 trolley		◇1 trolley	◇1 trolley	◇1 trolley	
York 8	33	d		07 29	07 40	07 44		07 48	07 55			08 12	08 25		08 40	08 43	08 44		08 57			09 11	09 28	09 40	09 44	
Ulleskelf	33	d																								
Church Fenton	33	d						08 05														09 23				
Selby		d	07 26	07a50			07 43				08 11			08 24		09a05		08 43			09 11					09 43
South Milford		d	07 35				07 52							08 34				08 53								09 52
Micklefield		d	07 41				07 57	08 13				08 27		08 41				08 56				09 30				09 58
East Garforth		d	07 46				08 01	08 17				08 31		08 45				09 01				09 34				10 02
Garforth		d	07 48				08 04	08 20	08 12			08 33	08 40	08 48				09 04	09 12			09 37				10 05
Cross Gates		d	07 53				08 10	08 25				08 38		08 52				09 08				09 42				10 10
Leeds 10		a	08 02		08 04	08 08	08 19	08 35	08 22		08 36	08 49	08 52	09 02	09 04		09 08	09 19	09 22		09 36	09 51	09 52	10 04	10 08	10 19
Bradford Interchange	37	a	08 28				08 43					09 12						09 43				10 12				10 43

			TP	TP	NT		NT	TP	TP	XC	TP	NT	NT	TP	NT		TP	TP	XC	NT	NT	TP	TP	NT	TP	
			◇1 trolley	◇1 trolley				◇1 trolley	◇1 trolley	◇1 trolley	◇1 trolley			◇1 trolley			◇1 trolley	◇1 trolley	◇1 trolley			◇1 trolley	◇1 trolley		◇1 trolley	
York 8	33	d	09 57		10 11		10 20	10 28	10 40	10 44	10 57	11 00	11 05		11 09		11 26	11 40	11 44		11 45	11 57		12 13	12 26	
Ulleskelf	33	d											11 15													
Church Fenton	33	d											11a19		11 21											
Selby		d		10 11			10a40					11a21		11 11						11 43	12a04		12 11			
South Milford		d																		11 52						
Micklefield		d			10 29										11 29					11 57				12 28		
East Garforth		d			10 33										11 33					12 02				12 32		
Garforth		d	10 12		10 35						11 12				11 35					12 05		12 12		12 35		
Cross Gates		d			10 40										11 40					12 09				12 40		
Leeds 10		a	10 22	10 36	10 49			10 52	11 04	11 07	11 22			11 36	11 49		11 52	12 04	12 08	12 19		12 22	12 36	12 49	12 52	
Bradford Interchange	37	a			11 11										12 11					12 43				13 12		

			TP	XC	NT	NT	TP	TP	NT	TP	TP		XC	NT	NT	TP	TP	NT	TP	TP	XC		NT	NT	TP	NT
			◇1 trolley	◇1 trolley			◇1 trolley	◇1 trolley		◇1 trolley	◇1 trolley		◇1 trolley			◇1 trolley	◇1 trolley		◇1 trolley	◇1 trolley	◇1 trolley				◇1 trolley	
York 8	33	d	12 40	12 44		12 47	12 57		13 09	13 24	13 40		13 44		13 44	13 57		14 13	14 26	14 40	14 44			14 47	14 57	15 01
Ulleskelf	33	d																								15 11
Church Fenton	33	d							13 21																	15a15
Selby		d			12 43	13a06		13 11						13 43	14a07		14 11						14 43	15a06		
South Milford		d			12 53									13 52									14 52			
Micklefield		d			12 58				13 29					13 57				14 29					14 56			
East Garforth		d			13 02				13 33					14 02				14 33					15 00			
Garforth		d			13 05		13 12		13 35					14 05		14 12		14 35					15 03		15 12	
Cross Gates		d			13 10				13 40					14 09				14 40					15 08			
Leeds 10		a	13 04	13 10	13 19		13 22	13 36	13 49	13 52	14 04		14 07	14 20		14 22	14 36	14 49	14 52	15 04	15 07		15 19		15 22	
Bradford Interchange	37	a			13 43				14 12					14 43				15 12					15 43			

			TP	NT	TP	TP	XC FX		XC FO	NT	TP	XC	TP	NT	NT	TP	TP		NT	TP	TP	NT	NT	TP	TP	TP
			◇1 trolley		◇1 trolley	◇1 trolley	◇1 trolley		◇1 trolley		◇1 trolley	◇1 trolley	◇1 trolley			◇1 trolley	◇1 trolley			◇1 trolley	◇1 trolley			◇1 trolley	◇1	◇1 trolley
York 8	33	d		15 08	15 26	15 40	15 44		15 44		15 57	16 04		16 09	16 12	16 26	16 40			16 57		17 13	17 19	17 26		17 41
Ulleskelf	33	d																								
Church Fenton	33	d		15 20										16 21									17 30			
Selby		d	15 11							15 41			16 10		16a36				16 43		17 11		17a45		17 32	
South Milford		d								15 52									16 53							
Micklefield		d		15 29						15 55				16 29					16 58			17 28				
East Garforth		d		15 33						15 59				16 33					17 02			17 32				
Garforth		d		15 35						16 02			16 27	16 35					17 05	17 12		17 35				
Cross Gates		d		15 40						16 07				16 40					17 10			17 40				
Leeds 10		a	15 36	15 49	15 52	16 04	16 07		16 08	16 19	16 22	16 32	16 37	16 49		16 52	17 04		17 19	17 22	17 36	17 49		17 52	17 58	18 04
Bradford Interchange	37	a		16 10						16 43				17 10								18 10				

York and Selby - Leeds

	XC		NT	TP	NT	NT	TP	NT	TP	TP	XC		NT	NT	NT	TP	TP	TP	XC	TP	NT		NT	TP
	◇1 ⌶			◇1 ⌶			◇1 ⌶		◇1 ⌶	◇1	◇1 ⌶					◇1	◇1	◇1	◇1	◇1				◇1
York 8 33 d	17 44			17 57		18 05	18 12	18 18		18 40	18 45				19 04	19 10		19 40	19 44	20 10	20 13		20 21	20 40
Ulleskelf 33 d						18 15																		
Church Fenton 33 d						18 23									19 21									
Selby d			17 38		18 00			18a42	18 29				18 46	19 00			19 30						20a42	
South Milford d			17 49										18 52											
Micklefield d			17 56			18 30							18 58		19 28						20 27			
East Garforth d			18 01			18 34							19 02		19 32						20 31			
Garforth d			18 03	18 12	18 18	18 37							19 04	19 15	19 35	19 22					20 34			
Cross Gates d			18 08			18 42							19 10		19 40						20 39			
Leeds 10 a	18 07		18 19	18 22	18 32	18 49	18 37		18 52	19 04	19 08		19 20	19 27	19 48	19 35	19 56	20 04	20 09	20 35	20 48			21 04
Bradford Interchange 37 a			18 43		18 58	19 09							19 44								21 10			

	XC	TP FO	TP FX	TP FX	NT	TP	TP		NT	NT	TP	NT
	◇1	◇1	◇1	◇1		◇1	◇1				◇1	
York 8 33 d	20 44		21 14		21 22	21 46			22 13	22 14	23 06	23 13
Ulleskelf 33 d					21 31							
Church Fenton 33 d					21 35							23 28
Selby d		21 06		21 16			22 07		22a32			
South Milford d		21 16		21 26			22 16					
Micklefield d					21 42					22 29		23 35
East Garforth d					21 45					22 34		23 39
Garforth d					21 47					22 36		23 42
Cross Gates d					21 52					22 40		23 47
Leeds 10 a	21 08	21 35	21 37	21 44	22 01	22 07	22 35			22 52	23 33	23 56
Bradford Interchange 37 a												

Saturdays

	GR	TP	TP	TP	TP	TP	NT	NT	TP		TP	XC	NT	TP	TP	NT	TP	NT	TP		XC	NT	TP	TP
	■ 1 ⊡	◇1	◇1	◇1	◇1	◇1			◇1		◇1 ⌶	◇1 ⌶		◇1	◇1		◇1		◇1 ⌶		◇1 ⌶		◇1 ⌶	◇1 ⌶
York 8 33 d	00 17	01 52	02 40	03 52	05 26	05 57	06 09	06 13	06 28			06 40		06 55		07 06	07 27	07 38	07 40		07 44		07 53	
Ulleskelf 33 d																07 15								
Church Fenton 33 d																07 21								
Selby d							06a30				06 36		06 42		07 07			07a57				07 42		08 11
South Milford d													06 51									07 52		
Micklefield d								06 28					06 58			07 28						07 57		
East Garforth d								06 32					07 02			07 32						08 02		
Garforth d						06 12		06 35					07 04	07 09		07 35						08 07	08 12	
Cross Gates d								06 40					07 09			07 40						08 10		
Leeds 10 a	00 50	02 18	03 06	04 34	05 52	06 22		06 49	06 53		07 00	07 01	07 19	07 20	07 33	07 49	07 51		08 03		08 08	08 19	08 22	08 36
Bradford Interchange 37 a								07 11					07 43			08 09						08 43		

	NT	TP	TP	NT	XC		NT	TP	TP	NT	TP	TP	XC	NT	NT		TP	TP	NT	TP	TP	NT	XC	NT
		◇1 ⌶	◇1 ⌶		◇1 ⌶			◇1 ⌶	◇1 ⌶		◇1 ⌶	◇1	◇1 ⌶				◇1 ⌶	◇1		◇1 ⌶	◇1 ⌶		◇1 ⌶	
York 8 33 d	08 12	08 25	08 40	08 43	08 44			08 57		09 11	09 25	09 40	09 46		09 50		09 57		10 11	10 28	10 40	10 43	10 45	
Ulleskelf 33 d																								
Church Fenton 33 d										09 22														
Selby d				09a05			08 43		09 11					09 43	10a09			10 11				11a03		10 42
South Milford d							08 53							09 53										10 52
Micklefield d	08 25						08 58			09 30				09 58					10 29					10 56
East Garforth d	08 29						09 02			09 34				10 02					10 33					11 00
Garforth d	08 32						09 05	09 12		09 37				10 05			10 12		10 35					11 03
Cross Gates d	08 37						09 10			09 42				10 10					10 41					11 08
Leeds 10 a	08 49	08 52	09 04		09 07		09 19	09 22	09 36	09 51	09 53	10 04	10 09	10 19			10 22	10 36	10 49	10 52	11 04		11 08	11 19
Bradford Interchange 37 a	09 12						09 43			10 11				10 43					11 12					11 43

	TP		NT	TP	NT	TP	TP	XC	NT	NT	TP		TP	NT	TP	TP	XC	NT	NT	TP	TP		NT	TP
	◇1 ⌶			◇1		◇1 ⌶	◇1 ⌶	◇1 ⌶			◇1 ⌶		◇1 ⌶		◇1 ⌶	◇1	◇1 ⌶			◇1 ⌶	◇1 ⌶			◇1 ⌶
York 8 33 d	10 57		11 05		11 09	11 26	11 40	11 45		11 45	11 57			12 13	12 26	12 40	12 45		12 47	12 57			13 09	13 24
Ulleskelf 33 d			11 15																					
Church Fenton 33 d			11a19		11 21																		13 21	
Selby d				11 11					11 43	12a04			12 11					12 44	13a06		13 11			
South Milford d									11 53									12 56						
Micklefield d					11 29				11 58					12 28				12 58					13 29	
East Garforth d					11 33				12 02					12 32				13 03					13 33	
Garforth d	11 12				11 35				12 05		12 12			12 35				13 06		13 12			13 35	
Cross Gates d					11 40				12 10					12 40				13 10					13 40	
Leeds 10 a	11 22			11 36	11 49	11 53	12 04	12 08	12 19		12 22		12 36	12 49	12 52	13 04	13 08	13 20		13 22	13 36		13 49	13 52
Bradford Interchange 37 a					12 12				12 43					13 12				13 43					14 12	

Table 40

York and Selby - Leeds

Saturdays

			TP ◇1 🛒	XC ◇1 🛒	NT	NT	TP ◇1 🛒	TP ◇1	NT		TP ◇1 🛒	TP ◇1 🛒	XC ◇1 🛒	NT	NT	TP ◇1 🛒	NT	TP ◇1	NT		TP ◇1 🛒	TP ◇1 🛒	XC ◇1 🛒	NT	TP ◇1 🛒	XC ◇1 🛒
York 8	33	d	13 40	13 44		13 44	13 57		14 13		14 26	14 40	14 44		14 47	14 57	15 01		15 09		15 26	15 40	15 45		15 57	16 06
Ulleskelf	33	d															15 11									
Church Fenton	33	d															15a15		15 21							
Selby		d			13 43	14a07		14 11						14 43	15a06			15 11						15 41		
South Milford		d			13 53									14 54										15 52		
Micklefield		d			13 58				14 29					14 57					15 29					15 56		
East Garforth		d			14 02				14 33					15 02					15 33					16 01		
Garforth		d			14 05		14 12		14 35					15 05		15 12			15 35					16 03	16 12	
Cross Gates		d			14 10				14 40					15 09					15 40					16 08		
Leeds 10		a	14 04	14 09	14 19		14 22	14 35	14 49		14 52	15 04	15 08	15 19		15 22		15 36	15 49		15 53	16 04	16 08	16 18	16 22	16 32
Bradford Interchange	37	a			14 43				15 12					15 43					16 10					16 43		

			TP ◇1 🛒	NT	NT		TP ◇1 🛒	TP ◇1 🛒	XC ◇1 🛒	NT	TP ◇1 🛒	TP ◇1	NT	NT	TP ◇1 🛒		TP ◇1	TP ◇1	XC ◇1 🛒	NT	TP ◇1	NT	TP ◇1	NT	TP ◇1	
York 8	33	d		16 09	16 12		16 26	16 40	16 44		16 57		17 12	17 19	17 26			17 40	17 44		17 57	18 05	18 12	18 18		
Ulleskelf	33	d																				18 16				
Church Fenton	33	d		16 21										17 30								18 20				
Selby		d	16 11		16a36					16 43		17 11		17a45			17 32			17 39				18a42	18 29	
South Milford		d								16 53										17 49						
Micklefield		d		16 29						16 58			17 29							17 56		18 28				
East Garforth		d		16 33						17 02			17 33							18 01		18 32				
Garforth		d		16 35						17 05	17 12		17 36							18 04	18 12	18 34				
Cross Gates		d		16 40						17 10			17 41							18 08		18 39				
Leeds 10		a	16 36	16 49			16 52	17 04	17 08	17 19	17 22	17 36	17 49		17 52		17 58	18 04	18 08	18 18	18 22	18 48	18 37		18 52	
Bradford Interchange	37	a		17 10						17 43			18 09							18 43		19 10				

			TP ◇1	XC ◇1 🛒	NT	NT	NT	TP ◇1	TP ◇1	TP ◇1	XC ◇1		NT	TP ◇1	NT	TP ◇1	TP ◇1	XC ◇1	TP ◇1	NT	TP ◇1		TP ◇1	NT	NT	TP ◇1
York 8	33	d	18 40	18 44			19 04	19 10		19 40	19 44		19 47	20 10	20 13		20 40	20 45	21 14	21 18	21 46			22 11	22 13	23 07
Ulleskelf	33	d																		21 27						
Church Fenton	33	d					19 21													21 33						
Selby		d			18 46	18 55			19 30				20a06			20 27							22 07	22a29		
South Milford		d			18 55											20 36							22 16			
Micklefield		d			18 58		19 28								20 27					21 41					22 28	
East Garforth		d			19 02		19 32								20 31					21 45					22 32	
Garforth		d			19 05	19 12	19 35	19 22							20 34					21 47					22 34	
Cross Gates		d			19 10		19 40								20 39					21 52					22 39	
Leeds 10		a	19 04	19 08	19 21	19 25	19 49	19 35	19 56	20 04	20 08			20 35	20 48	20 56	21 04	21 08	21 37	21 57	22 07		22 35		22 50	23 33
Bradford Interchange	37	a			19 44										21 10											

			NT
York 8	33	d	23 13
Ulleskelf	33	d	
Church Fenton	33	d	23 28
Selby		d	
South Milford		d	
Micklefield		d	23 35
East Garforth		d	23 39
Garforth		d	23 42
Cross Gates		d	23 47
Leeds 10		a	23 56
Bradford Interchange	37	a	

Sundays

until 19 June

			TP ◇1	TP ◇1	TP ◇1	TP ◇1	TP ◇1	TP ◇1	TP ◇1	NT	TP ◇1		XC ◇1 🛒	TP ◇1	NT	TP ◇1	XC ◇1 🛒	NT	TP ◇1	NT	TP ◇1		XC ◇1 🛒	TP ◇1	TP ◇1	NT
York 8	33	d	02 44	03 59	05 12	06 12	07 12	08 10	08 40	08 50	09 15		09 28		09 52	10 15	10 28	10 40	10 45	10 57	11 15		11 28		11 45	11 52
Ulleskelf	33	d																								
Church Fenton	33	d								09 02					10 04											12 04
Selby		d												09 33				10a58						11 29		
South Milford		d												09 42										11 38		
Micklefield		d								09 09					10 12					11 12						12 11
East Garforth		d								09 13					10 16					11 16						12 15
Garforth		d								09 16					10 18					11 18						12 18
Cross Gates		d								09 21					10 23					11 23						12 23
Leeds 10		a	03 10	04 25	05 38	06 38	07 38	08 37	09 03	09 30	09 38		09 52	10 00	10 32	10 38	10 51		11 08	11 32	11 38		11 51	11 56	12 08	12 32
Bradford Interchange	37	a								09 53					10 53					11 53						12 53

Table 40

York and Selby - Leeds

Sundays
until 19 June

		NT	TP	XC	TP	TP		NT	TP	TP	XC	NT	TP	NT	TP	TP		XC	TP	NT	NT	TP	TP	XC	TP
			◇1	◇1 🚲	◇1	◇1			◇1	◇1	◇1 🚲		◇1		◇1	◇1		◇1 🚲	◇1			◇1	◇1	◇1 🚲	◇1
York 8	33 d	12 05	12 15	12 28	.	12 45	.	12 52	13 15	.	13 40	13 40	13 45	13 52	14 15	14 33	.	14 41	14 45	14 49	14 52	15 15	.	15 39	15 45
Ulleskelf	33 d	.	.	.	.	.	.	.	.	.	.	.	.	.	.	.	.	.	.	.	.	.	.	.	.
Church Fenton	33 d	.	.	.	.	.	.	.	.	.	.	.	.	14 04	.	.	.	.	.	.	.	.	.	.	.
Selby	d	12a24	.	.	12 32	.	.	.	.	13 29	.	13a59	.	.	.	.	.	.	.	15a08	.	.	15 29	.	.
South Milford	d	.	.	.	.	.	.	.	.	13 38	.	.	.	.	.	.	.	.	.	.	.	.	15 38	.	.
Micklefield	d	.	.	.	.	.	.	13 07	.	.	.	.	.	14 11	.	.	.	.	.	.	15 07	.	.	.	.
East Garforth	d	.	.	.	.	.	.	13 11	.	.	.	.	.	14 15	.	.	.	.	.	.	15 11	.	.	.	.
Garforth	d	.	.	.	.	.	.	13 13	.	.	.	.	.	14 18	.	.	.	.	.	.	15 13	.	.	.	.
Cross Gates	d	.	.	.	.	.	.	13 18	.	.	.	.	.	14 23	.	.	.	.	.	.	15 18	.	.	.	.
Leeds 10	a	.	12 38	12 51	12 56	13 08	.	13 27	13 38	13 56	14 03	.	14 08	14 32	14 38	14 56	.	15 05	15 09	.	15 27	15 38	15 56	16 03	16 08
Bradford Interchange	37 a	.	.	.	.	.	.	13 53	.	.	.	.	.	14 53	.	.	.	.	.	.	15 53	.	.	.	.

		NT		NT	TP	TP	XC	TP	NT	NT	TP	TP		XC	TP	NT	TP	TP	XC	NT	TP	NT		NT	TP
					◇1	◇1	◇1 🚲	◇1			◇1	◇1		◇1 🚲	◇1		◇1	◇1	◇1 🚲	🚌	◇1				◇1
York 8	33 d	15 52	.	16 06	16 15	16 33	16 39	16 45	16 52	17 11	17 15	.	.	17 41	17 45	17 52	18 15	18 33	18 40	18 40	18 45	18 52	.	19 10	19 15
Ulleskelf	33 d	.	.	.	.	.	.	.	.	.	.	.	.	.	.	.	.	.	.	.	.	.	.	.	.
Church Fenton	33 d	16 04	.	.	.	.	.	.	.	.	.	.	.	.	.	18 04	.	.	.	19a10	.	.	.	.	.
Selby	d	.	.	16a24	.	.	.	.	.	17a30	.	17 29	.	.	.	.	.	.	.	.	.	.	.	19a35	.
South Milford	d	.	.	.	.	.	.	.	.	.	.	17 38	.	.	.	.	.	.	.	.	.	.	.	.	.
Micklefield	d	16 11	.	.	.	.	.	.	17 07	.	.	.	.	.	.	18 11	.	.	.	.	.	19 07	.	.	.
East Garforth	d	16 15	.	.	.	.	.	.	17 11	.	.	.	.	.	.	18 15	.	.	.	.	.	19 11	.	.	.
Garforth	d	16 18	.	.	.	.	.	.	17 13	.	.	.	.	.	.	18 18	.	.	.	.	.	19 13	.	.	.
Cross Gates	d	16 23	.	.	.	.	.	.	17 18	.	.	.	.	.	.	18 23	.	.	.	.	.	19 18	.	.	.
Leeds 10	a	16 32	.	.	16 38	16 56	17 01	17 08	17 27	.	17 38	17 56	.	18 04	18 08	18 32	18 38	18 57	19 04	.	19 08	19 27	.	.	19 38
Bradford Interchange	37 a	16 53	.	.	.	.	.	.	17 53	.	.	.	.	.	.	18 53	.	.	.	.	.	19 53	.	.	.

		TP	XC	TP	NT	TP	XC	TP		NT	TP	NT	TP	NT	NT	TP	GR	TP							
		◇1	◇1	◇1		◇1	◇1	◇1			◇1	🚌	◇1			◇1	1	◇1							
York 8	33 d	.	19 39	19 45	19 52	20 15	20 39	20 45	.	20 57	21 15	21 15	.	21 41	21 52	22 12	23 03	23 12	.	.	.	.	.	.	.
Ulleskelf	33 d	.	.	.	.	.	.	.	.	.	.	.	.	.	.	.	.	.	.	.	.	.	.	.	.
Church Fenton	33 d	.	.	.	20 04	.	.	.	.	.	.	21a45	.	.	22 04	.	.	.	.	.	.	.	.	.	.
Selby	d	19 29	.	.	.	.	.	.	.	.	.	.	21 31	22a00	.	.	.	.	.	.	.	.	.	.	.
South Milford	d	19 38	.	.	.	.	.	.	.	.	.	.	21 40	.	.	.	.	.	.	.	.	.	.	.	.
Micklefield	d	.	.	.	20 12	.	.	.	.	21 12	.	.	.	.	22 12	.	.	.	.	.	.	.	.	.	.
East Garforth	d	.	.	.	20 16	.	.	.	.	21 17	.	.	.	.	22 16	.	.	.	.	.	.	.	.	.	.
Garforth	d	.	.	.	20 18	.	.	.	.	21 19	.	.	.	.	22 19	.	.	.	.	.	.	.	.	.	.
Cross Gates	d	.	.	.	20 23	.	.	.	.	21 24	.	.	.	.	22 23	.	.	.	.	.	.	.	.	.	.
Leeds 10	a	19 54	20 05	20 08	20 32	20 38	21 02	21 08	.	21 33	21 38	.	21 59	.	22 32	22 36	23 34	23 38	.	.	.	.	.	.	.
Bradford Interchange	37 a	.	.	.	20 53	.	.	.	.	21 56	.	.	.	.	.	.	.	.	.	.	.	.	.	.	.

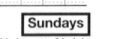

Sundays
26 June to 31 July

		TP	TP	TP	TP	TP	TP	TP	NT	TP		XC	TP	NT	TP	XC	NT	TP	NT	TP		XC	TP	TP	NT
		◇1	◇1	◇1	◇1	◇1	◇1	◇1		◇1		◇1 🚲	◇1		◇1	◇1 🚲		◇1		◇1		◇1 🚲	◇1	◇1	
York 8	33 d	02 44	03 59	05 12	06 12	07 12	08 10	08 40	08 50	09 15	.	09 28	.	09 52	10 15	10 28	10 40	10 45	10 57	11 15	.	11 28	.	11 45	11 52
Ulleskelf	33 d	.	.	.	.	.	.	.	.	.	.	.	.	.	.	.	.	.	.	.	.	.	.	.	.
Church Fenton	33 d	.	.	.	.	.	.	.	09 02	.	.	.	.	10 04	.	.	.	.	.	.	.	.	.	.	12 04
Selby	d	.	.	.	.	.	.	.	.	.	.	.	09 33	.	.	.	10a58	.	.	.	.	.	11 29	.	.
South Milford	d	.	.	.	.	.	.	.	.	.	.	.	09 42	.	.	.	.	.	.	.	.	.	11 38	.	.
Micklefield	d	.	.	.	.	.	.	.	09 09	.	.	.	.	10 12	.	.	.	.	11 12	.	.	.	.	.	12 11
East Garforth	d	.	.	.	.	.	.	.	09 13	.	.	.	.	10 16	.	.	.	.	11 16	.	.	.	.	.	12 15
Garforth	d	.	.	.	.	.	.	.	09 16	.	.	.	.	10 18	.	.	.	.	11 18	.	.	.	.	.	12 18
Cross Gates	d	.	.	.	.	.	.	.	09 21	.	.	.	.	10 23	.	.	.	.	11 23	.	.	.	.	.	12 23
Leeds 10	a	03 10	04 25	05 38	06 38	07 38	08 37	09 03	09 30	09 38	.	09 52	10 00	10 32	10 38	10 51	.	11 08	11 32	11 38	.	11 51	11 56	12 08	12 32
Bradford Interchange	37 a	.	.	.	.	.	.	.	09 53	.	.	.	.	10 53	.	.	.	.	11 53	.	.	.	.	.	12 53

		NT	TP	XC	TP	TP		NT	TP	TP	XC	NT	TP	NT	TP	TP		XC	TP	NT	NT	TP	TP	XC	TP
			◇1	◇1 🚲	◇1	◇1			◇1	◇1	◇1 🚲		◇1		◇1	◇1		◇1 🚲	◇1			◇1	◇1	◇1 🚲	◇1
York 8	33 d	12 05	12 15	12 28	.	12 45	.	12 52	13 15	.	13 40	13 40	13 45	13 52	14 15	14 33	.	14 41	14 45	14 49	14 52	15 15	.	15 39	15 45
Ulleskelf	33 d	.	.	.	.	.	.	.	.	.	.	.	.	.	.	.	.	.	.	.	.	.	.	.	.
Church Fenton	33 d	.	.	.	.	.	.	.	.	.	.	.	.	14 04	.	.	.	.	.	.	.	.	.	.	.
Selby	d	12a24	.	.	12 32	.	.	.	.	13 29	.	13a59	.	.	.	.	.	.	.	15a08	.	.	15 29	.	.
South Milford	d	.	.	.	.	.	.	.	.	13 38	.	.	.	.	.	.	.	.	.	.	.	.	15 38	.	.
Micklefield	d	.	.	.	.	.	.	13 07	.	.	.	.	.	14 11	.	.	.	.	.	.	15 07	.	.	.	.
East Garforth	d	.	.	.	.	.	.	13 11	.	.	.	.	.	14 15	.	.	.	.	.	.	15 11	.	.	.	.
Garforth	d	.	.	.	.	.	.	13 13	.	.	.	.	.	14 18	.	.	.	.	.	.	15 13	.	.	.	.
Cross Gates	d	.	.	.	.	.	.	13 18	.	.	.	.	.	14 23	.	.	.	.	.	.	15 18	.	.	.	.
Leeds 10	a	.	12 38	12 51	12 56	13 08	.	13 27	13 38	13 56	14 03	.	14 08	14 32	14 38	14 56	.	15 05	15 09	.	15 27	15 38	15 56	16 03	16 08
Bradford Interchange	37 a	.	.	.	.	.	.	13 53	.	.	.	.	.	14 53	.	.	.	.	.	.	15 53	.	.	.	.

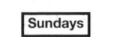

Table 40

York and Selby - Leeds

Sundays
26 June to 31 July

			NT		NT	TP	TP	XC	TP	NT	NT	TP	TP		XC	TP	NT	NT	TP	TP	XC	TP	NT		NT	TP
						◇1	◇1	◇1 🍴	◇1			◇1	◇1		◇1 🍴	◇1			◇1	◇1	◇1 🍴	◇1				◇1
York 8	33	d	15 52		16 06	16 15	16 33	16 39	16 45	16 52	17 11	17 15			17 41	17 45	17 52	18 10	18 15	18 33	18 40	18 45	18 52		19 10	19 15
Ulleskelf	33	d																								
Church Fenton	33	d	16 04														18 04	18a21								
Selby		d			16a24						17a30		17 29												19a35	
South Milford		d											17 38													
Micklefield		d	16 11							17 07							18 11						19 07			
East Garforth		d	16 15							17 11							18 15						19 11			
Garforth		d	16 18							17 13							18 18						19 13			
Cross Gates		d	16 23							17 18							18 23						19 18			
Leeds 10		a	16 32			16 38	16 56	17 01	17 08	17 27		17 38	17 56		18 04	18 08	18 32		18 38	18 57	19 04	19 08	19 27			19 38
Bradford Interchange	37	a	16 53							17 53							18 53						19 53			

			TP	XC	TP	NT	TP	XC	TP		NT	NT	TP	TP	NT	NT	TP	GR	TP							
			◇1	◇1	◇1		◇1	◇1	◇1				◇1	◇1			◇1	R 1 🍴	◇1							
York 8	33	d		19 39	19 45	19 52	20 15	20 39	20 45		20 50	20 57	21 15		21 41	21 52	22 12	23 03	23 12							
Ulleskelf	33	d																								
Church Fenton	33	d				20 04					21a01					22 04										
Selby		d	19 29											21 31	22a00											
South Milford		d	19 38											21 40												
Micklefield		d				20 12						21 12				22 12										
East Garforth		d				20 16						21 17				22 16										
Garforth		d				20 18						21 19				22 19										
Cross Gates		d				20 23						21 24				22 23										
Leeds 10		a	19 54	20 05	20 08	20 32	20 38	21 02	21 08			21 33	21 38	21 59		22 32	22 36	23 34	23 38							
Bradford Interchange	37	a				20 53						21 56														

Sundays
7 August to 11 September

			TP	TP	TP	TP	TP	TP	TP	NT	TP		XC	TP	NT	TP	XC	NT	TP	NT	TP		XC	TP	TP	NT
			◇1	◇1	◇1	◇1	◇1	◇1	◇1		◇1		◇1 🍴	◇1		◇1	◇1 🍴		◇1		◇1		◇1 🍴	◇1	◇1	
York 8	33	d	02 44	03 59	05 12	06 12	07 12	08 10	08 40	08 50	09 15		09 28		09 52	10 15	10 28	10 40	10 45	10 57	11 15		11 28		11 45	11 52
Ulleskelf	33	d																								
Church Fenton	33	d								09 02					10 04											12 04
Selby		d												09 33				10a58						11 29		
South Milford		d												09 42										11 38		
Micklefield		d								09 09					10 12					11 12						12 11
East Garforth		d								09 13					10 16					11 16						12 15
Garforth		d								09 16					10 18					11 18						12 18
Cross Gates		d								09 21					10 23					11 23						12 23
Leeds 10		a	03 10	04 25	05 38	06 38	07 38	08 37	09 03	09 30	09 38		09 54	10 00	10 32	10 38	10 51		11 08	11 32	11 38		11 51	11 56	12 08	12 32
Bradford Interchange	37	a								09 53					10 53					11 53						12 53

			NT	TP	XC	TP	TP		NT	TP	TP	XC	NT	TP	NT	TP	TP		XC	TP	NT	NT	TP	TP	XC	TP
				◇1	◇1 🍴	◇1	◇1			◇1	◇1	◇1 🍴		◇1		◇1	◇1		◇1 🍴	◇1			◇1	◇1	◇1 🍴	◇1
York 8	33	d	12 05	12 15	12 28		12 45		12 52	13 15		13 40	13 40	13 45	13 52	14 15	14 33		14 41	14 45	14 49	14 52	15 15		15 39	15 45
Ulleskelf	33	d																								
Church Fenton	33	d													14 04											
Selby		d	12a24			12 32					13 29		13a59								15a08			15 29		
South Milford		d									13 38													15 38		
Micklefield		d							13 07						14 11							15 07				
East Garforth		d							13 11						14 15							15 11				
Garforth		d							13 13						14 18							15 13				
Cross Gates		d							13 18						14 23							15 18				
Leeds 10		a		12 38	12 51	12 56	13 08		13 27	13 38	13 56	14 03		14 08	14 32	14 38	14 56		15 05	15 09		15 27	15 38	15 56	16 03	16 08
Bradford Interchange	37	a							13 53						14 53							15 53				

			NT		NT	TP	TP	XC	TP	NT	NT	TP	TP		XC	TP	NT	NT	TP	TP	XC	TP	NT		NT	TP
						◇1	◇1	◇1 🍴	◇1			◇1	◇1		◇1 🍴	◇1			◇1	◇1	◇1 🍴	◇1				◇1
York 8	33	d	15 52		16 06	16 15	16 33	16 39	16 45	16 52	17 11	17 15			17 41	17 45	17 52	18 10	18 15	18 33	18 40	18 45	18 52		19 10	19 15
Ulleskelf	33	d																								
Church Fenton	33	d	16 04														18 04	18a21								
Selby		d			16a24						17a30		17 29												19a35	
South Milford		d											17 38													
Micklefield		d	16 11							17 07							18 11						19 07			
East Garforth		d	16 15							17 11							18 15						19 11			
Garforth		d	16 18							17 13							18 18						19 13			
Cross Gates		d	16 23							17 18							18 23						19 18			
Leeds 10		a	16 32			16 38	16 56	17 01	17 08	17 27		17 38	17 56		18 04	18 08	18 32		18 38	18 57	19 04	19 08	19 27			19 38
Bradford Interchange	37	a	16 53							17 53							18 53						19 53			

Table 40

Sundays

7 August to 11 September

York and Selby - Leeds

		TP	XC	TP	NT	TP	XC	TP		NT	NT	TP	TP	NT	NT	TP	GR	TP
		◇1	◇1	◇1		◇1	◇1	◇1				◇1	◇1			◇1	1	◇1
York 8	33 d		19 39	19 45	19 52	20 15	20 39	20 45		20 50	20 57	21 15		21 41	21 52	22 12	23 03	23 12
Ulleskelf	33 d																	
Church Fenton	33 d				20 04					21a01					22 04			
Selby	d	19 29											21 31	22a00				
South Milford	d	19 38											21 40					
Micklefield	d				20 12						21 12				22 12			
East Garforth	d				20 16						21 17				22 16			
Garforth	d				20 18						21 19				22 19			
Cross Gates	d				20 23						21 24				22 23			
Leeds 10	a	19 54	20 05	20 08	20 32	20 38	21 02	21 08			21 33	21 38	21 59		22 32	22 36	23 34	23 38
Bradford Interchange	37 a				20 53						21 56							

Sundays

18 September to 23 October

		TP	TP	NT	TP	XC	TP	TP	NT	TP		XC	NT	TP	NT	TP	XC	TP	TP	NT		TP	XC	TP	TP
		◇1	◇1		◇1	◇1	◇1	◇1		◇1		◇1		◇1		◇1	◇1	◇1	◇1			◇1	◇1	◇1	◇1
York 8	33 d	08 10	08 30	08 50	09 15	09 28		09 45	09 52	10 15		10 28	10 40	10 45	10 57	11 15	11 28		11 45	11 52		12 15	12 28		12 45
Ulleskelf	33 d																								
Church Fenton	33 d			09 02					10 04											12 04					
Selby	d						09 33						10a58					11 29						12 32	
South Milford	d						09 42											11 38							
Micklefield	d			09 09					10 12						11 12					12 11					
East Garforth	d			09 13					10 16						11 16					12 15					
Garforth	d			09 16					10 18						11 18					12 18					
Cross Gates	d			09 21					10 23						11 23					12 23					
Leeds 10	a	08 37	08 53	09 30	09 38	09 54	10 00	10 08	10 32	10 38		10 51		11 08	11 32	11 38	11 51	11 56	12 08	12 32		12 38	12 51	12 56	13 08
Bradford Interchange	37 a			09 53					10 53						11 53					12 53					

		NT	TP	TP	XC	NT		TP	NT	TP	TP	XC	TP	NT	TP	TP		XC	TP	NT	NT	TP	TP	XC	TP
			◇1	◇1	◇1			◇1		◇1	◇1	◇1	◇1		◇1	◇1		◇1	◇1			◇1	◇1	◇1	◇1
York 8	33 d	12 52	13 15		13 40	13 40		13 45	13 52	14 15	14 33	14 41	14 45	14 52	15 15			15 38	15 45	15 52	16 06	16 15	16 33	16 39	16 45
Ulleskelf	33 d																								
Church Fenton	33 d								14 04											16 04					
Selby	d			13 29		13a59										15 29					16a24				
South Milford	d			13 38												15 38									
Micklefield	d	13 07							14 11					15 07						16 11					
East Garforth	d	13 11							14 15					15 11						16 15					
Garforth	d	13 13							14 18					15 13						16 18					
Cross Gates	d	13 18							14 23					15 18						16 23					
Leeds 10	a	13 27	13 37	13 56	14 03			14 08	14 32	14 38	14 56	15 05	15 08	15 27	15 38	15 56		16 03	16 08	16 32		16 38	16 56	17 01	17 08
Bradford Interchange	37 a	13 53							14 53					15 53						16 53					

		NT		TP	TP	XC	TP	NT	NT	TP	TP	XC		TP	NT	NT	TP	TP	XC	TP	NT	TP		XC	TP
				◇1	◇1	◇1	◇1			◇1	◇1	◇1		◇1			◇1	◇1	◇1	◇1		◇1		◇1	◇1
York 8	33 d	16 52		17 15		17 41	17 45	17 52	18 10	18 15	18 33	18 40		18 45	18 52	19 10	19 15		19 39	19 45	19 52	20 15		20 39	20 45
Ulleskelf	33 d																								
Church Fenton	33 d							18 04	18a21												20 04				
Selby	d				17 29											19a35		19 29							
South Milford	d				17 38													19 38							
Micklefield	d	17 07						18 11							19 07						20 12				
East Garforth	d	17 11						18 15							19 11						20 16				
Garforth	d	17 13						18 18							19 13						20 18				
Cross Gates	d	17 18						18 23							19 18						20 23				
Leeds 10	a	17 27		17 38	17 56	18 04	18 08	18 32		18 38	18 57	19 04		19 08	19 27		19 38	19 56	20 05	20 08	20 32	20 38		21 02	21 08
Bradford Interchange	37 a	17 53						18 53							19 53						20 53				

		NT	NT	TP	TP	NT	NT	TP		GR	TP
				◇1	◇1			◇1		1	◇1
York 8	33 d	20 50	20 57	21 15		21 41	21 52	22 12		23 03	23 12
Ulleskelf	33 d										
Church Fenton	33 d	21a01					22 04				
Selby	d				21 31	22a00					
South Milford	d				21 40						
Micklefield	d		21 12				22 12				
East Garforth	d		21 17				22 16				
Garforth	d		21 19				22 19				
Cross Gates	d		21 24				22 23				
Leeds 10	a		21 33	21 38	21 59		22 32	22 36		23 34	23 38
Bradford Interchange	37 a		21 56								

Table 40

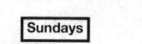

Sundays
from 30 October

York and Selby - Leeds

			TP ◇1	TP ◇1	NT	TP ◇1	XC ◇1 (trolley)	TP ◇1	NT	TP ◇1	XC ◇1 (trolley)		NT	TP ◇1	NT	TP ◇1	XC ◇1 (trolley)	TP ◇1	TP ◇1	NT	TP ◇1		XC ◇1 (trolley)	TP ◇1	TP ◇1	NT
York 8	33	d	08 10	08 40	08 50	09 15	09 28		09 52	10 15	10 28		10 40	10 45	10 57	11 15	11 28		11 45	11 52	12 15		12 28		12 45	12 52
Ulleskelf	33	d																								
Church Fenton	33	d			09 02				10 04											12 04						
Selby		d						09 33					10a58					11 29						12 32		
South Milford		d						09 42										11 38								
Micklefield		d			09 09				10 12						11 12					12 11						13 07
East Garforth		d			09 13				10 16						11 16					12 15						13 11
Garforth		d			09 16				10 18						11 18					12 18						13 13
Cross Gates		d			09 21				10 23						11 23					12 23						13 18
Leeds 10		a	08 37	09 03	09 30	09 38	09 54	10 00	10 32	10 38	10 51			11 08	11 32	11 38	11 51	11 56	12 08	12 32	12 38		12 51	12 56	13 08	13 27
Bradford Interchange	37	a			09 53				10 53						11 53					12 53						13 53

			TP ◇1	TP ◇1	XC ◇1 (trolley)	NT	TP ◇1		NT	TP ◇1	TP ◇1	XC ◇1 (trolley)	TP ◇1	NT	TP ◇1	TP ◇1	XC ◇1 (trolley)		TP ◇1	NT	NT	TP ◇1	TP ◇1	XC ◇1 (trolley)	TP ◇1	NT
York 8	33	d	13 15		13 40	13 40	13 45		13 52	14 15	14 33	14 41	14 45	14 52	15 15		15 39		15 45	15 52	16 06	16 15	16 33	16 39	16 45	16 52
Ulleskelf	33	d																								
Church Fenton	33	d							14 04											16 04						
Selby		d		13 29		13a59										15 29					16a24					
South Milford		d		13 38												15 38										
Micklefield		d							14 11					15 07						16 11						17 07
East Garforth		d							14 15					15 11						16 15						17 11
Garforth		d							14 18					15 13						16 18						17 13
Cross Gates		d							14 23					15 18						16 23						17 18
Leeds 10		a	13 38	13 56	14 03		14 08		14 32	14 38	14 56	15 05	15 09	15 27	15 38	15 56	16 03		16 08	16 32		16 38	16 56	17 01	17 08	17 27
Bradford Interchange	37	a							14 53					15 53						16 53						17 53

			TP ◇1		TP ◇1	XC ◇1 (trolley)	TP ◇1	NT	NT	TP ◇1	TP ◇1	XC ◇1 (trolley)	TP ◇1		NT	NT	TP ◇1	TP ◇1	XC ◇1	TP ◇1	NT	TP ◇1	XC ◇1		TP ◇1	NT
York 8	33	d	17 15			17 41	17 45	17 52	18 10	18 15	18 33	18 40	18 45		18 52	19 10	19 15		19 39	19 45	19 52	20 15	20 39		20 45	20 50
Ulleskelf	33	d																								
Church Fenton	33	d						18 04	18a21												20 04					21a01
Selby		d			17 29											19a35		19 29								
South Milford		d			17 38													19 38								
Micklefield		d						18 11							19 07						20 12					
East Garforth		d						18 15							19 11						20 16					
Garforth		d						18 18							19 13						20 18					
Cross Gates		d						18 23							19 18						20 23					
Leeds 10		a	17 38		17 56	18 04	18 08	18 32		18 38	18 57	19 04	19 08		19 27		19 38	19 54	20 05	20 08	20 32	20 38	21 02		21 08	
Bradford Interchange	37	a						18 53							19 53						20 53					

			NT	TP ◇1	TP ◇1	NT	NT	TP ◇1	GR R 1 (restaurant)		TP ◇1
York 8	33	d	20 57	21 15		21 41	21 52	22 12	23 03		23 12
Ulleskelf	33	d									
Church Fenton	33	d					22 04				
Selby		d			21 31	22a00					
South Milford		d			21 40						
Micklefield		d	21 12				22 12				
East Garforth		d	21 17				22 16				
Garforth		d	21 19				22 19				
Cross Gates		d	21 24				22 23				
Leeds 10		a	21 33	21 38	21 59		22 32	22 36	23 34		23 38
Bradford Interchange	37	a	21 56								

Leeds - Selby and York

Miles	Miles		TP	TP	TP	TP	TP	TP	TP	TP	TP		TP	TP	TP	NT	NT	TP	NT	GR	TP		NT	NT
					MX		MX		MX		MX		MO											
			◇1	◇1	◇1	◇1	◇1	◇1	◇1	◇1	◇1		◇1	◇1	◇1			◇1		1 ⊼⊘	◇1 ⊼			
			A	B		C		D		C														
—	—	Bradford Interchange 37 d																					07 02	07 20
0	0	**Leeds 10** d	23p40	23p42	23p45	23p53	00 32	00 54	00 54	01 06	02 08		02 34	06 04	06 35	06 38	06 48	06 55	06 58	07 10	07 23		07 29	07 41
4¼	4¼	Cross Gates d														06 44			07 05				07 36	
7¼	7¼	Garforth d														06 50	06 58		07 10				07 41	07 51
8	8	East Garforth d														06 52			07 12				07 43	
9	9	Micklefield d														06 56			07 16				07 47	
—	12¾	South Milford d																	07 20					
—	20¾	**Selby** a															07 20		07 31		07 43			
14¾	—	Church Fenton 33 a																						07 59
16½	—	Ulleskelf 33 a																						
25½	—	**York 8** 33 a	00 09	00 26	00 28	00 22	01 16	01 22	01 43	01 34	02 45		03 04	06 28	07 01	07 15		07 22		07 34			08 06	08 16

	TP	XC	NT	TP	NT	TP	TP		NT	TP	XC	TP	NT	TP	NT	TP	NT		TP	XC	TP	NT	TP	TP
	◇1 ⊼	◇1 ⊼		◇1 ⊼		◇1 ⊼	◇1 ⊼			◇1 ⊼	◇1 ⊼	◇1 ⊼		◇1 ⊼		◇1 ⊼			◇1 ⊼	◇1 ⊼	◇1 ⊼		◇1 ⊼	◇1 ⊼
Bradford Interchange 37 d			07 34		07 50				08 20				08 50				09 20					09 50		
Leeds 10 d	07 50	07 57	08 00	08 12	08 15	08 28	08 38		08 41	08 57	09 05	09 12	09 15	09 28	09 33	09 38	09 41		09 57	10 05	10 12	10 15	10 28	10 38
Cross Gates d			08 06		08 22				08 48				09 22				09 48					10 22		
Garforth d	08 00		08 12		08 27				08 53	09 05			09 27				09 53		10 05			10 27		
East Garforth d			08 14		08 29				08 56				09 29				09 56					10 29		
Micklefield d			08 18		08 33				08 59				09 33				09 59					10 33		
South Milford d			08 22		08 38								09 38									10 38		
Selby a			08 36		08 53		08 57						09 53			09 57						10 53		10 57
Church Fenton 33 a									09 05								10 05							
Ulleskelf 33 a																								
York 8 33 a	08 21	08 23		08 35		08 55			09 21	09 23	09 32	09 36		09 54	10 06		10 24		10 23	10 28	10 36		10 52	

	NT	TP	XC		TP	NT	TP	TP	NT	TP	XC	TP	NT		TP	TP	NT	TP	XC	TP	NT	TP	TP	
		◇1 ⊼	◇1 ⊼		◇1 ⊼		◇1 ⊼	◇1 ⊼		◇1 ⊼	◇1 ⊼	◇1 ⊼			◇1 ⊼	◇1 ⊼		◇1 ⊼	◇1 ⊼	◇1 ⊼		◇1 ⊼	◇1 ⊼	
Bradford Interchange 37 d	10 18					10 50			11 20				11 50				12 19				12 50			
Leeds 10 d	10 41	10 57	11 05		11 12	11 15	11 28	11 38	11 41	11 57	12 05	12 12	12 15		12 28	12 38	12 41	12 57	13 05	13 12	13 15	13 28	13 38	
Cross Gates d	10 48					11 22			11 48				12 22				12 48				13 22			
Garforth d	10 53	11 05				11 27			11 53	12 05			12 27				12 53	13 05			13 27			
East Garforth d	10 56					11 29			11 56				12 29				12 56				13 29			
Micklefield d	10 59					11 33			11 59				12 33				12 59				13 33			
South Milford d						11 38							12 38								13 38			
Selby a						11 54		11 57					12 50			12 57					13 51		13 57	
Church Fenton 33 a									12 05															
Ulleskelf 33 a																								
York 8 33 a	11 19	11 23	11 27		11 36		11 54		12 21	12 23	12 27	12 36			12 52		13 19	13 23	13 27	13 36		13 54		

	NT	TP	XC	TP	NT	TP	TP	NT	TP		XC	TP	NT	TP	TP	NT	TP	XC	TP		NT	TP	TP	NT
		◇1 ⊼	◇1 ⊼	◇1 ⊼		◇1 ⊼	◇1 ⊼		◇1 ⊼		◇1 ⊼	◇1 ⊼		◇1 ⊼	◇1 ⊼		◇1 ⊼	◇1 ⊼	◇1 ⊼			◇1 ⊼	◇1 ⊼	
Bradford Interchange 37 d	13 19				13 50			14 19					14 50			15 19					15 50			16 19
Leeds 10 d	13 42	13 57	14 05	14 12	14 15	14 28	14 38	14 41	14 57		15 05	15 12	15 15	15 28	15 38	15 41	15 56	16 05	16 12		16 15	16 28	16 38	16 41
Cross Gates d	13 49				14 22			14 48					15 22			15 48					16 22			16 48
Garforth d	13 54	14 05			14 27			14 53	15 05				15 27			15 53	16 05				16 27			16 53
East Garforth d	13 57				14 29			14 56					15 29			15 56					16 30			16 56
Micklefield d	14 00				14 33			14 59					15 33			15 59					16 34			16 59
South Milford d					14 38								15 38								16 39			
Selby a					14 51		14 57						15 53		15 57						16 54		17 00	
Church Fenton 33 a	14 06															16 05								
Ulleskelf 33 a																								
York 8 33 a	14 22	14 23	14 27	14 36		14 52		15 18	15 23		15 27	15 36		15 53		16 21	16 23	16 29	16 36			16 52		17 20

	TP	XC	TP	NT	TP		NT	TP	NT	NT	TP	XC	TP	NT	TP		XC	TP	NT	TP	XC	TP	NT	TP
	◇1 ⊼	◇1 ⊼	◇1 ⊼		◇1 ⊼			◇1 ⊼			◇1 ⊼	◇1 ⊼	◇1 ⊼		◇1 ⊼		◇1 ⊼	◇1 ⊼		◇1 ⊼	◇1 ⊼	◇1 ⊼		◇1 ⊼
Bradford Interchange 37 d				16 50					17 19					17 50					18 19				18 52	
Leeds 10 d	16 57	17 07	17 12	17 15	17 24		17 28	17 38	17 41	17 46	17 57	18 06	18 12	18 15	18 28		18 35	18 38	18 41	18 57	19 05	19 12	19 15	19 28
Cross Gates d			17 18	17 22			17 35		17 48	17 53				18 22					18 48				19 22	
Garforth d	17 05			17 28	17 34		17 40		17 53	17 58	18 05			18 27					18 53	19 05			19 27	
East Garforth d				17 30			17 42		17 56	18 01				18 29					18 56				19 29	
Micklefield d				17 34			17 46		17 59	18 05				18 33					18 59				19 33	
South Milford d				17 39						18 09				18 38				18 51						
Selby a				17 51				17 59		18 21				18 49				19 00						
Church Fenton 33 a							17 51												19 05					
Ulleskelf 33 a							17 57																	
York 8 33 a	17 21	17 29	17 37		17 55		18 10		18 19		18 23	18 30	18 35		18 51		19 02		19 21	19 23	19 30	19 36	19 53	19 55

A MO until 20 June

B MO from 27 June until 12 September, MO from 31 October

C MO from 19 September until 24 October

D MO until 12 September, MO from 31 October

Leeds - Selby and York

	TP		NT	TP	XC	TP	TP	NT	TP FX	TP FO	TP		NT	TP	TP	TP	NT	TP
	◇1 ⊼			◇1	◇1	◇1	◇1		◇1	◇1	◇1			◇1	◇1	◇1		◇1
Bradford Interchange 37 d			19 19					20 19									22 19	
Leeds 10 d	19 38		19 41	19 57	20 08	20 12	20 45	20 48	21 12	21 12	21 42		21 55	22 12	22 22	22 42	23 02	23 45
Cross Gates d			19 48					20 55					22 02				23 09	
Garforth d			19 53	20 05				21 00					22 07				23 14	
East Garforth d			19 55					21 02					22 10				23 17	
Micklefield d			19 59					21 06					22 14				23 21	
South Milford d	19 51								21 24	21 24					22 36			
Selby a	20 00								21 33	21 34					22 46			
Church Fenton 33 a								21 11									23 27	
Ulleskelf 33 a								21 15										
York 8 33 a			20 21	20 23	20 30	20 38	21 09	21 30			22 06		22 32	22 38		23 09	23 44	00 28

Saturdays

	TP	TP	TP	TP	TP	TP	NT	TP	GR		NT	TP	NT	TP	XC	NT	TP	NT	TP		TP	NT	TP	XC
	◇1	◇1	◇1	◇1	◇1	◇1		◇1	R 1 ⊼			◇1		◇1 ⊼	◇1 ⊼		◇1 ⊼		◇1 ⊼		◇1 ⊼		◇1 ⊼	◇1 ⊼
Bradford Interchange 37 d													07 20			07 34						08 20		
Leeds 10 d	23p45	00 34	00 37	02 16	05 34	06 35	06 38	06 55	07 10		07 14	07 23	07 41	07 50	07 57	08 00	08 12	08 12	08 28		08 38	08 41	08 57	09 05
Cross Gates d							06 44						07 48			08 06		08 20				08 48		
Garforth d							06 50						07 53	08 00		08 12		08 24				08 53	09 05	
East Garforth d							06 52						07 56			08 14		08 26				08 56		
Micklefield d							06 56						07 59			08 18		08 30				08 59		
South Milford d																08 22		08 36						
Selby a											07 37	07 43				08 36		08 54			08 57			
Church Fenton 33 a													08 05									09 05		
Ulleskelf 33 a																								
York 8 33 a	00 28	01 16	01 20	02 45	06 00	07 01	07 15	07 22	07 34				08 19	08 21	08 24		08 35		08 55			09 22	09 23	09 30

	TP	NT	TP	TP	NT		TP	XC	TP	NT	TP	TP	NT	TP	XC		TP	NT	TP	TP	NT	TP	XC	TP
	◇1 ⊼		◇1 ⊼	◇1			◇1 ⊼	◇1 ⊼	◇1 ⊼		◇1 ⊼	◇1 ⊼		◇1 ⊼	◇1 ⊼		◇1 ⊼		◇1	◇1 ⊼		◇1 ⊼	◇1 ⊼	◇1 ⊼
Bradford Interchange 37 d		08 50			09 20					09 50			10 18					10 50			11 20			
Leeds 10 d	09 12	09 15	09 28	09 38	09 41		09 57	10 05	10 12	10 15	10 28	10 38	10 41	10 57	11 05		11 12	11 15	11 28	11 38	11 41	11 57	12 05	12 12
Cross Gates d		09 22			09 48					10 22			10 48					11 22			11 48			
Garforth d		09 27			09 53		10 05			10 27			10 53	11 05				11 27			11 53	12 05		
East Garforth d		09 29			09 56					10 29			10 56					11 29			11 56			
Micklefield d		09 33			09 59					10 33			10 59					11 33			11 59			
South Milford d		09 38								10 38								11 38						
Selby a		09 53		09 57						10 53		10 57						11 55		11 57				
Church Fenton 33 a					10 05																12 05			
Ulleskelf 33 a																								
York 8 33 a	09 36		09 54		10 22		10 23	10 27	10 36		10 52		11 18	11 23	11 27		11 36		11 54		12 21	12 23	12 29	12 36

	NT		TP	TP	NT	TP	XC	TP	NT	TP	TP		NT	TP	XC	TP	NT	TP	TP	NT	TP		XC	TP
			◇1 ⊼	◇1		◇1 ⊼	◇1 ⊼	◇1 ⊼		◇1 ⊼	◇1			◇1 ⊼	◇1 ⊼	◇1 ⊼		◇1 ⊼	◇1 ⊼		◇1 ⊼		◇1 ⊼	◇1 ⊼
Bradford Interchange 37 d	11 50				12 19				12 50				13 19				13 50			14 19				
Leeds 10 d	12 15		12 28	12 38	12 41	12 57	13 05	13 12	13 15	13 28	13 38		13 42	13 57	14 05	14 12	14 15	14 28	14 38	14 41	14 57		15 05	15 12
Cross Gates d	12 22				12 48				13 22				13 49				14 22			14 48				
Garforth d	12 27				12 53	13 05			13 27				13 54	14 05			14 27			14 53	15 05			
East Garforth d	12 29				12 56				13 29				13 57				14 29			14 56				
Micklefield d	12 33				12 59				13 33				14 00				14 33			14 59				
South Milford d	12 38								13 38								14 38							
Selby a	12 50			12 57					13 52		13 57						14 51		14 57					
Church Fenton 33 a													14 06											
Ulleskelf 33 a																								
York 8 33 a			12 52		13 19	13 23	13 29	13 36		13 54			14 22	14 23	14 27	14 36		14 52		15 17	15 23		15 29	15 36

	NT	TP	TP	NT	TP	XC	TP		NT	TP	TP	NT	TP	XC	TP	NT	TP		TP	NT	TP	XC	TP	NT
		◇1 ⊼	◇1		◇1	◇1 ⊼	◇1 ⊼			◇1 ⊼	◇1		◇1 ⊼	◇1 ⊼	◇1		◇1		◇1		◇1	◇1 ⊼	◇1	
Bradford Interchange 37 d	14 50			15 19					15 50			16 19				16 50				17 19				17 50
Leeds 10 d	15 15	15 28	15 38	15 41	15 56	16 05	16 12		16 15	16 28	16 38	16 41	16 57	17 05	17 12	17 15	17 24		17 38	17 41	17 57	18 06	18 12	18 15
Cross Gates d	15 22			15 48					16 22			16 48				17 23				17 48				18 22
Garforth d	15 27			15 53	16 05				16 27			16 53	17 05			17 30	17 34			17 53	18 05			18 27
East Garforth d	15 29			15 56					16 30			16 56				17 32				17 56				18 29
Micklefield d	15 33			15 59					16 34			16 59				17 36				17 59				18 33
South Milford d	15 38								16 39							17 41								18 38
Selby a	15 53		15 57						16 54		17 00					17 55			17 59					18 50
Church Fenton 33 a				16 05																				
Ulleskelf 33 a																								
York 8 33 a		15 53		16 24	16 23	16 27	16 36			16 52		17 21	17 23	17 27	17 36		17 55			18 19	18 23	18 30	18 35	

Table 40

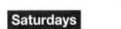

Leeds - Selby and York

		TP	XC	TP		NT	TP	XC	TP	NT	TP	TP	NT	TP		XC	TP	TP	NT	TP	TP	XC	TP	NT	
		◇1	◇1 🛒	◇1			◇1	◇1 🛒	◇1		◇1	◇1		◇1		◇1 🛒	◇1	◇1		◇1	◇1	◇1 🛒	◇1		
Bradford Interchange	37 d					18 19				18 52			19 18						20 20						
Leeds 10	d	18 28	18 35	18 38		18 41	18 57	19 05	19 12	19 16	19 28	19 38	19 41	19 57		20 08	20 12	20 45	20 48	21 08	21 12	21 15	21 42	22 00	
Cross Gates	d					18 48				19 22			19 48						20 55					22 07	
Garforth	d					18 53	19 05			19 28			19 53	20 05					21 00					22 12	
East Garforth	d					18 56				19 30			19 56						21 02					22 14	
Micklefield	d					18 59				19 34			19 59						21 06					22 18	
South Milford	d			18 51								19 51								21 21					
Selby	a			19 00								20 00								21 30					
Church Fenton	33 a					19 05													21 12						
Ulleskelf	33 a																		21 17						
York 8	33 a	18 52	18 59			19 19	19 23	19 29	19 36	19 54	19 56		20 18	20 23		20 32	20 38	21 09	21 31		21 41	21 57	22 06	22 36	

		TP	TP	TP	NT	TP
		◇1	◇1	◇1		◇1
Bradford Interchange	37 d				22 19	
Leeds 10	d	22 12	22 22	22 42	22 56	23 42
Cross Gates	d				23 03	
Garforth	d				23 08	
East Garforth	d				23 11	
Micklefield	d				23 15	
South Milford	d		22 36			
Selby	a		22 46			
Church Fenton	33 a				23 21	
Ulleskelf	33 a					
York 8	33 a	22 38		23 09	23 38	00 09

Sundays

until 19 June

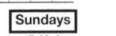

		TP	TP	TP	TP	TP	TP	TP	NT	XC		TP	TP	NT	TP	XC	TP	NT	TP	TP		NT	TP	XC	TP
		◇1	◇1	◇1	◇1	◇1	◇1	◇1		◇1		◇1	◇1		◇1	◇1	◇1		◇1	◇1			◇1	◇1	◇1
		A	A	A						🛒						🛒								🛒	
Bradford Interchange	37 d								08 31					09 20				10 02				11 02			
Leeds 10	d	23p42	00 15	00 54	02 35	05 55	07 40	08 40	08 54	09 08		09 12	09 40	09 50	10 04	10 08	10 22	10 27	10 40	11 12		11 25	11 40	12 08	12 12
Cross Gates	d								09 00					09 56				10 33				11 32			
Garforth	d								09 06					10 02				10 39				11 37			
East Garforth	d								09 08					10 04				10 41				11 39			
Micklefield	d								09 12					10 08				10 45				11 43			
South Milford	d																10 35								
Selby	a																10 44								
Church Fenton	33 a								09 18									10 51							
Ulleskelf	33 a																								
York 8	33 a	00 09	00 42	01 22	03 03	06 23	08 08	09 07	09 34	09 35		09 37	10 07	10 28	10 29	10 33		11 05	11 07	11 39		11 59	12 05	12 32	12 39

		NT	TP	TP	XC	TP		NT	TP	TP	XC	TP	NT	TP	TP	XC		TP	NT	TP	TP	XC	TP	NT	TP
			◇1	◇1	◇1 🛒	◇1			◇1	◇1	◇1 🛒	◇1		◇1	◇1	◇1 🛒		◇1		◇1	◇1	◇1 🛒	◇1		◇1
Bradford Interchange	37 d	12 02						13 02					14 02						15 02					16 03	
Leeds 10	d	12 25	12 40	13 01	13 08	13 12		13 25	13 40	13 57	14 08	14 12	14 25	14 40	15 00	15 08		15 12	15 25	15 40	15 57	16 08	16 12	16 25	16 40
Cross Gates	d	12 32						13 32					14 32						15 32					16 32	
Garforth	d	12 37						13 37					14 37						15 37					16 37	
East Garforth	d	12 39						13 39					14 39						15 39					16 39	
Micklefield	d	12 43						13 43					14 43						15 43					16 43	
South Milford	d			13 14											15 12										
Selby	a			13 23											15 22										
Church Fenton	33 a	12 48											14 48											16 48	
Ulleskelf	33 a																								
York 8	33 a	13 02	13 07		13 32	13 39		13 59	14 07	14 24	14 31	14 38	15 02	15 07		15 31		15 38	15 59	16 05	16 24	16 32	16 38	17 03	17 07

		TP		XC	TP	NT	TP	TP	XC	TP	NT	TP		TP	XC	TP	NT	TP	TP	XC	TP	NT		TP	TP
		◇1		◇1 🛒	◇1		◇1	◇1	◇1 🛒	◇1		◇1		◇1	◇1 🛒	◇1		◇1	◇1	◇1	◇1			◇1	◇1
Bradford Interchange	37 d					17 02					18 02						19 02					20 02			
Leeds 10	d	17 01		17 08	17 12	17 25	17 40	17 57	18 08	18 12	18 23	18 40		19 01	19 08	19 12	19 25	19 40	19 57	20 08	20 12	20 25		20 40	21 04
Cross Gates	d					17 32					18 30						19 32					20 32			
Garforth	d					17 37					18 35						19 37					20 37			
East Garforth	d					17 39					18 38						19 39					20 39			
Micklefield	d					17 43					18 41						19 43					20 43			
South Milford	d	17 14												19 14											
Selby	a	17 23												19 29					20 17						21 38
Church Fenton	33 a										18 47											20 48			
Ulleskelf	33 a																								
York 8	33 a			17 32	17 38	18 02	18 07	18 24	18 32	18 38	19 03	19 07			19 32	19 35	19 59	20 04		20 32	20 38	21 03		21 05	

A not 22 May

Table 40

Sundays
until 19 June

Leeds - Selby and York

			XC	TP	NT	TP	TP	TP	TP		NT	TP
			◇1	◇1		◇1	◇1	◇1	◇1			◇1
Bradford Interchange	37	d			21 02							
Leeds 10		d	21 08	21 12	21 26	21 40	22 12	22 22	22 40		22 43	23 40
Cross Gates		d			21 33						22 49	
Garforth		d			21 38						22 55	
East Garforth		d			21 40						22 57	
Micklefield		d			21 44						23 01	
South Milford		d						22 35				
Selby		a						22 44				
Church Fenton	33	a									23 07	
Ulleskelf	33	a										
York 8	33	a	21 32	21 38	22 00	22 08	22 40		23 11		23 23	00 09

Sundays
26 June to 31 July

			TP	TP	TP	TP	TP	TP	TP	NT	XC		TP	TP	NT	TP	XC	TP	NT	TP	TP		NT	TP	XC	TP
			◇1	◇1	◇1	◇1	◇1	◇1	◇1		◇1		◇1	◇1		◇1	◇1	◇1		◇1	◇1			◇1	◇1	◇1
Bradford Interchange	37	d								08 31					09 20				10 02				11 02			
Leeds 10		d	23p42	00 15	00 54	02 35	05 55	07 40	08 40	08 54	09 08		09 12	09 40	09 50	10 04	10 08	10 22	10 27	10 40	11 12		11 25	11 40	12 08	12 12
Cross Gates		d								09 00					09 56				10 33				11 32			
Garforth		d								09 06					10 02				10 39				11 37			
East Garforth		d								09 08					10 04				10 41				11 39			
Micklefield		d								09 12					10 08				10 45				11 43			
South Milford		d																10 35								
Selby		a																10 44								
Church Fenton	33	a								09 18									10 51							
Ulleskelf	33	a																								
York 8	33	a	00 09	00 42	01 22	03 03	06 23	08 08	09 07	09 34	09 35		09 37	10 07	10 28	10 29	10 33		11 05	11 07	11 39		11 59	12 05	12 32	12 39

			NT	TP	TP	XC	TP		NT	TP	TP	XC	TP	NT	TP	TP	XC		TP	NT	TP	TP	XC	TP	NT	TP
				◇1	◇1	◇1	◇1			◇1	◇1	◇1	◇1		◇1	◇1	◇1		◇1		◇1	◇1	◇1	◇1		◇1
Bradford Interchange	37	d	12 02						13 02					14 02						15 02					16 03	
Leeds 10		d	12 25	12 40	13 01	13 08	13 12		13 25	13 40	13 57	14 08	14 12	14 25	14 40	15 00	15 08		15 12	15 25	15 40	15 57	16 08	16 12	16 25	16 40
Cross Gates		d	12 32						13 32					14 32						15 32					16 32	
Garforth		d	12 37						13 37					14 37						15 37					16 37	
East Garforth		d	12 39						13 39					14 39						15 39					16 39	
Micklefield		d	12 43						13 43					14 43						15 43					16 43	
South Milford		d			13 14											15 12										
Selby		a			13 23											15 22										
Church Fenton	33	a	12 48											14 48											16 48	
Ulleskelf	33	a																								
York 8	33	a	13 02	13 07		13 32	13 39		13 59	14 07	14 24	14 31	14 38	15 02	15 07		15 31		15 38	15 59	16 05	16 24	16 32	16 38	17 03	17 07

			TP		XC	TP	NT	TP	TP	XC	TP	NT	TP		XC	TP	XC	TP	NT	TP	TP	XC	TP		NT	TP
			◇1		◇1	◇1		◇1	◇1	◇1	◇1		◇1		◇1	◇1	◇1	◇1		◇1	◇1	◇1	◇1			◇1
Bradford Interchange	37	d					17 02					18 02							19 02						20 02	
Leeds 10		d	17 01		17 08	17 12	17 25	17 40	17 57	18 08	18 12	18 23	18 40		18 57	19 01	19 08	19 12	19 25	19 40	19 57	20 08	20 12		20 25	20 40
Cross Gates		d					17 32					18 30							19 32						20 32	
Garforth		d					17 37					18 35							19 37						20 37	
East Garforth		d					17 39					18 38							19 39						20 39	
Micklefield		d					17 43					18 41							19 43						20 43	
South Milford		d	17 14													19 14										
Selby		a	17 23													19 29					20 17					
Church Fenton	33	a										18 47													20 48	
Ulleskelf	33	a																								
York 8	33	a			17 32	17 38	18 02	18 07	18 24	18 32	18 38	19 03	19 07		19 21		19 32	19 35	19 59	20 04		20 32	20 38		21 03	21 05

			TP	XC	TP	NT	TP	TP	TP		TP	NT	TP
			◇1	◇1	◇1		◇1	◇1	◇1		◇1		◇1
Bradford Interchange	37	d				21 02							
Leeds 10		d	21 04	21 08	21 12	21 26	21 40	22 12	22 22		22 40	22 43	23 42
Cross Gates		d				21 33						22 49	
Garforth		d				21 38						22 55	
East Garforth		d				21 40						22 57	
Micklefield		d				21 44						23 01	
South Milford		d							22 35				
Selby		a	21 38						22 44				
Church Fenton	33	a										23 07	
Ulleskelf	33	a											
York 8	33	a		21 32	21 38	22 00	22 08	22 40			23 11	23 23	00 26

Table 40

Sundays

7 August to 11 September

Leeds - Selby and York

	TP	TP	TP	TP	TP	TP	TP	NT	XC		TP	TP	NT	TP	XC	TP	NT	TP	XC		TP	NT	TP	XC
	◇1	◇1	◇1	◇1	◇1	◇1	◇1		◇1 🛒		◇1	◇1		◇1	◇1 🛒	◇1		◇1	◇1 🛒		◇1		◇1	◇1 🛒
Bradford Interchange 37 d								08 31					09 20				10 02					11 02		
Leeds 10 d	23p42	00 15	00 54	02 35	05 55	07 40	08 40	08 54	09 08		09 12	09 40	09b50	10 04	10 08	10 22	10 27	10 40	11 08		11 12	11 25	11 40	12 08
Cross Gates d								09 00					09 56				10 33					11 32		
Garforth d								09 06					10 02				10 39					11 37		
East Garforth d								09 08					10 04				10 41					11 39		
Micklefield d								09 12					10 08				10 45					11 43		
South Milford d																10 35								
Selby a																10 44								
Church Fenton 33 a								09 18									10 51							
Ulleskelf 33 a																								
York 8 33 a	00 09	00 42	01 22	03 03	06 23	08 08	09 07	09 34	09 35		09 37	10 07	10 28	10 29	10 33		11 05	11 07	11 35		11 39	11 59	12 05	12 32

	TP	NT	TP	TP	XC		TP	NT	TP	TP	XC	TP	NT	TP	TP		XC	NT	TP	TP	XC	TP	NT	TP
	◇1		◇1	◇1	◇1 🛒		◇1		◇1	◇1	◇1 🛒	◇1		◇1	◇1		◇1 🛒		◇1	◇1	◇1 🛒	◇1		◇1
Bradford Interchange 37 d		12 02						13 02					14 02					15 02					16 03	
Leeds 10 d	12 12	12 25	12 40	13 01	13 08		13 12	13 25	13 40	13 57	14 08	14 12	14 25	14 40	15 00		15 08	15 25	15 40	15 57	16 08	16 12	16 25	16 40
Cross Gates d		12 32						13 32					14 32					15 32					16 32	
Garforth d		12 37						13 37					14 37					15 37					16 37	
East Garforth d		12 39						13 39					14 39					15 39					16 39	
Micklefield d		12 43						13 43					14 43					15 43					16 43	
South Milford d				13 14											15 12									
Selby a				13 23											15 22									
Church Fenton 33 a		12 48											14 48										16 48	
Ulleskelf 33 a																								
York 8 33 a	12 39	13 02	13 07		13 32		13 39	13 59	14 07	14 24	14 31	14 38	15 02	15 07			15 31	15 59	16 05	16 24	16 32	16 38	17 03	17 07

	TP		XC	TP	NT	TP	TP	XC	TP	NT	TP		XC	TP	XC	TP	NT	TP	TP	XC	TP		NT	TP
	◇1		◇1 🛒	◇1		◇1	◇1	◇1 🛒	◇1		◇1		◇1 🛒	◇1	◇1 🛒	◇1		◇1	◇1	◇1	◇1			◇1
Bradford Interchange 37 d					17 02					18 02							19 02						20 02	
Leeds 10 d	17 01		17 08	17 12	17 25	17 40	17 57	18 08	18 12	18 23	18 40		18 57	19 01	19 08	19 12	19 25	19 40	19 57	20 08	20 12		20 25	20 40
Cross Gates d					17 32					18 30							19 32						20 32	
Garforth d					17 37					18 35							19 37						20 37	
East Garforth d					17 39					18 38							19 39						20 39	
Micklefield d					17 43					18 41							19 43						20 43	
South Milford d	17 14													19 14										
Selby a	17 23													19 29					20 17					
Church Fenton 33 a										18 47													20 48	
Ulleskelf 33 a																								
York 8 33 a			17 31	17 38	18 02	18 07	18 24	18 32	18 38	19 03	19 07		19 21		19 32	19 35	19 59	20 04		20 32	20 38		21 03	21 05

	TP	XC	TP	NT	TP	TP	TP		TP	NT	TP
	◇1	◇1 🛒	◇1		◇1	◇1	◇1		◇1		◇1
Bradford Interchange 37 d				21 02							
Leeds 10 d	21 04	21 08	21 12	21 26	21 40	22 12	22 22		22 40	22 43	23 42
Cross Gates d				21 33						22 49	
Garforth d				21 38						22 55	
East Garforth d				21 40						22 57	
Micklefield d				21 44						23 01	
South Milford d							22 35				
Selby a	21 38						22 44				
Church Fenton 33 a										23 07	
Ulleskelf 33 a											
York 8 33 a		21 32	21 38	22 00	22 08	22 40			23 11	23 23	00 26

Sundays

18 September to 23 October

	TP	TP	TP	NT	XC	TP	TP	NT	XC		TP	TP	NT	TP	XC	TP	NT	TP	XC		TP	NT	TP	TP
	◇1	1	◇1		◇1 🛒	◇1	◇1		◇1 🛒		◇1	◇1		◇1	◇1 🛒	◇1		◇1	◇1 🛒		◇1		◇1	◇1
Bradford Interchange 37 d				08 31				09 20					10 04				11 02					12 02		
Leeds 10 d	23p42	00 16	08 40	08 54	09 08	09 12	09 45	09 50	10 08		10 17	10 24	10 28	10 40	11 08	11 18	11 25	11 40	12 08		12 12	12 25	12 40	13 01
Cross Gates d				09 00				09 56					10 34				11 32					12 32		
Garforth d				09 06				10 02					10 40				11 37					12 37		
East Garforth d				09 08				10 04					10 42				11 39					12 39		
Micklefield d				09 12				10 08					10 46				11 43					12 43		
South Milford d												10 37												13 14
Selby a												10 46												13 23
Church Fenton 33 a				09 18									10 52									12 48		
Ulleskelf 33 a																								
York 8 33 a	00 09	00 43	09 08	09 34	09 35	09 37	10 11	10 28	10 33		10 41		11 08	11 08	11 35	11 41	11 59	12 05	12 32		12 38	13 02	13 07	

Table 40

Leeds - Selby and York

Sundays

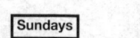

18 September to 23 October

	TP ◇1	NT	TP ◇1	TP ◇1	XC ◇1 (trolley)		TP ◇1	NT	TP ◇1	TP ◇1	XC ◇1 (trolley)	TP ◇1	NT	TP ◇1	TP ◇1		XC ◇1 (trolley)	TP ◇1	NT	TP ◇1	TP ◇1	XC ◇1 (trolley)	TP ◇1	NT
Bradford Interchange 37 d		13 02						14 02					15 02						16 03					17 02
Leeds 10 d	13 12	13 25	13 40	13 57	14 08		14 12	14 25	14 40	15 01	15 08	15 12	15 25	15 40	15 57		16 08	16 12	16 25	16 40	17 01	17 08	17 12	17 25
Cross Gates d		13 32						14 32					15 32						16 32					17 32
Garforth d		13 37						14 37					15 37						16 37					17 37
East Garforth d		13 39						14 39					15 39						16 39					17 39
Micklefield d		13 43						14 43					15 43						16 43					17 43
South Milford d										15 13											17 14			
Selby a										15 23											17 23			
Church Fenton 33 a								14 48											16 48					
Ulleskelf 33 a																								
York 8 33 a	13 39	13 59	14 06	14 24	14 31		14 38	15 02	15 07		15 31	15 38	15 59	16 05	16 24		16 32	16 38	17 03	17 07		17 32	17 38	18 02

	TP ◇1		TP ◇1	XC ◇1 (trolley)	TP ◇1	NT	TP ◇1	XC ◇1 (trolley)	TP ◇1	XC ◇1 (trolley)	TP ◇1		NT	TP ◇1	TP ◇1	XC ◇1	TP ◇1	NT	TP ◇1	TP ◇1	XC ◇1 (trolley)		TP ◇1	NT
Bradford Interchange 37 d						18 02							19 02					20 02						21 02
Leeds 10 d	17 40		17 57	18 08	18 12	18 23	18 40	18 57	19 01	19 08	19 12		19 25	19 40	19 57	20 08	20 12	20 25	20 40	21 04	21 08		21 12	21 26
Cross Gates d						18 30							19 32					20 32						21 33
Garforth d						18 35							19 37					20 37						21 38
East Garforth d						18 38							19 39					20 39						21 40
Micklefield d						18 41							19 43					20 43						21 44
South Milford d									19 14															
Selby a									19 30						20 17					21 38				
Church Fenton 33 a						18 47												20 48						
Ulleskelf 33 a																								
York 8 33 a	18 07		18 24	18 32	18 38	19 03	19 05	19 21		19 32	19 35		19 59	20 04		20 32	20 38	21 03	21 05		21 32		21 38	22 00

	TP ◇1	TP ◇1	TP ◇1	NT	TP ◇1	TP ◇1
Bradford Interchange 37 d						
Leeds 10 d	21 40	22 12	22 22	22 43	22 53	23 53
Cross Gates d				22 49		
Garforth d				22 55		
East Garforth d				22 57		
Micklefield d				23 01		
South Milford d			22 35			
Selby a			22 44			
Church Fenton 33 a				23 07		
Ulleskelf 33 a						
York 8 33 a	22 08	22 40		23 23	23 28	00 22

Sundays

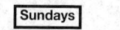

from 30 October

	TP ◇1	TP 1	TP ◇1	NT	XC ◇1 (trolley)	TP ◇1	TP ◇1	NT	XC ◇1 (trolley)		TP ◇1	NT	TP ◇1	XC ◇1 (trolley)	TP ◇1	NT	TP ◇1	XC ◇1 (trolley)	TP ◇1		NT	TP ◇1	TP ◇1	XC ◇1 (trolley)
Bradford Interchange 37 d				08 31				09 20				10 02				11 02					12 02			
Leeds 10 d	23p42	00 16	08 40	08 54	09 08	09 12	09 45	09 50	10 08		10 22	10 27	10 39	11 08	11 12	11 25	11 40	12 08	12 12		12 25	12 40	13 01	13 08
Cross Gates d				09 00				09 56				10 33				11 32					12 32			
Garforth d				09 06				10 02				10 39				11 37					12 37			
East Garforth d				09 08				10 04				10 41				11 39					12 39			
Micklefield d				09 12				10 08				10 45				11 43					12 43			
South Milford d											10 35												13 14	
Selby a											10 44												13 23	
Church Fenton 33 a				09 18								10 51									12 48			
Ulleskelf 33 a																								
York 8 33 a	00 09	00 43	09 08	09 34	09 35	09 37	10 11	10 28	10 33			11 05	11 07	11 35	11 39	11 59	12 05	12 32	12 39		13 02	13 07		13 32

	TP ◇1	NT	TP ◇1	TP ◇1	XC ◇1 (trolley)		TP ◇1	NT	TP ◇1	TP ◇1	XC ◇1 (trolley)	NT	TP ◇1	TP ◇1	XC ◇1 (trolley)		TP ◇1	NT	TP ◇1	TP ◇1	XC ◇1 (trolley)	TP ◇1	NT	TP ◇1
Bradford Interchange 37 d		13 02						14 02				15 02						16 03					17 02	
Leeds 10 d	13 12	13 25	13 40	13 57	14 08		14 12	14 25	14 40	15 00	15 08	15 25	15 40	15 57	16 08		16 12	16 25	16 40	17 01	17 08	17 12	17 25	17 40
Cross Gates d		13 32						14 32				15 32						16 32					17 32	
Garforth d		13 37						14 37				15 37						16 37					17 37	
East Garforth d		13 39						14 39				15 39						16 39					17 39	
Micklefield d		13 43						14 43				15 43						16 43					17 43	
South Milford d										15 12										17 14				
Selby a										15 22										17 23				
Church Fenton 33 a								14 48										16 48						
Ulleskelf 33 a																								
York 8 33 a	13 39	13 59	14 07	14 24	14 31		14 38	15 02	15 07		15 31	15 59	16 05	16 24	16 32		16 38	17 02	17 07		17 31	17 38	18 02	18 07

Table 40

Sundays

from 30 October

Leeds - Selby and York

			TP		XC	TP	NT	TP	XC	TP	XC	TP	NT		TP	TP	XC	TP	NT	TP	TP	XC	TP		NT	TP
			◇1		◇1 ⫧	◇1		◇1	◇1 ⫧	◇1	◇1 ⫧	◇1			◇1	◇1	◇1	◇1		◇1	◇1	◇1 ⫧	◇1			◇1
Bradford Interchange	37	d					18 02						19 02						20 02						21 02	
Leeds 10		d	17 57		18 08	18 12	18 23	18 40	18 57	19 01	19 08	19 12	19 25		19 40	19 57	20 08	20 12	20 25	20 40	21 04	21 08	21 12		21 26	21 40
Cross Gates		d					18 30						19 32						20 32						21 33	
Garforth		d					18 35						19 37						20 37						21 38	
East Garforth		d					18 38						19 39						20 39						21 40	
Micklefield		d					18 41						19 43						20 43						21 44	
South Milford		d								19 14																
Selby		a								19 29						20 17					21 38					
Church Fenton	33	a					18 47												20 48							
Ulleskelf	33	a																								
York 8	33	a	18 24		18 32	18 38	19 01	19 07	19 21		19 32	19 35	19 59		20 04		20 32	20 38	21 03	21 05		21 32	21 38		22 00	22 08

			TP	TP	TP	NT	TP
			◇1	◇1	◇1		◇1
Bradford Interchange	37	d					
Leeds 10		d	22 12	22 22	22 40	22 43	23 42
Cross Gates		d				22 49	
Garforth		d				22 55	
East Garforth		d				22 57	
Micklefield		d				23 01	
South Milford		d		22 35			
Selby		a		22 44			
Church Fenton	33	a				23 07	
Ulleskelf	33	a					
York 8	33	a	22 40		23 11	23 23	00 26

Leeds and Bradford - Huddersfield, Blackpool North, Rochdale and Manchester Victoria via Halifax and Brighouse

Miles	Miles	Miles	Miles	Miles				NT MX	NT MX	NT	NT	NT	NT	NT	GC	NT		NT	NT	NT	NT	NT	NT	NT	NT	NT
														A	R 1 ✕				B			C			D	
—	—	—	—	—	York 8	40	d											06 13						07 06		
—	—	—	—	—	Selby	40	d															06 42				07 26
0	0	—	—	0	**Leeds 10**	37,39	d	22p37	23p08	05 08	05 51	06 03	06 13			06 37		06 51		07 08	07 13	07 22	07 37	07 51		08 08
4	4	—	—	—	Bramley	37	d	22p44	23p15	05 15	05 58					06 44				07 15		07 29	07 44			08 15
5¾	5¾	—	—	—	New Pudsey	37	d	22p49	23p20	05 20	06 02	06 13				06 49		07 01		07 20		07 34	07 49	08 01		08 20
9½	9½	—	—	—	**Bradford Interchange**	37	a	22p57	23p29	05 28	06 13	06 21				06 57		07 11		07 28		07 43	07 57	08 09		08 28
—	—	—	—	—			d	23p00	23p31	05 32	06 14	06 24			06 51	07 00		07 14		07 31		07 45	08 00	08 12		08 32
17½	17½	0	—	—	**Halifax**		a	23p12	23p44	05 44	06 25	06 36			07 06	07 12		07 25		07 43		08 00	08 12	08 23		08 44
—	—	—	—	—			d	23p12	23p44	05 44	06 26	06 36		07 02	07 07	07 12		07 26		07 44		08 06	08 12	08 24		08 44
—	—	—	9¼	—	Dewsbury	39	d						06 29								07 29					
—	—	—	12¼	—	Mirfield	39	d						06 35								07 35					
—	—	5¼	16¼	—	Brighouse		d		23p55				06 49	07a12	07 18						07 49	08 16				
—	—	—	—	—	London Kings Cross 15 ⊖	26	a								10 13											
—	—	10½	—	—	**Huddersfield**	39	a		00 08													08 29				
21	21	—	22	—	Sowerby Bridge		d	23p19		05 51		06 43	06 59			07 19					07 59		08 19			
25	25	—	26	—	Mytholmroyd		d	23p25		05 57		06 49	07 05			07 25					08 05		08 25			
26¼	26¼	—	27¼	—	**Hebden Bridge**		a	23p28		06 00	06 37	06 52	07 08			07 28		07 37		07 55	08 08		08 28	08 35		08 56
—	—	—	—	—			d	23p28		06 00	06 38	06 52	07 08			07 28		07 38		07 56	08 08		08 28	08 36		08 56
—	39	—	—	—	Burnley Manchester Road	97	a				06 57							07 57						08 57		
—	45¼	—	—	—	Accrington	97	a				07 06							08 06						09 06		
—	51½	—	—	—	Blackburn	97	a				07 16							08 14						09 14		
—	63½	—	—	—	**Preston 8**	97	a				07 36							08 38						09 32		
—	78	—	—	—	Poulton-le-Fylde	97	a				07 54							08 56						09 50		
—	81	—	—	—	**Blackpool North**	97	a				08 05							09 05						10 01		
30½	—	—	—	—	Todmorden		d	23p36		06 08		06 59	07 15			07 36			07 44	08 04	08 15		08 36			09 04
32	—	—	—	—	Walsden		d	23p39		06 11		07 02				07 39			07 47				08 39			
36	—	—	—	—	Littleborough		d	23p45		06 17		07 09	07 23			07 45			07 53		08 23		08 45			
37	—	—	—	—	Smithy Bridge		d	23p48		06 20		07 11	07 25			07 48			07 56		08 25		08 48			
39¼	—	—	—	—	**Rochdale**		a	23p52		06 24		07 15	07 29			07 51			08 00	08 14	08 29		08 51			09 14
—	—	—	—	—			d	23p52		06 24		07 16	07 30			07 51			08 00	08 14	08 30		08 51		09 04	09 14
41	—	—	—	—	Castleton		d			06 27		07 19	07 33			07 54			08 03	08 17	08 33				09 07	
43¾	—	—	—	—	Mills Hill		d			06 32		07 24	07 38			07 59			08 08	08 22	08 37				09 12	
45¾	—	—	—	—	Moston		d			06 35		07 27	07 41			08 02			08 11	08 25	08 40				09 15	
49¾	—	—	—	—	**Manchester Victoria** ⇌		a	00 10		06 48		07 39	07 53			08 14			08 22	08 37	08 53		09 08		09 26	09 30

			NT	NT	NT	NT	NT	NT	NT	NT	NT		NT	GC	NT	NT	NT	NT	NT	NT	NT		NT	NT	NT
				C			D			C				R 1 ✕	D			C			D				
York 8	40	d				08 12							09 11							10 11					
Selby	40	d		07 43						08 43								09 43							
Leeds 10	37,39	d	08 13	08 23	08 37	08 51		09 07	09 13	09 23	09 37		09 53			10 07	10 13	10 23	10 37	10 53			11 07	11 13	11 37
Bramley	37	d		08 30	08 44			09 14		09 30	09 44					10 14		10 30	10 44				11 14		11 44
New Pudsey	37	d		08 35	08 49	09 00		09 19		09 35	09 49		10 02			10 20		10 35	10 49	11 02			11 19		11 49
Bradford Interchange	37	a		08 43	08 57	09 12		09 28		09 43	09 57		10 12			10 28		10 43	10 57	11 11			11 28		11 57
		d		08 46	09 00	09 13		09 32		09 46	10 00		10 14	10 22		10 32		10 46	11 00	11 12			11 31		12 00
Halifax		a		09 01	09 12	09 25		09 44		10 01	10 12		10 25	10 34		10 44		11 01	11 12	11 25			11 43		12 12
		d		09 06	09 12	09 25		09 44		10 06	10 12		10 26	10 38		10 44		11 06	11 12	11 25			11 44		12 12
Dewsbury	39	d	08 31						09 31								10 29							11 29	
Mirfield	39	d	08 38						09 37								10 35							11 35	
Brighouse		d	08 49	09 16					09 49	10 16				10 50			10 49	11 16						11 49	
London Kings Cross 15 ⊖	26	a												13 45											
Huddersfield	39	a		09 29						10 29								11 29							
Sowerby Bridge		d	08 59		09 19				09 59		10 19						10 59		11 19					11 59	12 19
Mytholmroyd		d	09 05		09 25				10 05		10 25						11 05		11 25					12 05	12 25
Hebden Bridge		a	09 08		09 28	09 37		09 56	10 08		10 28		10 37			10 56	11 08		11 28	11 37			11 55	12 08	12 28
		d	09 08		09 28	09 37		09 56	10 08		10 28		10 38			10 56	11 08		11 28	11 38			11 56	12 08	12 28
Burnley Manchester Road	97	a				09 56							10 57							11 57					
Accrington	97	a				10 06							11 06							12 06					
Blackburn	97	a				10 14							11 14							12 14					
Preston 8	97	a				10 32							11 32							12 32					
Poulton-le-Fylde	97	a				10 50							11 50							12 50					
Blackpool North	97	a				11 01							12 00							13 00					
Todmorden		d	09 15		09 36			10 04	10 15		10 36					11 04	11 15		11 36				12 03	12 15	12 36
Walsden		d			09 39						10 39								11 39						12 39
Littleborough		d	09 23		09 45				10 23		10 45						11 23		11 45					12 23	12 45
Smithy Bridge		d	09 25		09 48				10 25		10 48						11 25		11 48					12 25	12 48
Rochdale		a	09 29		09 51			10 14	10 29		10 51					11 14	11 29		11 51				12 13	12 29	12 51
		d	09 30		09 51		10 05	10 14	10 30		10 51				11 04	11 14	11 30		11 51		12 04		12 14	12 30	12 51
Castleton		d	09 33				10 08		10 33						11 07		11 33				12 07			12 33	
Mills Hill		d	09 37				10 13		10 38						11 12		11 38				12 12			12 38	
Moston		d	09 40				10 16		10 41						11 15		11 41				12 15			12 41	
Manchester Victoria ⇌		a	09 53		10 08		10 26	10 32	10 53		11 08				11 26	11 32	11 53		12 08		12 25		12 30	12 53	13 08

A To Leeds
B To Wigan Wallgate
C To Wakefield Westgate
D until 30 September. To Wigan Wallgate

For connections to Liverpool Lime Street please refer to Table 90

Leeds and Bradford - Huddersfield, Blackpool North, Rochdale and Manchester Victoria via Halifax and Brighouse

		NT	NT A	NT	NT	NT B	NT		NT	NT A	NT	NT	NT B	NT	NT	NT A	NT		NT	NT B	NT	NT	NT C	NT	NT
York [8]	40 d	11 09							12 13						13 09							14 13			
Selby	40 d					11 43							12 43							13 43					
Leeds [10]	37,39 d	11 53		12 07	12 13	12 23	12 37		12 53		13 07	13 13	13 23	13 37	13 53		14 07		14 13	14 23	14 37	14 53		15 07	15 13
Bramley	37 d			12 14		12 30	12 44				13 14		13 30	13 44			14 14			14 30	14 44			15 14	
New Pudsey	37 d	12 02		12 19		12 35	12 49		13 02		13 19		13 35	13 49	14 02		14 19			14 35	14 49	15 02		15 19	
Bradford Interchange	37 a	12 11		12 28		12 43	12 57		13 12		13 28		13 43	13 58	14 12		14 28			14 43	14 57	15 12		15 28	
	d	12 14		12 32		12 46	13 00		13 14		13 32		13 46	14 00	14 14		14 32			14 46	15 00	15 14		15 32	
Halifax	a	12 25		12 44		13 01	13 12		13 25		13 44		14 01	14 12	14 25		14 44			15 00	15 12	15 25		15 44	
	d	12 26		12 44		13 06	13 12		13 26		13 44		14 06	14 13	14 26		14 44			15 06	15 12	15 26		15 44	
Dewsbury	39 d				12 29							13 29							14 29						15 29
Mirfield	39 d				12 35							13 35							14 35						15 35
Brighouse	d				12 49	13 16						13 49	14 16						14 49	15 16					15 49
London Kings Cross [15] ⊖26	a																								
Huddersfield	39 a					13 29							14 29							15 29					
Sowerby Bridge	d				12 59		13 19					13 59		14 19					14 59		15 19				15 59
Mytholmroyd	d				13 05		13 25					14 05		14 25					15 05		15 25				16 05
Hebden Bridge	a	12 37		12 56	13 08		13 28		13 37		13 56	14 08		14 28	14 37		14 56		15 08		15 28	15 37		15 56	16 08
	d	12 38		12 56	13 08		13 28		13 38		13 56	14 08		14 29	14 38		14 56		15 08		15 28	15 38		15 56	16 08
Burnley Manchester Road	97 a	12 57							13 57						14 57							15 57			
Accrington	97 a	13 06							14 06						15 06							16 06			
Blackburn	97 a	13 14							14 14						15 14							16 14			
Preston [8]	97 a	13 32							14 32						15 32							16 32			
Poulton-le-Fylde	97 a	13 50							14 50						15 50							16 50			
Blackpool North	97 a	14 00							15 00						16 00							17 00			
Todmorden	d			13 04	13 15		13 36				14 04	14 15		14 36			15 04		15 15		15 36			16 04	16 15
Walsden	d						13 39							14 39							15 39				
Littleborough	d				13 23		13 45					14 23		14 46					15 23		15 45				16 23
Smithy Bridge	d				13 25		13 48					14 25		14 48					15 25		15 48				16 25
Rochdale	a			13 14	13 29		13 51				14 14	14 29		14 51			15 14		15 29		15 51			16 14	16 29
	d		13 04	13 14	13 30		13 51			14 04	14 14	14 30		14 52		15 04	15 14		15 30		15 51		16 04	16 14	16 30
Castleton	d		13 07		13 33					14 07		14 33				15 07			15 33				16 07		16 33
Mills Hill	d		13 12		13 38					14 12		14 38				15 12			15 38				16 12		16 38
Moston	d		13 15		13 41					14 15		14 41				15 15			15 41				16 15		16 41
Manchester Victoria	a		13 25	13 32	13 53		14 08			14 25	14 32	14 52		15 08		15 26	15 31		15 53		16 08		16 27	16 32	16 52

		GC [R] [1] ✕	NT B		NT	NT	NT D	NT	NT	NT B	NT	NT	NT D		NT	NT	NT B	NT	NT	NT	NT	NT	NT B		NT
York [8]	40 d					15 08						16 09							17 13						
Selby	40 d		14 43							15 41													17 38		18 00
Leeds [10]	37,39 d		15 23		15 37	15 52		16 07	16 13	16 22	16 37	16 51			17 07	17 13	17 23	17 37	17 51		18 08	18 13	18 22		18 37
Bramley	37 d		15 30		15 44			16 14		16 30	16 44				17 14		17 30	17 44			18 15		18 30		18 44
New Pudsey	37 d		15 35		15 49	16 01		16 19		16 35	16 49	17 01			17 19		17 35	17 49	18 01		18 20		18 35		18 49
Bradford Interchange	37 a		15 43		15 57	16 10		16 28		16 43	16 57	17 10			17 28		17 43	17 57	18 10		18 28		18 43		18 58
	d	15 37	15 46		16 00	16 13		16 32		16 46	17 00	17 12			17 31		17 46	18 00	18 12		18 32		18 46		19 00
Halifax	a	15 50	16 01		16 12	16 24		16 44		17 01	17 12	17 24			17 43		17 59	18 12	18 24		18 44		19 00		19 12
	d	15 51	16 06		16 12	16 25		16 44		17 06	17 12	17 24			17 44		18 06	18 12	18 24		18 44		19 06		19 12
Dewsbury	39 d								16 31							17 31						18 31			
Mirfield	39 d								16 38							17 38						18 38			
Brighouse	d	16 09	16 16						16 49	17 16						17 49	18 16					18 49	19 16		
London Kings Cross [15] ⊖26	a	19 05																							
Huddersfield	39 a		16 29							17 29							18 31						19 29		
Sowerby Bridge	d				16 19	16 32			16 59		17 19	17 31				17 59		18 19	18 31			18 59			19 19
Mytholmroyd	d				16 25				17 05		17 25					18 05		18 25				19 05			19 25
Hebden Bridge	a				16 28	16 38		16 56	17 08		17 28	17 37			17 56	18 08		18 28	18 37		18 56	19 08			19 28
	d				16 28	16 39		16 56	17 08		17 28	17 38			17 56	18 08		18 28	18 38		18 56	19 08			19 28
Burnley Manchester Road	97 a					16 57						17 57							18 57						
Accrington	97 a					17 06						18 06							19 06						
Blackburn	97 a					17 14						18 14							19 14						
Preston [8]	97 a					17 32						18 33							19 32						
Poulton-le-Fylde	97 a					17 56						18 50							19 50						
Blackpool North	97 a					18 06						18 58							20 00						
Todmorden	d				16 36			17 04	17 15		17 36				18 04	18 15		18 36			19 04	19 15			19 36
Walsden	d				16 39						17 39					18 19		18 39				19 19			19 39
Littleborough	d				16 45				17 23		17 45					18 25		18 45				19 25			19 45
Smithy Bridge	d				16 48				17 25		17 48					18 28		18 48				19 28			19 48
Rochdale	a				16 51			17 14	17 29		17 51				18 14	18 32		18 51			19 15	19 32			19 52
	d				16 51		17 03	17 14	17 30		17 51		18 02		18 14	18 32		18 51		19 00	19 15	19 32			19 52
Castleton	d						17 06		17 33				18 05			18 35				19 03		19 35			19 55
Mills Hill	d						17 11		17 38				18 10			18 40				19 08		19 40			20 00
Moston	d						17 14		17 41				18 13			18 43				19 11		19 43			20 03
Manchester Victoria	a				17 08		17 23	17 32	17 53		18 08		18 21		18 32	18 54		19 09		19 21	19 32	19 54			20 15

A until 30 September. To Wigan Wallgate
B To Wakefield Westgate
C To Wigan Wallgate
D To Blackburn

For connections to Liverpool Lime Street please refer to Table 90

Table 41

Leeds and Bradford - Huddersfield, Blackpool North, Rochdale and Manchester Victoria via Halifax and Brighouse

			NT	NT	NT A	NT	NT	NT	NT	NT	NT	NT	NT	NT
York 8	40	d	18 05						20 13					
Selby	40	d			18 46									
Leeds 10	37,39	d	18 51	19 08	19 22	19 37	20 08	20 37	20 51	21 08	21 37	22 08	22 37	23 08
Bramley	37	d		19 15	19 30	19 44	20 15	20 44		21 15	21 44	22 15	22 44	23 15
New Pudsey	37	d	19 01	19 20	19 35	19 49	20 20	20 49	21 01	21 20	21 49	22 20	22 49	23 20
Bradford Interchange	37	a	19 09	19 28	19 44	19 57	20 28	20 57	21 10	21 28	21 57	22 28	22 57	23 29
		d	19 11	19 32	19 46	20 00	20 31	21 00	21 13	21 31	22 00	22 31	23 00	23 31
Halifax		a	19 24	19 44	20 00	20 12	20 44	21 12	21 24	21 44	22 12	22 44	23 12	23 44
		d	19 24	19 44	20 06	20 12	20 44	21 12	21 25	21 44	22 12	22 44	23 12	23 44
Dewsbury	39	d												
Mirfield	39	d												
Brighouse		d			20 16		20 55			21 55		22 55		23 55
London Kings Cross 15 ⊖	26	a												
Huddersfield	39	a			20 29		21 08			22 08		23 08		00 08
Sowerby Bridge		d				20 19		21 19			22 19		23 19	
Mytholmroyd		d				20 25		21 25			22 25		23 25	
Hebden Bridge		a	19 36	19 56		20 28		21 28	21 36		22 28		23 28	
		d	19 36	19 56		20 28		21 28	21 37		22 28		23 28	
Burnley Manchester Road	97	a	19 56						21 56					
Accrington	97	a	20 05						22 05					
Blackburn	97	a	20 14						22 13					
Preston 8	97	a	20 32						22 31					
Poulton-le-Fylde	97	a	20 50						22 49					
Blackpool North	97	a	21 00						22 59					
Todmorden		d		20 04		20 36		21 36			22 36		23 36	
Walsden		d				20 39		21 39			22 39		23 39	
Littleborough		d				20 45		21 45			22 45		23 45	
Smithy Bridge		d				20 48		21 48			22 48		23 48	
Rochdale		a		20 14		20 52		21 52			22 52		23 52	
		d		20 14		20 52		21 52			22 52		23 52	
Castleton		d				20 55		21 55			22 55			
Mills Hill		d				21 00		22 00			23 00			
Moston		d				21 03		22 03			23 03			
Manchester Victoria		a		20 34		21 13		22 15			23 15		00 10	

Saturdays

			NT	NT	NT	NT	NT	GC R 1 ✕	NT	NT B	NT
York 8	40	d									06 13
Selby	40	d									
Leeds 10	37,39	d	22p37	23p08	05 37	05 51	06 16		06 37		06 51
Bramley	37	d	22p44	23p15	05 44	05 58	06 23		06 44		
New Pudsey	37	d	22p49	23p20	05 49	06 02	06 28		06 49		07 01
Bradford Interchange	37	a	22p57	23p29	05 57	06 13	06 36		06 57		07 11
		d	23p00	23p31	06 00	06 14	06 40	06 51	07 00		07 14
Halifax		a	23p12	23p44	06 12	06 25	06 52	07 02	07 12		07 25
		d	23p12	23p44	06 12	06 26	06 52	07 04	07 12		07 26
Dewsbury	39	d									
Mirfield	39	d									
Brighouse		d		23p55				07 17			
London Kings Cross 15 ⊖	26	a						10 09			
Huddersfield	39	a		00 08							
Sowerby Bridge		d	23p19		06 19		06 59		07 19		
Mytholmroyd		d	23p25		06 25		07 05		07 25		
Hebden Bridge		a	23p28		06 28	06 37	07 08		07 28		07 37
		d	23p28		06 28	06 38	07 08		07 28	07 33	07 38
Burnley Manchester Road	97	a				06 57					07 57
Accrington	97	a				07 06					08 06
Blackburn	97	a				07 16					08 14
Preston 8	97	a				07 36					08 38
Poulton-le-Fylde	97	a				07 54					08 56
Blackpool North	97	a				08 05					09 05
Todmorden		d	23p36		06 35		07 15		07 36	07 44	
Walsden		d	23p39		06 38				07 39	07 47	
Littleborough		d	23p45		06 45		07 23		07 45	07 53	
Smithy Bridge		d	23p48		06 47		07 25		07 48	07 56	
Rochdale		a	23p52		06 54		07 29		07 52	08 00	
		d	23p52		06 55		07 30		07 52	08 00	
Castleton		d			06 58		07 33		07 55	08 03	
Mills Hill		d			07 03		07 38		08 00	08 08	
Moston		d			07 06		07 41		08 03	08 11	
Manchester Victoria		a	00 10		07 17		07 53		08 14	08 22	

			NT	NT	NT A	NT	NT	NT C	NT	NT	NT A	NT	NT	NT C	NT
York 8	40	d					07 06						08 12		
Selby	40	d			06 42						07 42				
Leeds 10	37,39	d	07 08	07 13	07 22	07 37	07 51		08 08	08 13	08 23	08 37	08 51		09 07
Bramley	37	d	07 15		07 29	07 44			08 15		08 30	08 44			09 14
New Pudsey	37	d	07 20		07 34	07 49	08 01		08 20		08 35	08 49	09 00		09 19
Bradford Interchange	37	a	07 28		07 43	07 57	08 09		08 28		08 43	08 57	09 12		09 28
		d	07 31		07 45	08 00	08 12		08 32		08 46	09 00	09 13		09 32
Halifax		a	07 43		08 00	08 12	08 23		08 44		09 01	09 12	09 24		09 44
		d	07 44		08 06	08 12	08 24		08 44		09 06	09 12	09 24		09 44
Dewsbury	39	d		07 29						08 31					
Mirfield	39	d		07 35						08 38					
Brighouse		d		07 49	08 16					08 49	09 16				
London Kings Cross 15 ⊖	26	a													
Huddersfield	39	a			08 30						09 29				
Sowerby Bridge		d		07 59		08 19				08 59		09 19			
Mytholmroyd		d		08 05		08 25				09 05		09 25			
Hebden Bridge		a	07 55	08 08		08 28	08 35		08 56	09 08		09 28	09 37		09 56
		d	07 56	08 08		08 28	08 36		08 56	09 08		09 28	09 37		09 56
Burnley Manchester Road	97	a					08 57						09 56		
Accrington	97	a					09 06						10 06		
Blackburn	97	a					09 14						10 14		
Preston 8	97	a					09 32						10 32		
Poulton-le-Fylde	97	a					09 50						10 50		
Blackpool North	97	a					10 01						11 01		
Todmorden		d	08 04	08 15		08 36			09 04	09 15		09 36			10 04
Walsden		d				08 39						09 39			
Littleborough		d		08 23		08 45				09 23		09 45			
Smithy Bridge		d		08 25		08 48				09 25		09 48			
Rochdale		a	08 14	08 29		08 51			09 14	09 29		09 51			10 14
		d	08 14	08 30		08 51		09 04	09 14	09 30		09 51		10 05	10 14
Castleton		d	08 17	08 33				09 07		09 33				10 08	
Mills Hill		d	08 22	08 37				09 12		09 37				10 13	
Moston		d	08 25	08 40				09 15		09 40				10 16	
Manchester Victoria		a	08 37	08 53		09 08		09 26	09 32	09 53		10 07		10 26	10 32

A To Wakefield Westgate

B To Wigan Wallgate

C until 1 October. To Wigan Wallgate

For connections to Liverpool Lime Street please refer to Table 90

Table 41

Saturdays

Leeds and Bradford - Huddersfield, Blackpool North, Rochdale and Manchester Victoria via Halifax and Brighouse

			NT	NT	NT	NT	GC		NT	NT	NT	NT	NT	NT	NT	NT	NT		NT	NT	NT	NT	NT	NT	NT	NT
				A			B 1 ☕		B			A			B				A			B			A	
York 8	40	d				09 11								10 11							11 09					
Selby	40	d		08 43								09 43							10 42						11 43	
Leeds 10	37,39	d	09 13	09 23	09 37	09 53				10 07	10 13	10 23	10 37	10 53		11 07	11 13		11 23	11 37	11 53		12 07	12 13	12 23	12 37
Bramley	37	d		09 30	09 44					10 14		10 30	10 44			11 14			11 30	11 44			12 14		12 30	12 44
New Pudsey	37	d		09 35	09 49	10 02				10 19		10 35	10 49	11 02		11 19			11 35	11 49	12 02		12 19		12 35	12 49
Bradford Interchange	37	a		09 43	09 57	10 11				10 28		10 43	10 57	11 12		11 28			11 43	11 57	12 12		12 28		12 43	12 57
		d		09 46	10 00	10 14	10 22			10 32		10 46	11 00	11 14		11 31			11 46	12 00	12 14		12 32		12 46	13 00
Halifax		a		10 01	10 12	10 25	10 34			10 44		11 01	11 12	11 24		11 43			11 59	12 12	12 25		12 44		13 01	13 12
		d		10 06	10 12	10 26	10 38			10 44		11 06	11 12	11 26		11 44			12 06	12 12	12 26		12 44		13 06	13 12
Dewsbury	39	d	09 31								10 29						11 29							12 29		
Mirfield	39	d	09 37								10 35						11 35							12 35		
Brighouse		d	09 49	10 16			10 49				10 49	11 16					11 49		12 16					12 49	13 16	
London Kings Cross 15 ⊖	26	a					13 46																			
Huddersfield	39	a		10 29								11 29							12 30						13 29	
Sowerby Bridge		d	09 59		10 19						10 59		11 19				11 59			12 19				12 59		13 19
Mytholmroyd		d	10 05		10 25						11 05		11 25				12 05			12 25				13 05		13 25
Hebden Bridge		a	10 08		10 28	10 37				10 56	11 08		11 28	11 36		11 55	12 08			12 28	12 37		12 56	13 08		13 28
		d	10 08		10 28	10 38				10 56	11 08		11 28	11 38		11 56	12 08			12 28	12 38		12 56	13 08		13 28
Burnley Manchester Road	97	a				10 57								11 57							12 57					
Accrington	97	a				11 06								12 06							13 06					
Blackburn	97	a				11 14								12 14							13 14					
Preston 8	97	a				11 32								12 32							13 32					
Poulton-le-Fylde	97	a				11 50								12 50							13 50					
Blackpool North	97	a				12 00								13 00							14 00					
Todmorden		d	10 15		10 36					11 04	11 15		11 36			12 03	12 15			12 36			13 04	13 15		13 36
Walsden		d			10 39								11 39							12 39						13 39
Littleborough		d	10 23		10 45						11 23		11 45				12 23			12 45				13 23		13 45
Smithy Bridge		d	10 25		10 48						11 25		11 48				12 25			12 48				13 25		13 48
Rochdale		a	10 29		10 51					11 14	11 29		11 51			12 13	12 29			12 51			13 14	13 29		13 51
		d	10 30		10 51				11 04	11 14	11 30		11 51		12 04	12 14	12 30			12 51		13 04	13 14	13 30		13 51
Castleton		d	10 33						11 07		11 33				12 07		12 33					13 07		13 33		
Mills Hill		d	10 38						11 12		11 38				12 12		12 38					13 12		13 38		
Moston		d	10 41						11 15		11 41				12 15		12 41					13 15		13 41		
Manchester Victoria 🚌		a	10 53		11 07				11 26	11 32	11 53		12 07		12 25	12 32	12 53			13 07		13 25	13 32	13 53		14 07

			NT		NT	NT	NT	NT	NT	NT	NT	NT	NT		NT	NT	NT	GC	NT	NT	NT	NT	NT		NT	NT
					B			A			B				A			B 1 ☕	C			A				D
York 8	40	d	12 13							13 09							14 13								15 09	
Selby	40	d						12 44							13 43							14 43				
Leeds 10	37,39	d	12 53			13 07	13 13	13 23	13 37	13 53		14 07	14 13		14 23	14 37	14 53			15 07	15 13	15 23	15 37		15 52	
Bramley	37	d				13 14		13 30	13 44			14 14			14 30	14 44				15 14		15 30	15 44			
New Pudsey	37	d	13 02			13 19		13 35	13 49	14 02		14 19			14 35	14 49	15 02			15 19		15 35	15 49		16 01	
Bradford Interchange	37	a	13 12			13 28		13 43	13 58	14 12		14 28			14 43	14 58	15 12			15 28		15 43	15 57		16 10	
		d	13 14			13 32		13 46	14 00	14 14		14 32			14 46	15 01	15 14	15 22		15 32		15 46	16 00		16 13	
Halifax		a	13 25			13 44		14 01	14 12	14 25		14 44			15 00	15 13	15 25	15 33		15 44		15 59	16 12		16 24	
		d	13 26			13 44		14 06	14 13	14 26		14 44			15 06	15 13	15 26	15 35		15 44		16 06	16 12		16 25	
Dewsbury	39	d					13 29						14 29								15 29					
Mirfield	39	d					13 35						14 35								15 35					
Brighouse		d					13 49	14 16					14 49		15 16			15 46			15 49	16 16				
London Kings Cross 15 ⊖	26	a																18 45								
Huddersfield	39	a						14 29							15 29							16 29				
Sowerby Bridge		d					13 59		14 19				14 59			15 20					15 59		16 19		16 31	
Mytholmroyd		d					14 05		14 25				15 05			15 26					16 05		16 25			
Hebden Bridge		a	13 37			13 56	14 08		14 28	14 37		14 56	15 08			15 29	15 37			15 56	16 08		16 28		16 37	
		d	13 38			13 56	14 08		14 29	14 38		14 56	15 08			15 29	15 38			15 56	16 08		16 28		16 38	
Burnley Manchester Road	97	a	13 57							14 57							15 57								16 57	
Accrington	97	a	14 06							15 06							16 06								17 06	
Blackburn	97	a	14 14							15 14							16 14								17 14	
Preston 8	97	a	14 32							15 32							16 32								17 32	
Poulton-le-Fylde	97	a	14 50							15 50							16 50								17 56	
Blackpool North	97	a	15 00							16 00							17 00								18 06	
Todmorden		d				14 04	14 15		14 36			15 04	15 15			15 37				16 04	16 15		16 36			
Walsden		d							14 39							15 40							16 39			
Littleborough		d					14 23		14 46				15 23			15 46					16 23		16 45			
Smithy Bridge		d					14 25		14 48				15 25			15 49					16 25		16 48			
Rochdale		a				14 14	14 29		14 51			15 14	15 29			15 52				16 14	16 29		16 51			
		d			14 04	14 14	14 30		14 52		15 04	15 14	15 30			15 52			16 04	16 14	16 30		16 51			17 03
Castleton		d			14 07		14 33				15 07		15 33						16 07		16 33					17 06
Mills Hill		d			14 12		14 38				15 12		15 38						16 12		16 38					17 11
Moston		d			14 15		14 41				15 15		15 41						16 15		16 41					17 14
Manchester Victoria 🚌		a			14 25	14 32	14 53		15 08		15 26	15 32	15 53			16 08			16 25	16 32	16 53		17 07			17 23

A To Wakefield Westgate
B until 1 October. To Wigan Wallgate
C To Wigan Wallgate
D To Blackburn

For connections to Liverpool Lime Street please refer to Table 90

Table 41

Saturdays

Leeds and Bradford - Huddersfield, Blackpool North, Rochdale and Manchester Victoria via Halifax and Brighouse

		NT	NT	NT A	NT	NT	NT B	NT		NT	NT A	NT	NT	NT	NT	NT	NT A	NT		NT	NT	NT A	NT	NT	NT
York 8	40 d					16 09							17 12							18 05					
Selby	40 d			15 41							16 43						17 39					18 46			
Leeds 10	37,39 d	16 07	16 13	16 23	16 37	16 51		17 07		17 13	17 23	17 37	17 51		18 08	18 13	18 22	18 37		18 51	19 08	19 23	19 37	20 08	20 37
Bramley	37 d	16 14		16 30	16 44			17 14			17 30	17 44			18 15		18 30	18 44			19 15	19 31	19 44	20 15	20 44
New Pudsey	37 d	16 19		16 35	16 49	17 01		17 19			17 35	17 49	18 01		18 20		18 35	18 49		19 01	19 20	19 35	19 49	20 20	20 49
Bradford Interchange	37 a	16 28		16 43	16 57	17 10		17 28			17 43	17 57	18 09		18 28		18 43	18 58		19 10	19 28	19 44	19 57	20 28	20 57
	d	16 32		16 46	17 00	17 12		17 32			17 46	18 00	18 12		18 32		18 46	19 00		19 12	19 32	19 46	20 00	20 31	21 00
Halifax	a	16 44		17 01	17 12	17 24		17 44			17 59	18 12	18 23		18 44		19 00	19 12		19 23	19 44	19 59	20 12	20 44	21 12
	d	16 44		17 06	17 12	17 24		17 44			18 06	18 12	18 24		18 44		19 06	19 13		19 24	19 44	20 06	20 12	20 44	21 12
Dewsbury	39 d		16 31							17 31						18 31									
Mirfield	39 d		16 38							17 38						18 38									
Brighouse	d		16 49	17 16						17 49	18 16					18 49	19 16					20 16		20 55	
London Kings Cross 15 ⊖26	a																								
Huddersfield	39 a			17 29							18 30						19 29					20 29		21 08	
Sowerby Bridge	d		16 59		17 19	17 31				17 59		18 19	18 31			18 59		19 19					20 19		21 19
Mytholmroyd	d		17 05		17 25					18 05		18 25				19 05		19 25					20 25		21 25
Hebden Bridge	a	16 56	17 08		17 28	17 37		17 56		18 08		18 28	18 37		18 56	19 08		19 28		19 35	19 56		20 28		21 28
	d	16 56	17 08		17 28	17 38		17 56		18 08		18 28	18 38		18 56	19 08		19 28		19 36	19 56		20 28		21 28
Burnley Manchester Road	97 a					17 57							18 57							19 56					
Accrington	97 a					18 06							19 06							20 05					
Blackburn	97 a					18 14							19 14							20 14					
Preston 8	97 a					18 33							19 32							20 32					
Poulton-le-Fylde	97 a					18 50							19 50							20 50					
Blackpool North	97 a					19 00							20 00							21 00					
Todmorden	d	17 04	17 15		17 36			18 04		18 15		18 36			19 04	19 15		19 36			20 04		20 36		21 36
Walsden	d				17 39					18 19		18 39				19 19		19 39					20 39		21 39
Littleborough	d		17 23		17 45					18 25		18 45				19 25		19 45					20 45		21 45
Smithy Bridge	d		17 25		17 48					18 28		18 48				19 28		19 48					20 48		21 48
Rochdale	a	17 14	17 29		17 51			18 14		18 32		18 51			19 15	19 32		19 52			20 14		20 52		21 52
	d	17 14	17 30		17 51		18 02	18 14		18 32		18 51		19 02	19 15	19 32		19 52			20 14		20 52		21 52
Castleton	d		17 33				18 05			18 35				19 05		19 35		19 55					20 55		21 55
Mills Hill	d		17 38				18 10			18 40				19 10		19 40		20 00					21 00		22 00
Moston	d		17 41				18 13			18 43				19 13		19 43		20 03					21 03		22 03
Manchester Victoria ⛴	a	17 33	17 53		18 07		18 22	18 32		18 54		19 10		19 22	19 32	19 54		20 15			20 32		21 14		22 14

		NT	NT	NT		NT	NT	NT	NT
York 8	40 d	20 13							
Selby	40 d								
Leeds 10	37,39 d	20 51	21 08	21 37		22 08		22 37	23 00
Bramley	37 d		21 15	21 44		22 15		22 44	23 07
New Pudsey	37 d	21 01	21 20	21 49		22 20		22 49	23 12
Bradford Interchange	37 a	21 10	21 28	21 57		22 28		22 57	23 21
	d	21 13	21 31	22 00		22 31		23 00	23 23
Halifax	a	21 24	21 44	22 12		22 44		23 12	23 36
	d	21 25	21 44	22 12		22 44		23 12	23 36
Dewsbury	39 d								
Mirfield	39 d								
Brighouse	d		21 55			22 55			23 47
London Kings Cross 15 ⊖26	a								
Huddersfield	39 a		22 08			23 08			23 59
Sowerby Bridge	d			22 19				23 19	
Mytholmroyd	d			22 25				23 25	
Hebden Bridge	a	21 36		22 28				23 28	
	d	21 37		22 28				23 28	
Burnley Manchester Road	97 a	21 56							
Accrington	97 a	22 05							
Blackburn	97 a	22 13							
Preston 8	97 a	22 31							
Poulton-le-Fylde	97 a	22 49							
Blackpool North	97 a	22 59							
Todmorden	d			22 36				23 36	
Walsden	d			22 39				23 39	
Littleborough	d			22 45				23 45	
Smithy Bridge	d			22 48				23 48	
Rochdale	a			22 52				23 52	
	d			22 52			23 04	23 52	
Castleton	d			22 55			23 07		
Mills Hill	d			23 00			23 12		
Moston	d			23 03			23 15		
Manchester Victoria ⛴	a			23 14			23 27	00 08	

A To Wakefield Westgate

B To Blackburn

For connections to Liverpool Lime Street please refer to Table 90

Table 41

Sundays until 19 June

Leeds and Bradford - Huddersfield, Blackpool North, Rochdale and Manchester Victoria via Halifax and Brighouse

			NT	GC	NT	NT	NT	NT	NT	NT	NT		NT	NT	NT	GC	NT	NT	NT	NT	NT		NT	NT	NT	NT
			A	R 1 B ☕												R 1 ☕										
York 8	40	d								08 50				09 52			10 57			11 52			12 52			13 52
Selby	40	d																								
Leeds 10	37,39	d	22p37			08 21	08 45	09 02	09 18	09 35	09 54		10 12	10 35	10 54		11 35	11 54	12 12	12 35	12 54		13 35	13 54	14 12	14 35
Bramley	37	d	22p44			08 28		09 09	09 25		10 01		10 19		11 01			12 01	12 19		13 01			14 01	14 19	
New Pudsey	37	d	22p49			08 33	08 54	09 14	09 30	09 44	10 06		10 24	10 44	11 06		11 44	12 06	12 24	12 44	13 06		13 44	14 06	14 24	14 44
Bradford Interchange	37	a	22p57			08 41	09 03	09 22	09 38	09 53	10 14		10 32	10 53	11 14		11 53	12 14	12 32	12 53	13 14		13 53	14 14	14 32	14 53
		d	23p00	07 55		08 45	09 05	09 25	09 41	09 55	10 17		10 35	10 55	11 17	11 42	11 55	12 17	12 35	12 55	13 17		13 55	14 17	14 35	14 55
Halifax		a	23p12	08 06		08 57	09 17	09 37	09 54	10 07	10 29		10 48	11 07	11 29	11 54	12 07	12 29	12 48	13 07	13 29		14 07	14 29	14 48	15 07
		d	23p12	08 09		09 01	09 17	09 37	09 54	10 07	10 29		10 48	11 07	11 29	11 55	12 07	12 29	12 48	13 07	13 29		14 07	14 29	14 48	15 07
Dewsbury	39	d																								
Mirfield	39	d																								
Brighouse		d		08 20					10 04				10 58			12 06			12 58						14 58	
London Kings Cross 15 ⊖26		a		10 42												14 48										
Huddersfield	39	a							10 17				11 12						13 12						15 12	
Sowerby Bridge		d	23p19			09 06		09 44			10 36				11 36			12 36			13 36			14 36		
Mytholmroyd		d	23p25			09 12		09 50			10 42				11 42			12 42			13 42			14 42		
Hebden Bridge		a	23p28			09 17	09 29	09 53		10 19	10 45			11 19	11 45		12 19	12 45		13 19	13 45		14 19	14 45		15 19
		d	23p28			09 17	09 29	09 53		10 19	10 45			11 19	11 45		12 19	12 45		13 19	13 45		14 19	14 45		15 19
Burnley Manchester Road	97	a					09 50			10 38				11 38			12 38			13 38			14 38			15 38
Accrington	97	a					09 59			10 47				11 47			12 47			13 47			14 47			15 47
Blackburn	97	a					10 07			10 56				11 55			12 55			13 55			14 55			15 55
Preston 8	97	a					10 27			11 13				12 13			13 13			14 13			15 13			16 13
Poulton-le-Fylde	97	a					10 45			11 31				12 31			13 31			14 30			15 32			16 31
Blackpool North	97	a					10 53			11 39				12 38			13 38			14 38			15 39			16 38
Todmorden		d	23p36			09 24		10 00			10 52				11 52			12 52			13 52			14 52		
Walsden		d	23p39			09 27		10 03			10 55				11 55			12 55			13 55			14 55		
Littleborough		d	23p45			09 34		10 10			11 02				12 02			13 02			14 02			15 02		
Smithy Bridge		d	23p48			09 36		10 12			11 04				12 04			13 04			14 04			15 04		
Rochdale		a	23p52			09 41		10 16			11 08				12 08			13 08			14 08			15 08		
		d	23p52		08 53	09 41		10 17			11 09				12 09			13 09			14 09			15 09		
Castleton		d			08 56	09 44		10 20			11 12				12 12			13 12			14 12			15 12		
Mills Hill		d			09 01	09 49		10 25			11 17				12 17			13 17			14 17			15 17		
Moston		d			09 04	09 52		10 28			11 20				12 20			13 20			14 20			15 20		
Manchester Victoria		a	00 08		09 14	10 02		10 38			11 30				12 30			13 30			14 30			15 30		

			NT	GC	NT	NT	NT		NT	NT	NT	NT	NT	NT	NT	NT	NT		NT	NT	NT	NT	NT	NT		
				R 1 ☕																						
York 8	40	d			14 52				15 52		16 52			17 52		18 52				19 52		20 57				
Selby	40	d																								
Leeds 10	37,39	d	14 54		15 35	15 54	16 13		16 35	16 54	17 35	17 54	18 13	18 35	19 03	19 35	19 54		20 12	20 35	21 04	21 35	22 05	22 35		
Bramley	37	d	15 01			16 01	16 20			17 01		18 01	18 20		19 10		20 01		20 20		21 12	21 43	22 12	22 43		
New Pudsey	37	d	15 06		15 44	16 06	16 25		16 44	17 06	17 44	18 06	18 25	18 44	19 15	19 44	20 06		20 25	20 44	21 17	21 47	22 17	22 47		
Bradford Interchange	37	a	15 14		15 53	16 14	16 33		16 53	17 14	17 53	18 14	18 33	18 53	19 23	19 53	20 14		20 34	20 53	21 25	21 56	22 27	22 56		
		d	15 17	15 42	15 55	16 17	16 36		16 55	17 17	17 55	18 17	18 36	18 55	19 27	19 55	20 19		20 35	20 55	21 28	21 58	22 29	22 58		
Halifax		a	15 29	15 54	16 07	16 29	16 49		17 07	17 29	18 07	18 29	18 49	19 07	19 39	20 07	20 31		20 47	21 07	21 40	22 10	22 42	23 12		
		d	15 29	15 56	16 07	16 29	16 49		17 07	17 29	18 07	18 29	18 49	19 07	19 39	20 07	20 31		20 48	21 07	21 40	22 11	22 42	23 12		
Dewsbury	39	d																								
Mirfield	39	d																								
Brighouse		d		16 06			16 59						18 59						20 58				22 52	23a23		
London Kings Cross 15 ⊖26		a		18 51																						
Huddersfield	39	a					17 12						19 12						21 13				23 04			
Sowerby Bridge		d	15 36			16 36				17 36		18 36			19 46		20 38				21 47	22 17				
Mytholmroyd		d	15 42			16 42				17 42		18 42			19 52		20 44				21 53	22 23				
Hebden Bridge		a	15 45		16 19	16 45			17 19	17 45	18 19	18 45		19 19	19 55	20 19	20 47			21 19	21 57	22 27				
		d	15 45		16 19	16 45			17 19	17 45	18 19	18 45		19 19	19 55	20 19	20 47			21 19		22 27				
Burnley Manchester Road	97	a			16 38				17 38		18 38			19 38		20 38				21 38						
Accrington	97	a			16 47				17 47		18 47			19 47		20 47				21 47						
Blackburn	97	a			16 55				17 55		18 55			19 56		20 55				21 55						
Preston 8	97	a			17 13				18 13		19 13			20 14		21 13				22 13						
Poulton-le-Fylde	97	a			17 31				18 31		19 31			20 32		21 31				22 31						
Blackpool North	97	a			17 38				18 38		19 38			20 39		21 38				22 38						
Todmorden		d	15 52			16 52				17 52		18 52			20 02		20 54					22 34				
Walsden		d	15 55			16 55				17 55		18 55			20 05		20 57					22 37				
Littleborough		d	16 02			17 02				18 02		19 02			20 11		21 03					22 44				
Smithy Bridge		d	16 04			17 04				18 04		19 04			20 14		21 06					22 46				
Rochdale		a	16 08			17 08				18 08		19 08			20 18		21 10					22 50				
		d	16 09			17 09				18 09		19 09			20 19		21 11					22 51				
Castleton		d	16 12			17 12				18 12		19 12			20 22		21 14					22 54				
Mills Hill		d	16 17			17 17				18 17		19 17			20 27		21 19					22 59				
Moston		d	16 20			17 20				18 20		19 20			20 30		21 22					23 02				
Manchester Victoria		a	16 30			17 30				18 30		19 30			20 41		21 33					23 12				

A not 22 May

B R to Brighouse

For connections to Liverpool Lime Street please refer to Table 90

Table 41

Sundays

26 June to 31 July

Leeds and Bradford - Huddersfield, Blackpool North, Rochdale and Manchester Victoria via Halifax and Brighouse

Station	Table		NT	GC R 1 A	NT	NT	NT	NT	NT	NT	NT		NT	NT	NT	GC R 1	NT	NT	NT	NT	NT		NT	NT	NT	NT
York 8	40	d								08 50				09 52			10 57			11 52			12 52			13 52
Selby	40	d																								
Leeds 10	37,39	d	22p37			08 21	08 45	09 02	09 18	09 35	09 54		10 12	10 35	10 54		11 35	11 54	12 12	12 35	12 54		13 35	13 54	14 12	14 35
Bramley	37	d	22p44			08 28		09 09	09 25		10 01		10 19		11 01			12 01	12 19		13 01			14 01	14 19	
New Pudsey	37	d	22p49			08 33	08 54	09 14	09 30	09 44	10 06		10 24	10 44	11 06		11 44	12 06	12 24	12 44	13 06		13 44	14 06	14 24	14 44
Bradford Interchange	37	a	22p57			08 41	09 03	09 22	09 38	09 53	10 14		10 32	10 53	11 14		11 53	12 14	12 32	12 53	13 14		13 53	14 14	14 32	14 53
		d	23p00	07 55		08 45	09 05	09 25	09 41	09 55	10 17		10 35	10 55	11 17	11 42	11 55	12 17	12 35	12 55	13 17		13 55	14 17	14 35	14 55
Halifax		a	23p12	08 06		08 57	09 17	09 37	09 54	10 07	10 29		10 48	11 07	11 29	11 54	12 07	12 29	12 48	13 07	13 29		14 07	14 29	14 48	15 07
		d	23p12	08 09		09 01	09 17	09 37	09 54	10 07	10 29		10 48	11 07	11 29	11 55	12 07	12 29	12 48	13 07	13 29		14 07	14 29	14 48	15 07
Dewsbury	39	d																								
Mirfield	39	d																								
Brighouse		d		08 20					10 04				10 58			12 06			12 58						14 58	
London Kings Cross 15 ⊖26		a		11 03												14 48										
Huddersfield	39	a							10 17				11 12						13 12						15 12	
Sowerby Bridge		d	23p19			09 06		09 44			10 36				11 36			12 36			13 36			14 36		
Mytholmroyd		d	23p25			09 12		09 50			10 42				11 42			12 42			13 42			14 42		
Hebden Bridge		a	23p28			09 17	09 29	09 53		10 19	10 45			11 19	11 45		12 19	12 45		13 19	13 45		14 19	14 45		15 19
		d	23p28			09 17	09 29	09 53		10 19	10 45			11 19	11 45		12 19	12 45		13 19	13 45		14 19	14 45		15 19
Burnley Manchester Road	97	a					09 50			10 38				11 38			12 38			13 38			14 38			15 38
Accrington	97	a					09 59			10 47				11 47			12 47			13 47			14 47			15 47
Blackburn	97	a					10 07			10 56				11 55			12 55			13 55			14 55			15 55
Preston 8	97	a					10 27			11 13				12 13			13 13			14 13			15 13			16 13
Poulton-le-Fylde	97	a					10 45			11 31				12 31			13 31			14 30			15 32			16 31
Blackpool North	97	a					10 53			11 39				12 38			13 38			14 38			15 39			16 38
Todmorden		d	23p36			09 24		10 00			10 52				11 52			12 52			13 52			14 52		
Walsden		d	23p39			09 27		10 03			10 55				11 55			12 55			13 55			14 55		
Littleborough		d	23p45			09 34		10 10			11 02				12 02			13 02			14 02			15 02		
Smithy Bridge		d	23p48			09 36		10 12			11 04				12 04			13 04			14 04			15 04		
Rochdale		a	23p52			09 41		10 16			11 08				12 08			13 08			14 08			15 08		
		d	23p52		08 53	09 41		10 17			11 09				12 09			13 09			14 09			15 09		
Castleton		d			08 56	09 44		10 20			11 12				12 12			13 12			14 12			15 12		
Mills Hill		d			09 01	09 49		10 25			11 17				12 17			13 17			14 17			15 17		
Moston		d			09 04	09 52		10 28			11 20				12 20			13 20			14 20			15 20		
Manchester Victoria		a	00 08		09 14	10 02		10 38			11 30				12 30			13 30			14 30			15 30		

Station	Table		NT	GC R 1	NT	NT	NT		NT	NT	NT	NT	NT	NT	NT	NT	NT		NT	NT	NT	NT	NT	NT		
York 8	40	d			14 52				15 52		16 52			17 52		18 52				19 52		20 57				
Selby	40	d																								
Leeds 10	37,39	d	14 54		15 35	15 54	16 13		16 35	16 54	17 35	17 54	18 13	18 35	19 03	19 35	19 54		20 12	20 35	21 04	21 35	22 05	22 35		
Bramley	37	d	15 01			16 01	16 20			17 01		18 01	18 20		19 10		20 01		20 20		21 12	21 43	22 12	22 43		
New Pudsey	37	d	15 06		15 44	16 06	16 25		16 44	17 06	17 44	18 06	18 25	18 44	19 15	19 44	20 06		20 25	20 44	21 17	21 47	22 17	22 47		
Bradford Interchange	37	a	15 14		15 53	16 14	16 33		16 53	17 14	17 53	18 14	18 33	18 53	19 23	19 53	20 14		20 34	20 53	21 25	21 56	22 27	22 56		
		d	15 17	15 42	15 55	16 17	16 36		16 55	17 17	17 55	18 17	18 36	18 55	19 27	19 55	20 19		20 35	20 55	21 28	21 58	22 29	22 58		
Halifax		a	15 29	15 54	16 07	16 29	16 49		17 07	17 29	18 07	18 29	18 49	19 07	19 39	20 07	20 31		20 47	21 07	21 40	22 10	22 42	23 12		
		d	15 29	15 56	16 07	16 29	16 49		17 07	17 29	18 07	18 29	18 49	19 07	19 39	20 07	20 31		20 48	21 07	21 40	22 11	22 42	23 12		
Dewsbury	39	d																								
Mirfield	39	d																								
Brighouse		d		16 06			16 59						18 59						20 58				22 52	23a23		
London Kings Cross 15 ⊖26		a		18 51																						
Huddersfield	39	a					17 12						19 12						21 13				23 04			
Sowerby Bridge		d	15 36			16 36				17 36		18 36			19 46		20 38				21 47	22 17				
Mytholmroyd		d	15 42			16 42				17 42		18 42			19 52		20 44				21 53	22 23				
Hebden Bridge		a	15 45		16 19	16 45			17 19	17 45	18 19	18 45		19 19	19 55	20 19	20 47			21 19	21 57	22 27				
		d	15 45		16 19	16 45			17 19	17 45	18 19	18 45		19 19	19 55	20 19	20 47			21 19		22 27				
Burnley Manchester Road	97	a			16 38				17 38		18 38			19 38		20 38				21 38						
Accrington	97	a			16 47				17 47		18 47			19 47		20 47				21 47						
Blackburn	97	a			16 55				17 55		18 55			19 56		20 55				21 55						
Preston 8	97	a			17 13				18 13		19 13			20 14		21 13				22 13						
Poulton-le-Fylde	97	a			17 31				18 31		19 31			20 32		21 31				22 31						
Blackpool North	97	a			17 38				18 38		19 38			20 39		21 38				22 38						
Todmorden		d	15 52			16 52				17 52		18 52			20 02		20 54					22 34				
Walsden		d	15 55			16 55				17 55		18 55			20 05		20 57					22 37				
Littleborough		d	16 02			17 02				18 02		19 02			20 11		21 03					22 44				
Smithy Bridge		d	16 04			17 04				18 04		19 04			20 14		21 06					22 46				
Rochdale		a	16 08			17 08				18 08		19 08			20 18		21 10					22 50				
		d	16 09			17 09				18 09		19 09			20 19		21 11					22 51				
Castleton		d	16 12			17 12				18 12		19 12			20 22		21 14					22 54				
Mills Hill		d	16 17			17 17				18 17		19 17			20 27		21 19					22 59				
Moston		d	16 20			17 20				18 20		19 20			20 30		21 22					23 02				
Manchester Victoria		a	16 30			17 30				18 30		19 30			20 41		21 33					23 12				

A R to Brighouse

For connections to Liverpool Lime Street please refer to Table 90

Table 41

Sundays

7 August to 11 September

Leeds and Bradford - Huddersfield, Blackpool North, Rochdale and Manchester Victoria via Halifax and Brighouse

			NT	GC	NT	NT	NT	NT	NT	NT	NT		NT	NT	NT	GC	NT	NT	NT	NT	NT		NT	NT	NT	NT
				R 1 A ☕												R 1 ☕										
York 8	40	d								08 50				09 52			10 57			11 52			12 52			13 52
Selby	40	d																								
Leeds 10	37,39	d	22p37			08 21	08 45	09 02	09 18	09 35	09 54		10 12	10 35	10 54		11 35	11 54	12 12	12 35	12 54		13 35	13 54	14 12	14 35
Bramley	37	d	22p44			08 28		09 09	09 25		10 01		10 19		11 01			12 01	12 19		13 01			14 01	14 19	
New Pudsey	37	d	22p49			08 33	08 54	09 14	09 30	09 44	10 06		10 24	10 44	11 06		11 44	12 06	12 24	12 44	13 06		13 44	14 06	14 24	14 44
Bradford Interchange	37	a	22p57			08 41	09 03	09 22	09 38	09 53	10 14		10 32	10 53	11 14		11 53	12 14	12 32	12 53	13 14		13 53	14 14	14 32	14 53
		d	23p00	07 55		08 45	09 05	09 25	09 41	09 55	10 17		10 35	10 55	11 17	11 42	11 55	12 17	12 35	12 55	13 17		13 55	14 17	14 35	14 55
Halifax		a	23p12	08 06		08 57	09 17	09 37	09 54	10 07	10 29		10 48	11 07	11 29	11 54	12 07	12 29	12 48	13 07	13 29		14 07	14 29	14 48	15 07
		d	23p12	08 09		09 01	09 17	09 37	09 54	10 07	10 29		10 48	11 07	11 29	11 55	12 07	12 29	12 48	13 07	13 29		14 07	14 29	14 48	15 07
Dewsbury	39	d																								
Mirfield	39	d																								
Brighouse		d		08 20					10 04				10 58			12 06			12 58						14 58	
London Kings Cross 15 ⊖	26	a		10 42												14 48										
Huddersfield	39	a							10 17				11 12						13 12						15 12	
Sowerby Bridge		d	23p19			09 06		09 44			10 36				11 36			12 36			13 36			14 36		
Mytholmroyd		d	23p25			09 12		09 50			10 42				11 42			12 42			13 42			14 42		
Hebden Bridge		a	23p28			09 17	09 29	09 53		10 19	10 45			11 19	11 45		12 19	12 45		13 19	13 45		14 19	14 45		15 19
		d	23p28			09 17	09 29	09 53		10 19	10 45			11 19	11 45		12 19	12 45		13 19	13 45		14 19	14 45		15 19
Burnley Manchester Road	97	a					09 50			10 38				11 38			12 38			13 38			14 38			15 38
Accrington	97	a					09 59			10 47				11 47			12 47			13 47			14 47			15 47
Blackburn	97	a					10 07			10 56				11 55			12 55			13 55			14 55			15 55
Preston 8	97	a					10 27			11 13				12 13			13 13			14 13			15 13			16 13
Poulton-le-Fylde	97	a					10 45			11 31				12 31			13 31			14 30			15 32			16 31
Blackpool North	97	a					10 53			11 39				12 38			13 38			14 38			15 39			16 38
Todmorden		d	23p36			09 24		10 00			10 52				11 52			12 52			13 52			14 52		
Walsden		d	23p39			09 27		10 03			10 55				11 55			12 55			13 55			14 55		
Littleborough		d	23p45			09 34		10 10			11 02				12 02			13 02			14 02			15 02		
Smithy Bridge		d	23p48			09 36		10 12			11 04				12 04			13 04			14 04			15 04		
Rochdale		a	23p52			09 41		10 16			11 08				12 08			13 08			14 08			15 08		
		d	23p52		08 53	09 41		10 17			11 09				12 09			13 09			14 09			15 09		
Castleton		d			08 56	09 44		10 20			11 12				12 12			13 12			14 12			15 12		
Mills Hill		d			09 01	09 49		10 25			11 17				12 17			13 17			14 17			15 17		
Moston		d			09 04	09 52		10 28			11 20				12 20			13 20			14 20			15 20		
Manchester Victoria ⇌		a	00 08		09 14	10 02		10 38			11 30				12 30			13 30			14 30			15 30		

			NT	GC	NT	NT	NT		NT	NT	NT	NT	NT	NT	NT	NT	NT		NT	NT	NT	NT	NT	NT		
				R 1 ☕																						
York 8	40	d			14 52				15 52		16 52			17 52		18 52				19 52		20 57				
Selby	40	d																								
Leeds 10	37,39	d	14 54		15 35	15 54	16 13		16 35	16 54	17 35	17 54	18 13	18 35	19 03	19 35	19 54		20 12	20 35	21 04	21 35	22 05	22 35		
Bramley	37	d	15 01			16 01	16 20			17 01		18 01	18 20		19 10		20 01		20 20		21 12	21 43	22 12	22 43		
New Pudsey	37	d	15 06		15 44	16 06	16 25		16 44	17 06	17 44	18 06	18 25	18 44	19 15	19 44	20 06		20 25	20 44	21 17	21 47	22 17	22 47		
Bradford Interchange	37	a	15 14		15 53	16 14	16 33		16 53	17 14	17 53	18 14	18 33	18 53	19 23	19 53	20 14		20 34	20 53	21 25	21 56	22 27	22 56		
		d	15 17	15 42	15 55	16 17	16 36		16 55	17 17	17 55	18 17	18 36	18 55	19 27	19 55	20 19		20 35	20 55	21 28	21 58	22 29	22 58		
Halifax		a	15 29	15 54	16 07	16 29	16 49		17 07	17 29	18 07	18 29	18 49	19 07	19 39	20 07	20 31		20 47	21 07	21 40	22 10	22 42	23 12		
		d	15 29	15 56	16 07	16 29	16 49		17 07	17 29	18 07	18 29	18 49	19 07	19 39	20 07	20 31		20 48	21 07	21 40	22 11	22 42	23 12		
Dewsbury	39	d																								
Mirfield	39	d																								
Brighouse		d		16 06			16 59						18 59						20 58				22 52	23a23		
London Kings Cross 16 ⊖	26	a		18 51																						
Huddersfield	39	a					17 12						19 12						21 13				23 04			
Sowerby Bridge		d	15 36			16 36				17 36		18 36			19 46		20 38				21 47	22 17				
Mytholmroyd		d	15 42			16 42				17 42		18 42			19 52		20 44				21 53	22 23				
Hebden Bridge		a	15 45		16 19	16 45			17 19	17 45	18 19	18 45		19 19	19 55	20 19	20 47			21 19	21 57	22 27				
		d	15 45		16 19	16 45			17 19	17 45	18 19	18 45		19 19	19 55	20 19	20 47			21 19		22 27				
Burnley Manchester Road	97	a			16 38				17 38		18 38			19 38		20 38				21 38						
Accrington	97	a			16 47				17 47		18 47			19 47		20 47				21 47						
Blackburn	97	a			16 55				17 55		18 55			19 56		20 55				21 55						
Preston 8	97	a			17 13				18 13		19 13			20 14		21 13				22 13						
Poulton-le-Fylde	97	a			17 31				18 31		19 31			20 32		21 31				22 31						
Blackpool North	97	a			17 38				18 38		19 38			20 39		21 38				22 38						
Todmorden		d	15 52			16 52				17 52		18 52			20 02		20 54					22 34				
Walsden		d	15 55			16 55				17 55		18 55			20 05		20 57					22 37				
Littleborough		d	16 02			17 02				18 02		19 02			20 11		21 03					22 44				
Smithy Bridge		d	16 04			17 04				18 04		19 04			20 14		21 06					22 46				
Rochdale		a	16 08			17 08				18 08		19 08			20 18		21 10					22 50				
		d	16 09			17 09				18 09		19 09			20 19		21 11					22 51				
Castleton		d	16 12			17 12				18 12		19 12			20 22		21 14					22 54				
Mills Hill		d	16 17			17 17				18 17		19 17			20 27		21 19					22 59				
Moston		d	16 20			17 20				18 20		19 20			20 30		21 22					23 02				
Manchester Victoria ⇌		a	16 30			17 30				18 30		19 30			20 41		21 33					23 12				

A R to Brighouse

For connections to Liverpool Lime Street please refer to Table 90

Table 41

Sundays

18 September to 23 October

Leeds and Bradford - Huddersfield, Blackpool North, Rochdale and Manchester Victoria via Halifax and Brighouse

Station	Table		NT	NT	NT	NT	NT	NT	NT	NT	NT		NT	NT	GC R 1 ☕	NT	NT	NT	NT	NT	NT		NT	NT	NT	NT
York 8	40	d							08 50				09 52			10 57			11 52		12 52				13 52	
Selby	40	d																								
Leeds 10	37,39	d	22p37		08 21	08 45	09 02	09 18	09 35	09 54	10 12		10 35	10 54		11 35	11 54	12 12	12 35	12 54	13 35		13 54	14 12	14 35	14 54
Bramley	37	d	22p44		08 28		09 09	09 25		10 01	10 19			11 01			12 01	12 19		13 01			14 01	14 19		15 01
New Pudsey	37	d	22p49		08 33	08 54	09 14	09 30	09 44	10 06	10 24		10 44	11 06		11 44	12 06	12 24	12 44	13 06	13 44		14 06	14 24	14 44	15 06
Bradford Interchange	37	a	22p57		08 41	09 03	09 22	09 38	09 53	10 14	10 32		10 53	11 14		11 53	12 14	12 32	12 53	13 14	13 53		14 14	14 32	14 53	15 14
		d	23p00		08 45	09 05	09 25	09 44	09 55	10 17	10 35		10 55	11 17	11 42	11 55	12 17	12 35	12 55	13 17	13 55		14 17	14 35	14 55	15 17
Halifax		a	23p12		08 57	09 17	09 37	09 57	10 07	10 29	10 48		11 07	11 29	11 54	12 07	12 29	12 48	13 07	13 29	14 07		14 29	14 48	15 07	15 29
		d	23p12		09 01	09 17	09 37	09 59	10 07	10 29	10 48		11 07	11 29	11 55	12 07	12 29	12 48	13 07	13 29	14 07		14 29	14 48	15 07	15 29
Dewsbury	39	d																								
Mirfield	39	d																								
Brighouse		d						10 09			10 58				12 06			12 58						14 58		
London Kings Cross 15	⊖26	a													14 48											
Huddersfield	39	a						10 22			11 12							13 12						15 12		
Sowerby Bridge		d	23p19		09 06		09 44			10 36				11 36			12 36			13 36			14 40			15 36
Mytholmroyd		d	23p25		09 12		09 50			10 42				11 42			12 42			13 42			14 46			15 42
Hebden Bridge		a	23p28		09 17	09 29	09 53		10 19	10 45			11 19	11 45		12 19	12 45		13 19	13 45	14 19		14 49		15 19	15 45
		d	23p28		09 17	09 29	09 53		10 19	10 45			11 19	11 45		12 19	12 45		13 19	13 45	14 19		14 49		15 19	15 45
Burnley Manchester Road	97	a				09 50			10 38				11 38			12 38			13 38		14 38				15 38	
Accrington	97	a				09 59			10 47				11 47			12 47			13 47		14 47				15 47	
Blackburn	97	a				10 07			10 56				11 55			12 55			13 55		14 55				15 55	
Preston 8	97	a				10 27			11 13				12 13			13 13			14 13		15 13				16 13	
Poulton-le-Fylde	97	a				10 45			11 31				12 31			13 31			14 30		15 32				16 31	
Blackpool North	97	a				10 53			11 39				12 38			13 38			14 38		15 39				16 38	
Todmorden		d	23p36		09 24		10 00			10 52				11 52			12 52			13 52			14 57			15 52
Walsden		d	23p39		09 27		10 03			10 55				11 55			12 55			13 55			15 00			15 55
Littleborough		d	23p45		09 34		10 10			11 02				12 02			13 02			14 02			15 06			16 02
Smithy Bridge		d	23p48		09 36		10 12			11 04				12 04			13 04			14 04			15 09			16 04
Rochdale		a	23p52		09 41		10 16			11 08				12 08			13 08			14 08			15 13			16 08
		d	23p52	08 58	09 41		10 17			11 09				12 09			13 09			14 09			15 13			16 09
Castleton		d		09 01	09 44		10 20			11 12				12 12			13 12			14 12			15 16			16 12
Mills Hill		d		09 06	09 49		10 25			11 17				12 17			13 17			14 17			15 21			16 17
Moston		d		09 09	09 52		10 28			11 20				12 20			13 20			14 20			15 24			16 20
Manchester Victoria	⛴	a	00 08	09 19	10 02		10 38			11 30				12 30			13 30			14 30			15 37			16 30

Station	Table		GC R 1 ☕	NT	NT	NT	NT		NT	NT	NT	NT	NT	NT	NT	NT	NT		NT	NT	NT	NT	NT			
York 8	40	d		14 52			15 52			16 52			17 52		18 52				19 52		20 57					
Selby	40	d																								
Leeds 10	37,39	d		15 35	15 54	16 13	16 35		16 54	17 35	17 54	18 13	18 35	19 03	19 35	19 54	20 12		20 35	21 04	21 35	22 05	22 35			
Bramley	37	d			16 01	16 20			17 01		18 01	18 20		19 10		20 01	20 19			21 12	21 43	22 12	22 43			
New Pudsey	37	d		15 44	16 06	16 25	16 44		17 06	17 44	18 06	18 25	18 44	19 15	19 44	20 06	20 24		20 44	21 17	21 47	22 17	22 47			
Bradford Interchange	37	a		15 53	16 14	16 33	16 53		17 14	17 53	18 14	18 33	18 53	19 23	19 53	20 14	20 34		20 53	21 25	21 56	22 27	22 56			
		d	15 42	15 55	16 17	16 36	16 55		17 17	17 55	18 17	18 36	18 55	19 27	19 55	20 19	20 35		20 55	21 28	22 05	22 29	22 58			
Halifax		a	15 54	16 07	16 29	16 49	17 07		17 29	18 07	18 29	18 49	19 07	19 39	20 07	20 31	20 47		21 07	21 40	22 17	22 42	23 12			
		d	15 55	16 07	16 29	16 49	17 07		17 29	18 07	18 29	18 49	19 07	19 39	20 07	20 31	20 48		21 07	21 40	22 17	22 42	23 12			
Dewsbury	39	d																								
Mirfield	39	d																								
Brighouse		d	16 06			16 59						18 59					20 58					22 52	23a23			
London Kings Cross 15	⊖26	a	18 51																							
Huddersfield	39	a				17 12						19 12					21 12					23 04				
Sowerby Bridge		d			16 36				17 36		18 40			19 46		20 38				21 47	22 24					
Mytholmroyd		d			16 42				17 42		18 46			19 52		20 44				21 53	22 30					
Hebden Bridge		a		16 19	16 45		17 19		17 45	18 19	18 49		19 19	19 55	20 19	20 47			21 19	21 57	22 33					
		d		16 19	16 45		17 19		17 45	18 19	18 49		19 19	19 55	20 19	20 47			21 19		22 33					
Burnley Manchester Road	97	a		16 38			17 38			18 38			19 38		20 38				21 38							
Accrington	97	a		16 47			17 47			18 47			19 47		20 47				21 47							
Blackburn	97	a		16 55			17 55			18 55			19 56		20 55				21 55							
Preston 8	97	a		17 13			18 13			19 13			20 14		21 13				22 13							
Poulton-le-Fylde	97	a		17 31			18 31			19 31			20 32		21 31				22 31							
Blackpool North	97	a		17 38			18 38			19 38			20 39		21 38				22 38							
Todmorden		d			16 52				17 52		18 57			20 02		20 54					22 40					
Walsden		d			16 55				17 55		19 00			20 05		20 57					22 43					
Littleborough		d			17 02				18 02		19 06			20 11		21 03					22 50					
Smithy Bridge		d			17 04				18 04		19 09			20 14		21 06					22 52					
Rochdale		a			17 08				18 08		19 13			20 18		21 10					22 56					
		d			17 09				18 09		19 13			20 19		21 11					22 57					
Castleton		d			17 12				18 12		19 16			20 22		21 14					23 00					
Mills Hill		d			17 17				18 17		19 21			20 27		21 19					23 05					
Moston		d			17 20				18 20		19 24			20 30		21 22					23 08					
Manchester Victoria	⛴	a			17 30				18 30		19 37			20 41		21 33					23 17					

For connections to Liverpool Lime Street please refer to Table 90

Table 41

Sundays
from 30 October

Leeds and Bradford - Huddersfield, Blackpool North, Rochdale and Manchester Victoria via Halifax and Brighouse

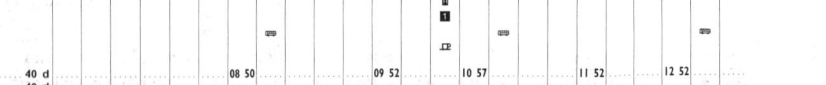

Station	Table		NT	NT	NT	NT	NT	NT	NT	NT	NT		NT	NT	NT	GC	NT	NT	NT	NT	NT		NT	NT	NT	NT
										bus						R 1 catering		bus							bus	
York 8	40	d							08 50					09 52			10 57				11 52			12 52		
Selby	40	d																								
Leeds 10	37,39	d	22p37		08 21	08 45	09 02	09 18	09 35		09 54		10 12	10 35	10 54		11 35		11 54	12 12	12 35		12 54	13 35		13 54
Bramley	37	d	22p44		08 28		09 09	09 25			10 01		10 19		11 01				12 01	12 19			13 01			14 01
New Pudsey	37	d	22p49		08 33	08 54	09 14	09 30	09 44		10 06		10 24	10 44	11 06		11 44		12 06	12 24	12 44		13 06	13 44		14 06
Bradford Interchange	37	a	22p57		08 41	09 03	09 22	09 38	09 53		10 14		10 32	10 53	11 14		11 53		12 14	12 32	12 53		13 14	13 53		14 14
		d	23p00		08 45	09 05	09 25	09 41	09 55		10 17		10 35	10 55	11 17	11 42	11 55		12 17	12 35	12 55		13 17	13 55		14 17
Halifax		a	23p12		08 57	09 17	09 37	09 54	10 07		10 29		10 48	11 07	11 29	11 54	12 07		12 29	12 48	13 07		13 29	14 07		14 29
		d	23p12		09 01	09 17	09 37	09 54	10 07		10 29		10 48	11 07	11 29	11 55	12 07		12 29	12 48	13 07		13 29	14 07		14 29
Dewsbury	39	d																								
Mirfield	39	d																								
Brighouse		d						10 04					10 58			12 06				12 58						
London Kings Cross 15 ⊖	26	a														14 48										
Huddersfield	39	a						10 17					11 12							13 12						
Sowerby Bridge		d	23p19		09 06		09 44				10 36				11 36				12 36				13 36			14 36
Mytholmroyd		d	23p25		09 12		09 50				10 42				11 42				12 42				13 42			14 42
Hebden Bridge		a	23p28		09 17	09 30	09 53		10 19		10 45			11 19	11 45		12 19		12 45		13 19		13 45	14 19		14 45
		d	23p28		09 17		09 53		10 19	10 30	10 45				11 45			12 30	12 45				13 45		14 30	14 45
Burnley Manchester Road	97	a							10 38	10 59								12 59							14 59	
Accrington	97	a							10 47	11 20								13 19							15 19	
Blackburn	97	a							10 56	11 37								13 37							15 37	
Preston 8	97	a							11 13	12 08								14 08							16 08	
Poulton-le-Fylde	97	a							11 31																	
Blackpool North	97	a							11 39	12 50								14 50							16 50	
Todmorden		d	23p36		09 24		10 00				10 52				11 52				12 52				13 52			14 52
Walsden		d	23p39		09 27		10 03				10 55				11 55				12 55				13 55			14 55
Littleborough		d	23p45		09 34		10 10				11 02				12 02				13 02				14 02			15 02
Smithy Bridge		d	23p48		09 36		10 12				11 04				12 04				13 04				14 04			15 04
Rochdale		a	23p52		09 41		10 16				11 08				12 08				13 08				14 08			15 08
		d	23p52	08 58	09 41		10 17				11 09				12 09				13 09				14 09			15 09
Castleton		d		09 01	09 44		10 20				11 12				12 12				13 12				14 12			15 12
Mills Hill		d		09 06	09 49		10 25				11 17				12 17				13 17				14 17			15 17
Moston		d		09 09	09 52		10 28				11 20				12 20				13 20				14 20			15 20
Manchester Victoria		a	00 08	09 19	10 02		10 38				11 30				12 30				13 30				14 30			15 30

Station	Table		NT	NT	NT	GC	NT		NT	NT	NT	NT	NT	NT	NT	NT	NT		NT	NT	NT	NT	NT	NT	NT	NT
						R 1 catering			bus				bus			bus							bus			
York 8	40	d		13 52			14 52					15 52			16 52					17 52		18 52				19 52
Selby	40	d																								
Leeds 10	37,39	d	14 12	14 35	14 54		15 35			15 54	16 13	16 35		16 54	17 35		17 54		18 13	18 35	19 03	19 35		19 54	20 12	20 35
Bramley	37	d	14 19		15 01					16 01	16 20			17 01			18 01		18 20		19 10			20 01	20 20	
New Pudsey	37	d	14 24	14 44	15 06		15 44			16 06	16 25	16 44		17 06	17 44		18 06		18 25	18 44	19 15	19 44		20 06	20 25	20 44
Bradford Interchange	37	a	14 32	14 53	15 14		15 53			16 14	16 33	16 53		17 14	17 53		18 14		18 33	18 53	19 23	19 53		20 14	20 34	20 53
		d	14 35	14 55	15 17	15 42	15 55			16 17	16 36	16 55		17 17	17 55		18 17		18 36	18 55	19 27	19 55		20 19	20 35	20 55
Halifax		a	14 48	15 07	15 29	15 54	16 07			16 29	16 49	17 07		17 29	18 07		18 29		18 49	19 07	19 39	20 07		20 31	20 47	21 07
		d	14 48	15 07	15 29	15 56	16 07			16 29	16 49	17 07		17 29	18 07		18 29		18 49	19 07	19 39	20 07		20 31	20 48	21 07
Dewsbury	39	d																								
Mirfield	39	d																								
Brighouse		d	14 58			16 06					16 59								18 59						20 58	
London Kings Cross 15 ⊖	26	a				18 51																				
Huddersfield	39	a	15 12								17 12								19 12						21 13	
Sowerby Bridge		d			15 36					16 36				17 36			18 36				19 46			20 38		
Mytholmroyd		d			15 42					16 42				17 42			18 42				19 52			20 44		
Hebden Bridge		a		15 19	15 45		16 19			16 45		17 19		17 45	18 19		18 45			19 19	19 55	20 19		20 47		21 19
		d			15 45				16 30	16 45			17 30	17 45		18 30	18 45				19 55		20 30	20 47		
Burnley Manchester Road	97	a							16 59				17 59			18 59							20 59			
Accrington	97	a							17 19				18 19			19 19							21 19			
Blackburn	97	a							17 37				18 37			19 37							21 37			
Preston 8	97	a							18 08				19 08			20 08							22 08			
Poulton-le-Fylde	97	a																								
Blackpool North	97	a							18 50				19 50			20 50							22 50			
Todmorden		d			15 52					16 52				17 52			18 52				20 02			20 54		
Walsden		d			15 55					16 55				17 55			18 55				20 05			20 57		
Littleborough		d			16 02					17 02				18 02			19 02				20 11			21 03		
Smithy Bridge		d			16 04					17 04				18 04			19 04				20 14			21 06		
Rochdale		a			16 08					17 08				18 08			19 08				20 18			21 10		
		d			16 09					17 09				18 09			19 09				20 19			21 11		
Castleton		d			16 12					17 12				18 12			19 12				20 22			21 14		
Mills Hill		d			16 17					17 17				18 17			19 17				20 27			21 19		
Moston		d			16 20					17 20				18 20			19 20				20 30			21 22		
Manchester Victoria		a			16 30					17 30				18 30			19 30				20 41			21 33		

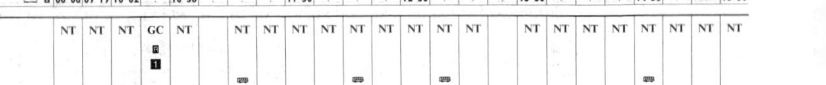

For connections to Liverpool Lime Street please refer to Table 90

Table 41

Sundays
from 30 October

Leeds and Bradford - Huddersfield, Blackpool North, Rochdale and Manchester Victoria via Halifax and Brighouse

Station			NT		NT	NT	NT
York 8	40	d			20 57		
Selby	40	d					
Leeds 10	37,39	d	21 04		21 35	22 05	22 35
Bramley	37	d	21 12		21 43	22 12	22 43
New Pudsey	37	d	21 17		21 47	22 17	22 47
Bradford Interchange	37	a	21 25		21 56	22 27	22 56
		d	21 28		21 58	22 29	22 58
Halifax		a	21 40		22 10	22 42	23 12
		d	21 40		22 11	22 42	23 12
Dewsbury	39	d					
Mirfield	39	d					
Brighouse		d				22 52	23a23
London Kings Cross 15 ⊖	26	a					
Huddersfield	39	a				23 04	
Sowerby Bridge		d	21 47		22 17		
Mytholmroyd		d	21 53		22 23		
Hebden Bridge		a	21 57		22 27		
		d			22 27		
Burnley Manchester Road	97	a					
Accrington	97	a					
Blackburn	97	a					
Preston 8	97	a					
Poulton-le-Fylde	97	a					
Blackpool North	97	a					
Todmorden		d			22 34		
Walsden		d			22 37		
Littleborough		d			22 44		
Smithy Bridge		d			22 46		
Rochdale		a			22 50		
		d			22 51		
Castleton		d			22 54		
Mills Hill		d			22 59		
Moston		d			23 02		
Manchester Victoria	⇌	a			23 12		

For connections to Liverpool Lime Street please refer to Table 90

Manchester Victoria, Rochdale, Blackpool North and Huddersfield - Bradford and Leeds via Brighouse and Halifax

Miles	Miles	Miles	Miles			NT MX	NT A	NT MX	NT	NT	NT	NT	NT	NT		NT	NT	NT	NT	NT	NT	NT B	NT	NT	
0	—	—	—	**Manchester Victoria**	d	22p28		23p20			05 51			06 17		06 43		06 58		07 17	07 48		08 00		
4	—	—	—	Moston	d	22p34		23p27						06 23				07 04		07 23			08 06		
6	—	—	—	Mills Hill	d	22p39		23p32						06 28				07 09		07 28			08 11		
8¾	—	—	—	Castleton	d	22p44		23p37						06 33				07 14		07 33			08 16		
10½	—	—	—	**Rochdale**	a	22p47		23p40			06 05			06 36		06 56		07 17		07 36	08 01		08 19		
—	—	—	—		d	22p48		23p41			06 05			06 37		06 56		07 18		07 37	08 01		08 20		
12¾	—	—	—	Smithy Bridge	d	22p52		23p45			06 09			06 41				07 22		07 41			08 24		
13¾	—	—	—	Littleborough	d	22p55		23p48			06 13			06 44				07 25		07 44			08 27		
17¾	—	—	—	Walsden	d	23p01		23p54			06 19			06 50				07 31		07 50					
19¼	—	—	—	Todmorden	d	23p05		23p58			06 22			06 54		07 08		07 35		07 54	08 13		08 34		
—	0	—	—	**Blackpool North** 97	d		20p40						05 29						06 28					07 29	
—	3	—	—	Poulton-le-Fylde 97	d		20p55						05 35						06 34					07 35	
—	17½	—	—	**Preston** 8 97	d		21p40						05 54						06 54					07 54	
—	29½	—	—	Blackburn 97	d		22p10						06 10						07 10					08 10	
—	35¾	—	—	Accrington 97	d		22p28						06 17						07 17					08 17	
—	42	—	—	Burnley Manchester Road 97	d		22p48						06 26						07 26					08 26	
23½	54¾	—	0	**Hebden Bridge**	a	23p11	23p18	00 04			06 29		06 49	07 00		07 14		07 41	07 49	08 00	08 19		08 41	08 49	
—	—	—	—		d	23p11	23p18	00 04	05 47	06 17	06 29		06 50	07 00		07 16		07 41	07 50	08 00	08 21		08 41	08 50	
24¾	56	—	1¼	Mytholmroyd	d	23p15	23p28	00 08	05 50	06 20	06 32			07 03		07 19		07 45		08 04			08 44		
28¾	60	—	5¼	Sowerby Bridge	d	23p20	23p43	00 13	05 56	06 26	06 38		06 57	07 09		07 25		07 50	07 57	08 09			08 50	08 57	
—	—	0	—	**Huddersfield** 39	d												07 29					08 22			
—	—	—	—	London Kings Cross 15 ⊖26	d																				
—	—	5¼	11	Brighouse	d												07 39	07 59				08 33	08 58		
—	—	—	15	Mirfield 39	a													08 06					09 06		
—	—	—	18	Dewsbury 39	a													08 11					09 12		
32¼	63½	10½	—	**Halifax**	a	23p29	23p57	00 20	06 02	06 32	06 45		07 03	07 16		07 32	07 50		08 03	08 16	08 33	08 43		09 03	
—	—	—	—		d	23p29	23p58	00 20	06 03	06 33	06 45	07 02	07 03	07 16		07 33	07 50		08 03	08 16	08 33	08 48		09 03	
40¼	71½	—	—	**Bradford Interchange**	a	23p43	00 22	00 34	06 16	06 46	07 00		07 17	07 31		07 47	08 03		08 17	08 31	08 47	09 01		09 17	
—	—	—	—		d	23p46	00 23	00 37	06 18	06 48	07 02		07 20	07 34		07 50	08 05		08 20	08 34	08 50	09 04		09 20	
43¾	75	—	—	New Pudsey 37	a	23p54	00 33		06 27	06 57	07 11		07 28	07 42		07 58	08 13		08 28	08 42	08 58	09 12		09 27	
45¾	77	—	—	Bramley 37	a	23p58	00 43		06 30	07 00	07 14			07 46		08 02	08 18			08 46	09 02	09 16			
49¾	81	—	27¼	**Leeds** 10 37,39	a	00 09	01 03	00 55	06 41	07 09	07 27	07 55	07 39	07 57		08 12	08 29	08 33	08 39	08 57	09 12	09 27	09 32	09 39	
—	—	—	—	Selby 40	a									08 36		08 53					09 53				
—	—	—	—	York 8 40	a						08 06		08 16						09 21					10 24	

		NT	NT C	NT	NT B	NT	NT	NT	NT	NT		NT B	NT	NT	NT	NT D	NT	NT B	NT	NT		NT	NT D	NT	NT B
Manchester Victoria	d	08 22	08 30	08 48		09 00		09 22	09 33	09 48			10 00		10 21	10 30	10 48		11 00			11 21	11 30	11 48	
Moston	d		08 36			09 06			09 39				10 06			10 36			11 06				11 36		
Mills Hill	d		08 40			09 11			09 44				10 11			10 40			11 11				11 40		
Castleton	d		08 45			09 16			09 49				10 16			10 45			11 16				11 45		
Rochdale	a	08 34	08 51	09 02		09 19		09 35	09 54	10 02			10 19		10 34	10 51	11 02		11 19			11 34	11 51	12 02	
	d	08 35		09 02		09 20		09 36		10 02			10 20		10 35		11 02		11 20			11 35		12 02	
Smithy Bridge	d	08 39				09 24		09 40					10 24		10 39				11 24			11 39			
Littleborough	d	08 42				09 27		09 43					10 27		10 42				11 27			11 42			
Walsden	d	08 48						09 49							10 48							11 48			
Todmorden	d	08 52		09 14		09 34		09 53		10 14			10 34		10 52		11 14		11 34			11 52		12 14	
Blackpool North 97	d						08 29							09 29						10 29					
Poulton-le-Fylde 97	d						08 35							09 35						10 35					
Preston 8 97	d						08 54							09 54						10 54					
Blackburn 97	d						09 10							10 10						11 10					
Accrington 97	d						09 17							10 17						11 17					
Burnley Manchester Road 97	d						09 26							10 26						11 28					
Hebden Bridge	a	08 58		09 20		09 41	09 49	09 59		10 20			10 41	10 49	10 58		11 20		11 41	11 49		11 58		12 20	
	d	09 00		09 21		09 41	09 50	10 00		10 21			10 41	10 50	11 00		11 21		11 41	11 50		12 00		12 21	
Mytholmroyd	d	09 03				09 44		10 03					10 44		11 03				11 44			12 03			
Sowerby Bridge	d	09 09				09 50		10 09					10 50		11 09				11 50			12 09			
Huddersfield 39	d				09 23							10 23						11 23							12 23
London Kings Cross 15 ⊖26	d																								
Brighouse	d				09 34	09 58						10 33	10 58					11 33	11 58						12 33
Mirfield 39	a					10 06							11 06						12 06						
Dewsbury 39	a					10 12							11 12						12 12						
Halifax	a	09 15		09 33	09 44		10 02	10 15		10 33		10 43		11 02	11 15		11 33	11 43		12 02		12 15		12 33	12 43
	d	09 16		09 33	09 49		10 03	10 16		10 33		10 49		11 03	11 16		11 33	11 49		12 03		12 16		12 33	12 49
Bradford Interchange	a	09 31		09 47	10 03		10 17	10 31		10 47		11 02		11 17	11 31		11 47	12 02		12 17		12 31		12 47	13 02
	d	09 34		09 50	10 05		10 18	10 34		10 50		11 05		11 20	11 34		11 50	12 05		12 19		12 34		12 50	13 05
New Pudsey 37	a	09 42		09 58	10 14		10 27	10 42		10 58		11 13		11 28	11 42		11 58	12 13		12 27		12 42		12 58	13 13
Bramley 37	a	09 46		10 02	10 17			10 46		11 02		11 17			11 46		12 02	12 17				12 46		13 02	13 17
Leeds 10 37,39	a	10 00		10 12	10 29	10 32	10 38	11 00		11 13		11 27	11 33	11 39	12 00		12 12	12 27	12 31	12 39		12 59		13 12	13 27
Selby 40	a			10 53						11 54							12 50							13 51	
York 8 40	a						11 19							12 21						13 19					

A MO from 31 October
B From Wakefield Westgate
C until 30 September. From Kirkby
D until 30 September. From Wigan Wallgate

For connections from Liverpool Lime Street please refer to Table 90

Manchester Victoria, Rochdale, Blackpool North and Huddersfield - Bradford and Leeds via Brighouse and Halifax

		NT	NT	NT	NT A	NT	GC R 1	NT B	NT	NT	NT	NT A	NT	NT B	NT	NT	NT	NT A	NT	NT B	NT	NT	NT
Manchester Victoria	d	12 00		12 21	12 30	12 48			13 00		13 21	13 30	13 48		14 00		14 21	14 30	14 48		15 00		15 21
Moston	d	12 06			12 36				13 06			13 36			14 06			14 36			15 06		
Mills Hill	d	12 11			12 40				13 11			13 40			14 11			14 40			15 11		
Castleton	d	12 16			12 45				13 16			13 45			14 16			14 45			15 16		
Rochdale	a	12 19		12 34	12 51	13 02			13 19		13 34	13 51	14 02		14 19		14 34	14 51	15 02		15 19		15 34
	d	12 20		12 35		13 02			13 20		13 35		14 02		14 20		14 35		15 02		15 20		15 35
Smithy Bridge	d	12 24		12 39					13 24		13 39				14 24		14 39				15 24		15 39
Littleborough	d	12 27		12 42					13 27		13 42				14 27		14 42				15 27		15 42
Walsden	d			12 48							13 48						14 48						15 48
Todmorden	d	12 34		12 52		13 14			13 34		13 52		14 14		14 34		14 52		15 14		15 34		15 52
Blackpool North	97 d		11 29							12 29						13 29						14 29	
Poulton-le-Fylde	97 d		11 35							12 35						13 35						14 35	
Preston 8	97 d		11 54							12 54						13 54						14 54	
Blackburn	97 d		12 10							13 10						14 10						15 10	
Accrington	97 d		12 17							13 17						14 17						15 17	
Burnley Manchester Road	97 d		12 26							13 26						14 26						15 26	
Hebden Bridge	a	12 41	12 49	12 58		13 20			13 41	13 49	13 58		14 20		14 41	14 49	14 58		15 20		15 41	15 49	16 00
	d	12 41	12 50	13 00		13 21			13 41	13 50	14 00		14 21		14 41	14 50	15 00		15 21		15 41	15 50	16 01
Mytholmroyd	d	12 44		13 03					13 44		14 03				14 44		15 03				15 44		16 04
Sowerby Bridge	d	12 50		13 09					13 50		14 09				14 50		15 09				15 50		16 10
Huddersfield	39 d							13 23						14 23						15 23			
London Kings Cross 15 ⊖	26 d						10 48																
Brighouse	d	12 58					13 31	13 35	13 58					14 33	14 58					15 33	15 58		
Mirfield	39 a	13 06							14 06						15 06						16 06		
Dewsbury	39 a	13 12							14 12						15 12						16 12		
Halifax	a		13 02	13 15		13 33	13 40	13 46		14 02	14 15		14 33	14 43		15 02	15 15		15 33	15 43		16 02	16 16
	d		13 03	13 16		13 33	13 42	13 49		14 03	14 16		14 33	14 49		15 03	15 16		15 33	15 49		16 03	16 17
Bradford Interchange	a		13 17	13 31		13 47	13 55	14 02		14 17	14 31		14 47	15 02		15 17	15 31		15 47	16 02		16 17	16 31
	d		13 19	13 34		13 50		14 05		14 19	14 34		14 50	15 05		15 19	15 34		15 50	16 05		16 19	16 34
New Pudsey	37 a		13 27	13 42		13 58		14 13		14 28	14 42		14 58	15 13		15 27	15 42		15 58	16 13		16 27	16 42
Bramley	37 a			13 46		14 02		14 17			14 46		15 02	15 17			15 46		16 02	16 17			16 46
Leeds 10	37,39 a	13 32	13 40	14 00		14 13		14 26	14 32	14 39	15 00		15 12	15 27	15 32	15 39	16 00		16 12	16 27	16 32	16 39	16 59
Selby	40 a					14 51							15 53						16 54				
York 8	40 a		14 22							15 18						16 21						17 20	

		NT A	NT	NT B	NT	NT	NT	NT A	NT	GC R 1	NT	NT B	NT	NT	NT	NT A	NT	NT	NT B	NT	NT	NT
Manchester Victoria	d	15 30	15 48		16 00		16 24	16 30	16 48				17 00		17 17	17 30	17 43			18 00		18 21
Moston	d	15 36			16 06			16 36					17 06		17 24	17 36	17 49					
Mills Hill	d	15 40			16 11			16 40					17 11		17 28	17 40	17 54			18 09		
Castleton	d	15 45			16 16			16 45					17 16		17 33	17 45	17 59			18 14		
Rochdale	a	15 51	16 02		16 19		16 37	16 51	17 02				17 19		17 37	17 51	18 02			18 18		18 35
	d		16 02		16 20		16 37		17 02		17 03		17 20		17 38		18 03	18 02		18 18		18 36
Smithy Bridge	d				16 24		16 41						17 24		17 42					18 22		18 40
Littleborough	d				16 27		16 45						17 27		17 45		18 08			18 26		18 43
Walsden	d						16 51								17 51					18 32		18 49
Todmorden	d		16 14		16 34		16 54		17 14				17 34		17 55		18 16			18 35		18 53
Blackpool North	97 d					15 29								16 29							17 14	
Poulton-le-Fylde	97 d					15 35								16 35							17 20	
Preston 8	97 d					15 54								16 54							17 44	
Blackburn	97 d					16 10					18a16			17 10				19a21			18 11	
Accrington	97 d					16 17								17 17							18 19	
Burnley Manchester Road	97 d					16 26								17 26							18 28	
Hebden Bridge	a		16 20		16 41	16 49	17 01		17 20				17 41	17 49	17 59		18 22			18 42	18 49	18 59
	d		16 21		16 41	16 50	17 01		17 21				17 41	17 50	17 59		18 23			18 42	18 50	19 00
Mytholmroyd	d				16 44		17 04						17 44		18 05					18 45		19 03
Sowerby Bridge	d				16 50		17 10						17 50		18 10					18 51		19 09
Huddersfield	39 d			16 23								17 23							18 23			
London Kings Cross 15 ⊖	26 d									14 48												
Brighouse	d			16 33	16 58					17 28		17 37	17 58						18 34	18 59		
Mirfield	39 a				17 06								18 07							19 07		
Dewsbury	39 a				17 12								18 13							19 13		
Halifax	a		16 33	16 46		17 02	17 17		17 33	17 38		17 50		18 02	18 15		18 35		18 45		19 03	19 15
	d		16 33	16 49		17 03	17 17		17 33	17 39		17 50		18 03	18 15		18 35		18 49		19 03	19 16
Bradford Interchange	a		16 47	17 02		17 17	17 31		17 47	17 55		18 03		18 17	18 31		18 49		19 02		19 17	19 31
	d		16 50	17 04		17 19	17 34		17 50			18 04		18 19	18 34		18 52		19 05		19 19	19 34
New Pudsey	37 a		16 58	17 13		17 28	17 42		17 58			18 12		18 28	18 40		19 00		19 13		19 27	19 42
Bramley	37 a		17 02	17 17			17 46		18 02			18 16			18 45		19 04		19 17			19 46
Leeds 10	37,39 a		17 12	17 27	17 31	17 39	17 57		18 12			18 31	18 34	18 39	18 56		19 13		19 28	19 33	19 39	19 56
Selby	40 a		17 51						18 49													
York 8	40 a					18 19								19 21			19 53				20 21	

A until 30 September. From Wigan Wallgate

B From Wakefield Westgate

For connections from Liverpool Lime Street please refer to Table 90

Manchester Victoria, Rochdale, Blackpool North and Huddersfield - Bradford and Leeds via Brighouse and Halifax

		NT	NT	NT	NT	NT	NT	NT		NT	NT	NT	NT FX	NT FO	GC ◇[1] A ☒	NT	NT
Manchester Victoria	d	18 48		19 00		19 21		20 21				21 21				22 28	23 20
Moston	d			19 06		19 27		20 27				21 27				22 34	23 27
Mills Hill	d			19 11		19 32		20 32				21 32				22 39	23 32
Castleton	d			19 16		19 37		20 37				21 37				22 44	23 37
Rochdale	a	19 01		19 19		19 40		20 40				21 40				22 47	23 40
	d	19 01		19 19		19 41		20 41				21 41				22 48	23 41
Smithy Bridge	d			19 23		19 45		20 45				21 45				22 52	23 45
Littleborough	d			19 27		19 48		20 48				21 48				22 55	23 48
Walsden	d					19 54		20 54				21 54				23 01	23 54
Todmorden	d	19 13		19 34		19 58		20 58				21 58				23 05	23 58
Blackpool North 97	d				18 29						20 29						
Poulton-le-Fylde 97	d				18 35						20 35						
Preston [8] 97	d				18 54						20 54						
Blackburn 97	d				19 10						21 10						
Accrington 97	d				19 17						21 17						
Burnley Manchester Road 97	d				19 26						21 28						
Hebden Bridge	a	19 20		19 41	19 49	20 04		21 04			21 50	22 04				23 11	00 04
	d	19 20		19 41	19 50	20 05		21 05			21 51	22 05				23 11	00 04
Mytholmroyd	d			19 44		20 08		21 08				22 08				23 15	00 08
Sowerby Bridge	d			19 50		20 14		21 14				22 14				23 20	00 13
Huddersfield 39	d		19 23				20 25			21 27			22 25	22 25			
London Kings Cross [15] ⊖26	d														19 48		
Brighouse	d		19 33	19 58			20 35			21 37			22 35	22 35	22 43		
Mirfield 39	a			20 07													
Dewsbury 39	a			20 12													
Halifax	a	19 32	19 43		20 03	20 20	20 45	21 20		21 47	22 03	22 20	22 45	22 45	22 53	23 29	00 20
	d	19 32	19 49		20 03	20 21	20 49	21 21		21 49	22 03	22 21	22 49	22 49	22 54	23 29	00 20
Bradford Interchange	a	19 48	20 02		20 17	20 35	21 02	21 35		22 02	22 17	22 35	23 02	23 02	23 07	23 43	00 34
	d	19 50	20 04		20 19	20 37	21 04	21 37		22 04	22 19	22 37	23 04	23 04		23 46	00 37
New Pudsey 37	a	19 59	20 13		20 28	20 46	21 13	21 46		22 13	22 28	22 46	23 13	23 13		23 54	
Bramley 37	a	20 03	20 16			20 49	21 16	21 49		22 16		22 49	23 16	23 16		23 58	
Leeds [10] 37,39	a	20 13	20 29	20 34	20 41	20 59	21 25	22 01		22 25	22 37	23 01	23 26	23 27		00 09	00 55
Selby 40	a																
York [8] 40	a				21 30						23 44						

Saturdays

		NT	NT	NT	NT	NT	NT	NT	NT	NT		NT	NT	NT	NT B	NT	NT	NT	NT C	NT		NT B	NT	NT	NT
Manchester Victoria	d	22p28	23p20		05 54		06 17	06 43		06 58			07 17	07 48		08 00		08 22	08 30	08 48			09 00		09 22
Moston	d	22p34	23p27				06 23			07 04			07 23			08 06			08 36				09 06		
Mills Hill	d	22p39	23p32				06 28			07 09			07 28			08 11			08 40				09 11		
Castleton	d	22p44	23p37				06 33			07 14			07 33			08 16			08 45				09 16		
Rochdale	a	22p47	23p40		06 08		06 36	06 56		07 17			07 36	08 01		08 19		08 35	08 51	09 02			09 19		09 35
	d	22p48	23p41		06 09		06 37	06 56		07 18			07 37	08 01		08 20		08 35		09 02			09 20		09 36
Smithy Bridge	d	22p52	23p45		06 13		06 41			07 22			07 41			08 24		08 39					09 24		09 40
Littleborough	d	22p55	23p48		06 16		06 44			07 25			07 44			08 27		08 42					09 27		09 43
Walsden	d	23p01	23p54		06 22		06 50			07 31			07 50					08 48							09 49
Todmorden	d	23p05	23p58		06 26		06 54	07 08		07 35			07 54	08 13		08 34		08 52		09 14			09 34		09 53
Blackpool North 97	d					05 29						06 28					07 29							08 29	
Poulton-le-Fylde 97	d					05 35						06 34					07 35							08 35	
Preston [8] 97	d					05 54						06 54					07 54							08 54	
Blackburn 97	d					06 10						07 10					08 10							09 10	
Accrington 97	d					06 17						07 17					08 17							09 17	
Burnley Manchester Road 97	d					06 26						07 26					08 26							09 26	
Hebden Bridge	a	23p11	00 04		06 32	06 49	07 00	07 14		07 41		07 49	08 00	08 19		08 41	08 49	09 00		09 20			09 41	09 49	09 59
	d	23p11	00 04	05 55	06 33	06 50	07 00	07 16		07 41		07 50	08 00	08 21		08 41	08 50	09 00		09 21			09 41	09 50	10 00
Mytholmroyd	d	23p15	00 08	05 58	06 36		07 04	07 19		07 45			08 04			08 44		09 03					09 44		10 03
Sowerby Bridge	d	23p20	00 13	06 04	06 42	06 57	07 09	07 25		07 50		07 57	08 09			08 50	08 57	09 09					09 50		10 09
Huddersfield 39	d								07 29						08 21							09 23			
London Kings Cross [15] ⊖26	d																								
Brighouse	d								07 39	07 59					08 33	08 58						09 34	09 58		
Mirfield 39	a									08 06						09 06							10 06		
Dewsbury 39	a									08 11						09 12							10 12		
Halifax	a	23p29	00 20	06 10	06 48	07 03	07 16	07 32	07 50			08 03	08 16	08 33	08 43		09 03	09 16		09 33		09 44		10 02	10 15
	d	23p29	00 20	06 11	06 49	07 03	07 16	07 33	07 50			08 03	08 16	08 33	08 49		09 03	09 16		09 33		09 48		10 03	10 16
Bradford Interchange	a	23p43	00 34	06 24	07 03	07 17	07 31	07 47	08 03			08 17	08 31	08 47	09 02		09 17	09 31		09 47		10 02		10 17	10 31
	d	23p46	00 37	06 26	07 05	07 20	07 34	07 50	08 05			08 20	08 34	08 50	09 04		09 20	09 34		09 50		10 04		10 18	10 34
New Pudsey 37	a	23p54		06 35	07 14	07 28	07 42	07 58	08 14			08 28	08 42	08 58	09 12		09 27	09 42		09 58		10 12		10 27	10 42
Bramley 37	a	23p58		06 38	07 17		07 46	08 02	08 18				08 46	09 02	09 16			09 46		10 02		10 16			10 46
Leeds [10] 37,39	a	00 09	00 55	06 49	07 27	07 39	07 57	08 11	08 30	08 31		08 39	08 56	09 12	09 27	09 32	09 39	09 58		10 12		10 27	10 32	10 38	11 00
Selby 40	a						08 36							09 53						10 53					
York [8] 40	a					08 19						09 22					10 22							11 18	

A ☒ from Brighouse ◇ from Brighouse

B From Wakefield Westgate

C until 1 October. From Kirkby

For connections from Liverpool Lime Street please refer to Table 90

Table 41

Saturdays

Manchester Victoria, Rochdale, Blackpool North and Huddersfield - Bradford and Leeds via Brighouse and Halifax

		NT A	NT	NT B	NT	NT		NT	NT C	NT	NT B	NT	NT	NT	NT C	NT		NT B	NT	NT	NT	NT C	NT	GC	NT B
Manchester Victoria	d	09 33	09 48		10 00			10 21	10 30	10 48		11 00		11 21	11 30	11 48			12 00		12 21	12 30	12 48		
Moston	d	09 39			10 06				10 36			11 06			11 36				12 06			12 36			
Mills Hill	d	09 44			10 11				10 40			11 11			11 40				12 11			12 40			
Castleton	d	09 49			10 16				10 45			11 16			11 45				12 16			12 45			
Rochdale	a	09 54	10 02		10 19			10 34	10 51	11 02		11 19		11 34	11 51	12 02			12 19		12 34	12 51	13 02		
	d		10 02		10 20			10 35		11 02		11 20		11 35		12 02			12 20		12 35		13 02		
Smithy Bridge	d				10 24			10 39				11 24		11 39					12 24		12 39				
Littleborough	d				10 27			10 42				11 27		11 42					12 27		12 42				
Walsden	d							10 48						11 48							12 48				
Todmorden	d		10 14		10 34			10 52		11 14		11 34		11 52		12 14			12 34		12 52		13 14		
Blackpool North 97	d					09 29							10 29							11 29					
Poulton-le-Fylde 97	d					09 35							10 35							11 35					
Preston 8 97	d					09 54							10 54							11 54					
Blackburn 97	d					10 10							11 10							12 10					
Accrington 97	d					10 18							11 17							12 17					
Burnley Manchester Road 97	d					10 26							11 28							12 26					
Hebden Bridge	a		10 20		10 41	10 50		10 58		11 20		11 41	11 49	11 58		12 20			12 41	12 49	12 58		13 20		
	d		10 21		10 41	10 50		11 00		11 21		11 41	11 50	12 00		12 21			12 41	12 50	13 00		13 21		
Mytholmroyd	d				10 44			11 03				11 44		12 03					12 44		13 03				
Sowerby Bridge	d				10 50			11 09				11 50		12 09					12 50		13 09				
Huddersfield 39	d			10 23							11 23							12 23							13 23
London Kings Cross 15 ⊖26	d																							10 48	
Brighouse	d			10 33	10 58						11 33	11 58						12 33	12 58					13 31	13 35
Mirfield 39	a				11 06							12 06							13 06						
Dewsbury 39	a				11 12							12 12							13 12						
Halifax	a		10 33	10 43		11 02		11 15		11 33	11 43		12 02	12 15		12 33		12 43		13 02	13 15		13 33	13 40	13 45
	d		10 33	10 49		11 03		11 16		11 33	11 49		12 03	12 16		12 33		12 49		13 03	13 16		13 33	13 42	13 49
Bradford Interchange	a		10 47	11 02		11 17		11 31		11 47	12 02		12 17	12 31		12 47		13 02		13 17	13 31		13 47	13 55	14 02
	d		10 50	11 05		11 20		11 34		11 50	12 05		12 19	12 34		12 50		13 05		13 19	13 34		13 50		14 05
New Pudsey 37	a		10 58	11 13		11 28		11 42		11 58	12 13		12 27	12 42		12 58		13 13		13 27	13 42		13 58		14 13
Bramley 37	a		11 02	11 17				11 46		12 02	12 17			12 46		13 02		13 17			13 46		14 02		14 17
Leeds 10 37,39	a		11 13	11 27	11 35	11 39		12 00		12 12	12 27	12 32	12 39	12 58		13 12		13 27	13 32	13 39	13 58		14 14		14 26
Selby 40	a		11 55							12 50						13 52							14 51		
York 8 40	a					12 21							13 19							14 22					

		NT		NT	NT	NT C	NT	NT B	NT	NT	NT	NT C		NT	NT B	NT	NT	NT	NT C	NT	NT B	NT		NT	NT
Manchester Victoria	d	13 00			13 21	13 30	13 48		14 00		14 21	14 30		14 48		15 00		15 21	15 30	15 48		16 00			16 24
Moston	d	13 06				13 36			14 06			14 36				15 06			15 36			16 06			
Mills Hill	d	13 11				13 40			14 11			14 40				15 11			15 40			16 11			
Castleton	d	13 16				13 45			14 16			14 45				15 16			15 45			16 16			
Rochdale	a	13 19			13 34	13 51	14 02		14 19		14 34	14 51		15 02		15 19		15 34	15 51	16 02		16 19			16 37
	d	13 20			13 35		14 02		14 20		14 35			15 02		15 20		15 35		16 02		16 20			16 37
Smithy Bridge	d	13 24			13 39				14 24		14 39					15 24		15 39				16 24			16 41
Littleborough	d	13 27			13 42				14 27		14 42					15 27		15 42				16 27			16 45
Walsden	d				13 48						14 48							15 48							16 51
Todmorden	d	13 34			13 52		14 14		14 34		14 52			15 14		15 34		15 52		16 14		16 34			16 54
Blackpool North 97	d			12 29						13 29							14 29							15 29	
Poulton-le-Fylde 97	d			12 35						13 35							14 35							15 35	
Preston 8 97	d			12 53						13 54							14 54							15 54	
Blackburn 97	d			13 09						14 10							15 10							16 10	
Accrington 97	d			13 16						14 17							15 17							16 17	
Burnley Manchester Road 97	d			13 25						14 26							15 26							16 26	
Hebden Bridge	a	13 41		13 49	13 58		14 20		14 41	14 49	14 58			15 20		15 41	15 49	16 00		16 20		16 41		16 49	17 01
	d	13 41		13 50	14 00		14 21		14 41	14 50	15 00			15 21		15 41	15 50	16 01		16 21		16 41		16 50	17 01
Mytholmroyd	d	13 44			14 03				14 44		15 03					15 44		16 04				16 44			17 04
Sowerby Bridge	d	13 50			14 09				14 50		15 09					15 50		16 10				16 50			17 10
Huddersfield 39	d							14 23							15 23						16 23				
London Kings Cross 15 ⊖26	d																								
Brighouse	d	13 58						14 33	14 58						15 33	15 58					16 33	16 58			
Mirfield 39	a	14 06							15 06							16 06						17 06			
Dewsbury 39	a	14 12							15 12							16 12						17 12			
Halifax	a			14 02	14 15		14 33	14 43		15 02	15 15			15 33	15 43		16 02	16 16		16 33	16 46			17 02	17 17
	d			14 03	14 16		14 33	14 49		15 03	15 16			15 33	15 49		16 03	16 17		16 33	16 49			17 03	17 17
Bradford Interchange	a			14 17	14 31		14 47	15 02		15 17	15 31			15 47	16 02		16 17	16 31		16 47	17 02			17 17	17 31
	d			14 19	14 34		14 50	15 05		15 19	15 34			15 50	16 05		16 19	16 34		16 50	17 04			17 19	17 34
New Pudsey 37	a			14 28	14 42		14 58	15 13		15 27	15 42			15 58	16 13		16 27	16 42		16 58	17 13			17 28	17 42
Bramley 37	a				14 46		15 02	15 17			15 46			16 02	16 17			16 46		17 02	17 17				17 46
Leeds 10 37,39	a	14 32		14 39	14 58		15 10	15 27	15 32	15 39	16 00			16 12	16 27	16 31	16 39	16 59		17 12	17 27	17 31		17 39	17 57
Selby 40	a						15 53							16 54						17 55					
York 8 40	a			15 17						16 24							17 21							18 19	

A From Blackburn

B From Wakefield Westgate

C until 1 October. From Wigan Wallgate

For connections from Liverpool Lime Street please refer to Table 90

Manchester Victoria, Rochdale, Blackpool North and Huddersfield - Bradford and Leeds via Brighouse and Halifax

	NT A	NT	NT	NT B	NT	NT	NT		NT A	NT	GC	NT	NT B	NT	NT	NT	NT		NT	NT	NT	NT	NT	NT
Manchester Victoria d	16 30	16 48			17 00		17 18		17 30	17 43				18 00		18 21	18 48			19 00		19 21		20 21
Moston d	16 36				17 06		17 24		17 36	17 49										19 06		19 27		20 27
Mills Hill d	16 40				17 11		17 29		17 40	17 54				18 09						19 10		19 32		20 32
Castleton d	16 45				17 16		17 34		17 45	17 59				18 14						19 15		19 37		20 37
Rochdale a	16 51	17 02			17 19		17 37		17 51	18 02				18 18		18 35	19 01			19 19		19 40		20 40
d		17 02	17 03		17 20		17 38			18 03		18 02		18 18		18 36	19 01			19 19		19 41		20 41
Smithy Bridge d					17 24		17 42							18 22		18 40				19 23		19 45		20 45
Littleborough d					17 27		17 46			18 08				18 26		18 43				19 27		19 48		20 48
Walsden d							17 52							18 32		18 49						19 54		20 54
Todmorden d		17 14			17 34		17 55			18 16				18 35		18 53	19 13			19 34		19 58		20 58
Blackpool North 97 d						16 29									17 14						18 29			
Poulton-le-Fylde 97 d						16 35									17 20						18 35			
Preston 8 97 d						16 54									17 44						18 54			
Blackburn 97 d			18a21			17 10						19a21			18 11						19 10			
Accrington 97 d						17 17									18 19						19 17			
Burnley Manchester Road 97 d						17 26									18 28						19 26			
Hebden Bridge a		17 20			17 41	17 49	18 02			18 22				18 42	18 49	18 59	19 19			19 41	19 49	20 04		21 04
d		17 21			17 41	17 50	18 02			18 23				18 42	18 50	19 00	19 20			19 41	19 50	20 05		21 05
Mytholmroyd d					17 44		18 05							18 45		19 03				19 44		20 08		21 08
Sowerby Bridge d					17 50		18 11							18 51		19 09				19 50		20 14		21 14
Huddersfield 39 d				17 23									18 23						19 23				20 25	
London Kings Cross 15 ⊖26 d											15 48													
Brighouse d				17 34	17 58						18 30		18 34	18 59					19 33	19 58			20 35	
Mirfield 39 a					18 07									19 07						20 07				
Dewsbury 39 a					18 12									19 13						20 12				
Halifax a		17 33		17 49		18 02	18 17			18 35	18 40		18 46		19 02	19 15	19 32		19 43		20 03	20 20	20 45	21 20
d		17 33		17 49		18 03	18 18			18 35	18 42		18 49		19 03	19 16	19 32		19 49		20 03	20 21	20 49	21 21
Bradford Interchange a		17 47		18 04		18 17	18 32			18 49	18 55		19 02		19 17	19 31	19 48		20 02		20 17	20 35	21 02	21 35
d		17 50		18 04		18 19	18 34			18 52			19 05		19 18	19 34	19 50		20 04		20 20	20 37	21 04	21 37
New Pudsey 37 a		17 58		18 13		18 28	18 43			19 00			19 13		19 27	19 42	19 58		20 13		20 28	20 46	21 13	21 46
Bramley 37 a		18 02		18 17			18 46			19 04			19 17			19 46	20 02		20 16			20 49	21 16	21 49
Leeds 10 37,39 a		18 12		18 28	18 31	18 39	18 56			19 13			19 28	19 33	19 39	19 58	20 12		20 30	20 33	20 39	20 59	21 25	21 59
Selby 40 a		18 50																						
York 8 40 a						19 19				19 54					20 18						21 31			

	NT	GC	NT		NT	NT	NT	NT	NT
Manchester Victoria d					21 21	22 21		22 54	23 20
Moston d					21 27	22 27			23 26
Mills Hill d					21 32	22 32			23 31
Castleton d					21 37	22 37			23 36
Rochdale a					21 40	22 42		23 07	23 41
d					21 41			23 07	
Smithy Bridge d					21 45			23 11	
Littleborough d					21 48			23 15	
Walsden d					21 54			23 21	
Todmorden d					21 58			23 24	
Blackpool North 97 d			20 29						
Poulton-le-Fylde 97 d			20 35						
Preston 8 97 d			20 54						
Blackburn 97 d			21 10						
Accrington 97 d			21 17						
Burnley Manchester Road 97 d			21 28						
Hebden Bridge a			21 50		22 04			23 31	
d			21 51		22 05			23 31	
Mytholmroyd d					22 08			23 34	
Sowerby Bridge d					22 14			23 40	
Huddersfield 39 d	21 27						22 25		
London Kings Cross 15 ⊖26 d		19 07							
Brighouse d	21 37	21 44					22 35		
Mirfield 39 a									
Dewsbury 39 a									
Halifax a	21 47	21 53	22 03		22 20		22 45	23 46	
d	21 49	21 55	22 03		22 21		22 49	23 47	
Bradford Interchange a	22 02	22 09	22 17		22 35		23 02	00 02	
d	22 04		22 19		22 37		23 04	00 04	
New Pudsey 37 a	22 13		22 28		22 46		23 13	00 12	
Bramley 37 a	22 16				22 49		23 16	00 15	
Leeds 10 37,39 a	22 24		22 37		23 01		23 26	00 27	
Selby 40 a									
York 8 40 a			23 38						

A until 1 October. From Wigan Wallgate

B From Wakefield Westgate

For connections from Liverpool Lime Street please refer to Table 90

Table 41

Sundays until 11 September

Manchester Victoria, Rochdale, Blackpool North and Huddersfield - Bradford and Leeds via Brighouse and Halifax

Station		NT A	NT	NT	NT	NT	NT	NT	NT	NT	NT	NT	NT	NT	NT	NT	NT	NT	GC R	NT	NT	NT	NT
Manchester Victoria	d	22p54	08 26			09 08		10 08			11 08			12 08			13 08				14 08		
Moston	d					09 15		10 15			11 15			12 15			13 15				14 15		
Mills Hill	d					09 19		10 19			11 19			12 19			13 19				14 19		
Castleton	d					09 24		10 24			11 24			12 24			13 24				14 24		
Rochdale	a	23p07	08 42			09 28		10 28			11 28			12 28			13 28				14 28		
	d	23p07				09 28		10 28			11 28			12 28			13 28				14 28		
Smithy Bridge	d	23p11				09 32		10 32			11 32			12 32			13 32				14 32		
Littleborough	d	23p15				09 36		10 36			11 36			12 36			13 36				14 36		
Walsden	d	23p21				09 42		10 42			11 42			12 42			13 42				14 42		
Todmorden	d	23p24				09 45		10 45			11 45			12 45			13 45				14 45		
Blackpool North 97	d						09 11			10 11			11 13			12 11				13 13			14 11
Poulton-le-Fylde 97	d						09 17			10 17			11 19			12 17				13 19			14 17
Preston 8 97	d						09 37			10 37			11 37			12 37				13 37			14 37
Blackburn 97	d						09 54			10 54			11 54			12 54				13 54			14 54
Accrington 97	d						10 01			11 01			12 01			13 01				14 01			15 01
Burnley Manchester Road 97	d						10 10			11 10			12 10			13 10				14 10			15 10
Hebden Bridge	a	23p31				09 52	10 32	10 52		11 32	11 52		12 32	12 52		13 32	13 52			14 32	14 52		15 32
	d	23p31				09 52	10 32	10 52		11 32	11 52		12 32	12 52		13 32	13 52			14 32	14 52		15 32
Mytholmroyd	d	23p34				09 55		10 55			11 55			12 55			13 55				14 55		
Sowerby Bridge	d	23p40				10 01		11 01			12 01			13 01			14 01				15 01		
Huddersfield 39	d				09 25				11 08						13 08							15 08	
London Kings Cross 15 ⊖26	d																		11 48				
Brighouse	d				09 35				11 18						13 18				14 24			15 18	
Mirfield 39	a																						
Dewsbury 39	a																						
Halifax	a	23p46			09 46	10 08	10 44	11 08	11 28	11 44	12 08		12 44	13 08	13 28	13 44	14 08		14 35	14 44	15 08	15 28	15 44
	d	23p47		09 05	09 46	10 08	10 45	11 08	11 29	11 45	12 08	12 29	12 45	13 08	13 29	13 46	14 08	14 29	14 37	14 45	15 08	15 29	15 46
Bradford Interchange	a	00 02		09 18	09 59	10 22	11 00	11 22	11 42	11 59	12 22	12 42	12 59	13 22	13 42	14 00	14 22	14 42	14 50	14 59	15 22	15 42	16 00
	d	00 04		09 20	10 02	10 25	11 02	11 25	11 44	12 02	12 25	12 44	13 02	13 25	13 44	14 02	14 25	14 44		15 02	15 25	15 44	16 03
New Pudsey 37	a	00 12		09 29	10 10	10 33	11 10	11 33	11 53	12 10	12 33	12 53	13 10	13 33	13 53	14 10	14 33	14 53		15 10	15 33	15 53	16 11
Bramley 37	a	00 15		09 32	10 14	10 37		11 37	11 56		12 37	12 56		13 37	13 56		14 37	14 56			15 37	15 56	
Leeds 10 37,39	a	00 27		09 42	10 24	10 46	11 21	11 48	12 05	12 22	12 46	13 06	13 22	13 46	14 06	14 22	14 48	15 06		15 22	15 46	16 06	16 22
Selby 40	a																						
York 8 40	a			10 28	11 05		11 59			13 02			13 59			15 02				15 59			17 03

Station		NT	NT	NT	NT	NT	NT	NT	NT	GC R	NT	NT	NT	NT	NT	NT	NT	NT	NT	NT	GC R	NT	NT
Manchester Victoria	d	15 08			16 08			17 08				18 08			19 08		20 08			21 08			22 08
Moston	d	15 15			16 15			17 15				18 15			19 15		20 15			21 15			22 15
Mills Hill	d	15 19			16 19			17 19				18 19			19 19		20 19			21 19			22 19
Castleton	d	15 24			16 24			17 24				18 24			19 24		20 24			21 24			22 24
Rochdale	a	15 28			16 28			17 28				18 28			19 28		20 28			21 28			22 28
	d	15 28			16 28			17 28				18 28			19 28		20 28			21 28			22 28
Smithy Bridge	d	15 32			16 32			17 32				18 32			19 32		20 32			21 32			22 32
Littleborough	d	15 36			16 36			17 36				18 36			19 36		20 36			21 36			22 36
Walsden	d	15 42			16 42			17 42				18 42			19 42		20 42			21 42			22 42
Todmorden	d	15 45			16 45			17 45				18 45			19 45		20 45			21 45			22 45
Blackpool North 97	d			15 13			16 11				17 11			18 11		19 13			20 11			21 13	
Poulton-le-Fylde 97	d			15 19			16 17				17 17			18 17		19 19			20 17			21 19	
Preston 8 97	d			15 37			16 37				17 37			18 37		19 37			20 37			21 39	
Blackburn 97	d			15 54			16 54				17 54			18 54		19 54			20 54			21 55	
Accrington 97	d			16 01			17 01				18 01			19 01		20 01			21 01			22 02	
Burnley Manchester Road 97	d			16 10			17 10				18 10			19 10		20 10			21 10			22 12	
Hebden Bridge	a	15 52		16 32	16 52		17 32	17 52			18 32	18 52		19 32	19 52	20 32	20 52		21 32	21 52		22 34	22 52
	d	15 52		16 32	16 52		17 32	17 52			18 32	18 52		19 32	19 52	20 32	20 52		21 32	21 52		22 34	22 52
Mytholmroyd	d	15 55			16 55			17 55				18 55			19 55		20 55			21 55			22 55
Sowerby Bridge	d	16 01			17 01			18 01				19 01			20 01		21 01			22 01			23 01
Huddersfield 39	d					17 08							19 08					21 08					
London Kings Cross 15 ⊖26	d									15 48											19 27		
Brighouse	d					17 17				18 24			19 18					21 18			22 06		
Mirfield 39	a																						
Dewsbury 39	a																						
Halifax	a	16 08		16 44	17 08	17 27	17 44	18 08		18 35	18 44	19 08	19 28	19 44	20 08	20 44	21 08	21 28	21 44	22 08	22 17	22 46	23 08
	d	16 08	16 29	16 45	17 08	17 29	17 45	18 08	18 29	18 37	18 45	19 08	19 29	19 45	20 08	20 45	21 08	21 29	21 45	22 09	22 19	22 47	23 08
Bradford Interchange	a	16 22	16 42	16 59	17 22	17 42	17 59	18 22	18 42	18 50	18 59	19 22	19 42	19 59	20 22	20 59	21 22	21 42	21 59	22 23	22 32	23 01	23 22
	d	16 26	16 44	17 02	17 25	17 44	18 02	18 25	18 44		19 02	19 25	19 44	20 02	20 25	21 02	21 26	21 44	22 02	22 26		23 04	23 25
New Pudsey 37	a	16 34	16 53	17 10	17 33	17 53	18 10	18 33	18 53		19 10	19 33	19 53	20 10	20 33	21 10	21 34	21 53	22 10	22 34		23 12	23 33
Bramley 37	a	16 38	16 56		17 37	17 56		18 37	18 56			19 37	19 56		20 37		21 38	21 56		22 38			23 37
Leeds 10 37,39	a	16 48	17 05	17 21	17 46	18 05	18 21	18 46	19 07		19 21	19 47	20 08	20 22	20 47	21 22	21 48	22 05	22 22	22 47		23 23	23 46
Selby 40	a																						
York 8 40	a			18 02			19 03				19 59			21 03		22 00							

A not 22 May

For connections from Liverpool Lime Street please refer to Table 90

Table 41

Sundays

18 September to 23 October

Manchester Victoria, Rochdale, Blackpool North and Huddersfield - Bradford and Leeds via Brighouse and Halifax

		NT	NT	NT	NT	NT	NT	NT	NT	NT	NT	NT	NT	NT	NT	NT	NT	NT	GC	NT	NT	NT	NT
Manchester Victoria	d	22p54	08 32			09 08		10 08			11 08			12 08			13 08				14 08		
Moston	d					09 15		10 15			11 15			12 15			13 15				14 15		
Mills Hill	d					09 19		10 19			11 19			12 19			13 19				14 19		
Castleton	d					09 24		10 24			11 24			12 24			13 24				14 24		
Rochdale	a	23p07	08 48			09 28		10 28			11 28			12 28			13 28				14 28		
	d	23p07				09 28		10 28			11 28			12 28			13 28				14 28		
Smithy Bridge	d	23p11				09 32		10 32			11 32			12 32			13 32				14 32		
Littleborough	d	23p15				09 36		10 36			11 36			12 36			13 36				14 36		
Walsden	d	23p21				09 42		10 42			11 42			12 42			13 42				14 42		
Todmorden	d	23p24				09 45		10 45			11 45			12 45			13 45				14 45		
Blackpool North 97	d						09 01			10 11			11 13			12 11				13 13			14 11
Poulton-le-Fylde 97	d						09 07			10 17			11 19			12 17				13 19			14 17
Preston 8 97	d						09 27			10 37			11 37			12 37				13 37			14 37
Blackburn 97	d						09 44			10 54			11 54			12 54				13 54			14 54
Accrington 97	d						09 51			11 01			12 01			13 01				14 01			15 01
Burnley Manchester Road 97	d						10 00			11 10			12 10			13 10				14 10			15 10
Hebden Bridge	a	23p31				09 52	10 22	10 52		11 32	11 52		12 32	12 52		13 32	13 52			14 32	14 52		15 32
	d	23p31				09 52	10 22	10 52		11 32	11 52		12 32	12 52		13 32	13 52			14 32	14 52		15 32
Mytholmroyd	d	23p34				09 55		10 55			11 55			12 55			13 55				14 55		
Sowerby Bridge	d	23p40				10 01		11 01			12 01			13 01			14 01				15 01		
Huddersfield 39	d				09 27				11 08						13 08							15 08	
London Kings Cross 15 ⊖26	d																		11 48				
Brighouse	d				09 37				11 18						13 18				14 23			15 18	
Mirfield 39	a																						
Dewsbury 39	a																						
Halifax	a	23p46			09 48	10 08	10 34	11 08	11 28	11 44	12 08		12 44	13 08	13 28	13 44	14 08		14 35	14 44	15 08	15 28	15 44
	d	23p47		09 05	09 48	10 08	10 45	11 08	11 29	11 45	12 08	12 29	12 45	13 08	13 29	13 46	14 08	14 29	14 37	14 45	15 08	15 29	15 46
Bradford Interchange	a	00 02		09 18	10 01	10 22	11 00	11 22	11 42	11 59	12 22	12 42	12 59	13 22	13 42	14 00	14 22	14 42	14 50	14 59	15 22	15 42	16 00
	d	00 04		09 20	10 04	10 25	11 02	11 25	11 44	12 02	12 25	12 44	13 02	13 25	13 44	14 02	14 25	14 44		15 02	15 25	15 44	16 03
New Pudsey 37	a	00 12		09 29	10 12	10 33	11 10	11 33	11 53	12 10	12 33	12 53	13 10	13 33	13 53	14 10	14 33	14 53		15 10	15 33	15 53	16 11
Bramley 37	a	00 15		09 32	10 16	10 37		11 37	11 56		12 37	12 56		13 37	13 56		14 37	14 56			15 37	15 56	
Leeds 10 37,39	a	00 27		09 42	10 25	10 46	11 21	11 48	12 05	12 22	12 46	13 06	13 22	13 46	14 06	14 22	14 48	15 06		15 22	15 46	16 06	16 22
Selby 40	a																						
York 8 40	a			10 28	11 08		11 59			13 02			13 59			15 02				15 59			17 03

		NT	NT	NT	NT	NT	NT	NT	NT	GC	NT	NT	NT	NT	NT	NT	NT	NT	NT	NT	GC ■ ⊐P	NT	NT
Manchester Victoria	d	15 08			16 08			17 08				18 08			19 08		20 08			21 08			22 08
Moston	d	15 15			16 15			17 15				18 15			19 15		20 15			21 15			22 15
Mills Hill	d	15 19			16 19			17 19				18 19			19 19		20 19			21 19			22 19
Castleton	d	15 24			16 24			17 24				18 24			19 24		20 24			21 24			22 24
Rochdale	a	15 28			16 28			17 28				18 28			19 28		20 28			21 28			22 28
	d	15 28			16 28			17 28				18 28			19 28		20 28			21 28			22 28
Smithy Bridge	d	15 32			16 32			17 32				18 32			19 32		20 32			21 32			22 32
Littleborough	d	15 36			16 36			17 36				18 36			19 36		20 36			21 36			22 36
Walsden	d	15 42			16 42			17 42				18 42			19 42		20 42			21 42			22 42
Todmorden	d	15 45			16 45			17 45				18 45			19 45		20 45			21 45			22 45
Blackpool North 97	d			15 13			16 11				17 11			18 11		19 13			20 11			21 13	
Poulton-le-Fylde 97	d			15 19			16 17				17 17			18 17		19 19			20 17			21 19	
Preston 8 97	d			15 37			16 37				17 37			18 37		19 37			20 37			21 39	
Blackburn 97	d			15 54			16 54				17 54			18 54		19 54			20 54			21 55	
Accrington 97	d			16 01			17 01				18 01			19 01		20 01			21 01			22 02	
Burnley Manchester Road 97	d			16 10			17 10				18 10			19 10		20 10			21 10			22 12	
Hebden Bridge	a	15 52		16 32	16 52		17 32	17 52			18 32	18 52		19 32	19 52	20 32	20 52		21 32	21 52		22 34	22 52
	d	15 52		16 32	16 52		17 32	17 52			18 32	18 52		19 32	19 52	20 32	20 52		21 32	21 52		22 34	22 52
Mytholmroyd	d	15 55			16 55			17 55				18 55			19 55		20 55			21 55			22 55
Sowerby Bridge	d	16 01			17 01			18 01				19 01			20 01		21 01			22 01			23 01
Huddersfield 39	d					17 08							19 08					21 08					
London Kings Cross 15 ⊖26	d									15 48											19 27		
Brighouse	d					17 17				18 23			19 18					21 18			22 06		
Mirfield 39	a																						
Dewsbury 39	a																						
Halifax	a	16 08		16 44	17 08	17 27	17 44	18 08		18 35	18 44	19 08	19 28	19 44	20 08	20 44	21 08	21 28	21 44	22 08	22 17	22 46	23 08
	d	16 08	16 29	16 45	17 08	17 29	17 45	18 08	18 29	18 37	18 45	19 08	19 29	19 45	20 08	20 45	21 08	21 30	21 45	22 09	22 19	22 47	23 08
Bradford Interchange	a	16 22	16 42	16 59	17 22	17 42	17 59	18 22	18 42	18 50	18 59	19 22	19 42	19 59	20 22	20 59	21 22	21 42	21 59	22 23	22 32	23 01	23 22
	d	16 26	16 44	17 02	17 25	17 44	18 02	18 25	18 44		19 02	19 25	19 44	20 02	20 25	21 02	21 26	21 44	22 02	22 26		23 04	23 25
New Pudsey 37	a	16 34	16 53	17 10	17 33	17 53	18 10	18 33	18 53		19 10	19 33	19 53	20 10	20 33	21 10	21 34	21 53	22 10	22 34		23 12	23 33
Bramley 37	a	16 38	16 56		17 37	17 56		18 37	18 56			19 37	19 56		20 37		21 38	21 56		22 38			23 37
Leeds 10 37,39	a	16 48	17 05	17 21	17 46	18 05	18 21	18 46	19 07		19 21	19 47	20 08	20 22	20 47	21 22	21 48	22 05	22 22	22 47		23 23	23 46
Selby 40	a																						
York 8 40	a			18 02			19 03				19 59			21 03		22 00							

For connections from Liverpool Lime Street please refer to Table 90

Table 41

Sundays
from 30 October

Manchester Victoria, Rochdale, Blackpool North and Huddersfield - Bradford and Leeds via Brighouse and Halifax

	NT	NT	NT	NT	NT	NT	NT	NT	NT		NT	NT	NT	NT	NT	NT	NT	NT	GC ■R ☕		NT	NT	NT	NT
Manchester Victoria d	22p54	08 32			09 08		10 08				11 08			12 08			13 08					14 08		
Moston d					09 15		10 15				11 15			12 15			13 15					14 15		
Mills Hill d					09 19		10 19				11 19			12 19			13 19					14 19		
Castleton d					09 24		10 24				11 24			12 24			13 24					14 24		
Rochdale a	23p07	08 48			09 28		10 28				11 28			12 28			13 28					14 28		
d	23p07				09 28		10 28				11 28			12 28			13 28					14 28		
Smithy Bridge d	23p11				09 32		10 32				11 32			12 32			13 32					14 32		
Littleborough d	23p15				09 36		10 36				11 36			12 36			13 36					14 36		
Walsden d	23p21				09 42		10 42				11 42			12 42			13 42					14 42		
Todmorden d	23p24				09 45		10 45				11 45			12 45			13 45					14 45		
Blackpool North 97 d																								
Poulton-le-Fylde 97 d																								
Preston [8] 97 d																								
Blackburn 97 d																								
Accrington 97 d																								
Burnley Manchester Road 97 d																								
Hebden Bridge a	23p31				09 52		10 52				11 52			12 52			13 52					14 52		
d	23p31				09 52	10 32	10 52		11 32		11 52		12 33	12 52		13 32	13 52				14 33	14 52		15 32
Mytholmroyd d	23p34				09 55		10 55				11 55			12 55			13 55					14 55		
Sowerby Bridge d	23p40				10 01		11 01				12 01			13 01			14 01					15 01		
Huddersfield 39 d				09 25				11 08							13 08								15 08	
London Kings Cross [15] ⊖26 d																			11 48					
Brighouse d				09 35				11 18							13 18				14 24				15 18	
Mirfield 39 a																								
Dewsbury 39 a																								
Halifax a	23p46			09 46	10 08	10 44	11 08	11 28	11 44		12 08		12 44	13 08	13 28	13 44	14 08		14 35		14 44	15 08	15 28	15 44
d	23p47		09 05	09 46	10 08	10 45	11 08	11 29	11 45		12 08	12 29	12 45	13 08	13 29	13 46	14 08	14 29	14 37		14 45	15 08	15 29	15 46
Bradford Interchange a	00 02		09 18	09 59	10 22	11 00	11 22	11 42	11 59		12 22	12 42	12 59	13 22	13 42	14 00	14 22	14 42	14 50		14 59	15 22	15 42	16 00
d	00 04		09 20	10 02	10 25	11 02	11 25	11 44	12 02		12 25	12 44	13 02	13 25	13 44	14 02	14 25	14 44			15 02	15 25	15 44	16 03
New Pudsey 37 a	00 12		09 29	10 10	10 33	11 10	11 33	11 53	12 10		12 33	12 53	13 10	13 33	13 53	14 10	14 33	14 53			15 10	15 33	15 53	16 11
Bramley 37 a	00 15		09 32	10 14	10 37		11 37	11 56			12 37	12 56		13 37	13 56		14 37	14 56				15 37	15 56	
Leeds [10] 37,39 a	00 27		09 42	10 24	10 46	11 21	11 48	12 05	12 22		12 46	13 06	13 22	13 46	14 06	14 22	14 48	15 06			15 22	15 46	16 06	16 22
Selby 40 a																								
York [8] 40 a			10 28	11 05		11 59			13 02				13 59			15 02					15 59			17 02

	NT	NT	NT	NT	NT		NT	NT	NT	GC ■R ☕	NT	NT	NT	NT	NT		NT	NT	NT	NT	NT	GC ■R ☕	NT	NT
Manchester Victoria d	15 08			16 08				17 08				18 08			19 08			20 08			21 08			22 08
Moston d	15 15			16 15				17 15				18 15			19 15			20 15			21 15			22 15
Mills Hill d	15 19			16 19				17 19				18 19			19 19			20 19			21 19			22 19
Castleton d	15 24			16 24				17 24				18 24			19 24			20 24			21 24			22 24
Rochdale a	15 28			16 28				17 28				18 28			19 28			20 28			21 28			22 28
d	15 28			16 28				17 28				18 28			19 28			20 28			21 28			22 28
Smithy Bridge d	15 32			16 32				17 32				18 32			19 32			20 32			21 32			22 32
Littleborough d	15 36			16 36				17 36				18 36			19 36			20 36			21 36			22 36
Walsden d	15 42			16 42				17 42				18 42			19 42			20 42			21 42			22 42
Todmorden d	15 45			16 45				17 45				18 45			19 45			20 45			21 45			22 45
Blackpool North 97 d																								
Poulton-le-Fylde 97 d																								
Preston [8] 97 d																								
Blackburn 97 d																								
Accrington 97 d																								
Burnley Manchester Road 97 d																								
Hebden Bridge a	15 52			16 52				17 52				18 52			19 52			20 52			21 52			22 52
d	15 52		16 33	16 52			17 32	17 52			18 32	18 52		19 32	19 52		20 33	20 52		21 32	21 52		22 34	22 52
Mytholmroyd d	15 55			16 55				17 55				18 55			19 55			20 55			21 55			22 55
Sowerby Bridge d	16 01			17 01				18 01				19 01			20 01			21 01			22 01			23 01
Huddersfield 39 d					17 08								19 08						21 08					
London Kings Cross [15] ⊖26 d										15 48												19 27		
Brighouse d					17 17					18 24			19 18						21 18			22 06		
Mirfield 39 a																								
Dewsbury 39 a																								
Halifax a	16 08		16 44	17 08	17 27		17 44	18 08		18 35	18 44	19 08	19 28	19 44	20 08		20 44	21 08	21 28	21 44	22 08	22 17	22 46	23 08
d	16 08	16 29	16 45	17 08	17 29		17 45	18 08	18 29	18 37	18 45	19 08	19 29	19 45	20 08		20 45	21 08	21 29	21 45	22 09	22 19	22 47	23 08
Bradford Interchange a	16 22	16 42	16 59	17 22	17 42		17 59	18 22	18 42	18 50	18 59	19 22	19 42	19 59	20 22		20 59	21 22	21 42	21 59	22 23	22 32	23 01	23 22
d	16 26	16 44	17 02	17 25	17 44		18 02	18 25	18 44		19 02	19 25	19 44	20 02	20 25		21 02	21 26	21 44	22 02	22 26		23 04	23 25
New Pudsey 37 a	16 34	16 53	17 10	17 33	17 53		18 10	18 33	18 53		19 10	19 33	19 53	20 10	20 33		21 10	21 34	21 53	22 10	22 34		23 12	23 33
Bramley 37 a	16 38	16 56		17 37	17 56			18 37	18 56			19 37	19 56		20 37			21 38	21 56		22 38			23 37
Leeds [10] 37,39 a	16 48	17 05	17 21	17 46	18 05		18 21	18 46	19 07		19 21	19 47	20 08	20 22	20 47		21 22	21 48	22 05	22 22	22 47		23 23	23 46
Selby 40 a																								
York [8] 40 a			18 02				19 01				19 59			21 03			22 00							

For connections from Liverpool Lime Street please refer to Table 90

Table 41

Sundays
from 30 October

Manchester Victoria, Rochdale, Blackpool North and Huddersfield - Bradford and Leeds via Brighouse and Halifax

			NT
			🚌
Manchester Victoria	🚢	d	
Moston		d	
Mills Hill		d	
Castleton		d	
Rochdale		a	
		d	
Smithy Bridge		d	
Littleborough		d	
Walsden		d	
Todmorden		d	
Blackpool North	97	d	20 40
Poulton-le-Fylde	97	d	20 55
Preston 8	97	d	21 40
Blackburn	97	d	22 10
Accrington	97	d	22 28
Burnley Manchester Road	97	d	22 48
Hebden Bridge		a	23 18
		d	23 18
Mytholmroyd		d	23 28
Sowerby Bridge		d	23 43
Huddersfield	39	d	
London Kings Cross 15 ⊖	26	d	
Brighouse		d	
Mirfield	39	a	
Dewsbury	39	a	
Halifax		a	23 57
		d	23 58
Bradford Interchange		a	00 22
		d	00 23
New Pudsey	37	a	00 33
Bramley	37	a	00 43
Leeds 10	37,39	a	01 03
Selby	40	a	
York 8	40	a	

For connections from Liverpool Lime Street please refer to Table 90

Mondays to Saturdays

until 1 October

Hull - Beverley, Bridlington and Scarborough

Miles			NT	TP ◇1	TP ◇1	NT	NT	NT	NT	TP ◇1 🛒	NT SX		NT SO	NT	NT	TP SO ◇1 🛒	TP SX ◇1 🛒	NT	NT	NT	TP ◇1 🛒		TP ◇1 🛒	NT	NT
0	**Hull**	d	06 23			06 54	07 14	07 36	07 52		08 14		08 14	08 37	09 17			09 47	10 14	10 44				11 14	11 44
4	Cottingham	d	06 30			07 01	07 21	07 43	07 59		08 21		08 21	08 44	09 24			09 54	10 21	10 51				11 21	11 51
8¼	**Beverley**	d	06 36			07 07	07 27	07a51	08 05		08 27		08 28	08a52	09 30			10 00	10 27	10 57				11 27	11 57
11¼	Arram	d				07 12			08 10																
16¼	Hutton Cranswick	d				07 19	07 36		08 17		08 36		08 37		09 39			10 09		11 06					12 06
19½	Driffield	d	06 48			07 24	07 42		08 22		08 42		08 42		09 45			10 15	10 39	11 12				11 39	12 12
21½	Nafferton	d				07 28	07 46		08 26		08 46		08 46		09 49			10 19		11 16					12 16
31	**Bridlington**	a	07 04			07 40	07 59		08 41		08 57		08 59		10 02			10 30	10 56	11 29				11 53	12 29
—		d				07 49					09 00		09 02					10 37						12 05	
34½	Bempton	d				07 56					09 07		09 09					10 44						12 12	
41¾	Hunmanby	d				08 06					09 17		09 19					10 54						12 22	
44½	Filey	d				08 11					09 22		09 24					10 59						12 27	
51	Seamer	d		07 21	08 06	08 22				09 21	09 34		09 36			10 21	10 21	11 10			11 21		12 21	12 38	
53¾	**Scarborough**	a		07 30	08 15	08 29				09 30	09 39		09 42			10 30	10 32	11 17			11 30		12 30	12 45	

		NT	NT	TP SO ◇1 🛒	TP SX ◇1 🛒	TP ◇1 🛒	NT		NT	NT	TP ◇1 🛒	NT	NT	NT	NT SX	TP ◇1 🛒	TP ◇1 🛒		NT SO	NT SX	NT	NT	TP SX ◇1 🛒	TP SO ◇1	TP SX ◇1 🛒
Hull	d	12 14	12 44				13 14		13 44	14 14		14 44	15 14	15 44	16 00				16 14	16 19	16 44	17 14			
Cottingham	d	12 21	12 51				13 21		13 51	14 21		14 51	15 21	15 51	16 07				16 21	16 26	16 51	17 21			
Beverley	d	12 27	12 57				13 27		13 57	14 27		14 57	15 27	15 57	16a15				16 27	16 32	16 57	17 27			
Arram	d		13 02											16 02											
Hutton Cranswick	d		13 09						14 06			15 06		16 09					16 36	16 41		17 36			
Driffield	d	12 39	13 14				13 39		14 12	14 39		15 12	15 39	16 14					16 41	16 46	17 09	17 42			
Nafferton	d		13 18						14 16			15 16		16 18					16 45	16 50		17 46			
Bridlington	a	12 56	13 33				13 53		14 29	14 55		15 27	15 56	16 33					16 56	17 01	17 26	18 00			
	d						14 05					15 31							17 04	17 04					
Bempton	d						14 12					15 38							17 10	17 10					
Hunmanby	d						14 22					15 48							17 20	17 20					
Filey	d						14 27					15 53							17 25	17 25					
Seamer	d			13 21	13 21	14 21	14 38				15 21	16 04				16 21	17 21		17 36	17 36			18 04	18 21	18 41
Scarborough	a			13 30	13 32	14 30	14 45				15 30	16 10				16 30	17 30		17 43	17 43			18 15	18 30	18 50

		NT	NT		NT SX	NT SO	NT	TP SO ◇1	TP SX ◇1 🛒	TP SO ◇1	TP SX ◇1 🛒	NT SX	NT SO		NT	NT	TP ◇1	NT	TP SX ◇1	TP SO ◇1	NT				
Hull	d	17 38	17 57		18 14	18 15	18 44					19 17	19 20		20 14	21 10		21 48			23 00				
Cottingham	d	17 45	18 04		18 21	18 22	18 51					19 24	19 27		20 21	21 17		21 55			23 07				
Beverley	d	17 51	18a12		18 27	18 29	18a58					19 30	19 34		20 27	21a25		22 01			23a15				
Arram	d	17 56													20 32										
Hutton Cranswick	d	18 03			18 36	18 38						19 39	19 43		20 39			22 10							
Driffield	d	18 08			18 42	18 43						19 44	19 47		20 44			22 16							
Nafferton	d	18 12			18 46	18 47						19 49	19 52		20 48			22 20							
Bridlington	a	18 24			19 02	19 01						20 00	20 04		21 02			22 33							
	d	18 30										20 03	20 20												
Bempton	d	18 37										20 10	20 27												
Hunmanby	d	18 47										20 20	20 37												
Filey	d	18 52										20 25	20 42												
Seamer	d	19 03						19 24	19 24	20 22	20 22	20 36	20 54				21 23		22 49	22 54					
Scarborough	a	19 09						19 32	19 32	20 31	20 31	20 42	21 04				21 32		22 58	23 03					

Mondays to Saturdays

from 3 October

		NT	TP ◇1	TP ◇1	NT	NT	NT	NT	TP ◇1 🛒	NT		NT	NT	TP SO ◇1 🛒	TP SX ◇1 🛒	NT	NT	NT	TP ◇1 🛒	TP ◇1 🛒		NT SX	NT SO	NT	NT
Hull	d	06 23			06 54	07 14	07 36	07 52		08 14		08 37	09 17			09 47	10 14	10 44				11 14	11 14	11 44	12 14
Cottingham	d	06 30			07 01	07 21	07 43	07 59		08 21		08 44	09 24			09 54	10 21	10 51				11 21	11 21	11 51	12 21
Beverley	d	06 37			07 08	07 28	07a52	08 06		08 28		08a52	09 31			10 01	10 28	10 58				11 28	11 28	11 58	12 28
Arram	d				07 12			08 10																	
Hutton Cranswick	d				07 19	07 37		08 17		08 37			09 40			10 10		11 07						12 07	
Driffield	d	06 49			07 25	07 42		08 23		08 42			09 45			10 15	10 40	11 12				11 40	11 40	12 12	12 40
Nafferton	d				07 29	07 46		08 27		08 46			09 49			10 19		11 16						12 16	
Bridlington	a	07 07			07 41	08 01		08 42		08 59			10 04			10 32	10 58	11 31				11 55	11 55	12 31	12 58
	d				07 47					09 02						10 36						12 05	12 05		
Bempton	d				07 54					09 09						10 43						12 12	12 12		
Hunmanby	d				08 04					09 19						10 53						12 22	12 22		
Filey	d				08 09					09 24						10 58						12 27	12 27		
Seamer	d		07 21	08 06	08 22				09 21	09 36				10 21	10 21	11 10			11 21	12 21		12 39	12 39		
Scarborough	a		07 30	08 15	08 30				09 30	09 44				10 30	10 32	11 17			11 30	12 30		12 45	12 46		

Table 43

Mondays to Saturdays

from 3 October

Hull - Beverley, Bridlington and Scarborough

		NT	TP SO ◇1 🛒	TP SX ◇1 🛒	TP ◇1 🛒	NT		NT	NT SO	NT SX	TP ◇1 🛒	NT	NT	NT	NT SX	TP ◇1 🛒		TP ◇1 🛒	NT SO	NT SX	NT	NT	TP SX ◇1 🛒	TP SO ◇1	TP SX ◇1 🛒
Hull	d	12 44				13 14		13 44	14 14	14 14		14 44	15 14	15 44	16 00				16 14	16 19	16 44	17 14			
Cottingham	d	12 51				13 21		13 51	14 21	14 21		14 51	15 21	15 51	16 07				16 21	16 26	16 51	17 21			
Beverley	d	12 58				13 28		13 58	14 28	14 28		14 58	15 28	15 58	16a15				16 27	16 32	16 58	17 28			
Arram	d	13 02												16 02											
Hutton Cranswick	d	13 09						14 07				15 07		16 09					16 36	16 41		17 37			
Driffield	d	13 15				13 40		14 12	14 40	14 40		15 12	15 40	16 15					16 42	16 47	17 10	17 42			
Nafferton	d	13 19						14 16				15 16		16 19					16 46	16 51		17 46			
Bridlington	a	13 34				13 55		14 31	14 57	14 58		15 28	15 58	16 34					16 59	17 02	17 28	18 01			
	d					14 05						15 31							17 04	17 04					
Bempton	d					14 12						15 38							17 10	17 11					
Hunmanby	d					14 22						15 48							17 20	17 21					
Filey	d					14 27						15 53							17 25	17 26					
Seamer	d		13 21	13 21	14 21	14 39					15 21	16 05				16 21		17 21	17 36	17 38			18 04	18 21	18 41
Scarborough	a		13 30	13 32	14 30	14 46					15 30	16 10				16 30		17 30	17 43	17 43			18 15	18 30	18 50

		NT		NT	NT SX	NT SO	NT	TP SO ◇1	TP SX ◇1 🛒	TP SO ◇1	TP SX ◇1 🛒	NT SX		NT SO	NT SO	NT SX	NT	TP ◇1	NT SX	NT SO	TP SX ◇1	TP SO ◇1		NT	
Hull	d	17 38		17 57	18 14	18 15	18 44					19 17		19 20	20 14	20 14	21 10		21 48	21 48				23 00	
Cottingham	d	17 45		18 04	18 21	18 22	18 51					19 24		19 27	20 21	20 21	21 17		21 55	21 55				23 07	
Beverley	d	17 51		18a13	18 27	18 29	18a58					19 30		19 33	20 28	20 28	21a26		22 01	22 02				23a15	
Arram	d	17 56													20 32	20 32									
Hutton Cranswick	d	18 03			18 36	18 38						19 39		19 42	20 39	20 39			22 11	22 11					
Driffield	d	18 08			18 43	18 44						19 44		19 47	20 45	20 45			22 17	22 17					
Nafferton	d	18 12			18 47	18 48						19 49		19 52	20 49	20 49			22 21	22 21					
Bridlington	a	18 24			19 03	19 02						20 00		20 03	21 02	21 04			22 35	22 35					
	d	18 30										20 03		20 20											
Bempton	d	18 37										20 10		20 27											
Hunmanby	d	18 47										20 20		20 37											
Filey	d	18 52										20 26		20 42											
Seamer	d	19 03						19 24	19 24	20 22	20 22	20 38		20 54				21 23			22 49	22 54			
Scarborough	a	19 09						19 32	19 32	20 31	20 31	20 48		21 04				21 32			22 58	23 03			

Sundays

until 31 July

		NT	TP ◇1	NT	TP ◇1	NT	NT	TP ◇1	NT	NT		TP ◇1	NT	NT	TP ◇1	NT	NT	NT	TP ◇1	NT		NT	NT	TP ◇1	TP ◇1
Hull	d	09 00		09 25		10 25	11 25		12 00	13 00			14 05	15 05		16 05	16 55	17 15		18 00		19 00	20 00		
Cottingham	d	09 07		09 32		10 32	11 32		12 07	13 07			14 12	15 12		16 12	17 02	17 22		18 07		19 07	20 06		
Beverley	d	09 13		09 38		10 38	11 38		12 13	13 13			14 18	15 18		16 18	17 09	17 28		18 13		19 13	20a12		
Arram	d			09 43																					
Hutton Cranswick	d			09 50		10 47			12 22				14 27			16 27		17 37				19 22			
Driffield	d	09 25		09 55		10 53	11 50		12 28	13 25			14 33	15 30		16 33	17 21	17 43		18 25		19 28			
Nafferton	d			09 59		10 57			12 32				14 37			16 37		17 47				19 32			
Bridlington	a	09 41		10 11		11 08	12 06		12 43	13 42			14 48	15 46		16 48	17 39	18 00		18 39		19 45			
	d			10 13		11 11			12 46				14 51			16 53				18 45					
Bempton	d			10 20		11 18			12 53				14 58			17 00				18 52					
Hunmanby	d			10 30		11 28			13 03				15 08			17 10				19 02					
Filey	d			10 35		11 33			13 08				15 13			17 15				19 07					
Seamer	d		10 20	10 46	11 13	11 44		12 25	13 20			14 24	15 24		16 24	17 26			18 24	19 19				20 26	21 25
Scarborough	a		10 30	10 54	11 22	11 50		12 34	13 25			14 33	15 30		16 33	17 32			18 33	19 24				20 35	21 34

		TP ◇1
Hull	d	
Cottingham	d	
Beverley	d	
Arram	d	
Hutton Cranswick	d	
Driffield	d	
Nafferton	d	
Bridlington	a	
	d	
Bempton	d	
Hunmanby	d	
Filey	d	
Seamer	d	22 51
Scarborough	a	22 59

Table 43

Hull - Beverley, Bridlington and Scarborough

Sundays

7 August to 11 September

		NT	TP	NT	TP	NT	NT	TP	NT	NT		TP	NT	NT	NT	NT	NT	TP	NT	NT		NT	TP	TP	TP
			◇1		◇1			◇1				◇1						◇1					◇1	◇1	◇1
Hull	d	09 00		09 25		10 25	11 25		12 00	13 00			14 05	15 05	16 05	16 55	17 15		18 00	19 00		20 00			
Cottingham	d	09 07		09 32		10 32	11 32		12 07	13 07			14 12	15 12	16 12	17 02	17 22		18 07	19 07		20 06			
Beverley	d	09 13		09 38		10 38	11 38		12 13	13 13			14 18	15 18	16 18	17 09	17 28		18 13	19 13		20a12			
Arram	d			09 43																					
Hutton Cranswick	d			09 50		10 47			12 22				14 27		16 27		17 37			19 22					
Driffield	d	09 25		09 55		10 53	11 50		12 28	13 25			14 33	15 30	16 33	17 21	17 43		18 25	19 28					
Nafferton	d			09 59		10 57			12 32				14 37		16 37		17 47			19 32					
Bridlington	a	09 41		10 11		11 08	12 06		12 43	13 42			14 48	15 46	16 48	17 39	18 00		18 39	19 45					
	d			10 13		11 11			12 46				14 51		16 53				18 45						
Bempton	d			10 20		11 18			12 53				14 58		17 00				18 52						
Hunmanby	d			10 30		11 28			13 03				15 08		17 10				19 02						
Filey	d			10 35		11 33			13 08				15 13		17 15				19 07						
Seamer	d		10 20	10 46	11 13	11 44		12 25	13 20			14 24	15 24		17 26			18 24	19 19				20 26	21 25	22 51
Scarborough	a		10 30	10 54	11 22	11 50		12 34	13 25			14 33	15 30		17 32			18 33	19 24				20 35	21 34	22 59

Sundays

18 September to 2 October

		NT	TP	NT	NT	NT	TP	NT	NT	TP		NT	NT	TP	NT	NT	NT	TP	NT	NT		NT	TP	TP	TP
			◇1				◇1			◇1				◇1				◇1					◇1	◇1	◇1
Hull	d	09 00		09 25	10 25	11 25		12 00	13 00			14 05	15 05		16 05	16 55	17 15		18 00	19 00		20 00			
Cottingham	d	09 07		09 32	10 32	11 32		12 07	13 07			14 12	15 12		16 12	17 02	17 22		18 07	19 07		20 06			
Beverley	d	09 13		09 38	10 38	11 38		12 13	13 13			14 18	15 18		16 18	17 09	17 28		18 13	19 13		20a12			
Arram	d			09 43																					
Hutton Cranswick	d			09 50	10 47			12 22				14 27			16 27		17 37			19 22					
Driffield	d	09 25		09 55	10 53	11 50		12 28	13 25			14 33	15 30		16 33	17 21	17 43		18 25	19 28					
Nafferton	d			09 59	10 57			12 32				14 37			16 37		17 47			19 32					
Bridlington	a	09 41		10 11	11 08	12 06		12 43	13 42			14 48	15 46		16 48	17 39	18 00		18 39	19 45					
	d			10 13	11 11			12 46				14 51			16 53				18 45						
Bempton	d			10 20	11 18			12 53				14 58			17 00				18 52						
Hunmanby	d			10 30	11 28			13 03				15 08			17 10				19 02						
Filey	d			10 35	11 33			13 08				15 13			17 15				19 07						
Seamer	d		10 20	10 46	11 44		12 25	13 20		14 24		15 24		16 24	17 26			18 24	19 19				20 26	21 25	22 51
Scarborough	a		10 30	10 54	11 50		12 34	13 25		14 33		15 30		16 33	17 32			18 33	19 24				20 35	21 34	22 59

Sundays

9 October to 23 October

		NT	TP	NT	NT	NT	TP	NT	NT	TP		NT	NT	TP	NT	NT	NT	TP	NT	NT		NT	TP	TP	TP
			◇1				◇1			◇1				◇1				◇1					◇1	◇1	◇1
Hull	d	09 00		09 25	10 25	11 25		12 00	13 00			14 05	15 05		16 05	16 55	17 15		18 00	19 00		20 00			
Cottingham	d	09 07		09 32	10 32	11 32		12 07	13 07			14 12	15 12		16 12	17 02	17 22		18 07	19 07		20 06			
Beverley	d	09 14		09 39	10 38	11 39		12 14	13 14			14 18	15 19		16 19	17 08	17 29		18 14	19 14		20a13			
Arram	d			09 43																					
Hutton Cranswick	d			09 50	10 47			12 23				14 27			16 28		17 38			19 23					
Driffield	d	09 26		09 56	10 53	11 51		12 28	13 26			14 33	15 31		16 33	17 20	17 43		18 26	19 28					
Nafferton	d			10 00	10 57			12 32				14 37			16 37		17 47			19 32					
Bridlington	a	09 41		10 12	11 08	12 07		12 45	13 44			14 50	15 47		16 49	17 37	18 01		18 40	19 46					
	d			10 15	11 11			12 47				14 52			16 53				18 45						
Bempton	d			10 22	11 18			12 54				14 59			17 00				18 52						
Hunmanby	d			10 32	11 28			13 04				15 09			17 10				19 02						
Filey	d			10 37	11 33			13 09				15 14			17 15				19 07						
Seamer	d		10 20	10 49	11 44		12 25	13 21		14 24		15 26		16 24	17 27			18 24	19 19				20 26	21 25	22 51
Scarborough	a		10 30	10 57	11 50		12 34	13 27		14 33		15 33		16 33	17 34			18 33	19 24				20 35	21 34	22 59

Sundays

from 30 October

		NT	TP	NT	NT	NT	TP	NT	NT	TP		NT	NT	NT	NT	NT	TP	NT	NT	NT		TP	TP	TP	
			◇1				◇1			◇1							◇1					◇1	◇1	◇1	
Hull	d	09 00		09 25	10 25	11 25		12 00	13 00			14 05	15 05	16 05	16 55	17 15		18 00	19 00	20 00					
Cottingham	d	09 07		09 32	10 32	11 32		12 07	13 07			14 12	15 12	16 12	17 02	17 22		18 07	19 07	20 06					
Beverley	d	09 14		09 39	10 38	11 39		12 14	13 14			14 18	15 19	16 19	17 08	17 29		18 14	19 14	20a13					
Arram	d			09 43																					
Hutton Cranswick	d			09 50	10 47			12 23				14 27		16 28		17 38			19 23						
Driffield	d	09 26		09 56	10 53	11 51		12 28	13 26			14 33	15 31	16 33	17 20	17 43		18 26	19 28						
Nafferton	d			10 00	10 57			12 32				14 37		16 37		17 47			19 32						
Bridlington	a	09 41		10 12	11 08	12 07		12 45	13 44			14 50	15 47	16 49	17 37	18 01		18 40	19 46						
	d			10 15	11 11			12 47				14 52		16 53				18 45							
Bempton	d			10 22	11 18			12 54				14 59		17 00				18 52							
Hunmanby	d			10 32	11 28			13 04				15 09		17 10				19 02							
Filey	d			10 37	11 33			13 09				15 14		17 15				19 07							
Seamer	d		10 20	10 49	11 44		12 25	13 21		14 24		15 26		17 27			18 24	19 19				20 26	21 25	22 51	
Scarborough	a		10 30	10 57	11 50		12 34	13 27		14 33		15 33		17 34			18 33	19 24				20 35	21 34	22 59	

Table 43

Mondays to Saturdays

until 1 October

Scarborough, Bridlington and Beverley - Hull

Miles			TP	TP	NT	NT	NT	NT	NT	NT	NT		TP	TP	TP	TP	NT	TP	TP	NT	NT		NT	NT	TP
			SX	SO		SX				SO	SX		SO	SX	SX	SO		SX	SO		SO		SX		
			◇1	◇1									◇1	◇1	◇1	◇1		◇1	◇1						◇1
			(trolley)										(trolley)	(trolley)	(trolley)	(trolley)		(trolley)							(trolley)
0	**Scarborough**	d	06 30	06 30						06 50	06 50		06 58	07 00	07 40	07 47		08 48	08 48					09 02	09 48
2¾	Seamer	d	06a35	06a35						06 55	06 55		07a03	07a05	07a45	07a52		08a53	08a53					09 07	09a53
9¼	Filey	d								07 04	07 04													09 16	
12	Hunmanby	d								07 09	07 09													09 21	
19¼	Bempton	d								07 19	07 19													09 31	
22¾	**Bridlington**	a								07 27	07 27													09 38	
—		d					06 46	07 14		07 32	07 34						08 08				09 03		09 05	09 41	
32¼	Nafferton	d					06 56	07 24		07 43	07 45						08 19				09 14		09 16	09 52	
24¼	Driffield	d					07 01	07 29		07 47	07 49						08 23				09 18		09 20	09 56	
37½	Hutton Cranswick	d					07 05	07 33		07 52	07 54						08 28				09 23		09 25	10 01	
42½	Arram	d								07 59	08 01										09 30		09 32		
45½	**Beverley**	d			06 38	06 58	07 15	07 43	07 57	08 06	08 07						08 38			09 00	09 36		09 37	10 11	
49¾	Cottingham	d			06 44	07 03	07 21	07 49	08 03	08 12	08 13						08 44			09 06	09 42		09 43	10 17	
53¾	**Hull**	a			06 53	07 12	07 33	07 59	08 13	08 23	08 23						08 54			09 15	09 53		09 53	10 27	

		NT	NT	TP	NT	NT	NT		NT	TP	TP	NT	TP	NT	NT	NT	TP		NT	TP	NT	NT	NT	NT	TP
					SX	SO				SX	SO										SO	SX	SX	SO	
				◇1						◇1	◇1		◇1				◇1			◇1					◇1
				(trolley)						(trolley)			(trolley)				(trolley)			(trolley)					(trolley)
Scarborough	d		10 00	10 48					11 28	11 48	11 48		12 48			13 28	13 48			14 48			14 54	14 54	15 48
Seamer	d		10 05	10a53					11 33	11a53	11a53		12a53			13 33	13a53			14a53			14 59	14 59	15a53
Filey	d		10 14						11 42							13 42							15 08	15 08	
Hunmanby	d		10 19						11 47							13 47							15 13	15 12	
Bempton	d		10 29						11 57							13 57							15 23	15 22	
Bridlington	a		10 36						12 04							14 04							15 30	15 30	
	d	10 11	10 41		11 11	11 11	11 41		12 11			12 41		13 11	13 41	14 11			14 41		15 11	15 11	15 36	15 38	
Nafferton	d		10 52				11 52					12 52			13 52				14 52				15 47	15 49	
Driffield	d	10 24	10 56		11 24	11 24	11 56		12 24			12 56		13 24	13 56	14 24			14 56		15 24	15 24	15 51	15 53	
Hutton Cranswick	d		11 01				12 01					13 01			14 01				15 01				15 56	15 58	
Arram	d						12 08																		
Beverley	d	10 37	11 11		11 37	11 37	12 13		12 37			13 11		13 37	14 11	14 37			15 11		15 37	15 37	16 06	16 08	
Cottingham	d	10 43	11 17		11 43	11 43	12 19		12 43			13 17		13 43	14 17	14 43			15 17		15 43	15 43	16 12	16 14	
Hull	a	10 53	11 27		11 53	11 54	12 29		12 54			13 27		13 53	14 27	14 53			15 30		15 52	15 53	16 24	16 25	

		NT	NT		NT	NT	NT	TP	TP	NT	NT	TP	NT		NT	NT	NT	TP	NT	TP	NT	TP	NT		NT
		SO	SX			SX	SO	SO	SX	SO	SX		SX		SO							SX			
								◇1	◇1			◇1						◇1		◇1		◇1			
									(trolley)																
Scarborough	d					16 23	16 23	16 48	16 48			17 48					17 53	18 48		19 48	20 03	20 48			
Seamer	d					16 28	16 28	16a53	16a53			17a53					17 58	18a53		19a53	20 08	20a53			
Filey	d					16 37	16 37										18 07				20 17				
Hunmanby	d					16 42	16 42										18 12				20 23				
Bempton	d					16 52	16 52										18 22				20 32				
Bridlington	a					16 59	17 00										18 29				20 40				
	d	16 09	16 09		16 41	17 06	17 06			17 34	17 34					18 15	18 41		19 10		20 42				21 28
Nafferton	d				16 52					17 45	17 45						18 52		19 21		20 53				21 39
Driffield	d	16 22	16 22		16 56	17 18	17 19			17 49	17 49					18 28	18 56		19 25		20 58				21 43
Hutton Cranswick	d				17 01					17 54	17 54						19 01		19 30		21 03				21 48
Arram	d				17 08																				
Beverley	d	16 35	16 35		17 13	17 32	17 32			18 04	18 04		18 20		18 21	18 41	19 11		19 40		21 12		21 40		21 58
Cottingham	d	16 41	16 41		17 19	17 38	17 38			18 10	18 10		18 26		18 26	18 47	19 17		19 46		21 18		21 46		22 04
Hull	a	16 50	16 51		17 30	17 49	17 49			18 20	18 21		18 36		18 36	18 58	19 27		19 58		21 28		21 57		22 14

		TP	NT
		◇1	
Scarborough	d	22 03	
Seamer	d	22a08	
Filey	d		
Hunmanby	d		
Bempton	d		
Bridlington	a		
	d		22 42
Nafferton	d		22 53
Driffield	d		22 58
Hutton Cranswick	d		23 03
Arram	d		
Beverley	d		23 12
Cottingham	d		23 18
Hull	a		23 28

Table 43

Mondays to Saturdays

from 3 October

Scarborough, Bridlington and Beverley - Hull

		TP	TP	NT	NT	NT	NT	NT	NT	NT		NT	NT	TP	TP	TP	TP	NT	NT	TP		TP	NT	NT	NT
		SX	SO	SO	SX	SX	SO	SX	SO	SX				SO	SX	SX	SO	SX	SO	SX		SO		SX	SO
		◇1	◇1											◇1	◇1	◇1	◇1			◇1		◇1			
		🛒												🛒	🛒	🛒	🛒			🛒					
Scarborough	d	06 30	06 30										06 50	06 58	07 00	07 40	07 47			08 48		08 48			
Seamer	d	06a35	06a35										06 55	07a03	07a05	07a45	07a52			08a53		08a53			
Filey	d												07 04												
Hunmanby	d												07 09												
Bempton	d												07 19												
Bridlington	a												07 27												
	d						06 44	06 44	07 12	07 14			07 32					08 06	08 06					09 03	09 05
Nafferton	d						06 54	06 55	07 23	07 24			07 43					08 17	08 17					09 14	09 16
Driffield	d						06 59	06 59	07 27	07 29			07 47					08 21	08 21					09 18	09 20
Hutton Cranswick	d						07 03	07 04	07 32	07 33			07 52					08 26	08 26					09 23	09 25
Arram	d												07 59											09 30	09 32
Beverley	d			06 37	06 38	06 58	07 14	07 15	07 42	07 43		07 57	08 06					08 36	08 36				09 00	09 36	09 37
Cottingham	d			06 43	06 44	07 03	07 20	07 21	07 48	07 49		08 03	08 12					08 42	08 42				09 06	09 42	09 43
Hull	a			06 53	06 53	07 15	07 33	07 33	07 59	07 59		08 13	08 23					08 53	08 54				09 15	09 53	09 53

		NT	TP	NT	NT	TP		NT	NT	NT	NT	NT	TP	TP	NT	TP		NT	NT	NT	NT	TP	NT	TP	NT
								SX	SO		SO	SX	SX	SO				SX	SO						
			◇1			◇1							◇1	◇1		◇1						◇1		◇1	
			🛒			🛒							🛒			🛒						🛒		🛒	
Scarborough	d	09 00	09 48		09 58	10 48					11 27	11 28	11 48	11 48		12 48					13 28	13 48		14 48	
Seamer	d	09 05	09a53		10 03	10a53					11 32	11 33	11a53	11a53		12a53					13 33	13a53		14a53	
Filey	d	09 14			10 12						11 41	11 42									13 42				
Hunmanby	d	09 20			10 17						11 46	11 47									13 47				
Bempton	d	09 30			10 27						11 56	11 57									13 57				
Bridlington	a	09 37			10 35						12 03	12 04									14 04				
	d	09 40		10 09	10 40			11 09	11 09	11 40	12 09	12 09			12 40			13 09	13 09	13 40	14 09		14 40		15 09
Nafferton	d	09 51			10 51					11 51					12 51					13 51			14 51		
Driffield	d	09 55		10 22	10 55			11 22	11 22	11 55	12 22	12 22			12 55			13 22	13 22	13 55	14 22		14 55		15 22
Hutton Cranswick	d	10 00			11 00					12 00					13 00					14 00			15 00		
Arram	d									12 07															
Beverley	d	10 10		10 36	11 10			11 36	11 37	12 12	12 36	12 36			13 10			13 36	13 36	14 10	14 36		15 10		15 36
Cottingham	d	10 16		10 42	11 16			11 42	11 43	12 18	12 42	12 42			13 16			13 42	13 43	14 16	14 42		15 16		15 42
Hull	a	10 27		10 53	11 27			11 53	11 54	12 29	12 54	12 54			13 27			13 53	13 53	14 26	14 53		15 30		15 53

		NT		NT	TP	NT	NT	NT	NT	NT	TP	TP		NT	NT	TP	NT	NT	NT	NT	TP	NT		TP	NT
		SX		SO		SO	SX		SX	SO	SO	SX		SX	SO		SX	SO							
					◇1						◇1	◇1				◇1					◇1			◇1	
					🛒							🛒													
Scarborough	d	14 54		14 54	15 48				16 21	16 21	16 48	16 48				17 48				17 53	18 48			19 48	20 01
Seamer	d	14 59		14 59	15a53				16 26	16 26	16a53	16a53				17a53				17 58	18a53			19a53	20 06
Filey	d	15 08		15 08					16 35	16 35										18 07					20 15
Hunmanby	d	15 13		15 12					16 40	16 40										18 12					20 23
Bempton	d	15 23		15 22					16 50	16 50										18 22					20 32
Bridlington	a	15 30		15 30					16 59	16 59										18 29					20 40
	d	15 36		15 38		16 09	16 09	16 40	17 04	17 04				17 32	17 32				18 13	18 40		19 09			20 42
Nafferton	d	15 47		15 49				16 51						17 43	17 43					18 51		19 20			20 53
Driffield	d	15 51		15 53		16 22	16 22	16 55	17 16	17 17				17 47	17 47				18 26	18 55		19 24			20 58
Hutton Cranswick	d	15 56		15 58				17 00						17 52	17 52					19 00		19 29			21 03
Arram	d							17 07																	
Beverley	d	16 07		16 08		16 35	16 35	17 12	17 30	17 30				18 03	18 03		18 20	18 21	18 40	19 10		19 39			21 12
Cottingham	d	16 13		16 14		16 41	16 41	17 18	17 36	17 36				18 09	18 09		18 26	18 26	18 46	19 16		19 45			21 18
Hull	a	16 24		16 25		16 50	16 51	17 30	17 49	17 49				18 20	18 22		18 36	18 36	18 58	19 27		19 58			21 28

		TP	NT	NT	TP	NT
		SX				
		◇1			◇1	
Scarborough	d	20 48			22 03	
Seamer	d	20a53			22a08	
Filey	d					
Hunmanby	d					
Bempton	d					
Bridlington	a					
	d			21 26		22 40
Nafferton	d			21 37		22 51
Driffield	d			21 41		22 56
Hutton Cranswick	d			21 46		23 01
Arram	d					
Beverley	d		21 40	21 57		23 11
Cottingham	d		21 46	22 03		23 17
Hull	a		21 57	22 14		23 28

Table 43

Sundays until 2 October

Scarborough, Bridlington and Beverley - Hull

		TP ◇1	NT	TP ◇1	NT	TP ◇1	NT	NT	TP ◇1	NT		NT	NT	TP ◇1	NT	NT	NT	TP ◇1	NT	NT		NT	NT	TP ◇1	TP ◇1
Scarborough	d	09 20		10 51	11 12	11 51	12 08		13 51	14 08		14 54		15 51	16 08			17 51		18 08			19 40	19 51	21 20
Seamer	d	09a25		10a56	11 17	11a56	12 13		13a56	14 13		14 59		15a56	16 13			17a56		18 13			19 45	19a56	21a25
Filey	d				11 26		12 22			14 22		15 08			16 22					18 22			19 54		
Hunmanby	d				11 31		12 27			14 27		15 13			16 27					18 27			19 59		
Bempton	d				11 41		12 37			14 37		15 23			16 37					18 37			20 09		
Bridlington	a				11 48		12 44			14 44		15 30			16 44					18 44			20 17		
	d		09 51		11 51		12 51	13 51		14 51		15 36	15 51		16 51	17 21	17 51		18 11	18 57		19 57	20 27		
Nafferton	d		10 02		12 01			14 02				15 47	16 02			17 32				19 08		20 08	20 38		
Driffield	d		10 06		12 06		13 04	14 06		15 04		15 51	16 06		17 04	17 36	18 04		18 24	19 12		20 12	20 42		
Hutton Cranswick	d		10 11		12 10			14 11				15 56	16 11			17 41				19 17		20 17	20 47		
Arram	d																			19 24					
Beverley	d		10 21		12 20		13 17	14 21		15 17		16 08	16 21		17 17	17 51	18 17		18 37	19 29		20 27	20 57		
Cottingham	d		10 27		12 25		13 23	14 27		15 23		16 14	16 27		17 23	17 57	18 23		18 43	19 35		20 33	21 03		
Hull	a		10 37		12 35		13 33	14 37		15 33		16 24	16 37		17 34	18 07	18 33		18 53	19 45		20 43	21 15		

Mondays to Fridays from 10 October

		TP ◇1 (trolley)	NT	NT	NT	NT	NT	NT	TP ◇1 (trolley)	TP ◇1 (trolley)		NT	TP ◇1 (trolley)	NT	NT	NT	TP ◇1 (trolley)	NT	NT	TP ◇1 (trolley)		NT	NT	NT	TP ◇1 (trolley)
Scarborough	d	06 30						06 50	07 00	07 40			08 48			09 00	09 48		09 58	10 48				11 28	11 48
Seamer	d	06a35						06 55	07a05	07a45			08a53			09 05	09a53		10 03	10a53				11 33	11a53
Filey	d							07 04								09 14			10 12					11 42	
Hunmanby	d							07 09								09 20			10 17					11 47	
Bempton	d							07 19								09 30			10 27					11 57	
Bridlington	a							07 27								09 37			10 35					12 04	
	d				06 44	07 14		07 32				08 06			09 03	09 40		10 09	10 40			11 09	11 40	12 09	
Nafferton	d				06 55	07 24		07 43				08 17			09 14	09 51			10 51				11 51		
Driffield	d				06 59	07 29		07 47				08 21			09 18	09 55		10 22	10 55			11 22	11 55	12 22	
Hutton Cranswick	d				07 04	07 33		07 52				08 26			09 23	10 00			11 00				12 00		
Arram	d							07 59							09 30								12 07		
Beverley	d		06 38	06 58	07 15	07 43	07 57	08 06				08 36		09 00	09 36	10 10		10 36	11 10			11 36	12 12	12 36	
Cottingham	d		06 44	07 03	07 21	07 49	08 03	08 12				08 42		09 06	09 42	10 16		10 42	11 16			11 42	12 18	12 42	
Hull	a		06 53	07 15	07 33	07 59	08 13	08 23				08 53		09 15	09 53	10 27		10 53	11 27			11 53	12 29	12 54	

		NT	TP ◇1 (trolley)	NT	NT	NT		TP ◇1 (trolley)	NT	TP ◇1 (trolley)	NT	NT	TP ◇1 (trolley)	NT	NT	NT		TP ◇1 (trolley)	NT	TP ◇1	NT	NT	NT	TP ◇1	NT
Scarborough	d		12 48			13 28		13 48		14 48		14 54	15 48			16 21		16 48		17 48			17 53	18 48	
Seamer	d		12a53			13 33		13a53		14a53		14 59	15a53			16 26		16a53		17a53			17 58	18a53	
Filey	d					13 42						15 08				16 35							18 07		
Hunmanby	d					13 47						15 13				16 40							18 12		
Bempton	d					13 57						15 23				16 50							18 22		
Bridlington	a					14 04						15 30				16 59							18 29		
	d	12 40		13 09	13 40	14 09			14 40		15 09	15 36		16 09	16 40	17 04			17 32			18 13	18 40		19 09
Nafferton	d	12 51			13 51				14 51			15 47			16 51				17 43				18 51		19 20
Driffield	d	12 55		13 22	13 55	14 22			14 55		15 22	15 51		16 22	16 55	17 16			17 47			18 26	18 55		19 24
Hutton Cranswick	d	13 00			14 00				15 00			15 56			17 00				17 52				19 00		19 29
Arram	d														17 07										
Beverley	d	13 10		13 36	14 10	14 36			15 10		15 36	16 07		16 35	17 12	17 30			18 03		18 20	18 40	19 10		19 39
Cottingham	d	13 16		13 42	14 16	14 42			15 16		15 42	16 13		16 41	17 18	17 36			18 09		18 26	18 46	19 16		19 45
Hull	a	13 27		13 53	14 26	14 53			15 30		15 53	16 24		16 51	17 30	17 49			18 20		18 36	18 58	19 27		19 58

		TP ◇1		NT	TP ◇1	NT	NT	TP ◇1	NT
Scarborough	d	19 48		20 01	20 48			22 03	
Seamer	d	19a53		20 06	20a53			22a08	
Filey	d			20 15					
Hunmanby	d			20 23					
Bempton	d			20 32					
Bridlington	a			20 40					
	d			20 42			21 26		22 40
Nafferton	d			20 53			21 37		22 51
Driffield	d			20 58			21 41		22 56
Hutton Cranswick	d			21 03			21 46		23 01
Arram	d								
Beverley	d			21 12		21 40	21 57		23 11
Cottingham	d			21 18		21 46	22 03		23 17
Hull	a			21 28		21 57	22 14		23 28

Network Diagram for Tables 44, 45, 48

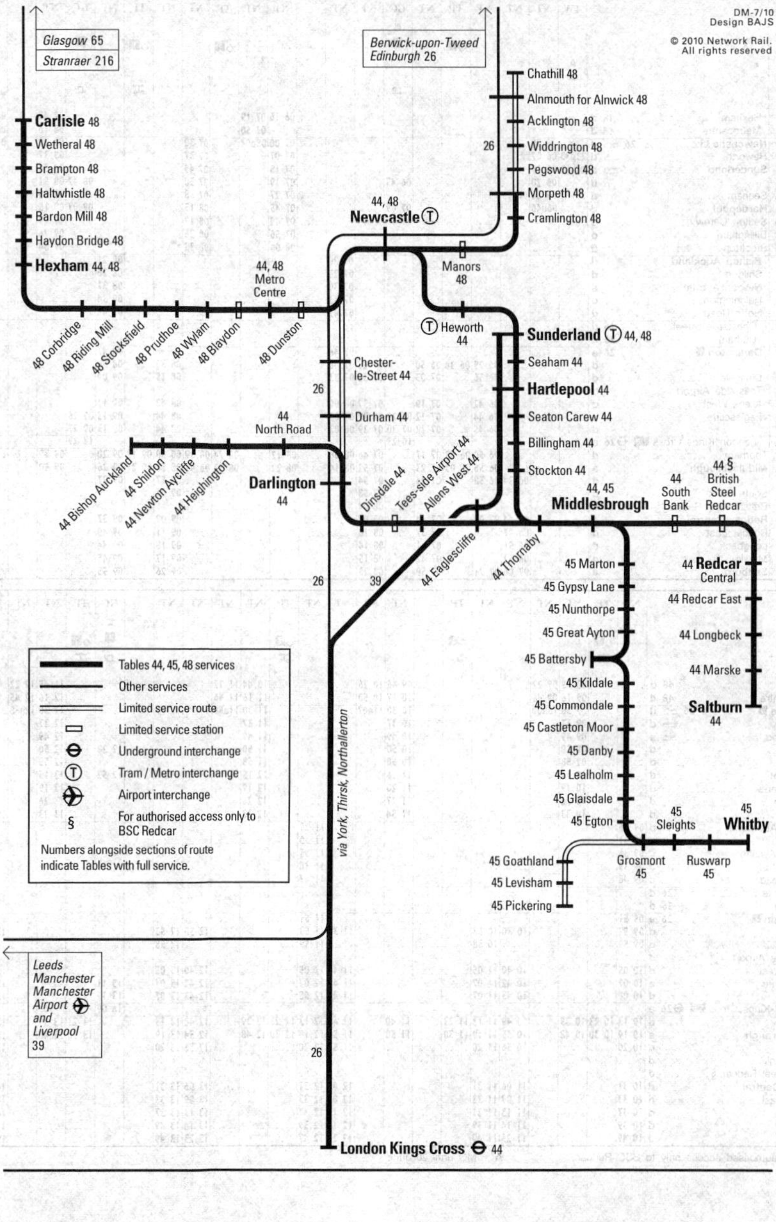

Table 44

Mondays to Fridays

until 30 September

Newcastle, Sunderland, Bishop Auckland and Darlington - Middlesbrough and Saltburn

Miles	Miles			TW	NT	NT	NT	TP	NT	GC	NT	NT		NT	NT	TP	NT	NT	TP	NT	GC	NT		SR	NT
				A 🚌				◇1		R 1 ⊡						◇1			◇1 ⊥		R 1 ⊡				
—	—	Hexham	48 d											06 16	07 19							07 42		08 11	
—	—	Metrocentre	48 d												07 50							08 16		08 44	
—	0	**Newcastle** 8	26 ⛴ d		06 00									07 00	08a04		07 30					08 30		08a57	
—	2¾	Heworth	⛴ d	23p33	06 07									07 07			07 37					08 37			
—	12	**Sunderland**	⛴ a	00∫13	06 19									07 18			07 49					08 50			
—	—		d		06 20					06 45				07 19			07 50				08 42	08 51			
—	17¼	Seaham	d		06 28									07 27			07 58					08 58			
—	30	**Hartlepool**	d		06a46					07 09				07 45			08 15				09 07	09 15			
—	32¼	Seaton Carew	d											07 49			08 19					09 19			
—	37¼	Billingham	d											07 56			08 26					09 26			
—	41¾	Stockton	d											08 04			08 33					09 34			
0	—	**Bishop Auckland**	d									07 20								08 21					
2¾	—	Shildon	d									07 25								08 26					
5	—	Newton Aycliffe	d									07 30								08 31					
6¼	—	Heighington	d									07 33								08 34					
10¾	—	North Road	d									07 42								08 43					
—	—	Chester-le-Street	26 d																						
—	—	Durham	26 d																						
12	—	**Darlington** 7	26 a									07 46								08 47					
—	—		d				06 29	06 36	06 58		07 25	07 48						08 30		08 59					09 30
15¾	—	Dinsdale	d				06 36		07 03		07 30	07 53						08 35		09 04					
17½	—	Tees-side Airport	d																						
20	—	Allens West	d				06 42		07 10		07 37	08 00						08 42		09 11					09 40
20¾	—	Eaglescliffe	a				06 44		07 12	07 29	07 39	08 02						08 44		09 13	09 26				09 42
—	—		d				06 45		07 12	07 30	07 39	08 02						08 44		09 13	09 27				09 43
—	—	London Kings Cross 15 ⊖	26 a							10 25											12 29				
23¾	44	Thornaby	d				06 50	06 53	07 17		07 46	08 08		08 12		08 24	08 39	08 50	09 12	09 20		09 39			09 48
27	47¼	**Middlesbrough**	a				06 56	07 03	07 23		07 52	08 14		08 22		08 32	08 47	08 56	09 21	09 26		09 50			09 55
—	—		d			06 34	06 58		07 24		07 54							08 57		09 27					09 56
29½	—	South Bank	d								07 58							09 01							
32¾	—	British Steel Redcar §	d								08 04														
34½	—	**Redcar Central**	d			06 44	07 08		07 34		08 07							09 09		09 37					10 06
35½	—	Redcar East	d			06 47			07 37		08 10							09 11		09 40					10 09
37	—	Longbeck	d			06 51			07 41		08 14							09 15		09 44					10 13
37½	—	Marske	d			06 52			07 42		08 15							09 17		09 45					10 14
39½	—	**Saltburn**	a			07 06	07 21		07 50		08 23							09 26		09 53					10 23

		NT	TP	NT	NT	NT	NT	TP		NT	SR	NT	NT	TP	NT	NT	NT	NT		GC	TP	NT	NT	NT	NT
			◇1 ⊥					◇1 ⊥						◇1 ⊥						R 1 ⊡	◇1 ⊥				
Hexham	48 d			08 45	09 22					09 46	10 26				10 44	11 22						11 45	12 22		
Metrocentre	48 d			09 16	09 46					10 17	10 50				11 16	11 46						12 16	12 45		
Newcastle 8	26 ⛴ d			09 30	10a00					10 30	11a07				11 30	11a59						12 30	12a58		
Heworth	⛴ d			09 37						10 37					11 37							12 37			
Sunderland	⛴ a			09 49						10 49					11 49							12 49			
	d			09 50						10 50					11 50					12 28		12 50			
Seaham	d			09 58						10 58					11 58							12 58			
Hartlepool	d			10 15						11 16					12 15					12 52		13 15			
Seaton Carew	d			10 19						11 20					12 19							13 19			
Billingham	d			10 26						11 27					12 26							13 26			
Stockton	d			10 33						11 34					12 33							13 33			
Bishop Auckland	d	09 26											11 25												13 25
Shildon	d	09 31											11 30												13 30
Newton Aycliffe	d	09 36											11 35												13 35
Heighington	d	09 39											11 38												13 38
North Road	d	09 48											11 47												13 47
Chester-le-Street	26 d																								
Durham	26 d																								
Darlington 7	26 a	09 51											11 51												13 51
	d	09 53				10 30	10 53					11 30	11 53				12 30	12 53						13 30	13 53
Dinsdale	d	09 59					10 58						11 59					12 58							13 58
Tees-side Airport	d																								
Allens West	d	10 05				10 40	11 05					11 40	12 05				12 40	13 05						13 40	14 05
Eaglescliffe	a	10 07				10 42	11 07					11 42	12 07				12 42	13 07		13 11				13 42	14 07
	d	10 08				10 43	11 07					11 43	12 08				12 43	13 07		13 12				13 43	14 07
London Kings Cross 15 ⊖	26 a																			16 09					
Thornaby	d	10 13	10 23	10 39		10 49	11 13	11 23		11 40		11 48	12 13	12 23	12 39		12 48	13 13			13 23	13 39		13 48	14 13
Middlesbrough	a	10 19	10 30	10 48		10 55	11 19	11 30		11 50		11 56	12 19	12 30	12 48		12 54	13 19			13 30	13 48		13 54	14 19
	d	10 20				10 56	11 20					11 56	12 20				12 56	13 20						13 56	14 20
South Bank	d																								
British Steel Redcar §	d																								
Redcar Central	d	10 31				11 06	11 31					12 06	12 31				13 06	13 31						14 06	14 31
Redcar East	d	10 33				11 09	11 33					12 09	12 33				13 09	13 33						14 09	14 33
Longbeck	d	10 37				11 13	11 37					12 13	12 37				13 13	13 37						14 13	14 37
Marske	d	10 39				11 14	11 39					12 14	12 39				13 14	13 39						14 14	14 39
Saltburn	a	10 49				11 23	11 49					12 24	12 47				13 23	13 49						14 24	14 52

§ For authorised access only to BSC Redcar

A MO until 20 June

Table 44

Mondays to Fridays

until 30 September

Newcastle, Sunderland, Bishop Auckland and Darlington - Middlesbrough and Saltburn

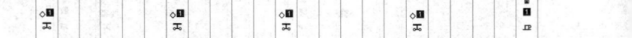

			TP	NT	NT		NT	NT	TP	NT	NT	NT	NT	TP	NT		SR	NT	NT	TP	NT	NT	NT	NT	GC	
			◇1						◇1					◇1						◇1					R 1	
Hexham	48	d		12 45	13 22					13 45	14 24				14 43		15 21				15 42		16 14			
Metrocentre	48	d		13 16	13 46					14 14	14 47				15 16		15 45				16 16		16 38			
Newcastle 8	26	d		13 30	14a00					14 30	15a01				15 30		15a54				16 30		16 53			
Heworth		d		13 37						14 37					15 37						16 37		17 00			
Sunderland		a		13 49						14 49					15 49						16 49		17 14			
		d		13 50						14 50					15 50						16 50		17 15		17 31	
Seaham		d		13 58						14 58					15 58						16 58		17 22			
Hartlepool		d		14 15						15 15					16 15						17 15		17 39		17 55	
Seaton Carew		d		14 19						15 19					16 19						17 19		17 43			
Billingham		d		14 26						15 26					16 26						17 26		17 50			
Stockton		d		14 33						15 33					16 33						17 33		17 57			
Bishop Auckland		d											15 25						16 24							
Shildon		d											15 30						16 29							
Newton Aycliffe		d											15 35						16 34							
Heighington		d											15 38						16 37							
North Road		d											15 47						16 46							
Chester-le-Street	26	d																								
Durham	26	d																								
Darlington 7	26	a											15 51						16 50							
		d					14 30	14 53				15 30	15 53					16 29	16 53			17 30		18 00		
Dinsdale		d						14 58					15 58					16 35	16 58			17 35		18 06		
Tees-side Airport		d																								
Allens West		d					14 40	15 05				15 40	16 05					16 42	17 05			17 42		18 12		
Eaglescliffe		a					14 42	15 07				15 42	16 07					16 44	17 07			17 44		18 14	18 17	
		d					14 43	15 07				15 43	16 07					16 44	17 07			17 44		18 15	18 20	
London Kings Cross 15	⊖26	a																							21 04	
Thornaby		d	14 23	14 37			14 49	15 13	15 23	15 39		15 48	16 13	16 23	16 39			16 50	17 13	17 22	17 39	17 50	18 03	18 21		
Middlesbrough		a	14 30	14 44			14 54	15 19	15 30	15 48		15 54	16 19	16 30	16 47			16 56	17 19	17 30	17 48	17 57	18 15	18 26		
		d					14 56	15 20				15 56	16 20					16 58	17 20			17 59		18 27		
South Bank		d											16 25											18 32		
British Steel Redcar §		d																								
Redcar Central		d					15 06	15 31				16 06	16 32					17 08	17 31			18 08		18 39		
Redcar East		d					15 09	15 33				16 09	16 35					17 11	17 33			18 11		18 42		
Longbeck		d					15 13	15 37				16 13	16 39					17 15	17 37			18 15		18 46		
Marske		d					15 14	15 39				16 14	16 40					17 16	17 39			18 16		18 47		
Saltburn		a					15 23	15 49				16 23	16 49					17 25	17 49			18 27		18 56		

			TP	NT	NT	NT	TP	NT	NT	NT	NT		TP	NT	SR	NT	NT	NT	TP	NT	NT		NT	NT	NT	NT
			◇1				◇1						◇1						◇1							
Hexham	48	d		16 45	17 22			17 45	18 23					18 44	19 27	20 28		21 14						22 23		23 20
Metrocentre	48	d		17 16	17 46			18 16	18 53					19 17	19 57	20 59		21 45						22 53		
Newcastle 8	26	d		17 30	17a57			18 30	19a04					19 28	20a12	21a10		21a56		20 30			21 18	23a08		23a57
Heworth		d		17 37				18 37						19 37						20 37			21 25			
Sunderland		a		17 50				18 49						19 50						20 49			21 37			
		d		17 50				18 50						19 50						20 50			21 38			
Seaham		d		17 58				18 58						19 58						20 58			21 46			
Hartlepool		d		18 15				19 15						20 15						21 15			22 03			
Seaton Carew		d		18 19				19 19						20 19						21 19			22 07			
Billingham		d		18 26				19 26						20 26						21 26			22 14			
Stockton		d		18 33				19 33						20 33						21 33			22 21			
Bishop Auckland		d				18 02					19 25										21 10					
Shildon		d				18 07					19 30										21 15					
Newton Aycliffe		d				18 12					19 35										21 20					
Heighington		d				18 15					19 38										21 23					
North Road		d				18 24					19 47										21 32					
Chester-le-Street	26	d																								
Durham	26	d																								
Darlington 7	26	a				18 28					19 51										21 36					
		d				18 30				19 30	19 53						20 32				21 38				22 38	
Dinsdale		d				18 35				19 35	19 59						20 35				21 43				22 43	
Tees-side Airport		d																								
Allens West		d				18 42				19 42	20 05						20 42				21 50				22 50	
Eaglescliffe		a				18 44				19 44	20 07						20 45				21 52				22 52	
		d				18 44				19 44	20 08						20 45				21 52				22 52	
London Kings Cross 15	⊖26	a																								
Thornaby		d	18 33	18 39		18 50	19 23	19 36		19 53	20 14		20 21	20 39			20 50		21 24	21 40	21 58		22 30		22 58	
Middlesbrough		a	18 40	18 48		18 56	19 32	19 47		19 59	20 21		20 30	20 50			20 58		21 32	21 48	22 05		22 36		23 04	
		d				18 58				20 00							20 59				22 06					
South Bank		d																								
British Steel Redcar §		d																								
Redcar Central		d				19 08				20 11							21 08				22 17					
Redcar East		d				19 11				20 13							21 11				22 19					
Longbeck		d				19 15				20 17							21 15				22 23					
Marske		d				19 16				20 19							21 16				22 25					
Saltburn		a				19 25				20 28							21 25				22 34					

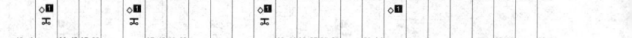

§ For authorised access only to BSC Redcar

from 3 October

Newcastle, Sunderland, Bishop Auckland and Darlington - Middlesbrough and Saltburn

Station		NT	NT	NT	TP	NT	GC	NT	NT	NT		NT	TP	NT	NT	TP	NT	GC	NT	SR		NT	NT	TP	NT
					◇1		R 1						◇1			◇1		R 1						◇1	
Hexham	48 d									06 14		07 19							07 40	08 11					08 43
Metrocentre	48 d											07 50							08 16	08 44					09 16
Newcastle 8	26 ⛴ d	06 00								07 00		08a04		07 30					08 30	08a57					09 30
Heworth	⛴ d	06 07								07 07				07 37					08 37						09 37
Sunderland	⛴ a	06 19								07 18				07 49					08 50						09 49
	d	06 20					06 45			07 19				07 50				08 42	08 51						09 50
Seaham	d	06 28								07 27				07 58					08 58						09 58
Hartlepool	d	06a46					07 09			07 45				08 15				09 07	09 15						10 15
Seaton Carew	d									07 49				08 19					09 19						10 19
Billingham	d									07 56				08 26					09 26						10 26
Stockton	d									08 04				08 33					09 34						10 33
Bishop Auckland	d								07 20								08 21						09 26		
Shildon	d								07 25								08 26						09 31		
Newton Aycliffe	d								07 30								08 31						09 36		
Heighington	d								07 33								08 34						09 39		
North Road	d								07 42								08 43						09 48		
Chester-le-Street	26 d																								
Durham	26 d																								
Darlington 7	26 a								07 46								08 47						09 51		
	d			06 29	06 36	06 58		07 25	07 48						08 30		08 59					09 30	09 53		
Dinsdale	d			06 36		07 03		07 30	07 53						08 35		09 04						09 59		
Tees-side Airport	d																								
Allens West	d			06 42		07 10		07 37	08 00						08 42		09 11					09 40	10 05		
Eaglescliffe	a			06 44		07 12	07 29	07 39	08 02						08 44		09 13	09 26				09 42	10 07		
	d			06 45		07 12	07 30	07 39	08 02						08 44		09 13	09 27				09 43	10 08		
London Kings Cross 15	⊖26 a						10 25											12 29							
Thornaby	d			06 50	06 53	07 17		07 46	08 08	08 12			08 24	08 39	08 50	09 12	09 20		09 39			09 48	10 13	10 23	10 39
Middlesbrough	a			06 56	07 03	07 23		07 52	08 14	08 22			08 32	08 47	08 56	09 21	09 26		09 50			09 55	10 19	10 30	10 48
	d		06 34	06 58		07 24		07 54							08 57		09 27					09 56	10 20		
South Bank	d							07 58							09 01										
British Steel Redcar §	d							08 04																	
Redcar Central	d		06 44	07 08		07 34		08 07							09 09		09 37					10 06	10 31		
Redcar East	d		06 47			07 37		08 10							09 11		09 40					10 09	10 33		
Longbeck	d		06 51			07 41		08 14							09 15		09 44					10 13	10 37		
Marske	d		06 52			07 42		08 15							09 17		09 45					10 14	10 39		
Saltburn	a		07 06	07 21		07 50		08 23							09 26		09 53					10 23	10 49		

Station		NT	NT	NT	TP	NT		SR	NT	NT	TP	NT	NT	NT	NT	GC		TP	NT	NT	NT	NT	TP	NT	NT
					◇1						◇1					R 1		◇1					◇1		
Hexham	48 d	09 22				09 43		10 26				10 42	11 20						11 43	12 19				12 43	13 20
Metrocentre	48 d	09 46				10 16		10 50				11 16	11 46						12 16	12 45				13 16	13 46
Newcastle 8	26 ⛴ d	10a00				10 30		11a07				11 30	11a59						12 30	12a58				13 30	13a59
Heworth	⛴ d					10 37						11 37							12 37					13 37	
Sunderland	⛴ a					10 49						11 49							12 49					13 49	
	d					10 50						11 50				12 28			12 50					13 50	
Seaham	d					10 58						11 58							12 58					13 58	
Hartlepool	d					11 16						12 15				12 52			13 15					14 15	
Seaton Carew	d					11 20						12 19							13 19					14 19	
Billingham	d					11 27						12 26							13 26					14 26	
Stockton	d					11 34						12 33							13 33					14 33	
Bishop Auckland	d									11 25												13 25			
Shildon	d									11 30												13 30			
Newton Aycliffe	d									11 35												13 35			
Heighington	d									11 38												13 38			
North Road	d									11 47												13 47			
Chester-le-Street	26 d																								
Durham	26 d																								
Darlington 7	26 a									11 51												13 51			
	d		10 30	10 53					11 30	11 53				12 30	12 53						13 30	13 53			
Dinsdale	d			10 58						11 59					12 58							13 58			
Tees-side Airport	d																								
Allens West	d		10 40	11 05					11 40	12 05				12 40	13 05						13 40	14 05			
Eaglescliffe	a		10 42	11 07					11 42	12 07				12 42	13 07	13 11					13 42	14 07			
	d		10 43	11 07					11 43	12 08				12 43	13 07	13 12					13 43	14 07			
London Kings Cross 15	⊖26 a															16 09									
Thornaby	d		10 49	11 13	11 23	11 40			11 48	12 13	12 23	12 39		12 48	13 13			13 23	13 39		13 48	14 13	14 23	14 37	
Middlesbrough	a		10 55	11 19	11 30	11 50			11 56	12 19	12 30	12 48		12 54	13 19			13 30	13 48		13 54	14 19	14 30	14 44	
	d		10 56	11 20					11 56	12 20				12 56	13 20						13 56	14 20			
South Bank	d																								
British Steel Redcar §	d																								
Redcar Central	d		11 06	11 31					12 06	12 31				13 06	13 31						14 06	14 31			
Redcar East	d		11 09	11 33					12 09	12 33				13 09	13 33						14 09	14 33			
Longbeck	d		11 13	11 37					12 13	12 37				13 13	13 37						14 13	14 37			
Marske	d		11 14	11 39					12 14	12 39				13 14	13 39						14 14	14 39			
Saltburn	a		11 23	11 49					12 24	12 47				13 23	13 49						14 24	14 52			

§ For authorised access only to BSC Redcar

Table 44

Mondays to Fridays

from 3 October

Newcastle, Sunderland, Bishop Auckland and Darlington - Middlesbrough and Saltburn

Station		NT	NT	TP	NT	NT	NT	NT	TP	NT	SR	NT	NT	TP	NT	NT	NT	NT	GC	TP	NT	NT
				◇1 ⚲					◇1 ⚲					◇1 ⚲					R 1 🍴	◇1 ⚲		
Hexham 48	d				13 43	14 24				14 43	15 21				15 42		16 12				16 43	17 20
Metrocentre 48	d				14 14	14 46				15 16	15 45				16 16		16 38				17 16	17 46
Newcastle 8 26 ⛴	d				14 30	15a03				15 30	15a54				16 30		16 53				17 30	17a59
Heworth ⛴	d				14 37					15 37					16 37		17 00				17 37	
Sunderland ⛴	a				14 49					15 49					16 49		17 14				17 50	
	d				14 50					15 50					16 50		17 15		17 31		17 50	
Seaham	d				14 58					15 58					16 58		17 22				17 58	
Hartlepool	d				15 15					16 15					17 15		17 39		17 55		18 15	
Seaton Carew	d				15 19					16 19					17 19		17 43				18 19	
Billingham	d				15 26					16 26					17 26		17 50				18 26	
Stockton	d				15 33					16 33					17 33		17 57				18 33	
Bishop Auckland	d							15 25					16 24									
Shildon	d							15 30					16 29									
Newton Aycliffe	d							15 35					16 34									
Heighington	d							15 38					16 37									
North Road	d							15 47					16 46									
Chester-le-Street 26	d																					
Durham 26	d																					
Darlington 7 26	a							15 51					16 50									
	d	14 30	14 53				15 30	15 53				16 29	16 53			17 30		18 00				
Dinsdale	d		14 58					15 58				16 35	16 58			17 35		18 06				
Tees-side Airport	d																					
Allens West	d	14 40	15 05				15 40	16 05				16 42	17 05			17 42		18 12				
Eaglescliffe	a	14 42	15 07				15 42	16 07				16 44	17 07			17 44		18 14	18 17			
	d	14 43	15 07				15 43	16 07				16 44	17 07			17 44		18 15	18 20			
London Kings Cross 15 ⊖26	a																		21 04			
Thornaby	d	14 49	15 13	15 23	15 39		15 48	16 13	16 23	16 39		16 50	17 13	17 22	17 39	17 50	18 03	18 21		18 33	18 39	
Middlesbrough	a	14 54	15 19	15 30	15 48		15 54	16 19	16 30	16 47		16 56	17 19	17 30	17 48	17 57	18 15	18 26		18 40	18 48	
	d	14 56	15 20				15 56	16 20				16 58	17 20			17 59		18 27				
South Bank	d							16 25										18 32				
British Steel Redcar §	d																					
Redcar Central	d	15 06	15 31				16 06	16 32				17 08	17 31			18 08		18 39				
Redcar East	d	15 09	15 33				16 09	16 35				17 11	17 33			18 11		18 42				
Longbeck	d	15 13	15 37				16 13	16 39				17 15	17 37			18 15		18 46				
Marske	d	15 14	15 39				16 14	16 40				17 16	17 39			18 16		18 47				
Saltburn	a	15 23	15 49				16 23	16 49				17 25	17 49			18 27		18 56				

Station		NT	TP	NT	NT	NT	NT	TP	NT	SR	NT	NT	NT	TP	NT	NT	NT	NT	NT	NT
			◇1 ⚲					◇1 ⚲						◇1						
Hexham 48	d			17 43	18 21				18 44	19 27	20 26		21 12					22 21		23 20
Metrocentre 48	d			18 16	18 53				19 17	19 57	20 59		21 45					22 53		
Newcastle 8 26 ⛴	d			18 30	19a05				19 28	20a12	21a10		21a56		20 30		21 18	23a07		23a59
Heworth ⛴	d			18 37					19 37						20 37		21 25			
Sunderland ⛴	a			18 49					19 50						20 49		21 37			
	d			18 50					19 50						20 50		21 38			
Seaham	d			18 58					19 58						20 58		21 46			
Hartlepool	d			19 15					20 15						21 15		22 03			
Seaton Carew	d			19 19					20 19						21 19		22 07			
Billingham	d			19 26					20 26						21 26		22 14			
Stockton	d			19 33					20 33						21 33		22 21			
Bishop Auckland	d	18 02					19 25									21 10				
Shildon	d	18 07					19 30									21 15				
Newton Aycliffe	d	18 12					19 35									21 20				
Heighington	d	18 15					19 38									21 23				
North Road	d	18 24					19 47									21 32				
Chester-le-Street 26	d																			
Durham 26	d																			
Darlington 7 26	a	18 28					19 51									21 36				
	d	18 30				19 30	19 53					20 32				21 38			22 38	
Dinsdale	d	18 35				19 35	19 59					20 35				21 43			22 43	
Tees-side Airport	d																			
Allens West	d	18 42				19 42	20 05					20 42				21 50			22 50	
Eaglescliffe	a	18 44				19 44	20 07					20 45				21 52			22 52	
	d	18 44				19 44	20 08					20 45				21 52			22 52	
London Kings Cross 15 ⊖26	a																			
Thornaby	d	18 50	19 23	19 36		19 53	20 14	20 21	20 39			20 50		21 24	21 40	21 58	22 30		22 58	
Middlesbrough	a	18 56	19 32	19 47		19 59	20 21	20 30	20 50			20 58		21 32	21 48	22 05	22 36		23 04	
	d	18 58				20 00						20 59				22 06				
South Bank	d																			
British Steel Redcar §	d																			
Redcar Central	d	19 08				20 11						21 08				22 17				
Redcar East	d	19 11				20 13						21 11				22 19				
Longbeck	d	19 15				20 17						21 15				22 23				
Marske	d	19 16				20 19						21 16				22 25				
Saltburn	a	19 25				20 28						21 25				22 34				

§ For authorised access only to BSC Redcar

Table 44

Saturdays
until 25 June

Newcastle, Sunderland, Bishop Auckland and Darlington - Middlesbrough and Saltburn

	NT	NT	NT	TP	NT	GC	NT	NT	NT		NT	TP	NT	NT	TP	NT	GC	NT	SR		NT	NT	TP	NT
				◇1		R 1						◇1			◇1		R 1						◇1	
Hexham 48 d									06 16		07 19							07 42	08 11					08 45
Metrocentre 48 d											07 51							08 16	08 44					09 16
Newcastle 8 26 d	06 00								07 00		08a04		07 30					08 30	08a57					09 30
Heworth d	06 07								07 07				07 37					08 37						09 37
Sunderland a	06 27								07 20				07 49					08 50						09 49
d	06 28					06 43			07 21				07 50				08 30	08 51						09 50
Seaham d	06 35								07 29				07 58					08 58						09 58
Hartlepool d	06a54					07 09			07 45				08 15				08 54	09 15						10 15
Seaton Carew d									07 49				08 19					09 19						10 19
Billingham d									07 56				08 26					09 26						10 26
Stockton d									08 04				08 33					09 34						10 33
Bishop Auckland d								07 20								08 21						09 26		
Shildon d								07 25								08 26						09 31		
Newton Aycliffe d								07 30								08 31						09 36		
Heighington d								07 33								08 34						09 40		
North Road d								07 42								08 43						09 48		
Chester-le-Street 26 d																								
Durham 26 d																								
Darlington 7 26 a								07 46								08 47						09 54		
d			06 28	06 36	06 58		07 28	07 48						08 23		08 59					09 30	09 55		
Dinsdale d			06 34		07 03		07 33	07 53						08 28		09 04						09 59		
Tees-side Airport d																								
Allens West d			06 40		07 10		07 40	08 00						08 35		09 11					09 40	10 05		
Eaglescliffe a			06 42		07 12	07 29	07 41	08 02						08 37		09 13	09 15				09 42	10 07		
d			06 43		07 12	07 30	07 41	08 02						08 37		09 13	09 17				09 43	10 08		
London Kings Cross 15 ⊖26 a						10 15											12 07							
Thornaby d			06 48	06 53	07 17		07 47	08 08	08 13			08 24	08 39	08 45	09 12	09 19		09 39			09 48	10 13	10 23	10 39
Middlesbrough a			06 54	07 03	07 23		07 53	08 14	08 23			08 32	08 47	08 51	09 21	09 26		09 50			09 54	10 17	10 30	10 48
d		06 34	06 58		07 25		07 55							08 53		09 27					09 56	10 20		
South Bank d							08 00							08 57										
British Steel Redcar § d																								
Redcar Central d		06 44	07 08		07 35		08 07							09 05		09 38					10 06	10 31		
Redcar East d		06 47			07 38		08 10							09 07		09 40					10 09	10 33		
Longbeck d		06 51			07 42		08 14							09 11		09 44					10 13	10 37		
Marske d		06 52			07 43		08 15							09 13		09 46					10 14	10 39		
Saltburn a		07 00	07 22		07 51		08 23							09 23		09 55					10 23	10 49		

	NT	NT	NT	TP	NT		SR	NT	NT	TP	NT	NT	NT	GC	NT		TP	NT	NT	NT	NT	TP	NT	NT
				◇1						◇1				R 1			◇1					◇1		
Hexham 48 d	09 22				09 46		10 26				10 44	11 22						11 45	12 22				12 45	13 22
Metrocentre 48 d	09 46				10 17		10 50				11 16	11 46						12 16	12 45				13 16	13 46
Newcastle 8 26 d	09a59				10 30		11a07				11 30	11a59						12 30	12a57				13 30	13a59
Heworth d					10 37						11 37							12 37					13 37	
Sunderland a					10 49						11 49							12 49					13 49	
d					10 50						11 50			12 18				12 50					13 50	
Seaham d					10 58						11 58							12 58					13 58	
Hartlepool d					11 16						12 15			12 43				13 15					14 15	
Seaton Carew d					11 20						12 19							13 19					14 19	
Billingham d					11 27						12 26							13 26					14 26	
Stockton d					11 34						12 33							13 33					14 33	
Bishop Auckland d									11 25												13 25			
Shildon d									11 30												13 30			
Newton Aycliffe d									11 35												13 35			
Heighington d									11 38												13 38			
North Road d									11 47												13 47			
Chester-le-Street 26 d																								
Durham 26 d																								
Darlington 7 26 a									11 51												13 51			
d		10 30	10 53					11 30	11 53				12 30		12 53					13 30	13 53			
Dinsdale d			10 58						11 59						12 58						13 58			
Tees-side Airport d																								
Allens West d		10 40	11 05					11 40	12 05				12 40		13 05					13 40	14 05			
Eaglescliffe a		10 42	11 07					11 42	12 07				12 42	13 04	13 07					13 42	14 07			
d		10 43	11 07					11 43	12 08				12 43	13 05	13 07					13 43	14 07			
London Kings Cross 15 ⊖26 a														15 53										
Thornaby d		10 48	11 13	11 23	11 40			11 48	12 13	12 23	12 39		12 48		13 13		13 23	13 39		13 48	14 13	14 23	14 39	
Middlesbrough a		10 54	11 19	11 30	11 50			11 56	12 19	12 30	12 49		12 54		13 19		13 30	13 48		13 55	14 19	14 30	14 46	
d		10 56	11 20					11 56	12 20				12 56		13 20					13 56	14 20			
South Bank d																								
British Steel Redcar § d																								
Redcar Central d		11 06	11 31					12 06	12 31				13 06		13 31					14 06	14 31			
Redcar East d		11 09	11 33					12 08	12 33				13 09		13 33					14 09	14 33			
Longbeck d		11 13	11 37					12 12	12 37				13 13		13 37					14 13	14 37			
Marske d		11 14	11 39					12 14	12 39				13 14		13 39					14 14	14 39			
Saltburn a		11 23	11 49					12 24	12 48				13 23		13 49					14 23	14 50			

§ For authorised access only to BSC Redcar

Newcastle, Sunderland, Bishop Auckland and Darlington - Middlesbrough and Saltburn

		NT		NT	TP	NT	NT	NT	NT	TP	NT	SR		NT	NT	TP	NT	NT	NT		GC	NT		TP	NT
					◇1 🛒					◇1 🛒						◇1					R 1 ✕			◇1 🛒	
Hexham 48	d					13 45	14 24				14 43	15 21					15 45		16 14						16 45
Metrocentre 48	d					14 16	14 48				15 16	15 45					16 16		16 38						17 16
Newcastle 8 26 ⛴	d					14 30	15a00				15 30	15a54					16 30		16 53						17 30
Heworth ⛴	d					14 37					15 37						16 37		17 00						17 37
Sunderland ⛴	a					14 49					15 49						16 49		17 14						17 50
	d					14 50					15 50						16 50		17 15		17 29				17 50
Seaham	d					14 58					15 58						16 58		17 22						17 58
Hartlepool	d					15 15					16 15						17 15		17 39		17 53				18 15
Seaton Carew	d					15 19					16 19						17 19		17 43						18 19
Billingham	d					15 26					16 26						17 26		17 50						18 26
Stockton	d					15 33					16 33						17 33		17 57						18 33
Bishop Auckland	d								15 25						16 23										
Shildon	d								15 30						16 28										
Newton Aycliffe	d								15 35						16 33										
Heighington	d								15 38						16 36										
North Road	d								15 47						16 45										
Chester-le-Street 26	d																								
Durham 26	d																								
Darlington 7 26	a								15 51						16 49										
	d	14 30		14 53				15 30	15 53					16 29	16 53			17 30				18 00			
Dinsdale	d			14 58					15 58					16 35	16 58			17 35				18 06			
Tees-side Airport	d																								
Allens West	d	14 40		15 05				15 40	16 05					16 42	17 05			17 42				18 12			
Eaglescliffe	a	14 42		15 07				15 42	16 07					16 44	17 07			17 44			18 11	18 14			
	d	14 43		15 07				15 43	16 07					16 44	17 07			17 44			18 12	18 15			
London Kings Cross 15 ⊖26	a																				21 24				
Thornaby	d	14 49		15 13	15 23	15 39		15 48	16 13	16 23	16 39			16 50	17 13	17 22	17 39	17 50	18 04			18 20		18 25	18 39
Middlesbrough	a	14 54		15 19	15 30	15 48		15 54	16 19	16 30	16 47			16 56	17 19	17 30	17 49	17 57	18 15			18 26		18 32	18 48
	d	14 56		15 20				15 56	16 20					16 58	17 20			17 59				18 27			
South Bank	d								16 25													18 32			
British Steel Redcar §	d																								
Redcar Central	d	15 06		15 31				16 06	16 32					17 08	17 31			18 08				18 39			
Redcar East	d	15 09		15 33				16 09	16 35					17 11	17 33			18 11				18 42			
Longbeck	d	15 13		15 37				16 13	16 39					17 15	17 37			18 15				18 46			
Marske	d	15 14		15 39				16 14	16 40					17 16	17 39			18 16				18 47			
Saltburn	a	15 23		15 49				16 23	16 49					17 25	17 48			18 27				18 56			

		NT	NT	TP	NT	NT	NT	NT		TP	NT	SR	NT	TP	NT	NT	NT	NT		NT	NT				
				◇1						◇1				◇1											
Hexham 48	d	17 22			17 45	18 23					18 45	19 26					20 28	21 14			22 14				
Metrocentre 48	d	17 45			18 16	18 52					19 18	19 56				20 47	20 59	21 45			22 45				
Newcastle 8 26 ⛴	d	17a59			18 30	19a03					19 30	20a11				21 00	21a10	21a57		21 50	23a00				
Heworth ⛴	d				18 37						19 37					21 08									
Sunderland ⛴	a				18 49						19 50					21 20									
	d				18 50						19 50					21 20									
Seaham	d				18 58						19 58					21 28									
Hartlepool	d				19 15						20 15					21 45									
Seaton Carew	d				19 19						20 19					21 49									
Billingham	d				19 26						20 26					21 56									
Stockton	d				19 33						20 33					22 03									
Bishop Auckland	d		18 02					19 25							21 10										
Shildon	d		18 07					19 30							21 15										
Newton Aycliffe	d		18 12					19 35							21 20										
Heighington	d		18 15					19 38							21 23										
North Road	d		18 24					19 47							21 32										
Chester-le-Street 26	d																			21 59					
Durham 26	d																			22 08					
Darlington 7 26	a		18 28					19 51							21 36					22 29					
	d		18 30				19 34	19 53					20 30		21 38					22 30					
Dinsdale	d		18 35				19 39	19 59					20 35		21 43										
Tees-side Airport	d																								
Allens West	d		18 42				19 46	20 05					20 42		21 50					22 41					
Eaglescliffe	a		18 44				19 48	20 07					20 44		21 52					22 43					
	d		18 44				19 48	20 08					20 44		21 52					22 43					
London Kings Cross 15 ⊖26	a																								
Thornaby	d		18 50	19 22	19 39		19 54	20 13		20 21	20 38		20 50	21 24	21 59	22 10				22 48					
Middlesbrough	a		18 56	19 32	19 48		20 00	20 20		20 30	20 48		20 57	21 32	22 05	22 18				22 57					
	d		18 58				20 02						20 58		22 06										
South Bank	d																								
British Steel Redcar §	d																								
Redcar Central	d		19 08				20 12						21 08		22 17										
Redcar East	d		19 11				20 15						21 11		22 19										
Longbeck	d		19 15				20 19						21 15		22 23										
Marske	d		19 16				20 20						21 16		22 25										
Saltburn	a		19 25				20 29						21 25		22 34										

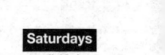

§ For authorised access only to BSC Redcar

Table 44

Saturdays

6 August to 1 October

Newcastle, Sunderland, Bishop Auckland and Darlington - Middlesbrough and Saltburn

		NT	NT	NT	TP	NT	GC	NT	NT	NT		NT	TP	NT	NT	TP	NT	GC	NT	SR		NT	NT	TP	NT
					◇1		R 1 ☕						◇1			◇1 🛒		R 1 ☕						◇1 🛒	
Hexham	48 d									06 16		07 19							07 42	08 11					08 45
Metrocentre	48 d											07 51							08 16	08 44					09 16
Newcastle 8	26 ⛴ d	06 00								07 00		08a04		07 30					08 30	08a57					09 30
Heworth	⛴ d	06 07								07 07				07 37					08 37						09 37
Sunderland	⛴ a	06 27								07 20				07 49					08 50						09 49
	d	06 28					06 43			07 21				07 50				08 30	08 51						09 50
Seaham	d	06 35								07 29				07 58					08 58						09 58
Hartlepool	d	06a54					07 09			07 45				08 15				08 54	09 15						10 15
Seaton Carew	d									07 49				08 19					09 19						10 19
Billingham	d									07 56				08 26					09 26						10 26
Stockton	d									08 04				08 33					09 34						10 33
Bishop Auckland	d								07 20								08 21						09 26		
Shildon	d								07 25								08 26						09 31		
Newton Aycliffe	d								07 30								08 31						09 36		
Heighington	d								07 33								08 34						09 40		
North Road	d								07 42								08 43						09 48		
Chester-le-Street	26 d																								
Durham	26 d																								
Darlington 7	26 a								07 46								08 47						09 54		
	d			06 28	06 36	06 58		07 28	07 48						08 23		08 59					09 30	09 55		
Dinsdale	d			06 34		07 03		07 33	07 53						08 28		09 04						09 59		
Tees-side Airport	d																								
Allens West	d			06 40		07 10		07 40	08 00						08 35		09 11					09 40	10 05		
Eaglescliffe	a			06 42		07 12	07 29	07 41	08 02						08 37		09 13	09 15				09 42	10 07		
	d			06 43		07 12	07 30	07 41	08 02						08 37		09 13	09 17				09 43	10 08		
London Kings Cross 15	⊖26 a						10 15											12 07							
Thornaby	d			06 48	06 53	07 17		07 47	08 08	08 13			08 24	08 39	08 45	09 12	09 19		09 39			09 48	10 13	10 23	10 39
Middlesbrough	a			06 54	07 03	07 23		07 53	08 14	08 23			08 32	08 47	08 51	09 21	09 26		09 50			09 54	10 17	10 30	10 48
	d		06 34	06 58		07 25		07 55							08 53		09 27					09 56	10 20		
South Bank	d							08 00							08 57										
British Steel Redcar §	d																								
Redcar Central	d		06 44	07 08		07 35		08 07							09 05		09 38					10 06	10 31		
Redcar East	d		06 47			07 38		08 10							09 07		09 40					10 09	10 33		
Longbeck	d		06 51			07 42		08 14							09 11		09 44					10 13	10 37		
Marske	d		06 52			07 43		08 15							09 13		09 46					10 14	10 39		
Saltburn	a		07 00	07 22		07 51		08 23							09 23		09 55					10 23	10 49		

		NT	NT	NT	TP	NT		SR	NT	NT	TP	NT	NT	NT	GC	NT		TP	NT	NT	NT	NT	TP	NT	NT
					◇1 🛒						◇1 🛒				R 1 ☕			◇1 🛒					◇1 🛒		
Hexham	48 d	09 22				09 46		10 26				10 44	11 22						11 45	12 22				12 45	13 22
Metrocentre	48 d	09 46				10 17		10 50				11 16	11 46						12 16	12 45				13 16	13 46
Newcastle 8	26 ⛴ d	09a59				10 30		11a07				11 30	11a59						12 30	12a57				13 30	13a59
Heworth	⛴ d					10 37						11 37							12 37					13 37	
Sunderland	⛴ a					10 49						11 49							12 49					13 49	
	d					10 50						11 50			12 18				12 50					13 50	
Seaham	d					10 58						11 58							12 58					13 58	
Hartlepool	d					11 16						12 15			12 43				13 15					14 15	
Seaton Carew	d					11 20						12 19							13 19					14 19	
Billingham	d					11 27						12 26							13 26					14 26	
Stockton	d					11 34						12 33							13 33					14 33	
Bishop Auckland	d									11 25												13 25			
Shildon	d									11 30												13 30			
Newton Aycliffe	d									11 35												13 35			
Heighington	d									11 38												13 38			
North Road	d									11 47												13 47			
Chester-le-Street	26 d																								
Durham	26 d																								
Darlington 7	26 a									11 51												13 51			
	d		10 30	10 53					11 30	11 53				12 30		12 53					13 30	13 53			
Dinsdale	d			10 58						11 59						12 58						13 58			
Tees-side Airport	d																								
Allens West	d		10 40	11 05					11 40	12 05				12 40		13 05					13 40	14 05			
Eaglescliffe	a		10 42	11 07					11 42	12 07				12 42	13 04	13 07					13 42	14 07			
	d		10 43	11 07					11 43	12 08				12 43	13 05	13 07					13 43	14 07			
London Kings Cross 15	⊖26 a														15 53										
Thornaby	d		10 48	11 13	11 23	11 40			11 48	12 13	12 23	12 39		12 48		13 13		13 23	13 39		13 48	14 13	14 23	14 39	
Middlesbrough	a		10 54	11 19	11 30	11 50			11 56	12 19	12 30	12 49		12 54		13 19		13 30	13 48		13 55	14 19	14 30	14 46	
	d		10 56	11 20					11 56	12 20				12 56		13 20					13 56	14 20			
South Bank	d																								
British Steel Redcar §	d																								
Redcar Central	d		11 06	11 31					12 06	12 31				13 06		13 31					14 06	14 31			
Redcar East	d		11 09	11 33					12 08	12 33				13 09		13 33					14 09	14 33			
Longbeck	d		11 13	11 37					12 12	12 37				13 13		13 37					14 13	14 37			
Marske	d		11 14	11 39					12 14	12 39				13 14		13 39					14 14	14 39			
Saltburn	a		11 23	11 49					12 24	12 48				13 23		13 49					14 23	14 50			

§ For authorised access only to BSC Redcar

Table 44

Saturdays

6 August to 1 October

Newcastle, Sunderland, Bishop Auckland and Darlington - Middlesbrough and Saltburn

	NT		NT	TP	NT	NT	NT	NT	TP	NT	SR		NT	NT	TP	NT	NT	NT	GC	NT	TP		NT	NT
				◇1					◇1						◇1				R 1		◇1			
Hexham 48 d					13 45	14 24				14 43	15 21					15 45		16 14					16 45	17 22
Metrocentre 48 d					14 16	14 48				15 16	15 45					16 16		16 38					17 16	17 45
Newcastle 8 26 ⛴ d					14 30	15a00				15 30	15a54					16 30		16 53					17 30	17a59
Heworth ⛴ d					14 37					15 37						16 37		17 00					17 37	
Sunderland ⛴ a					14 49					15 49						16 49		17 14					17 50	
d					14 50					15 50						16 50		17 15	17 29				17 50	
Seaham d					14 58					15 58						16 58		17 22					17 58	
Hartlepool d					15 15					16 15						17 15		17 39	17 53				18 15	
Seaton Carew d					15 19					16 19						17 19		17 43					18 19	
Billingham d					15 26					16 26						17 26		17 50					18 26	
Stockton d					15 33					16 33						17 33		17 57					18 33	
Bishop Auckland d								15 25						16 23										
Shildon d								15 30						16 28										
Newton Aycliffe d								15 35						16 33										
Heighington d								15 38						16 36										
North Road d								15 47						16 45										
Chester-le-Street 26 d																								
Durham 26 d																								
Darlington 7 26 a								15 51						16 49										
d	14 30		14 53				15 30	15 53					16 29	16 53			17 30			18 00				
Dinsdale d			14 58					15 58					16 35	16 58			17 35			18 06				
Tees-side Airport d																								
Allens West d	14 40		15 05				15 40	16 05					16 42	17 05			17 42			18 12				
Eaglescliffe a	14 42		15 07				15 42	16 07					16 44	17 07			17 44		18 11	18 14				
d	14 43		15 07				15 43	16 07					16 44	17 07			17 44		18 12	18 15				
London Kings Cross 15 ⊖26 a																			20 56					
Thornaby d	14 49		15 13	15 23	15 39		15 48	16 13	16 23	16 39			16 50	17 13	17 22	17 39	17 50	18 04		18 20	18 25		18 39	
Middlesbrough a	14 54		15 19	15 30	15 48		15 54	16 19	16 30	16 47			16 56	17 19	17 30	17 49	17 57	18 15		18 26	18 32		18 48	
d	14 56		15 20				15 56	16 20					16 58	17 20			17 59			18 27				
South Bank d								16 25												18 32				
British Steel Redcar § d																								
Redcar Central d	15 06		15 31				16 06	16 32					17 08	17 31			18 08			18 39				
Redcar East d	15 09		15 33				16 09	16 35					17 11	17 33			18 11			18 42				
Longbeck d	15 13		15 37				16 13	16 39					17 15	17 37			18 15			18 46				
Marske d	15 14		15 39				16 14	16 40					17 16	17 39			18 16			18 47				
Saltburn a	15 23		15 49				16 23	16 49					17 25	17 48			18 27			18 56				

	NT	TP	NT	NT	NT	NT	TP		NT	SR	NT	TP	NT	NT	NT	NT	NT		NT					
		◇1					◇1					◇1												
Hexham 48 d			17 45	18 23					18 45	19 26					20 28	21 14			22 14					
Metrocentre 48 d			18 16	18 52					19 18	19 56				20 47	20 59	21 45			22 45					
Newcastle 8 26 ⛴ d			18 30	19a03					19 30	20a11				21 00	21a10	21a57	21 50		23a00					
Heworth ⛴ d			18 37						19 37					21 08										
Sunderland ⛴ a			18 49						19 50					21 20										
d			18 50						19 50					21 20										
Seaham d			18 58						19 58					21 28										
Hartlepool d			19 15						20 15					21 45										
Seaton Carew d			19 19						20 19					21 49										
Billingham d			19 26						20 26					21 56										
Stockton d			19 33						20 33					22 03										
Bishop Auckland d	18 02					19 25							21 10											
Shildon d	18 07					19 30							21 15											
Newton Aycliffe d	18 12					19 35							21 20											
Heighington d	18 15					19 38							21 23											
North Road d	18 24					19 47							21 32											
Chester-le-Street 26 d																	21 59							
Durham 26 d																	22 08							
Darlington 7 26 a	18 28					19 51							21 36				22 29							
d	18 30				19 34	19 53					20 30		21 38				22 30							
Dinsdale d	18 35				19 39	19 59					20 35		21 43											
Tees-side Airport d																								
Allens West d	18 42				19 46	20 05					20 42		21 50				22 41							
Eaglescliffe a	18 44				19 48	20 07					20 44		21 52				22 43							
d	18 44				19 48	20 08					20 44		21 52				22 43							
London Kings Cross 15 ⊖26 a																								
Thornaby d	18 50	19 22	19 39		19 54	20 13	20 21		20 38		20 50	21 24	21 59	22 10			22 48							
Middlesbrough a	18 56	19 32	19 48		20 00	20 20	20 30		20 48		20 57	21 32	22 05	22 18			22 57							
d	18 58				20 02						20 58		22 06											
South Bank d																								
British Steel Redcar § d																								
Redcar Central d	19 08				20 12						21 08		22 17											
Redcar East d	19 11				20 15						21 11		22 19											
Longbeck d	19 15				20 19						21 15		22 23											
Marske d	19 16				20 20						21 16		22 25											
Saltburn a	19 25				20 29						21 25		22 34											

§ For authorised access only to BSC Redcar

Table 44

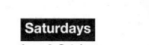

Saturdays
from 8 October

Newcastle, Sunderland, Bishop Auckland and Darlington - Middlesbrough and Saltburn

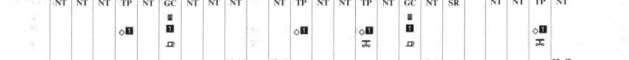

		NT	NT	NT	TP ◇1	NT	GC 1	NT	NT	NT		NT	TP ◇1	NT	NT	TP ◇1	NT	GC 1	NT	SR		NT	NT	TP ◇1	NT
Hexham	48 d									06 14		07 19							07 40	08 11					08 43
Metrocentre	48 d											07 51							08 16	08 44					09 16
Newcastle 8	26 ⛴ d	06 00								07 00		08a08		07 30					08 30	08a57					09 30
Heworth	⛴ d	06 07								07 07				07 37					08 37						09 37
Sunderland	⛴ a	06 27								07 20				07 49					08 50						09 49
	d	06 28					06 43			07 21				07 50				08 30	08 51						09 50
Seaham	d	06 35								07 29				07 58					08 58						09 58
Hartlepool	d	06a54					07 09			07 45				08 15				08 54	09 15						10 15
Seaton Carew	d									07 49				08 19					09 19						10 19
Billingham	d									07 56				08 26					09 26						10 26
Stockton	d									08 04				08 33					09 34						10 33
Bishop Auckland	d								07 20								08 21						09 26		
Shildon	d								07 25								08 26						09 31		
Newton Aycliffe	d								07 30								08 31						09 36		
Heighington	d								07 33								08 34						09 40		
North Road	d								07 42								08 43						09 48		
Chester-le-Street	26 d																								
Durham	26 d																								
Darlington 7	26 a								07 46								08 47						09 54		
	d			06 28	06 36	06 58		07 28	07 48						08 23		08 59					09 30	09 55		
Dinsdale	d			06 34		07 03		07 33	07 53						08 28		09 04						09 59		
Tees-side Airport	d																								
Allens West	d			06 40		07 10		07 40	08 00						08 35		09 11					09 40	10 05		
Eaglescliffe	a			06 42		07 12	07 29	07 41	08 02						08 37		09 13	09 15				09 42	10 07		
	d			06 43		07 12	07 30	07 41	08 02						08 37		09 13	09 17				09 43	10 08		
London Kings Cross 15 ⊖26	a						10 15											12 07							
Thornaby	d			06 48	06 53	07 17		07 47	08 08	08 13			08 24	08 39	08 45	09 12	09 19		09 39			09 48	10 13	10 23	10 39
Middlesbrough	a			06 54	07 03	07 23		07 53	08 14	08 23			08 32	08 47	08 51	09 21	09 26		09 50			09 54	10 17	10 30	10 48
	d		06 34	06 58		07 25		07 55							08 53		09 27					09 56	10 20		
South Bank	d							08 00							08 57										
British Steel Redcar §	d																								
Redcar Central	d		06 44	07 08		07 35		08 07							09 05		09 38					10 06	10 31		
Redcar East	d		06 47			07 38		08 10							09 07		09 40					10 09	10 33		
Longbeck	d		06 51			07 42		08 14							09 11		09 44					10 13	10 37		
Marske	d		06 52			07 43		08 15							09 13		09 46					10 14	10 39		
Saltburn	a		07 00	07 22		07 51		08 23							09 23		09 55					10 23	10 49		

		NT	NT	NT	TP ◇1	NT		SR	NT	NT	TP ◇1	NT	NT	NT	GC 1	NT		TP ◇1	NT	NT	NT	NT	TP ◇1	NT	NT
Hexham	48 d	09 22				09 44		10 26				10 42	11 20						11 43	12 19				12 43	13 20
Metrocentre	48 d	09 46				10 17		10 50				11 16	11 46						12 16	12 45				13 16	13 46
Newcastle 8	26 ⛴ d	10a03				10 30		11a07				11 30	11a59						12 30	12a57				13 30	13a58
Heworth	⛴ d					10 37						11 37							12 37					13 37	
Sunderland	⛴ a					10 49						11 49							12 49					13 49	
	d					10 50						11 50			12 18				12 50					13 50	
Seaham	d					10 58						11 58							12 58					13 58	
Hartlepool	d					11 16						12 15			12 43				13 15					14 15	
Seaton Carew	d					11 20						12 19							13 19					14 19	
Billingham	d					11 27						12 26							13 26					14 26	
Stockton	d					11 34						12 33							13 33					14 33	
Bishop Auckland	d									11 25												13 25			
Shildon	d									11 30												13 30			
Newton Aycliffe	d									11 35												13 35			
Heighington	d									11 38												13 38			
North Road	d									11 47												13 47			
Chester-le-Street	26 d																								
Durham	26 d																								
Darlington 7	26 a									11 51												13 51			
	d		10 30	10 53					11 30	11 53				12 30		12 53					13 30	13 53			
Dinsdale	d			10 58						11 59						12 58						13 58			
Tees-side Airport	d																								
Allens West	d		10 40	11 05					11 40	12 05				12 40		13 05					13 40	14 05			
Eaglescliffe	a		10 42	11 07					11 42	12 07				12 42	13 04	13 07					13 42	14 07			
	d		10 43	11 07					11 43	12 08				12 43	13 05	13 07					13 43	14 07			
London Kings Cross 15 ⊖26	a														15 53										
Thornaby	d		10 48	11 13	11 23	11 40			11 48	12 13	12 23	12 39		12 48		13 13		13 23	13 39		13 48	14 13	14 23	14 39	
Middlesbrough	a		10 54	11 19	11 30	11 50			11 56	12 19	12 30	12 49		12 54		13 19		13 30	13 48		13 55	14 19	14 30	14 46	
	d		10 56	11 20					11 56	12 20				12 56		13 20					13 56	14 20			
South Bank	d																								
British Steel Redcar §	d																								
Redcar Central	d		11 06	11 31					12 06	12 31				13 06		13 31					14 06	14 31			
Redcar East	d		11 09	11 33					12 08	12 33				13 09		13 33					14 09	14 33			
Longbeck	d		11 13	11 37					12 12	12 37				13 13		13 37					14 13	14 37			
Marske	d		11 14	11 39					12 14	12 39				13 14		13 39					14 14	14 39			
Saltburn	a		11 23	11 49					12 24	12 48				13 23		13 49					14 23	14 50			

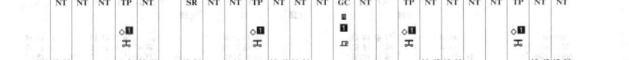

§ For authorised access only to BSC Redcar

Table 44

Saturdays
from 8 October

Newcastle, Sunderland, Bishop Auckland and Darlington - Middlesbrough and Saltburn

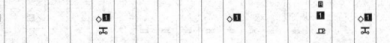

	NT		NT	TP	NT	NT	NT	NT	TP	NT	SR		NT	NT	TP	NT	NT	NT	GC	NT	TP		NT	NT
				◇1					◇1						◇1				R 1		◇1			
Hexham 48 d					13 43	14 24				14 43	15 21					15 43		16 12					16 43	17 20
Metrocentre 48 d					14 16	14 48				15 16	15 45					16 16		16 38					17 16	17 45
Newcastle 8 26 d					14 30	15a00				15 30	15a54					16 30		16 53					17 30	17a59
Heworth d					14 37					15 37						16 37		17 00					17 37	
Sunderland a					14 49					15 49						16 49		17 14					17 50	
d					14 50					15 50						16 50		17 15	17 29				17 50	
Seaham d					14 58					15 58						16 58		17 22					17 58	
Hartlepool d					15 15					16 15						17 15		17 39	17 53				18 15	
Seaton Carew d					15 19					16 19						17 19		17 43					18 19	
Billingham d					15 26					16 26						17 26		17 50					18 26	
Stockton d					15 33					16 33						17 33		17 57					18 33	
Bishop Auckland d								15 25						16 23										
Shildon d								15 30						16 28										
Newton Aycliffe d								15 35						16 33										
Heighington d								15 38						16 36										
North Road d								15 47						16 45										
Chester-le-Street 26 d																								
Durham 26 d																								
Darlington 7 26 a								15 51						16 49										
d	14 30		14 53				15 30	15 53					16 29	16 53			17 30			18 00				
Dinsdale d			14 58					15 58					16 35	16 58			17 35			18 06				
Tees-side Airport d																								
Allens West d	14 40		15 05				15 40	16 05					16 42	17 05			17 42			18 12				
Eaglescliffe a	14 42		15 07				15 42	16 07					16 44	17 07			17 44		18 11	18 14				
d	14 43		15 07				15 43	16 07					16 44	17 07			17 44		18 12	18 15				
London Kings Cross 15 ⊖26 a																			20 56					
Thornaby d	14 49		15 13	15 23	15 39		15 48	16 13	16 23	16 39			16 50	17 13	17 22	17 39	17 50	18 04		18 20	18 25		18 39	
Middlesbrough a	14 54		15 19	15 30	15 48		15 54	16 19	16 30	16 47			16 56	17 19	17 30	17 49	17 57	18 15		18 26	18 32		18 48	
d	14 56		15 20				15 56	16 20					16 58	17 20			17 59			18 27				
South Bank d								16 25												18 32				
British Steel Redcar § d																								
Redcar Central d	15 06		15 31				16 06	16 32					17 08	17 31			18 08			18 39				
Redcar East d	15 09		15 33				16 09	16 35					17 11	17 33			18 11			18 42				
Longbeck d	15 13		15 37				16 13	16 39					17 15	17 37			18 15			18 46				
Marske d	15 14		15 39				16 14	16 40					17 16	17 39			18 16			18 47				
Saltburn a	15 23		15 49				16 23	16 49					17 25	17 48			18 27			18 56				

	NT	TP	NT	NT	NT	NT	TP		NT	SR	NT	TP	NT	NT	NT	NT	NT		NT					
		◇1					◇1					◇1												
Hexham 48 d			17 43	18 21					18 43	19 26					20 26	21 12			22 13					
Metrocentre 48 d			18 16	18 52					19 18	19 56				20 47	20 59	21 45			22 45					
Newcastle 8 26 d			18 30	19a05					19 30	20a11				21 00	21a10	21a57	21 50		23a00					
Heworth d			18 37						19 37					21 08										
Sunderland a			18 49						19 50					21 20										
d			18 50						19 50					21 20										
Seaham d			18 58						19 58					21 28										
Hartlepool d			19 15						20 15					21 45										
Seaton Carew d			19 19						20 19					21 49										
Billingham d			19 26						20 26					21 56										
Stockton d			19 33						20 33					22 03										
Bishop Auckland d	18 02					19 25							21 10											
Shildon d	18 07					19 30							21 15											
Newton Aycliffe d	18 12					19 35							21 20											
Heighington d	18 15					19 38							21 23											
North Road d	18 24					19 47							21 32											
Chester-le-Street 26 d																	21 59							
Durham 26 d																	22 08							
Darlington 7 26 a	18 28					19 51							21 36				22 29							
d	18 30				19 34	19 53					20 30		21 38				22 30							
Dinsdale d	18 35				19 39	19 59					20 35		21 43											
Tees-side Airport d																								
Allens West d	18 42				19 46	20 05					20 42		21 50				22 41							
Eaglescliffe a	18 44				19 48	20 07					20 44		21 52				22 43							
d	18 44				19 48	20 08					20 44		21 52				22 43							
London Kings Cross 15 ⊖26 a																								
Thornaby d	18 50	19 22	19 39		19 54	20 13	20 21		20 38		20 50	21 24	21 59	22 10			22 48							
Middlesbrough a	18 56	19 32	19 48		20 00	20 20	20 30		20 48		20 57	21 32	22 05	22 18			22 57							
d	18 58				20 02						20 58		22 06											
South Bank d																								
British Steel Redcar § d																								
Redcar Central d	19 08				20 12						21 08		22 17											
Redcar East d	19 11				20 15						21 11		22 19											
Longbeck d	19 15				20 19						21 15		22 23											
Marske d	19 16				20 20						21 16		22 25											
Saltburn a	19 25				20 29						21 25		22 34											

§ For authorised access only to BSC Redcar

Table 44

Sundays
until 19 June

Newcastle, Sunderland, Bishop Auckland and Darlington - Middlesbrough and Saltburn

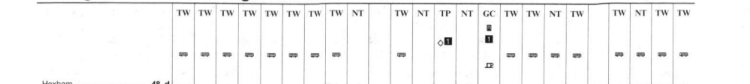

		TW	TW	TW	TW	TW	TW	TW	TW	NT		TW	NT	TP	NT	GC	TW	TW	NT	TW		TW	NT	TW	TW
														◇1		R 1 ☕									
		🚌	🚌	🚌	🚌	🚌	🚌	🚌	🚌			🚌					🚌	🚌	🚌	🚌		🚌	🚌	🚌	🚌
Hexham 48	d																								
Metrocentre 48	d																								
Newcastle 8 26 ⛴	d																		09 00				09 15		
Heworth ⛴	d	06 03	06 33	07 03	07 18	07 33	07 33	07 48	08 03			08 18					08 33	08 48	09 10	09 03		09 03	09 25	09 18	09 33
Sunderland ⛴	a	06 39	07 09	07 39	07 54	08 09	08 13	08 24	08 43			08 54					09 13	09 28	09 30	09 39		09 43	09 45	09 58	10 13
	d															09 12							09 45		
Seaham	d																						10a00		
Hartlepool	d															09 36									
Seaton Carew	d																								
Billingham	d																								
Stockton	d																								
Bishop Auckland	d														08 39										
Shildon	d														08 44										
Newton Aycliffe	d														08 49										
Heighington	d														08 53										
North Road	d														09 01										
Chester-le-Street 26	d																								
Durham 26	d																								
Darlington 7 26	a														09 09										
	d									08 17			08 45	09 00	09 11										
Dinsdale	d									08 23			08 50		09 16										
Tees-side Airport	d																								
Allens West	d									08 30			08 57		09 23										
Eaglescliffe	a									08 32			08 59		09 25	09 58									
	d									08 32			08 59		09 25	09 59									
London Kings Cross 15 ⊖26	a															12 44									
Thornaby	d									08 38			09 05	09 17	09 31										
Middlesbrough	a									08 44			09 10	09 27	09 40										
	d												09 12												
South Bank	d																								
British Steel Redcar §	d																								
Redcar Central	d												09 22												
Redcar East	d												09 25												
Longbeck	d												09 29												
Marske	d												09 30												
Saltburn	a												09 37												

		NT	TW	NT	TW	NT		NT	NT	TW	NT	TW	TW	NT	TW	TW		TP	NT	NT	NT	NT	GC	TW	TW
																		◇1					R 1 ☕		
			🚌		🚌					🚌	🚌	🚌	🚌		🚌	🚌					🚌			🚌	🚌
Hexham 48	d			09 59										10 59								11 59			
Metrocentre 48	d			10 30										11 30								12 30			
Newcastle 8 26 ⛴	d			10a40				10 04			10 35			11a40							11 35	12a40			
Heworth ⛴	d		09 48		10 03					10 18	10 45	10 33	10 48		11 03	11 18					11 45			11 33	11 48
Sunderland ⛴	a		10 28		10 43					10 58	11 05	11 13	11 28		11 43	11 58					12 05			12 13	12 28
	d										11 05										12 05		12 12		
Seaham	d					10 09					11a20									11 30	12a20				
Hartlepool	d					10 25														11 46			12 36		
Seaton Carew	d					10 30														11 51					
Billingham	d					10 37														11 58					
Stockton	d					10 44														12 05					
Bishop Auckland	d								10 17																
Shildon	d								10 22																
Newton Aycliffe	d								10 27																
Heighington	d								10 30																
North Road	d								10 39																
Chester-le-Street 26	d																								
Durham 26	d																								
Darlington 7 26	a							10 37	10 43																
	d	09 45						10 39	10 45										11 45						
Dinsdale	d	09 50							10 50										11 50						
Tees-side Airport	d																								
Allens West	d	09 57							10 57										11 57						
Eaglescliffe	a	09 59							10 59										11 59	12 11			12 58		
	d	09 59							10 59										11 59				12 59		
London Kings Cross 15 ⊖26	a																						15 46		
Thornaby	d	10 05				10 49		10 55	11 05									11 30	12 05						
Middlesbrough	a	10 10				10 58		11 03	11 13									11 39	12 10						
	d	10 12							11 14										12 12						
South Bank	d																								
British Steel Redcar §	d																								
Redcar Central	d	10 22							11 23										12 22						
Redcar East	d	10 25							11 26										12 25						
Longbeck	d	10 29							11 30										12 29						
Marske	d	10 30							11 31										12 30						
Saltburn	a	10 37							11 39										12 37						

§ For authorised access only to BSC Redcar

Table 44

Sundays
until 19 June

Newcastle, Sunderland, Bishop Auckland and Darlington - Middlesbrough and Saltburn

Station			TW		NT	TW	NT	TW	TW	NT	NT	TW	TW		TP	NT	NT	NT	GC	TW	TW	TW	TW		TW	NT
			🚌			🚌		🚌	🚌		🚌	🚌	🚌		◇1	🚌			R 1 ⊡	🚌	🚌	🚌	🚌		🚌	
Hexham	48	d								12 59								13 59								
Metrocentre	48	d								13 30								14 30								
Newcastle 8	26 ⛴	d								13a40	13 05					13 35		14a40								
Heworth	⛴	d	12 03			12 18		12 33	12 48		13 15	13 03	13 18			13 45				13 33	13 48	14 03	14 18		14 33	
Sunderland	⛴	a	12 43			12 58		13 13	13 28		13 35	13 43	13 58			14 05				14 13	14 28	14 43	14 58		15 13	
		d														14 05			14 12							
Seaham		d					12 29									14a20										
Hartlepool		d					12 45												14 36							
Seaton Carew		d					12 50																			
Billingham		d					12 57																			
Stockton		d					13 04																			
Bishop Auckland		d			12 17																					
Shildon		d			12 22																					
Newton Aycliffe		d			12 27																					
Heighington		d			12 30																					
North Road		d			12 39																					
Chester-le-Street	26	d																								
Durham	26	d																								
Darlington 7	26	a			12 44																					
		d			12 46												13 45									14 45
Dinsdale		d			12 51												13 50									14 50
Tees-side Airport		d																								
Allens West		d			12 58												13 57									14 57
Eaglescliffe		a			13 00												13 59		14 58							14 59
		d			13 00												13 59		14 59							14 59
London Kings Cross 15	⊖26	a																	17 46							
Thornaby		d			13 06		13 10								13 30		14 05									15 05
Middlesbrough		a			13 11		13 20								13 40		14 11									15 11
		d			13 13												14 12									15 12
South Bank		d																								
British Steel Redcar §		d																								
Redcar Central		d			13 23												14 22									15 22
Redcar East		d			13 26												14 25									15 25
Longbeck		d			13 30												14 29									15 29
Marske		d			13 31												14 30									15 30
Saltburn		a			13 38												14 37									15 37

Station			NT	TW	NT	NT	NT	TW	TW		NT	TW	TP	NT	TW	NT	TW	TW	NT		NT	NT	TW	TW	NT	TW
				🚌			🚌	🚌	🚌		🚌	🚌	◇1		🚌		🚌	🚌				🚌	🚌	🚌		🚌
Hexham	48	d			14 59											15 59									16 59	
Metrocentre	48	d			15 30											16 30									17 30	
Newcastle 8	26 ⛴	d			15a40		15 05				15 35					16a40						16 35			17a40	
Heworth	⛴	d		14 48			15 15	15 03	15 18		15 45	15 33			15 48		16 03	16 18				16 45	16 33	16 48		17 03
Sunderland	⛴	a		15 28			15 35	15 43	15 58		16 05	16 13			16 28		16 43	16 58				17 05	17 13	17 28		17 43
		d									16 05											17 05				
Seaham		d	14 29								16a20										16 29	17a20				
Hartlepool		d	14 45																		16 45					
Seaton Carew		d	14 50																		16 50					
Billingham		d	14 57																		16 57					
Stockton		d	15 04																		17 04					
Bishop Auckland		d												15 17												
Shildon		d												15 22												
Newton Aycliffe		d												15 27												
Heighington		d												15 30												
North Road		d												15 39												
Chester-le-Street	26	d																								
Durham	26	d																								
Darlington 7	26	a												15 43												
		d				15 01								15 45					16 45							
Dinsdale		d												15 50					16 50							
Tees-side Airport		d																								
Allens West		d												15 57					16 57							
Eaglescliffe		a												15 59					16 59							
		d												15 59					16 59							
London Kings Cross 15	⊖26	a																								
Thornaby		d	15 11			15 17							15 43	16 05					17 05		17 09					
Middlesbrough		a	15 20			15 23							15 52	16 10					17 11		17 18					
		d												16 12					17 12							
South Bank		d																								
British Steel Redcar §		d																								
Redcar Central		d												16 22					17 22							
Redcar East		d												16 25					17 25							
Longbeck		d												16 29					17 29							
Marske		d												16 30					17 30							
Saltburn		a												16 37					17 37							

§ For authorised access only to BSC Redcar

Table 44

Sundays
until 19 June

Newcastle, Sunderland, Bishop Auckland and Darlington - Middlesbrough and Saltburn

			TW	TP	NT		NT	NT	GC	TW	NT	TW	TW	TW	TW		NT	NT	NT	TW	NT	NT	TW	TW	TP	
			🚌	◇1					R 1 ⊡	🚌	🚌	🚌	🚌	🚌	🚌					🚌		🚌	🚌	🚌	◇1	
Hexham	48	d						17 59													18 59					
Metrocentre	48	d						18 30													19 30					
Newcastle 8	26	d						18a40			17 45										19a40	19 05				
Heworth		d	17 18							17 33	17 55	17 48	18 03	18 18	18 33					18 48		19 15	19 03	19 18		
Sunderland		a	17 58							18 13	18 15	18 28	18 43	18 58	19 13					19 28		19 35	19 43	19 58		
		d							18 12		18 15															
Seaham		d					17 30				18a30								18 42							
Hartlepool		d					17 46		18 36										18 58							
Seaton Carew		d					17 51												19 03							
Billingham		d					17 58												19 10							
Stockton		d					18 05												19 17							
Bishop Auckland		d			17 16													18 24								
Shildon		d			17 21													18 29								
Newton Aycliffe		d			17 26													18 34								
Heighington		d			17 29													18 37								
North Road		d			17 38													18 46								
Chester-le-Street	26	d																								
Durham	26	d																								
Darlington 7	26	a			17 42													18 52								
		d			17 45												18 45									
Dinsdale		d			17 50												18 50									
Tees-side Airport		d																								
Allens West		d			17 57												18 57									
Eaglescliffe		a			17 59		18 11		18 58								18 59									
		d			17 59				18 59								18 59									
London Kings Cross 15 ⊖	26	a							21 48																	
Thornaby		d		17 41	18 05												19 05		19 22						19 30	
Middlesbrough		a		17 50	18 10												19 10		19 31						19 40	
		d			18 12												19 12									
South Bank		d																								
British Steel Redcar §		d																								
Redcar Central		d			18 22												19 22									
Redcar East		d			18 25												19 25									
Longbeck		d			18 29												19 29									
Marske		d			18 30												19 30									
Saltburn		a			18 37												19 37									

			TW	NT	NT	TW	TW	NT	TW	TW	TW		TP	NT	NT	NT	TW	NT	TW	TW	TW		TW	TW	TW	NT
			🚌		🚌	🚌	🚌		🚌	🚌	🚌		◇1				🚌		🚌	🚌	🚌		🚌	🚌	🚌	
Hexham	48	d														21 01										
Metrocentre	48	d														21 31										
Newcastle 8	26	d			19 50									20 11		21a43		21 06								
Heworth		d	19 33		20 00	19 48	20 03		20 18	20 33	20 48						21 03		21 18	21 33	21 48		22 03	22 18	22 33	
Sunderland		a	20 13		20 20	20 28	20 43		20 58	21 13	21 28						21 43		21 58	22 13	22 28		22 43	22 58	23 13	
		d			20 20																					
Seaham		d			20a35										20 45											
Hartlepool		d													21 01											
Seaton Carew		d													21 06											
Billingham		d													21 13											
Stockton		d													21 20											
Bishop Auckland		d						20 04																		
Shildon		d						20 09																		
Newton Aycliffe		d						20 14																		
Heighington		d						20 17																		
North Road		d						20 26																		
Chester-le-Street	26	d																21 15								
Durham	26	d																21 24								
Darlington 7	26	a						20 30										21 44								
		d		19 45				20 32										21 45								22 45
Dinsdale		d		19 50				20 37										21 51								
Tees-side Airport		d																								
Allens West		d		19 57				20 44										21 58								
Eaglescliffe		a		19 59				20 45										22 00								22 56
		d		19 59				20 45										22 00								22 56
London Kings Cross 15 ⊖	26	a																								
Thornaby		d		20 05				20 52					20 58	21 04	21 24			22 05								23 02
Middlesbrough		a		20 10				20 57					21 08	21 16	21 34			22 10								23 10
		d		20 12				20 58										22 11								
South Bank		d																								
British Steel Redcar §		d																								
Redcar Central		d		20 22				21 08										22 21								
Redcar East		d		20 25				21 11										22 24								
Longbeck		d		20 29				21 15										22 28								
Marske		d		20 30				21 16										22 29								
Saltburn		a		20 37				21 25										22 37								

§ For authorised access only to BSC Redcar

Table 44

Sundays
until 19 June

Newcastle, Sunderland, Bishop Auckland and Darlington - Middlesbrough and Saltburn

			TW	TW	TW	TW
			🚌	🚌	🚌	🚌
Hexham	48	d				
Metrocentre	48	d				
Newcastle 8	26 ⛴	d				
Heworth	⛴	d	22 48	23 03	23 18	23 33
Sunderland	⛴	a	23 28	23 43	23 58	00 13
		d				
Seaham		d				
Hartlepool		d				
Seaton Carew		d				
Billingham		d				
Stockton		d				
Bishop Auckland		d				
Shildon		d				
Newton Aycliffe		d				
Heighington		d				
North Road		d				
Chester-le-Street	26	d				
Durham	26	d				
Darlington 7	26	a				
		d				
Dinsdale		d				
Tees-side Airport		d				
Allens West		d				
Eaglescliffe		a				
		d				
London Kings Cross 15	⊖26	a				
Thornaby		d				
Middlesbrough		a				
		d				
South Bank		d				
British Steel Redcar §		d				
Redcar Central		d				
Redcar East		d				
Longbeck		d				
Marske		d				
Saltburn		a				

Sundays
26 June to 11 September

			NT	NT	TP	NT	GC	NT	NT	NT	NT		NT	TP	NT	NT	NT	GC	NT	NT	NT		NT	NT	TP	NT
					◇1		R 1 🍴							◇1				R 1 🍴							◇1	
Hexham	48	d									09 59						10 59				11 59			12 59		
Metrocentre	48	d									10 30					10 48	11 30			11 48	12 30		12 48	13 30		
Newcastle 8	26 ⛴	d						09 00		09 45	10a40					11 00	11a40			12 00	12a40		13 00	13a40		
Heworth	⛴	d						09 07		09 52						11 06				12 06			13 06			
Sunderland	⛴	a						09 22		10 05						11 22				12 21			13 22			
		d					09 12			10 06						11 22		12 12		12 21						
Seaham		d								10 14						11 30				12 29						
Hartlepool		d					09 36			10 31						11 46		12 36		12 45						
Seaton Carew		d								10 35						11 51				12 50						
Billingham		d								10 42						11 58				12 57						
Stockton		d								10 49						12 05				13 04						
Bishop Auckland		d				08 39							10 17						12 17							
Shildon		d				08 44							10 22						12 22							
Newton Aycliffe		d				08 49							10 27						12 27							
Heighington		d				08 53							10 30						12 30							
North Road		d				09 01							10 39						12 39							
Chester-le-Street	26	d																								
Durham	26	d																								
Darlington 7	26	a				09 09							10 43						12 44							
		d	08 17	08 45	09 00	09 11			09 45				10 45		11 45				12 46							13 45
Dinsdale		d	08 23	08 50		09 16			09 50				10 50		11 50				12 51							13 50
Tees-side Airport		d																								
Allens West		d	08 30	08 57		09 23			09 57				10 57		11 57				12 58							13 57
Eaglescliffe		a	08 32	08 59		09 25	09 58		09 59				10 59		11 59	12 11		12 58	13 00							13 59
		d	08 32	08 59		09 25	09 59		09 59				10 59		11 59			12 59	13 00							13 59
London Kings Cross 15	⊖26	a					12 44											15 46								
Thornaby		d	08 38	09 05	09 17	09 31			10 05	10 55			11 05	11 30	12 05				13 06	13 10					13 30	14 05
Middlesbrough		a	08 44	09 10	09 27	09 40			10 10	11 04			11 13	11 39	12 10				13 11	13 20					13 40	14 11
		d		09 12					10 12				11 14		12 12				13 13							14 12
South Bank		d																								
British Steel Redcar §		d																								
Redcar Central		d		09 22					10 22				11 23		12 22				13 23							14 22
Redcar East		d		09 25					10 25				11 26		12 25				13 26							14 25
Longbeck		d		09 29					10 29				11 30		12 29				13 30							14 29
Marske		d		09 30					10 30				11 31		12 30				13 31							14 30
Saltburn		a		09 37					10 37				11 39		12 37				13 38							14 37

§ For authorised access only to BSC Redcar

Table 44

Sundays

26 June to 11 September

Newcastle, Sunderland, Bishop Auckland and Darlington - Middlesbrough and Saltburn

	GC R 1 ☕	NT	NT	NT	NT		NT	NT	TP ◇1	NT	NT	NT	NT	TP ◇1	NT		NT	NT	GC R 1 ☕	NT	NT	NT	NT	NT
Hexham 48 d				13 59			14 59						15 59					16 59				17 59		
Metrocentre 48 d			13 48	14 30	14 48		15 30					15 48	16 30				16 48	17 30			17 48	18 30		18 48
Newcastle 8 26 ⛴ d			14 00	14a40	15 00		15a40					16 00	16a40				17 00	17a40			18 00	18a40		19 00
Heworth ⛴ d			14 06		15 06							16 06					17 06				18 07			19 06
Sunderland ⛴ a			14 21		15 22							16 21					17 22				18 21			19 22
d	14 12		14 21									16 21					17 22		18 12		18 21			
Seaham d			14 29									16 29					17 30				18 29			
Hartlepool d	14 36		14 45									16 45					17 46		18 36		18 45			
Seaton Carew d			14 50									16 50					17 51				18 50			
Billingham d			14 57									16 57					17 58				18 57			
Stockton d			15 04									17 04					18 05				19 04			
Bishop Auckland d										15 17					17 16								18 24	
Shildon d										15 22					17 21								18 29	
Newton Aycliffe d										15 27					17 26								18 34	
Heighington d										15 30					17 29								18 37	
North Road d										15 39					17 38								18 46	
Chester-le-Street 26 d																								
Durham 26 d																								
Darlington 7 26 a										15 43					17 42								18 52	
d		14 45						15 01		15 45	16 45				17 45					18 45				
Dinsdale d		14 50								15 50	16 50				17 50					18 50				
Tees-side Airport d																								
Allens West d		14 57								15 57	16 57				17 57					18 57				
Eaglescliffe a	14 58	14 59								15 59	16 59				17 59		18 12		18 58	18 59				
d	14 59	14 59								15 59	16 59				17 59				18 59	18 59				
London Kings Cross 15 ⊖26 a	17 46																		21 48					
Thornaby d		15 05	15 10					15 17	15 43	16 05	17 05	17 09		17 41	18 05					19 05	19 09			
Middlesbrough a		15 11	15 18					15 23	15 52	16 10	17 11	17 18		17 50	18 10					19 10	19 18			
d		15 12								16 12	17 12				18 12					19 12				
South Bank d																								
British Steel Redcar § d																								
Redcar Central d		15 22								16 22	17 22				18 22					19 22				
Redcar East d		15 25								16 25	17 25				18 25					19 25				
Longbeck d		15 29								16 29	17 29				18 29					19 29				
Marske d		15 30								16 30	17 30				18 30					19 30				
Saltburn a		15 37								16 37	17 37				18 37					19 37				

	NT		TP ◇1	NT	NT	TP ◇1	NT	NT	NT	NT
Hexham 48 d	18 59							21 01		
Metrocentre 48 d	19 30							21 31		
Newcastle 8 26 ⛴ d	19a40						20 00	21a43	21 06	
Heworth ⛴ d							20 07			
Sunderland ⛴ a							20 21			
d							20 21			
Seaham d							20 29			
Hartlepool d							20 45			
Seaton Carew d							20 50			
Billingham d							20 57			
Stockton d							21 04			
Bishop Auckland d					20 04					
Shildon d					20 09					
Newton Aycliffe d					20 14					
Heighington d					20 17					
North Road d					20 26					
Chester-le-Street 26 d									21 15	
Durham 26 d									21 24	
Darlington 7 26 a					20 30				21 44	
d				19 45	20 32				21 45	22 45
Dinsdale d				19 50	20 37				21 51	
Tees-side Airport d										
Allens West d				19 57	20 44				21 58	
Eaglescliffe a				19 59	20 45				22 00	22 56
d				19 59	20 45				22 00	22 56
London Kings Cross 15 ⊖26 a										
Thornaby d			19 30	20 05	20 52	20 58	21 08		22 05	23 02
Middlesbrough a			19 40	20 10	20 57	21 08	21 20		22 10	23 10
d				20 12	20 58				22 11	
South Bank d										
British Steel Redcar § d										
Redcar Central d				20 22	21 08				22 21	
Redcar East d				20 25	21 11				22 24	
Longbeck d				20 29	21 15				22 28	
Marske d				20 30	21 16				22 29	
Saltburn a				20 37	21 25				22 37	

§ For authorised access only to BSC Redcar

Table 44

Sundays

18 September to 2 October

Newcastle, Sunderland, Bishop Auckland and Darlington - Middlesbrough and Saltburn

	NT	TP	GC	NT	NT	NT	NT	NT	TP		NT	NT	NT	GC	NT	NT	NT	NT	NT		TP	NT	GC	NT
		◇1	R 1 ☕						◇1					R 1 ☕							◇1		R 1 ☕	
Hexham 48 d							09 59						10 59				11 59		12 59					
Metrocentre 48 d							10 30					10 48	11 30			11 48	12 30	12 48	13 30					
Newcastle 8 26 ⇌ d				09 00		09 45	10a40					11 00	11a40			12 00	12a40	13 00	13a40					
Heworth ⇌ d				09 07		09 52						11 06				12 06		13 06						
Sunderland ⇌ a				09 22		10 05						11 22				12 21		13 22						
d			09 12			10 06						11 22		12 12		12 21							14 12	
Seaham d						10 14						11 30				12 29								
Hartlepool d			09 36			10 31						11 46		12 36		12 45							14 36	
Seaton Carew d						10 35						11 51				12 50								
Billingham d						10 42						11 58				12 57								
Stockton d						10 49						12 05				13 04								
Bishop Auckland d								10 17							12 17									
Shildon d								10 22							12 22									
Newton Aycliffe d								10 27							12 27									
Heighington d								10 30							12 30									
North Road d								10 39							12 39									
Chester-le-Street 26 d																								
Durham 26 d																								
Darlington 7 26 a								10 43							12 44									
d	08 45	09 00			09 45			10 45			11 45				12 46							13 45		14 45
Dinsdale d	08 50				09 50			10 50			11 50				12 51							13 50		14 50
Tees-side Airport d																								
Allens West d	08 57				09 57			10 57			11 57				12 58							13 57		14 57
Eaglescliffe a	08 59		09 58		09 59			10 59			11 59	12 11		12 58	13 00							13 59	14 58	14 59
d	08 59		09 59		09 59			10 59			11 59			12 59	13 00							13 59	14 59	14 59
London Kings Cross 15 ⊖26 a			12 44											15 46									17 46	
Thornaby d	09 05	09 17			10 05	10 55		11 05	11 30		12 05				13 06	13 10					13 30	14 05		15 05
Middlesbrough a	09 10	09 27			10 10	11 05		11 13	11 40		12 10				13 11	13 20					13 40	14 11		15 11
d	09 12				10 12			11 14			12 12				13 13							14 12		15 12
South Bank d																								
British Steel Redcar § d																								
Redcar Central d	09 22				10 22			11 23			12 22				13 23							14 22		15 22
Redcar East d	09 25				10 25			11 26			12 25				13 26							14 25		15 25
Longbeck d	09 29				10 29			11 30			12 29				13 30							14 29		15 29
Marske d	09 30				10 30			11 31			12 30				13 31							14 30		15 30
Saltburn a	09 37				10 37			11 39			12 37				13 38							14 37		15 37

	NT	NT	NT	NT	NT		TP	NT	NT	NT	NT	TP	NT	NT	NT		GC	NT	NT	NT	NT	NT	TP	NT
							◇1					◇1					R 1 ☕						◇1	
Hexham 48 d		13 59		14 59							15 59				16 59					17 59		18 59		
Metrocentre 48 d	13 48	14 30	14 48	15 30						15 48	16 30			16 48	17 30				17 48	18 30	18 48	19 30		
Newcastle 8 26 ⇌ d	14 00	14a40	15 00	15a40						16 00	16a40			17 00	17a40				18 00	18a40	19 00	19a40		
Heworth ⇌ d	14 06		15 06							16 06				17 06					18 07		19 06			
Sunderland ⇌ a	14 21		15 22							16 21				17 22					18 21		19 22			
d	14 21									16 21				17 22			18 12		18 21					
Seaham d	14 29									16 29				17 30					18 29					
Hartlepool d	14 45									16 45				17 46			18 36		18 45					
Seaton Carew d	14 50									16 50				17 51					18 50					
Billingham d	14 57									16 57				17 58					18 57					
Stockton d	15 04									17 04				18 05					19 04					
Bishop Auckland d								15 17					17 16											19 17
Shildon d								15 22					17 21											19 22
Newton Aycliffe d								15 27					17 26											19 27
Heighington d								15 30					17 29											19 30
North Road d								15 39					17 38											19 39
Chester-le-Street 26 d																								
Durham 26 d																								
Darlington 7 26 a								15 43					17 42											19 43
d					15 01			15 45	16 45				17 45					18 45						19 45
Dinsdale d								15 50	16 50				17 50					18 50						19 50
Tees-side Airport d																								
Allens West d								15 57	16 57				17 57					18 57						19 57
Eaglescliffe a								15 59	16 59				17 59	18 11			18 58	18 59						19 59
d								15 59	16 59				17 59				18 59	18 59						19 59
London Kings Cross 15 ⊖26 a																	21 48							
Thornaby d	15 10				15 17		15 43	16 05	17 05	17 09		17 41	18 05					19 05	19 09				19 30	20 05
Middlesbrough a	15 18				15 23		15 52	16 10	17 11	17 18		17 50	18 10					19 10	19 18				19 40	20 10
d								16 12	17 12				18 12					19 12						20 12
South Bank d																								
British Steel Redcar § d																								
Redcar Central d								16 22	17 22				18 22					19 22						20 22
Redcar East d								16 25	17 25				18 25					19 25						20 25
Longbeck d								16 29	17 29				18 29					19 29						20 29
Marske d								16 30	17 30				18 30					19 30						20 30
Saltburn a								16 37	17 37				18 37					19 37						20 37

§ For authorised access only to BSC Redcar

Table 44

Sundays
18 September to 2 October

Newcastle, Sunderland, Bishop Auckland and Darlington - Middlesbrough and Saltburn

	NT		TP ◇1	NT	NT	NT	NT
Hexham 48 d					21 01		
Metrocentre 48 d					21 31		
Newcastle [8] 26 ⛴ d				20 00	21a43	21 06	
Heworth ⛴ d				20 07			
Sunderland ⛴ a				20 21			
d				20 21			
Seaham d				20 29			
Hartlepool d				20 45			
Seaton Carew d				20 50			
Billingham d				20 57			
Stockton d				21 04			
Bishop Auckland d							
Shildon d							
Newton Aycliffe d							
Heighington d							
North Road d							
Chester-le-Street 26 d						21 15	
Durham 26 d						21 24	
Darlington [7] 26 a						21 44	
d	20 32					21 45	22 45
Dinsdale d	20 37					21 51	
Tees-side Airport d							
Allens West d	20 44					21 58	
Eaglescliffe a	20 46					22 00	22 56
d	20 46					22 00	22 56
London Kings Cross 15 ⊖26 a							
Thornaby d	20 52		20 58	21 08		22 05	23 02
Middlesbrough a	20 57		21 08	21 20		22 10	23 10
d	20 58					22 11	
South Bank d							
British Steel Redcar § d							
Redcar Central d	21 08					22 21	
Redcar East d	21 11					22 24	
Longbeck d	21 15					22 28	
Marske d	21 16					22 29	
Saltburn a	21 24					22 37	

Sundays
from 9 October

	NT	TP ◇1	GC R 1 (buffet)	NT	NT	NT	NT	NT	TP ◇1 A		TP ◇1 B	NT	NT	NT	GC R 1 (buffet)	NT	NT	NT	NT		NT	TP ◇1	NT	GC R 1 (buffet)
Hexham 48 d							09 59							10 59				11 55			12 59			
Metrocentre 48 d							10 33						10 48	11 33			11 48	12 30	12 48		13 33			
Newcastle [8] 26 ⛴ d				09 00		09 45	10a43						11 00	11a43			12 00	12a40	13 00		13a43			
Heworth ⛴ d				09 07		09 52							11 06				12 06		13 06					
Sunderland ⛴ a				09 22		10 05							11 22				12 21		13 22					
d			09 12			10 06							11 22		12 12		12 21							14 12
Seaham d						10 14							11 30				12 29							
Hartlepool d			09 36			10 31							11 46		12 36		12 45							14 36
Seaton Carew d						10 35							11 51				12 50							
Billingham d						10 42							11 58				12 57							
Stockton d						10 49							12 05				13 04							
Bishop Auckland d								10 17								12 17								
Shildon d								10 22								12 22								
Newton Aycliffe d								10 27								12 27								
Heighington d								10 30								12 30								
North Road d								10 39								12 39								
Chester-le-Street 26 d																								
Durham 26 d																								
Darlington [7] 26 a								10 43								12 44								
d	08 45	09 00			09 45			10 45				11 45				12 46							13 45	
Dinsdale d	08 50				09 50			10 50				11 50				12 51							13 50	
Tees-side Airport d																								
Allens West d	08 57				09 57			10 57				11 57				12 58							13 57	
Eaglescliffe a	08 59		09 58		09 59			10 59				11 59	12 11		12 58	13 00							13 59	14 58
d	08 59		09 59		09 59			10 59				11 59			12 59	13 00							13 59	14 59
London Kings Cross 15 ⊖26 a			12 44												15 46									17 46
Thornaby d	09 05	09 17			10 05	10 55		11 05	11 30		11 30	12 05				13 06	13 10					13 30	14 05	
Middlesbrough a	09 10	09 27			10 10	11 05		11 13	11 39		11 40	12 10				13 11	13 20					13 40	14 11	
d	09 12				10 12			11 14				12 12				13 13							14 12	
South Bank d																								
British Steel Redcar § d																								
Redcar Central d	09 22				10 22			11 23				12 22				13 23							14 22	
Redcar East d	09 25				10 25			11 26				12 25				13 26							14 25	
Longbeck d	09 29				10 29			11 30				12 29				13 30							14 29	
Marske d	09 30				10 30			11 31				12 30				13 31							14 30	
Saltburn a	09 37				10 37			11 39				12 37				13 38							14 37	

§ For authorised access only to BSC Redcar
A from 30 October
B 9 October, 16 October, 23 October

Table 44

Sundays
from 9 October

Newcastle, Sunderland, Bishop Auckland and Darlington - Middlesbrough and Saltburn

Station		NT	NT	NT	NT	NT		TP	NT	NT	NT	NT	TP	NT	NT	NT		GC	NT	NT	NT	NT	NT	TP	NT
								◇1					◇1					R 1 ☕						◇1	
Hexham	48 d			13 56		14 56						15 59				16 58					17 57		18 55		
Metrocentre	48 d		13 48	14 30	14 48	15 30					15 48	16 33			16 48	17 33				17 48	18 32	18 48	19 29		
Newcastle 8	26 ⛴ d		14 00	14a40	15 00	15a40					16 00	16a43			17 00	17a43				18 00	18a42	19 00	19a39		
Heworth	⛴ d		14 06		15 06						16 06				17 06					18 07		19 06			
Sunderland	⛴ a		14 21		15 22						16 21				17 22					18 21		19 22			
	d		14 21								16 21				17 22			18 12		18 21					
Seaham	d		14 29								16 29				17 30					18 29					
Hartlepool	d		14 45								16 45				17 46			18 36		18 45					
Seaton Carew	d		14 50								16 50				17 51					18 50					
Billingham	d		14 57								16 57				17 58					18 57					
Stockton	d		15 04								17 04				18 05					19 04					
Bishop Auckland	d								15 17					17 16											19 17
Shildon	d								15 22					17 21											19 22
Newton Aycliffe	d								15 27					17 26											19 27
Heighington	d								15 30					17 29											19 30
North Road	d								15 39					17 38											19 39
Chester-le-Street	26 d																								
Durham	26 d																								
Darlington 7	26 a								15 43					17 42											19 43
	d	14 45							15 45	16 45				17 45					18 45						19 45
Dinsdale	d	14 50							15 50	16 50				17 50					18 50						19 50
Tees-side Airport	d																								
Allens West	d	14 57							15 57	16 57				17 57					18 57						19 57
Eaglescliffe	a	14 59							15 59	16 59				17 59	18 11			18 58	18 59						19 59
	d	14 59							15 59	16 59				17 59				18 59	18 59						19 59
London Kings Cross 15	⊖26 a																	21 48							
Thornaby	d	15 05	15 10					15 43	16 05	17 05	17 09		17 41	18 05					19 05	19 09				19 30	20 05
Middlesbrough	a	15 11	15 18					15 52	16 10	17 11	17 18		17 50	18 10					19 10	19 18				19 40	20 10
	d	15 12							16 12	17 12				18 12					19 12						20 12
South Bank	d																								
British Steel Redcar §	d																								
Redcar Central	d	15 22							16 22	17 22				18 22					19 22						20 22
Redcar East	d	15 25							16 25	17 25				18 25					19 25						20 25
Longbeck	d	15 29							16 29	17 29				18 29					19 29						20 29
Marske	d	15 30							16 30	17 30				18 30					19 30						20 30
Saltburn	a	15 37							16 37	17 37				18 37					19 37						20 37

Station		NT		TP	NT	NT	NT	NT
				◇1				
Hexham	48 d					21 01		
Metrocentre	48 d					21 34		
Newcastle 8	26 ⛴ d				20 00	21a46	21 06	
Heworth	⛴ d				20 07			
Sunderland	⛴ a				20 21			
	d				20 21			
Seaham	d				20 29			
Hartlepool	d				20 45			
Seaton Carew	d				20 50			
Billingham	d				20 57			
Stockton	d				21 04			
Bishop Auckland	d							
Shildon	d							
Newton Aycliffe	d							
Heighington	d							
North Road	d							
Chester-le-Street	26 d						21 15	
Durham	26 d						21 24	
Darlington 7	26 a						21 44	
	d	20 32					21 45	22 45
Dinsdale	d	20 37					21 51	
Tees-side Airport	d							
Allens West	d	20 44					21 58	
Eaglescliffe	a	20 46					22 00	22 56
	d	20 46					22 00	22 56
London Kings Cross 15	⊖26 a							
Thornaby	d	20 52		20 58	21 08		22 05	23 02
Middlesbrough	a	20 57		21 08	21 20		22 10	23 10
	d	20 58					22 11	
South Bank	d							
British Steel Redcar §	d							
Redcar Central	d	21 08					22 21	
Redcar East	d	21 11					22 24	
Longbeck	d	21 15					22 28	
Marske	d	21 16					22 29	
Saltburn	a	21 24					22 37	

§ For authorised access only to BSC Redcar

Saltburn and Middlesbrough - Darlington, Bishop Auckland, Sunderland and Newcastle

Miles	Miles			TW	NT	TP	NT	NT	NT	NT	TP	NT		NT	NT	NT	NT	NT	NT	TP	NT	NT		TP	NT
				A 🚌		◇1 🛒					◇1 🛒									◇1 🛒				◇1 🛒	
0	—	**Saltburn**	d						06 22						07 12	07 27	07 54				08 31				09 31
2	—	Marske	d						06 26						07 16	07 31	07 58				08 35				09 35
2½	—	Longbeck	d						06 29						07 19	07 34	08 01				08 38				09 38
4	—	Redcar East	d						06 32						07 22	07 37	08 04				08 41				09 41
5	—	**Redcar Central**	d						06 35						07 25	07 40	08 07				08 44				09 44
6¾	—	British Steel Redcar §	d																						
10	—	South Bank	d																		08 51				
12½	0	**Middlesbrough**	a						06 45						07 36	07 50	08 19				08 56				09 55
—	—		d		05 45	05 55			06 47	06 51	07 12	07 32			07 37	07 52	08 20	08 32	08 44	08 50	09 08	09 32		09 50	09 56
15¾	3¼	Thornaby	d		05 50	06a00			06 52	06 56	07a17	07 37			07 42	07 57	08 25	08 37	08 50	08a55	09 13	09 37		09a55	10 01
—	—	London Kings Cross 15 ⊖26	d																						
18¾	—	Eaglescliffe	a		05 55				06 57						07 47	08 02	08 30		08 55		09 18				10 06
—	—		d		05 55				06 57						07 47	08 03	08 31		08 55		09 18				10 07
19½	—	Allens West	d		05 58				07 00						07 50	08 05	08 33		08 58		09 21				10 09
22	—	Tees-side Airport	d																						
23¾	—	Dinsdale	d		06 04				07 06						07 56	08 12	08 40		09 04		09 27				
27½	—	**Darlington 7** 26	a		06 14				07 19						08 07	08 22	08 50		09 14		09 39				10 23
—	—		d		06 14		06 47		07 20					07 48		08 22	08 52								
28¾	—	North Road	d				06 50							07 51			08 55								
33¼	—	Heighington	d				06 58							07 59			09 03								
34½	—	Newton Aycliffe	d				07 02							08 03			09 07								
36¾	—	Shildon	d				07 06							08 07			09 11								
39½	—	**Bishop Auckland**	a				07 14							08 15			09 18								
—	5½	Stockton	d							07 02		07 43						08 43				09 43			
—	10	Billingham	d							07 09		07 50						08 50				09 50			
—	15	Seaton Carew	d							07 15		07 56						08 56				09 56			
—	17¼	**Hartlepool**	d					07 03		07 21		08 02						09 01				10 02			
—	30	Seaham	d					07 18		07 36		08 17						09 15				10 17			
—	35¼	**Sunderland** 🚇	a					07 28		07 50		08 28						09 27				10 28			
—	—		d	00§10				07 30		07 55		08 30						09 30				10 30			
—	44½	Heworth 🚇	d	00a50				07 41		08 07		08 42						09 42				10 42			
—	47¼	**Newcastle 8** 26 🚇	a		06 55			07 51	08 05	08 18		08 52				09 06		09 51				10 51			
—	—	Metrocentre 48	a					08 00										10 02				11 01			
—	—	Hexham 48	a					08 38										10 36				11 36			

		NT	NT	GC	TP	NT	NT	NT		TP	NT	NT	NT	TP	NT	NT	NT	GC		TP	NT	NT	NT	TP FO	TP FX
				R 1 🍽	◇1 🛒					◇1 🛒				◇1 🛒				R 1 🍽		◇1 🛒				◇1	◇1 🛒
Saltburn	d	09 58				10 31	10 58				11 31	11 57			12 30	12 58					13 31	13 57			
Marske	d	10 02				10 35	11 02				11 35	12 01			12 34	13 02					13 35	14 02			
Longbeck	d	10 05				10 38	11 05				11 38	12 04			12 37	13 05					13 38	14 05			
Redcar East	d	10 08				10 41	11 08				11 41	12 07			12 40	13 08					13 41	14 08			
Redcar Central	d	10 11				10 44	11 11				11 45	12 10			12 43	13 11					13 44	14 11			
British Steel Redcar §	d																								
South Bank	d																								
Middlesbrough	a	10 22				10 54	11 21				11 55	12 21			12 54	13 21					13 54	14 21			
	d	10 22	10 32		10 50	10 55	11 22	11 31		11 50	11 56	12 22	12 32	12 50	12 55	13 22	13 32			13 50	13 55	14 22	14 32	14 50	14 50
Thornaby	d	10 27	10 37		10a55	11 00	11 27	11 36		11a55	12 01	12 27	12 37	12a55	13 00	13 27	13 37			13a55	14 00	14 27	14 37	14a55	14a55
London Kings Cross 15 ⊖26	d			07 49														11 23							
Eaglescliffe	a	10 32		10 47		11 05	11 32				12 06	12 32			13 05	13 32		14 03			14 05	14 32			
	d	10 33		10 48		11 06	11 33				12 06	12 33			13 06	13 33		14 04			14 06	14 33			
Allens West	d	10 35				11 08	11 35				12 09	12 35			13 08	13 35					14 08	14 35			
Tees-side Airport	d																								
Dinsdale	d	10 42					11 42					12 42				13 42						14 42			
Darlington 7 26	a	10 52				11 23	11 52				12 24	12 54			13 23	13 52					14 23	14 52			
	d	10 54										12 54										14 54			
North Road	d	10 57										12 57										14 57			
Heighington	d	11 05										13 05										15 05			
Newton Aycliffe	d	11 08										13 08										15 08			
Shildon	d	11 13										13 13										15 13			
Bishop Auckland	a	11 20										13 20										15 20			
Stockton	d		10 43					11 42					12 42				13 43						14 43		
Billingham	d		10 50					11 50					12 50				13 50						14 50		
Seaton Carew	d		10 56					11 56					12 56				13 56						14 56		
Hartlepool	d		11 02	11 14				12 02					13 02				14 02	14 23					15 02		
Seaham	d		11 17					12 17					13 17				14 17						15 17		
Sunderland 🚇	a		11 27	11 40				12 27					13 28				14 27	14 50					15 27		
	d		11 30					12 30					13 30				14 30						15 30		
Heworth 🚇	d		11 42					12 42					13 42				14 42						15 42		
Newcastle 8 26 🚇	a		11 51					12 52					13 51				14 51						15 51		
Metrocentre 48	a		12 01					13 01					14 01				15 02						16 01		
Hexham 48	a		12 36					13 36					14 36				15 37						16 36		

§ For authorised access only to BSC Redcar

A MO until 20 June

Table 44

Mondays to Fridays

until 30 September

Saltburn and Middlesbrough - Darlington, Bishop Auckland, Sunderland and Newcastle

		NT	NT	NT		TP	NT	NT	NT	TP	NT	NT	NT	TP
						◇1				◇1				◇1
Saltburn	d	14 31	14 58				15 31	15 58			16 27	16 58		
Marske	d	14 35	15 02				15 35	16 02			16 31	17 02		
Longbeck	d	14 38	15 05				15 38	16 05			16 34	17 05		
Redcar East	d	14 41	15 08				15 41	16 08			16 37	17 08		
Redcar Central	d	14 44	15 11				15 44	16 11			16 40	17 11		
British Steel Redcar §	d										16 43			
South Bank	d										16 49	17 18		
Middlesbrough	a	14 54	15 21				15 54	16 21			16 54	17 23		
	d	14 55	15 22	15 32		15 50	15 55	16 22	16 32	16 50	16 55	17 24	17 32	17 50
Thornaby	d	15 00	15 27	15 37		15a55	16 00	16 28	16 37	16a55	17 00	17 29	17 37	17a55
London Kings Cross 15 ⊖26	d													
Eaglescliffe	a	15 05	15 32				16 05	16 35			17 05	17 34		
	d	15 06	15 33				16 06	16 35			17 06	17 35		
Allens West	d	15 08	15 35				16 08	16 38			17 08	17 37		
Tees-side Airport	d													
Dinsdale	d		15 42				16 15	16 44			17 15	17 44		
Darlington 7 26	a	15 23	15 54				16 23	16 52			17 24	17 53		
	d		15 54								17 26			
North Road	d		15 57								17 29			
Heighington	d		16 05								17 37			
Newton Aycliffe	d		16 08								17 40			
Shildon	d		16 13								17 45			
Bishop Auckland	a		16 20								17 52			
Stockton	d			15 43					16 44				17 43	
Billingham	d			15 50					16 51				17 50	
Seaton Carew	d			15 56					16 57				17 56	
Hartlepool	d			16 02					17 03				18 02	
Seaham	d			16 17					17 18				18 18	
Sunderland ⛴	a			16 27					17 28				18 28	
	d			16 30					17 30				18 30	
Heworth ⛴	d			16 42					17 42				18 42	
Newcastle 8 26 ⛴	a			16 51					17 51				18 53	
Metrocentre 48	a			17 01					18 01					
Hexham 48	a			17 36					18 32					

			NT	NT	NT	TP	NT	NT	GC	NT	TP	
						◇1			R 1		◇1	
Saltburn	d		17 31	17 58			18 31	18 58				
Marske	d		17 35	18 02			18 35	19 02				
Longbeck	d		17 38	18 05			18 38	19 05				
Redcar East	d		17 41	18 08			18 41	19 08				
Redcar Central	d		17 44	18 11			18 44	19 11				
British Steel Redcar §	d											
South Bank	d											
Middlesbrough	a		17 54	18 21			18 54	19 21				
	d		17 55	18 22	18 32	18 50	18 55	19 22		19 40	19 50	
Thornaby	d		18 00	18 27	18 37	18a55	19 00	19 27		19 45	19 55	
London Kings Cross 15 ⊖26	d								16 48			
Eaglescliffe	a		18 05	18 32			19 05	19 32	19 33			
	d		18 06	18 33			19 06	19 33	19 34			
Allens West	d		18 08	18 35			19 08	19 35				
Tees-side Airport	d											
Dinsdale	d		18 15				19 15					
Darlington 7 26	a		18 23	18 50			19 23	19 52			20 17	
	d			18 54								
North Road	d			18 57								
Heighington	d			19 05								
Newton Aycliffe	d			19 08								
Shildon	d			19 13								
Bishop Auckland	a			19 20								
Stockton	d				18 43					19 51		
Billingham	d				18 50					19 58		
Seaton Carew	d				18 56					20 04		
Hartlepool	d				19 02				19 53	20 10		
Seaham	d				19 17					20 27		
Sunderland ⛴	a				19 27				20 21	20 37		
	d				19 29					20 38		
Heworth ⛴	d				19 42					20 53		
Newcastle 8 26 ⛴	a				19 51					21 04		
Metrocentre 48	a				20 01					21 12		
Hexham 48	a											

		NT	TP	NT	NT	GC	TP	NT	NT	NT FX
			◇1			R 1	◇1			
Saltburn	d	19 31		20 32				21 30	22 36	
Marske	d	19 35		20 36				21 34	22 40	
Longbeck	d	19 38		20 39				21 37	22 43	
Redcar East	d	19 41		20 42				21 40	22 46	
Redcar Central	d	19 44		20 45				21 43	22 49	
British Steel Redcar §	d									
South Bank	d									
Middlesbrough	a	19 54		20 55				21 53	22 59	
	d	19 55	20 50	20 56	21 01		21 50	21 54	23 00	23 09
Thornaby	d	20 00	20a55	21 01	21 06		21 55	21 59	23 05	
London Kings Cross 15 ⊖26	d					19 18				
Eaglescliffe	a	20 05		21 06		22 04		22 04	23 10	
	d	20 06		21 07		22 05		22 05	23 11	
Allens West	d	20 08		21 09				22 07	23 13	
Tees-side Airport	d									
Dinsdale	d	20 15		21 16				22 14	23 20	
Darlington 7 26	a	20 23		21 24			22 15	22 25	23 30	23 34
	d	20 32								
North Road	d	20 35								
Heighington	d	20 43								
Newton Aycliffe	d	20 46								
Shildon	d	20 51								
Bishop Auckland	a	20 58								
Stockton	d				21 12					
Billingham	d				21 19					
Seaton Carew	d				21 25					
Hartlepool	d				21 31	22 25				
Seaham	d				21 46					
Sunderland ⛴	a				21 57	22 51				
	d				21 58					
Heworth ⛴	d				22 09					
Newcastle 8 26 ⛴	a				22 19					
Metrocentre 48	a									
Hexham 48	a									

§ For authorised access only to BSC Redcar

Table 44

Mondays to Fridays

from 3 October

Saltburn and Middlesbrough - Darlington, Bishop Auckland, Sunderland and Newcastle

		NT	TP	NT	NT	NT	NT	TP	NT	NT	NT	NT	NT	NT	NT	TP	NT	NT	TP	NT	NT	NT	GC
			◇1					◇1								◇1			◇1				R 1
Saltburn	d					06 22					07 12	07 27	07 54				08 31			09 31	09 58		
Marske	d					06 26					07 16	07 31	07 58				08 35			09 35	10 02		
Longbeck	d					06 29					07 19	07 34	08 01				08 38			09 38	10 05		
Redcar East	d					06 32					07 22	07 37	08 04				08 41			09 41	10 08		
Redcar Central	d					06 35					07 25	07 40	08 07				08 44			09 44	10 11		
British Steel Redcar §	d																						
South Bank	d																08 51						
Middlesbrough	a					06 45					07 36	07 50	08 19				08 56			09 55	10 22		
	d	05 45	05 55			06 47	06 51	07 12	07 32		07 37	07 52	08 20	08 32	08 44	08 50	09 08	09 32	09 50	09 56	10 22	10 32	
Thornaby	d	05 50	06a00			06 52	06 56	07a17	07 37		07 42	07 57	08 25	08 37	08 50	08a55	09 13	09 37	09a55	10 01	10 27	10 37	
London Kings Cross 15 ⊖26	d																						07 49
Eaglescliffe	a	05 55				06 57					07 47	08 02	08 30		08 55		09 18			10 06	10 32		10 47
	d	05 55				06 57					07 47	08 03	08 31		08 55		09 18			10 07	10 33		10 48
Allens West	d	05 58				07 00					07 50	08 05	08 33		08 58		09 21			10 09	10 35		
Tees-side Airport	d																						
Dinsdale	d	06 04				07 06					07 56	08 12	08 40		09 04		09 27				10 42		
Darlington 7 26	a	06 14				07 19					08 07	08 22	08 50		09 14		09 39			10 23	10 52		
	d	06 14		06 47		07 20				07 48		08 22	08 52								10 54		
North Road	d			06 50						07 51			08 55								10 57		
Heighington	d			06 58						07 59			09 03								11 05		
Newton Aycliffe	d			07 02						08 03			09 07								11 08		
Shildon	d			07 06						08 07			09 11								11 13		
Bishop Auckland	a			07 14						08 15			09 18								11 20		
Stockton	d						07 02		07 43					08 43				09 43				10 43	
Billingham	d						07 09		07 50					08 50				09 50				10 50	
Seaton Carew	d						07 15		07 56					08 56				09 56				10 56	
Hartlepool	d				07 03		07 21		08 02					09 01				10 02				11 02	11 14
Seaham	d				07 18		07 36		08 17					09 15				10 17				11 17	
Sunderland ⛴	a				07 28		07 50		08 28					09 27				10 28				11 27	11 40
	d				07 30		07 55		08 30					09 30				10 30				11 30	
Heworth ⛴	d				07 41		08 07		08 42					09 42				10 42				11 42	
Newcastle 8 26 ⛴	a	06 55			07 51	08 05	08 18		08 52			09 06		09 51				10 51				11 51	
Metrocentre 48	a				08 00									10 02				11 01				12 01	
Hexham 48	a				08 39									10 36				11 38				12 38	

		TP	NT	NT	NT	TP	NT	NT	NT	TP	NT	NT	NT	GC	TP	NT	NT	NT	TP FO	TP FX	NT	NT	NT
		◇1				◇1				◇1				R 1	◇1				◇1	◇1			
Saltburn	d		10 31	10 58			11 31	11 57			12 30	12 58				13 31	13 57				14 31	14 58	
Marske	d		10 35	11 02			11 35	12 01			12 34	13 02				13 35	14 02				14 35	15 02	
Longbeck	d		10 38	11 05			11 38	12 04			12 37	13 05				13 38	14 05				14 38	15 05	
Redcar East	d		10 41	11 08			11 41	12 07			12 40	13 08				13 41	14 08				14 41	15 08	
Redcar Central	d		10 44	11 11			11 45	12 10			12 43	13 11				13 44	14 11				14 44	15 11	
British Steel Redcar §	d																						
South Bank	d																						
Middlesbrough	a		10 54	11 21			11 55	12 21			12 54	13 21				13 54	14 21				14 54	15 21	
	d	10 50	10 55	11 22	11 31	11 50	11 56	12 22	12 32	12 50	12 55	13 22	13 32		13 50	13 55	14 22	14 32	14 50	14 50	14 55	15 22	15 32
Thornaby	d	10a55	11 00	11 27	11 36	11a55	12 01	12 27	12 37	12a55	13 00	13 27	13 37		13a55	14 00	14 27	14 37	14a55	14a55	15 00	15 27	15 37
London Kings Cross 15 ⊖26	d													11 23									
Eaglescliffe	a		11 05	11 32			12 06	12 32			13 05	13 32		14 03		14 05	14 32				15 05	15 32	
	d		11 06	11 33			12 06	12 33			13 06	13 33		14 04		14 06	14 33				15 06	15 33	
Allens West	d		11 08	11 35			12 09	12 35			13 08	13 35				14 08	14 35				15 08	15 35	
Tees-side Airport	d																						
Dinsdale	d			11 42				12 42				13 42					14 42					15 42	
Darlington 7 26	a		11 23	11 52			12 24	12 54			13 23	13 52				14 23	14 52				15 23	15 54	
	d							12 54									14 54					15 54	
North Road	d							12 57									14 57					15 57	
Heighington	d							13 05									15 05					16 05	
Newton Aycliffe	d							13 08									15 08					16 08	
Shildon	d							13 13									15 13					16 13	
Bishop Auckland	a							13 20									15 20					16 20	
Stockton	d				11 42				12 42				13 43					14 43					15 43
Billingham	d				11 50				12 50				13 50					14 50					15 50
Seaton Carew	d				11 56				12 56				13 56					14 56					15 56
Hartlepool	d				12 02				13 02				14 02	14 23				15 02					16 02
Seaham	d				12 17				13 17				14 17					15 17					16 17
Sunderland ⛴	a				12 27				13 28				14 27	14 50				15 27					16 27
	d				12 30				13 30				14 30					15 30					16 30
Heworth ⛴	d				12 42				13 42				14 42					15 42					16 42
Newcastle 8 26 ⛴	a				12 52				13 51				14 51					15 51					16 51
Metrocentre 48	a				13 01				14 01				15 01					16 01					17 01
Hexham 48	a				13 38				14 38				15 39					16 38					17 38

§ For authorised access only to BSC Redcar

Table 44

Mondays to Fridays

from 3 October

Saltburn and Middlesbrough - Darlington, Bishop Auckland, Sunderland and Newcastle

		TP	NT	NT	NT	TP	NT	NT	NT	TP	NT	NT	NT	TP	NT	NT	GC	NT	TP	NT	TP	NT
		◇1 ⚲				◇1 ⚲				◇1				◇1			R 1 🍴		◇1		◇1	
Saltburn	d		15 31	15 58			16 27	16 58			17 31	17 58			18 31	18 58				19 31		20 32
Marske	d		15 35	16 02			16 31	17 02			17 35	18 02			18 35	19 02				19 35		20 36
Longbeck	d		15 38	16 05			16 34	17 05			17 38	18 05			18 38	19 05				19 38		20 39
Redcar East	d		15 41	16 08			16 37	17 08			17 41	18 08			18 41	19 08				19 41		20 42
Redcar Central	d		15 44	16 11			16 40	17 11			17 44	18 11			18 44	19 11				19 44		20 45
British Steel Redcar §	d						16 43															
South Bank	d						16 49	17 18														
Middlesbrough	a		15 54	16 21			16 54	17 23			17 54	18 21			18 54	19 21				19 54		20 55
	d	15 50	15 55	16 22	16 32	16 50	16 55	17 24	17 32	17 50	17 55	18 22	18 32	18 50	18 55	19 22		19 40	19 50	19 55	20 50	20 56
Thornaby	d	15a55	16 00	16 28	16 37	16a55	17 00	17 29	17 37	17a55	18 00	18 27	18 37	18a55	19 00	19 27		19 45	19 55	20 00	20a55	21 01
London Kings Cross 15 ⊖26	d																16 48					
Eaglescliffe	a		16 05	16 35			17 05	17 34			18 05	18 32			19 05	19 32	19 33			20 05		21 06
	d		16 06	16 35			17 06	17 35			18 06	18 33			19 06	19 33	19 34			20 06		21 07
Allens West	d		16 08	16 38			17 08	17 37			18 08	18 35			19 08	19 35				20 08		21 09
Tees-side Airport	d																					
Dinsdale	d		16 15	16 44			17 15	17 44			18 15				19 15					20 15		21 16
Darlington 7 26	a		16 23	16 52			17 24	17 53			18 23	18 50			19 23	19 52			20 17	20 23		21 24
	d						17 26					18 54								20 32		
North Road	d						17 29					18 57								20 35		
Heighington	d						17 37					19 05								20 43		
Newton Aycliffe	d						17 40					19 08								20 46		
Shildon	d						17 45					19 13								20 51		
Bishop Auckland	a						17 52					19 20								20 58		
Stockton	d				16 44				17 43				18 43					19 51				
Billingham	d				16 51				17 50				18 50					19 58				
Seaton Carew	d				16 57				17 56				18 56					20 04				
Hartlepool	d				17 03				18 02				19 02				19 53	20 10				
Seaham	d				17 18				18 18				19 17					20 27				
Sunderland ⛴	a				17 28				18 28				19 27				20 21	20 37				
	d				17 30				18 30				19 29					20 38				
Heworth ⛴	d				17 42				18 42				19 42					20 53				
Newcastle 8 26 ⛴	a				17 51				18 53				19 51					21 04				
Metrocentre 48	a				18 01								20 01					21 12				
Hexham 48	a				18 32																	

		NT	GC	TP	NT	NT	NT FX
			R 1 🍴	◇1			
Saltburn	d				21 30	22 36	
Marske	d				21 34	22 40	
Longbeck	d				21 37	22 43	
Redcar East	d				21 40	22 46	
Redcar Central	d				21 43	22 49	
British Steel Redcar §	d						
South Bank	d						
Middlesbrough	a				21 53	22 59	
	d	21 01		21 50	21 54	23 00	23 09
Thornaby	d	21 06		21 55	21 59	23 05	
London Kings Cross 15 ⊖26	d		19 18				
Eaglescliffe	a		22 04		22 04	23 10	
	d		22 05		22 05	23 11	
Allens West	d				22 07	23 13	
Tees-side Airport	d						
Dinsdale	d				22 14	23 20	
Darlington 7 26	a			22 15	22 25	23 30	23 34
	d						
North Road	d						
Heighington	d						
Newton Aycliffe	d						
Shildon	d						
Bishop Auckland	a						
Stockton	d	21 12					
Billingham	d	21 19					
Seaton Carew	d	21 25					
Hartlepool	d	21 31	22 25				
Seaham	d	21 46					
Sunderland ⛴	a	21 57	22 51				
	d	21 58					
Heworth ⛴	d	22 09					
Newcastle 8 26 ⛴	a	22 19					
Metrocentre 48	a						
Hexham 48	a						

§ For authorised access only to BSC Redcar

Table 44

Saturdays
until 25 June

Saltburn and Middlesbrough - Darlington, Bishop Auckland, Sunderland and Newcastle

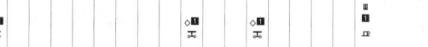

		NT	TP	NT	NT	NT	NT	TP	NT	NT		NT	NT	NT	NT	NT	TP	NT	NT	TP		NT	NT	NT	GC
			◇1					◇1 🚲									◇1 🚲			◇1 🚲					R 1 ☕
Saltburn	d					06 22						07 12	07 26	07 55				08 31				09 31	09 58		
Marske	d					06 26						07 16	07 30	07 59				08 35				09 35	10 02		
Longbeck	d					06 29						07 19	07 33	08 02				08 38				09 38	10 05		
Redcar East	d					06 32						07 22	07 36	08 05				08 41				09 41	10 08		
Redcar Central	d					06 35						07 25	07 39	08 08				08 44				09 44	10 11		
British Steel Redcar §	d																								
South Bank	d												07 46					08 51							
Middlesbrough	a					06 45						07 36	07 51	08 18				08 56				09 55	10 22		
	d	05 45	05 55			06 47	06 51	07 12	07 32			07 37	07 52	08 19	08 32	08 44	08 50	09 08	09 32	09 50		09 56	10 22	10 32	
Thornaby	d	05 50	06a00			06 52	06 56	07a17	07 37			07 42	07 57	08 24	08 37	08 50	08a55	09 13	09 37	09a55		10 01	10 27	10 37	
London Kings Cross 15 ⊖26	d																								07 47
Eaglescliffe	a	05 55				06 57						07 47	08 02	08 29		08 55		09 21				10 06	10 32		10 37
	d	05 55				06 57						07 47	08 03	08 30		08 55		09 21				10 07	10 33		10 38
Allens West	d	05 58				07 00						07 50	08 05	08 32		08 58		09 24				10 09	10 35		
Tees-side Airport	d																								
Dinsdale	d	06 04				07 06						07 56	08 12	08 39		09 04		09 30					10 42		
Darlington 7 26	a	06 13				07 20						08 07	08 22	08 50		09 14		09 42				10 23	10 52		
	d			06 47		07 21				07 48			08 22	08 52									10 54		
North Road	d			06 50						07 51				08 55									10 57		
Heighington	d			06 58						07 59				09 03									11 05		
Newton Aycliffe	d			07 01						08 03				09 07									11 08		
Shildon	d			07 06						08 07				09 11									11 13		
Bishop Auckland	a			07 14						08 15				09 18									11 20		
Stockton	d						07 02		07 43						08 43				09 43					10 43	
Billingham	d						07 09		07 50						08 50				09 50					10 50	
Seaton Carew	d						07 15		07 56						08 56				09 56					10 56	
Hartlepool	d				07 03		07 21		08 02						09 02				10 02					11 02	11 14
Seaham	d				07 18		07 36		08 17						09 16				10 17					11 17	
Sunderland ⛴	a				07 28		07 50		08 28						09 27				10 28					11 27	11 40
	d				07 30		07 55		08 30						09 30				10 30					11 30	
Heworth ⛴	d				07 41		08 07		08 42						09 42				10 42					11 42	
Newcastle 8 26 ⛴	a				07 51	08 05	08 18		08 52				09 01		09 51				10 51					11 51	
Metrocentre 48	a				08 00										10 02				11 01					12 01	
Hexham 48	a				08 37										10 36				11 36					12 36	

		TP	NT	NT	NT	TP		NT	NT	NT	TP	NT	NT	NT	GC	TP		NT	NT	NT	TP	NT	NT	NT	TP
		◇1 🚲				◇1 🚲					◇1 🚲				R 1 ☕	◇1 🚲					◇1 🚲				◇1 🚲
Saltburn	d		10 31	10 58				11 31	11 57			12 30	12 58					13 31	13 57			14 31	14 58		
Marske	d		10 35	11 02				11 35	12 01			12 34	13 02					13 35	14 02			14 35	15 02		
Longbeck	d		10 38	11 05				11 38	12 04			12 37	13 05					13 38	14 05			14 38	15 05		
Redcar East	d		10 41	11 08				11 41	12 07			12 40	13 08					13 41	14 08			14 41	15 08		
Redcar Central	d		10 44	11 11				11 44	12 10			12 43	13 11					13 44	14 11			14 44	15 11		
British Steel Redcar §	d																								
South Bank	d																								
Middlesbrough	a		10 54	11 21				11 54	12 21			12 54	13 21					13 54	14 21			14 54	15 21		
	d	10 50	10 55	11 22	11 32	11 50		11 55	12 22	12 32	12 50	12 55	13 22	13 32		13 50		13 55	14 22	14 32	14 50	14 55	15 22	15 32	15 50
Thornaby	d	10a55	11 00	11 27	11 36	11a55		12 00	12 27	12 37	12a55	13 00	13 27	13 37		13a55		14 00	14 27	14 37	14a55	15 00	15 27	15 37	15a55
London Kings Cross 15 ⊖26	d														11 20										
Eaglescliffe	a		11 05	11 32				12 05	12 32			13 08	13 32		13 59			14 05	14 32			15 05	15 32		
	d		11 06	11 33				12 06	12 33			13 09	13 33		14 00			14 06	14 33			15 06	15 33		
Allens West	d		11 08	11 35				12 08	12 35			13 11	13 35					14 08	14 35			15 08	15 35		
Tees-side Airport	d																								
Dinsdale	d			11 42					12 42				13 42						14 42				15 42		
Darlington 7 26	a		11 23	11 52				12 23	12 54			13 26	13 52					14 23	14 52			15 23	15 54		
	d								12 54										14 54				15 54		
North Road	d								12 57										14 57				15 57		
Heighington	d								13 05										15 05				16 05		
Newton Aycliffe	d								13 08										15 08				16 08		
Shildon	d								13 13										15 13				16 13		
Bishop Auckland	a								13 20										15 20				16 20		
Stockton	d				11 42					12 42				13 43						14 43				15 43	
Billingham	d				11 50					12 50				13 50						14 50				15 50	
Seaton Carew	d				11 56					12 56				13 56						14 56				15 56	
Hartlepool	d				12 02					13 02				14 02	14 22					15 02				16 02	
Seaham	d				12 17					13 17				14 17						15 17				16 17	
Sunderland ⛴	a				12 27					13 28				14 27	14 50					15 27				16 27	
	d				12 30					13 30				14 30						15 30				16 30	
Heworth ⛴	d				12 42					13 42				14 42						15 42				16 42	
Newcastle 8 26 ⛴	a				12 52					13 51				14 51						15 51				16 51	
Metrocentre 48	a				13 01					14 01				15 02						16 01				17 01	
Hexham 48	a				13 36					14 36				15 37						16 36				17 36	

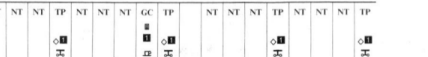

§ For authorised access only to BSC Redcar

Table 44

Saturdays

until 25 June

Saltburn and Middlesbrough - Darlington, Bishop Auckland, Sunderland and Newcastle

		NT		NT	NT	TP	NT	NT	NT	TP	NT	NT		NT	TP	NT	GC	NT	NT	NT	TP	NT		TP	NT
						◇1				◇1					◇1		R 1 ⊏P				◇1			◇1	
Saltburn	d	15 31		15 58			16 27	16 58			17 31	17 58				18 31		18 58		19 31					20 32
Marske	d	15 35		16 02			16 31	17 02			17 35	18 02				18 35		19 02		19 35					20 36
Longbeck	d	15 38		16 05			16 34	17 05			17 38	18 05				18 38		19 05		19 38					20 39
Redcar East	d	15 41		16 08			16 37	17 08			17 41	18 08				18 41		19 08		19 41					20 42
Redcar Central	d	15 44		16 11			16 40	17 11			17 44	18 11				18 44		19 11		19 44					20 45
British Steel Redcar §	d						16 43																		
South Bank	d						16 49	17 18																	
Middlesbrough	a	15 54		16 21			16 54	17 23			17 54	18 21				18 54		19 21		19 54					20 55
	d	15 55		16 22	16 32	16 50	16 55	17 24	17 32	17 50	17 55	18 22		18 32	18 50	18 55		19 22	19 40	19 55	20 10	20 45		20 50	20 56
Thornaby	d	16 00		16 27	16 37	16a55	17 00	17 29	17 37	17a55	18 00	18 27		18 37	18a55	19 00		19 27	19 45	20 00	20a15	20 50		20a55	21 01
London Kings Cross 15 ⊖26	d																16 48								
Eaglescliffe	a	16 05		16 32			17 05	17 34			18 05	18 32				19 05	19 28	19 32		20 05					21 06
	d	16 06		16 33			17 06	17 35			18 06	18 33				19 06	19 29	19 33		20 06					21 07
Allens West	d	16 08		16 35			17 08	17 37			18 08	18 35				19 08		19 35		20 08					21 09
Tees-side Airport	d																								
Dinsdale	d	16 15		16 42			17 15	17 44			18 15					19 15				20 15					21 16
Darlington 7 26	a	16 23		16 52			17 24	17 53			18 24	18 50				19 23		19 52		20 26					21 24
	d						17 26					18 54								20 32					
North Road	d						17 29					18 57								20 35					
Heighington	d						17 37					19 05								20 43					
Newton Aycliffe	d						17 40					19 08								20 46					
Shildon	d						17 45					19 13								20 51					
Bishop Auckland	a						17 52					19 21								20 58					
Stockton	d				16 43				17 43					18 43					19 51			20 56			
Billingham	d				16 50				17 50					18 50					19 58			21 03			
Seaton Carew	d				16 56				17 56					18 56					20 04			21 09			
Hartlepool	d				17 02				18 02					19 02			19 49		20 10			21 15			
Seaham	d				17 17				18 17					19 17					20 27			21 30			
Sunderland ⛴	a				17 27				18 27					19 27			20 21		20 37			21 40			
	d				17 30				18 30					19 30					20 38			21 43			
Heworth ⛴	d				17 42				18 42					19 42					20 53			21 54			
Newcastle 8 26 ⛴	a				17 51				18 51					19 51					21 04			22 04			
Metrocentre 48	a				18 01									20 01											
Hexham 48	a				18 32																				

		GC	TP	NT	NT
		R 1 ⊏P	◇1		
Saltburn	d			21 30	22 36
Marske	d			21 34	22 40
Longbeck	d			21 37	22 43
Redcar East	d			21 40	22 46
Redcar Central	d			21 43	22 49
British Steel Redcar §	d				
South Bank	d				
Middlesbrough	a			21 53	22 59
	d		21 50	21 54	23 00
Thornaby	d		21 55	21 59	23 05
London Kings Cross 15 ⊖26	d	19 20			
Eaglescliffe	a	22 03		22 04	23 10
	d	22 04		22 05	23 11
Allens West	d			22 07	23 13
Tees-side Airport	d				
Dinsdale	d			22 14	23 20
Darlington 7 26	a		22 15	22 24	23 30
	d				
North Road	d				
Heighington	d				
Newton Aycliffe	d				
Shildon	d				
Bishop Auckland	a				
Stockton	d				
Billingham	d				
Seaton Carew	d				
Hartlepool	d	22 24			
Seaham	d				
Sunderland ⛴	a	22 51			
	d				
Heworth ⛴	d				
Newcastle 8 26 ⛴	a				
Metrocentre 48	a				
Hexham 48	a				

§ For authorised access only to BSC Redcar

Table 44

Saturdays

6 August to 1 October

Saltburn and Middlesbrough - Darlington, Bishop Auckland, Sunderland and Newcastle

		NT	TP	NT	NT	NT	NT	TP	NT	NT	NT	NT	NT	NT	NT	TP	NT	NT	TP	NT	NT	NT	GC
			◇1					◇1 🛒								◇1 🛒			◇1 🛒				R 1 ☕
Saltburn	d					06 22					07 12	07 26	07 55				08 31			09 31	09 58		
Marske	d					06 26					07 16	07 30	07 59				08 35			09 35	10 02		
Longbeck	d					06 29					07 19	07 33	08 02				08 38			09 38	10 05		
Redcar East	d					06 32					07 22	07 36	08 05				08 41			09 41	10 08		
Redcar Central	d					06 35					07 25	07 39	08 08				08 44			09 44	10 11		
British Steel Redcar §	d																						
South Bank	d											07 46					08 51						
Middlesbrough	a					06 45					07 36	07 51	08 18				08 56			09 55	10 22		
	d	05 45	05 55			06 47	06 51	07 12	07 32		07 37	07 52	08 19	08 32	08 44	08 50	09 08	09 32	09 50	09 56	10 22	10 32	
Thornaby	d	05 50	06a00			06 52	06 56	07a17	07 37		07 42	07 57	08 24	08 37	08 50	08a55	09 13	09 37	09a55	10 01	10 27	10 37	
London Kings Cross 15 ⊖26	d																						07 47
Eaglescliffe	a	05 55				06 57					07 47	08 02	08 29		08 55		09 21			10 06	10 32		10 37
	d	05 55				06 57					07 47	08 03	08 30		08 55		09 21			10 07	10 33		10 38
Allens West	d	05 58				07 00					07 50	08 05	08 32		08 58		09 24			10 09	10 35		
Tees-side Airport	d																						
Dinsdale	d	06 04				07 06					07 56	08 12	08 39		09 04		09 30				10 42		
Darlington 7 26	a	06 13				07 20					08 07	08 22	08 50		09 14		09 42			10 23	10 52		
	d			06 47		07 21				07 48		08 22	08 52								10 54		
North Road	d			06 50						07 51			08 55								10 57		
Heighington	d			06 58						07 59			09 03								11 05		
Newton Aycliffe	d			07 01						08 03			09 07								11 08		
Shildon	d			07 06						08 07			09 11								11 13		
Bishop Auckland	a			07 14						08 15			09 18								11 20		
Stockton	d						07 02		07 43					08 43				09 43				10 43	
Billingham	d						07 09		07 50					08 50				09 50				10 50	
Seaton Carew	d						07 15		07 56					08 56				09 56				10 56	
Hartlepool	d				07 03		07 21		08 02					09 02				10 02				11 02	11 14
Seaham	d				07 18		07 36		08 17					09 16				10 17				11 17	
Sunderland ⛴	a				07 28		07 50		08 28					09 27				10 28				11 27	11 40
	d				07 30		07 55		08 30					09 30				10 30				11 30	
Heworth ⛴	d				07 41		08 07		08 42					09 42				10 42				11 42	
Newcastle 8 26 ⛴	a				07 51	08 05	08 18		08 52			09 01		09 51				10 51				11 51	
Metrocentre 48	a				08 00									10 02				11 01				12 01	
Hexham 48	a				08 37									10 36				11 36				12 36	

		TP	NT	NT	NT	TP	NT	NT	NT	TP	NT	NT	NT	GC	TP	NT	NT	NT	TP	NT	NT	NT	TP
		◇1 🛒				◇1 🛒				◇1 🛒				R 1 ☕	◇1 🛒				◇1 🛒				◇1 🛒
Saltburn	d		10 31	10 58			11 31	11 57			12 30	12 58				13 31	13 57			14 31	14 58		
Marske	d		10 35	11 02			11 35	12 01			12 34	13 02				13 35	14 02			14 35	15 02		
Longbeck	d		10 38	11 05			11 38	12 04			12 37	13 05				13 38	14 05			14 38	15 05		
Redcar East	d		10 41	11 08			11 41	12 07			12 40	13 08				13 41	14 08			14 41	15 08		
Redcar Central	d		10 44	11 11			11 44	12 10			12 43	13 11				13 44	14 11			14 44	15 11		
British Steel Redcar §	d																						
South Bank	d																						
Middlesbrough	a		10 54	11 21			11 54	12 21			12 54	13 21				13 54	14 21			14 54	15 21		
	d	10 50	10 55	11 22	11 32	11 50	11 55	12 22	12 32	12 50	12 55	13 22	13 32		13 50	13 55	14 22	14 32	14 50	14 55	15 22	15 32	15 50
Thornaby	d	10a55	11 00	11 27	11 36	11a55	12 00	12 27	12 37	12a55	13 00	13 27	13 37		13a55	14 00	14 27	14 37	14a55	15 00	15 27	15 37	15a55
London Kings Cross 15 ⊖26	d													11 20									
Eaglescliffe	a		11 05	11 32			12 05	12 32			13 08	13 32		13 59		14 05	14 32			15 05	15 32		
	d		11 06	11 33			12 06	12 33			13 09	13 33		14 00		14 06	14 33			15 06	15 33		
Allens West	d		11 08	11 35			12 08	12 35			13 11	13 35				14 08	14 35			15 08	15 35		
Tees-side Airport	d																						
Dinsdale	d			11 42				12 42				13 42					14 42				15 42		
Darlington 7 26	a		11 23	11 52			12 23	12 54			13 26	13 52				14 23	14 52			15 23	15 54		
	d							12 54									14 54				15 54		
North Road	d							12 57									14 57				15 57		
Heighington	d							13 05									15 05				16 05		
Newton Aycliffe	d							13 08									15 08				16 08		
Shildon	d							13 13									15 13				16 13		
Bishop Auckland	a							13 20									15 20				16 20		
Stockton	d				11 42				12 42				13 43					14 43				15 43	
Billingham	d				11 50				12 50				13 50					14 50				15 50	
Seaton Carew	d				11 56				12 56				13 56					14 56				15 56	
Hartlepool	d				12 02				13 02				14 02	14 22				15 02				16 02	
Seaham	d				12 17				13 17				14 17					15 17				16 17	
Sunderland ⛴	a				12 27				13 28				14 27	14 50				15 27				16 27	
	d				12 30				13 30				14 30					15 30				16 30	
Heworth ⛴	d				12 42				13 42				14 42					15 42				16 42	
Newcastle 8 26 ⛴	a				12 52				13 51				14 51					15 51				16 51	
Metrocentre 48	a				13 01				14 01				15 02					16 01				17 01	
Hexham 48	a				13 36				14 36				15 37					16 36				17 36	

§ For authorised access only to BSC Redcar

Table 44

Saturdays

6 August to 1 October

Saltburn and Middlesbrough - Darlington, Bishop Auckland, Sunderland and Newcastle

Station		NT		NT	NT	TP	NT	NT	NT	TP	NT	NT		NT	TP	NT	GC	NT	NT	NT	TP	NT		TP	NT
						◇1				◇1					◇1		R 1 (buffet)				◇1			◇1	
Saltburn	d	15 31		15 58			16 27	16 58			17 31	17 58				18 31		18 58		19 31					20 32
Marske	d	15 35		16 02			16 31	17 02			17 35	18 02				18 35		19 02		19 35					20 36
Longbeck	d	15 38		16 05			16 34	17 05			17 38	18 05				18 38		19 05		19 38					20 39
Redcar East	d	15 41		16 08			16 37	17 08			17 41	18 08				18 41		19 08		19 41					20 42
Redcar Central	d	15 44		16 11			16 40	17 11			17 44	18 11				18 44		19 11		19 44					20 45
British Steel Redcar §	d						16 43																		
South Bank	d						16 49	17 18																	
Middlesbrough	a	15 54		16 21			16 54	17 23			17 54	18 21				18 54		19 21		19 54					20 55
	d	15 55		16 22	16 32	16 50	16 55	17 24	17 32	17 50	17 55	18 22		18 32	18 50	18 55		19 22	19 40	19 55	20 10	20 45		20 50	20 56
Thornaby	d	16 00		16 27	16 37	16a55	17 00	17 29	17 37	17a55	18 00	18 27		18 37	18a55	19 00		19 27	19 45	20 00	20a15	20 50		20a55	21 01
London Kings Cross 15 ⊖26	d																16 48								
Eaglescliffe	a	16 05		16 32			17 05	17 34			18 05	18 32				19 05	19 28	19 32		20 05					21 06
	d	16 06		16 33			17 06	17 35			18 06	18 33				19 06	19 29	19 33		20 06					21 07
Allens West	d	16 08		16 35			17 08	17 37			18 08	18 35				19 08		19 35		20 08					21 09
Tees-side Airport	d																								
Dinsdale	d	16 15		16 42			17 15	17 44			18 15					19 15				20 15					21 16
Darlington 7 26	a	16 23		16 52			17 24	17 53			18 24	18 50				19 23		19 52		20 26					21 24
	d						17 26					18 54								20 32					
North Road	d						17 29					18 57								20 35					
Heighington	d						17 37					19 05								20 43					
Newton Aycliffe	d						17 40					19 08								20 46					
Shildon	d						17 45					19 13								20 51					
Bishop Auckland	a						17 52					19 21								20 58					
Stockton	d				16 43				17 43					18 43					19 51			20 56			
Billingham	d				16 50				17 50					18 50					19 58			21 03			
Seaton Carew	d				16 56				17 56					18 56					20 04			21 09			
Hartlepool	d				17 02				18 02					19 02			19 49		20 10			21 15			
Seaham	d				17 17				18 17					19 17					20 27			21 30			
Sunderland ⛴	a				17 27				18 27					19 27			20 21		20 37			21 40			
	d				17 30				18 30					19 30					20 38			21 43			
Heworth ⛴	d				17 42				18 42					19 42					20 53			21 54			
Newcastle 8 26 ⛴	a				17 51				18 51					19 51					21 04			22 04			
Metrocentre 48	a				18 01									20 01											
Hexham 48	a				18 32																				

Station		GC	TP	NT	NT
		R 1 (buffet)	◇1		
Saltburn	d			21 30	22 36
Marske	d			21 34	22 40
Longbeck	d			21 37	22 43
Redcar East	d			21 40	22 46
Redcar Central	d			21 43	22 49
British Steel Redcar §	d				
South Bank	d				
Middlesbrough	a			21 53	22 59
	d		21 50	21 54	23 00
Thornaby	d		21 55	21 59	23 05
London Kings Cross 15 ⊖26	d	19 20			
Eaglescliffe	a	22 03		22 04	23 10
	d	22 04		22 05	23 11
Allens West	d			22 07	23 13
Tees-side Airport	d				
Dinsdale	d			22 14	23 20
Darlington 7 26	a		22 15	22 24	23 30
	d				
North Road	d				
Heighington	d				
Newton Aycliffe	d				
Shildon	d				
Bishop Auckland	a				
Stockton	d				
Billingham	d				
Seaton Carew	d				
Hartlepool	d	22 24			
Seaham	d				
Sunderland ⛴	a	22 51			
	d				
Heworth ⛴	d				
Newcastle 8 26 ⛴	a				
Metrocentre 48	a				
Hexham 48	a				

§ For authorised access only to BSC Redcar

Table 44

Saturdays
from 8 October

Saltburn and Middlesbrough - Darlington, Bishop Auckland, Sunderland and Newcastle

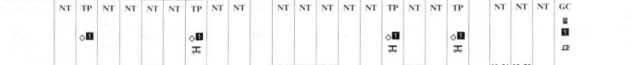

Station			NT	TP	NT	NT	NT	NT	TP	NT	NT	
				◇1					◇1 trolley			
Saltburn		d					06 22					
Marske		d					06 26					
Longbeck		d					06 29					
Redcar East		d					06 32					
Redcar Central		d					06 35					
British Steel Redcar §		d										
South Bank		d										
Middlesbrough		a					06 45					
		d	05 45	05 55			06 47	06 51	07 12	07 32		
Thornaby		d	05 50	06a00			06 52	06 56	07a17	07 37		
London Kings Cross 15 ⊖	26	d										
Eaglescliffe		a	05 55				06 57					
		d	05 55				06 57					
Allens West		d	05 58				07 00					
Tees-side Airport		d										
Dinsdale		d	06 04				07 06					
Darlington 7	26	a	06 13				07 20					
		d			06 47		07 21				07 48	
North Road		d			06 50						07 51	
Heighington		d			06 58						07 59	
Newton Aycliffe		d			07 01						08 03	
Shildon		d			07 06						08 07	
Bishop Auckland		a			07 14						08 15	
Stockton		d						07 02		07 43		
Billingham		d						07 09		07 50		
Seaton Carew		d						07 15		07 56		
Hartlepool		d				07 03		07 21		08 02		
Seaham		d				07 18		07 36		08 17		
Sunderland	⛴	a				07 28		07 50		08 28		
		d				07 30		07 55		08 30		
Heworth	⛴	d				07 41		08 07		08 42		
Newcastle 8	26 ⛴	a				07 51	08 05	08 18		08 52		
Metrocentre	48	a				08 00						
Hexham	48	a				08 40						

Station			NT	NT	NT	NT	NT	TP	NT	NT	TP		NT	NT	NT	GC
								◇1 trolley			◇1 trolley					R 1 restaurant
Saltburn		d	07 12	07 26	07 55				08 31				09 31	09 58		
Marske		d	07 16	07 30	07 59				08 35				09 35	10 02		
Longbeck		d	07 19	07 33	08 02				08 38				09 38	10 05		
Redcar East		d	07 22	07 36	08 05				08 41				09 41	10 08		
Redcar Central		d	07 25	07 39	08 08				08 44				09 44	10 11		
British Steel Redcar §		d														
South Bank		d		07 46					08 51							
Middlesbrough		a	07 36	07 51	08 18				08 56				09 55	10 22		
		d	07 37	07 52	08 19	08 32	08 44	08 50	09 08	09 32	09 50		09 56	10 22	10 32	
Thornaby		d	07 42	07 57	08 24	08 37	08 50	08a55	09 13	09 37	09a55		10 01	10 27	10 37	
London Kings Cross 15 ⊖	26	d														07 47
Eaglescliffe		a	07 47	08 02	08 29		08 55		09 21				10 06	10 32		10 37
		d	07 47	08 03	08 30		08 55		09 21				10 07	10 33		10 38
Allens West		d	07 50	08 05	08 32		08 58		09 24				10 09	10 35		
Tees-side Airport		d														
Dinsdale		d	07 56	08 12	08 39		09 04		09 30					10 42		
Darlington 7	26	a	08 07	08 22	08 50		09 14		09 42				10 23	10 52		
		d		08 22	08 52									10 54		
North Road		d			08 55									10 57		
Heighington		d			09 03									11 05		
Newton Aycliffe		d			09 07									11 08		
Shildon		d			09 11									11 13		
Bishop Auckland		a			09 18									11 20		
Stockton		d				08 43				09 43					10 43	
Billingham		d				08 50				09 50					10 50	
Seaton Carew		d				08 56				09 56					10 56	
Hartlepool		d				09 02				10 02					11 02	11 14
Seaham		d				09 16				10 17					11 17	
Sunderland	⛴	a				09 27				10 28					11 27	11 40
		d				09 30				10 30					11 30	
Heworth	⛴	d				09 42				10 42					11 42	
Newcastle 8	26 ⛴	a		09 01		09 51				10 51					11 51	
Metrocentre	48	a				10 02				11 01					12 01	
Hexham	48	a				10 37				11 38					12 38	

Station			TP	NT	NT	NT	TP		NT	NT	NT	TP
			◇1 trolley				◇1 trolley					◇1 trolley
Saltburn		d		10 31	10 58				11 31	11 57		
Marske		d		10 35	11 02				11 35	12 01		
Longbeck		d		10 38	11 05				11 38	12 04		
Redcar East		d		10 41	11 08				11 41	12 07		
Redcar Central		d		10 44	11 11				11 44	12 10		
British Steel Redcar §		d										
South Bank		d										
Middlesbrough		a		10 54	11 21				11 54	12 21		
		d	10 50	10 55	11 22	11 32	11 50		11 55	12 22	12 32	12 50
Thornaby		d	10a55	11 00	11 27	11 36	11a55		12 00	12 27	12 37	12a55
London Kings Cross 15 ⊖	26	d										
Eaglescliffe		a		11 05	11 32				12 05	12 32		
		d		11 06	11 33				12 06	12 33		
Allens West		d		11 08	11 35				12 08	12 35		
Tees-side Airport		d										
Dinsdale		d			11 42					12 42		
Darlington 7	26	a		11 23	11 52				12 23	12 54		
		d								12 54		
North Road		d								12 57		
Heighington		d								13 05		
Newton Aycliffe		d								13 08		
Shildon		d								13 13		
Bishop Auckland		a								13 20		
Stockton		d				11 42					12 42	
Billingham		d				11 50					12 50	
Seaton Carew		d				11 56					12 56	
Hartlepool		d				12 02					13 02	
Seaham		d				12 17					13 17	
Sunderland	⛴	a				12 27					13 28	
		d				12 30					13 30	
Heworth	⛴	d				12 42					13 42	
Newcastle 8	26 ⛴	a				12 52					13 51	
Metrocentre	48	a				13 01					14 01	
Hexham	48	a				13 38					14 38	

Station			NT	NT	NT	GC	TP		NT	NT	NT	TP	NT	NT	NT	TP
						R 1 restaurant	◇1 trolley					◇1 trolley				◇1 trolley
Saltburn		d	12 30	12 58					13 31	13 57			14 31	14 58		
Marske		d	12 34	13 02					13 35	14 02			14 35	15 02		
Longbeck		d	12 37	13 05					13 38	14 05			14 38	15 05		
Redcar East		d	12 40	13 08					13 41	14 08			14 41	15 08		
Redcar Central		d	12 43	13 11					13 44	14 11			14 44	15 11		
British Steel Redcar §		d														
South Bank		d														
Middlesbrough		a	12 54	13 21					13 54	14 21			14 54	15 21		
		d	12 55	13 22	13 32		13 50		13 55	14 22	14 32	14 50	14 55	15 22	15 32	15 50
Thornaby		d	13 00	13 27	13 37		13a55		14 00	14 27	14 37	14a55	15 00	15 27	15 37	15a55
London Kings Cross 15 ⊖	26	d				11 20										
Eaglescliffe		a	13 08	13 32		13 59			14 05	14 32			15 05	15 32		
		d	13 09	13 33		14 00			14 06	14 33			15 06	15 33		
Allens West		d	13 11	13 35					14 08	14 35			15 08	15 35		
Tees-side Airport		d														
Dinsdale		d		13 42						14 42				15 42		
Darlington 7	26	a	13 26	13 52					14 23	14 52			15 23	15 54		
		d								14 54				15 54		
North Road		d								14 57				15 57		
Heighington		d								15 05				16 05		
Newton Aycliffe		d								15 08				16 08		
Shildon		d								15 13				16 13		
Bishop Auckland		a								15 20				16 20		
Stockton		d			13 43						14 43				15 43	
Billingham		d			13 50						14 50				15 50	
Seaton Carew		d			13 56						14 56				15 56	
Hartlepool		d			14 02	14 22					15 02				16 02	
Seaham		d			14 17						15 17				16 17	
Sunderland	⛴	a			14 27	14 50					15 27				16 27	
		d			14 30						15 30				16 30	
Heworth	⛴	d			14 42						15 42				16 42	
Newcastle 8	26 ⛴	a			14 51						15 51				16 51	
Metrocentre	48	a			15 02						16 01				17 01	
Hexham	48	a			15 37						16 38				17 39	

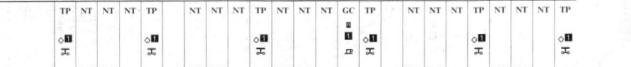

§ For authorised access only to BSC Redcar

Table 44

Saturdays

from 8 October

Saltburn and Middlesbrough - Darlington, Bishop Auckland, Sunderland and Newcastle

		NT		NT	NT	TP	NT	NT	NT	TP	NT	NT		NT	TP	NT	GC	NT	NT	NT	TP	NT		TP	NT
						◇[1]				◇[1]					◇[1]		[R] [1] ☕				◇[1]			◇[1]	
Saltburn	d	15 31		15 58			16 27	16 58			17 31	17 58				18 31		18 58		19 31					20 32
Marske	d	15 35		16 02			16 31	17 02			17 35	18 02				18 35		19 02		19 35					20 36
Longbeck	d	15 38		16 05			16 34	17 05			17 38	18 05				18 38		19 05		19 38					20 39
Redcar East	d	15 41		16 08			16 37	17 08			17 41	18 08				18 41		19 08		19 41					20 42
Redcar Central	d	15 44		16 11			16 40	17 11			17 44	18 11				18 44		19 11		19 44					20 45
British Steel Redcar §	d						16 43																		
South Bank	d						16 49	17 18																	
Middlesbrough	a	15 54		16 21			16 54	17 23			17 54	18 21				18 54		19 21		19 54					20 55
	d	15 55		16 22	16 32	16 50	16 55	17 24	17 32	17 50	17 55	18 22		18 32	18 50	18 55		19 22	19 40	19 55	20 10	20 45		20 50	20 56
Thornaby	d	16 00		16 27	16 37	16a55	17 00	17 29	17 37	17a55	18 00	18 27		18 37	18a55	19 00		19 27	19 45	20 00	20a15	20 50		20a55	21 01
London Kings Cross [15] ⊖26	d																16 48								
Eaglescliffe	a	16 05		16 32			17 05	17 34			18 05	18 32				19 05	19 28	19 32		20 05					21 06
	d	16 06		16 33			17 06	17 35			18 06	18 33				19 06	19 29	19 33		20 06					21 07
Allens West	d	16 08		16 35			17 08	17 37			18 08	18 35				19 08		19 35		20 08					21 09
Tees-side Airport	d																								
Dinsdale	d	16 15		16 42			17 15	17 44			18 15					19 15				20 15					21 16
Darlington [7] 26	a	16 23		16 52			17 24	17 53			18 24	18 50				19 23		19 52		20 26					21 24
	d						17 26					18 54								20 32					
North Road	d						17 29					18 57								20 35					
Heighington	d						17 37					19 05								20 43					
Newton Aycliffe	d						17 40					19 08								20 46					
Shildon	d						17 45					19 13								20 51					
Bishop Auckland	a						17 52					19 21								20 58					
Stockton	d				16 43				17 43					18 43					19 51			20 56			
Billingham	d				16 50				17 50					18 50					19 58			21 03			
Seaton Carew	d				16 56				17 56					18 56					20 04			21 09			
Hartlepool	d				17 02				18 02					19 02			19 49		20 10			21 15			
Seaham	d				17 17				18 17					19 17					20 27			21 30			
Sunderland ⛴	a				17 27				18 27					19 27			20 21		20 37			21 40			
	d				17 30				18 30					19 30					20 38			21 43			
Heworth ⛴	d				17 42				18 42					19 42					20 53			21 54			
Newcastle [8] 26 ⛴	a				17 51				18 51					19 51					21 04			22 04			
Metrocentre 48	a				18 01									20 01											
Hexham 48	a				18 32																				

		GC	TP	NT	NT
		[R] [1] ☕	◇[1]		
Saltburn	d			21 30	22 36
Marske	d			21 34	22 40
Longbeck	d			21 37	22 43
Redcar East	d			21 40	22 46
Redcar Central	d			21 43	22 49
British Steel Redcar §	d				
South Bank	d				
Middlesbrough	a			21 53	22 59
	d		21 50	21 54	23 00
Thornaby	d		21 55	21 59	23 05
London Kings Cross [15] ⊖26	d	19 20			
Eaglescliffe	a	22 03		22 04	23 10
	d	22 04		22 05	23 11
Allens West	d			22 07	23 13
Tees-side Airport	d				
Dinsdale	d			22 14	23 20
Darlington [7] 26	a		22 15	22 24	23 30
	d				
North Road	d				
Heighington	d				
Newton Aycliffe	d				
Shildon	d				
Bishop Auckland	a				
Stockton	d				
Billingham	d				
Seaton Carew	d				
Hartlepool	d	22 24			
Seaham	d				
Sunderland ⛴	a	22 51			
	d				
Heworth ⛴	d				
Newcastle [8] 26 ⛴	a				
Metrocentre 48	a				
Hexham 48	a				

§ For authorised access only to BSC Redcar

Table 44

Sundays
until 19 June

Saltburn and Middlesbrough - Darlington, Bishop Auckland, Sunderland and Newcastle

		TW	TW	TW	NT	TW	TW	NT	TW	TW		NT	NT	NT	TW	TW	NT	TW	TW	TP		TW	NT	TW	NT
																				◇1					
		bus	bus	bus		bus	bus		bus	bus			bus		bus	bus		bus	bus			bus	bus	bus	
Saltburn	d																09 44								
Marske	d																09 48								
Longbeck	d																09 51								
Redcar East	d																09 54								
Redcar Central	d																09 57								
British Steel Redcar §	d																								
South Bank	d																								
Middlesbrough	a																10 07								
	d							08 38				09 08		09 12			10 08			10 13					
Thornaby	d							08 43				09 13		09 17			10 13			10a18					
London Kings Cross 15 ⊖26	d																								
Eaglescliffe	a							08 48				09 18					10 18								
	d							08 49				09 19					10 19								10 36
Allens West	d							08 51				09 21					10 21								
Tees-side Airport	d																								
Dinsdale	d							08 58				09 28					10 28								
Darlington 7 26	a							09 07				09 37					10 37								
	d				08 05							09 38													
North Road	d				08 08							09 41													
Heighington	d				08 16							09 49													
Newton Aycliffe	d				08 19							09 52													
Shildon	d				08 24							09 57													
Bishop Auckland	a				08 31							10 02													
Stockton	d													09 23											10 41
Billingham	d													09 30											10 49
Seaton Carew	d													09 36											10 55
Hartlepool	d													09 42											11 00
Seaham	d													09a59									10 10		11a18
Sunderland ⛴	a																						10 30		
	d	06 50	07 20	07 50		08 20	08 35		08 50	09 05			09 12		09 20	09 35		09 50	10 05			10 20	10 30	10 35	
Heworth ⛴	d	07a28	08a00	08a30		09a00	09a15		09a30	09a45			09 32		10a00	10a15		10a00	10a45			10a23	10 50	11a15	
Newcastle 8 26 ⛴	a												09 50										11 10		
Metrocentre 48	a																								
Hexham 48	a																								

		NT	TW	TW	TW	TW		NT	NT	NT	TW	TW	TW	TW	NT	TP		TW	TW	NT	TW	GC	NT	NT	TW
																◇1						B 1			
			bus	bus	bus	bus		bus			bus	bus	bus	bus	bus			bus	bus	bus	bus				bus
Saltburn	d	10 44								11 44													12 44		
Marske	d	10 48								11 48													12 48		
Longbeck	d	10 51								11 51													12 51		
Redcar East	d	10 54								11 54													12 54		
Redcar Central	d	10 57								11 57													12 57		
British Steel Redcar §	d																								
South Bank	d																								
Middlesbrough	a	11 07								12 07													13 07		
	d	11 08							11 31	12 08						12 45							13 08	13 31	
Thornaby	d	11 13							11 36	12 13						12a50							13 13	13 36	
London Kings Cross 15 ⊖26	d																					09 48			
Eaglescliffe	a	11 18								12 18												12 28	13 18		
	d	11 19								12 19												12 29	13 19		
Allens West	d	11 21								12 21													13 21		
Tees-side Airport	d																								
Dinsdale	d	11 28								12 28													13 28		
Darlington 7 26	a	11 37								12 36													13 37		
	d	11 38																							
North Road	d	11 41																							
Heighington	d	11 49																							
Newton Aycliffe	d	11 52																							
Shildon	d	11 57																							
Bishop Auckland	a	12 02																							
Stockton	d								11 42															13 42	
Billingham	d								11 49															13 49	
Seaton Carew	d								11 55															13 55	
Hartlepool	d								12 01													12 52		14 01	
Seaham	d							11 30	12a18						12 30									14a18	
Sunderland ⛴	a							11 50							12 50							13 21			
	d		10 50	11 05	11 20	11 35		11 50			11 50	12 05	12 20	12 35	12 50			12 50	13 05	13 20	13 20				13 35
Heworth ⛴	d		11a30	11a45	12a00	12a15		12 10			12a30	12a45	13a00	13a15	13 10			13a30	13a45	13 40	14a00				14a15
Newcastle 8 26 ⛴	a							12 30							13 30					14 00					
Metrocentre 48	a																								
Hexham 48	a																								

§ For authorised access only to BSC Redcar

Table 44

Sundays
until 19 June

Saltburn and Middlesbrough - Darlington, Bishop Auckland, Sunderland and Newcastle

		NT		TW	TW	TW	TW	NT	TP	NT	TW	TW		NT	TW	NT	TW	NT	TW	TW	TW	TW		NT	TP
									◇1																◇1
Saltburn	d	13 44								14 44								15 44							
Marske	d	13 48								14 48								15 48							
Longbeck	d	13 51								14 51								15 51							
Redcar East	d	13 54								14 54								15 54							
Redcar Central	d	13 57								14 57								15 57							
British Steel Redcar §	d																								
South Bank	d																								
Middlesbrough	a	14 07								15 07								16 07							
	d	14 08							14 42	15 08						15 31		16 08							16 42
Thornaby	d	14 13							14a47	15 13						15 36		16 13							16a47
London Kings Cross 15 ⊖26	d																								
Eaglescliffe	a	14 18								15 18								16 18							
	d	14 19								15 19								16 19							
Allens West	d	14 21								15 21								16 21							
Tees-side Airport	d																								
Dinsdale	d	14 28								15 28								16 28							
Darlington 7 26	a	14 37								15 39								16 37							
	d	14 38																16 38							
North Road	d	14 41																16 41							
Heighington	d	14 49																16 49							
Newton Aycliffe	d	14 52																16 52							
Shildon	d	14 57																16 57							
Bishop Auckland	a	15 04																17 02							
Stockton	d															15 42									
Billingham	d															15 49									
Seaton Carew	d															15 55									
Hartlepool	d															16 01									
Seaham	d							14 30								16a18								16 30	
Sunderland ⛴	a							14 50																16 50	
	d			13 50	14 05	14 20	14 35	14 50			14 50	15 05		15 20	15 20		15 35		15 50	16 05	16 20	16 35		16 50	
Heworth ⛴	d			14a30	14a45	15a00	15a15	15 10			15a30	15a45		15 40	16a00		16a15		16a30	16a45	17a00	17a15		17 10	
Newcastle 8 26 ⛴	a							15 30						16 00										17 30	
Metrocentre 48	a																								
Hexham 48	a																								

		TW	TW	TW	GC	NT	NT	NT		TW	NT	NT	NT	TW	TW	TW	TW	NT		TP	NT	TW	NT	TW	TW
					1															◇1					
Saltburn	d						16 44						17 44								18 44				
Marske	d						16 48						17 48								18 48				
Longbeck	d						16 51						17 51								18 51				
Redcar East	d						16 54						17 54								18 54				
Redcar Central	d						16 57						17 57								18 57				
British Steel Redcar §	d																								
South Bank	d																								
Middlesbrough	a						17 07						18 07								19 07				
	d						17 08	17 22				17 45	18 08					18 40		18 45	19 08				
Thornaby	d						17 13	17 27				17 50	18 13					18 45		18a50	19 13				
London Kings Cross 15 ⊖26	d				13 48																				
Eaglescliffe	a				16 35		17 18	17 32					18 18					18 50			19 18				
	d				16 36	16 41	17 19	17 32					18 19					18 50			19 19				
Allens West	d						17 21	17 35					18 21					18 53			19 21				
Tees-side Airport	d																								
Dinsdale	d						17 28	17 41					18 28					19 01			19 28				
Darlington 7 26	a						17 37	17 52					18 37					19 14			19 37				
	d							17 54										19 15							
North Road	d							17 57										19 18							
Heighington	d							18 06										19 27							
Newton Aycliffe	d							18 09										19 30							
Shildon	d							18 13										19 34							
Bishop Auckland	a							18 20										19 44							
Stockton	d					16 46						17 56													
Billingham	d					16 53						18 03													
Seaton Carew	d					17 00						18 09													
Hartlepool	d				16 56	17 06						18 15													
Seaham	d					17a24					17 29	18a30											18 40		
Sunderland ⛴	a				17 22						17 49												19 00		
	d	16 50	17 05	17 20						17 35	17 49			17 50	18 05	18 20	18 35					18 50	19 00	19 05	19 20
Heworth ⛴	d	17a30	17a45	18a00						18a15	18 09			18a30	18a45	19a00	19a15					19a30	19 20	19a45	20a00
Newcastle 8 26 ⛴	a										18 29												19 40		
Metrocentre 48	a																								
Hexham 48	a																								

§ For authorised access only to BSC Redcar

Table 44

Sundays
until 19 June

Saltburn and Middlesbrough - Darlington, Bishop Auckland, Sunderland and Newcastle

		NT	TW	TW		TW	TW	GC	NT	TP	NT	TW	TW	NT		TW	TW	TW	TW	GC	NT	NT	TW	TP	
			🚌	🚌		🚌	🚌	[R] ☕		◇1		🚌	🚌	🚌		🚌	🚌	🚌	🚌	[R] ☕			🚌	◇1	
Saltburn	d										19 44										20 44	21 37			
Marske	d										19 48										20 48	21 41			
Longbeck	d										19 51										20 51	21 44			
Redcar East	d										19 54										20 54	21 47			
Redcar Central	d										19 57										20 57	21 50			
British Steel Redcar §	d																								
South Bank	d																								
Middlesbrough	a										20 11										21 07	22 00			
	d	19 31							19 40	20 06	20 12										21 08	22 02		22 06	
Thornaby	d	19 36							19 45	20a11	20 17										21 13	22 07		22a11	
London Kings Cross 15 ⊖26	d							16 48												18 27					
Eaglescliffe	a							19 35			20 22									21 06	21 18	22 12			
	d							19 39			20 22									21 07	21 19	22 12			
Allens West	d										20 25										21 21	22 15			
Tees-side Airport	d																								
Dinsdale	d										20 31										21 28	22 21			
Darlington 7 26	a	19 53									20 43										21 38	22 32			
	d																								
North Road	d																								
Heighington	d																								
Newton Aycliffe	d																								
Shildon	d																								
Bishop Auckland	a																								
Stockton	d								19 51																
Billingham	d								19 58																
Seaton Carew	d								20 04																
Hartlepool	d							19 59	20 10											21 27					
Seaham	d								20a27					20 40											
Sunderland 🚌	a							20 25						21 00						21 53					
	d		19 35	19 50		20 05	20 20					20 35	20 50	21 00		21 05	21 20	21 35	21 50				22 05		
Heworth 🚌	d		20a15	20a30		20a45	21a00					21a15	21a30	21 20		21a45	22a00	22a15	22a30				22a45		
Newcastle 8 26 🚌	a													21 40											
Metrocentre 48	a																								
Hexham 48	a																								

		TW	TW	NT	TW	TW	TW	TW
		🚌	🚌		🚌	🚌	🚌	🚌
Saltburn	d			22 44				
Marske	d			22 48				
Longbeck	d			22 51				
Redcar East	d			22 54				
Redcar Central	d			22 57				
British Steel Redcar §	d							
South Bank	d							
Middlesbrough	a			23 07				
	d			23 08				
Thornaby	d			23 13				
London Kings Cross 15 ⊖26	d							
Eaglescliffe	a			23 18				
	d			23 18				
Allens West	d			23 21				
Tees-side Airport	d							
Dinsdale	d			23 27				
Darlington 7 26	a			23 38				
	d							
North Road	d							
Heighington	d							
Newton Aycliffe	d							
Shildon	d							
Bishop Auckland	a							
Stockton	d							
Billingham	d							
Seaton Carew	d							
Hartlepool	d							
Seaham	d							
Sunderland 🚌	a							
	d	22 20	22 35		22 50	23 10	23 30	23 50
Heworth 🚌	d	23a00	23a15		23a30	23a44	00a10	00a06
Newcastle 8 26 🚌	a							
Metrocentre 48	a							
Hexham 48	a							

§ For authorised access only to BSC Redcar

Table 44

Sundays

26 June to 11 September

Saltburn and Middlesbrough - Darlington, Bishop Auckland, Sunderland and Newcastle

		NT	NT	NT	NT	NT	NT	TP	NT	NT		NT	NT	GC	GC	TP	NT	NT	NT	NT		TP	NT	NT	NT
								◇1						R 1 A ⊐P	R 1 B ⊐P	◇1						◇1			
Saltburn	d						09 44			10 44			11 44				12 44			13 44			14 44		
Marske	d						09 48			10 48			11 48				12 48			13 48			14 48		
Longbeck	d						09 51			10 51			11 51				12 51			13 51			14 51		
Redcar East	d						09 54			10 54			11 54				12 54			13 54			14 54		
Redcar Central	d						09 57			10 57			11 57				12 57			13 57			14 57		
British Steel Redcar §	d																								
South Bank	d																								
Middlesbrough	a						10 07			11 07			12 07				13 07			14 07			15 07		
	d		08 38	09 08		09 31	10 08	10 13		11 08		11 31	12 08			12 45	13 08		13 31	14 08		14 42	15 08		15 31
Thornaby	d		08 43	09 13		09 36	10 13	10a18		11 13		11 36	12 13			12a50	13 13		13 36	14 13		14a47	15 13		15 36
London Kings Cross 15 ⊖26	d													09 27	09 48										
Eaglescliffe	a		08 48	09 18			10 18			11 18			12 18	12 28	12 28		13 18			14 18			15 18		
	d		08 49	09 19			10 19		10 36	11 19			12 19	12 29	12 29		13 19			14 19			15 19		
Allens West	d		08 51	09 21			10 21			11 21			12 21				13 21			14 21			15 21		
Tees-side Airport	d																								
Dinsdale	d		08 58	09 28			10 28			11 28			12 28				13 28			14 28			15 28		
Darlington 7 26	a		09 07	09 37			10 37			11 37			12 36				13 37			14 37			15 39		
	d	08 05		09 38						11 38										14 38					
North Road	d	08 08		09 41						11 41										14 41					
Heighington	d	08 16		09 49						11 49										14 49					
Newton Aycliffe	d	08 19		09 52						11 52										14 52					
Shildon	d	08 24		09 57						11 57										14 57					
Bishop Auckland	a	08 31		10 02						12 02										15 04					
Stockton	d					09 42			10 41			11 42							13 42						15 42
Billingham	d					09 49			10 49			11 49							13 49						15 49
Seaton Carew	d					09 55			10 55			11 55							13 55						15 55
Hartlepool	d					10 01			11 00			12 01		12 52	12 52				14 01						16 01
Seaham	d					10 16			11 16			12 16							14 16						16 16
Sunderland ⛴	a					10 26			11 26			12 26		13 21	13 22				14 26						16 26
	d				09 28	10 28			11 28			12 28						13 28	14 28					15 28	16 28
Heworth ⛴	d				09 39	10 38			11 38			12 38						13 39	14 39					15 39	16 39
Newcastle 8 26 ⛴	a				09 50	10 48			11 48			12 48						13 49	14 48					15 48	16 48
Metrocentre 48	a				10 01	10 59			11 57			12 59						13 59	14 59					15 59	16 57
Hexham 48	a																								

		NT	NT	GC	TP	NT		NT	NT	NT	NT	TP	NT	NT	NT	GC		TP	NT	GC	NT	NT	TP	NT	
				R 1 ⊐P	◇1							◇1						◇1		R ⊐P			◇1		
Saltburn	d	15 44				16 44				17 44			18 44						19 44		20 44	21 37		22 44	
Marske	d	15 48				16 48				17 48			18 48						19 48		20 48	21 41		22 48	
Longbeck	d	15 51				16 51				17 51			18 51						19 51		20 51	21 44		22 51	
Redcar East	d	15 54				16 54				17 54			18 54						19 54		20 54	21 47		22 54	
Redcar Central	d	15 57				16 57				17 57			18 57						19 57		20 57	21 50		22 57	
British Steel Redcar §	d																								
South Bank	d																								
Middlesbrough	a	16 07				17 07				18 07			19 07						20 11		21 07	22 00		23 07	
	d	16 08			16 42	17 08		17 22	17 45	18 08	18 40	18 45	19 08		19 31			20 06	20 12		21 08	22 02	22 06	23 08	
Thornaby	d	16 13			16a47	17 13		17 27	17 50	18 13	18 45	18a50	19 13		19 36			20a11	20 17		21 13	22 07	22a11	23 13	
London Kings Cross 15 ⊖26	d			13 48												16 48				18 27					
Eaglescliffe	a	16 18		16 35		17 18		17 32		18 18	18 50		19 18			19 35			20 22	21 06	21 18	22 12		23 18	
	d	16 19	16 25	16 36		17 19		17 32		18 19	18 50		19 19			19 39			20 22	21 07	21 19	22 12		23 18	
Allens West	d	16 21				17 21		17 35		18 21	18 53		19 21						20 25		21 21	22 15		23 21	
Tees-side Airport	d																								
Dinsdale	d	16 28				17 28		17 41		18 28	19 01		19 28						20 31		21 28	22 21		23 27	
Darlington 7 26	a	16 37				17 37		17 52		18 37	19 14		19 37						20 43		21 38	22 32		23 38	
	d	16 38						17 54			19 15														
North Road	d	16 41						17 57			19 18														
Heighington	d	16 49						18 06			19 27														
Newton Aycliffe	d	16 52						18 09			19 30														
Shildon	d	16 57						18 13			19 34														
Bishop Auckland	a	17 02						18 20			19 44														
Stockton	d		16 31						17 56						19 42										
Billingham	d		16 38						18 03						19 49										
Seaton Carew	d		16 44						18 09						19 55										
Hartlepool	d		16 51	17 03					18 15						20 01	20 13				21 27					
Seaham	d		17 07						18 30						20 16										
Sunderland ⛴	a		17 22	17 27					18 41						20 26	20 39				21 53					
	d		17 28						18 43					19 28	20 29										
Heworth ⛴	d		17 39						18 54					19 39	20 40										
Newcastle 8 26 ⛴	a		17 48						19 05					19 52	20 47										
Metrocentre 48	a		17 59																						
Hexham 48	a																								

§ For authorised access only to BSC Redcar

A from 26 June until 31 July

B from 7 August until 11 September

Table 44

Sundays

18 September to 2 October

Saltburn and Middlesbrough - Darlington, Bishop Auckland, Sunderland and Newcastle

Station		NT	NT	NT	NT	NT	TP ◇1	NT	NT	NT	NT	GC R 1 ⊡	TP ◇1	NT	NT	NT	NT	TP ◇1	NT	NT	NT	NT	NT
Saltburn	d					09 44			10 44		11 44			12 44			13 44		14 44			15 44	
Marske	d					09 48			10 48		11 48			12 48			13 48		14 48			15 48	
Longbeck	d					09 51			10 51		11 51			12 51			13 51		14 51			15 51	
Redcar East	d					09 54			10 54		11 54			12 54			13 54		14 54			15 54	
Redcar Central	d					09 57			10 57		11 57			12 57			13 57		14 57			15 57	
British Steel Redcar §	d																						
South Bank	d																						
Middlesbrough	a					10 07			11 07		12 07			13 07			14 07		15 07			16 07	
	d	08 38	09 08		09 31	10 08	10 13		11 08	11 31	12 08		12 45	13 08		13 31	14 08	14 42	15 08		15 31	16 08	
Thornaby	d	08 43	09 13		09 36	10 13	10a18		11 13	11 36	12 13		12a50	13 13		13 36	14 13	14a47	15 13		15 36	16 13	
London Kings Cross 15 ⊖26	d											09 48											
Eaglescliffe	a	08 48	09 18			10 18			11 18		12 18	12 28		13 18			14 18		15 18			16 18	
	d	08 49	09 19			10 19		10 36	11 19		12 19	12 29		13 19			14 19		15 19			16 19	16 25
Allens West	d	08 51	09 21			10 21			11 21		12 21			13 21			14 21		15 21			16 21	
Tees-side Airport	d																						
Dinsdale	d	08 58	09 28			10 28			11 28		12 28			13 28			14 28		15 28			16 28	
Darlington 7 26	a	09 07	09 37			10 37			11 37		12 36			13 37			14 37		15 39			16 37	
	d		09 38						11 38								14 38					16 38	
North Road	d		09 41						11 41								14 41					16 41	
Heighington	d		09 49						11 49								14 49					16 49	
Newton Aycliffe	d		09 52						11 52								14 52					16 52	
Shildon	d		09 57						11 57								14 57					16 57	
Bishop Auckland	a		10 02						12 02								15 04					17 02	
Stockton	d				09 42			10 41		11 42						13 42					15 42		16 31
Billingham	d				09 49			10 49		11 49						13 49					15 49		16 38
Seaton Carew	d				09 55			10 55		11 55						13 55					15 55		16 44
Hartlepool	d				10 01			11 00		12 01		12 52				14 01					16 01		16 51
Seaham	d				10 16			11 16		12 16						14 16					16 16		17 07
Sunderland ⛴	a				10 26			11 26		12 26		13 22				14 26					16 26		17 22
	d			09 28	10 28			11 28		12 28					13 28	14 28				15 28	16 28		17 28
Heworth ⛴	d			09 39	10 38			11 38		12 38					13 39	14 39				15 39	16 39		17 39
Newcastle 8 26 ⛴	a			09 50	10 48			11 48		12 48					13 49	14 48				15 48	16 48		17 48
Metrocentre 48	a			10 01	10 59			11 57		12 59					13 59	14 59				15 59	16 57		17 59
Hexham 48	a																						

Station		GC R 1 ⊡	TP ◇1	NT	NT	NT	TP ◇1	NT	NT	NT	GC	TP ◇1	NT	GC R ⊡	NT	NT	TP ◇1	NT
Saltburn	d			16 44		17 44		18 44					19 44		20 44	21 37		22 44
Marske	d			16 48		17 48		18 48					19 48		20 48	21 41		22 48
Longbeck	d			16 51		17 51		18 51					19 51		20 51	21 44		22 51
Redcar East	d			16 54		17 54		18 54					19 54		20 54	21 47		22 54
Redcar Central	d			16 57		17 57		18 57					19 57		20 57	21 50		22 57
British Steel Redcar §	d																	
South Bank	d																	
Middlesbrough	a			17 07		18 07		19 07					20 11		21 07	22 00		23 07
	d		16 42	17 08	17 45	18 08	18 45	19 08		19 31		20 06	20 12		21 08	22 02	22 06	23 08
Thornaby	d		16a47	17 13	17 50	18 13	18a50	19 13		19 36		20a11	20 17		21 13	22 07	22a11	23 13
London Kings Cross 15 ⊖26	d	13 48									16 48			18 27				
Eaglescliffe	a	16 35		17 18		18 18		19 18			19 35		20 22	21 06	21 18	22 12		23 18
	d	16 36		17 19		18 19		19 19			19 39		20 22	21 07	21 19	22 12		23 18
Allens West	d			17 21		18 21		19 21					20 25		21 21	22 15		23 21
Tees-side Airport	d																	
Dinsdale	d			17 28		18 28		19 28					20 31		21 28	22 21		23 27
Darlington 7 26	a			17 37		18 37		19 37					20 43		21 38	22 32		23 38
	d					18 38												
North Road	d					18 41												
Heighington	d					18 49												
Newton Aycliffe	d					18 52												
Shildon	d					18 57												
Bishop Auckland	a					19 02												
Stockton	d				17 56					19 42								
Billingham	d				18 03					19 49								
Seaton Carew	d				18 09					19 55								
Hartlepool	d	17 03			18 15					20 01	20 13			21 27				
Seaham	d				18 30					20 16								
Sunderland ⛴	a	17 27			18 41					20 26	20 39			21 53				
	d				18 43				19 28	20 29								
Heworth ⛴	d				18 54				19 39	20 40								
Newcastle 8 26 ⛴	a				19 05				19 52	20 47								
Metrocentre 48	a																	
Hexham 48	a																	

§ For authorised access only to BSC Redcar

Table 44

Sundays

from 9 October

Saltburn and Middlesbrough - Darlington, Bishop Auckland, Sunderland and Newcastle

		NT	NT	NT	NT	NT	TP	NT	NT	NT		NT	GC	TP	NT	NT	NT	NT	TP	NT		NT	NT	NT	NT
							◇1						R 1 ⊐	◇1					◇1						
Saltburn	d					09 44			10 44			11 44			12 44			13 44		14 44				15 44	
Marske	d					09 48			10 48			11 48			12 48			13 48		14 48				15 48	
Longbeck	d					09 51			10 51			11 51			12 51			13 51		14 51				15 51	
Redcar East	d					09 54			10 54			11 54			12 54			13 54		14 54				15 54	
Redcar Central	d					09 57			10 57			11 57			12 57			13 57		14 57				15 57	
British Steel Redcar §	d																								
South Bank	d																								
Middlesbrough	a					10 07			11 07			12 07			13 07			14 07		15 07				16 07	
	d	08 38	09 08		09 31	10 08	10 13		11 08	11 31		12 08		12 45	13 08		13 31	14 08	14 42	15 08			15 31	16 08	
Thornaby	d	08 43	09 13		09 36	10 13	10a18		11 13	11 36		12 13		12a50	13 13		13 36	14 13	14a47	15 13			15 36	16 13	
London Kings Cross 15 ⊖26	d												09 48												
Eaglescliffe	a	08 48	09 18			10 18			11 18			12 18	12 28		13 18			14 18		15 18				16 18	
	d	08 49	09 19			10 19		10 36	11 19			12 19	12 29		13 19			14 19		15 19				16 19	16 25
Allens West	d	08 51	09 21			10 21			11 21			12 21			13 21			14 21		15 21				16 21	
Tees-side Airport	d																								
Dinsdale	d	08 58	09 28			10 28			11 28			12 28			13 28			14 28		15 28				16 28	
Darlington 7 26	a	09 07	09 37			10 37			11 37			12 36			13 37			14 37		15 39				16 37	
	d		09 38						11 38									14 38						16 38	
North Road	d		09 41						11 41									14 41						16 41	
Heighington	d		09 49						11 49									14 49						16 49	
Newton Aycliffe	d		09 52						11 52									14 52						16 52	
Shildon	d		09 57						11 57									14 57						16 57	
Bishop Auckland	a		10 02						12 02									15 04						17 02	
Stockton	d				09 42			10 41		11 42							13 42						15 42		16 31
Billingham	d				09 49			10 49		11 49							13 49						15 49		16 38
Seaton Carew	d				09 55			10 55		11 55							13 55						15 55		16 44
Hartlepool	d				10 01			11 00		12 01			12 52				14 01						16 01		16 51
Seaham	d				10 16			11 16		12 16							14 16						16 16		17 07
Sunderland 🚢	a				10 26			11 26		12 26			13 22				14 26						16 26		17 22
	d			09 28	10 28			11 28		12 28						13 28	14 28					15 28	16 28		17 28
Heworth 🚢	d			09 39	10 38			11 38		12 38						13 39	14 39					15 39	16 39		17 39
Newcastle 8 26 🚢	a			09 50	10 48			11 48		12 48						13 49	14 48					15 48	16 48		17 48
Metrocentre 48	a			10 01	10 59			11 57		12 59						13 59	14 59					15 59	16 57		17 59
Hexham 48	a																								

		GC	TP	NT	NT	NT		TP	NT	NT	NT	GC	TP	NT	GC	NT		NT	TP	NT
		R 1 ⊐	◇1					◇1					◇1		R ⊐				◇1	
Saltburn	d			16 44		17 44			18 44					19 44		20 44		21 37		22 44
Marske	d			16 48		17 48			18 48					19 48		20 48		21 41		22 48
Longbeck	d			16 51		17 51			18 51					19 51		20 51		21 44		22 51
Redcar East	d			16 54		17 54			18 54					19 54		20 54		21 47		22 54
Redcar Central	d			16 57		17 57			18 57					19 57		20 57		21 50		22 57
British Steel Redcar §	d																			
South Bank	d																			
Middlesbrough	a			17 07		18 07			19 07					20 11		21 07		22 00		23 07
	d		16 42	17 08	17 45	18 08		18 45	19 08		19 31		20 06	20 12		21 08		22 02	22 06	23 08
Thornaby	d		16a47	17 13	17 50	18 13		18a50	19 13		19 36		20a11	20 17		21 13		22 07	22a11	23 13
London Kings Cross 15 ⊖26	d	13 48										16 48			18 27					
Eaglescliffe	a	16 35		17 18		18 18			19 18			19 35		20 22	21 06	21 18		22 12		23 18
	d	16 36		17 19		18 19			19 19			19 39		20 22	21 07	21 19		22 12		23 18
Allens West	d			17 21		18 21			19 21					20 25		21 21		22 15		23 21
Tees-side Airport	d																			
Dinsdale	d			17 28		18 28			19 28					20 31		21 28		22 21		23 27
Darlington 7 26	a			17 37		18 37			19 37					20 43		21 38		22 32		23 38
	d					18 38														
North Road	d					18 41														
Heighington	d					18 49														
Newton Aycliffe	d					18 52														
Shildon	d					18 57														
Bishop Auckland	a					19 02														
Stockton	d				17 56						19 42									
Billingham	d				18 03						19 49									
Seaton Carew	d				18 09						19 55									
Hartlepool	d	17 03			18 15						20 01	20 13			21 27					
Seaham	d				18 30						20 16									
Sunderland 🚢	a	17 27			18 41						20 26	20 39			21 53					
	d				18 43					19 28	20 29									
Heworth 🚢	d				18 54					19 39	20 40									
Newcastle 8 26 🚢	a				19 05					19 52	20 47									
Metrocentre 48	a																			
Hexham 48	a																			

§ For authorised access only to BSC Redcar

Middlesbrough and Pickering - Whitby

Miles			NT	NT	NT	NY A 1	NT	NT	NY A 1 I	NT	NT		NT	NY B 1 J	NY C 1 J	NT	NT	NT
—	Newcastle 8 44	d			07 30			10 30			13 30		15 30				16 30	18 30
0	**Middlesbrough**	d	07 04	08 14	08 47		10 38	11 50		14 16	14 46		16 47			17 40	17b54	19 49
3	Marton	d	07 09	08 19	08 52		10 43	11 56		14 21	14 52		16 52			17 45	17 59	19 54
4	Gypsy Lane	d	07 12	08 23	08 55		10 46	12 00		14 24	14 55		16 55			17 48	18 02	19 57
4½	Nunthorpe	d	07 17	08a29	09a01		10 49	12a04		14 27	15a00		17a00			17 51	18a07	20a03
8½	Great Ayton	d	07 23				10 55			14 33						17 57		
11	Battersby	a	07 29				11 01			14 39						18 03		
—		d	07 36				11 05			14 43						18 07		
12¾	Kildale	d	07 41				11 10			14 48						18 12		
16¾	Commondale	d	07 48				11 17			14 55						18 19		
18½	Castleton Moor	d	07 52				11 20			14 58						18 22		
20	Danby	d	07 55				11 23			15 01						18 25		
23½	Lealholm	d	08 02				11 30			15 08						18 32		
25½	Glaisdale	a	08 07				11 34			15 12						18 36		
—		d	08 09				11 37			15 15						18 39		
27¼	Egton	d	08 13				11 40			15 18						18 42		
—	**Pickering** §	d				09 00			12 00					15 00	16 00			
—	Levisham §	d				09 19			12 20					15 20	16 20			
—	Goathland §	d				09 45			12 50					16 10	16 50			
28¾	Grosmont	d	08 17			10 10	11 44		13 10	15 22				16 35	17 10	18 46		
32	Sleights	d	08 26				11 53			15 31						18 55		
33½	Ruswarp	d	08 31				11 58			15 36						19 00		
35	**Whitby**	a	08 38			10 35	12 05		13 35	15 43				17 00	17 35	19 07		

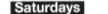

Saturdays

		NT	NT	NT	NT	NY D 1	NT	NT	NY D 1 I	NT		NT	NT	NY E 1 J	NY F 1 J	NT	NT	NT
Newcastle 8 44	d			07 30	08 30			10 30				13 30	15 30				16 30	18 30
Middlesbrough	d	07 04	08 14	08 47	09a50		10 38	11 50		14 16		14 46	16 47			17 40	17 54	19 49
Marton	d	07 09	08 19	08 52			10 43	11 56		14 21		14 52	16 52			17 45	17 59	19 54
Gypsy Lane	d	07 12	08 23	08 55			10 46	12 00		14 24		14 55	16 55			17 48	18 02	19 57
Nunthorpe	d	07 17	08a28	08a59			10 49	12a04		14 27		15a00	16a59			17 51	18a05	20a03
Great Ayton	d	07 23					10 55			14 33						17 57		
Battersby	a	07 29					11 01			14 39						18 03		
	d	07 36					11 05			14 43						18 07		
Kildale	d	07 41					11 10			14 48						18 12		
Commondale	d	07 48					11 17			14 55						18 19		
Castleton Moor	d	07 52					11 20			14 58						18 22		
Danby	d	07 55					11 23			15 01						18 25		
Lealholm	d	08 02					11 30			15 08						18 32		
Glaisdale	a	08 07					11 34			15 12						18 36		
	d	08 09					11 37			15 15						18 39		
Egton	d	08 13					11 40			15 18						18 42		
Pickering §	d					09 00			12 00					15 00	16 00			
Levisham §	d					09 19			12 20					15 20	16 20			
Goathland §	d					09 45			12 50					16 10	16 50			
Grosmont	d	08 17				10 10	11 44		13 10	15 22				16 35	17 10	18 46		
Sleights	d	08 26					11 53			15 31						18 55		
Ruswarp	d	08 31					11 58			15 36						19 00		
Whitby	a	08 38				10 35	12 05		13 35	15 43				17 00	17 35	19 07		

Sundays
until 19 June

		NT	NT	NT G	NT H	NT	NT	NT
Newcastle 8 44	d			09 45	10 04			21 06
Middlesbrough	d	08 47	09 48	11 06	11 06	14 17	15 25	22a10
Marton	d	08 52	09 53	11 12	11 12	14 23	15 30	
Gypsy Lane	d	08 55	09 56	11 15	11 15	14 26	15 33	
Nunthorpe	d	08 58	09 59	11 18	11 18	14 29	15 36	
Great Ayton	d	09 04	10 05	11 24	11 24	14 35	15 42	
Battersby	a	09 10	10 11	11 30	11 30	14 41	15 48	
	d	09 14	10 15	11 34	11 34	14 45	15 52	
Kildale	d	09 19	10 20	11 39	11 39	14 50	15 57	
Commondale	d	09 26	10 27	11 46	11 46	14 57	16 04	
Castleton Moor	d	09 29	10 30	11 49	11 49	15 00	16 07	
Danby	d	09 32	10 33	11 52	11 52	15 03	16 10	
Lealholm	d	09 39	10 40	11 59	11 59	15 10	16 17	
Glaisdale	a	09 43	10 44	12 03	12 03	15 14	16 21	
	d	09 46	10 50	12 06	12 06	15 17	16 26	
Egton	d	09 49	10 53	12 09	12 09	15 20	16 29	
Pickering §	d							
Levisham §	d							
Goathland §	d							
Grosmont	d	09 53	10 57	12 13	12 13	15 24	16 33	
Sleights	d	10 02	11 06	12 22	12 22	15 33	16 42	
Ruswarp	d	10 07	11 11	12 27	12 27	15 38	16 47	
Whitby	a	10 17	11 21	12 37	12 37	15 48	16 56	

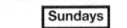

§ North Yorkshire Moors Railway. For full service between Grosmont and Pickering please refer to separate publicity
A until 28 October
B until 22 July, not from 30 May until 3 June, also from 5 September until 28 October
C from 30 May until 3 June, from 25 July until 2 September
D until 29 October
E from 11 June until 23 July, 10 September, 17 September, 24 September, 8 October, 22 October, 29 October
F 28 May, 4 June, from 30 July until 3 September, 1 October, 15 October
G 19 June
H not 19 June
I The Yorkshire Coast Express
J The Moors Explorer

Table 45

Middlesbrough and Pickering - Whitby

Sundays

26 June to 11 September

		NT	NT	NT	NT	NT	NT
Newcastle [8] 44	d			09 45			21 06
Middlesbrough	d	08 47	09 48	11 06	14 17	15 25	22a10
Marton	d	08 52	09 53	11 12	14 23	15 30	
Gypsy Lane	d	08 55	09 56	11 15	14 26	15 33	
Nunthorpe	d	08 58	09 59	11 18	14 29	15 36	
Great Ayton	d	09 04	10 05	11 24	14 35	15 42	
Battersby	a	09 10	10 11	11 30	14 41	15 48	
	d	09 14	10 15	11 34	14 45	15 52	
Kildale	d	09 19	10 20	11 39	14 50	15 57	
Commondale	d	09 26	10 27	11 46	14 57	16 04	
Castleton Moor	d	09 29	10 30	11 49	15 00	16 07	
Danby	d	09 32	10 33	11 52	15 03	16 10	
Lealholm	d	09 39	10 40	11 59	15 10	16 17	
Glaisdale	a	09 43	10 44	12 03	15 14	16 21	
	d	09 46	10 50	12 06	15 17	16 26	
Egton	d	09 49	10 53	12 09	15 20	16 29	
Pickering §	d						
Levisham §	d						
Goathland §	d						
Grosmont	d	09 53	10 57	12 13	15 24	16 33	
Sleights	d	10 02	11 06	12 22	15 33	16 42	
Ruswarp	d	10 07	11 11	12 27	15 38	16 47	
Whitby	a	10 17	11 21	12 37	15 48	16 56	

Sundays

18 September to 30 October

		NT	NY	NY	NY	NY	NT
					A	B	
			[1]	[1] C	[1] D	[1] D	
Newcastle [8] 44	d	09 45					21 06
Middlesbrough	d	11a05					22a10
Marton	d						
Gypsy Lane	d						
Nunthorpe	d						
Great Ayton	d						
Battersby	a						
	d						
Kildale	d						
Commondale	d						
Castleton Moor	d						
Danby	d						
Lealholm	d						
Glaisdale	a						
	d						
Egton	d						
Pickering §	d		09 00	12 00	*15 00*	16 00	
Levisham §	d		09 19	12 20	*15 20*	16 20	
Goathland §	d		09 45	12 50	16 10	16 50	
Grosmont	d		10 10	13 10	16 35	17 10	
Sleights	d						
Ruswarp	d						
Whitby	a		10 35	13 35	17 00	17 35	

Sundays

from 6 November

		NT	NT
Newcastle [8] 44	d	09 45	21 06
Middlesbrough	d	11a05	22a10
Marton	d		
Gypsy Lane	d		
Nunthorpe	d		
Great Ayton	d		
Battersby	a		
	d		
Kildale	d		
Commondale	d		
Castleton Moor	d		
Danby	d		
Lealholm	d		
Glaisdale	a		
	d		
Egton	d		
Pickering §	d		
Levisham §	d		
Goathland §	d		
Grosmont	d		
Sleights	d		
Ruswarp	d		
Whitby	a		

§ North Yorkshire Moors Railway. For full service between Grosmont and Pickering please refer to separate publicity

A not 2 October, 16 October

B 2 October, 16 October

C The Yorkshire Coast Express

D The Moors Explorer

Table 45

Mondays to Fridays

Whitby - Pickering and Middlesbrough

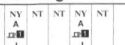

Miles			NT	NT	NT	NT	NY A 1 I	NT	NT	NY A 1 J	NT		NT	NT	NY B 1	NY C 1	NT	NT
0	**Whitby**	d				08 50	11 00		12 41	14 00				16 05	17 30	18 00		19 15
1½	Ruswarp	d				08 54			12 45					16 09				19 19
3	Sleights	d				08 59			12 50					16 14				19 24
6¼	Grosmont	d				09 07	11a20		12 58	14a20				16 22	17a50	18a20		19 32
—	Goathland §	a					11 45			14 45					18 15	18 45		
—	Levisham §	a					12 16			15 16					18 40	19 10		
—	**Pickering** §	a					12 40			15 40					19 00	19 30		
7¾	Egton	d				09 10			13 01					16 26				19 35
9½	Glaisdale	a				09 14			13 05					16 30				19 39
—		d				09 17			13 08					16 33				19 42
11½	Lealholm	d				09 22			13 13					16 38				19 47
15	Danby	d				09 28			13 19					16 45				19 53
16½	Castleton Moor	d				09 31			13 22					16 49				19 56
18¼	Commondale	d				09 35			13 26					16 52				20 00
22¼	Kildale	d				09 42			13 33					16 59				20 07
24	Battersby	a				09 47			13 38					17 04				20 12
—		d				09 51			13 42					17 09				20 16
26½	Great Ayton	d				09 56			13 47					17 14				20 21
30½	Nunthorpe	d	07 21	08 31	09 16	10 03		12 16	13 54		15 16		17 02	17 21			18 24	20 28
31	Gypsy Lane	d	07 23	08 33	09 18	10 05		12 18	13 56		15 18		17 04	17 23			18 26	20 30
32	Marton	d	07 25	08 36	09 21	10 08		12 21	13 59		15 21		17 06	17 25			18 29	20 33
35	**Middlesbrough**	a	07 31	08 43	09 29	10 17		12 28	14 07		15 28		17 15	17 35			18 35	20 41
—	Newcastle 8 44	a	08 52		10 51			13 51			16 51							

Saturdays

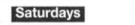

		NT	NT	NT	NT	NY D 1 I	NT	NT	NY D 1 J	NT		NT	NT	NY E 1	NY F 1	NT	NT
Whitby	d				08 50	11 00		12 41	14 00				16 05	17 30	18 00		19 15
Ruswarp	d				08 54			12 45					16 09				19 19
Sleights	d				08 59			12 50					16 14				19 24
Grosmont	d				09 07	11a20		12 58	14a20				16 22	17a50	18a20		19 32
Goathland §	a					11 45			14 45					18 15	18 45		
Levisham §	a					12 16			15 16					18 40	19 10		
Pickering §	a					12 40			15 40					19 00	19 30		
Egton	d				09 10			13 01					16 26				19 35
Glaisdale	a				09 14			13 05					16 30				19 39
	d				09 17			13 08					16 33				19 42
Lealholm	d				09 22			13 13					16 38				19 47
Danby	d				09 28			13 19					16 45				19 53
Castleton Moor	d				09 31			13 22					16 49				19 56
Commondale	d				09 35			13 26					16 52				20 00
Kildale	d				09 42			13 33					16 59				20 07
Battersby	a				09 47			13 38					17 04				20 12
	d				09 51			13 42					17 09				20 16
Great Ayton	d				09 56			13 47					17 14				20 21
Nunthorpe	d	07 21	08 31	09 16	10 03		12 16	13 54		15 16		17 02	17 21			18 24	20 28
Gypsy Lane	d	07 23	08 33	09 18	10 05		12 18	13 56		15 18		17 04	17 23			18 26	20 30
Marton	d	07 25	08 36	09 21	10 08		12 21	13 59		15 21		17 06	17 25			18 29	20 33
Middlesbrough	a	07 31	08 43	09 29	10 17		12 27	14 07		15 28		17 15	17 35			18 35	20 41
Newcastle 8 44	a	08 52		10 51			13 52			16 51							22 04

Sundays

until 19 June

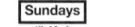

		NT	NT	NT	NT	NT G	NT H
Whitby	d	10 24	12 44	15 55	17 10	18 00	18 00
Ruswarp	d	10 28	12 48	15 59	17 14	18 04	18 04
Sleights	d	10 33	12 53	16 04	17 19	18 09	18 09
Grosmont	d	10 41	13 01	16 12	17 27	18 17	18 17
Goathland §	a						
Levisham §	a						
Pickering §	a						
Egton	d	10 44	13 04	16 15	17 30	18 20	18 20
Glaisdale	a	10 48	13 08	16 19	17 34	18 24	18 24
	d	10 53	13 11	16 24	17 37	18 27	18 27
Lealholm	d	10 58	13 16	16 29	17 42	18 32	18 32
Danby	d	11 04	13 22	16 35	17 48	18 38	18 38
Castleton Moor	d	11 07	13 25	16 38	17 51	18 41	18 41
Commondale	d	11 11	13 29	16 42	17 55	18 45	18 45
Kildale	d	11 18	13 36	16 49	18 02	18 52	18 52
Battersby	a	11 23	13 41	16 54	18 07	18 57	18 57
	d	11 39	13 45	16 58	18 11	19 01	19 01
Great Ayton	d	11 44	13 50	17 03	18 16	19 06	19 06
Nunthorpe	d	11 51	13 57	17 10	18 23	19 13	19 13
Gypsy Lane	d	11 53	13 59	17 12	18 25	19 15	19 15
Marton	d	11 56	14 02	17 15	18 28	19 18	19 18
Middlesbrough	a	12 02	14 12	17 22	18 39	19 30	19 30
Newcastle 8 44	a						20 47

§ North Yorkshire Moors Railway. For full service between Grosmont and Pickering please refer to separate publicity
A until 28 October
B until 22 July, not from 30 May until 3 June, also from 5 September until 28 October
C from 30 May until 3 June, from 25 July until 2 September
D until 29 October
E from 11 June until 23 July, 10 September, 17 September, 24 September, 8 October, 22 October, 29 October
F 28 May, 4 June, from 30 July until 3 September, 1 October, 15 October
G not 19 June
H 19 June
I The Moors Explorer
J The Yorkshire Coast Express

For connections to Darlington please refer to Table 44

Table 45

Whitby - Pickering and Middlesbrough

Sundays

26 June to 11 September

		NT	NT	NT	NT	NT
Whitby	d	10 24	12 44	15 55	17 10	18 00
Ruswarp	d	10 28	12 48	15 59	17 14	18 04
Sleights	d	10 33	12 53	16 04	17 19	18 09
Grosmont	d	10 41	13 01	16 12	17 27	18 17
Goathland §	a					
Levisham §	a					
Pickering §	a					
Egton	d	10 44	13 04	16 15	17 30	18 20
Glaisdale	a	10 48	13 08	16 19	17 34	18 24
	d	10 53	13 11	16 24	17 37	18 27
Lealholm	d	10 58	13 16	16 29	17 42	18 32
Danby	d	11 04	13 22	16 35	17 48	18 38
Castleton Moor	d	11 07	13 25	16 38	17 51	18 41
Commondale	d	11 11	13 29	16 42	17 55	18 45
Kildale	d	11 18	13 36	16 49	18 02	18 52
Battersby	a	11 23	13 41	16 54	18 07	18 57
	d	11 39	13 45	16 58	18 11	19 01
Great Ayton	d	11 44	13 50	17 03	18 16	19 06
Nunthorpe	d	11 51	13 57	17 10	18 23	19 13
Gypsy Lane	d	11 53	13 59	17 12	18 25	19 15
Marton	d	11 56	14 02	17 15	18 28	19 18
Middlesbrough	a	12 02	14 12	17 22	18 39	19 30
Newcastle 8 44	a					20 47

Sundays

18 September to 30 October

		NY	NY	NY	NY
				A	B
		1	1	1	1
		C	D		
Whitby	d	11 00	14 00	17 30	18 00
Ruswarp	d				
Sleights	d				
Grosmont	d	11a20	14a20	17a50	18a20
Goathland §	a	11 45	14 45	18 15	18 45
Levisham §	a	12 16	15 16	18 40	19 10
Pickering §	a	12 40	15 40	19 00	19 30
Egton	d				
Glaisdale	a				
	d				
Lealholm	d				
Danby	d				
Castleton Moor	d				
Commondale	d				
Kildale	d				
Battersby	a				
	d				
Great Ayton	d				
Nunthorpe	d				
Gypsy Lane	d				
Marton	d				
Middlesbrough	a				
Newcastle 8 44	a				

§ North Yorkshire Moors Railway. For full service between Grosmont and Pickering please refer to separate publicity

A not 2 October, 16 October
B 2 October, 16 October
C The Moors Explorer
D The Yorkshire Coast Express

For connections to Darlington please refer to Table 44

Table 48

Mondays to Fridays

until 30 September

Chathill and Morpeth - Newcastle - Metrocentre, Hexham and Carlisle

Miles	Miles			GR	NT	NT	GR	XC	NT	NT	NT	XC		NT	NT	NT	NT	GR	NT	NT	NT	NT		NT	NT
				R 1			R 1	◇1				◇1						R 1							
0	—	**Chathill**	d						07 07																
11¼	—	Alnmouth for Alnwick 26	d	06 19			06 52	07 08	07 19			07 59						08 58							
17½	—	Acklington	d						07 36																
22¾	—	Widdrington	d						07 44																
27½	—	Pegswood	d						07 50																
39½	—	**Morpeth** 26	d	06 35			07 07		07 54			08 13				08 49						09 49			
36¼	—	Cramlington	d						08 02							08 57						09 57			
45½	—	Manors	d						08 15							09 10						10 10			
46	—	**Newcastle** 8 26 ⛴	a	06 52			07 24	07 38	08 19			08 30				09 14		09 27				10 14			
—	—	Sunderland 26,44 ⛴	d							07 30	07 55				08 30						09 30				
—	—	**Newcastle** 8 ⛴	d		06 30	06 47				07 53	08a18			08 24	08a52		08 54		09 26	09 44	09 54	10 15		10 22	10 44
48¼	2¼	Dunston	d																		09 59				
49½	3½	**Metrocentre**	a							08 00				08 31			09 01		09 33	09 52	10 02	10 22		10 29	10 52
—	—		d							08 01				08 32			09 02		09 33		10 02			10 31	
—	5½	Blaydon	d							08 05															
—	9¾	Wylam	d		06 44					08 11				08 40			09 12				10 10				
—	12	Prudhoe	d		06 48	07 03				08 15				08 44			09 16		09 43		10 14			10 42	
—	14½	Stocksfield	d		06 53					08 20				08 48			09 21				10 18				
—	16¾	Riding Mill	d		06 57					08 24							09 25				10 23				
—	19¼	Corbridge	d		07 01					08 28							09 29				10 26				
—	22¼	**Hexham**	a		07 10	07 16				08 38				08 58			09 39		09 56		10 36			10 54	
—	—		d			07 16								08 59					09 56					10 54	
—	30	Haydon Bridge	d			07 25								09 08										11 04	
—	33¾	Bardon Mill	d			07 32								09 14										11 11	
—	38½	Haltwhistle	d			07 39								09 21					10 15					11 17	
—	50¾	Brampton (Cumbria)	d			07 54								09 37										11 33	
—	57½	Wetheral	d			08 03								09 46										11 42	
—	61¾	**Carlisle** 8	a			08 13								10 02					10 48					11 54	

		NT	NT	GR	XC	NT	NT	NT		NT	XC	NT	NT	NT	NT	GR	NT	NT		NT	NT	XC	NT	NT	NT
				R 1	◇1						◇1					R 1						◇1			
Chathill	d																								
Alnmouth for Alnwick 26	d			10 58							12 08					12 58						14 08			
Acklington	d																								
Widdrington	d																								
Pegswood	d																								
Morpeth 26	d		10 49		11 21					11 49					12 49						13 49				
Cramlington	d		10 57							11 57					12 57						13 57				
Manors	d		11 10							12 10					13 10						14 10				
Newcastle 8 26 ⛴	a		11 14	11 27	11 39					12 13	12 38				13 13	13 27					14 13	14 40			
Sunderland 26,44 ⛴	d	10 30						11 30						12 30						13 30					14 30
Newcastle 8 ⛴	d	10 54	11 15			11 22	11 42	11 54		12 14		12 22	12 43	12 54	13 15		13 22	13 44		13 54	14 15		14 24	14 44	14 56
Dunston	d																								
Metrocentre	a	11 01	11 22			11 31	11 51	12 01		12 22		12 31	12 52	13 01	13 22		13 31	13 51		14 01	14 22		14 31	14 51	15 02
	d	11 02				11 32		12 02				12 32		13 02			13 32			14 02			14 32		15 02
Blaydon	d																								
Wylam	d	11 10						12 10						13 10						14 10					15 10
Prudhoe	d	11 14				11 42		12 14				12 42		13 14			13 43			14 14			14 42		15 16
Stocksfield	d	11 18						12 18						13 18						14 18					15 18
Riding Mill	d	11 23						12 23						13 23						14 23					15 23
Corbridge	d	11 26						12 26						13 26						14 26					15 26
Hexham	a	11 36				11 55		12 36				12 55		13 36			13 55			14 36			14 55		15 37
	d					11 55						12 55					13 56						14 55		
Haydon Bridge	d											13 04											15 04		
Bardon Mill	d											13 11											15 11		
Haltwhistle	d					12 14						13 18					14 15						15 18		
Brampton (Cumbria)	d											13 33											15 33		
Wetheral	d											13 42											15 42		
Carlisle 8	a					12 47						13 54					14 49						15 54		

For connections from London Kings Cross please refer to Table 26

Table 48

Mondays to Fridays

until 30 September

Chathill and Morpeth - Newcastle - Metrocentre, Hexham and Carlisle

			NT	GR	NT		NT	NT	NT	NT	NT	NT	NT	XC	NT		NT	NT	NT	GR	NT	NT	NT	XC
				R 1										◇1						R 1				◇1
Chathill		d																						
Alnmouth for Alnwick	26	d		14 58										17 03						17 58				19 08
Acklington		d																						
Widdrington		d																						
Pegswood		d																						
Morpeth	26	d	14 49						15 49				16 49	17 18								18 26	19 01	
Cramlington		d	14 57						15 57				16 57									18 34	19 09	
Manors		d	15 10						16 10				17 10											
Newcastle 8	26 ⛴	a	15 14	15 27					16 14				17 15	17 36						18 27		18 49	19 25	19 38
Sunderland	26,44 ⛴	d						15 30				16 30							17 30					
Newcastle 8	⛴	d	15 15		15 23		15 44	15 54	16 15	16 22	16 44	16 54			17 16		17 24	17 44	17 54		18 24			
Dunston		d																17 50						
Metrocentre		a	15 22		15 31		15 51	16 01	16 22	16 33	16 53	17 01			17 23		17 31	17 53	18 01		18 31			
		d			15 31			16 02		16 33		17 02			17 24		17 32		18 02		18 32			
Blaydon		d															17 36							
Wylam		d						16 10		16 41		17 10			17 32		17 42		18 10		18 40			
Prudhoe		d			15 42			16 14		16 45		17 14			17 36		17 46		18 14		18 44			
Stocksfield		d						16 18		16 50		17 18					17 51		18 18		18 48			
Riding Mill		d						16 23		16 54		17 23					17 55		18 23		18 53			
Corbridge		d						16 26		16 58		17 26					17 59		18 26		18 56			
Hexham		a			15 55			16 36		17 03		17 36			17 51		18 09		18 32		19 02			
		d			15 55					17 03					17 52				18 33		19 03			
Haydon Bridge		d								17 12					18 01				18 42					
Bardon Mill		d								17 19					18 07				18 48					
Haltwhistle		d			16 17					17 26					18 14				18 55		19 22			
Brampton (Cumbria)		d								17 41					18 30				19 11					
Wetheral		d								17 50					18 39				19 20					
Carlisle 8		a			16 49					17 59					18 54				19 32		19 55			

			NT	NT	NT	GR	NT	NT	XC	NT	NT		GR	NT	NT
						R 1			◇1				R 1		
Chathill		d	19 08												
Alnmouth for Alnwick	26	d	19 20			19 36			21 08				22 10		
Acklington		d	19 28												
Widdrington		d	19 35												
Pegswood		d	19 41												
Morpeth	26	d	19 45			19 53							22 26		22 45
Cramlington		d	19 54												22 53
Manors		d													
Newcastle 8	26 ⛴	a	20 06			20 12			21 38				22 43		23 07
Sunderland	26,44 ⛴	d			19 29			20 38							
Newcastle 8	⛴	d		19 24	19 54		20 15	21 00		21 24	21 52			22 35	
Dunston		d													
Metrocentre		a		19 31	20 01		20 22	21 07		21 31	22 01			22 42	
		d		19 32			20 23			21 32				22 43	
Blaydon		d													
Wylam		d		19 40			20 31			21 40				22 51	
Prudhoe		d		19 44			20 35			21 44				22 55	
Stocksfield		d		19 48			20 39			21 48				22 59	
Riding Mill		d		19 53			20 44			21 53				23 04	
Corbridge		d		19 56			20 47			21 56				23 07	
Hexham		a		20 02			20 57			22 02				23 16	
		d		20 03						22 03					
Haydon Bridge		d		20 12						22 12					
Bardon Mill		d		20 18						22 18					
Haltwhistle		d		20 25						22 25					
Brampton (Cumbria)		d		20 41						22 41					
Wetheral		d		20 50						22 50					
Carlisle 8		a		21 04						23 01					

For connections from London Kings Cross please refer to Table 26

Table 48

Mondays to Fridays

from 3 October

Chathill and Morpeth - Newcastle - Metrocentre, Hexham and Carlisle

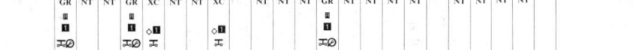

			GR	NT	NT	GR	XC	NT	NT	XC		NT	NT	NT	GR	NT	NT	NT	NT		NT	NT	NT	NT		
			R 1			R 1	◇1			◇1					R 1											
Chathill		d						07 07																		
Alnmouth for Alnwick	26	d	06 19			06 52	07 08	07 19		07 59					08 58											
Acklington		d						07 36																		
Widdrington		d						07 44																		
Pegswood		d						07 50																		
Morpeth	26	d	06 35			07 07		07 54		08 13			08 49						09 49					10 49		
Cramlington		d						08 02					08 57						09 57					10 57		
Manors		d						08 15					09 10						10 10					11 10		
Newcastle 8	26 ⛴	a	06 52			07 24	07 38	08 19		08 30			09 14		09 27				10 14					11 14		
Sunderland	26,44 ⛴	d							07 30									09 30					10 30			
Newcastle 8	⛴	d		06 30	06 47				07 53			08 24		08 54		09 26	09 44	09 54	10 15		10 22	10 44	10 54	11 15		
Dunston		d																09 59								
Metrocentre		a							08 00			08 31		09 01		09 33	09 52	10 02	10 22		10 29	10 52	11 01	11 22		
		d							08 01			08 32		09 02		09 33		10 02			10 32		11 02			
Blaydon		d							08 05																	
Wylam		d		06 44					08 11			08 40		09 12				10 10					11 10			
Prudhoe		d		06 48	07 03				08 15			08 44		09 16		09 43		10 14			10 42		11 14			
Stocksfield		d		06 53					08 20			08 48		09 21				10 18					11 18			
Riding Mill		d		06 57					08 24					09 25				10 23					11 23			
Corbridge		d		07 01					08 28					09 29				10 26					11 26			
Hexham		a		07 10	07 16				08 39			09 00		09 39		09 57		10 36			10 56		11 38			
		d			07 16							09 01				09 57					10 56					
Haydon Bridge		d			07 25							09 10									11 05					
Bardon Mill		d			07 32							09 16									11 12					
Haltwhistle		d			07 39							09 23				10 16					11 19					
Brampton (Cumbria)		d			07 54							09 39									11 34					
Wetheral		d			08 03							09 48									11 43					
Carlisle 8		a			08 13							09 57				10 50					11 58					

			GR	XC	NT	NT	NT		NT	XC	NT	NT	NT	NT	GR	NT	NT		NT	NT	XC	NT	NT	NT	NT	GR
			R 1	◇1						◇1					R 1						◇1					R 1
Chathill		d																								
Alnmouth for Alnwick	26	d	10 58							12 08					12 58						14 08					14 58
Acklington		d																								
Widdrington		d																								
Pegswood		d																								
Morpeth	26	d		11 21					11 49					12 49						13 49					14 49	
Cramlington		d							11 57					12 57						13 57					14 57	
Manors		d							12 10					13 10						14 10					15 10	
Newcastle 8	26 ⛴	a	11 27	11 39					12 13	12 38				13 13	13 27					14 13	14 40				15 14	15 27
Sunderland	26,44 ⛴	d					11 30						12 30						13 30					14 30		
Newcastle 8	⛴	d			11 22	11 42	11 54		12 14		12 22	12 43	12 54	13 15		13 22	13 44		13 54	14 15		14 24	14 44	14 54	15 15	
Dunston		d																								
Metrocentre		a			11 31	11 51	12 01		12 22		12 31	12 52	13 01	13 22		13 31	13 51		14 01	14 22		14 31	14 51	15 01	15 22	
		d			11 32		12 02				12 32		13 02			13 32			14 02			14 32		15 02		
Blaydon		d																								
Wylam		d					12 10						13 10						14 10					15 10		
Prudhoe		d			11 42		12 14				12 42		13 14			13 43			14 14			14 42		15 16		
Stocksfield		d					12 18						13 18						14 18					15 18		
Riding Mill		d					12 23						13 23						14 23					15 23		
Corbridge		d					12 26						13 26						14 26					15 26		
Hexham		a			11 57		12 38				12 57		13 38			13 55			14 38			14 55		15 39		
		d			11 57						12 57					13 56						14 55				
Haydon Bridge		d									13 06											15 04				
Bardon Mill		d									13 13											15 11				
Haltwhistle		d			12 16						13 20					14 15						15 18				
Brampton (Cumbria)		d									13 35											15 33				
Wetheral		d									13 44											15 42				
Carlisle 8		a			12 49						13 59					14 49						15 57				

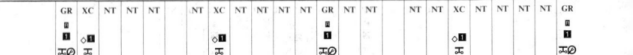

For connections from London Kings Cross please refer to Table 26

Table 48

Mondays to Fridays

from 3 October

Chathill and Morpeth - Newcastle - Metrocentre, Hexham and Carlisle

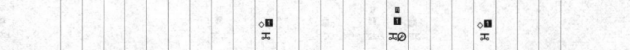

		NT		NT	NT	NT	NT	NT	NT	NT	XC	NT		NT	NT	NT	GR	NT	NT	NT	XC		NT	NT
											◇1 trolley						R 1 trolley ⊘				◇1 trolley			
Chathill	d																						19 08	
Alnmouth for Alnwick 26	d										17 03						17 58				19 08		19 20	
Acklington	d																						19 28	
Widdrington	d																						19 35	
Pegswood	d																						19 41	
Morpeth 26	d					15 49				16 49	17 18								18 26	19 01			19 45	
Cramlington	d					15 57				16 57									18 34	19 09			19 54	
Manors	d					16 10				17 10														
Newcastle 8 26 ⛴	a					16 14				17 15	17 36						18 27		18 49	19 25	19 38		20 06	
Sunderland 26,44 ⛴	d				15 30				16 30							17 30								
Newcastle 8 ⛴	d	15 23		15 44	15 54	16 15	16 22	16 44	16 54			17 16		17 24	17 44	17 54		18 24						19 24
Dunston	d														17 50									
Metrocentre	a	15 31		15 51	16 01	16 22	16 33	16 53	17 01			17 23		17 31	17 53	18 01		18 31						19 28
	d	15 31			16 02		16 33		17 02			17 24		17 32		18 02		18 32						19 32
Blaydon	d													17 36										
Wylam	d				16 10		16 41		17 10			17 32		17 42		18 10		18 40						19 40
Prudhoe	d	15 42			16 14		16 45		17 14			17 36		17 46		18 14		18 44						19 44
Stocksfield	d				16 18		16 50		17 18					17 51		18 18		18 48						19 48
Riding Mill	d				16 23		16 54		17 23					17 55		18 23		18 53						19 53
Corbridge	d				16 26		16 58		17 26					17 59		18 26		18 56						19 56
Hexham	a	15 56			16 38		17 03		17 38			17 51		18 11		18 32		19 04						20 01
	d	15 56					17 03					17 52				18 33		19 05						20 05
Haydon Bridge	d						17 12					18 01				18 42								20 14
Bardon Mill	d						17 19					18 07				18 48								20 20
Haltwhistle	d	16 17					17 26					18 14				18 55		19 24						20 27
Brampton (Cumbria)	d						17 41					18 30				19 11								20 43
Wetheral	d						17 50					18 39				19 20								20 52
Carlisle 8	a	16 52					17 59					18 54				19 35		20 00						21 09

		NT	GR	NT	NT	XC	NT	NT		GR	NT	NT
			R 1 trolley ⊘			◇1 trolley				R 1 🍽		
Chathill	d											
Alnmouth for Alnwick 26	d		19 36			21 08				22 10		
Acklington	d											
Widdrington	d											
Pegswood	d											
Morpeth 26	d		19 53							22 26		22 45
Cramlington	d											22 53
Manors	d											
Newcastle 8 26 ⛴	a		20 12			21 38				22 43		23 07
Sunderland 26,44 ⛴	d	19 29			20 38							
Newcastle 8 ⛴	d	19 54		20 15	21 00		21 24	21 52			22 35	
Dunston	d											
Metrocentre	a	20 01		20 22	21 07		21 31	22 01			22 42	
	d			20 23			21 32				22 43	
Blaydon	d											
Wylam	d			20 31			21 40				22 51	
Prudhoe	d			20 35			21 44				22 55	
Stocksfield	d			20 39			21 48				22 59	
Riding Mill	d			20 44			21 53				23 04	
Corbridge	d			20 47			21 56				23 07	
Hexham	a			20 59			22 02				23 18	
	d						22 03					
Haydon Bridge	d						22 12					
Bardon Mill	d						22 18					
Haltwhistle	d						22 25					
Brampton (Cumbria)	d						22 41					
Wetheral	d						22 50					
Carlisle 8	a						23 05					

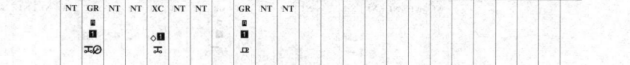

For connections from London Kings Cross please refer to Table 26

Table 48

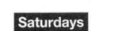

Saturdays
until 1 October

Chathill and Morpeth - Newcastle - Metrocentre, Hexham and Carlisle

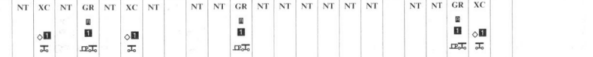

	NT	XC	NT	GR	NT	XC	NT		NT	NT	GR	NT	NT	NT	NT	NT	NT		NT	NT	GR	XC		
		◇1		R 1		◇1					R 1										R 1	◇1		
Chathill d			07 10																					
Alnmouth for Alnwick 26 d		07 08	07 22	07 25		08 00					08 58										10 58			
Acklington d			07 37																					
Widdrington d			07 45																					
Pegswood d			07 51																					
Morpeth 26 d			07 55	07 41		08 14			08 49						09 49					10 49		11 19		
Cramlington d			08 03						08 57						09 57					10 57				
Manors d			08 16						09 10						10 10					11 10				
Newcastle 8 26 a		07 38	08 20	07 58		08 32			09 14		09 27				10 14					11 13	11 27	11 38		
Sunderland 26,44 d					07 30									09 30					10 30					
Newcastle 8 d	06 30				07 53		08 24			08 54		09 24	09 44	09 54	10 15	10 22	10 44		10 54	11 15				
Dunston d														09 59										
Metrocentre a					08 00		08 31			09 01		09 32	09 52	10 02	10 22	10 29	10 53		11 01	11 22				
d					08 01		08 32			09 02		09 33		10 02		10 32			11 02					
Blaydon d					08 05					09 06														
Wylam d	06 44				08 11		08 40			09 12				10 10					11 10					
Prudhoe d	06 48				08 15		08 44			09 16		09 43		10 14		10 42			11 14					
Stocksfield d	06 53				08 20		08 48			09 21				10 18					11 18					
Riding Mill d	06 57				08 24					09 25				10 23					11 23					
Corbridge d	07 01				08 28					09 29				10 26					11 26					
Hexham a	07 07				08 37		08 58			09 39		09 56		10 36		10 55			11 36					
d	07 07						08 59					09 56				10 55								
Haydon Bridge d	07 16						09 08									11 04								
Bardon Mill d	07 23						09 14									11 11								
Haltwhistle d	07 30						09 21					10 15				11 18								
Brampton (Cumbria) d	07 45						09 37									11 33								
Wetheral d	07 54						09 46									11 42								
Carlisle 8 a	08 04						09 57					10 46				11 59								

	NT	NT	NT	NT	XC		NT	NT	NT	NT	GR	NT	NT	NT	NT		XC	NT	NT	NT	NT	GR	NT	NT
					◇1						R 1						◇1					R 1		
Chathill d																								
Alnmouth for Alnwick 26 d					12 08						12 58						14 09					14 58		
Acklington d																								
Widdrington d																								
Pegswood d																								
Morpeth 26 d				11 49						12 49					13 49						14 49			
Cramlington d				11 57						12 57					13 57						14 57			
Manors d				12 11						13 10					14 10						15 11			
Newcastle 8 26 a				12 13	12 38					13 13	13 27				14 15		14 39				15 14	15 27		
Sunderland 26,44 d			11 30						12 30					13 30						14 30				
Newcastle 8 d	11 22	11 44	11 54	12 15			12 22	12 44	12 54	13 14		13 22	13 44	13 54	14 15			14 24	14 44	14 56	15 15		15 24	15 44
Dunston d																								
Metrocentre a	11 31	11 52	12 01	12 23			12 31	12 52	13 01	13 22		13 31	13 51	14 01	14 23			14 31	14 51	15 02	15 22		15 31	15 51
d	11 32		12 02				12 32		13 02			13 32		14 02				14 32		15 02			15 32	
Blaydon d																								
Wylam d			12 10						13 10					14 10						15 10				
Prudhoe d	11 42		12 14				12 43		13 14			13 43		14 14				14 42		15 16			15 42	
Stocksfield d			12 18						13 18					14 18						15 18				
Riding Mill d			12 23						13 23					14 23						15 23				
Corbridge d			12 26						13 26					14 26						15 26				
Hexham a	11 55		12 36				12 55		13 36			13 55		14 36				14 55		15 37			15 55	
d	11 55						12 56					13 56						14 55					15 55	
Haydon Bridge d							13 05											15 04						
Bardon Mill d							13 11											15 11						
Haltwhistle d	12 14						13 18					14 15						15 18					16 15	
Brampton (Cumbria) d							13 33											15 33						
Wetheral d							13 42											15 42						
Carlisle 8 a	12 46						13 52					14 49						15 54					16 48	

For connections from London Kings Cross please refer to Table 26

Table 48

Saturdays

until 1 October

Chathill and Morpeth - Newcastle - Metrocentre, Hexham and Carlisle

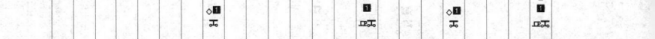

		NT	NT	NT	NT	NT	NT	XC	NT	NT	NT	NT	NT	GR	NT	NT	NT	XC	NT	NT	GR
								◇1						R 1				◇1			R 1
Chathill	d																18 36				
Alnmouth for Alnwick 26	d							17 01						17 58			18 48	19 08			20 07
Acklington	d																18 56				
Widdrington	d																19 03				
Pegswood	d																19 09				
Morpeth 26	d		15 49				16 49	17 16					17 52			18 50	19 13				20 24
Cramlington	d		15 57				16 57						18 00			18 58	19 22				
Manors	d		16 11				17 10														
Newcastle 8 26 ⛴	a		16 15				17 13	17 34					18 15	18 27		19 13	19 34	19 41			20 41
Sunderland 26,44 ⛴	d	15 30				16 30						17 30								19 30	
Newcastle 8 ⛴	d	15 54	16 15	16 22	16 46	16 54			17 16	17 24	17 43	17 54			18 24				19 25	19 54	
Dunston	d										17 50										
Metrocentre	a	16 01	16 22	16 31	16 53	17 01			17 23	17 31	17 53	18 01			18 31				19 33	20 01	
	d	16 02		16 31		17 02			17 24	17 32		18 02			18 32				19 34		
Blaydon	d									17 36											
Wylam	d	16 10		16 40		17 10			17 32	17 42		18 10			18 40				19 42		
Prudhoe	d	16 14		16 44		17 14			17 36	17 46		18 14			18 44				19 46		
Stocksfield	d	16 18		16 48		17 18				17 51		18 18			18 48				19 50		
Riding Mill	d	16 23		16 53		17 23				17 55		18 23			18 53				19 55		
Corbridge	d	16 26		16 56		17 26				17 59		18 26			18 56				19 58		
Hexham	a	16 36		17 02		17 36			17 51	18 09		18 32			19 02				20 04		
	d			17 03					17 52			18 33			19 03				20 05		
Haydon Bridge	d			17 12					18 01			18 42							20 14		
Bardon Mill	d			17 18					18 07			18 48							20 20		
Haltwhistle	d			17 25					18 14			18 55			19 22				20 27		
Brampton (Cumbria)	d			17 41					18 30			19 11							20 43		
Wetheral	d			17 50					18 39			19 20							20 52		
Carlisle 8	a			18 03					18 52			19 32			19 53				21 03		

		NT	NT	NT	NT	NT
Chathill	d					
Alnmouth for Alnwick 26	d					
Acklington	d					
Widdrington	d					
Pegswood	d					
Morpeth 26	d			21 15		
Cramlington	d			21 23		
Manors	d					
Newcastle 8 26 ⛴	a			21 39		
Sunderland 26,44 ⛴	d					
Newcastle 8 ⛴	d	20 15	20 30		21 24	21 52
Dunston	d					
Metrocentre	a	20 22	20 39		21 31	22 01
	d	20 23			21 32	22 02
Blaydon	d					
Wylam	d	20 31			21 40	22 10
Prudhoe	d	20 35			21 44	22a13
Stocksfield	d	20 39			21 48	
Riding Mill	d	20 44			21 53	
Corbridge	d	20 47			21 56	
Hexham	a	20 55			22 02	
	d				22 03	
Haydon Bridge	d				22 12	
Bardon Mill	d				22 18	
Haltwhistle	d				22 25	
Brampton (Cumbria)	d				22 41	
Wetheral	d				22 50	
Carlisle 8	a				23 01	

For connections from London Kings Cross please refer to Table 26

Table 48

Saturdays

from 8 October

Chathill and Morpeth - Newcastle - Metrocentre, Hexham and Carlisle

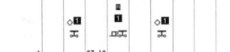

		NT	XC	NT	GR	NT	XC	NT		NT	NT	GR	NT	NT	NT	NT	NT	NT		NT	NT	GR	XC		
			◇1		R 1		◇1					R 1										R 1	◇1		
Chathill	d			07 10																					
Alnmouth for Alnwick 26	d		07 08	07 22	07 25		08 00					08 58										10 58			
Acklington	d			07 37																					
Widdrington	d			07 45																					
Pegswood	d			07 51																					
Morpeth 26	d			07 55	07 41		08 14			08 49						09 49					10 49		11 19		
Cramlington	d			08 03						08 57						09 57					10 57				
Manors	d			08 16						09 10						10 10					11 10				
Newcastle 8 26 ⛴	a		07 38	08 20	07 58		08 32			09 14		09 27				10 14					11 13	11 27	11 38		
Sunderland 26,44 ⛴	d					07 30									09 30					10 30					
Newcastle 8 ⛴	d	06 30				07 53		08 24			08 54		09 24	09 44	09 54	10 15	10 22	10 44		10 54	11 15				
Dunston	d														09 59										
Metrocentre	a					08 00		08 31			09 01		09 32	09 52	10 02	10 22	10 29	10 53		11 01	11 22				
	d					08 01		08 32			09 02		09 33		10 02		10 32			11 02					
Blaydon	d					08 05					09 06														
Wylam	d	06 44				08 11		08 40			09 12				10 10					11 10					
Prudhoe	d	06 48				08 15		08 44			09 16		09 42		10 14		10 42			11 14					
Stocksfield	d	06 53				08 20		08 48			09 21				10 18					11 18					
Riding Mill	d	06 57				08 24					09 25				10 23					11 23					
Corbridge	d	07 01				08 28					09 29				10 26					11 26					
Hexham	a	07 07				08 40		09 00			09 39		09 58		10 37		10 57			11 38					
	d	07 07						09 01					09 58				10 57								
Haydon Bridge	d	07 16						09 10									11 06								
Bardon Mill	d	07 23						09 16									11 13								
Haltwhistle	d	07 30						09 23					10 16				11 20								
Brampton (Cumbria)	d	07 45						09 39									11 35								
Wetheral	d	07 54						09 48									11 44								
Carlisle 8	a	08 04						10 02					10 53				11 58								

		NT	NT	NT	NT	XC		NT	NT	NT	NT	GR	NT	NT	NT	NT		XC	NT	NT	NT	NT	GR	NT	NT
						◇1						R 1						◇1					R 1		
Chathill	d																								
Alnmouth for Alnwick 26	d					12 08						12 58						14 09					14 58		
Acklington	d																								
Widdrington	d																								
Pegswood	d																								
Morpeth 26	d				11 49						12 49					13 49						14 49			
Cramlington	d				11 57						12 57					13 57						14 57			
Manors	d				12 11						13 10					14 10						15 11			
Newcastle 8 26 ⛴	a				12 13	12 38					13 13	13 27				14 15		14 39				15 14	15 27		
Sunderland 26,44 ⛴	d			11 30						12 30					13 30						14 30				
Newcastle 8 ⛴	d	11 22	11 44	11 54	12 15			12 22	12 44	12 54	13 14		13 22	13 44	13 54	14 15			14 24	14 44	14 56	15 15		15 24	15 44
Dunston	d																								
Metrocentre	a	11 31	11 52	12 01	12 23			12 31	12 52	13 01	13 22		13 31	13 51	14 01	14 23			14 31	14 51	15 02	15 22		15 31	15 51
	d	11 32		12 02				12 32		13 02			13 32		14 02				14 32		15 02			15 32	
Blaydon	d																								
Wylam	d			12 10						13 10					14 10						15 10				
Prudhoe	d	11 42		12 14				12 42		13 14			13 43		14 14				14 42		15 16			15 42	
Stocksfield	d			12 18						13 18					14 18						15 18				
Riding Mill	d			12 23						13 23					14 23						15 23				
Corbridge	d			12 26						13 26					14 26						15 26				
Hexham	a	11 57		12 38				12 57		13 38			13 55		14 38				14 55		15 37			15 57	
	d	11 57						12 57					13 56						14 55					15 57	
Haydon Bridge	d							13 06											15 04						
Bardon Mill	d							13 13											15 11						
Haltwhistle	d	12 16						13 20					14 15						15 18					16 17	
Brampton (Cumbria)	d							13 35											15 33						
Wetheral	d							13 44											15 42						
Carlisle 8	a	12 52						13 59					14 49						15 57					16 53	

For connections from London Kings Cross please refer to Table 26

Table 48

Saturdays
from 8 October

Chathill and Morpeth - Newcastle - Metrocentre, Hexham and Carlisle

		NT	NT	NT	NT	NT	NT	XC	NT	NT	NT	NT	NT	GR	NT	NT	NT	XC	NT	NT	GR
								◇1						R 1				◇1			R 1
Chathill	d																18 36				
Alnmouth for Alnwick 26	d							17 01						17 58			18 48	19 08			20 07
Acklington	d																18 56				
Widdrington	d																19 03				
Pegswood	d																19 09				
Morpeth 26	d		15 49				16 49	17 16					17 52			18 50	19 13				20 24
Cramlington	d		15 57				16 57						18 00			18 58	19 22				
Manors	d		16 11				17 10														
Newcastle 8 26	a		16 15				17 13	17 34					18 15	18 27		19 13	19 34	19 41			20 41
Sunderland 26,44	d	15 30				16 30						17 30								19 30	
Newcastle 8	d	15 54	16 15	16 22	16 46	16 54			17 16	17 24	17 43	17 54			18 24				19 25	19 54	
Dunston	d										17 50										
Metrocentre	a	16 01	16 22	16 31	16 53	17 01			17 23	17 31	17 53	18 01			18 31				19 31	20 01	
	d	16 02		16 31		17 02			17 24	17 32		18 02			18 32				19 32		
Blaydon	d									17 36											
Wylam	d	16 10		16 40		17 10			17 32	17 42		18 10			18 40				19 42		
Prudhoe	d	16 14		16 44		17 14			17 36	17 46		18 14			18 44				19 46		
Stocksfield	d	16 18		16 48		17 18				17 51		18 18			18 48				19 50		
Riding Mill	d	16 23		16 53		17 23				17 55		18 23			18 53				19 55		
Corbridge	d	16 26		16 56		17 26				17 59		18 26			18 56				19 58		
Hexham	a	16 38		17 02		17 39			17 51	18 12		18 32			19 02				20 06		
	d			17 03					17 52			18 33			19 03				20 07		
Haydon Bridge	d			17 12					18 01			18 42							20 16		
Bardon Mill	d			17 18					18 07			18 48							20 22		
Haltwhistle	d			17 25					18 14			18 55			19 22				20 29		
Brampton (Cumbria)	d			17 41					18 30			19 11							20 45		
Wetheral	d			17 50					18 39			19 20							20 54		
Carlisle 8	a			18 03					18 53			19 35			19 53				21 08		

		NT	NT	NT	NT	NT	NT
Chathill	d						
Alnmouth for Alnwick 26	d						
Acklington	d						
Widdrington	d						
Pegswood	d						
Morpeth 26	d			21 15			
Cramlington	d			21 23			
Manors	d						
Newcastle 8 26	a			21 39			
Sunderland 26,44	d					21 43	
Newcastle 8	d	20 15	20 30		21 24	22a04	21 52
Dunston	d						
Metrocentre	a	20 22	20 39		21 31		22 01
	d	20 23			21 32		22 02
Blaydon	d						
Wylam	d	20 31			21 40		22 10
Prudhoe	d	20 35			21 44		22a13
Stocksfield	d	20 39			21 48		
Riding Mill	d	20 44			21 53		
Corbridge	d	20 47			21 56		
Hexham	a	20 59			22 02		
	d				22 03		
Haydon Bridge	d				22 12		
Bardon Mill	d				22 18		
Haltwhistle	d				22 25		
Brampton (Cumbria)	d				22 41		
Wetheral	d				22 50		
Carlisle 8	a				23 05		

For connections from London Kings Cross please refer to Table 26

Table 48

Sundays
until 19 June

Chathill and Morpeth - Newcastle - Metrocentre, Hexham and Carlisle

			NT	NT	NT	NT	XC	NT	GR		NT	NT	NT	NT	GR	XC	NT	NT		NT	GR	NT
							◇1		R 1						R 1	◇1					R 1	
Chathill		d																				
Alnmouth for Alnwick	26	d					10 47		10 56							12 08					12 56	
Acklington		d																				
Widdrington		d																				
Pegswood		d																				
Morpeth	26	d					11 02								12 05							
Cramlington		d																				
Manors		d																				
Newcastle 8	26	a					11 19		11 27						12 23	12 35					13 27	
Sunderland	26,44	d											11 50									
Newcastle 8		d	09 10	09 53	10 10	10 30		10 50			11 10	11 30	12a30	11 50			12 10	12 30		12 50		13 10
Dunston		d																				
Metrocentre		a	09 17	10 01	10 17	10 37		10 59			11 17	11 37		11 57			12 17	12 37		12 59		13 17
		d	09 18		10 18						11 18						12 18					13 18
Blaydon		d																				
Wylam		d	09 26		10 26						11 26						12 26					13 26
Prudhoe		d	09 30		10 30						11 30						12 30					13 30
Stocksfield		d	09 34		10 34						11 34						12 34					13 34
Riding Mill		d	09 39		10 39						11 39						12 39					13 39
Corbridge		d	09 42		10 42						11 42						12 42					13 42
Hexham		a	09 48		10 48						11 48						12 48					13 48
		d	09 49		10 49						11 49						12 49					13 49
Haydon Bridge		d	09 58		10 58												12 58					
Bardon Mill		d	10 04		11 04												13 04					
Haltwhistle		d	10 11		11 11						12 08						13 11					14 08
Brampton (Cumbria)		d	10 27		11 27												13 27					
Wetheral		d	10 35		11 35												13 35					
Carlisle 8		a	10 44		11 49						12 38						13 45					14 38

			NT	NT	XC	NT	NT		NT	GR	NT	NT	NT	NT	NT		NT	GR	XC	NT	NT	NT
					◇1					R 1								R 1	◇1			
Chathill		d																				
Alnmouth for Alnwick	26	d			14 06					14 56								16 56	17 05			
Acklington		d																				
Widdrington		d																				
Pegswood		d																				
Morpeth	26	d																	17 20			
Cramlington		d																				
Manors		d																				
Newcastle 8	26	a			14 35					15 27								17 27	17 37			
Sunderland	26,44	d																				
Newcastle 8		d	13 30	13 50		14 10	14 30		14 50		15 10	15 30	15 50	16 10	16 30		16 50			17 10	17 30	17 50
Dunston		d																				
Metrocentre		a	13 37	13 59		14 17	14 37		14 59		15 17	15 37	15 59	16 19	16 37		16 57			17 17	17 37	17 59
		d				14 18					15 18			16 20						17 18		
Blaydon		d																				
Wylam		d				14 26					15 26			16 28						17 26		
Prudhoe		d				14 30					15 30			16 32						17 30		
Stocksfield		d				14 34					15 34			16 37						17 34		
Riding Mill		d				14 39					15 39			16 41						17 39		
Corbridge		d				14 42					15 42			16 45						17 42		
Hexham		a				14 48					15 48			16 51						17 48		
		d				14 49					15 49			16 51						17 49		
Haydon Bridge		d									15 58											
Bardon Mill		d									16 04											
Haltwhistle		d				15 08					16 11			17 10						18 08		
Brampton (Cumbria)		d									16 27											
Wetheral		d									16 35											
Carlisle 8		a				15 40					16 45			17 41						18 38		

For connections from London Kings Cross please refer to Table 26

Table 48

Sundays
until 19 June

Chathill and Morpeth - Newcastle - Metrocentre, Hexham and Carlisle

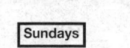

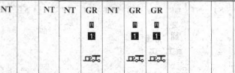

Station			NT		NT	NT	GR	NT	GR	GR
							R		R	R
							1		1	1
Chathill		d								
Alnmouth for Alnwick	26	d					18 56		21 07	22 06
Acklington		d								
Widdrington		d								
Pegswood		d								
Morpeth	26	d							21 24	
Cramlington		d								
Manors		d								
Newcastle 8	26	a					19 27		21 42	22 37
Sunderland	26,44	d								
Newcastle 8		d	18 10		18 30	18 50		20 15		
Dunston		d								
Metrocentre		a	18 17		18 37	18 59		20 22		
		d	18 18					20 23		
Blaydon		d								
Wylam		d	18 26					20 31		
Prudhoe		d	18 30					20 35		
Stocksfield		d	18 34					20 39		
Riding Mill		d	18 39					20 44		
Corbridge		d	18 42					20 47		
Hexham		a	18 48					20 53		
		d	18 49					20 54		
Haydon Bridge		d	18 58					21 03		
Bardon Mill		d	19 04					21 09		
Haltwhistle		d	19 11					21 16		
Brampton (Cumbria)		d	19 27					21 32		
Wetheral		d	19 35					21 40		
Carlisle 8		a	19 45					21 50		

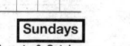

Sundays
26 June to 2 October

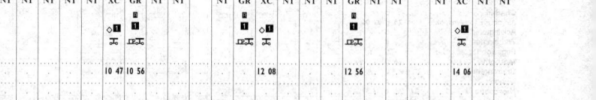

Station			NT	NT	NT	NT	NT	XC	GR	NT	NT		NT	GR	XC	NT	NT	NT	GR	NT	NT		NT	XC	NT	NT
									R					R					R							
								◇1	1					1	◇1				1					◇1		
Chathill		d																								
Alnmouth for Alnwick	26	d						10 47	10 56						12 08				12 56					14 06		
Acklington		d																								
Widdrington		d																								
Pegswood		d																								
Morpeth	26	d						11 02						12 05												
Cramlington		d																								
Manors		d																								
Newcastle 8	26	a						11 19	11 27					12 23	12 35				13 27					14 35		
Sunderland	26,44	d		09 28			10 28						11 28					12 28					13 28			
Newcastle 8		d	09 10	09 53	10 10	10 30	10 50			11 10	11 30		11 50			12 10	12 30	12 50		13 10	13 30		13 50		14 10	14 30
Dunston		d																								
Metrocentre		a	09 17	10 01	10 17	10 37	10 59			11 17	11 37		11 57			12 17	12 37	12 59		13 17	13 37		13 59		14 17	14 37
		d	09 18		10 18					11 18						12 18				13 18					14 18	
Blaydon		d																								
Wylam		d	09 26		10 26					11 26						12 26				13 26					14 26	
Prudhoe		d	09 30		10 30					11 30						12 30				13 30					14 30	
Stocksfield		d	09 34		10 34					11 34						12 34				13 34					14 34	
Riding Mill		d	09 39		10 39					11 39						12 39				13 39					14 39	
Corbridge		d	09 42		10 42					11 42						12 42				13 42					14 42	
Hexham		a	09 48		10 48					11 48						12 48				13 48					14 48	
		d	09 49		10 49					11 49						12 49				13 49					14 49	
Haydon Bridge		d	09 58		10 58											12 58										
Bardon Mill		d	10 04		11 04											13 04										
Haltwhistle		d	10 11		11 11					12 08						13 11				14 08					15 08	
Brampton (Cumbria)		d	10 27		11 27											13 27										
Wetheral		d	10 35		11 35											13 35										
Carlisle 8		a	10 44		11 49					12 38						13 45				14 38					15 40	

For connections from London Kings Cross please refer to Table 26

Table 48

Sundays

26 June to 2 October

Chathill and Morpeth - Newcastle - Metrocentre, Hexham and Carlisle

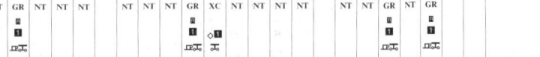

		NT	GR	NT	NT	NT	NT	NT	NT	GR	XC	NT	NT	NT	NT	NT	NT	GR	NT	GR
			R 1 🍴							R 1 🍴	◇1 🍴							R 1 🍴		R 1 🍴
Chathill	d																			
Alnmouth for Alnwick 26	d		14 56							16 56	17 05							18 56		21 07
Acklington	d																			
Widdrington	d																			
Pegswood	d																			
Morpeth 26	d										17 20									21 24
Cramlington	d																			
Manors	d																			
Newcastle 8 26 ⛴	a		15 27							17 27	17 37							19 27		21 42
Sunderland 26,44 ⛴	d	14 28				15 28			16 28					17 28						
Newcastle 8 ⛴	d	14 50		15 10	15 30	15 50	16 10	16 30	16 50			17 10	17 30	17 50	18 10	18 30	18 50		20 15	
Dunston	d																			
Metrocentre	a	14 59		15 17	15 37	15 59	16 19	16 37	16 57			17 17	17 37	17 59	18 17	18 37	18 59		20 22	
	d			15 18			16 20					17 18			18 18				20 23	
Blaydon	d																			
Wylam	d			15 26			16 28					17 26			18 26				20 31	
Prudhoe	d			15 30			16 32					17 30			18 30				20 35	
Stocksfield	d			15 34			16 37					17 34			18 34				20 39	
Riding Mill	d			15 39			16 41					17 39			18 39				20 44	
Corbridge	d			15 42			16 45					17 42			18 42				20 47	
Hexham	a			15 48			16 51					17 48			18 48				20 53	
	d			15 49			16 51					17 49			18 49				20 54	
Haydon Bridge	d			15 58											18 58				21 03	
Bardon Mill	d			16 04											19 04				21 09	
Haltwhistle	d			16 11			17 10					18 08			19 11				21 16	
Brampton (Cumbria)	d			16 27											19 27				21 32	
Wetheral	d			16 35											19 35				21 40	
Carlisle 8	a			16 45			17 41					18 38			19 45				21 50	

		GR
		R 1 🍴
Chathill	d	
Alnmouth for Alnwick 26	d	22 06
Acklington	d	
Widdrington	d	
Pegswood	d	
Morpeth 26	d	
Cramlington	d	
Manors	d	
Newcastle 8 26 ⛴	a	22 37
Sunderland 26,44 ⛴	d	
Newcastle 8 ⛴	d	
Dunston	d	
Metrocentre	a	
	d	
Blaydon	d	
Wylam	d	
Prudhoe	d	
Stocksfield	d	
Riding Mill	d	
Corbridge	d	
Hexham	a	
	d	
Haydon Bridge	d	
Bardon Mill	d	
Haltwhistle	d	
Brampton (Cumbria)	d	
Wetheral	d	
Carlisle 8	a	

For connections from London Kings Cross please refer to Table 26

Table 48

Sundays
from 9 October

Chathill and Morpeth - Newcastle - Metrocentre, Hexham and Carlisle

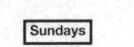

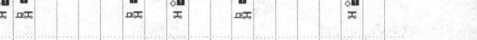

		NT	NT	NT	NT	NT	XC	GR	NT	NT		NT	GR	NT	XC	NT	NT	GR	NT	NT		NT	XC	NT	NT
							◇1	R 1					R 1		◇1			R 1					◇1		
Chathill	d																								
Alnmouth for Alnwick 26	d						10 47	10 56							12 08			12 56					14 06		
Acklington	d																								
Widdrington	d																								
Pegswood	d																								
Morpeth 26	d						11 02						12 05												
Cramlington	d																								
Manors	d																								
Newcastle 8 26 ⛴	a						11 19	11 27					12 23		12 35			13 27					14 35		
Sunderland 26,44 ⛴	d		09 28			10 28						11 28					12 28					13 28			
Newcastle 8 ⛴	d	09 10	09 53	10 10	10 30	10 50			11 06	11 30		11 50		12 06		12 30	12 50		13 07	13 30		13 50		14 10	14 30
Dunston	d																								
Metrocentre	a	09 17	10 01	10 17	10 37	10 59			11 13	11 37		11 57		12 13		12 37	12 59		13 14	13 37		13 59		14 17	14 37
	d	09 18		10 18					11 14					12 14					13 15					14 18	
Blaydon	d																								
Wylam	d	09 26		10 26					11 22					12 22					13 23					14 26	
Prudhoe	d	09 30		10 30					11 26					12 26					13 27					14 30	
Stocksfield	d	09 34		10 34					11 30					12 30					13 31					14 34	
Riding Mill	d	09 39		10 39					11 35					12 35					13 36					14 39	
Corbridge	d	09 42		10 42					11 38					12 38					13 39					14 42	
Hexham	a	09 48		10 48					11 44					12 44					13 45					14 48	
	d	09 49		10 49					11 45					12 45					13 46					14 49	
Haydon Bridge	d	09 58		10 58										12 54											
Bardon Mill	d	10 04		11 04										13 00											
Haltwhistle	d	10 11		11 11					12 04					13 07					14 05					15 08	
Brampton (Cumbria)	d	10 27		11 27										13 23											
Wetheral	d	10 35		11 35										13 31											
Carlisle 8	a	10 46		11 50					12 38					13 45					14 39					15 40	

		NT	GR	NT	NT	NT		NT	NT	NT	GR	XC	NT	NT	NT	NT		NT	NT	GR	NT	GR
			R 1								R 1	◇1								R 1		R 1
Chathill	d																					
Alnmouth for Alnwick 26	d		14 56								16 56	17 05								18 56		21 07
Acklington	d																					
Widdrington	d																					
Pegswood	d																					
Morpeth 26	d											17 20										21 24
Cramlington	d																					
Manors	d																					
Newcastle 8 26 ⛴	a		15 27								17 27	17 37								19 27		21 42
Sunderland 26,44 ⛴	d	14 28				15 28				16 28					17 28							
Newcastle 8 ⛴	d	14 50		15 07	15 30	15 50		16 10	16 30	16 50			17 10	17 30	17 50	18 10		18 30	18 50		20 15	
Dunston	d																					
Metrocentre	a	14 59		15 14	15 37	15 59		16 19	16 37	16 57			17 17	17 37	17 59	18 17		18 37	18 59		20 22	
	d			15 15				16 20					17 18			18 18					20 23	
Blaydon	d																					
Wylam	d			15 23				16 28					17 26			18 26					20 31	
Prudhoe	d			15 27				16 32					17 30			18 30					20 35	
Stocksfield	d			15 31				16 36					17 34			18 34					20 39	
Riding Mill	d			15 36				16 41					17 39			18 39					20 44	
Corbridge	d			15 39				16 44					17 42			18 42					20 47	
Hexham	a			15 45				16 50					17 48			18 48					20 53	
	d			15 46				16 51					17 49			18 49					20 54	
Haydon Bridge	d			15 55												18 58					21 03	
Bardon Mill	d			16 01												19 04					21 09	
Haltwhistle	d			16 08				17 10					18 08			19 11					21 16	
Brampton (Cumbria)	d			16 24												19 27					21 32	
Wetheral	d			16 32												19 35					21 40	
Carlisle 8	a			16 45				17 43					18 38			19 46					21 52	

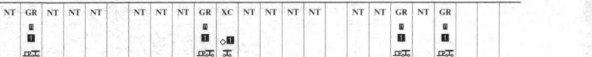

For connections from London Kings Cross please refer to Table 26

Table 48

Sundays
from 9 October

Chathill and Morpeth - Newcastle - Metrocentre, Hexham and Carlisle

			GR ◼ 1 ⚐
Chathill		d	
Alnmouth for Alnwick	26	d	22 06
Acklington		d	
Widdrington		d	
Pegswood		d	
Morpeth	26	d	
Cramlington		d	
Manors		d	
Newcastle ◼	26 ⛴	a	22 37
Sunderland	26,44 ⛴	d	
Newcastle ◼	⛴	d	
Dunston		d	
Metrocentre		a	
		d	
Blaydon		d	
Wylam		d	
Prudhoe		d	
Stocksfield		d	
Riding Mill		d	
Corbridge		d	
Hexham		a	
		d	
Haydon Bridge		d	
Bardon Mill		d	
Haltwhistle		d	
Brampton (Cumbria)		d	
Wetheral		d	
Carlisle ◼		a	

For connections from London Kings Cross please refer to Table 26

Carlisle, Hexham and Metrocentre - Newcastle - Morpeth and Chathill

Miles	Miles			NT	NT	NT	GR	XC	GR	NT	SR	NT		GR	NT	NT	NT	XC	NT	NT	NT	SR		GR	NT
							R 1	◇1	R 1					R 1				◇1						R 1	
0	—	**Carlisle** 8	d			06 25					07 17					08 28						09 37			
4¼	—	Wetheral	d			06 33					07 25					08 36									
11	—	Brampton (Cumbria)	d			06 43					07 35					08 46									
23¼	—	Haltwhistle	d			06 57					07 49					09 00						10 08			
28	—	Bardon Mill	d			07 05					07 57					09 08									
31¾	—	Haydon Bridge	d			07 10					08 02					09 13									
39½	—	**Hexham**	a			07 19					08 11					09 22						10 26			
—	—		d		06 16	07 19				07 42	08 11				08 45	09 22				09 46		10 26			
42½	—	Corbridge	d		06 20	07 24				07 46	08 16				08 49					09 50					
45	—	Riding Mill	d		06 25	07 27				07 51	08 20				08 54					09 55					
47¼	—	Stocksfield	d		06 29	07 31				07 55	08 24				08 58					09 59					
49¾	—	Prudhoe	d		06 33	07 37				07 59	08 29				09 02	09 34				10 03		10 38			
52	—	Wylam	d		06 37	07 41				08 03	08 33				09 06					10 07					
56¼	—	Blaydon	d							08 09	08 39														
58¼	—	**Metrocentre**	a			07 49				08 14	08 44				09 15	09 45				10 16		10 49			
—	—		d			07 50				08 16	08 44				09 16	09 46			10 01	10 17	10 31	10 50			11 00
59½	1¼	Dunston	d								08 47														
61¾	3½	**Newcastle** 8 ⛴	a		06 55	08 04				08 27	08 57				09 26	10 00			10 10	10 27	10 39	11 07			11 11
—	—	Sunderland 26,44 ⛴	a		07 18					08 50					09 49					10 49					
—	—	**Newcastle** 8 26 ⛴	d	05 55			06 25	07 35	07 41			07 58		08 41			09 15	09 35	10 15					10 41	11 15
—	4	Manors	d														09 17		10 17						11 17
—	13¼	Cramlington	d	06 07								08 07					09 28		10 28						11 28
—	20	**Morpeth** 26	d	06 15			06 38	07a47				08a18		08a56			09a36		10a36						11a36
—	22	Pegswood	d																						
—	26¾	Widdrington	d																						
—	32	Acklington	d																						
—	38¼	Alnmouth for Alnwick 26	d	06 32			06a52		08a07									09a58						11a07	
—	49½	**Chathill**	a	06 46																					

		NT	NT	NT	NT	NT	NT	NT		GR	NT	NT	NT	NT	XC	NT	NT	NT		NT	XC	GR	NT	NT	NT
										R 1					◇1						◇1	R 1			
Carlisle 8	d			10 28				11 34						12 28						13 30					
Wetheral	d													12 36						13 37					
Brampton (Cumbria)	d			10 46										12 46						13 47					
Haltwhistle	d			11 00				12 03						13 00						14 02					
Bardon Mill	d			11 08										13 08						14 09					
Haydon Bridge	d			11 13										13 13						14 15					
Hexham	a			11 22				12 21						13 22						14 24					
	d	10 44		11 22		11 45		12 22				12 45		13 22			13 45			14 24				14 43	
Corbridge	d	10 48				11 49						12 49					13 49							14 47	
Riding Mill	d	10 53				11 54						12 54					13 54							14 52	
Stocksfield	d	10 57				11 58						12 58					13 58							14 56	
Prudhoe	d	11 01		11 33		12 02		12 33				13 02		13 34			14 02			14 36				15 00	
Wylam	d	11 05				12 06						13 06					14 06							15 04	
Blaydon	d																								
Metrocentre	a	11 15		11 45		12 15		12 44				13 15		13 45			14 13			14 47				15 15	
	d	11 16	11 31	11 46	12 01	12 16	12 31	12 45			13 00	13 16	13 31	13 46		14 01	14 14	14 30		14 47			15 01	15 16	15 31
Dunston	d																								
Newcastle 8 ⛴	a	11 26	11 39	11 59	12 10	12 27	12 39	12 58			13 10	13 26	13 39	14 00		14 10	14 27	14 39		15 01			15 10	15 27	15 39
Sunderland 26,44 ⛴	a	11 49				12 49						13 49					14 49							15 49	
Newcastle 8 26 ⛴	d				12 15					12 44	13 15				13 38	14 15					14 36	14 43	15 15		
Manors	d				12 17						13 17					14 17							15 17		
Cramlington	d				12 28						13 28					14 28							15 28		
Morpeth 26	d				12a36						13a36					14a36					14a49		15a36		
Pegswood	d																								
Widdrington	d																								
Acklington	d																								
Alnmouth for Alnwick 26	d									13a10					14a01							15a09			
Chathill	a																								

For connections to London Kings Cross please refer to Table 26

Carlisle, Hexham and Metrocentre - Newcastle - Morpeth and Chathill

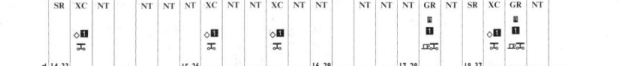

		SR	XC	NT	NT	NT	NT	XC	NT	NT	XC	NT	NT	NT	NT	NT	GR	NT	SR	XC	GR	NT
			◇ 1 trolley					◇ 1 trolley			◇ 1 trolley						R 1 restaurant/trolley			◇ 1 trolley	R 1 restaurant/trolley	
Carlisle 8	d	14 33					15 26						16 28			17 28			18 37			
Wetheral	d												16 36			17 36			18 45			
Brampton (Cumbria)	d												16 46			17 46			18 54			
Haltwhistle	d	15 03					15 55						17 00			18 01			19 09			
Bardon Mill	d												17 08			18 08						
Haydon Bridge	d												17 13			18 13						
Hexham	a	15 21					16 13						17 22			18 22			19 27			
	d	15 21			15 42		16 14			16 45			17 22		17 45	18 23		18 45	19 27			
Corbridge	d				15 46					16 49					17 49	18 27		18 49	19 32			
Riding Mill	d				15 51					16 54					17 54	18 32		18 54	19 36			
Stocksfield	d				15 55					16 58					17 58	18 36		18 58	19 40			
Prudhoe	d	15 32			16 00		16 25			17 02			17 34		18 02	18 40		19 02	19 45			
Wylam	d				16 04					17 06					18 06	18 44		19 06	19 49			
Blaydon	d																	19 12				
Metrocentre	a	15 44			16 15		16 38			17 15			17 45		18 15	18 52		19 17	19 57			
	d	15 45		16 01	16 16	16 31	16 38		17 01	17 16		17 29	17 46	18 06	18 16	18 53		19 18	19 57			20 31
Dunston	d													18 08								
Newcastle 8 ⛴	a	15 54		16 11	16 26	16 39	16 48		17 09	17 27		17 37	17 57	18 14	18 26	19 04		19 28	20 12			20 39
Sunderland 26,44 ⛴	a				16 49		17 14			17 50					18 49			19 50				
Newcastle 8 26 ⛴	d		15 37	16 15				16 37	17 15		17 37	17 38		18 25			18 43			19 38	19 44	
Manors	d			16 17					17 17			17 41		18 27								
Cramlington	d			16 28					17 28			17 52		18 38								
Morpeth 26	d			16a36					17 36			18a00		18a48							19a58	
Pegswood	d								17 40													
Widdrington	d								17 46													
Acklington	d								18 02													
Alnmouth for Alnwick 26	d		16a00					17a00	18 20		18a01						19a09			20a04		
Chathill	a								18 35													

		NT	XC	NT	NT	XC	GR	NT	NT	NT	GR FO	NT
			◇ 1			◇ 1	R 1 restaurant/trolley				R 1 trolley	
Carlisle 8	d	19 41								21 28		
Wetheral	d									21 36		
Brampton (Cumbria)	d									21 46		
Haltwhistle	d	20 10								22 01		
Bardon Mill	d									22 08		
Haydon Bridge	d									22 13		
Hexham	a	20 28								22 22		
	d	20 28			21 14					22 23		23 20
Corbridge	d	20 33			21 18					22 27		23 24
Riding Mill	d	20 37			21 23					22 32		
Stocksfield	d	20 41			21 27					22 36		
Prudhoe	d	20 46			21 31					22 40		23 34
Wylam	d	20 49			21 35					22 44		
Blaydon	d											
Metrocentre	a	20 58			21 44					22 53		
	d	20 59		21 22	21 45				22 15	22 53		
Dunston	d											
Newcastle 8 ⛴	a	21 10		21 30	21 56				22 25	23 08		23 57
Sunderland 26,44 ⛴	a											
Newcastle 8 26 ⛴	d		20 39			21 36	21 39	22 00			22 42	
Manors	d											
Cramlington	d							22 12				
Morpeth 26	d		20a54				21 55	22a21			22 56	
Pegswood	d											
Widdrington	d											
Acklington	d											
Alnmouth for Alnwick 26	d					21a59	22a09				23a11	
Chathill	a											

For connections to London Kings Cross please refer to Table 26

Table 48

Mondays to Fridays

from 3 October

Carlisle, Hexham and Metrocentre - Newcastle - Morpeth and Chathill

		NT	NT	NT	GR	XC	NT	SR	GR	NT		GR	NT	NT	NT	XC	NT	NT	NT	SR		GR	NT	NT	NT
					[R] [1]	◇[1]			[R] [1]			[R] [1]				◇[1]						[R] [1]			
Carlisle [8]	d			06 25				07 17						08 28						09 37					
Wetheral	d			06 33				07 25						08 36											
Brampton (Cumbria)	d			06 43				07 35						08 46											
Haltwhistle	d			06 57				07 49						09 00						10 08					
Bardon Mill	d			07 05				07 57						09 08											
Haydon Bridge	d			07 10				08 02						09 13											
Hexham	a			07 19				08 11						09 22						10 26					
	d		06 14	07 19			07 40	08 11					08 43	09 22				09 43		10 26				10 42	
Corbridge	d		06 18	07 24			07 44	08 16					08 47					09 47						10 46	
Riding Mill	d		06 23	07 27			07 49	08 20					08 52					09 52						10 51	
Stocksfield	d		06 27	07 31			07 53	08 24					08 56					09 56						10 55	
Prudhoe	d		06 31	07 37			07 57	08 29					09 00	09 34				10 00		10 38				10 59	
Wylam	d		06 35	07 41			08 01	08 33					09 04					10 04						11 03	
Blaydon	d						08 07	08 39																	
Metrocentre	a			07 49			08 14	08 44					09 15	09 45				10 16		10 49				11 15	
	d			07 50			08 16	08 44					09 16	09 46			10 01	10 16	10 31	10 50			11 00	11 16	11 31
Dunston	d							08 47																	
Newcastle [8] ⛴	a		06 55	08 04			08 27	08 57					09 26	10 00			10 10	10 27	10 39	11 07			11 11	11 26	11 39
Sunderland 26,44 ⛴	a		07 18				08 50						09 49					10 49						11 49	
Newcastle [8] 26 ⛴	d	05 55			06 25	07 35			07 41	07 58		08 41			09 15	09 35	10 15					10 41	11 15		
Manors	d														09 17		10 17						11 17		
Cramlington	d	06 07								08 07					09 28		10 28						11 28		
Morpeth 26	d	06 15			06 38	07a47				08a18		08a56			09a36		10a36						11a36		
Pegswood	d																								
Widdrington	d																								
Acklington	d																								
Alnmouth for Alnwick 26	d	06 32			06a52				08a07							09a58						11a07			
Chathill	a	06 46																							

		NT	NT	NT	NT	NT		GR	NT	NT	NT	NT	XC	NT	NT	NT		NT	XC	GR	NT	NT	NT	SR	XC
								[R] [1]					◇[1]						◇[1]	[R] [1]					◇[1]
Carlisle [8]	d	10 23				11 27						12 23						13 28						14 33	
Wetheral	d	10 31										12 31						13 36							
Brampton (Cumbria)	d	10 41										12 41						13 46							
Haltwhistle	d	10 55				11 56						12 55						14 00						15 03	
Bardon Mill	d	11 03										13 03						14 09							
Haydon Bridge	d	11 08										13 08						14 15							
Hexham	a	11 20				12 18						13 20						14 24						15 21	
	d	11 20		11 43		12 19				12 43		13 20			13 43			14 24				14 43		15 21	
Corbridge	d			11 47						12 47					13 47							14 47			
Riding Mill	d			11 52						12 52					13 52							14 52			
Stocksfield	d			11 56						12 56					13 56							14 56			
Prudhoe	d	11 31		12 00		12 30				13 00		13 32			14 00			14 33				15 00		15 32	
Wylam	d			12 04						13 04					14 04							15 04			
Blaydon	d																								
Metrocentre	a	11 45		12 15		12 44				13 15		13 45			14 13			14 45				15 15		15 44	
	d	11 46	12 01	12 16	12 31	12 45			13 00	13 16	13 31	13 46		14 01	14 14	14 30		14 46			15 01	15 16	15 31	15 45	
Dunston	d																								
Newcastle [8] ⛴	a	11 59	12 10	12 27	12 39	12 58			13 10	13 26	13 39	13 59		14 10	14 27	14 39		15 03			15 10	15 27	15 39	15 54	
Sunderland 26,44 ⛴	a			12 49						13 49					14 49							15 49			
Newcastle [8] 26 ⛴	d		12 15					12 44	13 15				13 38	14 15					14 36	14 43	15 15				15 37
Manors	d		12 17						13 17					14 17							15 17				
Cramlington	d		12 28						13 28					14 28							15 28				
Morpeth 26	d		12a36						13a36					14a36					14a49		15a36				
Pegswood	d																								
Widdrington	d																								
Acklington	d																								
Alnmouth for Alnwick 26	d							13a10					14a01							15a09					16a00
Chathill	a																								

For connections to London Kings Cross please refer to Table 26

Table 48

Mondays to Fridays

from 3 October

Carlisle, Hexham and Metrocentre - Newcastle - Morpeth and Chathill

		NT		NT	NT	NT	XC	NT	NT	XC	NT	NT		NT	NT	NT	GR	NT	SR	XC	GR	NT		NT	XC
							◇1			◇1							R 1			◇1	R 1				◇1
Carlisle 8	d					15 21						16 23				17 21			18 37					19 34	
Wetheral	d											16 31				17 29			18 45						
Brampton (Cumbria)	d											16 41				17 39			18 54						
Haltwhistle	d					15 50						16 55				17 54			19 09					20 03	
Bardon Mill	d											17 03				18 01									
Haydon Bridge	d											17 08				18 06									
Hexham	a					16 11						17 20				18 20			19 27					20 26	
	d			15 42		16 12			16 43			17 20			17 43	18 21		18 43	19 27					20 26	
Corbridge	d			15 46					16 47						17 47	18 25		18 47	19 32					20 31	
Riding Mill	d			15 51					16 52						17 52	18 30		18 52	19 36					20 35	
Stocksfield	d			15 55					16 56						17 56	18 34		18 56	19 40					20 39	
Prudhoe	d			16 00		16 23			17 00			17 32			18 00	18 38		19 00	19 45					20 44	
Wylam	d			16 04					17 04						18 04	18 42		19 04	19 49					20 47	
Blaydon	d																	19 10							
Metrocentre	a			16 15		16 38			17 15			17 45			18 15	18 53		19 17	19 57					20 58	
	d	16 01		16 16	16 31	16 38		17 01	17 16		17 29	17 46		18 06	18 16	18 53		19 18	19 57			20 31		20 59	
Dunston	d													18 08											
Newcastle 8	a	16 11		16 26	16 39	16 48		17 09	17 27		17 37	17 59		18 14	18 28	19 05		19 28	20 12			20 39		21 10	
Sunderland 26,44	a			16 49		17 14			17 50						18 49			19 50							
Newcastle 8 26	d	16 15					16 37	17 15		17 37	17 38			18 25			18 43			19 38	19 44				20 39
Manors	d	16 17						17 17			17 41			18 27											
Cramlington	d	16 28						17 28			17 52			18 38											
Morpeth 26	d	16a36						17 36			18a00			18a48							19a58				20a54
Pegswood	d							17 40																	
Widdrington	d							17 46																	
Acklington	d							18 02																	
Alnmouth for Alnwick 26	d						17a00	18 20		18a01							19a09			20a04					
Chathill	a							18 35																	

		NT	NT	XC	GR	NT	NT	NT		GR FO	NT
				◇1	R 1					R 1	
Carlisle 8	d							21 23			
Wetheral	d							21 31			
Brampton (Cumbria)	d							21 41			
Haltwhistle	d							21 56			
Bardon Mill	d							22 03			
Haydon Bridge	d							22 08			
Hexham	a							22 20			
	d		21 12					22 21			23 20
Corbridge	d		21 16					22 25			23 24
Riding Mill	d		21 21					22 30			
Stocksfield	d		21 25					22 34			
Prudhoe	d		21 29					22 38			23 34
Wylam	d		21 33					22 42			
Blaydon	d										
Metrocentre	a		21 44					22 53			
	d	21 22	21 45				22 15	22 53			
Dunston	d										
Newcastle 8	a	21 30	21 56				22 25	23 07			23 59
Sunderland 26,44	a										
Newcastle 8 26	d			21 36	21 39	22 00				22 42	
Manors	d										
Cramlington	d					22 12					
Morpeth 26	d				21 55	22a21				22 56	
Pegswood	d										
Widdrington	d										
Acklington	d										
Alnmouth for Alnwick 26	d			21a59	22a09					23a11	
Chathill	a										

For connections to London Kings Cross please refer to Table 26

Table 48

Saturdays
until 1 October

Carlisle, Hexham and Metrocentre - Newcastle - Morpeth and Chathill

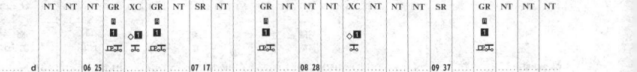

		NT	NT	NT	GR	XC	GR	NT	SR	NT		GR	NT	NT	NT	XC	NT	NT	NT	SR		GR	NT	NT	NT
					R 1	◇1	R 1					R 1				◇1						R 1			
Carlisle 8	d			06 25					07 17					08 28						09 37					
Wetheral	d			06 33					07 25					08 36											
Brampton (Cumbria)	d			06 43					07 35					08 46											
Haltwhistle	d			06 57					07 49					09 00						10 08					
Bardon Mill	d			07 05					07 57					09 08											
Haydon Bridge	d			07 10					08 02					09 13											
Hexham	a			07 19					08 11					09 22						10 26					
	d		06 16	07 19				07 42	08 11				08 45	09 22				09 46		10 26				10 44	
Corbridge	d		06 20	07 24				07 46	08 16				08 49					09 50						10 48	
Riding Mill	d		06 25	07 28				07 51	08 20				08 54					09 55						10 53	
Stocksfield	d		06 29	07 32				07 55	08 24				08 58					09 59						10 57	
Prudhoe	d		06 33	07 37				07 59	08 29				09 02	09 34				10 03		10 38				11 01	
Wylam	d		06 37	07 41				08 03	08 33				09 06					10 07						11 05	
Blaydon	d							08 09	08 39																
Metrocentre	a			07 50				08 14	08 44				09 15	09 45				10 16		10 49				11 15	
	d			07 51				08 16	08 44				09 16	09 46			10 01	10 17	10 31	10 50			10 59	11 16	11 31
Dunston	d								08 47																
Newcastle 8 ⛴	a		06 55	08 04				08 27	08 57				09 26	09 59			10 10	10 27	10 39	11 07			11 10	11 26	11 39
Sunderland 26,44 ⛴	a		07 20					08 50					09 49					10 49						11 49	
Newcastle 8 26 ⛴	d	05 55			06 30	07 38	07 42	11a51		07 58		08 41			09 15	09 35	10 14					10 39	11 15		
Manors	d														09 17		10 16						11 17		
Cramlington	d	06 07								08 09					09 28		10 27						11 28		
Morpeth 26	d	06 17			06 43	07a50				08a19		08a55			09a36		10a35						11a36		
Pegswood	d																								
Widdrington	d																								
Acklington	d																								
Alnmouth for Alnwick 26	d	06 35			06a57		08a08									09a58						11a05			
Chathill	a	06 50																							

		NT	NT	NT	NT	NT		GR	NT	NT	NT	NT	XC	NT	NT	NT		NT	XC	GR	NT	NT	NT	SR	XC
								R 1					◇1						◇1	R 1					◇1
Carlisle 8	d	10 28				11 34						12 28						13 29						14 33	
Wetheral	d	10 36										12 36						13 38							
Brampton (Cumbria)	d	10 46										12 46						13 48							
Haltwhistle	d	11 00				12 03						13 00						14 02						15 03	
Bardon Mill	d	11 08										13 08						14 10							
Haydon Bridge	d	11 13										13 13						14 15							
Hexham	a	11 22				12 21						13 22						14 23						15 21	
	d	11 22		11 45		12 22				12 45		13 22			13 45			14 24				14 43		15 21	
Corbridge	d			11 49						12 49					13 49							14 47			
Riding Mill	d			11 54						12 54					13 54							14 52			
Stocksfield	d			11 58						12 58					13 58							14 56			
Prudhoe	d	11 33		12 02		12 33				13 02		13 34			14 02			14 36				15 00		15 32	
Wylam	d			12 06						13 06					14 06							15 04			
Blaydon	d																								
Metrocentre	a	11 45		12 15		12 45				13 15		13 45			14 15			14 46				15 15		15 44	
	d	11 46	12 01	12 16	12 31	12 45			13 01	13 16	13 30	13 46		14 01	14 16	14 31		14 48			15 00	15 16	15 31	15 45	
Dunston	d																								
Newcastle 8 ⛴	a	11 59	12 10	12 27	12 39	12 57			13 10	13 26	13 39	13 59		14 10	14 27	14 39		15 00			15 10	15 27	15 39	15 54	
Sunderland 26,44 ⛴	a			12 49						13 49					14 49							15 49			
Newcastle 8 26 ⛴	d		12 15					12 40	13 15				13 35	14 15					14 35	14 40	15 15				15 34
Manors	d		12 17						13 17					14 17							15 17				
Cramlington	d		12 28						13 28					14 28							15 28				
Morpeth 26	d		12a35						13a37					14a37					14a47		15a35				
Pegswood	d																								
Widdrington	d																								
Acklington	d																								
Alnmouth for Alnwick 26	d							13a06					13a59							15a06					15a58
Chathill	a																								

For connections to London Kings Cross please refer to Table 26

Table 48

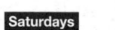

Saturdays
until 1 October

Carlisle, Hexham and Metrocentre - Newcastle - Morpeth and Chathill

Station		NT		NT	NT	NT	XC	NT	NT	NT	NT	XC		NT	NT	NT	GR	NT	SR	XC	GR	NT		NT	XC
							◇1 (trolley)					◇1 (trolley)					R 1 (restaurant, trolley)			◇1 (trolley)	R 1 (restaurant, trolley)				◇1 (trolley)
Carlisle 8	d					15 26					16 28					17 28			18 37						
Wetheral	d										16 36					17 36			18 44						
Brampton (Cumbria)	d										16 46					17 46			18 53						
Haltwhistle	d					15 55					17 00					18 01			19 08						
Bardon Mill	d										17 08					18 08									
Haydon Bridge	d										17 13					18 13									
Hexham	a					16 13					17 22					18 22			19 26						
	d			15 45		16 14				16 45	17 22				17 45	18 23		18 45	19 26						
Corbridge	d			15 49						16 49					17 49	18 27		18 49	19 31						
Riding Mill	d			15 54						16 54					17 54	18 32		18 54	19 35						
Stocksfield	d			15 58						16 58					17 58	18 36		18 58	19 39						
Prudhoe	d			16 02		16 25				17 02	17 34				18 02	18 40		19 02	19 44						
Wylam	d			16 06						17 06					18 06	18 44		19 06	19 48						
Blaydon	d																	19 12							
Metrocentre	a			16 15		16 38				17 15	17 44				18 15	18 52		19 17	19 56						
	d	16 01		16 16	16 30	16 38		16 50	17 07	17 16	17 45			18 06	18 16	18 52		19 18	19 56			20 15			
Dunston	d													18 08											
Newcastle 8 ⛴	a	16 10		16 26	16 38	16 48		16 58	17 15	17 27	17 59			18 14	18 26	19 03		19 28	20 11			20 23			
Sunderland 26,44 ⛴	a			16 49		17 14				17 50					18 49			19 50							
Newcastle 8 26 ⛴	d	16 15					16 35	17 00	17 22			17 37		18 19			18 42			19 37	19 45			20 20	20 38
Manors	d	16 17						17 03	17 24					18 21											
Cramlington	d	16 28						17 14	17 35					18 32										20 32	
Morpeth 26	d	16a36						17 22	17a42					18a40							19a59			20a41	20a51
Pegswood	d							17 25																	
Widdrington	d							17 31																	
Acklington	d							17 38																	
Alnmouth for Alnwick 26	d						16a59	17 46				18a00					19a08			20a03					
Chathill	a							17 59																	

Station		NT	NT	GR	NT	XC	NT	NT
				R 1 (restaurant, trolley)		◇1 (trolley)		
Carlisle 8	d		19 41					21 20
Wetheral	d							21 27
Brampton (Cumbria)	d							21 37
Haltwhistle	d		20 10					21 52
Bardon Mill	d							21 59
Haydon Bridge	d							22 04
Hexham	a		20 28					22 13
	d		20 28		21 14			22 14
Corbridge	d		20 33		21 18			22 18
Riding Mill	d		20 37		21 23			22 23
Stocksfield	d		20 41		21 27			22 27
Prudhoe	d		20 46		21 31			22 31
Wylam	d		20 49		21 35			22 35
Blaydon	d							
Metrocentre	a		20 58		21 44			22 44
	d	20 47	20 59		21 45		22 30	22 45
Dunston	d							
Newcastle 8 ⛴	a	20 55	21 10		21 57		22 39	23 00
Sunderland 26,44 ⛴	a	21 20						
Newcastle 8 26 ⛴	d			20 54		21 38		
Manors	d							
Cramlington	d							
Morpeth 26	d			21 09				
Pegswood	d							
Widdrington	d							
Acklington	d							
Alnmouth for Alnwick 26	d			21a24		22a01		
Chathill	a							

For connections to London Kings Cross please refer to Table 26

Table 48

Saturdays
from 8 October

Carlisle, Hexham and Metrocentre - Newcastle - Morpeth and Chathill

			NT	NT	NT	GR	XC	NT	SR	GR	NT		GR	NT	NT	NT	XC	NT	NT	NT	SR		GR	NT	NT	NT
						R 1	◇1			R 1			R 1				◇1						R 1			
Carlisle 8		d			06 25				07 17						08 28						09 37					
Wetheral		d			06 33				07 25						08 36											
Brampton (Cumbria)		d			06 43				07 35						08 46											
Haltwhistle		d			06 57				07 49						09 00						10 08					
Bardon Mill		d			07 05				07 57						09 08											
Haydon Bridge		d			07 10				08 02						09 13											
Hexham		a			07 19				08 11						09 22						10 26					
		d		06 14	07 19			07 40	08 11					08 43	09 22				09 44		10 26				10 42	
Corbridge		d		06 18	07 24			07 44	08 16					08 47					09 48						10 46	
Riding Mill		d		06 23	07 28			07 49	08 20					08 52					09 53						10 51	
Stocksfield		d		06 27	07 32			07 53	08 24					08 56					09 57						10 55	
Prudhoe		d		06 31	07 37			07 57	08 29					09 00	09 34				10 01		10 38				10 59	
Wylam		d		06 35	07 41			08 01	08 33					09 04					10 05						11 03	
Blaydon		d						08 07	08 39																	
Metrocentre		a			07 50			08 14	08 44					09 15	09 45				10 16		10 49				11 15	
		d			07 51			08 16	08 44					09 16	09 46			10 01	10 17	10 31	10 50			10 59	11 16	11 31
Dunston		d							08 47																	
Newcastle 8	⇌	a		06 55	08 08			08 27	08 57					09 26	10 03			10 10	10 27	10 39	11 07			11 10	11 26	11 39
Sunderland	26,44 ⇌	a		07 20				08 50						09 49					10 49						11 49	
Newcastle 8	26 ⇌	d	05 55			06 30	07 38			07 42	07 58		08 41			09 15	09 35	10 14					10 39	11 15		
Manors		d														09 17		10 16						11 17		
Cramlington		d	06 07								08 09					09 28		10 27						11 28		
Morpeth	26	d	06 17			06 43	07a50				08a19		08a55			09a36		10a35						11a36		
Pegswood		d																								
Widdrington		d																								
Acklington		d																								
Alnmouth for Alnwick	26	d	06 35			06a57				08a08							09a58						11a05			
Chathill		a	06 50																							

			NT	NT	NT	NT	NT		GR	NT	NT	NT	NT	XC	NT	NT	NT		NT	XC	GR	NT	NT	NT	SR	XC
									R 1					◇1						◇1	R 1					◇1
Carlisle 8		d	10 23				11 27						12 23						13 29						14 33	
Wetheral		d	10 31										12 31						13 38							
Brampton (Cumbria)		d	10 41										12 41						13 48							
Haltwhistle		d	10 55				11 56						12 55						14 02						15 03	
Bardon Mill		d	11 03										13 03						14 10							
Haydon Bridge		d	11 08										13 08						14 15							
Hexham		a	11 20				12 18						13 20						14 23						15 21	
		d	11 20		11 43		12 19				12 43		13 20			13 43			14 24				14 43		15 21	
Corbridge		d			11 47						12 47					13 47							14 47			
Riding Mill		d			11 52						12 52					13 52							14 52			
Stocksfield		d			11 56						12 56					13 56							14 56			
Prudhoe		d	11 31		12 00		12 30				13 00		13 32			14 00			14 36				15 00		15 32	
Wylam		d			12 04						13 04					14 04							15 04			
Blaydon		d																								
Metrocentre		a	11 45		12 15		12 45				13 15		13 45			14 15			14 46				15 15		15 44	
		d	11 46	12 01	12 16	12 31	12 45			13 01	13 16	13 30	13 46		14 01	14 16	14 31		14 48			15 00	15 16	15 31	15 45	
Dunston		d																								
Newcastle 8	⇌	a	11 59	12 10	12 27	12 39	12 57			13 10	13 26	13 39	13 58		14 10	14 27	14 39		15 00			15 10	15 27	15 39	15 54	
Sunderland	26,44 ⇌	a			12 49						13 49					14 49							15 49			
Newcastle 8	26 ⇌	d		12 15					12 40	13 15				13 35	14 15					14 35	14 40	15 15				15 34
Manors		d		12 17						13 17					14 17							15 17				
Cramlington		d		12 28						13 28					14 28							15 28				
Morpeth	26	d		12a35						13a37					14a37					14a47		15a35				
Pegswood		d																								
Widdrington		d																								
Acklington		d																								
Alnmouth for Alnwick	26	d							13a06					13a59							15a06					15a58
Chathill		a																								

For connections to London Kings Cross please refer to Table 26

Table 48

Saturdays
from 8 October

Carlisle, Hexham and Metrocentre - Newcastle - Morpeth and Chathill

			NT		NT	NT	NT	XC	NT	NT	NT	NT	XC		NT	NT	NT	GR	NT	SR	XC	GR	NT		NT	XC
								◇1 (bike symbol)					◇1 (bike symbol)					R 1 (bike symbol)			◇1 (bike symbol)	R 1 (bike symbol)				◇1 (bike symbol)
Carlisle 8		d					15 21					16 23					17 21			18 37						
Wetheral		d										16 31					17 29			18 44						
Brampton (Cumbria)		d										16 41					17 39			18 53						
Haltwhistle		d					15 50					16 55					17 54			19 08						
Bardon Mill		d										17 03					18 01									
Haydon Bridge		d										17 08					18 06									
Hexham		a					16 11					17 20					18 20			19 26						
		d			15 43		16 12				16 43	17 20				17 43	18 21		18 43	19 26						
Corbridge		d			15 47						16 47					17 47	18 25		18 47	19 31						
Riding Mill		d			15 52						16 52					17 52	18 30		18 52	19 35						
Stocksfield		d			15 56						16 56					17 56	18 34		18 56	19 39						
Prudhoe		d			16 00		16 23				17 00	17 32				18 00	18 38		19 00	19 44						
Wylam		d			16 04						17 04					18 04	18 42		19 04	19 48						
Blaydon		d																	19 10							
Metrocentre		a			16 15		16 38				17 15	17 44				18 15	18 52		19 17	19 56						
		d	16 01		16 16	16 30	16 38		16 50	17 07	17 16	17 45			18 06	18 16	18 52		19 18	19 56			20 15			
Dunston		d													18 08											
Newcastle 8	(ship symbol)	a	16 10		16 26	16 38	16 48		16 58	17 15	17 27	17 59			18 14	18 26	19 05		19 28	20 11			20 23			
Sunderland	26,44 (ship symbol)	a			16 49		17 14				17 50					18 49			19 50							
Newcastle 8	26 (ship symbol)	d	16 15					16 35	17 00	17 22			17 37		18 19			18 42			19 37	19 45			20 20	20 38
Manors		d	16 17						17 03	17 24					18 21											
Cramlington		d	16 28						17 14	17 35					18 32										20 32	
Morpeth	26	d	16a36						17 22	17a42					18a40							19a59			20a41	20a51
Pegswood		d							17 25																	
Widdrington		d							17 31																	
Acklington		d							17 38																	
Alnmouth for Alnwick	26	d						16a59	17 46				18a00					19a08			20a03					
Chathill		a							17 59																	

			NT	NT	GR	NT	XC	NT	NT
					R 1 (bike symbol)		◇1 (bike symbol)		
Carlisle 8		d		19 34					21 15
Wetheral		d							21 23
Brampton (Cumbria)		d							21 33
Haltwhistle		d		20 03					21 48
Bardon Mill		d							21 55
Haydon Bridge		d							22 00
Hexham		a		20 26					22 12
		d		20 26		21 12			22 13
Corbridge		d		20 31		21 16			22 17
Riding Mill		d		20 35		21 21			22 22
Stocksfield		d		20 39		21 25			22 26
Prudhoe		d		20 44		21 29			22 30
Wylam		d		20 47		21 33			22 34
Blaydon		d							
Metrocentre		a		20 58		21 44			22 45
		d	20 47	20 59		21 45		22 30	22 45
Dunston		d							
Newcastle 8	(ship symbol)	a	20 55	21 10		21 57		22 39	23 00
Sunderland	26,44 (ship symbol)	a	21 20						
Newcastle 8	26 (ship symbol)	d			20 54		21 38		
Manors		d							
Cramlington		d							
Morpeth	26	d			21 09				
Pegswood		d							
Widdrington		d							
Acklington		d							
Alnmouth for Alnwick	26	d			21a24		22a01		
Chathill		a							

For connections to London Kings Cross please refer to Table 26

Table 48

Sundays
until 19 June

Carlisle, Hexham and Metrocentre - Newcastle - Morpeth and Chathill

		XC	NT	NT	GR	NT	NT	NT	NT	NT		NT	GR	NT	NT	NT	XC	NT	NT	NT		XC	GR	NT	NT
		◇1			R 1								R 1				◇1					◇1	R 1		
Carlisle 8	d			09 05				10 05				11 12				12 05				13 12					
Wetheral	d			09 12				10 12								12 12									
Brampton (Cumbria)	d			09 22				10 22								12 22									
Haltwhistle	d			09 36				10 36				11 40				12 36				13 40					
Bardon Mill	d			09 44				10 44								12 44									
Haydon Bridge	d			09 49				10 49								12 49									
Hexham	a			09 58				10 58				11 58				12 58				13 58					
	d			09 59				10 59				11 59				12 59				13 59					
Corbridge	d			10 03				11 03				12 03				13 03				14 03					
Riding Mill	d			10 08				11 08				12 08				13 08				14 08					
Stocksfield	d			10 12				11 12				12 12				13 12				14 12					
Prudhoe	d			10 16				11 16				12 16				13 16				14 16					
Wylam	d			10 20				11 20				12 20				13 20				14 20					
Blaydon	d																								
Metrocentre	a			10 29				11 29				12 29				13 29				14 29					
	d		10 10	10 30		10 48	11 10	11 30	11 48	12 10		12 30		12 48	13 15	13 30		13 48	14 10	14 30				14 48	15 10
Dunston	d																								
Newcastle 8 ⛴	a		10 18	10 40		10 56	11 18	11 40	11 56	12 18		12 40		12 56	13 23	13 40		13 56	14 18	14 40				14 56	15 18
Sunderland 26,44 ⛴	a																								
Newcastle 8 26 ⛴	d	09 45			10 13								12 44				13 35					14 36	14 42		
Manors	d																								
Cramlington	d																								
Morpeth 26	d	09 58			10 29																	14a48			
Pegswood	d																								
Widdrington	d																								
Acklington	d																								
Alnmouth for Alnwick 26	d	10a11			10a43								13a10				13a59						15a08		
Chathill	a																								

		NT	XC	NT	NT	NT		XC	GR	NT	NT	NT	XC	NT	NT	NT		GR	NT	NT	NT	XC	GR	NT	XC
			◇1					◇1	R 1				◇1					R 1				◇1	R 1		◇1
Carlisle 8	d	14 12				15 05						16 12				17 12					18 05			20 15	
Wetheral	d					15 12															18 12				
Brampton (Cumbria)	d					15 22															18 22				
Haltwhistle	d	14 40				15 36						16 40				17 40					18 36			20 43	
Bardon Mill	d					15 44															18 44				
Haydon Bridge	d					15 49															18 49				
Hexham	a	14 58				15 58						16 58				17 58					18 58			21 01	
	d	14 59				15 59						16 59				17 59					18 59			21 01	
Corbridge	d	15 03				16 03						17 03				18 03					19 03			21 05	
Riding Mill	d	15 08				16 08						17 08				18 08					19 08			21 10	
Stocksfield	d	15 12				16 12						17 12				18 12					19 12			21 14	
Prudhoe	d	15 16				16 16						17 16				18 16					19 16			21 18	
Wylam	d	15 20				16 20						17 20				18 20					19 20			21 22	
Blaydon	d																								
Metrocentre	a	15 29				16 29						17 29				18 29					19 29			21 31	
	d	15 30		15 48	16 10	16 30				16 48	17 10	17 30		17 48	18 10	18 30			18 48	19 10	19 30			21 31	
Dunston	d																								
Newcastle 8 ⛴	a	15 40		15 58	16 18	16 40				16 56	17 18	17 40		17 58	18 18	18 40			18 56	19 18	19 40			21 43	
Sunderland 26,44 ⛴	a																								
Newcastle 8 26 ⛴	d		15 37					16 34	16 42				17 38					18 43				19 40	19 44		20 38
Manors	d																								
Cramlington	d																								
Morpeth 26	d																						19a58		20a52
Pegswood	d																								
Widdrington	d																								
Acklington	d																								
Alnmouth for Alnwick 26	d		16a01					16a58	17a08				18a01					19a10				20a04			
Chathill	a																								

For connections to London Kings Cross please refer to Table 26

Table 48

Sundays
until 19 June

Carlisle, Hexham and Metrocentre - Newcastle - Morpeth and Chathill

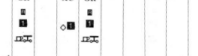

			GR	XC	GR
			R 1	◇1	R 1
Carlisle		d			
Wetheral		d			
Brampton (Cumbria)		d			
Haltwhistle		d			
Bardon Mill		d			
Haydon Bridge		d			
Hexham		a			
		d			
Corbridge		d			
Riding Mill		d			
Stocksfield		d			
Prudhoe		d			
Wylam		d			
Blaydon		d			
Metrocentre		a			
		d			
Dunston		d			
Newcastle		a			
Sunderland	26,44	a			
Newcastle	26	d	20 53	21 38	21 56
Manors		d			
Cramlington		d			
Morpeth	26	d	21 10		22 12
Pegswood		d			
Widdrington		d			
Acklington		d			
Alnmouth for Alnwick	26	d	21a24	22a04	22a27
Chathill		a			

Sundays
26 June to 26 June

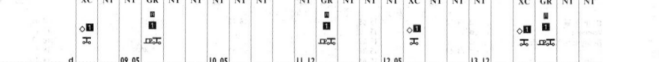

			XC	NT	NT	GR	NT	NT	NT	NT	NT	NT	GR	NT	NT	NT	XC	NT	NT	NT	XC	GR	NT	NT
			◇1			R 1							R 1				◇1				◇1	R 1		
Carlisle		d			09 05				10 05			11 12				12 05				13 12				
Wetheral		d			09 12				10 12							12 12								
Brampton (Cumbria)		d			09 22				10 22							12 22								
Haltwhistle		d			09 36				10 36			11 40				12 36				13 40				
Bardon Mill		d			09 44				10 44							12 44								
Haydon Bridge		d			09 49				10 49							12 49								
Hexham		a			09 58				10 58			11 58				12 58				13 58				
		d			09 59				10 59			11 59				12 59				13 59				
Corbridge		d			10 03				11 03			12 03				13 03				14 03				
Riding Mill		d			10 08				11 08			12 08				13 08				14 08				
Stocksfield		d			10 12				11 12			12 12				13 12				14 12				
Prudhoe		d			10 16				11 16			12 16				13 16				14 16				
Wylam		d			10 20				11 20			12 20				13 20				14 20				
Blaydon		d																						
Metrocentre		a			10 29				11 29			12 29				13 29				14 29				
		d		10 10	10 30		10 48	11 10	11 30	11 48	12 10	12 30		12 48	13 15	13 30		13 48	14 10	14 30			14 48	15 10
Dunston		d																						
Newcastle		a		10 18	10 40		10 56	11 18	11 40	11 56	12 18	12 40		12 56	13 23	13 40		13 56	14 18	14 40			14 56	15 18
Sunderland	26,44	a					11 22			12 21				13 22				14 21					15 22	
Newcastle	26	d	09 45			10 13							12 44				13 35				14 36	14 42		
Manors		d																						
Cramlington		d																						
Morpeth	26	d	09 58			10 29															14a48			
Pegswood		d																						
Widdrington		d																						
Acklington		d																						
Alnmouth for Alnwick	26	d	10a11			10a43							13a10				13a59					15a08		
Chathill		a																						

For connections to London Kings Cross please refer to Table 26

Table 48

Sundays

26 June to 26 June

Carlisle, Hexham and Metrocentre - Newcastle - Morpeth and Chathill

		NT	XC	NT	NT	NT		XC	GR	NT	NT	NT	XC	NT	NT	NT		GR	NT	NT	NT	XC	GR	NT	XC
									R									R					R		
			◇1					◇1	1				◇1					1				◇1	1		◇1
			⚲					⚲	⊐⚲				⚲					⊐⚲				⚲	⊐⚲		
Carlisle 8	d	14 12				15 05						16 12				17 12					18 05			20 15	
Wetheral	d					15 12															18 12				
Brampton (Cumbria)	d					15 22															18 22				
Haltwhistle	d	14 40				15 36						16 40				17 40					18 36			20 43	
Bardon Mill	d					15 44															18 44				
Haydon Bridge	d					15 49															18 49				
Hexham	a	14 58				15 58						16 58				17 58					18 58			21 01	
	d	14 59				15 59						16 59				17 59					18 59			21 01	
Corbridge	d	15 03				16 03						17 03				18 03					19 03			21 05	
Riding Mill	d	15 08				16 08						17 08				18 08					19 08			21 10	
Stocksfield	d	15 12				16 12						17 12				18 12					19 12			21 14	
Prudhoe	d	15 16				16 16						17 16				18 16					19 16			21 18	
Wylam	d	15 20				16 20						17 20				18 20					19 20			21 22	
Blaydon	d																								
Metrocentre	a	15 29				16 29						17 29				18 29					19 29			21 31	
	d	15 30		15 48	16 10	16 30				16 48	17 10	17 30		17 48	18 10	18 30			18 48	19 10	19 30			21 31	
Dunston	d																								
Newcastle 8 ⛴	a	15 40		15 58	16 18	16 40				16 56	17 18	17 40		17 58	18 18	18 40			18 56	19 18	19 40			21 43	
Sunderland 26,44 ⛴	a			16 21						17 22				18 21					19 22						
Newcastle 8 26 ⛴	d		15 37					16 34	16 42				17 38					18 43				19 40	19 44		20 38
Manors	d																								
Cramlington	d																								
Morpeth 26	d																						19a58		20a52
Pegswood	d																								
Widdrington	d																								
Acklington	d																								
Alnmouth for Alnwick 26	d		16a01					16a58	17a08				18a01					19a10				20a04			
Chathill	a																								

		GR		XC	GR
		R			R
		1		◇1	1
		⊐⚲			⊐⚲
Carlisle 8	d				
Wetheral	d				
Brampton (Cumbria)	d				
Haltwhistle	d				
Bardon Mill	d				
Haydon Bridge	d				
Hexham	a				
	d				
Corbridge	d				
Riding Mill	d				
Stocksfield	d				
Prudhoe	d				
Wylam	d				
Blaydon	d				
Metrocentre	a				
	d				
Dunston	d				
Newcastle 8 ⛴	a				
Sunderland 26,44 ⛴	a				
Newcastle 8 26 ⛴	d	20 53		21 38	21 56
Manors	d				
Cramlington	d				
Morpeth 26	d	21 10			22 12
Pegswood	d				
Widdrington	d				
Acklington	d				
Alnmouth for Alnwick 26	d	21a24		22a04	22a27
Chathill	a				

For connections to London Kings Cross please refer to Table 26

Table 48

Sundays
3 July to 31 July

Carlisle, Hexham and Metrocentre - Newcastle - Morpeth and Chathill

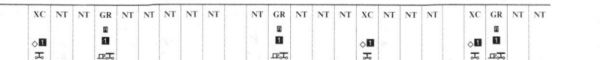

		XC	NT	NT	GR	NT	NT	NT	NT	NT		NT	GR	NT	NT	NT	XC	NT	NT	NT		XC	GR	NT	NT
		◇1			R 1								R 1				◇1					◇1	R 1		
Carlisle 8	d			09 05				10 05				11 12				12 05				13 12					
Wetheral	d			09 12				10 12								12 12									
Brampton (Cumbria)	d			09 22				10 22								12 22									
Haltwhistle	d			09 36				10 36				11 40				12 36				13 40					
Bardon Mill	d			09 44				10 44								12 44									
Haydon Bridge	d			09 49				10 49								12 49									
Hexham	a			09 58				10 58				11 58				12 58				13 58					
	d			09 59				10 59				11 59				12 59				13 59					
Corbridge	d			10 03				11 03				12 03				13 03				14 03					
Riding Mill	d			10 08				11 08				12 08				13 08				14 08					
Stocksfield	d			10 12				11 12				12 12				13 12				14 12					
Prudhoe	d			10 16				11 16				12 16				13 16				14 16					
Wylam	d			10 20				11 20				12 20				13 20				14 20					
Blaydon	d																								
Metrocentre	a			10 29				11 29				12 29				13 29				14 29					
	d		10 10	10 30		10 48	11 10	11 30	11 48	12 10		12 30		12 48	13 15	13 30		13 48	14 10	14 30				14 48	15 10
Dunston	d																								
Newcastle 8	a		10 18	10 40		10 56	11 18	11 40	11 56	12 18		12 40		12 56	13 23	13 40		13 56	14 18	14 40				14 56	15 18
Sunderland 26,44	a					11 22			12 21					13 22				14 21						15 22	
Newcastle 8 26	d	09 45			10 13								12 44				13 35					14 36	14 42		
Manors	d																								
Cramlington	d																								
Morpeth 26	d	09 58			10 29																	14a48			
Pegswood	d																								
Widdrington	d																								
Acklington	d																								
Alnmouth for Alnwick 26	d	10a11			10a43								13a10				13a59						15a08		
Chathill	a																								

		NT	XC	NT	NT	NT		XC	GR	NT	NT	NT	XC	NT	NT	NT		GR	NT	NT	NT	XC	GR	NT	XC
			◇1					◇1	R 1				◇1					R 1				◇1	R 1		◇1
Carlisle 8	d	14 12				15 05						16 12				17 12					18 05			20 15	
Wetheral	d					15 12															18 12				
Brampton (Cumbria)	d					15 22															18 22				
Haltwhistle	d	14 40				15 36						16 40				17 40					18 36			20 43	
Bardon Mill	d					15 44															18 44				
Haydon Bridge	d					15 49															18 49				
Hexham	a	14 58				15 58						16 58				17 58					18 58			21 01	
	d	14 59				15 59						16 59				17 59					18 59			21 01	
Corbridge	d	15 03				16 03						17 03				18 03					19 03			21 05	
Riding Mill	d	15 08				16 08						17 08				18 08					19 08			21 10	
Stocksfield	d	15 12				16 12						17 12				18 12					19 12			21 14	
Prudhoe	d	15 16				16 16						17 16				18 16					19 16			21 18	
Wylam	d	15 20				16 20						17 20				18 20					19 20			21 22	
Blaydon	d																								
Metrocentre	a	15 29				16 29						17 29				18 29					19 29			21 31	
	d	15 30		15 48	16 10	16 30				16 48	17 10	17 30		17 48	18 10	18 30			18 48	19 10	19 30			21 31	
Dunston	d																								
Newcastle 8	a	15 40		15 58	16 18	16 40				16 56	17 18	17 40		17 58	18 18	18 40			18 56	19 18	19 40			21 43	
Sunderland 26,44	a			16 21						17 22				18 21					19 22						
Newcastle 8 26	d		15 37					16 34	16 42				17 38					18 43				19 40	19 44		20 38
Manors	d																								
Cramlington	d																								
Morpeth 26	d																						19a58		20a52
Pegswood	d																								
Widdrington	d																								
Acklington	d																								
Alnmouth for Alnwick 26	d		16a01					16a58	17a08				18a01					19a10				20a04			
Chathill	a																								

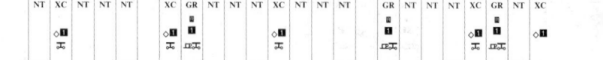

For connections to London Kings Cross please refer to Table 26

Table 48

Sundays

3 July to 31 July

Carlisle, Hexham and Metrocentre - Newcastle - Morpeth and Chathill

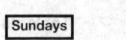

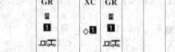

		GR		XC	GR
		R 1		◇1	R 1
Carlisle 8	d				
Wetheral	d				
Brampton (Cumbria)	d				
Haltwhistle	d				
Bardon Mill	d				
Haydon Bridge	d				
Hexham	a				
	d				
Corbridge	d				
Riding Mill	d				
Stocksfield	d				
Prudhoe	d				
Wylam	d				
Blaydon	d				
Metrocentre	a				
	d				
Dunston	d				
Newcastle 8	a				
Sunderland 26,44	a				
Newcastle 8 26	d	20 53		21 38	21 56
Manors	d				
Cramlington	d				
Morpeth 26	d	21 10			22 12
Pegswood	d				
Widdrington	d				
Acklington	d				
Alnmouth for Alnwick 26	d	21a24		22a04	22a27
Chathill	a				

Sundays

7 August to 11 September

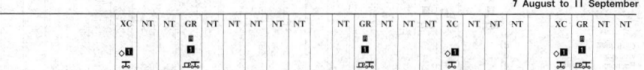

		XC	NT	NT	GR	NT	NT	NT	NT	NT		NT	GR
		◇1			R 1								R 1
Carlisle 8	d			09 05				10 05				11 12	
Wetheral	d			09 12				10 12					
Brampton (Cumbria)	d			09 22				10 22					
Haltwhistle	d			09 36				10 36				11 40	
Bardon Mill	d			09 44				10 44					
Haydon Bridge	d			09 49				10 49					
Hexham	a			09 58				10 58				11 58	
	d			09 59				10 59				11 59	
Corbridge	d			10 03				11 03				12 03	
Riding Mill	d			10 08				11 08				12 08	
Stocksfield	d			10 12				11 12				12 12	
Prudhoe	d			10 16				11 16				12 16	
Wylam	d			10 20				11 20				12 20	
Blaydon	d												
Metrocentre	a			10 29				11 29				12 29	
	d		10 10	10 30		10 48	11 10	11 30	11 48	12 10		12 30	
Dunston	d												
Newcastle 8	a		10 18	10 40		10 56	11 18	11 40	11 56	12 18		12 40	
Sunderland 26,44	a					11 22			12 21				
Newcastle 8 26	d	09 45			10 13								12 44
Manors	d												
Cramlington	d												
Morpeth 26	d	09 58			10 29								
Pegswood	d												
Widdrington	d												
Acklington	d												
Alnmouth for Alnwick 26	d	10a11			10a43								13a10
Chathill	a												

		NT	NT	NT	XC	NT	NT	NT		XC	GR	NT	NT
					◇1					◇1	R 1		
Carlisle 8	d			12 05				13 12					
Wetheral	d			12 12									
Brampton (Cumbria)	d			12 22									
Haltwhistle	d			12 36				13 40					
Bardon Mill	d			12 44									
Haydon Bridge	d			12 49									
Hexham	a			12 58				13 58					
	d			12 59				13 59					
Corbridge	d			13 03				14 03					
Riding Mill	d			13 08				14 08					
Stocksfield	d			13 12				14 12					
Prudhoe	d			13 16				14 16					
Wylam	d			13 20				14 20					
Blaydon	d												
Metrocentre	a			13 29				14 29					
	d	12 48	13 15	13 30		13 48	14 10	14 30				14 48	15 10
Dunston	d												
Newcastle 8	a	12 56	13 23	13 40		13 56	14 18	14 40				14 56	15 18
Sunderland 26,44	a	13 22				14 21						15 22	
Newcastle 8 26	d				13 35					14 36	14 42		
Manors	d												
Cramlington	d												
Morpeth 26	d									14a48			
Pegswood	d												
Widdrington	d												
Acklington	d												
Alnmouth for Alnwick 26	d				13a59						15a08		
Chathill	a												

For connections to London Kings Cross please refer to Table 26

Table 48

Sundays

7 August to 11 September

Carlisle, Hexham and Metrocentre - Newcastle - Morpeth and Chathill

			NT	XC	NT	NT	NT		XC	GR	NT	NT	NT	XC	NT	NT	NT		GR	NT	NT	NT	XC	GR	NT	XC
				◇1					◇1	R 1				◇1					R 1				◇1	R 1		◇1
Carlisle 8		d	14 12				15 05						16 12				17 12					18 05			20 15	
Wetheral		d					15 12															18 12				
Brampton (Cumbria)		d					15 22															18 22				
Haltwhistle		d	14 40				15 36						16 40				17 40					18 36			20 43	
Bardon Mill		d					15 44															18 44				
Haydon Bridge		d					15 49															18 49				
Hexham		a	14 58				15 58						16 58				17 58					18 58			21 01	
		d	14 59				15 59						16 59				17 59					18 59			21 01	
Corbridge		d	15 03				16 03						17 03				18 03					19 03			21 05	
Riding Mill		d	15 08				16 08						17 08				18 08					19 08			21 10	
Stocksfield		d	15 12				16 12						17 12				18 12					19 12			21 14	
Prudhoe		d	15 16				16 16						17 16				18 16					19 16			21 18	
Wylam		d	15 20				16 20						17 20				18 20					19 20			21 22	
Blaydon		d																								
Metrocentre		a	15 29				16 29						17 29				18 29					19 29			21 31	
		d	15 30		15 48	16 10	16 30				16 48	17 10	17 30		17 48	18 10	18 30			18 48	19 10	19 30			21 31	
Dunston		d																								
Newcastle 8		a	15 40		15 58	16 18	16 40				16 56	17 18	17 40		17 58	18 18	18 40			18 56	19 18	19 40			21 43	
Sunderland	26,44	a			16 21						17 22				18 21					19 22						
Newcastle 8	26	d		15 37					16 34	16 42				17 38					18 43				19 40	19 44		20 38
Manors		d																								
Cramlington		d																								
Morpeth	26	d																						19a58		20a52
Pegswood		d																								
Widdrington		d																								
Acklington		d																								
Alnmouth for Alnwick	26	d		16a01					16a58	17a08				18a01					19a10				20a04			
Chathill		a																								

			GR		XC	GR
			R 1		◇1	R 1
Carlisle 8		d				
Wetheral		d				
Brampton (Cumbria)		d				
Haltwhistle		d				
Bardon Mill		d				
Haydon Bridge		d				
Hexham		a				
		d				
Corbridge		d				
Riding Mill		d				
Stocksfield		d				
Prudhoe		d				
Wylam		d				
Blaydon		d				
Metrocentre		a				
		d				
Dunston		d				
Newcastle 8		a				
Sunderland	26,44	a				
Newcastle 8	26	d	20 53		21 38	21 56
Manors		d				
Cramlington		d				
Morpeth	26	d	21 10			22 12
Pegswood		d				
Widdrington		d				
Acklington		d				
Alnmouth for Alnwick	26	d	21a24		22a04	22a27
Chathill		a				

For connections to London Kings Cross please refer to Table 26

Table 48

Sundays

18 September to 2 October

Carlisle, Hexham and Metrocentre - Newcastle - Morpeth and Chathill

		XC	NT	NT	GR	NT	NT	NT	NT	NT		NT	GR	NT	NT	NT	XC	NT	NT	NT		GR	NT	NT	NT
		◇1			R 1								R 1				◇1					R 1			
Carlisle 8	d			09 05				10 05				11 12				12 05				13 12					14 12
Wetheral	d			09 12				10 12								12 12									
Brampton (Cumbria)	d			09 22				10 22								12 22									
Haltwhistle	d			09 36				10 36				11 40				12 36				13 40					14 40
Bardon Mill	d			09 44				10 44								12 44									
Haydon Bridge	d			09 49				10 49								12 49									
Hexham	a			09 58				10 58				11 58				12 58				13 58					14 58
	d			09 59				10 59				11 59				12 59				13 59					14 59
Corbridge	d			10 03				11 03				12 03				13 03				14 03					15 03
Riding Mill	d			10 08				11 08				12 08				13 08				14 08					15 08
Stocksfield	d			10 12				11 12				12 12				13 12				14 12					15 12
Prudhoe	d			10 16				11 16				12 16				13 16				14 16					15 16
Wylam	d			10 20				11 20				12 20				13 20				14 20					15 20
Blaydon	d																								
Metrocentre	a			10 29				11 29				12 29				13 29				14 29					15 29
	d		10 10	10 30		10 48	11 10	11 30	11 48	12 10		12 30		12 48	13 15	13 30		13 48	14 10	14 30			14 48	15 10	15 30
Dunston	d																								
Newcastle 8	a		10 18	10 40		10 56	11 18	11 40	11 56	12 18		12 40		12 56	13 23	13 40		13 56	14 18	14 40			14 56	15 18	15 40
Sunderland 26,44	a					11 22			12 21					13 22				14 21					15 22		
Newcastle 8 26	d	09 45			10 13								12 44				13 35					14 42			
Manors	d																								
Cramlington	d																								
Morpeth 26	d	09 58			10 29																				
Pegswood	d																								
Widdrington	d																								
Acklington	d																								
Alnmouth for Alnwick 26	d	10a11			10a43								13a10				13a59					15a08			
Chathill	a																								

		XC	NT	NT	NT	XC		GR	NT	NT	NT	XC	NT	NT	NT	GR		NT	NT	NT	XC	GR	NT	XC	GR
		◇1				◇1		R 1				◇1				R 1					◇1	R 1		◇1	R 1
Carlisle 8	d				15 05						16 12				17 12					18 05			20 15		
Wetheral	d				15 12															18 12					
Brampton (Cumbria)	d				15 22															18 22					
Haltwhistle	d				15 36						16 40				17 40					18 36			20 43		
Bardon Mill	d				15 44															18 44					
Haydon Bridge	d				15 49															18 49					
Hexham	a				15 58						16 58				17 58					18 58			21 01		
	d				15 59						16 59				17 59					18 59			21 01		
Corbridge	d				16 03						17 03				18 03					19 03			21 05		
Riding Mill	d				16 08						17 08				18 08					19 08			21 10		
Stocksfield	d				16 12						17 12				18 12					19 12			21 14		
Prudhoe	d				16 16						17 16				18 16					19 16			21 18		
Wylam	d				16 20						17 20				18 20					19 20			21 22		
Blaydon	d																								
Metrocentre	a				16 29						17 29				18 29					19 29			21 31		
	d		15 48	16 10	16 30				16 48	17 10	17 30		17 48	18 10	18 30			18 48	19 10	19 30			21 31		
Dunston	d																								
Newcastle 8	a		15 58	16 18	16 40				16 56	17 18	17 40		17 58	18 18	18 40			18 56	19 18	19 40			21 43		
Sunderland 26,44	a		16 21						17 22				18 21					19 22							
Newcastle 8 26	d	15 37				16 34		16 42				17 38				18 43					19 40	19 44		20 38	20 53
Manors	d																								
Cramlington	d																								
Morpeth 26	d																					19a58		20a52	21 10
Pegswood	d																								
Widdrington	d																								
Acklington	d																								
Alnmouth for Alnwick 26	d	16a01				16a58		17a08				18a01				19a10					20a04				21a24
Chathill	a																								

For connections to London Kings Cross please refer to Table 26

Table 48

Sundays

18 September to 2 October

Carlisle, Hexham and Metrocentre - Newcastle - Morpeth and Chathill

		XC		GR
		◇1		B 1
Carlisle 8	d			
Wetheral	d			
Brampton (Cumbria)	d			
Haltwhistle	d			
Bardon Mill	d			
Haydon Bridge	d			
Hexham	a			
	d			
Corbridge	d			
Riding Mill	d			
Stocksfield	d			
Prudhoe	d			
Wylam	d			
Blaydon	d			
Metrocentre	a			
	d			
Dunston	d			
Newcastle 8	a			
Sunderland 26,44	a			
Newcastle 8 26	d	21 38		21 56
Manors	d			
Cramlington	d			
Morpeth 26	d			22 12
Pegswood	d			
Widdrington	d			
Acklington	d			
Alnmouth for Alnwick 26	d	22a04		22a27
Chathill	a			

Sundays

9 October to 23 October

		XC	NT	NT	GR	NT	NT	NT	NT	NT		NT	GR	NT	NT	NT	XC	NT	NT	NT		GR	NT	NT	NT
		◇1			B 1								B 1				◇1					B 1			
Carlisle 8	d			09 05				10 05				11 08				12 05				13 09					14 09
Wetheral	d			09 12				10 12								12 12									
Brampton (Cumbria)	d			09 22				10 22								12 22									
Haltwhistle	d			09 36				10 36				11 36				12 36				13 37					14 37
Bardon Mill	d			09 44				10 44								12 44									
Haydon Bridge	d			09 49				10 49								12 49									
Hexham	a			09 58				10 58				11 54				12 58				13 55					14 55
	d			09 59				10 59				11 55				12 59				13 56					14 56
Corbridge	d			10 03				11 03				11 59				13 03				14 00					15 00
Riding Mill	d			10 08				11 08				12 04				13 08				14 05					15 05
Stocksfield	d			10 12				11 12				12 08				13 12				14 09					15 09
Prudhoe	d			10 16				11 16				12 12				13 16				14 13					15 13
Wylam	d			10 20				11 20				12 16				13 20				14 17					15 17
Blaydon	d																								
Metrocentre	a			10 33				11 33				12 29				13 33				14 29					15 29
	d		10 10	10 33		10 48	11 10	11 33	11 48	12 10		12 30		12 48	13 15	13 33		13 48	14 10	14 30			14 48	15 10	15 30
Dunston	d																								
Newcastle 8	a		10 18	10 43		10 56	11 18	11 43	11 56	12 18		12 40		12 56	13 23	13 43		13 56	14 18	14 40			14 56	15 18	15 40
Sunderland 26,44	a					11 22			12 21					13 22				14 21					15 22		
Newcastle 8 26	d	09 45			10 13								12 44				13 35					14 42			
Manors	d																								
Cramlington	d																								
Morpeth 26	d	09 58			10 29																				
Pegswood	d																								
Widdrington	d																								
Acklington	d																								
Alnmouth for Alnwick 26	d	10a11			10a43								13a10				13a59					15a08			
Chathill	a																								

For connections to London Kings Cross please refer to Table 26

Table 48

Sundays

9 October to 23 October

Carlisle, Hexham and Metrocentre - Newcastle - Morpeth and Chathill

		XC	NT	NT	NT	XC		GR	NT	NT	NT	XC	NT	NT	NT	GR		NT	NT	NT	XC	GR	NT	XC	GR
								R								R						R			R
		◇1				◇1		1				◇1				1					◇1	1		◇1	1
		🍴				🍴		🍴				🍴				🍴					🍴	🍴		🍴	🍴
Carlisle 8	d				15 05						16 11				17 10					18 01			20 15		
Wetheral	d				15 12															18 08					
Brampton (Cumbria)	d				15 22															18 18					
Haltwhistle	d				15 36						16 39				17 38					18 32			20 43		
Bardon Mill	d				15 44															18 40					
Haydon Bridge	d				15 49															18 45					
Hexham	a				15 58						16 57				17 56					18 54			21 01		
	d				15 59						16 58				17 57					18 55			21 01		
Corbridge	d				16 03						17 02				18 01					18 59			21 05		
Riding Mill	d				16 08						17 07				18 06					19 04			21 10		
Stocksfield	d				16 12						17 11				18 10					19 08			21 14		
Prudhoe	d				16 16						17 15				18 14					19 12			21 18		
Wylam	d				16 20						17 19				18 18					19 16			21 22		
Blaydon	d																								
Metrocentre	a				16 33						17 32				18 31					19 29			21 34		
	d		15 48	16 10	16 33				16 48	17 10	17 33		17 48	18 10	18 32			18 48	19 10	19 29			21 34		
Dunston	d																								
Newcastle 8 ⛴	a		15 58	16 18	16 43				16 56	17 18	17 43		17 58	18 18	18 42			18 56	19 18	19 39			21 46		
Sunderland 26,44 ⛴	a		16 21						17 22				18 21					19 22							
Newcastle 8 26 ⛴	d	15 37				16 34		16 42				17 38				18 43					19 40	19 44		20 38	20 53
Manors	d																								
Cramlington	d																								
Morpeth 26	d																					19a58		20a52	21 10
Pegswood	d																								
Widdrington	d																								
Acklington	d																								
Alnmouth for Alnwick 26	d	16a01				16a58		17a08				18a01				19a10					20a04				21a24
Chathill	a																								

		XC		GR
				R
		◇1		1
				🍴
Carlisle 8	d			
Wetheral	d			
Brampton (Cumbria)	d			
Haltwhistle	d			
Bardon Mill	d			
Haydon Bridge	d			
Hexham	a			
	d			
Corbridge	d			
Riding Mill	d			
Stocksfield	d			
Prudhoe	d			
Wylam	d			
Blaydon	d			
Metrocentre	a			
	d			
Dunston	d			
Newcastle 8 ⛴	a			
Sunderland 26,44 ⛴	a			
Newcastle 8 26 ⛴	d	21 38		21 56
Manors	d			
Cramlington	d			
Morpeth 26	d			22 12
Pegswood	d			
Widdrington	d			
Acklington	d			
Alnmouth for Alnwick 26	d	22a04		22a27
Chathill	a			

For connections to London Kings Cross please refer to Table 26

Table 48

Sundays
from 30 October

Carlisle, Hexham and Metrocentre - Newcastle - Morpeth and Chathill

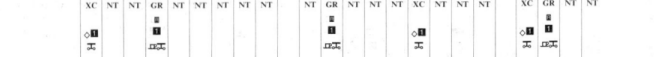

		XC	NT	NT	GR	NT	NT	NT	NT	NT		NT	GR	NT	NT	NT	XC	NT	NT	NT		XC	GR	NT	NT
		◇1			R 1								R 1				◇1					◇1	R 1		
Carlisle	d			09 05				10 05				11 08				12 05				13 09					
Wetheral	d			09 12				10 12								12 12									
Brampton (Cumbria)	d			09 22				10 22								12 22									
Haltwhistle	d			09 36				10 36				11 36				12 36				13 37					
Bardon Mill	d			09 44				10 44								12 44									
Haydon Bridge	d			09 49				10 49								12 49									
Hexham	a			09 58				10 58				11 54				12 58				13 55					
	d			09 59				10 59				11 55				12 59				13 56					
Corbridge	d			10 03				11 03				11 59				13 03				14 00					
Riding Mill	d			10 08				11 08				12 04				13 08				14 05					
Stocksfield	d			10 12				11 12				12 08				13 12				14 09					
Prudhoe	d			10 16				11 16				12 12				13 16				14 13					
Wylam	d			10 20				11 20				12 16				13 20				14 17					
Blaydon	d																								
Metrocentre	a			10 33				11 33				12 29				13 33				14 29					
	d		10 10	10 33		10 48	11 10	11 33	11 48	12 10		12 30		12 48	13 15	13 33		13 48	14 10	14 30				14 48	15 10
Dunston	d																								
Newcastle	a		10 18	10 43		10 56	11 18	11 43	11 56	12 18		12 40		12 56	13 23	13 43		13 56	14 18	14 40				14 56	15 18
Sunderland 26,44	a					11 22			12 21					13 22				14 21						15 22	
Newcastle 26	d	09 45			10 13								12 44				13 35					14 36	14 42		
Manors	d																								
Cramlington	d																								
Morpeth 26	d	09 58			10 29																	14a48			
Pegswood	d																								
Widdrington	d																								
Acklington	d																								
Alnmouth for Alnwick 26	d	10a11			10a43								13a10				13a59						15a08		
Chathill	a																								

		NT	XC	NT	NT	NT		XC	GR	NT	NT	NT	XC	NT	NT	NT		GR	NT	NT	NT	XC	GR	NT	XC
			◇1					◇1	R 1				◇1					R 1				◇1	R 1		◇1
Carlisle	d	14 09				15 05						16 11				17 10					18 01			20 15	
Wetheral	d					15 12															18 08				
Brampton (Cumbria)	d					15 22															18 18				
Haltwhistle	d	14 37				15 36						16 39				17 38					18 32			20 43	
Bardon Mill	d					15 44															18 40				
Haydon Bridge	d					15 49															18 45				
Hexham	a	14 55				15 58						16 57				17 56					18 54			21 01	
	d	14 56				15 59						16 58				17 57					18 55			21 01	
Corbridge	d	15 00				16 03						17 02				18 01					18 59			21 05	
Riding Mill	d	15 05				16 08						17 07				18 06					19 04			21 10	
Stocksfield	d	15 09				16 12						17 11				18 10					19 08			21 14	
Prudhoe	d	15 13				16 16						17 15				18 14					19 12			21 18	
Wylam	d	15 17				16 20						17 19				18 18					19 16			21 22	
Blaydon	d																								
Metrocentre	a	15 29				16 33						17 32				18 31					19 29			21 34	
	d	15 30		15 48	16 10	16 33				16 48	17 10	17 33		17 48	18 10	18 32			18 48	19 10	19 29			21 34	
Dunston	d																								
Newcastle	a	15 40		15 58	16 18	16 43				16 56	17 18	17 43		17 58	18 18	18 42			18 56	19 18	19 39			21 46	
Sunderland 26,44	a			16 21						17 22				18 21					19 22						
Newcastle 26	d		15 37					16 34	16 42				17 38					18 43				19 40	19 44		20 38
Manors	d																								
Cramlington	d																								
Morpeth 26	d																						19a58		20a52
Pegswood	d																								
Widdrington	d																								
Acklington	d																								
Alnmouth for Alnwick 26	d		16a01					16a58	17a08				18a01					19a10				20a04			
Chathill	a																								

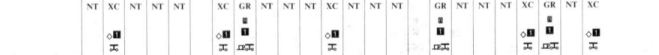

For connections to London Kings Cross please refer to Table 26

Table 48

Sundays
from 30 October

Carlisle, Hexham and Metrocentre - Newcastle - Morpeth and Chathill

Station	Table		GR	XC	GR
			R 1 (dining)	◇1	R 1 (dining)
Carlisle 8		d			
Wetheral		d			
Brampton (Cumbria)		d			
Haltwhistle		d			
Bardon Mill		d			
Haydon Bridge		d			
Hexham		a			
		d			
Corbridge		d			
Riding Mill		d			
Stocksfield		d			
Prudhoe		d			
Wylam		d			
Blaydon		d			
Metrocentre		a			
		d			
Dunston		d			
Newcastle 8	⇌	a			
Sunderland	26,44 ⇌	a			
Newcastle 8	26 ⇌	d	20 53	21 38	21 56
Manors		d			
Cramlington		d			
Morpeth	26	d	21 10		22 12
Pegswood		d			
Widdrington		d			
Acklington		d			
Alnmouth for Alnwick	26	d	21a24	22a04	22a27
Chathill		a			

For connections to London Kings Cross please refer to Table 26

Route Diagram for Table 49

DM-4/09(2)
Design BAJS

© Network Rail OPSU 2009.
All rights reserved

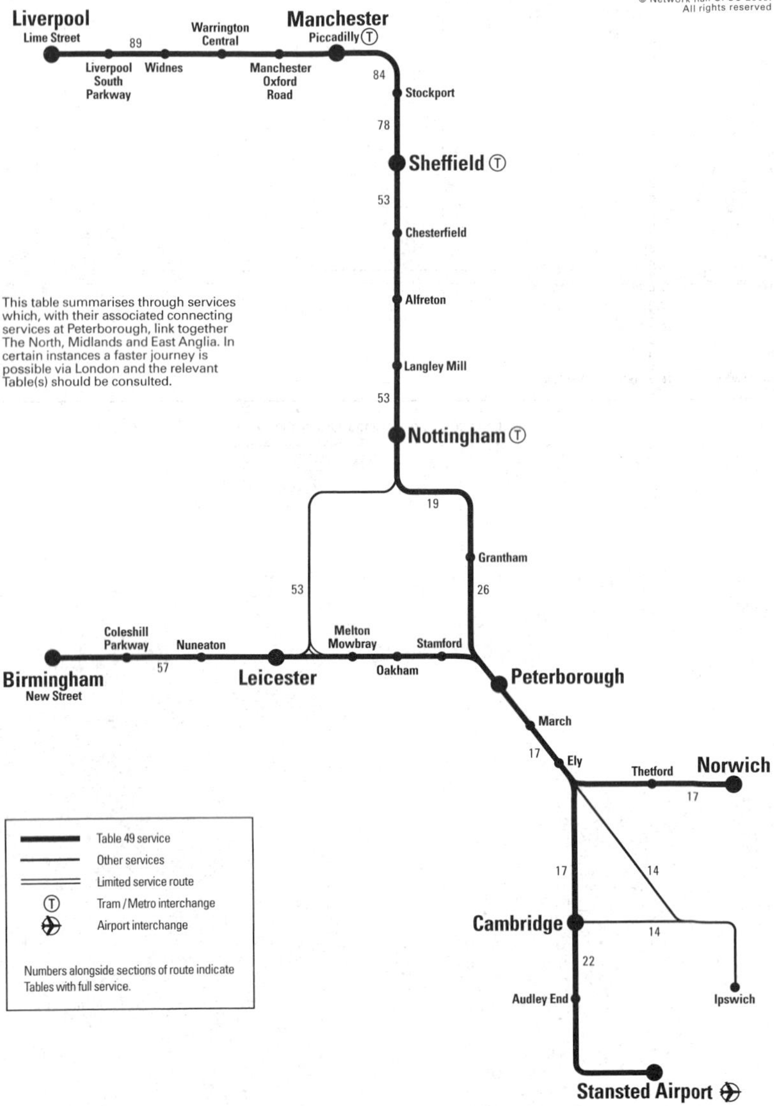

This table summarises through services which, with their associated connecting services at Peterborough, link together The North, Midlands and East Anglia. In certain instances a faster journey is possible via London and the relevant Table(s) should be consulted.

- Table 49 service
- Other services
- Limited service route
- Ⓣ Tram / Metro interchange
- Airport interchange

Numbers alongside sections of route indicate Tables with full service.

Stansted Airport - East Anglia - East Midlands - Birmingham and North West England

Miles	Miles	Miles	Miles			XC	XC	EM	EM	EM	EM	XC	EM	XC	EM	EM	XC	EM	XC	EM	XC	EM	XC
						◇1	◇1	◇	◇	◇	◇	◇1	◇	◇1	◇	◇	◇1	◇	◇1	◇	◇1	◇	◇1
							A					A		A		B	A		A		A		A
							🛒					🛒		🛒			🛒		🛒		🛒		🛒
0	0	—	0	**Norwich**	d						05 50		06 52		07 57			08 57		09 57		10 57	
30½	30½	—	30½	Thetford	d						06 23		07 20		08 24			09 24		10 24		11 24	
—	—	0	—	**Stansted Airport** ✈	d		05 15					06 06		07 21			08 21		09 21		10 21		11 25
—	—	10¾	—	Audley End	d		05 37					06 23		07 37			08 37		09 37		10 37		11 37
—	—	24¾	—	**Cambridge**	d	05 15	05 55					06 52		08 00			09 00		10 00		11 00		12 00
53¾	53¾	39½	53¾	Ely [6]	d	05 30	06 10				06 51	07 08	07 45	08 15	08 50		09 15	09 52	10 15	10 52	11 15	11 52	12 15
61¼	61¼	—	61¼	March	d	05 46	06 28				07 07	07 26	08 01	08 31	09 07		09 31		10 31		11 31		12 31
75¼	75¼	—	75¼	**Peterborough** [8]	a	06 08	06 50				07 25	07 51	08 24	08 50	09 25		09 50	10 26	10 50	11 25	11 50	12 24	12 50
—	—	—	—		d	06 10	06 52				07 27	07 52	08 26	08 52	09 27		09 52	10 28	10 52	11 26	11 52	12 25	12 52
87¾	—	—	—	Stamford	d	06 23	07 05					08 05		09 05			10 05		11 05		12 05		13 05
101¼	—	—	—	Oakham	d	06 39	07 21					08 21		09 21		09 52	10 21		11 21		12 21		13 21
112¾	—	—	—	Melton Mowbray	d	06 50	07 33					08 33		09 33		10a03	10 33		11 33		12 33		13 33
127¾	—	—	—	**Leicester**	d	07 10	07 49					08 49		09 49			10 49		11 49		12 49		13 49
146½	—	—	—	Nuneaton	a	07 29	08 15					09 08		10 08			11 08		12 08		13 08		14 08
158	—	—	—	Coleshill Parkway	a	07 45	08 32					09 25		10 25			11 25		12 25		13 25		14 25
167½	—	—	—	**Birmingham New Street** [12]	a	07 58	08 45					09 38		10 38			11 38		12 43		13 39		14 39
—	104½	—	—	Grantham [7]	d						07 58		08 55		09 58			11 00		11 58		12 58	
—	127¼	—	145	**Nottingham** [8] 🚋	a						08 40		09 36		10 36			11 35		12 36		13 36	
—	—	—	—		d			05 20	06 40	07 45	08 45		09 45		10 45			11 45		12 45		13 45	
—	139¼	—	157	Langley Mill	d																		
—	145½	—	163¼	Alfreton	d				07 02	08 07	09 07		10 07		11 07			12 07		13 07		14 07	
—	155¼	—	173¼	Chesterfield	d			05 49	07 13	08 18	09 18		10 18		11 18			12 18		13 18		14 19	
—	167¼	—	185½	**Sheffield** [7] 🚋	a			06 15	07 31	08 38	09 38		10 38		11 38			12 38		13 38		14 38	
—	—	—	—		d			06 20	07 35	08 42	09 42		10 42		11 42			12 42		13 42		14 42	
—	204½	—	222¼	Stockport	a			07 22	08 24	09 25	10 25		11 25		12 25			13 25		14 25		15 25	
—	210½	—	225¼	**Manchester Piccadilly** [10] 🚋	a			07 34	08 36	09 36	10 36		11 36		12 36			13 36		14 36		15 36	
—	211	—	228¾	Manchester Oxford Road	a			07 37	08 40	09 40	10 40		11 40		12 40			13 40		14 40		15 40	
—	226¾	—	244½	Warrington Central	a			07 53	08 57	09 57	10 57		11 57		12 57			13 57		14 57		15 57	
—	233	—	250¾	Widnes	a			08 01	09 05	10 05	11 05		12 05		13 05			14 05		15 05		16 05	
—	239¾	—	257½	Liverpool South Parkway [7]	a			08 18	09 15	10 15	11 15		12 15		13 15			14 15		15 15		16 15	
—	245¼	—	263	**Liverpool Lime Street** [10]	a			08 31	09 31	10 31	11 31		12 31		13 31			14 31		15 31		16 31	

		EM	XC	EM	XC	EM	XC	EM	XC	EM	XC	EM	XC	EM	EM	XC	EM	XC	NT	NT	EM	XC
		◇	◇1	◇	◇1	◇	◇1	◇	◇1	◇	◇1	◇	◇1	◇	◇1	◇1	◇	◇1				◇1
			A		A		A						A		C						E	
			🛒		🛒		🛒						🛒		🍴							
Norwich	d	11 57		12 57		13 57		14 57		15 52		16 57		17 54			18 57					
Thetford	d	12 24		13 24		14 24		15 24		16 27		17 27		18 27			19 24					
Stansted Airport ✈	d		12 25		13 25		14 25		15 25		16 25		17 18			18 21		19 21				20 21
Audley End	d		12 37		13 37		14 37		15 37		16 37		17 33			18 37		19 37				20 37
Cambridge	d		13 00		14 00		15 00		16 00		17 00		17 51			19 00		20 00				21 00
Ely [6]	d	12 52	13 15	13 52	14 15	14 52	15 15	15 52	16 15	16 52	17 15	17 52	18 06	18 52		19 15	19 52	20 15				21 15
March	d		13 31		14 31		15 31		16 31		17 31		18 25	19 08		19 31		20 31				21 31
Peterborough [8]	a	13 25	13 50	14 25	14 50	15 27	15 50	16 27	16 50	17 24	17 51	18 25	18 50	19 26		19 50	20 26	20 50				21 51
	d	13 26	13 52	14 26	14 52	15 27	15 52	16 28	16 52	17 27	17 52	18 26	18 52	19 26		19 52	20 28	20 52			21 30	21 52
Stamford	d		14 05		15 05		16 05		17 05		18 05		19 05			20 05		21 05			21 43	22 05
Oakham	d		14 21		15 21		16 21		17 21		18 21		19 21		19 43	20 21		21 21			21 58	22 21
Melton Mowbray	d		14 33		15 33		16 33		17 33		18 33		19 33		19a55	20 33		21 33			22 11	22 33
Leicester	d		14 49		15 49		16 49		17 49		18 49		19 49			20 49		21 49				22 49
Nuneaton	a		15 08		16 08		17 08		18 16		19 08		20 08			21 08		22 08				23 08
Coleshill Parkway	a		15 25		16 25		17 25		18 32		19 25		20 25			21 25		22 25				23 25
Birmingham New Street [12]	a		15 39		16 39		17 38		18 45		19 38		20 38			21 38		22 38				23 38
Grantham [7]	d	13 58		14 58		16 01		17 00		17 58		18 58		19 59			20 59					
Nottingham [8] 🚋	a	14 36		15 36		16 36		17 36		18 36		19 36		20 32			21 35				22 50	
	d	14 45		15 45		16 45		17 45		18 45		19 40							20 45	21 11		
Langley Mill	d							18 02												21 31		
Alfreton	d	15 07		16 07		17 07		18 09		19 07		20 01								21 39		
Chesterfield	d	15 20		16 18		17 18		18 21		19 18		20 12							21 28	22 00		
Sheffield [7] 🚋	a	15 38		16 38		17 34		18 39		19 39		20 28							21 54	22 19		
	d	15 42		16 42		17 40		18 43		19 42		20 32										
Stockport	a	16 25		17 25		18 25		19 25		20 25		21 20										
Manchester Piccadilly [10] 🚋	a	16 36		17 37		18 36		19 36		20 36		21 32										
Manchester Oxford Road	a	16 40		17 40		18 40		19 40		20 40												
Warrington Central	a	16 57		18 03		18 57		19 57		20 57												
Widnes	a	17 05		18 11		19 05		20 05		21 05												
Liverpool South Parkway [7]	a	17 15		18 21		19 18		20 16		21 19												
Liverpool Lime Street [10]	a	17 31		18 35		19 35		20 35		21 35												

A 🛒 from Peterborough
B From Corby, to Derby
C From St Pancras International
E From Spalding

For connections from Ipswich please refer to Table 14

Stansted Airport - East Anglia - East Midlands - Birmingham and North West England

		XC	EM	XC	EM	EM	EM	XC	EM	XC	
		◇1	◇	◇1	◇	◇	◇	◇1	◇	◇1	
				A				A		A	
Norwich	d						05 52		06 53		
Thetford	d						06 25		07 22		
Stansted Airport ✈	d			05 25				06 25		07 25	
Audley End	d			05 37				06 37		07 37	
Cambridge	d	05 15		05 55				06 56		08 00	
Ely 6	d	05 30		06 10			06 51	07 11	07 53	08 15	
March	d	05 46		06 28			07 07	07 29	08 08	08 31	
Peterborough 8	a	06 08		06 50			07 25	07 50	08 31	08 50	
	d	06 10		06 52			07 27	07 52	08 33	08 52	
Stamford	d	06 23		07 05				08 05		09 05	
Oakham	d	06 39		07 21				08 21		09 21	
Melton Mowbray	d	06 50		07 33				08 33		09 33	
Leicester	d	07 16		07 49				08 49		09 49	
Nuneaton	a	07 35		08 08				09 08		10 08	
Coleshill Parkway	a	07 51		08 24				09 25		10 25	
Birmingham New Street 12	a	08 04		08 38				09 38		10 38	
Grantham 7	d						07 58		09 07		
Nottingham 8	a						08 39		09 41		
	d		05 20		06 40	07 45	08 45		09 46		
Langley Mill	d										
Alfreton	d				07 02	08 07	09 07		10 08		
Chesterfield	d		05 49		07 13	08 18	09 18		10 19		
Sheffield 7	a		06 15		07 31	08 38	09 38		10 38		
	d		06 20		07 35	08 42	09 42		10 42		
Stockport	a		07 22		08 24	09 25	10 25		11 25		
Manchester Piccadilly 10	a		07 34		08 36	09 36	10 36		11 36		
Manchester Oxford Road	a		07 37		08 40	09 40	10 40		11 40		
Warrington Central	a		07 53		08 57	09 57	10 57		11 57		
Widnes	a		08 01		09 05	10 05	11 05		12 05		
Liverpool South Parkway 7	a		08 18		09 15	10 15	11 15		12 15		
Liverpool Lime Street 10	a		08 31		09 31	10 31	11 31		12 31		

		EM	XC	EM	XC	EM	XC	EM	XC	EM		XC	EM	XC	EM
		◇	◇1	◇	◇1	◇	◇1	◇	◇1	◇		◇1	◇	◇1	◇
			A		A		A		A			A		A	
Norwich	d	07 57		08 57		09 57		10 57		11 57			12 57		13 57
Thetford	d	08 24		09 24		10 24		11 24		12 24			13 24		14 24
Stansted Airport ✈	d		08 25		09 25		10 25		11 25			12 25		13 25	
Audley End	d		08 37		09 37		10 37		11 37			12 37		13 37	
Cambridge	d		09 00		10 00		11 00		12 00			13 00		14 00	
Ely 6	d	08 54	09 15	09 51	10 15	10 53	11 15	11 53	12 15	12 54		13 15	13 53	14 15	14 53
March	d	09 11	09 31		10 31		11 31		12 31			13 31		14 31	
Peterborough 8	a	09 28	09 50	10 25	10 50	11 24	11 50	12 24	12 50	13 26		13 50	14 25	14 50	15 25
	d	09 30	09 52	10 26	10 52	11 25	11 52	12 25	12 52	13 28		13 52	14 26	14 52	15 25
Stamford	d		10 05		11 05		12 05		13 05			14 05		15 05	
Oakham	d		10 21		11 21		12 21		13 21			14 21		15 21	
Melton Mowbray	d		10 33		11 33		12 33		13 33			14 33		15 33	
Leicester	d		10 49		11 49		12 49		13 49			14 49		15 49	
Nuneaton	a		11 08		12 08		13 08		14 08			15 08		16 08	
Coleshill Parkway	a		11 25		12 25		13 25		14 25			15 25		16 25	
Birmingham New Street 12	a		11 38		12 38		13 38		14 38			15 38		16 38	
Grantham 7	d	09 58		10 58		11 58		12 58		13 58			14 58		15 58
Nottingham 8	a	10 40		11 35		12 36		13 36		14 36			15 36		16 36
	d	10 45		11 45		12 45		13 45		14 45			15 45		16 45
Langley Mill	d														
Alfreton	d	11 07		12 07		13 07		14 07		15 07			16 07		17 07
Chesterfield	d	11 18		12 18		13 18		14 18		15 18			16 18		17 18
Sheffield 7	a	11 38		12 38		13 38		14 38		15 38			16 38		17 34
	d	11 42		12 42		13 42		14 42		15 42			16 42		17 40
Stockport	a	12 25		13 25		14 25		15 25		16 25			17 25		18 25
Manchester Piccadilly 10	a	12 36		13 36		14 36		15 36		16 36			17 37		18 36
Manchester Oxford Road	a	12 40		13 40		14 40		15 40		16 40			17 40		18 40
Warrington Central	a	12 57		13 57		14 57		15 57		16 57			18 03		18 57
Widnes	a	13 05		14 05		15 05		16 05		17 05			18 11		19 05
Liverpool South Parkway 7	a	13 15		14 15		15 15		16 15		17 15			18 21		19 18
Liverpool Lime Street 10	a	13 31		14 31		15 31		16 31		17 31			18 35		19 35

		XC	EM	XC	EM	XC		EM	XC	EM	XC	EM	XC	NT	NT	EM
		◇1	◇	◇1	◇	◇1		◇	◇1	◇	◇1	◇	◇1			
		A							A							B
Norwich	d		14 57		15 52			16 57		17 54		18 57				
Thetford	d		15 24		16 23			17 27		18 27		19 24				
Stansted Airport ✈	d	14 25		15 25		16 25			17 25		18 25		19 25			
Audley End	d	14 37		15 37		16 37			17 37		18 37		19 37			
Cambridge	d	15 00		16 00		17 00			18 00		19 00		20 00			
Ely 6	d	15 15	15 52	16 15	16 52	17 15		17 52	18 15	18 53	19 15	19 53	20 15			
March	d	15 31		16 31		17 31			18 33	19 09	19 31		20 31			
Peterborough 8	a	15 50	16 25	16 50	17 26	17 50		18 25	18 50	19 27	19 50	20 25	20 50			
	d	15 52	16 27	16 52	17 27	17 52		18 26	18 52	19 27	19 52	20 27	20 52			21 27
Stamford	d	16 05		17 05		18 05			19 05		20 05		21 05			
Oakham	d	16 21		17 21		18 21			19 21		20 21		21 21			
Melton Mowbray	d	16 33		17 33		18 33			19 33		20 33		21 33			
Leicester	d	16 49		17 49		18 49			19 49		20 49		21 49			
Nuneaton	a	17 08		18 08		19 08			20 08		21 08		22 08			
Coleshill Parkway	a	17 25		18 25		19 25			20 25		21 25		22 25			
Birmingham New Street 12	a	17 38		18 38		19 38			20 38		21 38		22 38			
Grantham 7	d		16 58		18 03			18 58		20 03		20 58				22 02
Nottingham 8	a		17 36		18 36			19 36		20 37		21 32				22 32
	d		17 45		18 45			19 40						20 39	21 15	
Langley Mill	d		18 03											21 02	21 31	
Alfreton	d		18 10		19 07			20 01						21 10	21 39	
Chesterfield	d		18 22		19 18			20 11						21 22	21 50	
Sheffield 7	a		18 39		19 39			20 27						21 40	22 13	
	d		18 42		19 42			20 31								
Stockport	a		19 25		20 25			21 20								
Manchester Piccadilly 10	a		19 36		20 36			21 32								
Manchester Oxford Road	a		19 40		20 40											
Warrington Central	a		19 57		20 57											
Widnes	a		20 05		21 05											
Liverpool South Parkway 7	a		20 15		21 19											
Liverpool Lime Street 10	a		20 30		21 35											

A from Peterborough

B From Spalding

For connections from Ipswich please refer to Table 14

Table 49

Sundays

Stansted Airport - East Anglia - East Midlands - Birmingham and North West England

		EM	EM	EM	EM	XC	EM	EM	XC	XC	XC	EM	EM	EM	XC	EM	XC	EM	XC	EM	XC	EM	EM
		◇	◇	◇	◇	◇ 1	◇	◇	◇ 1	◇ 1	◇ 1	◇	◇	◇	◇ 1	◇	◇ 1	◇	◇ 1	◇	◇ 1		◇
					A	B 🚲	C		B 🚲	B 🚲	B 🚲				B 🚲							D	
Norwich	d				09 33			10 47						13 49		14 49		15 53		16 53			17 53
Thetford	d				10 00			11 14						14 16		15 16		16 20		17 20			18 20
Stansted Airport ✈	d					10 25			11 25	12 25	13 25				14 25		15 25		16 25		17 25		
Audley End	d					10 39			11 39	12 39	13 39				14 39		15 39		16 39		17 39		
Cambridge	d					11 00			12 00	13 00	14 00				15 00		16 00		17 00		18 00		
Ely 6	d				10 32	11 15		11 39	12 15	13 15	14 15			14 45	15 15	15 48	16 15		17 15	17 48	18 15		18 48
March	d					11 31			12 31	13 31	14 31				15 31		16 31		17 31		18 31		
Peterborough 8	a				11 09	11 50		12 16	12 50	13 50	14 50			15 24	15 50	16 22	16 50	17 10	17 50	18 25	18 50		19 24
	d				11 11	11 52		12 18	12 52	13 52	14 52			15 26	15 52	16 24	16 52	17 11	17 52	18 26	18 52		19 26
Stamford	d					12 05			13 05	14 05	15 05				16 05		17 05		18 05		19 05		
Oakham	d					12 21			13 21	14 21	15 21				16 21		17 19		18 21		19 21		
Melton Mowbray	d					12 33			13 33	14 33	15 33				16 32		17 30		18 33		19 33		
Leicester	d					12 49			13 49	14 48	15 49				16 48		17 47		18 49		19 49		
Nuneaton	a					13 08			14 08	15 08	16 08				17 11		18 08		19 08		20 08		
Coleshill Parkway	a					13 24			14 24	15 24	16 24				17 27		18 24		19 24		20 24		
Birmingham New Street 12	a					13 38			14 37	15 39	16 39				17 40		18 39		19 37		20 39		
Grantham 7	d				11 56			12 54						15 59		16 56		17 55		18 58		19 37	19 57
Nottingham 8 🚊	a				12 29			13 33						16 28		17 25		18 29		19 33		20 14	20 31
	d	09 31	10 41	11 46	12 39		12 39	13 38				14 37	15 44	16 41		17 35		18 37		19 38			
Langley Mill	d				12 56		12 56	13 55				14 54		17 00		17 54		18 54					
Alfreton	d	09 53	11 03	12 08	13 04		13 04	14 03				15 02	16 06	17 08		18 02		19 02		20 00			
Chesterfield	d	10 08	11 15	12 18	13 17		13 17	14 18				15 13	16 23	17 22		18 17		19 13		20 10			
Sheffield 7 🚊	a	10 33	11 35	12 36	13 33		13 33	14 36				15 31	16 39	17 40		18 34		19 31		20 31			
	d	10 41	11 38	12 41	13 38		13 38	14 39				15 38	16 44	17 44		18 37		19 35		20 35			
Stockport	a	11 25	12 25	13 25	14 25		14 25	15 25				16 25	17 26	18 25		19 25		20 25		21 24			
Manchester Piccadilly 10 🚊	a	11 37	12 37	13 37	14 37		14 37	15 37				16 37	17 37	18 37		19 37		20 38		21 36			
Manchester Oxford Road	a	11 41	12 41	13 41	14 41		14 41	15 41				16 41	17 41	18 41		19 41							
Warrington Central	a	11 58	12 58	13 58	14 58		14 58	15 58				16 58	17 58	18 58		19 58							
Widnes	a	12 06	13 06	14 06	15 06		15 06	16 06				17 06	18 06	19 06		20 06							
Liverpool South Parkway 7	a	12 16	13 16	14 16	15 16		15 16	16 16				17 16	18 16	19 16		20 16							
Liverpool Lime Street 10	a	12 30	13 30	14 30	15 30		15 30	16 30				17 30	18 30	19 30		20 30							

		XC	EM	XC	NT	EM
		◇ 1	◇	◇ 1		◇
Norwich	d		18 56			20 52
Thetford	d		19 23			21 19
Stansted Airport ✈	d	18 25		19 25		
Audley End	d	18 39		19 39		
Cambridge	d	19 00		20 00		
Ely 6	d	19 15	19 48	20 15		21 44
March	d	19 31		20 31		
Peterborough 8	a	19 50	20 29	20 50		22 20
	d	19 52	20 31	20 52		22 22
Stamford	d	20 05		21 05		
Oakham	d	20 21		21 21		
Melton Mowbray	d	20 33		21 33		
Leicester	d	20 49		21 49		
Nuneaton	a	21 08		22 08		
Coleshill Parkway	a	21 24		22 24		
Birmingham New Street 12	a	21 37		22 38		
Grantham 7	d		21 03			22 55
Nottingham 8 🚊	a		21 35			23 29
	d				20 13	
Langley Mill	d				20 29	
Alfreton	d				20 37	
Chesterfield	d				20 48	
Sheffield 7 🚊	a				21 14	
	d					
Stockport	a					
Manchester Piccadilly 10 🚊	a					
Manchester Oxford Road	a					
Warrington Central	a					
Widnes	a					
Liverpool South Parkway 7	a					
Liverpool Lime Street 10	a					

A until 11 September
B 🚲 from Peterborough
C from 18 September
D until 11 September. From Skegness to Mansfield Woodhouse

For connections from Ipswich please refer to Table 14

North West England and Birmingham - East Midlands - East Anglia - Stansted Airport

Miles	Miles	Miles	Miles			EM MO ◇	EM MX ◇	EM ◇	EM A	EM ◇1 B ⊠(trolley)	XC ◇1	EM ◇	NT	XC ◇1 D (trolley)	NT	EM ◇ E	XC ◇1 D (trolley)	EM ◇	XC ◇1 F (trolley)	EM ◇
—	0	—	0	**Liverpool Lime Street** 10	d	21p22	21p37													06 47
—	5½	—	5½	Liverpool South Parkway 7 ✈	d		21p47													06 57
—	12¼	—	12¼	Widnes	d	21p39	21p55													07 07
—	18½	—	18½	Warrington Central	d	21p47	22p03													07 15
—	34¼	—	34¼	Manchester Oxford Road	d	22p07	22p24													07 38
—	34¾	—	34¾	**Manchester Piccadilly** 10 🚊	d	22p11	22p28													07 42
—	40¾	—	40¾	Stockport	d	22b28	22p37													07 54
—	77½	—	77½	**Sheffield** 7 🚊	a	23p25	23p35													08 36
—	—	—	—		d	23p29	23p37						05 05		06 00					08 38
—	89¾	—	89¾	Chesterfield	d	23p43	00 02						05 20		06 16					08 53
—	99¾	—	99¾	Alfreton	d	23p54									06 30					09 03
—	106	—	106	Langley Mill	d	00 02									06 37					
—	118	—	118	**Nottingham** 8 🚊	a	00 25	00 40						06 12		07 08					09 30
—	—	—	—		d			04 51	05 10			05 56				07 52		08 34		09 34
—	140¾	—	—	Grantham 7	d				05 51							08 27		09 10		10 11
0	—	—	—	**Birmingham New Street** 12	d						05 22			06 22			07 22		08 22	
9½	—	—	—	Coleshill Parkway	d						05 35			06 35			07 35		08 35	
21	—	—	—	Nuneaton	d						05 51			06 51			07 51		08 51	
39¾	—	—	—	**Leicester**	d						06 15			07 18			08 18		09 18	
54¾	—	—	—	Melton Mowbray	d			05 24		05 59	06 31	06 52		07 34			08 33		09 34	
66¼	—	—	—	Oakham	d			05 36		06a10	06 42	07 05		07 45			08 45		09 45	
79¾	—	—	—	Stamford	d			06 02			06 57	07 18		08 01			09 01		10 01	
92¼	170	—	187¾	**Peterborough** 8	a			06 17	06 25		07 10	07 33		08 16		08 57	09 16	09 39	10 16	10 40
—	—	—	—		d			06 27			07 12	07 35		08 18		08 59	09 18	09 40	10 18	10 44
106¼	184	—	201¾	March	a			06 42			07 31	07 50		08 33			09 34		10 33	
113¾	191½	0	209¼	Ely 6	a			07 01			07 53	08 11		08 52		09 41	09 51	10 13	10 52	11 16
—	—	14¾	—	**Cambridge**	a						08 09			09 08			10 08		11 08	
—	—	28¾	—	Audley End	a						08 24			09 23			10 23		11 23	
—	—	39½	—	**Stansted Airport** ✈	a						08 39			09 38			10 45		11 45	
137	214¾	—	232¾	Thetford	a			07 28				08 36				10 05		10 41		11 41
167½	245¼	—	263	**Norwich**	a			08 13				09 13				10 44		11 14		12 13

		XC ◇1 D (trolley)	EM ◇	XC ◇1 D (trolley)	EM ◇	XC ◇1 D (trolley)	EM ◇	XC ◇1 D (trolley)	EM ◇	XC ◇1 D (trolley)	EM ◇	XC ◇1 D (trolley)	EM ◇	EM ◇ G	XC ◇1 D (trolley)	EM ◇ H	EM ◇1 I (restaurant)	XC ◇1 D (trolley)	EM ◇
Liverpool Lime Street 10	d		07 43		08 52		09 52		10 52		11 52		12 52	13 52		13 52			14 52
Liverpool South Parkway 7 ✈	d		07 53		09 03		10 03		11 03		12 03		13 03	14 03		14 03			15 03
Widnes	d		08 05		09 11		10 11		11 11		12 11		13 11	14 11		14 11			15 11
Warrington Central	d		08 13		09 19		10 19		11 19		12 19		13 19	14 19		14 19			15 19
Manchester Oxford Road	d		08 39		09 39		10 39		11 39		12 39		13 39	14 39		14 39			15 39
Manchester Piccadilly 10 🚊	d		08 43		09 43		10 43		11 43		12 43		13 43	14 43		14 43			15 43
Stockport	d		08 54		09 54		10 54		11 54		12 54		13 54	14 54		14 54			15 54
Sheffield 7 🚊	a		09 35		10 35		11 34		12 35		13 35		14 35	15 35		15 35			16 34
	d		09 38		10 38		11 38		12 38		13 38		14 38	15 38		15 38			16 38
Chesterfield	d		09 53		10 52		11 53		12 53		13 52		14 53	15 53		15 53			16 56
Alfreton	d		10 04		11 03		12 03		13 03		14 03		15 07	16 04		16 04			17 07
Langley Mill	d																		
Nottingham 8 🚊	a		10 30		11 30		12 30		13 30		14 30		15 28	16 28		16 28			17 31
	d		10 34		11 34		12 34		13 34		14 34		15 34			16 34			17 34
Grantham 7	d		11 10		12 09		13 09		14 10		15 11		16 10			17 11			18 11
Birmingham New Street 12	d	09 22		10 22		11 22		12 22		13 22		14 22			15 22			16 22	
Coleshill Parkway	d	09 35		10 35		11 35		12 35		13 35		14 35			15 34			16 34	
Nuneaton	d	09 52		10 52		11 51		12 51		13 51		14 51			15 52			16 52	
Leicester	d	10 18		11 18		12 18		13 18		14 18		15 18			16 18			17 18	
Melton Mowbray	d	10 34		11 34		12 34		13 34		14 34		15 34			16 34		17 15	17 34	
Oakham	d	10 45		11 45		12 45		13 45		14 45		15 45			16 45		17a26	17 45	
Stamford	d	11 01		12 01		13 01		14 01		15 01		16 01			17 01			18 01	
Peterborough 8	a	11 17	11 40	12 16	12 40	13 16	13 39	14 16	14 39	15 16	15 38	16 16	16 39		17 16	17 40		18 16	18 39
	d	11 18	11 41	12 18	12 43	13 18	13 41	14 18	14 41	15 18	15 40	16 18	16 41		17 18	17 42		18 18	18 45
March	a	11 34		12 33		13 33		14 33		15 34		16 33			17 36			18 33	19 00
Ely 6	a	11 52	12 14	12 52	13 16	13 52	14 14	14 52	15 14	15 52	16 13	16 52	17 14		17 58	18 16		18 52	19 24
Cambridge	a	12 08		13 08		14 08		15 08		16 08		17 08			18 16			19 08	
Audley End	a	12 23		13 23		14 23		15 23		16 23		17 23			18 31			19 23	
Stansted Airport ✈	a	12 45		13 45		14 45		15 45		16 45		17 39			18 45			19 42	
Thetford	a		12 39		13 40		14 38		15 38		16 37		17 38			18 41			19 50
Norwich	a		13 13		14 09		15 13		16 14		17 13		18 13			19 15			20 22

A To Spalding
B To St Pancras International
D (trolley) to Stamford
E From Mansfield Woodhouse
F From Gloucester. (trolley) to Stamford
G until 29 July
H from 1 August
I From Derby to St Pancras International
b Previous night, arr. 2220

For connections to Ipswich please refer to Table 14

North West England and Birmingham - East Midlands - East Anglia - Stansted Airport

		XC	XC	EM	EM	XC	XC	EM	EM	EM	EM FX	EM FO	XC
		◇1	◇1	◇	◇	◇1	◇1	◇	◇	◇	◇	◇	◇1
Liverpool Lime Street 10	d			15 52	16 52			17 52	18 52	19 52	21 37	21 37	
Liverpool South Parkway 7 ✈	d			16 03	17 03			18 03	19 03	20 03	21 47	21 47	
Widnes	d			16 11	17 11			18 11	19 11	20 11	21 55	21 55	
Warrington Central	d			16 19	17 19			18 19	19 19	20 19	22 03	22 03	
Manchester Oxford Road	d			16 39	17 39			18 39	19 39	20 39	22 24	22 24	
Manchester Piccadilly 10	d			16 43	17 43			18 43	19 43	20 43	22 28	22 28	
Stockport	d			16 54	17 54			18 54	19 54	20 54	22 37	22 37	
Sheffield 7	a			17 37	18 41			19 33	20 36	21 35	23 35	23 35	
	d			17 44	18 45			19 38	20 41	21 39	23 37	23 37	
Chesterfield	d			18 02	19 01			19 53	20 58	21 55	00 02	00 02	
Alfreton	d			18 12	19 11			20 04	21 09	22 05			
Langley Mill	d									22 12			
Nottingham 8	a			18 34	19 38			20 31	21 38	22 38	00 40	00 41	
	d			18 35				20 34					
Grantham 7	d			19 07				21 10					
Birmingham New Street 12	d	16 52	17 22			18 22	19 22						20 22
Coleshill Parkway	d	17 05	17 34			18 34	19 35						20 35
Nuneaton	d	17 21	17 52			18 52	19 52						20 51
Leicester	d	17 51	18 18			19 18	20 18						21 18
Melton Mowbray	d	18 08	18 34			19 34	20 34						21 34
Oakham	d	18 20	18 45			19 45	20 45						21 45
Stamford	d	18 41	19 01			20 01	21 01						22 01
Peterborough 8	a	18 58	19 17	19 38		20 16	21 17	21 37					22 16
	d	19 00	19 19	19 40		20 18	21 19	21 38					22 18
March	a	19 15	19 34			20 34	21 35						22 35
Ely 8	a	19 33	19 53	20 13		20 53	21 53	22 11					22 54
Cambridge	a	19 51	20 08			21 08	22 09						23 11
Audley End	a		20 24			21 23	22 24						
Stansted Airport ✈	a		20 45			21 45	22 54						
Thetford	a			20 37				22 35					
Norwich	a			21 14				23 18					

Saturdays

		EM	EM	EM	XC	EM	XC	EM	EM	NT	EM	XC	EM	XC	EM	XC	EM	XC	EM	XC
		◇	◇		◇1	◇	◇1				◇	◇1	◇	◇1	◇	◇1	◇	◇1	◇	◇1
				B			D 🍴	E	F			D 🍴		G 🍴		D 🍴		D 🍴		D 🍴
Liverpool Lime Street 10	d	21p37													06 49		07 42		08 52	
Liverpool South Parkway 7 ✈	d	21p47													06 59		07 52		09 03	
Widnes	d	21p55													07 07		08 05		09 11	
Warrington Central	d	22p03													07 15		08 13		09 19	
Manchester Oxford Road	d	22p24													07 38		08 39		09 39	
Manchester Piccadilly 10	d	22p28													07 42		08 43		09 43	
Stockport	d	22p37													07 54		08 54		09 54	
Sheffield 7	a	23p35													08 36		09 35		10 35	
	d	23p37								05 54					08 39		09 38		10 38	
Chesterfield	d	00 02								06 20					08 53		09 53		10 53	
Alfreton	d									06 30					09 03		10 03		11 03	
Langley Mill	d									06 38										
Nottingham 8	a	00 41								07 04					09 30		10 30		11 29	
	d		05 04	05 10		05 54		06 53	06 55		07 45		08 32		09 34		10 34		11 34	
Grantham 7	d			05 51							08 20		09 03		10 08		11 10		12 07	
Birmingham New Street 12	d				05 22		06 22					07 22		08 22		09 22		10 22		11 22
Coleshill Parkway	d				05 35		06 35					07 35		08 35		09 35		10 35		11 35
Nuneaton	d				05 51		06 51					07 51		08 51		09 51		10 51		11 51
Leicester	d				06 15		07 15					08 15		09 15		10 15		11 15		12 15
Melton Mowbray	d		05 37		06 31	06 46	07 31					08 31		09 31		10 31		11 31		12 31
Oakham	d		05 49		06 43	06 58	07 43					08 43		09 43		10 43		11 43		12 43
Stamford	d		06 06		06 57	07 12	07 59					08 59		09 59		10 59		11 59		12 59
Peterborough 8	a		06 19	06 25	07 11	07 29	08 16	09 27	09 27		08 58	09 16	09 41	10 14	10 37	11 16	11 39	12 14	12 38	13 16
	d		06 27		07 13	07 35	08 18				09 00	09 18	09 43	10 18	10 41	11 18	11 41	12 18	12 40	13 18
March	a		06 42		07 31	07 50	08 33					09 33		10 33		11 33		12 33		13 33
Ely 8	a		07 01		07 52	08 11	08 52				09 33	09 52	10 14	10 52	11 17	11 52	12 12	12 52	13 13	13 52
Cambridge	a				08 08		09 07					10 07		11 07		12 07		13 07		14 07
Audley End	a				08 23		09 23					10 23		11 23		12 23		13 23		14 23
Stansted Airport ✈	a				08 45		09 45					10 45		11 45		12 45		13 45		14 45
Thetford	a		07 30			08 36					10 04		10 40		11 44		12 38		13 39	
Norwich	a		08 13			09 15					10 43		11 15		12 18		13 13		14 13	

A To Colchester
B To Spalding
D 🍴 to Stamford
E from 1 October
F until 24 September
G From Gloucester. 🍴 to Stamford

For connections to Ipswich please refer to Table 14

North West England and Birmingham - East Midlands - East Anglia - Stansted Airport

		EM	XC	EM	XC	EM	XC	EM	EM	XC	EM	XC	EM	XC	EM	EM	XC	XC	EM
		◇	◇1	◇	◇1	◇	◇1	◇	◇	◇1	◇	◇1	◇	◇1	◇	◇	◇1	◇1	◇
			B 🚲		B 🚲		B 🚲		C	B 🚲	D	B 🚲							
Liverpool Lime Street 10	d	09 52		10 52		11 52		12 52	13 52		13 52		14 52		15 52	16 52			17 52
Liverpool South Parkway 7 ✈	d	10 03		11 03		12 03		13 03	14 03		14 03		15 03		16 03	17 03			18 03
Widnes	d	10 11		11 11		12 11		13 11	14 11		14 11		15 11		16 11	17 11			18 11
Warrington Central	d	10 19		11 19		12 19		13 19	14 19		14 19		15 19		16 19	17 19			18 19
Manchester Oxford Road	d	10 39		11 39		12 39		13 39	14 39		14 39		15 39		16 39	17 39			18 39
Manchester Piccadilly 10	d	10 43		11 43		12 43		13 43	14 43		14 43		15 43		16 43	17 43			18 43
Stockport	d	10 54		11 54		12 54		13 54	14 54		14 54		15 54		16 54	17 54			18 54
Sheffield 7	a	11 35		12 35		13 35		14 35	15 36		15 36		16 35		17 37	18 35			19 35
	d	11 38		12 38		13 38		14 38	15 38		15 38		16 38		17 44	18 38			19 38
Chesterfield	d	11 53		12 53		13 53		14 53	15 53		15 53		16 53		18 01	18 53			19 53
Alfreton	d	12 03		13 03		14 03		15 04	16 04		16 04		17 04		18 11	19 03			20 04
Langley Mill	d																		
Nottingham 8	a	12 29		13 30		14 29		15 29	16 30		16 30		17 29		18 33	19 33			20 31
	d	12 34		13 34		14 34		15 34			16 34		17 34		18 34				20 34
Grantham 7	d	13 10		14 07		15 10		16 07			17 10		18 15		19 08				21 07
Birmingham New Street 12	d		12 22		13 22		14 22			15 22		16 22		17 22			18 22	19 22	
Coleshill Parkway	d		12 35		13 35		14 35			15 35		16 35		17 35			18 35	19 35	
Nuneaton	d		12 51		13 51		14 51			15 51		16 51		17 51			18 51	19 51	
Leicester	d		13 15		14 15		15 15			16 15		17 15		18 15			19 15	20 15	
Melton Mowbray	d		13 31		14 31		15 31			16 31		17 31		18 31			19 31	20 31	
Oakham	d		13 43		14 43		15 43			16 43		17 43		18 43			19 43	20 43	
Stamford	d		13 59		14 59		15 59			16 59		17 59		18 59			19 59	20 59	
Peterborough 8	a	13 39	14 16	14 41	15 16	15 39	16 16	16 40		17 16	17 39	18 14	18 45	19 16	19 39		20 14	21 16	21 36
	d	13 41	14 18	14 43	15 18	15 41	16 18	16 41		17 18	17 41	18 18	18 45	19 18	19 41		20 18	21 18	21 38
March	a		14 33		15 33		16 33			17 37		18 33	19 04	19 33			20 33	21 33	
Ely 6	a	14 14	14 52	15 14	15 52	16 14	16 52	17 13		17 59	18 14	18 52	19 22	19 51	20 14		20 51	21 51	22 12
Cambridge	a		15 07		16 07		17 07			18 16		19 08		20 07			21 07	22 07	
Audley End	a		15 23		16 23		17 23			18 33		19 24		20 23			21 23	22 23	
Stansted Airport ✈	a		15 45		16 45		17 45			18 53		19 45		20 45			21 45	22 45	
Thetford	a	14 38		15 40		16 38		17 39			18 38		19 47		20 36				22 41
Norwich	a	15 13		16 15		17 13		18 18			19 21		20 21		21 14				23 20

		EM	EM	EM	EM	EM	XC
		◇	◇	◇	◇	◇	◇1
					F	G	
Liverpool Lime Street 10	d	18 52	19 52	20 52	21 37	21 37	
Liverpool South Parkway 7 ✈	d	19 03	20 03	21 03	21 47	21 47	
Widnes	d	19 11	20 11	21 11	21 55	21 55	
Warrington Central	d	19 19	20 19	21 19	22 03	22 03	
Manchester Oxford Road	d	19 39	20 39	21 39	22 27	22 27	
Manchester Piccadilly 10	d	19 43	20 43	21 43	22 31	22 31	
Stockport	d	19 54	20 54	21 52	22 42	22 42	
Sheffield 7	a	20 35	21 34	22 31	23 39	23 39	
	d	20 41	21 38	22 35	23 42	23 42	
Chesterfield	d	20 59	21 54	22 51	23 57	23 57	
Alfreton	d	21 09	22 05	23 02			
Langley Mill	d		22 12				
Nottingham 8	a	21 33	22 33	23 32	00 27	00 34	
	d						
Grantham 7	d						
Birmingham New Street 12	d						20 22
Coleshill Parkway	d						20 35
Nuneaton	d						20 51
Leicester	d						21 15
Melton Mowbray	d						21 31
Oakham	d						21 43
Stamford	d						21 59
Peterborough 8	a						22 16
	d						22 18
March	a						22 33
Ely 6	a						22 53
Cambridge	a						23 10
Audley End	a						
Stansted Airport ✈	a						
Thetford	a						
Norwich	a						

B 🚲 to Stamford
C until 30 July
D from 6 August
E To Colchester
F from 17 September until 22 October
G until 10 September, from 29 October

For connections to Ipswich please refer to Table 14

North West England and Birmingham - East Midlands - East Anglia - Stansted Airport

		EM	EM	EM	EM	NT	EM	XC	EM	XC	EM	XC	EM	XC	EM	XC	EM	XC
		◇	◇		◇		◇	◇1	◇	◇1	◇	◇1	◇	◇1	◇	◇1	◇	◇1
		A	B	C	E		E	G 🚲		G 🚲		G 🚲		G 🚲		G 🚲		
Liverpool Lime Street 10	d	21p37	21p37												12 52		13 52	
Liverpool South Parkway 7 ✈	d	21p47	21p47												13 03		14 03	
Widnes	d	21p55	21p55												13 11		14 11	
Warrington Central	d	22p03	22p03												13 19		14 19	
Manchester Oxford Road	d	22p27	22p27												13 39		14 39	
Manchester Piccadilly 10 🚊	d	22p31	22p31										12 44		13 44		14 44	
Stockport	d	22p42	22p42										12 55		13 54		14 54	
Sheffield 7 🚊	a	23p39	23p39										13 37		14 39		15 37	
	d	23p42	23p42			09 00	10 49				12 49		13 49		14 46		15 43	
Chesterfield	d	23p57	23p57			09 17	11 04				13 03		14 03		15 00		15 57	
Alfreton	d					09 28	11 14				13 14		14 14		15 12		16 08	
Langley Mill	d					09 35									15 19		16 15	
Nottingham 8 🚊	a	00 27	00 34			09 53	11 39				13 39		14 39		15 38		16 33	
	d			09 41	09 52		11 45		12 37		13 49		14 43		15 49		16 45	
Grantham 7	d			10a15	10 29		12 18		13 12		14 22				16 22		17 19	
Birmingham New Street 12	d							11 22		12 22		13 22		14 22		15 22		16 22
Coleshill Parkway	d							11 35		12 35		13 34		14 35		15 35		16 35
Nuneaton	d							11 51		12 51		13 51		14 51		15 51		16 51
Leicester	d							12 15		13 15		14 15		15 15		16 15		17 15
Melton Mowbray	d							12 33		13 33		14 33		15 33		16 32		17 33
Oakham	d							12 45		13 45		14 45		15 45		16 43		17 45
Stamford	d							13 01		14 01		15 01		16 01		16 59		18 01
Peterborough 8	a				11 06		12 50	13 16	13 41	14 16	14 51	15 16	16 02	16 16	16 55	17 14	17 50	18 16
	d				11 09		12 53	13 18	13 43	14 18	14 53	15 18	16 03	16 18	16 59	17 18	17 56	18 18
March	a				11 25			13 33		14 33		15 33		16 33		17 33	18 11	18 33
Ely 6	a				11 48		13 32	13 52	14 16	14 52	15 29	15 52	16 38	16 52	17 32	17 52	18 31	18 52
Cambridge	a							14 08		15 08		16 08		17 07		18 07		19 07
Audley End	a							14 23		15 23		16 23		17 23		18 23		19 23
Stansted Airport ✈	a							14 43		15 43		16 43		17 43		18 43		19 43
Thetford	a				12 23		13 57		14 50		15 53		17 02		17 57		18 55	
Norwich	a				13 06		14 35		15 30		16 35		17 35		18 31		19 29	

		EM	XC	EM	EM	XC	XC	EM	EM	EM	XC	EM
		◇	◇1	◇	◇	◇1	◇1	◇	◇	◇	◇1	◇
Liverpool Lime Street 10	d	14 52		15 52	16 52			17 52	18 52	19 52		21 22
Liverpool South Parkway 7 ✈	d	15 03		16 03	17 03			18 03	19 03	20 03		
Widnes	d	15 11		16 11	17 11			18 11	19 11	20 11		21 39
Warrington Central	d	15 19		16 19	17 19			18 19	19 19	20 19		21 47
Manchester Oxford Road	d	15 39		16 39	17 39			18 39	19 39	20 39		22 07
Manchester Piccadilly 10 🚊	d	15 44		16 44	17 44			18 44	19 44	20 44		22 11
Stockport	d	15 54		16 54	17 54			18 54	19 54	20 54		22 28
Sheffield 7 🚊	a	16 36		17 36	18 37			19 34	20 34	21 36		23 25
	d	16 40		17 39	18 41			19 40	20 40	21 40		23 29
Chesterfield	d	16 56		17 54	18 56			19 55	20 55	21 56		23 43
Alfreton	d	17 07		18 04	19 06			20 06	21 06	22 07		23 54
Langley Mill	d	17 14		18 12	19 14			20 14	21 13	22 14		00 02
Nottingham 8 🚊	a	17 32		18 29	19 35			20 31	21 36	22 36		00 25
	d	17 36		18 47				20 44				
Grantham 7	d	18 17		19 27				21 19				
Birmingham New Street 12	d		17 22			18 22	19 22				20 22	
Coleshill Parkway	d		17 35			18 35	19 35				20 35	
Nuneaton	d		17 51			18 51	19 51				20 51	
Leicester	d		18 15			19 15	20 15				21 15	
Melton Mowbray	d		18 31			19 31	20 31				21 31	
Oakham	d		18 43			19 43	20 43				21 43	
Stamford	d		18 59			19 59	20 59				21 59	
Peterborough 8	a	18 46	19 14	19 56		20 14	21 14	21 49			22 14	
	d	18 48	19 18	19 58		20 18	21 18	21 51			22 18	
March	a		19 33			20 33	21 33				22 33	
Ely 6	a	19 21	19 52	20 31		20 52	21 52	22 24			22 52	
Cambridge	a		20 07			21 07	22 07				23 07	
Audley End	a		20 23			21 23	22 23					
Stansted Airport ✈	a		20 43			21 43	22 43					
Thetford	a	19 49		20 55				22 48				
Norwich	a	20 29		21 35				23 28				

A from 18 September until 23 October
B from 29 May until 11 September, from 30 October
C until 11 September. From Mansfield Woodhouse to Skegness
E until 11 September
G 🚲 to Stamford

For connections to Ipswich please refer to Table 14

Network Diagram for Tables 50, 55, 56, 57

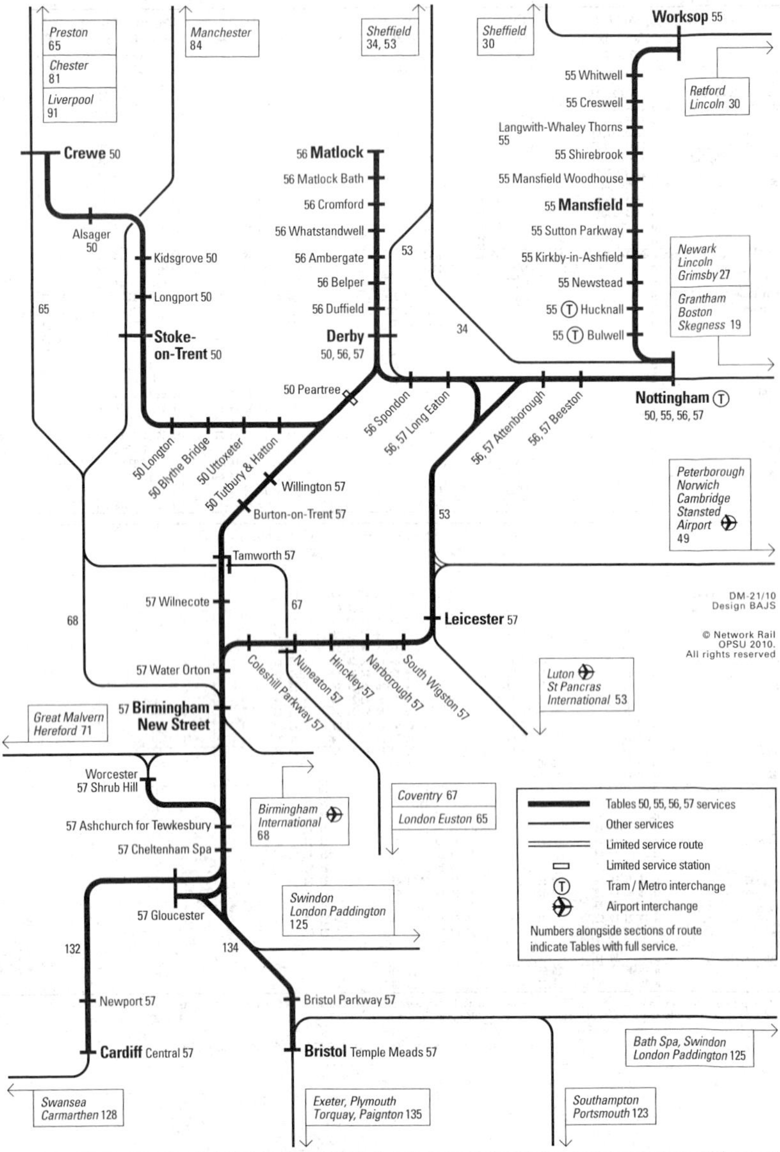

Table 50

Mondays to Fridays
until 23 September

Derby - Stoke-on-Trent and Crewe

Miles			NT A	NT A	LM ◇1 B	EM	NT A	LM ◇1 C	EM	NT A	LM ◇1 D	EM	NT A	LM ◇1 D	EM	NT A	LM ◇1 D	EM	NT A	LM ◇1 D	EM	NT A	LM ◇1 D
0	**Derby 6**	d				06 40			07 40			08 40			09 40			10 40			11 40		
1¼	Peartree	d							07 44														
11½	Tutbury & Hatton	d				06 54			07 56			08 56			09 56			10 56			11 56		
19¼	Uttoxeter	d				07 05			08 07			09 07			10 07			11 07			12 07		
30¼	Blythe Bridge	d				07 19			08 21			09 21			10 21			11 21			12 21		
33½	Longton	d				07 25			08 27			09 27			10 27			11 27			12 27		
35	**Stoke-on-Trent**	a				07 31			08 32			09 33			10 33			11 33			12 33		
—		d	06 30	07 17	07 26	07 33	07 57	08 13	08 34	08 58	09 13	09 34	09 58	10 13	10 34	10 58	11 13	11 34	11 58	12 13	12 34	12 58	13 13
39	Longport	d	06 34	07 21		07 38			08 39			09 39			10 39			11 39			12 39		
42¼	Kidsgrove	d	06a38	07a25	07 34	07 44	08a04	08 21	08 45	09a05	09 21	09 45	10a05	10 21	10 45	11a05	11 21	11 45	12a05	12 21	12 45	13a05	13 21
44½	Alsager	d			07 39	07 48		08 26	08 49		09 26	09 49		10 26	10 49		11 26	11 49		12 26	12 49		13 26
50¾	**Crewe 10**	a			07 49	07 59		08 38	08 59		09 38	09 59		10 38	10 59		11 38	11 59		12 38	12 59		13 38

		EM	NT A	LM ◇1 D	EM	NT A	LM ◇1 D	EM	NT A	LM ◇1 D	EM	NT A	LM ◇1 D	EM	NT A	EM	LM ◇1 D	NT A	EM	NT A	EM	NT A	LM ◇1 D
Derby 6	d	12 40			13 40			14 40			15 40			16 40		17 40			18 40		19 40		
Peartree	d													16 45		17 44							
Tutbury & Hatton	d	12 56			13 56			14 56			15 56			16 56		17 56			18 56		19 56		
Uttoxeter	d	13 07			14 07			15 07			16 07			17 07		18 07			19 07		20 07		
Blythe Bridge	d	13 21			14 21			15 21			16 21			17 21		18 21			19 21		20 21		
Longton	d	13 27			14 27			15 27			16 27			17 27		18 27			19 27		20 27		
Stoke-on-Trent	a	13 33			14 33			15 33			16 33			17 33		18 32			19 33		20 33		
	d	13 34	13 58	14 13	14 34	14 58	15 13	15 34	15 58	16 13	16 34	16 58	17 13	17 34	17 58	18 34	18 41	18 58	19 34	19 58	20 34	20 58	21 05
Longport	d	13 39			14 39			15 39			16 39			17 39		18 39			19 39		20 39		
Kidsgrove	d	13 45	14a05	14 21	14 45	15a05	15 21	15 45	16a05	16 21	16 45	17a05	17 21	17 46	18a05	18 45	18 49	19a05	19 45	20a05	20 45	21a05	21 14
Alsager	d	13 49		14 26	14 49		15 26	15 49		16 26	16 49		17 26	17 50		18 49	18 54		19 49		20 49		21 18
Crewe 10	a	13 59		14 38	14 59		15 38	15 59		16 38	16 59		17 38	17 59		18 59	19 05		19 59		20 59		21 27

		EM	NT A
Derby 6	d	20 40	
Peartree	d		
Tutbury & Hatton	d	20 56	
Uttoxeter	d	21 07	
Blythe Bridge	d	21 21	
Longton	d	21 27	
Stoke-on-Trent	a	21 33	
	d	21 34	22 18
Longport	d	21 39	
Kidsgrove	d	21 45	22a25
Alsager	d	21 49	
Crewe 10	a	21 59	

Mondays to Fridays
from 26 September

		NT A	NT A	LM ◇1 B	EM	NT A	LM ◇1 C	EM	NT A	LM ◇1 D	EM	NT A	LM ◇1 D	EM	NT A	LM ◇1 D	EM	NT A	LM ◇1 D	EM	NT A	LM ◇1 D	EM
Derby 6	d				06 40			07 40			08 40			09 40			10 40			11 40			12 40
Peartree	d							07 44															
Tutbury & Hatton	d				06 54			07 56			08 56			09 56			10 56			11 56			12 56
Uttoxeter	d				07 05			08 07			09 07			10 07			11 07			12 07			13 07
Blythe Bridge	d				07 19			08 21			09 21			10 21			11 21			12 21			13 21
Longton	d				07 25			08 27			09 27			10 27			11 27			12 27			13 27
Stoke-on-Trent	a				07 31			08 32			09 33			10 33			11 33			12 33			13 33
	d	06 30	07 17	07 26	07 33	07 57	08 13	08 34	08 58	09 13	09 34	09 58	10 13	10 34	10 58	11 13	11 34	11 58	12 13	12 34	12 58	13 13	13 34
Longport	d	06 34	07 21		07 38			08 39			09 39			10 39			11 39			12 39			13 39
Kidsgrove	d	06a38	07a25	07 34	07 44	08a04	08 21	08 45	09a05	09 21	09 45	10a05	10 21	10 45	11a05	11 21	11 45	12a05	12 21	12 45	13a05	13 21	13 45
Alsager	d			07 39	07 48		08 26	08 49		09 26	09 49		10 26	10 49		11 26	11 49		12 26	12 49		13 26	13 49
Crewe 10	a			07 49	08 04		08 38	08 59		09 38	09 59		10 38	10 59		11 38	11 59		12 38	12 59		13 38	13 59

		NT A	LM ◇1 D	EM	NT A	LM ◇1 D	EM	NT A	LM ◇1 D	EM	NT A	LM ◇1 D	EM	NT A	EM	LM ◇1 D	NT A	EM	NT A	EM	NT A	LM ◇1 D	EM	NT A
Derby 6	d			13 40			14 40			15 40			16 40		17 40			18 40		19 40			20 40	
Peartree	d												16 45		17 44									
Tutbury & Hatton	d			13 56			14 56			15 56			16 56		17 56			18 56		19 56			20 56	
Uttoxeter	d			14 07			15 07			16 07			17 07		18 07			19 07		20 07			21 07	
Blythe Bridge	d			14 21			15 21			16 21			17 21		18 21			19 21		20 21			21 21	
Longton	d			14 27			15 27			16 27			17 27		18 27			19 27		20 27			21 27	
Stoke-on-Trent	a			14 33			15 33			16 33			17 33		18 32			19 33		20 33			21 33	
	d	13 58	14 13	14 34	14 58	15 13	15 34	15 58	16 13	16 34	16 58	17 13	17 34	17 58	18 34	18 41	18 58	19 34	19 58	20 34	20 58	21 05	21 34	22 18
Longport	d			14 39			15 39			16 39			17 39		18 39			19 39		20 39			21 39	
Kidsgrove	d	14a05	14 21	14 45	15a05	15 21	15 45	16a05	16 21	16 45	17a05	17 21	17 46	18a05	18 45	18 49	19a05	19 45	20a05	20 45	21a05	21 14	21 45	22a25
Alsager	d		14 26	14 49		15 26	15 49		16 26	16 49		17 26	17 50		18 49	18 54		19 49		20 49		21 18	21 49	
Crewe 10	a		14 38	14 59		15 38	15 59		16 38	16 59		17 38	17 59		18 59	19 05		19 59		21 04		21 27	22 04	

A To Manchester Piccadilly
B From Bletchley
C From Northampton
D From London Euston

Table 50

Saturdays
until 24 September

		NT	LM	EM	NT	LM	EM	NT	LM	EM	NT	LM	EM	NT	LM	EM	NT	LM	EM	NT	LM	EM	NT
			◇1			◇1			◇1			◇1			◇1			◇1			◇1		
		A	B		A	C		A	D		A	D		A	D		A	D		A	D		A
Derby 6	d			06 40			07 40			08 40			09 40			10 40			11 40			12 40	
Peartree	d						07 44																
Tutbury & Hatton	d			06 56			07 56			08 56			09 56			10 56			11 56			12 56	
Uttoxeter	d			07 07			08 07			09 07			10 07			11 07			12 07			13 07	
Blythe Bridge	d			07 21			08 21			09 21			10 21			11 21			12 21			13 21	
Longton	d			07 28			08 27			09 27			10 27			11 27			12 27			13 27	
Stoke-on-Trent	a			07 34			08 32			09 33			10 33			11 33			12 33			13 33	
	d	06 57	07 13	07 34	07 57	08 13	08 34	08 58	09 13	09 34	09 58	10 13	10 34	10 58	11 13	11 34	11 58	12 13	12 34	12 58	13 13	13 34	13 58
Longport	d			07 39			08 39			09 39			10 39			11 39			12 39			13 39	
Kidsgrove	d	07a04	07 21	07 46	08a04	08 21	08 45	09a05	09 21	09 45	10a05	10 21	10 45	11a05	11 21	11 45	12a05	12 21	12 45	13a05	13 21	13 45	14a05
Alsager	d		07 26	07 50		08 26	08 49		09 26	09 49		10 26	10 49		11 26	11 49		12 26	12 49		13 26	13 49	
Crewe 10	a		07 36	07 59		08 37	08 59		09 38	09 59		10 38	10 59		11 38	11 59		12 38	12 59		13 38	13 59	

		LM	EM	NT	LM	EM	NT	LM	EM	NT	LM	EM	NT	EM	LM	NT	LM	EM	NT	LM	EM	NT	LM	EM	NT
		◇1			◇1			◇1			◇1				◇1		◇1			1			1		
		D		A	D		A	D		A	D		A		D	A	D		A	D		A	D		A
Derby 6	d		13 40			14 40			15 40			16 40		17 40				18 40			19 40			20 40	
Peartree	d													17 45											
Tutbury & Hatton	d		13 56			14 56			15 56			16 56		17 57				18 56			19 56			20 56	
Uttoxeter	d		14 07			15 07			16 07			17 07		18 07				19 07			20 07			21 07	
Blythe Bridge	d		14 21			15 21			16 21			17 21		18 21				19 21			20 21			21 21	
Longton	d		14 27			15 27			16 27			17 27		18 27				19 27			20 27			21 27	
Stoke-on-Trent	a		14 33			15 33			16 33			17 32		18 32				19 33			20 33			21 33	
	d	14 13	14 34	14 58	15 13	15 34	15 58	16 13	16 34	16 58	17 13	17 34	17 58	18 34	18 41	18 58	19 13	19 34	19 58	20 13	20 34	20 58	21 15	21 34	22 18
Longport	d		14 39			15 39			16 39			17 39		18 39				19 39			20 39			21 39	
Kidsgrove	d	14 21	14 45	15a05	15 21	15 45	16a05	16 21	16 45	17a05	17 21	17 45	18a05	18 45	18 49	19a05	19 21	19 45	20a05	20 21	20 45	21a05	21 23	21 45	22a25
Alsager	d	14 26	14 49		15 26	15 49		16 26	16 49		17 26	17 49		18 49	18 54		19 26	19 49		20 26	20 49		21 28	21 49	
Crewe 10	a	14 38	14 59		15 38	15 59		16 38	16 59		17 38	17 59		18 59	19 05		19 36	19 59		20 36	20 59		21 38	21 59	

Saturdays
from 1 October

		NT	LM	EM	NT	LM	EM	NT	LM	EM	NT	LM	EM	NT	LM	EM	NT	LM	EM	NT	LM	EM	NT	LM
			◇1			◇1			◇1			◇1			◇1			◇1			◇1			◇1
		A	B		A	C		A	D		A	D		A	D		A	D		A	D		A	A
Derby 6	d			06 40			07 40			08 40			09 40			10 40			11 40			12 40		
Peartree	d						07 44																	
Tutbury & Hatton	d			06 56			07 56			08 56			09 56			10 56			11 56			12 56		
Uttoxeter	d			07 07			08 07			09 07			10 07			11 07			12 07			13 07		
Blythe Bridge	d			07 21			08 21			09 21			10 21			11 21			12 21			13 21		
Longton	d			07 28			08 27			09 27			10 27			11 27			12 27			13 27		
Stoke-on-Trent	a			07 34			08 32			09 33			10 33			11 33			12 33			13 33		
	d	06 57	07 13	07 34	07 57	08 13	08 34	08 58	09 13	09 34	09 58	10 13	10 34	10 58	11 13	11 34	11 58	12 13	12 34	12 58	13 13	13 34	13 58	14 13
Longport	d			07 39			08 39			09 39			10 39			11 39			12 39			13 39		
Kidsgrove	d	07a04	07 21	07 46	08a04	08 21	08 45	09a05	09 21	09 45	10a05	10 21	10 45	11a05	11 21	11 45	12a05	12 21	12 45	13a05	13 21	13 45	14a05	14 21
Alsager	d		07 26	07 50		08 26	08 49		09 26	09 49		10 26	10 49		11 26	11 49		12 26	12 49		13 26	13 49		14 26
Crewe 10	a		07 36	08 04		08 37	08 59		09 38	09 59		10 38	10 59		11 38	11 59		12 38	12 59		13 38	13 59		14 38

A To Manchester Piccadilly
B From Bletchley
C From Northampton
D From London Euston

Table 50

Saturdays

Derby - Stoke-on-Trent and Crewe

		EM	NT	LM	EM	NT	LM	EM	NT	LM	EM	NT	EM	LM	NT	LM	EM	NT	LM	EM	NT	LM	EM	NT
				◇1			◇1			◇1				◇1		◇1			1			1		
			B	A		B	A		B	A		B		A	B	A		B	A		B	A		B
Derby 6	d	13 40			14 40			15 40			16 40		17 40				18 40			19 40			20 40	
Peartree	d												17 45											
Tutbury & Hatton	d	13 56			14 56			15 56			16 56		17 57				18 56			19 56			20 56	
Uttoxeter	d	14 07			15 07			16 07			17 07		18 07				19 07			20 07			21 07	
Blythe Bridge	d	14 21			15 21			16 21			17 21		18 21				19 21			20 21			21 21	
Longton	d	14 27			15 27			16 27			17 27		18 27				19 27			20 27			21 27	
Stoke-on-Trent	a	14 33			15 33			16 33			17 32		18 32				19 33			20 33			21 33	
	d	14 34	14 58	15 13	15 34	15 58	16 13	16 34	16 58	17 13	17 34	17 58	18 34	18 41	18 58	19 13	19 34	19 58	20 13	20 34	20 58	21 15	21 34	22 18
Longport	d	14 39			15 39			16 39			17 39		18 39				19 39			20 39			21 39	
Kidsgrove	d	14 45	15a05	15 21	15 45	16a05	16 21	16 45	17a05	17 21	17 45	18a05	18 45	18 49	19a05	19 21	19 45	20a05	20 21	20 45	21a05	21 23	21 45	22a25
Alsager	d	14 49		15 26	15 49		16 26	16 49		17 26	17 49		18 49	18 54		19 26	19 49		20 26	20 49		21 28	21 49	
Crewe 10	a	14 59		15 38	15 59		16 38	16 59		17 38	17 59		18 59	19 05		19 36	19 59		20 36	21 04		21 38	22 04	

Sundays

		LM	LM	EM	LM	NT	EM	EM	LM	EM	EM	LM	NT	EM	EM	LM	NT
		1	◇1		◇1				◇1			◇1				◇1	
		C	D		A	B			A			A	B			A	B
Derby 6	d			14 38			15 38	16 38		17 38	18 38			19 38	20 40		
Peartree	d																
Tutbury & Hatton	d			14 52			15 52	16 52		17 52	18 52			19 52	20 54		
Uttoxeter	d			15 03			16 03	17 03		18 03	19 03			20 03	21 05		
Blythe Bridge	d			15 17			16 17	17 17		18 17	19 17			20 17	21 19		
Longton	d			15 23			16 23	17 23		18 24	19 23			20 23	21 25		
Stoke-on-Trent	a			15 29			16 29	17 29		18 30	19 29			20 30	21 34		
	d	12 03	13 20	15 30	15 41	16 01	16 30	17 30	17 42	18 31	19 30	19 41	20 01	20 30	21 36	21 43	22 39
Longport	d			15 35			16 35	17 35		18 36	19 35			20 35	21 41		
Kidsgrove	d	12 11	13 28	15 41	15 52	16a08	16 41	17 41	17 50	18 41	19 41	19 52	20a08	20 41	21 47	21 54	22a46
Alsager	d	12 15	13 32	15 46	15 58		16 45	17 45	17 54	18 46	19 46	19 57		20 46	21 52	22 01	
Crewe 10	a	12 26	13 43	16 01	16 07		17 02	18 01	18 06	19 01	20 02	20 06		21 01	22 05	22 12	

A From London Euston
B To Manchester Piccadilly
C From Stafford
D From Northampton

Table 50

Crewe and Stoke-on-Trent - Derby

Mondays to Fridays
until 23 September

Miles	Station		XC ◇1 A	NT 1 B	EM	LM ◇1 C	EM	LM ◇1 C	EM	NT 1 D	LM ◇1 C	EM	NT 1 D	LM ◇1 C	EM	NT 1 D	LM ◇1 C	EM	NT 1 D	LM ◇1 C	EM	NT 1 D	LM ◇1 C
0	**Crewe** 10	d	05 47		06 07	06 35	06 58	07 33	08 07		08 33	09 07		09 33	10 07		10 33	11 07		11 33	12 07		12 33
6¼	Alsager	d			06 16	06 44	07 07	07 41	08 16		08 41	09 16		09 41	10 16		10 41	11 16		11 41	12 16		12 41
8¼	Kidsgrove	d		06 16	06 21	06 48	07 12	07 46	08 21	08 32	08 46	09 21	09 32	09 46	10 21	10 32	10 46	11 21	11 32	11 46	12 21	12 32	12 46
11¾	Longport	d			06 27		07 18		08 27			09 27			10 27			11 27			12 27		
15¾	**Stoke-on-Trent**	a	06 06	06 26	06 31	06 57	07 23	07 54	08 31	08 42	08 54	09 31	09 42	09 54	10 31	10 42	10 54	11 31	11 42	11 54	12 31	12 42	12 54
—		d			06 33		07 24		08 33			09 33			10 33			11 33			12 33		
17¼	Longton	d			06 39		07 30		08 39			09 39			10 39			11 39			12 39		
20½	Blythe Bridge	d			06 45		07 37		08 45			09 45			10 45			11 45			12 45		
31½	Uttoxeter	d			06 58		07 49		08 58			09 58			10 58			11 58			12 58		
39¼	Tutbury & Hatton	d			07 07		07 58		09 07			10 07			11 07			12 07			13 07		
49½	Peartree	d			07 20																		
50¾	**Derby** 6	a			07 24		08 16		09 24			10 24			11 24			12 24			13 24		

Station		EM	NT 1 D	LM ◇1 C	EM	NT 1 D	LM ◇1 C	EM	NT 1 D	LM ◇1 C	EM	NT 1 D	LM ◇1 C	EM	NT 1 D	LM ◇1 C	EM	LM ◇1 E	EM	NT 1 D	NT 1 D	EM	NT 1 D	NT 1 D
Crewe 10	d	13 07		13 33	14 07		14 33	15 07		15 33	16 07		16 33	17 07		17 33	18 07	18 33	19 07			20 45		
Alsager	d	13 16		13 41	14 16		14 41	15 16		15 41	16 16		16 41	17 16		17 41	18 16	18 41	19 16			20 58		
Kidsgrove	d	13 21	13 32	13 46	14 21	14 32	14 46	15 21	15 32	15 46	16 21	16 32	16 46	17 21	17 32	17 46	18 21	18 46	19 21	19 32	20 32	21 07	21 32	22 32
Longport	d	13 27			14 27			15 27			16 27			17 27			18 27		19 27			21 12		
Stoke-on-Trent	a	13 31	13 42	13 54	14 31	14 42	14 54	15 31	15 42	15 54	16 31	16 42	16 54	17 31	17 42	17 54	18 31	18 54	19 31	19 42	20 42	21 16	21 42	22 42
	d	13 33			14 33			15 33			16 33			17 33			18 33		19 33			21 18		
Longton	d	13 39			14 39			15 39			16 39			17 39			18 39		19 39			21 24		
Blythe Bridge	d	13 45			14 45			15 45			16 45			17 45			18 45		19 45			21 29		
Uttoxeter	d	13 58			14 58			15 58			16 58			17 58			18 58		19 58			21 42		
Tutbury & Hatton	d	14 07			15 07			16 07			17 07			18 07			19 07		20 07			21 51		
Peartree	d							16 18																
Derby 6	a	14 24			15 24			16 24			17 24			18 24			19 24		20 24			22 10		

Mondays to Fridays
from 26 September

Station		XC ◇1 A	NT 1 B	EM	LM ◇1 C	EM	LM ◇1 C	EM	NT 1 D	LM ◇1 C	EM	NT 1 D	LM ◇1 C	EM	NT 1 D	LM ◇1 C	EM	NT 1 D	LM ◇1 C	EM	NT 1 D	LM ◇1 C	EM
Crewe 10	d	05 47		06 07	06 35	06 58	07 33	08 07		08 33	09 07		09 33	10 07		10 33	11 07		11 33	12 07		12 33	13 07
Alsager	d			06 16	06 44	07 07	07 41	08 16		08 41	09 16		09 41	10 16		10 41	11 16		11 41	12 16		12 41	13 16
Kidsgrove	d		06 16	06 21	06 48	07 12	07 46	08 21	08 32	08 46	09 21	09 32	09 46	10 21	10 32	10 46	11 21	11 32	11 46	12 21	12 32	12 46	13 21
Longport	d			06 27		07 18		08 27			09 27			10 27			11 27			12 27			13 27
Stoke-on-Trent	a	06 06	06 26	06 31	06 57	07 23	07 54	08 31	08 42	08 54	09 31	09 42	09 54	10 31	10 42	10 54	11 31	11 42	11 54	12 31	12 42	12 54	13 31
	d			06 33		07 24		08 33			09 33			10 33			11 33			12 33			13 33
Longton	d			06 39		07 30		08 39			09 39			10 39			11 39			12 39			13 39
Blythe Bridge	d			06 45		07 37		08 45			09 45			10 45			11 45			12 45			13 45
Uttoxeter	d			06 58		07 49		08 58			09 58			10 58			11 58			12 58			13 58
Tutbury & Hatton	d			07 07		07 58		09 07			10 07			11 07			12 07			13 07			14 07
Peartree	d			07 20																			
Derby 6	a			07 27		08 17		09 26			10 26			11 26			12 26			13 26			14 26

Station		NT 1 D	LM ◇1 C	EM	NT 1 D	LM ◇1 C	EM	NT 1 D	LM ◇1 C	EM	NT 1 D	LM ◇1 C	EM	NT 1 D	LM ◇1 C	EM	LM ◇1 E	EM	NT 1 D	NT 1 D	EM	NT 1 D	NT 1 D
Crewe 10	d		13 33	14 07		14 33	15 07		15 33	16 07		16 33	17 07		17 33	18 07	18 33	19 07			20 45		
Alsager	d		13 41	14 16		14 41	15 16		15 41	16 16		16 41	17 16		17 41	18 16	18 41	19 16			20 58		
Kidsgrove	d	13 32	13 46	14 21	14 32	14 46	15 21	15 32	15 46	16 21	16 32	16 46	17 21	17 32	17 46	18 21	18 46	19 21	19 32	20 32	21 07	21 32	22 32
Longport	d			14 27			15 27			16 27			17 27			18 27		19 27			21 12		
Stoke-on-Trent	a	13 42	13 54	14 31	14 42	14 54	15 31	15 42	15 54	16 31	16 42	16 54	17 31	17 42	17 54	18 31	18 54	19 31	19 42	20 42	21 16	21 42	22 42
	d			14 33			15 33			16 33			17 33			18 33		19 33			21 18		
Longton	d			14 39			15 39			16 39			17 39			18 39		19 39			21 24		
Blythe Bridge	d			14 45			15 45			16 45			17 45			18 45		19 45			21 29		
Uttoxeter	d			14 58			15 58			16 58			17 58			18 58		19 58			21 42		
Tutbury & Hatton	d			15 07			16 07			17 07			18 07			19 07		20 07			21 51		
Peartree	d						16 18																
Derby 6	a			15 26			16 26			17 26			18 26			19 26		20 26			22 10		

Saturdays
until 24 September

Station		XC ◇1 A	NT 1 B	EM	LM ◇1 C	EM	NT 1 D	LM ◇1 C	EM	NT 1 D	LM ◇1 C	EM	NT 1 D	LM ◇1 C	EM	NT 1 D	LM ◇1 C	EM	NT 1 D	LM ◇1 C	EM	NT 1 D	LM ◇1 C
Crewe 10	d	05 47		06 07	06 38	07 07		07 38	08 07		08 33	09 07		09 33	10 07		10 33	11 07		11 33	12 07		12 33
Alsager	d			06 16	06 47	07 16		07 47	08 16		08 41	09 16		09 41	10 16		10 41	11 16		11 41	12 16		12 41
Kidsgrove	d		06 16	06 21	06 51	07 21	07 28	07 51	08 21	08 32	08 46	09 21	09 32	09 46	10 21	10 32	10 46	11 21	11 32	11 46	12 21	12 32	12 46
Longport	d			06 27		07 27			08 27			09 27			10 27			11 27			12 27		
Stoke-on-Trent	a	06 07	06 26	06 31	06 59	07 31	07 40	07 59	08 31	08 42	08 54	09 31	09 42	09 54	10 31	10 42	10 54	11 31	11 42	11 54	12 31	12 42	12 54
	d			06 33		07 33			08 33			09 33			10 33			11 33			12 33		
Longton	d			06 39		07 39			08 39			09 39			10 39			11 39			12 39		
Blythe Bridge	d			06 45		07 45			08 45			09 45			10 45			11 45			12 45		
Uttoxeter	d			06 58		07 58			08 58			09 58			10 58			11 58			12 58		
Tutbury & Hatton	d			07 07		08 07			09 07			10 07			11 07			12 07			13 07		
Peartree	d			07 19																			
Derby 6	a			07 23		08 22			09 23			10 23			11 23			12 23			13 23		

A From Manchester Piccadilly to Bournemouth
B From Macclesfield
C To London Euston
D From Manchester Piccadilly
E To Northampton

Table 50

Crewe and Stoke-on-Trent - Derby

Saturdays
until 24 September

		EM	NT ■1 A	LM ◇■1 B	EM	NT ■1 A		LM ◇■1 B	EM	NT ■1 A	LM ◇■1 B	EM	NT ■1 A	LM ◇■1 B	EM	LM ◇■1 C		EM	LM ◇■1 C	EM	NT ■1 A	NT ■1 A	EM	NT ■1 A	NT ■1 A
Crewe 10	d	13 07		13 33	14 07			14 33	15 07		15 33	16 07		16 33	17 07	17 33		18 07	18 33	19 07			20 45		
Alsager	d	13 16		13 41	14 16			14 41	15 16		15 41	16 16		16 41	17 16	17 41		18 16	18 41	19 16			20 54		
Kidsgrove	d	13 21	13 32	13 46	14 21	14 32		14 46	15 21	15 32	15 46	16 21	16 32	16 46	17 21	17 46		18 21	18 46	19 21	19 32	20 32	21 08	21 32	22 32
Longport	d	13 27			14 27				15 27			16 27			17 27			18 27		19 27			21 14		
Stoke-on-Trent	a	13 31	13 42	13 54	14 31	14 42		14 54	15 31	15 42	15 54	16 31	16 42	16 54	17 31	17 54		18 31	18 54	19 31	19 42	20 42	21 18	21 42	22 42
	d	13 33			14 33				15 33			16 33			17 33			18 33		19 33			21 19		
Longton	d	13 39			14 39				15 39			16 39			17 39			18 39		19 39			21 25		
Blythe Bridge	d	13 45			14 45				15 45			16 45			17 45			18 45		19 45			21 31		
Uttoxeter	d	13 58			14 58				15 58			16 58			17 58			18 58		19 58			21 44		
Tutbury & Hatton	d	14 07			15 07				16 07			17 07			18 07			19 07		20 07			21 53		
Peartree	d								16 19																
Derby 6	a	14 23			15 23				16 23			17 23			18 23			19 23		20 23			22 10		

Saturdays
from 1 October

		XC ◇■1 D	NT ■1 E	EM	LM ◇■1 B	EM	NT ■1 A	LM ◇■1 B	EM	NT ■1 A		LM ◇■1 B	EM	NT ■1 A	LM ◇■1 B	EM	NT ■1 A	LM ◇■1 B	EM	NT ■1 A		LM ◇■1 B	EM	NT ■1 A	LM ◇■1 B
Crewe 10	d	05 47		06 07	06 38	07 07		07 38	08 07			08 33	09 07		09 33	10 07		10 33	11 07			11 33	12 07		12 33
Alsager	d			06 16	06 47	07 16		07 47	08 16			08 41	09 16		09 41	10 16		10 41	11 16			11 41	12 16		12 41
Kidsgrove	d		06 16	06 21	06 51	07 21	07 28	07 51	08 21	08 32		08 46	09 21	09 32	09 46	10 21	10 32	10 46	11 21	11 32		11 46	12 21	12 32	12 46
Longport	d			06 27		07 27			08 27				09 27			10 27			11 27				12 27		
Stoke-on-Trent	a	06 07	06 26	06 31	06 59	07 31	07 40	07 59	08 31	08 42		08 54	09 31	09 42	09 54	10 31	10 42	10 54	11 31	11 42		11 54	12 31	12 42	12 54
	d			06 33		07 33			08 33				09 33			10 33			11 33				12 33		
Longton	d			06 39		07 39			08 39				09 39			10 39			11 39				12 39		
Blythe Bridge	d			06 45		07 45			08 45				09 45			10 45			11 45				12 45		
Uttoxeter	d			06 58		07 58			08 58				09 58			10 58			11 58				12 58		
Tutbury & Hatton	d			07 07		08 07			09 07				10 07			11 07			12 07				13 07		
Peartree	d			07 19																					
Derby 6	a			07 23		08 24			09 26				10 26			11 26			12 26				13 26		

		EM	NT ■1 A	LM ◇■1 B	EM	NT ■1 A		LM ◇■1 B	EM	NT ■1 A	LM ◇■1 B	EM	NT ■1 A	LM ◇■1 B	EM	LM ◇■1 C		EM	LM ◇■1 C	EM	NT ■1 A	NT ■1 A	EM	NT ■1 A	NT ■1 A
Crewe 10	d	13 07		13 33	14 07			14 33	15 07		15 33	16 07		16 33	17 07	17 33		18 07	18 33	19 07			20 45		
Alsager	d	13 16		13 41	14 16			14 41	15 16		15 41	16 16		16 41	17 16	17 41		18 16	18 41	19 16			20 54		
Kidsgrove	d	13 21	13 32	13 46	14 21	14 32		14 46	15 21	15 32	15 46	16 21	16 32	16 46	17 21	17 46		18 21	18 46	19 21	19 32	20 32	21b08	21 32	22 32
Longport	d	13 27			14 27				15 27			16 27			17 27			18 27		19 27			21 14		
Stoke-on-Trent	a	13 31	13 42	13 54	14 31	14 42		14 54	15 31	15 42	15 54	16 31	16 42	16 54	17 31	17 54		18 31	18 54	19 31	19 42	20 42	21 18	21 42	22 42
	d	13 33			14 33				15 33			16 33			17 33			18 33		19 33			21 19		
Longton	d	13 39			14 39				15 39			16 39			17 39			18 39		19 39			21 25		
Blythe Bridge	d	13 45			14 45				15 45			16 45			17 45			18 45		19 45			21 31		
Uttoxeter	d	13 58			14 58				15 58			16 58			17 58			18 58		19 58			21 44		
Tutbury & Hatton	d	14 07			15 07				16 07			17 07			18 07			19 07		20 07			21 53		
Peartree	d								16 19																
Derby 6	a	14 26			15 26				16 26			17 26			18 26			19 25		20 26			22 10		

Sundays

		LM ■1 F	LM ◇■1 B	LM ◇■1 B	EM	EM	NT ■1 A	LM ◇■1 B	EM	EM		LM ◇■1 B	EM	EM	NT ■1 A	LM ◇■1 B	EM	EM	NT ■1 A						
Crewe 10	d	10 37	11 38	13 38	14 04	15 05		15 38	16 08	17 08		17 38	18 08	19 08		19 36	20 08	21 16							
Alsager	d	10 46	11 46	13 46	14 13	15 14		15 46	16 17	17 17		17 46	18 17	19 17		19 44	20 20	21 25							
Kidsgrove	d	10 50	11 52	13 51	14 18	15 21	15 25	15 52	16 22	17 22		17 51	18 22	19 22	19 28	19 50	20 25	21 30	22 26						
Longport	d				14 24	15 26			16 29	17 29			18 29	19 29			20 33	21 36							
Stoke-on-Trent	a	10 57	11 59	13 58	14 29	15 30	15 37	15 59	16 35	17 33		17 58	18 34	19 33	19 40	19 57	20 37	21 40	22 36						
	d				14 29	15 32			16 35	17 35			18 35	19 35			20 39	21 42							
Longton	d				14 35	15 38			16 41	17 41			18 41	19 41			20 46	21 53							
Blythe Bridge	d				14 41	15 44			16 47	17 47			18 47	19 47			20 52	21 59							
Uttoxeter	d				14 53	15 56			16 59	17 59			18 59	19 59			21 04	22 12							
Tutbury & Hatton	d				15 02	16 06			17 08	18 08			19 08	20 08			21 13	22 21							
Peartree	d																								
Derby 6	a				15 21	16 25			17 27	18 27			19 27	20 27			21 33	22 40							

A From Manchester Piccadilly
B To London Euston
C To Northampton
D From Manchester Piccadilly to Bournemouth
E From Macclesfield
F To Stafford

Route Diagram for Table 51

DM-5/10
Design BAJS

© Network Rail OPSU 2010.
All rights reserved

This Table summarises through services which, with their associated connecting services at Birmingham New Street, link centres in the North and South of the country. In certain instances a faster journey is possible via London and the relevant Table(s) should be consulted.

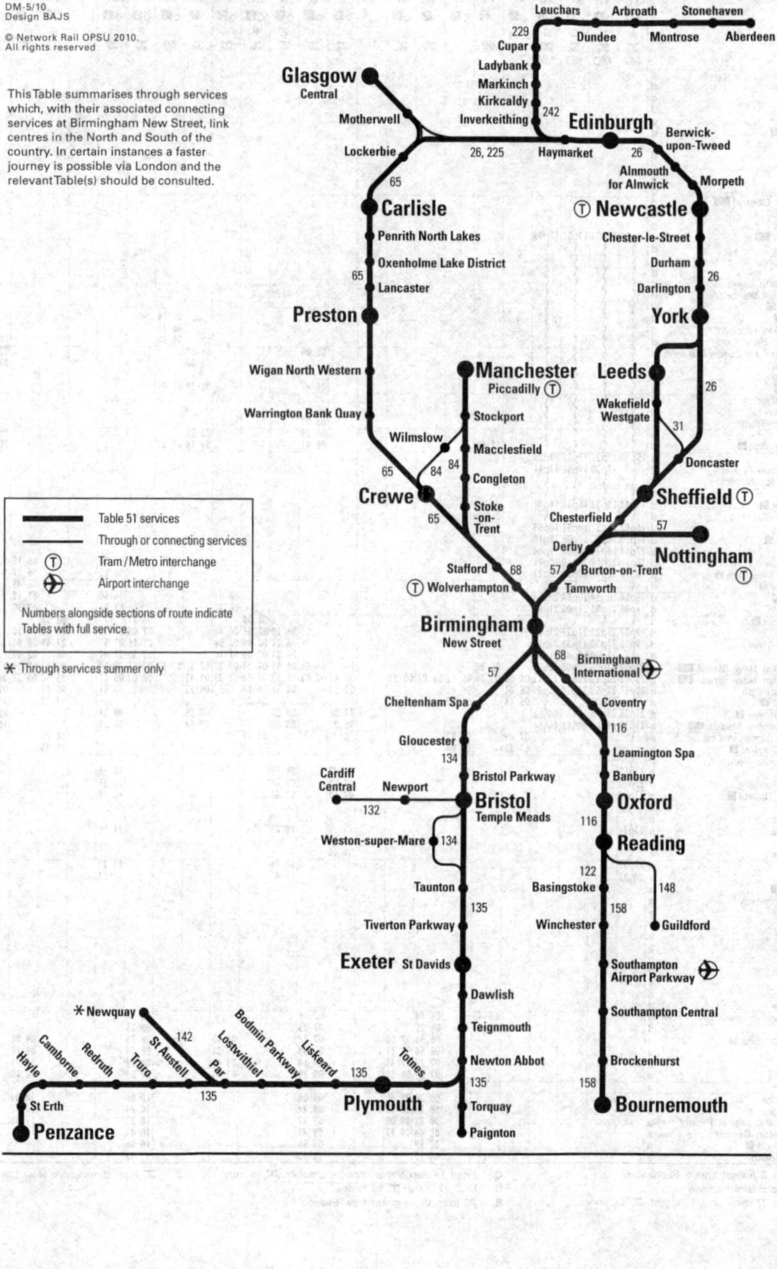

(thick line)	Table 51 services
(thin line)	Through or connecting services
Ⓣ	Tram / Metro interchange
(airport symbol)	Airport interchange

Numbers alongside sections of route indicate Tables with full service.

* Through services summer only

Scotland, The North East, North West England - The South West and South Coast

		XC	XC	XC	XC	XC	VT	XC	XC	XC	XC	XC	XC	XC	XC	XC	VT	XC	XC	XC	XC	XC	XC
		◇[1]	◇[1]	◇[1]	◇[1]	◇[1]	◇[1]	◇[1]	◇[1]	◇[1]	◇[1]	◇[1]	◇[1]	◇[1]	◇[1]	◇[1]	◇[1]	◇[1]	◇[1]	◇[1]	◇[1]	◇[1]	[1]
		A	B	C	D								E	F				E		F			
		🛒	🛒	🛒	🛒		⊠		🛒	🛒	🛒	🛒	🛒	🛒	🛒	🛒	⊠	🛒	🛒	🛒	🛒	🛒	
		MX	MO	MO	MX																		
Aberdeen	d																						
Stonehaven	d																						
Montrose	d																						
Arbroath	d																						
Dundee	d																						
Leuchars [3]	d																						
Cupar	d																						
Ladybank	d																						
Markinch	d																						
Kirkcaldy	d																						
Inverkeithing	d																						
Glasgow Central [15]	d																						
Motherwell	d																						
Haymarket	d																						
Edinburgh [10]	d	15p08	17p07	17p07	17p08																		
Haymarket	d																						
Lockerbie	d																						
Carlisle [8]	d																						
Penrith North Lakes	d																						
Oxenholme Lake District	d																						
Lancaster [6]	d																						
Preston [8]	d																06 16						
Wigan North Western	d																06 27						
Warrington Bank Quay	d																06 38						
M'chester Piccadilly [10] 🚊	d											05 00				06 00						07 06	
Stockport	d															06 08						07 16	
Wilmslow	d																						
Crewe [10]	d											05 47				06 38	07 01						
Macclesfield	d																						
Congleton	d																						
Stoke-on-Trent	d											06 07										07 44	
Stafford	d											06 25				06 58						08 02	
Wolverhampton [7] 🚊	d						05 00					06 41				07 15	07 32					08 16	
Dunbar	d	15p28	17p27	17p27	17p28																		
Berwick-upon-Tweed	d		17p50	17p50	17p51																		
Alnmouth for Alnwick	d																						
Morpeth	d																						
Newcastle [8]	d	16p42	18p38	18p38	18p41																		
Chester-le-Street	d																						
Durham	d	16p52	18p51	18p51	18p53																		
Darlington [7]	d	17p10	19p08	19p08	19p10																		
York [8]	d	17p44	19p39	19p39	19p44																		
Leeds [10]	d	18p11	20p10	20p10	20p11														06 00		06 15		
Wakefield Westgate [7]	d	18p23	20p22	20p22	20p23														06 12		06 27		
Doncaster [7]	d																				06 45		
Sheffield [7] 🚊	d	18p54	20p54	20p54	20p54										06 01				06 50		07 18		
Chesterfield	d	19p06	21p06	21p06	21p06										06 27				07 04		07 30		
Nottingham [8] 🚊	d													06 00				06 37		06 56			07 37
Derby [6]	d	19p27	21p27	21p27	21p28								06 10	06 36	06 48			07 06	07 26	07 36	07 50		08 06
Burton-on-Trent	d	19p38	21p38	21p38	21p39								06 21	06 48	06 59			07 18	07 37	07 49	08 01		08 18
Tamworth	d		21p49	21p49	21p50								06 32	07 00	07 10			07 30	07 49	08 01	08 12		08 30
Birmingham New Street [12]	a	20p09	22p06	22p08	22p09		05 26					06 58	06 51	07 24	07 27	07 31	07 55	07 55	08 09	08 24	08 29	08 32	08 53
Birmingham New Street [12]	d	20p12	22p12	22p12	22p12	05 00	05 29	05 42	06 03	06 33	06 42	07 03	07 12	07 30	07 33	07 42		08 03	08 12	08 30	08 33	08 42	
Cheltenham Spa	a	20p51	22p50	22p50	23p29	06 01		06 43			07 20		07 51	08 14		08 23			08 51	09 11		09 23	
Gloucester [7]	a		23p03			06 16		06 53						08 27						09 22			
Bristol Parkway [7]	a	21p25	23p55		00 02						07 56		08 25			08 55			09 24			09 55	
Bristol Temple Meads [10]	a	21p38	00 10	00 13	00 14						08 08		08 40			09 14			09 39			10 08	
Newport (South Wales)	a					07 09		07 52						09 12						10 09			
Cardiff Central [7]	a					07 26		08 08						09 30						10 25			
Weston-super-Mare	a																						
Taunton	a	22p15									08 42		09 15						10 16				
Tiverton Parkway	a	22p50									08 54		09 28						10 29				
Exeter St Davids [6]	a	23p04									09 10		09 43						10 46				
Dawlish	a																						
Teignmouth	a																						
Newton Abbot	a	23p24											10 03						11 08				
Torquay	a										09 39												
Paignton	a										09 46												
Totnes	a	23p37											10 16						11 22				
Plymouth	a	00 03											10 46						11 51				
Liskeard [6]	a																						
Bodmin Parkway	a																						
Lostwithiel	a																						
Par	a																						
St Austell	a																						
Truro	a																						
Redruth	a																						
Camborne	a																						
Hayle	a																						
St Erth	a																						
Penzance	a																						
Birmingham International ✈	d						05 40		06 14			07 14						08 14					
Coventry	d						05 51		06 25			07 25						08 25					
Leamington Spa [8]	d								06 38	07 00		07 38			08 05			08 38			09 00		
Banbury	a								06 56	07 21		07 54			08 21			08 54			09 18		
Oxford	a								07 14	07 41		08 14			08 41			09 14			09 41		
Reading [7]	a								07 39	08 10		08 39			09 09			09 39			10 10		
Guildford	a																						
Basingstoke	a								08 08	08 40		09 08						10 08			10 39		
Winchester	a								08 24	08 56		09 24						10 24			10 54		
Southampton Airport Pkway ✈	a								08 32	09 08		09 32						10 32			11 08		
Southampton Central ⛴	a								08 44	09 17		09 41						10 43			11 16		
Brockenhurst [3]	a								08 59			09 56						10 58					
Bournemouth	a								09 15			10 12						11 12					

A From 2 August until 9 September. 🛒 to Bristol Parkway
B From 27 June until 1 August. 🛒 to York
C From 19 September until 24 October. 🛒 to York
D Until 17 June. 🛒 to York
E 🛒 from Birmingham New Street
F 🛒 from Birmingham New Street to Gloucester

Scotland, The North East, North West England - The South West and South Coast

		VT	XC	XC	XC	XC	XC	XC	XC	VT	XC	XC	XC	XC	XC	XC	VT	XC	XC	XC	XC	XC	XC
				MX	MO																		
		◇1	◇1	◇1	◇1	◇1	◇1	◇1	1	◇1	◇1	◇1	◇1	◇1	◇1	1	◇1	◇1	◇1	◇1	◇1	◇1	1
						A							A							A			
		⊠	T	T	T	T	T	T		⊠	T	T	T	T	T		⊠	T	T	T	T	T	
Aberdeen	d																						
Stonehaven	d																						
Montrose	d																						
Arbroath	d																						
Dundee	d																						
Leuchars [3]	d																						
Cupar	d																						
Ladybank	d																						
Markinch	d																						
Kirkcaldy	d																						
Inverkeithing	d																						
Glasgow Central [15]	d									05 50													
Motherwell	d									06 04													
Haymarket	d																						
Edinburgh [10]	d																06 52		06 06		07 00		
Haymarket	d																06 56						
Lockerbie	d																						
Carlisle [8]	d									07 04							08 07						
Penrith North Lakes	d									07 19							08 22						
Oxenholme Lake District	d									07 42													
Lancaster [6]	d	06 58								07 57							08 57						
Preston [8]	d	07 17								08 17							09 17						
Wigan North Western	d	07 28								08 28							09 28						
Warrington Bank Quay	d	07 39								08 39							09 39						
M'chester Piccadilly [10]	d		07 26					08 07			08 27				09 07			09 27				10 07	
Stockport	d		07 35					08 16			08 35				09 16			09 35				10 16	
Wilmslow	d																						
Crewe [10]	d	08 01								09 01							10 01						
Macclesfield	d		07 49								08 49							09 49					
Congleton	d																						
Stoke-on-Trent	d		08 07					08 44			09 07				09 44			10 07				10 44	
Stafford	d		08 25					09 03			09 25				10 03			10 25				11 02	
Wolverhampton [7]	d	08 32	08 41					09 16		09 32	09 41				10 17		10 32	10 41				11 16	
Dunbar	d																						
Berwick-upon-Tweed	d																		06 46		07 39		
Alnmouth for Alnwick	d																		07 08		07 59		
Morpeth	d																				08 13		
Newcastle [8]	d						06 22					06 44		07 25					07 41		08 34		
Chester-le-Street	d																						
Durham	d						06 37					06 56		07 37					07 55		08 46		
Darlington [7]	d						06 54					07 14		07 54					08 12		09 04		
York [8]	d			06 32	06 32		07 23					07 44		08 24					08 44		09 35		
Leeds [10]	d			07 05	07 05							08 11							09 11				
Wakefield Westgate [7]	d			07 18	07 18							08 23							09 24				
Doncaster [7]	d						07 55							08 50							09 58		
Sheffield [7]	d			07 53	07 53		08 20					08 54		09 23					09 54		10 23		
Chesterfield	d			08 06	08 06		08 32					09 06							10 06				
Nottingham [8]	d					08 08			08 37				09 11			09 37				10 11			10 37
Derby [6]	d			08 28	08 28	08 36	08 54		09 06			09 27	09 36	09 53		10 06			10 28	10 37	10 53		11 06
Burton-on-Trent	d			08 38	08 38	08 49			09 18			09 38	09 49			10 18				10 49			11 18
Tamworth	d			08 49	08 49	09 01			09 30				10 01			10 30			10 48	11 01			11 30
Birmingham New Street [12]	a	08 55	08 58	09 09	09 09	09 24	09 27	09 39	09 53	09 55	09 58	10 07	10 24	10 27	10 39	10 53	10 55	10 58	11 10	11 24	11 27	11 32	11 53
Birmingham New Street [12]	d		09 03	09 12	09 12	09 30	09 33	09 42			10 03	10 12	10 30	10 33	10 42			11 03	11 12	11 30	11 33	11 42	
Cheltenham Spa	a			09 51	09 51	10 10		10 23				10 50	11 10		11 23				11 51	12 10		12 23	
Gloucester [7]	a					10 22							11 22							12 22			
Bristol Parkway [7]	a			10 25	10 26			10 55				11 26			11 55				12 28			12 55	
Bristol Temple Meads [10]	a			10 41	10 41			11 12				11 38			12 08				12 41			13 10	
Newport (South Wales)	a					11 11							12 10							13 11			
Cardiff Central [7]	a					11 27							12 28							13 29			
Weston-super-Mare	a							11 32															
Taunton	a			11 16	11 16			12 00				12 15							13 16				
Tiverton Parkway	a			11 29	11 29			12 13				12 28							13 29				
Exeter St Davids [6]	a			11 46	11 46			12 30				12 43							13 46				
Dawlish	a							12 43															
Teignmouth	a							12 48															
Newton Abbot	a			12 07	12 07			12 55				13 03							14 07				
Torquay	a							13 06															
Paignton	a							13 14															
Totnes	a			12 21	12 21							13 16							14 21				
Plymouth	a			12 50	12 50							13 43							14 50				
Liskeard [6]	a																						
Bodmin Parkway	a																						
Lostwithiel	a																						
Par	a																						
St Austell	a																						
Truro	a																						
Redruth	a																						
Camborne	a																						
Hayle	a																						
St Erth	a																						
Penzance	a																						
Birmingham International ✈	d		09 14								10 14							11 14					
Coventry	d		09 25								10 25							11 25					
Leamington Spa [8]	d		09 38				10 00				10 38			11 00				11 38			12 00		
Banbury	a		09 54				10 17				10 54			11 17				11 54			12 17		
Oxford	a		10 14				10 41				11 14			11 40				12 14			12 40		
Reading [7]	a		10 39				11 08				11 39			12 10				12 39			13 08		
Guildford	a																						
Basingstoke	a		11 08								12 08			12 39				13 08					
Winchester	a		11 24								12 24			12 54				13 24					
Southampton Airport Pkway ✈	a		11 32								12 32			13 08				13 32					
Southampton Central	a		11 43								12 41			13 17				13 41					
Brockenhurst [3]	a		11 58								12 56							13 56					
Bournemouth	a		12 12								13 10							14 10					

A T to Gloucester

Scotland, The North East, North West England - The South West and South Coast

	VT ◇[1] ⊠		XC ◇[1] 🛒	XC ◇[1] A 🛒	XC ◇[1] B 🛒	XC ◇[1] 🛒	XC ◇[1] 🛒	XC [1] 🛒	VT ◇[1] ⊠	XC ◇[1] 🛒	XC ◇[1] A 🛒		XC ◇[1] C 🛒	XC ◇[1] 🛒	XC ◇[1] 🛒	XC [1] 🛒	VT ◇[1] ☕	XC ◇[1] 🛒	XC ◇[1] A 🛒	XC ◇[1] C 🛒	XC ◇[1] 🛒		XC ◇[1] 🛒	XC [1] 🛒
Aberdeen d																								
Stonehaven d																								
Montrose d																								
Arbroath d																								
Dundee d											06 32													
Leuchars [3] d											06 46													
Cupar d											06 54													
Ladybank d											07 03													
Markinch d											07 11													
Kirkcaldy d											07 21													
Inverkeithing d											07 42													
Glasgow Central [15] d	08 00			06 01													10 00		07 50					
Motherwell d				06 16															08 05					
Haymarket d				06 57							08 01								08 50					
Edinburgh [10] d				07 07					08 52		08 10								09 08					
Haymarket d									08 57															
Lockerbie d																								
Carlisle [8] d	09 10								10 07								11 11							
Penrith North Lakes d																	11 26							
Oxenholme Lake District d									10 42															
Lancaster [6] d	09 57								10 57															
Preston [8] d	10 17								11 17								12 17							
Wigan North Western d	10 28								11 28								12 28							
Warrington Bank Quay d	10 39								11 39								12 39							
M'chester Piccadilly [10] d			10 27				11 07			11 27					12 07			12 27					13 07	
Stockport d			10 35				11 16			11 35					12 16			12 35					13 16	
Wilmslow d																								
Crewe [10] d	11 01								12 01								13 01							
Macclesfield d			10 49							11 49								12 49						
Congleton d																								
Stoke-on-Trent d			11 07				11 44			12 07					12 44			13 07					13 44	
Stafford d			11 25				12 03			12 25								13 25					14 02	
Wolverhampton [7] d	11 32		11 41				12 17		12 32	12 41					13 14		13 32	13 41					14 16	
Dunbar d				07 27															09 28					
Berwick-upon-Tweed d											08 50								09 51					
Alnmouth for Alnwick d																								
Morpeth d																								
Newcastle [8] d				08 43		09 35					09 41			10 35					10 43		11 35			
Chester-le-Street d																								
Durham d				08 56		09 47					09 55			10 47					10 55		11 47			
Darlington [7] d				09 13		10 05					10 12			11 04					11 12		12 05			
York [8] d				09 44		10 34					10 44			11 34					11 44		12 34			
Leeds [10] d				10 11							11 11								12 12					
Wakefield Westgate [7] d				10 23							11 24								12 24					
Doncaster [7] d						10 58								11 58							12 59			
Sheffield [7] d				10 54		11 23					11 54			12 23					12 54		13 23			
Chesterfield d				11 06							12 06								13 06					
Nottingham [8] d					11 08			11 37					12 08			12 37				13 11				13 37
Derby [6] d				11 27	11 36	11 53		12 06			12 28		12 36	12 53		13 06			13 28	13 36	13 53			14 06
Burton-on-Trent d					11 49			12 18					12 49			13 18			13 39	13 49				14 18
Tamworth d					12 01			12 30			12 48		13 01			13 30				14 01				14 30
Birmingham New Street [12] a	11 55		11 58	12 07	12 24	12 27	12 39	12 53	12 55	12 58	13 10		13 24	13 27	13 31	13 53	13 55	13 58	14 07	14 24	14 27		14 32	14 53
Birmingham New Street [12] d			12 03	12 12	12 30	12 33	12 42			13 03	13 12		13 30	13 33	13 42			14 03	14 12	14 30	14 33		14 42	
Cheltenham Spa a				12 50	13 10		13 23				13 55		14 10		14 23				14 50	15 10			15 23	
Gloucester [7] a					13 22								14 22							15 22				
Bristol Parkway [7] a				13 25			13 57				14 27				14 56				15 25				15 56	
Bristol Temple Meads [10] a				13 39			14 09				14 41				15 10				15 40				16 08	
Newport (South Wales) a					14 09								15 11							16 10				
Cardiff Central [7] a					14 27								15 29							16 29				
Weston-super-Mare a																								
Taunton a				14 15							15 16				15 44				16 15					
Tiverton Parkway a				14 28							15 29				15 57				16 28					
Exeter St Davids [6] a				14 43							15 46				16 13				16 43					
Dawlish a																								
Teignmouth a																								
Newton Abbot a				15 03							16 07								17 03					
Torquay a																								
Paignton a																								
Totnes a				15 16							16 21								17 16					
Plymouth a				15 43							16 50								17 43					
Liskeard [6] a																								
Bodmin Parkway a																								
Lostwithiel a																								
Par a																								
St Austell a																								
Truro a																								
Redruth a																								
Camborne a																								
Hayle a																								
St Erth a																								
Penzance a																								
Birmingham International ✈ d			12 14							13 14								14 14						
Coventry d			12 25							13 25								14 25						
Leamington Spa [8] d			12 38			13 00				13 38				14 00				14 38			15 00			
Banbury a			12 54			13 20				13 54				14 17				14 54			15 17			
Oxford a			13 14			13 40				14 14				14 40				15 14			15 42			
Reading [7] a			13 39			14 10				14 39				15 08				15 39			16 10			
Guildford a																								
Basingstoke a			14 08			14 39				15 08								16 08			16 39			
Winchester a			14 24			14 54				15 24								16 24			16 59			
Southampton Airport Pkway ✈ a			14 34			15 09				15 32								16 32						
Southampton Central ⛴ a			14 42			15 17				15 41								16 41			17 17			
Brockenhurst [3] a			14 56							15 56								16 56						
Bournemouth a			15 11							16 10								17 10						

A 🛒 from Edinburgh

B 🛒 to Gloucester

C 🛒 from Birmingham New Street to Gloucester

Scotland, The North East, North West England - The South West and South Coast

		VT	XC	XC	XC	XC	XC	XC	VT	XC	XC	XC	XC	XC	XC	VT	XC	XC	XC	XC	XC	XC	VT
		◇1	◇1	◇1	◇1	◇1	◇1	1	◇1	◇1	◇1	◇1	◇1	◇1	1	◇1	◇1	◇1	◇1	◇1	◇1	1	◇1
		A		B	C						B							B					
		⊠	🛒	🛒	🛒	🛒	🛒	🛒	☕	🛒	🛒		🛒	🛒	🛒	☕	🛒	🛒		🛒	🛒	🛒	☕
Aberdeen	d										08 20												
Stonehaven	d										08 38												
Montrose	d										08 59												
Arbroath	d										09 15												
Dundee	d										09 32												
Leuchars 3	d										09 47												
Cupar	d										09 54												
Ladybank	d										10 01												
Markinch	d										10 09												
Kirkcaldy	d										10 17												
Inverkeithing	d										10 32												
Glasgow Central 15	d			09 00					12 00									10 59					14 00
Motherwell	d			09 15														11 14					
Haymarket	d			09 58							10 54							11 57					
Edinburgh 10	d	10 51		10 10							11 05					12 51		12 08					
Haymarket	d	10 57														12 57							
Lockerbie	d																						
Carlisle 8	d	12 07							13 09							14 07							15 09
Penrith North Lakes	d															14 22							
Oxenholme Lake District	d	12 43																					15 44
Lancaster 6	d	12 57							13 58							14 57							
Preston 8	d	13 17							14 17							15 17							16 17
Wigan North Western	d	13 28							14 28							15 28							16 28
Warrington Bank Quay	d	13 39							14 39							15 39							16 39
M'chester Piccadilly 10 🚋	d		13 27				14 07			14 27				15 07			15 27				16 07		
Stockport	d		13 35				14 16			14 35				15 16			15 35				16 16		
Wilmslow	d																						
Crewe 10	d	14 01							15 01							16 01							17 01
Macclesfield	d		13 49							14 49							15 49						
Congleton	d																						
Stoke-on-Trent	d		14 07				14 44			15 07				15 44			16 07				16 44		
Stafford	d		14 25				15 03			15 25				16 03			16 25				17 03		
Wolverhampton 7 🚋	d	14 32	14 41				15 17		15 32	15 41				16 17		16 32	16 41				17 16		17 32
Dunbar	d										11 25												
Berwick-upon-Tweed	d			10 49							11 48							12 47					
Alnmouth for Alnwick	d										12 08												
Morpeth	d			11 21																			
Newcastle 8	d			11 44		12 35					12 41		13 35					13 41		14 33			
Chester-le-Street	d																						
Durham	d			11 56		12 47					12 53		13 47					13 53		14 48			
Darlington 7	d			12 13		13 04					13 11		14 05					14 11		15 05			
York 8	d			12 44		13 34					13 44		14 34					14 44		15 34			
Leeds 10	d			13 11							14 11							15 11					
Wakefield Westgate 7	d			13 23							14 23							15 23					
Doncaster 7	d					13 58							14 58							15 58			
Sheffield 7 🚋	d			13 54		14 23					14 54		15 23					15 54		16 23			
Chesterfield	d			14 07							15 06							16 06					
Nottingham 8 🚋	d				14 08			14 37				15 11			15 37				16 08			16 37	
Derby 6	d			14 29	14 36	14 53		15 06			15 28	15 36	15 53		16 06			16 28	16 36	16 53		17 06	
Burton-on-Trent	d				14 49			15 18			15 40	15 49			16 18				16 49			17 18	
Tamworth	d			14 49	15 01			15 30				16 01			16 30			16 48	17 01			17 30	
Birmingham New Street 12	a	14 55	14 58	15 07	15 24	15 27	15 39	15 53	15 55	15 58	16 04	16 24	16 27	16 39	16 53	16 55	16 58	17 09	17 25	17 28	17 39	17 53	17 55
Birmingham New Street 12	d		15 03	15 12	15 30	15 33	15 42			16 03	16 12	16 30	16 33	16 42			17 03	17 12	17 30	17 33	17 42		
Cheltenham Spa	a			15 51	16 10		16 23				16 51	17 13		17 23				17 50	18 18		18 23		
Gloucester 7	a				16 22							17 26							18 29				
Bristol Parkway 7	a			16 27			16 56				17 25			17 58				18 27			18 55		
Bristol Temple Meads 10	a			16 42			17 11				17 40			18 10				18 40			19 07		
Newport (South Wales)	a				17 11							18 10							19 16				
Cardiff Central 7	a				17 28							18 27							19 33				
Weston-super-Mare	a																						
Taunton	a			17 16			17 45				18 16							19 15					
Tiverton Parkway	a			17 29			17 57				18 29							19 28					
Exeter St Davids 6	a			17 44			18 13				18 44							19 43					
Dawlish	a						18 26																
Teignmouth	a						18 31																
Newton Abbot	a			18 11			18 38				19 06							20 04					
Torquay	a						18 49																
Paignton	a						18 57																
Totnes	a			18 24							19 19							20 17					
Plymouth	a			18 52							19 45							20 45					
Liskeard 6	a			19 23							20 11							21 13					
Bodmin Parkway	a			19 35							20 23							21 25					
Lostwithiel	a																	21 31					
Par	a			19 46							20 35							21 39					
St Austell	a			19 53							20 41							21 45					
Truro	a			20 10							21 00							22 03					
Redruth	a			20 25							21 15							22 14					
Camborne	a			20 32							21 22							22 21					
Hayle	a																	22 29					
St Erth	a			20 42							21 33							22 34					
Penzance	a			20 52							21 42							22 43					
Birmingham International ✈	d		15 14							16 14							17 14						
Coventry	d		15 25							16 25							17 25						
Leamington Spa 8	d		15 38			16 00				16 38			17 00				17 38			18 00			
Banbury	a		15 54			16 17				16 54			17 17				17 54			18 18			
Oxford	a		16 14			16 40				17 14			17 41				18 14			18 40			
Reading 7	a		16 39			17 08				17 39			18 10				18 39			19 08			
Guildford	a																						
Basingstoke	a		17 08							18 08			18 47				19 08						
Winchester	a		17 24							18 24							19 24						
Southampton Airport Pkway ✈	a		17 32							18 32							19 32						
Southampton Central ⛴	a		17 41							18 44			19 53				19 41						
Brockenhurst 3	a		17 56							18 58							19 56						
Bournemouth	a		18 15							19 13							20 12						

A until 15 July, from 12 September

B 🛒 from Edinburgh to Totnes

C 🛒 to Gloucester

Table 51

Scotland, The North East, North West England - The South West and South Coast

		XC	XC FO	XC FX	XC	XC	XC	XC	VT	XC	XC	XC FX	XC FO	XC	XC	XC	VT	XC	XC	XC	XC FO	XC FX
		◇1	◇1	◇1	◇1	◇1	◇1	1	B 1	◇1	◇1	◇1	◇1	◇1	◇1	1	◇1	◇1	◇1	◇1	◇1	◇1
							A		B	C	D				A			E	F	G		
		🚲	🚲	🚲		🚲	🚲	🚲	🛒	🚲	🚲			🚲	🚲	🚲	🛒	🚲	🚲	🚲		
Aberdeen	d																					
Stonehaven	d																					
Montrose	d																					
Arbroath	d																					
Dundee	d																					
Leuchars 3	d																					
Cupar	d																					
Ladybank	d																					
Markinch	d																					
Kirkcaldy	d																					
Inverkeithing	d																					
Glasgow Central 15	d										12 51						16 00					
Motherwell	d										13 06											
Haymarket	d																					
Edinburgh 10	d		13 06	13 06					14 51		14 08								15 08	15 08		
Haymarket	d								14 57													
Lockerbie	d																					
Carlisle 8	d								16 07								17 09					
Penrith North Lakes	d								16 21													
Oxenholme Lake District	d																17 44					
Lancaster 6	d								16 57													
Preston 8	d								17 17								18 17					
Wigan North Western	d								17 28								18 28					
Warrington Bank Quay	d								17 39								18 39					
M'chester Piccadilly 10	d	16 27					17 06			17 27					18 05			18 27				
Stockport	d	16 35								17 35					18 13			18 35				
Wilmslow	d									17 44												
Crewe 10	d								18 01	18 07							19 01					
Macclesfield	d	16 49					17 27								18 26							
Congleton	d																	18 54				
Stoke-on-Trent	d	17 07					17 44								18 44			19 07				
Stafford	d	17 25					18 04			18 28					19 02			19 25				
Wolverhampton 7	d	17 41					18 16		18 32	18 41					19 16		19 32	19 41				
Dunbar	d		13 28	13 28															15 28	15 28		
Berwick-upon-Tweed	d										14 49											
Alnmouth for Alnwick	d		14 08	14 08																		
Morpeth	d																					
Newcastle 8	d		14 42	14 42		15 03					15 41			16 35					16 42	16 42		
Chester-le-Street	d																					
Durham	d		14 52	14 52		15 16					15 53			16 47					16 52	16 52		
Darlington 7	d		15 12	15 12		15 33					16 10			17 04					17 10	17 10		
York 8	d		15 44	15 44		16 04					16 44			17 34					17 44	17 44		
Leeds 10	d		16 11	16 11		16 38					17 11								18 11	18 11		
Wakefield Westgate 7	d		16 23	16 23		16 50					17 23								18 23	18 23		
Doncaster 7	d													17 59								
Sheffield 7	d		16 54	16 54		17 23					17 54			18 23					18 54	18 54		
Chesterfield	d		17 06	17 06							18 07								19 06	19 06		
Nottingham 8	d				17 08			17 37				18 08	18 08			18 37					19 08	19 08
Derby 6	d		17 28	17 28	17 36	17 53		18 06			18 28	18 37	18 37	18 53		19 06			19 27	19 27	19 36	19 36
Burton-on-Trent	d		17 38	17 38	17 49			18 18				18 49	18 49			19 18			19 38	19 38	19 49	19 49
Tamworth	d				18 01			18 30			18 49	19 01	19 01			19 30					20 01	20 01
Birmingham New Street 12	a	17 58	18 08	18 07	18 25	18 28	18 38	18 54	18 55	18 58	19 09	19 24	19 24	19 28	19 32	19 53	19 55	19 58	20 09	20 09	20 24	20 24
Birmingham New Street 12	d	18 03	18 12	18 12	18 30	18 33	18 42			19 03	19 12	19 30	19 30	19 33	19 42			20 03	20 12	20 12	20 30	20 30
Cheltenham Spa	a		18 50	18 50	19 13		19 23				19 51	20 10	20 10		20 23				20 51	20 51	21 10	21 10
Gloucester 7	a				19 27							20 22	20 22								21 22	21 22
Bristol Parkway 7	a		19 27	19 27			19 56				20 27				20 56				21 25	21 25		
Bristol Temple Meads 10	a		19 39	19 39			20 10				20 41				21 08				21 38	21 38		
Newport (South Wales)	a				20 11		20 47					21 11	21 11								22 15	22 15
Cardiff Central 7	a				20 27		21 02					21 27	21 29								22 31	22 35
Weston-super-Mare	a																					
Taunton	a		20 16	20 16							21 16				21 44				22 15	22 15		
Tiverton Parkway	a		20 29	20 29							21 29				21 57				22 28	22 50		
Exeter St Davids 6	a		20 44	20 44							21 44				22 11				22 44	23 04		
Dawlish	a																					
Teignmouth	a																					
Newton Abbot	a		21 03	21 03							22 04				22 30				23 04	23 24		
Torquay	a																					
Paignton	a																					
Totnes	a		21 17	21 17							22 17				22 43				23 17	23 37		
Plymouth	a		21 44	21 44							22 45				23 15				23 44	00 03		
Liskeard 6	a																					
Bodmin Parkway	a																					
Lostwithiel	a																					
Par	a																					
St Austell	a																					
Truro	a																					
Redruth	a																					
Camborne	a																					
Hayle	a																					
St Erth	a																					
Penzance	a																					
Birmingham International ✈	d	18 14								19 14								20 14				
Coventry	d	18 25								19 25								20 25				
Leamington Spa 8	d	18 38				19 00				19 38				20 05				20 38				
Banbury	a	18 54				19 17				19 54				20 22				20 54				
Oxford	a	19 14				19 41				20 14				20 41				21 14				
Reading 7	a	19 39				20 08				20 39				21 07				21 40				
Guildford	a																					
Basingstoke	a	20 09								21 09								22 09				
Winchester	a	20 24								21 24								22 24				
Southampton Airport Pkway ✈	a	20 32								21 32								22 32				
Southampton Central ⛴	a	20 41								21 41								22 42				
Brockenhurst 3	a	20 58								21 56								22 56				
Bournemouth	a	21 15								22 16								23 21				

A 🚲 to Bristol Parkway
B until 15 July, from 12 September
C 🚲 to Oxford
D 🚲 from Edinburgh to Bristol Parkway
E 🚲 to Wolverhampton
F until 29 July, from 12 September. 🚲 to Bristol Parkway
G from 1 August until 9 September. 🚲 to Bristol Parkway

Scotland, The North East, North West England - The South West and South Coast

		XC	XC	LM	XC	VT	XC	XC	XC	XC		VT	XC	XC	XC	XC	XC	XC	VT	XC		XC	XC	XC
		◇1	◇1	◇1	1	1	◇1	◇1	◇1	◇1		◇1	1	◇1	◇1	◇1	◇1	◇1	◇1	◇1		1	◇1	◇1
		A	B				B	C								D	E	F					G	
		🛒	🛒			🍽	🛒	🛒		🛒		🍽				🛒	🛒	🛒	🍽				🛒	
Aberdeen	d																							
Stonehaven	d																							
Montrose	d																							
Arbroath	d																							
Dundee	d																							
Leuchars 3	d																							
Cupar	d																							
Ladybank	d																							
Markinch	d																							
Kirkcaldy	d																							
Inverkeithing	d																							
Glasgow Central 15	d							15 00				17 40											16 52	
Motherwell	d							15 14															17 14	
Haymarket	d							15 56															17 54	
Edinburgh 10	d					16 52		16 05								17 08	17 08		18 52				18 04	
Haymarket	d					16 56													18 57					
Lockerbie	d											18 33												
Carlisle 8	d					18 07						18 54							20 08					
Penrith North Lakes	d											19 09												
Oxenholme Lake District	d					18 42						19 32							20 42					
Lancaster 6	d					18 57						19 47							20 57					
Preston 8	d					19 16						20 08							21 17					
Wigan North Western	d					19 29						20 19							21 28					
Warrington Bank Quay	d					19 39						20 31							21 39					
M'chester Piccadilly 10	d		19 07				19 27		20 07					20 27						21 27				22 07
Stockport	d		19 16				19 35		20 16					20 35						21 35				22 16
Wilmslow	d																							
Crewe 10	d			19 55		20 01						20 53							22 01					
Macclesfield	d						19 49							20 49						21 49				22 29
Congleton	d																							
Stoke-on-Trent	d		19 44				20 07		20 44					21 07						22 08				22 47
Stafford	d		20 04	20 16			20 26		21 03			21 13		21 25						22 26				23 07
Wolverhampton 7	d		20 17	20 29		20 34	20 43		21 16			21 32		21 41					22 32	22 41				23 21
Dunbar	d															17 28	17 28						18 25	
Berwick-upon-Tweed	d															17 51	17 51						18 48	
Alnmouth for Alnwick	d							17 03															19 08	
Morpeth	d							17 18																
Newcastle 8	d	17 32						17 41		18 35						18 41	18 41	19 33					19 40	
Chester-le-Street	d	17 41																						
Durham	d	17 48						17 53		18 47						18 53	18 53	19 48					19 53	
Darlington 7	d	18 05						18 10		19 05						19 10	19 10	20 05					20 10	
York 8	d	18 34						18 45		19 34						19 44	19 44	20 34					20 44	
Leeds 10	d							19 11								20 11	20 11						21 11	
Wakefield Westgate 7	d							19 23								20 23	20 23						21 23	
Doncaster 7	d	18 58								19 58								21 02						
Sheffield 7	d	19 23						19 54		20 23						20 54	20 54	21 28					22 00	
Chesterfield	d							20 06								21 06	21 06	21 41					22 24	
Nottingham 8	d				19 37								20 37									21 37		
Derby 6	d	19 54			20 06			20 28		20 54			21 06			21 28	21 28	22 02				22 10	22 46	
Burton-on-Trent	d				20 18								21 19			21 39	21 39					22 21	22 56	
Tamworth	d				20 30			20 48					21 31			21 51	21 50					22 33	23 07	
Birmingham New Street 12	a	20 27	20 33	20 47	20 54	20 55	21 00	21 07	21 32	21 35		21 48	21 55	22 00		22 09	22 09	22 51	22 55	22 58		23 02	23 27	23 39
Birmingham New Street 12	d	20 33	20 42				21 03	21 12							22 03	22 12	22 12							
Cheltenham Spa	a		21 25					21 51								22 51	23 29							
Gloucester 7	a							22 02																
Bristol Parkway 7	a		22 01					22 32								23 23	00 02							
Bristol Temple Meads 10	a		22 14					22 45								23 40	00 14							
Newport (South Wales)	a																							
Cardiff Central 7	a																							
Weston-super-Mare	a																							
Taunton	a																							
Tiverton Parkway	a																							
Exeter St Davids 6	a																							
Dawlish	a																							
Teignmouth	a																							
Newton Abbot	a																							
Torquay	a																							
Paignton	a																							
Totnes	a																							
Plymouth	a																							
Liskeard 6	a																							
Bodmin Parkway	a																							
Lostwithiel	a																							
Par	a																							
St Austell	a																							
Truro	a																							
Redruth	a																							
Camborne	a																							
Hayle	a																							
St Erth	a																							
Penzance	a																							
Birmingham International ✈	d						21 14								22 14									
Coventry	d						21 25								22 25									
Leamington Spa 8	d	21 00					21 38								22 38									
Banbury	a	21 17					21 54								22 54									
Oxford	a	21 40					22 14								23 14									
Reading 7	a	22 16					22 41								23 52									
Guildford	a	22 59																						
Basingstoke	a						23 06																	
Winchester	a						23 24																	
Southampton Airport Pkway ✈	a						23 36																	
Southampton Central	a						23 43																	
Brockenhurst 3	a																							
Bournemouth	a																							

A 🛒 to Derby
B 🛒 to Wolverhampton
C 🛒 from Edinburgh to Tamworth
D from 20 June. 🛒 to York
E until 17 June. 🛒 to York
F 🛒 to Darlington
G 🛒 from Edinburgh to York

Table 51

Saturdays

Scotland, The North East, North West England - The South West and South Coast

Station		XC ◇1 A	XC ◇1 B	XC ◇1	XC ◇1	XC ◇1	XC ◇1	XC ◇1	XC ◇1	XC ◇1 C	XC ◇1 D	XC ◇1 E	XC ◇1 F	XC ◇1	VT ◇1	XC ◇1 G	XC ◇1 F	XC ◇1 E	XC ◇1 D	VT ◇1	XC ◇1	XC ◇1 E	XC ◇1 F
Aberdeen	d																						
Stonehaven	d																						
Montrose	d																						
Arbroath	d																						
Dundee	d																						
Leuchars [8]	d																						
Cupar	d																						
Ladybank	d																						
Markinch	d																						
Kirkcaldy	d																						
Inverkeithing	d																						
Glasgow Central [15]	d																						
Motherwell	d																						
Haymarket	d																						
Edinburgh [10]	d	15p08	17p08																				
Haymarket	d																						
Lockerbie	d																						
Carlisle [8]	d																						
Penrith North Lakes	d																						
Oxenholme Lake District	d																						
Lancaster [6]	d																						
Preston [8]	d														06 17								
Wigan North Western	d														06 28								
Warrington Bank Quay	d														06 39								
M'chester Piccadilly [10]	d								05 11					06 00								07 07	07 07
Stockport	d													06 08								07 16	07 16
Wilmslow	d																						
Crewe [10]	d								05 47						07 01								
Macclesfield	d													06 21									
Congleton	d																						
Stoke-on-Trent	d								06 08					06 39								07 44	07 44
Stafford	d								06 26					06 58								08 03	08 03
Wolverhampton [7]	d								06 41					07 15	07 32					08 06		08 18	08 18
Dunbar	d	15p28	17p28																				
Berwick-upon-Tweed	d		17p51																				
Alnmouth for Alnwick	d																						
Morpeth	d																						
Newcastle [8]	d	16p42	18p41																				
Chester-le-Street	d																						
Durham	d	16p52	18p53																				
Darlington [7]	d	17p10	19p10																				
York [8]	d	17p44	19p44																				
Leeds [10]	d	18p11	20p11														06 00	06 00			06 15		
Wakefield Westgate [7]	d	18p23	20p23														06 12	06 12			06 29		
Doncaster [7]	d																				06 47		
Sheffield [7]	d	18p54	20p54									05 45					06 50	06 50			07 18		
Chesterfield	d	19p06	21p06									05 57					07 03	07 03			07 30		
Nottingham [8]	d										05 57					06 37			06 56				
Derby [6]	d	19p27	21p28							06 10	06 36	06 46	06 47			07 06	07 25	07 25	07 36		07 51		
Burton-on-Trent	d	19p38	21p39							06 21	06 48	06 57	06 58			07 18	07 36	07 36	07 49		08 01		
Tamworth	d		21p50							06 32	07 00	07 08	07 09			07 30	07 48	07 48	08 01		08 12		
Birmingham New Street [12]	a	20p09	22p09						06 57	06 50	07 24	07 27	07 27	07 31	07 55	07 55	08 08	08 08	08 24	08 24	08 29	08 39	08 38
Birmingham New Street [12]	d	20p12	22p12	05 00	05 42	06 03	06 33	06 42	07 03	07 12	07 30	07 33	07 33	07 42		08 03	08 12	08 12	08 30	08 30	08 33	08 42	08 42
Cheltenham Spa	a	20p51	23p29	06 02	06 41			07 23		07 50	08 10			08 23			08 51	08 51	09 10			09 22	09 23
Gloucester [7]	a			06 13	06 54						08 22								09 22				
Bristol Parkway [7]	a	21p25	00 02					07 55		08 24				08 55			09 24	09 24				09 55	09 55
Bristol Temple Meads [10]	a	21p38	00 14					08 07		08 38				09 08			09 38	09 38				10 11	10 07
Newport (South Wales)	a			07 06	07 52						09 07								10 07				
Cardiff Central [7]	a			07 22	08 08						09 23								10 23				
Weston-super-Mare	a																						
Taunton	a	22p15						08 42		09 15							10 17	10 17				10 59	
Tiverton Parkway	a	22p50						08 54		09 28							10 30	10 30				11 12	
Exeter St Davids [6]	a	23p04						09 10		09 43							10 46	10 46				11 26	
Dawlish	a																	10 59					
Teignmouth	a																	11 06					
Newton Abbot	a	23p24								10 03							11 08	11 15				11 49	
Torquay	a							09 38										11 26					
Paignton	a							09 46										11 36					
Totnes	a	23p37								10 16							11 22					12 04	
Plymouth	a	00 03								10 44							11 51					12 34	
Liskeard [6]	a																					13 03	
Bodmin Parkway	a																					13 18	
Lostwithiel	a																						
Par	a																					13 32	
St Austell	a																						
Truro	a																						
Redruth	a																						
Camborne	a																						
Hayle	a																						
St Erth	a																						
Penzance	a																						
Birmingham International ✈	d					06 14			07 14							08 14				08 40			
Coventry	d					06 25			07 25							08 25				08 51			
Leamington Spa [8]	d					06 38	07 00		07 38			08 00	08 00			08 38					09 00		
Banbury	a					06 54	07 17		07 54			08 17	08 17			08 54					09 17		
Oxford	a					07 14	07 40		08 14			08 40	08 40			09 14					09 40		
Reading [7]	a					07 39	08 06		08 39			09 08	09 08			09 39					10 09		
Guildford	a																						
Basingstoke	a					08 08	08 40		09 08							10 08					10 39		
Winchester	a					08 24	08 55		09 24							10 24					10 54		
Southampton Airport Pkway ✈	a					08 32	09 08		09 32							10 32					11 08		
Southampton Central	a					08 41	09 17		09 40							10 43					11 17		
Brockenhurst [3]	a					08 56			09 57							10 58							
Bournemouth	a					09 14			10 11							11 12							

A from 6 August until 10 September. 🍴 to Bristol Parkway
B until 18 June. 🍴 to York
C 🍴 from Birmingham New Street
D 🍴 from Birmingham New Street to Gloucester
E until 10 September
F from 17 September
G 🍴 from Derby

Table 51

Saturdays

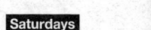

Scotland, The North East, North West England - The South West and South Coast

		XC	VT	XC	XC	XC	XC	XC	XC	VT	XC	XC	XC	XC	XC	XC	XC	VT	XC	XC	XC	XC	XC
		1	◇1	◇1	◇1	◇1	◇1	◇1	1	◇1	◇1	◇1	◇1	◇1	◇1	◇1	1	◇1	◇1	◇1	◇1	◇1	◇1
						A						B	C	A							A		
			☕	🛒	🛒	🛒	🛒	🛒		☕	🛒	🛒	🛒	🛒	🛒	🛒		☕	🛒	🛒	🛒	🛒	🛒
Aberdeen	d																						
Stonehaven	d																						
Montrose	d																						
Arbroath	d																						
Dundee	d																						
Leuchars 8	d																						
Cupar	d																						
Ladybank	d																						
Markinch	d																						
Kirkcaldy	d																						
Inverkeithing	d																						
Glasgow Central 15	d									05 50													
Motherwell	d									06 04													
Haymarket	d																						
Edinburgh 10	d																	06 52		06 06		07 00	
Haymarket	d																	06 56					
Lockerbie	d																						
Carlisle 8	d									07 03								08 07					
Penrith North Lakes	d									07 18								08 22					
Oxenholme Lake District	d									07 42													
Lancaster 6	d		06 58							07 57								08 57					
Preston 8	d		07 17							08 17								09 17					
Wigan North Western	d		07 28							08 28								09 28					
Warrington Bank Quay	d		07 39							08 39								09 39					
M'chester Piccadilly 10 ⛴	d			07 27				08 07			08 27					09 07			09 27				10 07
Stockport	d			07 35				08 16			08 35					09 16			09 35				10 16
Wilmslow	d																						
Crewe 10	d		08 01							09 01								10 01					
Macclesfield	d			07 49							08 49								09 49				
Congleton	d																						
Stoke-on-Trent	d			08 07				08 44			09 07					09 44			10 07				10 44
Stafford	d			08 26				09 03			09 26					10 03			10 26				11 03
Wolverhampton 7 ⛴	d		08 32	08 41				09 17		09 32	09 41					10 17		10 32	10 41				11 17
Dunbar	d																						
Berwick-upon-Tweed	d																			06 48		07 40	
Alnmouth for Alnwick	d																			07 08		08 00	
Morpeth	d																					08 14	
Newcastle 8	d						06 22					06 45			07 30					07 44		08 36	
Chester-le-Street	d																						
Durham	d						06 37					06 57			07 43					07 56		08 48	
Darlington 7	d						06 54					07 14			08 02					08 13		09 05	
York 8	d				06 40		07 24					07 44	07 44		08 34					08 44		09 35	
Leeds 10	d				07 10							08 12	08 12							09 11			
Wakefield Westgate 7	d				07 23							08 24	08 24							09 24			
Doncaster 7	d						07 52								08 58							09 58	
Sheffield 7 ⛴	d				07 56		08 20					08 54	08 54		09 23					09 54		10 23	
Chesterfield	d				08 08		08 32					09 06	09 06							10 06			
Nottingham 8 ⛴	d	07 37				08 08			08 37					09 08			09 37				10 08		
Derby 6	d	08 06			08 29	08 36	08 53		09 06			09 28	09 30	09 36	09 53		10 06			10 28	10 37	10 53	
Burton-on-Trent	d	08 18			08 40	08 49			09 18			09 39	09 41	09 49			10 18				10 49		
Tamworth	d	08 30			08 51	09 01			09 30					10 01			10 30			10 49	11 01		
Birmingham New Street 12	a	08 53	08 55	08 58	09 09	09 24	09 29	09 39	09 53	09 55	09 58	10 07	10 08	10 24	10 27	10 39	10 53	10 55	10 58	11 07	11 24	11 27	11 39
Birmingham New Street 12	d			09 03	09 12	09 30	09 33	09 42			10 03	10 12	10 12	10 30	10 33	10 42			11 03	11 12	11 30	11 33	11 42
Cheltenham Spa	a				09 50	10 10		10 23				10 50	10 52	11 10		11 23				11 50	12 10		12 23
Gloucester 7	a					10 22								11 22							12 22		
Bristol Parkway 7	a				10 29			10 57				11 24	11 25			11 55				12 29			12 55
Bristol Temple Meads 10	a				10 42			11 10				11 38	11 39			12 08				12 42			13 07
Newport (South Wales)	a					11 08								12 07							13 11		
Cardiff Central 7	a					11 24								12 23							13 27		
Weston-super-Mare	a							11 31															
Taunton	a				11 15			11 59				12 15	12 15							13 15			
Tiverton Parkway	a				11 28			12 12				12 28	12 29							13 28			
Exeter St Davids 6	a				11 43			12 27				12 43	12 44							13 43			
Dawlish	a							12 40															
Teignmouth	a							12 45															
Newton Abbot	a				12 03			12 52				13 03	13 10							14 03			
Torquay	a							13 03															
Paignton	a							13 11															
Totnes	a				12 16							13 16	13 23							14 16			
Plymouth	a				12 44							13 44	13 50							14 44			
Liskeard 6	a												14 15										
Bodmin Parkway	a												14 27										
Lostwithiel	a												14 33										
Par	a												14 42										
St Austell	a												14 49										
Truro	a												15 08										
Redruth	a												15 20										
Camborne	a												15 27										
Hayle	a												15 36										
St Erth	a												15 41										
Penzance	a												15 52										
Birmingham International ✈	d			09 14							10 14								11 14				
Coventry	d			09 25							10 25								11 25				
Leamington Spa 8	d			09 38			10 00				10 38				11 00				11 38			12 00	
Banbury	a			09 54			10 17				10 54				11 17				11 54			12 17	
Oxford	a			10 14			10 40				11 14				11 40				12 14			12 40	
Reading 7	a			10 39			11 09				11 39				12 09				12 39			13 08	
Guildford	a																						
Basingstoke	a			11 08							12 08				12 40				13 08				
Winchester	a			11 24							12 24				12 55				13 24				
Southampton Airport Pkway ✈	a			11 32							12 32				13 08				13 32				
Southampton Central ⛴	a			11 41							12 41				13 17				13 41				
Brockenhurst 3	a			11 57							12 57								13 57				
Bournemouth	a			12 11							13 11								14 11				

A 🛒 to Gloucester

B from 17 September

C until 10 September. 🛒 to Totnes

Table 51

Saturdays

Scotland, The North East, North West England - The South West and South Coast

		XC	VT	XC	XC	XC	XC	XC	XC	XC	VT	XC	XC	XC	XC	XC	XC	XC	XC	VT	XC	XC
		■	◇■	◇■	◇■	◇■	◇■	◇■	◇■	■	◇■	◇■	◇■	◇■	◇■	◇■	◇■	◇■	■	◇■	◇■	◇■
					A	B	C						A	B	D		E	F				A
			⊡	⊼	⊼	⊼	⊼	⊼	⊼	⊼	⊡	⊼	⊼	⊼	⊼	⊼	⊼	⊼	⊼	⊡	⊼	⊼
Aberdeen	d																					
Stonehaven	d																					
Montrose	d																					
Arbroath	d																					
Dundee	d												06§32	06§32								
Leuchars ■	d												06§46	06§46								
Cupar	d												06§54	06§54								
Ladybank	d												07§03	07§03								
Markinch	d												07§11	07§11								
Kirkcaldy	d												07§21	07§21								
Inverkeithing	d												07§38	07§38								
Glasgow Central ■	d		08 00		06§01	06§01														10 00		07§50
Motherwell	d				06§16	06§16																08§05
Haymarket	d				06§54	06§57							07§56	07§56								08§50
Edinburgh ■	d				07§07	07§07					08 52		08§05	08§05								09§06
Haymarket	d										08 57											
Lockerbie	d																					
Carlisle ■	d		09 09								10 07									11 10		
Penrith North Lakes	d																			11 25		
Oxenholme Lake District	d										10 42											
Lancaster ■	d		09 57								10 57											
Preston ■	d		10 17								11 17									12 17		
Wigan North Western	d		10 28								11 28									12 28		
Warrington Bank Quay	d		10 39								11 39									12 39		
M'chester Piccadilly ■	d			10 27					11 07			11 27					12§07	12§07			12 27	
Stockport	d			10 35					11 16			11 35					12§16	12§16			12 35	
Wilmslow	d																					
Crewe ■	d		11 01								12 01									13 01		
Macclesfield	d			10 49								11 49									12 49	
Congleton	d																					
Stoke-on-Trent	d			11 07					11 44			12 07					12§44	12§44			13 07	
Stafford	d			11 26					12 03			12 25					13§03	13§03			13 26	
Wolverhampton ■	d		11 32	11 41					12 17		12 32	12 41					13§16	13§16		13 32	13 41	
Dunbar	d				07§27	07§28																09§26
Berwick-upon-Tweed	d												08§46	08§46								09§49
Alnmouth for Alnwick	d																					
Morpeth	d																					
Newcastle ■	d				08§45	08§44		09 35					09§41	09§41		10 35						10§44
Chester-le-Street	d																					
Durham	d				08§57	08§57		09 47					09§55	09§55		10 47						10§56
Darlington ■	d				09§14	09§14		10 05					10§12	10§12		11 04						11§13
York ■	d				09§46	09§46		10 34					10§45	10§45		11 34						11§45
Leeds ■	d				10§12	10§12							11§11	11§11								12§11
Wakefield Westgate ■	d				10§24	10§24							11§23	11§23								12§24
Doncaster ■	d							10 58								11 58						
Sheffield ■	d				10§54	10§54		11 23					11§54	11§54		12 23						12§54
Chesterfield	d				11§06	11§08							12§07	12§07								13§06
Nottingham ■	d	10 37					11 11			11 37					12 08				12 37			
Derby ■	d	11 06			11§27	11§30	11 36	11 55		12 06			12§29	12§29	12f37	12 53			13 06			13§28
Burton-on-Trent	d	11 18			11§38	11§41	11 49			12 18					12 49				13 18			13§39
Tamworth	d	11 30					12 01			12 30			12§49	12§49	13 01				13 30			
Birmingham New Street ■	a	11 53	11 55	11 58	12§07	12§08	12 24	12 29	12 39	12 53	12 55	12 58	13§09	13§10	13 24	13 27	13§39	13§39	13 53	13 55	13 58	14§07
Birmingham New Street ■	d			12 03	12§12	12§12	12 30	12 33	12 42			13 03	13§12	13§12	13 30	13 33	13§42	13§42			14 03	14§12
Cheltenham Spa	a				12§50	12§52	13 10		13 25				13§51	13§51	14 10		14§23	14§23				14§50
Gloucester ■	a						13 22								14 22							
Bristol Parkway ■	a				13§24	13§26			13 57				14§26	14§26			14§57	14§57				15§23
Bristol Temple Meads ■	a				13§38	13§40			14 09				14§41	14§41			15§10	15§10				15§37
Newport (South Wales)	a						14 08								15 11							
Cardiff Central ■	a						14 24								15 27							
Weston-super-Mare	a																					
Taunton	a				14§15	14§15							15§16	15§16			15§52	15§52				16§15
Tiverton Parkway	a				14§28	14§29							15§29	15§29			16§07	16§07				16§28
Exeter St Davids ■	a				14§43	14§45							15§46	15§46			16§26	16§23				16§43
Dawlish	a					15§04												16§40				
Teignmouth	a					15§10												16§46				
Newton Abbot	a				15§03	15§18							16§07	16§07				16§54				17§03
Torquay	a					15§30												17§06				
Paignton	a					15§40												17§15				
Totnes	a				15§16								16§21	16§21								17§16
Plymouth	a				15§44								16§50	16§48								17§44
Liskeard ■	a													17§14								
Bodmin Parkway	a													17§27								
Lostwithiel	a																					
Par	a													17§40								
St Austell	a																					
Truro	a																					
Redruth	a																					
Camborne	a																					
Hayle	a																					
St Erth	a																					
Penzance	a																					
Birmingham International ✈	d			12 14								13 14									14 14	
Coventry	d			12 25								13 25									14 25	
Leamington Spa ■	d			12 38				13 02				13 38				14 00					14 38	
Banbury	a			12 54				13 19				13 54				14 17					14 54	
Oxford	a			13 14				13 40				14 14				14 40					15 14	
Reading ■	a			13 39				14 09				14 39				15 08					15 39	
Guildford	a																					
Basingstoke	a			14 08				14 40				15 08									16 08	
Winchester	a			14 24				14 55				15 24									16 24	
Southampton Airport Pkway ✈	a			14 33				15 08				15 32									16 32	
Southampton Central	a			14 41				15 17				15 41									16 41	
Brockenhurst ■	a			14 57								15 57									16 57	
Bournemouth	a			15 11								16 11									17 11	

A from 17 September. ⊼ from Edinburgh
B until 10 September. ⊼ from Edinburgh
C ⊼ to Gloucester
D ⊼ from Birmingham New Street to Gloucester
E from 17 September
F until 10 September

Table 51

Saturdays

Scotland, The North East, North West England - The South West and South Coast

		XC	XC	XC	XC	XC	VT	XC	XC	XC	XC	XC	XC	XC	VT	XC	XC	XC	XC	XC	XC	VT	XC
		◇1	◇1	◇1	◇1	1	◇1	◇1	◇1	◇1	◇1	◇1	◇1	1	◇1	◇1	◇1	◇1	◇1	◇1	1	◇1	◇1
		A	B				C		D	E		F	G				D						
Aberdeen	d																08 20						
Stonehaven	d																08 38						
Montrose	d																08 59						
Arbroath	d																09 15						
Dundee	d																09 32						
Leuchars 3	d																09 47						
Cupar	d																09 54						
Ladybank	d																10 01						
Markinch	d																10 08						
Kirkcaldy	d																10 17						
Inverkeithing	d																10 32						
Glasgow Central 15	d	07 50							09 00						12 00								
Motherwell	d	08 05							09 15														
Haymarket	d	08 50							09 57								10 52						
Edinburgh 10	d	09 06					10 52		10 05								11 05					12 52	
Haymarket	d						10 57															12 57	
Lockerbie	d																						
Carlisle 8	d						12 07								13 09							14 07	
Penrith North Lakes	d																					14 22	
Oxenholme Lake District	d						12 43																
Lancaster 6	d						12 57								13 58							14 57	
Preston 8	d						13 17								14 17							15 17	
Wigan North Western	d						13 28								14 28							15 28	
Warrington Bank Quay	d						13 39								14 39							15 39	
M'chester Piccadilly 10	d				13 07			13 27				14 07	14 07			14 27				15 07			15 27
Stockport	d				13 16			13 35				14 16	14 16			14 35				15 16			15 35
Wilmslow	d																						
Crewe 10	d						14 01								15 01							16 01	
Macclesfield	d							13 49								14 49							15 49
Congleton	d																						
Stoke-on-Trent	d				13 44			14 07				14 44	14 44			15 07				15 44			16 07
Stafford	d				14 03			14 26				15 03	15 03			15 26				16 03			16 25
Wolverhampton 7	d				14 17		14 32	14 41				15 17	15 17		15 32	15 41				16 17		16 32	16 41
Dunbar	d	09 26															11 25						
Berwick-upon-Tweed	d	09 49							10 48								11 48						
Alnmouth for Alnwick	d																12 08						
Morpeth	d								11 19														
Newcastle 8	d	10 48		11 35					11 42		12 35						12f44		13 35				
Chester-le-Street	d																						
Durham	d	10 56		11 47					11 55		12 47						12 56		13 47				
Darlington 7	d	11 13		12 05					12 12		13 04						13 13		14 05				
York 8	d	11 45		12 34					12 45		13 34						13 44		14 34				
Leeds 10	d	12 11							13 11								14 11						
Wakefield Westgate 7	d	12 24							13 23								14 24						
Doncaster 7	d			12 58							13 58								14 58				
Sheffield 7	d	12 54		13 23					13 54		14 23						14 54		15 23				
Chesterfield	d	13 06							14 07								15 06						
Nottingham 8	d		13 08			13 37				14 08				14 37				15 08			15 37		
Derby 6	d	13 28	13 36	13 53		14 06			14 29	14 36	14 53			15 06			15 28	15 36	15 53		16 06		
Burton-on-Trent	d	13 39	13 49			14 18				14 49				15 18			15 39	15 49			16 18		
Tamworth	d		14 01			14 30			14 48	15 01				15 30				16 01			16 30		
Birmingham New Street 12	a	14 07	14 24	14 27	14 39	14 53	14 55	14 58	15 08	15 24	15 27	15 39	15 39	15 53	15 55	15 58	16 07	16 24	16 27	16 39	16 53	16 55	16 58
Birmingham New Street 12	d	14 12	14 30	14 33	14 42			15 03	15 12	15 30	15 33	15 42	15 42			16 03	16 12	16 30	16 33	16 42			17 03
Cheltenham Spa	a	14 50	15 10		15 23				15 50	16 10		16 23	16 23				16 50	17 10		17 23			
Gloucester 7	a		15 22							16 22								17 22					
Bristol Parkway 7	a	15 24			15 55				16 29			16 55	16 55				17 24			17 55			
Bristol Temple Meads 10	a	15 38			16 08				16 42			17 07	17 07				17 38			18 07			
Newport (South Wales)	a		16 08							17 10								18 05					
Cardiff Central 7	a		16 25							17 26								18 21					
Weston-super-Mare	a																						
Taunton	a	16 15							17 17				17 41				18 15						
Tiverton Parkway	a								17 30				17 53				18 28						
Exeter St Davids 6	a	16 40							17 47				18 09				18 43						
Dawlish	a												18 21										
Teignmouth	a												18 26										
Newton Abbot	a								18 10				18 33				19 05						
Torquay	a												18 45										
Paignton	a												18 53										
Totnes	a	17 10							18 24								19 18						
Plymouth	a	17 37							18 52								19 44						
Liskeard 6	a	18 04							19 21								20 10						
Bodmin Parkway	a	18 16							19 33								20 22						
Lostwithiel	a																20 28						
Par	a	18 27							19 45								20 35						
St Austell	a	18 33							19 53								20 42						
Truro	a	18 50							20 11								20 59						
Redruth	a	19 08							20 24								21 12						
Camborne	a	19 15							20 31								21 18						
Hayle	a																21 26						
St Erth	a	19 25							20 43								21 31						
Penzance	a	19 36							20 54								21 43						
Birmingham International	d							15 14								16 14							17 14
Coventry	d							15 25								16 25							17 25
Leamington Spa 8	d			15 00				15 38			16 02					16 38			17 00				17 38
Banbury	a			15 19				15 54			16 18					16 54			17 17				17 54
Oxford	a			15 41				16 14			16 40					17 14			17 41				18 14
Reading 7	a			16 09				16 39			17 08					17 39			18 09				18 39
Guildford	a																						
Basingstoke	a			16 40				17 08								18 08			18 40				19 08
Winchester	a			16 55				17 24								18 24			18 55				19 24
Southampton Airport Pkway	a			17 08				17 32								18 32			19 08				19 32
Southampton Central	a			17 17				17 41								18 40			19 17				19 41
Brockenhurst 3	a							17 57								18 57							19 57
Bournemouth	a							18 11								19 11							20 11

A until 10 September. from Edinburgh to Totnes
B from Birmingham New Street to Gloucester
C until 9 July, from 17 September
D from Edinburgh to Totnes
E to Gloucester
F until 10 September
G from 17 September

Table 51

Saturdays

Scotland, The North East, North West England - The South West and South Coast

	XC	XC	XC	XC	XC	XC	VT	XC	XC	XC	XC	XC	XC	VT	XC	XC	XC	XC	XC	XC	XC
	◇1	◇1	◇1	◇1	◇1	1	◇1	◇1	◇1	◇1	◇1	◇1	1	◇1	◇1	◇1	◇1	◇1	◇1	◇1	◇1
	A	B												C	D	E	F			G	H
	🛒	🛒		🛒	🛒	🛒	🍴	🛒	🛒		🛒	🛒	🛒	🍴	🛒	🛒	🛒		🛒	🛒	🛒
Aberdeen d																					
Stonehaven d																					
Montrose d																					
Arbroath d																					
Dundee d																					
Leuchars [8] d																					
Cupar d																					
Ladybank d																					
Markinch d																					
Kirkcaldy d																					
Inverkeithing d																					
Glasgow Central [15] d	10 59	10 59					14 00									12 51	12 51				
Motherwell d	11 14	11 14														13 12	13 12				
Haymarket d	11 56	11 56																			
Edinburgh [10] d	12 09	12 09							13 08					14 52		14 08	14 08				
Haymarket d														14 57							
Lockerbie d																					
Carlisle [8] d							15 11							16 07							
Penrith North Lakes d														16 22							
Oxenholme Lake District d							15 46														
Lancaster [6] d														16 57							
Preston [8] d							16 17							17 17							
Wigan North Western d							16 28							17 28							
Warrington Bank Quay d							16 39							17 39							
M'chester Piccadilly [10] ⛴ d					16 07			16 27				17 06			17 27					18 05	18 05
Stockport d					16 16			16 35							17 36					18 13	18 13
Wilmslow d																					
Crewe [10] d							17 01							18 01							
Macclesfield d								16 49				17 26								18 26	18 26
Congleton d															17 54						
Stoke-on-Trent d					16 44			17 07				17 44			18 08					18 44	18 44
Stafford d					17 03			17 26				18 04			18 27					19 03	19 03
Wolverhampton [7] ⛴ d					17 17		17 32	17 41				18 17		18 32	18 41					19 17	19 17
Dunbar d									13 29												
Berwick-upon-Tweed d	12 48	12 48														14 49	14 49				
Alnmouth for Alnwick d									14 09												
Morpeth d																					
Newcastle [8] d	13 44	13 44		14 35					14 44		15 03					15 41	15 41		16 35		
Chester-le-Street d																					
Durham d	13 56	13 56		14 47					14 56		15 16					15 53	15 53		16 47		
Darlington [7] d	14 13	14 13		15 04					15 13		15 33					16 11	16 11		17 04		
York [8] d	14 44	14 44		15 34					15 45		16 06					16 44	16 44		17 34		
Leeds [10] d	15 12	15 12							16 12		16e40					17 11	17 11				
Wakefield Westgate [7] d	15 24	15 24							16 24		16 52					17 23	17 23				
Doncaster [7] d				15 58															17 58		
Sheffield [7] ⛴ d	15 54	15 54		16 23					16 54		17 23					17 54	17 54		18 23		
Chesterfield d	16 07	16 07							17 06							18 06	18 06				
Nottingham [8] ⛴ d			16 08			16 37				17 11			17 37					18 08			
Derby [6] d	16 28	16 28	16 36	16 53		17 06			17 28	17 36	17 53		18 06			18 28	18 28	18 36	18 53		
Burton-on-Trent d			16 49			17 18			17 39	17 49			18 18					18 49			
Tamworth d	16 48	16 48	17 01			17 30				18 01			18 30			18 47	18 47	19 01			
Birmingham New Street [12] a	17 07	17 07	17 24	17 27	17 39	17 53	17 55	17 58	18 07	18 24	18 27	18 38	18 54	18 55	18 58	19 07	19 07	19 24	19 27	19 33	19 33
Birmingham New Street [12] d	17 12	17 12	17 30	17 33	17 42			18 03	18 12	18 30	18 33	18 42			19 03	19 12	19 12	19 30	19 33	19 42	19 42
Cheltenham Spa a	17 50	17 50	18 17		18 23				18 50	19 10		19 23				19 50	19 50	20 10		20 23	20 23
Gloucester [7] a			18 29							19 22								20 22			
Bristol Parkway [7] a	18 29	18 29			18 55				19 27			19 55				20 29	20 29			20 55	20 55
Bristol Temple Meads [10] a	18 42	18 42			19 07				19 41			20 07				20 42	20 42			21 09	21 07
Newport (South Wales) a			19 12							20 05		20 55						21 11			
Cardiff Central [7] a			19 29							20 21		21 11						21 29			
Weston-super-Mare a																					
Taunton a	19 15	19 15							20 15							21 17	21 15				21 42
Tiverton Parkway a	19 28	19 28							20 28								21 28				21 55
Exeter St Davids [6] a	19 43	19 43							20 43								21 43				22 10
Dawlish a																					
Teignmouth a																					
Newton Abbot a	20 03	20 03							21 03								22 05				22 30
Torquay a																					
Paignton a																					
Totnes a	20 16	20 16							21 16								22 21				22 43
Plymouth a	20 43	20 43							21 44								22 49				23 10
Liskeard [6] a		21 24																			
Bodmin Parkway a		21 36																			
Lostwithiel a																					
Par a		21 48																			
St Austell a		21 54																			
Truro a		22 12																			
Redruth a		22 27																			
Camborne a		22 33																			
Hayle a																					
St Erth a		22 44																			
Penzance a		22 54																			
Birmingham International ✈ d								18 14							19 14						
Coventry d								18 25							19 25						
Leamington Spa [8] d				18 02				18 38			19 00				19 38				20 03		
Banbury a				18 18				18 54			19 17				19 54				20 19		
Oxford a				18 40				19 14			19 40				20 14				20 40		
Reading [7] a				19 08				19 39			20 08				20 39				21 08		
Guildford a																					
Basingstoke a								20 08							21 08						
Winchester a								20 24							21 24						
Southampton Airport Pkwy ✈ a								20 32							21 33						
Southampton Central ⛴ a								20 41							21 41						
Brockenhurst [3] a								20 57							21 57						
Bournemouth a								21 11							22 15						

A until 10 September. 🛒 from Edinburgh
B from 17 September. 🛒 from Edinburgh to Totnes
C until 9 July, from 17 September
D 🛒 to Oxford
E until 30 July. 🛒 from Edinburgh to Bristol Parkway
F from 6 August. 🛒 from Edinburgh to Bristol Parkway
G until 10 September
H from 17 September. 🛒 to Bristol Parkway

Table 51

Saturdays

Scotland, The North East, North West England - The South West and South Coast

		XC	VT	XC	XC	XC	XC	XC	XC	LM		XC	VT	XC	XC	XC	XC	VT	XC	XC		XC	XC	VT	XC
		[1]	◇[1]	◇[1]	◇[1]	◇[1]	◇[1]	◇[1]	◇[1]	◇[1]		[1]	◇[1]	◇[1]	◇[1]	◇[1]	◇[1]	◇[1]	[1]	◇[1]		◇[1]	◇[1]	◇[1]	◇[1]
				A	B		C	D						E	F							G			
		🛒	🍽	🛒	🛒		🛒	🛒	🛒				🍽	🛒	🛒	🛒		🍽				🛒		🍽	🛒
Aberdeen	d																								
Stonehaven	d																								
Montrose	d																								
Arbroath	d																								
Dundee	d																								
Leuchars [3]	d																								
Cupar	d																								
Ladybank	d																								
Markinch	d																								
Kirkcaldy	d																								
Inverkeithing	d																								
Glasgow Central [15]	d		16 00												15 00			18 00						18 40	
Motherwell	d														15 14										
Haymarket	d														15 56										
Edinburgh [10]	d				15 08								16 52		16 05							17 08			
Haymarket	d												16 57												
Lockerbie	d																								
Carlisle [8]	d		17 09										18 07					19 09						19 48	
Penrith North Lakes	d																							20 02	
Oxenholme Lake District	d		17 44										18 42											20 25	
Lancaster [6]	d												18 57					19 56						20 40	
Preston [8]	d		18 17										19 17					20 17						21 00	
Wigan North Western	d		18 28										19 28					20 28						21 11	
Warrington Bank Quay	d		18 39										19 39					20 39						21 22	
M'chester Piccadilly [10] 🚊	d			18 27					19 07					19 27			20 07			20 27			21 07		
Stockport	d			18 35					19 16					19 35			20 16			20 35					
Wilmslow	d																								
Crewe [10]	d		19 01							19 51			20 01					21 01						21 43	
Macclesfield	d													19 49						20 49					
Congleton	d			18 54																					
Stoke-on-Trent	d			19 07					19 44					20 07			20 44			21 07			21 45		
Stafford	d			19 25					20 03	20 12				20 26			21 03			21 27			22 03	22 08	
Wolverhampton [7] 🚊	d		19 32	19 41					20 17	20 28			20 32	20 41			21 16	21 33		21 41			22 16	22 23	
Dunbar	d				15 28																	17 28			
Berwick-upon-Tweed	d																					17 51			
Alnmouth for Alnwick	d														17 01										
Morpeth	d														17 16										
Newcastle [8]	d				16 41		17 32	17 32							17 43	18 35						18 44			19 17
Chester-le-Street	d						17 41	17 41																	
Durham	d				16 52		17 48	17 48							17 55	18 48						18 56			19 29
Darlington [7]	d				17 10		18 05	18 05							18 13	19 05						19 13			19 46
York [8]	d				17 44		18 34	18 34							18 44	19 34						19 44			20 23
Leeds [10]	d				18 11										19 11							20 11			
Wakefield Westgate [7]	d				18 23										19 24							20 23			
Doncaster [7]	d						18 58	18 58								19 58									
Sheffield [7] 🚊	d				18 54		19 24	19 24							19 54	20 23						20 54			21 23
Chesterfield	d				19 06										20 06							21 06			21 35
Nottingham [8] 🚊	d	18 37				19 08						19 37							20 37						
Derby [6]	d	19 06			19 27	19 36	19 54	19 54				20 06			20 28	20 53			21 06			21 28			21 56
Burton-on-Trent	d	19 18			19 38	19 49						20 18							21 19			21 39			22 07
Tamworth	d	19 30				20 01						20 30			20 48				21 31			21 50			22 18
Birmingham New Street [12]	a	19 53	19 55	19 58	20 09	20 24	20 28	20 27	20 33	20 47		20 54	20 55	20 58	21 07	21 27	21 32	21 54	21 54	21 58		22 08	22 32	22 40	22 44
Birmingham New Street [12]	d			20 03	20 12	20 30		20 33	20 42					21 03	21 12										
Cheltenham Spa	a				20 51	21 10			21 23						21 50										
Gloucester [7]	a					21 22									22 02										
Bristol Parkway [7]	a				21 25				21 58						22 32										
Bristol Temple Meads [10]	a				21 38				22 12						22 45										
Newport (South Wales)	a					22 16																			
Cardiff Central [7]	a					22 41																			
Weston-super-Mare	a																								
Taunton	a				22 15																				
Tiverton Parkway	a				22 28																				
Exeter St Davids [6]	a				22 44																				
Dawlish	a																								
Teignmouth	a																								
Newton Abbot	a				23 11																				
Torquay	a																								
Paignton	a																								
Totnes	a				23 27																				
Plymouth	a				23 54																				
Liskeard [6]	a																								
Bodmin Parkway	a																								
Lostwithiel	a																								
Par	a																								
St Austell	a																								
Truro	a																								
Redruth	a																								
Camborne	a																								
Hayle	a																								
St Erth	a																								
Penzance	a																								
Birmingham International ✈	d			20 14										21 14											
Coventry	d			20 25										21 25											
Leamington Spa [8]	d			20 38				21 00						21 38											
Banbury	a			20 54				21 19						21 54											
Oxford	a			21 14				21 41						22 16											
Reading [7]	a			21 39				22 10						22 41											
Guildford	a							22 59																	
Basingstoke	a			22 08										23 06											
Winchester	a			22 24										23 24											
Southampton Airport Pkway ✈	a			22 32										23 32											
Southampton Central ⛴	a			22 41										23 41											
Brockenhurst [3]	a			22 57																					
Bournemouth	a			23 21																					

A 🛒 to Oxford
B 🛒 to Bristol Parkway
C until 10 September
D from 17 September. 🛒 to Oxford
E 🛒 to Wolverhampton
F 🛒 from Edinburgh to Tamworth
G 🛒 to York

Table 51

Saturdays

Scotland, The North East, North West England - The South West and South Coast

		VT	XC	XC	XC	XC		XC	XC	XC
		◇1	◇1	1	1	◇1			◇1	
				A	B	C		D	E	D
								🚌		🚌
		☕				🚃			🚃	
Aberdeen	d									
Stonehaven	d									
Montrose	d									
Arbroath	d									
Dundee	d									
Leuchars 3	d									
Cupar	d									
Ladybank	d									
Markinch	d									
Kirkcaldy	d									
Inverkeithing	d									
Glasgow Central 15	d					16 52			16 52	
Motherwell	d					17 14			17 14	
Haymarket	d					17 56			17 56	
Edinburgh 10	d	18 52				18 05			18 05	
Haymarket	d	18 57								
Lockerbie	d									
Carlisle 8	d	20 07								
Penrith North Lakes	d	20 22								
Oxenholme Lake District	d	20 45								
Lancaster 6	d	21 00								
Preston 8	d	21 20								
Wigan North Western	d	21 31								
Warrington Bank Quay	d	21 42								
M'chester Piccadilly 10 ⛴	d		21 28							
Stockport	d		21 36							
Wilmslow	d									
Crewe 10	d	22 04								
Macclesfield	d		21 50							
Congleton	d									
Stoke-on-Trent	d		22 08							
Stafford	d	22 24	22 33							
Wolverhampton 7 ⛴	d	22 39	22 46							
Dunbar	d					18 25			18 25	
Berwick-upon-Tweed	d					18 48			18 48	
Alnmouth for Alnwick	d					19 08			19 08	
Morpeth	d									
Newcastle 8	d					19 44			19 44	
Chester-le-Street	d									
Durham	d					19 56			19 56	
Darlington 7	d					20 13			20 13	
York 8	d					20 45			20 45	
Leeds 10	d					21 11			21 11	
Wakefield Westgate 7	d					21 23			21 23	
Doncaster 7	d									
Sheffield 7 ⛴	d					21 54			21 54	
Chesterfield	d					22 06			22 06	
Nottingham 8 ⛴	d			21 37	21 37					
Derby 6	d			22b10	22b10	22 27		22 10	22 27	22 35
Burton-on-Trent	d			22 21	22 21	22 37		22 30		22 55
Tamworth	d			22 33	22 33	22 48		22 50		23s15
Birmingham New Street 12	a	22 58	23 02	23 02	23 03	23 06		23 25	23 35	23 50
Birmingham New Street 12	d									
Cheltenham Spa	a									
Gloucester 7	a									
Bristol Parkway 7	a									
Bristol Temple Meads 10	a									
Newport (South Wales)	a									
Cardiff Central 7	a									
Weston-super-Mare	a									
Taunton	a									
Tiverton Parkway	a									
Exeter St Davids 6	a									
Dawlish	a									
Teignmouth	a									
Newton Abbot	a									
Torquay	a									
Paignton	a									
Totnes	a									
Plymouth	a									
Liskeard 6	a									
Bodmin Parkway	a									
Lostwithiel	a									
Par	a									
St Austell	a									
Truro	a									
Redruth	a									
Camborne	a									
Hayle	a									
St Erth	a									
Penzance	a									
Birmingham International ✈	d									
Coventry	d									
Leamington Spa 8	d									
Banbury	a									
Oxford	a									
Reading 7	a									
Guildford	a									
Basingstoke	a									
Winchester	a									
Southampton Airport Pkway ✈	a									
Southampton Central ⛴	a									
Brockenhurst 3	a									
Bournemouth	a									

A from 25 June until 30 July

B from 6 August

C from 25 June. 🚃 from Edinburgh to York

D until 18 June

E until 18 June. 🚃 from Edinburgh to York

b Arr. 2204

Table 51

Sundays

Scotland, The North East, North West England - The South West and South Coast

		XC	XC	XC	XC	XC	XC	XC	XC	XC		XC	XC	XC	XC	XC	XC	XC	XC	XC		XC	XC	XC	XC
		◇1	◇1	◇1	◇1	◇1	◇1	◇1	◇1	◇1		◇1	◇1	◇1	◇1	◇1	◇1	◇1	◇1	◇1		◇1	◇1	◇1	◇1
		A	B	C	D	E	F	G	H	I		B	C	J	D	K	L	M	H	I		B	C	B	J
Aberdeen	d																								
Stonehaven	d																								
Montrose	d																								
Arbroath	d																								
Dundee	d																								
Leuchars 8	d																								
Cupar	d																								
Ladybank	d																								
Markinch	d																								
Kirkcaldy	d																								
Inverkeithing	d																								
Glasgow Central 15	d																								
Motherwell	d																								
Haymarket	d																								
Edinburgh 10	d																								
Haymarket	d																								
Lockerbie	d																								
Carlisle 8	d																								
Penrith North Lakes	d																								
Oxenholme Lake District	d																								
Lancaster 6	d																								
Preston 8	d																								
Wigan North Western	d																								
Warrington Bank Quay	d																								
M'chester Piccadilly 10	d								0827	0827		0827	0827						0927	0927		0927	0927		
Stockport	d								0836	0836		0836	0836						0936	0936		0936	0936		
Wilmslow	d								0843	0843		0843	0843												
Crewe 10	d								0905	0905		0905	0905												
Macclesfield	d																		0949	0949		0949	0949		
Congleton	d																								
Stoke-on-Trent	d																		1007	1007		1007	1007		
Stafford	d								0926	0926		0926	0926						1027	1027		1027	1027		
Wolverhampton 7	d								0941	0941		0941	0941						1043	1043		1043	1043		
Dunbar	d																								
Berwick-upon-Tweed	d																								
Alnmouth for Alnwick	d																								
Morpeth	d																								
Newcastle 8	d																								
Chester-le-Street	d																								
Durham	d																								
Darlington 7	d																								
York 8	d																								
Leeds 10	d														0810	0810								0810	0810
Wakefield Westgate 7	d														0823	0823								0823	0823
Doncaster 7	d																								
Sheffield 7	d														0854	0854								0854	0854
Chesterfield	d														0907	0907								0907	0907
Nottingham 8	d																								
Derby 6	d														0928	0928								09b36	0930
Burton-on-Trent	d																								
Tamworth	d														0948	0948									
Birmingham New Street 12	a								0958	0958		0958	0958		1009	1009			1059	1059		1059	1059	1047	1048
Birmingham New Street 12	d	0903	0903	0903	0912	0912	0912	0912	1003	1003		1003	1003	1012	1012	1012	1030	1030	1103	1103		1103	1103	1112	1112
Cheltenham Spa	a				0949	0949	0949	0949						1049	1055	1055	1110	1110						1151	1151
Gloucester 7	a							1001						1101			1121	1121						1203	1203
Bristol Parkway 7	a				1023	1022	1023	1111						1213	1128	1128								1317	1317
Bristol Temple Meads 10	a					1034	1035	1140						1235		1141								1336	1337
Newport (South Wales)	a																	1206							
Cardiff Central 7	a																	1226							
Weston-super-Mare	a																								
Taunton	a					1115	1115	1215						1315		1216								1416	1416
Tiverton Parkway	a					1128	1128	1226						1328		1227								1428	1428
Exeter St Davids 6	a					1142	1142	1242						1342		1245								1446	1446
Dawlish	a																								
Teignmouth	a																								
Newton Abbot	a					1203	1203	1303						1403		1307								1508	1508
Torquay	a																								
Paignton	a																								
Totnes	a					1216	1216	1316						1416		1321								1522	1522
Plymouth	a					1244	1244	1344						1445		1350								1553	1553
Liskeard 6	a					1317	1317																		
Bodmin Parkway	a					1329	1329																		
Lostwithiel	a																								
Par	a					1340	1340																		
St Austell	a					1347	1347																		
Truro	a					1404	1404																		
Redruth	a					1419	1418																		
Camborne	a					1426	1424																		
Hayle	a																								
St Erth	a					1437	1435																		
Penzance	a					1449	1449																		
Birmingham International	d	0914	0914	0914					1014	1014		1014	1014						1114	1114		1114	1114		
Coventry	d	0925	0925	09a33					1025	1025		1025	10a33						1125	1125		1125	11a28		
Leamington Spa 8	d	09a36	0938						10a35	10a35		1038							11a35	11a35		1138			
Banbury	a		0954									1054										1154			
Oxford	a		1014									1114										1214			
Reading 7	a		1042									1142										1242			
Guildford	a																								
Basingstoke	a		1109									1209										1309			
Winchester	a		1124									1224										1324			
Southampton Airport Pkwy	a		1133									1233										1333			
Southampton Central	a		1142									1242										1342			
Brockenhurst 3	a		1202									1302										1401			
Bournemouth	a		1226									1326										1426			

A from 19 June, from 18 September
B from 26 June until 31 July
C from 7 August until 11 September
D from 18 September until 23 October
E from 7 August until 11 September. to Totnes
F from 30 October. to Totnes
G until 31 July
H from 18 September until 23 October.
from Birmingham New Street
to Wolverhampton
I until 19 June, from 30 October
J until 19 June
K from 7 August until 11 September, from 30 October
L from 7 August until 23 October
M until 31 July, from 30 October
b Arr. 0928

Table 51

Sundays

Scotland, The North East, North West England - The South West and South Coast

		XC ◇1 A	XC ◇1 B	XC ◇1 C	XC ◇1 D	XC ◇1 E	VT ◇1	XC ◇1 F	XC ◇1 E	XC ◇1 G	XC ◇1 H	XC ◇1 E	XC ◇1 A	XC ◇1 B	XC ◇1 A	XC ◇1 G	XC ◇1 I	XC ◇1 J	XC ◇1 E	VT ◇1	XC ◇1 K	XC ◇1 L	XC ◇1 E
Aberdeen	d																						
Stonehaven	d																						
Montrose	d																						
Arbroath	d																						
Dundee	d																						
Leuchars 8	d																						
Cupar	d																						
Ladybank	d																						
Markinch	d																						
Kirkcaldy	d																						
Inverkeithing	d																						
Glasgow Central 15	d																						
Motherwell	d																						
Haymarket	d																						
Edinburgh 10	d																						
Haymarket	d																						
Lockerbie	d																						
Carlisle 8	d																						
Penrith North Lakes	d																						
Oxenholme Lake District	d																						
Lancaster 6	d																						
Preston 8	d						10 17													11 17			
Wigan North Western	d						10 28													11 28			
Warrington Bank Quay	d						10 39													11 39			
M'chester Piccadilly 10	d							10 27	10 27	10 27											11 27	11 27	11 27
Stockport	d							10 36	10 36	10 36											11 36	11 36	11 36
Wilmslow	d																						
Crewe 10	d						11 01													12 01			
Macclesfield	d							10 49	10 49	10 49											11 49	11 49	11 49
Congleton	d																						
Stoke-on-Trent	d							11 07	11 07	11 07											12 07	12 07	12 07
Stafford	d							11 28	11 28	11 28											12 25	12 25	12 25
Wolverhampton 7	d						11 32	11 42	11 42	11 42										12 32	12 41	12 41	12 41
Dunbar	d																						
Berwick-upon-Tweed	d																						
Alnmouth for Alnwick	d																						
Morpeth	d																						
Newcastle 8	d																						
Chester-le-Street	d																						
Durham	d																						
Darlington 7	d																						
York 8	d												09 28	09 28									
Leeds 10	d	09 00	09 00								09 00	09 00	10b00	10b00									
Wakefield Westgate 7	d	09 11	09 11								09 11	09 11	10 12	10 12									
Doncaster 7	d	09 32	09 32								09 32	09 32	10 30	10 30									
Sheffield 7	d	09 57	09 57								09 57	09 57	10 57	10 57									
Chesterfield	d	10 09	10 09								10 09	10 09	11 10	11 09									
Nottingham 8	d														11 10	11 10	11 10						
Derby 6	d	10 33	10 33								10 33	10 33	11 30	11 30	11 36	11 36	11 36						
Burton-on-Trent	d													11 42	11 48	11 48	11 48						
Tamworth	d														12 00	12 00	12 00						
Birmingham New Street 12	a	11 09	11 08				11 55	12 00	12 00	12 00	11 44	11 44	12 09	12 07	12 23	12 22	12 26			12 55	12 58	12 58	12 58
Birmingham New Street 12	d	11 12	11 12	11 30	11 30	11 33		12 03	12 03	12 03	12 12	12 12	12 12	12 12	12 30	12 30	12 30	12 30	12 33		13 03	13 03	13 03
Cheltenham Spa	a	11 50	11 50	12 10	12 10						12 50	12 50	12 50	12 50	13 10	13 10	13 10	13 10					
Gloucester 7	a			12 21	12 21						13 03	13 02			13 21	13 21	13 21	13 21					
Bristol Parkway 7	a	12 23	12 23								14 18	14 17	13 23	13 23									
Bristol Temple Meads 10	a		12 36								14 36	14 40		13 35									
Newport (South Wales)	a				13 06												14 06	14 06					
Cardiff Central 7	a				13 26												14 26	14 26					
Weston-super-Mare	a																						
Taunton	a		13 16								15 16	15 16		14 15									
Tiverton Parkway	a		13 28								15 28	15 30		14 28									
Exeter St Davids 6	a		13 45								15 45	15 46		14 44									
Dawlish	a																						
Teignmouth	a																						
Newton Abbot	a		14 07								16 07	16 07		15 04									
Torquay	a																						
Paignton	a																						
Totnes	a		14 21								16 21	16 21		15 17									
Plymouth	a		14 50								16 50	16 50		15 44									
Liskeard 6	a																						
Bodmin Parkway	a																						
Lostwithiel	a																						
Par	a																						
St Austell	a																						
Truro	a																						
Redruth	a																						
Camborne	a																						
Hayle	a																						
St Erth	a																						
Penzance	a																						
Birmingham International ✈	d							12 14	12 14	12 14											13 14	13 14	13 14
Coventry	d							12 25	12 25	12a27											13 25	13 25	13 25
Leamington Spa 8	d					12 00		12a35	12 38										13 00		13a36	13a36	13 38
Banbury	a					12 17			12 54										13 17				13 54
Oxford	a					12 38			13 14										13 41				14 14
Reading 7	a					13 09			13 42										14 10				14 42
Guildford	a																						
Basingstoke	a								14 09														15 09
Winchester	a								14 24														15 24
Southampton Airport Pkway ✈	a								14 33														15 33
Southampton Central	a								14 42														15 42
Brockenhurst 3	a								15 02														16 02
Bournemouth	a								15 26														16 26

A from 18 September until 23 October
B from 7 August until 11 September, from 30 October
C from 7 August until 23 October
D until 31 July, from 30 October
E from 26 June until 31 July
F until 19 June, from 18 September
G from 7 August until 11 September
H until 19 June
I from 30 October. Trolley service to Gloucester
J until 31 July. Trolley service to Gloucester
K until 19 June. Restaurant from Birmingham New Street; Trolley service to Wolverhampton
L from 18 September
b Arr. 0954

Table 51

Sundays

Scotland, The North East, North West England - The South West and South Coast

		XC	XC	XC	XC	XC	XC	XC	XC	XC	XC	XC	XC	XC	VT	XC	XC	XC	XC	XC	XC	XC
		◇1	◇1	◇1	◇1	◇1	◇1	◇1	◇1	◇1	◇1	◇1	◇1	◇1	◇1	◇1	◇1	◇1	◇1	◇1	◇1	◇1
		A	B	C	D	E	F	G	H	D	A	I	C	E			B	D	E	J	A	K
Aberdeen	d																					
Stonehaven	d																					
Montrose	d																					
Arbroath	d																					
Dundee	d																					
Leuchars	d																					
Cupar	d																					
Ladybank	d																					
Markinch	d																					
Kirkcaldy	d																					
Inverkeithing	d																					
Glasgow Central	d																					
Motherwell	d																					
Haymarket	d																					
Edinburgh	d																	08 50	08 50	08 50		
Haymarket	d																					
Lockerbie	d																					
Carlisle	d																					
Penrith North Lakes	d																					
Oxenholme Lake District	d																					
Lancaster	d														12 00							
Preston	d														12 17							
Wigan North Western	d														12 28							
Warrington Bank Quay	d														12 39							
M'chester Piccadilly	d	11 27														12 26						
Stockport	d	11 36														12 35						
Wilmslow	d																					
Crewe	d														13 01							
Macclesfield	d	11 49														12 49						
Congleton	d																					
Stoke-on-Trent	d	12 07														13 07						
Stafford	d	12 25														13 25						
Wolverhampton	d	12 41													13 32	13 41						
Dunbar	d																					
Berwick-upon-Tweed	d																	09 31	09 31	09 31		
Alnmouth for Alnwick	d																					
Morpeth	d																					
Newcastle	d				09 20	09 20							09 20				09 20	10 24	10 24	10 24		
Chester-le-Street	d																					
Durham	d				09 33	09 33							09 33				09 33	10 37	10 37	10 37		
Darlington	d				09 50	09 50							09 50				09 50	10 54	10 54	10 54		
York	d		09 28	09 28	10e28	10e28							10e28				10e28	11 28	11 28	11 28		
Leeds	d		10b00	10b00	11f00	11f00							11f00				11f00	12i00	12i00	12i00		
Wakefield Westgate	d		10 12	10 12	11 12	11 12							11 12				11 12	12 12	12 12	12 12		
Doncaster	d		10 30	10 30	11 30	11 30							11 30				11 30	12 30	12 30	12 30		
Sheffield	d		10 57	10 57	11 57	11 57							11 57				11 57	12 57	12 57	12 57		
Chesterfield	d		11 09	11 09	12 09	12 09							12 09				12 09	13 09	13 09	13 09		
Nottingham	d						12 10			12 10	12 10										13 06	13 06
Derby	d		11c35	11 30	12 30	12 30	12g36			12g36	12g36		12 30				12h36	13 32	13 32	13 32	13j36	13j36
Burton-on-Trent	d						12 48			12 48	12 48							13 43	13 43	13 43	13 47	13 48
Tamworth	d				12 49	12 49	13 00			13 00	13 01										14 00	14 00
Birmingham New Street	a	12 58	12 45	12 43	13 09	13 07	13 21			13 21	13 22		13 42		13 55	13 58	13 50	14 11	14 10	14 11	14 22	14 22
Birmingham New Street	d	13 03	13 12	13 12	13 12	13 12	13 30	13 30	13 30	13 30	13 30	13 33		13 42		14 03	14 12	14 12	14 12	14 12	14 30	14 30
Cheltenham Spa	a		13 50	13 50	13 50	13 50	14 12	14 12	14 12	14 12	14 12			14 23			14 50	14 51	14 51	14 51	15 10	15 10
Gloucester	a		14 02	14 02			14 22	14 22	14 22	14 22	14 22						15 02			15 03	15 21	15 21
Bristol Parkway	a		15 08	15 12	14 23	14 23								14 56			15 33	15 23	15 25	16 16		
Bristol Temple Meads	a		15 23	15 35		14 39								15 08			15 45		15 38	16 36		
Newport (South Wales)	a						15 08	15 07	15 08	15 14												16 06
Cardiff Central	a						15 31	15 31	15 31													16 26
Weston-super-Mare	a																					
Taunton	a			16 15		15 15											16 18		16 16	17 16		
Tiverton Parkway	a			16 26		15 28											16 32		16 27	17 30		
Exeter St Davids	a			16 43		15 43											16 46		16 46	17 46		
Dawlish	a																					
Teignmouth	a																					
Newton Abbot	a			17 03		16 03											17 07		17 07	18 07		
Torquay	a																					
Paignton	a																					
Totnes	a			17 16		16 16											17 20		17 21	18 21		
Plymouth	a			17 44		16 44											17 47		17 50	18 51		
Liskeard	a																			19 17		
Bodmin Parkway	a																			19 29		
Lostwithiel	a																					
Par	a																			19 40		
St Austell	a																			19 47		
Truro	a																			20 08		
Redruth	a																			20 19		
Camborne	a																			20 26		
Hayle	a																					
St Erth	a																			20 38		
Penzance	a																			20 47		
Birmingham International	d	13 14														14 14						
Coventry	d	13a27														14 25						
Leamington Spa	d											14 00				14 38						
Banbury	a											14 17				14 54						
Oxford	a											14 38				15 14						
Reading	a											15 09				15 42						
Guildford	a																					
Basingstoke	a															16 09						
Winchester	a															16 24						
Southampton Airport Pkway	a															16 33						
Southampton Central	a															16 42						
Brockenhurst	a															17 02						
Bournemouth	a															17 26						

A from 7 August until 11 September
B until 19 June
C from 26 June until 31 July
D from 18 September until 23 October
E from 7 August until 11 September, from 30 October
F from 30 October. to Gloucester
G from 26 June until 31 July. to Gloucester
H until 19 June. to Gloucester
I from 26 June until 31 July, from 18 September
J from 26 June until 31 July. to Totnes
K from 26 June until 31 July, from 18 September. to Gloucester
b Arr. 0952
c Arr. 1128
e Arr. 1018
f Arr. 1051
g Arr. 1230
h Arr. 1229
i Arr. 1151
j Arr. 1330

Scotland, The North East, North West England - The South West and South Coast

		XC	XC	XC	XC	XC	XC	XC	VT	XC	XC	XC	XC	XC	XC	XC	XC	XC	XC	XC	XC	XC	VT
		◇1	◇1	◇1	◇1	◇1	◇1	◇1	◇1	◇1	◇1	◇1	◇1	◇1	◇1	◇1	◇1	◇1	◇1	◇1	◇1	◇1	◇1
		A	B	C	D	E	F	G			H	C	I	D	D	J	K	A	B	C	L	G	
		🛒	🛒	🛒	🛒	🛒	🛒	🛒	🍽	🛒	🛒	🛒	🛒	🛒	🛒	🛒	🛒	🛒	🛒	🛒	🛒	🛒	🍽
Aberdeen	d																						
Stonehaven	d																						
Montrose	d																						
Arbroath	d																						
Dundee	d																						
Leuchars 3	d																						
Cupar	d																						
Ladybank	d																						
Markinch	d																						
Kirkcaldy	d																						
Inverkeithing	d																						
Glasgow Central 15	d																						11 58
Motherwell	d																						
Haymarket	d																						
Edinburgh 10	d								10 52		08 50	09 50	09 50	09 50									
Haymarket	d								10 57														
Lockerbie	d																						
Carlisle 8	d								12 07														13 10
Penrith North Lakes	d																						
Oxenholme Lake District	d								12 43														
Lancaster 6	d								12 57														13 58
Preston 8	d								13 17														14 17
Wigan North Western	d								13 28														14 28
Warrington Bank Quay	d								13 39														14 39
M'chester Piccadilly 10	d			13 07	13 07	13 07	13 07			13 27					14 07					14 07	14 07		
Stockport	d									13 36													
Wilmslow	d																						
Crewe 10	d								14 01														15 01
Macclesfield	d									13 49													
Congleton	d																						
Stoke-on-Trent	d			13 43	13 43	13 43	13 43			14 07					14 43					14 43	14 43		
Stafford	d									14 25													
Wolverhampton 7	d			14 15	14 15	14 15	14 15		14 33	14 41					15 15					15 15	15 15		15 32
Dunbar	d																						
Berwick-upon-Tweed	d										09 31												
Alnmouth for Alnwick	d											10 47	10 47	10 47									
Morpeth	d											11 02	11 02	11 02									
Newcastle 8	d										10 24	11c25	11c25	11c25									
Chester-le-Street	d																						
Durham	d										10 37	11 37	11 37	11 37									
Darlington 7	d										10 54	11 55	11 55	11 55									
York 8	d										11 28	12 28	12 28	12 28									
Leeds 10	d										12b00	13e00	13e00	13e00									
Wakefield Westgate 7	d										12 12	13 12	13 12	13 12									
Doncaster 7	d										12 30	13 30	13 30	13 30									
Sheffield 7	d										12 57	13 57	13 57	13 57				14 22					
Chesterfield	d										13 09	14 09	14 09	14 09				14 32					
Nottingham 8	d															14 10	14 10						
Derby 6	d	13 53									13 32	14 30	14 30	14 30		14f35	14f35	14 54					
Burton-on-Trent	d															14 48	14 48						
Tamworth	d											14 50	14 50	14 50		15 00	15 00						
Birmingham New Street 12	a	14 27		14 31	14 33	14 31	14 31		14 55	14 58	14 44	15 09	15 07	15 07	15 30	15 21	15 21	15 27		15 31	15 31		15 55
Birmingham New Street 12	d	14 33	14 30			14 42	14 42	14 33		15 03	15 12	15 12	15 12	15 12		15 30	15 30	15 33	15 30		15 42	15 33	
Cheltenham Spa	a		15 10			15 24	15 24				15 50	15 50	15 50	15 50		16 10	16 10		16 10		16 24		
Gloucester 7	a		15 21											16 02		16 21	16 21		16 21				
Bristol Parkway 7	a					15 56	15 59				16 24	16 23	16 23	17 21							16 57		
Bristol Temple Meads 10	a					16 09	16 11				16 37		16 35	17 36							17 09		
Newport (South Wales)	a		16 06														17 06		17 06				
Cardiff Central 7	a		16 26														17 27		17 27				
Weston-super-Mare	a																						
Taunton	a					16 45	16 45				17 16		17 15	18 19									
Tiverton Parkway	a					16 57	16 57				17 27		17 28	18 32									
Exeter St Davids 6	a					17 12	17 12				17 46		17 43	18 48									
Dawlish	a					17 25	17 25																
Teignmouth	a					17 30	17 30																
Newton Abbot	a					17 38	17 38				18 07		18 03	19 07									
Torquay	a					17 49	17 49																
Paignton	a					17 57	17 57																
Totnes	a										18 21		18 16	19 20									
Plymouth	a										18 51		18 44	19 48									
Liskeard 6	a										19 17		19 17										
Bodmin Parkway	a										19 29		19 29										
Lostwithiel	a																						
Par	a										19 40		19 40										
St Austell	a										19 47		19 47										
Truro	a										20 08		20 08										
Redruth	a										20 19		20 19										
Camborne	a										20 26		20 26										
Hayle	a																						
St Erth	a										20 38		20 38										
Penzance	a										20 47		20 47										
Birmingham International ✈	d									15 14													
Coventry	d									15 25													
Leamington Spa 8	d	15 00						15 00		15 38								16 00				16 00	
Banbury	a	15 18						15 18		15 54								16 17				16 17	
Oxford	a	15 41						15 41		16 14								16 41				16 41	
Reading 7	a	16 09						16 09		16 42								17 09				17 09	
Guildford	a																						
Basingstoke	a									17 09													
Winchester	a									17 24													
Southampton Airport Pkway ✈	a									17 33													
Southampton Central ⛴	a									17 40													
Brockenhurst 3	a									18 02													
Bournemouth	a									18 26													

A from 26 June
B until 19 June. 🛒 to Gloucester
C from 18 September until 23 October
D from 26 June until 31 July
E until 19 June, from 7 August until 11 September
F from 30 October
G until 19 June
H until 19 June. 🛒 to Totnes
I from 7 August until 11 September, from 30 October. 🛒 to Totnes
J from 7 August until 11 September
K from 26 June until 31 July, from 18 September. 🛒 to Gloucester
L until 19 June, from 7 August until 11 September, from 30 October
b Arr. 1151
c Arr. 1119
e Arr. 1251
f Arr. 1428

Table 51

Sundays

Scotland, The North East, North West England - The South West and South Coast

		XC	XC	XC	XC	XC	XC	XC	XC	XC	XC	XC	XC	XC	VT	XC	XC	XC	XC	XC	XC	XC
		◇1	◇1	◇1	◇1	◇1	◇1	◇1	◇1	◇1	◇1	◇1	◇1	◇1	◇1	◇1	◇1	◇1	◇1	◇1	◇1	◇1
			A	B	C	D	E	A	F	G	H	I	J	A			K	L	M	N	O	P
		🍴	🍴	🍴	🍴	🍴	🍴		🍴	🍴	🍴	🍴	🍴	🍴	🍴	🍴	🍴	🍴	🍴	🍴	🍴	🍴
Aberdeen	d																					
Stonehaven	d																					
Montrose	d																					
Arbroath	d																					
Dundee	d																					
Leuchars 3	d																					
Cupar	d																					
Ladybank	d																					
Markinch	d																					
Kirkcaldy	d																					
Inverkeithing	d																					
Glasgow Central 15	d																	10 55	10 55	10 55	10 55	
Motherwell	d																	11 10	11 10	11 10	11 10	
Haymarket	d																	11 51	11 51	11 51		
Edinburgh 10	d		09 50	11 05	11 05	11 05									12 52		11 05	12 08	12 08	12 08	12 08	
Haymarket	d														12 56							
Lockerbie	d																					
Carlisle 8	d														14 07							
Penrith North Lakes	d														14 22							
Oxenholme Lake District	d																					
Lancaster 6	d														14 57							
Preston 8	d														15 17							
Wigan North Western	d														15 28							
Warrington Bank Quay	d														15 39							
M'chester Piccadilly 10 🚌	d	14 27										15 07	15 07			15 27						
Stockport	d	14 36														15 36						
Wilmslow	d																					
Crewe 10	d														16 01							
Macclesfield	d	14 49														15 49						
Congleton	d																					
Stoke-on-Trent	d	15 07										15 43	15 43			16 07						
Stafford	d	15 25														16 25						
Wolverhampton 7 🚌	d	15 41										16 15	16 15		16 32	16 41						
Dunbar	d			11 25	11 25	11 26											11 25					
Berwick-upon-Tweed	d			11 48	11 48												11 48	12 47	12 47	12 47	12 47	
Alnmouth for Alnwick	d		10 47	12 08	12 08	12 08											12 08					
Morpeth	d		11 02																			
Newcastle 8	d		11 25	12 38	12 38	12 38					13 35						12 38	13 40	13 40	13 40	13 40	
Chester-le-Street	d																					
Durham	d		11 37	12 50	12 50	12 50					13 47						12 50	13 52	13 52	13 52	13 52	
Darlington 7	d		11 55	13 07	13 07	13 07					14 05						13 07	14 10	14 10	14 10	14 10	
York 8	d		12 28	13 40	13 40	13 40					14 34						13 40	14 41	14 41	14 41	14 41	
Leeds 10	d		13 00	14 10	14 10	14 10											14e10	15 10	15 10	15 10	15 10	
Wakefield Westgate 7	d		13 12	14 23	14 23	14 23											14 23	15 23	15 23	15 23	15 23	
Doncaster 7	d		13 30								14 59											
Sheffield 7 🚌	d		13 57	14 54	14 54	14 54					15 23						14 54	15 54	15 54	15 54	15 54	
Chesterfield	d		14 09	15 06	15 06	15 06											15 06	16 07	16 07	16 07	16 07	
Nottingham 8 🚌	d						15 05		15 05	15 05												16 05
Derby 6	d		14 34	15 28	15 28	15 28	15 35		15 35	15 35	15 54						15 30	16 29	16 29	16 29	16 29	16 35
Burton-on-Trent	d			15 39	15 39	15 38	15 48		15 48	15 48												16 48
Tamworth	d						16 00		16 00	16 00								16 48	16 48	16 48	16 48	17 00
Birmingham New Street 12	a	15 58	15 43	16 03	16 03	16 07	16 24		16 23	16 23	16 27	16 31	16 31		16 55	16 58	16 47	17 06	17 06	17 06	17 08	17 21
Birmingham New Street 12	d	16 03	16 12	16 12	16 12	16 12	16 30	16 30	16 30	16 30	16 33		16 42	16 33		17 03	17 12	17 12	17 12	17 12	17 12	17 30
Cheltenham Spa	a		16 50	16 50	16 50	16 50	17 10	17 10	17 10	17 10			17 24				17 50	17 50	17 50	17 50	17 52	18 10
Gloucester 7	a				17 02		17 21	17 21	17 21	17 21										18 02		18 21
Bristol Parkway 7	a		17 23	17 23	18 12	17 23							18 02				18 23	18 23	18 23	19 12	18 23	
Bristol Temple Meads 10	a		17 35	17 35	18 39								18 14				18 37	18 37	18 40	19 35		
Newport (South Wales)	a							18 06	18 07	18 07												
Cardiff Central 7	a							18 28	18 29	18 29												
Weston-super-Mare	a																					
Taunton	a		18 19	18 18	19 15												19 15	19 15	19 15	20 19		
Tiverton Parkway	a		18 32	18 31	19 28												19 28	19 28	19 28	20 32		
Exeter St Davids 6	a		18 48	18 46	19 48												19 48	19 48	19 48	20 48		
Dawlish	a																					
Teignmouth	a																					
Newton Abbot	a		19 07	19 06	20 07												20 07	20 07	20 07	21 07		
Torquay	a																					
Paignton	a																					
Totnes	a		19 20	19 19	20 20												20 20	20 20	20 20	21 21		
Plymouth	a		19 48	19 47	20 48												20 48	20 48	20 48	21 49		
Liskeard 6	a				21 12												21 12	21 12	21 12			
Bodmin Parkway	a				21 24												21 24	21 24	21 24			
Lostwithiel	a																					
Par	a				21 35												21 35	21 35	21 35			
St Austell	a				21 42												21 42	21 42	21 42			
Truro	a				21 59												21 59	21 59	21 59			
Redruth	a				22 11												22 11	22 11	22 11			
Camborne	a				22 17												22 17	22 17	22 17			
Hayle	a																					
St Erth	a				22 29												22 29	22 29	22 29			
Penzance	a				22 38												22 38	22 38	22 38			
Birmingham International ✈	d	16 14														17 14						
Coventry	d	16 25														17 25						
Leamington Spa 8	d	16 38									17 00			17 00		17 38						
Banbury	a	16 54									17 17			17 17		17 54						
Oxford	a	17 14									17 38			17 38		18 14						
Reading 7	a	17 39									18 09			18 09		18 42						
Guildford	a																					
Basingstoke	a	18 09														19 09						
Winchester	a	18 24														19 24						
Southampton Airport Pkwy ✈	a	18 33														19 33						
Southampton Central ⛴	a	18 42														19 40						
Brockenhurst 3	a	19 01														20 02						
Bournemouth	a	19 26														20 26						

A until 19 June
B from 7 August until 11 September, from 30 October
C from 26 June until 31 July. 🍴 to Totnes
D from 18 September until 23 October
E from 7 August until 11 September. 🍴 to Tamworth
F from 30 October
G from 26 June until 31 July, from 18 September until 23 October. 🍴 to Tamworth
H from 26 June
I from 26 June until 31 July, from 18 September until 23 October
J until 19 June, from 7 August until 11 September, from 30 October
K until 19 June. 🍴 to Totnes
L from 7 August until 11 September. 🍴 from Edinburgh to Totnes
M from 30 October. 🍴 from Edinburgh to Totnes
N from 26 June until 31 July. 🍴 from Edinburgh
O from 18 September until 23 October. 🍴 from Edinburgh
P from 7 August until 11 September

Table 51

Sundays

Scotland, The North East, North West England - The South West and South Coast

		XC	XC	XC	XC	XC	XC	XC	XC	XC	VT	XC	XC	XC	XC	XC	XC	XC	XC	XC	XC	XC	XC
		◇1	◇1	◇1	◇1	◇1	◇1	◇1	◇1	◇1	◇1	◇1	◇1	◇1	◇1	◇1	◇1	◇1	◇1	◇1	◇1	◇1	◇1
		A	B	C	D	E	F	G	H	H			H	I	J	K	L	A	M	D	N	O	H
Aberdeen	d																						
Stonehaven	d																						
Montrose	d																						
Arbroath	d																						
Dundee	d																						
Leuchars 3	d																						
Cupar	d																						
Ladybank	d																						
Markinch	d																						
Kirkcaldy	d																						
Inverkeithing	d																						
Glasgow Central 15	d										13 55			11 52	11 52	11 52							
Motherwell	d													12 07	12 07	12 07							
Haymarket	d													12 47	12 47	12 47							
Edinburgh 10	d												12 08	13 06	13 06	13 06			13 50				
Haymarket	d																						
Lockerbie	d																						
Carlisle 8	d										15 11												
Penrith North Lakes	d																						
Oxenholme Lake District	d										15 46												
Lancaster 6	d																						
Preston 8	d										16 17												
Wigan North Western	d										16 28												
Warrington Bank Quay	d										16 39												
M'chester Piccadilly 10	d					16 07	16 07	16 07	16 07			16 27									17 07	17 07	
Stockport	d											16 36											
Wilmslow	d																						
Crewe 10	d										17 01												
Macclesfield	d											16 49											
Congleton	d																						
Stoke-on-Trent	d					16 43	16 43	16 43	16 43			17 08									17 43	17 43	
Stafford	d											17 26											
Wolverhampton 7	d					17 15	17 15	17 15	17 15		17 32	17 41									18 15	18 15	
Dunbar	d													13 25	13 25	13 25							
Berwick-upon-Tweed	d												12 47						14 31				
Alnmouth for Alnwick	d													14 06	14 06	14 06							
Morpeth	d																						
Newcastle 8	d		14 35	14 35									13c40	14 40	14 40	14 40			15 23				
Chester-le-Street	d																						
Durham	d		14 47	14 47									13 52	14 52	14 52	14 52			15 36				
Darlington 7	d		15 04	15 04									14 10	15 09	15 09	15 09			15 53				
York 8	d		15 34	15 34									14 41	15 38	15 39	15 39			16 23				
Leeds 10	d												15 10	16g10	16g10	16g10							
Wakefield Westgate 7	d												15 23	16 22	16 22	16 22							
Doncaster 7	d		15 59	15 59															16 51				
Sheffield 7	d		16 24	16 24									15 54	16 54	16 54	16 54			17 24				
Chesterfield	d												16 07	17 06	17 06	17 06							
Nottingham 6	d	16 05															17 10	17 10					
Derby 6	d	16b35	16 55	16 55									16 36	17 28	17 28	17 28	17 36	17 36	17 55				
Burton-on-Trent	d	16 48												17 39	17 39	17 39	17 48	17 48					
Tamworth	d	17 00															18 00	18 00					
Birmingham New Street 12	a	17 21	17 28	17 28		17 31	17 32	17 31	17 31		17 55	17 58	17 48	18 05	18 03	18 03	18 22	18 21	18 27		18 31	18 31	
Birmingham New Street 12	d	17 30	17 33	17 33	17 30			17 42	17 42	17 33		18 03	18 12	18 12	18 12	18 12	18 30	18 30	18 33	18 30		18 42	18 33
Cheltenham Spa	a	18 10			18 10			18 24	18 24				18 50	18 50	18 50	18 50	19 11	19 11		19 11		19 24	
Gloucester 7	a	18 22			18 22											19 02	19 24	19 26		19 26			
Bristol Parkway 7	a							18 57	19 02				19 23	19 23	19 23	20 15						20 02	
Bristol Temple Meads 10	a							19 09	19 14				19 37		19 35	20 35						20 14	
Newport (South Wales)	a	19 07			19 07													20 11		20 11			
Cardiff Central 7	a	19 27			19 27													20 31		20 31			
Weston-super-Mare	a																					20 36	
Taunton	a												20 19		20 18	21 15						20 59	
Tiverton Parkway	a												20 30		20 31	21 28						21 12	
Exeter St Davids 6	a												20 48		20 46	21 43						21 28	
Dawlish	a																					21 42	
Teignmouth	a																					21 47	
Newton Abbot	a												21 07		21 06	22 03						21 55	
Torquay	a																					22 07	
Paignton	a																					22 13	
Totnes	a												21 21		21 19	22 19							
Plymouth	a												21 49		21 47	22 46							
Liskeard 6	a																						
Bodmin Parkway	a																						
Lostwithiel	a																						
Par	a																						
St Austell	a																						
Truro	a																						
Redruth	a																						
Camborne	a																						
Hayle	a																						
St Erth	a																						
Penzance	a																						
Birmingham International	d											18 14											
Coventry	d											18 25											
Leamington Spa 8	d		18 01	18 01						18 01		18 38							19 00				19 00
Banbury	a		18 19	18 19						18 19		18 54							19 17				19 17
Oxford	a		18 38	18 40						18 40		19 14							19 38				19 38
Reading 7	a		19 06	19 06						19 06		19 42							20 09				20 09
Guildford	a																						
Basingstoke	a											20 09											
Winchester	a											20 24											
Southampton Airport Pkway	a											20 33											
Southampton Central	a											20 42											
Brockenhurst 3	a											21 02											
Bournemouth	a											21 26											

A from 26 June until 31 July, from 18 September. to Gloucester
B from 30 October
C from 26 June until 23 October
D until 19 June. to Gloucester
E from 18 September until 23 October
F from 26 June until 31 July
G from 7 August until 11 September, from 30 October
H until 19 June
I from 18 September until 23 October. from Edinburgh
J from 7 August until 11 September, from 30 October. from Edinburgh
K from 26 June until 31 July. from Edinburgh to Bristol Parkway
L from 7 August until 11 September
M from 26 June
N from 26 June until 31 July, from 18 September until 23 October
O until 19 June, from 7 August until 11 September

Table 51

Scotland, The North East, North West England - The South West and South Coast

		VT	XC	XC	XC	XC	XC	XC	XC	XC	XC	XC	XC	XC	XC	VT	XC	XC	XC	XC	XC	XC	XC
		◇1	◇1	◇1	◇1	◇1	◇1	◇1	◇1	◇1	◇1	◇1	◇1	◇1	◇1	◇1	◇1	◇1	◇1	◇1	◇1	◇1	◇1
			A	B	C	D	E	F	G	H	I	J	K	L	I		A	M	C	D	N	H	O
Aberdeen	d				11 12	11 12	11 12											11 12					
Stonehaven	d				11 29	11 29	11 29											11 29					
Montrose	d				11 50	11 50	11 50											11 50					
Arbroath	d				12 06	12 06	12 06											12 06					
Dundee	d				12 25	12 25	12 25											12 25					
Leuchars 3	d				12 38	12 38	12 38											12 38					
Cupar	d				12 45	12 45	12 45											12 45					
Ladybank	d																						
Markinch	d																						
Kirkcaldy	d				13 03	13 03	13 03											13 03					
Inverkeithing	d				13 18	13 18	13 18											13 18					
Glasgow Central 15	d			11 52												15 57			13 49	13 49	13 49		
Motherwell	d			12 07															14 04	14 04	14 04		
Haymarket	d			12 47	13 37	13 37	13 37											13 37	14 43	14 43	14 43		
Edinburgh 10	d	14 52		13b06	14e08	14e08	14e08											14 08	15 07	15 07	15 07		
Haymarket	d	14 57																					
Lockerbie	d																						
Carlisle 8	d	16 07														17 09							
Penrith North Lakes	d	16 22																					
Oxenholme Lake District	d															17 44							
Lancaster 6	d	16 57																					
Preston 8	d	17 17														18 17							
Wigan North Western	d	17 28														18 28							
Warrington Bank Quay	d	17 39														18 39							
M'chester Piccadilly 10	d		17 27									18 07	18 07	18 07			18 27						
Stockport	d		17 36														18 36						
Wilmslow	d																						
Crewe 10	d	18 01														19 01							
Macclesfield	d		17 49														18 49						
Congleton	d																						
Stoke-on-Trent	d		18 08									18 43	18 43	18 43			19 07						
Stafford	d		18 26														19 25						
Wolverhampton 7	d	18 33	18 41									19 14	19 15	19 15		19 32	19 41						
Dunbar	d			13 25															15 27	15 27	15 27		
Berwick-upon-Tweed	d				14 47	14 47	14 47											14 47					
Alnmouth for Alnwick	d			14 06																			
Morpeth	d																						
Newcastle 8	d			14 40	15 39	15 39	15 39			16 35								15 39	16i40	16i40	16i40		17 35
Chester-le-Street	d																						
Durham	d			14 52	15 51	15 51	15 51			16 47								15 51	16 52	16 52	16 52		17 47
Darlington 7	d			15 09	16 08	16 08	16 08			17 05								16 08	17 09	17 09	17 09		18 05
York 8	d			15 39	16 39	16 39	16 39			17 34								16 39	17 41	17 41	17 41		18 34
Leeds 10	d			16c10	17f10	17f10	17f10											17 10	18 10	18 10	18 10		
Wakefield Westgate 7	d			16 22	17 22	17 22	17 22											17 22	18 22	18 22	18 22		
Doncaster 7	d									17 59													18 59
Sheffield 7	d			16 54	17 54	17 54	17 54			18 24								17 54	18 54	18 54	18 54		19 24
Chesterfield	d			17 06	18 06	18 06	18 06											18 06	19 06	19 06	19 06		
Nottingham 8	d							18 05	18 05													19 09	
Derby 6	d			17 28	18 26	18 26	18 26	18 35	18 35	18 55								18g35	19 28	19 28	19 28	19 33	19 55
Burton-on-Trent	d							18 48	18 48										19 39	19 39	19 39	19 48	
Tamworth	d				18 47	18 47	18 47	19 00	19 00													20 00	
Birmingham New Street 12	a	18 55	18 58	18 47	19 06	19 04	19 04	19 21	19 21	19 28		19 31	19 32	19 31		19 55	19 58	19 51	20 04	20 03	20 03	20 23	20 27
Birmingham New Street 12	d		19 03	19 12	19 12	19 12	19 12	19 30	19 30	19 33	19 30			19 42	19 33		20 03	20 12	20 12	20 12	20 12		20 33
Cheltenham Spa	a			19 50	19 50	19 50	19 50	20 10	20 10		20 10			20 24				20 50	20 50	20 50	20 50		
Gloucester 7	a						20 02	20 21	20 21		20 21										21 02		
Bristol Parkway 7	a			20 23	20 23	20 23	21 12							20 57				21 23	21 23	21 23	22 12		
Bristol Temple Meads 10	a			20 35		20 35	21 35							21 09				21 35		21 35	22 25		
Newport (South Wales)	a								21 06		21 06												
Cardiff Central 7	a								21 26		21 26												
Weston-super-Mare	a																						
Taunton	a			21 15		21 15	22 15											22 15		22 15			
Tiverton Parkway	a			21 28		21 28	22 28											22 28		22 28			
Exeter St Davids 6	a			21 43		21 43	22 45											22 45		22 45			
Dawlish	a																						
Teignmouth	a																						
Newton Abbot	a			22 03		22 03	23 06											23 07		23 06			
Torquay	a																						
Paignton	a																						
Totnes	a			22 19		22 19	23 20											23 20		23 20			
Plymouth	a			22 46		22 46	23 51											23 50		23 49			
Liskeard 6	a																						
Bodmin Parkway	a																						
Lostwithiel	a																						
Par	a																						
St Austell	a																						
Truro	a																						
Redruth	a																						
Camborne	a																						
Hayle	a																						
St Erth	a																						
Penzance	a																						
Birmingham International	d		19 14														20 14						
Coventry	d		19 25														20 25						
Leamington Spa 8	d		19 38							20 00					20 00		20 38						21 00
Banbury	a		19 54							20 18					20 18		20 54						21 17
Oxford	a		20 14							20 40					20 40		21 14						21 38
Reading 7	a		20 42							21 09					21 09		21 43						22 06
Guildford	a																						
Basingstoke	a		21 09														22 09						
Winchester	a		21 24														22 25						
Southampton Airport Pkway	a		21 33														22 33						
Southampton Central	a		21 43														22 42						
Brockenhurst 3	a		22 02																				
Bournemouth	a		22 26																				

- **A** to Oxford
- **B** until 19 June. from Edinburgh
- **C** from 18 September until 23 October. from Edinburgh
- **D** from 7 August until 11 September, from 30 October. from Edinburgh to Bristol Parkway
- **E** from 26 June until 31 July. from Edinburgh to Bristol Parkway
- **F** from 7 August until 11 September. to Tamworth
- **G** from 26 June until 31 July, from 18 September. to Tamworth
- **H** from 26 June
- **I** until 19 June
- **J** from 18 September until 23 October
- **K** from 26 June until 31 July
- **L** until 19 June, from 7 August until 11 September, from 30 October
- **M** until 19 June. from Edinburgh to Bristol Parkway
- **N** from 26 June until 31 July. from Edinburgh
- **O** from 7 August until 11 September

Table 51

Sundays

Scotland, The North East, North West England - The South West and South Coast

		XC	XC	XC	XC	XC	XC	VT	XC	XC	XC	XC	XC	XC	XC	XC	XC	XC	XC	XC	XC	XC
		◇1	◇1	◇1	◇1	◇1	◇1	◇1	◇1	◇1	◇1	◇1	◇1	◇1	◇1	◇1	◇1	◇1	◇1	◇1	◇1	◇1
		A	B	C	B	D	E		F	G	H	I	J	K	L	L	M	N	O	P	Q	R
Aberdeen	d																					
Stonehaven	d																					
Montrose	d																					
Arbroath	d																					
Dundee	d																					
Leuchars 3	d																					
Cupar	d																					
Ladybank	d																					
Markinch	d																					
Kirkcaldy	d																					
Inverkeithing	d																					
Glasgow Central 15	d									13 49	14 55	14 55	14 55	14 55					14 55			
Motherwell	d									14 04	15 11	15 11	15 11	15 11					15 11			
Haymarket	d									14 43	15 51	15 51	15 51	15 51					15 51			
Edinburgh 10	d							16 52		15 07	16 05	16 05	16 05	16 05					16 05	17 07	17 07	17 07
Haymarket	d							16 56														
Lockerbie	d																					
Carlisle 8	d							18 07														
Penrith North Lakes	d																					
Oxenholme Lake District	d							18 42														
Lancaster 6	d							18 57														
Preston 8	d							19 17														
Wigan North Western	d							19 28														
Warrington Bank Quay	d							19 39														
M'chester Piccadilly 10	d		19 07			19 07	19 07		19 27								20 07	20 07				
Stockport	d								19 36								20 16	20 16				
Wilmslow	d																					
Crewe 10	d							20 01														
Macclesfield	d								19 49								20 29	20 29				
Congleton	d																					
Stoke-on-Trent	d		19 43			19 43	19 43		20 07								20 47	20 47				
Stafford	d								20 27								21 09	21 09				
Wolverhampton 7	d		20 15			20 15	20 15	20 33	20 41								21 22	21 22				
Dunbar	d									15 27	16 25	16 25	16 25	16 25					16 25	17 27	17 27	17 27
Berwick-upon-Tweed	d																			17 50	17 50	17 50
Alnmouth for Alnwick	d										17 05	17 05	17 05	17 05					17 05			
Morpeth	d										17 20	17 20	17 20	17 20					17 20			
Newcastle 8	d	17 35			17 35					16 40	17 40	17 40	17 40	17 40		18 20			17 40	18 38	18 38	18 38
Chester-le-Street	d																					
Durham	d	17 47			17 47					16 52	17 52	17 52	17 52	17 52		18 32			17 52	18 51	18 51	18 51
Darlington 7	d	18 05			18 05					17 09	18 09	18 09	18 09	18 09		18 50			18 09	19 08	19 08	19 08
York 8	d	18 34			18 34					17 41	18 40	18 40	18 40	18 40		19 24			18 40	19 39	19 39	19 39
Leeds 10	d									18 10	19 10	19 10	19 10	19 10					19 10	20 10	20 10	20 10
Wakefield Westgate 7	d									18 22	19 22	19 22	19 22	19 22					19 22	20 22	20 22	20 22
Doncaster 7	d	18 59			18 59											19 50						
Sheffield 7	d	19 24			19 24					18 54	19 54	19 54	19 54	19 54		20 20			19 54	20 54	20 54	20 54
Chesterfield	d									19 06	20 06	20 06	20 06	20 06					20 06	21 06	21 06	21 06
Nottingham 8	d														20 10							
Derby 6	d	19 55			19 55					19f33	20 27	20 27	20 27	20 27	20 35	20 54			20 33	21 27	21 27	21 27
Burton-on-Trent	d														20 48					21 38	21 38	21 38
Tamworth	d										20 47	20 47	20 47	20 47	21 00					21 49	21 49	21 49
Birmingham New Street 12	a	20 27	20 31		20 27	20 31	20 31	20 50	21 00	20 47	21 06	21 04	21 04	21 06	21 18	21 35	21 39	21 39	21 50	22 06	22 06	22 08
Birmingham New Street 12	d	20 33		20 33	20 33	20 42	20 42		21 03	21 12	21 12	21 12	21 12	21 12				21 42	22 12	22 12	22 12	22 12
Cheltenham Spa	a					21 24	21 24			21 50	21 50	21 50	21 50	21 50				22 24	22 50	22 50	22 50	22 50
Gloucester 7	a									22 02	22 01	22 01	22 01	22 02							23 03	
Bristol Parkway 7	a					21 58	21 59			22 35	22 34	22 34		23 22				22 56	23 24	23 24	23 55	
Bristol Temple Meads 10	a						22 11			22 45	22 46	22 46	23 20	23 41				23 10	23 36	23 36	00 10	00 13
Newport (South Wales)	a																					
Cardiff Central 7	a																					
Weston-super-Mare	a																					
Taunton	a																					
Tiverton Parkway	a																					
Exeter St Davids 6	a																					
Dawlish	a																					
Teignmouth	a																					
Newton Abbot	a																					
Torquay	a																					
Paignton	a																					
Totnes	a																					
Plymouth	a																					
Liskeard 6	a																					
Bodmin Parkway	a																					
Lostwithiel	a																					
Par	a																					
St Austell	a																					
Truro	a																					
Redruth	a																					
Camborne	a																					
Hayle	a																					
St Erth	a																					
Penzance	a																					
Birmingham International	d								21 14													
Coventry	d								21 24													
Leamington Spa 8	d	21 00		21 00	21 00				21 35													
Banbury	a	21 17		21 17	21 17																	
Oxford	a	21 38		21 38	21 38				22 08													
Reading 7	a	22 07		22 07	22 10				22 35													
Guildford	a	22 42																				
Basingstoke	a																					
Winchester	a																					
Southampton Airport Pkway	a																					
Southampton Central	a																					
Brockenhurst 3	a																					
Bournemouth	a																					

A from 18 September. ⚲ to Oxford
B from 26 June until 31 July
C until 19 June
D from 18 September until 23 October. ⚲ to Wolverhampton
E until 19 June, from 7 August until 11 September, from 30 October. ⚲ to Wolverhampton
F ⚲ to Wolverhampton
G until 19 June. ⚲ from Edinburgh
H from 7 August until 11 September. ⚲ from Edinburgh to Tamworth
I from 30 October. ⚲ from Edinburgh to Tamworth
J from 18 September until 23 October. ⚲ from Edinburgh to Tamworth
K from 26 June until 31 July. ⚲ from Edinburgh to Tamworth
L from 26 June
M from 26 June until 31 July, from 18 September until 23 October
N until 19 June, from 7 August until 11 September, from 30 October
O until 19 June. ⚲ from Edinburgh to Derby
P from 7 August until 11 September, from 30 October. ⚲ to York
Q from 26 June until 31 July. ⚲ to York
R from 18 September until 23 October. ⚲ to York

Table 51

Sundays

Scotland, The North East, North West England - The South West and South Coast

		XC	XC	VT	XC	XC	VT	XC		XC	XC
		◇1	◇1	◇1	◇1	◇1	◇1	◇1		◇1	◇1
		A	A			B		C			D
			🛒	🍽		🛒	🍽	🛒			🛒
Aberdeen	d										
Stonehaven	d										
Montrose	d										
Arbroath	d										
Dundee	d										
Leuchars 3	d										
Cupar	d										
Ladybank	d										
Markinch	d										
Kirkcaldy	d										
Inverkeithing	d										
Glasgow Central 15	d			18 30				16 55			16 55
Motherwell	d							17 11			17 11
Haymarket	d							17 55			17 55
Edinburgh 10	d					17 07	18 52	18 07			18 07
Haymarket	d						18 57				
Lockerbie	d										
Carlisle 8	d			19 44			20 07				
Penrith North Lakes	d						20 22				
Oxenholme Lake District	d			20 19							
Lancaster 6	d			20 34			20 57				
Preston 8	d			20 55			21 17				
Wigan North Western	d			21 07			21 28				
Warrington Bank Quay	d			21 18			21 39				
M'chester Piccadilly 10 ⛴	d				21 07					22 07	
Stockport	d				21 16					22 16	
Wilmslow	d										
Crewe 10	d			21 40			22 01				
Macclesfield	d				21 29					22 29	
Congleton	d										
Stoke-on-Trent	d				21 47					22 47	
Stafford	d			22 02	22 06					23 05	
Wolverhampton 7 ⛴	d			22 18	22 22		22 32			23 19	
Dunbar	d					17 27		18 26			18 26
Berwick-upon-Tweed	d					17 50		18 50			18 50
Alnmouth for Alnwick	d										
Morpeth	d										
Newcastle 8	d		19 25			18 38		19 40			19 40
Chester-le-Street	d										
Durham	d		19 37			18 51		19 52			19 52
Darlington 7	d		19 54			19 08		20 09			20 09
York 8	d		20 24			19 39		20 39			20 39
Leeds 10	d					20 10		21 10			21 10
Wakefield Westgate 7	d					20 22		21 22			21 22
Doncaster 7	d		20 50								
Sheffield 7 ⛴	d		21 20			20 54		21 54			21 54
Chesterfield	d		21 32			21 06		22 06			22 06
Nottingham 8 ⛴	d	21 08									
Derby 6	d	21 35	21 53			21 44		22 27			22 38
Burton-on-Trent	d	21 48	22 04					22 38			
Tamworth	d	22 00	22 15					22 49			
Birmingham New Street 12	a	22 23	22 34	22 38	22 40	22 53	22 55	23 07		23 36	23 48
Birmingham New Street 12	d										
Cheltenham Spa	a										
Gloucester 7	a										
Bristol Parkway 7	a										
Bristol Temple Meads 10	a										
Newport (South Wales)	a										
Cardiff Central 7	a										
Weston-super-Mare	a										
Taunton	a										
Tiverton Parkway	a										
Exeter St Davids 6	a										
Dawlish	a										
Teignmouth	a										
Newton Abbot	a										
Torquay	a										
Paignton	a										
Totnes	a										
Plymouth	a										
Liskeard 6	a										
Bodmin Parkway	a										
Lostwithiel	a										
Par	a										
St Austell	a										
Truro	a										
Redruth	a										
Camborne	a										
Hayle	a										
St Erth	a										
Penzance	a										
Birmingham International ✈	d										
Coventry	d										
Leamington Spa 8	d										
Banbury	a										
Oxford	a										
Reading 7	a										
Guildford	a										
Basingstoke	a										
Winchester	a										
Southampton Airport Pkway ✈	a										
Southampton Central ⛴	a										
Brockenhurst 3	a										
Bournemouth	a										

A from 26 June
B until 19 June. 🛒 to York
C from 26 June. 🛒 from Edinburgh to York
D until 19 June. 🛒 from Edinburgh to York

South Coast and the South West - North West England, The North East and Scotland

		XC	XC	XC	XC	XC	XC	XC	XC	AW	XC	XC	XC	XC	XC	VT	XC	XC	XC	XC	XC	XC	VT
				MO	MO				MX	MO	MX	MO											
		◇1	◇1	◇1	◇1	◇1	◇1	◇1	◇1		◇1	◇1	◇1	◇1	1	◇1	◇1	◇1	1	◇1	◇1	1	◇1
		A	B	C	D	E	F	G				H		I									
		🍴	🍴	🍴	🍴								🍴	🍴	🍴	⊠	🍴	🍴		🍴	🍴	🍴	⊠
Bournemouth	d																						
Brockenhurst 3	d																						
Southampton Central ⛴	d																						
Southampton Airport Pkwy ✈	d																						
Winchester	d																						
Basingstoke	d																						
Guildford	d																						
Reading 7	d																						
Oxford	d																						
Banbury	d																						
Leamington Spa 8	d																						
Coventry	d																						
Birmingham International ✈	d									23p08													
Penzance	d	15p30																					
St Erth	d	15p38																					
Hayle	d																						
Camborne	d	15p51																					
Redruth	d	15p57																					
Truro	d	16p09																					
St Austell	d	16p25																					
Par	d	16p33																					
Lostwithiel	d																						
Bodmin Parkway	d	16p44																					
Liskeard 6	d	16p56																					
Plymouth	d	17p25	17p23	18p23																			
Totnes	d	17p51	17p49	18p49																			
Paignton	d																						
Torquay	d																						
Newton Abbot	d	18p03	18p03	19p03																			
Teignmouth	d																						
Dawlish	d																						
Exeter St Davids 6	d	18p24	18p25	19p25																			
Tiverton Parkway	d	18p36	18p38	19p38																			
Taunton	d	18p52	18p54	19p54																			
Weston-super-Mare	d																						
Cardiff Central 7	d										21p50												
Newport (South Wales)	d										22p05												
Bristol Temple Meads 10	d	19p30	19p30	20p30								22p10											
Bristol Parkway 7	d	19p40	19b45	20p40	20p40							22p24											
Gloucester 7	d		21p04								22p47	23p21											
Cheltenham Spa	d	20p12	21p13	21p12	21p12						22p58	23p29											
London Paddington	d																						
Birmingham New Street 12	a	20p50	21p52	21p51	21p51					23p19	00 04	00 16											
Birmingham New Street 12	d	21p03	22p03	22p03	22p03	22p30	22p30	22p30	23p09	23p24			05 57	06 00	06 19	06 19	06 22	06 30	06 49	06 57	07 03	07 19	07 20
Tamworth	d		22p20	22p20	22p20				23p28						06 39				07 06		07 19	07 38	
Burton-on-Trent	d								23p39						06 51				07 18		07 29	07 49	
Derby 6	a	22p31	22p45	22p45	22p45				23p55					06 33	07 05			07 11	07 34		07 42	08 05	
Nottingham 8 ⛴	a								00 18						07 41				08 08			08 33	
Chesterfield	a	23p06	23p06	23p06	23p06									06 53				07 31			08 02		
Sheffield 7 ⛴	a	23p22	23p22	23p22	23p22									07 07				07 48			08 17		
Doncaster 7	a																	08 24					
Wakefield Westgate 7	a													07 36							08 46		
Leeds 10	a	00 34	00 34	00 34	00 34									07 52							09 03		
York 8	a													08 23				08 46			09 32		
Darlington 7	a													08 55				09 16			09 58		
Durham	a													09 12				09 33			10 16		
Chester-le-Street	a																						
Newcastle 8	a													09 30				09 48			10 31		
Morpeth	a																						
Alnmouth for Alnwick	a													09 58									
Berwick-upon-Tweed	a													10 19									
Dunbar	a																				11 36		
Wolverhampton 7 ⛴	d					22p48	22p48	22p48		23c46			06 16			06 36	06 40			07 16			07 37
Stafford	a					23p00	23p00	23p00					06 29				06 53			07 29			
Stoke-on-Trent	a					23p20	23p20	23p20					06 50				07 13						
Congleton	a												07 02										
Macclesfield	a												07 11				07 30						
Crewe 10	a															07 07				07 50			08 07
Wilmslow	a																			08 08			
Stockport	a												07 27				07 45			08 20			
M'chester Piccadilly 10 ⛴	a					00 12	00 32	00 33					07 37				07 59			08 34			
Warrington Bank Quay	a															07 26							08 26
Wigan North Western	a															07 37							08 37
Preston 8	a															07 51							08 51
Lancaster 6	a															08 08							09 08
Oxenholme Lake District	a															08 21							
Penrith North Lakes	a																						09 44
Carlisle 8	a															09 01							09 59
Lockerbie	a																						
Haymarket	a															10 16							
Edinburgh 10	a													11 05		10 21					12 03		
Haymarket	a													11 14									
Motherwell	a													11 52									
Glasgow Central 15	a													12 14									11 16
Inverkeithing	a																						
Kirkcaldy	a																						
Markinch	a																						
Ladybank	a																						
Cupar	a																						
Leuchars 8	a																						
Dundee	a																						
Arbroath	a																						
Montrose	a																						
Stonehaven	a																						
Aberdeen	a																						

A MO until 20 June. 🍴 from Plymouth to Cheltenham Spa
B MO from 27 June until 1 August. 🍴 to Cheltenham Spa
C From 8 August until 12 September, from 31 October. 🍴 to Cheltenham Spa
D From 19 September until 24 October. 🍴 to Cheltenham Spa
E ThFO
F TWO until 15 June, TWO from 13 September
G TWO from 21 June until 7 September
H From 27 June until 1 August
I 🍴 to Berwick-upon-Tweed
b Previous night, arr. 1938
c Previous night, arr. 2340

South Coast and the South West - North West England, The North East and Scotland

		AW	XC	XC	XC	XC	XC	XC	XC	XC	VT	AW	XC	XC	XC	XC	XC	VT	AW	XC	XC	XC	XC
		◇	◇1	◇1	◇1	1	◇1	◇1	1	◇1	◇1	◇	◇1	◇1	◇1	1	◇1	◇1	◇	◇1	◇1	◇1	◇1
					A		B			A										C	D		B
		🛒	🛒	🛒	🛒		🛒		🛒	🛒	⊠	🛒	🛒	🛒	🛒	🛒	🛒	⊠	🛒	🛒	🛒	🛒	🛒
Bournemouth	d																					06 30	
Brockenhurst 3	d																					06 49	
Southampton Central ⛴	d				05 15									06 15								07 15	
Southampton Airport Pkway ✈	d				05 22									06 22								07 22	
Winchester	d				05 31									06 31								07 31	
Basingstoke	d				05 47									06 47								07 47	
Guildford	d									06 02													
Reading 7	d				06 11					06 41				07 11			07 41					08 11	
Oxford	d				06 36					07 07				07 36			08 07					08 36	
Banbury	d				06 54					07 26				07 54			08 27					08 54	
Leamington Spa 8	d				07 12					07 43				08 12			08 44					09 12	
Coventry	d				07 27									08 27								09 27	
Birmingham International ✈	d	07 09			07 38							08 09		08 38					09 09			09 38	
Penzance	d																						
St Erth	d																						
Hayle	d																						
Camborne	d																						
Redruth	d																						
Truro	d																						
St Austell	d																						
Par	d																						
Lostwithiel	d																						
Bodmin Parkway	d																						
Liskeard 6	d																						
Plymouth	d														05 20								06 25
Totnes	d														05 45								06 50
Paignton	d																						
Torquay	d																						
Newton Abbot	d														06 03								07 03
Teignmouth	d																						
Dawlish	d																						
Exeter St Davids 6	d														06 23								07 23
Tiverton Parkway	d														06 37								07 37
Taunton	d														06 51								07 51
Weston-super-Mare	d																						
Cardiff Central 7	d																			07 00	07 45		
Newport (South Wales)	d																			07 15	08 02		
Bristol Temple Meads 10	d						06 27						07 00		07 30					08 00			08 30
Bristol Parkway 7	d						06 40						07 10		07 40					08 10			08 40
Gloucester 7	d							07 10													08 46		
Cheltenham Spa	d						07 12	07 21					07 42		08 12					08 42	08 57		09 12
London Paddington	d																						
Birmingham New Street 12	a	07 20			07 48		07 56	08 16		08 15		08 20	08 26	08 48	08 56		09 18		09 20	09 26	09 45	09 48	09 56
Birmingham New Street 12	d	07 24	07 30	07 31	07 57	07 49	08 03		08 19	08 30	08 20	08 24	08 31	08 57	09 03	09 19	09 30	09 20	09 24	09 31	09 49	09 57	10 03
Tamworth	d					08 06	08 19		08 36							09 39					10 06		10 19
Burton-on-Trent	d					08 18	08 29		08 48						09 25	09 51					10 19		
Derby 6	a		08 11			08 34	08 42		09 05	09 11					09 39	10 05	10 09				10 34		10 40
Nottingham 8 🚌	a					09 05			09 35							10 33					11 05		
Chesterfield	a		08 32				09 02								10 02								11 02
Sheffield 7 🚌	a		08 45				09 17			09 43					10 17		10 41						11 17
Doncaster 7	a		09 18							10 18							11 18						
Wakefield Westgate 7	a						09 46								10 46								11 46
Leeds 10	a						10 02								11 02								12 01
York 8	a		09 45				10 28			10 45					11 27		11 47						12 27
Darlington 7	a		10 13				11 00			11 14					11 57		12 14						12 58
Durham	a		10 31				11 18			11 31					12 22		12 31						13 15
Chester-le-Street	a																						
Newcastle 8	a		10 46				11 35			11 47					12 35		12 47						13 30
Morpeth	a																						
Alnmouth for Alnwick	a																						14 01
Berwick-upon-Tweed	a						12 21																14 22
Dunbar	a														13 39								
Wolverhampton 7 🚌	d	07 43		07 49	08 15						08 37	08 43	08 49	09 15				09 37	09 43	09 49		10 15	
Stafford	a				08 29								09 00	09 29						10 00		10 29	
Stoke-on-Trent	a			08 18	08 54								09 19	09 54						10 19		10 54	
Congleton	a																						
Macclesfield	a			08 35	09 11									10 11								11 11	
Crewe 10	a										09 07							10 07					
Wilmslow	a																						
Stockport	a			08 49	09 27								09 49	10 27						10 49		11 27	
M'chester Piccadilly 10 🚌	a			08 59	09 39								09 59	10 39						10 59		11 39	
Warrington Bank Quay	a										09 26							10 26					
Wigan North Western	a										09 37							10 37					
Preston 8	a										09 51							10 51					
Lancaster 6	a										10 08							11 08					
Oxenholme Lake District	a										10 22												
Penrith North Lakes	a																	11 44					
Carlisle 8	a										11 02							12 00					
Lockerbie	a																						
Haymarket	a										12 14												
Edinburgh 10	a						13 06				12 21				14 10								15 06
Haymarket	a						13 15																15 14
Motherwell	a						13 52																15 51
Glasgow Central 15	a						14 12											13 17					16 23
Inverkeithing	a																						
Kirkcaldy	a																						
Markinch	a																						
Ladybank	a																						
Cupar	a																						
Leuchars 3	a																						
Dundee	a																						
Arbroath	a																						
Montrose	a																						
Stonehaven	a																						
Aberdeen	a																						

A 🛒 from Reading
B 🛒 to Berwick-upon-Tweed
C 🛒 from Bristol Temple Meads
D 🛒 from Newport (South Wales)

Table 51

South Coast and the South West - North West England, The North East and Scotland

		XC	XC	VT	AW	XC	XC	XC	XC	XC	XC	VT	AW	XC	XC	XC	XC	XC	VT	AW	XC	XC
		1	◇1	◇1	◇	◇1	◇1	◇1	◇1	1	◇1	◇1	◇	◇1	◇1	◇1	1	◇1	◇1	◇	◇1	◇1
				A			B									C						B
			🛒	⊠	🛒	🛒	🛒	🛒	🛒		🛒	☕	🛒	🛒	🛒	🛒	🛒	🛒	☕	🛒	🛒	🛒
Bournemouth	d							07 30							08 45							
Brockenhurst 3	d							07 49							09 00							
Southampton Central ⛴	d							08b15							09 15			09 46				
Southampton Airport Pkway ✈	d							08 22							09 22			09 53				
Winchester	d		08 01					08 31							09 31			10 03				
Basingstoke	d		08 18					08 47							09 47			10 19				
Guildford	d																					
Reading 7	d		08 41					09c11			09 41				10e11			10f41				
Oxford	d		09 07					09 36			10 07				10 36			11 07				
Banbury	d		09 26					09 54			10 25				10 54			11 25				
Leamington Spa 8	d		09 43					10 12			10 43				11 12			11 43				
Coventry	d							10 27							11 27							
Birmingham International ✈	d				10 09			10 38					11 09		11 38					12 09		
Penzance	d															06 28						
St Erth	d															06 36						
Hayle	d																					
Camborne	d															06 46						
Redruth	d															06 52						
Truro	d															07 04						
St Austell	d															07 20						
Par	d															07 28						
Lostwithiel	d																					
Bodmin Parkway	d															07 39						
Liskeard 6	d															07 53						
Plymouth	d								07 25							08 25						
Totnes	d								07 50							08 50						
Paignton	d					07 01																
Torquay	d					07 07																
Newton Abbot	d					07 18			08 03							09 03						
Teignmouth	d					07 25																
Dawlish	d					07 30																
Exeter St Davids 6	d					07 44			08 23							09 23						
Tiverton Parkway	d					07 57			08 37							09 37						
Taunton	d					08 12			08 51							09 51						
Weston-super-Mare	d					08 33																
Cardiff Central 7	d						08 45															10 45
Newport (South Wales)	d						09 02															11 00
Bristol Temple Meads 10	d					09 00			09 30					10 00		10 30					11 00	
Bristol Parkway 7	d					09 10			09 40					10 10		10 40					11 10	
Gloucester 7	d						09 46															11 46
Cheltenham Spa	d					09 42	09 57		10 12					10 42		11 12					11 42	11 57
London Paddington	d																					
Birmingham New Street 12	a		10 18		10 19	10 26	10 45	10 48	10 56		11 18		11 20	11 26	11 48	11 58		12 18		12 20	12 26	12 45
Birmingham New Street 12	d	10 19	10 30	10 20	10 24	10 31	10 49	10 57	11 03	11 19	11 30	11 20	11 24	11 31	11 57	12 03	12 19	12 30	12 20	12 24	12 31	12 49
Tamworth	d	10 36					11 06			11 39						12 19	12 36					13 06
Burton-on-Trent	d	10 48					11 19		11 25	11 51							12 49					13 19
Derby 6	a	11 05	11 08				11 34		11 39	12 05	12 07					12 41	13 05	13 09				13 34
Nottingham 8 🚌	a	11 33					12 05			12 33							13 33					14 05
Chesterfield	a								12 03							13 02						
Sheffield 7 🚌	a		11 43						12 17		12 41					13 17		13 41				
Doncaster 7	a		12 18								13 18							14 18				
Wakefield Westgate 7	a								12 46							13 46						
Leeds 10	a								13 03							14 02						
York 8	a		12 48						13 27		13 45					14 27		14 46				
Darlington 7	a		13 15						13 59		14 13					14 58		15 14				
Durham	a		13 33						14 16		14 30					15 15		15 31				
Chester-le-Street	a																					
Newcastle 8	a		13 46						14 31		14 46					15 33		15 46				
Morpeth	a								14 49													
Alnmouth for Alnwick	a															16 00						
Berwick-upon-Tweed	a															16 21						
Dunbar	a								15 40													
Wolverhampton 7 🚌	d			10 37	10 43	10 49		11 15				11 37	11 43	11 49	12 15				12 37	12 43	12 49	
Stafford	a					11 00		11 28						12 00	12 29						13 00	
Stoke-on-Trent	a					11 19		11 54						12 19	12 54						13 19	
Congleton	a																					
Macclesfield	a							12 11							13 11							
Crewe 10	a			11 07								12 07							13 07			
Wilmslow	a																					
Stockport	a					11 49		12 27						12 49	13 27						13 49	
M'chester Piccadilly 10 🚌	a					11 59		12 39						12 59	13 39						13 59	
Warrington Bank Quay	a			11 26								12 26							13 26			
Wigan North Western	a			11 37								12 37							13 37			
Preston 8	a			11 51								12 51							13 51			
Lancaster 6	a			12 08								13 08							14 08			
Oxenholme Lake District	a			12 22								13 22										
Penrith North Lakes	a																		14 44			
Carlisle 8	a			13 01								14 01							15 00			
Lockerbie	a																					
Haymarket	a			14 15															16 17			
Edinburgh 10	a			14 21					16 05							17 06			16 21			
Haymarket	a															17 15						
Motherwell	a															17 51						
Glasgow Central 15	a											15 17				18 16						
Inverkeithing	a																					
Kirkcaldy	a																					
Markinch	a																					
Ladybank	a																					
Cupar	a																					
Leuchars 3	a																					
Dundee	a																					
Arbroath	a																					
Montrose	a																					
Stonehaven	a																					
Aberdeen	a																					

A until 15 July, from 12 September
B 🛒 from Newport (South Wales)
C 🛒 from Plymouth to Berwick-upon-Tweed
b Arr. 0803
c Arr. 0904
e Arr. 1004
f Arr. 1035

South Coast and the South West - North West England, The North East and Scotland

		XC	XC	XC	XC	VT	AW	XC	XC	XC	XC	XC	VT	AW	XC	XC	XC	XC	XC	VT	AW	XC	XC
		◇1	◇1	1	◇1	◇1	◇	◇1	◇1	◇1	1	◇1	◇1	◇	◇1	◇1	◇1	◇1	1	◇1	◇	◇1	◇1
			A							B							A			C		D	E
		🛒	🛒		🛒	☕	🛒	🛒	🛒	🛒		🛒	☕	🛒	🛒	🛒	🛒	🛒		☕	🛒	🛒	🛒
Bournemouth	d	09 45							10 45							11 45							
Brockenhurst 3	d	10 00							11 00							12 00							
Southampton Central	d	10 15							11 15			11 46				12 15							
Southampton Airport Pkway	d	10 22							11 22			11 53				12 22							
Winchester	d	10 31							11 31			12 02				12 31							
Basingstoke	d	10 47							11 47			12 18				12 47							
Guildford	d																						
Reading 7	d	11b11			11 41				12f11			12i41				13j11		13 41					
Oxford	d	11 36			12 07				12 36			13 07				13 36		14 07					
Banbury	d	11 54			12 25				12 54			13 25				13 54		14 25					
Leamington Spa 8	d	12 12			12 43				13 12			13 43				14 12		14 41					
Coventry	d	12 27							13 27							14 27							
Birmingham International	d	12 38					13 09		13 38					14 09		14 38					15 09		
Penzance	d									08 28												09 40	
St Erth	d									08 36												09 48	
Hayle	d																					09 52	
Camborne	d									08 46												10 01	
Redruth	d									08 52												10 08	
Truro	d									09 04												10 19	
St Austell	d									09 20												10 35	
Par	d									09 28												10 43	
Lostwithiel	d																					10 50	
Bodmin Parkway	d									09 39												10 57	
Liskeard 6	d									09 51												11 09	
Plymouth	d		09 25							10g25							11 25					11l50	
Totnes	d		09 50							10 50							11 50					12 15	
Paignton	d							10 06															
Torquay	d							10 12															
Newton Abbot	d		10 03					10 23		11 03							12 03					12 28	
Teignmouth	d							10 30															
Dawlish	d							10 35															
Exeter St Davids 6	d		10 23					10 49		11 23							12 23					12 48	
Tiverton Parkway	d		10 37					11 02		11 37							12 37					13 02	
Taunton	d		10 51					11 17		11 51							12 51					13 16	
Weston-super-Mare	d																						
Cardiff Central 7	d																						13 45
Newport (South Wales)	d																						14 00
Bristol Temple Meads 10	d		11c30					12e00		12h30					13 00		13k30					14 00	
Bristol Parkway 7	d		11 40					12 10		12 40					13 10		13 40					14 10	
Gloucester 7	d																						14 46
Cheltenham Spa	d		12 12					12 42		13 12					13 42		14 12					14 42	14 57
London Paddington	d																						
Birmingham New Street 12	a	12 48	12 56		13 18		13 20	13 26	13 48	13 56		14 18		14 19	14 26	14 48	14 56	15 18			15 19	15 26	15 45
Birmingham New Street 12	d	12 57	13 03	13 19	13 30	13 20	13 24	13 31	13 57	14 03	14 19	14 30	14 20	14 24	14 31	14 57	15 03	15 30	15 19	15 20	15 26	15 31	15 49
Tamworth	d			13 39						14 19	14 39								15 39				16 06
Burton-on-Trent	d		13 28	13 51							14 51						15 26		15 51				16 19
Derby 6	a		13 40	14 05	14 08					14 42	15 05	15 08					15 39	16 08	16 05				16 34
Nottingham 8	a			14 33							15 33								16 33				17 05
Chesterfield	a		14 02							15 02							16 02						
Sheffield 7	a		14 17		14 41					15 17		15 41					16 17	16 41					
Doncaster 7	a				15 18							16 18						17 18					
Wakefield Westgate 7	a		14 46							15 46							16 49						
Leeds 10	a		15 01							16 02							17 04						
York 8	a		15 27		15 45					16 29		16 46					17 29	17 43					
Darlington 7	a		15 58		16 14					16 57		17 14					17 58	18 13					
Durham	a		16 16		16 31					17 14		17 31					18 15	18 31					
Chester-le-Street	a																						
Newcastle 8	a		16 31		16 47					17 31		17 46					18 34	18 46					
Morpeth	a																						
Alnmouth for Alnwick	a		17 00							18 01													
Berwick-upon-Tweed	a									18 22							19 20						
Dunbar	a		17 42														19 43						
Wolverhampton 7	d	13 15				13 37	13 43	13 49	14 15				14 37	14 43	14 49	15 15				15 37	15 44	15 50	
Stafford	a	13 29						14 00	14 29						15 00	15 29							
Stoke-on-Trent	a	13 54						14 19	14 54						15 19	15 54						16 18	
Congleton	a																						
Macclesfield	a	14 11							15 11							16 11							
Crewe 10	a					14 07							15 07							16 07			
Wilmslow	a																						
Stockport	a	14 27						14 49	15 27						15 49	16 27						16 47	
M'chester Piccadilly 10	a	14 39						14 59	15 39						15 59	16 39						16 59	
Warrington Bank Quay	a					14 26							15 26							16 26			
Wigan North Western	a					14 37							15 37							16 37			
Preston 8	a					14 51							15 51							16 51			
Lancaster 6	a					15 08							16 08							17 08			
Oxenholme Lake District	a					15 22														17 22			
Penrith North Lakes	a												16 44							17 48			
Carlisle 8	a					16 01							17 00							18 05			
Lockerbie	a																						
Haymarket	a												18 12										
Edinburgh 10	a		18 07							19 06			18 22				20 09						
Haymarket	a		18 14							19 14							20 16						
Motherwell	a									19 55													
Glasgow Central 15	a					17 14				20 15										19 20			
Inverkeithing	a		18 28														20 30						
Kirkcaldy	a		18 46																				
Markinch	a		18 56														21 02						
Ladybank	a		19 03														21 10						
Cupar	a		19 10														21 18						
Leuchars 3	a		19 17														21 26						
Dundee	a		19 32														21 42						
Arbroath	a		19 49																				
Montrose	a		20 03																				
Stonehaven	a		20 23																				
Aberdeen	a		20 43																				

A 🛒 to Dunbar
B 🛒 from Plymouth to Berwick-upon-Tweed
C until 15 July, from 12 September
D 🛒 from Plymouth
E 🛒 from Newport (South Wales)

b Arr. 1104
c Arr. 1124
e Arr. 1153
f Arr. 1204
g Arr. 1015
h Arr. 1224

i Arr. 1235
j Arr. 1304
k Arr. 1324
l Arr. 1139

South Coast and the South West - North West England, The North East and Scotland

	XC	XC	XC	VT	XC	AW	XC	XC	XC	XC	XC	VT	AW	XC	XC	XC	XC	XC	XC	VT	AW
	◇1	◇1	1	R 1	◇1	R	◇1	◇1	◇1	1	◇1	R 1	◇	◇1	1	◇1	◇1	1	◇1	◇1	◇
		A			B				C								D		E		
	🛒	🛒		🍴	🛒	🛒	🛒	🛒	🛒		🛒	🍴	🛒	🛒		🛒	🛒		🛒	🍴	🛒
Bournemouth d	12 45							13 45								14 45					
Brockenhurst 3 d	13 00							14 00								15 00					
Southampton Central d	13 15				13 46			14 15								15 15			15 47		
Southampton Airport Pkwy ✈ d	13 22							14 22								15 22					
Winchester d	13 31							14 31								15 31					
Basingstoke d	13 47				14 18			14 47								15 47			16 18		
Guildford d																					
Reading 7 d	14b11				14c41			15e11			15 41					16f11			16g41		
Oxford d	14 36				15 07			15 36			16 07					16 36			17 07		
Banbury d	14 54				15 25			15 54			16 26					16 54			17 28		
Leamington Spa 8 d	15 12				15 43			16 12			16 44					17 12			17 47		
Coventry d	15 27							16 27								17 27					
Birmingham International ✈ d	15 38					16 09		16 38					17 09			17 38					18 09
Penzance d																					
St Erth d																					
Hayle d																					
Camborne d																					
Redruth d																					
Truro d																					
St Austell d																					
Par d																					
Lostwithiel d																					
Bodmin Parkway d																					
Liskeard 6 d																					
Plymouth d		12 23							13 23								14 25				
Totnes d		12 49							13 49								14 50				
Paignton d														14 01							
Torquay d														14 07							
Newton Abbot d		13 03							14 03					14 18			15 03				
Teignmouth d														14 25							
Dawlish d														14 30							
Exeter St Davids 6 d		13 25							14 25					14 44			15 23				
Tiverton Parkway d		13 39							14 39					14 57			15 37				
Taunton d		13 54							14 54					15 12			15 51				
Weston-super-Mare d														15 38							
Cardiff Central 7 d																					
Newport (South Wales) d																					
Bristol Temple Meads 10 d		14 30					15 00		15 30					16 00			16 30				
Bristol Parkway 7 d		14 40					15 10		15 40					16 10			16 40				
Gloucester 7 d																					
Cheltenham Spa d		15 12					15 42		16 12					16 42			17 12				
London Paddington d																					
Birmingham New Street 12 a	15 48	15 56			16 18	16 20	16 26	16 48	16 58		17 18		17 19	17 26		17 48	17 56		18 18		18 20
Birmingham New Street 12 d	15 57	16 03	16 19	16 20	16 30	16 24	16 31	16 57	17 03	17 19	17 30	17 20	17 26	17 31	17 39	17 57	18 03	18 19	18 30	18 20	18 24
Tamworth d		16 20	16 39							17 39					18 00		18 19	18 39			
Burton-on-Trent d			16 51						17 26	17 51					18 12			18 51			
Derby 6 a		16 41	17 05		17 09				17 40	18 05	18 08				18 30		18 42	19 05	19 08		
Nottingham 8 a			17 33							18 33								19 33			
Chesterfield a		17 03							18 01								19 02		19 29		
Sheffield 7 a		17 19			17 44				18 18		18 44						19 19		19 47		
Doncaster 7 a											19 14								20 15		
Wakefield Westgate 7 a		17 47			18 13				18 47								19 50				
Leeds 10 a		18 03			18 31				19 02								20 05				
York 8 a		18 30			19 02				19 30		19 39						20 30		20 46		
Darlington 7 a		19 00			19 37				20 02		20 10						20 59		21 14		
Durham a		19 18			19 54				20 20		20 27						21 17		21 31		
Chester-le-Street a																					
Newcastle 8 a		19 34			20 09				20 36		20 43						21 32		21 46		
Morpeth a									20 54												
Alnmouth for Alnwick a		20 04															21 59				
Berwick-upon-Tweed a		20 26							21 25												
Dunbar a									21 50												
Wolverhampton 7 d	16 15			16 37		16 43	16 49	17 15				17 37	17 44	17 49		18 15				18 37	18 43
Stafford a	16 29						17 00	17 29						18 00		18 29					
Stoke-on-Trent a	16 54						17 19	17 54						18 19		18 54					
Congleton a																					
Macclesfield a	17 11							18 11								19 11					
Crewe 10 a				17 07								18 07								19 07	
Wilmslow a																					
Stockport a	17 27						17 49	18 27						18 49		19 27					
M'chester Piccadilly 10 a	17 39						17 59	18 39						18 59		19 39					
Warrington Bank Quay a				17 26								18 26								19 26	
Wigan North Western a				17 37								18 37								19 37	
Preston 8 a				17 51								18 51								19 51	
Lancaster 6 a				18 08								19 08								20 08	
Oxenholme Lake District a				18 22								19 22									
Penrith North Lakes a				18 48																20 44	
Carlisle 8 a				19 04								20 01								21 00	
Lockerbie a																					
Haymarket a				20 16																22 14	
Edinburgh 10 a		21 11		20 22	21 35				22 16								23 04			22 22	
Haymarket a		21 17																			
Motherwell a		22 01																			
Glasgow Central 15 a		22 27										21 17									
Inverkeithing a																					
Kirkcaldy a																					
Markinch a																					
Ladybank a																					
Cupar a																					
Leuchars 3 a																					
Dundee a																					
Arbroath a																					
Montrose a																					
Stonehaven a																					
Aberdeen a																					

A 🛒 to Berwick-upon-Tweed
B 🛒 from Reading
C 🛒 to Durham
D 🛒 to Wakefield Westgate
E 🛒 to Sheffield
b Arr. 1404
c Arr. 1435
e Arr. 1504
f Arr. 1604
g Arr. 1635

South Coast and the South West - North West England, The North East and Scotland

		XC	XC	XC	XC	XC	XC	VT	AW	XC	XC	XC	XC	AW	XC	XC	XC	VT	VT	VT	VT	XC	AW
		◇1	◇1	◇1	◇1	1	◇1	◇1	◇	◇1	◇1	◇1	◇1	◇	◇1	◇1	◇1	◇1	◇1	◇1	◇1	◇1	◇
							A				B	C	D		C	B	C	E	F	G	H		
		⊤		⊤	⊤		⊤	℗	⊤	⊤	⊤	⊤	⊤		⊤	⊤	⊤	℗	℗	℗	℗	⊤	
Bournemouth	d			15 45							16 45					17 45							
Brockenhurst 3	d			16 00							17 00					18 00							
Southampton Central	d			16 15							17 15		17 46			18 15							
Southampton Airport Pkway ✈	d			16 22							17 22					18 22							
Winchester	d			16 31							17 31		18 01			18 31							
Basingstoke	d			16 47							17 47		18 18			18 47							
Guildford	d																						
Reading 7	d			17b11			17 41				18f11		18h41			19i11						19 41	
Oxford	d			17 36			18 07				18 36		19 12			19 36						20 07	
Banbury	d			17 54			18 26				18 54		19 31			19 54						20 28	
Leamington Spa 8	d			18 12			18 43				19 12		19 50			20 12						20 46	
Coventry	d			18c27							19 27					20 27							
Birmingham International ✈	d			18 38					19 09		19 38			20 09		20 38							21 09
Penzance	d																						
St Erth	d																						
Hayle	d																						
Camborne	d																						
Redruth	d																						
Truro	d																						
St Austell	d																						
Par	d																						
Lostwithiel	d																						
Bodmin Parkway	d																						
Liskeard 6	d																						
Plymouth	d				15 23							16 25					17 23						
Totnes	d				15 49							16 50					17 49						
Paignton	d																						
Torquay	d																						
Newton Abbot	d				16 03							17 03					18 03						
Teignmouth	d																						
Dawlish	d																						
Exeter St Davids 6	d				16 25					16 53		17 23					18 25						
Tiverton Parkway	d				16 39					17 07		17 37					18 39						
Taunton	d				16 54					17 21		17 51					18 54						
Weston-super-Mare	d																						
Cardiff Central 7	d		16 45																				
Newport (South Wales)	d		17 00																				
Bristol Temple Meads 10	d	17 00			17 30					18e00		18g30			19 00		19 30						
Bristol Parkway 7	d	17 10			17 40					18 10		18 40			19 10		19 40						
Gloucester 7	d		17 46																				
Cheltenham Spa	d	17 42	17 58		18 12					18 42		19 12			19 42		20 12						
London Paddington	d																						
Birmingham New Street 12	a	18 26	18 45	18 48	18 55		19 18		19 20	19 26	19 48	19 56	20 18	20 20	20 28	20 48	20 52					21 22	21 19
Birmingham New Street 12	d	18 31	18 49	18 57	19 03	19 19	19 30	19 20	19 24	19 31	19 57	20 03	20 30	20 24	20 31	20 57	21 03	21 20	21 20	21 20	21 20		21 24
Tamworth	d		19 06			19 39						20 19					21 20						
Burton-on-Trent	d		19 19		19 26	19 51											21 31						
Derby 6	a		19 34		19 39	20 05	20 08					20 42	21 11				21 44						
Nottingham 8	a		20 03			20 33																	
Chesterfield	a				20 02							21 02	21 33				22 06						
Sheffield 7	a				20 18		20 48					21 18	21 51				22 24						
Doncaster 7	a						21 19						22 29										
Wakefield Westgate 7	a				20 46							21 46					22 59						
Leeds 10	a				21 05							22 02					23 15						
York 8	a						21 46						22 54										
Darlington 7	a						22 15																
Durham	a						22 32																
Chester-le-Street	a																						
Newcastle 8	a						22 51																
Morpeth	a																						
Alnmouth for Alnwick	a																						
Berwick-upon-Tweed	a																						
Dunbar	a																						
Wolverhampton 7	d	18 49		19 15				19 37	19 43	19 49	20 16			20 43	20 49	21 16		21 41	21 41	21 41	21 41		21 43
Stafford	a	19 00		19 27						20 00	20 29					21 31		21 53	21 53	21 53	21 53		
Stoke-on-Trent	a	19 19		19 54						20 19	20 54				21 17	21 54							
Congleton	a																						
Macclesfield	a			20 11							21 11					22 11							
Crewe 10	a							20 07										22 17	22 17	22 17	22 17		
Wilmslow	a																						
Stockport	a	19 48		20 27						20 48	21 27				21 46	22 25							
M'chester Piccadilly 10	a	20 00		20 39						20 58	21 40				21 59	22 35							
Warrington Bank Quay	a							20 26										22 36	22 36	22 36	22 40		23 49
Wigan North Western	a							20 37										22 46	22 46	22 51	22 50		
Preston 8	a							20 51										23 01	23 03	23 06	23 05		
Lancaster 6	a							21 08															
Oxenholme Lake District	a							21 22															
Penrith North Lakes	a																						
Carlisle 8	a							22 01															
Lockerbie	a																						
Haymarket	a																						
Edinburgh 10	a																						
Haymarket	a																						
Motherwell	a																						
Glasgow Central 15	a							23 18															
Inverkeithing	a																						
Kirkcaldy	a																						
Markinch	a																						
Ladybank	a																						
Cupar	a																						
Leuchars 3	a																						
Dundee	a																						
Arbroath	a																						
Montrose	a																						
Stonehaven	a																						
Aberdeen	a																						

A ⊤ to Derby
B ⊤ to Birmingham International
C ⊤ to Cheltenham Spa
D ⊤ to Leamington Spa
E until 17 June
F from 24 October
G from 12 September until 21 October
H from 20 June until 9 September
b Arr. 1704
c Arr. 1822
e Arr. 1754
f Arr. 1804
g Arr. 1824
h Arr. 1835
i Arr. 1904

South Coast and the South West - North West England, The North East and Scotland

		XC	XC	XC	XC	XC	XC	XC	XC	XC	XC	XC	XC	XC	XC
		◇1	◇1	◇1	◇1	◇1	◇1	◇1	◇1	◇1	◇1	◇1	◇1	◇1	◇1
			A (trolley)		B (trolley)		C	D	E						
Bournemouth	d		18 45							19 45					
Brockenhurst (3)	d		19 00							20 00					
Southampton Central	d		19 15							20 15					
Southampton Airport Pkwy	d		19 22							20 22					
Winchester	d		19 31							20 31					
Basingstoke	d		19 47							20 47					
Guildford	d														
Reading (7)	d		20c11			20 41				21e11				21 46	
Oxford	d		20 36			21 23				21 36				22 30	
Banbury	d		20 54			21 41				21 54				22 54	
Leamington Spa (8)	d		21 12			22 00				22 12				23 13	
Coventry	d		21 27							22 24				23 27	
Birmingham International	d		21 38							22 34				23 37	
Penzance	d														
St Erth	d														
Hayle	d														
Camborne	d														
Redruth	d														
Truro	d														
St Austell	d														
Par	d														
Lostwithiel	d														
Bodmin Parkway	d														
Liskeard (6)	d														
Plymouth	d				18 25										
Totnes	d				18 50										
Paignton	d												20 12		
Torquay	d												20 18		
Newton Abbot	d				19 03								20 29		
Teignmouth	d														
Dawlish	d														
Exeter St Davids (6)	d				19 23								20 50		
Tiverton Parkway	d				19 37								21 03		
Taunton	d				19 51								21 18		
Weston-super-Mare	d														
Cardiff Central (7)	d											21 05			21 50
Newport (South Wales)	d											21 21			22 05
Bristol Temple Meads (10)	d	20 00			20 30								22f00		
Bristol Parkway (7)	d	20 10			20 40								22 10		
Gloucester (7)	d	20b46										22 04			22 47
Cheltenham Spa	d	20 56			21 17							22 15	22 42		22 58
London Paddington	d														
Birmingham New Street (12)	a	21 46	21 48		22 09	22 30				22 45		23 36	23 44	23 58	00 04
Birmingham New Street (12)	d		21 57	22 03			22 30	22 30	22 30		23 09				
Tamworth	d			22 28							23 28				
Burton-on-Trent	d			22 39							23 39				
Derby (6)	a			22 54							23 55				
Nottingham (8)	a			23 27							00 18				
Chesterfield	a														
Sheffield (7)	a														
Doncaster (7)	a														
Wakefield Westgate (7)	a														
Leeds (10)	a														
York (8)	a														
Darlington (7)	a														
Durham	a														
Chester-le-Street	a														
Newcastle (8)	a														
Morpeth	a														
Alnmouth for Alnwick	a														
Berwick-upon-Tweed	a														
Dunbar	a														
Wolverhampton (7)	d		22 16				22 48	22 48	22 48						
Stafford	a		22 29				23 00	23 00	23 00						
Stoke-on-Trent	a		22 53				23 20	23 20	23 20						
Congleton	a														
Macclesfield	a		23 11												
Crewe (10)	a														
Wilmslow	a														
Stockport	a		23 25												
M'chester Piccadilly (10)	a		23 37				00 12	00 32	00 33						
Warrington Bank Quay	a														
Wigan North Western	a														
Preston (8)	a														
Lancaster (6)	a														
Oxenholme Lake District	a														
Penrith North Lakes	a														
Carlisle (8)	a														
Lockerbie	a														
Haymarket	a														
Edinburgh (10)	a														
Haymarket	a														
Motherwell	a														
Glasgow Central (15)	a														
Inverkeithing	a														
Kirkcaldy	a														
Markinch	a														
Ladybank	a														
Cupar	a														
Leuchars (3)	a														
Dundee	a														
Arbroath	a														
Montrose	a														
Stonehaven	a														
Aberdeen	a														

A (trolley) to Basingstoke
B (trolley) to Taunton
C WThFO
D MTO until 14 June, MTO from 12 September
E MTO from 20 June until 6 September
b Arr. 2038
c Arr. 2004
e Arr. 2104
f Arr. 2151

Table 51

Saturdays

South Coast and the South West - North West England, The North East and Scotland

		XC	XC	XC	XC	XC	XC	VT	XC	XC		XC	XC	XC	XC	VT	AW	XC	XC	XC		XC	XC	XC	XC
		◇1	◇1	◇1	◇1	◇1	1	◇1	◇1	◇1		1	◇1	◇1	1	◇1	◇	◇1	◇1	◇1		1	◇1	◇1	1
					A															B			A		
					T	T	T	B	T	T			T	T	T	B	T	T	T	T			T		T
Bournemouth	d																								
Brockenhurst 3	d																								
Southampton Central	d																			05 09					
Southampton Airport Pkwy	d																			05 16					
Winchester	d																			05 25					
Basingstoke	d																			05 41					
Guildford	d																								
Reading 7	d																			06b11					
Oxford	d																			06 38					
Banbury	d																			06 56					
Leamington Spa 8	d																			07 14					
Coventry	d																			07 27					
Birmingham International	d																07 09			07 38					
Penzance	d																								
St Erth	d																								
Hayle	d																								
Camborne	d																								
Redruth	d																								
Truro	d																								
St Austell	d																								
Par	d																								
Lostwithiel	d																								
Bodmin Parkway	d																								
Liskeard 6	d																								
Plymouth	d																								
Totnes	d																								
Paignton	d																								
Torquay	d																								
Newton Abbot	d																								
Teignmouth	d																								
Dawlish	d																								
Exeter St Davids 6	d																								
Tiverton Parkway	d																								
Taunton	d																								
Weston-super-Mare	d																								
Cardiff Central 7	d			21p50																					
Newport (South Wales)	d			22p05																					
Bristol Temple Meads 10	d																						06 15		
Bristol Parkway 7	d																						06 25		
Gloucester 7	d			22p47																			07c01	07 07	
Cheltenham Spa	d			22p58																			07 12	07 18	
London Paddington	d																								
Birmingham New Street 12	a			00 04													07 20			07 48			07 56	08 08	
Birmingham New Street 12	d	22p30	23p09		05 56	05 57	06 19	06 20	06 30	06 31		06 49	06 57	07 03	07 19	07 20	07 24	07 30	07 31	07 57		07 49	08 03		08 19
Tamworth	d		23p28		06 12		06 39		06 46			07 06		07 19	07 38			07 46				08 06	08 19		08 36
Burton-on-Trent	d		23p39		06 22		06 51		06 56			07 18		07 29	07 49			07 56				08 18	08 29		08 48
Derby 6	a		23p55		06 35		07 05		07 09			07 34		07 42	08 05			08 09				08 34	08 42		09 05
Nottingham 8	a		00 18				07 38					08 08			08 33							09 05			09 35
Chesterfield	a				06 55				07 29					08 02				08 29					09 02		
Sheffield 7	a				07 09				07 48					08 17				08 45					09 18		
Doncaster 7	a								08 23									09 18							
Wakefield Westgate 7	a				07 36									08 45									09 46		
Leeds 10	a				07 52									09 03									10 02		
York 8	a				08 24				08 47					09 30				09 45					10 27		
Darlington 7	a				08 56				09 16					09 58				10 15					10 58		
Durham	a				09 13				09 34					10 15				10 32					11 15		
Chester-le-Street	a																								
Newcastle 8	a				09 28				09 48					10 31				10 47					11 31		
Morpeth	a																								
Alnmouth for Alnwick	a				09 58																				
Berwick-upon-Tweed	a				10 19																		12 19		
Dunbar	a													11 37											
Wolverhampton 7	d	22p48				06 16		06 37		06 49			07 15			07 37	07 43		07 49	08 15					
Stafford	a	23p00				06 29				07 00			07 29						08 00	08 29					
Stoke-on-Trent	a	23p20				06 50				07 18									08 19	08 54					
Congleton	a					07 02																			
Macclesfield	a					07 11				07 36									08 36	09 11					
Crewe 10	a							07 07					07 50			08 07									
Wilmslow	a												08 09												
Stockport	a					07 27				07 49			08 21						08 49	09 27					
M'chester Piccadilly 10	a	00 12				07 38				07 59			08 36						08 59	09 39					
Warrington Bank Quay	a							07 26								08 27									
Wigan North Western	a							07 37								08 38									
Preston 8	a							07 51								08 52									
Lancaster 6	a							08 08								09 09									
Oxenholme Lake District	a							08 21																	
Penrith North Lakes	a															09 45									
Carlisle 8	a							09 00								10 01									
Lockerbie	a																								
Haymarket	a							10 16																	
Edinburgh 10	a				11 07			10 22						12 07									13 04		
Haymarket	a				11 15																		13 14		
Motherwell	a				11 52																		13 52		
Glasgow Central 15	a				12 13											11 17							14 13		
Inverkeithing	a																								
Kirkcaldy	a																								
Markinch	a																								
Ladybank	a																								
Cupar	a																								
Leuchars 3	a																								
Dundee	a																								
Arbroath	a																								
Montrose	a																								
Stonehaven	a																								
Aberdeen	a																								

A T to Berwick-upon-Tweed

B T from Reading

b Arr. 0559

c Arr. 0654

South Coast and the South West - North West England, The North East and Scotland

		XC	VT	AW	XC	XC	XC	XC	XC	VT	AW	XC	XC	XC	XC	XC	XC	VT	AW	XC	XC	XC	XC
		◇1	◇1	◇	◇1	◇1	◇1	◇1	1	◇1	◇	◇1	◇1	◇1	◇1	1	◇1	◇1	◇	◇1	◇1	◇1	◇1
		A											B		C			D			B		
		🛒	🍽	🛒	🛒	🛒	🛒	🛒	🛒	🍽	🛒	🛒	🛒	🛒	🛒		🛒	🍽	🛒	🛒	🛒	🛒	🛒
Bournemouth	d							06 25						06 37								07 45	
Brockenhurst 3	d							06 39						06 55								08 00	
Southampton Central	d					06 15		06 53						07e15			07 47					08 15	
Southampton Airport Pkway ✈	d					06 22		07 01						07 22			07 54					08 22	
Winchester	d					06 31		07 09						07 31			08 03					08 31	
Basingstoke	d					06 47		07 25						07 47			08 19					08 47	
Guildford	d	06 09																					
Reading 7	d	06 46				07b11		07 47						08f11			08 40					09j11	
Oxford	d	07 12				07 36		08 15						08 36			09 07					09 36	
Banbury	d	07 33				07 54		08 33						08 54			09 24					09 54	
Leamington Spa 8	d	07 51				08 12		08 50						09 12			09 42					10 12	
Coventry	d					08 27								09 27								10 27	
Birmingham International ✈	d			08 09		08 38					09 09			09 38					10 09			10 38	
Penzance	d																						
St Erth	d																						
Hayle	d																						
Camborne	d																						
Redruth	d																						
Truro	d																						
St Austell	d																						
Par	d																						
Lostwithiel	d																						
Bodmin Parkway	d																						
Liskeard 6	d																						
Plymouth	d						05 25								06 25								07 25
Totnes	d						05 50								06 50								07 50
Paignton	d																			07 00			
Torquay	d																			07 06			
Newton Abbot	d						06 03								07 03					07 18			08 03
Teignmouth	d																			07 25			
Dawlish	d																			07 30			
Exeter St Davids 6	d						06 23								07 23					07h47			08 23
Tiverton Parkway	d						06 37								07 37								08 37
Taunton	d						06 51								07 51					08 12			08 51
Weston-super-Mare	d																						
Cardiff Central 7	d											07 00	07 45								08 45		
Newport (South Wales)	d											07 15	08 00								09 00		
Bristol Temple Meads 10	d				07 00		07 30					08c00			08g30					09i00			09 30
Bristol Parkway 7	d				07 10		07 40					08 10			08 40					09 10			09 40
Gloucester 7	d												08 47								09 46		
Cheltenham Spa	d				07 42		08 12					08 42	08 58		09 12					09 42	09 57		10 12
London Paddington	d																						
Birmingham New Street 12	a	08 17		08 20	08 26	08 48	08 56	09 19			09 20	09 26	09 45	09 48	09 56		10 17		10 19	10 26	10 45	10 48	10 56
Birmingham New Street 12	d	08 30	08 20	08 24	08 31	08 57	09 03	09 30	09 19	09 20	09 24	09 31	09 49	09 57	10 03	10 19	10 30	10 20	10 24	10 31	10 49	10 57	11 03
Tamworth	d								09 39				10 06		10 19	10 36					11 06		
Burton-on-Trent	d						09 25		09 50				10 19			10 48					11 19		11 25
Derby 6	a	09 08					09 41	10 08	10 05				10 34		10 41	11 05	11 08				11 34		11 41
Nottingham 8	a								10 33				11 05			11 33					12 05		
Chesterfield	a						10 02								11 02								12 02
Sheffield 7	a	09 44					10 17	10 42							11 17		11 41						12 16
Doncaster 7	a	10 17						11 15									12 15						
Wakefield Westgate 7	a						10 46								11 46								12 46
Leeds 10	a						11 02								12 02								13 02
York 8	a	10 45					11 27	11 45							12 29		12 45						13 29
Darlington 7	a	11 13					11 58	12 13							12 58		13 13						13 58
Durham	a	11 30					12 15	12 30							13 17		13 30						14 15
Chester-le-Street	a																						
Newcastle 8	a	11 47					12 31	12 46							13 34		13 46						14 32
Morpeth	a																						14 47
Alnmouth for Alnwick	a														13 59								
Berwick-upon-Tweed	a														14 19								
Dunbar	a						13 37																15 39
Wolverhampton 7	d		08 37	08 43	08 49	09 15				09 37	09 43	09 49		10 15				10 37	10 43	10 49		11 15	
Stafford	a				09 00	09 29						10 00		10 29						11 00		11 29	
Stoke-on-Trent	a				09 19	09 54						10 19		10 54						11 19		11 54	
Congleton	a																						
Macclesfield	a					10 11								11 11								12 11	
Crewe 10	a		09 07							10 07								11 07					
Wilmslow	a																						
Stockport	a				09 49	10 27						10 49		11 27						11 49		12 27	
M'chester Piccadilly 10	a				09 59	10 39						10 59		11 39						11 59		12 39	
Warrington Bank Quay	a		09 26							10 26								11 26					
Wigan North Western	a		09 37							10 37								11 37					
Preston 8	a		09 51							10 51								11 51					
Lancaster 6	a		10 08							11 08								12 08					
Oxenholme Lake District	a		10 22															12 22					
Penrith North Lakes	a									11 44													
Carlisle 8	a		11 01							12 00								13 01					
Lockerbie	a																						
Haymarket	a		12 16															14 16					
Edinburgh 10	a		12 22				14 07								15 07			14 22					16 04
Haymarket	a														15 15								
Motherwell	a														15 52								
Glasgow Central 15	a									13 17					16 20								
Inverkeithing	a																						
Kirkcaldy	a																						
Markinch	a																						
Ladybank	a																						
Cupar	a																						
Leuchars 3	a																						
Dundee	a																						
Arbroath	a																						
Montrose	a																						
Stonehaven	a																						
Aberdeen	a																						

A 🛒 from Reading
B 🛒 from Newport (South Wales)
C 🛒 to Berwick-upon-Tweed
D until 9 July, from 17 September

b Arr. 0704
c Arr. 0751
e Arr. 0707
f Arr. 0804
g Arr. 0824

h Arr. 0741
i Arr. 0849
j Arr. 0904

Table 51

Saturdays

South Coast and the South West - North West England, The North East and Scotland

		XC	XC	VT	AW	XC	XC	XC	XC	XC	VT	AW	XC	XC	XC	XC	XC	XC	XC	XC	VT	AW
		◇1	1	◇1	◇	◇1	◇1	◇1	1	◇1	◇1	◇	◇1	◇1	◇1	◇1	◇1	◇1	1	◇1	◇1	◇
								A					B	C	D		E	F				
		🛒		⊡	🛒	🛒	🛒	🛒	🛒	🛒	⊡	🛒	⊡🛒	🛒	🛒	🛒	🛒	🛒		🛒	⊡	🛒
Bournemouth	d						08 45									09 45						
Brockenhurst 3	d						09 00									10 00						
Southampton Central	d						09 15			09 47						10 15						
Southampton Airport Pkwy	d						09 22			09 54						10 22						
Winchester	d						09 31			10 03						10 31						
Basingstoke	d						09 47			10 19						10 47						
Guildford	d																					
Reading 7	d	09 40					10b11			10 40						11e11				11 40		
Oxford	d	10 07					10 36			11 07						11 36				12 07		
Banbury	d	10 24					10 54			11 24						11 54				12 24		
Leamington Spa 8	d	10 42					11 12			11 42						12 12				12 42		
Coventry	d						11 27									12 27						
Birmingham International	d				11 09		11 38					12 09				12 38						13 09
Penzance	d							06 30														
St Erth	d							06 38														
Hayle	d							06 41														
Camborne	d							06 51														
Redruth	d							06 57														
Truro	d							07 09														
St Austell	d							07 25														
Par	d							07 32														
Lostwithiel	d							07 39														
Bodmin Parkway	d							07 46														
Liskeard 6	d							07 58														
Plymouth	d							08 25					08 39				09 18	09 25				
Totnes	d							08 50					09 04				09 43	09 50				
Paignton	d																					
Torquay	d																					
Newton Abbot	d							09 03					09 17				09 56	10 03				
Teignmouth	d																10 03					
Dawlish	d																10 09					
Exeter St Davids 6	d							09 23					09 41				10 25	10 23				
Tiverton Parkway	d							09 37					09 54				10 39	10 37				
Taunton	d							09 51					10 09				10 53	10 51				
Weston-super-Mare	d												10 33									
Cardiff Central 7	d														10 45							
Newport (South Wales)	d														11 00							
Bristol Temple Meads 10	d					10 00		10 30					11c00	11 00			11 30	11 30				
Bristol Parkway 7	d					10 10		10 40					11 10	11 10			11 40	11 40				
Gloucester 7	d														11 46							
Cheltenham Spa	d					10 42		11 12					11 42	11 42	11 57		12 12	12 12				
London Paddington	d																					
Birmingham New Street 12	a	11 18			11 20	11 26	11 48	11 56		12 18		12 20	12 26	12 26	12 45	12 48	12 56	12 56		13 18		13 20
Birmingham New Street 12	d	11 30	11 19	11 20	11 24	11 31	11 57	12 03	12 19	12 30	12 20	12 24	12 31	12 31	12 49	12 57	13 03	13 03	13 19	13 30	13 20	13 24
Tamworth	d		11 39					12 19	12 36						13 06				13 39			
Burton-on-Trent	d		11 51						12 49						13 19		13 25	13 25	13 51			
Derby 6	a	12 08	12 05					12 41	13 05	13 08					13 34		13 41	13 41	14 05	14 08		
Nottingham 8	a		12 33						13 33						14 05				14 33			
Chesterfield	a							13 02									14 02	14 02				
Sheffield 7	a	12 41						13 17		13 41							14 17	14 17		14 41		
Doncaster 7	a	13 17								14 18										15 18		
Wakefield Westgate 7	a							13 46									14 46	14 46				
Leeds 10	a							14 02									15 02	15 02				
York 8	a	13 45						14 27		14 45							15 29	15 29		15 45		
Darlington 7	a	14 13						14 58		15 13							15 58	15 58		16 13		
Durham	a	14 30						15 15		15 30							16 15	16 15		16 30		
Chester-le-Street	a																					
Newcastle 8	a	14 46						15 31		15 46							16 31	16 31		16 46		
Morpeth	a																					
Alnmouth for Alnwick	a							15 58									16 59	16 59				
Berwick-upon-Tweed	a							16 18														
Dunbar	a																17 38	17 38				
Wolverhampton 7	d			11 37	11 43	11 49	12 15				12 37	12 43	12 49	12 49	13 15						13 37	13 43
Stafford	a					12 00	12 29						13 00	13 00	13 29							
Stoke-on-Trent	a					12 19	12 54						13 18	13 19	13 54							
Congleton	a																					
Macclesfield	a						13 11								14 11							
Crewe 10	a			12 07							13 07										14 07	
Wilmslow	a																					
Stockport	a					12 49	13 27						13 49	13 49	14 27							
M'chester Piccadilly 10	a					12 59	13 39						13 59	13 59	14 39							
Warrington Bank Quay	a			12 26							13 26										14 26	
Wigan North Western	a			12 37							13 37										14 37	
Preston 8	a			12 51							13 51										14 51	
Lancaster 6	a			13 08							14 08										15 08	
Oxenholme Lake District	a			13 22																	15 22	
Penrith North Lakes	a										14 44											
Carlisle 8	a			14 01							15 00										16 01	
Lockerbie	a																					
Haymarket	a										16 16											
Edinburgh 10	a							17 07			16 22						18 05	18 05				
Haymarket	a							17 15									18 14	18 14				
Motherwell	a							17 52														
Glasgow Central 15	a			15 17				18 11													17 17	
Inverkeithing	a																18 28	18 28				
Kirkcaldy	a																18 46	18 46				
Markinch	a																18 56	18 56				
Ladybank	a																19 03	19 03				
Cupar	a																19 10	19 10				
Leuchars 8	a																19 17	19 17				
Dundee	a																19 32	19 32				
Arbroath	a																19 49	19 49				
Montrose	a																20 03	20 03				
Stonehaven	a																20 23	20 23				
Aberdeen	a																20 43	20 43				

A 🛒 from Plymouth to Berwick-upon-Tweed
B until 10 September. ⊡ from Birmingham New Street 🛒 to Cheltenham Spa
C from 17 September
D 🛒 from Newport (South Wales)
E until 10 September. 🛒 to Dunbar
F from 17 September. 🛒 to Dunbar
b Arr. 1004
c Arr. 1052
e Arr. 1104

Table 51

Saturdays

South Coast and the South West - North West England, The North East and Scotland

		XC	XC	XC	XC	XC	VT	AW	XC	XC	XC	XC	XC	XC	VT	AW	XC	XC	XC	XC	XC	XC	XC
		◇1	◇1	◇1	1	◇1	◇1	◇	◇1	◇1	◇1	◇1	◇1	1	◇1	◇	◇1	◇1	◇1	◇1	◇1	◇1	1
				A							B	C			D		E	F	G		H	I	
Bournemouth	d		10 45							11 45										12 45			
Brockenhurst 3	d		11 00							12 00										13 00			
Southampton Central	d		11 15			11 47				12 15										13 15			
Southampton Airport Pkway	d		11 22			11 54				12 22										13 22			
Winchester	d		11 31			12 03				12 31										13 31			
Basingstoke	d		11 47			12 19				12 47										13 47			
Guildford	d																						
Reading 7	d		12b11			12 40				13e11			13 40							14j11			
Oxford	d		12 36			13 07				13 36			14 07							14 36			
Banbury	d		12 54			13 24				13 54			14 24							14 54			
Leamington Spa 8	d		13 12			13 42				14 12			14 42							15 12			
Coventry	d		13 27							14 27										15 27			
Birmingham International	d		13 38					14 09		14 38						15 09				15 38			
Penzance	d			08 28													09 43						
St Erth	d			08 36													09 51						
Hayle	d																						
Camborne	d			08 46													10 01						
Redruth	d			08 52													10 07						
Truro	d			09 04													10 19						
St Austell	d			09 20													10 35						
Par	d			09 28							10 26						10 42						
Lostwithiel	d																10 49						
Bodmin Parkway	d			09 39							10f43						10 56						
Liskeard 6	d			09 51							10 55						11 09						
Plymouth	d			10c25							11g25	11 25					11i48					12 23	
Totnes	d			10 50							11 50	11 50					12 13					12 49	
Paignton	d	10 06																			12 34		
Torquay	d	10 12																			12 41		
Newton Abbot	d	10 23		11 03							12 03	12 03					12 25				12 53	13 03	
Teignmouth	d	10 30																			13 02		
Dawlish	d	10 35																			13 09		
Exeter St Davids 6	d	10 49		11 23							12 23	12 23					12 48				13 25	13 25	
Tiverton Parkway	d	11 02		11 37							12 37	12 37					13 02				13 39	13 39	
Taunton	d	11 17		11 51							12 51	12 51					13 16				13 54	13 54	
Weston-super-Mare	d																						
Cardiff Central 7	d																		13 45				
Newport (South Wales)	d																		14 00				
Bristol Temple Meads 10	d	12 00		12 30					13 00		13h30	13h30					14 00	14 00			14 30	14 30	
Bristol Parkway 7	d	12 10		12 40					13 10		13 40	13 40					14 10	14 10			14 40	14 40	
Gloucester 7	d																		14 46				
Cheltenham Spa	d	12 42		13 12					13 42		14 12	14 12					14 42	14 42	14 57		15 12	15 12	
London Paddington	d																						
Birmingham New Street 12	a	13 26	13 48	13 56		14 18		14 19	14 26	14 48	14 56	14 56	15 17			15 20	15 26	15 26	15 45	15 48	15 55	15 55	
Birmingham New Street 12	d	13 31	13 57	14 03	14 19	14 30	14 20	14 24	14 31	14 57	15 03	15 03	15 30	15 19	15 20	15 24	15 31	15 31	15 49	15 57	16 03	16 03	16 19
Tamworth	d			14 19	14 39									15 39					16 06		16 18	16 18	16 39
Burton-on-Trent	d				14 51						15 26	15 26		15 51					16 19				16 51
Derby 6	a			14 41	15 05	15 08					15 41	15 41	16 08	16 05					16 34		16 41	16 41	17 05
Nottingham 8	a				15 33									16 33					17 05				17 33
Chesterfield	a			15 02							16 02	16 02									17 01	17 01	
Sheffield 7	a			15 17		15 41					16 18	16 18	16 41								17 19	17 19	
Doncaster 7	a					16 18							17 16										
Wakefield Westgate 7	a			15 46							16 46	16 46									17 47	17 47	
Leeds 10	a			16 02							17 02	17 02									18 02	18 02	
York 8	a			16 27		16 46					17 27	17 27	17 38								18 30	18 30	
Darlington 7	a			16 58		17 13					17 58	17 58	18 13								19 00	19 00	
Durham	a			17 15		17 30					18 15	18 15	18 30								19 18	19 18	
Chester-le-Street	a																						
Newcastle 8	a			17 31		17 46					18 31	18 31	18 46								19 34	19 34	
Morpeth	a																						
Alnmouth for Alnwick	a			18 00																	20 03	20 03	
Berwick-upon-Tweed	a			18 20							19 18	19 18									20 24	20 24	
Dunbar	a										19 41	19 41											
Wolverhampton 7	d	13 49	14 15				14 37	14 43	14 49	15 15					15 37	15 43	15 49	15 49		16 15			
Stafford	a	14 00	14 29						15 00	15 29							16 00	16 00		16 29			
Stoke-on-Trent	a	14 19	14 54						15 19	15 54							16 19	16 19		16 54			
Congleton	a																						
Macclesfield	a		15 11							16 11										17 11			
Crewe 10	a						15 07								16 08								
Wilmslow	a																						
Stockport	a	14 49	15 27						15 49	16 27							16 49	16 49		17 27			
M'chester Piccadilly 10	a	14 59	15 39						15 59	16 39							16 59	16 59		17 39			
Warrington Bank Quay	a						15 26								16 26								
Wigan North Western	a						15 37								16 37								
Preston 8	a						15 51								16 51								
Lancaster 6	a						16 08								17 09								
Oxenholme Lake District	a														17 24								
Penrith North Lakes	a						16 45																
Carlisle 8	a						17 00								18 03								
Lockerbie	a																						
Haymarket	a						18 14																
Edinburgh 10	a			19 08			18 22				20 07	20 07									21 09	21 09	
Haymarket	a			19 15							20 19	20 19									21 16	21 16	
Motherwell	a			19 52																	21 58	21 58	
Glasgow Central 15	a			20 11											19 17						22 17	22 17	
Inverkeithing	a										20 34	20 34											
Kirkcaldy	a										20 51	20 51											
Markinch	a										21 01	21 01											
Ladybank	a										21 09	21 09											
Cupar	a										21 18	21 18											
Leuchars 3	a										21 27	21 26											
Dundee	a										21 44	21 44											
Arbroath	a																						
Montrose	a																						
Stonehaven	a																						
Aberdeen	a																						

A [catering symbol] from Plymouth to Berwick-upon-Tweed
B until 10 September. [catering symbol] from Plymouth to Dunbar
C from 17 September. [catering symbol] to Dunbar
D until 9 July, from 17 September
E from 17 September
F until 10 September
G [catering symbol] from Newport (South Wales)
H until 10 September. [catering symbol] to Berwick-upon-Tweed
I from 17 September. [catering symbol] to Berwick-upon-Tweed
b Arr. 1204
c Arr. 1015
e Arr. 1304
f Arr. 1037
g Arr. 1119
h Arr. 1324
i Arr. 1133
j Arr. 1404

Table 51

Saturdays

South Coast and the South West - North West England, The North East and Scotland

		XC	VT	XC	AW	XC	XC	XC	XC	XC	VT	AW	XC	XC	XC	XC	XC	VT	AW	XC	XC	XC
		◇[1]	◇[1]	◇[1]	R	◇[1]	◇[1]	◇[1]	◇[1]	[1]	◇[1]	◇	◇[1]	◇[1]	◇[1]	◇[1]	[1]	◇[1]	◇	◇[1]	◇[1]	◇[1]
		A		B																		
Bournemouth	d						13 45							14 45								15 45
Brockenhurst [3]	d						14 00							15 00								16 00
Southampton Central	d	13 47		13 47			14 15							15 15		15 47						16 15
Southampton Airport Pkway	d	13 54		13 54			14 22							15 22		15 54						16 22
Winchester	d	14 03		14 03			14 31							15 31		16 03						16 31
Basingstoke	d	14 19		14 19			14 47							15 47		16 19						16 47
Guildford	d																					
Reading [7]	d	14 40		14 40			15b11		15 40					16f11		16 40						17g11
Oxford	d	15 07		15 07			15 36		16 07					16 36		17 07						17 36
Banbury	d	15 24		15 24			15 54		16 24					16 54		17 24						17 54
Leamington Spa [8]	d	15 42		15 42			16 12		16 42					17 12		17 42						18 12
Coventry	d						16 27							17 27								18 27
Birmingham International	d				16 09		16 38					17 09		17 38					18 09			18 38
Penzance	d																					
St Erth	d																					
Hayle	d																					
Camborne	d																					
Redruth	d																					
Truro	d																					
St Austell	d																					
Par	d																					
Lostwithiel	d																					
Bodmin Parkway	d																					
Liskeard [6]	d																					
Plymouth	d							13 25							14 25							
Totnes	d							13 50							14 50							
Paignton	d												13 53									
Torquay	d												13 59									
Newton Abbot	d							14 03					14 10		15 03							
Teignmouth	d												14 17									
Dawlish	d												14 22									
Exeter St Davids [6]	d							14 23					14 36		15 23							
Tiverton Parkway	d							14 37					14 49		15 37							
Taunton	d							14 52					15 04		15 51							
Weston-super-Mare	d												15c30									
Cardiff Central [7]	d																				16 45	
Newport (South Wales)	d																				17 00	
Bristol Temple Meads [10]	d					15 00		15 30					16e00		16 30					17 00		
Bristol Parkway [7]	d					15 10		15 40					16 10		16 40					17 10		
Gloucester [7]	d																				17 46	
Cheltenham Spa	d					15 42		16 12					16 42		17 12					17 42	17 58	
London Paddington	d																					
Birmingham New Street [12]	a	16 17		16 17	16 20	16 26	16 48	16 56	17 17			17 20	17 26	17 48	17 56	18 18			18 20	18 26	18 45	18 48
Birmingham New Street [12]	d	16 30	16 20	16 30	16 24	16 31	16 57	17 03	17 30	17 19	17 20	17 24	17 31	17 57	18 03	18 30	18 19	18 20	18 24	18 31	18 49	18 57
Tamworth	d									17 39					18 19		18 39				19 06	
Burton-on-Trent	d							17 26		17 51							18 51				19 19	
Derby [6]	a	17 08		17 08				17 41	18 08	18 05					18 41	19 08	19 05				19 34	
Nottingham [8]	a									18 33							19 33				20 05	
Chesterfield	a							18 02							19 02	19 29						
Sheffield [7]	a	17 44		17 44				18 18	18 42						19 18	19 51						
Doncaster [7]	a								19 15							20 17						
Wakefield Westgate [7]	a	18 12		18 12				18 46							19 49							
Leeds [10]	a	18 31		18 31				19 01							20 05							
York [8]	a	18 59		18 59				19 29	19 40						20 32	20 46						
Darlington [7]	a	19 37		19 37				19 58	20 11						21 00	21 14						
Durham	a	19 54		19 54				20 16	20 28						21 17	21 32						
Chester-le-Street	a																					
Newcastle [8]	a	20 10		20 10				20 28	20 44						21 32	21 47						
Morpeth	a							20 51														
Alnmouth for Alnwick	a														22 01							
Berwick-upon-Tweed	a							21 24														
Dunbar	a							21 47														
Wolverhampton [7]	d		16 37		16 43	16 49	17 15				17 37	17 43	17 49	18 15				18 37	18 43	18 49		19 15
Stafford	a					17 00	17 29						18 00	18 29						19 00		19 29
Stoke-on-Trent	a					17 19	17 54						18 19	18 54						19 19		19 54
Congleton	a																					
Macclesfield	a						18 11							19 11								20 11
Crewe [10]	a		17 07								18 07							19 07				
Wilmslow	a																					
Stockport	a					17 49	18 27						18 49	19 27						19 49		20 27
M'chester Piccadilly [10]	a					17 59	18 39						18 59	19 39						19 59		20 39
Warrington Bank Quay	a		17 26								18 26							19 26				
Wigan North Western	a		17 37								18 37							19 37				
Preston [8]	a		17 51								18 51							19 54				
Lancaster [6]	a		18 08								19 08											
Oxenholme Lake District	a		18 22								19 22											
Penrith North Lakes	a		18 48																			
Carlisle [8]	a		19 04								20 01											
Lockerbie	a																					
Haymarket	a		20 16																			
Edinburgh [10]	a		20 22	21 35				22 14							23 10							
Haymarket	a																					
Motherwell	a																					
Glasgow Central [15]	a										21 17											
Inverkeithing	a																					
Kirkcaldy	a																					
Markinch	a																					
Ladybank	a																					
Cupar	a																					
Leuchars [3]	a																					
Dundee	a																					
Arbroath	a																					
Montrose	a																					
Stonehaven	a																					
Aberdeen	a																					

A from 17 September
B until 10 September. to Durham
b Arr. 1504
c Arr. 1523
e Arr. 1549
f Arr. 1605
g Arr. 1704

Table 51

Saturdays

South Coast and the South West - North West England, The North East and Scotland

		XC	XC	XC	VT	AW	XC	XC	XC	XC	XC	XC	VT	AW	XC	XC	XC	XC	XC	XC	XC	AW	XC
		◇1	1	◇1	◇1	◇	◇1	◇1	◇1	◇1	◇1	◇1	◇1	◇	◇1	◇1	◇1	◇1	◇1	◇1	◇1	◇	◇1
				A	B		C	D	E	F	G	H			I	J	K	L	G	D			D
		⊼		⊼	⊡	⊼	⊡⊼	⊼	⊼	⊼	⊼	⊼	⊡		⊼	⊼	⊼	⊼	⊼	⊼	⊼		
Bournemouth	d								16 45							17 45	17 45	17 45					
Brockenhurst 3	d								17 00							18 00	18 00	18 00					
Southampton Central	d								17 15			17 47				18 15	18 15	18 15					
Southampton Airport Pkway	d								17 22			17 54				18 22	18 22	18 22					
Winchester	d								17 31			18 03				18 31	18 31	18 31					
Basingstoke	d								17 47			18 19				18 47	18 47	18 47					
Guildford	d																						
Reading 7	d			17 40					18 11			18 40				19 11	19 11	19 11			19 40		
Oxford	d			18 07					18 36			19 07				19 36	19 36	19 36			20 07		
Banbury	d			18 24					18 54			19 24				19 54	19 54	19 54			20 29		
Leamington Spa 8	d			18 42					19 12			19 42				20 12	20 12	20 12			20 46		
Coventry	d								19 27							20 27	20 27	20 27					
Birmingham International	d					19 09			19 38					20 09		20 39	20 39	20 39				21 09	
Penzance	d																						
St Erth	d																						
Hayle	d																						
Camborne	d																						
Redruth	d																						
Truro	d																						
St Austell	d																						
Par	d																			16 27			
Lostwithiel	d																						
Bodmin Parkway	d																			16 37			
Liskeard 6	d																			16 51			
Plymouth	d	15 25									16 25								17 23	17h25			
Totnes	d	15 50									16 50								17 49	17 50			
Paignton	d									16 34													18 05
Torquay	d									16 41													18 12
Newton Abbot	d	16 03								16 53	17 03								18 03	18 03			18 23
Teignmouth	d									17 02													
Dawlish	d									17 09													
Exeter St Davids 6	d	16 23					16 53			17 25	17 23								18 25	18 23			18 50
Tiverton Parkway	d	16 37					17 07			17 39	17 37								18 39	18 37			19 04
Taunton	d	16 51					17 21			17 54	17 51								18 54	18 51			19 18
Weston-super-Mare	d																						
Cardiff Central 7	d																						
Newport (South Wales)	d																						
Bristol Temple Meads 10	d	17 30					18 00	18 00		18 30	18 30				19 00				19 30	19 30			20 00
Bristol Parkway 7	d	17 40					18 10	18 10		18 40	18 40				19 10				19 40	19 40			20 10
Gloucester 7	d																						
Cheltenham Spa	d	18 12					18 42	18 42		19 12	19 12				19 42				20 12	20 12			20 42
London Paddington	d																						
Birmingham New Street 12	a	18 56		19 18		19 20	19 26	19 26	19 48	19 58	19 56	20 18		20 20	20 26	20 48	20 48	20 48	20 53	20 54	21 18	21 19	21 38
Birmingham New Street 12	d	19 03	19 19	19 30	19 20	19 24	19 31	19 31	19 57	20 03	20 03	20 30	20 20	20 24	20 31	20 57	21 03	21 03	21 03	20 57		21 24	
Tamworth	d		19 39							20 20	20 19						21 20	21 20	21 20				
Burton-on-Trent	d	19 25	19 51															21 30	21 31				
Derby 6	a	19 39	20 05	20 08						20 42	20 42	21 25					21 42	21 43	21 44				
Nottingham 8	a		20 35																				
Chesterfield	a	20 04		20 29						21 04	21 02	21 45					22 02	22 07	22 07				
Sheffield 7	a	20 19		20 49						21 19	21 18	22 05					22 23	22 23	22 23				
Doncaster 7	a			21 21								22 30					22 51	22 51	22 51				
Wakefield Westgate 7	a	20 48								21 49	21 48						23 10	23 10	23 10				
Leeds 10	a	21 03								22 02	22 02						23 27	23 27	23 27				
York 8	a	21 57		21 45								22 55											
Darlington 7	a			22 13																			
Durham	a			22 31																			
Chester-le-Street	a																						
Newcastle 8	a			22 49																			
Morpeth	a																						
Alnmouth for Alnwick	a																						
Berwick-upon-Tweed	a																						
Dunbar	a																						
Wolverhampton 7	d				19 37	19 43	19 49	19 49	20 16				20 37	20 43	20 49	21 16				21 16		21 42	
Stafford	a						20 00	20 00	20 29				20 49		21 00	21 29				21 29			
Stoke-on-Trent	a						20 19	20 19	20 54						21 20	21 54				21 52			
Congleton	a																						
Macclesfield	a						20 36	20 36	21 11						21 38	22 11				22 10			
Crewe 10	a				20 07								21 09										
Wilmslow	a																						
Stockport	a						20 49	20 49	21 27						21 53	22 27				22 26			
M'chester Piccadilly 10	a						20 59	20 59	21 39						22 04	22 39				22 39			
Warrington Bank Quay	a				20 26																		
Wigan North Western	a				20 37																		
Preston 8	a				20 59																		
Lancaster 6	a																						
Oxenholme Lake District	a																						
Penrith North Lakes	a																						
Carlisle 8	a																						
Lockerbie	a																						
Haymarket	a																						
Edinburgh 10	a																						
Haymarket	a																						
Motherwell	a																						
Glasgow Central 15	a																						
Inverkeithing	a																						
Kirkcaldy	a																						
Markinch	a																						
Ladybank	a																						
Cupar	a																						
Leuchars 3	a																						
Dundee	a																						
Arbroath	a																						
Montrose	a																						
Stonehaven	a																						
Aberdeen	a																						

A ⊼ to Chesterfield
B until 9 July, from 17 September
C from 17 September. ⊡ from Birmingham New Street ⊼ to Cheltenham Spa
D until 10 September
E ⊼ to Birmingham International
F until 10 September. ⊼ to Cheltenham Spa
G from 17 September. ⊼ to Cheltenham Spa
H ⊼ to Leamington Spa
I ⊼ to Cheltenham Spa
J from 17 September. ⊼ to Birmingham International
K from 25 June until 30 July
L until 18 June, from 6 August until 10 September
h Arr. 1954

Table 51

Saturdays

South Coast and the South West - North West England, The North East and Scotland

		XC	XC	XC	XC	XC		XC	XC	XC	XC	XC	XC	XC
		◇1	◇1	◇1	◇1	◇1			◇1	◇1	◇1	◇1	1	
		A	B	C	A	D		E					F	G
								🚌						🚌
			🛒	🛒	🛒	🛒			🛒			🛒		
Bournemouth	d					18 45						19 45		
Brockenhurst 3	d					19 00						20 00		
Southampton Central ⛴	d					19 15						20 15		
Southampton Airport Pkway ✈	d					19 22						20 22		
Winchester	d					19 31						20 31		
Basingstoke	d					19 47						20 47		
Guildford	d													
Reading 7	d					20b11			20 40			21c11		
Oxford	d					20 36			21 07			21 36		
Banbury	d					20 54			21 25			21 54		
Leamington Spa 8	d					21 12			21 45			22 12		
Coventry	d					21 27			21 56			22 27		
Birmingham International ✈	d					21 38			22 11			22 38		
Penzance	d		16 25	16 25										
St Erth	d		16 35	16 35										
Hayle	d													
Camborne	d		16 46	16 46										
Redruth	d		16 53	16 53										
Truro	d		17 06	17 06										
St Austell	d		17 23	17 23										
Par	d													
Lostwithiel	d													
Bodmin Parkway	d		17 40	17 40										
Liskeard 6	d		17 53	17 53										
Plymouth	d		18 23	18 23	18 25									
Totnes	d		18 49	18 49	18 50									
Paignton	d													
Torquay	d													
Newton Abbot	d		19 03	19 03	19 03									
Teignmouth	d													
Dawlish	d													
Exeter St Davids 6	d		19 25	19 25	19 23									
Tiverton Parkway	d		19 39	19 39	19 37									
Taunton	d		19 54	19 54	19 51									
Weston-super-Mare	d													
Cardiff Central 7	d										20 50			
Newport (South Wales)	d										21 05			
Bristol Temple Meads 10	d	20 00	20 30	20 30	20 30									
Bristol Parkway 7	d	20 10	20 40	20 40	20 40									
Gloucester 7	d										21 49			
Cheltenham Spa	d	20 42	21 12	21 12	21 12						22 00			
London Paddington	d													
Birmingham New Street 12	a	21 38	21 53	21 53	21 53	21 48			22 22		22 42	22 48		
Birmingham New Street 12	d		21 56	21 56		21 57		22 20		22 31			22 49	22 49
Tamworth	d							22 55					23 08	23 29
Burton-on-Trent	d							23 15					23 19	23s49
Derby 6	a		22 30	22 32				23s45					23 33	00 09
Nottingham 8 🚌	a							00 49						
Chesterfield	a		22 52	22 53										
Sheffield 7 🚌	a		23 09	23 09										
Doncaster 7	a													
Wakefield Westgate 7	a													
Leeds 10	a		23 51	23 51										
York 8	a													
Darlington 7	a													
Durham	a													
Chester-le-Street	a													
Newcastle 8	a													
Morpeth	a													
Alnmouth for Alnwick	a													
Berwick-upon-Tweed	a													
Dunbar	a													
Wolverhampton 7 🚌	d					22 16				22 49				
Stafford	a					22 29				23 01				
Stoke-on-Trent	a					22 50				23 20				
Congleton	a													
Macclesfield	a					23 07				23 38				
Crewe 10	a													
Wilmslow	a													
Stockport	a					23 21				23 53				
M'chester Piccadilly 10 🚌	a					23 32				00 10				
Warrington Bank Quay	a													
Wigan North Western	a													
Preston 8	a													
Lancaster 6	a													
Oxenholme Lake District	a													
Penrith North Lakes	a													
Carlisle 8	a													
Lockerbie	a													
Haymarket	a													
Edinburgh 10	a													
Haymarket	a													
Motherwell	a													
Glasgow Central 15	a													
Inverkeithing	a													
Kirkcaldy	a													
Markinch	a													
Ladybank	a													
Cupar	a													
Leuchars 8	a													
Dundee	a													
Arbroath	a													
Montrose	a													
Stonehaven	a													
Aberdeen	a													

A from 17 September
B from 6 August until 10 September. 🛒 from Plymouth to Taunton
C until 30 July. 🛒 from Plymouth to Taunton
D 🛒 to Basingstoke
E until 18 June
F from 6 August
G until 30 July
b Arr. 2004
c Arr. 2104

Table 51

Sundays

South Coast and the South West - North West England, The North East and Scotland

	XC	XC	XC	VT	XC	XC	XC	XC	VT	XC	AW	XC	XC	XC	VT	XC	XC	XC	XC	XC	AW	AW
		◇1		◇1	◇1	◇1	◇1	◇1	◇1	◇1		◇1	◇1	◇1	◇1	◇1	◇1	◇1	◇1	◇1	◇	◇
	A	B	C			D	E	F			G	H	I	J		J	K	I	L	M	J	G
Bournemouth d																						
Brockenhurst 3 d																						
Southampton Central d																						
Southampton Airport Pkwy d																						
Winchester d																						
Basingstoke d																						
Guildford d																						
Reading 7 d																09 11						
Oxford d																09 37						
Banbury d																09 54						
Leamington Spa 8 d																10 12		10 12	10 18			
Coventry d																10 28		10 28	10 28	10 28		
Birmingham International d											09 51					10 40		10 40	10 40	10 40	10 48	10 48
Penzance d																						
St Erth d																						
Hayle d																						
Camborne d																						
Redruth d																						
Truro d																						
St Austell d																						
Par d																						
Lostwithiel d																						
Bodmin Parkway d																						
Liskeard 6 d																						
Plymouth d																						
Totnes d																						
Paignton d																						
Torquay d																						
Newton Abbot d																						
Teignmouth d																						
Dawlish d																						
Exeter St Davids 6 d																						
Tiverton Parkway d																						
Taunton d																						
Weston-super-Mare d																						
Cardiff Central 7 d																						
Newport (South Wales) d																						
Bristol Temple Meads 10 d																	09 15					
Bristol Parkway 7 d																	09 25					
Gloucester 7 d																	10 01					
Cheltenham Spa d																	10 12					
London Paddington d																						
Birmingham New Street 12 a											10 02					10 50	10 50	10 50	10 50	10 50	10 58	10 58
Birmingham New Street 12 d	22p20	22p31	22p49	08 45	09 01	09 03	09 03	09 03	09 20	10 01	10 05	10 03	10 03	10 03	10 20	11 01	11 03	11 01	11 01	11 01	11 05	11 05
Tamworth d	22p55		23p29			09 19						10 18										
Burton-on-Trent d	23p15		23b49			09 28						10 29					11 26					
Derby 6 a	23b45		00 09			09 42	10 11	10 12				10 41	11 26	11 32			11 42					
Nottingham 8 a	00 49																					
Chesterfield a						10 02	11 02	11 02				11 02	12 02	12 02			12 02					
Sheffield 7 a						10 16	11 17	11 17				11 17	12 18	12 18			12 18					
Doncaster 7 a																						
Wakefield Westgate 7 a						10 44	11 44	11 44				11 44	12 44	12 44			12 44					
Leeds 10 a						11 02	12 02	12 02				12 01	13 02	13 02			13 02					
York 8 a						11 35	12 32	12 32				12 32	13 32	13 32			13 32					
Darlington 7 a						12 02	13 00	13 00				13 00	14 00	14 00			14 00					
Durham a						12 19	13 17	13 17				13 17	14 17	14 17			14 17					
Chester-le-Street a																						
Newcastle 8 a						12 35	13 33	13 33				13 33	14 32	14 32			14 32					
Morpeth a													14 48	14 48			14 48					
Alnmouth for Alnwick a							13 59	13 59				13 59										
Berwick-upon-Tweed a							14 19	14 19				14 19										
Dunbar a						13 39							15 40	15 40			15 40					
Wolverhampton 7 d		22p49		09 04	09 19				09 37	10 19	10 22				10 37	11 19		11 19	11 19	11 19	11 27	11 27
Stafford a		23p01		09 16	09 32					10 32						11 31		11 31	11 31	11 31		
Stoke-on-Trent a		23p20								10 51						11 51		11 51	11 51	11 51		
Congleton a																						
Macclesfield a		23p38								11 08						12 09		12 09	12 09	12 09		
Crewe 10 a				09 35	09 54				10 06						11 07							
Wilmslow a					10 12																	
Stockport a		23p53			10 21					11 22						12 22		12 22	12 22	12 22		
M'chester Piccadilly 10 a		00 10			10 37					11 31						12 40		12 40	12 40	12 40		
Warrington Bank Quay a				09 54					10 26						11 26							
Wigan North Western a				10 05					10 37						11 37							
Preston 8 a				10 22					10 51						11 51							
Lancaster 6 a									11 07						12 08							
Oxenholme Lake District a									11 22						12 22							
Penrith North Lakes a																						
Carlisle 8 a									12 01						13 01							
Lockerbie a																						
Haymarket a															14 13							
Edinburgh 10 a						14 07	15 06	15 06				15 06	16 06	16 06	14 22		16 06					
Haymarket a							15 14	15 14				15 14										
Motherwell a							15 51	15 51				15 51										
Glasgow Central 15 a							16 14	16 14	13 17			16 14										
Inverkeithing a																						
Kirkcaldy a																						
Markinch a																						
Ladybank a																						
Cupar a																						
Leuchars 3 a																						
Dundee a																						
Arbroath a																						
Montrose a																						
Stonehaven a																						
Aberdeen a																						

A from 29 May until 19 June
B not 22 May
C from 29 May until 31 July
D from 7 August
E from 26 June until 31 July. trolley to Berwick-upon-Tweed
F until 19 June. trolley to Berwick-upon-Tweed
G until 19 June, from 7 August
H from 7 August. trolley to Berwick-upon-Tweed
I until 19 June
J from 26 June until 31 July
K from 7 August until 11 September, from 30 October
L from 18 September
M from 7 August until 11 September
b Previous night, stops to set down only

Table 51

Sundays

South Coast and the South West - North West England, The North East and Scotland

		XC	XC	VT	XC	XC	XC	XC	XC	XC	XC	XC	XC	XC	VT	AW	XC	XC	XC	XC	XC	XC	XC
		◇1	◇1	◇1	◇1	◇1	◇1	◇1	◇1	◇1	◇1	◇1	◇1	◇1	◇1	◇	◇1	◇1	◇1	◇1	◇1	◇1	◇1
		A	B		C	D	C	E	F	G	H	I	J	K			L	H	M	N	C	O	B
Bournemouth	d																				09 40		
Brockenhurst 3	d																				09 57		
Southampton Central	d						09 15														10 15		
Southampton Airport Pkwy	d						09 22														10 22		
Winchester	d						09 31														10 31		
Basingstoke	d						09 47														10 47		
Guildford	d																						
Reading 7	d						10 11														11 11		
Oxford	d						10 37														11 37		
Banbury	d						10 54														11 54		
Leamington Spa 8	d						11 12				11 12		11 18	11 18							12 12		
Coventry	d						11 28				11 28	11 28	11 29	11 30							12 28		
Birmingham International	d						11 40				11 40	11 40	11 42	11 43		12 08					12 40		
Penzance	d																						
St Erth	d																						
Hayle	d																						
Camborne	d																						
Redruth	d																						
Truro	d																						
St Austell	d																						
Par	d																						
Lostwithiel	d																						
Bodmin Parkway	d																						
Liskeard 8	d																						
Plymouth	d																						
Totnes	d																						
Paignton	d																						
Torquay	d																						
Newton Abbot	d																						
Teignmouth	d																						
Dawlish	d																						
Exeter St Davids 6	d																						
Tiverton Parkway	d																						
Taunton	d																						
Weston-super-Mare	d																						
Cardiff Central 7	d																	10 45	10 45				
Newport (South Wales)	d																	10 59	10 59				
Bristol Temple Meads 10	d				09 30			09 30	10 30													10 30	10 30
Bristol Parkway 7	d				09 43			09 48	10 40	10 40												10 43	10 43
Gloucester 7	d				11 01			11 01										11 51	11 51	11 52		12 00	12 02
Cheltenham Spa	d				11 12			11 12	11 12	11 12								12 03	12 03	12 03		12 12	12 12
London Paddington	d																						
Birmingham New Street 12	a				11 48		11 50	11 50	11 50	11 50	11 50	11 50	11 51	11 53		12 18		12 45	12 45	12 45	12 50	12 50	12 50
Birmingham New Street 12	d	11 03	11 03	11 20		11 49	12 01	12 03	12 03	12 03	12 01	12 01	12 01	12 01	12 20	12 24	12 30		12 49	12 49	13 01	13 03	13 03
Tamworth	d					12 06			12 19	12 19									13 06	13 06			
Burton-on-Trent	d					12 18													13 19	13 19		13 25	
Derby 6	a	12 27	12 28			12 34		13 23	12 43	12 43							13 09		13 32	13 32		13 44	14 25
Nottingham 8	a					13 02													13 59	13 59			
Chesterfield	a	13 02	13 02					14 02	13 02	13 03							13 29					14 02	15 02
Sheffield 7	a	13 17	13 17					14 17	13 17	13 17							13 43					14 17	15 17
Doncaster 7	a																14 13						
Wakefield Westgate 7	a	13 44	13 44					14 44	13 44	13 44												14 44	15 44
Leeds 10	a	14 02	14 02					15 02	14 02	14 02												15 02	16 02
York 8	a	14 31	14 31					15 31	14 31	14 31							14 41					15 31	16 32
Darlington 7	a	15 00	15 00					15 59	15 00	15 00							15 15					15 59	17 00
Durham	a	15 19	15 19					16 17	15 19	15 19							15 32					16 17	17 17
Chester-le-Street	a																						
Newcastle 8	a	15 35	15 35					16 32	15 35	15 35							15 47					16 32	17 33
Morpeth	a																						
Alnmouth for Alnwick	a	16 01	16 01					16 58	16 01	16 01												16 58	18 01
Berwick-upon-Tweed	a	16 21	16 21						16 21	16 21													18 22
Dunbar	a							17 39														17 39	
Wolverhampton 7	d			11 37			12 19				12 19	12 19	12 19	12 19	12 37	12 42					13 19		
Stafford	a						12 32				12 32	12 32	12 32	12 32							13 33		
Stoke-on-Trent	a						12 52				12 52	12 52	12 52	12 52							13 56		
Congleton	a																						
Macclesfield	a						13 10				13 10	13 10	13 10	13 10							14 14		
Crewe 10	a			12 07											13 07								
Wilmslow	a																						
Stockport	a						13 28				13 28	13 28	13 28	13 28							14 28		
M'chester Piccadilly 10	a						13 40				13 40	13 40	13 40	13 40							14 40		
Warrington Bank Quay	a			12 26											13 26								
Wigan North Western	a			12 37											13 37								
Preston 8	a			12 51											13 51								
Lancaster 6	a			13 08											14 08								
Oxenholme Lake District	a			13 22																			
Penrith North Lakes	a														14 44								
Carlisle 8	a			14 01											15 00								
Lockerbie	a																						
Haymarket	a														16 14								
Edinburgh 10	a	17 06	17 06					18 07	17 06	17 06					16 22							18 07	19 06
Haymarket	a	17 14	17 14					18 14	17 14	17 14												18 14	19 22
Motherwell	a	17 52	17 52						17 52	17 52													20 00
Glasgow Central 15	a	18 12	18 12	15 16					18 12	18 12													20 20
Inverkeithing	a							18 28														18 28	
Kirkcaldy	a							18 44														18 44	
Markinch	a							18 53														18 53	
Ladybank	a							19 01														19 01	
Cupar	a							19 07														19 07	
Leuchars 3	a							19 14														19 14	
Dundee	a							19 29														19 29	
Arbroath	a							19 46														19 46	
Montrose	a							20 00														20 00	
Stonehaven	a							20 23														20 23	
Aberdeen	a							20 43														20 43	

A from 26 June until 31 July. ✠ to Berwick-upon-Tweed
B until 19 June. ✠ to Berwick-upon-Tweed
C from 26 June until 31 July
D from 7 August
E until 19 June. ✠ to Dunbar
F from 7 August until 11 September, from 30 October. ✠ to Berwick-upon-Tweed
G from 18 September until 23 October. ✠ to Berwick-upon-Tweed
H until 19 June
I from 7 August until 11 September
J from 30 October
K from 18 September until 23 October
L from 26 June
M from 26 June until 31 July, from 30 October. ✠ from Newport (South Wales)
N from 7 August until 23 October
O from 26 June until 31 July. ✠ to Dunbar

Table 51

Sundays

South Coast and the South West - North West England, The North East and Scotland

		XC	XC	XC	XC	XC	VT	AW	AW	XC	XC	XC	XC	XC	XC	XC	XC	XC	XC	XC	XC	XC
		◇1	◇1	◇1	◇1	◇1	◇1	◇	◇	◇1	◇1	◇1	◇1	◇1	◇1	◇1	◇1	◇1	◇1	◇1	◇1	◇1
		A	B	C	D	E		F	G	H		I	J	K	L	E	F	M	D	N	O	P
		🛒	🛒	🛒	🛒	🛒	🍴	🛒	🛒	🛒	🛒	🛒	🛒	🛒	🛒		🛒	🛒	🛒	🛒	🛒	🛒
Bournemouth	d																10 40					
Brockenhurst 3	d																10 57					
Southampton Central ⛴	d																11 15					
Southampton Airport Pkway ✈	d																11 22					
Winchester	d																11 31					
Basingstoke	d																11 47					
Guildford	d																					
Reading 7	d																12 11					
Oxford	d																12 37					
Banbury	d																12 54					
Leamington Spa 8	d			12 12		12 18											13 12	13 12				
Coventry	d			12 28	12 28	12 29											13 26	13 26	13 26			
Birmingham International ✈	d			12 40	12 40	12 43		13 12	13 12								13 38	13 38	13 38			
Penzance	d																					
St Erth	d																					
Hayle	d																					
Camborne	d																					
Redruth	d																					
Truro	d																					
St Austell	d																					
Par	d																					
Lostwithiel	d																					
Bodmin Parkway	d																					
Liskeard 6	d																					
Plymouth	d	09 25																		09 25	09 25	10 25
Totnes	d	09 50																		09 50	09 50	10 50
Paignton	d																					
Torquay	d																					
Newton Abbot	d	10 03																		10 03	10 03	11 03
Teignmouth	d																					
Dawlish	d																					
Exeter St Davids 6	d	10 23																		10 23	10 23	11 23
Tiverton Parkway	d	10 37																		10 37	10 37	11 37
Taunton	d	10 51																		10 51	10 51	11 51
Weston-super-Mare	d																					
Cardiff Central 7	d											11 25	11 45	11 45	11 45							
Newport (South Wales)	d											11 39	11 59	11 59	11 59							
Bristol Temple Meads 10	d	11 30																		11 30	11 30	12 30
Bristol Parkway 7	d	11 40	11 40																	11 43	11 43	12 40
Gloucester 7	d											12c47	12 47	12 47	12 47	12 47				12 59	12 59	
Cheltenham Spa	d	12 12	12 12									12 58	12 58	12 58	12 58	12 58				13 12	13 12	13 12
London Paddington	d																					
Birmingham New Street 12	a	12 50	12 50	12 50	12 50	12 53		13 21	13 21			13 41	13 42	13 41	13 41	13 41	13 48	13 48	13 48	13 50	13 50	13 50
Birmingham New Street 12	d	13 03	13 03	13 01	13 01	13 01	13 20	13 24	13 24	13 30	13 31	13 49		13 49	13 49	13 49	14 01	14 01	14 01	14 03	14 03	14 03
Tamworth	d											14 06		14 06	14 06	14 06				14 19		14 19
Burton-on-Trent	d	13 25	13 25									14 19		14 18	14 19	14 19						
Derby 6	a	13 44	13 44							14 09		14 34		14 34	14 34	14 34				14 42	15 35	14 42
Nottingham 8 🚊	a											15 07		15 07	15 07	15 07						
Chesterfield	a	14 02	14 02							14 29										15 02	16 02	15 02
Sheffield 7 🚊	a	14 17	14 17							14 48										15 17	16 18	15 17
Doncaster 7	a									15 13												
Wakefield Westgate 7	a	14 44	14 44																	15 44	16 44	15 44
Leeds 10	a	15 02	15 02																	16 02	17 02	16 02
York 8	a	15 31	15 31							15 44										16 32	17 32	16 32
Darlington 7	a	15 59	15 59							16 12										17 00	18 00	17 00
Durham	a	16 17	16 17							16 30										17 17	18 17	17 17
Chester-le-Street	a																					
Newcastle 8	a	16 32	16 32							16 45										17 33	18 32	17 33
Morpeth	a																					
Alnmouth for Alnwick	a	16 58	16 58																	18 01		18 01
Berwick-upon-Tweed	a																			18 22	19 17	18 22
Dunbar	a	17 39	17 39																		19 40	
Wolverhampton 7 🚊	d			13 19	13 19	13 19	13 37	13 42	13 42		13 49						14 19	14 19	14 19			
Stafford	a			13 33	13 33	13 33											14 33	14 33	14 33			
Stoke-on-Trent	a			13 56	13 56	13 56					14 19						14 56	14 56	14 56			
Congleton	a																					
Macclesfield	a			14 14	14 14	14 14											15 14	15 14	15 14			
Crewe 10	a						14 07															
Wilmslow	a																					
Stockport	a			14 28	14 28	14 28											15 28	15 28	15 28			
M'chester Piccadilly 10 🚊	a			14 40	14 40	14 40					14 57						15 40	15 40	15 40			
Warrington Bank Quay	a						14 26															
Wigan North Western	a						14 37															
Preston 8	a						14 50															
Lancaster 6	a						15 08															
Oxenholme Lake District	a						15 22															
Penrith North Lakes	a																					
Carlisle 8	a						16 01															
Lockerbie	a																					
Haymarket	a																					
Edinburgh 10	a	18 07	18 07																	19 06	20 05	19 06
Haymarket	a	18 14	18 14																	19 22		19 22
Motherwell	a																			20 00		20 00
Glasgow Central 15	a						17 17													20 20		20 20
Inverkeithing	a	18 28	18 28																			
Kirkcaldy	a	18 44	18 44																			
Markinch	a	18 53	18 53																			
Ladybank	a	19 01	19 01																			
Cupar	a	19 07	19 07																			
Leuchars 3	a	19 14	19 14																			
Dundee	a	19 29	19 29																			
Arbroath	a	19 46	19 46																			
Montrose	a	20 00	20 00																			
Stonehaven	a	20 23	20 23																			
Aberdeen	a	20 43	20 43																			

A from 7 August until 11 September, from 30 October. 🛒 to Dunbar
B from 18 September until 23 October. 🛒 to Dunbar
C until 19 June, from 30 October
D from 7 August until 11 September
E from 18 September until 23 October
F from 26 June until 31 July
G until 19 June, from 7 August
H from 26 June
I from 7 August until 11 September. 🛒 from Newport (South Wales)
J until 19 June. 🛒 from Newport (South Wales)
K from 30 October. 🛒 from Newport (South Wales)
L from 26 June until 31 July. 🛒 from Newport (South Wales)
M until 19 June, from 18 September
N from 26 June until 31 July. 🛒 to Berwick-upon-Tweed
O until 19 June
P from 7 August until 11 September. 🛒 to Berwick-upon-Tweed

Table 51

Sundays

South Coast and the South West - North West England, The North East and Scotland

		XC	XC	VT	AW	XC	XC	XC	XC	XC	XC	XC	XC	XC	XC	XC	XC	XC	XC	XC	XC	VT	AW
		◇1	◇1	◇1	◇	◇1	◇1	◇1	◇1	◇1	◇1	◇1	◇1	◇1	◇1	◇1	◇1	◇1	◇1	◇1	◇1	◇1	
		A	B			C	D	E	F	G	H	I	C	J	K	C	L	M	N	O	P		C
		⊼	⊼	⊡	⊼	⊼	⊼	⊼	⊼		⊼		⊼	⊼	⊼	⊼	⊼	⊼	⊼	⊼	⊼	⊡	
Bournemouth	d												11 40										
Brockenhurst 3	d												11 57										
Southampton Central	d												12 15										
Southampton Airport Pkway ✈	d												12 22										
Winchester	d												12 31										
Basingstoke	d												12 47										
Guildford	d																						
Reading 7	d					12 54							13 11							13 40	13 40		
Oxford	d					13 17							13 37							14 06	14 12		
Banbury	d					13 35							13 54							14 25	14 31		
Leamington Spa 8	d					13 53							14 12	14 12						14 43	14 49		
Coventry	d												14 26	14 26	14 26								
Birmingham International ✈	d				14 07								14 38	14 38	14 38								15 07
Penzance	d																	09 30					
St Erth	d																	09 38					
Hayle	d																						
Camborne	d																	09 48					
Redruth	d																	09 54					
Truro	d																	10 06					
St Austell	d																	10 22					
Par	d																	10 30					
Lostwithiel	d																						
Bodmin Parkway	d																	10 41					
Liskeard 6	d																	10 53					
Plymouth	d	10 25														10 25	10 25	11 25					
Totnes	d	10 50														10 50	10 50	11 50					
Paignton	d						10 50																
Torquay	d						10 56																
Newton Abbot	d	11 03					11 08									11 03	11 03	12 03					
Teignmouth	d						11 15																
Dawlish	d						11 20																
Exeter St Davids 6	d	11 23					11 32									11 23	11 23	12 23					
Tiverton Parkway	d	11 37					11 46									11 37	11 38	12 37					
Taunton	d	11 53					12 00									11 51	11 53	12 51					
Weston-super-Mare	d						12 21																
Cardiff Central 7	d									12 45	12 45												
Newport (South Wales)	d									12 59	12 59												
Bristol Temple Meads 10	d	12 30					13b00									12 30	12 30	13 30					
Bristol Parkway 7	d	12 40	12 40				13 10									12 43	12 43	13 40	13 40				
Gloucester 7	d									13 51	13 51	13 51				14 00	14 02						
Cheltenham Spa	d	13 12	13 12				13 42			14 02	14 02	14 02				14 12	14 12	14 12	14 12				
London Paddington	d																						
Birmingham New Street 12	a	13 50	13 50		14 18	14 19	14 26			14 44	14 45	14 45	14 48	14 48	14 48	14 50	14 48	14 50	14 50	15 13	15 13		15 18
Birmingham New Street 12	d	14 03	14 03	14 20	14 24	14 30	14 31	14 30	14 31		14 49	14 49	15 01	15 01	15 01	15 03	15 03	15 03	15 03	15 30	15 30	15 20	15 24
Tamworth	d	14 19	14 19								15 08	15 08											
Burton-on-Trent	d										15 21	15 21				15 26		15 26	15 28				
Derby 6	a	14 42	14 42			15 04		15 04			15 35	15 35				15 42	16 19	15 42	15 42	16 02	16 02		
Nottingham 8	a										16 04	16 04											
Chesterfield	a	15 02	15 02													16 02	17 03	16 02	16 02				
Sheffield 7	a	15 17	15 17			15 47		15 47								16 18	17 17	16 18	16 18	16 48	16 48		
Doncaster 7	a					16 15		16 15												17 13	17 13		
Wakefield Westgate 7	a	15 44	15 44													16 44	17 46	16 44	16 44				
Leeds 10	a	16 02	16 02													17 02	18 02	17 02	17 02				
York 8	a	16 32	16 32			16 44		16 44								17 32	18 32	17 31	17 32	17 42	17 42		
Darlington 7	a	17 00	17 00			17 16		17 16								18 00	19 00	17 59	18 00	18 12	18 12		
Durham	a	17 17	17 17			17 34		17 34								18 17	19 17	18 16	18 17	18 30	18 30		
Chester-le-Street	a																						
Newcastle 8	a	17 33	17 33			17 48		17 48								18 32	19 35	18 32	18 32	18 46	18 46		
Morpeth	a																						
Alnmouth for Alnwick	a	18 01	18 01														20 04						
Berwick-upon-Tweed	a	18 22	18 22													19 17	20 24	19 17	19 17				
Dunbar	a															19 40		19 40	19 40				
Wolverhampton 7	d			14 37	14 43		14 49		14 49				15 19	15 19	15 19							15 37	15 43
Stafford	a												15 33	15 33	15 33								
Stoke-on-Trent	a						15 19		15 19				15 56	15 56	15 56								
Congleton	a																						
Macclesfield	a												16 14	16 14	16 14								
Crewe 10	a			15 07																		16 07	
Wilmslow	a																						
Stockport	a												16 28	16 28	16 28								
M'chester Piccadilly 10	a						16 00		16 00				16 40	16 40	16 40								
Warrington Bank Quay	a			15 26																		16 26	
Wigan North Western	a			15 37																		16 37	
Preston 8	a			15 51																		16 51	
Lancaster 6	a			16 08																		17 08	
Oxenholme Lake District	a																					17 22	
Penrith North Lakes	a			16 44																			
Carlisle 8	a			17 00																		18 01	
Lockerbie	a																						
Haymarket	a			18 13																			
Edinburgh 10	a	19 06	19 06	18 22												20 05	21 08	20 05	20 05				
Haymarket	a	19 22	19 22														21 15						
Motherwell	a	20 00	20 00														21 53						
Glasgow Central 15	a	20 20	20 20														22 14					19 17	
Inverkeithing	a																						
Kirkcaldy	a																						
Markinch	a																						
Ladybank	a																						
Cupar	a																						
Leuchars 3	a																						
Dundee	a																						
Arbroath	a																						
Montrose	a																						
Stonehaven	a																						
Aberdeen	a																						

A from 30 October. ⊼ to Berwick-upon-Tweed
B from 18 September until 23 October. ⊼ to Berwick-upon-Tweed
C from 26 June until 31 July
D from 7 August until 11 September, from 30 October
E from 7 August
F until 31 July, from 18 September until 23 October
G until 19 June
H from 26 June until 31 July, from 30 October. ⊼ from Newport (South Wales)
I from 7 August until 23 October
J until 19 June, from 18 September
K from 7 August until 11 September
L until 19 June. ⊼ to Berwick-upon-Tweed
M from 7 August until 11 September, from 30 October. ⊼ from Plymouth
N from 18 September until 23 October. ⊼ from Birmingham New Street
O from 26 June until 11 September
P from 18 September
b Arr. 1246

Table 51

Sundays

South Coast and the South West - North West England, The North East and Scotland

		AW	XC	XC	XC	XC	XC	XC	XC	XC	XC	XC	XC	XC	XC	XC	VT	AW	XC	XC	XC	XC
		◇	◇1	◇1	◇1	◇1	◇1	◇1	◇1	◇1	◇1	◇1	◇1	◇1	◇1	◇1	◇1	◇	◇1	◇1	◇1	◇1
		A	B	C	D	E	F	G	H		I	J	K	L	C	M			C	D	B	E
Bournemouth	d									12 40												
Brockenhurst 3	d									12 57												
Southampton Central	d									13 15												
Southampton Airport Pkwy	d									13 22												
Winchester	d									13 31												
Basingstoke	d									13 47												
Guildford	d																					
Reading 7	d									14 11					14 40	14 40						
Oxford	d									14 37					15 06	15 06						
Banbury	d									14 54					15 25	15 25						
Leamington Spa 8	d									15 12					15 43	15 43						
Coventry	d									15 26												
Birmingham International	d	15 07								15 38								16 07				
Penzance	d										09 30	09 30										
St Erth	d										09 38	09 38										
Hayle	d																					
Camborne	d										09 48	09 48										
Redruth	d										09 54	09 54										
Truro	d										10 06	10 06										
St Austell	d										10 22	10 22										
Par	d										10 30	10 30										
Lostwithiel	d																					
Bodmin Parkway	d										10 41	10 41										
Liskeard 6	d										10 53	10 53										
Plymouth	d				12 00						11 25	11 25	12 25						12 25	12 52		
Totnes	d										11 50	11 50	12 50						12 50			
Paignton	d			10 50																		
Torquay	d			10 56																		
Newton Abbot	d			11 08	12 36						12 03	12 03	13 03						13 03	13 27		
Teignmouth	d			11 15																		
Dawlish	d			11 20																		
Exeter St Davids 6	d			11 33	12 57						12 23	12 23	13 23						13 23	13 48		
Tiverton Parkway	d			11 47	13 10						12 37	12 37	13 37						13 37			
Taunton	d			12 01	13 25						12 51	12 51	13 51						13 51			
Weston-super-Mare	d			12 23																		
Cardiff Central 7	d					13 45	13 45		13 45													14 45
Newport (South Wales)	d					13 59	13 59		13 59													14 59
Bristol Temple Meads 10	d			13b00	14 00						13 30	13 30	14 30						15h00	15 00		
Bristol Parkway 7	d			13 13	14 10						13 43	13g48	14 40	14 40					15 10	15 10		
Gloucester 7	d			14 30		14 47	14 47	14 47	14 49		15 00	15 02										15 47
Cheltenham Spa	d			14 42	14 42	14 58	14 58	14 58	14 59		15 12	15 12	15 12	15 12					15 42	15 42		15 58
London Paddington	d																					
Birmingham New Street 12	a	15 18		15 26	15 27	15 42	15 41	15 41	15 43	15 48	15 50	15 50	15 50	15 50	16 12	16 12		16 18	16 26	16 26		16 41
Birmingham New Street 12	d	15 24	15 31	15 31	15 31		15 49	15 49	15 49	16 01	16 03	16 03	16 03	16 03		16 30	16 20	16 24	16 31	16 31	16 31	
Tamworth	d						16 06	16 06	16 06			16 19	16 19	16 19								
Burton-on-Trent	d						16 19	16 19	16 19													
Derby 6	a						16 34	16 34	16 34		17 20	16 42	16 42	16 42		17 04						
Nottingham 8	a						17 03	17 03	17 03													
Chesterfield	a										18 03	17 02	17 02	17 03								
Sheffield 7	a										18 19	17 17	17 17	17 17		17 48						
Doncaster 7	a															18 13						
Wakefield Westgate 7	a										18 47	17 46	17 46	17 46		18 33						
Leeds 10	a										19 04	18 02	18 02	18 02		18 51						
York 8	a										19 32	18 32	18 32	18 32		19 21						
Darlington 7	a										20 01	19 00	19 00	19 00		19 51						
Durham	a										20 18	19 17	19 17	19 17		20 08						
Chester-le-Street	a																					
Newcastle 8	a										20 33	19 35	19 35	19 35		20 24						
Morpeth	a										20 52											
Alnmouth for Alnwick	a											20 04	20 04	20 04								
Berwick-upon-Tweed	a										21 24	20 24	20 24	20 24								
Dunbar	a										21 49											
Wolverhampton 7	d	15 43	15 49	15 49	15 49					16 19							16 37	16 43	16 49	16 49	16 49	
Stafford	a									16 34												
Stoke-on-Trent	a		16 19	16 19	16 19					16 56									17 19	17 19	17 19	
Congleton	a																					
Macclesfield	a									17 14												
Crewe 10	a																17 07					
Wilmslow	a																					
Stockport	a									17 28												
M'chester Piccadilly 10	a		16 59	17 00	16 59					17 40									17 56	17 56	17 56	
Warrington Bank Quay	a																17 26					
Wigan North Western	a																17 37					
Preston 8	a																17 51					
Lancaster 6	a																18 08					
Oxenholme Lake District	a																18 22					
Penrith North Lakes	a																18 48					
Carlisle 8	a																19 04					
Lockerbie	a																					
Haymarket	a																					
Edinburgh 10	a										22 16	21 08	21 08	21 08			20 22					
Haymarket	a											21 15	21 15	21 15								
Motherwell	a											21 53	21 53	21 53								
Glasgow Central 15	a											22 14	22 14	22 14								
Inverkeithing	a																					
Kirkcaldy	a																					
Markinch	a																					
Ladybank	a																					
Cupar	a																					
Leuchars 3	a																					
Dundee	a																					
Arbroath	a																					
Montrose	a																					
Stonehaven	a																					
Aberdeen	a																					

A until 19 June, from 7 August
B from 26 June until 31 July, from 18 September until 23 October
C until 19 June
D from 7 August until 11 September, from 30 October
E until 19 June. from Newport (South Wales)
F from 26 June until 31 July, from 30 October. from Newport (South Wales)
G from 7 August until 11 September
H from 18 September until 23 October. from Newport (South Wales)
I until 19 June. from Plymouth
J from 26 June until 31 July. from Plymouth to Berwick-upon-Tweed
K from 7 August until 11 September, from 30 October. to Berwick-upon-Tweed
L from 18 September until 23 October. to Berwick-upon-Tweed
M from 26 June

South Coast and the South West - North West England, The North East and Scotland

		XC	XC	XC	XC	XC	XC	XC	XC	XC	XC	VT	AW	AW	XC	XC	XC	XC	XC	XC	XC	XC	XC
		◇1	◇1	◇1	◇1	◇1	◇1	◇1	◇1	◇1	◇1	◇1	◇	◇	◇1	◇1	◇1	◇1	◇1	◇1	◇1	◇1	◇1
		A	B		C	D	E	F	G	H	I		J	K	L	M	N	O	P	B		Q	R
		✠		✠	✠	✠	✠	✠	✠	✠	✠	🍴	✠	✠	✠	✠	✠		✠		✠	✠	✠
Bournemouth	d			13 40																	14 40		
Brockenhurst 3	d			13 57																	14 57		
Southampton Central	d			14 15																	15 15		
Southampton Airport Pkway	d			14 22																	15 22		
Winchester	d			14 31																	15 31		
Basingstoke	d			14 47																	15 47		
Guildford	d																						
Reading 7	d			15 11						15 40	15 40										16 11		
Oxford	d			15 37						16 06	16 06										16 37		
Banbury	d			15 54						16 25	16 25										16 54		
Leamington Spa 8	d			16 12						16 43	16 43										17 12		
Coventry	d			16 26																	17 26		
Birmingham International	d			16 38									17 07	17 07							17 38		
Penzance	d								11 25														
St Erth	d								11 35														
Hayle	d																						
Camborne	d								11 46														
Redruth	d								11 53														
Truro	d								12 06														
St Austell	d								12 23														
Par	d								12 31														
Lostwithiel	d																						
Bodmin Parkway	d					12 41		12 41	12 42													12 41	
Liskeard 6	d					12 54		12 54	12 55													12 54	
Plymouth	d				12 25	13 23		13 23	13 23													13 23	14 23
Totnes	d				12 52	13 49		13 49	13 49													13 49	14 49
Paignton	d																						
Torquay	d																						
Newton Abbot	d				13 05	14 03		14 03	14 03													14 03	15 03
Teignmouth	d																						
Dawlish	d																						
Exeter St Davids 6	d				13 27	14 25		14 25	14 25													14 25	15 25
Tiverton Parkway	d					14 39		14 39	14 39													14 39	15 38
Taunton	d				13 53	14 54		14 54	14 54													14 54	15 54
Weston-super-Mare	d																						
Cardiff Central 7	d	14 45															15 45	15 45					
Newport (South Wales)	d	14 59															15 59	15 59	15 59				
Bristol Temple Meads 10	d				14 30	15 30		15 30	15 30						16 00							15 30	16 30
Bristol Parkway 7	d				14 47	15 40	15 40	15 40	15 40						16 10							15 45	16 40
Gloucester 7	d	15 47	15 47		16 01												16 47	16 47	16 47	16 47		17 02	
Cheltenham Spa	d	15 58	15 58		16 12	16 12	16 12	16 12	16 12						16 42		16 58	16 58	16 58	16 58		17 12	17 12
London Paddington	d																						
Birmingham New Street 12	a	16 41	16 41	16 48	16 51	16 50	16 50	16 50	16 50	17 12	17 12		17 18	17 18	17 26		17 41	17 41	17 41	17 41	17 48	17 49	17 49
Birmingham New Street 12	d	16 49	16 49	17 01	17 03	17 03	17 03	17 03	17 03		17 30	17 20	17 24	17 24	17 31	17 31		17 49	17 49	17 49	18 01	18 03	18 03
Tamworth	d	17 06	17 06															18 06	18 06	18 06		18 20	18 20
Burton-on-Trent	d	17 19	17 18		17 28	17 28	17 28		17 28									18 19	18 19	18 19			
Derby 6	a	17 35	17 35		17 42	17 42	17 42	18 25	17 42		18 04							18 34	18 34	18 34		18 42	18 42
Nottingham 8	a	18 00	18 02															19 04	19 04	19 04			
Chesterfield	a				18 03	18 03	18 03	19 04	18 03													19 04	19 04
Sheffield 7	a				18 19	18 19	18 19	19 20	18 19		18 46											19 20	19 20
Doncaster 7	a										19 15												
Wakefield Westgate 7	a				18 47	18 47	18 47	19 48	18 47													19 48	19 48
Leeds 10	a				19 04	19 04	19 04	20 05	19 04													20 05	20 05
York 8	a				19 32	19 32	19 32	20 32	19 32		19 44											20 32	20 32
Darlington 7	a				20 02	20 02	20 02	21 02	20 02		20 12											21 02	21 02
Durham	a				20 20	20 20	20 20	21 20	20 20		20 30											21 20	21 20
Chester-le-Street	a																						
Newcastle 8	a				20 36	20 36	20 36	21 36	20 36		20 45											21 36	21 36
Morpeth	a				20 52	20 52	20 52		20 52														
Alnmouth for Alnwick	a							22 04														22 04	22 04
Berwick-upon-Tweed	a				21 25	21 25	21 25		21 25														
Dunbar	a				21 48	21 48	21 48		21 48														
Wolverhampton 7	d			17 19								17 37	17 43	17 43	17 49	17 49					18 19		
Stafford	a			17 35																	18 35		
Stoke-on-Trent	a			17 56											18 19	18 19					18 56		
Congleton	a																						
Macclesfield	a			18 14																	19 15		
Crewe 10	a											18 07											
Wilmslow	a																						
Stockport	a			18 28																	19 28		
M'chester Piccadilly 10	a			18 40											18 56	18 56					19 40		
Warrington Bank Quay	a											18 26											
Wigan North Western	a											18 37											
Preston 8	a											18 51											
Lancaster 6	a											19 08											
Oxenholme Lake District	a											19 22											
Penrith North Lakes	a																						
Carlisle 8	a											20 01											
Lockerbie	a																						
Haymarket	a																						
Edinburgh 10	a				22 16	22 16	22 16	23 09	22 16		22 23											23 09	23 09
Haymarket	a																						
Motherwell	a																						
Glasgow Central 15	a											21 17											
Inverkeithing	a																						
Kirkcaldy	a																						
Markinch	a																						
Ladybank	a																						
Cupar	a																						
Leuchars 3	a																						
Dundee	a																						
Arbroath	a																						
Montrose	a																						
Stonehaven	a																						
Aberdeen	a																						

A from 26 June until 31 July, from 18 Sept. ✠ from Newport (South Wales)
B from 7 August until 11 September
C from 26 June until 31 July. ✠ to Durham
D from 7 August until 11 Sept. ✠ from Plymouth
E from 18 September until 23 October. ✠ from Birmingham New Street
F until 19 June. ✠ to Wakefield Westgate
G from 30 October. ✠ from Plymouth
H until 19 June
I from 26 June
J from 26 June until 31 July
K until 19 June, from 7 August
L until 19 June, from 7 August until 11 September, from 30 October
M from 26 June until 31 July, from 18 September until 23 October
N until 19 June. ✠ from Newport (South Wales)
O from 26 June until 31 July, from 30 October
P from 18 September until 23 October
Q from 26 June until 31 July. ✠ to Wakefield Westgate
R from 7 August until 11 September, from 30 October. ✠ to Wakefield Westgate

Table 51

Sundays

South Coast and the South West - North West England, The North East and Scotland

	XC	XC	XC	XC	VT	AW	XC	XC	XC	XC	XC	XC	XC	XC	XC	XC	XC	XC	VT	AW	AW	AW
																			R			
	◇1	◇1	◇1	◇1	◇1	◇	◇1	◇1	◇1	◇1	◇1	◇1	◇1	◇1	◇1	◇1	◇1	◇1	1	◇	◇	◇
	A	B	B	C			D	E	B	F	G		H	I	J	K	B	L		H	M	N
	🍴	🍴	🍴	🍴	☕	🍴	🍴	🍴				🍴	🍴	🍴	🍴	🍴	🍴	🍴	☕	🍴	🍴	🍴
Bournemouth d												15 40										
Brockenhurst [3] d												15 57										
Southampton Central ⛴ d												16 15										
Southampton Airport Pkwy ✈ d												16 22										
Winchester d												16 31										
Basingstoke d												16 47										
Guildford d																						
Reading [7] d			16 40	16 40								17f11					17 40	17 40				
Oxford d			17 06	17 06								17 37					18 06	18 06				
Banbury d			17 25	17 25								17 54					18 25	18 25				
Leamington Spa [8] d			17 43	17 43								18 12					18 43	18 43				
Coventry d												18 26										
Birmingham International ✈ d						18 07						18 38								19 07	19 07	19 07
Penzance d							12 30															
St Erth d							12 40															
Hayle d							12 44															
Camborne d							12 56															
Redruth d							13 02															
Truro d							13 14															
St Austell d							13 30															
Par d							13 38															
Lostwithiel d							13 45															
Bodmin Parkway d							13 52															
Liskeard [8] d							14 04															
Plymouth d		14 23					14b35						14 23	15 23		15 25						
Totnes d		14 49					15 00						14 49	15 49		15 50						
Paignton d																						
Torquay d																						
Newton Abbot d		15 03					15 12						15 03	16 03		16 03						
Teignmouth d																						
Dawlish d																						
Exeter St Davids [6] d		15 25					15 33						15 25	16 25		16 23						
Tiverton Parkway d		15 38					15 46						15 38	16 38		16 37						
Taunton d		15 54					16 01						15 54	16 54		16 51						
Weston-super-Mare d							16 30															
Cardiff Central [7] d									16 45	16 45												
Newport (South Wales) d									16 59	16 59												
Bristol Temple Meads [10] d		16 30					17 00						16 30	17 30		17 30						
Bristol Parkway [7] d	16 40	16 40					17 10						16 45	17 40	17 40	17 40						
Gloucester [7] d									17 47	17 47	17 47		17 59									
Cheltenham Spa d	17 12	17 12					17 42		17 58	17 58	17 58		18 12	18 12	18 12	18 12						
London Paddington d																						
Birmingham New Street [12] a	17 49	17 51	18 11	18 09		18 18	18 27		18 41	18 41	18 41	18 48	18 51	18 51	18 51	18 50	19 11	19 11		19 18	19 18	19 18
Birmingham New Street [12] d	18 03	18 03		18 30	18 20	18 24	18 31	18 31		18 49	18 49	19 01	19 03	19 03	19 03	19 03		19 30	19 20	19 24	19 24	19 24
Tamworth d	18 20									19 08	19 08											
Burton-on-Trent d										19 20	19 20		19 26	19 26	19 27							
Derby [6] a	18 42	19 22		19 03						19 33	19 33		19 39	19 39	19 39	20 29		20 02				
Nottingham [8] ⛴ a										19 56	19 56											
Chesterfield a	19 04	20 01											20 01	20 01	20 02	21 00						
Sheffield [7] ⛴ a	19 20	20 17		19 39									20 17	20 17	20 18	21 16		20 38				
Doncaster [7] a				20 16														21 19				
Wakefield Westgate [7] a	19 48	20 46											20 46	20 46	20 46	21 47						
Leeds [10] a	20 05	21 03											21 03	21 03	21 03	22 04						
York [8] a	20 32	21 32		20 45									21 32	21 32	21 32			21 44				
Darlington [7] a	21 02	22 23		21 15														22 22				
Durham a	21 20	22 42		21 33														22 40				
Chester-le-Street a																						
Newcastle [8] a	21 36	23 15		21 51														23 10				
Morpeth a																						
Alnmouth for Alnwick a	22 04																					
Berwick-upon-Tweed a																						
Dunbar a																						
Wolverhampton [7] ⛴ d					18 37	18 43	18 49	18 49				19 19							19 37	19 43	19 43	19 43
Stafford a												19 37										
Stoke-on-Trent a							19 19	19 19				19 56										
Congleton a																						
Macclesfield a												20 14										
Crewe [10] a					19 07														20 07			
Wilmslow a																						
Stockport a												20 28										
M'chester Piccadilly [10] ⛴ a							19 58	19 58				20 40										
Warrington Bank Quay a					19 26														20 26			
Wigan North Western a					19 37														20 37			
Preston [8] a					19 51														20 51			
Lancaster [6] a					20 08														21 08			
Oxenholme Lake District a																			21 22			
Penrith North Lakes a					20 44																	
Carlisle [8] a					21 00														22 01			
Lockerbie a																			22 22			
Haymarket a					22 13																	
Edinburgh [10] a	23 09				22 21																	
Haymarket a																						
Motherwell a																			23 07			
Glasgow Central [15] a																			23 22			
Inverkeithing a																						
Kirkcaldy a																						
Markinch a																						
Ladybank a																						
Cupar a																						
Leuchars [3] a																						
Dundee a																						
Arbroath a																						
Montrose a																						
Stonehaven a																						
Aberdeen a																						

A from 18 September until 23 October. 🍴 to Wakefield Westgate
B until 19 June
C from 26 June
D until 19 Jun, from 7 Aug until 11 Sept, from 30 Oct 🍴 from Plymouth to Cheltenham Spa
E from 26 June until 31 July, from 18 September until 23 October
F from 26 June until 31 July, from 18 September
G from 7 August until 11 September
H from 26 June until 31 July
I from 7 August until 11 September, from 30 October
J from 18 September until 23 October
K until 19 June. 🍴 to Cheltenham Spa
L from 26 June. 🍴 to Derby
M from 18 September
N until 19 June, from 7 August until 11 September

Table 51

Sundays

South Coast and the South West - North West England, The North East and Scotland

		XC	XC	XC	XC	XC	XC	XC	XC	XC	XC	XC	VT	AW	XC	XC	XC	XC	XC	XC	XC	XC
		◇1	◇1	◇1	◇1	◇1	◇1	◇1	◇1	◇1	◇1	◇1	◇1	◇	◇1	◇1	◇1	◇1	◇1	◇1	◇1	◇1
		A	B	C	D	E	F	G	H	I	C				A	J	K	C	D	E	G	F
Bournemouth	d						16 40															17 40
Brockenhurst 3	d						16 57															17 57
Southampton Central	d						17 15															18 15
Southampton Airport Pkway	d						17 22															18 22
Winchester	d						17 31															18 31
Basingstoke	d						17 47															18 47
Guildford	d																					
Reading 7	d						18b11					18 40										19e11
Oxford	d						18 37					19 06										19 37
Banbury	d						18 54					19 25										19 54
Leamington Spa 8	d						19 12					19 43										20 12
Coventry	d						19 26					19 54										20 26
Birmingham International	d						19 38					20 04		20 07								20 38
Penzance	d																					
St Erth	d																					
Hayle	d																					
Camborne	d																					
Redruth	d																					
Truro	d																					
St Austell	d																					
Par	d																					
Lostwithiel	d																					
Bodmin Parkway	d																					
Liskeard 6	d																					
Plymouth	d							15 25	16 25		16 25										16 25	
Totnes	d							15 50	16 50		16 51										16 51	
Paignton	d																					
Torquay	d																					
Newton Abbot	d							16 03	17 03		17 04										17 04	
Teignmouth	d																					
Dawlish	d																					
Exeter St Davids 6	d							16 23	17 23		17 25										17 25	
Tiverton Parkway	d							16 37	17 37		17 41										17 41	
Taunton	d							16 51	17 51		17 54										17 54	
Weston-super-Mare	d																					
Cardiff Central 7	d			17 45	17 45													18 45	18 45			
Newport (South Wales)	d			17 59	17 59													18 59	18 59			
Bristol Temple Meads 10	d	18 00						17 30	18 30		18 30				19 00						18 30	
Bristol Parkway 7	d	18 10						17 43	18 40	18 40	18 40				19 10						18c48	
Gloucester 7	d			18 47	18 47	18 47		18 59										19 50	19 50	19 50	20 02	
Cheltenham Spa	d	18 42		18 58	18 58	18 58		19 12	19 12	19 12	19 12				19 42			20 00	20 00	20 00	20 12	
London Paddington	d																					
Birmingham New Street 12	a	19 26		19 42	19 41	19 41	19 48	19 50	19 50	19 52	19 53	20 15		20 18	20 26			20 42	20 42	20 42	20 51	20 48
Birmingham New Street 12	d	19 31	19 31		19 49	19 49	20 01	20 03	20 03	20 03	20 03		20 20	20 24	20 31	20 31	20 31		20 49	20 49	21 00	21 01
Tamworth	d				20 06	20 06		20 19	20 19	20 19									21 06	21 06	21 17	
Burton-on-Trent	d				20 19	20 19													21 19	21 19	21 28	
Derby 6	a				20 34	20 34		20 42	20 42	20 43	21 26								21 34	21 34	21 41	
Nottingham 8	a				21 01	21 01													22 00	22 00		
Chesterfield	a							21 02	21 02	21 03	22 02										22 03	
Sheffield 7	a							21 16	21 16	21 17	22 18										22 19	
Doncaster 7	a																					
Wakefield Westgate 7	a							21 47	21 47	21 47	22 45										22 46	
Leeds 10	a							22 04	22 04	22 04	23 03										23 03	
York 8	a																					
Darlington 7	a																					
Durham	a																					
Chester-le-Street	a																					
Newcastle 8	a																					
Morpeth	a																					
Alnmouth for Alnwick	a																					
Berwick-upon-Tweed	a																					
Dunbar	a																					
Wolverhampton 7	d	19 49	19 49				20 19						20 38	20 43	20 52	20 52	20 52					21 19
Stafford	a						20 36						20 51									21 36
Stoke-on-Trent	a	20 19	20 19				20 56								21 19	21 19	21 19					21 56
Congleton	a																					
Macclesfield	a						21 15															22 14
Crewe 10	a												21 10									
Wilmslow	a																					
Stockport	a						21 28															22 28
M'chester Piccadilly 10	a	21 00	21 00				21 40								21 56	21 56	21 56					22 40
Warrington Bank Quay	a																					
Wigan North Western	a																					
Preston 8	a																					
Lancaster 6	a																					
Oxenholme Lake District	a																					
Penrith North Lakes	a																					
Carlisle 8	a																					
Lockerbie	a																					
Haymarket	a																					
Edinburgh 10	a																					
Haymarket	a																					
Motherwell	a																					
Glasgow Central 15	a																					
Inverkeithing	a																					
Kirkcaldy	a																					
Markinch	a																					
Ladybank	a																					
Cupar	a																					
Leuchars 3	a																					
Dundee	a																					
Arbroath	a																					
Montrose	a																					
Stonehaven	a																					
Aberdeen	a																					

A until 19 June, from 7 August until 11 September, from 30 October
B from 26 June until 31 July, from 18 September until 23 October
C until 19 June
D from 26 June until 31 July, from 18 September
E from 7 August until 11 September
F to Birmingham International
G from 26 June until 31 July. to Cheltenham Spa
H from 7 August until 11 September, from 30 October. to Cheltenham Spa
I from 18 September until 23 October. to Cheltenham Spa
J from 18 September until 23 October
K from 26 June until 31 July
b Arr. 1804
c Arr. 1841
e Arr. 1904

Table 51

Sundays

South Coast and the South West - North West England, The North East and Scotland

		XC	XC	XC	XC	XC	VT	AW	XC	XC	XC	XC	XC	XC	XC	XC	AW	XC	XC	XC	XC	AW	XC
		◇1	◇1	◇1	◇1	◇1	◇1	◇	◇1	◇1	◇1	◇1	◇1	◇1	◇1	◇1		◇1	◇1	◇1	◇1	◇	◇1
		A	B	C		D			E	F	G	H	I	J	A				E	F	K		L
Bournemouth	d											18 40						19 40					
Brockenhurst 3	d											18 57						19 57					
Southampton Central	d											19 15						20 15					
Southampton Airport Pkwy	d											19 22						20 22					
Winchester	d											19 31						20 31					
Basingstoke	d											19 47						20 47					
Guildford	d																						
Reading 7	d				19 40							20c11				20 40		21f11					
Oxford	d				20 06							20 37				21 06		21 37					
Banbury	d				20 25							20 54				21 25		21 54					
Leamington Spa 8	d				20 43							21 12				21 43		22 12					
Coventry	d				20 54							21 26				21 54		22 23					
Birmingham International	d				21 04			21 07				21 38				22 04	22 11	22 33				22 40	
Penzance	d		15 30	15 30																			
St Erth	d		15 38	15 38																			
Hayle	d																						
Camborne	d		15 51	15 51																			
Redruth	d		15 57	15 57																			
Truro	d		16 09	16 09																			
St Austell	d		16 25	16 25																			
Par	d		16 33	16 33																			
Lostwithiel	d																						
Bodmin Parkway	d		16 44	16 44																			
Liskeard 8	d		16 56	16 56																			
Plymouth	d		17 25	17 26							18 23		17 23	18 23							18 23		
Totnes	d		17 51	17 52							18 49		17 49	18 49							18 49		
Paignton	d					18 18																	
Torquay	d					18 24																	
Newton Abbot	d		18 03	18 04		18 35					19 03		18 03	19 03							19 03		
Teignmouth	d																						
Dawlish	d																						
Exeter St Davids 6	d		18 24	18 23		18 56					19 25		18 25	19 25							19 25		
Tiverton Parkway	d		18 36	18 38		19 09					19 38		18 38	19 38							19 38		
Taunton	d		18 52	18 52		19 23					19 54		18 54	19 54							19 54		
Weston-super-Mare	d																						
Cardiff Central 7	d								19 45										20 45				
Newport (South Wales)	d								20 00										20 59				
Bristol Temple Meads 10	d		19 30	19 30		20 00					20 30		19 30	20 30							20 30		
Bristol Parkway 7	d	19 40	19 40	19 40		20 10					20 40		19e45	20 40	20 40						20 43		21 45
Gloucester 7	d								20 50	20 50			21 04						21 48	21 48	22 03		
Cheltenham Spa	d	20 12	20 12	20 12		20 42			21 01	21 01	21 12		21 13	21 12	21 12				21 59	21 59	22 12		22 20
London Paddington	d																						
Birmingham New Street 12	a	20 50	20 50	20 50	21 15	21 20		21 18	21 45	21 45	21 51	21 48	21 52	21 51	21 51	22 15	22 21	22 42	22 42	22 42	22 50	22 50	23 07
Birmingham New Street 12	d	21 03	21 03	21 03			21 20	21 24				22 01	22 03	22 03	22 03		22 24					22 55	
Tamworth	d	21 19		21 19									22 20	22 20	22 20								
Burton-on-Trent	d	21 29		21 29																			
Derby 6	a	21 42	22 31	21 42									22 45	22 45	22 45								
Nottingham 8	a																						
Chesterfield	a	22 02	23 06	22 02									23 06	23 06	23 06								
Sheffield 7	a	22 18	23 22	22 18									23 22	23 22	23 22								
Doncaster 7	a																						
Wakefield Westgate 7	a	22 43		22 43																			
Leeds 10	a	23 01	00 34	23 01									00 34	00 34	00 34								
York 8	a																						
Darlington 7	a																						
Durham	a																						
Chester-le-Street	a																						
Newcastle 8	a																						
Morpeth	a																						
Alnmouth for Alnwick	a																						
Berwick-upon-Tweed	a																						
Dunbar	a																						
Wolverhampton 7	d						21 38	21 43				22 19					22 42					23 15	
Stafford	a						21 56					22 36										23 30	
Stoke-on-Trent	a											22 55											
Congleton	a																						
Macclesfield	a											23 12											
Crewe 10	a						22 17	23 03														23 55	
Wilmslow	a																						
Stockport	a											23 27											
M'chester Piccadilly 10	a											23 41											
Warrington Bank Quay	a						22 36																
Wigan North Western	a						22 47																
Preston 8	a						23 07																
Lancaster 6	a																						
Oxenholme Lake District	a																						
Penrith North Lakes	a																						
Carlisle 8	a																						
Lockerbie	a																						
Haymarket	a																						
Edinburgh 10	a																						
Haymarket	a																						
Motherwell	a																						
Glasgow Central 15	a																						
Inverkeithing	a																						
Kirkcaldy	a																						
Markinch	a																						
Ladybank	a																						
Cupar	a																						
Leuchars 8	a																						
Dundee	a																						
Arbroath	a																						
Montrose	a																						
Stonehaven	a																						
Aberdeen	a																						

A from 18 September until 23 October. to Cheltenham Spa
B until 19 June. from Plymouth to Cheltenham Spa
C from 7 August until 11 September, from 30 October. from Plymouth to Cheltenham Spa
D until 19 June, from 7 August until 11 September, from 30 October
E until 31 July, from 18 September
F from 7 August until 11 September
G until 19 June
H to Basingstoke
I from 26 June until 31 July. to Cheltenham Spa
J from 7 August until 11 September, from 30 October. to Cheltenham Spa
K from 26 June until 31 July
L from 18 September until 23 October

Table 51

Sundays

South Coast and the South West - North West England, The North East and Scotland

		XC ◇1	AW	XC ◇1 A		XC ◇1 B	XC ◇1 C
Bournemouth	d						
Brockenhurst 3	d						
Southampton Central	d						
Southampton Airport Pkway ✈	d						
Winchester	d						
Basingstoke	d						
Guildford	d						
Reading 7	d	21 40					
Oxford	d	22 06					
Banbury	d	22 25					
Leamington Spa 8	d	22 43					
Coventry	d	22 54					
Birmingham International ✈	d	23 04	23 08				
Penzance	d						
St Erth	d						
Hayle	d						
Camborne	d						
Redruth	d						
Truro	d						
St Austell	d						
Par	d						
Lostwithiel	d						
Bodmin Parkway	d						
Liskeard 6	d						
Plymouth	d						
Totnes	d						
Paignton	d						
Torquay	d						
Newton Abbot	d						
Teignmouth	d						
Dawlish	d						
Exeter St Davids 6	d						
Tiverton Parkway	d						
Taunton	d						
Weston-super-Mare	d						
Cardiff Central 7	d						
Newport (South Wales)	d						
Bristol Temple Meads 10	d			22 10			22 10
Bristol Parkway 7	d			22 20		22 20	22 24
Gloucester 7	d						23 21
Cheltenham Spa	d			22 52		22 52	23 29
London Paddington	d						
Birmingham New Street 12	a	23 14	23 19	23 39		23 39	00 16
Birmingham New Street 12	d		23 24				
Tamworth	d						
Burton-on-Trent	d						
Derby 6	a						
Nottingham 8	a						
Chesterfield	a						
Sheffield 7	a						
Doncaster 7	a						
Wakefield Westgate 7	a						
Leeds 10	a						
York 8	a						
Darlington 7	a						
Durham	a						
Chester-le-Street	a						
Newcastle 8	a						
Morpeth	a						
Alnmouth for Alnwick	a						
Berwick-upon-Tweed	a						
Dunbar	a						
Wolverhampton 7	d		23b46				
Stafford	a						
Stoke-on-Trent	a						
Congleton	a						
Macclesfield	a						
Crewe 10	a						
Wilmslow	a						
Stockport	a						
M'chester Piccadilly 10	a						
Warrington Bank Quay	a						
Wigan North Western	a						
Preston 8	a						
Lancaster 6	a						
Oxenholme Lake District	a						
Penrith North Lakes	a						
Carlisle 8	a						
Lockerbie	a						
Haymarket	a						
Edinburgh 10	a						
Haymarket	a						
Motherwell	a						
Glasgow Central 15	a						
Inverkeithing	a						
Kirkcaldy	a						
Markinch	a						
Ladybank	a						
Cupar	a						
Leuchars 3	a						
Dundee	a						
Arbroath	a						
Montrose	a						
Stonehaven	a						
Aberdeen	a						

A until 19 June, from 7 August until 11 September, from 30 October

B from 18 September until 23 October

C from 26 June until 31 July

b Arr. 2340

Network Diagram for Table 52

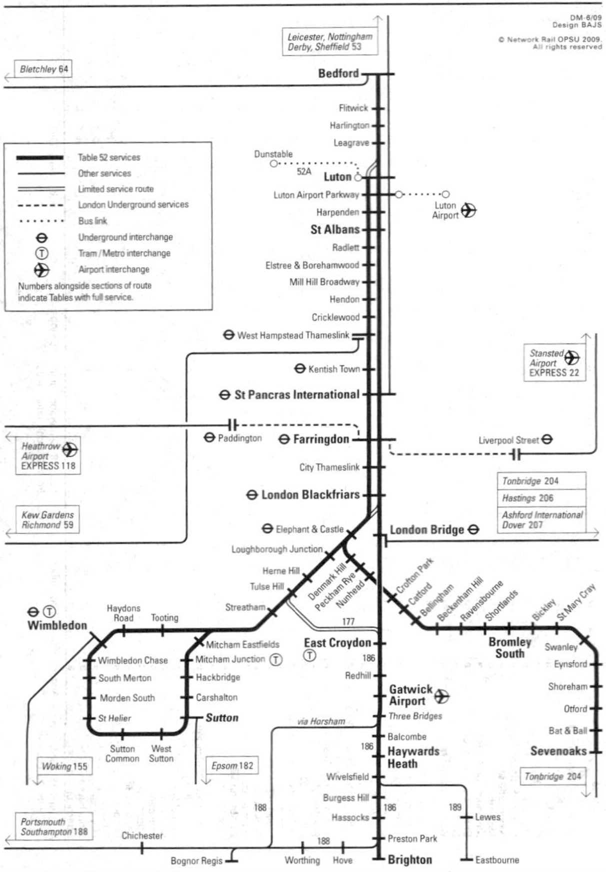

Table 52

Mondays to Fridays

Bedford, Luton, St. Albans and City of London - South London, Gatwick Airport and Brighton

Miles	Miles	Miles	Miles			FC	FC	FC	FC	FC	FC	FC	FC	FC	FC	SE	FC	FC	FC	FC	FC	FC	FC
						MX			MX		MX		MX			MX	MX						
						1			1				1									1	1
							A	B		C		A		B	C			D	E	E	D	E	D
0	0	—	—	**Bedford** 7	d	22p52	23p12	23p12	23p12	23p12		23p32	23p32	23p32	23p32			00 02	00 02	01 02	01 02	02 02	02 02
9½	—	—	—	Flitwick	d	23p02	23p22	23p22	23p22	23p22		23p42	23p42	23p42	23p42			00 12	00 12	01 12	01 12	02 12	02 12
12½	—	—	—	Harlington	d	23p06	23p26	23p26	23p26	23p26		23p46	23p46	23p46	23p46			00 16	00 16	01 16	01 16	02 16	02 16
17	—	—	—	Leagrave	d	23p11	23p31	23p31	23p31	23p32		23p51	23p51	23p51	23p52			00 21	00 21	01 21	01 21	02 21	02 21
19½	19½	—	—	**Luton** 10	d	23p16	23p36	23p36	23p36	23p36		23p56	23p56	23p56	23p56			00 26	00 26	01 26	01 26	02 26	02 26
20½	—	—	—	Luton Airport Parkway 7 ✈	d	23p18	23p38	23p38	23p38	23p38		23p58	23p58	23p58	23p58			00 28	00 28	01 28	01 28	02 28	02 28
25	—	—	—	Harpenden	d	23p24	23p44	23p44	23p44	23p44		00 04	00 04	00 04	00 04			00 34	00 34	01 34	01 34	02 34	02 34
29¾	—	—	—	**St Albans City**	d	23p30	23p50	23p50	23p50	23p50		00 10	00 10	00 10	00 10			00 40	00 40	01 40	01 40	02 40	02 40
34¼	—	—	—	Radlett	d	23p36	23p55	23p56	23p56	23p56		00 15	00 16	00 16	00 16			00 46	00 46	01 46	01 46	02 46	02 46
37¼	—	—	—	Elstree & Borehamwood	d	23p40	00 01	00 01	00 01	00 01		00 20	00 20	00 20	00 20			00 50	00 50	01 50	01 50	02 50	02 50
40½	—	—	—	Mill Hill Broadway	d	23p44	00 04	00 04	00 04	00 04		00 24	00 24	00 24	00 24			00 54	00 54	01 54	01 54	02 54	02 54
42¾	—	—	—	Hendon	d	23p48	00 07	00 08	00 08	00 08		00 27	00 28	00 28	00 28			00 58	00 58	01 58	01 58	02 58	02 58
44¾	—	—	—	Cricklewood	d	23p51	00 11	00 11	00 11	00 11		00 31	00 31	00 31	00 31			01 01	01 01	02 01	02 01	03 01	03 01
45¾	—	—	—	West Hampstead Thameslink ⊖	d	23p54	00 13	00 14	00 14	00 14		00 33	00 34	00 34	00 34			01 04	01 03	02 03	02 04	03 03	03 04
48¼	—	—	—	Kentish Town ⊖	d	00 02	00 18	00 20	00 20	00 20		00 38	00 40	00 40	00 40			01 10	01 12	02 10	02 10	03 10	03 10
49¾	—	—	—	**St Pancras International** 15 ⊖	a	00 06		00 26	00 26	00 26			00 46	00 46	00 46			01 16			02 16		03 16
50	0	—	—	**St Pancras International** 15 ⊖	a		00 24					00 44							01 16	02 16		03 16	
—	—	—	—		d																		
51	0	—	—	Farringdon 3 ⊖	d																		
51¾	0	—	—	City Thameslink 3	d																		
52¼	0	0	0	**London Blackfriars** 3 ⊖	d																		
1	1	—	—	Elephant & Castle ⊖	d																		
3	3	—	—	Loughborough Jn	d																		
4	4	—	—	Herne Hill 4	d																		
53	—	—	—	**London Bridge** 4	a																		
—	—	—	—		d						23p28						23p58						
—	5	5	5	Tulse Hill 3	d						23p40						00 10						
—	62	62	0	Streatham 4	d						23p44						00 14						
—	—	—	1	Mitcham Eastfields	d																		
—	—	2	—	Mitcham Junction	d																		
—	—	4	—	Hackbridge	d																		
—	—	4¾	—	Carshalton	d																		
—	8	—	—	Tooting	d						23p48						00 18						
—	9¼	—	—	Haydons Road	d						23p51						00 21						
—	10½	—	—	**Wimbledon** 6 ⊖	d						23p55						00 25						
—	11½	—	—	Wimbledon Chase	d						23p58						00 28						
—	12	—	—	South Merton	d						00 01						00 30						
—	12½	—	—	Morden South	d						00 03						00 32						
—	13	—	—	St Helier	d						00 05						00 34						
—	14	—	—	Sutton Common	d						00 08						00 36						
—	15	—	—	West Sutton	d						00 11						00 39						
—	16	12½	6	**Sutton (Surrey)** 4	a						00 14						00 43						
63¼	—	—	10	**East Croydon**	d																		
—	—	—	—	Denmark Hill 4	d											23p52							
—	—	—	—	Peckham Rye 4	d											23p55							
—	—	—	—	Nunhead 4	d											23p57							
—	—	—	—	Crofton Park	d											23p59							
—	—	—	—	Catford	d											00 03							
—	—	—	—	Bellingham	d											00 05							
—	—	—	—	Beckenham Hill	d											00 07							
—	—	—	—	Ravensbourne	d											00 09							
—	—	—	—	Shortlands	d											00 11							
—	—	—	—	Bromley South 4	d											00 14							
—	—	—	—	Bickley 4	d											00a17							
—	—	—	—	St Mary Cray	d																		
—	—	—	—	Swanley 4	d																		
—	—	—	—	Eynsford	d																		
—	—	—	—	Shoreham (Kent)	d																		
—	—	—	—	Otford 4	d																		
—	—	—	—	Bat & Ball	d																		
—	—	—	—	Sevenoaks 4	a																		
73¾	—	—	—	Redhill	d																		
79½	—	—	—	**Gatwick Airport** 10 ✈	d																		
82¼	—	—	—	Three Bridges 4	d																		
86¾	—	—	—	Balcombe	d																		
90¾	—	—	—	**Haywards Heath** 3	d																		
93¾	—	—	—	Wivelsfield 4	d																		
94½	—	—	—	Burgess Hill 4	d																		
96½	—	—	—	Hassocks 4	d																		
102¼	—	—	—	Preston Park	d																		
103¾	—	—	—	**Brighton** 10	a																		

A MO from 8 August until 24 October
B MO until 20 June, MO from 31 October
C MO from 27 June until 1 August
D until 29 July, MX from 2 August until 14 October, from 18 October
E MO from 1 August until 17 October

Bedford, Luton, St. Albans and City of London - South London, Gatwick Airport and Brighton

		FC	FC	FC	SE	FC	FC	SN	FC	SE	FC	FC	SN	FC	SE	FC	EM	SN	FC	FC	FC	FC	FC
		1	1	1		1					1			1			◇1		1		1		1
		A	B																				
Bedford 7	d	03 02	03 02	04 10		04 20					05 00			05 20			05 36		05 40		05 54		05 58
Flitwick	d	03 12	03 12	04 20		04 30					05 10			05 30					05 50		06 04		06 08
Harlington	d	03 16	03 16	04 24		04 34					05 14			05 34					05 54				06 12
Leagrave	d	03 21	03 21	04 29		04 39					05 19			05 39					05 59				06 17
Luton 10	d	03 26	03 26	04 34		04 44			05 08		05 24			05 44		05 48			06 04	06 06	06 14		06 22
Luton Airport Parkway 7 ✈	d	03 28	03 28	04 36		04 46			05 10		05 26			05 46		05 50	05 54		06 06	06 08			06 24
Harpenden	d	03 34	03 34	04 42		04 52			05 16		05 32			05 52		05 56			06 12	06 14	06 20		06 30
St Albans City	d	03 40	03 40	04 48		04 58			05 22		05 38			05 58		06 02			06 18	06 20	06 26		06 36
Radlett	d	03 46	03 46			05 04			05 28							06 07				06 25			
Elstree & Borehamwood	d	03 50	03 50			05 08			05 32							06 12				06 29			
Mill Hill Broadway	d	03 54	03 54			05 12			05 36							06 16				06 34			
Hendon	d	03 58	03 58			05 16			05 40							06 19				06 37			
Cricklewood	d	04 01	04 01			05 19			05 43							06 23				06 41			
West Hampstead Thameslink ⊖	d	04 03	04 04	05 04		05 22			05 46		05 54	06 04		06 14		06 26			06 30	06 44			06 50
Kentish Town ⊖	d	04 10	04 10			05 26			05 50			06 08				06 30				06 48			
St Pancras International 15 ⊖	a		04 16														06 17					←	
St Pancras International 15 ⊖	a	04 16		05 12		05 32			05 54		06 02	06 12		06 22		06 34			06 38	06 52	06 45	06 52	06 57
	d			05 12		05 32	05 38		05 54		06 02	06 12		06 22		06 34			06 38	06 52	06 46	06 52	06 58
Farringdon 3 ⊖	d			05 17		05 37	05 42		05 58		06 07	06 17		06 27		06 39			06 43	→	06 51	06 57	07 03
City Thameslink 3	d			05 21	05 26	05 41	05 45		06 01	06 07	06 11	06 21		06 31	06 39	06 43			06 47		06 54	07 01	07 05
London Blackfriars 3 ⊖	d			05 24	05 28	05 44	05 48		06 06	06 10	06 14	06 24		06 34	06 42	06 46			06 50		06 58	07 04	07 08
Elephant & Castle ⊖	d				05 32		05 51		06 09	06 16		06 27			06 46	06 49					07 02	07 07	
Loughborough Jn.	d								06 13			06 31				06 53						07 11	
Herne Hill 4	d						05 58		06 16			06 34				06 57						07 16	
London Bridge 4	a			05 30		05 50					06 20			06 41					06 56				07 15
	d			05 30		05 50		06 00			06 20		06 30	06 42				06 58	07 00				07 16
Tulse Hill 3	d						06 02	06 18	06 22			06 42	06 48			07 02		07 16				07 20	
Streatham 4	d						06 05	06 21	06 25			06 46	06 51			07 05		07 19				07 23	
Mitcham Eastfields	d								06 29			06 50										07 27	
Mitcham Junction	d								06 32			06 53										07 30	
Hackbridge	d								06 35			06 56										07 33	
Carshalton	d								06 38			06 59										07 36	
Tooting	d						06 09	06 25					06 55			07 10		07 23					
Haydons Road	d						06 12	06 28					06 58			07 13		07 26					
Wimbledon 6 ⊖	d						06 15	06a31					07a01			07 17		07a30					
Wimbledon Chase	d						06 18									07 20							
South Merton	d						06 20									07 22							
Morden South	d						06 22									07 24							
St Helier	d						06 24									07 26							
Sutton Common	d						06 27									07 28							
West Sutton	d						06 29									07 31							
Sutton (Surrey) 4	a						06 33		06 43			07 04				07 35						07 39	
East Croydon	d			05 52		06 06					06 36			06 56					07 15				07 31
Denmark Hill 4	d				05 39					06 22					06 52						07 09		
Peckham Rye 4	d				05 41					06 25					06 55						07 12		
Nunhead 4	d				05 44					06 27					06 57						07 14		
Crofton Park	d				05 47					06 30					07 00						07 17		
Catford	d				05 49					06 33					07 03						07 20		
Bellingham	d				05 52					06 35					07 05						07 22		
Beckenham Hill	d				05 54					06 37					07 07						07 24		
Ravensbourne	d				05 56					06 39					07 09						07 26		
Shortlands	d				05 58					06 41					07 11						07 28		
Bromley South 4	d				06 01					06 44					07 14						07 31		
Bickley 4	d				06 03					06 47					07 17						07 34		
St Mary Cray	d				06 08					06 51					07 21						07 38		
Swanley 4	d				06 12					06 56					07 26						07 44		
Eynsford	d				06 17					07 00					07 30						07 48		
Shoreham (Kent)	d				06 20					07 04					07 34						07 52		
Otford 4	d				06 23					07 07					07 37						07 55		
Bat & Ball	d				06 26					07 10					07 40						07 58		
Sevenoaks 4	a				06 29					07 14					07 43						08 01		
Redhill	d																						
Gatwick Airport 10 ✈	d			06 10		06 22					06 52			07 12					07 32				07 47
Three Bridges 4	d			06 14		06 27					06 57			07 17					07 37				07 52
Balcombe	d			06 20		06 34																	07 58
Haywards Heath 3	d			06 26		06 40					07 06			07 26					07 46				08 04
Wivelsfield 4	d			06 30		06 44					07 10			07 30					07 50				08 08
Burgess Hill 4	d			06 32		06 46					07 12			07 32					07 52				08 10
Hassocks 4	d			06 35		06 49					07 15			07 36					07 55				08 13
Preston Park	d			06 42		06 56					07 22			07 43									08 20
Brighton 10	a			06 47		07 00					07 27			07 47					08 05				08 25

A MO from 1 August until 17 October

B until 29 July, MX from 2 August until 14 October, from 18 October

Bedford, Luton, St. Albans and City of London - South London, Gatwick Airport and Brighton

		EM	FC	FC	FC	FC	FC	SN	FC	FC	FC	EM	FC	FC	FC	FC	FC	EM	FC	FC	FC	SN	FC
		◇1		1			1		1			◇1	1					◇1		1			
Bedford 7	d			06 14			06 18		06 22		06 26	06 32	06 36			06 40				06 56			
Flitwick	d			06 24					06 32		06 36		06 46			06 50				07 06			
Harlington	d								06 36		06 40					06 54							
Leagrave	d						06 35		06 41		06 45					06 59							
Luton 10	d	06 24		06 34		06 36	06 40		06 46		06 50		06 56			07 04			07 10	07 16			
Luton Airport Parkway 7 ✈	d					06 38	06 42		06 48		06 52					07 06		07 07	07 12				
Harpenden	d			06 40		06 44	06 48		06 54		06 58		07 02			07 12			07 18	07 22			
St Albans City	d		06 40	06 46		06 50	06 54		07 00		07 04		07 08		07 12	07 18			07 24	07 28			07 32
Radlett	d		06 45			06 55					07 09				07 17				07 29				07 37
Elstree & Borehamwood	d		06 49			07 01					07 13				07 21				07 33				07 41
Mill Hill Broadway	d		06 54			07 06					07 17				07 26				07 37				07 46
Hendon	d		06 57			07 09									07 29								07 49
Cricklewood	d		07 01			07 13									07 33								07 53
West Hampstead Thameslink ⊖	d		07 04			07 16	07 08				07 24				07 36				07 44				07 59
Kentish Town ⊖	d		07 08			07 20									07 40								08 03
St Pancras International 15 ⊖	a	06 49			←					←		07 10		←			←	07 34			←		
St Pancras International 15 ⊖	a		07 12	07 05	07 12	07 24	07 16		07 20	07 24	07 31		07 27	07 31	07 44	07 38	07 44		07 51	07 47	07 51		08 07
	d		07 12	07 06	07 12	07 24	07 16		07 20	07 24	07 32		07 28	07 32	07 44	07 38	07 44		07 52	07 48	07 52		08 08
Farringdon 3 ⊖	d		→	07 11	07 17	→	07 21		07 25	07 29	→		07 33	07 37	→	07 43	07 49		→	07 53	07 57		→
City Thameslink 3	d			07 15	07 21		07 25		07 29	07 33			07 37	07 41		07 47	07 53			07 57	08 01		
London Blackfriars 3 ⊖	d			07 18	07 24		07 28		07 32	07 36			07 40	07 44		07 50	07 56			08 00	08 04		
Elephant & Castle ⊖	d			07 21	07 28		07 33			07 40			07 44	07 47		07 54	08 00				08 07		
Loughborough Jn.	d			07 25			07 37							07 51							08 11		
Herne Hill 4	d			07 31			07 41			07a46				07 56							08 15		
London Bridge 4	a								07 41														
	d							07 29	07 42													08 06	
Tulse Hill 3	d			07 37			07 45	07 47						08 05						08 13	08 20	08 25	
Streatham 4	d			07 40			07 48	07 51						08 09							08 24	08 28	
Mitcham Eastfields	d						07 52														08 28		
Mitcham Junction	d						07 55														08 31		
Hackbridge	d						07 58														08 34		
Carshalton	d						08 01														08 37		
Tooting	d			07 44				07 55						08 12								08 33	
Haydons Road	d			07 47				07 58						08 15								08 36	
Wimbledon 6 ⊖	d			07 51				08a01						08 19								08a38	
Wimbledon Chase	d			07 54										08 22									
South Merton	d			07 56										08 24									
Morden South	d			07 58										08 26									
St Helier	d			08 00										08 28									
Sutton Common	d			08 02										08 30									
West Sutton	d			08 05										08 33									
Sutton (Surrey) 4	a			08 08			08 04							08 37							08 40		
East Croydon	d								07 56											08 26			
Denmark Hill 4	d				07 34								07 50			08 00	08 09						
Peckham Rye 4	d				07 36								07 53			08 03	08 12						
Nunhead 4	d				07 39								07 56			08 06	08 14						
Crofton Park	d				07 42											08 09	08 17						
Catford	d				07 44								08 00			08 12	08 20						
Bellingham	d				07 47								08 02			08 15	08 22						
Beckenham Hill	d				07 49											08 17	08 24						
Ravensbourne	d				07 51											08 19	08 26						
Shortlands	d				07 54											08 22	08 30						
Bromley South 4	d				07 57								08a10			08 25	08 33						
Bickley 4	d				08 00											08a28	08 35						
St Mary Cray	d				08 04												08 40						
Swanley 4	d				08 10												08 44						
Eynsford	d				08 15												08 49						
Shoreham (Kent)	d				08 18												08 52						
Otford 4	d				08 21												08 55						
Bat & Ball	d				08 24												08 58						
Sevenoaks 4	a				08 27												09 01						
Redhill	d																						
Gatwick Airport 10 ✈	d								08 11											08 41			
Three Bridges 4	d								08 15											08 45			
Balcombe	d								08 21											08 51			
Haywards Heath 3	d								08 27											08 57			
Wivelsfield 4	d								08 31											09 01			
Burgess Hill 4	d								08 33											09 03			
Hassocks 4	d								08 36											09 06			
Preston Park	d								08 43											09 13			
Brighton 10	a								08 48											09 18			

Bedford, Luton, St. Albans and City of London - South London, Gatwick Airport and Brighton

		FC ■	EM ◇■	FC ■	FC	FC	EM ◇■	FC ■	FC ■	FC	FC ■	FC ■	FC	EM ◇■	FC	FC ■	FC ■	FC	FC	FC	FC ■	EM ◇■
Bedford 7	d	07 00	07 08	07 12					07 16	07 22	07 28					07 32	07 44				07 48	07 55
Flitwick	d	07 10							07 26	07 32	07 38					07 42					07 58	
Harlington	d	07 14							07 30	07 36						07 46					08 02	
Leagrave	d	07 19		07 28					07 35	07 41						07 51	08 00				08 07	
Luton 10	d	07 24	07 24	07 32		07 30			07 40	07 46	07 48			07 56		07 56	08 04		08 02		08 12	
Luton Airport Parkway 7 ✈	d	07 26				07 32	07 41		07 42	07 48						07 58			08 04		08 14	08 12
Harpenden	d	07 32		07 38		07 38			07 48	07 54	07 54					08 04	08 10		08 10		08 20	
St Albans City	d	07 38		07 44		07 44		07 50	07 55	08 00	08 00				08 06	08 10	08 16		08 16	08 22	08 26	
Radlett	d					07 49		07 55		08 05					08 11				08 21	08 27		
Elstree & Borehamwood	d					07 53		07 59		08 10					08 15				08 25	08 31		
Mill Hill Broadway	d					07 57		08 04							08 20				08 29	08 36		
Hendon	d							08 07							08 23					08 39		
Cricklewood	d							08 11							08 27					08 43		
West Hampstead Thameslink ⊖	d					08 04		08 15		08 20					08 31				08 36	08 47		
Kentish Town ⊖	d							08 19							08 35					08 51		
St Pancras International 15 ⊖	a		07 51		←		08 07					←	←	08 26				←				08 38
St Pancras International 15 ⊖	a	07 58		08 03	08 07	08 11		08 23	08 15	08 27	08 19	08 23	08 27		08 39	08 30	08 35	08 39	08 43	08 55	08 47	
	d	08 00		08 04	08 08	08 12		08 24	08 16	08 28	08 20	08 24	08 28		08 40	08 32	08 36	08 40	08 44	08 56	08 48	
Farringdon 3 ⊖	d	08 05		08 09	08 13	08 17		→	08 21	→	08 25	08 29	08 33		→	08 37	08 41	08 45	08 49	→	08 53	
City Thameslink 3	d	08 07		08 13	08 17	08 21			08 25		08 29	08 33	08 37			08 41	08 45	08 49	08 53		08 57	
London Blackfriars 3 ⊖	d	08 10		08a16	08 20	08 24			08 28		08 32	08 36	08 40			08 44	08 48	08 52	08 56		09 00	
Elephant & Castle ⊖	d					08 27			08 32				08 44			08 47	08a52	08 56	09 00			
Loughborough Jn	d					08 31										08 51			09 04			
Herne Hill 4	d					08 36						08 46				08 57			09 11			
London Bridge 4	a	08 16																			09 11	
	d	08 18																			09 12	
Tulse Hill 3	d					08 40						08 50				09 01			09 16			
Streatham 4	d					08 44						08 54				09 05			09 20			
Mitcham Eastfields	d											08 58							09 24			
Mitcham Junction	d											09 01							09 27			
Hackbridge	d											09 04							09 30			
Carshalton	d											09 07							09 33			
Tooting	d					08 48										09 10						
Haydons Road	d					08 51										09 13						
Wimbledon 6 ⊖	d					08 55										09 17						
Wimbledon Chase	d					08 58										09 20						
South Merton	d					09 00										09 22						
Morden South	d					09 02										09 24						
St Helier	d					09 04										09 26						
Sutton Common	d					09 06										09 28						
West Sutton	d					09 09										09 31						
Sutton (Surrey) 4	a					09 12						09 10				09 37			09 36			
East Croydon	d	08 37									08 56										09 25	
Denmark Hill 4	d								08 38				08 52					09 02				
Peckham Rye 4	d								08 41				08 55									
Nunhead 4	d								08 43				08 57									
Crofton Park	d								08 46				09 00									
Catford	d								08 49				09 03					09 09				
Bellingham	d								08 51				09 05									
Beckenham Hill	d								08 53				09 07									
Ravensbourne	d								08 55				09 09									
Shortlands	d								08 57				09 11									
Bromley South 4	d				08a37				09 00				09 14					09 18				
Bickley 4	d								09 03				09 17					09 20				
St Mary Cray	d								09 07				09 21					09 25				
Swanley 4	d								09 12				09 26					09 36				
Eynsford	d								09 16				09 30					09 40				
Shoreham (Kent)	d								09 20				09 34					09 44				
Otford 4	d								09 23				09 37					09 47				
Bat & Ball	d								09 26				09 40					09 50				
Sevenoaks 4	a								09 29				09 45					09 53				
Redhill	d																					
Gatwick Airport 10 ✈	d	08 52									09 13										09 41	
Three Bridges 4	d	08 57									09 17										09 45	
Balcombe	d																				09 51	
Haywards Heath 3	d	09 08									09 26										09 57	
Wivelsfield 4	d										09 30										10 01	
Burgess Hill 4	d	09 13									09 33										10 03	
Hassocks 4	d										09 36										10 06	
Preston Park	d										09 43										10 13	
Brighton 10	a	09 25									09 48										10 18	

Bedford, Luton, St. Albans and City of London - South London, Gatwick Airport and Brighton

		EM ◇■	FC ■	FC	FC	FC	FC ■	FC	FC	FC ■	FC	EM ◇■	FC	FC	FC ■	FC	FC	FC	FC ■	FC	FC	EM ◇■	FC
Bedford 7	d		07 58				08 04			08 24		08 29			08 40				08 54			09 02	
Flitwick	d		08 08				08 14			08 34					08 50				09 04				
Harlington	d						08 18			08 38					08 54				09 08				
Leagrave	d						08 23			08 43					08 59				09 13				
Luton 10	d	08 15	08 20		08 20		08 28			08 48			08 54		09 04			09 14	09 18			09 19	
Luton Airport Parkway 7 ✈	d				08 22		08 30			08 50			08 56		09 06			09 16	09 20				
Harpenden	d		08 26		08 28		08 36			08 56			09 02		09 12			09 22	09 26				
St Albans City	d		08 32		08 34	08 42	08 44		08 58	09 04			09 08	09 14	09 18			09 29	09 32				09 44
Radlett	d				08 39	08 47			09 03				09 13	09 19				09 34					09 49
Elstree & Borehamwood	d				08 43	08 51			09 07				09 17	09 23				09 38					09 53
Mill Hill Broadway	d					08 56			09 12					09 28				09 43					09 58
Hendon	d					08 59			09 15					09 31				09 46					10 01
Cricklewood	d					09 03			09 19					09 35				09 50					10 05
West Hampstead Thameslink ⊖	d				08 52	09 07			09 22				09 26	09 39				09 54					10 09
Kentish Town ⊖	d					09 11			09 26					09 43			09 54	10 00					10 13
St Pancras International 15 ⊖	a	08 43		←				←			←	09 06				←				←	←	09 44	
St Pancras International 15 ⊖	a		08 51	08 55	08 59	09 15	09 03	09 15	09 30	09 23	09 30		09 33	09 48	09 39	09 48	10 00	10 04	09 52	10 00	10 04		10 18
	d		08 52	08 56	09 00	09 16	09 04	09 16	09 30	09 24	09 30		09 34	09 48	09 40	09 48	10 00	10 04	09 54	10 00	10 04		10 18
Farringdon 3 ⊖	d		08 57	09 01	09 05	→	09 09	09 21	→	09 29	09 35		09 39	→	09 44	09 53	→	→	09 59	10 05	10 09		→
City Thameslink 3	d		09 01	09 05	09 09		09 13	09 25		09 32	09 39		09 43		09 47	09 57			10 02	10 09	10 13		
London Blackfriars 3 ⊖	d		09 04	09 08	09 12		09 16	09 28		09 34	09 42		09 46		09 50	10 00			10 05	10 12	10 16		
Elephant & Castle ⊖	d		09a09	09 12	09 16			09 31			09 46		09 49			10 03				10 16	10 19		
Loughborough Jn	d			09 16				09 35					09 53			10 07					10 23		
Herne Hill 4	d			09 25				09 41					09 57			10 11					10 27		
London Bridge 4	a						09 26			09 41					09 56				10 11				
	d						09 27			09 42					09 57				10 12				
Tulse Hill 3	d			09 31				09 46					10 01			10 16					10 31		
Streatham 4	d			09 35				09 50					10 05			10 20					10 35		
Mitcham Eastfields	d							09 54								10 24							
Mitcham Junction	d							09 57								10 27							
Hackbridge	d							10 00								10 30							
Carshalton	d							10 03								10 33							
Tooting	d			09 40									10 10								10 40		
Haydons Road	d			09 43									10 13								10 43		
Wimbledon 6 ⊖	d			09 47									10 17								10 47		
Wimbledon Chase	d			09 50									10 20								10 50		
South Merton	d			09 52									10 22								10 52		
Morden South	d			09 54									10 24								10 54		
St Helier	d			09 56									10 26								10 56		
Sutton Common	d			09 58									10 28								10 58		
West Sutton	d			10 01									10 31								11 01		
Sutton (Surrey) 4	a			10 05				10 06					10 35			10 36					11 05		
East Croydon	d						09 41			09 55					10 11				10 25				
Denmark Hill 4	d				09 22						09 52									10 22			
Peckham Rye 4	d				09 25						09 55									10 25			
Nunhead 4	d				09 27						09 57									10 27			
Crofton Park	d				09 30						10 00									10 30			
Catford	d				09 33						10 03									10 33			
Bellingham	d				09 35						10 05									10 35			
Beckenham Hill	d				09 37						10 07									10 37			
Ravensbourne	d				09 39						10 09									10 39			
Shortlands	d				09 41						10 11									10 41			
Bromley South 4	d				09 44						10 14									10 44			
Bickley 4	d				09 47						10 17									10 47			
St Mary Cray	d				09 51						10 21									10 51			
Swanley 4	d				09 56						10 26									10 56			
Eynsford	d				10 00						10 30									11 00			
Shoreham (Kent)	d				10 04						10 34									11 04			
Otford 4	d				10 07						10 37									11 07			
Bat & Ball	d				10 10						10 40									11 10			
Sevenoaks 4	a				10 13						10 43									11 13			
Redhill	d																						
Gatwick Airport 10 ✈	d						09 57			10 11					10 27				10 41				
Three Bridges 4	d						10 02			10 15					10 32				10 45				
Balcombe	d									10 21													
Haywards Heath 3	d						10 11			10 27					10 41				10 55				
Wivelsfield 4	d									10 31									10 59				
Burgess Hill 4	d									10 33									11 01				
Hassocks 4	d									10 36									11 04				
Preston Park	d									10 43									11 11				
Brighton 10	a						10 25			10 48					10 55				11 16				

Bedford, Luton, St. Albans and City of London - South London, Gatwick Airport and Brighton

		FC 1	EM ◇1	FC 1	FC	FC	FC	FC 1	FC	FC	FC	FC 1	FC 1	FC	EM ◇1	FC	FC	FC 1	FC	FC	FC	FC 1
Bedford 7	d	09 10	09 18	09 18				09 24				09 40	09 48		09 49			09 54				10 10
Flitwick	d	09 20		09 28				09 34				09 50	09 58					10 04				10 20
Harlington	d	09 24						09 38				09 54						10 08				10 24
Leagrave	d	09 29						09 43				09 59						10 13				10 29
Luton 10	d	09 34		09 38			09 44	09 48				10 04	10 08		10 04		10 14	10 18				10 34
Luton Airport Parkway 7 ✈	d	09 36	09 34	09 41			09 46	09 50				10 06	10 11				10 16	10 20				10 36
Harpenden	d	09 42		09 48			09 52	09 56				10 12	10 18				10 22	10 26				10 42
St Albans City	d	09 48		09 54			09 59	10 02			10 14	10 18	10 24				10 29	10 32			10 44	10 48
Radlett	d						10 04				10 19						10 34				10 49	
Elstree & Borehamwood	d						10 08				10 23						10 38				10 53	
Mill Hill Broadway	d						10 13				10 28						10 43				10 58	
Hendon	d						10 16				10 31						10 46				11 01	
Cricklewood	d						10 20				10 35						10 50				11 05	
West Hampstead Thameslink ⊖	d						10 24				10 39						10 54				11 09	
Kentish Town ⊖	d					10 26	10 30				10 43					10 56	11 00				11 13	
St Pancras International 15 ⊖	a		10 00		←				←	←				←	10 29				←	←		
St Pancras International 15 ⊖	a	10 09		10 13	10 18	10 30	10 34	10 23	10 30	10 34	10 48	10 39	10 44	10 48		11 00	11 04	10 52	11 00	11 04	11 18	11 09
	d	10 10		10 14	10 18	10 30	10 34	10 24	10 30	10 34	10 48	10 40	10 44	10 48		11 00	11 04	10 54	11 00	11 04	11 18	11 10
Farringdon 3 ⊖	d	10 14		10 19	10 23	→	→	10 29	10 35	10 39	→	10 44	10 49	10 53		→	→	10 59	11 05	11 09	→	11 14
City Thameslink 3	d	10 17		10 22	10 27			10 32	10 39	10 43		10 47	10 52	10 57				11 02	11 09	11 13		11 17
London Blackfriars 3 ⊖	d	10 20		10 26	10 30			10 35	10 42	10 46		10 50	10 56	11 00				11 05	11 12	11 16		11 20
Elephant & Castle ⊖	d			10a30	10 33				10 46	10 49			11a00	11 03					11 16	11 19		
Loughborough Jn.	d				10 37					10 53				11 07						11 23		
Herne Hill 4	d				10 41					10 57				11 11						11 27		
London Bridge 4	a	10 26						10 41				10 56						11 11				11 26
	d	10 27						10 42				10 57						11 12				11 27
Tulse Hill 3	d				10 46					11 01				11 16						11 31		
Streatham 4	d				10 50					11 05				11 20						11 35		
Mitcham Eastfields	d				10 54									11 24								
Mitcham Junction	d				10 57									11 27								
Hackbridge	d				11 00									11 30								
Carshalton	d				11 03									11 33								
Tooting	d									11 10										11 40		
Haydons Road	d									11 13										11 43		
Wimbledon 6 ⊖	d									11 17										11 47		
Wimbledon Chase	d									11 20										11 50		
South Merton	d									11 22										11 52		
Morden South	d									11 24										11 54		
St Helier	d									11 26										11 56		
Sutton Common	d									11 28										11 58		
West Sutton	d									11 31										12 01		
Sutton (Surrey) 4	a				11 06					11 35				11 36						12 05		
East Croydon	d	10 41						10 55				11 11						11 25				11 41
Denmark Hill 4	d								10 52										11 22			
Peckham Rye 4	d								10 55										11 25			
Nunhead 4	d								10 57										11 27			
Crofton Park	d								11 00										11 30			
Catford	d								11 03										11 33			
Bellingham	d								11 05										11 35			
Beckenham Hill	d								11 07										11 37			
Ravensbourne	d								11 09										11 39			
Shortlands	d								11 11										11 41			
Bromley South 4	d								11 14										11 44			
Bickley 4	d								11 17										11 47			
St Mary Cray	d								11 21										11 51			
Swanley 4	d								11 26										11 56			
Eynsford	d								11 30										12 00			
Shoreham (Kent)	d								11 34										12 04			
Otford 4	d								11 37										12 07			
Bat & Ball	d								11 40										12 10			
Sevenoaks 4	a								11 43										12 13			
Redhill	d																					
Gatwick Airport 10 ✈	d	10 57						11 11				11 27						11 41				11 57
Three Bridges 4	d	11 02						11 15				11 32						11 45				12 02
Balcombe	d							11 21														
Haywards Heath 3	d	11 11						11 27				11 41						11 55				12 11
Wivelsfield 4	d							11 31										11 59				
Burgess Hill 4	d							11 33										12 01				
Hassocks 4	d							11 36										12 04				
Preston Park	d							11 43										12 11				
Brighton 10	a	11 25						11 48				11 55						12 16				12 25

Bedford, Luton, St. Albans and City of London - South London, Gatwick Airport and Brighton

		EM ◇1	FC	FC	FC	FC	FC 1	FC	FC	FC	FC 1	FC	EM ◇1	FC	FC	FC 1	FC	FC	FC	FC 1	FC	EM ◇1	FC
Bedford 7	d	10 18	10 18				10 24				10 40		10 49			10 54				11 10		11 18	
Flitwick	d		10 28				10 34				10 50					11 04				11 20			
Harlington	d						10 38				10 54					11 08				11 24			
Leagrave	d						10 43				10 59					11 13				11 29			
Luton 10	d		10 38			10 44	10 48				11 04		11 05		11 14	11 18				11 34			
Luton Airport Parkway 7 ✈	d	10 34	10 41			10 46	10 50				11 06				11 16	11 20				11 36		11 34	
Harpenden	d		10 48			10 52	10 56				11 12				11 22	11 26				11 42			
St Albans City	d		10 54			10 59	11 02			11 14	11 18				11 29	11 32			11 44	11 48			
Radlett	d					11 04				11 19					11 34				11 49				
Elstree & Borehamwood	d					11 08				11 23					11 38				11 53				
Mill Hill Broadway	d					11 13				11 28					11 43				11 58				
Hendon	d					11 16				11 31					11 46				12 01				
Cricklewood	d					11 20				11 35					11 50				12 05				
West Hampstead Thameslink ⊖	d					11 24				11 39					11 54				12 09				
Kentish Town ⊖	d				11 26	11 30				11 43				11 56	12 00				12 13				12 26
St Pancras International 15 ⊖	a	11 01		←				←	←			←	11 29				←	←			←	12 00	
St Pancras International 15 ⊖	a		11 14	11 18	11 30	11 34	11 22	11 30	11 34	11 48	11 39	11 48		12 00	12 04	11 52	12 00	12 04	12 18	12 09	12 18		12 30
	d		11 14	11 18	11 30	11 34	11 24	11 30	11 34	11 48	11 40	11 48		12 00	12 04	11 54	12 00	12 04	12 18	12 10	12 18		12 30
Farringdon 3 ⊖	d		11 19	11 23	→	→	11 29	11 35	11 39	→	11 44	11 53		→	→	11 59	12 05	12 09	→	12 14	12 23		→
City Thameslink 3	d		11 22	11 27			11 32	11 39	11 43		11 47	11 57				12 02	12 09	12 13		12 17	12 27		
London Blackfriars 3 ⊖	d		11 26	11 30			11 35	11 42	11 46		11 50	12 00				12 05	12 12	12 16		12 20	12 30		
Elephant & Castle ⊖	d		11a30	11 33				11 46	11 49			12 03					12 16	12 19			12 33		
Loughborough Jn.	d			11 37					11 53			12 07						12 23			12 37		
Herne Hill 4	d			11 41					11 57			12 11						12 27			12 41		
London Bridge 4	a						11 41				11 56					12 11				12 26			
	d						11 42				11 57					12 12				12 27			
Tulse Hill 3	d			11 46					12 01			12 16						12 31			12 46		
Streatham 4	d			11 50					12 05			12 20						12 35			12 50		
Mitcham Eastfields	d			11 54								12 24									12 54		
Mitcham Junction	d			11 57								12 27									12 57		
Hackbridge	d			12 00								12 30									13 00		
Carshalton	d			12 03								12 33									13 03		
Tooting	d								12 10									12 40					
Haydons Road	d								12 13									12 43					
Wimbledon 6 ⊖	d								12 17									12 47					
Wimbledon Chase	d								12 20									12 50					
South Merton	d								12 22									12 52					
Morden South	d								12 24									12 54					
St Helier	d								12 26									12 56					
Sutton Common	d								12 28									12 58					
West Sutton	d								12 31									13 01					
Sutton (Surrey) 4	a			12 06					12 35			12 36						13 05			13 06		
East Croydon	d						11 55				12 11					12 25				12 41			
Denmark Hill 4	d							11 52									12 22						
Peckham Rye 4	d							11 55									12 25						
Nunhead 4	d							11 57									12 27						
Crofton Park	d							12 00									12 30						
Catford	d							12 03									12 33						
Bellingham	d							12 05									12 35						
Beckenham Hill	d							12 07									12 37						
Ravensbourne	d							12 09									12 39						
Shortlands	d							12 11									12 41						
Bromley South 4	d							12 14									12 44						
Bickley 4	d							12 17									12 47						
St Mary Cray	d							12 21									12 51						
Swanley 4	d							12 26									12 56						
Eynsford	d							12 30									13 00						
Shoreham (Kent)	d							12 34									13 04						
Otford 4	d							12 37									13 07						
Bat & Ball	d							12 40									13 10						
Sevenoaks 4	a							12 43									13 13						
Redhill	d																						
Gatwick Airport 10 ✈	d						12 11				12 27					12 41				12 57			
Three Bridges 4	d						12 15				12 32					12 45				13 02			
Balcombe	d						12 21																
Haywards Heath 3	d						12 27				12 41					12 55				13 11			
Wivelsfield 4	d						12 31									12 59							
Burgess Hill 4	d						12 33									13 01							
Hassocks 4	d						12 36									13 04							
Preston Park	d						12 43									13 11							
Brighton 10	a						12 48				12 55					13 16				13 25			

Bedford, Luton, St. Albans and City of London - South London, Gatwick Airport and Brighton

		FC	FC 1	FC	FC	FC	FC 1	FC	EM ◇1 ☕	FC	FC	FC 1	FC	FC	FC	FC 1	FC	EM ◇1 ☕	FC	FC	FC 1	FC	FC
Bedford 7	d		11 24				11 40		11 49			11 54				12 10		12 18			12 24		
Flitwick	d		11 34				11 50					12 04				12 20					12 34		
Harlington	d		11 38				11 54					12 08				12 24					12 38		
Leagrave	d		11 43				11 59					12 13				12 29					12 43		
Luton 10	d	11 44	11 48				12 04		12 05		12 14	12 18				12 34				12 44	12 48		
Luton Airport Parkway 7 ✈	d	11 46	11 50				12 06				12 16	12 20				12 36		12 34		12 46	12 50		
Harpenden	d	11 52	11 56				12 12				12 22	12 26				12 42				12 52	12 56		
St Albans City	d	11 59	12 02			12 14	12 18				12 29	12 32			12 44	12 48				12 59	13 02		
Radlett	d	12 04				12 19					12 34				12 49					13 04			
Elstree & Borehamwood	d	12 08				12 23					12 38				12 53					13 08			
Mill Hill Broadway	d	12 13				12 28					12 43				12 58					13 13			
Hendon	d	12 16				12 31					12 46				13 01					13 16			
Cricklewood	d	12 20				12 35					12 50				13 05					13 20			
West Hampstead Thameslink ⊖	d	12 24				12 39					12 54				13 09					13 24			
Kentish Town ⊖	d	12 30				12 43				12 56	13 00				13 13				13 26	13 30			
St Pancras International 15 ⊖	a			←	←			←	12 29				←	←			←	13 00				←	←
St Pancras International 15 ⊖	a	12 34	12 22	12 30	12 34	12 48	12 39	12 48		13 00	13 04	12 52	13 00	13 04	13 18	13 09	13 18		13 30	13 34	13 22	13 30	13 34
	d	12 34	12 24	12 30	12 34	12 48	12 40	12 48		13 00	13 04	12 54	13 00	13 04	13 18	13 10	13 18		13 30	13 34	13 24	13 30	13 34
Farringdon 3 ⊖	d	→	12 29	12 35	12 39	→	12 44	12 53		→	→	12 59	13 05	13 09	→	13 14	13 23		→	→	13 29	13 35	13 39
City Thameslink 3	d		12 32	12 39	12 43		12 47	12 57				13 02	13 09	13 13		13 17	13 27				13 32	13 39	13 43
London Blackfriars 3 ⊖	d		12 35	12 42	12 46		12 50	13 00				13 05	13 12	13 16		13 20	13 30				13 35	13 42	13 46
Elephant & Castle ⊖	d			12 46	12 49			13 03					13 16	13 19			13 33					13 46	13 49
Loughborough Jn	d				12 53			13 07						13 23			13 37						13 53
Herne Hill 4	d				12 57			13 11						13 27			13 41						13 57
London Bridge 4	a		12 41				12 56					13 11				13 26					13 41		
	d		12 42				12 57					13 12				13 27					13 42		
Tulse Hill 3	d				13 01			13 16						13 31			13 46						14 01
Streatham 4	d				13 05			13 20						13 35			13 50						14 05
Mitcham Eastfields	d							13 24									13 54						
Mitcham Junction	d							13 27									13 57						
Hackbridge	d							13 30									14 00						
Carshalton	d							13 33									14 03						
Tooting	d				13 10									13 40									14 10
Haydons Road	d				13 13									13 43									14 13
Wimbledon 6 ⊖ ⇌	d				13 17									13 47									14 17
Wimbledon Chase	d				13 20									13 50									14 20
South Merton	d				13 22									13 52									14 22
Morden South	d				13 24									13 54									14 24
St Helier	d				13 26									13 56									14 26
Sutton Common	d				13 28									13 58									14 28
West Sutton	d				13 31									14 01									14 31
Sutton (Surrey) 4	a				13 35			13 36						14 05			14 06						14 35
East Croydon ⇌	d		12 55				13 11					13 25				13 41					13 55		
Denmark Hill 4	d			12 52									13 22									13 52	
Peckham Rye 4	d			12 55									13 25									13 55	
Nunhead 4	d			12 57									13 27									13 57	
Crofton Park	d			13 00									13 30									14 00	
Catford	d			13 03									13 33									14 03	
Bellingham	d			13 05									13 35									14 05	
Beckenham Hill	d			13 07									13 37									14 07	
Ravensbourne	d			13 09									13 39									14 09	
Shortlands	d			13 11									13 41									14 11	
Bromley South 4	d			13 14									13 44									14 14	
Bickley 4	d			13 17									13 47									14 17	
St Mary Cray	d			13 21									13 51									14 21	
Swanley 4	d			13 26									13 56									14 26	
Eynsford	d			13 30									14 00									14 30	
Shoreham (Kent)	d			13 34									14 04									14 34	
Otford 4	d			13 37									14 07									14 37	
Bat & Ball	d			13 40									14 10									14 40	
Sevenoaks 4	a			13 43									14 13									14 43	
Redhill	d																						
Gatwick Airport 10 ✈	d		13 11				13 27					13 41				13 57					14 11		
Three Bridges 4	d		13 15				13 32					13 45				14 02					14 15		
Balcombe	d		13 21																		14 21		
Haywards Heath 3	d		13 27				13 41					13 55				14 11					14 27		
Wivelsfield 4	d		13 31									13 59									14 31		
Burgess Hill 4	d		13 33									14 01									14 33		
Hassocks 4	d		13 36									14 04									14 36		
Preston Park	d		13 43									14 11									14 43		
Brighton 10	a		13 48				13 55					14 16				14 25					14 48		

Bedford, Luton, St. Albans and City of London - South London, Gatwick Airport and Brighton

		FC	FC 1	FC	EM ◇1 ☕	FC	FC	FC 1	FC	FC	FC	FC 1	FC	EM ◇1 ☕	FC	FC	FC 1	FC	FC	FC	FC 1	FC
Bedford 7	d		12 40		12 49			12 54				13 10		13 18			13 24				13 40	
Flitwick	d		12 50					13 04				13 20					13 34				13 50	
Harlington	d		12 54					13 08				13 24					13 38				13 54	
Leagrave	d		12 59					13 13				13 29					13 43				13 59	
Luton 10	d		13 04		13 05		13 14	13 18				13 34				13 44	13 48				14 04	
Luton Airport Parkway 7 ✈	d		13 06				13 16	13 20				13 36		13 34		13 46	13 50				14 06	
Harpenden	d		13 12				13 22	13 26				13 42				13 52	13 56				14 12	
St Albans City	d	13 14	13 18				13 29	13 32			13 44	13 48				13 59	14 02			14 14	14 18	
Radlett	d	13 19					13 34				13 49					14 04				14 19		
Elstree & Borehamwood	d	13 23					13 38				13 53					14 08				14 23		
Mill Hill Broadway	d	13 28					13 43				13 58					14 13				14 28		
Hendon	d	13 31					13 46				14 01					14 16				14 31		
Cricklewood	d	13 35					13 50				14 05					14 20				14 35		
West Hampstead Thameslink ⊖	d	13 39					13 54				14 09					14 24				14 39		
Kentish Town ⊖	d	13 43				13 56	14 00				14 13				14 26	14 30				14 43		
St Pancras International 15 ⊖	a			←	13 29				←	←			←	14 01				←	←			←
St Pancras International 15 ⊖	a	13 48	13 39	13 48		14 00	14 04	13 52	14 00	14 04	14 18	14 09	14 18		14 30	14 34	14 22	14 30	14 34	14 48	14 39	14 48
	d	13 48	13 40	13 48		14 00	14 04	13 54	14 00	14 04	14 18	14 10	14 18		14 30	14 34	14 24	14 30	14 34	14 48	14 40	14 48
Farringdon 3 ⊖	d	→	13 44	13 53		→	→	13 59	14 05	14 09	→	14 14	14 23		→	→	14 29	14 35	14 39	→	14 44	14 53
City Thameslink 3	d		13 47	13 57				14 02	14 09	14 13		14 17	14 27				14 32	14 39	14 43		14 47	14 57
London Blackfriars 3 ⊖	d		13 50	14 00				14 05	14 12	14 16		14 20	14 30				14 35	14 42	14 46		14 50	15 00
Elephant & Castle ⊖	d			14 03					14 16	14 19			14 33					14 46	14 49			15 03
Loughborough Jn	d			14 07						14 23			14 37						14 53			15 07
Herne Hill 4	d			14 11						14 27			14 41						14 57			15 11
London Bridge 4	a		13 56					14 11				14 26					14 41				14 56	
	d		13 57					14 12				14 27					14 42				14 57	
Tulse Hill 3	d			14 16						14 31			14 46						15 01			15 16
Streatham 4	d			14 20						14 35			14 50						15 05			15 20
Mitcham Eastfields	d			14 24									14 54									15 24
Mitcham Junction	d			14 27									14 57									15 27
Hackbridge	d			14 30									15 00									15 30
Carshalton	d			14 33									15 03									15 33
Tooting	d									14 40									15 10			
Haydons Road	d									14 43									15 13			
Wimbledon 6 ⊖ ⇌	d									14 47									15 17			
Wimbledon Chase	d									14 50									15 20			
South Merton	d									14 52									15 22			
Morden South	d									14 54									15 24			
St Helier	d									14 56									15 26			
Sutton Common	d									14 58									15 28			
West Sutton	d									15 01									15 31			
Sutton (Surrey) 4	a			14 36						15 05			15 06						15 35			15 36
East Croydon ⇌	d		14 11					14 25				14 41					14 55				15 11	
Denmark Hill 4	d								14 22									14 52				
Peckham Rye 4	d								14 25									14 55				
Nunhead 4	d								14 27									14 57				
Crofton Park	d								14 30									15 00				
Catford	d								14 33									15 03				
Bellingham	d								14 35									15 05				
Beckenham Hill	d								14 37									15 07				
Ravensbourne	d								14 39									15 09				
Shortlands	d								14 41									15 11				
Bromley South 4	d								14 44									15 14				
Bickley 4	d								14 47									15 17				
St Mary Cray	d								14 51									15 21				
Swanley 4	d								14 56									15 26				
Eynsford	d								15 00									15 30				
Shoreham (Kent)	d								15 04									15 34				
Otford 4	d								15 07									15 37				
Bat & Ball	d								15 10									15 40				
Sevenoaks 4	a								15 13									15 43				
Redhill	d																					
Gatwick Airport 10 ✈	d		14 27					14 41				14 57					15 11				15 27	
Three Bridges 4	d		14 32					14 45				15 02					15 15				15 32	
Balcombe	d																15 21					
Haywards Heath 3	d		14 41					14 55				15 11					15 27				15 41	
Wivelsfield 4	d							14 59									15 31					
Burgess Hill 4	d							15 01									15 33					
Hassocks 4	d							15 04									15 36					
Preston Park	d							15 11									15 43					
Brighton 10	a		14 55					15 16				15 25					15 48				15 55	

Bedford, Luton, St. Albans and City of London - South London, Gatwick Airport and Brighton

		EM ◇1	FC	FC	FC 1	FC	FC	FC	FC 1	FC	EM ◇1	FC	FC	FC 1	FC	FC	FC	FC 1	FC	EM ◇1	FC	FC	FC 1
Bedford 7	d	13 49			13 54				14 10		14 18			14 24				14 40		14 49			14 54
Flitwick	d				14 04				14 20					14 34				14 50					15 04
Harlington	d				14 08				14 24					14 38				14 54					15 08
Leagrave	d				14 13				14 29					14 43				15 00					15 13
Luton 10	d	14 05		14 14	14 18				14 34				14 44	14 48				15 04		15 05		15 14	15 18
Luton Airport Parkway 7 ✈	d			14 16	14 20				14 36		14 34		14 46	14 50				15 06				15 16	15 20
Harpenden	d			14 22	14 26				14 42				14 52	14 56				15 12				15 22	15 26
St Albans City	d			14 29	14 32			14 44	14 48				14 59	15 02			15 14	15 18				15 29	15 32
Radlett	d			14 34				14 49					15 04				15 19					15 34	
Elstree & Borehamwood	d			14 38				14 53					15 08				15 23					15 38	
Mill Hill Broadway	d			14 43				14 58					15 13				15 28					15 43	
Hendon	d			14 46				15 01					15 16				15 31					15 46	
Cricklewood	d			14 50				15 05					15 20				15 35					15 50	
West Hampstead Thameslink ⊖	d			14 54				15 09					15 24				15 39					15 54	
Kentish Town ⊖	d		14 56	15 00				15 13				15 26	15 30				15 43				15 56	16 00	
St Pancras International 15 ⊖	a	14 29				←	←			←	14 59				←	←			←	15 29			
St Pancras International 15 ⊖	a		15 00	15 04	14 52	15 00	15 04	15 18	15 09	15 18		15 30	15 34	15 22	15 30	15 34	15 48	15 39	15 48		16 00	16 04	15 52
	d		15 00	15 04	14 54	15 00	15 04	15 18	15 10	15 18		15 30	15 34	15 24	15 30	15 34	15 48	15 40	15 48		16 00	16 04	15 54
Farringdon 3 ⊖	d		→	→	14 59	15 05	15 09	→	15 14	15 23		→	→	15 29	15 35	15 39	→	15 44	15 53		→	→	15 59
City Thameslink 3	d				15 02	15 09	15 13		15 17	15 27				15 32	15 39	15 43		15 47	15 57				16 02
London Blackfriars 3 ⊖	d				15 05	15 12	15 16		15 20	15 30				15 35	15 42	15 46		15 50	16 00				16 05
Elephant & Castle ⊖	d					15 16	15 19			15 33					15 46	15 49			16 03				
Loughborough Jn.	d						15 23			15 37						15 53			16 07				
Herne Hill 4	d						15 27			15 41						15 57			16 11				
London Bridge 4	a				15 11				15 26					15 41				15 56					16 11
	d				15 12				15 27					15 42				15 57					16 12
Tulse Hill 3	d						15 31			15 46						16 01			16 16				
Streatham 4	d						15 35			15 50						16 05			16 20				
Mitcham Eastfields	d									15 54									16 24				
Mitcham Junction	d									15 57									16 27				
Hackbridge	d									16 00									16 30				
Carshalton	d									16 03									16 33				
Tooting	d						15 40									16 10							
Haydons Road	d						15 43									16 13							
Wimbledon 6 ⊖ ⛴	d						15 47									16 17							
Wimbledon Chase	d						15 50									16 20							
South Merton	d						15 52									16 22							
Morden South	d						15 54									16 24							
St Helier	d						15 56									16 26							
Sutton Common	d						15 58									16 28							
West Sutton	d						16 01									16 31							
Sutton (Surrey) 4	a						16 05			16 06						16 35			16 36				
East Croydon ⛴	d				15 25				15 41					15 55				16 11					16 25
Denmark Hill 4	d					15 22									15 52								
Peckham Rye 4	d					15 25									15 55								
Nunhead 4	d					15 27									15 57								
Crofton Park	d					15 30									16 00								
Catford	d					15 33									16 03								
Bellingham	d					15 35									16 05								
Beckenham Hill	d					15 37									16 07								
Ravensbourne	d					15 39									16 09								
Shortlands	d					15 41									16 11								
Bromley South 4	d					15 44									16 14								
Bickley 4	d					15 47									16 17								
St Mary Cray	d					15 51									16 21								
Swanley 4	d					15 56									16 26								
Eynsford	d					16 00									16 30								
Shoreham (Kent)	d					16 04									16 34								
Otford 4	d					16 07									16 37								
Bat & Ball	d					16 10									16 40								
Sevenoaks 4	a					16 13									16 43								
Redhill	d																						
Gatwick Airport 10 ✈	d				15 41				15 57					16 11				16 27					16 41
Three Bridges 4	d				15 45				16 02					16 15				16 32					16 46
Balcombe	d													16 21									
Haywards Heath 3	d				15 55				16 11					16 27				16 41					16 55
Wivelsfield 4	d				15 59									16 31									16 59
Burgess Hill 4	d				16 01									16 33									17 01
Hassocks 4	d				16 04									16 36									17 04
Preston Park	d				16 11									16 43									17 11
Brighton 10	a				16 16				16 25					16 48				16 55					17 16

Bedford, Luton, St. Albans and City of London - South London, Gatwick Airport and Brighton

		FC	FC	FC	FC	FC 1	FC	FC	EM ◇1	FC	FC	FC 1	FC	FC	FC	FC 1	EM ◇1	FC 1	FC	SN	FC	FC
Bedford 7	d					15 10			15 18			15 24				15 40	15 49	15 52				15 56
Flitwick	d					15 20						15 34				15 50		16 02				16 06
Harlington	d					15 24						15 38				15 54						16 10
Leagrave	d					15 29						15 43				15 59						16 15
Luton 10	d					15 34					15 44	15 48				16 04	16 05	16 14			16 16	16 20
Luton Airport Parkway 7 ✈	d					15 36			15 34		15 46	15 50				16 06		16 17			16 18	16 22
Harpenden	d					15 42					15 52	15 56				16 12					16 24	16 28
St Albans City	d				15 44	15 48					15 59	16 02			16 14	16 18		16 25			16 30	16 34
Radlett	d				15 49						16 04				16 19						16 35	
Elstree & Borehamwood	d				15 53						16 08				16 23						16 39	
Mill Hill Broadway	d				15 58						16 13				16 28						16 44	
Hendon	d				16 01						16 16				16 31						16 47	
Cricklewood	d				16 05						16 20				16 35						16 51	
West Hampstead Thameslink ⊖	d				16 09						16 24				16 42						16 54	16 48
Kentish Town ⊖	d			16 09	16 13					16 24	16 30				16 46						16 58	
St Pancras International 15 ⊖	a	←	←				←	←	15 59				←	←			16 29		←			
St Pancras International 15 ⊖	a	16 00	16 04	16 13	16 18	16 09	16 13	16 18		16 28	16 34	16 23	16 28	16 34	16 50	16 40		16 45	16 50		17 02	16 58
	d	16 00	16 04	16 14	16 18	16 10	16 14	16 18		16 28	16 34	16 24	16 28	16 34	16 52	16 40		16 46	16 52		17 02	16 58
Farringdon 3 ⊖	d	16 05	16 09	→	→	16 14	16 19	16 23		→	→	16 29	16 33	16 39	→	16 45		16 51	16 57		→	17 03
City Thameslink 3	d	16 09	16 13			16 17	16 23	16 27				16 33	16 37	16 43		16 49		16 55	17 01			17 07
London Blackfriars 3 ⊖	d	16 12	16 16			16 20	16 26	16 30				16 36	16 42	16 46		16 52		17 00	17 04			17 10
Elephant & Castle ⊖	d	16 16	16 19				16 30	16 33					16 46	16 49		16 56		17 04	17 08			17 14
Loughborough Jn.	d		16 23					16 37						16 53		17 00			17 12			
Herne Hill 4	d		16 27					16 41						16 57		17a04			17 16			
London Bridge 4	a					16 26						16 42										
	d					16 27						16 43								17 06		
Tulse Hill 3	d		16 32					16 46						17 02					17 20	17 24		
Streatham 4	d		16 36					16 50						17 06					17 24	17 28		
Mitcham Eastfields	d							16 56											17 28	17 32		
Mitcham Junction	d							16 59											17 31	17 35		
Hackbridge	d							17 02											17 34	17 38		
Carshalton	d							17 05											17 37	17 41		
Tooting	d		16 40											17 10								
Haydons Road	d		16 43											17 13								
Wimbledon 6 ⊖ ⛴	d		16 47											17 19								
Wimbledon Chase	d		16 50											17 22								
South Merton	d		16 52											17 24								
Morden South	d		16 54											17 26								
St Helier	d		16 56											17 28								
Sutton Common	d		16 58											17 30								
West Sutton	d		17 01											17 33								
Sutton (Surrey) 4	a		17 05					17 08						17 39					17 40	17 44		
East Croydon ⛴	d					16 41						17 00						17 26				
Denmark Hill 4	d	16 22					16 39						16 52									17 20
Peckham Rye 4	d	16 25					16 42						16 55									17 23
Nunhead 4	d	16 27					16 44						16 57									17 26
Crofton Park	d	16 30					16 47						17 00									17 29
Catford	d	16 33					16 50						17 03									17 32
Bellingham	d	16 35					16 52						17 05									17 35
Beckenham Hill	d	16 37					16 54						17 07									17 37
Ravensbourne	d	16 39					16 56						17 09									17 39
Shortlands	d	16 41					16 58						17 11									17 43
Bromley South 4	d	16 44					17 01						17 14									17 46
Bickley 4	d	16 47					17a04						17 17									
St Mary Cray	d	16 51											17 21									
Swanley 4	d	16 56											17 30									17 55
Eynsford	d	17 00											17 34									18 00
Shoreham (Kent)	d	17 04											17 38									18 03
Otford 4	d	17 07											17 41									18 06
Bat & Ball	d	17 10											17 44									18 14
Sevenoaks 4	a	17 14											17 49									18 23
Redhill	d																					
Gatwick Airport 10 ✈	d					16 57						17 16						17 41				
Three Bridges 4	d					17 02						17 21						17 46				
Balcombe	d											17 27						17 52				
Haywards Heath 3	d					17 11						17 33						17 58				
Wivelsfield 4	d											17 37										
Burgess Hill 4	d					17 16						17 40						18 03				
Hassocks 4	d											17 44						18 07				
Preston Park	d											17 51						18 15				
Brighton 10	a					17 27						17 55						18 20				

Bedford, Luton, St. Albans and City of London - South London, Gatwick Airport and Brighton

		FC	FC	FC 1	EM ◇1	FC 1	FC	FC	SN	FC	FC 1	FC	FC 1	EM ◇1	FC 1	FC	FC	FC	FC	FC	SN	FC	FC 1
Bedford 7	d			16 10	16 18	16 22					16 26		16 36	16 49									16 58
Flitwick	d			16 20		16 32					16 36		16 46										17 08
Harlington	d			16 24							16 40		16 50										17 12
Leagrave	d			16 29							16 45		16 55										17 17
Luton 10	d			16 34		16 42				16 46	16 50		17 00	17 05				17 10				17 18	17 22
Luton Airport Parkway 7 ✈	d			16 36	16 34	16 45				16 48	16 52		17 02					17 12				17 20	17 24
Harpenden	d			16 42						16 54	16 58		17 08					17 18				17 26	17 30
St Albans City	d		16 44	16 48		16 54				17 00	17 04		17 14				17 20	17 24				17 32	17 36
Radlett	d		16 49							17 05							17 25					17 37	
Elstree & Borehamwood	d		16 53							17 09							17 29					17 41	
Mill Hill Broadway	d		16 58							17 14							17 34					17 46	
Hendon	d		17 01							17 17							17 37					17 49	
Cricklewood	d		17 05							17 21							17 41					17 53	
West Hampstead Thameslink ⊖	d		17 10							17 24	17 18		17 28				17 44					17 56	17 50
Kentish Town ⊖	d		17 14					17 18		17 28						17 44	17 48					18 00	
St Pancras International 15 ⊖	a	←			17 00		←					←		17 29					←	←			
St Pancras International 15 ⊖	a	17 02	17 18	17 10		17 14	17 18	17 22		17 32	17 26	17 32	17 36			17 48	17 52	17 44	17 48	17 52		18 04	17 58
	d	17 02	17 18	17 10		17 14	17 18	17 22		17 32	17 28	17 32	17 36		17 40	17 48	17 52	17 44	17 48	17 52		18 04	17 58
Farringdon 3 ⊖	d	17 07	→	17 15		17 19	17 23	17 27		→	17 33	17 37	17 41		17 45	→	→	17 49	17 53	17 57		→	18 03
City Thameslink 3	d	17 11		17 19		17 23	17 27	17 31			17 37	17 41	17 45		17 49			17 53	17 57	18 01			18 07
London Blackfriars 3 ⊖	d	17 14		17 22		17 26	17 30	17 36			17 40	17 44	17 48		17 52			17 56	18 00	18 04			18 10
Elephant & Castle ⊖	d	17 18				17 30	17 34	17 40				17 48	17 52		17 56			18 00	18 05	18 08			18 14
Loughborough Jn.	d	17 22					17 38					17 52								18 12			
Herne Hill 4	d	17 26				17 36	17 44					17 57						18a06		18 18			18 21
London Bridge 4	a																						
	d								17 37												18 08		
Tulse Hill 3	d	17 31					17 48		17 55			18 02								18 22	18 27		
Streatham 4	d	17 36					17 52		17 58			18 06								18 26	18 30		
Mitcham Eastfields	d						17 56		18 02											18 30	18 34		
Mitcham Junction	d						17 59		18 05											18 33	18 37		
Hackbridge	d						18 02		18 09											18 36	18 41		
Carshalton	d						18 05		18 11											18 39	18 43		
Tooting	d	17 40										18 10											
Haydons Road	d	17 43										18 13											
Wimbledon 5 ⊖ ⇌	d	17 49										18 19											
Wimbledon Chase	d	17 52										18 22											
South Merton	d	17 54										18 24											
Morden South	d	17 56										18 26											
St Helier	d	17 58										18 28											
Sutton Common	d	18 00										18 30											
West Sutton	d	18 03										18 33											
Sutton (Surrey) 4	a	18 07					18 08		18 15			18 37								18 42	18 47		
East Croydon ⇌	d			17 47							18 09				18 26								
Denmark Hill 4	d							17 47											18 15				
Peckham Rye 4	d							17 50											18 18				
Nunhead 4	d							17 52											18 20				
Crofton Park	d							17 55											18 23				
Catford	d							17 58											18 26				
Bellingham	d							18 01											18 29				
Beckenham Hill	d							18 03											18 31				
Ravensbourne	d							18 05											18 33				
Shortlands	d							18 07											18 35				
Bromley South 4	d					17 48		18 10					18 11						18 38				18 31
Bickley 4	d					17 50		18 12											18 40				
St Mary Cray	d					17 55		18 22					18 18						18 45				18 38
Swanley 4	d					17a59		18 26					18 22						18 53				18a42
Eynsford	d							18 31											18 57				
Shoreham (Kent)	d							18 34											19 01				
Otford 4	d							18 38					18a30						19 04				
Bat & Ball	d							18 41											19 07				
Sevenoaks 4	a							18 50											19 14				
Redhill	d			18 03											18 39								
Gatwick Airport 10 ✈	d			18 14							18 25				18 50								
Three Bridges 4	d			18 19							18 30				18a56								
Balcombe	d			18 25																			
Haywards Heath 3	d			18 31							18 39												
Wivelsfield 4	d										18 43												
Burgess Hill 4	d			18 36							18 46												
Hassocks 4	d			18 40							18 50												
Preston Park	d			18 48							18 57												
Brighton 10	a			18 53							19 03												

Bedford, Luton, St. Albans and City of London - South London, Gatwick Airport and Brighton

		FC	FC	FC 1	FC	EM ◇1	FC	FC 1	FC	EM ◇1	FC	FC 1	FC 1	FC 1	FC	EM ◇1	FC	EM ◇1	FC	FC 1	FC	FC	FC 1
Bedford 7	d			17 08		17 18		17 22				17 36	17 42			17 49				17 54		18 04	18 10
Flitwick	d			17 18				17 32				17 46								18 04			18 20
Harlington	d			17 22				17 36				17 50								18 08			18 24
Leagrave	d			17 27				17 41				17 55								18 13			18 29
Luton 10	d			17 32			17 38	17 46		17 51		18 00				18 05	18 06	18 15		18 18		18 22	18 34
Luton Airport Parkway 7 ✈	d			17 34		17 30	17 40	17 48				18 02	18 00				18 08			18 20		18 25	18 36
Harpenden	d			17 40			17 46	17 54				18 08					18 14			18 26		18 30	18 42
St Albans City	d		17 42	17 46			17 52	18 00			18 06	18 14					18 20		18 26	18 32		18 36	18 48
Radlett	d		17 47				17 57				18 11						18 25		18 31			18 41	
Elstree & Borehamwood	d		17 51				18 01				18 15						18 29		18 35			18 45	
Mill Hill Broadway	d		17 56				18 06				18 20						18 33		18 40			18 49	
Hendon	d						18 09				18 23								18 43				
Cricklewood	d						18 13				18 27								18 47				
West Hampstead Thameslink ⊖	d		18 04				18 16				18 30						18 40		18 50	18 46		18 56	
Kentish Town ⊖	d						18 20				18 34								18 54				
St Pancras International 15 ⊖	a	←			←	18 04			←	18 19				←	←	18 29		18 39			←		
St Pancras International 15 ⊖	a	18 04	18 11	18 08	18 11		18 24	18 20	18 24		18 38	18 34	18 28	18 34	18 38		18 48		18 59	18 54	18 59	19 04	19 09
	d	18 04	18 12	18 08	18 12		18 24	18 20	18 24		18 38	18 34	18 30	18 34	18 38		18 48		19 00	18 54	19 00	19 04	19 10
Farringdon 3 ⊖	d	18 09	→	18 13	18 17		→	18 25	18 29		→	→	18 35	18 39	18 43		18 53		→	18 59	19 05	19 09	19 14
City Thameslink 3	d	18 13		18 17	18 21			18 29	18 33				18 39	18 43	18 47		18 57			19 03	19 09	19 13	19 17
London Blackfriars 3 ⊖	d	18 16		18 20	18 24			18 32	18 36				18 42	18 46	18 50		19 00			19 05	19 12	19 16	19 20
Elephant & Castle ⊖	d	18 20			18 28			18 36	18 40				18 46		18 54		19 04				19 16	19 19	
Loughborough Jn.	d	18 24							18 44						18 58		19 08					19 23	
Herne Hill 4	d	18 28							18 48						19 02		19 12					19 27	
London Bridge 4	a			18 27										18 54						19 11			19 26
	d			18 27										18 57						19 12			19 27
Tulse Hill 3	d	18 32							18 52						19 07		19 16					19 31	
Streatham 4	d	18 36							18 56						19 11		19 20					19 35	
Mitcham Eastfields	d								19 00								19 24						
Mitcham Junction	d								19 03								19 27						
Hackbridge	d								19 06								19 30						
Carshalton	d								19 09								19 33						
Tooting	d	18 40													19 16							19 40	
Haydons Road	d	18 43													19 19							19 43	
Wimbledon 5 ⊖ ⇌	d	18 47													19 23							19 49	
Wimbledon Chase	d	18 50													19 26							19 52	
South Merton	d	18 52													19 28							19 54	
Morden South	d	18 54													19 30							19 56	
St Helier	d	18 56													19 32							19 58	
Sutton Common	d	18 58													19 34							20 00	
West Sutton	d	19 01													19 37							20 03	
Sutton (Surrey) 4	a	19 07							19 12						19 40		19 36					20 07	
East Croydon ⇌	d			18 41				18 56						19 11						19 25			19 41
Denmark Hill 4	d				18 34								18 52								19 22		
Peckham Rye 4	d				18 38								18 55								19 25		
Nunhead 4	d				18 40								18 57								19 27		
Crofton Park	d				18 43								19 00								19 30		
Catford	d				18 46								19 03								19 33		
Bellingham	d				18 49								19 05								19 35		
Beckenham Hill	d				18 51								19 07								19 37		
Ravensbourne	d				18 53								19 09								19 39		
Shortlands	d				18 57								19 13								19 41		
Bromley South 4	d				19 00								19 16								19 44		
Bickley 4	d				19 03								19 19								19 47		
St Mary Cray	d				19 10								19 23								19 51		
Swanley 4	d				19 15								19 28								19 56		
Eynsford	d				19 19								19 32								20 00		
Shoreham (Kent)	d				19 23								19 36								20 04		
Otford 4	d				19 26								19 39								20 07		
Bat & Ball	d				19 29								19 42								20 10		
Sevenoaks 4	a				19 37								19 50								20 13		
Redhill	d																						
Gatwick Airport 10 ✈	d			18 57				19 11						19 27						19 41			19 57
Three Bridges 4	d			19 02										19 32						19 45			20 02
Balcombe	d			19 08				19 19												19 51			
Haywards Heath 3	d			19 14				19 31						19 41						19 57			20 11
Wivelsfield 4	d																			20 01			
Burgess Hill 4	d			19 19				19 36						19 46						20 03			20 16
Hassocks 4	d			19 23				19 40						19 49						20 06			20 19
Preston Park	d							19 48												20 13			
Brighton 10	a			19 33				19 53						19 59						20 18			20 29

Bedford, Luton, St. Albans and City of London - South London, Gatwick Airport and Brighton

		EM ◇1	FC	FC	FC 1	FC	FC	FC 1	EM ◇1	FC	FC	FC 1	FC	FC	EM ◇1	FC	FC 1	FC	FC	EM ◇1	FC 1	FC
Bedford [7]	d	18 18			18 24		18 36	18 40	18 49			18 54			19 18		19 22			19 49	19 52	
Flitwick	d				18 34			18 50				19 04					19 32				20 02	
Harlington	d				18 38			18 54				19 08					19 36				20 06	
Leagrave	d				18 43			18 59				19 13					19 41				20 11	
Luton [10]	d			18 44	18 48		18 54	19 04	19 05		19 14	19 18		19 24			19 46		19 50	20 05	20 16	
Luton Airport Parkway [7] ✈	d	18 34		18 46	18 50		18 57	19 06			19 16	19 20		19 27	19 34		19 48		19 52		20 18	
Harpenden	d			18 52	18 56		19 02	19 12			19 22	19 26		19 32			19 54		19 58		20 24	
St Albans City	d		18 52	18 58	19 02		19 08	19 18		19 22	19 28	19 32		19 38		19 52	20 00		20 04		20 30	
Radlett	d		18 57	19 03			19 13			19 27	19 33			19 43		19 57			20 09			
Elstree & Borehamwood	d		19 01	19 07			19 17			19 31	19 37			19 47		20 01			20 13			
Mill Hill Broadway	d			19 12							19 42								20 17			
Hendon	d			19 15							19 45								20 20			
Cricklewood	d			19 19							19 49								20 24			
West Hampstead Thameslink ⊖	d		19 10	19 22			19 26			19 40	19 52			19 56		20 10	20 14		20 26		20 44	
Kentish Town ⊖	d			19 26							19 56							20 26	20 30			20 56
St Pancras International [15] ⊖	a	19 00				←			19 31				←		20 01					20 29		
St Pancras International [15] ⊖	a		19 18	19 30	19 23	19 30	19 34	19 39		19 48	20 00	19 52	20 00	20 04		20 18	20 22	20 30	20 35		20 52	21 00
	d		19 18	19 30	19 24	19 30	19 34	19 40		19 48	20 00	19 54	20 00	20 04		20 18	20 24	20 30	20 36		20 54	21 00
Farringdon [3] ⊖	d		19 23	→	19 29	19 35	19 39	19 44		19 53	→	19 59	20 05	20 09		20 23	20 29	20 35	20 40		20 59	21 05
City Thameslink [3]	d		19 27		19 32	19 39	19 43	19 47		19 57		20 02	20 09	20 13		20 27	20 32	20 39	20 43		21 02	21 09
London Blackfriars [3] ⊖	d		19 30		19 35	19 42	19 46	19 50		20 00		20 05	20 12	20 16		20 30	20 35	20 42	20 46		21 05	21 12
Elephant & Castle ⊖	d		19 33			19 46	19 49			20 03			20 16	20 19		20 33		20 46	20 49			21 16
Loughborough Jn.	d		19 37				19 53			20 07				20 23		20 37			20 53			
Herne Hill [4]	d		19 41				19 57			20 11				20 27		20 41			20 57			
London Bridge [4]	a				19 41			19 56				20 11					20 41				21 11	
	d				19 42			19 57				20 12					20 42				21 12	
Tulse Hill [3]	d		19 46				20 01			20 16				20 31		20 46			21 01			
Streatham [4]	d		19 50				20 05			20 20				20 35		20 50			21 05			
Mitcham Eastfields	d		19 54							20 24						20 54						
Mitcham Junction	d		19 57							20 27						20 57						
Hackbridge	d		20 00							20 30						21 00						
Carshalton	d		20 03							20 33						21 03						
Tooting	d						20 10							20 40					21 10			
Haydons Road	d						20 13							20 43					21 13			
Wimbledon [6] ⊖ ⇌	d						20 19							20 49					21 19			
Wimbledon Chase	d						20 22							20 52					21 22			
South Merton	d						20 24							20 54					21 24			
Morden South	d						20 26							20 56					21 26			
St Helier	d						20 28							20 58					21 28			
Sutton Common	d						20 30							21 00					21 30			
West Sutton	d						20 33							21 03					21 33			
Sutton (Surrey) [4]	a		20 06				20 39			20 36				21 09		21 06			21 39			
East Croydon ⇌	d				19 55			20 11				20 25					20 55				21 25	
Denmark Hill [4]	d					19 52							20 22					20 52				21 22
Peckham Rye [4]	d					19 55							20 25					20 55				21 25
Nunhead [4]	d					19 57							20 27					20 57				21 27
Crofton Park	d					20 00							20 30					21 00				21 30
Catford	d					20 03							20 33					21 03				21 33
Bellingham	d					20 05							20 35					21 05				21 35
Beckenham Hill	d					20 07							20 37					21 07				21 37
Ravensbourne	d					20 09							20 39					21 09				21 39
Shortlands	d					20 11							20 41					21 11				21 41
Bromley South [4]	d					20 14							20 44					21 14				21 44
Bickley [4]	d					20 17							20 47					21 17				21 47
St Mary Cray	d					20 21							20 51					21 21				21 51
Swanley [4]	d					20 26							20 56					21 26				21 56
Eynsford	d					20 30							21 00					21 30				22 00
Shoreham (Kent)	d					20 34							21 04					21 34				22 04
Otford [4]	d					20 37							21 07					21 37				22 07
Bat & Ball	d					20 40							21 10					21 40				22 10
Sevenoaks [4]	a					20 43							21 13					21 43				22 13
Redhill	d																					
Gatwick Airport [10] ✈	d				20 11			20 27				20 41					21 11				21 41	
Three Bridges [4]	d				20 15			20 32				20 45					21 15				21 45	
Balcombe	d											20 51									21 53	
Haywards Heath [3]	d				20 25			20 41				20 57					21 25				21 59	
Wivelsfield [4]	d				20 29							21 01					21 29				22 03	
Burgess Hill [4]	d				20 31			20 46				21 03					21 31				22 05	
Hassocks [4]	d				20 34							21 06					21 34				22 08	
Preston Park	d				20 41							21 13					21 41				22 15	
Brighton [10]	a				20 46			20 57				21 18					21 46				22 20	

Bedford, Luton, St. Albans and City of London - South London, Gatwick Airport and Brighton

		FC	EM ◇1	FC 1	FC	EM ◇1	FC 1	FC	FC 1	EM ◇1	FC	EM ◇1	SE	FC 1	FC	FC 1	EM ◇1	SE	FC	EM ◇1	SE	FC 1	FC
Bedford [7]	d		20 18	20 22		20 51	20 52		21 22	21 25		21 44		21 52		22 16	22 19			22 47		22 52	
Flitwick	d			20 32			21 02		21 32					22 02		22 26						23 02	
Harlington	d			20 36			21 06		21 36					22 06		22 30						23 06	
Leagrave	d			20 41			21 11		21 41					22 11		22 35						23 11	
Luton [10]	d	20 20		20 46	20 50	21 05	21 16	21 20	21 46		21 50	22 01		22 16	22 20	22 40	22 34		22 46	23 05		23 16	
Luton Airport Parkway [7] ✈	d	20 22	20 34	20 48	20 52		21 18	21 22	21 48	21 41	21 52			22 18	22 22	22 42	22 38		22 48			23 18	
Harpenden	d	20 28		20 54	20 58		21 24	21 28	21 54		21 58			22 24	22 28	22 48			22 54			23 24	
St Albans City	d	20 34		21 00	21 04		21 30	21 34	22 00		22 04			22 30	22 34	22 54			23 00			23 30	
Radlett	d	20 39			21 09			21 39			22 10				22 40				23 06			23 36	
Elstree & Borehamwood	d	20 43			21 13			21 43			22 14				22 44				23 10			23 40	
Mill Hill Broadway	d	20 47			21 17			21 47			22 18				22 48				23 14			23 44	
Hendon	d	20 50			21 20			21 50			22 22				22 52				23 18			23 48	
Cricklewood	d	20 54			21 24			21 54			22 25				22 55				23 21			23 51	
West Hampstead Thameslink ⊖	d	20 56		21 14	21 26		21 44	21 56	22 14		22 28			22 44	22 58	23 12			23 23			23 54	
Kentish Town ⊖	d	21 00			21 30			22 00			22 34				23 04				23 31			00 02	
St Pancras International [15] ⊖	a		20 59			21 30			22 23	22 06	22 40	22 29		22 53	23 10	23 24	23 01		23 37	23 34		00 06	
St Pancras International [15] ⊖	a	21 05		21 22	21 35		21 52	22 05															
	d	21 06		21 24	21 36		21 54	22 06															
Farringdon [3] ⊖	d	21 10		21 29	21 40		21 59	22 10															
City Thameslink [3]	d	21 13		21 32	21 43		22 02	22 13															
London Blackfriars [3] ⊖	d	21 16		21 35	21 46		22 05	22 16															
Elephant & Castle ⊖	d	21 19			21 49			22 19															
Loughborough Jn.	d	21 23			21 53			22 23															
Herne Hill [4]	d	21 27			21 57			22 27															
London Bridge [4]	a			21 41			22 11																
	d			21 42			22 12																23 01
Tulse Hill [3]	d	21 31			22 01			22 31															23 11
Streatham [4]	d	21 35			22 05			22 35															23 15
Mitcham Eastfields	d																						
Mitcham Junction	d																						
Hackbridge	d																						
Carshalton	d																						
Tooting	d	21 40			22 10			22 40															23 20
Haydons Road	d	21 43			22 13			22 43															23 23
Wimbledon [6] ⊖ ⇌	d	21 49			22 19			22 49															23 26
Wimbledon Chase	d	21 52			22 22			22 52															23 29
South Merton	d	21 54			22 24			22 54															23 31
Morden South	d	21 56			22 26			22 56															23 33
St Helier	d	21 58			22 28			22 58															23 35
Sutton Common	d	22 00			22 30			23 00															23 38
West Sutton	d	22 03			22 33			23 03															23 40
Sutton (Surrey) [4]	a	22 09			22 39			23 09															23 45
East Croydon ⇌	d			21 55			22 25																
Denmark Hill [4]	d												21 52					22 22			22 52		
Peckham Rye [4]	d												21 55					22 25			22 55		
Nunhead [4]	d												21 57					22 27			22 57		
Crofton Park	d												22 00					22 30			23 00		
Catford	d												22 03					22 33			23 03		
Bellingham	d												22 05					22 35			23 05		
Beckenham Hill	d												22 07					22 37			23 07		
Ravensbourne	d												22 09					22 39			23 09		
Shortlands	d												22 11					22 41			23 11		
Bromley South [4]	d												22 14					22 44			23 14		
Bickley [4]	d												22 17					22 47			23a17		
St Mary Cray	d												22 21					22 51					
Swanley [4]	d												22 26					22 56					
Eynsford	d												22 30					23 00					
Shoreham (Kent)	d												22 34					23 04					
Otford [4]	d												22 37					23 07					
Bat & Ball	d												22 40					23 10					
Sevenoaks [4]	a												22 43					23 13					
Redhill	d																						
Gatwick Airport [10] ✈	d			22 11			22 41																
Three Bridges [4]	d			22 15			22 45																
Balcombe	d						22 53																
Haywards Heath [3]	d			22 25			22 59																
Wivelsfield [4]	d			22 29			23 03																
Burgess Hill [4]	d			22 31			23 05																
Hassocks [4]	d			22 34			23 08																
Preston Park	d			22 41			23 15																
Brighton [10]	a			22 46			23 20																

Bedford, Luton, St. Albans and City of London - South London, Gatwick Airport and Brighton

		FC 1	SE	FC	FC 1	SE	FC
Bedford 7	d	23 12			23 32		
Flitwick	d	23 22			23 42		
Harlington	d	23 26			23 46		
Leagrave	d	23 31			23 51		
Luton 10	d	23 36			23 56		
Luton Airport Parkway 7 ✈	d	23 38			23 58		
Harpenden	d	23 44			00 04		
St Albans City	d	23 50			00 10		
Radlett	d	23 56			00 16		
Elstree & Borehamwood	d	00 01			00 20		
Mill Hill Broadway	d	00 04			00 24		
Hendon	d	00 08			00 28		
Cricklewood	d	00 11			00 31		
West Hampstead Thameslink ⊖	d	00 14			00 34		
Kentish Town ⊖	d	00 20			00 40		
St Pancras International 15 ⊖	a	00 26			00 46		
St Pancras International 15 ⊖	a						
	d						
Farringdon 3 ⊖	d						
City Thameslink 3	d						
London Blackfriars 3 ⊖	d						
Elephant & Castle ⊖	d						
Loughborough Jn	d						
Herne Hill 4	d						
London Bridge 4	a						
	d			23 28			23 58
Tulse Hill 3	d			23 40			00 10
Streatham 4	d			23 44			00 14
Mitcham Eastfields	d						
Mitcham Junction	d						
Hackbridge	d						
Carshalton	d						
Tooting	d			23 48			00 18
Haydons Road	d			23 51			00 21
Wimbledon 8 ⊖	d			23 55			00 25
Wimbledon Chase	d			23 58			00 28
South Merton	d			00 01			00 30
Morden South	d			00 03			00 32
St Helier	d			00 05			00 34
Sutton Common	d			00 08			00 36
West Sutton	d			00 11			00 39
Sutton (Surrey) 4	a			00 14			00 43
East Croydon	d						
Denmark Hill 4	d		23 22			23 52	
Peckham Rye 4	d		23 25			23 55	
Nunhead 4	d		23 27			23 57	
Crofton Park	d		23 30			23 59	
Catford	d		23 33			00 03	
Bellingham	d		23 35			00 05	
Beckenham Hill	d		23 37			00 07	
Ravensbourne	d		23 39			00 09	
Shortlands	d		23 41			00 11	
Bromley South 4	d		23 44			00 14	
Bickley 4	d		23a47			00a17	
St Mary Cray	d						
Swanley 4	d						
Eynsford	d						
Shoreham (Kent)	d						
Otford 4	d						
Bat & Ball	d						
Sevenoaks 4	a						
Redhill	d						
Gatwick Airport 10 ✈	d						
Three Bridges 4	d						
Balcombe	d						
Haywards Heath 3	d						
Wivelsfield 4	d						
Burgess Hill 4	d						
Hassocks 4	d						
Preston Park	d						
Brighton 10	a						

Brighton, Gatwick Airport and South London - City of London, St. Albans, Luton and Bedford

Miles	Miles	Miles	Miles	Miles			FC MX	FC MX 1	FC A	FC B	EM MX ◇1	FC C	FC MX	FC MX 1	FC C		FC A	FC B	FC MX 1	FC MO 1	FC MX	FC MX 1	FC 1 D	FC 1 E	EM MX ◇1
0	-	-	-	-	Brighton 10	d													23p37	23p44					
1½	-	-	-	-	Preston Park	d													23p41						
7¼	-	-	-	-	Hassocks 4	d													23p47	23p52					
9¼	-	-	-	-	Burgess Hill 4	d													23p51	23p56					
10	-	-	-	-	Wivelsfield 4	d													23p53						
13	-	-	-	-	Haywards Heath 3	d													23p59	00 01					
17	-	-	-	-	Balcombe	d													00 04						
21½	-	-	-	-	Three Bridges 4	d													00 10	00 10					
24¼	-	-	-	-	Gatwick Airport 10 ✈	d													00 15	00 15					
30	-	-	-	-	Redhill	d													00 22	00 22					
40½	-	-	0	-	East Croydon	d													00a35	00a35					
-	-	-	-	-	Sevenoaks 4	d																			
-	-	-	-	-	Bat & Ball	d																			
-	-	-	-	-	Otford 4	d																			
-	-	-	-	-	Shoreham (Kent)	d																			
-	-	-	-	-	Eynsford	d																			
-	-	-	-	-	Swanley 4	d																			
-	-	-	-	-	St Mary Cray 4	d																			
-	-	-	-	-	Bickley	d																			
-	-	-	-	-	Bromley South	d																			
-	-	-	-	-	Shortlands 4	d																			
-	-	-	-	-	Ravensbourne	d																			
-	-	-	-	-	Beckenham Hill	d																			
-	-	-	-	-	Bellingham	d																			
-	-	-	-	-	Catford	d																			
-	-	-	-	-	Crofton Park	d																			
-	-	-	-	-	Nunhead 4	d																			
-	-	-	-	-	Peckham Rye 4	d																			
-	-	-	-	-	Denmark Hill 4	d																			
-	0	0	-	0	Sutton (Surrey) 4	d																			
-	1	-	-	-	West Sutton	d																			
-	2	-	-	-	Sutton Common	d																			
-	3	-	-	-	St Helier	d																			
-	3½	-	-	-	Morden South	d																			
-	4	-	-	-	South Merton	d																			
-	4½	-	-	-	Wimbledon Chase	d																			
-	5½	-	-	-	Wimbledon 8 ⊖	d																			
-	6¾	-	-	-	Haydons Road	d																			
-	8	-	-	-	Tooting	d																			
-	-	-	-	1¾	Carshalton	d																			
-	-	-	-	2	Hackbridge	d																			
-	-	-	-	4	Mitcham Junction	d																			
-	-	-	-	5	Mitcham Eastfields	d																			
-	9½	6	-	6	Streatham 4	d																			
-	11	7½	5	-	Tulse Hill 3	d																			
50¾	-	-	-	-	London Bridge 4 ⊖	a																			
-	-	-	-	-		d																			
-	-	-	-	-	West Croydon	d																			
-	12	8½	-	-	Herne Hill 4	d																			
-	13	9½	-	-	Loughborough Jn	d																			
-	15	11½	-	-	Elephant & Castle	d																			
51½	16	12½	10	-	London Blackfriars 3 ⊖	d																			
52	-	-	-	-	City Thameslink 3	d																			
52¾	3	-	-	-	Farringdon 3 ⊖	d																			
53¾	0	-	-	-	St Pancras International 15 ⊖	d	22p48	23p02	23p04	23p04	23p15		23p18	23p32			23p32	23p32			23p48	00 02		00 02	00 15
-	-	-	-	-	St Pancras International 15 ⊖	a																			
-	-	-	-	-		d						23p02			23p32								00 02		
55½	-	-	-	-	Kentish Town ⊖	d	22p53		23p09	23p09		23p09	23p23		23p37		23p37	23p37			23p53		00 06	00 07	
58	-	-	-	-	West Hampstead Thameslink ⊖	d	22p57	23p10	23p13	23p13		23p13	23p27	23p40	23p41		23p41	23p41			23p57	00 10	00 10	00 11	
59	-	-	-	-	Cricklewood	d	23p00		23p16	23p16		23p16	23p30		23p44		23p44	23p44			00 01		00 13	00 14	
61	-	-	-	-	Hendon	d	23p03		23p19	23p19		23p19	23p33		23p47		23p47	23p47			00 03		00 16	00 17	
63¼	-	-	-	-	Mill Hill Broadway	d	23p07		23p23	23p23		23p23	23p37		23p51		23p51	23p51			00 07		00 20	00 21	
66½	-	-	-	-	Elstree & Borehamwood	d	23p11		23p27	23p27		23p27	23p41		23p55		23p55	23p55			00 11		00 24	00 25	
69½	-	-	-	-	Radlett	d	23p16		23p32	23p32		23p32	23p46		00 01		00 01	00 01			00 16		00 29	00 30	
74	-	-	-	-	St Albans City	d	23p22	23p26	23p38	23p38		23p38	23p52	23p56	00 06		00 06	00 06			00 22	00 26	00 35	00 36	
78¾	-	-	-	-	Harpenden	d	23p28	23p32	23p44	23p44		23p44	23p58	00 02	00 12		00 12	00 12			00 28	00 32	00 41	00 42	
83¼	-	-	-	-	Luton Airport Parkway 7 ✈	d	23p34	23p38	23p50	23p50		23p50	00 04	00 08	00 18		00 18	00 18			00 34	00 38	00 47	00 48	00 44
84¼	30¼	-	-	-	Luton 10	d	23p37	23p41	23p53	23p53	23p46	23p53	00 07	00 11	00 21		00 21	00 22			00 37	00 41	00 50	00 51	00 47
86¾	-	-	-	-	Leagrave	d	23p41	23p45	23p56	23p56		23p56	00 11	00 15	00 25		00 25	00 26			00 41	00 45	00 54	00 55	
91¾	-	-	-	-	Harlington	d	23p46	23p50	00 02	00 02		00 02	00 16	00 20	00 30		00 30	00 32			00 46	00 50	00 59	01 00	
94¼	-	-	-	-	Flitwick	d	23p50	23p54	00 06	00 07		00 06	00 20	00 24	00 34		00 34	00 36			00 50	00 54	01 03	01 04	
103¾	49¾	-	-	-	Bedford 7	a	00 04	00 08	00 20	00 20	00 11	00 20	00 34	00 38	00 48		00 48	00 48			01 04	01 08	01 17	01 18	01 12

A MO until 20 June, MO from 31 October
B MO from 27 June until 1 August
C MO from 8 August until 24 October
D MO from 1 August until 17 October
E MO until 25 July, MO from 24 October

Brighton, Gatwick Airport and South London - City of London, St. Albans, Luton and Bedford

		FC MX	FC 1 A	FC 1 B	FC A	FC B	FC A	FC B	FC 1 B	FC 1 A	FC 1 A	FC 1 B	FC A	FC B	FC	SE	SE	EM ◇1 ⊡	FC 1	FC	FC 1	SE
Brighton 10	d																					
Preston Park	d																					
Hassocks 4	d																					
Burgess Hill 4	d																					
Wivelsfield 4	d																					
Haywards Heath 3	d																					
Balcombe	d																					
Three Bridges 4	d														04 25				04 55			
Gatwick Airport 10 ✈	d														04 30				05 00		05 27	
Redhill	d																				05 35	
East Croydon	d														04 47				05 17		05 47	
Sevenoaks 4	d																					
Bat & Ball	d																					
Otford 4	d																					
Shoreham (Kent)	d																					
Eynsford	d																					
Swanley 4	d																					
St Mary Cray 4	d																					
Bickley	d															04 41	05 02					05 41
Bromley South	d															04 44	05 05					05 44
Shortlands 4	d															04 47	05 08					05 47
Ravensbourne	d															04 49						05 49
Beckenham Hill	d															04 51						05 51
Bellingham	d															04 53						05 53
Catford	d															04 56						05 56
Crofton Park	d															04 58						05 58
Nunhead 4	d															05 01						06 01
Peckham Rye 4	d															05 04						06 04
Denmark Hill 4	d															05 07						06 07
Sutton (Surrey) 4	d																					
West Sutton	d																					
Sutton Common	d																					
St Helier	d																					
Morden South	d																					
South Merton	d																					
Wimbledon Chase	d																					
Wimbledon 6 ⊖	d																					
Haydons Road	d																					
Tooting	d																					
Carshalton	d																					
Hackbridge	d																					
Mitcham Junction	d																					
Mitcham Eastfields	d																					
Streatham 4	d																			05 46		
Tulse Hill 3	d																			05 50		
London Bridge 4 ⊖	a																		05 34		06 02	
	d																		05 34		06 02	
West Croydon	d																					
Herne Hill 4	d																05 23			05 54		
Loughborough Jn.	d																					
Elephant & Castle	d															05 13	05 29			06 00		06 13
London Blackfriars 3 ⊖	d														05 14	05 17	05 33		05 42	06 04	06 12	06 17
City Thameslink 3	d														05 16	05a19	05a35		05 44	06 06	06 14	06a19
Farringdon 3 ⊖	d														05 20				05 48	06 10	06 18	
St Pancras International 15 ⊖	d	00 18		00 36		01 06		01 32	02 32			03 52		04 52				06 10				
St Pancras International 15 ⊖	a														05 23				05 51	06 13	06 21	
	d		00 36		01 06		01 32			02 32	03 52		04 52		05 24				05 52	06 14	06 22	
Kentish Town ⊖	d	00 23	00 41	00 41	01 11	01 11	01 37	01 37	02 37	02 37	03 57	03 57	04 57	04 57	05 28				05 56	06 18		
West Hampstead Thameslink ⊖	d	00 27	00 45	00 45	01 15	01 15	01 41	01 41	02 41	02 41	04 01	04 01	05 01	05 01	05 32				06 00	06 22		
Cricklewood	d	00 30	00 48	00 48	01 18	01 18	01 44	01 44	02 44	02 44	04 04	04 04	05 04	05 04	05 35				06 03	06 25		
Hendon	d	00 33	00 51	00 51	01 21	01 21	01 47	01 47	02 47	02 47	04 07	04 07	05 07	05 07	05 38				06 06	06 28		
Mill Hill Broadway	d	00 37	00 55	00 55	01 25	01 25	01 51	01 51	02 51	02 51	04 11	04 11	05 11	05 11	05 42				06 10	06 32		
Elstree & Borehamwood	d	00 41	00 59	00 59	01 29	01 29	01 55	01 55	02 55	02 55	04 15	04 15	05 15	05 15	05 46				06 14	06 36		
Radlett	d	00 46	01 04	01 04	01 34	01 34	02 00	02 00	03 00	03 00	04 20	04 20	05 20	05 20	05 51				06 18	06 40		
St Albans City	d	00 52	01 10	01 10	01 40	01 40	02 06	02 06	03 06	03 06	04 26	04 26	05 26	05 26	05 58				06 24	06a47	06 42	
Harpenden	d	00 58	01 16	01 16	01 46	01 46	02 12	02 12	03 12	03 12	04 32	04 32	05 32	05 32	06 04				06 30		06 48	
Luton Airport Parkway 7 ✈	d	01 04	01 22	01 22	01 52	01 52	02 18	02 18	03 18	03 18	04 38	04 38	05 38	05 38	06 10				06 36		06 54	
Luton 10	d	01 07	01 25	01 25	01 55	01 55	02 21	02 21	03 21	03 21	04 41	04 41	05 41	05 41	06 13			06 33	06 39		06 59	
Leagrave	d	01 11	01 29	01 29	01 59	01 59	02 25	02 25	03 25	03 25	04 45	04 45	05 45	05 45	06 16				06 42		07 02	
Harlington	d	01 16	01 34	01 34	02 04	02 04	02 30	02 30	03 30	03 30	04 50	04 50	05 50	05 50	06 22				06 48		07 08	
Flitwick	d	01 20	01 38	01 38	02 08	02 08	02 34	02 34	03 34	03 34	04 54	04 54	05 54	05 54	06 26				06 52		07 12	
Bedford 7	a	01 34	01 52	01 52	02 22	02 22	02 48	02 48	03 48	03 48	05 08	05 08	06 08	06 08	06 40			06 47	07 04		07 24	

A MO from 1 August until 17 October

B until 29 July, MX from 2 August until 14 October, from 18 October

Brighton, Gatwick Airport and South London - City of London, St. Albans, Luton and Bedford

		EM ◇1 ⊡	FC 1	EM ◇1 ⊡	EM ◇1 ⊡	FC	SE	FC 1	FC	EM ◇1 ⊡	FC 1	SN 1	FC	SE	SE 1	FC 1	SN 1	EM ◇1 ⊡	FC	SE	SE	FC 1
Brighton 10	d		05 09					05 39			05 49	06 01				06 07	06 17					06 24
Preston Park	d		05 13					05 43			05 53					06 11						06 28
Hassocks 4	d		05 19					05 49			05 59	06 09				06 18	06 26					06 35
Burgess Hill 4	d		05 23					05 53			06 03	06 12				06 22	06 30					06 39
Wivelsfield 4	d		05 25					05 55			06 05	06 15				06 25						
Haywards Heath 3	d		05 30					06 00			06 10	06 27				06 30	06 35					06 44
Balcombe	d		05 36					06 06								06 35						06 50
Three Bridges 4	d		05 41					06 11			06 20	06 36				06 41	06a45					06 56
Gatwick Airport 10 ✈	d		05 46					06 16			06 25	06 41				06 46						07 01
Redhill	d										06 33					06 56						07 11
East Croydon	d		06 02					06 32			06 44	06a56				07 09						07 24
Sevenoaks 4	d						05 40							06 13							06 42	
Bat & Ball	d						05 43							06 16							06 48	
Otford 4	d						05 46							06 19	06 38						06 51	
Shoreham (Kent)	d						05 49							06 22							06 54	
Eynsford	d						05 53							06 26							06 58	
Swanley 4	d						05 58							06 31	06 48						07 03	
St Mary Cray 4	d						06 02							06 35							07 07	
Bickley	d						06 06							06 39						07 05	07 11	
Bromley South	d						06 10							06 42	06 57					07 08	07 14	
Shortlands 4	d						06 13							06 45						07 11	07 17	
Ravensbourne	d						06 15							06 47							07 19	
Beckenham Hill	d						06 17							06 49							07 21	
Bellingham	d						06 19							06 51							07 23	
Catford	d						06 22							06 54							07 26	
Crofton Park	d						06 25							06 57							07 29	
Nunhead 4	d						06 27							06 59							07 31	
Peckham Rye 4	d						06 30							07 02							07 34	
Denmark Hill 4	d						06 33							07 05							07 37	
Sutton (Surrey) 4	d								06 05				06 34						06 46			
West Sutton	d								06 09										06 49			
Sutton Common	d								06 11										06 51			
St Helier	d								06 14										06 54			
Morden South	d								06 16										06 56			
South Merton	d								06 18										06 58			
Wimbledon Chase	d								06 20										07 00			
Wimbledon 6 ⊖	d								06 28										07 06			
Haydons Road	d								06 30										07 08			
Tooting	d								06 33										07 11			
Carshalton	d												06 37									
Hackbridge	d												06 39									
Mitcham Junction	d												06 42									
Mitcham Eastfields	d												06 45									
Streatham 4	d					06 06			06 38				06 49						07 16			
Tulse Hill 3	d					06 10			06 42				06 53						07 20			
London Bridge 4 ⊖	a		06 15					06 46			06 58					07 23						
	d		06 16					06 46			06 58					07 24						
West Croydon	d																					
Herne Hill 4	d					06 16			06 46				06 57						07 24	07 31		07 41
Loughborough Jn.	d					06 19			06 49				07 00						07 27	07 34		
Elephant & Castle	d					06 24	06 40		06 54				07 06	07 12	07 16				07 32	07 38	07 44	07 48
London Blackfriars 3 ⊖	d		06 24			06 30	06 48	06 52	07 00		07 06		07 12	07 18	07 24	07 30			07 36	07 42	07 48	07 54
City Thameslink 3	d		06 26			06 32	06 50	06 54	07 02		07 08		07 14	07 20	07 26	07 33			07 38	07 44	07 50	07 56
Farringdon 3 ⊖	d		06 30			06 36	06 54	06 58	07 06		07 12		07 18	07 24	07 30	07 36			07 42	07 48	07 54	08 00
St Pancras International 15 ⊖	d	06 37		06 55	07 00					07 30								08 00				
St Pancras International 15 ⊖	a		06 33			06 39	06 57	07 01	07 09		07 15		07 21	07 27	07 33	07 39			07 45	07 51	07 57	08 03
	d		06 34			06 40	06 58	07 02	07 10		07 18		07 22	07 28	07 34	07 40			07 46	07 52	07 58	08 04
Kentish Town ⊖	d					06 44	07 02							07 32							08 02	
West Hampstead Thameslink ⊖	d		06 42			06 48	07 06	07 10	07 18		07 26		07 30	07 36					07 54	08 00	08 06	
Cricklewood	d					06 51	07 09							07 39							08 09	
Hendon	d					06 54	07 12							07 42							08 12	
Mill Hill Broadway	d					06 58	07 16							07 46							08 16	
Elstree & Borehamwood	d					07 02	07 20		07 28				07 40	07 50						08 10	08 20	
Radlett	d					07 06	07 24		07 32				07 44	07 54						08 14	08 24	
St Albans City	d		06 56			07 12	07a32	07 26	07 38		07 42		07a52	08a02	07 54				08 10	08a22	08 30	08 24
Harpenden	d		07 02			07 18		07 32	07 44		07 48				08 00				08 16		08 36	08 32
Luton Airport Parkway 7 ✈	d		07 08	07a15		07 24		07 38	07 50	07 51	07 54				08 06	08 10			08 22		08 42	08 38
Luton 10	d	06a58	07 11		07 23	07 27		07 41	07a54		07 59				08 09	08a12		08 23	08 25		08a46	08 41
Leagrave	d		07 14			07 30		07 44			08 02				08 12				08 28			08 44
Harlington	d		07 20			07 36		07 50			08 08				08 18				08 34			08 50
Flitwick	d		07 24			07 40		07 54			08 12				08 22				08 38			08 54
Bedford 7	a		07 36		07 38	07 52		08 06		08 06	08 24				08 34			08 37	08 50			09 06

Brighton, Gatwick Airport and South London - City of London, St. Albans, Luton and Bedford

		SN ■	SN ■	FC	SE	SE	SE ■	FC	EM ◇■	FC ■	SN ■	SE ■	SE	EM ◇■	FC	SE	SE ■	FC	SE ■	FC ■	SN ■	SE
Brighton 10	d		06 37							07 00										07 24	07 33	
Preston Park	d	06 36								07 04										07 28	07 37	
Hassocks 4	d	06 43								07 10	07 21									07 35		
Burgess Hill 4	d	06 47								07 14										07 39	07 46	
Wivelsfield 4	d	06 50								07 18	07 26										07 49	
Haywards Heath 3	d		07 00							07 23	07 31									07 46	07 54	
Balcombe	d																				07 59	
Three Bridges 4	d									07 32										07 56	08 05	
Gatwick Airport 10 ✈	d		07 12							07 38										08 01		
Redhill	d																			08 09		
East Croydon	d		07a27							07 54	07a57									08 21	08a24	
Sevenoaks 4	d					07 11										07 36						07 53
Bat & Ball	d					07 14										07 39						07 56
Otford 4	d					07 18	07 23									07 43						08 00
Shoreham (Kent)	d					07 21										07 46						08 03
Eynsford	d					07 24										07 49						08 06
Swanley 4	d					07 30	07 32									07 54	07 55					08 11
St Mary Cray 4	d					07 34										07 59	08 00					08 16
Bickley	d				07 35	07 39							07 55			08 03						08 20
Bromley South	d				07 38	07 42	07 40						07 58			08 08	08 06		08 18			08 26
Shortlands 4	d				07 41	07 44							08 00			08 10			08 20			08 29
Ravensbourne	d					07 47										08 13			08 23			
Beckenham Hill	d					07 49										08 15			08 25			
Bellingham	d					07 51							08 05			08 17			08 27			08 33
Catford	d					07 53							08 08			08 20			08 30			08 36
Crofton Park	d					07 56							08 10									08 39
Nunhead 4	d					07 58							08 14									08 41
Peckham Rye 4	d					08 01							08 16						08 36			08 44
Denmark Hill 4	d					08 04							08 19			08 26			08 39			08 47
Sutton (Surrey) 4	d			07 06				07 37							07 40			08 09				
West Sutton	d			07 09											07 43							
Sutton Common	d			07 11											07 45							
St Helier	d			07 14											07 48							
Morden South	d			07 16											07 50							
South Merton	d			07 18											07 52							
Wimbledon Chase	d			07 20											07 54							
Wimbledon 6 ⊖	d			07 26											07 58							
Haydons Road	d			07 28											08 00							
Tooting	d			07 31											08 03							
Carshalton	d							07 40										08 12				
Hackbridge	d							07 42										08 14				
Mitcham Junction	d							07 45										08 17				
Mitcham Eastfields	d							07 48										08 20				
Streatham 4	d			07 38				07 52							08 09			08 24				
Tulse Hill 3	d			07 42				07 57							08 13			08 28		08 36		
London Bridge 4 ⊖	a																					
	d																					
West Croydon	d																					
Herne Hill 4	d			07 46	07 57			08 01				08 12			08 20			08 31				
Loughborough Jn.	d			07 49	08 00			08 04				08 16			08 23			08 35				
Elephant & Castle	d			07 54	08 05	08 13	08 00	08 09				08 21	08 25		08 28	08 35	08 31	08 40	08 45	08 50		08 54
London Blackfriars 3 ⊖	d			07 58	08 09	08 17	08 04	08 13		08 21		08 25	08 29		08 33	08 42	08 37	08 46	08 50	08 54		08 58
City Thameslink 3	d			08 00	08 11	08 19	08 06	08 15		08 23		08 27	08 31		08 35	08 44	08 39	08 48	08 52	08 56		09 00
Farringdon 3 ⊖	d			08 04	08 15	08 23	08 10	08 19		08 27		08 31	08 35		08 39	08 48	08 43	08 52	08 56	09 00		09 04
St Pancras International 15 ⊖	d								08 30					09 00								
St Pancras International 15 ⊖	a			08 07	08 19	08 27	08 13	08 23		08 31		08 35	08 39		08 43	08 51	08 47	08 55	08 59	09 03		09 07
	d			08 10	08 20	08 28	08 16	08 24		08 32		08 36	08 40		08 44	08 52	08 48	08 56	09 00	09 04		09 08
Kentish Town ⊖	d			08 14				08 28							08 48	08a58		09 00				09a14
West Hampstead Thameslink ⊖	d			08 18	08 28	08a37		08 33							08 52			09 04				
Cricklewood	d			08 21				08 36							08 55			09 07				
Hendon	d			08 24				08 39							08 58			09 10				
Mill Hill Broadway	d			08 28				08 43							09 02			09 14				
Elstree & Borehamwood	d			08 32	08 38			08 47					08 56		09 06			09 18				
Radlett	d			08 36	08 42			08 51					09 00		09 10			09 22				
St Albans City	d			08a44	08 50		08 36	08a58		08 52		08 57	09 06		09 16		09 10	09a29	09 20	09 25		
Harpenden	d				08 55		08 44					09 04	09 12		09 22		09 16			09 32		
Luton Airport Parkway 7 ✈	d				09 01		08 50		08 51	09 00		09 10	09 18		09 28		09 22		09 29	09 38		
Luton 10	d				09a04		08 53			09 04		09 13	09a22	09 23	09a32		09 27		09 32	09 41		
Leagrave	d						08 56					09 16					09 30			09 44		
Harlington	d						09 02					09 22					09 36			09 50		
Flitwick	d						09 06			09 14		09 26					09 40		09 44	09 56		
Bedford 7	a						09 18		09 07	09 26		09 38		09 37			09 52		09 58	10 08		

Brighton, Gatwick Airport and South London - City of London, St. Albans, Luton and Bedford

		FC	SE ■	EM ◇■	FC ■	FC	SE	FC ■	SE ■	SE	EM ◇■	FC	FC ■	SE	FC	FC ■	EM ◇■	FC	FC ■	FC	SE	FC ■	EM ◇■
Brighton 10	d				07 50			08 02					08 16			08 36			09 00			09 07	
Preston Park	d				07 54			08 06					08 20			08 40						09 11	
Hassocks 4	d				08 00			08 12					08 26			08 46			09 08			09 17	
Burgess Hill 4	d							08 16					08 30			08 50			09 12			09 21	
Wivelsfield 4	d							08 18					08 34									09 23	
Haywards Heath 3	d				08 09			08 23					08 39			09 00			09 17			09 32	
Balcombe	d				08 15											09 06						09 37	
Three Bridges 4	d							08 34					08 48			09 12			09 26			09 42	
Gatwick Airport 10 ✈	d				08 23			08 38					08 53			09 16			09 31			09 46	
Redhill	d																						
East Croydon	d				08 39			08 54					09 09			09 32			09 47			10 02	
Sevenoaks 4	d								08 24					08 43							09 13		
Bat & Ball	d								08 27					08 46							09 16		
Otford 4	d								08 31					08 49							09 21		
Shoreham (Kent)	d								08 34					08 52							09 24		
Eynsford	d								08 37					08 56							09 28		
Swanley 4	d								08 42					09 01							09 33		
St Mary Cray 4	d								08 46					09 05							09 37		
Bickley	d								08 51	08 55				09 09							09 42		
Bromley South	d						08 44		08 54	08 58				09 12							09 45		
Shortlands 4	d						08 46		08 56	09 00				09 15							09 48		
Ravensbourne	d						08 49			09 03				09 17							09 50		
Beckenham Hill	d						08 51			09 05				09 19							09 52		
Bellingham	d						08 53		09 01	09 07				09 21							09 54		
Catford	d						08 56		09 04	09 09				09 24							09 57		
Crofton Park	d						08 58			09 12				09 26							09 59		
Nunhead 4	d						09 01			09 14				09 29							10 02		
Peckham Rye 4	d						09 04		09 09	09 17				09 31							10 04		
Denmark Hill 4	d						09 07		09 12	09 19				09 34							10 07		
Sutton (Surrey) 4	d	08 08				08 39						08 41			09 13			09 11		09 38			
West Sutton	d	08 11										08 44						09 14					
Sutton Common	d	08 13										08 46						09 16					
St Helier	d	08 16										08 49						09 19					
Morden South	d	08 18										08 51						09 21					
South Merton	d	08 20										08 53						09 23					
Wimbledon Chase	d	08 22										08 55						09 25					
Wimbledon 6 ⊖	d	08 28										08 58						09 28					
Haydons Road	d	08 30										09 00						09 30					
Tooting	d	08 33										09 03						09 33					
Carshalton	d					08 42									09 16					09 41			
Hackbridge	d					08 44									09 18					09 43			
Mitcham Junction	d					08 47									09 21					09 46			
Mitcham Eastfields	d					08 50									09 24					09 49			
Streatham 4	d	08 39				08 54						09 08			09 28			09 38		09 53			
Tulse Hill 3	d	08 43				08 58						09 16			09 32			09 42		09 57			
London Bridge 4 ⊖	a							09 08								09 46			10 00			10 15	
	d							09 09								09 46			10 00			10 16	
West Croydon	d																						
Herne Hill 4	d	08 47	08 52		08 57	09 02						09 20			09 35			09 47		10 01			
Loughborough Jn.	d	08 50	08 55			09 05						09 23			09 39			09 50		10 04			
Elephant & Castle	d	08 58	09 02		09 06	09 10	09 14		09 20	09 26		09 30	09 34	09 42	09 46			09 55		10 09	10 14		
London Blackfriars 3 ⊖	d	09 02	09 06		09 10	09 14	09 18	09 22	09 26	09 30		09 34	09 38	09 46	09 50	09 54		10 00	10 08	10 13	10 18	10 24	
City Thameslink 3	d	09 04	09 08		09 12	09 16	09 20	09 25	09 28	09 32		09 36	09 40	09 48	09 52	09 56		10 02	10 10	10 15	10 20	10 26	
Farringdon 3 ⊖	d	09 08	09 12		09 16	09 20	09 24	09 28	09 32	09 36		09 40	09 44	09 52	09 56	10 00		10 06	10 14	10 19	10 24	10 30	
St Pancras International 15 ⊖	d			09 30							10 00						10 30						11 00
St Pancras International 15 ⊖	a	09 11	09 15		09 19	09 23	09 27	09 32	09 35	09 39		09 43	09 47	09 55	09 59	10 03		10 09	10 17	10 22	10 27	10 33	
	d	09 12	09 16		09 20	09 24	09 28	09 32	09 36	09 40		09 44	09 48	09 56	10 00	10 04		10 10	10 18	10 23	10 28	10 34	
Kentish Town ⊖	d	09 16					09 34			09a46		09 49		10 00	10a06			10 14		10 27	10a34		
West Hampstead Thameslink ⊖	d	09 20				09 31	09 40					09 54		10 04				10 18		10 32			
Cricklewood	d	09 23					09 43					09 57		10 07				10 21		10 35			
Hendon	d	09 26					09 46					10 00		10 10				10 24		10 38			
Mill Hill Broadway	d	09 30					09 50					10 04		10 14				10 28		10 42			
Elstree & Borehamwood	d	09 34				09 42	09 54					10 08		10 18				10 32		10 46			
Radlett	d	09 40				09 46	09 58					10 12		10 22				10 36		10 50			
St Albans City	d	09 46			09 40	09 52	10 04	09 52	09 57			10 18	10 10	10a29		10 25		10 44	10 40	10a57		10 55	
Harpenden	d	09 54			09 46	09 58	10 12		10 04			10 24	10 16			10 32		10 52	10 46			11 00	
Luton Airport Parkway 7 ✈	d	10 00	09 44	09 51	09 52	10 04	10 18	10 01	10 10			10 30	10 22			10 38	10 51	10 58	10 52			11 06	
Luton 10	d	10a04	09 47		09 56	10 07	10a20	10 04	10 13		10 23	10a34	10 25			10 41		11a02	10 55			11 09	11 23
Leagrave	d		09 50		10 00	10 10			10 16				10 28			10 44			10 58			11 14	
Harlington	d				10 05	10 16			10 22				10 34			10 50			11 04			11 20	
Flitwick	d		10 01		10 09	10 22		10 14	10 26				10 38			10 54			11 08			11 24	
Bedford 7	a		10 13	10 07	10 22	10 34		10 28	10 38		10 37		10 50			11 06	11 06		11 20			11 36	11 37

Brighton, Gatwick Airport and South London - City of London, St. Albans, Luton and Bedford

Station		FC	FC [1]	FC	SE	FC [1]		EM ◇[1]	FC	SE	FC [1]	FC	FC [1]	EM ◇[1]	FC	SE		FC [1]	FC	FC [1]	EM ◇[1]	FC	SE	FC [1]	FC
Brighton [10]	d		09 34			09 37					10 04		10 07					10 34		10 37				11 04	
Preston Park	d					09 41							10 11							10 41					
Hassocks [4]	d					09 47							10 17							10 47					
Burgess Hill [4]	d					09 51							10 21							10 51					
Wivelsfield [4]	d					09 53							10 23							10 53					
Haywards Heath [3]	d		09 47			09 58					10 17		10 32					10 47		11 02				11 17	
Balcombe	d												10 37												
Three Bridges [4]	d		09 56			10 10					10 26		10 42					10 56		11 12				11 26	
Gatwick Airport [10] ✈	d		10 01			10 16					10 31		10 46					11 01		11 16				11 31	
Redhill	d																								
East Croydon	d		10 17			10 32					10 47		11 02					11 17		11 32				11 47	
Sevenoaks [4]	d				09 42					10 02						10 32							11 02		
Bat & Ball	d				09 46					10 05						10 35							11 05		
Otford [4]	d				09 50					10 08						10 38							11 08		
Shoreham (Kent)	d				09 53					10 11						10 41							11 11		
Eynsford	d				09 56					10 15						10 45							11 15		
Swanley [4]	d				10 01					10 20						10 50							11 20		
St Mary Cray [4]	d				10 05					10 24						10 54							11 24		
Bickley	d				10 10					10 28						10 58							11 28		
Bromley South	d				10 15					10 31						11 01							11 31		
Shortlands [4]	d				10 18					10 34						11 04							11 34		
Ravensbourne	d				10 20					10 36						11 06							11 36		
Beckenham Hill	d				10 22					10 38						11 08							11 38		
Bellingham	d				10 24					10 40						11 10							11 40		
Catford	d				10 27					10 43						11 13							11 43		
Crofton Park	d				10 29					10 45						11 15							11 45		
Nunhead [4]	d				10 32					10 48						11 18							11 48		
Peckham Rye [4]	d				10 34					10 50						11 20							11 50		
Denmark Hill [4]	d				10 37					10 54						11 24							11 54		
Sutton (Surrey) [4]	d	09 37		10 08					10 07			10 38			10 37				11 08			11 07			11 38
West Sutton	d	09 40							10 10						10 40							11 10			
Sutton Common	d	09 42							10 12						10 42							11 12			
St Helier	d	09 45							10 15						10 45							11 15			
Morden South	d	09 47							10 17						10 47							11 17			
South Merton	d	09 49							10 19						10 49							11 19			
Wimbledon Chase	d	09 51							10 21						10 51							11 21			
Wimbledon [6] ⊖	d	09 58							10 28						10 58							11 28			
Haydons Road	d	10 00							10 30						11 00							11 30			
Tooting	d	10 03							10 33						11 03							11 33			
Carshalton	d			10 11								10 41							11 11						11 41
Hackbridge	d			10 13								10 43							11 13						11 43
Mitcham Junction	d			10 16								10 46							11 16						11 46
Mitcham Eastfields	d			10 19								10 49							11 19						11 49
Streatham [4]	d	10 08		10 23					10 38			10 53			11 08				11 23			11 38			11 53
Tulse Hill [3]	d	10 12		10 27					10 42			10 57			11 12				11 27			11 42			11 57
London Bridge [4] ⊖	a		10 30			10 45					11 00		11 15					11 30		11 45				12 00	
	d		10 30			10 45					11 00		11 15					11 30		11 45				12 00	
West Croydon	d																								
Herne Hill [4]	d	10 16		10 31					10 46			11 01			11 16				11 31			11 46			12 01
Loughborough Jn	d	10 19		10 34					10 49			11 04			11 19				11 34			11 49			12 04
Elephant & Castle	d	10 24		10 39	10 44				10 54	11 00		11 09			11 24	11 30			11 39			11 54	12 00		12 09
London Blackfriars [3] ⊖	d	10 30	10 38	10 43	10 48	10 54			11 00	11 04	11 08	11 13	11 24		11 30	11 34		11 38	11 43	11 54		12 00	12 04	12 08	12 13
City Thameslink [3]	d	10 32	10 40	10 45	10 50	10 56			11 02	11 06	11 10	11 15	11 26		11 32	11 36		11 40	11 45	11 56		12 02	12 06	12 10	12 15
Farringdon [3] ⊖	d	10 36	10 44	10 49	10 54	11 00			11 06	11 10	11 14	11 19	11 30		11 36	11 40		11 44	11 49	12 00		12 06	12 10	12 14	12 19
St Pancras International [15] ⊖	d							11 30						12 00							12 30				
St Pancras International [15] ⊖	a	10 39	10 47	10 52	10 57	11 03			11 09	11 13	11 17	11 22	11 33		11 39	11 43		11 47	11 52	12 03		12 09	12 13	12 17	12 22
	d	10 40	10 48	10 53	10 58	11 04			11 10	11 14	11 18	11 23	11 34		11 40	11 44		11 48	11 53	12 04		12 10	12 14	12 18	12 23
Kentish Town ⊖	d	10 44		10 57	11a03				11 14	11a20		11 27			11 44	11a50			11 57			12 14	12a20		12 27
West Hampstead Thameslink ⊖	d	10 50		11 02					11 20			11 32			11 50				12 02			12 20			12 32
Cricklewood	d	10 53		11 05					11 23			11 35			11 53				12 05			12 23			12 35
Hendon	d	10 56		11 08					11 26			11 38			11 56				12 08			12 26			12 38
Mill Hill Broadway	d	11 00		11 12					11 30			11 42			12 00				12 12			12 30			12 42
Elstree & Borehamwood	d	11 04		11 16					11 34			11 46			12 04				12 16			12 34			12 46
Radlett	d	11 10		11 20					11 38			11 50			12 08				12 20			12 38			12 50
St Albans City	d	11 16	11 10	11a27		11 25			11 44		11 40	11a57	11 55		12 14			12 10	12a27	12 25		12 44		12 40	12a57
Harpenden	d	11 22	11 16			11 32			11 50		11 46		12 02		12 20			12 16		12 32		12 50		12 46	
Luton Airport Parkway [7] ✈	d	11 28	11 22			11 38		11 51	11 56		11 52		12 08		12 26			12 22		12 38	12 51	12 56		12 52	
Luton [10]	d	11a32	11 25			11 41			12a00		11 55		12 11	12 23	12a30			12 25		12 41		13a00		12 55	
Leagrave	d		11 28			11 44					11 58		12 14					12 28		12 44				12 58	
Harlington	d		11 34			11 50					12 04		12 20					12 34		12 50				13 04	
Flitwick	d		11 38			11 54					12 08		12 24					12 38		12 54				13 08	
Bedford [7]	a		11 50			12 06		12 06			12 20		12 36	12 37				12 50		13 06	13 06			13 20	

Brighton, Gatwick Airport and South London - City of London, St. Albans, Luton and Bedford

Station		FC [1]		EM ◇[1]	FC	SE	FC [1]	FC	FC [1]	EM ◇[1]	FC	SE		FC [1]	FC	FC [1]	EM ◇[1]	FC	SE	FC [1]	FC	FC [1]		EM ◇[1]	FC
Brighton [10]	d	11 07					11 34		11 37					12 04		12 07				12 34		12 37			
Preston Park	d	11 11							11 41							12 11						12 41			
Hassocks [4]	d	11 17							11 47							12 17						12 47			
Burgess Hill [4]	d	11 21							11 51							12 21						12 51			
Wivelsfield [4]	d	11 23							11 53							12 23						12 53			
Haywards Heath [3]	d	11 32					11 47		12 02					12 17		12 32				12 47		13 02			
Balcombe	d	11 37														12 37									
Three Bridges [4]	d	11 42					11 56		12 12					12 26		12 42				12 56		13 12			
Gatwick Airport [10] ✈	d	11 46					12 01		12 16					12 31		12 46				13 01		13 16			
Redhill	d																								
East Croydon	d	12 02					12 17		12 32					12 47		13 02				13 17		13 32			
Sevenoaks [4]	d					11 32						12 02							12 32						
Bat & Ball	d					11 35						12 05							12 35						
Otford [4]	d					11 38						12 08							12 38						
Shoreham (Kent)	d					11 41						12 11							12 41						
Eynsford	d					11 45						12 15							12 45						
Swanley [4]	d					11 50						12 20							12 50						
St Mary Cray [4]	d					11 54						12 24							12 54						
Bickley	d					11 58						12 28							12 58						
Bromley South	d					12 01						12 31							13 01						
Shortlands [4]	d					12 04						12 34							13 04						
Ravensbourne	d					12 06						12 36							13 06						
Beckenham Hill	d					12 08						12 38							13 08						
Bellingham	d					12 10						12 40							13 10						
Catford	d					12 13						12 43							13 13						
Crofton Park	d					12 15						12 45							13 15						
Nunhead [4]	d					12 18						12 48							13 18						
Peckham Rye [4]	d					12 20						12 50							13 20						
Denmark Hill [4]	d					12 24						12 54							13 24						
Sutton (Surrey) [4]	d				11 37			12 08			12 07				12 38			12 37			13 08				13 07
West Sutton	d				11 40						12 10							12 40							13 10
Sutton Common	d				11 42						12 12							12 42							13 12
St Helier	d				11 45						12 15							12 45							13 15
Morden South	d				11 47						12 17							12 47							13 17
South Merton	d				11 49						12 19							12 49							13 19
Wimbledon Chase	d				11 51						12 21							12 51							13 21
Wimbledon [6] ⊖	d				11 58						12 28							12 58							13 28
Haydons Road	d				12 00						12 30							13 00							13 30
Tooting	d				12 03						12 33							13 03							13 33
Carshalton	d							12 11							12 41						13 11				
Hackbridge	d							12 13							12 43						13 13				
Mitcham Junction	d							12 16							12 46						13 16				
Mitcham Eastfields	d							12 19							12 49						13 19				
Streatham [4]	d				12 08			12 23			12 38				12 53			13 08			13 23				13 38
Tulse Hill [3]	d				12 12			12 27			12 42				12 57			13 12			13 27				13 42
London Bridge [4] ⊖	a	12 15					12 30		12 45					13 00		13 15				13 30		13 45			
	d	12 15					12 30		12 45					13 00		13 15				13 30		13 45			
West Croydon	d																								
Herne Hill [4]	d				12 16			12 31			12 46				13 01			13 16			13 31				13 46
Loughborough Jn	d				12 19			12 34			12 49				13 04			13 19			13 34				13 49
Elephant & Castle	d				12 24	12 30		12 39			12 54	13 00			13 09			13 24	13 30		13 39				13 54
London Blackfriars [3] ⊖	d	12 24			12 30	12 34	12 38	12 43	12 54		13 00	13 04		13 08	13 13	13 24		13 30	13 34	13 38	13 43	13 54			14 00
City Thameslink [3]	d	12 26			12 32	12 36	12 40	12 45	12 56		13 02	13 06		13 10	13 15	13 26		13 32	13 36	13 40	13 45	13 56			14 02
Farringdon [3] ⊖	d	12 30			12 36	12 40	12 44	12 49	13 00		13 06	13 10		13 14	13 19	13 30		13 36	13 40	13 44	13 49	14 00			14 06
St Pancras International [15] ⊖	d			13 00						13 30							14 00							14 30	
St Pancras International [15] ⊖	a	12 33			12 39	12 43	12 47	12 52	13 03		13 09	13 13		13 17	13 22	13 33		13 39	13 43	13 47	13 52	14 03			14 09
	d	12 34			12 40	12 44	12 48	12 53	13 04		13 10	13 14		13 18	13 23	13 34		13 40	13 44	13 48	13 53	14 04			14 10
Kentish Town ⊖	d				12 44	12a50		12 57			13 14	13a20			13 27			13 44	13a50		13 57				14 14
West Hampstead Thameslink ⊖	d				12 50			13 02			13 20				13 32			13 50			14 02				14 20
Cricklewood	d				12 53			13 05			13 23				13 35			13 53			14 05				14 23
Hendon	d				12 56			13 08			13 26				13 38			13 56			14 08				14 26
Mill Hill Broadway	d				13 00			13 12			13 30				13 42			14 00			14 12				14 30
Elstree & Borehamwood	d				13 04			13 16			13 34				13 46			14 04			14 16				14 34
Radlett	d				13 08			13 20			13 38				13 50			14 08			14 20				14 38
St Albans City	d	12 55			13 14		13 10	13a27	13 25		13 45			13 40	13a57	13 55		14 14		14 10	14a27	14 25			14 44
Harpenden	d	13 02			13 20		13 16		13 32		13 50			13 46		14 02		14 20		14 16		14 32			14 50
Luton Airport Parkway [7] ✈	d	13 08			13 26		13 22		13 38	13 51	13 56			13 52		14 08		14 26		14 22		14 38		14 51	14 56
Luton [10]	d	13 11		13 23	13a30		13 25		13 41		14a00			13 55		14 11	14 23	14a30		14 25		14 41			15a00
Leagrave	d	13 14					13 28		13 44					13 58		14 14				14 28		14 44			
Harlington	d	13 20					13 34		13 50					14 04		14 20				14 34		14 50			
Flitwick	d	13 24					13 38		13 54					14 08		14 24				14 38		14 54			
Bedford [7]	a	13 36		13 37			13 50		14 06	14 06				14 20		14 36	14 37			14 50		15 06		15 06	

Brighton, Gatwick Airport and South London - City of London, St. Albans, Luton and Bedford

		SE	FC ■1	FC	FC ■1	EM ◇■1	FC	SE	FC ■1	FC	FC ■1	EM ◇■1	FC	SE	FC ■1	FC	FC ■1	EM ◇■1	FC	SE	FC ■1	FC	FC ■1
Brighton 10	d		13 04		13 07				13 34		13 37				14 04		14 07				14 34		14 37
Preston Park	d				13 11						13 41						14 11						14 41
Hassocks 4	d				13 17						13 47						14 17						14 47
Burgess Hill 4	d				13 21						13 51						14 21						14 51
Wivelsfield 4	d				13 23						13 53						14 23						14 53
Haywards Heath 3	d		13 17		13 32				13 47		14 02				14 17		14 32				14 47		15 02
Balcombe	d				13 37												14 37						
Three Bridges 4	d		13 26		13 42				13 56		14 12				14 26		14 42				14 56		15 12
Gatwick Airport 10 ✈	d		13 31		13 46				14 01		14 16				14 31		14 46				15 01		15 16
Redhill	d																						
East Croydon	d		13 47		14 02				14 17		14 32				14 47		15 02				15 17		15 32
Sevenoaks 4	d	13 02						13 32						14 02						14 32			
Bat & Ball	d	13 05						13 35						14 05						14 35			
Otford 4	d	13 08						13 38						14 08						14 38			
Shoreham (Kent)	d	13 11						13 41						14 11						14 41			
Eynsford	d	13 15						13 45						14 15						14 45			
Swanley 4	d	13 20						13 50						14 20						14 50			
St Mary Cray 4	d	13 24						13 54						14 24						14 54			
Bickley	d	13 28						13 58						14 28						14 58			
Bromley South	d	13 31						14 01						14 31						15 01			
Shortlands 4	d	13 34						14 04						14 34						15 04			
Ravensbourne	d	13 36						14 06						14 36						15 06			
Beckenham Hill	d	13 38						14 08						14 38						15 08			
Bellingham	d	13 40						14 10						14 40						15 10			
Catford	d	13 43						14 13						14 43						15 13			
Crofton Park	d	13 45						14 15						14 45						15 15			
Nunhead 4	d	13 48						14 18						14 48						15 18			
Peckham Rye 4	d	13 50						14 20						14 50						15 20			
Denmark Hill 4	d	13 54						14 24						14 54						15 24			
Sutton (Surrey) 4	d			13 38			13 37			14 08			14 07			14 38			14 37			15 08	
West Sutton	d						13 40						14 10						14 40				
Sutton Common	d						13 42						14 12						14 42				
St Helier	d						13 45						14 15						14 45				
Morden South	d						13 47						14 17						14 47				
South Merton	d						13 49						14 19						14 49				
Wimbledon Chase	d						13 51						14 21						14 51				
Wimbledon 6 ⊖	d						13 58						14 28						14 58				
Haydons Road	d						14 00						14 30						15 00				
Tooting	d						14 03						14 33						15 03				
Carshalton	d			13 41						14 11						14 41						15 11	
Hackbridge	d			13 43						14 13						14 43						15 13	
Mitcham Junction	d			13 46						14 16						14 46						15 16	
Mitcham Eastfields	d			13 49						14 19						14 49						15 19	
Streatham 4	d			13 53			14 08			14 23			14 38			14 53			15 08			15 23	
Tulse Hill 3	d			13 57			14 12			14 27			14 42			14 57			15 12			15 27	
London Bridge 4 ⊖	a		14 00		14 15				14 30		14 45				15 00		15 15				15 30		15 45
	d		14 00		14 15				14 30		14 45				15 00		15 15				15 30		15 45
West Croydon	d																						
Herne Hill 4	d			14 01			14 16			14 31			14 46			15 01			15 16			15 31	
Loughborough Jn	d			14 04			14 19			14 34			14 49			15 04			15 19			15 34	
Elephant & Castle	d	14 00		14 09			14 24	14 30		14 39			14 54	15 00		15 09			15 24	15 30		15 39	
London Blackfriars 3 ⊖	d	14 04	14 08	14 13	14 24		14 30	14 34	14 38	14 43	14 54		15 00	15 04	15 08	15 13	15 24		15 30	15 34	15 38	15 43	15 54
City Thameslink 3	d	14 06	14 10	14 15	14 26		14 32	14 36	14 40	14 45	14 56		15 02	15 06	15 10	15 15	15 26		15 32	15 36	15 40	15 45	15 56
Farringdon 3 ⊖	d	14 10	14 14	14 19	14 30		14 36	14 40	14 44	14 49	15 00		15 06	15 10	15 14	15 19	15 30		15 36	15 40	15 44	15 49	16 00
St Pancras International 15 ⊖	d					15 00						15 30						16 00					
St Pancras International 15 ⊖	a	14 13	14 17	14 22	14 33		14 39	14 43	14 47	14 52	15 03		15 09	15 13	15 17	15 22	15 33		15 39	15 43	15 47	15 52	16 03
	d	14 14	14 18	14 23	14 34		14 40	14 44	14 48	14 53	15 04		15 10	15 14	15 18	15 23	15 34		15 40	15 44	15 48	15 53	16 04
Kentish Town ⊖	d	14a20		14 27			14 44	14a50		14 57			15 14	15a20		15 27			15 44	15a50		15 57	
West Hampstead Thameslink ⊖	d			14 32			14 50			15 02			15 20			15 32			15 50			16 02	
Cricklewood	d			14 35			14 53			15 05			15 23			15 35			15 53			16 05	
Hendon	d			14 38			14 56			15 08			15 26			15 38			15 56			16 08	
Mill Hill Broadway	d			14 42			15 00			15 12			15 30			15 42			16 00			16 12	
Elstree & Borehamwood	d			14 46			15 04			15 16			15 34			15 46			16 04			16 16	
Radlett	d			14 50			15 08			15 20			15 38			15 50			16 08			16 20	
St Albans City	d		14 40	14a57	14 55		15 14		15 10	15a27	15 25		15 44		15 40	15a57	15 55		16 14		16 10	16a27	16 25
Harpenden	d		14 46		15 02		15 20		15 16		15 32		15 50		15 46		16 00		16 20		16 16		16 32
Luton Airport Parkway 7 ✈	d		14 52		15 08		15 26		15 22		15 38	15 51	15 56		15 52		16 06		16 26		16 22		16 38
Luton 10	d		14 55		15 11	15 23	15a30		15 25		15 41		16a00		15 55		16 09	16 22	16a30		16 25		16 41
Leagrave	d		14 58		15 14				15 28		15 44				15 58		16 12				16 28		16 44
Harlington	d		15 04		15 20				15 34		15 50				16 04		16 18				16 34		16 50
Flitwick	d		15 08		15 24				15 38		15 54				16 08		16 22				16 38		16 54
Bedford 7	a		15 20		15 36	15 37			15 50		16 06	16 06			16 20		16 36	16 37			16 50		17 06

Table 52 Mondays to Fridays

Brighton, Gatwick Airport and South London - City of London, St. Albans, Luton and Bedford

		EM ◇■1	FC	SE	FC ■1	FC	FC ■1	EM ◇■1	FC ■1	FC	SE ■1	FC	FC ■1	EM ◇■1	EM ◇■1	FC ■1	FC	FC	SE ■1	FC ■1 A	SE	FC ■1
Brighton 10	d				15 04				15 07				15 34			15 37						16 04
Preston Park	d								15 11							15 41						
Hassocks 4	d								15 17							15 47						
Burgess Hill 4	d								15 21							15 51						
Wivelsfield 4	d								15 23							15 53						
Haywards Heath 3	d				15 17				15 32				15 47			15 58						16 17
Balcombe	d								15 37													
Three Bridges 4	d				15 26				15 42				15 56			16 07						16 26
Gatwick Airport 10 ✈	d				15 31				15 46				16 01			16 11						16 31
Redhill	d																					
East Croydon	d				15 47				16 02				16 17			16 28						16 47
Sevenoaks 4	d			15 02							15 32								16 02		16 22	
Bat & Ball	d			15 05							15 35								16 05		16 25	
Otford 4	d			15 08							15 38								16 08		16 28	
Shoreham (Kent)	d			15 11							15 41								16 11			
Eynsford	d			15 15							15 45								16 15			
Swanley 4	d			15 20							15 50								16 20		16 37	
St Mary Cray 4	d			15 24							15 54								16 24		16 41	
Bickley	d			15 28							15 58								16 28			
Bromley South	d			15 31							16 01								16 31		16 47	
Shortlands 4	d			15 34							16 04								16 34			
Ravensbourne	d			15 36							16 06								16 36			
Beckenham Hill	d			15 38							16 08								16 38			
Bellingham	d			15 40							16 10								16 40		16 52	
Catford	d			15 43							16 13								16 43		16 55	
Crofton Park	d			15 45							16 15								16 45			
Nunhead 4	d			15 48							16 18								16 48		16 59	
Peckham Rye 4	d			15 50							16 20								16 50		17 02	
Denmark Hill 4	d			15 54							16 24								16 54		17 05	
Sutton (Surrey) 4	d		15 07			15 38				15 37		16 08						16 07		16 38		
West Sutton	d		15 10							15 40								16 10				
Sutton Common	d		15 12							15 42								16 12				
St Helier	d		15 15							15 45								16 15				
Morden South	d		15 17							15 47								16 17				
South Merton	d		15 19							15 49								16 19				
Wimbledon Chase	d		15 21							15 51								16 21				
Wimbledon 6 ⊖	d		15 28							15 58								16 30				
Haydons Road	d		15 30							16 00								16 32				
Tooting	d		15 33							16 03								16 35				
Carshalton	d					15 41						16 11								16 41		
Hackbridge	d					15 43						16 13								16 43		
Mitcham Junction	d					15 46						16 16								16 46		
Mitcham Eastfields	d					15 49						16 19								16 49		
Streatham 4	d		15 38			15 53				16 08		16 23						16 40		16 53		
Tulse Hill 3	d		15 42			15 57				16 12		16 27	16 33					16 46		16 57		
London Bridge 4 ⊖	a				16 00				16 15													
	d				16 00				16 16													
West Croydon	d																					
Herne Hill 4	d		15 46			16 01				16 16		16 31						16 50		17 01		
Loughborough Jn	d		15 49			16 04				16 19		16 34						16 53				
Elephant & Castle	d		15 54	16 00		16 09	16 18			16 24	16 30	16 39	16 44				16 56	17 00	17 04	17 08	17 12	
London Blackfriars 3 ⊖	d		16 00	16 04	16 08	16 14	16 22		16 26	16 30	16 38	16 44	16 52			16 56	17 00	17 04	17 08	17 12	17 16	17 22
City Thameslink 3	d		16 02	16 06	16 10	16 16	16 24		16 28	16 32	16 40	16 46	16 54			16 58	17 02	17 06	17 10	17 14	17 18	17 24
Farringdon 3 ⊖	d		16 06	16 10	16 13	16 19	16 27		16 31	16 35	16 43	16 49	16 57			17 01	17 05	17 09	17 13	17 17	17 23	17 27
St Pancras International 15 ⊖	d	16 30						17 00						17 15	17 30							
St Pancras International 15 ⊖	a		16 09	16 13	16 17	16 23	16 31		16 35	16 39	16 47	16 53	17 01			17 05	17 09	17 13	17 17	17 21	17 27	17 31
	d		16 10	16 14	16 18	16 24	16 32		16 36	16 40	16 48	16 54	17 02			17 06	17 10	17 14	17 18	17 22	17 28	17 32
Kentish Town ⊖	d		16 14	16a20		16 28				16 44		16 58						17 18			17 32	
West Hampstead Thameslink ⊖	d		16 20			16 32				16 48		17 02					17 18	17 24			17 36	
Cricklewood	d		16 23			16 35				16 51		17 05						17 27			17 39	
Hendon	d		16 26			16 38				16 54		17 08						17 30			17 42	
Mill Hill Broadway	d		16 30			16 43				16 59		17 13					17 25	17 34			17 47	
Elstree & Borehamwood	d		16 34			16 47				17 04		17 17					17 30	17 39			17 51	
Radlett	d		16 38			16 52				17 08		17 22					17 34	17 46			17 56	
St Albans City	d		16 46		16 40	16a59	16 52		16 56	17 14	17 08	17a29	17 22			17 26	17 40	17a52	17 38	17 44	18a03	17 52
Harpenden	d		16 54		16 46		16 58		17 04	17 20	17 14		17 28			17 34	17 46			17 50		17 58
Luton Airport Parkway 7 ✈	d	16 51	17 00		16 52				17 10	17 26	17 20					17 40	17 52		17 46	17 56		
Luton 10	d	16 55	17a04		16 55		17 04		17 13	17a30	17 23		17 34	17a40		17 43	17a55		17 49	17 59		18 04
Leagrave	d				16 59				17 17		17 27					17 47				18 03		
Harlington	d				17 04				17 22		17 32					17 52				18 08		
Flitwick	d				17 08		17 14		17 26		17 36		17 44			17 56			18 00	18 12		18 16
Bedford 7	a	17 09			17 20		17 26	17 33	17 38		17 50		17 58		18 07	18 08			18 12	18 24		18 28

A ■1 to City Thameslink

Brighton, Gatwick Airport and South London - City of London, St. Albans, Luton and Bedford

		FC ■	EM ◇■	EM ◇■	FC	FC ■	SE	FC	FC ■	SE ■		EM ◇■	FC	SE ■	EM ◇■	SE ■	FC	FC	FC ■	FC ■		EM ◇■	FC	SE ■	FC
Brighton 10	d	16 07				16 24			16 30										17 03	17 07					
Preston Park	d	16 11							16 34											17 11					
Hassocks 4	d	16 17							16 40											17 17					
Burgess Hill 4	d	16 21							16 44										17 13	17 21					
Wivelsfield 4	d								16 46																
Haywards Heath 3	d	16 26				16 38			16 50										17 18	17 26					
Balcombe	d	16 31							16 57																
Three Bridges 4	d	16 37				16 47			17 03										17 27						
Gatwick Airport 10 ✈	d	16 42				16 53			17 08										17 31	17 39					
Redhill	d																								
East Croydon	d	16 58				17 09			17 23										17 47	17 58					
Sevenoaks 4	d						16 32							17 02										17 32	
Bat & Ball	d						16 35							17 05										17 35	
Otford 4	d						16 38							17 08										17 38	
Shoreham (Kent)	d						16 41							17 11										17 41	
Eynsford	d						16 45							17 15										17 45	
Swanley 4	d						16 50							17 20										17 50	
St Mary Cray 4	d						16 54							17 24										17 54	
Bickley	d						16 58							17 28		17 42								17 58	
Bromley South	d						17 01							17 31		17 45								18 01	
Shortlands 4	d						17 04							17 34										18 04	
Ravensbourne	d						17 06							17 36										18 06	
Beckenham Hill	d						17 08							17 38										18 08	
Bellingham	d						17 10							17 40										18 10	
Catford	d						17 13							17 43										18 13	
Crofton Park	d						17 15							17 45										18 15	
Nunhead 4	d						17 18							17 48										18 18	
Peckham Rye 4	d						17 20							17 50										18 20	
Denmark Hill 4	d						17 24							17 54										18 23	
Sutton (Surrey) 4	d				16 37			17 08					17 11					17 42					17 41		18 08
West Sutton	d				16 40								17 14										17 44		
Sutton Common	d				16 42								17 16										17 46		
St Helier	d				16 45								17 19										17 49		
Morden South	d				16 47								17 21										17 51		
South Merton	d				16 49								17 23										17 53		
Wimbledon Chase	d				16 51								17 25										17 55		
Wimbledon 6 ⊖	d				17 00								17 30										18 00		
Haydons Road	d				17 02								17 32										18 02		
Tooting	d				17 05								17 35										18 05		
Carshalton	d							17 11										17 45							18 11
Hackbridge	d							17 13										17 47							18 13
Mitcham Junction	d							17 16										17 50							18 16
Mitcham Eastfields	d							17 19										17 53							18 19
Streatham 4	d				17 10			17 23					17 40					17 57					18 10		18 23
Tulse Hill 3	d	17 12			17 16			17 27					17 44					18 01		18 12			18 16		18 27
London Bridge 4 ⊖	a					17 27													18 13						
	d					17 27													18 13						
West Croydon	d																								
Herne Hill 4	d				17 20			17 31		17 43			17 48					18 06					18 20		18 31
Loughborough Jn.	d				17 23			17 34		17 46			17 51					18 09					18 23		18 34
Elephant & Castle	d	17 22			17 28		17 34	17 39		17 52			17 56	18 00		18 05	18 09	18 14		18 22			18 28	18 32	18 40
London Blackfriars 3 ⊖	d	17 26			17 32	17 36	17 40	17 46	17 52	17 56			18 00	18 06		18 10	18 14	18 18	18 22	18 26			18 32	18 36	18 44
City Thameslink 3	d	17 28			17 34	17 38	17 42	17 48	17 54	17 58			18 02	18 08		18 12	18 16	18 20	18 24	18 28			18 34	18 38	18 46
Farringdon 3 ⊖	d	17 31			17 37	17 41	17 45	17 51	17 57	18 01			18 05	18 11		18 15	18 19	18 23	18 27	18 31			18 37	18 41	18 49
St Pancras International 15 ⊖	d		17 45	18 00								18 25			18 30							19 00			
St Pancras International 15 ⊖	a	17 35			17 41	17 45	17 49	17 55	18 01	18 05			18 09	18 15		18 19	18 23	18 27	18 31	18 35			18 41	18 45	18 53
	d	17 36			17 42	17 46	17 50	17 56	18 02	18 06			18 10	18 16		18 20	18 24	18 28	18 32	18 36			18 42	18 46	18 54
Kentish Town ⊖	d				17 46			18 00					18 14					18 32					18 46		
West Hampstead Thameslink ⊖	d				17 50		17 58	18 04					18 18				18 32	18 36					18 52	18 53	19 02
Cricklewood	d				17 53			18 07					18 21					18 39					18 55		
Hendon	d				17 56			18 10					18 24					18 42					18 58		
Mill Hill Broadway	d				18 01		18 06	18 15					18 29				18 40	18 47					19 02		19 10
Elstree & Borehamwood	d				18 05		18 10	18 19					18 33				18 44	18 51					19 07		19 14
Radlett	d				18 10		18 14	18 24					18 40				18 48	18 56					19 12		19 18
St Albans City	d	17 56			18 16	18 06	18 20	18a31	18 22	18 26			18 46	18 36		18 42	18 54	19a03	18 52	18 56			19 18	19 06	19 24
Harpenden	d	18 04			18 22	18 14	18 26		18 28	18 34			18 52			18 48	19 00		18 58	19 04			19 24	19 14	19 30
Luton Airport Parkway 7 ✈	d	18 10	18a09		18 28	18 20	18 32			18 40			18 58	18 48	18 54	18 54	19 06			19 10			19 30	19 20	19 36
Luton 10	d	18 13		18 23	18a32	18 23	18 37		18 34	18 43		18a50	19a02	18 51		18 57	19 09		19 04	19 13		19 23	19a34	19 23	19 39
Leagrave	d	18 17				18 27	18 41			18 47						19 01	19 13			19 17				19 27	19 43
Harlington	d	18 22				18 32	18 46			18 52						19 06	19 18			19 22				19 32	19 48
Flitwick	d	18 26				18 36	18 50		18 46	18 56				19 00		19 10	19 22		19 14	19 26				19 36	19 52
Bedford 7	a	18 38		18 38		18 48	19 04		18 58	19 08				19 12	19 09	19 22	19 34		19 26	19 38		19 39		19 48	20 04

Table 52 — Mondays to Fridays

Brighton, Gatwick Airport and South London - City of London, St. Albans, Luton and Bedford

		FC	FC ■	FC ■	EM ◇■	FC		SE ■ A	FC ■	FC	FC ■	EM ◇■	FC	SE	FC ■	FC		FC ■	EM ◇■	FC	SE	FC ■	SN ◇■	FC	FC ■
Brighton 10	d		17 24	17 37					18 04		18 07				18 34			18 37					18 59		19 07
Preston Park	d		17 28	17 41							18 11							18 41					19 03		19 11
Hassocks 4	d		17 34	17 47							18 17							18 47					19 09		19 17
Burgess Hill 4	d		17 38	17 51					18 14		18 21							18 51					19 13		19 21
Wivelsfield 4	d		17 40	17 53							18 23							18 53					19 15		19 23
Haywards Heath 3	d		17 46	18 02					18 18		18 32				18 47			19 02					19 21		19 32
Balcombe	d			18 07							18 37														19 37
Three Bridges 4	d		17 55	18 13							18 42				18 56			19 12				19 27	19a31		19 42
Gatwick Airport 10 ✈	d		18 00	18 17					18 31		18 46				19 01			19 16				19 31			19 46
Redhill	d																								
East Croydon	d		18 17	18 33					18 47		19 02				19 17			19 32				19 47			20 02
Sevenoaks 4	d							18 02						18 32							19 02				
Bat & Ball	d							18 05						18 35							19 05				
Otford 4	d							18 08						18 38							19 08				
Shoreham (Kent)	d							18 11						18 41							19 11				
Eynsford	d							18 15						18 45							19 15				
Swanley 4	d							18 20						18 50							19 20				
St Mary Cray 4	d							18 24						18 54							19 24				
Bickley	d							18 28						18 58							19 28				
Bromley South	d							18 31						19 01							19 31				
Shortlands 4	d							18 34						19 04							19 34				
Ravensbourne	d							18 36						19 06							19 36				
Beckenham Hill	d							18 38						19 08							19 38				
Bellingham	d							18 40						19 10							19 40				
Catford	d							18 43						19 13							19 43				
Crofton Park	d							18 45						19 15							19 45				
Nunhead 4	d							18 48						19 18							19 48				
Peckham Rye 4	d							18 50						19 20							19 50				
Denmark Hill 4	d							18 54						19 24							19 54				
Sutton (Surrey) 4	d					18 09				18 38			18 43			19 08				19 13				19 42	
West Sutton	d					18 12							18 46							19 16					
Sutton Common	d					18 14							18 48							19 18					
St Helier	d					18 17							18 51							19 21					
Morden South	d					18 19							18 53							19 23					
South Merton	d					18 21							18 55							19 25					
Wimbledon Chase	d					18 23							18 57							19 27					
Wimbledon 6 ⊖	d					18 28							19 00							19 30					
Haydons Road	d					18 30							19 02							19 32					
Tooting	d					18 33							19 05							19 35					
Carshalton	d									18 41						19 11								19 45	
Hackbridge	d									18 43						19 13								19 47	
Mitcham Junction	d									18 46						19 16								19 50	
Mitcham Eastfields	d									18 49						19 19								19 53	
Streatham 4	d					18 40				18 53			19 10			19 23				19 40				19 57	
Tulse Hill 3	d		18 33			18 44				18 57			19 14			19 27				19 44				20 01	
London Bridge 4 ⊖	a			18 46					19 00		19 15				19 30			19 45				20 00			20 15
	d			18 46					19 00		19 17				19 30			19 45				20 00			20 15
West Croydon	d																								
Herne Hill 4	d					18 48				19 01			19 17			19 31				19 47				20 05	
Loughborough Jn.	d					18 51				19 04			19 20			19 34				19 50				20 08	
Elephant & Castle	d	18 44	18 48			18 56		19 00		19 09			19 25	19 30		19 39				19 55	20 00			20 13	
London Blackfriars 3 ⊖	d	18 48	18 52	18 56		19 00		19 06	19 10	19 18	19 24		19 30	19 34	19 38	19 46		19 54		20 00	20 04	20 08		20 18	20 24
City Thameslink 3	d	18 50	18 54	18 58		19 02		19 08	19 12	19 20	19 26		19 32	19 36	19 40	19 48		19 56		20 02	20 06	20 10		20 20	20 26
Farringdon 3 ⊖	d	18 53	18 57	19 01		19 05		19 11	19 15	19 23	19 30		19 36	19 40	19 44	19 52		20 00		20 06	20 10	20 14		20 24	20 30
St Pancras International 15 ⊖	d				19 30							20 00							20 30						
St Pancras International 15 ⊖	a	18 57	19 01	19 05		19 09		19 15	19 19	19 27	19 33		19 39	19 43	19 47	19 55		20 03		20 09	20 13	20 17		20 27	20 33
	d	18 58	19 02	19 06		19 10		19 16	19 20	19 28	19 34		19 40	19 44	19 48	19 56		20 04		20 10	20 14	20 18		20 28	20 34
Kentish Town ⊖	d	19 02				19 14				19 32			19 44	19a50		20 00				20 14	20a20			20 32	
West Hampstead Thameslink ⊖	d	19 06				19 18			19 28	19 36	19 41		19 50			20 04		20 11		20 18				20 36	20 41
Cricklewood	d	19 09				19 21				19 39			19 53			20 07				20 21				20 39	
Hendon	d	19 12				19 24				19 42			19 56			20 10				20 24				20 42	
Mill Hill Broadway	d	19 17				19 28				19 46			20 00			20 14				20 28				20 46	
Elstree & Borehamwood	d	19 21				19 32			19 38	19 50			20 04			20 18				20 32				20 50	
Radlett	d	19 26				19 36				19 54			20 08			20 22				20 38				20 54	
St Albans City	d	19a33	19 22	19 26		19 42		19 36	19 46	20a01	19 55		20 14		20 10	20a29		20 25		20 44		20 40		21a01	20 55
Harpenden	d		19 28	19 34		19 48		19 44	19 52		20 02		20 20		20 16			20 32		20 50		20 46			21 02
Luton Airport Parkway 7 ✈	d			19 40	19 51	19 54			19 58		20 08		20 26		20 22			20 38	20 51	20 56		20 52			21 08
Luton 10	d		19 34	19 43		19a58		19 50	20 01		20 11	20 23	20a30		20 25			20 41		21a00		20 55			21 11
Leagrave	d			19 47				19 54	20 04		20 14				20 28			20 44				20 58			21 14
Harlington	d			19 52					20 10		20 20				20 34			20 50				21 04			21 20
Flitwick	d		19 46	19 56					20 14		20 24				20 38			20 54				21 08			21 24
Bedford 7	a		19 58	20 08	20 07			20 12	20 26		20 36	20 37			20 50			21 06	21 06			21 20			21 36

A ■ from London Blackfriars

Brighton, Gatwick Airport and South London - City of London, St. Albans, Luton and Bedford

		EM ◇1	FC	SE	FC 1	FC	FC 1	FC	SE	FC 1	SE	FC	SE	EM ◇1	FC 1	SE	EM ◇1	FC	FC 1	FC	FC 1	FC 1
Brighton 10	d				19 34		19 37			20 04					20 07				20 34		20 37	21 11
Preston Park	d						19 41								20 11						20 41	
Hassocks 4	d						19 47								20 17						20 47	21 19
Burgess Hill 4	d						19 51								20 21						20 51	21 23
Wivelsfield 4	d						19 53								20 23						20 53	
Haywards Heath 3	d				19 47		20 02			20 17					20 32				20 47		21 02	21 32
Balcombe	d														20 37							21 37
Three Bridges 4	d				19 56		20 12			20 26					20 42				20 56		21 12	21 42
Gatwick Airport 10 ✈	d				20 01		20 16			20 31					20 46				21 01		21 16	21 46
Redhill	d																					
East Croydon	d				20 17		20 32			20 47					21 02				21 17		21 32	22a02
Sevenoaks 4	d			19 32					20 02		20 32		21 02			21 32						
Bat & Ball	d			19 35					20 05		20 35		21 05			21 35						
Otford 4	d			19 38					20 08		20 38		21 08			21 38						
Shoreham (Kent)	d			19 41					20 11		20 41		21 11			21 41						
Eynsford	d			19 45					20 15		20 45		21 15			21 45						
Swanley 4	d			19 50					20 20		20 50		21 20			21 50						
St Mary Cray 4	d			19 54					20 24		20 54		21 24			21 54						
Bickley	d			19 58					20 28		20 58		21 28			21 58						
Bromley South	d			20 01					20 31		21 01		21 31			22 01						
Shortlands 4	d			20 04					20 34		21 04		21 34			22 04						
Ravensbourne	d			20 06					20 36		21 06		21 36			22 06						
Beckenham Hill	d			20 08					20 38		21 08		21 38			22 08						
Bellingham	d			20 10					20 40		21 10		21 40			22 10						
Catford	d			20 13					20 43		21 13		21 43			22 13						
Crofton Park	d			20 15					20 45		21 15		21 45			22 15						
Nunhead 4	d			20 18					20 48		21 18		21 48			22 18						
Peckham Rye 4	d			20 20					20 50		21 20		21 50			22 20						
Denmark Hill 4	d			20 24					20 54		21a23		21a53			22a23						
Sutton (Surrey) 4	d		19 38			20 10		20 07				20 40						20 37		21 10		
West Sutton	d		19 41					20 10										20 40				
Sutton Common	d		19 43					20 12										20 42				
St Helier	d		19 46					20 15										20 45				
Morden South	d		19 48					20 17										20 47				
South Merton	d		19 50					20 19										20 49				
Wimbledon Chase	d		19 52					20 21										20 51				
Wimbledon 6 ⊖	d		19 56					20 26										20 56				
Haydons Road	d		19 58					20 28										20 58				
Tooting	d		20 01					20 31										21 01				
Carshalton	d					20 13						20 43								21 13		
Hackbridge	d					20 15						20 45								21 15		
Mitcham Junction	d					20 18						20 48								21 18		
Mitcham Eastfields	d					20 21						20 51								21 21		
Streatham 4	d		20 06			20 25		20 36				20 55						21 06		21 25		
Tulse Hill 3	d		20 12			20 29		20 42				20 59						21 12		21 29		
London Bridge 4 ⊖	a				20 30		20 45			21 00					21 15				21 30		21 45	
	d				20 30		20 45			21 00					21 15				21 30		21 45	
West Croydon	d																					
Herne Hill 4	d		20 16			20 35		20 46				21 05						21 16		21 35		
Loughborough Jn	d		20 19			20 38		20 49				21 08						21 19		21 38		
Elephant & Castle	d		20 24	20 30		20 43		20 54	21 00			21 13						21 24		21 43		
London Blackfriars 3 ⊖	d		20 30	20 34	20 38	20 48	20 54	21 00	21 04	21 08		21 18			21 24			21 30	21 38	21 48	21 54	
City Thameslink 3	d		20 32	20 36	20 40	20 50	20 56	21 02	21 06	21 10		21 20			21 26			21 32	21 40	21 50	21 56	
Farringdon 3 ⊖	d		20 36	20 40	20 44	20 54	21 00	21 06	21 10	21 14		21 24			21 30			21 36	21 44	21 54	22 00	
St Pancras International 15 ⊖	d	21 00												21 30			22 00					
St Pancras International 15 ⊖	a		20 39	20 43	20 47	20 57	21 03	21 09	21 13	21 17		21 27			21 33			21 39	21 47	21 57	22 03	
	d		20 40	20 44	20 48	20 58	21 04	21 10	21 14	21 18		21 28			21 34			21 40	21 48	21 58	22 04	
Kentish Town ⊖	d		20 44	20a50		21 02		21 14	21a20			21 32						21 44		22 02		
West Hampstead Thameslink ⊖	d		20 48			21 06	21 11	21 18				21 36			21 41			21 48		22 06	22 11	
Cricklewood	d		20 51			21 09		21 21				21 39						21 51		22 09		
Hendon	d		20 54			21 12		21 24				21 42						21 54		22 12		
Mill Hill Broadway	d		20 58			21 16		21 28				21 46						21 58		22 16		
Elstree & Borehamwood	d		21 02			21 20		21 32				21 50						22 02		22 20		
Radlett	d		21 08			21 24		21 38				21 54						22 08		22 24		
St Albans City	d		21 14		21 10	21a31	21 25	21 44		21 40		22a01			21 55			22 14	22 10	22a31	22 25	
Harpenden	d		21 20		21 16		21 32	21 50		21 46					22 02			22 20	22 16		22 32	
Luton Airport Parkway 7 ✈	d		21 26		21 22		21 38	21 56		21 52				21 53	22 08			22 26	22 22		22 38	
Luton 10	d	21 23	21a30		21 25		21 41	22a00		21 55					22 11		22 24	22a30	22 25		22 41	
Leagrave	d				21 28		21 44			21 58					22 14				22 28		22 44	
Harlington	d				21 34		21 50			22 04					22 20				22 34		22 50	
Flitwick	d				21 38		21 54			22 08					22 24				22 38		22 54	
Bedford 7	a	21 37			21 50		22 06			22 22				22 08	22 36		22 39		22 50		23 06	

Table 52 Mondays to Fridays

Brighton, Gatwick Airport and South London - City of London, St. Albans, Luton and Bedford

		SN 1	FC 1	SE	FC 1	EM ◇1	FC	SE	FC 1	FC 1	FC	FC 1	FC 1	EM ◇1	FC	FC 1	FC 1	FC
Brighton 10	d	21 34	21 37		22 07					22 33			23 11				23 37	
Preston Park	d		21 41		22 11					22 37							23 41	
Hassocks 4	d		21 47		22 17					22 43			23 19				23 47	
Burgess Hill 4	d		21 51		22 21					22 47			23 23				23 51	
Wivelsfield 4	d		21 53		22 23					22 49							23 53	
Haywards Heath 3	d	21 47	22 02		22 32					22 54			23 28				23 59	
Balcombe	d				22 37					23 00							00 04	
Three Bridges 4	d	21 56	22 12		22 42					23 12			23 38				00 10	
Gatwick Airport 10 ✈	d	22 02	22 16		22 46					23 16			23 43				00 15	
Redhill	d																00 22	
East Croydon	d	22a17	22a32		23a02					23a32			00a02				00a35	
Sevenoaks 4	d			22 02				22 32										
Bat & Ball	d			22 05				22 35										
Otford 4	d			22 08				22 38										
Shoreham (Kent)	d			22 11				22 41										
Eynsford	d			22 15				22 45										
Swanley 4	d			22 20				22 50										
St Mary Cray 4	d			22 24				22 54										
Bickley	d			22 28				22 58										
Bromley South	d			22 31				23 01										
Shortlands 4	d			22 34				23 04										
Ravensbourne	d			22 36				23 06										
Beckenham Hill	d			22 38				23 08										
Bellingham	d			22 40				23 10										
Catford	d			22 43				23 13										
Crofton Park	d			22 45				23 15										
Nunhead 4	d			22 48				23 18										
Peckham Rye 4	d			22 50				23 20										
Denmark Hill 4	d			22a53				23a23										
Sutton (Surrey) 4	d						21 10											
West Sutton	d						21 13											
Sutton Common	d						21 15											
St Helier	d						21 18											
Morden South	d						21 20											
South Merton	d						21 22											
Wimbledon Chase	d						21 24											
Wimbledon 6 ⊖	d						21 36											
Haydons Road	d						21 38											
Tooting	d						21 41											
Carshalton	d																	
Hackbridge	d																	
Mitcham Junction	d																	
Mitcham Eastfields	d																	
Streatham 4	d						21 46											
Tulse Hill 3	d						21 50											
London Bridge 4 ⊖	a																	
	d																	
West Croydon	d																	
Herne Hill 4	d						21 54											
Loughborough Jn	d						21 57											
Elephant & Castle	d						22 02											
London Blackfriars 3 ⊖	d						22 08											
City Thameslink 3	d						22 10											
Farringdon 3 ⊖	d						22 14											
St Pancras International 15 ⊖	d					22 25			22 32		22 48	23 02		23 15	23 18	23 32		23 48
St Pancras International 15 ⊖	a						22 17											
	d						22 18											
Kentish Town ⊖	d						22 22				22 53				23 23			23 53
West Hampstead Thameslink ⊖	d						22 26		22 40		22 57	23 10			23 27	23 40		23 57
Cricklewood	d						22 29				23 00				23 30			00 01
Hendon	d						22 32				23 03				23 33			00 03
Mill Hill Broadway	d						22 36				23 07				23 37			00 07
Elstree & Borehamwood	d						22 40				23 11				23 41			00 11
Radlett	d						22 44				23 16				23 46			00 16
St Albans City	d						22 50		22 56		23 22	23 26			23 52	23 56		00 22
Harpenden	d						22 56		23 02		23 28	23 32			23 58	00 02		00 28
Luton Airport Parkway 7 ✈	d					22 48	23 02		23 08		23 34	23 38			00 04	00 08		00 34
Luton 10	d						23 05		23 11		23 37	23 41		23 46	00 07	00 11		00 37
Leagrave	d						23 09		23 15		23 41	23 45			00 11	00 15		00 41
Harlington	d						23 14		23 21		23 46	23 50			00 16	00 20		00 46
Flitwick	d						23 18		23 25		23 50	23 54			00 20	00 24		00 50
Bedford 7	a					23 03	23 30		23 38		00 04	00 08		00 11	00 34	00 38		01 04

Table 52

Saturdays

Bedford, Luton, St.Albans - London

Station		FC 1	FC 1	FC 1	FC	FC	FC 1	FC 1	FC	FC	FC	FC	EM ◇1	FC 1	FC	FC 1	FC	FC 1	FC	FC 1	EM ◇1	FC	FC 1
Bedford 7	d	22p52	23p12	23p32	00 02	01 02	02 02	03 02	03 42	04 12	04 42	05 12	05 32	05 38	05 42	06 08		06 24		06 38	06 49		06 54
Flitwick	d	23p02	23p22	23p42	00 12	01 12	02 12	03 12	03 52	04 22	04 52	05 22		05 48	05 52	06 18		06 34		06 48			07 04
Harlington	d	23p06	23p26	23p46	00 16	01 16	02 16	03 16	03 56	04 26	04 56	05 26		05 52	05 56	06 22		06 38		06 52			07 08
Leagrave	d	23p11	23p31	23p51	00 21	01 21	02 21	03 21	04 01	04 31	05 01	05 31		05 57	06 01	06 27		06 43		06 57			07 13
Luton 10	d	23p16	23p36	23p56	00 26	01 26	02 26	03 26	04 06	04 36	05 06	05 36		06 02	06 06	06 32	06 40	06 48		07 02	07 04	07 10	07 18
Luton Airport Parkway 7 ✈	d	23p18	23p38	23p58	00 28	01 28	02 28	03 28	04 08	04 38	05 08	05 38	05 55	06 04	06 08	06 34	06 42	06 50		07 04		07 12	07 20
Harpenden	d	23p24	23p44	00 04	00 34	01 34	02 34	03 34	04 14	04 44	05 14	05 44		06 10	06 14	06 40	06 48	06 56		07 10		07 18	07 26
St Albans City	d	23p30	23p50	00 10	00 40	01 40	02 40	03 40	04 20	04 50	05 20	05 50		06 16	06 20	06 46	06 54	07 02		07 16		07 24	07 32
Radlett	d	23p36	23p56	00 16	00 46	01 46	02 46	03 46	04 26	04 56	05 26	05 56			06 25		06 59					07 29	
Elstree & Borehamwood	d	23p40	00 01	00 20	00 50	01 50	02 50	03 50	04 30	05 00	05 30	06 00			06 30		07 03			07 23		07 33	
Mill Hill Broadway	d	23p44	00 04	00 24	00 54	01 54	02 54	03 54	04 34	05 04	05 34	06 04			06 34		07 07					07 37	
Hendon	d	23p48	00 08	00 28	00 58	01 58	02 58	03 58	04 38	05 08	05 38	06 08			06 38		07 10					07 40	
Cricklewood	d	23p51	00 11	00 31	01 01	02 01	03 01	04 01	04 41	05 11	05 41	06 11			06 41		07 14		←			07 44	
West Hampstead Thameslink ⊖	d	23p54	00 14	00 34	01 04	02 04	03 04	04 04	04 45	05 14	05 44	06 14		06 30	06 44	06 58	07 18	07 14	07 18	07 32		07 48	07 44
Kentish Town ⊖	a	00 02	00 20	00 40	01 10	02 10	03 10	04 10	04 50	05 20	05 50	06 20			06 50		→		07 24			→	
St Pancras International 15 ⊖	a	00 06	00 26	00 46	01 16	02 16	03 16	04 16	04 56	05 26	05 56	06 26	06 21	06 40	06 56	07 07		07 24		07 41	07 31		07 54
	d																						
St Pancras International 15 ⊖	a																						
	d																						
Farringdon 3 ⊖	d																						
City Thameslink 3	d																						
London Blackfriars 3 ⊖	a																						
London Bridge 4	a																						

Station		FC	FC 1	EM ◇1	FC	FC 1	FC	FC 1	EM ◇1	FC	FC 1	FC	FC 1	EM ◇1	FC	FC 1	FC	FC 1	EM ◇1	FC	FC 1	FC	FC 1
Bedford 7	d		07 08	07 19		07 24		07 38	07 49		07 54		08 08	08 19		08 24		08 38	08 49		08 54		09 08
Flitwick	d		07 18			07 34		07 48			08 04		08 18			08 34		08 48			09 04		09 18
Harlington	d		07 22			07 38		07 52			08 08		08 22			08 38		08 52			09 08		09 22
Leagrave	d		07 27			07 43		07 57			08 13		08 27			08 43		08 57			09 13		09 27
Luton 10	d		07 32		07 40	07 48		08 02	08 05	08 10	08 18		08 32		08 40	08 48		09 02	09 05	09 10	09 18		09 32
Luton Airport Parkway 7 ✈	d		07 34	07 35	07 42	07 50		08 04		08 12	08 20		08 34	08 35	08 42	08 50		09 04		09 12	09 20		09 34
Harpenden	d		07 40		07 48	07 56		08 10		08 18	08 26		08 40		08 48	08 56		09 10		09 18	09 26		09 40
St Albans City	d		07 46		07 54	08 02		08 16		08 24	08 32		08 46		08 54	09 02		09 16		09 24	09 32		09 46
Radlett	d				07 59					08 29					08 59					09 29			
Elstree & Borehamwood	d		07 53		08 03			08 23		08 33			08 53		09 03			09 23		09 33			09 53
Mill Hill Broadway	d				08 07					08 37					09 07					09 37			
Hendon	d				08 10					08 40					09 10					09 40			
Cricklewood	d	←			08 14		←			08 44		←			09 14		←			09 44		←	
West Hampstead Thameslink ⊖	d	07 48	08 02		08 18	08 14	08 18	08 32		08 48	08 44	08 48	09 02		09 18	09 14	09 18	09 32		09 48	09 45	09 48	10 02
Kentish Town ⊖	a	07 54			→		08 24			→		08 54			→		09 24			→		09 54	
St Pancras International 15 ⊖	a		08 11	08 00		08 24		08 41	08 31		08 54		09 11	09 01		09 24		09 41	09 29		09 54		10 11
	d																						
St Pancras International 15 ⊖	a																						
	d																						
Farringdon 3 ⊖	d																						
City Thameslink 3	d																						
London Blackfriars 3 ⊖	a																						
London Bridge 4	a																						

Station		EM ◇1	FC	FC 1	FC	FC 1	EM ◇1	FC	FC 1	FC	FC 1	EM ◇1	FC 1	FC 1	EM ◇1	FC 1	FC 1	EM ◇1	FC	FC 1	FC	FC 1
Bedford 7	d	09 19		09 24		09 40	09 49		09 54		10 08	10 19	10 24	10 38	10 49	10 54	11 08	11 19		11 24		11 38
Flitwick	d			09 34		09 50			10 04		10 18		10 34	10 48		11 04	11 18			11 34		11 48
Harlington	d			09 38		09 54			10 08		10 22		10 38	10 52		11 08	11 22			11 38		11 52
Leagrave	d			09 43		09 59			10 13		10 27		10 43	10 57		11 13	11 27			11 43		11 57
Luton 10	d		09 40	09 48		10 04	10 05	10 10	10 18		10 32		10 48	11 02	11 05	11 18	11 32		11 40	11 48		12 02
Luton Airport Parkway 7 ✈	d	09 35	09 42	09 50		10 06		10 12	10 20		10 34	10 35	10 50	11 04		11 20	11 34	11 35	11 42	11 50		12 04
Harpenden	d		09 48	09 56		10 12		10 18	10 26		10 40		10 56	11 10		11 26	11 40		11 48	11 56		12 10
St Albans City	d		09 54	10 02		10 18		10 24	10 32		10 46		11 02	11 16		11 32	11 46		11 54	12 02		12 16
Radlett	d		09 59					10 29											11 59			
Elstree & Borehamwood	d		10 03			10 25		10 33			10 53			11 23			11 53		12 03			12 23
Mill Hill Broadway	d		10 07					10 37											12 07			
Hendon	d		10 10					10 40											12 10			
Cricklewood	d		10 14		←			10 44		←									12 14		←	
West Hampstead Thameslink ⊖	d		10 18	10 14	10 18	10 34		10 48	10 44	10 48	11 01		11 14	11 32		11 44	12 02		12 18	12 14	12 18	12 32
Kentish Town ⊖	a		→		10 24			→		10 54									→		12 24	
St Pancras International 15 ⊖	a	10 00		10 24		10 43	10 29		10 54		11 11	11 01	11 24	11 41	11 29	11 54	12 11	12 01		12 24		12 41
	d																					
St Pancras International 15 ⊖	a																					
	d																					
Farringdon 3 ⊖	d																					
City Thameslink 3	d																					
London Blackfriars 3 ⊖	a																					
London Bridge 4	a																					

Please refer to separate pages within this table for services operating between South London and Brighton

At weekends please use local bus and tube services to travel to/from St Pancras International and London Bridge when no trains are operating. See local publicity for details of alternative routes and services that are available across central London

Table 52

Saturdays

Bedford, Luton, St.Albans - London

Station		EM ◇1	FC	FC 1	FC	FC 1	EM ◇1	FC	FC 1	FC	FC 1	EM ◇1	FC	FC 1	FC	FC 1	EM ◇1	FC	FC 1	FC	FC 1	EM ◇1	FC
Bedford 7	d	11 49		11 54		12 08	12 19		12 24		12 38	12 49		12 54		13 08	13 19		13 24		13 38	13 49	
Flitwick	d			12 04		12 18			12 34		12 48			13 04		13 18			13 34		13 48		
Harlington	d			12 08		12 22			12 38		12 52			13 08		13 22			13 38		13 52		
Leagrave	d			12 13		12 27			12 43		12 57			13 13		13 27			13 43		13 57		
Luton 10	d	12 05	12 10	12 18		12 32		12 40	12 48		13 02	13 05	13 10	13 18		13 32		13 40	13 48		14 02	14 05	14 10
Luton Airport Parkway 7 ✈	d		12 12	12 20		12 34	12 35	12 42	12 50		13 04		13 12	13 20		13 34	13 35	13 42	13 50		14 04		14 12
Harpenden	d		12 18	12 26		12 40		12 48	12 56		13 10		13 18	13 26		13 40		13 48	13 56		14 10		14 18
St Albans City	d		12 24	12 32		12 46		12 54	13 02		13 16		13 24	13 32		13 46		13 54	14 02		14 16		14 24
Radlett	d		12 29					12 59					13 29					13 59					14 29
Elstree & Borehamwood	d		12 33			12 53		13 03			13 23		13 33			13 53		14 03			14 23		14 33
Mill Hill Broadway	d		12 37					13 07					13 37					14 07					14 37
Hendon	d		12 40					13 10					13 40					14 10					14 40
Cricklewood	d		12 44		←			13 14		←			13 44		←			14 14		←			14 44
West Hampstead Thameslink ⊖	d		12 48	12 44	12 48	13 02		13 18	13 14	13 18	13 32		13 48	13 44	13 48	14 02		14 18	14 15	14 18	14 32		14 48
Kentish Town ⊖	a		→		12 54			→		13 24			→		13 54			→		14 24			→
St Pancras International 15 ⊖	a	12 29		12 54		13 11	13 01		13 24		13 41	13 29		13 54		14 11	14 01		14 25		14 41	14 29	
	d																						
St Pancras International 15 ⊖	a																						
	d																						
Farringdon 3 ⊖	d																						
City Thameslink 3	d																						
London Blackfriars 3 ⊖	a																						
London Bridge 4	a																						

Station		FC 1	FC	FC 1	EM ◇1	FC	FC 1	FC	FC 1	EM ◇1	FC	FC 1	FC	FC 1	EM ◇1	FC	FC 1	FC	FC 1	EM ◇1	FC	FC 1
Bedford 7	d	13 54		14 08	14 19		14 24		14 38	14 49		14 54		15 08	15 19		15 24		15 38	15 49		15 54
Flitwick	d	14 04		14 18			14 34		14 48			15 04		15 18			15 34		15 48			16 04
Harlington	d	14 08		14 22			14 38		14 52			15 08		15 22			15 38		15 52			16 08
Leagrave	d	14 13		14 27			14 43		14 57			15 13		15 27			15 43		15 57			16 13
Luton 10	d	14 18		14 32		14 40	14 48		15 02	15 05	15 10	15 18		15 32		15 40	15 48		16 02	16 05	16 10	16 18
Luton Airport Parkway 7 ✈	d	14 20		14 34	14 35	14 42	14 50		15 04		15 12	15 20		15 34	15 35	15 42	15 50		16 04		16 12	16 20
Harpenden	d	14 26		14 40		14 48	14 56		15 10		15 18	15 26		15 40		15 48	15 56		16 10		16 18	16 26
St Albans City	d	14 32		14 46		14 54	15 02		15 16		15 24	15 32		15 46		15 54	16 02		16 16		16 24	16 32
Radlett	d					14 59					15 29					15 59					16 29	
Elstree & Borehamwood	d			14 53		15 03			15 23		15 33			15 53		16 03			16 23		16 33	
Mill Hill Broadway	d					15 07					15 37					16 07					16 37	
Hendon	d					15 10					15 40					16 10					16 40	
Cricklewood	d		←			15 14		←			15 44		←			16 14		←			16 44	
West Hampstead Thameslink ⊖	d	14 44	14 48	15 02		15 18	15 14	15 18	15 32		15 48	15 45	15 48	16 02		16 18	16 14	16 18	16 32		16 48	16 44
Kentish Town ⊖	a		14 54			→		15 24			→		15 54			→		16 24			→	
St Pancras International 15 ⊖	a	14 54		15 11	15 01		15 24		15 41	15 29		15 54		16 11	16 01		16 24		16 41	16 29		16 54
	d																					
St Pancras International 15 ⊖	a																					
	d																					
Farringdon 3 ⊖	d																					
City Thameslink 3	d																					
London Blackfriars 3 ⊖	a																					
London Bridge 4	a																					

Station		FC	FC 1	EM ◇1	FC	FC 1	FC	FC 1	EM ◇1	FC	FC 1	FC	FC 1	EM ◇1	FC	FC 1	FC	FC 1	EM ◇1	FC	FC 1	FC	FC 1
Bedford 7	d		16 08	16 19		16 24		16 38	16 49		16 54		17 08	17 19		17 24		17 38	17 49		17 54		18 08
Flitwick	d		16 18			16 34		16 48			17 04		17 18			17 34		17 48			18 04		18 18
Harlington	d		16 22			16 38		16 52			17 08		17 22			17 38		17 52			18 08		18 22
Leagrave	d		16 27			16 43		16 57			17 13		17 27			17 43		17 57			18 13		18 27
Luton 10	d		16 32		16 40	16 48		17 02	17 05	17 10	17 18		17 32		17 40	17 48		18 02	18 05	18 10	18 18		18 32
Luton Airport Parkway 7 ✈	d		16 34	16 35	16 42	16 50		17 04		17 12	17 20		17 34	17 35	17 42	17 50		18 04		18 12	18 20		18 34
Harpenden	d		16 40		16 48	16 56		17 10		17 18	17 26		17 40		17 48	17 56		18 10		18 18	18 26		18 40
St Albans City	d		16 46		16 54	17 02		17 16		17 24	17 32		17 46		17 54	18 02		18 16		18 24	18 32		18 46
Radlett	d				16 59					17 29					17 59					18 29			
Elstree & Borehamwood	d		16 53		17 03			17 23		17 33			17 53		18 03			18 23		18 33			18 53
Mill Hill Broadway	d				17 07					17 37					18 07					18 37			
Hendon	d				17 10					17 40					18 10					18 40			
Cricklewood	d	←			17 14		←			17 44		←			18 14		←			18 44		←	
West Hampstead Thameslink ⊖	d	16 48	17 02		17 18	17 14	17 18	17 32		17 48	17 44	17 48	18 02		18 18	18 14	18 18	18 32		18 48	18 44	18 48	19 02
Kentish Town ⊖	a	16 54			→		17 24			→		17 54			→		18 24			→		18 54	
St Pancras International 15 ⊖	a		17 11	17 01		17 24		17 41	17 28		17 54		18 11	18 01		18 24		18 41	18 29		18 54		19 11
	d																						
St Pancras International 15 ⊖	a																						
	d																						
Farringdon 3 ⊖	d																						
City Thameslink 3	d																						
London Blackfriars 3 ⊖	a																						
London Bridge 4	a																						

Please refer to separate pages within this table for services operating between South London and Brighton

At weekends please use local bus and tube services to travel to/from St Pancras International and London Bridge when no trains are operating. See local publicity for details of alternative routes and services that are available across central London

Table 52

Bedford, Luton, St.Albans - London

Saturdays

		EM	FC	EM	FC	FC	EM	FC	FC	EM	FC	FC	FC	FC	EM	FC	FC	FC	FC	EM	FC	FC	FC
		◇1	1	◇1		1	◇1		1	◇1		1	1		◇1		1	1		◇1		1	1
												A	B	B		A	A	B	B		A	A	B
Bedford 7	d	18 19	18 22	18 49		18 52	19 18		19 22	19 49		19 52	19 52		20 18		20 22	20 22		20 49		20 52	20 52
Flitwick	d		18 32			19 02			19 32			20 02	20 02				20 32	20 32				21 02	21 02
Harlington	d		18 36			19 06			19 36			20 06	20 06				20 36	20 36				21 06	21 06
Leagrave	d		18 41			19 11			19 41			20 11	20 11				20 41	20 41				21 11	21 11
Luton 10	d		18 46	19 05	18 50	19 16		19 20	19 46	20 05	19 50	20 16	20 16	20 20		20 20	20 46	20 46	20 50	21 03	20 50	21 16	21 16
Luton Airport Parkway 7 ✈	d	18 35	18 48		18 52	19 18	19 30	19 22	19 48		19 52	20 18	20 18	20 22	20 30	20 22	20 48	20 48	20 52		20 52	21 18	21 18
Harpenden	d		18 54		18 58	19 24		19 28	19 54		19 58	20 24	20 24	20 28		20 28	20 54	20 54	20 58		20 58	21 24	21 24
St Albans City	d		19 00		19 04	19 30		19 34	20 00		20 04	20 30	20 30	20 34		20 34	21 00	21 00	21 04		21 04	21 30	21 30
Radlett	d				19 09			19 39			20 09			20 39		20 39			21 09		21 09		
Elstree & Borehamwood	d				19 14			19 44			20 14			20 44		20 44			21 14		21 14		
Mill Hill Broadway	d				19 18			19 48			20 18			20 48		20 48			21 18		21 18		
Hendon	d				19 21			19 51			20 21			20 51		20 51			21 21		21 21		
Cricklewood	d				19 25			19 55			20 25			20 55		20 55			21 25		21 25		
West Hampstead Thameslink ⊖	d		19 14		19 28	19 44		19 58	20 14		20 28	20 44	20 44	20 58		20 58	21 14	21 14	21 28		21 28	21 44	21 44
Kentish Town ⊖	a				19 34			20 04			20 34			21 04		21 04			21 34		21 34		
St Pancras International 15 ⊖	a	18 59	19 24	19 29	19 40	19 54	20 02	20 10	20 24	20 29	20 40	20 54			21 01	21 11	21 24			21 29	21 41	21 54	
	d																						
St Pancras International 15 ⊖	a												20 55	21 11				21 25	21 41				21 55
	d																						
Farringdon 3 ⊖	d																						
City Thameslink 3	d																						
London Blackfriars 3 ⊖	a																						
London Bridge 4	a																						

		EM	FC	FC	FC	FC	EM	FC	FC	FC	EM	FC	FC	FC	FC	EM	FC	FC	FC	FC	FC	FC
		◇1		1	1		◇1		1	1	◇1					◇1			1	1	1	1
			A	A	B	B		A	A	B		B	A	B	A		B	A	B	A	B	A
Bedford 7	d	21 22		21 22	21 22		21 47		21 52	21 52	22 03			22 12	22 12	22 37	22 42	22 42	23 12	23 12	23 42	23 42
Flitwick	d			21 32	21 32				22 02	22 02				22 22	22 22		22 52	22 52	23 22	23 22	23 52	23 52
Harlington	d			21 36	21 36				22 06	22 06				22 26	22 26		22 56	22 56	23 26	23 26	23 56	23 56
Leagrave	d			21 41	21 41				22 11	22 11				22 31	22 31		23 01	23 01	23 31	23 31	00 01	00 01
Luton 10	d		21 20	21 46	21 46	21 50	22 03	21 50	22 16	22 16	22 18	22 20	22 20	22 36	22 36	22 59	23 06	23 06	23 36	23 36	00 06	00 06
Luton Airport Parkway 7 ✈	d	21 38	21 22	21 48	21 48	21 52		21 52	22 18	22 18	22 21	22 22	22 22	22 38	22 38		23 08	23 08	23 38	23 38	00 08	00 08
Harpenden	d		21 28	21 54	21 54	21 58		21 58	22 24	22 24		22 28	22 28	22 44	22 44		23 14	23 14	23 44	23 44	00 14	00 14
St Albans City	d		21 34	22 00	22 00	22 04		22 04	22 30	22 30		22 34	22 34	22 50	22 50		23 20	23 20	23 50	23 50	00 20	00 20
Radlett	d		21 39			22 09		22 10				22 39	22 40	22 56	22 56		23 26	23 26	23 56	23 56	00 26	00 26
Elstree & Borehamwood	d		21 44			22 14		22 14				22 44	22 44	23 00	23 00		23 30	23 30	23 59	00 01	00 30	00 30
Mill Hill Broadway	d		21 48			22 18		22 18				22 48	22 48	23 04	23 04		23 34	23 34	00 03	00 04	00 34	00 34
Hendon	d		21 51			22 21		22 22				22 51	22 52	23 08	23 08		23 38	23 38	00 08	00 08	00 38	00 38
Cricklewood	d		21 55			22 25		22 25				22 55	22 55	23 11	23 11		23 41	23 41	00 11	00 11	00 41	00 41
West Hampstead Thameslink ⊖	d		21 58	22 14	22 14	22 28		22 28	22 44	22 44		22 58	22 58	23 14	23 14		23 44	23 44	00 14	00 14	00 44	00 44
Kentish Town ⊖	a		22 04			22 34		22 34				23 04	23 04	23 19	23 20		23 49	23 50	00 19	00 20	00 49	00 50
St Pancras International 15 ⊖	a	22 05	22 10	22 24			22 29	22 40	22 54		22 48		23 10		23 26	23 35		23 56		00 26		00 56
	d																					
St Pancras International 15 ⊖	a				22 25	22 41				22 55		23 11		23 25			23 55		00 25		00 55	
	d																					
Farringdon 3 ⊖	d																					
City Thameslink 3	d																					
London Blackfriars 3 ⊖	a																					
London Bridge 4	a																					

Please refer to separate pages within this table for services operating between South London and Brighton

At weekends please use local bus and tube services to travel to/from St Pancras International and London Bridge when no trains are operating. See local publicity for details of alternative routes and services that are available across central London

Table 52

Bedford, Luton, St.Albans - London

Sundays
until 19 June

		FC	FC	FC	FC	FC	FC	FC	FC	EM	FC	FC	FC	EM	FC	FC	FC	EM	FC	FC	FC	EM	FC
		1	1					1		◇1	1		1	◇1	1		1	◇1	1		1	◇1	1
		C	C																				
Bedford 7	d	23p12	23p42							08 13			08 36	08 45			09 06	09 14			09 36	09 43	
Flitwick	d	23p22	23p52	05 52	06 22	06 52	07 22	08 00			08 30		08 46				09 16				09 46		
Harlington	d	23p26	23p56	05 56	06 26	06 56	07 26	08 04			08 34		08 50				09 20				09 50		
Leagrave	d	23p31	00 01	06 01	06 31	07 01	07 31	08 09			08 39		08 56				09 25				09 55		
Luton 10	d	23p36	00 06	06 06	06 36	07 06	07 36	08 14	08 18	08 32	08 44	08 48	09 00		09 14	09 18	09 30	09 39	09 44	09 48	10 00		10 14
Luton Airport Parkway 7 ✈	d	23p38	00 08	06 08	06 38	07 08	07 38	08 16	08 20		08 46	08 50	09 02	09 09	09 16	09 20	09 32		09 46	09 50	10 02	10 09	10 16
Harpenden	d	23p44	00 14	06 14	06 44	07 14	07 44	08 22	08 26		08 52	08 56	09 08		09 22	09 26	09 38		09 52	09 56	10 08		10 22
St Albans City	d	23p50	00 20	06 20	06 50	07 20	07 50	08 28	08 32		08 58	09 02	09 14		09 28	09 32	09 44		09 58	10 02	10 14		10 28
Radlett	d	23p56	00 26	06 26	06 56	07 26	07 56		08 37			09 07				09 37				10 07			
Elstree & Borehamwood	d	00 01	00 30	06 30	07 00	07 30	08 00		08 41			09 11				09 41				10 11			
Mill Hill Broadway	d	00 04	00 34	06 34	07 04	07 34	08 04		08 45			09 15				09 45				10 15			
Hendon	d	00 08	00 38	06 38	07 08	07 38	08 08		08 48			09 18				09 48				10 18			
Cricklewood	d	00 11	00 41	06 41	07 11	07 41	08 11		08 52			09 22				09 52				10 22			
West Hampstead Thameslink ⊖	d	00 14	00 44	06 44	07 14	07 44	08 14	08 42	08 54		09 12	09 24	09 30		09 42	09 54	10 00		10 12	10 24	10 30		10 42
Kentish Town ⊖	a	00 20	00 50	06 50	07 20	07 50	08 20		09 01			09 31				10 01				10 31			
St Pancras International 15 ⊖	a	00 26	00 56	06 56	07 26	07 56	08 26	08 54		09 13	09 24		09 38	09 43	09 54		10 08	10 19	10 24		10 38	10 47	10 54
	d																						
St Pancras International 15 ⊖	a																						
	d																						
Farringdon 3 ⊖	d																						
City Thameslink 3	d																						
London Blackfriars 3 ⊖	a																						
London Bridge 4	a																						

A until 30 July, from 29 October **B** from 6 August until 22 October **C** not 22 May

Please refer to separate pages within this table for services operating between South London and Brighton

At weekends please use local bus and tube services to travel to/from St Pancras International and London Bridge when no trains are operating. See local publicity for details of alternative routes and services that are available across central London

Table 52

Bedford, Luton, St.Albans - London

Sundays until 19 June

		FC	FC ■	EM ◇■	FC ■	FC	FC ■	EM ◇■	FC ■	FC	FC ■	EM ◇■	FC ■	FC	FC ■	EM ◇■	FC ■	FC	FC ■	EM ◇■	FC ■	FC	FC ■
Bedford ■	d		10 06	10 12			10 36	10 44			11 06	11 15			11 36	11 45			12 06	12 14			12 36
Flitwick	d		10 16				10 46				11 16				11 46				12 16				12 46
Harlington	d		10 20				10 50				11 20				11 50				12 20				12 50
Leagrave	d		10 25				10 55				11 25				11 55				12 25				12 55
Luton ■	d	10 18	10 30	10 36	10 44	10 48	11 00		11 14	11 18	11 30	11 39	11 44	11 48	12 00		12 14	12 18	12 30	12 39	12 44	12 48	13 00
Luton Airport Parkway ■ ✈	d	10 20	10 32		10 46	10 50	11 02	11 09	11 16	11 20	11 32		11 46	11 50	12 02	12 09	12 16	12 20	12 32		12 46	12 50	13 02
Harpenden	d	10 26	10 38		10 52	10 56	11 08		11 22	11 26	11 38		11 52	11 56	12 08		12 22	12 26	12 38		12 52	12 56	13 08
St Albans City	d	10 32	10 44		10 58	11 02	11 14		11 28	11 32	11 44		11 58	12 02	12 14		12 28	12 32	12 44		12 58	13 02	13 14
Radlett	d	10 37				11 07				11 37				12 07				12 37				13 07	
Elstree & Borehamwood	d	10 41				11 11				11 41				12 11				12 41				13 11	
Mill Hill Broadway	d	10 45				11 15				11 45				12 15				12 45				13 15	
Hendon	d	10 48				11 18				11 48				12 18				12 48				13 18	
Cricklewood	d	10 52				11 22				11 52				12 22				12 52				13 22	
West Hampstead Thameslink ⊖	d	10 54	11 00		11 12	11 24	11 30		11 42	11 54	12 00		12 12	12 24	12 30		12 42	12 54	13 00		13 12	13 24	13 30
Kentish Town ⊖	a	11 01				11 31				12 01				12 31				13 01				13 31	
St Pancras International ■ ⊖	a		11 08	11 15	11 24		11 38	11 47	11 54		12 08	12 15	12 24		12 38	12 45	12 54		13 08	13 16	13 24		13 38
	d																						
St Pancras International ■ ⊖	a																						
	d																						
Farringdon ■ ⊖	d																						
City Thameslink ■	d																						
London Blackfriars ■ ⊖	a																						
London Bridge ■	a																						

		EM ◇■	FC ■	FC	FC ■	EM ◇■	FC ■	FC	FC ■	EM ◇■	FC ■	FC	FC ■	EM ◇■	FC ■	FC	FC ■	EM ◇■	FC ■	FC	FC ■	EM ◇■
Bedford ■	d	12 45			13 06	13 15			13 36	13 46			14 06	14 20			14 36	14 44			15 06	15 14
Flitwick	d				13 16				13 46				14 16				14 46				15 16	
Harlington	d				13 20				13 50				14 20				14 50				15 20	
Leagrave	d				13 25				13 55				14 25				14 55				15 25	
Luton ■	d		13 14	13 18	13 30	13 38	13 44	13 48	14 00		14 14	14 18	14 30	14 37	14 44	14 48	15 00		15 14	15 18	15 30	15 33
Luton Airport Parkway ■ ✈	d	13 10	13 16	13 20	13 32		13 46	13 50	14 02	14 10	14 16	14 20	14 32		14 46	14 50	15 02	15 02	15 16	15 20	15 32	
Harpenden	d		13 22	13 26	13 38		13 52	13 56	14 08		14 22	14 26	14 38		14 52	14 56	15 08		15 22	15 26	15 38	
St Albans City	d		13 28	13 32	13 44		13 58	14 02	14 14		14 28	14 32	14 44		14 58	15 02	15 14		15 28	15 32	15 44	
Radlett	d			13 37				14 07				14 37				15 07				15 37		
Elstree & Borehamwood	d			13 41				14 11				14 41				15 11				15 41		
Mill Hill Broadway	d			13 45				14 15				14 45				15 15				15 45		
Hendon	d			13 48				14 18				14 48				15 18				15 48		
Cricklewood	d			13 52				14 22				14 52				15 22				15 52		
West Hampstead Thameslink ⊖	d		13 42	13 54	14 00		14 12	14 24	14 30		14 42	14 54	15 00		15 12	15 24	15 30		15 42	15 54	16 00	
Kentish Town ⊖	a			14 01				14 31				15 01				15 31				16 01		
St Pancras International ■ ⊖	a	13 48	13 54		14 08	14 15	14 24		14 38	14 44	14 54		15 08	15 08	15 24		15 38	15 35	15 54		16 08	16 04
	d																					
St Pancras International ■ ⊖	a																					
	d																					
Farringdon ■ ⊖	d																					
City Thameslink ■	d																					
London Blackfriars ■ ⊖	a																					
London Bridge ■	a																					

		FC ■	FC	FC ■	EM ◇■	EM ◇■	FC ■	FC	FC ■	FC ■	FC	EM ◇■	FC ■	FC ■	FC	FC ■	EM ◇■	FC ■	FC	FC ■	EM ◇■	FC ■	EM ◇■
Bedford ■	d			15 36	15 44				16 06	16 20		16 32	16 36	16 50		17 06	17 09	17 20		17 36	17 40	17 50	18 11
Flitwick	d			15 46					16 16	16 30			16 46	17 00		17 16		17 30		17 46		18 00	
Harlington	d			15 50					16 20	16 34			16 50	17 04		17 20		17 34		17 50		18 04	
Leagrave	d			15 55					16 25	16 39			16 55	17 09		17 25		17 39		17 55		18 09	
Luton ■	d	15 44	15 48	16 00		16 09	16 14	16 18	16 30	16 44	16 48		17 00	17 14	17 18	17 30	17 27	17 44	17 48	18 00		18 14	18 29
Luton Airport Parkway ■ ✈	d	15 46	15 50	16 02	16 02		16 16	16 20	16 32	16 46	16 50	16 53	17 02	17 16	17 20	17 32		17 46	17 50	18 02	17 59	18 16	
Harpenden	d	15 52	15 56	16 08			16 22	16 26	16 38	16 52	16 56		17 08	17 22	17 26	17 38		17 52	17 56	18 08		18 22	
St Albans City	d	15 58	16 02	16 14			16 28	16 32	16 44	16 58	17 02		17 14	17 28	17 32	17 44		17 58	18 02	18 14		18 28	
Radlett	d		16 07					16 37			17 07				17 37				18 07				
Elstree & Borehamwood	d		16 11					16 41			17 11				17 41				18 11				
Mill Hill Broadway	d		16 15					16 45			17 15				17 45				18 15				
Hendon	d		16 18					16 48			17 18				17 48				18 18				
Cricklewood	d		16 22					16 52			17 22				17 52				18 22				
West Hampstead Thameslink ⊖	d	16 12	16 24	16 30			16 42	16 54	17 00	17 12	17 24		17 30	17 42	17 54	18 00		18 12	18 24	18 30		18 42	
Kentish Town ⊖	a		16 31					17 01			17 31				18 01				18 31				
St Pancras International ■ ⊖	a	16 24		16 38	16 33	16 42	16 54		17 08	17 24		17 27	17 38	17 54		18 08	17 59	18 24		18 38	18 29	18 54	18 59
	d																						
St Pancras International ■ ⊖	a																						
	d																						
Farringdon ■ ⊖	d																						
City Thameslink ■	d																						
London Blackfriars ■ ⊖	a																						
London Bridge ■	a																						

Please refer to separate pages within this table for services operating between South London and Brighton

At weekends please use local bus and tube services to travel to/from St Pancras International and London Bridge when no trains are operating. See local publicity for details of alternative routes and services that are available across central London

Table 52

Bedford, Luton, St.Albans - London

Sundays until 19 June

		FC	FC ■	EM ◇■	FC	FC ■	EM ◇■	FC	FC ■	EM ◇■	FC	FC ■	EM ◇■	FC	FC	EM ◇■	FC	EM ◇■	FC	EM ◇■	FC	FC
Bedford ■	d		18 20	18 40		18 50	19 10		19 20	19 40		19 50	20 06		20 10	20 40	20 40	21 08	21 10	21 37	21 42	22 10
Flitwick	d		18 30			19 00			19 30			20 00			20 20		20 50		21 20		21 52	22 20
Harlington	d		18 34			19 04			19 34			20 04			20 24		20 54		21 24		21 56	22 24
Leagrave	d		18 39			19 09			19 39			20 09			20 29		20 59		21 29		22 01	22 29
Luton ■	d	18 18	18 44		18 48	19 14	19 29	19 18	19 44		19 48	20 14	20 26	20 18	20 34		21 04	21 23	21 34	21 52	22 06	22 34
Luton Airport Parkway ■ ✈	d	18 20	18 46	18 59	18 50	19 16		19 20	19 46	19 59	19 50	20 16		20 20	20 36	20 55	21 06		21 36		22 08	22 36
Harpenden	d	18 26	18 52		18 56	19 22		19 26	19 52		19 56	20 22		20 26	20 42		21 12		21 42		22 14	22 42
St Albans City	d	18 32	18 58		19 02	19 28		19 32	19 58		20 02	20 28		20 32	20 48		21 18		21 48		22 20	22 48
Radlett	d	18 38			19 08			19 38			20 08			20 38	20 54		21 24		21 54		22 26	22 54
Elstree & Borehamwood	d	18 42			19 12			19 42			20 12			20 42	20 58		21 28		21 58		22 30	22 58
Mill Hill Broadway	d	18 46			19 16			19 46			20 16			20 46	21 02		21 32		22 02		22 34	23 02
Hendon	d	18 50			19 20			19 50			20 20			20 50	21 06		21 36		22 06		22 38	23 06
Cricklewood	d	18 53			19 23			19 53			20 23			20 53	21 09		21 39		22 09		22 41	23 09
West Hampstead Thameslink ⊖	d	18 56	19 12		19 26	19 42		19 56	20 12		20 26	20 42		20 56	21 12		21 42		22 12		22 44	23 12
Kentish Town ⊖	a	19 02			19 32			20 02			20 32			21 02	21 18		21 48		22 18		22 50	23 18
St Pancras International ■ ⊖	a	19 08	19 24	19 29	19 38	19 54	19 59	20 08	20 24	20 29	20 38	20 54	20 57	21 08	21 24	21 27	21 54	21 57	22 24	22 27	22 56	23 24
	d																					
St Pancras International ■ ⊖	a																					
	d																					
Farringdon ■ ⊖	d																					
City Thameslink ■	d																					
London Blackfriars ■ ⊖	a																					
London Bridge ■	a																					

		EM ◇■	EM ◇■	FC	FC	FC
Bedford ■	d	22 24	22 31	22 42	23 12	23 32
Flitwick	d			22 52	23 22	23 42
Harlington	d			22 56	23 26	23 46
Leagrave	d			23 01	23 31	23 51
Luton ■	d	22 40	22 50	23 06	23 36	23 56
Luton Airport Parkway ■ ✈	d			23 08	23 38	23 58
Harpenden	d			23 14	23 44	00 04
St Albans City	d			23 20	23 50	00 10
Radlett	d			23 26	23 56	00 16
Elstree & Borehamwood	d			23 30	00 01	00 20
Mill Hill Broadway	d			23 34	00 04	00 24
Hendon	d			23 38	00 08	00 28
Cricklewood	d			23 41	00 11	00 31
West Hampstead Thameslink ⊖	d			23 44	00 14	00 34
Kentish Town ⊖	a			23 50	00 20	00 40
St Pancras International ■ ⊖	a	23 13	23 27	23 56	00 26	00 46
	d					
St Pancras International ■ ⊖	a					
	d					
Farringdon ■ ⊖	d					
City Thameslink ■	d					
London Blackfriars ■ ⊖	a					
London Bridge ■	a					

Sundays 26 June to 31 July

		FC ■	FC ■	FC	FC	FC	FC	FC ■	FC	EM ◇■	FC ■	FC	FC ■	EM ◇■	FC ■	FC	FC ■	EM ◇■	FC ■	FC	FC ■	EM ◇■	FC ■
Bedford ■	d	23p12	23p42							08 15			08 36	08 45			09 06	09 14			09 36	09 44	
Flitwick	d	23p22	23p52	05 52	06 22	06 52	07 22	08 00			08 30		08 46				09 16				09 46		
Harlington	d	23p26	23p56	05 56	06 26	06 56	07 26	08 04			08 34		08 50				09 20				09 50		
Leagrave	d	23p31	00 01	06 01	06 31	07 01	07 31	08 09			08 39		08 56				09 26				09 56		
Luton ■	d	23p36	00 06	06 06	06 36	07 06	07 36	08 14	08 18	08 32	08 44	08 48	09 00		09 14	09 18	09 30	09 39	09 44	09 48	10 00		10 14
Luton Airport Parkway ■ ✈	d	23p38	00 08	06 08	06 38	07 08	07 38	08 16	08 20		08 46	08 50	09 02	09 09	09 16	09 20	09 32		09 46	09 50	10 02	10 11	10 16
Harpenden	d	23p44	00 14	06 14	06 44	07 14	07 44	08 22	08 26		08 52	08 56	09 08		09 22	09 26	09 38		09 52	09 56	10 08		10 22
St Albans City	d	23p50	00 20	06 20	06 50	07 20	07 50	08 28	08 32		08 58	09 02	09 14		09 28	09 32	09 44		09 58	10 02	10 14		10 28
Radlett	d	23p56	00 26	06 26	06 56	07 26	07 56		08 37			09 07				09 37				10 07			
Elstree & Borehamwood	d	00 01	00 30	06 30	07 00	07 30	08 00		08 41			09 11				09 41				10 11			
Mill Hill Broadway	d	00 04	00 34	06 34	07 04	07 34	08 04		08 45			09 15				09 45				10 15			
Hendon	d	00 08	00 38	06 38	07 08	07 38	08 08		08 48			09 18				09 48				10 18			
Cricklewood	d	00 11	00 41	06 41	07 11	07 41	08 11		08 52			09 22				09 52				10 22			
West Hampstead Thameslink ⊖	d	00 14	00 44	06 44	07 14	07 44	08 14	08 42	08 53		09 12	09 24	09 30		09 42	09 54	10 00		10 12	10 24	10 30		10 42
Kentish Town ⊖	a	00 20	00 50	06 50	07 20	07 50	08 20		09 01			09 31				10 01				10 31			
St Pancras International ■ ⊖	a	00 26	00 56	06 56	07 26	07 56	08 26	08 54		09 13	09 24		09 38	09 50	09 54		10 08	10 19	10 24		10 38	10 49	10 54
	d																						
St Pancras International ■ ⊖	a																						
	d																						
Farringdon ■ ⊖	d																						
City Thameslink ■	d																						
London Blackfriars ■ ⊖	a																						
London Bridge ■	a																						

Please refer to separate pages within this table for services operating between South London and Brighton

At weekends please use local bus and tube services to travel to/from St Pancras International and London Bridge when no trains are operating. See local publicity for details of alternative routes and services that are available across central London

Table 52

Bedford, Luton, St.Albans - London

Sundays
26 June to 31 July

		FC	FC ■	EM ◇■ ☕	FC ■	FC		FC ■	EM ◇■ ☕	FC ■	FC	FC ■	EM ◇■ ☕	FC ■	FC	FC ■		EM ◇■ ☕	FC ■	FC	FC ■	EM ◇■ ☕	FC ■	FC	FC ■
Bedford [7]	d		10 06	10 15				10 36	10 45			11 06	11 15			11 36		11 45			12 06	12 17			12 36
Flitwick	d		10 16					10 46				11 16				11 46					12 16				12 46
Harlington	d		10 20					10 50				11 20				11 50					12 20				12 50
Leagrave	d		10 26					10 56				11 26				11 56					12 26				12 56
Luton [10]	d	10 18	10 30	10 36	10 44	10 48		11 00		11 14	11 18	11 30	11 39	11 44	11 48	12 00			12 14	12 18	12 30	12 41	12 44	12 48	13 00
Luton Airport Parkway [7] ✈	d	10 20	10 32		10 46	10 50		11 02	11 11	11 16	11 20	11 32		11 46	11 50	12 02		12 09	12 16	12 20	12 32		12 46	12 50	13 02
Harpenden	d	10 26	10 38		10 52	10 56		11 08		11 22	11 26	11 38		11 52	11 56	12 08			12 22	12 26	12 38		12 52	12 56	13 08
St Albans City	d	10 32	10 44		10 58	11 02		11 14		11 28	11 32	11 44		11 58	12 02	12 14			12 28	12 32	12 44		12 58	13 02	13 14
Radlett	d	10 37				11 07					11 37				12 07					12 37				13 07	
Elstree & Borehamwood	d	10 41				11 11					11 41				12 11					12 41				13 11	
Mill Hill Broadway	d	10 45				11 15					11 45				12 15					12 45				13 15	
Hendon	d	10 48				11 18					11 48				12 18					12 48				13 18	
Cricklewood	d	10 52				11 22					11 52				12 22					12 52				13 22	
West Hampstead Thameslink ⊖	d	10 54	11 00		11 11	11 24		11 30		11 42	11 54	12 00		12 12	12 24	12 30			12 42	12 54	13 00		13 12	13 24	13 30
Kentish Town ⊖	a	11 01				11 31					12 01				12 31					13 01				13 31	
St Pancras International [15] ⊖	a		11 08	11 20	11 24			11 38	11 49	11 54		12 08	12 18	12 24		12 38		12 49	12 54		13 08	13 16	13 24		13 38
	d																								
St Pancras International [15] ⊖	a																								
	d																								
Farringdon [3] ⊖	d																								
City Thameslink [3]	d																								
London Blackfriars [3] ⊖	a																								
London Bridge [4]	a																								

		EM ◇■ ☕		FC ■	FC	FC ■	EM ◇■ ☕	FC ■	FC	FC ■	EM ◇■ ☕	FC ■		FC	FC ■	EM ◇■ ☕	FC ■	FC	FC ■	EM ◇■ ☕	FC ■	FC		FC ■	EM ◇■ ☕
Bedford [7]	d	12 45				13 06	13 15			13 36	13 45				14 06	14 20			14 36	14 44				15 06	15 14
Flitwick	d					13 16				13 46					14 16				14 46					15 16	
Harlington	d					13 20				13 50					14 20				14 50					15 20	
Leagrave	d					13 26				13 56					14 26				14 56					15 26	
Luton [10]	d			13 14	13 18	13 30	13 39	13 44	13 48	14 00		14 14		14 18	14 30	14 37	14 44	14 48	15 00		15 14	15 18		15 30	15 33
Luton Airport Parkway [7] ✈	d	13 10		13 16	13 20	13 32		13 46	13 50	14 02	14 11	14 16		14 20	14 32		14 46	14 50	15 02	15 02	15 16	15 20		15 32	
Harpenden	d			13 22	13 26	13 38		13 52	13 56	14 08		14 22		14 26	14 38		14 52	14 56	15 08		15 22	15 26		15 38	
St Albans City	d			13 28	13 32	13 44		13 58	14 02	14 14		14 28		14 32	14 44		14 58	15 02	15 14		15 28	15 32		15 44	
Radlett	d				13 37				14 07					14 37				15 07				15 37			
Elstree & Borehamwood	d				13 41				14 11					14 41				15 11				15 41			
Mill Hill Broadway	d				13 45				14 15					14 45				15 15				15 45			
Hendon	d				13 48				14 18					14 48				15 18				15 48			
Cricklewood	d				13 52				14 22					14 52				15 22				15 52			
West Hampstead Thameslink ⊖	d			13 42	13 53	14 00		14 12	14 24	14 30		14 42		14 54	15 00		15 12	15 23	15 30		15 42	15 54		16 00	
Kentish Town ⊖	a				14 01				14 31					15 01				15 31				16 01			
St Pancras International [15] ⊖	a	13 48		13 54		14 08	14 19	14 24		14 38	14 44	14 54			15 08	15 08	15 24		15 38	15 35	15 54			16 08	16 04
	d																								
St Pancras International [15] ⊖	a																								
	d																								
Farringdon [3] ⊖	d																								
City Thameslink [3]	d																								
London Blackfriars [3] ⊖	a																								
London Bridge [4]	a																								

		FC ■	FC	FC ■	EM ◇■ ☕	EM ◇■ ☕	FC ■	FC		FC ■	FC ■	FC	EM ◇■ ☕	FC ■	FC ■	FC	FC ■	EM ◇■ ☕		FC ■	FC	FC ■	EM ◇■ ☕	FC ■	EM ◇■ ☕
Bedford [7]	d			15 36	15 44					16 06	16 20		16 32	16 36	16 50		17 06	17 09		17 20		17 36	17 40	17 50	18 11
Flitwick	d			15 46						16 16	16 30			16 46	17 00		17 16			17 30		17 46		18 00	
Harlington	d			15 50						16 20	16 34			16 50	17 04		17 20			17 34		17 50		18 04	
Leagrave	d			15 56						16 26	16 40			16 56	17 10		17 26			17 40		17 56		18 10	
Luton [10]	d	15 44	15 48	16 00		16 09	16 14	16 18		16 30	16 44	16 48		17 00	17 14	17 18	17 30	17 33		17 44	17 48	18 00		18 14	18 29
Luton Airport Parkway [7] ✈	d	15 46	15 50	16 02	16 02		16 16	16 20		16 32	16 46	16 50	16 54	17 02	17 16	17 20	17 32			17 46	17 50	18 02	18 03	18 16	
Harpenden	d	15 52	15 56	16 08			16 22	16 26		16 38	16 52	16 56		17 08	17 22	17 26	17 38			17 52	17 56	18 08		18 22	
St Albans City	d	15 58	16 02	16 14			16 28	16 32		16 44	16 58	17 02		17 14	17 28	17 32	17 44			17 58	18 02	18 14		18 28	
Radlett	d		16 07					16 37				17 07				17 37					18 07				
Elstree & Borehamwood	d		16 11					16 41				17 11				17 41					18 11				
Mill Hill Broadway	d		16 15					16 45				17 15				17 45					18 15				
Hendon	d		16 18					16 48				17 18				17 48					18 18				
Cricklewood	d		16 22					16 52				17 22				17 52					18 22				
West Hampstead Thameslink ⊖	d	16 12	16 24	16 30			16 42	16 54		17 00	17 12	17 24		17 30	17 42	17 54	18 00			18 12	18 24	18 30		18 42	
Kentish Town ⊖	a		16 31					17 01				17 31				18 01					18 31				
St Pancras International [15] ⊖	a	16 24		16 38	16 33	16 42	16 54			17 08	17 24		17 27	17 38	17 54		18 08	17 59		18 24		18 38	18 31	18 54	18 59
	d																								
St Pancras International [15] ⊖	a																								
	d																								
Farringdon [3] ⊖	d																								
City Thameslink [3]	d																								
London Blackfriars [3] ⊖	a																								
London Bridge [4]	a																								

Please refer to separate pages within this table for services operating between South London and Brighton

At weekends please use local bus and tube services to travel to/from St Pancras International and London Bridge when no trains are operating. See local publicity for details of alternative routes and services that are available across central London

Table 52

Bedford, Luton, St.Albans - London

Sundays
26 June to 31 July

		FC	FC ■	EM ◇■ ☕		FC	FC ■	EM ◇■ ☕	FC	FC ■	EM ◇■ ☕	FC	FC ■	EM ◇■ ☕		FC	FC	EM ◇■ ☕	FC	EM ◇■ ☕	FC	EM ◇■ ☕	FC	FC
Bedford [7]	d		18 20	18 40			18 50	19 10		19 20	19 40		19 50	20 06			20 10	20 40	20 42	21 08	21 10	21 37	21 42	22 10
Flitwick	d		18 30				19 00			19 30			20 00				20 20		20 52		21 20		21 52	22 20
Harlington	d		18 34				19 04			19 34			20 04				20 24		20 56		21 24		21 56	22 24
Leagrave	d		18 40				19 10			19 40			20 10				20 30		21 02		21 30		22 02	22 30
Luton [10]	d	18 18	18 44			18 48	19 14	19 29	19 18	19 44		19 48	20 14	20 26		20 18	20 34		21 06	21 23	21 34	21 52	22 06	22 34
Luton Airport Parkway [7] ✈	d	18 20	18 46	18 59		18 50	19 16		19 20	19 46	19 59	19 50	20 16			20 20	20 36	20 55	21 08		21 36		22 08	22 36
Harpenden	d	18 26	18 52			18 56	19 22		19 26	19 52		19 56	20 22			20 26	20 42		21 14		21 42		22 14	22 42
St Albans City	d	18 32	18 58			19 02	19 28		19 32	19 58		20 02	20 28			20 32	20 48		21 20		21 48		22 20	22 48
Radlett	d	18 38				19 08			19 38			20 08				20 38	20 54		21 26		21 54		22 26	22 54
Elstree & Borehamwood	d	18 42				19 12			19 42			20 12				20 42	20 58		21 30		21 58		22 30	22 58
Mill Hill Broadway	d	18 46				19 16			19 46			20 16				20 46	21 02		21 34		22 02		22 34	23 02
Hendon	d	18 50				19 20			19 50			20 20				20 50	21 06		21 38		22 06		22 38	23 06
Cricklewood	d	18 53				19 23			19 53			20 23				20 53	21 09		21 41		22 09		22 41	23 09
West Hampstead Thameslink ⊖	d	18 56	19 12			19 26	19 42		19 56	20 12		20 26	20 42			20 56	21 12		21 44		22 12		22 44	23 12
Kentish Town ⊖	a	19 02				19 32			20 02			20 32				21 02	21 18		21 50		22 18		22 50	23 18
St Pancras International [15] ⊖	a	19 08	19 24	19 29		19 38	19 54	19 59	20 08	20 24	20 29	20 38	20 54	20 57		21 08	21 24	21 27	21 56	21 57	22 24	22 27	22 56	23 24
	d																							
St Pancras International [15] ⊖	a																							
	d																							
Farringdon [3] ⊖	d																							
City Thameslink [3]	d																							
London Blackfriars [3] ⊖	a																							
London Bridge [4]	a																							

		EM ◇■ ☕	EM ◇■ ☕	FC	FC	FC
Bedford [7]	d	22 24	22 31	22 42	23 12	23 32
Flitwick	d			22 52	23 22	23 42
Harlington	d			22 56	23 26	23 46
Leagrave	d			23 02	23 32	23 52
Luton [10]	d	22 40	22 50	23 06	23 36	23 56
Luton Airport Parkway [7] ✈	d			23 09	23 38	23 58
Harpenden	d			23 14	23 44	00 04
St Albans City	d			23 20	23 50	00 10
Radlett	d			23 26	23 56	00 16
Elstree & Borehamwood	d			23 30	00 01	00 20
Mill Hill Broadway	d			23 34	00 04	00 24
Hendon	d			23 38	00 08	00 28
Cricklewood	d			23 41	00 11	00 31
West Hampstead Thameslink ⊖	d			23 44	00 14	00 34
Kentish Town ⊖	a			23 50	00 20	00 40
St Pancras International [15] ⊖	a	23 13	23 27	23 56	00 26	00 46
	d					
St Pancras International [15] ⊖	a					
	d					
Farringdon [3] ⊖	d					
City Thameslink [3]	d					
London Blackfriars [3] ⊖	a					
London Bridge [4]	a					

Sundays
7 August to 11 September

		FC ■	FC ■	FC	FC	FC	FC	FC ■	FC	EM ◇■ ☕		FC ■	FC	FC ■	EM ◇■ ☕	FC ■	FC	FC ■	EM ◇■ ☕	FC ■		FC	FC ■	EM ◇■ ☕	FC ■
Bedford [7]	d	23p12	23p42							08 13				08 36	08 45			09 06	09 14				09 36	09 44	
Flitwick	d	23p22	23p52	05 52	06 22	06 52	07 22	08 00				08 30		08 46				09 16					09 46		
Harlington	d	23p26	23p56	05 56	06 26	06 56	07 26	08 04				08 34		08 50				09 20					09 50		
Leagrave	d	23p31	00 01	06 01	06 31	07 01	07 31	08 10				08 39		08 55				09 25					09 55		
Luton [10]	d	23p36	00 06	06 06	06 36	07 06	07 36	08 14	08 20	08 32		08 44	08 50	09 00		09 14	09 20	09 30	09 39	09 44		09 50	10 00		10 14
Luton Airport Parkway [7] ✈	d	23p38	00 08	06 08	06 38	07 08	07 38	08 16	08 22			08 46	08 52	09 02	09 07	09 16	09 22	09 32		09 46		09 52	10 02	10 11	10 16
Harpenden	d	23p44	00 14	06 14	06 44	07 14	07 44	08 22	08 28			08 52	08 58	09 08		09 22	09 28	09 38		09 52		09 58	10 08		10 22
St Albans City	d	23p50	00 20	06 20	06 50	07 20	07 50	08 28	08 34			08 58	09 04	09 15		09 28	09 34	09 45		09 58		10 04	10 15		10 28
Radlett	d	23p56	00 26	06 26	06 56	07 26	07 56		08 39				09 09				09 39					10 09			
Elstree & Borehamwood	d	23p59	00 30	06 30	07 00	07 30	08 00		08 44				09 14				09 44					10 14			
Mill Hill Broadway	d	00 03	00 34	06 34	07 04	07 34	08 04		08 48				09 18				09 48					10 18			
Hendon	d	00 08	00 38	06 38	07 08	07 38	08 08	08 39	08 51				09 21				09 51					10 21			
Cricklewood	d	00 11	00 41	06 41	07 11	07 41	08 11		08 55				09 25				09 55					10 25			
West Hampstead Thameslink ⊖	d	00 14	00 44	06 43	07 13	07 43	08 13	08 43	08 57			09 12	09 27	09 32		09 41	09 57	10 02		10 11		10 27	10 32		10 41
Kentish Town ⊖	a	00 19	00 49	06 48	07 18	07 48	08 18	08 48	09 03				09 33				10 03					10 33			
St Pancras International [15] ⊖	a									09 13					09 50				10 20					10 47	
	d																								
St Pancras International [15] ⊖	a	00 25	00 55	06 54	07 24	07 54	08 24	08 54	09 09			09 24	09 39	09 43		09 54	10 09	10 13		10 24		10 39	10 43		10 54
	d																								
Farringdon [3] ⊖	d																								
City Thameslink [3]	d																								
London Blackfriars [3] ⊖	a																								
London Bridge [4]	a																								

Please refer to separate pages within this table for services operating between South London and Brighton

At weekends please use local bus and tube services to travel to/from St Pancras International and London Bridge when no trains are operating. See local publicity for details of alternative routes and services that are available across central London

Bedford, Luton, St.Albans - London

Sundays

7 August to 11 September

		FC	FC 1	EM ◇1 ⊡	FC 1	FC		FC 1	EM ◇1 ⊡	FC 1	FC	FC 1	EM ◇1 ⊡	FC 1	FC	FC 1		EM ◇1 ⊡	FC 1	FC	FC 1	EM ◇1 ⊡	FC 1	FC	FC 1
Bedford 7	d		10 06	10 15				10 36	10 45			11 06	11 15			11 36		11 45			12 06	12 15			12 36
Flitwick	d		10 16					10 46				11 16				11 46					12 16				12 46
Harlington	d		10 20					10 50				11 20				11 50					12 20				12 50
Leagrave	d		10 25					10 55				11 25				11 55					12 25				12 55
Luton 10	d	10 20	10 30	10 37	10 44	10 50		11 00		11 14	11 20	11 30	11 39	11 44	11 50	12 00			12 14	12 20	12 30	12 40	12 44	12 50	13 00
Luton Airport Parkway 7 ✈	d	10 22	10 32		10 46	10 52		11 02	11 10	11 16	11 22	11 32		11 46	11 52	12 02		12 09	12 16	12 22	12 32		12 46	12 52	13 02
Harpenden	d	10 28	10 38		10 52	10 58		11 08		11 22	11 28	11 38		11 52	11 58	12 08			12 22	12 28	12 38		12 52	12 58	13 08
St Albans City	d	10 34	10 45		10 58	11 04		11 15		11 28	11 34	11 45		11 58	12 04	12 15			12 28	12 34	12 45		12 58	13 04	13 15
Radlett	d	10 39				11 09					11 39				12 09					12 39				13 09	
Elstree & Borehamwood	d	10 44				11 14					11 44				12 14					12 44				13 14	
Mill Hill Broadway	d	10 48				11 18					11 48				12 18					12 48				13 18	
Hendon	d	10 51				11 21					11 51				12 21					12 51				13 21	
Cricklewood	d	10 55				11 25					11 55				12 25					12 55				13 25	
West Hampstead Thameslink ⊖	d	10 57	11 02		11 11	11 27		11 32		11 41	11 57	12 02		12 11	12 27	12 32			12 41	12 57	13 02		13 11	13 27	13 32
Kentish Town ⊖	a	11 03				11 33					12 03				12 33					13 03				13 33	
St Pancras International 15 ⊖	a			11 20					11 49				12 20					12 50				13 20			
	d																								
St Pancras International 15 ⊖	a	11 09	11 13		11 24	11 39		11 43		11 54	12 09	12 13		12 24	12 39	12 43			12 54	13 09	13 13		13 24	13 39	13 43
	d																								
Farringdon 3 ⊖	d																								
City Thameslink 3	d																								
London Blackfriars 3 ⊖	a																								
London Bridge 4	a																								

		EM ◇1 ⊡		FC 1	FC	FC 1	EM ◇1 ⊡	FC 1	FC	FC 1	EM ◇1 ⊡	FC 1		FC	FC 1	EM ◇1 ⊡	FC 1	FC	FC 1	EM ◇1 ⊡	FC 1	FC		FC 1	EM ◇1 ⊡
Bedford 7	d	12 45				13 06	13 16			13 36	13 45				14 06	14 18			14 36	14 45				15 06	15 15
Flitwick	d					13 16				13 46					14 16				14 46					15 16	
Harlington	d					13 20				13 50					14 20				14 50					15 20	
Leagrave	d					13 25				13 55					14 25				14 55					15 25	
Luton 10	d			13 14	13 20	13 30	13 37	13 44	13 50	14 00		14 14		14 20	14 30	14 37	14 44	14 50	15 00		15 14	15 20		15 30	15 32
Luton Airport Parkway 7 ✈	d	13 10		13 16	13 22	13 32		13 46	13 52	14 02	14 09	14 16		14 22	14 32		14 46	14 52	15 02	15 02	15 16	15 22		15 32	
Harpenden	d			13 22	13 28	13 38		13 52	13 58	14 08		14 22		14 28	14 38		14 52	14 58	15 08		15 22	15 28		15 38	
St Albans City	d			13 28	13 34	13 45		13 58	14 04	14 15		14 28		14 34	14 45		14 58	15 04	15 15		15 28	15 34		15 45	
Radlett	d				13 39				14 09					14 39				15 09				15 39			
Elstree & Borehamwood	d				13 44				14 14					14 44				15 14				15 44			
Mill Hill Broadway	d				13 48				14 18					14 48				15 18				15 48			
Hendon	d				13 51				14 21					14 51				15 21				15 51			
Cricklewood	d				13 55				14 25					14 55				15 25				15 55			
West Hampstead Thameslink ⊖	d			13 41	13 57	14 02		14 11	14 27	14 32		14 41		14 57	15 02		15 11	15 27	15 32		15 41	15 57		16 02	
Kentish Town ⊖	a				14 03				14 33					15 03				15 33				16 03			
St Pancras International 15 ⊖	a	13 48					14 19				14 44					15 08				15 36					16 04
	d																								
St Pancras International 15 ⊖	a			13 54	14 09	14 13		14 24	14 39	14 43		14 54		15 09	15 13		15 24	15 39	15 43		15 54	16 09		16 13	
	d																								
Farringdon 3 ⊖	d																								
City Thameslink 3	d																								
London Blackfriars 3 ⊖	a																								
London Bridge 4	a																								

		FC 1	FC	FC 1	EM ◇1 ⊡	EM ◇1 ⊡	FC 1	FC		FC 1	FC 1	EM ◇1 ⊡	FC	FC 1	FC 1	FC	FC 1	EM ◇1 ⊡		FC 1	FC	FC 1	EM ◇1 ⊡	FC 1	FC
Bedford 7	d			15 36	15 45					16 06	16 20	16 33		16 36	16 50		17 06	17 07		17 20		17 36	17 40	17 50	
Flitwick	d			15 46						16 16	16 30			16 46	17 00		17 16			17 30		17 46		18 00	
Harlington	d			15 50						16 20	16 34			16 50	17 04		17 20			17 34		17 50		18 04	
Leagrave	d			15 55						16 25	16 39			16 55	17 09		17 25			17 39		17 55		18 09	
Luton 10	d	15 44	15 50	16 00		16 09	16 14	16 20		16 30	16 44		16 50	17 00	17 14	17 20	17 30	17 25		17 44	17 50	18 00		18 14	18 20
Luton Airport Parkway 7 ✈	d	15 46	15 52	16 02	16 03		16 16	16 22		16 32	16 46	16 53	16 52	17 02	17 16	17 22	17 32			17 46	17 52	18 02	17 59	18 16	18 22
Harpenden	d	15 52	15 58	16 08			16 22	16 28		16 38	16 52		16 58	17 08	17 22	17 28	17 38			17 52	17 58	18 08		18 22	18 28
St Albans City	d	15 58	16 04	16 15			16 28	16 34		16 45	16 58		17 04	17 15	17 28	17 34	17 45			17 58	18 04	18 15		18 28	18 34
Radlett	d		16 09					16 39					17 09			17 39					18 09				18 39
Elstree & Borehamwood	d		16 14					16 44					17 14			17 44					18 14				18 44
Mill Hill Broadway	d		16 18					16 48					17 18			17 48					18 18				18 48
Hendon	d		16 21					16 51					17 21			17 51					18 21				18 51
Cricklewood	d		16 25					16 55					17 25			17 55					18 25				18 55
West Hampstead Thameslink ⊖	d	16 11	16 27	16 32			16 41	16 57		17 02	17 12		17 27	17 32	17 42	17 57	18 02			18 12	18 27	18 32		18 42	18 57
Kentish Town ⊖	a		16 33					17 03					17 33			18 03					18 33				19 03
St Pancras International 15 ⊖	a				16 34	16 42						17 27						17 59					18 29		
	d																								
St Pancras International 15 ⊖	a	16 24	16 39	16 43			16 54	17 09		17 13	17 24		17 39	17 43	17 54	18 09	18 13			18 24	18 39	18 43		18 54	19 09
	d																								
Farringdon 3 ⊖	d																								
City Thameslink 3	d																								
London Blackfriars 3 ⊖	a																								
London Bridge 4	a																								

Please refer to separate pages within this table for services operating between South London and Brighton

At weekends please use local bus and tube services to travel to/from St Pancras International and London Bridge when no trains are operating. See local publicity for details of alternative routes and services that are available across central London

Bedford, Luton, St.Albans - London

Sundays

7 August to 11 September

		EM ◇1 ⊡	FC 1	FC		EM ◇1 ⊡	FC 1	FC	EM ◇1 ⊡	FC 1	FC	EM ◇1 ⊡	FC 1	FC		EM ◇1 ⊡	FC	EM ◇1 ⊡	FC	EM ◇1 ⊡	FC	EM ◇1 ⊡	FC	FC	
Bedford 7	d	18 11	18 20			18 40	18 50		19 10	19 20		19 40	19 50			20 06	20 10	20 40	20 40	21 08	21 10	21 37	21 42	22 10	
Flitwick	d		18 30				19 00			19 30			20 00				20 20		20 50		21 20		21 52	22 20	
Harlington	d		18 34				19 04			19 34			20 04				20 24		20 54		21 24		21 56	22 24	
Leagrave	d		18 39				19 09			19 39			20 09				20 29		20 59		21 29		22 01	22 29	
Luton 10	d	18 29	18 44	18 50			19 14	19 20	19 29	19 44	19 50		20 14	20 20		20 26	20 34		21 04	21 23	21 34	21 52	22 06	22 34	
Luton Airport Parkway 7 ✈	d		18 46	18 52		18 59	19 16	19 22		19 46	19 52	19 59	20 16	20 22			20 36	20 55	21 06		21 36		22 08	22 36	
Harpenden	d		18 52	18 58			19 22	19 28		19 52	19 58		20 22	20 28			20 42		21 12		21 42		22 14	22 42	
St Albans City	d		18 58	19 04			19 28	19 34		19 58	20 04		20 28	20 34			20 48		21 18		21 48		22 20	22 48	
Radlett	d			19 09				19 39			20 09			20 39			20 54		21 24		21 54		22 25	22 54	
Elstree & Borehamwood	d			19 14				19 44			20 14			20 44			20 58		21 28		21 58		22 30	22 58	
Mill Hill Broadway	d			19 18				19 48			20 18			20 48			21 02		21 32		22 02		22 34	23 02	
Hendon	d			19 21				19 51			20 21			20 51			21 06		21 36		22 06		22 37	23 06	
Cricklewood	d			19 25				19 55			20 25			20 55			21 09		21 39		22 09		22 41	23 09	
West Hampstead Thameslink ⊖	d		19 12	19 27			19 42	19 57		20 12	20 27		20 42	20 57			21 12		21 42		22 12		22 43	23 12	
Kentish Town ⊖	a			19 33				20 03			20 33			21 03			21 18		21 48		22 18		22 48	23 18	
St Pancras International 15 ⊖	a	18 59				19 29			19 59			20 29				20 57		21 27		21 57		22 27			
	d																								
St Pancras International 15 ⊖	a		19 24	19 39			19 54	20 09		20 24	20 39		20 54	21 09			21 24		21 54		22 24		22 54	23 24	
	d																								
Farringdon 3 ⊖	d																								
City Thameslink 3	d																								
London Blackfriars 3 ⊖	a																								
London Bridge 4	a																								

		EM ◇1 ⊡	EM ◇1 ⊡	FC	FC	FC
Bedford 7	d	22 24	22 31	22 42	23 12	23 32
Flitwick	d			22 52	23 22	23 42
Harlington	d			22 56	23 26	23 46
Leagrave	d			23 01	23 31	23 51
Luton 10	d	22 40	22 50	23 06	23 36	23 56
Luton Airport Parkway 7 ✈	d			23 08	23 38	23 58
Harpenden	d			23 14	23 44	00 04
St Albans City	d			23 20	23 50	00 10
Radlett	d			23 25	23 55	00 15
Elstree & Borehamwood	d			23 30	00 01	00 20
Mill Hill Broadway	d			23 34	00 04	00 24
Hendon	d			23 37	00 07	00 27
Cricklewood	d			23 41	00 11	00 31
West Hampstead Thameslink ⊖	d			23 43	00 13	00 33
Kentish Town ⊖	a			23 48	00 18	00 38
St Pancras International 15 ⊖	a	23 13	23 27			
	d					
St Pancras International 15 ⊖	a			23 54	00 24	00 44
	d					
Farringdon 3 ⊖	d					
City Thameslink 3	d					
London Blackfriars 3 ⊖	a					
London Bridge 4	a					

Sundays

18 September to 23 October

		FC 1	FC 1	FC	FC	FC	FC	FC 1	FC	EM ◇1 ⊡		FC 1	FC	EM ◇1 ⊡	FC 1	FC	FC 1	EM ◇1 ⊡	FC 1	FC		FC 1	EM ◇1 ⊡	FC 1	FC
Bedford 7	d	23p12	23p42							08 15				08 45	08 52		09 06	09 14	09 22			09 36	09 42	09 52	
Flitwick	d	23p22	23p52	05 52	06 22	06 52	07 22	08 00				08 30			09 02		09 16		09 32			09 46		10 02	
Harlington	d	23p26	23p56	05 56	06 26	06 56	07 26	08 04				08 34			09 06		09 20		09 36			09 50		10 06	
Leagrave	d	23p31	00 01	06 01	06 31	07 01	07 31	08 10				08 39			09 11		09 25		09 41			09 55		10 11	
Luton 10	d	23p36	00 06	06 06	06 36	07 06	07 36	08 14	08 20	08 34		08 44	08 48		09 15	09 20	09 30	09 39	09 46	09 50		10 00		10 16	10 20
Luton Airport Parkway 7 ✈	d	23p38	00 08	06 08	06 38	07 08	07 38	08 16	08 22			08 46	08 50	09 07	09 18	09 22	09 32		09 48	09 52		10 02	10 10	10 18	10 22
Harpenden	d	23p44	00 14	06 14	06 44	07 14	07 44	08 22	08 28			08 52	08 56		09 23	09 28	09 38		09 54	09 58		10 08		10 24	10 28
St Albans City	d	23p50	00 20	06 20	06 50	07 20	07 50	08 28	08 34			08 58	09 02		09 29	09 34	09 45		10 00	10 04		10 15		10 30	10 34
Radlett	d	23p56	00 26	06 26	06 56	07 26	07 56		08 39				09 08			09 39				10 09					10 39
Elstree & Borehamwood	d	23p59	00 30	06 30	07 00	07 30	08 00		08 44				09 12			09 44				10 14					10 44
Mill Hill Broadway	d	00 03	00 34	06 34	07 04	07 34	08 04		08 48				09 16			09 48				10 18					10 48
Hendon	d	00 08	00 38	06 38	07 08	07 38	08 08	08 39	08 51				09 20			09 51				10 21					10 51
Cricklewood	d	00 11	00 41	06 41	07 11	07 41	08 11		08 55				09 23			09 55				10 25					10 55
West Hampstead Thameslink ⊖	d	00 14	00 44	06 43	07 13	07 43	08 13	08 42	08 57			09 13	09 26		09 43	09 57	10 02		10 14	10 27		10 32		10 44	10 57
Kentish Town ⊖	a	00 19	00 49	06 48	07 18	07 48	08 18	08 48	09 03				09 31			10 03			10 19	10 33					11 03
St Pancras International 15 ⊖	a									09 13				09 50				10 20					10 49		
	d																								
St Pancras International 15 ⊖	a	00 25	00 55	06 54	07 24	07 54	08 24	08 54	09 09			09 23	09 39		09 54	10 09	10 13		10 24	10 39		10 43		10 54	11 09
	d																								
Farringdon 3 ⊖	d																								
City Thameslink 3	d																								
London Blackfriars 3 ⊖	a																								
London Bridge 4	a																								

Please refer to separate pages within this table for services operating between South London and Brighton

At weekends please use local bus and tube services to travel to/from St Pancras International and London Bridge when no trains are operating. See local publicity for details of alternative routes and services that are available across central London

Table 52

Sundays

18 September to 23 October

Bedford, Luton, St.Albans - London

	FC 1	EM ◇1	FC 1	FC	FC 1	EM ◇1	FC 1	FC	FC 1	EM ◇1	FC 1	FC	FC 1	EM ◇1	FC 1	FC	FC 1	EM ◇1	FC 1	FC	FC 1	EM ◇1
Bedford 7 d	10 06	10 15	10 22		10 36	10 45	10 52		11 06	11 15	11 22		11 36	11 45	11 52		12 06	12 15	12 22		12 36	12 45
Flitwick d	10 16		10 32		10 46		11 02		11 16		11 32		11 46		12 02		12 16		12 32		12 46	
Harlington d	10 20		10 36		10 50		11 06		11 20		11 36		11 50		12 06		12 20		12 36		12 50	
Leagrave d	10 25		10 41		10 55		11 11		11 25		11 41		11 55		12 11		12 25		12 41		12 55	
Luton 10 d	10 30	10 37	10 46	10 50	11 00		11 16	11 20	11 30	11 39	11 46	11 50	12 00		12 16	12 20	12 30	12 40	12 46	12 50	13 00	
Luton Airport Parkway 7 ✈ d	10 32		10 48	10 52	11 02	11 10	11 18	11 22	11 32		11 48	11 52	12 02	12 09	12 18	12 22	12 32		12 48	12 52	13 02	13 10
Harpenden d	10 38		10 54	10 58	11 08		11 24	11 28	11 38		11 54	11 58	12 08		12 24	12 28	12 38		12 54	12 58	13 08	
St Albans City d	10 45		11 00	11 04	11 15		11 30	11 34	11 45		12 00	12 04	12 15		12 30	12 34	12 45		13 00	13 04	13 15	
Radlett d				11 09				11 39				12 09				12 39				13 09		
Elstree & Borehamwood d				11 14				11 44				12 14				12 44				13 14		
Mill Hill Broadway d				11 18				11 48				12 18				12 48				13 18		
Hendon d				11 21				11 51				12 21				12 51				13 21		
Cricklewood d				11 25				11 55				12 25				12 55				13 25		
West Hampstead Thameslink ⊖ d	11 02		11 14	11 27	11 32		11 44	11 57	12 02		12 14	12 27	12 32		12 44	12 57	13 02		13 14	13 27	13 32	
Kentish Town ⊖ a				11 33				12 03				12 33				13 03				13 33		
St Pancras International 15 ⊖ a		11 20				11 49				12 20				12 45				13 20				13 48
d																						
St Pancras International 15 ⊖ a	11 13		11 24	11 39	11 43		11 54	12 09	12 13		12 24	12 39	12 43		12 54	13 09	13 13		13 24	13 39	13 43	
d																						
Farringdon 3 ⊖ d																						
City Thameslink 3 d																						
London Blackfriars 3 ⊖ a																						
London Bridge 4 a																						

	FC 1	FC	FC 1	EM ◇1	FC 1	FC	FC 1	EM ◇1	FC 1	FC	FC 1	FC 1	EM ◇1	FC	FC 1	FC 1	EM ◇1	FC	FC 1	FC 1	EM ◇1
Bedford 7 d	12 52		13 06	13 16	13 22		13 36	13 46	13 52		14 06	14 22	14 26		14 36	14 52	14 54		15 06	15 22	15 25
Flitwick d	13 02		13 16		13 32		13 46		14 02		14 16	14 32			14 46	15 02			15 16	15 32	
Harlington d	13 06		13 20		13 36		13 50		14 06		14 20	14 36			14 50	15 06			15 20	15 36	
Leagrave d	13 11		13 25		13 41		13 55		14 11		14 25	14 41			14 55	15 11			15 25	15 41	
Luton 10 d	13 16	13 20	13 30	13 37	13 46	13 50	14 00		14 16	14 20	14 30	14 46	14 49	14 50	15 00	15 16		15 20	15 30	15 46	15 42
Luton Airport Parkway 7 ✈ d	13 18	13 22	13 32		13 48	13 52	14 02	14 09	14 18	14 22	14 32	14 48		14 52	15 02	15 18	15 11	15 22	15 32	15 48	
Harpenden d	13 24	13 28	13 38		13 54	13 58	14 08		14 24	14 28	14 38	14 54		14 58	15 08	15 24		15 28	15 38	15 54	
St Albans City d	13 30	13 34	13 45		14 00	14 04	14 15		14 30	14 34	14 45	15 00		15 04	15 15	15 30		15 34	15 45	16 00	
Radlett d		13 39				14 09				14 39				15 09				15 39			
Elstree & Borehamwood d		13 44				14 14				14 44				15 14				15 44			
Mill Hill Broadway d		13 48				14 18				14 48				15 18				15 48			
Hendon d		13 51				14 21				14 51				15 21				15 51			
Cricklewood d		13 55				14 25				14 55				15 25				15 55			
West Hampstead Thameslink ⊖ d	13 44	13 57	14 02		14 14	14 27	14 32		14 44	14 57	15 02	15 14		15 27	15 32	15 44		15 57	16 02	16 14	
Kentish Town ⊖ a		14 03				14 33				15 03				15 33				16 03			
St Pancras International 15 ⊖ a				14 19				14 44					15 20				15 45				16 15
d																					
St Pancras International 15 ⊖ a	13 54	14 09	14 13		14 24	14 39	14 43		14 54	15 09	15 13	15 24		15 39	15 43	15 54		16 09	16 13	16 24	
d																					
Farringdon 3 ⊖ d																					
City Thameslink 3 d																					
London Blackfriars 3 ⊖ a																					
London Bridge 4 a																					

	FC	FC 1	EM ◇1	EM ◇1	FC 1	FC	FC 1	FC 1	EM ◇1	FC	FC 1	FC 1	FC	FC 1	EM ◇1	FC 1	FC	FC 1	EM ◇1	FC 1	FC	EM ◇1
Bedford 7 d		15 36	15 46		15 52		16 06	16 20	16 32		16 36	16 50		17 06	17 07	17 20		17 36	17 40	17 50		18 11
Flitwick d		15 46			16 02		16 16	16 30			16 46	17 00		17 16		17 30		17 46		18 00		
Harlington d		15 50			16 06		16 20	16 34			16 50	17 04		17 20		17 34		17 50		18 04		
Leagrave d		15 55			16 11		16 25	16 39			16 55	17 09		17 25		17 39		17 55		18 10		
Luton 10 d	15 50	16 00		16 09	16 16	16 20	16 30	16 44		16 50	17 00	17 14	17 20	17 30	17 25	17 44	17 50	18 00		18 14	18 20	18 29
Luton Airport Parkway 7 ✈ d	15 52	16 02	16 03		16 18	16 22	16 32	16 46	16 53	16 52	17 02	17 16	17 22	17 32		17 46	17 52	18 02	17 59	18 17	18 22	
Harpenden d	15 58	16 08			16 24	16 28	16 38	16 52		16 58	17 08	17 22	17 28	17 38		17 52	17 58	18 08		18 22	18 28	
St Albans City d	16 04	16 15			16 30	16 34	16 45	16 58		17 04	17 15	17 28	17 34	17 45		17 58	18 04	18 15		18 28	18 34	
Radlett d	16 09					16 39				17 09			17 39				18 09				18 39	
Elstree & Borehamwood d	16 14					16 44				17 14			17 44				18 14				18 44	
Mill Hill Broadway d	16 18					16 48				17 18			17 48				18 18				18 48	
Hendon d	16 21					16 51		17 09		17 21		17 39	17 51				18 21			18 39	18 51	
Cricklewood d	16 25					16 55				17 25			17 55				18 25				18 55	
West Hampstead Thameslink ⊖ d	16 27	16 32			16 44	16 57	17 02	17 12		17 27	17 32	17 42	17 57	18 02		18 12	18 27	18 32		18 44	18 57	
Kentish Town ⊖ a	16 33					17 03		17 18		17 33		17 48	18 03			18 17	18 33				19 03	
St Pancras International 15 ⊖ a			16 34	16 42					17 27						17 59				18 29			18 59
d																						
St Pancras International 15 ⊖ a	16 39	16 43			16 54	17 09	17 13	17 24		17 39	17 43	17 54	18 09	18 13		18 23	18 39	18 43		18 54	19 09	
d																						
Farringdon 3 ⊖ d																						
City Thameslink 3 d																						
London Blackfriars 3 ⊖ a																						
London Bridge 4 a																						

Please refer to separate pages within this table for services operating between South London and Brighton

At weekends please use local bus and tube services to travel to/from St Pancras International and London Bridge when no trains are operating. See local publicity for details of alternative routes and services that are available across central London

Table 52

Sundays

18 September to 23 October

Bedford, Luton, St.Albans - London

	FC 1	FC	EM ◇1	FC 1	FC	EM ◇1	FC 1	FC	EM ◇1	FC 1	FC	EM ◇1	FC	EM ◇1	FC	EM ◇1	FC	EM ◇1	FC	FC	EM ◇1
Bedford 7 d	18 20		18 40	18 50		19 10	19 20		19 40	19 50		20 06	20 10	20 40	20 40	21 08	21 10	21 37	21 42	22 10	22 24
Flitwick d	18 30			19 00			19 30			20 00			20 20		20 50		21 20		21 52	22 20	
Harlington d	18 34			19 04			19 34			20 04			20 24		20 54		21 24		21 56	22 24	
Leagrave d	18 40			19 10			19 40			20 10			20 29		20 59		21 29		22 01	22 29	
Luton 10 d	18 44	18 50		19 14	19 20	19 29	19 44	19 50		20 14	20 20	20 26	20 34		21 04	21 23	21 34	21 52	22 06	22 34	22 40
Luton Airport Parkway 7 ✈ d	18 47	18 52	18 59	19 17	19 22		19 47	19 52	19 59	20 17	20 22		20 36	20 55	21 06		21 36		22 08	22 36	
Harpenden d	18 52	18 58		19 22	19 28		19 52	19 58		20 22	20 28		20 42		21 12		21 42		22 14	22 42	
St Albans City d	18 58	19 04		19 28	19 34		19 58	20 04		20 28	20 34		20 48		21 18		21 48		22 20	22 48	
Radlett d		19 09			19 39			20 09			20 39		20 54		21 24		21 54		22 25	22 54	
Elstree & Borehamwood d		19 14			19 44			20 14			20 44		20 58		21 28		21 58		22 30	22 58	
Mill Hill Broadway d		19 18			19 48			20 18			20 48		21 02		21 32		22 02		22 34	23 02	
Hendon d	19 09	19 21		19 39	19 51		20 09	20 21		20 39	20 51		21 06		21 36		22 06		22 37	23 06	
Cricklewood d		19 25			19 55			20 25			20 55		21 09		21 39		22 09		22 41	23 09	
West Hampstead Thameslink ⊖ d	19 14	19 27		19 44	19 57		20 14	20 27		20 43	20 57		21 12		21 42		22 12		22 43	23 12	
Kentish Town ⊖ a		19 33			20 03			20 33			21 03		21 18		21 48		22 18		22 48	23 18	
St Pancras International 15 ⊖ a			19 29			19 59			20 29			20 57		21 27		21 57		22 27			23 13
d																					
St Pancras International 15 ⊖ a	19 24	19 39		19 54	20 09		20 24	20 39		20 54	21 09		21 24		21 54		22 24		22 54	23 24	
d																					
Farringdon 3 ⊖ d																					
City Thameslink 3 d																					
London Blackfriars 3 ⊖ a																					
London Bridge 4 a																					

	EM ◇1	FC	FC	FC
Bedford 7 d	22 31	22 42	23 12	23 32
Flitwick d		22 52	23 22	23 42
Harlington d		22 56	23 26	23 46
Leagrave d		23 01	23 31	23 51
Luton 10 d	22 50	23 06	23 36	23 56
Luton Airport Parkway 7 ✈ d		23 08	23 38	23 58
Harpenden d		23 14	23 44	00 04
St Albans City d		23 20	23 50	00 10
Radlett d		23 25	23 55	00 15
Elstree & Borehamwood d		23 30	00 01	00 20
Mill Hill Broadway d		23 34	00 04	00 24
Hendon d		23 37	00 07	00 27
Cricklewood d		23 41	00 11	00 31
West Hampstead Thameslink ⊖ d		23 43	00 13	00 33
Kentish Town ⊖ a		23 48	00 18	00 38
St Pancras International 15 ⊖ a	23 27			
d				
St Pancras International 15 ⊖ a		23 54	00 24	00 44
d				
Farringdon 3 ⊖ d				
City Thameslink 3 d				
London Blackfriars 3 ⊖ a				
London Bridge 4 a				

Sundays

from 30 October

	FC 1	FC 1	FC	FC	FC	FC	FC 1	FC	EM ◇1	FC 1	FC	EM ◇1	FC 1	FC	FC 1	EM ◇1	FC 1	FC	FC 1	EM ◇1	FC 1	FC
Bedford 7 d	23p12	23p42	05 42	06 12	06 42	07 12	07 50		08 15	08 20		08 45	08 50		09 06	09 14	09 20		09 36	09 45	09 50	
Flitwick d	23p22	23p52	05 52	06 22	06 52	07 22	08 00			08 30			09 00		09 16		09 30		09 46		10 00	
Harlington d	23p26	23p56	05 56	06 26	06 56	07 26	08 04			08 34			09 04		09 20		09 34		09 50		10 04	
Leagrave d	23p31	00 01	06 01	06 31	07 01	07 31	08 09			08 39			09 10		09 25		09 39		09 55		10 09	
Luton 10 d	23p36	00 06	06 06	06 36	07 06	07 36	08 14	08 18	08 34	08 44	08 48		09 14	09 18	09 30	09 39	09 44	09 48	10 00		10 14	10 18
Luton Airport Parkway 7 ✈ d	23p38	00 08	06 08	06 38	07 08	07 38	08 16	08 20		08 46	08 50	09 11	09 16	09 20	09 32		09 46	09 50	10 02	10 10	10 16	10 20
Harpenden d	23p44	00 14	06 14	06 44	07 14	07 44	08 22	08 26		08 52	08 56		09 22	09 26	09 38		09 52	09 56	10 08		10 22	10 26
St Albans City d	23p50	00 20	06 20	06 50	07 20	07 50	08 28	08 32		08 58	09 02		09 28	09 32	09 44		09 58	10 02	10 14		10 28	10 32
Radlett d	23p56	00 26	06 26	06 56	07 26	07 56		08 37			09 07			09 37				10 07				10 37
Elstree & Borehamwood d	00 01	00 30	06 30	07 00	07 30	08 00		08 41			09 11			09 41				10 11				10 41
Mill Hill Broadway d	00 04	00 34	06 34	07 04	07 34	08 04		08 45			09 15			09 45				10 15				10 45
Hendon d	00 08	00 38	06 38	07 08	07 38	08 08		08 48			09 18			09 48				10 18				10 48
Cricklewood d	00 11	00 41	06 41	07 11	07 41	08 11		08 52			09 22			09 52				10 22				10 52
West Hampstead Thameslink ⊖ d	00 14	00 44	06 44	07 14	07 44	08 14	08 42	08 54		09 12	09 23		09 42	09 53	09 58		10 12	10 23	10 28		10 42	10 53
Kentish Town ⊖ a	00 20	00 50	06 50	07 20	07 50	08 20		09 00			09 31			10 01				10 31				11 01
St Pancras International 15 ⊖ a	00 26	00 56	06 56	07 26	07 56	08 26	08 54	09 09	09 13	09 24	09 39	09 50	09 54		10 08	10 20	10 24		10 38	10 49	10 54	
d																						
St Pancras International 15 ⊖ a																						
d																						
Farringdon 3 ⊖ d																						
City Thameslink 3 d																						
London Blackfriars 3 ⊖ a																						
London Bridge 4 a																						

Please refer to separate pages within this table for services operating between South London and Brighton

At weekends please use local bus and tube services to travel to/from St Pancras International and London Bridge when no trains are operating. See local publicity for details of alternative routes and services that are available across central London

Table 52

Sundays from 30 October

Bedford, Luton, St.Albans - London

		FC 1	EM ◇1	FC 1	FC	FC 1	EM ◇1	FC 1	FC	FC 1	EM ◇1	FC 1	FC	FC 1	EM ◇1	FC 1	FC	FC 1	EM ◇1	FC 1	FC	FC 1	EM ◇1
Bedford 7	d	10 06	10 16	10 20		10 36	10 45	10 50		11 06	11 16	11 20		11 36	11 45	11 50		12 06	12 15	12 20		12 36	12 46
Flitwick	d	10 16		10 30		10 46		11 00		11 16		11 30		11 46		12 00		12 16		12 30		12 46	
Harlington	d	10 20		10 34		10 50		11 04		11 20		11 34		11 50		12 04		12 20		12 34		12 50	
Leagrave	d	10 25		10 39		10 55		11 09		11 25		11 39		11 55		12 09		12 25		12 39		12 55	
Luton 10	d	10 30	10 39	10 44	10 48	11 00		11 14	11 18	11 30	11 39	11 44	11 48	12 00		12 14	12 18	12 30	12 40	12 44	12 48	13 00	
Luton Airport Parkway 7 ✈	d	10 32		10 46	10 50	11 02	11 10	11 16	11 20	11 32		11 46	11 50	12 02	12 09	12 16	12 20	12 32		12 46	12 50	13 02	13 10
Harpenden	d	10 38		10 52	10 56	11 08		11 22	11 26	11 38		11 52	11 56	12 08		12 22	12 26	12 38		12 52	12 56	13 08	
St Albans City	d	10 44		10 58	11 02	11 14		11 28	11 32	11 44		11 58	12 02	12 14		12 28	12 32	12 44		12 58	13 02	13 14	
Radlett	d				11 07				11 37				12 07				12 37				13 07		
Elstree & Borehamwood	d				11 11				11 41				12 11				12 41				13 11		
Mill Hill Broadway	d				11 15				11 45				12 15				12 45				13 15		
Hendon	d				11 18				11 48				12 18				12 48				13 18		
Cricklewood	d				11 22				11 52				12 22				12 52				13 22		
West Hampstead Thameslink ⊖	d	10 58		11 12	11 23	11 28		11 42	11 53	11 58		12 12	12 23	12 28		12 42	12 53	12 58		13 12	13 23	13 28	
Kentish Town ⊖	a				11 31				12 01				12 31				13 01				13 31		
St Pancras International 15 ⊖	a	11 08	11 20	11 24		11 38	11 49	11 54		12 08	12 20	12 24		12 38	12 50	12 54		13 08	13 20	13 24		13 38	13 48
	d																						
St Pancras International 15 ⊖	a																						
	d																						
Farringdon 3 ⊖	d																						
City Thameslink 3	d																						
London Blackfriars 3 ⊖	a																						
London Bridge 4	a																						

		FC 1	FC	FC 1	EM ◇1	FC 1	FC	FC 1	EM ◇1	FC 1	FC	FC 1	FC 1	EM ◇1	FC	FC 1	FC 1	EM ◇1	FC	FC 1	FC 1	EM ◇1
Bedford 7	d	12 50		13 06	13 15	13 20		13 36	13 46	13 50		14 06	14 20	14 25		14 36	14 50	14 53		15 06	15 20	15 25
Flitwick	d	13 00		13 16		13 30		13 46		14 00		14 16	14 30			14 46	15 00			15 16	15 30	
Harlington	d	13 04		13 20		13 34		13 50		14 04		14 20	14 34			14 50	15 04			15 20	15 34	
Leagrave	d	13 09		13 25		13 39		13 55		14 09		14 25	14 39			14 55	15 09			15 25	15 39	
Luton 10	d	13 14	13 18	13 30	13 39	13 44	13 48	14 00		14 14	14 18	14 30	14 44	14 49	14 48	15 00	15 14		15 18	15 30	15 44	15 46
Luton Airport Parkway 7 ✈	d	13 16	13 20	13 32		13 46	13 50	14 02	14 10	14 16	14 20	14 32	14 46		14 50	15 02	15 16	15 15	15 20	15 32	15 46	
Harpenden	d	13 22	13 26	13 38		13 52	13 56	14 08		14 22	14 26	14 38	14 52		14 56	15 08	15 22		15 26	15 38	15 52	
St Albans City	d	13 28	13 32	13 44		13 58	14 02	14 14		14 28	14 32	14 44	14 58		15 02	15 14	15 28		15 32	15 44	15 58	
Radlett	d		13 37				14 07				14 37				15 07				15 37			
Elstree & Borehamwood	d		13 41				14 11				14 41				15 11				15 41			
Mill Hill Broadway	d		13 45				14 15				14 45				15 15				15 45			
Hendon	d		13 48				14 18				14 48				15 18				15 48			
Cricklewood	d		13 52				14 22				14 52				15 22				15 52			
West Hampstead Thameslink ⊖	d	13 42	13 53	13 58		14 12	14 23	14 28		14 42	14 53	14 58	15 12		15 23	15 28	15 42		15 53	15 58	16 12	
Kentish Town ⊖	a		14 01				14 31				15 01				15 31				16 01			
St Pancras International 15 ⊖	a	13 54		14 08	14 19	14 24		14 38	14 44	14 54		15 08	15 24	15 20		15 38	15 54	15 45		16 08	16 24	16 15
	d																					
St Pancras International 15 ⊖	a																					
	d																					
Farringdon 3 ⊖	d																					
City Thameslink 3	d																					
London Blackfriars 3 ⊖	a																					
London Bridge 4	a																					

		FC	FC 1	EM ◇1	EM ◇1	FC 1	FC	FC 1	FC 1	FC	EM ◇1	FC 1	FC 1	FC	EM ◇1	FC 1	FC 1	FC	EM ◇1	FC 1	FC 1	EM ◇1	FC
Bedford 7	d		15 36	15 42		15 50		16 06	16 20		16 31	16 36	16 50		17 04	17 08	17 20		17 35	17 38	17 50	18 05	
Flitwick	d		15 46			16 00		16 16	16 30			16 46	17 00			17 18	17 30			17 48	18 00		
Harlington	d		15 50			16 04		16 20	16 34			16 50	17 04			17 22	17 34			17 52	18 04		
Leagrave	d		15 55			16 09		16 25	16 39			16 55	17 09			17 27	17 39			17 57	18 09		
Luton 10	d	15 48	16 00		16 16	16 14	16 18	16 30	16 44	16 48		17 00	17 14	17 18	17 27	17 32	17 44	17 48		18 02	18 14	18 29	18 18
Luton Airport Parkway 7 ✈	d	15 50	16 02	16 03		16 16	16 20	16 32	16 46	16 50	16 54	17 02	17 16	17 20		17 34	17 46	17 50	17 59	18 04	18 16		18 20
Harpenden	d	15 56	16 08			16 22	16 26	16 38	16 52	16 56		17 08	17 22	17 26		17 40	17 52	17 56		18 10	18 22		18 26
St Albans City	d	16 02	16 14			16 28	16 32	16 44	16 58	17 02		17 14	17 28	17 32		17 46	17 58	18 02		18 16	18 28		18 32
Radlett	d	16 07					16 37			17 07				17 37				18 07					18 38
Elstree & Borehamwood	d	16 11					16 41			17 11				17 41				18 11					18 42
Mill Hill Broadway	d	16 15					16 45			17 15				17 45				18 15					18 46
Hendon	d	16 18					16 48			17 18				17 48				18 18					18 50
Cricklewood	d	16 22					16 52			17 22				17 52				18 22					18 53
West Hampstead Thameslink ⊖	d	16 23	16 28			16 42	16 53	16 58	17 12	17 23		17 28	17 42	17 53		18 01	18 12	18 23		18 30	18 42		18 56
Kentish Town ⊖	a	16 31					17 01			17 31				18 01				18 31					19 02
St Pancras International 15 ⊖	a		16 38	16 34	16 42	16 54		17 08	17 24		17 27	17 38	17 54		17 59	18 10	18 24		18 29	18 40	18 54	18 59	19 08
	d																						
St Pancras International 15 ⊖	a																						
	d																						
Farringdon 3 ⊖	d																						
City Thameslink 3	d																						
London Blackfriars 3 ⊖	a																						
London Bridge 4	a																						

Please refer to separate pages within this table for services operating between South London and Brighton

At weekends please use local bus and tube services to travel to/from St Pancras International and London Bridge when no trains are operating. See local publicity for details of alternative routes and services that are available across central London

Table 52

Sundays from 30 October

Bedford, Luton, St.Albans - London

		FC 1	EM ◇1	FC	FC 1	EM ◇1	FC	FC 1	EM ◇1	FC	FC 1	EM ◇1	FC	FC	EM ◇1	FC	EM ◇1	FC	EM ◇1	FC	FC	EM ◇1
Bedford 7	d	18 20	18 39		18 50	19 09		19 20	19 37		19 50	20 03		20 10	20 36	20 40	21 06	21 10	21 37	21 42	22 10	22 24
Flitwick	d	18 30			19 00			19 30			20 00			20 20		20 50		21 20		21 52	22 20	
Harlington	d	18 34			19 04			19 34			20 04			20 24		20 54		21 24		21 56	22 24	
Leagrave	d	18 39			19 09			19 39			20 09			20 29		20 59		21 29		22 01	22 29	
Luton 10	d	18 44		18 48	19 14	19 29	19 18	19 44		19 48	20 14	20 29	20 18	20 34		21 04	21 25	21 34	21 56	22 06	22 34	22 42
Luton Airport Parkway 7 ✈	d	18 46	18 59	18 50	19 16		19 20	19 46	19 59	19 50	20 16		20 20	20 36	20 57	21 06		21 36		22 08	22 36	
Harpenden	d	18 52		18 56	19 22		19 26	19 52		19 56	20 22		20 26	20 42		21 12		21 42		22 14	22 42	
St Albans City	d	18 58		19 02	19 28		19 32	19 58		20 02	20 28		20 32	20 48		21 18		21 48		22 20	22 48	
Radlett	d			19 08			19 38			20 08			20 38	20 54		21 24		21 54		22 26	22 54	
Elstree & Borehamwood	d			19 12			19 42			20 12			20 42	20 58		21 28		21 58		22 30	22 58	
Mill Hill Broadway	d			19 16			19 46			20 16			20 46	21 02		21 32		22 02		22 34	23 02	
Hendon	d			19 20			19 50			20 20			20 50	21 06		21 36		22 06		22 38	23 06	
Cricklewood	d			19 23			19 53			20 23			20 53	21 09		21 39		22 09		22 41	23 09	
West Hampstead Thameslink ⊖	d	19 12		19 26	19 42		19 56	20 12		20 26	20 42		20 56	21 12		21 42		22 12		22 44	23 12	
Kentish Town ⊖	a			19 32			20 02			20 32			21 02	21 18		21 48		22 18		22 50	23 18	
St Pancras International 15 ⊖	a	19 24	19 29	19 38	19 54	19 59	20 08	20 24	20 29	20 38	20 54	20 57	21 08	21 24	21 27	21 54	21 57	22 24	22 31	22 56	23 24	23 15
	d																					
St Pancras International 15 ⊖	a																					
	d																					
Farringdon 3 ⊖	d																					
City Thameslink 3	d																					
London Blackfriars 3 ⊖	a																					
London Bridge 4	a																					

		EM ◇1	FC	FC	FC
Bedford 7	d	22 31	22 42	23 12	23 32
Flitwick	d		22 52	23 22	23 42
Harlington	d		22 56	23 26	23 46
Leagrave	d		23 01	23 31	23 51
Luton 10	d	22 50	23 06	23 36	23 56
Luton Airport Parkway 7 ✈	d		23 08	23 38	23 58
Harpenden	d		23 14	23 44	00 04
St Albans City	d		23 20	23 50	00 10
Radlett	d		23 26	23 56	00 16
Elstree & Borehamwood	d		23 30	00 01	00 20
Mill Hill Broadway	d		23 34	00 04	00 24
Hendon	d		23 38	00 08	00 28
Cricklewood	d		23 41	00 11	00 31
West Hampstead Thameslink ⊖	d		23 44	00 14	00 34
Kentish Town ⊖	a		23 50	00 20	00 40
St Pancras International 15 ⊖	a	23 27	23 56	00 26	00 46
	d				
St Pancras International 15 ⊖	a				
	d				
Farringdon 3 ⊖	d				
City Thameslink 3	d				
London Blackfriars 3 ⊖	a				
London Bridge 4	a				

Please refer to separate pages within this table for services operating between South London and Brighton

At weekends please use local bus and tube services to travel to/from St Pancras International and London Bridge when no trains are operating. See local publicity for details of alternative routes and services that are available across central London

London, St.Albans, Luton - Bedford

		FC	FC	EM	FC	FC	FC	FC	EM	FC		FC	FC	FC	FC	FC	FC	FC	FC	FC		EM	FC	FC	FC
			1	◇1		1		1	◇1			1			1							◇1		1	
London Bridge 4 ⊖	d																								
Elephant & Castle	d																								
London Blackfriars 3 ⊖	a																								
	d																								
City Thameslink 3	d																								
Farringdon 3 ⊖	d																								
St Pancras International 15 ⊖	a																								
	d	22p48	23p02	23p15	23p18	23p32	23p48	00 02	00 15	00 18		00 36	01 06	01 32	02 32	03 52	04 32	05 02	05 32	06 02		06 10		06 20	06 32
Kentish Town	d	22p53			23p23		23p53			00 23		00 41	01 11	01 37	02 37	03 57	04 37	05 07	05 37	06 07					06 37
West Hampstead Thameslink	d	22p57	23p10		23p27	23p40	23p57	00 10		00 27		00 45	01 15	01 41	02 41	04 01	04 41	05 11	05 41	06 11				06 28	06 41
Cricklewood	d	23p00			23p30		00 01			00 30		00 48	01 18	01 44	02 44	04 04	04 44	05 14	05 44	06 14					06 44
Hendon	d	23p03			23p33		00 03			00 33		00 51	01 21	01 47	02 47	04 07	04 47	05 17	05 47	06 17					06 47
Mill Hill Broadway	d	23p07			23p37		00 07			00 37		00 55	01 25	01 51	02 51	04 11	04 51	05 21	05 51	06 21					06 51
Elstree & Borehamwood	d	23p11			23p41		00 11			00 41		00 59	01 29	01 55	02 55	04 15	04 55	05 25	05 55	06 25				06 38	06 55
Radlett	d	23p16			23p46		00 16			00 46		01 04	01 34	02 00	03 00	04 20	05 00	05 30	06 00	06 30					07 00
St Albans City	d	23p22	23p26		23p52	23p56	00 22	00 26		00 52		01 10	01 40	02 06	03 06	04 26	05 06	05 36	06 06	06 36				06 46	07 06
Harpenden	d	23p28	23p32		23p58	00 02	00 28	00 32		00 58		01 16	01 46	02 12	03 12	04 32	05 12	05 42	06 12	06 42				06 52	07 12
Luton Airport Parkway 7 ✈	d	23p34	23p38		00 04	00 08	00 34	00 38	00 44	01 04		01 22	01 52	02 18	03 18	04 38	05 18	05 48	06 18	06 48			←	06 58	07 18
Luton 10	d	23p37	23p41	23p46	00 07	00 11	00 37	00 41	00 47	01 07		01 25	01 55	02 21	03 21	04 41	05 21	05 51	06 21	06 51		06 33	06 51	07 01	07a22
Leagrave	d	23p41	23p45		00 11	00 15	00 41	00 45		01 11		01 29	01 59	02 25	03 25	04 45	05 25	05 55	06 25	→			06 55	07 04	
Harlington	d	23p46	23p50		00 16	00 20	00 46	00 50		01 16		01 34	02 04	02 30	03 30	04 50	05 30	06 00	06 30				07 00	07 10	
Flitwick	d	23p50	23p54		00 20	00 24	00 50	00 55		01 20		01 38	02 08	02 34	03 34	04 54	05 34	06 04	06 34				07 04	07 14	
Bedford 7	a	00 04	00 08	00 11	00 34	00 38	01 04	01 08	01 12	01 34		01 52	02 22	02 48	03 48	05 08	05 48	06 18	06 48			06 47	07 18	07 26	

		EM	FC	EM	EM	FC		FC	FC	EM	FC	FC	FC	EM	FC	FC		FC	FC	EM	FC	FC	FC	EM	FC
		◇1	1	◇1	◇1	1			1	◇1	1		1	◇1	1	1			1	◇1	1		1	◇1	1
London Bridge 4 ⊖	d																								
Elephant & Castle	d																								
London Blackfriars 3 ⊖	a																								
	d																								
City Thameslink 3	d																								
Farringdon 3 ⊖	d																								
St Pancras International 15 ⊖	a																								
	d	06 37	06 50	06 55	07 00			07 04	07 20	07 30	07 34		07 50	08 00		08 04			08 20	08 30	08 34		08 50	09 00	
Kentish Town	d							07 09				07 42						08 12				08 42			
West Hampstead Thameslink	d		06 58					07 13	07 28		07 40	07 46	07 58			08 10		08 16	08 28		08 40	08 46	08 58		
Cricklewood	d							07 16				07 49						08 19				08 49			
Hendon	d							07 19				07 52						08 22				08 52			
Mill Hill Broadway	d							07 23				07 56						08 26				08 56			
Elstree & Borehamwood	d		07 08					07 27	07 38			08 00	08 08					08 30	08 38			09 00	09 08		
Radlett	d							07 32				08 04						08 34				09 04			
St Albans City	d		07 16					07 38	07 45		07 55	08 10	08 15			08 25		08 40	08 45		08 55	09 10	09 15		
Harpenden	d		07 22					07 44	07 52		08 02	08 16	08 22			08 32		08 46	08 52		09 02	09 16	09 22		
Luton Airport Parkway 7 ✈	d		07 28	07a15		←		07 50	07 58	07 51	08 08	08 22	08 28		←	08 38		08 52	08 58	08 51	09 08	09 22	09 28		←
Luton 10	d	06a58	07 31		07 23	07 31		07a54	08 01		08 11	08a26	08 31	08 23	08 31	08 41		08a56	09 01		09 11	09a26	09 31	09 23	09 31
Leagrave	d		→			07 34			08 04		08 14		→		08 34	08 44			09 04		09 14		→		09 34
Harlington	d					07 40			08 10		08 20				08 40	08 50			09 10		09 20				09 40
Flitwick	d					07 44			08 14		08 24				08 44	08 54			09 14		09 24				09 44
Bedford 7	a				07 38	07 56			08 26	08 06	08 36			08 37	08 56	09 06			09 26	09 06	09 36			09 37	09 56

		FC		FC	FC	EM	FC	FC	FC	EM	FC	FC		FC	FC	EM	FC	FC	FC	EM	FC	FC		FC	FC
		1			1	◇1	1		1	◇1	1	1			1	◇1	1		1	◇1	1	1			1
London Bridge 4 ⊖	d																								
Elephant & Castle	d																								
London Blackfriars 3 ⊖	a																								
	d																								
City Thameslink 3	d																								
Farringdon 3 ⊖	d																								
St Pancras International 15 ⊖	a																								
	d	09 04			09 20	09 30	09 34		09 50	10 00		10 04			10 20	10 30	10 34		10 50	11 00		11 04			11 20
Kentish Town	d			09 12				09 42						10 12				10 42						11 12	
West Hampstead Thameslink	d	09 10		09 16	09 28		09 40	09 46	09 58			10 10		10 16	10 28		10 40	10 46	10 58			11 10		11 16	11 28
Cricklewood	d			09 19				09 49						10 19				10 49						11 19	
Hendon	d			09 22				09 52						10 22				10 52						11 22	
Mill Hill Broadway	d			09 26				09 56						10 26				10 56						11 26	
Elstree & Borehamwood	d			09 30	09 38			10 00	10 08					10 30	10 38			11 00	11 08					11 30	11 38
Radlett	d			09 34				10 04						10 34				11 04						11 34	
St Albans City	d	09 25		09 40	09 45		09 55	10 10	10 15			10 25		10 40	10 45		10 55	11 10	11 15			11 25		11 40	11 45
Harpenden	d	09 32		09 46	09 52		10 02	10 16	10 22			10 32		10 46	10 52		11 02	11 16	11 22			11 32		11 46	11 52
Luton Airport Parkway 7 ✈	d	09 38		09 52	09 58	09 51	10 08	10 22	10 28		←	10 38		10 52	10 58	10 51	11 08	11 22	11 28		←	11 38		11 52	11 58
Luton 10	d	09 41		09a56	10 01		10 11	10a26	10 31	10 23	10 31	10 41		10a56	11 01		11 11	11a26	11 31	11 23	11 31	11 41		11a56	12 01
Leagrave	d	09 44			10 04		10 14		→		10 34	10 44			11 04		11 14		→		11 34	11 44			12 04
Harlington	d	09 50			10 10		10 20				10 40	10 50			11 10		11 20				11 40	11 50			12 10
Flitwick	d	09 54			10 14		10 24				10 44	10 54			11 14		11 24				11 44	11 54			12 14
Bedford 7	a	10 06			10 26	10 06	10 36			10 37	10 56	11 06			11 26	11 06	11 36			11 37	11 56	12 06			12 26

Please refer to separate pages within this table for services operating between Brighton and South London

At weekends please use local bus and tube services to travel to/from St Pancras International and London Bridge when no trains are operating. See local publicity for details of alternative routes and services that are available across central London

London, St.Albans, Luton - Bedford

		EM	FC	FC	FC	EM	FC	FC		FC	FC	EM	FC	FC	FC	EM	FC	FC		FC	FC	EM	FC	FC	FC
		◇1	1		1	◇1	1	1			1	◇1	1		1	◇1	1	1			1	◇1	1		1
London Bridge 4 ⊖	d																								
Elephant & Castle	d																								
London Blackfriars 3 ⊖	a																								
	d																								
City Thameslink 3	d																								
Farringdon 3 ⊖	d																								
St Pancras International 15 ⊖	a																								
	d	11 30	11 34		11 50	12 00		12 04			12 20	12 30	12 34		12 50	13 00		13 04			13 20	13 30	13 34		13 50
Kentish Town	d			11 42						12 12				12 42						13 12				13 42	
West Hampstead Thameslink	d		11 40	11 46	11 58			12 10		12 16	12 28		12 40	12 46	12 58			13 10		13 16	13 28		13 40	13 46	13 58
Cricklewood	d			11 49						12 19				12 49						13 19				13 49	
Hendon	d			11 52						12 22				12 52						13 22				13 52	
Mill Hill Broadway	d			11 56						12 26				12 56						13 26				13 56	
Elstree & Borehamwood	d			12 00	12 08					12 30	12 38			13 00	13 08					13 30	13 38			14 00	14 08
Radlett	d			12 04						12 34				13 04						13 34				14 04	
St Albans City	d		11 55	12 10	12 15			12 25		12 40	12 45		12 55	13 10	13 15			13 25		13 40	13 45		13 55	14 10	14 15
Harpenden	d		12 02	12 16	12 22			12 32		12 46	12 52		13 02	13 16	13 22			13 32		13 46	13 52		14 02	14 16	14 22
Luton Airport Parkway 7 ✈	d	11 51	12 08	12 22	12 28		←	12 38		12 52	12 58	12 51	13 08	13 22	13 28		←	13 38		13 52	13 58	13 51	14 08	14 22	14 28
Luton 10	d		12 11	12a26	12 31	12 23	12 31	12 41		12a56	13 01		13 11	13a26	13 31	13 23	13 31	13 41		13a56	14 01		14 11	14a26	14 31
Leagrave	d		12 14		→		12 34	12 44			13 04		13 14		→		13 34	13 44			14 04		14 14		→
Harlington	d		12 20				12 40	12 50			13 10		13 20				13 40	13 50			14 10		14 20		
Flitwick	d		12 24				12 44	12 54			13 14		13 24				13 44	13 54			14 14		14 24		
Bedford 7	a	12 06	12 36			12 37	12 56	13 06			13 26	13 06	13 36			13 37	13 56	14 06			14 26	14 06	14 36		

		EM	FC	FC		FC	FC	EM	FC	FC	FC	EM	FC	FC		FC	FC	EM	FC	FC	FC	EM	FC	FC	
		◇1	1	1			1	◇1	1		1	◇1	1	1			1	◇1	1		1	◇1	1	1	
London Bridge 4 ⊖	d																								
Elephant & Castle	d																								
London Blackfriars 3 ⊖	a																								
	d																								
City Thameslink 3	d																								
Farringdon 3 ⊖	d																								
St Pancras International 15 ⊖	a																								
	d	14 00		14 04			14 20	14 30	14 34		14 50	15 00		15 04			15 20	15 30	15 34		15 50	16 00		16 04	
Kentish Town	d					14 12				14 42						15 12				15 42					
West Hampstead Thameslink	d			14 10		14 16	14 28		14 40	14 46	14 58			15 10		15 16	15 28		15 40	15 46	15 58			16 10	
Cricklewood	d					14 19				14 49						15 19				15 49					
Hendon	d					14 22				14 52						15 22				15 52					
Mill Hill Broadway	d					14 26				14 56						15 26				15 56					
Elstree & Borehamwood	d					14 30	14 38			15 00	15 08					15 30	15 38			16 00	16 08				
Radlett	d					14 34				15 04						15 34				16 04					
St Albans City	d			14 25		14 40	14 45		14 55	15 10	15 15			15 25		15 40	15 45		15 55	16 10	16 15			16 25	
Harpenden	d			14 32		14 46	14 52		15 02	15 16	15 22			15 32		15 46	15 52		16 02	16 16	16 22			16 32	
Luton Airport Parkway 7 ✈	d		←	14 38		14 52	14 58	14 51	15 08	15 22	15 28		←	15 38		15 52	15 58	15 51	16 08	16 22	16 28		←	16 38	
Luton 10	d	14 23	14 31	14 41		14a56	15 01		15 11	15a26	15 31	15 23	15 31	15 41		15a56	16 01		16 11	16a26	16 31	16 23	16 31	16 41	
Leagrave	d		14 34	14 44			15 04		15 14		→		15 34	15 44			16 04		16 14		→		16 34	16 44	
Harlington	d		14 40	14 50			15 10		15 20				15 40	15 50			16 10		16 20				16 40	16 50	
Flitwick	d		14 44	14 54			15 14		15 24				15 44	15 54			16 14		16 24				16 44	16 54	
Bedford 7	a	14 37	14 56	15 06			15 26	15 06	15 36			15 37	15 56	16 06			16 26	16 06	16 36			16 37	16 56	17 06	

		FC	FC	EM	FC	FC	FC	EM	FC	FC		FC	FC	EM	FC	FC	FC	EM	FC	FC		FC	FC	EM	FC
			1	◇1	1		1	◇1	1	1			1	◇1	1		1	◇1	1	1			1	◇1	1
London Bridge 4 ⊖	d																								
Elephant & Castle	d																								
London Blackfriars 3 ⊖	a																								
	d																								
City Thameslink 3	d																								
Farringdon 3 ⊖	d																								
St Pancras International 15 ⊖	a																								
	d		16 20	16 30	16 34		16 50	17 00		17 04			17 20	17 30	17 34		17 50	18 00		18 04			18 20	18 30	18 34
Kentish Town	d	16 12				16 42						17 12				17 42						18 12			
West Hampstead Thameslink	d	16 16	16 28		16 40	16 46	16 58			17 10		17 16	17 28		17 40	17 46	17 58			18 10		18 16	18 28		18 40
Cricklewood	d	16 19				16 49						17 19				17 49						18 19			
Hendon	d	16 22				16 52						17 22				17 52						18 22			
Mill Hill Broadway	d	16 26				16 56						17 26				17 56						18 26			
Elstree & Borehamwood	d	16 30	16 38			17 00	17 08					17 30	17 38			18 00	18 08					18 30	18 38		
Radlett	d	16 34				17 04						17 34				18 04						18 34			
St Albans City	d	16 40	16 45		16 55	17 10	17 15			17 25		17 40	17 45		17 55	18 10	18 15			18 25		18 40	18 45		18 55
Harpenden	d	16 46	16 52		17 02	17 16	17 22			17 32		17 46	17 52		18 02	18 16	18 22			18 32		18 46	18 52		19 02
Luton Airport Parkway 7 ✈	d	16 52	16 58	16 51	17 08	17 22	17 28		←	17 38		17 52	17 58	17 51	18 08	18 22	18 28		←	18 38		18 52	18 58	18 51	19 08
Luton 10	d	16a56	17 01		17 11	17a26	17 31	17 23	17 31	17 41		17a56	18 01		18 11	18a26	18 31	18 23	18 31	18 41		18a56	19 01		19 11
Leagrave	d		17 04		17 14		→		17 34	17 44			18 04		18 14		→		18 34	18 44			19 04		19 14
Harlington	d		17 10		17 20				17 40	17 50			18 10		18 20				18 40	18 50			19 10		19 20
Flitwick	d		17 14		17 24				17 44	17 54			18 14		18 24				18 44	18 54			19 14		19 24
Bedford 7	a		17 26	17 06	17 36			17 37	17 56	18 06			18 26	18 06	18 36			18 37	18 56	19 06			19 26	19 06	19 36

Please refer to separate pages within this table for services operating between Brighton and South London

At weekends please use local bus and tube services to travel to/from St Pancras International and London Bridge when no trains are operating. See local publicity for details of alternative routes and services that are available across central London

London, St.Albans, Luton - Bedford

		FC	FC 1	EM ◇1	FC 1	FC 1	FC	FC 1	EM ◇1	FC 1	FC	EM ◇1	FC	FC 1	FC	EM ◇1	FC 1	FC	EM ◇1	FC	FC 1 A	FC 1 B	FC A
London Bridge 4 ⊖	d																						
Elephant & Castle	d																						
London Blackfriars 3 ⊖	a																						
	d																						
City Thameslink 3	d																						
Farringdon 3 ⊖	d																						
St Pancras International 15 ⊖	a																						
	d		18 50	19 00		19 04		19 20	19 30	19 34	19 48	20 00		20 04	20 18	20 30	20 34	20 48	21 00		21 04	21 04	21 18
Kentish Town	d	18 42					19 12				19 53				20 23			20 53					21 23
West Hampstead Thameslink	d	18 46	18 58			19 10	19 16	19 28		19 40	19 57			20 10	20 27		20 40	20 57			21 10	21 12	21 27
Cricklewood	d	18 49					19 19				20 00				20 30			21 00					21 30
Hendon	d	18 52					19 22				20 03				20 33			21 03					21 33
Mill Hill Broadway	d	18 56					19 26				20 07				20 37			21 07					21 37
Elstree & Borehamwood	d	19 00	19 08				19 30	19 38			20 11				20 41			21 11					21 41
Radlett	d	19 04					19 34				20 16				20 46			21 16					21 46
St Albans City	d	19 10	19 15			19 25	19 40	19 45		19 55	20 22			20 25	20 52		20 55	21 22			21 25	21 28	21 52
Harpenden	d	19 16	19 22			19 32	19 46	19 52		20 02	20 28			20 32	20 58		21 02	21 28			21 32	21 33	21 58
Luton Airport Parkway 7 ✈	d	19 22	19 28		←	19 38	19 52	19 58	19 51	20 08	20 34		←	20 38	21 04	20 51	21 08	21 34		←	21 38	21 39	22 04
Luton 10	d	19a26	19 31	19 23	19 31	19 41	19a56	20 01		20 11	20 37	20 23	20 37	20 41	21 07		21 11	21 37	21 23	21 37	21 41	21 42	22 07
Leagrave	d		→		19 34	19 44		20 04		20 14	→		20 40	20 44	21 10		21 14	→		21 40	21 44	21 46	22 10
Harlington	d				19 40	19 50		20 10		20 20			20 46	20 50	21 16		21 20			21 46	21 50	21 51	22 16
Flitwick	d				19 44	19 54		20 14		20 24			20 50	20 54	21 20		21 24			21 50	21 54	21 55	22 20
Bedford 7	a			19 37	19 56	20 06		20 26	20 06	20 36		20 37	21 02	21 06	21 32	21 06	21 36		21 38	22 02	22 06	22 07	22 32

		FC B	EM ◇1	FC 1 A	FC 1 B	FC C	FC B	FC D	EM ◇1 E	EM ◇1 F	FC C	FC B	FC D	FC 1 D	FC 1 C	FC 1 B	FC A	FC B	EM ◇1 A	EM ◇1 B	FC 1 B	FC 1 A
London Bridge 4 ⊖	d																					
Elephant & Castle	d																					
London Blackfriars 3 ⊖	a																					
	d																					
City Thameslink 3	d																					
Farringdon 3 ⊖	d																					
St Pancras International 15 ⊖	a																					
	d	21 18	21 30	21 34	21 34	21 48	21 48	21 48	22 00	22 00				22 04	22 04	22 04	22 18	22 18	22 25	22 25	22 32	22 32
Kentish Town	d	21 23				21 53	21 53	21 53									22 23	22 23				
West Hampstead Thameslink	d	21 27		21 40	21 42	21 57	21 57	21 57						22 10	22 10	22 12	22 27	22 27			22 40	22 40
Cricklewood	d	21 30				22 00	22 00	22 00									22 30	22 30				
Hendon	d	21 33				22 03	22 03	22 03									22 33	22 33				
Mill Hill Broadway	d	21 37				22 07	22 07	22 07									22 37	22 37				
Elstree & Borehamwood	d	21 41				22 11	22 11	22 11									22 41	22 41				
Radlett	d	21 46				22 16	22 16	22 16									22 46	22 46				
St Albans City	d	21 52		21 55	21 58	22 22	22 22	22 22						22 25	22 25	22 28	22 52	22 52			22 56	22 56
Harpenden	d	21 58		22 02	22 04	22 27	22 28	22 28						22 32	22 32	22 34	22 58	22 58			23 02	23 02
Luton Airport Parkway 7 ✈	d	22 04	21 51	22 08	22 10	22 33	22 34	22 34			←	←	←	22 38	22 38	22 40	23 04	23 04	22 46	22 47	23 08	23 08
Luton 10	d	22 07		22 11	22 13	22 36	22 37	22 37	22 24	22 25	22 36	22 37	22 37	22 41	22 41	22 43	23 07	23 07			23 11	23 11
Leagrave	d	22 10		22 14	22 16	→	→	→			22 40	22 40	22 40	22 44	22 45	22 46	23 11	23 11			23 15	23 15
Harlington	d	22 16		22 20	22 22						22 46	22 46	22 46	22 50	22 50	22 52	23 16	23 16			23 19	23 20
Flitwick	d	22 20		22 24	22 26						22 50	22 50	22 50	22 54	22 54	22 56	23 20	23 20			23 23	23 24
Bedford 7	a	22 32	22 09	22 36	22 38				22 41	22 41	23 02	23 02	23 02	23 06	23 07	23 08	23 34	23 34	23 01	23 02	23 38	23 38

Please refer to separate pages within this table for services operating between Brighton and South London

At weekends please use local bus and tube services to travel to/from St Pancras International and London Bridge when no trains are operating. See local publicity for details of alternative routes and services that are available across central London

London, St.Albans, Luton - Bedford

		FC A	FC B	FC 1 G	FC 1 H	FC 1 I	FC 1 J	FC 1 C	FC A	FC B	FC 1 H	FC 1 G	FC 1 J	FC 1 I	FC 1 C	FC A	FC B
London Bridge 4 ⊖	d																
Elephant & Castle	d																
London Blackfriars 3 ⊖	a																
	d																
City Thameslink 3	d																
Farringdon 3 ⊖	d																
St Pancras International 15 ⊖	a																
	d	22 48	22 48	23 02	23 02	23 02	23 02	23 02	23 18	23 18	23 32	23 32	23 32	23 32	23 32	23 48	23 48
Kentish Town	d	22 53	22 53						23 23	23 23						23 53	23 53
West Hampstead Thameslink	d	22 57	22 57	23 10	23 10	23 10	23 10	23 10	23 27	23 27	23 40	23 40	23 39	23 40	23 40	23 57	23 57
Cricklewood	d	23 00	23 00			23 13	23 13	23 13	23 30	23 30			23 43	23 43	23 43	00 01	00 01
Hendon	d	23 03	23 03			23 16	23 16	23 16	23 33	23 33			23 46	23 46	23 46	00 03	00 03
Mill Hill Broadway	d	23 07	23 07			23 20	23 20	23 20	23 37	23 37			23 50	23 50	23 50	00 07	00 07
Elstree & Borehamwood	d	23 11	23 11			23 24	23 24	23 24	23 41	23 41			23 54	23 54	23 54	00 11	00 11
Radlett	d	23 16	23 16			23 28	23 28	23 28	23 46	23 46			23 58	23 58	23 58	00 16	00 16
St Albans City	d	23 22	23 22	23 26	23 26	23 34	23 34	23 34	23 52	23 52	23 56	23 56	00 04	00 04	00 04	00 22	00 22
Harpenden	d	23 28	23 28	23 32	23 32	23 40	23 40	23 40	23 58	23 58	00 02	00 02	00 10	00 10	00 10	00 28	00 28
Luton Airport Parkway 7 ✈	d	23 34	23 34	23 38	23 38	23 46	23 46	23 46	00 04	00 04	00 08	00 08	00 16	00 16	00 16	00 34	00 34
Luton 10	d	23 37	23 37	23 41	23 41	23 49	23 49	23 49	00 07	00 07	00 11	00 11	00 19	00 19	00 19	00 37	00 37
Leagrave	d	23 41	23 41	23 45	23 45	23 53	23 53	23 53	00 11	00 11	00 15	00 15	00 23	00 23	00 23	00 41	00 41
Harlington	d	23 46	23 46	23 49	23 50	23 58	23 58	23 58	00 16	00 16	00 20	00 20	00 28	00 28	00 28	00 46	00 46
Flitwick	d	23 50	23 50	23 53	23 54	00 02	00 02	00 02	00 20	00 20	00 24	00 24	00 32	00 32	00 32	00 50	00 50
Bedford 7	a	00 04	00 04	00 08	00 08	00 15	00 15	00 16	00 34	00 34	00 38	00 38	00 45	00 45	00 46	01 04	01 04

A until 30 July, from 29 October
B from 6 August until 22 October
C from 25 June until 30 July
D until 18 June, from 29 October
E until 30 July
F from 6 August
G from 17 September until 22 October
H from 29 October
I until 18 June
J from 6 August until 10 September

Please refer to separate pages within this table for services operating between Brighton and South London

At weekends please use local bus and tube services to travel to/from St Pancras International and London Bridge when no trains are operating. See local publicity for details of alternative routes and services that are available across central London

London, St.Albans, Luton - Bedford

Sundays
until 19 June

		FC	FC	FC	FC	FC	FC	FC	FC	FC	FC	FC	FC	FC	FC	FC	EM	FC	EM	FC	FC	EM	FC
		A	1 A	A	1 A	A	1										◇1 ☕	1	◇1 ☕		1	◇1 ☕	1
London Bridge 4 ⊖	d																						
Elephant & Castle	d																						
London Blackfriars 3 ⊖	a																						
	d																						
City Thameslink 3	d																						
Farringdon 3 ⊖	d																						
St Pancras International 15 ⊖	a																						
	d	22p48	23p02	23p18	23p32	23p48	00 02	00 18	00 36	01 06	01 32	06 02	07 02	07 32	08 02	08 32	09 00	09 18	09 30		09 48	10 00	10 03
Kentish Town	d	22p53		23p23		23p53		00 23	00 41	01 11	01 37	06 07	07 07	07 37	08 07	08 37				09 38			
West Hampstead Thameslink	d	22p57	23p10	23p27	23p40	23p57	00 10	00 27	00 45	01 15	01 41	06 11	07 11	07 41	08 11	08 41		09 26		09 43	09 56		10 10
Cricklewood	d	23p00	23p13	23p30	23p43	00 01	00 13	00 30	00 48	01 18	01 44	06 14	07 14	07 44	08 14	08 44				09 46			
Hendon	d	23p03	23p16	23p33	23p46	00 03	00 16	00 33	00 51	01 21	01 47	06 17	07 17	07 47	08 17	08 47				09 49			
Mill Hill Broadway	d	23p07	23p20	23p37	23p50	00 07	00 20	00 37	00 55	01 25	01 51	06 21	07 21	07 51	08 21	08 51				09 53			
Elstree & Borehamwood	d	23p11	23p24	23p41	23p54	00 11	00 24	00 41	00 59	01 29	01 55	06 25	07 25	07 55	08 25	08 55				09 57			
Radlett	d	23p16	23p28	23p46	23p58	00 16	00 28	00 46	01 04	01 34	02 00	06 30	07 30	08 00	08 30	09 00				10 01			
St Albans City	d	23p22	23p34	23p52	00 04	00 22	00 34	00 52	01 10	01 40	02 06	06 36	07 36	08 06	08 36	09 06		09 42		10 07	10 12		10 26
Harpenden	d	23p28	23p40	23p58	00 10	00 28	00 40	00 58	01 16	01 46	02 12	06 42	07 42	08 12	08 42	09 12		09 48		10 13	10 18		10 32
Luton Airport Parkway 7 ✈	d	23p34	23p46	00 04	00 16	00 34	00 46	01 04	01 22	01 52	02 18	06 48	07 48	08 18	08 48	09 18	09 28	09 54		10 19	10 24	10 29	10 38
Luton 10	d	23p37	23p49	00 07	00 19	00 37	00 49	01 07	01 25	01 55	02 21	06 51	07 56	08 26	08 56	09 26		09 57	10 02	10a22	10 27		10a42
Leagrave	d	23p41	23p53	00 11	00 23	00 41	00 53	01 11	01 29	01 59	02 25	06 55	07 59	08 29	08 59	09 30		10 00			10 30		
Harlington	d	23p46	23p58	00 16	00 28	00 46	00 58	01 16	01 34	02 04	02 30	07 00	08 07	08 37	09 07	09 35		10 06			10 36		
Flitwick	d	23p50	00 02	00 20	00 32	00 50	01 03	01 20	01 38	02 08	02 34	07a07	08 11	08 41	09 11	09 39		10 10			10 40		
Bedford 7	a	00 04	00 15	00 34	00 45	01 04	01 15	01 34	01 52	02 22	02 48		08 23	08 53	09 23	09 53	09 51	10 23	10 21		10 53	10 53	

		FC	FC	EM	FC	FC	FC	EM	FC	FC	FC	EM	FC	FC	FC	EM	FC	FC	FC	EM	FC	FC	FC
			1	◇1 ☕	1		1	◇1 ☕	1		1	◇1 ☕	1		1	◇1 ☕	1		1	◇1 ☕	1		1
London Bridge 4 ⊖	d																						
Elephant & Castle	d																						
London Blackfriars 3 ⊖	a																						
	d																						
City Thameslink 3	d																						
Farringdon 3 ⊖	d																						
St Pancras International 15 ⊖	a																						
	d		10 18	10 30	10 33		10 48	11 00	11 03		11 18	11 30	11 33		11 48	12 00	12 03		12 18	12 30	12 33		12 48
Kentish Town	d	10 10				10 40				11 10				11 40				12 10				12 40	
West Hampstead Thameslink	d	10 14	10 26		10 40	10 44	10 56		11 10	11 14	11 26		11 40	11 44	11 56		12 10	12 14	12 26		12 40	12 44	12 56
Cricklewood	d	10 17				10 47				11 17				11 47				12 17				12 47	
Hendon	d	10 20				10 50				11 20				11 50				12 20				12 50	
Mill Hill Broadway	d	10 24				10 54				11 24				11 54				12 24				12 54	
Elstree & Borehamwood	d	10 28				10 58				11 28				11 58				12 28				12 58	
Radlett	d	10 32				11 02				11 32				12 02				12 32				13 02	
St Albans City	d	10 38	10 42		10 56	11 08	11 12		11 26	11 38	11 42		11 56	12 08	12 12		12 26	12 38	12 42		12 56	13 08	13 12
Harpenden	d	10 44	10 48		11 02	11 14	11 18		11 32	11 44	11 48		12 02	12 14	12 18		12 32	12 44	12 48		13 02	13 14	13 18
Luton Airport Parkway 7 ✈	d	10 50	10 54		11 08	11 20	11 24	11 29	11 38	11 50	11 54	11 59	12 08	12 20	12 24	12 29	12 38	12 50	12 54	12 59	13 08	13 20	13 24
Luton 10	d	10a53	10 57	11 02	11a14	11a23	11 27	11 32	11a42	11a53	11 57	12 02	12a12	12a23	12 27	12 33	12a42	12a53	12 57	13 03	13a12	13a23	13 27
Leagrave	d		11 00				11 30				12 00				12 30				13 00				13 30
Harlington	d		11 06				11 36				12 06				12 36				13 06				13 36
Flitwick	d		11 10				11 40				12 10				12 40				13 10				13 40
Bedford 7	a		11 23	11 24			11 53	11 56			12 23	12 26			12 53	12 57			13 23	13 26			13 53

		EM	FC	FC	FC	EM	FC	FC	FC	EM	FC	FC	FC	EM	FC	FC	FC	EM	FC	FC	FC	EM
		◇1 ☕	1		1	◇1 ☕	1		1	◇1 ☕	1		1	◇1 ☕	1		1	◇1 ☕	1		1	◇1 ☕
London Bridge 4 ⊖	d																					
Elephant & Castle	d																					
London Blackfriars 3 ⊖	a																					
	d																					
City Thameslink 3	d																					
Farringdon 3 ⊖	d																					
St Pancras International 15 ⊖	a																					
	d	13 00	13 03		13 18	13 30	13 33		13 48	14 00	14 03		14 18	14 30	14 33		14 48	15 00	15 03		15 18	15 30
Kentish Town	d			13 10				13 40				14 10				14 40				15 10		
West Hampstead Thameslink	d		13 10	13 14	13 26		13 40	13 44	13 56		14 10	14 14	14 26		14 40	14 44	14 56		15 10	15 14	15 26	
Cricklewood	d			13 17				13 47				14 17				14 47				15 17		
Hendon	d			13 20				13 50				14 20				14 50				15 20		
Mill Hill Broadway	d			13 24				13 54				14 24				14 54				15 24		
Elstree & Borehamwood	d			13 28				13 58				14 28				14 58				15 28		
Radlett	d			13 32				14 02				14 32				15 02				15 32		
St Albans City	d		13 26	13 38	13 42		13 56	14 08	14 12		14 26	14 38	14 42		14 56	15 08	15 12		15 26	15 38	15 42	
Harpenden	d		13 32	13 44	13 48		14 02	14 14	14 18		14 32	14 44	14 48		15 02	15 14	15 18		15 32	15 44	15 48	
Luton Airport Parkway 7 ✈	d	13 29	13 38	13 50	13 54	13 58	14 08	14 20	14 24	14 29	14 38	14 50	14 54		15 08	15 20	15 24	15 29	15 38	15 50	15 54	
Luton 10	d	13 33	13a42	13a53	13 57	14 02	14a12	14a23	14 27		14a42	14a53	14 57	15 01	15a12	15a23	15 27		15 41	15a53	15 57	16 01
Leagrave	d				14 00				14 30				15 00				15 30		15 44		16 00	
Harlington	d				14 06				14 36				15 06				15 36		15 50		16 06	
Flitwick	d				14 10				14 40				15 10				15 40		15 54		16 10	
Bedford 7	a	13 57			14 23	14 19			14 53	14 47			15 23	15 17			15 53	15 47	16 06		16 22	16 17

A not 22 May

Please refer to separate pages within this table for services operating between Brighton and South London

At weekends please use local bus and tube services to travel to/from St Pancras International and London Bridge when no trains are operating. See local publicity for details of alternative routes and services that are available across central London

Table 52

London, St.Albans, Luton - Bedford

Sundays
until 19 June

		FC	FC	FC	EM	FC	FC	FC	EM	FC	FC	FC	FC	EM	FC	FC	FC	EM	FC	FC	FC	FC	EM
		1		1	◇1 ☕	1		1	◇1 ☕	1	1		1	◇1 ☕	1		1	◇1 ☕	1	1		1	◇1 ☕
London Bridge 4 ⊖	d																						
Elephant & Castle	d																						
London Blackfriars 3 ⊖	a																						
	d																						
City Thameslink 3	d																						
Farringdon 3 ⊖	d																						
St Pancras International 15 ⊖	a																						
	d	15 33		15 48	16 00	16 03		16 18	16 30		16 33		16 48	17 00	17 03		17 18	17 30		17 33		17 48	18 00
Kentish Town	d		15 40				16 10					16 40				17 10					17 40		
West Hampstead Thameslink	d	15 40	15 44	15 56		16 10	16 14	16 26			16 40	16 44	16 56		17 10	17 14	17 26			17 40	17 44	17 56	
Cricklewood	d		15 47				16 17					16 47				17 17					17 47		
Hendon	d		15 50				16 20					16 50				17 20					17 50		
Mill Hill Broadway	d		15 54				16 24					16 54				17 24					17 54		
Elstree & Borehamwood	d		15 58				16 28					16 58				17 28					17 58		
Radlett	d		16 02				16 32					17 02				17 32					18 02		
St Albans City	d	15 56	16 08	16 12		16 26	16 38	16 42			16 56	17 08	17 12		17 26	17 38	17 42			17 56	18 08	18 12	
Harpenden	d	16 02	16 14	16 18		16 32	16 44	16 48			17 02	17 14	17 18		17 32	17 44	17 48			18 02	18 14	18 18	
Luton Airport Parkway 7 ✈	d	16 08	16 20	16 24	16 29	16 38	16 50	16 54		←	17 08	17 20	17 24	17 21	17 38	17 50	17 54		←	18 08	18 20	18 24	18 21
Luton 10	d	16 11	16a23	16 27		16 41	16a53	16 57	16 52	16 57	17 11	17a23	17 27		17 41	17a53	17 57	17 52	17 57	18 11	18a23	18 27	
Leagrave	d	16 14		16 30		16 44		→		17 00	17 14		17 30		17 44		→		18 00	18 14		18 30	
Harlington	d	16 20		16 36		16 50				17 06	17 20		17 36		17 50				18 06	18 20		18 36	
Flitwick	d	16 24		16 40		16 54				17 10	17 24		17 40		17 54				18 10	18 24		18 40	
Bedford 7	a	16 36		16 52	16 47	17 06			17 15	17 22	17 36		17 52	17 45	18 06			18 15	18 22	18 36		18 52	18 45

		FC	FC	FC	EM	FC	FC	FC	FC	EM	FC	FC	EM	FC	FC	FC	EM	FC	FC	EM	FC	FC
		1		1	◇1 ☕	1	1			◇1 ☕	1		◇1 ☕		1		◇1 ☕	1		◇1 ☕		1
London Bridge 4 ⊖	d																					
Elephant & Castle	d																					
London Blackfriars 3 ⊖	a																					
	d																					
City Thameslink 3	d																					
Farringdon 3 ⊖	d																					
St Pancras International 15 ⊖	a																					
	d	18 03		18 18	18 30		18 33		18 48	19 00	19 03	19 18	19 30		19 33	19 48	20 00	20 03	20 18	20 30		20 33
Kentish Town	d		18 10					18 40	18 53			19 23				19 53			20 23			
West Hampstead Thameslink	d	18 10	18 14	18 26			18 40	18 44	18 57		19 10	19 27			19 40	19 57		20 10	20 27			20 40
Cricklewood	d		18 17					18 47	19 00			19 30				20 00			20 30			
Hendon	d		18 20					18 50	19 03			19 33				20 03			20 33			
Mill Hill Broadway	d		18 24					18 54	19 07			19 37				20 07			20 37			
Elstree & Borehamwood	d		18 28					18 58	19 11			19 41				20 11			20 41			
Radlett	d		18 32					19 02	19 16			19 46				20 16			20 46			
St Albans City	d	18 26	18 38	18 42			18 56	19 08	19 22		19 26	19 52			19 56	20 22		20 26	20 52			20 56
Harpenden	d	18 32	18 44	18 48			19 02	19 14	19 28		19 32	19 58			20 02	20 28		20 32	20 58			21 02
Luton Airport Parkway 7 ✈	d	18 38	18 50	18 54		←	19 08	19 20	19 34	19 21	19 38	20 04		←	20 08	20 34	20 23	20 38	21 04		←	21 08
Luton 10	d	18 41	18a53	18 57	18 52	18 57	19 11	19a23	19 37		19 41	20 07	19 52	20 07	20 11	20 37		20 41	21 07	20 54	21 07	21 11
Leagrave	d	18 44		→		19 00	19 14		19 40		19 44	→		20 10	20 14	20 40		20 44	→		21 10	21 14
Harlington	d	18 50				19 06	19 20		19 46		19 50			20 16	20 20	20 46		20 50			21 16	21 20
Flitwick	d	18 54				19 10	19 24		19 50		19 54			20 20	20 24	20 50		20 54			21 20	21 24
Bedford 7	a	19 06			19 15	19 22	19 36		20 02	19 45	20 06		20 15	20 32	20 36	21 02	20 47	21 06		21 17	21 32	21 36

		FC	EM	FC	FC	EM	FC	FC	FC	FC	EM	FC	EM	FC	FC
			◇1 ☕	1		◇1 ☕		1			◇1 ☕		◇1 ☕		
London Bridge 4 ⊖	d														
Elephant & Castle	d														
London Blackfriars 3 ⊖	a														
	d														
City Thameslink 3	d														
Farringdon 3 ⊖	d														
St Pancras International 15 ⊖	a														
	d	20 48	21 00	21 03	21 18	21 30		21 33	21 48	22 04	22 30	22 34	23 00	23 04	23 32
Kentish Town	d	20 53			21 23				21 53	22 09		22 39		23 09	23 37
West Hampstead Thameslink	d	20 57		21 10	21 27			21 40	21 57	22 13		22 43		23 13	23 41
Cricklewood	d	21 00			21 30				22 00	22 16		22 46		23 16	23 44
Hendon	d	21 03			21 33				22 03	22 19		22 49		23 19	23 47
Mill Hill Broadway	d	21 07			21 37				22 07	22 23		22 53		23 23	23 51
Elstree & Borehamwood	d	21 11			21 41				22 11	22 27		22 57		23 27	23 55
Radlett	d	21 16			21 46				22 16	22 32		23 02		23 32	00 01
St Albans City	d	21 22		21 26	21 52			21 56	22 22	22 38		23 08		23 38	00 06
Harpenden	d	21 28		21 32	21 58			22 02	22 28	22 44		23 14		23 44	00 12
Luton Airport Parkway 7 ✈	d	21 34	21 23	21 38	22 04		←	22 08	22 34	22 50	22 53	23 20	23 27	23 50	00 18
Luton 10	d	21 37		21 41	22 07	21 54	22 07	22 11	22 37	22 53		23 23		23 53	00 21
Leagrave	d	21 40		21 44	→		22 10	22 14	22 40	22 56		23 26		23 56	00 25
Harlington	d	21 46		21 50			22 16	22 20	22 46	23 02		23 32		00 02	00 30
Flitwick	d	21 50		21 54			22 20	22 24	22 50	23 06		23 36		00 06	00 34
Bedford 7	a	22 02	21 47	22 06		22 17	22 32	22 36	23 02	23 20	23 17	23 50	23 50	00 20	00 48

Please refer to separate pages within this table for services operating between Brighton and South London

At weekends please use local bus and tube services to travel to/from St Pancras International and London Bridge when no trains are operating. See local publicity for details of alternative routes and services that are available across central London

London, St.Albans, Luton - Bedford

		FC	FC	FC	FC	FC	FC	FC	FC	FC		FC	FC	FC	FC	FC	FC	EM	FC	FC		EM	FC	FC	FC
			■1		■1		■1											◇■1		■1		◇■1			■1
London Bridge ■4 ⊖	d																								
Elephant & Castle	d																								
London Blackfriars ■3 ⊖	a																								
	d																								
City Thameslink ■3	d																								
Farringdon ■3 ⊖	d																								
St Pancras International ■15 ⊖	a																								
	d	22p48	23p02	23p18	23p32	23p48	00 02	00 18	00 36	01 06		01 32	06 02	07 02	07 32	08 02	08 32	09 00	09 03	09 18		09 30	09 35		09 48
Kentish Town	d	22p53		23p23		23p53		00 23	00 41	01 11		01 37	06 07	07 07	07 37	08 07	08 37		09 07				09 39	09 40	
West Hampstead Thameslink	d	22p57	23p10	23p27	23p40	23p57	00 10	00 27	00 45	01 15		01 41	06 11	07 11	07 41	08 11	08 41		09 11	09 26			09 44	09 44	09 56
Cricklewood	d	23p00	23p13	23p30	23p43	00 01	00 13	00 30	00 48	01 18		01 44	06 14	07 14	07 44	08 14	08 44		09 14				09 47	09 47	
Hendon	d	23p03	23p16	23p33	23p46	00 03	00 16	00 33	00 51	01 21		01 47	06 17	07 17	07 47	08 17	08 47		09 17				09 50	09 50	
Mill Hill Broadway	d	23p07	23p20	23p37	23p50	00 07	00 20	00 37	00 55	01 25		01 51	06 21	07 21	07 51	08 21	08 51		09 21				09 54	09 54	
Elstree & Borehamwood	d	23p11	23p24	23p41	23p54	00 11	00 24	00 41	00 59	01 29		01 55	06 25	07 25	07 55	08 25	08 55		09 25				09 58	09 58	
Radlett	d	23p16	23p28	23p46	23p58	00 16	00 28	00 46	01 04	01 34		02 00	06 30	07 30	08 00	08 30	09 00		09 30				10 02	10 02	
St Albans City	d	23p22	23p34	23p52	00 04	00 22	00 34	00 52	01 10	01 40		02 06	06 36	07 36	08 06	08 36	09 06		09 36	09 42			10 08	10 08	10 12
Harpenden	d	23p28	23p40	23p58	00 10	00 28	00 40	00 58	01 16	01 46		02 12	06 42	07 42	08 12	08 42	09 12		09 42	09 48			10 14	10 14	10 18
Luton Airport Parkway ■7 ✈	d	23p34	23p46	00 04	00 16	00 34	00 46	01 04	01 22	01 52		02 18	06 48	07 48	08 18	08 48	09 18	09 29	09 48	09 54			10 20	10 20	10 24
Luton ■10	d	23p37	23p49	00 07	00 19	00 37	00 49	01 07	01 25	01 55		02 21	06 51	07 56	08 26	08 56	09 26		09 57	09 57		10 04	10a23	10a23	10 27
Leagrave	d	23p41	23p53	00 11	00 23	00 41	00 53	01 11	01 29	01 59		02 25	06 54	07 59	08 29	08 59	09 29		10 00	10 00					10 30
Harlington	d	23p46	23p58	00 16	00 28	00 46	00 58	01 16	01 34	02 04		02 30	07 00	08 07	08 37	09 07	09 37		10 06	10 06					10 36
Flitwick	d	23p50	00 02	00 20	00 32	00 50	01 03	01 20	01 38	02 08		02 34	07a07	08 11	08 41	09 11	09 41		10 11	10 11					10 41
Bedford ■7	a	00 04	00 16	00 34	00 46	01 04	01 16	01 34	01 52	02 22		02 48		08 23	08 53	09 23	09 53	09 54	10 23	10 23		10 24			10 53

		EM	FC	FC	FC	EM		FC	FC	FC	EM	FC	FC	FC	EM	FC		FC	FC	EM	FC	FC	FC	EM	FC
		◇■1	■1		■1	◇■1		■1		■1	◇■1	■1		■1	◇■1	■1			■1	◇■1	■1		■1	◇■1	■1
London Bridge ■4 ⊖	d																								
Elephant & Castle	d																								
London Blackfriars ■3 ⊖	a																								
	d																								
City Thameslink ■3	d																								
Farringdon ■3 ⊖	d																								
St Pancras International ■15 ⊖	a																								
	d	10 00	10 03		10 18	10 30		10 33		10 48	11 00	11 03		11 18	11 30	11 33			11 48	12 00	12 03		12 18	12 30	12 33
Kentish Town	d			10 10					10 40				11 10					11 40				12 10			
West Hampstead Thameslink	d		10 10	10 14	10 26			10 40	10 44	10 56		11 10	11 14	11 26		11 40		11 44	11 56		12 10	12 14	12 26		12 40
Cricklewood	d			10 17					10 47				11 17					11 47				12 17			
Hendon	d			10 20					10 50				11 20					11 50				12 20			
Mill Hill Broadway	d			10 24					10 54				11 24					11 54				12 24			
Elstree & Borehamwood	d			10 28					10 58				11 28					11 58				12 28			
Radlett	d			10 32					11 02				11 32					12 02				12 32			
St Albans City	d		10 26	10 38	10 42			10 56	11 08	11 12		11 26	11 38	11 42		11 56		12 08	12 12		12 26	12 38	12 42		12 56
Harpenden	d		10 32	10 44	10 48			11 02	11 14	11 18		11 32	11 44	11 48		12 02		12 14	12 18		12 32	12 44	12 48		13 02
Luton Airport Parkway ■7 ✈	d	10 29	10 38	10 50	10 54			11 08	11 20	11 24	11 29	11 38	11 50	11 54	11 59	12 08		12 20	12 24	12 29	12 38	12 50	12 54	12 59	13 08
Luton ■10	d		10a42	10a53	10 57	11 02		11a12	11a23	11 27	11 32	11a42	11a53	11 57	12 02	12a12		12a23	12 27	12 33	12a42	12a53	12 57	13 03	13a12
Leagrave	d				11 00					11 30				12 00					12 30				13 00		
Harlington	d				11 06					11 36				12 06					12 36				13 06		
Flitwick	d				11 11					11 41				12 11					12 41				13 11		
Bedford ■7	a	10 53			11 23	11 23				11 53	11 53			12 23	12 23				12 53	12 54			13 23	13 26	

		FC		FC	EM	FC	FC	FC	EM	FC	FC	FC		EM	FC	FC	FC	EM	FC	FC	FC	FC		EM	FC
				■1	◇■1	■1		■1	◇■1	■1		■1		◇■1	■1		■1	◇■1	■1	■1		■1		◇■1	■1
London Bridge ■4 ⊖	d																								
Elephant & Castle	d																								
London Blackfriars ■3 ⊖	a																								
	d																								
City Thameslink ■3	d																								
Farringdon ■3 ⊖	d																								
St Pancras International ■15 ⊖	a																								
	d			12 48	13 00	13 03		13 18	13 30	13 33		13 48		14 00	14 03		14 18	14 30		14 33		14 48		15 00	15 03
Kentish Town	d	12 40					13 10				13 40					14 10					14 40				
West Hampstead Thameslink	d	12 44		12 56		13 10	13 14	13 26		13 40	13 44	13 56			14 10	14 14	14 26			14 40	14 44	14 56			15 10
Cricklewood	d	12 47					13 17				13 47					14 17					14 47				
Hendon	d	12 50					13 20				13 50					14 20					14 50				
Mill Hill Broadway	d	12 54					13 24				13 54					14 24					14 54				
Elstree & Borehamwood	d	12 58					13 28				13 58					14 28					14 58				
Radlett	d	13 02					13 32				14 02					14 32					15 02				
St Albans City	d	13 08		13 12		13 26	13 38	13 42		13 56	14 08	14 12			14 26	14 38	14 42			14 56	15 08	15 12			15 26
Harpenden	d	13 14		13 18		13 32	13 44	13 48		14 02	14 14	14 18			14 32	14 44	14 48			15 02	15 14	15 18			15 32
Luton Airport Parkway ■7 ✈	d	13 20		13 24	13 29	13 38	13 50	13 54	14 00	14 08	14 20	14 24		14 23	14 38	14 50	14 54		←	15 08	15 20	15 24		15 23	15 38
Luton ■10	d	13a23		13 27	13 33	13a42	13a53	13 57	14 04	14a12	14a23	14 27			14a42	14a53	14 57	14 54	14 57	15a12	15a23	15 27			15 41
Leagrave	d			13 30				14 00				14 30					→		15 00			15 30			15 44
Harlington	d			13 36				14 06				14 36							15 06			15 36			15 50
Flitwick	d			13 41				14 11				14 41							15 11			15 41			15 55
Bedford ■7	a			13 53	13 54			14 23	14 23			14 53		14 46				15 17	15 23			15 53		15 47	16 07

Please refer to separate pages within this table for services operating between Brighton and South London

At weekends please use local bus and tube services to travel to/from St Pancras International and London Bridge when no trains are operating. See local publicity for details of alternative routes and services that are available across central London

Table 52

Sundays
26 June to 31 July

London, St.Albans, Luton - Bedford

		FC	FC	EM	FC	FC	FC	FC		EM	FC	FC	FC	EM	FC	FC	FC	FC		EM	FC	FC	FC	EM	FC
			■1	◇■1	■1	■1		■1		◇■1	■1		■1	◇■1	■1	■1		■1		◇■1	■1		■1	◇■1	■1
London Bridge ■4 ⊖	d																								
Elephant & Castle	d																								
London Blackfriars ■3 ⊖	a																								
	d																								
City Thameslink ■3	d																								
Farringdon ■3 ⊖	d																								
St Pancras International ■15 ⊖	a																								
	d		15 18	15 30		15 33		15 48		16 00	16 03		16 18	16 30		16 33		16 48		17 00	17 03		17 18	17 30	
Kentish Town	d	15 10					15 40					16 10					16 40					17 10			
West Hampstead Thameslink	d	15 14	15 26			15 40	15 44	15 56			16 10	16 14	16 26			16 40	16 44	16 56			17 10	17 14	17 26		
Cricklewood	d	15 17					15 47					16 17					16 47					17 17			
Hendon	d	15 20					15 50					16 20					16 50					17 20			
Mill Hill Broadway	d	15 24					15 54					16 24					16 54					17 24			
Elstree & Borehamwood	d	15 28					15 58					16 28					16 58					17 28			
Radlett	d	15 32					16 02					16 32					17 02					17 32			
St Albans City	d	15 38	15 42			15 56	16 08	16 12			16 26	16 38	16 42			16 56	17 08	17 12			17 26	17 38	17 42		
Harpenden	d	15 44	15 48			16 02	16 14	16 18			16 32	16 44	16 48			17 02	17 14	17 18			17 32	17 44	17 48		
Luton Airport Parkway ■7 ✈	d	15 50	15 54		←	16 08	16 20	16 24		16 23	16 38	16 50	16 54		←	17 08	17 20	17 24		17 21	17 38	17 50	17 54		←
Luton ■10	d	15a53	15 57	15 54	15 57	16 11	16a23	16 27			16 41	16a53	16 57	16 52	16 57	17 11	17a23	17 27			17 41	17a53	17 57	17 52	17 57
Leagrave	d		→		16 00	16 14		16 30			16 44		→		17 00	17 14		17 30			17 44		→		18 00
Harlington	d				16 06	16 20		16 36			16 50				17 06	17 20		17 36			17 50				18 06
Flitwick	d				16 11	16 25		16 41			16 55				17 11	17 25		17 41			17 55				18 11
Bedford ■7	a			16 17	16 23	16 37		16 53		16 47	17 07			17 15	17 23	17 37		17 53		17 45	18 07			18 15	18 23

		FC	FC	FC		EM	FC	FC	FC	EM	FC	FC	FC	FC		EM	FC	FC	EM	FC	FC	FC	EM	FC	
		■1		■1		◇■1	■1		■1	◇■1	■1	■1				◇■1	■1		◇■1		■1		◇■1	■1	
London Bridge ■4 ⊖	d																								
Elephant & Castle	d																								
London Blackfriars ■3 ⊖	a																								
	d																								
City Thameslink ■3	d																								
Farringdon ■3 ⊖	d																								
St Pancras International ■15 ⊖	a																								
	d	17 33		17 48		18 00	18 03		18 18	18 30		18 33		18 48		19 00	19 03	19 18	19 30		19 33	19 48	20 00	20 03	
Kentish Town	d		17 40					18 10					18 40	18 53				19 23				19 53			
West Hampstead Thameslink	d	17 40	17 44	17 56			18 10	18 14	18 26			18 40	18 44	18 57			19 10	19 27			19 40	19 57		20 10	
Cricklewood	d		17 47					18 17					18 47	19 00				19 30				20 00			
Hendon	d		17 50					18 20					18 50	19 03				19 33				20 03			
Mill Hill Broadway	d		17 54					18 24					18 54	19 07				19 37				20 07			
Elstree & Borehamwood	d		17 58					18 28					18 58	19 11				19 41				20 11			
Radlett	d		18 02					18 32					19 02	19 16				19 46				20 16			
St Albans City	d	17 56	18 08	18 12			18 26	18 38	18 42			18 56	19 08	19 22			19 26	19 52			19 56	20 22		20 26	
Harpenden	d	18 02	18 14	18 18			18 32	18 44	18 48			19 02	19 14	19 28			19 32	19 58			20 02	20 28		20 32	
Luton Airport Parkway ■7 ✈	d	18 08	18 20	18 24		18 21	18 38	18 50	18 54		←	19 08	19 20	19 34		19 21	19 38	20 04		←	20 08	20 34	20 23	20 38	
Luton ■10	d	18 11	18a23	18 27			18 41	18a53	18 57	18 52	18 57	19 11	19a23	19 37			19 41	20 07	19 52	20 07	20 11	20 37		20 41	
Leagrave	d	18 14		18 30			18 44		→		19 00	19 14		19 40			19 44	→		20 10	20 14	20 40		20 44	
Harlington	d	18 20		18 36			18 50				19 06	19 20		19 46			19 50			20 16	20 20	20 46		20 50	
Flitwick	d	18 25		18 41			18 55				19 11	19 25		19 51			19 55			20 21	20 25	20 51		20 55	
Bedford ■7	a	18 37		18 53		18 45	19 07			19 15	19 23	19 37		20 02		19 45	20 07		20 15	20 32	20 37	21 02	20 47	21 07	

		FC	EM	FC	FC	FC	EM	FC	FC	EM		FC	FC	FC	FC	EM	FC	EM	FC	FC
			◇■1		■1		◇■1	■1		◇■1			■1			◇■1		◇■1		
London Bridge ■4 ⊖	d																			
Elephant & Castle	d																			
London Blackfriars ■3 ⊖	a																			
	d																			
City Thameslink ■3	d																			
Farringdon ■3 ⊖	d																			
St Pancras International ■15 ⊖	a																			
	d	20 18	20 30		20 33	20 48	21 00	21 03	21 18	21 30			21 33	21 48	22 04	22 30	22 34	23 00	23 04	23 32
Kentish Town	d	20 23				20 53			21 23					21 53	22 09		22 39		23 09	23 37
West Hampstead Thameslink	d	20 27			20 40	20 57		21 10	21 27				21 40	21 57	22 13		22 43		23 13	23 41
Cricklewood	d	20 30				21 00			21 30					22 00	22 16		22 46		23 16	23 44
Hendon	d	20 33				21 03			21 33					22 03	22 19		22 49		23 19	23 47
Mill Hill Broadway	d	20 37				21 07			21 37					22 07	22 23		22 53		23 23	23 51
Elstree & Borehamwood	d	20 41				21 11			21 41					22 11	22 27		22 57		23 27	23 55
Radlett	d	20 46				21 16			21 46					22 16	22 32		23 02		23 32	00 01
St Albans City	d	20 52			20 56	21 22		21 26	21 52				21 56	22 22	22 38		23 08		23 38	00 06
Harpenden	d	20 58			21 02	21 28		21 32	21 58				22 02	22 28	22 44		23 14		23 44	00 12
Luton Airport Parkway ■7 ✈	d	21 04		←	21 08	21 34	21 23	21 38	22 04			←	22 08	22 34	22 50	22 53	23 20	23 27	23 50	00 18
Luton ■10	d	21 07	20 54	21 07	21 11	21 37		21 41	22 07	21 54		22 07	22 11	22 37	22 53		23 23		23 53	00 22
Leagrave	d	→		21 10	21 14	21 40		21 44	→			22 10	22 14	22 40	22 56		23 26		23 56	00 26
Harlington	d			21 16	21 20	21 46		21 50				22 16	22 20	22 46	23 02		23 32		00 02	00 32
Flitwick	d			21 21	21 25	21 51		21 55				22 21	22 25	22 51	23 07		23 37		00 07	00 36
Bedford ■7	a		21 17	21 32	21 37	22 02	21 47	22 07		22 17		22 32	22 37	23 02	23 20	23 19	23 50	23 54	00 20	00 48

Please refer to separate pages within this table for services operating between Brighton and South London

At weekends please use local bus and tube services to travel to/from St Pancras International and London Bridge when no trains are operating. See local publicity for details of alternative routes and services that are available across central London

London, St.Albans, Luton - Bedford

		FC	FC ■1	FC	FC ■1	FC	FC ■1	FC	FC	FC		FC	FC	FC	FC	FC	FC	EM ◇■1	FC	EM ◇■1		FC	FC	FC ■1	EM ◇■1
London Bridge 4 ⊖	d																								
Elephant & Castle	d																								
London Blackfriars 3 ⊖	a																								
	d																								
City Thameslink 3	d																								
Farringdon 3 ⊖	d																								
St Pancras International 15 ⊖	a																								
	d	22p48	23p02	23p18	23p32	23p48	00 02	00 19	00 37	01 07		01 33	06 02	07 02	07 32	08 02	08 36	09 00	09 06	09 30		09 32	09 36	09 47	10 00
Kentish Town	d	22p53		23p23		23p53		00 23	00 41	01 11		01 37	06 07	07 07	07 37	08 07	08 41						09 40		
West Hampstead Thameslink	d	22p57	23p10	23p27	23p39	23p57	00 10	00 27	00 45	01 15		01 41	06 11	07 11	07 41	08 11	08 45		09 16			09 40	09 44	09 56	
Cricklewood	d	23p00	23p13	23p30	23p43	00 01	00 13	00 30	00 48	01 18		01 44	06 14	07 14	07 44	08 14	08 48		09 19				09 47		
Hendon	d	23p03	23p16	23p33	23p46	00 03	00 16	00 33	00 51	01 21		01 47	06 17	07 17	07 47	08 17	08 51		09 22				09 50		
Mill Hill Broadway	d	23p07	23p20	23p37	23p50	00 07	00 20	00 37	00 55	01 25		01 51	06 21	07 21	07 51	08 21	08 55		09 26				09 54		
Elstree & Borehamwood	d	23p11	23p24	23p41	23p54	00 11	00 24	00 41	00 59	01 29		01 55	06 25	07 25	07 55	08 25	08 59		09 30				09 58		
Radlett	d	23p16	23p28	23p46	23p58	00 16	00 28	00 46	01 04	01 34		02 00	06 30	07 30	08 00	08 30	09 04		09 35				10 02		
St Albans City	d	23p22	23p34	23p52	00 04	00 22	00 34	00 52	01 10	01 40		02 06	06 36	07 36	08 06	08 36	09 10		09 41			09 56	10 08	10 12	
Harpenden	d	23p28	23p40	23p58	00 10	00 28	00 40	00 58	01 16	01 46		02 12	06 42	07 42	08 12	08 42	09 16		09 47			10 02	10 14	10 18	
Luton Airport Parkway 7 ✈	d	23p34	23p46	00 04	00 16	00 34	00 46	01 04	01 22	01 52		02 18	06 48	07 48	08 18	08 48	09 22	09 28	09 53			10 08	10 20	10 24	10 31
Luton 10	d	23p37	23p49	00 07	00 19	00 37	00 49	01 07	01 25	01 55		02 21	06 51	07 56	08 26	08 56	09 26		09 55	10 02		10a12	10a23	10 27	
Leagrave	d	23p41	23p53	00 11	00 23	00 41	00 53	01 11	01 29	01 59		02 25	06 55	07 59	08 29	09 02	09 30		09 59					10 30	
Harlington	d	23p46	23p58	00 16	00 28	00 46	00 58	01 16	01 34	02 04		02 30	07 00	08 07	08 37	09 07	09 35		10 04					10 36	
Flitwick	d	23p50	00 02	00 20	00 32	00 50	01 03	01 20	01 38	02 08		02 34	07a07	08 11	08 41	09 11	09 39		10 08					10 40	
Bedford 7	a	00 04	00 15	00 34	00 45	01 04	01 15	01 34	01 52	02 22		02 48		08 23	08 53	09 23	09 53	09 55	10 23	10 25				10 53	10 56

		FC ■1	FC	FC ■1	EM ◇■1	FC ■1		FC	FC ■1	EM ◇■1	FC ■1	FC	FC ■1	EM ◇■1	FC ■1	FC		FC ■1	EM ◇■1	FC ■1	FC	FC ■1	EM ◇■1	FC ■1	FC
London Bridge 4 ⊖	d																								
Elephant & Castle	d																								
London Blackfriars 3 ⊖	a																								
	d																								
City Thameslink 3	d																								
Farringdon 3 ⊖	d																								
St Pancras International 15 ⊖	a																								
	d	10 02	10 06	10 17	10 30	10 32		10 36	10 47	11 00	11 02	11 06	11 17	11 30	11 32	11 36		11 47	12 00	12 02	12 06	12 17	12 30	12 32	12 36
Kentish Town	d		10 10					10 40				11 10				11 40					12 10				12 40
West Hampstead Thameslink	d	10 10	10 14	10 26		10 40		10 44	10 56		11 10	11 14	11 26		11 40	11 44		11 56		12 10	12 14	12 26		12 40	12 44
Cricklewood	d		10 17					10 47				11 17				11 47					12 17				12 47
Hendon	d		10 20					10 50				11 20				11 50					12 20				12 50
Mill Hill Broadway	d		10 24					10 54				11 24				11 54					12 24				12 54
Elstree & Borehamwood	d		10 28					10 58				11 28				11 58					12 28				12 58
Radlett	d		10 32					11 02				11 32				12 02					12 32				13 02
St Albans City	d	10 26	10 38	10 42		10 56		11 08	11 12		11 26	11 38	11 42		11 56	12 08		12 12		12 26	12 38	12 42		12 56	13 08
Harpenden	d	10 32	10 44	10 48		11 02		11 14	11 18		11 32	11 44	11 48		12 02	12 14		12 18		12 32	12 44	12 48		13 02	13 14
Luton Airport Parkway 7 ✈	d	10 38	10 50	10 54		11 08		11 20	11 24	11 31	11 38	11 50	11 54	12 03	12 08	12 20		12 24	12 31	12 38	12 50	12 54	13 03	13 08	13 20
Luton 10	d	10a42	10a53	10 57	11 02	11a12		11a23	11 27	11 35	11a42	11a53	11 57	12 07	12a12	12a23		12 27	12 35	12a42	12a53	12 57	13 06	13a12	13a23
Leagrave	d			11 00					11 30				12 00					12 30				13 00			
Harlington	d			11 06					11 36				12 06					12 36				13 06			
Flitwick	d			11 10					11 40				12 10					12 40				13 10			
Bedford 7	a			11 23	11 26				11 53	11 55			12 23	12 27				12 53	12 56			13 23	13 28		

		FC ■1		EM ◇■1	FC ■1	FC	FC ■1	EM ◇■1	FC ■1	FC	FC ■1	EM ◇■1		FC ■1	FC	FC ■1	EM ◇■1	FC ■1	FC	FC ■1	EM ◇■1	FC ■1		FC	FC ■1
London Bridge 4 ⊖	d																								
Elephant & Castle	d																								
London Blackfriars 3 ⊖	a																								
	d																								
City Thameslink 3	d																								
Farringdon 3 ⊖	d																								
St Pancras International 15 ⊖	a																								
	d	12 47		13 00	13 02	13 06	13 17	13 30	13 32	13 36	13 47	14 00		14 02	14 06	14 17	14 30	14 32	14 36	14 47	15 00	15 02		15 06	15 17
Kentish Town	d					13 10				13 40					14 10				14 40					15 10	
West Hampstead Thameslink	d	12 56			13 10	13 14	13 26		13 40	13 44	13 56			14 10	14 14	14 26		14 40	14 44	14 56		15 10		15 14	15 26
Cricklewood	d					13 17				13 47					14 17				14 47					15 17	
Hendon	d					13 20				13 50					14 20				14 50					15 20	
Mill Hill Broadway	d					13 24				13 54					14 24				14 54					15 24	
Elstree & Borehamwood	d					13 28				13 58					14 28				14 58					15 28	
Radlett	d					13 32				14 02					14 32				15 02					15 32	
St Albans City	d	13 12			13 26	13 38	13 42		13 56	14 08	14 12			14 26	14 38	14 42		14 56	15 08	15 12		15 26		15 38	15 42
Harpenden	d	13 18			13 32	13 44	13 48		14 02	14 14	14 18			14 32	14 44	14 48		15 02	15 14	15 18		15 32		15 44	15 48
Luton Airport Parkway 7 ✈	d	13 24		13 33	13 38	13 50	13 54	14 00	14 08	14 20	14 24	14 29		14 38	14 50	14 54		15 08	15 20	15 24	15 29	15 38		15 50	15 54
Luton 10	d	13 27		13 37	13a42	13a53	13 57	14 04	14a12	14a23	14 27			14a42	14a53	14 57	15 01	15a12	15a23	15 27		15 41		15a53	15 57
Leagrave	d	13 30					14 01				14 30					15 00				15 30		15 44			16 00
Harlington	d	13 36					14 08				14 36					15 06				15 36		15 50			16 06
Flitwick	d	13 40					14 13				14 40					15 10				15 40		15 54			16 10
Bedford 7	a	13 53		13 57			14 26	14 19			14 53	14 47				15 23	15 17			15 53	15 47	16 06			16 22

Please refer to separate pages within this table for services operating between Brighton and South London

At weekends please use local bus and tube services to travel to/from St Pancras International and London Bridge when no trains are operating. See local publicity for details of alternative routes and services that are available across central London

Table 52

London, St.Albans, Luton - Bedford

Sundays

7 August to 11 September

		EM ◇■1	FC ■1	FC	FC ■1	EM ◇■1	FC ■1	FC		FC ■1	EM ◇■1	FC ■1	FC ■1	FC	FC ■1	EM ◇■1	FC ■1	FC		FC ■1	EM ◇■1	FC ■1	FC ■1	FC	FC ■1
London Bridge 4 ⊖	d																								
Elephant & Castle	d																								
London Blackfriars 3 ⊖	a																								
	d																								
City Thameslink 3	d																								
Farringdon 3 ⊖	d																								
St Pancras International 15 ⊖	a																								
	d	15 30	15 32	15 36	15 47	16 00	16 02	16 06		16 17	16 30		16 32	16 36	16 47	17 00	17 02	17 06		17 17	17 30		17 32	17 36	17 47
Kentish Town	d			15 40				16 10						16 40				17 10						17 40	
West Hampstead Thameslink	d		15 40	15 44	15 56		16 10	16 14		16 26			16 40	16 44	16 56		17 10	17 14		17 26			17 40	17 44	17 56
Cricklewood	d			15 47				16 17						16 47				17 17						17 47	
Hendon	d			15 50				16 20						16 50				17 20						17 50	
Mill Hill Broadway	d			15 54				16 24						16 54				17 24						17 54	
Elstree & Borehamwood	d			15 58				16 28						16 58				17 28						17 58	
Radlett	d			16 02				16 32						17 02				17 32						18 02	
St Albans City	d		15 56	16 08	16 12		16 26	16 38		16 42			16 56	17 08	17 12		17 26	17 38		17 42			17 56	18 08	18 12
Harpenden	d		16 02	16 14	16 18		16 32	16 44		16 48			17 02	17 14	17 18		17 32	17 44		17 48			18 02	18 14	18 18
Luton Airport Parkway 7 ✈	d		16 08	16 20	16 24	16 29	16 38	16 50		16 54		←	17 08	17 20	17 24	17 21	17 38	17 50		17 54		←	18 08	18 20	18 24
Luton 10	d	16 01	16 11	16a23	16 27		16 41	16a53		16 57	16 52	16 57	17 11	17a23	17 27		17 41	17a53		17 57	17 52	17 57	18 11	18a23	18 27
Leagrave	d		16 14		16 30		16 44			→		17 00	17 14		17 30		17 44			→		18 00	18 14		18 30
Harlington	d		16 20		16 36		16 50					17 06	17 20		17 36		17 50					18 06	18 20		18 36
Flitwick	d		16 24		16 40		16 54					17 10	17 24		17 40		17 54					18 10	18 24		18 40
Bedford 7	a	16 17	16 36		16 52	16 47	17 06				17 15	17 22	17 36		17 52	17 45	18 06				18 15	18 22	18 36		18 52

		EM ◇■1	FC ■1	FC		FC ■1	EM ◇■1	FC ■1	FC ■1	FC	FC	EM ◇■1	FC ■1	FC		FC	EM ◇■1	FC	FC ■1	FC	EM ◇■1	FC ■1	FC	EM ◇■1	
London Bridge 4 ⊖	d																								
Elephant & Castle	d																								
London Blackfriars 3 ⊖	a																								
	d																								
City Thameslink 3	d																								
Farringdon 3 ⊖	d																								
St Pancras International 15 ⊖	a																								
	d	18 00	18 02	18 06		18 17	18 30		18 32	18 36	18 47	19 00	19 02	19 06		19 17	19 30		19 32	19 47	20 00	20 02	20 17	20 30	
Kentish Town	d			18 10						18 40	18 51			19 10		19 21				19 52			20 22		
West Hampstead Thameslink	d		18 10	18 14		18 26			18 40	18 44	18 55		19 10	19 14		19 25			19 40	19 56		20 10	20 26		
Cricklewood	d			18 17						18 47	18 58			19 17		19 28				19 59			20 29		
Hendon	d			18 20						18 50	19 01			19 20		19 31				20 02			20 32		
Mill Hill Broadway	d			18 24						18 54	19 05			19 24		19 35				20 06			20 36		
Elstree & Borehamwood	d			18 28						18 58	19 09			19 28		19 39				20 10			20 40		
Radlett	d			18 32						19 02	19 14			19 32		19 44				20 15			20 45		
St Albans City	d		18 26	18 38		18 42			18 56	19 08	19 20		19 26	19 38		19 50			19 56	20 21		20 26	20 51		
Harpenden	d		18 32	18 44		18 48			19 02	19 14	19 26		19 32	19 44		19 56			20 02	20 27		20 32	20 57		
Luton Airport Parkway 7 ✈	d	18 21	18 38	18 50		18 54		←	19 08	19 20	19 32	19 21	19 38	19 50		20 02		←	20 08	20 33	20 23	20 38	21 03		
Luton 10	d		18 41	18a53		18 57	18 52	18 57	19 11	19a23	19 35		19 41	19a53		20 05	19 52	20 05	20 11	20 36		20 41	21 06	20 54	
Leagrave	d		18 44			→		19 00	19 14		19 38		19 44			→		20 08	20 14	20 39		20 44	→		
Harlington	d		18 50					19 06	19 20		19 44		19 50					20 14	20 20	20 45		20 50			
Flitwick	d		18 54					19 10	19 24		19 48		19 54					20 18	20 24	20 49		20 54			
Bedford 7	a	18 45	19 06				19 15	19 22	19 36		20 02	19 45	20 06				20 15	20 32	20 36	21 02	20 47	21 06		21 17	

		FC	FC ■1	FC	EM ◇■1	FC ■1	FC	EM ◇■1	FC	FC ■1		FC	FC ■1		FC	FC	EM ◇■1	FC	EM ◇■1	FC	FC
London Bridge 4 ⊖	d																				
Elephant & Castle	d																				
London Blackfriars 3 ⊖	a																				
	d																				
City Thameslink 3	d																				
Farringdon 3 ⊖	d																				
St Pancras International 15 ⊖	a																				
	d		20 32	20 47	21 00	21 02	21 17	21 30		21 32			21 32		21 47	22 02	22 30	22 32	23 00	23 02	23 32
Kentish Town	d			20 52			21 22								21 52	22 09		22 39		23 09	23 37
West Hampstead Thameslink	d		20 40	20 56		21 10	21 26			21 40			21 40		21 56	22 13		22 43		23 13	23 41
Cricklewood	d			20 59			21 29								21 59	22 16		22 46		23 16	23 44
Hendon	d			21 02			21 32								22 02	22 19		22 49		23 19	23 47
Mill Hill Broadway	d			21 06			21 36								22 06	22 23		22 53		23 23	23 51
Elstree & Borehamwood	d			21 10			21 40								22 10	22 27		22 57		23 27	23 55
Radlett	d			21 15			21 45								22 15	22 32		23 02		23 32	00 01
St Albans City	d		20 56	21 21		21 26	21 51			21 56			21 56		22 21	22 38		23 08		23 38	00 06
Harpenden	d		21 02	21 27		21 32	21 57			22 02			22 02		22 27	22 44		23 14		23 44	00 12
Luton Airport Parkway 7 ✈	d	←	21 08	21 33	21 23	21 38	22 03		←	22 08		←	22 08		22 33	22 50	22 53	23 20	23 27	23 50	00 18
Luton 10	d	21 06	21 11	21 36		21 41	22 06	21 54	22 06	22 11		22 06	22 11		22 36	22 53		23 23		23 53	00 21
Leagrave	d	21 09	21 14	21 39		21 44	→		22 09	22 14		22 09	22 14		22 39	22 56		23 26		23 56	00 25
Harlington	d	21 15	21 20	21 45		21 50			22 15	22 20		22 15	22 20		22 45	23 02		23 32		00 02	00 30
Flitwick	d	21 19	21 24	21 49		21 54			22 19	22 24		22 19	22 24		22 49	23 06		23 36		00 06	00 34
Bedford 7	a	21 32	21 36	22 02	21 47	22 06		22 17	22 32	22 36		22 32	22 36		23 02	23 20	23 17	23 50	23 50	00 20	00 48

Please refer to separate pages within this table for services operating between Brighton and South London

At weekends please use local bus and tube services to travel to/from St Pancras International and London Bridge when no trains are operating. See local publicity for details of alternative routes and services that are available across central London

London, St.Albans, Luton - Bedford

Sundays

18 September to 23 October

	FC	FC 1	FC	FC 1	FC	FC 1	FC	FC	FC	FC	FC	FC	FC	FC	FC	EM ◇1	FC	EM ◇1	FC 1	FC	EM ◇1	FC 1
London Bridge 4 ⊖ d																						
Elephant & Castle d																						
London Blackfriars 3 ⊖ a																						
d																						
City Thameslink 3 d																						
Farringdon 3 ⊖ d																						
St Pancras International 15 ⊖ a																						
d	22p48	23p02	23p18	23p32	23p48	00 02	00 19	00 37	01 07	01 33	06 02	07 02	07 32	08 02	08 36	09 00	09 06	09 30	09 32	09 36	10 00	10 02
Kentish Town d	22p53		23p23		23p53		00 23	00 41	01 11	01 37	06 07	07 07	07 37	08 07	08 41					09 40		
West Hampstead Thameslink d	22p57	23p10	23p27	23p40	23p57	00 11	00 27	00 45	01 15	01 41	06 11	07 11	07 41	08 11	08 45		09 16		09 40	09 44		10 10
Cricklewood d	23p00		23p30		00 01		00 30	00 48	01 18	01 44	06 14	07 14	07 44	08 14	08 48		09 19			09 47		
Hendon d	23p03		23p33		00 03		00 33	00 51	01 21	01 47	06 17	07 17	07 47	08 17	08 51		09 22			09 50		
Mill Hill Broadway d	23p07		23p37		00 07		00 37	00 55	01 25	01 51	06 21	07 21	07 51	08 21	08 55		09 26			09 54		
Elstree & Borehamwood d	23p11		23p41		00 11		00 41	00 59	01 29	01 55	06 25	07 25	07 55	08 25	08 59		09 30			09 58		
Radlett d	23p16		23p46		00 16		00 46	01 04	01 34	02 00	06 30	07 30	08 00	08 30	09 04		09 35			10 02		
St Albans City d	23p22	23p26	23p52	23p56	00 22	00 27	00 52	01 10	01 40	02 06	06 36	07 36	08 06	08 36	09 10		09 41		09 55	10 08		10 26
Harpenden d	23p28	23p32	23p58	00 02	00 28	00 33	00 58	01 16	01 46	02 12	06 42	07 42	08 12	08 42	09 16		09 47		10 02	10 14		10 32
Luton Airport Parkway 7 ✈ d	23p34	23p38	00 04	00 08	00 34	00 39	01 04	01 22	01 52	02 18	06 48	07 48	08 18	08 48	09 22	09 28	09 53		10 08	10 20	10 31	10 38
Luton 10 d	23p37	23p41	00 07	00 11	00 37	00 42	01 07	01 25	01 55	02 21	06 51	07 56	08 26	08 56	09 26		09 55	10 02	10a11	10a23		10 41
Leagrave d	23p41	23p45	00 11	00 15	00 41	00 46	01 11	01 29	01 59	02 25	06 55	07 59	08 29	09 02	09 30		09 59					10 44
Harlington d	23p46	23p49	00 16	00 20	00 46	00 51	01 16	01 34	02 04	02 30	07 00	08 07	08 37	09 07	09 35		10 04					10 50
Flitwick d	23p50	23p53	00 20	00 24	00 50	00 56	01 20	01 38	02 08	02 34	07a07	08 11	08 41	09 11	09 39		10 08					10 54
Bedford 7 a	00 04	00 08	00 34	00 38	01 04	01 09	01 34	01 52	02 22	02 48		08 23	08 53	09 23	09 53	09 55	10 23	10 25			10 55	11 06

	FC	FC 1	EM ◇1	FC 1	FC	FC 1	EM ◇1	FC 1	FC	FC 1	EM ◇1	FC 1	FC	FC 1	EM ◇1	FC 1	FC	FC 1	EM ◇1	FC 1	FC	FC 1
London Bridge 4 ⊖ d																						
Elephant & Castle d																						
London Blackfriars 3 ⊖ a																						
d																						
City Thameslink 3 d																						
Farringdon 3 ⊖ d																						
St Pancras International 15 ⊖ a																						
d	10 06	10 17	10 30	10 32	10 36	10 47	11 00	11 02	11 06	11 17	11 30	11 32	11 36	11 47	12 00	12 02	12 06	12 17	12 30	12 32	12 36	12 47
Kentish Town d	10 10				10 40				11 10				11 40				12 10				12 40	
West Hampstead Thameslink d	10 14	10 26		10 40	10 44	10 56		11 10	11 14	11 26		11 40	11 44	11 56		12 10	12 14	12 26		12 40	12 44	12 56
Cricklewood d	10 17				10 47				11 17				11 47				12 17				12 47	
Hendon d	10 20				10 50				11 20				11 50				12 20				12 50	
Mill Hill Broadway d	10 24				10 54				11 24				11 54				12 24				12 54	
Elstree & Borehamwood d	10 28				10 58				11 28				11 58				12 28				12 58	
Radlett d	10 32				11 02				11 32				12 02				12 32				13 02	
St Albans City d	10 38	10 42		10 55	11 08	11 12		11 26	11 38	11 42		11 56	12 08	12 12		12 26	12 38	12 42		12 56	13 08	13 12
Harpenden d	10 44	10 48		11 02	11 14	11 18		11 32	11 44	11 48		12 02	12 14	12 18		12 32	12 44	12 48		13 02	13 14	13 18
Luton Airport Parkway 7 ✈ d	10 50	10 54		11 08	11 20	11 24	11 31	11 38	11 50	11 54	12 03	12 08	12 20	12 24	12 31	12 38	12 50	12 54	13 03	13 08	13 20	13 24
Luton 10 d	10a53	10 57	11 02	11 13	11a23	11 27	11 35	11 41	11a53	11 57	12 07	12 11	12a23	12 27	12 35	12 41	12a53	12 57	13 06	13 11	13a23	13 27
Leagrave d		11 00		11 16		11 30		11 44		12 00		12 14		12 30		12 44		13 00		13 14		13 30
Harlington d		11 06		11 22		11 36		11 50		12 06		12 20		12 36		12 50		13 06		13 20		13 36
Flitwick d		11 10		11 26		11 40		11 54		12 10		12 24		12 40		12 54		13 10		13 24		13 40
Bedford 7 a		11 23	11 26	11 38		11 53	11 55	12 06		12 23	12 28	12 36		12 53	12 56	13 06		13 23	13 28	13 36		13 53

	EM ◇1	FC 1	FC	FC 1	EM ◇1	FC 1	FC	FC 1	EM ◇1	FC 1	FC	FC 1	EM ◇1	FC 1	FC	FC 1	EM ◇1	FC 1	FC	FC 1	EM ◇1
London Bridge 4 ⊖ d																					
Elephant & Castle d																					
London Blackfriars 3 ⊖ a																					
d																					
City Thameslink 3 d																					
Farringdon 3 ⊖ d																					
St Pancras International 15 ⊖ a																					
d	13 00	13 02	13 06	13 17	13 30	13 32	13 36	13 47	14 00	14 02	14 06	14 17	14 30	14 32	14 36	14 47	15 00	15 02	15 06	15 17	15 30
Kentish Town d			13 10				13 40				14 10				14 40				15 10		
West Hampstead Thameslink d		13 10	13 14	13 26		13 40	13 44	13 56		14 10	14 14	14 26		14 40	14 44	14 56		15 10	15 14	15 26	
Cricklewood d			13 17				13 47				14 17				14 47				15 17		
Hendon d			13 20				13 50				14 20				14 50				15 20		
Mill Hill Broadway d			13 24				13 54				14 24				14 54				15 24		
Elstree & Borehamwood d			13 28				13 58				14 28				14 58				15 28		
Radlett d			13 32				14 02				14 32				15 02				15 32		
St Albans City d		13 26	13 38	13 42		13 56	14 08	14 12		14 26	14 38	14 42		14 56	15 08	15 12		15 26	15 38	15 42	
Harpenden d		13 32	13 44	13 48		14 02	14 14	14 18		14 32	14 44	14 48		15 02	15 14	15 18		15 32	15 44	15 48	
Luton Airport Parkway 7 ✈ d	13 32	13 38	13 50	13 54	14 00	14 08	14 20	14 24	14 29	14 38	14 50	14 54		15 08	15 20	15 24	15 29	15 38	15 50	15 54	
Luton 10 d	13 36	13 41	13a53	13 57	14 04	14 11	14a23	14 27		14 41	14a53	14 57	15 01	15 11	15a23	15 27		15 41	15a53	15 57	16 01
Leagrave d		13 44		14 00		14 14		14 30		14 44		15 00		15 14		15 30		15 44		16 00	
Harlington d		13 50		14 06		14 20		14 36		14 50		15 06		15 20		15 36		15 50		16 06	
Flitwick d		13 54		14 10		14 24		14 40		14 54		15 10		15 24		15 40		15 54		16 10	
Bedford 7 a	13 59	14 06		14 23	14 19	14 38		14 53	14 47	15 06		15 23	15 17	15 36		15 53	15 47	16 06		16 22	16 17

Please refer to separate pages within this table for services operating between Brighton and South London

At weekends please use local bus and tube services to travel to/from St Pancras International and London Bridge when no trains are operating. See local publicity for details of alternative routes and services that are available across central London

London, St.Albans, Luton - Bedford

Sundays

18 September to 23 October

	FC 1	FC	FC 1	EM ◇1	FC 1	FC	FC 1	EM ◇1	FC 1	FC 1	FC	FC 1	EM ◇1	FC 1	FC	FC 1	EM ◇1	FC 1	FC 1	FC	FC 1	EM ◇1
London Bridge 4 ⊖ d																						
Elephant & Castle d																						
London Blackfriars 3 ⊖ a																						
d																						
City Thameslink 3 d																						
Farringdon 3 ⊖ d																						
St Pancras International 15 ⊖ a																						
d	15 32	15 36	15 47	16 00	16 02	16 06	16 17	16 30		16 32	16 36	16 47	17 00	17 02	17 06	17 17	17 30		17 32	17 36	17 47	18 00
Kentish Town d		15 40				16 10					16 40				17 10					17 40		
West Hampstead Thameslink d	15 40	15 44	15 56		16 10	16 14	16 26			16 40	16 44	16 56		17 10	17 14	17 26			17 40	17 44	17 56	
Cricklewood d		15 47				16 17					16 47				17 17					17 47		
Hendon d		15 50				16 20					16 50				17 20					17 50		
Mill Hill Broadway d		15 54				16 24					16 54				17 24					17 54		
Elstree & Borehamwood d		15 58				16 28					16 58				17 28					17 58		
Radlett d		16 02				16 32					17 02				17 32					18 02		
St Albans City d	15 56	16 08	16 12		16 26	16 38	16 42			16 56	17 08	17 12		17 26	17 38	17 42			17 56	18 08	18 12	
Harpenden d	16 02	16 14	16 18		16 32	16 44	16 48			17 02	17 14	17 18		17 32	17 44	17 48			18 02	18 14	18 18	
Luton Airport Parkway 7 ✈ d	16 08	16 20	16 24	16 29	16 38	16 50	16 54		←	17 08	17 20	17 24	17 21	17 38	17 50	17 54		←	18 08	18 20	18 24	18 21
Luton 10 d	16 11	16a23	16 27		16 41	16a53	16 57	16 52	16 57	17 11	17a23	17 27		17 41	17a53	17 57	17 52	17 57	18 11	18a23	18 27	
Leagrave d	16 14		16 30		16 44		→		17 00	17 14		17 30		17 44		→		18 00	18 14		18 30	
Harlington d	16 20		16 36		16 50				17 06	17 20		17 36		17 50				18 06	18 20		18 36	
Flitwick d	16 24		16 40		16 54				17 10	17 24		17 40		17 54				18 10	18 24		18 40	
Bedford 7 a	16 36		16 52	16 47	17 06			17 15	17 22	17 36		17 52	17 45	18 06			18 15	18 22	18 34		18 52	18 45

	FC 1	FC	FC 1	EM ◇1	FC 1	FC 1	FC	FC	EM ◇1	FC 1	FC	FC	EM ◇1	FC	FC 1	FC	EM ◇1	FC 1	FC	EM ◇1	FC
London Bridge 4 ⊖ d																					
Elephant & Castle d																					
London Blackfriars 3 ⊖ a																					
d																					
City Thameslink 3 d																					
Farringdon 3 ⊖ d																					
St Pancras International 15 ⊖ a																					
d	18 02	18 06	18 17	18 30		18 32	18 36	18 47	19 00	19 02	19 06	19 17	19 30		19 32	19 47	20 00	20 02	20 17	20 30	
Kentish Town d		18 10					18 40	18 51			19 10	19 21				19 52			20 22		
West Hampstead Thameslink d	18 10	18 14	18 26			18 40	18 44	18 55		19 10	19 14	19 25			19 40	19 56		20 10	20 26		
Cricklewood d		18 17					18 47	18 58			19 17	19 28				19 59			20 29		
Hendon d		18 20					18 50	19 01			19 20	19 31				20 02			20 32		
Mill Hill Broadway d		18 24					18 54	19 05			19 24	19 35				20 06			20 36		
Elstree & Borehamwood d		18 28					18 58	19 09			19 28	19 39				20 10			20 40		
Radlett d		18 32					19 02	19 14			19 32	19 44				20 15			20 45		
St Albans City d	18 26	18 38	18 42			18 56	19 08	19 20		19 26	19 38	19 50			19 56	20 21		20 26	20 51		
Harpenden d	18 32	18 44	18 48			19 02	19 14	19 26		19 32	19 44	19 56			20 02	20 27		20 32	20 57		
Luton Airport Parkway 7 ✈ d	18 38	18 50	18 54		←	19 08	19 20	19 32	19 21	19 38	19 50	20 02		←	20 08	20 33	20 23	20 38	21 03		←
Luton 10 d	18 41	18a53	18 57	18 52	18 57	19 11	19a23	19 35		19 41	19a53	20 05	19 52	20 05	20 11	20 36		20 41	21 06	20 54	21 06
Leagrave d	18 44		→		19 00	19 14		19 38		19 44		→		20 08	20 14	20 39		20 44	→		21 09
Harlington d	18 50				19 06	19 20		19 44		19 50				20 14	20 20	20 45		20 50			21 15
Flitwick d	18 54				19 10	19 24		19 48		19 54				20 18	20 24	20 49		20 54			21 19
Bedford 7 a	19 06			19 15	19 22	19 34		19 58	19 45	20 06			20 15	20 30	20 36	21 01	20 47	21 06		21 17	21 31

	FC 1	FC	EM ◇1	FC 1	FC	EM ◇1	FC	FC 1	FC	FC	EM ◇1	FC	EM ◇1	FC	FC
London Bridge 4 ⊖ d															
Elephant & Castle d															
London Blackfriars 3 ⊖ a															
d															
City Thameslink 3 d															
Farringdon 3 ⊖ d															
St Pancras International 15 ⊖ a															
d	20 32	20 47	21 00	21 02	21 17	21 30		21 32	21 47	22 02	22 30	22 32	23 00	23 02	23 32
Kentish Town d		20 52			21 22				21 52	22 09		22 39		23 09	23 37
West Hampstead Thameslink d	20 40	20 56		21 10	21 26			21 40	21 56	22 13		22 43		23 13	23 41
Cricklewood d		20 59			21 29				21 59	22 16		22 46		23 16	23 44
Hendon d		21 02			21 32				22 02	22 19		22 49		23 19	23 47
Mill Hill Broadway d		21 06			21 36				22 06	22 23		22 53		23 23	23 51
Elstree & Borehamwood d		21 10			21 40				22 10	22 27		22 57		23 27	23 55
Radlett d		21 15			21 45				22 15	22 32		23 02		23 32	00 01
St Albans City d	20 56	21 21		21 26	21 51			21 56	22 21	22 38		23 08		23 38	00 06
Harpenden d	21 02	21 27		21 32	21 57			22 02	22 27	22 44		23 14		23 44	00 12
Luton Airport Parkway 7 ✈ d	21 08	21 33	21 23	21 38	22 03		←	22 08	22 33	22 50	22 53	23 20	23 27	23 50	00 18
Luton 10 d	21 11	21 36		21 41	22 06	21 54	22 06	22 11	22 36	22 53		23 23		23 53	00 21
Leagrave d	21 14	21 39		21 44	→		22 09	22 14	22 39	22 56		23 26		23 56	00 25
Harlington d	21 20	21 45		21 50			22 15	22 20	22 45	23 02		23 32		00 02	00 30
Flitwick d	21 24	21 49		21 54			22 19	22 24	22 49	23 06		23 36		00 06	00 34
Bedford 7 a	21 36	22 01	21 47	22 06		22 17	22 31	22 36	23 01	23 20	23 17	23 50	23 50	00 20	00 48

Please refer to separate pages within this table for services operating between Brighton and South London

At weekends please use local bus and tube services to travel to/from St Pancras International and London Bridge when no trains are operating. See local publicity for details of alternative routes and services that are available across central London

Table 52

Sundays from 30 October

London, St.Albans, Luton - Bedford

		FC	FC 1	FC	FC 1	FC	FC 1	FC	FC	FC		FC	FC	FC	FC	FC	FC	EM ◇1	FC	EM ◇1		FC	FC 1	EM ◇1	FC 1
London Bridge 4 ⊖	d																								
Elephant & Castle	d																								
London Blackfriars 3 ⊖	a																								
	d																								
City Thameslink 3	d																								
Farringdon 3 ⊖	d																								
St Pancras International 15 ⊖	a																								
	d	22p48	23p02	23p18	23p32	23p48	00 02	00 18	00 36	01 06		01 32	06 02	07 02	07 32	08 02	08 32	09 00	09 03	09 30		09 33	09 48	10 00	10 03
Kentish Town	d	22p53		23p23		23p53		00 23	00 41	01 11		01 37	06 07	07 07	07 37	08 07	08 37		09 07			09 37			
West Hampstead Thameslink	d	22p57	23p10	23p27	23p40	23p57	00 10	00 27	00 45	01 15		01 41	06 11	07 11	07 41	08 11	08 41		09 11			09 41	09 56		10 10
Cricklewood	d	23p00		23p30		00 01		00 30	00 48	01 18		01 44	06 14	07 14	07 44	08 14	08 44		09 14			09 44			
Hendon	d	23p03		23p33		00 03		00 33	00 51	01 21		01 47	06 17	07 17	07 47	08 17	08 47		09 17			09 47			
Mill Hill Broadway	d	23p07		23p37		00 07		00 37	00 55	01 25		01 51	06 21	07 21	07 51	08 21	08 51		09 21			09 51			
Elstree & Borehamwood	d	23p11		23p41		00 11		00 41	00 59	01 29		01 55	06 25	07 25	07 55	08 25	08 55		09 25			09 55			
Radlett	d	23p16		23p46		00 16		00 46	01 04	01 34		02 00	06 30	07 30	08 00	08 30	09 00		09 30			10 00			
St Albans City	d	23p22	23p26	23p52	23p56	00 22	00 26	00 52	01 10	01 40		02 06	06 36	07 36	08 06	08 36	09 06		09 36			10 06	10 12		10 26
Harpenden	d	23p28	23p32	23p58	00 02	00 28	00 32	00 58	01 16	01 46		02 12	06 42	07 42	08 12	08 42	09 12		09 42			10 12	10 18		10 32
Luton Airport Parkway 7 ✈	d	23p34	23p38	00 04	00 08	00 34	00 38	01 04	01 22	01 52		02 18	06 48	07 48	08 18	08 48	09 18	09 28	09 48			10 18	10 24	10 29	10 38
Luton 10	d	23p37	23p41	00 07	00 11	00 37	00 41	01 07	01 25	01 55		02 21	06 51	07 51	08 21	08 51	09 21		09 51	10 00		10 21	10 27		10 41
Leagrave	d	23p41	23p45	00 11	00 15	00 41	00 45	01 11	01 29	01 59		02 25	06 55	07 55	08 25	08 55	09 25		09 55			10 25	10 30		10 44
Harlington	d	23p46	23p50	00 16	00 20	00 46	00 50	01 16	01 34	02 04		02 30	07 00	08 00	08 30	09 00	09 30		10 00			10 30	10 36		10 50
Flitwick	d	23p50	23p54	00 20	00 24	00 50	00 55	01 20	01 38	02 08		02 34	07 04	08 04	08 34	09 04	09 34		10 04			10 34	10 40		10 54
Bedford 7	a	00 04	00 08	00 34	00 38	01 04	01 08	01 34	01 52	02 22		02 48	07 18	08 18	08 48	09 18	09 48	09 52	10 17	10 20		10 48	10 52	10 53	11 06

		FC	FC 1	EM ◇1	FC 1	FC		FC 1	EM ◇1	FC 1	FC	FC 1	EM ◇1	FC 1	FC	FC 1		EM ◇1	FC 1	FC	FC 1	EM ◇1	FC 1	FC	FC 1
London Bridge 4 ⊖	d																								
Elephant & Castle	d																								
London Blackfriars 3 ⊖	a																								
	d																								
City Thameslink 3	d																								
Farringdon 3 ⊖	d																								
St Pancras International 15 ⊖	a																								
	d		10 18	10 30	10 33			10 48	11 00	11 03		11 18	11 30	11 33		11 48		12 00	12 03		12 18	12 30	12 33		12 48
Kentish Town	d	10 10				10 40					11 10				11 40					12 10				12 40	
West Hampstead Thameslink	d	10 14	10 26		10 40	10 44		10 56		11 10	11 14	11 26		11 40	11 44	11 56			12 10	12 14	12 26		12 40	12 44	12 56
Cricklewood	d	10 17				10 47					11 17				11 47					12 17				12 47	
Hendon	d	10 20				10 50					11 20				11 50					12 20				12 50	
Mill Hill Broadway	d	10 24				10 54					11 24				11 54					12 24				12 54	
Elstree & Borehamwood	d	10 28				10 58					11 28				11 58					12 28				12 58	
Radlett	d	10 32				11 02					11 32				12 02					12 32				13 02	
St Albans City	d	10 38	10 42		10 56	11 08		11 12		11 26	11 38	11 42		11 56	12 08	12 12			12 26	12 38	12 42		12 56	13 08	13 12
Harpenden	d	10 44	10 48		11 02	11 14		11 18		11 32	11 44	11 48		12 02	12 14	12 18			12 32	12 44	12 48		13 02	13 14	13 18
Luton Airport Parkway 7 ✈	d	10 50	10 54		11 08	11 20		11 24	11 29	11 38	11 50	11 54	11 58	12 08	12 20	12 24		12 29	12 38	12 50	12 54	12 59	13 08	13 20	13 24
Luton 10	d	10a53	10 57	11 02	11 11	11a23		11 27	11 32	11 41	11a53	11 57	12 02	12 11	12a23	12 27		12 33	12 41	12a53	12 57	13 03	13 11	13a23	13 27
Leagrave	d		11 00		11 14			11 30		11 44		12 00		12 14		12 30			12 44		13 00		13 14		13 30
Harlington	d		11 06		11 20			11 36		11 50		12 06		12 20		12 36			12 50		13 06		13 20		13 36
Flitwick	d		11 10		11 24			11 40		11 54		12 10		12 24		12 40			12 54		13 10		13 24		13 40
Bedford 7	a		11 22	11 26	11 36			11 52	11 55	12 06		12 22	12 25	12 36		12 52		12 56	13 06		13 22	13 26	13 36		13 52

		EM ◇1		FC 1	FC	FC 1	EM ◇1	FC 1	FC	FC 1	EM ◇1	FC 1		FC	FC 1	EM ◇1	FC 1	FC	FC 1	EM ◇1	FC 1	FC		FC 1	EM ◇1
London Bridge 4 ⊖	d																								
Elephant & Castle	d																								
London Blackfriars 3 ⊖	a																								
	d																								
City Thameslink 3	d																								
Farringdon 3 ⊖	d																								
St Pancras International 15 ⊖	a																								
	d	13 00		13 03		13 18	13 30	13 33		13 48	14 00	14 03			14 18	14 30	14 33		14 48	15 00	15 03			15 18	15 30
Kentish Town	d				13 10				13 40					14 10				14 40				15 10			
West Hampstead Thameslink	d			13 10	13 14	13 26		13 40	13 44	13 56		14 10		14 14	14 26		14 40	14 44	14 56		15 10	15 14		15 26	
Cricklewood	d				13 17				13 47					14 17				14 47				15 17			
Hendon	d				13 20				13 50					14 20				14 50				15 20			
Mill Hill Broadway	d				13 24				13 54					14 24				14 54				15 24			
Elstree & Borehamwood	d				13 28				13 58					14 28				14 58				15 28			
Radlett	d				13 32				14 02					14 32				15 02				15 32			
St Albans City	d			13 26	13 38	13 42		13 56	14 08	14 12		14 26		14 38	14 42		14 56	15 08	15 12		15 26	15 38		15 42	
Harpenden	d			13 32	13 44	13 48		14 02	14 14	14 18		14 32		14 44	14 48		15 02	15 14	15 18		15 32	15 44		15 48	
Luton Airport Parkway 7 ✈	d	13 29		13 38	13 50	13 54	14 00	14 08	14 20	14 24	14 23	14 38		14 50	14 54		15 08	15 20	15 24	15 29	15 38	15 50		15 54	
Luton 10	d	13 33		13 41	13a53	13 57	14 04	14 11	14a23	14 27		14 41		14a53	14 57	15 01	15 11	15a23	15 27		15 41	15a53		15 57	16 00
Leagrave	d			13 44		14 00		14 14		14 30		14 44			15 00		15 14		15 30		15 44			16 00	
Harlington	d			13 50		14 06		14 20		14 36		14 50			15 06		15 20		15 36		15 50			16 06	
Flitwick	d			13 54		14 10		14 24		14 40		14 54			15 10		15 24		15 40		15 54			16 10	
Bedford 7	a	13 56		14 06		14 22	14 22	14 36		14 52	14 49	15 06			15 22	15 23	15 36		15 52	15 53	16 06			16 22	16 23

Please refer to separate pages within this table for services operating between Brighton and South London

At weekends please use local bus and tube services to travel to/from St Pancras International and London Bridge when no trains are operating. See local publicity for details of alternative routes and services that are available across central London

Table 52

Sundays from 30 October

London, St.Albans, Luton - Bedford

		FC 1	FC	FC 1	EM ◇1	FC 1	FC	FC 1		EM ◇1	FC 1	FC 1	FC	FC 1	EM ◇1	FC 1	FC	FC 1		EM ◇1	FC 1	FC 1	FC	FC 1	EM ◇1
London Bridge 4 ⊖	d																								
Elephant & Castle	d																								
London Blackfriars 3 ⊖	a																								
	d																								
City Thameslink 3	d																								
Farringdon 3 ⊖	d																								
St Pancras International 15 ⊖	a																								
	d	15 33		15 48	16 00	16 03		16 18		16 30		16 33		16 48	17 00	17 03		17 18		17 30		17 33		17 48	18 00
Kentish Town	d		15 40				16 10						16 40				17 10						17 40		
West Hampstead Thameslink	d	15 40	15 44	15 56		16 10	16 14	16 26				16 40	16 44	16 56		17 10	17 14	17 26				17 40	17 44	17 56	
Cricklewood	d		15 47				16 17						16 47				17 17						17 47		
Hendon	d		15 50				16 20						16 50				17 20						17 50		
Mill Hill Broadway	d		15 54				16 24						16 54				17 24						17 54		
Elstree & Borehamwood	d		15 58				16 28						16 58				17 28						17 58		
Radlett	d		16 02				16 32						17 02				17 32						18 02		
St Albans City	d	15 56	16 08	16 12		16 26	16 38	16 42				16 56	17 08	17 12		17 26	17 38	17 42				17 56	18 08	18 12	
Harpenden	d	16 02	16 14	16 18		16 32	16 44	16 48				17 02	17 14	17 18		17 32	17 44	17 48				18 02	18 14	18 18	
Luton Airport Parkway 7 ✈	d	16 08	16 20	16 24	16 29	16 38	16 50	16 54			←	17 08	17 20	17 24	17 21	17 38	17 50	17 54			←	18 08	18 20	18 24	18 21
Luton 10	d	16 11	16a23	16 27		16 41	16a53	16 57		16 52	16 57	17 11	17a23	17 27		17 41	17a53	17 57		17 52	17 57	18 11	18a23	18 27	
Leagrave	d	16 14		16 30		16 44		→			17 00	17 14		17 30		17 44		→			18 00	18 14		18 30	
Harlington	d	16 20		16 36		16 50					17 06	17 20		17 36		17 50					18 06	18 20		18 36	
Flitwick	d	16 24		16 40		16 54					17 10	17 24		17 40		17 54					18 10	18 24		18 40	
Bedford 7	a	16 36		16 52	16 53	17 06				17 17	17 22	17 36		17 52	17 49	18 06				18 19	18 22	18 36		18 52	18 47

		FC 1	FC	FC 1		EM ◇1	FC 1	FC 1	FC	FC	EM ◇1	FC 1	FC	EM ◇1		FC	FC 1	FC	EM ◇1	FC 1	FC	EM ◇1	FC	FC 1	
London Bridge 4 ⊖	d																								
Elephant & Castle	d																								
London Blackfriars 3 ⊖	a																								
	d																								
City Thameslink 3	d																								
Farringdon 3 ⊖	d																								
St Pancras International 15 ⊖	a																								
	d	18 03		18 18		18 30		18 33		18 48	19 00	19 03	19 18	19 30			19 33	19 48	20 00	20 03	20 18	20 30		20 33	
Kentish Town	d		18 10						18 40	18 53			19 23					19 53			20 23				
West Hampstead Thameslink	d	18 10	18 14	18 26				18 40	18 44	18 57		19 10	19 27				19 40	19 57		20 10	20 27			20 40	
Cricklewood	d		18 17						18 47	19 00			19 30					20 00			20 30				
Hendon	d		18 20						18 50	19 03			19 33					20 03			20 33				
Mill Hill Broadway	d		18 24						18 54	19 07			19 37					20 07			20 37				
Elstree & Borehamwood	d		18 28						18 58	19 11			19 41					20 11			20 41				
Radlett	d		18 32						19 02	19 16			19 46					20 16			20 46				
St Albans City	d	18 26	18 38	18 42				18 56	19 08	19 22		19 26	19 52				19 56	20 22		20 26	20 52			20 56	
Harpenden	d	18 32	18 44	18 48				19 02	19 14	19 28		19 32	19 58				20 02	20 28		20 32	20 58			21 02	
Luton Airport Parkway 7 ✈	d	18 38	18 50	18 54			←	19 08	19 20	19 34	19 21	19 38	20 04			←	20 08	20 34	20 23	20 38	21 04		←	21 08	
Luton 10	d	18 41	18a53	18 57		18 52	18 57	19 11	19a23	19 37		19 41	20 07	19 52		20 07	20 11	20 37		20 41	21 07	20 54	21 07	21 11	
Leagrave	d	18 44		→			19 00	19 14		19 40		19 44	→			20 10	20 14	20 40		20 44	→		21 10	21 14	
Harlington	d	18 50					19 06	19 20		19 46		19 50				20 16	20 20	20 46		20 50			21 16	21 20	
Flitwick	d	18 54					19 10	19 24		19 50		19 54				20 20	20 24	20 50		20 54			21 20	21 24	
Bedford 7	a	19 06				19 19	19 22	19 36		20 02	19 49	20 06		20 19		20 32	20 36	21 02	20 51	21 06		21 22	21 32	21 36	

		FC	EM ◇1	FC 1	FC	EM ◇1	FC	FC 1	FC	FC		EM ◇1	FC	EM ◇1	FC	FC
London Bridge 4 ⊖	d															
Elephant & Castle	d															
London Blackfriars 3 ⊖	a															
	d															
City Thameslink 3	d															
Farringdon 3 ⊖	d															
St Pancras International 15 ⊖	a															
	d	20 48	21 00	21 03	21 18	21 30		21 33	21 48	22 04		22 30	22 34	23 00	23 04	23 32
Kentish Town	d	20 53			21 23				21 53	22 09			22 39		23 09	23 37
West Hampstead Thameslink	d	20 57		21 10	21 27			21 40	21 57	22 13			22 43		23 13	23 41
Cricklewood	d	21 00			21 30				22 00	22 16			22 46		23 16	23 44
Hendon	d	21 03			21 33				22 03	22 19			22 49		23 19	23 47
Mill Hill Broadway	d	21 07			21 37				22 07	22 23			22 53		23 23	23 51
Elstree & Borehamwood	d	21 11			21 41				22 11	22 27			22 57		23 27	23 55
Radlett	d	21 16			21 46				22 16	22 32			23 02		23 32	00 01
St Albans City	d	21 22		21 26	21 52			21 56	22 22	22 38			23 08		23 38	00 06
Harpenden	d	21 28		21 32	21 58			22 02	22 28	22 44			23 14		23 44	00 12
Luton Airport Parkway 7 ✈	d	21 34	21 23	21 38	22 04		←	22 08	22 34	22 50		22 53	23 20	23 27	23 50	00 18
Luton 10	d	21 37		21 41	22 07	21 54	22 07	22 11	22 37	22 53			23 23		23 53	00 21
Leagrave	d	21 40		21 44	→		22 10	22 14	22 40	22 56			23 26		23 56	00 25
Harlington	d	21 46		21 50			22 16	22 20	22 46	23 02			23 32		00 02	00 30
Flitwick	d	21 50		21 54			22 20	22 24	22 50	23 06			23 36		00 06	00 34
Bedford 7	a	22 02	21 51	22 06		22 21	22 32	22 36	23 02	23 20		23 21	23 50	23 50	00 20	00 48

Please refer to separate pages within this table for services operating between Brighton and South London

At weekends please use local bus and tube services to travel to/from St Pancras International and London Bridge when no trains are operating. See local publicity for details of alternative routes and services that are available across central London

South London, Gatwick Airport - Brighton

Station		FC [1]	FC	FC [1]	SE	FC	FC	SN	SN	FC	FC [1]	FC	SE	FC [1]	FC	FC [1]	FC	SE	FC [1]	FC	FC [1]	FC	SE
					A				B				C					C					C
St Pancras International [15] ⊖	d																						
Farringdon [3] ⊖	d																						
City Thameslink [3]	d																						
London Blackfriars [3] ⊖	a																						
	d																						
Elephant & Castle ⊖	d																						
Loughborough Jn.	d																						
Herne Hill [4]	d														06 42					07 12			
Denmark Hill [4]	d				23p52								06 22					06 52					07 22
Peckham Rye [4]	d				23p55								06 25					06 55					07 25
Nunhead [4]	d				23p57								06 27					06 57					07 27
Crofton Park	d				23p59								06 30					07 00					07 30
Catford	d				00 03								06 33					07 03					07 33
Bellingham	d				00 05								06 35					07 05					07 35
Beckenham Hill	d				00 07								06 37					07 07					07 37
Ravensbourne	d				00 09								06 39					07 09					07 39
Shortlands	d				00 11								06 41					07 11					07 41
Bromley South [4]	d				00 14								06 44					07 14					07 44
Bickley [4]	d				00a17								06 47					07 17					07 47
St Mary Cray	d												06 51					07 21					07 51
Swanley [4]	d												06 56					07 26					07 56
Eynsford	d												07 00					07 30					08 00
Shoreham (Kent)	d												07 04					07 34					08 04
Otford [4]	d												07 07					07 37					08 07
Bat & Ball	d												07 10					07 40					08 10
Sevenoaks [4]	a												07 13					07 43					08 13
London Bridge [4]	a																						
	d	23p12	23p28	23p42		23p58	00 12	00 36		00 42	05 52	06 21		06 27		06 42	06 45		06 57		07 12	07 15	
Tulse Hill [3]	d		23p40			00 10						06 31			06 46		07 01			07 16		07 31	
Streatham [4]	d		23p44			00 14						06 35			06 50		07 05			07 20		07 35	
Mitcham Eastfields	d								00 38						06 54					07 24			
Mitcham Junction	d								00 41						06 57					07 27			
Hackbridge	d								00 45						07 00					07 30			
Carshalton	d								00 47						07 03					07 33			
Tooting	d		23p48			00 18						06 40					07 10					07 40	
Haydons Road	d		23p51			00 21						06 43					07 13					07 43	
Wimbledon [6] ⊖	d		23p55			00 25						06 47					07 17					07 47	
Wimbledon Chase	d		23p58			00 28						06 50					07 20					07 50	
South Merton	d		00 01			00 30						06 52					07 22					07 52	
Morden South	d		00 03			00 32						06 54					07 24					07 54	
St Helier	d		00 05			00 34						06 56					07 26					07 56	
Sutton Common	d		00 08			00 36						06 58					07 28					07 58	
West Sutton	d		00 11			00 39						07 01					07 31					08 01	
Sutton (Surrey) [4]	a		00 14			00 43			00 51			07 05			07 06		07 35			07 36		08 05	
East Croydon	d	23p25		23p57			00 27	01a03		00 57	06 05			06 41		06 55			07 11		07 25		
Redhill	d																						
Gatwick Airport [10] ✈	d	23p41		00 19			00 49			01 22	06 20			06 57		07 11			07 27		07 41		
Three Bridges [4]	d	23p47		00a24			00a54			01a28	06 25			07 02		07 15			07 32		07 45		
Balcombe	d	23p53														07 21							
Haywards Heath [3]	d	23p59									06 34			07 11		07 27			07 41		07 55		
Wivelsfield [4]	d	00 03														07 31					07 59		
Burgess Hill [4]	d	00 05									06 40					07 33					08 01		
Hassocks [4]	d	00 08														07 36					08 04		
Preston Park	d	00 15														07 43					08 11		
Brighton [10]	a	00 20									06 52			07 24		07 48			07 54		08 16		

A From London Victoria to Orpington **B** From London Victoria **C** From London Victoria

Please refer to separate pages within this table for services operating between Bedford and London

At weekends please use local bus and tube services to travel to/from St Pancras International and London Bridge when no trains are operating. See local publicity for details of alternative routes and services that are available across central London

South London, Gatwick Airport - Brighton

Station		FC [1]	FC	FC [1]	FC	SE	FC [1]	FC	FC [1]	FC	SE	FC [1]	FC	FC [1]	FC	SE	FC [1]	FC	FC [1]	FC	SE	FC [1]	FC
						A					A					A					A		
St Pancras International [15] ⊖	d																						
Farringdon [3] ⊖	d																						
City Thameslink [3]	d																						
London Blackfriars [3] ⊖	a																						
	d																						
Elephant & Castle ⊖	d																						
Loughborough Jn.	d																						
Herne Hill [4]	d		07 42					08 12					08 42					09 12					09 42
Denmark Hill [4]	d					07 52					08 22					08 52					09 22		
Peckham Rye [4]	d					07 55					08 25					08 55					09 25		
Nunhead [4]	d					07 57					08 27					08 57					09 27		
Crofton Park	d					08 00					08 30					09 00					09 30		
Catford	d					08 03					08 33					09 03					09 33		
Bellingham	d					08 05					08 35					09 05					09 35		
Beckenham Hill	d					08 07					08 37					09 07					09 37		
Ravensbourne	d					08 09					08 39					09 09					09 39		
Shortlands	d					08 11					08 41					09 11					09 41		
Bromley South [4]	d					08 14					08 44					09 14					09 44		
Bickley [4]	d					08 17					08 47					09 17					09 47		
St Mary Cray	d					08 21					08 51					09 21					09 51		
Swanley [4]	d					08 26					08 56					09 26					09 56		
Eynsford	d					08 30					09 00					09 30					10 00		
Shoreham (Kent)	d					08 34					09 04					09 34					10 04		
Otford [4]	d					08 37					09 07					09 37					10 07		
Bat & Ball	d					08 40					09 10					09 40					10 10		
Sevenoaks [4]	a					08 43					09 13					09 43					10 13		
London Bridge [4]	a																						
	d	07 27		07 42	07 45		07 57		08 12	08 15		08 27		08 42	08 45		08 57		09 12	09 15		09 27	
Tulse Hill [3]	d		07 46		08 01			08 16		08 31			08 46		09 01			09 16		09 31			09 46
Streatham [4]	d		07 50		08 05			08 20		08 35			08 50		09 05			09 20		09 35			09 50
Mitcham Eastfields	d		07 54					08 24					08 54					09 24					09 54
Mitcham Junction	d		07 57					08 27					08 57					09 27					09 57
Hackbridge	d		08 00					08 30					09 00					09 30					10 00
Carshalton	d		08 03					08 33					09 03					09 33					10 03
Tooting	d				08 10					08 40					09 10					09 40			
Haydons Road	d				08 13					08 43					09 13					09 43			
Wimbledon [6] ⊖	d				08 17					08 47					09 17					09 47			
Wimbledon Chase	d				08 20					08 50					09 20					09 50			
South Merton	d				08 22					08 52					09 22					09 52			
Morden South	d				08 24					08 54					09 24					09 54			
St Helier	d				08 26					08 56					09 26					09 56			
Sutton Common	d				08 28					08 58					09 28					09 58			
West Sutton	d				08 31					09 01					09 31					10 01			
Sutton (Surrey) [4]	a		08 06		08 35			08 36		09 05			09 06		09 35			09 36		10 05			10 06
East Croydon	d	07 41		07 55			08 11		08 25			08 40		08 55			09 11		09 25			09 41	
Redhill	d																						
Gatwick Airport [10] ✈	d	07 57		08 11			08 27		08 41			08 57		09 11			09 27		09 41			09 57	
Three Bridges [4]	d	08 02		08 15			08 32		08 45			09 02		09 15			09 32		09 45			10 02	
Balcombe	d			08 21										09 21									
Haywards Heath [3]	d	08 11		08 27			08 41		08 55			09 11		09 27			09 41		09 55			10 11	
Wivelsfield [4]	d			08 31					08 59					09 31					09 59				
Burgess Hill [4]	d			08 33					09 01					09 33					10 01				
Hassocks [4]	d			08 36					09 04					09 36					10 04				
Preston Park	d			08 43					09 11					09 43					10 11				
Brighton [10]	a	08 24		08 48			08 55		09 16			09 25		09 48			09 55		10 16			10 25	

A From London Victoria

Please refer to separate pages within this table for services operating between Bedford and London

At weekends please use local bus and tube services to travel to/from St Pancras International and London Bridge when no trains are operating. See local publicity for details of alternative routes and services that are available across central London

Table 52

Saturdays

South London, Gatwick Airport - Brighton

		FC 1	FC	SE	FC 1	FC	FC 1	FC	SE	FC 1	FC	FC 1	FC	SE	FC 1	FC	FC 1	FC	SE	FC 1	FC	FC 1
				A					A					A					A			
St Pancras International 15 ⊖	d																					
Farringdon 3 ⊖	d																					
City Thameslink 3	d																					
London Blackfriars 3 ⊖	a																					
	d																					
Elephant & Castle ⊖	d																					
Loughborough Jn	d																					
Herne Hill 4	d					10 12					10 42					11 12					11 42	
Denmark Hill 4	d			09 52					10 22					10 52					11 22			
Peckham Rye 4	d			09 55					10 25					10 55					11 25			
Nunhead 4	d			09 57					10 27					10 57					11 27			
Crofton Park	d			10 00					10 30					11 00					11 30			
Catford	d			10 03					10 33					11 03					11 33			
Bellingham	d			10 05					10 35					11 05					11 35			
Beckenham Hill	d			10 07					10 37					11 07					11 37			
Ravensbourne	d			10 09					10 39					11 09					11 39			
Shortlands	d			10 11					10 41					11 11					11 41			
Bromley South 4	d			10 14					10 44					11 14					11 44			
Bickley 4	d			10 17					10 47					11 17					11 47			
St Mary Cray	d			10 21					10 51					11 21					11 51			
Swanley 4	d			10 26					10 56					11 26					11 56			
Eynsford	d			10 30					11 00					11 30					12 00			
Shoreham (Kent)	d			10 34					11 04					11 34					12 04			
Otford 4	d			10 37					11 07					11 37					12 07			
Bat & Ball	d			10 40					11 10					11 40					12 10			
Sevenoaks 4	a			10 43					11 13					11 43					12 13			
London Bridge 4	a																					
	d	09 42	09 45		09 57		10 12	10 15		10 27		10 42	10 45		10 57		11 12	11 15		11 27		11 42
Tulse Hill 3	d		10 01			10 16		10 31			10 46		11 01			11 16		11 31			11 46	
Streatham 4	d		10 05			10 20		10 35			10 50		11 05			11 20		11 35			11 50	
Mitcham Eastfields	d					10 24					10 54					11 24					11 54	
Mitcham Junction	d					10 27					10 57					11 27					11 57	
Hackbridge	d					10 30					11 00					11 30					12 00	
Carshalton	d					10 33					11 03					11 33					12 03	
Tooting	d		10 10					10 40					11 10					11 40				
Haydons Road	d		10 13					10 43					11 13					11 43				
Wimbledon 6 ⊖ ⇌	d		10 17					10 47					11 17					11 47				
Wimbledon Chase	d		10 20					10 50					11 20					11 50				
South Merton	d		10 22					10 52					11 22					11 52				
Morden South	d		10 24					10 54					11 24					11 54				
St Helier	d		10 26					10 56					11 26					11 56				
Sutton Common	d		10 28					10 58					11 28					11 58				
West Sutton	d		10 31					11 01					11 31					12 01				
Sutton (Surrey) 4	a		10 35			10 36		11 05			11 06		11 35			11 36		12 05			12 06	
East Croydon ⇌	d	09 55			10 11		10 25			10 41		10 55			11 11		11 25			11 41		11 55
Redhill	d																					
Gatwick Airport 10 ✈	d	10 11			10 27		10 41			10 57		11 11			11 27		11 41			11 57		12 11
Three Bridges 4	d	10 15			10 32		10 45			11 02		11 15			11 32		11 45			12 02		12 15
Balcombe	d	10 21										11 21										12 21
Haywards Heath 3	d	10 27			10 41		10 55			11 11		11 27			11 41		11 55			12 11		12 27
Wivelsfield 4	d	10 31					10 59					11 31					11 59					12 31
Burgess Hill 4	d	10 33					11 01					11 33					12 01					12 33
Hassocks 4	d	10 36					11 04					11 36					12 04					12 36
Preston Park	d	10 43					11 11					11 43					12 11					12 43
Brighton 10	a	10 48			10 55		11 16			11 25		11 48			11 55		12 16			12 25		12 48

A From London Victoria

Please refer to separate pages within this table for services operating between Bedford and London

At weekends please use local bus and tube services to travel to/from St Pancras International and London Bridge when no trains are operating. See local publicity for details of alternative routes and services that are available across central London

Table 52

Saturdays

South London, Gatwick Airport - Brighton

		FC	SE	FC 1	FC	FC 1	FC	SE	FC 1	FC	FC 1	FC	SE	FC 1	FC	FC 1	FC	SE	FC 1	FC	FC 1	FC	SE
			A					A					A					A					A
St Pancras International 15 ⊖	d																						
Farringdon 3 ⊖	d																						
City Thameslink 3	d																						
London Blackfriars 3 ⊖	a																						
	d																						
Elephant & Castle ⊖	d																						
Loughborough Jn	d																						
Herne Hill 4	d				12 12					12 42					13 12					13 42			
Denmark Hill 4	d		11 52					12 22					12 52					13 22					13 52
Peckham Rye 4	d		11 55					12 25					12 55					13 25					13 55
Nunhead 4	d		11 57					12 27					12 57					13 27					13 57
Crofton Park	d		12 00					12 30					13 00					13 30					14 00
Catford	d		12 03					12 33					13 03					13 33					14 03
Bellingham	d		12 05					12 35					13 05					13 35					14 05
Beckenham Hill	d		12 07					12 37					13 07					13 37					14 07
Ravensbourne	d		12 09					12 39					13 09					13 39					14 09
Shortlands	d		12 11					12 41					13 11					13 41					14 11
Bromley South 4	d		12 14					12 44					13 14					13 44					14 14
Bickley 4	d		12 17					12 47					13 17					13 47					14 17
St Mary Cray	d		12 21					12 51					13 21					13 51					14 21
Swanley 4	d		12 26					12 56					13 26					13 56					14 26
Eynsford	d		12 30					13 00					13 30					14 00					14 30
Shoreham (Kent)	d		12 34					13 04					13 34					14 04					14 34
Otford 4	d		12 37					13 07					13 37					14 07					14 37
Bat & Ball	d		12 40					13 10					13 40					14 10					14 40
Sevenoaks 4	a		12 43					13 13					13 43					14 13					14 43
London Bridge 4	a																						
	d	11 45		11 57		12 12	12 15		12 27		12 42	12 45		12 57		13 12	13 15		13 27		13 42	13 45	
Tulse Hill 3	d	12 01			12 16		12 31			12 46		13 01			13 16		13 31			13 46		14 01	
Streatham 4	d	12 05			12 20		12 35			12 50		13 05			13 20		13 35			13 50		14 05	
Mitcham Eastfields	d				12 24					12 54					13 24					13 54			
Mitcham Junction	d				12 27					12 57					13 27					13 57			
Hackbridge	d				12 30					13 00					13 30					14 00			
Carshalton	d				12 33					13 03					13 33					14 03			
Tooting	d	12 10					12 40					13 10					13 40					14 10	
Haydons Road	d	12 13					12 43					13 13					13 43					14 13	
Wimbledon 6 ⊖ ⇌	d	12 17					12 47					13 17					13 47					14 17	
Wimbledon Chase	d	12 20					12 50					13 20					13 50					14 20	
South Merton	d	12 22					12 52					13 22					13 52					14 22	
Morden South	d	12 24					12 54					13 24					13 54					14 24	
St Helier	d	12 26					12 56					13 26					13 56					14 26	
Sutton Common	d	12 28					12 58					13 28					13 58					14 28	
West Sutton	d	12 31					13 01					13 31					14 01					14 31	
Sutton (Surrey) 4	a	12 35			12 36		13 05			13 06		13 35			13 36		14 05			14 06		14 35	
East Croydon ⇌	d			12 11		12 25			12 41		12 55			13 11		13 25			13 41		13 55		
Redhill	d																						
Gatwick Airport 10 ✈	d			12 27		12 41			12 57		13 11			13 27		13 41			13 57		14 11		
Three Bridges 4	d			12 32		12 45			13 02		13 15			13 32		13 45			14 02		14 15		
Balcombe	d										13 21										14 21		
Haywards Heath 3	d			12 41		12 55			13 11		13 27			13 41		13 55			14 11		14 27		
Wivelsfield 4	d					12 59					13 31					13 59					14 31		
Burgess Hill 4	d					13 01					13 33					14 01					14 33		
Hassocks 4	d					13 04					13 36					14 04					14 36		
Preston Park	d					13 11					13 43					14 11					14 43		
Brighton 10	a			12 55		13 16			13 25		13 48			13 55		14 16			14 25		14 48		

A From London Victoria

Please refer to separate pages within this table for services operating between Bedford and London

At weekends please use local bus and tube services to travel to/from St Pancras International and London Bridge when no trains are operating. See local publicity for details of alternative routes and services that are available across central London

South London, Gatwick Airport - Brighton

		FC	FC	FC	FC	SE	FC	FC	FC	FC	SE	FC	FC	FC	FC	SE	FC	FC	FC	FC	SE	FC
		1		1			1		1			1		1			1		1			1
						A					A					A					A	
St Pancras International 15 ⊖	d																					
Farringdon 3 ⊖	d																					
City Thameslink 3	d																					
London Blackfriars 3 ⊖	a																					
	d																					
Elephant & Castle ⊖	d																					
Loughborough Jn.	d																					
Herne Hill 4	d		14 12					14 42					15 12					15 42				
Denmark Hill 4	d					14 22					14 52					15 22					15 52	
Peckham Rye 4	d					14 25					14 55					15 25					15 55	
Nunhead 4	d					14 27					14 57					15 27					15 57	
Crofton Park	d					14 30					15 00					15 30					16 00	
Catford	d					14 33					15 03					15 33					16 03	
Bellingham	d					14 35					15 05					15 35					16 05	
Beckenham Hill	d					14 37					15 07					15 37					16 07	
Ravensbourne	d					14 39					15 09					15 39					16 09	
Shortlands	d					14 41					15 11					15 41					16 11	
Bromley South 4	d					14 44					15 14					15 44					16 14	
Bickley 4	d					14 47					15 17					15 47					16 17	
St Mary Cray	d					14 51					15 21					15 51					16 21	
Swanley 4	d					14 56					15 26					15 56					16 26	
Eynsford	d					15 00					15 30					16 00					16 30	
Shoreham (Kent)	d					15 04					15 34					16 04					16 34	
Otford 4	d					15 07					15 37					16 07					16 37	
Bat & Ball	d					15 10					15 40					16 10					16 40	
Sevenoaks 4	a					15 13					15 43					16 13					16 43	
London Bridge 4	a																					
	d	13 57		14 12	14 15		14 27		14 42	14 45		14 57		15 12	15 15		15 27		15 42	15 45		15 57
Tulse Hill 3	d		14 16		14 31			14 46		15 01			15 16		15 31			15 46		16 01		
Streatham 4	d		14 20		14 35			14 50		15 05			15 20		15 35			15 50		16 05		
Mitcham Eastfields	d		14 24					14 54					15 24					15 54				
Mitcham Junction	d		14 27					14 57					15 27					15 57				
Hackbridge	d		14 30					15 00					15 30					16 00				
Carshalton	d		14 33					15 03					15 33					16 03				
Tooting	d				14 40					15 10					15 40					16 10		
Haydons Road	d				14 43					15 13					15 43					16 13		
Wimbledon 6 ⊖	d				14 47					15 17					15 47					16 17		
Wimbledon Chase	d				14 50					15 20					15 50					16 20		
South Merton	d				14 52					15 22					15 52					16 22		
Morden South	d				14 54					15 24					15 54					16 24		
St Helier	d				14 56					15 26					15 56					16 26		
Sutton Common	d				14 58					15 28					15 58					16 28		
West Sutton	d				15 01					15 31					16 01					16 31		
Sutton (Surrey) 4	a		14 36		15 05			15 06		15 35			15 36		16 05			16 06		16 35		
East Croydon	d	14 11		14 25			14 41		14 55			15 11		15 25			15 41		15 55			16 11
Redhill	d																					
Gatwick Airport 10 ✈	d	14 27		14 41			14 57		15 11			15 27		15 41			15 57		16 11			16 27
Three Bridges 4	d	14 32		14 45			15 02		15 15			15 32		15 45			16 02		16 15			16 32
Balcombe	d								15 21										16 21			
Haywards Heath 3	d	14 41		14 55			15 11		15 27			15 41		15 55			16 11		16 27			16 41
Wivelsfield 4	d			14 59					15 31					15 59					16 31			
Burgess Hill 4	d			15 01					15 33					16 01					16 33			
Hassocks 4	d			15 04					15 36					16 04					16 36			
Preston Park	d			15 11					15 43					16 11					16 43			
Brighton 10	a	14 55		15 16			15 25		15 48			15 55		16 16			16 25		16 48			16 55

A From London Victoria

Please refer to separate pages within this table for services operating between Bedford and London

At weekends please use local bus and tube services to travel to/from St Pancras International and London Bridge when no trains are operating. See local publicity for details of alternative routes and services that are available across central London

South London, Gatwick Airport - Brighton

		FC	FC	FC	SE	FC	FC	FC	FC	SE	FC	FC	FC	FC	SE	FC	FC	FC	FC	SE	FC	FC	FC
			1			1		1			1		1			1		1			1		1
					A					A					A					A			
St Pancras International 15 ⊖	d																						
Farringdon 3 ⊖	d																						
City Thameslink 3	d																						
London Blackfriars 3 ⊖	a																						
	d																						
Elephant & Castle ⊖	d																						
Loughborough Jn.	d																						
Herne Hill 4	d	16 12					16 42					17 12					17 42					18 12	
Denmark Hill 4	d				16 22					16 52					17 22					17 52			
Peckham Rye 4	d				16 25					16 55					17 25					17 55			
Nunhead 4	d				16 27					16 57					17 27					17 57			
Crofton Park	d				16 30					17 00					17 30					18 00			
Catford	d				16 33					17 03					17 33					18 03			
Bellingham	d				16 35					17 05					17 35					18 05			
Beckenham Hill	d				16 37					17 07					17 37					18 07			
Ravensbourne	d				16 39					17 09					17 39					18 09			
Shortlands	d				16 41					17 11					17 41					18 11			
Bromley South 4	d				16 44					17 14					17 44					18 14			
Bickley 4	d				16 47					17 17					17 47					18 17			
St Mary Cray	d				16 51					17 21					17 51					18 21			
Swanley 4	d				16 56					17 26					17 56					18 26			
Eynsford	d				17 00					17 30					18 00					18 30			
Shoreham (Kent)	d				17 04					17 34					18 04					18 34			
Otford 4	d				17 07					17 37					18 07					18 37			
Bat & Ball	d				17 10					17 40					18 10					18 40			
Sevenoaks 4	a				17 13					17 43					18 13					18 43			
London Bridge 4	a																						
	d		16 12	16 15		16 27		16 42	16 45		16 57		17 12	17 15		17 27		17 42	17 45		17 57		18 12
Tulse Hill 3	d	16 16		16 31			16 46		17 01			17 16		17 31			17 46		18 01			18 16	
Streatham 4	d	16 20		16 35			16 50		17 05			17 20		17 35			17 50		18 05			18 20	
Mitcham Eastfields	d	16 24					16 54					17 24					17 54					18 24	
Mitcham Junction	d	16 27					16 57					17 27					17 57					18 27	
Hackbridge	d	16 30					17 00					17 30					18 00					18 30	
Carshalton	d	16 33					17 03					17 33					18 03					18 33	
Tooting	d			16 40					17 10					17 40					18 10				
Haydons Road	d			16 43					17 13					17 43					18 13				
Wimbledon 6 ⊖	d			16 47					17 17					17 47					18 17				
Wimbledon Chase	d			16 50					17 20					17 50					18 20				
South Merton	d			16 52					17 22					17 52					18 22				
Morden South	d			16 54					17 24					17 54					18 24				
St Helier	d			16 56					17 26					17 56					18 26				
Sutton Common	d			16 58					17 28					17 58					18 28				
West Sutton	d			17 01					17 31					18 01					18 31				
Sutton (Surrey) 4	a	16 36		17 05			17 06		17 35			17 36		18 05			18 06		18 35			18 36	
East Croydon	d		16 25			16 41		16 55			17 11		17 25			17 41		17 55			18 11		18 25
Redhill	d																						
Gatwick Airport 10 ✈	d		16 41			16 57		17 11			17 27		17 41			17 57		18 11			18 27		18 41
Three Bridges 4	d		16 45			17 02		17 15			17 32		17 45			18 02		18 15			18 32		18 45
Balcombe	d							17 21										18 21					
Haywards Heath 3	d		16 55			17 11		17 27			17 41		17 55			18 11		18 27			18 41		18 55
Wivelsfield 4	d		16 59					17 31					17 59					18 31					18 59
Burgess Hill 4	d		17 01					17 33					18 01					18 33					19 01
Hassocks 4	d		17 04					17 36					18 04					18 36					19 04
Preston Park	d		17 11					17 43					18 11					18 43					19 11
Brighton 10	a		17 16			17 25		17 48			17 55		18 16			18 25		18 48			18 55		19 16

A From London Victoria

Please refer to separate pages within this table for services operating between Bedford and London

At weekends please use local bus and tube services to travel to/from St Pancras International and London Bridge when no trains are operating. See local publicity for details of alternative routes and services that are available across central London

South London, Gatwick Airport - Brighton

		FC	SE A	FC [1]	FC	FC [1]	FC	SE A	FC [1]	FC	FC [1]	FC	SE A	FC [1]	FC	FC [1]	FC	SE A	FC [1]	FC [1]	FC	SE A	FC [1]
St Pancras International 15 ⊖	d																						
Farringdon 3 ⊖	d																						
City Thameslink 3	d																						
London Blackfriars 3 ⊖	a																						
	d																						
Elephant & Castle ⊖	d																						
Loughborough Jn.	d																						
Herne Hill 4	d				18 42					19 12					19 42								
Denmark Hill 4	d		18 22					18 52					19 22					19 52				20 22	
Peckham Rye 4	d		18 25					18 55					19 25					19 55				20 25	
Nunhead 4	d		18 27					18 57					19 27					19 57				20 27	
Crofton Park	d		18 30					19 00					19 30					20 00				20 30	
Catford	d		18 33					19 03					19 33					20 03				20 33	
Bellingham	d		18 35					19 05					19 35					20 05				20 35	
Beckenham Hill	d		18 37					19 07					19 37					20 07				20 37	
Ravensbourne	d		18 39					19 09					19 39					20 09				20 39	
Shortlands	d		18 41					19 11					19 41					20 11				20 41	
Bromley South 4	d		18 44					19 14					19 44					20 14				20 44	
Bickley 4	d		18 47					19 17					19 47					20 17				20 47	
St Mary Cray	d		18 51					19 21					19 51					20 21				20 51	
Swanley 4	d		18 56					19 26					19 56					20 26				20 56	
Eynsford	d		19 00					19 30					20 00					20 30				21 00	
Shoreham (Kent)	d		19 04					19 34					20 04					20 34				21 04	
Otford 4	d		19 07					19 37					20 07					20 37				21 07	
Bat & Ball	d		19 10					19 40					20 10					20 40				21 10	
Sevenoaks 4	a		19 13					19 43					20 13					20 43				21 13	
London Bridge 4	a																						
	d	18 15		18 27		18 42	18 45		18 57		19 12	19 15		19 27		19 42	19 45		19 57	20 12	20 15		20 42
Tulse Hill 3	d	18 31			18 46		19 01			19 16		19 31			19 46		20 01				20 31		
Streatham 4	d	18 35			18 50		19 05			19 20		19 35			19 51		20 05				20 35		
Mitcham Eastfields	d				18 54					19 24					19 55								
Mitcham Junction	d				18 57					19 27					19 58								
Hackbridge	d				19 00					19 30					20 01								
Carshalton	d				19 03					19 33					20 04								
Tooting	d	18 40					19 10					19 40					20 10				20 40		
Haydons Road	d	18 43					19 13					19 43					20 13				20 43		
Wimbledon 6 ⊖ 🚋	d	18 47					19 17					19 47					20 17				20 47		
Wimbledon Chase	d	18 50					19 20					19 50					20 20				20 50		
South Merton	d	18 52					19 22					19 52					20 22				20 52		
Morden South	d	18 54					19 24					19 54					20 24				20 54		
St Helier	d	18 56					19 26					19 56					20 26				20 56		
Sutton Common	d	18 58					19 28					19 58					20 28				20 58		
West Sutton	d	19 01					19 31					20 01					20 31				21 01		
Sutton (Surrey) 4	a	19 05			19 06		19 39			19 36		20 05			20 07		20 37				21 05		
East Croydon 🚋	d			18 41		18 55			19 11		19 25			19 41		19 55			20 11	20 25			20 54
Redhill	d																						
Gatwick Airport 10 ✈	d			18 57		19 11			19 27		19 41			19 57		20 11			20 27	20 41			21 11
Three Bridges 4	d			19 02		19 15			19 32		19 45			20 02		20 15			20 32	20 45			21 15
Balcombe	d					19 21										20 21				20 51			
Haywards Heath 3	d			19 11		19 27			19 41		19 55			20 11		20 27			20 41	20 57			21 25
Wivelsfield 4	d					19 31					19 59					20 31				21 01			21 29
Burgess Hill 4	d					19 33					20 01					20 33				21 03			21 31
Hassocks 4	d					19 36					20 04					20 36				21 06			21 34
Preston Park	d					19 43					20 11					20 43				21 13			21 41
Brighton 10	a			19 25		19 48			19 54		20 16			20 25		20 48			20 55	21 18			21 46

A From London Victoria

Please refer to separate pages within this table for services operating between Bedford and London

At weekends please use local bus and tube services to travel to/from St Pancras International and London Bridge when no trains are operating. See local publicity for details of alternative routes and services that are available across central London

South London, Gatwick Airport - Brighton

		FC	SE A	FC [1]	FC	SE A	FC [1]	FC	SE A	FC [1]	FC	SE A	FC [1]	FC	SE B	FC [1]	FC	SE B	FC [1]	FC	SE B
St Pancras International 15 ⊖	d																				
Farringdon 3 ⊖	d																				
City Thameslink 3	d																				
London Blackfriars 3 ⊖	a																				
	d																				
Elephant & Castle ⊖	d																				
Loughborough Jn.	d																				
Herne Hill 4	d																				
Denmark Hill 4	d		20 52			21 22			21 52			22 22			22 52			23 22			23 52
Peckham Rye 4	d		20 55			21 25			21 55			22 25			22 55			23 25			23 55
Nunhead 4	d		20 57			21 27			21 57			22 27			22 57			23 27			23 57
Crofton Park	d		21 00			21 30			22 00			22 30			23 00			23 30			23 58
Catford	d		21 03			21 33			22 03			22 33			23 03			23 33			00 03
Bellingham	d		21 05			21 35			22 05			22 35			23 05			23 35			00 05
Beckenham Hill	d		21 07			21 37			22 07			22 37			23 07			23 37			00 07
Ravensbourne	d		21 09			21 39			22 09			22 39			23 09			23 39			00 09
Shortlands	d		21 11			21 41			22 11			22 41			23 11			23 41			00 11
Bromley South 4	d		21 14			21 44			22 14			22 44			23 14			23 44			00 14
Bickley 4	d		21 17			21 47			22 17			22 47			23a17			23a47			00a17
St Mary Cray	d		21 21			21 51			22 21			22 51									
Swanley 4	d		21 26			21 56			22 26			22 56									
Eynsford	d		21 30			22 00			22 30			23 00									
Shoreham (Kent)	d		21 34			22 04			22 34			23 04									
Otford 4	d		21 37			22 07			22 37			23 07									
Bat & Ball	d		21 40			22 10			22 40			23 10									
Sevenoaks 4	a		21 43			22 13			22 43			23 13									
London Bridge 4	a																				
	d	20 45		21 12	21 15		21 42	21 45		22 12	22 15		22 42	22 45		23 12	23 15		23 42	23 45	
Tulse Hill 3	d	21 01			21 31			22 01			22 31			23 01			23 31			00 01	
Streatham 4	d	21 05			21 35			22 05			22 35			23 05			23 35			00 05	
Mitcham Eastfields	d																				
Mitcham Junction	d																				
Hackbridge	d																				
Carshalton	d																				
Tooting	d	21 10			21 40			22 10			22 40			23 10			23 40			00 10	
Haydons Road	d	21 13			21 43			22 13			22 43			23 13			23 43			00 13	
Wimbledon 6 ⊖ 🚋	d	21 17			21 47			22 17			22 47			23 17			23 47			00 17	
Wimbledon Chase	d	21 20			21 50			22 20			22 50			23 20			23 50			00 20	
South Merton	d	21 22			21 52			22 22			22 52			23 22			23 52			00 22	
Morden South	d	21 24			21 54			22 24			22 54			23 24			23 54			00 24	
St Helier	d	21 26			21 56			22 26			22 56			23 26			23 56			00 26	
Sutton Common	d	21 28			21 58			22 28			22 58			23 28			23 58			00 28	
West Sutton	d	21 31			22 01			22 31			23 01			23 31			00 01			00 31	
Sutton (Surrey) 4	a	21 37			22 05			22 39			23 05			23 35			00 05			00 35	
East Croydon 🚋	d			21 25			21 55			22 25			22 55			23 25			23 57		
Redhill	d																				
Gatwick Airport 10 ✈	d			21 41			22 11			22 41			23 11			23 41			00 19		
Three Bridges 4	d			21 45			22 15			22 45			23 15			23 47			00a24		
Balcombe	d			21 53						22 53						23 53					
Haywards Heath 3	d			21 59			22 25			22 59			23 25			23 59					
Wivelsfield 4	d			22 03			22 29			23 03			23 29			00 03					
Burgess Hill 4	d			22 05			22 31			23 05			23 31			00 05					
Hassocks 4	d			22 08			22 34			23 08			23 34			00 08					
Preston Park	d			22 15			22 41			23 15			23 41			00 15					
Brighton 10	a			22 20			22 46			23 20			23 46			00 20					

A From London Victoria

B From London Victoria to Orpington

Please refer to separate pages within this table for services operating between Bedford and London

At weekends please use local bus and tube services to travel to/from St Pancras International and London Bridge when no trains are operating. See local publicity for details of alternative routes and services that are available across central London

Table 52

Sundays
until 4 September

South London, Gatwick Airport - Brighton

		FC 1 A	FC A	FC 1 A	FC A	SE B	FC 1	SN	FC 1	FC 1		SN	FC 1	SE C	SN	FC 1	SE C	SN	FC 1	SE C		SN	FC 1	SE C	SN
St Pancras International 15 ⊖	d																								
Farringdon 3 ⊖	d																								
City Thameslink 3	d																								
London Blackfriars 3 ⊖	a																								
	d																								
Elephant & Castle ⊖	d																								
Loughborough Jn.	d																								
Herne Hill 4	d																								
Denmark Hill 4	d					23p52								07 48			08 18			08 48				09 18	
Peckham Rye 4	d					23p55								07 51			08 21			08 51				09 21	
Nunhead 4	d					23p57								07 53			08 23			08 53				09 23	
Crofton Park	d					23p58								07 56			08 26			08 56				09 26	
Catford	d					00 03								07 59			08 29			08 59				09 29	
Bellingham	d					00 05								08 01			08 31			09 01				09 31	
Beckenham Hill	d					00 07								08 03			08 33			09 03				09 33	
Ravensbourne	d					00 09								08 05			08 35			09 05				09 35	
Shortlands	d					00 11								08 07			08 37			09 07				09 37	
Bromley South 4	d					00 14								08 10			08 40			09 10				09 40	
Bickley 4	d					00a17								08 13			08 43			09 13				09 43	
St Mary Cray	d													08 17			08 47			09 17				09 47	
Swanley 4	d													08 22			08 52			09 22				09 52	
Eynsford	d													08 26			08 56			09 26				09 56	
Shoreham (Kent)	d													08 30			09 00			09 30				10 00	
Otford 4	d													08 33			09 03			09 33				10 03	
Bat & Ball	d													08 36			09 06			09 36				10 06	
Sevenoaks 4	a													08 39			09 09			09 39				10 09	
London Bridge 4	a																								
	d	23p12	23p15	23p42	23p45		00 12	00 36	00 42	07 12		07 21	07 42		07 51	08 12		08 21	08 42			08 51	09 12		09 21
Tulse Hill 3	d		23p31		00 01							07 39			08 09			08 39				09 09			09 39
Streatham 4	d		23p35		00 05							07 42			08 12			08 42				09 12			09 42
Mitcham Eastfields	d																								
Mitcham Junction	d																								
Hackbridge	d																								
Carshalton	d																								
Tooting	d		23p40		00 10																				
Haydons Road	d		23p43		00 13																				
Wimbledon 6 ⊖ ⇌	d		23p47		00 17																				
Wimbledon Chase	d		23p50		00 20																				
South Merton	d		23p52		00 22																				
Morden South	d		23p54		00 24																				
St Helier	d		23p56		00 26																				
Sutton Common	d		23p58		00 28																				
West Sutton	d		00 01		00 31																				
Sutton (Surrey) 4	a		00 05		00 35																				
East Croydon ⇌	d	23p25		23p57			00 27	01a03	00 57	07 24		08a01	07 54		08a30	08 24		09a01	08 54			09a30	09 24		10a01
Redhill	d																								
Gatwick Airport 10 ✈	d	23p41		00 19			00 49		01 20	07 41			08 11			08 41			09 11				09 41		
Three Bridges 4	d	23p47		00a24			00a54		01a24	07 47			08 17			08 47			09 17				09 47		
Balcombe	d	23p53																							
Haywards Heath 3	d	23p59								07 56			08 26			08 56			09 26				09 56		
Wivelsfield 4	d	00 03																							
Burgess Hill 4	d	00 05								08 01			08 31			09 01			09 31				10 01		
Hassocks 4	d	00 08								08 05			08 35			09 05			09 35				10 05		
Preston Park	d	00 15																							
Brighton 10	a	00 20								08 15			08 44			09 15			09 44				10 15		

A not 22 May

B not 22 May. From London Victoria to Orpington

C From London Victoria

Please refer to separate pages within this table for services operating between Bedford and London

At weekends please use local bus and tube services to travel to/from St Pancras International and London Bridge when no trains are operating. See local publicity for details of alternative routes and services that are available across central London

Table 52

Sundays
until 4 September

South London, Gatwick Airport - Brighton

		FC	FC 1	SE A	SN	FC		FC 1	SE A	SN	FC	FC 1	SE A	SN	FC	FC 1		SE A	SN	FC	FC 1	SE A	SN	FC	FC 1
St Pancras International 15 ⊖	d																								
Farringdon 3 ⊖	d																								
City Thameslink 3	d																								
London Blackfriars 3 ⊖	a																								
	d																								
Elephant & Castle ⊖	d																								
Loughborough Jn.	d																								
Herne Hill 4	d																								
Denmark Hill 4	d			09 48					10 18				10 48					11 18				11 48			
Peckham Rye 4	d			09 51					10 21				10 51					11 21				11 51			
Nunhead 4	d			09 53					10 23				10 53					11 23				11 53			
Crofton Park	d			09 56					10 26				10 56					11 26				11 56			
Catford	d			09 59					10 29				10 59					11 29				11 59			
Bellingham	d			10 01					10 31				11 01					11 31				12 01			
Beckenham Hill	d			10 03					10 33				11 03					11 33				12 03			
Ravensbourne	d			10 05					10 35				11 05					11 35				12 05			
Shortlands	d			10 07					10 37				11 07					11 37				12 07			
Bromley South 4	d			10 10					10 40				11 10					11 40				12 10			
Bickley 4	d			10 13					10 43				11 13					11 43				12 13			
St Mary Cray	d			10 17					10 47				11 17					11 47				12 17			
Swanley 4	d			10 22					10 52				11 22					11 52				12 22			
Eynsford	d			10 26					10 56				11 26					11 56				12 26			
Shoreham (Kent)	d			10 30					11 00				11 30					12 00				12 30			
Otford 4	d			10 33					11 03				11 33					12 03				12 33			
Bat & Ball	d			10 36					11 06				11 36					12 06				12 36			
Sevenoaks 4	a			10 39					11 09				11 39					12 09				12 39			
London Bridge 4	a																								
	d	09 32	09 42		09 51	10 02		10 12		10 21	10 32	10 42		10 51	11 02	11 12			11 21	11 32	11 42		11 51	12 02	12 12
Tulse Hill 3	d	09 43			10 09	10 13				10 39	10 43			11 09	11 13				11 39	11 43			12 09	12 13	
Streatham 4	d	09 46			10 12	10 16				10 42	10 46			11 12	11 16				11 42	11 46			12 12	12 16	
Mitcham Eastfields	d																								
Mitcham Junction	d																								
Hackbridge	d																								
Carshalton	d																								
Tooting	d	09 50				10 20					10 50				11 20					11 50				12 20	
Haydons Road	d	09 53				10 23					10 53				11 23					11 53				12 23	
Wimbledon 6 ⊖ ⇌	d	09 58				10 28					10 58				11 28					11 58				12 28	
Wimbledon Chase	d	10 01				10 31					11 01				11 31					12 01				12 31	
South Merton	d	10 03				10 33					11 03				11 33					12 03				12 33	
Morden South	d	10 05				10 35					11 05				11 35					12 05				12 35	
St Helier	d	10 07				10 37					11 07				11 37					12 07				12 37	
Sutton Common	d	10 09				10 39					11 09				11 39					12 09				12 39	
West Sutton	d	10 12				10 42					11 12				11 42					12 12				12 42	
Sutton (Surrey) 4	a	10 16				10 46					11 16				11 46					12 16				12 46	
East Croydon ⇌	d		09 54		10a30			10 24		11a01		10 54		11a30		11 24			12a01		11 54		12a30		12 24
Redhill	d																								
Gatwick Airport 10 ✈	d		10 11					10 41				11 11				11 41					12 11				12 41
Three Bridges 4	d		10 17					10 47				11 17				11 47					12 17				12 47
Balcombe	d																								
Haywards Heath 3	d		10 26					10 56				11 26				11 56					12 26				12 56
Wivelsfield 4	d																								
Burgess Hill 4	d		10 31					11 01				11 31				12 01					12 31				13 01
Hassocks 4	d		10 35					11 05				11 35				12 05					12 35				13 05
Preston Park	d																								
Brighton 10	a		10 44					11 15				11 44				12 15					12 44				13 15

A From London Victoria

Please refer to separate pages within this table for services operating between Bedford and London

At weekends please use local bus and tube services to travel to/from St Pancras International and London Bridge when no trains are operating. See local publicity for details of alternative routes and services that are available across central London

Table 52

Sundays until 4 September

South London, Gatwick Airport - Brighton

		SE A	SN	FC	FC 1	SE A	SN	FC	FC 1	SE A	SN	FC	FC 1	SE A	SN	FC	FC 1	SE A	SN	FC	FC 1	SE A
St Pancras International 15 ⊖	d																					
Farringdon 3 ⊖	d																					
City Thameslink 3	d																					
London Blackfriars 3 ⊖	a																					
	d																					
Elephant & Castle ⊖	d																					
Loughborough Jn	d																					
Herne Hill 4	d																					
Denmark Hill 4	d	12 18				12 48				13 18				13 48				14 18				14 48
Peckham Rye 4	d	12 21				12 51				13 21				13 51				14 21				14 51
Nunhead 4	d	12 23				12 53				13 23				13 53				14 23				14 53
Crofton Park	d	12 26				12 56				13 26				13 56				14 26				14 56
Catford	d	12 29				12 59				13 29				13 59				14 29				14 59
Bellingham	d	12 31				13 01				13 31				14 01				14 31				15 01
Beckenham Hill	d	12 33				13 03				13 33				14 03				14 33				15 03
Ravensbourne	d	12 35				13 05				13 35				14 05				14 35				15 05
Shortlands	d	12 37				13 07				13 37				14 07				14 37				15 07
Bromley South 4	d	12 40				13 10				13 40				14 10				14 40				15 10
Bickley 4	d	12 43				13 13				13 43				14 13				14 43				15 13
St Mary Cray	d	12 47				13 17				13 47				14 17				14 47				15 17
Swanley 4	d	12 52				13 22				13 52				14 22				14 52				15 22
Eynsford	d	12 56				13 26				13 56				14 26				14 56				15 26
Shoreham (Kent)	d	13 00				13 30				14 00				14 30				15 00				15 30
Otford 4	d	13 03				13 33				14 03				14 33				15 03				15 33
Bat & Ball	d	13 06				13 36				14 06				14 36				15 06				15 36
Sevenoaks 4	a	13 09				13 39				14 09				14 39				15 09				15 39
London Bridge 4	a																					
	d		12 21	12 32	12 42		12 51	13 02	13 12		13 21	13 32	13 42		13 51	14 02	14 12		14 21	14 32	14 42	
Tulse Hill 3	d		12 39	12 43			13 09	13 13			13 39	13 43			14 09	14 13			14 39	14 43		
Streatham 4	d		12 42	12 46			13 12	13 16			13 42	13 46			14 12	14 16			14 42	14 46		
Mitcham Eastfields	d																					
Mitcham Junction	d																					
Hackbridge	d																					
Carshalton	d																					
Tooting	d			12 50				13 20				13 50				14 20				14 50		
Haydons Road	d			12 53				13 23				13 53				14 23				14 53		
Wimbledon 6 ⊖	d			12 58				13 28				13 58				14 28				14 58		
Wimbledon Chase	d			13 01				13 31				14 01				14 31				15 01		
South Merton	d			13 03				13 33				14 03				14 33				15 03		
Morden South	d			13 05				13 35				14 05				14 35				15 05		
St Helier	d			13 07				13 37				14 07				14 37				15 07		
Sutton Common	d			13 09				13 39				14 09				14 39				15 09		
West Sutton	d			13 12				13 42				14 12				14 42				15 12		
Sutton (Surrey) 4	a			13 16				13 46				14 16				14 46				15 16		
East Croydon	d		13a01		12 54		13a30		13 24		14a01		13 54		14a30		14 24		15a01		14 54	
Redhill	d																					
Gatwick Airport 10 ✈	d				13 11				13 41				14 11				14 41				15 11	
Three Bridges 4	d				13 17				13 47				14 17				14 47				15 17	
Balcombe	d																					
Haywards Heath 3	d				13 26				13 56				14 26				14 56				15 26	
Wivelsfield 4	d																					
Burgess Hill 4	d				13 31				14 01				14 31				15 01				15 31	
Hassocks 4	d				13 35				14 05				14 35				15 05				15 35	
Preston Park	d																					
Brighton 10	a				13 44				14 15				14 44				15 15				15 44	

A From London Victoria

Please refer to separate pages within this table for services operating between Bedford and London

At weekends please use local bus and tube services to travel to/from St Pancras International and London Bridge when no trains are operating. See local publicity for details of alternative routes and services that are available across central London

Table 52

Sundays until 4 September

South London, Gatwick Airport - Brighton

		SN	FC	FC 1	SE A	SN	FC	FC 1	SE A	SN	FC	FC 1	SE A	SN	FC	FC 1	SE A	SN	FC	FC 1	SE A	SN	FC
St Pancras International 15 ⊖	d																						
Farringdon 3 ⊖	d																						
City Thameslink 3	d																						
London Blackfriars 3 ⊖	a																						
	d																						
Elephant & Castle ⊖	d																						
Loughborough Jn	d																						
Herne Hill 4	d																						
Denmark Hill 4	d				15 18				15 48				16 18				16 48				17 18		
Peckham Rye 4	d				15 21				15 51				16 21				16 51				17 21		
Nunhead 4	d				15 23				15 53				16 23				16 53				17 23		
Crofton Park	d				15 26				15 56				16 26				16 56				17 26		
Catford	d				15 29				15 59				16 29				16 59				17 29		
Bellingham	d				15 31				16 01				16 31				17 01				17 31		
Beckenham Hill	d				15 33				16 03				16 33				17 03				17 33		
Ravensbourne	d				15 35				16 05				16 35				17 05				17 35		
Shortlands	d				15 37				16 07				16 37				17 07				17 37		
Bromley South 4	d				15 40				16 10				16 40				17 10				17 40		
Bickley 4	d				15 43				16 13				16 43				17 13				17 43		
St Mary Cray	d				15 47				16 17				16 47				17 17				17 47		
Swanley 4	d				15 52				16 22				16 52				17 22				17 52		
Eynsford	d				15 56				16 26				16 56				17 26				17 56		
Shoreham (Kent)	d				16 00				16 30				17 00				17 30				18 00		
Otford 4	d				16 03				16 33				17 03				17 33				18 03		
Bat & Ball	d				16 06				16 36				17 06				17 36				18 06		
Sevenoaks 4	a				16 09				16 39				17 09				17 39				18 09		
London Bridge 4	a																						
	d	14 51	15 02	15 12		15 21	15 32	15 42		15 51	16 02	16 12		16 21	16 32	16 42		16 51	17 02	17 12		17 21	17 32
Tulse Hill 3	d	15 09	15 13			15 39	15 43			16 09	16 13			16 39	16 43			17 09	17 13			17 39	17 43
Streatham 4	d	15 12	15 16			15 42	15 46			16 12	16 16			16 42	16 46			17 12	17 16			17 42	17 46
Mitcham Eastfields	d																						
Mitcham Junction	d																						
Hackbridge	d																						
Carshalton	d																						
Tooting	d		15 20				15 50				16 20				16 50				17 20				17 50
Haydons Road	d		15 23				15 53				16 23				16 53				17 23				17 53
Wimbledon 6 ⊖	d		15 28				15 58				16 28				16 58				17 28				17 58
Wimbledon Chase	d		15 31				16 01				16 31				17 01				17 31				18 01
South Merton	d		15 33				16 03				16 33				17 03				17 33				18 03
Morden South	d		15 35				16 05				16 35				17 05				17 35				18 05
St Helier	d		15 37				16 07				16 37				17 07				17 37				18 07
Sutton Common	d		15 39				16 09				16 39				17 09				17 39				18 09
West Sutton	d		15 42				16 12				16 42				17 12				17 42				18 12
Sutton (Surrey) 4	a		15 46				16 16				16 46				17 16				17 46				18 16
East Croydon	d	15a30		15 24		16a01		15 54		16a30		16 24		17a01		16 54		17a30		17 24		18a01	
Redhill	d																						
Gatwick Airport 10 ✈	d			15 41				16 11				16 41				17 11				17 41			
Three Bridges 4	d			15 47				16 17				16 47				17 17				17 47			
Balcombe	d																						
Haywards Heath 3	d			15 56				16 26				16 56				17 26				17 56			
Wivelsfield 4	d																						
Burgess Hill 4	d			16 01				16 31				17 01				17 31				18 01			
Hassocks 4	d			16 05				16 35				17 05				17 35				18 05			
Preston Park	d																						
Brighton 10	a			16 15				16 44				17 15				17 44				18 15			

A From London Victoria

Please refer to separate pages within this table for services operating between Bedford and London

At weekends please use local bus and tube services to travel to/from St Pancras International and London Bridge when no trains are operating. See local publicity for details of alternative routes and services that are available across central London

Sundays
until 4 September

South London, Gatwick Airport - Brighton

Station		FC	SE	SN		FC	FC	SE	SN	FC	FC	SE	SN	FC		FC	SE	SN	FC	FC	SE	SN	FC	FC
		1					1				1					1				1				1
			A					A				A					A				A			
St Pancras International	d																							
Farringdon	d																							
City Thameslink	d																							
London Blackfriars	a																							
	d																							
Elephant & Castle	d																							
Loughborough Jn.	d																							
Herne Hill	d																							
Denmark Hill	d		17 48					18 18				18 48					19 18				19 48			
Peckham Rye	d		17 51					18 21				18 51					19 21				19 51			
Nunhead	d		17 53					18 23				18 53					19 23				19 53			
Crofton Park	d		17 56					18 26				18 56					19 26				19 56			
Catford	d		17 59					18 29				18 59					19 29				19 59			
Bellingham	d		18 01					18 31				19 01					19 31				20 01			
Beckenham Hill	d		18 03					18 33				19 03					19 33				20 03			
Ravensbourne	d		18 05					18 35				19 05					19 35				20 05			
Shortlands	d		18 07					18 37				19 07					19 37				20 07			
Bromley South	d		18 10					18 40				19 10					19 40				20 10			
Bickley	d		18 13					18 43				19 13					19 43				20 13			
St Mary Cray	d		18 17					18 47				19 17					19 47				20 17			
Swanley	d		18 22					18 52				19 22					19 52				20 22			
Eynsford	d		18 26					18 56				19 26					19 56				20 26			
Shoreham (Kent)	d		18 30					19 00				19 30					20 00				20 30			
Otford	d		18 33					19 03				19 33					20 03				20 33			
Bat & Ball	d		18 36					19 06				19 36					20 06				20 36			
Sevenoaks	a		18 39					19 09				19 39					20 09				20 39			
London Bridge	a																							
	d	17 42		17 51		18 02	18 12		18 21	18 32	18 42		18 51	19 02		19 12		19 21	19 32	19 42		19 51	20 02	20 12
Tulse Hill	d			18 09		18 13			18 39	18 43			19 09	19 13				19 39	19 43			20 09	20 13	
Streatham	d			18 12		18 16			18 42	18 46			19 12	19 16				19 42	19 46			20 12	20 16	
Mitcham Eastfields	d																							
Mitcham Junction	d																							
Hackbridge	d																							
Carshalton	d																							
Tooting	d					18 20				18 50				19 20					19 50				20 20	
Haydons Road	d					18 23				18 53				19 23					19 53				20 23	
Wimbledon	d					18 28				18 58				19 28					19 58				20 28	
Wimbledon Chase	d					18 31				19 01				19 31					20 01				20 31	
South Merton	d					18 33				19 03				19 33					20 03				20 33	
Morden South	d					18 35				19 05				19 35					20 05				20 35	
St Helier	d					18 37				19 07				19 37					20 07				20 37	
Sutton Common	d					18 39				19 09				19 39					20 09				20 39	
West Sutton	d					18 42				19 12				19 42					20 12				20 42	
Sutton (Surrey)	a					18 46				19 16				19 46					20 16				20 46	
East Croydon	d	17 54		18a30			18 24		19a01		18 54		19a30			19 24		20a01		19 54		20a30		20 24
Redhill	d																							
Gatwick Airport	d	18 11					18 41				19 11					19 41				20 11				20 41
Three Bridges	d	18 17					18 47				19 17					19 47				20 17				20 47
Balcombe	d																							
Haywards Heath	d	18 26					18 56				19 26					19 56				20 26				20 56
Wivelsfield	d																							
Burgess Hill	d	18 31					19 01				19 31					20 01				20 31				21 01
Hassocks	d	18 35					19 05				19 35					20 05				20 35				21 05
Preston Park	d																							
Brighton	a	18 44					19 15				19 44					20 15				20 44				21 15

A From London Victoria

Please refer to separate pages within this table for services operating between Bedford and London

At weekends please use local bus and tube services to travel to/from St Pancras International and London Bridge when no trains are operating. See local publicity for details of alternative routes and services that are available across central London

Table 52

Sundays
until 4 September

South London, Gatwick Airport - Brighton

Station		SE	SN	FC	FC	SE	SN	FC	FC	SE		SN	FC	SE	SN	FC	SE	SN	FC	SE		SN	SN	FC	SE
					1				1				1			1			1					1	
		A				A				A				A			A			B					B
St Pancras International	d																								
Farringdon	d																								
City Thameslink	d																								
London Blackfriars	a																								
	d																								
Elephant & Castle	d																								
Loughborough Jn.	d																								
Herne Hill	d																								
Denmark Hill	d	20 18				20 48				21 18				21 48			22 18			22 48					23 18
Peckham Rye	d	20 21				20 51				21 21				21 51			22 21			22 51					23 21
Nunhead	d	20 23				20 53				21 23				21 53			22 23			22 53					23 23
Crofton Park	d	20 26				20 56				21 26				21 56			22 26			22 56					23 26
Catford	d	20 29				20 59				21 29				21 59			22 29			22 59					23 29
Bellingham	d	20 31				21 01				21 31				22 01			22 31			23 01					23 31
Beckenham Hill	d	20 33				21 03				21 33				22 03			22 33			23 03					23 33
Ravensbourne	d	20 35				21 05				21 35				22 05			22 35			23 05					23 35
Shortlands	d	20 37				21 07				21 37				22 07			22 37			23 07					23 37
Bromley South	d	20 40				21 10				21 40				22 10			22 40			23 10					23 40
Bickley	d	20 43				21 13				21 43				22 13			22 43			23a13					23a43
St Mary Cray	d	20 47				21 17				21 47				22 17			22 47								
Swanley	d	20 52				21 22				21 52				22 22			22 52								
Eynsford	d	20 56				21 26				21 56				22 26			22 56								
Shoreham (Kent)	d	21 00				21 30				22 00				22 30			23 00								
Otford	d	21 03				21 33				22 03				22 33			23 03								
Bat & Ball	d	21 06				21 36				22 06				22 36			23 06								
Sevenoaks	a	21 09				21 39				22 09				22 39			23 09								
London Bridge	a																								
	d		20 21	20 32	20 42		20 51	21 02	21 12			21 21	21 42		21 51	22 12		22 21	22 42			22 51	23 09	23 12	
Tulse Hill	d		20 39	20 43			21 09	21 13				21 39			22 09			22 39				23 09			
Streatham	d		20 42	20 46			21 12	21 16				21 42			22 12			22 42				23 12			
Mitcham Eastfields	d																								
Mitcham Junction	d																								
Hackbridge	d																								
Carshalton	d																								
Tooting	d			20 50				21 20																	
Haydons Road	d			20 53				21 23																	
Wimbledon	d			20 58				21 28																	
Wimbledon Chase	d			21 01				21 31																	
South Merton	d			21 03				21 33																	
Morden South	d			21 05				21 35																	
St Helier	d			21 07				21 37																	
Sutton Common	d			21 09				21 39																	
West Sutton	d			21 12				21 42																	
Sutton (Surrey)	a			21 16				21 46																	
East Croydon	d		21a01		20 54		21a30		21 24			22a01	21 54		22a30	22 24		23a00	22 54			23a30	23a38	23 24	
Redhill	d																								
Gatwick Airport	d				21 11				21 41				22 11			22 41			23 11					23 41	
Three Bridges	d				21 17				21 47				22 17			22 47			23 17					23 47	
Balcombe	d																								
Haywards Heath	d				21 26				21 56				22 26			22 56			23 26					23 56	
Wivelsfield	d																								
Burgess Hill	d				21 31				22 01				22 31			23 01			23 31					00 01	
Hassocks	d				21 35				22 05				22 35			23 05			23 35					00 05	
Preston Park	d																								
Brighton	a				21 44				22 15				22 44			23 15			23 44					00 15	

A From London Victoria

B From London Victoria to Orpington

Please refer to separate pages within this table for services operating between Bedford and London

At weekends please use local bus and tube services to travel to/from St Pancras International and London Bridge when no trains are operating. See local publicity for details of alternative routes and services that are available across central London

Table 52

Sundays
until 4 September

South London, Gatwick Airport - Brighton

Station		SN	FC 1
St Pancras International 15 ⊖	d		
Farringdon 3 ⊖	d		
City Thameslink 3	d		
London Blackfriars 3 ⊖	a		
	d		
Elephant & Castle ⊖	d		
Loughborough Jn	d		
Herne Hill 4	d		
Denmark Hill 4	d		
Peckham Rye 4	d		
Nunhead 4	d		
Crofton Park	d		
Catford	d		
Bellingham	d		
Beckenham Hill	d		
Ravensbourne	d		
Shortlands	d		
Bromley South 4	d		
Bickley 4	d		
St Mary Cray	d		
Swanley 4	d		
Eynsford	d		
Shoreham (Kent)	d		
Otford 4	d		
Bat & Ball	d		
Sevenoaks 4	a		
London Bridge 4	a		
	d	23 21	23 42
Tulse Hill 3	d	23 39	
Streatham 4	d	23 42	
Mitcham Eastfields	d		
Mitcham Junction	d		
Hackbridge	d		
Carshalton	d		
Tooting	d		
Haydons Road	d		
Wimbledon 6 ⊖	d		
Wimbledon Chase	d		
South Merton	d		
Morden South	d		
St Helier	d		
Sutton Common	d		
West Sutton	d		
Sutton (Surrey) 4	a		
East Croydon	d	00a01	23 57
Redhill	d		
Gatwick Airport 10	d		00 19
Three Bridges 4	d		00a24
Balcombe	d		
Haywards Heath 3	d		
Wivelsfield 4	d		
Burgess Hill 4	d		
Hassocks 4	d		
Preston Park	d		
Brighton 10	a		

Please refer to separate pages within this table for services operating between Bedford and London

At weekends please use local bus and tube services to travel to/from St Pancras International and London Bridge when no trains are operating. See local publicity for details of alternative routes and services that are available across central London

Table 52

Sundays
from 11 September

South London, Gatwick Airport - Brighton

Station		FC 1	FC	FC 1	FC	SE A	FC 1	SN	FC 1	FC 1		SN	FC 1	SE B	SN	FC 1	SE B	SN	FC 1	SE B		SN	FC 1	SE B	SN
St Pancras International 15 ⊖	d																								
Farringdon 3 ⊖	d																								
City Thameslink 3	d																								
London Blackfriars 3 ⊖	a																								
	d																								
Elephant & Castle ⊖	d																								
Loughborough Jn	d																								
Herne Hill 4	d																								
Denmark Hill 4	d					23p52								07 48			08 18			08 48				09 18	
Peckham Rye 4	d					23p55								07 51			08 21			08 51				09 21	
Nunhead 4	d					23p57								07 53			08 23			08 53				09 23	
Crofton Park	d					23p58								07 56			08 26			08 56				09 26	
Catford	d					00 03								07 59			08 29			08 59				09 29	
Bellingham	d					00 05								08 01			08 31			09 01				09 31	
Beckenham Hill	d					00 07								08 03			08 33			09 03				09 33	
Ravensbourne	d					00 09								08 05			08 35			09 05				09 35	
Shortlands	d					00 11								08 07			08 37			09 07				09 37	
Bromley South 4	d					00 14								08 10			08 40			09 10				09 40	
Bickley 4	d					00a17								08 13			08 43			09 13				09 43	
St Mary Cray	d													08 17			08 47			09 17				09 47	
Swanley 4	d													08 22			08 52			09 22				09 52	
Eynsford	d													08 26			08 56			09 26				09 56	
Shoreham (Kent)	d													08 30			09 00			09 30				10 00	
Otford 4	d													08 33			09 03			09 33				10 03	
Bat & Ball	d													08 36			09 06			09 36				10 06	
Sevenoaks 4	a													08 39			09 09			09 39				10 09	
London Bridge 4	a																								
	d	23p12	23p15	23p42	23p45		00 12	00 36	00 42	07 12		07 21	07 42		07 51	08 12		08 21	08 42			08 51	09 12		09 21
Tulse Hill 3	d		23p31		00 01							07 39			08 09			08 39				09 09			09 39
Streatham 4	d		23p35		00 05							07 42			08 12			08 42				09 12			09 42
Mitcham Eastfields	d																								
Mitcham Junction	d																								
Hackbridge	d																								
Carshalton	d																								
Tooting	d		23p40		00 10																				
Haydons Road	d		23p43		00 13																				
Wimbledon 6 ⊖	d		23p47		00 17																				
Wimbledon Chase	d		23p50		00 20																				
South Merton	d		23p52		00 22																				
Morden South	d		23p54		00 24																				
St Helier	d		23p56		00 26																				
Sutton Common	d		23p58		00 28																				
West Sutton	d		00 01		00 31																				
Sutton (Surrey) 4	a		00 05		00 35																				
East Croydon	d	23p25		23p57			00 27	01a03	00 57	07 27		08a01	07 57		08a30	08 27		09a01	08 57			09a30	09 27		10a01
Redhill	d																								
Gatwick Airport 10	d	23p41		00 19			00 49		01 20	07 50			08 20			08 50			09 20				09 50		
Three Bridges 4	d	23p47		00a24			00a54		01a24	07 54			08 24			08 54			09 24				09 54		
Balcombe	d	23p53																							
Haywards Heath 3	d	23p59								08 03			08 33			09 03			09 33				10 03		
Wivelsfield 4	d	00 03																							
Burgess Hill 4	d	00 05								08 08			08 38			09 08			09 38				10 08		
Hassocks 4	d	00 08								08 12			08 42			09 12			09 42				10 12		
Preston Park	d	00 15																							
Brighton 10	a	00 20								08 22			08 52			09 22			09 52				10 22		

A From London Victoria to Orpington
B From London Victoria

Please refer to separate pages within this table for services operating between Bedford and London

At weekends please use local bus and tube services to travel to/from St Pancras International and London Bridge when no trains are operating. See local publicity for details of alternative routes and services that are available across central London

Table 52

Sundays
from 11 September

South London, Gatwick Airport - Brighton

		FC	FC 1	SE	SN	FC		FC 1	SE	SN	FC	FC 1	SE	SN	FC	FC 1		SE	SN	FC	FC 1	SE	SN	FC	FC 1
				A					A				A					A				A			
St Pancras International 15 ⊖	d																								
Farringdon 3 ⊖	d																								
City Thameslink 3	d																								
London Blackfriars 3 ⊖	a																								
	d																								
Elephant & Castle ⊖	d																								
Loughborough Jn.	d																								
Herne Hill 4	d																								
Denmark Hill 4	d			09 48					10 18				10 48					11 18				11 48			
Peckham Rye 4	d			09 51					10 21				10 51					11 21				11 51			
Nunhead 4	d			09 53					10 23				10 53					11 23				11 53			
Crofton Park	d			09 56					10 26				10 56					11 26				11 56			
Catford	d			09 59					10 29				10 59					11 29				11 59			
Bellingham	d			10 01					10 31				11 01					11 31				12 01			
Beckenham Hill	d			10 03					10 33				11 03					11 33				12 03			
Ravensbourne	d			10 05					10 35				11 05					11 35				12 05			
Shortlands	d			10 07					10 37				11 07					11 37				12 07			
Bromley South 4	d			10 10					10 40				11 10					11 40				12 10			
Bickley 4	d			10 13					10 43				11 13					11 43				12 13			
St Mary Cray	d			10 17					10 47				11 17					11 47				12 17			
Swanley 4	d			10 22					10 52				11 22					11 52				12 22			
Eynsford	d			10 26					10 56				11 26					11 56				12 26			
Shoreham (Kent)	d			10 30					11 00				11 30					12 00				12 30			
Otford 4	d			10 33					11 03				11 33					12 03				12 33			
Bat & Ball	d			10 36					11 06				11 36					12 06				12 36			
Sevenoaks 4	a			10 39					11 09				11 39					12 09				12 39			
London Bridge 4	a																								
	d	09 32	09 42		09 51	10 02		10 12		10 21	10 32	10 42		10 51	11 02	11 12			11 21	11 32	11 42		11 51	12 02	12 12
Tulse Hill 3	d	09 43			10 09	10 13				10 39	10 43			11 09	11 13				11 39	11 43			12 09	12 13	
Streatham 4	d	09 46			10 12	10 16				10 42	10 46			11 12	11 16				11 42	11 46			12 12	12 16	
Mitcham Eastfields	d																								
Mitcham Junction	d																								
Hackbridge	d																								
Carshalton	d																								
Tooting	d	09 50				10 20					10 50				11 20					11 50				12 20	
Haydons Road	d	09 53				10 23					10 53				11 23					11 53				12 23	
Wimbledon 6 ⊖ ⇌	d	09 58				10 28					10 58				11 28					11 58				12 28	
Wimbledon Chase	d	10 01				10 31					11 01				11 31					12 01				12 31	
South Merton	d	10 03				10 33					11 03				11 33					12 03				12 33	
Morden South	d	10 05				10 35					11 05				11 35					12 05				12 35	
St Helier	d	10 07				10 37					11 07				11 37					12 07				12 37	
Sutton Common	d	10 09				10 39					11 09				11 39					12 09				12 39	
West Sutton	d	10 12				10 42					11 12				11 42					12 12				12 42	
Sutton (Surrey) 4	a	10 16				10 46					11 16				11 46					12 16				12 46	
East Croydon ⇌	d		09 57		10a30			10 27		11a01		10 57		11a30		11 27			12a01		11 57		12a30		12 27
Redhill	d																								
Gatwick Airport 10 ✈	d		10 20					10 50				11 20				11 50					12 20				12 50
Three Bridges 4	d		10 24					10 54				11 24				11 54					12 24				12 54
Balcombe	d																								
Haywards Heath 3	d		10 33					11 03				11 33				12 03					12 33				13 03
Wivelsfield 4	d																								
Burgess Hill 4	d		10 38					11 08				11 38				12 08					12 38				13 08
Hassocks 4	d		10 42					11 12				11 42				12 12					12 42				13 12
Preston Park	d																								
Brighton 10	a		10 52					11 22				11 52				12 22					12 52				13 22

A From London Victoria

Please refer to separate pages within this table for services operating between Bedford and London

At weekends please use local bus and tube services to travel to/from St Pancras International and London Bridge when no trains are operating. See local publicity for details of alternative routes and services that are available across central London

Table 52

Sundays
from 11 September

South London, Gatwick Airport - Brighton

		SE		SN	FC	FC 1	SE	SN	FC	FC 1	SE	SN		FC	FC 1	SE	SN	FC	FC 1	SE	SN	FC		FC 1	SE
		A					A				A					A				A					A
St Pancras International 15 ⊖	d																								
Farringdon 3 ⊖	d																								
City Thameslink 3	d																								
London Blackfriars 3 ⊖	a																								
	d																								
Elephant & Castle ⊖	d																								
Loughborough Jn.	d																								
Herne Hill 4	d																								
Denmark Hill 4	d	12 18					12 48				13 18					13 48				14 18					14 48
Peckham Rye 4	d	12 21					12 51				13 21					13 51				14 21					14 51
Nunhead 4	d	12 23					12 53				13 23					13 53				14 23					14 53
Crofton Park	d	12 26					12 56				13 26					13 56				14 26					14 56
Catford	d	12 29					12 59				13 29					13 59				14 29					14 59
Bellingham	d	12 31					13 01				13 31					14 01				14 31					15 01
Beckenham Hill	d	12 33					13 03				13 33					14 03				14 33					15 03
Ravensbourne	d	12 35					13 05				13 35					14 05				14 35					15 05
Shortlands	d	12 37					13 07				13 37					14 07				14 37					15 07
Bromley South 4	d	12 40					13 10				13 40					14 10				14 40					15 10
Bickley 4	d	12 43					13 13				13 43					14 13				14 43					15 13
St Mary Cray	d	12 47					13 17				13 47					14 17				14 47					15 17
Swanley 4	d	12 52					13 22				13 52					14 22				14 52					15 22
Eynsford	d	12 56					13 26				13 56					14 26				14 56					15 26
Shoreham (Kent)	d	13 00					13 30				14 00					14 30				15 00					15 30
Otford 4	d	13 03					13 33				14 03					14 33				15 03					15 33
Bat & Ball	d	13 06					13 36				14 06					14 36				15 06					15 36
Sevenoaks 4	a	13 09					13 39				14 09					14 39				15 09					15 39
London Bridge 4	a																								
	d			12 21	12 32	12 42		12 51	13 02	13 12		13 21		13 32	13 42		13 51	14 02	14 12		14 21	14 32		14 42	
Tulse Hill 3	d			12 39	12 43			13 09	13 13			13 39		13 43			14 09	14 13			14 39	14 43			
Streatham 4	d			12 42	12 46			13 12	13 16			13 42		13 46			14 12	14 16			14 42	14 46			
Mitcham Eastfields	d																								
Mitcham Junction	d																								
Hackbridge	d																								
Carshalton	d																								
Tooting	d				12 50				13 20					13 50				14 20				14 50			
Haydons Road	d				12 53				13 23					13 53				14 23				14 53			
Wimbledon 6 ⊖ ⇌	d				12 58				13 28					13 58				14 28				14 58			
Wimbledon Chase	d				13 01				13 31					14 01				14 31				15 01			
South Merton	d				13 03				13 33					14 03				14 33				15 03			
Morden South	d				13 05				13 35					14 05				14 35				15 05			
St Helier	d				13 07				13 37					14 07				14 37				15 07			
Sutton Common	d				13 09				13 39					14 09				14 39				15 09			
West Sutton	d				13 12				13 42					14 12				14 42				15 12			
Sutton (Surrey) 4	a				13 16				13 46					14 16				14 46				15 16			
East Croydon ⇌	d			13a01		12 57		13a30		13 27		14a01			13 57		14a30		14 27		15a01			14 57	
Redhill	d																								
Gatwick Airport 10 ✈	d					13 20				13 50					14 20				14 50					15 20	
Three Bridges 4	d					13 24				13 54					14 24				14 54					15 24	
Balcombe	d																								
Haywards Heath 3	d					13 33				14 03					14 33				15 03					15 33	
Wivelsfield 4	d																								
Burgess Hill 4	d					13 38				14 08					14 38				15 08					15 38	
Hassocks 4	d					13 42				14 12					14 42				15 12					15 42	
Preston Park	d																								
Brighton 10	a					13 52				14 22					14 52				15 22					15 52	

A From London Victoria

Please refer to separate pages within this table for services operating between Bedford and London

At weekends please use local bus and tube services to travel to/from St Pancras International and London Bridge when no trains are operating. See local publicity for details of alternative routes and services that are available across central London

Table 52

Sundays from 11 September

South London, Gatwick Airport - Brighton

		SN	FC	FC 1	SE A	SN	FC	FC 1	SE A	SN	FC	FC 1	SE A	SN	FC	FC 1	SE A	SN	FC	FC 1	SE A	SN	FC
St Pancras International ⊖	d																						
Farringdon ⊖	d																						
City Thameslink	d																						
London Blackfriars ⊖	a																						
	d																						
Elephant & Castle ⊖	d																						
Loughborough Jn	d																						
Herne Hill	d																						
Denmark Hill	d				15 18				15 48				16 18				16 48				17 18		
Peckham Rye	d				15 21				15 51				16 21				16 51				17 21		
Nunhead	d				15 23				15 53				16 23				16 53				17 23		
Crofton Park	d				15 26				15 56				16 26				16 56				17 26		
Catford	d				15 29				15 59				16 29				16 59				17 29		
Bellingham	d				15 31				16 01				16 31				17 01				17 31		
Beckenham Hill	d				15 33				16 03				16 33				17 03				17 33		
Ravensbourne	d				15 35				16 05				16 35				17 05				17 35		
Shortlands	d				15 37				16 07				16 37				17 07				17 37		
Bromley South	d				15 40				16 10				16 40				17 10				17 40		
Bickley	d				15 43				16 13				16 43				17 13				17 43		
St Mary Cray	d				15 47				16 17				16 47				17 17				17 47		
Swanley	d				15 52				16 22				16 52				17 22				17 52		
Eynsford	d				15 56				16 26				16 56				17 26				17 56		
Shoreham (Kent)	d				16 00				16 30				17 00				17 30				18 00		
Otford	d				16 03				16 33				17 03				17 33				18 03		
Bat & Ball	d				16 06				16 36				17 06				17 36				18 06		
Sevenoaks	a				16 09				16 39				17 09				17 39				18 09		
London Bridge	a																						
	d	14 51	15 02	15 12		15 21	15 32	15 42		15 51	16 02	16 12		16 21	16 32	16 42		16 51	17 02	17 12		17 21	17 32
Tulse Hill	d	15 09	15 13			15 39	15 43			16 09	16 13			16 39	16 43			17 09	17 13			17 39	17 43
Streatham	d	15 12	15 16			15 42	15 46			16 12	16 16			16 42	16 46			17 12	17 16			17 42	17 46
Mitcham Eastfields	d																						
Mitcham Junction	d																						
Hackbridge	d																						
Carshalton	d																						
Tooting	d		15 20				15 50				16 20				16 50				17 20				17 50
Haydons Road	d		15 23				15 53				16 23				16 53				17 23				17 53
Wimbledon ⊖	d		15 28				15 58				16 28				16 58				17 28				17 58
Wimbledon Chase	d		15 31				16 01				16 31				17 01				17 31				18 01
South Merton	d		15 33				16 03				16 33				17 03				17 33				18 03
Morden South	d		15 35				16 05				16 35				17 05				17 35				18 05
St Helier	d		15 37				16 07				16 37				17 07				17 37				18 07
Sutton Common	d		15 39				16 09				16 39				17 09				17 39				18 09
West Sutton	d		15 42				16 12				16 42				17 12				17 42				18 12
Sutton (Surrey)	a		15 46				16 16				16 46				17 16				17 46				18 16
East Croydon	d	15a30		15 27		16a01		15 57		16a30		16 27		17a01		16 57		17a30		17 27		18a01	
Redhill	d																						
Gatwick Airport ✈	d			15 50				16 20				16 50				17 20				17 50			
Three Bridges	d			15 54				16 24				16 54				17 24				17 54			
Balcombe	d																						
Haywards Heath	d			16 03				16 33				17 03				17 33				18 03			
Wivelsfield	d																						
Burgess Hill	d			16 08				16 38				17 08				17 38				18 08			
Hassocks	d			16 12				16 42				17 12				17 42				18 12			
Preston Park	d																						
Brighton	a			16 22				16 52				17 22				17 52				18 22			

A From London Victoria

Please refer to separate pages within this table for services operating between Bedford and London

At weekends please use local bus and tube services to travel to/from St Pancras International and London Bridge when no trains are operating. See local publicity for details of alternative routes and services that are available across central London

Table 52

Sundays from 11 September

South London, Gatwick Airport - Brighton

		FC 1	SE A	SN	FC	FC 1	SE A	SN	FC	FC 1	SE A	SN	FC	FC 1	SE A	SN	FC	FC 1	SE A	SN	FC	FC 1
St Pancras International ⊖	d																					
Farringdon ⊖	d																					
City Thameslink	d																					
London Blackfriars ⊖	a																					
	d																					
Elephant & Castle ⊖	d																					
Loughborough Jn	d																					
Herne Hill	d																					
Denmark Hill	d		17 48				18 18				18 48				19 18				19 48			
Peckham Rye	d		17 51				18 21				18 51				19 21				19 51			
Nunhead	d		17 53				18 23				18 53				19 23				19 53			
Crofton Park	d		17 56				18 26				18 56				19 26				19 56			
Catford	d		17 59				18 29				18 59				19 29				19 59			
Bellingham	d		18 01				18 31				19 01				19 31				20 01			
Beckenham Hill	d		18 03				18 33				19 03				19 33				20 03			
Ravensbourne	d		18 05				18 35				19 05				19 35				20 05			
Shortlands	d		18 07				18 37				19 07				19 37				20 07			
Bromley South	d		18 10				18 40				19 10				19 40				20 10			
Bickley	d		18 13				18 43				19 13				19 43				20 13			
St Mary Cray	d		18 17				18 47				19 17				19 47				20 17			
Swanley	d		18 22				18 52				19 22				19 52				20 22			
Eynsford	d		18 26				18 56				19 26				19 56				20 26			
Shoreham (Kent)	d		18 30				19 00				19 30				20 00				20 30			
Otford	d		18 33				19 03				19 33				20 03				20 33			
Bat & Ball	d		18 36				19 06				19 36				20 06				20 36			
Sevenoaks	a		18 39				19 09				19 39				20 09				20 39			
London Bridge	a																					
	d	17 42		17 51	18 02	18 12		18 21	18 32	18 42		18 51	19 02	19 12		19 21	19 32	19 42		19 51	20 02	20 12
Tulse Hill	d			18 09	18 13			18 39	18 43			19 09	19 13			19 39	19 43			20 09	20 13	
Streatham	d			18 12	18 16			18 42	18 46			19 12	19 16			19 42	19 46			20 12	20 16	
Mitcham Eastfields	d																					
Mitcham Junction	d																					
Hackbridge	d																					
Carshalton	d																					
Tooting	d				18 20				18 50				19 20				19 50				20 20	
Haydons Road	d				18 23				18 53				19 23				19 53				20 23	
Wimbledon ⊖	d				18 28				18 58				19 28				19 58				20 28	
Wimbledon Chase	d				18 31				19 01				19 31				20 01				20 31	
South Merton	d				18 33				19 03				19 33				20 03				20 33	
Morden South	d				18 35				19 05				19 35				20 05				20 35	
St Helier	d				18 37				19 07				19 37				20 07				20 37	
Sutton Common	d				18 39				19 09				19 39				20 09				20 39	
West Sutton	d				18 42				19 12				19 42				20 12				20 42	
Sutton (Surrey)	a				18 46				19 16				19 46				20 16				20 46	
East Croydon	d	17 57		18a30		18 27		19a01		18 57		19a30		19 27		20a01		19 57		20a30		20 27
Redhill	d																					
Gatwick Airport ✈	d	18 20				18 50				19 20				19 50				20 20				20 50
Three Bridges	d	18 24				18 54				19 24				19 54				20 24				20 54
Balcombe	d																					
Haywards Heath	d	18 33				19 03				19 33				20 03				20 33				21 03
Wivelsfield	d																					
Burgess Hill	d	18 38				19 08				19 38				20 08				20 38				21 08
Hassocks	d	18 42				19 12				19 42				20 12				20 42				21 12
Preston Park	d																					
Brighton	a	18 52				19 22				19 52				20 22				20 52				21 22

A From London Victoria

Please refer to separate pages within this table for services operating between Bedford and London

At weekends please use local bus and tube services to travel to/from St Pancras International and London Bridge when no trains are operating. See local publicity for details of alternative routes and services that are available across central London

Sundays
from 11 September

South London, Gatwick Airport - Brighton

		SE A	SN	FC	FC [1]	SE A	SN	FC	FC [1]	SE A	SN	FC [1]	SE A	SN	FC [1]	SE A	SN	FC [1]	SE B	SN	SN	FC [1]	SE B
St Pancras International [15] ⊖	d																						
Farringdon [3] ⊖	d																						
City Thameslink [3]	d																						
London Blackfriars [3] ⊖	a																						
	d																						
Elephant & Castle ⊖	d																						
Loughborough Jn.	d																						
Herne Hill [4]	d																						
Denmark Hill [4]	d	20 18				20 48				21 18			21 48			22 18			22 48				23 18
Peckham Rye [4]	d	20 21				20 51				21 21			21 51			22 21			22 51				23 21
Nunhead [4]	d	20 23				20 53				21 23			21 53			22 23			22 53				23 23
Crofton Park	d	20 26				20 56				21 26			21 56			22 26			22 56				23 26
Catford	d	20 29				20 59				21 29			21 59			22 29			22 59				23 29
Bellingham	d	20 31				21 01				21 31			22 01			22 31			23 01				23 31
Beckenham Hill	d	20 33				21 03				21 33			22 03			22 33			23 03				23 33
Ravensbourne	d	20 35				21 05				21 35			22 05			22 35			23 05				23 35
Shortlands	d	20 37				21 07				21 37			22 07			22 37			23 07				23 37
Bromley South [4]	d	20 40				21 10				21 40			22 10			22 40			23 10				23 40
Bickley [4]	d	20 43				21 13				21 43			22 13			22 43			23a13				23a43
St Mary Cray	d	20 47				21 17				21 47			22 17			22 47							
Swanley [4]	d	20 52				21 22				21 52			22 22			22 52							
Eynsford	d	20 56				21 26				21 56			22 26			22 56							
Shoreham (Kent)	d	21 00				21 30				22 00			22 30			23 00							
Otford [4]	d	21 03				21 33				22 03			22 33			23 03							
Bat & Ball	d	21 06				21 36				22 06			22 36			23 06							
Sevenoaks [4]	a	21 09				21 39				22 09			22 39			23 09							
London Bridge [4]	a																						
	d		20 21	20 32	20 42		20 51	21 02	21 12		21 21	21 42		21 51	22 12		22 21	22 42		22 51	23 09	23 12	
Tulse Hill [3]	d		20 39	20 43			21 09	21 13			21 39			22 09			22 39			23 09			
Streatham [4]	d		20 42	20 46			21 12	21 16			21 42			22 12			22 42			23 12			
Mitcham Eastfields	d																						
Mitcham Junction	d																						
Hackbridge	d																						
Carshalton	d																						
Tooting	d			20 50				21 20															
Haydons Road	d			20 53				21 23															
Wimbledon [6] ⊖	d			20 58				21 28															
Wimbledon Chase	d			21 01				21 31															
South Merton	d			21 03				21 33															
Morden South	d			21 05				21 35															
St Helier	d			21 07				21 37															
Sutton Common	d			21 09				21 39															
West Sutton	d			21 12				21 42															
Sutton (Surrey) [4]	a			21 16				21 46															
East Croydon	d		21a01		20 57		21a30		21 27		22a01	21 57		22a30	22 27		23a00	22 57		23a30	23a38	23 27	
Redhill	d																						
Gatwick Airport [10] ✈	d				21 20				21 50			22 20			22 50			23 20				23 50	
Three Bridges [4]	d				21 24				21 54			22 24			22 54			23 24				23 54	
Balcombe	d																						
Haywards Heath [3]	d				21 33				22 03			22 33			23 03			23 33				00 03	
Wivelsfield [4]	d																						
Burgess Hill [4]	d				21 38				22 08			22 38			23 08			23 38				00 08	
Hassocks [4]	d				21 42				22 12			22 42			23 12			23 42				00 12	
Preston Park	d																						
Brighton [10]	a				21 52				22 22			22 52			23 22			23 52				00 22	

A From London Victoria

B From London Victoria to Orpington

Please refer to separate pages within this table for services operating between Bedford and London

At weekends please use local bus and tube services to travel to/from St Pancras International and London Bridge when no trains are operating. See local publicity for details of alternative routes and services that are available across central London

Sundays
from 11 September

South London, Gatwick Airport - Brighton

		SN	FC [1]
St Pancras International [15] ⊖	d		
Farringdon [3] ⊖	d		
City Thameslink [3]	d		
London Blackfriars [3] ⊖	a		
	d		
Elephant & Castle ⊖	d		
Loughborough Jn.	d		
Herne Hill [4]	d		
Denmark Hill [4]	d		
Peckham Rye [4]	d		
Nunhead [4]	d		
Crofton Park	d		
Catford	d		
Bellingham	d		
Beckenham Hill	d		
Ravensbourne	d		
Shortlands	d		
Bromley South [4]	d		
Bickley [4]	d		
St Mary Cray	d		
Swanley [4]	d		
Eynsford	d		
Shoreham (Kent)	d		
Otford [4]	d		
Bat & Ball	d		
Sevenoaks [4]	a		
London Bridge [4]	a		
	d	23 21	23 42
Tulse Hill [3]	d	23 39	
Streatham [4]	d	23 42	
Mitcham Eastfields	d		
Mitcham Junction	d		
Hackbridge	d		
Carshalton	d		
Tooting	d		
Haydons Road	d		
Wimbledon [6] ⊖	d		
Wimbledon Chase	d		
South Merton	d		
Morden South	d		
St Helier	d		
Sutton Common	d		
West Sutton	d		
Sutton (Surrey) [4]	a		
East Croydon	d	00a01	23 57
Redhill	d		
Gatwick Airport [10] ✈	d		00 19
Three Bridges [4]	d		00a24
Balcombe	d		
Haywards Heath [3]	d		
Wivelsfield [4]	d		
Burgess Hill [4]	d		
Hassocks [4]	d		
Preston Park	d		
Brighton [10]	a		

Please refer to separate pages within this table for services operating between Bedford and London

At weekends please use local bus and tube services to travel to/from St Pancras International and London Bridge when no trains are operating. See local publicity for details of alternative routes and services that are available across central London

Brighton, Gatwick Airport - South London

		FC 1	FC 1	SN ◇1 A	FC 1	SN ◇1 A	SE B	SE C	SN ◇1 A	FC 1	SN ◇1 A	FC 1	SE C	FC 1	SE C	FC	FC 1	FC 1	FC	SE C	FC	FC 1	FC 1
Brighton 10	d	23p11	23p37	05 21	05 24	05 50			05 56	06 04	06 10	06 24		06 37			07 04	07 07				07 34	07 37
Preston Park	d		23p41		05 28				06 00		06 14	06 28		06 41				07 11					07 41
Hassocks 4	d	23p19	23p47		05 34				06 06		06 20	06 34		06 47				07 17					07 47
Burgess Hill 4	d	23p23	23p51	05 31	05 38					06 14	06 24	06 38		06 51				07 21					07 51
Wivelsfield 4	d		23p53		05 40				06 11		06 26	06 40		06 53				07 23					07 53
Haywards Heath 3	d	23p28	23p59	05 37	05 45	06 11			06 16	06 18	06 40	06 45		07 02			07 17	07 32				07 47	08 02
Balcombe	d		00 04		05 51							06 51						07 37					
Three Bridges 4	d	23p38	00 10	05 46	05 56	06 20			06 31		06 49	06 56		07 12			07 26	07 42				07 56	08 12
Gatwick Airport 10 ✈	d	23p43	00 15	05 53	06 01	06 25			06 38	06 31	06 55	07 01		07 16			07 31	07 46				08 01	08 16
Redhill	d		00 22																				
East Croydon	d	00 04	00 36	06a10	06 17	06a40			06a53	06 47	07a10	07 17		07 32			07 47	08 02				08 17	08 32
Sutton (Surrey) 4	d															07 07			07 08		07 37		
West Sutton	d															07 10					07 40		
Sutton Common	d															07 12					07 42		
St Helier	d															07 15					07 45		
Morden South	d															07 17					07 47		
South Merton	d															07 19					07 49		
Wimbledon Chase	d															07 21					07 51		
Wimbledon 6	d															07 30					08 00		
Haydons Road	d															07 32					08 02		
Tooting	d															07 35					08 05		
Carshalton	d																		07 11				
Hackbridge	d																		07 13				
Mitcham Junction	d																		07 16				
Mitcham Eastfields	d																		07 19				
Streatham 4	d															07 40			07 23		08 10		
Tulse Hill 3	d															07 47			07 27		08 17		
London Bridge 4 ⊖	a	00 19	00 52		06 32					07 02		07 32		07 47		08 00	08 02	08 17			08 30	08 32	08 47
	d																						
Sevenoaks 4	d							05 55					06 25		06 55					07 25			
Bat & Ball	d							05 58					06 28		06 58					07 28			
Otford 4	d							06 01					06 31		07 01					07 31			
Shoreham (Kent)	d							06 04					06 34		07 04					07 34			
Eynsford	d							06 08					06 38		07 08					07 38			
Swanley 4	d							06 13					06 43		07 13					07 43			
St Mary Cray 4	d							06 17					06 47		07 17					07 47			
Bickley	d						05 51	06 21					06 51		07 21					07 51			
Bromley South	d						05 54	06 24					06 54		07 24					07 54			
Shortlands 4	d						05 57	06 27					06 57		07 27					07 57			
Ravensbourne	d						05 59	06 29					06 59		07 29					07 59			
Beckenham Hill	d						06 01	06 31					07 01		07 31					08 01			
Bellingham	d						06 03	06 33					07 03		07 33					08 03			
Catford	d						06 06	06 36					07 06		07 36					08 06			
Crofton Park	d						06 08	06 38					07 08		07 38					08 08			
Nunhead 4	d						06 11	06 41					07 11		07 41					08 11			
Peckham Rye 4	d						06 13	06 43					07 13		07 43					08 13			
Denmark Hill 4	d						06a16	06a46					07a16		07a46					08a16			
Herne Hill 4	d																		07a31				
Loughborough Jn	d																						
Elephant & Castle	d																						
London Blackfriars 3 ⊖	a																						
	d																						
City Thameslink 3	d																						
Farringdon 3 ⊖	d																						
St Pancras International 15 ⊖	a																						

A To London Victoria B From Orpington to London Victoria C To London Victoria

Please refer to separate pages within this table for services operating between London and Bedford

At weekends please use local bus and tube services to travel to/from St Pancras International and London Bridge when no trains are operating. See local publicity for details of alternative routes and services that are available across central London

Brighton, Gatwick Airport - South London

		FC	SE A	FC	FC 1	FC 1	FC	SE A	FC	FC 1	FC 1	FC	SE A	FC	FC 1	FC 1	FC	SE A	FC	FC 1	FC 1	FC	SE A
Brighton 10	d				08 04	08 07				08 34	08 37				09 04	09 07				09 34	09 37		
Preston Park	d					08 11					08 41					09 11					09 41		
Hassocks 4	d					08 17					08 47					09 17					09 47		
Burgess Hill 4	d					08 21					08 51					09 21					09 51		
Wivelsfield 4	d					08 23					08 53					09 23					09 53		
Haywards Heath 3	d				08 17	08 32				08 47	09 02				09 17	09 32				09 47	10 02		
Balcombe	d					08 37										09 37							
Three Bridges 4	d				08 26	08 42				08 56	09 12				09 26	09 42				09 56	10 12		
Gatwick Airport 10 ✈	d				08 31	08 46				09 01	09 16				09 31	09 46				10 01	10 16		
Redhill	d																						
East Croydon	d				08 47	09 02				09 17	09 32				09 47	10 02				10 17	10 32		
Sutton (Surrey) 4	d	07 38		08 07			08 08		08 37			08 38		09 07			09 08		09 37			09 38	
West Sutton	d			08 10					08 40					09 10					09 40				
Sutton Common	d			08 12					08 42					09 12					09 42				
St Helier	d			08 15					08 45					09 15					09 45				
Morden South	d			08 17					08 47					09 17					09 47				
South Merton	d			08 19					08 49					09 19					09 49				
Wimbledon Chase	d			08 21					08 51					09 21					09 51				
Wimbledon 6	d			08 30					09 00					09 30					10 00				
Haydons Road	d			08 32					09 02					09 32					10 02				
Tooting	d			08 35					09 05					09 35					10 05				
Carshalton	d	07 41					08 11					08 41					09 11					09 41	
Hackbridge	d	07 43					08 13					08 43					09 13					09 43	
Mitcham Junction	d	07 46					08 16					08 46					09 16					09 46	
Mitcham Eastfields	d	07 49					08 19					08 49					09 19					09 49	
Streatham 4	d	07 53		08 40			08 23		09 10			08 53		09 40			09 23		10 10			09 53	
Tulse Hill 3	d	07 57		08 47			08 27		09 17			08 57		09 47			09 27		10 17			09 57	
London Bridge 4 ⊖	a			09 00	09 02	09 17			09 30	09 32	09 47			10 00	10 02	10 17			10 30	10 32	10 47		
	d																						
Sevenoaks 4	d		07 55					08 25					08 55					09 25					09 55
Bat & Ball	d		07 58					08 28					08 58					09 28					09 58
Otford 4	d		08 01					08 31					09 01					09 31					10 01
Shoreham (Kent)	d		08 04					08 34					09 04					09 34					10 04
Eynsford	d		08 08					08 38					09 08					09 38					10 08
Swanley 4	d		08 13					08 43					09 13					09 43					10 13
St Mary Cray 4	d		08 17					08 47					09 17					09 47					10 17
Bickley	d		08 21					08 51					09 21					09 51					10 21
Bromley South	d		08 24					08 54					09 24					09 54					10 24
Shortlands 4	d		08 27					08 57					09 27					09 57					10 27
Ravensbourne	d		08 29					08 59					09 29					09 59					10 29
Beckenham Hill	d		08 31					09 01					09 31					10 01					10 31
Bellingham	d		08 33					09 03					09 33					10 03					10 33
Catford	d		08 36					09 06					09 36					10 06					10 36
Crofton Park	d		08 38					09 08					09 38					10 08					10 38
Nunhead 4	d		08 41					09 11					09 41					10 11					10 41
Peckham Rye 4	d		08 43					09 13					09 43					10 13					10 43
Denmark Hill 4	d		08a46					09a16					09a46					10a16					10a46
Herne Hill 4	d	08a01					08a31					09a01					09a31					10a01	
Loughborough Jn	d																						
Elephant & Castle	d																						
London Blackfriars 3 ⊖	a																						
	d																						
City Thameslink 3	d																						
Farringdon 3 ⊖	d																						
St Pancras International 15 ⊖	a																						

A To London Victoria

Please refer to separate pages within this table for services operating between London and Bedford

At weekends please use local bus and tube services to travel to/from St Pancras International and London Bridge when no trains are operating. See local publicity for details of alternative routes and services that are available across central London

Table 52

Saturdays

Brighton, Gatwick Airport - South London

		FC	FC 1	FC 1	FC	SE	FC	FC 1	FC 1	FC	SE	FC	FC 1	FC 1	FC	SE	FC	FC 1	FC 1	FC	SE	FC
						A					A					A					A	
Brighton 10	d		10 04	10 07				10 34	10 37				11 04	11 07				11 34	11 37			
Preston Park	d			10 11					10 41					11 11					11 41			
Hassocks 4	d			10 17					10 47					11 17					11 47			
Burgess Hill 4	d			10 21					10 51					11 21					11 51			
Wivelsfield 4	d			10 23					10 53					11 23					11 53			
Haywards Heath 3	d		10 17	10 32				10 47	11 02				11 17	11 32				11 47	12 02			
Balcombe	d			10 37										11 37								
Three Bridges 4	d		10 26	10 42				10 56	11 12				11 26	11 42				11 56	12 12			
Gatwick Airport 10 ✈	d		10 31	10 46				11 01	11 16				11 31	11 46				12 01	12 16			
Redhill	d																					
East Croydon	d		10 47	11 02				11 17	11 32				11 47	12 02				12 17	12 32			
Sutton (Surrey) 4	d	10 07			10 08		10 37			10 38		11 07			11 08		11 37			11 38		12 07
West Sutton	d	10 10					10 40					11 10					11 40					12 10
Sutton Common	d	10 12					10 42					11 12					11 42					12 12
St Helier	d	10 15					10 45					11 15					11 45					12 15
Morden South	d	10 17					10 47					11 17					11 47					12 17
South Merton	d	10 19					10 49					11 19					11 49					12 19
Wimbledon Chase	d	10 21					10 51					11 21					11 51					12 21
Wimbledon 6	d	10 30					11 00					11 30					12 00					12 30
Haydons Road	d	10 32					11 02					11 32					12 02					12 32
Tooting	d	10 35					11 05					11 35					12 05					12 35
Carshalton	d				10 11					10 41					11 11					11 41		
Hackbridge	d				10 13					10 43					11 13					11 43		
Mitcham Junction	d				10 16					10 46					11 16					11 46		
Mitcham Eastfields	d				10 19					10 49					11 19					11 49		
Streatham 4	d	10 40			10 23		11 10			10 53		11 40			11 23		12 10			11 53		12 40
Tulse Hill 3	d	10 47			10 27		11 17			10 57		11 47			11 27		12 17			11 57		12 47
London Bridge 4 ⊖	a	11 00	11 02	11 17			11 30	11 32	11 47			12 00	12 02	12 17			12 30	12 32	12 47			13 00
	d																					
Sevenoaks 4	d					10 25					10 55					11 25					11 55	
Bat & Ball	d					10 28					10 58					11 28					11 58	
Otford 4	d					10 31					11 01					11 31					12 01	
Shoreham (Kent)	d					10 34					11 04					11 34					12 04	
Eynsford	d					10 38					11 08					11 38					12 08	
Swanley 4	d					10 43					11 13					11 43					12 13	
St Mary Cray 4	d					10 47					11 17					11 47					12 17	
Bickley	d					10 51					11 21					11 51					12 21	
Bromley South	d					10 54					11 24					11 54					12 24	
Shortlands 4	d					10 57					11 27					11 57					12 27	
Ravensbourne	d					10 59					11 29					11 59					12 29	
Beckenham Hill	d					11 01					11 31					12 01					12 31	
Bellingham	d					11 03					11 33					12 03					12 33	
Catford	d					11 06					11 36					12 06					12 36	
Crofton Park	d					11 08					11 38					12 08					12 38	
Nunhead 4	d					11 11					11 41					12 11					12 41	
Peckham Rye 4	d					11 13					11 43					12 13					12 43	
Denmark Hill 4	d					11a16					11a46					12a16					12a46	
Herne Hill 4	d				10a31					11a01					11a31					12a01		
Loughborough Jn	d																					
Elephant & Castle	d																					
London Blackfriars 3 ⊖	a																					
	d																					
City Thameslink 3	d																					
Farringdon 3 ⊖	d																					
St Pancras International 15 ⊖	a																					

A To London Victoria

Please refer to separate pages within this table for services operating between London and Bedford

At weekends please use local bus and tube services to travel to/from St Pancras International and London Bridge when no trains are operating. See local publicity for details of alternative routes and services that are available across central London

Table 52

Saturdays

Brighton, Gatwick Airport - South London

		FC 1	FC 1	FC	SE	FC	FC 1	FC 1	FC	SE	FC	FC 1	FC 1	FC	SE	FC	FC 1	FC 1	FC	SE	FC	FC 1	FC 1
					A					A					A					A			
Brighton 10	d	12 04	12 07				12 34	12 37				13 04	13 07				13 34	13 37				14 04	14 07
Preston Park	d		12 11					12 41					13 11					13 41					14 11
Hassocks 4	d		12 17					12 47					13 17					13 47					14 17
Burgess Hill 4	d		12 21					12 51					13 21					13 51					14 21
Wivelsfield 4	d		12 23					12 53					13 23					13 53					14 23
Haywards Heath 3	d	12 17	12 32				12 47	13 02				13 17	13 32				13 47	14 02				14 17	14 32
Balcombe	d		12 37										13 37										14 37
Three Bridges 4	d	12 26	12 42				12 56	13 12				13 26	13 42				13 56	14 12				14 26	14 42
Gatwick Airport 10 ✈	d	12 31	12 46				13 01	13 16				13 31	13 46				14 01	14 16				14 31	14 46
Redhill	d																						
East Croydon	d	12 47	13 02				13 17	13 32				13 47	14 02				14 17	14 32				14 47	15 02
Sutton (Surrey) 4	d			12 08		12 37			12 38		13 07			13 08		13 37			13 38		14 07		
West Sutton	d					12 40					13 10					13 40					14 10		
Sutton Common	d					12 42					13 12					13 42					14 12		
St Helier	d					12 45					13 15					13 45					14 15		
Morden South	d					12 47					13 17					13 47					14 17		
South Merton	d					12 49					13 19					13 49					14 19		
Wimbledon Chase	d					12 51					13 21					13 51					14 21		
Wimbledon 6	d					13 00					13 30					14 00					14 30		
Haydons Road	d					13 02					13 32					14 02					14 32		
Tooting	d					13 05					13 35					14 05					14 35		
Carshalton	d			12 11					12 41					13 11					13 41				
Hackbridge	d			12 13					12 43					13 13					13 43				
Mitcham Junction	d			12 16					12 46					13 16					13 46				
Mitcham Eastfields	d			12 19					12 49					13 19					13 49				
Streatham 4	d			12 23		13 10			12 53		13 40			13 23		14 10			13 53		14 40		
Tulse Hill 3	d			12 27		13 17			12 57		13 47			13 27		14 17			13 57		14 47		
London Bridge 4 ⊖	a	13 02	13 17			13 30	13 32	13 47			14 00	14 02	14 17			14 30	14 32	14 47			15 00	15 02	15 17
	d																						
Sevenoaks 4	d				12 25					12 55					13 25					13 55			
Bat & Ball	d				12 28					12 58					13 28					13 58			
Otford 4	d				12 31					13 01					13 31					14 01			
Shoreham (Kent)	d				12 34					13 04					13 34					14 04			
Eynsford	d				12 38					13 08					13 38					14 08			
Swanley 4	d				12 43					13 13					13 43					14 13			
St Mary Cray 4	d				12 47					13 17					13 47					14 17			
Bickley	d				12 51					13 21					13 51					14 21			
Bromley South	d				12 54					13 24					13 54					14 24			
Shortlands 4	d				12 57					13 27					13 57					14 27			
Ravensbourne	d				12 59					13 29					13 59					14 29			
Beckenham Hill	d				13 01					13 31					14 01					14 31			
Bellingham	d				13 03					13 33					14 03					14 33			
Catford	d				13 06					13 36					14 06					14 36			
Crofton Park	d				13 08					13 38					14 08					14 38			
Nunhead 4	d				13 11					13 41					14 11					14 41			
Peckham Rye 4	d				13 13					13 43					14 13					14 43			
Denmark Hill 4	d				13a16					13a46					14a16					14a46			
Herne Hill 4	d			12a31					13a01					13a31					14a01				
Loughborough Jn	d																						
Elephant & Castle	d																						
London Blackfriars 3 ⊖	a																						
	d																						
City Thameslink 3	d																						
Farringdon 3 ⊖	d																						
St Pancras International 15 ⊖	a																						

A To London Victoria

Please refer to separate pages within this table for services operating between London and Bedford

At weekends please use local bus and tube services to travel to/from St Pancras International and London Bridge when no trains are operating. See local publicity for details of alternative routes and services that are available across central London

Table 52

Brighton, Gatwick Airport - South London

		FC	SE	FC	FC	FC	FC	SE	FC	FC	FC	FC	SE	FC	FC	FC	FC	SE	FC	FC	FC	FC
					1	1				1	1				1	1				1	1	
			A					A					A					A				
Brighton [10]	d				14 34	14 37				15 04	15 07				15 34	15 37				16 04	16 07	
Preston Park	d					14 41					15 11					15 41					16 11	
Hassocks [4]	d					14 47					15 17					15 47					16 17	
Burgess Hill [4]	d					14 51					15 21					15 51					16 21	
Wivelsfield [4]	d					14 53					15 23					15 53					16 23	
Haywards Heath [3]	d				14 47	15 02				15 17	15 32				15 47	16 02				16 17	16 32	
Balcombe	d										15 37										16 37	
Three Bridges [4]	d				14 56	15 12				15 26	15 42				15 56	16 12				16 26	16 42	
Gatwick Airport [10] ✈	d				15 01	15 16				15 31	15 46				16 01	16 16				16 31	16 46	
Redhill	d																					
East Croydon	d				15 17	15 32				15 47	16 02				16 17	16 32				16 47	17 02	
Sutton (Surrey) [4]	d	14 08		14 37			14 38		15 07			15 08		15 37			15 38		16 07			16 08
West Sutton	d			14 40					15 10					15 40					16 10			
Sutton Common	d			14 42					15 12					15 42					16 12			
St Helier	d			14 45					15 15					15 45					16 15			
Morden South	d			14 47					15 17					15 47					16 17			
South Merton	d			14 49					15 19					15 49					16 19			
Wimbledon Chase	d			14 51					15 21					15 51					16 21			
Wimbledon [3]	d			15 00					15 30					16 00					16 30			
Haydons Road	d			15 02					15 32					16 02					16 32			
Tooting	d			15 05					15 35					16 05					16 35			
Carshalton	d	14 11					14 41					15 11					15 41					16 11
Hackbridge	d	14 13					14 43					15 13					15 43					16 13
Mitcham Junction	d	14 16					14 46					15 16					15 46					16 16
Mitcham Eastfields	d	14 19					14 49					15 19					15 49					16 19
Streatham [4]	d	14 23		15 10			14 53		15 40			15 23		16 10			15 53		16 40			16 23
Tulse Hill [3]	d	14 27		15 17			14 57		15 47			15 27		16 17			15 57		16 47			16 27
London Bridge [4] ⊖	a			15 30	15 32	15 47			16 00	16 02	16 17			16 30	16 32	16 47			17 00	17 02	17 17	
	d																					
Sevenoaks [4]	d		14 25					14 55					15 25					15 55				
Bat & Ball	d		14 28					14 58					15 28					15 58				
Otford [4]	d		14 31					15 01					15 31					16 01				
Shoreham (Kent)	d		14 34					15 04					15 34					16 04				
Eynsford	d		14 38					15 08					15 38					16 08				
Swanley [4]	d		14 43					15 13					15 43					16 13				
St Mary Cray [4]	d		14 47					15 17					15 47					16 17				
Bickley	d		14 51					15 21					15 51					16 21				
Bromley South	d		14 54					15 24					15 54					16 24				
Shortlands [4]	d		14 57					15 27					15 57					16 27				
Ravensbourne	d		14 59					15 29					15 59					16 29				
Beckenham Hill	d		15 01					15 31					16 01					16 31				
Bellingham	d		15 03					15 33					16 03					16 33				
Catford	d		15 06					15 36					16 06					16 36				
Crofton Park	d		15 08					15 38					16 08					16 38				
Nunhead [4]	d		15 11					15 41					16 11					16 41				
Peckham Rye [4]	d		15 13					15 43					16 13					16 43				
Denmark Hill [4]	d		15a16					15a46					16a16					16a46				
Herne Hill [4]	d	14a31					15a01					15a31					16a01					16a31
Loughborough Jn	d																					
Elephant & Castle	d																					
London Blackfriars [3] ⊖	a																					
	d																					
City Thameslink [3]	d																					
Farringdon [3] ⊖	d																					
St Pancras International [15] ⊖	a																					

A To London Victoria

Please refer to separate pages within this table for services operating between London and Bedford

At weekends please use local bus and tube services to travel to/from St Pancras International and London Bridge when no trains are operating. See local publicity for details of alternative routes and services that are available across central London

Table 52

Brighton, Gatwick Airport - South London

		SE	FC	FC	FC	FC	SE	FC	FC	FC	FC	SE	FC	FC	FC	FC	SE	FC	FC	FC	FC	SE	FC
				1	1				1	1				1	1				1	1			
		A					A					A					A					A	
Brighton [10]	d			16 34	16 37				17 04	17 07				17 34	17 37				18 04	18 07			
Preston Park	d				16 41					17 11					17 41					18 11			
Hassocks [4]	d				16 47					17 17					17 47					18 17			
Burgess Hill [4]	d				16 51					17 21					17 51					18 21			
Wivelsfield [4]	d				16 53					17 23					17 53					18 23			
Haywards Heath [3]	d			16 47	17 02				17 17	17 32				17 47	18 02				18 17	18 32			
Balcombe	d									17 37										18 37			
Three Bridges [4]	d			16 56	17 12				17 26	17 42				17 56	18 12				18 26	18 42			
Gatwick Airport [10] ✈	d			17 01	17 16				17 31	17 46				18 01	18 16				18 31	18 46			
Redhill	d																						
East Croydon	d			17 17	17 32				17 47	18 02				18 17	18 32				18 47	19 02			
Sutton (Surrey) [4]	d		16 37			16 38		17 07			17 08		17 37			17 38		18 07			18 08		18 37
West Sutton	d		16 40					17 10					17 40					18 10					18 40
Sutton Common	d		16 42					17 12					17 42					18 12					18 42
St Helier	d		16 45					17 15					17 45					18 15					18 45
Morden South	d		16 47					17 17					17 47					18 17					18 47
South Merton	d		16 49					17 19					17 49					18 19					18 49
Wimbledon Chase	d		16 51					17 21					17 51					18 21					18 51
Wimbledon [3]	d		17 00					17 30					18 00					18 30					19 00
Haydons Road	d		17 02					17 32					18 02					18 32					19 02
Tooting	d		17 05					17 35					18 05					18 35					19 05
Carshalton	d					16 41					17 11					17 41					18 11		
Hackbridge	d					16 43					17 13					17 43					18 13		
Mitcham Junction	d					16 46					17 16					17 46					18 16		
Mitcham Eastfields	d					16 49					17 19					17 49					18 19		
Streatham [4]	d		17 10			16 53		17 40			17 23		18 10			17 53		18 40			18 23		19 10
Tulse Hill [3]	d		17 17			16 57		17 47			17 27		18 17			17 57		18 47			18 27		19 17
London Bridge [4] ⊖	a		17 30	17 32	17 47			18 00	18 02	18 17			18 30	18 32	18 47			19 00	19 02	19 17			19 30
	d																						
Sevenoaks [4]	d	16 25					16 55					17 25					17 55					18 25	
Bat & Ball	d	16 28					16 58					17 28					17 58					18 28	
Otford [4]	d	16 31					17 01					17 31					18 01					18 31	
Shoreham (Kent)	d	16 34					17 04					17 34					18 04					18 34	
Eynsford	d	16 38					17 08					17 38					18 08					18 38	
Swanley [4]	d	16 43					17 13					17 43					18 13					18 43	
St Mary Cray [4]	d	16 47					17 17					17 47					18 17					18 47	
Bickley	d	16 51					17 21					17 51					18 21					18 51	
Bromley South	d	16 54					17 24					17 54					18 24					18 54	
Shortlands [4]	d	16 57					17 27					17 57					18 27					18 57	
Ravensbourne	d	16 59					17 29					17 59					18 29					18 59	
Beckenham Hill	d	17 01					17 31					18 01					18 31					19 01	
Bellingham	d	17 03					17 33					18 03					18 33					19 03	
Catford	d	17 06					17 36					18 06					18 36					19 06	
Crofton Park	d	17 08					17 38					18 08					18 38					19 08	
Nunhead [4]	d	17 11					17 41					18 11					18 41					19 11	
Peckham Rye [4]	d	17 13					17 43					18 13					18 43					19 13	
Denmark Hill [4]	d	17a16					17a46					18a16					18a46					19a16	
Herne Hill [4]	d					17a01					17a31					18a01					18a31		
Loughborough Jn	d																						
Elephant & Castle	d																						
London Blackfriars [3] ⊖	a																						
	d																						
City Thameslink [3]	d																						
Farringdon [3] ⊖	d																						
St Pancras International [15] ⊖	a																						

A To London Victoria

Please refer to separate pages within this table for services operating between London and Bedford

At weekends please use local bus and tube services to travel to/from St Pancras International and London Bridge when no trains are operating. See local publicity for details of alternative routes and services that are available across central London

Table 52

Saturdays

Brighton, Gatwick Airport - South London

		FC	FC	FC	SE	FC	FC	FC	FC	SE	FC	FC	FC	SN	SE	FC	FC	FC	SE	FC	FC	FC	SE
		1	1				1	1				1	1	◇1			1	1			1	1	
					A					A				B	A				A				A
Brighton	d	18 34	18 37				19 04	19 07				19 34	19 37	19 54			20 04	20 07			20 34	20 37	
Preston Park	d		18 41					19 11					19 41	19 57				20 11				20 41	
Hassocks	d		18 47					19 17					19 47	20 04				20 17				20 47	
Burgess Hill	d		18 51					19 21					19 51	20 07				20 21				20 51	
Wivelsfield	d		18 53					19 23					19 53	20 10				20 23				20 53	
Haywards Heath	d	18 47	19 02				19 17	19 32				19 47	20 02	20 22			20 18	20 32			20 47	21 02	
Balcombe	d							19 37										20 37					
Three Bridges	d	18 56	19 12				19 26	19 42				19 56	20 12	20 32			20 26	20 42			20 56	21 12	
Gatwick Airport	d	19 01	19 16				19 31	19 46				20 01	20 16	20 38			20 31	20 46			21 01	21 16	
Redhill	d													20 48									
East Croydon	d	19 17	19 32				19 47	20 02				20 17	20 32	20a59			20 47	21 02			21 17	21 32	
Sutton (Surrey)	d			18 38		19 07			19 08		19 37					20 08				20 37			
West Sutton	d					19 10					19 40					20 11				20 40			
Sutton Common	d					19 12					19 42					20 13				20 42			
St Helier	d					19 15					19 45					20 16				20 45			
Morden South	d					19 17					19 47					20 18				20 47			
South Merton	d					19 19					19 49					20 20				20 49			
Wimbledon Chase	d					19 21					19 51					20 22				20 51			
Wimbledon	d					19 30					20 00					20 30				21 00			
Haydons Road	d					19 32					20 02					20 32				21 02			
Tooting	d					19 35					20 05					20 35				21 05			
Carshalton	d			18 41					19 11														
Hackbridge	d			18 43					19 13														
Mitcham Junction	d			18 46					19 16														
Mitcham Eastfields	d			18 49					19 19														
Streatham	d			18 53		19 40			19 23		20 10					20 40				21 10			
Tulse Hill	d			18 57		19 47			19 27		20 17					20 47				21 17			
London Bridge	a	19 32	19 47			20 00	20 02	20 17			20 30	20 32	20 47			21 00	21 02	21 17		21 30	21 32	21 47	
	d																						
Sevenoaks	d				18 55					19 25					19 55				20 25				20 55
Bat & Ball	d				18 58					19 28					19 58				20 28				20 58
Otford	d				19 01					19 31					20 01				20 31				21 01
Shoreham (Kent)	d				19 04					19 34					20 04				20 34				21 04
Eynsford	d				19 08					19 38					20 08				20 38				21 08
Swanley	d				19 13					19 43					20 13				20 43				21 13
St Mary Cray	d				19 17					19 47					20 17				20 47				21 17
Bickley	d				19 21					19 51					20 21				20 51				21 21
Bromley South	d				19 24					19 54					20 24				20 54				21 24
Shortlands	d				19 27					19 57					20 27				20 57				21 27
Ravensbourne	d				19 29					19 59					20 29				20 59				21 29
Beckenham Hill	d				19 31					20 01					20 31				21 01				21 31
Bellingham	d				19 33					20 03					20 33				21 03				21 33
Catford	d				19 36					20 06					20 36				21 06				21 36
Crofton Park	d				19 38					20 08					20 38				21 08				21 38
Nunhead	d				19 41					20 11					20 41				21 11				21 41
Peckham Rye	d				19 43					20 13					20 43				21 13				21 43
Denmark Hill	d				19a46					20a16					20a46				21a16				21a46
Herne Hill	d			19a01					19a31														
Loughborough Jn.	d																						
Elephant & Castle	d																						
London Blackfriars	a																						
	d																						
City Thameslink	d																						
Farringdon	d																						
St Pancras International	a																						

A To London Victoria

B To London Victoria

Please refer to separate pages within this table for services operating between London and Bedford

At weekends please use local bus and tube services to travel to/from St Pancras International and London Bridge when no trains are operating. See local publicity for details of alternative routes and services that are available across central London

Table 52

Saturdays

Brighton, Gatwick Airport - South London

		SN	FC	FC	SE	FC	FC	SE	SN	FC	FC	SE	FC	FC	FC
		◇1		1			1		◇1		1		1	1	1
		A			B			B	A			B			
Brighton	d	21 00		21 07			21 37		22 00		22 07		22 33	23 11	23 37
Preston Park	d	21 04		21 11			21 41		22 04		22 11		22 37		23 41
Hassocks	d	21 10		21 17			21 47		22 10		22 17		22 43	23 19	23 47
Burgess Hill	d	21 14		21 21			21 51		22 14		22 21		22 47	23 23	23 51
Wivelsfield	d	21 16		21 23			21 53		22 16		22 23		22 49		23 53
Haywards Heath	d	21 22		21 32			22 02		22 22		22 32		22 54	23 28	23 59
Balcombe	d			21 37							22 37		23 00		00 04
Three Bridges	d	21 32		21 42			22 12		22 32		22 42		23 12	23 38	00 10
Gatwick Airport	d	21 38		21 46			22 16		22 38		22 46		23 16	23 43	00 15
Redhill	d	21 48							22 47						00 22
East Croydon	d	21a59		22 02			22 32		22a59		23 02		23 32	00 04	00 36
Sutton (Surrey)	d		21 07			21 37				22 07					
West Sutton	d		21 10			21 40				22 10					
Sutton Common	d		21 12			21 42				22 12					
St Helier	d		21 15			21 45				22 15					
Morden South	d		21 17			21 47				22 17					
South Merton	d		21 19			21 49				22 19					
Wimbledon Chase	d		21 21			21 51				22 21					
Wimbledon	d		21 30			22 00				22 30					
Haydons Road	d		21 32			22 02				22 32					
Tooting	d		21 35			22 05				22 35					
Carshalton	d														
Hackbridge	d														
Mitcham Junction	d														
Mitcham Eastfields	d														
Streatham	d		21 40			22 10				22 40					
Tulse Hill	d		21 47			22 17				22 47					
London Bridge	a		22 00	22 17		22 30	22 47			23 00	23 17		23 47	00 19	00 52
	d														
Sevenoaks	d				21 25			21 55				22 25			
Bat & Ball	d				21 28			21 58				22 28			
Otford	d				21 31			22 01				22 31			
Shoreham (Kent)	d				21 34			22 04				22 34			
Eynsford	d				21 38			22 08				22 38			
Swanley	d				21 43			22 13				22 43			
St Mary Cray	d				21 47			22 17				22 47			
Bickley	d				21 51			22 21				22 51			
Bromley South	d				21 54			22 24				22 54			
Shortlands	d				21 57			22 27				22 57			
Ravensbourne	d				21 59			22 29				22 59			
Beckenham Hill	d				22 01			22 31				23 01			
Bellingham	d				22 03			22 33				23 03			
Catford	d				22 06			22 36				23 06			
Crofton Park	d				22 08			22 38				23 08			
Nunhead	d				22 11			22 41				23 11			
Peckham Rye	d				22 13			22 43				23 13			
Denmark Hill	d				22a16			22a46				23a16			
Herne Hill	d														
Loughborough Jn.	d														
Elephant & Castle	d														
London Blackfriars	a														
	d														
City Thameslink	d														
Farringdon	d														
St Pancras International	a														

A To London Victoria

B To London Victoria

Please refer to separate pages within this table for services operating between London and Bedford

At weekends please use local bus and tube services to travel to/from St Pancras International and London Bridge when no trains are operating. See local publicity for details of alternative routes and services that are available across central London

Brighton, Gatwick Airport - South London

Sundays
until 4 September

		FC	FC	FC	FC	SN	FC	SE	SN	FC		SE	FC	SE	SE	SN	FC	SE	FC	SE		SN	FC	SE	FC
		1	1	1	1	◇1	1		◇1	1			1			◇1	1		1			◇1	1		1
		A	A			B		C	B			C		C	D	B		D		D		B		D	
Brighton 10	d	23p11	23p37	05 45	06 11	06 16	06 44		07 04	07 14			07 44			08 00	08 14		08 44			09 00	09 14		09 44
Preston Park	d		23p41			06 19			07 07							08 03						09 03			
Hassocks 4	d	23p19	23p47	05 53	06 19	06 26	06 52		07 14	07 22			07 52			08 10	08 22		08 52			09 10	09 22		09 52
Burgess Hill 4	d	23p23	23p51	05 56	06 26	06 29	06 56		07 17	07 26			07 56			08 13	08 26		08 56			09 13	09 26		09 56
Wivelsfield 4	d		23p53			06 32			07 20							08 16						09 16			
Haywards Heath 3	d	23p28	23p59	06 01	06 31	06 40	07 01		07 25	07 31			08 01			08 25	08 31		09 01			09 25	09 31		10 01
Balcombe	d		00 04						07 30							08 30						09 30			
Three Bridges 4	d	23p38	00 10	06 10	06 40	06 49	07 11		07 36	07 41			08 11			08 36	08 41		09 11			09 36	09 41		10 11
Gatwick Airport 10	d	23p43	00 15	06 15	06 45	06 54	07 16		07 42	07 46			08 16			08 42	08 46		09 16			09 42	09 46		10 16
Redhill	d		00 22						07 49							08 49						09 49			
East Croydon	d	00 04	00 36	06 32	07 02	07a10	07 32		08a00	08 02			08 32			09a00	09 02		09 32			10a00	10 02		10 32
Sutton (Surrey) 4	d																								
West Sutton	d																								
Sutton Common	d																								
St Helier	d																								
Morden South	d																								
South Merton	d																								
Wimbledon Chase	d																								
Wimbledon 6	d																								
Haydons Road	d																								
Tooting	d																								
Carshalton	d																								
Hackbridge	d																								
Mitcham Junction	d																								
Mitcham Eastfields	d																								
Streatham 4	d																								
Tulse Hill 3	d																								
London Bridge 4 ⊖	a	00 19	00 52	06 59	07 15		07 45			08 15			08 45				09 15		09 45				10 15		10 45
	d																								
Sevenoaks 4	d														07 54			08 24		08 54				09 24	
Bat & Ball	d														07 57			08 27		08 57				09 27	
Otford 4	d														08 00			08 30		09 00				09 30	
Shoreham (Kent)	d														08 03			08 33		09 03				09 33	
Eynsford	d														08 07			08 37		09 07				09 37	
Swanley 4	d														08 12			08 42		09 12				09 42	
St Mary Cray 4	d														08 16			08 46		09 16				09 46	
Bickley	d							06 50				07 20		07 50	08 20			08 50		09 20				09 50	
Bromley South	d							06 53				07 23		07 53	08 23			08 53		09 23				09 53	
Shortlands 4	d							06 56				07 26		07 56	08 26			08 56		09 26				09 56	
Ravensbourne	d							06 58				07 28		07 58	08 28			08 58		09 28				09 58	
Beckenham Hill	d							07 00				07 30		08 00	08 30			09 00		09 30				10 00	
Bellingham	d							07 02				07 32		08 02	08 32			09 02		09 32				10 02	
Catford	d							07 05				07 35		08 05	08 35			09 05		09 35				10 05	
Crofton Park	d							07 07				07 37		08 07	08 37			09 07		09 37				10 07	
Nunhead 4	d							07 10				07 40		08 10	08 40			09 10		09 40				10 10	
Peckham Rye 4	d							07 12				07 42		08 12	08 42			09 12		09 42				10 12	
Denmark Hill 4	d							07a15				07a45		08a15	08a45			09a15		09a45				10a15	
Herne Hill 4	d																								
Loughborough Jn	d																								
Elephant & Castle	d																								
London Blackfriars 3 ⊖	a																								
	d																								
City Thameslink 3	d																								
Farringdon 3 ⊖	d																								
St Pancras International 15 ⊖	a																								

A not 22 May
B To London Victoria
C From Orpington to London Victoria
D To London Victoria

Please refer to separate pages within this table for services operating between London and Bedford

At weekends please use local bus and tube services to travel to/from St Pancras International and London Bridge when no trains are operating. See local publicity for details of alternative routes and services that are available across central London

Brighton, Gatwick Airport - South London

Sundays
until 4 September

		SE	SN	SE	FC	FC		SE	FC	FC	SN	SE	FC	FC	SE	FC		FC	SN	SE	FC	FC	SE	FC	FC
			◇1			1				1	◇1			1				1	◇1			1			1
		A	B	A				A			B	A			A				B	A			A		
Brighton 10	d		10 00			10 14				10 44	11 00			11 14				11 44	12 00			12 14			12 44
Preston Park	d		10 03								11 03								12 03						
Hassocks 4	d		10 10			10 22				10 52	11 10			11 22				11 52	12 10			12 22			12 52
Burgess Hill 4	d		10 13			10 26				10 56	11 13			11 26				11 56	12 13			12 26			12 56
Wivelsfield 4	d		10 16								11 16								12 16						
Haywards Heath 3	d		10 25			10 31				11 01	11 25			11 31				12 01	12 25			12 31			13 01
Balcombe	d		10 30								11 30								12 30						
Three Bridges 4	d		10 36			10 41				11 11	11 36			11 41				12 11	12 36			12 41			13 11
Gatwick Airport 10	d		10 42			10 46				11 16	11 42			11 46				12 16	12 42			12 46			13 16
Redhill	d		10 49								11 49								12 49						
East Croydon	d		11a00			11 02				11 32	12a00			12 02				12 32	13a00			13 02			13 32
Sutton (Surrey) 4	d				10 28				10 58				11 28			11 58					12 28			12 58	
West Sutton	d				10 31				11 01				11 31			12 01					12 31			13 01	
Sutton Common	d				10 33				11 03				11 33			12 03					12 33			13 03	
St Helier	d				10 36				11 06				11 36			12 06					12 36			13 06	
Morden South	d				10 38				11 08				11 38			12 08					12 38			13 08	
South Merton	d				10 40				11 10				11 40			12 10					12 40			13 10	
Wimbledon Chase	d				10 42				11 12				11 42			12 12					12 42			13 12	
Wimbledon 6	d				10 45				11 15				11 45			12 15					12 45			13 15	
Haydons Road	d				10 48				11 18				11 48			12 18					12 48			13 18	
Tooting	d				10 51				11 21				11 51			12 21					12 51			13 21	
Carshalton	d																								
Hackbridge	d																								
Mitcham Junction	d																								
Mitcham Eastfields	d																								
Streatham 4	d				10 55				11 25				11 55			12 25					12 55			13 25	
Tulse Hill 3	d				10 59				11 29				11 59			12 29					12 59			13 29	
London Bridge 4 ⊖	a				11 10	11 15			11 40	11 45			12 10	12 15		12 40		12 45			13 10	13 15		13 40	13 45
	d																								
Sevenoaks 4	d	09 54		10 24				10 54				11 24			11 54					12 24			12 54		
Bat & Ball	d	09 57		10 27				10 57				11 27			11 57					12 27			12 57		
Otford 4	d	10 00		10 30				11 00				11 30			12 00					12 30			13 00		
Shoreham (Kent)	d	10 03		10 33				11 03				11 33			12 03					12 33			13 03		
Eynsford	d	10 07		10 37				11 07				11 37			12 07					12 37			13 07		
Swanley 4	d	10 12		10 42				11 12				11 42			12 12					12 42			13 12		
St Mary Cray 4	d	10 16		10 46				11 16				11 46			12 16					12 46			13 16		
Bickley	d	10 20		10 50				11 20				11 50			12 20					12 50			13 20		
Bromley South	d	10 23		10 53				11 23				11 53			12 23					12 53			13 23		
Shortlands 4	d	10 26		10 56				11 26				11 56			12 26					12 56			13 26		
Ravensbourne	d	10 28		10 58				11 28				11 58			12 28					12 58			13 28		
Beckenham Hill	d	10 30		11 00				11 30				12 00			12 30					13 00			13 30		
Bellingham	d	10 32		11 02				11 32				12 02			12 32					13 02			13 32		
Catford	d	10 35		11 05				11 35				12 05			12 35					13 05			13 35		
Crofton Park	d	10 37		11 07				11 37				12 07			12 37					13 07			13 37		
Nunhead 4	d	10 40		11 10				11 40				12 10			12 40					13 10			13 40		
Peckham Rye 4	d	10 42		11 12				11 42				12 12			12 42					13 12			13 42		
Denmark Hill 4	d	10a45		11a15				11a45				12a15			12a45					13a15			13a45		
Herne Hill 4	d																								
Loughborough Jn	d																								
Elephant & Castle	d																								
London Blackfriars 3 ⊖	a																								
	d																								
City Thameslink 3	d																								
Farringdon 3 ⊖	d																								
St Pancras International 15 ⊖	a																								

A To London Victoria
B To London Victoria

Please refer to separate pages within this table for services operating between London and Bedford

At weekends please use local bus and tube services to travel to/from St Pancras International and London Bridge when no trains are operating. See local publicity for details of alternative routes and services that are available across central London

Table 52

Sundays until 4 September

Brighton, Gatwick Airport - South London

		SN ◇1 A	SE B	FC	FC 1	SE B	FC	FC 1	SN ◇1 A	SE B	FC	FC 1	SE B	FC	FC 1	SN ◇1 A	SE B	FC	FC 1	SE B	FC	FC 1
Brighton 10	d	13 00			13 14			13 44	14 00			14 14			14 44	15 00			15 14			15 44
Preston Park	d	13 03							14 03							15 03						
Hassocks 4	d	13 10			13 22			13 52	14 10			14 22			14 52	15 10			15 22			15 52
Burgess Hill 4	d	13 13			13 26			13 56	14 13			14 26			14 56	15 13			15 26			15 56
Wivelsfield 4	d	13 16							14 16							15 16						
Haywards Heath 3	d	13 25			13 31			14 01	14 25			14 31			15 01	15 25			15 31			16 01
Balcombe	d	13 30							14 30							15 30						
Three Bridges 4	d	13 36			13 41			14 11	14 36			14 41			15 11	15 36			15 41			16 11
Gatwick Airport 10 ✈	d	13 42			13 46			14 16	14 42			14 46			15 16	15 42			15 46			16 16
Redhill	d	13 49							14 49							15 49						
East Croydon	d	14a00			14 02			14 32	15a00			15 02			15 32	16a00			16 02			16 32
Sutton (Surrey) 4	d			13 28			13 58				14 28			14 58				15 28			15 58	
West Sutton	d			13 31			14 01				14 31			15 01				15 31			16 01	
Sutton Common	d			13 33			14 03				14 33			15 03				15 33			16 03	
St Helier	d			13 36			14 06				14 36			15 06				15 36			16 06	
Morden South	d			13 38			14 08				14 38			15 08				15 38			16 08	
South Merton	d			13 40			14 10				14 40			15 10				15 40			16 10	
Wimbledon Chase	d			13 42			14 12				14 42			15 12				15 42			16 12	
Wimbledon 6	d			13 45			14 15				14 45			15 15				15 45			16 15	
Haydons Road	d			13 48			14 18				14 48			15 18				15 48			16 18	
Tooting	d			13 51			14 21				14 51			15 21				15 51			16 21	
Carshalton	d																					
Hackbridge	d																					
Mitcham Junction	d																					
Mitcham Eastfields	d																					
Streatham 4	d			13 55			14 25				14 55			15 25				15 55			16 25	
Tulse Hill 3	d			13 59			14 29				14 59			15 29				15 59			16 29	
London Bridge 4 ⊖	a			14 10	14 15		14 40	14 45			15 10	15 15		15 40	15 45			16 10	16 15		16 40	16 45
	d																					
Sevenoaks 4	d		13 24			13 54				14 24			14 54				15 24			15 54		
Bat & Ball	d		13 27			13 57				14 27			14 57				15 27			15 57		
Otford 4	d		13 30			14 00				14 30			15 00				15 30			16 00		
Shoreham (Kent)	d		13 33			14 03				14 33			15 03				15 33			16 03		
Eynsford	d		13 37			14 07				14 37			15 07				15 37			16 07		
Swanley 4	d		13 42			14 12				14 42			15 12				15 42			16 12		
St Mary Cray 4	d		13 46			14 16				14 46			15 16				15 46			16 16		
Bickley	d		13 50			14 20				14 50			15 20				15 50			16 20		
Bromley South	d		13 53			14 23				14 53			15 23				15 53			16 23		
Shortlands 4	d		13 56			14 26				14 56			15 26				15 56			16 26		
Ravensbourne	d		13 58			14 28				14 58			15 28				15 58			16 28		
Beckenham Hill	d		14 00			14 30				15 00			15 30				16 00			16 30		
Bellingham	d		14 02			14 32				15 02			15 32				16 02			16 32		
Catford	d		14 05			14 35				15 05			15 35				16 05			16 35		
Crofton Park	d		14 07			14 37				15 07			15 37				16 07			16 37		
Nunhead 4	d		14 10			14 40				15 10			15 40				16 10			16 40		
Peckham Rye 4	d		14 12			14 42				15 12			15 42				16 12			16 42		
Denmark Hill 4	d		14a15			14a45				15a15			15a45				16a15			16a45		
Herne Hill 4	d																					
Loughborough Jn.	d																					
Elephant & Castle	d																					
London Blackfriars 3 ⊖	a																					
	d																					
City Thameslink 3	d																					
Farringdon 3 ⊖	d																					
St Pancras International 15 ⊖	a																					

A To London Victoria

B To London Victoria

Please refer to separate pages within this table for services operating between London and Bedford

At weekends please use local bus and tube services to travel to/from St Pancras International and London Bridge when no trains are operating. See local publicity for details of alternative routes and services that are available across central London

Table 52

Sundays until 4 September

Brighton, Gatwick Airport - South London

		SN ◇1 A	SE B	FC	FC 1	SE B	FC	FC 1	SN ◇1 A	SE B	FC	FC 1	SE B	FC	FC 1	SN ◇1 A	SE B	FC	FC 1	SE B	FC	FC 1	SN ◇1 A
Brighton 10	d	16 00			16 14			16 44	17 00			17 14			17 44	18 00			18 14			18 44	19 00
Preston Park	d	16 03							17 03							18 03							19 03
Hassocks 4	d	16 10			16 22			16 52	17 10			17 22			17 52	18 10			18 22			18 52	19 10
Burgess Hill 4	d	16 13			16 26			16 56	17 13			17 26			17 56	18 13			18 26			18 56	19 13
Wivelsfield 4	d	16 16							17 16							18 16							19 16
Haywards Heath 3	d	16 25			16 31			17 01	17 25			17 31			18 01	18 25			18 31			19 01	19 25
Balcombe	d	16 30							17 30							18 30							19 30
Three Bridges 4	d	16 36			16 41			17 11	17 36			17 41			18 11	18 36			18 41			19 11	19 36
Gatwick Airport 10 ✈	d	16 42			16 46			17 16	17 42			17 46			18 16	18 42			18 46			19 16	19 42
Redhill	d	16 49							17 49							18 49							19 49
East Croydon	d	17a00			17 02			17 32	18a00			18 02			18 32	19a00			19 02			19 32	20a00
Sutton (Surrey) 4	d			16 28			16 58				17 28			17 58				18 28			18 58		
West Sutton	d			16 31			17 01				17 31			18 01				18 31			19 01		
Sutton Common	d			16 33			17 03				17 33			18 03				18 33			19 03		
St Helier	d			16 36			17 06				17 36			18 06				18 36			19 06		
Morden South	d			16 38			17 08				17 38			18 08				18 38			19 08		
South Merton	d			16 40			17 10				17 40			18 10				18 40			19 10		
Wimbledon Chase	d			16 42			17 12				17 42			18 12				18 42			19 12		
Wimbledon 6	d			16 45			17 15				17 45			18 15				18 45			19 15		
Haydons Road	d			16 48			17 18				17 48			18 18				18 48			19 18		
Tooting	d			16 51			17 21				17 51			18 21				18 51			19 21		
Carshalton	d																						
Hackbridge	d																						
Mitcham Junction	d																						
Mitcham Eastfields	d																						
Streatham 4	d			16 55			17 25				17 55			18 25				18 55			19 25		
Tulse Hill 3	d			16 59			17 29				17 59			18 29				18 59			19 29		
London Bridge 4 ⊖	a			17 10	17 15		17 40	17 45			18 10	18 15		18 40	18 45			19 10	19 15		19 40	19 45	
	d																						
Sevenoaks 4	d		16 24			16 54				17 24			17 54				18 24			18 54			
Bat & Ball	d		16 27			16 57				17 27			17 57				18 27			18 57			
Otford 4	d		16 30			17 00				17 30			18 00				18 30			19 00			
Shoreham (Kent)	d		16 33			17 03				17 33			18 03				18 33			19 03			
Eynsford	d		16 37			17 07				17 37			18 07				18 37			19 07			
Swanley 4	d		16 42			17 12				17 42			18 12				18 42			19 12			
St Mary Cray 4	d		16 46			17 16				17 46			18 16				18 46			19 16			
Bickley	d		16 50			17 20				17 50			18 20				18 50			19 20			
Bromley South	d		16 53			17 23				17 53			18 23				18 53			19 23			
Shortlands 4	d		16 56			17 26				17 56			18 26				18 56			19 26			
Ravensbourne	d		16 58			17 28				17 58			18 28				18 58			19 28			
Beckenham Hill	d		17 00			17 30				18 00			18 30				19 00			19 30			
Bellingham	d		17 02			17 32				18 02			18 32				19 02			19 32			
Catford	d		17 05			17 35				18 05			18 35				19 05			19 35			
Crofton Park	d		17 07			17 37				18 07			18 37				19 07			19 37			
Nunhead 4	d		17 10			17 40				18 10			18 40				19 10			19 40			
Peckham Rye 4	d		17 12			17 42				18 12			18 42				19 12			19 42			
Denmark Hill 4	d		17a15			17a45				18a15			18a45				19a15			19a45			
Herne Hill 4	d																						
Loughborough Jn.	d																						
Elephant & Castle	d																						
London Blackfriars 3 ⊖	a																						
	d																						
City Thameslink 3	d																						
Farringdon 3 ⊖	d																						
St Pancras International 15 ⊖	a																						

A To London Victoria

B To London Victoria

Please refer to separate pages within this table for services operating between London and Bedford

At weekends please use local bus and tube services to travel to/from St Pancras International and London Bridge when no trains are operating. See local publicity for details of alternative routes and services that are available across central London

Brighton, Gatwick Airport - South London

		SE	FC	FC	SE	FC	FC	SN	SE	FC	FC	SE	FC	FC	SN	SE	FC	FC	FC	SE	SN	FC
				1			1	◇1			1			1	◇1			1	1		◇1	1
		A			A			B	A			A			B	A				A	B	
Brighton 10	d			19 14			19 44	20 00			20 14			20 44	21 04			21 14	21 44		22 04	22 14
Preston Park	d							20 03							21 07						22 07	
Hassocks 4	d			19 22			19 52	20 10			20 22			20 52	21 14			21 22	21 52		22 14	22 22
Burgess Hill 4	d			19 26			19 56	20 13			20 26			20 56	21 17			21 26	21 56		22 17	22 26
Wivelsfield 4	d							20 16							21 20						22 20	
Haywards Heath 3	d			19 31			20 01	20 25			20 31			21 01	21 25			21 31	22 01		22 25	22 31
Balcombe	d							20 30							21 30						22 30	
Three Bridges 4	d			19 41			20 11	20 36			20 41			21 11	21 36			21 41	22 11		22 36	22 41
Gatwick Airport 10 ✈	d			19 46			20 16	20 42			20 46			21 16	21 42			21 46	22 16		22 42	22 46
Redhill	d							20 49							21 49						22 49	
East Croydon	d			20 02			20 32	21a00			21 02			21 32	22a00			22 02	22 32		23a00	23 02
Sutton (Surrey) 4	d		19 28			19 58				20 28			20 58				21 28					
West Sutton	d		19 31			20 01				20 31			21 01				21 31					
Sutton Common	d		19 33			20 03				20 33			21 03				21 33					
St Helier	d		19 36			20 06				20 36			21 06				21 36					
Morden South	d		19 38			20 08				20 38			21 08				21 38					
South Merton	d		19 40			20 10				20 40			21 10				21 40					
Wimbledon Chase	d		19 42			20 12				20 42			21 12				21 42					
Wimbledon 6	d		19 45			20 15				20 45			21 15				21 45					
Haydons Road	d		19 48			20 18				20 48			21 18				21 48					
Tooting	d		19 51			20 21				20 51			21 21				21 51					
Carshalton	d																					
Hackbridge	d																					
Mitcham Junction	d																					
Mitcham Eastfields	d																					
Streatham 4	d		19 55			20 25				20 55			21 25				21 55					
Tulse Hill 3	d		19 59			20 29				20 59			21 29				21 59					
London Bridge 4 ⊖	a		20 10	20 15		20 40	20 45			21 10	21 15		21 40	21 45			22 10	22 15	22 45			23 15
	d																					
Sevenoaks 4	d	19 24			19 54				20 24			20 54				21 24				21 54		
Bat & Ball	d	19 27			19 57				20 27			20 57				21 27				21 57		
Otford 4	d	19 30			20 00				20 30			21 00				21 30				22 00		
Shoreham (Kent)	d	19 33			20 03				20 33			21 03				21 33				22 03		
Eynsford	d	19 37			20 07				20 37			21 07				21 37				22 07		
Swanley 4	d	19 42			20 12				20 42			21 12				21 42				22 12		
St Mary Cray 4	d	19 46			20 16				20 46			21 16				21 46				22 16		
Bickley	d	19 50			20 20				20 50			21 20				21 50				22 20		
Bromley South	d	19 53			20 23				20 53			21 23				21 53				22 23		
Shortlands 4	d	19 56			20 26				20 56			21 26				21 56				22 26		
Ravensbourne	d	19 58			20 28				20 58			21 28				21 58				22 28		
Beckenham Hill	d	20 00			20 30				21 00			21 30				22 00				22 30		
Bellingham	d	20 02			20 32				21 02			21 32				22 02				22 32		
Catford	d	20 05			20 35				21 05			21 35				22 05				22 35		
Crofton Park	d	20 07			20 37				21 07			21 37				22 07				22 37		
Nunhead 4	d	20 10			20 40				21 10			21 40				22 10				22 40		
Peckham Rye 4	d	20 12			20 42				21 12			21 42				22 12				22 42		
Denmark Hill 4	d	20a15			20a45				21a15			21a45				22a15				22a45		
Herne Hill 4	d																					
Loughborough Jn	d																					
Elephant & Castle	d																					
London Blackfriars 3 ⊖	a																					
	d																					
City Thameslink 3	d																					
Farringdon 3 ⊖	d																					
St Pancras International 15 ⊖	a																					

A To London Victoria

B To London Victoria

Please refer to separate pages within this table for services operating between London and Bedford

At weekends please use local bus and tube services to travel to/from St Pancras International and London Bridge when no trains are operating. See local publicity for details of alternative routes and services that are available across central London

Brighton, Gatwick Airport - South London

		SE	FC	SE	FC	FC
			1		1	1
		A		A		
Brighton 10	d		22 44		23 14	23 44
Preston Park	d					
Hassocks 4	d		22 52		23 22	23 52
Burgess Hill 4	d		22 56		23 26	23 56
Wivelsfield 4	d					
Haywards Heath 3	d		23 01		23 31	00 01
Balcombe	d					
Three Bridges 4	d		23 11		23 40	00 10
Gatwick Airport 10 ✈	d		23 16		23 45	00 15
Redhill	d					00 22
East Croydon	d		23 32		00 04	00 36
Sutton (Surrey) 4	d					
West Sutton	d					
Sutton Common	d					
St Helier	d					
Morden South	d					
South Merton	d					
Wimbledon Chase	d					
Wimbledon 6	d					
Haydons Road	d					
Tooting	d					
Carshalton	d					
Hackbridge	d					
Mitcham Junction	d					
Mitcham Eastfields	d					
Streatham 4	d					
Tulse Hill 3	d					
London Bridge 4 ⊖	a		23 45		00 19	00 52
	d					
Sevenoaks 4	d	22 24		22 54		
Bat & Ball	d	22 27		22 57		
Otford 4	d	22 30		23 00		
Shoreham (Kent)	d	22 33		23 03		
Eynsford	d	22 37		23 07		
Swanley 4	d	22 42		23 12		
St Mary Cray 4	d	22 46		23 16		
Bickley	d	22 50		23 20		
Bromley South	d	22 53		23 23		
Shortlands 4	d	22 56		23 26		
Ravensbourne	d	22 58		23 28		
Beckenham Hill	d	23 00		23 30		
Bellingham	d	23 02		23 32		
Catford	d	23 05		23 35		
Crofton Park	d	23 07		23 37		
Nunhead 4	d	23 10		23 40		
Peckham Rye 4	d	23 12		23 42		
Denmark Hill 4	d	23a15		23a45		
Herne Hill 4	d					
Loughborough Jn	d					
Elephant & Castle	d					
London Blackfriars 3 ⊖	a					
	d					
City Thameslink 3	d					
Farringdon 3 ⊖	d					
St Pancras International 15 ⊖	a					

A To London Victoria

Please refer to separate pages within this table for services operating between London and Bedford

At weekends please use local bus and tube services to travel to/from St Pancras International and London Bridge when no trains are operating. See local publicity for details of alternative routes and services that are available across central London

Table 52

Sundays
from 11 September

Brighton, Gatwick Airport - South London

		FC 1	FC 1	FC 1	FC 1	SN ◇1 A	FC 1	SE B	SN ◇1 A	FC 1	SE B	FC 1	SE B	SE C	SN ◇1 A	FC 1	SE C	FC 1	SE C	SN ◇1 A	FC 1	SE C	FC 1
Brighton 10	d	23p11	23p37	05 45	06 11	06 16	06 44		07 00	07 14		07 44			08 00	08 14		08 44		09 00	09 14		09 44
Preston Park	d		23p41			06 19			07 03						08 03					09 03			
Hassocks 4	d	23p19	23p47	05 53	06 19	06 26	06 52		07 10	07 22		07 52			08 10	08 22		08 52		09 10	09 22		09 52
Burgess Hill 4	d	23p23	23p51	05 56	06 26	06 29	06 56		07 13	07 26		07 56			08 13	08 26		08 56		09 13	09 26		09 56
Wivelsfield 4	d		23p53			06 32			07 16						08 16					09 16			
Haywards Heath 3	d	23p28	23p59	06 01	06 31	06 40	07 01		07 21	07 31		08 01			08 21	08 31		09 01		09 21	09 31		10 01
Balcombe	d		00 04						07 26						08 26					09 26			
Three Bridges 4	d	23p38	00 10	06 10	06 40	06 49	07 10		07 32	07 40		08 10			08 32	08 40		09 10		09 32	09 40		10 10
Gatwick Airport 10 ✈	d	23p43	00 15	06 15	06 45	06 54	07 15		07 38	07 45		08 15			08 38	08 45		09 15		09 38	09 45		10 15
Redhill	d		00 22						07 46						08 46					09 46			
East Croydon	d	00 04	00 36	06 32	07 02	07a10	07 32		07a58	08 02		08 32			08a58	09 02		09 32		09a58	10 02		10 32
Sutton (Surrey) 4	d																						
West Sutton	d																						
Sutton Common	d																						
St Helier	d																						
Morden South	d																						
South Merton	d																						
Wimbledon Chase	d																						
Wimbledon 6	d																						
Haydons Road	d																						
Tooting	d																						
Carshalton	d																						
Hackbridge	d																						
Mitcham Junction	d																						
Mitcham Eastfields	d																						
Streatham 4	d																						
Tulse Hill 3	d																						
London Bridge 4 ⊖	a	00 19	00 52	06 59	07 15		07 45			08 15		08 45				09 15		09 45			10 15		10 45
	d																						
Sevenoaks 4	d													07 54			08 24		08 54			09 24	
Bat & Ball	d													07 57			08 27		08 57			09 27	
Otford 4	d													08 00			08 30		09 00			09 30	
Shoreham (Kent)	d													08 03			08 33		09 03			09 33	
Eynsford	d													08 07			08 37		09 07			09 37	
Swanley 4	d													08 12			08 42		09 12			09 42	
St Mary Cray 4	d													08 16			08 46		09 16			09 46	
Bickley	d							06 50			07 20		07 50	08 20			08 50		09 20			09 50	
Bromley South	d							06 53			07 23		07 53	08 23			08 53		09 23			09 53	
Shortlands 4	d							06 56			07 26		07 56	08 26			08 56		09 26			09 56	
Ravensbourne	d							06 58			07 28		07 58	08 28			08 58		09 28			09 58	
Beckenham Hill	d							07 00			07 30		08 00	08 30			09 00		09 30			10 00	
Bellingham	d							07 02			07 32		08 02	08 32			09 02		09 32			10 02	
Catford	d							07 05			07 35		08 05	08 35			09 05		09 35			10 05	
Crofton Park	d							07 07			07 37		08 07	08 37			09 07		09 37			10 07	
Nunhead 4	d							07 10			07 40		08 10	08 40			09 10		09 40			10 10	
Peckham Rye 4	d							07 12			07 42		08 12	08 42			09 12		09 42			10 12	
Denmark Hill 4	d							07a15			07a45		08a15	08a45			09a15		09a45			10a15	
Herne Hill 4	d																						
Loughborough Jn	d																						
Elephant & Castle	d																						
London Blackfriars 3 ⊖	a																						
	d																						
City Thameslink 3	d																						
Farringdon 3 ⊖	d																						
St Pancras International 15 ⊖	a																						

A To London Victoria B From Orpington to London Victoria C To London Victoria

Please refer to separate pages within this table for services operating between London and Bedford

At weekends please use local bus and tube services to travel to/from St Pancras International and London Bridge when no trains are operating. See local publicity for details of alternative routes and services that are available across central London

Table 52

Sundays
from 11 September

Brighton, Gatwick Airport - South London

		SE A	SN ◇1 B	SE A	FC	FC 1	SE A	FC	FC 1	SN ◇1 B	SE A	FC	FC 1	SE A	FC	FC 1	SN ◇1 B	SE A	FC	FC 1	SE A	FC	FC 1
Brighton 10	d		10 00			10 14			10 44	11 00			11 14			11 44	12 00			12 14			12 44
Preston Park	d		10 03							11 03							12 03						
Hassocks 4	d		10 10			10 22			10 52	11 10			11 22			11 52	12 10			12 22			12 52
Burgess Hill 4	d		10 13			10 26			10 56	11 13			11 26			11 56	12 13			12 26			12 56
Wivelsfield 4	d		10 16							11 16							12 16						
Haywards Heath 3	d		10 21			10 31			11 01	11 21			11 31			12 01	12 21			12 31			13 01
Balcombe	d		10 26							11 26							12 26						
Three Bridges 4	d		10 32			10 40			11 10	11 32			11 40			12 10	12 32			12 40			13 10
Gatwick Airport 10 ✈	d		10 38			10 45			11 15	11 38			11 45			12 15	12 38			12 45			13 15
Redhill	d		10 46							11 46							12 46						
East Croydon	d		10a58			11 02			11 32	11a58			12 02			12 32	12a58			13 02			13 32
Sutton (Surrey) 4	d				10 28			10 58				11 28			11 58				12 28			12 58	
West Sutton	d				10 31			11 01				11 31			12 01				12 31			13 01	
Sutton Common	d				10 33			11 03				11 33			12 03				12 33			13 03	
St Helier	d				10 36			11 06				11 36			12 06				12 36			13 06	
Morden South	d				10 38			11 08				11 38			12 08				12 38			13 08	
South Merton	d				10 40			11 10				11 40			12 10				12 40			13 10	
Wimbledon Chase	d				10 42			11 12				11 42			12 12				12 42			13 12	
Wimbledon 6	d				10 45			11 15				11 45			12 15				12 45			13 15	
Haydons Road	d				10 48			11 18				11 48			12 18				12 48			13 18	
Tooting	d				10 51			11 21				11 51			12 21				12 51			13 21	
Carshalton	d																						
Hackbridge	d																						
Mitcham Junction	d																						
Mitcham Eastfields	d																						
Streatham 4	d				10 55			11 25				11 55			12 25				12 55			13 25	
Tulse Hill 3	d				10 59			11 29				11 59			12 29				12 59			13 29	
London Bridge 4 ⊖	a				11 10	11 15		11 40	11 45			12 10	12 15		12 40	12 45			13 10	13 15		13 40	13 45
	d																						
Sevenoaks 4	d	09 54		10 24			10 54				11 24			11 54				12 24			12 54		
Bat & Ball	d	09 57		10 27			10 57				11 27			11 57				12 27			12 57		
Otford 4	d	10 00		10 30			11 00				11 30			12 00				12 30			13 00		
Shoreham (Kent)	d	10 03		10 33			11 03				11 33			12 03				12 33			13 03		
Eynsford	d	10 07		10 37			11 07				11 37			12 07				12 37			13 07		
Swanley 4	d	10 12		10 42			11 12				11 42			12 12				12 42			13 12		
St Mary Cray 4	d	10 16		10 46			11 16				11 46			12 16				12 46			13 16		
Bickley	d	10 20		10 50			11 20				11 50			12 20				12 50			13 20		
Bromley South	d	10 23		10 53			11 23				11 53			12 23				12 53			13 23		
Shortlands 4	d	10 26		10 56			11 26				11 56			12 26				12 56			13 26		
Ravensbourne	d	10 28		10 58			11 28				11 58			12 28				12 58			13 28		
Beckenham Hill	d	10 30		11 00			11 30				12 00			12 30				13 00			13 30		
Bellingham	d	10 32		11 02			11 32				12 02			12 32				13 02			13 32		
Catford	d	10 35		11 05			11 35				12 05			12 35				13 05			13 35		
Crofton Park	d	10 37		11 07			11 37				12 07			12 37				13 07			13 37		
Nunhead 4	d	10 40		11 10			11 40				12 10			12 40				13 10			13 40		
Peckham Rye 4	d	10 42		11 12			11 42				12 12			12 42				13 12			13 42		
Denmark Hill 4	d	10a45		11a15			11a45				12a15			12a45				13a15			13a45		
Herne Hill 4	d																						
Loughborough Jn	d																						
Elephant & Castle	d																						
London Blackfriars 3 ⊖	a																						
	d																						
City Thameslink 3	d																						
Farringdon 3 ⊖	d																						
St Pancras International 15 ⊖	a																						

A To London Victoria B To London Victoria

Please refer to separate pages within this table for services operating between London and Bedford

At weekends please use local bus and tube services to travel to/from St Pancras International and London Bridge when no trains are operating. See local publicity for details of alternative routes and services that are available across central London

Table 52

Sundays
from 11 September

Brighton, Gatwick Airport - South London

		SN		SE	FC	FC	SE	FC	FC	SN	SE	FC		FC	SE	FC	FC	SN	SE	FC	FC	SE		FC	FC
		◇1				1			1	◇1				1			1	◇1			1				1
		A		B			B			A	B				B			A	B			B			
Brighton 10	d	13 00				13 14			13 44	14 00				14 14			14 44	15 00			15 14				15 44
Preston Park	d	13 03								14 03								15 03							
Hassocks 4	d	13 10				13 22			13 52	14 10				14 22			14 52	15 10			15 22				15 52
Burgess Hill 4	d	13 13				13 26			13 56	14 13				14 26			14 56	15 13			15 26				15 56
Wivelsfield 4	d	13 16								14 16								15 16							
Haywards Heath 3	d	13 21				13 31			14 01	14 21				14 31			15 01	15 21			15 31				16 01
Balcombe	d	13 26								14 26								15 26							
Three Bridges 4	d	13 32				13 40			14 10	14 32				14 40			15 10	15 32			15 40				16 10
Gatwick Airport 10 ✈	d	13 38				13 45			14 15	14 38				14 45			15 15	15 38			15 45				16 15
Redhill	d	13 46								14 46								15 46							
East Croydon	d	13a58				14 02			14 32	14a58				15 02			15 32	15a58			16 02				16 32
Sutton (Surrey) 4	d				13 28			13 58				14 28				14 58				15 28				15 58	
West Sutton	d				13 31			14 01				14 31				15 01				15 31				16 01	
Sutton Common	d				13 33			14 03				14 33				15 03				15 33				16 03	
St Helier	d				13 36			14 06				14 36				15 06				15 36				16 06	
Morden South	d				13 38			14 08				14 38				15 08				15 38				16 08	
South Merton	d				13 40			14 10				14 40				15 10				15 40				16 10	
Wimbledon Chase	d				13 42			14 12				14 42				15 12				15 42				16 12	
Wimbledon 6	d				13 45			14 15				14 45				15 15				15 45				16 15	
Haydons Road	d				13 48			14 18				14 48				15 18				15 48				16 18	
Tooting	d				13 51			14 21				14 51				15 21				15 51				16 21	
Carshalton	d																								
Hackbridge	d																								
Mitcham Junction	d																								
Mitcham Eastfields	d																								
Streatham 4	d				13 55			14 25				14 55				15 25				15 55				16 25	
Tulse Hill 3	d				13 59			14 29				14 59				15 29				15 59				16 29	
London Bridge 4 ⊖	a				14 10	14 15		14 40	14 45			15 10		15 15		15 40	15 45			16 10	16 15			16 40	16 45
	d																								
Sevenoaks 4	d			13 24			13 54				14 24				14 54				15 24			15 54			
Bat & Ball	d			13 27			13 57				14 27				14 57				15 27			15 57			
Otford 4	d			13 30			14 00				14 30				15 00				15 30			16 00			
Shoreham (Kent)	d			13 33			14 03				14 33				15 03				15 33			16 03			
Eynsford	d			13 37			14 07				14 37				15 07				15 37			16 07			
Swanley 4	d			13 42			14 12				14 42				15 12				15 42			16 12			
St Mary Cray 4	d			13 46			14 16				14 46				15 16				15 46			16 16			
Bickley	d			13 50			14 20				14 50				15 20				15 50			16 20			
Bromley South	d			13 53			14 23				14 53				15 23				15 53			16 23			
Shortlands 4	d			13 56			14 26				14 56				15 26				15 56			16 26			
Ravensbourne	d			13 58			14 28				14 58				15 28				15 58			16 28			
Beckenham Hill	d			14 00			14 30				15 00				15 30				16 00			16 30			
Bellingham	d			14 02			14 32				15 02				15 32				16 02			16 32			
Catford	d			14 05			14 35				15 05				15 35				16 05			16 35			
Crofton Park	d			14 07			14 37				15 07				15 37				16 07			16 37			
Nunhead 4	d			14 10			14 40				15 10				15 40				16 10			16 40			
Peckham Rye 4	d			14 12			14 42				15 12				15 42				16 12			16 42			
Denmark Hill 4	d			14a15			14a45				15a15				15a45				16a15			16a45			
Herne Hill 4	d																								
Loughborough Jn.	d																								
Elephant & Castle	d																								
London Blackfriars 3 ⊖	a																								
	d																								
City Thameslink 3	d																								
Farringdon 3 ⊖	d																								
St Pancras International 15 ⊖	a																								

A To London Victoria

B To London Victoria

Please refer to separate pages within this table for services operating between London and Bedford

At weekends please use local bus and tube services to travel to/from St Pancras International and London Bridge when no trains are operating. See local publicity for details of alternative routes and services that are available across central London

Table 52

Sundays
from 11 September

Brighton, Gatwick Airport - South London

		SN	SE	FC	FC	SE	FC	FC		SN	SE	FC	FC	SE	FC	FC	SN	SE		FC	FC	SE	FC	FC	SN
		◇1			1			1		◇1			1			1	◇1				1			1	◇1
		A	B			B				A	B			B			A	B				B			A
Brighton 10	d	16 00			16 14			16 44		17 00			17 14			17 44	18 00				18 14			18 44	19 00
Preston Park	d	16 03								17 03							18 03								19 03
Hassocks 4	d	16 10			16 22			16 52		17 10			17 22			17 52	18 10				18 22			18 52	19 10
Burgess Hill 4	d	16 13			16 26			16 56		17 13			17 26			17 56	18 13				18 26			18 56	19 13
Wivelsfield 4	d	16 16								17 16							18 16								19 16
Haywards Heath 3	d	16 21			16 31			17 01		17 21			17 31			18 01	18 21				18 31			19 01	19 21
Balcombe	d	16 26								17 26							18 26								19 26
Three Bridges 4	d	16 32			16 40			17 10		17 32			17 40			18 10	18 32				18 40			19 10	19 32
Gatwick Airport 10 ✈	d	16 38			16 45			17 15		17 38			17 45			18 15	18 38				18 45			19 15	19 38
Redhill	d	16 46								17 46							18 46								19 46
East Croydon	d	16a58			17 02			17 32		17a58			18 02			18 32	18a58				19 02			19 32	19a58
Sutton (Surrey) 4	d			16 28			16 58					17 28			17 58					18 28			18 58		
West Sutton	d			16 31			17 01					17 31			18 01					18 31			19 01		
Sutton Common	d			16 33			17 03					17 33			18 03					18 33			19 03		
St Helier	d			16 36			17 06					17 36			18 06					18 36			19 06		
Morden South	d			16 38			17 08					17 38			18 08					18 38			19 08		
South Merton	d			16 40			17 10					17 40			18 10					18 40			19 10		
Wimbledon Chase	d			16 42			17 12					17 42			18 12					18 42			19 12		
Wimbledon 6	d			16 45			17 15					17 45			18 15					18 45			19 15		
Haydons Road	d			16 48			17 18					17 48			18 18					18 48			19 18		
Tooting	d			16 51			17 21					17 51			18 21					18 51			19 21		
Carshalton	d																								
Hackbridge	d																								
Mitcham Junction	d																								
Mitcham Eastfields	d																								
Streatham 4	d			16 55			17 25					17 55			18 25					18 55			19 25		
Tulse Hill 3	d			16 59			17 29					17 59			18 29					18 59			19 29		
London Bridge 4 ⊖	a			17 10	17 15		17 40	17 45				18 10	18 15		18 40	18 45				19 10	19 15		19 40	19 45	
	d																								
Sevenoaks 4	d		16 24			16 54					17 24			17 54				18 24				18 54			
Bat & Ball	d		16 27			16 57					17 27			17 57				18 27				18 57			
Otford 4	d		16 30			17 00					17 30			18 00				18 30				19 00			
Shoreham (Kent)	d		16 33			17 03					17 33			18 03				18 33				19 03			
Eynsford	d		16 37			17 07					17 37			18 07				18 37				19 07			
Swanley 4	d		16 42			17 12					17 42			18 12				18 42				19 12			
St Mary Cray 4	d		16 46			17 16					17 46			18 16				18 46				19 16			
Bickley	d		16 50			17 20					17 50			18 20				18 50				19 20			
Bromley South	d		16 53			17 23					17 53			18 23				18 53				19 23			
Shortlands 4	d		16 56			17 26					17 56			18 26				18 56				19 26			
Ravensbourne	d		16 58			17 28					17 58			18 28				18 58				19 28			
Beckenham Hill	d		17 00			17 30					18 00			18 30				19 00				19 30			
Bellingham	d		17 02			17 32					18 02			18 32				19 02				19 32			
Catford	d		17 05			17 35					18 05			18 35				19 05				19 35			
Crofton Park	d		17 07			17 37					18 07			18 37				19 07				19 37			
Nunhead 4	d		17 10			17 40					18 10			18 40				19 10				19 40			
Peckham Rye 4	d		17 12			17 42					18 12			18 42				19 12				19 42			
Denmark Hill 4	d		17a15			17a45					18a15			18a45				19a15				19a45			
Herne Hill 4	d																								
Loughborough Jn	d																								
Elephant & Castle	d																								
London Blackfriars 3 ⊖	a																								
	d																								
City Thameslink 3	d																								
Farringdon 3 ⊖	d																								
St Pancras International 15 ⊖	a																								

A To London Victoria

B To London Victoria

Please refer to separate pages within this table for services operating between London and Bedford

At weekends please use local bus and tube services to travel to/from St Pancras International and London Bridge when no trains are operating. See local publicity for details of alternative routes and services that are available across central London

Table 52

Sundays
from 11 September

Brighton, Gatwick Airport - South London

		SE	FC	FC	SE	FC	FC	SN	SE	FC	FC	SE	FC	FC	SN	SE	FC	FC	FC	SE	SN	FC
				■1			■1	◇■1			■1			■1	◇■1			■1	■1		◇■1	■1
		A			A			B	A			A			B	A				A	B	
Brighton ■10	d			19 14			19 44	20 00			20 14			20 44	21 00			21 14	21 44		22 00	22 14
Preston Park	d							20 03							21 03						22 03	
Hassocks ■4	d			19 22			19 52	20 10			20 22			20 52	21 10			21 22	21 52		22 10	22 22
Burgess Hill ■4	d			19 26			19 56	20 13			20 26			20 56	21 13			21 26	21 56		22 13	22 26
Wivelsfield ■4	d							20 16							21 16						22 16	
Haywards Heath ■3	d			19 31			20 01	20 21			20 31			21 01	21 21			21 31	22 01		22 21	22 31
Balcombe	d							20 26							21 26						22 26	
Three Bridges ■4	d			19 40			20 10	20 32			20 40			21 10	21 32			21 40	22 10		22 32	22 40
Gatwick Airport ■10 ✈	d			19 45			20 15	20 38			20 45			21 15	21 38			21 45	22 15		22 38	22 45
Redhill	d							20 46							21 46						22 46	
East Croydon	d			20 02			20 32	20a58			21 02			21 32	21a58			22 02	22 32		22a58	23 02
Sutton (Surrey) ■4	d		19 28			19 58				20 28			20 58				21 28					
West Sutton	d		19 31			20 01				20 31			21 01				21 31					
Sutton Common	d		19 33			20 03				20 33			21 03				21 33					
St Helier	d		19 36			20 06				20 36			21 06				21 36					
Morden South	d		19 38			20 08				20 38			21 08				21 38					
South Merton	d		19 40			20 10				20 40			21 10				21 40					
Wimbledon Chase	d		19 42			20 12				20 42			21 12				21 42					
Wimbledon ■6	d		19 45			20 15				20 45			21 15				21 45					
Haydons Road	d		19 48			20 18				20 48			21 18				21 48					
Tooting	d		19 51			20 21				20 51			21 21				21 51					
Carshalton	d																					
Hackbridge	d																					
Mitcham Junction	d																					
Mitcham Eastfields	d																					
Streatham ■4	d		19 55			20 25				20 55			21 25				21 55					
Tulse Hill ■3	d		19 59			20 29				20 59			21 29				21 59					
London Bridge ■4 ⊖	a		20 10	20 15		20 40	20 45			21 10	21 15		21 40	21 45			22 10	22 15	22 45			23 15
	d																					
Sevenoaks ■4	d	19 24			19 54				20 24			20 54				21 24				21 54		
Bat & Ball	d	19 27			19 57				20 27			20 57				21 27				21 57		
Otford ■4	d	19 30			20 00				20 30			21 00				21 30				22 00		
Shoreham (Kent)	d	19 33			20 03				20 33			21 03				21 33				22 03		
Eynsford	d	19 37			20 07				20 37			21 07				21 37				22 07		
Swanley ■4	d	19 42			20 12				20 42			21 12				21 42				22 12		
St Mary Cray ■4	d	19 46			20 16				20 46			21 16				21 46				22 16		
Bickley	d	19 50			20 20				20 50			21 20				21 50				22 20		
Bromley South	d	19 53			20 23				20 53			21 23				21 53				22 23		
Shortlands ■4	d	19 56			20 26				20 56			21 26				21 56				22 26		
Ravensbourne	d	19 58			20 28				20 58			21 28				21 58				22 28		
Beckenham Hill	d	20 00			20 30				21 00			21 30				22 00				22 30		
Bellingham	d	20 02			20 32				21 02			21 32				22 02				22 32		
Catford	d	20 05			20 35				21 05			21 35				22 05				22 35		
Crofton Park	d	20 07			20 37				21 07			21 37				22 07				22 37		
Nunhead ■4	d	20 10			20 40				21 10			21 40				22 10				22 40		
Peckham Rye ■4	d	20 12			20 42				21 12			21 42				22 12				22 42		
Denmark Hill ■4	d	20a15			20a45				21a15			21a45				22a15				22a45		
Herne Hill ■4	d																					
Loughborough Jn.	d																					
Elephant & Castle	d																					
London Blackfriars ■3 ⊖	a																					
	d																					
City Thameslink ■3	d																					
Farringdon ■3 ⊖	d																					
St Pancras International ■15 ⊖	a																					

A To London Victoria

B To London Victoria

Please refer to separate pages within this table for services operating between London and Bedford

At weekends please use local bus and tube services to travel to/from St Pancras International and London Bridge when no trains are operating. See local publicity for details of alternative routes and services that are available across central London

Table 52

Sundays
from 11 September

Brighton, Gatwick Airport - South London

		SE	FC	SE	FC	FC
			■1		■1	■1
		A		A		
Brighton ■10	d		22 44		23 14	23 44
Preston Park	d					
Hassocks ■4	d		22 52		23 22	23 52
Burgess Hill ■4	d		22 56		23 26	23 56
Wivelsfield ■4	d					
Haywards Heath ■3	d		23 01		23 31	00 01
Balcombe	d					
Three Bridges ■4	d		23 10		23 40	00 10
Gatwick Airport ■10 ✈	d		23 15		23 45	00 15
Redhill	d					00 22
East Croydon	d		23 32		00 04	00 36
Sutton (Surrey) ■4	d					
West Sutton	d					
Sutton Common	d					
St Helier	d					
Morden South	d					
South Merton	d					
Wimbledon Chase	d					
Wimbledon ■6	d					
Haydons Road	d					
Tooting	d					
Carshalton	d					
Hackbridge	d					
Mitcham Junction	d					
Mitcham Eastfields	d					
Streatham ■4	d					
Tulse Hill ■3	d					
London Bridge ■4 ⊖	a		23 45		00 19	00 52
	d					
Sevenoaks ■4	d	22 24		22 54		
Bat & Ball	d	22 27		22 57		
Otford ■4	d	22 30		23 00		
Shoreham (Kent)	d	22 33		23 03		
Eynsford	d	22 37		23 07		
Swanley ■4	d	22 42		23 12		
St Mary Cray ■4	d	22 46		23 16		
Bickley	d	22 50		23 20		
Bromley South	d	22 53		23 23		
Shortlands ■4	d	22 56		23 26		
Ravensbourne	d	22 58		23 28		
Beckenham Hill	d	23 00		23 30		
Bellingham	d	23 02		23 32		
Catford	d	23 05		23 35		
Crofton Park	d	23 07		23 37		
Nunhead ■4	d	23 10		23 40		
Peckham Rye ■4	d	23 12		23 42		
Denmark Hill ■4	d	23a15		23a45		
Herne Hill ■4	d					
Loughborough Jn.	d					
Elephant & Castle	d					
London Blackfriars ■3 ⊖	a					
	d					
City Thameslink ■3	d					
Farringdon ■3 ⊖	d					
St Pancras International ■15 ⊖	a					

A To London Victoria

Please refer to separate pages within this table for services operating between London and Bedford

At weekends please use local bus and tube services to travel to/from St Pancras International and London Bridge when no trains are operating. See local publicity for details of alternative routes and services that are available across central London

Table 52A

Mondays to Fridays

Luton - Dunstable

Bus Service

		FC	FC	FC	FC	FC	FC	FC	FC	FC	FC	FC	FC	FC	FC	FC	FC	FC	FC	FC	FC	FC	FC	FC	FC
Luton	d	05 57	06 15	06 40	07 10	07 32	07 53	08 06	08 27	08 47	09 08	09 27	09 34	09 52	10 04	10 22	10 34	10 52	11 04	11 22	11 34	11 52	12 04	12 22	12 34
Dunstable	a	06 20	06 50	07 10	07 45	08 05	08 25	08 45	09 00	09 25	09 40	09 55	10 10	10 25	10 40	10 55	11 10	11 25	11 40	11 55	12 10	12 29	12 40	12 55	13 10
		FC	FC	FC	FC	FC	FC	FC	FC	FC	FC	FC	FC	FC	FC	FC	FC	FC	FC	FC	FC	FC	FC	FC	FC
Luton	d	12 52	13 04	13 22	13 34	13 52	14 04	14 22	14 34	14 52	15 04	15 22	15 36	15 52	16 04	16 22	16 37	16 50	17 07	17 25	17 40	17 57	18 27	18 43	19 15
Dunstable	a	13 25	13 40	13 55	14 10	14 29	14 40	14 55	15 10	15 25	15 40	15 55	16 10	16 25	16 40	16 59	17 14	17 34	17 46	18 00	18 12	18 32	18 55	19 08	19 42
		FC	FC	FC	FC	FC	FC	FC	FC																
Luton	d	19 30	20 02	20 32	21 00	21 17	21 45	22 15	22 45																
Dunstable	a	19 54	20 32	21 02	21 20	21 41	22 09	22 37	23 08																

Saturdays

		FC	FC	FC	FC	FC	FC	FC	FC	FC	FC	FC	FC	FC	FC	FC	FC	FC	FC	FC	FC	FC	FC	FC	FC
Luton	d	05 55	06 30	07 07	07 37	08 07	08 37	09 07	09 27	09 42	10 02	10 22	10 42	11 02	11 22	11 42	12 02	12 22	12 42	13 02	13 22	13 42	14 02	14 22	14 42
Dunstable	a	06 13	06 48	07 35	08 05	08 40	09 10	09 40	09 57	10 15	10 35	10 55	11 15	11 35	11 55	12 15	12 39	12 55	13 15	13 35	13 55	14 15	14 39	14 55	15 15
		FC	FC	FC	FC	FC	FC	FC	FC	FC	FC	FC	FC	FC	FC	FC									
Luton	d	15 02	15 22	15 42	16 02	16 13	16 22	16 42	17 12	17 42	19 00	19 30	20 02	20 30	21 17	21 45									
Dunstable	a	15 35	15 55	16 15	16 31	16 47	17 00	17 11	17 45	18 11	19 18	19 54	21 02	21 02	21 41	21 59									

Sundays

		FC	FC	FC	FC	FC
Luton	d	18 42	19 42	20 42	21 42	22 42
Dunstable	a	19 04	20 04	21 04	22 04	23 06

Table 52A

Mondays to Fridays

Dunstable - Luton

Bus Service

		FC	FC	FC	FC	FC	FC	FC	FC	FC	FC	FC	FC	FC	FC	FC	FC	FC	FC	FC	FC	FC	FC	FC	FC
Dunstable	d	05 15	05 45	05 50	06 00	06 05	06 25	06 40	06 50	07 15	07 30	07 36	07 53	08 00	08 08	08 10	08 18	08 28	08 30	08 49	09 00	09 05	09 17	09 30	09 35
Luton	a	05 40	06 04	06 04	06 15	06 30	06 40	07 06	07 04	07 32	08 04	07 53	08 12	08 36	08 27	08 46	08 37	08 47	09 06	09 08	09 34	09 27	09 34	10 04	09 52
		FC	FC	FC	FC	FC	FC	FC	FC	FC	FC	FC	FC	FC	FC	FC	FC	FC	FC	FC	FC	FC	FC	FC	FC
Dunstable	d	09 47	10 00	10 05	10 17	10 30	10 35	10 47	11 00	11 05	11 17	11 30	11 35	11 47	12 00	12 05	12 17	12 30	12 35	12 47	13 00	13 05	13 17	13 35	13 47
Luton	a	10 04	10 34	10 22	10 34	11 04	10 52	11 07	11 34	11 22	11 34	12 04	11 52	12 04	12 34	12 22	12 34	13 04	12 52	13 04	13 34	13 22	13 34	13 52	14 04
		FC	FC	FC	FC	FC	FC	FC	FC	FC	FC	FC	FC	FC	FC	FC	FC	FC	FC	FC	FC	FC	FC	FC	FC
		FC	FC	FC	FC	FC	FC	FC	FC	FC	FC	FC	FC	FC	FC	FC	FC	FC	FC	FC	FC	FC	FC	FC	FC
Dunstable	d	14 00	14 05	14 17	14 30	14 35	14 47	15 00	15 05	15 19	15 35	15 40	15 47	16 05	16 10	16 20	16 33	16 40	16 50	17 08	17 10	17 20	17 23	17 40	17 40
Luton	a	14 34	14 22	14 34	15 04	14 52	15 04	15 34	15 22	15 36	15 52	16 15	16 04	16 22	16 47	16 37	16 50	17 17	17 07	17 25	17 47	17 59	17 40	17 57	18 17
Dunstable	d	18 10	18 20	18 45	19 15	20 15	20 45	21 45	23 08																
Luton	a	18 27	18 51	19 16	19 44	20 35	21 10	22 07	23 31																

Saturdays

		FC	FC	FC	FC	FC	FC	FC	FC	FC	FC	FC	FC	FC	FC	FC	FC	FC	FC	FC	FC	FC	FC	FC	FC
Dunstable	d	06 00	06 15	06 20	06 50	07 00	07 15	07 40	07 50	08 10	08 20	08 40	08 50	09 05	09 10	09 25	09 30	09 45	10 00	10 05	10 25	10 30	11 45	12 00	12 05
Luton	a	06 26	06 30	06 44	07 07	07 34	07 28	08 10	08 07	08 40	08 37	09 10	09 07	09 27	09 34	09 42	10 04	10 02	10 34	10 22	10 42	11 02	12 02	12 34	12 22
		FC	FC	FC	FC	FC	FC	FC	FC	FC	FC	FC	FC	FC	FC	FC	FC	FC	FC	FC	FC	FC	FC	FC	FC
Dunstable	d	12 25	12 30	12 45	13 00	13 05	13 25	13 30	13 45	14 00	14 05	14 25	14 30	14 45	15 00	15 05	15 25	15 30	15 45	16 00	16 05	16 25	16 40	16 55	17 10
Luton	a	12 42	13 04	13 02	13 34	13 22	13 42	14 04	14 02	14 34	14 22	14 42	15 04	15 02	15 34	15 22	15 42	16 04	16 02	16 34	16 22	16 42	17 14	17 12	17 44
		FC	FC	FC	FC	FC	FC	FC																	
Dunstable	d	17 23	17 40	18 00	18 45	19 15	20 45	23 08																	
Luton	a	17 40	18 10	18 33	19 16	19 44	21 10	23 31																	

No Sunday Service Dunstable to Luton

Route Diagram for Table 53

DM-7/09(2)
Design BAJS

© Network Rail OPSU 2009.
All rights reserved

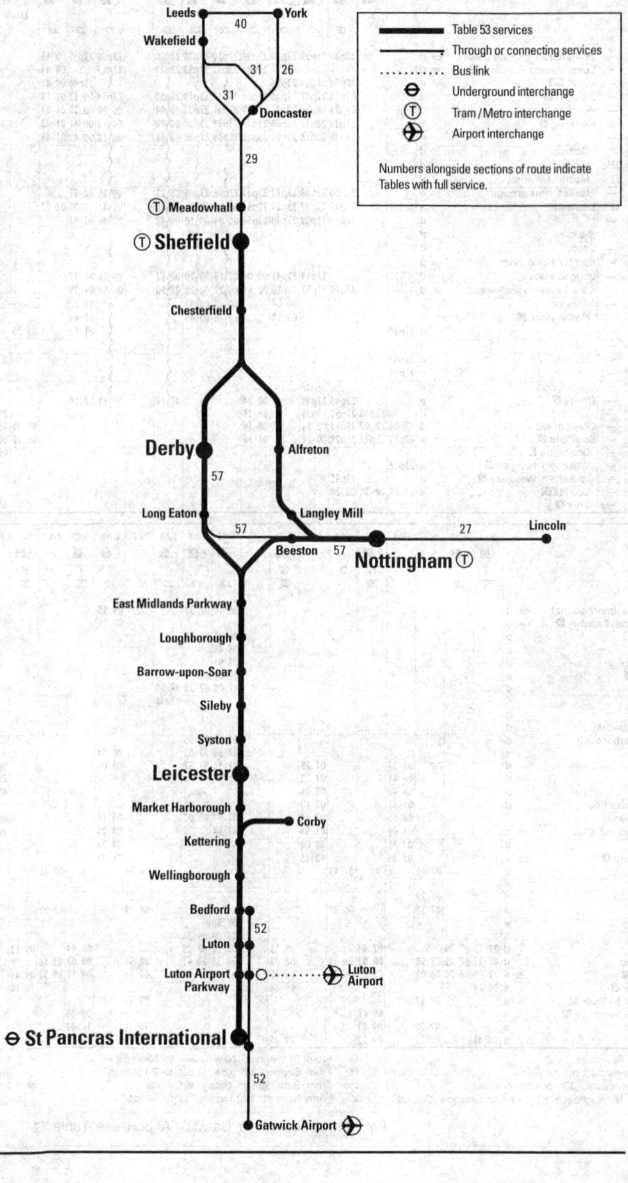

Table 53

Mondays to Fridays

until 23 September

London - East Midlands - Sheffield

Miles	Miles	Miles			NT	XC	EM	EM	EM	EM	EM	EM	EM		EM	EM	EM	EM	XC	NT	EM	XC	NT		EM
					MO	MO	MO	MO	MX	MX	MO	MO	MO		MO	MX	MX								
						◇1	◇1	◇1	◇1	◇1	◇1	◇1	◇1		◇1	◇1	◇1	◇	◇1		◇1	◇1			◇
						A												D	E			F			D
							⊏P	⊏P	⊏P	⊏P	⊏P	⊏P	⊏P		⊏P	⊏P	⊏P		⊥o		⊏P	⊥o			
0	0	—	**St Pancras International** ⊖	d			20p30	21p30	22p00	22p25	22p30	22p30	23p00		23p00	23p15	00 15								
29¼	29¼	—	Luton Airport Parkway 7 ✈	d						22p48	22p53	22p53	23p27		23p27		00 44								
30¼	30¼	—	Luton 10	d			20p54	21p54	22p24							23p46	00 47								
49¾	49¾	—	Bedford 7	d			21p18	22p17	22p40	23p04	23p17	23p19	23p50		23p54	00 12	01 12								
65¼	65¼	—	Wellingborough	d			21p31	22p30	22p53	23p17	23p31	23p32	00 04		00 08	00 25	01 33								
72	72	0	Kettering 4	a			21p38	22p37	23p00	23p25	23p37	23p38	00 10		00 14	00 41	01 43								
—	—	—		d			21p39	22p38	23p01	23p26	23p38	23p39	00 11		00 15	00 42	01 43								
—	—	7½	Corby	d																					
—	—	21¾	Oakham	d																					
—	—	33¼	Melton Mowbray	d																					
83	83	—	**Market Harborough**	d			21p50	22p48	23p12	23p37	23p48	23p49	00 21		00 25	00 52									
99¼	99¼	48½	**Leicester**	a			22p11	23p07	23p29	23p53	00 07	00 08	00 40		00 44	01 05	02 07								
—	—	—		d			22p13	23p09	23p30	23p55	00 09	00 10	00 42		00 46	01 07									
103	103	—	Syston	d																					
105¾	105¾	—	Sileby	d																					
107¾	107¾	—	Barrow Upon Soar	d																					
111¾	111¾	—	Loughborough	d				23p19	23p41	00 06	00 19	00 20	00 52		00 56	01 17									
117½	117½	—	East Midlands Parkway ✈	d			22p29	23p32	23p50	00 14	00 27	00 28	01 00		01 04	01 25									
123¼	—	—	Beeston	a					00 04		00 40	00 41				01 38									
126½	—	—	**Nottingham 8**	a					00 12		00 48	00 49				01 45									
—	—	—		d	21p20											01 52		05 20					06 23		06 40
—	—	—	Lincoln	a																					
138½	—	—	Langley Mill	d	21p41																		06 38		
144¾	—	—	Alfreton	d	21p49																		06 46		07 02
—	120½	—	Long Eaton	a				23p38																	
—	128½	—	**Derby 6**	a			22p43	23p49		00 34			01 19		01 23	02 10									
—	—	—		d		22p46	22p52	23p55		00 35									05 56		06 20	06 34			
155	152¾	—	Chesterfield	d	22p08	23p07	23p13	00 14		00 58								05 49	06 15	06 26	06 42	06 54	06 58		07 13
167¼	165	—	**Sheffield 7**	a	22p32	23p22	23p28	00 28		01 13								06 15	06 28	06 46	07 13	07 07	07 18		07 31
—	—	—	Doncaster 7	a															06 57						
—	—	—	Wakefield Kirkgate 4	a	23p26															07 27			07 57		
—	—	—	Wakefield Westgate 7	a			23p55															07 36			
—	—	—	Leeds 10	a	00 05	00 34	00 28													07 51		07 52	08 21		
—	—	—	York 8	a															07 28			08 23			

		XC	EM	NT	EM	XC	EM	EM	XC		EM	EM	EM	NT	EM	XC	EM	XC	EM		EM	EM	EM	EM	EM
		◇1	◇1			◇1	◇		◇1		◇1	◇1	◇1		◇1	◇1	◇	◇1			◇1		◇1	◇1	◇1
		G				H	D		G							I	J	K	L			M			
		⊥o	⊏P			⊥o			⊥o		⊏P	⊏P	⊏P		⊏P	⊥o		⊥o			⊏P		⊏P	⊏P	⊏P
St Pancras International ⊖	d										06 10	06 37			06 55						07 00		07 25	07 30	07 55
Luton Airport Parkway 7 ✈	d														07 16									07 51	
Luton 10	d										06 33	06 59									07 23				
Bedford 7	d										06 48										07 38			08 07	
Wellingborough	d										07 01										07 51			08 20	
Kettering 4	a										07 07	07 27									08 00			08 26	
	d										07 08	07 28	07 38								08 01			08 27	
Corby	d												07a48												
Oakham	d																								
Melton Mowbray	d																								
Market Harborough	d										07 18	07 38									08 12		08 21	08 37	
Leicester	a										07 35	07 53			08 04						08 29		08 36	08 52	09 02
	d				06 33			07 25			07 36	07 57			08 06				08 25		08 30		08 38	08 54	09 04
Syston	d				06 41			07 32											08 32						
Sileby	d				06 46			07 36											08 36						
Barrow Upon Soar	d				06 51			07 40											08 40						
Loughborough	d				06 56			07 45			07 47	08 07			08 16				08 45		08 41	←	08 48	09 04	
East Midlands Parkway ✈	d				07 06			07 54			07 54				08 24				08 54		08 50	08 54	08 56		
Beeston	a				07 16			08 06							08 31				→			09 02		09 16	
Nottingham 8	a				07 23			08 15							08 39						09 02	09 13		09 26	
	d			07 13			07 45							08 11			08 45					09 21			
Lincoln	a																					10 18			
Langley Mill	d			07 29										08 31											
Alfreton	d			07 37			08 07							08 39			09 07								
Long Eaton	a										07 58												08 59		
Derby 6	a										08 09	08 24											09 15		09 26
	d	07 13	07 20			07 44			08 13		08 18	08 28				08 44		09 13					09 18		09 28
Chesterfield	d	07 32	07 42	07 50		08 03	08 18		08 32		08 38	08 47		08 51		09 03	09 18						09 37		09 47
Sheffield 7	a	07 48	08 00	08 08		08 17	08 38		08 45		08 52	09 04		09 16		09 17	09 38	09 43					09 52		10 00
Doncaster 7	a	08 24							09 18									10 18							
Wakefield Kirkgate 4	a			08 57										09 57											
Wakefield Westgate 7	a					08 46										09 46									
Leeds 10	a			09 20		09 03								10 18		10 02									
York 8	a	08 46				09 32			09 45							10 28		10 45							

A From Penzance
D To Liverpool Lime Street
E To Newcastle. ⊥o from Sheffield
F From Birmingham New Street to Glasgow Central
G From Birmingham New Street to Newcastle
H From Birmingham New Street to Edinburgh
I From Bath Spa to Glasgow Central
J From Norwich to Liverpool Lime Street
K From Guildford to Newcastle
L To Lincoln
M From Leicester

For connections from Gatwick Airport see Table 52

Table 53

Mondays to Fridays

until 23 September

London - East Midlands - Sheffield

		EM	EM	NT	XC		EM	XC	EM	EM	EM	EM	EM	EM	EM		EM	NT	XC	EM	XC	EM	EM	EM	EM
		◇1	◇1		◇1		◇	◇1		◇1	◇1		◇1	◇1	◇1		1		◇1	◇	◇1		◇1	◇1	
					A		B	C	D			E							F	B	G	D			E
		☕	☕		🛒			🛒		☕	☕		☕	☕	☕				🛒		🛒		☕	☕	
St Pancras International ⊖	d		08 00							08 15	08 25		08 30	08 55	09 00								09 15	09 25	
Luton Airport Parkway 7 ✈	d												08 51												
Luton 10	d		08 23												09 23										
Bedford 7	d		08 38										09 07		09 38										
Wellingborough	d		08 51										09 20		09 51										
Kettering 4	a		09 00										09 27		10 00										
	d	08 32	09 01										09 27												
Corby	d	08a42	09a10														09 30								
Oakham	d																09 52								
Melton Mowbray	d																10 04								
Market Harborough	d									09 12			09 37										10 12		
Leicester	a									09 29	09 34		09 53	10 02									10 29	10 34	
	d								09 25	09 30	09 35		09 54	10 04								10 25	10 30	10 35	
Syston	d								09 32													10 32			
Sileby	d								09 36													10 36			
Barrow Upon Soar	d								09 40													10 40			
Loughborough	d								09 45		09 45	←	10 04									10 45		10 46	←
East Midlands Parkway ✈	d								09 54	09 46	09 52	09 54					10 28					10 54	10 46	10 53	10 54
Beeston	a								↦			10 02	10 16									↦			11 02
Nottingham 8	a									09 59		10 13	10 25										10 59		11 14
	d			09 15			09 45					10 29						10 15		10 45					11 17
Lincoln	a											11 31													12 21
Langley Mill	d			09 32														10 32							
Alfreton	d			09 40			10 07											10 40		11 07					
Long Eaton	a										09 56													10 56	
Derby 6	a										10 09			10 26			10 40							11 09	
	d				09 44			10 11			10 18			10 28					10 44		11 11			11 18	
Chesterfield	d			09 52	10 03		10 18				10 37			10 47				10 52	11 03	11 18				11 37	
Sheffield 7	a			10 16	10 17		10 38	10 41			10 52			11 02				11 16	11 17	11 38	11 43			11 52	
Doncaster 7	a							11 18													12 18				
Wakefield Kirkgate 4	a			10 57														11 57							
Wakefield Westgate 7	a				10 46														11 46						
Leeds 10	a			11 18	11 02													12 18	12 01						
York 8	a				11 27			11 47											12 27		12 48				

			EM	EM	EM	NT	XC	EM	XC	EM	EM		EM	EM	EM	EM	EM	NT	XC	EM	XC		EM	EM	EM
			◇1	◇1	◇1		◇1	◇	◇1		◇1		◇1		◇1	◇1	◇1		◇1	◇	◇1			◇1	◇1
							A	B	C	D				E					H	B	I		D		
			☕	☕	☕		🛒		🛒		☕		☕		☕	☕	☕		🛒		🛒			☕	☕
St Pancras International ⊖	d		09 30	09 55	10 00						10 15		10 25		10 30	10 55	11 00							11 15	11 25
Luton Airport Parkway 7 ✈	d		09 51												10 51										
Luton 10	d				10 23												11 23								
Bedford 7	d		10 07		10 38										11 07		11 38								
Wellingborough	d		10 20		10 51										11 20		11 51								
Kettering 4	a		10 26		11 00										11 26		12 00								
	d		10 27		11 01										11 27		12 01								
Corby	d				11a10												12a10								
Oakham	d																								
Melton Mowbray	d																								
Market Harborough	d		10 37								11 12				11 37									12 12	
Leicester	a		10 54	11 02							11 29		11 33		11 52	12 02								12 29	12 33
	d		10 54	11 04						11 25	11 30		11 35		11 54	12 04							12 25	12 30	12 35
Syston	d									11 32													12 32		
Sileby	d									11 36													12 36		
Barrow Upon Soar	d									11 40													12 40		
Loughborough	d		11 04							11 45			11 45	←	12 04								12 46		12 45
East Midlands Parkway ✈	d									11 54	11 46		11 53	11 54									12 58	12 46	12 53
Beeston	a		11 16							↦				12 02	12 16								↦		
Nottingham 8	a		11 25								11 59			12 13	12 26									12 59	
	d					11 15		11 45						12 27				12 15		12 45					
Lincoln	a													13 20											
Langley Mill	d					11 31												12 32							
Alfreton	d					11 39		12 07										12 40		13 07					
Long Eaton	a												11 56												12 56
Derby 6	a			11 26									12 09			12 26									13 09
	d			11 28			11 44		12 11				12 18			12 28			12 44		13 11				13 18
Chesterfield	d			11 47		11 52	12 04	12 18					12 37			12 47		12 52	13 03	13 18					13 37
Sheffield 7	a			12 04		12 16	12 17	12 38	12 41				12 52			13 04		13 16	13 17	13 38	13 41				13 52
Doncaster 7	a								13 18												14 18				
Wakefield Kirkgate 4	a					12 57												13 57							
Wakefield Westgate 7	a						12 46												13 46						
Leeds 10	a					13 18	13 03											14 18	14 02						
York 8	a						13 27		13 45										14 27		14 46				

A From Plymouth to Edinburgh
B From Norwich to Liverpool Lime Street
C From Reading to Newcastle
D To Lincoln
E From Leicester
F From Plymouth to Glasgow Central
G From Winchester to Newcastle
H From Penzance to Glasgow Central
I From Southampton Central to Newcastle

For connections from Gatwick Airport see Table 52

Table 53

Mondays to Fridays

until 23 September

London - East Midlands - Sheffield

		EM	EM	EM	EM	NT	XC	EM	XC	EM	EM	EM	EM	EM	EM	EM	NT	XC	EM	XC	EM	EM	EM
			◇1	◇1	◇1		◇1	◇	◇1		◇1	◇1		◇1	◇1	◇1		◇1	◇	◇1		◇1	◇1
		A					B	C	D	E			A					F	C	G	E		
St Pancras International ⊖	d		11 30	11 55	12 00						12 15	12 25		12 30	12 55	13 00						13 15	13 25
Luton Airport Parkway 7 ✈	d		11 51											12 51									
Luton 10	d				12 23											13 23							
Bedford 7	d		12 07		12 38									13 07		13 38							
Wellingborough	d		12 20		12 51									13 20		13 51							
Kettering 4	a		12 26		13 00									13 26		14 00							
	d		12 27		13 01									13 27		14 01							
Corby	d				13a10											14a10							
Oakham	d																						
Melton Mowbray	d																						
Market Harborough	d		12 37								13 12			13 37								14 12	
Leicester	a		12 53	13 02							13 30	13 33		13 54	14 02							14 29	14 33
	d		12 54	13 04						13 25	13 30	13 35		13 54	14 04						14 25	14 30	14 35
Syston	d									13 32											14 32		
Sileby	d									13 36											14 36		
Barrow Upon Soar	d									13 40											14 40		
Loughborough	d	←	13 04							13 45		13 45	←	14 04							14 45		14 45
East Midlands Parkway ✈	d	12 58								13 54	13 45	13 53	13 54								14 54	14 46	14 53
Beeston	a	13 07	13 16							→			14 02	14 16							→		
Nottingham 8 ⛴	a	13 14	13 25								13 59		14 13	14 26								14 59	
	d	13 17				13 15		13 45					14 29				14 15		14 45				
Lincoln	a	14 23											15 22										
Langley Mill	d					13 32											14 30						
Alfreton	d					13 40		14 07									14 38		15 07				
Long Eaton	a											13 56											14 56
Derby 6	a			13 26								14 09			14 26								15 13
	d			13 28			13 44		14 11			14 18			14 28			14 44		15 11			15 15
Chesterfield	d			13 47		13 52	14 03	14 19				14 37			14 47		14 52	15 03	15 20				15 34
Sheffield 7 ⛴	a			14 00		14 16	14 17	14 38	14 41			14 52			15 03		15 16	15 17	15 38	15 41			15 52
Doncaster 7	a								15 18											16 18			
Wakefield Kirkgate 4	a					14 57											15 57						
Wakefield Westgate 7	a						14 46											15 46					
Leeds 10	a					15 18	15 01										16 18	16 02					
York 8	a						15 27		15 45									16 29		16 46			

		EM	EM	EM	EM	NT	XC	EM	XC	EM	EM	EM	EM	EM	EM	EM	NT	XC	EM	XC	EM	EM
			◇1	◇1	◇1		◇1	◇	◇1		◇1	◇1		◇1	◇1	◇1		◇1	◇	◇1		◇1
		A					H	C	D	I			J					K	C	L	E	
St Pancras International ⊖	d		13 30	13 55	14 00						14 15	14 25		14 30	14 55	15 00						15 15
Luton Airport Parkway 7 ✈	d		13 51											14 51								
Luton 10	d				14 23											15 23						
Bedford 7	d		14 07		14 38									15 07		15 38						
Wellingborough	d		14 20		14 51									15 20		15 51						
Kettering 4	a		14 26		15 00									15 26		16 00						
	d		14 27		15 01									15 27		16 01						
Corby	d				15a10											16a10						
Oakham	d																					
Melton Mowbray	d																					
Market Harborough	d		14 37								15 12			15 37								16 12
Leicester	a		14 54	15 02							15 29	15 33		15 54	16 02							16 29
	d		14 54	15 04						15 25	15 30	15 35		15 54	16 04						16 25	16 30
Syston	d									15 32											16 32	
Sileby	d									15 36											16 36	
Barrow Upon Soar	d									15 40											16 40	
Loughborough	d	←	15 04							15 45		15 45	←	16 04							16 45	
East Midlands Parkway ✈	d	14 54								15 54	15 46	15 53	15 54								16 54	16 46
Beeston	a	15 02	15 16							→			16 02	16 16							→	
Nottingham 8 ⛴	a	15 13	15 26								15 59		16 13	16 25								16 59
	d	15 27				15 15		15 45					16 14				16 15		16 45			
Lincoln	a	16 25											17 18									
Langley Mill	d					15 32											16 32					
Alfreton	d					15 40		16 07									16 40		17 07			
Long Eaton	a											15 56										
Derby 6	a			15 26								16 09			16 26							
	d			15 28			15 44		16 10			16 17			16 28			16 42		17 11		
Chesterfield	d			15 47		15 53	16 03	16 18				16 36			16 47		16 55	17 04	17 18			
Sheffield 7 ⛴	a			16 00		16 16	16 17	16 38	16 41			16 52			17 04		17 17	17 19	17 34	17 44		
Doncaster 7	a								17 18													
Wakefield Kirkgate 4	a					16 57											17 57					
Wakefield Westgate 7	a						16 49											17 47		18 13		
Leeds 10	a					17 18	17 04										18 18	18 03		18 31		
York 8	a						17 29		17 43									18 30		19 02		

A From Leicester
B From Plymouth to Aberdeen
C From Norwich to Liverpool Lime Street
D From Reading to Newcastle
E To Lincoln
F From Penzance to Glasgow Central
G From Southampton Central to Newcastle
H From Plymouth to Dundee
I To Sleaford
J From Leicester to Sleaford
K From Plymouth to Glasgow Central
L From Southampton Central to Edinburgh

For connections from Gatwick Airport see Table 52

Table 53

Mondays to Fridays

until 23 September

London - East Midlands - Sheffield

		EM	EM	EM	EM	EM	NT	XC	EM		XC	EM	EM	EM	EM	EM	EM	NT	XC		EM	XC	EM	EM	
		◇[1]		◇[1]	◇[1]	◇[1]		◇[1]	◇		◇[1]		◇[1]	◇[1]		◇[1]	◇[1]		◇[1]		◇	◇[1]		◇[1]	
			A					B	C		D	E			A				F		C	G	H		
		🍴		🍴	🍴	🍴		🛒			🛒		🍴	🍴		🍴	🍴		🛒			🛒		🍴	
St Pancras International ⊖	d	15 25		15 30	15 55	16 00							16 15	16 25		16 30	16 55							17 00	
Luton Airport Parkway [7] ✈	d			15 51												16 51									
Luton [10]	d					16 22										16 55									
Bedford [7]	d			16 07		16 38										17 10								17 35	
Wellingborough	d			16 20		16 50										17 23								17 48	
Kettering [4]	a			16 26		16 59										17 29								17 56	
	d			16 27		17 00										17 30								18 04	18 08
Corby	d					17a09																			18a18
Oakham	d																								
Melton Mowbray	d																								
Market Harborough	d			16 37									17 12			17 40									
Leicester	a	16 33		16 54	17 02								17 29	17 35		17 55	18 02							18 30	
	d	16 35		16 54	17 04							17 25	17 30	17 35		17 55	18 04						18 25	18 32	
Syston	d											17 32											18 32		
Sileby	d											17 36											18 36		
Barrow Upon Soar	d											17 40											18 40		
Loughborough	d	16 45	←	17 04								17 45		17 45	←	18 05							18 45	18 43	
East Midlands Parkway ✈	d	16 53	16 54									17 54	17 46	17 52	17 54								18 54	18 50	
Beeston	a		17 02	17 16								→			18 02	18 17							→		
Nottingham [8] 🚊	a		17 13	17 26									17 59		18 13	18 27									
	d		17 17				17 15		17 45						18 15			18 15			18 45				
Lincoln	a		18 26												19 25										
Langley Mill	d						17 31		18 02									18 32							
Alfreton	d						17 39		18 09									18 40			19 07				
Long Eaton	a	16 56												18 00										18 55	
Derby [6]	a	17 09			17 26									18 14			18 26							19 09	
	d	17 18			17 28			17 41			18 11			18 18			18 28		18 44			19 11		19 18	
Chesterfield	d	17 37			17 47		17 52	18 02	18 21					18 42			18 50	18 52	19 03		19 18	19 30		19 37	
Sheffield [7] 🚊	a	17 52			18 02		18 15	18 18	18 39		18 44			18 58			19 04	19 17	19 19		19 39	19 47		19 52	
Doncaster [7]	a										19 14											20 15			
Wakefield Kirkgate [4]	a						18 58											19 58							
Wakefield Westgate [7]	a							18 47											19 50						
Leeds [10]	a						19 23	19 02										20 19	20 05						
York [8]	a							19 30			19 39								20 30			20 46			

		EM	EM	EM	EM		NT	XC	EM	EM	EM	EM	XC	EM	EM		EM	XC	EM	EM	NT	XC	EM	EM	EM
		◇[1]		◇[1]	◇[1]			◇[1]	◇	◇[1]	◇[1]		◇[1]	◇[1]	◇[1]		◇[1]	◇[1]	◇[1]	◇[1]		◇[1]		◇[1]	
			A					I	J				D					I				K	H		A
		🍴		🍴	🍴			🛒		🍴	🍴			🍴	🍴		🍴		🍴	🍴				🍴	
St Pancras International ⊖	d	17 15		17 30	17 55					17 45	18 00			18 15	18 25		18 30		18 55	19 00				19 15	
Luton Airport Parkway [7] ✈	d									18 10							18 54								
Luton [10]	d	17 41									18 23				18 51					19 23					
Bedford [7]	d			18 09							18 38						19 11			19 40					
Wellingborough	d			18 22						18 35	18 51			19 02			19 24			19 53					
Kettering [4]	a			18 28						18 45	19 05			19 09			19 30			20 04					
	d			18 29						18 47	19 10			19 10			19 32			20 05					
Corby	d										19 20									20a14					
Oakham	d										19 43														
Melton Mowbray	d										19a55														
Market Harborough	d	18 19		18 39						19 00					19 28				19 54					20 12	
Leicester	a	18 36		18 54	19 04					19 21				19 34	19 45		19 56		20 11					20 30	
	d	18 37		18 56	19 04					19 25		19 25		19 36	19 46		19 57		20 13				20 25	20 30	
Syston	d											19 32											20 32		
Sileby	d											19 36											20 36		
Barrow Upon Soar	d											19 40											20 40		
Loughborough	d		←	19 06						19 36		19 45		19 47	19 57				20 23				20 45		←
East Midlands Parkway ✈	d	18 53	18 54	19 13						19 44		19 54		19 55			20 12		20 31				20 54	20 45	20 54
Beeston	a	19 02	19 07	19 18								20 07					20 17						→		21 03
Nottingham [8] 🚊	a	19 10	19 15	19 27						19 58		20 15		20 08			20 28							21 05	21 15
	d						19 15		19 40	20 07				20 15			20 29				20 45				
Lincoln	a																21 22								
Langley Mill	d						19 32							20 33											
Alfreton	d						19 40		20 01					20 41											
Long Eaton	a									20 22					20 06										
Derby [6]	a				19 28					20 35					20 19				20 46		21 05				
	d				19 28			19 42					20 11		20 21			20 44	20 48		21 06	21 12			
Chesterfield	d				19 47		19 52	20 03	20 12					20 53	20 41			21 03	21 09		21 28	21 34			
Sheffield [7] 🚊	a				20 04		20 15	20 18	20 28				20 48	21 14	20 56			21 18	21 25		21 54	21 51			
Doncaster [7]	a												21 19									22 29			
Wakefield Kirkgate [4]	a						20 57																		
Wakefield Westgate [7]	a							20 46						21 59				21 46							
Leeds [10]	a						21 19	21 05						22 19				22 02							
York [8]	a												21 46									22 54			

- **A** From Leicester
- **B** From Plymouth to Edinburgh
- **C** From Norwich to Liverpool Lime Street
- **D** From Reading to Newcastle
- **E** To Lincoln
- **F** From Plymouth to Edinburgh. 🛒 to Wakefield Westgate
- **G** From Southampton Central to Newcastle. 🛒 to Sheffield
- **H** To Nottingham
- **I** From Plymouth
- **J** From Norwich to Manchester Piccadilly
- **K** From Southampton Central

For connections from Gatwick Airport see Table 52

Table 53

Mondays to Fridays

until 23 September

London - East Midlands - Sheffield

		EM	EM	EM	EM	NT	EM	XC	EM	EM	EM	EM	EM	EM	EM	EM	EM	EM	EM	EM	EM
		◇1	◇1	◇1	◇1		◇1	◇1		◇1		◇1	◇1	◇1	◇1	◇1	◇1	◇1	◇1	◇1	◇1
								A	B		C										
		☕	☕	☕	☕		☕			☕		☕	☕	☕	☕	☕	☕	☕	☕	☕	☕
St Pancras International ⊖	d	19 25	19 30	19 55	20 00		20 15			20 25		20 30	20 55	21 00	21 25		21 30	22 00		22 25	23 15
Luton Airport Parkway [7] ✈	d		19 51									20 51					21 53			22 48	
Luton [10]	d				20 23									21 23				22 24			23 46
Bedford [7]	d		20 07		20 38							21 07		21 38			22 09	22 40		23 04	00 12
Wellingborough	d		20 20		20 51							21 20		21 51			22 22	22 53		23 17	00 25
Kettering [4]	a	20 16			21 00							21 26		21 57			22 30	23 00		23 25	00 41
	d	20 17			21 01							21 27		21 58		22 05	22 31	23 01	23 05	23 26	00 42
Corby	d				21a10											22a15			23a15		
Oakham	d																				
Melton Mowbray	d																				
Market Harborough	d	20 27	20 37				21 11					21 37		22 08	22 23		22 42	23 12		23 37	00 52
Leicester	a	20 42	20 54	21 04			21 25			21 33		21 53	22 02	22 26	22 40		23 01	23 29		23 53	01 05
	d	20 43	20 54	21 04			21 26		21 25	21 35		21 54	22 04	22 28	22 41		23 02	23 30		23 55	01 07
Syston	d								21 32												
Sileby	d								21 36												
Barrow Upon Soar	d								21 40												
Loughborough	d	20 54	21 04						21 45	21 45	←	22 04		22 38	22 52		23 13	23 41		00 06	01 17
East Midlands Parkway ✈	d	21 01					21 43		21 54	21 53	21 54			22 46	23 01		23 24	23 50		00 14	01 25
Beeston	a		21 18						↪		22 07	22 16						00 04			01 38
Nottingham [8]	a		21 29				21 58				22 15	22 26			23 12			00 12			01 45
	d		21 43			21 11															01 52
Lincoln	a																				
Langley Mill	d		22 01			21 31															
Alfreton	d		22 09			21 39															
Long Eaton	a	21 05								21 58							23 37				
Derby [6]	a	21 16		21 32						22 10			22 26	22 59			23 50			00 34	02 10
	d			21 34				21 45					22 28							00 35	
Chesterfield	d		22 21	21 55		22 00		22 07					22 47							00 58	
Sheffield [7]	a		22 37	22 15		22 19		22 24					23 03							01 13	
Doncaster [7]	a																				
Wakefield Kirkgate [4]	a																				
Wakefield Westgate [7]	a		23 21	22 46				22 59													
Leeds [10]	a		23 40	23 05				23 15													
York [8]	a																				

Mondays to Fridays

from 26 September

		NT	XC	EM	EM	EM	EM	EM	EM	EM	EM	EM	EM	EM	EM	XC	NT	EM	XC	NT	EM	XC	EM
		MO	MO	MO	MO	MO	V	MX	MX	MO	MO	MO	MX	MX									
			◇1	◇1	◇1	◇1	◇1	◇1	◇1	◇1	◇1	◇1	◇1	◇1	◇	◇1		◇1	◇1		◇	◇1	◇1
			A												F	G			H		F	I	
				☕	☕	☕	☕	☕	☕	☕	☕	☕	☕	☕		🛒		☕	🛒			🛒	☕
St Pancras International ⊖	d			20p30	20p30	21p30	21p30	22p00	22p25	22p30	22p30	23p00	23p15	00 15									
Luton Airport Parkway [7] ✈	d			⌇	⌇	⌇	⌇		22p48	22p53	22p53	23p27		00 44									
Luton [10]	d			20p54	20p54	21p54	21p54	22p24		⌇	⌇		23p46	00 47									
Bedford [7]	d			21p18	21p23	22p17	22p21	22p40	23p04	23p17	23p21	23p50	00 12	01 12									
Wellingborough	d			21p31	21p36	22p30	22p34	22p53	23p17	23p31	23p34	00 04	00 25	01 33									
Kettering [4]	a			21p38	21p43	22p37	22p41	23p00	23p25	23p37	23p41	00 10	00 41	01 43									
	d			21p39	21p44	22p38	22p42	23p01	23p26	23p38	23p42	00 11	00 42	01 43									
Corby	d			⌇	⌇	⌇	⌇			⌇	⌇												
Oakham	d			⌇	⌇	⌇	⌇			⌇	⌇												
Melton Mowbray	d			⌇	⌇	⌇	⌇			⌇	⌇												
Market Harborough	d			21p50	21p55	22p48	22p52	23p12	23p37	23p48	23p52	00 21	00 52										
Leicester	a			22p11	22p16	23p07	23p11	23p29	23p53	00 07	00 11	00 40	01 05	02 07									
	d			22p13	22p18	23p09	23p13	23p30	23p55	00 09	00 12	00 42	01 07										
Syston	d			⌇	⌇	⌇	⌇			⌇	⌇												
Sileby	d			⌇	⌇	⌇	⌇			⌇	⌇												
Barrow Upon Soar	d			⌇	⌇	⌇	⌇			⌇	⌇												
Loughborough	d			⌇	⌇	23p19	23p23	23p41	00 06	00 19	00 23	00 52	01 17										
East Midlands Parkway ✈	d			22p29	22p34	23p32	23p36	23p50	00 14	00 27	00 30	01 00	01 25										
Beeston	a			⌇	⌇	⌇	⌇	00 04		00 40	00 44		01 38										
Nottingham [8]	a			⌇	⌇	⌇	⌇	00 12		00 48	00 52		01 45										
	d	21p20		⌇	⌇	⌇	⌇						01 52		05 20					06 23	06 40		
Lincoln	a			⌇	⌇	⌇	⌇																
Langley Mill	d	21p41		⌇	⌇	⌇	⌇													06 38			
Alfreton	d	21p49		⌇	⌇	⌇	⌇													06 46	07 02		
Long Eaton	a			⌇	⌇	23p38	23p42																
Derby [6]	a			22p43	22p46	23p49	23p53		00 34			01 19	02 10										
	d		22p46	22p52	22p52	23p55	23p55		00 35							05 56		06 20	06 34			07 13	07 20
Chesterfield	d	22p08	23p07	23p13	23p13	00 14	00 14		00 58						05 49	06 15	06 26	06 42	06 54	06 58	07 13	07 32	07 42
Sheffield [7]	a	22p32	23p22	23p28	23p28	00 28	00 28		01 13						06 15	06 28	06 46	07 13	07 07	07 18	07 31	07 48	08 00
Doncaster [7]	a			⌇	⌇											06 57						08 24	
Wakefield Kirkgate [4]	a	23p26		⌇	⌇												07 27			07 57			
Wakefield Westgate [7]	a			23p55	23p55														07 36				
Leeds [10]	a	00 05	00 34	00 28	00 28												07 51		07 52	08 21			
York [8]	a															07 28			08 23			08 46	

A From Plymouth
B To Nottingham
C From Leicester
F To Liverpool Lime Street
G To Newcastle. 🛒 from Sheffield
H From Birmingham New Street to Glasgow Central
I From Birmingham New Street to Newcastle

For connections from Gatwick Airport see Table 52

Table 53

Mondays to Fridays

from 26 September

London - East Midlands - Sheffield

		NT	EM	XC	EM	EM		XC	EM	EM	EM	NT	EM	XC	EM	XC		EM	EM	EM	EM	EM	EM	EM	EM
				◇1	◇			◇1	◇1	◇1	◇1		◇1	◇1	◇	◇1			◇1		◇1	◇1	◇1	◇1	◇1
				A	B			C						D	E	F		G		H					
				🛒				🛒	☕	☕	☕		☕	🛒		🛒			☕		☕	☕	☕	☕	☕
St Pancras International ⊖	d								06 10	06 37			06 55						07 00		07 25	07 30	07 55		08 00
Luton Airport Parkway 7 ✈	d												07 16									07 51			
Luton 10	d								06 33	06 59									07 23						08 23
Bedford 7	d								06 48										07 38			08 07			08 38
Wellingborough	d								07 01										07 51			08 20			08 51
Kettering 4	a								07 07	07 27									08 00			08 26			09 00
	d								07 08	07 28	07 38								08 01			08 27		08 32	09 01
Corby	d										07a48													08a42	09a10
Oakham	d																								
Melton Mowbray	d																								
Market Harborough	d								07 18	07 38									08 12		08 21	08 37			
Leicester	a								07 35	07 53			08 04						08 29		08 36	08 52	09 02		
	d		06 33			07 25			07 36	07 57			08 06					08 25	08 30		08 38	08 54	09 04		
Syston	d		06 41			07 32												08 32							
Sileby	d		06 46			07 36												08 36							
Barrow Upon Soar	d		06 51			07 40												08 40							
Loughborough	d		06 56			07 45			07 47	08 07			08 16					08 45	08 41	←	08 48	09 04			
East Midlands Parkway ✈	d		07 06			07 54			07 54				08 24					08 54	08 50	08 54	08 56				
Beeston	a		07 16			08 06							08 31					→		09 02		09 16			
Nottingham 8 🚋	a		07 23			08 15							08 39						09 02	09 13		09 26			
	d	07 13			07 45							08 11			08 45					09 19					
Lincoln	a																			10 19					
Langley Mill	d	07 29										08 31													
Alfreton	d	07 37			08 07							08 39			09 07										
Long Eaton	a								07 58												08 59				
Derby 6	a								08 09	08 24											09 15		09 26		
	d			07 44				08 13	08 18	08 28				08 44		09 13					09 18		09 28		
Chesterfield	d	07 50		08 03	08 18			08 32	08 38	08 47		08 51		09 03	09 18						09 37		09 47		
Sheffield 7 🚋	a	08 08		08 17	08 38			08 45	08 52	09 04		09 16		09 17	09 38	09 43					09 52		10 00		
Doncaster 7	a							09 18								10 18									
Wakefield Kirkgate 4	a	08 57										09 57													
Wakefield Westgate 7	a			08 46										09 46											
Leeds 10	a	09 20		09 03								10 18		10 02											
York 8	a			09 32				09 45						10 28		10 45									

		NT		XC	EM	XC	EM	EM	EM	EM	EM	EM		EM	EM	NT	XC	EM	XC	EM	EM	EM		EM	EM
				◇1	◇	◇1		◇1	◇1		◇1	◇1		◇1			◇1	◇	◇1		◇1	◇1			◇1
				I	E	J	G			H							K	E	L	G				H	
				🛒		🛒		☕	☕		☕	☕		☕			🛒		🛒		☕	☕			☕
St Pancras International ⊖	d							08 15	08 25		08 30	08 55		09 00							09 15	09 25			09 30
Luton Airport Parkway 7 ✈	d										08 51														09 51
Luton 10	d													09 23											
Bedford 7	d										09 07			09 38											10 07
Wellingborough	d										09 20			09 51											10 20
Kettering 4	a										09 27			10 00											10 26
	d										09 27														10 27
Corby	d														09 30										
Oakham	d														09 52										
Melton Mowbray	d														10 04										
Market Harborough	d							09 12			09 37										10 12				10 37
Leicester	a							09 29	09 34		09 53	10 02									10 29	10 34			10 54
	d						09 25	09 30	09 35		09 54	10 04								10 25	10 30	10 35			10 54
Syston	d						09 32													10 32					
Sileby	d						09 36													10 36					
Barrow Upon Soar	d						09 40													10 40					
Loughborough	d						09 45		09 45	←	10 04									10 45		10 46		←	11 04
East Midlands Parkway ✈	d						09 54	09 46	09 52	09 54					10 28					10 54	10 46	10 53		10 54	
Beeston	a						→			10 02	10 16									→				11 02	11 16
Nottingham 8 🚋	a							09 59		10 13	10 25										10 59			11 14	11 25
	d	09 15			09 45					10 29						10 15		10 45						11 17	
Lincoln	a									11 33														12 23	
Langley Mill	d	09 32														10 32									
Alfreton	d	09 40			10 07											10 40		11 07							
Long Eaton	a								09 56													10 56			
Derby 6	a								10 09			10 26			10 40							11 09			
	d			09 44		10 11			10 18			10 28					10 44		11 11			11 18			
Chesterfield	d	09 52		10 03	10 18				10 37			10 47				10 52	11 03	11 18				11 37			
Sheffield 7 🚋	a	10 16		10 17	10 38	10 41			10 52			11 02				11 16	11 17	11 38	11 43			11 52			
Doncaster 7	a					11 18													12 18						
Wakefield Kirkgate 4	a	10 57														11 57									
Wakefield Westgate 7	a			10 46													11 46								
Leeds 10	a	11 18		11 02												12 18	12 01								
York 8	a			11 27		11 47											12 27		12 48						

A From Birmingham New Street to Edinburgh
B To Liverpool Lime Street
C From Birmingham New Street to Newcastle
D From Bath Spa to Glasgow Central
E From Norwich to Liverpool Lime Street
F From Guildford to Newcastle
G To Lincoln
H From Leicester
I From Plymouth to Edinburgh
J From Reading to Newcastle
K From Plymouth to Glasgow Central
L From Winchester to Newcastle

For connections from Gatwick Airport see Table 52

Table 53

Mondays to Fridays

from 26 September

London - East Midlands - Sheffield

		EM	EM	NT	XC	EM	XC	EM		EM	EM	EM	EM	EM	EM	NT	XC	EM		XC	EM	EM	EM	EM	EM
		◇1	◇1		◇1	◇	◇1			◇1	◇1		◇1	◇1	◇1		◇1	◇		◇1		◇1	◇1		◇1
					A	B	C	D				E					F	B		G	D			E	
		☕	☕		🛒		🛒			☕	☕		☕	☕	☕		🛒			🛒		☕	☕		☕
St Pancras International ⊖	d	09 55	10 00							10 15	10 25		10 30	10 55	11 00							11 15	11 25		11 30
Luton Airport Parkway 7 ✈	d												10 51												11 51
Luton 10	d		10 23												11 23										
Bedford 7	d		10 38										11 07		11 38										12 07
Wellingborough	d		10 51										11 20		11 51										12 20
Kettering 4	a		11 00										11 26		12 00										12 26
	d		11 01										11 27		12 01										12 27
Corby	d		11a10												12a10										
Oakham	d																								
Melton Mowbray	d																								
Market Harborough	d									11 12			11 37									12 12			12 37
Leicester	a	11 02								11 29	11 33		11 52	12 02								12 29	12 33		12 53
	d	11 04						11 25		11 30	11 35		11 54	12 04							12 25	12 30	12 35		12 54
Syston	d							11 32													12 32				
Sileby	d							11 36													12 36				
Barrow Upon Soar	d							11 40													12 40				
Loughborough	d							11 45			11 45	←	12 04								12 46		12 45	←	13 04
East Midlands Parkway ✈	d							11 54		11 46	11 53	11 54									12 58	12 46	12 53	12 58	
Beeston	a							↪				12 02	12 16								↪			13 07	13 16
Nottingham 8 ⛴	a									11 59		12 13	12 26									12 59		13 14	13 25
	d			11 15		11 45						12 27				12 15		12 45						13 17	
Lincoln	a											13 22												14 26	
Langley Mill	d			11 31												12 32									
Alfreton	d			11 39		12 07										12 40		13 07							
Long Eaton	a										11 56												12 56		
Derby 6	a	11 26									12 09			12 26									13 09		
	d	11 28			11 44		12 11				12 18			12 28			12 44			13 11			13 18		
Chesterfield	d	11 47		11 52	12 04	12 18					12 37			12 47		12 52	13 03	13 18					13 37		
Sheffield 7 ⛴	a	12 04		12 16	12 17	12 38	12 41				12 52			13 04		13 16	13 17	13 38		13 41			13 52		
Doncaster 7	a						13 18													14 18					
Wakefield Kirkgate 4	a			12 57												13 57									
Wakefield Westgate 7	a				12 46												13 46								
Leeds 10	a			13 18	13 03											14 18	14 02								
York 8	a				13 27		13 45										14 27			14 46					

		EM	EM	NT		XC	EM	XC	EM	EM	EM	EM	EM	EM		EM	NT	XC	EM	XC	EM	EM	EM	EM	
		◇1	◇1			◇1	◇	◇1		◇1	◇1		◇1	◇1		◇1		◇1	◇	◇1		◇1	◇1		
						H	B	C	D			E						F	B	G	D			E	
		☕	☕			🛒		🛒		☕	☕		☕	☕		☕		🛒		🛒		☕	☕		
St Pancras International ⊖	d	11 55	12 00							12 15	12 25		12 30	12 55		13 00						13 15	13 25		
Luton Airport Parkway 7 ✈	d												12 51												
Luton 10	d		12 23													13 23									
Bedford 7	d		12 38										13 07			13 38									
Wellingborough	d		12 51										13 20			13 51									
Kettering 4	a		13 00										13 26			14 00									
	d		13 01										13 27			14 01									
Corby	d		13a10													14a10									
Oakham	d																								
Melton Mowbray	d																								
Market Harborough	d									13 12			13 37									14 12			
Leicester	a	13 02								13 30	13 33		13 54	14 02								14 29	14 33		
	d	13 04							13 25	13 30	13 35		13 54	14 04							14 25	14 30	14 35		
Syston	d								13 32												14 32				
Sileby	d								13 36												14 36				
Barrow Upon Soar	d								13 40												14 40				
Loughborough	d								13 45		13 45	←	14 04								14 45		14 45	←	
East Midlands Parkway ✈	d								13 54	13 45	13 53	13 54									14 54	14 46	14 53	14 54	
Beeston	a								↪			14 02	14 16								↪			15 02	
Nottingham 8 ⛴	a									13 59		14 13	14 26									14 59		15 13	
	d			13 15			13 45					14 29					14 15		14 45					15 27	
Lincoln	a											15 24												16 27	
Langley Mill	d			13 32													14 30								
Alfreton	d			13 40			14 07										14 38		15 07						
Long Eaton	a										13 56												14 56		
Derby 6	a	13 26									14 09			14 26									15 13		
	d	13 28				13 44		14 11			14 18			14 28				14 44		15 11			15 15		
Chesterfield	d	13 47		13 52		14 03	14 19				14 37			14 47			14 52	15 03	15 20				15 34		
Sheffield 7 ⛴	a	14 00		14 16		14 17	14 38	14 41			14 52			15 03			15 16	15 17	15 38	15 41			15 52		
Doncaster 7	a							15 18												16 18					
Wakefield Kirkgate 4	a			14 57													15 57								
Wakefield Westgate 7	a					14 46												15 46							
Leeds 10	a			15 18		15 01											16 18	16 02							
York 8	a					15 27		15 45										16 29		16 46					

A From Plymouth to Edinburgh
B From Norwich to Liverpool Lime Street
C From Reading to Newcastle
D To Lincoln
E From Leicester
F From Penzance to Glasgow Central
G From Southampton Central to Newcastle
H From Plymouth to Aberdeen

For connections from Gatwick Airport see Table 52

Table 53

London - East Midlands - Sheffield

Mondays to Fridays

from 26 September

Station		EM ◇1 🍴	EM ◇1 🍴	EM ◇1 🍴	NT	XC ◇1 A 🛒	EM ◇ B	XC ◇1 C 🛒	EM D	EM ◇1 🍴	EM ◇1 🍴	EM E	EM ◇1 🍴	EM ◇1 🍴	EM ◇1 🍴	NT	XC ◇1 F 🛒	EM ◇ B	XC ◇1 G 🛒	EM H	EM ◇1 🍴	EM ◇1 🍴	EM I
St Pancras International ⊖	d	13 30	13 55	14 00						14 15	14 25		14 30	14 55	15 00						15 15	15 25	
Luton Airport Parkway [7] ✈	d	13 51											14 51										
Luton [10]	d			14 23											15 23								
Bedford [7]	d	14 07		14 38									15 07		15 38								
Wellingborough	d	14 20		14 51									15 20		15 51								
Kettering [4]	a	14 26		15 00									15 26		16 00								
	d	14 27		15 01									15 27		16 01								
Corby	d			15a10											16a10								
Oakham	d																						
Melton Mowbray	d																						
Market Harborough	d	14 37								15 12			15 37								16 12		
Leicester	a	14 54	15 02							15 29	15 33		15 54	16 02							16 29	16 33	
	d	14 54	15 04						15 25	15 30	15 35		15 54	16 04						16 25	16 30	16 35	
Syston	d								15 32											16 32			
Sileby	d								15 36											16 36			
Barrow Upon Soar	d								15 40											16 40			
Loughborough	d	15 04							15 45		15 45	←	16 04							16 45		16 45	←
East Midlands Parkway ✈	d								15 54	15 46	15 53	15 54								16 54	16 46	16 53	16 54
Beeston	a	15 16							→			16 02	16 16							→			17 02
Nottingham [8] ⛴	a	15 26								15 59		16 13	16 25								16 59		17 13
	d				15 15		15 45					16 14				16 15		16 45					17 17
Lincoln	a											17 19											18 28
Langley Mill	d				15 32											16 32							
Alfreton	d				15 40		16 07									16 40		17 07					
Long Eaton	a										15 56											16 56	
Derby [6]	a		15 26								16 09			16 26								17 09	
	d		15 28			15 44		16 10			16 17			16 28			16 42		17 11			17 18	
Chesterfield	d		15 47		15 53	16 03	16 18				16 36			16 47		16 55	17 04	17 18				17 37	
Sheffield [7] ⛴	a		16 00		16 16	16 17	16 38	16 41			16 52			17 04		17 17	17 19	17 34	17 44			17 52	
Doncaster [7]	a							17 18															
Wakefield Kirkgate [4]	a				16 57											17 57							
Wakefield Westgate [7]	a					16 49											17 47		18 13				
Leeds [10]	a				17 18	17 04										18 18	18 03		18 31				
York [8]	a					17 29		17 43									18 30		19 02				

Station		EM ◇1 🍴	EM ◇1 🍴	EM ◇1 🍴	NT	XC ◇1 J 🛒	EM ◇ B	XC ◇1 C 🛒	EM H	EM ◇1 🍴	EM ◇1 🍴	EM I	EM ◇1 🍴	EM ◇1 🍴	NT	XC ◇1 K 🛒	EM ◇ B	XC ◇1 L 🛒	EM M	EM ◇1 🍴		EM ◇1 🍴	EM I
St Pancras International ⊖	d	15 30	15 55	16 00						16 15	16 25		16 30	16 55						17 00		17 15	
Luton Airport Parkway [7] ✈	d	15 51											16 51										
Luton [10]	d			16 22									16 55									17 41	
Bedford [7]	d	16 07		16 38									17 10							17 35			
Wellingborough	d	16 20		16 50									17 23							17 48			
Kettering [4]	a	16 26		16 59									17 29							17 56			
	d	16 27		17 00									17 30							18 04	18 08		
Corby	d			17a09																	18a18		
Oakham	d																						
Melton Mowbray	d																						
Market Harborough	d	16 37								17 12			17 40									18 19	
Leicester	a	16 54	17 02							17 29	17 35		17 55	18 02						18 30		18 36	
	d	16 54	17 04						17 25	17 30	17 35		17 55	18 04					18 25	18 32		18 37	
Syston	d								17 32										18 32				
Sileby	d								17 36										18 36				
Barrow Upon Soar	d								17 40										18 40				
Loughborough	d	17 04							17 45		17 45	←	18 05						18 45	18 43			←
East Midlands Parkway ✈	d								17 54	17 46	17 52	17 54							18 54	18 50		18 53	18 54
Beeston	a	17 16							→			18 02	18 17						→			19 02	19 07
Nottingham [8] ⛴	a	17 26								17 59		18 13	18 27									19 10	19 15
	d				17 15		17 45					18 15			18 15		18 45						
Lincoln	a											19 27											
Langley Mill	d				17 31		18 02								18 32								
Alfreton	d				17 39		18 09								18 40		19 07						
Long Eaton	a										18 00									18 55			
Derby [6]	a		17 26								18 14			18 26						19 09			
	d		17 28			17 41		18 11			18 18			18 28		18 44		19 11		19 18			
Chesterfield	d		17 47		17 52	18 02	18 21				18 42			18 50	18 52	19 03	19 18	19 30		19 37			
Sheffield [7] ⛴	a		18 02		18 15	18 18	18 39	18 44			18 58			19 04	19 17	19 19	19 39	19 47		19 52			
Doncaster [7]	a							19 14										20 15					
Wakefield Kirkgate [4]	a				18 58										19 58								
Wakefield Westgate [7]	a					18 47										19 50							
Leeds [10]	a				19 23	19 02									20 19	20 05							
York [8]	a					19 30		19 39								20 30		20 46					

A From Plymouth to Dundee
B From Norwich to Liverpool Lime Street
C From Reading to Newcastle
D To Sleaford
E From Leicester to Sleaford
F From Plymouth to Glasgow Central
G From Southampton Central to Edinburgh
H To Lincoln
I From Leicester
J From Plymouth to Edinburgh
K From Plymouth to Edinburgh. 🛒 to Wakefield Westgate
L From Southampton Central to Newcastle. 🛒 to Sheffield
M To Nottingham

For connections from Gatwick Airport see Table 52

Table 53

Mondays to Fridays

from 26 September

London - East Midlands - Sheffield

Station		EM	EM	NT	XC	EM	EM	EM	EM	XC	EM	EM	EM	XC	EM	EM	NT	XC	EM	EM	EM	EM
		◇1	◇1		◇1	◇	◇1	◇1		◇1	◇1	◇1	◇1	◇1	◇1	◇1		◇1		◇1		◇1
					A	B				C				A				D	E		F	
		☕	☕		🛒		☕	☕			☕	☕	☕		☕	☕				☕		☕
St Pancras International ⊖	d	17 30	17 55				17 45	18 00			18 15	18 25	18 30		18 55	19 00				19 15		19 25
Luton Airport Parkway 7 ✈	d						18 10						18 54									
Luton 10	d							18 23				18 51				19 23						
Bedford 7	d	18 09						18 38					19 11			19 40						
Wellingborough	d	18 22					18 35	18 51			19 02		19 24			19 53						
Kettering 4	a	18 28					18 45	19 05			19 09		19 30			20 04						20 16
	d	18 29					18 47	19 10			19 10		19 32			20 05						20 17
Corby	d							19 20								20a14						
Oakham	d							19 43														
Melton Mowbray	d							19a55														
Market Harborough	d	18 39					19 00					19 28			19 54					20 12		20 27
Leicester	a	18 54	19 04				19 21				19 34	19 45	19 56		20 11					20 30		20 42
	d	18 56	19 04				19 25		19 25		19 36	19 46	19 57		20 13				20 25	20 30		20 43
Syston	d								19 32										20 32			
Sileby	d								19 36										20 36			
Barrow Upon Soar	d								19 40										20 40			
Loughborough	d	19 06					19 36		19 45		19 47	19 57			20 23				20 45		←	20 54
East Midlands Parkway ✈	d	19 13					19 44		19 54		19 55		20 12		20 31				20 54	20 45	20 54	21 01
Beeston	a	19 18							20 07				20 17						↦		21 03	
Nottingham 8	a	19 27					19 58		20 15		20 08		20 28							21 05	21 15	
	d			19 15		19 40	20 07				20 15		20 29				20 45					
Lincoln	a												21 22									
Langley Mill	d			19 32							20 33											
Alfreton	d			19 40		20 01					20 41											
Long Eaton	a						20 22					20 06										21 05
Derby 6	a		19 28				20 35					20 19			20 46		21 05					21 16
	d		19 28		19 42					20 11		20 21		20 44	20 48		21 06	21 12				
Chesterfield	d		19 47	19 52	20 03	20 12					20 53	20 41		21 03	21 09		21 28	21 34				
Sheffield 7	a		20 04	20 15	20 18	20 28				20 48	21 14	20 56		21 18	21 25		21 54	21 51				
Doncaster 7	a									21 19								22 29				
Wakefield Kirkgate 4	a			20 57																		
Wakefield Westgate 7	a				20 46						21 59			21 46								
Leeds 10	a			21 19	21 05						22 19			22 02								
York 8	a									21 46								22 54				

Station		EM	EM	EM	NT	EM	XC	EM	EM	EM	EM	EM	EM	EM	EM	EM	EM	EM	EM	EM
		◇1	◇1	◇1		◇1	◇1		◇1		◇1	◇1	◇1	◇1	◇1	◇1	◇1	◇1	◇1	◇1
							A	E		F										
		☕	☕	☕		☕			☕		☕	☕	☕	☕	☕	☕	☕	☕	☕	☕
St Pancras International ⊖	d	19 30	19 55	20 00		20 15			20 25		20 30	20 55	21 00	21 25		21 30	22 00		22 25	23 15
Luton Airport Parkway 7 ✈	d	19 51									20 51					21 53			22 48	
Luton 10	d			20 23									21 23				22 24			23 46
Bedford 7	d	20 07		20 38							21 07		21 38			22 09	22 40		23 04	00 12
Wellingborough	d	20 20		20 51							21 20		21 51			22 22	22 53		23 17	00 25
Kettering 4	a			21 00							21 26		21 57			22 30	23 00		23 25	00 41
	d			21 01							21 27		21 58		22 05	22 31	23 01	23 05	23 26	00 42
Corby	d			21a10											22a15			23a15		
Oakham	d																			
Melton Mowbray	d																			
Market Harborough	d	20 37				21 11					21 37		22 08	22 23		22 42	23 12		23 37	00 52
Leicester	a	20 54	21 04			21 25			21 33		21 53	22 02	22 26	22 40		23 01	23 29		23 53	01 05
	d	20 54	21 04			21 26		21 25	21 35		21 54	22 04	22 28	22 41		23 02	23 30		23 55	01 07
Syston	d							21 32												
Sileby	d							21 36												
Barrow Upon Soar	d							21 40												
Loughborough	d	21 04						21 45	21 45	←	22 04		22 38	22 52		23 13	23 41		00 06	01 17
East Midlands Parkway ✈	d					21 43		21 54	21 53	21 54			22 46	23 01		23 24	23 50		00 14	01 25
Beeston	a	21 18						↦		22 07	22 16						00 04			01 38
Nottingham 8	a	21 29				21 58				22 15	22 26			23 12			00 12			01 45
	d	21 43			21 11															01 52
Lincoln	a																			
Langley Mill	d	22 01			21 31															
Alfreton	d	22 09			21 39															
Long Eaton	a								21 58							23 37				
Derby 6	a		21 32						22 10			22 26	22 59			23 50			00 34	02 10
	d		21 34				21 45					22 28							00 35	
Chesterfield	d	22 21	21 55		22 00		22 07					22 47							00 58	
Sheffield 7	a	22 37	22 15		22 19		22 24					23 03							01 13	
Doncaster 7	a																			
Wakefield Kirkgate 4	a																			
Wakefield Westgate 7	a	23 21	22 46				22 59													
Leeds 10	a	23 40	23 05				23 15													
York 8	a																			

A From Plymouth
B From Norwich to Manchester Piccadilly
C From Reading to Newcastle
D From Southampton Central
E To Nottingham
F From Leicester

For connections from Gatwick Airport see Table 52

Table 53

Saturdays

until 24 September

London - East Midlands - Sheffield

		EM	EM	EM	EM	EM	XC	EM	XC	EM		XC	EM	NT	EM	XC	EM	EM	XC	EM		EM	EM	EM	NT
		◇1	◇1	◇1	◇1	◇	◇1	◇1	◇1	◇		◇1	◇1			◇1	◇		◇1	◇1		◇1	◇1	◇1	
						A	B		C	A		D				E	A		D			F	G		
		⊡	⊡	⊡	⊡		⊼	⊡	⊼			⊼	⊡			⊼			⊼	⊡		⊡	⊡	⊡	
St Pancras International ⊖	d	22p00	22p25	23p15	00 15															06 10		06 37	06 37		
Luton Airport Parkway 7 ✈	d		22p48		00 44																				
Luton 10	d	22p24		23p46	00 47															06 33		06 59	06 59		
Bedford 7	d	22p40	23p04	00 12	01 12															06 48					
Wellingborough	d	22p53	23p17	00 25	01 33															07 01					
Kettering 4	a	23p00	23p25	00 41	01 43															07 07		07 27	07 27		
	d	23p01	23p26	00 42	01 43															07 08		07 28	07 28	07 38	
Corby	d																							07a48	
Oakham	d																								
Melton Mowbray	d																								
Market Harborough	d	23p12	23p37	00 52																07 18		07 38	07 38		
Leicester	a	23p29	23p53	01 05	02 07															07 35		07 53	07 53		
	d	23p30	23p55	01 07											06 36			07 25		07 36		07 55	07 55		
Syston	d														06 43			07 32							
Sileby	d														06 47			07 36							
Barrow Upon Soar	d														06 51			07 40							
Loughborough	d	23p41	00 06	01 17											06 56			07 46		07 47		08 05	08 05		
East Midlands Parkway ✈	d	23p50	00 14	01 25											07 06			07 57				08 13	08 13		
Beeston	a	00 04		01 38											07 15			08 04							
Nottingham 8 ⛴	a	00 12		01 45											07 24			08 13							
	d			01 52		05 20				06 40				07 15			07 45								08 11
Lincoln	a																								
Langley Mill	d													07 30											08 31
Alfreton	d									07 02				07 38			08 07								08 39
Long Eaton	a																			07 55					
Derby 6	a		00 34	02 10																08 09		08 26	08 26		
	d		00 35				05 55	06 26	06 37			07 11	07 20			07 44			08 11	08 18		08 28	08 28		
Chesterfield	d		00 58			05 49	06 31	06 45	06 56	07 13		07 30	07 42	07 50		08 03	08 18		08 30	08 37		08 47	08 47		08 51
Sheffield 7 ⛴	a		01 13			06 15	06 44	07 09	07 09	07 31		07 48	07 59	08 08		08 17	08 38		08 45	08 52		09 07	09 07		09 15
Doncaster 7	a						07 16					08 23							09 18			09 53	09 53		
Wakefield Kirkgate 4	a													08 57											09 57
Wakefield Westgate 7	a								07 36							08 45									
Leeds 10	a								07 52					09 20		09 03									10 18
York 8	a						07 43		08 24			08 47				09 30			09 45			10 14	10 16		

		EM	XC	EM	XC	EM		EM	EM	EM	EM	EM	EM	NT	XC	EM		XC	EM	EM	EM	EM	EM	EM	EM
		◇1	◇1	◇	◇1			◇1	◇1		◇1	◇1	◇1		◇1	◇		◇1		◇1	◇1		◇1	◇1	◇1
			H	I	J	K				L					M	I		N	K			L			
		⊡	⊼		⊼			⊡	⊡		⊡	⊡	⊡		⊼			⊼		⊡	⊡		⊡	⊡	⊡
St Pancras International ⊖	d	06 55						07 00			07 30	07 55	08 00							08 15	08 25		08 30	08 55	09 00
Luton Airport Parkway 7 ✈	d	07 16									07 51												08 51		
Luton 10	d							07 23					08 23												09 23
Bedford 7	d							07 38			08 07		08 38										09 07		09 38
Wellingborough	d							07 51			08 20		08 51										09 20		09 51
Kettering 4	a							08 00			08 27		09 00										09 26		10 00
	d							08 01			08 27		09 01										09 27		10 01
Corby	d												09a10												10a10
Oakham	d																								
Melton Mowbray	d																								
Market Harborough	d							08 12			08 37									09 12			09 37		
Leicester	a	08 04						08 29			08 53	09 02								09 29	09 33		09 52	10 02	
	d	08 06				08 25		08 30	08 38		08 54	09 04							09 25	09 30	09 35		09 54	10 04	
Syston	d					08 32													09 32						
Sileby	d					08 36													09 36						
Barrow Upon Soar	d					08 40													09 40						
Loughborough	d	08 18				08 45		08 41	08 49	←	09 04								09 45		09 45	←	10 04		
East Midlands Parkway ✈	d					08 57		08 50	08 56	08 57									09 54	09 46	09 53	09 54			
Beeston	a	08 31				→				09 05	09 16								→			10 02	10 16		
Nottingham 8 ⛴	a	08 42						09 03		09 14	09 26									09 59		10 13	10 26		
	d			08 45						09 23				09 15		09 46						10 29			
Lincoln	a									10 17												11 30			
Langley Mill	d													09 32											
Alfreton	d			09 07										09 40		10 08									
Long Eaton	a								09 00												09 56				
Derby 6	a								09 14			09 26									10 09				10 26
	d		08 44		09 11				09 18			09 28			09 44			10 10			10 18				10 28
Chesterfield	d		09 03	09 18					09 37			09 47		09 52	10 03	10 19					10 37				10 47
Sheffield 7 ⛴	a		09 18	09 38	09 44				09 52			10 00		10 15	10 17	10 38		10 42			10 52				11 00
Doncaster 7	a				10 17													11 15							
Wakefield Kirkgate 4	a													10 57											
Wakefield Westgate 7	a		09 46												10 46										
Leeds 10	a		10 02											11 18	11 02										
York 8	a		10 27		10 45										11 27			11 45							

A To Liverpool Lime Street
B To Newcastle. ⊼ from Sheffield
C From Birmingham New Street to Glasgow Central
D From Birmingham New Street to Newcastle
E From Birmingham New Street to Edinburgh
F Until 10 September. To Scarborough
G 17 September, 24 September
H From Bristol Temple Meads to Glasgow Central
I From Norwich to Liverpool Lime Street
J From Guildford to Newcastle
K To Lincoln
L From Leicester
M From Plymouth to Edinburgh
N From Bournemouth to Newcastle

For connections from Gatwick Airport see Table 52

Table 53

Saturdays
until 24 September

London - East Midlands - Sheffield

		NT		XC	EM	XC	EM	EM	EM	EM	EM	EM		EM	NT	XC	EM	XC	EM	EM	EM	EM		EM	EM
				◇1	◇	◇1		◇1	◇1		◇1	◇1		◇1		◇1	◇	◇1		◇1	◇1			◇1	◇1
				A	B	C	D			E						F	B	G	D			E			
				🛒		🛒		☕	☕		☕	☕		☕		🛒		🛒		☕	☕			☕	☕
St Pancras International ⊖	d							09 15	09 25		09 30	09 55		10 00						10 15	10 25			10 30	10 55
Luton Airport Parkway 7 ✈	d										09 51													10 51	
Luton 10	d													10 23											
Bedford 7	d										10 07			10 38										11 07	
Wellingborough	d										10 20			10 51										11 20	
Kettering 4	a										10 26			11 00										11 26	
	d										10 27			11 01										11 27	
Corby	d													11a10											
Oakham	d																								
Melton Mowbray	d																								
Market Harborough	d							10 12			10 37									11 12				11 37	
Leicester	a							10 29	10 33		10 54	11 02								11 29	11 33			11 54	12 02
	d						10 25	10 30	10 35		10 54	11 04							11 25	11 30	11 35			11 54	12 04
Syston	d						10 32												11 32						
Sileby	d						10 36												11 36						
Barrow Upon Soar	d						10 40												11 40						
Loughborough	d						10 45		10 45	←	11 04								11 45		11 45	←		12 04	
East Midlands Parkway ✈	d						10 54	10 46	10 53	10 54									11 54	11 46	11 53	11 54			
Beeston	a						→			11 02	11 16								→			12 02		12 16	
Nottingham 8 🚊	a							10 59		11 13	11 26									11 59		12 13		12 26	
	d	10 15			10 45					11 17					11 15		11 45					12 27			
Lincoln	a									12 27												13 18			
Langley Mill	d	10 32													11 31										
Alfreton	d	10 40			11 07										11 39		12 07								
Long Eaton	a								10 56												11 56				
Derby 6	a								11 09			11 26									12 09				12 26
	d			10 44		11 11			11 18			11 28				11 44		12 10			12 18				12 28
Chesterfield	d	10 52		11 03	11 18				11 37			11 47			11 52	12 03	12 18				12 37				12 47
Sheffield 7 🚊	a	11 15		11 17	11 38	11 41			11 52			12 00			12 16	12 16	12 38	12 41			12 52				13 04
Doncaster 7	a					12 15												13 17							
Wakefield Kirkgate 4	a	11 57													12 57										
Wakefield Westgate 7	a			11 46												12 46									
Leeds 10	a	12 18		12 02											13 18	13 02									
York 8	a			12 29		12 45										13 29		13 45							

		EM	NT	XC	EM	XC	EM	EM		EM	EM	EM	EM	EM	NT	XC	EM	XC		EM	EM	EM	EM	EM	EM
		◇1		◇1	◇	◇1		◇1		◇1		◇1	◇1	◇1		◇1	◇	◇1			◇1	◇1		◇1	◇1
				H	B	C	D				E					I	B	G		D			E		
		☕		🛒		🛒		☕		☕		☕	☕	☕		🛒		🛒			☕	☕		☕	☕
St Pancras International ⊖	d	11 00						11 15		11 25		11 30	11 55	12 00							12 15	12 25		12 30	12 55
Luton Airport Parkway 7 ✈	d											11 51												12 51	
Luton 10	d	11 23												12 23											
Bedford 7	d	11 38										12 07		12 38										13 07	
Wellingborough	d	11 51										12 20		12 51										13 20	
Kettering 4	a	12 00										12 26		13 00										13 26	
	d	12 01										12 27		13 01										13 27	
Corby	d	12a10												13a10											
Oakham	d																								
Melton Mowbray	d																								
Market Harborough	d							12 12				12 37									13 12			13 37	
Leicester	a							12 29		12 33		12 54	13 02								13 29	13 33		13 52	14 02
	d						12 25	12 30		12 35		12 54	13 04							13 25	13 30	13 35		13 54	14 04
Syston	d						12 32													13 32					
Sileby	d						12 36													13 36					
Barrow Upon Soar	d						12 40													13 40					
Loughborough	d						12 45			12 45	←	13 04								13 45		13 45	←	14 04	
East Midlands Parkway ✈	d						12 54	12 46		12 53	12 54									13 54	13 46	13 53	13 54		
Beeston	a						→				13 02	13 16								→			14 02	14 16	
Nottingham 8 🚊	a							12 59			13 13	13 27									13 59		14 13	14 26	
	d		12 15		12 45						13 17				13 15		13 45						14 29		
Lincoln	a										14 23												15 22		
Langley Mill	d		12 32												13 32										
Alfreton	d		12 40		13 07										13 40		14 07								
Long Eaton	a									12 56												13 56			
Derby 6	a									13 09			13 26									14 09			14 26
	d			12 44		13 11				13 18			13 28			13 44		14 11				14 18			14 28
Chesterfield	d		12 52	13 03	13 18					13 37			13 47		13 52	14 03	14 18					14 37			14 47
Sheffield 7 🚊	a		13 15	13 17	13 38	13 41				13 52			14 00		14 15	14 17	14 38	14 41				14 52			15 00
Doncaster 7	a					14 18												15 18							
Wakefield Kirkgate 4	a		13 57												14 57										
Wakefield Westgate 7	a			13 46												14 46									
Leeds 10	a		14 18	14 02											15 18	15 02									
York 8	a			14 27		14 45										15 29		15 45							

A From Plymouth to Glasgow Central
B From Norwich to Liverpool Lime Street
C From Southampton Central to Newcastle
D To Lincoln
E From Leicester
F From Plymouth to Edinburgh
G From Reading to Newcastle
H From Penzance to Glasgow Central
I From Plymouth to Aberdeen

For connections from Gatwick Airport see Table 52

Table 53

Saturdays

until 24 September

London - East Midlands - Sheffield

		EM	NT	XC	EM	XC	EM	EM	EM	EM	EM	EM	EM	NT	XC	EM	XC	EM	EM	EM	EM	EM
		◇1		◇1	◇	◇1		◇1	◇1		◇1	◇1	◇1		◇1	◇	◇1		◇1	◇1		◇1
				A	B	C	D			E					F	B	G	D			E	
		⊐P		⊥		⊥		⊐P	⊐P		⊐P	⊐P	⊐P		⊥		⊥		⊐P	⊐P		⊐P
St Pancras International ⊖	d	13 00						13 15	13 25		13 30	13 55	14 00						14 15	14 25		14 30
Luton Airport Parkway 7 ✈	d										13 51											14 51
Luton 10	d	13 23											14 23									
Bedford 7	d	13 38									14 07		14 38									15 07
Wellingborough	d	13 51									14 20		14 51									15 20
Kettering 4	a	14 00									14 26		15 00									15 26
	d	14 01									14 27		15 01									15 27
Corby	d	14a10											15a10									
Oakham	d																					
Melton Mowbray	d																					
Market Harborough	d							14 12			14 37								15 12			15 37
Leicester	a							14 29	14 33		14 54	15 02							15 29	15 33		15 53
	d						14 25	14 30	14 35		14 54	15 04						15 25	15 30	15 35		15 54
Syston	d						14 32											15 32				
Sileby	d						14 36											15 36				
Barrow Upon Soar	d						14 40											15 40				
Loughborough	d						14 45		14 45	←	15 04							15 45		15 45	←	16 04
East Midlands Parkway ✈	d						14 54	14 46	14 53	14 54								15 54	15 46	15 53	15 54	
Beeston	a						→			15 02	15 16							→			16 02	16 16
Nottingham 8	a							14 59		15 13	15 26								16 01		16 13	16 26
	d		14 15		14 45					15 23				15 15		15 45					16 14	
Lincoln	a									16 21											17 16	
Langley Mill	d		14 30											15 32								
Alfreton	d		14 38		15 07									15 40		16 07						
Long Eaton	a								14 56											15 56		
Derby 6	a								15 09			15 26								16 09		
	d			14 44		15 11			15 18			15 28			15 44		16 10			16 18		
Chesterfield	d		14 52	15 03	15 18				15 37			15 47		15 53	16 03	16 18				16 37		
Sheffield 7	a		15 15	15 17	15 38	15 41			15 52			16 00		16 14	16 18	16 38	16 41			16 52		
Doncaster 7	a					16 18											17 16					
Wakefield Kirkgate 4	a		15 57											16 57								
Wakefield Westgate 7	a			15 46											16 46							
Leeds 10	a		16 18	16 02										17 18	17 02							
York 8	a			16 27		16 46									17 27		17 38					

		EM	EM	NT	XC	EM	XC	EM	EM	EM	EM	EM	EM	EM	NT	XC	EM	XC	EM	EM	EM	EM	EM
		◇1	◇1		◇1	◇	◇1		◇1	◇1		◇1	◇1	◇1		◇1	◇	◇1		◇1	◇1		◇1
					H	B	I	D			E					J	B	G	D			E	
		⊐P	⊐P		⊥		⊥		⊐P	⊐P		⊐P	⊐P	⊐P		⊥		⊥		⊐P	⊐P		⊐P
St Pancras International ⊖	d	14 55	15 00						15 15	15 25		15 30	15 55	16 00						16 15	16 25		16 30
Luton Airport Parkway 7 ✈	d											15 51											16 51
Luton 10	d		15 23											16 23									
Bedford 7	d		15 38									16 07		16 38									17 07
Wellingborough	d		15 51									16 20		16 51									17 20
Kettering 4	a		16 00									16 26		17 00									17 26
	d		16 01									16 27		17 01									17 27
Corby	d		16a10											17a10									
Oakham	d																						
Melton Mowbray	d																						
Market Harborough	d								16 12			16 37								17 12			17 37
Leicester	a	16 02							16 29	16 33		16 54	17 02							17 29	17 33		17 52
	d	16 04						16 25	16 30	16 35		16 54	17 04						17 25	17 30	17 35		17 54
Syston	d							16 32											17 32				
Sileby	d							16 36											17 36				
Barrow Upon Soar	d							16 40											17 40				
Loughborough	d							16 45		16 45	←	17 04							17 45		17 45	←	18 04
East Midlands Parkway ✈	d							16 54	16 45	16 52	16 54								17 54	17 46	17 53	17 54	
Beeston	a							→			17 02	17 16							→			18 02	18 16
Nottingham 8	a								16 59		17 13	17 26								17 59		18 12	18 26
	d			16 15		16 45					17 13				17 15		17 45					18 15	
Lincoln	a										18 22											19 25	
Langley Mill	d			16 32											17 32		18 03						
Alfreton	d			16 40		17 07									17 40		18 10						
Long Eaton	a									16 56											17 56		
Derby 6	a	16 26								17 09			17 26								18 09		
	d	16 28			16 42		17 11			17 18			17 28			17 44		18 10			18 18		
Chesterfield	d	16 47		16 54	17 02	17 18				17 37			17 47		17 52	18 03	18 22				18 39		
Sheffield 7	a	17 00		17 17	17 19	17 34	17 44			17 52			18 04		18 16	18 18	18 39	18 42			18 59		
Doncaster 7	a																	19 15					
Wakefield Kirkgate 4	a			17 57											18 59								
Wakefield Westgate 7	a				17 47		18 12									18 46							
Leeds 10	a			18 18	18 02		18 31								19 23	19 01							
York 8	a				18 30		18 59									19 29		19 40					

A From Penzance to Glasgow Central
B From Norwich to Liverpool Lime Street
C From Southampton Central to Newcastle
D To Lincoln
E From Leicester
F From Newquay to Dundee
G From Reading to Newcastle
H From Plymouth to Glasgow Central
I From Southampton Central to Edinburgh
J From Plymouth to Edinburgh

For connections from Gatwick Airport see Table 52

Table 53

Saturdays
until 24 September

London - East Midlands - Sheffield

		EM	EM	NT	XC	EM		XC	EM	EM	EM	EM	EM	EM	EM	NT		XC	EM	XC	EM	EM	EM	EM	EM
		◇1	◇1		◇1	◇		◇1		◇1	◇1		◇1	◇1	◇1			◇1	◇	◇1		◇1	◇1		◇1
					A	B		C	D			E						F	G	H	I			E	
		☕	☕		🛒			🛒		☕	☕		☕	☕	☕			🛒		🛒		☕	☕		☕
St Pancras International ⊖	d	16 55	17 00							17 15	17 25		17 30	17 55	18 00							18 15	18 25		18 30
Luton Airport Parkway 7 ✈	d												17 51												18 51
Luton 10	d		17 23												18 23										
Bedford 7	d		17 38										18 07		18 38										19 07
Wellingborough	d		17 51										18 20		18 51										19 20
Kettering 4	a		18 00										18 26		19 00										19 26
	d		18 01										18 27		19 01										19 27
Corby	d		18a10												19a10										
Oakham	d																								
Melton Mowbray	d																								
Market Harborough	d									18 12			18 37									19 12			19 37
Leicester	a	18 02								18 29	18 33		18 52	19 02								19 29	19 33		19 52
	d	18 04							18 25	18 30	18 35		18 54	19 04							19 25	19 30	19 35		19 54
Syston	d								18 32												19 32				
Sileby	d								18 36												19 36				
Barrow Upon Soar	d								18 40												19 40				
Loughborough	d								18 45		18 45	←	19 04								19 45		19 45	←	20 04
East Midlands Parkway ✈	d								18 54	18 46	18 53	18 54									19 54	19 46	19 53	19 54	
Beeston	a								→			19 02	19 16								→			20 05	20 16
Nottingham 8	a									18 59		19 14	19 26									20 00		20 15	20 26
	d			18 15		18 45							19 29			19 15			19 40			20 15		20 29	
Lincoln	a												20 25											21 23	
Langley Mill	d			18 32												19 32						20 33			
Alfreton	d			18 40		19 07										19 40			20 01			20 41			
Long Eaton	a										18 56												19 56		
Derby 6	a	18 26									19 09			19 26									20 09		
	d	18 28			18 44			19 10			19 18			19 28				19 44		20 11			20 18		
Chesterfield	d	18 47		18 55	19 03	19 18		19 30			19 37			19 47		19 52		20 05	20 11	20 30		20 53	20 37		
Sheffield 7	a	19 04		19 15	19 18	19 39		19 51			19 52			20 00		20 15		20 19	20 27	20 49		21 14	20 54		
Doncaster 7	a							20 17												21 21					
Wakefield Kirkgate 4	a			19 58												20 57									
Wakefield Westgate 7	a				19 49													20 48				21 59			
Leeds 10	a			20 20	20 05											21 19		21 03				22 21			
York 8	a				20 32			20 46										21 57		21 45					

		EM		EM	XC	NT	XC	EM	EM	EM	EM	NT		EM	EM	EM	XC	XC	XC	EM	EM	EM		EM	EM
		◇1		◇1	◇1		◇1		◇1	◇1				◇1	◇1	◇1	◇1	◇1	◇1		◇1	◇1			◇1
					F		J	I			E						K	L	M	D				E	N
		☕		☕					☕	☕				☕	☕	☕	🛒	🛒			☕	☕			☕
St Pancras International ⊖	d	18 55		19 00					19 15	19 25				19 30	19 55	20 00					20 15	20 25			20 30
Luton Airport Parkway 7 ✈	d													19 51											20 51
Luton 10	d			19 23												20 23									
Bedford 7	d			19 38										20 07		20 38									21 07
Wellingborough	d			19 51										20 20		20 51									21 20
Kettering 4	a			20 00										20 26		21 00									21 26
	d			20 01										20 27		21 01									21 27
Corby	d			20a10												21a10									
Oakham	d																								
Melton Mowbray	d																								
Market Harborough	d								20 12					20 37							21 12				21 37
Leicester	a	20 02							20 29	20 33				20 52	21 04						21 29	21 33			21 52
	d	20 04						20 25	20 30	20 35				20 54	21 06					21 25	21 30	21 35			21 54
Syston	d							20 32												21 32					
Sileby	d							20 36												21 36					
Barrow Upon Soar	d							20 40												21 40					
Loughborough	d							20 45		20 45	←			21 04						21 45		21 45		←	22 04
East Midlands Parkway ✈	d							20 54	20 46	20 53	20 54									21 54	21 46	21 53		21 54	22 12
Beeston	a							→			21 05			21 16						→				22 06	22 17
Nottingham 8	a								20 59		21 15			21 26							22 01			22 14	22 27
	d					20 39					21 25	21 15													
Lincoln	a										22 40														
Langley Mill	d					21 02						21 31													
Alfreton	d					21 10						21 39													
Long Eaton	a									20 56												21 59			
Derby 6	a	20 26								21 10					21 32							22 10			
	d	20 28			20 44		21 26								21 34		21 44	21 45	21 48						
Chesterfield	d	20 47			21 05	21 22	21 46					21 50			21 56		22 03	22 08	22 08						
Sheffield 7	a	21 00			21 19	21 40	22 05					22 13			22 16		22 23	22 23	22 23						
Doncaster 7	a						22 30										22 51	22 51	22 51						
Wakefield Kirkgate 4	a																								
Wakefield Westgate 7	a				21 49										22 44		23 10	23 10	23 10						
Leeds 10	a				22 03										23 04		23 27	23 27	23 27						
York 8	a						22 55																		

A From Plymouth to Edinburgh
B From Norwich to Liverpool Lime Street
C From Southampton Central to Newcastle
D To Nottingham
E From Leicester
F From Plymouth
G From Norwich to Manchester Piccadilly
H From Reading to Newcastle. 🛒 to Chesterfield
I To Lincoln
J From Southampton Central
K from 25 June until 30 July. From Bournemouth
L until 18 June, from 6 August until 10 September. From Bournemouth
M 17 September, 24 September. From Plymouth
N until 30 July

For connections from Gatwick Airport see Table 52

Table 53

Saturdays
until 24 September

London - East Midlands - Sheffield

		EM	EM	XC	XC	EM	EM	EM		EM	EM	EM	EM	EM	EM	EM	EM	EM		EM	EM				
		◇1	◇1	◇1	◇1	◇1	◇1	◇1		◇1	◇1	◇1	◇1	◇1	◇1	◇1	◇1	◇1		◇1	◇1				
		A	B	C	D	E	B	A		B	A		B	A		B	F	E		B	A				
		🍴	🍴			🍴	🍴	🍴		🍴	🍴	🍴	🍴	🍴	🍴	🍴	🍴	🍴		🍴	🍴				
St Pancras International ⊖	d	20 30	20 55			20 55	21 00	21 00		21 25	21 25		21 30	21 30		22 00	22 00	22 00		22 25	22 25				
Luton Airport Parkway 7 ✈	d	20 51											21 51	21 51						22 46	22 46				
Luton 10	d						21 23	21 23								22 24	22 25	22 25							
Bedford 7	d	21 07					21 38	21 38					22 10	22 10		22 42	22 42	22 42		23 02	23 02				
Wellingborough	d	21 20					21 51	21 51					22 22	22 22		22 55	22 55	22 55		23 14	23 14				
Kettering 4	a	21 26					22 00	22 00					22 29	22 29		23 02	23 02	23 02		23 21	23 21				
	d	21 27					22 01	22 01				22 05	22 30	22 30	23 00	23 03	23 03	23 03		23 22	23 22				
Corby	d											22a15			23a10										
Oakham	d																								
Melton Mowbray	d																								
Market Harborough	d	21 37					22 12	22 12		22 20	22 20		22 40	22 40		23 14	23 14	23 14		23 32	23 32				
Leicester	a	21 52	22 02			22 02	22 29	22 29		22 36	22 36		22 54	22 54		23 31	23 31	23 31		23 46	23 46				
	d	21 54	22 04			22 04	22 30	22 30		22 37	22 37		22 54	22 54		23 32	23 32	23 32		23 46	23 46				
Syston	d																								
Sileby	d																								
Barrow Upon Soar	d																								
Loughborough	d						22 41			22 48						23 44				23 59					
East Midlands Parkway ✈	d	22 14								22 55	22 57		23 12	23 16		23 52	23 53	23 53		00 02	00 09				
Beeston	a	22 20														23 59	00 02	00 01							
Nottingham 8 ⛴	a	22 28								23 06	23 08					00 08	00 11	00 11							
	d																								
Lincoln	a																								
Langley Mill	d																								
Alfreton	d																								
Long Eaton	a												23 15	23 20						00 06	00 13				
Derby 6	a		22 26			22 38	23 02	23 10					23 26	23 31						00 17	00 24				
	d		22 28	22 32	22 33	22 40																			
Chesterfield	d		22 47	22 53	22 54	22 58																			
Sheffield 7 ⛴	a		23 00	23 09	23 09	23 12																			
Doncaster 7	a																								
Wakefield Kirkgate 4	a																								
Wakefield Westgate 7	a																								
Leeds 10	a			23 50	23 51																				
York 8	a																								

Saturdays
from 1 October

		EM	EM	EM	EM	EM	XC	EM	XC	EM		XC	EM	NT	EM	XC	EM	EM	XC	EM		EM	EM	NT	EM
		◇1	◇1	◇1	◇1	◇	◇1	◇1	◇1	◇		◇1	◇1			◇1	◇		◇1	◇1		◇1	◇1		◇1
						G	H		I	G		J				K	G		J						
		🍴	🍴	🍴	🍴		🛒	🍴	🛒			🛒	🍴			🛒			🛒	🍴		🍴	🍴		🍴
St Pancras International ⊖	d	22p00	22p25	23p15	00 15															06 10		06 37			06 55
Luton Airport Parkway 7 ✈	d		22p48		00 44																				07 16
Luton 10	d	22p24		23p46	00 47															06 33		06 59			
Bedford 7	d	22p40	23p04	00 12	01 12															06 48					
Wellingborough	d	22p53	23p17	00 25	01 33															07 01					
Kettering 4	a	23p00	23p25	00 41	01 43															07 07		07 27			
	d	23p01	23p26	00 42	01 43															07 08		07 28	07 38		
Corby	d																						07a48		
Oakham	d																								
Melton Mowbray	d																								
Market Harborough	d	23p12	23p37	00 52																07 18		07 38			
Leicester	a	23p29	23p53	01 05	02 07															07 35		07 53			08 04
	d	23p30	23p55	01 07											06 36			07 25		07 36		07 55			08 06
Syston	d														06 43			07 32							
Sileby	d														06 47			07 36							
Barrow Upon Soar	d														06 51			07 40							
Loughborough	d	23p41	00 06	01 17											06 56			07 46		07 47		08 05			08 18
East Midlands Parkway ✈	d	23p50	00 14	01 25											07 06			07 57				08 13			
Beeston	a	00 04		01 38											07 15			08 04							08 31
Nottingham 8 ⛴	a	00 12		01 45											07 24			08 13							08 42
	d			01 52		05 20				06 40				07 15			07 45							08 11	
Lincoln	a																								
Langley Mill	d													07 30										08 31	
Alfreton	d									07 02				07 38			08 07							08 39	
Long Eaton	a																			07 55					
Derby 6	a		00 34	02 10																08 09		08 26			
	d		00 35				05 55	06 26	06 37			07 11	07 20			07 44			08 11	08 18		08 28			
Chesterfield	d		00 58			05 49	06 31	06 45	06 56	07 13		07 30	07 42	07 50		08 03	08 18		08 30	08 37		08 47		08 51	
Sheffield 7 ⛴	a		01 13			06 15	06 44	07 09	07 09	07 31		07 48	07 59	08 08		08 17	08 38		08 45	08 52		09 07		09 15	
Doncaster 7	a						07 16					08 23							09 18			09 53			
Wakefield Kirkgate 4	a													08 57										09 57	
Wakefield Westgate 7	a								07 36							08 45									
Leeds 10	a								07 52					09 20		09 03								10 18	
York 8	a						07 43		08 24			08 47				09 30			09 45			10 16			

- **A** from 6 August until 24 September
- **B** until 30 July
- **C** from 6 August until 10 September. From Penzance
- **D** until 30 July. From Penzance
- **E** from 6 August until 10 September
- **F** 17 September, 24 September
- **G** To Liverpool Lime Street
- **H** To Newcastle. 🛒 from Sheffield
- **I** From Birmingham New Street to Glasgow Central
- **J** From Birmingham New Street to Newcastle
- **K** From Birmingham New Street to Edinburgh

For connections from Gatwick Airport see Table 52

Table 53

Saturdays

from 1 October

London - East Midlands - Sheffield

		XC	EM	XC	EM	EM		EM	EM	EM	EM	EM	NT	XC	EM	XC		EM	EM	EM	EM	EM	EM	EM	NT
		◇1	◇	◇1		◇1		◇1		◇1	◇1	◇1		◇1	◇	◇1			◇1	◇1		◇1	◇1	◇1	
		A	B	C	D				E					F	B	G		D			E				
		🛒		🛒		☕		☕		☕	☕	☕		🛒		🛒			☕	☕		☕	☕	☕	
St Pancras International ⊖	d					07 00				07 30	07 55	08 00							08 15	08 25		08 30	08 55	09 00	
Luton Airport Parkway 7 ✈	d									07 51												08 51			
Luton 10	d					07 23						08 23												09 23	
Bedford 7	d					07 38				08 07		08 38										09 07		09 38	
Wellingborough	d					07 51				08 20		08 51										09 20		09 51	
Kettering 4	a					08 00				08 27		09 00										09 26		10 00	
	d					08 01				08 27		09 01										09 27		10 01	
Corby	d											09a10												10a10	
Oakham	d																								
Melton Mowbray	d																								
Market Harborough	d					08 12				08 37									09 12			09 37			
Leicester	a					08 29				08 53	09 02								09 29	09 33		09 52	10 02		
	d				08 25	08 30		08 38		08 54	09 04							09 25	09 30	09 35		09 54	10 04		
Syston	d				08 32													09 32							
Sileby	d				08 36													09 36							
Barrow Upon Soar	d				08 40													09 40							
Loughborough	d				08 45	08 41		08 49	←	09 04								09 45		09 45	←	10 04			
East Midlands Parkway ✈	d				08 57	08 50		08 56	08 57									09 54	09 46	09 53	09 54				
Beeston	a				→				09 05	09 16								→			10 02	10 16			
Nottingham 8	a					09 03			09 14	09 26									09 59		10 13	10 26			
	d		08 45						09 23				09 15		09 46						10 29				10 15
Lincoln	a								10 18												11 32				
Langley Mill	d												09 32												10 32
Alfreton	d		09 07										09 40		10 08										10 40
Long Eaton	a							09 00												09 56					
Derby 6	a							09 14			09 26									10 09			10 26		
	d	08 44		09 11				09 18			09 28			09 44		10 10				10 18			10 28		
Chesterfield	d	09 03	09 18					09 37			09 47		09 52	10 03	10 19					10 37			10 47		10 52
Sheffield 7	a	09 18	09 38	09 44				09 52			10 00		10 15	10 17	10 38	10 42				10 52			11 00		11 15
Doncaster 7	a			10 17												11 15									
Wakefield Kirkgate 4	a												10 57												11 57
Wakefield Westgate 7	a	09 46												10 46											
Leeds 10	a	10 02											11 18	11 02											12 18
York 8	a	10 27		10 45										11 27		11 45									

		XC		EM	XC	EM	EM	EM	EM	EM	EM	EM		NT	XC	EM	XC	EM	EM	EM	EM	EM		EM	EM
		◇1		◇	◇1		◇1	◇1		◇1	◇1	◇1			◇1	◇	◇1		◇1	◇1		◇1		◇1	◇1
		H		B	I	D			E						F	B	J	D			E				
		🛒			🛒		☕	☕		☕	☕	☕			🛒		🛒		☕	☕		☕		☕	☕
St Pancras International ⊖	d						09 15	09 25		09 30	09 55	10 00							10 15	10 25		10 30		10 55	11 00
Luton Airport Parkway 7 ✈	d									09 51												10 51			
Luton 10	d											10 23													11 23
Bedford 7	d									10 07		10 38										11 07			11 38
Wellingborough	d									10 20		10 51										11 20			11 51
Kettering 4	a									10 26		11 00										11 26			12 00
	d									10 27		11 01										11 27			12 01
Corby	d											11a10													12a10
Oakham	d																								
Melton Mowbray	d																								
Market Harborough	d						10 12			10 37									11 12			11 37			
Leicester	a						10 29	10 33		10 54	11 02								11 29	11 33		11 54		12 02	
	d					10 25	10 30	10 35		10 54	11 04							11 25	11 30	11 35		11 54		12 04	
Syston	d					10 32												11 32							
Sileby	d					10 36												11 36							
Barrow Upon Soar	d					10 40												11 40							
Loughborough	d					10 45		10 45	←	11 04								11 45		11 45	←	12 04			
East Midlands Parkway ✈	d					10 54	10 46	10 53	10 54									11 54	11 46	11 53	11 54				
Beeston	a					→			11 02	11 16								→			12 02	12 16			
Nottingham 8	a						10 59		11 13	11 26									11 59		12 13	12 26			
	d			10 45					11 17					11 15		11 45					12 27				
Lincoln	a								12 29												13 20				
Langley Mill	d													11 31											
Alfreton	d			11 07										11 39		12 07									
Long Eaton	a							10 56												11 56					
Derby 6	a							11 09			11 26									12 09				12 26	
	d	10 44			11 11			11 18			11 28				11 44		12 10			12 18				12 28	
Chesterfield	d	11 03		11 18				11 37			11 47			11 52	12 03	12 18				12 37				12 47	
Sheffield 7	a	11 17		11 38	11 41			11 52			12 00			12 16	12 16	12 38	12 41			12 52				13 04	
Doncaster 7	a				12 15												13 17								
Wakefield Kirkgate 4	a													12 57											
Wakefield Westgate 7	a	11 46													12 46										
Leeds 10	a	12 02												13 18	13 02										
York 8	a	12 29			12 45										13 29		13 45								

A From Bristol Temple Meads to Glasgow Central
B From Norwich to Liverpool Lime Street
C From Guildford to Newcastle
D To Lincoln
E From Leicester
F From Plymouth to Edinburgh
G From Bournemouth to Newcastle
H From Plymouth to Glasgow Central
I From Southampton Central to Newcastle
J From Reading to Newcastle

For connections from Gatwick Airport see Table 52

Table 53

Saturdays
from 1 October

London - East Midlands - Sheffield

		NT	XC	EM	XC	EM	EM	EM		EM	EM	EM	EM	NT	XC	EM	XC	EM		EM	EM	EM	EM	EM	EM
			◇1	◇	◇1		◇1	◇1			◇1	◇1	◇1		◇1	◇	◇1			◇1	◇1		◇1	◇1	◇1
			A	B	C	D				E					F	B	G	D				E			
			🛒		🛒		🍽	🍽			🍽	🍽	🍽		🛒		🛒			🍽	🍽		🍽	🍽	🍽
St Pancras International ⊖	d						11 15	11 25			11 30	11 55	12 00							12 15	12 25		12 30	12 55	13 00
Luton Airport Parkway 7 ✈	d										11 51												12 51		
Luton 10	d												12 23												13 23
Bedford 7	d										12 07		12 38										13 07		13 38
Wellingborough	d										12 20		12 51										13 20		13 51
Kettering 4	a										12 26		13 00										13 26		14 00
	d										12 27		13 01										13 27		14 01
Corby	d												13a10												14a10
Oakham	d																								
Melton Mowbray	d																								
Market Harborough	d						12 12				12 37									13 12			13 37		
Leicester	a						12 29	12 33			12 54	13 02								13 29	13 33		13 52	14 02	
	d					12 25	12 30	12 35			12 54	13 04						13 25		13 30	13 35		13 54	14 04	
Syston	d					12 32												13 32							
Sileby	d					12 36												13 36							
Barrow Upon Soar	d					12 40												13 40							
Loughborough	d					12 45		12 45		←	13 04							13 45			13 45	←	14 04		
East Midlands Parkway ✈	d					12 54	12 46	12 53		12 54								13 54		13 46	13 53	13 54			
Beeston	a					→				13 02	13 16							→				14 02	14 16		
Nottingham 8 🚊	a						12 59			13 13	13 27									13 59		14 13	14 26		
	d	12 15		12 45						13 17				13 15		13 45						14 29			
Lincoln	a									14 26												15 24			
Langley Mill	d	12 32												13 32											
Alfreton	d	12 40		13 07										13 40		14 07									
Long Eaton	a							12 56													13 56				
Derby 6	a							13 09				13 26									14 09			14 26	
	d		12 44		13 11			13 18				13 28			13 44		14 11				14 18			14 28	
Chesterfield	d	12 52	13 03	13 18				13 37				13 47		13 52	14 03	14 18					14 37			14 47	
Sheffield 7 🚊	a	13 15	13 17	13 38	13 41			13 52				14 00		14 15	14 17	14 38	14 41				14 52			15 00	
Doncaster 7	a				14 18												15 18								
Wakefield Kirkgate 4	a	13 57												14 57											
Wakefield Westgate 7	a		13 46												14 46										
Leeds 10	a	14 18	14 02											15 18	15 02										
York 8	a		14 27		14 45										15 29		15 45								

		NT	XC	EM		XC	EM	EM	EM	EM	EM	EM	EM	NT		XC	EM	XC	EM	EM	EM	EM	EM	EM	
			◇1	◇		◇1		◇1	◇1		◇1	◇1	◇1			◇1	◇	◇1		◇1	◇1		◇1	◇1	
			A	B		C	D			E						H	B	G	D			E			
			🛒			🛒		🍽	🍽		🍽	🍽	🍽			🛒		🛒		🍽	🍽		🍽	🍽	
St Pancras International ⊖	d							13 15	13 25		13 30	13 55	14 00							14 15	14 25		14 30	14 55	
Luton Airport Parkway 7 ✈	d										13 51												14 51		
Luton 10	d												14 23												
Bedford 7	d										14 07		14 38										15 07		
Wellingborough	d										14 20		14 51										15 20		
Kettering 4	a										14 26		15 00										15 26		
	d										14 27		15 01										15 27		
Corby	d												15a10												
Oakham	d																								
Melton Mowbray	d																								
Market Harborough	d							14 12			14 37									15 12			15 37		
Leicester	a							14 29	14 33		14 54	15 02								15 29	15 33		15 53	16 02	
	d						14 25	14 30	14 35		14 54	15 04							15 25	15 30	15 35		15 54	16 04	
Syston	d						14 32												15 32						
Sileby	d						14 36												15 36						
Barrow Upon Soar	d						14 40												15 40						
Loughborough	d						14 45		14 45	←	15 04								15 45		15 45	←	16 04		
East Midlands Parkway ✈	d						14 54	14 46	14 53	14 54									15 54	15 46	15 53	15 54			
Beeston	a						→			15 02	15 16								→			16 02	16 16		
Nottingham 8 🚊	a							14 59		15 13	15 26									16 01		16 13	16 26		
	d	14 15		14 45						15 23				15 15			15 45					16 14			
Lincoln	a									16 23												17 17			
Langley Mill	d	14 30												15 32											
Alfreton	d	14 38		15 07										15 40			16 07								
Long Eaton	a								14 56												15 56				
Derby 6	a								15 09			15 26									16 09			16 26	
	d		14 44			15 11			15 18			15 28				15 44		16 10			16 18			16 28	
Chesterfield	d	14 52	15 03	15 18					15 37			15 47		15 53		16 03	16 18				16 37			16 47	
Sheffield 7 🚊	a	15 15	15 17	15 38		15 41			15 52			16 00		16 14		16 18	16 38	16 41			16 52			17 00	
Doncaster 7	a					16 18												17 16							
Wakefield Kirkgate 4	a	15 57												16 57											
Wakefield Westgate 7	a		15 46													16 46									
Leeds 10	a	16 18	16 02											17 18		17 02									
York 8	a		16 27			16 46										17 27		17 38							

A From Penzance to Glasgow Central
B From Norwich to Liverpool Lime Street
C From Southampton Central to Newcastle
D To Lincoln
E From Leicester
F From Plymouth to Aberdeen
G From Reading to Newcastle
H From Plymouth to Dundee

For connections from Gatwick Airport see Table 52

Table 53

Saturdays
from 1 October

London - East Midlands - Sheffield

		EM	NT	XC	EM	XC	EM	EM	EM	EM		EM	EM	EM	NT	XC	EM	XC	EM	EM		EM	EM	EM	EM
		◇1		◇1	◇	◇1		◇1	◇1			◇1	◇1	◇1		◇1	◇	◇1		◇1		◇1		◇1	◇1
				A	B	C	D			E						F	B	G	D				E		
		☕		🛒		🛒		☕	☕			☕	☕	☕		🛒		🛒		☕		☕		☕	☕
St Pancras International ⊖	d	15 00						15 15	15 25			15 30	15 55	16 00						16 15		16 25		16 30	16 55
Luton Airport Parkway 7 ✈	d											15 51												16 51	
Luton 10	d	15 23												16 23											
Bedford 7	d	15 38										16 07		16 38										17 07	
Wellingborough	d	15 51										16 20		16 51										17 20	
Kettering 4	a	16 00										16 26		17 00										17 26	
	d	16 01										16 27		17 01										17 27	
Corby	d	16a10												17a10											
Oakham	d																								
Melton Mowbray	d																								
Market Harborough	d							16 12				16 37								17 12				17 37	
Leicester	a							16 29	16 33			16 54	17 02							17 29		17 33		17 52	18 02
	d						16 25	16 30	16 35			16 54	17 04						17 25	17 30		17 35		17 54	18 04
Syston	d						16 32												17 32						
Sileby	d						16 36												17 36						
Barrow Upon Soar	d						16 40												17 40						
Loughborough	d						16 45		16 45	←		17 04							17 45			17 45	←	18 04	
East Midlands Parkway ✈	d						16 54	16 45	16 52	16 54									17 54	17 46		17 53	17 54		
Beeston	a						↪			17 02		17 16							↪				18 02	18 16	
Nottingham 8 🚊	a							16 59		17 13		17 26								17 59			18 12	18 26	
	d		16 15		16 45					17 13					17 15		17 45						18 15		
Lincoln	a									18 24													19 27		
Langley Mill	d		16 32												17 32		18 03								
Alfreton	d		16 40		17 07										17 40		18 10								
Long Eaton	a								16 56													17 56			
Derby 6	a								17 09				17 26									18 09			18 26
	d			16 42		17 11			17 18				17 28			17 44		18 10				18 18			18 28
Chesterfield	d		16 54	17 02	17 18				17 37				17 47		17 52	18 03	18 22					18 39			18 47
Sheffield 7 🚊	a		17 17	17 19	17 34	17 44			17 52				18 04		18 16	18 18	18 39	18 42				18 59			19 04
Doncaster 7	a																	19 15							
Wakefield Kirkgate 4	a		17 57												18 59										
Wakefield Westgate 7	a			17 47		18 12										18 46									
Leeds 10	a		18 18	18 02		18 31									19 23	19 01									
York 8	a			18 30		18 59										19 29		19 40							

		EM	NT	XC	EM	XC		EM	EM	EM	EM	EM	EM	EM	NT	XC		EM	XC	EM	EM	EM	EM	EM	EM
		◇1		◇1	◇	◇1			◇1	◇1		◇1	◇1	◇1		◇1		◇	◇1		◇1	◇1		◇1	◇1
				F	B	H		I			E					J		K	L	D			E		
		☕		🛒		🛒			☕	☕		☕	☕	☕		🛒			🛒		☕	☕		☕	☕
St Pancras International ⊖	d	17 00							17 15	17 25		17 30	17 55	18 00							18 15	18 25		18 30	18 55
Luton Airport Parkway 7 ✈	d											17 51												18 51	
Luton 10	d	17 23												18 23											
Bedford 7	d	17 38										18 07		18 38										19 07	
Wellingborough	d	17 51										18 20		18 51										19 20	
Kettering 4	a	18 00										18 26		19 00										19 26	
	d	18 01										18 27		19 01										19 27	
Corby	d	18a10												19a10											
Oakham	d																								
Melton Mowbray	d																								
Market Harborough	d								18 12			18 37									19 12			19 37	
Leicester	a								18 29	18 33		18 52	19 02								19 29	19 33		19 52	20 02
	d							18 25	18 30	18 35		18 54	19 04							19 25	19 30	19 35		19 54	20 04
Syston	d							18 32												19 32					
Sileby	d							18 36												19 36					
Barrow Upon Soar	d							18 40												19 40					
Loughborough	d							18 45		18 45	←	19 04								19 45		19 45	←	20 04	
East Midlands Parkway ✈	d							18 54	18 46	18 53	18 54									19 54	19 46	19 53	19 54		
Beeston	a							↪			19 02	19 16								↪			20 05	20 16	
Nottingham 8 🚊	a								18 59		19 14	19 26									20 00		20 15	20 26	
	d		18 15		18 45							19 29			19 15			19 40			20 15		20 29		
Lincoln	a											20 25											21 23		
Langley Mill	d		18 32												19 32						20 33				
Alfreton	d		18 40		19 07										19 40			20 01			20 41				
Long Eaton	a									18 56												19 56			
Derby 6	a									19 09			19 26									20 09			20 26
	d			18 44		19 10				19 18			19 28			19 44			20 11			20 18			20 28
Chesterfield	d		18 55	19 03	19 18	19 30				19 37			19 47		19 52	20 05		20 11	20 30		20 53	20 37			20 47
Sheffield 7 🚊	a		19 15	19 18	19 39	19 51				19 52			20 00		20 15	20 19		20 27	20 49		21 14	20 54			21 00
Doncaster 7	a					20 17													21 21						
Wakefield Kirkgate 4	a		19 58												20 57										
Wakefield Westgate 7	a			19 49												20 48					21 59				
Leeds 10	a		20 20	20 05											21 19	21 03					22 21				
York 8	a			20 32		20 46										21 57			21 45						

A From Plymouth to Glasgow Central
B From Norwich to Liverpool Lime Street
C From Southampton Central to Edinburgh
D To Lincoln
E From Leicester
F From Plymouth to Edinburgh
G From Reading to Newcastle
H From Southampton Central to Newcastle
I To Nottingham
J From Plymouth
K From Norwich to Manchester Piccadilly
L From Reading to Newcastle.
🛒 to Chesterfield

For connections from Gatwick Airport see Table 52

Table 53

Saturdays
from 1 October

London - East Midlands - Sheffield

		EM	XC	NT	XC	EM	EM	EM	EM	NT	EM	EM	EM	XC	EM	EM	EM	EM	EM	EM	EM	EM
		◇1	◇1		◇1		◇1	◇1			◇1	◇1	◇1	◇1		◇1	◇1		◇1	◇1	◇1	◇1
			A		B	C			D					A	E			D	F	G	F	F
		☕					☕	☕			☕	☕	☕			☕	☕		☕	☕	☕	☕
St Pancras International ⊖	d	19 00					19 15	19 25			19 30	19 55	20 00			20 15	20 25		20 30	20 30	20 55	21 00
Luton Airport Parkway 7 ✈	d										19 51								20 51	20 51		
Luton 10	d	19 23											20 23									21 23
Bedford 7	d	19 38									20 07		20 38						21 07	21 07		21 38
Wellingborough	d	19 51									20 20		20 51						21 20	21 20		21 51
Kettering 4	a	20 00									20 26		21 00						21 26	21 26		22 00
	d	20 01									20 27		21 01						21 27	21 27		22 01
Corby	d	20a10											21a10									
Oakham	d																					
Melton Mowbray	d																					
Market Harborough	d						20 12				20 37					21 12			21 37	21 37		22 12
Leicester	a						20 29	20 33			20 52	21 04				21 29	21 33		21 52	21 52	22 02	22 29
	d					20 25	20 30	20 35			20 54	21 06			21 25	21 30	21 35		21 54	21 54	22 04	22 30
Syston	d					20 32									21 32							
Sileby	d					20 36									21 36							
Barrow Upon Soar	d					20 40									21 40							
Loughborough	d					20 45		20 45	←		21 04				21 45		21 45	←	22 04			22 41
East Midlands Parkway ✈	d					20 54	20 46	20 53	20 54						21 54	21 46	21 53	21 54	22 12	22 14		
Beeston	a					→			21 05		21 16				→			22 06	22 17	22 20		
Nottingham 8 🚢	a						20 59		21 15		21 26					22 01		22 14	22 27	22 28		
	d			20 39					21 25	21 15												
Lincoln	a								22 40													
Langley Mill	d			21 02						21 31												
Alfreton	d			21 10						21 39												
Long Eaton	a							20 56									21 59					
Derby 6	a							21 10				21 32					22 10				22 26	23 02
	d		20 44		21 26							21 34		21 48							22 28	
Chesterfield	d		21 05	21 22	21 46					21 50		21 56		22 08							22 47	
Sheffield 7 🚢	a		21 19	21 40	22 05					22 13		22 16		22 23							23 00	
Doncaster 7	a				22 30									22 51								
Wakefield Kirkgate 4	a																					
Wakefield Westgate 7	a		21 49									22 44		23 10								
Leeds 10	a		22 03									23 04		23 27								
York 8	a				22 55																	

		EM	EM	EM	EM	EM	EM	EM	EM	EM	EM	EM
		◇1	◇1	◇1	◇1	◇1	◇1	◇1	◇1	◇1	◇1	◇1
		G	F	G		F	G		F	G	F	G
		☕	☕	☕	☕	☕	☕	☕	☕	☕	☕	☕
St Pancras International ⊖	d	21 00	21 25	21 25		21 30	21 30		22 00	22 00	22 25	22 25
Luton Airport Parkway 7 ✈	d					21 51	21 51				22 46	22 46
Luton 10	d	21 23							22 25	22 25		
Bedford 7	d	21 38				22 10	22 10		22 42	22 42	23 02	23 02
Wellingborough	d	21 51				22 22	22 22		22 55	22 55	23 14	23 14
Kettering 4	a	22 00				22 29	22 29		23 02	23 02	23 21	23 21
	d	22 01			22 05	22 30	22 30	23 00	23 03	23 03	23 22	23 22
Corby	d				22a15			23a10				
Oakham	d											
Melton Mowbray	d											
Market Harborough	d	22 12	22 20	22 20		22 40	22 40		23 14	23 14	23 32	23 32
Leicester	a	22 29	22 36	22 36		22 54	22 54		23 31	23 31	23 46	23 46
	d	22 30	22 37	22 37		22 54	22 54		23 32	23 32	23 46	23 46
Syston	d											
Sileby	d											
Barrow Upon Soar	d											
Loughborough	d		22 48						23 44		23 59	23 59
East Midlands Parkway ✈	d		22 55	22 57		23 12	23 16		23 52	23 53	00 02	00 09
Beeston	a								23 59	00 02		
Nottingham 8 🚢	a		23 06	23 08					00 08	00 11		
	d											
Lincoln	a											
Langley Mill	d											
Alfreton	d											
Long Eaton	a					23 15	23 20				00 06	00 13
Derby 6	a	23 10				23 26	23 31				00 17	00 24
	d											
Chesterfield	d											
Sheffield 7 🚢	a											
Doncaster 7	a											
Wakefield Kirkgate 4	a											
Wakefield Westgate 7	a											
Leeds 10	a											
York 8	a											

A From Plymouth
B From Southampton Central
C To Lincoln
D From Leicester
E To Nottingham
F from 29 October
G from 1 October until 22 October

For connections from Gatwick Airport see Table 52

Table 53

Sundays
until 19 June

London - East Midlands - Sheffield

		EM	EM	EM	EM	NT	XC	EM	EM	NT	EM	XC	EM	EM	EM	NT	EM	XC	EM	EM	EM	NT	EM
		◇1	◇1	◇	◇1		◇1	◇1	◇		◇1	◇1	◇1	◇1	◇		◇1	◇1	◇1	◇1	◇		◇1
		A	A	B			C		B			D			B			C			E		
		☕	☕		☕		🛒	☕			☕	🛒	☕	☕			☕	🛒	☕	☕			☕
St Pancras International ⊖	d	22p00	22p25								09 00		09 30				10 00		10 30				11 00
Luton Airport Parkway 7 ✈	d		22p46								09 28						10 29						11 29
Luton 10	d	22p24											10 02						11 02				11 32
Bedford 7	d	22p42	23p02								09 51		10 21				10 53		11 24				11 56
Wellingborough	d	22p55	23p14								10 05		10 35				11 07		11 37				12 09
Kettering 4	a	23p02	23p21								10 13		10 41				11 14		11 44				12 15
	d	23p03	23p22		09 55						10 14		10 43	10 55			11 15		11 45	11 55			12 16
Corby	d				10a05									11a05						12a05			
Oakham	d																						
Melton Mowbray	d																						
Market Harborough	d	23p14	23p32								10 25		10 53				11 26		11 54				12 26
Leicester	a	23p31	23p46								10 45		11 12				11 47		12 14				12 45
	d	23p32	23p46					10 10			10 47		11 15				11 48		12 16				12 47
Syston	d																						
Sileby	d																						
Barrow Upon Soar	d																						
Loughborough	d	23p44						10 21			10 58		11 25				11 59		12 27				12 57
East Midlands Parkway ✈	d	23p52	00 02					10 29			11 06		11 33				12 08		12 34				13 05
Beeston	a	23p59									11 12												13 10
Nottingham 8 🚊	a	00 08									11 20						12 22						13 18
	d			09 31		10 06			10 41	11 15					11 46	12 19					12 39	13 09	
Lincoln	a																						
Langley Mill	d					10 27				11 31						12 35					12 56	13 27	
Alfreton	d			09 53		10 35			11 03	11 39					12 08	12 43					13 04	13 35	
Long Eaton	a		00 06					10 32					11 36						12 38				
Derby 6	a		00 17					10 46					11 48						12 49				
	d						10 44	10 48				11 43	11 49					12 44	12 50				
Chesterfield	d			10 08		10 54	11 03	11 09	11 15	11 51		12 03	12 10		12 18	12 54		13 03	13 12		13 17	13 46	
Sheffield 7 🚊	a			10 33		11 15	11 17	11 28	11 35	12 15		12 18	12 29		12 36	13 16		13 17	13 28		13 33	14 07	
Doncaster 7	a							11 56															
Wakefield Kirkgate 4	a					11 52				12 52						13 52						14 52	
Wakefield Westgate 7	a						11 44					12 44						13 44					
Leeds 10	a					12 18	12 02			13 18		13 02				14 18		14 02				15 18	
York 8	a						12 32	12 20				13 32						14 31					

		XC	EM	EM	EM	NT	EM	XC	EM	EM	EM	NT	EM	XC	EM	EM	EM	EM	NT	XC	EM	EM	EM
		◇1	◇1	◇1	◇		◇1	◇1	◇	◇1	◇1		◇1	◇1	◇1	◇1	◇	◇1		◇1	◇1	◇1	◇
		F			E			G	B					H			B			I			E
		🛒	☕	☕			☕	🛒		☕	☕		☕	🛒	☕	☕		☕		🛒	☕	☕	
St Pancras International ⊖	d		11 30				12 00			12 30			13 00		13 30			14 00			14 30		
Luton Airport Parkway 7 ✈	d		11 59				12 29			12 59			13 29		13 58			14 29					
Luton 10	d		12 02				12 33			13 03			13 33		14 02						15 01		
Bedford 7	d		12 26				12 57			13 27			13 57		14 19			14 47			15 17		
Wellingborough	d		12 40				13 10			13 40			14 10		14 33			15 00			15 31		
Kettering 4	a		12 47				13 16			13 48			14 16		14 40			15 07			15 38		
	d		12 48	12 55			13 17			13 49	13 55		14 17		14 43	14 55		15 08			15 39	15 45	
Corby	d			13a05							14a05					15a05						15a55	
Oakham	d																						
Melton Mowbray	d																						
Market Harborough	d		12 58				13 27			14 00			14 27		14 54			15 18			15 50		
Leicester	a		13 17				13 46			14 20			14 46		15 16			15 37			16 11		
	d		13 19				13 48			14 22			14 48		15 18			15 39			16 13		
Syston	d																						
Sileby	d																						
Barrow Upon Soar	d																						
Loughborough	d		13 29				13 58			14 33			14 58		15 29			15 49			16 24		
East Midlands Parkway ✈	d		13 37				14 06			14 41			15 06		15 37			15 57			16 32		
Beeston	a						14 12						15 11					16 04					
Nottingham 8 🚊	a						14 20						15 18					16 10					
	d				13 38	14 19			14 37			15 12					15 44		16 14				16 41
Lincoln	a																						
Langley Mill	d				13 55	14 35			14 54			15 34							16 30				17 00
Alfreton	d				14 03	14 43			15 02			15 44					16 06		16 38				17 08
Long Eaton	a		13 40							14 45					15 41						16 36		
Derby 6	a		13 52							14 59					15 53						16 48		
	d	13 44	13 54					14 44		15 01				15 44	15 58					16 44	16 56		
Chesterfield	d	14 03	14 13		14 18	14 54		15 03	15 13	15 22		15 53		16 03	16 19		16 23		16 50	17 04	17 17		17 22
Sheffield 7 🚊	a	14 17	14 26		14 36	15 15		15 17	15 31	15 40		16 15		16 18	16 33		16 39		17 15	17 17	17 32		17 40
Doncaster 7	a																						
Wakefield Kirkgate 4	a					15 52						16 52							17 52				
Wakefield Westgate 7	a	14 44						15 44						16 44						17 46	18 06		
Leeds 10	a	15 02				16 18		16 02				17 18		17 02					18 18	18 02	18 24		
York 8	a	15 31						16 32						17 32						18 32			

A not 22 May
B To Liverpool Lime Street
C From Birmingham New Street to Glasgow Central
D From Birmingham New Street to Edinburgh
E From Norwich to Liverpool Lime Street
F From Bristol Temple Meads to Aberdeen
G From Bristol Temple Meads to Glasgow Central
H From Plymouth to Edinburgh
I From Plymouth to Glasgow Central

For connections from Gatwick Airport see Table 52

Table 53

Sundays
until 19 June

London - East Midlands - Sheffield

		EM		NT	XC	EM	EM	EM	EM	EM	EM	EM		NT	XC	EM	EM	EM	EM	EM	EM	NT		XC	EM
		◇1			◇1	◇1	◇1	◇	◇1	◇1	◇1	◇1			◇1	◇	◇1	◇1	◇1	◇1	◇1			◇1	◇
					A			B							C	D								E	D
		☕			🛒	☕	☕		☕	☕	☕	☕			🛒		☕	☕	☕	☕	☕			🛒	
St Pancras International ⊖	d	15 00				15 30			16 00	16 25	16 30						16 55	17 00	17 25	17 30					
Luton Airport Parkway 7 ✈	d	15 29							16 29									17 21							
Luton 10	d					16 01					16 52									17 52					
Bedford 7	d	15 47				16 17			16 47		17 15							17 45		18 15					
Wellingborough	d	16 01				16 31			17 00		17 28							17 58		18 28					
Kettering 4	a	16 08				16 38			17 07		17 35							18 05		18 35					
	d	16 09				16 39	16 45		17 08		17 36	17 50						18 06		18 36	18 50				
Corby	d						16a55					18a00									19a00				
Oakham	d																								
Melton Mowbray	d																								
Market Harborough	d	16 20				16 50			17 18		17 46							18 16		18 46					
Leicester	a	16 41				17 11			17 37	17 47	18 08						18 21	18 35	18 44	19 05					
	d	16 43				17 12			17 39	17 49	18 10						18 22	18 37	18 46	19 07					
Syston	d																								
Sileby	d																								
Barrow Upon Soar	d																								
Loughborough	d	16 54				17 24			17 49		18 20							18 47		19 17					
East Midlands Parkway ✈	d	17 02				17 32			17 57	18 05	18 28						18 36	18 55	19 00	19 25					
Beeston	a								18 06									19 01							
Nottingham 8	a	17 14							18 14								18 52	19 07							
	d			17 14				17 35						18 14		18 37						19 19			19 38
Lincoln	a																								
Langley Mill	d			17 30				17 54						18 30		18 54						19 35			
Alfreton	d			17 38				18 02						18 38		19 02						19 43			20 00
Long Eaton	a					17 36					18 31									19 30					
Derby 6	a					17 48				18 17	18 47								19 14	19 45					
	d				17 44	17 50				18 24					18 43				19 18					19 41	
Chesterfield	d			17 51	18 03			18 17		18 45				18 50	19 05	19 13			19 37			19 54		20 02	20 10
Sheffield 7	a			18 15	18 19	18 29		18 34		18 59				19 16	19 20	19 31			19 53			20 15		20 17	20 31
Doncaster 7	a																								
Wakefield Kirkgate 4	a			18 52										19 52								20 52			
Wakefield Westgate 7	a				18 47										19 48									20 46	
Leeds 10	a			19 18	19 04									20 18	20 05							21 16		21 03	
York 8	a				19 32										20 32									21 32	

		EM	EM	EM	EM	EM	NT	EM	EM	XC	EM	EM	EM	XC	NT	EM	EM	EM	XC	EM	EM	EM	EM	EM	EM
		◇1	◇1	◇1	◇1	◇1		◇1	◇1	◇1	◇1	◇1	◇1	◇1		◇1	◇1	◇1	◇1	◇1	◇1	◇1	◇1	◇1	◇1
										F				F					G						
		☕	☕	☕	☕	☕		☕	☕		☕	☕	☕			☕	☕	☕		☕	☕	☕	☕	☕	☕
St Pancras International ⊖	d	17 55	18 00	18 25	18 30			18 55	19 00		19 25	19 30				19 55	20 00	20 25		20 30		21 00	21 30	22 30	23 00
Luton Airport Parkway 7 ✈	d		18 21						19 21								20 23					21 23		22 53	23 27
Luton 10	d				18 52							19 52								20 54			21 54		
Bedford 7	d		18 45		19 15				19 45			20 15					20 48			21 18		21 47	22 17	23 17	23 50
Wellingborough	d		18 58		19 28				19 58			20 28					21 00			21 31		22 00	22 30	23 31	00 04
Kettering 4	a		19 05		19 35				20 05			20 35					21 07			21 38		22 07	22 37	23 37	00 10
	d		19 06		19 36	19 45			20 06			20 36	20 46				21 08			21 39	21 55	22 08	22 38	23 38	00 11
Corby	d					19a55							20a56								22a05				
Oakham	d																								
Melton Mowbray	d																								
Market Harborough	d		19 16		19 46				20 16			20 46					21 18			21 50		22 18	22 48	23 48	00 21
Leicester	a	19 20	19 35	19 48	20 05			20 17	20 35		20 47	21 05				21 17	21 37	21 47		22 11		22 37	23 07	00 07	00 40
	d	19 22	19 37	19 50	20 07			20 20	20 37		20 49	21 07				21 19	21 39	21 49		22 13		22 39	23 09	00 09	00 42
Syston	d																								
Sileby	d																								
Barrow Upon Soar	d																								
Loughborough	d		19 47		20 17				20 47			21 17				21 30	21 49	22 01				22 49	23 19	00 19	00 52
East Midlands Parkway ✈	d	19 40	19 55	20 09	20 25			20 35	20 55		21 05	21 25				21 39	21 57	22 09		22 29		22 57	23 32	00 27	01 00
Beeston	a		20 01						21 02								22 03					23 10		00 40	
Nottingham 8	a	19 52	20 08					20 48	21 12							21 52	22 11					23 18		00 48	
	d						20 13								21 20										
Lincoln	a																								
Langley Mill	d						20 29								21 41										
Alfreton	d						20 37								21 49										
Long Eaton	a				20 28							21 28											23 38		
Derby 6	a			20 21	20 45						21 17	21 40						22 21		22 43			23 49		01 19
	d			20 24						20 44	21 24			21 42					22 46	22 52			23 55		
Chesterfield	d			20 45			20 48			21 01	21 45			22 03	22 08				23 07	23 13			00 14		
Sheffield 7	a			20 59			21 14			21 16	22 00			22 18	22 32				23 22	23 28			00 28		
Doncaster 7	a																								
Wakefield Kirkgate 4	a														23 26										
Wakefield Westgate 7	a			21 27						21 47				22 45						23 55					
Leeds 10	a			21 45						22 04				23 03	00 05				00 34	00 28					
York 8	a																								

A From Penzance to Edinburgh
B From Norwich to Liverpool Lime Street
C From Newquay to Edinburgh. 🛒 to Wakefield Westgate
D From Norwich to Manchester Piccadilly
E From Plymouth to Newcastle
F From Plymouth
G From Penzance

For connections from Gatwick Airport see Table 52

Table 53

Sundays

26 June to 31 July

London - East Midlands - Sheffield

		EM ◇1 🍴	EM ◇1 🍴	EM ◇ A	EM ◇1 🍴	NT	XC ◇1 B ☕	EM ◇1 🍴	EM ◇ A	NT	EM ◇1 🍴	XC ◇1 C ☕	EM ◇1 🍴	EM ◇1 🍴	EM ◇ A	NT	EM ◇1 🍴	XC ◇1 B ☕	EM ◇1 🍴	EM ◇1 🍴	EM ◇ D	XC ◇1 E ☕	NT
St Pancras International ⊖	d	22p00	22p25								09 00		09 30				10 00		10 30				
Luton Airport Parkway 7 ✈	d		22p46								09 29						10 29						
Luton 10	d	22p24											10 04						11 02				
Bedford 7	d	22p42	23p02								09 54		10 24				10 53		11 24				
Wellingborough	d	22p55	23p14								10 08		10 37				11 07		11 37				
Kettering 4	a	23p02	23p21								10 16		10 43				11 14		11 44				
	d	23p03	23p22		09 55						10 17		10 44	10 55			11 15		11 45	11 55			
Corby	d				10a05									11a05						12a05			
Oakham	d																						
Melton Mowbray	d																						
Market Harborough	d	23p14	23p32								10 28		10 54				11 26		11 54				
Leicester	a	23p31	23p46								10 48		11 13				11 47		12 14				
	d	23p32	23p46					10 10			10 50		11 15				11 48		12 16				
Syston	d																						
Sileby	d																						
Barrow Upon Soar	d																						
Loughborough	d	23p44						10 21			11 01		11 25				11 59		12 27				
East Midlands Parkway ✈	d	23p52	00 02					10 29			11 09		11 33				12 08		12 34				
Beeston	a	23p59									11 15												
Nottingham 8 🚊	a	00 08									11 24						12 22						
	d			09 31		10 06			10 41	11 15					11 46	12 19					12 39		13 09
Lincoln	a																						
Langley Mill	d					10 27				11 31						12 35					12 56		13 27
Alfreton	d			09 53		10 35			11 03	11 39					12 08	12 43					13 04		13 35
Long Eaton	a		00 06					10 32					11 36						12 38				
Derby 6	a		00 17					10 46					11 48						12 49				
	d						10 44	10 48				11 44	11 49					12 44	12 50			13 11	
Chesterfield	d			10 08		10 54	11 03	11 09	11 15	11 51		12 03	12 10		12 18	12 54		13 03	13 12		13 17	13 30	13 46
Sheffield 7 🚊	a			10 33		11 15	11 17	11 28	11 35	12 15		12 18	12 29		12 36	13 16		13 17	13 28		13 33	13 43	14 07
Doncaster 7	a							11 56														14 13	
Wakefield Kirkgate 4	a					11 52				12 52						13 52							14 52
Wakefield Westgate 7	a						11 44					12 44						13 44					
Leeds 10	a					12 18	12 02			13 18		13 02				14 18		14 02					15 18
York 8	a						12 32	12 20				13 32						14 31				14 41	

A To Liverpool Lime Street
B From Birmingham New Street to Glasgow Central
C From Birmingham New Street to Edinburgh
D From Norwich to Liverpool Lime Street
E From Birmingham New Street to Newcastle

		EM ◇1 🍴	XC ◇1 A ☕	EM ◇1 🍴	EM ◇1 🍴	EM ◇ B	EM ◇1 🍴	XC ◇1 C ☕	NT	XC ◇1 D ☕	EM ◇ E	EM ◇1 🍴	EM ◇1 🍴	XC ◇1 F ☕	NT	EM ◇1 🍴	XC ◇1 G ☕	EM ◇1 🍴	EM ◇1 🍴	EM ◇ E	EM ◇1 🍴	XC ◇1 F ☕	NT
St Pancras International ⊖	d	11 00		11 30			12 00					12 30				13 00		13 30			14 00		
Luton Airport Parkway 7 ✈	d	11 29		11 59			12 29					12 59				13 29		14 00			14 23		
Luton 10	d	11 32		12 02			12 33					13 03				13 33		14 04					
Bedford 7	d	11 53		12 23			12 54					13 26				13 54		14 23			14 46		
Wellingborough	d	12 06		12 37			13 07					13 40				14 07		14 37			15 00		
Kettering 4	a	12 12		12 44			13 13					13 48				14 13		14 44			15 07		
	d	12 13		12 45	12 55		13 14					13 49	13 55			14 14		14 47	14 55		15 08		
Corby	d				13a05								14a05						15a05				
Oakham	d																						
Melton Mowbray	d																						
Market Harborough	d	12 23		12 55			13 24					14 00				14 24		14 58			15 18		
Leicester	a	12 42		13 16			13 43					14 20				14 43		15 19			15 37		
	d	12 44		13 19			13 45					14 22				14 45		15 21			15 39		
Syston	d																						
Sileby	d																						
Barrow Upon Soar	d																						
Loughborough	d	12 54		13 29			13 55					14 33				14 55		15 32			15 49		
East Midlands Parkway ✈	d	13 02		13 37			14 03					14 41				15 03		15 40			15 57		
Beeston	a	13 07					14 09									15 09					16 03		
Nottingham 8 🚊	a	13 17					14 17									15 18					16 10		
	d					13 38			14 19		14 37				15 12					15 44			16 14
Lincoln	a																						
Langley Mill	d					13 55			14 35		14 54				15 34								16 30
Alfreton	d					14 03			14 43		15 02				15 44					16 06			16 38
Long Eaton	a			13 40								14 45						15 44					
Derby 6	a			13 52								14 59						15 56					
	d		13 44	13 54				14 11		14 44		15 01		15 11			15 44	15 58				16 11	
Chesterfield	d		14 03	14 13		14 18		14 30	14 54	15 03	15 13	15 22			15 53		16 03	16 19		16 23			16 50
Sheffield 7 🚊	a		14 17	14 26		14 36		14 48	15 15	15 17	15 31	15 40		15 47	16 15		16 18	16 33		16 39		16 48	17 15
Doncaster 7	a							15 13						16 15								17 13	
Wakefield Kirkgate 4	a								15 52						16 52								17 52
Wakefield Westgate 7	a		14 44							15 44							16 44						
Leeds 10	a		15 02						16 18	16 02					17 18		17 02						18 18
York 8	a		15 31					15 44		16 32				16 44			17 32					17 42	

A From Bristol Temple Meads to Aberdeen
B From Norwich to Liverpool Lime Street
C From Birmingham New Street to Newcastle
D From Plymouth to Glasgow Central
E To Liverpool Lime Street
F From Reading to Newcastle
G From Plymouth to Edinburgh
H From Penzance to Glasgow Central
I From Reading to Edinburgh
J From Newquay to Edinburgh. ☕ to Wakefield Westgate
K From Norwich to Manchester Piccadilly

For connections from Gatwick Airport see Table 52

Table 53

Sundays

26 June to 31 July

London - East Midlands - Sheffield

		XC		EM	EM	EM	EM	XC	NT	XC	EM	EM		EM	EM	XC	EM	EM	EM	NT	XC	EM		EM	EM
		◇1		◇1	◇1	◇	◇1	◇1		◇1	◇1	◇1		◇	◇1	◇1	◇1	◇1	◇1		◇1	◇		◇1	◇1
		H				B		F		G				B		I					J	K			
		🛒		🍴	🍴		🍴	🛒		🛒	🍴	🍴			🍴	🛒	🍴	🍴	🍴		🛒			🍴	🍴
St Pancras International ⊖	d			14 30			15 00				15 30				16 00		16 25	16 30						16 55	17 00
Luton Airport Parkway 7 ✈	d						15 23								16 23										17 21
Luton 10	d			14 54							15 54							16 52							
Bedford 7	d			15 17			15 47				16 17				16 47			17 15							17 45
Wellingborough	d			15 30			16 01				16 31				17 00			17 28							17 58
Kettering 4	a			15 37			16 08				16 38				17 07			17 35							18 05
	d			15 38	15 45		16 09				16 39	16 45			17 08			17 36	17 50						18 06
Corby	d				15a55							16a55							18a00						
Oakham	d																								
Melton Mowbray	d																								
Market Harborough	d			15 49			16 20				16 50				17 18			17 46							18 16
Leicester	a			16 10			16 41				17 11				17 37		17 47	18 08						18 21	18 35
	d			16 12			16 43				17 12				17 39		17 49	18 10						18 22	18 37
Syston	d																								
Sileby	d																								
Barrow Upon Soar	d																								
Loughborough	d			16 23			16 54				17 24				17 49			18 20							18 47
East Midlands Parkway ✈	d			16 31			17 02				17 32				17 57		18 05	18 28						18 36	18 55
Beeston	a														18 06										19 01
Nottingham 8 🚊	a						17 14								18 14									18 52	19 07
	d					16 41			17 14					17 35						18 14		18 37			
Lincoln	a																								
Langley Mill	d					17 00			17 30					17 54						18 30		18 54			
Alfreton	d					17 08			17 38					18 02						18 38		19 02			
Long Eaton	a			16 35							17 36							18 31							
Derby 6	a			16 47							17 48						18 17	18 47							
	d	16 44		16 56				17 11		17 43	17 50					18 09	18 24				18 43				
Chesterfield	d	17 03		17 17		17 22			17 51	18 04				18 17			18 45			18 50	19 05	19 13			
Sheffield 7 🚊	a	17 17		17 32		17 40		17 48	18 15	18 19	18 29			18 34		18 46	18 59			19 16	19 20	19 31			
Doncaster 7	a							18 13								19 15									
Wakefield Kirkgate 4	a								18 52											19 52					
Wakefield Westgate 7	a	17 46		18 06				18 33		18 47											19 48				
Leeds 10	a	18 02		18 24				18 51	19 18	19 04										20 18	20 05				
York 8	a	18 32						19 21		19 32						19 44					20 32				

A From Bristol Temple Meads to Aberdeen
B From Norwich to Liverpool Lime Street
C From Birmingham New Street to Newcastle
D From Plymouth to Glasgow Central
E To Liverpool Lime Street
F From Reading to Newcastle
G From Plymouth to Edinburgh
H From Penzance to Glasgow Central
I From Reading to Edinburgh
J From Newquay to Edinburgh.
🛒 to Wakefield Westgate
K From Norwich to Manchester Piccadilly

		XC	EM	EM	EM	NT	XC	EM		EM	EM	XC	EM	EM	EM	NT	EM	EM		XC	EM	EM	EM	XC	NT
		◇1	◇1	◇1	◇1		◇1	◇		◇1	◇1	◇1	◇1	◇1	◇1		◇1	◇1		◇1	◇1	◇1	◇1	◇1	
		A					B	C				A								B				B	
		🛒	🍴	🍴	🍴		🛒			🍴	🍴		🍴	🍴	🍴		🍴	🍴			🍴	🍴	🍴		
St Pancras International ⊖	d		17 25	17 30						17 55	18 00		18 25	18 30			18 55	19 00			19 25	19 30			
Luton Airport Parkway 7 ✈	d										18 21							19 21							
Luton 10	d			17 52										18 52								19 52			
Bedford 7	d			18 15							18 45			19 15				19 45				20 15			
Wellingborough	d			18 28							18 58			19 28				19 58				20 28			
Kettering 4	a			18 35							19 05			19 35				20 05				20 35			
	d			18 36	18 50						19 06			19 36	19 45			20 06				20 36	20 46		
Corby	d				19a00										19a55								20a56		
Oakham	d																								
Melton Mowbray	d																								
Market Harborough	d			18 46							19 16			19 46				20 16				20 46			
Leicester	a		18 44	19 05						19 19	19 35		19 48	20 05			20 17	20 35			20 47	21 05			
	d		18 46	19 07						19 20	19 37		19 50	20 07			20 20	20 37			20 49	21 07			
Syston	d																								
Sileby	d																								
Barrow Upon Soar	d																								
Loughborough	d			19 17							19 47			20 17				20 47				21 17			
East Midlands Parkway ✈	d		19 00	19 25						19 38	19 55		20 08	20 25			20 35	20 55			21 05	21 25			
Beeston	a										20 01							21 02							
Nottingham 8 🚊	a									19 50	20 08						20 48	21 12							
	d					19 19		19 38								20 13									21 20
Lincoln	a																								
Langley Mill	d					19 35										20 29									21 41
Alfreton	d					19 43		20 00								20 37									21 49
Long Eaton	a			19 30										20 28								21 28			
Derby 6	a		19 14	19 45									20 20	20 45							21 17	21 40			
	d	19 05	19 18				19 41					20 05	20 24							20 44	21 24			21 43	
Chesterfield	d		19 37			19 54	20 02	20 10					20 45			20 48				21 03	21 45			22 04	22 08
Sheffield 7 🚊	a	19 39	19 53			20 15	20 17	20 31				20 38	20 59			21 14				21 16	22 00			22 19	22 32
Doncaster 7	a	20 16										21 19													
Wakefield Kirkgate 4	a					20 52																			23 26
Wakefield Westgate 7	a						20 46						21 27							21 47				22 46	
Leeds 10	a					21 16	21 03						21 45							22 04				23 03	00 05
York 8	a	20 45					21 32					21 44													

A From Reading to Newcastle
B From Plymouth
C From Norwich to Manchester Piccadilly

For connections from Gatwick Airport see Table 52

Table 53

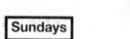

Sundays
26 June to 31 July

London - East Midlands - Sheffield

		EM	EM	EM	XC	EM	EM	EM	EM	EM	EM
		◇1	◇1	◇1	◇1	◇1	◇1	◇1	◇1	◇1	◇1
					B						
		☕	☕	☕		☕	☕	☕	☕	☕	☕
St Pancras International ⊖	d	19 55	20 00	20 25		20 30		21 00	21 30	22 30	23 00
Luton Airport Parkway 7 ✈	d		20 23					21 23		22 53	23 27
Luton 10	d					20 54			21 54		
Bedford 7	d		20 48			21 18		21 47	22 17	23 19	23 54
Wellingborough	d		21 00			21 31		22 00	22 30	23 32	00 08
Kettering 4	a		21 07			21 38		22 07	22 37	23 38	00 14
	d		21 08			21 39	21 55	22 08	22 38	23 39	00 15
Corby	d						22a05				
Oakham	d										
Melton Mowbray	d										
Market Harborough	d		21 18			21 50		22 18	22 48	23 49	00 25
Leicester	a	21 17	21 37	21 47		22 11		22 37	23 07	00 08	00 44
	d	21 19	21 39	21 49		22 13		22 39	23 09	00 10	00 46
Syston	d										
Sileby	d										
Barrow Upon Soar	d										
Loughborough	d	21 30	21 49	22 01				22 49	23 19	00 20	00 56
East Midlands Parkway ✈	d	21 39	21 57	22 09		22 29		22 57	23 32	00 28	01 04
Beeston	a		22 03					23 10		00 41	
Nottingham 8	a	21 52	22 11					23 18		00 49	
	d										
Lincoln	a										
Langley Mill	d										
Alfreton	d										
Long Eaton	a								23 38		
Derby 6	a			22 21		22 43			23 49		01 23
	d				22 46	22 52			23 55		
Chesterfield	d				23 07	23 13			00 14		
Sheffield 7	a				23 22	23 28			00 28		
Doncaster 7	a										
Wakefield Kirkgate 4	a										
Wakefield Westgate 7	a					23 55					
Leeds 10	a				00 34	00 28					
York 8	a										

A From Reading to Newcastle
B From Plymouth
C From Norwich to Manchester Piccadilly

Sundays
7 August to 11 September

		EM	EM	XC	EM	EM	NT	XC	EM	EM	NT	EM	XC	EM	EM	EM	NT	EM	XC	EM	EM	EM	XC
		◇1	◇1	◇1	◇	◇1		◇1	◇	◇1		◇1	◇1	◇	◇1	◇1		◇1	◇1	◇	◇1	◇1	◇1
				A	B			C	B				D	B					E	F			G
		☕	☕	🍴		☕		🍴		☕		☕	🍴		☕	☕		☕	🍴		☕	☕	🍴
St Pancras International ⊖	d	22p00	22p25									09 00			09 30			10 00			10 30		
Luton Airport Parkway 7 ✈	d		22p47									09 28						10 31					
Luton 10	d	22p25													10 02						11 02		
Bedford 7	d	22p42	23p03									09 55			10 25			10 56			11 27		
Wellingborough	d	22p55	23p15									10 09			10 38			11 10			11 39		
Kettering 4	a	23p02	23p22									10 16			10 45			11 17			11 46		
	d	23p03	23p23			09 55						10 17			10 46	10 55		11 18			11 46	11 55	
Corby	d					10a05										11a05						12a05	
Oakham	d																						
Melton Mowbray	d																						
Market Harborough	d	23p14	23p33									10 28			10 56			11 29			11 56		
Leicester	a	23p31	23p47									10 48			11 15			11 50			12 16		
	d	23p32	23p47							10 21		10 50			11 20			11 51			12 21		
Syston	d																						
Sileby	d																						
Barrow Upon Soar	d																						
Loughborough	d																						
East Midlands Parkway ✈	d	23p53	00 09							10 42		11 10			11 40			12 12			12 41		
Beeston	a	00 01										11 17											
Nottingham 8	a	00 11										11 25						12 23					
	d				09 31		10 06		10 41		11 15			11 46			12 19			12 39			
Lincoln	a																						
Langley Mill	d						10 27				11 31						12 35			12 56			
Alfreton	d				09 53		10 35		11 03		11 39			12 08			12 43			13 04			
Long Eaton	a		00 13							10 47					11 45						12 45		
Derby 6	a		00 24							10 57					11 56						12 56		
	d			09 44				10 44		11 05			11 44		12 05				12 44		13 05		13 11
Chesterfield	d			10 03	10 08		10 54	11 03	11 15	11 26	11 51		12 03	12 18	12 25		12 54		13 03	13 17	13 25		13 30
Sheffield 7	a			10 16	10 33		11 15	11 17	11 35	11 42	12 15		12 18	12 36	12 40		13 16		13 17	13 33	13 42		13 43
Doncaster 7	a									12 06													14 13
Wakefield Kirkgate 4	a						11 52				12 52						13 52						
Wakefield Westgate 7	a			10 44				11 44					12 44						13 44				
Leeds 10	a			11 02			12 18	12 01			13 18		13 02				14 18		14 02				
York 8	a			11 35				12 32		12 29			13 32						14 31				14 41

A From Birmingham New Street to Edinburgh
B To Liverpool Lime Street
C From Birmingham New Street to Glasgow Central
D From Bristol Temple Meads to Edinburgh
E From Bristol Temple Meads to Glasgow Central
F From Norwich to Liverpool Lime Street
G From Birmingham New Street to Newcastle
H From Plymouth to Aberdeen
I From Plymouth to Glasgow Central
J From Penzance to Edinburgh
K From Reading to Newcastle

For connections from Gatwick Airport see Table 52

Table 53

Sundays

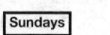

7 August to 11 September

London - East Midlands - Sheffield

		NT	EM	XC	EM	EM		EM	XC	NT	EM	XC	EM	EM	EM	XC		NT	EM	XC	EM	EM	EM	EM	XC
			◇1 ☕	◇1 H 🛒	◇ F	◇1 ☕		◇1 ☕	◇1 G 🛒		◇1 ☕	◇1 I 🛒	◇ B	◇1 ☕	◇1 ☕	◇1 G 🛒			◇1 ☕	◇1 J 🛒	◇1 ☕	◇1 ☕	◇ B	◇1 ☕	◇1 K 🛒
St Pancras International ⊖	d		11 00			11 30					12 00			12 30					13 00		13 30			14 00	
Luton Airport Parkway 7 ✈	d		11 31			12 02					12 31			13 03					13 33		14 00			14 29	
Luton 10	d		11 35			12 06					12 35			13 06					13 37		14 04				
Bedford 7	d		11 55			12 28					12 56			13 28					13 57		14 19			14 47	
Wellingborough	d		12 08			12 40					13 10			13 42					14 11		14 33			15 00	
Kettering 4	a		12 15			12 47					13 16			13 50					14 17		14 40			15 07	
	d		12 16			12 48		12 55			13 17			13 51	13 55				14 18		14 44	14 55		15 08	
Corby	d							13a05							14a05							15a05			
Oakham	d																								
Melton Mowbray	d																								
Market Harborough	d		12 26			12 58					13 27			14 02					14 28		14 55			15 18	
Leicester	a		12 45			13 17					13 46			14 22					14 47		15 16			15 37	
	d		12 46			13 22					13 48			14 24					14 49		15 18			15 39	
Syston	d																								
Sileby	d																								
Barrow Upon Soar	d																								
Loughborough	d										14 06			14 35					14 59		15 29			15 49	
East Midlands Parkway ✈	d		13 06			13 43					14 13			14 43					15 07		15 37			15 57	
Beeston	a		13 12								14 19								15 12					16 05	
Nottingham 8 ⛴	a		13 19								14 26								15 19					16 12	
	d	13 09			13 38					14 19			14 37					15 12					15 44		
Lincoln	a																								
Langley Mill	d	13 27			13 55					14 35			14 54					15 34							
Alfreton	d	13 35			14 03					14 43			15 02					15 44					16 06		
Long Eaton	a					13 47								14 47							15 41				
Derby 6	a					13 59								14 59							15 53				
	d			13 44		14 04			14 11			14 44		15 01		15 11				15 44	15 58				16 11
Chesterfield	d	13 46		14 03	14 18	14 24			14 30	14 54		15 03	15 13	15 22				15 53		16 03	16 19		16 23		
Sheffield 7 ⛴	a	14 07		14 17	14 36	14 44			14 48	15 15		15 17	15 31	15 40		15 47		16 15		16 18	16 33		16 39		16 48
Doncaster 7	a								15 13							16 15									17 13
Wakefield Kirkgate 4	a	14 52								15 52								16 52							
Wakefield Westgate 7	a			14 44								15 44								16 44					
Leeds 10	a	15 18		15 02						16 18		16 02						17 18		17 02					
York 8	a			15 31					15 44			16 32				16 44				17 31					17 42

A From Birmingham New Street to Edinburgh
B To Liverpool Lime Street
C From Birmingham New Street to Glasgow Central
D From Bristol Temple Meads to Edinburgh
E From Bristol Temple Meads to Glasgow Central
F From Norwich to Liverpool Lime Street
G From Birmingham New Street to Newcastle
H From Plymouth to Aberdeen
I From Plymouth to Glasgow Central
J From Penzance to Edinburgh
K From Reading to Newcastle

		NT		XC	EM	EM	EM	EM	XC	NT	XC	EM		EM	EM	EM	XC	EM	EM	EM	NT	XC		EM	EM
				◇1 A 🛒	◇1 ☕	◇1 ☕	◇ B	◇1 ☕	◇1 C 🛒		◇1 D 🛒	◇1 ☕		◇1 ☕	◇ B	◇1 ☕	◇1 E 🛒	◇1 ☕	◇1 ☕	◇1 ☕		◇1 F 🛒		◇ G	◇1 ☕
St Pancras International ⊖	d				14 30			15 00				15 30				16 00		16 25	16 30						16 55
Luton Airport Parkway 7 ✈	d							15 29								16 29									
Luton 10	d				15 01							16 01							16 52						
Bedford 7	d				15 17			15 47				16 17				16 47			17 15						
Wellingborough	d				15 31			16 01				16 31				17 00			17 28						
Kettering 4	a				15 38			16 08				16 38				17 07			17 35						
	d				15 39	15 45		16 09				16 39		16 45		17 08			17 36	17 50					
Corby	d					15a55								16a55						18a00					
Oakham	d																								
Melton Mowbray	d																								
Market Harborough	d				15 53			16 20				16 50				17 18			17 46						
Leicester	a				16 17			16 41				17 11				17 37		17 47	18 08						18 21
	d				16 19			16 43				17 12				17 39		17 49	18 10						18 22
Syston	d																								
Sileby	d																								
Barrow Upon Soar	d																								
Loughborough	d				16 30			16 54				17 24				17 49			18 20						
East Midlands Parkway ✈	d				16 38			17 02				17 32				17 57		18 05	18 28						18 36
Beeston	a															18 06									
Nottingham 8 ⛴	a							17 14								18 14									18 52
	d	16 14					16 41			17 14					17 35						18 14			18 37	
Lincoln	a																								
Langley Mill	d	16 30					17 00			17 30					17 54						18 30			18 54	
Alfreton	d	16 38					17 08			17 38					18 02						18 38			19 02	
Long Eaton	a				16 42							17 36							18 31						
Derby 6	a				16 55							17 48						18 17	18 47						
	d			16 44	16 56				17 11		17 43	17 50					18 09	18 24				18 43			
Chesterfield	d	16 50		17 03	17 17		17 22			17 51	18 04				18 17			18 45			18 50	19 05		19 13	
Sheffield 7 ⛴	a	17 15		17 17	17 32		17 40		17 48	18 15	18 19	18 29			18 34		18 46	18 59			19 16	19 20		19 31	
Doncaster 7	a								18 13								19 15								
Wakefield Kirkgate 4	a	17 52								18 52											19 52				
Wakefield Westgate 7	a			17 46	18 06				18 33		18 47											19 48			
Leeds 10	a	18 18		18 02	18 24				18 51	19 18	19 04										20 18	20 05			
York 8	a			18 32					19 21		19 32						19 44					20 32			

A From Plymouth to Glasgow Central
B From Norwich to Liverpool Lime Street
C From Reading to Newcastle
D From Newquay to Edinburgh
E From Reading to Edinburgh
F From Plymouth to Edinburgh. 🛒 to Wakefield Westgate
G From Norwich to Manchester Piccadilly
H From Plymouth
I From Penzance

For connections from Gatwick Airport see Table 52

Table 53

Sundays

7 August to 11 September

London - East Midlands - Sheffield

		EM	XC	EM	EM	EM	NT	XC		EM	EM	EM	XC	EM	EM	EM	NT	EM		EM	XC	EM	EM	EM	XC
		◇1	◇1	◇1	◇1	◇1		◇1		◇	◇1	◇1	◇1	◇1	◇1	◇1		◇1		◇1	◇1	◇1	◇1	◇1	◇1
			C					H		G			C								H				I
		ꟷ	⚲	ꟷ	ꟷ	ꟷ		⚲			ꟷ	ꟷ		ꟷ	ꟷ	ꟷ		ꟷ		ꟷ		ꟷ	ꟷ	ꟷ	
St Pancras International ⊖	d	17 00		17 25	17 30						17 55	18 00		18 25	18 30			18 55		19 00		19 25	19 30		
Luton Airport Parkway 7 ✈	d	17 21										18 21								19 21					
Luton 10	d				17 52										18 52								19 52		
Bedford 7	d	17 45			18 15							18 45			19 15					19 45			20 15		
Wellingborough	d	17 58			18 28							18 58			19 28					19 58			20 28		
Kettering 4	a	18 05			18 35							19 05			19 35					20 05			20 35		
	d	18 06			18 36	18 50						19 06			19 36	19 45				20 06			20 36	20 46	
Corby	d					19a00										19a55								20a56	
Oakham	d																								
Melton Mowbray	d																								
Market Harborough	d	18 16			18 46							19 16			19 46					20 16			20 46		
Leicester	a	18 35		18 44	19 05						19 20	19 35		19 47	20 05			20 17		20 35		20 47	21 05		
	d	18 37		18 46	19 07						19 21	19 37		19 49	20 07			20 20		20 37		20 49	21 07		
Syston	d																								
Sileby	d																								
Barrow Upon Soar	d																								
Loughborough	d	18 47			19 17							19 47			20 17					20 47			21 17		
East Midlands Parkway ✈	d	18 55		19 00	19 25						19 39	19 55		20 08	20 25			20 35		20 55		21 05	21 25		
Beeston	a	19 01										20 01								21 02					
Nottingham 8 ⇌	a	19 07									19 51	20 08						20 48		21 12					
	d						19 19			19 38							20 13								
Lincoln	a																								
Langley Mill	d						19 35										20 29								
Alfreton	d						19 43			20 00							20 37								
Long Eaton	a				19 30										20 28								21 28		
Derby 6	a			19 14	19 45									20 20	20 45							21 17	21 40		
	d		19 05	19 18				19 41					20 05	20 24							20 44	21 24			21 44
Chesterfield	d			19 37			19 54	20 02		20 10				20 45			20 48				21 03	21 45			22 03
Sheffield 7 ⇌	a		19 39	19 53			20 15	20 17		20 31			20 38	20 59			21 14				21 16	22 00			22 18
Doncaster 7	a		20 16										21 19												
Wakefield Kirkgate 4	a						20 52																		
Wakefield Westgate 7	a							20 46						21 27							21 47				22 43
Leeds 10	a						21 16	21 03						21 45							22 04				23 01
York 8	a		20 45					21 32					21 44												

A From Plymouth to Glasgow Central
B From Norwich to Liverpool Lime Street
C From Reading to Newcastle
D From Newquay to Edinburgh
E From Reading to Edinburgh
F From Plymouth to Edinburgh. ⚲ to Wakefield Westgate
G From Norwich to Manchester Piccadilly
H From Plymouth
I From Penzance

		NT	EM	EM		EM	XC	EM	EM	EM	EM	EM	EM
			◇1	◇1		◇1	◇1	◇1	◇1	◇1	◇1	◇1	◇1
							A						
			ꟷ	ꟷ		ꟷ		ꟷ	ꟷ	ꟷ	ꟷ	ꟷ	ꟷ
St Pancras International ⊖	d		19 55	20 00		20 25		20 30		21 00	21 30	22 30	23 00
Luton Airport Parkway 7 ✈	d			20 23						21 23		22 53	23 27
Luton 10	d							20 54			21 54		
Bedford 7	d			20 48				21 18		21 47	22 17	23 17	23 50
Wellingborough	d			21 00				21 31		22 00	22 30	23 31	00 04
Kettering 4	a			21 07				21 38		22 07	22 37	23 37	00 10
	d			21 08				21 39	21 55	22 08	22 38	23 38	00 11
Corby	d								22a05				
Oakham	d												
Melton Mowbray	d												
Market Harborough	d			21 18				21 50		22 18	22 48	23 48	00 21
Leicester	a		21 17	21 37		21 47		22 11		22 37	23 07	00 07	00 40
	d		21 19	21 39		21 49		22 13		22 39	23 09	00 09	00 42
Syston	d												
Sileby	d												
Barrow Upon Soar	d												
Loughborough	d		21 30	21 49		22 01				22 49	23 19	00 19	00 52
East Midlands Parkway ✈	d		21 39	21 57		22 09		22 29		22 57	23 32	00 27	01 00
Beeston	a			22 03						23 10		00 40	
Nottingham 8 ⇌	a		21 52	22 11						23 18		00 48	
	d	21 20											
Lincoln	a												
Langley Mill	d	21 41											
Alfreton	d	21 49											
Long Eaton	a										23 38		
Derby 6	a					22 21		22 43			23 49		01 19
	d						22 46	22 52			23 55		
Chesterfield	d	22 08					23 07	23 13			00 14		
Sheffield 7 ⇌	a	22 32					23 22	23 28			00 28		
Doncaster 7	a												
Wakefield Kirkgate 4	a	23 26											
Wakefield Westgate 7	a							23 55					
Leeds 10	a	00 05					00 34	00 28					
York 8	a												

A From Plymouth
B From Birmingham New Street to Edinburgh
C To Liverpool Lime Street
D From Birmingham New Street to Glasgow Central
E From Bristol Parkway to Glasgow Central
F From Birmingham New Street to Newcastle

For connections from Gatwick Airport see Table 52

Table 53

Sundays

18 September to 23 October

London - East Midlands - Sheffield

		EM ◇1 P	EM ◇1 P	XC ◇1 B T	EM ◇ C	EM ◇1 P	NT	XC ◇1 D T	EM ◇ C	EM ◇1 P		NT	EM ◇1 P	EM ◇ C	EM ◇1 P	EM ◇1 P	NT	EM ◇1 P	XC ◇1 E T	EM ◇ C		EM ◇1 P	EM ◇1 P	XC ◇1 F T	NT
St Pancras International ⊖	d	22p00	22p25										09 00		09 30			10 00				10 30			
Luton Airport Parkway 7 ✈	d		22p47										09 28					10 31							
Luton 10	d	22p25													10 02							11 02			
Bedford 7	d	22p42	23p03										09 55		10 25			10 56				11 27			
Wellingborough	d	22p55	23p15										10 09		10 38			11 09				11 39			
Kettering 4	a	23p02	23p22										10 17		10 45			11 16				11 46			
	d	23p03	23p23			09 55							10 18		10 46	10 55		11 17				11 46	11 55		
Corby	d					10a05										11a05							12a05		
Oakham	d																								
Melton Mowbray	d																								
Market Harborough	d	23p14	23p33										10 29		10 56			11 28				11 56			
Leicester	a	23p31	23p47										10 48		11 15			11 49				12 16			
	d	23p32	23p47							10 21			10 50		11 20			11 50				12 19			
Syston	d																								
Sileby	d																								
Barrow Upon Soar	d																								
Loughborough	d																								
East Midlands Parkway ✈	d	23p53	00 09							10 42			11 10		11 40			12 11				12 43			
Beeston	a	00 02											11 18												
Nottingham 8 🚌	a	00 11											11 26					12 23							
	d				09 31		10 06		10 41			11 15		11 46			12 19			12 39					13 09
Lincoln	a																								
Langley Mill	d						10 27					11 31					12 35			12 56					13 27
Alfreton	d				09 53		10 35		11 03			11 39		12 08			12 43			13 04					13 35
Long Eaton	a		00 13							10 47					11 45							12 47			
Derby 6	a		00 24							10 57					11 56							12 58			
	d			09 44				10 44		11 05					12 05				12 44			13 05		13 11	
Chesterfield	d			10 03	10 08		10 54	11 03	11 15	11 26		11 51		12 18	12 25		12 54		13 04	13 17		13 25		13 30	13 46
Sheffield 7 🚌	a			10 16	10 33		11 15	11 17	11 35	11 42		12 15		12 36	12 40		13 16		13 17	13 33		13 42		13 43	14 07
Doncaster 7	a									12 06														14 13	
Wakefield Kirkgate 4	a						11 52					12 52					13 52								14 52
Wakefield Westgate 7	a			10 44				11 44											13 44						
Leeds 10	a			11 02			12 18	12 01				13 18					14 18		14 02						15 18
York 8	a			11 35				12 32		12 29									14 31					14 41	

A From Plymouth
B From Birmingham New Street to Edinburgh
C To Liverpool Lime Street
D From Birmingham New Street to Glasgow Central
E From Bristol Parkway to Glasgow Central
F From Birmingham New Street to Newcastle

		EM ◇1 P	XC ◇1 A T	EM ◇ B	EM ◇1 P	EM ◇1 P		XC ◇1 C T	NT	EM ◇1 P	XC ◇1 D T	EM ◇ E	EM ◇1 P	EM ◇1 P	XC ◇1 C T	NT		EM ◇1 P	XC ◇1 F T	EM ◇1 P	EM ◇1 P	EM ◇ E	EM ◇1 P	NT	XC ◇1 D T
St Pancras International ⊖	d	11 00			11 30					12 00			12 30					13 00		13 30			14 00		
Luton Airport Parkway 7 ✈	d	11 31			12 03					12 31			13 03					13 32		14 00			14 29		
Luton 10	d	11 35			12 07					12 35			13 06					13 36		14 04					
Bedford 7	d	11 55			12 29					12 56			13 28					13 59		14 19			14 47		
Wellingborough	d	12 08			12 41					13 10			13 42					14 13		14 33			15 00		
Kettering 4	a	12 15			12 48					13 16			13 50					14 19		14 40			15 07		
	d	12 16			12 49	12 55				13 17			13 51	13 55				14 20		14 43	14 55		15 08		
Corby	d					13a05								14a05							15a05				
Oakham	d																								
Melton Mowbray	d																								
Market Harborough	d	12 26			12 59					13 27			14 02					14 30		14 54			15 18		
Leicester	a	12 45			13 18					13 46			14 22					14 49		15 15			15 37		
	d	12 46			13 23					13 48			14 24					14 51		15 17			15 39		
Syston	d																								
Sileby	d																								
Barrow Upon Soar	d																								
Loughborough	d									14 06			14 35					15 01		15 28			15 49		
East Midlands Parkway ✈	d	13 06			13 43					14 13			14 43					15 09		15 36			15 57		
Beeston	a	13 12								14 19								15 14					16 05		
Nottingham 8 🚌	a	13 22								14 26								15 21					16 12		
	d			13 38					14 19			14 37				15 12						15 44		16 14	
Lincoln	a																								
Langley Mill	d			13 55					14 35			14 54				15 34								16 30	
Alfreton	d			14 03					14 43			15 02				15 44						16 06		16 38	
Long Eaton	a				13 47								14 47							15 40					
Derby 6	a				13 59								14 59							15 52					
	d		13 44		14 04			14 11			14 44		15 01		15 11				15 44	15 57					16 44
Chesterfield	d		14 03	14 18	14 24			14 30	14 54		15 03	15 13	15 22			15 53			16 03	16 18		16 23		16 50	17 04
Sheffield 7 🚌	a		14 17	14 36	14 44			14 48	15 15		15 17	15 31	15 40		15 47	16 15			16 18	16 33		16 39		17 15	17 17
Doncaster 7	a							15 13							16 15										
Wakefield Kirkgate 4	a								15 52							16 52								17 52	
Wakefield Westgate 7	a		14 44								15 44								16 44						17 46
Leeds 10	a		15 02						16 18		16 02					17 18			17 02					18 18	18 02
York 8	a		15 31					15 44			16 32				16 44				17 32						18 32

A From Bristol Parkway to Aberdeen
B From Norwich to Liverpool Lime Street
C From Birmingham New Street to Newcastle
D From Bristol Parkway to Glasgow Central
E To Liverpool Lime Street
F From Bristol Parkway to Edinburgh
G From Reading to Newcastle
H From Reading to Edinburgh
I From Bristol Parkway to Edinburgh. T to Wakefield Westgate
J From Norwich to Manchester Piccadilly

For connections from Gatwick Airport see Table 52

Table 53

Sundays

18 September to 23 October

London - East Midlands - Sheffield

		EM ◇1 ☕		EM ◇1 ☕	EM ◇ B	EM ◇1 ☕	XC ◇1 G 🛒	NT	XC ◇1 F 🛒	EM ◇1 ☕	EM ◇1 ☕	EM ◇ B		EM ◇1 ☕	XC ◇1 H 🛒	EM ◇1 ☕	EM ◇1 ☕	EM ◇1 ☕	NT	XC ◇1 I 🛒	EM ◇ J	EM ◇1 ☕		EM ◇1 ☕	XC ◇1 G 🛒
St Pancras International ⊖	d	14 30				15 00				15 30				16 00		16 25	16 30					16 55		17 00	
Luton Airport Parkway 7 ✈	d					15 29								16 29										17 21	
Luton 10	d	15 01								16 01							16 52								
Bedford 7	d	15 17				15 47				16 17				16 47			17 15							17 45	
Wellingborough	d	15 31				16 01				16 31				17 00			17 28							17 58	
Kettering 4	a	15 38				16 08				16 38				17 07			17 35							18 05	
	d	15 39		15 45		16 09				16 39	16 45			17 08			17 36	17 50						18 06	
Corby	d			15a55							16a55							18a00							
Oakham	d																								
Melton Mowbray	d																								
Market Harborough	d	15 53				16 20				16 50				17 18			17 46							18 16	
Leicester	a	16 17				16 41				17 11				17 37		17 47	18 08					18 21		18 35	
	d	16 19				16 43				17 12				17 39		17 49	18 10					18 22		18 37	
Syston	d																								
Sileby	d																								
Barrow Upon Soar	d																								
Loughborough	d	16 30				16 54				17 24				17 49			18 20							18 47	
East Midlands Parkway ✈	d	16 38				17 02				17 32				17 57		18 05	18 28					18 36		18 55	
Beeston	a													18 06										19 01	
Nottingham 8	a					17 14								18 14								18 52		19 07	
	d				16 41			17 14				17 35							18 14		18 37				
Lincoln	a																								
Langley Mill	d				17 00			17 30				17 54							18 30		18 54				
Alfreton	d				17 08			17 38				18 02							18 38		19 02				
Long Eaton	a	16 42								17 36							18 31								
Derby 6	a	16 55								17 48						18 17	18 47								
	d	16 56					17 11		17 43	17 50					18 09	18 24				18 43					19 05
Chesterfield	d	17 17			17 22			17 51	18 04			18 17				18 45			18 50	19 05	19 13				
Sheffield 7	a	17 32			17 40		17 48	18 15	18 19	18 29		18 34			18 46	18 59			19 16	19 20	19 31				19 39
Doncaster 7	a						18 13								19 15										20 16
Wakefield Kirkgate 4	a							18 52											19 52						
Wakefield Westgate 7	a	18 06					18 33		18 47											19 48					
Leeds 10	a	18 24					18 51	19 18	19 04										20 18	20 05					
York 8	a						19 21		19 32						19 44					20 32					20 45

A From Bristol Parkway to Aberdeen
B From Norwich to Liverpool Lime Street
C From Birmingham New Street to Newcastle
D From Bristol Parkway to Glasgow Central
E To Liverpool Lime Street
F From Bristol Parkway to Edinburgh
G From Reading to Newcastle
H From Reading to Edinburgh
I From Bristol Parkway to Edinburgh. 🛒 to Wakefield Westgate
J From Norwich to Manchester Piccadilly

		EM ◇1 ☕	EM ◇1 ☕	EM ◇1 ☕	NT	XC ◇1 A 🛒	EM ◇ B	EM ◇1 ☕		EM ◇1 ☕	XC ◇1 C	EM ◇1 ☕	EM ◇1 ☕	EM ◇1 ☕	NT	EM ◇1 ☕	EM ◇1 ☕	XC ◇1 A		EM ◇1 ☕	EM ◇1 ☕	EM ◇1 ☕	XC ◇1 A	NT	EM ◇1 ☕
St Pancras International ⊖	d	17 25	17 30					17 55		18 00		18 25	18 30			18 55	19 00			19 25	19 30				19 55
Luton Airport Parkway 7 ✈	d									18 21							19 21								
Luton 10	d		17 52										18 52								19 52				
Bedford 7	d		18 15							18 45			19 15				19 45				20 15				
Wellingborough	d		18 28							18 58			19 28				19 58				20 28				
Kettering 4	a		18 35							19 05			19 35				20 05				20 35				
	d		18 36	18 50						19 06			19 36	19 45			20 06				20 36	20 46			
Corby	d			19a00										19a55								20a56			
Oakham	d																								
Melton Mowbray	d																								
Market Harborough	d		18 46							19 16			19 46				20 16				20 46				
Leicester	a	18 44	19 05					19 20		19 35		19 47	20 05			20 17	20 35			20 47	21 05				21 17
	d	18 46	19 07					19 21		19 37		19 49	20 07			20 20	20 37			20 49	21 07				21 19
Syston	d																								
Sileby	d																								
Barrow Upon Soar	d																								
Loughborough	d		19 17							19 47			20 17				20 47				21 17				21 30
East Midlands Parkway ✈	d	19 00	19 25					19 39		19 55		20 08	20 25			20 35	20 55			21 05	21 25				21 39
Beeston	a									20 01							21 02								
Nottingham 8	a							19 51		20 08						20 48	21 12								21 52
	d				19 19		19 38								20 13									21 20	
Lincoln	a																								
Langley Mill	d				19 35										20 29									21 41	
Alfreton	d				19 43		20 00								20 37									21 49	
Long Eaton	a		19 30										20 28								21 28				
Derby 6	a	19 14	19 45									20 20	20 45							21 17	21 40				
	d	19 18				19 41					20 05	20 24						20 44		21 24			21 44		
Chesterfield	d	19 37			19 54	20 03	20 10					20 45			20 48			21 04		21 45			22 03	22 08	
Sheffield 7	a	19 53			20 15	20 18	20 31				20 38	20 59			21 14			21 17		22 00			22 18	22 32	
Doncaster 7	a										21 19														
Wakefield Kirkgate 4	a				20 52																			23 26	
Wakefield Westgate 7	a					20 46						21 27						21 47					22 43		
Leeds 10	a				21 16	21 03						21 45						22 04					23 01	00 05	
York 8	a					21 32					21 44														

A From Bristol Parkway
B From Norwich to Manchester Piccadilly
C From Reading to Newcastle

For connections from Gatwick Airport see Table 52

Table 53

Sundays

18 September to 23 October

London - East Midlands - Sheffield

		EM	EM	XC	EM	EM	EM	EM	EM	EM
		◇1	◇1	◇1	◇1	◇1	◇1	◇1	◇1	◇1
				A						
		☕	☕		☕	☕	☕	☕	☕	☕
St Pancras International ⊖	d	20 00	20 25		20 30		21 00	21 30	22 30	23 00
Luton Airport Parkway 7 ✈	d	20 23					21 23		22 53	23 27
Luton 10	d				20 54			21 54		
Bedford 7	d	20 48			21 18		21 47	22 17	23 17	23 50
Wellingborough	d	21 00			21 31		22 00	22 30	23 31	00 04
Kettering 4	a	21 07			21 38		22 07	22 37	23 37	00 10
	d	21 08			21 39	21 55	22 08	22 38	23 38	00 11
Corby	d					22a05				
Oakham	d									
Melton Mowbray	d									
Market Harborough	d	21 18			21 50		22 18	22 48	23 48	00 21
Leicester	a	21 37	21 47		22 11		22 37	23 07	00 07	00 40
	d	21 39	21 49		22 13		22 39	23 09	00 09	00 42
Syston	d									
Sileby	d									
Barrow Upon Soar	d									
Loughborough	d	21 49	22 01				22 49	23 19	00 19	00 52
East Midlands Parkway ✈	d	21 57	22 09		22 29		22 57	23 32	00 27	01 00
Beeston	a	22 03					23 10		00 40	
Nottingham 8 🚢	a	22 11					23 18		00 48	
	d									
Lincoln	a									
Langley Mill	d									
Alfreton	d									
Long Eaton	a							23 38		
Derby 6	a		22 21		22 43			23 49		01 19
	d			22 46	22 52			23 55		
Chesterfield	d			23 07	23 13			00 14		
Sheffield 7 🚢	a			23 22	23 28			00 28		
Doncaster 7	a									
Wakefield Kirkgate 4	a									
Wakefield Westgate 7	a				23 55					
Leeds 10	a			00 34	00 28					
York 8	a									

A From Bristol Parkway
B From Norwich to Manchester Piccadilly
C From Reading to Newcastle

Sundays

from 30 October

		EM	EM	XC	EM	EM	NT	XC	EM	EM
		◇1	◇1	◇1	◇	◇1		◇1	◇1	◇
				A	B			C		B
		☕	☕	🛒		☕		🛒	☕	
St Pancras International ⊖	d	22p00	22p25							
Luton Airport Parkway 7 ✈	d		22p46							
Luton 10	d	22p25								
Bedford 7	d	22p42	23p02							
Wellingborough	d	22p55	23p14							
Kettering 4	a	23p02	23p21							
	d	23p03	23p22			09 55				
Corby	d					10a05				
Oakham	d									
Melton Mowbray	d									
Market Harborough	d	23p14	23p32							
Leicester	a	23p31	23p46							
	d	23p32	23p46						10 10	
Syston	d									
Sileby	d									
Barrow Upon Soar	d									
Loughborough	d	23p44							10 21	
East Midlands Parkway ✈	d	23p52	00 02						10 29	
Beeston	a	23p59								
Nottingham 8 🚢	a	00 08								
	d				09 31		10 06			10 41
Lincoln	a									
Langley Mill	d						10 27			
Alfreton	d				09 53		10 35			11 03
Long Eaton	a		00 06						10 32	
Derby 6	a		00 17						10 46	
	d			09 44				10 44	10 48	
Chesterfield	d			10 03	10 08		10 54	11 03	11 09	11 15
Sheffield 7 🚢	a			10 16	10 33		11 15	11 17	11 28	11 35
Doncaster 7	a								11 56	
Wakefield Kirkgate 4	a						11 52			
Wakefield Westgate 7	a			10 44				11 44		
Leeds 10	a			11 02			12 18	12 01		
York 8	a			11 35				12 32	12 20	

		NT	EM	XC	EM	EM	EM	NT	EM	XC	EM	EM	EM	XC
			◇1	◇1	◇	◇1	◇1		◇1	◇1	◇	◇1	◇1	◇1
				D	B					E	B			F
			☕	🛒		☕	☕		☕	🛒		☕	☕	🛒
St Pancras International ⊖	d		09 00			09 30			10 00			10 30		
Luton Airport Parkway 7 ✈	d		09 28						10 29					
Luton 10	d					10 00						11 02		
Bedford 7	d		09 52			10 20			10 53			11 27		
Wellingborough	d		10 06			10 34			11 07			11 39		
Kettering 4	a		10 14			10 40			11 14			11 46		
	d		10 15			10 41	10 55		11 15			11 46	11 55	
Corby	d						11a05						12a05	
Oakham	d													
Melton Mowbray	d													
Market Harborough	d		10 26			10 51			11 26			11 56		
Leicester	a		10 46			11 10			11 47			12 16		
	d		10 48			11 13			11 48			12 19		
Syston	d													
Sileby	d													
Barrow Upon Soar	d													
Loughborough	d		10 59			11 23			11 59			12 29		
East Midlands Parkway ✈	d		11 07			11 31			12 08			12 37		
Beeston	a		11 13											
Nottingham 8 🚢	a		11 21						12 22					
	d	11 15			11 46			12 19			12 39			
Lincoln	a													
Langley Mill	d	11 31						12 35			12 56			
Alfreton	d	11 39			12 08			12 43			13 04			
Long Eaton	a					11 34						12 40		
Derby 6	a					11 46						12 51		
	d			11 44		12 05				12 44		13 05		13 11
Chesterfield	d	11 51		12 03	12 18	12 25		12 54		13 03	13 17	13 25		13 30
Sheffield 7 🚢	a	12 15		12 18	12 36	12 40		13 16		13 17	13 33	13 42		13 43
Doncaster 7	a													14 13
Wakefield Kirkgate 4	a	12 52						13 52						
Wakefield Westgate 7	a			12 44						13 44				
Leeds 10	a	13 18		13 02				14 18		14 02				
York 8	a			13 32						14 31				14 41

A From Birmingham New Street to Edinburgh
B To Liverpool Lime Street
C From Birmingham New Street to Glasgow Central
D From Bristol Temple Meads to Edinburgh
E From Bristol Temple Meads to Glasgow Central
F From Birmingham New Street to Newcastle
G From Plymouth to Aberdeen
H From Norwich to Liverpool Lime Street
I From Plymouth to Glasgow Central
J From Penzance to Edinburgh

For connections from Gatwick Airport see Table 52

Table 53

Sundays

from 30 October

London - East Midlands - Sheffield

		NT	EM	XC	EM	EM		EM	XC	NT	EM	XC	EM	EM	EM	XC		NT	EM	XC	EM	EM	EM	NT	EM
			◇1	◇1	◇	◇1		◇1	◇1		◇1	◇1	◇	◇1	◇1	◇1			◇1	◇1	◇1	◇1	◇		◇1
				G	H				F			I	B			F				J			B		
			🍴	☕		🍴		🍴	☕		🍴	☕		🍴	🍴	☕			🍴	☕	🍴	🍴			🍴
St Pancras International ⊖	d		11 00			11 30					12 00			12 30					13 00		13 30				14 00
Luton Airport Parkway 7 ✈	d		11 29			11 58					12 29			12 59					13 29		14 00				14 23
Luton 10	d		11 32			12 02					12 33			13 03					13 33		14 04				
Bedford 7	d		11 55			12 26					12 56			13 26					13 56		14 22				14 49
Wellingborough	d		12 09			12 40					13 10			13 40					14 10		14 36				15 03
Kettering 4	a		12 15			12 47					13 16			13 48					14 16		14 43				15 09
	d		12 16			12 48		12 55			13 17			13 49	13 55				14 17		14 44	14 55			15 10
Corby	d							13a05							14a05							15a05			
Oakham	d																								
Melton Mowbray	d																								
Market Harborough	d		12 26			12 58					13 27			14 00					14 27		14 55				15 20
Leicester	a		12 45			13 17					13 46			14 20					14 46		15 16				15 40
	d		12 47			13 19					13 48			14 22					14 48		15 18				15 41
Syston	d																								
Sileby	d																								
Barrow Upon Soar	d																								
Loughborough	d		12 57			13 30					13 58			14 33					14 58		15 29				15 52
East Midlands Parkway ✈	d		13 05			13 37					14 06			14 41					15 06		15 37				15 59
Beeston	a		13 10								14 12								15 11						16 08
Nottingham 8 🚊	a		13 20								14 20								15 18						16 15
	d	13 09			13 38					14 19			14 37					15 12					15 44	16 14	
Lincoln	a																								
Langley Mill	d	13 27			13 55					14 35			14 54					15 34						16 30	
Alfreton	d	13 35			14 03					14 43			15 02					15 44					16 06	16 38	
Long Eaton	a					13 41								14 45							15 41				
Derby 6	a					13 52								14 59							15 53				
	d			13 44		14 04			14 11			14 44		15 01		15 11				15 44	15 58				
Chesterfield	d	13 46		14 03	14 18	14 24			14 30	14 54		15 03	15 13	15 22				15 53		16 03	16 19		16 23	16 50	
Sheffield 7 🚊	a	14 07		14 17	14 36	14 44			14 48	15 15		15 17	15 31	15 40		15 47		16 15		16 18	16 33		16 39	17 15	
Doncaster 7	a								15 13							16 15									
Wakefield Kirkgate 4	a	14 52								15 52								16 52						17 52	
Wakefield Westgate 7	a			14 44								15 44								16 44					
Leeds 10	a	15 18		15 02						16 18		16 02						17 18		17 02				18 18	
York 8	a			15 31					15 44			16 32				16 44				17 31					

A From Birmingham New Street to Edinburgh
B To Liverpool Lime Street
C From Birmingham New Street to Glasgow Central
D From Bristol Temple Meads to Edinburgh
E From Bristol Temple Meads to Glasgow Central
F From Birmingham New Street to Newcastle
G From Plymouth to Aberdeen
H From Norwich to Liverpool Lime Street
I From Plymouth to Glasgow Central
J From Penzance to Edinburgh

		EM		XC	EM	EM	XC	NT	EM	EM	XC	EM		EM	EM	XC	EM	EM	EM	NT	XC	EM		EM	EM
		◇1		◇1	◇1	◇	◇1		◇1	◇1	◇1	◇		◇1	◇1	◇1	◇1	◇1	◇1		◇1	◇		◇1	◇1
				A		B	C				D	B				E					F	G			
		🍴		☕	🍴		☕		🍴	🍴	☕			🍴	🍴	☕	🍴	🍴	🍴		☕			🍴	🍴
St Pancras International ⊖	d				14 30				15 00					15 30	16 00		16 25	16 30						16 55	17 00
Luton Airport Parkway 7 ✈	d								15 29						16 29										17 21
Luton 10	d				15 01									16 00				16 52							
Bedford 7	d				15 23				15 53					16 23	16 53			17 17							17 49
Wellingborough	d				15 37				16 07					16 37	17 06			17 31							18 02
Kettering 4	a				15 44				16 15					16 45	17 13			17 37							18 09
	d	15 45			15 45				16 16	16 45				16 46	17 14			17 38	17 50						18 10
Corby	d	15a55								16a55									18a00						
Oakham	d																								
Melton Mowbray	d																								
Market Harborough	d				15 56				16 27					16 57	17 24			17 48							18 20
Leicester	a				16 17				16 48					17 23	17 43		17 52	18 09						18 25	18 39
	d				16 19				16 49					17 25	17 45		17 54	18 10						18 27	18 41
Syston	d																								
Sileby	d																								
Barrow Upon Soar	d																								
Loughborough	d				16 30				17 00					17 36	17 55			18 23							18 51
East Midlands Parkway ✈	d				16 38				17 09					17 45	18 03		18 10	18 30						18 41	18 59
Beeston	a														18 08										19 05
Nottingham 8 🚊	a								17 20						18 16									18 57	19 11
	d					16 41		17 14				17 35								18 14		18 37			
Lincoln	a																								
Langley Mill	d					17 00		17 30				17 54								18 30		18 54			
Alfreton	d					17 08		17 38				18 02								18 38		19 02			
Long Eaton	a				16 42									17 48				18 34							
Derby 6	a				16 55									18 01			18 22	18 48							
	d			16 44	16 56		17 11				17 43			18 02		18 09	18 24				18 43				
Chesterfield	d			17 03	17 17	17 22		17 51			18 04	18 17					18 45			18 50	19 05	19 13			
Sheffield 7 🚊	a			17 17	17 32	17 40	17 48	18 15			18 19	18 34		18 41		18 46	18 59			19 16	19 20	19 31			
Doncaster 7	a						18 13									19 15									
Wakefield Kirkgate 4	a							18 52												19 52					
Wakefield Westgate 7	a			17 46	18 06		18 33				18 47										19 48				
Leeds 10	a			18 02	18 24		18 51	19 18			19 04									20 18	20 05				
York 8	a			18 32			19 21				19 32					19 44					20 32				

A From Plymouth to Glasgow Central
B From Norwich to Liverpool Lime Street
C From Reading to Newcastle
D From Penzance to Edinburgh
E From Reading to Edinburgh
F From Plymouth to Edinburgh. ☕ to Wakefield Westgate
G From Norwich to Manchester Piccadilly
H From Plymouth
I From Penzance

For connections from Gatwick Airport see Table 52

Table 53

Sundays
from 30 October

London - East Midlands - Sheffield

		XC	EM	EM	EM	NT	XC	EM		EM	EM	XC	EM	EM	EM	NT	EM	EM		XC	EM	EM	EM	XC	NT
		◇1	◇1	◇1	◇1		◇1	◇		◇1	◇1	◇1	◇1	◇1	◇1		◇1	◇1		◇1	◇1	◇1	◇1	◇1	
		C					H	G				C								H				I	
		🛒	☕	☕	☕		🛒			☕	☕		☕	☕	☕		☕	☕			☕	☕	☕		
St Pancras International ⊖	d		17 25	17 30						17 55	18 00		18 25	18 30			18 55	19 00			19 25	19 30			
Luton Airport Parkway 7 ✈	d										18 21							19 21							
Luton 10	d			17 52										18 52								19 52			
Bedford 7	d			18 19							18 47			19 19				19 49				20 19			
Wellingborough	d			18 33							19 01			19 33				20 02				20 32			
Kettering 4	a			18 39							19 07			19 39				20 09				20 38			
	d			18 40	18 50						19 08			19 40	19 45			20 10				20 39	20 46		
Corby	d				19a00										19a55								20a56		
Oakham	d																								
Melton Mowbray	d																								
Market Harborough	d			18 50							19 18			19 50				20 20				20 49			
Leicester	a		18 47	19 10						19 20	19 38		19 52	20 10			20 19	20 39			20 52	21 09			
	d		18 48	19 11						19 22	19 39		19 54	20 11			20 21	20 41			20 54	21 10			
Syston	d																								
Sileby	d																								
Barrow Upon Soar	d																								
Loughborough	d			19 22							19 50			20 22				20 51				21 22			
East Midlands Parkway ✈	d		19 04	19 29						19 36	19 57		20 10	20 29			20 35	20 59			21 10	21 29			
Beeston	a										20 04							21 04							
Nottingham 8 ⛴	a									19 46	20 11						20 46	21 12							
	d					19 19		19 38								20 13									21 20
Lincoln	a																								
Langley Mill	d					19 35										20 29									21 41
Alfreton	d					19 43		20 00								20 37									21 49
Long Eaton	a			19 33										20 33								21 33			
Derby 6	a		19 16	19 44									20 22	20 44							21 22	21 45			
	d	19 05	19 18				19 41					20 05	20 24							20 44	21 24			21 44	
Chesterfield	d		19 37			19 54	20 02	20 10					20 45			20 48				21 03	21 45			22 03	22 08
Sheffield 7 ⛴	a	19 39	19 53			20 15	20 17	20 31				20 38	20 59			21 14				21 16	22 00			22 18	22 32
Doncaster 7	a	20 16										21 19													
Wakefield Kirkgate 4	a					20 52																			23 26
Wakefield Westgate 7	a						20 46						21 27							21 47				22 43	
Leeds 10	a					21 16	21 03						21 45							22 04				23 01	00 05
York 8	a	20 45					21 32					21 44													

A From Plymouth to Glasgow Central
B From Norwich to Liverpool Lime Street
C From Reading to Newcastle
D From Penzance to Edinburgh
E From Reading to Edinburgh
F From Plymouth to Edinburgh. 🛒 to Wakefield Westgate
G From Norwich to Manchester Piccadilly
H From Plymouth
I From Penzance

		EM	EM	EM		XC	EM	EM	EM	EM	EM	EM
		◇1	◇1	◇1		◇1	◇1	◇1	◇1	◇1	◇1	◇1
						A						
		☕	☕	☕			☕	☕	☕	☕	☕	☕
St Pancras International ⊖	d	19 55	20 00	20 25			20 30		21 00	21 30	22 30	23 00
Luton Airport Parkway 7 ✈	d		20 23						21 23		22 53	23 27
Luton 10	d						20 54			21 54		
Bedford 7	d		20 52				21 23		21 51	22 21	23 21	23 50
Wellingborough	d		21 05				21 36		22 05	22 34	23 34	00 04
Kettering 4	a		21 11				21 43		22 11	22 41	23 41	00 10
	d		21 12				21 44	21 55	22 12	22 42	23 42	00 11
Corby	d							22a05				
Oakham	d											
Melton Mowbray	d											
Market Harborough	d		21 22				21 55		22 22	22 52	23 52	00 21
Leicester	a	21 20	21 42	21 48			22 16		22 42	23 11	00 11	00 40
	d	21 22	21 43	21 49			22 18		22 43	23 13	00 12	00 42
Syston	d											
Sileby	d											
Barrow Upon Soar	d											
Loughborough	d	21 33	21 54	22 00					22 54	23 23	00 23	00 52
East Midlands Parkway ✈	d	21 42	22 01	22 07			22 34		23 01	23 36	00 30	01 00
Beeston	a		22 08						23 15		00 44	
Nottingham 8 ⛴	a	21 55	22 16						23 23		00 52	
	d											
Lincoln	a											
Langley Mill	d											
Alfreton	d											
Long Eaton	a									23 42		
Derby 6	a			22 19			22 46			23 53		01 19
	d					22 46	22 52			23 55		
Chesterfield	d					23 07	23 13			00 14		
Sheffield 7 ⛴	a					23 22	23 28			00 28		
Doncaster 7	a											
Wakefield Kirkgate 4	a											
Wakefield Westgate 7	a						23 55					
Leeds 10	a					00 34	00 28					
York 8	a											

A From Plymouth

For connections from Gatwick Airport see Table 52

Table 53

Mondays to Fridays

until 23 September

Sheffield - East Midlands - London

Miles	Miles	Miles	Station		EM MX A	EM MX ◇1 ☕	EM MO ◇ B	EM MX ◇ B	EM ◇1 ☕	EM ◇1 ⊠🛒	EM ◇1 ⊠🛒	EM ◇1 ⊠🛒	EM	NT	EM ◇1 ⊠🛒	EM ◇1 ⊠	EM ◇1 ☕	EM ◇1 ⊠🛒	EM ◇1 ⊠🛒	EM ◇1 ⊠🛒	NT	XC ◇1 C 🛒	EM
—	—	—	York 8	d																			
—	—	—	Leeds 10	d																			
—	—	—	Wakefield Westgate 7	d																			
—	—	—	Wakefield Kirkgate 4	d																			
—	—	—	Doncaster 7	d																			
0	0	—	**Sheffield 7**	d		23p21	23p29	23p37						05 05		05 29			05 56		06 00	06 01	
12¼	12¼	—	Chesterfield	d		23p45	23p43	00 02						05 20		05 41			06 09		06 16	06 27	
—	36½	—	**Derby 6**	a		00 11										06 02			06 30			06 47	
—	—	—		d						04 55	05 17					06 04			06 32				
—	44	—	Long Eaton	d							05 27								06 42				
22½	—	—	Alfreton	d			23p54														06 30		
34½	—	—	Langley Mill	d			00 02														06 37		
—	—	—	Lincoln	d																			
40¾	—	—	**Nottingham 8**	a			00 25	00 40						06 12							07 08		
—	—	—		d	23p10							05 34	05 43					06 28		06 49			
44	—	—	Beeston	d	23p16													06 34		06 55			
—	—	—	East Midlands Parkway	d	23p25					05 06		05 45				06 17		06 40		07 02			
55½	53¼	—	Loughborough	d	23p34					05 14		05 53	06 05			06 25			06 52				06 53
59½	57¼	—	Barrow Upon Soar	d									06 09										06 57
61½	59¼	—	Sileby	d									06 14										07 03
64¼	62	—	Syston	d									06 20										07 08
68	65¾	0	**Leicester**	a	00 02					05 24	05 42	06 05	06 28			06 37		06 54	07 04	07 16			07 19
—	—	—		d					04 44	05 26	05 44	06 07				06 39		06 57	07 06	07 17			
84¼	82	—	Market Harborough	d						05 41	05 58	06 22				06 54		07 12		07 32			
—	—	15¼	Melton Mowbray	d											05 59								
—	—	26¾	Oakham	d											06 11								
—	—	41	Corby	d											06 34		07 08						
95¼	93	48½	Kettering 4	a					05 04	05 50	06 07	06 32			06 43	07 04	07 17	07 21	07 28	07 41			
—	—	—		d					05 05	05 51	06 09	06 33			06 44	07 06		07 22	07 29	07 42			
102¼	100	—	Wellingborough	d					05 23	05 59	06 17	06 41			06 53	07 14		07 30	07 38	07 50			
117½	115¼	—	Bedford 7	d					05 36		06 32				07 08				07 55				
137	134¾	—	Luton 10	d						06 24					07 24			07 56		08 15			
138	135¾	—	Luton Airport Parkway 7	d					05 54			07 07				07 41			08 12				
167¼	165	—	**St Pancras International** ⊖	a					06 17	06 49	07 10	07 34			07 51	08 07		08 26	08 38	08 43			

Station		EM ◇1 ⊠	EM ◇1 ☕	EM ◇1 ☕	EM ◇1 ⊠🛒	XC ◇1 D 🛒	EM ◇1 ☕	EM	EM ◇1 ⊠	NT	XC ◇1 E 🛒	EM ◇1 ⊠	EM ◇1 ☕	EM ◇1 F ☕	EM ◇1 ⊠	EM ◇1 G ☕	XC ◇1 D 🛒	EM H	NT	XC ◇1 I 🛒	EM ◇1 ☕	EM ◇1 ☕	EM ◇1 ☕
York 8	d																06 32			07 23			
Leeds 10	d	05 25				06 00				06 05	06 15			06 34			07 05		07 05				
Wakefield Westgate 7	d	05 37				06 12					06 27			06 46			07 18						
Wakefield Kirkgate 4	d									06 21									07 25				
Doncaster 7	d	05 57									06 45									07 55			
Sheffield 7	d	06 27			06 47	06 50				07 03	07 18	07 27		07 32	07 41		07 53		08 05	08 20		08 27	
Chesterfield	d	06 39			06 59	07 04				07 20	07 30	07 39		07 45	07 55		08 06		08 24	08 32		08 39	
Derby 6	a	07 03			07 19	07 25					07 49	07 59			08 14		08 26			08 52		08 59	
	d	07 05			07 20		07 26					08 00			08 16							09 01	
Long Eaton	d						07 36								08 26								
Alfreton	d									07 33				07 58					08 35				
Langley Mill	d									07 40				08 06					08 42				
Lincoln	d												07 08					07 26					
Nottingham 8	a									08 02			07 57	08 21				08 30	09 02				
	d		07 10					07 31	07 50				08 02	08 28				08 32					09 02
Beeston	d		07 17					07 37					08 08			←		08 38					09 08
East Midlands Parkway	d		07 25		07 33			07 46	08 01					08 39	08 32	08 39		08 46					
Loughborough	d	07 22			07 41		07 47	07 55					08 22	→	08 40			08 55					09 20
Barrow Upon Soar	d							07 59										08 59					
Sileby	d							08 04										09 03					
Syston	d							08 09										09 08					
Leicester	a	07 34	07 41		07 52		07 59	08 21	08 17			08 23	08 32		08 52	08 57		09 22				09 23	09 31
	d	07 35	07 42		07 54		08 01		08 18			08 25	08 33		08 52	08 57						09 25	09 33
Market Harborough	d		07 58				08 16						08 47			09 12							09 47
Melton Mowbray	d																						
Oakham	d																						
Corby	d			08 02																	09 17		
Kettering 4	a	07 57	08 08	08 11	08 14		08 26						08 56								09 26		09 56
	d	07 59	08 09		08 16		08 28						08 56								09 27		09 56
Wellingborough	d	08 07			08 24		08 39						09 04								09 35		10 04
Bedford 7	d		08 29				09 02						09 18								09 49		10 18
Luton 10	d						09 19														10 04		
Luton Airport Parkway 7	d												09 34										10 34
St Pancras International ⊖	a	08 55	09 06		09 10		09 44		09 29			09 34	10 00		10 05	10 17					10 29	10 34	11 01

A From 2 August until 23 September
B From Liverpool Lime Street
C To Reading
D To Plymouth
E To Southampton Central
F To St Pancras International
G From Leeds
H From Sleaford
I From Newcastle to Reading

For connections to Gatwick Airport see Table 52

Table 53

Mondays to Fridays

until 23 September

Sheffield - East Midlands - London

		EM	EM	XC	EM	EM	NT	XC	EM	EM	EM	EM	EM	EM	EM	XC	NT	XC	EM	EM	EM	EM	EM
		◇	◇1	◇1	◇1			◇1	◇1	◇1	◇1	◇1	◇1		◇	◇1		◇1	◇1	◇1	◇1	◇	◇1
		A		B				C							A	D		E				A	
			☕	🛒	☕			🛒	☕	☕	☕	☕	☕			🛒		🛒	☕	☕	☕		☕
York 8	d			07 44				08 24								08 44		09 35					
Leeds 10	d			08 11			08 02									09 11	09 05						
Wakefield Westgate 7	d			08 23												09 24							
Wakefield Kirkgate 4	d						08 23										09 23						
Doncaster 7	d							08 50										09 58					
Sheffield 7	d	08 38	08 47	08 54			09 05	09 23		09 27		09 35			09 38	09 54	10 05	10 23		10 27		10 38	10 47
Chesterfield	d	08 53	08 59	09 06			09 22			09 39		09 47			09 53	10 06	10 22			10 39		10 52	10 59
Derby 6	a		09 19	09 26				09 52		09 59		10 16				10 26		10 52		10 59			11 19
	d		09 20							10 01		10 20								11 01			11 20
Long Eaton	d		09 30									10 30											11 30
Alfreton	d	09 03					09 33								10 04		10 33					11 03	
Langley Mill	d						09 40										10 40						
Lincoln	d					08 35								09 32									
Nottingham 8	a	09 30				09 30	10 01							10 30	10 30		11 00					11 30	
	d				09 28	09 32					10 02		10 28	10 32							11 02		
Beeston	d					09 38					10 08			10 38							11 08		
East Midlands Parkway	d		09 35		09 39	09 46						10 35	10 39	10 46									11 35
Loughborough	d		09 42			09 55					10 20	10 42		10 55							11 20		11 42
Barrow Upon Soar	d					09 59								10 59									
Sileby	d					10 03								11 03									
Syston	d					10 08								11 08									
Leicester	a		09 54		09 57	10 21				10 23	10 33	10 54	10 57	11 21						11 23	11 31		11 54
	d		09 55		09 57					10 25	10 33	10 55	10 57							11 25	11 33		11 55
Market Harborough	d				10 12						10 47		11 12								11 47		
Melton Mowbray	d																						
Oakham	d																						
Corby	d																		11 17				
Kettering 4	a										10 55								11 26		11 56		
	d								10 27		10 56								11 27		11 56		
Wellingborough	d								10 35		11 04								11 35		12 04		
Bedford 7	d								10 49		11 18								11 49		12 18		
Luton 10	d								11 05										12 05				
Luton Airport Parkway 7	d										11 34										12 34		
St Pancras International	a		11 04		11 18				11 29	11 34	12 00	12 05	12 13						12 29	12 33	13 00		13 04

		XC	EM	EM	NT	XC	EM	EM	EM	EM	EM	XC	EM	EM	NT	XC	EM	EM	EM	EM	EM	EM
		◇1	◇1			◇1	◇1	◇1	◇1	◇	◇1	◇1	◇1			◇1	◇1	◇1	◇1	◇1	◇1	
		F				C				A		G				H						
		🛒	☕			🛒	☕	☕	☕		☕	🛒	☕			🛒	☕	☕	☕	☕	☕	
York 8	d	09 44				10 34						10 44				11 34						
Leeds 10	d	10 11			10 05							11 11			11 05							
Wakefield Westgate 7	d	10 23										11 24										
Wakefield Kirkgate 4	d				10 23										11 23							
Doncaster 7	d					10 58										11 58						
Sheffield 7	d	10 54			11 05	11 23		11 27		11 38	11 47	11 54			12 05	12 23		12 27		12 35		
Chesterfield	d	11 06			11 22			11 39		11 53	11 59	12 06			12 22			12 39		12 48		
Derby 6	a	11 26				11 52		11 59			12 19	12 26				12 52		12 59		13 15		
	d							12 01			12 20							13 01		13 20		
Long Eaton	d										12 30									13 30		
Alfreton	d				11 33					12 03					12 33							
Langley Mill	d				11 40										12 40							
Lincoln	d			10 36										11 42								12 30
Nottingham 8	a			11 30	12 02					12 30				12 30	13 00							13 30
	d		11 28	11 32					12 02				12 28	12 32					13 02		13 28	13 32
Beeston	d			11 38					12 08					12 38					13 08			13 38
East Midlands Parkway	d		11 39	11 46							12 35		12 39	12 46						13 35	13 39	13 46
Loughborough	d			11 55					12 20		12 42			12 55					13 20	13 42		13 55
Barrow Upon Soar	d			11 59										12 59								13 59
Sileby	d			12 03										13 03								14 03
Syston	d			12 08										13 08								14 08
Leicester	a		11 57	12 21				12 23	12 31		12 53		12 57	13 21				13 23	13 32	13 54	13 57	14 21
	d		11 57					12 25	12 33		12 55		12 57					13 25	13 33	13 55	13 57	
Market Harborough	d		12 12						12 47				13 12						13 47		14 12	
Melton Mowbray	d																					
Oakham	d																					
Corby	d						12 17										13 17					
Kettering 4	a						12 26		12 56								13 26		13 56			
	d						12 27		12 56								13 27		13 56			
Wellingborough	d						12 35		13 04								13 35		14 04			
Bedford 7	d						12 49		13 18								13 49		14 18			
Luton 10	d						13 05										14 05					
Luton Airport Parkway 7	d								13 34										14 34			
St Pancras International	a		13 13				13 29	13 34	14 01		14 05		14 13				14 29	14 34	14 59	15 04	15 13	

A From Liverpool Lime Street to Norwich
B From Newcastle to Plymouth
C From Newcastle to Southampton Central
D From Edinburgh to Plymouth
E From Edinburgh to Reading
F From Glasgow Central to Plymouth
G From Dundee to Plymouth
H From Newcastle to Reading

For connections to Gatwick Airport see Table 52

Table 53

Sheffield - East Midlands - London

Mondays to Fridays

until 23 September

		EM	XC	NT	XC	EM	EM		EM	EM	EM	XC	EM	EM	NT	XC	EM		EM	EM	EM	EM	XC	EM	EM
		◇ A	◇1 B		◇1 C	◇1	◇1		◇1	◇ A	◇1	◇1 D	◇1			◇1 E	◇1		◇1	◇1	◇1	◇ A	◇1 F	◇1	
York 8	d		11 44		12 34							12 44				13 34							13 44		
Leeds 10	d		12 12	12 05								13 11			13 05								14 11		
Wakefield Westgate 7	d		12 24									13 23											14 23		
Wakefield Kirkgate 4	d			12 23											13 23										
Doncaster 7	d				12 59											13 58									
Sheffield 7	d	12 38	12 54	13 05	13 23		13 27			13 38	13 47	13 54			14 05	14 23			14 27		14 35	14 38	14 54		
Chesterfield	d	12 53	13 06	13 22			13 39			13 52	13 59	14 07			14 22				14 39		14 47	14 53	15 06		
Derby 6	a		13 26		13 52		13 59				14 19	14 26				14 52			14 59		15 16		15 26		
	d						14 01				14 20								15 01		15 20				
Long Eaton	d										14 30										15 30				
Alfreton	d	13 03		13 33						14 03					14 33							15 07			
Langley Mill	d			13 40											14 40										
Lincoln	d													13 40											14 35
Nottingham 8	a	13 30		14 00						14 30				14 30	15 00							15 28			15 29
	d								14 02				14 28	14 32						15 02				15 28	15 32
Beeston	d								14 08					14 38						15 08					15 38
East Midlands Parkway	d										14 35		14 39	14 46							15 35			15 39	15 46
Loughborough	d								14 20		14 42			14 55						15 20	15 42				15 55
Barrow Upon Soar	d													14 59											15 59
Sileby	d													15 03											16 03
Syston	d													15 08											16 08
Leicester	a						14 23		14 31		14 53		14 57	15 21					15 23	15 31	15 53			15 57	16 21
	d						14 25		14 33		14 55		14 57						15 25	15 33	15 54			15 57	
Market Harborough	d								14 47				15 12							15 47				16 12	
Melton Mowbray	d																								
Oakham	d																								
Corby	d					14 17											15 17								
Kettering 4	a					14 26			14 56								15 26			15 56					
	d					14 27			14 56								15 27			15 56					
Wellingborough	d					14 35			15 04								15 35			16 04					
Bedford 7	d					14 49			15 18								15 49			16 18					
Luton 10	d					15 05											16 05								
Luton Airport Parkway 7	d								15 34											16 34					
St Pancras International	a					15 29	15 34		15 59		16 05		16 13				16 29		16 34	17 00	17 06			17 17	

		NT	XC		EM	EM	EM	EM	EM	XC	EM	EM	EM		EM	NT	XC	EM	EM	EM	EM	EM	EM		XC FO
			◇1 C		◇1	◇1	◇1	◇ G	◇1	◇1 D	◇1	◇1	◇1				◇1 E	◇1	◇1	◇1	◇1		◇ A		◇1 H
York 8	d		14 34							14 44							15 34								15 44
Leeds 10	d	14 05								15 11						15 05									16 11
Wakefield Westgate 7	d									15 23															16 22
Wakefield Kirkgate 4	d	14 23														15 23									
Doncaster 7	d		14 58														15 58								
Sheffield 7	d	15 05	15 23			15 27		15 38	15 47	15 54						16 05	16 23	16 27		16 35			16 38		16 54
Chesterfield	d	15 22				15 39		15 53		16 06						16 22		16 39		16 50			16 56		17 06
Derby 6	a		15 52			15 59			16 16	16 26							16 52	16 59		17 16					17 26
	d					16 01			16 18				16 34					17 01		17 18					
Long Eaton	d								16 28											17 28					
Alfreton	d	15 33						16 04								16 33							17 07		
Langley Mill	d	15 40														16 40									
Lincoln	d														15 30							16 34			
Nottingham 8	a	16 00						16 28							16 30	17 00						17 30	17 31		
	d						16 02				16 28				16 32				17 02		17 28	17 32			
Beeston	d						16 08								16 38				17 08			17 38			
East Midlands Parkway	d								16 32		16 39		16 47		16 48					17 32	17 39	17 48			
Loughborough	d						16 20		16 40						16 57				17 20	17 40		17 57			
Barrow Upon Soar	d														17 01							18 01			
Sileby	d														17 05							18 05			
Syston	d														17 09							18 09			
Leicester	a					16 23	16 31		16 51		16 55				17 21			17 23	17 31	17 52	17 57	18 22			
	d					16 25	16 33		16 53		16 57							17 25	17 33	17 53	17 57				
Market Harborough	d						16 47				17 12								17 47		18 12				
Melton Mowbray	d												17 12												
Oakham	d												17 24												
Corby	d				16 17							17 17	17 52												
Kettering 4	a				16 26		16 56		17 14			17 26	18 01						17 56	18 14					
	d				16 27		16 56		17 15			17 27	18 27						17 56	18 15					
Wellingborough	d				16 35		17 04					17 35	18 35						18 04						
Bedford 7	d				16 49		17 18					17 49	18 49						18 18						
Luton 10	d				17 05						17 51	18 05	19 05					18 15							
Luton Airport Parkway 7	d						17 30												18 34						
St Pancras International	a				17 29	17 33	18 04		18 08		18 19	18 29	19 31					18 39	19 00	19 06	19 19				

A From Liverpool Lime Street to Norwich
B From Glasgow Central to Plymouth
C From Newcastle to Southampton Central
D From Glasgow Central to Penzance
E From Newcastle to Reading
F From Aberdeen to Penzance
G From Liverpool Lime Street
H From Edinburgh to Plymouth

For connections to Gatwick Airport see Table 52

Table 53

Mondays to Fridays

until 23 September

Sheffield - East Midlands - London

		XC FX	NT	XC	EM	EM	EM	EM	EM		EM	NT	XC	EM	EM	EM	EM	EM	EM		EM	XC	NT	XC	EM
		◇1 A		◇1 B	◇1	◇1	◇1	◇1			◇ C		◇1 B	◇1	◇1	◇1	◇1	◇1			◇ D	◇1 A		◇1 E	◇1
York 8	d	15 44		16 04									17 34									17 44		18 34	
Leeds 10	d	16 11	16 05	16 40								17 05										18 11	18 05		
Wakefield Westgate 7	d	16 22		16 52																		18 23			
Wakefield Kirkgate 4	d		16 23									17 23											18 23		
Doncaster 7	d												17 59											18 58	
Sheffield 7	d	16 54	17 05	17 23	17 27		17 35				17 44	18 05	18 23		18 27		18 35				18 45	18 54	19 05	19 23	
Chesterfield	d	17 06	17 22		17 39		17 50				18 02	18 22			18 39		18 47				19 01	19 06	19 22		
Derby 6	a	17 27		17 52	17 59		18 16						18 52		18 59		19 14					19 26		19 53	
	d				18 01		18 18								19 01		19 18								
Long Eaton	d						18 28										19 28								
Alfreton	d		17 33								18 12	18 33									19 11		19 33		
Langley Mill	d		17 40									18 40											19 40		
Lincoln	d								17 28										18 35						
Nottingham 8	a		18 00						18 32		18 34	18 57							19 29		19 38		20 00		
	d					18 02		18 28	18 33							19 02		19 28	19 32						
Beeston	d					18 08			18 39							19 08			19 38						
East Midlands Parkway	d						18 32	18 39	18 48								19 32	19 39	19 46						
Loughborough	d					18 20	18 40		18 56							19 20	19 40		19 55						
Barrow Upon Soar	d								19 01										19 59						
Sileby	d								19 05										20 03						
Syston	d								19 10										20 08						
Leicester	a				18 23	18 31	18 51	18 55	19 22						19 23	19 31	19 51	19 57	20 20						
	d				18 25	18 33	18 53	18 57							19 25	19 33	19 53	19 57							
Market Harborough	d					18 47		19 12								19 47		20 12							
Melton Mowbray	d																								
Oakham	d																								
Corby	d													18 57											19 43
Kettering 4	a					18 56								19 06		19 56									19 52
	d					18 56								19 27		19 56									20 27
Wellingborough	d					19 04								19 35		20 04									20 35
Bedford 7	d					19 18								19 49		20 18									20 51
Luton 10	d													20 05											21 05
Luton Airport Parkway 7	d					19 34										20 34									
St Pancras International	a				19 34	20 01	20 05	20 11						20 29	20 34	20 59	21 06	21 15							21 30

		EM	EM	EM	XC		EM	NT	XC	EM	EM	EM	EM	EM	EM		EM	XC	XC	EM	EM	XC	EM	EM	EM
		◇1	◇1	◇ C	◇1 F				◇1 G	◇1	◇1	◇1	◇1	◇1			◇ D	◇1 H	◇1 G	◇ D	◇1	◇1 I	◇1	J	K
York 8	d				18 45				19 34									19 44	20 34			20 44			
Leeds 10	d				19 11			19 05										20 11				21 11			
Wakefield Westgate 7	d				19 23													20 23				21 23			
Wakefield Kirkgate 4	d							19 24																	
Doncaster 7	d								19 58										21 02						
Sheffield 7	d	19 27		19 38	19 54			20 04	20 23				20 39				20 41	20 54	21 28	21 39	21 44	22 00			
Chesterfield	d	19 39		19 53	20 06			20 22					20 53				20 58	21 06	21 41	21 55	22 00	22 24			
Derby 6	a	19 59			20 27				20 53				21 18					21 26	22 00		22 21	22 44			
	d	20 01											21 20												
Long Eaton	d																								
Alfreton	d			20 04				20 33									21 09			22 05					
Langley Mill	d							20 40												22 12					
Lincoln	d																								
Nottingham 8	a			20 31				21 01									21 38			22 38					
	d		20 02				20 32					21 02		21 28	21 32									23 10	23 10
Beeston	d		20 08				20 38					21 08			21 38									23 16	23 16
East Midlands Parkway	d		20 16				20 46					21 15	21 33		21 46									23 25	23 25
Loughborough	d		20 24				20 55					21 22	21 41	21 47	21 55									23 33	23 34
Barrow Upon Soar	d						20 59								21 59										
Sileby	d						21 03								22 03										
Syston	d						21 08								22 08										
Leicester	a	20 23	20 34				21 22					21 32	21 52	21 58	22 21									23 58	00 02
	d	20 25	20 36									21 33	21 55	22 00											
Market Harborough	d		20 50									21 47		22 14											
Melton Mowbray	d																								
Oakham	d																								
Corby	d									20 43	21 43												22 43		
Kettering 4	a		20 59							20 52	21 52	21 56		22 23									22 52		
	d		20 59							21 18		21 57		22 24											
Wellingborough	d		21 07							21 27		22 05		22 32											
Bedford 7	d		21 25							21 44		22 19		22 47											
Luton 10	d									22 01		22 34		23 05											
Luton Airport Parkway 7	d		21 41									22 38													
St Pancras International	a	21 37	22 06							22 29		23 01	23 06	23 34											

A *From Edinburgh to Plymouth*
B From Newcastle to Reading
C From Liverpool Lime Street to Norwich
D From Liverpool Lime Street
E From Newcastle to Guildford
F From Glasgow Central to Bristol Temple Meads
G From Newcastle to Birmingham New Street
H From Edinburgh to Bristol Temple Meads
I From Glasgow Central to Birmingham New Street
J until 29 July
K from 1 August until 23 September

For connections to Gatwick Airport see Table 52

Sheffield - East Midlands - London

Mondays to Fridays
until 23 September

		EM	EM FX	EM FO
		◇1	◇	◇
			A	A
		☕		
York 8	d			
Leeds 10	d			
Wakefield Westgate 7	d			
Wakefield Kirkgate 4	d			
Doncaster 7	d			
Sheffield 7	d	23 21	23 37	23 37
Chesterfield	d	23 45	00 02	00 02
Derby 6	a	00 11		
	d			
Long Eaton	d			
Alfreton	d			
Langley Mill	d			
Lincoln	d			
Nottingham 8	a		00 40	00 41
	d			
Beeston	d			
East Midlands Parkway ✈	d			
Loughborough	d			
Barrow Upon Soar	d			
Sileby	d			
Syston	d			
Leicester	a			
	d			
Market Harborough	d			
Melton Mowbray	d			
Oakham	d			
Corby	d			
Kettering 4	a			
	d			
Wellingborough	d			
Bedford 7	d			
Luton 10	d			
Luton Airport Parkway 7 ✈	d			
St Pancras International ⊖	a			

Mondays to Fridays
from 26 September

		EM MX	EM MX	EM MO	EM MX	EM	EM	EM	EM	EM
			◇1	◇	◇	◇1	◇1	◇1	◇1	
		B		A	A					
			☕			☕	⊠🛒	⊠🛒	⊠🛒	
York 8	d									
Leeds 10	d									
Wakefield Westgate 7	d									
Wakefield Kirkgate 4	d									
Doncaster 7	d									
Sheffield 7	d		23p21	23p29	23p37					
Chesterfield	d		23p45	23p43	00 02					
Derby 6	a		00 11							
	d						04 55	05 17		
Long Eaton	d							05 27		
Alfreton	d			23p54						
Langley Mill	d			00 02						
Lincoln	d									
Nottingham 8	a			00 25	00 40					
	d	23p10							05 34	05 43
Beeston	d	23p16								
East Midlands Parkway ✈	d	23p25					05 06		05 45	
Loughborough	d	23p34					05 14		05 53	06 05
Barrow Upon Soar	d									06 09
Sileby	d									06 14
Syston	d									06 20
Leicester	a	00 02					05 24	05 42	06 05	06 28
	d					04 44	05 26	05 44	06 07	
Market Harborough	d						05 41	05 58	06 22	
Melton Mowbray	d									
Oakham	d									
Corby	d									
Kettering 4	a					05 04	05 50	06 07	06 32	
	d					05 05	05 51	06 09	06 33	
Wellingborough	d					05 23	05 59	06 17	06 41	
Bedford 7	d					05 36		06 32		
Luton 10	d						06 24			
Luton Airport Parkway 7 ✈	d					05 54			07 07	
St Pancras International ⊖	a					06 17	06 49	07 10	07 34	

		NT	EM	EM	EM	EM	EM	EM	NT	XC	EM	EM	EM	EM
			◇1	◇1	◇1	◇1	◇1	◇1		◇1		◇1	◇1	◇1
										C				
			⊠🛒	⊠	☕	⊠🛒	⊠🛒	⊠🛒		🛒		⊠	☕	☕
York 8	d													
Leeds 10	d											05 25		
Wakefield Westgate 7	d											05 37		
Wakefield Kirkgate 4	d													
Doncaster 7	d											05 57		
Sheffield 7	d	05 05		05 29			05 56		06 00	06 01		06 27		
Chesterfield	d	05 20		05 41			06 09		06 16	06 27		06 39		
Derby 6	a			06 02			06 30			06 47		07 03		
	d			06 04			06 32					07 05		
Long Eaton	d						06 42							
Alfreton	d								06 30					
Langley Mill	d								06 37					
Lincoln	d													
Nottingham 8	a	06 12							07 08					
	d					06 28		06 49					07 10	
Beeston	d					06 34		06 55					07 17	
East Midlands Parkway ✈	d			06 17		06 40		07 02					07 25	
Loughborough	d			06 25			06 52				06 53	07 22		
Barrow Upon Soar	d										06 57			
Sileby	d										07 03			
Syston	d										07 08			
Leicester	a			06 37		06 54	07 04	07 16			07 19	07 34	07 41	
	d			06 39		06 57	07 06	07 17				07 35	07 42	
Market Harborough	d			06 54		07 12		07 32					07 58	
Melton Mowbray	d		05 59											
Oakham	d		06 11											
Corby	d		06 34		07 08									08 02
Kettering 4	a		06 43	07 04	07 17	07 21	07 28	07 41				07 57	08 08	08 11
	d		06 44	07 06		07 22	07 29	07 42				07 59	08 09	
Wellingborough	d		06 53	07 14		07 30	07 38	07 50				08 07		
Bedford 7	d		07 08				07 55						08 29	
Luton 10	d		07 24			07 56		08 15						
Luton Airport Parkway 7 ✈	d			07 41			08 12							
St Pancras International ⊖	a		07 51	08 07		08 26	08 38	08 43				08 55	09 06	

A From Liverpool Lime Street

B From 27 September until 21 October

C To Reading

For connections to Gatwick Airport see Table 52

Table 53

Mondays to Fridays

from 26 September

Sheffield - East Midlands - London

		EM	XC	EM	EM	EM	NT	XC	EM	EM	EM	EM	EM	XC	EM	NT	XC	EM	EM	EM	EM	EM	XC
		◇1	◇1	◇1		◇1		◇1	◇1	◇1	◇1	◇1	◇1	◇1			◇1	◇1	◇1	◇1	◇	◇1	◇1
			A					B			C		D	A	E		F				G		H
		⊠⚯	⚯	⊡		⊠		⚯	⊠	⊡	⊡	⊠	⊡	⚯			⚯	⊡	⊡	⊡		⊡	⚯
York 8	d													06 32			07 23						07 44
Leeds 10	d		06 00				06 05	06 15			06 34			07 05		07 05							08 11
Wakefield Westgate 7	d		06 12					06 27			06 46			07 18									08 23
Wakefield Kirkgate 4	d						06 21									07 25							
Doncaster 7	d							06 45									07 55						
Sheffield 7	d	06 47	06 50				07 03	07 18	07 27		07 32	07 41		07 53		08 05	08 20		08 27		08 38	08 47	08 54
Chesterfield	d	06 59	07 04				07 20	07 30	07 39		07 45	07 55		08 06		08 24	08 32		08 39		08 53	08 59	09 06
Derby 6	a	07 19	07 25					07 49	07 59			08 14		08 26			08 52		08 59			09 19	09 26
	d	07 20		07 26					08 00			08 16							09 01			09 20	
Long Eaton	d			07 36								08 26										09 30	
Alfreton	d						07 33				07 58					08 35					09 03		
Langley Mill	d						07 40				08 06					08 42							
Lincoln	d									07 08					07 26								
Nottingham 8	a						08 02			07 57	08 21				08 32	09 02					09 30		
	d				07 31	07 50				08 02	08 28				08 32					09 02			
Beeston	d				07 37					08 08			←		08 38					09 08			
East Midlands Parkway	d	07 33			07 46	08 01					08 39	08 32	08 39		08 46							09 35	
Loughborough	d	07 41		07 47	07 55					08 22	→	08 40			08 55					09 20		09 42	
Barrow Upon Soar	d				07 59										08 59								
Sileby	d				08 04										09 03								
Syston	d				08 09										09 08								
Leicester	a	07 52		07 59	08 21	08 17			08 23	08 32		08 52	08 57		09 22				09 23	09 31		09 54	
	d	07 54		08 01		08 18			08 25	08 33		08 52	08 57						09 25	09 33		09 55	
Market Harborough	d			08 16						08 47			09 12							09 47			
Melton Mowbray	d																						
Oakham	d																						
Corby	d																	09 17					
Kettering 4	a	08 14		08 26						08 56								09 26		09 56			
	d	08 16		08 28						08 56								09 27		09 56			
Wellingborough	d	08 24		08 39						09 04								09 35		10 04			
Bedford 7	d			09 02						09 18								09 49		10 18			
Luton 10	d			09 19														10 04					
Luton Airport Parkway 7 ✈	d									09 34										10 34			
St Pancras International ⊖	a	09 10		09 44		09 29			09 34	10 00		10 05	10 17					10 29	10 34	11 01		11 04	

		EM	EM	NT	XC	EM	EM	EM	EM	EM	EM	XC	EM	NT	XC	EM	EM	EM	EM	EM	XC	EM
		◇1			◇1	◇1	◇1	◇1	◇1	◇1	◇	◇1			◇1	◇1	◇1	◇1	◇	◇1	◇1	◇1
					I						G	J			K				G		L	
		⊡			⚯	⊡	⊡	⊡	⊡	⊡		⚯			⚯	⊡	⊡	⊡		⊡	⚯	⊡
York 8	d				08 24							08 44			09 35						09 44	
Leeds 10	d			08 02								09 11		09 05							10 11	
Wakefield Westgate 7	d											09 24									10 23	
Wakefield Kirkgate 4	d			08 23										09 23								
Doncaster 7	d				08 50										09 58							
Sheffield 7	d			09 05	09 23		09 27		09 35		09 38	09 54		10 05	10 23		10 27		10 38	10 47	10 54	
Chesterfield	d			09 22			09 39		09 47		09 53	10 06		10 22			10 39		10 52	10 59	11 06	
Derby 6	a				09 52		09 59		10 16			10 26			10 52		10 59			11 19	11 26	
	d						10 01		10 20								11 01			11 20		
Long Eaton	d								10 30											11 30		
Alfreton	d			09 33							10 04			10 33					11 03			
Langley Mill	d			09 40										10 40								
Lincoln	d		08 35										09 32									
Nottingham 8	a		09 32	10 01							10 30		10 32	11 00					11 30			
	d	09 28	09 32					10 02		10 28			10 32					11 02				11 28
Beeston	d		09 38					10 08					10 38					11 08				
East Midlands Parkway	d	09 39	09 46						10 35	10 39			10 46							11 35		11 39
Loughborough	d		09 55					10 20	10 42				10 55					11 20		11 42		
Barrow Upon Soar	d		09 59										10 59									
Sileby	d		10 03										11 03									
Syston	d		10 08										11 08									
Leicester	a	09 57	10 21				10 23	10 33	10 54	10 57			11 21				11 23	11 31		11 54		11 57
	d	09 57					10 25	10 33	10 55	10 57							11 25	11 33		11 55		11 57
Market Harborough	d	10 12						10 47		11 12								11 47				12 12
Melton Mowbray	d																					
Oakham	d																					
Corby	d															11 17						
Kettering 4	a							10 55								11 26		11 56				
	d					10 27		10 56								11 27		11 56				
Wellingborough	d					10 35		11 04								11 35		12 04				
Bedford 7	d					10 49		11 18								11 49		12 18				
Luton 10	d					11 05										12 05						
Luton Airport Parkway 7 ✈	d							11 34										12 34				
St Pancras International ⊖	a	11 18				11 29	11 34	12 00	12 05	12 13						12 29	12 33	13 00		13 04		13 13

A To Plymouth
B To Southampton Central
C To St Pancras International
D From Leeds
E From Sleaford
F From Newcastle to Reading
G From Liverpool Lime Street to Norwich
H From Newcastle to Plymouth
I From Newcastle to Southampton Central
J From Edinburgh to Plymouth
K From Edinburgh to Reading
L From Glasgow Central to Plymouth

For connections to Gatwick Airport see Table 52

Table 53

Mondays to Fridays

from 26 September

Sheffield - East Midlands - London

		EM	NT	XC	EM	EM	EM	EM	EM	XC	EM	EM	NT	XC	EM	EM	EM	EM	EM	EM	XC	EM	NT
				◇1	◇1	◇1	◇1	◇	◇1	◇1	◇1			◇1	◇1	◇1	◇1	◇1	◇1	◇	◇1		
				A				B		C				D						B	E		
York [8]	d			10 34						10 44				11 34							11 44		
Leeds [10]	d		10 05							11 11			11 05								12 12		12 05
Wakefield Westgate [7]	d									11 24											12 24		
Wakefield Kirkgate [4]	d		10 23										11 23										12 23
Doncaster [7]	d			10 58										11 58									
Sheffield [7]	d		11 05	11 23		11 27		11 38	11 47	11 54			12 05	12 23		12 27		12 35		12 38	12 54		13 05
Chesterfield	d		11 22			11 39		11 53	11 59	12 06			12 22			12 39		12 48		12 53	13 06		13 22
Derby [6]	a			11 52		11 59			12 19	12 26				12 52		12 59		13 15			13 26		
	d					12 01			12 20							13 01		13 20					
Long Eaton	d								12 30									13 30					
Alfreton	d		11 33					12 03					12 33							13 03			13 33
Langley Mill	d		11 40										12 40										13 40
Lincoln	d	10 36										11 42										12 30	
Nottingham [8]	a	11 32	12 02					12 30				12 32	13 00							13 30		13 32	14 00
	d	11 32					12 02				12 28	12 32					13 02		13 28			13 32	
Beeston	d	11 38					12 08					12 38					13 08					13 38	
East Midlands Parkway	d	11 46							12 35		12 39	12 46						13 35	13 39			13 46	
Loughborough	d	11 55					12 20		12 42			12 55					13 20	13 42				13 55	
Barrow Upon Soar	d	11 59										12 59										13 59	
Sileby	d	12 03										13 03										14 03	
Syston	d	12 08										13 08										14 08	
Leicester	a	12 21				12 23	12 31		12 53		12 57	13 21				13 23	13 32	13 54	13 57			14 21	
	d					12 25	12 33		12 55		12 57					13 25	13 33	13 55	13 57				
Market Harborough	d						12 47				13 12						13 47		14 12				
Melton Mowbray	d																						
Oakham	d																						
Corby	d				12 17										13 17								
Kettering [4]	a				12 26		12 56								13 26		13 56						
	d				12 27		12 56								13 27		13 56						
Wellingborough	d				12 35		13 04								13 35		14 04						
Bedford [7]	d				12 49		13 18								13 49		14 18						
Luton [10]	d				13 05										14 05								
Luton Airport Parkway [7]	d						13 34										14 34						
St Pancras International	a				13 29	13 34	14 01		14 05		14 13				14 29	14 34	14 59	15 04	15 13				

		XC	EM	EM	EM	EM	EM	XC	EM	EM	NT	XC	EM	EM	EM	EM	EM	XC	EM	EM	NT	XC
		◇1	◇1	◇1	◇1	◇	◇1	◇1	◇1			◇1	◇1	◇1	◇1	◇1	◇	◇1	◇1			◇1
		A				B		F				D					B	G				A
York [8]	d	12 34						12 44				13 34						13 44				14 34
Leeds [10]	d							13 11			13 05							14 11			14 05	
Wakefield Westgate [7]	d							13 23										14 23				
Wakefield Kirkgate [4]	d										13 23										14 23	
Doncaster [7]	d	12 59										13 58										14 58
Sheffield [7]	d	13 23		13 27		13 38	13 47	13 54			14 05	14 23		14 27		14 35	14 38	14 54			15 05	15 23
Chesterfield	d			13 39		13 52	13 59	14 07			14 22			14 39		14 47	14 53	15 06			15 22	
Derby [6]	a	13 52		13 59			14 19	14 26				14 52		14 59		15 16		15 26				15 52
	d			14 01			14 20							15 01		15 20						
Long Eaton	d						14 30									15 30						
Alfreton	d					14 03					14 33						15 07				15 33	
Langley Mill	d										14 40										15 40	
Lincoln	d									13 40										14 35		
Nottingham [8]	a					14 30				14 32	15 00						15 28			15 31	16 00	
	d				14 02				14 28	14 32					15 02				15 28	15 32		
Beeston	d				14 08					14 38					15 08					15 38		
East Midlands Parkway	d						14 35		14 39	14 46						15 35			15 39	15 46		
Loughborough	d				14 20		14 42			14 55					15 20	15 42				15 55		
Barrow Upon Soar	d									14 59										15 59		
Sileby	d									15 03										16 03		
Syston	d									15 08										16 08		
Leicester	a			14 23	14 31		14 53		14 57	15 21				15 23	15 31	15 53			15 57	16 21		
	d			14 25	14 33		14 55		14 57					15 25	15 33	15 54			15 57			
Market Harborough	d				14 47				15 12						15 47				16 12			
Melton Mowbray	d																					
Oakham	d																					
Corby	d		14 17										15 17									
Kettering [4]	a		14 26		14 56								15 26		15 56							
	d		14 27		14 56								15 27		15 56							
Wellingborough	d		14 35		15 04								15 35		16 04							
Bedford [7]	d		14 49		15 18								15 49		16 18							
Luton [10]	d		15 05										16 05									
Luton Airport Parkway [7]	d				15 34										16 34							
St Pancras International	a		15 29	15 34	15 59		16 05		16 13				16 29	16 34	17 00	17 06			17 17			

A From Newcastle to Southampton Central
B From Liverpool Lime Street to Norwich
C From Dundee to Plymouth
D From Newcastle to Reading
E From Glasgow Central to Plymouth
F From Glasgow Central to Penzance
G From Aberdeen to Penzance

For connections to Gatwick Airport see Table 52

Table 53

Mondays to Fridays

from 26 September

Sheffield - East Midlands - London

		EM	EM	EM	EM	EM	XC	EM	EM	EM	EM	NT	XC	EM	EM	EM	EM	EM	XC	XC	EM	NT	XC
																			FO	FX			
		◇1	◇1	◇1	◇	◇1	◇1	◇1	◇1	◇1			◇1	◇1	◇1	◇1	◇1	◇	◇1	◇1			◇1
					A		B						C					A	D	D			C
		☕	☕	☕		☕	🛒	☕	☕	☕			🛒	☕	☕	☕	☕		🛒	🛒			🛒
York 8	d						14 44						15 34						15 44	15 44			16 04
Leeds 10	d						15 11					15 05							16 11	16 11		16 05	16 40
Wakefield Westgate 7	d						15 23												16 22	16 22			16 52
Wakefield Kirkgate 4	d											15 23										16 23	
Doncaster 7	d												15 58										
Sheffield 7 🚊	d		15 27		15 38	15 47	15 54					16 05	16 23	16 27		16 35		16 38	16 54	16 54		17 05	17 23
Chesterfield	d		15 39		15 53		16 06					16 22		16 39		16 50		16 56	17 06	17 06		17 22	
Derby 6	a		15 59			16 16	16 26						16 52	16 59		17 16			17 26	17 27			17 52
	d		16 01			16 18				16 34				17 01		17 18							
Long Eaton	d					16 28										17 28							
Alfreton	d				16 04							16 33						17 07				17 33	
Langley Mill	d											16 40										17 40	
Lincoln	d										15 30										16 34		
Nottingham 8 🚊	a				16 28						16 32	17 00						17 31			17 32	18 00	
	d			16 02				16 28			16 32				17 02		17 28				17 32		
Beeston	d			16 08							16 38				17 08						17 38		
East Midlands Parkway ✈	d					16 32		16 39		16 47	16 48					17 32	17 39				17 48		
Loughborough	d			16 20		16 40					16 57				17 20	17 40					17 57		
Barrow Upon Soar	d										17 01										18 01		
Sileby	d										17 05										18 05		
Syston	d										17 09										18 09		
Leicester	a		16 23	16 31		16 51		16 55			17 22			17 23	17 31	17 52	17 57				18 22		
	d		16 25	16 33		16 53		16 57						17 25	17 33	17 53	17 57						
Market Harborough	d			16 47				17 12							17 47		18 12						
Melton Mowbray	d									17 12													
Oakham	d									17 24													
Corby	d	16 17							17 17	17 52													
Kettering 4	a	16 26		16 56		17 14			17 26	18 01					17 56	18 14							
	d	16 27		16 56		17 15			17 27	18 27					17 56	18 15							
Wellingborough	d	16 35		17 04					17 35	18 35					18 04								
Bedford 7	d	16 49		17 18					17 49	18 49					18 18								
Luton 10	d	17 05						17 51	18 05	19 05				18 15									
Luton Airport Parkway 7 ✈	d			17 30											18 34								
St Pancras International ⊖	a	17 29	17 33	18 04		18 08		18 19	18 29	19 31				18 39	19 00	19 06	19 19						

		EM	EM	EM	EM	EM	EM	NT	XC	EM	EM	EM	EM	EM	EM	EM	XC	NT	XC	EM	EM	EM	EM
		◇1	◇1	◇1	◇1		◇		◇1	◇1	◇1	◇1	◇1	◇1		◇	◇1		◇1	◇1	◇1	◇1	◇
							A		C							E	D		F				A
		☕	☕	☕	☕				🛒	☕	☕	☕	☕	☕			🛒		🛒	☕	☕	☕	
York 8	d								17 34								17 44		18 34				
Leeds 10	d							17 05									18 11	18 05					
Wakefield Westgate 7	d																18 23						
Wakefield Kirkgate 4	d							17 23										18 23					
Doncaster 7	d								17 59										18 58				
Sheffield 7 🚊	d	17 27		17 35			17 44	18 05	18 23		18 27		18 35			18 45	18 54	19 05	19 23		19 27		19 38
Chesterfield	d	17 39		17 50			18 02	18 22			18 39		18 47			19 01	19 06	19 22			19 39		19 53
Derby 6	a	17 59		18 16					18 52		18 59		19 14				19 26		19 53		19 59		
	d	18 01		18 18							19 01		19 18								20 01		
Long Eaton	d			18 28									19 28										
Alfreton	d						18 12	18 33								19 11		19 33					20 04
Langley Mill	d							18 40										19 40					
Lincoln	d					17 28									18 35								
Nottingham 8 🚊	a					18 33	18 34	18 57							19 31	19 38		20 00					20 31
	d		18 02		18 28	18 33						19 02		19 28	19 32							20 02	
Beeston	d		18 08			18 39						19 08			19 38							20 08	
East Midlands Parkway ✈	d			18 32	18 39	18 48							19 32	19 39	19 46							20 16	
Loughborough	d		18 20	18 40		18 56						19 20	19 40		19 55							20 24	
Barrow Upon Soar	d					19 01									19 59								
Sileby	d					19 05									20 03								
Syston	d					19 10									20 08								
Leicester	a	18 23	18 31	18 51	18 55	19 23					19 23	19 31	19 51	19 57	20 20						20 23	20 34	
	d	18 25	18 33	18 53	18 57						19 25	19 33	19 53	19 57							20 25	20 36	
Market Harborough	d		18 47		19 12							19 47		20 12								20 50	
Melton Mowbray	d																						
Oakham	d																						
Corby	d									18 57										19 43			
Kettering 4	a		18 56							19 06		19 56								19 52		20 59	
	d		18 56							19 27		19 56								20 27		20 59	
Wellingborough	d		19 04							19 35		20 04								20 35		21 07	
Bedford 7	d		19 18							19 49		20 18								20 51		21 25	
Luton 10	d									20 05										21 05			
Luton Airport Parkway 7 ✈	d		19 34									20 34										21 41	
St Pancras International ⊖	a	19 34	20 01	20 05	20 11					20 29	20 34	20 59	21 06	21 15						21 30	21 37	22 06	

A From Liverpool Lime Street to Norwich
B From Glasgow Central to Penzance
C From Newcastle to Reading
D From Edinburgh to Plymouth
E From Liverpool Lime Street
F From Newcastle to Guildford

For connections to Gatwick Airport see Table 52

Table 53

Mondays to Fridays

from 26 September

Sheffield - East Midlands - London

		XC		EM	NT	XC	EM	EM	EM	EM	EM	EM	EM	XC	XC	EM	EM	XC	EM	EM	EM		EM	EM FX	EM FO
		◇1				◇1	◇1	◇1	◇1	◇1	◇1		◇	◇1	◇1	◇	◇1	◇1	◇1				◇1	◇	◇
		A				B							C	D	B	C		E		F	G			C	C
		ꝏ				ꝏ	⊏P	⊏P	⊏P	⊏P	⊏P						⊏P		⊏P				⊏P		
York 8	d	18 45				19 34								19 44	20 34			20 44							
Leeds 10	d	19 11			19 05									20 11				21 11							
Wakefield Westgate 7	d	19 23												20 23				21 23							
Wakefield Kirkgate 4	d				19 24																				
Doncaster 7	d					19 58									21 02										
Sheffield 7 ⇌	d	19 54			20 04	20 23				20 39			20 41	20 54	21 28	21 39	21 44	22 00					23 21	23 37	23 37
Chesterfield	d	20 06			20 22					20 53			20 58	21 06	21 41	21 55	22 00	22 24					23 45	00 02	00 02
Derby 6	a	20 27				20 53				21 18				21 26	22 00		22 21	22 44					00 11		
	d									21 20															
Long Eaton	d																								
Alfreton	d				20 33								21 09			22 05									
Langley Mill	d				20 40											22 12									
Lincoln	d																								
Nottingham 8 ⇌	a				21 01								21 38			22 38								00 40	00 41
	d			20 32					21 02		21 28	21 32								23 10	23 10				
Beeston	d			20 38					21 08			21 38								23 16	23 16				
East Midlands Parkway ✈	d			20 46					21 15	21 33		21 46								23 25	23 25				
Loughborough	d			20 55					21 22	21 41	21 47	21 55								23 33	23 34				
Barrow Upon Soar	d			20 59								21 59													
Sileby	d			21 03								22 03													
Syston	d			21 08								22 08													
Leicester	a			21 22					21 32	21 52	21 58	22 21								23 58	00 02				
	d								21 33	21 55	22 00														
Market Harborough	d								21 47		22 14														
Melton Mowbray	d																								
Oakham	d																								
Corby	d						20 43	21 43											22 43						
Kettering 4	a						20 52	21 52	21 56		22 23								22 52						
	d						21 18		21 57		22 24														
Wellingborough	d						21 27		22 05		22 32														
Bedford 7	d						21 44		22 19		22 47														
Luton 10	d						22 01		22 34		23 05														
Luton Airport Parkway 7 ✈	d								22 38																
St Pancras International ⊖	a						22 29		23 01	23 06	23 34														

A From Glasgow Central to Bristol Temple Meads
B From Newcastle to Birmingham New Street
C From Liverpool Lime Street
D From Edinburgh to Bristol Temple Meads
E From Glasgow Central to Birmingham New Street
F from 24 October
G from 26 September until 21 October

For connections to Gatwick Airport see Table 52

Table 53

Saturdays

until 24 September

Sheffield - East Midlands - London

		EM	EM	EM	EM	EM	EM	EM	EM	XC		EM	NT	EM	EM	EM	EM	EM	XC	EM		EM	NT	XC	EM
			◇1	◇	◇1	◇1	◇1	◇1	◇1	◇1		◇1			◇1	◇1	◇1	◇1	◇1	◇1				◇1	◇1
		A		B						C									D				E	F	
			☕		☕	☕	☕	☕	☕	🛒		☕			☕	☕	☕	☕	🛒	☕				🛒	☕
York 8	d																								
Leeds 10	d																		06 00					06 15	
Wakefield Westgate 7	d																		06 12					06 29	
Wakefield Kirkgate 4	d																								
Doncaster 7	d																							06 47	
Sheffield 7 🚋	d		23p21	23p37			05 27			05 45			05 54		06 25				06 50				07 03	07 18	
Chesterfield	d		23p45	00 02			05 39			05 57			06 20		06 37				07 03				07 20	07 30	
Derby 6	a		00 11				05 59			06 36					06 59				07 24					07 49	
	d					05 25	06 01		06 18						07 01			07 18							
Long Eaton	d					05 35			06 28									07 28							
Alfreton	d												06 30										07 33		
Langley Mill	d												06 38										07 40		
Lincoln	d																								
Nottingham 8 🚋	a			00 41									07 04										08 02		
	d	23p10						06 02				06 28					07 02			07 28		07 31			
Beeston	d	23p16						06 08									07 08					07 37			
East Midlands Parkway ✈	d	23p25				05 39			06 32			06 39						07 32		07 39		07 46			
Loughborough	d	23p34				05 47		06 20	06 40					06 50			07 20	07 40				07 55			
Barrow Upon Soar	d													06 57								07 59			
Sileby	d													07 05								08 03			
Syston	d													07 10								08 08			
Leicester	a	00 02				05 57	06 23	06 31	06 51			06 55		07 21	07 23		07 31	07 51		07 55		08 21			
	d				04 40	05 59	06 25	06 33	06 53			06 57			07 25		07 33	07 53		07 57					
Market Harborough	d					06 14		06 47				07 12					07 47			08 12					
Melton Mowbray	d																								
Oakham	d																								
Corby	d															07 08									08 15
Kettering 4	a				05 00	06 23		06 56	07 15							07 20	07 56								08 24
	d				05 01	06 26		06 56	07 26								07 56								08 26
Wellingborough	d				05 09	06 34		07 04	07 34								08 04								08 34
Bedford 7	d				05 32	06 49		07 19	07 49								08 19								08 49
Luton 10	d					07 04			08 05																09 05
Luton Airport Parkway 7 ✈	d				05 55			07 35									08 35								
St Pancras International ⊖	a				06 21	07 31	07 34	08 00	08 31			08 19			08 34		09 01	09 06		09 19					09 29

		EM	EM	EM	EM	XC		EM	NT	XC	EM	EM	EM	EM	EM	EM		EM	XC	XC	EM	NT	XC	EM	EM
		◇1	◇1	◇1	◇1	◇1				◇1	◇1	◇1	◇1	◇1	◇	◇1		◇1	◇1	◇1			◇1	◇1	◇1
						G		H		I				J	K			L	M	N			O		
		☕	☕	⊠	☕	🛒				🛒	☕	☕	☕	☕		☕		☕	🛒	🛒			🛒	☕	☕
York 8	d					06 40				07 24									07 44	07 44			08 34		
Leeds 10	d				06 34	07 10			07 05					07 34					08 12	08 12		08 05			
Wakefield Westgate 7	d				06 46	07 23								07 46					08 24	08 24					
Wakefield Kirkgate 4	d								07 25													08 23			
Doncaster 7	d									07 52													08 58		
Sheffield 7 🚋	d	07 27			07 32	07 56			08 05	08 20		08 27		08 31	08 39	08 47			08 54	08 54		09 05	09 23		09 27
Chesterfield	d	07 39			07 45	08 08			08 24	08 32		08 39		08 45	08 53	08 59			09 06	09 06		09 23			09 39
Derby 6	a	07 59				08 27				08 52		08 59				09 19			09 26	09 28			09 52		09 59
	d	08 01		08 18								09 01				09 20									10 01
Long Eaton	d			08 28												09 30									
Alfreton	d				07 56				08 35					08 56	09 03							09 33			
Langley Mill	d				08 04				08 42													09 41			
Lincoln	d		07 08					07 26													08 35				
Nottingham 8 🚋	a		07 58		08 23			08 30	09 02					09 21	09 30						09 30	10 02			
	d		08 02		08 28			08 32					09 02	09 28							09 32				
Beeston	d		08 08					08 38					09 08					←			09 38				
East Midlands Parkway ✈	d			08 32	08 39			08 46						09 39		09 35		09 39			09 46				
Loughborough	d		08 20	08 40				08 55					09 20	→		09 42					09 55				
Barrow Upon Soar	d							08 59													09 59				
Sileby	d							09 03													10 03				
Syston	d							09 08													10 08				
Leicester	a	08 23	08 31	08 51	08 55			09 18				09 23	09 31			09 54		09 57			10 21				10 23
	d	08 25	08 33	08 53	08 57							09 25	09 33			09 55		09 57							10 25
Market Harborough	d		08 47		09 12								09 47					10 12							
Melton Mowbray	d																								
Oakham	d																								
Corby	d										09 17													10 17	
Kettering 4	a		08 56								09 26		09 56											10 26	
	d		08 56								09 27		09 56											10 27	
Wellingborough	d		09 04								09 35		10 04											10 35	
Bedford 7	d		09 19								09 49		10 19											10 49	
Luton 10	d										10 05													11 05	
Luton Airport Parkway 7 ✈	d		09 35										10 35												
St Pancras International ⊖	a	09 34	10 00	10 06	10 19						10 29	10 34	11 01			11 05		11 19						11 29	11 37

A from 6 August until 24 September
B From Liverpool Lime Street
C Until 10 September. To Reading
D To Paignton
E From Barnsley
F To Southampton Central
G To Plymouth
H From Sleaford
I From Newcastle to Reading
J To St Pancras International
K From Liverpool Lime Street to Norwich
L From Leeds
M 17 September, 24 September. From Newcastle to Plymouth
N Until 10 September. To Penzance
O From Newcastle to Southampton Central

For connections to Gatwick Airport see Table 52

Table 53

Saturdays
until 24 September

Sheffield - East Midlands - London

		EM		EM	EM	XC	EM	EM	NT	XC	EM	EM		EM	EM	EM	XC	XC	EM	EM	NT	XC		EM	EM
		◇1		◇	◇1	◇1	◇1			◇1	◇1	◇1		◇1	◇	◇1	◇1	◇1	◇1			◇1		◇1	◇1
				A		B				C					A		D	E				F			
		☕			☕	🛒	☕			🛒	☕	☕		☕		☕	🛒	🛒	☕			🛒		☕	☕
York 8	d					08 44				09 35							09 46	09 46				10 34			
Leeds 10	d					09 11			09 05								10 12	10 12			10 05				
Wakefield Westgate 7	d					09 24											10 24	10 24							
Wakefield Kirkgate 4	d								09 23												10 23				
Doncaster 7	d									09 58												10 58			
Sheffield 7 🚊	d			09 38	09 47	09 54			10 04	10 23		10 27			10 38	10 47	10 54	10 54			11 05	11 23			11 27
Chesterfield	d			09 53	09 59	10 06			10 21			10 39			10 53	10 59	11 06	11 08			11 22				11 39
Derby 6	a				10 19	10 26				10 52		10 59				11 19	11 26	11 28				11 52			11 59
	d				10 20							11 01				11 20									12 01
Long Eaton	d				10 30											11 30									
Alfreton	d			10 03					10 32						11 03						11 33				
Langley Mill	d								10 40												11 40				
Lincoln	d							09 19												10 36					
Nottingham 8 🚊	a			10 30				10 25	11 00						11 29					11 29	12 02				
	d	10 02					10 28	10 32						11 02					11 28	11 32					
Beeston	d	10 08						10 38						11 08						11 38					
East Midlands Parkway ✈	d				10 35		10 39	10 46								11 35			11 39	11 46					
Loughborough	d	10 20			10 42			10 55						11 20		11 42				11 55					
Barrow Upon Soar	d							10 59												11 59					
Sileby	d							11 03												12 03					
Syston	d							11 08												12 08					
Leicester	a	10 31			10 54		10 57	11 20				11 23		11 31		11 54			11 57	12 19					12 23
	d	10 33			10 55		10 57					11 25		11 33		11 55			11 57						12 25
Market Harborough	d	10 47					11 12							11 47					12 12						
Melton Mowbray	d																								
Oakham	d																								
Corby	d										11 17													12 17	
Kettering 4	a	10 56									11 26			11 56										12 26	
	d	10 56									11 27			11 56										12 27	
Wellingborough	d	11 04									11 35			12 04										12 35	
Bedford 7	d	11 19									11 49			12 19										12 49	
Luton 10	d										12 05													13 05	
Luton Airport Parkway 7 ✈	d	11 35												12 35											
St Pancras International ⊖	a	12 01			12 05		12 19				12 29	12 34		13 01		13 05			13 19					13 29	13 34

		EM	EM	EM	XC	EM	EM	NT		XC	EM	EM	EM	EM	EM	XC	EM	EM		NT	XC	EM	EM	EM	EM
		◇1	◇	◇1	◇1	◇1				◇1	◇1	◇1	◇1	◇	◇1	◇1	◇1				◇1	◇1	◇1	◇1	◇
			A		G					H				A		I					F				A
		☕		☕	🛒	☕				🛒	☕	☕	☕		☕	🛒	☕				🛒	☕	☕	☕	
York 8	d				10 45					11 34						11 45					12 34				
Leeds 10	d				11 11			11 05								12 11				12 05					
Wakefield Westgate 7	d				11 23											12 24									
Wakefield Kirkgate 4	d							11 23												12 23					
Doncaster 7	d									11 58											12 58				
Sheffield 7 🚊	d		11 38	11 47	11 54			12 06		12 23		12 27		12 38	12 47	12 54				13 05	13 23		13 27		13 38
Chesterfield	d		11 53	11 59	12 07			12 23				12 39		12 53	12 59	13 06				13 22			13 39		13 53
Derby 6	a			12 19	12 26					12 52		12 59			13 19	13 26					13 52		13 59		
	d			12 20								13 01			13 20								14 01		
Long Eaton	d			12 30											13 30										
Alfreton	d		12 03					12 34						13 03						13 34					14 03
Langley Mill	d							12 41												13 41					
Lincoln	d						11 42											12 30							
Nottingham 8 🚊	a		12 29				12 30	13 01						13 30				13 30		14 00					14 29
	d	12 02				12 28	12 32						13 02				13 28	13 32						14 02	
Beeston	d	12 08					12 38						13 08					13 38						14 08	
East Midlands Parkway ✈	d			12 35		12 39	12 46								13 35		13 39	13 46							
Loughborough	d	12 20		12 42			12 55						13 20		13 42			13 55						14 20	
Barrow Upon Soar	d						12 59											13 59							
Sileby	d						13 03											14 03							
Syston	d						13 08											14 08							
Leicester	a	12 31		12 54		12 57	13 19					13 23	13 31		13 54		13 57	14 19					14 23	14 31	
	d	12 33		12 55		12 57						13 25	13 33		13 55		13 57						14 25	14 33	
Market Harborough	d	12 47				13 12							13 47				14 12							14 47	
Melton Mowbray	d																								
Oakham	d																								
Corby	d										13 17											14 17			
Kettering 4	a	12 56									13 26		13 56									14 26		14 56	
	d	12 56									13 27		13 56									14 27		14 56	
Wellingborough	d	13 04									13 35		14 04									14 35		15 04	
Bedford 7	d	13 19									13 49		14 19									14 49		15 19	
Luton 10	d										14 05											15 05			
Luton Airport Parkway 7 ✈	d	13 35											14 35											15 35	
St Pancras International ⊖	a	14 01		14 05		14 19					14 29	14 34	15 01		15 05		15 19					15 29	15 34	16 01	

A From Liverpool Lime Street to Norwich
B From Edinburgh to Plymouth
C From Edinburgh to Reading
D 17 September, 24 September. From Glasgow Central to Plymouth
E Until 10 September. From Glasgow Central to Paignton
F From Newcastle to Southampton Central
G From Dundee to Plymouth
H From Newcastle to Reading
I From Glasgow Central to Plymouth

For connections to Gatwick Airport see Table 52

Table 53

Saturdays

until 24 September

Sheffield - East Midlands - London

		EM	XC	EM	EM	NT	XC	EM	EM	EM	EM	EM	XC	EM	EM	NT	XC	EM	EM	EM	EM	EM
		◇1	◇1	◇1			◇1	◇1	◇1	◇1	◇	◇1	◇1	◇1			◇1	◇1	◇1	◇1	◇	◇1
			A				B				C		D				E				F	
		☕	🛒	☕			🛒	☕	☕	☕		☕	🛒	☕			🛒	☕	☕	☕		☕
York 8	d		12 45				13 34						13 44				14 34					
Leeds 10	d		13 11			13 05							14 11			14 05						
Wakefield Westgate 7	d		13 23										14 24									
Wakefield Kirkgate 4	d					13 23										14 23						
Doncaster 7	d						13 58										14 58					
Sheffield 7	d	13 47	13 54			14 05	14 23		14 27		14 38	14 47	14 54			15 05	15 23		15 27		15 38	15 47
Chesterfield	d	13 59	14 07			14 22			14 39		14 53	14 59	15 06			15 22			15 39		15 53	15 59
Derby 6	a	14 19	14 26				14 52		14 59			15 19	15 26				15 52		15 59			16 19
	d	14 20							15 01			15 20							16 01			16 20
Long Eaton	d	14 30										15 30										16 30
Alfreton	d					14 33					15 04					15 33					16 04	
Langley Mill	d					14 40										15 40						
Lincoln	d				13 40										14 35							
Nottingham 8	a				14 30	15 00					15 29				15 30	16 02					16 30	
	d			14 28	14 32					15 02				15 28	15 32					16 02		
Beeston	d				14 38					15 08					15 38					16 08		
East Midlands Parkway	d	14 35		14 39	14 46							15 35		15 39	15 46							16 35
Loughborough	d	14 42			14 55					15 20		15 42			15 55					16 19		16 42
Barrow Upon Soar	d				14 59										15 59							
Sileby	d				15 03										16 03							
Syston	d				15 08										16 08							
Leicester	a	14 54		14 57	15 21				15 23	15 31		15 54		15 57	16 21				16 23	16 31		16 54
	d	14 55		14 57					15 25	15 33		15 55		15 57					16 25	16 33		16 55
Market Harborough	d			15 12						15 47				16 12						16 47		
Melton Mowbray	d																					
Oakham	d																					
Corby	d							15 17										16 17				
Kettering 4	a							15 26		15 56								16 26		16 56		
	d							15 27		15 56								16 27		16 56		
Wellingborough	d							15 35		16 04								16 35		17 04		
Bedford 7	d							15 49		16 19								16 49		17 19		
Luton 10	d							16 05										17 05				
Luton Airport Parkway 7	d									16 35										17 35		
St Pancras International	a	16 06		16 19				16 29	16 34	17 01		17 05		17 19				17 28	17 34	18 01		18 05

		XC	EM	EM	NT	XC	EM	EM	EM	EM	EM	EM	XC	EM	NT	XC	EM	EM	EM	EM	EM	EM	EM
		◇1	◇1			◇1	◇1	◇1	◇1	◇1	◇1	◇	◇1			◇1	◇1	◇1	◇1	◇1	◇1		◇
		G				B						C	H			B							C
		🛒	☕			🛒	☕	☕	☕	☕	☕		🛒			🛒	☕	☕	☕	☕	☕		
York 8	d	14 44				15 34							15 45			16 06							
Leeds 10	d	15 12			15 05								16 12		16 05	16 40							
Wakefield Westgate 7	d	15 24											16 24			16 52							
Wakefield Kirkgate 4	d				15 23										16 23								
Doncaster 7	d					15 58																	
Sheffield 7	d	15 54			16 04	16 23		16 27		16 35		16 38	16 54		17 05	17 23		17 27		17 35			17 44
Chesterfield	d	16 07			16 21			16 39		16 47		16 53	17 06		17 22			17 39		17 51			18 01
Derby 6	a	16 27				16 52		16 59		17 16			17 26			17 52		17 59		18 16			
	d							17 01		17 18								18 01		18 18			
Long Eaton	d									17 28										18 28			
Alfreton	d				16 32							17 04			17 33								18 11
Langley Mill	d				16 40										17 40								
Lincoln	d			15 27										16 34								17 26	
Nottingham 8	a			16 30	17 00							17 29		17 30	18 00							18 31	18 33
	d		16 28	16 32					17 02		17 28			17 32					18 02		18 28	18 32	
Beeston	d			16 38					17 08					17 38					18 08			18 38	
East Midlands Parkway	d		16 39	16 48						17 32	17 39			17 48						18 32	18 39	18 47	
Loughborough	d			16 57					17 20	17 40				17 57					18 20	18 40		18 55	
Barrow Upon Soar	d			17 01										18 01								19 00	
Sileby	d			17 05										18 05								19 04	
Syston	d			17 10										18 10								19 09	
Leicester	a		16 57	17 22				17 23	17 31	17 51	17 55			18 22				18 23	18 31	18 51	18 55	19 22	
	d		16 57					17 25	17 33	17 53	17 57							18 25	18 33	18 53	18 57		
Market Harborough	d		17 12						17 47		18 12								18 47		19 12		
Melton Mowbray	d																						
Oakham	d																						
Corby	d						17 17										18 17						
Kettering 4	a						17 26		17 56								18 26		18 56				
	d						17 27		17 56								18 27		18 56				
Wellingborough	d						17 35		18 04								18 35		19 04				
Bedford 7	d						17 49		18 19								18 49		19 18				
Luton 10	d						18 05										19 05						
Luton Airport Parkway 7	d								18 35										19 30				
St Pancras International	a		18 19				18 29	18 34	18 59	19 08	19 19						19 29	19 34	20 02	20 05	20 19		

A From Glasgow Central to Penzance
B From Newcastle to Reading
C From Liverpool Lime Street to Norwich
D From Aberdeen to Penzance
E From Newcastle to Southampton Central
F From Liverpool Lime Street
G From Glasgow Central to Plymouth
H From Edinburgh to Plymouth

For connections to Gatwick Airport see Table 52

Table 53

Saturdays
until 24 September

Sheffield - East Midlands - London

		XC	NT	XC	EM	EM		EM	EM	EM	XC	EM	EM	NT	XC	EM		EM	EM	EM	XC	EM	EM	EM	NT
		◇1		◇1	◇1	◇1		◇1	◇	◇1	◇1	◇1			◇1	◇1		◇1	◇1	◇	◇1		◇1	◇1	
		A		B					C	D	E				F					G	H				
		🛒		🛒	☕	☕		☕		☕	🛒	☕			🛒	☕		☕	☕		🛒		☕	☕	
York 8	d	16 44		17 34						17 50	17 44				18 34						18 44				
Leeds 10	d	17 11	17 05								18 11			18 05							19 11				19 05
Wakefield Westgate 7	d	17 23									18 23										19 24				
Wakefield Kirkgate 4	d		17 23											18 23											19 24
Doncaster 7	d			17 58						18 18					18 58										
Sheffield 7	d	17 54	18 06	18 23		18 27			18 38	18 47	18 54			19 07	19 24			19 27		19 38	19 54				20 05
Chesterfield	d	18 06	18 23			18 39			18 53		19 06			19 23				19 39		19 53	20 06				20 22
Derby 6	a	18 26		18 52		18 59				19 19	19 26				19 53			19 59			20 26				
	d					19 01				19 21								20 01							
Long Eaton	d									19 31															
Alfreton	d		18 34						19 03					19 33						20 04					20 33
Langley Mill	d		18 41											19 41											20 40
Lincoln	d												18 34												
Nottingham 8	a		18 58						19 33				19 29	20 01						20 31					21 00
	d							19 02				19 28	19 32						20 02			20 32		20 45	
Beeston	d							19 08					19 38						20 08			20 38		20 51	
East Midlands Parkway ✈	d									19 35		19 41	19 46						20 16			20 46		20 57	
Loughborough	d							19 20		19 41			19 55						20 24			20 55		21 05	
Barrow Upon Soar	d												19 59									20 59			
Sileby	d												20 03									21 03			
Syston	d												20 08									21 08			
Leicester	a					19 23		19 31		19 54		19 58	20 20					20 23	20 34			21 19		21 15	
	d					19 25		19 33		19 54		20 00						20 25	20 36					21 17	
Market Harborough	d							19 47				20 15							20 50					21 31	
Melton Mowbray	d																								
Oakham	d																								
Corby	d				19 17											19 43							20 43		
Kettering 4	a				19 26			19 56		20 16						19 52			20 59				20 52	21 40	
	d				19 27			19 56		20 17						20 26			20 59				21 24	21 40	
Wellingborough	d				19 35			20 04								20 35			21 07				21 32	21 49	
Bedford 7	d				19 49			20 18								20 49			21 22				21 47	22 03	
Luton 10	d				20 05											21 03							22 03	22 18	
Luton Airport Parkway 7 ✈	d							20 30											21 38					22 21	
St Pancras International ⊖	a				20 29	20 34		21 01		21 06		21 15				21 29		21 38	22 05				22 29	22 48	

		XC		EM	EM	EM	EM	EM	XC	XC	EM	XC		EM	EM	EM	EM	EM	EM	EM
		◇1		◇1	◇1	◇1		◇	◇1	◇1	◇	◇1		◇1		◇	◇1	◇1	◇	◇
		F						C	I	F	C	J				C	K	L	M	N
		🛒		☕	☕	☕				🛒				☕			☕	☕		
York 8	d	19 34							19 44	20 23		20 45								
Leeds 10	d								20 11			21 11								
Wakefield Westgate 7	d								20 23			21 23								
Wakefield Kirkgate 4	d																			
Doncaster 7	d	19 58																		
Sheffield 7	d	20 23		20 27				20 41	20 54	21 23	21 38	21 54				22 35	23 20	23 30	23 42	23 42
Chesterfield	d			20 39				20 59	21 06	21 35	21 54	22 06				22 51	23 33	23 43	23 57	23 57
Derby 6	a	20 52		21 00					21 27	21 55		22 25					00 08	00 18		
	d			21 01																
Long Eaton	d																			
Alfreton	d							21 09			22 05					23 02				
Langley Mill	d										22 12									
Lincoln	d																			
Nottingham 8	a							21 33			22 33					23 32			00 27	00 34
	d					21 18	21 32								23 10					
Beeston	d						21 38								23 17					
East Midlands Parkway ✈	d			21 14			21 46								23 25					
Loughborough	d			21 23		21 32	21 55								23 33					
Barrow Upon Soar	d						21 59													
Sileby	d						22 03													
Syston	d						22 13													
Leicester	a			21 39		21 43	22 21								23 59					
	d					21 45														
Market Harborough	d					21 59														
Melton Mowbray	d																			
Oakham	d																			
Corby	d				21 43									22 43						
Kettering 4	a				21 52	22 14								22 52						
	d					22 15														
Wellingborough	d					22 22														
Bedford 7	d					22 37														
Luton 10	d					22 59														
Luton Airport Parkway 7 ✈	d																			
St Pancras International ⊖	a					23 35														

A From Glasgow Central to Taunton
B From Newcastle to Reading
C From Liverpool Lime Street
D From Scarborough
E From Edinburgh to Plymouth
F From Newcastle to Birmingham New Street
G From Liverpool Lime Street to Norwich
H From Glasgow Central to Bristol Temple Meads
I From Edinburgh to Birmingham New Street
J From Glasgow Central to Birmingham New Street
K until 30 July
L from 6 August until 24 September
M 17 September, 24 September. From Liverpool Lime Street
N Until 10 September. From Liverpool Lime Street

For connections to Gatwick Airport see Table 52

Table 53

Saturdays
from 1 October

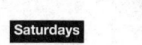

Sheffield - East Midlands - London

		EM	EM	EM	EM	EM	EM	EM	EM	EM		NT	EM	EM	EM	EM	EM	XC	EM	EM		NT	XC	EM	EM
			◇1	◇	◇1	◇1	◇1	◇1	◇1	◇1				◇1	◇1	◇1	◇1	◇1	◇1				◇1	◇1	◇1
		A		B														C				D	E		
			☕		☕	☕	☕	☕	☕	☕				☕	☕	☕	☕	🛒	☕				🛒	☕	☕
York [8]	d																								
Leeds [10]	d																	06 00					06 15		
Wakefield Westgate [7]	d																	06 12					06 29		
Wakefield Kirkgate [4]	d																								
Doncaster [7]	d																						06 47		
Sheffield [7]	d		23p21	23p37			05 27					05 54		06 25				06 50				07 03	07 18		07 27
Chesterfield	d		23p45	00 02			05 39					06 20		06 37				07 03				07 20	07 30		07 39
Derby [6]	a		00 11				05 59							06 59				07 24					07 49		07 59
	d					05 25	06 01		06 18					07 01			07 18								08 01
Long Eaton	d					05 35			06 28								07 28								
Alfreton	d											06 30										07 33			
Langley Mill	d											06 38										07 40			
Lincoln	d																								
Nottingham [8]	a			00 41								07 04										08 02			
	d	23p10						06 02		06 28						07 02			07 28	07 31					
Beeston	d	23p16						06 08								07 08				07 37					
East Midlands Parkway	d	23p25				05 39			06 32	06 39							07 32		07 39	07 46					
Loughborough	d	23p34				05 47		06 20	06 40				06 50			07 20	07 40			07 55					
Barrow Upon Soar	d												06 57							07 59					
Sileby	d												07 05							08 03					
Syston	d												07 10							08 08					
Leicester	a	00 02				05 57	06 23	06 31	06 51	06 55			07 21	07 23		07 31	07 51		07 55	08 21					08 23
	d				04 40	05 59	06 25	06 33	06 53	06 57				07 25		07 33	07 53		07 57						08 25
Market Harborough	d					06 14		06 47		07 12						07 47			08 12						
Melton Mowbray	d																								
Oakham	d																								
Corby	d														07 08									08 15	
Kettering [4]	a				05 00	06 23		06 56	07 15						07 20	07 56								08 24	
	d				05 01	06 26		06 56	07 26							07 56								08 26	
Wellingborough	d				05 09	06 34		07 04	07 34							08 04								08 34	
Bedford [7]	d				05 32	06 49		07 19	07 49							08 19								08 49	
Luton [10]	d					07 04			08 05															09 05	
Luton Airport Parkway [7]	d				05 55			07 35								08 35									
St Pancras International	a				06 21	07 31	07 34	08 00	08 31	08 19				08 34		09 01	09 06		09 19					09 29	09 34

		EM	EM	EM	XC	EM		NT	XC	EM	EM	EM	EM	EM	EM	EM		XC	EM	NT	XC	EM	EM	EM	EM
		◇1	◇1	◇1	◇1				◇1	◇1	◇1	◇1	◇1	◇	◇1	◇1		◇1			◇1	◇1	◇1	◇1	◇
					C	F			G				H	I		J		K			L				I
		☕	⊠	☕	🛒				🛒	☕	☕	☕	☕		☕	☕		🛒			🛒	☕	☕	☕	
York [8]	d				06 40				07 24									07 44			08 34				
Leeds [10]	d			06 34	07 10			07 05					07 34					08 12		08 05					
Wakefield Westgate [7]	d			06 46	07 23								07 46					08 24							
Wakefield Kirkgate [4]	d							07 25												08 23					
Doncaster [7]	d								07 52												08 58				
Sheffield [7]	d			07 32	07 56			08 05	08 20		08 27		08 31	08 39	08 47			08 54		09 05	09 23		09 27		09 38
Chesterfield	d			07 45	08 08			08 24	08 32		08 39		08 45	08 53	08 59			09 06		09 23			09 39		09 53
Derby [6]	a				08 27				08 52		08 59				09 19			09 26			09 52		09 59		
	d		08 18								09 01				09 20								10 01		
Long Eaton	d		08 28												09 30										
Alfreton	d			07 56				08 35					08 56	09 03						09 33					10 03
Langley Mill	d			08 04				08 42												09 41					
Lincoln	d	07 08				07 26													08 35						
Nottingham [8]	a	07 58		08 23		08 32		09 02					09 21	09 30					09 32	10 02					10 30
	d	08 02		08 28		08 32						09 02	09 28						09 32					10 02	
Beeston	d	08 08				08 38						09 08				←			09 38					10 08	
East Midlands Parkway	d		08 32	08 39		08 46							09 39		09 35	09 39			09 46						
Loughborough	d	08 20	08 40			08 55						09 20	→		09 42				09 55					10 20	
Barrow Upon Soar	d					08 59													09 59						
Sileby	d					09 03													10 03						
Syston	d					09 08													10 08						
Leicester	a	08 31	08 51	08 55		09 18					09 23	09 31			09 54	09 57			10 21				10 23	10 31	
	d	08 33	08 53	08 57							09 25	09 33			09 55	09 57							10 25	10 33	
Market Harborough	d	08 47		09 12								09 47				10 12								10 47	
Melton Mowbray	d																								
Oakham	d																								
Corby	d									09 17												10 17			
Kettering [4]	a	08 56								09 26		09 56										10 26		10 56	
	d	08 56								09 27		09 56										10 27		10 56	
Wellingborough	d	09 04								09 35		10 04										10 35		11 04	
Bedford [7]	d	09 19								09 49		10 19										10 49		11 19	
Luton [10]	d									10 05												11 05			
Luton Airport Parkway [7]	d	09 35										10 35												11 35	
St Pancras International	a	10 00	10 06	10 19						10 29	10 34	11 01			11 05	11 19						11 29	11 37	12 01	

A from 1 October until 22 October
B From Liverpool Lime Street
C To Plymouth
D From Barnsley
E To Southampton Central
F From Sleaford
G From Newcastle to Reading
H To St Pancras International
I From Liverpool Lime Street to Norwich
J From Leeds
K From Newcastle to Plymouth
L From Newcastle to Southampton Central

For connections to Gatwick Airport see Table 52

Table 53

Saturdays from 1 October

Sheffield - East Midlands - London

		EM		XC	EM	EM	NT	XC	EM	EM	EM	EM		EM	XC	EM	EM	NT	XC	EM	EM	EM		EM	EM
		◇1		◇1	◇1			◇1	◇1	◇1	◇1	◇		◇1	◇1	◇1			◇1	◇1	◇1	◇1		◇	◇1
				A				B				C			D				E					C	
		☕		🛒	☕			🛒	☕	☕	☕			☕	🛒	☕			🛒	☕	☕	☕			☕
York [8]	d			08 44				09 35							09 46				10 34						
Leeds [10]	d			09 11			09 05								10 12			10 05							
Wakefield Westgate [7]	d			09 24											10 24										
Wakefield Kirkgate [4]	d						09 23											10 23							
Doncaster [7]	d							09 58											10 58						
Sheffield [7]	d	09 47		09 54			10 04	10 23		10 27		10 38		10 47	10 54			11 05	11 23		11 27			11 38	11 47
Chesterfield	d	09 59		10 06			10 21			10 39		10 53		10 59	11 06			11 22			11 39			11 53	11 59
Derby [6]	a	10 19		10 26				10 52		10 59				11 19	11 26				11 52		11 59				12 19
	d	10 20								11 01				11 20							12 01				12 20
Long Eaton	d	10 30												11 30											12 30
Alfreton	d						10 32					11 03						11 33						12 03	
Langley Mill	d						10 40											11 40							
Lincoln	d					09 31											10 36								
Nottingham [8]	a					10 32	11 00					11 29					11 31	12 02						12 29	
	d				10 28	10 32					11 02					11 28	11 32					12 02			
Beeston	d					10 38					11 08						11 38					12 08			
East Midlands Parkway	d	10 35			10 39	10 46								11 35		11 39	11 46								12 35
Loughborough	d	10 42				10 55					11 20			11 42			11 55					12 20			12 42
Barrow Upon Soar	d					10 59											11 59								
Sileby	d					11 03											12 03								
Syston	d					11 08											12 08								
Leicester	a	10 54			10 57	11 20				11 23	11 31			11 54		11 57	12 19				12 23	12 31			12 54
	d	10 55			10 57					11 25	11 33			11 55		11 57					12 25	12 33			12 55
Market Harborough	d				11 12						11 47					12 12						12 47			
Melton Mowbray	d																								
Oakham	d																								
Corby	d								11 17											12 17					
Kettering [4]	a								11 26		11 56									12 26		12 56			
	d								11 27		11 56									12 27		12 56			
Wellingborough	d								11 35		12 04									12 35		13 04			
Bedford [7]	d								11 49		12 19									12 49		13 19			
Luton [10]	d								12 05											13 05					
Luton Airport Parkway [7]	d										12 35											13 35			
St Pancras International	a	12 05			12 19				12 29	12 34	13 01			13 05		13 19				13 29	13 34	14 01			14 05

		XC	EM	EM	NT	XC	EM	EM		EM	EM	EM	XC	EM	EM	NT	XC	EM		EM	EM	EM	EM	XC	EM
		◇1	◇1			◇1	◇1	◇1		◇1	◇	◇1	◇1	◇1			◇1	◇1		◇1	◇1	◇	◇1	◇1	◇1
		F				G					C		D				E					C		H	
		🛒	☕			🛒	☕	☕		☕		☕	🛒	☕			🛒	☕		☕	☕		☕	🛒	☕
York [8]	d	10 45				11 34							11 45				12 34							12 45	
Leeds [10]	d	11 11			11 05								12 11			12 05								13 11	
Wakefield Westgate [7]	d	11 23											12 24											13 23	
Wakefield Kirkgate [4]	d				11 23											12 23									
Doncaster [7]	d					11 58											12 58								
Sheffield [7]	d	11 54			12 06	12 23		12 27			12 38	12 47	12 54			13 05	13 23			13 27		13 38	13 47	13 54	
Chesterfield	d	12 07			12 23			12 39			12 53	12 59	13 06			13 22				13 39		13 53	13 59	14 07	
Derby [6]	a	12 26				12 52		12 59				13 19	13 26				13 52			13 59			14 19	14 26	
	d							13 01				13 20								14 01			14 20		
Long Eaton	d											13 30											14 30		
Alfreton	d				12 34						13 03					13 34						14 03			
Langley Mill	d				12 41											13 41									
Lincoln	d			11 42											12 30										
Nottingham [8]	a			12 30	13 01						13 30				13 32	14 00						14 29			
	d		12 28	12 32						13 02				13 28	13 32						14 02				14 28
Beeston	d			12 38						13 08					13 38						14 08				
East Midlands Parkway	d		12 39	12 46								13 35		13 39	13 46								14 35		14 39
Loughborough	d			12 55						13 20		13 42			13 55						14 20		14 42		
Barrow Upon Soar	d			12 59											13 59										
Sileby	d			13 03											14 03										
Syston	d			13 08											14 08										
Leicester	a		12 57	13 19				13 23		13 31		13 54		13 57	14 19					14 23	14 31		14 54		14 57
	d		12 57					13 25		13 33		13 55		13 57						14 25	14 33		14 55		14 57
Market Harborough	d		13 12							13 47				14 12							14 47				15 12
Melton Mowbray	d																								
Oakham	d																								
Corby	d						13 17											14 17							
Kettering [4]	a						13 26			13 56								14 26			14 56				
	d						13 27			13 56								14 27			14 56				
Wellingborough	d						13 35			14 04								14 35			15 04				
Bedford [7]	d						13 49			14 19								14 49			15 19				
Luton [10]	d						14 05											15 05							
Luton Airport Parkway [7]	d									14 35											15 35				
St Pancras International	a		14 19				14 29	14 34		15 01		15 05		15 19				15 29		15 34	16 01		16 06		16 19

A From Edinburgh to Plymouth
B From Edinburgh to Reading
C From Liverpool Lime Street to Norwich
D From Glasgow Central to Plymouth
E From Newcastle to Southampton Central
F From Dundee to Plymouth
G From Newcastle to Reading
H From Glasgow Central to Penzance

For connections to Gatwick Airport see Table 52

Table 53

Saturdays

from 1 October

Sheffield - East Midlands - London

		EM	NT	XC	EM	EM	EM	EM	EM	XC	EM	EM	NT	XC	EM	EM	EM	EM	EM	XC	EM	EM
				◇1	◇1	◇1	◇1	◇	◇1	◇1	◇1			◇1	◇1	◇1	◇1	◇	◇1	◇1	◇1	
				A				B		C				D				B		E		
				⚭	⊐	⊐	⊐		⊐	⚭	⊐			⚭	⊐	⊐	⊐		⊐	⚭	⊐	
York 8	d			13 34						13 44				14 34						14 44		
Leeds 10	d		13 05							14 11			14 05							15 12		
Wakefield Westgate 7	d									14 24										15 24		
Wakefield Kirkgate 4	d		13 23										14 23									
Doncaster 7	d			13 58										14 58								
Sheffield 7	d		14 05	14 23		14 27		14 38	14 47	14 54			15 05	15 23		15 27		15 38	15 47	15 54		
Chesterfield	d		14 22			14 39		14 53	14 59	15 06			15 22			15 39		15 53	15 59	16 07		
Derby 6	a			14 52		14 59			15 19	15 26				15 52		15 59			16 19	16 27		
	d					15 01			15 20							16 01			16 20			
Long Eaton	d								15 30										16 30			
Alfreton	d		14 33					15 04					15 33					16 04				
Langley Mill	d		14 40										15 40									
Lincoln	d	13 40										14 35										15 27
Nottingham 8	a	14 32	15 00					15 29				15 32	16 02					16 30				16 32
	d	14 32					15 02				15 28	15 32					16 02				16 28	16 32
Beeston	d	14 38					15 08					15 38					16 08					16 38
East Midlands Parkway	d	14 46							15 35		15 39	15 46							16 35		16 39	16 48
Loughborough	d	14 55					15 20		15 42			15 55					16 19		16 42			16 57
Barrow Upon Soar	d	14 59										15 59										17 01
Sileby	d	15 03										16 03										17 05
Syston	d	15 08										16 08										17 10
Leicester	a	15 21				15 23	15 31		15 54		15 57	16 21				16 23	16 31		16 54		16 57	17 22
	d					15 25	15 33		15 55		15 57					16 25	16 33		16 55		16 57	
Market Harborough	d						15 47				16 12						16 47				17 12	
Melton Mowbray	d																					
Oakham	d																					
Corby	d				15 17										16 17							
Kettering 4	a				15 26		15 56								16 26		16 56					
	d				15 27		15 56								16 27		16 56					
Wellingborough	d				15 35		16 04								16 35		17 04					
Bedford 7	d				15 49		16 19								16 49		17 19					
Luton 10	d				16 05										17 05							
Luton Airport Parkway 7	d						16 35										17 35					
St Pancras International	a				16 29	16 34	17 01		17 05		17 19				17 28	17 34	18 01		18 05		18 19	

		NT	XC	EM	EM	EM	EM	EM	EM	XC	EM	NT	XC	EM	EM	EM	EM	EM	EM	EM	XC	NT	XC
			◇1	◇1	◇1	◇1	◇1	◇1	◇	◇1			◇1	◇1	◇1	◇1	◇1	◇1		◇	◇1		◇1
			A						B	F			A							B	G		A
			⚭	⊐	⊐	⊐	⊐	⊐		⚭			⚭	⊐	⊐	⊐	⊐	⊐			⚭		⚭
York 8	d		15 34							15 45			16 06								16 44		17 34
Leeds 10	d	15 05								16 12		16 05	16 40								17 11	17 05	
Wakefield Westgate 7	d									16 24			16 52								17 23		
Wakefield Kirkgate 4	d	15 23										16 23										17 23	
Doncaster 7	d		15 58																				17 58
Sheffield 7	d	16 04	16 23		16 27		16 35		16 38	16 54		17 05	17 23		17 27		17 35			17 44	17 54	18 06	18 23
Chesterfield	d	16 21			16 39		16 47		16 53	17 06		17 22			17 39		17 51			18 01	18 06	18 23	
Derby 6	a		16 52		16 59		17 16			17 26			17 52		17 59		18 16				18 26		18 52
	d				17 01		17 18								18 01		18 18						
Long Eaton	d						17 28										18 28						
Alfreton	d	16 32							17 04			17 33								18 11		18 34	
Langley Mill	d	16 40										17 40										18 41	
Lincoln	d										16 34								17 26				
Nottingham 8	a	17 00							17 29		17 30	18 00							18 32	18 33		18 58	
	d					17 02		17 28			17 32					18 02		18 28	18 32				
Beeston	d					17 08					17 38					18 08			18 38				
East Midlands Parkway	d						17 32	17 39			17 48						18 32	18 39	18 47				
Loughborough	d					17 20	17 40				17 57					18 20	18 40		18 55				
Barrow Upon Soar	d										18 01								19 00				
Sileby	d										18 05								19 04				
Syston	d										18 10								19 09				
Leicester	a				17 23	17 31	17 51	17 55			18 22				18 23	18 31	18 51	18 55	19 22				
	d				17 25	17 33	17 53	17 57							18 25	18 33	18 53	18 57					
Market Harborough	d					17 47		18 12								18 47		19 12					
Melton Mowbray	d																						
Oakham	d																						
Corby	d			17 17										18 17									
Kettering 4	a			17 26		17 56								18 26		18 56							
	d			17 27		17 56								18 27		18 56							
Wellingborough	d			17 35		18 04								18 35		19 04							
Bedford 7	d			17 49		18 19								18 49		19 18							
Luton 10	d			18 05										19 05									
Luton Airport Parkway 7	d					18 35										19 30							
St Pancras International	a			18 29	18 34	18 59	19 08	19 19						19 29	19 34	20 02	20 05	20 19					

A From Newcastle to Reading
B From Liverpool Lime Street to Norwich
C From Aberdeen to Penzance
D From Newcastle to Southampton Central
E From Glasgow Central to Penzance
F From Edinburgh to Plymouth
G From Glasgow Central to Plymouth

For connections to Gatwick Airport see Table 52

Table 53

Saturdays
from 1 October

Sheffield - East Midlands - London

Station		EM	EM	EM	EM	EM		XC	EM	EM	NT	XC	EM
		◇**1**	◇**1**	◇**1**	◇	◇**1**		◇**1**	◇**1**			◇**1**	◇**1**
					A			B				C	
		☕	☕	☕		☕		🚲	☕			🚲	☕
York **8**	d					17 50		17 44				18 34	
Leeds **10**	d							18 11			18 05		
Wakefield Westgate **7**	d							18 23					
Wakefield Kirkgate **4**	d										18 23		
Doncaster **7**	d					18 18						18 58	
Sheffield 7 🚌	d		18 27		18 38	18 47		18 54			19 07	19 24	
Chesterfield	d		18 39		18 53			19 06			19 23		
Derby 6	a		18 59			19 19		19 26				19 53	
	d		19 01			19 21							
Long Eaton	d					19 31							
Alfreton	d				19 03						19 33		
Langley Mill	d										19 41		
Lincoln	d									18 34			
Nottingham 8 🚌	a				19 33					19 31	20 01		
	d			19 02					19 28	19 32			
Beeston	d			19 08						19 38			
East Midlands Parkway ✈	d					19 35			19 41	19 46			
Loughborough	d			19 20		19 41				19 55			
Barrow Upon Soar	d									19 59			
Sileby	d									20 03			
Syston	d									20 08			
Leicester	a		19 23	19 31		19 54			19 58	20 20			
	d		19 25	19 33		19 54			20 00				
Market Harborough	d			19 47					20 15				
Melton Mowbray	d												
Oakham	d												
Corby	d	19 17											19 43
Kettering **4**	a	19 26		19 56		20 16							19 52
	d	19 27		19 56		20 17							20 26
Wellingborough	d	19 35		20 04									20 35
Bedford **7**	d	19 49		20 18									20 49
Luton **10**	d	20 05											21 03
Luton Airport Parkway **7** ✈	d			20 30									
St Pancras International ⊖	a	20 29	20 34	21 01		21 06			21 15				21 29

Station		EM	EM	EM		XC	EM	EM	EM	NT	XC	EM	EM
		◇**1**	◇**1**	◇		◇**1**		◇**1**	◇**1**		◇**1**	◇**1**	◇**1**
				D		E					F		
		☕	☕			🚲		☕	☕		🚲	☕	☕
York **8**	d					18 44					19 34		
Leeds **10**	d					19 11				19 05			
Wakefield Westgate **7**	d					19 24							
Wakefield Kirkgate **4**	d									19 24			
Doncaster **7**	d										19 58		
Sheffield 7 🚌	d	19 27		19 38		19 54				20 05	20 23	20 27	
Chesterfield	d	19 39		19 53		20 06				20 22		20 39	
Derby 6	a	19 59				20 26					20 52	21 00	
	d	20 01										21 01	
Long Eaton	d												
Alfreton	d			20 04						20 33			
Langley Mill	d									20 40			
Lincoln	d												
Nottingham 8 🚌	a			20 31						21 00			
	d		20 02				20 32		20 45				
Beeston	d		20 08				20 38		20 51				
East Midlands Parkway ✈	d		20 16				20 46		20 57			21 14	
Loughborough	d		20 24				20 55		21 05			21 23	
Barrow Upon Soar	d						20 59						
Sileby	d						21 03						
Syston	d						21 08						
Leicester	a	20 23	20 34				21 19		21 15			21 39	
	d	20 25	20 36						21 17				
Market Harborough	d		20 50						21 31				
Melton Mowbray	d												
Oakham	d												
Corby	d							20 43					21 43
Kettering **4**	a		20 59					20 52	21 40				21 52
	d		20 59					21 24	21 40				
Wellingborough	d		21 07					21 32	21 49				
Bedford **7**	d		21 22					21 47	22 03				
Luton **10**	d							22 03	22 18				
Luton Airport Parkway **7** ✈	d		21 38						22 21				
St Pancras International ⊖	a	21 38	22 05					22 29	22 48				

Station		EM		EM	EM	XC	XC	EM	XC	EM	EM	EM		EM	EM	EM	EM
		◇**1**			◇	◇**1**	◇**1**	◇	◇**1**	◇**1**		◇		◇**1**	◇**1**	◇	◇
					A	G	F	A	H			A		I	J	K	L
		☕					🚲			☕				☕	☕		
York **8**	d					19 44	20 23		20 45								
Leeds **10**	d					20 11			21 11								
Wakefield Westgate **7**	d					20 23			21 23								
Wakefield Kirkgate **4**	d																
Doncaster **7**	d																
Sheffield 7 🚌	d				20 41	20 54	21 23	21 38	21 54			22 35		23 20	23 30	23 42	23 42
Chesterfield	d				20 59	21 06	21 35	21 54	22 06			22 51		23 33	23 43	23 57	23 57
Derby 6	a					21 27	21 55		22 25					00 08	00 18		
	d																
Long Eaton	d																
Alfreton	d				21 09			22 05				23 02					
Langley Mill	d							22 12									
Lincoln	d																
Nottingham 8 🚌	a				21 33			22 33				23 32				00 27	00 34
	d	21 18		21 32							23 10						
Beeston	d			21 38							23 17						
East Midlands Parkway ✈	d			21 46							23 25						
Loughborough	d	21 32		21 55							23 33						
Barrow Upon Soar	d			21 59													
Sileby	d			22 03													
Syston	d			22 13													
Leicester	a	21 43		22 21							23 59						
	d	21 45															
Market Harborough	d	21 59															
Melton Mowbray	d																
Oakham	d																
Corby	d									22 43							
Kettering **4**	a	22 14								22 52							
	d	22 15															
Wellingborough	d	22 22															
Bedford **7**	d	22 37															
Luton **10**	d	22 59															
Luton Airport Parkway **7** ✈	d																
St Pancras International ⊖	a	23 35															

A From Liverpool Lime Street
B From Edinburgh to Plymouth
C From Newcastle to Guildford
D From Liverpool Lime Street to Norwich
E From Glasgow Central to Bristol Temple Meads
F From Newcastle to Birmingham New Street
G From Edinburgh to Birmingham New Street
H From Glasgow Central to Birmingham New Street
I from 29 October
J from 1 October until 22 October
K from 1 October until 22 October. From Liverpool Lime Street
L from 29 October. From Liverpool Lime Street

For connections to Gatwick Airport see Table 52

Table 53

Sundays until 19 June

Sheffield - East Midlands - London

		EM	EM	EM	EM	EM	EM	EM	EM	XC		EM	NT	EM	EM	XC	EM	NT	EM	EM		EM	EM	XC	NT
		◇1	◇	◇1	◇1	◇1	◇1	◇1	◇1	◇1		◇1		◇1	◇1	◇1	◇1		◇1	◇1		◇1	◇	◇1	
		A	B							C						C							D	E	
		☕		☕	☕	☕	☕	☕	☕	🛒		☕		☕	☕	🛒	☕		☕	☕		☕		🛒	
York 8	d																							09 28	
Leeds 10	d									08 10						09 00		09 05				09 44		10 00	10 02
Wakefield Westgate 7	d									08 23						09 11						09 57		10 12	
Wakefield Kirkgate 4	d																	09 21							10 18
Doncaster 7	d															09 32								10 30	
Sheffield 7	d	23p20	23p42						08 13	08 54			09 00		09 17	09 57		10 07		10 17		10 26	10 49	10 57	11 03
Chesterfield	d	23p33	23p57						08 25	09 07			09 17		09 29	10 09		10 23		10 29		10 41	11 04	11 09	11 20
Derby 6	a	00 08							08 42	09 29					09 49	10 32				10 49				11 28	
	d			06 48		07 52			08 44						09 51					10 51					
Long Eaton	d								08 54						10 01					11 01					
Alfreton	d												09 28					10 33					11 14		11 30
Langley Mill	d												09 35					10 41							11 38
Lincoln	d																								
Nottingham 8	a		00 34										09 53					10 59				11 11	11 39		11 54
	d				07 28		08 18					09 14					10 15					11 18			
Beeston	d						08 24										10 22								
East Midlands Parkway	d			07 00	07 38	08 03	08 31		08 58			09 25			10 05		10 30			11 05		11 30			
Loughborough	d					08 11	08 38		09 06			09 33			10 13		10 38			11 13		11 38			
Barrow Upon Soar	d																								
Sileby	d																								
Syston	d																								
Leicester	a			07 16	07 52	08 22	08 49		09 17			09 46			10 23		10 51			11 23		11 51			
	d			07 18	07 54	08 23	08 51		09 18			09 48			10 25		10 53			11 25		11 53			
Market Harborough	d			07 36	08 11	08 40	09 08		09 35			10 06			10 39		11 08			11 39		12 08			
Melton Mowbray	d																								
Oakham	d																								
Corby	d							09 30						10 25					11 25						
Kettering 4	a			07 46	08 20	08 49	09 17	09 39	09 44			10 16		10 34	10 48		11 18		11 34	11 48		12 18			
	d			07 47	08 21	08 50	09 18		09 47			10 17			10 51		11 19			11 49		12 19			
Wellingborough	d			07 59	08 32	09 02	09 29		10 00			10 25			10 59		11 27			11 57		12 27			
Bedford 7	d			08 13	08 45	09 14	09 43		10 12			10 44			11 15		11 45			12 14		12 45			
Luton 10	d			08 32		09 39			10 36						11 39					12 39					
Luton Airport Parkway 7	d				09 09		10 09					11 09					12 09					13 10			
St Pancras International	a			09 13	09 43	10 19	10 47		11 15			11 47			12 15		12 45			13 16		13 48			

		EM	EM	XC	EM	NT		EM	EM	EM	NT	EM	XC	EM	EM	NT		EM	EM	XC	EM	EM	EM	EM	EM
		◇1	◇1	◇1	◇1			◇1	◇1	◇1		◇	◇1	◇1	◇1			◇1	◇	◇1	◇1	◇1	◇1	◇1	◇
				F								D	G						H	I					J
		☕	☕	🛒	☕			☕	☕	☕			🛒	☕	☕			☕		🛒	☕	☕	☕	☕	
York 8	d			10 28									11 28							12 28					
Leeds 10	d		10 15	11 00		10 57					11 29		12 00			12 29				13 00					
Wakefield Westgate 7	d		10 28	11 12									12 12							13 12					
Wakefield Kirkgate 4	d					11 13					11 46					12 46									
Doncaster 7	d			11 30									12 30							13 30					
Sheffield 7	d		11 06	11 57		12 00			12 23		12 31	12 49	12 57		13 20	13 31			13 49	13 57	14 04				14 46
Chesterfield	d		11 25	12 09		12 18			12 36		12 49	13 03	13 09		13 32	13 48			14 03	14 09	14 16				15 00
Derby 6	a		11 47	12 29					12 55				13 31		13 51					14 29	14 36				
	d		11 48						12 57						13 53						14 38				
Long Eaton	d								13 07						14 03						14 48				
Alfreton	d					12 28					12 59	13 14				13 59			14 14						15 12
Langley Mill	d					12 36					13 07					14 06									15 19
Lincoln	d																								
Nottingham 8	a					12 53					13 25	13 39				14 22			14 39						15 38
	d				12 15					13 14								14 23					15 10	15 36	
Beeston	d				12 22					13 21								14 29					15 16		
East Midlands Parkway	d		12 01		12 30				13 11	13 30					14 07			14 35			14 56		15 23	15 46	
Loughborough	d		12 09		12 38				13 19	13 38					14 15			14 43			15 04		15 30		
Barrow Upon Soar	d																								
Sileby	d																								
Syston	d																								
Leicester	a		12 21		12 52				13 29	13 51					14 25			14 54			15 14		15 42	16 02	
	d		12 23		12 53				13 31	13 53					14 27			14 56			15 16		15 44	16 03	
Market Harborough	d		12 38		13 08				13 45	14 08					14 41			15 10					15 58		
Melton Mowbray	d																								
Oakham	d																								
Corby	d	12 30						13 30						14 25								15 25			
Kettering 4	a	12 39	12 48		13 18			13 39	13 54	14 17				14 34	14 49			15 19				15 34	16 07		
	d		12 49		13 19				13 55	14 18					14 50			15 20					16 08		
Wellingborough	d		12 57		13 27				14 02	14 27					14 58			15 27					16 15		
Bedford 7	d		13 15		13 46				14 20	14 44					15 14			15 44					16 32		
Luton 10	d		13 38						14 37						15 33						16 09				
Luton Airport Parkway 7	d				14 10					15 02								16 02					16 53		
St Pancras International	a		14 15		14 44				15 08	15 35					16 04			16 33			16 42		17 27	17 31	

A not 22 May
B not 22 May. From Liverpool Lime Street
C To Plymouth
D To Norwich
E To Bristol Temple Meads
F From Newcastle to Plymouth
G From Edinburgh to Penzance
H From Manchester Piccadilly to Norwich
I From Edinburgh to Plymouth
J From Liverpool Lime Street to Norwich

For connections to Gatwick Airport see Table 52

Table 53

Sundays
until 19 June

Sheffield - East Midlands - London

		XC		EM	EM	NT	EM	EM	EM	XC	EM	NT		EM	EM	EM	EM	EM	XC	EM	NT	EM	EM	EM	EM
		◇1		◇1	◇1		◇1	◇1	◇	◇1	◇1			◇1	◇1	◇1	◇1	◇	◇1	◇1		◇1	◇1	◇1	◇1
		A							B	C								B	D						
		🛒		🍴	🍴		🍴	🍴		🛒	🍴			🍴	🍴	🍴	🍴		🛒	🍴		🍴	🍴	🍴	🍴
York [8]	d	13 40								14 41									15 39						
Leeds [10]	d	14 10			13 59	14 05				15 10		15 05							16 10		16 04				
Wakefield Westgate [7]	d	14 23			14 12					15 23									16 22						
Wakefield Kirkgate [4]	d					14 21						15 22									16 22				
Doncaster [7]	d																								
Sheffield [7]	d	14 54			15 02	15 07	15 32		15 43	15 54		16 07				16 29		16 40	16 54		17 07			17 29	
Chesterfield	d	15 06			15 15	15 24	15 44		15 57	16 07		16 23				16 43		16 56	17 06		17 23			17 43	
Derby [6]	a	15 26			15 38		16 05			16 26						17 04			17 27					18 04	
	d				15 38		16 09								16 47	17 09							17 47	18 07	
Long Eaton	d														16 57								17 57		
Alfreton	d					15 34			16 08			16 33						17 07			17 33				
Langley Mill	d					15 42			16 15			16 41						17 14			17 41				
Lincoln	d																								
Nottingham [8]	a					16 00			16 33			16 59						17 32			17 59				
	d							16 18			16 45						17 20			17 39					18 10
Beeston	d							16 24									17 26								18 19
East Midlands Parkway	d				15 52		16 21	16 31			16 55				17 01	17 21	17 32			17 50			18 01	18 20	18 25
Loughborough	d				16 01			16 39							17 09		17 40						18 09		18 33
Barrow Upon Soar	d																								
Sileby	d																								
Syston	d																								
Leicester	a				16 13		16 35	16 50			17 11				17 20	17 38	17 50			18 07			18 19	18 39	18 43
	d				16 15		16 37	16 52			17 12				17 22	17 40	17 52			18 09			18 21	18 40	18 45
Market Harborough	d				16 32			17 06							17 36		18 06						18 35		19 05
Melton Mowbray	d																								
Oakham	d																								
Corby	d			16 25										17 20								18 20			
Kettering [4]	a			16 34	16 42			17 15						17 29	17 45		18 15					18 29	18 44		19 14
	d				16 43			17 16							17 46		18 16						18 45		19 15
Wellingborough	d				16 51			17 23							17 53		18 23						18 52		19 22
Bedford [7]	d				17 09			17 40							18 11		18 40						19 10		19 40
Luton [10]	d				17 27										18 29								19 29		
Luton Airport Parkway [7]	d							17 59									18 59								19 59
St Pancras International ⊖	a				17 59		18 04	18 29			18 34				18 59	19 04	19 29			19 34			19 59	20 04	20 29

		EM	XC	EM	EM	NT	EM	EM	XC	EM	EM	NT	EM	EM	XC	NT	EM	EM	EM	EM	XC	EM	XC	EM	EM
		◇	◇1	◇1	◇1		◇1	◇	◇1	◇1	◇1		◇1	◇	◇1		◇1	◇1	◇1	◇	◇1	◇	◇1	◇1	◇
		B	E					F	G					B	G					F	H	F	A		B
			🛒	🍴	🍴		🍴		🛒	🍴	🍴		🍴		🛒		🍴	🍴	🍴					🍴	
York [8]	d		16 39				17 40		17 41						18 40						19 39		20 39		
Leeds [10]	d		17 10			17 05			18 10			18 05			19 10	19 04					20 10		21 10		
Wakefield Westgate [7]	d		17 22						18 22						19 22						20 22		21 22		
Wakefield Kirkgate [4]	d					17 21						18 22				19 21									
Doncaster [7]	d						18 06																		
Sheffield [7]	d	17 39	17 54			18 07	18 32	18 41	18 54			19 07	19 31	19 40	19 54	20 06		20 24		20 40	20 54	21 40	21 54	22 35	23 29
Chesterfield	d	17 54	18 06			18 25	18 44	18 56	19 06			19 25	19 44	19 55	20 06	20 23		20 38		20 55	21 06	21 56	22 06	22 49	23 43
Derby [6]	a		18 26				19 08		19 26				20 04		20 29			20 57			21 26		22 25	23 26	
	d						19 09						20 06					20 59							
Long Eaton	d						19 20						20 16												
Alfreton	d	18 04				18 36		19 06				19 36		20 06		20 34				21 06		22 07			23 54
Langley Mill	d	18 12				18 43		19 14				19 43		20 14		20 41				21 13		22 14			00 02
Lincoln	d																								
Nottingham [8]	a	18 29				19 00		19 35				19 59		20 31		20 57				21 36		22 36			00 25
	d				18 43						19 46								21 12						
Beeston	d										19 52														
East Midlands Parkway	d				18 53		19 25				19 58		20 21					21 11	21 23						
Loughborough	d				19 01		19 32				20 06		20 30						21 30						
Barrow Upon Soar	d																								
Sileby	d																								
Syston	d																								
Leicester	a				19 12		19 44				20 16		20 42					21 28	21 41						
	d				19 14		19 45				20 18		20 44					21 30	21 42						
Market Harborough	d				19 30		20 03				20 32		20 59					21 45	21 56						
Melton Mowbray	d																								
Oakham	d																								
Corby	d			19 20						20 20							21 25								
Kettering [4]	a			19 29	19 39		20 12			20 29	20 41		21 09				21 34	21 55	22 05						
	d				19 40		20 13				20 42		21 10					21 56	22 06						
Wellingborough	d				19 47		20 21				20 49		21 18					22 04	22 14						
Bedford [7]	d				20 06		20 40				21 08		21 37					22 24	22 31						
Luton [10]	d				20 26						21 23		21 52					22 40	22 50						
Luton Airport Parkway [7]	d						20 55																		
St Pancras International ⊖	a				20 57		21 27				21 57		22 27					23 13	23 27						

A From Edinburgh to Penzance
B From Liverpool Lime Street to Norwich
C From Edinburgh to Plymouth
D From Glasgow Central to Plymouth
E From Aberdeen to Plymouth
F From Liverpool Lime Street
G From Glasgow Central to Bristol Temple Meads
H From Edinburgh to Birmingham New Street

For connections to Gatwick Airport see Table 52

Table 53

Sundays

26 June to 31 July

Sheffield - East Midlands - London

		EM	EM	EM	EM	EM	EM	EM	EM	XC		EM	NT	EM	EM	XC	EM	NT	EM	EM		EM	EM	XC	NT
		◇1	◇	◇1	◇1	◇1	◇1	◇1	◇1	◇1		◇1		◇1	◇1	◇1	◇1		◇1	◇1		◇1	◇	◇1	
			B							C						C							D	C	
		🍴		🍴	🍴	🍴	🍴	🍴	🍴	🍴		🍴		🍴	🍴	🍴	🍴		🍴	🍴		🍴		🍴	
York 8	d																							09 28	
Leeds 10	d									08 10						09 00		09 05				09 44		10 00	10 02
Wakefield Westgate 7	d									08 23						09 11						09 57		10 12	
Wakefield Kirkgate 4	d																	09 21							10 18
Doncaster 7	d															09 32								10 30	
Sheffield 7	d	23p20	23p42						08 13	08 54			09 00		09 17	09 57		10 07		10 17		10 26	10 49	10 57	11 03
Chesterfield	d	23p33	23p57						08 25	09 07			09 17		09 29	10 09		10 23		10 29		10 41	11 04	11 09	11 20
Derby 6	a	00 08							08 42	09 28					09 49	10 32				10 52				11 28	
	d			06 50		07 52			08 49						09 51					10 54					
Long Eaton	d								09 00						10 01					11 04					
Alfreton	d												09 28					10 33					11 14		11 30
Langley Mill	d												09 35					10 41							11 38
Lincoln	d																								
Nottingham 8	a		00 34										09 53					10 59				11 11	11 39		11 54
	d				07 28		08 19					09 15					10 15					11 18			
Beeston	d						08 25										10 22								
East Midlands Parkway	d			07 02	07 38	08 03	08 32		09 05			09 26			10 05		10 30			11 08		11 30			
Loughborough	d					08 11	08 39					09 34			10 13		10 38			11 16		11 38			
Barrow Upon Soar	d																								
Sileby	d																								
Syston	d																								
Leicester	a			07 18	07 52	08 22	08 50		09 19			09 47			10 23		10 51			11 26		11 51			
	d			07 20	07 54	08 23	08 52		09 21			09 49			10 25		10 53			11 28		11 53			
Market Harborough	d			07 38	08 11	08 40	09 09		09 38			10 07			10 39		11 08			11 42		12 08			
Melton Mowbray	d																								
Oakham	d																								
Corby	d							09 30						10 25					11 25						
Kettering 4	a			07 48	08 20	08 49	09 18	09 39	09 47			10 17		10 34	10 48		11 18		11 34	11 51		12 18			
	d			07 49	08 21	08 50	09 19		09 50			10 18			10 51		11 19			11 52		12 19			
Wellingborough	d			08 01	08 32	09 02	09 30		10 02			10 26			10 59		11 27			12 00		12 27			
Bedford 7	d			08 15	08 45	09 14	09 44		10 15			10 45			11 15		11 45			12 17		12 45			
Luton 10	d			08 32		09 39			10 36						11 39					12 41					
Luton Airport Parkway 7	d				09 09		10 11					11 11					12 09					13 10			
St Pancras International ⊖	a			09 13	09 50	10 19	10 49		11 20			11 49			12 18		12 49			13 16		13 48			

A From Glasgow Central to Birmingham New Street
B From Liverpool Lime Street
C To Plymouth
D To Norwich
b Arr. 2102
c Arr. 0952

For connections to Gatwick Airport see Table 52

Table 53

Sundays

26 June to 31 July

Sheffield - East Midlands - London

		EM	EM	XC	EM	NT		EM	EM	EM	NT	EM	XC	EM	EM	NT		EM	EM	XC	EM	XC	EM	EM	EM
		◇1	◇1	◇1	◇1			◇1	◇1	◇1		◇	◇1	◇1	◇1			◇1	◇	◇1	◇1	◇1	◇1	◇1	◇1
				A								B	C						D	E		F			
		☕	☕	🛒	☕			☕	☕	☕			🛒	☕	☕			☕		🛒	☕	🛒	☕	☕	☕
York 8	d			10 28									11 28							12 28					
Leeds 10	d		10 15	11 00		10 57					11 29		12 00			12 29				13 00					
Wakefield Westgate 7	d		10 28	11 12									12 12							13 12					
Wakefield Kirkgate 4	d					11 13					11 46					12 46									
Doncaster 7	d			11 30									12 30							13 30					
Sheffield 7 🚊	d		11 06	11 57		12 00			12 23		12 31	12 49	12 57		13 20	13 31			13 49	13 57	14 04	14 22			
Chesterfield	d		11 25	12 09		12 18			12 36		12 49	13 03	13 09		13 32	13 48			14 03	14 09	14 16	14 32			
Derby 6	a		11 47	12 29					12 55				13 31		13 51					14 29	14 40	14 51			
	d		11 48						12 57						13 53						14 42				
Long Eaton	d								13 07						14 03						14 52				
Alfreton	d					12 28					12 59	13 14				13 59			14 14						
Langley Mill	d					12 36					13 07					14 06									
Lincoln	d																								
Nottingham 8 🚊	a					12 53					13 25	13 39				14 22			14 39						
	d				12 14					13 14								14 23						15 11	15 36
Beeston	d				12 21					13 21								14 29						15 17	
East Midlands Parkway ✈	d		12 01		12 29				13 11	13 30					14 07			14 35			14 56			15 24	15 46
Loughborough	d		12 09		12 37				13 19	13 38					14 15			14 43			15 04			15 31	
Barrow Upon Soar	d																								
Sileby	d																								
Syston	d																								
Leicester	a		12 21		12 51				13 29	13 51					14 25			14 54			15 14			15 42	16 02
	d		12 23		12 52				13 31	13 53					14 27			14 56			15 16			15 44	16 03
Market Harborough	d		12 38		13 07				13 45	14 08					14 41			15 10						15 58	
Melton Mowbray	d																								
Oakham	d																								
Corby	d	12 30						13 30						14 25									15 25		
Kettering 4	a	12 39	12 48		13 17			13 39	13 54	14 17				14 34	14 49			15 19					15 34	16 07	
	d		12 49		13 18				13 55	14 18					14 50			15 20						16 08	
Wellingborough	d		12 57		13 26				14 02	14 27					14 58			15 27						16 15	
Bedford 7	d		13 15		13 45				14 20	14 44					15 14			15 44						16 32	
Luton 10	d		13 39						14 37						15 33						16 09				
Luton Airport Parkway 7 ✈	d				14 11					15 02								16 02						16 54	
St Pancras International ⊖	a		14 19		14 44				15 08	15 35					16 04			16 33			16 42			17 27	17 31

		EM		XC	EM	EM	NT	XC	EM	EM	EM	XC		EM	NT	EM	EM	XC	EM	EM	EM	XC		EM	NT
		◇		◇1	◇1	◇1		◇1	◇1	◇1	◇	◇1		◇1		◇1	◇1	◇1	◇1	◇1	◇	◇1		◇1	
		G		C				H			G	I						H			G	I			
				🛒	☕	☕		🛒	☕	☕		🛒		☕		☕	☕	🛒	☕	☕		🛒		☕	
York 8	d			13 40				14 34				14 41						15 34				15 39			
Leeds 10	d			14 10		13 59	14 05					15 10			15 05							16 10			16 04
Wakefield Westgate 7	d			14 23		14 12						15 23										16 22			
Wakefield Kirkgate 4	d						14 21								15 22										16 22
Doncaster 7	d							14 59										15 59							
Sheffield 7 🚊	d	14 46		14 54		15 02	15 07	15 23	15 32		15 43	15 54			16 07			16 24	16 29		16 40	16 54			17 07
Chesterfield	d	15 00		15 06		15 15	15 24		15 44		15 57	16 07			16 23				16 43		16 56	17 06			17 23
Derby 6	a			15 26		15 38		15 53	16 05			16 26						16 54	17 04			17 27			
	d					15 38			16 09								16 47		17 09						
Long Eaton	d																16 57								
Alfreton	d	15 12					15 34				16 08				16 33						17 07				17 33
Langley Mill	d	15 19					15 42				16 15				16 41						17 14				17 41
Lincoln	d																								
Nottingham 8 🚊	a	15 38					16 00				16 33				16 59						17 32				17 59
	d									16 18				16 45						17 20				17 39	
Beeston	d									16 24										17 26					
East Midlands Parkway ✈	d					15 52			16 21	16 31				16 55			17 01		17 21	17 32				17 50	
Loughborough	d					16 01				16 39							17 09			17 40					
Barrow Upon Soar	d																								
Sileby	d																								
Syston	d																								
Leicester	a					16 13			16 35	16 50				17 11			17 20		17 38	17 50				18 07	
	d					16 15			16 37	16 52				17 12			17 22		17 40	17 52				18 09	
Market Harborough	d					16 32				17 06							17 36			18 06					
Melton Mowbray	d																								
Oakham	d																								
Corby	d				16 25											17 20									
Kettering 4	a				16 34	16 42				17 15						17 29	17 45			18 15					
	d					16 43				17 16							17 46			18 16					
Wellingborough	d					16 51				17 23							17 53			18 23					
Bedford 7	d					17 09				17 40							18 11			18 40					
Luton 10	d					17 33											18 29								
Luton Airport Parkway 7 ✈	d									18 03										18 59					
St Pancras International ⊖	a					17 59			18 04	18 31				18 34			18 59		19 04	19 29				19 34	

A From Newcastle to Birmingham New Street
B To Norwich
C From Edinburgh to Penzance
D From Manchester Piccadilly to Norwich
E From Edinburgh to Plymouth
F To Reading
G From Liverpool Lime Street to Norwich
H From Newcastle to Reading
I From Glasgow Central to Plymouth

For connections to Gatwick Airport see Table 52

Table 53

Sundays

26 June to 31 July

Sheffield - East Midlands - London

		EM	EM	XC	EM	EM	EM	XC		EM	EM	NT	XC	EM	EM	XC	EM	EM		NT	XC	EM	EM	XC	NT
		◇1	◇1	◇1	◇1	◇1	◇	◇1		◇1	◇1		◇1	◇1	◇	◇1	◇1	◇1			◇1	◇1	◇	◇1	
				A			B	C					D		E	F					D		B	F	
		☕	☕	🛒	☕	☕		🛒		☕	☕		🛒	☕		🛒	☕	☕			🛒	☕		🛒	
York 8	d			16 23				16 39					17 34	17 40		17 41					18 34			18 40	
Leeds 10	d							17b10				17 05				18 10				18 05				19 10	19 04
Wakefield Westgate 7	d							17 22								18 22								19 22	
Wakefield Kirkgate 4	d											17 21								18 22					19 21
Doncaster 7	d			16 51									17 59	18 06							18 59				
Sheffield 7	d			17 24	17 29		17 39	17 54				18 07	18 24	18 32	18 41	18 54				19 07	19 24	19 31	19 40	19 54	20 06
Chesterfield	d				17 43		17 54	18 06				18 25		18 44	18 56	19 06				19 25		19 44	19 55	20 06	20 23
Derby 6	a			17 53	18 04			18 26					18 54	19 08		19 26					19 54	20 04		20 26	
	d		17 47		18 07									19 09								20 06			
Long Eaton	d		17 57											19 20								20 16			
Alfreton	d						18 04					18 36			19 06					19 36			20 06		20 34
Langley Mill	d						18 12					18 43			19 14					19 43			20 14		20 41
Lincoln	d																								
Nottingham 8	a						18 29					19 00			19 35					19 59			20 31		20 57
	d					18 10					18 43							19 46							
Beeston	d					18 19												19 52							
East Midlands Parkway	d		18 01		18 20	18 25					18 53			19 25				19 58				20 21			
Loughborough	d		18 09			18 33					19 01			19 32				20 06				20 30			
Barrow Upon Soar	d																								
Sileby	d																								
Syston	d																								
Leicester	a		18 19		18 39	18 43					19 12			19 44				20 16				20 42			
	d		18 21		18 40	18 45					19 14			19 45				20 18				20 44			
Market Harborough	d		18 35			19 05					19 30			20 03				20 32				20 59			
Melton Mowbray	d																								
Oakham	d																								
Corby	d	18 20								19 20							20 20								
Kettering 4	a	18 29	18 44			19 14				19 29	19 39			20 12			20 29	20 41				21 09			
	d		18 45			19 15					19 40			20 13				20 42				21 10			
Wellingborough	d		18 52			19 22					19 47			20 21				20 49				21 18			
Bedford 7	d		19 10			19 40					20 06			20 40				21 08				21 37			
Luton 10	d		19 29								20 26							21 23				21 52			
Luton Airport Parkway 7	d					19 59								20 55											
St Pancras International	a		19 59		20 04	20 29					20 57			21 27				21 57				22 27			

		XC	EM	EM		EM	EM	XC	XC	EM	XC	EM	EM
		◇1	◇1	◇1		◇1	◇	◇1	◇1	◇	◇1	◇1	◇
		G					E	H	G	E	I		E
		🛒	☕	☕		☕			🛒			☕	
York 8	d	19 24						19 39	20 24		20 39		
Leeds 10	d							20 10			21 10		
Wakefield Westgate 7	d							20 22			21 22		
Wakefield Kirkgate 4	d												
Doncaster 7	d	19 50							20 50				
Sheffield 7	d	20 20		20 24			20 40	20 54	21 20	21 40	21 54	22 35	23 29
Chesterfield	d			20 38			20 55	21 06	21 32	21 56	22 06	22 49	23 43
Derby 6	a	20 50		20 57				21 26	21 52		22 25	23 26	
	d			20 59									
Long Eaton	d												
Alfreton	d						21 06			22 07			23 54
Langley Mill	d						21 13			22 14			00 02
Lincoln	d												
Nottingham 8	a						21 36			22 36			00 25
	d					21 13							
Beeston	d												
East Midlands Parkway	d			21 11		21 23							
Loughborough	d					21 30							
Barrow Upon Soar	d												
Sileby	d												
Syston	d												
Leicester	a			21 28		21 41							
	d			21 30		21 42							
Market Harborough	d			21 45		21 56							
Melton Mowbray	d												
Oakham	d												
Corby	d		21 25										
Kettering 4	a		21 34	21 55		22 05							
	d			21 56		22 06							
Wellingborough	d			22 04		22 14							
Bedford 7	d			22 24		22 31							
Luton 10	d			22 40		22 50							
Luton Airport Parkway 7	d												
St Pancras International	a			23 13		23 27							

A From Edinburgh to Reading
B From Liverpool Lime Street to Norwich
C From Aberdeen to Plymouth
D From Newcastle to Reading
E From Liverpool Lime Street
F From Glasgow Central to Bristol Temple Meads
G From Newcastle to Birmingham New Street
H From Edinburgh to Bristol Temple Meads
I From Glasgow Central to Birmingham New Street

For connections to Gatwick Airport see Table 52

Table 53

Sundays

7 August to 11 September

Sheffield - East Midlands - London

		EM	EM	EM	EM	EM	EM	EM	EM	XC	EM	NT	EM	EM	XC	EM	NT	EM	EM	EM	EM	XC	NT
		◇1	◇	◇1	◇1	◇1	◇1	◇1	◇1	◇1	◇1		◇1	◇1	◇1	◇1		◇1	◇1	◇1	◇	◇1	
			A							B					B						C	B	
York 8	d																					09 28	
Leeds 10	d									08 10					09 00		09 05			09 44		10 00	10 02
Wakefield Westgate 7	d									08 23					09 11					09 57		10 12	
Wakefield Kirkgate 4	d																09 21						10 18
Doncaster 7	d														09 32							10 30	
Sheffield 7	d	23p30	23p42						08 11	08 54		09 00		09 17	09 57		10 07		10 17	10 26	10 49	10 57	11 03
Chesterfield	d	23p43	23p57						08 23	09 07		09 17		09 29	10 09		10 23		10 29	10 41	11 04	11 09	11 20
Derby 6	a	00 18							08 42	09 28				09 48	10 32				10 49			11 28	
	d			06 40		07 46			08 44					09 50					10 50				
Long Eaton	d								08 54					10 00					11 00				
Alfreton	d											09 28					10 33				11 14		11 30
Langley Mill	d											09 35					10 41						11 38
Lincoln	d																						
Nottingham 8	a		00 34									09 53					10 59			11 12	11 39		11 54
	d				07 20		08 17				09 12					10 14				11 18			
Beeston	d						08 23									10 21							
East Midlands Parkway	d			06 54	07 30	07 59	08 29		09 00		09 23			10 06		10 30			11 06	11 30			
Loughborough	d																						
Barrow Upon Soar	d																						
Sileby	d																						
Syston	d																						
Leicester	a			07 16	07 52	08 22	08 52		09 22		09 47			10 25		10 51			11 25	11 51			
	d			07 18	07 54	08 23	08 53		09 23		09 49			10 26		10 52			11 27	11 52			
Market Harborough	d			07 36	08 11	08 40	09 10		09 40		10 07			10 40		11 07			11 41	12 07			
Melton Mowbray	d																						
Oakham	d																						
Corby	d							09 30					10 25					11 25					
Kettering 4	a			07 46	08 20	08 49	09 19	09 39	09 49		10 17		10 34	10 49		11 17		11 34	11 50	12 17			
	d			07 47	08 21	08 50	09 20		09 50		10 18			10 50		11 18			11 51	12 18			
Wellingborough	d			07 59	08 32	09 02	09 32		10 03		10 26			10 58		11 26			11 58	12 26			
Bedford 7	d			08 13	08 45	09 14	09 44		10 15		10 45			11 15		11 45			12 15	12 45			
Luton 10	d			08 32		09 39			10 37					11 39					12 40				
Luton Airport Parkway 7	d				09 07		10 11				11 10					12 09				13 10			
St Pancras International	a			09 13	09 50	10 20	10 47		11 20		11 49			12 20		12 50			13 20	13 48			

		EM	EM	XC	EM	NT	EM	EM	EM	NT	EM	XC	EM	EM	NT	EM	EM	XC	EM	XC	EM	EM	EM
		◇1	◇1	◇1	◇1		◇1	◇1	◇1		◇	◇1	◇1	◇1		◇1	◇	◇1	◇1	◇1	◇1	◇1	◇1
				D							C	E					F	G		H			
York 8	d			10 28								11 28						12 28					
Leeds 10	d		10 15	11 00		10 57				11 29		12 00			12 29			13 00					
Wakefield Westgate 7	d		10 28	11 12								12 12						13 12					
Wakefield Kirkgate 4	d					11 13				11 46					12 46								
Doncaster 7	d			11 30								12 30						13 30					
Sheffield 7	d		11 06	11 57		12 00		12 19		12 31	12 49	12 57		13 20	13 31		13 49	13 57	14 04	14 22			
Chesterfield	d		11 25	12 09		12 18		12 31		12 49	13 03	13 09		13 32	13 48		14 03	14 09	14 16	14 32			
Derby 6	a		11 47	12 29				12 51				13 31		13 51				14 29	14 36	14 51			
	d		11 48					12 52						13 53					14 38				
Long Eaton	d							13 02						14 03					14 48				
Alfreton	d					12 28				12 59	13 14				13 59		14 14						
Langley Mill	d					12 36				13 07					14 06								
Lincoln	d																						
Nottingham 8	a					12 53				13 25	13 39				14 22		14 39						
	d				12 14				13 12							14 24						15 10	15 36
Beeston	d				12 21				13 19							14 30						15 16	
East Midlands Parkway	d		12 02		12 29			13 08	13 27					14 07		14 36			14 56			15 23	15 46
Loughborough	d													14 15		14 44			15 04			15 30	
Barrow Upon Soar	d																						
Sileby	d																						
Syston	d																						
Leicester	a		12 22		12 51			13 27	13 51					14 25		14 54			15 14			15 42	16 02
	d		12 23		12 52			13 29	13 52					14 27		14 56			15 16			15 44	16 03
Market Harborough	d		12 38		13 07			13 43	14 07					14 41		15 10						15 58	
Melton Mowbray	d																						
Oakham	d																						
Corby	d	12 30					13 30						14 25								15 25		
Kettering 4	a	12 39	12 49		13 17		13 39	13 52	14 17				14 34	14 50		15 19					15 34	16 07	
	d		12 50		13 18			13 53	14 18					14 51		15 20						16 08	
Wellingborough	d		12 58		13 26			14 00	14 26					14 58		15 27						16 15	
Bedford 7	d		13 16		13 45			14 18	14 45					15 15		15 45						16 32	
Luton 10	d		13 37					14 37						15 32					16 09				
Luton Airport Parkway 7	d				14 09				15 02							16 03						16 53	
St Pancras International	a		14 19		14 44			15 08	15 36					16 04		16 34			16 42			17 27	17 31

A From Liverpool Lime Street
B To Plymouth
C To Norwich
D From Newcastle to Plymouth
E From Edinburgh to Plymouth
F From Manchester Piccadilly to Norwich
G From Edinburgh to Penzance
H To Reading

For connections to Gatwick Airport see Table 52

Table 53

Sundays

7 August to 11 September

Sheffield - East Midlands - London

		EM		XC	EM	EM	NT	XC	EM	EM	EM	XC		EM	NT	EM	EM	XC	EM	EM	EM	XC		EM	NT
		◇		◇1	◇1	◇1		◇1	◇1	◇1	◇	◇1		◇1		◇1	◇1	◇1	◇1	◇1	◇	◇1		◇1	
		A		B				C			A	D						C			A	E			
				🛒	☕	☕		🛒	☕	☕		🛒		☕		☕	☕	🛒	☕	☕		🛒		☕	
York [8]	d			13 40				14 34				14 41						15 34				15 39			
Leeds [10]	d			14 10		13 59	14 05					15 10			15 05							16 10			16 04
Wakefield Westgate [7]	d			14 23		14 12						15 23										16 22			
Wakefield Kirkgate [4]	d						14 21								15 22										16 22
Doncaster [7]	d							14 59										15 59							
Sheffield [7]	d	14 46		14 54		15 02	15 07	15 23	15 32		15 43	15 54			16 07			16 24	16 29		16 40	16 54			17 07
Chesterfield	d	15 00		15 06		15 15	15 24		15 44		15 57	16 07			16 23				16 43		16 56	17 06			17 23
Derby [6]	a			15 26		15 38		15 53	16 09			16 26						16 54	17 04			17 27			
	d					15 38			16 14								16 47		17 09						
Long Eaton	d																16 57								
Alfreton	d	15 12					15 34				16 08				16 33						17 07				17 33
Langley Mill	d	15 19					15 42				16 15				16 41						17 14				17 41
Lincoln	d																								
Nottingham [8]	a	15 38					16 00				16 33				16 59						17 32				17 59
	d									16 18				16 45						17 20				17 39	
Beeston	d									16 24										17 26					
East Midlands Parkway	d					15 52			16 25	16 31				16 55			17 01		17 21	17 32				17 50	
Loughborough	d					16 01				16 39							17 09			17 40					
Barrow Upon Soar	d																								
Sileby	d																								
Syston	d																								
Leicester	a					16 13			16 40	16 50				17 12			17 20		17 38	17 50				18 07	
	d					16 15			16 41	16 52				17 13			17 22		17 40	17 52				18 09	
Market Harborough	d					16 30				17 06							17 36			18 06					
Melton Mowbray	d																								
Oakham	d																								
Corby	d				16 25											17 20									
Kettering [4]	a				16 34	16 40				17 15						17 29	17 45			18 15					
	d					16 41				17 16							17 46			18 16					
Wellingborough	d					16 49				17 23							17 53			18 23					
Bedford [7]	d					17 07				17 40							18 11			18 40					
Luton [10]	d					17 25											18 29								
Luton Airport Parkway [7]	d									17 59										18 59					
St Pancras International	a					17 59			18 04	18 29				18 34			18 59		19 04	19 29				19 34	

		EM	EM	XC	EM	EM	EM	XC		EM	EM	NT	XC	EM	EM	XC	EM	EM		NT	XC	EM	EM	XC	NT
		◇1	◇1	◇1	◇1	◇1	◇	◇1		◇1	◇1		◇1	◇1	◇	◇1	◇1	◇1			◇1	◇1	◇	◇1	
				F			A	G					C		H	E					C		A	I	
		☕	☕	🛒	☕	☕		🛒		☕	☕		🛒	☕		🛒	☕	☕			🛒	☕		🛒	
York [8]	d			16 23				16 39					17 34	17 40		17 41					18 34			18 40	
Leeds [10]	d							17 10				17 05				18 10				18 05				19 10	19 04
Wakefield Westgate [7]	d							17 22								18 22								19 22	
Wakefield Kirkgate [4]	d											17 21								18 22					19 21
Doncaster [7]	d			16 51									17 59	18 06							18 59				
Sheffield [7]	d			17 24	17 29		17 39	17 54				18 07	18 24	18 32	18 41	18 54				19 07	19 24	19 31	19 40	19 54	20 06
Chesterfield	d				17 43		17 54	18 06				18 25		18 44	18 56	19 06				19 25		19 44	19 55	20 06	20 23
Derby [6]	a			17 53	18 04			18 26					18 54	19 08		19 26					19 54	20 04		20 26	
	d		17 47		18 07									19 09								20 06			
Long Eaton	d		17 57											19 20								20 16			
Alfreton	d						18 04					18 36			19 06					19 36			20 06		20 34
Langley Mill	d						18 12					18 43			19 14					19 43			20 14		20 41
Lincoln	d																								
Nottingham [8]	a						18 29					19 00			19 35					19 59			20 31		20 57
	d					18 10					18 43							19 46							
Beeston	d					18 19												19 52							
East Midlands Parkway	d		18 01		18 20	18 25					18 53			19 25				19 58				20 21			
Loughborough	d		18 09			18 33					19 01			19 32				20 06				20 30			
Barrow Upon Soar	d																								
Sileby	d																								
Syston	d																								
Leicester	a		18 19		18 39	18 43					19 12			19 44				20 16				20 42			
	d		18 21		18 40	18 45					19 14			19 45				20 18				20 44			
Market Harborough	d		18 35			19 05					19 30			20 03				20 32				20 59			
Melton Mowbray	d																								
Oakham	d																								
Corby	d	18 20								19 20							20 20								
Kettering [4]	a	18 29	18 44			19 14				19 29	19 39			20 12			20 29	20 41				21 09			
	d		18 45			19 15					19 40			20 13				20 42				21 10			
Wellingborough	d		18 52			19 22					19 47			20 21				20 49				21 18			
Bedford [7]	d		19 10			19 40					20 06			20 40				21 08				21 37			
Luton [10]	d		19 29								20 26							21 23				21 52			
Luton Airport Parkway [7]	d					19 59								20 55											
St Pancras International	a		19 59		20 04	20 29					20 57			21 27				21 57				22 27			

A From Liverpool Lime Street to Norwich
B From Edinburgh to Plymouth
C From Newcastle to Reading
D From Glasgow Central to Penzance
E From Glasgow Central to Plymouth
F From Edinburgh to Reading
G From Aberdeen to Plymouth
H From Liverpool Lime Street
I From Glasgow Central to Bristol Temple Meads

For connections to Gatwick Airport see Table 52

Table 53

Sundays

7 August to 11 September

Sheffield - East Midlands - London

		XC	EM	EM	EM	EM	XC	XC	EM	XC	EM	EM
		◇1	◇1	◇1	◇1	◇	◇1	◇1	◇	◇1	◇1	◇
		A				B	C	A	B	D		B
		✕	☕	☕	☕			✕			☕	
York 8	d	19 24					19 39	20 24		20 39		
Leeds 10	d						20 10			21 10		
Wakefield Westgate 7	d						20 22			21 22		
Wakefield Kirkgate 4	d											
Doncaster 7	d	19 50						20 50				
Sheffield 7	d	20 20		20 24		20 40	20 54	21 20	21 40	21 54	22 35	23 29
Chesterfield	d			20 38		20 55	21 06	21 32	21 56	22 06	22 49	23 43
Derby 6	a	20 50		20 57			21 26	21 52		22 25	23 26	
	d			20 59								
Long Eaton	d											
Alfreton	d					21 06			22 07			23 54
Langley Mill	d					21 13			22 14			00 02
Lincoln	d											
Nottingham 8	a					21 36			22 36			00 25
	d				21 13							
Beeston	d											
East Midlands Parkway ✈	d			21 11	21 23							
Loughborough	d				21 31							
Barrow Upon Soar	d											
Sileby	d											
Syston	d											
Leicester	a			21 28	21 41							
	d			21 30	21 43							
Market Harborough	d			21 45	21 57							
Melton Mowbray	d											
Oakham	d											
Corby	d		21 25									
Kettering 4	a		21 34	21 55	22 06							
	d			21 56	22 07							
Wellingborough	d			22 04	22 14							
Bedford 7	d			22 24	22 31							
Luton 10	d			22 40	22 50							
Luton Airport Parkway 7 ✈	d											
St Pancras International ⊖	a			23 13	23 27							

Sundays

18 September to 23 October

		EM	EM	EM	EM	EM	EM	EM	EM	XC	NT	EM	EM	EM	XC	EM	NT	EM	EM	EM	XC	NT	EM
		◇1	◇	◇1	◇1	◇1	◇1	◇1	◇1	◇1		◇1	◇1	◇1	◇1	◇1		◇1	◇1	◇1	◇1		◇1
			B							E					E						E		
		☕		☕	☕	☕	☕	☕	☕	✕		☕	☕	☕	✕	☕		☕	☕	☕	✕		☕
York 8	d																				09 28		
Leeds 10	d									08 10					09 00		09 05			09 44	10 00	10 02	
Wakefield Westgate 7	d									08 23					09 11					09 57	10 12		
Wakefield Kirkgate 4	d																09 21					10 18	
Doncaster 7	d														09 32						10 30		
Sheffield 7	d	23p30	23p42						08 11	08 54	09 00			09 17	09 57		10 07		10 17	10 26	10 57	11 03	
Chesterfield	d	23p43	23p57						08 23	09 07	09 17			09 29	10 09		10 23		10 29	10 41	11 09	11 20	
Derby 6	a	00 18							08 42	09 28				09 48	10 32				10 49		11 28		
	d			06 42		07 46			08 44					09 50					10 50				
Long Eaton	d								08 54					10 00					11 00				
Alfreton	d										09 28						10 33					11 30	
Langley Mill	d										09 35						10 41					11 38	
Lincoln	d																						
Nottingham 8	a		00 27								09 53						10 59			11 12		11 54	
	d															10 14				11 18			
Beeston	d															10 21							
East Midlands Parkway ✈	d			06 56	07 30	07 59	08 28		09 00			09 24		10 06		10 30			11 06	11 30			
Loughborough	d																						
Barrow Upon Soar	d																						
Sileby	d																						
Syston	d																						
Leicester	a			07 18	07 52	08 22	08 50		09 22			09 47		10 25		10 51			11 25	11 51			
	d			07 20	07 54	08 23	08 51		09 23			09 49		10 26		10 52			11 27	11 52			
Market Harborough	d			07 38	08 11	08 40	09 08		09 40			10 07		10 40		11 07			11 41	12 07			
Melton Mowbray	d																						
Oakham	d																						
Corby	d							09 30					10 25					11 25					12 30
Kettering 4	a			07 48	08 20	08 49	09 17	09 39	09 49			10 17	10 34	10 49		11 17		11 34	11 50	12 17			12 39
	d			07 49	08 21	08 50	09 18		09 50			10 18		10 50		11 18			11 51	12 18			
Wellingborough	d			08 01	08 32	09 02	09 30		10 03			10 26		10 58		11 26			11 58	12 26			
Bedford 7	d			08 15	08 45	09 14	09 42		10 15			10 45		11 15		11 45			12 15	12 45			
Luton 10	d			08 34		09 39			10 37					11 39					12 40				
Luton Airport Parkway 7 ✈	d				09 07		10 10					11 10				12 09				13 10			
St Pancras International ⊖	a			09 13	09 50	10 20	10 49		11 20			11 49		12 20		12 45			13 20	13 48			

A From Newcastle to Birmingham New Street
B From Liverpool Lime Street
C From Edinburgh to Bristol Temple Meads
D From Glasgow Central to Birmingham New Street
E To Bristol Parkway

For connections to Gatwick Airport see Table 52

Table 53

Sundays

18 September to 23 October

Sheffield - East Midlands - London

		EM ◇1	XC ◇1 A	EM ◇1	NT	EM ◇1		EM ◇1	EM ◇1	NT	EM ◇ B	XC ◇1 C	EM ◇1	EM ◇1	NT	EM ◇1		EM ◇ D	XC ◇1 C	EM ◇1	XC ◇1 E	EM ◇1	EM ◇1	EM ◇1	EM ◇ F
York 8	d		10 28									11 28							12 28						
Leeds 10	d	10 15	11 00		10 57					11 29		12 00			12 29				13 00						
Wakefield Westgate 7	d	10 28	11 12									12 12							13 12						
Wakefield Kirkgate 4	d				11 13					11 46					12 46										
Doncaster 7	d		11 30									12 30							13 30						
Sheffield 7	d	11 06	11 57		12 00			12 23		12 31	12 49	12 57		13 20	13 31			13 49	13 57	14 04	14 22				14 46
Chesterfield	d	11 25	12 09		12 18			12 36		12 49	13 03	13 09		13 32	13 48			14 03	14 09	14 16	14 32				15 00
Derby 6	a	11 47	12 29					12 56				13 31		13 52					14 29	14 36	14 51				
	d	11 48						13 01						13 54						14 38					
Long Eaton	d							13 11						14 04						14 48					
Alfreton	d				12 28					12 59	13 14				13 59			14 14							15 12
Langley Mill	d				12 36					13 07					14 06										15 19
Lincoln	d																								
Nottingham 8	a				12 53					13 25	13 39				14 22			14 39							15 38
	d			12 14					13 12							14 24							15 10	15 36	
Beeston	d			12 21					13 19							14 30							15 16		
East Midlands Parkway	d	12 02		12 29				13 17	13 27					14 09		14 36				14 56			15 23	15 46	
Loughborough	d													14 17		14 44				15 04			15 30		
Barrow Upon Soar	d																								
Sileby	d																								
Syston	d																								
Leicester	a	12 22		12 52				13 36	13 51					14 27		14 55				15 14			15 42	16 02	
	d	12 23		12 53				13 37	13 53					14 29		14 57				15 16			15 44	16 03	
Market Harborough	d	12 38		13 08				13 51	14 08					14 43		15 11							15 58		
Melton Mowbray	d																								
Oakham	d																								
Corby	d					13 30							14 25									15 25			
Kettering 4	a	12 49		13 18		13 39		14 00	14 18				14 34	14 52		15 20						15 34	16 07		
	d	12 50		13 19				14 01	14 19					14 55		15 21							16 08		
Wellingborough	d	12 58		13 27				14 09	14 29					15 02		15 28							16 15		
Bedford 7	d	13 16		13 46				14 26	14 54					15 25		15 46							16 32		
Luton 10	d	13 37						14 49						15 42						16 09					
Luton Airport Parkway 7	d			14 09					15 11							16 03							16 53		
St Pancras International	a	14 19		14 44				15 20	15 45					16 15		16 34				16 42			17 27	17 31	

		XC ◇1 C		EM ◇1	EM ◇1	NT	XC ◇1 G	EM ◇1	EM ◇1	EM ◇ F	XC ◇1 H	EM ◇1		NT	EM ◇1	EM ◇1	XC ◇1 G	EM ◇1	EM ◇1	EM ◇ F	XC ◇1 H	EM ◇1		NT	EM ◇1
York 8	d	13 40					14 34				14 41						15 34				15 38				
Leeds 10	d	14 10			13 59	14 05					15 10			15 05							16 10			16 04	
Wakefield Westgate 7	d	14 23			14 12						15 23										16 22				
Wakefield Kirkgate 4	d					14 21								15 22										16 22	
Doncaster 7	d						14 59										15 59								
Sheffield 7	d	14 54			15 02	15 07	15 23	15 32		15 43	15 54			16 07			16 24	16 29		16 40	16 54			17 07	
Chesterfield	d	15 06			15 15	15 24		15 44		15 57	16 07			16 23				16 43		16 56	17 06			17 23	
Derby 6	a	15 26			15 38		15 53	16 09			16 26						16 54	17 04			17 27				
	d				15 38			16 14								16 47		17 09							
Long Eaton	d															16 57									
Alfreton	d					15 34				16 08				16 33						17 07				17 33	
Langley Mill	d					15 42				16 15				16 41						17 14				17 41	
Lincoln	d																								
Nottingham 8	a					16 00				16 33				16 59						17 32				17 59	
	d								16 18			16 45							17 20			17 39			
Beeston	d								16 24										17 26						
East Midlands Parkway	d				15 52			16 25	16 31			16 55				17 01		17 21	17 32			17 50			
Loughborough	d				16 01				16 39							17 09			17 40						
Barrow Upon Soar	d																								
Sileby	d																								
Syston	d																								
Leicester	a				16 13			16 40	16 50			17 12				17 20		17 38	17 50			18 07			
	d				16 15			16 41	16 52			17 13				17 22		17 40	17 52			18 09			
Market Harborough	d				16 30				17 06							17 36			18 06						
Melton Mowbray	d																								
Oakham	d																								
Corby	d			16 25											17 20										18 20
Kettering 4	a			16 34	16 40				17 15						17 29	17 45			18 15						18 29
	d				16 41				17 16							17 46			18 16						
Wellingborough	d				16 49				17 23							17 53			18 23						
Bedford 7	d				17 07				17 40							18 11			18 40						
Luton 10	d				17 25											18 29									
Luton Airport Parkway 7	d								17 59										18 59						
St Pancras International	a				17 59			18 04	18 29			18 34				18 59		19 04	19 29			19 34			

A From Newcastle to Bristol Parkway
B To Norwich
C From Edinburgh to Bristol Parkway
D From Manchester Piccadilly to Norwich
E To Reading
F From Liverpool Lime Street to Norwich
G From Newcastle to Reading
H From Glasgow Central to Bristol Parkway

For connections to Gatwick Airport see Table 52

Table 53

Sundays

18 September to 23 October

Sheffield - East Midlands - London

		EM	XC	EM	EM	EM	XC	EM	EM	NT	XC	EM	EM	XC	EM	EM	NT	XC	EM	EM	XC	NT	XC
		◇1	◇1	◇1	◇1	◇	◇1	◇1	◇1		◇1	◇1	◇	◇1	◇1	◇1		◇1	◇1	◇	◇1		◇1
			A			B	C				D		E	F				G		B	H		I
		☕	🛒	☕	☕		🛒	☕	☕		🛒	☕		🛒	☕	☕		🛒	☕		🛒		🛒
York 8	d		16 23				16 39				17 34	17 40		17 41				18 34			18 40		19 24
Leeds 10	d						17 10			17 05				18 10			18 05				19 10	19 04	
Wakefield Westgate 7	d						17 22							18 22							19 22		
Wakefield Kirkgate 4	d									17 21							18 22					19 21	
Doncaster 7	d		16 51								17 59	18 06						18 59					19 50
Sheffield 7	d		17 24	17 29		17 39	17 54			18 07	18 24	18 32	18 41	18 54			19 07	19 24	19 31	19 40	19 54	20 06	20 20
Chesterfield	d			17 43		17 54	18 06			18 25		18 44	18 56	19 06			19 25		19 44	19 55	20 06	20 23	
Derby 6	a		17 53	18 04			18 26				18 54	19 08		19 26				19 54	20 04		20 26		20 50
	d	17 47		18 07								19 09							20 06				
Long Eaton	d	17 57										19 20							20 16				
Alfreton	d					18 04				18 36			19 06				19 36			20 06		20 34	
Langley Mill	d					18 12				18 43			19 14				19 43			20 14		20 41	
Lincoln	d																						
Nottingham 8	a					18 29				19 00			19 35				19 59			20 31		20 57	
	d				18 10				18 43							19 46							
Beeston	d				18 19											19 52							
East Midlands Parkway	d	18 01		18 20	18 25				18 53			19 25				19 58			20 21				
Loughborough	d	18 09			18 33				19 01			19 32				20 06			20 30				
Barrow Upon Soar	d																						
Sileby	d																						
Syston	d																						
Leicester	a	18 19		18 39	18 43				19 12			19 44				20 16			20 42				
	d	18 21		18 40	18 45				19 14			19 45				20 18			20 44				
Market Harborough	d	18 35			19 05				19 30			20 03				20 32			20 59				
Melton Mowbray	d																						
Oakham	d																						
Corby	d							19 20							20 20								
Kettering 4	a	18 44			19 14			19 29	19 39			20 12			20 29	20 41			21 09				
	d	18 45			19 15				19 40			20 13				20 42			21 10				
Wellingborough	d	18 52			19 22				19 47			20 21				20 49			21 18				
Bedford 7	d	19 10			19 40				20 06			20 40				21 08			21 37				
Luton 10	d	19 29							20 26							21 23			21 52				
Luton Airport Parkway 7	d				19 59							20 55											
St Pancras International	a	19 59		20 04	20 29				20 57			21 27				21 57			22 27				

		EM	EM	EM	EM	XC	XC	EM	XC	EM	EM
		◇1	◇1	◇1	◇	◇1	◇1	◇	◇1	◇1	◇
					E	J	I	E	K		E
		☕	☕	☕			🛒			☕	
York 8	d					19 39	20 24		20 39		
Leeds 10	d					20 10			21 10		
Wakefield Westgate 7	d					20 22			21 22		
Wakefield Kirkgate 4	d										
Doncaster 7	d						20 50				
Sheffield 7	d		20 24		20 40	20 54	21 20	21 40	21 54	22 35	23 29
Chesterfield	d		20 38		20 55	21 06	21 32	21 56	22 06	22 49	23 43
Derby 6	a		20 57			21 26	21 52		22 25	23 26	
	d		20 59								
Long Eaton	d										
Alfreton	d				21 06			22 07			23 54
Langley Mill	d				21 13			22 14			00 02
Lincoln	d										
Nottingham 8	a				21 36			22 36			00 25
	d			21 13							
Beeston	d										
East Midlands Parkway	d		21 11	21 23							
Loughborough	d			21 31							
Barrow Upon Soar	d										
Sileby	d										
Syston	d										
Leicester	a		21 28	21 41							
	d		21 30	21 43							
Market Harborough	d		21 45	21 57							
Melton Mowbray	d										
Oakham	d										
Corby	d	21 25									
Kettering 4	a	21 34	21 55	22 06							
	d		21 56	22 07							
Wellingborough	d		22 04	22 14							
Bedford 7	d		22 24	22 31							
Luton 10	d		22 40	22 50							
Luton Airport Parkway 7	d										
St Pancras International	a		23 13	23 27							

A From Edinburgh to Reading
B From Liverpool Lime Street to Norwich
C From Aberdeen to Bristol Parkway
D From Newcastle to Reading
E From Liverpool Lime Street
F From Glasgow Central to Bristol Parkway
G From Newcastle to Guildford
H From Glasgow Central to Bristol Temple Meads
I From Newcastle to Birmingham New Street
J From Edinburgh to Bristol Temple Meads
K From Glasgow Central to Birmingham New Street

For connections to Gatwick Airport see Table 52

Table 53

Sundays

from 30 October

Sheffield - East Midlands - London

		EM	EM	EM	EM	EM	EM	EM	EM	XC		EM	NT	EM	EM	XC	EM	NT	EM	EM		EM	XC	NT	EM
		◇1	◇	◇1	◇1	◇1	◇1	◇1	◇1	◇1		◇1		◇1	◇1	◇1	◇1		◇1	◇1		◇1	◇1		◇1
			A							B						B							B		
		☕		☕	☕	☕	☕	☕	☕	🛒		☕		☕	☕	🛒	☕		☕	☕		☕	🛒		☕
York 8	d																						09 28		
Leeds 10	d									08 10						09 00		09 05				09 44	10 00	10 02	
Wakefield Westgate 7	d									08 23						09 11						09 57	10 12		
Wakefield Kirkgate 4	d																	09 21						10 18	
Doncaster 7	d															09 32							10 30		
Sheffield 7	d	23p20	23p42						08 13	08 54			09 00		09 17	09 57		10 07		10 17		10 26	10 57	11 03	
Chesterfield	d	23p33	23p57						08 25	09 07			09 17		09 29	10 09		10 23		10 29		10 41	11 09	11 20	
Derby 6	a	00 08							08 42	09 28					09 49	10 32				10 50			11 28		
	d			06 50		07 52			08 47						09 51					10 52					
Long Eaton	d								08 58						10 01					11 02					
Alfreton	d												09 28					10 33						11 30	
Langley Mill	d												09 35					10 41						11 38	
Lincoln	d																								
Nottingham 8	a		00 34										09 53					10 59				11 11		11 54	
	d				07 28		08 19					09 15					10 15					11 18			
Beeston	d						08 25										10 22								
East Midlands Parkway	d			07 02	07 38	08 03	08 32		09 02			09 26			10 05		10 30			11 06		11 30			
Loughborough	d					08 11	08 39		09 10			09 34			10 13		10 38			11 14		11 38			
Barrow Upon Soar	d																								
Sileby	d																								
Syston	d																								
Leicester	a			07 18	07 52	08 22	08 50		09 21			09 47			10 23		10 51			11 24		11 51			
	d			07 20	07 54	08 23	08 52		09 22			09 49			10 25		10 53			11 26		11 53			
Market Harborough	d			07 38	08 11	08 40	09 09		09 39			10 07			10 39		11 08			11 40		12 08			
Melton Mowbray	d																								
Oakham	d																								
Corby	d							09 30						10 25					11 25						12 30
Kettering 4	a			07 48	08 20	08 49	09 18	09 39	09 48			10 17		10 34	10 48		11 18		11 34	11 49		12 18			12 39
	d			07 49	08 21	08 50	09 19		09 51			10 18			10 51		11 19			11 50		12 19			
Wellingborough	d			08 01	08 32	09 02	09 30		10 04			10 26			10 58		11 27			11 58		12 27			
Bedford 7	d			08 15	08 45	09 14	09 45		10 16			10 45			11 16		11 45			12 15		12 46			
Luton 10	d			08 34		09 39			10 39						11 39					12 40					
Luton Airport Parkway 7	d				09 11		10 10					11 10					12 09					13 10			
St Pancras International	a			09 13	09 50	10 20	10 49		11 20			11 49			12 20		12 50			13 20		13 48			

		EM	XC	EM	NT	EM		EM	EM	NT	EM	XC	EM	EM	EM	NT		EM	XC	EM	XC	EM	EM	EM	EM
		◇1	◇1	◇1		◇1		◇1	◇1		◇	◇1	◇1	◇1	◇1			◇	◇1	◇1	◇1	◇1	◇1	◇1	◇
			C								D	E						F	G		H				I
		☕	🛒	☕		☕		☕	☕			🛒	☕	☕	☕				🛒	☕	🛒	☕	☕	☕	
York 8	d		10 28									11 28							12 28						
Leeds 10	d	10 15	11 00		10 57					11 29		12 00				12 29			13 00						
Wakefield Westgate 7	d	10 28	11 12									12 12							13 12						
Wakefield Kirkgate 4	d				11 13					11 46						12 46									
Doncaster 7	d		11 30									12 30							13 30						
Sheffield 7	d	11 06	11 57		12 00			12 23		12 31	12 49	12 57		13 20		13 31		13 49	13 57	14 04	14 22				14 46
Chesterfield	d	11 25	12 09		12 18			12 36		12 49	13 03	13 09		13 32		13 48		14 03	14 09	14 16	14 32				15 00
Derby 6	a	11 47	12 29					12 57				13 31		13 52					14 29	14 36	14 51				
	d	11 48						13 02						13 54						14 38					
Long Eaton	d							13 12						14 04						14 48					
Alfreton	d				12 28					12 59	13 14					13 59		14 14							15 12
Langley Mill	d				12 36					13 07						14 06									15 19
Lincoln	d																								
Nottingham 8	a				12 53					13 25	13 39					14 22		14 39							15 38
	d			12 15					13 14						14 17								15 10	15 33	
Beeston	d			12 22					13 21						14 23								15 16		
East Midlands Parkway	d	12 01		12 30				13 16	13 30					14 09	14 32					14 56			15 22	15 43	
Loughborough	d	12 09		12 38				13 24	13 38					14 17	14 40					15 04			15 30		
Barrow Upon Soar	d																								
Sileby	d																								
Syston	d																								
Leicester	a	12 21		12 52				13 34	13 51					14 27	14 51					15 14			15 42	16 02	
	d	12 23		12 53				13 36	13 53					14 29	14 53					15 16			15 43	16 03	
Market Harborough	d	12 38		13 08				13 50	14 08					14 43	15 07								15 57		
Melton Mowbray	d																								
Oakham	d																								
Corby	d					13 30							14 25									15 25			
Kettering 4	a	12 48		13 18		13 39		13 59	14 18				14 34	14 52	15 16							15 34	16 06		
	d	12 49		13 19				14 00	14 19					14 55	15 17								16 07		
Wellingborough	d	12 57		13 27				14 07	14 29					15 02	15 24								16 15		
Bedford 7	d	13 15		13 46				14 25	14 53					15 25	15 42								16 31		
Luton 10	d	13 39						14 49						15 46						16 16					
Luton Airport Parkway 7	d			14 10					15 15						16 03								16 54		
St Pancras International	a	14 19		14 44				15 20	15 45					16 15	16 34					16 42			17 27	17 31	

A From Liverpool Lime Street
B To Plymouth
C From Newcastle to Plymouth
D To Norwich
E From Edinburgh to Plymouth
F From Manchester Piccadilly to Norwich
G From Edinburgh to Penzance
H To Reading
I From Liverpool Lime Street to Norwich

For connections to Gatwick Airport see Table 52

Table 53

Sundays
from 30 October

Sheffield - East Midlands - London

		XC		EM	EM	NT	XC	EM	EM	EM	XC	EM		NT	EM	EM	XC	EM	EM	EM	XC	EM		NT	EM
		◇1		◇1	◇1		◇1	◇1	◇1	◇	◇1	◇1			◇1	◇1	◇1	◇1	◇1	◇	◇1	◇1			◇1
		A					B			C	D						B			C	E				
		🛒		🍴	🍴		🛒	🍴	🍴		🛒	🍴			🍴	🍴	🛒	🍴	🍴		🛒	🍴			🍴
York 8	d	13 40					14 34				14 41						15 34				15 39				
Leeds 10	d	14 10			13 59	14 05					15 10			15 05							16 10			16 04	
Wakefield Westgate 7	d	14 23			14 12						15 23										16 22				
Wakefield Kirkgate 4	d					14 21								15 22										16 22	
Doncaster 7	d						14 59										15 59								
Sheffield 7	d	14 54			15 02	15 07	15 23	15 32		15 43	15 54			16 07			16 24	16 29		16 40	16 54			17 07	
Chesterfield	d	15 06			15 15	15 24		15 44		15 57	16 07			16 23				16 43		16 56	17 06			17 23	
Derby 6	a	15 26			15 35		15 53	16 04			16 26						16 54	17 03			17 27				
	d				15 35			16 05								16 37		17 04							
Long Eaton	d															16 47									
Alfreton	d					15 34				16 08				16 33						17 07				17 33	
Langley Mill	d					15 42				16 15				16 41						17 14				17 41	
Lincoln	d																								
Nottingham 8	a					16 00				16 33				16 59						17 32				17 59	
	d								16 10			16 39							17 18			17 32			
Beeston	d								16 16										17 24						
East Midlands Parkway	d				15 49			16 17	16 23			16 50				16 56		17 17	17 30			17 45			
Loughborough	d				15 58				16 30							17 03			17 38						
Barrow Upon Soar	d																								
Sileby	d																								
Syston	d																								
Leicester	a				16 10			16 34	16 42			17 06				17 15		17 34	17 49			18 02			
	d				16 12			16 36	16 43			17 08				17 16		17 35	17 51			18 04			
Market Harborough	d				16 27				17 00							17 30			18 05						
Melton Mowbray	d																								
Oakham	d																								
Corby	d			16 25											17 20										18 20
Kettering 4	a			16 34	16 37				17 09						17 29	17 39			18 14						18 29
	d				16 38				17 10							17 40			18 15						
Wellingborough	d				16 46				17 18							17 48			18 22						
Bedford 7	d				17 04				17 35							18 05			18 39						
Luton 10	d				17 27											18 29									
Luton Airport Parkway 7	d								17 59										18 59						
St Pancras International	a				17 59			18 04	18 29			18 34				18 59		19 04	19 29			19 34			

		EM	XC	EM	EM	EM	XC	EM		EM	NT	XC	EM	EM	XC	EM	EM	NT		XC	EM	EM	XC	NT	XC
		◇1	◇1	◇1	◇1	◇	◇1	◇1		◇1		◇1	◇1	◇	◇1	◇1	◇1			◇1	◇1	◇	◇1		◇1
			F			C	G					B		H	E					I		C	J		K
		🍴	🛒	🍴	🍴		🛒	🍴		🍴		🛒	🍴		🛒	🍴	🍴			🛒	🍴		🛒		🛒
York 8	d		16 23				16 39					17 34	17 40		17 41					18 34			18 40		19 24
Leeds 10	d						17 10				17 05				18 10			18 05					19 10	19 04	
Wakefield Westgate 7	d						17 22								18 22								19 22		
Wakefield Kirkgate 4	d										17 21							18 22						19 21	
Doncaster 7	d		16 51									17 59	18 06							18 59					19 50
Sheffield 7	d		17 24	17 29		17 39	17 54				18 07	18 24	18 32	18 41	18 54			19 07		19 24	19 31	19 40	19 54	20 06	20 20
Chesterfield	d			17 43		17 54	18 06				18 25		18 44	18 56	19 06			19 25			19 44	19 55	20 06	20 23	
Derby 6	a		17 53	18 03			18 26					18 54	19 05		19 26					19 54	20 04		20 26		20 50
	d	17 45		18 04									19 07								20 06				
Long Eaton	d	17 55											19 17								20 16				
Alfreton	d					18 04					18 36			19 06				19 36				20 06		20 34	
Langley Mill	d					18 12					18 43			19 14				19 43				20 14		20 41	
Lincoln	d																								
Nottingham 8	a					18 29					19 00			19 35				19 59				20 31		20 57	
	d				18 10					18 40							19 44								
Beeston	d				18 17												19 50								
East Midlands Parkway	d	17 59		18 17	18 26					18 51			19 21				19 57				20 21				
Loughborough	d	18 07			18 33					18 58			19 29				20 04				20 30				
Barrow Upon Soar	d																								
Sileby	d																								
Syston	d																								
Leicester	a	18 18		18 34	18 44					19 10			19 40				20 15				20 42				
	d	18 20		18 35	18 45					19 11			19 42				20 16				20 44				
Market Harborough	d	18 34			19 02					19 27			20 00				20 30				20 59				
Melton Mowbray	d																								
Oakham	d																								
Corby	d							19 20								20 20									
Kettering 4	a	18 43			19 11			19 29		19 36			20 09			20 29	20 39				21 09				
	d	18 44			19 12					19 37			20 10				20 40				21 10				
Wellingborough	d	18 51			19 20					19 45			20 17				20 48				21 18				
Bedford 7	d	19 09			19 37					20 03			20 36				21 06				21 37				
Luton 10	d	19 29								20 29							21 25				21 56				
Luton Airport Parkway 7	d				19 59								20 57												
St Pancras International	a	19 59		20 04	20 29					20 57			21 27				21 57				22 31				

A From Edinburgh to Plymouth
B From Newcastle to Reading
C From Liverpool Lime Street to Norwich
D From Glasgow Central to Penzance
E From Glasgow Central to Plymouth
F From Edinburgh to Reading
G From Aberdeen to Plymouth
H From Liverpool Lime Street
I From Newcastle to Guildford
J From Glasgow Central to Bristol Temple Meads
K From Newcastle to Birmingham New Street

For connections to Gatwick Airport see Table 52

Table 53

Sundays
from 30 October

Sheffield - East Midlands - London

		EM	EM	EM	EM	XC	XC	EM	XC	EM	EM
		◇	◇	◇	◇	◇	◇	◇	◇	◇	◇
					A	B	C	A	D		A
York	d					19 39	20 24		20 39		
Leeds	d					20 10			21 10		
Wakefield Westgate	d					20 22			21 22		
Wakefield Kirkgate	d										
Doncaster	d						20 50				
Sheffield	d		20 24		20 40	20 54	21 20	21 40	21 54	22 35	23 29
Chesterfield	d		20 38		20 55	21 06	21 32	21 56	22 06	22 49	23 43
Derby	a		20 57			21 26	21 52		22 25	23 26	
	d		20 59								
Long Eaton	d										
Alfreton	d				21 06			22 07			23 54
Langley Mill	d				21 13			22 14			00 02
Lincoln	d										
Nottingham	a				21 36			22 36			00 25
	d			21 13							
Beeston	d										
East Midlands Parkway	d		21 11	21 23							
Loughborough	d			21 31							
Barrow Upon Soar	d										
Sileby	d										
Syston	d										
Leicester	a		21 28	21 41							
	d		21 30	21 43							
Market Harborough	d		21 45	21 57							
Melton Mowbray	d										
Oakham	d										
Corby	d	21 25									
Kettering	a	21 34	21 55	22 06							
	d		21 56	22 07							
Wellingborough	d		22 04	22 14							
Bedford	d		22 24	22 31							
Luton	d		22 42	22 50							
Luton Airport Parkway	d										
St Pancras International	a		23 15	23 27							

A From Liverpool Lime Street
B From Edinburgh to Bristol Temple Meads
C From Newcastle to Birmingham New Street
D From Glasgow Central to Birmingham New Street

For connections to Gatwick Airport see Table 52

Table 55

Mondays to Fridays

Nottingham - Mansfield - Worksop

Miles			EM	EM	EM	EM	EM	EM	EM	EM	EM	EM	EM	EM	EM	EM	EM	EM	EM	EM	EM	EM	EM
0	**Nottingham** 8	d	05 40	06 05	07 00	08 25	08 53	09 25	09 55	10 25	10 55	11 25	11 55	12 25	12 55	13 25	13 55	14 25	14 55	15 25	15 55	16 25	16 55
5½	Bulwell	d	05 49	06 14	07 10	08 36	09 02		10 06		11 06		12 06		13 06		14 06		15 06		16 06		17 06
8¼	Hucknall	d	05 54	06 19	07 15	08 41	09 07	09 39	10 11	10 39	11 11	11 39	12 11	12 39	13 11	13 39	14 11	14 39	15 11	15 39	16 11	16 39	17 12
10¾	Newstead	d	05 59	06 24	07 21	08 46	09 12	09 44		10 44		11 44		12 44		13 44		14 44		15 44		16 44	17 17
13¾	Kirkby In Ashfield	d	06 05	06 30	07 31	08 52	09 18	09 49	10 19	10 49	11 19	11 49	12 19	12 49	13 19	13 49	14 19	14 49	15 19	15 49	16 19	16 49	17 23
14½	Sutton Parkway	d	06 08	06 33	07 34	08 55	09 21	09 52	10 22	10 52	11 22	11 52	12 22	12 52	13 22	13 52	14 22	14 52	15 22	15 52	16 22	16 52	17 27
17¼	**Mansfield**	d	06 13	06 38	07 40	09 00	09 26	09 57	10 27	10 57	11 27	11 57	12 27	12 57	13 27	13 57	14 27	14 57	15 27	15 57	16 27	16 57	17 32
18¾	Mansfield Woodhouse	d	06 18	06 47	07 45	09 04	09a33	10 02	10a34	11 02	11a34	12 02	12a34	13 02	13a34	14 02	14a34	15 02	15a34	16 02	16a34	17 02	17a39
21½	Shirebrook	d	06 24	06 54	07 51	09 11		10 08		11 08		12 08		13 08		14 08		15 08		16 08		17 08	
22¼	Langwith - Whaley Thorns	d	06 28	06 58	07 55	09 15		10 12		11 12		12 12		13 12		14 12		15 12		16 12		17 12	
25½	Creswell (Derbys)	d	06 32	07 02	07 59	09 19		10 16		11 16		12 16		13 16		14 16		15 16		16 16		17 16	
26¾	Whitwell	d	06 36	07 05	08 03	09 22		10 20		11 20		12 20		13 20		14 20		15 20		16 20		17 20	
31½	**Worksop**	a	06 48	07 20	08 18	09 33		10 33		11 33		12 33		13 33		14 33		15 33		16 33		17 33	

		EM	EM	EM	EM	EM	EM
Nottingham 8	d	17 25	17 55	18 55	19 55	20 55	22 05
Bulwell	d	17 39	18 11	19 05	20 05	21 05	22 19
Hucknall	d	17 44	18 16	19 10	20 16	21 16	22 24
Newstead	d	17 49	18 21	19 15	20 21	21 21	22 29
Kirkby In Ashfield	d	17 55	18 27	19 21	20 27	21 27	22 34
Sutton Parkway	d	17 58	18 30	19 24	20 30	21 30	22 37
Mansfield	d	18 03	18 35	19 29	20 35	21 35	22 42
Mansfield Woodhouse	d	18 08	18 39	19 33	20 39	21 40	22 47
Shirebrook	d	18 14	18 46	19 40	20 46	21 46	22 53
Langwith - Whaley Thorns	d	18 18	18 50	19 44	20 50	21 50	22 57
Creswell (Derbys)	d	18 22	18 54	19 48	20 54	21 54	23 01
Whitwell	d	18 26	18 57	19 51	20 57	21 58	23 05
Worksop	a	18 37	19 07	20 03	21 09	22 06	23 13

Saturdays

		EM	EM	EM	EM	EM	EM	EM	EM	EM	EM	EM	EM	EM	EM	EM	EM	EM	EM	EM	EM	EM	EM
Nottingham 8	d	05 40	06 05	06 59	08 25	08 53	09 25	09 55	10 25	10 55	11 25	11 55	12 25	12 55	13 25	13 55	14 25	14 55	15 25	15 55	16 25	16 55	17 25
Bulwell	d	05 49	06 14	07 09	08 36	09 02		10 06		11 06		12 06		13 06		14 06		15 06		16 06		17 06	17 39
Hucknall	d	05 54	06 19	07 14	08 41	09 07	09 39	10 11	10 39	11 11	11 39	12 11	12 39	13 11	13 39	14 11	14 39	15 11	15 39	16 11	16 39	17 12	17 44
Newstead	d	05 59	06 24	07 20	08 46	09 12	09 44		10 44		11 44		12 44		13 44		14 44		15 44		16 44	17 17	17 49
Kirkby In Ashfield	d	06 05	06 30	07 31	08 52	09 18	09 49	10 19	10 49	11 19	11 49	12 19	12 49	13 19	13 49	14 19	14 49	15 19	15 49	16 19	16 49	17 23	17 55
Sutton Parkway	d	06 08	06 33	07 34	08 55	09 21	09 52	10 22	10 52	11 22	11 52	12 22	12 52	13 22	13 52	14 22	14 52	15 22	15 52	16 22	16 52	17 27	17 58
Mansfield	d	06 13	06 38	07 40	09 00	09 26	09 57	10 27	10 57	11 27	11 57	12 27	12 57	13 27	13 57	14 27	14 57	15 27	15 57	16 27	16 57	17 32	18 03
Mansfield Woodhouse	d	06 18	06 47	07 45	09 04	09a33	10 02	10a34	11 02	11a34	12 02	12a34	13 02	13a34	14 02	14a34	15 02	15a34	16 02	16a34	17 02	17a39	18 08
Shirebrook	d	06 24	06 54	07 51	09 11		10 08		11 08		12 08		13 08		14 08		15 08		16 08		17 08		18 14
Langwith - Whaley Thorns	d	06 28	06 58	07 55	09 15		10 12		11 12		12 12		13 12		14 12		15 12		16 12		17 12		18 18
Creswell (Derbys)	d	06 32	07 02	07 59	09 19		10 16		11 16		12 16		13 16		14 16		15 16		16 16		17 16		18 22
Whitwell	d	06 36	07 05	08 03	09 22		10 20		11 20		12 20		13 20		14 20		15 20		16 20		17 20		18 26
Worksop	a	06 48	07 20	08 12	09 33		10 33		11 33		12 33		13 33		14 33		15 33		16 33		17 33		18 37

		EM	EM	EM	EM	EM	EM
Nottingham 8	d	17 55	18 55	19 55	20 55	22 05	23 05
Bulwell	d	18 11	19 05	20 05	21 05	22 19	23 18
Hucknall	d	18 16	19 10	20 16	21 16	22 24	23 23
Newstead	d	18 21	19 15	20 21	21 21	22 29	23 28
Kirkby In Ashfield	d	18 27	19 21	20 27	21 27	22 34	23 33
Sutton Parkway	d	18 30	19 24	20 30	21 30	22 37	23 36
Mansfield	d	18 35	19 29	20 35	21 35	22 42	23 41
Mansfield Woodhouse	d	18 39	19 33	20 39	21 40	22 47	23a46
Shirebrook	d	18 46	19 40	20 46	21 46	22 53	
Langwith - Whaley Thorns	d	18 50	19 44	20 50	21 50	22 57	
Creswell (Derbys)	d	18 54	19 48	20 54	21 54	23 01	
Whitwell	d	18 57	19 51	20 57	21 58	23 05	
Worksop	a	19 07	20 03	21 09	22 06	23 13	

Sundays

		EM A (bus)	EM B	EM	EM	EM	EM	EM	EM	EM
Nottingham 8	d	07 20	08 07	09 36	11 26	13 26	15 25	16 53	18 30	20 28
Bulwell	d	07 40	08 16	09 46	11 36	13 36	15 34	17 02	18 39	20 37
Hucknall	d	07 45	08 21	09 51	11 41	13 41	15 39	17 07	18 44	20 42
Newstead	d	07 55	08 26	09 56	11 46	13 46	15 44	17 12	18 49	20 47
Kirkby In Ashfield	d	08 08	08 32	10 01	11 51	13 51	15 50	17 18	18 55	20 53
Sutton Parkway	d	08 15	08 35	10 04	11 54	13 54	15 53	17 21	18 58	20 56
Mansfield	d	08 30	08 40	10 09	11 59	13 59	15 58	17 26	19 03	21 01
Mansfield Woodhouse	d	08a40	08a47	10a16	12a06	14a06	16a04	17a31	19a09	21a05
Shirebrook	d									
Langwith - Whaley Thorns	d									
Creswell (Derbys)	d									
Whitwell	d									
Worksop	a									

A from 18 September until 23 October

B until 11 September, from 30 October

Table 55

Mondays to Fridays

Worksop - Mansfield - Nottingham

Miles	Station		EM	EM	EM	EM	EM	EM	EM	EM	EM
0	**Worksop**	d	05 50		06 56		07 38	08 38		09 38	
4¾	Whitwell	d	05 59		07 05		07 47	08 47		09 47	
6	Creswell (Derbys)	d	06 02		07 08		07 50	08 50		09 50	
9¼	Langwith - Whaley Thorns	d	06 06		07 13		07 55	08 55		09 55	
10	Shirebrook	d	06 10		07 16		07 58	08 58		09 58	
12¾	Mansfield Woodhouse	d	06 17	07 07	07 25	07 39	08 06	09 06	09 37	10 07	10 37
14¼	**Mansfield**	d	06 22	07 11	07 29	07 43	08 10	09 10	09 40	10 10	10 40
17	Sutton Parkway	d	06 27	07 16	07 35	07 48	08 15	09 15	09 46	10 16	10 46
17¾	Kirkby In Ashfield	d	06 30	07 19	07 38	07 52	08 18	09 18	09 49	10 19	10 49
20¾	Newstead	d	06 35	07 26	07 43	07 57	08 23	09 23	09 54		10 54
23¼	Hucknall	d	06 39	07 31	07 48	08 02	08 28	09 27	09 58	10 26	10 58
26	Bulwell	d	06 43	07 35	07 53	08 06	08 32	09 31		10 30	
31½	**Nottingham** 8	a	06 58	07 48	08 04	08 18	08 44	09 44	10 14	10 44	11 14

Miles	Station		EM	EM	EM	EM	EM	EM	EM	EM	EM	EM	EM	EM
0	**Worksop**	d	10 38		11 38		12 38		13 38		14 38		15 38	
4¾	Whitwell	d	10 47		11 47		12 47		13 47		14 47		15 47	
6	Creswell (Derbys)	d	10 50		11 50		12 50		13 50		14 50		15 50	
9¼	Langwith - Whaley Thorns	d	10 55		11 55		12 55		13 55		14 55		15 55	
10	Shirebrook	d	10 58		11 58		12 58		13 58		14 58		15 58	
12¾	Mansfield Woodhouse	d	11 07	11 37	12 07	12 37	13 07	13 37	14 07	14 37	15 07	15 37	16 07	16 37
14¼	**Mansfield**	d	11 10	11 40	12 10	12 40	13 10	13 40	14 10	14 40	15 10	15 40	16 10	16 40
17	Sutton Parkway	d	11 16	11 46	12 16	12 46	13 16	13 46	14 16	14 46	15 16	15 46	16 16	16 46
17¾	Kirkby In Ashfield	d	11 19	11 49	12 19	12 49	13 19	13 49	14 19	14 49	15 19	15 49	16 19	16 49
20¾	Newstead	d		11 54		12 54		13 54		14 54		15 54		16 54
23¼	Hucknall	d	11 26	11 58	12 26	12 58	13 26	13 58	14 26	14 58	15 26	15 58	16 26	16 58
26	Bulwell	d	11 30		12 30		13 30		14 30		15 30		16 30	
31½	**Nottingham** 8	a	11 44	12 14	12 44	13 19	13 44	14 14	14 44	15 14	15 44	16 14	16 44	17 14

Station		EM	EM	EM	EM	EM	EM	EM	EM
Worksop	d	16 42		17 45	18 41	19 21	20 15	21 20	22 20
Whitwell	d	16 51		17 54	18 50	19 30	20 24	21 29	22 29
Creswell (Derbys)	d	16 54		17 57	18 53	19 33	20 27	21 32	22 32
Langwith - Whaley Thorns	d	16 59		18 01	18 58	19 37	20 31	21 37	22 37
Shirebrook	d	17 02		18 07	19 01	19 41	20 35	21 40	22 40
Mansfield Woodhouse	d	17 10	17 43	18 14	19 09	19 48	20 43	21 48	22 48
Mansfield	d	17 14	17 46	18 18	19 13	19 52	20 50	21 53	22 52
Sutton Parkway	d	17 19	17 52	18 24	19 18	19 57	20 55	21 58	22 57
Kirkby In Ashfield	d	17 22	17 55	18 27	19 21	20 00	20 58	22 01	23 00
Newstead	d		17 59	18 31	19 26	20 05	21 03	22 06	23 05
Hucknall	d	17 30	18 04	18 36	19 30	20 09	21 07	22 10	23 09
Bulwell	d	17 34		18 40	19 34	20 14	21 14	22 14	23 13
Nottingham 8	a	17 48	18 20	18 51	19 47	20 36	21 26	22 26	23 26

Saturdays

Station		EM	EM	EM	EM	EM	EM	EM	EM	EM
Worksop	d	05 50	06 56	07 38	08 38		09 38		10 38	
Whitwell	d	05 59	07 05	07 47	08 47		09 47		10 47	
Creswell (Derbys)	d	06 02	07 08	07 50	08 50		09 50		10 50	
Langwith - Whaley Thorns	d	06 06	07 13	07 55	08 55		09 55		10 55	
Shirebrook	d	06 10	07 16	07 58	08 58		09 58		10 58	
Mansfield Woodhouse	d	06 17	07 25	08 06	09 06	09 37	10 07	10 37	11 07	11 37
Mansfield	d	06 22	07 29	08 10	09 10	09 40	10 10	10 40	11 10	11 40
Sutton Parkway	d	06 27	07 35	08 15	09 15	09 46	10 16	10 46	11 16	11 46
Kirkby In Ashfield	d	06 30	07 38	08 18	09 18	09 49	10 19	10 49	11 19	11 49
Newstead	d	06 35	07 43	08 23	09 23	09 54		10 54		11 54
Hucknall	d	06 39	07 48	08 28	09 27	09 58	10 26	10 58	11 26	11 58
Bulwell	d	06 43	07 53	08 32	09 31		10 30		11 30	
Nottingham 8	a	06 58	08 05	08 44	09 44	10 15	10 44	11 14	11 44	12 14

Station		EM	EM	EM	EM	EM	EM	EM	EM	EM	EM	EM	EM	EM
Worksop	d	11 38		12 38		13 38		14 38		15 38		16 42		17 45
Whitwell	d	11 47		12 47		13 47		14 47		15 47		16 51		17 54
Creswell (Derbys)	d	11 50		12 50		13 50		14 50		15 50		16 54		17 57
Langwith - Whaley Thorns	d	11 55		12 55		13 55		14 55		15 55		16 59		18 01
Shirebrook	d	11 58		12 58		13 58		14 58		15 58		17 02		18 07
Mansfield Woodhouse	d	12 07	12 37	13 07	13 37	14 07	14 37	15 07	15 37	16 07	16 37	17 10	17 43	18 14
Mansfield	d	12 10	12 40	13 10	13 40	14 10	14 40	15 10	15 40	16 10	16 40	17 14	17 46	18 18
Sutton Parkway	d	12 16	12 46	13 16	13 46	14 16	14 46	15 16	15 46	16 16	16 46	17 19	17 52	18 24
Kirkby In Ashfield	d	12 19	12 49	13 19	13 49	14 19	14 49	15 19	15 49	16 19	16 49	17 22	17 55	18 27
Newstead	d		12 54		13 54		14 54		15 54		16 54		17 59	18 31
Hucknall	d	12 26	12 58	13 26	13 58	14 26	14 58	15 26	15 58	16 26	16 58	17 30	18 04	18 36
Bulwell	d	12 30		13 30		14 30		15 30		16 30		17 34		18 40
Nottingham 8	a	12 44	13 15	13 44	14 14	14 44	15 14	15 44	16 15	16 44	17 14	17 48	18 20	18 51

Station		EM	EM	EM	EM	EM
Worksop	d	18 41	19 21	20 15	21 19	22 20
Whitwell	d	18 50	19 30	20 24	21 28	22 29
Creswell (Derbys)	d	18 53	19 33	20 27	21 31	22 32
Langwith - Whaley Thorns	d	18 58	19 37	20 31	21 36	22 37
Shirebrook	d	19 01	19 41	20 35	21 39	22 40
Mansfield Woodhouse	d	19 09	19 48	20 43	21 47	22 48
Mansfield	d	19 13	19 52	20 50	21 52	22 52
Sutton Parkway	d	19 18	19 57	20 55	21 57	22 57
Kirkby In Ashfield	d	19 21	20 00	20 58	22 00	23 00
Newstead	d	19 26	20 05	21 03	22 05	23 05
Hucknall	d	19 30	20 09	21 07	22 09	23 09
Bulwell	d	19 34	20 14	21 14	22 13	23 13
Nottingham 8	a	19 47	20 32	21 27	22 25	23 26

Sundays

Station		EM A	EM B	EM	EM	EM	EM	EM	EM	EM
Worksop	d									
Whitwell	d									
Creswell (Derbys)	d									
Langwith - Whaley Thorns	d									
Shirebrook	d									
Mansfield Woodhouse	d	*08 52*	*08 45*	*10 30*	*12 12*	*14 10*	16 09	17 36	19 20	21 10
Mansfield	d	08 55	08 57	10 33	12 15	14 13	16 12	17 39	19 23	21 13
Sutton Parkway	d	09 01	09 12	10 39	12 21	14 19	16 18	17 45	19 29	21 19
Kirkby In Ashfield	d	09 04	09 19	10 42	12 24	14 22	16 21	17 48	19 32	21 22
Newstead	d	09 08	09 32	10 46	12 28	14 26	16 25	17 52	19 36	21 26
Hucknall	d	09 13	09 42	10 51	12 33	14 31	16 30	17 57	19 41	21 31
Bulwell	d	09 17	09 47	10 55	12 37	14 35	16 34	18 01	19 45	21 35
Nottingham 8	a	09 29	10 07	11 07	12 49	14 47	16 46	18 13	19 57	21 47

A until 11 September, from 30 October

B from 18 September until 23 October

Table 56

Mondays to Fridays

until 23 September

Nottingham - Derby - Matlock

Miles			EM MX	EM	XC	EM	EM	XC	EM	EM	XC	EM	EM	EM	XC	EM	EM	XC	EM	EM	XC	EM	EM
			◇1 ☕		◇1		◇1 ⊠🛒	◇1	◇1 ⊠🛒	◇1 ☕	◇1	◇1 ☕			1	◇1 ☕	◇1 ☕	◇1 🛒			1	◇1 ☕	◇1 ☕
0	**Nottingham 8**	d	01 52		06 00	06 18	06 28	06 37	06 49		06 56	07 10	07 18	07 31	07 37		08 02	08 08	08 15	08 32	08 37		09 02
3¼	Beeston	d			06 06	06 24	06a33	06 43	06a54		07 07	07a16	07 24	07a37	07 43		08a07		08 24	08a38	08 43		09a07
4¾	Attenborough	d			06 10	06 27					07 11		07 27						08 27				
7¾	Long Eaton	d			06 18	06 35					07 18		07 35		07 51	07 59			08 35		08 51	09 00	
13½	Spondon	d			06 25	06 42							07 42						08 42		08 57		
16	**Derby 6**	a	02 10		06 30	06 49		07 00			07 31		07 48		08 02	08 09		08 32	08 49		09 02	09 15	
—		d		05 40		06 50				07 20			07 50						08 50				
21¼	Duffield	d		05 47		06 57							07 57						08 57				
23¾	Belper	d		05 52		07 02				07a27			08 02						09 02				
26½	Ambergate	d		05 58		07 08							08 08						09 08				
28½	Whatstandwell	d		06 02		07 12							08 12						09 12				
31½	Cromford	d		06 07		07 17							08 17						09 17				
32¼	Matlock Bath	d		06 11		07 20							08 20						09 19				
33¼	**Matlock**	a		06 14		07 24							08 24						09 24				

		XC	EM	EM	XC	EM	EM	XC	EM	EM	XC	EM	EM	XC	EM	EM	XC	EM	EM	XC	EM	EM	XC
		◇1 🛒			1	◇1 ☕	◇1 ☕	◇1 🛒			1	◇1 ☕	◇1 ☕	◇1 🛒			1 🛒	◇1 ☕	◇1 ☕	◇1			1 🛒
Nottingham 8	d	09 11	09 18	09 32	09 37		10 02	10 11	10 18	10 32	10 37		11 02	11 08	11 18	11 32	11 37		12 02	12 08	12 18	12 32	12 37
Beeston	d		09 24	09a38	09 43		10a07		10 24	10a38	10 43		11a07		11 24	11a38	11 43		12a07		12 24	12a38	12 43
Attenborough	d		09 27						10 27						11 27						12 27		
Long Eaton	d		09 35		09 51	09 56			10 35		10 51	10 56			11 35		11 51	11 57			12 35		12 51
Spondon	d																						
Derby 6	a	09 31	09 48		10 02	10 09		10 33	10 49		11 02	11 09		11 31	11 48		12 02	12 09		12 33	12 48		13 02
	d		09 50						10 50						11 54						12 50		
Duffield	d		09 57						10 57						12 01						12 57		
Belper	d		10 02						11 02						12 06						13 02		
Ambergate	d		10 08						11 08						12 12						13 08		
Whatstandwell	d		10 12						11 12						12 16						13 12		
Cromford	d		10 17						11 17						12 21						13 17		
Matlock Bath	d		10 20						11 20						12 24						13 20		
Matlock	a		10 24						11 24						12 28						13 24		

		EM	EM	XC	EM	EM	XC	EM	EM	XC	EM	EM	XC	EM	EM	XC	EM	EM	XC	EM	EM	XC
		◇1 ☕	◇1 ☕	◇1			1 🛒	◇1 ☕	◇1 ☕	◇1 🛒			1 🛒	◇1 ☕	◇1 ☕	◇1			1 🛒	◇1 ☕	◇1 ☕	◇1
Nottingham 8	d		13 02	13 11	13 18	13 32	13 37		14 02	14 08	14 18	14 32	14 37		15 02	15 11	15 18	15 32	15 37		16 02	16 08
Beeston	d		13a07		13 24	13a38	13 43		14a07		14 24	14a38	14 43		15a07		15 24	15a38	15 43		16a07	
Attenborough	d				13 27						14 27						15 27					
Long Eaton	d	12 57			13 35		13 51	13 57			14 35		14 51	14 57			15 35		15 51	15 57		
Spondon	d																					
Derby 6	a	13 09		13 31	13 48		14 02	14 09		14 31	14 47		15 02	15 13		15 31	15 48		16 02	16 09		16 31
	d				13 50						14 54						15 50					
Duffield	d				13 57						15 01						15 57					
Belper	d				14 02						15 06						16 02					
Ambergate	d				14 08						15 12						16 08					
Whatstandwell	d				14 12						15 16						16 12					
Cromford	d				14 17						15 21						16 17					
Matlock Bath	d				14 20						15 24						16 20					
Matlock	a				14 24						15 28						16 24					

		EM	EM	XC	EM	EM	EM	XC	EM	EM	XC	EM	EM	XC	EM	EM	XC	EM	EM	XC	EM	EM	XC
				1 🛒	◇1 ☕		◇1 ☕	◇1			1 🛒	◇1 ☕	◇1 ☕	◇1			1 🛒	◇1 ☕	◇1 ☕	◇1			1
Nottingham 8	d	16 18	16 32	16 37		16 50	17 02	17 08	17 18	17 32	17 37		18 02	18 08	18 18	18 33	18 37		19 02	19 08	19 18	19 32	19 37
Beeston	d	16 24	16 38	16 43		16 55	17a07		17 24	17 38	17 43		18a07		18 24	18a39	18 43		19a07		19 24	19a38	19 43
Attenborough	d	16 27	16a41			16 58			17 27	17a41					18 27						19 27		19 46
Long Eaton	d	16 35		16 51	16 57	17 07			17 35		17 51	18 01			18 37		18 51	18 56			19 35		19 53
Spondon	d								17 42		17 57												
Derby 6	a	16 48		17 02	17 09	17 23		17 31	17 49		18 02	18 14		18 33	18 48		19 02	19 09		19 32	19 48		20 02
	d	16 50							17 50						18 50						19 50		
Duffield	d	16 57							17 57						18 57						19 57		
Belper	d	17 02							18 02						19 02						20 02		
Ambergate	d	17 08							18 08						19 08						20 08		
Whatstandwell	d	17 12							18 12						19 12						20 12		
Cromford	d	17 17							18 17						19 17						20 17		
Matlock Bath	d	17 20							18 20						19 20						20 20		
Matlock	a	17 24							18 24						19 24						20 24		

		EM	EM	EM	EM	EM	XC	NT	EM	EM	EM	EM	XC	EM	EM	EM	EM	EM	EM
		◇1 ☕	◇1 ☕	◇1 ☕			1		◇1 ☕	◇1 ☕			1	◇1 ☕					◇1 ☕
Nottingham 8	d	20 02		20 07	20 11	20 32	20 37	20 45	21 02		21 16	21 32	21 37			22 16	23 10	23 15	
Beeston	d	20a07			20 17	20a38	20 43		21a07		21 22	21a38	21 43			22 22	23a16	23 21	
Attenborough	d				20 20						21 25		21 46			22 25		23 24	
Long Eaton	d		20 07	20 23	20 28		20 51			21 06	21 33		21 53	21 59		22 33		23 33	23 38
Spondon	d												21 59						
Derby 6	a		20 19	20 35	20 44		21 02	21 05		21 16	21 49		22 04	22 10		22 49		23 48	23 50
	d				20 56										22 16				
Duffield	d				21 03										22 23				
Belper	d				21 08										22 28				
Ambergate	d				21 14										22 34				
Whatstandwell	d				21 18										22 38				
Cromford	d				21 23										22 43				
Matlock Bath	d				21 27										22 47				
Matlock	a				21 30										22 50				

For connections from St Pancras International please refer to Table 53

Table 56

Mondays to Fridays

from 26 September

Nottingham - Derby - Matlock

		EM MX	EM	XC	EM	EM	XC	EM	EM	XC		EM	EM	EM	XC	EM	EM	XC	EM	EM		XC	EM	EM	XC
		◇■1		◇■1		◇■1	◇■1	◇■1	◇■1	◇■1		◇■1			■1	◇■1	◇■1	◇■1				■1	◇■1	◇■1	◇■1
		⊡				⊠🚲		⊠🚲	⊡			⊡				⊡	⊡	🚲					⊡	⊡	🚲
Nottingham ■	d	01 52		06 00	06 18	06 28	06 37	06 49		06 56		07 10	07 18	07 31	07 37		08 02	08 08	08 15	08 32		08 37		09 02	09 11
Beeston	d			06 06	06 24	06a33	06 43	06a54		07 07		07a16	07 24	07a37	07 43		08a07		08 24	08a38		08 43		09a07	
Attenborough	d			06 10	06 27					07 11			07 27						08 27						
Long Eaton	d			06 18	06 35					07 18			07 35		07 51	07 59			08 35			08 51	09 00		
Spondon	d			06 25	06 42								07 42						08 42			08 57			
Derby ■	a	02 10		06 30	06 49		07 00			07 31			07 48		08 02	08 09		08 32	08 49			09 02	09 15		09 31
	d		05 40		06 50				07 20				07 50						08 50						
Duffield	d		05 47		06 57								07 57						08 57						
Belper	d		05 52		07 02				07a27				08 02						09 02						
Ambergate	d		05 58		07 08								08 08						09 08						
Whatstandwell	d		06 02		07 12								08 12						09 12						
Cromford	d		06 07		07 17								08 17						09 17						
Matlock Bath	d		06 11		07 20								08 20						09 19						
Matlock	a		06 16		07 25								08 25						09 26						

		EM	EM	XC	EM	EM		XC	EM	EM	XC	EM	EM	XC	EM	EM		XC	EM	EM	XC	EM	EM	XC	EM
				■1	◇■1	◇■1		◇■1			■1	◇■1	◇■1	◇■1				■1	◇■1	◇■1	◇■1			■1	◇■1
					⊡	⊡		🚲				⊡	⊡	🚲				🚲	⊡	⊡				🚲	⊡
Nottingham ■	d	09 18	09 32	09 37		10 02		10 11	10 18	10 32	10 37		11 02	11 08	11 18	11 32		11 37		12 02	12 08	12 18	12 32	12 37	
Beeston	d	09 24	09a38	09 43		10a07			10 24	10a38	10 43		11a07		11 24	11a38		11 43		12a07		12 24	12a38	12 43	
Attenborough	d	09 27							10 27						11 27							12 27			
Long Eaton	d	09 35		09 51	09 56				10 35		10 51	10 56			11 35			11 51	11 57			12 35		12 51	12 57
Spondon	d																								
Derby ■	a	09 48		10 02	10 09			10 33	10 49		11 02	11 09		11 31	11 48			12 02	12 09		12 33	12 48		13 02	13 09
	d	09 50							10 50						11 54							12 50			
Duffield	d	09 57							10 57						12 01							12 57			
Belper	d	10 02							11 02						12 06							13 02			
Ambergate	d	10 08							11 08						12 12							13 08			
Whatstandwell	d	10 12							11 12						12 16							13 12			
Cromford	d	10 17							11 17						12 21							13 17			
Matlock Bath	d	10 20							11 20						12 24							13 20			
Matlock	a	10 26							11 26						12 30							13 26			

		EM		XC	EM	EM	XC	EM	EM	XC	EM	EM		XC	EM	EM	XC	EM	EM	XC	EM	EM		XC	EM
		◇■1		◇■1			■1	◇■1	◇■1	◇■1				■1	◇■1	◇■1	◇■1			■1	◇■1	◇■1		◇■1	
		⊡					🚲	⊡	⊡	🚲				🚲	⊡	⊡				🚲	⊡	⊡			
Nottingham ■	d	13 02		13 11	13 18	13 32	13 37		14 02	14 08	14 18	14 32		14 37		15 02	15 11	15 18	15 32	15 37		16 02		16 08	16 18
Beeston	d	13a07			13 24	13a38	13 43		14a07		14 24	14a38		14 43		15a07		15 24	15a38	15 43		16a07			16 24
Attenborough	d				13 27						14 27							15 27							16 27
Long Eaton	d				13 35		13 51	13 57			14 35			14 51	14 57			15 35		15 51	15 57				16 35
Spondon	d																								
Derby ■	a			13 31	13 48		14 02	14 09		14 31	14 47			15 02	15 13		15 31	15 48		16 02	16 09			16 31	16 48
	d				13 50						14 54							15 50							16 50
Duffield	d				13 57						15 01							15 57							16 57
Belper	d				14 02						15 06							16 02							17 02
Ambergate	d				14 08						15 12							16 08							17 08
Whatstandwell	d				14 12						15 16							16 12							17 12
Cromford	d				14 17						15 21							16 17							17 17
Matlock Bath	d				14 20						15 24							16 20							17 20
Matlock	a				14 26						15 29							16 26							17 26

		EM	XC	EM	EM	EM	XC	EM		EM	XC	EM	EM	XC	EM	EM	XC	EM		EM	XC	EM	EM	XC	EM
			■1	◇■1		◇■1	◇■1				■1	◇■1	◇■1	◇■1			■1	◇■1		◇■1	◇■1			■1	◇■1
			🚲	⊡		⊡					🚲	⊡	⊡				🚲	⊡		⊡					⊡
Nottingham ■	d	16 32	16 37		16 50	17 02	17 08	17 18		17 32	17 37		18 02	18 08	18 18	18 33	18 37			19 02	19 08	19 18	19 32	19 37	20 02
Beeston	d	16 38	16 43		16 55	17a07		17 24		17 38	17 43		18a07		18 24	18a39	18 43			19a07		19 24	19a38	19 43	20a07
Attenborough	d	16a41			16 58			17 27		17a41					18 27							19 27		19 46	
Long Eaton	d		16 51	16 57	17 07			17 35			17 51	18 01			18 37		18 51	18 56				19 35		19 53	
Spondon	d							17 42			17 57														
Derby ■	a		17 02	17 09	17 23		17 31	17 49			18 02	18 14		18 33	18 48		19 02	19 09			19 32	19 48		20 02	
	d							17 50							18 50							19 50			
Duffield	d							17 57							18 57							19 57			
Belper	d							18 02							19 02							20 02			
Ambergate	d							18 08							19 08							20 08			
Whatstandwell	d							18 12							19 12							20 12			
Cromford	d							18 17							19 17							20 17			
Matlock Bath	d							18 20							19 20							20 20			
Matlock	a							18 26							19 26							20 26			

		EM	EM	EM		EM	XC	NT	EM	EM	EM	EM	XC	EM		EM	EM	EM	EM	EM					
		◇■1	◇■1				■1		◇■1	◇■1			■1	◇■1						◇■1					
		⊡	⊡						⊡	⊡				⊡						⊡					
Nottingham ■	d		20 07	20 11		20 32	20 37	20 45	21 02		21 16	21 32	21 37				22 16	23 10	23 15						
Beeston	d			20 17		20a38	20 43		21a07		21 22	21a38	21 43				22 22	23a16	23 21						
Attenborough	d			20 20							21 25		21 46				22 25		23 24						
Long Eaton	d	20 07	20 23	20 28			20 51			21 06	21 33		21 53	21 59			22 33		23 33	23 38					
Spondon	d												21 59												
Derby ■	a	20 19	20 35	20 44			21 02	21 05		21 16	21 49		22 04	22 10			22 49		23 48	23 50					
	d			20 56												22 16									
Duffield	d			21 03												22 23									
Belper	d			21 08												22 28									
Ambergate	d			21 14												22 34									
Whatstandwell	d			21 18												22 38									
Cromford	d			21 23												22 43									
Matlock Bath	d			21 27												22 47									
Matlock	a			21 32												22 52									

For connections from St Pancras International please refer to Table 53

Table 56

Saturdays

until 24 September

Nottingham - Derby - Matlock

		EM	EM	XC	EM	EM	XC	EM	XC	EM		EM	EM	XC	EM	EM	XC	EM	EM	XC		EM	EM	XC	EM
		◇1		◇1	◇1		◇1	◇1	◇1	◇1				1	◇1	◇1	◇1			1		◇1	◇1	◇1	
		🍴			🍴			🍴		🍴					🍴	🍴	🛒					🍴	🍴	🛒	
Nottingham 8	d	01 52		05 57	06 02	06 18	06 37		06 56	07 02		07 18	07 31	07 37		08 02	08 08	08 18	08 32	08 37			09 02	09 08	09 18
Beeston	d			06 03	06a07	06 24	06 43		07 02	07a07		07 24	07a37	07 43		08a07		08 24	08a38	08 43			09a07		09 24
Attenborough	d			06 06		06 27			07 06			07 27						08 27							09 27
Long Eaton	d			06 17		06 34			07 14			07 35		07 51	07 56			08 35		08 51		09 01			09 35
Spondon	d			06 24		06 43			07 24									08 42							
Derby 6	a	02 10		06 32		06 48	07 01		07 30			07 49		08 02	08 09		08 31	08 48		09 02		09 14		09 31	09 48
	d		05 40			06 50		07 20				07 50						08 50							09 50
Duffield	d		05 47			06 57						07 57						08 57							09 57
Belper	d		05 52			07 02		07a27				08 02						09 02							10 02
Ambergate	d		05 58			07 08						08 08						09 08							10 08
Whatstandwell	d		06 02			07 12						08 12						09 12							10 12
Cromford	d		06 07			07 17						08 17						09 17							10 17
Matlock Bath	d		06 11			07 20						08 20						09 21							10 20
Matlock	a		06 14			07 24						08 24						09 24							10 24

		EM	XC	EM	EM	XC		EM	EM	XC	EM	EM	XC	EM	EM	XC		EM	EM	XC	EM	EM	XC	EM	EM
			1	◇1	◇1	◇1				1	◇1	◇1	◇1			1		◇1	◇1	◇1			1	◇1	◇1
				🍴	🍴	🛒					🍴	🍴	🛒			🛒		🍴	🍴				🛒	🍴	🍴
Nottingham 8	d	09 32	09 37		10 02	10 08		10 18	10 32	10 37		11 02	11 11	11 18	11 32	11 37			12 02	12 08	12 18	12 32	12 37		13 02
Beeston	d	09a38	09 43		10a07			10 24	10a38	10 43		11a07		11 24	11a38	11 43			12a07		12 24	12a38	12 43		13a07
Attenborough	d							10 27						11 27							12 27				
Long Eaton	d		09 51	09 57				10 35		10 51	10 57			11 36		11 51		11 57			12 36		12 51	12 57	
Spondon	d																								
Derby 6	a		10 02	10 09		10 31		10 49		11 02	11 09		11 31	11 48		12 02		12 09		12 31	12 48		13 02	13 09	
	d							10 50						11 50							12 50				
Duffield	d							10 57						11 57							12 57				
Belper	d							11 02						12 02							13 02				
Ambergate	d							11 08						12 08							13 08				
Whatstandwell	d							11 12						12 12							13 12				
Cromford	d							11 17						12 17							13 17				
Matlock Bath	d							11 20						12 20							13 20				
Matlock	a							11 24						12 24							13 24				

		XC		EM	EM	XC	EM	EM	EM	XC	EM	EM		XC	EM	EM	XC	EM	EM	XC	EM	EM		XC	EM
		◇1				1	◇1		◇1	◇1				1	◇1	◇1	◇1			1	◇1	◇1		◇1	
								A																	
						🛒	🍴		🍴	🛒				🛒	🍴	🍴	🛒			🛒	🍴	🍴			
Nottingham 8	d	13 08		13 18	13 32	13 37		13 52	14 02	14 08	14 18	14 32		14 37		15 02	15 08	15 18	15 32	15 37		16 02		16 08	16 18
Beeston	d			13 24	13a38	13 43		13 59	14a07		14 24	14a38		14 43		15a07		15 24	15a38	15 43		16a07			16 24
Attenborough	d			13 27							14 27							15 27							16 27
Long Eaton	d			13 36		13 51	13 57	14 08			14 36			14 51	14 57			15 36		15 51	15 57				16 36
Spondon	d																								
Derby 6	a	13 31		13 48		14 02	14 09	14 20		14 32	14 48			15 02	15 09		15 31	15 48		16 02	16 09			16 31	16 48
	d			13 50							14 50							15 50							16 50
Duffield	d			13 57							14 57							15 57							16 57
Belper	d			14 02							15 02							16 02							17 02
Ambergate	d			14 08							15 08							16 08							17 08
Whatstandwell	d			14 12							15 12							16 12							17 12
Cromford	d			14 17							15 17							16 17							17 17
Matlock Bath	d			14 20							15 20							16 20							17 20
Matlock	a			14 24							15 24							16 24							17 24

		EM	XC	EM	EM	XC	EM	EM		XC	EM	EM	XC	EM	EM	XC	EM	EM		XC	EM	EM	XC	EM	EM
			1	◇1	◇1	◇1				1	◇1	◇1	◇1			1	◇1	◇1		◇1			1	◇1	◇1
			🛒	🍴	🍴					🛒	🍴	🍴				🛒	🍴	🍴						🍴	🍴
Nottingham 8	d	16 32	16 37		17 02	17 11	17 18	17 32		17 37		18 02	18 08	18 19	18 32	18 37		19 02		19 08	19 18	19 32	19 37		20 02
Beeston	d	16 38	16 43		17a07		17 24	17 38		17 43		18a07		18 24	18a38	18 43		19a07			19 24	19a38	19 43		20a07
Attenborough	d	16a41					17 27	17a41						18 27							19 27		19 46		
Long Eaton	d		16 51	16 56			17 35			17 51	17 57			18 37		18 51	18 57				19 35		19 53	19 57	
Spondon	d						17 42													19 27					
Derby 6	a		17 02	17 09		17 31	17 48			18 02	18 09		18 31	18 48		19 02	19 09			19 32	19 48		20 02	20 09	
	d						17 50							18 50							19 50				
Duffield	d						17 57							18 57							19 57				
Belper	d						18 02							19 02							20 02				
Ambergate	d						18 08							19 08							20 08				
Whatstandwell	d						18 12							19 12							20 12				
Cromford	d						18 17							19 17							20 17				
Matlock Bath	d						18 20							19 20							20 20				
Matlock	a						18 24							19 24							20 24				

A from 23 July until 10 September

For connections from St Pancras International please refer to Table 53

Table 56

Nottingham - Derby - Matlock

Saturdays
until 24 September

		EM	EM	XC 1		EM ◇1 ☕	EM ◇1 ☕	EM	EM	XC 1	EM ◇1 ☕	EM	EM	EM		EM ◇1 A ☕	EM ◇1 B ☕	EM							
Nottingham 8 🚊	d	20 09	20 32	20 37		20 45		21 08	21 32	21 37			22 15	23 10				23 15							
Beeston	d	20 15	20a37	20 43		20a50		21 14	21a38	21 43			22 21	23a17				23 21							
Attenborough	d	20 18						21 17		21 46			22 24					23 24							
Long Eaton	d	20 27		20 51			20 57	21 26		21 53	21 59		22 33			23 16	23 21	23 32							
Spondon	d									21 59															
Derby 6	a	20 42		21 02			21 10	21 41		22 04	22 10		22 48			23 26	23 31	23 47							
	d	20 50										22 16													
Duffield	d	20 57										22 23													
Belper	d	21 02										22 28													
Ambergate	d	21 08										22 35													
Whatstandwell	d	21 12										22 39													
Cromford	d	21 17										22 44													
Matlock Bath	d	21 20										22 47													
Matlock	a	21 24										22 50													

Saturdays
from 1 October

		EM ◇1 ☕	EM	XC ◇1	EM ◇1 ☕	EM	XC ◇1	EM ◇1 ☕	XC ◇1	EM ◇1 ☕		EM	EM	XC 1	EM ◇1 ☕	EM ◇1 ☕	XC ◇1 🛒	EM	EM	XC 1		EM ◇1 ☕	EM ◇1 ☕	XC ◇1 🛒	EM
Nottingham 8 🚊	d	01 52		05 57	06 02	06 18	06 37		06 56	07 02		07 18	07 31	07 37		08 02	08 08	08 18	08 32	08 37			09 02	09 08	09 18
Beeston	d			06 03	06a07	06 24	06 43		07 02	07a07		07 24	07a37	07 43		08a07		08 24	08a38	08 43			09a07		09 24
Attenborough	d			06 06		06 27			07 06			07 27						08 27							09 27
Long Eaton	d			06 17		06 34			07 14			07 35		07 51	07 56			08 35		08 51		09 01			09 35
Spondon	d			06 24		06 43			07 24									08 42							
Derby 6	a	02 10		06 32		06 48	07 01		07 30			07 49		08 02	08 09		08 31	08 48		09 02		09 14		09 31	09 48
	d		05 40			06 50		07 20				07 50						08 50							09 50
Duffield	d		05 47			06 57						07 57						08 57							09 57
Belper	d		05 52			07 02		07a27				08 02						09 02							10 02
Ambergate	d		05 58			07 08						08 08						09 08							10 08
Whatstandwell	d		06 02			07 12						08 12						09 12							10 12
Cromford	d		06 07			07 17						08 17						09 17							10 17
Matlock Bath	d		06 11			07 20						08 20						09 21							10 20
Matlock	a		06 16			07 25						08 25						09 26							10 26

		EM	XC 1	EM ◇1 ☕	EM ◇1 ☕	XC ◇1 🛒		EM	EM	XC 1	EM ◇1 ☕	EM ◇1 ☕	XC ◇1 🛒	EM	EM	XC 1 🛒		EM ◇1 ☕	EM ◇1 ☕	XC ◇1	EM	EM	XC 1 🛒	EM ◇1 ☕	EM ◇1 ☕
Nottingham 8 🚊	d	09 32	09 37		10 02	10 08		10 18	10 32	10 37		11 02	11 11	11 18	11 32	11 37			12 02	12 08	12 18	12 32	12 37		13 02
Beeston	d	09a38	09 43		10a07			10 24	10a38	10 43		11a07		11 24	11a38	11 43			12a07		12 24	12a38	12 43		13a07
Attenborough	d							10 27						11 27							12 27				
Long Eaton	d		09 51	09 57				10 35		10 51	10 57			11 36		11 51		11 57			12 36		12 51	12 57	
Spondon	d																								
Derby 6	a		10 02	10 09		10 31		10 49		11 02	11 09		11 31	11 48		12 02		12 09		12 31	12 48		13 02	13 09	
	d							10 50						11 50							12 50				
Duffield	d							10 57						11 57							12 57				
Belper	d							11 02						12 02							13 02				
Ambergate	d							11 08						12 08							13 08				
Whatstandwell	d							11 12						12 12							13 12				
Cromford	d							11 17						12 17							13 17				
Matlock Bath	d							11 20						12 20							13 20				
Matlock	a							11 26						12 26							13 26				

		XC ◇1		EM	EM	XC 1 🛒	EM ◇1 ☕	EM ◇1 ☕	XC ◇1 🛒	EM	EM	XC 1 🛒		EM ◇1 ☕	EM ◇1 ☕	XC ◇1 🛒	EM	EM	XC 1 🛒	EM ◇1 ☕	EM ◇1 ☕	XC ◇1		EM	EM
Nottingham 8 🚊	d	13 08		13 18	13 32	13 37		14 02	14 08	14 18	14 32	14 37			15 02	15 08	15 18	15 32	15 37		16 02	16 08		16 18	16 32
Beeston	d			13 24	13a38	13 43		14a07		14 24	14a38	14 43			15a07		15 24	15a38	15 43		16a07			16 24	16 38
Attenborough	d			13 27						14 27							15 27							16 27	16a41
Long Eaton	d			13 36		13 51	13 57			14 36		14 51		14 57			15 36		15 51	15 57				16 36	
Spondon	d																								
Derby 6	a	13 31		13 48		14 02	14 09		14 32	14 48		15 02		15 09		15 31	15 48		16 02	16 09		16 31		16 48	
	d			13 50						14 50							15 50							16 50	
Duffield	d			13 57						14 57							15 57							16 57	
Belper	d			14 02						15 02							16 02							17 02	
Ambergate	d			14 08						15 08							16 08							17 08	
Whatstandwell	d			14 12						15 12							16 12							17 12	
Cromford	d			14 17						15 17							16 17							17 17	
Matlock Bath	d			14 20						15 20							16 20							17 20	
Matlock	a			14 26						15 26							16 26							17 26	

A until 30 July

B from 6 August until 24 September

For connections from St Pancras International please refer to Table 53

Table 56

Nottingham - Derby - Matlock

Saturdays
from 1 October

Station		XC [1] 🛒	EM ◇[1] ☕	EM ◇[1] ☕	XC ◇[1]	EM	EM	XC [1] 🛒		EM ◇[1] ☕	EM ◇[1] ☕	XC ◇[1]	EM	EM	XC [1] 🛒	EM ◇[1] ☕	EM ◇[1] ☕	XC ◇[1]		EM	EM	XC [1]	EM ◇[1] ☕	EM ◇[1] ☕	EM
Nottingham [8]	d	16 37		17 02	17 11	17 18	17 32	17 37			18 02	18 08	18 19	18 32	18 37		19 02	19 08		19 18	19 32	19 37		20 02	20 09
Beeston	d	16 43		17a07		17 24	17 38	17 43			18a07		18 24	18a38	18 43		19a07			19 24	19a38	19 43		20a07	20 15
Attenborough	d					17 27	17a41						18 27							19 27		19 46			20 18
Long Eaton	d	16 51	16 56			17 35		17 51		17 57			18 37		18 51	18 57				19 35		19 53	19 57		20 27
Spondon	d					17 42												19 27							
Derby [6]	a	17 02	17 09		17 31	17 48		18 02		18 09		18 31	18 48		19 02	19 09		19 32		19 48		20 02	20 09		20 42
	d					17 50							18 50							19 50					20 50
Duffield	d					17 57							18 57							19 57					20 57
Belper	d					18 02							19 02							20 02					21 02
Ambergate	d					18 08							19 08							20 08					21 08
Whatstandwell	d					18 12							19 12							20 12					21 12
Cromford	d					18 17							19 17							20 17					21 17
Matlock Bath	d					18 20							19 20							20 20					21 20
Matlock	a					18 26							19 26							20 26					21 26

Station		EM	XC [1]	EM ◇[1] ☕		EM ◇[1] ☕	EM	EM	XC [1]	EM ◇[1] ☕	EM	EM	EM	EM ◇[1] A ☕		EM ◇[1] B ☕	EM
Nottingham [8]	d	20 32	20 37	20 45			21 08	21 32	21 37			22 15	23 10				23 15
Beeston	d	20a37	20 43	20a50			21 14	21a38	21 43			22 21	23a17				23 21
Attenborough	d						21 17		21 46			22 24					23 24
Long Eaton	d		20 51			20 57	21 26		21 53	21 59		22 33		23 16		23 21	23 32
Spondon	d								21 59								
Derby [6]	a		21 02			21 10	21 41		22 04	22 10		22 48		23 26		23 31	23 47
	d										22 16						
Duffield	d										22 23						
Belper	d										22 28						
Ambergate	d										22 35						
Whatstandwell	d										22 39						
Cromford	d										22 44						
Matlock Bath	d										22 47						
Matlock	a										22 52						

Sundays
until 19 June

Station		EM ◇[1] C ☕	EM ◇[1] ☕	EM	EM ◇[1] ☕	EM ◇[1] ☕	XC ◇[1] 🛒	EM ◇[1] ☕	EM	XC ◇[1] 🛒		EM ◇[1] ☕	EM ◇[1] ☕	XC ◇[1] 🛒	EM ◇[1] ☕	EM	EM ◇[1] ☕	XC ◇[1] 🛒	EM	EM ◇[1] ☕		EM ◇[1] ☕	EM	XC ◇[1] 🛒	EM ◇[1] ☕
Nottingham [8]	d		08 18	09 28	10 15		11 10		11 22	12 10		12 15		13 05	13 14	13 19		14 10	14 14	14 23			14 58	15 05	15 10
Beeston	d		08a23	09 34	10a21				11 29			12a21			13a20	13 25			14 19	14a28			15 03		15a15
Attenborough	d			09 37					11 32							13 28			14 23				15 06		
Long Eaton	d	00 07		09 45		10 32		11 37	11 36				12 39			13 35	13 41		14 32			14 46	15 14		
Spondon	d																								
Derby [6]	a	00 17		09 56		10 46	11 34	11 48	11 49	12 30			12 49	13 25		13 47	13 52	14 28	14 44			14 59	15 27	15 30	
	d			09 58					11 54							13 57							15 30		
Duffield	d			10 05					12 01							14 04							15 36		
Belper	d			10 10					12 06							14 09							15 41		
Ambergate	d			10 16					12 12							14 15							15 47		
Whatstandwell	d			10 20					12 16							14 19							15 51		
Cromford	d			10 25					12 21							14 24							15 56		
Matlock Bath	d			10 29					12 24							14 27							16 00		
Matlock	a			10 32					12 27							14 30							16 04		

Station		EM ◇[1] ☕	XC ◇[1] 🛒	EM ◇[1] ☕	EM ◇[1] ☕	EM	EM	XC ◇[1] 🛒	EM ◇[1] ☕	EM ◇[1] ☕	XC ◇[1] 🛒	EM ◇[1] ☕	EM ◇[1] ☕	EM	XC ◇[1]	EM ◇[1] ☕	EM	EM ◇[1] ☕	XC ◇[1]	EM ◇[1] ☕	EM	XC ◇[1]	EM ◇[1] ☕	EM	EM ◇[1] ☕
Nottingham [8]	d		16 10	16 18		16 22	17 00	17 10	17 20		18 05	18 10		18 23	19 09		19 23	19 46	20 10		20 22	21 08		21 25	
Beeston	d			16a23		16 28	17 06		17a25			18a18		18 29			19 28	19a51			20 28			21 31	
Attenborough	d					16 31	17 09							18 32			19 31				20 31			21 34	
Long Eaton	d	15 42			16 36	16 39	17 17			17 37			18 32	18 41		19 31	19 39			20 29	20 41		21 29	21 41	23 39
Spondon	d																								
Derby [6]	a	15 53	16 30		16 48	16 51	17 27	17 33		17 48	18 32		18 47	18 52	19 29	19 45	19 50		20 31	20 45	20 53	21 30	21 40	21 53	23 49
	d						17 29										19 52							21 56	
Duffield	d						17 36										19 59							22 04	
Belper	d						17 41										20 04							22 09	
Ambergate	d						17 47										20 10							22 15	
Whatstandwell	d						17 51										20 14							22 19	
Cromford	d						17 56										20 19							22 24	
Matlock Bath	d						17 59										20 23							22 27	
Matlock	a						18 02										20 26							22 30	

A from 29 October **B** from 1 October until 22 October **C** not 22 May

For connections from St Pancras International please refer to Table 53

Table 56

Sundays

26 June to 31 July

		EM	EM	EM	EM	EM	XC	EM	EM	XC		EM	EM	XC	EM	EM	EM	XC	EM	EM		EM	EM	XC	EM
		◇1	◇1		◇1	◇1	◇1	◇1		◇1		◇1	◇1	◇1	◇1		◇1	◇1		◇1		◇1		◇1	◇1
		☕	☕		☕	☕	🛒	☕		🛒		☕	☕	🛒	☕		☕	🛒		☕		☕		🛒	☕
Nottingham 8 🚊	d		08 19	09 28	10 15		11 10		11 22	12 10		12 14		13 06	13 14	13 19		14 10	14 14	14 23			14 58	15 05	15 11
Beeston	d		08a24	09 34	10a21				11 29			12a20			13a20	13 25			14 19	14a28			15 03		15a16
Attenborough	d			09 37					11 32							13 28			14 23				15 06		
Long Eaton	d	00 07		09 45		10 32		11 37	11 36				12 39			13 35	13 41		14 32			14 46	15 14		
Spondon	d																								
Derby 6	a	00 17		09 56		10 46	11 34	11 48	11 49	12 29			12 49	13 30		13 47	13 52	14 28	14 44			14 59	15 27	15 31	
	d			09 58					11 54							13 57							15 30		
Duffield	d			10 05					12 01							14 04							15 36		
Belper	d			10 10					12 06							14 09							15 41		
Ambergate	d			10 16					12 12							14 15							15 47		
Whatstandwell	d			10 20					12 16							14 19							15 51		
Cromford	d			10 25					12 21							14 24							15 56		
Matlock Bath	d			10 29					12 24							14 27							16 00		
Matlock	a			10 32					12 27							14 30							16 04		

		EM	XC	EM	EM	EM	EM	XC	EM	EM	XC	EM	EM	EM	XC	EM	EM	EM	XC	EM	EM	XC	EM	EM	EM
		◇1	◇1	◇1	◇1			◇1	◇1	◇1	◇1	◇1	◇1		◇1	◇1		◇1	◇1	◇1		◇1	◇1		◇1
		☕	🛒	☕	☕			🛒	☕	☕	🛒	☕	☕		🛒	☕		☕		☕			☕		☕
Nottingham 8 🚊	d		16 05	16 18		16 22	17 00	17 10	17 20		18 05	18 10		18 23	19 09		19 23	19 46	20 10		20 22	21 08		21 25	
Beeston	d			16a23		16 28	17 06		17a25			18a18		18 29			19 28	19a51			20 28			21 31	
Attenborough	d					16 31	17 09							18 32			19 31				20 31			21 34	
Long Eaton	d	15 45			16 35	16 39	17 17			17 37			18 32	18 41		19 31	19 39			20 29	20 41		21 29	21 41	23 39
Spondon	d																								
Derby 6	a	15 56	16 28		16 47	16 51	17 27	17 30		17 48	18 31		18 47	18 52	19 29	19 45	19 50		20 29	20 45	20 53	21 31	21 40	21 53	23 49
	d						17 29										19 52							21 56	
Duffield	d						17 36										19 59							22 04	
Belper	d						17 41										20 04							22 09	
Ambergate	d						17 47										20 10							22 15	
Whatstandwell	d						17 51										20 14							22 19	
Cromford	d						17 56										20 19							22 24	
Matlock Bath	d						17 59										20 23							22 27	
Matlock	a						18 02										20 26							22 30	

7 August to 23 October

		EM	EM	EM	EM	EM	XC	EM	EM	XC	EM	EM	EM	XC	EM	EM	EM	XC	EM	EM	EM	EM	XC	EM	EM
		◇1	◇1		◇1	◇1	◇1		◇1	◇1	◇1	◇1	◇1	◇1	◇1		◇1	◇1		◇1	◇1		◇1	◇1	◇1
			A									A	B												B
		☕	☕		☕	☕	🛒		☕	🛒	☕	☕	☕	🛒	☕		☕	🛒		☕	☕		🛒		☕
Nottingham 8 🚊	d		08 17	09 28	10 14		11 10	11 22		12 10	12 14			13 06	13 12	13 19		14 10	14 14	14 24		14 58	15 05	15 10	
Beeston	d		08a22	09 34	10a20			11 29			12a20				13a18	13 25			14 19	14a29		15 03		15a15	
Attenborough	d			09 37				11 32								13 28			14 23			15 06			
Long Eaton	d	00 14		09 45		10 47		11 36	11 46			12 46	12 48			13 35	13 48		14 32		14 48	15 14			15 41
Spondon	d																								
Derby 6	a	00 24		09 56		10 57	11 34	11 49	11 56	12 30		12 56	12 58	13 30		13 47	13 59	14 28	14 44		14 59	15 27	15 31		15 52
	d			09 58				11 54								13 48						15 30			
Duffield	d			10 05				12 01								13 56						15 36			
Belper	d			10 10				12 06								14 01						15 41			
Ambergate	d			10 16				12 12								14 07						15 47			
Whatstandwell	d			10 20				12 16								14 11						15 51			
Cromford	d			10 25				12 21								14 16						15 56			
Matlock Bath	d			10 29				12 24								14 18						16 00			
Matlock	a			10 32				12 27								14 21						16 04			

		EM	XC	EM	EM	EM	EM	XC	EM	EM	XC	EM	EM	EM	XC	EM	EM	EM	XC	EM	EM	XC	EM	EM	EM
		◇1	◇1	◇1		◇1		◇1	◇1	◇1	◇1	◇1	◇1		◇1	◇1		◇1	◇1	◇1		◇1	◇1		◇1
		A																					☕		☕
		☕	🛒	☕		☕		🛒	☕	☕	🛒	☕	☕		🛒	☕		☕		☕				☕	
Nottingham 8 🚊	d		16 05	16 18	16 22		17 00	17 10	17 20		18 05	18 10		18 23	19 09		19 23	19 46	20 10		20 22	21 08		21 25	
Beeston	d			16a23	16 28		17 06		17a25			18a18		18 29			19 28	19a51			20 28			21 31	
Attenborough	d				16 31		17 09							18 32			19 31				20 31			21 34	
Long Eaton	d	15 42			16 39	16 43	17 17			17 37			18 32	18 41		19 31	19 39			20 29	20 41		21 29	21 41	23 39
Spondon	d																								
Derby 6	a	15 53	16 28		16 51	16 55	17 27	17 30		17 48	18 31		18 47	18 52	19 29	19 45	19 50		20 29	20 45	20 53	21 31	21 40	21 53	23 49
	d						17 29										19 52							21 56	
Duffield	d						17 36										19 59							22 04	
Belper	d						17 41										20 04							22 09	
Ambergate	d						17 47										20 10							22 15	
Whatstandwell	d						17 51										20 14							22 19	
Cromford	d						17 56										20 19							22 24	
Matlock Bath	d						17 59										20 23							22 27	
Matlock	a						18 02										20 26							22 30	

from 30 October

		EM	EM	EM	EM	EM	XC	EM	EM	XC		EM	EM	XC	EM	EM	EM	XC	EM	EM		EM	EM	XC	EM
		◇1	◇1		◇1	◇1	◇1	◇1		◇1		◇1	◇1	◇1	◇1		◇1	◇1	◇1			◇1		◇1	◇1
		☕	☕		☕	☕	🛒	☕		🛒		☕	☕	🛒	☕		☕	🛒	☕			☕		🛒	☕
Nottingham 8 🚊	d		08 19	09 28	10 15		11 10		11 22	12 10		12 15		13 06	13 14	13 19		14 10	14 17	14 23			14 57	15 05	15 10
Beeston	d		08a24	09 34	10a21				11 29			12a21			13a20	13 25			14a22	14 28			15 02		15a15
Attenborough	d			09 37					11 32							13 28				14 32			15 05		
Long Eaton	d	00 07		09 45		10 32		11 35	11 36				12 41			13 35	13 42			14 41		14 46	15 14		
Spondon	d																								
Derby 6	a	00 17		09 56		10 46	11 34	11 46	11 49	12 30			12 51	13 30		13 47	13 52	14 28		14 52		14 59	15 27	15 31	
	d			09 58					11 54							13 48							15 30		
Duffield	d			10 05					12 01							13 56							15 36		
Belper	d			10 10					12 06							14 01							15 41		
Ambergate	d			10 16					12 12							14 07							15 47		
Whatstandwell	d			10 20					12 16							14 11							15 51		
Cromford	d			10 25					12 21							14 16							15 56		
Matlock Bath	d			10 29					12 24							14 18							16 00		
Matlock	a			10 32					12 27							14 21							16 04		

A from 7 August until 11 September

B from 18 September until 23 October

For connections from St Pancras International please refer to Table 53

Table 56

Sundays

from 30 October

Nottingham - Derby - Matlock

		EM	XC	EM	EM	EM		XC	EM	EM	EM	XC	EM
		◇1	◇1	◇1		◇1		◇1	◇1		◇1	◇1	◇1
		☕	🍴	☕		☕		🍴	☕		☕	🍴	☕
Nottingham 8 🚌	d		16 05	16 10	16 22			17 10	17 18	17 23		18 05	18 10
Beeston	d			16a15	16 28				17a23	17 29			18a16
Attenborough	d				16 31					17 32			
Long Eaton	d	15 42			16 39	16 43				17 40	17 49		
Spondon	d												
Derby 6	a	15 53	16 28		16 51	16 55		17 30		17 51	18 01	18 31	
	d									17 52			
Duffield	d									18 00			
Belper	d									18 05			
Ambergate	d									18 11			
Whatstandwell	d									18 15			
Cromford	d									18 20			
Matlock Bath	d									18 22			
Matlock	a									18 25			

		EM	EM	XC		EM	EM	EM	XC	EM	EM	XC	EM
		◇1		◇1		◇1		◇1	◇1	◇1		◇1	◇1
		☕		🍴		☕		☕		☕			☕
Nottingham 8 🚌	d		18 23	19 09			19 23	19 44	20 10		20 22	21 08	
Beeston	d		18 29				19 28	19a49			20 28		
Attenborough	d		18 32				19 31				20 31		
Long Eaton	d	18 35	18 41			19 34	19 39			20 34	20 41		21 34
Spondon	d												
Derby 6	a	18 48	18 52	19 29		19 44	19 50		20 29	20 44	20 53	21 31	21 45
	d						19 52						
Duffield	d						19 59						
Belper	d						20 04						
Ambergate	d						20 10						
Whatstandwell	d						20 14						
Cromford	d						20 19						
Matlock Bath	d						20 23						
Matlock	a						20 26						

		EM		EM
				◇1
				☕
Nottingham 8 🚌	d	21 25		
Beeston	d	21 31		
Attenborough	d	21 34		
Long Eaton	d	21 41		23 43
Spondon	d			
Derby 6	a	21 53		23 53
	d	21 56		
Duffield	d	22 04		
Belper	d	22 09		
Ambergate	d	22 15		
Whatstandwell	d	22 19		
Cromford	d	22 24		
Matlock Bath	d	22 27		
Matlock	a	22 30		

For connections from St Pancras International please refer to Table 53

Table 56

Mondays to Fridays

until 23 September

Matlock - Derby - Nottingham

Miles			EM	EM	XC	EM	EM	EM	XC	EM	EM		EM	EM	EM	XC	EM	EM	XC	EM	EM		XC	EM	EM
			MX	MX	MX	MO	MO																		
				◇1	◇1	◇1	◇1	◇1			◇1				◇1	1	◇1		1				1	◇1	◇1
						A	B																		
				[P]		[P]	[P]	⊠🛒			⊠🛒				⊠🛒	🛒	[P]						🛒	⊠	[P]
0	**Matlock**	d	22p55										06 22												
1	Matlock Bath	d	22p57										06 24												
1¾	Cromford	d	23p00										06 27												
4¾	Whatstandwell	d	23p05										06 32												
6¾	Ambergate	d	23p10										06 37												
9½	Belper	d	23p17										06 44												
12	Duffield	d	23p21										06 48												
17¼	**Derby** 6	a	23p29										06 56												
—		d	23p31		23p59			05 17	06 00	06 24	06 32				07 01	07 10	07 26	07 33	07 40		07 53		08 10	08 16	
19¾	Spondon	d								06 29						07 18			07 45						
25½	Long Eaton	d	23p41					05a26		06 36	06a41					07 25	07a35	07 42	07 49		08 03		08 19	08a25	
28½	Attenborough	d	23p48							06 44				07 13		07 31		07 52			08 13				
30	Beeston	d	23p51	00 05		00∫41	00∫42		06 15	06 47				07 16		07 35		07 55	07 58	08 06	08 16		08 27		08 32
33¼	**Nottingham** 8	a	00 02	00 12	00 18	00∫48	00∫49		06 21	06 57				07 23	07 29	07 41		08 05	08 08	08 15	08 26		08 33		08 39

		EM	XC	EM	EM	XC	EM		EM	XC	EM	EM	XC	EM	EM	XC	EM		EM	XC	EM	EM	XC	EM	EM
			1		◇1	1	◇1			◇1		◇1	1	◇1		◇1			◇1	1	◇1		◇1		◇1
					[P]	🛒	[P]					[P]	🛒	[P]		🛒			[P]		[P]		🛒		[P]
Matlock	d	07 36							08 36						09 36							10 36			
Matlock Bath	d	07 38							08 38						09 38							10 38			
Cromford	d	07 41							08 41						09 41							10 41			
Whatstandwell	d	07 46							08 46						09 46							10 46			
Ambergate	d	07 51							08 51						09 51							10 51			
Belper	d	07 58							08 58						09 58							10 58			
Duffield	d	08 02							09 02						10 02							11 02			
Derby 6	a	08 10							09 10						10 10							11 10			
	d	08 20	08 40			09 10	09 20		09 24	09 40			10 10	10 20	10 24	10 40				11 10	11 20	11 24	11 40		
Spondon	d	08 25																							
Long Eaton	d	08 32				09 19	09a29		09 33				10 19	10a29	10 33					11 19	11a29	11 33			
Attenborough	d	08 39				09 26			09 40						10 40							11 40			
Beeston	d	08 42		09 02	09 17	09 29			09 43		10 02	10 17	10 27		10 43		11 02		11 17	11 27		11 43		12 02	12 17
Nottingham 8	a	08 50	09 05	09 13	09 26	09 35			09 53	10 05	10 13	10 25	10 33		10 53	11 06	11 14		11 25	11 33		11 53	12 05	12 13	12 26

		XC	EM		EM	XC	EM	EM	XC	EM	EM	XC	EM		EM	XC	EM	EM	XC	EM	EM	XC	EM		EM
		1	◇1			◇1		◇1	1	◇1		◇1			◇1	1	◇1		◇1		◇1	1	◇1		
			[P]			🛒		[P]	🛒	[P]		🛒			[P]		[P]		🛒		[P]		[P]		
Matlock	d				11 36						12 36							13 36							14 36
Matlock Bath	d				11 38						12 38							13 38							14 38
Cromford	d				11 41						12 41							13 41							14 41
Whatstandwell	d				11 46						12 46							13 46							14 46
Ambergate	d				11 51						12 51							13 51							14 51
Belper	d				11 58						12 58							13 58							14 58
Duffield	d				12 02						13 02							14 02							15 02
Derby 6	a				12 10						13 10							14 10							15 10
	d	12 10	12 20		12 24	12 40			13 10	13 20	13 24	13 40				14 10	14 20	14 24	14 40			15 10	15 20		15 24
Spondon	d																								
Long Eaton	d	12 19	12a29		12 33				13 19	13a29	13 33					14 19	14a29	14 33				15 19	15a29		15 33
Attenborough	d				12 40						13 40							14 40							15 40
Beeston	d	12 27			12 43		13 07	13 17	13 27		13 43		14 02		14 16	14 27		14 43		15 02	15 17	15 27			15 43
Nottingham 8	a	12 33			12 53	13 05	13 14	13 25	13 33		13 53	14 05	14 13		14 26	14 33		14 53	15 05	15 13	15 26	15 33			15 53

		XC	EM	EM	XC	EM	EM	XC	EM		EM	XC	EM	EM	XC	EM	EM	EM	XC		EM	EM	XC	EM	EM
		◇1		◇1	1	◇1		◇1			◇1	1	◇1		◇1			◇1	1		◇1		◇1	◇1	
		🛒		[P]		[P]		🛒			[P]		[P]		🛒			[P]			[P]			[P]	
Matlock	d						15 36							16 36								17 36			
Matlock Bath	d						15 38							16 38								17 38			
Cromford	d						15 41							16 41								17 41			
Whatstandwell	d						15 46							16 46								17 46			
Ambergate	d						15 51							16 51								17 51			
Belper	d						15 58							16 58								17 58			
Duffield	d						16 02							17 02								18 02			
Derby 6	a						16 10							17 10								18 10			
	d	15 40			16 10	16 18	16 24	16 40				17 10	17 18	17 24	17 40		17 47		18 10		18 18	18 24	18 40		
Spondon	d													17 29			17 53								
Long Eaton	d				16 19	16a27	16 33					17 19	17a28	17 36			18 01		18 19		18a27	18 33			
Attenborough	d						16 40							17 43			18 09					18 40			
Beeston	d		16 02	16 17	16 27		16 43		17 02		17 17	17 27		17 46		18 02	18 12	18 18	18 27			18 43		19 03	19 07
Nottingham 8	a	16 05	16 13	16 25	16 33		16 54	17 05	17 13		17 26	17 33		17 54	18 05	18 13	18 22	18 27	18 33			18 54	19 05	19 10	19 15

A Until 20 June and then from 8 August until 19 September

B From 27 June until 1 August

For connections to St Pancras International please refer to Table 53

Table 56

Mondays to Fridays

until 23 September

Matlock - Derby - Nottingham

		EM	XC	EM	EM		XC	EM	EM	XC	EM	XC	EM	EM	EM		XC	EM	EM	EM	XC	EM	XC		
		◇1	1	◇1			◇1		◇1	1		◇1		◇1			◇1			◇1	◇1		◇1		
		☕		☕					☕					☕						☕					
Matlock	d				18 36						19 36				20 36			21 37				22 55			
Matlock Bath	d				18 38						19 38				20 38			21 39				22 57			
Cromford	d				18 41						19 41				20 41			21 42				23 00			
Whatstandwell	d				18 46						19 46				20 46			21 47				23 05			
Ambergate	d				18 51						19 51				20 51			21 52				23 10			
Belper	d				18 58						19 58				20 58			21 59				23 17			
Duffield	d				19 02						20 02				21 02			22 03				23 21			
Derby 6	a				19 10						20 10				21 10			22 11				23 29			
	d		19 10	19 18	19 24		19 40			20 10	20 24	20 40			21 24		21 40				22 59	23 31	23 59		
Spondon	d																21 45				23 04				
Long Eaton	d		19 19	19a27	19 33					20 19	20 33	20 49			21 33		21 52				23 11	23 41			
Attenborough	d				19 40						20 40				21 40		21 58				23 17	23 48			
Beeston	d	19 19	19 26		19 43			20 07	20 18	20 27	20 43	20 58	21 03	21 19	21 43		22 02		22 07	22 17	23 20	23 51			
Nottingham 8	a	19 27	19 33		19 53		20 03	20 15	20 28	20 33	20 53	21 05	21 15	21 29	21 54		22 08		22 15	22 26	23 27	00 02	00 18		

Mondays to Fridays

from 26 September

		EM	EM	XC	EM	EM	EM	XC	EM	EM		EM	EM	EM	XC	EM	EM	XC	EM	EM		XC	EM	EM	EM
		MX	MX	MX	MO	MO																			
			◇1	◇1	◇1	◇1	◇1			◇1				◇1	1	◇1		1				1	◇1	◇1	
					A	B																			
			☕		☕	☕	⊠🍴			⊠🍴				⊠🍴	🍴	☕						🍴	⊠	☕	
Matlock	d	22p55										06 20													07 35
Matlock Bath	d	22p57										06 22													07 37
Cromford	d	23p00										06 25													07 40
Whatstandwell	d	23p05										06 30													07 45
Ambergate	d	23p10										06 36													07 50
Belper	d	23p17										06 44													07 58
Duffield	d	23p21										06 48													08 02
Derby 6	a	23p29										06 56													08 10
	d	23p31		23p59			05 17	06 00	06 24	06 32				07 01	07 10	07 26	07 33	07 40		07 53		08 10	08 16		08 20
Spondon	d								06 29						07 18			07 45							08 25
Long Eaton	d	23p41					05a26		06 36	06a41					07 25	07a35	07 42	07 49		08 03		08 19	08a25		08 32
Attenborough	d	23p48							06 44				07 13		07 31		07 52			08 13					08 39
Beeston	d	23p51	00 05		00 41	00 45		06 15	06 47				07 16		07 35		07 55	07 58	08 06	08 16		08 27		08 32	08 42
Nottingham 8	a	00 02	00 12	00 18	00 48	00 52		06 21	06 57				07 23	07 29	07 41		08 05	08 08	08 15	08 26		08 33		08 39	08 50

		XC	EM	EM	XC	EM		EM	XC	EM	EM	XC	EM	EM	XC	EM		EM	XC	EM	EM	XC	EM	EM	XC
		1		◇1	1	◇1			◇1		◇1	1	◇1		◇1			◇1	1	◇1		◇1		◇1	1
				☕	🍴	☕					☕	🍴	☕		🍴			☕		☕		🍴		☕	
Matlock	d							08 35						09 35							10 35				
Matlock Bath	d							08 37						09 37							10 37				
Cromford	d							08 40						09 40							10 40				
Whatstandwell	d							08 45						09 45							10 45				
Ambergate	d							08 50						09 50							10 50				
Belper	d							08 58						09 58							10 58				
Duffield	d							09 02						10 02							11 02				
Derby 6	a							09 10						10 10							11 10				
	d	08 40			09 10	09 20		09 24	09 40			10 10	10 20	10 24	10 40				11 10	11 20	11 24	11 40			12 10
Spondon	d																								
Long Eaton	d				09 19	09a29		09 33				10 19	10a29	10 33					11 19	11a29	11 33				12 19
Attenborough	d				09 26			09 40						10 40							11 40				
Beeston	d		09 02	09 17	09 29			09 43		10 02	10 17	10 27		10 43		11 02		11 17	11 27		11 43		12 02	12 17	12 27
Nottingham 8	a	09 05	09 13	09 26	09 35			09 53	10 05	10 13	10 25	10 33		10 53	11 06	11 14		11 25	11 33		11 53	12 05	12 13	12 26	12 33

		EM		EM	XC	EM	EM	XC	EM	EM	XC	EM		EM	XC	EM	EM	XC	EM	EM	XC	EM		EM	XC
		◇1			◇1		◇1	1	◇1		◇1			◇1	1	◇1		◇1		◇1	1	◇1			◇1
		☕			🍴		☕	🍴	☕		🍴			☕		☕		🍴		☕		☕			🍴
Matlock	d			11 35						12 35							13 35							14 35	
Matlock Bath	d			11 37						12 37							13 37							14 37	
Cromford	d			11 40						12 40							13 40							14 40	
Whatstandwell	d			11 45						12 45							13 45							14 45	
Ambergate	d			11 50						12 50							13 50							14 50	
Belper	d			11 58						12 58							13 58							14 58	
Duffield	d			12 02						13 02							14 02							15 02	
Derby 6	a			12 10						13 10							14 10							15 10	
	d	12 20		12 24	12 40			13 10	13 20	13 24	13 40				14 10	14 20	14 24	14 40			15 10	15 20		15 24	15 40
Spondon	d																								
Long Eaton	d	12a29		12 33				13 19	13a29	13 33					14 19	14a29	14 33				15 19	15a29		15 33	
Attenborough	d			12 40						13 40							14 40							15 40	
Beeston	d			12 43		13 07	13 17	13 27		13 43		14 02		14 16	14 27		14 43		15 02	15 17	15 27			15 43	
Nottingham 8	a			12 53	13 05	13 14	13 25	13 33		13 53	14 05	14 13		14 26	14 33		14 53	15 05	15 13	15 26	15 33			15 53	16 05

A From 26 September until 24 October

B From 31 October

For connections to St Pancras International please refer to Table 53

Table 56

Mondays to Fridays

from 26 September

Matlock - Derby - Nottingham

		EM	EM	XC	EM	EM	XC	EM		EM	XC	EM	EM	XC	EM	EM	EM	XC		EM	EM	XC	EM	EM	EM
			◇1 ☕	1	◇1 ☕		◇1 🛒			◇1 ☕	1	◇1 ☕		◇1 🛒			◇1 ☕	1		◇1 ☕		◇1	◇1 ☕		◇1 ☕
Matlock	d					15 35							16 35								17 35				
Matlock Bath	d					15 37							16 37								17 37				
Cromford	d					15 40							16 40								17 40				
Whatstandwell	d					15 45							16 45								17 45				
Ambergate	d					15 50							16 50								17 50				
Belper	d					15 58							16 58								17 58				
Duffield	d					16 02							17 02								18 02				
Derby 6	a					16 10							17 10								18 10				
	d			16 10	16 18	16 24	16 40				17 10	17 18	17 24	17 40		17 47		18 10		18 18	18 24	18 40			
Spondon	d												17 29			17 53									
Long Eaton	d			16 19	16a27	16 33					17 19	17a28	17 36			18 01		18 19		18a27	18 33				
Attenborough	d					16 40							17 43			18 09					18 40				
Beeston	d	16 02	16 17	16 27		16 43		17 02		17 17	17 27		17 46		18 02	18 12	18 18	18 27			18 43		19 03	19 07	19 19
Nottingham 8 🚊	a	16 13	16 25	16 33		16 54	17 05	17 13		17 26	17 33		17 54	18 05	18 13	18 22	18 27	18 33			18 54	19 05	19 10	19 15	19 27

		XC	EM	EM		XC	EM	EM	XC	EM	XC	EM	EM	EM		XC	EM	EM	EM	XC	EM	XC			
		1	◇1 ☕			◇1		◇1 ☕	1		◇1		◇1 ☕			◇1			◇1 ☕	◇1		◇1			
Matlock	d			18 35						19 35				20 35			21 36				22 55				
Matlock Bath	d			18 37						19 37				20 37			21 38				22 57				
Cromford	d			18 40						19 40				20 40			21 41				23 00				
Whatstandwell	d			18 45						19 45				20 45			21 46				23 05				
Ambergate	d			18 50						19 50				20 50			21 51				23 10				
Belper	d			18 58						19 58				20 58			21 59				23 17				
Duffield	d			19 02						20 02				21 02			22 03				23 21				
Derby 6	a			19 10						20 10				21 10			22 11				23 29				
	d	19 10	19 18	19 24		19 40			20 10	20 24	20 40			21 24		21 40				22 59	23 31	23 59			
Spondon	d															21 45				23 04					
Long Eaton	d	19 19	19a27	19 33					20 19	20 33	20 49			21 33		21 52				23 11	23 41				
Attenborough	d			19 40						20 40				21 40		21 58				23 17	23 48				
Beeston	d	19 26		19 43			20 07	20 18	20 27	20 43	20 58	21 03	21 19	21 43		22 02		22 07	22 17	23 20	23 51				
Nottingham 8 🚊	a	19 33		19 53		20 03	20 15	20 28	20 33	20 53	21 05	21 15	21 29	21 54		22 08		22 15	22 26	23 27	00 02	00 18			

Saturdays

until 24 September

		EM	EM	XC	EM	EM	EM	EM	EM	XC		EM	EM	XC	EM	EM	XC	EM	EM	EM		XC	EM	EM	XC
			◇1	◇1	◇1	◇1				1		◇1		1			1	◇1	◇1			1		◇1	1
																A									
			☕		☕	☕				🛒		☕					🛒	⊠	☕					☕	🛒
Matlock	d	22p55						06 22												07 36					
Matlock Bath	d	22p57						06 24												07 38					
Cromford	d	23p00						06 27												07 41					
Whatstandwell	d	23p05						06 32												07 46					
Ambergate	d	23p10						06 38												07 51					
Belper	d	23p17						06 44												07 58					
Duffield	d	23p21						06 48												08 02					
Derby 6	a	23p29						06 56												08 10					
	d	23p31		23p59	05 25	06 18	06 24			07 10		07 18	07 33	07 39		07 53	08 10	08 18		08 24		08 39			09 10
Spondon	d						06 29			07 15				07 44						08 29					
Long Eaton	d	23p41			05a34	06a27	06 35			07 22		07a27	07 42	07 52		08 03	08 19	08a27		08 36					09 19
Attenborough	d	23p48					06 44		07 12	07 28			07 51							08 43					09 26
Beeston	d	23p51	00 05				06 47		07 15	07 32			07 54	07 59	08 04	08 12	08 27		08 31	08 46			09 05	09 17	09 29
Nottingham 8 🚊	a	00 02	00 12	00 18			06 57		07 24	07 38			08 05	08 08	08 13	08 19	08 34		08 42	08 53		09 05	09 14	09 26	09 35

		EM	EM	XC	EM	EM		XC	EM	EM	XC	EM	EM	XC	EM	EM		XC	EM	EM	XC	EM	EM	XC	EM
		◇1		◇1		◇1		1	◇1		◇1		◇1	1	◇1			◇1		◇1	1	◇1		◇1	
		☕				☕		🛒	☕		🛒		☕		☕			🛒		☕		☕		🛒	
Matlock	d		08 36							09 36						10 36							11 36		
Matlock Bath	d		08 38							09 38						10 38							11 38		
Cromford	d		08 41							09 41						10 41							11 41		
Whatstandwell	d		08 46							09 46						10 46							11 46		
Ambergate	d		08 51							09 51						10 51							11 51		
Belper	d		08 58							09 58						10 58							11 58		
Duffield	d		09 02							10 02						11 02							12 02		
Derby 6	a		09 10							10 10						11 10							12 10		
	d	09 20	09 24	09 40				10 10	10 20	10 24	10 40			11 10	11 20	11 24		11 40			12 10	12 20	12 24	12 40	
Spondon	d																								
Long Eaton	d	09a29	09 33					10 19	10a29	10 33				11 19	11a29	11 33					12 19	12a29	12 33		
Attenborough	d		09 40							10 40						11 40							12 40		
Beeston	d		09 43		10 02	10 17		10 27		10 43		11 02	11 17	11 27		11 43			12 02	12 16	12 27		12 43		13 02
Nottingham 8 🚊	a		09 54	10 05	10 13	10 26		10 33		10 53	11 05	11 13	11 26	11 33		11 53		12 05	12 13	12 26	12 33		12 53	13 05	13 13

A from 23 July until 10 September

For connections to St Pancras International please refer to Table 53

Table 56

Saturdays
until 24 September

Matlock - Derby - Nottingham

		EM ◇1 ☕		XC 1 🛒	EM ◇1 ☕	EM	XC ◇1 🛒	EM	EM ◇1 ☕	XC 1	EM ◇1 ☕	EM		XC ◇1 🛒	EM	EM ◇1 ☕	XC 1	EM ◇1 ☕	EM	XC ◇1 🛒	EM	EM ◇1 ☕		XC 1	EM ◇1 ☕
Matlock	d					12 36						13 36							14 36						
Matlock Bath	d					12 38						13 38							14 38						
Cromford	d					12 41						13 41							14 41						
Whatstandwell	d					12 46						13 46							14 46						
Ambergate	d					12 51						13 51							14 51						
Belper	d					12 58						13 58							14 58						
Duffield	d					13 02						14 02							15 02						
Derby 6	a					13 10						14 10							15 10						
	d			13 10	13 20	13 24	13 40			14 10	14 20	14 24		14 40			15 10	15 20	15 24	15 40				16 10	16 20
Spondon	d																								
Long Eaton	d			13 19	13a29	13 33				14 19	14a30	14 33					15 19	15a29	15 33					16 19	16a29
Attenborough	d					13 40						14 40							15 40						
Beeston	d	13 16		13 27		13 43		14 02	14 17	14 27		14 43			15 02	15 17	15 27		15 43		16 02	16 17		16 27	
Nottingham 8	a	13 27		13 33		13 53	14 05	14 13	14 26	14 33		14 53		15 05	15 13	15 26	15 33		15 53	16 05	16 13	16 26		16 33	

		EM	XC ◇1 🛒	EM	EM ◇1 ☕	XC 1	EM ◇1 ☕	EM		XC ◇1 🛒	EM	EM ◇1 ☕	XC 1	EM ◇1 ☕	EM	XC ◇1	EM	EM ◇1 ☕		XC 1	EM ◇1 ☕	EM	XC ◇1	EM	EM ◇1 ☕
Matlock	d	15 36						16 36							17 36							18 36			
Matlock Bath	d	15 38						16 38							17 38							18 38			
Cromford	d	15 41						16 41							17 41							18 41			
Whatstandwell	d	15 46						16 46							17 46							18 46			
Ambergate	d	15 51						16 51							17 51							18 51			
Belper	d	15 58						16 58							17 58							18 58			
Duffield	d	16 02						17 02							18 02							19 02			
Derby 6	a	16 10						17 10							18 10							19 10			
	d	16 24	16 40			17 10	17 18	17 24		17 40			18 10	18 18	18 24	18 40				19 10	19 21	19 25	19 40		
Spondon	d							17 29																	
Long Eaton	d	16 33				17 19	17a27	17 36					18 19	18a27	18 33					19 19	19a30	19 34			
Attenborough	d	16 40						17 43							18 40							19 41			
Beeston	d	16 43		17 02	17 17	17 27		17 46			18 02	18 16	18 27		18 43		19 02	19 17		19 27		19 44		20 05	20 16
Nottingham 8	a	16 52	17 05	17 13	17 26	17 33		17 53		18 05	18 12	18 26	18 33		18 54	19 06	19 14	19 26		19 33		19 51	20 05	20 15	20 26

		XC 1	EM	XC ◇1		EM	EM ◇1 ☕	EM	XC ◇1	EM	EM	EM ◇1 A ☕	EM ◇1 B ☕	XC ◇1 C		XC 1 D	EM
Matlock	d		19 36					20 36		21 36							22 55
Matlock Bath	d		19 38					20 38		21 38							22 57
Cromford	d		19 41					20 41		21 41							23 00
Whatstandwell	d		19 46					20 46		21 46							23 05
Ambergate	d		19 51					20 51		21 51							23 11
Belper	d		19 58					20 58		21 58							23 17
Duffield	d		20 02					21 02		22 02							23 21
Derby 6	a		20 10					21 10		22 10							23 29
	d	20 10	20 24	20 40				21 24	21 40					23 00		23 00	23 31
Spondon	d								21 45					23 05		23 05	
Long Eaton	d	20 19	20 33	20 49				21 33	21 52					23 12		23 12	23 41
Attenborough	d		20 40					21 40	21 58					23 18		23 18	23 48
Beeston	d	20 27	20 43	20 57		21 05	21 17	21 43	22 02		22 06	22 18	22 21	23 22		23 22	23 52
Nottingham 8	a	20 35	20 53	21 04		21 15	21 26	21 53	22 08		22 14	22 27	22 28	23 28		23 28	23 57

Saturdays
from 1 October

		EM	EM ◇1 ☕	XC ◇1	EM ◇1 ☕	EM ◇1 ☕	EM	EM	EM	XC 1 🛒		EM ◇1 ☕	EM	XC 1	EM	XC 1 🛒	EM ◇1 ⊠	EM ◇1 ☕	EM	XC 1		EM	EM ◇1 ☕	XC 1 🛒	EM ◇1 ☕
Matlock	d	22p55						06 20											07 35						
Matlock Bath	d	22p57						06 22											07 37						
Cromford	d	23p00						06 25											07 40						
Whatstandwell	d	23p05						06 30											07 45						
Ambergate	d	23p10						06 36											07 50						
Belper	d	23p17						06 44											07 58						
Duffield	d	23p21						06 48											08 02						
Derby 6	a	23p29						06 56											08 10						
	d	23p31		23p59	05 25	06 18	06 24			07 10		07 18	07 33	07 39		08 10	08 18		08 24	08 39				09 10	09 20
Spondon	d						06 29			07 15				07 44					08 29						
Long Eaton	d	23p41			05a34	06a27	06 35			07 22		07a27	07 42	07 52		08 19	08a27		08 36					09 19	09a29
Attenborough	d	23p48					06 44		07 12	07 28			07 51						08 43					09 26	
Beeston	d	23p51	00 05				06 47		07 15	07 32			07 54	07 59	08 04	08 27		08 31	08 46			09 05	09 17	09 29	
Nottingham 8	a	00 02	00 12	00 18			06 57		07 24	07 38			08 05	08 08	08 13	08 34		08 42	08 53	09 05		09 14	09 26	09 35	

A until 30 July
B from 6 August until 24 September
C from 25 June until 24 September
D until 18 June

For connections to St Pancras International please refer to Table 53

Table 56

Matlock - Derby - Nottingham

Saturdays
from 1 October

		EM	XC ◇1	EM	EM ◇1 ☕	XC 1 🛒		EM ◇1 ☕	EM	XC ◇1 🛒	EM	EM ◇1 ☕	XC 1	EM ◇1 ☕	EM	XC ◇1 🛒		EM	EM ◇1 ☕	XC 1	EM ◇1 ☕	EM	XC ◇1 🛒	EM	EM ◇1 ☕
Matlock	d	08 35							09 35						10 35							11 35			
Matlock Bath	d	08 37							09 37						10 37							11 37			
Cromford	d	08 40							09 40						10 40							11 40			
Whatstandwell	d	08 45							09 45						10 45							11 45			
Ambergate	d	08 50							09 50						10 50							11 50			
Belper	d	08 58							09 58						10 58							11 58			
Duffield	d	09 02							10 02						11 02							12 02			
Derby 6	a	09 10							10 10						11 10							12 10			
	d	09 24	09 40			10 10		10 20	10 24	10 40			11 10	11 20	11 24	11 40				12 10	12 20	12 24	12 40		
Spondon	d																								
Long Eaton	d	09 33				10 19		10a29	10 33				11 19	11a29	11 33					12 19	12a29	12 33			
Attenborough	d	09 40							10 40						11 40							12 40			
Beeston	d	09 43		10 02	10 17	10 27			10 43		11 02	11 17	11 27		11 43			12 02	12 16	12 27		12 43		13 02	13 16
Nottingham 8	a	09 54	10 05	10 13	10 26	10 33			10 53	11 05	11 13	11 26	11 33		11 53	12 05		12 13	12 26	12 33		12 53	13 05	13 13	13 27

		XC 1 🛒		EM ◇1 ☕	EM	XC ◇1 🛒	EM	EM ◇1 ☕	XC 1	EM ◇1 ☕	EM	XC ◇1 🛒		EM	EM ◇1 ☕	XC 1	EM ◇1 ☕	EM	XC ◇1 🛒	EM	EM ◇1 ☕	XC 1		EM ◇1 ☕	EM
Matlock	d				12 35						13 35							14 35							15 35
Matlock Bath	d				12 37						13 37							14 37							15 37
Cromford	d				12 40						13 40							14 40							15 40
Whatstandwell	d				12 45						13 45							14 45							15 45
Ambergate	d				12 50						13 50							14 50							15 50
Belper	d				12 58						13 58							14 58							15 58
Duffield	d				13 02						14 02							15 02							16 02
Derby 6	a				13 10						14 10							15 10							16 10
	d	13 10		13 20	13 24	13 40			14 10	14 20	14 24	14 40				15 10	15 20	15 24	15 40			16 10		16 20	16 24
Spondon	d																								
Long Eaton	d	13 19		13a29	13 33				14 19	14a30	14 33					15 19	15a29	15 33				16 19		16a29	16 33
Attenborough	d				13 40						14 40							15 40							16 40
Beeston	d	13 27			13 43		14 02	14 17	14 27		14 43			15 02	15 17	15 27		15 43		16 02	16 17	16 27			16 43
Nottingham 8	a	13 33			13 53	14 05	14 13	14 26	14 33		14 53	15 05		15 13	15 26	15 33		15 53	16 05	16 13	16 26	16 33			16 52

		XC ◇1 🛒	EM	EM ◇1 ☕	XC 1	EM ◇1 ☕	EM	XC ◇1 🛒		EM	EM ◇1 ☕	XC 1	EM ◇1 ☕	EM	XC ◇1	EM	EM ◇1 ☕	XC 1		EM ◇1 ☕	EM	XC ◇1	EM	EM ◇1 ☕	XC 1
Matlock	d						16 35							17 35							18 35				
Matlock Bath	d						16 37							17 37							18 37				
Cromford	d						16 40							17 40							18 40				
Whatstandwell	d						16 45							17 45							18 45				
Ambergate	d						16 50							17 50							18 50				
Belper	d						16 58							17 58							18 58				
Duffield	d						17 02							18 02							19 02				
Derby 6	a						17 10							18 10							19 10				
	d	16 40			17 10	17 18	17 24	17 40				18 10	18 18	18 24	18 40			19 10		19 21	19 25	19 40			20 10
Spondon	d						17 29																		
Long Eaton	d				17 19	17a27	17 36					18 19	18a27	18 33				19 19		19a30	19 34				20 19
Attenborough	d						17 43							18 40							19 41				
Beeston	d		17 02	17 17	17 27		17 46			18 02	18 16	18 27		18 43		19 02	19 17	19 27			19 44		20 05	20 16	20 27
Nottingham 8	a	17 05	17 13	17 26	17 33		17 53	18 05		18 12	18 26	18 33		18 54	19 06	19 14	19 26	19 33			19 51	20 05	20 15	20 26	20 35

		EM	XC ◇1	EM		EM ◇1 ☕	EM	XC ◇1	EM	EM	EM ◇1 A ☕	EM ◇1 B ☕	XC ◇1	EM
Matlock	d	19 35					20 35		21 35					22 55
Matlock Bath	d	19 37					20 37		21 37					22 57
Cromford	d	19 40					20 40		21 40					23 00
Whatstandwell	d	19 45					20 45		21 45					23 05
Ambergate	d	19 50					20 50		21 50					23 11
Belper	d	19 58					20 58		21 58					23 17
Duffield	d	20 02					21 02		22 02					23 21
Derby 6	a	20 10					21 10		22 10					23 29
	d	20 24	20 40				21 24	21 40					23 00	23 31
Spondon	d							21 45					23 05	
Long Eaton	d	20 33	20 49				21 33	21 52					23 12	23 41
Attenborough	d	20 40					21 40	21 58					23 18	23 48
Beeston	d	20 43	20 57	21 05		21 17	21 43	22 02		22 06	22 18	22 21	23 22	23 52
Nottingham 8	a	20 53	21 04	21 15		21 26	21 53	22 08		22 14	22 27	22 28	23 28	23 57

A from 29 October

B from 1 October until 22 October

For connections to St Pancras International please refer to Table 53

Table 56

Matlock - Derby - Nottingham

Sundays
until 19 June

		EM	XC	EM	EM	EM	EM	EM	EM	EM		XC	XC	EM	EM	EM	XC	EM	EM	EM	XC	EM	EM	XC	EM
		◇[1]			◇[1]		◇[1]	◇[1]	◇[1]			◇[1]	◇[1]	◇[1]	◇[1]		◇[1]	◇[1]	◇[1]	◇[1]	◇[1]	◇[1]		◇[1]	◇[1]
		A	A																						
			🚌																						
		☕			☕		☕	☕	☕					☕	☕			☕	☕	☕		☕			☕
Matlock	d									10 42						12 38							14 39		
Matlock Bath	d									10 44						12 40							14 41		
Cromford	d									10 47						12 43							14 44		
Whatstandwell	d									10 52						12 48							14 49		
Ambergate	d									10 57						12 53							14 53		
Belper	d									11 03						13 00							15 00		
Duffield	d									11 07						13 04							15 04		
Derby [6]	a									11 15						13 12							15 12		
	d			08 18	08 44	09 18	09 51	10 51		11 19		11 41	12 38	12 57		13 25	13 41	13 53		14 38	14 43		15 15	15 44	
Spondon	d		00s01																						
Long Eaton	d		00s12	08 28	08a53	09 28	10a00	11a00		11 29				13a06		13 35		14a02		14a47			15 25		
Attenborough	d		00s23	08 35		09 34				11 36						13 42							15 32		
Beeston	d	00 01	00s29	08 39		09 37			11 13	11 39					13 11	13 45			14 13			15 12	15 35		16 05
Nottingham [8] 🚊	a	00 08	00 49	08 46		09 44			11 20	11 45		12 00	13 03		13 18	13 53	14 00		14 20		15 05	15 18	15 40	16 03	16 10

		EM	XC	EM	EM	XC	EM	EM	EM	XC	EM	EM	EM	XC	EM	EM	EM	XC	EM	EM	XC	EM	EM	EM	EM
			◇[1]	◇[1]		◇[1]	◇[1]	◇[1]		◇[1]	◇[1]	◇[1]		◇[1]	◇[1]	◇[1]		◇[1]	◇[1]		◇[1]	◇[1]			◇[1]
				☕			☕	☕			☕	☕			☕	☕			☕			☕			☕
Matlock	d				16 38								18 40							20 39				22 46	
Matlock Bath	d				16 40								18 42							20 41				22 48	
Cromford	d				16 43								18 45							20 44				22 51	
Whatstandwell	d				16 48								18 50							20 49				22 56	
Ambergate	d				16 53								18 55							20 53				23 01	
Belper	d				17 00								19 02							21 00				23 09	
Duffield	d				17 04								19 06							21 04				23 13	
Derby [6]	a				17 12								19 14							21 12				23 20	
	d	16 30	16 41	16 47	17 21	17 43	17 47		18 21	18 41		19 09	19 22	19 37		20 06	20 29	20 37		21 21	21 41		22 30		
Spondon	d																								
Long Eaton	d	16 39		16a56	17 31		17a56		18 31			19a19	19 32			20a15	20 38			21 31			22 40		
Attenborough	d	16 46			17 38				18 38				19 39				20 47			21 38			22 46		
Beeston	d	16 49			17 41			18 06	18 41		19 02		19 42		20 02		20 50		21 03	21 41		22 04	22 49		23 11
Nottingham [8] 🚊	a	16 56	17 02		17 47	18 02		18 14	18 48	19 03	19 07		19 48	19 56	20 08		20 56	21 00	21 12	21 47	22 00	22 11	22 57		23 18

Sundays
26 June to 31 July

		EM	EM	EM	EM	EM	EM	EM	EM	XC		XC	EM	EM	EM	XC	EM	EM	EM	XC		EM	EM	XC	EM
		◇[1]		◇[1]		◇[1]	◇[1]	◇[1]		◇[1]		◇[1]	◇[1]	◇[1]		◇[1]	◇[1]	◇[1]	◇[1]	◇[1]		◇[1]		◇[1]	◇[1]
		☕		☕		☕	☕	☕					☕	☕		🛒	☕	☕	☕	🛒		☕		🛒	☕
Matlock	d								10 42						12 38								14 39		
Matlock Bath	d								10 44						12 40								14 41		
Cromford	d								10 47						12 43								14 44		
Whatstandwell	d								10 52						12 48								14 49		
Ambergate	d								10 57						12 53								14 53		
Belper	d								11 03						13 00								15 00		
Duffield	d								11 07						13 04								15 04		
Derby [6]	a								11 15						13 12								15 12		
	d		08 18	08 49	09 18	09 51	10 54		11 19	11 41		12 38	12 57		13 25	13 38	13 53		14 42	14 46			15 15	15 44	
Spondon	d																								
Long Eaton	d		08 28	08a59	09 28	10a00	11a03		11 29				13a06		13 35		14a02		14a51				15 25		
Attenborough	d		08 35		09 34				11 36						13 42								15 32		
Beeston	d	00 01	08 39		09 37			11 16	11 39					13 08	13 45			14 10				15 10	15 35		16 04
Nottingham [8] 🚊	a	00 08	08 46		09 44			11 24	11 45	12 02		13 02		13 17	13 53	13 59		14 17		15 07		15 18	15 40	16 04	16 10

		EM	XC	EM	EM	XC	EM	EM	EM	XC	EM	EM	EM	XC	EM	EM	EM	XC	EM	EM	XC	EM	EM	EM	EM
			◇[1]	◇[1]		◇[1]	◇[1]	◇[1]		◇[1]	◇[1]	◇[1]		◇[1]	◇[1]	◇[1]		◇[1]	◇[1]		◇[1]	◇[1]			◇[1]
			🛒	☕		🛒	☕	☕			☕	☕			☕	☕			☕			☕			☕
Matlock	d				16 38								18 40							20 39				22 46	
Matlock Bath	d				16 40								18 42							20 41				22 48	
Cromford	d				16 43								18 45							20 44				22 51	
Whatstandwell	d				16 48								18 50							20 49				22 56	
Ambergate	d				16 53								18 55							20 53				23 01	
Belper	d				17 00								19 02							21 00				23 09	
Duffield	d				17 04								19 06							21 04				23 13	
Derby [6]	a				17 12								19 14							21 12				23 20	
	d	16 30	16 41	16 47	17 21	17 41	17 47		18 21	18 41		19 09	19 22	19 37		20 06	20 29	20 37		21 21	21 41		22 30		
Spondon	d																								
Long Eaton	d	16 39		16a56	17 31		17a56		18 31			19a19	19 32			20a15	20 38			21 31			22 40		
Attenborough	d	16 46			17 38				18 38				19 39				20 47			21 38			22 46		
Beeston	d	16 49			17 41			18 06	18 41		19 02		19 42		20 02		20 50		21 03	21 41		22 04	22 49		23 11
Nottingham [8] 🚊	a	16 56	17 03		17 47	18 00		18 14	18 48	19 04	19 07		19 48	19 56	20 08		20 56	21 01	21 12	21 47	22 00	22 11	22 57		23 18

A not 22 May

For connections to St Pancras International please refer to Table 53

Table 56

Sundays

7 August to 23 October

	EM	EM	EM	EM	EM	EM	EM	EM	EM		XC	EM	EM	EM	EM	EM	XC	EM	EM		EM	EM	XC	XC
	◇1		◇1		◇1	◇1	◇1	◇1			◇1	◇1	◇1	◇1	◇1		◇1	◇1	◇1		◇1	◇1	◇1	◇1
		A					A	B				A	B	A	B			A	B				A	B
	☕		☕		☕	☕	☕	☕			🛒	☕	☕	☕	☕			☕	☕		☕	☕	🛒	
Matlock d									10 42							12 38								
Matlock Bath d									10 44							12 40								
Cromford d									10 47							12 43								
Whatstandwell d									10 52							12 48								
Ambergate d									10 57							12 53								
Belper d									11 03							13 00								
Duffield d									11 07							13 04								
Derby 6 a									11 15							13 12								
d		08 18	08 44	09 18	09 50	10 50			11 19		12 38	12 52	13 01			13 25	13 38	13 53	13 54			14 38	14 41	14 41
Spondon d																								
Long Eaton d		08 28	08a53	09 28	09a59	10a59			11 29			13a01	13a10			13 35		14a02	14a03			14a47		
Attenborough d		08 35		09 34					11 36							13 42								
Beeston d	00 03	08 39		09 37			11 18	11 19	11 39					13 13	13 13	13 45					14 20			
Nottingham 8 ⇌ a	00 11	08 46		09 44			11 25	11 26	11 45		13 02			13 19	13 22	13 53	13 59				14 26		15 07	15 07

	EM	EM	EM	XC	EM		EM	XC	XC	EM	EM	XC	XC	EM	EM		EM	XC	XC	EM	EM	EM	XC	EM
	◇1	◇1		◇1	◇1			◇1	◇1	◇1		◇1	◇1	◇1	◇1			◇1	◇1	◇1	◇1		◇1	◇1
	A	B						B	A			B	A					B	A					
Matlock d			14 39								16 38											18 40		
Matlock Bath d			14 41								16 40											18 42		
Cromford d			14 44								16 43											18 45		
Whatstandwell d			14 49								16 48											18 50		
Ambergate d			14 53								16 53											18 55		
Belper d			15 00								17 00											19 02		
Duffield d			15 04								17 04											19 06		
Derby 6 a			15 12								17 12											19 14		
d			15 15	15 44			16 30	16 41	16 41	16 47	17 21	17 41	17 43	17 47			18 21	18 41	18 41		19 09	19 22	19 37	
Spondon d																								
Long Eaton d			15 25				16 39			16a56	17 31			17a56			18 31				19a19	19 32		
Attenborough d			15 32				16 46				17 38						18 38					19 39		
Beeston d	15 13	15 15	15 35		16 06		16 49				17 41				18 06		18 41			19 02		19 42		20 02
Nottingham 8 ⇌ a	15 19	15 21	15 40	16 04	16 12		16 56	17 03	17 03		17 47	18 00	18 02		18 14		18 48	19 04	19 04	19 07		19 48	19 56	20 08

	EM		EM	XC	EM	EM	XC	EM	EM	EM	EM
	◇1			◇1	◇1		◇1	◇1			◇1
	☕				☕			☕			☕
Matlock d						20 39				22 46	
Matlock Bath d						20 41				22 48	
Cromford d						20 44				22 51	
Whatstandwell d						20 49				22 56	
Ambergate d						20 53				23 01	
Belper d						21 00				23 09	
Duffield d						21 04				23 13	
Derby 6 a						21 12				23 20	
d	20 06		20 29	20 37		21 21	21 41		22 30		
Spondon d											
Long Eaton d	20a15		20 38			21 31			22 40		
Attenborough d			20 47			21 38			22 46		
Beeston d			20 50		21 03	21 41		22 04	22 49		23 11
Nottingham 8 ⇌ a			20 56	21 01	21 12	21 47	22 00	22 11	22 57		23 18

from 30 October

	EM	EM	EM	EM	EM	EM	EM	XC	EM		EM	EM	XC	EM	EM	EM	XC	EM	EM		XC	EM	EM	EM
	◇1	◇1		◇1	◇1	◇1		◇1	◇1		◇1		◇1	◇1	◇1	◇1	◇1	◇1			◇1	◇1		◇1
	☕	☕		☕	☕	☕		🛒	☕		☕		🛒	☕	☕	☕	🛒	☕			🛒	☕		☕
Matlock d							10 42					12 38							14 39					
Matlock Bath d							10 44					12 40							14 41					
Cromford d							10 47					12 43							14 44					
Whatstandwell d							10 52					12 48							14 49					
Ambergate d							10 57					12 53							14 53					
Belper d							11 03					13 00							15 00					
Duffield d							11 07					13 04							15 04					
Derby 6 a							11 15					13 12							15 12					
d		08 47	09 18	09 51	10 52		11 19	12 38	13 02			13 25	13 38	13 54		14 38	14 41		15 15		15 44		16 30	16 37
Spondon d																								
Long Eaton d		08a57	09 28	10a00	11a01		11 29		13a11			13 35		14a03		14a47			15 25				16 39	16a46
Attenborough d			09 34				11 36					13 42							15 32				16 46	
Beeston d	00 01		09 37			11 14	11 39				13 11	13 45			14 13			15 12	15 35			16 09	16 49	
Nottingham 8 ⇌ a	00 08		09 44			11 21	11 45	13 02			13 20	13 53	13 59		14 20		15 07	15 18	15 40		16 04	16 15	16 56	

	XC	EM	XC	EM	EM		EM	XC	EM	EM	EM	XC	EM	EM	EM		XC	EM	EM	XC	EM	EM	EM	EM
	◇1		◇1	◇1	◇1			◇1	◇1	◇1		◇1	◇1	◇1			◇1	◇1		◇1	◇1			◇1
	🛒		🛒	☕	☕				☕	☕			☕	☕				☕			☕			☕
Matlock d		16 38									18 40								20 39				22 46	
Matlock Bath d		16 40									18 42								20 41				22 48	
Cromford d		16 43									18 45								20 44				22 51	
Whatstandwell d		16 48									18 50								20 49				22 56	
Ambergate d		16 53									18 55								20 53				23 01	
Belper d		17 00									19 02								21 00				23 09	
Duffield d		17 04									19 06								21 04				23 13	
Derby 6 a		17 12									19 14								21 12				23 20	
d	16 41	17 21	17 41	17 45			18 21	18 41		19 07	19 22	19 37		20 06	20 29		20 37		21 21	21 41		22 30		
Spondon d																								
Long Eaton d		17 31		17a54			18 31			19a16	19 32			20a15	20 38				21 31			22 40		
Attenborough d		17 38					18 38				19 43				20 47				21 38			22 46		
Beeston d		17 41			18 08		18 41		19 06		19 46		20 05		20 50			21 05	21 41		22 09	22 49		23 16
Nottingham 8 ⇌ a	17 03	17 47	18 00		18 16		18 48	19 04	19 11		19 52	19 56	20 11		20 56		21 01	21 12	21 47	22 00	22 16	22 57		23 23

A from 7 August until 11 September

B from 18 September until 23 October

For connections to St Pancras International please refer to Table 53

Nottingham, Derby and Leicester Birmingham - Cardiff and Bristol

Miles	Miles	Miles	Station		XC MO ◇1 A	XC MO ◇1 B	AW MX	XC MX ◇1 C	XC MO 1	AW D	GW ◇1 E [restaurant]	XC ◇1	GW F		GW ◇1 E [restaurant]	XC ◇1	GW G	XC ◇1 H [trolley]	GW ◇1 E [restaurant]	AW D	XC ◇1 I [trolley]	XC 1	XC ◇1 J [trolley]		XC ◇1 K [trolley]
0	—	—	**Nottingham [8]**	d																			06 00		
3¼	—	—	Beeston	d																			06 06		
4¾	—	—	Attenborough	d																			06 10		
7¾	—	—	Long Eaton	d																			06 18		
16	—	—	**Derby [6]**	a																			06 30		
—	—	—		d	21p27	21p27		21p28													06 10		06 36		06 48
22¼	—	—	Willington	d																					
27	—	—	Burton-on-Trent	d	21p38	21p38		21p39													06 21		06 48		06 59
40	—	—	Tamworth	d	21p49	21p49		21p50													06 32		07 00		07 10
41¾	—	—	Wilnecote	d																			07 04		
—	0	—	**Leicester**	d					23p19													06 16			
—	1¾	—	South Wigston	d					23p25													06 22			
—	4¾	—	Narborough	d					23p29													06 27			
—	13½	—	Hinckley	d					23p38													06 35			
—	18¾	—	Nuneaton	d					23p46													06 42			
—	29¼	—	Coleshill Parkway	d					00 02													06 59			
—	31	—	Water Orton	d																					
56¾	38¾	0	**Birmingham New Street [12]**	a	22p06	22p08		22p09	00 14												06 51	07 15	07 24		07 27
—	—	—		d	22p12	22p12		22p12				05 00				05 42		06 42			07 12		07 30		
83¾	—	—	Worcester Shrub Hill [7]	d							05 21						06 47		07 08						
98½	—	39¼	Ashchurch for Tewkesbury	d												06 34	07 03								
105¾	—	46½	Cheltenham Spa	d	22p52	22p52	23p00	23p31		05 37	05 53	06 03	06 23		06 30	06 43	07 13	07 22	07 29	07 45	07 52		08 16		
112¼	—	—	Gloucester [7]	a	23p03		23p12			05 48	06 03	06 16	06 34		06 40	06 53	07 24		07 39	07 57			08 27		
—	—	87	Bristol Parkway [7]	a	23p55			00 02					07 23				08 19	07 56			08 25				
—	—	92¾	**Bristol Temple Meads [10]**	a	00 10	00 13		00 14					07 40				08 36	08 08			08 40				
157	—	—	Newport (South Wales)	a			00 05			06 41		07 09				07 52				08 50			09 12		
168¾	—	—	**Cardiff Central [7]**	a			00 29			07 00		07 26				08 08				09 07			09 29		

Station		XC ◇1 L [trolley]	XC 1	XC ◇1 M	XC ◇1 N	GW ◇1 E [restaurant]	AW D	XC ◇1 O [trolley]	XC 1		XC ◇1 J [trolley]	XC ◇1 P [trolley]	XC ◇1 L [trolley]	XC ◇1 Q [trolley]	XC 1	GW R	GW S	GW T	XC MX ◇1 U [trolley]		XC MO ◇1 U [trolley]	XC 1	XC ◇1 V [trolley]	XC ◇1 W [trolley]	XC ◇1 Q [trolley]
Nottingham [8]	d			06 37							06 56				07 37								08 08		
Beeston	d			06 43							07 07				07 43										
Attenborough	d										07 11														
Long Eaton	d										07 18				07 51										
Derby [6]	a			07 00							07 31				08 02								08 32		
	d			07 06				07 26			07 36	07 50			08 06				08 28		08 28		08 36	08 54	
Willington	d										07 43														
Burton-on-Trent	d			07 18				07 37			07 49	08 01			08 18				08 38		08 38		08 49		
Tamworth	d			07 30				07 49			08 01	08 12			08 30				08 49		08 49		09 01		
Wilnecote	d										08 05				08 34										
Leicester	d		06 43		07 10				07 24					07 49								08 16			08 49
South Wigston	d		06 49											07 55											
Narborough	d		06 54						07 33					08 00								08 25			
Hinckley	d		07 02						07 42					08 08								08 34			
Nuneaton	d		07 10		07 30				07 50					08 17								08 41			09 10
Coleshill Parkway	d		07 26		07 46				08 05					08 32								08 57			09 25
Water Orton	d		07 30						08 09																
Birmingham New Street [12]	a		07 44	07 55	07 58			08 09	08 19		08 24	08 29		08 45	08 53				09 09		09 09	09 14	09 24	09 27	09 38
	d	07 42						08 12			08 30		08 42						09 12		09 12		09 30		
Worcester Shrub Hill [7]	d															08 57	09 06								
Ashchurch for Tewkesbury	d															09 24	09 24								
Cheltenham Spa	d	08 25				08 31	08 45	08 52			09 12		09 25			09 34	09 34	09 40	09 52		09 52		10 11		
Gloucester [7]	a					08 40	08 58				09 22					09 42	09 42	09 51					10 22		
Bristol Parkway [7]	a	08 55						09 24					09 55			10 22	10 22		10 25		10 26				
Bristol Temple Meads [10]	a	09 14						09 39					10 08			10 38	10 38		10 41		10 41				
Newport (South Wales)	a						09 51				10 09												11 11		
Cardiff Central [7]	a						10 07				10 25												11 27		

- **A** From 27 June until 1 August. From Edinburgh
- **B** From 19 September until 24 October. From Edinburgh
- **C** Until 17 June. From Edinburgh
- **D** To Maesteg
- **E** To London Paddington
- **F** To Westbury
- **G** To Weymouth
- **H** To Paignton
- **I** To Plymouth. [trolley] from Birmingham New Street
- **J** [trolley] from Birmingham New Street to Gloucester
- **K** From Sheffield to Reading
- **L** From Manchester Piccadilly
- **M** To Bournemouth
- **N** From Cambridge
- **O** From Leeds to Plymouth
- **P** From Leeds to Southampton Central
- **Q** From Stansted Airport
- **R** until 9 September. From Great Malvern to Westbury
- **S** from 12 September. From Great Malvern to Westbury
- **T** To Swindon
- **U** From York to Plymouth
- **V** [trolley] to Gloucester
- **W** From Newcastle to Reading

Nottingham, Derby and Leicester Birmingham - Cardiff and Bristol

		XC	XC	GW	AW		XC	XC	XC	XC	XC	XC	XC	GW	GW		AW	XC	XC	XC	XC	XC	XC	XC	GW
														R											
		◇1	1	◇1			◇1	1	◇1	◇1	◇1	◇1	1					◇1	1	◇1	◇1	◇1	◇1	1	◇1
		A		B	C		D		E	F	G	H		I	J		C	K		E	L	G	H		B
		[trolley]		[buffet]			[trolley]		[trolley]	[trolley]	[trolley]	[trolley]						[trolley]		[trolley]	[trolley]	[trolley]	[trolley]		[buffet]
Nottingham 8	d		08 37						09 11				09 37							10 11				10 37	
Beeston	d		08 43										09 43											10 43	
Attenborough	d																								
Long Eaton	d		08 51										09 51											10 51	
Derby 6	a		09 02						09 31				10 02							10 33				11 02	
	d		09 06				09 27		09 36	09 53			10 06					10 28		10 37	10 53			11 06	
Willington	d																								
Burton-on-Trent	d		09 18				09 38		09 49				10 18							10 49				11 18	
Tamworth	d		09 30						10 01				10 30					10 48		11 01				11 30	
Wilnecote	d		09 34										10 34											11 34	
Leicester	d							09 16			09 49								10 16			10 49			
South Wigston	d																		10 22						
Narborough	d							09 25											10 27						
Hinckley	d							09 34											10 35						
Nuneaton	d							09 42			10 10								10 42			11 10			
Coleshill Parkway	d							09 57			10 25								10 59			11 25			
Water Orton	d							10 01																	
Birmingham New Street 12	a		09 53				10 07	10 14	10 24	10 27	10 38		10 53					11 10	11 14	11 24	11 27	11 38		11 53	
	d	09 42					10 12		10 30			10 42						11 12		11 30			11 42		
Worcester Shrub Hill 7	d													11 06											
Ashchurch for Tewkesbury	d													11 24											
Cheltenham Spa	d	10 25		10 31	10 45		10 52		11 11			11 25		11 32	11 40		11 45	11 52		12 11			12 25		12 31
Gloucester 7	a			10 40	10 57				11 22					11 42	11 51		11 57			12 22					12 40
Bristol Parkway 7	a	10 55					11 26					11 55		12 22				12 28					12 55		
Bristol Temple Meads 10	a	11 12					11 38					12 08		12 35				12 41					13 10		
Newport (South Wales)	a				11 50				12 10								12 50			13 11					
Cardiff Central 7	a				12 10				12 26								13 07			13 29					

			XC	XC	XC	XC	XC	XC	XC	GW	GW		AW	XC	XC	XC	XC	XC	XC	XC	GW		AW	XC	XC
			◇1	1	◇1	◇1	◇1	◇1	1					◇1	1	◇1	◇1	◇1	◇1	1	◇1			◇1	1
			M		E	F	G	H		N	J		C	O		P	Q	G	R		S		C	M	
			[trolley]		[trolley]	[trolley]	[trolley]	[trolley]	[trolley]					[trolley]		[trolley]	[trolley]	[trolley]	[trolley]	[trolley]	[buffet]			[trolley]	
Nottingham 8	d				11 08				11 37							12 08				12 37					
Beeston	d								11 43											12 43					
Attenborough	d																								
Long Eaton	d								11 51											12 51					
Derby 6	a				11 31				12 02							12 33				13 02					
	d		11 27		11 36	11 53			12 06					12 28		12 36	12 53			13 06				13 28	
Willington	d																			13 12					
Burton-on-Trent	d				11 49				12 18							12 49				13 18				13 39	
Tamworth	d				12 01				12 30					12 48		13 01				13 30					
Wilnecote	d								12 34																
Leicester	d			11 16			11 49								12 16			12 49							13 16
South Wigston	d														12 22										
Narborough	d			11 25											12 27										13 25
Hinckley	d			11 34											12 35										13 34
Nuneaton	d			11 42			12 10								12 42			13 10							13 42
Coleshill Parkway	d			11 57			12 25								12 59			13 25							13 57
Water Orton	d			12 01																					14 01
Birmingham New Street 12	a		12 07	12 14	12 24	12 27	12 39		12 53					13 10	13 14	13 24	13 27	13 39		13 53				14 07	14 14
	d		12 12		12 30			12 42						13 12		13 30			13 42					14 12	
Worcester Shrub Hill 7	d									13 06															
Ashchurch for Tewkesbury	d									13 24															
Cheltenham Spa	d		12 52		13 11			13 25		13 34	13 40		13 45	13 56		14 11			14 25		14 31		14 45	14 52	
Gloucester 7	a				13 22					13 42	13 51		13 57			14 22					14 40		14 56		
Bristol Parkway 7	a		13 25					13 57		14 22				14 27					14 56					15 25	
Bristol Temple Meads 10	a		13 39					14 09		14 38				14 41					15 10					15 40	
Newport (South Wales)	a				14 09								14 50			15 11							15 50		
Cardiff Central 7	a				14 27								15 07			15 29							16 10		

A From Manchester Piccadilly to Paignton
B To London Paddington
C To Maesteg
D From Newcastle to Plymouth
E [trolley] to Gloucester
F From Newcastle to Southampton Central
G From Stansted Airport
H From Manchester Piccadilly
I From Great Malvern to Brighton
J To Swindon
K From Edinburgh to Plymouth
L From Edinburgh to Reading
M From Glasgow Central to Plymouth
N From Great Malvern to Weymouth
O From Dundee to Plymouth
P [trolley] from Birmingham New Street to Gloucester
Q From Newcastle to Reading
R From Manchester Piccadilly to Exeter St Davids
S To London Paddington. **The Cheltenham Spa Express**

Nottingham, Derby and Leicester
Birmingham - Cardiff and Bristol

		XC ◇1 A (trolley)	XC ◇1 B (trolley)	XC ◇1 C (trolley)	XC ◇1 D (trolley)	XC 1 (trolley)	GW E		GW F	XC ◇1 G (trolley)	XC 1	XC ◇1 H (trolley)	XC ◇1 I (trolley)	XC ◇1 C (trolley)	XC ◇1 J (trolley)	XC 1 (trolley)	GW ◇1 K (cup)		AW L	XC ◇1 M (trolley)	XC 1	XC ◇1	XC ◇1 B (trolley)	XC ◇1 C (trolley)	XC ◇1 D (trolley)
Nottingham 8 (bus)	d	13 11				13 37						14 08				14 37						15 11			
Beeston	d					13 43										14 43									
Attenborough	d																								
Long Eaton	d					13 51										14 51									
Derby 6	a	13 31				14 02						14 31				15 02						15 31			
	d	13 36	13 53			14 06				14 29		14 36	14 53			15 06				15 28		15 36	15 53		
Willington	d															15 12									
Burton-on-Trent	d	13 49				14 18						14 49				15 18				15 40		15 49			
Tamworth	d	14 01				14 30				14 49		15 01				15 30						16 01			
Wilnecote	d					14 34																			
Leicester	d			13 49							14 16			14 49							15 16			15 49	
South Wigston	d										14 22														
Narborough	d										14 27										15 25				
Hinckley	d										14 35										15 34				
Nuneaton	d			14 10							14 42			15 10							15 42			16 10	
Coleshill Parkway	d			14 25							14 59			15 25							15 57			16 25	
Water Orton	d																				16 01				
Birmingham New Street 12	a	14 24	14 27	14 39		14 53				15 07	15 14	15 24	15 27	15 39		15 53				16 04	16 14	16 24	16 27	16 39	
	d	14 30			14 42					15 12		15 30			15 42					16 12		16 30			16 42
Worcester Shrub Hill 7	d						15 06																		
Ashchurch for Tewkesbury	d						15 24															17 05			
Cheltenham Spa	d	15 11			15 25		15 34		15 40	15 53		16 11			16 25		16 31		16 45	16 52		17 15			17 25
Gloucester 7	a	15 22					15 42		15 51			16 22					16 40		16 56			17 26			
Bristol Parkway 7	a				15 56		16 22			16 27					16 56					17 25					17 58
Bristol Temple Meads 10	a				16 08		16 38			16 42					17 11					17 40					18 10
Newport (South Wales)	a	16 10										17 11							17 50			18 10			
Cardiff Central 7	a	16 29										17 28							18 10			18 27			

		XC 1 (trolley)	GW N		GW O	AW L	XC ◇1 G (trolley)	XC 1	XC ◇1	XC ◇1 I (trolley)	XC ◇1 C (trolley)	XC ◇1 D (trolley)	XC 1 (trolley)		GW ◇1 K (cup)	AW L	XC FO ◇1 P (trolley)	XC FO ◇1 Q (trolley)	XC FX ◇1 R (trolley)	XC 1	XC ◇1	XC ◇1 I (trolley)	XC ◇1 S (trolley)		XC ◇1 C
Nottingham 8 (bus)	d	15 37							16 08				16 37								17 08				
Beeston	d	15 43											16 43												
Attenborough	d																								
Long Eaton	d	15 51											16 51												
Derby 6	a	16 02							16 31				17 02								17 31				
	d	16 06					16 28		16 36	16 53			17 06				17 28	17 28	17 28		17 36	17 53			
Willington	d												17 12												
Burton-on-Trent	d	16 18							16 49				17 18				17 38	17 38	17 38		17 49				
Tamworth	d	16 30					16 48		17 01				17 30								18 01				
Wilnecote	d	16 34																							
Leicester	d							16 16			16 49									17 16					17 49
South Wigston	d							16 22												17 22					17 55
Narborough	d							16 27												17 27					18 01
Hinckley	d							16 35												17 35					18 09
Nuneaton	d							16 42			17 10									17 42					18 17
Coleshill Parkway	d							16 59			17 25									17 59					18 33
Water Orton	d																								
Birmingham New Street 12	a	16 53					17 09	17 14	17 25	17 28	17 38		17 53				18 08	18 08	18 07	18 14	18 25	18 28			18 45
	d						17 12		17 30			17 42					18 12	18 12	18 12		18 30		18 42		
Worcester Shrub Hill 7	d				17 06																				
Ashchurch for Tewkesbury	d				17 25				18 09																
Cheltenham Spa	d		17 30		17 40	17 45	17 52		18 18			18 25			18 34	18 45	18 52	18 52	18 52		19 15		19 25		
Gloucester 7	a		17 39		17 50	17 57			18 29						18 45	18 56					19 27				
Bristol Parkway 7	a		18 20				18 27					18 55					19 27	19 27	19 27				19 56		
Bristol Temple Meads 10	a		18 37				18 40					19 07					19 38	19 39	19 39				20 10		
Newport (South Wales)	a					18 51			19 16							19 50					20 11		20 47		
Cardiff Central 7	a					19 09			19 33							20 09					20 27		21 02		

A (trolley) from Birmingham New Street to Gloucester
B From Newcastle to Southampton Central
C From Stansted Airport
D From Manchester Piccadilly
E From Great Malvern to Weymouth
F To Swindon
G From Glasgow Central to Penzance
H (trolley) to Gloucester
I From Newcastle to Reading
J From Manchester Piccadilly to Paignton
K To London Paddington
L To Maesteg
M From Aberdeen to Penzance
N To Westbury
O From Great Malvern to Southampton Central
P Until 9 September. From Edinburgh to Plymouth
Q From 16 September. From Edinburgh to Plymouth
R From Edinburgh to Plymouth
S From Manchester Piccadilly. (trolley) to Bristol Parkway

Nottingham, Derby and Leicester Birmingham - Cardiff and Bristol

		XC 1 🍴	GW A	AW B	XC ◇1 C 🍴	XC 1	GW D	XC FX ◇1	XC FO ◇1		XC ◇1 E 🍴	XC ◇1 F	XC ◇1 G 🍴	XC 1 🍴	GW 1 D	XC ◇1 H 🍴	XC 1	GW	XC FO ◇1		XC FX ◇1	XC ◇1 I	XC ◇1 F 🍴	XC ◇1 J	XC 1
Nottingham 8	d	17 37						18 08	18 08					18 37					19 08		19 08				19 37
Beeston	d	17 43												18 43											19 43
Attenborough	d																								19 46
Long Eaton	d	17 51												18 51											19 53
Derby 6	a	18 02						18 33	18 33					19 02					19 32		19 32				20 02
	d	18 06			18 28			18 37	18 37		18 53			19 06		19 27			19 36		19 36	19 54			20 06
Willington	d	18 13																							
Burton-on-Trent	d	18 18						18 49	18 49					19 18		19 38			19 49		19 49				20 18
Tamworth	d	18 30			18 49			19 01	19 01					19 30					20 01		20 01				20 30
Wilnecote	d	18 34												19 34											20 34
Leicester	d					18 16						18 49					19 16						19 49		
South Wigston	d					18 25											19 22								
Narborough	d					18 30											19 27								
Hinckley	d					18 38											19 35								
Nuneaton	d					18 46						19 10					19 42						20 10		
Coleshill Parkway	d					19 02						19 25					19 59						20 25		
Water Orton	d																								
Birmingham New Street 12	a	18 54			19 09	19 14		19 24	19 24		19 28	19 38		19 53		20 09	20 15		20 24		20 24	20 27	20 38		20 54
	d				19 12			19 30	19 30				19 42			20 12			20 30		20 30			20 42	
Worcester Shrub Hill 7	d		19 07																						
Ashchurch for Tewkesbury	d		19 24																						
Cheltenham Spa	d		19 34	19 45	19 53		20 00	20 11	20 11				20 25		20 48	20 52		21 00	21 11		21 11			21 27	
Gloucester 7	a		19 42	19 56			20 10	20 22	20 22						20 58			21 11	21 22		21 22				
Bristol Parkway 7	a		20 22		20 27								20 56			21 25		21 52						22 01	
Bristol Temple Meads 10	a		20 38		20 41								21 08			21 38		22 10						22 14	
Newport (South Wales)	a			20 51				21 11	21 11										22 15		22 15				
Cardiff Central 7	a			21 10				21 27	21 29										22 31		22 35				

		XC ◇1 K 🍴	XC 1	XC ◇1 L 🍴	XC ◇1 F		XC 1	XC 1	GW D	GW M	GW	GW		XC ◇1 N	AW FX	AW FO	XC ◇1 O		XC ◇1 F	XC ◇1 L	LM FO	XC 1	XC 1	XC ◇1 P	XC ◇1 F
Nottingham 8	d						20 37															21 37			
Beeston	d						20 43															21 43			
Attenborough	d																					21 46			
Long Eaton	d						20 51															21 53			
Derby 6	a						21 02															22 04			
	d	20 28		20 54			21 06							21 28			21 28			22 02		22 10		22 46	
Willington	d						21 14																		
Burton-on-Trent	d						21 19							21 39			21 39					22 21		22 56	
Tamworth	d	20 48					21 31							21 51			21 50					22 33		23 07	
Wilnecote	d						21 35															22 37			
Leicester	d		20 18		20 49			21 16											21 49				22 27		22 49
South Wigston	d		20 22					21 22															22 33		
Narborough	d		20 26					21 27															22 38		
Hinckley	d		20 35					21 35															22 46		
Nuneaton	d		20 42		21 10			21 42											22 10				22 54		23 10
Coleshill Parkway	d		20 59		21 25			21 59											22 25				23 10		23 25
Water Orton	d																								
Birmingham New Street 12	a	21 07	21 15	21 35	21 38		21 55	22 11						22 09			22 09		22 38	22 51		23 02	23 23	23 27	23 38
	d	21 12												22 12			22 12				23 00				
Worcester Shrub Hill 7	d									21 32	22 20	22 28									23 46				
Ashchurch for Tewkesbury	d									21 52	22 36	22 51									00 01				
Cheltenham Spa	d	21 52							22 00	22 06	22 46	23 05		22 52	23 00	23 00	23 31				00 09				
Gloucester 7	a	22 02							22 11	22 21	23 02	23 18			23 12	23 12					00 20				
Bristol Parkway 7	a	22 32								23 04				23 23			00 02								
Bristol Temple Meads 10	a	22 45								23 19				23 40			00 14								
Newport (South Wales)	a														00 05	00 07									
Cardiff Central 7	a														00 29	00 35									

A From Great Malvern to Weymouth
B To Maesteg
C From Glasgow Central to Plymouth. 🍴 to Bristol Parkway
D To Swindon
E From Newcastle to Reading
F From Stansted Airport
G From Manchester Piccadilly to Plymouth. 🍴 to Bristol Parkway
H From Edinburgh to Plymouth. 🍴 to Bristol Parkway
I From Newcastle to Guildford
J From Manchester Piccadilly
K From Glasgow Central. 🍴 to Tamworth
L From Newcastle
M From Great Malvern
N from 20 June. From Edinburgh
O until 17 June. From Edinburgh
P From Glasgow Central

Table 57

Saturdays

Nottingham, Derby and Leicester Birmingham - Cardiff and Bristol

		AW	XC ◇1 A	LM	GW B	XC ◇1	XC ◇1	GW C	GW D	XC ◇1 E 🛒		XC 1	GW ◇1 F ☕	AW G	XC ◇1 H 🛒	XC ◇1 I 🛒	XC ◇1 J 🛒	XC ◇1 K 🛒	XC ◇1 L 🛒	XC 1		XC ◇1 M 🛒	XC ◇1 N	AW G	XC ◇1 O 🛒
Nottingham 8 🚌	d															05 57						06 37			
Beeston	d															06 03						06 43			
Attenborough	d															06 06									
Long Eaton	d															06 17									
Derby 6	a															06 32						07 01			
	d		21p28												06 10	06 36	06 46	06 47				07 06			07 25
Willington	d																								
Burton-on-Trent	d		21p39												06 21	06 48	06 57	06 58				07 18			07 36
Tamworth	d		21p50												06 32	07 00	07 08	07 09				07 30			07 48
Wilnecote	d															07 04									
Leicester	d											05 49								06 49			07 16		
South Wigston	d											05 55								06 55					
Narborough	d											06 00								07 00					
Hinckley	d											06 08								07 08					
Nuneaton	d											06 15								07 15			07 36		
Coleshill Parkway	d											06 31								07 31			07 52		
Water Orton	d																			07 35					
Birmingham New Street 12	a		22p09									06 43			06 50	07 24	07 27	07 27		07 47		07 55	08 04		08 08
	d		22p12	23p00		05 00	05 42			06 42					07 12	07 30			07 42						08 12
Worcester Shrub Hill 7	d			23b46					06 47																
Ashchurch for Tewkesbury	d			00 01			06 33		07 03																
Cheltenham Spa	d	23p00	23p31	00 09	05 30	06 04	06 43	06 48	07 13	07 25			07 30	07 45	07 52	08 11			08 25					08 45	08 52
Gloucester 7	a	23p12		00 20	05 40	06 13	06 54	06 58	07 24				07 40	07 57		08 22								08 57	
Bristol Parkway 7	a		00 02					07 39	08 19	07 55					08 24				08 55						09 24
Bristol Temple Meads 10	a		00 14					07 54	08 34	08 07					08 38				09 08						09 38
Newport (South Wales)	a	00 07				07 06	07 52							08 50		09 07								09 50	
Cardiff Central 7	a	00 35				07 22	08 08							09 10		09 23								10 07	

		GW ◇1 F ☕	XC ◇1 I 🛒	XC ◇1 P 🛒	XC ◇1 Q 🛒	XC ◇1 R 🛒		XC ◇1 S 🛒	XC 1	GW T	XC ◇1 U 🛒	XC 1	GW B	XC ◇1 V 🛒	XC ◇1 W 🛒	XC ◇1 Q 🛒		XC ◇1 X 🛒	XC 1	AW G	XC ◇1 Y 🛒	XC ◇1 Z 🛒	XC 1	GW ◇1 F ☕	XC ◇1 V 🛒
Nottingham 8 🚌	d		06 56						07 37					08 08					08 37						09 08
Beeston	d		07 02						07 43										08 43						
Attenborough	d		07 06																						
Long Eaton	d		07 14						07 51										08 51						
Derby 6	a		07 30						08 02					08 31					09 02						09 31
	d		07 36	07 51					08 06		08 29			08 36	08 53				09 06		09 28	09 30			09 36
Willington	d		07 43																						
Burton-on-Trent	d		07 49	08 01					08 18		08 40			08 49					09 18		09 39	09 41			09 49
Tamworth	d		08 01	08 12					08 30		08 51			09 01					09 30						10 01
Wilnecote	d		08 05						08 34										09 34						
Leicester	d				07 49							08 16				08 49							09 16		
South Wigston	d											08 22													
Narborough	d											08 27											09 25		
Hinckley	d											08 35											09 34		
Nuneaton	d				08 10							08 43				09 10							09 42		
Coleshill Parkway	d				08 25							09 01				09 25							09 57		
Water Orton	d																						10 02		
Birmingham New Street 12	a		08 24	08 29	08 38				08 53		09 09	09 14		09 24	09 29	09 38			09 53		10 07	10 08	10 14		10 24
	d		08 30			08 42		08 42			09 12			09 30				09 42			10 12	10 12			10 30
Worcester Shrub Hill 7	d									09 08															
Ashchurch for Tewkesbury	d									09 25															
Cheltenham Spa	d	08 59	09 11			09 24		09 25		09 35	09 52		10 01	10 11				10 25		10 45	10 52	10 53		11 00	11 11
Gloucester 7	a	09 09	09 22							09 44			10 11	10 22						10 56				11 10	11 22
Bristol Parkway 7	a					09 55		09 55		10 24	10 29							10 57			11 24	11 25			
Bristol Temple Meads 10	a					10 11		10 07		10 39	10 42							11 10			11 38	11 39			
Newport (South Wales)	a		10 07											11 08						11 50					12 07
Cardiff Central 7	a		10 23											11 24						12 07					12 23

A until 18 June. From Edinburgh
B To Swindon
C To Weston-super-Mare
D To Weymouth
E To Paignton
F To London Paddington
G To Maesteg
H To Plymouth. 🛒 from Birmingham New Street
I 🛒 from Birmingham New Street to Gloucester
J until 10 September. From Sheffield to Reading
K from 17 September. To Reading
L From Manchester Piccadilly
M To Bournemouth. 🛒 from Derby
N From Cambridge
O From Leeds to Paignton
P From Leeds to Southampton Central
Q From Stansted Airport
R until 10 September. From Manchester Piccadilly to Newquay
S from 17 September. From Manchester Piccadilly
T To Westbury
U From York to Plymouth
V 🛒 to Gloucester
W From Newcastle to Reading
X From Manchester Piccadilly to Paignton
Y from 17 September. From Newcastle to Plymouth
Z until 10 September. From York to Penzance
b Previous night, arr. 2337

Table 57

Saturdays

Nottingham, Derby and Leicester
Birmingham - Cardiff and Bristol

		XC		XC	XC	XC	GW	AW	XC	XC	GW	XC		XC	XC	XC	XC	XC	XC	XC	GW	XC		XC	XC
							R																		
		◇1		◇1	◇1	1			◇1	1		◇1		◇1	◇1	◇1	1	◇1	◇1	1	◇1	◇1		◇1	◇1
		A		B	C		D	E	F		G	H		I	B	C		J	K		L	H		A	B
		🛒		🛒	🛒				🛒			🛒		🛒	🛒	🛒		🛒	🛒		🍴	🛒		🛒	🛒
Nottingham 8	d					09 37						10 08					10 37					11 11			
Beeston	d					09 43											10 43								
Attenborough	d																								
Long Eaton	d					09 51											10 51								
Derby 6	a					10 02						10 31					11 02					11 31			
	d	09 53				10 06			10 28			10 37		10 53			11 06	11 27	11 30			11 36		11 55	
Willington	d																								
Burton-on-Trent	d					10 18						10 49					11 18	11 38	11 41			11 49			
Tamworth	d					10 30			10 49			11 01					11 30					12 01			
Wilnecote	d					10 34											11 34								
Leicester	d			09 49						10 16					10 49					11 16					11 49
South Wigston	d									10 22															
Narborough	d									10 27										11 25					
Hinckley	d									10 35										11 34					
Nuneaton	d			10 10						10 43					11 10					11 42					12 10
Coleshill Parkway	d			10 25						10 59					11 25					11 57					12 25
Water Orton	d																			12 02					
Birmingham New Street 12	a	10 27		10 38		10 53			11 07	11 14		11 24		11 27	11 38		11 53	12 07	12 08	12 14		12 24		12 29	12 38
	d				10 42				11 12			11 30				11 42		12 12	12 12			12 30			
Worcester Shrub Hill 7	d						11 06																		
Ashchurch for Tewkesbury	d						11 24																		
Cheltenham Spa	d				11 25		11 34	11 45	11 52		12 01	12 11				12 25		12 52	12 53		13 00	13 11			
Gloucester 7	a						11 44	11 57			12 11	12 22									13 10	13 22			
Bristol Parkway 7	a				11 55		12 24		12 29							12 55		13 24	13 26						
Bristol Temple Meads 10	a				12 08		12 39		12 42							13 07		13 38	13 40						
Newport (South Wales)	a							12 50				13 11										14 08			
Cardiff Central 7	a							13 07				13 27										14 24			

		GW	XC	XC	AW	XC	XC	XC		GW	XC	XC	XC	XC	XC	AW	XC	XC		XC	GW	XC	XC	XC	XC
			◇1	1		◇1	◇1	1			◇1	◇1	◇1	◇1	1		◇1	◇1		1	◇1	◇1	◇1	◇1	◇1
		M	C		E	N	O			G	P	Q	B	R		E	J	S			L	P	A	B	C
			🛒	🛒		🛒	🛒				🛒	🛒	🛒	🛒	🛒		🛒	🛒			🍴	🛒	🛒	🛒	🛒
Nottingham 8	d			11 37							12 08				12 37							13 08			
Beeston	d			11 43											12 43										
Attenborough	d																								
Long Eaton	d			11 51											12 51										
Derby 6	a			12 02							12 31				13 02							13 31			
	d			12 06		12 29	12 29				12 37	12 53			13 06		13 28	13 28				13 36	13 53		
Willington	d														13 12										
Burton-on-Trent	d			12 18							12 49				13 18		13 39	13 39				13 49			
Tamworth	d			12 30		12 49	12 49				13 01				13 30							14 01			
Wilnecote	d			12 34																					
Leicester	d							12 16					12 49							13 16				13 49	
South Wigston	d							12 22																	
Narborough	d							12 27												13 25					
Hinckley	d							12 35												13 34					
Nuneaton	d							12 43					13 10							13 42				14 10	
Coleshill Parkway	d							12 59					13 25							13 57				14 25	
Water Orton	d																			14 01					
Birmingham New Street 12	a			12 53		13 09	13 10	13 14			13 24	13 27	13 38		13 53		14 07	14 07		14 14		14 24	14 27	14 38	
	d		12 42			13 12	13 12				13 30			13 42			14 12	14 12				14 30			14 42
Worcester Shrub Hill 7	d	12 54																							
Ashchurch for Tewkesbury	d	13 10																							
Cheltenham Spa	d	13 20	13 26		13 45	13 52	13 53			14 01	14 11			14 25		14 45	14 52	14 52			15 00	15 11			15 25
Gloucester 7	a	13 32			13 57					14 11	14 22					14 56					15 10	15 22			
Bristol Parkway 7	a	14 20	13 57			14 26	14 26							14 57			15 23	15 24							15 55
Bristol Temple Meads 10	a	14 36	14 09			14 41	14 41							15 10			15 37	15 38							16 08
Newport (South Wales)	a				14 50						15 11					15 50						16 08			
Cardiff Central 7	a				15 09						15 27					16 07						16 25			

A From Newcastle to Southampton Central
B From Stansted Airport
C From Manchester Piccadilly
D From Great Malvern to Brighton.
R to Bristol Parkway
E To Maesteg
F From Edinburgh to Plymouth
G To Swindon
H 🛒 to Gloucester
I From Edinburgh to Reading
J from 17 September. From Glasgow Central to Plymouth
K until 10 September. From Glasgow Central to Paignton
L To London Paddington
M From Worcester Foregate Street to Weymouth
N from 17 September. From Dundee to Plymouth
O until 10 September. From Dundee to Newquay
P 🛒 from Birmingham New Street to Gloucester
Q From Newcastle to Reading
R From Manchester Piccadilly to Exeter St Davids
S until 10 September. From Glasgow Central to Penzance

Nottingham, Derby and Leicester Birmingham - Cardiff and Bristol

		XC	GW	XC	XC	GW	XC	XC	XC	XC	XC	AW	XC	XC	GW	XC	XC	XC	XC	XC	GW	AW
		1		◇1	1		◇1	◇1	◇1	◇1	1		◇1	1	◇1	◇1	◇1	◇1	◇1	1		
			A	B		C	D	E	F	G		H	I		J		K	F	G		L	H
		[trolley]		[trolley]			[trolley]	[trolley]	[trolley]	[trolley]	[trolley]		[trolley]		[restaurant]	[trolley]	[trolley]	[trolley]	[trolley]	[trolley]		
Nottingham 8	d	13 37					14 08				14 37					15 08				15 37		
Beeston	d	13 43									14 43									15 43		
Attenborough	d																					
Long Eaton	d	13 51									14 51									15 51		
Derby 6	a	14 02					14 32				15 02					15 31				16 02		
	d	14 06		14 29			14 36	14 53			15 06		15 28			15 36	15 53			16 06		
Willington	d										15 12											
Burton-on-Trent	d	14 18					14 49				15 18		15 39			15 49				16 18		
Tamworth	d	14 30		14 48			15 01				15 30					16 01				16 30		
Wilnecote	d	14 34																		16 34		
Leicester	d				14 16				14 49					15 16				15 49				
South Wigston	d				14 22																	
Narborough	d				14 27									15 25								
Hinckley	d				14 35									15 34								
Nuneaton	d				14 43				15 10					15 42				16 10				
Coleshill Parkway	d				14 59				15 25					15 57				16 25				
Water Orton	d													16 01								
Birmingham New Street 12	a	14 53		15 08	15 14		15 24	15 27	15 38		15 53		16 07	16 14		16 24	16 27	16 38		16 53		
	d			15 12			15 30			15 42			16 12			16 30			16 42			
Worcester Shrub Hill 7	d		15 06																		17 08	
Ashchurch for Tewkesbury	d		15 24																		17 24	
Cheltenham Spa	d		15 34	15 52		16 01	16 11			16 25		16 45	16 52		17 00	17 11			17 25		17 34	17 45
Gloucester 7	a		15 42			16 11	16 22					16 56			17 10	17 22					17 44	17 56
Bristol Parkway 7	a		16 24	16 29						16 55			17 24						17 55		18 24	
Bristol Temple Meads 10	a		16 39	16 42						17 07			17 38						18 07		18 39	
Newport (South Wales)	a						17 10					17 50				18 05						18 50
Cardiff Central 7	a						17 26					18 10				18 21						19 10

		XC	XC	GW	XC	XC	XC	XC	XC	AW	XC	XC	GW	XC	XC	XC	XC	XC	GW	AW	XC	XC	GW
		◇1	1		◇1	◇1	◇1	◇1	1		◇1	1	◇1	◇1	◇1	◇1	◇1	1			◇1	1	
		M		C		E	F	G		H	N		J		E	F	G		A	H	O		P
		[trolley]				[trolley]	[trolley]	[trolley]	[trolley]		[trolley]		[restaurant]		[trolley]		[trolley]	[trolley]			[trolley]		
Nottingham 8	d				16 08				16 37					17 11				17 37					
Beeston	d								16 43									17 43					
Attenborough	d																						
Long Eaton	d								16 51									17 51					
Derby 6	a				16 31				17 02					17 31				18 02					
	d	16 28			16 36	16 53			17 06		17 28			17 36	17 53			18 06			18 28		
Willington	d								17 12									18 13					
Burton-on-Trent	d				16 49				17 18		17 39			17 49				18 18					
Tamworth	d	16 48			17 01				17 30					18 01				18 30			18 47		
Wilnecote	d																	18 34					
Leicester	d		16 16				16 49					17 16				17 49						18 16	
South Wigston	d		16 22									17 22										18 22	
Narborough	d		16 27									17 27										18 27	
Hinckley	d		16 35									17 35										18 35	
Nuneaton	d		16 43				17 10					17 42				18 10						18 43	
Coleshill Parkway	d		16 59				17 25					17 59				18 25						18 59	
Water Orton	d																						
Birmingham New Street 12	a	17 07	17 14		17 24	17 27	17 38		17 53		18 07	18 14		18 24	18 27	18 38		18 54			19 07	19 14	
	d	17 12			17 30			17 42			18 12			18 30			18 42				19 12		
Worcester Shrub Hill 7	d																		19 07				
Ashchurch for Tewkesbury	d				18 08														19 24				
Cheltenham Spa	d	17 52		18 01	18 18			18 25		18 45	18 52		19 00	19 11			19 25		19 34	19 45	19 52		20 01
Gloucester 7	a			18 11	18 29					18 56			19 10	19 22					19 42	19 56			20 11
Bristol Parkway 7	a	18 29						18 55			19 27						19 55		20 24		20 29		
Bristol Temple Meads 10	a	18 42						19 07			19 41						20 07		20 39		20 42		
Newport (South Wales)	a				19 12					19 50				20 05			20 55			20 50			
Cardiff Central 7	a				19 29					20 11				20 21			21 11			21 09			

A From Great Malvern to Weymouth
B From Glasgow Central to Penzance
C To Swindon
D [trolley] to Gloucester
E From Newcastle to Reading
F From Stansted Airport
G From Manchester Piccadilly
H To Maesteg
I From Aberdeen to Penzance
J To London Paddington
K From Newcastle to Southampton Central
L From Great Malvern to Westbury
M From Glasgow Central to Plymouth
N From Edinburgh to Plymouth
O From Glasgow Central to Taunton. [trolley] to Bristol Parkway
P To Westbury

Table 57

Saturdays

Nottingham, Derby and Leicester
Birmingham - Cardiff and Bristol

		XC	XC	XC	XC	XC		XC	XC	XC	GW	XC	XC	XC	XC	GW		XC	XC	XC	XC	XC	XC	XC	XC
		◇1	◇1	◇1	◇1	◇1		1	◇1	1		◇1	◇1	◇1	◇1			◇1	1	◇1	1	◇1	◇1	1	◇1
			A	B	C	D			E				F	G	B	H		I		J		K	B		L
			🛒		🛒	🛒		🛒	🛒				🛒	🛒	🛒			🛒		🛒		🛒			
Nottingham 8 🚢	d	18 08						18 37				19 08							19 37					20 37	
Beeston	d							18 43											19 43					20 43	
Attenborough	d																		19 46						
Long Eaton	d							18 51											19 53					20 51	
Derby 6	a	18 31						19 02				19 32							20 02					21 02	
	d	18 36	18 53					19 06	19 27			19 36	19 54	19 54					20 06	20 28		20 53		21 06	21 28
Willington	d																							21 14	
Burton-on-Trent	d	18 49						19 18	19 38			19 49							20 18					21 19	21 39
Tamworth	d	19 01						19 30				20 01							20 30	20 48				21 31	21 50
Wilnecote	d							19 34											20 34					21 35	
Leicester	d			18 49						19 16					19 49						20 16		20 49		
South Wigston	d									19 22											20 22				
Narborough	d									19 27											20 27				
Hinckley	d									19 35											20 35				
Nuneaton	d			19 10						19 43					20 10						20 43		21 10		
Coleshill Parkway	d			19 25						19 59					20 25						20 59		21 25		
Water Orton	d																								
Birmingham New Street 12	a	19 24	19 27	19 38				19 53	20 09	20 15		20 24	20 27	20 28	20 38				20 54	21 07	21 14	21 27	21 38	21 54	22 08
	d	19 30			19 42	19 42			20 12			20 30						20 42		21 12					
Worcester Shrub Hill 7	d																								
Ashchurch for Tewkesbury	d																								
Cheltenham Spa	d	20 11			20 25	20 25			20 52		21 02	21 11				21 19		21 25		21 52					
Gloucester 7	a	20 22									21 12	21 22				21 29				22 02					
Bristol Parkway 7	a				20 55	20 55			21 25		21 53							21 58		22 32					
Bristol Temple Meads 10	a				21 07	21 09			21 38		22 05							22 12		22 45					
Newport (South Wales)	a	21 11										22 16													
Cardiff Central 7	a	21 29										22 41													

		XC		GW	XC	XC	XC	XC	XC	XC	XC	XC		XC
		1			◇1	◇1	1	1	◇1	1		◇1		
				M	B	K	N	O	P		Q	R		Q
											🚌			🚌
						🛒								
Nottingham 8 🚢	d						21 37	21 37						
Beeston	d						21 43	21 43						
Attenborough	d						21 46	21 46						
Long Eaton	d						21 53	21 53						
Derby 6	a						22 04	22 04						
	d					21 56	22 10	22 10	22 27		22 10	22 27		22 35
Willington	d													
Burton-on-Trent	d					22 07	22 21	22 21	22 37		22 30			22 55
Tamworth	d					22 18	22 33	22 33	22 48		22 50			23s15
Wilnecote	d						22 37	22 37			22 55			
Leicester	d	21 16			21 49					22 16				
South Wigston	d	21 22								22 22				
Narborough	d	21 27								22 27				
Hinckley	d	21 35								22 35				
Nuneaton	d	21 43			22 10					22 44				
Coleshill Parkway	d	21 59			22 25					22 59				
Water Orton	d													
Birmingham New Street 12	a	22 14			22 38	22 44	23 02	23 03	23 06	23 13	23 25	23 35		23 50
	d													
Worcester Shrub Hill 7	d			21 31										
Ashchurch for Tewkesbury	d			21 51										
Cheltenham Spa	d			22 01										
Gloucester 7	a			22 10										
Bristol Parkway 7	a													
Bristol Temple Meads 10	a													
Newport (South Wales)	a													
Cardiff Central 7	a													

- **A** From Newcastle to Reading
- **B** From Stansted Airport
- **C** from 17 September. From Manchester Piccadilly to Plymouth. 🛒 to Bristol Parkway
- **D** until 10 September. From Manchester Piccadilly
- **E** From Edinburgh to Plymouth. 🛒 to Bristol Parkway
- **F** from 17 September. From Newcastle to Guildford
- **G** until 10 September. From Newcastle
- **H** To Swindon
- **I** From Manchester Piccadilly
- **J** From Glasgow Central. 🛒 to Tamworth
- **K** From Newcastle
- **L** From Edinburgh
- **M** From Great Malvern
- **N** from 25 June until 30 July
- **O** from 6 August
- **P** from 25 June. From Glasgow Central
- **Q** until 18 June
- **R** until 18 June. From Glasgow Central

Table 57

Sundays
until 19 June

Nottingham, Derby and Leicester Birmingham - Cardiff and Bristol

		GW	GW	XC	GW	XC	XC	GW	XC	GW		XC	AW	XC	XC	GW	XC	XC	XC	GW		XC	XC	AW	XC
				◇1		◇1	◇1	◇1	◇1			◇1		◇1	1		◇1	◇1	1	◇1		◇1	◇1		◇1
			A	B		B		C	D					D		A	E	F		C		E	G		H
		bus		trolley		trolley		restaurant	trolley			trolley		trolley			trolley	trolley		restaurant		trolley	trolley		trolley
Nottingham 8	d																								
Beeston	d																								
Attenborough	d																								
Long Eaton	d																								
Derby 6	a																								
	d								09 30					10 33				11 35							12 36
Willington	d																								
Burton-on-Trent	d																								
Tamworth	d																								
Wilnecote	d																								
Leicester	d														11 19				12 19				12 49		
South Wigston	d																		12 24						
Narborough	d														11 28				12 29						
Hinckley	d														11 36				12 38						
Nuneaton	d														11 44				12 46				13 09		
Coleshill Parkway	d														11 59				13 01				13 25		
Water Orton	d																								
Birmingham New Street 12	a								10 48					11 44	12 15			12 45	13 15				13 38		13 50
	d			09 12		10 12	10 30		11 12			11 30		12 12			12 30	13 12				13 30			14 12
Worcester Shrub Hill 7	d																								
Ashchurch for Tewkesbury	d																								
Cheltenham Spa	d	08 45	09 24	09 52	10 05	10 52	11 11	11 46	11 52	12 00		12 11	12 18	12 52		13 04	13 11	13 52		13 56		14 12		14 18	14 52
Gloucester 7	a	09 13	09 34	10 01	10 16	11 01	11 21	11 56	12 03	12 11		12 21	12 28	13 03		13 15	13 21	14 02		14 07		14 22		14 29	15 02
Bristol Parkway 7	a	10 45		11 11		12 13			13 17					14 18				15 08							15 33
Bristol Temple Meads 10	a			11 40		12 35			13 37					14 36				15 23							15 45
Newport (South Wales)	a						12 06					13 06	13 33				14 06					15 08		15 31	
Cardiff Central 7	a						12 26					13 26	13 52				14 26					15 31		15 51	

		XC	GW	XC	XC	XC		XC	XC	GW	XC	XC	AW	XC	GW	XC		XC	XC	XC	XC	GW	XC	XC	GW
		1		◇1	◇1	◇1		◇1	1	◇1	◇1	◇1		◇1		◇1		1	◇1	◇1	◇1	◇1	◇1	1	
			I	E	G	J		K		C	E	G		L	A	M				G	L	C	K		
				trolley	trolley	trolley		trolley		restaurant	trolley	trolley		trolley		trolley			trolley	trolley	trolley	restaurant	trolley		
Nottingham 8	d																								
Beeston	d																								
Attenborough	d																								
Long Eaton	d																								
Derby 6	a																								
	d							13 32								14 34							15 30		
Willington	d																								
Burton-on-Trent	d																								
Tamworth	d																								
Wilnecote	d																								
Leicester	d	13 19			13 49				14 19			14 48						15 19		15 49				16 19	
South Wigston	d								14 24															16 24	
Narborough	d	13 28							14 29									15 28						16 29	
Hinckley	d	13 36							14 38									15 37						16 38	
Nuneaton	d	13 44			14 09				14 46			15 09						15 45		16 09				16 46	
Coleshill Parkway	d	13 59			14 25				15 01			15 25						15 59		16 25				17 01	
Water Orton	d																								
Birmingham New Street 12	a	14 16			14 37			14 44	15 15			15 39				15 43		16 15		16 39			16 47	17 15	
	d			14 30		14 42		15 12			15 30			15 42		16 12			16 30		16 42		17 12		
Worcester Shrub Hill 7	d		14 36																						17 38
Ashchurch for Tewkesbury	d		14 52																						17 56
Cheltenham Spa	d		15 01	15 11		15 25		15 52		15 59	16 11		16 18	16 25	16 33	16 52			17 11		17 25	17 46	17 52		18 06
Gloucester 7	a		15 15	15 21						16 09	16 21		16 29		16 45				17 21			17 56			18 15
Bristol Parkway 7	a		16 09			15 56		16 24						16 57		17 23					18 02		18 23		18 57
Bristol Temple Meads 10	a		16 24			16 09		16 37						17 09		17 35					18 14		18 37		19 10
Newport (South Wales)	a			16 06							17 06		17 37						18 06						
Cardiff Central 7	a			16 26							17 27		17 55						18 28						

A To Swindon
B To Plymouth
C To London Paddington
D From Leeds to Plymouth
E trolley to Gloucester
F From York
G From Stansted Airport
H From Newcastle to Plymouth
I To Weston-super-Mare
J From Manchester Piccadilly to Paignton
K From Edinburgh to Penzance
L From Manchester Piccadilly
M From Edinburgh to Plymouth

Table 57

Sundays
until 19 June

Nottingham, Derby and Leicester Birmingham - Cardiff and Bristol

Station		XC ◇1 A 🛒		XC ◇1 B 🛒	XC ◇1 C 🛒	AW	XC ◇1 D 🛒	XC 1	GW	XC ◇1 A 🛒	XC ◇1 B	XC ◇1 E 🛒		GW ◇1 F 🍽	XC ◇1 G 🛒	XC 1	XC ◇1 A 🛒	XC ◇1 B	AW	XC ◇1 C 🛒	XC ◇1 H 🛒	XC 1		XC ◇1 B	GW
Nottingham 8 🚌	d																								
Beeston	d																								
Attenborough	d																								
Long Eaton	d																								
Derby 6	a																								
	d						16 36								17 28						18 35				
Willington	d																								
Burton-on-Trent	d																								
Tamworth	d																								
Wilnecote	d																								
Leicester	d			16 48				17 16			17 47					18 16		18 49				19 19		19 49	
South Wigston	d							17 23														19 24			
Narborough	d							17 28								18 25						19 29			
Hinckley	d							17 36								18 33						19 38			
Nuneaton	d			17 12				17 44			18 09					18 41		19 09				19 45		20 09	
Coleshill Parkway	d			17 28				17 59			18 25					18 57		19 25				20 01		20 25	
Water Orton	d																								
Birmingham New Street 12	a			17 40			17 48	18 15			18 39				18 47	19 15		19 37			19 51	20 15		20 39	
	d	17 30			17 42		18 12			18 30		18 42			19 12		19 30			19 42	20 12				
Worcester Shrub Hill 7	d								18 40																20 37
Ashchurch for Tewkesbury	d								18 56																20 53
Cheltenham Spa	d	18 11			18 25	18 35	18 52		19 07	19 13		19 25		19 46	19 52		20 11		20 18	20 25	20 52				21 03
Gloucester 7	a	18 22				18 46			19 16	19 26				19 56			20 21		20 29						21 13
Bristol Parkway 7	a				19 02		19 23		19 56			20 02			20 23					20 57	21 23				21 53
Bristol Temple Meads 10	a				19 14		19 37		20 10			20 14			20 35					21 09	21 35				22 07
Newport (South Wales)	a	19 07				19 54				20 11							21 06		21 31						
Cardiff Central 7	a	19 27				20 12				20 31							21 26		21 49						

Station		XC ◇1 C	XC 1	GW I	XC ◇1 J 🛒	XC ◇1 B	GW	XC ◇1 C		XC ◇1 J	XC 1	XC ◇1 B	XC ◇1 K	XC ◇1 J	XC 1
Nottingham 8 🚌	d														
Beeston	d														
Attenborough	d														
Long Eaton	d														
Derby 6	a														
	d				19 33					20 33			21 44	22 38	
Willington	d														
Burton-on-Trent	d														
Tamworth	d														
Wilnecote	d														
Leicester	d		20 08			20 49					21 19	21 49			23 19
South Wigston	d		20 15								21 25				23 25
Narborough	d		20 20								21 29				23 29
Hinckley	d		20 29								21 38				23 38
Nuneaton	d		20 36			21 09					21 46	22 09			23 46
Coleshill Parkway	d		20 52			21 25					22 01	22 25			00 02
Water Orton	d														
Birmingham New Street 12	a		21 06		20 47	21 37				21 50	22 18	22 38	22 53	23 48	00 14
	d	20 42			21 12			21 42		22 12					
Worcester Shrub Hill 7	d														
Ashchurch for Tewkesbury	d														
Cheltenham Spa	d	21 25		21 46	21 52		22 01	22 25		22 52					
Gloucester 7	a			21 56	22 02		22 12								
Bristol Parkway 7	a	21 59			22 35			22 56		23 24					
Bristol Temple Meads 10	a	22 11			22 45			23 10		23 36					
Newport (South Wales)	a														
Cardiff Central 7	a														

A 🛒 to Gloucester
B From Stansted Airport
C From Manchester Piccadilly
D From Edinburgh to Plymouth
E From Manchester Piccadilly to Paignton
F To London Paddington
G From Glasgow Central to Plymouth
H From Aberdeen to Plymouth. 🛒 to Bristol Parkway
I To Swindon
J From Glasgow Central
K From Edinburgh

Sundays

26 June to 31 July

Nottingham, Derby and Leicester Birmingham - Cardiff and Bristol

		GW	XC	XC	XC	XC	AW	XC	XC	XC		XC	XC	GW	XC	XC	XC	AW	XC	XC		GW	XC	XC	XC
			◇[1]	◇[1]	◇[1]	◇[1]		◇[1]	[1]	◇[1]		◇[1]	[1]	◇[1]	◇[1]	◇[1]	◇[1]		◇[1]	[1]			◇[1]	◇[1]	◇[1]
		A	B		C			C		D		E		F	D	G	H		I				D	J	G
		🚌	🛒		🛒	🛒		🛒		🛒		🛒		🍽	🛒	🛒	🛒		🛒				🛒	🛒	🛒
Nottingham [8] 🚊	d																						13 06		
Beeston	d																								
Attenborough	d																								
Long Eaton	d																								
Derby [6]	a																						13 30		
	d				09 36			10 33				11 30					12 30		13 32				13 36	13 53	
Willington	d																								
Burton-on-Trent	d																		13 43				13 48		
Tamworth	d																						14 00		
Wilnecote	d																								
Leicester	d								11 19				12 19			12 49				13 19					13 49
South Wigston	d												12 24												
Narborough	d								11 28				12 29							13 28					
Hinckley	d								11 36				12 38							13 36					
Nuneaton	d								11 44				12 46			13 09				13 44					14 09
Coleshill Parkway	d								11 59				13 01			13 25				13 59					14 25
Water Orton	d																								
Birmingham New Street [12]	a				10 47			11 44	12 15			12 43	13 15			13 38	13 42		14 11	14 16			14 22	14 27	14 37
	d		09 12	10 30	11 12	11 30		12 12		12 30		13 12			13 30				14 12				14 30		
Worcester Shrub Hill [7]	d																					14 36			
Ashchurch for Tewkesbury	d																					14 52			
Cheltenham Spa	d	09 35	09 52	11 11	11 52	12 11	12 18	12 52		13 11		13 52		13 56	14 12			14 18	14 52			15 01	15 11		
Gloucester [7]	a	09 53	10 01	11 21	12 03	12 21	12 28	13 02		13 21		14 02		14 07	14 22			14 29	15 03			15 10	15 21		
Bristol Parkway [7]	a		11 11		13 17			14 17				15 12							16 16						
Bristol Temple Meads [10]	a		11 40		13 36			14 40				15 35							16 36						
Newport (South Wales)	a			12 06		13 06	13 33			14 06					15 07			15 31					16 06		
Cardiff Central [7]	a			12 26		13 26	13 52			14 26					15 31			15 51					16 26		

		GW	XC	XC	XC	XC		XC	AW	GW	XC	XC	GW	XC	XC	XC		GW	XC	XC	XC	XC	XC	AW	XC
		◇[1]	◇[1]	[1]	◇[1]	◇[1]		◇[1]			◇[1]	[1]		◇[1]	◇[1]	◇[1]		◇[1]	◇[1]	[1]	◇[1]	◇[1]	◇[1]		◇[1]
		F	K		D	L		G		M	I			N	O	G		F	P		D	O	G		Q
		🍽	🛒		🛒	🛒		🛒			🛒			🛒	🛒	🛒		🍽	🛒		🛒	🛒	🛒		🛒
Nottingham [8] 🚊	d				14 10									15 05							16 05				
Beeston	d																								
Attenborough	d																								
Long Eaton	d																								
Derby [6]	a				14 28									15 31							16 28				
	d		14 30		14 35	14 54					15 28			15 35	15 54				16 29		16 35	16 55			17 28
Willington	d																								
Burton-on-Trent	d				14 48						15 39			15 48							16 48				17 39
Tamworth	d		14 50		15 00									16 00					16 48		17 00				
Wilnecote	d													16 04											
Leicester	d			14 19				14 48				15 19				15 49				16 19			16 48		
South Wigston	d			14 24																16 24					
Narborough	d			14 29								15 28								16 29					
Hinckley	d			14 38								15 37								16 38					
Nuneaton	d			14 46				15 09				15 45				16 09				16 46			17 12		
Coleshill Parkway	d			15 01				15 25				15 59				16 25				17 01			17 28		
Water Orton	d																								
Birmingham New Street [12]	a		15 07	15 15	15 21	15 27		15 39			16 03	16 15		16 23	16 27	16 39			17 06	17 15	17 21	17 28	17 40		18 03
	d		15 12		15 30						16 12			16 30					17 12		17 30				18 12
Worcester Shrub Hill [7]	d												16 40												
Ashchurch for Tewkesbury	d												16 58												
Cheltenham Spa	d	15 46	15 52		16 11				16 18	16 33	16 52		17 08	17 11				17 46	17 52		18 11			18 35	18 52
Gloucester [7]	a	15 56	16 02		16 21				16 29	16 43	17 02		17 17	17 21				17 56	18 02		18 22			18 46	19 02
Bristol Parkway [7]	a		17 21								18 12								19 12						20 15
Bristol Temple Meads [10]	a		17 36								18 39								19 35						20 35
Newport (South Wales)	a				17 06				17 37					18 07							19 07			19 54	
Cardiff Central [7]	a				17 27				17 55					18 29							19 27			20 12	

A To Stroud
B To Plymouth
C From Leeds to Plymouth
D 🛒 to Gloucester
E From York to Plymouth
F To London Paddington
G From Stansted Airport
H From Newcastle
I From Edinburgh to Penzance
J To Reading
K From Edinburgh to Plymouth
L From Sheffield to Reading
M To Swindon
N 🛒 to Wilnecote
O From Newcastle to Reading
P From Glasgow Central to Plymouth
Q From Glasgow Central to Plymouth. 🛒 to Bristol Parkway

Table 57

Sundays

26 June to 31 July

Nottingham, Derby and Leicester
Birmingham - Cardiff and Bristol

		XC		GW	XC	XC	XC	GW	XC	XC	XC	XC		XC	AW	XC	XC	XC	XC	XC	XC	GW		XC	XC
		1			◇1	◇1	◇1	◇1	◇1	1	◇1	◇1		◇1		◇1	1	◇1	◇1	◇1	1			◇1	◇1
					A	B	C	D	E		F	G		C		H			G	C		I		J	
					[trolley]	[trolley]		[restaurant]	[trolley]		[trolley]	[trolley]				[trolley]		[trolley]	[trolley]					[trolley]	
Nottingham 8	d				17 10						18 05							19 09							20 10
Beeston	d																								
Attenborough	d																								
Long Eaton	d																								
Derby 6	a				17 30						18 31							19 29							20 29
	d				17 36	17 55			18 26		18 35	18 55				19 28		19 33	19 55					20 27	20 35
Willington	d																								
Burton-on-Trent	d				17 48						18 48					19 39		19 48							20 48
Tamworth	d				18 00				18 47		19 00							20 00						20 47	21 00
Wilnecote	d																	20 04							
Leicester	d	17 16					17 47			18 16				18 49			19 19			19 49	20 08				
South Wigston	d	17 23															19 24				20 15				
Narborough	d	17 28								18 25							19 29				20 20				
Hinckley	d	17 36								18 33							19 38				20 29				
Nuneaton	d	17 44					18 09			18 41				19 09			19 45			20 09	20 36				
Coleshill Parkway	d	17 59					18 25			18 57				19 25			20 01			20 25	20 52				
Water Orton	d																								
Birmingham New Street 12	a	18 15			18 21	18 27	18 39		19 04	19 15	19 21	19 28		19 37		20 03	20 15	20 23	20 27	20 39	21 06			21 06	21 18
	d				18 30				19 12		19 30					20 12								21 12	
Worcester Shrub Hill 7	d			18 40																					
Ashchurch for Tewkesbury	d			18 56																					
Cheltenham Spa	d			19 07	19 13			19 46	19 52		20 11				20 18	20 52						21 46		21 52	
Gloucester 7	a			19 16	19 26			19 56	20 02		20 21				20 29	21 02						21 56		22 02	
Bristol Parkway 7	a								21 12							22 12								23 22	
Bristol Temple Meads 10	a								21 35							22 25								23 41	
Newport (South Wales)	a				20 11						21 06				21 31										
Cardiff Central 7	a				20 31						21 26				21 49										

		XC	XC	GW	XC	XC	XC	XC		XC	XC	XC
		◇1	◇1		◇1	1	◇1	◇1		◇1	◇1	1
		K	C		L			K		C	H	
		[trolley]						[trolley]				
Nottingham 8	d						21 08					
Beeston	d											
Attenborough	d											
Long Eaton	d											
Derby 6	a						21 31					
	d	20 54			21 27		21 35	21 53			22 27	
Willington	d											
Burton-on-Trent	d				21 38		21 48	22 04			22 38	
Tamworth	d				21 49		22 00	22 15			22 49	
Wilnecote	d						22 04					
Leicester	d		20 49			21 19				21 49		23 19
South Wigston	d					21 25						23 25
Narborough	d					21 29						23 29
Hinckley	d					21 38						23 38
Nuneaton	d		21 09			21 46				22 09		23 46
Coleshill Parkway	d		21 25			22 01				22 25		00 02
Water Orton	d											
Birmingham New Street 12	a	21 35	21 37		22 06	22 18	22 23	22 34		22 38	23 07	00 14
	d				22 12							
Worcester Shrub Hill 7	d			21 36								
Ashchurch for Tewkesbury	d			21 52								
Cheltenham Spa	d			22 02	22 52							
Gloucester 7	a			22 12	23 03							
Bristol Parkway 7	a				23 55							
Bristol Temple Meads 10	a				00 10							
Newport (South Wales)	a											
Cardiff Central 7	a											

A [trolley] to Gloucester
B From Edinburgh to Reading
C From Stansted Airport
D To London Paddington
E From Aberdeen to Plymouth. [trolley] to Bristol Parkway
F [trolley] to Tamworth
G From Newcastle to Reading
H From Glasgow Central
I To Swindon
J From Glasgow Central. [trolley] to Tamworth
K From Newcastle
L From Edinburgh

Table 57

Sundays

7 August to 11 September

Nottingham, Derby and Leicester
Birmingham - Cardiff and Bristol

		GW	XC	GW	XC	XC	GW	XC	GW	XC		GW	XC	XC	XC	GW	XC	XC	XC	XC		XC	XC	XC	GW
			◇1		◇1	◇1	◇1	◇1		◇1			◇1	1	◇1	◇1	◇1	1	◇1	◇1		◇1	◇1	1	
		A	B	C	D		E	D				A	F			E	G			H			I		J
			🛒		🛒	🛒	🍽	🛒		🛒			🛒		🛒	🍽	🛒		🛒	🛒		🛒	🛒		
Nottingham 8 🚌	d														11 10				12 10						
Beeston	d																								
Attenborough	d																								
Long Eaton	d																								
Derby 6	a														11 34				12 30						
	d				09 28			10 33					11 30		11 36		12 30		12 36				13 32		
Willington	d																								
Burton-on-Trent	d												11 42		11 48				12 48				13 43		
Tamworth	d				09 48										12 00		12 49		13 01						
Wilnecote	d																								
Leicester	d													11 19				12 19		12 49				13 19	
South Wigston	d																	12 24							
Narborough	d													11 28				12 29						13 28	
Hinckley	d													11 36				12 38						13 36	
Nuneaton	d													11 44				12 46		13 09				13 44	
Coleshill Parkway	d													11 59				13 01		13 25				13 59	
Water Orton	d																								
Birmingham New Street 12	a				10 09			11 08					12 07	12 15	12 22		13 07	13 15	13 22	13 38			14 10	14 16	
	d		09 12		10 12	10 30		11 12		11 30			12 12		12 30		13 12		13 30			13 42	14 12		
Worcester Shrub Hill 7	d																								14 36
Ashchurch for Tewkesbury	d																								14 52
Cheltenham Spa	d	09 24	09 52	10 05	10 57	11 11	11 46	11 52	12 00	12 11		12 24	12 52		13 11	13 46	13 52		14 12			14 24	14 52		15 01
Gloucester 7	a	09 34		10 15		11 21	11 56		12 10	12 21		12 34			13 21	13 57			14 22						15 10
Bristol Parkway 7	a		10 22	10 55	11 28			12 23	12 51				13 23				14 23					14 56	15 25		15 49
Bristol Temple Meads 10	a		10 34	11 08	11 41			12 36	13 10				13 35				14 39					15 08	15 38		16 09
Newport (South Wales)	a																								
Cardiff Central 7	a																								

		XC	XC	XC	XC	GW		XC	XC	XC	XC	XC	XC	GW	XC	XC		GW	XC	XC	XC	XC	GW	XC	XC
		◇1	◇1	◇1	◇1	◇1		◇1	1	◇1	◇1	◇1	◇1		◇1	1			◇1	◇1	◇1	◇1	◇1	◇1	1
			K	H	L	E		M			N	H	O	A	I				P	Q	H	O	E	R	
		🛒	🛒	🛒	🛒	🍽		🛒		🛒	🛒	🛒	🛒		🛒				🛒	🛒	🛒	🛒	🍽	🛒	
Nottingham 8 🚌	d	13 06								14 10									15 05						
Beeston	d																								
Attenborough	d																								
Long Eaton	d																								
Derby 6	a	13 30								14 28									15 31						
	d	13 36	13 53					14 30		14 35	14 54				15 28				15 35	15 54				16 29	
Willington	d																								
Burton-on-Trent	d	13 47								14 48					15 39				15 48						
Tamworth	d	14 00						14 50		15 00									16 00					16 48	
Wilnecote	d																		16 04						
Leicester	d			13 49					14 19			14 48				15 19					15 49				16 19
South Wigston	d								14 24																16 24
Narborough	d								14 29							15 28									16 29
Hinckley	d								14 38							15 37									16 38
Nuneaton	d			14 09					14 46			15 09				15 45					16 09				16 46
Coleshill Parkway	d			14 25					15 01			15 25				15 59					16 25				17 01
Water Orton	d																								
Birmingham New Street 12	a	14 22	14 27	14 37				15 07	15 15	15 21	15 27	15 39			16 03	16 15			16 24	16 27	16 39			17 06	17 15
	d	14 30			14 42			15 12		15 30			15 42		16 12				16 30			16 42		17 12	
Worcester Shrub Hill 7	d																	16 40							
Ashchurch for Tewkesbury	d																	16 58							
Cheltenham Spa	d	15 11			15 25	15 46		15 52		16 11			16 25	16 33	16 52			17 08	17 11			17 25	17 46	17 52	
Gloucester 7	a	15 21				15 56				16 21				16 43				17 16	17 21				17 56		
Bristol Parkway 7	a				15 56			16 23					16 57		17 23			17 57				18 02		18 23	
Bristol Temple Meads 10	a				16 09			16 35					17 09		17 35			18 10				18 14		18 37	
Newport (South Wales)	a																								
Cardiff Central 7	a																								

- **A** To Swindon
- **B** To Penzance
- **C** To Taunton
- **D** From Leeds to Plymouth
- **E** To London Paddington
- **F** From York to Plymouth
- **G** From Newcastle to Plymouth
- **H** From Stansted Airport
- **I** From Edinburgh to Plymouth
- **J** To Weston-super-Mare
- **K** To Reading
- **L** From Manchester Piccadilly to Paignton
- **M** From Edinburgh to Penzance
- **N** From Sheffield to Reading
- **O** From Manchester Piccadilly
- **P** 🛒 to Wilnecote
- **Q** From Newcastle to Reading
- **R** From Glasgow Central to Penzance

Table 57

Sundays

7 August to 11 September

Nottingham, Derby and Leicester Birmingham - Cardiff and Bristol

		XC		XC	XC	XC	XC	XC	GW	XC	XC	XC		XC	GW	XC	XC	XC	XC	XC	XC	XC		XC	XC
		◇1		◇1	◇1	◇1	◇1	1		◇1	◇1	◇1		◇1	◇1	◇1	1	◇1	◇1	◇1	◇1	◇1		1	◇1
				A	B	C	D				E	B		F	G	H		I	A	B	C	J			
		🚲		🚲	🚲	🚲	🚲			🚲	🚲			🚲	🛒	🚲		🚲	🚲		🚲	🚲			🚲
Nottingham [8] ⇌	d	16 05								17 10								18 05							19 09
Beeston	d																								
Attenborough	d																								
Long Eaton	d																								
Derby [6]	a	16 28								17 30								18 31							19 29
	d	16 35		16 55			17 28			17 36	17 55					18 26		18 35	18 55			19 28			19 33
Willington	d																								
Burton-on-Trent	d	16 48					17 39			17 48								18 48				19 39			19 48
Tamworth	d	17 00								18 00						18 47		19 00							20 00
Wilnecote	d																								20 04
Leicester	d				16 48			17 16				17 47					18 16			18 49				19 19	
South Wigston	d							17 23																19 24	
Narborough	d							17 28									18 25							19 29	
Hinckley	d							17 36									18 33							19 38	
Nuneaton	d				17 12			17 44				18 09					18 41			19 09				19 45	
Coleshill Parkway	d				17 28			17 59				18 25					18 57			19 25				20 01	
Water Orton	d																								
Birmingham New Street [12]	a	17 21		17 28	17 40		18 03	18 15		18 22	18 27	18 39				19 04	19 15	19 21	19 28	19 37		20 03		20 15	20 23
	d	17 30				17 42	18 12			18 30				18 42		19 12		19 30			19 42	20 12			
Worcester Shrub Hill [7]	d								18 40																
Ashchurch for Tewkesbury	d								18 56																
Cheltenham Spa	d	18 11				18 25	18 52		19 07	19 13				19 25	19 46	19 52		20 11			20 25	20 52			
Gloucester [7]	a	18 21							19 16	19 24					19 56			20 21							
Bristol Parkway [7]	a					18 57	19 23		19 56					20 02		20 23					20 57	21 23			
Bristol Temple Meads [10]	a					19 09	19 35		20 10					20 14		20 35					21 09	21 35			
Newport (South Wales)	a																								
Cardiff Central [7]	a																								

		XC	XC	GW	XC	XC	GW	XC		XC	XC	XC	GW	XC	XC	XC	XC	XC		XC	XC	XC			
		◇1	◇1		◇1	1		◇1		◇1	◇1	◇1		◇1	◇1	1	◇1	◇1		◇1	◇1	1			
		A	B		C		K	L			M	B		C	N			M		B	O				
		🚲						🚲			🚲							🚲							
Nottingham [8] ⇌	d									20 10							21 08								
Beeston	d																								
Attenborough	d																								
Long Eaton	d																								
Derby [6]	a									20 29							21 31								
	d	19 55						20 27		20 35	20 54				21 27		21 35	21 53			22 27				
Willington	d																								
Burton-on-Trent	d									20 48					21 38		21 48	22 04			22 38				
Tamworth	d							20 47		21 00					21 49		22 00	22 15			22 49				
Wilnecote	d																22 04								
Leicester	d		19 49			20 08						20 49				21 19				21 49		23 19			
South Wigston	d					20 15										21 25						23 25			
Narborough	d					20 20										21 29						23 29			
Hinckley	d					20 29										21 38						23 38			
Nuneaton	d		20 09			20 36						21 09				21 46				22 09		23 46			
Coleshill Parkway	d		20 25			20 52						21 25				22 01				22 25		00 02			
Water Orton	d																								
Birmingham New Street [12]	a	20 27	20 39			21 06		21 06		21 18	21 35	21 37			22 06	22 18	22 23	22 34		22 38	23 07	00 14			
	d				20 42			21 12						21 42	22 12										
Worcester Shrub Hill [7]	d			20 37																					
Ashchurch for Tewkesbury	d			20 53																					
Cheltenham Spa	d			21 03	21 25		21 46	21 52					22 01	22 25	22 52										
Gloucester [7]	a			21 13			21 56	22 01					22 12												
Bristol Parkway [7]	a			21 53	21 59			22 34						22 56	23 24										
Bristol Temple Meads [10]	a			22 07	22 11			22 46						23 10	23 36										
Newport (South Wales)	a																								
Cardiff Central [7]	a																								

A From Newcastle to Reading
B From Stansted Airport
C From Manchester Piccadilly
D From Glasgow Central to Plymouth
E From Edinburgh to Reading
F From Manchester Piccadilly to Paignton
G To London Paddington
H From Aberdeen to Plymouth. 🚲 to Bristol Parkway
I 🚲 to Tamworth
J From Glasgow Central to Plymouth. 🚲 to Bristol Parkway
K To Swindon
L From Glasgow Central. 🚲 to Tamworth
M From Newcastle
N From Edinburgh
O From Glasgow Central

Table 57

Sundays

18 September to 23 October

Nottingham, Derby and Leicester Birmingham - Cardiff and Bristol

		GW	GW	XC	GW	XC	XC	GW	XC	GW		XC	XC	XC	GW	XC	XC	XC	XC	XC		GW	XC	XC	GW
				◇1		◇1	◇1		◇1			◇1	1	◇1		◇1	◇1	1	◇1	◇1			◇1	1	
		A			A	B		A	B					C	A		D			E		A	F		
				🛒		🛒	🛒		🛒			🛒		🛒		🛒	🛒		🛒	🛒			🛒		
Nottingham 8	d															11 10			12 10						
Beeston	d																								
Attenborough	d																								
Long Eaton	d																								
Derby 6	a															11 34			12 30						
	d					09 28			10 33					11 30		11 36	12 30		12 36				13 32		
Willington	d																								
Burton-on-Trent	d															11 48			12 48				13 43		
Tamworth	d					09 48										12 00	12 49		13 00						
Wilnecote	d																								
Leicester	d												11 19					12 19		12 49				13 19	
South Wigston	d																	12 24							
Narborough	d												11 28					12 29						13 28	
Hinckley	d												11 36					12 38						13 36	
Nuneaton	d												11 44					12 46		13 09				13 44	
Coleshill Parkway	d												11 59					13 01		13 25				13 59	
Water Orton	d																								
Birmingham New Street 12	a					10 09			11 09				12 15	12 13		12 23	13 09	13 15	13 21	13 38			14 11	14 16	
	d			09 12		10 12	10 30		11 12			11 30		12 16		12 30	13 12		13 30				14 12		
Worcester Shrub Hill 7	d																								14 36
Ashchurch for Tewkesbury	d																								14 52
Cheltenham Spa	d	09 24	09 45	09 52	10 24	10 57	11 11	11 24	11 52	12 00		12 11		12 57	13 01	13 11	13 52		14 12			14 46	14 52		15 01
Gloucester 7	a	09 34	09 55		10 34		11 21	11 34		12 10		12 21			13 11	13 21			14 22			14 56			15 10
Bristol Parkway 7	a		10 37	10 23		11 28			12 23	12 52				13 29			14 23						15 23		15 51
Bristol Temple Meads 10	a																								
Newport (South Wales)	a																		15 14						
Cardiff Central 7	a																								

		XC	XC	XC	GW	XC		XC	XC	XC	XC	AW	GW	XC	XC	GW		XC	XC	XC	GW	XC	XC	XC	XC
		◇1	◇1	◇1	◇1	◇1		1	◇1	◇1	◇1			◇1	1			◇1	◇1	◇1	◇1	◇1	1	◇1	◇1
		G	H	E	I	F			G	J	E		A	F				K	L	E	I	M		G	L
		🛒	🛒	🛒	☕	🛒			🛒	🛒	🛒			🛒				🛒	🛒	🛒	☕	🛒		🛒	🛒
Nottingham 8	d	13 06							14 10									15 05						16 05	
Beeston	d																								
Attenborough	d																								
Long Eaton	d																								
Derby 6	a	13 30							14 28									15 31						16 28	
	d	13 36	13 53			14 30			14 35	14 54				15 31				15 35	15 54			16 29		16 35	16 55
Willington	d																								
Burton-on-Trent	d	13 48							14 48					15 43				15 48						16 48	
Tamworth	d	14 00				14 50			15 00									16 00				16 48		17 00	
Wilnecote	d																	16 04							
Leicester	d			13 49				14 19			14 48				15 19					15 49			16 19		
South Wigston	d							14 24															16 24		
Narborough	d							14 29							15 28								16 29		
Hinckley	d							14 38							15 37								16 38		
Nuneaton	d			14 09				14 46			15 09				15 45					16 09			16 46		
Coleshill Parkway	d			14 25				15 01			15 25				15 59					16 25			17 01		
Water Orton	d																								
Birmingham New Street 12	a	14 22	14 27	14 37		15 09		15 15	15 21	15 27	15 39			16 04	16 15			16 23	16 27	16 39		17 08	17 15	17 21	17 28
	d	14 30				15 12			15 30					16 12				16 30				17 12		17 30	
Worcester Shrub Hill 7	d															16 40									
Ashchurch for Tewkesbury	d															16 58									
Cheltenham Spa	d	15 11			15 46	15 52			16 11			16 18	16 33	16 53		17 08		17 11			17 46	17 53		18 11	
Gloucester 7	a	15 21			15 56				16 21			16 29	16 43			17 16		17 21			17 56			18 22	
Bristol Parkway 7	a					16 23								17 25		17 57						18 23			
Bristol Temple Meads 10	a																								
Newport (South Wales)	a	16 06							17 06			17 37						18 07						19 07	
Cardiff Central 7	a	16 26							17 27			17 55						18 29						19 27	

A To Swindon
B From Leeds
C From York
D From Newcastle
E From Stansted Airport
F From Edinburgh
G 🛒 to Gloucester
H To Reading
I To London Paddington
J From Sheffield to Reading
K 🛒 to Wilnecote
L From Newcastle to Reading
M From Glasgow Central

Table 57

Sundays

18 September to 23 October

Nottingham, Derby and Leicester Birmingham - Cardiff and Bristol

		XC		AW	XC	XC	GW	XC	XC	XC	GW	XC		XC	XC	XC	XC	AW	XC	XC	XC	XC		XC	GW
		◇1			◇1	1		◇1	◇1	◇1	◇1	◇1		1	◇1	◇1	◇1		◇1	1	◇1	◇1		◇1	
		A			B			C	D	A	E	F			G	H	A		B			I		A	
		⊤			⊤			⊤	⊤		⊡	⊤			⊤	⊤			⊤		⊤	⊤			
Nottingham 8	d							17 10							18 05						19 09				
Beeston	d																								
Attenborough	d																								
Long Eaton	d																								
Derby 6	a							17 30							18 31						19 29				
	d				17 28			17 36	17 55			18 26			18 35	18 55			19 28		19 33	19 55			
Willington	d																								
Burton-on-Trent	d				17 39			17 48							18 48				19 39		19 48				
Tamworth	d							18 00				18 47			19 00						20 00				
Wilnecote	d																				20 04				
Leicester	d	16 48				17 16				17 47				18 16			18 49			19 19				19 49	
South Wigston	d					17 23														19 24					
Narborough	d					17 28								18 25						19 29					
Hinckley	d					17 36								18 33						19 38					
Nuneaton	d	17 12				17 44				18 09				18 41			19 09			19 45				20 09	
Coleshill Parkway	d	17 28				17 59				18 25				18 57			19 25			20 01				20 25	
Water Orton	d																								
Birmingham New Street 12	a	17 40			18 05	18 15		18 21	18 27	18 39		19 06		19 15	19 21	19 28	19 37		20 04	20 15	20 23	20 27		20 39	
	d				18 12			18 30				19 12			19 30				20 12						
Worcester Shrub Hill 7	d						18 40																		20 37
Ashchurch for Tewkesbury	d						18 56																		20 53
Cheltenham Spa	d			18 35	18 52		19 07	19 13			19 46	19 52			20 11			20 18	20 52						21 03
Gloucester 7	a			18 46			19 16	19 26			19 56				20 21			20 29							21 13
Bristol Parkway 7	a				19 23		19 57					20 23							21 23						21 53
Bristol Temple Meads 10	a																								
Newport (South Wales)	a			19 54				20 11							21 06			21 31							
Cardiff Central 7	a			20 12				20 31							21 26			21 49							

		XC	XC	GW	XC	XC	XC	XC		GW	XC	XC	XC	XC	XC	XC	XC
		◇1	1		◇1	◇1	◇1	◇1			◇1	1	◇1	◇1	◇1	◇1	1
		J		K	L		M	A			N			M	A	B	
					⊤		⊤							⊤			
Nottingham 8	d					20 10							21 08				
Beeston	d																
Attenborough	d																
Long Eaton	d																
Derby 6	a					20 29							21 31				
	d				20 27	20 35	20 54				21 27		21 35	21 53		22 27	
Willington	d																
Burton-on-Trent	d					20 48					21 38		21 48	22 04		22 38	
Tamworth	d				20 47	21 00					21 49		22 00	22 15		22 49	
Wilnecote	d												22 04				
Leicester	d		20 08					20 49				21 19			21 49		23 19
South Wigston	d		20 15									21 25					23 25
Narborough	d		20 20									21 29					23 29
Hinckley	d		20 29									21 38					23 38
Nuneaton	d		20 36					21 09				21 46			22 09		23 46
Coleshill Parkway	d		20 52					21 25				22 01			22 25		00 02
Water Orton	d																
Birmingham New Street 12	a		21 06		21 04	21 18	21 35	21 37			22 08	22 18	22 23	22 34	22 38	23 07	00 14
	d	20 42			21 12						22 12						
Worcester Shrub Hill 7	d																
Ashchurch for Tewkesbury	d																
Cheltenham Spa	d	21 25		21 46	21 52					22 01	22 52						
Gloucester 7	a			21 56	22 01					22 12							
Bristol Parkway 7	a	21 58															
Bristol Temple Meads 10	a				23 20						00 13						
Newport (South Wales)	a																
Cardiff Central 7	a																

A From Stansted Airport
B From Glasgow Central
C ⊤ to Gloucester
D From Edinburgh to Reading
E To London Paddington
F From Aberdeen
G ⊤ to Tamworth
H From Newcastle to Reading
I From Newcastle to Guildford
J From Manchester Piccadilly
K To Swindon
L From Glasgow Central. ⊤ to Tamworth
M From Newcastle
N From Edinburgh

Table 57

Sundays
from 30 October

Nottingham, Derby and Leicester
Birmingham - Cardiff and Bristol

		GW	XC	GW	GW	XC	XC	GW	XC	GW		XC	AW	XC	XC	GW	XC	XC	XC	XC		XC	AW	XC	GW
			◇[1]			◇[1]	◇[1]		◇[1]			◇[1]		◇[1]	[1]		◇[1]	◇[1]	[1]	◇[1]		◇[1]		◇[1]	
		A	B	C	A	D		A	D					E		A	F	G		F		H			A
			🛒			🛒			🛒			🛒		🛒			🛒	🛒		🛒		🛒		🛒	
Nottingham [8] 🚌	d																11 10			12 10					
Beeston	d																								
Attenborough	d																								
Long Eaton	d																								
Derby [6]	a																11 34			12 30					
	d					09 28			10 33					11 30			11 36	12 30		12 36					
Willington	d																								
Burton-on-Trent	d													11 42			11 48			12 48					
Tamworth	d					09 48											12 00	12 49		13 00					
Wilnecote	d																								
Leicester	d														11 19				12 19			12 49			
South Wigston	d																		12 24						
Narborough	d														11 28				12 29						
Hinckley	d														11 36				12 38						
Nuneaton	d														11 44				12 46			13 09			
Coleshill Parkway	d														11 59				13 01			13 25			
Water Orton	d																								
Birmingham New Street [12]	a					10 09			11 08					12 07	12 15		12 26	13 07	13 15	13 21		13 38			
	d		09 12			10 12	10 30		11 12			11 30		12 12			12 30	13 12		13 30				13 42	
Worcester Shrub Hill [7]	d																								
Ashchurch for Tewkesbury	d																								
Cheltenham Spa	d	09 24	09 52	10 05	10 24	10 57	11 11	11 24	11 52	12 00		12 11	12 18	12 52		13 01	13 11	13 52		14 12			14 18	14 24	14 46
Gloucester [7]	a	09 34		10 15	10 34		11 21	11 34		12 10		12 21	12 28			13 11	13 21			14 22			14 29		14 56
Bristol Parkway [7]	a		10 23	10 55		11 28			12 23	12 51				13 23				14 23						14 56	
Bristol Temple Meads [10]	a		10 35	11 08		11 41			12 36	13 10				13 35				14 39						15 08	
Newport (South Wales)	a						12 06					13 06	13 33				14 06			15 08			15 31		
Cardiff Central [7]	a						12 26					13 26	13 52				14 26			15 31			15 51		

		XC	XC	GW	XC	XC		XC	XC	GW	XC	XC	XC	XC	XC	AW		XC	GW	XC	XC	GW	XC	XC	XC
		◇[1]	[1]		◇[1]	◇[1]		◇[1]	◇[1]		◇[1]	[1]	◇[1]	◇[1]	◇[1]			◇[1]		◇[1]	[1]		◇[1]	◇[1]	◇[1]
		I		J	F	K		H	L	A	M		F	N	H			O	A	I				P	H
		🛒			🛒	🛒		🛒	🛒		🛒		🛒	🛒	🛒			🛒		🛒			🛒	🛒	🛒
Nottingham [8] 🚌	d				13 06								14 10										15 05		
Beeston	d																								
Attenborough	d																								
Long Eaton	d																								
Derby [6]	a				13 30								14 28										15 31		
	d	13 32			13 36	13 53					14 30		14 35	14 54						15 28			15 35	15 54	
Willington	d																								
Burton-on-Trent	d	13 43			13 48								14 48							15 39			15 48		
Tamworth	d				14 00						14 50		15 00										16 00		
Wilnecote	d																						16 04		
Leicester	d		13 19					13 49				14 19			14 48						15 19				15 49
South Wigston	d											14 24													
Narborough	d		13 28									14 29									15 28				
Hinckley	d		13 36									14 38									15 37				
Nuneaton	d		13 44					14 09				14 46			15 09						15 45				16 09
Coleshill Parkway	d		13 59					14 25				15 01			15 25						15 59				16 25
Water Orton	d																								
Birmingham New Street [12]	a	14 10	14 16		14 22	14 27		14 37			15 07	15 15	15 21	15 27	15 39					16 03	16 15		16 23	16 27	16 39
	d	14 12			14 30				14 42		15 12		15 30					15 42		16 12			16 30		
Worcester Shrub Hill [7]	d			14 36																		16 40			
Ashchurch for Tewkesbury	d			14 52																		16 58			
Cheltenham Spa	d	14 52		15 01	15 11				15 25	15 46	15 52		16 11			16 18		16 25	16 33	16 52		17 08	17 11		
Gloucester [7]	a			15 10	15 21					15 57			16 21			16 29			16 43			17 16	17 21		
Bristol Parkway [7]	a	15 25		15 49					15 59		16 23							16 57		17 23		17 57			
Bristol Temple Meads [10]	a	15 38		16 09					16 11		16 35							17 09		17 35		18 10			
Newport (South Wales)	a				16 06								17 06			17 37							18 07		
Cardiff Central [7]	a				16 26								17 27			17 55							18 29		

A To Swindon
B To Penzance
C To Taunton
D From Leeds to Plymouth
E From York to Plymouth
F 🛒 to Gloucester
G From Newcastle to Plymouth
H From Stansted Airport
I From Edinburgh to Plymouth
J To Weston-super-Mare
K To Reading
L From Manchester Piccadilly to Paignton
M From Edinburgh to Penzance
N From Sheffield to Reading
O From Manchester Piccadilly
P From Newcastle to Reading

Nottingham, Derby and Leicester Birmingham - Cardiff and Bristol

		XC ◇1 A 🛒		GW B	XC ◇1 C 🛒	XC 1	XC ◇1 D 🛒	XC ◇1 E 🛒	XC ◇1 A 🛒	AW	XC ◇1 F 🛒	XC 1		GW	XC ◇1 D 🛒	XC ◇1 G 🛒	XC ◇1 E	XC ◇1 H 🛒	XC 1	GW B	XC ◇1 I 🛒	XC ◇1 J 🛒		XC ◇1 E	AW
Nottingham 8	d						16 05								17 10						18 05				
Beeston	d																								
Attenborough	d																								
Long Eaton	d																								
Derby 6	a						16 28								17 30						18 31				
	d				16 29		16 35				17 28				17 36	17 55		18 26			18 35	18 55			
Willington	d																								
Burton-on-Trent	d						16 48				17 39				17 48						18 48				
Tamworth	d				16 48		17 00								18 00			18 47			19 00				
Wilnecote	d																								
Leicester	d					16 19		16 48				17 16					17 47		18 16					18 49	
South Wigston	d					16 24						17 23													
Narborough	d					16 29						17 28							18 25						
Hinckley	d					16 38						17 36							18 33						
Nuneaton	d					16 46		17 12				17 44					18 09		18 41					19 09	
Coleshill Parkway	d					17 01		17 28				17 59					18 25		18 57					19 25	
Water Orton	d																								
Birmingham New Street 12	a				17 06	17 15	17 21	17 40			18 03	18 15			18 21	18 27	18 39	19 04	19 15		19 21	19 28		19 37	
	d	16 42			17 12		17 30		17 42		18 12				18 30			19 12			19 30				
Worcester Shrub Hill 7	d													18 40											
Ashchurch for Tewkesbury	d													18 56											
Cheltenham Spa	d	17 25		17 46	17 52		18 11		18 25	18 35	18 52			19 07	19 13			19 52		20 05	20 11				20 18
Gloucester 7	a			17 57			18 22			18 46				19 16	19 26					20 14	20 21				20 29
Bristol Parkway 7	a	18 02			18 23				18 57		19 23			19 56				20 23							
Bristol Temple Meads 10	a	18 14			18 40				19 09		19 35			20 10				20 35							
Newport (South Wales)	a						19 07			19 54					20 11						21 06				21 31
Cardiff Central 7	a						19 27			20 12					20 31						21 26				21 49

		XC ◇1 A 🛒	XC ◇1 K 🛒	XC 1	XC ◇1 🛒	XC ◇1 L 🛒	XC ◇1 E	GW		XC ◇1 A	XC 1	GW B	XC ◇1 M 🛒	XC ◇1	XC ◇1 N 🛒	XC ◇1 E	GW	XC ◇1 A	XC ◇1 O	XC 1	XC ◇1	XC ◇1 N 🛒	XC ◇1 E	XC ◇1 P	XC 1
Nottingham 8	d				19 09									20 10							21 08				
Beeston	d																								
Attenborough	d																								
Long Eaton	d																								
Derby 6	a				19 29									20 29							21 31				
	d		19 28		19 33	19 55							20 27	20 35	20 54				21 27		21 35	21 53		22 27	
Willington	d																								
Burton-on-Trent	d		19 39		19 48									20 48					21 38		21 48	22 04		22 38	
Tamworth	d				20 00								20 47	21 00					21 49		22 00	22 15		22 49	
Wilnecote	d				20 04																22 04				
Leicester	d			19 19			19 49				20 08					20 49				21 19			21 49		23 19
South Wigston	d			19 24							20 15									21 25					23 25
Narborough	d			19 29							20 20									21 29					23 29
Hinckley	d			19 38							20 29									21 38					23 38
Nuneaton	d			19 45			20 09				20 36					21 09				21 46			22 09		23 46
Coleshill Parkway	d			20 01			20 25				20 52					21 25				22 01			22 25		00 02
Water Orton	d																								
Birmingham New Street 12	a		20 03	20 15	20 23	20 27	20 39				21 06		21 04	21 18	21 35	21 37			22 06	22 18	22 23	22 34	22 38	23 07	00 14
	d	19 42	20 12							20 42			21 12					21 42	22 12						
Worcester Shrub Hill 7	d							20 37																	
Ashchurch for Tewkesbury	d							20 53																	
Cheltenham Spa	d	20 25	20 52					21 03		21 25		21 46	21 52				22 01	22 25	22 52						
Gloucester 7	a							21 13				21 56	22 01				22 12								
Bristol Parkway 7	a	20 57	21 23					21 53		21 59			22 35					22 56	23 24						
Bristol Temple Meads 10	a	21 09	21 35					22 07		22 11			22 47					23 10	23 36						
Newport (South Wales)	a																								
Cardiff Central 7	a																								

A From Manchester Piccadilly
B To Swindon
C From Glasgow Central to Penzance
D 🛒 to Gloucester
E From Stansted Airport
F From Glasgow Central to Plymouth
G From Edinburgh to Reading
H From Aberdeen to Plymouth. 🛒 to Bristol Parkway
I 🛒 to Tamworth
J From Newcastle to Reading
K From Glasgow Central to Plymouth. 🛒 to Bristol Parkway
L From Newcastle to Guildford
M From Glasgow Central. 🛒 to Tamworth
N From Newcastle
O From Edinburgh
P From Glasgow Central

Table 57

Mondays to Fridays

Bristol and Cardiff - Birmingham Leicester, Derby and Nottingham

Miles	Miles	Miles	Station		XC MX ◇1	XC MX ◇1	XC MO ◇1 A	XC ◇1 B	XC 1	XC ◇1 C 🛒	GW	XC 1 🛒	XC ◇1 B 🛒	XC ◇1 D 🛒	XC 1	XC 1	XC ◇1 E 🛒	XC 1 🛒	XC ◇1 B 🛒	XC ◇1 D 🛒	XC 1	XC 1	XC ◇1 F 🛒
0	—	—	**Cardiff Central 7**	d		21p50																	
11¾	—	—	Newport (South Wales)	d		22p05																	
—	—	0	**Bristol Temple Meads 10**	d			22p10																06 27
—	—	5¾	Bristol Parkway 7	d			22p24																06 40
56½	—	—	Gloucester 7	d		22p47	23p21				06 01												
63	—	46¼	Cheltenham Spa	d		22p58	23p29				06 11												07 12
70¼	—	53½	Ashchurch for Tewkesbury	d							06 20												
85	—	—	Worcester Shrub Hill 7	a							06 40												
112	0	92¾	**Birmingham New Street 12**	a		00 04	00 16																07 56
—	—	—		d	23p09			05 22	05 52	06 00		06 19	06 22	06 30	06 49	06 52	07 03	07 19	07 22	07 30	07 49	07 52	08 03
119¾	7¾	—	Water Orton	d																			
—	9½	—	Coleshill Parkway	d				05 35	06 05				06 35			07 05			07 35			08 05	
—	20	—	Nuneaton	d				05 51	06 21				06 51			07 21			07 51			08 21	
—	25¼	—	Hinckley	d					06 28							07 29			07 57			08 29	
—	34	—	Narborough	d					06 36							07 37			08 05			08 37	
—	37	—	South Wigston	d					06 41							07 42			08 10			08 42	
—	38¾	—	**Leicester**	a				06 12	06 49				07 15			07 48			08 15			08 48	
127	—	—	Wilnecote	d	23p24							06 34						07 34					
128¾	—	—	Tamworth	d	23p28							06 39			07 06		07 19	07 38			08 06		08 19
141¾	—	—	Burton-on-Trent	d	23p39							06 51			07 18		07 29	07 49			08 18		08 29
146½	—	—	Willington	d	23p45													07 56					
152¾	—	—	**Derby 6**	a	23p55					06 33		07 05		07 11	07 34		07 42	08 05		08 11	08 34		08 42
—	—	—		d	23p59							07 10			07 40			08 10			08 40		
161	—	—	Long Eaton	d								07 25			07 49			08 19					
164	—	—	Attenborough	d								07 31											
165½	—	—	Beeston	d								07 35			07 58			08 27					
168¾	—	—	**Nottingham 6** ⛴	a	00 18							07 41			08 08			08 33			09 05		

Station		XC ◇1 G 🛒	GW H	XC 1 🛒	XC ◇1 I 🛒	XC ◇1 J 🛒	XC ◇1	XC 1	XC ◇1 K 🛒	XC 1 🛒	XC ◇1 B 🛒	XC ◇1 L 🛒	XC ◇1 M 🛒	XC ◇1 N 🛒	XC 1	XC ◇1 O 🛒	XC 1	XC ◇1 B 🛒	XC ◇1 P 🛒	GW Q	XC ◇1 R 🛒	XC ◇1 N 🛒	XC 1
Cardiff Central 7	d						06 40					07 00		07 45								08 45	
Newport (South Wales)	d						06 55					07 15		08 02								09 02	
Bristol Temple Meads 10	d				07 00				07 30			08 00				08 30			09 00	08 41			
Bristol Parkway 7	d				07 10				07 40			08 10				08 40			09 10	08 52			
Gloucester 7	d	07 10	07 15				07 46							08 46						09 38		09 46	
Cheltenham Spa	d	07 21	07 25		07 42		07 57		08 12			08 42		08 57		09 12			09 42	09 48		09 57	
Ashchurch for Tewkesbury	d	07 29	07 34				08 05													09 56			
Worcester Shrub Hill 7	a		07 54																	10 14			
Birmingham New Street 12	a	08 16			08 26		08 45		08 56			09 26		09 45		09 56			10 26			10 45	
	d	08 22		08 19		08 30	08 49	08 52	09 03	09 19	09 22		09 30	09 49	09 52	10 03	10 19	10 22			10 30	10 49	10 52
Water Orton	d							09 03															11 03
Coleshill Parkway	d	08 35						09 07			09 35				10 07			10 35					11 07
Nuneaton	d	08 51						09 22			09 52				10 23			10 52					11 23
Hinckley	d							09 30							10 30								11 30
Narborough	d							09 39							10 38								11 39
South Wigston	d														10 43								
Leicester	a	09 16						09 49			10 15				10 49			11 14					11 48
Wilnecote	d									09 34													
Tamworth	d			08 36			09 06			09 39				10 06		10 19	10 36					11 06	
Burton-on-Trent	d			08 48			09 19		09 25	09 51				10 19			10 48					11 19	
Willington	d			08 54													10 54						
Derby 6	a			09 05		09 11	09 34		09 39	10 05			10 09	10 34		10 40	11 05				11 08	11 34	
	d			09 10			09 40			10 10				10 40			11 10					11 40	
Long Eaton	d			09 19						10 19							11 19						
Attenborough	d			09 26																			
Beeston	d			09 29						10 27							11 27						
Nottingham 6 ⛴	a			09 35			10 05			10 33				11 05			11 33					12 05	

A From 27 June until 1 August
B To Stansted Airport
C To Glasgow Central
D To Newcastle
E To Edinburgh
F From Bath Spa to Glasgow Central
G To Stansted Airport. 🛒 from Birmingham New Street
H To Great Malvern
I To Manchester Piccadilly
J From Guildford to Newcastle
K From Plymouth to Edinburgh
L To Manchester Piccadilly. 🛒 from Bristol Temple Meads
M From Reading to Newcastle
N 🛒 from Newport (South Wales)
O From Plymouth to Glasgow Central
P From Paignton to Manchester Piccadilly
Q From Warminster to Great Malvern
R From Winchester to Newcastle

Bristol and Cardiff - Birmingham Leicester, Derby and Nottingham

Station		XC ◇1 A	XC 1	XC ◇1 B	XC ◇1 C		XC ◇1 D	XC ◇1 E	XC 1	XC ◇1 F	XC 1	XC ◇1 B	XC ◇1 C	GW ◇ G	XC ◇1 H		XC ◇1 E	XC 1	XC ◇1 I	XC 1	XC ◇1 B	XC ◇1 J	XC ◇1 D	XC ◇1 E	XC 1
Cardiff Central 7	d							09 45									10 45							11 45	
Newport (South Wales)	d							10 00									11 00							12 02	
Bristol Temple Meads 10	d	09 30			10 00					10 30			11 00	10 41					11 30			12 00			
Bristol Parkway 7	d	09 40			10 10					10 40			11 10	10 52					11 40			12 10			
Gloucester 7	d							10 46						11 36			11 46							12 46	
Cheltenham Spa	d	10 12			10 42			10 57		11 12			11 42	11 48			11 57		12 12			12 42		12 57	
Ashchurch for Tewkesbury	d													11 56										13 05	
Worcester Shrub Hill 7	a													12 14											
Birmingham New Street 12	a	10 56			11 26			11 45		11 58			12 26				12 45		12 56			13 26		13 45	
	d	11 03	11 19	11 22			11 30	11 49	11 52	12 03	12 19	12 22			12 30		12 49	12 52	13 03	13 19	13 22		13 30	13 49	13 52
Water Orton	d																	13 03							
Coleshill Parkway	d			11 35					12 07			12 35						13 07			13 35				14 07
Nuneaton	d			11 51					12 23			12 51						13 23			13 51				14 23
Hinckley	d								12 30									13 30							14 30
Narborough	d								12 38									13 39							14 38
South Wigston	d								12 43																14 43
Leicester	a			12 15					12 49			13 15						13 50			14 14				14 49
Wilnecote	d		11 34																	13 34					
Tamworth	d		11 39					12 06		12 19	12 36						13 06			13 39				14 06	
Burton-on-Trent	d	11 25	11 51					12 19			12 49						13 19		13 28	13 51				14 19	
Willington	d										12 56														
Derby 6	a	11 39	12 05				12 07	12 34		12 41	13 05				13 09		13 34		13 40	14 05			14 08	14 34	
	d		12 10					12 40			13 10						13 40			14 10				14 40	
Long Eaton	d		12 19								13 19									14 19					
Attenborough	d																								
Beeston	d		12 27								13 27									14 27					
Nottingham 8 ⛴	a		12 33					13 05			13 33						14 05			14 33				15 05	

Station			XC ◇1 F	XC 1	XC ◇1 B	XC ◇1 C	GW ◇ K	XC ◇1 H	XC ◇1 E	XC 1	XC ◇1 L		XC 1	XC ◇1 B	XC ◇1 M	XC ◇1 D	XC ◇1 E	XC 1	XC ◇1 N	XC 1	XC 1		XC ◇1 B	XC ◇1 C	GW ◇ G
Cardiff Central 7	d								12 45								13 45								
Newport (South Wales)	d								13 01								14 00								
Bristol Temple Meads 10	d		12 30			13 00	12 41				13 30				14 00				14 30					15 00	14 41
Bristol Parkway 7	d		12 40			13 10	12 52				13 40				14 10				14 40					15 10	14 52
Gloucester 7	d						13 38		13 46								14 46								15 37
Cheltenham Spa	d		13 12			13 42	13 48		13 57		14 12				14 42		14 57		15 12					15 42	15 48
Ashchurch for Tewkesbury	d						13 56																		15 56
Worcester Shrub Hill 7	a						14 14																		16 15
Birmingham New Street 12	a		13 56			14 26			14 45		14 56				15 26		15 45		15 56					16 26	
	d		14 03	14 19	14 22			14 30	14 49	14 52	15 03		15 19	15 22		15 30	15 49	15 52	16 03	16 09	16 19		16 22		
Water Orton	d									15 03										16 19					
Coleshill Parkway	d				14 35					15 07				15 34				16 07		16 23			16 34		
Nuneaton	d				14 51					15 23				15 52				16 23		16 39			16 52		
Hinckley	d									15 30								16 30		16 46					
Narborough	d									15 39								16 39		16 55					
South Wigston	d																	16 43							
Leicester	a				15 15					15 48				16 15				16 50		17 06			17 15		
Wilnecote	d			14 34									15 34								16 34				
Tamworth	d		14 19	14 39					15 06				15 39				16 06		16 19		16 39				
Burton-on-Trent	d			14 51					15 19		15 26		15 51				16 19				16 51				
Willington	d																								
Derby 6	a		14 42	15 05				15 08	15 34		15 39		16 05			16 08	16 34		16 41		17 05				
	d			15 10					15 40				16 10				16 40				17 10				
Long Eaton	d			15 19									16 19								17 19				
Attenborough	d																								
Beeston	d			15 27									16 27								17 27				
Nottingham 8 ⛴	a			15 33					16 05				16 33				17 05				17 33				

A From Plymouth to Edinburgh
B To Stansted Airport
C To Manchester Piccadilly
D From Reading to Newcastle
E trolley service from Newport (South Wales)
F From Penzance to Glasgow Central
G From Southampton Central to Great Malvern
H From Southampton Central to Newcastle
I From Plymouth to Aberdeen
J From Paignton to Manchester Piccadilly
K From Brighton to Great Malvern
L From Plymouth to Dundee
M From Penzance to Manchester Piccadilly
N From Plymouth to Glasgow Central

Table 57

Bristol and Cardiff - Birmingham Leicester, Derby and Nottingham

		XC	XC	XC	XC	XC	XC		XC	XC	XC	XC	XC	XC	XC	XC	XC		XC	GW	XC	XC	XC	XC	XC
		◇1	◇1	◇1	◇1	1	1		◇1	◇1	◇1	1	◇1	1	◇1	1	◇1		◇1		◇1	◇1	1	◇1	1
		A	B	C	D				E	F	G				D		E		H	I	J			K	
		trolley	trolley		trolley					trolley	trolley				trolley				trolley		trolley			trolley	
Cardiff Central 7	d		14 45										15 45									16 45			
Newport (South Wales)	d		15 01										16 00									17 00			
Bristol Temple Meads 10	d				15 30					16 00					16 30				17 00	16 41				17 30	
Bristol Parkway 7	d				15 40					16 10					16 40				17 10	16 52				17 40	
Gloucester 7	d		15 46										16 46							17 38		17 46			
Cheltenham Spa	d		15 57		16 12					16 42			16 57		17 12				17 42	17 48		17 58		18 12	
Ashchurch for Tewkesbury	d																			17 56					
Worcester Shrub Hill 7	a																			18 19					
Birmingham New Street 12	a		16 45		16 58					17 26			17 45		17 56				18 26			18 45		18 55	
	d	16 30	16 49	16 52	17 03	17 09	17 19		17 22		17 30	17 39	17 49	17 52	18 03	18 19	18 22				18 30	18 49	18 52	19 03	19 19
Water Orton	d					17 23						17 50		18 03											
Coleshill Parkway	d			17 05		17 27			17 34					18 07			18 34						19 07		
Nuneaton	d			17 21		17 44			17 52					18 23			18 52						19 23		
Hinckley	d			17 28		17 51								18 30									19 30		
Narborough	d			17 38										18 39									19 38		
South Wigston	d					18 03								18 44									19 43		
Leicester	a			17 51		18 09			18 15					18 50			19 15						19 49		
Wilnecote	d						17 34									18 34									19 34
Tamworth	d		17 06				17 39					18 00	18 06		18 19	18 39						19 06			19 39
Burton-on-Trent	d		17 19		17 26		17 51					18 12	18 19			18 51						19 19		19 26	19 51
Willington	d											18 18													
Derby 6	a	17 09	17 34		17 40		18 05				18 08	18 30	18 34		18 42	19 05					19 08	19 34		19 39	20 05
	d		17 40				18 10						18 40			19 10						19 40			20 10
Long Eaton	d						18 19									19 19									20 19
Attenborough	d																								
Beeston	d						18 27									19 26									20 27
Nottingham 8 (tram)	a		18 05				18 33						19 05			19 33						20 03			20 33

		XC	XC	XC	XC	XC	XC	XC	XC	GW	XC	XC	XC	XC	XC	XC	XC	XC	GW	GW	XC	XC	XC	XC	XC
		◇1	◇1	◇1	◇1	1	◇1	◇1	◇1		◇1	◇1	◇1	1	◇1	◇1	◇1	◇1		◇1	1	◇1	◇1	◇1	◇1
		E	L	G	M		N	C	O	I	P		N					Q		R				A	
			trolley	trolley	trolley		trolley		trolley				trolley							restaurant					
Cardiff Central 7	d				17 45							18 45				19 50							21 05		21 50
Newport (South Wales)	d				18 00							19 01				20 05							21 21		22 05
Bristol Temple Meads 10	d		18 00				18 30		19 00	18 41			19 30		20 00			20 30	20 41					22 00	
Bristol Parkway 7	d		18 10				18 40		19 10	18 52			19 40		20 10			20 40	20 52					22 10	
Gloucester 7	d				18 46					19 38		19 46			20 46	20 58			21 35	21 53			22 04		22 47
Cheltenham Spa	d		18 42		18 57		19 12		19 42	19 48		19 58	20 12		20 56	21 09		21 17	21 46	22 04			22 15	22 42	22 58
Ashchurch for Tewkesbury	d									19 56		20 05							21 55				22 23		
Worcester Shrub Hill 7	a									20 15									22 15	22 24					
Birmingham New Street 12	a		19 26		19 45		19 56		20 28			20 45	20 52		21 46	21 52		22 09					23 36	23 44	00 04
	d	19 22		19 30	19 49	19 52	20 03	20 22			20 30	20 49	21 03	20 52			22 03				22 22	23 09			
Water Orton	d					20 03																			
Coleshill Parkway	d	19 35				20 07		20 35						21 05							22 37				
Nuneaton	d	19 52				20 23		20 51						21 21							22 53				
Hinckley	d					20 30								21 29							23 01				
Narborough	d					20 39								21 37							23 09				
South Wigston	d					20 44								21 42							23 14				
Leicester	a	20 16				20 50		21 15						21 48							23 20				
Wilnecote	d											21 04										23 24			
Tamworth	d				20 06		20 19					21 08	21 20				22 28					23 28			
Burton-on-Trent	d				20 19							21 20	21 31				22 39					23 39			
Willington	d																					23 45			
Derby 6	a			20 08	20 34		20 42				21 11	21 34	21 44				22 54					23 55			
	d				20 40							21 40					22 59					23 59			
Long Eaton	d				20 49							21 52					23 11								
Attenborough	d											21 58					23 17								
Beeston	d				20 58							22 02					23 20								
Nottingham 8 (tram)	a				21 05							22 08					23 27					00 18			

- **A** From Southampton Central to Edinburgh
- **B** trolley from Newport (South Wales)
- **C** To Cambridge
- **D** From Plymouth to Edinburgh
- **E** To Stansted Airport
- **F** From Paignton to Manchester Piccadilly
- **G** From Reading to Newcastle
- **H** To Manchester Piccadilly
- **I** From Warminster to Great Malvern
- **J** From Southampton Central to Newcastle
- **K** From Plymouth to Leeds
- **L** From Exeter St Davids to Manchester Piccadilly
- **M** trolley from Newport (South Wales) to Cheltenham Spa
- **N** From Plymouth to Leeds. trolley to Cheltenham Spa
- **O** To Manchester Piccadilly. trolley to Cheltenham Spa
- **P** From Southampton Central to York
- **Q** From Plymouth
- **R** From London Paddington
- **A** From Paignton

Table 57

Saturdays

Bristol and Cardiff - Birmingham Leicester, Derby and Nottingham

		XC	XC	XC	GW	XC	XC	XC	XC	XC		XC	XC	XC	XC	XC	XC	XC	XC	XC		XC	GW	XC	XC
		◇[1]	◇[1]	◇[1]		[1]	◇[1]	[1]	◇[1]	◇[1]		[1]	[1]	◇[1]	[1]	◇[1]	◇[1]	[1]	[1]	◇[1]		◇[1]		[1]	◇[1]
				B			C		B	D				E		B	D			C		F			G
							[trolley]	[trolley]	[trolley]	[trolley]				[trolley]	[trolley]	[trolley]	[trolley]			[trolley]		[trolley]		[trolley]	[trolley]
Cardiff Central [7]	d		21p50																						
Newport (South Wales)	d		22p05																						
Bristol Temple Meads [10]	d																			06 15					07 00
Bristol Parkway [7]	d																			06 25					07 10
Gloucester [7]	d		22p47		05 50															07 01		07 07	07 15		
Cheltenham Spa	d		22p58		06 00															07 12		07 18	07 25		07 42
Ashchurch for Tewkesbury	d				06 09																	07 25	07 34		
Worcester Shrub Hill [7]	a				06 33																		07 52		
Birmingham New Street [12]	a		00 04																	07 56		08 08			08 26
	d	23p09		05 22		05 52	05 56	06 19	06 22	06 30		06 49	06 52	07 03	07 19	07 22	07 30	07 49	07 52	08 03		08 22		08 19	
Water Orton	d												07 02												
Coleshill Parkway	d			05 35		06 04			06 35				07 06			07 35			08 05			08 35			
Nuneaton	d			05 51		06 23			06 51				07 22			07 51			08 21			08 51			
Hinckley	d					06 30							07 29						08 29						
Narborough	d					06 38							07 37						08 37						
South Wigston	d					06 43							07 42						08 42						
Leicester	a			06 13		06 49			07 13				07 48			08 13			08 48			09 13			
Wilnecote	d	23p24						06 34							07 34										
Tamworth	d	23p28					06 12	06 39		06 46		07 06		07 19	07 38		07 46	08 06		08 19				08 36	
Burton-on-Trent	d	23p39					06 22	06 51		06 56		07 18		07 29	07 49		07 56	08 18		08 29				08 48	
Willington	d	23p45													07 54									08 55	
Derby [6]	a	23p55					06 35	07 05		07 09		07 34		07 42	08 05		08 09	08 34		08 42				09 05	
	d	23p59						07 10				07 39			08 10			08 39						09 10	
Long Eaton	d							07 22				07 52			08 19									09 19	
Attenborough	d							07 28																09 26	
Beeston	d							07 32				07 59			08 27									09 29	
Nottingham [8]	a	00 18						07 38				08 08			08 33			09 05						09 35	

B To Stansted Airport
C To Glasgow Central
D To Newcastle
E To Edinburgh
F To Stansted Airport. [trolley] from Birmingham New Street
G To Manchester Piccadilly

Table 57

Saturdays

Bristol and Cardiff - Birmingham Leicester, Derby and Nottingham

		XC	XC	XC	XC	XC		XC	XC	XC	XC	XC	XC	XC	XC	XC		GW	XC	XC	XC	XC	XC	XC	XC
		◇1	◇1	1	◇1	1		◇1	◇1	◇1	◇1	1	◇1	1	◇1	◇1			◇1	◇1	1	◇1	1	◇1	◇1
		A			B			C	D	E	F		G		C	H		I	J	F		B		C	D
		🛒			🛒	🛒		🛒	🛒	🛒	🛒		🛒		🛒	🛒			🛒	🛒		🛒		🛒	🛒
Cardiff Central 7	d		06 40						07 00		07 45									08 45					
Newport (South Wales)	d		06 55						07 15		08 00									09 00					
Bristol Temple Meads 10	d				07 30				08 00				08 30			09 00		08 41				09 30			10 00
Bristol Parkway 7	d				07 40				08 10				08 40			09 10		08 52				09 40			10 10
Gloucester 7	d		07 46								08 47							09 38		09 46					
Cheltenham Spa	d		07 57		08 12				08 42		08 58		09 12			09 42		09 48		09 57		10 12			10 42
Ashchurch for Tewkesbury	d		08 04															09 57							
Worcester Shrub Hill 7	a																	10 14							
Birmingham New Street 12	a		08 45		08 56				09 26		09 45		09 56			10 26				10 45		10 56			11 26
	d	08 30	08 49	08 52	09 03	09 19		09 22		09 30	09 49	09 52	10 03	10 19	10 22				10 30	10 49	10 52	11 03	11 19	11 22	
Water Orton	d			09 03																	11 03				
Coleshill Parkway	d			09 07				09 35				10 07			10 35						11 07			11 35	
Nuneaton	d			09 23				09 51				10 23			10 51						11 23			11 51	
Hinckley	d			09 30								10 30									11 30				
Narborough	d			09 39								10 39									11 39				
South Wigston	d											10 43													
Leicester	a			09 48				10 13				10 49			11 13						11 48			12 13	
Wilnecote	d					09 34																	11 34		
Tamworth	d		09 06			09 39					10 06		10 19	10 36						11 06			11 39		
Burton-on-Trent	d		09 19		09 25	09 50					10 19			10 48						11 19		11 25	11 51		
Willington	d													10 54											
Derby 6	a	09 08	09 34		09 41	10 05				10 08	10 34		10 41	11 05					11 08	11 34		11 41	12 05		
	d		09 40			10 10					10 40			11 10						11 40			12 10		
Long Eaton	d					10 19								11 19									12 19		
Attenborough	d																								
Beeston	d					10 27								11 27									12 27		
Nottingham 8 🚊	a		10 05			10 33					11 05			11 33						12 05			12 33		

		XC		XC	XC	XC	XC	XC	XC	GW	XC	XC		XC	XC	XC	XC	XC	XC	XC	XC	XC		XC	XC
		◇1		◇1	1	◇1	1	◇1	◇1	◇	◇1	◇1		1	◇1	1	◇1	◇1	◇1	◇1	1	◇1		1	◇1
		K		F		L		C	M	N	J	F			O		C	H	K	F		L			C
		🛒		🛒		🛒	🛒	🛒	🛒		🛒	🛒			🛒		🛒	🛒	🛒	🛒		🛒			🛒
Cardiff Central 7	d			09 45								10 45								11 45					
Newport (South Wales)	d			10 00								11 00								12 00					
Bristol Temple Meads 10	d					10 30			11 00	10 41					11 30			12 00				12 30			
Bristol Parkway 7	d					10 40			11 10	10 52					11 40			12 10				12 40			
Gloucester 7	d			10 46						11 38		11 46								12 46					
Cheltenham Spa	d			10 57		11 12			11 42	11 48		11 57			12 12			12 42		12 57		13 12			
Ashchurch for Tewkesbury	d									11 58										13 05					
Worcester Shrub Hill 7	a									12 15															
Birmingham New Street 12	a			11 45		11 56			12 26			12 45			12 56			13 26		13 45		13 56			
	d	11 30		11 49	11 52	12 03	12 19	12 22			12 30	12 49		12 52	13 03	13 19	13 22		13 30	13 49	13 52	14 03		14 19	14 22
Water Orton	d													13 03											
Coleshill Parkway	d				12 07			12 35						13 07			13 35				14 07				14 35
Nuneaton	d				12 23			12 51						13 23			13 51				14 23				14 51
Hinckley	d				12 30									13 30							14 30				
Narborough	d				12 39									13 39							14 39				
South Wigston	d				12 43																14 43				
Leicester	a				12 49			13 13						13 48			14 13				14 49				15 13
Wilnecote	d															13 34								14 34	
Tamworth	d			12 06		12 19	12 36					13 06				13 39				14 06		14 19		14 39	
Burton-on-Trent	d			12 19			12 49					13 19			13 25	13 51				14 19				14 51	
Willington	d						12 56																		
Derby 6	a	12 08		12 35		12 41	13 05				13 08	13 34			13 41	14 05			14 08	14 34		14 41		15 05	
	d			12 40			13 10					13 40				14 10				14 40				15 10	
Long Eaton	d						13 19									14 19								15 19	
Attenborough	d																								
Beeston	d						13 27									14 27								15 27	
Nottingham 8 🚊	a			13 05			13 33					14 05				14 33				15 05				15 33	

A From Guildford to Newcastle
B From Plymouth to Edinburgh
C To Stansted Airport
D To Manchester Piccadilly
E From Bournemouth to Newcastle
F 🛒 from Newport (South Wales)
G From Plymouth to Glasgow Central
H From Paignton to Manchester Piccadilly
I From Warminster to Great Malvern
J From Southampton Central to Newcastle
K From Reading to Newcastle
L From Penzance to Glasgow Central
M From Plymouth to Manchester Piccadilly. 🛒 to Cheltenham Spa
N From Southampton Central to Worcester Foregate Street
O From Plymouth to Aberdeen

Bristol and Cardiff - Birmingham Leicester, Derby and Nottingham

		XC	GW	XC	XC	XC	XC	XC		XC	XC	XC	XC	XC	XC	XC	XC	XC		GW	XC	XC	XC	XC	XC
		◇[1]	◇	◇[1]	◇[1]	[1]	◇[1]	[1]		◇[1]	◇[1]	◇[1]	◇[1]	[1]	◇[1]	[1]	◇[1]	◇[1]		◇	◇[1]	◇[1]	[1]	◇[1]	[1]
		A	B	C	D		E			F	G	H	D		I		F	A		J	C	D		K	
		🍴		🍴	🍴		🍴			🍴	🍴	🍴	🍴		🍴		🍴	🍴			🍴	🍴		🍴	
Cardiff Central [7]	d				12 45								13 45									14 45			
Newport (South Wales)	d				13 00								14 00									15 00			
Bristol Temple Meads [10]	d	13 00	12 41				13 30				14 00				14 30			15 00		14 41				15 30	
Bristol Parkway [7]	d	13 10	12 52				13 40				14 10				14 40			15 10		14 52				15 40	
Gloucester [7]	d		13 38		13 46								14 46							15 38		15 46			
Cheltenham Spa	d	13 42	13 48		13 57		14 12				14 42		14 57		15 12			15 42		15 48		15 57		16 12	
Ashchurch for Tewkesbury	d		13 57																	15 57					
Worcester Shrub Hill [7]	a		14 15																	16 14					
Birmingham New Street [12]	a	14 26			14 45		14 56				15 26		15 45		15 55			16 26				16 45		16 56	
	d			14 30	14 49	14 52	15 03	15 19		15 22		15 30	15 49	15 52	16 03	16 19	16 22				16 30	16 49	16 52	17 03	17 19
Water Orton	d					15 03																	17 03		
Coleshill Parkway	d					15 07				15 35				16 07			16 35						17 07		
Nuneaton	d					15 23				15 51				16 23			16 51						17 23		
Hinckley	d					15 30								16 30									17 30		
Narborough	d					15 39								16 39									17 39		
South Wigston	d													16 43											
Leicester	a					15 48				16 13				16 49			17 13						17 48		
Wilnecote	d							15 34								16 34									17 34
Tamworth	d				15 06			15 39					16 06		16 18	16 39						17 06			17 39
Burton-on-Trent	d				15 19		15 26	15 51					16 19			16 51						17 19		17 26	17 51
Willington	d																								
Derby [6]	a			15 08	15 34		15 41	16 05				16 08	16 34		16 41	17 05					17 08	17 34		17 41	18 05
	d				15 40			16 10					16 40			17 10						17 40			18 10
Long Eaton	d							16 19								17 19									18 19
Attenborough	d																								
Beeston	d							16 27								17 27									18 27
Nottingham [8] 🚋	a				16 05			16 33					17 05			17 33						18 05			18 33

		XC	XC	XC		XC	XC	XC	XC	XC	XC	GW	XC	XC		XC	XC	XC	XC	XC	XC	XC	XC	XC	
		◇[1]	◇[1]	◇[1]		◇[1]	[1]	◇[1]	[1]	◇[1]	◇[1]		◇[1]	◇[1]		[1]	◇[1]	[1]	◇[1]	◇[1]	◇[1]	◇[1]	[1]	◇[1]	
		F	L	H				K		F	A	M	C				N		F	O	H	P		Q	
			🍴	🍴				🍴			🍴		🍴				🍴			🍴	🍴	🍴		🍴	
Cardiff Central [7]	d					15 45								16 45								17 45			
Newport (South Wales)	d					16 00								17 00								18 00			
Bristol Temple Meads [10]	d		16 00					16 30			17 00	16 41					17 30			18 00				18 30	
Bristol Parkway [7]	d		16 10					16 40			17 10	16 52					17 40			18 10				18 40	
Gloucester [7]	d					16 46						17 38		17 46								18 46			
Cheltenham Spa	d		16 42			16 57		17 12			17 42	17 48		17 58			18 12			18 42		18 57		19 12	
Ashchurch for Tewkesbury	d											17 57													
Worcester Shrub Hill [7]	a											18 15													
Birmingham New Street [12]	a		17 26			17 45		17 56			18 26			18 45			18 56			19 26		19 45		19 56	
	d	17 22		17 30		17 49	17 52	18 03	18 19	18 22			18 30	18 49		18 52	19 03	19 19	19 22		19 30	19 49	19 52	20 03	
Water Orton	d																						20 03		
Coleshill Parkway	d	17 35					18 05			18 35						19 05			19 35				20 07		
Nuneaton	d	17 51					18 21			18 51						19 21			19 51				20 23		
Hinckley	d						18 29									19 29							20 30		
Narborough	d						18 37									19 37							20 39		
South Wigston	d						18 42									19 42							20 43		
Leicester	a	18 13					18 48			19 13						19 48			20 13				20 49		
Wilnecote	d								18 34									19 34							
Tamworth	d					18 06		18 19	18 39					19 06				19 39				20 06		20 19	
Burton-on-Trent	d					18 19			18 51					19 19			19 25	19 51				20 19			
Willington	d					18 26																			
Derby [6]	a			18 08		18 34		18 41	19 05				19 08	19 34			19 39	20 05			20 08	20 34		20 42	
	d					18 40			19 10					19 40				20 10				20 40			
Long Eaton	d								19 19									20 19				20 49			
Attenborough	d																								
Beeston	d								19 27									20 27				20 57			
Nottingham [8] 🚋	a					19 06			19 33					20 05				20 35				21 04			

A To Manchester Piccadilly
B From Brighton to Great Malvern
C From Southampton Central to Newcastle
D 🍴 from Newport (South Wales)
E From Newquay to Dundee
F To Stansted Airport
G From Penzance to Manchester Piccadilly
H From Reading to Newcastle
I From Plymouth to Glasgow Central
J From Southampton Central to Great Malvern
K From Plymouth to Edinburgh
L From Paignton to Manchester Piccadilly
M From Warminster to Great Malvern
N From Plymouth to York
O From Exeter St Davids to Manchester Piccadilly. 🍴 to Cheltenham Spa
P 🍴 from Newport (South Wales) to Cheltenham Spa
Q from 17 September. From Plymouth to Leeds. 🍴 to Cheltenham Spa

Table 57

Saturdays

Bristol and Cardiff - Birmingham Leicester, Derby and Nottingham

		XC	XC	XC	GW	XC	XC	XC	XC	XC	XC	XC	XC	XC	XC	XC	XC	XC	GW	XC	XC	XC	XC	XC
		◇1	◇1	◇1		◇1	◇1	1	◇1	◇1	◇1	◇1	◇1	◇1	◇1	◇1	◇1	◇1			1	◇1	1	Q
		A	B	C	D	E			F	G	H	I	J	K	L	M	N	O		N 🚌			P	🚌
		🛒		🛒					🛒	🛒	🛒	🛒				🛒								
Cardiff Central 7	d						18 45										20 00	20 00				20 50		
Newport (South Wales)	d						19 00										20 15	20 15				21 05		
Bristol Temple Meads 10	d	18 30		19 00	18 41				19 30			19 30	20 00	20 30	20 30	20 30			20 41					
Bristol Parkway 7	d	18 40		19 10	18 52				19 40			19 40	20 10	20 40	20 40	20 40			20 52					
Gloucester 7	d				19 38		19 46										21 07	21 07	21 38			21 49		
Cheltenham Spa	d	19 12		19 42	19 48		19 57		20 12			20 12	20 42	21 12	21 12	21 12	21 18	21 18	21 49			22 00		
Ashchurch for Tewkesbury	d				19 57												21 25	21 25	21 57					
Worcester Shrub Hill 7	a				20 15														22 18					
Birmingham New Street 12	a	19 58		20 26			20 40		20 54			20 53	21 38	21 53	21 53	21 53	22 07	22 07				22 42		
	d	20 03	20 22			20 30	20 49	20 52		21 03	21 03	21 03		21 56	21 56			22 10		22 20	22 22		22 49	22 49
Water Orton	d																							
Coleshill Parkway	d		20 35					21 05													22 35			
Nuneaton	d		20 51					21 21													22 51			
Hinckley	d							21 29													22 59			
Narborough	d							21 37													23 07			
South Wigston	d							21 42													23 12			
Leicester	a		21 13					21 48													23 18			
Wilnecote	d						21 04																23 04	23 19
Tamworth	d	20 20					21 08			21 20	21 20	21 20						22 27		22 55			23 08	23 29
Burton-on-Trent	d						21 20				21 30	21 31						22 39		23 15			23 19	23s49
Willington	d																	22 45		23 30				
Derby 6	a	20 42				21 25	21 34			21 42	21 43	21 44		22 30	22 32			22 55		23s45			23 33	00 09
	d						21 40											23 00						
Long Eaton	d						21 52											23 12		00s12				
Attenborough	d						21 58											23 18		00s23				
Beeston	d						22 02											23 22		00s29				
Nottingham 8 🚌	a						22 08											23 28		00 49				

A until 10 September. From Paignton to Leeds. 🛒 to Cheltenham Spa
B To Cambridge
C To Manchester Piccadilly. 🛒 to Cheltenham Spa
D From Weymouth to Great Malvern
E From Southampton Central to York
F until 10 September. From Newquay to Manchester Piccadilly
G from 25 June until 30 July. From Bournemouth to Leeds
H until 18 June, from 6 August until 10 September. From Bournemouth to Leeds
I from 17 September. From Plymouth to Leeds. 🛒 to Cheltenham Spa
J From Paignton
K from 6 August until 10 September. From Penzance to Leeds
L until 30 July. From Penzance to Leeds
M from 17 September. From Plymouth
N until 18 June
O from 25 June
P from 6 August
Q until 30 July

Table 57

Sundays

until 19 June

Bristol and Cardiff - Birmingham
Leicester, Derby and Nottingham

		XC	XC	XC	XC	XC	XC	XC	XC	XC		XC	XC	XC	XC	XC	XC	XC	XC	GW		XC	XC	XC	XC
				◇■	■	◇■	■	◇■	◇■	◇■		■	◇■	◇■	◇■	■	◇■	◇■	◇■			■	◇■	◇■	◇■
		A	A	B		C		B	D	E			D	F	B		D	F	G				D	F	H
		🚌	🚌	⊼		⊼		⊼	⊼	⊼			⊼	⊼	⊼		⊼	⊼	⊼				⊼	⊼	⊼
Cardiff Central 7	d													10 45				11 45						12 45	
Newport (South Wales)	d													10 59				11 59						12 59	
Bristol Temple Meads 10	d									09 30					10 30				11 30						12 30
Bristol Parkway 7	d									09 48					10 43				11 43						12 43
Gloucester 7	d									11 01				11 50	12 02			12 47	12 59	13 37				13 51	14 02
Cheltenham Spa	d									11 12				12 03	12 12			12 58	13 12	13 48				14 02	14 12
Ashchurch for Tewkesbury	d																			13 57					
Worcester Shrub Hill 7	a																			14 23					
Birmingham New Street 12	a									11 50				12 45	12 50			13 42	13 50					14 44	14 48
	d	22p20	22p49	09 03	09 52	10 03	10 52	11 03	11 22	12 03		11 52	12 22		13 03	12 52	13 22		14 03			13 52	14 22		15 03
Water Orton	d																								
Coleshill Parkway	d				10 05		11 05		11 35			12 05	12 35			13 05	13 34					14 05	14 35		
Nuneaton	d				10 21		11 21		11 51			12 21	12 51			13 21	13 51					14 21	14 51		
Hinckley	d				10 29		11 28					12 29				13 29						14 28			
Narborough	d				10 37		11 37					12 37				13 37						14 37			
South Wigston	d				10 42							12 42										14 42			
Leicester	a				10 51		11 51		12 12			12 50	13 13			13 50	14 12					14 51	15 12		
Wilnecote	d		23p19																						
Tamworth	d	22p55	23p29																						
Burton-on-Trent	d	23p15	23b49																						
Willington	d	23p30																							
Derby 6	a	23b45	00 09	10 12		11 26		12 28		13 23					14 25				15 35						16 19
	d																								
Long Eaton	d	00s12																							
Attenborough	d	00s23																							
Beeston	d	00s29																							
Nottingham 8 ⛴	a	00 49																							

		XC	XC	XC	XC	XC		XC	XC	XC	XC	XC	XC	XC	XC	GW		XC	XC	XC	XC	XC	GW	XC	XC
		■	◇■	◇■	◇■	◇■		■	◇■	◇■	◇■	◇■	■	◇■	◇■			◇■	◇■	■	◇■	◇■		◇■	◇■
			D	I	F	J			D	K	F	L		D	M			F	N		D	O			P
			⊼	⊼	⊼	⊼				⊼	⊼	⊼			⊼			⊼	⊼			⊼			⊼
Cardiff Central 7	d				13 45						14 45							15 45						16 45	
Newport (South Wales)	d				13 59						14 59							15 59						16 59	
Bristol Temple Meads 10	d			13 00		13 30				15 00		15 30			16 00	15 34			16 30			17 00	16 41		17 30
Bristol Parkway 7	d			13 13		13 43				15 10		15 40			16 10	15 46			16 40			17 10	16 52		17 40
Gloucester 7	d			14 30	14 47	15 00					15 47					16 35		16 47					17 35	17 47	
Cheltenham Spa	d			14 42	14 58	15 12				15 42	15 58	16 12			16 42	16 47		16 58	17 12			17 42	17 46	17 58	18 12
Ashchurch for Tewkesbury	d															16 55							17 54		
Worcester Shrub Hill 7	a															17 14							18 14		
Birmingham New Street 12	a			15 26	15 42	15 50				16 26	16 41	16 50			17 26			17 41	17 51			18 27		18 41	18 50
	d	14 52	15 22			16 03		15 52	16 22			17 03	16 52	17 22					18 03	17 52	18 22				19 03
Water Orton	d																								
Coleshill Parkway	d	15 05	15 35					16 05	16 35				17 05	17 35						18 05	18 35				
Nuneaton	d	15 21	15 51					16 21	16 51				17 21	17 51						18 21	18 51				
Hinckley	d	15 29						16 29					17 29							18 29					
Narborough	d	15 37						16 37					17 37							18 37					
South Wigston	d							16 42					17 42							18 42					
Leicester	a	15 49	16 13					16 51	17 15				17 50	18 12						18 51	19 12				
Wilnecote	d																								
Tamworth	d																								
Burton-on-Trent	d																								
Willington	d																								
Derby 6	a					17 20						18 25							19 22						20 29
	d																								
Long Eaton	d																								
Attenborough	d																								
Beeston	d																								
Nottingham 8 ⛴	a																								

A not 22 May
B To Glasgow Central
C To Edinburgh
D To Stansted Airport
E To Aberdeen
F ⊼ from Newport (South Wales)
G From Plymouth to Edinburgh
H From Plymouth to Glasgow Central
I From Paignton to Manchester Piccadilly
J From Penzance to Edinburgh
K From Plymouth to Manchester Piccadilly
L From Newquay to Edinburgh
M To Manchester Piccadilly
N From Plymouth to Newcastle
O From Penzance to Manchester Piccadilly. ⊼ to Cheltenham Spa
P From Plymouth to Leeds. ⊼ to Cheltenham Spa
b Previous night, stops to set down only

Table 57

Sundays until 19 June

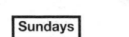

Bristol and Cardiff - Birmingham Leicester, Derby and Nottingham

		XC		XC	XC	XC	XC	XC	XC	XC	GW	XC		XC	XC	XC	XC	XC	XC	XC	XC				
		1		◇1	◇1	◇1	1	◇1	◇1	◇1		◇1		◇1	1	◇1	◇1	◇1	1	◇1	◇1				
				A	B			C	D	B				E		F		G							
					🛒					🛒				🛒		🛒		🛒							
Cardiff Central 7	d					17 45						18 45					19 45			20 45					
Newport (South Wales)	d					17 59						18 59					20 00			20 59					
Bristol Temple Meads 10	d				18 00			18 30		19 00	18 41			19 30		20 00		20 30			22 10				
Bristol Parkway 7	d				18 10			18 40		19 10	18 52			19 40		20 10		20 40			22 20				
Gloucester 7	d					18 47					19 37	19 50					20 50			21 48					
Cheltenham Spa	d				18 42	18 58		19 12		19 42	19 48	20 00		20 12		20 42	21 01	21 12		21 59	22 52				
Ashchurch for Tewkesbury	d										19 57														
Worcester Shrub Hill 7	a										20 21														
Birmingham New Street 12	a				19 26	19 42		19 53		20 26		20 42		20 50		21 20	21 45	21 51		22 42	23 39				
	d	18 52		19 22			19 52	20 03	20 22					21 03	20 52				21 52						
Water Orton	d																								
Coleshill Parkway	d	19 05		19 35			20 05		20 35						21 05				22 05						
Nuneaton	d	19 21		19 51			20 21		20 51						21 21				22 26						
Hinckley	d	19 29					20 29								21 29				22 33						
Narborough	d	19 37					20 37								21 37				22 41						
South Wigston	d	19 42					20 42								21 42				22 46						
Leicester	a	19 50		20 12			20 50		21 13						21 52				22 52						
Wilnecote	d																								
Tamworth	d																								
Burton-on-Trent	d																								
Willington	d																								
Derby 6	a							21 26						22 31											
	d																								
Long Eaton	d																								
Attenborough	d																								
Beeston	d																								
Nottingham 8 ⛴	a																								

Sundays 26 June to 31 July

		XC	XC	XC	XC	XC	XC	XC	XC	XC		XC	XC	XC	XC	XC	XC	XC	XC	XC		GW	XC	XC	XC
			◇1	1	◇1	1	◇1	◇1	◇1	1		◇1	◇1	◇1	◇1	1	◇1	◇1	◇1	◇1			1	◇1	◇1
			H		I		H	A				A	J	K	L		A	J	K	M				A	N
		🚌	🛒		🛒		🛒	🛒	🛒			🛒	🛒	🛒	🛒		🛒	🛒	🛒	🛒				🛒	🛒
Cardiff Central 7	d													10 45					11 45						
Newport (South Wales)	d													10 59					11 59						
Bristol Temple Meads 10	d								09 30						10 30					11 30					
Bristol Parkway 7	d								09 43						10 43					11 43					
Gloucester 7	d								11 01					11 51	12 00				12 47	12 59		13 37			
Cheltenham Spa	d								11 12					12 03	12 12				12 58	13 12		13 48			
Ashchurch for Tewkesbury	d																					13 57			
Worcester Shrub Hill 7	a																					14 25			
Birmingham New Street 12	a								11 48					12 45	12 50				13 41	13 50					
	d	22p49	09 03	09 52	10 03	10 52	11 03	11 22		11 52		12 22	12 30	12 49	13 03	12 52	13 22	13 30	13 49	14 03			13 52	14 22	14 30
Water Orton	d																								
Coleshill Parkway	d			10 05		11 05		11 35		12 05		12 35				13 05	13 34						14 05	14 35	
Nuneaton	d			10 21		11 21		11 51		12 21		12 51				13 21	13 51						14 21	14 51	
Hinckley	d			10 29		11 28				12 29						13 29							14 28		
Narborough	d			10 37		11 37				12 37						13 37							14 37		
South Wigston	d			10 42						12 42													14 42		
Leicester	a			10 51		11 51		12 12		12 50		13 13				13 50	14 12						14 51	15 12	
Wilnecote	d	23p19																							
Tamworth	d	23p29												13 06					14 06	14 19					
Burton-on-Trent	d	23b49												13 19	13 25				14 19						
Willington	d																								
Derby 6	a	00 09	10 11		11 32		12 27						13 09	13 32	13 44			14 09	14 34	14 42					15 04
	d													13 38					14 46						
Long Eaton	d																								
Attenborough	d																								
Beeston	d																								
Nottingham 8 ⛴	a													13 59					15 07						

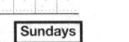

A To Stansted Airport
B To Manchester Piccadilly
C From Plymouth to Leeds
D To Cambridge
E From Penzance to Leeds. 🛒 to Cheltenham Spa
F From Paignton
G From Plymouth
H To Glasgow Central
I To Edinburgh
J To Newcastle
K 🛒 from Newport (South Wales)
L To Aberdeen
M From Plymouth to Glasgow Central
N From Reading to Newcastle
b Previous night, stops to set down only

Table 57

Sundays

26 June to 31 July

Bristol and Cardiff - Birmingham Leicester, Derby and Nottingham

		XC	XC	XC	XC	XC		XC	XC	XC	XC	XC	XC	GW	XC	XC		XC	XC	XC	XC	GW	XC	XC	XC
		◇1	◇1	1	◇1	◇1		◇1	◇1	1	◇1	◇1	◇1		◇1	1		◇1	◇1	◇1	◇1		1	◇1	◇1
		A	B		C	D		A	E		C	D	A		B			C	F		G			C	D
		🚲	🚲		🚲	🚲		🚲	🚲			🚲	🚲		🚲				🚲		🚲				🚲
Cardiff Central 7	d	12 45						13 45					14 45							15 45					
Newport (South Wales)	d	12 59						13 59					14 59							15 59					
Bristol Temple Meads 10	d		12 30						13 30						14 30						15 30				
Bristol Parkway 7	d		12 43						13 48						14 47						15 45				
Gloucester 7	d	13 51	14 00					14 47	15 02				15 47	15 52	16 01					16 47	17 02	17 37			
Cheltenham Spa	d	14 02	14 12					14 58	15 12				15 58	16 03	16 12					16 58	17 12	17 46			
Ashchurch for Tewkesbury	d													16 12								17 54			
Worcester Shrub Hill 7	a													16 33								18 14			
Birmingham New Street 12	a	14 45	14 50					15 41	15 50				16 41		16 51					17 41	17 49				
	d	14 49	15 03	14 52	15 22	15 30		15 49	16 03	15 52	16 22	16 30	16 49		17 03	16 52		17 22	17 30	17 49	18 03		17 52	18 22	18 30
Water Orton	d																								
Coleshill Parkway	d			15 05	15 35					16 05	16 35					17 05		17 35					18 05	18 35	
Nuneaton	d			15 21	15 51					16 21	16 51					17 21		17 51					18 21	18 51	
Hinckley	d			15 29						16 29						17 29							18 29		
Narborough	d			15 37						16 37						17 37							18 37		
South Wigston	d									16 42						17 42							18 42		
Leicester	a			15 49	16 13					16 51	17 15					17 50		18 13					18 51	19 12	
Wilnecote	d	15 04																							
Tamworth	d	15 08						16 06	16 19				17 06							18 06	18 20				
Burton-on-Trent	d	15 21	15 26					16 19					17 19		17 28					18 19					
Willington	d																								
Derby 6	a	15 35	15 42			16 02		16 34	16 42			17 04	17 35		17 42				18 04	18 34	18 42				19 03
	d	15 44						16 41					17 41							18 41					
Long Eaton	d																								
Attenborough	d																								
Beeston	d																								
Nottingham 8 🚌	a	16 04						17 03					18 00							19 04					

		XC		XC	XC	XC	XC	XC	XC	XC	XC	XC		XC	GW	XC	XC	XC	XC	XC	XC	XC			
		◇1		◇1	1	◇1	◇1	◇1	◇1	1	◇1	◇1		◇1		1	◇1	◇1	1	◇1	◇1	◇1			
				H		C	D		I		J			I				I			K				
				🚲			🚲		🚲					🚲				🚲			🚲				
Cardiff Central 7	d	16 45						17 45				18 45					19 45			20 45					
Newport (South Wales)	d	16 59						17 59				18 59					20 00			20 59					
Bristol Temple Meads 10	d			16 30					17 30					18 30				19 30			20 30	22 10			
Bristol Parkway 7	d			16 45					17 43					18 48				19 45			20 43	22 24			
Gloucester 7	d	17 47		17 59				18 47	18 59			19 50		20 02	20 25		20 50	21 04		21 48	22 03	23 21			
Cheltenham Spa	d	17 58		18 12				18 58	19 12			20 00		20 12	20 35		21 01	21 13		21 59	22 12	23 29			
Ashchurch for Tewkesbury	d														20 44										
Worcester Shrub Hill 7	a														21 02										
Birmingham New Street 12	a	18 41		18 51				19 41	19 50			20 42		20 51			21 45	21 52		22 42	22 50	00 16			
	d	18 49		19 03	18 52	19 22	19 30	19 49	20 03	19 52	20 22	20 49		21 00		20 52		22 03	21 52						
Water Orton	d																								
Coleshill Parkway	d				19 05	19 35				20 05	20 35					21 05			22 05						
Nuneaton	d				19 21	19 51				20 21	20 51					21 21			22 26						
Hinckley	d				19 29					20 29						21 29			22 33						
Narborough	d				19 37					20 37						21 37			22 41						
South Wigston	d				19 42					20 42						21 42			22 46						
Leicester	a				19 50	20 12				20 50	21 13					21 52			22 52						
Wilnecote	d	19 04																							
Tamworth	d	19 08						20 06	20 19			21 06		21 17				22 20							
Burton-on-Trent	d	19 20		19 26				20 19				21 19		21 28											
Willington	d																								
Derby 6	a	19 33		19 39			20 02	20 34	20 42			21 34		21 41				22 45							
	d	19 37						20 37				21 41													
Long Eaton	d																								
Attenborough	d																								
Beeston	d																								
Nottingham 8 🚌	a	19 56						21 01				22 00													

A 🚲 from Newport (South Wales)
B From Plymouth to Edinburgh
C To Stansted Airport
D From Reading to Newcastle
E From Penzance to Glasgow Central
F From Reading to Edinburgh
G From Newquay to Edinburgh
H From Plymouth to York
I From Plymouth to Leeds. 🚲 to Cheltenham Spa
J To Cambridge
K From Plymouth

Table 57

Sundays

7 August to 11 September

Bristol and Cardiff - Birmingham
Leicester, Derby and Nottingham

		XC	XC	XC	XC	XC	XC	XC	XC	XC		XC	XC	XC	XC	XC	XC	XC	XC	XC		XC	XC	XC	GW
		◇1	1	◇1	◇1	1	◇1	◇1	◇1	1		◇1	◇1	◇1	◇1	1	◇1	◇1	◇1	◇1		1	◇1	◇1	
		A		B	A		C		B			C	D		E		C	D	F	G			C	H	
		🚲		🚲	🚲		🚲	🚲	🚲			🚲	🚲		🚲		🚲	🚲	🚲	🚲			🚲	🚲	
Cardiff Central 7	d																		11 25						
Newport (South Wales)	d																		11 39						
Bristol Temple Meads 10	d				09 15				10 30						11 30					12 30				13 00	12 41
Bristol Parkway 7	d				09 25				10 40						11 40					12 40				13 10	12 52
Gloucester 7	d				10 01									11 52					12 47						13 37
Cheltenham Spa	d				10 12				11 12					12 03	12 12				12 56	13 12				13 42	13 48
Ashchurch for Tewkesbury	d																								13 57
Worcester Shrub Hill 7	a																								14 23
Birmingham New Street 12	a				10 50				11 50					12 45	12 50				13 40	13 50				14 26	
	d	09 03	09 52	10 03	11 03	10 52	11 22	11 49	12 03	11 52		12 22	12 30	12 49	13 03	12 52	13 22	13 30	13 49	14 03		13 52	14 22		
Water Orton	d																								
Coleshill Parkway	d		10 05			11 05	11 35			12 05		12 35				13 05	13 34					14 05	14 35		
Nuneaton	d		10 21			11 21	11 51			12 21		12 51				13 21	13 51					14 21	14 51		
Hinckley	d		10 29			11 28				12 29						13 29						14 28			
Narborough	d		10 37			11 37				12 37						13 37						14 37			
South Wigston	d		10 42							12 42												14 42			
Leicester	a		10 51			11 51	12 12			12 50		13 13				13 50	14 12					14 51	15 12		
Wilnecote	d																								
Tamworth	d	09 19		10 18				12 06	12 19					13 06					14 06	14 19					
Burton-on-Trent	d	09 28		10 29	11 26			12 18						13 19	13 25				14 19						
Willington	d																								
Derby 6	a	09 42		10 41	11 42			12 34	12 43				13 09	13 32	13 44			14 09	14 34	14 42					
	d							12 38						13 38					14 41						
Long Eaton	d																								
Attenborough	d																								
Beeston	d																								
Nottingham 8	a							13 02						13 59					15 07						

		XC	XC	XC	XC	XC		XC	XC	XC	XC	XC	XC	XC	XC	XC		GW	XC	XC	XC	XC	XC	XC	XC
		◇1	◇1	◇1	1	◇1		◇1	◇1	◇1	◇1	1	◇1	◇1	◇1	◇1			◇1	1	◇1	◇1	◇1	◇1	◇1
		D		I		C		J	K		G		C	J	K				L		C	M	N		O
		🚲		🚲		🚲		🚲	🚲		🚲			🚲	🚲				🚲			🚲	🚲		🚲
Cardiff Central 7	d																								
Newport (South Wales)	d																								
Bristol Temple Meads 10	d			13 30				14 00			14 30			15 00				14 41	15 30			16 00			16 30
Bristol Parkway 7	d			13 40				14 10			14 40			15 10				14 53	15 40			16 10			16 40
Gloucester 7	d		13 51							14 47						15 47		15 52						16 47	
Cheltenham Spa	d		14 02	14 12				14 42		14 58	15 12			15 42		15 58		16 03	16 12			16 42		16 58	17 12
Ashchurch for Tewkesbury	d																	16 12							
Worcester Shrub Hill 7	a																	16 33							
Birmingham New Street 12	a		14 45	14 50				15 27		15 41	15 50			16 26		16 41			16 50			17 26		17 41	17 49
	d	14 30	14 49	15 03	14 52	15 22			15 30	15 49	16 03	15 52	16 22		16 30	16 49			17 03	16 52	17 22		17 30	17 49	18 03
Water Orton	d																								
Coleshill Parkway	d				15 05	15 35						16 05	16 35							17 05	17 35				
Nuneaton	d				15 21	15 51						16 21	16 51							17 21	17 51				
Hinckley	d				15 29							16 29								17 29					
Narborough	d				15 37							16 37								17 37					
South Wigston	d											16 42								17 42					
Leicester	a				15 49	16 13						16 51	17 15							17 50	18 13				
Wilnecote	d		15 04																						
Tamworth	d		15 08							16 06	16 19					17 06								18 06	18 20
Burton-on-Trent	d		15 21	15 26						16 19						17 18			17 28					18 19	
Willington	d																								
Derby 6	a	15 04	15 35	15 42					16 02	16 34	16 42				17 04	17 35			17 42				18 04	18 34	18 42
	d		15 44							16 41						17 43								18 41	
Long Eaton	d																								
Attenborough	d																								
Beeston	d																								
Nottingham 8	a		16 04							17 03						18 02								19 04	

- **A** To Edinburgh
- **B** To Glasgow Central
- **C** To Stansted Airport
- **D** To Newcastle
- **E** From Plymouth to Aberdeen
- **F** 🚲 from Newport (South Wales)
- **G** From Plymouth to Glasgow Central
- **H** From Paignton to Manchester Piccadilly
- **I** From Penzance to Edinburgh
- **J** From Plymouth to Manchester Piccadilly
- **K** From Reading to Newcastle
- **L** From Newquay to Edinburgh
- **M** To Manchester Piccadilly
- **N** From Reading to Edinburgh
- **O** From Plymouth to Edinburgh

Table 57

Sundays

7 August to 11 September

Bristol and Cardiff - Birmingham Leicester, Derby and Nottingham

		XC 1		XC ◇1 A	XC ◇1 B ☕	GW	XC ◇1 C ☕	XC ◇1	XC ◇1 D ☕	XC 1	XC ◇1 A	XC ◇1 E ☕		XC ◇1 C ☕	XC ◇1	XC ◇1 F ☕	XC 1	XC ◇1 G	XC ◇1 E ☕	GW	XC ◇1	XC ◇1 H ☕		XC 1	XC ◇1 I ☕
Cardiff Central 7	d																								
Newport (South Wales)	d																								
Bristol Temple Meads 10	d				17 00	16 41			17 30			18 00				18 30			19 00	18 41		19 30			20 00
Bristol Parkway 7	d				17 10	16 54			17 40			18 10				18 40			19 10	18 52		19 40			20 10
Gloucester 7	d					17 37		17 46							18 47					19 37	19 50				
Cheltenham Spa	d				17 42	17 46		17 58	18 12			18 42			18 58	19 12			19 42	19 48	20 00	20 12			20 42
Ashchurch for Tewkesbury	d					17 54														19 57					
Worcester Shrub Hill 7	a					18 14														20 21					
Birmingham New Street 12	a				18 27			18 41	18 51			19 26			19 41	19 50			20 26		20 42	20 50			21 20
	d	17 52		18 22			18 30	18 49	19 03	18 52	19 22			19 30	19 49	20 03	19 52	20 22			20 49	21 03		20 52	
Water Orton	d																								
Coleshill Parkway	d	18 05		18 35						19 05	19 35						20 05	20 35						21 05	
Nuneaton	d	18 21		18 51						19 21	19 51						20 21	20 51						21 21	
Hinckley	d	18 29								19 29							20 29							21 29	
Narborough	d	18 37								19 37							20 37							21 37	
South Wigston	d	18 42								19 42							20 42							21 42	
Leicester	a	18 51		19 12						19 50	20 12						20 50	21 13						21 52	
Wilnecote	d							19 04																	
Tamworth	d							19 08							20 06	20 19					21 06	21 19			
Burton-on-Trent	d							19 20	19 26						20 19						21 19	21 29			
Willington	d																								
Derby 6	a						19 03	19 33	19 39					20 02	20 34	20 42					21 34	21 42			
	d							19 37							20 37						21 41				
Long Eaton	d																								
Attenborough	d																								
Beeston	d																								
Nottingham 8 🚋	a							19 56							21 01						22 00				

		XC ◇1	XC ◇1 F ☕	XC 1	XC ◇1	XC ◇1
Cardiff Central 7	d					
Newport (South Wales)	d					
Bristol Temple Meads 10	d		20 30			22 10
Bristol Parkway 7	d		20 40			22 20
Gloucester 7	d	20 50			21 48	
Cheltenham Spa	d	21 01	21 12		21 59	22 52
Ashchurch for Tewkesbury	d					
Worcester Shrub Hill 7	a					
Birmingham New Street 12	a	21 45	21 51		22 42	23 39
	d		22 03	21 52		
Water Orton	d					
Coleshill Parkway	d			22 05		
Nuneaton	d			22 26		
Hinckley	d			22 33		
Narborough	d			22 41		
South Wigston	d			22 46		
Leicester	a			22 52		
Wilnecote	d					
Tamworth	d		22 20			
Burton-on-Trent	d					
Willington	d					
Derby 6	a		22 45			
	d					
Long Eaton	d					
Attenborough	d					
Beeston	d					
Nottingham 8 🚋	a					

A To Stansted Airport
B From Penzance to Manchester Piccadilly. ☕ to Cheltenham Spa
C From Reading to Newcastle
D From Plymouth to York
E To Manchester Piccadilly
F From Plymouth to Leeds. ☕ to Cheltenham Spa
G To Cambridge
H From Penzance to Leeds. ☕ to Cheltenham Spa
I From Paignton

Table 57

Sundays

18 September to 23 October

Bristol and Cardiff - Birmingham Leicester, Derby and Nottingham

		XC	XC	XC	XC	XC	XC	XC	XC	XC		XC	XC	XC	XC	XC	XC	XC	XC	GW		XC	XC	XC	XC
		◇1	1	◇1	1	◇1	◇1	◇1	1	◇1		◇1	◇1	◇1	1	◇1	◇1	◇1	◇1			1	◇1	◇1	◇1
		A		B		C		B		C		D		E		C	D		B				C	D	
		🛒		🛒		🛒	🛒	🛒		🛒		🛒		🛒		🛒	🛒		🛒				🛒	🛒	
Cardiff Central 7	d																			11 40					
Newport (South Wales)	d																			11 55					
Bristol Temple Meads 10	d																								
Bristol Parkway 7	d							10 40						11 40					12 40	12 52					
Gloucester 7	d												11 51					12 47		13 37					13 51
Cheltenham Spa	d							11 12					12 03	12 12				12 58	13 12	13 48					14 02
Ashchurch for Tewkesbury	d																			13 57					
Worcester Shrub Hill 7	a																			14 23					
Birmingham New Street 12	a							11 50					12 45	12 50				13 41	13 50						14 45
	d	09 03	09 52	10 03	10 52	11 22	11 49	12 03	11 52	12 22		12 30	12 49	13 03	12 52	13 22	13 30	13 49	14 03			13 52	14 22	14 30	14 49
Water Orton	d																								
Coleshill Parkway	d		10 05		11 05	11 35			12 05	12 35					13 05	13 34						14 05	14 35		
Nuneaton	d		10 21		11 21	11 51			12 21	12 51					13 21	13 51						14 21	14 51		
Hinckley	d		10 29		11 28				12 29						13 29							14 28			
Narborough	d		10 37		11 37				12 37						13 37							14 37			
South Wigston	d		10 42						12 42													14 42			
Leicester	a		10 51		11 51	12 12			12 50	13 13					13 50	14 12						14 51	15 12		
Wilnecote	d																								15 04
Tamworth	d	09 19		10 18			12 06	12 19					13 06					14 06	14 19						15 08
Burton-on-Trent	d	09 28		10 29			12 18						13 19	13 25				14 19							15 21
Willington	d																								
Derby 6	a	09 42		10 41			12 34	12 43				13 09	13 32	13 44			14 09	14 34	14 42					15 04	15 35
	d						12 38						13 38					14 41							15 44
Long Eaton	d																								
Attenborough	d																								
Beeston	d																								
Nottingham 8 🚊	a						13 02						13 59					15 07							16 04

		XC	XC	XC	XC	XC		XC	XC	XC	XC	GW	XC	XC	XC	XC		XC	XC	GW	XC	XC	XC	XC	XC
		◇1	1	◇1	◇1	◇1		1	◇1	◇1	◇1		◇1	1	◇1	◇1		◇1	◇1		1	◇1	◇1	◇1	◇1
		F		C	G	B			C	H	G		F		C	I			A			C	H		J
		🛒		🛒	🛒	🛒				🛒	🛒		🛒			🛒		🛒	🛒				🛒		🛒
Cardiff Central 7	d				13 45						14 45													16 45	
Newport (South Wales)	d				13 59						14 59							15 59						16 59	
Bristol Temple Meads 10	d																								
Bristol Parkway 7	d	13 40				14 40						15 05	15 40						16 40	16 52					17 40
Gloucester 7	d				14 49						15 47	15 52						16 47		17 35				17 47	
Cheltenham Spa	d	14 12			14 59	15 12					15 58	16 03	16 12					16 58	17 12	17 46				17 58	18 12
Ashchurch for Tewkesbury	d											16 12								17 54					
Worcester Shrub Hill 7	a											16 33								18 14					
Birmingham New Street 12	a	14 50			15 43	15 50					16 41		16 50					17 41	17 49					18 41	18 51
	d	15 03	14 52	15 22	15 49	16 03		15 52	16 22	16 30	16 49		17 03	16 52	17 22	17 30		17 49	18 03		17 52	18 22	18 30	18 49	19 03
Water Orton	d																								
Coleshill Parkway	d		15 05	15 35				16 05	16 35					17 05	17 35						18 05	18 35			
Nuneaton	d		15 21	15 51				16 21	16 51					17 21	17 51						18 21	18 51			
Hinckley	d		15 29					16 29						17 29							18 29				
Narborough	d		15 37					16 37						17 37							18 37				
South Wigston	d							16 42						17 42							18 42				
Leicester	a		15 49	16 13				16 51	17 15					17 50	18 13						18 51	19 12			
Wilnecote	d																							19 04	
Tamworth	d				16 06	16 19					17 06							18 06	18 20					19 08	
Burton-on-Trent	d	15 28			16 19						17 19		17 28					18 19						19 20	19 27
Willington	d																								
Derby 6	a	15 42			16 34	16 42				17 04	17 35		17 42			18 04		18 34	18 42				19 03	19 33	19 39
	d				16 41						17 41							18 41						19 37	
Long Eaton	d																								
Attenborough	d																								
Beeston	d																								
Nottingham 8 🚊	a				17 03						18 00							19 04						19 56	

A To Edinburgh
B To Glasgow Central
C To Stansted Airport
D To Newcastle
E To Aberdeen
F To Edinburgh. 🛒 from Birmingham New Street
G 🛒 from Newport (South Wales)
H From Reading to Newcastle
I From Reading to Edinburgh
J To York

Table 57

Sundays

18 September to 23 October

Bristol and Cardiff - Birmingham
Leicester, Derby and Nottingham

		XC 1		XC ◇1 A	XC ◇1 B 🍴	XC ◇1	XC ◇1 C 🍴	GW	XC 1	XC ◇1 D	XC ◇1	XC ◇1 C 🍴		XC 1	XC ◇1	XC ◇1 C 🍴	XC 1	XC ◇1	XC ◇1	XC ◇1					
Cardiff Central 7	d					17 45					18 45				19 45			20 45							
Newport (South Wales)	d					17 59					18 59				20 00			20 59							
Bristol Temple Meads 10	d																								
Bristol Parkway 7	d						18 40	18 52				19 40				20 40			21 45	22 20					
Gloucester 7	d					18 47		19 38			19 50				20 50			21 48							
Cheltenham Spa	d					18 58	19 12	19 48			20 00	20 12			21 01	21 12		21 59	22 20	22 52					
Ashchurch for Tewkesbury	d							19 57																	
Worcester Shrub Hill 7	a							20 21																	
Birmingham New Street 12	a					19 41	19 52				20 42	20 50			21 45	21 51		22 42	23 07	23 39					
	d	18 52		19 22	19 30	19 49	20 03		19 52	20 22	20 49	21 03		20 52		22 03	21 52								
Water Orton	d																								
Coleshill Parkway	d	19 05		19 35					20 05	20 35				21 05			22 05								
Nuneaton	d	19 21		19 51					20 21	20 51				21 21			22 26								
Hinckley	d	19 29							20 29					21 29			22 33								
Narborough	d	19 37							20 37					21 37			22 41								
South Wigston	d	19 42							20 42					21 42			22 46								
Leicester	a	19 50		20 12					20 50	21 13				21 52			22 52								
Wilnecote	d																								
Tamworth	d					20 06	20 19				21 06	21 19				22 20									
Burton-on-Trent	d					20 19					21 19	21 29													
Willington	d																								
Derby 6	a				20 02	20 34	20 43				21 34	21 42				22 45									
	d					20 37					21 41														
Long Eaton	d																								
Attenborough	d																								
Beeston	d																								
Nottingham 8 🚢	a					21 01					22 00														

Sundays

from 30 October

		XC ◇1 E 🍴	XC 1	XC ◇1 F 🍴	XC ◇1 E 🍴	XC 1	XC ◇1 A 🍴	XC ◇1 🍴	XC ◇1 F 🍴	XC 1		XC ◇1 A 🍴	XC ◇1 G 🍴	XC ◇1 H 🍴	XC ◇1 I 🍴	XC 1	XC ◇1 A 🍴	XC ◇1 G 🍴	XC ◇1 H 🍴	XC ◇1 J 🍴		XC 1	XC ◇1 A 🍴	XC ◇1 K 🍴	GW
Cardiff Central 7	d													10 45					11 45						
Newport (South Wales)	d													10 59					11 59						
Bristol Temple Meads 10	d				09 15				10 30						11 30					12 30				13 00	12 41
Bristol Parkway 7	d				09 25				10 40						11 40					12 40				13 10	12 52
Gloucester 7	d				10 01									11 51					12 47						13 37
Cheltenham Spa	d				10 12				11 12					12 03	12 12				12 58	13 12				13 42	13 48
Ashchurch for Tewkesbury	d																								13 57
Worcester Shrub Hill 7	a																								14 23
Birmingham New Street 12	a				10 50				11 50					12 45	12 50				13 41	13 50				14 26	
	d	09 03	09 52	10 03	11 03	10 52	11 22	11 49	12 03	11 52		12 22	12 30	12 49	13 03	12 52	13 22	13 30	13 49	14 03		13 52	14 22		
Water Orton	d																								
Coleshill Parkway	d		10 05			11 05	11 35			12 05		12 35				13 05	13 34					14 05	14 35		
Nuneaton	d		10 21			11 21	11 51			12 21		12 51				13 21	13 51					14 21	14 51		
Hinckley	d		10 29			11 28				12 29						13 29						14 28			
Narborough	d		10 37			11 37				12 37						13 37						14 37			
South Wigston	d		10 42							12 42												14 42			
Leicester	a		10 51			11 51	12 12			12 50		13 13				13 50	14 12					14 51	15 12		
Wilnecote	d																								
Tamworth	d	09 19		10 18				12 06	12 19					13 06					14 06	14 19					
Burton-on-Trent	d	09 28		10 29	11 26			12 18						13 19	13 25				14 18						
Willington	d																								
Derby 6	a	09 42		10 41	11 42			12 34	12 43				13 09	13 32	13 44			14 09	14 34	14 42					
	d							12 38						13 38					14 41						
Long Eaton	d																								
Attenborough	d																								
Beeston	d																								
Nottingham 8 🚢	a							13 02						13 59					15 07						

A To Stansted Airport
B From Reading to Newcastle
C To Leeds. 🍴 to Cheltenham Spa
D To Cambridge
E To Edinburgh
F To Glasgow Central
G To Newcastle
H 🍴 from Newport (South Wales)
I From Plymouth to Aberdeen
J From Plymouth to Glasgow Central
K From Paignton to Manchester Piccadilly

Table 57

Sundays

from 30 October

Bristol and Cardiff - Birmingham
Leicester, Derby and Nottingham

		XC	XC	XC	XC	XC		XC	XC	XC	XC	XC	XC	XC	XC	GW		XC	XC	XC	XC	XC	XC	XC	XC
		◇1	◇1	◇1	1	◇1		◇1	◇1	◇1	1	◇1	◇1	◇1	◇1			◇1	1	◇1	◇1	◇1	◇1	◇1	1
		A	B	C		D		E	B	F		D	E	G	B			C		D	H	I		J	
		🚲	🚲	🚲		🚲		🚲	🚲	🚲			🚲	🚲	🚲			🚲			🚲	🚲		🚲	
Cardiff Central 7	d		12 45						13 45						14 45								15 45		
Newport (South Wales)	d		12 59						13 59						14 59								15 59		
Bristol Temple Meads 10	d			13 30				14 00		14 30			15 00			14 41		15 30			16 00			16 30	
Bristol Parkway 7	d			13 40				14 10		14 40			15 10			14 53		15 40			16 10			16 40	
Gloucester 7	d		13 51						14 47						15 47	15 52							16 47		
Cheltenham Spa	d		14 02	14 12				14 42	14 58	15 12			15 42		15 58	16 03		16 12			16 42		16 58	17 12	
Ashchurch for Tewkesbury	d															16 12									
Worcester Shrub Hill 7	a															16 33									
Birmingham New Street 12	a		14 45	14 50				15 27	15 41	15 50			16 26		16 41			16 50			17 26		17 41	17 49	
	d	14 30	14 49	15 03	14 52	15 22			15 49	16 03	15 52	16 22		16 30	16 49			17 03	16 52	17 22		17 30	17 49	18 03	17 52
Water Orton	d																								
Coleshill Parkway	d				15 05	15 35					16 05	16 35							17 05	17 35					18 05
Nuneaton	d				15 21	15 51					16 21	16 51							17 21	17 51					18 21
Hinckley	d				15 29						16 29								17 29						18 29
Narborough	d				15 37						16 37								17 37						18 37
South Wigston	d										16 42								17 42						18 42
Leicester	a				15 49	16 13					16 51	17 15							17 47	18 13					18 51
Wilnecote	d		15 04																						
Tamworth	d		15 08						16 06	16 19					17 06								18 06	18 20	
Burton-on-Trent	d		15 21	15 26					16 19						17 19			17 28					18 19		
Willington	d																								
Derby 6	a	15 04	15 35	15 42					16 34	16 42				17 04	17 35			17 42				18 04	18 34	18 42	
	d		15 44						16 41						17 41								18 41		
Long Eaton	d																								
Attenborough	d																								
Beeston	d																								
Nottingham 8 🚢	a		16 04						17 03						18 00								19 04		

		XC		XC	GW	XC	XC	XC	XC	XC	XC	XC		XC	XC	XC	XC	XC	GW	XC	XC	XC		XC	XC
		◇1		◇1		◇1	◇1	◇1	1	◇1	◇1	◇1		◇1	◇1	1	◇1	◇1		◇1	◇1	1		◇1	◇1
		D		K		G		L		D	H	G			M		N	H			O			P	
				🚲		🚲		🚲			🚲	🚲			🚲			🚲			🚲			🚲	
Cardiff Central 7	d						16 45							17 45						18 45					19 45
Newport (South Wales)	d						16 59							17 59						18 59					20 00
Bristol Temple Meads 10	d			17 00	16 41			17 30			18 00				18 30			19 00	18 41		19 30			20 00	
Bristol Parkway 7	d			17 10	16 54			17 40			18 10				18 40			19 10	18 52		19 40			20 10	
Gloucester 7	d				17 37		17 47							18 47					19 37	19 50					20 50
Cheltenham Spa	d			17 42	17 46		17 58	18 12			18 42			18 58	19 12			19 42	19 48	20 00	20 12			20 42	21 01
Ashchurch for Tewkesbury	d				17 54														19 57						
Worcester Shrub Hill 7	a				18 14														20 21						
Birmingham New Street 12	a			18 27			18 41	18 51			19 26			19 41	19 50			20 26		20 42	20 50			21 20	21 45
	d	18 22				18 30	18 49	19 03	18 52	19 22		19 30		19 49	20 03	19 52	20 22			20 49	21 03	20 52			
Water Orton	d																								
Coleshill Parkway	d	18 35							19 05	19 35						20 05	20 35					21 05			
Nuneaton	d	18 51							19 21	19 51						20 21	20 51					21 21			
Hinckley	d								19 29							20 29						21 29			
Narborough	d								19 37							20 37						21 37			
South Wigston	d								19 42							20 42						21 42			
Leicester	a	19 12							19 50	20 13						20 50	21 13					21 52			
Wilnecote	d						19 04																		
Tamworth	d						19 08							20 06	20 19					21 06	21 19				
Burton-on-Trent	d						19 20	19 26						20 19						21 19	21 29				
Willington	d																								
Derby 6	a					19 03	19 33	19 39				20 02		20 34	20 42					21 34	21 42				
	d						19 37							20 37						21 41					
Long Eaton	d																								
Attenborough	d																								
Beeston	d																								
Nottingham 8 🚢	a						19 56							21 01						22 00					

A To Newcastle
B 🚲 from Newport (South Wales)
C From Penzance to Edinburgh
D To Stansted Airport
E From Plymouth to Manchester Piccadilly
F From Plymouth to Glasgow Central
G From Reading to Newcastle
H To Manchester Piccadilly
I From Reading to Edinburgh
J From Plymouth to Edinburgh
K From Penzance to Manchester Piccadilly. 🚲 to Cheltenham Spa
L From Plymouth to York
M From Plymouth to Leeds. 🚲 to Cheltenham Spa
N To Cambridge
O From Penzance to Leeds. 🚲 to Cheltenham Spa
P From Paignton

Table 57

Sundays
from 30 October

Bristol and Cardiff - Birmingham Leicester, Derby and Nottingham

		XC	XC	XC	XC
		◇1	1	◇1	◇1
		A			
		⚲			
Cardiff Central 7	d			20 45	
Newport (South Wales)	d			20 59	
Bristol Temple Meads 10	d	20 30			22 10
Bristol Parkway 7	d	20 40			22 20
Gloucester 7	d			21 48	
Cheltenham Spa	d	21 12		21 59	22 52
Ashchurch for Tewkesbury	d				
Worcester Shrub Hill 7	a				
Birmingham New Street 12	a	21 51		22 42	23 39
	d	22 03	21 52		
Water Orton	d				
Coleshill Parkway	d		22 05		
Nuneaton	d		22 26		
Hinckley	d		22 33		
Narborough	d		22 41		
South Wigston	d		22 46		
Leicester	a		22 52		
Wilnecote	d				
Tamworth	d	22 20			
Burton-on-Trent	d				
Willington	d				
Derby 6	a	22 45			
	d				
Long Eaton	d				
Attenborough	d				
Beeston	d				
Nottingham 8 🚌	a				

A From Plymouth to Leeds. ⚲ to Cheltenham Spa

Network Diagram for Tables 59, 60, 61, 62, 64, 66

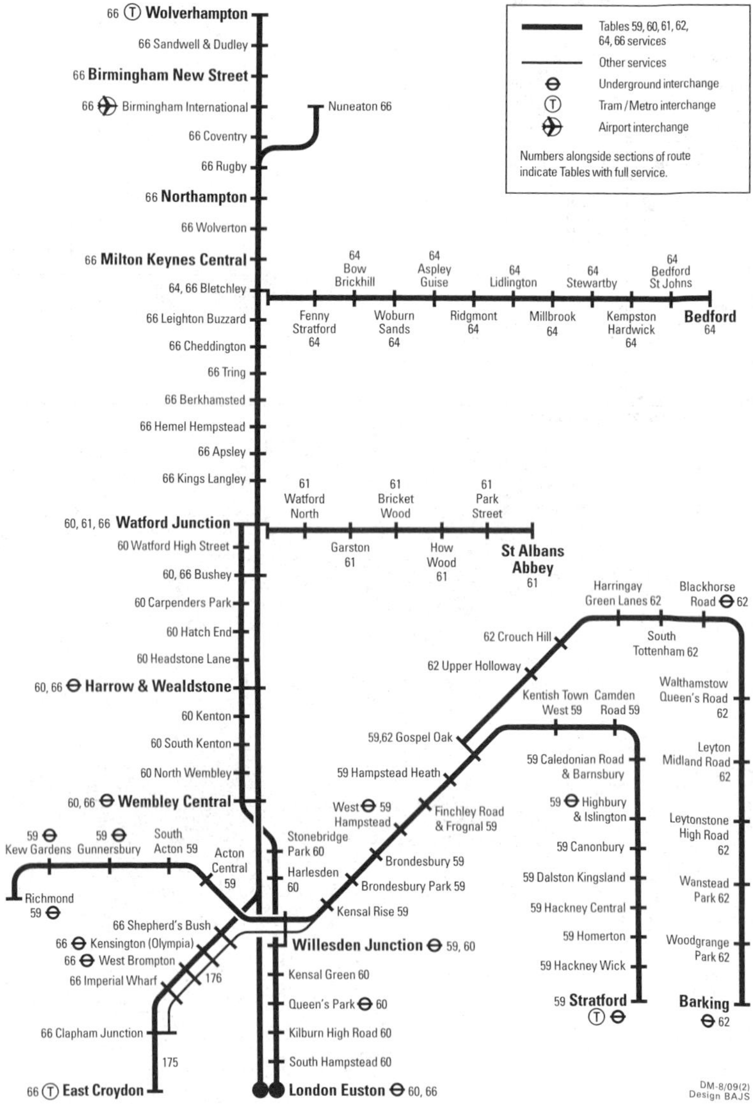

DM-8/09(2)
Design BAJS

© Network Rail OPSU 2009.
All rights reserved

Table 59

Mondays to Fridays

Stratford - Highbury and Islington, West Hampstead, Willesden Junction and Richmond

Miles				LO MX	LO	LO	LO	LO	LO	LO	LO	LO		LO	LO	LO	LO	LO	LO	LO	LO	LO		LO	LO	LO
0	**Stratford** 7	⊖	d	23p45		05 47		06 05	06 12	06 20	06 27	06 35		06 42	06 50	06 55	07 00	07 12	07 20	07 27	07 35	07 42		07 50	07 57	08 05
1	Hackney Wick		d	23p48		05 50		06 08	06 15	06 23	06 30	06 38		06 45	06 53	06 58	07 03	07 15	07 23	07 30	07 38	07 45		07 53	08 00	08 08
1¾	Homerton		d	23p51		05 53		06 11	06 18	06 26	06 33	06 41		06 48	06 56	07 01	07 06	07 18	07 26	07 33	07 42	07 48		07 56	08 03	08 11
2½	Hackney Central		d	23p53		05 55		06 13	06 20	06 28	06 35	06 43		06 50	06 58	07 03	07 08	07 20	07 28	07 35	07 43	07 50		07 58	08 05	08 13
3¼	Dalston Kingsland		d	23p55		05 57		06 15	06 22	06 30	06 37	06 45		06 52	07 00	07 05	07 10	07 22	07 30	07 37	07 45	07 52		08 00	08 07	08 15
4¼	Canonbury		d	23p57		05 59		06 17	06 24	06 32	06 39	06 47		06 54	07 02	07 07	07 12	07 24	07 32	07 39	07 47	07 54		08 02	08 09	08 17
4¾	**Highbury & Islington**	⊖	d	23p59		06 02		06 20	06 27	06 35	06 42	06 50		06 57	07 05	07 10	07 15	07 27	07 35	07 42	07 50	07 57		08 05	08 12	08 20
5¼	Caledonian Rd & Barnsbury		d	00 02		06 04		06 22	06 29	06 37	06 44	06 52		06 59	07 07	07 12	07 17	07 29	07 37	07 44	07 52	07 59		08 07	08 14	08 22
6¼	Camden Road		d	00 05		06 07		06 25	06 32	06 40	06 47	06 55		07 02	07 10	07 15	07 20	07 32	07 40	07 47	07 55	08 02		08 10	08 17	08 25
6½	Kentish Town West		d	00 07		06 09		06 27	06 34	06 42	06 49	06 57		07 04	07 12	07 17	07 22	07 34	07 42	07 49	07 57	08 04		08 12	08 19	08 27
7½	**Gospel Oak**		d	00 10		06 12		06 30	06 37	06 45	06 52	07 00		07 07	07 15	07 20	07 25	07 37	07 45	07 52	08 00	08 07		08 15	08 22	08 30
8	Hampstead Heath		d	00 12		06 14		06 32	06 39	06 47	06 54	07 02		07 09	07 17	07 22	07 27	07 39	07 47	07 54	08 02	08 09		08 17	08 24	08 32
9	Finchley Road & Frognal		d	00 14		06 16		06 34	06 41	06 49	06 56	07 04		07 11	07 19	07 24	07 29	07 41	07 49	07 56	08 04	08 11		08 19	08 26	08 34
9½	West Hampstead	⊖	d	00 16		06 18		06 36	06 43	06 51	06 58	07 06		07 13	07 21	07 26	07 31	07 43	07 51	07 58	08 06	08 13		08 21	08 28	08 36
10	Brondesbury		d	00 18		06 20		06 38	06 45	06 53	07 00	07 08		07 15	07 23	07 28	07 33	07 45	07 53	08 00	08 08	08 15		08 23	08 30	08 38
10¼	Brondesbury Park		d	00 19		06 21		06 39	06 46	06 54	07 01	07 09		07 16	07 24	07 29	07 34	07 46	07 54	08 01	08 09	08 16		08 24	08 31	08 39
11	Kensal Rise		d	00a21		06 23		06 41	06 48	06 56	07 03	07 11		07 18	07 26	07 31	07 36	07 48	07 56	08 03	08 11	08 18		08 26	08 33	08 41
12	**Willesden Jn. High Level**	⊖	a			06 27		06 45	06 52	07 00	07 07	07 15		07 22	07 30	07 35	07 40	07 52	08 00	08 07	08 15	08 22		08 30	08 37	08 45
—			d		06 09	06 28	06 41		06 53		07 08			07 23		07 36		07 53		08 08		08 23			08 38	
13½	Acton Central		d		06 14	06 33	06 46		06 58		07 13			07 28		07 41		07 58		08 13		08 28			08 43	
14½	South Acton		d		06 16	06 36	06 49		07 01		07 16			07 31		07 44		08 01		08 16		08 31			08 46	
15¼	Gunnersbury	⊖	d		06 20	06 39	06 54		07 04		07 19			07 35		07 51		08 05		08 19		08 35			08 49	
16¼	Kew Gardens	⊖	d		06 23	06 42	06 57		07 07		07 22			07 38		07 54		08 08		08 22		08 38			08 52	
17½	**Richmond**	⊖	a		06 31	06 49	07 05		07 14		07 29			07 45		08 00		08 15		08 29		08 45			08 59	

			LO	LO	LO	LO	LO	LO		LO	LO	LO	LO	LO	LO	LO	LO	LO		LO	LO	LO	LO	LO	LO	LO
Stratford 7	⊖	d	08 12	08 20	08 27	08 35	08 42	08 50		08 57	09 05	09 15	09 25	09 35	09 45	09 55	10 05	10 15		10 25	10 35	10 45	10 55	11 05	11 15	11 25
Hackney Wick		d	08 15	08 23	08 30	08 38	08 45	08 53		09 00	09 08	09 18	09 28	09 38	09 48	09 58	10 08	10 18		10 28	10 38	10 48	10 58	11 08	11 18	11 28
Homerton		d	08 18	08 26	08 33	08 41	08 48	08 56		09 03	09 11	09 21	09 31	09 41	09 51	10 01	10 11	10 21		10 31	10 41	10 51	11 01	11 11	11 21	11 31
Hackney Central		d	08 20	08 28	08 35	08 43	08 50	08 58		09 05	09 13	09 23	09 33	09 43	09 53	10 03	10 13	10 23		10 33	10 43	10 53	11 03	11 13	11 23	11 33
Dalston Kingsland		d	08 22	08 30	08 37	08 45	08 52	09 00		09 07	09 15	09 25	09 35	09 45	09 55	10 05	10 15	10 25		10 35	10 45	10 55	11 05	11 15	11 25	11 35
Canonbury		d	08 24	08 32	08 39	08 47	08 54	09 02		09 09	09 17	09 27	09 37	09 47	09 57	10 07	10 17	10 27		10 37	10 47	10 57	11 07	11 17	11 27	11 37
Highbury & Islington	⊖	d	08 27	08 35	08 42	08 50	08 57	09 05		09 12	09 20	09 30	09 40	09 50	10 00	10 10	10 20	10 30		10 40	10 50	11 00	11 10	11 20	11 30	11 40
Caledonian Rd & Barnsbury		d	08 29	08 37	08 44	08 52	08 59	09 07		09 14	09 22	09 32	09 42	09 52	10 02	10 12	10 22	10 32		10 42	10 52	11 02	11 12	11 22	11 32	11 42
Camden Road		d	08 32	08 40	08 47	08 55	09 02	09 10		09 17	09 25	09 35	09 45	09 55	10 05	10 15	10 25	10 35		10 45	10 55	11 05	11 15	11 25	11 35	11 45
Kentish Town West		d	08 34	08 42	08 49	08 57	09 04	09 12		09 19	09 27	09 37	09 47	09 57	10 07	10 17	10 27	10 37		10 47	10 57	11 07	11 17	11 27	11 37	11 47
Gospel Oak		d	08 37	08 45	08 52	09 00	09 07	09 15		09 22	09 30	09 40	09 50	10 00	10 10	10 20	10 30	10 40		10 50	11 00	11 10	11 20	11 31	11 40	11 50
Hampstead Heath		d	08 39	08 47	08 54	09 02	09 09	09 17		09 24	09 32	09 42	09 52	10 02	10 12	10 22	10 32	10 42		10 52	11 02	11 12	11 22	11 33	11 42	11 52
Finchley Road & Frognal		d	08 41	08 49	08 56	09 04	09 11	09 19		09 26	09 34	09 44	09 54	10 04	10 14	10 24	10 34	10 44		10 54	11 04	11 14	11 24	11 35	11 44	11 54
West Hampstead	⊖	d	08 43	08 51	08 58	09 06	09 13	09 21		09 28	09 36	09 46	09 56	10 06	10 16	10 26	10 36	10 46		10 56	11 06	11 16	11 26	11 37	11 46	11 56
Brondesbury		d	08 45	08 53	09 00	09 08	09 15	09 23		09 30	09 38	09 48	09 58	10 08	10 18	10 28	10 38	10 48		10 58	11 08	11 18	11 28	11 39	11 48	11 58
Brondesbury Park		d	08 46	08 54	09 01	09 09	09 16	09 24		09 31	09 39	09 49	09 59	10 09	10 19	10 29	10 39	10 49		10 59	11 09	11 19	11 29	11 40	11 49	11 59
Kensal Rise		d	08 48	08 56	09 03	09 11	09 18	09 26		09 33	09 41	09 51	10 01	10 11	10 21	10 31	10 41	10 51		11 01	11 11	11 21	11 31	11 42	11 51	12 01
Willesden Jn. High Level	⊖	a	08 52	09 00	09 07	09 15	09 22	09 30		09 37	09 45	09 55	10 05	10 15	10 25	10 35	10 45	10 55		11 05	11 15	11 25	11 35	11 45	11 55	12 05
		d	08 53		09 08		09 23			09 38		09 56	10 06		10 26	10 36		10 56		11 06		11 26	11 36		11 56	12 06
Acton Central		d	08 58		09 13		09 28			09 43		10 01	10 11		10 31	10 41		11 01		11 11		11 31	11 41		12 01	12 11
South Acton		d	09 01		09 16		09 31			09 46		10 04	10 14		10 34	10 44		11 04		11 14		11 34	11 44		12 04	12 14
Gunnersbury	⊖	d	09 04		09 19		09 35			09 49		10 07	10 17		10 37	10 47		11 07		11 17		11 37	11 47		12 07	12 17
Kew Gardens	⊖	d	09 07		09 22		09 38			09 52		10 10	10 20		10 40	10 50		11 10		11 20		11 40	11 50		12 10	12 20
Richmond	⊖	a	09 14		09 29		09 45			09 59		10 17	10 27		10 47	10 57		11 17		11 27		11 47	11 57		12 17	12 27

			LO	LO		LO	LO		LO	LO	LO	LO	LO		LO	LO	LO	LO	LO	LO	LO	LO	LO		LO
Stratford 7	⊖	d	11 35	11 45		11 55	12 05	and at the same minutes past each hour until	15 05	15 15	15 25	15 35	15 42		15 50	15 57	16 12	16 20	16 27	16 35	16 42	16 50	16 57		17 05
Hackney Wick		d	11 38	11 48		11 58	12 08		15 08	15 18	15 28	15 38	15 45		15 53	16 00	16 15	16 23	16 30	16 38	16 45	16 53	17 00		17 08
Homerton		d	11 41	11 51		12 01	12 11		15 11	15 21	15 31	15 41	15 48		15 56	16 03	16 18	16 26	16 33	16 41	16 48	16 56	17 03		17 11
Hackney Central		d	11 43	11 53		12 03	12 13		15 13	15 23	15 33	15 43	15 50		15 58	16 05	16 20	16 28	16 35	16 43	16 50	16 58	17 05		17 13
Dalston Kingsland		d	11 45	11 55		12 05	12 15		15 15	15 25	15 35	15 45	15 52		16 00	16 07	16 22	16 30	16 37	16 45	16 52	17 00	17 07		17 15
Canonbury		d	11 47	11 57		12 07	12 17		15 17	15 27	15 37	15 47	15 54		16 02	16 09	16 24	16 32	16 39	16 47	16 54	17 02	17 09		17 17
Highbury & Islington	⊖	d	11 50	12 00		12 10	12 20		15 20	15 30	15 40	15 50	15 57		16 05	16 12	16 27	16 35	16 42	16 50	16 57	17 05	17 12		17 20
Caledonian Rd & Barnsbury		d	11 52	12 02		12 12	12 22		15 22	15 32	15 42	15 52	15 59		16 07	16 14	16 29	16 37	16 44	16 52	16 59	17 07	17 14		17 22
Camden Road		d	11 55	12 05		12 15	12 25		15 25	15 35	15 45	15 55	16 02		16 10	16 17	16 32	16 40	16 47	16 55	17 02	17 10	17 17		17 25
Kentish Town West		d	11 57	12 07		12 17	12 27		15 27	15 37	15 47	15 57	16 04		16 12	16 19	16 34	16 42	16 49	16 57	17 04	17 12	17 19		17 27
Gospel Oak		d	12 00	12 10		12 20	12 30		15 30	15 40	15 50	16 02	16 07		16 15	16 22	16 37	16 45	16 52	17 00	17 07	17 15	17 22		17 30
Hampstead Heath		d	12 02	12 12		12 22	12 32		15 32	15 42	15 52	16 04	16 09		16 17	16 24	16 39	16 47	16 54	17 02	17 09	17 17	17 24		17 32
Finchley Road & Frognal		d	12 04	12 14		12 24	12 34		15 34	15 44	15 54	16 06	16 11		16 19	16 26	16 41	16 49	16 56	17 04	17 11	17 19	17 26		17 34
West Hampstead	⊖	d	12 06	12 16		12 26	12 36		15 36	15 46	15 56	16 08	16 13		16 21	16 28	16 43	16 51	16 58	17 06	17 13	17 21	17 28		17 36
Brondesbury		d	12 08	12 18		12 28	12 38		15 38	15 48	15 58	16 10	16 15		16 23	16 30	16 45	16 53	17 00	17 08	17 15	17 23	17 30		17 38
Brondesbury Park		d	12 09	12 19		12 29	12 39		15 39	15 49	15 59	16 11	16 16		16 24	16 31	16 46	16 54	17 01	17 09	17 16	17 24	17 31		17 39
Kensal Rise		d	12 11	12 21		12 31	12 41		15 41	15 51	16 01	16 13	16 18		16 26	16 33	16 48	16 56	17 03	17 11	17 18	17 26	17 33		17 41
Willesden Jn. High Level	⊖	a	12 15	12 25		12 35	12 45		15 45	15 55	16 05	16 16	16 22		16 30	16 37	16 52	17 00	17 07	17 15	17 22	17 30	17 37		17 45
		d		12 26		12 36				15 56	16 06		16 23			16 38	16 53		17 08		17 23		17 38		
Acton Central		d		12 31		12 41				16 01	16 11		16 28			16 43	16 58		17 13		17 28		17 43		
South Acton		d		12 34		12 44				16 04	16 14		16 31			16 46	17 01		17 16		17 31		17 46		
Gunnersbury	⊖	d		12 37		12 47				16 07	16 17		16 34			16 49	17 05		17 19		17 35		17 49		
Kew Gardens	⊖	d		12 40		12 50				16 10	16 20		16 37			16 52	17 08		17 22		17 38		17 52		
Richmond	⊖	a		12 47		12 57				16 17	16 27		16 44			16 59	17 15		17 29		17 45		17 59		

Stratford - Highbury and Islington, West Hampstead, Willesden Junction and Richmond

		LO	LO	LO	LO	LO	LO	LO	LO		LO	LO	LO	LO	LO	LO	LO	LO	LO		LO	LO	LO	LO	LO
Stratford 7 ⊖	d	17 12	17 21	17 27	17 36	17 42	17 50	17 57	18 05		18 12	18 20	18 27	18 35	18 42	18 50	18 57	19 05	19 15		19 25	19 37	19 45	19 55	20 05
Hackney Wick	d	17 15	17 23	17 30	17 38	17 45	17 53	18 00	18 08		18 15	18 23	18 30	18 38	18 45	18 53	19 00	19 08	19 18		19 28	19 40	19 48	19 58	20 08
Homerton	d	17 18	17 26	17 33	17 41	17 48	17 56	18 03	18 11		18 18	18 26	18 33	18 41	18 48	18 56	19 03	19 11	19 21		19 31	19 43	19 51	20 01	20 11
Hackney Central	d	17 20	17 28	17 35	17 43	17 50	17 58	18 05	18 13		18 20	18 28	18 35	18 43	18 50	18 58	19 05	19 13	19 23		19 33	19 45	19 53	20 03	20 13
Dalston Kingsland	d	17 22	17 30	17 37	17 45	17 52	18 00	18 07	18 15		18 22	18 31	18 37	18 45	18 52	19 00	19 07	19 15	19 25		19 35	19 47	19 55	20 05	20 15
Canonbury	d	17 24	17 32	17 39	17 47	17 54	18 02	18 09	18 17		18 24	18 32	18 39	18 47	18 54	19 02	19 09	19 17	19 27		19 37	19 49	19 57	20 07	20 17
Highbury & Islington ⊖	d	17 27	17 35	17 42	17 50	17 57	18 05	18 12	18 20		18 27	18 35	18 42	18 50	18 57	19 05	19 12	19 20	19 30		19 40	19 52	20 00	20 10	20 20
Caledonian Rd & Barnsbury	d	17 29	17 37	17 44	17 52	17 59	18 07	18 14	18 22		18 29	18 37	18 44	18 52	18 59	19 07	19 14	19 22	19 32		19 42	19 54	20 02	20 12	20 22
Camden Road	d	17 32	17 40	17 47	17 55	18 02	18 10	18 17	18 25		18 32	18 40	18 47	18 55	19 02	19 10	19 17	19 25	19 35		19 45	19 57	20 05	20 15	20 25
Kentish Town West	d	17 34	17 42	17 49	17 57	18 04	18 12	18 19	18 27		18 34	18 42	18 49	18 57	19 04	19 12	19 19	19 27	19 37		19 47	19 59	20 07	20 17	20 27
Gospel Oak	d	17 37	17 45	17 52	18 00	18 07	18 15	18 22	18 30		18 37	18 45	18 52	19 00	19 07	19 15	19 24	19 30	19 40		19 50	20 01	20 10	20 20	20 30
Hampstead Heath	d	17 39	17 47	17 54	18 02	18 09	18 17	18 24	18 32		18 39	18 47	18 54	19 02	19 09	19 17	19 26	19 32	19 42		19 52	20 03	20 12	20 22	20 32
Finchley Road & Frognal	d	17 41	17 49	17 56	18 04	18 11	18 19	18 26	18 34		18 41	18 49	18 56	19 04	19 11	19 19	19 28	19 34	19 44		19 54	20 05	20 14	20 24	20 34
West Hampstead ⊖	d	17 43	17 51	17 58	18 06	18 13	18 21	18 28	18 36		18 43	18 51	18 58	19 06	19 13	19 21	19 30	19 36	19 46		19 56	20 07	20 16	20 26	20 36
Brondesbury	d	17 45	17 53	18 00	18 08	18 15	18 23	18 30	18 38		18 45	18 53	19 00	19 08	19 15	19 23	19 32	19 38	19 48		19 58	20 09	20 18	20 28	20 38
Brondesbury Park	d	17 46	17 54	18 01	18 09	18 16	18 24	18 31	18 39		18 46	18 54	19 01	19 09	19 16	19 24	19 33	19 39	19 49		19 59	20 10	20 19	20 29	20 39
Kensal Rise	d	17 48	17 56	18 03	18 11	18 18	18 26	18 33	18 41		18 48	18 56	19 03	19 11	19 18	19 26	19 35	19 41	19 51		20 01	20 12	20 21	20 31	20 41
Willesden Jn. High Level ⊖	a	17 52	18 00	18 07	18 15	18 22	18 30	18 37	18 45		18 52	19 00	19 07	19 15	19 22	19 30	19 39	19 45	19 55		20 08	20 16	20 25	20 35	20 45
	d	17 53		18 08		18 23		18 38			18 53		19 08		19 23		19 40		19 56		20 09		20 26	20 36	
Acton Central	d	17 58		18 13		18 28		18 43			18 58		19 13		19 28		19 45		20 01		20 14		20 31	20 41	
South Acton	d	18 01		18 16		18 31		18 46			19 01		19 16		19 31		19 48		20 04		20 17		20 34	20 44	
Gunnersbury ⊖	d	18 06		18 19		18 35		18 51			19 05		19 21		19 35		19 51		20 07		20 20		20 37	20 47	
Kew Gardens ⊖	d	18 09		18 22		18 38		18 54			19 08		19 24		19 38		19 54		20 10		20 23		20 40	20 50	
Richmond ⊖	a	18 16		18 29		18 45		19 01			19 15		19 31		19 45		20 01		20 17		20 30		20 47	20 57	

		LO	LO	LO	LO		LO	LO	LO	LO	LO	LO	LO	LO	LO		LO	LO
Stratford 7 ⊖	d	20 15	20 25	20 35	20 45		20 55	21 05	21 15	21 25	21 35	21 45	21 55	22 15	22 45		23 15	23 45
Hackney Wick	d	20 18	20 28	20 38	20 48		20 58	21 08	21 18	21 28	21 38	21 48	21 58	22 18	22 48		23 18	23 48
Homerton	d	20 21	20 31	20 41	20 51		21 01	21 11	21 21	21 31	21 41	21 51	22 01	22 21	22 51		23 21	23 51
Hackney Central	d	20 23	20 33	20 43	20 53		21 03	21 13	21 23	21 33	21 43	21 53	22 03	22 23	22 53		23 23	23 53
Dalston Kingsland	d	20 25	20 35	20 45	20 55		21 05	21 15	21 25	21 35	21 45	21 55	22 05	22 25	22 55		23 25	23 55
Canonbury	d	20 27	20 37	20 47	20 57		21 07	21 17	21 27	21 37	21 47	21 57	22 07	22 27	22 57		23 27	23 57
Highbury & Islington ⊖	d	20 30	20 40	20 50	21 00		21 10	21 20	21 30	21 40	21 50	22 00	22 10	22 30	23 00		23 30	23 59
Caledonian Rd & Barnsbury	d	20 32	20 42	20 52	21 02		21 12	21 22	21 32	21 42	21 52	22 02	22 12	22 32	23 02		23 32	00 02
Camden Road	d	20 35	20 48	20 55	21 05		21 15	21 25	21 35	21 45	21 55	22 05	22 15	22 35	23 05		23 35	00 05
Kentish Town West	d	20 37	20 51	20 57	21 07		21 17	21 27	21 37	21 47	21 57	22 07	22 17	22 37	23 07		23 37	00 07
Gospel Oak	d	20 40	20 54	21 00	21 10		21 20	21 30	21 40	21 50	22 00	22 10	22 20	22 40	23 10		23 40	00 10
Hampstead Heath	d	20 42	20 56	21 02	21 12		21 22	21 32	21 42	21 52	22 02	22 12	22 22	22 42	23 12		23 42	00 12
Finchley Road & Frognal	d	20 44	20 58	21 04	21 14		21 24	21 34	21 44	21 54	22 04	22 14	22 24	22 44	23 14		23 44	00 14
West Hampstead ⊖	d	20 46	21 00	21 06	21 16		21 26	21 36	21 46	21 56	22 06	22 16	22 26	22 46	23 16		23 46	00 16
Brondesbury	d	20 48	21 01	21 08	21 18		21 28	21 38	21 48	21 58	22 08	22 18	22 28	22 48	23 18		23 48	00 18
Brondesbury Park	d	20 49	21 03	21 09	21 19		21 29	21 39	21 49	21 59	22 09	22 19	22 29	22 49	23 19		23 49	00 19
Kensal Rise	d	20 51	21 05	21 11	21 21		21 31	21 41	21 51	22 01	22 11	22 21	22 31	22 51	23 21		23a51	00a21
Willesden Jn. High Level ⊖	a	20 55	21 09	21 15	21 25		21 35	21 45	21 55	22 05	22 15	22 25	22 35	22 55	23 25			
	d	20 57	21 10		21 26		21 36		21 56	22 06		22 26	22 36	22 56	23 26			
Acton Central	d	21 02	21 15		21 31		21 41		22 01	22 11		22 31	22 41	23 01	23 31			
South Acton	d	21 05	21 17		21 34		21 44		22 04	22 14		22 34	22 44	23 04	23 34			
Gunnersbury ⊖	d	21 08	21 22		21 37		21 47		22 07	22 17		22 37	22 47	23 07	23 37			
Kew Gardens ⊖	d	21 11	21 25		21 40		21 50		22 10	22 20		22 40	22 50	23 10	23 40			
Richmond ⊖	a	21 18	21 31		21 47		21 57		22 17	22 27		22 47	22 57	23 17	23 47			

Saturdays

		LO	LO	LO	LO	LO	LO	LO	LO	LO		LO		LO	LO	LO	LO	LO	LO	LO	LO	LO		LO
Stratford 7 ⊖	d	23p45		05 45	05 55	06 05	06 15	06 25	06 35	06 45		17 45		17 55	18 05	18 15	18 25	18 35	18 45	18 55	19 05	19 15		19 25
Hackney Wick	d	23p48		05 48	05 58	06 08	06 18	06 28	06 38	06 48		17 48		17 58	18 08	18 18	18 28	18 38	18 48	18 58	19 08	19 18		19 28
Homerton	d	23p51		05 51	06 01	06 11	06 21	06 31	06 41	06 51		17 51		18 01	18 11	18 21	18 31	18 41	18 51	19 01	19 11	19 21		19 31
Hackney Central	d	23p53		05 53	06 03	06 13	06 23	06 33	06 43	06 53		17 53		18 03	18 13	18 23	18 33	18 43	18 53	19 03	19 13	19 23		19 33
Dalston Kingsland	d	23p55		05 55	06 05	06 15	06 25	06 35	06 45	06 55		17 55		18 05	18 15	18 25	18 35	18 45	18 55	19 05	19 15	19 25		19 35
Canonbury	d	23p57		05 57	06 07	06 17	06 27	06 37	06 47	06 57		17 57		18 07	18 17	18 27	18 37	18 47	18 57	19 07	19 17	19 27		19 37
Highbury & Islington ⊖	d	23p59		06 00	06 10	06 20	06 30	06 40	06 50	07 00		18 00		18 10	18 20	18 30	18 40	18 50	19 00	19 10	19 20	19 30		19 40
Caledonian Rd & Barnsbury	d	00 02		06 02	06 12	06 22	06 32	06 42	06 52	07 02		18 02		18 12	18 22	18 32	18 42	18 52	19 02	19 12	19 22	19 32		19 42
Camden Road	d	00 05		06 05	06 15	06 25	06 35	06 45	06 55	07 05	and at the same minutes past each hour until	18 05		18 15	18 25	18 35	18 45	18 55	19 05	19 15	19 25	19 35		19 45
Kentish Town West	d	00 07		06 07	06 17	06 27	06 37	06 47	06 57	07 07		18 07		18 17	18 27	18 37	18 47	18 57	19 07	19 17	19 27	19 37		19 47
Gospel Oak	d	00 10		06 11	06 20	06 30	06 40	06 50	07 00	07 10		18 10		18 20	18 30	18 40	18 50	19 00	19 10	19 20	19 30	19 40		19 50
Hampstead Heath	d	00 12		06 13	06 22	06 32	06 42	06 52	07 02	07 12		18 12		18 22	18 32	18 42	18 52	19 02	19 12	19 22	19 32	19 42		19 52
Finchley Road & Frognal	d	00 14		06 15	06 24	06 34	06 44	06 54	07 04	07 14		18 14		18 24	18 34	18 44	18 54	19 04	19 14	19 24	19 34	19 44		19 54
West Hampstead ⊖	d	00 16		06 17	06 26	06 36	06 46	06 56	07 06	07 16		18 16		18 26	18 36	18 46	18 56	19 06	19 16	19 26	19 36	19 46		19 56
Brondesbury	d	00 18		06 19	06 28	06 38	06 48	06 58	07 08	07 18		18 18		18 28	18 38	18 48	18 58	19 08	19 18	19 28	19 38	19 48		19 58
Brondesbury Park	d	00 19		06 20	06 29	06 39	06 49	06 59	07 09	07 19		18 19		18 29	18 39	18 49	18 59	19 09	19 19	19 29	19 39	19 49		19 59
Kensal Rise	d	00a21		06 22	06 31	06 41	06 51	07 01	07 11	07 21		18 21		18 31	18 41	18 51	19 01	19 11	19 21	19 31	19 41	19 51		20 01
Willesden Jn. High Level ⊖	a			06 25	06 35	06 45	06 55	07 05	07 15	07 25		18 25		18 35	18 45	18 55	19 05	19 15	19 25	19 35	19 45	19 55		20 05
	d		06 06	06 26	06 36		06 56	07 06		07 26		18 26		18 36		18 56	19 06		19 26	19 36		19 56		20 06
Acton Central	d		06 11	06 31	06 41		07 01	07 11		07 31		18 31		18 41		19 01	19 11		19 31	19 41		20 01		20 11
South Acton	d		06 14	06 34	06 44		07 04	07 14		07 34		18 34		18 44		19 04	19 14		19 34	19 44		20 04		20 14
Gunnersbury ⊖	d		06 19	06 37	06 47		07 07	07 17		07 37		18 37		18 47		19 07	19 17		19 37	19 47		20 07		20 17
Kew Gardens ⊖	d		06 22	06 40	06 50		07 10	07 20		07 40		18 40		18 50		19 10	19 20		19 40	19 50		20 10		20 20
Richmond ⊖	a		06 29	06 47	06 57		07 17	07 27		07 47		18 47		18 57		19 17	19 28		19 47	19 57		20 17		20 27

Table 59

Saturdays

Stratford - Highbury and Islington, West Hampstead, Willesden Junction and Richmond

		LO	LO	LO	LO	LO	LO	LO	LO		LO	LO	LO	LO	LO	LO	LO	LO	LO		LO	LO
Stratford 7	⊖ d	19 35	19 45	19 55	20 05	20 15	20 25	20 35	20 45		20 55	21 05	21 15	21 25	21 35	21 45	21 55	22 15	22 45		23 15	23 45
Hackney Wick	d	19 38	19 48	19 58	20 08	20 18	20 28	20 38	20 48		20 58	21 08	21 18	21 28	21 38	21 48	21 58	22 18	22 48		23 18	23 48
Homerton	d	19 41	19 51	20 01	20 11	20 21	20 31	20 41	20 51		21 01	21 11	21 21	21 31	21 41	21 51	22 01	22 21	22 51		23 21	23 51
Hackney Central	d	19 43	19 53	20 03	20 13	20 23	20 33	20 43	20 53		21 03	21 13	21 23	21 33	21 43	21 53	22 03	22 23	22 53		23 23	23 53
Dalston Kingsland	d	19 45	19 55	20 05	20 15	20 25	20 35	20 45	20 55		21 05	21 15	21 25	21 35	21 45	21 55	22 05	22 25	22 55		23 25	23 55
Canonbury	d	19 47	19 57	20 07	20 17	20 27	20 37	20 47	20 57		21 07	21 17	21 27	21 37	21 47	21 57	22 07	22 27	22 57		23 27	23 57
Highbury & Islington	⊖ d	19 50	20 00	20 10	20 20	20 30	20 40	20 50	21 00		21 10	21 20	21 30	21 40	21 50	22 00	22 10	22 30	23 00		23 30	23 59
Caledonian Rd & Barnsbury	d	19 52	20 02	20 12	20 22	20 32	20 42	20 52	21 02		21 12	21 22	21 32	21 42	21 52	22 02	22 12	22 32	23 02		23 32	00 02
Camden Road	d	19 55	20 05	20 15	20 25	20 35	20 45	20 55	21 05		21 15	21 25	21 35	21 45	21 55	22 05	22 15	22 35	23 05		23 35	00 05
Kentish Town West	d	19 57	20 07	20 17	20 27	20 37	20 47	20 57	21 07		21 17	21 27	21 37	21 47	21 57	22 07	22 17	22 37	23 07		23 37	00 07
Gospel Oak	d	20 00	20 10	20 20	20 30	20 40	20 50	21 00	21 10		21 20	21 30	21 40	21 50	22 00	22 10	22 20	22 40	23 10		23 40	00 10
Hampstead Heath	d	20 02	20 12	20 22	20 32	20 42	20 52	21 02	21 12		21 22	21 32	21 42	21 52	22 02	22 12	22 22	22 42	23 12		23 42	00 12
Finchley Road & Frognal	d	20 04	20 14	20 24	20 34	20 44	20 54	21 04	21 14		21 24	21 34	21 44	21 54	22 04	22 14	22 24	22 44	23 14		23 44	00 14
West Hampstead	⊖ d	20 06	20 16	20 26	20 36	20 46	20 56	21 06	21 16		21 26	21 36	21 46	21 56	22 06	22 16	22 26	22 46	23 16		23 46	00 16
Brondesbury	d	20 08	20 18	20 28	20 38	20 48	20 58	21 08	21 18		21 28	21 38	21 48	21 58	22 08	22 18	22 28	22 48	23 18		23 48	00 18
Brondesbury Park	d	20 09	20 19	20 29	20 39	20 49	20 59	21 09	21 19		21 29	21 39	21 49	21 59	22 09	22 19	22 29	22 49	23 19		23 49	00 19
Kensal Rise	d	20 11	20 21	20 31	20 41	20 51	21 01	21 11	21 21		21 31	21 41	21 51	22 01	22 11	22 21	22 31	22 51	23 21		23 51	00a21
Willesden Jn. High Level	⊖ a	20 15	20 25	20 35	20 45	20 55	21 05	21 15	21 25		21 35	21 45	21 55	22 05	22 15	22 25	22 35	22 55	23 25		23 54	
	d		20 26	20 36		20 56	21 06		21 26		21 36		21 56	22 06		22 26	22 36	22 56	23 26			
Acton Central	d		20 31	20 41		21 01	21 11		21 31		21 41		22 01	22 11		22 31	22 41	23 01	23 31			
South Acton	d		20 34	20 44		21 04	21 14		21 34		21 44		22 04	22 14		22 34	22 44	23 04	23 34			
Gunnersbury	⊖ d		20 37	20 47		21 07	21 17		21 37		21 47		22 07	22 17		22 37	22 47	23 07	23 37			
Kew Gardens	⊖ d		20 40	20 50		21 10	21 20		21 40		21 50		22 10	22 20		22 40	22 50	23 10	23 40			
Richmond	⊖ a		20 47	20 57		21 17	21 27		21 47		21 57		22 17	22 27		22 47	22 57	23 17	23 47			

Sundays

		LO A	LO	LO	LO	LO	LO	LO	LO	LO		LO	LO	LO	LO	LO	LO	LO	LO		LO		LO	LO
Stratford 7	⊖ d	23p45				09 15	09 30	09 45	10 00	10 20		10 35		10 45	10 55	11 05	11 15	11 25	11 35	and at the same minutes past each hour until	20 35		20 45	21 00
Hackney Wick	d	23p48				09 18	09 33	09 48	10 03	10 23		10 38		10 48	10 58	11 08	11 18	11 28	11 38		20 38		20 48	21 03
Homerton	d	23p51				09 21	09 36	09 51	10 06	10 26		10 41		10 51	11 01	11 11	11 21	11 31	11 41		20 41		20 51	21 06
Hackney Central	d	23p53				09 23	09 38	09 53	10 08	10 28		10 43		10 53	11 03	11 13	11 23	11 33	11 43		20 43		20 53	21 08
Dalston Kingsland	d	23p55				09 25	09 40	09 55	10 10	10 30		10 45		10 55	11 05	11 15	11 25	11 35	11 45		20 45		20 55	21 10
Canonbury	d	23p57				09 27	09 42	09 57	10 12	10 32		10 47		10 57	11 07	11 17	11 27	11 37	11 47		20 47		20 57	21 12
Highbury & Islington	⊖ d	23p59				09 30	09 45	10 00	10 15	10 35		10 50		11 00	11 10	11 20	11 30	11 40	11 50		20 50		21 00	21 15
Caledonian Rd & Barnsbury	d	00 02				09 32	09 47	10 02	10 17	10 37		10 52		11 02	11 12	11 22	11 32	11 42	11 52		20 52		21 02	21 17
Camden Road	d	00 05				09 35	09 50	10 05	10 20	10 40		10 55		11 05	11 15	11 25	11 35	11 45	11 55		20 55		21 05	21 20
Kentish Town West	d	00 07				09 37	09 52	10 07	10 22	10 42		10 57		11 07	11 17	11 27	11 37	11 47	11 57		20 57		21 07	21 22
Gospel Oak	d	00 10			09 25	09 40	09 55	10 10	10 25	10 45		11 00		11 10	11 20	11 30	11 40	11 50	12 00		21 00		21 10	21 25
Hampstead Heath	d	00 12			09 27	09 42	09 57	10 12	10 27	10 47		11 02		11 12	11 22	11 32	11 42	11 52	12 02		21 02		21 12	21 27
Finchley Road & Frognal	d	00 14			09 29	09 44	09 59	10 14	10 29	10 49		11 04		11 14	11 24	11 34	11 44	11 54	12 04		21 04		21 14	21 29
West Hampstead	⊖ d	00 16			09 31	09 46	10 01	10 16	10 31	10 51		11 06		11 16	11 26	11 36	11 46	11 56	12 06		21 06		21 16	21 31
Brondesbury	d	00 18			09 33	09 48	10 03	10 18	10 33	10 53		11 08		11 18	11 28	11 38	11 48	11 58	12 08		21 08		21 18	21 33
Brondesbury Park	d	00 19			09 34	09 49	10 04	10 19	10 34	10 54		11 09		11 19	11 29	11 39	11 49	11 59	12 09		21 09		21 19	21 34
Kensal Rise	d	00a21			09 36	09 51	10 06	10 21	10 36	10 56		11 11		11 21	11 31	11 41	11 51	12 01	12 11		21 11		21 21	21 36
Willesden Jn. High Level	⊖ a				09 40	09 55	10 10	10 25	10 40	11 00		11 15		11 25	11 35	11 45	11 55	12 05	12 15		21 15		21 25	21 40
	d		08 56	09 26	09 41	09 56	10 11	10 26	10 41	11 01			11 16	11 26	11 36		11 56	12 06					21 26	21 44
Acton Central	d		09 01	09 31	09 46	10 01	10 16	10 31	10 46	11 06			11 21	11 31	11 41		12 01	12 11					21 31	21 49
South Acton	d		09 03	09 34	09 49	10 04	10 19	10 34	10 49	11 09			11 24	11 34	11 44		12 04	12 14					21 34	21 52
Gunnersbury	⊖ d		09 06	09 37	09 52	10 07	10 22	10 37	10 52	11 12			11 27	11 37	11 47		12 07	12 17					21 37	21 55
Kew Gardens	⊖ d		09 09	09 40	09 55	10 10	10 25	10 40	10 55	11 15			11 30	11 40	11 50		12 10	12 20					21 40	21 58
Richmond	⊖ a		09 17	09 47	10 04	10 17	10 34	10 47	11 04	11 22			11 37	11 47	11 57		12 17	12 27					21 47	22 02

		LO	LO	LO	LO	LO	LO
Stratford 7	⊖ d	21 15	21 30	21 45	22 00		
Hackney Wick	d	21 18	21 33	21 48	22 03		
Homerton	d	21 21	21 36	21 51	22 06		
Hackney Central	d	21 23	21 38	21 53	22 08		
Dalston Kingsland	d	21 25	21 40	21 55	22 10		
Canonbury	d	21 27	21 42	21 57	22 12		
Highbury & Islington	⊖ d	21 30	21 45	22 00	22 15		
Caledonian Rd & Barnsbury	d	21 32	21 47	22 02	22 17		
Camden Road	d	21 35	21 50	22 05	22 20		
Kentish Town West	d	21 37	21 52	22 07	22 22		
Gospel Oak	d	21 40	21 55	22 10	22 25	22 55	23 30
Hampstead Heath	d	21 42	21 57	22 12	22 27	22 57	23 32
Finchley Road & Frognal	d	21 44	21 59	22 14	22 29	22 59	23 34
West Hampstead	⊖ d	21 46	22 01	22 16	22 31	23 01	23 36
Brondesbury	d	21 48	22 03	22 18	22 33	23 03	23 38
Brondesbury Park	d	21 49	22 04	22 19	22 34	23 04	23 39
Kensal Rise	d	21 51	22 06	22 21	22 36	23 06	23a41
Willesden Jn. High Level	⊖ a	21 55	22 10	22 25	22 40	23 10	
	d	21 56	22 11	22 26	22 41	23 11	
Acton Central	d	22 01	22 16	22 31	22 46	23 16	
South Acton	d	22 04	22 19	22 34	22 49	23 19	
Gunnersbury	⊖ d	22 07	22 22	22 37	22 52	23 22	
Kew Gardens	⊖ d	22 10	22 25	22 40	22 55	23 25	
Richmond	⊖ a	22 17	22 33	22 47	23 02	23 32	

A not 22 May

Table 59

Mondays to Fridays

Richmond - Willesden Junction, West Hampstead, Highbury and Islington and Stratford

Miles	Station		LO MX	LO	LO	LO	LO	LO	LO	LO	LO	LO	LO	LO	LO	LO	LO	LO	LO	LO	LO	LO	LO
0	**Richmond**	⊖ d	23p00			05 54	06 09		06 21		06 39		06 53		07 09		07 24		07 39		07 53		08 08
1½	Kew Gardens	⊖ d	23p03			05 57	06 12		06 24		06 42		06 56		07 12		07 27		07 42		07 56		08 11
2½	Gunnersbury	⊖ d	23p06			06 00	06 15		06 27		06 45		06 59		07 15		07 30		07 45		07 59		08 14
3¼	South Acton	d	23p09			06 03	06 18		06 30		06 48		07 02		07 18		07 33		07 48		08 02		08 17
4	Acton Central	d	23p12			06 06	06 21		06 36		06 51		07 06		07 21		07 36		07 51		08 06		08 21
5¾	**Willesden Jn. High Level**	⊖ a	23p17			06 11	06 26		06 41		06 56		07 11		07 26		07 41		07 56		08 11		08 26
—		d	23p18			06 12	06 27	06 35	06 42	06 51	06 57	07 05	07 12	07 20	07 27	07 35	07 42	07 50	07 57	08 06	08 12	08 20	08 27
6¾	Kensal Rise	d	23p20		06 02	06 14	06 29	06 37	06 44	06 52	06 59	07 07	07 14	07 22	07 29	07 37	07 44	07 52	07 59	08 08	08 14	08 22	08 29
7½	Brondesbury Park	d	23p22		06 04	06 16	06 31	06 39	06 46	06 54	07 01	07 09	07 16	07 24	07 31	07 39	07 46	07 54	08 01	08 10	08 16	08 24	08 31
7¾	Brondesbury	d	23p24		06 06	06 18	06 33	06 41	06 48	06 56	07 03	07 11	07 18	07 26	07 33	07 41	07 48	07 56	08 03	08 12	08 18	08 26	08 33
8¼	West Hampstead	⊖ d	23p26		06 08	06 20	06 35	06 43	06 50	06 58	07 05	07 13	07 20	07 28	07 35	07 43	07 50	07 58	08 05	08 14	08 20	08 28	08 35
8¾	Finchley Road & Frognal	d	23p27		06 09	06 21	06 36	06 44	06 51	06 59	07 06	07 14	07 21	07 29	07 36	07 44	07 51	07 59	08 06	08 15	08 21	08 29	08 36
9¾	Hampstead Heath	d	23p30		06 12	06 24	06 39	06 47	06 54	07 02	07 09	07 17	07 24	07 32	07 39	07 47	07 54	08 02	08 09	08 18	08 24	08 32	08 39
10¼	**Gospel Oak**	d	23p32		06 14	06 26	06 41	06 49	06 56	07 04	07 11	07 19	07 26	07 34	07 41	07 49	07 56	08 04	08 11	08 20	08 26	08 34	08 41
11	Kentish Town West	d	23p34		06 16	06 28	06 43	06 51	06 58	07 06	07 13	07 21	07 28	07 36	07 43	07 51	07 58	08 06	08 13	08 22	08 28	08 36	08 43
11¼	Camden Road	d	23p38	06 11	06 20	06 32	06 47	06 55	07 02	07 10	07 17	07 25	07 32	07 40	07 47	07 55	08 02	08 10	08 17	08 26	08 32	08 40	08 47
12½	Caledonian Rd & Barnsbury	d	23p41	06 14	06 23	06 35	06 50	06 58	07 05	07 13	07 20	07 28	07 35	07 43	07 50	07 58	08 05	08 13	08 20	08 29	08 35	08 43	08 50
13	**Highbury & Islington**	⊖ d	23p44	06 16	06 26	06 38	06 53	07 01	07 08	07 16	07 23	07 31	07 38	07 46	07 53	08 01	08 08	08 16	08 23	08 32	08 38	08 46	08 53
13½	Canonbury	⊖ d	23p46	06 18	06 28	06 40	06 55	07 03	07 10	07 18	07 25	07 33	07 40	07 48	07 55	08 03	08 10	08 18	08 25	08 34	08 40	08 48	08 55
14½	Dalston Kingsland	d	23p48	06 20	06 30	06 42	06 57	07 05	07 12	07 20	07 27	07 35	07 42	07 50	07 57	08 05	08 12	08 20	08 27	08 36	08 42	08 50	08 57
15¼	Hackney Central	d	23p50	06 22	06 32	06 44	06 59	07 07	07 14	07 22	07 29	07 37	07 44	07 52	07 59	08 07	08 14	08 22	08 29	08 38	08 44	08 52	08 59
16	Homerton	d	23p52	06 24	06 34	06 46	07 01	07 09	07 16	07 24	07 31	07 39	07 46	07 54	08 01	08 09	08 16	08 24	08 31	08 40	08 46	08 54	09 01
16¾	Hackney Wick	d	23p54	06 26	06 36	06 48	07 03	07 11	07 18	07 26	07 33	07 41	07 48	07 56	08 03	08 11	08 18	08 26	08 33	08 42	08 48	08 56	09 03
17¾	**Stratford** 7	⊖ a	00 02	06 35	06 45	06 56	07 11	07 18	07 26	07 33	07 41	07 48	07 56	08 03	08 11	08 18	08 26	08 33	08 41	08 49	08 56	09 03	09 11

Station		LO	LO	LO	LO	LO	LO	LO	LO	LO	LO	LO	LO	LO	LO	LO	LO	LO	LO	LO	LO	LO	LO
Richmond	⊖ d	08 22		08 38		08 53		09 08		09 27	09 38		09 57	10 08		10 28	10 38		10 57	11 08		11 28	11 38
Kew Gardens	⊖ d	08 25		08 41		08 56		09 11		09 30	09 41		10 00	10 11		10 31	10 41		11 00	11 11		11 31	11 41
Gunnersbury	⊖ d	08 28		08 44		08 59		09 14		09 33	09 44		10 03	10 14		10 34	10 44		11 03	11 14		11 34	11 44
South Acton	d	08 31		08 47		09 02		09 17		09 36	09 47		10 06	10 17		10 37	10 47		11 06	11 17		11 37	11 47
Acton Central	d	08 36		08 51		09 06		09 20		09 40	09 50		10 10	10 20		10 40	10 50		11 10	11 20		11 40	11 50
Willesden Jn. High Level	⊖ a	08 41		08 56		09 11		09 25		09 45	09 55		10 15	10 25		10 45	10 55		11 15	11 25		11 45	11 55
	d	08 42	08 50	08 57	09 06	09 13	09 20	09 26	09 36	09 46	09 56	10 06	10 16	10 26	10 36	10 46	10 56	11 06	11 16	11 26	11 36	11 46	11 56
Kensal Rise	d	08 44	08 52	08 59	09 08	09 15	09 22	09 28	09 38	09 48	09 58	10 08	10 18	10 28	10 38	10 48	10 58	11 08	11 18	11 28	11 38	11 48	11 58
Brondesbury Park	d	08 46	08 54	09 01	09 10	09 17	09 24	09 30	09 40	09 50	10 00	10 10	10 20	10 30	10 40	10 50	11 00	11 10	11 20	11 30	11 40	11 50	12 00
Brondesbury	d	08 48	08 56	09 03	09 12	09 19	09 26	09 32	09 42	09 52	10 02	10 12	10 22	10 32	10 42	10 52	11 02	11 12	11 22	11 32	11 42	11 52	12 02
West Hampstead	⊖ d	08 50	08 58	09 05	09 14	09 21	09 28	09 34	09 44	09 54	10 04	10 14	10 24	10 34	10 44	10 54	11 04	11 14	11 24	11 34	11 44	11 54	12 04
Finchley Road & Frognal	d	08 51	08 59	09 06	09 15	09 22	09 29	09 35	09 45	09 55	10 05	10 15	10 25	10 35	10 45	10 55	11 05	11 15	11 25	11 35	11 45	11 55	12 05
Hampstead Heath	d	08 54	09 02	09 09	09 18	09 25	09 32	09 38	09 48	09 58	10 08	10 18	10 28	10 38	10 48	10 58	11 08	11 18	11 28	11 38	11 48	11 58	12 08
Gospel Oak	d	08 56	09 04	09 11	09 20	09 27	09 34	09 40	09 50	10 00	10 10	10 20	10 30	10 40	10 50	11 00	11 10	11 20	11 30	11 40	11 50	12 00	12 10
Kentish Town West	d	08 58	09 06	09 13	09 22	09 29	09 36	09 42	09 52	10 02	10 12	10 22	10 32	10 42	10 52	11 02	11 12	11 22	11 32	11 42	11 52	12 02	12 12
Camden Road	d	09 02	09 10	09 17	09 26	09 33	09 40	09 46	09 56	10 06	10 16	10 26	10 36	10 46	10 56	11 06	11 16	11 26	11 36	11 46	11 56	12 06	12 16
Caledonian Rd & Barnsbury	d	09 05	09 13	09 20	09 29	09 36	09 43	09 49	09 59	10 09	10 19	10 29	10 39	10 49	10 59	11 09	11 19	11 29	11 39	11 49	11 59	12 09	12 19
Highbury & Islington	⊖ d	09 08	09 16	09 23	09 32	09 39	09 46	09 52	10 02	10 12	10 22	10 32	10 42	10 52	11 02	11 12	11 22	11 32	11 42	11 52	12 02	12 12	12 22
Canonbury	⊖ d	09 10	09 18	09 25	09 34	09 41	09 48	09 54	10 04	10 14	10 24	10 34	10 44	10 54	11 04	11 14	11 24	11 34	11 44	11 54	12 04	12 14	12 24
Dalston Kingsland	d	09 12	09 20	09 27	09 36	09 43	09 50	09 56	10 06	10 16	10 26	10 36	10 46	10 56	11 06	11 16	11 26	11 36	11 46	11 56	12 06	12 16	12 26
Hackney Central	d	09 14	09 22	09 29	09 38	09 45	09 52	09 58	10 08	10 18	10 28	10 38	10 48	10 58	11 08	11 18	11 28	11 38	11 48	11 58	12 08	12 18	12 28
Homerton	d	09 16	09 24	09 31	09 40	09 47	09 54	10 00	10 10	10 20	10 30	10 40	10 50	11 00	11 10	11 20	11 30	11 40	11 50	12 00	12 10	12 20	12 30
Hackney Wick	d	09 18	09 26	09 33	09 42	09 49	09 56	10 02	10 12	10 22	10 32	10 42	10 52	11 02	11 12	11 22	11 32	11 42	11 52	12 02	12 12	12 22	12 32
Stratford 7	⊖ a	09 26	09 33	09 41	09 51	09 57	10 03	10 10	10 20	10 30	10 40	10 50	11 00	11 10	11 20	11 30	11 40	11 49	12 00	12 10	12 20	12 30	12 40

Station		LO	LO	LO	LO	LO	LO	LO	LO	LO	LO	LO	LO	LO	LO	LO	LO	LO	LO	LO	LO	LO
Richmond	⊖ d		11 58	12 08		12 28	12 38		12 58	13 08		13 28	13 38		13 58	14 10		14 28	14 38		14 58	15 08
Kew Gardens	⊖ d		12 01	12 11		12 31	12 41		13 01	13 11		13 31	13 41		14 01	14 13		14 31	14 41		15 01	15 11
Gunnersbury	⊖ d		12 04	12 14		12 34	12 44		13 04	13 14		13 34	13 44		14 04	14 16		14 34	14 44		15 04	15 14
South Acton	d		12 07	12 17		12 37	12 47		13 07	13 17		13 37	13 47		14 07	14 19		14 37	14 47		15 07	15 17
Acton Central	d		12 10	12 20		12 40	12 50		13 10	13 20		13 40	13 50		14 10	14 22		14 40	14 50		15 10	15 20
Willesden Jn. High Level	⊖ a		12 15	12 25		12 45	12 55		13 15	13 25		13 45	13 55		14 15	14 27		14 45	14 55		15 15	15 25
	d	12 06	12 16	12 26	12 36	12 46	12 56	13 06	13 16	13 26	13 36	13 46	13 56	14 06	14 16	14 28	14 36	14 46	14 56	15 06	15 16	15 26
Kensal Rise	d	12 08	12 18	12 28	12 38	12 48	12 58	13 08	13 18	13 28	13 38	13 48	13 58	14 08	14 18	14 30	14 38	14 48	14 58	15 08	15 18	15 28
Brondesbury Park	d	12 10	12 20	12 30	12 40	12 50	13 00	13 10	13 20	13 30	13 40	13 50	14 00	14 10	14 20	14 32	14 40	14 50	15 00	15 10	15 20	15 30
Brondesbury	d	12 12	12 22	12 32	12 42	12 52	13 02	13 12	13 22	13 32	13 42	13 52	14 02	14 12	14 22	14 34	14 42	14 52	15 02	15 12	15 22	15 32
West Hampstead	⊖ d	12 14	12 24	12 34	12 44	12 54	13 04	13 14	13 24	13 34	13 44	13 54	14 04	14 14	14 24	14 36	14 44	14 54	15 04	15 14	15 24	15 34
Finchley Road & Frognal	d	12 15	12 25	12 35	12 45	12 55	13 05	13 15	13 25	13 35	13 45	13 55	14 05	14 15	14 25	14 37	14 45	14 55	15 05	15 15	15 25	15 35
Hampstead Heath	d	12 18	12 28	12 38	12 48	12 58	13 08	13 18	13 28	13 38	13 48	13 58	14 08	14 18	14 28	14 40	14 48	14 58	15 08	15 18	15 28	15 38
Gospel Oak	d	12 20	12 30	12 40	12 50	13 00	13 10	13 20	13 30	13 40	13 50	14 00	14 10	14 20	14 30	14 42	14 50	15 00	15 10	15 20	15 30	15 40
Kentish Town West	d	12 22	12 32	12 42	12 52	13 02	13 12	13 22	13 32	13 42	13 52	14 02	14 12	14 22	14 32	14 44	14 52	15 02	15 12	15 22	15 32	15 42
Camden Road	d	12 26	12 36	12 46	12 56	13 06	13 16	13 26	13 36	13 46	13 56	14 06	14 16	14 26	14 36	14 48	14 56	15 06	15 16	15 27	15 36	15 46
Caledonian Rd & Barnsbury	d	12 29	12 39	12 49	12 59	13 09	13 19	13 29	13 39	13 49	13 59	14 09	14 19	14 29	14 39	14 51	14 59	15 09	15 19	15 30	15 39	15 49
Highbury & Islington	⊖ d	12 32	12 42	12 52	13 02	13 12	13 22	13 32	13 42	13 52	14 02	14 12	14 22	14 32	14 42	14 54	15 02	15 12	15 22	15 33	15 42	15 52
Canonbury	⊖ d	12 34	12 44	12 54	13 04	13 14	13 24	13 34	13 44	13 54	14 04	14 14	14 24	14 34	14 44	14 56	15 04	15 14	15 24	15 35	15 44	15 54
Dalston Kingsland	d	12 36	12 46	12 56	13 06	13 16	13 26	13 36	13 46	13 56	14 06	14 16	14 26	14 36	14 46	14 58	15 06	15 16	15 26	15 37	15 46	15 56
Hackney Central	d	12 38	12 48	12 58	13 08	13 18	13 28	13 38	13 48	13 58	14 08	14 18	14 28	14 38	14 48	15 00	15 08	15 18	15 28	15 39	15 48	15 58
Homerton	d	12 40	12 50	13 00	13 10	13 20	13 30	13 40	13 50	14 00	14 10	14 20	14 30	14 40	14 50	15 02	15 10	15 20	15 30	15 41	15 50	16 00
Hackney Wick	d	12 42	12 52	13 02	13 12	13 22	13 32	13 42	13 52	14 02	14 12	14 22	14 32	14 42	14 52	15 04	15 12	15 22	15 32	15 43	15 52	16 02
Stratford 7	⊖ a	12 50	13 00	13 10	13 20	13 30	13 40	13 50	14 00	14 10	14 20	14 30	14 40	14 50	15 00	15 12	15 20	15 30	15 40	15 51	16 00	16 11

Richmond - Willesden Junction, West Hampstead, Highbury and Islington and Stratford

			LO	LO	LO	LO	LO	LO	LO	LO		LO	LO	LO	LO	LO	LO	LO	LO	LO		LO	LO	LO	LO	LO
Richmond	⊖	d		15 26	15 38		15 51		16 09			16 24		16 39		16 53		17 09		17 23			17 37		17 53	
Kew Gardens	⊖	d		15 29	15 41		15 54		16 12			16 27		16 42		16 56		17 12		17 26			17 40		17 56	
Gunnersbury	⊖	d		15 32	15 44		15 57		16 15			16 30		16 45		16 59		17 15		17 29			17 43		17 59	
South Acton		d		15 35	15 47		16 00		16 18			16 33		16 48		17 02		17 18		17 32			17 46		18 02	
Acton Central		d		15 38	15 50		16 06		16 21			16 36		16 51		17 06		17 21		17 36			17 51		18 06	
Willesden Jn. High Level	⊖	a		15 44	15 55		16 11		16 26			16 41		16 56		17 11		17 26		17 41			17 56		18 11	
		d	15 36	15 45	15 56	16 05	16 12	16 20	16 27	16 35		16 42	16 50	16 57	17 05	17 12	17 20	17 27	17 35	17 42		17 50	17 57	18 05	18 12	18 20
Kensal Rise		d	15 38	15 47	15 58	16 07	16 14	16 22	16 29	16 37		16 44	16 52	16 59	17 07	17 14	17 22	17 29	17 37	17 44		17 52	17 59	18 07	18 14	18 22
Brondesbury Park		d	15 40	15 49	16 00	16 09	16 16	16 24	16 31	16 40		16 46	16 54	17 01	17 09	17 16	17 24	17 31	17 39	17 46		17 54	18 01	18 09	18 16	18 24
Brondesbury		d	15 42	15 51	16 02	16 11	16 18	16 26	16 33	16 41		16 48	16 56	17 03	17 11	17 18	17 26	17 33	17 41	17 48		17 56	18 03	18 11	18 18	18 26
West Hampstead	⊖	d	15 44	15 53	16 04	16 13	16 20	16 28	16 35	16 43		16 50	16 58	17 05	17 13	17 20	17 28	17 35	17 43	17 50		17 58	18 05	18 13	18 20	18 28
Finchley Road & Frognal		d	15 45	15 54	16 05	16 14	16 21	16 29	16 36	16 44		16 51	16 59	17 06	17 14	17 21	17 29	17 36	17 44	17 51		17 59	18 06	18 14	18 21	18 29
Hampstead Heath		d	15 48	15 57	16 08	16 17	16 24	16 32	16 39	16 47		16 54	17 02	17 09	17 17	17 24	17 32	17 39	17 47	17 54		18 02	18 09	18 17	18 24	18 32
Gospel Oak		d	15 50	16 00	16 10	16 19	16 26	16 34	16 41	16 49		16 56	17 04	17 11	17 19	17 26	17 34	17 41	17 49	17 56		18 04	18 11	18 19	18 26	18 34
Kentish Town West		d	15 52	16 02	16 12	16 21	16 28	16 36	16 43	16 51		16 58	17 06	17 13	17 21	17 28	17 36	17 43	17 51	17 58		18 06	18 13	18 21	18 28	18 36
Camden Road		d	15 56	16 05	16 16	16 25	16 32	16 40	16 47	16 55		17 02	17 10	17 17	17 25	17 32	17 40	17 47	17 55	18 02		18 10	18 17	18 25	18 32	18 40
Caledonian Rd & Barnsbury		d	15 59	16 08	16 19	16 28	16 35	16 43	16 50	16 58		17 05	17 13	17 20	17 28	17 35	17 43	17 50	17 58	18 05		18 13	18 20	18 28	18 35	18 44
Highbury & Islington	⊖	d	16 02	16 11	16 22	16 31	16 38	16 46	16 53	17 01		17 08	17 16	17 23	17 31	17 38	17 46	17 53	18 01	18 08		18 16	18 23	18 31	18 38	18 46
Canonbury	⊖	d	16 04	16 13	16 24	16 33	16 40	16 48	16 55	17 03		17 10	17 18	17 25	17 33	17 40	17 48	17 55	18 03	18 10		18 18	18 25	18 33	18 40	18 48
Dalston Kingsland		d	16 06	16 15	16 26	16 35	16 42	16 50	16 57	17 05		17 12	17 20	17 27	17 35	17 42	17 50	17 57	18 05	18 12		18 20	18 27	18 35	18 42	18 50
Hackney Central		d	16 08	16 17	16 28	16 37	16 44	16 52	16 59	17 07		17 14	17 22	17 29	17 37	17 44	17 52	17 59	18 07	18 14		18 22	18 29	18 37	18 44	18 52
Homerton		d	16 10	16 19	16 30	16 39	16 46	16 54	17 01	17 09		17 16	17 24	17 31	17 39	17 46	17 54	18 01	18 09	18 16		18 24	18 31	18 39	18 46	18 54
Hackney Wick		d	16 12	16 21	16 32	16 41	16 48	16 56	17 03	17 11		17 18	17 26	17 33	17 41	17 48	17 56	18 03	18 11	18 18		18 26	18 33	18 41	18 48	18 56
Stratford 7	⊖	a	16 20	16 30	16 42	16 49	16 57	17 05	17 11	17 20		17 27	17 35	17 41	17 50	17 56	18 05	18 11	18 20	18 26		18 35	18 42	18 50	18 56	19 05

			LO	LO	LO	LO		LO	LO	LO	LO	LO	LO	LO	LO	LO		LO	LO	LO	LO	LO	LO	LO	LO	LO
Richmond	⊖	d	18 08		18 23			18 37		18 54		19 11		19 26	19 42			19 56	20 11		20 26	20 40		20 58	21 10	
Kew Gardens	⊖	d	18 11		18 26			18 40		18 57		19 14		19 29	19 45			19 59	20 14		20 29	20 43		21 01	21 13	
Gunnersbury	⊖	d	18 14		18 29			18 43		19 00		19 17		19 32	19 48			20 02	20 17		20 32	20 46		21 04	21 16	
South Acton		d	18 17		18 32			18 46		19 03		19 20		19 35	19 51			20 05	20 20		20 35	20 49		21 07	21 19	
Acton Central		d	18 21		18 36			18 51		19 06		19 23		19 40	19 54			20 08	20 23		20 40	20 52		21 10	21 23	
Willesden Jn. High Level	⊖	a	18 26		18 41			18 56		19 11		19 28		19 45	19 59			20 15	20 28		20 45	20 57		21 15	21 28	
		d	18 27	18 35	18 42	18 50		18 57	19 05	19 12	19 20	19 29	19 36	19 46	20 00	20 06		20 16	20 29	20 36	20 46	20 59	21 06	21 16	21 29	21 36
Kensal Rise		d	18 29	18 37	18 44	18 52		18 59	19 07	19 14	19 22	19 31	19 38	19 48	20 02	20 08		20 18	20 31	20 38	20 48	21 01	21 08	21 18	21 31	21 38
Brondesbury Park		d	18 31	18 39	18 46	18 54		19 01	19 09	19 16	19 24	19 33	19 40	19 50	20 04	20 10		20 20	20 33	20 40	20 50	21 03	21 10	21 20	21 33	21 40
Brondesbury		d	18 33	18 41	18 48	18 56		19 03	19 11	19 18	19 26	19 35	19 42	19 52	20 06	20 12		20 22	20 35	20 42	20 52	21 05	21 12	21 22	21 35	21 42
West Hampstead	⊖	d	18 35	18 43	18 50	18 58		19 05	19 13	19 20	19 28	19 37	19 44	19 54	20 08	20 14		20 24	20 37	20 44	20 54	21 07	21 14	21 24	21 37	21 44
Finchley Road & Frognal		d	18 36	18 44	18 51	18 59		19 06	19 14	19 21	19 29	19 38	19 45	19 55	20 09	20 15		20 25	20 38	20 45	20 55	21 08	21 15	21 25	21 38	21 45
Hampstead Heath		d	18 39	18 47	18 54	19 02		19 09	19 17	19 24	19 32	19 41	19 48	19 58	20 12	20 18		20 28	20 41	20 48	20 58	21 11	21 18	21 28	21 41	21 48
Gospel Oak		d	18 41	18 49	18 56	19 04		19 11	19 19	19 26	19 34	19 43	19 50	20 00	20 14	20 20		20 30	20 43	20 50	21 00	21 13	21 20	21 30	21 43	21 50
Kentish Town West		d	18 43	18 51	18 58	19 06		19 13	19 21	19 28	19 36	19 45	19 52	20 02	20 16	20 22		20 32	20 45	20 52	21 02	21 15	21 22	21 32	21 45	21 52
Camden Road		d	18 47	18 55	19 02	19 10		19 17	19 25	19 32	19 40	19 49	19 56	20 06	20 20	20 26		20 36	20 49	20 56	21 06	21 19	21 26	21 36	21 49	21 56
Caledonian Rd & Barnsbury		d	18 50	18 58	19 05	19 13		19 20	19 28	19 35	19 43	19 52	19 59	20 09	20 23	20 29		20 39	20 52	20 59	21 09	21 22	21 29	21 39	21 52	21 59
Highbury & Islington	⊖	d	18 53	19 01	19 08	19 16		19 23	19 31	19 38	19 46	19 55	20 02	20 12	20 26	20 32		20 42	20 55	21 02	21 12	21 25	21 32	21 42	21 55	22 02
Canonbury	⊖	d	18 55	19 03	19 10	19 18		19 25	19 33	19 40	19 48	19 57	20 04	20 14	20 28	20 34		20 44	20 57	21 04	21 14	21 27	21 34	21 44	21 57	22 04
Dalston Kingsland		d	18 57	19 05	19 12	19 20		19 27	19 35	19 42	19 50	19 59	20 06	20 16	20 30	20 36		20 46	20 59	21 06	21 16	21 29	21 36	21 46	21 59	22 06
Hackney Central		d	18 59	19 07	19 14	19 22		19 29	19 37	19 44	19 52	20 01	20 08	20 18	20 32	20 38		20 48	21 01	21 08	21 18	21 31	21 38	21 48	22 01	22 08
Homerton		d	19 01	19 09	19 16	19 24		19 31	19 39	19 46	19 54	20 03	20 10	20 20	20 34	20 40		20 50	21 03	21 10	21 20	21 33	21 40	21 50	22 03	22 10
Hackney Wick		d	19 03	19 11	19 18	19 26		19 33	19 41	19 48	19 56	20 05	20 12	20 22	20 36	20 42		20 52	21 05	21 12	21 22	21 35	21 42	21 52	22 05	22 12
Stratford 7	⊖	a	19 11	19 21	19 26	19 35		19 43	19 50	19 57	20 04	20 13	20 20	20 30	20 44	20 50		21 00	21 13	21 20	21 30	21 43	21 50	22 00	22 13	22 20

				LO	LO	LO	LO	LO	LO	LO
Richmond	⊖	d		21 28	21 38		21 56	22 28	23 00	23 28
Kew Gardens	⊖	d		21 31	21 41		21 59	22 31	23 03	23 31
Gunnersbury	⊖	d		21 34	21 44		22 02	22 34	23 06	23 34
South Acton		d		21 37	21 47		22 05	22 37	23 09	23 37
Acton Central		d		21 40	21 50		22 10	22 40	23 12	23 40
Willesden Jn. High Level	⊖	a		21 45	21 55		22 15	22 45	23 17	23 45
		d		21 46	21 56	22 06	22 16	22 46	23 18	
Kensal Rise		d		21 48	21 58	22 08	22 18	22 48	23 20	
Brondesbury Park		d		21 50	22 00	22 10	22 20	22 50	23 22	
Brondesbury		d		21 52	22 02	22 12	22 22	22 52	23 24	
West Hampstead	⊖	d		21 54	22 04	22 14	22 24	22 54	23 26	
Finchley Road & Frognal		d		21 55	22 05	22 15	22 25	22 55	23 27	
Hampstead Heath		d		21 58	22 08	22 18	22 28	22 58	23 30	
Gospel Oak		d		22 00	22 10	22 20	22 30	23 00	23 32	
Kentish Town West		d		22 02	22 12	22 22	22 32	23 02	23 34	
Camden Road		d		22 06	22 16	22 26	22 36	23 06	23 38	
Caledonian Rd & Barnsbury		d		22 09	22 19	22 29	22 39	23 09	23 41	
Highbury & Islington	⊖	d		22 12	22 22	22 32	22 42	23 12	23 44	
Canonbury	⊖	d		22 14	22 24	22 34	22 44	23 14	23 46	
Dalston Kingsland		d		22 16	22 26	22 36	22 46	23 16	23 48	
Hackney Central		d		22 18	22 28	22 38	22 48	23 18	23 50	
Homerton		d		22 20	22 30	22 40	22 50	23 20	23 52	
Hackney Wick		d		22 22	22 32	22 42	22 52	23 22	23 54	
Stratford 7	⊖	a		22 30	22 40	22 50	23 00	23 30	00 02	

Table 59

Saturdays

Richmond - Willesden Junction, West Hampstead, Highbury and Islington and Stratford

Station			LO	LO	LO	LO	LO	LO	LO	LO	LO	LO	LO	LO	LO	LO	LO	LO	LO	LO	LO		LO
Richmond	⊖	d	23p00		05 58	06 10		06 28	06 40		06 58	07 10		07 28	07 40		07 58	08 08		08 28	08 38		21 38
Kew Gardens	⊖	d	23p03		06 01	06 13		06 31	06 43		07 01	07 13		07 31	07 43		08 01	08 11		08 31	08 41		21 41
Gunnersbury	⊖	d	23p06		06 04	06 16		06 34	06 46		07 04	07 16		07 34	07 46		08 04	08 14		08 34	08 44		21 44
South Acton		d	23p09		06 07	06 19		06 37	06 49		07 07	07 19		07 37	07 49		08 07	08 17		08 37	08 47		21 47
Acton Central		d	23p12		06 10	06 23		06 40	06 53		07 10	07 23		07 40	07 52		08 10	08 20		08 40	08 50		21 50
Willesden Jn. High Level	⊖	a	23p17		06 15	06 28		06 45	06 58		07 15	07 28		07 45	07 57		08 15	08 25		08 45	08 55		21 55
		d	23p18		06 16	06 29	06 36	06 46	06 59	07 06	07 16	07 29	07 36	07 46	07 58	08 06	08 16	08 26	08 36	08 46	08 56		21 56
Kensal Rise		d	23p20	06 01	06 18	06 31	06 38	06 48	07 01	07 08	07 18	07 31	07 38	07 48	08 00	08 08	08 18	08 28	08 38	08 48	08 58		21 58
Brondesbury Park		d	23p22	06 03	06 20	06 33	06 40	06 50	07 03	07 10	07 20	07 33	07 40	07 50	08 02	08 10	08 20	08 30	08 40	08 50	09 00	and at the same minutes past each hour until	22 00
Brondesbury		d	23p24	06 05	06 22	06 35	06 42	06 52	07 05	07 12	07 22	07 35	07 42	07 52	08 04	08 12	08 22	08 32	08 42	08 52	09 02		22 02
West Hampstead	⊖	d	23p26	06 07	06 24	06 37	06 44	06 54	07 07	07 14	07 24	07 37	07 44	07 54	08 06	08 14	08 24	08 34	08 44	08 54	09 04		22 04
Finchley Road & Frognal		d	23p27	06 08	06 25	06 38	06 45	06 55	07 08	07 15	07 25	07 38	07 45	07 55	08 07	08 15	08 25	08 35	08 45	08 55	09 05		22 05
Hampstead Heath		d	23p30	06 11	06 28	06 41	06 48	06 58	07 11	07 18	07 28	07 41	07 48	07 58	08 10	08 18	08 28	08 38	08 48	08 58	09 08		22 08
Gospel Oak		d	23p32	06 13	06 30	06 43	06 50	07 00	07 13	07 20	07 30	07 43	07 50	08 00	08 12	08 20	08 30	08 40	08 50	09 00	09 10		22 10
Kentish Town West		d	23p34	06 15	06 32	06 45	06 52	07 02	07 15	07 22	07 32	07 45	07 52	08 02	08 14	08 22	08 32	08 42	08 52	09 02	09 12		22 12
Camden Road		d	23p38	06 19	06 36	06 49	06 56	07 06	07 19	07 26	07 36	07 49	07 56	08 06	08 18	08 26	08 36	08 46	08 56	09 06	09 16		22 16
Caledonian Rd & Barnsbury		d	23p41	06 22	06 39	06 52	06 59	07 09	07 22	07 29	07 39	07 52	07 59	08 09	08 21	08 29	08 39	08 49	08 59	09 09	09 19		22 19
Highbury & Islington	⊖	d	23p44	06 25	06 42	06 55	07 02	07 12	07 25	07 32	07 42	07 55	08 02	08 12	08 24	08 32	08 42	08 52	09 02	09 12	09 22		22 22
Canonbury	⊖	d	23p46	06 27	06 44	06 57	07 04	07 14	07 27	07 34	07 44	07 57	08 04	08 14	08 26	08 34	08 44	08 54	09 04	09 14	09 24		22 24
Dalston Kingsland		d	23p48	06 29	06 46	06 59	07 06	07 16	07 29	07 36	07 46	07 59	08 06	08 16	08 28	08 36	08 46	08 56	09 06	09 16	09 26		22 26
Hackney Central		d	23p50	06 31	06 48	07 01	07 08	07 18	07 31	07 38	07 48	08 01	08 08	08 18	08 30	08 38	08 48	08 58	09 08	09 18	09 28		22 28
Homerton		d	23p52	06 33	06 50	07 03	07 10	07 20	07 33	07 40	07 50	08 03	08 10	08 20	08 32	08 40	08 50	09 00	09 10	09 20	09 30		22 30
Hackney Wick		d	23p54	06 35	06 52	07 05	07 12	07 22	07 35	07 42	07 52	08 05	08 12	08 22	08 34	08 42	08 52	09 02	09 12	09 22	09 32		22 32
Stratford 7	⊖	a	00 02	06 43	07 01	07 13	07 20	07 30	07 43	07 50	08 01	08 13	08 20	08 30	08 43	08 50	09 01	09 11	09 20	09 30	09 41		22 41

Station			LO	LO	LO	LO	LO
Richmond	⊖	d		21 58	22 28	23 00	23 28
Kew Gardens	⊖	d		22 01	22 31	23 03	23 31
Gunnersbury	⊖	d		22 04	22 34	23 06	23 34
South Acton		d		22 07	22 37	23 09	23 37
Acton Central		d		22 10	22 40	23 12	23 40
Willesden Jn. High Level	⊖	a		22 15	22 45	23 17	23 45
		d	22 06	22 16	22 46	23 18	
Kensal Rise		d	22 08	22 18	22 48	23 20	
Brondesbury Park		d	22 10	22 20	22 50	23 22	
Brondesbury		d	22 12	22 22	22 52	23 24	
West Hampstead	⊖	d	22 14	22 24	22 54	23 26	
Finchley Road & Frognal		d	22 15	22 25	22 55	23 27	
Hampstead Heath		d	22 18	22 28	22 58	23 30	
Gospel Oak		d	22 20	22 30	23 00	23 32	
Kentish Town West		d	22 22	22 32	23 02	23 34	
Camden Road		d	22 26	22 36	23 06	23 38	
Caledonian Rd & Barnsbury		d	22 29	22 39	23 09	23 41	
Highbury & Islington	⊖	d	22 32	22 42	23 12	23 44	
Canonbury	⊖	d	22 34	22 44	23 14	23 46	
Dalston Kingsland		d	22 36	22 46	23 16	23 48	
Hackney Central		d	22 38	22 48	23 18	23 50	
Homerton		d	22 40	22 50	23 20	23 52	
Hackney Wick		d	22 42	22 52	23 22	23 54	
Stratford 7	⊖	a	22 50	23 01	23 30	00 02	

Sundays

Station			LO A	LO	LO	LO	LO	LO	LO	LO	LO	LO	LO	LO	LO	LO	LO	LO	LO	LO	LO	LO
Richmond	⊖	d	23p00		08 59	09 15	09 29	09 45	09 59	10 10		10 29	10 40		10 59	11 10		11 29	11 40		11 59	12 10
Kew Gardens	⊖	d	23p03		09 02	09 18	09 32	09 48	10 02	10 13		10 32	10 43		11 02	11 13		11 32	11 43		12 02	12 13
Gunnersbury	⊖	d	23p06		09 05	09 21	09 35	09 51	10 05	10 16		10 35	10 46		11 05	11 16		11 35	11 46		12 05	12 16
South Acton		d	23p09		09 08	09 24	09 38	09 54	10 08	10 19		10 38	10 49		11 08	11 19		11 38	11 49		12 08	12 19
Acton Central		d	23p12		09 11	09 27	09 41	09 57	10 11	10 22		10 41	10 52		11 11	11 22		11 41	11 52		12 11	12 22
Willesden Jn. High Level	⊖	a	23p17		09 16	09 32	09 46	10 02	10 16	10 27		10 46	10 57		11 16	11 27		11 46	11 57		12 16	12 27
		d	23p18		09 17	09 33	09 47	10 03	10 17	10 28	10 41	10 47	10 58	11 06	11 17	11 28	11 41	11 47	11 58	12 06	12 17	12 28
Kensal Rise		d	23p20	09 04	09 19	09 35	09 49	10 05	10 19	10 30	10 43	10 49	11 00	11 08	11 19	11 30	11 43	11 49	12 00	12 08	12 19	12 30
Brondesbury Park		d	23p22	09 06	09 21	09 37	09 51	10 07	10 21	10 32	10 45	10 51	11 02	11 10	11 21	11 32	11 45	11 51	12 02	12 10	12 21	12 32
Brondesbury		d	23p24	09 08	09 23	09 39	09 53	10 09	10 23	10 34	10 47	10 53	11 04	11 12	11 23	11 34	11 47	11 53	12 04	12 12	12 23	12 34
West Hampstead	⊖	d	23p26	09 10	09 25	09 41	09 55	10 11	10 25	10 36	10 49	10 55	11 06	11 14	11 25	11 36	11 49	11 55	12 06	12 14	12 25	12 36
Finchley Road & Frognal		d	23p27	09 11	09 26	09 42	09 56	10 12	10 26	10 37	10 50	10 56	11 07	11 15	11 26	11 37	11 50	11 56	12 07	12 15	12 26	12 37
Hampstead Heath		d	23p30	09 14	09 30	09 45	09 59	10 15	10 29	10 40	10 53	10 59	11 10	11 18	11 29	11 40	11 53	11 59	12 10	12 18	12 29	12 40
Gospel Oak		d	23p32	09 16	09 32	09 47	10 01	10 17	10 31	10 42	10 55	11 01	11 12	11 20	11 31	11 42	11 55	12 01	12 12	12 20	12 31	12 42
Kentish Town West		d	23p34	09 18	09 34	09 49	10 03	10 19	10 33	10 44	10 57	11 03	11 14	11 22	11 33	11 44	11 57	12 03	12 14	12 22	12 33	12 44
Camden Road		d	23p38	09 22	09 37	09 53	10 07	10 23	10 37	10 48	11 01	11 07	11 18	11 26	11 37	11 48	12 01	12 07	12 18	12 26	12 37	12 48
Caledonian Rd & Barnsbury		d	23p41	09 25	09 40	09 56	10 10	10 26	10 40	10 51	11 04	11 10	11 21	11 29	11 40	11 51	12 04	12 10	12 21	12 29	12 40	12 51
Highbury & Islington	⊖	d	23p44	09 28	09 43	09 59	10 13	10 29	10 43	10 54	11 07	11 13	11 24	11 32	11 43	11 54	12 07	12 13	12 24	12 32	12 43	12 54
Canonbury	⊖	d	23p46	09 30	09 45	10 01	10 15	10 31	10 45	10 56	11 09	11 15	11 26	11 34	11 45	11 56	12 09	12 15	12 26	12 34	12 45	12 56
Dalston Kingsland		d	23p48	09 32	09 47	10 03	10 17	10 33	10 47	10 58	11 11	11 17	11 28	11 36	11 47	11 58	12 11	12 17	12 28	12 36	12 47	12 58
Hackney Central		d	23p50	09 34	09 49	10 05	10 19	10 35	10 49	11 00	11 13	11 19	11 30	11 38	11 49	12 00	12 13	12 19	12 30	12 38	12 49	13 00
Homerton		d	23p52	09 36	09 51	10 07	10 21	10 37	10 51	11 02	11 15	11 21	11 32	11 40	11 51	12 02	12 15	12 21	12 32	12 40	12 51	13 02
Hackney Wick		d	23p54	09 38	09 53	10 09	10 23	10 39	10 53	11 04	11 17	11 23	11 34	11 42	11 53	12 04	12 17	12 23	12 34	12 42	12 53	13 04
Stratford 7	⊖	a	00 02	09 46	10 01	10 17	10 32	10 47	11 01	11 12	11 25	11 30	11 42	11 50	12 00	12 12	12 25	12 30	12 42	12 50	13 00	13 12

A not 22 May

Table 59

Sundays

Richmond - Willesden Junction, West Hampstead, Highbury and Islington and Stratford

		LO		LO	LO	LO	LO		LO	LO	LO	LO	LO	LO	LO	LO	LO		LO
Richmond ⊖	d				19 29	19 40	19 59		20 10	20 29	20 40	20 59	21 17	21 29	21 47	21 59	22 28		23 00
Kew Gardens ⊖	d				19 32	19 43	20 02		20 13	20 32	20 43	21 02	21 20	21 32	21 50	22 02	22 31		23 03
Gunnersbury ⊖	d				19 35	19 46	20 05		20 16	20 35	20 46	21 05	21 23	21 35	21 53	22 05	22 34		23 06
South Acton	d				19 38	19 49	20 08		20 19	20 38	20 49	21 08	21 26	21 38	21 56	22 08	22 37		23 09
Acton Central	d				19 41	19 52	20 11		20 22	20 41	20 52	21 11	21 29	21 41	21 59	22 11	22 40		23 12
Willesden Jn. High Level ⊖	a				19 46	19 57	20 16		20 27	20 46	20 57	21 16	21 34	21 46	22 04	22 16	22 45		23 17
	d	12 36		19 36	19 47	19 58	20 17		20 28	20 47	20 58	21 17	21 35	21 47	22 05	22 17	22 46		23 18
Kensal Rise	d	12 38		19 38	19 49	20 00	20 19		20 30	20 49	21 00	21 19	21 37	21 49	22 07	22 19	22 48		23 20
Brondesbury Park	d	12 40	and at	19 40	19 51	20 02	20 21		20 32	20 51	21 02	21 21	21 39	21 51	22 09	22 21	22 50		23 22
Brondesbury	d	12 42	the same	19 42	19 53	20 04	20 23		20 34	20 53	21 04	21 23	21 41	21 53	22 11	22 23	22 52		23 24
West Hampstead ⊖	d	12 44	minutes	19 44	19 55	20 06	20 25		20 36	20 55	21 06	21 25	21 43	21 55	22 13	22 25	22 54		23 26
Finchley Road & Frognal	d	12 45	past	19 45	19 56	20 07	20 26		20 37	20 56	21 07	21 26	21 44	21 56	22 14	22 26	22 55		23 27
Hampstead Heath	d	12 48	each	19 48	19 59	20 10	20 29		20 40	20 59	21 10	21 29	21 47	21 59	22 17	22 29	22 58		23 30
Gospel Oak	d	12 50	hour until	19 50	20 01	20 12	20 31		20 42	21 01	21 12	21 31	21 49	22 01	22a22	22a36	23a03		23a35
Kentish Town West	d	12 52		19 52	20 03	20 14	20 33		20 44	21 03	21 14	21 33	21 51	22 03					
Camden Road	d	12 56		19 56	20 07	20 18	20 37		20 48	21 07	21 18	21 37	21 55	22 07					
Caledonian Rd & Barnsbury	d	12 59		19 59	20 10	20 21	20 40		20 51	21 10	21 21	21 40	21 58	22 10					
Highbury & Islington ⊖	d	13 02		20 02	20 13	20 24	20 43		20 54	21 13	21 24	21 43	22 01	22 13					
Canonbury ⊖	d	13 04		20 04	20 15	20 26	20 45		20 56	21 15	21 26	21 45	22 03	22 15					
Dalston Kingsland	d	13 06		20 06	20 17	20 28	20 47		20 58	21 17	21 28	21 47	22 05	22 17					
Hackney Central	d	13 08		20 08	20 19	20 30	20 49		21 00	21 19	21 30	21 49	22 07	22 19					
Homerton	d	13 10		20 10	20 21	20 32	20 51		21 02	21 21	21 32	21 51	22 09	22 21					
Hackney Wick	d	13 12		20 12	20 23	20 34	20 53		21 04	21 23	21 34	21 53	22 11	22 23					
Stratford 7 ⊖	a	13 20		20 20	20 30	20 42	21 01		21 12	21 30	21 39	22 01	22 19	22 31					

London, Queen's Park and Harrow & Wealdstone - Watford Junction

Miles			LO MO	LO MX	LO MX	LO	LO	LO	LO	LO	LO	LO		LO	LO		LO	LO	LO	LO	LO		LO	LO
0	**London Euston** 15 ⊖	d	23p17	23p27	23p57	05 37	06 07	06 37	06 57	07 17	07 37	07 57		08 17	08 37	and at the same minutes past each hour until	15 37	15 57	16 17	16 37	16 57		17 17	17 37
2½	South Hampstead	d	23p23	23p33	00 03	05 43	06 13	06 43	07 03	07 23	07 43	08 03		08 23	08 43		15 43	16 03	16 23	16 43	17 03		17 23	17 43
3	Kilburn High Road	d	23p24	23p34	00 04	05 44	06 14	06 44	07 04	07 24	07 44	08 04		08 24	08 44		15 44	16 04	16 24	16 44	17 04		17 24	17 44
3¾	**Queen's Park (London)** ⊖	d	23p26	23p36	00 06	05 46	06 16	06 46	07 06	07 26	07 46	08 06		08 26	08 46		15 46	16 06	16 27	16 47	17 07		17 27	17 47
4½	Kensal Green	d	23p28	23p38	00 08	05 48	06 18	06 48	07 08	07 28	07 48	08 08		08 28	08 48		15 48	16 08	16 29	16 49	17 09		17 29	17 49
5½	**Willesden Jn Low Level**	d	23p31	23p41	00 11	05 51	06 21	06 51	07 11	07 31	07 51	08 11		08 31	08 51		15 51	16 11	16 32	16 52	17 12		17 32	17 52
6	Harlesden	d	23p33	23p43	00 13	05 53	06 23	06 53	07 13	07 33	07 53	08 13		08 33	08 53		15 53	16 13	16 34	16 54	17 14		17 34	17 54
7	Stonebridge Park	d	23p35	23p45	00 15	05 55	06 25	06 55	07 15	07 35	07 55	08 15		08 35	08 55		15 55	16 15	16 36	16 56	17 16		17 36	17 56
8	Wembley Central	d	23p38	23p48	00 18	05 58	06 28	06 58	07 18	07 38	07 58	08 18		08 38	08 58		15 58	16 18	16 39	16 59	17 19		17 39	17 59
9	North Wembley	d	23p40	23p50	00 20	06 00	06 30	07 00	07 20	07 40	08 00	08 20		08 40	09 00		16 00	16 20	16 41	17 01	17 21		17 41	18 01
9½	South Kenton	d	23p42	23p52	00 22	06 02	06 32	07 02	07 22	07 42	08 02	08 22		08 42	09 02		16 02	16 22	16 43	17 03	17 23		17 43	18 03
10¼	Kenton	d	23p44	23p54	00 24	06 04	06 34	07 04	07 24	07 44	08 04	08 24		08 44	09 04		16 04	16 24	16 45	17 05	17 25		17 45	18 05
11¼	**Harrow & Wealdstone**	d	23p46	23p56	00 26	06 06	06 36	07 06	07 26	07 46	08 06	08 26		08 46	09 06		16 06	16 26	16 48	17 08	17 28		17 48	18 08
12½	Headstone Lane	d	23p49	23p59	00 29	06 09	06 39	07 09	07 29	07 49	08 09	08 29		08 49	09 09		16 09	16 29	16 51	17 11	17 31		17 51	18 11
13¼	Hatch End	d	23p51	00 01	00 31	06 11	06 41	07 11	07 31	07 51	08 11	08 31		08 51	09 11		16 11	16 31	16 53	17 13	17 33		17 53	18 13
14¾	Carpenders Park	d	23p54	00 04	00 34	06 14	06 44	07 14	07 34	07 54	08 14	08 34		08 54	09 14		16 14	16 34	16 56	17 16	17 36		17 56	18 16
16	Bushey	d	23p57	00 07	00 37	06 17	06 47	07 17	07 37	07 57	08 17	08 37		08 57	09 17		16 17	16 37	16 59	17 19	17 39		17 59	18 19
16¾	Watford High Street	d	23p59	00 10	00 40	06 20	06 50	07 20	07 40	08 00	08 20	08 40		09 00	09 20		16 20	16 40	17 01	17 21	17 41		18 01	18 21
17¾	**Watford Junction**	a	00 04	00 14	00 44	06 24	06 54	07 24	07 44	08 04	08 28	08 44		09 04	09 24		16 24	16 44	17 08	17 28	17 48		18 08	18 28

		LO	LO	LO	LO	LO	LO	LO		LO	LO	LO	LO	LO	LO	LO	LO	LO		LO
London Euston 15 ⊖	d	17 57	18 17	18 37	18 57	19 17	19 37	19 57		20 17	20 37	20 57	21 17	21 37	21 57	22 27	22 57	23 27		23 57
South Hampstead	d	18 03	18 23	18 43	19 03	19 23	19 43	20 03		20 23	20 43	21 03	21 23	21 43	22 03	22 33	23 03	23 33		00 03
Kilburn High Road	d	18 04	18 24	18 44	19 04	19 24	19 44	20 04		20 24	20 44	21 04	21 24	21 44	22 04	22 34	23 04	23 34		00 04
Queen's Park (London) ⊖	d	18 07	18 27	18 47	19 07	19 26	19 46	20 06		20 26	20 46	21 06	21 26	21 46	22 06	22 36	23 06	23 36		00 06
Kensal Green	d	18 09	18 29	18 49	19 09	19 28	19 48	20 08		20 28	20 48	21 08	21 28	21 48	22 08	22 38	23 08	23 38		00 08
Willesden Jn Low Level	d	18 12	18 32	18 52	19 12	19 31	19 51	20 11		20 31	20 51	21 11	21 31	21 51	22 11	22 41	23 11	23 41		00 11
Harlesden	d	18 14	18 34	18 54	19 14	19 33	19 53	20 13		20 33	20 53	21 13	21 33	21 53	22 13	22 43	23 13	23 43		00 13
Stonebridge Park	d	18 16	18 36	18 56	19 16	19 35	19 55	20 15		20 35	20 55	21 15	21 35	21 55	22 15	22 45	23 15	23 45		00 15
Wembley Central	d	18 19	18 39	18 59	19 19	19 38	19 58	20 18		20 38	20 58	21 18	21 38	21 58	22 18	22 48	23 18	23 48		00 18
North Wembley	d	18 21	18 41	19 01	19 21	19 40	20 00	20 20		20 40	21 00	21 20	21 40	22 00	22 20	22 50	23 20	23 50		00 20
South Kenton	d	18 23	18 43	19 03	19 23	19 42	20 02	20 22		20 42	21 02	21 22	21 42	22 02	22 22	22 52	23 22	23 52		00 22
Kenton	d	18 25	18 45	19 05	19 25	19 44	20 04	20 24		20 44	21 04	21 24	21 44	22 04	22 24	22 54	23 24	23 54		00 24
Harrow & Wealdstone	d	18 28	18 48	19 08	19 28	19 46	20 06	20 26		20 46	21 06	21 26	21 46	22 06	22 26	22 56	23 26	23 56		00 26
Headstone Lane	d	18 31	18 51	19 11	19 31	19 49	20 09	20 29		20 49	21 09	21 29	21 49	22 09	22 29	22 59	23 29	23 59		00 29
Hatch End	d	18 33	18 53	19 13	19 33	19 51	20 11	20 31		20 51	21 11	21 31	21 51	22 11	22 31	23 01	23 31	00 01		00 31
Carpenders Park	d	18 36	18 56	19 16	19 36	19 54	20 14	20 34		20 54	21 14	21 34	21 54	22 14	22 34	23 04	23 34	00 04		00 34
Bushey	d	18 39	18 59	19 19	19 39	19 57	20 17	20 37		20 57	21 17	21 37	21 57	22 17	22 37	23 07	23 37	00 07		00 37
Watford High Street	d	18 41	19 01	19 21	19 41	20 00	20 20	20 40		21 00	21 20	21 40	22 00	22 20	22 40	23 10	23 40	00 10		00 40
Watford Junction	a	18 48	19 08	19 28	19 48	20 04	20 28	20 45		21 08	21 28	21 44	22 04	22 25	22 44	23 14	23 44	00 14		00 44

Saturdays

		LO	LO	LO	LO	LO	LO	LO		LO		LO	LO	LO	LO	LO		LO	LO		LO	LO	LO
London Euston 15 ⊖	d	23p27	23p57	05 37	06 07	06 37	06 57	07 17	and at the same minutes past each hour until	14 17		14 37	14 57	15 17	15 37	15 57	and at the same minutes past each hour until	19 57	20 17		20 37	20 57	21 17
South Hampstead	d	23p33	00 03	05 43	06 13	06 43	07 03	07 23		14 23		14 43	15 03	15 23	15 43	16 03		20 03	20 23		20 43	21 03	21 23
Kilburn High Road	d	23p34	00 04	05 44	06 14	06 44	07 04	07 24		14 24		14 44	15 04	15 24	15 44	16 04		20 04	20 24		20 44	21 04	21 24
Queen's Park (London) ⊖	d	23p36	00 06	05 46	06 16	06 46	07 06	07 26		14 26		14 46	15 06	15 26	15 46	16 06		20 06	20 26		20 46	21 06	21 26
Kensal Green	d	23p38	00 08	05 48	06 18	06 48	07 08	07 28		14 28		14 48	15 08	15 28	15 48	16 08		20 08	20 28		20 48	21 08	21 28
Willesden Jn Low Level	d	23p41	00 11	05 51	06 21	06 51	07 11	07 31		14 31		14 51	15 11	15 31	15 51	16 11		20 11	20 31		20 51	21 11	21 31
Harlesden	d	23p43	00 13	05 53	06 23	06 53	07 13	07 33		14 33		14 53	15 13	15 33	15 53	16 13		20 13	20 33		20 53	21 13	21 33
Stonebridge Park	d	23p45	00 15	05 55	06 25	06 55	07 15	07 35		14 35		14 55	15 15	15 35	15 55	16 15		20 15	20 35		20 55	21 15	21 35
Wembley Central	d	23p48	00 18	05 58	06 28	06 58	07 18	07 38		14 38		14 58	15 18	15 38	15 58	16 18		20 18	20 38		20 58	21 18	21 38
North Wembley	d	23p50	00 20	06 00	06 30	07 00	07 20	07 40		14 40		15 00	15 20	15 40	16 00	16 20		20 20	20 40		21 00	21 20	21 40
South Kenton	d	23p52	00 22	06 02	06 32	07 02	07 22	07 42		14 42		15 02	15 22	15 42	16 02	16 22		20 22	20 42		21 02	21 22	21 42
Kenton	d	23p54	00 24	06 04	06 34	07 04	07 24	07 44		14 44		15 04	15 24	15 44	16 04	16 24		20 24	20 44		21 04	21 24	21 44
Harrow & Wealdstone	d	23p56	00 26	06 06	06 36	07 06	07 26	07 46		14 46		15 06	15 26	15 46	16 06	16 26		20 26	20 46		21 06	21 26	21 46
Headstone Lane	d	23p59	00 29	06 09	06 39	07 09	07 29	07 49		14 49		15 09	15 29	15 49	16 09	16 29		20 29	20 49		21 09	21 29	21 49
Hatch End	d	00 01	00 31	06 11	06 41	07 11	07 31	07 51		14 51		15 11	15 31	15 51	16 11	16 31		20 31	20 51		21 11	21 31	21 51
Carpenders Park	d	00 04	00 34	06 14	06 44	07 14	07 34	07 54		14 54		15 14	15 34	15 54	16 14	16 34		20 34	20 54		21 14	21 34	21 54
Bushey	d	00 07	00 37	06 17	06 47	07 17	07 37	07 57		14 57		15 17	15 37	15 57	16 17	16 37		20 37	20 57		21 17	21 37	21 57
Watford High Street	d	00 10	00 40	06 20	06 50	07 20	07 40	08 00		15 00		15 20	15 40	16 00	16 20	16 40		20 40	21 00		21 20	21 40	22 00
Watford Junction	a	00 14	00 44	06 24	06 55	07 24	07 44	08 04		15 04		15 24	15 44	16 08	16 28	16 48		20 48	21 04		21 24	21 44	22 08

		LO	LO	LO	LO	LO	LO
London Euston 15 ⊖	d	21 37	21 57	22 27	22 57	23 27	23 57
South Hampstead	d	21 43	22 03	22 33	23 03	23 33	00 03
Kilburn High Road	d	21 44	22 04	22 34	23 04	23 34	00 04
Queen's Park (London) ⊖	d	21 46	22 06	22 36	23 06	23 36	00 06
Kensal Green	d	21 48	22 08	22 38	23 08	23 38	00 08
Willesden Jn Low Level	d	21 51	22 11	22 41	23 11	23 41	00 11
Harlesden	d	21 53	22 13	22 43	23 13	23 43	00 13
Stonebridge Park	d	21 55	22 15	22 45	23 15	23 45	00 15
Wembley Central	d	21 58	22 18	22 48	23 18	23 48	00 18
North Wembley	d	22 00	22 20	22 50	23 20	23 50	00 20
South Kenton	d	22 02	22 22	22 52	23 22	23 52	00 22
Kenton	d	22 04	22 24	22 54	23 24	23 54	00 24
Harrow & Wealdstone	d	22 06	22 26	22 56	23 26	23 56	00 26
Headstone Lane	d	22 09	22 29	22 59	23 29	23 59	00 29
Hatch End	d	22 11	22 31	23 01	23 31	00 01	00 31
Carpenders Park	d	22 14	22 34	23 04	23 34	00 04	00 34
Bushey	d	22 17	22 37	23 07	23 37	00 07	00 37
Watford High Street	d	22 20	22 40	23 10	23 40	00 10	00 40
Watford Junction	a	22 24	22 44	23 14	23 44	00 15	00 44

Stations Queen's Park to Harrow & Wealdstone inclusive are also served by London Underground Bakerloo Line Services

Table 60

Sundays

London, Queen's Park and Harrow & Wealdstone - Watford Junction

			LO A	LO A	LO		LO	LO	LO	LO	LO	LO	LO	LO		LO	LO	LO	LO	LO	LO	LO
London Euston 15	⊖	d	23p27	23p57	06 47		08 17	08 47	09 17	09 37	09 57	10 17	10 37	10 57		14 57	15 17	15 37	15 57	16 17	16 37	16 57
South Hampstead		d	23p33	00 03	06 53		08 23	08 53	09 23	09 43	10 03	10 23	10 43	11 03		15 03	15 23	15 43	16 03	16 23	16 43	17 03
Kilburn High Road		d	23p34	00 04	06 54		08 24	08 54	09 24	09 44	10 04	10 24	10 44	11 04		15 04	15 24	15 44	16 04	16 24	16 44	17 04
Queen's Park (London)	⊖	d	23p36	00 06	06 56		08 26	08 56	09 26	09 46	10 06	10 26	10 46	11 06		15 06	15 26	15 46	16 06	16 26	16 46	17 06
Kensal Green		d	23p38	00 08	06 58		08 28	08 58	09 28	09 48	10 08	10 28	10 48	11 08		15 08	15 28	15 48	16 08	16 28	16 48	17 08
Willesden Jn Low Level		d	23p41	00 11	07 01		08 31	09 01	09 31	09 51	10 11	10 31	10 51	11 11		15 11	15 31	15 51	16 11	16 31	16 51	17 11
Harlesden		d	23p43	00 13	07 03	and every 30 minutes until	08 33	09 03	09 33	09 53	10 13	10 33	10 53	11 13	and at the same minutes past each hour until	15 13	15 33	15 53	16 13	16 33	16 53	17 13
Stonebridge Park		d	23p45	00 15	07 05		08 35	09 05	09 35	09 55	10 15	10 35	10 55	11 15		15 15	15 35	15 55	16 15	16 35	16 55	17 15
Wembley Central		d	23p48	00 18	07 08		08 38	09 08	09 38	09 58	10 18	10 38	10 58	11 18		15 18	15 38	15 58	16 18	16 38	16 58	17 18
North Wembley		d	23p50	00 20	07 10		08 40	09 10	09 40	10 00	10 20	10 40	11 00	11 20		15 20	15 40	16 00	16 20	16 40	17 00	17 20
South Kenton		d	23p52	00 22	07 12		08 42	09 12	09 42	10 02	10 22	10 42	11 02	11 22		15 22	15 42	16 02	16 22	16 42	17 02	17 22
Kenton		d	23p54	00 24	07 14		08 44	09 14	09 44	10 04	10 24	10 44	11 04	11 24		15 24	15 44	16 04	16 24	16 44	17 04	17 24
Harrow & Wealdstone		d	23p56	00 26	07 16		08 46	09 16	09 46	10 06	10 26	10 46	11 06	11 26		15 26	15 46	16 06	16 26	16 46	17 06	17 26
Headstone Lane		d	23p59	00 29	07 19		08 49	09 19	09 49	10 09	10 29	10 49	11 09	11 29		15 29	15 49	16 09	16 29	16 49	17 09	17 29
Hatch End		d	00 01	00 31	07 21		08 51	09 21	09 51	10 11	10 31	10 51	11 11	11 31		15 31	15 51	16 11	16 31	16 51	17 11	17 31
Carpenders Park		d	00 04	00 34	07 24		08 54	09 24	09 54	10 14	10 34	10 54	11 14	11 34		15 34	15 54	16 14	16 34	16 54	17 14	17 34
Bushey		d	00 07	00 37	07 27		08 57	09 27	09 57	10 17	10 37	10 57	11 17	11 37		15 37	15 57	16 17	16 37	16 57	17 17	17 37
Watford High Street		d	00 10	00 40	07 30		09 00	09 30	10 00	10 20	10 40	11 00	11 20	11 40		15 40	16 00	16 20	16 40	17 00	17 20	17 40
Watford Junction		a	00 15	00 44	07 34		09 04	09 35	10 04	10 24	10 45	11 04	11 24	11 44		15 44	16 08	16 28	16 48	17 08	17 24	17 44

			LO	LO	LO	LO	LO	LO	LO	LO	LO	LO	LO	LO	LO	LO	LO	LO	LO	LO
London Euston 15	⊖	d	17 17	17 37	17 57	18 17	18 37	18 57	19 17	19 37	19 57	20 17	20 37	20 57	21 17	21 37	21 57	22 17	22 47	23 17
South Hampstead		d	17 23	17 43	18 03	18 23	18 43	19 03	19 23	19 43	20 03	20 23	20 43	21 03	21 23	21 43	22 03	22 23	22 53	23 23
Kilburn High Road		d	17 24	17 44	18 04	18 24	18 44	19 04	19 24	19 44	20 04	20 24	20 44	21 04	21 24	21 44	22 04	22 24	22 54	23 24
Queen's Park (London)	⊖	d	17 26	17 46	18 06	18 26	18 46	19 06	19 26	19 46	20 06	20 26	20 46	21 06	21 26	21 46	22 06	22 26	22 56	23 26
Kensal Green		d	17 28	17 48	18 08	18 28	18 48	19 08	19 28	19 48	20 08	20 28	20 48	21 08	21 28	21 48	22 08	22 28	22 58	23 28
Willesden Jn Low Level		d	17 31	17 51	18 11	18 31	18 51	19 11	19 31	19 51	20 11	20 31	20 51	21 11	21 31	21 51	22 11	22 31	23 01	23 31
Harlesden		d	17 33	17 53	18 13	18 33	18 53	19 13	19 33	19 53	20 13	20 33	20 53	21 13	21 33	21 53	22 13	22 33	23 03	23 33
Stonebridge Park		d	17 35	17 55	18 15	18 35	18 55	19 15	19 35	19 55	20 15	20 35	20 55	21 15	21 35	21 55	22 15	22 35	23 05	23 35
Wembley Central		d	17 38	17 58	18 18	18 38	18 58	19 18	19 38	19 58	20 18	20 38	20 58	21 18	21 38	21 58	22 18	22 38	23 08	23 38
North Wembley		d	17 40	18 00	18 20	18 40	19 00	19 20	19 40	20 00	20 20	20 40	21 00	21 20	21 40	22 00	22 20	22 40	23 10	23 40
South Kenton		d	17 42	18 02	18 22	18 42	19 02	19 22	19 42	20 02	20 22	20 42	21 02	21 22	21 42	22 02	22 22	22 42	23 12	23 42
Kenton		d	17 44	18 04	18 24	18 44	19 04	19 24	19 44	20 04	20 24	20 44	21 04	21 24	21 44	22 04	22 24	22 44	23 14	23 44
Harrow & Wealdstone		d	17 46	18 06	18 26	18 46	19 06	19 26	19 46	20 06	20 26	20 46	21 06	21 26	21 46	22 06	22 26	22 46	23 16	23 46
Headstone Lane		d	17 49	18 09	18 29	18 49	19 09	19 29	19 49	20 09	20 29	20 49	21 09	21 29	21 49	22 09	22 29	22 49	23 19	23 49
Hatch End		d	17 51	18 11	18 31	18 51	19 11	19 31	19 51	20 11	20 31	20 51	21 11	21 31	21 51	22 11	22 31	22 51	23 21	23 51
Carpenders Park		d	17 54	18 14	18 34	18 54	19 14	19 34	19 54	20 14	20 34	20 54	21 14	21 34	21 54	22 14	22 34	22 54	23 24	23 54
Bushey		d	17 57	18 17	18 37	18 57	19 17	19 37	19 57	20 17	20 37	20 57	21 17	21 37	21 57	22 17	22 37	22 57	23 27	23 57
Watford High Street		d	18 00	18 20	18 40	19 00	19 20	19 40	20 00	20 20	20 40	21 00	21 20	21 40	22 00	22 20	22 40	23 00	23 30	23 59
Watford Junction		a	18 08	18 28	18 48	19 08	19 28	19 48	20 08	20 28	20 48	21 04	21 24	21 45	22 04	22 24	22 44	23 04	23 34	00 04

A not 22 May

Stations Queen's Park to Harrow & Wealdstone inclusive are also served by London Underground Bakerloo Line Services

Watford Junction - Harrow & Wealdstone, Queen's Park and London

Miles			LO MX	LO MO	LO	LO	LO	LO	LO	LO	LO		LO	LO	LO	LO	LO	LO	LO	LO	LO		LO	
0	**Watford Junction**	d	23p21	23p21	05 11	05 41	06 11	06 40	07 00	07 20	07 40		08 00	08 20	08 40	09 00	09 21	09 41	10 01	10 21	10 41		11 01	
1	Watford High Street	d	23p24	23p24	05 14	05 44	06 14	06 43	07 03	07 23	07 43		08 03	08 23	08 43	09 03	09 24	09 44	10 04	10 24	10 44		11 04	
13	Bushey	d	23p26	23p26	05 16	05 46	06 16	06 45	07 05	07 25	07 45		08 05	08 25	08 45	09 05	09 26	09 46	10 06	10 26	10 46		11 06	
3	Carpenders Park	d	23p29	23p29	05 19	05 49	06 19	06 48	07 08	07 28	07 48		08 08	08 28	08 48	09 08	09 29	09 49	10 09	10 29	10 49		11 09	
4½	Hatch End	d	23p32	23p32	05 22	05 52	06 22	06 51	07 11	07 31	07 51		08 11	08 31	08 51	09 11	09 32	09 52	10 12	10 32	10 52		11 12	
5¼	Headstone Lane	d	23p34	23p34	05 24	05 54	06 24	06 53	07 13	07 33	07 53		08 13	08 33	08 53	09 13	09 34	09 54	10 14	10 34	10 54		11 14	and at the same minutes past each hour until
6½	**Harrow & Wealdstone**	d	23p37	23p37	05 27	05 57	06 27	06 56	07 16	07 36	07 56		08 16	08 36	08 56	09 16	09 37	09 57	10 17	10 37	10 57		11 17	
7½	Kenton	d	23p39	23p39	05 29	05 59	06 29	06 59	07 19	07 39	07 59		08 19	08 39	08 59	09 19	09 39	09 59	10 19	10 39	10 59		11 19	
8¼	South Kenton	d	23p41	23p41	05 31	06 01	06 31	07 01	07 21	07 41	08 01		08 21	08 41	09 01	09 21	09 41	10 01	10 21	10 41	11 01		11 21	
8¾	North Wembley	d	23p43	23p43	05 33	06 03	06 33	07 03	07 23	07 43	08 03		08 23	08 43	09 03	09 23	09 43	10 03	10 23	10 43	11 03		11 23	
9¾	Wembley Central	d	23p45	23p45	05 35	06 05	06 35	07 05	07 25	07 45	08 05		08 25	08 45	09 05	09 25	09 45	10 05	10 25	10 45	11 05		11 25	
10¾	Stonebridge Park	d	23p48	23p48	05 38	06 08	06 38	07 08	07 28	07 48	08 08		08 28	08 48	09 08	09 28	09 48	10 08	10 28	10 48	11 08		11 28	
11¾	Harlesden	d	23p50	23p50	05 40	06 10	06 40	07 10	07 30	07 50	08 10		08 30	08 50	09 10	09 30	09 50	10 10	10 30	10 50	11 10		11 30	
12¼	**Willesden Jn Low Level**	d	23p52	23p52	05 42	06 12	06 42	07 13	07 33	07 53	08 13		08 33	08 53	09 13	09 33	09 52	10 12	10 32	10 52	11 12		11 32	
13¼	Kensal Green	d	23p55	23p55	05 45	06 15	06 45	07 15	07 35	07 55	08 15		08 35	08 55	09 15	09 35	09 55	10 15	10 35	10 55	11 15		11 35	
14	**Queen's Park (London)** ⊖	d	23p57	23p57	05 47	06 17	06 47	07 18	07 38	07 58	08 18		08 38	08 58	09 18	09 38	09 57	10 17	10 37	10 57	11 17		11 37	
14¾	Kilburn High Road	d	23p59	23p59	05 49	06 19	06 49	07 20	07 40	08 00	08 20		08 40	09 00	09 20	09 40	09 59	10 19	10 39	10 59	11 19		11 39	
15¼	South Hampstead	d	00 01	00 01	05 51	06 21	06 51	07 22	07 42	08 02	08 22		08 42	09 02	09 22	09 42	10 01	10 21	10 41	11 01	11 21		11 41	
17¾	**London Euston 15** ⊖	a	00 09	00 12	05 59	06 32	06 58	07 29	07 52	08 12	08 32		08 52	09 12	09 29	09 52	10 11	10 30	10 49	11 11	11 30		11 50	

		LO	LO	LO	LO	LO	LO		LO	LO	LO	LO	LO	LO	LO	LO	LO		LO	LO	LO	LO	LO	LO	LO
Watford Junction	d	15 01	15 21	15 41	16 01	16 21	16 41		17 01	17 21	17 41	18 01	18 21	18 41	19 01	19 21	19 41		20 01	20 21	20 41	21 01	21 21	21 41	22 01
Watford High Street	d	15 04	15 24	15 44	16 04	16 24	16 44		17 04	17 24	17 44	18 04	18 24	18 44	19 04	19 24	19 44		20 04	20 24	20 44	21 04	21 24	21 44	22 04
Bushey	d	15 06	15 26	15 46	16 06	16 26	16 46		17 06	17 26	17 46	18 06	18 26	18 46	19 06	19 26	19 46		20 06	20 26	20 46	21 06	21 26	21 46	22 06
Carpenders Park	d	15 09	15 29	15 49	16 09	16 29	16 49		17 09	17 29	17 49	18 09	18 29	18 49	19 09	19 29	19 49		20 09	20 29	20 49	21 09	21 29	21 49	22 09
Hatch End	d	15 12	15 32	15 52	16 12	16 32	16 52		17 12	17 32	17 52	18 12	18 32	18 52	19 12	19 32	19 52		20 12	20 32	20 52	21 12	21 32	21 52	22 12
Headstone Lane	d	15 14	15 34	15 54	16 14	16 34	16 54		17 14	17 34	17 54	18 14	18 34	18 54	19 14	19 34	19 54		20 14	20 34	20 54	21 14	21 34	21 54	22 14
Harrow & Wealdstone	d	15 17	15 37	15 57	16 17	16 37	16 57		17 17	17 37	17 57	18 17	18 37	18 57	19 17	19 37	19 57		20 17	20 37	20 57	21 17	21 37	21 57	22 17
Kenton	d	15 19	15 39	15 59	16 19	16 39	16 59		17 19	17 39	17 59	18 19	18 39	18 59	19 19	19 39	19 59		20 19	20 39	20 59	21 19	21 39	21 59	22 19
South Kenton	d	15 21	15 41	16 01	16 21	16 41	17 01		17 21	17 41	18 01	18 21	18 41	19 01	19 21	19 41	20 01		20 21	20 41	21 01	21 21	21 41	22 01	22 21
North Wembley	d	15 23	15 43	16 03	16 23	16 43	17 03		17 23	17 43	18 03	18 23	18 43	19 03	19 23	19 43	20 03		20 23	20 43	21 03	21 23	21 43	22 03	22 23
Wembley Central	d	15 25	15 45	16 05	16 25	16 45	17 05		17 25	17 45	18 05	18 25	18 45	19 05	19 25	19 45	20 05		20 25	20 45	21 05	21 25	21 45	22 05	22 25
Stonebridge Park	d	15 28	15 48	16 08	16 28	16 48	17 08		17 28	17 48	18 08	18 28	18 48	19 08	19 28	19 48	20 08		20 28	20 48	21 08	21 28	21 48	22 08	22 28
Harlesden	d	15 30	15 50	16 10	16 30	16 50	17 10		17 30	17 50	18 10	18 30	18 50	19 10	19 30	19 50	20 10		20 30	20 50	21 10	21 30	21 50	22 10	22 30
Willesden Jn Low Level	d	15 32	15 52	16 12	16 32	16 52	17 12		17 32	17 52	18 12	18 32	18 52	19 12	19 32	19 52	20 12		20 32	20 52	21 12	21 32	21 52	22 12	22 32
Kensal Green	d	15 35	15 55	16 15	16 35	16 55	17 15		17 35	17 55	18 15	18 35	18 55	19 15	19 35	19 55	20 15		20 35	20 55	21 15	21 35	21 55	22 15	22 35
Queen's Park (London) ⊖	d	15 37	15 57	16 17	16 37	16 57	17 17		17 37	17 57	18 17	18 37	18 57	19 17	19 37	19 57	20 17		20 37	20 57	21 17	21 37	21 57	22 17	22 37
Kilburn High Road	d	15 39	15 59	16 19	16 39	16 59	17 19		17 39	17 59	18 19	18 39	18 59	19 19	19 39	19 59	20 19		20 39	20 59	21 19	21 39	21 59	22 19	22 39
South Hampstead	d	15 41	16 01	16 21	16 41	17 01	17 21		17 41	18 01	18 21	18 41	19 01	19 21	19 41	20 01	20 21		20 41	21 01	21 21	21 41	22 01	22 21	22 41
London Euston 15 ⊖	a	15 50	16 11	16 30	16 49	17 11	17 30		17 53	18 13	18 30	18 50	19 11	19 30	19 52	20 10	20 30		20 48	21 11	21 30	21 51	22 11	22 30	22 50

		LO	LO		LO
Watford Junction	d	22 21	22 51		23 21
Watford High Street	d	22 24	22 54		23 24
Bushey	d	22 26	22 56		23 26
Carpenders Park	d	22 29	22 59		23 29
Hatch End	d	22 32	23 02		23 32
Headstone Lane	d	22 34	23 04		23 34
Harrow & Wealdstone	d	22 37	23 07		23 37
Kenton	d	22 39	23 09		23 39
South Kenton	d	22 41	23 11		23 41
North Wembley	d	22 43	23 13		23 43
Wembley Central	d	22 45	23 15		23 45
Stonebridge Park	d	22 48	23 18		23 48
Harlesden	d	22 50	23 20		23 50
Willesden Jn Low Level	d	22 52	23 22		23 52
Kensal Green	d	22 55	23 25		23 55
Queen's Park (London) ⊖	d	22 57	23 27		23 57
Kilburn High Road	d	22 59	23 29		23 59
South Hampstead	d	23 01	23 31		00 01
London Euston 15 ⊖	a	23 10	23 39		00 09

Saturdays

		LO	LO	LO	LO	LO	LO	LO	LO	LO		LO	LO	LO	LO	LO	LO	LO	LO	LO		LO		LO
Watford Junction	d	23p21	05 11	05 41	06 11	06 41	07 01	07 21	07 41	08 01		08 21	08 41	09 01	09 21	09 41	10 01	10 21	10 41	11 01		21 01		21 21
Watford High Street	d	23p24	05 14	05 44	06 14	06 44	07 04	07 24	07 44	08 04		08 24	08 44	09 04	09 24	09 44	10 04	10 24	10 44	11 04		21 04		21 24
Bushey	d	23p26	05 16	05 46	06 16	06 46	07 06	07 26	07 46	08 06		08 26	08 46	09 06	09 26	09 46	10 06	10 26	10 46	11 06		21 06		21 26
Carpenders Park	d	23p29	05 19	05 49	06 19	06 49	07 09	07 29	07 49	08 09		08 29	08 49	09 09	09 29	09 49	10 09	10 29	10 49	11 09		21 09		21 29
Hatch End	d	23p32	05 22	05 52	06 22	06 52	07 12	07 32	07 52	08 12		08 32	08 52	09 12	09 32	09 52	10 12	10 32	10 52	11 12		21 12		21 32
Headstone Lane	d	23p34	05 24	05 54	06 24	06 54	07 14	07 34	07 54	08 14		08 34	08 54	09 14	09 34	09 54	10 14	10 34	10 54	11 14	and at the same minutes past each hour until	21 14		21 34
Harrow & Wealdstone	d	23p37	05 27	05 57	06 27	06 57	07 17	07 37	07 57	08 17		08 37	08 57	09 17	09 37	09 57	10 17	10 37	10 57	11 17		21 17		21 37
Kenton	d	23p39	05 29	05 59	06 29	06 59	07 19	07 39	07 59	08 19		08 39	08 59	09 19	09 39	09 59	10 19	10 39	10 59	11 19		21 19		21 39
South Kenton	d	23p41	05 31	06 01	06 31	07 01	07 21	07 41	08 01	08 21		08 41	09 01	09 21	09 41	10 01	10 21	10 41	11 01	11 21		21 21		21 41
North Wembley	d	23p43	05 33	06 03	06 33	07 03	07 23	07 43	08 03	08 23		08 43	09 03	09 23	09 43	10 03	10 23	10 43	11 03	11 23		21 23		21 43
Wembley Central	d	23p45	05 35	06 05	06 35	07 05	07 25	07 45	08 05	08 25		08 45	09 05	09 25	09 45	10 05	10 25	10 45	11 05	11 25		21 25		21 45
Stonebridge Park	d	23p48	05 38	06 08	06 38	07 08	07 28	07 48	08 08	08 28		08 48	09 08	09 28	09 48	10 08	10 28	10 48	11 08	11 28		21 28		21 48
Harlesden	d	23p50	05 40	06 10	06 40	07 10	07 30	07 50	08 10	08 30		08 50	09 10	09 30	09 50	10 10	10 30	10 50	11 10	11 30		21 30		21 50
Willesden Jn Low Level	d	23p52	05 42	06 12	06 42	07 12	07 32	07 52	08 12	08 32		08 52	09 12	09 32	09 52	10 12	10 32	10 52	11 12	11 32		21 32		21 52
Kensal Green	d	23p55	05 45	06 15	06 45	07 15	07 35	07 55	08 15	08 35		08 55	09 15	09 35	09 55	10 15	10 35	10 55	11 15	11 35		21 35		21 55
Queen's Park (London) ⊖	d	23p57	05 47	06 17	06 47	07 17	07 37	07 57	08 17	08 37		08 57	09 17	09 37	09 57	10 17	10 37	10 57	11 17	11 37		21 37		21 57
Kilburn High Road	d	23p59	05 49	06 19	06 49	07 19	07 39	07 59	08 19	08 39		08 59	09 19	09 39	09 59	10 19	10 39	10 59	11 19	11 39		21 39		21 59
South Hampstead	d	00 01	05 51	06 21	06 51	07 21	07 41	08 01	08 21	08 41		09 01	09 21	09 41	10 01	10 21	10 41	11 01	11 21	11 41		21 41		22 01
London Euston 15 ⊖	a	00 09	06 00	06 31	06 59	07 30	07 49	08 13	08 30	08 50		09 12	09 30	09 50	10 13	10 30	10 49	11 13	11 30	11 50		21 50		22 10

Stations Harrow & Wealdstone to Queen's Park inclusive are also served by London Underground Bakerloo Line Services

Table 60

Saturdays

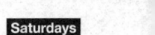

Watford Junction - Harrow & Wealdstone, Queen's Park and London

		LO	LO	LO	LO	LO
Watford Junction	d	21 41	22 01	22 21	22 51	23 21
Watford High Street	d	21 44	22 04	22 24	22 54	23 24
Bushey	d	21 46	22 06	22 26	22 56	23 26
Carpenders Park	d	21 49	22 09	22 29	22 59	23 29
Hatch End	d	21 52	22 12	22 32	23 02	23 32
Headstone Lane	d	21 54	22 14	22 34	23 04	23 34
Harrow & Wealdstone	d	21 57	22 17	22 37	23 07	23 37
Kenton	d	21 59	22 19	22 39	23 09	23 39
South Kenton	d	22 01	22 21	22 41	23 11	23 41
North Wembley	d	22 03	22 23	22 43	23 13	23 43
Wembley Central	d	22 05	22 25	22 45	23 15	23 45
Stonebridge Park	d	22 08	22 28	22 48	23 17	23 48
Harlesden	d	22 10	22 30	22 50	23 19	23 50
Willesden Jn Low Level	d	22 12	22 32	22 52	23 21	23 52
Kensal Green	d	22 15	22 35	22 55	23 23	23 55
Queen's Park (London) ⊖	d	22 17	22 37	22 57	23 25	23 57
Kilburn High Road	d	22 19	22 39	22 59	23 27	23 59
South Hampstead	d	22 21	22 41	23 01	23 29	00 01
London Euston 15 ⊖	a	22 30	22 53	23 11	23 38	00 08

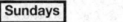

Sundays

		LO A	LO		LO	LO	LO	LO	LO	LO	LO	LO	LO	LO		LO	LO	LO	LO	LO	LO
Watford Junction	d	23p21	06 51		09 21	09 41	10 01	10 21	10 41	11 01	11 21	11 41	12 01	12 21		18 21	18 41	19 01	19 21	19 41	20 01
Watford High Street	d	23p24	06 54		09 24	09 44	10 04	10 24	10 44	11 04	11 24	11 44	12 04	12 24		18 24	18 44	19 04	19 24	19 44	20 04
Bushey	d	23p26	06 56		09 26	09 46	10 06	10 26	10 46	11 06	11 26	11 46	12 06	12 26		18 26	18 46	19 06	19 26	19 46	20 06
Carpenders Park	d	23p29	06 59		09 29	09 49	10 09	10 29	10 49	11 09	11 29	11 49	12 09	12 29		18 29	18 49	19 09	19 29	19 49	20 09
Hatch End	d	23p32	07 02		09 32	09 52	10 12	10 32	10 52	11 12	11 32	11 52	12 12	12 32		18 32	18 52	19 12	19 32	19 52	20 12
Headstone Lane	d	23p34	07 04		09 34	09 54	10 14	10 34	10 54	11 14	11 34	11 54	12 14	12 34	and at	18 34	18 54	19 14	19 34	19 54	20 14
Harrow & Wealdstone	d	23p37	07 07	and	09 37	09 57	10 17	10 37	10 57	11 17	11 37	11 57	12 17	12 37	the same	18 37	18 57	19 17	19 37	19 57	20 17
Kenton	d	23p39	07 09	every 30	09 39	09 59	10 19	10 39	10 59	11 19	11 39	11 59	12 19	12 39	minutes	18 39	18 59	19 19	19 39	19 59	20 19
South Kenton	d	23p41	07 11	minutes	09 41	10 01	10 21	10 41	11 01	11 21	11 41	12 01	12 21	12 41	past	18 41	19 01	19 21	19 41	20 01	20 21
North Wembley	d	23p43	07 13	until	09 43	10 03	10 23	10 43	11 03	11 23	11 43	12 03	12 23	12 43	each	18 43	19 03	19 23	19 43	20 03	20 23
Wembley Central	d	23p45	07 15		09 45	10 05	10 25	10 45	11 05	11 25	11 45	12 05	12 25	12 45	hour until	18 45	19 05	19 25	19 45	20 05	20 25
Stonebridge Park	d	23p48	07 18		09 48	10 08	10 28	10 48	11 08	11 28	11 48	12 08	12 28	12 48		18 48	19 08	19 28	19 48	20 08	20 28
Harlesden	d	23p50	07 20		09 50	10 10	10 30	10 50	11 10	11 30	11 50	12 10	12 30	12 50		18 50	19 10	19 30	19 50	20 10	20 30
Willesden Jn Low Level	d	23p52	07 22		09 52	10 12	10 32	10 52	11 12	11 32	11 52	12 12	12 32	12 52		18 52	19 12	19 32	19 52	20 12	20 32
Kensal Green	d	23p55	07 25		09 55	10 15	10 35	10 55	11 15	11 35	11 55	12 15	12 35	12 55		18 55	19 15	19 35	19 55	20 15	20 35
Queen's Park (London) ⊖	d	23p57	07 27		09 57	10 17	10 37	10 57	11 17	11 37	11 57	12 17	12 37	12 57		18 57	19 17	19 37	19 57	20 17	20 37
Kilburn High Road	d	23p59	07 29		09 59	10 19	10 39	10 59	11 19	11 39	11 59	12 19	12 39	12 59		18 59	19 19	19 39	19 59	20 19	20 39
South Hampstead	d	00 01	07 31		10 01	10 21	10 41	11 01	11 21	11 41	12 01	12 21	12 41	13 01		19 01	19 21	19 41	20 01	20 21	20 41
London Euston 15 ⊖	a	00 08	07 40		10 10	10 30	10 50	11 13	11 30	11 50	12 11	12 31	12 50	13 10		19 10	19 31	19 49	20 10	20 31	20 49

		LO	LO	LO	LO	LO	LO	LO	LO	LO
Watford Junction	d	20 21	20 41	21 01	21 21	21 41	22 01	22 21	22 51	23 21
Watford High Street	d	20 24	20 44	21 04	21 24	21 44	22 04	22 24	22 54	23 24
Bushey	d	20 26	20 46	21 06	21 26	21 46	22 06	22 26	22 56	23 26
Carpenders Park	d	20 29	20 49	21 09	21 29	21 49	22 09	22 29	22 59	23 29
Hatch End	d	20 32	20 52	21 12	21 32	21 52	22 12	22 32	23 02	23 32
Headstone Lane	d	20 34	20 54	21 14	21 34	21 54	22 14	22 34	23 04	23 34
Harrow & Wealdstone	d	20 37	20 57	21 17	21 37	21 57	22 17	22 37	23 07	23 37
Kenton	d	20 39	20 59	21 19	21 39	21 59	22 19	22 39	23 09	23 39
South Kenton	d	20 41	21 01	21 21	21 41	22 01	22 21	22 41	23 11	23 41
North Wembley	d	20 43	21 03	21 23	21 43	22 03	22 23	22 43	23 13	23 43
Wembley Central	d	20 45	21 05	21 25	21 45	22 05	22 25	22 45	23 15	23 45
Stonebridge Park	d	20 48	21 08	21 28	21 48	22 08	22 28	22 48	23 18	23 48
Harlesden	d	20 50	21 10	21 30	21 50	22 10	22 30	22 50	23 20	23 50
Willesden Jn Low Level	d	20 52	21 12	21 32	21 52	22 12	22 32	22 52	23 22	23 52
Kensal Green	d	20 55	21 15	21 35	21 55	22 15	22 35	22 55	23 25	23 55
Queen's Park (London) ⊖	d	20 57	21 17	21 37	21 57	22 17	22 37	22 57	23 27	23 57
Kilburn High Road	d	20 59	21 19	21 39	21 59	22 19	22 39	22 59	23 29	23 59
South Hampstead	d	21 01	21 21	21 41	22 01	22 21	22 41	23 01	23 31	00 01
London Euston 15 ⊖	a	21 13	21 30	21 51	22 10	22 30	22 49	23 10	23 40	00 12

A not 22 May

Stations Harrow & Wealdstone to Queen's Park inclusive are also served by London Underground Bakerloo Line Services

Table 61

Watford Junction - St. Albans

Mondays to Fridays
until 21 October

Miles			LM	LM	LM	LM	LM	LM	LM	LM	LM	LM	LM	LM	LM	LM	LM	LM	LM	LM	LM	LM	LM
			1	1	1	1	1	1	1	1	1	1	1	1	1	1	1	1	1	1	1	1	1
0	**Watford Junction**	d	05 57	06 39	07 21	08 04	09 01	09 46	10 31	11 16	12 01	12 46	13 31	14 16	15 01	15 46	16 31	17 21	18 10	18 55	19 38	20 31	21 31
0¾	Watford North	d	05 59	06 41	07 23	08 06	09 03	09 48	10 33	11 18	12 03	12 48	13 33	14 18	15 03	15 48	16 33	17 23	18 12	18 57	19 40	20 33	21 33
1¾	Garston (Hertfordshire)	d	06 02	06 44	07 26	08 09	09 06	09 51	10 36	11 21	12 06	12 51	13 36	14 21	15 06	15 51	16 36	17 26	18 15	19 00	19 43	20 36	21 36
3¼	Bricket Wood	d	06 05	06 47	07 29	08 12	09 09	09 54	10 39	11 24	12 09	12 54	13 39	14 24	15 09	15 54	16 39	17 29	18 18	19 03	19 46	20 39	21 39
4½	How Wood	d	06 07	06 49	07 31	08 14	09 11	09 56	10 41	11 26	12 11	12 56	13 41	14 26	15 11	15 56	16 41	17 31	18 20	19 05	19 48	20 41	21 41
5	Park Street	d	06 09	06 51	07 33	08 16	09 13	09 58	10 43	11 28	12 13	12 58	13 43	14 28	15 13	15 58	16 43	17 33	18 22	19 07	19 50	20 43	21 43
6½	**St Albans Abbey**	a	06 13	06 55	07 37	08 20	09 17	10 02	10 47	11 32	12 17	13 02	13 47	14 32	15 17	16 02	16 47	17 37	18 26	19 11	19 54	20 47	21 47

Mondays to Fridays
from 24 October

		LM	LM	LM	LM	LM	LM	LM	LM	LM	LM	LM	LM	LM	LM	LM	LM	LM	LM	LM	LM
		1	1	1	1	1	1	1	1	1	1	1	1	1	1	1	1	1	1	1	1
Watford Junction	d	05 46	06 32	07 18	08 04	08 53	09 39	10 25	11 25	12 25	13 25	14 15	15 01	15 48	16 35	17 21	18 08	18 54	19 40	20 30	21 31
Watford North	d	05 48	06 34	07 20	08 06	08 55	09 41	10 27	11 27	12 27	13 27	14 17	15 03	15 50	16 37	17 23	18 10	18 56	19 42	20 32	21 33
Garston (Hertfordshire)	d	05 51	06 37	07 23	08 09	08 58	09 44	10 30	11 30	12 30	13 30	14 20	15 06	15 53	16 40	17 26	18 13	18 59	19 45	20 35	21 36
Bricket Wood	d	05 54	06 40	07 26	08 12	09 01	09 47	10 33	11 33	12 33	13 33	14 23	15 09	15 56	16 43	17 29	18 16	19 02	19 48	20 38	21 39
How Wood	d	05 56	06 42	07 28	08 14	09 03	09 49	10 35	11 35	12 35	13 35	14 25	15 11	15 58	16 45	17 31	18 18	19 04	19 50	20 40	21 41
Park Street	d	05 58	06 44	07 30	08 16	09 05	09 51	10 37	11 37	12 37	13 37	14 27	15 13	16 00	16 47	17 33	18 20	19 06	19 52	20 42	21 43
St Albans Abbey	a	06 04	06 50	07 36	08 22	09 11	09 57	10 43	11 43	12 43	13 43	14 33	15 19	16 06	16 53	17 39	18 26	19 12	19 58	20 48	21 49

Saturdays
until 22 October

		LM	LM	LM	LM	LM	LM	LM	LM	LM	LM	LM	LM	LM	LM	LM	LM	LM	LM	LM	LM	LM
		1	1	1	1	1	1	1	1	1	1	1	1	1	1	1	1	1	1	1	1	1
Watford Junction	d	06 01	06 45	07 31	08 15	09 01	09 46	10 31	11 16	12 01	12 46	13 31	14 16	15 01	15 46	16 31	17 16	18 01	18 46	19 31	20 31	21 31
Watford North	d	06 03	06 47	07 33	08 17	09 03	09 48	10 33	11 18	12 03	12 48	13 33	14 18	15 03	15 48	16 33	17 18	18 03	18 48	19 33	20 33	21 33
Garston (Hertfordshire)	d	06 06	06 50	07 36	08 20	09 06	09 51	10 36	11 21	12 06	12 51	13 36	14 21	15 06	15 51	16 36	17 21	18 06	18 51	19 36	20 36	21 36
Bricket Wood	d	06 09	06 53	07 39	08 23	09 09	09 54	10 39	11 24	12 09	12 54	13 39	14 24	15 09	15 54	16 39	17 24	18 09	18 54	19 39	20 39	21 39
How Wood	d	06 11	06 55	07 41	08 25	09 11	09 56	10 41	11 26	12 11	12 56	13 41	14 26	15 11	15 56	16 41	17 26	18 11	18 56	19 41	20 41	21 41
Park Street	d	06 13	06 57	07 43	08 27	09 13	09 58	10 43	11 28	12 13	12 58	13 43	14 28	15 13	15 58	16 43	17 28	18 13	18 58	19 43	20 43	21 43
St Albans Abbey	a	06 17	07 01	07 47	08 31	09 17	10 02	10 47	11 32	12 17	13 02	13 47	14 32	15 17	16 02	16 47	17 32	18 17	19 02	19 47	20 47	21 47

Saturdays
from 29 October

		LM	LM	LM	LM	LM	LM	LM	LM	LM	LM	LM	LM	LM	LM	LM	LM	LM	LM	LM	LM
		1	1	1	1	1	1	1	1	1	1	1	1	1	1	1	1	1	1	1	1
Watford Junction	d	05 49	06 35	07 21	08 07	08 53	09 39	10 25	11 25	12 25	13 25	14 15	15 01	15 48	16 35	17 21	18 08	18 54	19 40	20 30	21 31
Watford North	d	05 51	06 37	07 23	08 09	08 55	09 41	10 27	11 27	12 27	13 27	14 17	15 03	15 50	16 37	17 23	18 10	18 56	19 42	20 32	21 33
Garston (Hertfordshire)	d	05 54	06 40	07 26	08 12	08 58	09 44	10 30	11 30	12 30	13 30	14 20	15 06	15 53	16 40	17 26	18 13	18 59	19 45	20 35	21 36
Bricket Wood	d	05 57	06 43	07 29	08 15	09 01	09 47	10 33	11 33	12 33	13 33	14 23	15 09	15 56	16 43	17 29	18 16	19 02	19 48	20 38	21 39
How Wood	d	05 59	06 45	07 31	08 17	09 03	09 49	10 35	11 35	12 35	13 35	14 25	15 11	15 58	16 45	17 31	18 18	19 04	19 50	20 40	21 41
Park Street	d	06 01	06 47	07 33	08 19	09 05	09 51	10 37	11 37	12 37	13 37	14 27	15 13	16 00	16 47	17 33	18 20	19 06	19 52	20 42	21 43
St Albans Abbey	a	06 07	06 53	07 39	08 25	09 11	09 57	10 43	11 43	12 43	13 43	14 33	15 19	16 06	16 53	17 39	18 26	19 12	19 58	20 48	21 49

Sundays
until 23 October

		LM	LM	LM	LM	LM	LM	LM	LM	LM	LM	LM	LM	LM	LM	LM
		1	1	1	1	1	1	1	1	1	1	1	1	1	1	1
Watford Junction	d	08 07	09 07	10 20	11 20	12 07	13 07	14 07	15 07	16 07	17 07	18 07	19 07	20 07	21 02	22 04
Watford North	d	08 09	09 09	10 22	11 22	12 09	13 09	14 09	15 09	16 09	17 09	18 09	19 09	20 09	21 04	22 06
Garston (Hertfordshire)	d	08 12	09 12	10 25	11 25	12 12	13 12	14 12	15 12	16 12	17 12	18 12	19 12	20 12	21 07	22 09
Bricket Wood	d	08 15	09 15	10 28	11 28	12 15	13 15	14 15	15 15	16 15	17 15	18 15	19 15	20 15	21 10	22 12
How Wood	d	08 17	09 17	10 30	11 30	12 17	13 17	14 17	15 17	16 17	17 17	18 17	19 17	20 17	21 12	22 14
Park Street	d	08 19	09 19	10 32	11 32	12 19	13 19	14 19	15 19	16 19	17 19	18 19	19 19	20 19	21 14	22 16
St Albans Abbey	a	08 23	09 23	10 36	11 36	12 23	13 23	14 23	15 23	16 23	17 23	18 23	19 23	20 23	21 18	22 20

Sundays
from 30 October

		LM	LM	LM	LM	LM	LM	LM	LM	LM	LM	LM	LM	LM	LM	LM
		1	1	1	1	1	1	1	1	1	1	1	1	1	1	1
Watford Junction	d	08 07	09 07	10 20	11 20	12 07	13 07	14 07	15 07	16 07	17 07	18 07	19 07	20 07	21 02	22 04
Watford North	d	08 09	09 09	10 22	11 22	12 09	13 09	14 09	15 09	16 09	17 09	18 09	19 09	20 09	21 04	22 06
Garston (Hertfordshire)	d	08 12	09 12	10 25	11 25	12 12	13 12	14 12	15 12	16 12	17 12	18 12	19 12	20 12	21 07	22 09
Bricket Wood	d	08 15	09 15	10 28	11 28	12 15	13 15	14 15	15 15	16 15	17 15	18 15	19 15	20 15	21 10	22 12
How Wood	d	08 17	09 17	10 30	11 30	12 17	13 17	14 17	15 17	16 17	17 17	18 17	19 17	20 17	21 12	22 14
Park Street	d	08 19	09 19	10 32	11 32	12 19	13 19	14 19	15 19	16 19	17 19	18 19	19 19	20 19	21 14	22 16
St Albans Abbey	a	08 25	09 25	10 38	11 38	12 25	13 25	14 25	15 25	16 25	17 25	18 25	19 25	20 25	21 20	22 22

For connections from London Euston please refer to Table 66

Table 61

St. Albans - Watford Junction

Mondays to Fridays
until 21 October

Miles			LM 1	LM 1	LM 1	LM 1	LM 1	LM 1	LM 1	LM 1	LM 1	LM 1	LM 1	LM 1	LM 1	LM 1	LM 1	LM 1	LM 1	LM 1	LM 1	LM 1	LM 1
0	**St Albans Abbey**	d	06 18	07 00	07 42	08 25	09 22	10 07	10 52	11 37	12 22	13 07	13 52	14 37	15 22	16 07	16 52	17 42	18 32	19 16	20 00	20 52	21 52
1½	Park Street	d	06 21	07 03	07 45	08 28	09 25	10 10	10 55	11 40	12 25	13 10	13 55	14 40	15 25	16 10	16 55	17 45	18 35	19 19	20 03	20 55	21 55
2¼	How Wood	d	06 23	07 05	07 47	08 30	09 27	10 12	10 57	11 42	12 27	13 12	13 57	14 42	15 27	16 12	16 57	17 47	18 37	19 21	20 05	20 57	21 57
3	Bricket Wood	d	06 26	07 08	07 50	08 33	09 30	10 15	11 00	11 45	12 30	13 15	14 00	14 45	15 30	16 15	17 00	17 50	18 40	19 24	20 08	21 00	22 00
4¾	Garston (Hertfordshire)	d	06 29	07 11	07 53	08 36	09 33	10 18	11 03	11 48	12 33	13 18	14 03	14 48	15 33	16 18	17 03	17 53	18 43	19 27	20 11	21 03	22 03
5½	Watford North	d	06 31	07 13	07 55	08 38	09 35	10 20	11 05	11 50	12 35	13 20	14 05	14 50	15 35	16 20	17 05	17 55	18 45	19 29	20 13	21 05	22 05
6½	**Watford Junction**	a	06 34	07 16	07 58	08 41	09 38	10 23	11 08	11 53	12 38	13 23	14 08	14 53	15 38	16 24	17 08	17 58	18 48	19 32	20 16	21 08	22 08

Mondays to Fridays
from 24 October

		LM 1	LM 1	LM 1	LM 1	LM 1	LM 1	LM 1	LM 1	LM 1	LM 1	LM 1	LM 1	LM 1	LM 1	LM 1	LM 1	LM 1	LM 1	LM 1	LM 1
St Albans Abbey	d	06 09	06 55	07 41	08 27	09 16	10 02	10 48	11 48	12 48	13 48	14 38	15 24	16 11	16 58	17 44	18 31	19 17	20 03	20 53	21 54
Park Street	d	06 12	06 58	07 44	08 30	09 19	10 05	10 51	11 51	12 51	13 51	14 41	15 27	16 14	17 01	17 47	18 34	19 20	20 06	20 56	21 57
How Wood	d	06 14	07 00	07 46	08 32	09 21	10 07	10 53	11 53	12 53	13 53	14 43	15 29	16 16	17 03	17 49	18 36	19 22	20 08	20 58	21 59
Bricket Wood	d	06 17	07 03	07 49	08 35	09 24	10 10	10 56	11 56	12 56	13 56	14 46	15 32	16 19	17 06	17 52	18 39	19 25	20 11	21 01	22 02
Garston (Hertfordshire)	d	06 20	07 06	07 52	08 38	09 27	10 13	10 59	11 59	12 59	13 59	14 49	15 35	16 22	17 09	17 55	18 42	19 28	20 14	21 04	22 05
Watford North	d	06 22	07 08	07 54	08 40	09 29	10 15	11 01	12 01	13 01	14 01	14 51	15 37	16 24	17 11	17 57	18 44	19 30	20 16	21 06	22 07
Watford Junction	a	06 27	07 13	07 59	08 45	09 34	10 20	11 06	12 06	13 06	14 06	14 56	15 42	16 29	17 16	18 02	18 49	19 35	20 21	21 10	22 12

Saturdays
until 22 October

		LM 1	LM 1	LM 1	LM 1	LM 1	LM 1	LM 1	LM 1	LM 1	LM 1	LM 1	LM 1	LM 1	LM 1	LM 1	LM 1	LM 1	LM 1	LM 1	LM 1	LM 1
St Albans Abbey	d	06 22	07 06	07 52	08 36	09 22	10 07	10 52	11 37	12 22	13 07	13 52	14 37	15 22	16 07	16 52	17 37	18 22	19 07	19 52	20 52	21 52
Park Street	d	06 25	07 09	07 55	08 39	09 25	10 10	10 55	11 40	12 25	13 10	13 55	14 40	15 25	16 10	16 55	17 40	18 25	19 10	19 55	20 55	21 55
How Wood	d	06 27	07 11	07 57	08 41	09 27	10 12	10 57	11 42	12 27	13 12	13 57	14 42	15 27	16 12	16 57	17 42	18 27	19 12	19 57	20 57	21 57
Bricket Wood	d	06 30	07 14	08 00	08 44	09 30	10 15	11 00	11 45	12 30	13 15	14 00	14 45	15 30	16 15	17 00	17 45	18 30	19 15	20 00	21 00	22 00
Garston (Hertfordshire)	d	06 33	07 17	08 03	08 47	09 33	10 18	11 03	11 48	12 33	13 18	14 03	14 48	15 33	16 18	17 03	17 48	18 33	19 18	20 03	21 03	22 03
Watford North	d	06 35	07 19	08 05	08 49	09 35	10 20	11 05	11 50	12 35	13 20	14 05	14 50	15 35	16 20	17 05	17 50	18 35	19 20	20 05	21 05	22 05
Watford Junction	a	06 38	07 22	08 08	08 52	09 38	10 23	11 08	11 53	12 38	13 23	14 08	14 53	15 38	16 23	17 08	17 53	18 38	19 23	20 08	21 08	22 08

Saturdays
from 29 October

		LM 1	LM 1	LM 1	LM 1	LM 1	LM 1	LM 1	LM 1	LM 1	LM 1	LM 1	LM 1	LM 1	LM 1	LM 1	LM 1	LM 1	LM 1	LM 1	LM 1
St Albans Abbey	d	06 12	06 58	07 44	08 30	09 16	10 02	10 48	11 48	12 48	13 48	14 38	15 24	16 11	16 58	17 44	18 31	19 17	20 03	20 53	21 54
Park Street	d	06 15	07 01	07 47	08 33	09 19	10 05	10 51	11 51	12 51	13 51	14 41	15 27	16 14	17 01	17 47	18 34	19 20	20 06	20 56	21 57
How Wood	d	06 17	07 03	07 49	08 35	09 21	10 07	10 53	11 53	12 53	13 53	14 43	15 29	16 16	17 03	17 49	18 36	19 22	20 08	20 58	21 59
Bricket Wood	d	06 20	07 06	07 52	08 38	09 24	10 10	10 56	11 56	12 56	13 56	14 46	15 32	16 19	17 06	17 52	18 39	19 25	20 11	21 01	22 02
Garston (Hertfordshire)	d	06 23	07 09	07 55	08 41	09 27	10 13	10 59	11 59	12 59	13 59	14 49	15 35	16 22	17 09	17 55	18 42	19 28	20 14	21 04	22 05
Watford North	d	06 25	07 11	07 57	08 43	09 29	10 15	11 01	12 01	13 01	14 01	14 51	15 37	16 24	17 11	17 57	18 44	19 30	20 16	21 06	22 07
Watford Junction	a	06 30	07 16	08 02	08 48	09 34	10 20	11 06	12 06	13 06	14 06	14 56	15 42	16 29	17 16	18 02	18 49	19 35	20 21	21 10	22 12

Sundays
until 23 October

		LM 1	LM 1	LM 1	LM 1	LM 1	LM 1	LM 1	LM 1	LM 1	LM 1	LM 1	LM 1	LM 1	LM 1	LM 1
St Albans Abbey	d	08 28	09 28	10 42	11 42	12 28	13 28	14 28	15 28	16 28	17 28	18 28	19 28	20 28	21 23	22 25
Park Street	d	08 31	09 31	10 45	11 45	12 31	13 31	14 31	15 31	16 31	17 31	18 31	19 31	20 31	21 26	22 28
How Wood	d	08 33	09 33	10 47	11 47	12 33	13 33	14 33	15 33	16 33	17 33	18 33	19 33	20 33	21 28	22 30
Bricket Wood	d	08 36	09 36	10 50	11 50	12 36	13 36	14 36	15 36	16 36	17 36	18 36	19 36	20 36	21 31	22 33
Garston (Hertfordshire)	d	08 39	09 39	10 53	11 53	12 39	13 39	14 39	15 39	16 39	17 39	18 39	19 39	20 39	21 34	22 36
Watford North	d	08 41	09 41	10 55	11 55	12 41	13 41	14 41	15 41	16 41	17 41	18 41	19 41	20 41	21 36	22 38
Watford Junction	a	08 44	09 44	10 58	11 58	12 44	13 44	14 44	15 44	16 44	17 44	18 44	19 44	20 44	21 39	22 41

Sundays
from 30 October

		LM 1	LM 1	LM 1	LM 1	LM 1	LM 1	LM 1	LM 1	LM 1	LM 1	LM 1	LM 1	LM 1	LM 1	LM 1
St Albans Abbey	d	08 30	09 30	10 43	11 43	12 30	13 30	14 30	15 30	16 30	17 30	18 30	19 30	20 30	21 25	22 27
Park Street	d	08 33	09 33	10 46	11 46	12 33	13 33	14 33	15 33	16 33	17 33	18 33	19 33	20 33	21 28	22 30
How Wood	d	08 35	09 35	10 48	11 48	12 35	13 35	14 35	15 35	16 35	17 35	18 35	19 35	20 35	21 30	22 32
Bricket Wood	d	08 38	09 38	10 51	11 51	12 38	13 38	14 38	15 38	16 38	17 38	18 38	19 38	20 38	21 33	22 35
Garston (Hertfordshire)	d	08 41	09 41	10 54	11 54	12 41	13 41	14 41	15 41	16 41	17 41	18 41	19 41	20 41	21 36	22 38
Watford North	d	08 43	09 43	10 56	11 56	12 43	13 43	14 43	15 43	16 43	17 43	18 43	19 43	20 43	21 38	22 40
Watford Junction	a	08 48	09 48	11 00	12 01	12 47	13 47	14 47	15 47	16 47	17 47	18 47	19 47	20 48	21 43	22 45

For connections to London Euston please refer to Table 66

Table 62

Mondays to Fridays

Gospel Oak - Barking

Miles			LO MX	LO	LO	LO	LO	LO	LO	LO	LO		LO	LO	LO	LO	LO	LO	LO	LO	LO		LO	
0	**Gospel Oak**	d	23p35	06 20	06 35	06 50	07 05	07 20	07 35	07 50	08 05		08 20	08 35	08 50	09 05	09 20	09 35	09 50	10 05	10 20		10 35	and at the same minutes past each hour until
1¼	Upper Holloway	d	23p39	06 24	06 39	06 54	07 09	07 24	07 39	07 54	08 09		08 24	08 39	08 54	09 09	09 24	09 39	09 54	10 09	10 24		10 39	
2	Crouch Hill	d	23p42	06 27	06 42	06 57	07 12	07 27	07 42	07 57	08 12		08 27	08 42	08 57	09 12	09 27	09 42	09 57	10 12	10 27		10 42	
3	Harringay Green Lanes	d	23p45	06 30	06 45	07 00	07 15	07 30	07 45	08 00	08 15		08 30	08 45	09 00	09 15	09 30	09 45	10 00	10 15	10 30		10 45	
4¼	South Tottenham	d	23p48	06 33	06 48	07 03	07 18	07 33	07 48	08 03	08 18		08 33	08 48	09 03	09 18	09 33	09 48	10 03	10 18	10 33		10 48	
5¾	Blackhorse Road ⊖	d	23p51	06 36	06 51	07 06	07 21	07 36	07 51	08 06	08 21		08 36	08 51	09 06	09 21	09 36	09 51	10 06	10 21	10 36		10 51	
6½	Walthamstow Queen's Road	d	23p54	06 39	06 54	07 09	07 24	07 39	07 54	08 09	08 24		08 39	08 54	09 09	09 24	09 39	09 54	10 09	10 24	10 39		10 54	
7½	Leyton Midland Road	d	23p57	06 42	06 57	07 12	07 27	07 42	07 57	08 12	08 27		08 42	08 57	09 12	09 27	09 42	09 57	10 12	10 27	10 42		10 57	
8¼	Leytonstone High Road	d	23p59	06 45	07 00	07 15	07 30	07 45	08 00	08 15	08 30		08 45	09 00	09 15	09 30	09 45	10 00	10 15	10 30	10 45		11 00	
9½	Wanstead Park	d	00 03	06 48	07 03	07 18	07 33	07 48	08 03	08 18	08 33		08 48	09 03	09 18	09 33	09 48	10 03	10 18	10 33	10 48		11 03	
10½	Woodgrange Park	d	00 05	06 50	07 05	07 20	07 35	07 50	08 05	08 20	08 35		08 50	09 05	09 20	09 35	09 50	10 05	10 20	10 35	10 50		11 05	
12¼	**Barking** ⊖	a	00 12	06 57	07 11	07 27	07 41	07 56	08 11	08 26	08 42		08 56	09 11	09 26	09 41	09 56	10 12	10 26	10 41	10 56		11 11	

		LO	LO	LO	LO	LO	LO		LO	LO	LO	LO	LO	LO	LO	LO	LO		LO	LO	LO
Gospel Oak	d	18 35	18 50	19 05	19 20	19 35	19 50		20 05	20 20	20 35	20 50	21 05	21 20	21 35	21 50	22 05		22 35	23 05	23 35
Upper Holloway	d	18 39	18 54	19 09	19 24	19 39	19 54		20 09	20 24	20 39	20 54	21 09	21 24	21 39	21 54	22 09		22 39	23 09	23 39
Crouch Hill	d	18 42	18 57	19 12	19 27	19 42	19 57		20 12	20 27	20 42	20 57	21 12	21 27	21 42	21 57	22 12		22 42	23 12	23 42
Harringay Green Lanes	d	18 45	19 00	19 15	19 30	19 45	20 00		20 15	20 30	20 45	21 00	21 15	21 30	21 45	22 00	22 15		22 45	23 15	23 45
South Tottenham	d	18 48	19 03	19 18	19 33	19 48	20 03		20 18	20 33	20 48	21 03	21 18	21 33	21 48	22 03	22 18		22 48	23 18	23 48
Blackhorse Road ⊖	d	18 51	19 06	19 21	19 36	19 51	20 06		20 21	20 36	20 51	21 06	21 21	21 36	21 51	22 06	22 21		22 51	23 21	23 51
Walthamstow Queen's Road	d	18 54	19 09	19 24	19 39	19 54	20 09		20 24	20 39	20 54	21 09	21 24	21 39	21 54	22 09	22 24		22 54	23 24	23 54
Leyton Midland Road	d	18 57	19 12	19 27	19 42	19 57	20 12		20 27	20 42	20 57	21 12	21 27	21 42	21 57	22 12	22 27		22 57	23 27	23 57
Leytonstone High Road	d	19 00	19 15	19 30	19 45	20 00	20 15		20 30	20 45	21 00	21 15	21 30	21 45	22 00	22 15	22 30		23 00	23 30	23 59
Wanstead Park	d	19 03	19 18	19 33	19 48	20 03	20 18		20 33	20 48	21 03	21 18	21 33	21 48	22 03	22 18	22 33		23 03	23 33	00 03
Woodgrange Park	d	19 05	19 20	19 35	19 50	20 05	20 20		20 35	20 50	21 05	21 20	21 35	21 50	22 05	22 20	22 35		23 05	23 35	00 05
Barking ⊖	a	19 11	19 26	19 41	19 57	20 11	20 26		20 42	20 56	21 11	21 26	21 41	21 56	22 11	22 26	22 41		23 11	23 41	00 12

Saturdays

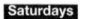

		LO	LO A	LO	LO	LO	LO		LO		LO	LO	LO	LO	LO	LO	LO		LO		LO	LO	LO
Gospel Oak	d	23p35	06 20	06 35	06 50	07 05	07 20	and at the same minutes past each hour until	10 20		10 35	10 50	11 06	11 20	11 35	11 50	12 05	and at the same minutes past each hour until	15 05		15 20	15 35	15 50
Upper Holloway	d	23p39	06 24	06 39	06 54	07 09	07 24		10 24		10 39	10 54	11 10	11 24	11 39	11 54	12 09		15 09		15 24	15 39	15 54
Crouch Hill	d	23p42	06 27	06 42	06 57	07 12	07 27		10 27		10 42	10 57	11 13	11 27	11 42	11 57	12 12		15 12		15 27	15 42	15 57
Harringay Green Lanes	d	23p45	06 30	06 45	07 00	07 15	07 30		10 30		10 45	11 00	11 16	11 30	11 45	12 00	12 15		15 15		15 30	15 45	16 00
South Tottenham	d	23p48	06 33	06 48	07 03	07 18	07 33		10 33		10 48	11 03	11 19	11 33	11 48	12 03	12 18		15 18		15 33	15 48	16 03
Blackhorse Road ⊖	d	23p51	06 36	06 51	07 06	07 21	07 36		10 36		10 51	11 06	11 22	11 36	11 51	12 06	12 21		15 21		15 36	15 51	16 06
Walthamstow Queen's Road	d	23p54	06 39	06 54	07 09	07 24	07 39		10 39		10 54	11 09	11 25	11 39	11 54	12 09	12 24		15 24		15 39	15 54	16 09
Leyton Midland Road	d	23p57	06 42	06 57	07 12	07 27	07 42		10 42		10 57	11 12	11 28	11 42	11 57	12 12	12 27		15 27		15 42	15 57	16 12
Leytonstone High Road	d	23p59	06 45	07 00	07 15	07 30	07 45		10 45		11 00	11 15	11 31	11 45	12 00	12 15	12 30		15 30		15 45	16 00	16 15
Wanstead Park	d	00 03	06 48	07 03	07 18	07 33	07 48		10 48		11 03	11 18	11 34	11 48	12 03	12 18	12 33		15 33		15 48	16 03	16 18
Woodgrange Park	d	00 05	06 50	07 05	07 20	07 35	07 50		10 50		11 05	11 20	11 36	11 50	12 05	12 20	12 35		15 35		15 50	16 05	16 20
Barking ⊖	a	00 12	06 57	07 09	07 24	07 39	07 54		10 54		11 09	11 24	11 40	11 54	12 09	12 24	12 39		15 39		15 54	16 09	16 24

		LO	LO	LO	LO	LO	LO		LO	LO	LO		LO	LO	LO	LO A
Gospel Oak	d	16 05	16 20	16 35	16 50	17 05	17 20		17 35	17 50	18 05	and at the same minutes past each hour until	22 05	22 35	23 05	23 35
Upper Holloway	d	16 09	16 24	16 39	16 54	17 09	17 24		17 39	17 54	18 09		22 09	22 39	23 09	23 39
Crouch Hill	d	16 12	16 27	16 42	16 57	17 12	17 27		17 42	17 57	18 12		22 12	22 42	23 12	23 42
Harringay Green Lanes	d	16 15	16 30	16 45	17 00	17 15	17 30		17 45	18 00	18 15		22 15	22 45	23 15	23 45
South Tottenham	d	16 18	16 33	16 48	17 03	17 18	17 33		17 48	18 03	18 18		22 18	22 48	23 18	23 48
Blackhorse Road ⊖	d	16 21	16 36	16 51	17 06	17 21	17 36		17 51	18 06	18 21		22 21	22 51	23 21	23 51
Walthamstow Queen's Road	d	16 24	16 39	16 54	17 09	17 24	17 39		17 54	18 09	18 24		22 24	22 54	23 24	23 54
Leyton Midland Road	d	16 27	16 42	16 57	17 12	17 27	17 42		17 57	18 12	18 27		22 27	22 57	23 27	23 57
Leytonstone High Road	d	16 30	16 45	17 00	17 15	17 30	17 45		18 00	18 15	18 30		22 30	23 00	23 30	23 59
Wanstead Park	d	16 33	16 48	17 03	17 18	17 33	17 48		18 03	18 18	18 33		22 33	23 03	23 33	00 03
Woodgrange Park	d	16 35	16 50	17 05	17 20	17 35	17 50		18 05	18 20	18 35		22 35	23 05	23 35	00 05
Barking ⊖	a	16 42	16 57	17 12	17 27	17 42	17 54		18 09	18 24	18 39		22 39	23 09	23 39	00 12

Sundays

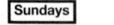

		LO B	LO	LO	LO	LO		LO	LO		LO	LO	LO	LO	LO	LO	LO
Gospel Oak	d	23p35	08 55	09 10	09 25	09 40	and at the same minutes past each hour until	20 40	20 55		21 10	21 25	21 40	21 55	22 10	22 40	23 10
Upper Holloway	d	23p39	08 59	09 14	09 29	09 44		20 44	20 59		21 14	21 29	21 44	21 59	22 14	22 44	23 14
Crouch Hill	d	23p42	09 02	09 17	09 32	09 47		20 47	21 02		21 17	21 32	21 47	22 02	22 17	22 47	23 17
Harringay Green Lanes	d	23p45	09 05	09 20	09 35	09 50		20 50	21 05		21 20	21 35	21 50	22 05	22 20	22 50	23 20
South Tottenham	d	23p48	09 08	09 23	09 38	09 53		20 53	21 08		21 23	21 38	21 53	22 08	22 23	22 53	23 23
Blackhorse Road ⊖	d	23p51	09 11	09 26	09 41	09 56		20 56	21 11		21 26	21 41	21 56	22 11	22 26	22 56	23 26
Walthamstow Queen's Road	d	23p54	09 14	09 29	09 44	09 59		20 59	21 14		21 29	21 44	21 59	22 14	22 29	22 59	23 29
Leyton Midland Road	d	23p57	09 17	09 32	09 47	10 02		21 02	21 17		21 32	21 47	22 02	22 17	22 32	23 02	23 32
Leytonstone High Road	d	23p59	09 20	09 35	09 50	10 05		21 05	21 20		21 35	21 50	22 05	22 20	22 35	23 05	23 35
Wanstead Park	d	00 03	09 23	09 38	09 53	10 08		21 08	21 23		21 38	21 53	22 08	22 23	22 38	23 08	23 38
Woodgrange Park	d	00 05	09 25	09 40	09 55	10 10		21 10	21 25		21 40	21 55	22 10	22 25	22 40	23 10	23 40
Barking ⊖	a	00 12	09 29	09 44	09 59	10 14		21 14	21 29		21 47	21 59	22 14	22 29	22 44	23 14	23 44

A not 10 December

B not 22 May

Table 62

Mondays to Fridays

Barking - Gospel Oak

Miles			LO MO	LO MX	LO	LO	LO	LO	LO	LO	LO	LO	LO	LO	LO	LO	LO	LO	LO	LO	LO	LO	LO
0	**Barking** ⊖	d	23p38	23p47	06 17	06 32	06 47	07 02	07 17	07 32	07 47	08 02	08 17	08 32	08 47	09 02	09 17	09 32	09 47	10 02	10 17	10 32	10 47
1¾	Woodgrange Park	d	23p41	23p50	06 20	06 35	06 50	07 05	07 20	07 35	07 50	08 05	08 20	08 35	08 50	09 05	09 20	09 35	09 50	10 05	10 20	10 35	10 50
2¾	Wanstead Park	d	23p44	23p53	06 23	06 38	06 53	07 08	07 23	07 38	07 53	08 08	08 23	08 38	08 53	09 08	09 23	09 38	09 53	10 08	10 23	10 38	10 53
4	Leytonstone High Road	d	23p48	23p57	06 27	06 42	06 57	07 12	07 27	07 42	07 57	08 12	08 27	08 42	08 57	09 12	09 27	09 42	09 57	10 12	10 27	10 42	10 57
4¾	Leyton Midland Road	d	23p50	23p59	06 29	06 44	06 59	07 14	07 29	07 44	07 59	08 14	08 29	08 44	08 59	09 14	09 29	09 44	09 59	10 14	10 29	10 44	10 59
5¾	Walthamstow Queen's Road	d	23p53	00 02	06 32	06 47	07 02	07 17	07 32	07 47	08 02	08 17	08 32	08 47	09 02	09 17	09 32	09 47	10 02	10 17	10 32	10 47	11 02
6½	Blackhorse Road ⊖	d	23p56	00 05	06 35	06 50	07 05	07 20	07 35	07 50	08 05	08 20	08 35	08 50	09 05	09 20	09 35	09 50	10 05	10 20	10 35	10 50	11 05
8¼	South Tottenham	d	23p59	00 09	06 39	06 54	07 09	07 24	07 39	07 54	08 09	08 24	08 39	08 54	09 09	09 24	09 39	09 54	10 09	10 24	10 39	10 54	11 09
9¼	Harringay Green Lanes	d	00 03	00 12	06 42	06 57	07 12	07 27	07 42	07 57	08 12	08 27	08 42	08 57	09 12	09 27	09 42	09 57	10 12	10 27	10 42	10 57	11 12
10¼	Crouch Hill	d	00 06	00 15	06 45	07 00	07 15	07 30	07 45	08 00	08 15	08 30	08 45	09 00	09 15	09 30	09 45	10 00	10 19	10 30	10 45	11 00	11 15
11	Upper Holloway	d	00 08	00 17	06 47	07 02	07 17	07 32	07 47	08 02	08 17	08 32	08 47	09 02	09 17	09 32	09 47	10 02	10 22	10 32	10 47	11 02	11 17
12¼	**Gospel Oak**	a	00 13	00 24	06 54	07 09	07 23	07 39	07 53	08 08	08 23	08 38	08 53	09 08	09 23	09 38	09 53	10 08	10 29	10 38	10 54	11 08	11 23

		LO	LO	LO	LO	LO	LO	LO	LO	LO	LO	LO	LO	LO	LO	LO	LO	LO	LO	LO	LO	LO	LO
Barking ⊖	d	11 02	11 17	11 32	11 47	12 02	12 17	12 32	12 47	13 02	13 17	13 32	13 47	14 02	14 17	14 32	14 47	15 02	15 17	15 32	15 47	16 02	16 17
Woodgrange Park	d	11 05	11 20	11 35	11 50	12 05	12 20	12 35	12 50	13 05	13 20	13 35	13 50	14 05	14 20	14 35	14 50	15 05	15 20	15 35	15 50	16 05	16 20
Wanstead Park	d	11 08	11 23	11 38	11 53	12 08	12 23	12 38	12 53	13 08	13 23	13 38	13 53	14 08	14 23	14 38	14 53	15 08	15 23	15 38	15 53	16 08	16 23
Leytonstone High Road	d	11 12	11 27	11 42	11 57	12 12	12 27	12 42	12 57	13 12	13 27	13 42	13 57	14 12	14 27	14 42	14 57	15 12	15 27	15 42	15 57	16 12	16 27
Leyton Midland Road	d	11 14	11 29	11 44	11 59	12 14	12 29	12 44	12 59	13 14	13 29	13 44	13 59	14 14	14 29	14 44	14 59	15 14	15 29	15 44	15 59	16 14	16 29
Walthamstow Queen's Road	d	11 17	11 32	11 47	12 02	12 17	12 32	12 47	13 02	13 17	13 32	13 47	14 02	14 17	14 32	14 47	15 02	15 17	15 32	15 47	16 02	16 17	16 32
Blackhorse Road ⊖	d	11 20	11 35	11 50	12 05	12 20	12 35	12 50	13 05	13 20	13 35	13 50	14 05	14 20	14 35	14 50	15 05	15 20	15 35	15 50	16 05	16 20	16 35
South Tottenham	d	11 24	11 39	11 54	12 09	12 24	12 39	12 54	13 09	13 24	13 39	13 54	14 09	14 24	14 39	14 54	15 09	15 24	15 39	15 54	16 09	16 24	16 39
Harringay Green Lanes	d	11 27	11 42	11 57	12 12	12 27	12 42	12 57	13 12	13 27	13 42	13 57	14 12	14 27	14 42	14 57	15 12	15 27	15 42	15 57	16 12	16 27	16 42
Crouch Hill	d	11 30	11 45	12 00	12 15	12 30	12 45	13 00	13 15	13 30	13 45	14 00	14 15	14 30	14 45	15 00	15 15	15 30	15 45	16 00	16 15	16 30	16 45
Upper Holloway	d	11 32	11 47	12 02	12 17	12 32	12 47	13 02	13 17	13 32	13 47	14 02	14 17	14 32	14 47	15 02	15 17	15 32	15 47	16 02	16 17	16 32	16 47
Gospel Oak	a	11 38	11 55	12 08	12 23	12 38	12 54	13 08	13 23	13 38	13 53	14 08	14 23	14 38	14 53	15 08	15 24	15 38	15 53	16 08	16 23	16 40	16 53

		LO	LO	LO	LO	LO	LO	LO	LO	LO	LO	LO	LO	LO	LO	LO	LO	LO	LO	LO	LO	LO
Barking ⊖	d	16 32	16 47	17 02	17 17	17 32	17 47	18 02	18 17	18 32	18 47	19 02	19 17	19 32	19 47	20 02	20 17	20 32	20 47	21 02	21 17	21 32
Woodgrange Park	d	16 35	16 50	17 05	17 20	17 35	17 50	18 05	18 20	18 35	18 50	19 05	19 20	19 35	19 50	20 05	20 20	20 35	20 50	21 05	21 20	21 35
Wanstead Park	d	16 38	16 53	17 08	17 23	17 38	17 53	18 08	18 23	18 38	18 53	19 08	19 23	19 38	19 53	20 08	20 23	20 38	20 53	21 08	21 23	21 38
Leytonstone High Road	d	16 42	16 57	17 12	17 27	17 42	17 57	18 12	18 27	18 42	18 57	19 12	19 27	19 42	19 57	20 12	20 27	20 42	20 57	21 12	21 27	21 42
Leyton Midland Road	d	16 44	16 59	17 14	17 29	17 44	17 59	18 14	18 29	18 44	18 59	19 14	19 29	19 44	19 59	20 14	20 29	20 44	20 59	21 14	21 29	21 44
Walthamstow Queen's Road	d	16 47	17 02	17 17	17 32	17 47	18 02	18 17	18 32	18 47	19 02	19 17	19 32	19 47	20 02	20 17	20 32	20 47	21 02	21 17	21 32	21 47
Blackhorse Road ⊖	d	16 50	17 05	17 20	17 35	17 50	18 05	18 20	18 35	18 50	19 05	19 20	19 35	19 50	20 05	20 20	20 35	20 50	21 05	21 20	21 35	21 50
South Tottenham	d	16 54	17 09	17 24	17 39	17 54	18 09	18 24	18 39	18 54	19 09	19 24	19 39	19 54	20 09	20 24	20 39	20 54	21 09	21 24	21 39	21 54
Harringay Green Lanes	d	16 57	17 12	17 27	17 42	17 57	18 12	18 27	18 42	18 57	19 12	19 27	19 42	19 57	20 12	20 27	20 42	20 57	21 12	21 27	21 42	21 57
Crouch Hill	d	17 00	17 15	17 30	17 45	18 00	18 15	18 30	18 45	19 00	19 15	19 30	19 45	20 00	20 15	20 30	20 45	21 00	21 15	21 30	21 45	22 00
Upper Holloway	d	17 02	17 17	17 32	17 47	18 02	18 17	18 32	18 47	19 02	19 17	19 32	19 47	20 02	20 17	20 32	20 47	21 02	21 17	21 32	21 47	22 02
Gospel Oak	a	17 08	17 23	17 38	17 53	18 08	18 23	18 38	18 53	19 09	19 26	19 38	19 53	20 08	20 23	20 38	20 53	21 08	21 24	21 38	21 54	22 08

		LO	LO	LO	LO	LO	LO
Barking ⊖	d	21 47	22 02	22 17	22 47	23 17	23 47
Woodgrange Park	d	21 50	22 05	22 20	22 50	23 20	23 50
Wanstead Park	d	21 53	22 08	22 23	22 53	23 23	23 53
Leytonstone High Road	d	21 57	22 12	22 27	22 57	23 27	23 57
Leyton Midland Road	d	21 59	22 14	22 29	22 59	23 29	23 59
Walthamstow Queen's Road	d	22 02	22 17	22 32	23 02	23 32	00 02
Blackhorse Road ⊖	d	22 05	22 20	22 35	23 05	23 35	00 05
South Tottenham	d	22 09	22 24	22 39	23 09	23 39	00 09
Harringay Green Lanes	d	22 12	22 27	22 42	23 12	23 42	00 12
Crouch Hill	d	22 15	22 30	22 45	23 15	23 45	00 15
Upper Holloway	d	22 17	22 32	22 47	23 17	23 47	00 17
Gospel Oak	a	22 23	22 38	22 53	23 25	23 53	00 24

Saturdays

		LO	LO	LO	LO	LO	LO	LO	LO	LO	LO	LO	LO	LO	LO	LO	LO	LO	LO	LO	LO	LO	LO
Barking ⊖	d	23p47	06 17	06 32	06 47	07 02	07 17	07 32	07 47	08 02	08 17	08 32	08 47	09 02	09 17	09 32	09 47	10 02	10 17	10 32	10 47	11 02	11 17
Woodgrange Park	d	23p50	06 20	06 35	06 50	07 05	07 20	07 35	07 50	08 05	08 20	08 35	08 50	09 05	09 20	09 35	09 50	10 05	10 20	10 35	10 50	11 05	11 20
Wanstead Park	d	23p53	06 23	06 38	06 53	07 08	07 23	07 38	07 53	08 08	08 23	08 38	08 53	09 08	09 23	09 38	09 53	10 08	10 23	10 38	10 53	11 08	11 23
Leytonstone High Road	d	23p57	06 27	06 42	06 57	07 12	07 27	07 42	07 57	08 12	08 27	08 42	08 57	09 12	09 27	09 42	09 57	10 12	10 27	10 42	10 57	11 12	11 27
Leyton Midland Road	d	23p59	06 29	06 44	06 59	07 14	07 29	07 44	07 59	08 14	08 29	08 44	08 59	09 14	09 29	09 44	09 59	10 14	10 29	10 44	10 59	11 14	11 29
Walthamstow Queen's Road	d	00 02	06 32	06 47	07 02	07 17	07 32	07 47	08 02	08 17	08 32	08 47	09 02	09 17	09 32	09 47	10 02	10 17	10 32	10 47	11 02	11 17	11 32
Blackhorse Road ⊖	d	00 05	06 35	06 50	07 05	07 20	07 35	07 50	08 05	08 20	08 35	08 50	09 05	09 20	09 35	09 50	10 05	10 20	10 35	10 50	11 05	11 20	11 35
South Tottenham	d	00 09	06 39	06 54	07 09	07 24	07 39	07 54	08 09	08 24	08 39	08 54	09 09	09 24	09 39	09 54	10 09	10 24	10 39	10 54	11 09	11 24	11 39
Harringay Green Lanes	d	00 12	06 42	06 57	07 12	07 27	07 42	07 57	08 12	08 27	08 42	08 57	09 12	09 27	09 42	09 57	10 12	10 27	10 42	10 57	11 12	11 27	11 42
Crouch Hill	d	00 15	06 45	07 00	07 15	07 30	07 45	08 00	08 15	08 30	08 45	09 00	09 15	09 30	09 45	10 00	10 15	10 30	10 45	11 00	11 15	11 30	11 45
Upper Holloway	d	00 17	06 47	07 02	07 17	07 32	07 47	08 02	08 17	08 32	08 47	09 02	09 17	09 32	09 47	10 02	10 17	10 32	10 47	11 02	11 17	11 32	11 47
Gospel Oak	a	00 24	06 54	07 08	07 23	07 38	07 53	08 08	08 23	08 38	08 53	09 08	09 23	09 38	09 53	10 08	10 23	10 39	10 53	11 09	11 23	11 39	11 53

		LO	LO	LO	LO	LO	LO	LO		LO	LO	LO	LO	LO	LO	LO	LO	LO A
Barking ⊖	d	11 32	11 47	12 02	12 17	12 32	12 47	13 02	and at the same minutes past each hour until	21 02	21 17	21 32	21 47	22 02	22 17	22 47	23 17	23 47
Woodgrange Park	d	11 35	11 50	12 05	12 20	12 35	12 50	13 05		21 05	21 20	21 35	21 50	22 05	22 20	22 50	23 20	23 50
Wanstead Park	d	11 38	11 53	12 08	12 23	12 38	12 53	13 08		21 08	21 23	21 38	21 53	22 08	22 23	22 53	23 23	23 53
Leytonstone High Road	d	11 42	11 57	12 12	12 27	12 42	12 57	13 12		21 12	21 27	21 42	21 57	22 12	22 27	22 57	23 27	23 57
Leyton Midland Road	d	11 44	11 59	12 14	12 29	12 44	12 59	13 14		21 14	21 29	21 44	21 59	22 14	22 29	22 59	23 29	23 59
Walthamstow Queen's Road	d	11 47	12 02	12 17	12 32	12 47	13 02	13 17		21 17	21 32	21 47	22 02	22 17	22 32	23 02	23 32	00 02
Blackhorse Road ⊖	d	11 50	12 05	12 20	12 35	12 50	13 05	13 20		21 20	21 35	21 50	22 05	22 20	22 35	23 05	23 35	00 05
South Tottenham	d	11 54	12 09	12 24	12 39	12 54	13 09	13 24		21 24	21 39	21 54	22 09	22 24	22 39	23 09	23 39	00 09
Harringay Green Lanes	d	11 57	12 12	12 27	12 42	12 57	13 12	13 27		21 27	21 42	21 57	22 12	22 27	22 42	23 12	23 42	00 12
Crouch Hill	d	12 00	12 15	12 30	12 45	13 00	13 15	13 30		21 30	21 45	22 00	22 15	22 30	22 45	23 15	23 45	00 15
Upper Holloway	d	12 02	12 17	12 32	12 47	13 02	13 17	13 32		21 32	21 47	22 02	22 17	22 32	22 47	23 17	23 47	00 17
Gospel Oak	a	12 09	12 23	12 39	12 53	13 08	13 23	13 38		21 38	21 53	22 08	22 22	22 38	22 52	23 22	23 52	00 24

A not 10 December

Table 62

Sundays

Barking - Gospel Oak

			LO A	LO	LO	LO	LO		LO	LO	LO	LO	LO	LO
Barking	⊖	d	23p47	08 53	09 08	09 23	09 38	and at the same minutes past each hour until	21 38	21 53	22 08	22 38	23 08	23 38
Woodgrange Park		d	23p50	08 56	09 11	09 26	09 41		21 41	21 56	22 11	22 41	23 11	23 41
Wanstead Park		d	23p53	08 59	09 14	09 29	09 44		21 44	21 59	22 14	22 44	23 14	23 44
Leytonstone High Road		d	23p57	09 03	09 18	09 33	09 48		21 48	22 03	22 18	22 48	23 18	23 48
Leyton Midland Road		d	23p59	09 05	09 20	09 35	09 50		21 50	22 05	22 20	22 50	23 20	23 50
Walthamstow Queen's Road		d	00 02	09 08	09 23	09 38	09 53		21 53	22 08	22 23	22 53	23 23	23 53
Blackhorse Road	⊖	d	00 05	09 11	09 26	09 41	09 56		21 56	22 11	22 26	22 56	23 26	23 56
South Tottenham		d	00 09	09 15	09 30	09 45	10 00		22 00	22 15	22 30	23 00	23 30	23 59
Harringay Green Lanes		d	00 12	09 18	09 33	09 48	10 03		22 03	22 18	22 33	23 03	23 33	00 03
Crouch Hill		d	00 15	09 21	09 36	09 51	10 06		22 06	22 21	22 36	23 06	23 36	00 06
Upper Holloway		d	00 17	09 23	09 38	09 53	10 08		22 08	22 23	22 38	23 08	23 38	00 08
Gospel Oak		a	00 24	09 28	09 43	09 58	10 13		22 13	22 28	22 43	23 13	23 43	00 13

A not 22 May

Table 64

Mondays to Fridays

Bletchley - Bedford

Miles			LM	LM	LM	LM	LM	LM	LM	LM	LM	LM	LM	LM	LM	LM	LM	LM
0	**Bletchley**	d	05 41	06 37	07 32	08 39	10 01	11 01	12 01	13 01	14 01	15 01	15 47	16 47	17 31	18 31	20 01	21 01
1	Fenny Stratford	d	05 44	06 40	07 35	08 42	10 04	11 04	12 04	13 04	14 04	15 04	15 50	16 50	17 34	18 34	20 04	21 04
2	Bow Brickhill	d	05 48	06 44	07 39	08 46	10 08	11 08	12 08	13 08	14 08	15 08	15 54	16 54	17 38	18 38	20 08	21 08
4	Woburn Sands	d	05 52	06 48	07 43	08 50	10 12	11 12	12 12	13 12	14 12	15 12	15 58	16 58	17 42	18 42	20 12	21 12
5	Aspley Guise	d	05 55	06 51	07 46	08 53	10 15	11 15	12 15	13 15	14 15	15 15	16 01	17 01	17 45	18 45	20 15	21 15
6¾	Ridgmont	d	05 58	06 54	07 49	08 56	10 18	11 18	12 18	13 18	14 18	15 18	16 04	17 04	17 48	18 48	20 18	21 18
8½	Lidlington	d	06 02	06 58	07 53	09 00	10 22	11 22	12 22	13 22	14 22	15 22	16 08	17 08	17 52	18 52	20 22	21 22
10	Millbrook (Bedfordshire)	d	06 05	07 01	07 56	09 03	10 25	11 25	12 25	13 25	14 25	15 25	16 11	17 11	17 55	18 55	20 25	21 25
11¼	Stewartby	d	06 09	07 05	08 00	09 07	10 29	11 29	12 29	13 29	14 29	15 29	16 15	17 15	17 59	18 59	20 29	21 29
13	Kempston Hardwick	d	06 12	07 08	08 03	09 10	10 32	11 32	12 32	13 32	14 32	15 32	16 18	17 18	18 02	19 02	20 32	21 32
16	Bedford St Johns	d	06 19	07 15	08 10	09 17	10 39	11 39	12 39	13 39	14 39	15 39	16 25	17 25	18 09	19 09	20 39	21 39
16¾	**Bedford [7]**	a	06 25	07 21	08 16	09 23	10 45	11 45	12 45	13 45	14 45	15 45	16 31	17 31	18 15	19 15	20 45	21 45

Saturdays

		LM	LM	LM	LM	LM	LM	LM	LM	LM	LM	LM	LM	LM	LM	LM	LM
Bletchley	d	05 41	06 37	07 32	08 39	10 01	11 01	12 01	13 01	14 01	15 01	15 47	16 47	17 31	18 31	20 01	21 01
Fenny Stratford	d	05 44	06 40	07 35	08 42	10 04	11 04	12 04	13 04	14 04	15 04	15 50	16 50	17 34	18 34	20 04	21 04
Bow Brickhill	d	05 48	06 44	07 39	08 46	10 08	11 08	12 08	13 08	14 08	15 08	15 54	16 54	17 38	18 38	20 08	21 08
Woburn Sands	d	05 52	06 48	07 43	08 50	10 12	11 12	12 12	13 12	14 12	15 12	15 58	16 58	17 42	18 42	20 12	21 12
Aspley Guise	d	05 55	06 51	07 46	08 53	10 15	11 15	12 15	13 15	14 15	15 15	16 01	17 01	17 45	18 45	20 15	21 15
Ridgmont	d	05 58	06 54	07 49	08 56	10 18	11 18	12 18	13 18	14 18	15 18	16 04	17 04	17 48	18 48	20 18	21 18
Lidlington	d	06 02	06 58	07 53	09 00	10 22	11 22	12 22	13 22	14 22	15 22	16 08	17 08	17 52	18 52	20 22	21 22
Millbrook (Bedfordshire)	d	06 05	07 01	07 56	09 03	10 25	11 25	12 25	13 25	14 25	15 25	16 11	17 11	17 55	18 55	20 25	21 25
Stewartby	d	06 09	07 05	08 00	09 07	10 29	11 29	12 29	13 29	14 29	15 29	16 15	17 15	17 59	18 59	20 29	21 29
Kempston Hardwick	d	06 12	07 08	08 03	09 10	10 32	11 32	12 32	13 32	14 32	15 32	16 18	17 18	18 02	19 02	20 32	21 32
Bedford St Johns	d	06 19	07 15	08 10	09 17	10 39	11 39	12 39	13 39	14 39	15 39	16 25	17 25	18 09	19 09	20 39	21 39
Bedford [7]	a	06 25	07 21	08 16	09 23	10 45	11 45	12 45	13 45	14 45	15 45	16 31	17 31	18 15	19 15	20 45	21 45

Table 64

Mondays to Fridays

Bedford - Bletchley

Miles			LM	LM	LM	LM	LM	LM	LM	LM	LM	LM	LM	LM	LM	LM	LM	LM
0	**Bedford [7]**	d	06 31	07 31	08 31	09 33	10 55	11 55	12 55	13 55	14 55	15 55	16 37	17 37	18 25	19 35	20 55	21 56
0¾	Bedford St Johns	d	06 34	07 34	08 34	09 36	10 58	11 58	12 58	13 58	14 58	15 58	16 40	17 40	18 28	19 38	20 58	21 59
3¾	Kempston Hardwick	d	06 41	07 41	08 41	09 43	11 05	12 05	13 05	14 05	15 05	16 05	16 47	17 47	18 35	19 45	21 05	22 06
5½	Stewartby	d	06 44	07 44	08 44	09 46	11 08	12 08	13 08	14 08	15 08	16 08	16 50	17 50	18 38	19 48	21 08	22 09
6¾	Millbrook (Bedfordshire)	d	06 48	07 48	08 48	09 50	11 12	12 12	13 12	14 12	15 12	16 12	16 54	17 54	18 42	19 52	21 12	22 13
8¼	Lidlington	d	06 51	07 51	08 51	09 53	11 15	12 15	13 15	14 15	15 15	16 15	16 57	17 57	18 45	19 55	21 15	22 16
10	Ridgmont	d	06 56	07 56	08 56	09 58	11 20	12 20	13 20	14 20	15 20	16 20	17 02	18 02	18 50	20 00	21 20	22 21
11¾	Aspley Guise	d	06 59	07 59	08 59	10 01	11 23	12 23	13 23	14 23	15 23	16 23	17 05	18 05	18 53	20 03	21 23	22 24
12¾	Woburn Sands	d	07 02	08 02	09 02	10 04	11 26	12 26	13 26	14 26	15 26	16 26	17 08	18 08	18 56	20 06	21 26	22 27
14¾	Bow Brickhill	d	07 06	08 06	09 06	10 08	11 30	12 30	13 30	14 30	15 30	16 30	17 12	18 12	19 00	20 10	21 30	22 31
15¾	Fenny Stratford	d	07 09	08 09	09 09	10 11	11 33	12 33	13 33	14 33	15 33	16 33	17 15	18 15	19 03	20 13	21 33	22 34
16¾	**Bletchley**	a	07 14	08 14	09 14	10 16	11 38	12 38	13 38	14 38	15 38	16 38	17 20	18 20	19 08	20 18	21 38	22 39

Saturdays

		LM	LM	LM	LM	LM	LM	LM	LM	LM	LM	LM	LM	LM	LM	LM	LM
Bedford [7]	d	06 31	07 31	08 31	09 33	10 55	11 55	12 55	13 55	14 55	15 55	16 37	17 37	18 25	19 35	20 55	21 56
Bedford St Johns	d	06 34	07 34	08 34	09 36	10 58	11 58	12 58	13 58	14 58	15 58	16 40	17 40	18 28	19 38	20 58	21 59
Kempston Hardwick	d	06 41	07 41	08 41	09 43	11 05	12 05	13 05	14 05	15 05	16 05	16 47	17 47	18 35	19 45	21 05	22 06
Stewartby	d	06 44	07 44	08 44	09 46	11 08	12 08	13 08	14 08	15 08	16 08	16 50	17 50	18 38	19 48	21 08	22 09
Millbrook (Bedfordshire)	d	06 48	07 48	08 48	09 50	11 12	12 12	13 12	14 12	15 12	16 12	16 54	17 54	18 42	19 52	21 12	22 13
Lidlington	d	06 51	07 51	08 51	09 53	11 15	12 15	13 15	14 15	15 15	16 15	16 57	17 57	18 45	19 55	21 15	22 16
Ridgmont	d	06 56	07 56	08 56	09 58	11 20	12 20	13 20	14 20	15 20	16 20	17 02	18 02	18 50	20 00	21 20	22 21
Aspley Guise	d	06 59	07 59	08 59	10 01	11 23	12 23	13 23	14 23	15 23	16 23	17 05	18 05	18 53	20 03	21 23	22 24
Woburn Sands	d	07 02	08 02	09 02	10 04	11 26	12 26	13 26	14 26	15 26	16 26	17 08	18 08	18 56	20 06	21 26	22 27
Bow Brickhill	d	07 06	08 06	09 06	10 08	11 30	12 30	13 30	14 30	15 30	16 30	17 12	18 12	19 00	20 10	21 30	22 31
Fenny Stratford	d	07 09	08 09	09 09	10 11	11 33	12 33	13 33	14 33	15 33	16 33	17 15	18 15	19 03	20 13	21 33	22 34
Bletchley	a	07 14	08 14	09 14	10 16	11 38	12 38	13 38	14 38	15 38	16 38	17 20	18 20	19 08	20 18	21 38	22 39

No Sunday Service

For connections to Milton Keynes Central please refer to Table 66

Route Diagram for Table 65

London-Scotland
See Tables 400-404 for Sleeper trains.

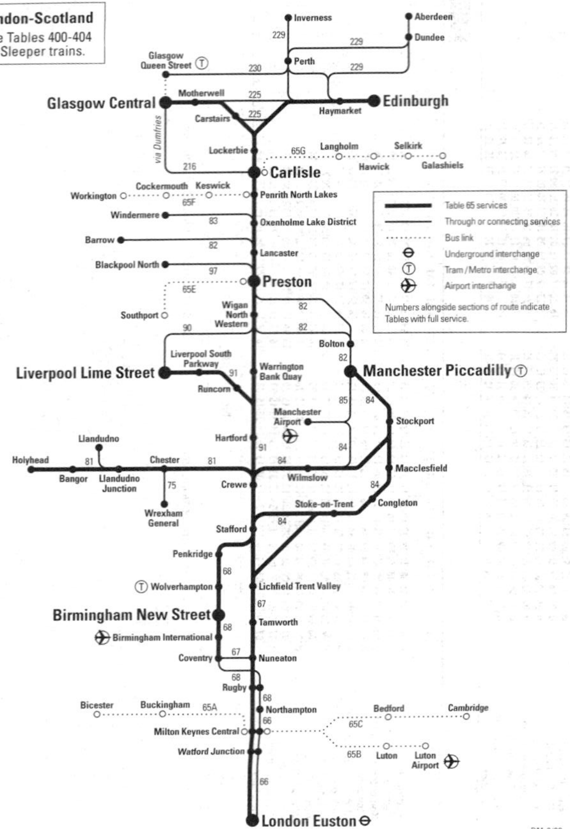

DM-9/09
Design BAJS
© Network Rail OPSU 2009. All rights reserved

London and West Midlands - North West England and Scotland

Miles	Miles	Miles	Miles	Miles	Station		AW	XC	XC	XC	VT	VT	VT	TP	TP	SR	SR	SR	SR	SR	VT	VT
							MO				MO	MX	MO		MX	MO					MO	MO
												▣				▣	▣	▣	▣	▣		
							◇	◇1	◇1	◇1	◇1	1	◇1	◇1	◇1						◇1	◇1
								A	B	C				D			E	F	G	H		
																🛏	🛏	🛏	🛏	🛏		
											☕	☕	☕			☕	☕	☕	☕	☕	☕	☕
0	—	—	—	—	**London Euston** 15 ⊖	d					19p25	19p30				20p55	21p15	21p15	21p15	21p15	21p21	21p25
17½	—	—	—	—	Watford Junction	d										21b17	21b33	21b33	21b33	21b33		
49¾	—	—	—	—	Milton Keynes Central	d																22p14
82½	0	—	—	—	Rugby	d																
97	—	—	—	—	Nuneaton	d															22p52	
110	—	—	—	—	Tamworth Low Level	d																
116¼	—	0	—	—	Lichfield Trent Valley	d																
—	11½	—	—	—	Coventry	d																
—	22	—	—	—	Birmingham International ✈	d																
—	30½	—	—	—	**Birmingham New Street** 12	d		22p30	22p30	22p30												
—	43¼	—	—	—	Wolverhampton 7	d		22p48	22p48	22p48												
—	53¼	—	—	—	Penkridge	d																
133½	59½	—	—	—	**Stafford**	a		23p00	23p00	23p00											23p16	
—	—	—	—	—		d		23p01	23p01	23p01											23p17	
—	75¾	30¼	—	—	**Stoke-on-Trent**	a		23p20	23p20	23p20												23p29
—	87½	42	—	—	Congleton	a																
—	95¾	50¼	—	—	Macclesfield	a																23p45
158	—	—	0	—	**Crewe** 10	a															23p37	
—	—	—	—	—		d	22p29									23b39	23b52	23b52	23b54	23b54	23p39	
—	—	—	—	—	Chester	a	22p50															
—	—	—	—	—	Wrexham General	a																
—	—	—	—	—	Llandudno	a																
—	—	—	—	—	Bangor (Gwynedd)	a	00 12															
—	—	—	—	—	Holyhead	a	00 49															
—	—	—	—	—	Wilmslow	a																
—	107¼	62¼	—	—	Stockport	a																23p59
—	113	68	—	—	**Manchester Piccadilly** 10	a		00 12	00 32	00 33												00 12
169¾	—	—	11¾	—	Hartford	a																
182	—	—	—	—	Warrington Bank Quay	a					21p16	21p15										
—	—	—	—	—		d					21p16	21p15										
—	—	—	22½	—	Runcorn	a															23p56	
—	—	—	30	—	Liverpool South Parkway 7 ✈	a																
—	—	—	35½	—	**Liverpool Lime Street** 10	a															00 23	
—	—	—	—	—		d																
—	—	—	—	—	Manchester Airport ✈	d								22p00	22p29							
—	—	—	—	—	**Manchester Piccadilly** 10	d								22p16	22p46							
—	—	79¼	—	—	Bolton	d							←	22p33	23p07							
193¾	—	—	—	—	Wigan North Western	a					21p27	21p26	21p27	22p48								
—	—	—	—	—		d					21p27	21p26	21p27	22p51								
209	—	99¼	—	—	**Preston** 8	a					→	21p39	21p40	23p09	23p33							
—	—	—	—	—	**Preston** 8	d						21p41	21p42	23p13	23p35	00u30	00u52	00u52	00u52	00u52		
—	—	—	—	—	Blackpool North	a									00 02							
230	—	—	—	—	**Lancaster** 6	a						21p55	21p56	23p28								
—	—	—	—	—		d						21p56	21p57	23p29								
—	—	—	—	—	Barrow-in-Furness	a								00 32								
249	—	—	—	—	Oxenholme Lake District	a						22p09	22p10									
—	—	—	—	—		d						22p09	22p11									
—	—	—	—	—	Windermere	a																
281¼	—	—	—	—	Penrith North Lakes	d						22p35	22p36									
299	—	—	—	—	**Carlisle** 8	a						22p50	22p51			01 53	02 15	02 15	02 15	02 15		
—	—	—	—	—		d						22p51	22p53			01 55	02 16	02 16	02 16	02 16		
324¼	—	—	0	—	Lockerbie	d																
372½	—	—	—	0	Carstairs	a																
388½	—	—	—	—	Motherwell	a																
401¼	—	—	—	—	**Glasgow Central** 15	a						00 06	00 02									
—	—	—	75	26¼	Haymarket	a																
—	—	—	76¼	27½	**Edinburgh** 10	a										03 58	03 58	03 58	03 58	03 58		
—	—	—	—	97¼	Perth	a										05s40	05s40		05s40			
—	—	—	135½	—	Dundee	a											06s08		06s08			
—	—	—	206¾	—	Aberdeen	a											07 35		07 35			
—	—	—	—	215¼	Inverness	a										08 31	08 31		08 31			

A ThFO
B TWO until 15 June, TWO from 13 September
C TWO from 21 June until 7 September
D MX from 19 July
E TWThO from 21 June until 8 September. ☕ to Edinburgh ☕ from Edinburgh 🛏 to Edinburgh 🛏 from Edinburgh
F TWThO from 21 June until 8 September
G TWThO until 16 June, TWThO from 13 September. ☕ to Edinburgh ☕ from Edinburgh 🛏 to Edinburgh 🛏 from Edinburgh
H TWThO until 16 June, TWThO from 13 September
b Previous night, stops to pick up only

OVERNIGHT SLEEPERS. For sleeper trains, operated by First ScotRail, please refer to Tables 400 - 404

London and West Midlands - North West England and Scotland

		AW MX	AW MO	VT MO	VT MX	LM MX	TP	SR MO	SR	NT MX	TP	TP	NT	LM	LM	TP	TP MO	TP MX	TP	VT	TP
		◇	◇	◇1	◇1	1	◇1				◇1	1		1	1	1	◇1	◇1	◇1	◇1	◇1
									A			B	C	D	E	B	F	G	B		
London Euston	d			21p51	22p00			23p27	23p50												
Watford Junction	d							23c47	00u10												
Milton Keynes Central	d			22p38	22p31																
Rugby	d			23p18	22p54																
Nuneaton	d			23p29	23p04																
Tamworth Low Level	d				23b15																
Lichfield Trent Valley	d				23b22																
Coventry	d																				
Birmingham International	d		22p40																		
Birmingham New Street	d	22p55	22p55			23p09															
Wolverhampton	d	23p13	23p15			23p36															
Penkridge	d					23p46															
Stafford	a	23p30	23p30	23b53	23b38	23p52															
	d	23p30	23p31			23p53															
Stoke-on-Trent	a																				
Congleton	a																				
Macclesfield	a																				
Crewe	a	23p55	23p55	00s12	00s03	00 16															
	d	23p57	00 10							00 44				05 34	05 40					05 57	
Chester	a	00 18	00 31																		
Wrexham General	a																				
Llandudno	a																				
Bangor (Gwynedd)	a	01 45	01 41																		
Holyhead	a	02 15	02 17																		
Wilmslow	a																				
Stockport	a			00s41	00s26																
Manchester Piccadilly	a			00 53	00 35																
Hartford	a																				
Warrington Bank Quay	a							02 42	03 09											06 13	
	d							02 44	03 11											06 14	
Runcorn	a													05 58	05 58						
Liverpool South Parkway	a													06 10	06 10						
Liverpool Lime Street	a													06 22	06 22						
	d																				
Manchester Airport	d						00 01			01 20	04 00										05 45
Manchester Piccadilly	d						00 16			01a36	04 15						05 46	05 46	05 46		06 03
Bolton	d						00s31				04s29										06 19
Wigan North Western	a										04 44						06 15	06 15	06 15	06 24	
	d										04 44						06 15	06 15	06 15	06 25	
Preston	a						01s05	03 12	03 39		05s04						06 35	06 35	06 35	06 37	06 42
Preston	d							03 16	03 48			05 22	05 22			06 34	06 37	06 37	06 37	06 40	06 44
Blackpool North	a						01 30				05 33						07 05	07 06	07 09		
Lancaster	a											05 39	05 42			06 50				06 54	06 59
	d												05 42							06 54	07 00
Barrow-in-Furness	a												06 47								
Oxenholme Lake District	a																			07 08	07 15
	d																			07 10	07 15
Windermere	a																				
Penrith North Lakes	d																			07 35	
Carlisle	a							05s04	05s16				09 22							07 50	07 55
	d																			07 51	07 56
Lockerbie	d																			08 10	08 16
Carstairs	a							06s20	06s20												
Motherwell	a							06s56	06s56												
Glasgow Central	a							07 20	07 20											09 14	
Haymarket	a																				09s17
Edinburgh	a								07 16												09 22
Perth	a																				
Dundee	a																				
Aberdeen	a																				
Inverness	a																				

A TWThO until 20 October. to Carstairs; from Carstairs; to Carstairs; from Carstairs
B until 15 July
C from 18 July
D from 20 June until 9 September
E until 17 June, from 12 September
F From 18 July until 5 September
G From 19 July until 2 September, from 6 September
b Previous night, stops to set down only
c Previous night, stops to pick up only

OVERNIGHT SLEEPERS. For sleeper trains, operated by First ScotRail, please refer to Tables 400 - 404

London and West Midlands - North West England and Scotland

		LM	VT	VT	TP	AW	XC	NT	TP	TP	NT	LM	AW	LM	VT	XC	TP	TP	AW	VT	TP	VT	VT
		1	◇1	◇1	◇1		◇1		◇1	◇1		1	◇	◇1	◇1	◇1	◇1	◇1		◇1		◇1	◇1
									A	B							C FX	D FO			A		
London Euston	d																			05 27		05 39	06 17
Watford Junction	d																			05u45		05u44	
Milton Keynes Central	d																			06 10		06 23	06 47
Rugby	d																					06 46	
Nuneaton	d																			06 39			
Tamworth Low Level	d																						
Lichfield Trent Valley	d																						
Coventry	d																						
Birmingham International	d																						
Birmingham New Street	d			05 30			05 57							06 01	06 19	06 22							
Wolverhampton	d			05 48			06 16							06 19	06 36	06 40							
Penkridge	d													06 29									
Stafford	a			06 01			06 29							06 35		06 53				07 03			
	d			06 02			06 30							06 36		06 55				07 03			
Stoke-on-Trent	a						06 50									07 13							07 45
Congleton	a						07 02																
Macclesfield	a						07 11									07 30							08 01
Crewe	a			06 21										06 56	07 07					07 22		07 30	
	d	06 02	06 11	06 23		06 27						06 32	06 54	06 57	07 09				07 23	07 24		07 32	
Chester	a			06 43									07 14						07 46				
Wrexham General	a																						
Llandudno	a																						
Bangor (Gwynedd)	a			07 49									08 33										
Holyhead	a			08 23									09 20										
Wilmslow	a		06 26			06 44																	
Stockport	a		06 36			06 55	07 27									07 45							08 16
Manchester Piccadilly	a		06 49			07 07	07 37									07 59							08 28
Hartford	a	06 14										06 46		07 09									
Warrington Bank Quay	a														07 26							07 48	
	d														07 27							07 51	
Runcorn	a	06 27										06 59		07 23						07 41			
Liverpool South Parkway	a	06 36										07 08		07 32									
Liverpool Lime Street	a	06 49										07 22		07 43						08 01			
	d										06 57												
Manchester Airport	d				06 18												07 00	07 00					
Manchester Piccadilly	d				06 33												07 15	07 15					
Bolton	d				06 50			07 01									07 31	07 31					
Wigan North Western	a							07 19			07 30				07 37							08 00	
	d										07 31				07 38							08 01	
Preston	a				07 11						07 56				07 51		07 57	07 55				08 13	
Preston	d				07 14				07 20	07 20					07 53		07 59	07 59			08 08	08 16	
Blackpool North	a																08 29	08 29					
Lancaster	a				07 30				07 36	07 36					08 08						08 25	08 29	
	d				07 30					07 36					08 08							08 30	
Barrow-in-Furness	a									08 40													
Oxenholme Lake District	a														08 21							08 42	
	d														08 22							08 44	
Windermere	a																						
Penrith North Lakes	d				08 07																		
Carlisle	a				08 24										09 01							09 21	
	d				08 25										09 01							09 22	
Lockerbie	d																						
Carstairs	a																						
Motherwell	a																						
Glasgow Central	a				09 45																	10 31	
Haymarket	a														10 16								
Edinburgh	a														10 21								
Perth	a																						
Dundee	a																						
Aberdeen	a																						
Inverness	a																						

A until 15 July
B from 18 July
C Until 14 July, from 18 July
D Until 15 July

OVERNIGHT SLEEPERS. For sleeper trains, operated by First ScotRail, please refer to Tables 400 - 404

London and West Midlands - North West England and Scotland

		TP	NT		NT	LM	XC	LM	VT	VT	XC	VT	TP		AW	LM	VT	VT	VT	XC	NT	TP	VT		NT
		◇1				◇1	◇1	1	◇1	◇1	◇1	◇1	◇1			◇1	◇1	◇1	◇1	◇1		◇1	◇1		
			A																						
		⌶					⌶		⊠	⊠	⌶	⊠	⌶				⊠	⊠	⊠	⌶		⌶	⊠		
London Euston ⊖	d									06 36		06 55					07 07	07 10	07 20				07 30		
Watford Junction	d									06u51															
Milton Keynes Central	d											07 27						07 41	07 50						
Rugby	d																								
Nuneaton	d																								
Tamworth Low Level	d																								
Lichfield Trent Valley	d																								
Coventry	d																			07 27					
Birmingham International ✈	d															07 17				07 38					
Birmingham New Street	d					06 36	06 57	07 01	07 20		07 31					07 36				07 57					
Wolverhampton ⛴	d					06 53	07 16	07 19	07 37		07 49					07 53				08 15					
Penkridge	d							07 30								08 03									
Stafford	a					07 08	07 29	07 36								08 09	08 22			08 29					
	d					07 08	07 30	07 36								08 09	08 23			08 30					
Stoke-on-Trent	a										08 18	08 24							08 48	08 54					
Congleton	a																								
Macclesfield	a										08 35	08 41								09 11					
Crewe	a					07 33	07 50	07 56	08 07	08 10						08 30		08 47							
	d					07 34	07 52	07 58	08 09	08 11					08 23	08 31		08 49							
Chester	a														08 46			09 12							
Wrexham General	a																								
Llandudno	a																								
Bangor (Gwynedd)	a																								
Holyhead	a																								
Wilmslow	a						08 08			08 27															
Stockport	a						08 20			08 37	08 49	08 55							09 16	09 27					
Manchester Piccadilly ⛴	a						08 34			08 49	08 59	09 07							09 28	09 39					
Hartford	a					07 47		08 09																	
Warrington Bank Quay	a								08 26														09 14		
	d								08 27														09 14		
Runcorn	a					08 00		08 22								08 50	08 55								
Liverpool South Parkway ✈	a					08 09		08 31								08 59									
Liverpool Lime Street	a					08 21		08 44								09 10	09 15								
	d				07 57																				08 57
Manchester Airport ✈	d	07 25											07 56									08 25			
Manchester Piccadilly ⛴	d	07 45											08 15									08 46			
Bolton	d	07 59											08 32									09 07			
Wigan North Western	a				08 30				08 37														09 25		09 30
	d				08 31				08 38														09 25		09 31
Preston	a	08 22			08 56				08 51				08 58									09 33	09 38		09 54
Preston	d	08 24	08 38						08 53				08 59								09 34	09 38	09 41		09 55
Blackpool North	a												09 25								10 01	10 05			10 21
Lancaster	a	08 39	08 58						09 08														09 54		
	d	08 40	08 58						09 08														09 55		
Barrow-in-Furness	a		10 04																						
Oxenholme Lake District	a	08 54																							
	d	08 54																							
Windermere	a																								
Penrith North Lakes	d	09 20							09 45														10 31		
Carlisle	a	09 34	12 39						09 59														10 46		
	d	09 36							10 01														10 47		
Lockerbie	d	09 55																							
Carstairs	a																								
Motherwell	a																								
Glasgow Central	a								11 16														12 01		
Haymarket	a	10s56																							
Edinburgh	a	11 04																							
Perth	a																								
Dundee	a																								
Aberdeen	a																								
Inverness	a																								

A from 18 July

OVERNIGHT SLEEPERS. For sleeper trains, operated by First ScotRail, please refer to Tables 400 - 404

Table 65 — Mondays to Fridays

London and West Midlands - North West England and Scotland

		LM	VT	VT	XC	VT	TP		AW		LM	VT	VT	VT	XC	TP	TP	NT	VT		TP		NT	LM	VT
		◇1	◇1	◇1	◇1	◇1	◇1				1	◇1	◇1	◇1	◇1	◇1	1		◇1		◇1			1	◇1
																A	B								
			⊠	⊠	⌶	⊠	⌶					⊠	⊠	⊠	⌶				⊠		⌶				⊠
London Euston ⊖	d			07 35		08 00						08 07	08 10	08 20					08 30						
Watford Junction	d																								
Milton Keynes Central	d			08 06									08 41	08 50											
Rugby	d																								
Nuneaton	d																								
Tamworth Low Level	d																								
Lichfield Trent Valley	d																								
Coventry	d														08 27										
Birmingham International ✈	d														08 38										
Birmingham New Street	d	08 01	08 20		08 31						08 36				08 57									09 01	09 20
Wolverhampton ⛴	d	08 19	08 37		08 49						08 53				09 15									09 19	09 37
Penkridge	d	08 29									09 03														
Stafford	a	08 35			09 00						09 09	09 22			09 29									09 34	
	d	08 36			09 01						09 09	09 23			09 30									09 35	
Stoke-on-Trent	a				09 19	09 26								09 48	09 54										
Congleton	a																								
Macclesfield	a					09 42									10 11										
Crewe	a	08 56	09 07	09 10							09 30		09 47											09 56	10 07
	d	08 58	09 09	09 11					09 23		09 31		09 49											09 57	10 09
Chester	a								09 46				10 09												
Wrexham General	a																								
Llandudno	a																								
Bangor (Gwynedd)	a												11 27												
Holyhead	a																								
Wilmslow	a			09 27																					
Stockport	a			09 36	09 49	09 56								10 16	10 27										
Manchester Piccadilly ⛴	a			09 49	09 59	10 09								10 28	10 39										
Hartford	a	09 11																						10 10	
Warrington Bank Quay	a		09 26																10 14						10 26
	d		09 27																10 14						10 27
Runcorn	a	09 22									09 50	09 55												10 22	
Liverpool South Parkway ✈	a	09 31									09 59													10 31	
Liverpool Lime Street	a	09 43									10 10	10 15												10 44	
	d																						09 57		
Manchester Airport ✈	d						09 00														09 29				
Manchester Piccadilly ⛴	d						09 16														09 46				
Bolton	d						09 33														10 07				
Wigan North Western	a		09 37																10 25				10 30		10 37
	d		09 38																10 25				10 31		10 38
Preston	a		09 51				09 55												10 38		10 33		10 54		10 51
Preston	d		09 53				09 58	10 07								10 07	10 07	10 34	10 41		10 38	10 45	10 55		10 53
Blackpool North	a																	11 01			11 05		11 21		
Lancaster	a		10 08				10 13	10 22								10 22	10 22		10 54			11 00			11 08
	d		10 08				10 14									10 23	10 23		10 55			11 01			11 08
Barrow-in-Furness	a															11 17	11 17								
Oxenholme Lake District	a		10 22																11 08			11 17			
	d		10 23																11 08			11 18			
Windermere	a																					11 39			
Penrith North Lakes	d																								11 45
Carlisle	a		11 02				11 07												11 46						12 00
	d		11 04				11 10												11 47						12 01
Lockerbie	d						11 29																		
Carstairs	a																								
Motherwell	a																								
Glasgow Central	a						12 28												13 01						13 17
Haymarket	a		12 14																						
Edinburgh	a		12 21																						
Perth	a																								
Dundee	a																								
Aberdeen	a																								
Inverness	a																								

A from 12 September

B from 18 July until 9 September

OVERNIGHT SLEEPERS. For sleeper trains, operated by First ScotRail, please refer to Tables 400 - 404

Table 65

London and West Midlands - North West England and Scotland

Station		VT	XC	TP	AW	LM	XC	LM	NT	TP	VT A	VT	VT	VT	VT	VT	VT	NT	VT A	VT B	VT	XC	VT
London Euston ⊖	d	08 40									08 43	09 00	09 07	09 10	09 10	09 20	09 30				09 40		10 00
Watford Junction	d																						
Milton Keynes Central	d										09 13			09 40	09 41	09 50							
Rugby	d																						
Nuneaton	d																						
Tamworth Low Level	d																						
Lichfield Trent Valley	d																						
Coventry	d						09 27				09 42												
Birmingham International	d						09 38				09 53												
Birmingham New Street	d		09 31			09 36	09 57	10 01			10 20									10 20		10 31	
Wolverhampton	d		09 49			09 53	10 15	10 19			10 37									10 37		10 49	
Penkridge	d					10 03																	
Stafford	a		10 00			10 09	10 29	10 34					10 22									11 00	
	d		10 01			10 09	10 30	10 35					10 23									11 01	
Stoke-on-Trent	a		10 19				10 54					10 24				10 48						11 19	11 24
Congleton	a																						
Macclesfield	a						11 11					10 41											11 41
Crewe	a	10 10				10 30		10 56			11 07			10 47	10 47					11 07	11 10		
	d	10 11			10 23	10 31		10 57			11 09			10 49	10 49					11 09	11 11		
Chester	a				10 46									11 09	11 09								
Wrexham General	a																						
Llandudno	a																						
Bangor (Gwynedd)	a														12 16								
Holyhead	a														12 50								
Wilmslow	a	10 27																			11 27		
Stockport	a	10 36	10 49				11 27					10 55				11 16					11 36	11 49	11 55
Manchester Piccadilly	a	10 49	10 59				11 39					11 07				11 28					11 49	11 59	12 07
Hartford	a							11 11															
Warrington Bank Quay	a										11 26						11 14			11 26			
	d										11 27						11 14			11 27			
Runcorn	a					10 50		11 21					10 55										
Liverpool South Parkway	a					10 59		11 30															
Liverpool Lime Street	a					11 10		11 43					11 15										
	d																	10 57					
Manchester Airport	d			10 00						10 29													
Manchester Piccadilly	d			10 16						10 46													
Bolton	d			10 33						11 07													
Wigan North Western	a										11 37						11 25	11 30	11 37	11 37			
	d										11 38						11 25	11 31	11 38	11 38			
Preston	a			10 55						11 33	→						11 38	11 54	11 51	11 51			
Preston	d			10 58					11 34	11 38							11 41	11 55	11 53	11 53			
Blackpool North	a								12 00	12 05								12 21					
Lancaster	a			11 13													11 54		12 08	12 08			
	d			11 14													11 55		12 08	12 08			
Barrow-in-Furness	a																						
Oxenholme Lake District	a			11 28															12 22	12 22			
	d			11 28															12 24	12 24			
Windermere	a																						
Penrith North Lakes	d			11 53													12 30						
Carlisle	a			12 10													12 45		13 01	13 01			
	d			12 11													12 47		13 03	13 03			
Lockerbie	d			12 30																			
Carstairs	a																						
Motherwell	a																						
Glasgow Central	a																14 01						
Haymarket	a			13s32															14 15	14 15			
Edinburgh	a			13 39															14 21	14 21			
Perth	a																						
Dundee	a																						
Aberdeen	a																						
Inverness	a																						

A from 18 July until 9 September

B until 15 July, from 12 September

OVERNIGHT SLEEPERS. For sleeper trains, operated by First ScotRail, please refer to Tables 400 - 404

Table 65

London and West Midlands - North West England and Scotland

Station		TP A	TP B	AW	LM	VT	VT	VT	XC	NT	TP	VT C	VT D	NT	LM	VT	VT	XC	VT	TP	AW	LM
London Euston ⊖	d					10 07	10 10	10 20				10 30	10 30				10 40		11 00			
Watford Junction	d																					
Milton Keynes Central	d						10 41	10 50														
Rugby	d																					
Nuneaton	d																					
Tamworth Low Level	d																					
Lichfield Trent Valley	d																					
Coventry	d								10 27													
Birmingham International	d								10 38													
Birmingham New Street	d				10 36				10 57						11 01	11 20		11 31				11 36
Wolverhampton	d				10 53				11 15						11 19	11 37		11 49				11 53
Penkridge	d				11 03																	12 03
Stafford	a				11 09	11 22			11 28						11 34			12 00				12 09
	d				11 09	11 23			11 30						11 35			12 01				12 09
Stoke-on-Trent	a							11 48	11 54									12 19	12 24			
Congleton	a																					
Macclesfield	a								12 11										12 41			
Crewe	a				11 30		11 47								11 56	12 07	12 10					12 30
	d			11 23	11 31		11 49								11 57	12 09	12 11				12 23	12 31
Chester	a			11 46			12 12														12 46	
Wrexham General	a																					
Llandudno	a																					
Bangor (Gwynedd)	a																					
Holyhead	a																					
Wilmslow	a																12 27					
Stockport	a							12 16	12 27								12 36	12 49	12 55			
Manchester Piccadilly	a							12 28	12 39								12 49	12 59	13 07			
Hartford	a														12 10							
Warrington Bank Quay	a											12 14	12 14			12 26						
	d											12 14	12 14			12 27						
Runcorn	a				11 50	11 55									12 23							12 50
Liverpool South Parkway	a				11 59										12 32							12 59
Liverpool Lime Street	a				12 10	12 15									12 44							13 10
	d													11 57								
Manchester Airport	d	11 00	11 00								11 29									12 00		
Manchester Piccadilly	d	11 16	11 16								11 46									12 16		
Bolton	d	11 33	11 33								12 07									12 33		
Wigan North Western	a											12 25	12 25	12 30		12 37						
	d											12 25	12 25	12 31		12 38						
Preston	a	11 57	11 57								12 33	12 39	12 39	12 54		12 51				12 55		
Preston	d	11 58	11 58							12 34	12 38	12 42	12 42	12 55		12 53				12 58		
Blackpool North	a									13 00	13 05			13 21								
Lancaster	a	12 14	12 14									13 00	13 00			13 08				13 13		
	d		12 14										13 00			13 08				13 14		
Barrow-in-Furness	a		13 10																			
Oxenholme Lake District	a												13 15			13 22				13 28		
	d												13 17			13 24				13 28		
Windermere	a																					
Penrith North Lakes	d												13 42							13 53		
Carlisle	a												13 57			14 01				14 10		
	d												13 58			14 03				14 11		
Lockerbie	d																			14 30		
Carstairs	a												14 45									
Motherwell	a																					
Glasgow Central	a												15 24			15 17						
Haymarket	a																			15s31		
Edinburgh	a																			15 39		
Perth	a																					
Dundee	a																					
Aberdeen	a																					
Inverness	a																					

A until 15 July, to Bolton

B from 18 July, to Bolton

C until 15 July, from 12 September

D from 18 July until 9 September

OVERNIGHT SLEEPERS. For sleeper trains, operated by First ScotRail, please refer to Tables 400 - 404

London and West Midlands - North West England and Scotland

		VT	VT	VT	XC	TP	NT		TP	VT	NT	LM	VT	VT	XC	VT	TP			AW	LM	VT	VT	VT	XC
		◇1	◇1	◇1	◇1	◇1			◇1	1		1	◇1	◇1	◇1	◇1	◇1				1	◇1	◇1	◇1	◇1
		☕	☕	☕	🛒				🛒	⊠			☕	☕	🛒	☕	🛒					☕	☕	☕	🛒
London Euston 15 ⊖	d	11 07	11 10	11 20						11 30				11 40		12 00						12 07	12 10	12 20	
Watford Junction	d																								
Milton Keynes Central	d		11 41	11 50																			12 41	12 50	
Rugby	d																								
Nuneaton	d																								
Tamworth Low Level	d																								
Lichfield Trent Valley	d																								
Coventry	d				11 27																				12 27
Birmingham International ✈	d				11 38																				12 38
Birmingham New Street 12	d				11 57							12 01	12 20		12 31						12 36				12 57
Wolverhampton 7	d				12 15							12 19	12 37		12 49						12 53				13 15
Penkridge	d																				13 03				
Stafford	a	12 22			12 29							12 34			13 00						13 09	13 22			13 29
	d	12 23			12 30							12 35			13 01						13 09	13 23			13 30
Stoke-on-Trent	a			12 48	12 54										13 19	13 24								13 48	13 54
Congleton	a																								
Macclesfield	a				13 11											13 41									14 11
Crewe 10	a		12 47									12 56	13 07	13 10							13 30		13 47		
	d		12 49									12 57	13 09	13 11						13 23	13 31		13 49		
Chester	a		13 12																	13 46			14 12		
Wrexham General	a																								
Llandudno	a																								
Bangor (Gwynedd)	a																								
Holyhead	a																								
Wilmslow	a													13 27											
Stockport	a			13 16	13 27									13 36	13 49	13 55								14 16	14 27
Manchester Piccadilly 10	a			13 28	13 39									13 49	13 59	14 07								14 28	14 39
Hartford	a											13 11													
Warrington Bank Quay	a									13 14			13 26												
	d									13 14			13 27												
Runcorn	a	12 55										13 21									13 50	13 55			
Liverpool South Parkway 7 ✈	a											13 30									13 59				
Liverpool Lime Street 10	a	13 15										13 43									14 10	14 15			
	d										12 57														
Manchester Airport ✈	d								12 29								13 00								
Manchester Piccadilly 10	d								12 46								13 16								
Bolton	d								13 07								13 33								
Wigan North Western	a									13 25	13 30		13 37												
	d									13 25	13 31		13 38												
Preston 8	a								13 33	13 38	13 54		13 51				13 55								
Preston 8	d					13 04	13 34		13 38	13 41	13 55		13 53				13 58	14 04							
Blackpool North	a						14 00		14 05		14 21														
Lancaster 6	a					13 19				13 54			14 08				14 13	14 19							
	d					13 20				13 55			14 08				14 14								
Barrow-in-Furness	a																								
Oxenholme Lake District	a					13 36				14 08															
	d					13 37				14 08															
Windermere	a					13 56																			
Penrith North Lakes	d												14 45												
Carlisle 8	a									14 46			15 00				15 06								
	d									14 47			15 02				15 07								
Lockerbie	d																15 27								
Carstairs	a																								
Motherwell	a																								
Glasgow Central 15	a									16 00							16 30								
Haymarket	a												16 17												
Edinburgh 10	a												16 21												
Perth	a																								
Dundee	a																								
Aberdeen	a																								
Inverness	a																								

OVERNIGHT SLEEPERS. For sleeper trains, operated by First ScotRail, please refer to Tables 400 - 404

London and West Midlands - North West England and Scotland

		TP	NT	TP		VT	NT	LM	VT	VT	XC	VT	TP	AW		LM	VT	VT	VT	XC	NT	TP	TP	VT
		◇1		◇1		◇1		1	◇1	◇1	◇1	◇1	◇1			1	◇1	◇1	◇1	◇1		◇1	◇1	◇1
		A		🛒		☕			☕	☕	🛒	☕	🛒				☕	☕	☕	🛒		B 🛒	C 🛒 FO	⊠
London Euston 15 ⊖	d					12 30				12 40		13 00					13 07	13 10	13 20					13 30
Watford Junction	d																							
Milton Keynes Central	d																	13 41	13 50					
Rugby	d																							
Nuneaton	d																							
Tamworth Low Level	d																							
Lichfield Trent Valley	d																							
Coventry	d																			13 27				
Birmingham International ✈	d																			13 38				
Birmingham New Street 12	d							13 01	13 20		13 31					13 36				13 57				
Wolverhampton 7	d							13 19	13 37		13 49					13 53				14 15				
Penkridge	d															14 03								
Stafford	a							13 34			14 00					14 09	14 22			14 29				
	d							13 35			14 01					14 09	14 23			14 30				
Stoke-on-Trent	a										14 19	14 24							14 48	14 54				
Congleton	a																							
Macclesfield	a											14 41								15 11				
Crewe 10	a							13 56	14 07	14 10						14 30		14 47						
	d							13 57	14 09	14 11				14 23		14 31		14 49						
Chester	a													14 46				15 12						
Wrexham General	a																							
Llandudno	a																							
Bangor (Gwynedd)	a																							
Holyhead	a																							
Wilmslow	a									14 27														
Stockport	a									14 36	14 49	14 55							15 16	15 27				
Manchester Piccadilly 10	a									14 49	14 59	15 07							15 28	15 39				
Hartford	a							14 11																
Warrington Bank Quay	a					14 14			14 26															15 14
	d					14 14			14 27															15 14
Runcorn	a							14 21								14 50	14 55							
Liverpool South Parkway 7 ✈	a							14 30								14 59								
Liverpool Lime Street 10	a							14 43								15 10	15 15							
	d						13 57																	
Manchester Airport ✈	d			13 29									14 00									14 29	14 29	
Manchester Piccadilly 10	d			13 46									14 16									14 46	14 46	
Bolton	d			14 07									14 33									15 07	15 07	
Wigan North Western	a					14 25	14 30		14 37															15 25
	d					14 25	14 31		14 38															15 25
Preston 8	a			14 33		14 38	14 54		14 51				14 55									15 33	15 33	15 38
Preston 8	d	14 04	14 34	14 38		14 41	14 55		14 53				14 58								15 34	15 38	15 38	15 41
Blackpool North	a		15 00	15 05			15 21														16 00	16 05	16 07	
Lancaster 6	a	14 19				15 00			15 08				15 13											
	d	14 20							15 09				15 14											
Barrow-in-Furness	a	15 16																						
Oxenholme Lake District	a								15 22				15 28											16 04
	d								15 24				15 28											16 06
Windermere	a																							
Penrith North Lakes	d												15 53											16 31
Carlisle 8	a								16 01				16 10											16 46
	d								16 03				16 11											16 47
Lockerbie	d												16 30											
Carstairs	a																							
Motherwell	a																							
Glasgow Central 15	a								17 14															18 01
Haymarket	a												17s31											
Edinburgh 10	a												17 40											
Perth	a																							
Dundee	a																							
Aberdeen	a																							
Inverness	a																							

A from 18 July

B until 23 June, FX from 27 June until 8 September, from 12 September

C From 24 June until 9 September

OVERNIGHT SLEEPERS. For sleeper trains, operated by First ScotRail, please refer to Tables 400 - 404

London and West Midlands - North West England and Scotland

		NT	LM	VT	TP	TP	VT	VT	XC	AW		LM	XC	LM	NT	TP	VT	VT	VT	VT		VT	VT	VT	NT
							FO																FX	FO	
			1	◇1	◇1	◇1	◇	◇1	◇1			1	◇1	1		◇1	◇1	◇1	◇1	◇1		◇1	◇1	1	
					A	B											C								
London Euston 15 ⊖	d						13 33	13 40									13 43	14 00	14 07	14 10		14 20	14 30	14 30	
Watford Junction	d																								
Milton Keynes Central	d																14 13			14 41		14 50			
Rugby	d																								
Nuneaton	d																								
Tamworth Low Level	d																								
Lichfield Trent Valley	d																								
Coventry	d												14 27				14 42								
Birmingham International ✈	d												14 38				14 53								
Birmingham New Street 12	d		14 01	14 20					14 31			14 36	14 57	15 01			15 20								
Wolverhampton 7	d		14 19	14 37					14 49			14 53	15 15	15 19			15 37								
Penkridge	d											15 03													
Stafford	a		14 34						15 00			15 09	15 29	15 34					15 22						
	d		14 35						15 01			15 09	15 30	15 35					15 23						
Stoke-on-Trent	a								15 19				15 54					15 24				15 48			
Congleton	a																								
Macclesfield	a												16 11					15 41							
Crewe 10	a		14 56	15 07			15 16	15 10				15 30		15 56			16 07			15 47					
	d		14 57	15 09			15 19	15 11		15 23		15 31		15 57			16 09			15 49					
Chester	a									15 46										16 12					
Wrexham General	a																								
Llandudno	a																								
Bangor (Gwynedd)	a																								
Holyhead	a																								
Wilmslow	a							15 27																	
Stockport	a							15 36	15 49				16 27					15 55				16 16			
Manchester Piccadilly 10	a							15 49	15 59				16 39					16 07				16 28			
Hartford	a		15 11											16 10											
Warrington Bank Quay	a			15 26			15 38										16 26						16 16	16 16	
	d			15 27			15 39										16 27						16 17	16 17	
Runcorn	a		15 21									15 50		16 22					15 55						
Liverpool South Parkway 7 ✈	a		15 30									15 59		16 31											
Liverpool Lime Street 10	a		15 43									16 10		16 45					16 15						
	d	14 57																							
Manchester Airport ✈	d				15 00	15 00										15 29									15 57
Manchester Piccadilly 10	d				15 16	15 16										15 46									
Bolton	d				15 33	15 33										16 07									
Wigan North Western	a	15 30		15 37			15 49										16 37						16 28	16 28	16 30
	d	15 31		15 38			15 50										16 38						16 29	16 29	16 30
Preston 8	a	15 54		15 51	15 55	15 57	16 03									16 35	→						16 42	16 42	16 54
Preston 8	d	15 55		15 53	15 58	15 58	16 06								16 34	16 38							16 43	16 43	16 56
Blackpool North	a	16 21													17 00	17 07									17 21
Lancaster 8	a			16 08	16 13	16 14	16 26																17 00	17 00	
	d			16 08		16 15																		17 00	
Barrow-in-Furness	a					17 18																			
Oxenholme Lake District	a																							17 15	
	d																							17 16	
Windermere	a																								
Penrith North Lakes	d			16 45																				17 42	
Carlisle 8	a			17 00																				18 00	
	d			17 02																				18 00	
Lockerbie	d																								
Carstairs	a																								
Motherwell	a																								
Glasgow Central 15	a																							19 14	
Haymarket	a			18 12																					
Edinburgh 10	a			18 22																					
Perth	a																								
Dundee	a																								
Aberdeen	a																								
Inverness	a																								

A until 15 July. to Bolton

B from 18 July. to Bolton

C from 18 July until 9 September

OVERNIGHT SLEEPERS. For sleeper trains, operated by First ScotRail, please refer to Tables 400 - 404

Table 65

Mondays to Fridays

London and West Midlands - North West England and Scotland

		VT	VT	VT	XC	VT		TP		AW	LM	VT	VT	VT	XC	TP		TP	NT	VT	NT	LM	VT	VT	XC
		◇1	◇1	◇1	◇1	◇1		◇1			1	◇1	◇1	◇1	◇1	◇1		◇1		◇1		1	1	◇1	◇1
		A	B																						
London Euston 15 ⊖	d			14 40		15 00						15 07	15 10	15 20						15 30				15 40	
Watford Junction	d																								
Milton Keynes Central	d												15 41	15 50											
Rugby	d																								
Nuneaton	d																								
Tamworth Low Level	d																								
Lichfield Trent Valley	d																								
Coventry	d														15 27										
Birmingham International ✈	d														15 38										
Birmingham New Street 12	d		15 20		15 31						15 36				15 57							16 01	16 20		16 31
Wolverhampton 7	d		15 37		15 50						15 53				16 15							16 19	16 37		16 49
Penkridge	d										16 03														
Stafford	a										16 09	16 22			16 29							16 34			17 00
	d										16 09	16 23			16 30							16 35			17 01
Stoke-on-Trent	a				16 18	16 24								16 48	16 54										17 19
Congleton	a																								
Macclesfield	a					16 41									17 11										
Crewe 10	a		16 07	16 11							16 30		16 47									16 56	17 07	17 10	
	d		16 09	16 12						16 23	16 31		16 49									16 57	17 09	17 11	
Chester	a									16 46			17 12												
Wrexham General	a																								
Llandudno	a																								
Bangor (Gwynedd)	a																								
Holyhead	a																								
Wilmslow	a			16 27																				17 27	
Stockport	a			16 36	16 47	16 54								17 16	17 27									17 36	17 49
Manchester Piccadilly 10	a			16 49	16 59	17 07								17 28	17 39									17 49	17 59
Hartford	a																					17 11			
Warrington Bank Quay	a		16 26																	17 14			17 26		
	d		16 27																	17 14			17 27		
Runcorn	a										16 50	16 55										17 21			
Liverpool South Parkway 7 ✈	a										16 59											17 30			
Liverpool Lime Street 10	a										17 10	17 15										17 43			
	d																				16 57				
Manchester Airport ✈	d							16 00										16 29							
Manchester Piccadilly 10	d							16 16										16 46							
Bolton	d	←						16 33										17 06							
Wigan North Western	a	16 37	16 37																	17 25	17 30		17 37		
	d	16 38	16 38																	17 25	17 31		17 38		
Preston 8	a	16 51	16 51					16 55										17 30		17 38	17 54		17 51		
Preston 8	d	16 53	16 53					17 00	17 04							17 04		17 32	17 35	17 41	17 55		17 53		
Blackpool North	a																	18 02	18 06		18 24				
Lancaster 8	a	17 08	17 08					17 15	17 23							17 23				17 54			18 08		
	d	17 08	17 08					17 16	17 25							17 25				17 55			18 08		
Barrow-in-Furness	a																								
Oxenholme Lake District	a	17 22	17 22					17 30	17 43							17 43				18 08			18 22		
	d	17 23	17 23					17 30	17 49							17 49				18 08			18 23		
Windermere	a								18 08							18 08									
Penrith North Lakes	d	17 49	17 49																				18 49		
Carlisle 8	a	18 05	18 05					18 10												18 47			19 04		
	d	18 06	18 06					18 11												18 47			19 04		
Lockerbie	d							18 30																	
Carstairs	a																								
Motherwell	a																								
Glasgow Central 15	a	19 19	19 19																	19 57					
Haymarket	a							19s31															20 16		
Edinburgh 10	a							19 39															20 22		
Perth	a																								
Dundee	a																								
Aberdeen	a																								
Inverness	a																								

A from 18 July until 9 September

B until 15 July, from 12 September

OVERNIGHT SLEEPERS. For sleeper trains, operated by First ScotRail, please refer to Tables 400 - 404

Table 65

Mondays to Fridays

London and West Midlands - North West England and Scotland

		VT		TP		NT	AW	LM	VT	VT	VT	XC		LM	TP	VT	NT	TP	VT	VT	VT	XC		TP	
		◇1		◇1				1	◇1	◇1	◇1	◇1		1	◇1	◇1		◇1	1	◇1	◇1	◇1		◇1	
															A										
		☕		⊤					☕	☕	☕	⊤				⊠		⊤	☕	☕	☕	⊤		⊤	
London Euston 15 ⊖	d	16 00							16 07	16 10	16 20					16 30				16 33	16 40				
Watford Junction	d																								
Milton Keynes Central	d									16u40	16u50														
Rugby	d																			17 22					
Nuneaton	d																								
Tamworth Low Level	d																								
Lichfield Trent Valley	d																								
Coventry	d											16 27													
Birmingham International ✈	d											16 38													
Birmingham New Street 12	d							16 36				16 57		17 01					17 20			17 31			
Wolverhampton 7	d							16 53				17 15		17 19					17 37			17 49			
Penkridge	d							17 03						17 29											
Stafford	a							17 09	17 22			17 29		17 35						17 52		18 00			
	d							17 09	17 23			17 30		17 36						17 56		18 01			
Stoke-on-Trent	a	17 24									17 48	17 54										18 19			
Congleton	a																								
Macclesfield	a	17 41										18 11													
Crewe 10	a							17 30		17 47				17 56					18 07	18 16	18 10				
	d						17 23	17 31		17 49				18 01					18 09	18 18	18 11				
Chester	a						17 46			18 08															
Wrexham General	a																								
Llandudno	a																								
Bangor (Gwynedd)	a									19 21															
Holyhead	a																								
Wilmslow	a																				18 27				
Stockport	a	17 55									18 16	18 27									18 37	18 49			
Manchester Piccadilly 10	a	18 07									18 28	18 39									18 49	18 59			
Hartford	a													18 13											
Warrington Bank Quay	a																		18 26	18 35					
	d																		18 27	18 36					
Runcorn	a							17 50	17 55					18 23											
Liverpool South Parkway 7 ✈	a							17 59						18 32											
Liverpool Lime Street 10	a							18 10	18 15					18 44											
	d					17 19																			
Manchester Airport ✈	d			17 00														17 29						18 00	
Manchester Piccadilly 10	d			17 15														17 46						18 16	
Bolton	d			17 32														18 07						18 33	
Wigan North Western	a					18 04													18 37	18 46					
	d																		18 38	18 47					
Preston 8	a			17 55												18 30		18 38	18 51	19 01				18 55	
Preston 8	d			17 58	18 08										18 08	18 30	18 34	18 40	18 53					19 00	19 04
Blackpool North	a																18 58	19 09							
Lancaster 8	a			18 13	18 23										18 23				19 08					19 15	19 20
	d			18 14	18 24														19 08					19 16	19 20
Barrow-in-Furness	a				19 30																				20 24
Oxenholme Lake District	a			18 28															19 22					19 30	
	d			18 28															19 24					19 32	
Windermere	a																								
Penrith North Lakes	d			18 53																				19 57	
Carlisle 8	a			19 10															20 01					20 14	
	d			19 13															20 03					20 15	
Lockerbie	d																								
Carstairs	a																								
Motherwell	a			20s15																					
Glasgow Central 15	a			20 33												20 38			21 17						
Haymarket	a																							21s31	
Edinburgh 10	a																							21 39	
Perth	a																								
Dundee	a																								
Aberdeen	a																								
Inverness	a																								

A until 15 July

OVERNIGHT SLEEPERS. For sleeper trains, operated by First ScotRail, please refer to Tables 400 - 404

Table 65

Mondays to Fridays

London and West Midlands - North West England and Scotland

		AW	LM	TP	NT	VT	VT	VT		VT	VT	VT	XC	LM	NT	TP	VT	VT		TP	TP	NT	VT	VT	VT
			◇1	◇1		◇1	◇1	◇1		◇1	◇1	◇1	◇1	1		◇1	◇1	◇1		◇1	◇1		◇1	◇1	◇1
				A																B	C				
						⊠	⊠	⊠		⊠	⊠	⊠	⊤			⊤	⊠	☕		⊤			⊠	⊠	⊠
London Euston 15 ⊖	d					16 57	17 00	17 07		17 10	17 10	17 20					17 30						17 33	17 40	17 57
Watford Junction	d																								
Milton Keynes Central	d									17u40	17u40	17u50													
Rugby	d																						18 23		
Nuneaton	d									18 12	18 12														
Tamworth Low Level	d					18 00																			19 00
Lichfield Trent Valley	d					18 07																			19 08
Coventry	d												17 27												
Birmingham International ✈	d												17 38												
Birmingham New Street 12	d		17 36										17 57	18 01				18 20							
Wolverhampton 7	d		17 53										18 15	18 19				18 37							
Penkridge	d		18 03											18 29											
Stafford	a		18 09					18 23					18 29	18 35									18 52		
	d		18 09					18 24					18 30	18 35									18 55		
Stoke-on-Trent	a						18 24					18 49	18 54												
Congleton	a																								
Macclesfield	a						18 41						19 11												
Crewe 10	a		18 30					18 42		18 53	18 53			19 00				19 07					19 14	19 10	
	d	18 23	18 31					18 44		18 56	18 56			19 02				19 09					19 16	19 11	
Chester	a	18 46								19 15	19 15														
Wrexham General	a																								
Llandudno	a																								
Bangor (Gwynedd)	a										20 27														
Holyhead	a										20 59														
Wilmslow	a																							19 27	
Stockport	a						18 55					19 16	19 27											19 36	
Manchester Piccadilly 10	a						19 07					19 28	19 39											19 49	
Hartford	a		18 44																						
Warrington Bank Quay	a					18 49											19 14	19 26							19 49
	d					18 50											19 14	19 27							19 50
Runcorn	a		18 56					19 02						19 22									19 33		
Liverpool South Parkway 7 ✈	a		19 05											19 31											
Liverpool Lime Street 10	a		19 17					19 22						19 44									19 51		
	d																					19 23			
Manchester Airport ✈	d															18 29				19 00	19 00				
Manchester Piccadilly 10	d															18 46				19 16	19 16				
Bolton	d															19 07				19 33	19 33				
Wigan North Western	a					19 00											19 25	19 37				19 54			20 00
	d					19 01											19 25	19 38				19 55			20 01
Preston 8	a					19 14										19 33	19 38	19 51		19 55	19 55	20 18			20 14
Preston 8	d			19 04	19 08	19 15									19 34	19 38	19 41	19 53		19 58	19 58	20 19			20 15
Blackpool North	a				19 33										20 00	20 05						20 44			
Lancaster 8	a			19 20		19 30											19 54	20 08		20 13	20 13				20 30
	d					19 30											19 55	20 08			20 14				20 30
Barrow-in-Furness	a																				21 18				
Oxenholme Lake District	a					19 43											20 08								
	d					19 45											20 08								
Windermere	a																								
Penrith North Lakes	d					20 10												20 45							
Carlisle 8	a					20 25											20 46	21 00							21 17
	d					20 25											20 47	21 02							21 18
Lockerbie	d					20 44																			21 37
Carstairs	a																								
Motherwell	a					21 26																			22 21
Glasgow Central 15	a					21 47											22 01								22 39
Haymarket	a																	22 14							
Edinburgh 10	a																	22 22							
Perth	a																								
Dundee	a																								
Aberdeen	a																								
Inverness	a																								

A until 15 July

B until 15 July. ⊤ to Bolton

C from 18 July

OVERNIGHT SLEEPERS. For sleeper trains, operated by First ScotRail, please refer to Tables 400 - 404

London and West Midlands - North West England and Scotland

		XC	VT	AW	LM	VT	VT	VT	XC	LM	NT	TP	VT	VT	TP	TP	NT	VT	VT	XC	AW
		◇1	◇1		1	◇1	◇1	◇1	◇1	1		◇1	◇1	◇1	◇1	◇1		◇1	◇1	◇1	
							A								B	C					
		⌶	⊠			⊠	⊠	⊠	⌶				⊠	ᴿ				⊠	⊠	⌶	
London Euston 15 ⊖	d		18 00			18 07	18 10	18 20					18 30					18 33	18 40		
Watford Junction	d																				
Milton Keynes Central	d						18u40	18u50													
Rugby	d																	19 23			
Nuneaton	d						19 13														
Tamworth Low Level	d																				
Lichfield Trent Valley	d																				
Coventry	d								18 27												
Birmingham International ✈	d								18 38												
Birmingham New Street 12	d	18 31			18 36				18 57	19 01				19 20						19 31	
Wolverhampton 7	d	18 49			18 53				19 15	19 19				19 37						19 49	
Penkridge	d				19 03					19 29											
Stafford	a	19 00			19 09	19 23			19 27	19 36								19 53		20 00	
	d	19 01			19 09	19 24			19 29	19 36								19 56		20 01	
Stoke-on-Trent	a	19 19	19 24					19 48	19 54											20 19	
Congleton	a																				
Macclesfield	a		19 41						20 11												
Crewe 10	a				19 30	19 42	19 53			20 01				20 07				20 15	20 11		
	d			19 23	19 31	19 44	19 56							20 09				20 17	20 12		20 23
Chester	a			19 46			20 15														20 46
Wrexham General	a						20 38														
Llandudno	a																				
Bangor (Gwynedd)	a						21 25														
Holyhead	a						21 59														
Wilmslow	a																		20 27		
Stockport	a	19 48	19 55					20 16	20 27										20 36	20 48	
Manchester Piccadilly 10	a	20 00	20 07					20 28	20 39										20 49	20 58	
Hartford	a				19 47																
Warrington Bank Quay	a												20 14	20 26							
	d												20 14	20 27							
Runcorn	a				19 57	20 01												20 34			
Liverpool South Parkway 7 ✈	a				20 06																
Liverpool Lime Street 10	a				20 18	20 19												20 53			
	d																20 25				
Manchester Airport ✈	d											19 29			20 00	20 00					
Manchester Piccadilly 10	d											19 46			20 16	20 16					
Bolton	d											20 07			20 33	20 33					
Wigan North Western	a												20 25	20 37			20 57				
	d												20 25	20 38			20 57				
Preston 8	a											20 33	20 38	20 51	20 57	20 57	21 22				
Preston 8	d										20 34	20 38	20 41	20 53	20 58	20 58	21 24				
Blackpool North	a										21 00	21 06					21 53				
Lancaster 6	a												20 54	21 08	21 13	21 13					
	d												20 55	21 08		21 14					
Barrow-in-Furness	a															22 19					
Oxenholme Lake District	a												21 08	21 22							
	d												21 09	21 24							
Windermere	a																				
Penrith North Lakes	d												21 34								
Carlisle 8	a												21 49	22 01							
	d												21 51	22 03							
Lockerbie	d																				
Carstairs	a																				
Motherwell	a																				
Glasgow Central 15	a												23 04	23 18							
Haymarket	a																				
Edinburgh 10	a																				
Perth	a																				
Dundee	a																				
Aberdeen	a																				
Inverness	a																				

A ⊠ to Chester
B until 15 July
C from 18 July

OVERNIGHT SLEEPERS. For sleeper trains, operated by First ScotRail, please refer to Tables 400 - 404

London and West Midlands - North West England and Scotland

		LM	XC	VT	TP	VT	VT	VT	VT	VT	VT	VT	AW	VT	XC	VT	AW	LM	VT	VT	XC	NT	NT
						FO						FO											
		1	◇1	◇1	◇1	◇	1	1	1	1	1	◇		◇1	◇1	◇1		1	◇1	◇1	◇1		
			A																		A	B	
			⌶	⊠		ᴿ	ᴿ	ᴿ	ᴿ	ᴿ	ᴿ	ᴿ		ᴿ		ᴿ			ᴿ	ᴿ	⌶		
London Euston 15 ⊖	d			18 43		18 46	19 00	19 07	19 10	19 20	19 30			19 40		20 00			20 07	20 10			
Watford Junction	d																						
Milton Keynes Central	d			19 13					19u40	19u50										20 40			
Rugby	d					19 39																	
Nuneaton	d							20 03											21 03				
Tamworth Low Level	d					19s59								20 43									
Lichfield Trent Valley	d					20s07								20 50									
Coventry	d		19 27	19 42																	20 27		
Birmingham International ✈	d		19 38	19 53																	20 38		
Birmingham New Street 12	d	19 36	19 57	20 20											20 31			20 36			20 57		
Wolverhampton 7	d	19 53	20 16	20 36											20 49			20 53			21 16		
Penkridge	d	20 03																21 03					
Stafford	a	20 09	20 29	20 49		20s35		20 26						21 02				21 09	21 27		21 31		
	d	20 09	20 30	20 52				20 27						21 04				21 09	21 27		21 32		
Stoke-on-Trent	a		20 54				20 24			20 48					21 17	21 23					21 54		
Congleton	a																						
Macclesfield	a		21 11				20 41									21 40					22 11		
Crewe 10	a	20 30		21 15		21s01			20 48					21 21				21 30		21 48			
	d	20 31							20 50				21 00	21 23			21 23	21 31		21 50			
Chester	a								21 10				21 23				21 46			22 15			
Wrexham General	a																						
Llandudno	a																						
Bangor (Gwynedd)	a								22 22														
Holyhead	a								22 56														
Wilmslow	a													21 38									
Stockport	a		21 27				20 55			21 16					21 46	21 55					22 25		
Manchester Piccadilly 10	a		21 40				21 07			21 28				21 57	21 59	22 07					22 35		
Hartford	a	20 45																21 43					
Warrington Bank Quay	a					21s20					21 15												
	d										21 15												
Runcorn	a	20 56						21 01										21 54	21 59				
Liverpool South Parkway 7 ✈	a	21 05																22 05					
Liverpool Lime Street 10	a	21 16						21 21										22 15	22 20				
	d																						
Manchester Airport ✈	d				20 29																		
Manchester Piccadilly 10	d				20 46																		
Bolton	d				21 07							←											
Wigan North Western	a					21s31					21 26	21s31											
	d										21 26												
Preston 8	a				21 33	→					21 39	21 47											
Preston 8	d				21 38						21 41											21 51	22 32
Blackpool North	a				22 06																		22 59
Lancaster 6	a										21 55											22 11	
	d										21 56											22 11	
Barrow-in-Furness	a																					23 16	
Oxenholme Lake District	a										22 09												
	d										22 09												
Windermere	a																						
Penrith North Lakes	d										22 35												
Carlisle 8	a										22 50												
	d										22 51												
Lockerbie	d																						
Carstairs	a																						
Motherwell	a																						
Glasgow Central 15	a										00 06												
Haymarket	a																						
Edinburgh 10	a																						
Perth	a																						
Dundee	a																						
Aberdeen	a																						
Inverness	a																						

A ⌶ to Birmingham International
B from 18 July

OVERNIGHT SLEEPERS. For sleeper trains, operated by First ScotRail, please refer to Tables 400 - 404

London and West Midlands - North West England and Scotland

		TP	VT	VT	VT	VT	VT	TP	TP	AW	LM	LM	VT	VT	XC	TP	VT	VT	AW	SR	SR	SR
																				🛏	🛏	🛏
		◇1	◇1	◇1	◇1	◇1	◇1	◇1	◇1		1	1	◇1	◇1	◇1	◇1	◇1	◇1				
			A			B	C	D	E		F	C	F	C			B	C		G	H	F
			☕	☕	☕	☕	☕						☕	☕			☕	☕		☕	☕	☕
London Euston 15 ⊖	d		20 30	20 40	21 00								21 07	21 07			21 10	21 10		21 15	21 15	21 15
Watford Junction	d																21u25	21u25		21u33	21u33	21u33
Milton Keynes Central	d				21 31								21 38	21 38								
Rugby	d																22 04	22 04				
Nuneaton	d												22 08	22 08								
Tamworth Low Level	d		21 34																			
Lichfield Trent Valley	d		21 42																			
Coventry	d														21 27							
Birmingham International ✈	d														21 38							
Birmingham New Street 12	d					21 20	21 20				21 36	21 36			21 57							
Wolverhampton 7	d					21 41	21 41				21 53	21 53			22 16							
Penkridge	d										22 03	22 03										
Stafford	a					21 53	21 53				22 09	22 09			22 29		22 34	22 34				
	d					21 55	21 55				22 09	22 09			22 30		22 34	22 34				
Stoke-on-Trent	a				22 28										22 53							
Congleton	a																					
Macclesfield	a				22 44										23 11							
Crewe 10	a			22 12		22 17	22 17				22 30	22 30	22 46	22 46			22 53	22 53				
	d			22 13		22 18	22 18			22 23	22 31	22 31	22 48	22 48			22 54	22 54	23 23	23u52	23u52	23u54
Chester	a									22 45									23 44			
Wrexham General	a																					
Llandudno	a																					
Bangor (Gwynedd)	a																					
Holyhead	a																					
Wilmslow	a			22 29																		
Stockport	a			22 38	22 58										23 25							
Manchester Piccadilly 10	a			22 48	23 11										23 37							
Hartford	a										22 43	22 49										
Warrington Bank Quay	a		22 22			22 36	22 40										23 12	23 17				
	d		22 23			22 36	22 40										23 12	23 17				
Runcorn	a										22 56	23 01	23 05	23 10								
Liverpool South Parkway 7 ✈	a										23 07	23 12										
Liverpool Lime Street 10	a										23 23	23 26	23 24	23 29								
	d																					
Manchester Airport ✈	d	21 29						22 00	22 00							22 29						
Manchester Piccadilly 10	d	21 46						22 16	22 16							22 46						
Bolton	d	22 07						22 33	22 33							23 07						
Wigan North Western	a		22 33			22 46	22 50	22 48	22 48								23 23	23 28				
	d		22 34			22 46	22 50	22 51	22 51								23 23	23 28				
Preston 8	a	22 33	22 53			23 01	23 05	23 09	23 09							23 33	23 39	23 44				
Preston 8	d	22 35						23 13	23 13							23 35				00u52	00u52	00u52
Blackpool North	a	23 02														00 02						
Lancaster 6	a							23 28	23 28													
	d							23 29														
Barrow-in-Furness	a							00 32														
Oxenholme Lake District	a																					
	d																					
Windermere	a																					
Penrith North Lakes	d																					
Carlisle 8	a																			02 15	02 15	02 15
	d																			02 16	02 16	02 16
Lockerbie	d																					
Carstairs	a																					
Motherwell	a																					
Glasgow Central 15	a																					
Haymarket	a																					
Edinburgh 10	a																			03 58	03 58	03 58
Perth	a																			05s40		05s40
Dundee	a																			06s08		
Aberdeen	a																			07 35		
Inverness	a																			08 31		08 31

A until 9 September
B until 17 June
C from 20 June until 9 September
D from 18 July
E until 15 July
F until 17 June, from 12 September
G MTWO from 20 June until 7 September. ☕ to Edinburgh ☕ from Edinburgh 🛏 to Edinburgh 🛏 from Edinburgh
H MTWO from 20 June until 7 September

OVERNIGHT SLEEPERS. For sleeper trains, operated by First ScotRail, please refer to Tables 400 - 404

London and West Midlands - North West England and Scotland

		SR	VT	XC	XC	XC	LM	AW	VT	LM	SR	SR	SR
		🛏									🛏	🛏	🛏
			◇1	◇1	◇1	◇1	◇1	◇	◇1	1		FO	FO
		A		B	C	D					E	F	G
		☕	☕						☕		☕	☕	☕
London Euston 15 ⊖	d	21 15	21 40						22 00		23 50	23 50	23 50
Watford Junction	d	21u33									00u10	00u10	00u10
Milton Keynes Central	d								22 31				
Rugby	d								22 54				
Nuneaton	d								23 04				
Tamworth Low Level	d								23s15				
Lichfield Trent Valley	d								23s22				
Coventry	d												
Birmingham International ✈	d												
Birmingham New Street 12	d			22 30	22 30	22 30	22 36	22 55		23 09			
Wolverhampton 7	d			22 48	22 48	22 48	22 57	23 13		23 36			
Penkridge	d						23 07			23 46			
Stafford	a			23 00	23 00	23 00	23 13	23 30	23s38	23 52			
	d			23 01	23 01	23 01	23 13	23 30		23 53			
Stoke-on-Trent	a		23 06	23 20	23 20	23 20							
Congleton	a												
Macclesfield	a		23 23										
Crewe 10	a						23 43	23 55	00s03	00 16			
	d	23u54						23 57					
Chester	a							00 18					
Wrexham General	a												
Llandudno	a												
Bangor (Gwynedd)	a							01 45					
Holyhead	a							02 15					
Wilmslow	a												
Stockport	a		23 37						00s26				
Manchester Piccadilly 10	a		23 46	00 12	00 32	00 33			00 35				
Hartford	a												
Warrington Bank Quay	a										03 09	03 15	03 16
	d										03 11	03 17	03 18
Runcorn	a												
Liverpool South Parkway 7 ✈	a												
Liverpool Lime Street 10	a												
	d												
Manchester Airport ✈	d												
Manchester Piccadilly 10	d												
Bolton	d												
Wigan North Western	a												
	d												
Preston 8	a										03 39	03 46	03 46
Preston 8	d	00u52									03 48	03 55	03 56
Blackpool North	a												
Lancaster 6	a												
	d												
Barrow-in-Furness	a												
Oxenholme Lake District	a												
	d												
Windermere	a												
Penrith North Lakes	d												
Carlisle 8	a	02 15									05s16	05s16	05s16
	d	02 16											
Lockerbie	d												
Carstairs	a										06s20	06s21	06s21
Motherwell	a										06s56	06s56	06s56
Glasgow Central 15	a										07 20	07 20	07 20
Haymarket	a												
Edinburgh 10	a	03 58									07 16		
Perth	a	SR 🛏											
Dundee	a	06s08											
Aberdeen	a	07 35											
Inverness	a												

A MTWO until 15 June, MTWO from 12 September. ☕ to Edinburgh ☕ from Edinburgh 🛏 to Edinburgh 🛏 from Edinburgh
B WThFO
C MTO until 14 June, MTO from 12 September
D MTO from 20 June until 6 September
E MTWO until 19 October. ☕ to Carstairs ☕ from Carstairs 🛏 to Carstairs 🛏 from Carstairs
F Until 17 June, FO from 16 September
G From 24 June until 9 September

OVERNIGHT SLEEPERS. For sleeper trains, operated by First ScotRail, please refer to Tables 400 - 404

Table 65

Saturdays until 10 September

London and West Midlands - North West England and Scotland

	VT	TP	TP	SR	SR	XC	AW	VT	LM	TP	SR	SR	NT	TP	TP	LM	TP	VT	TP	LM	VT	TP
	1	◇1	◇1			◇1	◇	◇1	1	◇1				◇1	◇1	1	1	◇1	◇1	1	◇1	◇1
		A		B	C						C	B					D					
London Euston 15 d	19p30			21p15	21p15			22p00			23p50	23p50										
Watford Junction d				21b33	21b33						00u10	00u10										
Milton Keynes Central d								22p31														
Rugby d								22p54														
Nuneaton d								23p04														
Tamworth Low Level d								23c15														
Lichfield Trent Valley d								23c22														
Coventry d																						
Birmingham International d																						
Birmingham New Street 12 d						22p30	22p55		23p09												05 30	
Wolverhampton 7 d						22p48	23p13		23p36												05 48	
Penkridge d									23p46													
Stafford a						23p00	23p30	23c38	23p52												06 00	
d						23p01	23p30		23p53												06 01	
Stoke-on-Trent a						23p20																
Congleton a																						
Macclesfield a																						
Crewe 10 a							23p55	00s03	00 16												06 20	
d				23b52	23b54		23p57						00 44			05 48		05 57		06 12	06 23	
Chester a							00 18														06 43	
Wrexham General a																						
Llandudno a																						
Bangor (Gwynedd) a							01 45														07 49	
Holyhead a							02 15														08 23	
Wilmslow a																						
Stockport a								00s26														
Manchester Piccadilly 10 a						00 12		00 35														
Hartford a																						
Warrington Bank Quay a	21p15										03 15	03 16						06 13				
d	21p15										03 17	03 18						06 14				
Runcorn a																06 07				06 31		
Liverpool South Parkway 7 a																06 15				06 39		
Liverpool Lime Street 10 a																06 26				06 53		
d																						
Manchester Airport d		22p00	22p29							00 01			01 20	04 00					05 45			06 18
Manchester Piccadilly 10 d		22p16	22p46							00 16			01a36	04 15	05 43				06 03			06 33
Bolton d		22p33	23p07							00s31				04s29	05 59				06 19			06 50
Wigan North Western a	21p26	22p48																06 24				
d	21p26	22p51																06 25				
Preston 8 a	21p39	23p09	23p33							01s05	03 46	03 46		05s04	06 26			06 37	06 42			07 11
Preston 8 d	21p41	23p13	23p35	00u52	00u52						03 55	03 56			06 37		06 34	06 40	06 44			07 14
Blackpool North a			00 02							01 30				05 33	07 06							
Lancaster 6 a	21p55	23p28															06 50	06 54	06 59			07 30
d	21p56	23p29																06 54	07 00			07 30
Barrow-in-Furness a		00 32																				
Oxenholme Lake District a	22p09																	07 08	07 15			
d	22p09																	07 10	07 15			
Windermere a																						
Penrith North Lakes d	22p35																	07 37				08 07
Carlisle 8 a	22p50			02 15	02 15						05s16	05s16						07 50	07 55			08 24
d	22p51			02 16	02 16													07 51	07 56			08 25
Lockerbie d																		08 10	08 16			
Carstairs a											06s21	06s21										
Motherwell a											06s56	06s56										
Glasgow Central 15 a	00 06										07 20	07 20						09 13				09 45
Haymarket a																			09s17			
Edinburgh 10 a				03 58	03 58														09 22			
Perth a				05s40	05s40																	
Dundee a																						
Aberdeen a																						
Inverness a				08 31	08 31																	

A from 23 July until 10 September
B from 25 June until 10 September
C until 18 June
D until 16 July
b Previous night, stops to pick up only
c Previous night, stops to set down only

OVERNIGHT SLEEPERS. For sleeper trains, operated by First ScotRail, please refer to Tables 400 - 404

Table 65

Saturdays until 10 September

London and West Midlands - North West England and Scotland

	AW	XC	NT	TP	TP	NT	LM	LM	AW	VT	XC	TP	TP	AW	LM	XC	TP	VT	NT	NT	LM	VT
		◇1		◇1	◇1		◇1	◇1	◇	◇1	◇1	◇1	◇1		◇1	◇1	◇1	◇1			◇1	◇1
				A	B							B	A						B			
London Euston 15 d																		06 05				
Watford Junction d																		06u20				
Milton Keynes Central d																		06 41				
Rugby d																		07 03				
Nuneaton d																						
Tamworth Low Level d																						
Lichfield Trent Valley d																						
Coventry d																						
Birmingham International d																						
Birmingham New Street 12 d		05 57						06 01		06 20	06 31				06 36	06 57					07 01	07 20
Wolverhampton 7 d		06 16						06 18		06 37	06 49				06 54	07 15					07 18	07 37
Penkridge d								06 29													07 30	
Stafford a		06 29						06 35			07 00				07 08	07 29		07 33			07 36	
d		06 30						06 36			07 01				07 08	07 31		07 34			07 38	
Stoke-on-Trent a		06 50									07 18											
Congleton a		07 02																				
Macclesfield a		07 11									07 36											
Crewe 10 a								06 56		07 07					07 33	07 50		07 53			07 58	08 07
d	06 27						06 32	06 57	07 03	07 09				07 23	07 35	07 54		07 55			08 00	08 09
Chester a									07 23					07 46								
Wrexham General a																						
Llandudno a																						
Bangor (Gwynedd) a									08 36													
Holyhead a									09 21													
Wilmslow a	06 44															08 09						
Stockport a	06 55	07 27									07 49					08 21						
Manchester Piccadilly 10 a	07 07	07 38									07 59					08 36						
Hartford a							06 46	07 10							07 48						08 11	
Warrington Bank Quay a										07 26								08 11				08 27
d										07 27								08 12				08 28
Runcorn a							06 59	07 20							08 02						08 24	
Liverpool South Parkway 7 a							07 08	07 30							08 11						08 33	
Liverpool Lime Street 10 a							07 22	07 42							08 24						08 46	
d						06 57														07 57		
Manchester Airport d												07 00	07 00				07 25					
Manchester Piccadilly 10 d												07 15	07 15				07 45					
Bolton d			07 01									07 31	07 31				07 59					
Wigan North Western a			07 19			07 30				07 37								08 22		08 30		08 38
d						07 31				07 38								08 23		08 31		08 39
Preston 8 a						07 54				07 51		07 57	07 55				08 22	08 36		08 54		08 52
Preston 8 d				07 20	07 20	07 55				07 53		07 59	07 59				08 24	08 37	08 42	08 55		08 54
Blackpool North a						08 21						08 29	08 29							09 21		
Lancaster 6 a				07 36	07 36					08 08							08 39	08 52	09 02			09 09
d					07 36					08 08							08 40	08 52	09 03			09 09
Barrow-in-Furness a					08 40														10 07			
Oxenholme Lake District a										08 21								09 05				
d										08 22								09 06				
Windermere a																						
Penrith North Lakes d																		09 32				09 46
Carlisle 8 a										09 00							09 30	09 47	12 39			10 01
d										09 02							09 30	09 48				10 04
Lockerbie d																	09 50					
Carstairs a																						
Motherwell a																						
Glasgow Central 15 a																		11 03				11 17
Haymarket a										10 16							10s48					
Edinburgh 10 a										10 22							10 55					
Perth a																						
Dundee a																						
Aberdeen a																						
Inverness a																						

A until 16 July
B from 23 July until 10 September

OVERNIGHT SLEEPERS. For sleeper trains, operated by First ScotRail, please refer to Tables 400 - 404

Table 65

Saturdays
until 10 September

London and West Midlands - North West England and Scotland

Station		VT		XC	VT	TP	AW	LM	VT	VT	XC	TP		NT	VT	TP	NT	LM	VT	VT	XC	VT			TP
		◇1		◇1	◇1	◇1		◇1	◇1	◇1	◇1	◇1			◇1	◇1		◇1	◇1	◇1	◇1	◇1			◇1
												A				B									C
		▭		⌶	▭	⌶			▭	▭	⌶	⌶			▭				▭	▭	▭	▭			⌶
London Euston 15 ⊖	d	06 36			06 55				07 07	07 20					07 30					07 35		08 00			
Watford Junction	d	06u51																							
Milton Keynes Central	d				07 27					07 50										08 06					
Rugby	d																								
Nuneaton	d																								
Tamworth Low Level	d																								
Lichfield Trent Valley	d																								
Coventry	d										07 27														
Birmingham International ✈	d										07 38														
Birmingham New Street 12	d			07 31				07 36			07 57							08 01	08 20		08 31				
Wolverhampton 7	d			07 49				07 53			08 15							08 19	08 37		08 49				
Penkridge	d							08 03										08 29							
Stafford	a			08 00				08 09	08 22		08 29							08 35			09 00				
	d			08 01				08 09	08 23		08 30							08 36			09 01				
Stoke-on-Trent	a			08 19	08 24					08 48	08 54										09 19	09 24			
Congleton	a																								
Macclesfield	a			08 36	08 41						09 11											09 41			
Crewe 10	a	08 10						08 30	08 41									08 56	09 07	09 10					
	d	08 11					08 23	08 31	08 43									08 58	09 09	09 11					
Chester	a						08 46																		
Wrexham General	a																								
Llandudno	a																								
Bangor (Gwynedd)	a																								
Holyhead	a																								
Wilmslow	a	08 27																		09 27					
Stockport	a	08 37		08 49	08 55					09 16	09 27									09 36	09 49	09 55			
Manchester Piccadilly 10 ⇌	a	08 49		08 59	09 07					09 28	09 39									09 49	09 59	10 07			
Hartford	a																	09 11							
Warrington Bank Quay	a														09 14				09 26						
	d														09 14				09 27						
Runcorn	a							08 50	09 00									09 21							
Liverpool South Parkway 7 ✈	a							08 59										09 30							
Liverpool Lime Street 10	a							09 12	09 21									09 43							
	d																08 57								
Manchester Airport ✈	d					07 56						08 25													09 00
Manchester Piccadilly 10 ⇌	d					08 15						08 46													09 16
Bolton	d					08 32						09 07													09 33
Wigan North Western	a														09 25		09 30		09 37						
	d														09 25		09 31		09 38						
Preston 8	a					08 58						09 30			09 38		09 54		09 51						09 55
Preston 8	d					08 59						09 32		09 34	09 41	09 45	09 55		09 53					10 08	09 58
Blackpool North	a					09 25								10 01			10 21							10 35	
Lancaster 6	a											09 47			09 54	10 00			10 08						10 13
	d											09 48			09 55	10 01			10 08						10 14
Barrow-in-Furness	a															11 04									
Oxenholme Lake District	a											10 04							10 22						
	d											10 05							10 24						
Windermere	a											10 26													
Penrith North Lakes	d														10 31										10 53
Carlisle 8	a														10 46				11 01						11 10
	d														10 47				11 03						11 11
Lockerbie	d																								11 30
Carstairs	a																								
Motherwell	a																								
Glasgow Central 15	a														12 01										12 32
Haymarket	a																		12 16						
Edinburgh 10	a																		12 22						
Perth	a																								
Dundee	a																								
Aberdeen	a																								
Inverness	a																								

A ⌶ to Bolton
B from 23 July until 10 September
C ⌶ to Preston

OVERNIGHT SLEEPERS. For sleeper trains, operated by First ScotRail, please refer to Tables 400 - 404

Table 65

Saturdays
until 10 September

London and West Midlands - North West England and Scotland

Station		AW	LM	VT	VT	VT	XC	TP		NT	TP	VT	TP	NT	LM	VT	VT	XC		TP	AW	LM	XC	LM	NT
			◇1	◇1	◇1	◇1	◇1	◇1			◇1	◇1	◇1		◇1	◇1	◇1	◇1		◇1		◇1	◇1	◇1	
								A																	
				▭	▭	▭	⌶				⌶	▭				▭	▭	▭		⌶			⌶		
London Euston 15 ⊖	d			08 07	08 10	08 20						08 30					08 40								
Watford Junction	d																								
Milton Keynes Central	d				08 41	08 50																			
Rugby	d																								
Nuneaton	d																								
Tamworth Low Level	d																								
Lichfield Trent Valley	d																								
Coventry	d						08 27																09 27		
Birmingham International ✈	d						08 38																09 38		
Birmingham New Street 12	d		08 36				08 57								09 01	09 20		09 31				09 36	09 57	10 01	
Wolverhampton 7	d		08 53				09 15								09 19	09 37		09 49				09 53	10 15	10 19	
Penkridge	d		09 03																			10 03			
Stafford	a		09 09	09 22			09 29								09 34			10 00				10 09	10 29	10 35	
	d		09 09	09 23			09 30								09 35			10 01				10 09	10 30	10 35	
Stoke-on-Trent	a					09 48	09 54											10 19					10 54		
Congleton	a																								
Macclesfield	a						10 11																11 11		
Crewe 10	a		09 30		09 48										09 56	10 07	10 10					10 30		10 56	
	d	09 23	09 31		09 50										09 57	10 09	10 11				10 23	10 31		10 57	
Chester	a	09 46			10 12																10 46				
Wrexham General	a																								
Llandudno	a																								
Bangor (Gwynedd)	a																								
Holyhead	a																								
Wilmslow	a																10 27								
Stockport	a					10 16	10 27										10 36	10 49					11 27		
Manchester Piccadilly 10 ⇌	a					10 28	10 39										10 49	10 59					11 39		
Hartford	a														10 10									11 11	
Warrington Bank Quay	a											10 14				10 26									
	d											10 14				10 27									
Runcorn	a		09 50	09 55											10 22							10 50		11 21	
Liverpool South Parkway 7 ✈	a		09 59												10 31							10 59		11 30	
Liverpool Lime Street 10	a		10 10	10 15											10 44							11 10		11 43	
	d													09 57											
Manchester Airport ✈	d										09 29									10 00					
Manchester Piccadilly 10 ⇌	d										09 46									10 16					
Bolton	d										10 07									10 33					
Wigan North Western	a											10 25		10 30		10 37									
	d											10 25		10 31		10 38									
Preston 8	a										10 33	10 38		10 54		10 51				10 55					
Preston 8	d							10 04		10 34	10 38	10 41	10 45	10 55		10 53				10 58					11 34
Blackpool North	a									11 01	11 05			11 21											12 00
Lancaster 6	a							10 19				10 54	11 00			11 08				11 13					
	d											10 55	11 01			11 08				11 14					
Barrow-in-Furness	a																								
Oxenholme Lake District	a											11 08	11 17							11 28					
	d											11 08	11 18							11 28					
Windermere	a												11 39												
Penrith North Lakes	d															11 45				11 53					
Carlisle 8	a											11 46				12 00				12 10					
	d											11 47				12 03				12 11					
Lockerbie	d																			12 30					
Carstairs	a																								
Motherwell	a																								
Glasgow Central 15	a											13 01				13 17									
Haymarket	a																			13s33					
Edinburgh 10	a																			13 40					
Perth	a																								
Dundee	a																								
Aberdeen	a																								
Inverness	a																								

A until 16 July

OVERNIGHT SLEEPERS. For sleeper trains, operated by First ScotRail, please refer to Tables 400 - 404

London and West Midlands - North West England and Scotland

Station		TP	VT A	VT	VT	VT	VT	VT	NT	VT A	VT B	VT	XC	VT	TP C	TP D	AW	LM	VT	VT	VT	XC
London Euston 15	d		08 43	08 50	09 00	09 07	09 20	09 30				09 40		10 00					10 07	10 10	10 20	
Watford Junction	d			09 05																		
Milton Keynes Central	d		09 13	09 25			09 50													10 41	10 50	
Rugby	d																					
Nuneaton	d																					
Tamworth Low Level	d																					
Lichfield Trent Valley	d																					
Coventry	d		09 42																			10 27
Birmingham International	d		09 53																			10 38
Birmingham New Street 12	d		10 20								10 20		10 31					10 36				10 57
Wolverhampton 7	d		10 37								10 37		10 49					10 53				11 15
Penkridge	d																	11 03				
Stafford	a					10 22							11 00					11 09	11 22			11 29
	d					10 23							11 01					11 09	11 23			11 30
Stoke-on-Trent	a				10 24		10 48						11 19	11 24							11 48	11 54
Congleton	a																					
Macclesfield	a				10 41									11 41								12 11
Crewe 10	a		11 07	10 32							11 07	11 10						11 30		11 48		
	d		11 09	10 43							11 09	11 11					11 23	11 31		11 50		
Chester	a			11 10													11 46			12 12		
Wrexham General	a																					
Llandudno	a																					
Bangor (Gwynedd)	a			12 19																		
Holyhead	a			12 55																		
Wilmslow	a											11 27										
Stockport	a				10 55		11 16					11 36	11 49	11 55							12 16	12 27
Manchester Piccadilly 10	a				11 07		11 28					11 49	11 59	12 07							12 28	12 39
Hartford	a																					
Warrington Bank Quay	a		11 26					11 14			11 26											
	d		11 27					11 14			11 27											
Runcorn	a					10 55												11 50	11 55			
Liverpool South Parkway 7	a																	11 59				
Liverpool Lime Street 10	a					11 15												12 10	12 15			
	d								10 57													
Manchester Airport	d	10 29													11 00	11 00						
Manchester Piccadilly 10	d	10 46													11 16	11 16						
Bolton	d	11 07													11 33	11 33						
Wigan North Western	a		11 37					11 25	11 30	11 37	11 37											
	d		11 38					11 25	11 31	11 38	11 38											
Preston 8	a	11 33	→					11 38	11 54	11 51	11 51				11 57	11 57						
Preston 8	d	11 38						11 41	11 55	11 53	11 53				11 58	11 58						
Blackpool North	a	12 05							12 21													
Lancaster 6	a							11 54		12 08	12 08				12 14	12 14						
	d							11 55		12 08	12 08					12 14						
Barrow-in-Furness	a															13 10						
Oxenholme Lake District	a									12 22	12 22											
	d									12 24	12 24											
Windermere	a																					
Penrith North Lakes	d							12 30														
Carlisle 8	a							12 45		13 01	13 01											
	d							12 47		13 03	13 03											
Lockerbie	d																					
Carstairs	a																					
Motherwell	a																					
Glasgow Central 15	a							14 01														
Haymarket	a									14 16	14 16											
Edinburgh 10	a									14 22	14 22											
Perth	a																					
Dundee	a																					
Aberdeen	a																					
Inverness	a																					

A from 16 July until 10 September
B until 9 July
C until 16 July. to Bolton
D from 23 July until 10 September. to Bolton

OVERNIGHT SLEEPERS. For sleeper trains, operated by First ScotRail, please refer to Tables 400 - 404

London and West Midlands - North West England and Scotland

Station		NT	TP	VT	NT	LM	VT	VT	XC	VT	TP	AW	LM	VT	VT	VT	XC	TP	NT	TP	VT	NT	LM
London Euston 15	d			10 30				10 40		11 00				11 07	11 10	11 20					11 30		
Watford Junction	d																						
Milton Keynes Central	d														11 41	11 50							
Rugby	d																						
Nuneaton	d																						
Tamworth Low Level	d																						
Lichfield Trent Valley	d																						
Coventry	d																11 27						
Birmingham International	d																11 38						
Birmingham New Street 12	d					11 01	11 20		11 31				11 36				11 57						12 01
Wolverhampton 7	d					11 19	11 37		11 49				11 53				12 15						12 19
Penkridge	d												12 03										
Stafford	a					11 35			12 00				12 09	12 22			12 29						12 35
	d					11 35			12 01				12 09	12 23			12 30						12 35
Stoke-on-Trent	a								12 19	12 24						12 48	12 54						
Congleton	a																						
Macclesfield	a									12 41							13 11						
Crewe 10	a					11 56	12 07	12 10					12 30		12 47								12 56
	d					11 57	12 09	12 11				12 23	12 31		12 49								12 57
Chester	a											12 46			13 12								
Wrexham General	a																						
Llandudno	a																						
Bangor (Gwynedd)	a																						
Holyhead	a																						
Wilmslow	a							12 27															
Stockport	a							12 36	12 49	12 55						13 16	13 27						
Manchester Piccadilly 10	a							12 49	12 59	13 07						13 28	13 39						
Hartford	a					12 10																	13 11
Warrington Bank Quay	a			12 14			12 26														13 14		
	d			12 14			12 27														13 14		
Runcorn	a					12 22							12 50	12 55									13 21
Liverpool South Parkway 7	a					12 31							12 59										13 30
Liverpool Lime Street 10	a					12 44							13 10	13 15									13 43
	d				11 57																	12 57	
Manchester Airport	d		11 29								12 00									12 29			
Manchester Piccadilly 10	d		11 46								12 16									12 46			
Bolton	d		12 07								12 33									13 07			
Wigan North Western	a			12 25	12 30		12 37														13 25	13 30	
	d			12 25	12 31		12 38														13 25	13 31	
Preston 8	a		12 33	12 38	12 54		12 51				12 55									13 33	13 38	13 54	
Preston 8	d	12 34	12 38	12 41	12 55		12 53				12 58							13 04	13 34	13 38	13 41	13 55	
Blackpool North	a	13 00	13 05		13 21														14 00	14 05		14 21	
Lancaster 6	a			12 54			13 08				13 13							13 19			13 54		
	d			12 55			13 08				13 14							13 20			13 55		
Barrow-in-Furness	a																						
Oxenholme Lake District	a			13 08			13 22				13 28							13 36			14 08		
	d			13 09			13 24				13 28							13 37			14 08		
Windermere	a																	13 56					
Penrith North Lakes	d										13 53												
Carlisle 8	a			13 46			14 01				14 10										14 46		
	d			13 47			14 03				14 11										14 47		
Lockerbie	d										14 30												
Carstairs	a																						
Motherwell	a																						
Glasgow Central 15	a			15 01			15 17														16 01		
Haymarket	a										15s31												
Edinburgh 10	a										15 39												
Perth	a																						
Dundee	a																						
Aberdeen	a																						
Inverness	a																						

OVERNIGHT SLEEPERS. For sleeper trains, operated by First ScotRail, please refer to Tables 400 - 404

Table 65

Saturdays
until 10 September

London and West Midlands - North West England and Scotland

		VT	VT	XC	VT	TP	TP	AW	LM	VT	VT	VT	XC	NT	TP	VT	NT	LM	VT	VT	XC	VT
		◇1	◇1	◇1	◇1	◇1	◇1		◇1	◇1	◇1	◇1	◇1		◇1	◇1		◇1	◇1	◇1	◇1	◇1
						A	B															
		⊡	⊡	⊡	⊡	✠	✠			⊡	⊡	⊡	✠		✠	⊡			⊡	⊡	⊡	⊡
London Euston 15 ⊖	d		11 40		12 00					12 07	12 10	12 20				12 30				12 40		13 00
Watford Junction	d																					
Milton Keynes Central	d										12 41	12 50										
Rugby	d																					
Nuneaton	d																					
Tamworth Low Level	d																					
Lichfield Trent Valley	d																					
Coventry	d												12 27									
Birmingham International ✈	d												12 38									
Birmingham New Street 12	d	12 20		12 31					12 36				12 57					13 01	13 20		13 31	
Wolverhampton 7 ⛴	d	12 37		12 49					12 53				13 15					13 19	13 37		13 49	
Penkridge	d								13 03													
Stafford	a			13 00					13 09	13 22			13 29					13 35			14 00	
	d			13 01					13 09	13 23			13 30					13 35			14 01	
Stoke-on-Trent	a			13 18	13 24							13 48	13 54								14 19	14 24
Congleton	a																					
Macclesfield	a				13 41								14 11									14 41
Crewe 10	a	13 07	13 10						13 30		13 47							13 56	14 07	14 10		
	d	13 09	13 11					13 23	13 31		13 49							13 57	14 09	14 11		
Chester	a							13 46			14 12											
Wrexham General	a																					
Llandudno	a																					
Bangor (Gwynedd)	a																					
Holyhead	a																					
Wilmslow	a		13 27																	14 27		
Stockport	a		13 36	13 49	13 55							14 16	14 27							14 36	14 49	14 55
Manchester Piccadilly 10 ⛴	a		13 49	13 59	14 07							14 28	14 39							14 49	14 59	15 07
Hartford	a																	14 11				
Warrington Bank Quay	a	13 26														14 14			14 26			
	d	13 27														14 14			14 27			
Runcorn	a								13 50	13 55								14 21				
Liverpool South Parkway 7 ✈	a								13 59									14 30				
Liverpool Lime Street 10	a								14 10	14 15								14 43				
	d																13 57					
Manchester Airport ✈	d					13 00	13 00								13 29							
Manchester Piccadilly 10 ⛴	d					13 16	13 16								13 46							
Bolton	d					13 33	13 33								14 07							
Wigan North Western	a	13 37														14 25	14 30		14 37			
	d	13 38														14 25	14 31		14 38			
Preston 8	a	13 51				13 53	13 55								14 33	14 38	14 54		14 51			
Preston 8	d	13 53				14 00	13 58							14 34	14 38	14 41	14 55		14 53			
Blackpool North	a													15 00	15 05		15 21					
Lancaster 6	a	14 08				14 13	14 13									14 54			15 08			
	d	14 08				14 14	14 14									14 55			15 09			
Barrow-in-Furness	a																					
Oxenholme Lake District	a						14 28												15 22			
	d						14 28												15 24			
Windermere	a																					
Penrith North Lakes	d	14 45														15 30						
Carlisle 8	a	15 00				15 06	15 06									15 45			16 01			
	d	15 02				15 07	15 07									15 47			16 03			
Lockerbie	d					15 27	15 27															
Carstairs	a																					
Motherwell	a																					
Glasgow Central 15	a					16 28	16 30									17 01			17 17			
Haymarket	a	16 16																				
Edinburgh 10	a	16 22																				
Perth	a																					
Dundee	a																					
Aberdeen	a																					
Inverness	a																					

A from 25 June until 10 September
B until 18 June

OVERNIGHT SLEEPERS. For sleeper trains, operated by First ScotRail, please refer to Tables 400 - 404

Table 65

Saturdays
until 10 September

London and West Midlands - North West England and Scotland

		TP		AW	LM	VT	VT	VT	XC	TP	NT	TP	VT	NT	LM	VT	VT	XC	TP	TP	AW	LM
		◇1			◇1	◇1	◇1	◇1	◇1	◇1		◇1	◇1		◇1	◇1	◇1	◇1	◇1	◇1		◇1
										A									B	C		
		✠				⊡	⊡	⊡	✠			✠	⊡			⊡	⊡	⊡	✠	✠		
London Euston 15 ⊖	d					13 07	13 10	13 20					13 30				13 40					
Watford Junction	d																					
Milton Keynes Central	d						13 41	13 50														
Rugby	d																					
Nuneaton	d																					
Tamworth Low Level	d																					
Lichfield Trent Valley	d																					
Coventry	d								13 27													
Birmingham International ✈	d								13 38													
Birmingham New Street 12	d				13 36				13 57						14 01	14 20		14 31				14 36
Wolverhampton 7 ⛴	d				13 53				14 15						14 19	14 37		14 49				14 53
Penkridge	d				14 03																	15 03
Stafford	a				14 09	14 22			14 29						14 35			15 00				15 09
	d				14 09	14 23			14 30						14 35			15 01				15 09
Stoke-on-Trent	a							14 48	14 54									15 19				
Congleton	a																					
Macclesfield	a								15 11													
Crewe 10	a				14 30		14 48								14 56	15 07	15 10					15 30
	d			14 23	14 31		14 50								14 57	15 09	15 11				15 23	15 31
Chester	a			14 46			15 12														15 46	
Wrexham General	a																					
Llandudno	a																					
Bangor (Gwynedd)	a																					
Holyhead	a																					
Wilmslow	a																15 27					
Stockport	a							15 16	15 27								15 36	15 49				
Manchester Piccadilly 10 ⛴	a							15 28	15 39								15 49	15 59				
Hartford	a														15 11							
Warrington Bank Quay	a												15 14			15 26						
	d												15 14			15 27						
Runcorn	a				14 50	14 55									15 21							15 50
Liverpool South Parkway 7 ✈	a				14 59										15 30							15 59
Liverpool Lime Street 10	a				15 10	15 15									15 43							16 10
	d													14 57								
Manchester Airport ✈	d	14 00										14 29							15 00	15 00		
Manchester Piccadilly 10 ⛴	d	14 16										14 46							15 16	15 16		
Bolton	d	14 33										15 07							15 33	15 33		
Wigan North Western	a												15 25	15 30		15 37						
	d												15 25	15 31		15 38						
Preston 8	a	14 55										15 33	15 38	15 54		15 51			15 55	15 55		
Preston 8	d	14 58	15 04							15 04	15 34	15 38	15 41	15 55		15 53			15 58	15 58		
Blackpool North	a										16 00	16 05		16 21								
Lancaster 6	a	15 13	15 20							15 20			15 54			16 08			16 13	16 14		
	d	15 14	15 20										15 56			16 09				16 15		
Barrow-in-Furness	a		16 16																	17 18		
Oxenholme Lake District	a	15 28											16 08									
	d	15 28											16 09									
Windermere	a																					
Penrith North Lakes	d	15 53														16 45						
Carlisle 8	a	16 10											16 46			17 00						
	d	16 11											16 47			17 03						
Lockerbie	d	16 30																				
Carstairs	a																					
Motherwell	a																					
Glasgow Central 15	a												18 01									
Haymarket	a	17s31														18 14						
Edinburgh 10	a	17 40														18 22						
Perth	a																					
Dundee	a																					
Aberdeen	a																					
Inverness	a																					

A until 16 July
B until 16 July. ✠ to Bolton
C from 23 July until 10 September. ✠ to Bolton

OVERNIGHT SLEEPERS. For sleeper trains, operated by First ScotRail, please refer to Tables 400 - 404

Table 65

Saturdays until 10 September

London and West Midlands - North West England and Scotland

		XC ◇1	LM ◇1	NT	TP ◇1	VT ◇1 A	VT ◇1	VT ◇1	VT ◇1	VT ◇1	VT ◇1	NT	VT ◇1 A	VT ◇1 B	VT ◇1	XC ◇1	VT ◇1	TP ◇1		AW	LM ◇1	VT ◇1	VT ◇1
London Euston 15 ⊖	d					13 43	14 00	14 07	14 10	14 20	14 30				14 40		15 00					15 07	15 10
Watford Junction	d																						
Milton Keynes Central	d					14 13			14 41	14 50													15 41
Rugby	d																						
Nuneaton	d																						
Tamworth Low Level	d																						
Lichfield Trent Valley	d																						
Coventry	d	14 27				14 42																	
Birmingham International ✈	d	14 38				14 53																	
Birmingham New Street 12	d	14 57	15 01			15 20								15 20		15 31					15 36		
Wolverhampton 7	d	15 15	15 19			15 37								15 37		15 49					15 53		
Penkridge	d																				16 03		
Stafford	a	15 29	15 35					15 22								16 00					16 09	16 22	
	d	15 30	15 35					15 23								16 01					16 09	16 23	
Stoke-on-Trent	a	15 54					15 24			15 48						16 19	16 24						
Congleton	a																						
Macclesfield	a	16 11					15 41										16 41						
Crewe 10	a		15 56			16 08			15 47					16 08	16 11						16 30		16 47
	d		15 57			16 09			15 49					16 09	16 12					16 23	16 31		16 49
Chester	a								16 10											16 46			17 12
Wrexham General	a																						
Llandudno	a																						
Bangor (Gwynedd)	a								17 17														
Holyhead	a								17 51														
Wilmslow	a														16 27								
Stockport	a	16 27					15 55			16 16					16 36	16 49	16 54						
Manchester Piccadilly 10	a	16 39					16 07			16 28					16 49	16 59	17 07						
Hartford	a		16 10																				
Warrington Bank Quay	a					16 26					16 14			16 26									
	d					16 27					16 14			16 27									
Runcorn	a		16 23					15 55													16 50	16 55	
Liverpool South Parkway 7 ✈	a		16 32																		16 59		
Liverpool Lime Street 10	a		16 44					16 15													17 10	17 15	
	d											15 57											
Manchester Airport ✈	d				15 29													16 00					
Manchester Piccadilly 10	d				15 46													16 16					
Bolton	d				16 07								←					16 33					
Wigan North Western	a					16 37					16 25	16 30	16 37	16 37									
	d					16 38					16 25	16 31	16 38	16 38									
Preston 8	a				16 33	→					16 38	16 54	16 51	16 51				16 55					
Preston 8	d			16 34	16 38						16 41	16 55	16 53	16 53				17 00	17 04				
Blackpool North	a			17 00	17 07							17 21											
Lancaster 6	a										16 54		17 09	17 09				17 15	17 20				
	d										16 55		17 10	17 10				17 16	17 21				
Barrow-in-Furness	a																						
Oxenholme Lake District	a												17 24	17 24				17 30	17 37				
	d												17 25	17 25				17 30	17 38				
Windermere	a																		18 00				
Penrith North Lakes	d										17 30												
Carlisle 8	a										17 45		18 03	18 03				18 10					
	d										17 47		18 04	18 04				18 11					
Lockerbie	d																	18 30					
Carstairs	a																						
Motherwell	a																						
Glasgow Central 15	a										19 01		19 17	19 17									
Haymarket	a																	19s31					
Edinburgh 10	a																	19 39					
Perth	a																						
Dundee	a																						
Aberdeen	a																						
Inverness	a																						

A from 16 July until 10 September **B** until 9 July

OVERNIGHT SLEEPERS. For sleeper trains, operated by First ScotRail, please refer to Tables 400 - 404

Table 65

Saturdays until 10 September

London and West Midlands - North West England and Scotland

		VT ◇1	XC ◇1	TP ◇1	NT	VT ◇1	NT	LM ◇1	VT ◇1	VT ◇1	XC ◇1	VT ◇1	TP ◇1	NT	AW	LM ◇1	VT ◇1	VT ◇1	VT ◇1	XC ◇1	LM ◇1	TP ◇1 A	TP ◇1 B
London Euston 15 ⊖	d	15 20				15 30				15 40		16 00					16 07	16 10	16 20				
Watford Junction	d																						
Milton Keynes Central	d	15 50																16 41	16 50				
Rugby	d																						
Nuneaton	d																						
Tamworth Low Level	d																						
Lichfield Trent Valley	d																						
Coventry	d		15 27																	16 27			
Birmingham International ✈	d		15 38																	16 38			
Birmingham New Street 12	d		15 57					16 01	16 20		16 31					16 36				16 57	17 01		
Wolverhampton 7	d		16 15					16 19	16 37		16 49					16 53				17 15	17 19		
Penkridge	d															17 03					17 29		
Stafford	a		16 29					16 35			17 00					17 09	17 22			17 29	17 35		
	d		16 30					16 35			17 01					17 09	17 23			17 30	17 36		
Stoke-on-Trent	a	16 48	16 54								17 19	17 24							17 48	17 54			
Congleton	a																						
Macclesfield	a		17 11									17 41								18 11			
Crewe 10	a							16 56	17 07	17 10						17 30		17 47			17 56		
	d							16 57	17 09	17 11					17 23	17 31		17 49			18 00		
Chester	a														17 46			18 09					
Wrexham General	a																						
Llandudno	a																						
Bangor (Gwynedd)	a																	19 21					
Holyhead	a																	19 55					
Wilmslow	a									17 27													
Stockport	a	17 16	17 27							17 36	17 49	17 55							18 16	18 27			
Manchester Piccadilly 10	a	17 28	17 39							17 49	17 59	18 07							18 28	18 39			
Hartford	a							17 11													18 13		
Warrington Bank Quay	a					17 14			17 26														
	d					17 14			17 27														
Runcorn	a							17 21								17 50	17 55				18 23		
Liverpool South Parkway 7 ✈	a							17 30								17 59					18 32		
Liverpool Lime Street 10	a							17 43								18 10	18 15				18 44		
	d						16 57							17 19									
Manchester Airport ✈	d			16 29									17 00										
Manchester Piccadilly 10	d			16 46									17 15										
Bolton	d			17 06									17 32										
Wigan North Western	a					17 25	17 30		17 37					18 04									
	d					17 25	17 31		17 38														
Preston 8	a			17 30		17 38	17 54		17 51				17 55										
Preston 8	d			17 32	17 35	17 41	17 55		17 53				17 58									18 02	18 02
Blackpool North	a			18 02	18 06		18 24																
Lancaster 6	a					17 54			18 08				18 13									18 18	18 18
	d					17 55			18 08				18 14										18 18
Barrow-in-Furness	a																						19 26
Oxenholme Lake District	a					18 08			18 22				18 28										
	d					18 08			18 23				18 28										
Windermere	a																						
Penrith North Lakes	d								18 49				18 53										
Carlisle 8	a					18 46			19 04				19 10										
	d					18 47			19 04				19 11										
Lockerbie	d												19 30										
Carstairs	a																						
Motherwell	a												20s15										
Glasgow Central 15	a					20 01							20 33										
Haymarket	a								20 16														
Edinburgh 10	a								20 22														
Perth	a																						
Dundee	a																						
Aberdeen	a																						
Inverness	a																						

A until 16 July **B** from 23 July until 10 September

OVERNIGHT SLEEPERS. For sleeper trains, operated by First ScotRail, please refer to Tables 400 - 404

London and West Midlands - North West England and Scotland

		NT	VT	VT	TP	VT	VT	XC	VT	TP	TP	AW	LM	VT	VT	VT	XC	LM	NT	TP	VT	VT
			◇1	◇1	◇1	◇1	◇1	◇1	◇1	◇1	◇1		◇1	◇1	◇1	◇1	◇1	◇1		◇1	◇1	◇1
										A	B											
			☕	☕	trolley	☕	☕	trolley	☕	trolley	trolley			☕	☕	☕	trolley			trolley	☕	☕
London Euston 15 ⊖	d		16 30	16 33			16 40		17 00					17 07	17 10	17 20					17 30	
Watford Junction	d														17 41	17 50						
Milton Keynes Central	d																					
Rugby	d													18 03								
Nuneaton	d																					
Tamworth Low Level	d			17 38																		
Lichfield Trent Valley	d			17 45																		
Coventry	d																17 27					
Birmingham International ✈	d																17 38					
Birmingham New Street 12	d					17 20		17 31					17 36				17 57	18 01				18 20
Wolverhampton 7	d					17 37		17 49					17 53				18 15	18 19				18 37
Penkridge	d												18 03					18 29				
Stafford	a			17 59				18 00					18 09	18 26			18 29	18 35				
	d			17 59				18 01					18 09	18 27			18 30	18 35				
Stoke-on-Trent	a							18 19	18 24							18 48	18 54					
Congleton	a																19 11					
Macclesfield	a								18 41													
Crewe 10	a					18 07	18 10						18 30		18 48			18 56				19 07
	d					18 09	18 11					18 23	18 33		18 50			18 59				19 09
Chester	a											18 46			19 10							
Wrexham General	a																					
Llandudno	a														20 22							
Bangor (Gwynedd)	a														20 56							
Holyhead	a																					
Wilmslow	a						18 27															
Stockport	a						18 36	18 49	18 55							19 16	19 27					
Manchester Piccadilly 10	a						18 49	18 59	19 07							19 28	19 39					
Hartford	a												18 43					19 12				
Warrington Bank Quay	a		18 14			18 26															19 14	19 26
	d		18 14			18 27															19 14	19 27
Runcorn	a			18 31									18 52	18 59				19 22				
Liverpool South Parkway 7 ✈	a												19 02					19 31				
Liverpool Lime Street 10	a			18 51									19 14	19 17				19 44				
	d																					
Manchester Airport ✈	d				17 29					18 00	18 00									18 29		
Manchester Piccadilly 10	d				17 46					18 16	18 16									18 46		
Bolton	d				18 07					18 33	18 33									19 07		
Wigan North Western	a		18 25			18 37															19 25	19 37
	d		18 25			18 38															19 25	19 38
Preston 8	a		18 38		18 38	18 51				18 55	18 55									19 33	19 38	19 54
Preston 8	d	18 34	18 41		18 40	18 53				18 58	18 58								19 34	19 38	19 41	
Blackpool North	a	19 00			19 09														20 00	20 05		
Lancaster 6	a		18 54			19 08				19 13	19 13										19 54	
	d		18 55			19 08					19 14										19 55	
Barrow-in-Furness	a										20 20											
Oxenholme Lake District	a		19 08			19 22															20 08	
	d		19 09			19 24															20 08	
Windermere	a																					
Penrith North Lakes	d		19 34																		20 34	
Carlisle 8	a		19 49			20 01															20 49	
	d		19 51			20 03															20 50	
Lockerbie	d																					
Carstairs	a																					
Motherwell	a																					
Glasgow Central 15	a		21 01			21 17															22 01	
Haymarket	a																					
Edinburgh 10	a																					
Perth	a																					
Dundee	a																					
Aberdeen	a																					
Inverness	a																					

A until 16 July. trolley to Bolton

B from 23 July until 10 September. trolley to Bolton

OVERNIGHT SLEEPERS. For sleeper trains, operated by First ScotRail, please refer to Tables 400 - 404

Table 65

Saturdays

until 10 September

London and West Midlands - North West England and Scotland

		VT	XC	LM	XC	TP	TP	AW	NT	LM	NT	TP	VT	VT	VT	VT	VT	VT	VT	VT	TP	TP	NT
		◇1	◇1	◇1	◇1	◇1	◇1			◇1		◇1	◇1	◇1	◇1	◇1	◇1	◇1	◇1	◇1	◇1	◇1	
						A	B						C						C	D	A	B	
		☕	☕		trolley								☕	☕	☕	☕	☕	☕	☕	☕			
London Euston 15 ⊖	d	17 40											17 43	18 00	18 07	18 10	18 20	18 30					
Watford Junction	d																						
Milton Keynes Central	d												18 13			18 41	18 50						
Rugby	d																						
Nuneaton	d																						
Tamworth Low Level	d																						
Lichfield Trent Valley	d																						
Coventry	d				18 27								18 42										
Birmingham International ✈	d				18 38								18 53										
Birmingham New Street 12	d		18 31	18 36	18 57					19 01			19 20							19 20			
Wolverhampton 7	d		18 49	18 53	19 15					19 19			19 37							19 37			
Penkridge	d			19 03						19 29													
Stafford	a		19 00	19 09	19 29					19 35					19 22								
	d		19 01	19 09	19 30					19 36					19 23								
Stoke-on-Trent	a		19 19		19 54									19 24			19 48						
Congleton	a																						
Macclesfield	a				20 11									19 41									
Crewe 10	a	19 10		19 30						19 58			20 07			19 48				20 07			
	d	19 11						19 23		19 58			20 09			19 50				20 09			
Chester	a							19 46								20 12							
Wrexham General	a																						
Llandudno	a																						
Bangor (Gwynedd)	a																						
Holyhead	a																						
Wilmslow	a	19 27																					
Stockport	a	19 36	19 49		20 27									19 55			20 16						
Manchester Piccadilly 10	a	19 49	19 59		20 39									20 07			20 28						
Hartford	a									20 11													
Warrington Bank Quay	a												20 26					20 14		20 26			
	d												20 27					20 14		20 27			
Runcorn	a									20 24					19 55								
Liverpool South Parkway 7 ✈	a									20 33													
Liverpool Lime Street 10	a									20 46					20 15								
	d								19 23														20 25
Manchester Airport ✈	d					19 00	19 00					19 29									20 00	20 00	
Manchester Piccadilly 10	d					19 16	19 16					19 46									20 16	20 16	
Bolton	d					19 33	19 33					20 07							←		20 33	20 33	
Wigan North Western	a								19 54				20 37					20 25	20 37	20 37			20 57
	d								19 55				20 38					20 25	20 38	20 38			20 57
Preston 8	a					19 58	19 58		20 18			20 33	→					20 38	20 59	20 59	20 57	20 57	21 22
Preston 8	d					20 02	20 02		20 19		20 34	20 38						20 41			21 02	21 02	21 24
Blackpool North	a								20 44		21 00	21 06											21 53
Lancaster 6	a					20 17	20 17											20 54			21 17	21 17	
	d						20 18											20 55				21 18	
Barrow-in-Furness	a						21 20															22 21	
Oxenholme Lake District	a																	21 08					
	d																	21 09					
Windermere	a																						
Penrith North Lakes	d																	21 34					
Carlisle 8	a																	21 49					
	d																	21 51					
Lockerbie	d																						
Carstairs	a																						
Motherwell	a																	22 44					
Glasgow Central 15	a																	23 04					
Haymarket	a																						
Edinburgh 10	a																						
Perth	a																						
Dundee	a																						
Aberdeen	a																						
Inverness	a																						

A until 16 July

B from 23 July until 10 September

C from 16 July until 10 September

D until 9 July

OVERNIGHT SLEEPERS. For sleeper trains, operated by First ScotRail, please refer to Tables 400 - 404

Table 65

Saturdays
until 10 September

London and West Midlands - North West England and Scotland

		VT	VT	XC		VT	AW	VT	VT	XC	TP	AW	VT	LM		VT	VT	XC	LM	XC	AW	VT	VT	LM
		◇1	◇1	◇1		◇1		◇1	◇1	◇1	◇1	◇	◇1	◇1		◇1	◇1	◇1	◇1	◇1		◇1	◇1	◇1
										A														
London Euston 15 ⊖	d	18 33	18 40			19 00		19 07	19 20				19 30			19 40						20 11	20 20	
Watford Junction	d																							
Milton Keynes Central	d								19 50														21 05	
Rugby	d																					21 15		
Nuneaton	d							20 03															21 33	
Tamworth Low Level	d	19 38																						
Lichfield Trent Valley	d	19 46																						
Coventry	d									19 27														
Birmingham International ✈	d									19 38														
Birmingham New Street 12	d			19 31						19 57				20 01			20 20	20 31	20 36	20 57				21 36
Wolverhampton 7	d			19 49						20 16				20 22			20 37	20 49	20 53	21 16				21 59
Penkridge	d													20 31					21 03					22 09
Stafford	a	19 58		20 00				20 26		20 29				20 37			20 49	21 00	21 09	21 29		21 46		22 16
	d	19 59		20 01				20 27		20 30				20 38			20 50	21 01	21 09	21 30		21 46		22 16
Stoke-on-Trent	a			20 19		20 24			20 48	20 54								21 20		21 52			22 05	
Congleton	a																							
Macclesfield	a			20 36		20 41				21 11								21 38		22 10			22 21	
Crewe 10	a		20 10					20 45					21 01	20 58		21 18	21 09		21 30			22 05		22 40
	d		20 11				20 23	20 47				21 00	21 03	21 06		21 19					21 23	22 06		
Chester	a						20 46					21 21									21 46			
Wrexham General	a																							
Llandudno	a																							
Bangor (Gwynedd)	a											22 42												
Holyhead	a											23 18												
Wilmslow	a		20 27													21 34								
Stockport	a		20 36	20 49		20 55			21 16	21 27						21 44		21 53		22 26			22 35	
Manchester Piccadilly 10	a		20 49	20 59		21 07			21 28	21 39						21 53		22 04		22 39			22 51	
Hartford	a													21 19										
Warrington Bank Quay	a												21 19											
	d												21 20											
Runcorn	a	20 32						21 05						21 29								22 24		
Liverpool South Parkway 7 ✈	a													21 38										
Liverpool Lime Street 10	a	20 52						21 25						21 50								22 46		
	d																							
Manchester Airport ✈	d										20 29													
Manchester Piccadilly 10	d										20 46													
Bolton	d										21 07													
Wigan North Western	a												21 32											
	d												21 32											
Preston 8	a										21 33		21 48											
Preston 8	d										21 38													
Blackpool North	a										22 06													
Lancaster 6	a																							
	d																							
Barrow-in-Furness	a																							
Oxenholme Lake District	a																							
	d																							
Windermere	a																							
Penrith North Lakes	d																							
Carlisle 8	a																							
	d																							
Lockerbie	d																							
Carstairs	a																							
Motherwell	a																							
Glasgow Central 15	a																							
Haymarket	a																							
Edinburgh 10	a																							
Perth	a																							
Dundee	a																							
Aberdeen	a																							
Inverness	a																							

A to Birmingham International

OVERNIGHT SLEEPERS. For sleeper trains, operated by First ScotRail, please refer to Tables 400 - 404

Table 65

Saturdays
until 10 September

London and West Midlands - North West England and Scotland

		XC	NT	AW	NT	TP	TP	TP	VT	VT		TP	XC	LM	AW
		◇1				◇1	◇1	◇1	◇1	◇1		◇1	◇1	◇1	
			A				A	B							
London Euston 15 ⊖	d								20 31	21 00					
Watford Junction	d								20u46						
Milton Keynes Central	d									21 45					
Rugby	d								21 36						
Nuneaton	d														
Tamworth Low Level	d								21 53						
Lichfield Trent Valley	d								22 00						
Coventry	d	21 27													
Birmingham International ✈	d	21 38													
Birmingham New Street 12	d	21 57											22 31	22 36	
Wolverhampton 7	d	22 16											22 49	22 56	
Penkridge	d													23 06	
Stafford	a	22 29								22 32			23 01	23 13	
	d	22 30								22 34			23 02	23 13	
Stoke-on-Trent	a	22 50											23 20		
Congleton	a														
Macclesfield	a	23 07											23 38		
Crewe 10	a								22 35	22 58				23 37	
	d			22 23					22 37	22 59					23 21
Chester	a			22 45											23 42
Wrexham General	a														
Llandudno	a														
Bangor (Gwynedd)	a														
Holyhead	a														
Wilmslow	a									23 14					
Stockport	a	23 21								23 23			23 53		
Manchester Piccadilly 10	a	23 32								23 35			00 10		
Hartford	a														
Warrington Bank Quay	a								22 53						
	d								22 54						
Runcorn	a														
Liverpool South Parkway 7 ✈	a														
Liverpool Lime Street 10	a														
	d														
Manchester Airport ✈	d					21 29	22 00	22 00				22 29			
Manchester Piccadilly 10	d					21 46	22 16	22 16				22 46			
Bolton	d					22 07	22 33	22 33				23 07			
Wigan North Western	a								23 04						
	d								23 05						
Preston 8	a					22 33	22 54	22 54	23 19			23 33			
Preston 8	d		21 59		22 32	22 35	22 55	22 55				23 35			
Blackpool North	a				22 59	23 02						00 02			
Lancaster 6	a		22 19				23 11	23 11							
	d		22 19				23 11								
Barrow-in-Furness	a		23 24				00 15								
Oxenholme Lake District	a														
	d														
Windermere	a														
Penrith North Lakes	d														
Carlisle 8	a														
	d														
Lockerbie	d														
Carstairs	a														
Motherwell	a														
Glasgow Central 15	a														
Haymarket	a														
Edinburgh 10	a														
Perth	a														
Dundee	a														
Aberdeen	a														
Inverness	a														

A from 23 July until 10 September

B until 16 July

OVERNIGHT SLEEPERS. For sleeper trains, operated by First ScotRail, please refer to Tables 400 - 404

London and West Midlands - North West England and Scotland

	VT	TP	TP	SR	XC	AW	VT	LM	TP	SR	NT	TP	TP	LM	VT	TP	LM	VT	TP	AW	XC	NT
London Euston d	19p30			21p15			22p00			23p50												
Watford Junction d				21b33						00u10												
Milton Keynes Central d							22p31															
Rugby d							22p54															
Nuneaton d							23p04															
Tamworth Low Level d							23c15															
Lichfield Trent Valley d							23c22															
Coventry d																						
Birmingham International d																						
Birmingham New Street d					22p30	22p55		23p09										05 30			05 57	
Wolverhampton d					22p48	23p13		23p36										05 48			06 16	
Penkridge d								23p46														
Stafford a					23p00	23p30	23c38	23p52										06 00			06 29	
Stafford d					23p01	23p30		23p53										06 01			06 30	
Stoke-on-Trent a					23p20																06 50	
Congleton a																					07 02	
Macclesfield a																					07 11	
Crewe a						23p55	00s03	00 16										06 20				
Crewe d				23b54		23p57					00 44			05 48	05 57		06 12	06 23		06 27		
Chester a						00 18												06 43				
Wrexham General a																						
Llandudno a																						
Bangor (Gwynedd) a						01 45												07 49				
Holyhead a						02 15												08 23				
Wilmslow a																				06 44		
Stockport a							00s26													06 55	07 27	
Manchester Piccadilly a					00 12		00 35													07 07	07 38	
Hartford a																						
Warrington Bank Quay a	21p15									03 15					06 13							
Warrington Bank Quay d	21p15									03 17					06 14							
Runcorn a														06 07			06 31					
Liverpool South Parkway a														06 15			06 39					
Liverpool Lime Street a														06 26			06 53					
Liverpool Lime Street d																						
Manchester Airport d		22p00	22p29						00 01		01 20	04 00				05 45			06 18			
Manchester Piccadilly d		22p16	22p46						00 16		01a36	04 15	05 43			06 03			06 33			
Bolton d		22p33	23p07						00s31			04s29	05 59			06 19			06 50			07 01
Wigan North Western a	21p26	22p48													06 24							07 19
Wigan North Western d	21p26	22p51													06 25							
Preston a	21p39	23p09	23p33						01s05	03 46		05s04	06 26		06 37	06 42			07 11			
Preston d	21p41	23p13	23p35	00u52						03 55			06 37		06 40	06 44			07 14			
Blackpool North a			00 02						01 30			05 33	07 06									
Lancaster a	21p55	23p28													06 54	06 59			07 30			
Lancaster d	21p56	23p29													06 54	07 00			07 30			
Barrow-in-Furness a		00 32																				
Oxenholme Lake District a	22p09														07 08	07 15						
Oxenholme Lake District d	22p09														07 10	07 15						
Windermere a																						
Penrith North Lakes d	22p35														07 37				08 07			
Carlisle a	22p50			02 15						05s16					07 50	07 55			08 24			
Carlisle d	22p51			02 16											07 51	07 56			08 25			
Lockerbie d															08 10	08 16						
Carstairs a										06s21												
Motherwell a										06s56												
Glasgow Central a	00 06									07 20					09 13				09 45			
Haymarket a																09s17						
Edinburgh a				03 58												09 22						
Perth a				05s40																		
Dundee a																						
Aberdeen a																						
Inverness a				08 31																		

b Previous night, stops to pick up only

c Previous night, stops to set down only

OVERNIGHT SLEEPERS. For sleeper trains, operated by First ScotRail, please refer to Tables 400 - 404

London and West Midlands - North West England and Scotland

	TP	NT	LM	LM	AW	VT	XC	TP	AW	LM	XC	TP	VT	NT	NT	LM	VT	VT	XC	VT	TP	AW
London Euston d													06 05					06 36		06 55		
Watford Junction d													06u20					06u51				
Milton Keynes Central d													06 41							07 27		
Rugby d													07 03									
Nuneaton d																						
Tamworth Low Level d																						
Lichfield Trent Valley d																						
Coventry d																						
Birmingham International d																						
Birmingham New Street d				06 01		06 20	06 31			06 36	06 57					07 01	07 20		07 31			
Wolverhampton d				06 18		06 37	06 49			06 54	07 15					07 18	07 37		07 49			
Penkridge d				06 29												07 30						
Stafford a				06 35			07 00			07 08	07 29		07 33			07 36			08 00			
Stafford d				06 36			07 01			07 08	07 31		07 34			07 38			08 01			
Stoke-on-Trent a							07 18												08 19	08 24		
Congleton a																						
Macclesfield a							07 36												08 36	08 41		
Crewe a				06 56		07 07				07 33	07 50		07 53			07 58	08 07	08 10				
Crewe d			06 32	06 57	07 03	07 09			07 23	07 35	07 54		07 55			08 00	08 09	08 11				08 23
Chester a					07 23				07 46													08 46
Wrexham General a																						
Llandudno a																						
Bangor (Gwynedd) a					08 36																	
Holyhead a					09 21																	
Wilmslow a											08 09							08 27				
Stockport a							07 49				08 21							08 37	08 49	08 55		
Manchester Piccadilly a							07 59				08 36							08 49	08 59	09 07		
Hartford a			06 46	07 10						07 48						08 11						
Warrington Bank Quay a						07 26							08 11				08 27					
Warrington Bank Quay d						07 27							08 12				08 28					
Runcorn a			06 59	07 20						08 02						08 24						
Liverpool South Parkway a			07 08	07 30						08 11						08 33						
Liverpool Lime Street a			07 22	07 42						08 24						08 46						
Liverpool Lime Street d		06 57													07 57							
Manchester Airport d								07 00				07 25									07 56	
Manchester Piccadilly d								07 15				07 45									08 15	
Bolton d								07 31				07 59									08 32	
Wigan North Western a		07 30				07 37							08 22		08 30		08 38					
Wigan North Western d		07 31				07 38							08 23		08 31		08 39					
Preston a		07 54				07 51		07 57				08 22	08 36		08 54		08 52				08 58	
Preston d	07 20	07 55				07 53		07 59				08 24	08 37	08 42	08 55		08 54				08 59	
Blackpool North a		08 21						08 29							09 21						09 25	
Lancaster a	07 36					08 08						08 39	08 52	09 02			09 09					
Lancaster d	07 36					08 08						08 40	08 52	09 03			09 09					
Barrow-in-Furness a	08 40													10 07								
Oxenholme Lake District a						08 21							09 05									
Oxenholme Lake District d						08 22							09 06									
Windermere a																						
Penrith North Lakes d													09 32				09 46					
Carlisle a						09 00						09 30	09 47	12 39			10 01					
Carlisle d						09 02						09 30	09 48				10 04					
Lockerbie d												09 50										
Carstairs a																						
Motherwell a																						
Glasgow Central a													11 03				11 17					
Haymarket a						10 16						10s48										
Edinburgh a						10 22						10 55										
Perth a																						
Dundee a																						
Aberdeen a																						
Inverness a																						

OVERNIGHT SLEEPERS. For sleeper trains, operated by First ScotRail, please refer to Tables 400 - 404

Table 65

Saturdays from 17 September

London and West Midlands - North West England and Scotland

		LM	VT	VT	XC	TP	NT	VT	TP	NT	LM	VT	VT	XC	VT	TP		AW	LM	VT	VT	VT
		◇1	◇1	◇1	◇1	◇1		◇1	◇1		◇1	◇1	◇1	◇1	◇1	◇1			◇1	◇1	◇1	◇1
						A										B						
			⊡	⊡	⊼	⊼		⊡				⊡	⊡	⊡	⊡	⊼				⊡	⊡	⊡
London Euston 15 ⊖	d		07 07	07 20				07 30					07 35		08 00					08 07	08 10	08 20
Watford Junction	d																					
Milton Keynes Central	d			07 50									08 06								08 41	08 50
Rugby	d																					
Nuneaton	d																					
Tamworth Low Level	d																					
Lichfield Trent Valley	d																					
Coventry	d				07 27																	
Birmingham International ✈	d				07 38																	
Birmingham New Street 12	d	07 36			07 57						08 01	08 20		08 31					08 36			
Wolverhampton 7 ⇌	d	07 53			08 15						08 19	08 37		08 49					08 53			
Penkridge	d	08 03									08 29								09 03			
Stafford	a	08 09	08 22		08 29						08 35			09 00					09 09	09 22		
	d	08 09	08 23		08 30						08 36			09 01					09 09	09 23		
Stoke-on-Trent	a			08 48	08 54									09 19	09 24							09 48
Congleton	a																					
Macclesfield	a				09 11										09 41							
Crewe 10	a	08 30	08 41								08 56	09 07	09 10						09 30		09 48	
	d	08 31	08 43								08 58	09 09	09 11					09 23	09 31		09 50	
Chester	a																	09 46			10 12	
Wrexham General	a																					
Llandudno	a																					
Bangor (Gwynedd)	a																					
Holyhead	a																					
Wilmslow	a												09 27									
Stockport	a			09 16	09 27								09 36	09 49	09 55							10 16
Manchester Piccadilly 10 ⇌	a			09 28	09 39								09 49	09 59	10 07							10 28
Hartford	a										09 11											
Warrington Bank Quay	a							09 14				09 26										
	d							09 14				09 27										
Runcorn	a	08 50	09 00								09 21								09 50	09 55		
Liverpool South Parkway 7 ✈	a	08 59									09 30								09 59			
Liverpool Lime Street 10	a	09 12	09 21								09 43								10 10	10 15		
	d									08 57												
Manchester Airport ✈	d					08 25										09 00						
Manchester Piccadilly 10 ⇌	d					08 46										09 16						
Bolton	d					09 07										09 33						
Wigan North Western	a							09 25		09 30		09 37										
	d							09 25		09 31		09 38										
Preston 8	a					09 30		09 38		09 54		09 51				09 55						
Preston 8	d					09 32	09 34	09 41	09 45	09 55		09 53				10 08	09 58					
Blackpool North	a						10 01			10 21						10 35						
Lancaster 6	a					09 47		09 54	10 00			10 08					10 13					
	d					09 48		09 55	10 01			10 08					10 14					
Barrow-in-Furness	a								11 04													
Oxenholme Lake District	a					10 04						10 22										
	d					10 05						10 24										
Windermere	a					10 26																
Penrith North Lakes	d							10 31									10 53					
Carlisle 8	a							10 46				11 01					11 10					
	d							10 47				11 03					11 11					
Lockerbie	d																11 30					
Carstairs	a																					
Motherwell	a																					
Glasgow Central 15	a							12 01									12 32					
Haymarket	a											12 16										
Edinburgh 10	a											12 22										
Perth	a																					
Dundee	a																					
Aberdeen	a																					
Inverness	a																					

A ⊼ to Bolton

B ⊼ to Preston

OVERNIGHT SLEEPERS. For sleeper trains, operated by First ScotRail, please refer to Tables 400 - 404

Table 65

Saturdays from 17 September

London and West Midlands - North West England and Scotland

		XC	NT	TP	VT	TP	NT	LM	VT	VT	XC	TP	AW	LM	VT	VT	VT	VT	XC	NT	TP	VT	NT
		◇1		◇1	◇1	◇1		◇1	◇1	◇1	◇1	◇1		◇1	◇1	◇1	◇1	◇1	◇1		◇1	◇1	
		⊼		⊼	⊡				⊡	⊡	⊡	⊼			⊡	⊡	⊡	⊡	⊼		⊼	⊡	
London Euston 15 ⊖	d				08 30					08 40					08 50	09 00	09 07	09 20				09 30	
Watford Junction	d														09 05								
Milton Keynes Central	d														09 25			09 50					
Rugby	d																						
Nuneaton	d																						
Tamworth Low Level	d																						
Lichfield Trent Valley	d																						
Coventry	d	08 27																	09 27				
Birmingham International ✈	d	08 38																	09 38				
Birmingham New Street 12	d	08 57						09 01	09 20		09 31			09 36					09 57				
Wolverhampton 7 ⇌	d	09 15						09 19	09 37		09 49			09 53					10 15				
Penkridge	d													10 03									
Stafford	a	09 29						09 34			10 00			10 09			10 22		10 29				
	d	09 30						09 35			10 01			10 09			10 23		10 30				
Stoke-on-Trent	a	09 54									10 19					10 24		10 48	10 54				
Congleton	a																						
Macclesfield	a	10 11														10 41			11 11				
Crewe 10	a							09 56	10 07	10 10				10 30	10 32								
	d							09 57	10 09	10 11			10 23	10 31	10 43								
Chester	a												10 46		11 10								
Wrexham General	a																						
Llandudno	a																						
Bangor (Gwynedd)	a														12 19								
Holyhead	a														12 55								
Wilmslow	a									10 27													
Stockport	a	10 27								10 36	10 49					10 55		11 16	11 27				
Manchester Piccadilly 10 ⇌	a	10 39								10 49	10 59					11 07		11 28	11 39				
Hartford	a							10 10															
Warrington Bank Quay	a				10 14				10 26													11 14	
	d				10 14				10 27													11 14	
Runcorn	a							10 22						10 50			10 55						
Liverpool South Parkway 7 ✈	a							10 31						10 59									
Liverpool Lime Street 10	a							10 44						11 10			11 15						
	d						09 57																10 57
Manchester Airport ✈	d			09 29								10 00									10 29		
Manchester Piccadilly 10 ⇌	d			09 46								10 16									10 46		
Bolton	d			10 07								10 33									11 07		
Wigan North Western	a				10 25		10 30		10 37													11 25	11 30
	d				10 25		10 31		10 38													11 25	11 31
Preston 8	a			10 33	10 38		10 54		10 51			10 55									11 33	11 38	11 54
Preston 8	d		10 34	10 38	10 41	10 45	10 55		10 53			10 58								11 34	11 38	11 41	11 55
Blackpool North	a		11 01	11 05			11 21													12 00	12 05		12 21
Lancaster 6	a				10 54	11 00			11 08			11 13										11 54	
	d				10 55	11 01			11 08			11 14										11 55	
Barrow-in-Furness	a																						
Oxenholme Lake District	a				11 08	11 17						11 28											
	d				11 08	11 18						11 28											
Windermere	a					11 39																	
Penrith North Lakes	d								11 45			11 53										12 30	
Carlisle 8	a				11 46				12 00			12 10										12 45	
	d				11 47				12 03			12 11										12 47	
Lockerbie	d											12 30											
Carstairs	a																						
Motherwell	a																						
Glasgow Central 15	a				13 01				13 17													14 01	
Haymarket	a											13s33											
Edinburgh 10	a											13 40											
Perth	a																						
Dundee	a																						
Aberdeen	a																						
Inverness	a																						

OVERNIGHT SLEEPERS. For sleeper trains, operated by First ScotRail, please refer to Tables 400 - 404

Table 65

London and West Midlands - North West England and Scotland

		LM	VT	VT	XC	VT	TP	AW	LM	VT	VT	VT	XC	NT	TP	VT	NT	LM	VT	VT	XC	VT
		◇1	◇1	◇1	◇1	◇1	◇1		◇1	◇1	◇1	◇1	◇1		◇1	◇1		◇1	◇1	◇1	◇1	◇1
			☕	☕	☕	☕	A 🛒			☕	☕	☕	🛒		🛒	☕			☕	☕	☕	☕
London Euston 15 ⊖	d			09 40		10 00				10 07	10 10	10 20				10 30				10 40		11 00
Watford Junction	d																					
Milton Keynes Central	d										10 41	10 50										
Rugby	d																					
Nuneaton	d																					
Tamworth Low Level	d																					
Lichfield Trent Valley	d																					
Coventry	d												10 27									
Birmingham International ✈	d												10 38									
Birmingham New Street 12	d	10 01	10 20		10 31				10 36				10 57					11 01	11 20		11 31	
Wolverhampton 7	d	10 19	10 37		10 49				10 53				11 15					11 19	11 37		11 49	
Penkridge	d								11 03													
Stafford	a	10 35			11 00				11 09	11 22			11 29					11 35			12 00	
	d	10 35			11 01				11 09	11 23			11 30					11 35			12 01	
Stoke-on-Trent	a				11 19	11 24						11 48	11 54								12 19	12 24
Congleton	a																					
Macclesfield	a					11 41							12 11									12 41
Crewe 10	a	10 56	11 07	11 10					11 30		11 48							11 56	12 07	12 10		
	d	10 57	11 09	11 11				11 23	11 31		11 50							11 57	12 09	12 11		
Chester	a							11 46			12 12											
Wrexham General	a																					
Llandudno	a																					
Bangor (Gwynedd)	a																					
Holyhead	a																					
Wilmslow	a			11 27																12 27		
Stockport	a			11 36	11 49	11 55						12 16	12 27							12 36	12 49	12 55
Manchester Piccadilly 10	a			11 49	11 59	12 07						12 28	12 39							12 49	12 59	13 07
Hartford	a	11 11																12 10				
Warrington Bank Quay	a		11 26													12 14			12 26			
	d		11 27													12 14			12 27			
Runcorn	a	11 21							11 50	11 55								12 22				
Liverpool South Parkway 7 ✈	a	11 30							11 59									12 31				
Liverpool Lime Street 10	a	11 43							12 10	12 15								12 44				
	d																11 57					
Manchester Airport ✈	d						11 00								11 29							
Manchester Piccadilly 10	d						11 16								11 46							
Bolton	d						11 33								12 07							
Wigan North Western	a		11 37													12 25	12 30		12 37			
	d		11 38													12 25	12 31		12 38			
Preston 8	a		11 51				11 57								12 33	12 38	12 54		12 51			
Preston 8	d		11 53				11 58							12 34	12 38	12 41	12 55		12 53			
Blackpool North	a													13 00	13 05		13 21					
Lancaster 6	a		12 08				12 14									12 54			13 08			
	d		12 08				12 14									12 55			13 08			
Barrow-in-Furness	a						13 10															
Oxenholme Lake District	a		12 22													13 08			13 22			
	d		12 24													13 09			13 24			
Windermere	a																					
Penrith North Lakes	d																					
Carlisle 8	a		13 01													13 46			14 01			
	d		13 03													13 47			14 03			
Lockerbie	d																					
Carstairs	a																					
Motherwell	a																					
Glasgow Central 15	a															15 01			15 17			
Haymarket	a		14 16																			
Edinburgh 10	a		14 22																			
Perth	a																					
Dundee	a																					
Aberdeen	a																					
Inverness	a																					

A 🛒 to Bolton

OVERNIGHT SLEEPERS. For sleeper trains, operated by First ScotRail, please refer to Tables 400 - 404

Table 65

London and West Midlands - North West England and Scotland

		TP	AW	LM	VT	VT	VT	XC	TP	NT	TP	VT	NT	LM	VT	VT	XC	VT	TP	AW	LM	VT	VT
		◇1		◇1	◇1	◇1	◇1	◇1	◇1		◇1	◇1		◇1	◇1	◇1	◇1	◇1	◇1		◇1	◇1	◇1
		🛒			☕	☕	☕	🛒			🛒	☕			☕	☕	☕	☕	🛒			☕	☕
London Euston 15 ⊖	d				11 07	11 10	11 20					11 30				11 40		12 00				12 07	12 10
Watford Junction	d																						
Milton Keynes Central	d					11 41	11 50																12 41
Rugby	d																						
Nuneaton	d																						
Tamworth Low Level	d																						
Lichfield Trent Valley	d																						
Coventry	d							11 27															
Birmingham International ✈	d							11 38															
Birmingham New Street 12	d			11 36				11 57						12 01	12 20		12 31				12 36		
Wolverhampton 7	d			11 53				12 15						12 19	12 37		12 49				12 53		
Penkridge	d			12 03																	13 03		
Stafford	a			12 09	12 22			12 29						12 35			13 00				13 09	13 22	
	d			12 09	12 23			12 30						12 35			13 01				13 09	13 23	
Stoke-on-Trent	a						12 48	12 54									13 19	13 24					
Congleton	a																						
Macclesfield	a							13 11										13 41					
Crewe 10	a			12 30		12 47								12 56	13 07	13 10					13 30		13 47
	d		12 23	12 31		12 49								12 57	13 09	13 11				13 23	13 31		13 49
Chester	a		12 46			13 12														13 46			14 12
Wrexham General	a																						
Llandudno	a																						
Bangor (Gwynedd)	a																						
Holyhead	a																						
Wilmslow	a															13 27							
Stockport	a						13 16	13 27								13 36	13 49	13 55					
Manchester Piccadilly 10	a						13 28	13 39								13 49	13 59	14 07					
Hartford	a													13 11									
Warrington Bank Quay	a											13 14			13 26								
	d											13 14			13 27								
Runcorn	a			12 50	12 55									13 21							13 50	13 55	
Liverpool South Parkway 7 ✈	a			12 59										13 30							13 59		
Liverpool Lime Street 10	a			13 10	13 15									13 43							14 10	14 15	
	d												12 57										
Manchester Airport ✈	d	12 00									12 29								13 00				
Manchester Piccadilly 10	d	12 16									12 46								13 16				
Bolton	d	12 33									13 07								13 33				
Wigan North Western	a											13 25	13 30		13 37								
	d											13 25	13 31		13 38								
Preston 8	a	12 55									13 33	13 38	13 54		13 51				13 55				
Preston 8	d	12 58							13 04	13 34	13 38	13 41	13 55		13 53				13 58				
Blackpool North	a									14 00	14 05		14 21										
Lancaster 6	a	13 13							13 19			13 54			14 08				14 13				
	d	13 14							13 20			13 55			14 08				14 14				
Barrow-in-Furness	a																						
Oxenholme Lake District	a	13 28							13 36			14 08							14 28				
	d	13 28							13 37			14 08							14 28				
Windermere	a								13 56														
Penrith North Lakes	d	13 53													14 45								
Carlisle 8	a	14 10										14 46			15 00				15 06				
	d	14 11										14 47			15 02				15 07				
Lockerbie	d	14 30																	15 27				
Carstairs	a																						
Motherwell	a																						
Glasgow Central 15	a											16 01							16 30				
Haymarket	a	15s31													16 16								
Edinburgh 10	a	15 39													16 22								
Perth	a																						
Dundee	a																						
Aberdeen	a																						
Inverness	a																						

OVERNIGHT SLEEPERS. For sleeper trains, operated by First ScotRail, please refer to Tables 400 - 404

London and West Midlands - North West England and Scotland

Station		VT	XC	NT	TP	VT	NT	LM	VT	VT	XC	VT	TP		AW	LM	VT	VT	VT	XC	NT	TP	VT
		◇1	◇1		◇1	◇1		◇1	◇1	◇1	◇1	◇1	◇1			◇1	◇1	◇1	◇1	◇1		◇1	◇1
		🍴	🛒		🛒	🍴			🍴	🍴	🍴	🍴	🛒				🍴	🍴	🍴	🛒		🛒	🍴
London Euston 15 ⊖	d	12 20				12 30				12 40		13 00					13 07	13 10	13 20				13 30
Watford Junction	d																						
Milton Keynes Central	d	12 50																13 41	13 50				
Rugby	d																						
Nuneaton	d																						
Tamworth Low Level	d																						
Lichfield Trent Valley	d																						
Coventry	d		12 27																	13 27			
Birmingham International ✈	d		12 38																	13 38			
Birmingham New Street 12	d		12 57					13 01	13 20		13 31					13 36				13 57			
Wolverhampton 7	d		13 15					13 19	13 37		13 49					13 53				14 15			
Penkridge	d															14 03							
Stafford	a		13 29					13 35			14 00					14 09	14 22			14 29			
	d		13 30					13 35			14 01					14 09	14 23			14 30			
Stoke-on-Trent	a	13 48	13 54								14 19	14 24							14 48	14 54			
Congleton	a																						
Macclesfield	a		14 11									14 41								15 11			
Crewe 10	a							13 56	14 07	14 10						14 30		14 48					
	d							13 57	14 09	14 11					14 23	14 31		14 50					
Chester	a														14 46			15 12					
Wrexham General	a																						
Llandudno	a																						
Bangor (Gwynedd)	a																						
Holyhead	a																						
Wilmslow	a									14 27													
Stockport	a	14 16	14 27							14 36	14 49	14 55							15 16	15 27			
Manchester Piccadilly 10	a	14 28	14 39							14 49	14 59	15 07							15 28	15 39			
Hartford	a							14 11															
Warrington Bank Quay	a					14 14			14 26														15 14
	d					14 14			14 27														15 14
Runcorn	a							14 21								14 50	14 55						
Liverpool South Parkway 7 ✈	a							14 30								14 59							
Liverpool Lime Street 10	a							14 43								15 10	15 15						
	d						13 57																
Manchester Airport ✈	d				13 29								14 00									14 29	
Manchester Piccadilly 10	d				13 46								14 16									14 46	
Bolton	d				14 07								14 33									15 07	
Wigan North Western	a					14 25	14 30		14 37														15 25
	d					14 25	14 31		14 38														15 25
Preston 8	a				14 33	14 38	14 54		14 51				14 55									15 33	15 38
Preston 8	d			14 34	14 38	14 41	14 55		14 53				14 58	15 04							15 34	15 38	15 41
Blackpool North	a			15 00	15 05		15 21														16 00	16 05	
Lancaster 6	a					14 54			15 08				15 13	15 20									15 54
	d					14 55			15 09				15 14	15 20									15 56
Barrow-in-Furness	a													16 16									
Oxenholme Lake District	a								15 22				15 28										16 08
	d								15 24				15 28										16 09
Windermere	a																						
Penrith North Lakes	d					15 30							15 53										
Carlisle 8	a					15 45			16 01				16 10										16 46
	d					15 47			16 03				16 11										16 47
Lockerbie	d												16 30										
Carstairs	a																						
Motherwell	a																						
Glasgow Central 15	a					17 01			17 17														18 01
Haymarket	a												17s31										
Edinburgh 10	a												17 40										
Perth	a																						
Dundee	a																						
Aberdeen	a																						
Inverness	a																						

OVERNIGHT SLEEPERS. For sleeper trains, operated by First ScotRail, please refer to Tables 400 - 404

London and West Midlands - North West England and Scotland

Station		NT	LM	VT	VT	XC	VT	TP	AW	LM	VT	VT	VT	XC	NT	TP	VT	NT	LM	VT	VT	XC
			◇1	◇1	◇1	◇1	◇1	◇1		◇1	◇1	◇1	◇1	◇1		◇1	◇1		◇1	◇1	◇1	◇1
								A														
				🍴	🍴	🍴	🍴	🛒			🍴	🍴	🍴	🛒		🛒	🍴			🍴	🍴	🍴
London Euston 15 ⊖	d				13 40		14 00				14 07	14 10	14 20				14 30				14 40	
Watford Junction	d																					
Milton Keynes Central	d											14 41	14 50									
Rugby	d																					
Nuneaton	d																					
Tamworth Low Level	d																					
Lichfield Trent Valley	d																					
Coventry	d													14 27								
Birmingham International ✈	d													14 38								
Birmingham New Street 12	d		14 01	14 20		14 31				14 36				14 57					15 01	15 20		15 31
Wolverhampton 7	d		14 19	14 37		14 49				14 53				15 15					15 19	15 37		15 49
Penkridge	d									15 03												
Stafford	a		14 35			15 00				15 09	15 22			15 29					15 35			16 00
	d		14 35			15 01				15 09	15 23			15 30					15 35			16 01
Stoke-on-Trent	a					15 19	15 24						15 48	15 54								16 19
Congleton	a																					
Macclesfield	a						15 41							16 11								
Crewe 10	a		14 56	15 07	15 10					15 30		15 47							15 56	16 08	16 11	
	d		14 57	15 09	15 11				15 23	15 31		15 49							15 57	16 09	16 12	
Chester	a								15 46			16 10										
Wrexham General	a																					
Llandudno	a																					
Bangor (Gwynedd)	a											17 17										
Holyhead	a											17 51										
Wilmslow	a				15 27																16 27	
Stockport	a				15 36	15 49	15 55						16 16	16 27							16 36	16 49
Manchester Piccadilly 10	a				15 49	15 59	16 07						16 28	16 39							16 49	16 59
Hartford	a		15 11																16 10			
Warrington Bank Quay	a			15 26													16 14			16 26		
	d			15 27													16 14			16 27		
Runcorn	a		15 21							15 50	15 55								16 23			
Liverpool South Parkway 7 ✈	a		15 30							15 59									16 32			
Liverpool Lime Street 10	a		15 43							16 10	16 15								16 44			
	d	14 57																15 57				
Manchester Airport ✈	d							15 00								15 29						
Manchester Piccadilly 10	d							15 16								15 46						
Bolton	d							15 33								16 07						
Wigan North Western	a	15 30		15 37													16 25	16 30		16 37		
	d	15 31		15 38													16 25	16 31		16 38		
Preston 8	a	15 54		15 51				15 55								16 33	16 38	16 54		16 51		
Preston 8	d	15 55		15 53				15 58							16 34	16 38	16 41	16 55		16 53		
Blackpool North	a	16 21													17 00	17 07		17 21				
Lancaster 6	a			16 08				16 14									16 54			17 09		
	d			16 09				16 15									16 55			17 10		
Barrow-in-Furness	a							17 18														
Oxenholme Lake District	a																			17 24		
	d																			17 25		
Windermere	a																					
Penrith North Lakes	d			16 45													17 30					
Carlisle 8	a			17 00													17 45			18 03		
	d			17 03													17 47			18 04		
Lockerbie	d																					
Carstairs	a																					
Motherwell	a																					
Glasgow Central 15	a																19 01			19 17		
Haymarket	a			18 14																		
Edinburgh 10	a			18 22																		
Perth	a																					
Dundee	a																					
Aberdeen	a																					
Inverness	a																					

A 🛒 to Bolton

OVERNIGHT SLEEPERS. For sleeper trains, operated by First ScotRail, please refer to Tables 400 - 404

Table 65

Saturdays
from 17 September

London and West Midlands - North West England and Scotland

		VT	TP		AW	LM	VT	VT	VT	XC	TP	NT	VT	NT	LM	VT	VT	XC	VT	TP	NT	AW	LM
		◇1	◇1			◇1	◇1	◇1	◇1	◇1	◇1		◇1		◇1	◇1	◇1	◇1	◇1	◇1			◇1
London Euston 15 ⊖	d	15 00					15 07	15 10	15 20				15 30				15 40		16 00				
Watford Junction	d																						
Milton Keynes Central	d							15 41	15 50														
Rugby	d																						
Nuneaton	d																						
Tamworth Low Level	d																						
Lichfield Trent Valley	d																						
Coventry	d									15 27													
Birmingham International ✈	d									15 38													
Birmingham New Street 12	d					15 36				15 57					16 01	16 20		16 31					16 36
Wolverhampton 7	d					15 53				16 15					16 19	16 37		16 49					16 53
Penkridge	d					16 03																	17 03
Stafford	a					16 09	16 22			16 29					16 35			17 00					17 09
	d					16 09	16 23			16 30					16 35			17 01					17 09
Stoke-on-Trent	a	16 24							16 48	16 54								17 19	17 24				
Congleton	a																						
Macclesfield	a	16 41								17 11									17 41				
Crewe 10	a					16 30		16 47							16 56	17 07	17 10						17 30
	d				16 23	16 31		16 49							16 57	17 09	17 11					17 23	17 31
Chester	a				16 46			17 12														17 46	
Wrexham General	a																						
Llandudno	a																						
Bangor (Gwynedd)	a																						
Holyhead	a																						
Wilmslow	a																17 27						
Stockport	a	16 54							17 16	17 27							17 36	17 49	17 55				
Manchester Piccadilly 10	a	17 07							17 28	17 39							17 49	17 59	18 07				
Hartford	a														17 11								
Warrington Bank Quay	a												17 14			17 26							
	d												17 14			17 27							
Runcorn	a					16 50	16 55								17 21								17 50
Liverpool South Parkway 7 ✈	a					16 59									17 30								17 59
Liverpool Lime Street 10	a					17 10	17 15								17 43								18 10
	d													16 57							17 19		
Manchester Airport ✈	d		16 00								16 29									17 00			
Manchester Piccadilly 10	d		16 16								16 46									17 15			
Bolton	d		16 33								17 06									17 32			
Wigan North Western	a												17 25	17 30		17 37					18 04		
	d												17 25	17 31		17 38							
Preston 8	a		16 55								17 30		17 38	17 54		17 51				17 55			
Preston 8	d		17 00	17 04							17 32	17 35	17 41	17 55		17 53				17 58			
Blackpool North	a										18 02	18 06		18 24									
Lancaster 6	a		17 15	17 20									17 54			18 08				18 13			
	d		17 16	17 21									17 55			18 08				18 14			
Barrow-in-Furness	a																						
Oxenholme Lake District	a		17 30	17 37									18 08			18 22				18 28			
	d		17 30	17 38									18 08			18 23				18 28			
Windermere	a			18 00																			
Penrith North Lakes	d															18 49				18 53			
Carlisle 8	a		18 10										18 46			19 04				19 10			
	d		18 11										18 47			19 04				19 11			
Lockerbie	d		18 30																	19 30			
Carstairs	a																						
Motherwell	a																			20s15			
Glasgow Central 15	a												20 01							20 33			
Haymarket	a		19s31													20 16							
Edinburgh 10	a		19 39													20 22							
Perth	a																						
Dundee	a																						
Aberdeen	a																						
Inverness	a																						

OVERNIGHT SLEEPERS. For sleeper trains, operated by First ScotRail, please refer to Tables 400 - 404

Table 65

Saturdays
from 17 September

London and West Midlands - North West England and Scotland

		VT	VT	VT	XC	LM	TP	NT	VT	VT	TP	VT	VT	XC	VT	TP	AW	LM	VT	VT	VT	XC
		◇1	◇1	◇1	◇1	◇1	◇1		◇1	◇1	◇1	◇1	◇1	◇1	◇1	◇1		◇1	◇1	◇1	◇1	◇1
																A						
London Euston 15 ⊖	d	16 07	16 10	16 20					16 30	16 33			16 40		17 00				17 07	17 10	17 20	
Watford Junction	d																					
Milton Keynes Central	d		16 41	16 50																17 41	17 50	
Rugby	d																					
Nuneaton	d																		18 03			
Tamworth Low Level	d									17 38												
Lichfield Trent Valley	d									17 45												
Coventry	d				16 27																	17 27
Birmingham International ✈	d				16 38																	17 38
Birmingham New Street 12	d				16 57	17 01						17 20		17 31				17 36				17 57
Wolverhampton 7	d				17 15	17 19						17 37		17 49				17 53				18 15
Penkridge	d					17 29												18 03				
Stafford	a	17 22			17 29	17 35				17 59				18 00				18 09	18 26			18 29
	d	17 23			17 30	17 36				17 59				18 01				18 09	18 27			18 30
Stoke-on-Trent	a			17 48	17 54									18 19	18 24						18 48	18 54
Congleton	a																					
Macclesfield	a				18 11										18 41							19 11
Crewe 10	a		17 47			17 56						18 07	18 10					18 30		18 48		
	d		17 49			18 00						18 09	18 11				18 23	18 33		18 50		
Chester	a		18 09														18 46			19 10		
Wrexham General	a																					
Llandudno	a																					
Bangor (Gwynedd)	a		19 21																	20 22		
Holyhead	a		19 55																	20 56		
Wilmslow	a												18 27									
Stockport	a			18 16	18 27								18 36	18 49	18 55						19 16	19 27
Manchester Piccadilly 10	a			18 28	18 39								18 49	18 59	19 07						19 28	19 39
Hartford	a					18 13												18 43				
Warrington Bank Quay	a								18 14			18 26										
	d								18 14			18 27										
Runcorn	a	17 55				18 23				18 31								18 52	18 59			
Liverpool South Parkway 7 ✈	a					18 32												19 02				
Liverpool Lime Street 10	a	18 15				18 44				18 51								19 14	19 17			
	d																					
Manchester Airport ✈	d										17 29					18 00						
Manchester Piccadilly 10	d										17 46					18 16						
Bolton	d										18 07					18 33						
Wigan North Western	a								18 25			18 37										
	d								18 25			18 38										
Preston 8	a								18 38		18 38	18 51				18 55						
Preston 8	d						18 02	18 34	18 41		18 40	18 53				18 58						
Blackpool North	a							19 00			19 09											
Lancaster 6	a						18 18		18 54			19 08				19 13						
	d						18 18		18 55			19 08				19 14						
Barrow-in-Furness	a						19 26									20 20						
Oxenholme Lake District	a								19 08			19 22										
	d								19 09			19 24										
Windermere	a																					
Penrith North Lakes	d								19 34													
Carlisle 8	a								19 49			20 01										
	d								19 51			20 03										
Lockerbie	d																					
Carstairs	a																					
Motherwell	a																					
Glasgow Central 15	a								21 01			21 17										
Haymarket	a																					
Edinburgh 10	a																					
Perth	a																					
Dundee	a																					
Aberdeen	a																					
Inverness	a																					

A to Bolton

OVERNIGHT SLEEPERS. For sleeper trains, operated by First ScotRail, please refer to Tables 400 - 404

London and West Midlands - North West England and Scotland

		LM	NT	TP	VT	VT	VT	XC	VT	LM		TP	AW	NT	VT	VT	VT	XC	LM	NT		TP	VT	VT	TP
		◇1		◇1 ⊼	◇1 ⊡	◇1 ⊡	◇1 ⊡	◇1 ⊡	◇1 ⊡	◇1		◇1			◇1 ⊡	◇1 ⊡	◇1 ⊡	◇1 ⊼	◇1			◇1	◇1 ⊡	◇1 ⊡	◇1
London Euston 15 ⊖	d				17 30		17 40		18 00						18 07	18 10	18 20						18 30		
Watford Junction	d																								
Milton Keynes Central	d															18 41	18 50								
Rugby	d																								
Nuneaton	d																								
Tamworth Low Level	d																								
Lichfield Trent Valley	d																								
Coventry	d																	18 27							
Birmingham International ✈	d																	18 38							
Birmingham New Street 12	d	18 01				18 20		18 31		18 36								18 57	19 01					19 20	
Wolverhampton 7 ⇌	d	18 19				18 37		18 49		18 53								19 15	19 19					19 37	
Penkridge	d	18 29								19 03									19 29						
Stafford	a	18 35						19 00		19 09					19 22			19 29	19 35						
	d	18 35						19 01		19 09					19 23			19 30	19 36						
Stoke-on-Trent	a							19 19	19 24								19 48	19 54							
Congleton	a																								
Macclesfield	a								19 41									20 11							
Crewe 10	a	18 56				19 07	19 10			19 30						19 48			19 58					20 07	
	d	18 59				19 09	19 11						19 23			19 50			19 58					20 09	
Chester	a												19 46			20 12									
Wrexham General	a																								
Llandudno	a																								
Bangor (Gwynedd)	a																								
Holyhead	a																								
Wilmslow	a						19 27																		
Stockport	a						19 36	19 49	19 55								20 16	20 27							
Manchester Piccadilly 10 ⇌	a						19 49	19 59	20 07								20 28	20 39							
Hartford	a	19 12																	20 11						
Warrington Bank Quay	a				19 14	19 26																	20 14	20 26	
	d				19 14	19 27																	20 14	20 27	
Runcorn	a	19 22													19 55				20 24						
Liverpool South Parkway 7 ✈	a	19 31																	20 33						
Liverpool Lime Street 10	a	19 44													20 15				20 46						
	d													19 23											
Manchester Airport ✈	d			18 29								19 00										19 29			20 00
Manchester Piccadilly 10 ⇌	d			18 46								19 16										19 46			20 16
Bolton	d			19 07								19 33										20 07			20 33
Wigan North Western	a				19 25	19 37								19 54									20 25	20 37	
	d				19 25	19 38								19 55									20 25	20 38	
Preston 8	a			19 33	19 38	19 54						19 58		20 18								20 33	20 38	20 59	20 57
Preston 8	d		19 34	19 38	19 41							20 02		20 19						20 34		20 38	20 41		21 02
Blackpool North	a		20 00	20 05										20 44						21 00		21 06			
Lancaster 6	a				19 54							20 17											20 54		21 17
	d				19 55							20 18											20 55		21 18
Barrow-in-Furness	a											21 20													22 21
Oxenholme Lake District	a				20 08																		21 08		
	d				20 08																		21 09		
Windermere	a																								
Penrith North Lakes	d				20 34																		21 34		
Carlisle 8	a				20 49																		21 49		
	d				20 50																		21 51		
Lockerbie	d																								
Carstairs	a																								
Motherwell	a																						22 44		
Glasgow Central 15	a				22 01																		23 04		
Haymarket	a																								
Edinburgh 10	a																								
Perth	a																								
Dundee	a																								
Aberdeen	a																								
Inverness	a																								

OVERNIGHT SLEEPERS. For sleeper trains, operated by First ScotRail, please refer to Tables 400 - 404

London and West Midlands - North West England and Scotland

		NT	VT	VT	XC	VT		AW	VT	VT	XC	TP	AW	VT	LM	VT		VT	XC	LM	XC	AW	VT	VT	LM
			◇1 ⊡	◇1 ⊡	◇1 ⊡	◇1 ⊡			◇1 ⊡	◇1 ⊡	◇1 A ⊼	◇1	◇	◇1 ⊡	◇1	◇1 ⊡		◇1 ⊡	◇1 ⊡	◇1	◇1 A ⊼		◇1 ⊡	◇1 ⊡	◇1
London Euston 15 ⊖	d		18 33	18 40		19 00			19 07	19 20				19 30		19 40							20 11	20 20	
Watford Junction	d																								
Milton Keynes Central	d									19 50														21 05	
Rugby	d																						21 15		
Nuneaton	d								20 03															21 33	
Tamworth Low Level	d		19 38																						
Lichfield Trent Valley	d		19 46																						
Coventry	d										19 27										20 27				
Birmingham International ✈	d										19 38										20 39				
Birmingham New Street 12	d				19 31						19 57				20 01			20 20	20 31	20 36	20 57				21 36
Wolverhampton 7 ⇌	d				19 49						20 16				20 20			20 37	20 49	20 53	21 16				21 59
Penkridge	d														20 29					21 03					22 09
Stafford	a		19 58		20 00				20 26		20 29				20 36			20 49	21 00	21 09	21 29		21 46		22 16
	d		19 59		20 01				20 27		20 30				20 36			20 50	21 01	21 09	21 30		21 46		22 16
Stoke-on-Trent	a				20 19	20 24				20 48	20 54								21 20		21 54			22 05	
Congleton	a																								
Macclesfield	a				20 36	20 41					21 11								21 38		22 11			22 21	
Crewe 10	a			20 10					20 45					21 01	20 57	21 18		21 09		21 30			22 05		22 40
	d			20 11				20 23	20 47				21 00	21 03	21 05	21 19						21 23	22 06		
Chester	a							20 46					21 21									21 46			
Wrexham General	a																								
Llandudno	a																								
Bangor (Gwynedd)	a												22 42												
Holyhead	a												23 18												
Wilmslow	a			20 27												21 34									
Stockport	a			20 36	20 49	20 55				21 16	21 27					21 44			21 53		22 27			22 35	
Manchester Piccadilly 10 ⇌	a			20 49	20 59	21 07				21 28	21 39					21 53			22 04		22 39			22 51	
Hartford	a														21 19										
Warrington Bank Quay	a													21 19											
	d													21 20											
Runcorn	a		20 32						21 05						21 29								22 24		
Liverpool South Parkway 7 ✈	a														21 38										
Liverpool Lime Street 10	a		20 52						21 25						21 50								22 46		
	d	20 25																							
Manchester Airport ✈	d											20 29													
Manchester Piccadilly 10 ⇌	d											20 46													
Bolton	d											21 07													
Wigan North Western	a	20 57												21 32											
	d	20 57												21 32											
Preston 8	a	21 22										21 33		21 48											
Preston 8	d	21 24										21 38													
Blackpool North	a	21 53										22 06													
Lancaster 6	a																								
	d																								
Barrow-in-Furness	a																								
Oxenholme Lake District	a																								
	d																								
Windermere	a																								
Penrith North Lakes	d																								
Carlisle 8	a																								
	d																								
Lockerbie	d																								
Carstairs	a																								
Motherwell	a																								
Glasgow Central 15	a																								
Haymarket	a																								
Edinburgh 10	a																								
Perth	a																								
Dundee	a																								
Aberdeen	a																								
Inverness	a																								

A ⊼ to Birmingham International

OVERNIGHT SLEEPERS. For sleeper trains, operated by First ScotRail, please refer to Tables 400 - 404

Table 65

Saturdays
from 17 September

London and West Midlands - North West England and Scotland

		XC	NT	AW	NT	TP	TP	VT	VT	TP	XC	LM	AW
		◇1				◇1	◇1	◇1	◇1	◇1	◇1	◇1	
London Euston 15 ⊖	d							20 31	21 00				
Watford Junction	d							20u46					
Milton Keynes Central	d								21 45				
Rugby	d							21 36					
Nuneaton	d												
Tamworth Low Level	d							21 53					
Lichfield Trent Valley	d							22 00					
Coventry	d	21 27											
Birmingham International ✈	d	21 38											
Birmingham New Street 12	d	21 57									22 31	22 36	
Wolverhampton 7	d	22 16									22 49	22 56	
Penkridge	d											23 06	
Stafford	a	22 29							22 32		23 01	23 13	
	d	22 30							22 34		23 02	23 13	
Stoke-on-Trent	a	22 50									23 20		
Congleton	a												
Macclesfield	a	23 07									23 38		
Crewe 10	a							22 35	22 58			23 37	
	d			22 23				22 37	22 59				23 21
Chester	a			22 45									23 42
Wrexham General	a												
Llandudno	a												
Bangor (Gwynedd)	a												
Holyhead	a												
Wilmslow	a								23 14				
Stockport	a	23 21							23 23		23 53		
Manchester Piccadilly 10	a	23 32							23 35		00 10		
Hartford	a												
Warrington Bank Quay	a							22 53					
	d							22 54					
Runcorn	a												
Liverpool South Parkway 7 ✈	a												
Liverpool Lime Street 10	a												
	d												
Manchester Airport ✈	d					21 29	22 00			22 29			
Manchester Piccadilly 10	d					21 46	22 16			22 46			
Bolton	d					22 07	22 33			23 07			
Wigan North Western	a							23 04					
	d							23 05					
Preston 8	a					22 33	22 54	23 19		23 33			
Preston 8	d		21 59		22 32	22 35	22 55			23 35			
Blackpool North	a				22 59	23 02				00 02			
Lancaster 6	a		22 19				23 11						
	d		22 19				23 11						
Barrow-in-Furness	a		23 24				00 15						
Oxenholme Lake District	a												
	d												
Windermere	a												
Penrith North Lakes	d												
Carlisle 8	a												
	d												
Lockerbie	d												
Carstairs	a												
Motherwell	a												
Glasgow Central 15	a												
Haymarket	a												
Edinburgh 10	a												
Perth	a												
Dundee	a												
Aberdeen	a												
Inverness	a												

OVERNIGHT SLEEPERS. For sleeper trains, operated by First ScotRail, please refer to Tables 400 - 404

Table 65

Sundays

London and West Midlands - North West England and Scotland

		TP	TP	XC	TP	TP	AW	AW	NT	TP	NT	TP	TP	AW	AW	AW	NT	TP	VT	XC	AW	AW	NT	TP
		◇1	◇1	◇1	◇1	◇1	◇			◇1		◇1	◇1		◇			◇1	◇1	◇1				◇1
		A	B	B	C	D	D		E		F	D		C	D		D	F			D	C	E	C
London Euston 15 ⊖	d																							
Watford Junction	d																							
Milton Keynes Central	d																							
Rugby	d																							
Nuneaton	d																							
Tamworth Low Level	d																							
Lichfield Trent Valley	d																							
Coventry	d																							
Birmingham International ✈	d																							
Birmingham New Street 12	d			22p31															08 45	09 01				
Wolverhampton 7	d			22p49															09 04	09 19				
Penkridge	d																							
Stafford	a			23p01															09 16	09 32				
	d			23p02															09 17	09 33				
Stoke-on-Trent	a			23p20																				
Congleton	a																							
Macclesfield	a			23p38																				
Crewe 10	a																		09 35	09 54				
	d						08 27	08 29						09 24	09 27	09 28			09 37	09 56	09 57	10 07		
Chester	a						08 50							09 42	09 45						10 22	10 32		
Wrexham General	a																							
Llandudno	a																							
Bangor (Gwynedd)	a						10 11							11 04	11 04									
Holyhead	a						10 48							11 49	11 49									
Wilmslow	a							08 47								09 46				10 12				
Stockport	a			23p53																10 21				
Manchester Piccadilly 10	a			00 10				09 06								10 12				10 37				
Hartford	a																							
Warrington Bank Quay	a																		09 54					
	d																		09 54					
Runcorn	a																							
Liverpool South Parkway 7 ✈	a																							
Liverpool Lime Street 10	a																							
	d																							
Manchester Airport ✈	d	22p00	22p29		07 30	07 55				08 47		08 47	09 00											09 29
Manchester Piccadilly 10	d	22p16	22p46		07 46	08 11				09 03		09 03	09 16											09 46
Bolton	d	22p33	23p07		08 06	08 30				09 23		09 23	09 33											10 05
Wigan North Western	a										09 57								10 05					
	d																		10 05					
Preston 8	a	22p54	23p33		08 31	08 56				09 49		09 49	09 57						10 22					10 32
Preston 8	d	22p55	23p35		08 32	08 57			09 05	09 51		10 07	10 00				10 00	10 11					10 29	10 34
Blackpool North	a		00 02		08 58	09 25				10 18													10 53	11 00
Lancaster 6	a	23p11									10 57	10 22	10 15					10 27						
	d	23p11									10 58	10 23	10 16											
Barrow-in-Furness	a	00 15																						
Oxenholme Lake District	a											10 39	10 30											
	d											10 40	10 30											
Windermere	a											10 58												
Penrith North Lakes	d												10 55											
Carlisle 8	a								12 17				11 12				13 05							
	d												11 13											
Lockerbie	d												11 32											
Carstairs	a																							
Motherwell	a																							
Glasgow Central 15	a																							
Haymarket	a												12s32											
Edinburgh 10	a												12 39											
Perth	a																							
Dundee	a																							
Aberdeen	a																							
Inverness	a																							

A from 24 July
B not 22 May
C from 18 September
D until 11 September
E until 23 October
F until 17 July

OVERNIGHT SLEEPERS. For sleeper trains, operated by First ScotRail, please refer to Tables 400 - 404

Table 65

London and West Midlands - North West England and Scotland

		TP	VT	VT	TP	VT	VT	VT	LM	XC	VT	AW	NT	TP	TP	VT	AW	VT	TP	TP	AW	VT	VT
		A										A		B			C		D	E			
London Euston 15 ⊖	d			08 10			08 15	08 20								08 45						09 15	09 20
Watford Junction	d																						
Milton Keynes Central	d			08 56				09 06								09 32							10 07
Rugby	d															10 09							
Nuneaton	d						09 44															10 45	
Tamworth Low Level	d																						
Lichfield Trent Valley	d																						
Coventry	d																						
Birmingham International ✈	d																						
Birmingham New Street 12	d		09 20						09 42	10 01								10 20					
Wolverhampton 7	d		09 37						09 59	10 19								10 37					
Penkridge	d								10 10														
Stafford	a						10 08		10 16	10 32												11 09	
	d						10 08		10 16	10 33												11 09	
Stoke-on-Trent	a							10 19		10 51													11 20
Congleton	a																						
Macclesfield	a							10 36		11 08													11 37
Crewe 10	a		10 06	10 17			10 28		10 37							10 55		11 07				11 30	
	d		10 08	10 19		10 21	10 30		10 38		10 42	10 57				10 57	11 05	11 09			11 27	11 32	
Chester	a										11 02	11 22					11 30				11 48		
Wrexham General	a																						
Llandudno	a																						
Bangor (Gwynedd)	a										12 09										13 10		
Holyhead	a										12 43										13 46		
Wilmslow	a			10 33																			
Stockport	a			10 43				10 51		11 22													11 51
Manchester Piccadilly 10	a			10 55				11 04		11 31													12 04
Hartford	a								10 50														
Warrington Bank Quay	a		10 26			10 37										11 14		11 26					
	d		10 26			10 37										11 14		11 27					
Runcorn	a						10 47		11 00													11 49	
Liverpool South Parkway 7 ✈	a								11 09														
Liverpool Lime Street 10	a						11 09		11 20													12 10	
	d																						
Manchester Airport ✈	d	09 30			10 00										10 30				11 00	11 00			
Manchester Piccadilly 10	d	09 46			10 16										10 46				11 16	11 16			
Bolton	d	10 05			10 33										11 05				11 33	11 33			
Wigan North Western	a		10 37			10 48										11 25		11 37					
	d		10 37			10 48										11 25		11 38					
Preston 8	a	10 32	10 51		10 57	11 02									11 32	11 38		11 51	11 57	11 57			
Preston 8	d	10 34	10 52		10 58	11 04							11 15	11 18	11 34	11 40		11 53	11 58	11 58			
Blackpool North	a	11 00											11 39		12 00								
Lancaster 6	a		11 07		11 13	11 20								11 33		11 54		12 08	12 13	12 13			
	d		11 08		11 14									11 34		11 55		12 08		12 14			
Barrow-in-Furness	a													12 37						13 17			
Oxenholme Lake District	a		11 22		11 28											12 08		12 22					
	d		11 23		11 28											12 08		12 24					
Windermere	a																						
Penrith North Lakes	d				11 53											12 34							
Carlisle 8	a		12 01		12 11											12 49		13 01					
	d		12 02		12 11											12 50		13 03					
Lockerbie	d				12 30																		
Carstairs	a																						
Motherwell	a																						
Glasgow Central 15	a		13 17		13 35											14 01							
Haymarket	a																	14 13					
Edinburgh 10	a																	14 22					
Perth	a																						
Dundee	a																						
Aberdeen	a																						
Inverness	a																						

A until 11 September
B from 18 September until 23 October
C from 18 September
D until 17 July
E from 24 July until 11 September

OVERNIGHT SLEEPERS. For sleeper trains, operated by First ScotRail, please refer to Tables 400 - 404

Table 65

London and West Midlands - North West England and Scotland

		LM	XC	LM	AW	NT	NT	TP	VT	VT	TP	AW	VT	VT	LM	XC	XC	XC	AW	NT	TP	VT
						A	B									C	A	D		B		
London Euston 15 ⊖	d								09 45				10 15	10 20								10 45
Watford Junction	d																					
Milton Keynes Central	d								10 33					11 07								11 33
Rugby	d								11 09													12 09
Nuneaton	d												11 47									
Tamworth Low Level	d																					
Lichfield Trent Valley	d																					
Coventry	d		10 28													11 28	11 29	11 30				
Birmingham International ✈	d		10 40													11 40	11 42	11 43				
Birmingham New Street 12	d	10 42	11 01							11 20					11 42	12 01	12 01	12 01				
Wolverhampton 7	d	10 59	11 19							11 37					11 59	12 19	12 19	12 19				
Penkridge	d	11 10													12 10							
Stafford	a	11 16	11 31										12 13		12 16	12 32	12 32	12 32				
	d	11 16	11 32	11 44									12 13		12 17	12 33	12 33	12 33				
Stoke-on-Trent	a		11 51	12 02										12 24		12 52	12 52	12 52				
Congleton	a																					
Macclesfield	a		12 09											12 40		13 10	13 10	13 10				
Crewe 10	a	11 37		12 26					11 55	12 07			12 33		12 37							12 56
	d	11 38			11 57				11 57	12 09		12 27	12 35		12 38				12 54			12 58
Chester	a				12 20							12 48							13 15			
Wrexham General	a																					
Llandudno	a																					
Bangor (Gwynedd)	a											14 18										
Holyhead	a											14 53										
Wilmslow	a																					
Stockport	a		12 22											12 55		13 28	13 28	13 28				
Manchester Piccadilly 10	a		12 40											13 08		13 40	13 40	13 40				
Hartford	a	11 50													12 50							
Warrington Bank Quay	a								12 14	12 26												13 15
	d								12 14	12 27												13 15
Runcorn	a	12 01											12 52		13 01							
Liverpool South Parkway 7 ✈	a	12 10													13 10							
Liverpool Lime Street 10	a	12 21											13 14		13 21							
	d																					
Manchester Airport ✈	d							11 30			12 00										12 30	
Manchester Piccadilly 10	d							11 46			12 16										12 46	
Bolton	d							12 05			12 33										13 05	
Wigan North Western	a								12 25	12 37												13 26
	d								12 25	12 38												13 26
Preston 8	a							12 32	12 38	12 51	12 57										13 32	13 40
Preston 8	d					12 10	12 14	12 34	12 40	12 53	12 58									13 14	13 34	13 42
Blackpool North	a					12 50	12 38	13 00												13 38	14 00	
Lancaster 6	a								12 54	13 08	13 13											13 56
	d								12 55	13 08	13 14											13 57
Barrow-in-Furness	a																					
Oxenholme Lake District	a								13 08	13 22	13 28											14 10
	d								13 08	13 24	13 28											14 10
Windermere	a																					
Penrith North Lakes	d								13 34		13 53											14 36
Carlisle 8	a								13 49	14 01	14 10											14 51
	d								13 50	14 03	14 11											14 52
Lockerbie	d										14 30											
Carstairs	a																					
Motherwell	a																					
Glasgow Central 15	a								15 02	15 16												16 05
Haymarket	a										15s29											
Edinburgh 10	a										15 37											
Perth	a																					
Dundee	a																					
Aberdeen	a																					
Inverness	a																					

A from 30 October
B until 23 October
C until 11 September
D from 18 September until 23 October

OVERNIGHT SLEEPERS. For sleeper trains, operated by First ScotRail, please refer to Tables 400 - 404

Table 65

London and West Midlands - North West England and Scotland

		VT	VT	VT	TP	AW	LM	VT		VT	XC	XC	AW	TP	TP	TP		NT		NT	TP	VT	VT	VT	XC
		◇1	◇1	◇1	◇1	◇	◇1	◇1		◇1	◇1	◇1		◇1	◇1	◇1					◇1	◇1	◇1	◇1	◇1
					A						B	A		C	D	B		E		F					
		⊡	⊡	⊡	⊼	⊼		⊡		⊡	⊼	⊼				⊼		🚌				⊡	⊡	⊡	⊼
London Euston 15 ⊖	d		11 15	11 20				12 02		12 15												12 25		12 35	
Watford Junction	d																								
Milton Keynes Central	d		12 03	12 08						12 48															
Rugby	d																								
Nuneaton	d																								
Tamworth Low Level	d																								
Lichfield Trent Valley	d																								
Coventry	d										12 28	12 29													
Birmingham International ✈	d										12 40	12 43													
Birmingham New Street 12	d	12 20					12 35				13 01	13 01											13 20		13 31
Wolverhampton 7	d	12 37					12 52				13 19	13 19											13 37		13 49
Penkridge	d						13 03																		
Stafford	a		12 53				13 09	13 24			13 33	13 33													
	d		12 53				13 09	13 25			13 34	13 34													
Stoke-on-Trent	a			13 09						13 50	13 56	13 56													14 19
Congleton	a																								
Macclesfield	a			13 26							14 14	14 14													
Crewe 10	a	13 07	13 13				13 30	13 43															14 07	14 12	
	d	13 09	13 15			13 27	13 31	13 45					13 57										14 09	14 13	
Chester	a					13 47							14 20												
Wrexham General	a																								
Llandudno	a																								
Bangor (Gwynedd)	a					15 12																			
Holyhead	a					15 57																			
Wilmslow	a																							14 29	
Stockport	a			13 41						14 18	14 28	14 28												14 38	
Manchester Piccadilly 10	a			13 53						14 29	14 40	14 40												14 50	14 57
Hartford	a						13 43																		
Warrington Bank Quay	a	13 26																				14 16	14 26		
	d	13 27																				14 16	14 27		
Runcorn	a		13 32				13 54	14 02																	
Liverpool South Parkway 7 ✈	a						14 03																		
Liverpool Lime Street 10	a		13 54				14 14	14 24																	
	d																								
Manchester Airport ✈	d				12 58											13 00					13 30				
Manchester Piccadilly 10	d				13 16											13 16					13 46				
Bolton	d				13 33											13 33					14 05				
Wigan North Western	a	13 37																				14 27	14 37		
	d	13 38																				14 27	14 38		
Preston 8	a	13 51			13 57											13 57					14 32	14 40	14 50		
Preston 8	d	13 53			14 00									14 04	14 04	14 00	14 04	14 10		14 14	14 34	14 42	14 53		
Blackpool North	a																	14 50		14 38	15 00				
Lancaster 6	a	14 08			14 15									14 20	14 20	14 15	14 20					14 56	15 08		
	d	14 08			14 16										14 20	14 16	14 20					14 58	15 09		
Barrow-in-Furness	a														15 16		15 24								
Oxenholme Lake District	a				14 30											14 30							15 22		
	d				14 30											14 30							15 23		
Windermere	a																								
Penrith North Lakes	d	14 45			14 55											14 55						15 32			
Carlisle 8	a	15 00			15 12											15 12						15 47	16 01		
	d	15 03			15 17											15 17						15 48	16 03		
Lockerbie	d																								
Carstairs	a																								
Motherwell	a																								
Glasgow Central 15	a				16 35											16 35						17 00	17 17		
Haymarket	a	16 14																							
Edinburgh 10	a	16 22																							
Perth	a																								
Dundee	a																								
Aberdeen	a																								
Inverness	a																								

A from 18 September until 23 October
B until 11 September, from 30 October
C until 17 July
D from 18 September
E from 30 October
F until 23 October

OVERNIGHT SLEEPERS. For sleeper trains, operated by First ScotRail, please refer to Tables 400 - 404

Table 65

London and West Midlands - North West England and Scotland

		VT	TP	TP		AW	LM	VT	VT	XC	AW	NT	TP	VT		VT	VT	XC	VT	TP	TP	TP	AW	LM
		◇1	◇1	◇1		◇	◇1	◇1	◇1	◇1			◇1	◇1		◇1	◇1	◇1	◇1	◇1	◇1	◇1	◇	◇1
			A	B								C								A	D	E		
		⊡	⊼	⊼		⊼		⊡	⊡	⊼				⊡		⊡	⊡	⊼	⊡				⊼	
London Euston 15 ⊖	d	12 55						13 02	13 15					13 25			13 35		13 55					
Watford Junction	d																							
Milton Keynes Central	d								13 48															
Rugby	d																							
Nuneaton	d																							
Tamworth Low Level	d																							
Lichfield Trent Valley	d																							
Coventry	d									13 26														
Birmingham International ✈	d									13 38														
Birmingham New Street 12	d						13 35			14 01						14 20		14 31						14 35
Wolverhampton 7	d						13 52			14 19						14 37		14 49						14 52
Penkridge	d						14 03																	15 03
Stafford	a						14 10	14 21		14 33														15 10
	d						14 10	14 22		14 34														15 10
Stoke-on-Trent	a	14 26							14 50	14 56								15 19	15 25					
Congleton	a																							
Macclesfield	a	14 42								15 14									15 42					
Crewe 10	a						14 30	14 43								15 07	15 12							15 30
	d					14 27	14 31	14 45			14 57					15 09	15 13						15 27	15 31
Chester	a					14 47					15 20												15 47	
Wrexham General	a																							
Llandudno	a																							
Bangor (Gwynedd)	a					16 18																	17 12	
Holyhead	a					16 53																	17 57	
Wilmslow	a																15 29							
Stockport	a	14 56							15 18	15 28							15 38		15 56					
Manchester Piccadilly 10	a	15 09							15 29	15 40							15 50	16 00	16 09					
Hartford	a						14 43																	15 43
Warrington Bank Quay	a													15 16		15 26								
	d													15 16		15 27								
Runcorn	a						14 54	15 02																15 54
Liverpool South Parkway 7 ✈	a						15 03																	16 03
Liverpool Lime Street 10	a						15 14	15 24																16 14
	d																							
Manchester Airport ✈	d		13 58	14 00									14 30							14 58	15 00	15 00		
Manchester Piccadilly 10	d		14 16	14 16									14 46							15 16	15 16	15 16		
Bolton	d		14 33	14 33									15 05							15 33	15 33	15 33		
Wigan North Western	a													15 27		15 37								
	d													15 27		15 38								
Preston 8	a		14 57	14 57									15 32	15 40		15 51				15 57	15 57	15 57		
Preston 8	d		15 00	15 00								15 14	15 34	15 42		15 53				16 00	16 00	16 00		
Blackpool North	a											15 39	16 00											
Lancaster 6	a		15 15	15 15										15 56		16 08				16 15	16 15	16 15		
	d		15 16	15 16										15 58		16 08				16 16		16 16		
Barrow-in-Furness	a																			17 19		17 19		
Oxenholme Lake District	a		15 30	15 30										16 10										
	d		15 30	15 30										16 11										
Windermere	a																							
Penrith North Lakes	d		15 55	15 55												16 45								
Carlisle 8	a		16 12	16 12										16 48		17 00								
	d		16 13	16 13										16 49		17 02								
Lockerbie	d		16 32	16 32																				
Carstairs	a																							
Motherwell	a																							
Glasgow Central 15	a													18 01										
Haymarket	a		17s30	17s30												18 13								
Edinburgh 10	a		17 39	17 39												18 22								
Perth	a																							
Dundee	a																							
Aberdeen	a																							
Inverness	a																							

A from 18 September until 23 October
B until 11 September, from 30 October
C until 23 October
D until 17 July
E from 24 July until 11 September, from 30 October

OVERNIGHT SLEEPERS. For sleeper trains, operated by First ScotRail, please refer to Tables 400 - 404

Table 65

Sundays

London and West Midlands - North West England and Scotland

		VT	VT	XC	AW	NT	NT	TP	VT	VT	VT	XC	XC	VT	TP	TP	AW	LM	VT	VT	VT	VT	XC
		◇1	◇1	◇1				◇1	◇1	◇1	◇1	◇1	◇1	◇1	◇1	◇1	◇	◇1	◇1	◇1	◇1	◇1	◇1
					A	B	C					D	E		F	G			H	I			
		🍴	🍴	☕					🍴	🍴	🍴	☕	☕	🍴	☕	☕	☕		🍴	🍴	🍴	🍴	☕
London Euston [15] ⊖	d	14 02	14 15						14 25		14 35			14 55					15 02	15 02	15 05	15 15	
Watford Junction	d																						
Milton Keynes Central	d		14 48																		15 39	15 48	
Rugby	d																						
Nuneaton	d																						
Tamworth Low Level	d																						
Lichfield Trent Valley	d																						
Coventry	d			14 26																			15 26
Birmingham International ✈	d			14 38																			15 38
Birmingham New Street [12]	d			15 01						15 20		15 31	15 31					15 35					16 01
Wolverhampton [7] ⛴	d			15 19						15 37		15 49	15 49					15 52					16 19
Penkridge	d																	16 03					
Stafford	a	15 24		15 33														16 09	16 20	16 21			16 34
	d	15 25		15 34														16 09	16 21	16 22			16 34
Stoke-on-Trent	a		15 50	15 56								16 19	16 19	16 24								16 50	16 56
Congleton	a																						
Macclesfield	a			16 14										16 42									17 14
Crewe [10]	a	15 43								16 07	16 12							16 30			16 50		
	d	15 45			15 57					16 09	16 13						16 27	16 31			16 52		
Chester	a				16 20												16 47				17 14		
Wrexham General	a																						
Llandudno	a																						
Bangor (Gwynedd)	a																18 18						
Holyhead	a																18 54						
Wilmslow	a										16 29												
Stockport	a		16 18	16 28							16 38			16 56								17 18	17 28
Manchester Piccadilly [10] ⛴	a		16 29	16 40							16 50	16 59	17 00	17 09								17 29	17 40
Hartford	a																	16 43					
Warrington Bank Quay	a								16 16	16 26													
	d								16 16	16 27													
Runcorn	a	16 02																16 54	16 57	16 57			
Liverpool South Parkway [7] ✈	a																	17 03					
Liverpool Lime Street [10]	a	16 24																17 14	17 16	17 16			
	d																						
Manchester Airport ✈	d							15 30							15 58	16 00							
Manchester Piccadilly [10] ⛴	d							15 46							16 16	16 16							
Bolton	d							16 05							16 33	16 33							
Wigan North Western	a								16 27	16 37													
	d								16 27	16 38													
Preston [8]	a							16 32	16 40	16 51					16 57	16 57							
Preston [8]	d					16 10	16 14	16 34	16 42	16 53					17 00	17 00							
Blackpool North	a					16 50	16 38	17 00															
Lancaster [6]	a								16 56	17 08					17 15	17 15							
	d								16 57	17 08					17 16	17 16							
Barrow-in-Furness	a																						
Oxenholme Lake District	a									17 22					17 30	17 30							
	d									17 23					17 30	17 30							
Windermere	a																						
Penrith North Lakes	d								17 32						17 55	17 55							
Carlisle [8]	a								17 47	18 01					18 12	18 12							
	d								17 48	18 03					18 13	18 13							
Lockerbie	d																						
Carstairs	a																						
Motherwell	a																						
Glasgow Central [15]	a								19 00	19 17													
Haymarket	a														19s29	19s29							
Edinburgh [10]	a														19 36	19 36							
Perth	a																						
Dundee	a																						
Aberdeen	a																						
Inverness	a																						

A until 11 September
B from 30 October
C until 23 October
D from 26 June
E until 19 June
F from 18 September until 23 October
G until 11 September, from 30 October
H until 10 July, from 18 September
I from 17 July until 11 September

OVERNIGHT SLEEPERS. For sleeper trains, operated by First ScotRail, please refer to Tables 400 - 404

Table 65

Sundays

London and West Midlands - North West England and Scotland

		TP	NT	TP	VT	VT	VT	XC	VT	TP		TP	AW	AW	LM	VT	VT	VT	XC	TP	TP	TP	TP
		◇1		◇1	◇1	◇1	◇1	◇1	◇1	◇1		◇1	◇	◇	◇1	◇1	◇1	◇1	◇1	◇1	◇1	◇1	◇1
		A	B							C		D	A	E						F	E	G	H
					🍴	🍴	🍴	☕	🍴	☕		☕				🍴	🍴	🍴	☕			☕	☕
London Euston [15] ⊖	d				15 25		15 35		15 55							16 02	16 05	16 15					
Watford Junction	d																						
Milton Keynes Central	d																16 39	16 48					
Rugby	d																						
Nuneaton	d																						
Tamworth Low Level	d																						
Lichfield Trent Valley	d																						
Coventry	d																		16 26				
Birmingham International ✈	d																		16 38				
Birmingham New Street [12]	d					16 20		16 31							16 35				17 01				
Wolverhampton [7] ⛴	d					16 37		16 49							16 52				17 19				
Penkridge	d														17 03								
Stafford	a														17 09	17 24			17 35				
	d														17 09	17 25			17 36				
Stoke-on-Trent	a							17 19	17 25									17 50	17 56				
Congleton	a																						
Macclesfield	a								17 42										18 14				
Crewe [10]	a					17 07	17 12								17 30		17 50						
	d					17 09	17 13						17 27	17 27	17 31		17 52						
Chester	a												17 48	17 46			18 14						
Wrexham General	a																						
Llandudno	a																						
Bangor (Gwynedd)	a													19 12									
Holyhead	a													19 54									
Wilmslow	a						17 29																
Stockport	a						17 38		17 56									18 18	18 28				
Manchester Piccadilly [10] ⛴	a						17 50	17 56	18 09									18 29	18 40				
Hartford	a														17 43								
Warrington Bank Quay	a				17 16	17 26																	
	d				17 16	17 27																	
Runcorn	a														17 54	17 57							
Liverpool South Parkway [7] ✈	a														18 03								
Liverpool Lime Street [10]	a														18 14	18 16							
	d																						
Manchester Airport ✈	d			16 30						16 58		17 00										17 00	
Manchester Piccadilly [10] ⛴	d			16 46						17 16		17 16										17 16	
Bolton	d			17 05						17 33		17 33										17 33	
Wigan North Western	a				17 27	17 37																	
	d				17 27	17 38																	
Preston [8]	a			17 32	17 40	17 51				17 57		17 57										17 57	
Preston [8]	d	17 04	17 14	17 34	17 42	17 53				18 06	18 08	18 06								18 06	18 06	18 08	18 08
Blackpool North	a		17 38	18 00																			
Lancaster [6]	a	17 21			17 56	18 08				18 22	18 23	18 22								18 22	18 22	18 23	18 23
	d	17 21			17 57	18 08				18 22	18 24										18 22	18 24	18 24
Barrow-in-Furness	a									19 26											19 26		
Oxenholme Lake District	a	17 39			18 10	18 22					18 38											18 38	18 38
	d	17 39			18 10	18 23					18 38											18 38	18 38
Windermere	a	17 58																					
Penrith North Lakes	d					18 49					19 03											19 03	19 03
Carlisle [8]	a				18 48	19 04					19 18											19 18	19 18
	d				18 49	19 04					19 21											19 21	19 21
Lockerbie	d										19 40											19 40	19 40
Carstairs	a																						
Motherwell	a										20s27											20s27	20s27
Glasgow Central [15]	a				20 01						20 45											20 45	20 45
Haymarket	a																						
Edinburgh [10]	a					20 22																	
Perth	a																						
Dundee	a																						
Aberdeen	a																						
Inverness	a																						

A until 11 September
B until 23 October
C from 18 September until 23 October. ☕ to Preston
D until 19 June. ☕ to Preston
E from 18 September
F until 19 June
G from 26 June until 11 September, from 30 October
H from 26 June until 11 September

OVERNIGHT SLEEPERS. For sleeper trains, operated by First ScotRail, please refer to Tables 400 - 404

London and West Midlands - North West England and Scotland

		TP		NT	TP	TP	NT	TP	VT	VT	VT	XC		VT	TP	TP	AW	LM	VT	VT	VT	XC		NT
		◇1			◇1	◇1		◇1	◇1	◇1	◇1	◇1		◇1	◇1	◇1	◇	◇1	◇1	◇1	◇1	◇1		
		A		B 🚌	C	D	E								F	G								B 🚌
		⊼							⊡	⊡	⊡	⊼		⊡	⊼	⊼			⊡	⊡	⊡	⊼		
London Euston 15 ⊖	d								16 25		16 35			16 55					17 02	17 05	17 15			
Watford Junction	d																							
Milton Keynes Central	d																			17 39	17 48			
Rugby	d																							
Nuneaton	d																			18 10				
Tamworth Low Level	d																							
Lichfield Trent Valley	d																							
Coventry	d																					17 26		
Birmingham International ✈	d																					17 38		
Birmingham New Street 12	d									17 20		17 31						17 35				18 01		
Wolverhampton 7 ⇌	d									17 37		17 49						17 52				18 19		
Penkridge	d																	18 03						
Stafford	a																	18 09	18 24			18 35		
	d																	18 09	18 25			18 36		
Stoke-on-Trent	a											18 19		18 25							18 50	18 56		
Congleton	a																							
Macclesfield	a													18 42								19 15		
Crewe 10	a									18 07	18 12							18 30		18 53				
	d									18 09	18 13						18 27	18 31		18 56				
Chester	a																18 47			19 14				
Wrexham General	a																							
Llandudno	a																							
Bangor (Gwynedd)	a																20 08			20 27				
Holyhead	a																20 44			20 59				
Wilmslow	a										18 29													
Stockport	a										18 38			18 56							19 18	19 28		
Manchester Piccadilly 10 ⇌	a										18 50	18 56		19 09							19 29	19 40		
Hartford	a																	18 43						
Warrington Bank Quay	a								18 16	18 26														
	d								18 17	18 27														
Runcorn	a																	18 54	18 57					
Liverpool South Parkway 7 ✈	a																	19 03						
Liverpool Lime Street 10	a																	19 14	19 19					
	d																							
Manchester Airport ✈	d	17 00						17 30							17 58	18 00								
Manchester Piccadilly 10 ⇌	d	17 16						17 46							18 16	18 16								
Bolton	d	17 33						18 05							18 33	18 33								
Wigan North Western	a								18 27	18 37														
	d								18 28	18 38														
Preston 8	a	17 57						18 32	18 40	18 51					18 57	18 57								
Preston 8	d	18 00	18 12	18 10	18 12	18 12	18 14	18 34	18 42	18 53					19 00	19 00								19 10
Blackpool North	a			18 50			18 38	19 00																19 50
Lancaster 6	a	18 15	18 28		18 28	18 28			18 56	19 08					19 15	19 15								
	d	18 16				18 28			18 58	19 08					19 16	19 16								
Barrow-in-Furness	a					19 32																		
Oxenholme Lake District	a	18 30							19 10	19 22					19 30	19 30								
	d	18 30							19 11	19 24					19 30	19 30								
Windermere	a																							
Penrith North Lakes	d	18 55							19 36						19 55	19 55								
Carlisle 8	a	19 12							19 51	20 01					20 12	20 12								
	d	19 21							19 53	20 03					20 13	20 13								
Lockerbie	d	19 40													20 32	20 32								
Carstairs	a																							
Motherwell	a	20s27																						
Glasgow Central 15	a	20 45							21 08	21 17														
Haymarket	a														21s30	21s30								
Edinburgh 10	a														21 39	21 39								
Perth	a																							
Dundee	a																							
Aberdeen	a																							
Inverness	a																							

A until 19 June
B from 30 October
C from 26 June until 17 July
D from 24 July until 11 September
E until 23 October
F from 18 September until 23 October
G until 11 September, from 30 October

OVERNIGHT SLEEPERS. For sleeper trains, operated by First ScotRail, please refer to Tables 400 - 404

London and West Midlands - North West England and Scotland

		NT	TP	VT	VT	VT	XC	VT	TP		TP	TP	AW	LM	VT	VT	VT	XC	NT		NT	TP	VT	VT	VT
			◇1	◇1	◇1	◇1	◇1	◇1	◇1		◇1	◇1		◇1	◇1	◇1	◇1	◇1				◇1	◇1	■ 1	◇1
		A							B		C	D							E 🚌		A				
				⊡	⊡	⊡		⊡							⊡	⊡	⊡	⊼					⊡	⊡	⊡
London Euston 15 ⊖	d			17 25		17 35		17 55							18 02	18 05	18 15						18 25		18 35
Watford Junction	d																								
Milton Keynes Central	d															18 39	18 48								
Rugby	d																								
Nuneaton	d																								
Tamworth Low Level	d																								
Lichfield Trent Valley	d																								
Coventry	d																	18 26							
Birmingham International ✈	d																	18 38							
Birmingham New Street 12	d				18 20		18 31							18 35				19 01						19 20	
Wolverhampton 7 ⇌	d				18 37		18 49							18 52				19 19						19 37	
Penkridge	d													19 03											
Stafford	a													19 10	19 24			19 37							
	d													19 10	19 25			19 38							
Stoke-on-Trent	a						19 19	19 25									19 50	19 56							
Congleton	a																								
Macclesfield	a							19 42										20 14							
Crewe 10	a				19 07	19 12								19 30		19 50								20 07	20 12
	d				19 09	19 13							19 27	19 31		19 52								20 09	20 13
Chester	a												19 48			20 11									
Wrexham General	a																								
Llandudno	a																								
Bangor (Gwynedd)	a															21 23									
Holyhead	a															21 57									
Wilmslow	a					19 29																			20 29
Stockport	a					19 38		19 56									20 18	20 28							20 38
Manchester Piccadilly 10 ⇌	a					19 50	19 58	20 09									20 29	20 40							20 50
Hartford	a													19 43											
Warrington Bank Quay	a			19 16	19 26																		20 16	20 26	
	d			19 16	19 27																		20 16	20 27	
Runcorn	a													19 54	19 58										
Liverpool South Parkway 7 ✈	a													20 03											
Liverpool Lime Street 10	a													20 14	20 16										
	d																								
Manchester Airport ✈	d		18 30						18 58		19 00	19 00										19 30			
Manchester Piccadilly 10 ⇌	d		18 46						19 16		19 16	19 16										19 46			
Bolton	d		19 05						19 33		19 33	19 33										20 05			
Wigan North Western	a			19 27	19 37																		20 27	20 37	
	d			19 27	19 38																		20 27	20 38	
Preston 8	a		19 32	19 40	19 51				19 57		19 57	19 57										20 32	20 40	20 51	
Preston 8	d	19 14	19 34	19 42	19 53				20 00		20 00	20 00							20 10		20 15	20 34	20 42	20 53	
Blackpool North	a	19 38	20 00																20 50		20 39	21 00			
Lancaster 6	a			19 56	20 08				20 15		20 15	20 15											20 56	21 08	
	d			19 57	20 08				20 16			20 16											20 57	21 08	
Barrow-in-Furness	a								21 20			21 20													
Oxenholme Lake District	a			20 10																			21 10	21 22	
	d			20 10																			21 11	21 24	
Windermere	a																								
Penrith North Lakes	d			20 36	20 45																		21 36		
Carlisle 8	a			20 51	21 00																		21 51	22 01	
	d			20 52	21 02																		21 52	22 03	
Lockerbie	d																							22 23	
Carstairs	a																								
Motherwell	a																						22 48	23 07	
Glasgow Central 15	a			22 07																			23 09	23 22	
Haymarket	a				22 13																				
Edinburgh 10	a				22 21																				
Perth	a																								
Dundee	a																								
Aberdeen	a																								
Inverness	a																								

A until 23 October
B from 18 September until 23 October
C until 17 July
D from 24 July until 11 September, from 30 October
E from 30 October

OVERNIGHT SLEEPERS. For sleeper trains, operated by First ScotRail, please refer to Tables 400 - 404

London and West Midlands - North West England and Scotland

	XC	VT	AW	LM	VT	VT	VT	VT	XC	VT	NT	TP	VT	VT	XC	XC	VT	AW	VT	VT	VT	XC
	◇1	◇1		◇1	◇1	◇1	◇1	◇1	◇1	◇1		◇1	◇1	◇1	◇1	◇1	◇1	◇	◇1	◇1	◇1	◇1
					A	B			C		D				E	F						C
	⊥	⊐			⊐	⊐	⊐	⊐	⊥	⊐			⊐	⊐	⊥		⊐		⊐	⊐	⊐	⊥
London Euston 15 ⊖ d		18 55			19 02	19 02	19 05	19 15					19 25	19 35			19 55		20 02	20 05	20 15	
Watford Junction d																						
Milton Keynes Central d							19 39	19 48												20 38	20 48	
Rugby d																						
Nuneaton d					20 01	20 02													21 01			
Tamworth Low Level d																						
Lichfield Trent Valley d																						
Coventry d									19 26													20 26
Birmingham International ✈ d									19 38													20 38
Birmingham New Street 12 d	19 31			19 35					20 01	20 20					20 31	20 31						21 01
Wolverhampton 7 d	19 49			19 52					20 19	20 38					20 52	20 52						21 19
Penkridge d				20 03																		
Stafford a				20 09	20 25	20 26			20 36	20 51										21 31		21 36
d				20 09	20 30	20 30			20 37	20 52										21 33		21 37
Stoke-on-Trent a	20 19	20 25						20 50	20 56						21 19	21 19	21 25				21 50	21 56
Congleton a																						
Macclesfield a		20 42							21 15								21 42					22 14
Crewe 10 a				20 30	20 48	20 48	20 53			21 10				21 13					21 44	21 53		
d			20 27	20 31	20 50	20 50	20 55							21 14				21 27	21 46	21 55		
Chester a			20 48				21 14											21 46				
Wrexham General a																						
Llandudno a																						
Bangor (Gwynedd) a							22 22											23 10				
Holyhead a							22 56											23 55				
Wilmslow a														21 30								
Stockport a		20 56						21 18	21 28					21 39			21 56				22 18	22 28
Manchester Piccadilly 10 a	21 00	21 09						21 29	21 40					21 50	21 56	21 56	22 09				22 29	22 40
Hartford a				20 43																		
Warrington Bank Quay a													21 16									
d													21 16									
Runcorn a				20 54	21 07	21 07													22 03	22 12		
Liverpool South Parkway 7 ✈ a				21 03																		
Liverpool Lime Street 10 a				21 14	21 28	21 28													22 23	22 33		
d																						
Manchester Airport ✈ d												20 30										
Manchester Piccadilly 10 d												20 46										
Bolton d												21 05										
Wigan North Western a													21 27									
d													21 27									
Preston 8 a												21 32	21 40									
Preston 8 d											21 14	21 34	21 42									
Blackpool North a											21 38	22 00										
Lancaster 6 a													21 56									
d													21 57									
Barrow-in-Furness a																						
Oxenholme Lake District a													22 10									
d													22 11									
Windermere a																						
Penrith North Lakes d													22 36									
Carlisle 8 a													22 51									
d													22 53									
Lockerbie d																						
Carstairs a																						
Motherwell a																						
Glasgow Central 15 a													00 02									
Haymarket a																						
Edinburgh 10 a																						
Perth a																						
Dundee a																						
Aberdeen a																						
Inverness a																						

A until 10 July, from 18 September
B from 17 July until 11 September
C ⊥ to Birmingham International
D until 23 October
E until 19 June, from 7 August
F from 26 June until 31 July

OVERNIGHT SLEEPERS. For sleeper trains, operated by First ScotRail, please refer to Tables 400 - 404

London and West Midlands - North West England and Scotland

	AW	AW	NT	NT	TP	VT	VT	VT	LM	XC	AW	VT	AW	SR	VT	VT	AW	VT	SR
														⊞					⊞
					◇1	◇1	◇1	◇1	◇1	◇1	◇	◇1			◇1	◇1	◇	◇1	
	A	B	C	D															
						⊐	⊐	⊐				⊐		⊐	⊐	⊐		⊐	⊐
London Euston 15 ⊖ d						20 25		20 35				20 50		20 55	21 21	21 25		21 51	23 27
Watford Junction d														21u17					23u47
Milton Keynes Central d												21 37				22 14		22 38	
Rugby d												22 01						23 18	
Nuneaton d															22 52			23 29	
Tamworth Low Level d						21 32													
Lichfield Trent Valley d						21 39													
Coventry d										21 26									
Birmingham International ✈ d										21 38							22 40		
Birmingham New Street 12 d							21 20		21 35	22 01							22 55		
Wolverhampton 7 d							21 38		21 58	22 19							23 15		
Penkridge d									22 08										
Stafford a							21 56	21 59	22 16	22 36					23 16		23 30	23s53	
d							21 57	22 00	22 16	22 37					23 17		23 31		
Stoke-on-Trent a										22 55						23 29			
Congleton a																			
Macclesfield a										23 12						23 45			
Crewe 10 a						22 10	22 17	22 20	22 39			22 49			23 37		23 55	00s12	
d	21 57	22 00				22 13	22 18	22 21			22 29	22 51	23 38	23u39	23 39		00 10		
Chester a	22 18	22 21									22 50		23 59				00 31		
Wrexham General a																			
Llandudno a																			
Bangor (Gwynedd) a											00 12						01 41		
Holyhead a											00 49						02 17		
Wilmslow a								22 36											
Stockport a								22 45		23 27						23 59		00s41	
Manchester Piccadilly 10 a								22 57		23 41						00 12		00 53	
Hartford a																			
Warrington Bank Quay a						22 29	22 36					23 08							02 42
d						22 30	22 36					23 08							02 44
Runcorn a															23 56				
Liverpool South Parkway 7 ✈ a																			
Liverpool Lime Street 10 a															00 23				
d																			
Manchester Airport ✈ d					21 30														
Manchester Piccadilly 10 d					21 46														
Bolton d					22 05														
Wigan North Western a						22 40	22 47					23 19							
d						22 41	22 47					23 19							
Preston 8 a					22 28	22 58	23 07					23 41							03 12
Preston 8 d			22 10	22 14	22 29									00u30					03 16
Blackpool North a			22 50	22 38	22 55														
Lancaster 6 a																			
d																			
Barrow-in-Furness a																			
Oxenholme Lake District a																			
d																			
Windermere a																			
Penrith North Lakes d																			
Carlisle 8 a														01 53					05s04
d														01 55					
Lockerbie d																			
Carstairs a																			06s20
Motherwell a																			06s56
Glasgow Central 15 a																			07 20
Haymarket a																			
Edinburgh 10 a														03 58					
Perth a														05s40					
Dundee a																			
Aberdeen a																			
Inverness a														08 31					

A until 11 September
B from 18 September
C from 30 October
D until 23 October

OVERNIGHT SLEEPERS. For sleeper trains, operated by First ScotRail, please refer to Tables 400 - 404

Scotland and North West England - West Midlands and London

Miles	Miles	Miles	Miles	Miles			NT MO	TP MX	TP MO	NT MX	SR MO	SR MO	SR MX	SR MX	TP	AW	TP	TP	LM	XC MTO	XC	VT	SR MO
								◇1	◇1		🛏 A	🛏 B	🛏 C	🛏 D	◇1		◇1 E	◇1	1	◇1 ⌶	◇1 F ⌶	◇1 ⊠	🛏
—	0	—	—	—	Inverness	d																	20p25
—	—	0	—	—	Aberdeen	d																	
—	—	71¼	—	—	Dundee	d																	
—	118	—	—	—	Perth	d																	23b00
—	130¼	187¼	—	—	**Edinburgh** 10	d																	01 06
—	131½	188½	—	—	Haymarket	d																	
0	—	—	—	—	**Glasgow Central** 15	d					23p15	23p15	23p40	23p40									
12¾	—	—	—	—	Motherwell	d					23b31	23b31	23b56	23b56									
28¾	158	—	—	—	Carstairs	d					23b47	23b47	00u16	00u16									
77	—	263½	—	—	Lockerbie	d																	
102¼	—	—	—	—	**Carlisle** 8	a																	02 51
—	—	—	—	—		d					01u12	01u12	01u41	01u41									02 53
120	—	—	—	—	Penrith North Lakes	d																	
—	—	—	—	—	Windermere	d																	
152¼	—	—	—	—	Oxenholme Lake District	a																	
—	—	—	—	—		d																	
—	—	—	—	—	Barrow-in-Furness	d											04 35						
171¼	—	—	—	—	Lancaster 6	a											05 28						
—	—	—	—	—		d																	
—	—	—	—	—	Blackpool North	d	22p44	22p44	23p03	23p13					03 36								
192¼	—	—	—	—	**Preston** 8	a	23p08	23p08	23p28	23p40	03 02	03 02	03 03	03 07									04s41
—	—	—	0	—	**Preston** 8	d	23p09	23p10	23p28	23p42	03 07	03 07	03 08	03 13	04u01			05 16					
207½	—	—	—	—	Wigan North Western	a	23p29																
—	—	—	—	—		d	23p30																
—	—	—	—	—	Blackrod	d			23p49	00 04													
—	—	—	—	—	Lostock	d			23p56	00 13													
—	—	—	20	—	Bolton	a		23p34	00 02	00 18					04c30			05 42					
—	—	—	31¼	—	**Manchester Piccadilly** 10	a		23p53	00 18						04 48			06 01					
—	—	—	—	—	Manchester Airport ✈	a		00 22	00 32						05 07			06 18					
—	0	—	—	—	**Liverpool Lime Street** 10	a	00 18																
—	—	—	—	—		d																	
—	5½	—	—	—	Liverpool South Parkway ✈	d																	
—	13	—	—	—	Runcorn	d																	
219¼	—	—	—	—	Warrington Bank Quay	a					03 34	03 34	03 34	03 40									
—	—	—	—	—		d					03 36	03 36	03 36	03 41									
231½	23¾	—	—	—	Hartford	d																	
—	—	—	—	0	**Manchester Piccadilly** 10	d														05 00	05 00	05 05	
—	—	—	37	5¾	Stockport	d																05 13	
—	—	—	—	—	Wilmslow	d																	
—	—	—	—	—	Holyhead	d																	
—	—	—	—	—	Bangor (Gwynedd)	d																	
—	—	—	—	—	Llandudno Junction	d																	
—	—	—	—	—	Wrexham General	d																	
—	—	—	—	—	Chester	d										04 22							
243½	35½	—	—	—	**Crewe** 10	a										04 44				05 43	05 44	05 34	05s37
—	—	—	—	—		d										04 59			05 18	05 47	05 47	05 36	
—	—	—	49	17¾	Macclesfield	d																	
—	—	—	57	25¾	Congleton	d																	
—	—	—	68¾	37¼	**Stoke-on-Trent**	d														06 07	06 07		
267¼	—	—	—	53½	**Stafford**	a										05 24				06 24	06 24	05 53	
—	—	—	—	—		d										05 25				06 25 →	06 25 →	05 55	
—	—	—	—	59¼	Penkridge	a																	
—	—	—	—	69¾	Wolverhampton 7	a										05 39							
—	—	—	—	82½	**Birmingham New Street** 12	a										06 01							
—	—	—	—	91	Birmingham International ✈	a																	
—	—	—	—	101½	Coventry	a																	
285	—	—	99¼	—	Lichfield Trent Valley	a													06 06				
291¼	—	—	—	—	Tamworth Low Level	a													06 13				
304¼	—	—	—	—	Nuneaton	a													06 29			06 17	
318¾	—	—	—	113	Rugby	a					05 27	05 26							06 47			06 30	
351½	—	—	—	—	Milton Keynes Central	a																06 51	
383½	—	—	—	—	Watford Junction	a					06s23	06s23	06s19	06s19									
401¼	—	—	—	—	**London Euston** 15 ⊖	a					06 46	06 46	06 43	06 43								07 28	07 47

A From 20 June until 1 August
B Until 13 June, MO from 8 August
C From 21 June until 9 September
D Until 17 June, MX from 13 September
E from 18 July
F WThFO
b Previous night, stops to pick up only
c Stops to pick up only
e Arr. 0047

OVERNIGHT SLEEPERS. For sleeper trains, operated by First ScotRail, please refer to Tables 400 - 404

Scotland and North West England - West Midlands and London

		SR	SR	SR	VT	XC MTO	XC	VT	LM	VT	VT	XC	VT	LM	VT	VT	TP	VT	TP	TP	NT	VT
		🛏 MX A	🛏 B	🛏 MX C	◇1 ⊠	◇1 ⌶	◇1 D ⌶	◇1 ⊠	1	◇1 ⊠	◇1 ⊠	◇1 ⌶	◇1 ⊠	1	◇1 ⊠	◇1 ⊠	◇1 ⌶	◇1 ⊠	◇1 E ⌶	◇1 F ⌶		◇1 ⊠
Inverness	d	20p46		20p46																		
Aberdeen	d		21p40																			
Dundee	d		23b06																			
Perth	d	23b21		23b21																		
Edinburgh 10	d	01 24		01 24																		
Haymarket	d																					
Glasgow Central 15	d																					
Motherwell	d																					
Carstairs	d																					
Lockerbie	d																					
Carlisle 8	a	02 53		02 53																		
	d	02 54		02 55																		
Penrith North Lakes	d																					
Windermere	d																					
Oxenholme Lake District	a																					
	d																					
Barrow-in-Furness	d																		05 31			
Lancaster 6	a																		06 23			
	d															05 35			06 23	06 23		
Blackpool North	d																05 39				06 19	
Preston 8	a	04s32		04s29												05 52	06 03		06 42	06 42	06 46	
Preston 8	d							05 33								06 00	06 05	06 16	06 44	06 44	06 48	
Wigan North Western	a							05 44								06 11		06 27				
	d							05 45								06 11		06 27				
Blackrod	d																06 22				07 10	
Lostock	d																06 30				07 20	
Bolton	a																06 34		07 08	07 08	07 25	
Manchester Piccadilly 10	a																06 56		07 27	07 27		
Manchester Airport ✈	a																07 17		07 47	07 47		
Liverpool Lime Street 10	a																					
	d				05 27						06 05											
Liverpool South Parkway ✈	d																					
Runcorn	d				05 43						06 21											
Warrington Bank Quay	a							05 55								06 22		06 38				
	d							05 56								06 22		06 38				
Hartford	d																					
Manchester Piccadilly 10	d									05 55		06 00	06 10									06 27
Stockport	d									06 03		06 08	06 18									06 35
Wilmslow	d									06 11												
Holyhead	d														04 48							
Bangor (Gwynedd)	d														05 14							
Llandudno Junction	d														05 32							
Wrexham General	d																					
Chester	d														06e26							
Crewe 10	a	05s34		05s33	06 00					06 27		06 32			06 47	06 42		06 58				
	d				06 02				06 20	06 29		06 38		06 47	06 53			07 01				
Macclesfield	d												06 31									06 48
Congleton	d																					
Stoke-on-Trent	d					←	←						06 48									07 06
Stafford	a				06 20	06 24	06 24		06 40		06 52	06 57		07 10								07 27
	d				06 21	06 25	06 25		06 41		06 53	06 58		07 12								07 28
Penkridge	a								06 46					07 17								
Wolverhampton 7	a					06 39	06 39		06 57			07 12		07 28				07 31				07 43
Birmingham New Street 12	a					06 58	06 58		07 18			07 31		07 48				07 55				08 05
Birmingham International ✈	a					07 13	07 13															08 19
Coventry	a					07 24	07 24															08 30
Lichfield Trent Valley	a							06 40			07 07											
Tamworth Low Level	a							06 46			07 14											
Nuneaton	a									07 06					07 32							
Rugby	a				06 52			07 06					07 28									
Milton Keynes Central	a				07 12																	
Watford Junction	a																					09s15
London Euston 15 ⊖	a	07 47		07 47	07 50			07 57		08 07	08 22		08 22		08 33							09 34

A Until 17 June, MX from 13 September
B TWThO until 16 June, TWThO from 25 October
C From 21 June until 9 September
D WThFO
E from 18 July. ⌶ from Preston
F until 15 July. ⌶ from Preston
b Previous night, stops to pick up only

OVERNIGHT SLEEPERS. For sleeper trains, operated by First ScotRail, please refer to Tables 400 - 404

Scotland and North West England - West Midlands and London

		VT ◇1 ⊠	LM 1	VT ◇1 ⊠	LM 1	VT ◇1 ⊠	TP ◇1 🍴	XC ◇1 🍴	LM 1	VT ◇1 ⊠	VT ◇1 ⊠	VT ◇1 A ⊠	VT ◇1 ⊠	XC ◇1 🍴	VT ◇1 ⊠	LM 1	VT ◇1 ⊠	LM 1	VT ◇1 ⊠	XC ◇1 🍴	LM 1	VT ◇1 ⊠	NT
Inverness	d																						
Aberdeen	d																						
Dundee	d																						
Perth	d																						
Edinburgh 10	d																						
Haymarket	d																						
Glasgow Central 15	d					04 28																	
Motherwell	d																						
Carstairs	d																						
Lockerbie	d																						
Carlisle 8	a					05 42																	
	d					05 43																	
Penrith North Lakes	d					05 57																	
Windermere	d																						
Oxenholme Lake District	a					06 20																	
	d					06 20																	
Barrow-in-Furness	d																						
Lancaster 6	a					06 35																	
	d					06 35							06 58										
Blackpool North	d						06 40																06 53
Preston 8	a					06 53	07 07						07 15										07 15
Preston 8	d					06 56	07 09						07 17										07 17
Wigan North Western	a					07 06							07 28										
	d					07 08							07 28										
Blackrod	d																						07 40
Lostock	d						07 30																07 49
Bolton	a						07 34																07 54
Manchester Piccadilly 10	a						07 56																08 18
Manchester Airport ✈	a						08 17																
Liverpool Lime Street 10	a																						
	d		06 30						07 04							07 34	07 48				08 04		
Liverpool South Parkway ✈	d		06 40						07 14							07 44					08 15		
Runcorn	d		06 48						07 22							07 52	08 04				08 24		
Warrington Bank Quay	a					07 17							07 39										
	d					07 18							07 39										
Hartford	d		07 02						07 36							08 04							
Manchester Piccadilly 10	d	06 35		06 43				07 06		07 15				07 26	07 35				07 55	08 07		08 15	08 20
Stockport	d	06 43		06 51				07 16		07 23				07 35	07 43				08 04	08 16		08 23	08 35
Wilmslow	d			06 59															08 11				
Holyhead	d										05 51												
Bangor (Gwynedd)	d										06 18												
Llandudno Junction	d										06 36												
Wrexham General	d											07 00											
Chester	d											07 35											
Crewe 10	a		07 14	07 15					07 48			07 54	07 58			08 19			08 27		08 47		
	d		07 16	07 17					07 49			07 57	08 01			08 22			08 29		08 49		
Macclesfield	d	06 56												07 49	07 56								
Congleton	d																						
Stoke-on-Trent	d	07 12			←			07 44		07 50				08 07	08 12			←		08 44		08 50	
Stafford	a		07 40	07 34	07 40			08 01	08 10					08 24		08 42	08 35	08 42		09 02	09 09		
	d		07 41	07 35	07 41			08 02	08 10					08 25		08 43	08 36	08 43		09 03	09 10		
Penkridge	a		→		07 46				08 16							→		08 48			09 15		
Wolverhampton 7	a				07 57			08 15	08 26				08 31	08 39				08 58		09 15	09 27		
Birmingham New Street 12	a				08 17			08 32	08 47				08 55	08 58				09 18		09 39	09 47		
Birmingham International ✈	a													09 13									
Coventry	a													09 24									
Lichfield Trent Valley	a																						
Tamworth Low Level	a																						
Nuneaton	a														08 44								
Rugby	a	07 52										08 45											
Milton Keynes Central	a									08s46												09 46	
Watford Junction	a														09s31								
London Euston 15 ⊖	a	08 45		08 52		09 04				09 23		09 38			09 52		09 56		10 04			10 23	

A ⊠ from Chester

OVERNIGHT SLEEPERS. For sleeper trains, operated by First ScotRail, please refer to Tables 400 - 404

Scotland and North West England - West Midlands and London

		NT	TP ◇1 A 🍴	TP ◇1 B 🍴	TP ◇1 C 🍴	NT	VT ◇1 ⊠	VT ◇1 ⊠	TP ◇1 🍴	TP ◇1 🍴	VT ◇1 ⊠	NT D	XC ◇1 🍴	VT ◇1 ⊠	LM 1	VT ◇1 ⊠	LM 1	VT ◇1 ⊠	XC ◇1 🍴	LM 1	VT ◇1 ⊠	NT	TP ◇1 A 🍴
Inverness	d																						
Aberdeen	d																						
Dundee	d																						
Perth	d																						
Edinburgh 10	d								05 36														
Haymarket	d								05u40														
Glasgow Central 15	d						05 40				05 50												
Motherwell	d										06 04												
Carstairs	d																						
Lockerbie	d																						
Carlisle 8	a						06 46		06 58		07 02												
	d						06 49		06 58		07 04												
Penrith North Lakes	d										07 19												
Windermere	d																						
Oxenholme Lake District	a						07 22				07 42												
	d						07 24				07 42												
Barrow-in-Furness	d		06 20									07 00											07 29
Lancaster 6	a		07 21				07 37		07 47		07 56	08 04											08 26
	d		07 22		07 22		07 38		07 47		07 57	08 05											08 27
Blackpool North	d	07 02		07 10		07 18				07 36													
Preston 8	a	07 28	07 41	07 37	07 41	07 46	07 56		08 07	08 03	08 15	08 30											08 45
Preston 8	d	07 30	07 47		07 47	07 47	07 58		08 12		08 17											08 17	08 47
Wigan North Western	a	07 50					08 09				08 28												
	d	07 50					08 09				08 28												
Blackrod	d					08 10																08 41	
Lostock	d					08 20																08 50	
Bolton	a		08 08		08 08	08 25			08 34													08 55	09 08
Manchester Piccadilly 10	a		08 27		08 27				08 56													09 18	09 27
Manchester Airport ✈	a		08 47		08 47				09 19														09 47
Liverpool Lime Street 10	a	08 35																					
	d														08 34	08 48				09 04			
Liverpool South Parkway ✈	d														08 44					09 15			
Runcorn	d														08 52	09 04				09 25			
Warrington Bank Quay	a						08 20				08 39												
	d						08 20				08 39												
Hartford	d														09 06								
Manchester Piccadilly 10	d												08 27	08 35				08 55	09 07		09 15	09 21	
Stockport	d												08 35	08 43				09 04	09 16		09 23	09 35	
Wilmslow	d																	09 11					
Holyhead	d							06 55															
Bangor (Gwynedd)	d							07 22															
Llandudno Junction	d							07 40															
Wrexham General	d																						
Chester	d							08 35															
Crewe 10	a							08 54			08 58				09 20			09 27		09 44			
	d							08 56			09 01				09 22			09 29		09 49			
Macclesfield	d												08 49	08 56									
Congleton	d																						
Stoke-on-Trent	d												09 07	09 12			←		09 44		09 50		
Stafford	a												09 24		09 42	09 35	09 42		10 02	10 09			
	d												09 25		09 43	09 36	09 43		10 03	10 10			
Penkridge	a														→					10 15			
Wolverhampton 7	a										09 31		09 39				09 56		10 15	10 27			
Birmingham New Street 12	a										09 55		09 58				10 17		10 39	10 47			
Birmingham International ✈	a												10 13										
Coventry	a												10 24										
Lichfield Trent Valley	a																						
Tamworth Low Level	a																						
Nuneaton	a																						
Rugby	a																						
Milton Keynes Central	a							10 01													10 46		
Watford Junction	a																						
London Euston 15 ⊖	a						10 12	10 38						10 42		10 56		11 04			11 23		

A from 18 July. 🍴 from Preston
B until 15 July
C until 15 July. 🍴 from Preston
D from 18 July

OVERNIGHT SLEEPERS. For sleeper trains, operated by First ScotRail, please refer to Tables 400 - 404

Scotland and North West England - West Midlands and London

		TP	NT	VT	SR	NT	TP	VT	VT	XC	VT	LM	VT	LM	VT	XC	LM	VT	NT	TP	NT	VT
		◇1		◇1			◇1	◇1	◇1	◇1	◇1	1	◇1	1	◇1	◇1	1	◇1		◇1		◇1
		A ⌶		⊠			B ⌶	⊠	⊠	⌶	⊠		⊠		⊠	⌶		⊠		⌶		⊠
Inverness	d																					
Aberdeen	d																					
Dundee	d																					
Perth	d																					
Edinburgh 10	d								06 52													
Haymarket	d								06 56													
Glasgow Central 15	d			06 30	07 08															07 10		07 37
Motherwell	d			06 44																		07 52
Carstairs	d																					
Lockerbie	d			07 25																08 07		
Carlisle 8	a			07 43	09 37				08 05											08 30		08 46
	d			07 46					08 07											08 31		08 49
Penrith North Lakes	d			08 00					08 22											08 46		
Windermere	d																					
Oxenholme Lake District	a			08 22																09 09		09 22
	d			08 23																09 11		09 23
Barrow-in-Furness	d																					
Lancaster 6	a			08 37					08 56											09 26		09 37
	d	08 27		08 38					08 57											09 26		09 38
Blackpool North	d		08 20				08 44														09 20	
Preston 8	a	08 45	08 47	08 56			09 08		09 15											09 45	09 47	09 56
Preston 8	d	08 47	08 49	08 58		09 04	09 10		09 17										09 23	09 47	09 49	09 58
Wigan North Western	a			09 09		09 24			09 28													10 09
	d			09 09		09 24			09 28													10 09
Blackrod	d		09 10																		10 10	
Lostock	d		09 20																09 50		10 20	
Bolton	a	09 08	09 25				09 34												09 55	10 08	10 25	
Manchester Piccadilly 10	a	09 27					09 56												10 18	10 27		
Manchester Airport	a	09 47					10 17													10 47		
Liverpool Lime Street 10	a					10 02																
	d					10 16						09 34	09 48				10 04					
Liverpool South Parkway	d					10a27						09 44					10 15					
Runcorn	d											09 52	10 04				10 25					
Warrington Bank Quay	a			09 20					09 39													10 20
	d			09 20					09 39													10 20
Hartford	d											10 04										
Manchester Piccadilly 10	d									09 27	09 35				09 55	10 07		10 15	10 21			
Stockport	d									09 35	09 43				10 04	10 16		10 23	10 35			
Wilmslow	d														10 11							
Holyhead	d																					
Bangor (Gwynedd)	d																					
Llandudno Junction	d																					
Wrexham General	d																					
Chester	d							09 35														
Crewe 10	a							09 54	09 58			10 19			10 27		10 45					
	d							09 56	10 01			10 22			10 29		10 49					
Macclesfield	d									09 49	09 56											
Congleton	d																					
Stoke-on-Trent	d									10 07	10 12			←		10 44		10 50				
Stafford	a									10 24		10 42	10 35	10 42		11 01	11 09					
	d									10 25		10 43	10 36	10 43		11 02	11 10					
Penkridge	a											→					11 15					
Wolverhampton 7	a								10 31	10 39				10 56		11 15	11 27					
Birmingham New Street 12	a								10 55	10 58				11 18		11 32	11 47					
Birmingham International	a									11 13												
Coventry	a									11 24												
Lichfield Trent Valley	a																					
Tamworth Low Level	a																					
Nuneaton	a																					
Rugby	a																					
Milton Keynes Central	a							11 01										11 46				
Watford Junction	a																					
London Euston 15	a			11 12				11 38			11 42		11 56		12 04			12 23				12 12

A until 15 July. ⌶ from Preston

B not 9 December

OVERNIGHT SLEEPERS. For sleeper trains, operated by First ScotRail, please refer to Tables 400 - 404

Scotland and North West England - West Midlands and London

		VT	NT	TP	TP	VT	XC	VT	VT FO	TP	NT	TP	NT	LM	VT	LM	VT	VT	XC	LM	NT	TP	VT
		◇1		◇1	◇1	◇1	◇1	◇1	◇	◇1		◇1		1	◇1	1	◇1	◇1	◇1	1		◇1	◇1
		⊠		⌶	⌶	⊠	⌶	⊠	⊏	A ⌶	B	C ⌶			⊠		⊠	⊠	⌶			⌶	⊏
Inverness	d																						
Aberdeen	d																						
Dundee	d																						
Perth	d																						
Edinburgh 10	d			07 42																			
Haymarket	d			07u46																			
Glasgow Central 15	d					08 00												08 40					
Motherwell	d																						
Carstairs	d																						
Lockerbie	d																						
Carlisle 8	a			08 59		09 08												09 47					
	d			09 00		09 10												09 49					
Penrith North Lakes	d																	10 03					
Windermere	d																						
Oxenholme Lake District	a																						
	d																						
Barrow-in-Furness	d									09 23	10 16												
Lancaster 6	a					09 56				10 25	11 20							10 37					
	d					09 57				10 26		10 26						10 38					
Blackpool North	d		09 37		09 43								10 20								10 37	10 44	
Preston 8	a		10 02	10 04	10 07	10 15				10 45		10 45	10 47					10 56			11 02	11 08	
Preston 8	d		10 04	10 12		10 17			10 36	10 47		10 47	10 49					10 58			11 04	11 10	
Wigan North Western	a		10 24			10 28			10 47									11 09			11 24		
	d		10 24			10 28			10 47									11 09			11 24		
Blackrod	d												11 10										
Lostock	d												11 20										
Bolton	a			10 35						11 08		11 08	11 25									11 34	
Manchester Piccadilly 10	a			10 56						11 27		11 27										11 56	
Manchester Airport	a			11 17						11 50		11 50										12 17	
Liverpool Lime Street 10	a		11 02																		12 02		
	d		11 16											10 34	10 48					11 04	12 16		
Liverpool South Parkway	d		11a27											10 44						11 15	12a27		
Runcorn	d													10 52	11 04					11 25			
Warrington Bank Quay	a					10 39			10 58									11 20					
	d					10 39			10 58									11 20					
Hartford	d													11 04									
Manchester Piccadilly 10	d						10 27	10 35									10 55		11 07				11 15
Stockport	d						10 35	10 43									11 04		11 16				11 23
Wilmslow	d																11 11						
Holyhead	d	08 55																					
Bangor (Gwynedd)	d	09 22																					
Llandudno Junction	d	09 40																					
Wrexham General	d																						
Chester	d	10 35																					
Crewe 10	a	10 54				10 58								11 19			11 27			11 45			
	d	10 56				11 01								11 22			11 29			11 49			
Macclesfield	d						10 49	10 56															
Congleton	d																						
Stoke-on-Trent	d						11 07	11 12								←			11 44				11 50
Stafford	a						11 24							11 43	11 33	11 43			12 02	12 09			
	d						11 25							11 43	11 34	11 43			12 03	12 10			
Penkridge	a													→						12 15			
Wolverhampton 7	a					11 31	11 39									11 57			12 15	12 27			
Birmingham New Street 12	a					11 55	11 58									12 17			12 39	12 47			
Birmingham International	a						12 13																
Coventry	a						12 24																
Lichfield Trent Valley	a																						
Tamworth Low Level	a																						
Nuneaton	a																						
Rugby	a																						
Milton Keynes Central	a	12 01																					12 46
Watford Junction	a																						
London Euston 15	a	12 38						12 42	12 51						12 56		13 03	13 12					13 23

A from 18 July. ⌶ from Preston

B from 18 July

C until 15 July. ⌶ from Preston

OVERNIGHT SLEEPERS. For sleeper trains, operated by First ScotRail, please refer to Tables 400 - 404

Scotland and North West England - West Midlands and London

		VT	VT	XC	VT	LM	VT	LM	VT	XC	LM	VT	NT	TP	NT	VT	VT	VT	TP	NT	TP	TP
		◇1	◇1	◇1	◇1	1	◇1	1	◇1	◇1	1	◇1		◇1		◇1	◇1	◇1	◇1		◇1	◇1
														A		B	B	C	D			E
		⌂	⊠	⊥	⌂		⌂		⌂	⊥		⌂		⊥		⊠	⊠	⊠			⊥	
Inverness	d																					
Aberdeen	d																					
Dundee	d																					
Perth	d																					
Edinburgh [10]	d		08 52																			
Haymarket	d		08 57																			
Glasgow Central [15]	d															09 23	09 40	09 40				
Motherwell	d																					
Carstairs	d																					
Lockerbie	d																					
Carlisle [8]	a		10 05													10 43	10 47	10 47				
	d		10 07													10 45	10 49	10 49				
Penrith North Lakes	d																					
Windermere	d													10 49								
Oxenholme Lake District	a		10 41											11 08			11 22	11 22				
	d		10 42											11 09			11 23	11 23				
Barrow-in-Furness	d																		11 25			
Lancaster [6]	a		10 56											11 26		11 30		11 37	12 18			
	d		10 57											11 26		11 38		11 38	12 18			12 18
Blackpool North	d														11 20					11 37	11 44	
Preston [8]	a		11 15											11 45	11 47	11 56	11 50	11 56	12 37	12 02	12 08	12 37
Preston [8]	d		11 17										11 23	11 47	11 49	11 58	11 53	11 58		12 04	12 10	
Wigan North Western	a		11 28													12 09		12 09		12 24		
	d		11 28													12 09		12 09		12 24		
Blackrod	d														12 10							
Lostock	d												11 50		12 20							
Bolton	a												11 55	12 08	12 25						12 34	
Manchester Piccadilly [10]	a												12 18	12 27							12 56	
Manchester Airport ✈	a													12 47							13 17	
Liverpool Lime Street [10]	a																			13 02		
	d					11 34	11 48				12 04									13 16		
Liverpool South Parkway ✈	d					11 44					12 15									13a27		
Runcorn	d					11 52	12 04				12 25											
Warrington Bank Quay	a		11 39													12 20		12 20				
	d		11 39													12 20		12 20				
Hartford	d					12 04																
Manchester Piccadilly [10]	d			11 27	11 35				11 55	12 07		12 15	12 21									
Stockport	d			11 35	11 43				12 04	12 16		12 23	12 35									
Wilmslow	d								12 11													
Holyhead	d																					
Bangor (Gwynedd)	d																					
Llandudno Junction	d																					
Wrexham General	d																					
Chester	d	11 35																				
Crewe [10]	a	11 54	11 58			12 19			12 27		12 45											
	d	11 56	12 01			12 22			12 29		12 49											
Macclesfield	d			11 49	11 56																	
Congleton	d																					
Stoke-on-Trent	d			12 07	12 12			←		12 44		12 50										
Stafford	a			12 24		12 42	12 35	12 42			13 09											
	d			12 25		12 43	12 36	12 43			13 10											
Penkridge	a					→					13 15											
Wolverhampton [7]	a		12 31	12 39				12 56		13 13	13 27											
Birmingham New Street [12]	a		12 55	12 58				13 17		13 31	13 47											
Birmingham International ✈	a			13 13																		
Coventry	a			13 24																		
Lichfield Trent Valley	a																					
Tamworth Low Level	a																					
Nuneaton	a																					
Rugby	a																					
Milton Keynes Central	a	13 01										13 46										
Watford Junction	a																					
London Euston [15] ⊖	a	13 38			13 42		13 56		14 04			14 23				14 12	14 03	14 12				

A ⊥ from Preston
B from 18 July until 9 September
C until 15 July, from 12 September
D from 18 July
E until 15 July

OVERNIGHT SLEEPERS. For sleeper trains, operated by First ScotRail, please refer to Tables 400 - 404

Scotland and North West England - West Midlands and London

		VT	VT	XC	LM	VT	VT	XC	LM	VT	NT	TP FO	TP	NT	VT	VT	NT	TP	VT	XC	VT	VT	LM
		◇1	◇1	◇1	1	◇1	◇1	◇1	1	◇1		◇1	◇1		◇1	◇1		◇1	◇1	◇1	◇1	◇1	1
																			A			B	
		⌂	⌂	⊥		⌂	⌂	⊥		⌂		⊥	⊥		⊠	⌂		⊥	⊠	⊥	⌂	⊠	
Inverness	d																						
Aberdeen	d																						
Dundee	d																						
Perth	d																						
Edinburgh [10]	d											09 52							10 51			10 51	
Haymarket	d											09u56							10 57			10 57	
Glasgow Central [15]	d		10 00										10 10		10 40								
Motherwell	d																						
Carstairs	d																						
Lockerbie	d											11 01											
Carlisle [8]	a		11 10									11 22	11 26		11 47				12 05			12 05	
	d		11 11									11 31	11 31		11 49				12 07			12 07	
Penrith North Lakes	d		11 26									11 46	11 46										
Windermere	d																						
Oxenholme Lake District	a											12 09	12 09		12 22				12 41			12 41	
	d											12 10	12 10		12 23				12 43			12 43	
Barrow-in-Furness	d																						
Lancaster [6]	a											12 26	12 26		12 37				12 56			12 56	
	d											12 26	12 26		12 38				12 57			12 57	
Blackpool North	d													12 20			12 37	12 44					
Preston [8]	a		12 15									12 45	12 45	12 47	12 56		13 02	13 08	13 15			13 15	
Preston [8]	d		12 17								12 23	12 47	12 47	12 49	12 58		13 04	13 10	13 17			13 17	
Wigan North Western	a		12 28												13 09		13 24		13 28			13 28	
	d		12 28												13 09		13 24		13 28			13 28	
Blackrod	d													13 10									
Lostock	d										12 50			13 20									
Bolton	a										12 55	13 08	13 08	13 25				13 34					
Manchester Piccadilly [10]	a										13 18	13 27	13 27					13 56					
Manchester Airport ✈	a											13 47	13 47					14 17					
Liverpool Lime Street [10]	a																14 02						
	d				12 34				13 04								14 16						13 34
Liverpool South Parkway ✈	d				12 44				13 15								14a27						13 44
Runcorn	d				12 52				13 25														13 52
Warrington Bank Quay	a		12 39												13 20				13 39			13 39	
	d		12 39												13 20				13 39			13 39	
Hartford	d				13 06																		14 04
Manchester Piccadilly [10]	d			12 27		12 35	12 55	13 07		13 15	13 21									13 27	13 35		
Stockport	d			12 35		12 43	13 04	13 16		13 23	13 35									13 35	13 43		
Wilmslow	d						13 11																
Holyhead	d																						
Bangor (Gwynedd)	d															12 24							
Llandudno Junction	d															12 42							
Wrexham General	d																						
Chester	d	12 35														13 35							
Crewe [10]	a	12 54	12 58		13 20		13 27		13 45							13 54			13 58			13 58	14 19
	d	12 56	13 01		13 22		13 29		13 49							13 56			14 01			14 01	14 22
Macclesfield	d			12 49		12 56														13 49	13 56		
Congleton	d																						
Stoke-on-Trent	d			13 07		13 12		13 44		13 50										14 07	14 12		
Stafford	a			13 24	13 42			14 01	14 09											14 24			14 46
	d			13 25	13 43			14 02	14 10											14 25			14 46
Penkridge	a								14 15														→
Wolverhampton [7]	a		13 31	13 39	13 56			14 15	14 27										14 31	14 39		14 33	
Birmingham New Street [12]	a		13 55	13 58	14 17			14 32	14 47										14 55	14 58		15 05	
Birmingham International ✈	a			14 13																15 13		15 19	
Coventry	a			14 24																15 24		15 30	
Lichfield Trent Valley	a																						
Tamworth Low Level	a																						
Nuneaton	a																						
Rugby	a																						
Milton Keynes Central	a	14 01								14 46						15 01						16s15	
Watford Junction	a																						
London Euston [15] ⊖	a	14 38				14 42	15 04			15 23					15 12	15 38					15 42	16 34	

A until 15 July, from 12 September
B from 18 July until 9 September

OVERNIGHT SLEEPERS. For sleeper trains, operated by First ScotRail, please refer to Tables 400 - 404

Scotland and North West England - West Midlands and London

		VT	LM	VT	XC		LM	VT	NT	TP	NT	VT	VT	VT	NT		TP	VT	VT	SR	TP	NT	XC	VT	LM
		◇1	1	◇1	◇1		1	◇1		◇1		◇1	◇1	◇1			◇1	◇1	◇1		◇1		◇1	◇1	1
										A		B	C	B							D	D			
		⊡		⊡	⊼			⊡		⊼		⊠	⊠	⊡			⊼	⊡	⊡				⊼	⊡	
Inverness	d																								
Aberdeen	d																								
Dundee	d																								
Perth	d																								
Edinburgh	d																								
Haymarket	d																								
Glasgow Central	d											11 40	11 40						12 00	12 12					
Motherwell	d																								
Carstairs	d																								
Lockerbie	d																								
Carlisle	a											12 46	12 46						13 08	14 32					
	d											12 49	12 49						13 09						
Penrith North Lakes	d											13 03	13 03												
Windermere	d									12 51															
Oxenholme Lake District	a									13 07															
	d									13 09															
Barrow-in-Furness	d																				13 25	14 16			
Lancaster	a									13 26			13 37						13 56		14 18	15 20			
	d									13 26			13 39	13 39					13 58		14 18				
Blackpool North	d										13 20				13 37		13 44								
Preston	a									13 45	13 47	13 50	13 56	13 56	14 02		14 08		14 15		14 37				
Preston	d								13 23	13 47	13 49	13 53	13 59	13 59	14 04		14 10		14 17						
Wigan North Western	a												14 09	14 09	14 24				14 28						
	d												14 10	14 10	14 24				14 28						
Blackrod	d										14 10														
Lostock	d								13 50		14 20														
Bolton	a								13 55	14 08	14 25						14 34								
Manchester Piccadilly	a								14 18	14 27							14 56								
Manchester Airport	a									14 47							15 17								
Liverpool Lime Street	a														15 02										
	d	13 48					14 04								15 16										14 34
Liverpool South Parkway	d						14 15								15a27										14 44
Runcorn	d	14 04					14 25																		14 52
Warrington Bank Quay	a												14 20	14 20					14 39						
	d												14 21	14 21					14 39						
Hartford	d																								15 04
Manchester Piccadilly	d			13 55	14 07			14 15	14 21														14 27	14 35	
Stockport	d			14 04	14 16			14 23	14 35														14 35	14 43	
Wilmslow	d			14 11																					
Holyhead	d																								
Bangor (Gwynedd)	d																								
Llandudno Junction	d																								
Wrexham General	d																								
Chester	d																	14 35							
Crewe	a			14 27			14 45											14 54	14 58						15 19
	d			14 29			14 49											14 56	15 01						15 22
Macclesfield	d																						14 49	14 56	
Congleton	d																								
Stoke-on-Trent	d		←		14 44			14 50															15 07	15 12	
Stafford	a	14 35	14 46		15 02		15 09																15 24		15 42
	d	14 36	14 46		15 03		15 10																15 25		15 43
Penkridge	a						15 15																		→
Wolverhampton	a		14 59		15 15		15 27												15 31				15 39		
Birmingham New Street	a		15 20		15 39		15 47												15 55				15 58		
Birmingham International	a																						16 13		
Coventry	a																						16 24		
Lichfield Trent Valley	a																								
Tamworth Low Level	a																								
Nuneaton	a																								
Rugby	a																								
Milton Keynes Central	a							15 46										16 01							
Watford Junction	a																								
London Euston	a	15 56		16 04				16 23				16 03	16 11	16 11				16 38						16 42	

A ⊼ from Preston
B until 15 July, from 12 September
C from 18 July until 9 September
D from 18 July

OVERNIGHT SLEEPERS. For sleeper trains, operated by First ScotRail, please refer to Tables 400 - 404

Scotland and North West England - West Midlands and London

			VT	LM	VT	XC	LM	VT	NT	TP	NT		VT	NT	TP	VT	VT	VT	TP	XC	VT		LM	VT	LM
			◇1	1	◇1	◇1	1	◇1		◇1			◇1		◇1	◇1	◇1	◇1	◇1	◇1	◇1		1	◇1	1
																			A						
			⊡		⊡	⊼		⊡		⊼			⊠		⊼	⊡	⊡	⊡		⊼	⊡			⊡	
Inverness	d																								
Aberdeen	d																								
Dundee	d																								
Perth	d																								
Edinburgh	d									12 12								12 51							
Haymarket	d									12u16								12 57							
Glasgow Central	d												12 40												
Motherwell	d																								
Carstairs	d																								
Lockerbie	d									13 11															
Carlisle	a									13 33			13 47					14 05							
	d									13 33			13 49					14 07							
Penrith North Lakes	d																	14 22							
Windermere	d																								
Oxenholme Lake District	a									14 09			14 22												
	d									14 09			14 24												
Barrow-in-Furness	d																								
Lancaster	a									14 26			14 37					14 56							
	d									14 26			14 38					14 57	15 08						
Blackpool North	d										14 20			14 37	14 44										
Preston	a									14 45	14 47		14 56	15 02	15 08			15 15	15 26						
Preston	d								14 23	14 47	14 49		14 58	15 04	15 10			15 17							
Wigan North Western	a												15 09	15 24				15 28							
	d												15 09	15 24				15 28							
Blackrod	d										15 10														
Lostock	d								14 50		15 20														
Bolton	a								14 55	15 08	15 25				15 34										
Manchester Piccadilly	a								15 18	15 27					15 56										
Manchester Airport	a									15 47					16 17										
Liverpool Lime Street	a													16 02											
	d		14 48				15 04							16 16									15 34	15 48	
Liverpool South Parkway	d						15 15							16a27									15 44		
Runcorn	d		15 04				15 25																15 52	16 04	
Warrington Bank Quay	a												15 20					15 39							
	d												15 20					15 39							
Hartford	d																						16 04		
Manchester Piccadilly	d				14 55	15 07		15 15	15 21											15 27	15 35				
Stockport	d				15 04	15 16		15 23	15 35											15 35	15 43				
Wilmslow	d				15 11																				
Holyhead	d																13 58								
Bangor (Gwynedd)	d																14 25								
Llandudno Junction	d																14 43								
Wrexham General	d																								
Chester	d															15 35	15 35								
Crewe	a				15 27		15 45									15 54	15 54	15 58					16 19		
	d				15 29		15 49									15 56	15 57	16 01					16 22		
Macclesfield	d																			15 49	15 56				
Congleton	d																								
Stoke-on-Trent	d			←		15 44		15 50												16 07	16 12				←
Stafford	a		15 35	15 42		16 02	16 09													16 24			16 46	16 35	16 46
	d		15 36	15 43		16 03	16 10													16 25			16 46	16 36	16 46
Penkridge	a						16 15																→		
Wolverhampton	a			15 56		16 15	16 26											16 31		16 39					16 59
Birmingham New Street	a			16 17		16 39	16 47											16 55		16 58					17 20
Birmingham International	a																			17 13					
Coventry	a																			17 24					
Lichfield Trent Valley	a																								
Tamworth Low Level	a																								
Nuneaton	a																								
Rugby	a																								
Milton Keynes Central	a							16 46								17s01	17 01								
Watford Junction	a																								
London Euston	a		16 56		17 04			17 23					17 12			17 38	17 38				17 42			17 56	

A until 15 July

OVERNIGHT SLEEPERS. For sleeper trains, operated by First ScotRail, please refer to Tables 400 - 404

Table 65

Mondays to Fridays

Scotland and North West England - West Midlands and London

	VT	XC	LM	VT	NT	TP	NT	VT	VT	TP	NT	TP	TP	NT	VT	VT	XC	VT	NT	LM	VT	LM
	◇1	◇1	1	◇1		◇1		◇1	◇1	◇1 A		◇1	1 B	A	◇1	◇1	◇1	◇1	A	1	◇1	1
	⊏	✕		⊏		✕		⊠	⊏			✕			⊏	⊏	✕	⊏			⊏	
Inverness d																						
Aberdeen d																						
Dundee d																						
Perth d																						
Edinburgh 10 d																						
Haymarket d																						
Glasgow Central 15 d						12 54		13 40								14 00						
Motherwell d																						
Carstairs d																						
Lockerbie d						13 56																
Carlisle 8 a						14 18		14 46								15 08						
d						14 18		14 49								15 09						
Penrith North Lakes d						14 34																
Windermere d																						
Oxenholme Lake District a						14 58		15 22								15 44						
d						14 59		15 24								15 44						
Barrow-in-Furness d										15 25				16 20					17 43			
Lancaster 6 a						15 13				16 18				17 26					18 38			
d						15 14			15 39	16 18			16 18									
Blackpool North d							15 20				15 37	15 44										
Preston 8 a						15 34	15 47	15 50	15 56	16 37	16 02	16 08	16 37			16 15						
Preston 8 d					15 23	15 47	15 49	15 53	15 59		16 04	16 10				16 17						
Wigan North Western a									16 09		16 24					16 28						
d									16 10		16 24					16 28						
Blackrod d							16 10															
Lostock d					15 50		16 20															
Bolton a					15 55	16 08	16 25					16 34										
Manchester Piccadilly 10 ⇌ a					16 18	16 27						16 56										
Manchester Airport ✈ a						16 47						17 17										
Liverpool Lime Street 10 a											17 05											
d			16 04																	16 34	16 48	
Liverpool South Parkway ✈ d			16 15																	16 44		
Runcorn d			16 25																	16 52	17 04	
Warrington Bank Quay a									16 20							16 39						
d									16 21							16 39						
Hartford d																				17 06		
Manchester Piccadilly 10 ⇌ d	15 55	16 07		16 15	16 21												16 27	16 35				
Stockport d	16 04	16 16		16 23	16 35												16 35	16 43				
Wilmslow d	16 11																					
Holyhead d																						
Bangor (Gwynedd) d																						
Llandudno Junction d																						
Wrexham General d																						
Chester d															16 35							
Crewe 10 a	16 27		16 45												16 54	16 58				17 19		
d	16 29		16 49												16 56	17 01				17 22		
Macclesfield d																	16 49	16 56				
Congleton d																						
Stoke-on-Trent d		16 44		16 50													17 07	17 12				←
Stafford a		17 02	17 10														17 24			17 42	17 35	17 42
d		17 03	17 10														17 25			17 43	17 36	17 43
Penkridge a			17 15																	→		
Wolverhampton 7 ⇌ a		17 15	17 27													17 31	17 39					17 56
Birmingham New Street 12 a		17 39	17 47													17 55	17 58					18 17
Birmingham International ✈ a																	18 13					
Coventry a																	18 24					
Lichfield Trent Valley a																						
Tamworth Low Level a																						
Nuneaton a																						
Rugby a																						
Milton Keynes Central a				17 46											18 01						18 23	
Watford Junction a																						
London Euston 15 ⊖ a	18 03			18 23				18 01	18 09						18 38			18 42			18 59	

A from 18 July

B until 15 July

OVERNIGHT SLEEPERS. For sleeper trains, operated by First ScotRail, please refer to Tables 400 - 404

Table 65

Mondays to Fridays

Scotland and North West England - West Midlands and London

	VT	XC	LM	VT	NT	TP FX	TP	NT	VT	NT	TP	VT	VT	VT	TP	XC	VT	LM	VT	LM	VT
	◇1	◇1	1	◇1		◇1 A	◇1		◇1		◇1	◇1	1 B	1 C	◇1	◇1	◇1	1	◇1	1	◇1
	⊏	✕		⊠		✕	✕		⊠		✕	⊠	⊏	⊏	✕	✕	⊠		⊠		⊠
Inverness d																					
Aberdeen d																					
Dundee d																					
Perth d																					
Edinburgh 10 d							14 07						14 51	14 51							
Haymarket d							14u11						14 57	14 57							
Glasgow Central 15 d									14 40												
Motherwell d																					
Carstairs d																					
Lockerbie d							15 06														
Carlisle 8 a							15 28		15 47				16 05	16 05							
d							15 28		15 49				16 07	16 07							
Penrith North Lakes d							15 44						16 21	16 21							
Windermere d																					
Oxenholme Lake District a							16 08		16 22												
d							16 08		16 24												
Barrow-in-Furness d																					
Lancaster 6 a							16 23		16 37				16 56	16 56							
d						16 18	16 23		16 38				16 57	16 57							
Blackpool North d								16 20		16 35	16 40				17 20						
Preston 8 a						16 37	16 42	16 47	16 56	17 02	17 08		17 15	17 15	17 45						
Preston 8 d					16 23	16 47		16 49	16 58	17 04	17 10		17 17	17 17	17 47						
Wigan North Western a									17 09	17 24			17 28	17 28							
d									17 09	17 24			17 28	17 28							
Blackrod d								17 10													
Lostock d					16 50			17 20													
Bolton a					16 55	17 08		17 25			17 34				18 08						
Manchester Piccadilly 10 ⇌ a					17 21	17 29					17 57				18 27						
Manchester Airport ✈ a						17 48					18 16				18 47						
Liverpool Lime Street 10 a										18 02											
d			17 04															17 34	17 48		
Liverpool South Parkway ✈ d			17 15															17 44			
Runcorn d			17 25															17 52	18 04		
Warrington Bank Quay a									17 20				17 39	17 39							
d									17 20				17 39	17 39							
Hartford d																		18 06			
Manchester Piccadilly 10 ⇌ d	16 55	17 06		17 15	17 23											17 27	17 35				17 55
Stockport d	17 04			17 23	17 32											17 35	17 43				18 04
Wilmslow d	17 11															17 44					18 11
Holyhead d																					
Bangor (Gwynedd) d																					
Llandudno Junction d																					
Wrexham General d																					
Chester d												17 35									
Crewe 10 a	17 27		17 47									17 54	17 59	17 59		18 05		18 20			18 27
d	17 29		17 49									17 56	18 01	18 01		18 07		18 22			18 29
Macclesfield d		17 27															17 56				
Congleton d																					
Stoke-on-Trent d		17 44		17 50													18 12			←	
Stafford a		18 03	18 09													18 27		18 42	18 35	18 42	
d		18 04	18 10													18 28		18 43	18 36	18 43	
Penkridge a			18 15															→			
Wolverhampton 7 ⇌ a		18 15	18 27										18 31	18 33		18 39				18 56	
Birmingham New Street 12 a		18 38	18 48										18 55	19 05		18 58				19 17	
Birmingham International ✈ a														19 19		19 13					
Coventry a														19 30		19 24					
Lichfield Trent Valley a																					
Tamworth Low Level a																					
Nuneaton a																					
Rugby a																					
Milton Keynes Central a				18 47								19 01									19 31
Watford Junction a	18s48													20s15					19s42		
London Euston 15 ⊖ a	19 08			19 23					19 13			19 38		20 34			19 42		20 02		20 06

A Until 14 July. ✕ from Preston ◇ from Preston

B until 15 July, from 12 September

C from 18 July until 9 September

OVERNIGHT SLEEPERS. For sleeper trains, operated by First ScotRail, please refer to Tables 400 - 404

Scotland and North West England - West Midlands and London

		VT	XC	LM	NT	TP	VT	TP	SR		VT	NT	XC	LM	VT	VT	VT	XC	LM		NT	VT	TP	TP	VT
		◇1 ⊠	◇1 ⌶	1		◇1 A ⌶	◇1 ⊏	◇1 ⌶			◇1 ⊠		◇1 B ⌶	1	◇1 ⊠	◇1 ⊠	◇1 ⊠	◇1 B ⌶	1			◇1 ⊠	◇1 ⌶	◇1	◇1 ⊏
Inverness	d																								
Aberdeen	d																								
Dundee	d																								
Perth	d																								
Edinburgh 10	d							16 12																	
Haymarket	d							16u16																	
Glasgow Central 15	d						16 00		16 12													16 40			
Motherwell	d																					16 54			
Carstairs	d																								
Lockerbie	d							17 11																	
Carlisle 8	a						17 08	17 33	18 35													17 49			
	d						17 09	17 33														17 51			
Penrith North Lakes	d							17 48														18 05			
Windermere	d					17 06																		18 15	
Oxenholme Lake District	a					17 25	17 44															18 27		18 34	
	d					17 30	17 44															18 29		18 36	
Barrow-in-Furness	d																								
Lancaster 6	a					17 47		18 26														18 43		18 52	
	d	17 36				17 48		18 26														18 44		18 52	
Blackpool North	d				17 37							18 20									18 37		18 44		
Preston 8	a	17 54			18 02	18 06	18 15	18 45				18 47									19 02	19 02	19 07	19 11	
Preston 8	d	17 56			18 04	18 08	18 17	18 47				18 49									19 04	19 05	19 10	19 16	
Wigan North Western	a	18 07			18 24		18 28														19 24	19 16			
	d	18 08			18 24		18 28														19 24	19 16			
Blackrod	d											19 10													
Lostock	d					18 30						19 20													
Bolton	a					18 34		19 08				19 25											19 34	19 42	
Manchester Piccadilly 10	a					18 56		19 27															19 56	20 01	
Manchester Airport ✈	a					19 17		19 47															20 17	20 24	
Liverpool Lime Street 10	a				19 03																20 02				
	d			18 04										18 34		18 48			19 11						
Liverpool South Parkway ✈	d			18 15										18 44					19 21						
Runcorn	d			18 24										18 52		19 04			19 29						
Warrington Bank Quay	a	18 19					18 39															19 27			
	d	18 19					18 39															19 27			
Hartford	d													19 04											
Manchester Piccadilly 10	d		18 05								18 15		18 27		18 35		18 55	19 07							19 15
Stockport	d		18 13								18 23		18 35		18 43		19 04	19 16							19 23
Wilmslow	d																19 11								
Holyhead	d																								
Bangor (Gwynedd)	d																								
Llandudno Junction	d																								
Wrexham General	d																								
Chester	d																								
Crewe 10	a			18 47			18 59							19 16		19 21	19 27		19 53						
	d			18 49			19 01							19 18		19 23	19 29		19 55						
Macclesfield	d		18 26												18 56										19 36
Congleton	d												18 54												
Stoke-on-Trent	d		18 44								18 50		19 07		19 12			19 44							19 52
Stafford	a		19 01	19 09									19 24	19 41		19 41		20 03	20 15						
	d		19 02	19 10									19 25	19 42		19 42		20 04	20 16						
Penkridge	a			19 15										19 47											
Wolverhampton 7	a		19 15	19 27			19 31						19 39	19 57				20 16	20 29						
Birmingham New Street 12	a		19 32	19 47			19 55						19 58	20 18				20 33	20 47						
Birmingham International ✈	a												20 13												
Coventry	a												20 24												
Lichfield Trent Valley	a																								
Tamworth Low Level	a																								
Nuneaton	a																								
Rugby	a																								
Milton Keynes Central	a										19 46						20 32					20 45			20 48
Watford Junction	a															20s46									
London Euston 15 ⊖	a	20 11									20 23				20 42	21 05	21 06					21 24			21 26

A ⌶ from Preston

B ⌶ to Wolverhampton

OVERNIGHT SLEEPERS. For sleeper trains, operated by First ScotRail, please refer to Tables 400 - 404

Scotland and North West England - West Midlands and London

		VT	VT	TP	TP		TP	NT	XC	LM	VT	VT	VT	XC	LM		NT	VT	TP	TP	TP	VT	NT	VT	XC
		◇1 ⊏	1 ⊏	◇1 A ⌶	◇1 B ⌶		◇1 C ⌶		◇1 D ⌶	1	◇1 ⊏	◇1 ⊏	◇1 ⊏	◇1	1			◇1 ⊏	◇1	◇1 C	◇1 ⌶	◇1 ⊏		◇1 ⊠	◇1
Inverness	d																								
Aberdeen	d																								
Dundee	d																								
Perth	d																								
Edinburgh 10	d		16 52																		18 12				
Haymarket	d		16 56																		18u16				
Glasgow Central 15	d				17 06		17 06											17 40						18 40	
Motherwell	d																								
Carstairs	d																								
Lockerbie	d				18 06		18 06											18 33			19 11				
Carlisle 8	a		18 05		18 28		18 28											18 52			19 34			19 47	
	d		18 07		18 28		18 29											18 54			19 34			19 49	
Penrith North Lakes	d				18 44		18 44											19 09			19 49				
Windermere	d																								
Oxenholme Lake District	a		18 41		19 08		19 08											19 32			20 13			20 22	
	d		18 42		19 09		19 09											19 32			20 13			20 24	
Barrow-in-Furness	d																								
Lancaster 6	a		18 56		19 26													19 47			20 26			20 37	
	d		18 57	19 13	19 26													19 47		20 02	20 26			20 38	
Blackpool North	d							19 20									19 37		19 44				20 20		
Preston 8	a		19 15	19 37	19 45		19 41	19 47									20 02	20 05	20 08	20 20	20 45		20 47	20 56	
Preston 8	d		19 16	19 47			19 47	19 49					19 58				20 04	20 08	20 10		20 47		20 49	20 58	
Wigan North Western	a		19 28										20 09				20 24	20 19						21 09	
	d		19 29										20 09				20 24	20 19						21 09	
Blackrod	d							20 10															21 10		
Lostock	d							20 20															21 20		
Bolton	a			20 08			20 08	20 25											20 34		21 08		21 25		
Manchester Piccadilly 10	a			20 27			20 27												20 56		21 27				
Manchester Airport ✈	a			20 47			20 47												21 17		21 47				
Liverpool Lime Street 10	a																21 02								
	d									19 34	19 48				20 04										
Liverpool South Parkway ✈	d									19 44					20 15										
Runcorn	d									19 52	20 04				20 24										
Warrington Bank Quay	a		19 39										20 20					20 30						21 20	
	d		19 39										20 20					20 31						21 20	
Hartford	d									20 04															
Manchester Piccadilly 10	d								19 27			19 55		20 07								20 15			20 27
Stockport	d								19 35			20 04		20 16								20 23			20 35
Wilmslow	d											20 11													
Holyhead	d																								
Bangor (Gwynedd)	d																								
Llandudno Junction	d																								
Wrexham General	d																								
Chester	d	19 35																							
Crewe 10	a	19 54	19 59							20 16	20 21	20 27	20 39		20 45			20 50							
	d	19 56	20 01							20 18	20 23	20 29	20 41		20 47			20 53							
Macclesfield	d								19 49													20 36			20 49
Congleton	d																								
Stoke-on-Trent	d								20 07					20 44								20 53			21 07
Stafford	a								20 25	20 38		20 47		21 02	21 08			21 11							21 24
	d								20 26	20 42		20 48		21 03	21 10			21 13							21 25
Penkridge	a									20 47					21 15										
Wolverhampton 7	a		20 33						20 40	20 57				21 15	21 26			21 29							21 39
Birmingham New Street 12	a		20 55						21 00	21 18				21 32	21 47			21 48							22 00
Birmingham International ✈	a								21 13																
Coventry	a								21 24																
Lichfield Trent Valley	a																								
Tamworth Low Level	a																								
Nuneaton	a										21 02														
Rugby	a												21 27												
Milton Keynes Central	a	21 03										21 35	21 47									21 50		22 39	
Watford Junction	a										21s48											22s11		23s14	
London Euston 15 ⊖	a	21 42									22 09	22 12	22 22									22 33		23 38	

A until 15 July. 1 from Preston ⌶ from Preston
◇ from Preston

B from 18 July

C until 15 July

D ⌶ to Wolverhampton

OVERNIGHT SLEEPERS. For sleeper trains, operated by First ScotRail, please refer to Tables 400 - 404

Table 65

Scotland and North West England - West Midlands and London

		LM	VT	VT	VT	NT	TP	VT	TP	TP	NT	XC	LM	TP	VT FO	VT FO	VT FX	VT FX	XC	NT	TP FO	NT
		1	◇1	◇1	◇1		◇1	◇1	◇1 A	◇1 B		◇1	1	◇1	◇1 C	◇1 D	◇1 E	◇1 F	◇1		◇1	
Inverness	d																					
Aberdeen	d																					
Dundee	d																					
Perth	d																					
Edinburgh 10	d							18 52													20 12	
Haymarket	d							18 57													20u16	
Glasgow Central 15	d														20 10	20 10	20 10	20 10				
Motherwell	d																					
Carstairs	d																20 36	20 36				
Lockerbie	d														21 05	21 05	21 05	21 05			21 11	
Carlisle 8	a							20 06							21 25	21 25	21 25	21 25			21 34	
	d							20 08							21 26	21 26	21 26	21 26			21 34	
Penrith North Lakes	d														21 40	21 40	21 41	21 41				
Windermere	d																					
Oxenholme Lake District	a							20 42							22 04	22 04	22 04	22 04			22 10	
	d							20 42							22 04	22 04	22 05	22 05			22 10	
Barrow-in-Furness	d									20 08												
Lancaster 6	a							20 57		21 10					22 19	22 19	22 19	22 19			22 26	
	d							20 57	21 03	21 10					22 19	22 19	22 20	22 20			22 26	
Blackpool North	d					20 37	20 45				21 20			21 44						22 14		22 20
Preston 8	a					21 01	21 09	21 15	21 22	21 29	21 47			22 08	22 36	22 37	22 37	22 37		22 41	22 45	22 47
Preston 8	d					21 04	21 10	21 17	21 31	21 31	21 49			22 10	22 40	22 40	22 40	22 40		22 43	22 47	22 49
Wigan North Western	a					21 23		21 28	21 47	21 47					22 51	22 51	22 51	22 51		23 02		
	d					21 23		21 28	21 48	21 48					22 52	22 52	22 52	22 52		23 03		
Blackrod	d										22 10											23 10
Lostock	d										22 20											23 20
Bolton	a						21 34				22 25			22 34							23 06	23 25
Manchester Piccadilly 10	a						21 56		22 30	22 30				22 56							23 31	
Manchester Airport	a						22 17		22 47	22 47				23 17								
Liverpool Lime Street 10	a					22 16														23 54		
	d	20 34		20 48									21 34									
Liverpool South Parkway	d	20 44											21 44									
Runcorn	d	20 52		21 04									21 52									
Warrington Bank Quay	a							21 39							23 02	23 02	23 02	23 02				
	d							21 39							23 03	23 03	23 03	23 03				
Hartford	d	21 04											22 04									
Manchester Piccadilly 10	d		21 15									21 27							22 07			
Stockport	d		21 23									21 35							22 16			
Wilmslow	d																					
Holyhead	d																					
Bangor (Gwynedd)	d				20 20																	
Llandudno Junction	d				20 38																	
Wrexham General	d																					
Chester	d				21 35																	
Crewe 10	a	21 16		21 21	21 54			21 59					22 18		23 24	23 29	23 24	23 29				
	d	21 18		21 24	21 56			22 01					22 20									
Macclesfield	d		21 36									21 49							22 29			
Congleton	d																					
Stoke-on-Trent	d		21 53									22 08							22 47			
Stafford	a	21 38		21 42								22 25	22 40						23 06			
	d	21 41		21 44								22 26	22 41						23 07			
Penkridge	a	21 46											22 46									
Wolverhampton 7	a	21 57			22 27			22 32				22 39	22 57						23 19			
Birmingham New Street 12	a	22 17			22 50			22 55				22 58	23 18						23 39			
Birmingham International	a																					
Coventry	a																					
Lichfield Trent Valley	a			21 57																		
Tamworth Low Level	a			22 03																		
Nuneaton	a			22 16																		
Rugby	a			22 30																		
Milton Keynes Central	a		22 52	22 58																		
Watford Junction	a		23s25	23s30																		
London Euston 15	a		23 48	23 56																		

A until 15 July
B from 18 July
C until 17 June
D From 24 June until 9 September
E Until 16 June
F From 20 June until 8 September

OVERNIGHT SLEEPERS. For sleeper trains, operated by First ScotRail, please refer to Tables 400 - 404

Table 65

Scotland and North West England - West Midlands and London

		TP	NT	TP	NT	TP	NT	SR	SR	SR	SR	SR	SR	SR	SR FO
		1 A	B	◇1		◇1		FX C	FO D	FX E	FO F	E	G	C	
Inverness	d											20 46		20 46	20 46
Aberdeen	d												21 40		
Dundee	d												23u06		
Perth	d											23u21		23u21	23u21
Edinburgh 10	d											01 24		01b24	01b21
Haymarket	d														
Glasgow Central 15	d							23 40	23 40	23 40	23 40				
Motherwell	d							23u56	23u56	23u56	23u56				
Carstairs	d							00u16	00u16	00u16	00u16				
Lockerbie	d														
Carlisle 8	a											02 53		02 53	03 03
	d							01u41	01u41	01u41	01u41	02 54		02 55	03 11
Penrith North Lakes	d														
Windermere	d					22 45									
Oxenholme Lake District	a					23 04									
	d					23 06									
Barrow-in-Furness	d		21 43												
Lancaster 6	a		22 45			23 23									
	d	22 42	22 46		23 07	23 24									
Blackpool North	d			22 44			23 13								
Preston 8	a	23 02	23 11	23 08	23 28	23 45	23 40	03 03	03 05	03 07	03 07	04s32		04s29	04s32
Preston 8	d			23 10			23 42	03 08	03 10	03 13	03 14				
Wigan North Western	a														
	d														
Blackrod	d						00 04								
Lostock	d						00 13								
Bolton	a			23 34			00 18								
Manchester Piccadilly 10	a			23 53											
Manchester Airport	a			00 22											
Liverpool Lime Street 10	a														
	d														
Liverpool South Parkway	d														
Runcorn	d														
Warrington Bank Quay	a							03 34	03 38	03 40	03 40				
	d							03 36	03 40	03 41	03 42				
Hartford	d														
Manchester Piccadilly 10	d														
Stockport	d														
Wilmslow	d														
Holyhead	d														
Bangor (Gwynedd)	d														
Llandudno Junction	d														
Wrexham General	d														
Chester	d														
Crewe 10	a											05s34		05s33	05s34
	d														
Macclesfield	d														
Congleton	d														
Stoke-on-Trent	d														
Stafford	a														
	d														
Penkridge	a														
Wolverhampton 7	a														
Birmingham New Street 12	a														
Birmingham International	a														
Coventry	a														
Lichfield Trent Valley	a														
Tamworth Low Level	a														
Nuneaton	a														
Rugby	a														
Milton Keynes Central	a														
Watford Junction	a							06s19	06s29	06s19	06s27				
London Euston 15	a							06 43	06 53	06 43	06 50	07 47		07 47	07 47

A until 15 July
B from 18 July
C From 20 June until 8 September
D From 24 June until 9 September
E Until 16 June, FX from 12 September
F Until 17 June, FO from 16 September
G MTWO until 15 June, MTWO from 24 October

OVERNIGHT SLEEPERS. For sleeper trains, operated by First ScotRail, please refer to Tables 400 - 404

Scotland and North West England - West Midlands and London

		TP	NT	SR	SR	SR	TP	AW	TP	TP	XC	VT	XC	VT	LM	VT	VT	TP	XC	VT	VT	LM	VT
		◇1		A	B		◇1		◇1 C	◇1	◇1	◇1	◇1	◇1	◇1	◇1	◇1	◇1	◇1	◇1	◇1	◇1	◇1
Inverness	d					20p46																	
Aberdeen	d																						
Dundee	d																						
Perth	d					23b21																	
Edinburgh 10	d					01 21																	
Haymarket	d																						
Glasgow Central 15	d			23p40	23p40																		
Motherwell	d			23b56	23b56																		
Carstairs	d			00u16	00u16																		
Lockerbie	d																						
Carlisle 8	a					03 03																	
	d			01u41	01u41	03 11																	
Penrith North Lakes	d																						
Windermere	d																						
Oxenholme Lake District	a																						
	d																						
Barrow-in-Furness	d								04 35														
Lancaster 6	a								05 28														
	d																05 40						
Blackpool North	d	22p44	23p13				03 36											05 39					
Preston 8	a	23p08	23p40	03 05	03 07	04s32											05 55	06 03					
Preston 8	d	23p10	23p42	03 10	03 14		04u01			05 16							05 58	06 05					06 17
Wigan North Western	a																06 09						06 28
	d																06 09						06 28
Blackrod	d		00 04															06 22					
Lostock	d		00 13															06 30					
Bolton	a	23p34	00 18				04e30			05 42								06 34					
Manchester Piccadilly 10	a	23p53					04 48			06 01								06 56					
Manchester Airport	a	00 22					05 07			06 18								07 17					
Liverpool Lime Street 10	a																						
	d													05 47									
Liverpool South Parkway	d																						
Runcorn	d													06 03									
Warrington Bank Quay	a			03 38	03 40												06 20						06 39
	d			03 40	03 42												06 20						06 39
Hartford	d																						
Manchester Piccadilly 10	d										05 11	05 25				05 55			06 00	06 10	06 35		
Stockport	d											05 34				06 03			06 08	06 18	06 43		
Wilmslow	d											05 41				06 11							
Holyhead	d																						
Bangor (Gwynedd)	d																						
Llandudno Junction	d																						
Wrexham General	d																						
Chester	d							04 22															
Crewe 10	a					05s34		04 44			05 41	05 57				06 27							06 58
	d							04 59			05 47	06 00			06 20	06 29						06 47	07 01
Macclesfield	d																		06 21	06 31	06 56		
Congleton	d																						
Stoke-on-Trent	d										06 08		←						06 39	06 48	07 12		
Stafford	a							05 24			06 25	06 17	06 25	06 34	06 41				06 57			07 10	
	d							05 25			06 26	06 19	06 26	06 35	06 41				06 58			07 12	
Penkridge	a										→				06 47							07 17	
Wolverhampton 7	a							05 39					06 39		06 57				07 12			07 28	07 32
Birmingham New Street 12	a							05 58					06 57		07 17				07 31			07 47	07 55
Birmingham International	a												07 13										
Coventry	a												07 24										
Lichfield Trent Valley	a																			07 11			
Tamworth Low Level	a																			07 17			
Nuneaton	a													06 57									
Rugby	a											06 49									07 52		
Milton Keynes Central	a											07 11				07 31	07 37						
Watford Junction	a			06s29	06s27							07s32		07s44									
London Euston 15	a			06 53	06 50	07 47						07 52		08 05		08 09	08 14			08 27	08 46		

A from 25 June until 10 September
B until 18 June
C from 23 July until 10 September
b Previous night, stops to pick up only
e Stops to pick up only

OVERNIGHT SLEEPERS. For sleeper trains, operated by First ScotRail, please refer to Tables 400 - 404

Scotland and North West England - West Midlands and London

		TP	TP	NT	LM	VT	LM	VT	VT	TP	XC	VT	VT	LM	VT	VT	XC	VT	LM	VT	LM	VT	XC
		◇1 A	◇1 B		◇1	◇1	◇1	◇1	◇1	◇1	◇1	◇1	◇1	◇1	◇1	◇1	◇1	◇1	◇1	◇1	◇1	◇1	◇1
Inverness	d																						
Aberdeen	d																						
Dundee	d																						
Perth	d																						
Edinburgh 10	d																						
Haymarket	d																						
Glasgow Central 15	d								04 26														
Motherwell	d																						
Carstairs	d																						
Lockerbie	d																						
Carlisle 8	a								05 43														
	d								05 44														
Penrith North Lakes	d								05 59														
Windermere	d																						
Oxenholme Lake District	a								06 21														
	d								06 22														
Barrow-in-Furness	d	05 31																					
Lancaster 6	a	06 23							06 36														
	d	06 23	06 23						06 37							06 58							
Blackpool North	d			06 19						06 40													
Preston 8	a	06 42	06 42	06 46					06 55	07 07						07 15							
Preston 8	d	06 44	06 44	06 48					06 58	07 09						07 17							
Wigan North Western	a								07 09							07 28							
	d								07 10							07 28							
Blackrod	d			07 10																			
Lostock	d			07 20						07 30													
Bolton	a	07 08	07 08	07 25						07 34													
Manchester Piccadilly 10	a	07 27	07 27							07 56													
Manchester Airport	a	07 47	07 47							08 17													
Liverpool Lime Street 10	a																						
	d				06 32	06 45								07 04	07 19				07 34	07 48			
Liverpool South Parkway	d				06 42									07 14					07 44				
Runcorn	d				06 50	07 01								07 22	07 36				07 52	08 04			
Warrington Bank Quay	a								07 20							07 39							
	d								07 20							07 39							
Hartford	d				07 02									07 36					08 04				
Manchester Piccadilly 10	d							06 55			07 07	07 15					07 27	07 35				07 55	08 07
Stockport	d							07 04			07 16	07 23					07 35	07 43				08 04	08 16
Wilmslow	d							07 11														08 11	
Holyhead	d																						
Bangor (Gwynedd)	d																						
Llandudno Junction	d																						
Wrexham General	d																						
Chester	d												07 17										
Crewe 10	a				07 14	07 18		07 27					07 36	07 47	07 52	07 58			08 19			08 27	
	d				07 16	07 20		07 29					07 39	07 49	07 55	08 01			08 22			08 29	
Macclesfield	d																07 49	07 56					
Congleton	d																						
Stoke-on-Trent	d						←				07 44	07 50					08 07	08 12			←		08 44
Stafford	a				07 40	07 38	07 40				08 02			08 10	08 14		08 25		08 42	08 35	08 42		09 02
	d				07 41	07 39	07 41				08 03			08 10	08 16		08 26		08 43	08 36	08 43		09 03
Penkridge	a				→		07 46							08 16					→		08 48		
Wolverhampton 7	a						07 57				08 17			08 28		08 31	08 39				08 58		09 15
Birmingham New Street 12	a						08 17				08 39			08 47		08 55	08 58				09 18		09 39
Birmingham International	a																09 13						
Coventry	a																09 24						
Lichfield Trent Valley	a														08 30								
Tamworth Low Level	a														08 36								
Nuneaton	a																			08 58			
Rugby	a																						
Milton Keynes Central	a											08 46											
Watford Junction	a																						
London Euston 15	a					08 59		09 04	09 12			09 23	09 30		09 46			09 42		10 00		10 04	

A from 23 July until 10 September
B until 16 July

OVERNIGHT SLEEPERS. For sleeper trains, operated by First ScotRail, please refer to Tables 400 - 404

Table 65

Saturdays until 10 September

Scotland and North West England - West Midlands and London

		LM	VT	NT	NT	TP	TP	NT	VT	VT	TP	VT	XC	VT	LM	VT	LM	VT	XC	LM	VT	NT
		◇1	◇1			◇1	◇1		◇1	◇1	◇1	◇1	◇1	◇1	◇1	◇1	◇1	◇1	◇1	◇1	◇1	
						A	B															
			⊏⊐			⌶	⌶		⊏⊐	⊏⊐	⌶	⊏⊐	⌶	⊏⊐		⊏⊐		⊏⊐	⌶		⊏⊐	
Inverness	d																					
Aberdeen	d																					
Dundee	d																					
Perth	d																					
Edinburgh 10	d																					
Haymarket	d																					
Glasgow Central 15	d								05 40			05 50										
Motherwell	d											06 04										
Carstairs	d																					
Lockerbie	d																					
Carlisle 8	a								06 46			07 02										
	d								06 49			07 03										
Penrith North Lakes	d											07 18										
Windermere	d																					
Oxenholme Lake District	a								07 22			07 41										
	d								07 24			07 42										
Barrow-in-Furness	d					06 20																
Lancaster 6	a					07 21			07 37			07 56										
	d					07 22	07 22		07 38			07 57										
Blackpool North	d			06 53	07 02			07 18			07 44											
Preston 8	a			07 15	07 28	07 41	07 41	07 46	07 56		08 11	08 15										
Preston 8	d			07 17	07 30	07 47	07 47	07 47	07 58		08 12	08 17										08 17
Wigan North Western	a				07 50				08 09			08 28										
	d				07 50				08 09			08 28										
Blackrod	d			07 40				08 10														08 41
Lostock	d			07 49				08 20														08 50
Bolton	a			07 54		08 08	08 08	08 25			08 34											08 55
Manchester Piccadilly 10	a			08 18		08 27	08 27				08 56											09 18
Manchester Airport ✈	a					08 47	08 47				09 19											
Liverpool Lime Street 10	a				08 34																	
	d	08 04													08 34	08 48				0[illegible] 04		
Liverpool South Parkway ✈	d	08 15													08 44					09 15		
Runcorn	d	08 24													08 52	09 04				09 2[illegible]		
Warrington Bank Quay	a								08 20			08 39										
	d								08 20			08 39										
Hartford	d														09 06							
Manchester Piccadilly 10	d		08 15	08 20									08 27	08 35				08 55	09 07		09 15	09 21
Stockport	d		08 23	08 35									08 35	08 43				09 04	09 16		09 23	09 35
Wilmslow	d																	09 11				
Holyhead	d									06 52												
Bangor (Gwynedd)	d									07 20												
Llandudno Junction	d									07 38												
Wrexham General	d																					
Chester	d									08 35												
Crewe 10	a	08 47								08 54		08 58			09 20			09 27		09 44		
	d	08 49								08 56		09 01			09 22			09 29		09 49		
Macclesfield	d												08 49	08 56								
Congleton	d																					
Stoke-on-Trent	d		08 50										09 07	09 12			←		09 44		09 50	
Stafford	a	09 09											09 25		09 42	09 35	09 42		10 02	10 10		
	d	09 10											09 26		09 43	09 36	09 43		10 03	10 10		
Penkridge	a	09 15													→					10 16		
Wolverhampton 7	a	09 27										09 31	09 39				09 56		10 15	10 27		
Birmingham New Street 12	a	09 47										09 55	09 58				10 17		10 39	10 47		
Birmingham International ✈	a												10 13									
Coventry	a												10 24									
Lichfield Trent Valley	a																					
Tamworth Low Level	a																					
Nuneaton	a															09 58						
Rugby	a																					
Milton Keynes Central	a		09 46							10 01												
Watford Junction	a																				10 46	
London Euston 15 ⊖	a		10 23						10 12	10 37				10 42		11 01		11 04			11 23	

A from 23 July until 10 September. ⌶ from Preston B until 16 July. ⌶ from Preston

OVERNIGHT SLEEPERS. For sleeper trains, operated by First ScotRail, please refer to Tables 400 - 404

Table 65

Saturdays until 10 September

Scotland and North West England - West Midlands and London

		TP	TP	NT	VT	SR	VT	NT	TP	VT	XC	VT	LM	VT	LM	VT	XC	LM	VT	NT	TP	NT	VT
		◇1	◇1		◇1		◇1		◇1	◇1	◇1	◇1	◇1	◇1	◇1	◇1	◇1	◇1	◇1		◇1		◇1
		A	B																				
		⌶	⌶		⊏⊐		⊏⊐		⌶	⊏⊐	⌶	⊏⊐		⊏⊐		⊏⊐	⌶		⊏⊐		⌶		⊏⊐
Inverness	d																						
Aberdeen	d																						
Dundee	d																						
Perth	d																						
Edinburgh 10	d									06 52													
Haymarket	d									06 56													
Glasgow Central 15	d				06 30	07 08															07 10		07 35
Motherwell	d				06 44																		07 52
Carstairs	d																						
Lockerbie	d				07 25																08 07		
Carlisle 8	a				07 43	09 37				08 05											08 30		08 46
	d				07 46					08 07											08 31		08 49
Penrith North Lakes	d				08 00					08 22											08 46		
Windermere	d																						
Oxenholme Lake District	a				08 22																09 09		09 22
	d				08 23																09 12		09 23
Barrow-in-Furness	d	07 29																					
Lancaster 6	a	08 26			08 37					08 56											09 26		09 37
	d	08 27	08 27		08 38					08 57											09 27		09 38
Blackpool North	d			08 20				08 38	08 44													09 20	
Preston 8	a	08 45	08 45	08 47	08 56			09 02	09 08	09 15											09 45	09 47	09 56
Preston 8	d	08 47	08 47	08 49	08 58			09 04	09 10	09 17										09 23	09 47	09 49	09 58
Wigan North Western	a				09 09			09 24		09 28													10 09
	d				09 09			09 24		09 28													10 09
Blackrod	d			09 10																		10 10	
Lostock	d			09 20																09 50		10 20	
Bolton	a	09 08	09 08	09 25					09 34											09 55	10 08	10 25	
Manchester Piccadilly 10	a	09 27	09 27						09 56											10 18	10 27		
Manchester Airport ✈	a	09 47	09 47						10 17												10 47		
Liverpool Lime Street 10	a							10 02															
	d							10 16					09 34	09 48				10 04					
Liverpool South Parkway ✈	d							10a27					09 44					10 15					
Runcorn	d												09 52	10 04				10 25					
Warrington Bank Quay	a				09 20					09 39													10 20
	d				09 20					09 39													10 20
Hartford	d												10 04										
Manchester Piccadilly 10	d										09 27	09 35				09 55	10 07		10 15	10 21			
Stockport	d										09 35	09 43				10 04	10 16		10 23	10 35			
Wilmslow	d															10 11							
Holyhead	d						07 55																
Bangor (Gwynedd)	d						08 22																
Llandudno Junction	d						08 40																
Wrexham General	d																						
Chester	d						09 35																
Crewe 10	a						09 54			09 58			10 19			10 27		10 45					
	d						09 56			10 01			10 22			10 29		10 49					
Macclesfield	d										09 49	09 56											
Congleton	d																						
Stoke-on-Trent	d										10 07	10 12			←		10 44		10 50				
Stafford	a										10 25		10 42	10 35	10 42		11 02	11 09					
	d										10 26		10 43	10 36	10 43		11 03	11 10					
Penkridge	a												→					11 15					
Wolverhampton 7	a									10 31	10 39				10 56		11 16	11 27					
Birmingham New Street 12	a									10 55	10 58				11 17		11 39	11 47					
Birmingham International ✈	a										11 13												
Coventry	a										11 24												
Lichfield Trent Valley	a																						
Tamworth Low Level	a																						
Nuneaton	a																						
Rugby	a																						
Milton Keynes Central	a						11 01												11 46				
Watford Junction	a																						
London Euston 15 ⊖	a				11 12		11 38					11 42		11 56		12 04			12 23				12 12

A from 23 July until 10 September. ⌶ from Preston B until 16 July. ⌶ from Preston

OVERNIGHT SLEEPERS. For sleeper trains, operated by First ScotRail, please refer to Tables 400 - 404

Table 65

Saturdays
until 10 September

Scotland and North West England - West Midlands and London

		VT	NT	TP	TP	VT	TP	XC	VT	LM	VT	LM	VT	XC	LM	VT	NT	TP	NT	TP	NT	VT	NT
		◇1		◇1	◇1	◇1	◇1	◇1	◇1	◇1	◇1	◇1	◇1	◇1	◇1	◇1		◇1		◇1		◇1	
																		A	B	C			
		⊡		🛒	🛒	⊡		🛒	⊡		⊡		⊡	🛒		⊡		🛒		🛒		⊡	
Inverness	d																						
Aberdeen	d																						
Dundee	d																						
Perth	d																						
Edinburgh 10	d			07 42																			
Haymarket	d			07u46																			
Glasgow Central 15	d					08 00																08 40	
Motherwell	d																						
Carstairs	d																						
Lockerbie	d																						
Carlisle 8	a			08 59		09 08																09 46	
	d			09 00		09 09																09 49	
Penrith North Lakes	d																					10 03	
Windermere	d						09 38																
Oxenholme Lake District	a						09 57																
	d						09 58																
Barrow-in-Furness	d																	09 23	10 16				
Lancaster 6	a					09 56	10 16											10 25	11 21			10 37	
	d					09 57	10 16											10 26		10 26		10 38	
Blackpool North	d		09 37		09 43																10 20		10 37
Preston 8	a		10 02	10 05	10 07	10 15	10 35											10 45		10 45	10 47	10 56	11 02
Preston 8	d		10 04		10 12	10 17											10 23	10 47		10 47	10 49	10 58	11 04
Wigan North Western	a		10 24			10 28																11 09	11 24
	d		10 24			10 28																11 09	11 24
Blackrod	d																				11 10		
Lostock	d																10 50				11 20		
Bolton	a				10 35												10 55	11 08		11 08	11 25		
Manchester Piccadilly 10	a				10 56												11 18	11 27		11 27			
Manchester Airport ✈	a				11 17													11 47		11 47			
Liverpool Lime Street 10	a		11 02																				12 02
	d		11 16							10 34	10 48				11 04								12 16
Liverpool South Parkway ✈	d		11a27							10 44					11 15								12a27
Runcorn	d									10 52	11 04				11 25								
Warrington Bank Quay	a					10 39																11 20	
	d					10 39																11 20	
Hartford	d									11 04													
Manchester Piccadilly 10	d							10 27	10 35				10 55	11 07		11 15	11 21						
Stockport	d							10 35	10 43				11 04	11 16		11 23	11 35						
Wilmslow	d												11 11										
Holyhead	d	08 55																					
Bangor (Gwynedd)	d	09 22																					
Llandudno Junction	d	09 40																					
Wrexham General	d																						
Chester	d	10 35																					
Crewe 10	a	10 54				10 58				11 19			11 27		11 45								
	d	10 56				11 01				11 22			11 29		11 49								
Macclesfield	d							10 49	10 56														
Congleton	d																						
Stoke-on-Trent	d							11 07	11 12			←		11 44		11 50							
Stafford	a							11 25		11 42	11 35	11 42		12 02	12 09								
	d							11 26		11 43	11 36	11 43		12 03	12 10								
Penkridge	a									→					12 15								
Wolverhampton 7	a					11 31		11 39				11 56		12 16	12 27								
Birmingham New Street 12	a					11 55		11 58				12 17		12 39	12 47								
Birmingham International ✈	a							12 13															
Coventry	a							12 24															
Lichfield Trent Valley	a																						
Tamworth Low Level	a																						
Nuneaton	a																						
Rugby	a																						
Milton Keynes Central	a	12 01														12 46							
Watford Junction	a																						
London Euston 15 ⊖	a	12 38							12 42		12 56		13 04			13 23						13 12	

A from 23 July until 10 September. 🛒 from Preston
B from 23 July until 10 September
C until 16 July. 🛒 from Preston

OVERNIGHT SLEEPERS. For sleeper trains, operated by First ScotRail, please refer to Tables 400 - 404

Table 65

Saturdays
until 10 September

Scotland and North West England - West Midlands and London

		TP	VT	VT	XC	VT	LM	VT	LM	VT	XC	LM	VT	NT	TP	NT	VT	TP	NT	TP	VT	VT
		◇1	◇1	◇1	◇1	◇1	◇1	◇1	◇1	◇1	◇1	◇1	◇1		◇1		◇1	◇1		◇1	◇1	◇1
															A			B				
		🛒	⊡	⊡	🛒	⊡		⊡		⊡	🛒		⊡		🛒		⊡			🛒	⊡	⊡
Inverness	d																					
Aberdeen	d																					
Dundee	d																					
Perth	d																					
Edinburgh 10	d			08 52																		
Haymarket	d			08 57																		
Glasgow Central 15	d																09 40					10 00
Motherwell	d																					
Carstairs	d																					
Lockerbie	d																					
Carlisle 8	a			10 05													10 47					11 08
	d			10 07													10 49					11 10
Penrith North Lakes	d																					11 25
Windermere	d														10 49							
Oxenholme Lake District	a			10 41											11 08		11 22					
	d			10 42											11 09		11 23					
Barrow-in-Furness	d																	11 11				
Lancaster 6	a			10 56											11 26		11 37	12 04				
	d			10 57											11 26		11 38	12 04				
Blackpool North	d	10 44														11 15			11 37	11 44		
Preston 8	a	11 08		11 15											11 45	11 42	11 56	12 23	12 02	12 08		12 15
Preston 8	d	11 10		11 17										11 23	11 47	11 49	11 58		12 04	12 10		12 17
Wigan North Western	a			11 28													12 09		12 24			12 28
	d			11 28													12 09		12 24			12 28
Blackrod	d															12 10						
Lostock	d													11 50		12 20						
Bolton	a	11 34												11 55	12 08	12 25				12 34		
Manchester Piccadilly 10	a	11 56												12 18	12 27					12 56		
Manchester Airport ✈	a	12 17													12 47					13 17		
Liverpool Lime Street 10	a																		13 02			
	d						11 34	11 48				12 04							13 16			
Liverpool South Parkway ✈	d						11 44					12 15							13a27			
Runcorn	d						11 52	12 04				12 25										
Warrington Bank Quay	a			11 39													12 20					12 39
	d			11 39													12 20					12 39
Hartford	d						12 04															
Manchester Piccadilly 10	d				11 27	11 35				11 55	12 07		12 15	12 21								
Stockport	d				11 35	11 43				12 04	12 16		12 23	12 35								
Wilmslow	d									12 11												
Holyhead	d																					
Bangor (Gwynedd)	d																					
Llandudno Junction	d																					
Wrexham General	d																					
Chester	d		11 35																		12 35	
Crewe 10	a		11 54	11 58			12 19			12 27		12 45									12 54	12 58
	d		11 56	12 01			12 22			12 29		12 49									12 57	13 01
Macclesfield	d				11 49	11 56																
Congleton	d																					
Stoke-on-Trent	d				12 07	12 12			←		12 44		12 50									
Stafford	a				12 24		12 42	12 35	12 42		13 02	13 09										
	d				12 25		12 43	12 36	12 43		13 03	13 10										
Penkridge	a						→					13 15										
Wolverhampton 7	a			12 31	12 39				12 56		13 15	13 27										13 31
Birmingham New Street 12	a			12 55	12 58				13 17		13 39	13 47										13 55
Birmingham International ✈	a				13 13																	
Coventry	a				13 24																	
Lichfield Trent Valley	a																					
Tamworth Low Level	a																					
Nuneaton	a																					
Rugby	a																					
Milton Keynes Central	a		13 01										13 46								14 01	
Watford Junction	a																					
London Euston 15 ⊖	a		13 38			13 42		13 56		14 04			14 23				14 12				14 38	

A 🛒 from Preston
B from 23 July until 10 September

OVERNIGHT SLEEPERS. For sleeper trains, operated by First ScotRail, please refer to Tables 400 - 404

Table 65

Scotland and North West England - West Midlands and London

Saturdays
until 10 September

	XC ◇1 🛒	VT ◇1 ☕	LM ◇1	VT ◇1 ☕	LM ◇1	VT ◇1 ☕	XC ◇1 🛒	LM ◇1	VT ◇1 ☕	NT	TP ◇1 A 🛒	TP ◇1 A 🛒	TP ◇1 A 🛒	TP ◇1 B	TP ◇1 C 🛒	TP ◇1 C 🛒	NT	VT ◇1 ☕	VT ◇1 ☕	NT	TP ◇1 🛒	VT ◇1 D ☕
Inverness d																						
Aberdeen d																						
Dundee d																						
Perth d																						
Edinburgh 10 d												09 52			09 52							
Haymarket d												09u56			09u56							
Glasgow Central 15 d											10 10		10 10			10 10		10 40				
Motherwell d																						
Carstairs d																						
Lockerbie d												11 01			11 01							
Carlisle 8 a											11 26	11 23	11 26		11 23	11 26		11 47				
d											11 26	11 23	11 26		11 31			11 49				
Penrith North Lakes d											11 41		11 41		11 46							
Windermere d																						
Oxenholme Lake District a											12 05		12 05		12 09			12 22				
d											12 05		12 05		12 10			12 23				
Barrow-in-Furness d																						
Lancaster 6 a												12 14			12 26			12 37				
d												12 14		12 18	12 26			12 38				
Blackpool North d																	12 20			12 37	12 44	
Preston 8 a											12 37	12 34	12 37	12 37	12 45		12 47	12 56		13 02	13 08	
Preston 8 d										12 23		12 47			12 47		12 49	12 58		13 04	13 10	
Wigan North Western a																		13 09		13 24		
d																		13 09		13 24		
Blackrod d																	13 10					
Lostock d										12 50							13 20					
Bolton a										12 55		13 08			13 08		13 25				13 34	
Manchester Piccadilly 10 a										13 18		13 27			13 27						13 56	
Manchester Airport ✈ a												13 47			13 47						14 17	
Liverpool Lime Street 10 a																				14 02		
d			12 34	12 48				13 04												14 16		
Liverpool South Parkway ✈ d			12 44					13 15												14a27		
Runcorn d			12 52	13 04				13 25														
Warrington Bank Quay a																		13 20				
d																		13 20				
Hartford d			13 06																			
Manchester Piccadilly 10 d	12 27	12 35				12 55	13 07		13 15	13 21												
Stockport d	12 35	12 43				13 04	13 16		13 23	13 35												
Wilmslow d						13 11																
Holyhead d																			11 55			
Bangor (Gwynedd) d																			12 21			
Llandudno Junction d																			12 39			
Wrexham General d																						
Chester d																			13 35			13 35
Crewe 10 a			13 20			13 27		13 45											13 54			13 54
d			13 22			13 29		13 49											13 56			13 56
Macclesfield d	12 49	12 56																				
Congleton d																						
Stoke-on-Trent d	13 07	13 12			←		13 44		13 50													
Stafford a	13 25		13 42	13 35	13 42		14 02	14 09														
d	13 26		13 43	13 36	13 43		14 03	14 10														
Penkridge a			→					14 15														
Wolverhampton 7 a	13 39				13 56		14 16	14 27														
Birmingham New Street 12 a	13 58				14 17		14 39	14 47														
Birmingham International ✈ a	14 13																					
Coventry a	14 24																					
Lichfield Trent Valley a																						
Tamworth Low Level a																						
Nuneaton a																						
Rugby a																						
Milton Keynes Central a									14 46										15 01			15 01
Watford Junction a																						
London Euston 15 ⊖ a		14 42		14 56		15 04			15 23									15 12	15 38			15 38

A from 25 June until 10 September
B until 16 July
C until 18 June
D until 9 July

OVERNIGHT SLEEPERS. For sleeper trains, operated by First ScotRail, please refer to Tables 400 - 404

Table 65

Scotland and North West England - West Midlands and London

Saturdays
until 10 September

	VT ◇1 A ☕	XC ◇1 🛒	VT ◇1 ☕	VT ◇1 B ☕	LM ◇1	VT ◇1 ☕	LM ◇1	VT ◇1 ☕	XC ◇1 🛒	LM ◇1	VT ◇1 ☕	NT	TP ◇1 C 🛒	NT	VT ◇1 ☕	NT	TP ◇1 🛒	VT ◇1 ☕	VT ◇1 ☕	SR	TP ◇1 D
Inverness d																					
Aberdeen d																					
Dundee d																					
Perth d																					
Edinburgh 10 d	10 52			10 52																	
Haymarket d	10 57			10 57																	
Glasgow Central 15 d															11 40				12 00	12 12	
Motherwell d																					
Carstairs d																					
Lockerbie d																					
Carlisle 8 a	12 05			12 05											12 46				13 08	14 32	
d	12 07			12 07											12 49				13 09		
Penrith North Lakes d															13 03						
Windermere d													12 51								
Oxenholme Lake District a	12 41			12 41									13 07								
d	12 43			12 43									13 09								
Barrow-in-Furness d																					
Lancaster 6 a	12 56			12 56									13 26		13 37				13 56		
d	12 57			12 57									13 26		13 38				13 58		14 18
Blackpool North d														13 20		13 37	13 44				
Preston 8 a	13 15			13 15									13 45	13 47	13 56	14 02	14 08		14 15		14 37
Preston 8 d	13 17			13 17								13 23	13 47	13 49	13 58	14 04	14 10		14 17		
Wigan North Western a	13 28			13 28											14 09	14 24			14 28		
d	13 28			13 28											14 09	14 24			14 28		
Blackrod d														14 10							
Lostock d												13 50		14 20							
Bolton a												13 55	14 08	14 25			14 34				
Manchester Piccadilly 10 a												14 18	14 27				14 56				
Manchester Airport ✈ a													14 47				15 17				
Liverpool Lime Street 10 a																15 02					
d					13 34	13 48				14 04						15 16					
Liverpool South Parkway ✈ d					13 44					14 15						15a27					
Runcorn d					13 52	14 04				14 25											
Warrington Bank Quay a	13 39			13 39											14 20				14 39		
d	13 39			13 39											14 20				14 39		
Hartford d					14 04																
Manchester Piccadilly 10 d		13 27	13 35					13 55	14 07		14 15	14 21									
Stockport d		13 35	13 43					14 04	14 16		14 23	14 35									
Wilmslow d								14 11													
Holyhead d																					
Bangor (Gwynedd) d																					
Llandudno Junction d																					
Wrexham General d																					
Chester d																		14 35			
Crewe 10 a	13 58			13 58	14 19			14 27		14 45								14 54	14 58		
d	14 01			14 01	14 22			14 29		14 49								14 56	15 01		
Macclesfield d		13 49	13 56																		
Congleton d																					
Stoke-on-Trent d		14 07	14 12				←		14 44		14 50										
Stafford a		14 25			14 46	14 35	14 46		15 02	15 09											
d		14 26			14 46	14 36	14 46		15 03	15 10											
Penkridge a					→					15 15											
Wolverhampton 7 a	14 31	14 39		14 31			14 59		15 16	15 27									15 31		
Birmingham New Street 12 a	14 55	14 58		15 05			15 18		15 39	15 47									15 55		
Birmingham International ✈ a		15 13		15 19																	
Coventry a		15 24		15 30																	
Lichfield Trent Valley a																					
Tamworth Low Level a																					
Nuneaton a																					
Rugby a																					
Milton Keynes Central a											15 46							16 01			
Watford Junction a				16s15																	
London Euston 15 ⊖ a			15 42	16 34		15 56		16 04			16 23				16 12			16 38			

A until 9 July
B from 16 July until 10 September
C 🛒 from Preston
D until 16 July

OVERNIGHT SLEEPERS. For sleeper trains, operated by First ScotRail, please refer to Tables 400 - 404

Scotland and North West England - West Midlands and London

		XC	VT	LM	VT	LM	VT	XC	LM	VT	NT	TP	TP	NT	NT	VT	NT	TP	VT	VT	XC	VT	LM
		◇1	◇1	◇1	◇1	◇1	◇1	◇1	◇1	◇1		◇1	◇1			◇1		◇1	◇1	◇1	◇1	◇1	◇1
												A		B									
		⊥	⊡		⊡		⊡	⊥		⊡		⊥	⊥			⊡		⊥	⊡	⊡	⊥	⊡	
Inverness	d																						
Aberdeen	d																						
Dundee	d																						
Perth	d																						
Edinburgh [10]	d												12 08							12 52			
Haymarket	d												12u12							12 57			
Glasgow Central [15]	d															12 40							
Motherwell	d																						
Carstairs	d																						
Lockerbie	d												13 06										
Carlisle [8]	a												13 30			13 47				14 05			
	d												13 30			13 49				14 07			
Penrith North Lakes	d																			14 22			
Windermere	d																						
Oxenholme Lake District	a												14 07			14 22							
	d												14 07			14 24							
Barrow-in-Furness	d											13 25		14 16									
Lancaster [6]	a											14 18	14 22	15 20		14 37				14 56			
	d											14 18	14 22			14 38				14 57			
Blackpool North	d														14 20		14 37	14 44					
Preston [8]	a											14 37	14 41		14 47	14 56	15 02	15 08		15 15			
Preston [8]	d										14 23		14 47		14 49	14 58	15 04	15 10		15 17			
Wigan North Western	a															15 09	15 24			15 28			
	d															15 09	15 24			15 28			
Blackrod	d														15 10								
Lostock	d										14 50				15 20								
Bolton	a										14 55		15 08		15 25			15 34					
Manchester Piccadilly [10]	a										15 18		15 27					15 56					
Manchester Airport	a												15 47					16 17					
Liverpool Lime Street [10]	a																16 02						
	d			14 34	14 48				15 04								16 16						15 34
Liverpool South Parkway	d			14 44					15 15								16a27						15 44
Runcorn	d			14 52	15 04				15 25														15 52
Warrington Bank Quay	a															15 20				15 39			
	d															15 20				15 39			
Hartford	d			15 04																			16 04
Manchester Piccadilly [10]	d	14 27	14 35				14 55	15 07		15 15	15 21										15 27	15 35	
Stockport	d	14 35	14 43				15 04	15 16		15 23	15 35										15 35	15 43	
Wilmslow	d						15 11																
Holyhead	d																						
Bangor (Gwynedd)	d																						
Llandudno Junction	d																						
Wrexham General	d																						
Chester	d																		15 35				
Crewe [10]	a			15 19			15 27		15 45										15 54	15 58			16 19
	d			15 22			15 29		15 49										15 56	16 01			16 22
Macclesfield	d	14 49	14 56																		15 49	15 56	
Congleton	d																						
Stoke-on-Trent	d	15 07	15 12			←		15 44		15 50											16 07	16 12	
Stafford	a	15 25		15 42	15 35	15 42		16 02	16 09												16 24		16 46
	d	15 26		15 43	15 36	15 43		16 03	16 10												16 25		16 46
Penkridge	a			→					16 15														→
Wolverhampton [7]	a	15 39				15 56		16 16	16 27											16 31	16 39		
Birmingham New Street [12]	a	15 58				16 17		16 39	16 47											16 55	16 58		
Birmingham International	a	16 13																			17 13		
Coventry	a	16 24																			17 24		
Lichfield Trent Valley	a																						
Tamworth Low Level	a																						
Nuneaton	a																						
Rugby	a																						
Milton Keynes Central	a									16 46									17 01				
Watford Junction	a																						
London Euston [15]	a		16 42		16 56		17 04			17 23						17 12			17 38			17 42	

A from 23 July until 10 September. ⊥ from Preston **B** from 23 July until 10 September

OVERNIGHT SLEEPERS. For sleeper trains, operated by First ScotRail, please refer to Tables 400 - 404

Scotland and North West England - West Midlands and London

		VT	LM	VT	XC	LM	VT	NT	TP	NT	VT	VT	NT	TP	VT	XC	VT	LM	VT	LM	VT	XC	LM
		◇1	◇1	◇1	◇1	◇1	◇1		◇1		◇1	◇1		◇1	◇1	◇1	◇1	◇1	◇1	◇1	◇1	◇1	◇1
		⊡		⊡	⊥		⊡		⊥		⊡	⊡		⊥	⊡	⊥	⊡		⊡		⊡	⊥	
Inverness	d																						
Aberdeen	d																						
Dundee	d																						
Perth	d																						
Edinburgh [10]	d																						
Haymarket	d																						
Glasgow Central [15]	d								12 54		13 40				14 00								
Motherwell	d																						
Carstairs	d																						
Lockerbie	d								13 56														
Carlisle [8]	a								14 18		14 46				15 09								
	d								14 28		14 49				15 11								
Penrith North Lakes	d								14 44														
Windermere	d																						
Oxenholme Lake District	a								15 09		15 22				15 45								
	d								15 09		15 23				15 46								
Barrow-in-Furness	d																						
Lancaster [6]	a								15 26		15 37												
	d								15 26		15 38												
Blackpool North	d									15 20			15 37	15 44									
Preston [8]	a								15 45	15 47	15 56		16 02	16 08	16 15								
Preston [8]	d							15 23	15 47	15 49	15 58		16 04	16 10	16 17								
Wigan North Western	a										16 09		16 24		16 28								
	d										16 09		16 24		16 28								
Blackrod	d									16 10													
Lostock	d							15 50		16 20													
Bolton	a							15 55	16 08	16 25				16 34									
Manchester Piccadilly [10]	a							16 18	16 27					16 56									
Manchester Airport	a								16 47					17 17									
Liverpool Lime Street [10]	a												17 05										
	d	15 48				16 04												16 34	16 48				17 04
Liverpool South Parkway	d					16 15												16 44					17 15
Runcorn	d	16 04				16 25												16 52	17 04				17 25
Warrington Bank Quay	a										16 20				16 39								
	d										16 20				16 39								
Hartford	d																	17 06					
Manchester Piccadilly [10]	d			15 55	16 07		16 15	16 21								16 27	16 35				16 55	17 06	
Stockport	d			16 04	16 16		16 23	16 35								16 35	16 43				17 04		
Wilmslow	d			16 11																	17 11		
Holyhead	d											14 38											
Bangor (Gwynedd)	d											15 07											
Llandudno Junction	d											15 27											
Wrexham General	d																						
Chester	d											16 24											
Crewe [10]	a			16 27		16 45						16 47			16 58			17 20			17 27		17 47
	d			16 29		16 49						16 56			17 01			17 22			17 29		17 49
Macclesfield	d															16 49	16 56					17 26	
Congleton	d																						
Stoke-on-Trent	d		←		16 44		16 50									17 07	17 12			←		17 44	
Stafford	a	16 35	16 46		17 02	17 09										17 25		17 42	17 35	17 42		18 03	18 09
	d	16 36	16 46		17 03	17 10										17 26		17 43	17 36	17 43		18 04	18 10
Penkridge	a					17 15												→					18 15
Wolverhampton [7]	a		16 59		17 16	17 27									17 31	17 39				17 56		18 16	18 27
Birmingham New Street [12]	a		17 18		17 39	17 47									17 55	17 58				18 17		18 38	18 47
Birmingham International	a															18 13							
Coventry	a															18 24							
Lichfield Trent Valley	a																						
Tamworth Low Level	a																						
Nuneaton	a																						
Rugby	a																						
Milton Keynes Central	a						17 46					18 01											
Watford Junction	a																						
London Euston [15]	a	17 55		18 04			18 23				18 12	18 38					18 42		18 56		19 04		

OVERNIGHT SLEEPERS. For sleeper trains, operated by First ScotRail, please refer to Tables 400 - 404

Table 65

Saturdays
until 10 September

Scotland and North West England - West Midlands and London

		VT		NT	TP	NT	VT	NT	TP	VT	XC	VT		VT	TP	TP	LM	VT	LM	VT	XC	LM		VT	NT
		◇1			◇1		◇1		◇1	◇1	◇1	◇1		◇1	◇1	◇1	◇1	◇1	◇1	◇1	◇1	◇1		◇1	
										A				B	C	D									
		☕			🍴		☕		🍴	☕	🍴	☕		☕				☕		☕	🍴			☕	
Inverness	d																								
Aberdeen	d																								
Dundee	d																								
Perth	d																								
Edinburgh 10	d				14 07					14 52				14 52											
Haymarket	d				14u11					14 57				14 57											
Glasgow Central 15	d						14 40																		
Motherwell	d																								
Carstairs	d																								
Lockerbie	d				15 06																				
Carlisle 8	a				15 28		15 46			16 05				16 05											
	d				15 28		15 49			16 07				16 07											
Penrith North Lakes	d				15 44					16 22				16 22											
Windermere	d																								
Oxenholme Lake District	a				16 08		16 22																		
	d				16 08		16 24																		
Barrow-in-Furness	d														16 22										
Lancaster 6	a				16 26		16 37			16 56				16 56	17 19										
	d				16 26		16 38			16 57				16 57	17 20	17 20									
Blackpool North	d					16 20		16 35	16 40																
Preston 8	a				16 45	16 47	16 56	17 02	17 08	17 15				17 15	17 39	17 39									
Preston 8	d			16 23	16 47	16 49	16 58	17 04	17 10	17 17				17 17											17 23
Wigan North Western	a						17 09	17 24		17 28				17 28											
	d						17 09	17 24		17 28				17 28											
Blackrod	d					17 10																			
Lostock	d			16 50		17 20																			17 50
Bolton	a			16 55	17 08	17 25			17 34																17 55
Manchester Piccadilly 10	a			17 18	17 27				17 56																18 18
Manchester Airport ✈	a				17 48				18 17																
Liverpool Lime Street 10	a							18 02																	
	d																17 34	17 48				18 04			
Liverpool South Parkway ✈	d																17 44					18 15			
Runcorn	d																17 52	18 04				18 24			
Warrington Bank Quay	a						17 20			17 39				17 39											
	d						17 20			17 39				17 39											
Hartford	d																18 06								
Manchester Piccadilly 10	d	17 15		17 21							17 27	17 35								17 55	18 05			18 15	18 21
Stockport	d	17 23		17 35							17 36	17 43								18 04	18 13			18 23	18 35
Wilmslow	d																			18 11					
Holyhead	d																								
Bangor (Gwynedd)	d																								
Llandudno Junction	d																								
Wrexham General	d																								
Chester	d																								
Crewe 10	a									17 59				17 59			18 20			18 27		18 46			
	d									18 01				18 01			18 22			18 29		18 49			
Macclesfield	d											17 56													
Congleton	d										17 54										18 26				
Stoke-on-Trent	d	17 50									18 08	18 12							←		18 44			18 50	
Stafford	a										18 26						18 42	18 34	18 42		19 02	19 09			
	d										18 27						18 43	18 36	18 43		19 03	19 10			
Penkridge	a																→					19 15			
Wolverhampton 7	a									18 31	18 40			18 31					18 56		19 16	19 27			
Birmingham New Street 12	a									18 55	18 58			19 05					19 17		19 33	19 47			
Birmingham International ✈	a										19 13			19 19											
Coventry	a										19 24			19 30											
Lichfield Trent Valley	a																								
Tamworth Low Level	a																								
Nuneaton	a																								
Rugby	a													19 42											
Milton Keynes Central	a	18 46												20 05										19 46	
Watford Junction	a													20s34											
London Euston 15 ⊖	a	19 23					19 12					19 42		20 56				19 56		20 04				20 25	

A until 9 July
B from 16 July until 10 September
C from 23 July until 10 September
D until 16 July

OVERNIGHT SLEEPERS. For sleeper trains, operated by First ScotRail, please refer to Tables 400 - 404

Table 65

Saturdays
until 10 September

Scotland and North West England - West Midlands and London

		TP	VT	NT	TP	VT	SR	TP		TP	TP	NT	XC	VT	LM	VT	LM	VT		VT	XC	LM	NT	TP	VT
		◇1	◇1		◇1	◇1		◇1		◇1	◇1		◇1	◇1	◇1	◇1	◇1	◇1		◇1	◇1	◇1		◇1	◇1
					A			B		C															
		🍴	☕		🍴	☕					🍴		🍴	☕		☕		☕		☕	🍴				☕
Inverness	d																								
Aberdeen	d																								
Dundee	d																								
Perth	d																								
Edinburgh 10	d										16 12														16 52
Haymarket	d										16u16														16 57
Glasgow Central 15	d		15 40			16 00	16 12													16 40					
Motherwell	d																			16 54					
Carstairs	d																								
Lockerbie	d										17 11														
Carlisle 8	a		16 46			17 08	18 35				17 33									17 49					18 05
	d		16 49			17 09					17 33									17 52					18 07
Penrith North Lakes	d		17 03								17 48														
Windermere	d				17 06																				
Oxenholme Lake District	a				17 25	17 44														18 25					18 41
	d				17 30	17 44														18 26					18 42
Barrow-in-Furness	d							17 21																	
Lancaster 6	a		17 37		17 47			18 16			18 26									18 40					18 56
	d		17 38		17 48			18 17		18 17	18 26									18 41					18 57
Blackpool North	d	17 20		17 37								18 20											18 37	18 42	
Preston 8	a	17 45	17 56	18 02	18 06	18 15		18 35		18 37	18 45	18 47								18 59			19 00	19 07	19 15
Preston 8	d	17 47	17 58	18 04	18 08	18 17					18 47	18 49								19 01			19 04	19 09	19 17
Wigan North Western	a		18 09	18 24		18 28														19 12			19 24		19 28
	d		18 09	18 24		18 28														19 12			19 24		19 28
Blackrod	d											19 10													
Lostock	d				18 30							19 20													
Bolton	a	18 08			18 34						19 08	19 25												19 34	
Manchester Piccadilly 10	a	18 27			18 56						19 27													19 56	
Manchester Airport ✈	a	18 47			19 17						19 51													20 17	
Liverpool Lime Street 10	a			19 02																			20 02		
	d														18 34	18 48						19 04			
Liverpool South Parkway ✈	d														18 44							19 14			
Runcorn	d														18 52	19 04						19 23			
Warrington Bank Quay	a		18 20			18 39														19 23					19 39
	d		18 20			18 39														19 23					19 39
Hartford	d														19 04										
Manchester Piccadilly 10	d												18 27	18 35				18 55			19 07				
Stockport	d												18 35	18 43				19 04			19 16				
Wilmslow	d																	19 11							
Holyhead	d																								
Bangor (Gwynedd)	d																								
Llandudno Junction	d																								
Wrexham General	d																								
Chester	d																								
Crewe 10	a					18 59									19 19			19 27				19 49			19 59
	d					19 01									19 22			19 29				19 51			20 01
Macclesfield	d													18 56											
Congleton	d												18 54												
Stoke-on-Trent	d												19 07	19 12			←				19 44				
Stafford	a												19 25		19 42	19 35	19 42				20 02	20 11			
	d												19 25		19 43	19 36	19 43				20 03	20 12			
Penkridge	a														→		19 48								
Wolverhampton 7	a					19 31							19 39				19 59				20 16	20 28			20 31
Birmingham New Street 12	a					19 55							19 58				20 17				20 33	20 47			20 55
Birmingham International ✈	a												20 13												
Coventry	a												20 24												
Lichfield Trent Valley	a																								
Tamworth Low Level	a																								
Nuneaton	a																								
Rugby	a																								
Milton Keynes Central	a																			20 41					
Watford Junction	a																			21s15					
London Euston 15 ⊖	a		20 15											20 57		21 15		21 18		21 38					

A 🍴 from Preston
B from 23 July until 10 September
C until 16 July

OVERNIGHT SLEEPERS. For sleeper trains, operated by First ScotRail, please refer to Tables 400 - 404

Table 65

Saturdays
until 10 September

Scotland and North West England - West Midlands and London

		TP	TP	NT	XC	VT	LM	VT	LM	VT	NT	TP	XC	VT	TP	NT	XC	LM	TP	VT	XC	VT
			◇1		◇1	◇1	◇1	◇1	◇1	◇1		◇1	◇1	◇1	◇1		◇1	◇1	◇1	◇1	◇1	◇1
		A			B														A			
			🛒		🛒	🍴		🍴		🍴				🍴	🛒					🍴		🍴
Inverness	d																					
Aberdeen	d																					
Dundee	d																					
Perth	d																					
Edinburgh 10	d														18 12							
Haymarket	d														18u16							
Glasgow Central 15	d		17 06							17 40				18 00								18 40
Motherwell	d																					
Carstairs	d																					
Lockerbie	d		18 06							18 32					19 11							
Carlisle 8	a		18 28							18 50				19 08	19 34							19 46
	d		18 28							18 52				19 09	19 34							19 48
Penrith North Lakes	d		18 44							19 06					19 49							20 02
Windermere	d																					
Oxenholme Lake District	a		19 08							19 28					20 13							20 24
	d		19 09							19 29					20 13							20 25
Barrow-in-Furness	d																					
Lancaster 6	a		19 26							19 43				19 55	20 26							20 39
	d	19 13	19 26							19 44				19 56	20 26				20 35			20 40
Blackpool North	d			19 20							19 37	19 43				20 20						
Preston 8	a	19 33	19 45	19 47						20 02	20 02	20 07		20 15	20 45	20 47			20 53			20 58
Preston 8	d		19 47	19 49						20 04	20 04	20 09		20 17	20 47	20 49						21 00
Wigan North Western	a									20 15	20 24			20 28								21 11
	d									20 15	20 24			20 28								21 11
Blackrod	d			20 10												21 10						
Lostock	d			20 20												21 20						
Bolton	a		20 08	20 25								20 34			21 08	21 25						
Manchester Piccadilly 10	a		20 27									20 56			21 27							
Manchester Airport	a		20 47									21 17			21 47							
Liverpool Lime Street 10	a										21 02											
	d						19 34	19 48										20 34				
Liverpool South Parkway	d						19 44											20 44				
Runcorn	d						19 52	20 04										20 52				
Warrington Bank Quay	a									20 26				20 39								21 22
	d									20 26				20 39								21 22
Hartford	d						20 04											21 03				
Manchester Piccadilly 10	d				19 27	19 35							20 07				20 27			20 35	21 07	
Stockport	d				19 35	19 43							20 16				20 35			20 43		
Wilmslow	d																					
Holyhead	d																					
Bangor (Gwynedd)	d																					
Llandudno Junction	d																					
Wrexham General	d																					
Chester	d																					
Crewe 10	a						20 16	20 21		20 45				20 59				21 16				21 41
	d						20 22	20 23		20 47				21 01				21 17				21 43
Macclesfield	d				19 49	19 56											20 49			20 56		
Congleton	d																					
Stoke-on-Trent	d				20 07	20 12			←				20 44				21 07			21 12	21 45	
Stafford	a				20 25		20 42	20 41	20 42				21 02				21 26	21 42			22 02	22 07
	d				20 26		20 43	20 42	20 43				21 03				21 27	21 42			22 03	22 08
Penkridge	a						→		20 48									21 48				
Wolverhampton 7	a				20 39				20 57				21 15	21 31			21 39	21 58			22 14	22 22
Birmingham New Street 12	a				20 58				21 17				21 32	21 54			21 58	22 20			22 32	22 40
Birmingham International	a				21 13																	
Coventry	a				21 24																	
Lichfield Trent Valley	a																					
Tamworth Low Level	a																					
Nuneaton	a																					
Rugby	a																					
Milton Keynes Central	a					21 10				21 50										22 12		
Watford Junction	a																			22s42		
London Euston 15	a					22 00		22 19		22 44										23 04		

A until 16 July

B 🛒 to Wolverhampton

OVERNIGHT SLEEPERS. For sleeper trains, operated by First ScotRail, please refer to Tables 400 - 404

Table 65

Saturdays
until 10 September

Scotland and North West England - West Midlands and London

		NT	TP	TP	VT	NT	XC	LM	TP	TP	NT	NT	TP	NT	TP	NT
			◇1	◇1	◇1		◇1	◇1	◇1	◇1			1		◇1	
			A											A		
					🍴											
Inverness	d															
Aberdeen	d															
Dundee	d															
Perth	d															
Edinburgh 10	d				18 52											
Haymarket	d				18 57											
Glasgow Central 15	d															
Motherwell	d															
Carstairs	d															
Lockerbie	d															
Carlisle 8	a				20 05											
	d				20 07											
Penrith North Lakes	d				20 22											
Windermere	d								21 40							
Oxenholme Lake District	a				20 45				21 59							
	d				20 45				22 01							
Barrow-in-Furness	d		19 33											21 43		
Lancaster 6	a		20 34		20 59				22 17					22 45		
	d		20 35		21 00				22 17				22 42	22 46		
Blackpool North	d	20 37		20 42		21 20				21 44	22 14	22 20			22 44	23 02
Preston 8	a	21 01	20 53	21 06	21 18	21 47			22 38	22 08	22 41	22 47	23 02	23 11	23 08	23 29
Preston 8	d	21 04	21 10		21 20	21 49				22 10	22 43	22 49			23 10	23 31
Wigan North Western	a	21 23			21 31						23 02					
	d	21 23			21 31						23 03					
Blackrod	d					22 10						23 10				23 52
Lostock	d					22 20						23 20				00 02
Bolton	a		21 34			22 25				22 34		23 25			23 34	00 07
Manchester Piccadilly 10	a		21 56							22 56					23 53	
Manchester Airport	a		22 17							23 17					00 22	
Liverpool Lime Street 10	a	22 14									23 54					
	d							21 34								
Liverpool South Parkway	d							21 44								
Runcorn	d							21 52								
Warrington Bank Quay	a				21 42											
	d				21 42											
Hartford	d							22 04								
Manchester Piccadilly 10	d						21 28									
Stockport	d						21 36									
Wilmslow	d															
Holyhead	d															
Bangor (Gwynedd)	d															
Llandudno Junction	d															
Wrexham General	d															
Chester	d															
Crewe 10	a				22 02			22 21								
	d				22 04			22 23								
Macclesfield	d						21 50									
Congleton	d															
Stoke-on-Trent	d						22 08									
Stafford	a				22 23		22 32	22 47								
	d				22 24		22 33	22 47								
Penkridge	a							22 53								
Wolverhampton 7	a				22 38		22 45	23 03								
Birmingham New Street 12	a				22 59		23 02	23 21								
Birmingham International	a															
Coventry	a															
Lichfield Trent Valley	a															
Tamworth Low Level	a															
Nuneaton	a															
Rugby	a															
Milton Keynes Central	a															
Watford Junction	a															
London Euston 15	a															

A from 23 July until 10 September

OVERNIGHT SLEEPERS. For sleeper trains, operated by First ScotRail, please refer to Tables 400 - 404

Table 65

Scotland and North West England - West Midlands and London

		TP	NT	SR	SR	TP	AW	TP	TP	XC	VT	XC	VT	LM	VT	VT	TP	XC	VT	VT	LM	VT	TP
Inverness	d				20p46																		
Aberdeen	d																						
Dundee	d																						
Perth	d				23b21																		
Edinburgh	d				01 21																		
Haymarket	d																						
Glasgow Central	d			23p40																			
Motherwell	d			23b56																			
Carstairs	d			00u16																			
Lockerbie	d																						
Carlisle	a				03 03																		
	d			01u41	03 11																		
Penrith North Lakes	d																						
Windermere	d																						
Oxenholme Lake District	a																						
	d																						
Barrow-in-Furness	d							04 35															05 31
Lancaster	a							05 28															06 23
	d															05 40							06 23
Blackpool North	d	22p44	23p13			03 36											05 39						
Preston	a	23p08	23p40	03 07	04s32											05 55	06 03						06 42
Preston	d	23p10	23p42	03 14		04u01			05 16							05 58	06 05					06 17	06 44
Wigan North Western	a															06 09						06 28	
	d															06 09						06 28	
Blackrod	d		00 04														06 22						
Lostock	d		00 13														06 30						
Bolton	a	23p34	00 18			04e30			05 42								06 34						07 08
Manchester Piccadilly	a	23p53				04 48			06 01								06 56						07 27
Manchester Airport	a	00 22				05 07			06 18								07 17						07 47
Liverpool Lime Street	a																						
	d												05 47										
Liverpool South Parkway	d																						
Runcorn	d												06 03										
Warrington Bank Quay	a			03 40												06 20						06 39	
	d			03 42												06 20						06 39	
Hartford	d																						
Manchester Piccadilly	d									05 11	05 25				05 55			06 00	06 10	06 35			
Stockport	d										05 34				06 03			06 08	06 18	06 43			
Wilmslow	d										05 41				06 11								
Holyhead	d																						
Bangor (Gwynedd)	d																						
Llandudno Junction	d																						
Wrexham General	d																						
Chester	d						04 22																
Crewe	a				05s34		04 44			05 41	05 57				06 27							06 58	
	d						04 59			05 47	06 00			06 20	06 29						06 47	07 01	
Macclesfield	d																	06 21	06 31	06 56			
Congleton	d																						
Stoke-on-Trent	d									06 08		←						06 39	06 48	07 12			
Stafford	a						05 24			06 25	06 17	06 25	06 34	06 41				06 57			07 10		
	d						05 25			06 26	06 19	06 26	06 35	06 41				06 58			07 12		
Penkridge	a									→				06 47							07 17		
Wolverhampton	a						05 39					06 39		06 57				07 12			07 28	07 32	
Birmingham New Street	a						05 58					06 57		07 17				07 31			07 47	07 55	
Birmingham International	a											07 13											
Coventry	a											07 24											
Lichfield Trent Valley	a																		07 11				
Tamworth Low Level	a																		07 17				
Nuneaton	a												06 57										
Rugby	a										06 49									07 52			
Milton Keynes Central	a										07 11				07 31	07 37							
Watford Junction	a			06s27							07s32		07s44										
London Euston	a			06 50	07 47						07 52		08 05		08 09	08 14			08 27	08 46			

b Previous night, stops to pick up only

e Stops to pick up only

OVERNIGHT SLEEPERS. For sleeper trains, operated by First ScotRail, please refer to Tables 400 - 404

Table 65

Scotland and North West England - West Midlands and London

		NT	LM	VT	LM	VT	VT	TP	XC	VT	VT	LM	VT	VT	XC	VT	LM	VT	LM	VT	XC	LM	VT
Inverness	d																						
Aberdeen	d																						
Dundee	d																						
Perth	d																						
Edinburgh	d																						
Haymarket	d																						
Glasgow Central	d						04 26																
Motherwell	d																						
Carstairs	d																						
Lockerbie	d																						
Carlisle	a						05 43																
	d						05 44																
Penrith North Lakes	d						05 59																
Windermere	d																						
Oxenholme Lake District	a						06 21																
	d						06 22																
Barrow-in-Furness	d																						
Lancaster	a						06 36																
	d						06 37							06 58									
Blackpool North	d	06 19						06 40															
Preston	a	06 46					06 55	07 07						07 15									
Preston	d	06 48					06 58	07 09						07 17									
Wigan North Western	a						07 09							07 28									
	d						07 10							07 28									
Blackrod	d	07 10																					
Lostock	d	07 20						07 30															
Bolton	a	07 25						07 34															
Manchester Piccadilly	a							07 56															
Manchester Airport	a							08 17															
Liverpool Lime Street	a																						
	d		06 32	06 45								07 04	07 19				07 34	07 48				08 04	
Liverpool South Parkway	d		06 42									07 14					07 44					08 15	
Runcorn	d		06 50	07 01								07 22	07 36				07 52	08 04				08 24	
Warrington Bank Quay	a						07 20							07 39									
	d						07 20							07 39									
Hartford	d		07 02									07 36					08 04						
Manchester Piccadilly	d					06 55			07 07	07 15					07 27	07 35				07 55	08 07		08 15
Stockport	d					07 04			07 16	07 23					07 35	07 43				08 04	08 16		08 23
Wilmslow	d					07 11														08 11			
Holyhead	d																						
Bangor (Gwynedd)	d																						
Llandudno Junction	d																						
Wrexham General	d																						
Chester	d										07 17												
Crewe	a		07 14	07 18		07 27					07 36	07 47	07 52	07 58			08 19			08 27		08 47	
	d		07 16	07 20		07 29					07 39	07 49	07 55	08 01			08 22			08 29		08 49	
Macclesfield	d														07 49	07 56							
Congleton	d																						
Stoke-on-Trent	d				←				07 44	07 50					08 07	08 12			←		08 44		08 50
Stafford	a		07 40	07 38	07 40				08 02			08 10	08 14		08 25		08 42	08 35	08 42		09 02	09 09	
	d		07 41	07 39	07 41				08 03			08 10	08 16		08 26		08 43	08 36	08 43		09 03	09 10	
Penkridge	a		→		07 46							08 16					→		08 48			09 15	
Wolverhampton	a				07 57				08 16			08 28		08 31	08 39				08 58		09 15	09 27	
Birmingham New Street	a				08 17				08 38			08 47		08 55	08 58				09 18		09 39	09 47	
Birmingham International	a														09 13								
Coventry	a														09 24								
Lichfield Trent Valley	a												08 30										
Tamworth Low Level	a												08 36										
Nuneaton	a																	08 58					
Rugby	a																						
Milton Keynes Central	a									08 46													09 46
Watford Junction	a																						
London Euston	a			08 59		09 04	09 12			09 23	09 30		09 46			09 42		10 00		10 04			10 23

OVERNIGHT SLEEPERS. For sleeper trains, operated by First ScotRail, please refer to Tables 400 - 404

Table 65

Saturdays
from 17 September

Scotland and North West England - West Midlands and London

		NT	NT	TP	NT	VT	VT	TP	VT	XC	VT	LM	VT	LM	VT	XC	LM	VT	NT	TP	NT	VT
				◇1		◇1	◇1	◇1	◇1	◇1	◇1	◇1	◇1	◇1	◇1	◇1	◇1	◇1		◇1		◇1
				A																A		
				⊼		⊏	⊏	⊼	⊏	⊼	⊏		⊏		⊏	⊼		⊏		⊼		⊏
Inverness	d																					
Aberdeen	d																					
Dundee	d																					
Perth	d																					
Edinburgh 10	d																					
Haymarket	d																					
Glasgow Central 15	d					05 40			05 50													06 30
Motherwell	d								06 04													06 44
Carstairs	d																					
Lockerbie	d																					07 25
Carlisle 8	a					06 46			07 02													07 43
	d					06 49			07 03													07 46
Penrith North Lakes	d								07 18													08 00
Windermere	d																					
Oxenholme Lake District	a					07 22			07 41													08 22
	d					07 24			07 42													08 23
Barrow-in-Furness	d			06 20																07 29		
Lancaster 6	a			07 21		07 37			07 56											08 26		08 37
	d			07 22		07 38			07 57											08 27		08 38
Blackpool North	d	06 53	07 02		07 18			07 44													08 20	
Preston 8	a	07 15	07 28	07 41	07 46	07 56		08 11	08 15											08 45	08 47	08 56
Preston 8	d	07 17	07 30	07 47	07 47	07 58		08 12	08 17										08 17	08 47	08 49	08 58
Wigan North Western	a		07 50			08 09			08 28													09 09
	d		07 50			08 09			08 28													09 09
Blackrod	d	07 40			08 10														08 41		09 10	
Lostock	d	07 49			08 20														08 50		09 20	
Bolton	a	07 54		08 08	08 25			08 34											08 55	09 08	09 25	
Manchester Piccadilly 10 ⇌	a	08 18		08 27				08 56											09 18	09 27		
Manchester Airport ✈	a			08 47				09 19												09 47		
Liverpool Lime Street 10	a		08 34																			
	d											08 34	08 48				09 04					
Liverpool South Parkway ✈	d											08 44					09 15					
Runcorn	d											08 52	09 04				09 24					
Warrington Bank Quay	a					08 20			08 39													09 20
	d					08 20			08 39													09 20
Hartford	d											09 06										
Manchester Piccadilly 10 ⇌	d	08 20								08 27	08 35				08 55	09 07		09 15	09 21			
Stockport	d	08 35								08 35	08 43				09 04	09 16		09 23	09 35			
Wilmslow	d														09 11							
Holyhead	d						06 52															
Bangor (Gwynedd)	d						07 20															
Llandudno Junction	d						07 38															
Wrexham General	d																					
Chester	d						08 35															
Crewe 10	a						08 54		08 58			09 20			09 27		09 44					
	d						08 56		09 01			09 22			09 29		09 49					
Macclesfield	d									08 49	08 56											
Congleton	d																					
Stoke-on-Trent	d									09 07	09 12			←		09 44		09 50				
Stafford	a									09 25		09 42	09 35	09 42		10 02	10 10					
	d									09 26		09 43	09 36	09 43		10 03	10 10					
Penkridge	a											→					10 16					
Wolverhampton 7 ⇌	a								09 31	09 39				09 56		10 15	10 27					
Birmingham New Street 12	a								09 55	09 58				10 17		10 39	10 47					
Birmingham International ✈	a									10 13												
Coventry	a									10 24												
Lichfield Trent Valley	a																					
Tamworth Low Level	a																					
Nuneaton	a												09 58									
Rugby	a																					
Milton Keynes Central	a						10 01											10 46				
Watford Junction	a																					
London Euston 15 ⊖	a					10 12	10 37				10 42		11 01		11 04			11 23				11 12

A ⊼ from Preston

OVERNIGHT SLEEPERS. For sleeper trains, operated by First ScotRail, please refer to Tables 400 - 404

Table 65

Saturdays
from 17 September

Scotland and North West England - West Midlands and London

		SR	VT	NT	TP	VT	XC	VT	LM	VT	LM	VT	XC	LM	VT	NT	TP	NT	VT	VT	NT	TP	TP
			◇1		◇1	◇1	◇1	◇1	◇1	◇1	◇1	◇1	◇1	◇1	◇1		◇1		◇1	◇1		◇1	◇1
			⊏		⊼	⊏	⊼	⊏		⊏		⊏	⊼		⊏		⊼		⊏	⊏		⊼	⊼
Inverness	d																						
Aberdeen	d																						
Dundee	d																						
Perth	d																						
Edinburgh 10	d					06 52																07 42	
Haymarket	d					06 56																07u46	
Glasgow Central 15	d	07 08															07 10		07 35				
Motherwell	d																		07 52				
Carstairs	d																						
Lockerbie	d																08 07						
Carlisle 8	a	09 37				08 05											08 30		08 46			08 59	
	d					08 07											08 31		08 49			09 00	
Penrith North Lakes	d					08 22											08 46						
Windermere	d																						
Oxenholme Lake District	a																09 09		09 22				
	d																09 12		09 23				
Barrow-in-Furness	d																						
Lancaster 6	a					08 56											09 26		09 37				
	d					08 57											09 27		09 38				
Blackpool North	d			08 38	08 44													09 20			09 37		09 43
Preston 8	a			09 02	09 08	09 15											09 45	09 47	09 56		10 02	10 05	10 07
Preston 8	d			09 04	09 10	09 17										09 23	09 47	09 49	09 58		10 04	10 12	
Wigan North Western	a			09 24		09 28													10 09		10 24		
	d			09 24		09 28													10 09		10 24		
Blackrod	d																	10 10					
Lostock	d															09 50		10 20					
Bolton	a				09 34											09 55	10 08	10 25					10 35
Manchester Piccadilly 10 ⇌	a				09 56											10 18	10 27						10 56
Manchester Airport ✈	a				10 17												10 47						11 17
Liverpool Lime Street 10	a			10 02																	11 02		
	d			10 16					09 34	09 48				10 04							11 16		
Liverpool South Parkway ✈	d			10a27					09 44					10 15							11a27		
Runcorn	d								09 52	10 04				10 25									
Warrington Bank Quay	a					09 39													10 20				
	d					09 39													10 20				
Hartford	d								10 04														
Manchester Piccadilly 10 ⇌	d						09 27	09 35				09 55	10 07		10 15	10 21							
Stockport	d						09 35	09 43				10 04	10 16		10 23	10 35							
Wilmslow	d											10 11											
Holyhead	d		07 55																	08 55			
Bangor (Gwynedd)	d		08 22																	09 22			
Llandudno Junction	d		08 40																	09 40			
Wrexham General	d																						
Chester	d		09 35																	10 35			
Crewe 10	a		09 54			09 58			10 19			10 27		10 45						10 54			
	d		09 56			10 01			10 22			10 29		10 49						10 56			
Macclesfield	d						09 49	09 56															
Congleton	d																						
Stoke-on-Trent	d						10 07	10 12			←		10 44		10 50								
Stafford	a						10 25		10 42	10 35	10 42		11 02	11 09									
	d						10 26		10 43	10 36	10 43		11 03	11 10									
Penkridge	a								→					11 15									
Wolverhampton 7 ⇌	a					10 31	10 39				10 56		11 16	11 27									
Birmingham New Street 12	a					10 55	10 58				11 17		11 39	11 47									
Birmingham International ✈	a						11 13																
Coventry	a						11 24																
Lichfield Trent Valley	a																						
Tamworth Low Level	a																						
Nuneaton	a																						
Rugby	a																						
Milton Keynes Central	a		11 01												11 46					12 01			
Watford Junction	a																						
London Euston 15 ⊖	a		11 38					11 42		11 56		12 04			12 23				12 12	12 38			

OVERNIGHT SLEEPERS. For sleeper trains, operated by First ScotRail, please refer to Tables 400 - 404

Table 65

Saturdays
from 17 September

Scotland and North West England - West Midlands and London

		VT	TP	XC	VT	LM	VT	LM	VT	XC	LM	VT	NT	TP	NT	NT	VT	NT	TP	VT	VT	XC
		◇1	◇1	◇1	◇1	◇1	◇1	◇1	◇1	◇1	◇1	◇1		◇1			◇1		◇1	◇1	◇1	◇1
		☕		⊼	☕		☕		☕	⊼		☕		A ⊼			☕		⊼	☕	☕	⊼
Inverness	d																					
Aberdeen	d																					
Dundee	d																					
Perth	d																					
Edinburgh 10	d																				08 52	
Haymarket	d																				08 57	
Glasgow Central 15	d	08 00															08 40					
Motherwell	d																					
Carstairs	d																					
Lockerbie	d																					
Carlisle 8	a	09 08															09 46				10 05	
	d	09 09															09 49				10 07	
Penrith North Lakes	d																10 03					
Windermere	d		09 38																			
Oxenholme Lake District	a		09 57																		10 41	
	d		09 58																		10 42	
Barrow-in-Furness	d													09 23	10 16							
Lancaster 6	a	09 56	10 16											10 25	11 21		10 37				10 56	
	d	09 57	10 16											10 26			10 38				10 57	
Blackpool North	d															10 20		10 37	10 44			
Preston 8	a	10 15	10 35											10 45		10 47	10 56	11 02	11 08		11 15	
Preston 8	d	10 17											10 23	10 47		10 49	10 58	11 04	11 10		11 17	
Wigan North Western	a	10 28															11 09	11 24			11 28	
	d	10 28															11 09	11 24			11 28	
Blackrod	d															11 10						
Lostock	d												10 50			11 20						
Bolton	a												10 55	11 08		11 25			11 34			
Manchester Piccadilly 10	a												11 18	11 27					11 56			
Manchester Airport	a													11 47					12 17			
Liverpool Lime Street 10	a																	12 02				
	d					10 34	10 48				11 04							12 16				
Liverpool South Parkway	d					10 44					11 15							12a27				
Runcorn	d					10 52	11 04				11 25											
Warrington Bank Quay	a	10 39															11 20				11 39	
	d	10 39															11 20				11 39	
Hartford	d					11 04																
Manchester Piccadilly 10	d			10 27	10 35				10 55	11 07		11 15	11 21									11 27
Stockport	d			10 35	10 43				11 04	11 16		11 23	11 35									11 35
Wilmslow	d								11 11													
Holyhead	d																					
Bangor (Gwynedd)	d																					
Llandudno Junction	d																					
Wrexham General	d																					
Chester	d																			11 35		
Crewe 10	a	10 58				11 19			11 27		11 45									11 54	11 58	
	d	11 01				11 22			11 29		11 49									11 56	12 01	
Macclesfield	d			10 49	10 56																	11 49
Congleton	d																					
Stoke-on-Trent	d			11 07	11 12			←		11 44		11 50										12 07
Stafford	a			11 25		11 42	11 35	11 42		12 02	12 09											12 24
	d			11 26		11 43	11 36	11 43		12 03	12 10											12 25
Penkridge	a					→					12 15											
Wolverhampton 7	a	11 31		11 39				11 56		12 16	12 27										12 31	12 39
Birmingham New Street 12	a	11 55		11 58				12 17		12 39	12 47										12 55	12 58
Birmingham International	a			12 13																		13 13
Coventry	a			12 24																		13 24
Lichfield Trent Valley	a																					
Tamworth Low Level	a																					
Nuneaton	a																					
Rugby	a																					
Milton Keynes Central	a											12 46								13 01		
Watford Junction	a																					
London Euston 15	a				12 42		12 56		13 04			13 23					13 12			13 38		

A ⊼ from Preston

OVERNIGHT SLEEPERS. For sleeper trains, operated by First ScotRail, please refer to Tables 400 - 404

Table 65

Saturdays
from 17 September

Scotland and North West England - West Midlands and London

		VT	LM	VT	LM	VT	XC	LM	VT	NT	TP	NT	VT	TP	NT	TP	VT	VT	XC	VT	LM	VT	LM
		◇1	◇1	◇1	◇1	◇1	◇1	◇1	◇1		◇1		◇1	◇1		◇1	◇1	◇1	◇1	◇1	◇1	◇1	◇1
		☕		☕		☕	⊼		☕		A ⊼		☕			⊼	☕	☕	⊼	☕		☕	
Inverness	d																						
Aberdeen	d																						
Dundee	d																						
Perth	d																						
Edinburgh 10	d																						
Haymarket	d																						
Glasgow Central 15	d												09 40					10 00					
Motherwell	d																						
Carstairs	d																						
Lockerbie	d																						
Carlisle 8	a												10 47					11 08					
	d												10 49					11 10					
Penrith North Lakes	d																	11 25					
Windermere	d										10 49												
Oxenholme Lake District	a										11 08		11 22										
	d										11 09		11 23										
Barrow-in-Furness	d													11 25									
Lancaster 6	a										11 26		11 37	12 18									
	d										11 26		11 38	12 18									
Blackpool North	d											11 15			11 37	11 44							
Preston 8	a										11 45	11 42	11 56	12 37	12 02	12 08		12 15					
Preston 8	d									11 23	11 47	11 49	11 58		12 04	12 10		12 17					
Wigan North Western	a												12 09		12 24			12 28					
	d												12 09		12 24			12 28					
Blackrod	d											12 10											
Lostock	d									11 50		12 20											
Bolton	a									11 55	12 08	12 25				12 34							
Manchester Piccadilly 10	a									12 18	12 27					12 56							
Manchester Airport	a										12 47					13 17							
Liverpool Lime Street 10	a														13 02								
	d		11 34	11 48				12 04							13 16						12 34	12 48	
Liverpool South Parkway	d		11 44					12 15							13a27						12 44		
Runcorn	d		11 52	12 04				12 25													12 52	13 04	
Warrington Bank Quay	a												12 20					12 39					
	d												12 20					12 39					
Hartford	d		12 04																		13 06		
Manchester Piccadilly 10	d	11 35				11 55	12 07		12 15	12 21									12 27	12 35			
Stockport	d	11 43				12 04	12 16		12 23	12 35									12 35	12 43			
Wilmslow	d					12 11																	
Holyhead	d																						
Bangor (Gwynedd)	d																						
Llandudno Junction	d																						
Wrexham General	d																						
Chester	d																12 35						
Crewe 10	a		12 19			12 27		12 45									12 54	12 58			13 20		
	d		12 22			12 29		12 49									12 57	13 01			13 22		
Macclesfield	d	11 56																	12 49	12 56			
Congleton	d																						
Stoke-on-Trent	d	12 12			←		12 44		12 50										13 07	13 12			←
Stafford	a		12 42	12 35	12 42		13 02	13 09											13 25		13 42	13 35	13 42
	d		12 43	12 36	12 43		13 03	13 10											13 26		13 43	13 36	13 43
Penkridge	a		→					13 15													→		
Wolverhampton 7	a				12 56		13 15	13 27										13 31	13 39				13 56
Birmingham New Street 12	a				13 17		13 39	13 47										13 55	13 58				14 17
Birmingham International	a																		14 13				
Coventry	a																		14 24				
Lichfield Trent Valley	a																						
Tamworth Low Level	a																						
Nuneaton	a																						
Rugby	a																						
Milton Keynes Central	a								13 46								14 01						
Watford Junction	a																						
London Euston 15	a	13 42		13 56		14 04			14 23				14 12				14 38			14 42		14 56	

A ⊼ from Preston

OVERNIGHT SLEEPERS. For sleeper trains, operated by First ScotRail, please refer to Tables 400 - 404

Scotland and North West England - West Midlands and London

		VT ◇1 ☕	XC ◇1 🛒	LM ◇1	VT ◇1 ☕	NT	TP ◇1 🛒	TP ◇1 🛒	NT	VT ◇1 ☕	NT	TP ◇1 🛒	VT ◇1 ☕	VT ◇1 ☕	XC ◇1 🛒	VT ◇1 ☕	LM ◇1	VT ◇1 ☕	LM ◇1	VT ◇1 ☕	XC ◇1 🛒	LM ◇1	VT ◇1 ☕
Inverness	d																						
Aberdeen	d																						
Dundee	d																						
Perth	d																						
Edinburgh 10	d						09 52							10 52									
Haymarket	d						09u56							10 57									
Glasgow Central 15	d							10 10		10 40													
Motherwell	d																						
Carstairs	d																						
Lockerbie	d						11 01																
Carlisle 8	a						11 23	11 26		11 47				12 05									
	d						11 31			11 49				12 07									
Penrith North Lakes	d						11 46																
Windermere	d																						
Oxenholme Lake District	a						12 09			12 22				12 41									
	d						12 10			12 23				12 43									
Barrow-in-Furness	d																						
Lancaster 6	a						12 26			12 37				12 56									
	d						12 26			12 38				12 57									
Blackpool North	d								12 20		12 37	12 44											
Preston 8	a						12 45		12 47	12 56	13 02	13 08		13 15									
Preston 8	d					12 23	12 47		12 49	12 58	13 04	13 10		13 17									
Wigan North Western	a									13 09	13 24			13 28									
	d									13 09	13 24			13 28									
Blackrod	d								13 10														
Lostock	d					12 50			13 20														
Bolton	a					12 55	13 08		13 25			13 34											
Manchester Piccadilly 10	a					13 18	13 27					13 56											
Manchester Airport ✈	a						13 47					14 17											
Liverpool Lime Street 10	a										14 02												
	d			13 04							14 16						13 34	13 48				14 04	
Liverpool South Parkway ✈	d			13 15							14a27						13 44					14 15	
Runcorn	d			13 25													13 52	14 04				14 25	
Warrington Bank Quay	a									13 20				13 39									
	d									13 20				13 39									
Hartford	d																14 04						
Manchester Piccadilly 10	d	12 55	13 07		13 15	13 21									13 27	13 35				13 55	14 07		14 15
Stockport	d	13 04	13 16		13 23	13 35									13 35	13 43				14 04	14 16		14 23
Wilmslow	d	13 11																		14 11			
Holyhead	d																						
Bangor (Gwynedd)	d																						
Llandudno Junction	d																						
Wrexham General	d																						
Chester	d												13 35										
Crewe 10	a	13 27		13 45									13 54	13 58			14 19			14 27		14 45	
	d	13 29		13 49									13 56	14 01			14 22			14 29		14 49	
Macclesfield	d														13 49	13 56							
Congleton	d																						
Stoke-on-Trent	d		13 44		13 50										14 07	14 12			←		14 44		14 50
Stafford	a		14 02	14 09											14 25		14 46	14 35	14 46		15 02	15 09	
	d		14 03	14 10											14 26		14 46	14 36	14 46		15 03	15 10	
Penkridge	a			14 15													↪					15 15	
Wolverhampton 7	a		14 16	14 27										14 31	14 39				14 59		15 16	15 27	
Birmingham New Street 12	a		14 39	14 47										14 55	14 58				15 18		15 39	15 47	
Birmingham International ✈	a														15 13								
Coventry	a														15 24								
Lichfield Trent Valley	a																						
Tamworth Low Level	a																						
Nuneaton	a																						
Rugby	a																						
Milton Keynes Central	a				14 46								15 01										15 46
Watford Junction	a																						
London Euston 15 ⊖	a	15 04			15 23					15 12			15 38			15 42		15 56		16 04			16 23

OVERNIGHT SLEEPERS. For sleeper trains, operated by First ScotRail, please refer to Tables 400 - 404

Scotland and North West England - West Midlands and London

		NT	TP ◇1 A 🛒	NT	VT ◇1 ☕	NT	TP ◇1 🛒	VT ◇1 ☕	VT ◇1 ☕	SR	XC ◇1 🛒	VT ◇1 ☕	LM ◇1	VT ◇1 ☕	LM ◇1	VT ◇1 ☕	XC ◇1 🛒	LM ◇1	VT ◇1 ☕	NT	TP ◇1 A 🛒	TP ◇1 🛒
Inverness	d																					
Aberdeen	d																					
Dundee	d																					
Perth	d																					
Edinburgh 10	d																					12 08
Haymarket	d																					12u12
Glasgow Central 15	d				11 40				12 00	12 12												
Motherwell	d																					
Carstairs	d																					
Lockerbie	d																					13 06
Carlisle 8	a				12 46				13 08	14 32												13 30
	d				12 49				13 09													13 30
Penrith North Lakes	d				13 03																	
Windermere	d		12 51																			
Oxenholme Lake District	a		13 07																			14 07
	d		13 09																			14 07
Barrow-in-Furness	d																				13 25	
Lancaster 6	a		13 26		13 37				13 56												14 18	14 22
	d		13 26		13 38				13 58												14 18	14 22
Blackpool North	d			13 20		13 37	13 44															
Preston 8	a		13 45	13 47	13 56	14 02	14 08		14 15												14 37	14 41
Preston 8	d	13 23	13 47	13 49	13 58	14 04	14 10		14 17											14 23		14 47
Wigan North Western	a				14 09	14 24			14 28													
	d				14 09	14 24			14 28													
Blackrod	d			14 10																		
Lostock	d	13 50		14 20																14 50		
Bolton	a	13 55	14 08	14 25			14 34													14 55		15 08
Manchester Piccadilly 10	a	14 18	14 27				14 56													15 18		15 27
Manchester Airport ✈	a		14 47				15 17															15 47
Liverpool Lime Street 10	a					15 02																
	d					15 16							14 34	14 48				15 04				
Liverpool South Parkway ✈	d					15a27							14 44					15 15				
Runcorn	d												14 52	15 04				15 25				
Warrington Bank Quay	a				14 20				14 39													
	d				14 20				14 39													
Hartford	d												15 04									
Manchester Piccadilly 10	d	14 21									14 27	14 35				14 55	15 07		15 15	15 21		
Stockport	d	14 35									14 35	14 43				15 04	15 16		15 23	15 35		
Wilmslow	d															15 11						
Holyhead	d																					
Bangor (Gwynedd)	d																					
Llandudno Junction	d																					
Wrexham General	d																					
Chester	d							14 35														
Crewe 10	a							14 54	14 58				15 19			15 27		15 45				
	d							14 56	15 01				15 22			15 29		15 49				
Macclesfield	d										14 49	14 56										
Congleton	d																					
Stoke-on-Trent	d										15 07	15 12			←		15 44		15 50			
Stafford	a										15 25		15 42	15 35	15 42		16 02	16 09				
	d										15 26		15 43	15 36	15 43		16 03	16 10				
Penkridge	a												↪					16 15				
Wolverhampton 7	a								15 31		15 39				15 56		16 16	16 27				
Birmingham New Street 12	a								15 55		15 58				16 17		16 39	16 47				
Birmingham International ✈	a										16 13											
Coventry	a										16 24											
Lichfield Trent Valley	a																					
Tamworth Low Level	a																					
Nuneaton	a																					
Rugby	a																					
Milton Keynes Central	a							16 01											16 46			
Watford Junction	a																					
London Euston 15 ⊖	a				16 12			16 38				16 42		16 56		17 04			17 23			

A 🛒 from Preston

OVERNIGHT SLEEPERS. For sleeper trains, operated by First ScotRail, please refer to Tables 400 - 404

Table 65

Scotland and North West England - West Midlands and London

		NT	NT	VT	NT	TP	VT	VT	XC	VT	LM	VT	LM	VT	XC	LM	VT	NT	TP	NT	VT	VT	NT
				◇1 ⊡		◇1 ⊼	◇1 ⊡	◇1 ⊡	◇1 ⊼	◇1 ⊡	◇1	◇1 ⊡	◇1	◇1 ⊡	◇1 ⊼	◇1	◇1 ⊡		◇1 ⊼		◇1 ⊡	◇1 ⊡	
Inverness	d																						
Aberdeen	d																						
Dundee	d																						
Perth	d																						
Edinburgh 10	d							12 52															
Haymarket	d							12 57															
Glasgow Central 15	d			12 40															12 54		13 40		
Motherwell	d																						
Carstairs	d																						
Lockerbie	d																		13 56				
Carlisle 8	a			13 47				14 05											14 18		14 46		
	d			13 49				14 07											14 28		14 49		
Penrith North Lakes	d							14 22											14 44				
Windermere	d																						
Oxenholme Lake District	a			14 22															15 09		15 22		
	d			14 24															15 09		15 23		
Barrow-in-Furness	d	14 16																					
Lancaster 6	a	15 20		14 37				14 56											15 26		15 37		
	d			14 38				14 57											15 26		15 38		
Blackpool North	d		14 20		14 37	14 44														15 20			15 37
Preston 8	a		14 47	14 56	15 02	15 08		15 15											15 45	15 47	15 56		16 02
Preston 8	d		14 49	14 58	15 04	15 10		15 17										15 23	15 47	15 49	15 58		16 04
Wigan North Western	a			15 09	15 24			15 28													16 09		16 24
	d			15 09	15 24			15 28													16 09		16 24
Blackrod	d		15 10																	16 10			
Lostock	d		15 20															15 50		16 20			
Bolton	a		15 25			15 34												15 55	16 08	16 25			
Manchester Piccadilly 10	a					15 56												16 18	16 27				
Manchester Airport ✈	a					16 17													16 47				
Liverpool Lime Street 10	a				16 02																		17 05
	d				16 16						15 34	15 48				16 04							
Liverpool South Parkway ✈	d				16a27						15 44					16 15							
Runcorn	d										15 52	16 04				16 25							
Warrington Bank Quay	a			15 20				15 39													16 20		
	d			15 20				15 39													16 20		
Hartford	d										16 04												
Manchester Piccadilly 10	d								15 27	15 35				15 55	16 07		16 15	16 21					
Stockport	d								15 35	15 43				16 04	16 16		16 23	16 35					
Wilmslow	d													16 11									
Holyhead	d																					14 38	
Bangor (Gwynedd)	d																					15 07	
Llandudno Junction	d																					15 27	
Wrexham General	d																						
Chester	d						15 35															16 24	
Crewe 10	a						15 54	15 58			16 19			16 27		16 45						16 47	
	d						15 56	16 01			16 22			16 29		16 49						16 56	
Macclesfield	d								15 49	15 56													
Congleton	d																						
Stoke-on-Trent	d								16 07	16 12			←		16 44		16 50						
Stafford	a								16 24		16 46	16 35	16 46		17 02	17 09							
	d								16 25		16 46	16 36	16 46		17 03	17 10							
Penkridge	a										→					17 15							
Wolverhampton 7	a							16 31	16 39				16 59		17 16	17 27							
Birmingham New Street 12	a							16 55	16 58				17 18		17 39	17 47							
Birmingham International ✈	a								17 13														
Coventry	a								17 24														
Lichfield Trent Valley	a																						
Tamworth Low Level	a																						
Nuneaton	a																						
Rugby	a																						
Milton Keynes Central	a						17 01										17 46					18 01	
Watford Junction	a																						
London Euston 15 ⊖	a			17 12			17 38			17 42		17 55		18 04			18 23				18 12	18 38	

OVERNIGHT SLEEPERS. For sleeper trains, operated by First ScotRail, please refer to Tables 400 - 404

Table 65

Scotland and North West England - West Midlands and London

		TP	VT	XC	VT	LM	VT	LM	VT	XC	LM	VT	NT	TP	NT	VT	NT	TP	VT	TP	XC	VT
		◇1 ⊼	◇1 ⊡	◇1 ⊼	◇1 ⊡	◇1	◇1 ⊡	◇1	◇1 ⊡	◇1 ⊼	◇1	◇1 ⊡		◇1 ⊼		◇1 ⊡		◇1 ⊼	◇1 ⊡	◇1 ⊼	◇1 ⊼	◇1 ⊡
Inverness	d																					
Aberdeen	d																					
Dundee	d																					
Perth	d																					
Edinburgh 10	d													14 07					14 52			
Haymarket	d													14u11					14 57			
Glasgow Central 15	d		14 00													14 40						
Motherwell	d																					
Carstairs	d																					
Lockerbie	d													15 06								
Carlisle 8	a		15 09											15 28		15 46			16 05			
	d		15 11											15 28		15 49			16 07			
Penrith North Lakes	d													15 44					16 22			
Windermere	d																					
Oxenholme Lake District	a		15 45											16 08		16 22						
	d		15 46											16 08		16 24						
Barrow-in-Furness	d																			16 22		
Lancaster 6	a													16 26		16 37			16 56	17 19		
	d													16 26		16 38			16 57	17 20		
Blackpool North	d	15 44													16 20		16 35	16 40				
Preston 8	a	16 08	16 15											16 45	16 47	16 56	17 02	17 08	17 15	17 39		
Preston 8	d	16 10	16 17										16 23	16 47	16 49	16 58	17 04	17 10	17 17			
Wigan North Western	a		16 28													17 09	17 24		17 28			
	d		16 28													17 09	17 24		17 28			
Blackrod	d														17 10							
Lostock	d												16 50		17 20							
Bolton	a	16 34											16 55	17 08	17 25			17 34				
Manchester Piccadilly 10	a	16 56											17 18	17 27				17 56				
Manchester Airport ✈	a	17 17												17 48				18 17				
Liverpool Lime Street 10	a																18 02					
	d					16 34	16 48				17 04											
Liverpool South Parkway ✈	d					16 44					17 15											
Runcorn	d					16 52	17 04				17 25											
Warrington Bank Quay	a		16 39													17 20			17 39			
	d		16 39													17 20			17 39			
Hartford	d					17 06																
Manchester Piccadilly 10	d			16 27	16 35				16 55	17 06		17 15	17 21								17 27	17 35
Stockport	d			16 35	16 43				17 04			17 23	17 35								17 36	17 43
Wilmslow	d								17 11													
Holyhead	d																					
Bangor (Gwynedd)	d																					
Llandudno Junction	d																					
Wrexham General	d																					
Chester	d																					
Crewe 10	a		16 58			17 20			17 27		17 47								17 59			
	d		17 01			17 22			17 29		17 49								18 01			
Macclesfield	d			16 49	16 56					17 26												17 56
Congleton	d																				17 54	
Stoke-on-Trent	d			17 07	17 12			←		17 44		17 50									18 08	18 12
Stafford	a			17 25		17 42	17 35	17 42		18 03	18 09										18 26	
	d			17 26		17 43	17 36	17 43		18 04	18 10										18 27	
Penkridge	a					→					18 15											
Wolverhampton 7	a		17 31	17 39				17 56		18 16	18 27								18 31		18 40	
Birmingham New Street 12	a		17 55	17 58				18 17		18 38	18 47								18 55		18 58	
Birmingham International ✈	a			18 13																	19 13	
Coventry	a			18 24																	19 24	
Lichfield Trent Valley	a																					
Tamworth Low Level	a																					
Nuneaton	a																					
Rugby	a																					
Milton Keynes Central	a											18 46										
Watford Junction	a																					
London Euston 15 ⊖	a				18 42		18 56		19 04			19 23				19 12						19 42

OVERNIGHT SLEEPERS. For sleeper trains, operated by First ScotRail, please refer to Tables 400 - 404

Scotland and North West England - West Midlands and London

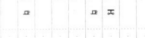

		LM	VT	LM	VT	XC	LM	VT	NT	TP	VT	NT	TP	VT	SR	TP	TP	NT	XC	VT	LM	VT	LM
		◇1	◇1	◇1	◇1	◇1	◇1	◇1		◇1	◇1		◇1	◇1		◇1	◇1		◇1	◇1	◇1	◇1	◇1
			⊏		⊏	⊼		⊏		⊼	⊏		A ⊼	⊏			⊼		⊼	⊏		⊏	
Inverness	d																						
Aberdeen	d																						
Dundee	d																						
Perth	d																						
Edinburgh 10	d																16 12						
Haymarket	d																16u16						
Glasgow Central 15	d										15 40			16 00	16 12								
Motherwell	d																						
Carstairs	d																						
Lockerbie	d																17 11						
Carlisle 8	a										16 46			17 08	18 35		17 33						
	d										16 49			17 09			17 33						
Penrith North Lakes	d										17 03						17 48						
Windermere	d												17 06										
Oxenholme Lake District	a												17 25	17 44									
	d												17 30	17 44									
Barrow-in-Furness	d															17 21							
Lancaster 6	a										17 37		17 47			18 16	18 26						
	d										17 38		17 48			18 17	18 26						
Blackpool North	d									17 20		17 37						18 20					
Preston 8	a									17 45	17 56	18 02	18 06	18 15		18 35	18 45	18 47					
Preston 8	d								17 23	17 47	17 58	18 04	18 08	18 17			18 47	18 49					
Wigan North Western	a										18 09	18 24		18 28									
	d										18 09	18 24		18 28									
Blackrod	d																	19 10					
Lostock	d								17 50				18 30					19 20					
Bolton	a								17 55	18 08			18 34				19 08	19 25					
Manchester Piccadilly 10	a								18 18	18 27			18 56				19 27						
Manchester Airport	a									18 47			19 17				19 51						
Liverpool Lime Street 10	a											19 02											
	d	17 34	17 48				18 04														18 34	18 48	
Liverpool South Parkway	d	17 44					18 15														18 44		
Runcorn	d	17 52	18 04				18 24														18 52	19 04	
Warrington Bank Quay	a										18 20			18 39									
	d										18 20			18 39									
Hartford	d	18 06																			19 04		
Manchester Piccadilly 10	d				17 55	18 05		18 15	18 21										18 27	18 35			
Stockport	d				18 04	18 13		18 23	18 35										18 35	18 43			
Wilmslow	d				18 11																		
Holyhead	d																						
Bangor (Gwynedd)	d																						
Llandudno Junction	d																						
Wrexham General	d																						
Chester	d																						
Crewe 10	a	18 20			18 27		18 46							18 59							19 19		
	d	18 22			18 29		18 49							19 01							19 22		
Macclesfield	d					18 26														18 56			
Congleton	d																		18 54				
Stoke-on-Trent	d			←		18 44		18 50											19 07	19 12			←
Stafford	a	18 42	18 34	18 42		19 02	19 09												19 25		19 42	19 35	19 42
	d	18 43	18 36	18 43		19 03	19 10												19 25		19 43	19 36	19 43
Penkridge	a	→					19 15														→		19 48
Wolverhampton 7	a			18 56		19 16	19 27							19 31					19 39				19 59
Birmingham New Street 12	a			19 17		19 33	19 47							19 55					19 58				20 17
Birmingham International	a																		20 13				
Coventry	a																		20 24				
Lichfield Trent Valley	a																						
Tamworth Low Level	a																						
Nuneaton	a																						
Rugby	a																						
Milton Keynes Central	a							19 46															
Watford Junction	a																						
London Euston 15	a		19 56		20 04			20 25			20 15									20 57		21 15	

A ⊼ from Preston

OVERNIGHT SLEEPERS. For sleeper trains, operated by First ScotRail, please refer to Tables 400 - 404

Scotland and North West England - West Midlands and London

		VT	VT	XC	LM	NT	TP	VT	TP	NT	XC	VT	LM	VT	LM	VT	NT	TP	XC	VT	TP	NT	XC
		◇1	◇1	◇1	◇1		◇1	◇1	◇1		◇1	◇1	◇1	◇1	◇1	◇1		◇1	◇1	◇1	◇1		◇1
		⊏	⊏	⊼				⊏	⊼		A ⊼	⊏		⊏		⊏				⊏	⊼		
Inverness	d																						
Aberdeen	d																						
Dundee	d																						
Perth	d																						
Edinburgh 10	d							16 52													18 12		
Haymarket	d							16 57													18u16		
Glasgow Central 15	d		16 40						17 06							17 40				18 00			
Motherwell	d		16 54																				
Carstairs	d																						
Lockerbie	d								18 06							18 32					19 11		
Carlisle 8	a		17 49					18 05	18 28							18 50				19 08	19 34		
	d		17 52					18 07	18 28							18 52				19 09	19 34		
Penrith North Lakes	d								18 44							19 06					19 49		
Windermere	d																						
Oxenholme Lake District	a		18 25					18 41	19 08							19 28					20 13		
	d		18 26					18 42	19 09							19 29					20 13		
Barrow-in-Furness	d																						
Lancaster 6	a		18 40					18 56	19 26							19 43				19 55	20 26		
	d		18 41					18 57	19 26							19 44				19 56	20 26		
Blackpool North	d					18 37	18 42			19 20							19 37	19 43				20 20	
Preston 8	a		18 59			19 00	19 07	19 15	19 45	19 47						20 02	20 02	20 07		20 15	20 45	20 47	
Preston 8	d		19 01			19 04	19 09	19 17	19 47	19 49						20 04	20 04	20 09		20 17	20 47	20 49	
Wigan North Western	a		19 12			19 24		19 28								20 15	20 24			20 28			
	d		19 12			19 24		19 28								20 15	20 24			20 28			
Blackrod	d									20 10												21 10	
Lostock	d									20 20												21 20	
Bolton	a						19 34		20 08	20 25								20 34			21 08	21 25	
Manchester Piccadilly 10	a						19 56		20 27									20 56			21 27		
Manchester Airport	a						20 17		20 47									21 17			21 47		
Liverpool Lime Street 10	a					20 02											21 02						
	d				19 04								19 34	19 48									
Liverpool South Parkway	d				19 14								19 44										
Runcorn	d				19 23								19 52	20 04									
Warrington Bank Quay	a		19 23					19 39								20 26				20 39			
	d		19 23					19 39								20 26				20 39			
Hartford	d												20 04										
Manchester Piccadilly 10	d	18 55		19 07							19 27	19 35							20 07				20 27
Stockport	d	19 04		19 16							19 35	19 43							20 16				20 35
Wilmslow	d	19 11																					
Holyhead	d																						
Bangor (Gwynedd)	d																						
Llandudno Junction	d																						
Wrexham General	d																						
Chester	d																						
Crewe 10	a	19 27			19 49			19 59					20 16			20 45				20 59			
	d	19 29			19 51			20 01					20 22			20 47				21 01			
Macclesfield	d										19 49	19 56											20 49
Congleton	d																						
Stoke-on-Trent	d			19 44							20 07	20 12			←				20 44				21 07
Stafford	a			20 02	20 11						20 25		20 42	20 35	20 42				21 02				21 26
	d			20 03	20 12						20 26		20 43	20 36	20 43				21 03				21 27
Penkridge	a												→		20 48								
Wolverhampton 7	a			20 16	20 28			20 31			20 39				20 57				21 15	21 31			21 39
Birmingham New Street 12	a			20 33	20 47			20 55			20 58				21 17				21 32	21 54			21 58
Birmingham International	a										21 13												
Coventry	a										21 24												
Lichfield Trent Valley	a																						
Tamworth Low Level	a																						
Nuneaton	a																						
Rugby	a																						
Milton Keynes Central	a		20 41									21 10				21 50							
Watford Junction	a		21s15																				
London Euston 15	a	21 18	21 38									22 00		22 14		22 44							

A ⊼ to Wolverhampton

OVERNIGHT SLEEPERS. For sleeper trains, operated by First ScotRail, please refer to Tables 400 - 404

Table 65

Saturdays
from 17 September

Scotland and North West England - West Midlands and London

		LM	VT	XC	VT	NT	TP	TP	VT	NT	XC	LM	TP	TP	NT	NT	TP	NT	TP	NT
		◇1	◇1	◇1	◇1		◇1	◇1	◇1		◇1	◇1	◇1	◇1			1		◇1	
			☕		☕				☕											
Inverness	d																			
Aberdeen	d																			
Dundee	d																			
Perth	d																			
Edinburgh 10	d								18 52											
Haymarket	d								18 57											
Glasgow Central 15	d				18 40															
Motherwell	d																			
Carstairs	d																			
Lockerbie	d																			
Carlisle 8	a				19 46				20 05											
	d				19 48				20 07											
Penrith North Lakes	d				20 02				20 22											
Windermere	d												21 40							
Oxenholme Lake District	a				20 24				20 45				21 59							
	d				20 25				20 45				22 01							
Barrow-in-Furness	d						19 33											21 43		
Lancaster 6	a				20 39		20 34		20 59				22 17					22 45		
	d				20 40		20 35		21 00				22 17				22 42	22 46		
Blackpool North	d					20 37		20 42		21 20				21 44	22 14	22 20			22 44	23 02
Preston 8	a				20 58	21 01	20 53	21 06	21 18	21 47			22 38	22 08	22 41	22 47	23 02	23 11	23 08	23 29
Preston 8	d				21 00	21 04	21 10		21 20	21 49				22 10	22 43	22 49			23 10	23 31
Wigan North Western	a				21 11	21 23			21 31						23 02					
	d				21 11	21 23			21 31						23 03					
Blackrod	d									22 10						23 10				23 52
Lostock	d									22 20						23 20				00 02
Bolton	a						21 34			22 25				22 34		23 25			23 34	00 07
Manchester Piccadilly 10	a						21 56							22 56					23 53	
Manchester Airport ✈	a						22 17							23 17					00 22	
Liverpool Lime Street 10	a					22 14									23 54					
	d	20 34										21 34								
Liverpool South Parkway ✈	d	20 44										21 44								
Runcorn	d	20 52										21 52								
Warrington Bank Quay	a				21 22				21 42											
	d				21 22				21 42											
Hartford	d	21 03										22 04								
Manchester Piccadilly 10	d		20 35	21 07							21 28									
Stockport	d		20 43								21 36									
Wilmslow	d																			
Holyhead	d																			
Bangor (Gwynedd)	d																			
Llandudno Junction	d																			
Wrexham General	d																			
Chester	d																			
Crewe 10	a	21 16			21 41				22 02			22 21								
	d	21 17			21 43				22 04			22 23								
Macclesfield	d		20 56								21 50									
Congleton	d																			
Stoke-on-Trent	d		21 12	21 45							22 08									
Stafford	a	21 42		22 02	22 07				22 23		22 32	22 47								
	d	21 42		22 03	22 08				22 24		22 33	22 47								
Penkridge	a	21 48										22 53								
Wolverhampton 7	a	21 58		22 14	22 22				22 38		22 45	23 03								
Birmingham New Street 12	a	22 20		22 32	22 40				22 59		23 02	23 21								
Birmingham International ✈	a																			
Coventry	a																			
Lichfield Trent Valley	a																			
Tamworth Low Level	a																			
Nuneaton	a																			
Rugby	a																			
Milton Keynes Central	a		22 12																	
Watford Junction	a		22s42																	
London Euston 15 ⊖	a		23 04																	

OVERNIGHT SLEEPERS. For sleeper trains, operated by First ScotRail, please refer to Tables 400 - 404

Table 65

Sundays

Scotland and North West England - West Midlands and London

		TP	NT	TP	VT	TP	NT	VT	VT	XC	XC	VT	VT	TP	TP	VT	XC	XC	VT	NT	NT	LM	LM
		◇1		◇1	◇1	◇1		◇1	◇1	◇1	◇1	◇1	◇1	◇1	◇1	◇1	◇1	◇1	◇1			◇1	1
		A	A	B		C				D	E				C		F	E					
					☕			☕	☕	⊼	☕⊼	☕	☕			☕	☕⊼	☕⊼	☕				
Inverness	d																						
Aberdeen	d																						
Dundee	d																						
Perth	d																						
Edinburgh 10	d																						
Haymarket	d																						
Glasgow Central 15	d																						
Motherwell	d																						
Carstairs	d																						
Lockerbie	d																						
Carlisle 8	a																						
	d																						
Penrith North Lakes	d																						
Windermere	d																						
Oxenholme Lake District	a																						
	d																						
Barrow-in-Furness	d														09 17								
Lancaster 6	a														10 17								
	d														10 21								
Blackpool North	d	22p44	23p02	07 48		08 14	08 20							08 44						08 50	09 20		
Preston 8	a	23p08	23p29	08 12		08 38	08 47							09 08	10 40					09 14	09 47		
Preston 8	d	23p10	23p31	08 14		08 42	08 49						09 00	09 10						09 15	09 49		
Wigan North Western	a												09 10							09 35			
	d												09 11							09 36			
Blackrod	d		23p52				09 10														10 10		
Lostock	d		00 02				09 20														10 20		
Bolton	a	23p34	00 07	08 37		09 05	09 25							09 34							10 25		
Manchester Piccadilly 10	a	23p53		08 59		09 28								09 56									
Manchester Airport ✈	a	00 22		09 19		09 50								10 17									
Liverpool Lime Street 10	a																			10 24			
	d								08 15			08 38							09 38				
Liverpool South Parkway ✈	d																						
Runcorn	d								08 35			08 54							09 54				
Warrington Bank Quay	a												09 21										
	d												09 22										
Hartford	d																						
Manchester Piccadilly 10	d				08 05			08 20		08 27	08 27					09 20	09 27	09 27					
Stockport	d				08 14			08 28		08 36	08 36					09 27	09 36	09 36					
Wilmslow	d				08 22					08 43	08 43												
Holyhead	d																						
Bangor (Gwynedd)	d																						
Llandudno Junction	d																						
Wrexham General	d																						
Chester	d																						
Crewe 10	a				08 39				08 52	09 01	09 01	09 11	09 41						10 12				
	d				08 43				08 53	09 05	09 05	09 13	09 43						10 14			10 20	10 37
Macclesfield	d							08 42								09 40	09 49	09 49					
Congleton	d																						
Stoke-on-Trent	d							08 59								09 57	10 07	10 07					10 58
Stafford	a				09 01					09 25	09 25	09 31					10 26	10 26	10 32			10 41	11 17
	d				09 02					09 26	09 26	09 32					10 27	10 27	10 33			10 41	
Penkridge	a																					10 48	
Wolverhampton 7	a									09 40	09 40						10 42	10 42				11 00	
Birmingham New Street 12	a									09 58	09 58						10 59	10 59				11 17	
Birmingham International ✈	a									10 13	10 13						11 13	11 13					
Coventry	a									10 24	10 33						11 24	11 28					
Lichfield Trent Valley	a																						
Tamworth Low Level	a																						
Nuneaton	a											09 54							10 55				
Rugby	a												10 31										
Milton Keynes Central	a								10 17				11 06			11 16			11 46				
Watford Junction	a				10s35			10s41				11s16	11s43										
London Euston 15 ⊖	a				10 57			11 02	11 06			11 37	12 05			12 08			12 32				

A not 22 May
B until 11 September
C from 18 September
D until 31 July, from 18 September

E from 7 August until 11 September.
☕ from Birmingham New Street
⊼ to Wolverhampton

F until 31 July, from 18 September.
☕ from Birmingham New Street
⊼ to Wolverhampton

OVERNIGHT SLEEPERS. For sleeper trains, operated by First ScotRail, please refer to Tables 400 - 404

Table 65

Sundays

Scotland and North West England - West Midlands and London

		VT	TP	NT	VT	VT	TP	TP	NT	XC	XC	VT	VT	VT	TP	NT	VT	VT	VT	NT	XC	XC	VT
		◇1	◇1		◇1	◇1	◇1	◇1		◇1	◇1	◇1	◇1	◇1	◇1		◇1	◇1	◇1		◇1	◇1	◇1
							A	B		C	D										E	D	
Inverness	d																						
Aberdeen	d																						
Dundee	d																						
Perth	d																						
Edinburgh 10	d																						
Haymarket	d																						
Glasgow Central 15	d																						
Motherwell	d																						
Carstairs	d																						
Lockerbie	d																						
Carlisle 8	a																						
	d																						
Penrith North Lakes	d																						
Windermere	d																						
Oxenholme Lake District	a																						
	d																						
Barrow-in-Furness	d						09 17																
Lancaster 6	a						10 17																
	d						10 21	10 21															
Blackpool North	d		09 44	09 50					10 20						10 44	10 50				11 20			
Preston 8	a		10 08	10 14			10 40	10 40	10 47						11 08	11 14				11 47			
Preston 8	d	10 00	10 10	10 15		10 17	10 47	10 47	10 49					10 58	11 10	11 15			11 17	11 49			
Wigan North Western	a	10 10		10 36		10 28								11 09		11 35			11 28				
	d	10 11		10 36		10 28								11 09		11 36			11 28				
Blackrod	d								11 10											12 10			
Lostock	d								11 20											12 20			
Bolton	a		10 34				11 08	11 08	11 25						11 34					12 25			
Manchester Piccadilly 10	a		10 56				11 27	11 27							11 56								
Manchester Airport	a		11 17				11 47	11 47							12 17								
Liverpool Lime Street 10	a			11 24												12 24							
	d												10 38										
Liverpool South Parkway	d																						
Runcorn	d												10 54										
Warrington Bank Quay	a	10 21				10 39								11 20					11 39				
	d	10 22				10 39								11 20					11 39				
Hartford	d																						
Manchester Piccadilly 10	d				10 20					10 27	10 27	10 35					11 15				11 27	11 27	11 35
Stockport	d				10 29					10 36	10 36	10 42					11 23				11 36	11 36	11 43
Wilmslow	d				10 36																		
Holyhead	d																						
Bangor (Gwynedd)	d																						
Llandudno Junction	d																						
Wrexham General	d																						
Chester	d																	11 28					
Crewe 10	a	10 41			10 53	10 59							11 12					11 47	11 59				
	d	10 43			10 55	11 01							11 14					11 49	12 01				
Macclesfield	d									10 49	10 49	10 55									11 49	11 49	11 56
Congleton	d																						
Stoke-on-Trent	d									11 07	11 07	11 12					11 51				12 07	12 07	12 13
Stafford	a									11 27	11 27		11 34								12 24	12 24	
	d									11 28	11 28		11 36								12 25	12 25	
Penkridge	a																						
Wolverhampton 7	a					11 31				11 41	11 41								12 32		12 40	12 40	
Birmingham New Street 12	a					11 55				12 00	12 00								12 55		12 58	12 58	
Birmingham International	a									12 13	12 13										13 13	13 13	
Coventry	a									12 24	12 27										13 24	13 27	
Lichfield Trent Valley	a																						
Tamworth Low Level	a																						
Nuneaton	a												11 58					12 31					
Rugby	a	11 31										11 56											
Milton Keynes Central	a	12 06										12 20					12 50	13 03					
Watford Junction	a				12s35								12s50										
London Euston 15 ⊖	a	12 45			12 56							12 59	13 11	13 21			13 28	13 44					13 47

A from 24 July until 11 September
B until 17 July
C until 31 July, from 18 September
D from 7 August until 11 September. from Birmingham New Street; to Wolverhampton
E until 31 July, from 18 September. from Birmingham New Street; to Wolverhampton

OVERNIGHT SLEEPERS. For sleeper trains, operated by First ScotRail, please refer to Tables 400 - 404

Table 65

Sundays

Scotland and North West England - West Midlands and London

		LM	VT	LM	VT	VT	TP	NT	VT	VT	VT	TP	TP	NT	XC	VT	NT	LM	VT	LM	VT	VT
		1	◇1	1	◇1	◇1	◇1		◇1	◇1	◇1	◇1	◇1		◇1	◇1		1	◇1	1	◇1	◇1
												A	B				A					
Inverness	d																					
Aberdeen	d																					
Dundee	d																					
Perth	d																					
Edinburgh 10	d																					
Haymarket	d																					
Glasgow Central 15	d					09 37																10 34
Motherwell	d																					10 49
Carstairs	d																					
Lockerbie	d																					
Carlisle 8	a					10 44																11 44
	d					10 46																11 46
Penrith North Lakes	d					11 00																12 00
Windermere	d																					
Oxenholme Lake District	a					11 22																12 22
	d					11 23																12 24
Barrow-in-Furness	d											11 25					12 45					
Lancaster 6	a					11 37						12 26					13 50					12 37
	d					11 38					12 00	12 26	12 26									12 38
Blackpool North	d						11 44	11 50						12 20								
Preston 8	a					11 56	12 08	12 14			12 15	12 45	12 45	12 47								12 56
Preston 8	d					11 58	12 10	12 15			12 17	12 47	12 47	12 49								12 58
Wigan North Western	a					12 09		12 35			12 28											13 09
	d					12 09		12 36			12 28											13 09
Blackrod	d													13 10								
Lostock	d													13 20								
Bolton	a						12 34					13 08	13 08	13 25								
Manchester Piccadilly 10	a						12 56					13 27	13 27									
Manchester Airport	a						13 17					13 47	13 47									
Liverpool Lime Street 10	a							13 24														
	d	11 34	11 48															12 34	12 48			
Liverpool South Parkway	d	11 44																12 44				
Runcorn	d	11 52	12 04															12 52	13 04			
Warrington Bank Quay	a					12 20					12 39											13 20
	d					12 20					12 39											13 20
Hartford	d	12 04																13 03				
Manchester Piccadilly 10	d				11 55				12 15						12 26	12 35					12 55	
Stockport	d				12 05				12 23						12 35	12 44					13 05	
Wilmslow	d				12 12																13 12	
Holyhead	d									10 55												
Bangor (Gwynedd)	d									11 22												
Llandudno Junction	d									11 40												
Wrexham General	d																					
Chester	d									12 33												
Crewe 10	a	12 20			12 28					12 52	12 59							13 19			13 28	
	d	12 22			12 30					12 56	13 01							13 22			13 30	
Macclesfield	d														12 49	12 57						
Congleton	d																					
Stoke-on-Trent	d			←					12 51						13 07	13 14				←		
Stafford	a	12 41	12 35	12 41											13 24			13 42	13 35	13 42		
	d	12 42	12 36	12 42											13 25			13 43	13 36	13 43		
Penkridge	a	→		12 48														→		13 48		
Wolverhampton 7	a			12 59							13 31				13 40					13 58		
Birmingham New Street 12	a			13 16							13 55				13 58					14 15		
Birmingham International	a														14 13							
Coventry	a														14 24							
Lichfield Trent Valley	a																					
Tamworth Low Level	a																					
Nuneaton	a																					
Rugby	a																					
Milton Keynes Central	a								13 49	14 02												
Watford Junction	a																					
London Euston 15 ⊖	a		14 01		14 09	14 16			14 27	14 43						14 47			15 01		15 09	15 15

A from 24 July
B until 17 July

OVERNIGHT SLEEPERS. For sleeper trains, operated by First ScotRail, please refer to Tables 400 - 404

Table 65

Sundays

Scotland and North West England - West Midlands and London

		TP	NT	XC	XC	VT	VT	VT	TP	NT	XC	VT	LM	VT	LM	VT	VT	TP	NT	XC	XC	VT	VT
		◇1		◇1	◇1	◇1	◇1	◇1	◇1		◇1	◇1	1	◇1	1	◇1	◇1	◇1		◇1	◇1	◇1	◇1
				A	B															B	A		
				✕	✕	⊡	⊡	⊡	✕		✕	⊡		⊡		⊡	⊡			✕	✕	⊡	⊡
Inverness	d																						
Aberdeen	d																						
Dundee	d																						
Perth	d																						
Edinburgh 10	d							10 52	11 10														
Haymarket	d							10 57	11u14														
Glasgow Central 15	d																11 36						
Motherwell	d																						
Carstairs	d																						
Lockerbie	d								12 09														
Carlisle 8	a							12 05	12 30								12 47						
	d							12 07	12 30								12 49						
Penrith North Lakes	d								12 46														
Windermere	d																						
Oxenholme Lake District	a							12 41	13 10								13 22						
	d							12 43	13 11								13 23						
Barrow-in-Furness	d																						
Lancaster 6	a							12 56	13 26								13 37						
	d							12 57	13 26								13 38						
Blackpool North	d	12 44	12 50							13 20								13 44	13 50				
Preston 8	a	13 08	13 14					13 15	13 45	13 47							13 56	14 08	14 14				
Preston 8	d	13 10	13 15					13 17	13 47	13 49							13 58	14 10	14 15				
Wigan North Western	a		13 35					13 28									14 09		14 35				
	d		13 36					13 28									14 09		14 36				
Blackrod	d									14 10													
Lostock	d									14 20													
Bolton	a	13 34							14 08	14 25								14 34					
Manchester Piccadilly 10 ⇌	a	13 56							14 27									14 56					
Manchester Airport ✈	a	14 17							14 47									15 17					
Liverpool Lime Street 10	a		14 24																15 24				
	d												13 34	13 48									
Liverpool South Parkway ✈	d												13 44										
Runcorn	d												13 52	14 04									
Warrington Bank Quay	a							13 39									14 20						
	d							13 39									14 20						
Hartford	d												14 03										
Manchester Piccadilly 10 ⇌	d			13 07	13 07	13 15					13 27	13 35				13 55				14 07	14 07	14 15	
Stockport	d					13 22					13 36	13 42				14 04						14 22	
Wilmslow	d															14 11							
Holyhead	d						11 50																12 50
Bangor (Gwynedd)	d						12 17																13 18
Llandudno Junction	d						12 35																13 36
Wrexham General	d																						
Chester	d						13 30																14 33
Crewe 10	a						13 50	13 59					14 18			14 27							14 52
	d						13 51	14 01					14 22			14 29							14 54
Macclesfield	d										13 49	13 55											
Congleton	d																						
Stoke-on-Trent	d			13 43	13 43	13 50					14 07	14 12			←					14 43	14 43	14 50	
Stafford	a										14 24		14 42	14 35	14 42								
	d										14 25		14 43	14 36	14 43								
Penkridge	a												→		14 48								
Wolverhampton 7 ⇌	a			14 13	14 13			14 32			14 40				14 58					15 13	15 13		
Birmingham New Street 12	a			14 31	14 33			14 55			14 58				15 15					15 30	15 31		
Birmingham International ✈	a										15 13												
Coventry	a										15 24												
Lichfield Trent Valley	a																						
Tamworth Low Level	a																						
Nuneaton	a						14 31																
Rugby	a																						
Milton Keynes Central	a					14 49	15s04															15 49	16 04
Watford Junction	a																						
London Euston 15 ⊖	a					15 27	15 45					15 47		16 01		16 09	16 15					16 27	16 44

A until 19 June, from 7 August

B from 26 June until 31 July

OVERNIGHT SLEEPERS. For sleeper trains, operated by First ScotRail, please refer to Tables 400 - 404

Table 65

Sundays

Scotland and North West England - West Midlands and London

		VT	TP	TP	NT	XC	VT	LM	VT	LM	VT	VT	TP	NT	XC	VT	VT	VT	TP	NT	XC	VT
		◇1	◇1	◇1		◇1	◇1	1	◇1	1	◇1	◇1	◇1		◇1	◇1	◇1	◇1	◇1		◇1	◇1
			A	B																		
		⊡				✕	⊡		⊡		⊡	⊡			✕	⊡	⊡	⊡	✕		✕	⊡
Inverness	d																					
Aberdeen	d																					
Dundee	d																					
Perth	d																					
Edinburgh 10	d																	12 52	13 07			
Haymarket	d																	12 56	13u11			
Glasgow Central 15	d	11 58										12 42										
Motherwell	d																					
Carstairs	d																					
Lockerbie	d																		14 08			
Carlisle 8	a	13 09										13 51						14 05	14 30			
	d	13 10										13 54						14 07	14 30			
Penrith North Lakes	d																	14 22	14 46			
Windermere	d																					
Oxenholme Lake District	a											14 27							15 10			
	d											14 28							15 11			
Barrow-in-Furness	d		13 25																			
Lancaster 6	a	13 56	14 26									14 42						14 56	15 26			
	d	13 58	14 26	14 26								14 43						14 57	15 26			
Blackpool North	d				14 20								14 44	14 50						15 20		
Preston 8	a	14 15	14 45	14 46	14 47							15 01	15 08	15 14				15 15	15 45	15 47		
Preston 8	d	14 17	14 47	14 47	14 49							15 03	15 10	15 15				15 17	15 47	15 49		
Wigan North Western	a	14 28										15 14		15 35				15 28				
	d	14 28										15 14		15 36				15 28				
Blackrod	d				15 10															16 10		
Lostock	d				15 20															16 20		
Bolton	a		15 08	15 08	15 25								15 34						16 08	16 25		
Manchester Piccadilly 10 ⇌	a		15 27	15 27									15 56						16 27			
Manchester Airport ✈	a		15 47	15 47									16 17						16 47			
Liverpool Lime Street 10	a													16 24								
	d							14 34	14 48													
Liverpool South Parkway ✈	d							14 44														
Runcorn	d							14 52	15 04													
Warrington Bank Quay	a	14 39										15 25						15 39				
	d	14 39										15 25						15 39				
Hartford	d							15 03														
Manchester Piccadilly 10 ⇌	d					14 27	14 35				14 55				15 07	15 15					15 27	15 35
Stockport	d					14 36	14 42				15 04					15 22					15 36	15 42
Wilmslow	d										15 11											
Holyhead	d																13 55					
Bangor (Gwynedd)	d																14 22					
Llandudno Junction	d																14 40					
Wrexham General	d																					
Chester	d																15 33					
Crewe 10	a	14 59						15 20			15 27						15 52	15 59				
	d	15 01						15 22			15 29						15 54	16 01				
Macclesfield	d					14 49	14 55														15 49	15 55
Congleton	d																					
Stoke-on-Trent	d					15 07	15 12			←					15 43	15 50					16 07	16 12
Stafford	a					15 24		15 42	15 35	15 42											16 24	
	d					15 25		15 43	15 36	15 43											16 25	
Penkridge	a							→		15 48												
Wolverhampton 7 ⇌	a	15 31				15 40				15 58					16 13			16 32			16 40	
Birmingham New Street 12	a	15 55				15 58				16 15					16 31			16 55			16 58	
Birmingham International ✈	a					16 13															17 13	
Coventry	a					16 24															17 24	
Lichfield Trent Valley	a																					
Tamworth Low Level	a																					
Nuneaton	a																					
Rugby	a																					
Milton Keynes Central	a															16 49	17 03					
Watford Junction	a																					
London Euston 15 ⊖	a						16 47		17 01		17 09	17 20				17 27	17 44					17 47

A from 24 July

B until 17 July

OVERNIGHT SLEEPERS. For sleeper trains, operated by First ScotRail, please refer to Tables 400 - 404

Table 65

Sundays

Scotland and North West England - West Midlands and London

Station		LM	VT	LM	VT	VT	TP	XC	XC	VT	VT	NT	VT	TP	TP	NT	TP	NT	XC	VT	LM	VT	LM
								A	B					C	D	E	F						
Inverness	d																						
Aberdeen	d																						
Dundee	d																						
Perth	d																						
Edinburgh	d																						
Haymarket	d																						
Glasgow Central	d					13 36							13 55										
Motherwell	d																						
Carstairs	d																						
Lockerbie	d																						
Carlisle	a					14 46							15 09										
	d					14 49							15 11			15 35							
Penrith North Lakes	d																						
Windermere	d																						
Oxenholme Lake District	a					15 22							15 46										
	d					15 23							15 46										
Barrow-in-Furness	d													15 32	15 34								
Lancaster	a					15 37								16 23	16 26								
	d					15 38								16 24	16 26		16 27						
Blackpool North	d						15 44					15 50						16 20					
Preston	a					15 56	16 08					16 14	16 15	16 42	16 45	18 29	16 45	16 47					
Preston	d					15 58	16 10					16 15	16 17	16 47	16 47		16 47	16 49					
Wigan North Western	a					16 09						16 35	16 28										
	d					16 09						16 36	16 28										
Blackrod	d																	17 10					
Lostock	d																	17 20					
Bolton	a						16 34							17 08	17 08		17 08	17 25					
Manchester Piccadilly	a						16 56							17 27	17 27		17 27						
Manchester Airport	a						17 17							17 47	17 47		17 47						
Liverpool Lime Street	a											17 24											
	d	15 34	15 48								16 18										16 34	16 48	
Liverpool South Parkway	d	15 44																			16 44		
Runcorn	d	15 52	16 04								16 34										16 52	17 04	
Warrington Bank Quay	a					16 20							16 39										
	d					16 20							16 39										
Hartford	d	16 03																			17 03		
Manchester Piccadilly	d				15 55			16 07	16 07	16 15									16 27	16 35			
Stockport	d				16 04					16 23									16 36	16 42			
Wilmslow	d				16 11																		
Holyhead	d																						
Bangor (Gwynedd)	d																						
Llandudno Junction	d																						
Wrexham General	d																						
Chester	d																						
Crewe	a	16 18			16 27						16 51		16 59								17 18		
	d	16 22			16 29						16 54		17 01								17 22		
Macclesfield	d																		16 49	16 55			
Congleton	d																						
Stoke-on-Trent	d			←				16 43	16 43	16 50									17 08	17 12			←
Stafford	a	16 42	16 36	16 42															17 25		17 42	17 35	17 42
	d	16 43	16 37	16 43															17 26		17 43	17 36	17 43
Penkridge	a	→		16 48																	→		17 48
Wolverhampton	a			16 58				17 13	17 13				17 31						17 40				17 58
Birmingham New Street	a			17 15				17 31	17 32				17 55						17 58				18 15
Birmingham International	a																		18 13				
Coventry	a																		18 24				
Lichfield Trent Valley	a										17 26												
Tamworth Low Level	a																						
Nuneaton	a																						
Rugby	a																						
Milton Keynes Central	a									17 49	18 04												
Watford Junction	a																						
London Euston	a		18 01		18 09	18 15				18 27	18 44									18 47		19 01	

A until 19 June, from 7 August
B from 26 June until 31 July
C from 24 July until 11 September
D from 18 September
E until 11 September
F until 17 July

OVERNIGHT SLEEPERS. For sleeper trains, operated by First ScotRail, please refer to Tables 400 - 404

Table 65

Sundays

Scotland and North West England - West Midlands and London

Station		VT	VT	TP	NT	XC	VT	VT	VT	TP	TP	TP	TP	NT	XC	VT	LM	VT	LM	VT	VT	TP	TP
										A	B	C										D	D
Inverness	d																						
Aberdeen	d																						
Dundee	d																						
Perth	d																						
Edinburgh	d								14 52														
Haymarket	d								14 57														
Glasgow Central	d		14 36										15 06								15 36		
Motherwell	d																						
Carstairs	d																						
Lockerbie	d												16 07										
Carlisle	a		15 46						16 05				16 28								16 46		
	d		15 49						16 07				16 28								16 49		
Penrith North Lakes	d								16 22				16 44								17 03		
Windermere	d																					16 58	
Oxenholme Lake District	a		16 22										17 08									17 15	
	d		16 23										17 09									17 16	
Barrow-in-Furness	d										16 17												
Lancaster	a		16 37						16 56		17 17		17 23								17 37	17 31	
	d		16 38						16 57	17 17	17 17	17 17	17 24								17 38	17 32	
Blackpool North	d			16 44	16 50									17 20									17 40
Preston	a		16 56	17 08	17 14				17 15	17 37	17 37	17 37	17 42	17 47							17 56	17 51	18 04
Preston	d		16 58	17 10	17 15				17 17		17 47		17 47	17 49							17 58	18 10	
Wigan North Western	a		17 09		17 35				17 28												18 09		
	d		17 09		17 36				17 28												18 09		
Blackrod	d													18 10									
Lostock	d													18 20									
Bolton	a			17 34							18 08		18 08	18 25								18 34	
Manchester Piccadilly	a			17 56							18 27		18 27									18 56	
Manchester Airport	a			18 17							18 47		18 47									19 17	
Liverpool Lime Street	a				18 24																		
	d																17 34	17 48					
Liverpool South Parkway	d																17 44						
Runcorn	d																17 52	18 04					
Warrington Bank Quay	a		17 20						17 39												18 20		
	d		17 20						17 39												18 20		
Hartford	d																18 03						
Manchester Piccadilly	d	16 55				17 07	17 15								17 27	17 35				17 55			
Stockport	d	17 04					17 22								17 36	17 42				18 04			
Wilmslow	d	17 11																		18 11			
Holyhead	d																						
Bangor (Gwynedd)	d																						
Llandudno Junction	d																						
Wrexham General	d																						
Chester	d							17 35															
Crewe	a	17 27						17 53	17 59								18 20			18 27			
	d	17 29						17 55	18 01								18 22			18 29			
Macclesfield	d														17 49	17 55							
Congleton	d																						
Stoke-on-Trent	d					17 43	17 50								18 08	18 12			←				
Stafford	a														18 25		18 42	18 35	18 42				
	d														18 26		18 43	18 36	18 43				
Penkridge	a																→		18 48				
Wolverhampton	a					18 13			18 32						18 40				18 58				
Birmingham New Street	a					18 31			18 55						18 58				19 15				
Birmingham International	a														19 13								
Coventry	a														19 24								
Lichfield Trent Valley	a																						
Tamworth Low Level	a																						
Nuneaton	a																						
Rugby	a																						
Milton Keynes Central	a						18 49	19 02															
Watford Junction	a																						
London Euston	a	19 09	19 15				19 27	19 43								19 47		20 01		20 09	20 15		

A until 17 July
B from 24 July until 11 September. from Preston
C until 17 July. from Preston
D until 11 September

OVERNIGHT SLEEPERS. For sleeper trains, operated by First ScotRail, please refer to Tables 400 - 404

Table 65

Sundays

Scotland and North West England - West Midlands and London

		TP ◇■ A	NT	XC ◇■ B ⌶	XC ◇■ C ⌶	VT ◇■ ☕	VT ◇■ ☕	VT ◇■ ☕	TP ◇■ ⌶	NT D ⌶	NT	XC ◇■ ⌶	VT ◇■ ☕	LM ■	VT ◇■ ☕	LM ■	VT ◇■ ☕	VT ◇■ ☕	TP ◇■	NT	XC ◇■ ⌶	VT ◇■ ☕
Inverness	d																					
Aberdeen	d																					
Dundee	d																					
Perth	d																					
Edinburgh 10	d								16 10													16 52
Haymarket	d								16u14													16 56
Glasgow Central 15	d							15 57										16 40				
Motherwell	d																	16 54				
Carstairs	d																					
Lockerbie	d								17 09													
Carlisle 8	a							17 08	17 30									17 49				18 05
	d							17 09	17 30	17 41								17 51				18 07
Penrith North Lakes	d								17 45									18 05				
Windermere	d																					
Oxenholme Lake District	a							17 44	18 10									18 27				18 41
	d							17 44	18 10									18 28				18 42
Barrow-in-Furness	d																					
Lancaster 6	a								18 26									18 42				18 56
	d								18 26									18 43				18 57
Blackpool North	d	17 44	17 50								18 20								18 44	18 50		
Preston 8	a	18 08	18 14					18 15	18 45	20 47	18 47							19 01	19 08	19 14		19 15
Preston 8	d	18 10	18 15					18 17	18 47		18 49							19 03	19 10	19 15		19 17
Wigan North Western	a		18 35					18 28										19 14		19 35		19 28
	d		18 36					18 28										19 14		19 36		19 28
Blackrod	d										19 10											
Lostock	d										19 20											
Bolton	a	18 34							19 08		19 25								19 34			
Manchester Piccadilly 10	a	18 56							19 27										19 56			
Manchester Airport	a	19 17							19 47										20 17			
Liverpool Lime Street 10	a		19 24																	20 24		
	d													18 34	18 48							
Liverpool South Parkway	d													18 44								
Runcorn	d													18 52	19 04							
Warrington Bank Quay	a							18 39										19 25				19 39
	d							18 39										19 25				19 39
Hartford	d													19 03								
Manchester Piccadilly 10	d			18 07	18 07	18 15						18 27	18 35				18 55				19 07	
Stockport	d					18 22						18 36	18 42				19 04					
Wilmslow	d																19 11					
Holyhead	d																					
Bangor (Gwynedd)	d																					
Llandudno Junction	d																					
Wrexham General	d																					
Chester	d						18 35															
Crewe 10	a						18 53	18 59						19 20			19 27					19 59
	d						18 55	19 01						19 22			19 29					20 01
Macclesfield	d											18 49	18 55									
Congleton	d																					
Stoke-on-Trent	d			18 43	18 43	18 50						19 07	19 12			←					19 43	
Stafford	a											19 24		19 42	19 35	19 42						
	d											19 25		19 43	19 36	19 43						
Penkridge	a													↪		19 48						
Wolverhampton 7	a			19 13	19 13			19 31				19 40				19 58					20 13	20 32
Birmingham New Street 12	a			19 31	19 32			19 55				19 58				20 15					20 31	20 50
Birmingham International	a											20 13										
Coventry	a											20 24										
Lichfield Trent Valley	a																					
Tamworth Low Level	a																					
Nuneaton	a																					
Rugby	a																					
Milton Keynes Central	a					19 49	20 03															
Watford Junction	a																					
London Euston 15	a					20 27	20 44						20 47		21 01		21 09	21 21				

A from 18 September
B until 19 June, from 7 August
C from 26 June until 31 July
D until 23 October

OVERNIGHT SLEEPERS. For sleeper trains, operated by First ScotRail, please refer to Tables 400 - 404

Table 65

Sundays

Scotland and North West England - West Midlands and London

		TP ◇■ A	VT ◇■ ☕	TP ◇■ B	TP ◇■ C ⌶	TP ◇■ D ⌶	TP ◇■ ⌶	NT	XC ◇■ E ⌶	LM ■	VT ◇■ ☕	VT ◇■ ☕	VT ◇■ ☕	TP ◇■	NT A	XC ◇■	AW ◇ ⌶	VT ◇■ ☕	LM ■	VT ◇■ ☕	VT ◇■ ☕	NT	TP ◇■ ⌶
Inverness	d																						
Aberdeen	d																						
Dundee	d																						
Perth	d																						
Edinburgh 10	d																						18 10
Haymarket	d																						18u14
Glasgow Central 15	d						17 06						17 36										
Motherwell	d																						
Carstairs	d																						
Lockerbie	d												18 32										19 09
Carlisle 8	a						18 27						18 50										19 30
	d						18 27						18 52										19 30
Penrith North Lakes	d						18 42						19 06										19 45
Windermere	d																						
Oxenholme Lake District	a						19 07						19 28										20 10
	d						19 07						19 29										20 10
Barrow-in-Furness	d	18 17			18 17										20 02								
Lancaster 6	a	19 17			19 17		19 22						19 43		21 07								20 26
	d	19 17		19 17	19 17	19 17	19 22						19 44										20 26
Blackpool North	d							19 20						19 44								19 50	
Preston 8	a	19 37		19 37	19 37	19 37	19 42	19 47					20 02	20 08								20 14	20 45
Preston 8	d				19 47		19 47	19 49					20 04	20 10								20 15	20 47
Wigan North Western	a												20 15									20 35	
	d												20 15									20 36	
Blackrod	d							20 10															
Lostock	d							20 20															
Bolton	a				20 08		20 08	20 25						20 34									21 08
Manchester Piccadilly 10	a				20 27		20 27							20 56									21 27
Manchester Airport	a				20 47		20 47							21 17									21 47
Liverpool Lime Street 10	a																					21 24	
	d									19 34		19 48							20 34		20 48		
Liverpool South Parkway	d									19 44									20 44				
Runcorn	d									19 52		20 04							20 52		21 04		
Warrington Bank Quay	a												20 26										
	d												20 26										
Hartford	d									20 03									21 03				
Manchester Piccadilly 10	d		19 15						19 27		19 35					20 07		20 20		20 55			
Stockport	d		19 22						19 36		19 41					20 16		20 27		21 03			
Wilmslow	d																						
Holyhead	d																18 25						
Bangor (Gwynedd)	d																19 04						
Llandudno Junction	d																19 24						
Wrexham General	d																						
Chester	d																20 27						
Crewe 10	a									20 16		20 22	20 45				20 48		21 16		21 21		
	d									20 18		20 24	20 47				20 52		21 17		21 23		
Macclesfield	d								19 49		19 54					20 29		20 40		21 15			
Congleton	d																						
Stoke-on-Trent	d		19 50						20 07		20 11					20 47		20 57		21 33			
Stafford	a								20 26	20 38		20 41				21 08	21 16		21 37		21 42		
	d								20 27	20 39		20 43				21 09	21 16		21 38		21 43		
Penkridge	a									20 44									21 44				
Wolverhampton 7	a								20 39	20 55						21 21	21 34		21 55				
Birmingham New Street 12	a								21 00	21 15						21 39	21 52		22 15				
Birmingham International	a								21 13								22 09						
Coventry	a								21 23														
Lichfield Trent Valley	a																				21 59		
Tamworth Low Level	a																				22 05		
Nuneaton	a																				22 17		
Rugby	a																				22 31		
Milton Keynes Central	a		20 46									21 36	21 55					22 03		22 45	23 04		
Watford Junction	a												22s31							23s26	23s34		
London Euston 15	a		21 31								21 58	22 28	22 53					22 56		23 48	23 54		

A from 24 July
B until 17 July
C from 24 July until 11 September, from 30 October. ⌶ from Preston
D until 17 July. ⌶ from Preston
E ⌶ to Wolverhampton

OVERNIGHT SLEEPERS. For sleeper trains, operated by First ScotRail, please refer to Tables 400 - 404

Table 65

Scotland and North West England - West Midlands and London

		NT	VT	TP	TP	NT	XC	VT	TP	NT	LM	NT	TP	TP	TP	VT	XC	NT	TP	SR	SR	SR
			◇1	◇1 A	◇1		◇1	◇1	◇1 B		1		◇1 C	◇1 D	◇1 E	◇1	◇1		◇1	F	G	
Inverness	d																					20 25
Aberdeen	d																					
Dundee	d																					
Perth	d																					23u00
Edinburgh 10	d							18 52					19 57		19 57							01 06
Haymarket	d							18 57					20u01		20u01							
Glasgow Central 15	d		18 30													20 08				23 15	23 15	
Motherwell	d																			23u31	23u31	
Carstairs	d																			23u47	23u47	
Lockerbie	d															21 00						
Carlisle 8	a		19 43					20 05					21 14		21 14	21 21						02 51
	d		19 44					20 07					21 14		21 14	21 24				01u12	01u12	02 53
Penrith North Lakes	d							20 22								21 39						
Windermere	d			20 40					20 40													
Oxenholme Lake District	a		20 19	20 59					20 59							22 02						
	d		20 19	21 01					21 01							22 03						
Barrow-in-Furness	d																					
Lancaster 6	a		20 34	21 18				20 56	21 17				22 04		22 04	22 17						
	d		20 34					20 57	21 23				22 04		22 04	22 18						
Blackpool North	d	20 20			20 44	20 50				21 20		21 50		21 56				22 44	23 03			
Preston 8	a	20 47	20 52		21 08	21 14		21 15	21 41	21 47		22 14	22 24	22 20	22 24	22 35		23 08	23 28	03 02	03 02	04s41
Preston 8	d	20 49	20 55		21 10	21 15		21 17		21 49		22 15		22 29	22 34	22 38		23 09	23 28	03 07	03 07	
Wigan North Western	a		21 06			21 35		21 28				22 35				22 49		23 29				
	d		21 07			21 36		21 28				22 36				22 50		23 30				
Blackrod	d	21 10								22 10									23 49			
Lostock	d	21 20								22 20									23 56			
Bolton	a	21 25			21 34					22 25				22 50	22 59				00 02			
Manchester Piccadilly 10	a				21 56									23 15	23 23				00 18			
Manchester Airport	a				22 17									23 31	23 39				00 32			
Liverpool Lime Street 10	a					22 24						23 24						00 18				
	d										21 34											
Liverpool South Parkway	d										21 44											
Runcorn	d										21 52											
Warrington Bank Quay	a		21 18					21 39								23 00				03 34	03 34	
	d		21 18					21 39								23 01				03 36	03 36	
Hartford	d										22 03											
Manchester Piccadilly 10	d						21 07										22 07					
Stockport	d						21 16										22 16					
Wilmslow	d																					
Holyhead	d																					
Bangor (Gwynedd)	d																					
Llandudno Junction	d																					
Wrexham General	d																					
Chester	d																					
Crewe 10	a		21 38					21 59			22 18					23 20						05s37
	d		21 40					22 01			22 22											
Macclesfield	d						21 29										22 29					
Congleton	d																					
Stoke-on-Trent	d						21 47										22 47					
Stafford	a		22 01				22 06				22 42						23 04					
	d		22 02				22 06				22 45						23 05					
Penkridge	a										22 50											
Wolverhampton 7	a		22 17				22 20	22 31			23 00						23 18					
Birmingham New Street 12	a		22 38				22 40	22 55			23 17						23 36					
Birmingham International	a																					
Coventry	a																					
Lichfield Trent Valley	a																					
Tamworth Low Level	a																					
Nuneaton	a																					
Rugby	a																			05 27	05 26	
Milton Keynes Central	a																					
Watford Junction	a																			06s23	06s23	
London Euston 15	a																			06 46	06 46	07 47

A from 24 July
B until 17 July
C until 19 June, from 18 September
D until 19 June, from 18 September. from Preston
E from 26 June until 11 September
F from 19 June until 31 July
G until 12 June, from 7 August

OVERNIGHT SLEEPERS. For sleeper trains, operated by First ScotRail, please refer to Tables 400 - 404

Mondays to Fridays

Milton Keynes Central - Buckingham and Bicester

Bus Service

		VT	VT	VT	VT	VT	VT	VT	VT	VT	VT	VT	VT	VT	VT	VT	VT	VT	VT	VT	VT	VT	VT
Milton Keynes Central	d	05 45	06 15	06 45	07 15	07 35	08 05	08 45	09 15	09 45	10 15	10 45	11 15	11 45	12 15	12 45	13 15	13 45	14 15	14 45	15 15	15 45	16 15
Buckingham Tesco	d	06 05	06 35	07 05	07 35	07 55	08 25	09 05	09 35	10 05	10 35	11 05	11 35	12 05	12 35	13 05	13 35	14 05	14 35	15 05	15 35	16 05	16 35
Bicester Bure Place	a	06 25	06 55	07 25	07 55	08 15	08 45	09 25	09 55	10 25	10 55	11 25	11 55	12 25	12 55	13 25	13 55	14 25	14 55	15 25	15 55	16 25	16 55

		VT	VT	VT	VT	VT		VT	VT
Milton Keynes Central	d	16 45	17 15	17 45	18 15	18 45		19 45	20 45
Buckingham Tesco	d	17 05	17 35	18 05	18 35	19 05		20 05	21 05
Bicester Bure Place	a	17 25	17 55	18 25	18 55	19 25		20 25	21 25

Saturdays

		VT	VT	VT	VT	VT	VT	VT	VT	VT	VT	VT	VT	VT	VT	VT	VT	VT	VT	VT	VT	VT	VT
Milton Keynes Central	d	05 50	06 20	06 50	07 20	07 45	08 15	08 45	09 15	09 45	10 15	10 45	11 15	11 45	12 15	12 45	13 15	13 45	14 15	14 45	15 15	15 45	16 15
Buckingham Tesco	d	06 10	06 40	07 10	07 40	08 05	08 35	09 05	09 35	10 05	10 35	11 05	11 35	12 05	12 35	13 05	13 35	14 05	14 35	15 05	15 35	16 05	16 35
Bicester Bure Place	a	06 30	07 00	07 30	08 00	08 25	08 55	09 25	09 55	10 25	10 55	11 25	11 55	12 25	12 55	13 25	13 55	14 25	14 55	15 25	15 55	16 25	16 55

		VT	VT	VT	VT	VT		VT	VT
Milton Keynes Central	d	16 45	17 15	17 45	18 15	18 45		19 45	20 45
Buckingham Tesco	d	17 05	17 35	18 05	18 35	19 05		20 05	21 05
Bicester Bure Place	a	17 25	17 55	18 25	18 55	19 25		20 25	21 25

Sundays

		VT	VT	VT	VT	VT	VT	VT	VT	VT	VT	VT	VT	VT	VT	VT	VT	VT	VT	VT	VT	VT	VT
Milton Keynes Central	d	06 45	07 45	08 45	09 45	10 15	10 45	11 15	11 45	12 15	12 45	13 15	13 45	14 15	14 45	15 15	15 45	16 15	16 45	17 15	17 45	18 15	18 45
Buckingham Tesco	d	07 05	08 05	09 05	10 05	10 35	11 05	11 35	12 05	12 35	13 05	13 35	14 05	14 35	15 05	15 35	16 05	16 35	17 05	17 35	18 05	18 35	19 05
Bicester Bure Place	a	07 25	08 25	09 25	10 25	10 55	11 25	11 55	12 25	12 55	13 25	13 55	14 25	14 55	15 25	15 55	16 25	16 55	17 25	17 55	18 25	18 55	19 25

		VT	VT	VT
Milton Keynes Central	d	19 45	20 40	21 35
Buckingham Tesco	d	20 05	21 00	21 55
Bicester Bure Place	a	20 25	21 20	22 15

Bicester and Buckingham - Milton Keynes Central

Mondays to Fridays

		VT MO	VT	VT	VT	VT	VT	VT	VT	VT	VT	VT	VT	VT	VT	VT	VT	VT	VT	VT	VT	VT	VT
Bicester Bure Place	d	23p30	07 35	08 05	08 35	09 05	09 35	10 05	10 35	11 05	11 35	12 05	12 35	13 05	13 35	14 05	14 35	15 05	15 35	16 05	16 35	17 05	17 35
Buckingham Tesco	d	23p50	07 55	08 25	08 55	09 25	09 55	10 25	10 55	11 25	11 55	12 25	12 55	13 25	13 55	14 25	14 55	15 25	15 55	16 25	16 55	17 25	17 55
Milton Keynes Central	a	00 10	08 15	08 45	09 15	09 45	10 15	10 45	11 15	11 45	12 15	12 45	13 15	13 45	14 15	14 45	15 15	15 45	16 15	16 45	17 15	17 45	18 15

		VT	VT	VT	VT	VT		VT	VT	VT
Bicester Bure Place	d	18 05	18 35	19 05	19 30	20 00		20 30	21 30	22 30
Buckingham Tesco	d	18 25	18 55	19 25	19 50	20 20		20 50	21 50	22 50
Milton Keynes Central	a	18 45	19 15	19 45	20 10	20 40		21 10	22 10	23 10

Saturdays

		VT	VT	VT	VT	VT	VT	VT	VT	VT	VT	VT	VT	VT	VT	VT	VT	VT	VT	VT	VT	VT	VT
Bicester Bure Place	d	07 35	08 05	08 35	09 05	09 35	10 05	10 35	11 05	11 35	12 05	12 35	13 05	13 35	14 05	14 45	15 05	15 35	16 05	16 35	17 05	17 35	18 05
Buckingham Tesco	d	07 55	08 25	08 55	09 25	09 55	10 25	10 55	11 25	11 55	12 25	12 55	13 25	13 55	14 25	15 05	15 25	15 55	16 25	16 55	17 25	17 55	18 25
Milton Keynes Central	a	08 15	08 45	09 15	09 45	10 15	10 45	11 15	11 45	12 15	12 45	13 15	13 45	14 15	14 45	15 25	15 45	16 15	16 45	17 15	17 45	18 15	18 45

		VT	VT	VT	VT	VT		VT	VT
Bicester Bure Place	d	18 35	19 05	19 30	20 00	20 30		21 30	22 30
Buckingham Tesco	d	18 55	19 25	19 50	20 20	20 50		21 50	22 50
Milton Keynes Central	a	19 15	19 45	20 10	20 40	21 10		22 10	23 10

Sundays

		VT	VT	VT	VT	VT	VT	VT	VT	VT	VT	VT	VT	VT	VT	VT	VT	VT	VT	VT	VT	VT	VT
Bicester Bure Place	d	08 35	09 35	10 35	11 35	12 05	12 35	13 05	13 35	14 05	14 45	15 05	15 35	16 05	16 35	17 05	17 35	18 05	18 35	19 05	19 30	20 00	20 30
Buckingham Tesco	d	08 55	09 55	10 55	11 55	12 25	12 55	13 25	13 55	14 25	15 05	15 25	15 55	16 25	16 55	17 25	17 55	18 25	18 55	19 25	19 50	20 20	20 50
Milton Keynes Central	a	09 15	10 15	11 15	12 15	12 45	13 15	13 45	14 15	14 45	15 25	15 45	16 15	16 45	17 15	17 45	18 15	18 45	19 15	19 45	20 10	20 40	21 10

		VT	VT	VT
Bicester Bure Place	d	21 30	22 30	23 30
Buckingham Tesco	d	21 50	22 50	23 50
Milton Keynes Central	a	22 10	23 10	00 10

This is the X5 service operated by Stagecoach East

Sunday service operates on Bank Holidays. Please check with local operator before travelling

Table 65B

Mondays to Fridays

Milton Keynes Central - London Luton Airport

Bus Service

		VT	VT	VT	VT	VT	VT	VT	VT	VT	VT	VT	VT	VT	VT	VT	VT	VT
Milton Keynes Central	d	06 40	07 50	08 55	09 55	10 55	11 55	12 55	13 55	14 55	15 55	16 55	17 25	17 55	18 55	19 55	20 55	21 55
Milton Keynes The Point	d	06 45	07 55	09 00	10 00	11 00	12 00	13 00	14 00	15 00	16 00	17 00	17 30	18 00	19 00	20 00	21 00	22 00
Luton	d	07 25	08 40	09 40	10 40	11 40	12 40	13 40	14 40	15 40	16 40	17 40	18 10	18 40	19 40	20 40	21 40	22 40
London Luton Airport	a	07 35	08 55	09 50	10 50	11 50	12 50	13 50	14 50	15 50	16 50	17 50	18 20	18 50	19 50	20 50	21 50	22 50

Saturdays

		VT	VT	VT	VT	VT	VT	VT	VT	VT	VT	VT	VT	VT	VT	VT
Milton Keynes Central	d	06 40	07 50	08 55	09 55	10 55	11 55	12 55	13 55	14 55	15 55	16 55	17 55	18 55	19 55	20 55
Milton Keynes The Point	d	06 45	08 00	09 00	10 00	11 00	12 00	13 00	14 00	15 00	16 00	17 00	18 00	19 00	20 00	21 00
Luton	d	07 25	08 40	09 40	10 40	11 40	12 40	13 40	14 40	15 40	16 40	17 40	18 40	19 40	20 40	21 40
London Luton Airport	a	07 35	08 55	09 50	10 50	11 50	12 50	13 50	14 50	15 50	16 50	17 50	18 50	19 50	20 50	21 50

Sundays

		VT	VT	VT	VT	VT	VT	VT	VT	VT	VT	VT	VT	VT
Milton Keynes Central	d	09 20	10 20	11 20	12 20	13 20	14 20	15 20	16 20	17 20	18 20	19 20	20 20	21 20
Milton Keynes The Point	d	09 25	10 25	11 25	12 25	13 25	14 25	15 25	16 25	17 25	18 25	19 25	20 25	21 25
Luton	d	10 05	11 05	12 05	13 05	14 05	15 05	16 05	17 05	18 05	19 05	20 05	21 05	22 05
London Luton Airport	a	10 15	11 15	12 15	13 15	14 15	15 15	16 15	17 15	18 15	19 15	20 15	21 15	22 15

Table 65B

Mondays to Fridays

London Luton Airport - Milton Keynes Central

Bus Service

		VT	VT	VT	VT	VT	VT	VT	VT	VT	VT	VT	VT	VT	VT	VT	VT
London Luton Airport	d	05 50	06 50	07 50	09 05	10 05	11 05	12 05	13 05	14 05	15 05	16 05	17 05	18 05	19 05	20 05	21 05
Luton	d	06 05	07 00	08 10	09 15	10 15	11 15	12 15	13 15	14 15	15 15	16 15	17 15	18 15	19 15	20 15	21 15
Luton Galaxy Centre	d																
Milton Keynes The Point	d	06 45	07 40	08 55	09 55	10 55	11 55	12 55	13 55	14 55	15 55	16 55	17 55	18 55	19 55	20 55	21 55
Milton Keynes Central	a	06 50	07 45	09 00	10 00	11 00	12 00	13 00	14 00	15 00	16 00	17 00	18 00	19 00	20 00	21 00	22 00

Saturdays

		VT	VT	VT	VT	VT	VT	VT	VT	VT	VT	VT	VT	VT	VT	VT
London Luton Airport	d	05 50	06 50	07 50	09 05	10 05	11 05	12 05	13 05	14 05	15 05	16 05	17 05	18 05	19 05	20 05
Luton	d	06 05	07 00	08 05	09 15	10 15	11 15	12 15	13 15	14 15	15 15	16 15	17 15	18 15	19 15	20 15
Luton Galaxy Centre	d															
Milton Keynes The Point	d	06 45	07 40	08 50	09 55	10 55	11 55	12 55	13 55	14 55	15 55	16 55	17 55	18 55	19 55	20 55
Milton Keynes Central	a	06 50	07 45	09 00	10 00	11 00	12 00	13 00	14 00	15 00	16 00	17 00	18 00	19 00	20 00	21 00

Sundays

		VT	VT	VT	VT	VT	VT	VT	VT	VT	VT	VT	VT	VT
London Luton Airport	d	08 20	09 20	10 20	11 20	12 20	13 20	14 20	15 20	16 20	17 20	18 20	19 20	20 20
Luton	d	08 30	09 30	10 30	11 30	12 30	13 30	14 30	15 30	16 30	17 30	18 30	19 30	20 30
Luton Galaxy Centre	d													
Milton Keynes The Point	d	09 10	10 10	11 10	12 10	13 10	14 10	15 10	16 10	17 10	18 10	19 10	20 10	21 10
Milton Keynes Central	a	09 15	10 15	11 15	12 15	13 15	14 15	15 15	16 15	17 15	18 15	19 15	20 15	21 15

Sunday service operates on Bank Holidays. Please check with local operator before travelling

Mondays to Fridays

Milton Keynes Central - Bedford and Cambridge

Bus Service

		VT MX	VT MO	VT	VT	VT	VT	VT	VT	VT		VT	VT	VT	VT	VT	VT	VT	VT	VT		VT	VT	VT	VT
Milton Keynes Central	d	23p10	23p59	07 00	07 45	08 15	08 45	09 15	09 45	10 15		10 45	11 15	11 45	12 15	12 45	13 15	13 45	14 15	14 45		15 15	15 45	16 15	16 45
Bedford Bus Station	a	00 10	00 50	08 15	08 45	09 15	09 45	10 15	10 45	11 15		11 45	12 15	12 45	13 15	13 45	14 15	14 45	15 15	15 45		16 15	16 45	17 15	17 45
St Neots Cambridge Street	a																								
Cambridge Parkside	a																								
Milton Keynes Central	d	17 15	17 45	18 15	18 45	19 15		19 45	20 10	20 40	21 10	22 10	23 10												
Bedford Bus Station	a	18 15	18 43	19 10	19 43	20 05		20 40	20 50	21 30	22 10	23 10	00 10												
St Neots Cambridge Street	a																								
Cambridge Parkside	a																								

Saturdays

		VT	VT	VT	VT	VT	VT	VT	VT	VT		VT	VT	VT	VT	VT	VT	VT	VT	VT		VT	VT	VT	VT
Milton Keynes Central	d	23p10	07 15	07 50	08 15	08 45	09 15	09 45	10 15	10 45		11 15	11 45	12 15	12 45	13 15	13 45	14 15	14 45	15 15		15 45	16 15	16 45	17 15
Bedford Bus Station	a	00 10	08 15	08 45	09 15	09 45	10 15	10 45	11 15	11 45		12 15	12 45	13 15	13 45	14 15	14 45	15 15	15 45	16 15		16 45	17 15	17 45	18 15
St Neots Cambridge Street	a																								
Cambridge Parkside	a																								
Milton Keynes Central	d	17 45	18 15	18 45	19 15	19 45		20 10	20 45	21 10	22 10	23 10													
Bedford Bus Station	a	18 43	19 10	19 43	20 05	20 43		20 50	21 43	21 50	22 50	23 50													
St Neots Cambridge Street	a																								
Cambridge Parkside	a																								

Sundays

		VT	VT	VT	VT	VT	VT	VT	VT	VT		VT	VT	VT	VT	VT	VT	VT	VT	VT		VT	VT	VT	VT
Milton Keynes Central	d	09 15	10 15	11 15	12 15	12 45	13 15	13 45	14 15	14 45		15 15	15 45	16 15	16 45	17 15	17 45	18 15	18 45	19 45		20 10	20 40	21 10	22 10
Bedford Bus Station	a	10 15	11 15	12 15	13 15	13 45	14 15	14 45	15 15	15 45		16 15	16 45	17 15	17 45	18 15	18 45	19 05	19 45	20 40		20 50	21 30	21 50	22 50
St Neots Cambridge Street	a																								
Cambridge Parkside	a																								
Milton Keynes Central	d	23 10	23 59																						
Bedford Bus Station	a	23 50	00 50																						
St Neots Cambridge Street	a																								
Cambridge Parkside	a																								

Cambridge and Bedford - MKC Bus Service

Mondays to Fridays

		VT	VT	VT	VT	VT	VT	VT	VT	VT		VT	VT	VT	VT	VT	VT	VT	VT	VT		VT	VT	VT	VT
Cambridge Parkside	d																								
St Neots Square	d																								
Bedford Bus Station	d	05 00	05 30	06 00	06 30	06 50	07 15	07 50	08 20	08 50		09 30	10 00	10 30	11 00	11 30	12 00	12 30	13 00	13 30		14 00	14 30	15 00	15 30
Milton Keynes Central	a	05 45	06 15	06 45	07 15	07 35	08 05	08 35	09 10	09 35		10 15	10 45	11 15	11 45	12 15	12 45	13 15	13 45	14 15		14 45	15 15	15 45	16 15
Cambridge Parkside	d																								
St Neots Square	d																								
Bedford Bus Station	d	16 00	16 30	17 00	17 30	18 00		18 30	19 00	19 30	20 00														
Milton Keynes Central	a	16 45	17 15	17 45	18 15	18 45		19 10	19 40	20 10	20 40														

Saturdays

		VT	VT	VT	VT	VT	VT	VT	VT	VT		VT	VT	VT	VT	VT	VT	VT	VT	VT		VT	VT	VT	VT
Cambridge Parkside	d																								
St Neots Square	d																								
Bedford Bus Station	d	05 05	05 35	06 05	06 35	07 00	07 30	08 00	08 30	09 00		09 30	10 00	10 30	11 00	11 30	12 00	12 30	13 00	13 30		14 00	14 30	15 00	15 30
Milton Keynes Central	a	05 50	06 20	06 50	07 20	07 45	08 15	08 45	09 15	09 45		10 15	10 45	11 15	11 45	12 15	12 45	13 15	13 45	14 15		14 45	15 15	15 45	16 15
Cambridge Parkside	d																								
St Neots Square	d																								
Bedford Bus Station	d	16 00	16 30	17 00	17 30	18 00		18 30	19 00	19 30	20 00														
Milton Keynes Central	a	16 45	17 15	17 45	18 15	18 45		19 10	19 40	20 10	20 40														

Sundays

		VT	VT	VT	VT	VT	VT	VT	VT	VT		VT	VT	VT	VT	VT	VT	VT	VT	VT		VT	VT	VT	VT
Cambridge Parkside	d																								
St Neots Square	d																								
Bedford Bus Station	d	06 00	07 00	08 00	09 00	09 30	10 00	10 30	11 00	11 30		12 00	12 30	13 00	13 30	14 00	14 30	15 00	15 30	16 00		16 30	17 00	17 30	18 00
Milton Keynes Central	a	06 45	07 45	08 45	09 45	10 15	10 45	11 15	11 45	12 15		12 45	13 15	13 45	14 15	14 45	15 15	15 45	16 15	16 45		17 15	17 45	18 15	18 45
Cambridge Parkside	d																								
St Neots Square	d																								
Bedford Bus Station	d	18 30	19 00	20 00	21 00																				
Milton Keynes Central	a	19 10	19 45	20 45	21 45																				

Sunday service operates on Bank Holidays. Please check with local operator before travelling

Table 65F

Mondays to Fridays

Penrith - Keswick, Cockermouth and Workington

Bus Service

		VT	VT	VT	VT	VT	VT	VT	VT	VT	VT	VT	VT	VT	VT	VT	VT	VT
		Bus	Bus	Bus	Bus	Bus	Bus	Bus	Bus	Bus	Bus	Bus	Bus	Bus	Bus	Bus	Bus	Bus
Penrith North Lakes	d	07.22	08.02	08.22	09.22	10.22	11.22	12.22	13.22	14.22	15.22	16.22	17.22	18.30	19.30	20.35	21.40	22.55
Keswick (Bus Station)	a	07.53	08.40	09.00	10.00	11.00	12.00	13.00	14.00	15.00	16.00	17.00	18.00	19.00	20.00	21.05	22.10	23.25
Cockermouth (Main Street)	a	08.32		09.39	10.39	11.39	12.39	13.39	14.39	15.39	16.39	17.39	18.39	19.39	20.39	21.40	22.40	23.45
Workington (Bus Station)	a	08.57		10.04	11.04	12.04	13.04	14.04	15.04	16.04	17.04	18.04	19.04	20.04	20.58	21.58	22.58	00.13

Saturdays

		VT	VT	VT	VT	VT	VT	VT	VT	VT	VT	VT	VT	VT	VT	VT	VT	VT
		Bus	Bus	Bus	Bus	Bus	Bus	Bus	Bus	Bus	Bus	Bus	Bus	Bus	Bus	Bus	Bus	Bus
Penrith North Lakes	d	07.22	08.22	08.35	09.22	10.22	11.22	12.22	13.22	14.22	15.22	16.22	17.22	18.30	19.30	20.35	21.40	22.55
Keswick (Bus Station)	a	07.53	09.00	09.17	10.00	11.00	12.00	13.00	14.00	15.00	16.00	17.00	18.00	19.00	20.00	21.05	22.10	23.25
Cockermouth (Main Street)	a	08.32	09.39		10.39	11.39	12.39	13.39	14.39	15.39	16.39	17.39	18.39	19.39	20.39	21.40	22.40	23.55
Workington (Bus Station)	a	08.57	10.04		11.04	12.04	13.04	14.04	15.04	16.04	17.04	18.04	19.04	20.04	20.58	21.58	22.58	00.13

Sundays

		VT	VT	VT	VT	VT	VT
		Bus	Bus	Bus	Bus	Bus	Bus
Penrith North Lakes	d	09.20	11.20	13.20	15.20	17.20	19.20
Keswick (Bus Station)	a	23.15	11.55	13.55	15.55	17.55	19.55
Cockermouth (Main Street)	a	23.45	12.31	14.31	16.31	18.31	20.31
Workington (Bus Station)	a	00.03	12.52	14.52	16.52	18.52	20.52

Table 65F

Mondays to Fridays

Workington, Cockermouth and Keswick - Penrith

Bus Service

		VT	VT	VT	VT	VT	VT	VT	VT	VT	VT	VT	VT	VT	VT	VT	VT	VT
		Bus	Bus	Bus	Bus	Bus	Bus	Bus	Bus	Bus	Bus	Bus	Bus	Bus	Bus	Bus	Bus	Bus
Workington (Bus Station)	d	05.20	06.20	06.55	07.55	09.20	10.20	11.20	12.20	13.20	14.20	15.20	16.20	17.20		18.20	19.15	21.15
Cockermouth (Main Street)	d	05.41	06.41	07.16	08.16	09.41	10.41	11.41	12.41	13.41	14.41	15.41	16.41	17.41		18.41	19.37	21.37
Keswick (Bus Station)	d	06.15	07.15	07.55	08.55	10.20	11.20	12.20	13.20	14.20	15.20	16.20	17.20	18.20	18.40	19.20	20.10	22.06
Penrith North Lakes	a	06.45	07.45	08.36	09.36	11.01	12.01	13.01	14.01	15.01	16.01	17.01	18.01	19.01	19.15	19.55	20.45	22.33

Saturdays

		VT	VT	VT	VT	VT	VT	VT	VT	VT	VT	VT	VT	VT	VT	VT	VT	VT
		Bus	Bus	Bus	Bus	Bus	Bus	Bus	Bus	Bus	Bus	Bus	Bus	Bus	Bus	Bus	Bus	Bus
Workington (Bus Station)	d	05.20	06.20	06.55	07.55	09.20	10.20	11.20	12.20	13.20	14.20	15.20	16.20	17.20		18.20	19.15	21.15
Cockermouth (Main Street)	d	05.41	06.41	07.16	08.16	09.41	10.41	11.41	12.41	13.41	14.41	15.41	16.41	17.41		18.41	19.37	21.37
Keswick (Bus Station)	d	06.15	07.15	07.55	08.55	10.20	11.20	12.20	13.20	14.20	15.20	16.20	17.20	18.20	18.40	19.20	20.10	22.06
Penrith North Lakes	a	06.45	07.45	08.36	09.36	11.01	12.01	13.01	14.01	15.01	16.01	17.01	18.01	19.01	19.15	19.55	20.45	22.33

Sundays

		VT	VT	VT	VT	VT	VT	VT
		Bus	Bus	Bus	Bus	Bus	Bus	Bus
Workington (Bus Station)	d	07.15	09.15	11.15	13.15	15.15	17.15	
Cockermouth (Main Street)	d	07.36	09.36	11.36	13.36	15.36	17.36	
Keswick (Bus Station)	d	08.15	10.15	12.15	14.15	16.15	18.15	18.40
Penrith North Lakes	a	08.50	10.50	12.50	14.50	16.50	18.50	19.15

This is an amalgamation of the X4/X5/X50 services operated by Stagecaoch in Cumbria

Sunday service operates on Bank Holidays.
Please check with local operator before travelling

Table 66

Mondays to Fridays

London - Watford Junction, Milton Keynes Central, Northampton and West Midlands

Miles	Miles	Miles			LM MX ◇1	VT MO ◇1 ☕	VT MO ◇1 ☕	VT MX ◇1 ☕	LM MX ◇1	LM MO ◇1	LM MX ◇1	VT MO ◇1 ☕	VT MX ◇1 ☕	LM MO ◇1	LM MX 1	LM ◇1	LM MO ◇1	LM MX ◇1	LM 1	SN 1	LM ◇1	VT ◇1 ⊠	LM ◇1
0	0	—	**London Euston 15** ⊖	d	21p46	21p55	22p25	22p30	22p54	22p58	23p24	23p25	23p30	23p34	23p34	00 04	00 34	00 34	01 34			05 27	05 30
—	—	0	East Croydon 🚊	d																			
—	—	—	Clapham Junction	d																			
—	—	8¾	Imperial Wharf	d																05 07			
—	—	9¼	West Brompton ⊖	d																05 10			
—	—	11¼	Kensington (Olympia) ⊖	d																05 14			
—	—	12½	Shepherd's Bush	d																05 17			
8	—	16¾	Wembley Central ⊖	d													00 43	00 45	01 45				
11½	11½	—	Harrow & Wealdstone ⊖	d						23p10				23p46	23p46	00 16	00 48	00 50	01 50	05 33			05 43
16	—	—	Bushey	d											23p51			00 55					
17½	17½	—	**Watford Junction**	a					23p09	23p17	23p39			23p53	23p54	00 22	00 54	00 57	01 56	05 40			05 50
—	—	—		d		22b09	22b39	22b45	23p10	23p17	23p40	23b40		23p53	23p54	00 23	00 58	00 58	01 57			05u45	05 50
21	—	—	Kings Langley	d					23p14	23p22				23p58	23p59		01 02	01 02					05 55
23	—	—	Apsley	d					23p18	23p25				00 01	00 02		01 06	01 06					05 59
24½	—	—	Hemel Hempstead	d					23p21	23p28	23p47			00 04	00 05	00 30	01 09	01 09	02 04				06 01
28	—	—	Berkhamsted	d					23p26	23p33	23p52			00 09	00 09	00 35	01 14	01 14	02 09				06 06
31¾	—	—	Tring	d					23p33	23p38				00 14	00 14	00 40	01 18	01 18	02 13				06 13
36	—	—	Cheddington	d						23p43				00 19	00 19		01 24	01 24					06 18
40¼	—	—	Leighton Buzzard	d	22p18				23p40	23p50	00 05			00 26	00 25	00 49	01 30	01 30	02 22				06 23
46¾	—	—	Bletchley	d					23p47	23p57	00 12			00 33	00 32	00 56	01 37	01 37	02 29		05 17		06 30
49¾	49¾	—	**Milton Keynes Central 10**	a	22p32	22p42	23p11	23p28	23p55	00 06	00 20	00 11	00 27	00 42	00 40	01 04	01 45	01 45	02 37		05 21	06 09	06 35
—	—	—		d	22p32	22p44	23p12	23p29	23p55	00 06	00 20	00 12	00 28	00 42		01 04	01 46	01 46			05 21	06 10	06 36
52½	52½	—	Wolverton	d	22p36				23p59	00 10	00 24			00 46		01 08	01 49	01 49			05 25		06 39
65¾	—	—	**Northampton**	a	22p49				00 12	00 24	00 37			01 00		01 21	02 03	02 03			05 37		06 52
84½	82½	—	**Rugby**	a	23p17	23p20	23p46	23p58				00s46	01s00								06 02		07 17
—	—	—	Nuneaton	a																	06 16	06 38	
96	—	—	Coventry	a	23p29	23p31	23p57	00 10				00s57	01s13										07 29
106¾	—	—	Birmingham International ✈	a	23p47	23p42	00 08	00 21				01s08	01s24										07 45
115¼	—	—	**Birmingham New Street 12**	a	00 04	23p54	00 21	00 32				01s21	01s36										08 03
120½	—	—	Sandwell & Dudley	a																			
128	—	—	Wolverhampton 7 🚊	a		00 15	00 43	01 03				01 52	02 07										

		VT ◇1 ⊠	SN 1	VT ◇1 ⊠	LM 1	SN 1	VT ◇1 ⊠	VT ◇1 ⊠	LM ◇1	LM 1	VT ◇1 ⊠	VT ◇1 ⊠	LM ◇1	VT ◇1 ⊠	SN 1	VT ◇1 ⊠	LM 1	VT ◇1 ⊠	LM ◇1	VT ◇1 ⊠	VT ◇1 ⊠	LM 1	LM 1
London Euston 15 ⊖	d	05 39		06 03	06 04		06 17	06 23	06 24	06 34	06 36	06 43	06 53	06 55		07 03	07 04	07 10	07 13	07 20	07 23	07 24	07 34
East Croydon 🚊	d																						
Clapham Junction	d		05 30			05 55									06 38								
Imperial Wharf	d		05 39			06 00									06 42								
West Brompton ⊖	d		05 41			06 03									06 45								
Kensington (Olympia) ⊖	d		05 44			06 07									06 49								
Shepherd's Bush	d		05 47			06 10									06 52								
Wembley Central ⊖	d		06s00			06 23									07s07								
Harrow & Wealdstone ⊖	d		06 07		06 16	06 28				06 47					07 12		07 17						07 46
Bushey	d																						
Watford Junction	a		06 14		06 22	06 35			06 39	06 53			07 08		07 19		07 24					07 40	07 52
	d	06u02	06 14		06 23			06u37	06 41	06 54			07 10		07 19		07 24				07u37	07 42	07 53
Kings Langley	d				06 27					06 58							07 29						07 58
Apsley	d				06 31					07 02							07 32						08 01
Hemel Hempstead	d		06 22		06 34				06 48	07 05			07 17		07 27		07 35					07 49	08 04
Berkhamsted	d		06 26		06 39				06 53	07 10			07 22		07 32		07 40					07 54	08 09
Tring	d		06 33		06a46				06 59	07 16					07 39		07a47					08 01	08a16
Cheddington	d								07 05	07 21												08 06	
Leighton Buzzard	d		06 42						07 10	07 26			07 35		07 51				07 42			08 11	
Bletchley	d		06 49						07 17	07 33			07 43		07 58				07 50			08 18	
Milton Keynes Central 10	a	06 22	06 55				06 47		07 22	07 38		07 13	07 48	07 25	08 03			07 40	07 54	07 50		08 23	
	d	06 22							07 23			07 13	07 48						07 54				
Wolverton	d								07 26				07 52						07 58				
Northampton	a								07 42				08 05						08 11				
Rugby	a	06 44		06 51					08 04				08 38			07 51							
Nuneaton	a								08 17														
Coventry	a			07 02				07 22				07 42	08 49			08 02					08 22		
Birmingham International ✈	a			07 13				07 33				07 53	09 04			08 12					08 33		
Birmingham New Street 12	a			07 27				07 45				08 08	09 16			08 27					08 45		
Sandwell & Dudley	a							07 57													08 57		
Wolverhampton 7 🚊	a							08 11													09 11		

b Previous night, stops to pick up only

London - Watford Junction, Milton Keynes Central, Northampton and West Midlands

		VT ◇1 ☒	VT ◇1 ☒	LM ◇1	LM ◇1		SN 1	VT ◇1 ☒	LM 1	VT ◇1 ☒	LM ◇1	VT ◇1 ☒	VT ◇1 ☒	LM 1	LM 1		VT ◇1 A ☒	VT ◇1 B ☒	LM ◇1	LM ◇1	SN 1	VT ◇1 ☒	LM 1	VT ◇1 ☒	LM ◇1
London Euston 15 ⊖	d	07 35	07 43	07 47	07 54			08 03	08 05	08 10	08 13	08 20	08 23	08 24	08 34		08 43	08 43	08 46	08 54		09 03	09 05	09 10	09 13
East Croydon	d																				08 07				
Clapham Junction	d						07 39														08 39				
Imperial Wharf	d						07 44														08 44				
West Brompton ⊖	d						07 47														08 47				
Kensington (Olympia) ⊖	d						07 50														08 50				
Shepherd's Bush	d						07 53														08 53				
Wembley Central ⊖	d						08s08														09s08				
Harrow & Wealdstone ⊖	d						08 13		08 21					08 36	08 46						09 13		09 17		
Bushey	d								08 26						08 51								09 22		
Watford Junction	a			08 01	08 11		08 20		08 29					08 43	08 54				09 00	09 09	09 20		09 25		
	d			08 02	08 12		08 20		08 29				08u37	08 44	08 55				09 01	09 11	09 20		09 26		
Kings Langley	d								08 34						08 59								09 30		
Apsley	d								08 38						09 03								09 34		
Hemel Hempstead	d				08 19		08 28		08 40					08 51	09 06					09 18	09 28		09 37		
Berkhamsted	d				08 24		08 32		08 45					08 56	09 11					09 23	09 32		09 42		
Tring	d						08 37		08a52					09 02	09a17						09 39		09a48		
Cheddington	d													09 07											
Leighton Buzzard	d				08 37		08 48				08 42			09 12						09 36	09 48				09 42
Bletchley	d				08 44		08 55				08 50			09 20						09 43	09 55				09 50
Milton Keynes Central 10	a	08 05	08 13	08 25	08 49		09 01			08 40	08 54	08 50		09 26			09 13	09 13	09 24	09 48	10 01			09 40	09 54
	d		08 13	08 31	08 50						08 54						09 13	09 13	09 25	09 49					09 54
Wolverton	d				08 53						08 58									09 52					09 58
Northampton	a			08 44	09 08						09 11								09 40	10 05					10 11
Rugby	a			09 04	09 38			08 51											10 04	10 38		09 51			
Nuneaton	a			09 16															10 16						
Coventry	a		08 42		09 49			09 02					09 22				09 42	09 42		10 49		10 02			
Birmingham International ✈	a		08 53		10 04			09 12					09 33				09 53	09 53		11 04		10 13			
Birmingham New Street 12	a		09 08		10 16			09 27					09 45				10 08	10 08		11 16		10 27			
Sandwell & Dudley	a												09 57												
Wolverhampton 7	a												10 11					10 37							

			VT ◇1 ☒	VT ◇1 ☒	LM 1	LM 1	VT ◇1 ☒	LM ◇1	LM ◇1	SN 1	VT ◇1 ☒		LM 1	VT ◇1 ☒	LM ◇1	VT ◇1 ☒	VT ◇1 ☒	LM 1	LM 1	VT ◇1 ☒	LM ◇1		LM ◇1	SN 1	VT ◇1
London Euston 15 ⊖	d		09 20	09 23	09 24	09 34	09 43	09 46	09 54		10 03		10 05	10 10	10 13	10 20	10 23	10 24	10 34	10 43	10 46		10 54		11 03
East Croydon	d									09 08														10 10	
Clapham Junction	d									09 39														10 39	
Imperial Wharf	d									09 44														10 44	
West Brompton ⊖	d									09 47														10 47	
Kensington (Olympia) ⊖	d									09 50														10 50	
Shepherd's Bush	d									09 53														10 53	
Wembley Central ⊖	d									10s08														11s08	
Harrow & Wealdstone ⊖	d					09 48				10 13			10 17						10 46					11 13	
Bushey	d					09 53							10 22						10 51						
Watford Junction	a				09 39	09 56		10 00	10 09	10 20			10 25					10 39	10 54		11 00		11 10	11 20	
	d			09u37	09 41	09 57		10 01	10 11	10 20			10 26				10u37	10 41	10 55		11 01		11 11	11 20	
Kings Langley	d					10 01							10 30						10 59						
Apsley	d					10 05							10 34						11 03						
Hemel Hempstead	d				09 48	10 08			10 18	10 28			10 37					10 48	11 06				11 18	11 28	
Berkhamsted	d				09 53	10 13			10 23	10 32			10 42					10 53	11 11				11 23	11 32	
Tring	d				09 59	10a19				10 39			10a48					10 59	11a17					11 39	
Cheddington	d				10 04													11 04							
Leighton Buzzard	d				10 09				10 38	10 48					10 42			11 09					11 36	11 48	
Bletchley	d				10 16				10 45	10 57					10 50			11 16					11 43	11 55	
Milton Keynes Central 10	a		09 50		10 21		10 13	10 24	10 50	11 02				10 40	10 54	10 50		11 21		11 13	11 24		11 48	12 01	
	d						10 13	10 25	10 51						10 54					11 13	11 25		11 49		
Wolverton	d								10 55						10 59								11 52		
Northampton	a							10 40	11 09						11 13						11 40		12 06		
Rugby	a							11 04	11 38		10 51										12 04		12 38		11 51
Nuneaton	a							11 16													12 16				
Coventry	a			10 22			10 42		11 49		11 02						11 22			11 42			12 49		12 02
Birmingham International ✈	a			10 33			10 53		12 04		11 13						11 33			11 53			13 04		12 13
Birmingham New Street 12	a			10 45			11 08		12 16		11 27						11 45			12 08			13 16		12 27
Sandwell & Dudley	a			10 57													11 57								
Wolverhampton 7	a			11 11													12 11								

A until 15 July, from 12 September **B** from 18 July until 9 September

London - Watford Junction, Milton Keynes Central, Northampton and West Midlands

		LM	VT	LM	VT	VT	LM		LM	VT	LM	LM	SN	VT	LM	VT	LM		VT	VT	LM	LM	VT	LM	LM
		1	◇1	◇1	◇1	◇1	1		1	◇1	◇1	◇1	1	◇1	1	◇1	◇1		◇1	◇1	1	1	◇1	◇1	◇1
			☕		☕	☕				☕				☕		☕			☕	☕			☕		
London Euston 15	⊖ d	11 04	11 10	11 13	11 20	11 23	11 24		11 34	11 43	11 46	11 54		12 03	12 04	12 10	12 13		12 20	12 23	12 24	12 34	12 43	12 46	12 54
East Croydon	d												11 11												
Clapham Junction	d												11 39												
Imperial Wharf	d												11 44												
West Brompton	⊖ d												11 47												
Kensington (Olympia)	⊖ d												11 50												
Shepherd's Bush	d												11 53												
Wembley Central	⊖ d												12s08												
Harrow & Wealdstone	⊖ d	11 17							11 46				12 13		12 17							12 46			
Bushey	d	11 22							11 51						12 22							12 51			
Watford Junction	a	11 25					11 39		11 54		12 00	12 09	12 20		12 25						12 40	12 54		13 00	13 09
	d	11 26				11u37	11 41		11 55		12 01	12 11	12 20		12 26					12u37	12 41	12 55		13 01	13 11
Kings Langley	d	11 30							11 59						12 30							12 59			
Apsley	d	11 34							12 03						12 34							13 03			
Hemel Hempstead	d	11 37					11 48		12 06			12 18	12 28		12 37						12 48	13 06			13 18
Berkhamsted	d	11 42					11 53		12 11			12 23	12 32		12 42						12 53	13 11			13 23
Tring	d	11a48					11 59		12a17				12 39		12a48						12 59	13a17			
Cheddington	d						12 04														13 04				
Leighton Buzzard	d			11 42			12 09					12 36	12 48				12 42				13 09				13 36
Bletchley	d			11 50			12 16					12 43	12 55				12 50				13 16				13 43
Milton Keynes Central 10	a		11 40	11 54	11 50		12 21			12 13	12 24	12 48	13 01			12 40	12 54		12 50		13 21		13 13	13 24	13 48
	d			11 54						12 13	12 25	12 49					12 54						13 13	13 25	13 49
Wolverton	d			11 58								12 52					12 58								13 52
Northampton	a			12 11							12 40	13 05					13 11							13 40	14 05
Rugby	a										13 04	13 38		12 51										14 04	14 38
Nuneaton	a										13 16													14 16	
Coventry	a					12 22				12 42		13 49		13 02						13 22			13 42		14 49
Birmingham International	✈ a					12 33				12 53		14 04		13 13						13 33			13 53		15 04
Birmingham New Street 12	a					12 45				13 08		14 16		13 27						13 45			14 08		15 16
Sandwell & Dudley	a					12 57														13 57					
Wolverhampton 7	a					13 11														14 11					

		SN	VT		LM	VT	LM	VT	VT	LM	LM	VT	VT		LM	LM	SN	VT	LM	VT	LM	VT	VT		LM
		1	◇1		1	◇1	◇1	◇1	◇1	1	1	◇1	◇1		◇1	◇1	1	◇1	1	◇1	◇1	◇1	◇1		1
												A	B												
			☕			☕		☕	☕			☕	☕					☕		☕		☕	☕		
London Euston 15	⊖ d		13 03		13 04	13 10	13 13	13 20	13 23	13 24	13 34	13 43	13 43		13 46	13 54		14 03	14 04	14 10	14 13	14 20	14 23		14 24
East Croydon	d	12 10															13 10								
Clapham Junction	d	12 39															13 39								
Imperial Wharf	d	12 44															13 44								
West Brompton	⊖ d	12 47															13 47								
Kensington (Olympia)	⊖ d	12 50															13 50								
Shepherd's Bush	d	12 53															13 53								
Wembley Central	⊖ d	13s08															14s08								
Harrow & Wealdstone	⊖ d	13 13			13 17						13 47						14 13		14 17						
Bushey	d				13 22						13 52								14 22						
Watford Junction	a	13 20			13 25					13 40	13 54				14 00	14 10	14 20		14 25						14 39
	d	13 20			13 26				13u37	13 41	13 55				14 01	14 11	14 20		14 26				14u37		14 41
Kings Langley	d				13 30						13 59								14 30						
Apsley	d				13 34						14 03								14 34						
Hemel Hempstead	d	13 28			13 37					13 48	14 06					14 18	14 28		14 37						14 48
Berkhamsted	d	13 32			13 42					13 53	14 11					14 23	14 32		14 42						14 53
Tring	d	13 39			13a48					13 59	14a17						14 39		14a48						14 59
Cheddington	d									14 04															15 04
Leighton Buzzard	d	13 48					13 42			14 09						14 36	14 48				14 42				15 09
Bletchley	d	13 55					13 50			14 16						14 43	14 55				14 50				15 16
Milton Keynes Central 10	a	14 01				13 40	13 54	13 50		14 23		14 13	14 13		14 24	14 48	15 01			14 40	14 54	14 50			15 21
	d						13 54					14 13	14 13		14 25	14 49					14 54				
Wolverton	d						13 58									14 52					14 58				
Northampton	a						14 11								14 40	15 05					15 11				
Rugby	a		13 51												15 04	15 38		14 51							
Nuneaton	a														15 16										
Coventry	a		14 02						14 22			14 42	14 42			15 49		15 02					15 22		
Birmingham International	✈ a		14 13						14 33			14 53	14 53			16 04		15 13					15 33		
Birmingham New Street 12	a		14 27						14 45			15 08	15 08			16 16		15 27					15 45		
Sandwell & Dudley	a								14 57														15 57		
Wolverhampton 7	a								15 11				15 37										16 11		

A until 15 July, from 12 September

B from 18 July until 9 September

London - Watford Junction, Milton Keynes Central, Northampton and West Midlands

		LM	VT	LM	LM	SN	VT	LM	VT		LM	VT	VT	LM	LM	VT	LM	LM	SN		VT	LM	VT	LM	VT
		1	◇1 ☕	◇1	◇1	1	◇1 ☕	1	◇1 ☕		◇1	◇1 ☕	◇1 ☕	1	1	◇1 ☕	◇1	◇1	1		◇1 ☕	1	◇1 ☕	◇1	◇1 ☕
London Euston 15 ⊖	d	14 34	14 43	14 46	14 54		15 03	15 04	15 10		15 13	15 20	15 23	15 24	15 34	15 43	15 46	15 54			16 03	16 04	16 10	16 13	16 20
East Croydon 🚊	d					14 10													15 10						
Clapham Junction	d					14 39													15 39						
Imperial Wharf	d					14 44													15 44						
West Brompton ⊖	d					14 47													15 47						
Kensington (Olympia) ⊖	d					14 50													15 50						
Shepherd's Bush	d					14 53													15 53						
Wembley Central ⊖	d					15s08													16s08						
Harrow & Wealdstone ⊖	d	14 46				15 13		15 17							15 47				16 13			16 17			
Bushey	d	14 51						15 22							15 51							16 22			
Watford Junction	a	14 54		15 00	15 09	15 20		15 25						15 39	15 54		16 00	16 09	16 20			16 25			
	d	14 55		15 01	15 11	15 20		15 26					15u37	15 41	15 55		16 01	16 11	16 20			16 26			
Kings Langley	d	14 59						15 30							15 59							16 30			
Apsley	d	15 03						15 34							16 03							16 34			
Hemel Hempstead	d	15 06			15 18	15 28		15 37						15 48	16 06			16 18	16 28			16 37			
Berkhamsted	d	15 11			15 23	15 32		15 42						15 53	16 11			16 23	16 32			16 42			
Tring	d	15a17				15 39		15a48						15 59	16a17				16 39			16a48			
Cheddington	d													16 04											
Leighton Buzzard	d				15 36	15 48					15 42			16 09				16 36	16 48					16 42	
Bletchley	d				15 43	15 55					15 50			16 16				16 43	16 56					16 50	
Milton Keynes Central 10	a		15 13	15 24	15 48	16 01			15 40		15 54	15 50		16 21		16 13	16 24	16 48	17 00					16 54	
	d		15 13	15 25	15 49						15 54					16 13	16 25	16 49						16 54	
Wolverton	d				15 52						15 58							16 52						16 58	
Northampton	a			15 40	16 05						16 11						16 40	17 05						17 12	
Rugby	a			16 04	16 38		15 51										17 04	17 38			16 51				
Nuneaton	a			16 16													17 16								
Coventry	a		15 42		16 49		16 02						16 22			16 42		17 49			17 02				
Birmingham International ✈	a		15 53		17 04		16 13						16 33			16 53		18 04			17 13				
Birmingham New Street 12	a		16 08		17 19		16 27						16 45			17 08		18 17			17 27				
Sandwell & Dudley	a												16 57												
Wolverhampton 7 🚊	a												17 11												

		VT	LM	VT	LM		VT	LM	LM	SN	VT	LM	VT	LM	LM		VT	VT	LM	LM	VT	LM	LM	VT	LM
		◇1 ☕	1	◇1 ☕	1		◇1 ☕	◇1	1	1	◇1 ⊠	1	◇1 ⊠	◇1	1		◇1 ⊠	◇1 ⊠	1	1	◇1 ⊠	1	1	◇1 ⊠	◇1
London Euston 15 ⊖	d	16 23	16 24	16 33	16 34		16 43	16 48	16 54		17 03	17 05	17 10	17 13	17 14		17 20	17 23	17 24	17 30	17 33	17 34	17 41	17 43	17 46
East Croydon 🚊	d									16 10															
Clapham Junction	d									16 39															
Imperial Wharf	d									16 44															
West Brompton ⊖	d									16 47															
Kensington (Olympia) ⊖	d									16 50															
Shepherd's Bush	d									16 53															
Wembley Central ⊖	d									17s08															
Harrow & Wealdstone ⊖	d				16 46				17 06	17 13		17 19			17 26							17 46			
Bushey	d				16 51				17 11						17 31							17 52	17 56		
Watford Junction	a		16 39		16 54				17 14	17 20		17 26			17 34				17 43	17 48		17 55	18 00		
	d	16u37	16 41		16 55				17 14	17 21		17 27			17 34			17u37	17 44	17 49			18 01		
Kings Langley	d				16 59							17 31			17 39								18 05		
Apsley	d				17 03				17 20						17 42					17 55					
Hemel Hempstead	d		16 48		17 06				17 23	17 28		17 36							17 51	17 58			18 10		
Berkhamsted	d		16 53		17 11				17 28	17 33		17 41							17 56				18 15		
Tring	d		16 59		17a19				17a36	17 38		17 46			17a52					18 05			18a22		
Cheddington	d		17 04									17 51								18 10					
Leighton Buzzard	d		17 09					17 19		17 47				17 42					18 09						18 19
Bletchley	d		17 16							17 54		18 01							18 16	18 22					
Milton Keynes Central 10	a		17 22					17 28		17 59		18 06		17 52					18 21	18 28					18 31
	d						17u13	17 29					17u40	17 52					18 23					18u13	18 32
Wolverton	d							17 33						17 56					18 26						18 36
Northampton	a							17 46						18 10					18 39						18 49
Rugby	a			17 21							17 51			18 38					19 04		18 21				19 17
Nuneaton	a												18 11												
Coventry	a	17 22					17 42				18 02			18 49				18 22						18 42	19 29
Birmingham International ✈	a	17 33					17 53				18 13			19 04				18 33						18 53	19 45
Birmingham New Street 12	a	17 45					18 08				18 27			19 17				18 45						19 08	20 03
Sandwell & Dudley	a	17 57																18 57							
Wolverhampton 7 🚊	a	18 11																19 11							

London - Watford Junction, Milton Keynes Central, Northampton and West Midlands

		LM	SN	VT	LM	VT	LM	LM	VT	LM	VT	LM	VT	LM	LM	VT	VT FO	LM	LM	SN	VT	LM
		◇1	1	◇1 ⊠	◇1	◇1 ⊠	1	◇1	◇1 ⊠	1	◇1 ⊠	◇1	◇1 ⊠	1	1	◇1 ⊠	◇ ☕	◇1	1	1	R 1 ☕	1
London Euston 15 ⊖	d	17 51		18 03	18 05	18 10	18 12	18 13	18 20	18 21	18 23	18 29	18 33	18 34	18 40	18 43	18 46	18 49	18 54		19 03	19 04
East Croydon	d		17 10																	18 10		
Clapham Junction	d		17 39																	18 39		
Imperial Wharf	d		17 44																	18 44		
West Brompton ⊖	d		17 47																	18 47		
Kensington (Olympia) ⊖	d		17 50																	18 50		
Shepherd's Bush	d		17 53																	18 53		
Wembley Central ⊖	d		18s08																	19s08		
Harrow & Wealdstone ⊖	d	18 04	18 13		18 18					18 34				18 46					19 06	19 13		19 17
Bushey	d						18 27							18 52	18 57							19 22
Watford Junction	a	18 10	18 20		18 25		18 30			18 40		18 46		18 55	19 00				19 12	19 20		19 25
	d	18 11	18 20		18 25		18 31			18 41	18u37	18 47		18 56	19 01				19 13	19 21		19 26
Kings Langley	d				18 30					18 46					19 05							19 30
Apsley	d				18 33							18 53			19 09							19 34
Hemel Hempstead	d	18 18	18 28				18 38			18 51				19 03	19 12				19 20	19 28		19 37
Berkhamsted	d	18 23	18 32				18 43					18 59			19 16				19 25	19 33		19 42
Tring	d		18 38		18 43		18a53			18 59				19 12	19a26				19 30	19 40		19a48
Cheddington	d				18 48							19 08		19 17								
Leighton Buzzard	d		18 47		18 53			18 42		19 07				19 24				19 19	19 38	19 52		
Bletchley	d	18 41	18 54		19 01							19 18		19a31				19 25	19 46	20 01		
Milton Keynes Central 10	a	18 45	19 00		19 06			18 52		19 19		19 23				19 13		19 30	19 52	20 06		
	d	18 46			19 07	18u40		18 54				19 23				19 13		19 31				
Wolverton	d	18 49			19 10			18 57				19 27						19 35				
Northampton	a	19 03			19 25			19 10				19 39						19 48				
Rugby	a			18 51				19 38				20 04	19 22				19 38	20 17			19 51	
Nuneaton	a					19 12						20 16										
Coventry	a			19 02				19 49			19 22					19 42		20 29			20 02	
Birmingham International ✈	a			19 13				20 04			19 33					19 53		20 45			20 13	
Birmingham New Street 12	a			19 27				20 16			19 45					20 06		21 01			20 27	
Sandwell & Dudley	a										19 58											
Wolverhampton 7	a										20 12					20 36						

		VT	VT	LM	VT	VT	LM	LM	VT	LM	LM	SN	VT	LM	VT	VT	LM	VT	LM	LM	VT	LM	LM
		R 1 ☕	R 1 ☕	◇1	R 1 ☕	R 1 ☕	1	1	◇1 ☕	◇1	◇1	1	◇1 ☕	1	◇1 ☕	◇1 ☕	◇1	◇1 ☕	1	1	◇1 ☕	◇1	◇1
London Euston 15 ⊖	d	19 07	19 10	19 13	19 20	19 23	19 24	19 34	19 43	19 46	19 54		20 03	20 04	20 07	20 10	20 13	20 23	20 24	20 34	20 43	20 46	20 54
East Croydon	d											19 10											
Clapham Junction	d											19 39											
Imperial Wharf	d											19 44											
West Brompton ⊖	d											19 47											
Kensington (Olympia) ⊖	d											19 50											
Shepherd's Bush	d											19 53											
Wembley Central ⊖	d											20s08											
Harrow & Wealdstone ⊖	d							19 46				20 13		20 17						20 46			
Bushey	d							19 51						20 22						20 51			
Watford Junction	a						19 40	19 54			20 10	20 20		20 25					20 40	20 54			21 10
	d					19u37	19 42	19 55			20 11	20 20		20 26				20u37	20 42	20 55			21 11
Kings Langley	d							19 59						20 30						20 59			
Apsley	d							20 03						20 34						21 03			
Hemel Hempstead	d						19 49	20 06			20 18	20 28		20 37					20 49	21 06			21 18
Berkhamsted	d						19 54	20 11			20 23	20 32		20 42					20 55	21 11			21 23
Tring	d						20 01	20a17				20 39		20a48					21 00	21a17			
Cheddington	d						20 06												21 05				
Leighton Buzzard	d			19 43			20 12			20 18	20 36	20 48					20 42		21 10			21 18	21 36
Bletchley	d						20 19				20 43	20 55					20 50		21 17				21 43
Milton Keynes Central 10	a			19 55			20 24		20 13	20 28	20 49	21 01				20 40	20 54		21 22		21 13	21 27	21 48
	d			19 56					20 13	20 30	20 49						20 55				21 13	21 29	21 49
Wolverton	d			19 59						20 33	20 53						20 59					21 32	21 52
Northampton	a			20 11						20 47	21 06						21 13					21 46	22 05
Rugby	a										21 38		20 51									22 17	
Nuneaton	a	20 02													21 02								
Coventry	a				20 22				20 42		21 49		21 02					21 22			21 42	22 29	
Birmingham International ✈	a				20 33				20 53		22 04		21 13					21 33			21 53	22 45	
Birmingham New Street 12	a				20 45				21 06		22 16		21 25					21 46			22 06	23 02	
Sandwell & Dudley	a				20 58				21 23									21 58			22 23		
Wolverhampton 7	a				21 12				21 38				21 56					22 12			22 38		

London - Watford Junction, Milton Keynes Central, Northampton and West Midlands

		VT	VT	SN	LM	VT	VT	LM	SR	LM	LM	VT	LM	LM	SN	VT	LM	LM	VT	LM	LM	SN
		◇1	◇1	1	1	◇1	◇1	◇1	A	1	1	◇1	◇1	◇1	1	◇1	1	◇1	◇1	1	◇1	1
		☕	☕			☕	☕		🛏 ☕			☕				☕			☕			
London Euston 15 ⊖	d	21 00	21 03		21 04	21 07	21 10	21 13	21 15	21 24	21 34	21 43	21 46	21 54		22 00	22 04	22 24	22 30	22 34	22 54	
East Croydon	d																					
Clapham Junction	d			20 39											21 39							22 39
Imperial Wharf	d			20 44											21 44							22 44
West Brompton ⊖	d			20 47											21 47							22 47
Kensington (Olympia) ⊖	d			20 50											21 50							22 50
Shepherd's Bush	d			20 53											21 53							22 53
Wembley Central ⊖	d			21s08																		
Harrow & Wealdstone ⊖	d			21 13	21 17						21 46				22 16		22 19			22 49		23 16
Bushey	d				21 22						21 51									22 54		
Watford Junction	a			21 20	21 25					21 39	21 53			22 09	22 23		22 25	22 39		22 57	23 09	23 23
	d			21 20	21 26		21u25			21 41	21 54	21u58		22 11			22 26	22 40	22u45	22 58	23 10	
Kings Langley	d				21 30						21 58						22 30			23 02	23 14	
Apsley	d				21 34						22 02						22 33			23 06	23 18	
Hemel Hempstead	d			21 28	21 36					21 48	22 05			22 18			22 36	22 47		23 09	23 21	
Berkhamsted	d			21 32	21 41					21 53	22 10			22 23			22 40	22 52		23 14	23 26	
Tring	d			21 39	21 48						22 16			22 28			22 45			23 18	23 33	
Cheddington	d				21 53						22 22									23 24		
Leighton Buzzard	d			21 50	21 57			21 45		22 07	22 26		22 18	22 37			22 54	23 05		23 30	23 40	
Bletchley	d			21 58	22a04			21 53		22 14	22 33			22 44			23 03	23 12		23 37	23 47	
Milton Keynes Central 10	a	21 30	21 33	22 03		21 37		21 57		22 20	22 38	22 17	22 32	22 52		22 30	23 11	23 20	23 28	23 45	23 55	
	d		21 34			21 38		21 58				22 17	22 32	22 55		22 31		23 21	23 29		23 55	
Wolverton	d							22 02					22 36	22 59				23 24			23 59	
Northampton	a							22 16					22 49	23 12				23 38			00 12	
Rugby	a		21 56				22 02	22 40					23 17			22 52			23 58			
Nuneaton	a					22 07										23 03						
Coventry	a		22 06					22 52				22 46	23 29						00 10			
Birmingham International ✈	a		22 18					23 07				23 00	23 47						00 21			
Birmingham New Street 12	a		22 29					23 19				23 16	00 04						00 32			
Sandwell & Dudley	a		22 41									23 33										
Wolverhampton 7	a		22 56									23 47							01 03			

		LM	VT	VT	LM	SR
			FX	FO		
		◇1	◇1	◇1	1	
			☕	☕		🛏 ☕
London Euston 15 ⊖	d	23 24	23 30	23 30	23 34	23 50
East Croydon	d					
Clapham Junction	d					
Imperial Wharf	d					
West Brompton ⊖	d					
Kensington (Olympia) ⊖	d					
Shepherd's Bush	d					
Wembley Central ⊖	d					
Harrow & Wealdstone ⊖	d				23 46	
Bushey	d				23 51	
Watford Junction	a	23 39			23 54	
	d	23 40			23 54	
Kings Langley	d				23 59	
Apsley	d				00 02	
Hemel Hempstead	d	23 47			00 05	
Berkhamsted	d	23 52			00 09	
Tring	d				00 14	
Cheddington	d				00 19	
Leighton Buzzard	d	00 05			00 25	
Bletchley	d	00 12			00 32	
Milton Keynes Central 10	a	00 20	00 27	00 27	00 40	
	d	00 20	00 28	00 28		
Wolverton	d	00 24				
Northampton	a	00 37				
Rugby	a		01s00	01s05		
Nuneaton	a					
Coventry	a		01s13	01s18		
Birmingham International ✈	a		01s24	01s29		
Birmingham New Street 12	a		01s36	01s41		
Sandwell & Dudley	a					
Wolverhampton 7	a		02 07	02 10		

A until 9 September, FO from 16 September until 14 October, from 21 October

Table 66

London - Watford Junction, Milton Keynes Central, Northampton and West Midlands

		LM	VT	LM	LM	VT	LM	LM	LM	LM		SN	LM	LM	SN	VT	VT	LM	SN	VT		VT	SN	VT	LM
		◇1	◇1	◇1	◇1	◇1	1	◇1	◇1	1		1	◇1	◇1	1	◇1	◇1	◇1	1	◇1		◇1	1	◇1	1
			☕			☕										☕	☕			☕		☕		☕	
London Euston 15 ⊖	d	21p46	22p30	22p54	23p24	23p30	23p34	00 04	00 34	01 34				05 34		06 05	06 23	06 24		06 36		06 55		07 03	07 04
East Croydon	d																						06 10		
Clapham Junction	d											05 08			05 38				06 09				06 39		
Imperial Wharf	d											05 12			05 42				06 13				06 44		
West Brompton ⊖	d											05 15			05 45				06 16				06 47		
Kensington (Olympia) ⊖	d											05 19			05 49				06 20				06 50		
Shepherd's Bush	d											05 22			05 52				06 23				06 53		
Wembley Central ⊖	d								00 45	01 45					06s07				06 38				07s07		
Harrow & Wealdstone ⊖	d						23p46	00 16	00 50	01 50		05 40		05 46	06 12				06 43				07 12		07 16
Bushey	d						23p51		00 55																07 21
Watford Junction	a			23p09	23p39		23p54	00 22	00 57	01 56		05 47		05 52	06 19			06 39	06 50				07 19		07 24
	d		22b45	23p10	23p40		23p54	00 23	00 58	01 57				05 52	06 19	06u20	06u37	06 41					07 19		07 24
Kings Langley	d			23p14			23p59		01 02					05 57											07 29
Apsley	d			23p18			00 02		01 06					06 01											07 32
Hemel Hempstead	d			23p21	23p47		00 05	00 30	01 09	02 04				06 03	06 27			06 48					07 27		07 35
Berkhamsted	d			23p26	23p52		00 09	00 35	01 14	02 09				06 08	06 31			06 53					07 32		07 40
Tring	d			23p33			00 14	00 40	01 18	02 13				06 13	06 37			06 59					07 39		07 47
Cheddington	d						00 19		01 24					06 18				07 05							07 52
Leighton Buzzard	d	22p18		23p40	00 05		00 25	00 49	01 30	02 22				06 25	06 47			07 10					07 48		07 57
Bletchley	d			23p47	00 12		00 32	00 56	01 37	02 29			05 17	06 32	06 55			07 17					07 55		08 04
Milton Keynes Central 10	a	22p32	23p28	23p55	00 20	00 27	00 40	01 04	01 45	02 37			05 21	06 37	07 00	06 39		07 22				07 25	08 00		08 09
	d	22p32	23p29	23p55	00 20	00 28		01 04	01 46				05 21	06 37		06 41		07 23							08 10
Wolverton	d	22p36		23p59	00 24			01 08	01 49				05 25	06 41				07 26							08 13
Northampton	a	22p49		00 12	00 37			01 21	02 03				05 37	06 53				07 39							08 29
Rugby	a	23p17	23p58			01s05							06 01			07 02		08 04						07 51	
Nuneaton	a												06 16					08 16							
Coventry	a	23p29	00 10			01s18											07 22							08 02	
Birmingham International ✈	a	23p47	00 21			01s29											07 33							08 13	
Birmingham New Street 12	a	00 04	00 32			01s41											07 45							08 27	
Sandwell & Dudley	a																07 57								
Wolverhampton 7	a		01 03			02 10											08 11								

		VT	VT	LM	LM	VT		VT	LM	LM	SN	VT	LM	VT	VT	VT		LM	LM	VT	VT	LM		VT	LM
		◇1	◇1	1	1	◇1		◇1	◇1	◇1	1	◇1	1	◇1	◇1	◇1		1	1	◇1	◇1	◇1		◇1	◇1
																				A	B				
		☕	☕			☕		☕				☕		☕	☕	☕				☕	☕			☕	
London Euston 15 ⊖	d	07 20	07 23	07 24	07 34	07 35		07 43	07 46	07 54		08 03	08 04	08 10	08 20	08 23		08 24	08 34	08 43	08 43	08 46		08 50	08 54
East Croydon	d										07 10														
Clapham Junction	d										07 39														
Imperial Wharf	d										07 44														
West Brompton ⊖	d										07 47														
Kensington (Olympia) ⊖	d										07 50														
Shepherd's Bush	d										07 53														
Wembley Central ⊖	d										08s07														
Harrow & Wealdstone ⊖	d				07 46						08 12		08 16						08 46						
Bushey	d												08 21						08 51						
Watford Junction	a			07 39	07 52				08 00	08 09	08 19		08 24					08 39	08 54					09 04	09 09
	d		07u37	07 42	07 53				08 01	08 11	08 19		08 25			08u37		08 41	08 55					09 05	09 11
Kings Langley	d				07 58								08 29						08 59						
Apsley	d				08 01								08 33						09 03						
Hemel Hempstead	d			07 49	08 04					08 18	08 27		08 36					08 48	09 06						09 18
Berkhamsted	d			07 54	08 09					08 23	08 31		08 41					08 53	09 11						09 23
Tring	d			08 01	08a16						08 37		08a47					08 59	09a17						
Cheddington	d			08 06														09 04							
Leighton Buzzard	d			08 11						08 36	08 47							09 09							09 36
Bletchley	d			08 18						08 43	08 55							09 16							09 43
Milton Keynes Central 10	a	07 50		08 23		08 05		08 13	08 24	08 48	09 00			08 40	08 50			09 21		09 13	09 13	09 21		09 24	09 48
	d							08 13	08 25	08 49										09 13	09 13	09 23			09 49
Wolverton	d									08 52															09 52
Northampton	a								08 41	09 09												09 39			10 09
Rugby	a								09 04			08 51										10 04	10 17		
Nuneaton	a								09 16													10 16			
Coventry	a		08 22					08 42				09 02				09 22				09 42	09 42		10 29		
Birmingham International ✈	a		08 33					08 53				09 13				09 33				09 53	09 53		10 45		
Birmingham New Street 12	a		08 45					09 08				09 27				09 45				10 08	10 08		11 01		
Sandwell & Dudley	a		08 57													09 57									
Wolverhampton 7	a		09 11													10 11					10 37				

A until 9 July, from 17 September

B from 16 July until 10 September

b Previous night, stops to pick up only

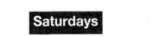

London - Watford Junction, Milton Keynes Central, Northampton and West Midlands

		SN		VT	LM	LM	VT	VT	LM	LM	VT	LM			LM	SN	VT	LM	VT	LM	VT	VT	LM		LM
		1		◇1 ☕	1	◇1	◇1 ☕	◇1 ☕	1	1	◇1 ☕	◇1			◇1	1	◇1 ☕	1	◇1 ☕	◇1	◇1 ☕	◇1 ☕	1		1
London Euston 15 ⊖	d			09 03	09 04	09 13	09 20	09 23	09 24	09 34	09 43	09 46			09 54		10 03	10 04	10 10	10 13	10 20	10 23	10 24		10 34
East Croydon	d	08 10														09 10									
Clapham Junction	d	08 39														09 39									
Imperial Wharf	d	08 44														09 44									
West Brompton ⊖	d	08 47														09 47									
Kensington (Olympia) ⊖	d	08 50														09 50									
Shepherd's Bush	d	08 53														09 53									
Wembley Central ⊖	d	09s07														10s07									
Harrow & Wealdstone ⊖	d	09 12			09 16					09 46						10 12		10 16							10 46
Bushey	d				09 21					09 51								10 21							10 51
Watford Junction	a	09 19			09 24				09 39	09 54		10 00			10 09	10 19		10 24					10 39		10 54
	d	09 19			09 25			09u37	09 41	09 55		10 01			10 11	10 19		10 25				10u37	10 41		10 55
Kings Langley	d				09 29					09 59								10 29							10 59
Apsley	d				09 33					10 03								10 33							11 03
Hemel Hempstead	d	09 27			09 36				09 48	10 06					10 18	10 27		10 36					10 48		11 06
Berkhamsted	d	09 33			09 41				09 53	10 11					10 23	10 31		10 41					10 53		11 11
Tring	d	09 38			09a47				09 59	10a17						10 37		10a47					10 59		11a17
Cheddington	d								10 04														11 04		
Leighton Buzzard	d	09 47				09 42			10 09						10 36	10 47				10 42			11 09		
Bletchley	d	09 55				09 50			10 16						10 43	10 55				10 50			11 16		
Milton Keynes Central 10	a	10 00				09 54	09 50		10 21		10 13	10 24			10 48	11 00			10 40	10 54	10 50		11 21		
	d					09 54					10 13	10 25			10 49					10 54					
Wolverton	d					09 58									10 52					10 58					
Northampton	a					10 13						10 40			11 09					11 13					
Rugby	a			09 52								11 04	11 17				10 51								
Nuneaton	a											11 16													
Coventry	a			10 03				10 22			10 42		11 29				11 02					11 22			
Birmingham International ✈	a			10 14				10 33			10 53		11 45				11 13					11 33			
Birmingham New Street 12	a			10 27				10 45			11 08		12 01				11 27					11 45			
Sandwell & Dudley	a							10 57														11 57			
Wolverhampton 7	a							11 11														12 11			

		VT	LM		LM	SN	VT	LM	VT		LM	VT	VT	LM	LM	VT	LM		LM		SN	VT	LM	VT	LM
		◇1 ☕	◇1		◇1	1	◇1 ☕	1	◇1 ☕		◇1	◇1 ☕	◇1 ☕	1	1	◇1 ☕	◇1		◇1		1	◇1 ☕	1	◇1 ☕	◇1
London Euston 15 ⊖	d	10 43	10 46		10 54		11 03	11 04	11 10		11 13	11 20	11 23	11 24	11 34	11 43	11 46		11 54			12 03	12 04	12 10	12 13
East Croydon	d					10 10															11 10				
Clapham Junction	d					10 39															11 39				
Imperial Wharf	d					10 44															11 44				
West Brompton ⊖	d					10 47															11 47				
Kensington (Olympia) ⊖	d					10 50															11 50				
Shepherd's Bush	d					10 53															11 53				
Wembley Central ⊖	d					11s08															12s07				
Harrow & Wealdstone ⊖	d					11 13		11 17							11 46						12 12		12 16		
Bushey	d							11 22							11 51								12 21		
Watford Junction	a		11 00		11 09	11 20		11 25						11 39	11 54		12 00		12 09		12 19		12 24		
	d		11 01		11 11	11 20		11 25					11u37	11 41	11 55		12 01		12 11		12 19		12 25		
Kings Langley	d							11 30							11 59								12 29		
Apsley	d							11 33							12 03								12 33		
Hemel Hempstead	d				11 18	11 28		11 36						11 48	12 06				12 18		12 28		12 36		
Berkhamsted	d				11 23	11 33		11 41						11 53	12 11				12 23		12 32		12 41		
Tring	d					11 38		11a47						11 59	12a17						12 37		12a47		
Cheddington	d													12 04											
Leighton Buzzard	d				11 36	11 47					11 42			12 09					12 36		12 47				12 42
Bletchley	d				11 43	11 55					11 50			12 16					12 43		12 55				12 50
Milton Keynes Central 10	a	11 13	11 24		11 48	12 00			11 40		11 54	11 50		12 21		12 13	12 24		12 48		13 00			12 40	12 54
	d	11 13	11 25		11 49						11 54					12 13	12 25		12 49						12 54
Wolverton	d				11 52						11 58								12 52						12 58
Northampton	a		11 41		12 09						12 13						12 41		13 09						13 13
Rugby	a		12 04	12 17			11 51										13 04	13 17				12 51			
Nuneaton	a		12 16														13 16								
Coventry	a	11 42		12 29			12 02						12 22			12 42		13 29				13 02			
Birmingham International ✈	a	11 53		12 45			12 13						12 33			12 53		13 45				13 13			
Birmingham New Street 12	a	12 08		13 01			12 27						12 45			13 08		14 01				13 27			
Sandwell & Dudley	a												12 57												
Wolverhampton 7	a												13 11												

Table 66

Saturdays

London - Watford Junction, Milton Keynes Central, Northampton and West Midlands

		VT	VT	LM	LM		VT	LM		LM	SN	VT	LM	VT	LM		VT	VT	LM	LM	VT	VT	LM		LM
		◇1	◇1	1	1		◇1	◇1		◇1	1	◇1	1	◇1	◇1		◇1	◇1	1	1	◇1	◇1	◇1		◇1
																					A	B			
		☕	☕				☕					☕		☕			☕	☕			☕	☕			
London Euston 15 ⊖	d	12 20	12 23	12 24	12 34		12 43	12 46		12 54		13 03	13 04	13 10	13 13		13 20	13 23	13 24	13 34	13 43	13 43	13 46		13 54
East Croydon	d										12 10														
Clapham Junction	d										12 39														
Imperial Wharf	d										12 44														
West Brompton ⊖	d										12 47														
Kensington (Olympia) ⊖	d										12 50														
Shepherd's Bush	d										12 53														
Wembley Central ⊖	d										13s07														
Harrow & Wealdstone ⊖	d				12 46						13 12		13 16							13 46					
Bushey	d				12 51								13 21							13 51					
Watford Junction	a			12 39	12 54			13 00		13 09	13 19		13 24						13 39	13 54			14 00		14 09
	d		12u37	12 41	12 55			13 01		13 11	13 19		13 25					13u37	13 41	13 55			14 01		14 11
Kings Langley	d				12 59								13 29							13 59					
Apsley	d				13 03								13 33							14 03					
Hemel Hempstead	d			12 48	13 06					13 18	13 27		13 36						13 48	14 06					14 18
Berkhamsted	d			12 53	13 11					13 23	13 32		13 41						13 53	14 11					14 23
Tring	d			12 59	13a17						13 37		13a47						13 59	14a17					
Cheddington	d			13 04															14 04						
Leighton Buzzard	d			13 09						13 36	13 47				13 42				14 09						14 36
Bletchley	d			13 16						13 43	13 55				13 50				14 16						14 43
Milton Keynes Central 10	a	12 50		13 21			13 13	13 24		13 48	14 00			13 40	13 54		13 50		14 21		14 13	14 13	14 24		14 48
	d						13 13	13 25		13 49					13 54						14 13	14 13	14 25		14 49
Wolverton	d									13 52					13 58										14 52
Northampton	a							13 41		14 09					14 13								14 41		15 09
Rugby	a							14 04	14 17			13 51											15 04	15 17	
Nuneaton	a							14 16															15 16		
Coventry	a		13 22				13 42		14 29			14 02						14 22			14 42	14 42		15 29	
Birmingham International ✈	a		13 33				13 53		14 45			14 13						14 33			14 53	14 53		15 45	
Birmingham New Street 12	a		13 45				14 08		15 01			14 27						14 45			15 08	15 08		16 01	
Sandwell & Dudley	a		13 57															14 57							
Wolverhampton 7	a		14 11															15 11				15 37			

			SN	VT	LM	VT	LM	VT	VT	LM	LM		VT	LM		LM	SN	VT	LM	VT	LM		VT	VT	LM
			1	◇1	1	◇1	◇1	◇1	◇1	1	1		◇1	◇1		◇1	1	◇1	1	◇1	◇1		◇1	◇1	1
				☕		☕		☕	☕				☕					☕		☕			☕	☕	
London Euston 15 ⊖	d			14 03	14 04	14 10	14 13	14 20	14 23	14 24	14 34		14 43	14 46		14 54		15 03	15 04	15 10	15 13		15 20	15 23	15 24
East Croydon	d		13 10														14 10								
Clapham Junction	d		13 39														14 39								
Imperial Wharf	d		13 44														14 44								
West Brompton ⊖	d		13 47														14 47								
Kensington (Olympia) ⊖	d		13 50														14 50								
Shepherd's Bush	d		13 53														14 53								
Wembley Central ⊖	d		14s08														15s07								
Harrow & Wealdstone ⊖	d		14 13		14 17						14 46						15 12		15 16						
Bushey	d				14 22						14 51								15 21						
Watford Junction	a		14 20		14 25					14 39	14 54			15 00		15 09	15 19		15 24						15 39
	d		14 20		14 26				14u37	14 41	14 55			15 01		15 11	15 19		15 25					15u37	15 41
Kings Langley	d				14 30						14 59								15 29						
Apsley	d				14 34						15 03								15 33						
Hemel Hempstead	d		14 28		14 37					14 48	15 06					15 18	15 27		15 36						15 48
Berkhamsted	d		14 32		14 42					14 53	15 11					15 23	15 32		15 41						15 53
Tring	d		14 37		14a48					14 59	15a17						15 37		15a47						15 59
Cheddington	d									15 04															16 04
Leighton Buzzard	d		14 47				14 42			15 09						15 36	15 47				15 42				16 09
Bletchley	d		14 55				14 50			15 16						15 43	15 55				15 50				16 16
Milton Keynes Central 10	a		15 00			14 40	14 54	14 50		15 21			15 13	15 24		15 48	16 00			15 40	15 54		15 50		16 21
	d						14 54						15 13	15 25		15 49					15 54				
Wolverton	d						14 58									15 52					15 58				
Northampton	a						15 13							15 41		16 09					16 13				
Rugby	a			14 51										16 04	16 17			15 51							
Nuneaton	a													16 16											
Coventry	a			15 02					15 22				15 42		16 29			16 02						16 22	
Birmingham International ✈	a			15 13					15 33				15 53		16 45			16 13						16 33	
Birmingham New Street 12	a			15 27					15 45				16 08		17 01			16 27						16 45	
Sandwell & Dudley	a								15 57															16 57	
Wolverhampton 7	a								16 11															17 11	

A until 9 July, from 17 September

B from 16 July until 10 September

Table 66

Saturdays

London - Watford Junction, Milton Keynes Central, Northampton and West Midlands

		LM	VT	LM		LM	SN		VT	LM	VT	LM	VT	VT	LM	LM	VT		LM		LM	SN	VT	LM	VT
		1	◇1	◇1		◇1	1		◇1	1	◇1	◇1	◇1	◇1	1	1	◇1		◇1		◇1	1	◇1	1	◇1
			🍴						🍴		🍴		🍴	🍴			🍴						🍴		🍴
London Euston 15 ⊖	d	15 34	15 43	15 46		15 54			16 03	16 04	16 10	16 13	16 20	16 23	16 24	16 34	16 43		16 46		16 54		17 03	17 04	17 07
East Croydon	d						15 10															16 10			
Clapham Junction	d						15 39															16 39			
Imperial Wharf	d						15 44															16 44			
West Brompton ⊖	d						15 47															16 47			
Kensington (Olympia) ⊖	d						15 50															16 50			
Shepherd's Bush	d						15 53															16 53			
Wembley Central ⊖	d						16s07															17s07			
Harrow & Wealdstone ⊖	d	15 46					16 12			16 16						16 46						17 12		17 16	
Bushey	d	15 51								16 21						16 51								17 21	
Watford Junction	a	15 54		16 00		16 09	16 19			16 24					16 39	16 54			17 00		17 09	17 19		17 24	
	d	15 55		16 01		16 11	16 19			16 25				16u37	16 41	16 55			17 01		17 11	17 19		17 25	
Kings Langley	d	15 59								16 29						16 59								17 29	
Apsley	d	16 03								16 33						17 03								17 33	
Hemel Hempstead	d	16 06				16 18	16 27			16 36					16 48	17 06					17 18	17 27		17 36	
Berkhamsted	d	16 11				16 23	16 32			16 41					16 53	17 11					17 23	17 32		17 41	
Tring	d	16a17					16 37			16a47					16 59	17a17						17 37		17a47	
Cheddington	d														17 04										
Leighton Buzzard	d					16 36	16 47					16 42			17 09						17 36	17 47			
Bletchley	d					16 43	16 55					16 50			17 16						17 43	17 55			
Milton Keynes Central 10	a		16 13	16 24		16 48	17 00				16 40	16 54	16 50		17 21		17 13		17 24		17 48	18 00			
	d		16 13	16 25		16 49						16 54					17 13		17 25		17 49				
Wolverton	d					16 52						16 58									17 52				
Northampton	a			16 41		17 09						17 13							17 41		18 09				
Rugby	a			17 04	17 17				16 51										18 04	18 17			17 51		
Nuneaton	a			17 16															18 16						18 02
Coventry	a		16 42		17 29				17 02					17 22			17 42			18 29			18 02		
Birmingham International ✈	a		16 53		17 45				17 13					17 33			17 53			18 45			18 13		
Birmingham New Street 12	a		17 08		18 01				17 27					17 45			18 08			19 01			18 27		
Sandwell & Dudley	a													17 57											
Wolverhampton 7	a													18 11											

		VT	LM		VT	VT	LM	LM	VT	VT	LM	LM			LM	SN	VT	LM	VT	LM	VT	VT	LM		LM
		◇1	◇1		◇1	◇1	1	1	◇1	◇1	◇1	1			◇1	1	◇1	1	◇1	◇1	◇1	◇1	1		1
									A	B															
		🍴			🍴	🍴			🍴	🍴							🍴		🍴		🍴	🍴			
London Euston 15 ⊖	d	17 10	17 13		17 20	17 23	17 24	17 34	17 43	17 43	17 46	17 46			17 54		18 03	18 04	18 10	18 13	18 20	18 23	18 24		18 34
East Croydon	d															17 10									
Clapham Junction	d															17 39									
Imperial Wharf	d															17 44									
West Brompton ⊖	d															17 47									
Kensington (Olympia) ⊖	d															17 50									
Shepherd's Bush	d															17 53									
Wembley Central ⊖	d															18s07									
Harrow & Wealdstone ⊖	d							17 46								18 12		18 16							18 46
Bushey	d							17 51										18 21							18 51
Watford Junction	a						17 39	17 54			18 00	18 00			18 09	18 19		18 24					18 39		18 54
	d					17u37	17 41	17 55			18 01	18 01			18 11	18 19		18 25				18u37	18 41		18 55
Kings Langley	d							17 59										18 29							18 59
Apsley	d							18 03										18 33							19 03
Hemel Hempstead	d						17 48	18 06							18 18	18 27		18 36					18 48		19 06
Berkhamsted	d						17 53	18 11							18 23	18 32		18 41					18 53		19 11
Tring	d						17 59	18a17								18 37		18a47					18 59		19a17
Cheddington	d						18 04																19 04		
Leighton Buzzard	d		17 42				18 09								18 36	18 47				18 42			19 09		
Bletchley	d		17 50				18 16								18 43	18 55				18 50			19 16		
Milton Keynes Central 10	a	17 40	17 54		17 50		18 21		18 13	18 13	18 24	18 24			18 48	19 00			18 40	18 54	18 50		19 21		
	d		17 54						18 13	18 13	18 25	18 25			18 49					18 54					
Wolverton	d		17 58												18 52					18 58					
Northampton	a		18 13								18 40	18 40			19 09					19 13					
Rugby	a											19 04	19 17				18 51								
Nuneaton	a											19 16													
Coventry	a					18 22			18 42	18 42			19 29				19 02					19 22			
Birmingham International ✈	a					18 33			18 53	18 53			19 45				19 13					19 33			
Birmingham New Street 12	a					18 45			19 08	19 08			20 01				19 25					19 45			
Sandwell & Dudley	a					18 57											19 53					19 58			
Wolverhampton 7	a					19 11				19 37							20 08					20 12			

A until 9 July, from 17 September

B from 16 July until 10 September

Table 66

Saturdays

London - Watford Junction, Milton Keynes Central, Northampton and West Midlands

		VT	LM		LM	LM	SN	VT	LM	VT	LM	LM	VT	VT	LM	VT	LM	SN	LM	VT	VT	VT	VT
		◇1	1		◇1	◇1	1	◇1	1	◇1	◇1	1	◇1	◇1	1	◇1	◇1	1	1	◇1	◇1	◇1	◇1
		☕						☕		☕			☕	☕		☕				☕	☕	☕	☕
London Euston 15 ⊖	d	18 43	18 46		18 46	18 54		19 03	19 04	19 07	19 13	19 14	19 20	19 23	19 30	19 43	19 45		20 02	20 11	20 20	20 25	20 31
East Croydon	d						18 10											19 10					
Clapham Junction	d						18 39											19 38					
Imperial Wharf	d						18 44											19 42					
West Brompton ⊖	d						18 47											19 45					
Kensington (Olympia) ⊖	d						18 50											19 48					
Shepherd's Bush	d						18 53											19 50					
Wembley Central ⊖	d						19 08																
Harrow & Wealdstone ⊖	d						19 13		19 17						19 42			20 08					
Bushey	d								19 22						19 47								
Watford Junction	a		19 00		19 00	19 09	19 21		19 25			19 30			19 50		20 00	20 15	20 18				
	d		19 01		19 01	19 11			19 26			19 32		19u37	19 51		20 01		20 19			20u40	20u46
Kings Langley	d								19 30						19 55		20 05						
Apsley	d								19 34						19 59		20 09						
Hemel Hempstead	d					19 18						19 39			20 02		20 12		20 26				
Berkhamsted	d					19 23			19 40			19 45			20 07		20 17		20 31				
Tring	d								19a46			19 50			20 11		20 22						
Cheddington	d											19 55					20 27						
Leighton Buzzard	d					19 36					19 42	20 00			20 20		20 32		20 42				
Bletchley	d					19 43					19 50	20 06			20a26		20 40		20 49				
Milton Keynes Central 10	a	19 13	19 24		19 26	19 48					19 54	20 12	19 50			20 20	20 44		20 54		21 03		
	d	19 13	19 25		19 27	19 49					19 54					20 20	20 47				21 05		
Wolverton	d					19 52					19 58						20 50						
Northampton	a		19 40		19 41	20 05					20 11						21 04						
Rugby	a		20 04	20 17				19 51												21 15			21 34
Nuneaton	a		20 16							20 02											21 32		
Coventry	a	19 42		20 29				20 02						20 22		20 49						21 36	
Birmingham International ✈	a	19 53		20 45				20 13						20 33		21 00						21 50	
Birmingham New Street 12	a	20 08		21 01				20 25						20 45		21 12						22 04	
Sandwell & Dudley	a							20 53						20 58								22 24	
Wolverhampton 7	a							21 08						21 12		21 38						22 38	

		LM	LM	SN	VT	VT	LM	LM	VT	LM	SN	LM	SN	LM	LM
		◇1	1	1	◇1	◇1	◇1	◇1	◇1	◇1	1	◇1	1	◇1	◇1
					☕	☕			☕						
London Euston 15 ⊖	d	20 34	20 40		21 00	21 03	21 08	21 28	21 43	21 54		22 34		23 04	23 44
East Croydon	d														
Clapham Junction	d			20 25							21 39		22 39		
Imperial Wharf	d			20 29							21 44		22 44		
West Brompton ⊖	d			20 32							21 47		22 47		
Kensington (Olympia) ⊖	d			20 36							21 50		22 50		
Shepherd's Bush	d			20 39							21 53		22 53		
Wembley Central ⊖	d														
Harrow & Wealdstone ⊖	d		20 52	21 02						22 06	22 13		23 12	23 16	23 56
Bushey	d														
Watford Junction	a	20 49	20 58	21 09			21 24	21 43		22 12	22 20	22 49	23 19	23 23	00 02
	d	20 50	21 00			21u18	21 25	21 44	21u58	22 13		22 50		23 24	00 02
Kings Langley	d		21 04							22 17				23 28	00 07
Apsley	d		21 08							22 21				23 32	00 11
Hemel Hempstead	d	20 57					21 32	21 51		22 24		22 57		23 35	00 13
Berkhamsted	d	21 02					21 37	21 56		22 29		23 02		23 40	00 18
Tring	d		21 18							22 33				23 44	00 24
Cheddington	d	21 10								22 39				23 49	00 29
Leighton Buzzard	d	21 15					21 50	22 07		22 45		23 13		23 56	00 34
Bletchley	d	21 22	21 30				21 57	22 14		22 52		23 20		00 03	00 41
Milton Keynes Central 10	a	21 30	21 38		21 43	21 50	22 05	22 22	22 29	23 00		23 28		00 11	00 48
	d	21 30				21 50	22 06	22 22	22 30	23 01		23 28		00 11	00 48
Wolverton	d	21 34					22 10	22 26		23 04		23 32		00 15	00 52
Northampton	a	21 50					22 27	22 43		23 18		23 49		00 28	01 10
Rugby	a					22 11			22 51						
Nuneaton	a														
Coventry	a					22 22			23 02						
Birmingham International ✈	a					22 33			23 13						
Birmingham New Street 12	a					22 45			23 25						
Sandwell & Dudley	a					22 56			23 36						
Wolverhampton 7	a					23 10			23 50						

Table 66

Sundays
until 10 July

London - Watford Junction, Milton Keynes Central, Northampton and West Midlands

		LM	LM	LM	LM	LM	LM	LM	LM	VT		VT	VT	LM	SN	VT	VT	LM	VT	VT		LM	SN	VT	VT
		◇1	◇1	◇1			◇1	◇1	◇1	◇1		◇1	◇1	◇1	1	◇1	◇1	◇1	◇1	◇1		◇1	1	◇1	◇1
		A	A																						
					🚌	🚌																			
										☕		☕	☕			☕	☕		☕	☕				☕	☕
London Euston 15 ⊖	d	23p04	23p44	00 15			06 53	07 23	07 53	08 10		08 15	08 20	08 23		08 45	08 50	08 53	09 15	09 20		09 23		09 45	09 50
East Croydon	d																								
Clapham Junction	d														08 15								09 15		
Imperial Wharf	d														08 19								09 19		
West Brompton ⊖	d														08 22								09 22		
Kensington (Olympia) ⊖	d														08 26								09 26		
Shepherd's Bush	d														08 29								09 29		
Wembley Central ⊖	d			00 28																					
Harrow & Wealdstone ⊖	d	23p16	23p56	00 32			07 08	07 38	08 06					08 35	08 48			09 05				09 35	09 48		
Bushey	d																								
Watford Junction	a	23p23	00 02	00 38			07 14	07 44	08 12					08 42	08 56			09 12				09 42	09 58		
	d	23p24	00 02	00 39	02 50	02 55	07 15	07 45	08 13					08 42			09u05	09 12				09 42			10u06
Kings Langley	d	23p28	00 07	00 43		03 11		07 49						08 47								09 47			
Apsley	d	23p32	00 11	00 47		03 22		07 53						08 50								09 50			
Hemel Hempstead	d	23p35	00 13	00 50	03 16	03 28	07 22	07 56	08 20					08 53				09 20				09 53			
Berkhamsted	d	23p40	00 18	00 55		03 39	07 27	08 01	08 25					08 58				09 24				09 58			
Tring	d	23p44	00 24	00 59		03 55	07 31		08 29									09 29							
Cheddington	d	23p49	00 29	01 05		04 16	07 37		08 35									09 34							
Leighton Buzzard	d	23p56	00 34	01 09	03 53	04 37	07 44	08 14	08 39					09 11				09 41				10 11			
Bletchley	d	00 03	00 41	01 16	04 19	05 03	07 51	08 21	08 46					09 18				09 49				10 18			
Milton Keynes Central 10	a	00 11	00 48	01 22	04 34	05 18	07 59	08 29	08 50	08 55			09 05	09 27		09 31	09 37	09 57		10 06		10 27		10 32	10 38
	d	00 11	00 48	01 23			07 59	08 29	08 50					09 27		09 32	09 38	09 58				10 27		10 33	10 39
Wolverton	d	00 15	00 52	01 26			08 03	08 33	08 54					09 31				10 01				10 31			
Northampton	a	00 28	01 10	01 40			08 16	08 46	09 09					09 45				10 16				10 45			
Rugby	a															10 07	10 12							11 07	11 13
Nuneaton	a											09 43							10 44						
Coventry	a																10 23								11 25
Birmingham International ✈	a																10 34								11 36
Birmingham New Street 12	a																10 47								11 49
Sandwell & Dudley	a																10 59								12 01
Wolverhampton 7	a																11 13								12 15

		LM	VT	VT	LM	SN		VT	VT	LM	VT	VT	LM	SN	VT	LM		LM	VT	VT	SN	LM	VT	LM	LM
		◇1	◇1	◇1	◇1	1		◇1	◇1	◇1	◇1	◇1	◇1	1	◇1	◇1		1	◇1	◇1	1	◇1	◇1	◇1	1
			☕	☕				☕	☕		☕	☕			☕				☕	☕			☕		
London Euston 15 ⊖	d	09 53	10 15	10 20	10 23			10 45	10 50	10 53	11 15	11 20	11 23		11 45	11 53		12 14	12 15	12 18		12 34	12 38	12 50	12 54
East Croydon	d																								
Clapham Junction	d					10 15								11 15							12 05				
Imperial Wharf	d					10 19								11 19							12 09				
West Brompton ⊖	d					10 22								11 22							12 12				
Kensington (Olympia) ⊖	d					10 26								11 26							12 16				
Shepherd's Bush	d					10 29								11 29							12 19				
Wembley Central ⊖	d																								
Harrow & Wealdstone ⊖	d	10 05			10 35	10 48				11 05			11 35	11 48		12 05		12 26			12 36				13 06
Bushey	d																	12 31							
Watford Junction	a	10 12			10 42	10 56				11 12			11 42	11 56		12 12		12 34			12 44	12 50		13 06	13 13
	d	10 12			10 42				11u04	11 12			11 42		12u01	12 12		12 35		12u32		12 51		13 06	13 13
Kings Langley	d				10 47								11 47					12 39							
Apsley	d				10 50								11 50					12 43							
Hemel Hempstead	d	10 20			10 53					11 20			11 53			12 20		12 46				12 58			13 21
Berkhamsted	d	10 24			10 58					11 24			11 58			12 24		12 50				13 03			13 25
Tring	d	10 29								11 29						12 29		12a57							13 30
Cheddington	d	10 34								11 34						12 34									13 35
Leighton Buzzard	d	10 41			11 11					11 41			12 12			12 41						13 16		13 26	13 42
Bletchley	d	10 49			11 18					11 49			12 19			12 49						13 23			13 50
Milton Keynes Central 10	a	10 57		11 06	11 27			11 32	11 37	11 57	12 02	12 08	12 27		12 26	12 57			12 48			13 29	13 11	13 36	13 56
	d	10 58			11 27			11 33	11 39	11 58			12 27		12 27	12 58						13 29	13 11	13 36	
Wolverton	d	11 01			11 31					12 01			12 31			13 01						13 33			
Northampton	a	11 16			11 45					12 16			12 45			13 16						13 46		13 51	
Rugby	a							12 07	12 13						12 46									14 17	
Nuneaton	a		11 46																					14 29	
Coventry	a								12 24						12 56					13 20			13 40		
Birmingham International ✈	a								12 35						13 07					13 31			13 51		
Birmingham New Street 12	a								12 48						13 22					13 44			14 05		
Sandwell & Dudley	a								13 00											13 56					
Wolverhampton 7	a								13 14											14 10					

A not 22 May

Table 66

Sundays
until 10 July

London - Watford Junction, Milton Keynes Central, Northampton and West Midlands

		VT		LM	VT	VT	SN	LM	VT	LM	LM	VT		LM	VT	VT	SN	LM	VT	LM	LM	VT		VT	LM
		◇[1] ☕		[1]	◇[1] ☕	◇[1] ☕	[1]	◇[1]	◇[1] ☕	◇[1]	[1]	◇[1] ☕		[1]	◇[1] ☕	◇[1] ☕	[1]	◇[1]	◇[1] ☕	◇[1]	[1]	◇[1] ☕		◇[1] ☕	[1]
London Euston [15] ⊖	d	12 58		13 14	13 15	13 18		13 34	13 38	13 50	13 54	13 58		14 14	14 15	14 18		14 34	14 38	14 50	14 54	14 58		15 05	15 14
East Croydon 🚋	d																								
Clapham Junction	d						13 05										14 05								
Imperial Wharf	d						13 09										14 09								
West Brompton ⊖	d						13 12										14 12								
Kensington (Olympia) ⊖	d						13 16										14 16								
Shepherd's Bush	d						13 19										14 19								
Wembley Central ⊖	d																								
Harrow & Wealdstone ⊖	d			13 26			13 36				14 06			14 26			14 36				15 06				15 26
Bushey	d			13 31										14 31											15 31
Watford Junction	a			13 34			13 44	13 50		14 06	14 13			14 34			14 44	14 50		15 06	15 13				15 34
	d			13 35		13u32		13 51		14 06	14 13			14 35		14u32		14 51		15 06	15 13				15 35
Kings Langley	d			13 39										14 39											15 39
Apsley	d			13 43										14 43											15 43
Hemel Hempstead	d			13 46				13 58			14 21			14 46				14 58			15 21				15 46
Berkhamsted	d			13 50				14 03			14 25			14 50				15 03			15 25				15 50
Tring	d			13a57							14 30			14a57							15 30				15a57
Cheddington	d										14 35										15 35				
Leighton Buzzard	d							14 16		14 26	14 42							15 16		15 26	15 42				
Bletchley	d							14 23			14 50							15 23			15 50				
Milton Keynes Central [10]	a				13 48			14 29	14 11	14 36	14 56				14 48			15 29	15 11	15 36	15 56			15 38	
	d							14 29	14 11	14 36								15 29	15 11	15 36					
Wolverton	d							14 33										15 33							
Northampton	a							14 46		14 52								15 46		15 51					
Rugby	a	13 49								15 19		14 49								16 17		15 49			
Nuneaton	a																			16 29					
Coventry	a	14 00				14 20			14 40			15 00				15 20			15 40			16 00			
Birmingham International ✈	a	14 11				14 31			14 51			15 11				15 31			15 51			16 11			
Birmingham New Street [12]	a	14 25				14 44			15 05			15 25				15 44			16 05			16 25			
Sandwell & Dudley	a					14 56										15 56									
Wolverhampton [7] 🚋	a					15 10										16 10									

		VT	VT	SN	LM	VT	LM	LM		VT	VT	LM	VT	VT	SN	LM	VT	LM		LM	VT	VT	LM	VT	VT
		◇[1] ☕	◇[1] ☕	[1]	◇[1]	◇[1] ☕	◇[1]	[1]		◇[1] ☕	◇[1] ☕	[1]	◇[1] ☕	◇[1] ☕	[1]	◇[1]	◇[1] ☕	◇[1]		[1]	◇[1] ☕	◇[1] ☕	[1]	◇[1] ☕	◇[1] ☕
London Euston [15] ⊖	d	15 15	15 18		15 34	15 38	15 50	15 54		15 58	16 05	16 14	16 15	16 18		16 34	16 38	16 50		16 54	16 58	17 05	17 14	17 15	17 18
East Croydon 🚋	d																								
Clapham Junction	d			15 05											16 05										
Imperial Wharf	d			15 09											16 09										
West Brompton ⊖	d			15 12											16 12										
Kensington (Olympia) ⊖	d			15 16											16 16										
Shepherd's Bush	d			15 19											16 19										
Wembley Central ⊖	d																								
Harrow & Wealdstone ⊖	d			15 36				16 06				16 26			16 36					17 06			17 26		
Bushey	d											16 31											17 31		
Watford Junction	a			15 44	15 50		16 06	16 13				16 34			16 44	16 50		17 06		17 13			17 34		
	d		15u32		15 51		16 06	16 13				16 35		16u32		16 51		17 06		17 13			17 35		17u32
Kings Langley	d											16 39											17 39		
Apsley	d											16 43											17 43		
Hemel Hempstead	d				15 58			16 21				16 46				16 58				17 21			17 46		
Berkhamsted	d				16 03			16 25				16 50				17 03				17 25			17 50		
Tring	d							16 30				16a57								17 30			17a57		
Cheddington	d							16 35												17 35					
Leighton Buzzard	d				16 16		16 26	16 42								17 16		17 26		17 42					
Bletchley	d				16 23			16 50								17 23				17 50					
Milton Keynes Central [10]	a	15 48			16 29	16 11	16 36	16 56			16 38		16 48			17 29	17 11	17 36		17 56		17 38		17 48	
	d				16 29	16 11	16 36									17 29	17 11	17 36				17 39			
Wolverton	d				16 33											17 33									
Northampton	a				16 46		16 52									17 46		17 54							
Rugby	a						17 19			16 49								18 17			17 49				
Nuneaton	a																	18 29				18 09			
Coventry	a		16 20			16 40				17 00				17 20			17 40				18 00				18 20
Birmingham International ✈	a		16 31			16 51				17 11				17 31			17 51				18 11				18 31
Birmingham New Street [12]	a		16 44			17 05				17 25				17 44			18 05				18 25				18 44
Sandwell & Dudley	a		16 56											17 56											18 56
Wolverhampton [7] 🚋	a		17 10											18 10											19 10

Table 66

Sundays
until 10 July

London - Watford Junction, Milton Keynes Central, Northampton and West Midlands

		SN	LM	VT		LM	LM	VT	VT	LM	VT	VT	SN	LM		VT	LM	LM	VT	VT	VT	LM	VT	VT	
		1	◇1	◇1		◇1	1	◇1	◇1	1	◇1	◇1	1	◇1		◇1	◇1	1	◇1	◇1	◇1	1	◇1	◇1	
				☕				☕	☕		☕	☕				☕			☕	☕	☕		☕	☕	
London Euston 15 ⊖	d		17 34	17 38		17 50	17 54	17 58	18 05	18 14	18 15	18 18		18 34		18 38	18 50	18 54	18 58	19 02	19 05	19 14	19 15	19 18	
East Croydon 🚊	d																								
Clapham Junction	d	17 05											18 05												
Imperial Wharf	d	17 09											18 09												
West Brompton ⊖	d	17 12											18 12												
Kensington (Olympia) ⊖	d	17 16											18 16												
Shepherd's Bush	d	17 19											18 19												
Wembley Central ⊖	d																								
Harrow & Wealdstone ⊖	d	17 36					18 06			18 26			18 36					19 06				19 26			
Bushey	d									18 31												19 31			
Watford Junction	a	17 44	17 50			18 06	18 13			18 34			18 44	18 50			19 06	19 13				19 34			
	d		17 51			18 06	18 13			18 35		18u32		18 51			19 06	19 13				19 35		19u32	
Kings Langley	d									18 39												19 39			
Apsley	d									18 43												19 43			
Hemel Hempstead	d		17 58				18 21			18 46				18 58				19 21				19 46			
Berkhamsted	d		18 03				18 25			18 50				19 03				19 25				19 50			
Tring	d						18 30			18a57								19 30				19a57			
Cheddington	d						18 35											19 35							
Leighton Buzzard	d		18 16			18 26	18 42							19 16			19 26	19 42							
Bletchley	d		18 23				18 50							19 23				19 50							
Milton Keynes Central 10	a		18 29	18 11		18 36	18 56		18 38		18 48			19 28		19 11	19 36	19 56			19 38		19 48		
	d		18 29	18 11		18 36								19 28		19 11	19 36								
Wolverton	d		18 33											19 33											
Northampton	a		18 46			18 52								19 46			19 54								
Rugby	a					19 19		18 49									20 17		19 49						
Nuneaton	a																20 29			20 00					
Coventry	a			18 40				19 00				19 20				19 40			20 00					20 20	
Birmingham International ✈	a			18 51				19 11				19 31				19 51			20 11					20 31	
Birmingham New Street 12	a			19 05				19 24				19 44				20 05			20 23					20 44	
Sandwell & Dudley	a							19 48				19 56							20 35					20 56	
Wolverhampton 7 🚊	a							20 02				20 10							20 46					21 10	

		SN	LM	VT	LM	LM	VT	VT	VT	LM		VT	VT	SN	LM	VT	VT	VT	SR	LM		VT	VT	LM	SN
																			R						
		1	◇1	◇1	◇1	1	◇1	◇1	◇1	1		◇1	◇1	1	◇1	◇1	◇1	◇1	🛏	◇1		◇1	◇1	◇1	1
				☕			☕	☕	☕			☕	☕			☕	☕	☕	☕			☕	☕		
London Euston 15 ⊖	d		19 34	19 38	19 50	19 54	19 58	20 02	20 05	20 14		20 15	20 18		20 34	20 38	20 50	20 54	20 55	21 02		21 21	21 25	21 28	
East Croydon 🚊	d																								
Clapham Junction	d	19 05												20 05											21 15
Imperial Wharf	d	19 09												20 09											21 19
West Brompton ⊖	d	19 12												20 12											21 22
Kensington (Olympia) ⊖	d	19 16												20 16											21 26
Shepherd's Bush	d	19 19												20 19											21 29
Wembley Central ⊖	d																								
Harrow & Wealdstone ⊖	d	19 36				20 06				20 26				20 36										21 40	21 47
Bushey	d									20 31															
Watford Junction	a	19 43	19 50		20 06	20 13				20 34				20 44	20 50					21 22				21 47	21 54
	d		19 51		20 06	20 13				20 35			20u32		20 52			21u10		21 23				21 47	
Kings Langley	d									20 39														21 52	
Apsley	d									20 43														21 55	
Hemel Hempstead	d		19 58			20 21				20 46					20 59					21 30				21 58	
Berkhamsted	d		20 03			20 25				20 50					21 04					21 35				22 03	
Tring	d					20 30				20a57										21 39					
Cheddington	d					20 35														21 45					
Leighton Buzzard	d		20 16		20 26	20 42									21 17					21 49				22 16	
Bletchley	d		20 23			20 50									21 24					21 56				22 23	
Milton Keynes Central 10	a		20 29	20 11	20 36	20 56			20 38			20 48			21 30	21 16	21 35	21 41		22 04			22 13	22 32	
	d		20 29	20 11	20 36										21 30	21 16	21 37	21 43		22 05				22 32	
Wolverton	d		20 33												21 34					22 08				22 36	
Northampton	a		20 46		20 56										21 47					22 22				22 50	
Rugby	a				21 19		20 49										21 59	22 05							
Nuneaton	a							21 00														22 51			
Coventry	a			20 40			21 00						21 20			21 46		22 16							
Birmingham International ✈	a			20 51			21 11						21 31			21 57		22 27							
Birmingham New Street 12	a			21 04			21 24						21 44			22 09		22 39							
Sandwell & Dudley	a			21 15			21 36						21 56			22 24		22 52							
Wolverhampton 7 🚊	a			21 31			21 51						22 10			22 38		23 06							

Table 66

Sundays
until 10 July

London - Watford Junction, Milton Keynes Central, Northampton and West Midlands

Station		VT	VT	LM	VT	LM		SN	LM	VT	SR	LM
		◇1	◇1	◇1	◇1	◇1		1	◇1	◇1	R	◇1
		☕	☕		☕					☕	☕	
London Euston 15 ⊖	d	21 51	21 55	21 58	22 25	22 28			22 58	23 25	23 27	23 34
East Croydon 🚋	d											
Clapham Junction	d							22 15				
Imperial Wharf	d							22 19				
West Brompton ⊖	d							22 22				
Kensington (Olympia) ⊖	d							22 26				
Shepherd's Bush	d							22 29				
Wembley Central ⊖	d											
Harrow & Wealdstone ⊖	d			22 10		22 40		22 48	23 10			23 46
Bushey	d											
Watford Junction	a			22 17		22 47		22 56	23 17			23 53
	d		22u09	22 17	22u39	22 47			23 17	23u40		23 53
Kings Langley	d					22 52			23 22			23 58
Apsley	d					22 55			23 25			00 01
Hemel Hempstead	d			22 25		22 58			23 28			00 04
Berkhamsted	d			22 29		23 03			23 33			00 09
Tring	d			22 34					23 38			00 14
Cheddington	d			22 39					23 43			00 19
Leighton Buzzard	d			22 46		23 16			23 50			00 26
Bletchley	d			22 54		23 23			23 57			00 33
Milton Keynes Central 10	a	22 36	22 42	23 02	23 11	23 32			00 06	00 11		00 42
	d	22 38	22 44	23 03	23 12	23 32			00 06	00 12		00 42
Wolverton	d			23 06		23 36			00 10			00 46
Northampton	a			23 21		23 50			00 24			01 00
Rugby	a	23 16	23 20		23 46					00s46		
Nuneaton	a	23 28										
Coventry	a		23 31		23 57					00s57		
Birmingham International ✈	a		23 42		00 08					01s08		
Birmingham New Street 12	a		23 54		00 21					01s21		
Sandwell & Dudley	a											
Wolverhampton 7 🚋	a		00 15		00 43					01 52		

Sundays
17 July to 11 September

Station		LM	LM	LM	LM	LM	LM	LM	LM	VT		VT	VT	LM	SN	VT	VT	LM	VT	VT		LM	SN	VT	VT
		◇1	◇1	◇1			◇1	◇1	◇1	◇1		◇1	◇1	◇1	1	◇1	◇1	◇1	◇1	◇1		◇1	1	◇1	◇1
					🚌	🚌				☕		☕	☕			☕	☕		☕	☕				☕	☕
London Euston 15 ⊖	d	23p04	23p44	00 15			06 53	07 23	07 53	08 10		08 15	08 20	08 23		08 45	08 50	08 53	09 15	09 20		09 23		09 45	09 50
East Croydon 🚋	d																								
Clapham Junction	d														08 15								09 15		
Imperial Wharf	d														08 19								09 19		
West Brompton ⊖	d														08 22								09 22		
Kensington (Olympia) ⊖	d														08 26								09 26		
Shepherd's Bush	d														08 29								09 29		
Wembley Central ⊖	d			00 28																					
Harrow & Wealdstone ⊖	d	23p16	23p56	00 32			07 08	07 38	08 06					08 35	08 48			09 05				09 35	09 48		
Bushey	d																								
Watford Junction	a	23p23	00 02	00 38			07 14	07 44	08 12					08 42	08 56			09 12				09 42	09 58		
	d	23p24	00 02	00 39	02 50	02 55	07 15	07 45	08 13					08 42			09u05	09 12				09 42			10u06
Kings Langley	d	23p28	00 07	00 43		03 11		07 49						08 47								09 47			
Apsley	d	23p32	00 11	00 47		03 22		07 53						08 50								09 50			
Hemel Hempstead	d	23p35	00 13	00 50	03 16	03 28	07 22	07 56	08 20					08 53				09 20				09 53			
Berkhamsted	d	23p40	00 18	00 55		03 39	07 27	08 01	08 25					08 58				09 24				09 58			
Tring	d	23p44	00 24	00 59		03 55	07 31		08 29									09 29							
Cheddington	d	23p49	00 29	01 05		04 16	07 37		08 35									09 34							
Leighton Buzzard	d	23p56	00 34	01 09	03 53	04 37	07 44	08 14	08 39					09 11				09 41				10 11			
Bletchley	d	00 03	00 41	01 16	04 19	05 03	07 51	08 21	08 46					09 18				09 49				10 18			
Milton Keynes Central 10	a	00 11	00 48	01 22	04 34	05 18	07 59	08 29	08 50	08 55			09 05	09 27		09 31	09 37	09 57		10 06		10 27		10 32	10 38
	d	00 11	00 48	01 23			07 59	08 29	08 50					09 27		09 32	09 38	09 58				10 27		10 33	10 39
Wolverton	d	00 15	00 52	01 26			08 03	08 33	08 54					09 31				10 01				10 31			
Northampton	a	00 28	01 10	01 40			08 16	08 46	09 09					09 45				10 16				10 45			
Rugby	a															10 07	10 12							11 07	11 13
Nuneaton	a											09 43							10 44						
Coventry	a																10 23								11 25
Birmingham International ✈	a																10 34								11 36
Birmingham New Street 12	a																10 47								11 49
Sandwell & Dudley	a																10 59								12 01
Wolverhampton 7 🚋	a																11 13								12 15

Table 66

Sundays

17 July to 11 September

London - Watford Junction, Milton Keynes Central, Northampton and West Midlands

		LM	VT	VT	LM	SN		VT	VT	LM	VT	VT	LM	SN	VT	LM		LM	VT	VT	SN	LM	VT	LM	LM
		◇1	◇1	◇1	◇1	1		◇1	◇1	◇1	◇1	◇1	◇1	1	◇1	◇1		1	◇1	◇1	1	◇1	◇1	◇1	1
			☕	☕				☕	☕		☕	☕			☕				☕	☕			☕		
London Euston 15 ⊖	d	09 53	10 15	10 20	10 23			10 45	10 50	10 53	11 15	11 20	11 23		11 45	11 53		12 14	12 15	12 18		12 34	12 38	12 50	12 54
East Croydon 🚢	d																								
Clapham Junction	d					10 15								11 15							12 05				
Imperial Wharf	d					10 19								11 19							12 09				
West Brompton ⊖	d					10 22								11 22							12 12				
Kensington (Olympia) ⊖	d					10 26								11 26							12 16				
Shepherd's Bush	d					10 29								11 29							12 19				
Wembley Central ⊖	d																								
Harrow & Wealdstone ⊖	d	10 05			10 35	10 48				11 05			11 35	11 48		12 05		12 26			12 36				13 06
Bushey	d																	12 31							
Watford Junction	a	10 12			10 42	10 56				11 12			11 42	11 56		12 12		12 34			12 44	12 50		13 06	13 13
	d	10 12			10 42				11u04	11 12			11 42		12u01	12 12		12 35		12u32		12 51		13 06	13 13
Kings Langley	d				10 47								11 47					12 39							
Apsley	d				10 50								11 50					12 43							
Hemel Hempstead	d	10 20			10 53					11 20			11 53			12 20		12 46				12 58			13 21
Berkhamsted	d	10 24			10 58					11 24			11 58			12 24		12 50				13 03			13 25
Tring	d	10 29								11 29						12 29		12a57							13 30
Cheddington	d	10 34								11 34						12 34									13 35
Leighton Buzzard	d	10 41			11 11					11 41			12 12			12 41						13 16		13 26	13 42
Bletchley	d	10 49			11 18					11 49			12 19			12 49						13 23			13 50
Milton Keynes Central 10	a	10 57		11 06	11 27			11 32	11 37	11 57	12 02	12 08	12 27		12 26	12 57			12 48			13 29	13 11	13 36	13 56
	d	10 58			11 27			11 33	11 39	11 58			12 27		12 27	12 58						13 29	13 11	13 36	
Wolverton	d	11 01			11 31					12 01			12 31			13 01						13 33			
Northampton	a	11 16			11 45					12 16			12 45			13 16						13 46		13 51	
Rugby	a							12 07	12 13						12 46									14 17	
Nuneaton	a		11 46																					14 29	
Coventry	a								12 24						12 56					13 20			13 40		
Birmingham International ✈	a								12 35						13 07					13 31			13 51		
Birmingham New Street 12	a								12 48						13 22					13 44			14 05		
Sandwell & Dudley	a								13 00											13 56					
Wolverhampton 7 🚢	a								13 14											14 10					

		VT		LM	VT	VT	SN	LM	VT	LM	LM	VT		LM	VT	VT	SN	LM	VT	LM	LM	VT		VT	LM
		◇1		1	◇1	◇1	1	◇1	◇1	◇1	1	◇1		1	◇1	◇1	1	◇1	◇1	◇1	1	◇1		◇1	1
		☕			☕	☕			☕			☕			☕	☕			☕			☕		☕	
London Euston 15 ⊖	d	12 58		13 14	13 15	13 18		13 34	13 38	13 50	13 54	13 58		14 14	14 15	14 18		14 34	14 38	14 50	14 54	14 58		15 05	15 14
East Croydon 🚢	d																								
Clapham Junction	d						13 05										14 05								
Imperial Wharf	d						13 09										14 09								
West Brompton ⊖	d						13 12										14 12								
Kensington (Olympia) ⊖	d						13 16										14 16								
Shepherd's Bush	d						13 19										14 19								
Wembley Central ⊖	d																								
Harrow & Wealdstone ⊖	d			13 26			13 36				14 06			14 26			14 36				15 06				15 26
Bushey	d			13 31										14 31											15 31
Watford Junction	a			13 34			13 44	13 50		14 06	14 13			14 34			14 44	14 50		15 06	15 13				15 34
	d			13 35		13u32		13 51		14 06	14 13			14 35		14u32		14 51		15 06	15 13				15 35
Kings Langley	d			13 39										14 39											15 39
Apsley	d			13 43										14 43											15 43
Hemel Hempstead	d			13 46				13 58			14 21			14 46				14 58			15 21				15 46
Berkhamsted	d			13 50				14 03			14 25			14 50				15 03			15 25				15 50
Tring	d			13a57							14 30			14a57							15 30				15a57
Cheddington	d										14 35										15 35				
Leighton Buzzard	d							14 16		14 26	14 42							15 16		15 26	15 42				
Bletchley	d							14 23			14 50							15 23			15 50				
Milton Keynes Central 10	a				13 48			14 29	14 11	14 36	14 56				14 48			15 29	15 11	15 36	15 56			15 38	
	d							14 29	14 11	14 36								15 29	15 11	15 36					
Wolverton	d							14 33										15 33							
Northampton	a							14 46		14 52								15 46		15 51					
Rugby	a	13 49								15 19		14 49								16 17		15 49			
Nuneaton	a																			16 29					
Coventry	a	14 00				14 20			14 40			15 00				15 20			15 40			15 59			
Birmingham International ✈	a	14 11				14 31			14 51			15 11				15 31			15 51			16 10			
Birmingham New Street 12	a	14 25				14 44			15 05			15 25				15 44			16 05			16 24			
Sandwell & Dudley	a					14 56										15 56									
Wolverhampton 7 🚢	a					15 10										16 10									

Table 66

Sundays

17 July to 11 September

London - Watford Junction, Milton Keynes Central, Northampton and West Midlands

		VT	VT	SN	LM	VT	LM	LM		VT	VT	LM	VT	VT	SN	LM	VT	LM		LM	VT	VT	LM	VT	VT
		◇1 ☕	◇1 ☕	1	◇1	◇1 ☕	◇1	1		◇1 ☕	◇1 ☕	1	◇1 ☕	◇1 ☕	1	◇1	◇1 ☕	◇1		1	◇1 ☕	◇1 ☕	1	◇1 ☕	◇1 ☕
London Euston 15 ⊖	d	15 15	15 18		15 34	15 38	15 50	15 54		15 58	16 05	16 14	16 15	16 18		16 34	16 38	16 50		16 54	16 58	17 05	17 14	17 15	17 18
East Croydon	d																								
Clapham Junction	d			15 05											16 05										
Imperial Wharf	d			15 09											16 09										
West Brompton ⊖	d			15 12											16 12										
Kensington (Olympia) ⊖	d			15 16											16 16										
Shepherd's Bush	d			15 19											16 19										
Wembley Central ⊖	d																								
Harrow & Wealdstone ⊖	d			15 36				16 06				16 26			16 36					17 06			17 26		
Bushey	d											16 31											17 31		
Watford Junction	a			15 44	15 50		16 06	16 13				16 34			16 44	16 50		17 06		17 13			17 34		
	d		15u32		15 51		16 06	16 13				16 35		16u32		16 51		17 06		17 13			17 35		17u32
Kings Langley	d											16 39											17 39		
Apsley	d											16 43											17 43		
Hemel Hempstead	d				15 58			16 21				16 46				16 58				17 21			17 46		
Berkhamsted	d				16 03			16 25				16 50				17 03				17 25			17 50		
Tring	d							16 30				16a57								17 30			17a57		
Cheddington	d							16 35												17 35					
Leighton Buzzard	d				16 16		16 26	16 42								17 16		17 26		17 42					
Bletchley	d				16 23			16 50								17 23				17 50					
Milton Keynes Central 10	a	15 48			16 29	16 11	16 36	16 56			16 38		16 48			17 29	17 11	17 36		17 56		17 38		17 48	
	d				16 29	16 11	16 36									17 29	17 11	17 36				17 39			
Wolverton	d				16 33											17 33									
Northampton	a				16 46		16 52									17 46		17 54							
Rugby	a						17 19			16 49								18 17			17 49				
Nuneaton	a																	18 29				18 09			
Coventry	a		16 20			16 40				17 00				17 20			17 40				18 00				18 20
Birmingham International ✈	a		16 31			16 51				17 11				17 31			17 51				18 11				18 31
Birmingham New Street 12	a		16 44			17 05				17 25				17 44			18 05				18 25				18 44
Sandwell & Dudley	a		16 56											17 56											18 56
Wolverhampton 7	a		17 10											18 10											19 10

		SN	LM	VT		LM	LM	VT	VT	LM	VT	VT	SN	LM		VT	LM	LM	VT	VT	VT	LM	VT	VT	
		1	◇1	◇1 ☕		◇1	1	◇1 ☕	◇1 ☕	1	◇1 ☕	◇1 ☕	1	◇1		◇1 ☕	◇1	1	◇1 ☕	◇1 ☕	◇1 ☕	1	◇1 ☕	◇1 ☕	
London Euston 15 ⊖	d		17 34	17 38		17 50	17 54	17 58	18 05	18 14	18 15	18 18		18 34		18 38	18 50	18 54	18 58	19 02	19 05	19 14	19 15	19 18	
East Croydon	d																								
Clapham Junction	d	17 05											18 05												
Imperial Wharf	d	17 09											18 09												
West Brompton ⊖	d	17 12											18 12												
Kensington (Olympia) ⊖	d	17 16											18 16												
Shepherd's Bush	d	17 19											18 19												
Wembley Central ⊖	d																								
Harrow & Wealdstone ⊖	d	17 36					18 06			18 26			18 36					19 06				19 26			
Bushey	d									18 31												19 31			
Watford Junction	a	17 44	17 50			18 06	18 13			18 34			18 44	18 50			19 06	19 13				19 34			
	d		17 51			18 06	18 13			18 35		18u32		18 51			19 06	19 13				19 35		19u32	
Kings Langley	d									18 39												19 39			
Apsley	d									18 43												19 43			
Hemel Hempstead	d		17 58				18 21			18 46				18 58				19 21				19 46			
Berkhamsted	d		18 03				18 25			18 50				19 03				19 25				19 50			
Tring	d						18 30			18a57								19 30				19a57			
Cheddington	d						18 35											19 35							
Leighton Buzzard	d		18 16			18 26	18 42							19 16			19 26	19 42							
Bletchley	d		18 23				18 50							19 23				19 50							
Milton Keynes Central 10	a		18 29	18 11		18 36	18 56		18 38		18 48			19 28		19 11	19 36	19 56			19 38		19 48		
	d		18 29	18 11		18 36								19 28		19 11	19 36								
Wolverton	d		18 33											19 33											
Northampton	a		18 46			18 52								19 46			19 54								
Rugby	a					19 19		18 49									20 17		19 49						
Nuneaton	a																20 29			20 01					
Coventry	a			18 40				19 00				19 20				19 40			19 59					20 20	
Birmingham International ✈	a			18 51				19 11				19 31				19 51			20 10					20 31	
Birmingham New Street 12	a			19 05				19 24				19 44				20 05			20 22					20 44	
Sandwell & Dudley	a							19 48				19 56							20 35					20 56	
Wolverhampton 7	a							20 02				20 10							20 46					21 10	

Table 66

Sundays

17 July to 11 September

London - Watford Junction, Milton Keynes Central, Northampton and West Midlands

		SN	LM	VT	LM	LM	VT	VT	VT	LM	VT	VT	SN	LM	VT	VT	VT	SR	LM	VT	VT	LM	SN
		1	◇1	◇1	◇1	1	◇1	◇1	◇1	1	◇1	◇1	1	◇1	◇1	◇1	◇1	R	◇1	◇1	◇1	◇1	1
				☕			☕	☕	☕		☕	☕			☕	☕	☕	🛏 ☕		☕	☕		
London Euston 15 ⊖	d		19 34	19 38	19 50	19 54	19 58	20 02	20 05	20 14	20 15	20 18		20 34	20 38	20 50	20 54	20 55	21 02	21 21	21 25	21 28	
East Croydon	d																						
Clapham Junction	d	19 05											20 05										21 15
Imperial Wharf	d	19 09											20 09										21 19
West Brompton ⊖	d	19 12											20 12										21 22
Kensington (Olympia) ⊖	d	19 16											20 16										21 26
Shepherd's Bush	d	19 19											20 19										21 29
Wembley Central ⊖	d																						
Harrow & Wealdstone ⊖	d	19 36				20 06				20 26			20 36									21 40	21 47
Bushey	d									20 31													
Watford Junction	a	19 43	19 50		20 06	20 13				20 34			20 44	20 50					21 22			21 47	21 54
	d		19 51		20 06	20 13				20 35		20u32		20 52			21u10		21 23			21 47	
Kings Langley	d									20 39												21 52	
Apsley	d									20 43												21 55	
Hemel Hempstead	d		19 58			20 21				20 46				20 59					21 30			21 58	
Berkhamsted	d		20 03			20 25				20 50				21 04					21 35			22 03	
Tring	d					20 30				20a57									21 39				
Cheddington	d					20 35													21 45				
Leighton Buzzard	d		20 16		20 26	20 42								21 17					21 49			22 16	
Bletchley	d		20 23			20 50								21 24					21 56			22 23	
Milton Keynes Central 10	a		20 29	20 11	20 36	20 56			20 38		20 48			21 30	21 16	21 35	21 41		22 04		22 13	22 32	
	d		20 29	20 11	20 36									21 30	21 16	21 37	21 43		22 05			22 32	
Wolverton	d		20 33											21 34					22 08			22 36	
Northampton	a		20 46		20 56									21 47					22 22			22 50	
Rugby	a				21 19		20 49									21 59	22 05						
Nuneaton	a							21 00												22 51			
Coventry	a			20 40			21 00					21 20			21 46		22 16						
Birmingham International ✈	a			20 51			21 11					21 31			21 57		22 27						
Birmingham New Street 12	a			21 04			21 24					21 44			22 09		22 39						
Sandwell & Dudley	a			21 15			21 36					21 56			22 24		22 52						
Wolverhampton 7	a			21 31			21 51					22 10			22 38		23 06						

		VT	VT	LM	VT	LM	SN	LM	VT	SR	LM
		◇1	◇1	◇1	◇1	◇1	1	◇1	◇1	R	◇1
		☕	☕		☕				☕	🛏 ☕	
London Euston 15 ⊖	d	21 51	21 55	21 58	22 25	22 28		22 58	23 25	23 27	23 34
East Croydon	d										
Clapham Junction	d						22 15				
Imperial Wharf	d						22 19				
West Brompton ⊖	d						22 22				
Kensington (Olympia) ⊖	d						22 26				
Shepherd's Bush	d						22 29				
Wembley Central ⊖	d										
Harrow & Wealdstone ⊖	d			22 10		22 40	22 48	23 10			23 46
Bushey	d										
Watford Junction	a			22 17		22 47	22 56	23 17			23 53
	d		22u09	22 17	22u39	22 47		23 17	23u40		23 53
Kings Langley	d					22 52		23 22			23 58
Apsley	d					22 55		23 25			00 01
Hemel Hempstead	d			22 25		22 58		23 28			00 04
Berkhamsted	d			22 29		23 03		23 33			00 09
Tring	d			22 34				23 38			00 14
Cheddington	d			22 39				23 43			00 19
Leighton Buzzard	d			22 46		23 16		23 50			00 26
Bletchley	d			22 54		23 23		23 57			00 33
Milton Keynes Central 10	a	22 36	22 42	23 02	23 11	23 32		00 06	00 11		00 42
	d	22 38	22 44	23 03	23 12	23 32		00 06	00 12		00 42
Wolverton	d			23 06		23 36		00 10			00 46
Northampton	a			23 21		23 50		00 24			01 00
Rugby	a	23 16	23 20		23 46				00s46		
Nuneaton	a	23 28									
Coventry	a		23 31		23 57				00s57		
Birmingham International ✈	a		23 42		00 08				01s08		
Birmingham New Street 12	a		23 54		00 21				01s21		
Sandwell & Dudley	a										
Wolverhampton 7	a		00 15		00 43				01 52		

Table 66

Sundays

18 September to 23 October

London - Watford Junction, Milton Keynes Central, Northampton and West Midlands

		LM	LM	LM	LM	LM	LM	LM	LM	VT		VT	VT	LM	SN	VT	VT	LM	VT	VT		LM	SN	VT	VT
		◇1	◇1	◇1			◇1	◇1	◇1	◇1		◇1	◇1	◇1	1	◇1	◇1	◇1	◇1	◇1		◇1	1	◇1	◇1
					🚌	🚌																			
										☕		☕	☕			☕	☕		☕	☕				☕	☕
London Euston 15 ⊖	d	23p04	23p44	00 15			06 53	07 23	07 53	08 10		08 15	08 20	08 23		08 45	08 50	08 53	09 15	09 20		09 23		09 45	09 50
East Croydon 🚊	d																								
Clapham Junction	d														08 15								09 15		
Imperial Wharf	d														08 19								09 19		
West Brompton ⊖	d														08 22								09 22		
Kensington (Olympia) ⊖	d														08 26								09 26		
Shepherd's Bush	d														08 29								09 29		
Wembley Central ⊖	d			00 28																					
Harrow & Wealdstone ⊖	d	23p16	23p56	00 32			07 08	07 38	08 06					08 35	08 48			09 05				09 35	09 48		
Bushey	d																								
Watford Junction	a	23p23	00 02	00 38			07 14	07 44	08 12					08 42	08 56			09 12				09 42	09 58		
	d	23p24	00 02	00 39	02 50	02 55	07 15	07 45	08 13					08 42			09u05	09 12				09 42			10u06
Kings Langley	d	23p28	00 07	00 43		03 11		07 49						08 47								09 47			
Apsley	d	23p32	00 11	00 47		03 22		07 53						08 50								09 50			
Hemel Hempstead	d	23p35	00 13	00 50	03 16	03 28	07 22	07 56	08 20					08 53				09 20				09 53			
Berkhamsted	d	23p40	00 18	00 55		03 39	07 27	08 01	08 25					08 58				09 24				09 58			
Tring	d	23p44	00 24	00 59		03 55	07 31		08 29									09 29							
Cheddington	d	23p49	00 29	01 05		04 16	07 37		08 35									09 34							
Leighton Buzzard	d	23p56	00 34	01 09	03 53	04 37	07 44	08 14	08 39					09 11				09 41				10 11			
Bletchley	d	00 03	00 41	01 16	04 19	05 03	07 51	08 21	08 46					09 18				09 49				10 18			
Milton Keynes Central 10	a	00 11	00 48	01 22	04 34	05 18	07 59	08 29	08 50	08 55			09 05	09 27		09 31	09 37	09 57		10 06		10 27		10 32	10 38
	d	00 11	00 48	01 23			07 59	08 29	08 50					09 27		09 32	09 38	09 58				10 27		10 33	10 39
Wolverton	d	00 15	00 52	01 26			08 03	08 33	08 54					09 31				10 01				10 31			
Northampton	a	00 28	01 10	01 40			08 16	08 46	09 09					09 45				10 16				10 45			
Rugby	a															10 07	10 12							11 07	11 13
Nuneaton	a											09 43							10 44						
Coventry	a																10 23								11 25
Birmingham International ✈	a																10 34								11 36
Birmingham New Street 12	a																10 47								11 49
Sandwell & Dudley	a																10 59								12 01
Wolverhampton 7 🚊	a																11 13								12 15

		LM	VT	VT	LM	SN		VT	VT	LM	VT	VT	LM	SN	VT	LM		LM	VT	VT	SN	LM	VT	LM	LM
		◇1	◇1	◇1	◇1	1		◇1	◇1	◇1	◇1	◇1	◇1	1	◇1	◇1		1	◇1	◇1	1	◇1	◇1	◇1	1
			☕	☕				☕	☕		☕	☕			☕				☕	☕			☕		
London Euston 15 ⊖	d	09 53	10 15	10 20	10 23			10 45	10 50	10 53	11 15	11 20	11 23		11 45	11 53		12 14	12 15	12 18		12 34	12 38	12 50	12 54
East Croydon 🚊	d																								
Clapham Junction	d					10 15								11 15							12 05				
Imperial Wharf	d					10 19								11 19							12 09				
West Brompton ⊖	d					10 22								11 22							12 12				
Kensington (Olympia) ⊖	d					10 26								11 26							12 16				
Shepherd's Bush	d					10 29								11 29							12 19				
Wembley Central ⊖	d																								
Harrow & Wealdstone ⊖	d	10 05			10 35	10 48				11 05			11 35	11 48		12 05		12 26			12 36				13 06
Bushey	d																	12 31							
Watford Junction	a	10 12			10 42	10 56				11 12			11 42	11 56		12 12		12 34			12 44	12 50		13 06	13 13
	d	10 12			10 42				11u04	11 12			11 42		12u01	12 12		12 35		12u32		12 51		13 06	13 13
Kings Langley	d				10 47								11 47					12 39							
Apsley	d				10 50								11 50					12 43							
Hemel Hempstead	d	10 20			10 53					11 20			11 53			12 20		12 46				12 58			13 21
Berkhamsted	d	10 24			10 58					11 24			11 58			12 24		12 50				13 03			13 25
Tring	d	10 29								11 29						12 29		12a57							13 30
Cheddington	d	10 34								11 34						12 34									13 35
Leighton Buzzard	d	10 41			11 11					11 41			12 12			12 41						13 16		13 26	13 42
Bletchley	d	10 49			11 18					11 49			12 19			12 49						13 23			13 50
Milton Keynes Central 10	a	10 57		11 06	11 27			11 32	11 37	11 57	12 02	12 08	12 27		12 26	12 57			12 48			13 29	13 11	13 36	13 56
	d	10 58			11 27			11 33	11 39	11 58			12 27		12 27	12 58						13 29	13 11	13 36	
Wolverton	d	11 01			11 31					12 01			12 31			13 01						13 33			
Northampton	a	11 16			11 45					12 16			12 45			13 16						13 46		13 51	
Rugby	a							12 07	12 13						12 46									14 17	
Nuneaton	a		11 46																					14 29	
Coventry	a								12 24						12 56					13 20			13 40		
Birmingham International ✈	a								12 35						13 07					13 31			13 51		
Birmingham New Street 12	a								12 48						13 22					13 44			14 05		
Sandwell & Dudley	a								13 00											13 56					
Wolverhampton 7 🚊	a								13 14											14 10					

Table 66

Sundays

18 September to 23 October

London - Watford Junction, Milton Keynes Central, Northampton and West Midlands

		VT ◇1 ☕		LM 1	VT ◇1 ☕	VT ◇1 ☕	SN 1	LM ◇1	VT ◇1 ☕	LM ◇1	LM 1	VT ◇1 ☕		LM 1	VT ◇1 ☕	VT ◇1 ☕	SN 1	LM ◇1	VT ◇1 ☕	LM ◇1	LM 1	VT ◇1 ☕		VT ◇1 ☕	LM 1
London Euston 15 ⊖	d	12 58		13 14	13 15	13 18		13 34	13 38	13 50	13 54	13 58		14 14	14 15	14 18		14 34	14 38	14 50	14 54	14 58		15 05	15 14
East Croydon 🚢	d																								
Clapham Junction	d						13 05										14 05								
Imperial Wharf	d						13 09										14 09								
West Brompton ⊖	d						13 12										14 12								
Kensington (Olympia) ⊖	d						13 16										14 16								
Shepherd's Bush	d						13 19										14 19								
Wembley Central ⊖	d																								
Harrow & Wealdstone ⊖	d			13 26			13 36				14 06			14 26			14 36				15 06				15 26
Bushey	d			13 31										14 31											15 31
Watford Junction	a			13 34			13 44	13 50		14 06	14 13			14 34			14 44	14 50		15 06	15 13				15 34
	d			13 35		13u32		13 51		14 06	14 13			14 35		14u32		14 51		15 06	15 13				15 35
Kings Langley	d			13 39										14 39											15 39
Apsley	d			13 43										14 43											15 43
Hemel Hempstead	d			13 46				13 58			14 21			14 46				14 58			15 21				15 46
Berkhamsted	d			13 50				14 03			14 25			14 50				15 03			15 25				15 50
Tring	d			13a57							14 30			14a57							15 30				15a57
Cheddington	d										14 35										15 35				
Leighton Buzzard	d							14 16		14 26	14 42							15 16		15 26	15 42				
Bletchley	d							14 23			14 50							15 23			15 50				
Milton Keynes Central 10	a				13 48			14 29	14 11	14 36	14 56				14 48			15 29	15 11	15 36	15 56			15 38	
	d							14 29	14 11	14 36								15 29	15 11	15 36					
Wolverton	d							14 33										15 33							
Northampton	a							14 46		14 52								15 46		15 51					
Rugby	a	13 49								15 19		14 49								16 17		15 49			
Nuneaton	a																			16 29					
Coventry	a	14 00				14 20			14 40			15 00				15 20			15 40			16 00			
Birmingham International ✈	a	14 11				14 31			14 51			15 11				15 31			15 51			16 11			
Birmingham New Street 12	a	14 25				14 44			15 05			15 25				15 44			16 05			16 25			
Sandwell & Dudley	a					14 56										15 56									
Wolverhampton 7 🚢	a					15 10										16 10									

		VT ◇1 ☕	VT ◇1 ☕	SN 1	LM ◇1	VT ◇1 ☕	LM ◇1	LM 1		VT ◇1 ☕	VT ◇1 ☕	LM 1	VT ◇1 ☕	VT ◇1 ☕	SN 1	LM ◇1	VT ◇1 ☕	LM ◇1		LM 1	VT ◇1 ☕	VT ◇1 ☕	LM 1	VT ◇1 ☕	VT ◇1 ☕
London Euston 15 ⊖	d	15 15	15 18		15 34	15 38	15 50	15 54		15 58	16 05	16 14	16 15	16 18		16 34	16 38	16 50		16 54	16 58	17 05	17 14	17 15	17 18
East Croydon 🚢	d																								
Clapham Junction	d			15 05											16 05										
Imperial Wharf	d			15 09											16 09										
West Brompton ⊖	d			15 12											16 12										
Kensington (Olympia) ⊖	d			15 16											16 16										
Shepherd's Bush	d			15 19											16 19										
Wembley Central ⊖	d																								
Harrow & Wealdstone ⊖	d			15 36				16 06				16 26			16 36					17 06			17 26		
Bushey	d											16 31											17 31		
Watford Junction	a			15 44	15 50		16 06	16 13				16 34			16 44	16 50		17 06		17 13			17 34		
	d		15u32		15 51		16 06	16 13				16 35		16u32		16 51		17 06		17 13			17 35		17u32
Kings Langley	d											16 39											17 39		
Apsley	d											16 43											17 43		
Hemel Hempstead	d				15 58			16 21				16 46				16 58				17 21			17 46		
Berkhamsted	d				16 03			16 25				16 50				17 03				17 25			17 50		
Tring	d							16 30				16a57								17 30			17a57		
Cheddington	d							16 35												17 35					
Leighton Buzzard	d				16 16		16 26	16 42								17 16		17 26		17 42					
Bletchley	d				16 23			16 50								17 23				17 50					
Milton Keynes Central 10	a	15 48			16 29	16 11	16 36	16 56			16 38		16 48			17 29	17 11	17 36		17 56		17 38		17 48	
	d				16 29	16 11	16 36									17 29	17 11	17 36				17 39			
Wolverton	d				16 33											17 33									
Northampton	a				16 46		16 52									17 46		17 54							
Rugby	a						17 19			16 49								18 17			17 49				
Nuneaton	a																	18 29				18 09			
Coventry	a		16 20			16 40				17 00				17 20			17 40				18 00				18 20
Birmingham International ✈	a		16 31			16 51				17 11				17 31			17 51				18 11				18 31
Birmingham New Street 12	a		16 44			17 05				17 25				17 44			18 05				18 25				18 44
Sandwell & Dudley	a		16 56											17 56											18 56
Wolverhampton 7 🚢	a		17 10											18 10											19 10

Table 66

Sundays

18 September to 23 October

London - Watford Junction, Milton Keynes Central, Northampton and West Midlands

		SN	LM	VT		LM	LM	VT	VT	LM	VT	VT	SN	LM		VT	LM	LM	VT	VT	VT	LM	VT	VT	
		1	◇1	◇1		◇1	1	◇1	◇1	1	◇1	◇1	1	◇1		◇1	◇1	1	◇1	◇1	◇1	1	◇1	◇1	
				☕				☕	☕		☕	☕				☕			☕	☕	☕		☕	☕	
London Euston 15 ⊖	d		17 34	17 38		17 50	17 54	17 58	18 05	18 14	18 15	18 18		18 34		18 38	18 50	18 54	18 58	19 02	19 05	19 14	19 15	19 18	
East Croydon 🚋	d																								
Clapham Junction	d	17 05											18 05												
Imperial Wharf	d	17 09											18 09												
West Brompton ⊖	d	17 12											18 12												
Kensington (Olympia) ⊖	d	17 16											18 16												
Shepherd's Bush	d	17 19											18 19												
Wembley Central ⊖	d																								
Harrow & Wealdstone ⊖	d	17 36					18 06			18 26			18 36					19 06				19 26			
Bushey	d									18 31												19 31			
Watford Junction	a	17 44	17 50			18 06	18 13			18 34			18 44	18 50			19 06	19 13				19 34			
	d		17 51			18 06	18 13			18 35		18u32		18 51			19 06	19 13				19 35		19u32	
Kings Langley	d									18 39												19 39			
Apsley	d									18 43												19 43			
Hemel Hempstead	d		17 58				18 21			18 46				18 58				19 21				19 46			
Berkhamsted	d		18 03				18 25			18 50				19 03				19 25				19 50			
Tring	d						18 30			18a57								19 30				19a57			
Cheddington	d						18 35											19 35							
Leighton Buzzard	d		18 16			18 26	18 42							19 16			19 26	19 42							
Bletchley	d		18 23				18 50							19 23				19 50							
Milton Keynes Central 10	a		18 29	18 11		18 36	18 56		18 38		18 48			19 28		19 11	19 36	19 56			19 38		19 48		
	d		18 29	18 11		18 36								19 28		19 11	19 36								
Wolverton	d		18 33											19 33											
Northampton	a		18 46			18 52								19 46			19 54								
Rugby	a					19 19		18 49									20 17		19 49						
Nuneaton	a																20 29			20 00					
Coventry	a			18 40				19 00				19 20				19 40			20 00					20 20	
Birmingham International ✈	a			18 51				19 11				19 31				19 51			20 11					20 31	
Birmingham New Street 12	a			19 05				19 24				19 44				20 05			20 23					20 44	
Sandwell & Dudley	a							19 48				19 56							20 35					20 56	
Wolverhampton 7 🚋	a							20 02				20 10							20 46					21 10	

		SN	LM	VT	LM	LM	VT	VT	VT	LM		VT	VT	SN	LM	VT	VT	VT	SR	LM		VT	VT	LM	SN
																			R						
		1	◇1	◇1	◇1	1	◇1	◇1	◇1	1		◇1	◇1	1	◇1	◇1	◇1	◇1		◇1		◇1	◇1	◇1	1
																			🛏						
				☕			☕	☕	☕			☕	☕			☕	☕	☕	☕			☕	☕		
London Euston 15 ⊖	d		19 34	19 38	19 50	19 54	19 58	20 02	20 05	20 14		20 15	20 18		20 34	20 38	20 50	20 54	20 55	21 02		21 21	21 25	21 28	
East Croydon 🚋	d																								
Clapham Junction	d	19 05												20 05											21 15
Imperial Wharf	d	19 09												20 09											21 19
West Brompton ⊖	d	19 12												20 12											21 22
Kensington (Olympia) ⊖	d	19 16												20 16											21 26
Shepherd's Bush	d	19 19												20 19											21 29
Wembley Central ⊖	d																								
Harrow & Wealdstone ⊖	d	19 36				20 06				20 26				20 36										21 40	21 47
Bushey	d									20 31															
Watford Junction	a	19 43	19 50		20 06	20 13				20 34				20 44	20 50					21 22				21 47	21 54
	d		19 51		20 06	20 13				20 35			20u32		20 52			21u10		21 23				21 47	
Kings Langley	d									20 39														21 52	
Apsley	d									20 43														21 55	
Hemel Hempstead	d		19 58			20 21				20 46					20 59					21 30				21 58	
Berkhamsted	d		20 03			20 25				20 50					21 04					21 35				22 03	
Tring	d					20 30				20a57										21 39					
Cheddington	d					20 35														21 45					
Leighton Buzzard	d		20 16		20 26	20 42									21 17					21 49				22 16	
Bletchley	d		20 23			20 50									21 24					21 56				22 23	
Milton Keynes Central 10	a		20 29	20 11	20 36	20 56			20 38			20 48			21 30	21 16	21 35	21 41		22 04			22 13	22 32	
	d		20 29	20 11	20 36										21 30	21 16	21 37	21 43		22 05				22 32	
Wolverton	d		20 33												21 34					22 08				22 36	
Northampton	a		20 46		20 56										21 47					22 22				22 50	
Rugby	a				21 19		20 49										21 59	22 05							
Nuneaton	a							21 00														22 51			
Coventry	a			20 40			21 00						21 20			21 46		22 16							
Birmingham International ✈	a			20 51			21 11						21 31			21 57		22 27							
Birmingham New Street 12	a			21 04			21 24						21 44			22 09		22 39							
Sandwell & Dudley	a			21 15			21 36						21 56			22 24		22 52							
Wolverhampton 7 🚋	a			21 31			21 51						22 10			22 38		23 06							

Table 66

Sundays
18 September to 23 October

London - Watford Junction, Milton Keynes Central, Northampton and West Midlands

		VT	VT	LM	VT	LM		SN	LM	VT	SR	LM
											8	
		◇1	◇1	◇1	◇1	◇1		1	◇1	◇1		◇1
											🛏	
		☕	☕		☕					☕	☕	
London Euston 15 ⊖	d	21 51	21 55	21 58	22 25	22 28			22 58	23 25	23 27	23 34
East Croydon 🚆	d											
Clapham Junction	d							22 15				
Imperial Wharf	d							22 19				
West Brompton ⊖	d							22 22				
Kensington (Olympia) ⊖	d							22 26				
Shepherd's Bush	d							22 29				
Wembley Central ⊖	d											
Harrow & Wealdstone ⊖	d			22 10		22 40		22 48	23 10			23 46
Bushey	d											
Watford Junction	a			22 17		22 47		22 56	23 17			23 53
	d		22u09	22 17	22u39	22 47			23 17	23u40		23 53
Kings Langley	d					22 52			23 22			23 58
Apsley	d					22 55			23 25			00 01
Hemel Hempstead	d			22 25		22 58			23 28			00 04
Berkhamsted	d			22 29		23 03			23 33			00 09
Tring	d			22 34					23 38			00 14
Cheddington	d			22 39					23 43			00 19
Leighton Buzzard	d			22 46		23 16			23 50			00 26
Bletchley	d			22 54		23 23			23 57			00 33
Milton Keynes Central 10	a	22 36	22 42	23 02	23 11	23 32			00 06	00 11		00 42
	d	22 38	22 44	23 03	23 12	23 32			00 06	00 12		00 42
Wolverton	d			23 06		23 36			00 10			00 46
Northampton	a			23 21		23 50			00 24			01 00
Rugby	a	23 16	23 20		23 46					00s46		
Nuneaton	a	23 28										
Coventry	a		23 31		23 57					00s57		
Birmingham International ✈	a		23 42		00 08					01s08		
Birmingham New Street 12	a		23 54		00 21					01s21		
Sandwell & Dudley	a											
Wolverhampton 7 🚆	a		00 15		00 43					01 52		

Sundays
from 30 October

		LM	LM	LM	LM	LM	LM	LM	LM	VT		VT	VT	LM	SN	VT	VT	LM	VT	VT		LM	SN	VT	VT
		◇1	◇1	◇1			◇1	◇1	◇1	◇1		◇1	◇1	◇1	1	◇1	◇1	◇1	◇1	◇1		◇1	1	◇1	◇1
					🚌	🚌																			
										☕		☕	☕			☕	☕		☕	☕				☕	☕
London Euston 15 ⊖	d	23p04	23p44	00 15			06 53	07 23	07 53	08 10		08 15	08 20	08 23		08 45	08 50	08 53	09 15	09 20		09 23		09 45	09 50
East Croydon 🚆	d																								
Clapham Junction	d														08 15								09 15		
Imperial Wharf	d														08 19								09 19		
West Brompton ⊖	d														08 22								09 22		
Kensington (Olympia) ⊖	d														08 26								09 26		
Shepherd's Bush	d														08 29								09 29		
Wembley Central ⊖	d			00 24																					
Harrow & Wealdstone ⊖	d	23p16	23p56	00 29			07 05	07 35	08 06					08 35	08 48			09 05				09 35	09 48		
Bushey	d																								
Watford Junction	a	23p23	00 02	00 35			07 12	07 42	08 12					08 42	08 56			09 12				09 42	09 58		
	d	23p24	00 02	00 35	02 50	02 55	07 12	07 42	08 13					08 42			09u05	09 12				09 42			10u06
Kings Langley	d	23p28	00 07	00 40		03 11		07 47						08 47								09 47			
Apsley	d	23p32	00 11	00 44		03 22		07 50						08 50								09 50			
Hemel Hempstead	d	23p35	00 13	00 46	03 16	03 28	07 20	07 53	08 20					08 53				09 20				09 53			
Berkhamsted	d	23p40	00 18	00 51		03 39	07 24	07 58	08 25					08 58				09 24				09 58			
Tring	d	23p44	00 24	00 56		03 55	07 29		08 29									09 29							
Cheddington	d	23p49	00 29	01 01		04 16	07 34		08 35									09 34							
Leighton Buzzard	d	23p56	00 34	01 06	03 53	04 37	07 41	08 11	08 39					09 11				09 41				10 11			
Bletchley	d	00 03	00 41	01 13	04 19	05 03	07 49	08 18	08 46					09 18				09 49				10 18			
Milton Keynes Central 10	a	00 11	00 48	01 19	04 34	05 18	07 57	08 27	08 50	08 55			09 05	09 27		09 31	09 37	09 57		10 06		10 27		10 32	10 38
	d	00 11	00 48	01 19			07 58	08 27	08 50					09 27		09 32	09 38	09 58				10 27		10 33	10 39
Wolverton	d	00 15	00 52	01 23			08 01	08 31	08 54					09 31				10 01				10 31			
Northampton	a	00 28	01 10	01 36			08 16	08 45	09 09					09 45				10 16				10 45			
Rugby	a															10 07	10 12							11 07	11 13
Nuneaton	a											09 43							10 44						
Coventry	a																10 23								11 25
Birmingham International ✈	a																10 34								11 36
Birmingham New Street 12	a																10 47								11 49
Sandwell & Dudley	a																10 59								12 01
Wolverhampton 7 🚆	a																11 13								12 15

Table 66

Sundays
from 30 October

London - Watford Junction, Milton Keynes Central, Northampton and West Midlands

		LM	VT	VT	LM	SN		VT	VT	LM	VT	VT	LM	SN	VT	LM		LM	VT	VT	SN	LM	VT	LM	LM
		◇1	◇1	◇1	◇1	1		◇1	◇1	◇1	◇1	◇1	◇1	1	◇1	◇1		1	◇1	◇1	1	◇1	◇1	◇1	1
			☕	☕				☕	☕		☕	☕			☕				☕	☕			☕		
London Euston 15 ⊖	d	09 53	10 15	10 20	10 23			10 45	10 50	10 53	11 15	11 20	11 23		11 45	11 53		12 14	12 15	12 18		12 34	12 38	12 50	12 54
East Croydon 🚋	d																								
Clapham Junction	d					10 15								11 15							12 05				
Imperial Wharf	d					10 19								11 19							12 09				
West Brompton ⊖	d					10 22								11 22							12 12				
Kensington (Olympia) ⊖	d					10 26								11 26							12 16				
Shepherd's Bush	d					10 29								11 29							12 19				
Wembley Central ⊖	d																								
Harrow & Wealdstone ⊖	d	10 05			10 35	10 48				11 05			11 35	11 48		12 05		12 26			12 36				13 06
Bushey	d																	12 31							
Watford Junction	a	10 12			10 42	10 56				11 12			11 42	11 56		12 12		12 34			12 44	12 50		13 06	13 13
	d	10 12			10 42				11u04	11 12			11 42		12u01	12 12		12 35		12u32		12 51		13 06	13 13
Kings Langley	d				10 47								11 47					12 39							
Apsley	d				10 50								11 50					12 43							
Hemel Hempstead	d	10 20			10 53					11 20			11 53			12 20		12 46				12 58			13 21
Berkhamsted	d	10 24			10 58					11 24			11 58			12 24		12 50				13 03			13 25
Tring	d	10 29								11 29						12 29		12a57							13 30
Cheddington	d	10 34								11 34						12 34									13 35
Leighton Buzzard	d	10 41			11 11					11 41			12 12			12 41						13 16		13 26	13 42
Bletchley	d	10 49			11 18					11 49			12 19			12 49						13 23			13 50
Milton Keynes Central 10	a	10 57		11 06	11 27			11 32	11 37	11 57	12 02	12 08	12 27		12 26	12 57			12 48			13 29	13 11	13 36	13 56
	d	10 58			11 27			11 33	11 39	11 58			12 27		12 27	12 58						13 29	13 11	13 36	
Wolverton	d	11 01			11 31					12 01			12 31			13 01						13 33			
Northampton	a	11 16			11 45					12 16			12 45			13 16						13 46		13 51	
Rugby	a							12 07	12 13						12 46									14 17	
Nuneaton	a		11 46																					14 29	
Coventry	a								12 24						12 56					13 20			13 40		
Birmingham International ✈	a								12 35						13 07					13 31			13 51		
Birmingham New Street 12	a								12 48						13 22					13 44			14 05		
Sandwell & Dudley	a								13 00											13 56					
Wolverhampton 7 🚋	a								13 14											14 10					

		VT		LM	VT	VT	SN	LM	VT	LM	LM	VT		LM	VT	VT	SN	LM	VT	LM	LM	VT		VT	LM
		◇1		1	◇1	◇1	1	◇1	◇1	◇1	1	◇1		1	◇1	◇1	1	◇1	◇1	◇1	1	◇1		◇1	1
		☕			☕	☕			☕			☕			☕	☕			☕			☕		☕	
London Euston 15 ⊖	d	12 58		13 14	13 15	13 18		13 34	13 38	13 50	13 54	13 58		14 14	14 15	14 18		14 34	14 38	14 50	14 54	14 58		15 05	15 14
East Croydon 🚋	d																								
Clapham Junction	d						13 05										14 05								
Imperial Wharf	d						13 09										14 09								
West Brompton ⊖	d						13 12										14 12								
Kensington (Olympia) ⊖	d						13 16										14 16								
Shepherd's Bush	d						13 19										14 19								
Wembley Central ⊖	d																								
Harrow & Wealdstone ⊖	d			13 26			13 36				14 06			14 26			14 36				15 06				15 26
Bushey	d			13 31										14 31											15 31
Watford Junction	a			13 34			13 44	13 50		14 06	14 13			14 34			14 44	14 50		15 06	15 13				15 34
	d			13 35		13u32		13 51		14 06	14 13			14 35		14u32		14 51		15 06	15 13				15 35
Kings Langley	d			13 39										14 39											15 39
Apsley	d			13 43										14 43											15 43
Hemel Hempstead	d			13 46				13 58			14 21			14 46				14 58			15 21				15 46
Berkhamsted	d			13 50				14 03			14 25			14 50				15 03			15 25				15 50
Tring	d			13a57							14 30			14a57							15 30				15a57
Cheddington	d										14 35										15 35				
Leighton Buzzard	d							14 16		14 26	14 42							15 16		15 26	15 42				
Bletchley	d							14 23			14 50							15 23			15 50				
Milton Keynes Central 10	a				13 48			14 29	14 11	14 36	14 56				14 48			15 29	15 11	15 36	15 56			15 38	
	d							14 29	14 11	14 36								15 29	15 11	15 36					
Wolverton	d							14 33										15 33							
Northampton	a							14 46		14 52								15 46		15 51					
Rugby	a	13 49								15 19		14 49								16 17		15 49			
Nuneaton	a																			16 29					
Coventry	a	14 00				14 20			14 40			15 00				15 20			15 40			16 00			
Birmingham International ✈	a	14 11				14 31			14 51			15 11				15 31			15 51			16 11			
Birmingham New Street 12	a	14 25				14 44			15 05			15 25				15 44			16 05			16 25			
Sandwell & Dudley	a					14 56										15 56									
Wolverhampton 7 🚋	a					15 10										16 10									

Table 66

Sundays
from 30 October

London - Watford Junction, Milton Keynes Central, Northampton and West Midlands

		VT	VT	SN	LM	VT	LM	LM		VT	VT	LM	VT	VT	SN	LM	VT	LM		LM	VT	VT	LM	VT	VT
		◇1	◇1	1	◇1	◇1	◇1	1		◇1	◇1	1	◇1	◇1	1	◇1	◇1	◇1		1	◇1	◇1	1	◇1	◇1
		☕	☕			☕				☕	☕		☕	☕			☕				☕	☕		☕	☕
London Euston 15 ⊖	d	15 15	15 18		15 34	15 38	15 50	15 54		15 58	16 05	16 14	16 15	16 18		16 34	16 38	16 50		16 54	16 58	17 05	17 14	17 15	17 18
East Croydon 🚢	d																								
Clapham Junction	d			15 05											16 05										
Imperial Wharf	d			15 09											16 09										
West Brompton ⊖	d			15 12											16 12										
Kensington (Olympia) ⊖	d			15 16											16 16										
Shepherd's Bush	d			15 19											16 19										
Wembley Central ⊖	d																								
Harrow & Wealdstone ⊖	d			15 36				16 06				16 26			16 36					17 06			17 26		
Bushey	d											16 31											17 31		
Watford Junction	a			15 44	15 50		16 06	16 13				16 34			16 44	16 50		17 06		17 13			17 34		
	d		15u32		15 51		16 06	16 13				16 35		16u32		16 51		17 06		17 13			17 35		17u32
Kings Langley	d											16 39											17 39		
Apsley	d											16 43											17 43		
Hemel Hempstead	d				15 58			16 21				16 46				16 58				17 21			17 46		
Berkhamsted	d				16 03			16 25				16 50				17 03				17 25			17 50		
Tring	d							16 30				16a57								17 30			17a57		
Cheddington	d							16 35												17 35					
Leighton Buzzard	d				16 16		16 26	16 42								17 16		17 26		17 42					
Bletchley	d				16 23			16 50								17 23				17 50					
Milton Keynes Central 10	a	15 48			16 29	16 11	16 36	16 56			16 38		16 48			17 29	17 11	17 36		17 56		17 38		17 48	
	d				16 29	16 11	16 36									17 29	17 11	17 36				17 39			
Wolverton	d				16 33											17 33									
Northampton	a				16 46		16 52									17 46		17 54							
Rugby	a						17 19			16 49								18 17			17 49				
Nuneaton	a																	18 29				18 09			
Coventry	a		16 20			16 40				17 00				17 20			17 40				18 00				18 20
Birmingham International ✈	a		16 31			16 51				17 11				17 31			17 51				18 11				18 31
Birmingham New Street 12	a		16 44			17 05				17 25				17 44			18 05				18 25				18 44
Sandwell & Dudley	a		16 56											17 56											18 56
Wolverhampton 7 🚢	a		17 10											18 10											19 10

		SN	LM	VT		LM	LM	VT	VT	LM	VT	VT	SN	LM		VT	LM	LM	VT	VT	VT	LM	VT	VT	
		1	◇1	◇1		◇1	1	◇1	◇1	1	◇1	◇1	1	◇1		◇1	◇1	1	◇1	◇1	◇1	1	◇1	◇1	
				☕				☕	☕		☕	☕				☕			☕	☕	☕		☕	☕	
London Euston 15 ⊖	d		17 34	17 38		17 50	17 54	17 58	18 05	18 14	18 15	18 18		18 34		18 38	18 50	18 54	18 58	19 02	19 05	19 14	19 15	19 18	
East Croydon 🚢	d																								
Clapham Junction	d	17 05											18 05												
Imperial Wharf	d	17 09											18 09												
West Brompton ⊖	d	17 12											18 12												
Kensington (Olympia) ⊖	d	17 16											18 16												
Shepherd's Bush	d	17 19											18 19												
Wembley Central ⊖	d																								
Harrow & Wealdstone ⊖	d	17 36					18 06			18 26			18 36					19 06				19 26			
Bushey	d									18 31												19 31			
Watford Junction	a	17 44	17 50			18 06	18 13			18 34			18 44	18 50			19 06	19 13				19 34			
	d		17 51			18 06	18 13			18 35		18u32		18 51			19 06	19 13				19 35		19u32	
Kings Langley	d									18 39												19 39			
Apsley	d									18 43												19 43			
Hemel Hempstead	d		17 58				18 21			18 46				18 58				19 21				19 46			
Berkhamsted	d		18 03				18 25			18 50				19 03				19 25				19 50			
Tring	d						18 30			18a57								19 30				19a57			
Cheddington	d						18 35											19 35							
Leighton Buzzard	d		18 16			18 26	18 42							19 16			19 26	19 42							
Bletchley	d		18 23				18 50							19 23				19 50							
Milton Keynes Central 10	a		18 29	18 11		18 36	18 56		18 38		18 48			19 28		19 11	19 36	19 56			19 38		19 48		
	d		18 29	18 11		18 36								19 28		19 11	19 36								
Wolverton	d		18 33											19 33											
Northampton	a		18 46			18 52								19 46			19 54								
Rugby	a					19 19		18 49									20 17		19 49						
Nuneaton	a																20 29			20 00					
Coventry	a			18 40				19 00				19 20				19 40			20 00					20 20	
Birmingham International ✈	a			18 51				19 11				19 31				19 51			20 11					20 31	
Birmingham New Street 12	a			19 05				19 24				19 44				20 05			20 23					20 44	
Sandwell & Dudley	a							19 48				19 56							20 35					20 56	
Wolverhampton 7 🚢	a							20 02				20 10							20 46					21 10	

Table 66

Sundays
from 30 October

London - Watford Junction, Milton Keynes Central, Northampton and West Midlands

		SN	LM	VT	LM	LM	VT	VT	VT	LM		VT	VT	SN	LM	VT	VT	VT	SR	LM		VT	VT	LM	SN
		1	◇1	◇1 ☕	◇1	1	◇1 ☕	◇1 ☕	◇1 ☕	1		◇1 ☕	◇1 ☕	1	◇1	◇1 ☕	◇1 ☕	◇1 ☕	R 🛏 ☕	◇1		◇1 ☕	◇1 ☕	◇1	1
London Euston 15 ⊖	d		19 34	19 38	19 50	19 54	19 58	20 02	20 05	20 14		20 15	20 18		20 34	20 38	20 50	20 54	20 55	21 02		21 21	21 25	21 28	
East Croydon 🚊	d																								
Clapham Junction	d	19 05												20 05											21 15
Imperial Wharf	d	19 09												20 09											21 19
West Brompton ⊖	d	19 12												20 12											21 22
Kensington (Olympia) ⊖	d	19 16												20 16											21 26
Shepherd's Bush	d	19 19												20 19											21 29
Wembley Central ⊖	d																								
Harrow & Wealdstone ⊖	d	19 36				20 06				20 26				20 36										21 40	21 47
Bushey	d									20 31															
Watford Junction	a	19 43	19 50		20 06	20 13				20 34				20 44	20 50					21 22				21 47	21 54
	d		19 51		20 06	20 13				20 35			20u32		20 52			21u10		21 23				21 47	
Kings Langley	d									20 39														21 52	
Apsley	d									20 43														21 55	
Hemel Hempstead	d		19 58			20 21				20 46					20 59					21 30				21 58	
Berkhamsted	d		20 03			20 25				20 50					21 04					21 35				22 03	
Tring	d					20 30				20a57										21 39					
Cheddington	d					20 35														21 45					
Leighton Buzzard	d		20 16		20 26	20 42									21 17					21 49				22 16	
Bletchley	d		20 23			20 50									21 24					21 56				22 23	
Milton Keynes Central 10	a		20 29	20 11	20 36	20 56			20 38			20 48			21 30	21 16	21 35	21 41		22 04			22 13	22 32	
	d		20 29	20 11	20 36										21 30	21 16	21 37	21 43		22 05				22 32	
Wolverton	d		20 33												21 34					22 08				22 36	
Northampton	a		20 46		20 56										21 47					22 22				22 50	
Rugby	a				21 19		20 49										21 59	22 05							
Nuneaton	a							21 00														22 51			
Coventry	a			20 40			21 00						21 20			21 46		22 16							
Birmingham International ✈	a			20 51			21 11						21 31			21 57		22 27							
Birmingham New Street 12	a			21 04			21 24						21 44			22 09		22 39							
Sandwell & Dudley	a			21 15			21 36						21 56			22 24		22 52							
Wolverhampton 7 🚊	a			21 31			21 51						22 10			22 38		23 06							

		VT	VT	LM	VT	LM		SN	LM	VT	SR	LM
		◇1 ☕	◇1 ☕	◇1	◇1 ☕	◇1		1	◇1	◇1 ☕	R 🛏 ☕	◇1
London Euston 15 ⊖	d	21 51	21 55	21 58	22 25	22 28			22 58	23 25	23 27	23 34
East Croydon 🚊	d											
Clapham Junction	d							22 15				
Imperial Wharf	d							22 19				
West Brompton ⊖	d							22 22				
Kensington (Olympia) ⊖	d							22 26				
Shepherd's Bush	d							22 29				
Wembley Central ⊖	d											
Harrow & Wealdstone ⊖	d			22 10		22 40		22 48	23 10			23 46
Bushey	d											
Watford Junction	a			22 17		22 47		22 56	23 17			23 53
	d		22u09	22 17	22u39	22 47			23 17	23u40		23 53
Kings Langley	d					22 52			23 22			23 58
Apsley	d					22 55			23 25			00 01
Hemel Hempstead	d			22 25		22 58			23 28			00 04
Berkhamsted	d			22 29		23 03			23 33			00 09
Tring	d			22 34					23 38			00 14
Cheddington	d			22 39					23 43			00 19
Leighton Buzzard	d			22 46		23 16			23 50			00 26
Bletchley	d			22 54		23 23			23 57			00 33
Milton Keynes Central 10	a	22 36	22 42	23 02	23 11	23 32			00 06	00 11		00 42
	d	22 38	22 44	23 03	23 12	23 32			00 06	00 12		00 42
Wolverton	d			23 06		23 36			00 10			00 46
Northampton	a			23 21		23 50			00 24			01 00
Rugby	a	23 16	23 20		23 46					00s46		
Nuneaton	a	23 28										
Coventry	a		23 31		23 57					00s57		
Birmingham International ✈	a		23 42		00 08					01s08		
Birmingham New Street 12	a		23 54		00 21					01s21		
Sandwell & Dudley	a											
Wolverhampton 7 🚊	a		00 15		00 43					01 52		

West Midlands, Northampton, Milton Keynes Central and Watford Junction - London

Miles	Miles	Miles		SN	SN	SN	LM	VT	LM	VT	LM	LM	VT	VT	LM	LM	LM	SN	LM	LM	SR	LM
				MX	MO	MX	MX	MX	MO	MO	TO		MO	MX							MX	
				1	1	1	◇1	◇1	◇1	◇1	◇1	◇1	◇1	◇1	1	◇1	◇1	1	◇1	1	R	1
												A										
								☕		☕			☕	☕							🛏 ☕	
0	—	—	Wolverhampton 7 d					21p45		22p05			22p37	22p45								
7½	—	—	Sandwell & Dudley d					21p56		22p15			22p47	22p55								
12¾	—	—	**Birmingham New Street** 12 d				21p33	22p10		22g30			23p00	23h10								
21¼	—	—	Birmingham International ✈ d				21p45	22p20		22p40			23p10	23p20								
32	—	—	Coventry d				22p01	22p31		22p51			23p21	23p31								
—	—	—	Nuneaton d																			
43½	0	—	**Rugby** d				22p12	22p43		23p04			23p34	23p44								
62¼	—	—	**Northampton** d				22e55		22p55		23p30	23p46	23f53	00s05		04 15	04 48		05 05			
75¼	30	—	Wolverton d				23p07		23p11		23p44	23p58				04 27	05 00		05 17			
78¼	32¾	—	**Milton Keynes Central** 10 a				23p12	23f05	23p14	23p36	23p50	00 03	00s12	00s23		04 30	05 03		05 20			
—	—	—	d	22p11			23p13		23p15	23p37	23p50	00 04			03 30	04 31	05 04		05 21			05 54
81¼	—	—	Bletchley d	22p15			23p18		23p20		23p55	00 09			03 35	04 36	05 09		05 26	05 38		05 59
87¾	—	—	Leighton Buzzard d	22p22			23p24		23p26		00 02	00 15			03 41	04 42	05 15		05 33	05 45		06 05
92	—	—	Cheddington d				23p29		23p31		00 08	00 24					05 20			05 50		
96¼	—	—	Tring d	22p34			23p38		23p40		00 14	00 29			03 53	04 54	05 29			05 56		
100	—	—	Berkhamsted d	22p39			23p43		23p45		00 18	00 34			03 58	04 59	05 34		05 47	06 01		06 17
103½	—	—	Hemel Hempstead d	22p43			23p47		23p49		00 22	00 38			04 02	05 03	05 38		05 52	06 05		06 22
105	—	—	Apsley d				23p50										05 41			06 08		
107	—	—	Kings Langley d				23p53										05 44			06 11		
110½	65	—	**Watford Junction** a	22p53			23p58	23f37	23p56	00s06	00 29	00 45	00s42	00s52	04 09	05 10	05 49		05 59	06 16		06 29
—	—	—	d	22p54	23p17	23p29	23p58		23p57		00 30	00 46			04 10	05 11	05 50	05 54	06 01	06 17		06 30
112	—	—	Bushey d				00 01															
116½	71	—	Harrow & Wealdstone ⊖ d	23p01	23p23	23p35	00 06		00 03		00 36	00 52			04 16	05 17	05 56	06 00		06 23		
119¾	—	0	Wembley Central ⊖ d								00 40	00 56			04 20	05 21		06 05				
—	—	4¼	Shepherd's Bush a	23p21	23p45	23p53												06 19				
—	—	5½	Kensington (Olympia) ⊖ a	23p23	23p47	23p56												06 21				
—	—	7½	West Brompton ⊖ a	23p26	23p50	23p59												06 24				
—	—	8	Imperial Wharf a	23p28	23p53	00 02												06 27				
—	—	—	Clapham Junction d	23b40	00 05	00a07												06a32				
—	—	16¾	East Croydon 🚆 a	00 01	00 22																	
128	82½	—	**London Euston** 15 ⊖ a				00 21	00 04	00 17	00 26	00 53	01 09	01 04	01 14	04 35	05 36	06 13		06 22	06 40	06 43	06 49

	LM	SR	LM	VT	LM	SN	LM	VT	LM	LM	LM	LM	VT	VT	VT	VT	SN	LM	VT	LM	LM	LM
		MO																				
	1	R	1	◇1	1	1	◇	◇1	1	1	1	◇1	◇1	◇1	◇1	◇1	1	◇1	◇1	1	1	1
		🛏 ☕		⊠				⊠					⊠	⊠	⊠	⊠			⊠			
Wolverhampton 7 d				05 00				05 24							05 45	06 04						
Sandwell & Dudley d								05 34							05 56	06 15						
Birmingham New Street 12 d				05 29				05 50							06 10	06 30		05 53				
Birmingham International ✈ d				05 40				06 00							06 20	06 40		06 05				
Coventry d				05 51				06 11							06 31	06 51		06 21				
Nuneaton d														06 18								
Rugby d	05 20	05 29		06 03								06 13	06 20	06 32				06 32	06 53			
Northampton d	05 45						06 17					06 38	06 42					07 00				
Wolverton d	05 57						06 29					06 50						07 12				
Milton Keynes Central 10 a	06 00			06 22			06 33	06 38				06 54		06 51	06 59			07 15	07 12			
d	06 02		06 20	06 23			06 34	06 38			06 48	06 55		06 52	06 59		07 01	07 17	07 14			07 21
Bletchley d	06 07		06 25				06 39		06 34		06 53	07 00					07 05			07 13		07 26
Leighton Buzzard d	06 14		06 31				06 46		06 41		06 59	07 07					07 13	07 26				07 33
Cheddington d			06 37								07 05											07 38
Tring d			06 42		06 24				06 52	07 00	07 11						07 22			07 28		07 45
Berkhamsted d			06 47		06 28				06 56	07 05	07 16						07 26			07 32		07 49
Hemel Hempstead d			06 52		06 33				07 01	07 09	07 20						07 31			07 37		07 54
Apsley d					06 36				07 04		07 24											07 57
Kings Langley d					06 39				07 07		07 27											08 00
Watford Junction a	06 31	06s23	06 59	06s43	06 44		07 04		07 12	07 17	07 31					07s36	07 38			07 44		08 05
d	06 33		07 00		06 45	06 53	07 05		07 12	07 19	07 32						07 38			07 45	07 55	08 05
Bushey d					06 48				07 15	07 22	07 34										07 59	
Harrow & Wealdstone ⊖ d			07 06		06 53	06 59			07 20		07 40						07 45				08 05	
Wembley Central ⊖ d						07 04											07u49					
Shepherd's Bush a						07 19											08 04					
Kensington (Olympia) ⊖ a						07 21											08 06					
West Brompton ⊖ a						07 24											08 09					
Imperial Wharf a						07 27											08 12					
Clapham Junction d						07a32											08 36					
East Croydon 🚆 a																	09 04					
London Euston 15 ⊖ a	06 50	06 46	07 20	07 02	07 07		07 22	07 13	07 34	07 40	07 54	07 40	07 30	07 28	07 34	07 53		08 02	07 50	08 05	08 18	08 24

A WThFO
b Previous night, arr. 2333
e Previous night, arr. 2233
f Previous night, stops to set down only
g Previous night, arr. 2224
h Previous night, arr. 2304

Table 66

Mondays to Fridays

West Midlands, Northampton, Milton Keynes Central and Watford Junction - London

		LM	VT	LM	LM		LM	LM	VT	VT	VT	VT	VT	LM	VT		LM	LM	SN	LM	VT	VT	LM	LM	VT
		◇1	◇1 ⊠	1	1		1	1	◇1 ⊠	◇1 ⊠	◇1 ⊠	◇1 ⊠	◇1 ⊠	◇1	◇1 ⊠		1	1	1	◇1	◇1 ⊠	◇1 ⊠	◇1	1	◇1 ⊠
Wolverhampton 7 ⛴	d		06 27									06 45			07 04										07 45
Sandwell & Dudley	d		06 37									06 56			07 15										07 56
Birmingham New Street 12	d		06 50									07 10			07b30					06 53					08 10
Birmingham International ✈	d		07 00									07 20								07 05		07 41			08 20
Coventry	d		07 11									07 31								07 21		07 52			08 31
Nuneaton	d									07 07			07 33												
Rugby	d							07 02	07 08		07 29									07 32	07 55				
Northampton	d	07 13						07 32						07 39						08 05			08 25		
Wolverton	d	07 25												07 51						08 17			08 37		
Milton Keynes Central 10	a	07 29	07s40					07 46						07 54						08 21			08 41		
	d	07 30						07 46						07 55			07 59		08 13	08 21			08 41		
Bletchley	d			07 39				07 51									08 04		08 17	08 27			08 46		
Leighton Buzzard	d	07 39		07 46				07 58						08 05			08 11		08 24	08 34			08 53		
Cheddington	d							08 04																	
Tring	d						08 04	08 10										08 25	08 34					08 48	
Berkhamsted	d			07 59				08 15										08 29	08 39					08 53	
Hemel Hempstead	d			08 03				08 19									08 28	08 34	08 43					08 57	
Apsley	d						08 13											08 37							
Kings Langley	d						08 16											08 40							
Watford Junction	a			08 10			08 20	08 26									08 35	08 45	08 51					09 04	09s15
	d			08 11	08 15		08 22	08 28									08 36	08 46	08 51					09 05	
Bushey	d				08 19													08 48						09 08	
Harrow & Wealdstone ⊖	d			08 17	08 24		08 29	08 34										08 54	08 58					09 13	
Wembley Central ⊖	d																		09u05						
Shepherd's Bush	a																		09 18						
Kensington (Olympia) ⊖	a																		09 20						
West Brompton ⊖	a																		09 23						
Imperial Wharf	a																		09 26						
Clapham Junction	d																		09 34						
East Croydon ⛴	a																		09 57						
London Euston 15 ⊖	a	08 11	08 14	08 33	08 38		08 42	08 49	07 57	08 07	08 22	08 30	08 33	08 39	08 42		08 55	09 08		09 10	08 45	08 49	09 27	09 27	09 34

			LM	LM	LM	VT	VT	VT	LM	SN	VT		LM	VT	LM	VT	VT	LM	LM	VT	LM		VT	LM	SN
			1	1	◇1	◇1 ⊠	◇1 ⊠	◇1 ⊠	1	1	◇1 ⊠		◇1	◇1 ⊠	◇1	◇1 ⊠	◇1 ⊠	1	1	◇1 ⊠	◇1		◇1 ⊠	1	1
Wolverhampton 7 ⛴	d																08 45								
Sandwell & Dudley	d																08 56								
Birmingham New Street 12	d					07 50					08 30		07 53				09 10						08 50		
Birmingham International ✈	d					08 00					08 40		08 05				09 20						09 00		
Coventry	d					08 11					08 51		08 21				09 31						09 11		
Nuneaton	d				08 02			08 46													09 02				
Rugby	d				08 20	08 23							08 32	08 46							09 20		09 23		
Northampton	d				08 47								09 05		09 25						09 50				
Wolverton	d												09 17		09 37										
Milton Keynes Central 10	a				09 01						09 18		09 20		09 41						10 04				
	d			08 47	09 01					09 13	09 19		09 22		09 41	09 47			09 47	10 02	10 05				10 13
Bletchley	d			08 52						09 17			09 27		09 46				09 52						10 17
Leighton Buzzard	d			08 58						09 24			09 33		09 53				09 58						10 24
Cheddington	d			09 04															10 04						
Tring	d		09 01	09 10					09 26	09 34								09 56	10 10					10 26	10 34
Berkhamsted	d		09 05	09 15					09 30	09 39			09 46					10 00	10 15					10 30	10 39
Hemel Hempstead	d		09 10	09 19					09 35	09 43			09 51					10 05	10 19					10 35	10 43
Apsley	d		09 13						09 38									10 08						10 38	
Kings Langley	d		09 16						09 41									10 11						10 41	
Watford Junction	a		09 20	09 26	09 27			09s31	09 46	09 51			09 58				10s15	10 16	10 26		10 30			10 46	10 51
	d		09 21	09 27	09 28				09 46	09 51			09 59					10 16	10 27		10 31			10 46	10 51
Bushey	d		09 23						09 49									10 19						10 49	
Harrow & Wealdstone ⊖	d		09 28	09 33					09 54	09 58								10 24						10 54	10 59
Wembley Central ⊖	d									10u05															11u04
Shepherd's Bush	a									10 21															11 19
Kensington (Olympia) ⊖	a									10 23															11 21
West Brompton ⊖	a									10 26															11 23
Imperial Wharf	a									10 29															11 26
Clapham Junction	d									10 34															11 34
East Croydon ⛴	a									10 57															11 57
London Euston 15 ⊖	a		09 42	09 47	09 44	09 13	09 23	09 52	10 08		09 54		10 18	09 38	10 27	10 23	10 34	10 38	10 46	10 38	10 49		10 14	11 08	

West Midlands, Northampton, Milton Keynes Central and Watford Junction - London

Station		VT	LM	LM	VT	VT	LM		LM	VT	LM	VT	LM	SN	VT	LM	LM		VT	VT	LM	LM	VT	LM	VT
		◇1 ⊠	◇1	◇1	◇1 ⊠	◇1 ⊠	1		1	◇1 ⊠	◇1	◇1 ⊠	1	1	◇1 ⊠	◇1	◇1		◇1 ⊠	◇1 ⊠	1	1	◇1 ⊠	◇1	◇1 ⊠
Wolverhampton 7	d					09 45														10 45					
Sandwell & Dudley	d					09 56														10 56					
Birmingham New Street 12	d	09 30	08 53			10 10						09 50			10 30	09 53				11 10					10 50
Birmingham International ✈	d	09 40	09 05			10 20						10 00			10 40	10 05				11 20					11 00
Coventry	d	09 51	09 21			10 31						10 11			10 51	10 21				11 31					11 11
Nuneaton	d										10 02													11 02	
Rugby	d		09 32								10 20	10 24				10 32								11 20	11 24
Northampton	d		10 05	10 25							10 50					11 05	11 25							11 50	
Wolverton	d		10 17	10 37												11 17	11 37								
Milton Keynes Central 10	a	10 18	10 20	10 41							11 04				11 18	11 20	11 41							12 04	
	d	10 19	10 22	10 41	10 47				10 47	11 02	11 05			11 13	11 19	11 22	11 41		11 47			11 47	12 02	12 05	
Bletchley	d		10 27	10 46					10 52					11 17		11 27	11 46					11 52			
Leighton Buzzard	d		10 33	10 53					10 58					11 24		11 33	11 53					11 58			
Cheddington	d								11 04													12 04			
Tring	d						10 56		11 10				11 26	11 34							11 56	12 10			
Berkhamsted	d		10 46				11 00		11 15				11 30	11 39		11 46					12 00	12 15			
Hemel Hempstead	d		10 51				11 05		11 19				11 35	11 43		11 51					12 05	12 19			
Apsley	d						11 08						11 38								12 08				
Kings Langley	d						11 11						11 41								12 11				
Watford Junction	a		10 58			11s15	11 16		11 26		11 31		11 46	11 51		11 58				12s15	12 16	12 26		12 30	
	d		10 59				11 16		11 27		11 31		11 46	11 51		11 59					12 16	12 27		12 31	
Bushey	d						11 19						11 49								12 19				
Harrow & Wealdstone ⊖	d						11 24						11 54	11 59							12 24				
Wembley Central ⊖	d													12u04											
Shepherd's Bush	a													12 19											
Kensington (Olympia) ⊖	a													12 21											
West Brompton ⊖	a													12 24											
Imperial Wharf	a													12 27											
Clapham Junction	d													12 34											
East Croydon	a													12 57											
London Euston 15 ⊖	a	10 54	11 17	11 27	11 23	11 34	11 38		11 46	11 38	11 49	11 14	12 08		11 54	12 17	12 27		12 23	12 34	12 38	12 45	12 38	12 49	12 14

Station		LM	SN		VT	LM	LM	VT	VT	LM	LM	VT	LM		VT	LM	SN	VT	LM	VT	LM	VT	VT		LM
		1	1		◇1 ☕	◇1	◇1	◇1 ☕	◇1 ☕	1	1	◇1 ☕	◇1		◇1 ☕	1	1	◇1 ☕	◇1	◇1 ☕	◇1	◇1 ☕	◇1 ☕		1
Wolverhampton 7	d								11 45														12 45		
Sandwell & Dudley	d								11 56														12 56		
Birmingham New Street 12	d				11 30	10 53			12 10						11 50			12 30	11 53	12 50			13 10		
Birmingham International ✈	d				11 40	11 05			12 20						12 00			12 40	12 05	13 00			13 20		
Coventry	d				11 51	11 21			12 31						12 11			12 51	12 21	13 11			13 31		
Nuneaton	d												12 02												
Rugby	d					11 32							12 20		12 24				12 32	13 24					
Northampton	d					12 05	12 25						12 50						13 05		13 25				
Wolverton	d					12 17	12 37												13 17		13 37				
Milton Keynes Central 10	a				12 18	12 20	12 41						13 04					13 18	13 20		13 41				
	d		12 13		12 19	12 22	12 41	12 46			12 47	13 02	13 05				13 13	13 20	13 22		13 41	13 47			
Bletchley	d		12 17			12 27	12 46				12 52						13 17		13 27		13 46				
Leighton Buzzard	d		12 24			12 33	12 53				12 58						13 24		13 33		13 53				
Cheddington	d										13 04														
Tring	d	12 26	12 34							12 56	13 10					13 26	13 34								13 56
Berkhamsted	d	12 30	12 39			12 46				13 00	13 15					13 30	13 39		13 46						14 00
Hemel Hempstead	d	12 35	12 43			12 51				13 05	13 19					13 35	13 43		13 51						14 05
Apsley	d	12 38								13 08						13 38									14 08
Kings Langley	d	12 41								13 11						13 41									14 11
Watford Junction	a	12 46	12 51			12 58			13s15	13 16	13 26		13 31			13 46	13 51		13 58				14s15		14 16
	d	12 46	12 51			12 59				13 16	13 27		13 31			13 46	13 51		13 59						14 16
Bushey	d	12 49								13 19						13 49									14 19
Harrow & Wealdstone ⊖	d	12 54	12 59							13 24						13 54	13 59								14 24
Wembley Central ⊖	d		13u04														14u04								
Shepherd's Bush	a		13 19														14 19								
Kensington (Olympia) ⊖	a		13 21														14 21								
West Brompton ⊖	a		13 24														14 24								
Imperial Wharf	a		13 27														14 27								
Clapham Junction	d		13 34														14 34								
East Croydon	a		13 57														14 57								
London Euston 15 ⊖	a	13 08			12 54	13 17	13 27	13 23	13 34	13 38	13 45	13 38	13 49		13 14	14 08		13 55	14 17	14 14	14 27	14 23	14 34		14 38

West Midlands, Northampton, Milton Keynes Central and Watford Junction - London

		LM	VT	LM	LM	SN	VT	LM	LM		VT	VT	LM	LM	VT	LM	VT	LM	SN		VT	LM	LM	VT	VT
		■1	◇1	◇1	■1	■1	◇1	◇1	◇1		◇1	◇1	■1	■1	◇1	◇1	◇1	■1	■1		◇1	◇1	◇1	◇1	◇1
																									A
			⊐P				⊐P				⊐P	⊐P			⊐P		⊐P				⊐P			⊐P	☒
Wolverhampton 7 ⇌	d											13 45													14 45
Sandwell & Dudley	d											13 56													14 56
Birmingham New Street 12	d						13 30	12 53				14 10					13 50				14 30	13 53			15 10
Birmingham International ✈	d						13 40	13 05				14 20					14 00				14 40	14 05			15 20
Coventry	d						13 51	13 21				14 31					14 11				14 51	14 21			15 31
Nuneaton	d			13 02												14 02									
Rugby	d			13 25				13 32								14 20	14 24					14 32			
Northampton	d			13 50				14 05	14 25							14 50						15 05	15 25		
Wolverton	d							14 17	14 37													15 17	15 37		
Milton Keynes Central 10	a			14 04			14 18	14 20	14 41							15 04					15 18	15 20	15 41		
	d	13 47	14 02	14 05		14 13	14 19	14 22	14 41		14 47			14 47	15 02	15 05			15 13		15 19	15 22	15 41	15 47	
Bletchley	d	13 52				14 17		14 27	14 46					14 52					15 17			15 27	15 46		
Leighton Buzzard	d	13 58				14 24		14 33	14 53					14 58					15 24			15 33	15 53		
Cheddington	d	14 04												15 04											
Tring	d	14 10			14 26	14 34							14 56	15 10				15 26	15 34						
Berkhamsted	d	14 15			14 30	14 39		14 46					15 00	15 15				15 30	15 39			15 46			
Hemel Hempstead	d	14 19			14 35	14 43		14 51					15 05	15 19				15 35	15 43			15 51			
Apsley	d				14 38								15 08					15 38							
Kings Langley	d				14 41								15 11					15 41							
Watford Junction	a	14 26		14 31	14 46	14 51		14 58				15s15	15 16	15 26		15 30		15 46	15 51			15 58			16s15
	d	14 27		14 31	14 46	14 51		14 59					15 16	15 27		15 31		15 46	15 51			15 59			
Bushey	d				14 49								15 19					15 49							
Harrow & Wealdstone ⊖	d				14 54	14 59							15 24					15 54	15 59						
Wembley Central ⊖	d					15u04													16u05						
Shepherd's Bush	a					15 22													16 19						
Kensington (Olympia) ⊖	a					15 24													16 21						
West Brompton ⊖	a					15 26													16 24						
Imperial Wharf	a					15 29													16 27						
Clapham Junction	d					15 34													16 34						
East Croydon ⇌	a					15 57													16 58						
London Euston 15 ⊖	a	14 45	14 38	14 49	15 08		14 54	15 17	15 27		15 23	15 34	15 38	15 45	15 38	15 49	15 14	16 08			15 54	16 17	16 27	16 23	16 34

		VT	LM	LM	VT		LM	VT	LM	SN	VT	LM	LM	VT	VT		LM	LM	VT	LM	VT	VT	LM	SN	VT
		◇1	■1	■1	◇1		◇1	◇1	■1	■1	◇1	◇1	◇1	◇1	◇1		■1	■1	◇1	◇1	◇1	◇1	■1	■1	◇1
		B																							
		⊐P			⊐P			⊐P			⊐P			⊐P	⊐P				⊐P		⊐P	⊐P			⊐P
Wolverhampton 7 ⇌	d	14 45													15 45										
Sandwell & Dudley	d	14 56													15 56										
Birmingham New Street 12	d	15 10						14 50			15 30	14 53			16 10						15 50				16 30
Birmingham International ✈	d	15 20						15 00			15 40	15 05			16 20						16 00				16 40
Coventry	d	15 31						15 11			15 51	15 21			16 31						16 11				16 51
Nuneaton	d						15 02													16 02					
Rugby	d						15 20	15 24				15 32								16 20	16 24				
Northampton	d						15 50					16 05	16 25							16 50					
Wolverton	d											16 17	16 37												
Milton Keynes Central 10	a						16 04				16 18	16 20	16 41							17 04					17 18
	d			15 47	16 02		16 05			16 13	16 19	16 22	16 41	16 47				16 47	17 02	17 05				17 13	17 19
Bletchley	d			15 52						16 17		16 27	16 46					16 52						17 17	
Leighton Buzzard	d			15 58						16 24		16 33	16 53					16 58						17 24	
Cheddington	d			16 04														17 04							
Tring	d		15 56	16 10					16 26	16 34							16 56	17 10					17 26	17 34	
Berkhamsted	d		16 00	16 15					16 30	16 39		16 46					17 00	17 15					17 30	17 39	
Hemel Hempstead	d		16 05	16 19					16 35	16 43		16 51					17 05	17 19					17 35	17 43	
Apsley	d		16 08						16 38								17 08						17 38		
Kings Langley	d		16 11						16 41								17 11						17 41		
Watford Junction	a	16s15	16 16	16 26			16 30		16 46	16 51		16 58			17s15		17 16	17 26		17 30			17 46	17 51	
	d		16 16	16 27			16 31		16 46	16 51		16 59					17 16	17 27		17 31			17 46	17 51	
Bushey	d		16 19						16 49								17 19						17 49		
Harrow & Wealdstone ⊖	d		16 24						16 54	16 59							17 24						17 54	17 59	
Wembley Central ⊖	d									17u05														18u05	
Shepherd's Bush	a									17 19														18 19	
Kensington (Olympia) ⊖	a									17 21														18 21	
West Brompton ⊖	a									17 24														18 24	
Imperial Wharf	a									17 27														18 27	
Clapham Junction	d									17 33														18 34	
East Croydon ⇌	a									17 59														19 02	
London Euston 15 ⊖	a	16 34	16 38	16 45	16 38		16 49	16 14	17 08		16 54	17 18	17 27	17 23	17 34		17 38	17 47	17 38	17 49	17 14	17 38	18 10		17 54

A from 18 July until 9 September

B until 15 July, from 12 September

West Midlands, Northampton, Milton Keynes Central and Watford Junction - London

			LM	LM	VT	VT	LM	LM	VT	LM	VT		LM	SN	VT	LM	VT	VT	LM	VT	LM		LM	VT	VT
			◇1	◇1	◇1	◇1	1	1	◇1	◇1	◇1		1	1	◇1	◇1	◇1	◇1	◇1	◇1	1		1	◇1	◇1
					☕	☕			☕		☕				⊠		☕	☕		⊠				⊠	⊠
Wolverhampton 7	d					16 45														17 45					
Sandwell & Dudley	d					16 56														17 56					
Birmingham New Street 12	d		15 53			17 10					16 50				17 30	16 53			17 13	18 10					
Birmingham International ✈	d		16 05			17 20					17 00				17 40	17 05			17 26	18 20					
Coventry	d		16 21			17 31					17 11				17 51	17 21			17 41	18 31					
Nuneaton	d									17 02															
Rugby	d		16 32							17 20	17 24					17 32			17 52						
Northampton	d		17 05	17 25						17 50						18 05			18 25						
Wolverton	d		17 17	17 37												18 17			18 37						
Milton Keynes Central 10	a		17 20	17 41						18 04					18 18	18 20			18 41						
	d		17 22	17 41	17 47			17 47	18 02	18 05				18 13	18 19	18 22	18 24		18 41				18 47	18 48	19 02
Bletchley	d		17 27	17 46				17 52						18 17		18 27			18 46				18 52		
Leighton Buzzard	d		17 33	17 53				17 58						18 24		18 33			18 53				18 58		
Cheddington	d							18 04															19 06		
Tring	d						17 59	18 10					18 27	18 34							19 00		19 12		
Berkhamsted	d		17 46				18 03	18 15					18 31	18 39		18 46					19 04		19 17		
Hemel Hempstead	d		17 51				18 08	18 19					18 36	18 43		18 51					19 09		19 21		
Apsley	d						18 11						18 39								19 12				
Kings Langley	d						18 14						18 42								19 15				
Watford Junction	a		17 59			18s15	18 19	18 26		18 31			18 46	18 51		18 58				19s16	19 20		19 28		
	d		18 00				18 19	18 27		18 31			18 47	18 51		18 59					19 20		19 29		
Bushey	d						18 22						18 49								19 23				
Harrow & Wealdstone ⊖	d						18 27						18 54	18 59							19 28				
Wembley Central ⊖	d													19u05											
Shepherd's Bush	a													19 18											
Kensington (Olympia) ⊖	a													19 20											
West Brompton ⊖	a													19 23											
Imperial Wharf	a													19 25											
Clapham Junction	d													19a30											
East Croydon	a																								
London Euston 15 ⊖	a		18 18	18 27	18 23	18 34	18 41	18 45	18 38	18 49	18 14		19 09		18 54	19 18	18 59	19 08	19 29	19 34	19 42		19 47	19 23	19 38

		LM	VT	LM	SN	VT	VT		LM	VT	LM	VT	VT	VT	LM	LM	LM		VT	LM	SN	VT	VT	LM	VT
		◇1	◇1	1	1	◇1	◇1		◇1	◇1	◇1	◇1	R 1	◇1	1	1	◇1		◇1	1	1	◇1	◇1	◇1	◇1
													A	B											
			⊠			⊠	⊠			⊠		⊠	☕	⊠					⊠			☕	⊠		⊠
Wolverhampton 7	d												18 45	18 45											
Sandwell & Dudley	d												18 56	18 56											
Birmingham New Street 12	d		17 50			18 30			17 53				19 10	19 10					18 50			19 30		18 53	
Birmingham International ✈	d		18 00			18 40			18 05				19 20	19 20					19 00			19 40		19 05	
Coventry	d		18 11			18 51			18 21				19 31	19 31					19 11			19 51		19 21	
Nuneaton	d	18 02															19 02								
Rugby	d	18 20	18 24						18 32								19 20		19 24					19 32	
Northampton	d	18 50							19 05		19 25						19 51							20 05	
Wolverton	d								19 17		19 37													20 17	
Milton Keynes Central 10	a	19 04				19 18			19 20		19 41						20 05					20 18		20 20	
	d	19 05			19 15	19 19			19 22	19 32	19 41	19 47				19 47	20 09				20 13	20 19		20 22	20 33
Bletchley	d				19 19				19 27		19 46					19 52					20 17			20 27	
Leighton Buzzard	d				19 26				19 33		19 53					19 58					20 24			20 33	
Cheddington	d															20 04									
Tring	d			19 29	19 36										19 56	20 10				20 26	20 34				
Berkhamsted	d			19 33	19 41				19 46						20 00	20 15				20 30	20 39			20 46	
Hemel Hempstead	d			19 38	19 45				19 51						20 05	20 19				20 35	20 43			20 51	
Apsley	d			19 41											20 08					20 38					
Kings Langley	d			19 44											20 11					20 41					
Watford Junction	a	19 31		19 49	19 54				19 59				20s15	20s15	20 16	20 26	20 31			20 46	20 51			20 58	
	d	19 31		19 49	19 54				19 59						20 16	20 27	20 32			20 46	20 51			20 59	
Bushey	d			19 52											20 19					20 49					
Harrow & Wealdstone ⊖	d			19 57	20 02										20 24					20 54	20 59				
Wembley Central ⊖	d				20u06																21u04				
Shepherd's Bush	a				20 21																21 22				
Kensington (Olympia) ⊖	a				20 23																21 24				
West Brompton ⊖	a				20 25																21 27				
Imperial Wharf	a				20 28																21 29				
Clapham Junction	d				20a33																21a34				
East Croydon	a																								
London Euston 15 ⊖	a	19 50	19 14	20 11		19 54	20 02		20 19	20 06	20 27	20 23	20 34	20 34	20 38	20 51	20 49		20 14	21 08		20 54	21 05	21 17	21 06

A from 18 July until 9 September

B until 15 July, from 12 September

Table 66

Mondays to Fridays

West Midlands, Northampton, Milton Keynes Central and Watford Junction - London

		VT	LM		VT	LM	LM	VT	VT	VT	LM	VT	SN		LM	VT	VT	VT	VT	LM	VT	SN	LM		SN
		◇1	◇1		◇1	1	1	◇1	◇1	◇1	1	◇1	1		◇1	◇1	◇1	◇1	◇1	◇1	◇1	1	1		1
		☕			⊠			☕	☕	☕		☕				☕	☕	☕	☕		☕				
Wolverhampton 7 ⇌	d								19 45												20 47				
Sandwell & Dudley	d								19 56												20 57				
Birmingham New Street 12	d	19 50							20 10						19 53	20 50					21 10				
Birmingham International ✈	d	20 00							20 20						20 05	21 00					21 20				
Coventry	d	20 11							20 31						20 21	21 11					21 31				
Nuneaton	d											21 03													
Rugby	d	20 23													20 32	21 23		21 28							
Northampton	d		20 25												21 05					21 37					
Wolverton	d		20 37												21 17					21 49					
Milton Keynes Central 10	a		20 41						20 58						21 20			21 47		21 52	21 58				
	d		20 41		20 46		20 47	20 50	20 59	21 04			21 13		21 22		21 36	21 49	21 52	21 53	21 59		22 05		22 11
Bletchley	d		20 46				20 52						21 17		21 27					21 58			22 10		22 15
Leighton Buzzard	d		20 53				20 58						21 24		21 33					22 04			22 17		22 22
Cheddington	d						21 06													22 10			22 23		
Tring	d					20 56	21 11				21 26		21 34							22 16			22 28		22 34
Berkhamsted	d					21 00	21 16				21 30		21 39		21 46					22 20			22 33		22 39
Hemel Hempstead	d					21 05	21 20				21 35		21 43		21 51					22 25			22 37		22 43
Apsley	d					21 08					21 38												22 41		
Kings Langley	d					21 11					21 41												22 44		
Watford Junction	a					21 16	21 27		21s19		21 46	21s48	21 51		21 58				22s11	22 32	22s20		22 48		22 53
	d					21 16	21 27				21 46		21 51		21 59					22 33		22 27	22 49		22 54
Bushey	d					21 19					21 49												22 51		
Harrow & Wealdstone ⊖	d					21 24					21 54		21 59									22 33	22 57		23 01
Wembley Central ⊖	d																								
Shepherd's Bush	a												22 23									22 49			23 21
Kensington (Olympia) ⊖	a												22 25									22 51			23 23
West Brompton ⊖	a												22 27									22 54			23 26
Imperial Wharf	a												22 30									22 56			23 28
Clapham Junction	d												22a34									23a01			23 40
East Croydon ⇌	a																								00 01
London Euston 15 ⊖	a	21 14	21 29		21 24	21 38	21 46	21 26	21 38	21 42	22 08	22 09			22 20	22 12	22 12	22 22	22 33	22 52	22 43		23 12		

		LM	VT	VT	SN	LM	VT	VT	LM MO		LM MX	VT
		◇1	◇1	◇1	1	◇1	◇1	◇1	◇1		◇1	◇1
			⊠	☕			☕	☕				☕
Wolverhampton 7 ⇌	d							21 45				22 45
Sandwell & Dudley	d							21 56				22 55
Birmingham New Street 12	d	20 53				21 33		22 10				23 10
Birmingham International ✈	d	21 05				21 45		22 20				23 20
Coventry	d	21 21				22 01		22 31				23 31
Nuneaton	d						22 17					
Rugby	d	21 32				22 12	22 34	22 43				23 44
Northampton	d	22 05				22 55			23 30		23 46	00s05
Wolverton	d	22 17				23 07			23 44		23 58	
Milton Keynes Central 10	a	22 20				23 12	22 58	23s05	23 50		00 03	00s23
	d	22 22	22 41	22 53		23 13	22 59		23 50		00 04	
Bletchley	d	22 27				23 18			23 55		00 09	
Leighton Buzzard	d	22 33				23 24			00 02		00 15	
Cheddington	d					23 29			00 08		00 24	
Tring	d					23 38			00 14		00 29	
Berkhamsted	d	22 48				23 43			00 18		00 34	
Hemel Hempstead	d	22 53				23 47			00 22		00 38	
Apsley	d					23 50						
Kings Langley	d					23 53						
Watford Junction	a	23 00	23s14	23s25		23 58	23s30	23s37	00 29		00 45	00s52
	d	23 01			23 29	23 58			00 30		00 46	
Bushey	d					00 01						
Harrow & Wealdstone ⊖	d				23 35	00 06			00 36		00 52	
Wembley Central ⊖	d								00 40		00 56	
Shepherd's Bush	a				23 53							
Kensington (Olympia) ⊖	a				23 56							
West Brompton ⊖	a				23 59							
Imperial Wharf	a				00 02							
Clapham Junction	d				00a07							
East Croydon ⇌	a											
London Euston 15 ⊖	a	23 21	23 38	23 48		00 21	23 56	00 04	00 53		01 09	01 14

Table 66

Saturdays

West Midlands, Northampton, Milton Keynes Central and Watford Junction - London

		SN	SN	LM	VT	LM	VT	LM	LM	SN	LM	SR	SR	LM	VT	SN	LM	LM	LM	VT	VT	VT	VT
												R	R										
		1	1	◇1	◇1	◇1	◇1	1	1	1	◇1			1	◇1	1	◇1	1	1	◇1	◇1	◇1	◇1
												A	B										
												🛏	🛏										
					☕		☕					☕	☕		☕					☕	☕	☕	☕
Wolverhampton 7	d				21p45		22p45													05 45		06 06	
Sandwell & Dudley	d				21p56		22p55													05 56		06 17	
Birmingham New Street 12	d			21p33	22p10		23f10								05 50					06 10		06 30	
Birmingham International	d			21p45	22p20		23p20								06 00					06 20		06 40	
Coventry	d			22p01	22p31		23p31								06 10					06 31		06 51	
Nuneaton	d																						06 59
Rugby	d			22p12	22p43		23p44								06 24						06 51		
Northampton	d			22c55		23p46	00s05				05 16						06 05						
Wolverton	d			23p07		23p58					05 28						06 17						
Milton Keynes Central 10	a			23p12	23e05	00 03	00s23				05 31						06 20			06 58	07 11		
	d	22p11		23p13		00 04		03 40	04 35		05 32						06 22		06 47	06 59	07 12		
Bletchley	d	22p15		23p18		00 09		03 45	04 40		05 37			06 10			06 27	06 40	06 52				
Leighton Buzzard	d	22p22		23p24		00 15		03 51	04 46		05 43			06 17			06 33	06 47	06 58				
Cheddington	d			23p29		00 24					05 49								07 04				
Tring	d	22p34		23p38		00 29		04 03	04 58		05 55			06 26			06 43	06 56	07 10				
Berkhamsted	d	22p39		23p43		00 34		04 08	05 03		06 00			06 31			06 47	07 01	07 15				
Hemel Hempstead	d	22p43		23p47		00 38		04 12	05 07		06 04			06 35			06 52	07 05	07 19				
Apsley	d			23p50							06 07			06 38				07 08					
Kings Langley	d			23p53							06 10			06 41				07 11					
Watford Junction	a	22p53		23p58	23e37	00 45	00s52	04 19	05 14		06 15			06 46			06 59	07 16	07 26	07s19	07s32	07s36	07s44
	d	22p54	23p29	23p58		00 46		04 20	05 15	05 52	06 16			06 47		06 55	07 01	07 17	07 27				
Bushey	d			00 01							06 18			06 49				07 20					
Harrow & Wealdstone ⊖	d	23p01	23p35	00 06		00 52		04 26	05 21	05 58	06 24			06 55		07 01		07 25					
Wembley Central ⊖	d					00 56		04 34	05 25							07 06							
Shepherd's Bush	a	23p21	23p53							06 20						07 19							
Kensington (Olympia) ⊖	a	23p23	23p56							06 22						07 21							
West Brompton ⊖	a	23p26	23p59							06 25						07 24							
Imperial Wharf	a	23p28	00 02							06 28						07 27							
Clapham Junction	d	23b40	00a07							06 34						07 34							
East Croydon	a	00 01								06 57						07 57							
London Euston 15 ⊖	a			00 21	00 04	01 09	01 14	04 46	05 41		06 38	06 50	06 53	07 09	07 16		07 20	07 39	07 45	07 38	07 52	07 55	08 05

		LM	SN	LM	VT	VT	VT	VT	LM	LM	LM	VT	LM	SN	VT	LM	LM	VT	LM	VT	LM	LM	LM
		1	1	◇1	◇1	◇1	◇1	◇1	1	1	◇1	◇1	1	1	◇1	◇1	◇1	◇1	1	◇1	1	◇1	◇1
					☕	☕	☕	☕				☕			☕			☕		☕			
Wolverhampton 7	d					06 27		06 45							07 04					07 44			
Sandwell & Dudley	d					06 37		06 56							07 15					07 56			
Birmingham New Street 12	d					06 50		07 10							07 30					08 10		07 33	
Birmingham International	d					07 00		07 20							07 40					08 20		07 45	
Coventry	d					07 11		07 31							07 52					08 31		08 01	
Nuneaton	d																						08 02
Rugby	d					07 23						07 54										08 12	08 20
Northampton	d			07 05							07 33					08 05	08 25					08 50	
Wolverton	d			07 17							07 45					08 17	08 37						
Milton Keynes Central 10	a			07 20							07 49				08 18	08 20	08 41					09 04	
	d		07 13	07 21	07 32		07 38			07 44	07 49			08 13	08 19	08 22	08 41	08 47			08 47	09 05	
Bletchley	d	07 10	07 17	07 26						07 49	07 54			08 17		08 27	08 46				08 52		
Leighton Buzzard	d	07 17	07 24	07 32						07 55	08 01			08 24		08 33	08 53				08 58		
Cheddington	d									08 01											09 04		
Tring	d	07 26	07 34						07 56	08 07			08 26	08 34					08 56		09 10		
Berkhamsted	d	07 31	07 39	07 45					08 00	08 11			08 30	08 39		08 46			09 00		09 15		
Hemel Hempstead	d	07 35	07 43	07 50					08 05	08 16			08 35	08 43		08 51			09 05		09 19		
Apsley	d	07 38							08 08				08 38						09 08				
Kings Langley	d	07 41							08 11				08 41						09 11				
Watford Junction	a	07 46	07 51	07 57				08s15	08 16	08 23	08 20		08 46	08 51		08 58			09 16	09s17	09 26	09 33	
	d	07 47	07 52	07 59					08 16	08 24	08 20		08 46	08 52		08 59			09 16		09 27	09 34	
Bushey	d	07 49							08 19				08 49						09 19				
Harrow & Wealdstone ⊖	d	07 55	07 59						08 24				08 54	08 59					09 24				
Wembley Central ⊖	d		08u04											09u04									
Shepherd's Bush	a		08 19											09 19									
Kensington (Olympia) ⊖	a		08 21											09 21									
West Brompton ⊖	a		08 24											09 24									
Imperial Wharf	a		08 27											09 27									
Clapham Junction	d		08 34											09 34									
East Croydon	a		08 57											09 57									
London Euston 15 ⊖	a	08 09		08 17	08 09	08 14	08 14	08 34	08 38	08 42	08 38	08 46	09 08		08 54	09 17	09 27	09 23	09 38	09 35	09 45	09 50	

A until 18 June, from 17 September
B from 25 June until 10 September
b Previous night, arr. 2333
c Previous night, arr. 2233
e Previous night, stops to set down only
f Previous night, arr. 2304

Table 66

Saturdays

West Midlands, Northampton, Milton Keynes Central and Watford Junction - London

		VT		LM	SN	VT	VT	LM	LM	VT	VT	LM		LM	VT	LM	VT	LM	SN	VT	VT	LM		LM	VT
		◇1		1	1	◇1	◇1	◇1	◇1	◇1	◇1	1		1	◇1	◇1	◇1	1	1	◇1	◇1	◇1		◇1	◇1
		☕				☕	☕			☕	☕				☕		☕			☕	☕				☕
Wolverhampton 7	d					08 06					08 45														
Sandwell & Dudley	d										08 56														
Birmingham New Street 12	d	07 50				08 30					09 10						08 50			09 30					
Birmingham International	d	08 00				08 40					09 20						09 00			09 40					
Coventry	d	08 11				08 51					09 31						09 11			09 51					
Nuneaton	d						08 59									09 02					09 59				
Rugby	d	08 23														09 20	09 23								
Northampton	d							09 05	09 25							09 50						10 05		10 25	
Wolverton	d							09 17	09 37													10 17		10 37	
Milton Keynes Central 10	a					09 18		09 20	09 41							10 04				10 18		10 20		10 41	
	d				09 13	09 19		09 22	09 41	09 47				09 47	10 02	10 05			10 13	10 19		10 22		10 41	10 47
Bletchley	d				09 17			09 27	09 46					09 52					10 17			10 27		10 46	
Leighton Buzzard	d				09 24			09 33	09 53					09 58					10 24			10 33		10 53	
Cheddington	d													10 04											
Tring	d			09 26	09 34							09 56		10 10				10 26	10 34						
Berkhamsted	d			09 30	09 39			09 46				10 00		10 15				10 30	10 39			10 46			
Hemel Hempstead	d			09 35	09 43			09 51				10 05		10 19				10 35	10 43			10 51			
Apsley	d			09 38								10 08						10 38							
Kings Langley	d			09 41								10 11						10 41							
Watford Junction	a			09 46	09 51			09 58			10s15	10 16		10 26		10 30		10 46	10 51			10 58			
	d			09 46	09 52			09 59				10 16		10 27		10 31		10 46	10 52			10 59			
Bushey	d			09 49								10 19						10 49							
Harrow & Wealdstone ⊖	d			09 54	09 59							10 24						10 54	10 59						
Wembley Central ⊖	d				10u04														11u04						
Shepherd's Bush	a				10 19														11 19						
Kensington (Olympia) ⊖	a				10 21														11 21						
West Brompton ⊖	a				10 24														11 24						
Imperial Wharf	a				10 27														11 27						
Clapham Junction	d				10 34														11 34						
East Croydon	a				10 57														11 57						
London Euston 15 ⊖	a	09 14		10 08		09 55	10 00	10 17	10 27	10 23	10 34	10 38		10 45	10 37	10 49	10 14	11 08		10 54	11 01	11 17		11 27	11 23

		VT	LM	LM	VT	LM	VT	LM		SN	VT	LM	LM	VT	VT	LM	LM	VT		LM	LM	VT	LM	SN	VT
		◇1	1	1	◇1	◇1	◇1	1		1	◇1	◇1	◇1	◇1	◇1	1	1	◇1		◇1	◇1	◇1	1	1	◇1
		☕			☕		☕				☕			☕	☕			☕				☕			☕
Wolverhampton 7	d	09 45													10 45										
Sandwell & Dudley	d	09 56													10 56										
Birmingham New Street 12	d	10 10					09 50				10 30				11 10					10 33		10 50			11 30
Birmingham International	d	10 20					10 00				10 40				11 20					10 45		11 00			11 40
Coventry	d	10 31					10 11				10 51				11 31					11 01		11 11			11 51
Nuneaton	d					10 02															11 02				
Rugby	d					10 20	10 23													11 12	11 20	11 23			
Northampton	d					10 50						11 05	11 25							11 50					
Wolverton	d											11 17	11 37												
Milton Keynes Central 10	a					11 04					11 18	11 20	11 41							12 04					12 17
	d			10 47	11 02	11 05				11 13	11 19	11 22	11 41	11 47			11 47	12 02		12 05				12 13	12 18
Bletchley	d			10 52						11 17		11 27	11 46				11 52							12 17	
Leighton Buzzard	d			10 58						11 24		11 33	11 53				11 58							12 24	
Cheddington	d			11 04													12 04								
Tring	d		10 56	11 10				11 26		11 34						11 56	12 10						12 26	12 34	
Berkhamsted	d		11 00	11 15				11 30		11 39		11 46				12 00	12 15						12 30	12 39	
Hemel Hempstead	d		11 05	11 19				11 35		11 43		11 51				12 05	12 19						12 35	12 43	
Apsley	d		11 08					11 38								12 08							12 38		
Kings Langley	d		11 11					11 41								12 11							12 41		
Watford Junction	a	11s15	11 16	11 26		11 30		11 46		11 51		11 58			12s15	12 16	12 26			12 30			12 46	12 51	
	d		11 16	11 27		11 31		11 46		11 52		11 59				12 16	12 27			12 31			12 46	12 52	
Bushey	d		11 19					11 49								12 19							12 49		
Harrow & Wealdstone ⊖	d		11 24					11 54		11 59						12 24							12 54	12 59	
Wembley Central ⊖	d									12u04														13u04	
Shepherd's Bush	a									12 19														13 19	
Kensington (Olympia) ⊖	a									12 21														13 21	
West Brompton ⊖	a									12 24														13 24	
Imperial Wharf	a									12 27														13 27	
Clapham Junction	d									12 34														13 34	
East Croydon	a									12 57														13 57	
London Euston 15 ⊖	a	11 34	11 38	11 45	11 38	11 49	11 14	12 08			11 54	12 17	12 27	12 23	12 34	12 38	12 45	12 38		12 49		12 14	13 08		12 53

Table 66

Saturdays

West Midlands, Northampton, Milton Keynes Central and Watford Junction - London

		LM ◇1	LM ◇1	VT ◇1 ☕		VT ◇1 ☕	LM 1	LM 1	VT ◇1 ☕	LM ◇1	VT ◇1 ☕	LM 1	SN 1	VT ◇1 ☕		LM ◇1	LM ◇1	VT ◇1 ☕	VT ◇1 ☕	LM 1	LM 1	VT ◇1 ☕	LM ◇1	VT ◇1 ☕
Wolverhampton 7	d					11 45													12 45					
Sandwell & Dudley	d					11 56													12 56					
Birmingham New Street 12	d					12 10					11 50			12 30					13 10					12 50
Birmingham International	d					12 20					12 00			12 40					13 20					13 00
Coventry	d					12 31					12 11			12 51					13 31					13 11
Nuneaton	d									12 02													13 02	
Rugby	d									12 20	12 23												13 20	13 23
Northampton	d	12 05	12 25							12 50						13 05	13 25						13 50	
Wolverton	d	12 17	12 37													13 17	13 37							
Milton Keynes Central 10	a	12 20	12 41							13 04				13 18		13 20	13 41						14 04	
	d	12 22	12 41	12 47				12 47	13 02	13 05			13 13	13 19		13 22	13 41	13 47			13 47	14 02	14 05	
Bletchley	d	12 27	12 46					12 52					13 17			13 27	13 46				13 52			
Leighton Buzzard	d	12 33	12 53					12 58					13 24			13 33	13 53				13 58			
Cheddington	d							13 04													14 04			
Tring	d						12 56	13 10				13 26	13 34							13 56	14 10			
Berkhamsted	d	12 46					13 00	13 15				13 30	13 39			13 46				14 00	14 15			
Hemel Hempstead	d	12 51					13 05	13 19				13 35	13 43			13 51				14 05	14 19			
Apsley	d						13 08					13 38								14 08				
Kings Langley	d						13 11					13 41								14 11				
Watford Junction	a	12 58				13s15	13 16	13 26		13 30		13 46	13 51			13 58			14s15	14 16	14 26		14 30	
	d	12 59					13 16	13 27		13 31		13 46	13 52			13 59				14 16	14 27		14 31	
Bushey	d						13 19					13 49								14 19				
Harrow & Wealdstone ⊖	d						13 24					13 54	13 59							14 24				
Wembley Central ⊖	d												14u04											
Shepherd's Bush	a												14 19											
Kensington (Olympia) ⊖	a												14 21											
West Brompton ⊖	a												14 24											
Imperial Wharf	a												14 27											
Clapham Junction	d												14 34											
East Croydon	a												14 57											
London Euston 15 ⊖	a	13 17	13 27	13 23		13 34	13 38	13 45	13 38	13 49	13 14	14 08		13 54		14 17	14 27	14 23	14 34	14 38	14 45	14 38	14 49	14 14

		LM 1	SN 1	VT ◇1 ☕	LM ◇1	LM ◇1	VT ◇1 ☕	VT ◇1 ☕	LM 1	LM 1		VT ◇1 ☕	LM ◇1	VT ◇1 ☕	LM 1	SN 1	VT ◇1 ☕	LM ◇1	LM ◇1	VT ◇1 ☕		VT ◇1 ☕	LM 1	LM 1	VT ◇1 ☕
Wolverhampton 7	d							13 45														14 45			
Sandwell & Dudley	d							13 56														14 56			
Birmingham New Street 12	d			13 30				14 10						13 50			14 30					15 10			
Birmingham International	d			13 40				14 20						14 00			14 40					15 20			
Coventry	d			13 51				14 31						14 11			14 51					15 31			
Nuneaton	d												14 02												
Rugby	d												14 20	14 23											
Northampton	d				14 05	14 25							14 50					15 05	15 25						
Wolverton	d				14 17	14 37												15 17	15 37						
Milton Keynes Central 10	a			14 18	14 20	14 41							15 04				15 18	15 20	15 41						
	d		14 13	14 19	14 22	14 41	14 47			14 47		15 02	15 05			15 13	15 19	15 22	15 41	15 47				15 47	16 02
Bletchley	d		14 17		14 27	14 46				14 52						15 17		15 27	15 46					15 52	
Leighton Buzzard	d		14 24		14 33	14 53				14 58						15 24		15 33	15 53					15 58	
Cheddington	d									15 04														16 04	
Tring	d	14 26	14 34						14 56	15 10					15 26	15 34							15 56	16 10	
Berkhamsted	d	14 30	14 39		14 46				15 00	15 15					15 30	15 39		15 46					16 00	16 15	
Hemel Hempstead	d	14 35	14 43		14 51				15 05	15 19					15 35	15 43		15 51					16 05	16 19	
Apsley	d	14 38							15 08						15 38								16 08		
Kings Langley	d	14 41							15 11						15 41								16 11		
Watford Junction	a	14 46	14 51		14 58			15s15	15 16	15 26			15 30		15 46	15 51		15 58				16s15	16 16	16 26	
	d	14 46	14 52		14 59				15 16	15 27			15 31		15 46	15 52		15 59					16 16	16 27	
Bushey	d	14 49							15 19						15 49								16 19		
Harrow & Wealdstone ⊖	d	14 54	14 59						15 24						15 54	15 59							16 24		
Wembley Central ⊖	d		15u04													16u04									
Shepherd's Bush	a		15 19													16 19									
Kensington (Olympia) ⊖	a		15 21													16 21									
West Brompton ⊖	a		15 24													16 24									
Imperial Wharf	a		15 27													16 27									
Clapham Junction	d		15 34													16 34									
East Croydon	a		15 57													16 57									
London Euston 15 ⊖	a	15 08		14 54	15 18	15 27	15 23	15 34	15 38	15 45		15 38	15 49	15 14	16 08		15 54	16 18	16 27	16 23		16 34	16 38	16 45	16 38

Table 66

Saturdays

West Midlands, Northampton, Milton Keynes Central and Watford Junction - London

		LM	LM	VT	LM	SN		VT	LM	LM	VT	VT	LM	LM	VT	LM	LM		VT	LM	SN	VT	LM	LM	VT
		◇1	◇1	◇1	1	1		◇1	◇1	◇1	◇1	◇1	1	1	◇1	◇1	◇1		◇1	1	1	◇1	◇1	◇1	◇1
				☕				☕			☕	☕			☕				☕			☕			☕
Wolverhampton 7 🚊	d											15 45													
Sandwell & Dudley	d											15 56													
Birmingham New Street 12	d	14 33		14 50				15 30				16 10				15 33			15 50			16 30			
Birmingham International ✈	d	14 45		15 00				15 40				16 20				15 45			16 00			16 40			
Coventry	d	15 01		15 11				15 51				16 31				16 01			16 11			16 51			
Nuneaton	d		15 02														16 02								
Rugby	d	15 12	15 20	15 23												16 12	16 20		16 23						
Northampton	d	15 50							16 05	16 25						16 50							17 05	17 25	
Wolverton	d								16 17	16 37													17 17	17 37	
Milton Keynes Central 10	a	16 04						16 18	16 20	16 41						17 04						17 18	17 20	17 41	
	d	16 05				16 13		16 19	16 22	16 41	16 47			16 47	17 02	17 05					17 13	17 19	17 22	17 41	17 47
Bletchley	d					16 17			16 27	16 46				16 52							17 17		17 27	17 46	
Leighton Buzzard	d					16 24			16 33	16 53				16 58							17 24		17 33	17 53	
Cheddington	d													17 04											
Tring	d				16 26	16 34							16 56	17 10						17 26	17 34				
Berkhamsted	d				16 30	16 39			16 46				17 00	17 15						17 30	17 39		17 46		
Hemel Hempstead	d				16 35	16 43			16 51				17 05	17 19						17 35	17 43		17 51		
Apsley	d				16 38								17 08							17 38					
Kings Langley	d				16 41								17 11							17 41					
Watford Junction	a	16 30			16 46	16 51			16 58			17s15	17 16	17 26		17 30				17 46	17 51		17 58		
	d	16 31			16 46	16 52			16 59				17 16	17 27		17 31				17 46	17 52		17 59		
Bushey	d				16 49								17 19							17 49					
Harrow & Wealdstone ⊖	d				16 54	16 59							17 24							17 54	17 59				
Wembley Central ⊖	d					17u04															18u04				
Shepherd's Bush	a					17 19															18 19				
Kensington (Olympia) ⊖	a					17 21															18 21				
West Brompton ⊖	a					17 24															18 24				
Imperial Wharf	a					17 27															18 27				
Clapham Junction	d					17 34															18 34				
East Croydon 🚊	a					17 57															18 57				
London Euston 15 ⊖	a	16 49		16 14	17 08	.		16 54	17 17	17 27	17 23	17 34	17 38	17 45	17 38	17 49			17 14	18 08	.	17 52	18 17	18 27	18 23

		VT	LM		LM	VT	LM	LM	VT	LM	SN	VT	LM		VT	VT	LM	LM	LM	LM	VT	SN	LM		SN
		◇1	1		1	◇1	◇1	◇1	◇1	1	1	◇1	◇1		◇1	◇1	1	◇1	◇1	◇1	◇1	1	1		1
		☕				☕			☕			☕			☕	☕					☕				
Wolverhampton 7 🚊	d	16 45														17 45									
Sandwell & Dudley	d	16 56														17 56									
Birmingham New Street 12	d	17 10					16 33		16 50			17 30				18 10			17 33		17 50				
Birmingham International ✈	d	17 20					16 45		17 00			17 40				18 20			17 45		18 00				
Coventry	d	17 31					17 01		17 11			17 51				18 31			18 01		18 11				
Nuneaton	d							17 02												18 02					
Rugby	d						17 12	17 20	17 23										18 12	18 20	18 23				
Northampton	d						17 50						18 05					18 31	18 50						
Wolverton	d												18 17					18 43							
Milton Keynes Central 10	a						18 05					18 18	18 20					18 46	19 04						
	d				17 47	18 02	18 05				18 13	18 19	18 22		18 47			18 47	19 05						19 13
Bletchley	d				17 52						18 17		18 27					18 52							19 17
Leighton Buzzard	d				17 58						18 24		18 33					18 58							19 24
Cheddington	d				18 04													19 04							
Tring	d		17 56		18 10					18 26	18 34						18 56	19 10					19 24		19 34
Berkhamsted	d		18 00		18 15					18 30	18 39		18 46				19 00	19 15					19 28		19 39
Hemel Hempstead	d		18 05		18 19					18 35	18 43		18 51				19 05	19 19					19 33		19 43
Apsley	d		18 08							18 38							19 08						19 36		
Kings Langley	d		18 11							18 41							19 11						19 39		
Watford Junction	a	18s15	18 16		18 26		18 31			18 46	18 51		18 58			19s15	19 16	19 26	19 30				19 44		19 50
	d		18 16		18 27		18 31			18 46	18 52		18 59				19 16	19 27	19 31			19 31	19 44		19 51
Bushey	d		18 19							18 49							19 19						19 47		
Harrow & Wealdstone ⊖	d		18 24							18 54	18 59						19 24					19 38	19 52		19 58
Wembley Central ⊖	d										19u04											19 43			
Shepherd's Bush	a										19 19											19 57			20 19
Kensington (Olympia) ⊖	a										19 21											19 59			20 21
West Brompton ⊖	a										19 24											20 02			20 24
Imperial Wharf	a										19 27											20 05			20 27
Clapham Junction	d										19 34											20a10			20 34
East Croydon 🚊	a										19 57														20 59
London Euston 15 ⊖	a	18 34	18 38	.	18 45	18 38	18 49		18 14	19 08	.	18 54	19 17	.	19 23	19 34	19 38	19 45	19 49		19 14	.	20 06	.	.

Table 66

Saturdays

West Midlands, Northampton, Milton Keynes Central and Watford Junction - London

		VT	VT	LM	VT	LM	LM	VT	VT
		◇1	◇1	◇1	◇1	1	◇1	◇1	◇1
								A	B
		☕	☕		☕			☕	☕
Wolverhampton [7]	d							18 45	18 45
Sandwell & Dudley	d							18 56	18 56
Birmingham New Street [12]	d	18 30	18 50					19 10	19 10
Birmingham International ✈	d	18 40	19 00					19 20	19 20
Coventry	d	18 51	19 11					19 31	19 31
Nuneaton	d								
Rugby	d		19 23					19 44	19 44
Northampton	d			19 05			19 31		
Wolverton	d			19 17			19 43		
Milton Keynes Central [10]	a	19 18		19 20			19 46	20 04	20 05
	d	19 19		19 22	19 47		19 47	20 05	20 07
Bletchley	d			19 27			19 52		
Leighton Buzzard	d			19 33			19 58		
Cheddington	d						20 05		
Tring	d					19 58	20 10		
Berkhamsted	d			19 46		20 02	20 15		
Hemel Hempstead	d			19 51		20 07	20 19		
Apsley	d					20 10			
Kings Langley	d					20 13			
Watford Junction	a			19 58		20 18	20 26	20s31	20s34
	d			20 03		20 19	20 27		
Bushey	d								
Harrow & Wealdstone ⊖	d					20 25			
Wembley Central ⊖	d								
Shepherd's Bush	a								
Kensington (Olympia) ⊖	a								
West Brompton ⊖	a								
Imperial Wharf	a								
Clapham Junction	d								
East Croydon	a								
London Euston [15] ⊖	a	19 54	20 15	20 21	20 25	20 39	20 45	20 52	20 55

		SN	LM	VT	LM	LM	VT	VT	SN	LM	LM	VT	VT	VT	SN
		1	◇1	◇1	◇1	1	◇1	◇1	1	◇1	◇1	◇1	◇1	◇1	1
				☕			☕	☕				☕	☕	☕	
Wolverhampton [7]	d						19 45						20 45		
Sandwell & Dudley	d						19 56						20 56		
Birmingham New Street [12]	d						20 10						21 10		
Birmingham International ✈	d						20 20						21 20		
Coventry	d						20 31						21 31		
Nuneaton	d														
Rugby	d						20 43						21 43		
Northampton	d		20 00		20 30					21 00	21 18				
Wolverton	d		20 12							21 12					
Milton Keynes Central [10]	a		20 15		20 46		21 04			21 15	21 33		22 04		
	d		20 16	20 43	20 47	20 50	21 05	21 11		21 16	21 34	21 52	22 05	22 13	
Bletchley	d		20 21			20 55					21 39				
Leighton Buzzard	d		20 27		20 55						21 45				
Cheddington	d				21 02						21 50				
Tring	d				21 07	21 12					21 57				
Berkhamsted	d					21 17				21 38	22 02				
Hemel Hempstead	d				21 14	21 21				21 42	22 06				
Apsley	d				21 17						22 09				
Kings Langley	d				21 20						22 13				
Watford Junction	a		20 50	21s15	21 25	21 30	21s34			21 49	22 17		22s34	22s42	
	d	20 43	20 51		21 26	21 31			21 43	21 51	22 18				22 48
Bushey	d														
Harrow & Wealdstone ⊖	d	20 50				21 37			21 50						22 55
Wembley Central ⊖	d														
Shepherd's Bush	a	21 07							22 07						23 14
Kensington (Olympia) ⊖	a	21 09							22 09						23 16
West Brompton ⊖	a	21 12							22 12						23 19
Imperial Wharf	a	21 15							22 15						23 21
Clapham Junction	d	21a20							22a20						23a26
East Croydon	a														
London Euston [15] ⊖	a		21 09	21 38	21 44	21 52	21 56	22 00		22 11	22 36	22 44	22 55	23 04	

		LM	VT	SN	LM	LM	LM	LM
		◇1	◇1	1	◇1	◇1	◇1	◇1
					C	D	C	D
			☕					
Wolverhampton [7]	d		21 07					
Sandwell & Dudley	d		21 17					
Birmingham New Street [12]	d		21 30					
Birmingham International ✈	d		21 40					
Coventry	d		21 51					
Nuneaton	d							
Rugby	d		22 03					
Northampton	d	22 05			22 55	22 55	23 30	23 30
Wolverton	d	22 17			23 07	23 07	23 42	23 42
Milton Keynes Central [10]	a	22 20	22 28		23 10	23 10	23 45	23 45
	d	22 21	22 29		23 11	23 11	23 46	23 46
Bletchley	d	22 26			23 16	23 16	23 51	23 51
Leighton Buzzard	d	22 32			23 22	23 22	23 57	23 57
Cheddington	d	22 37			23 27	23 27		
Tring	d	22 46			23 36	23 36		
Berkhamsted	d	22 51			23 41	23 41		
Hemel Hempstead	d	22 55			23 45	23 45		
Apsley	d	22 58			23 49	23 49		
Kings Langley	d	23 02			23 52	23 52		
Watford Junction	a	23 06	23s11		23 56	23 56	00 19	00 19
	d	23 07		23 25	23 57	23 57	00 20	00 20
Bushey	d							
Harrow & Wealdstone ⊖	d	23 13		23 31	00 03	00 03		
Wembley Central ⊖	d							
Shepherd's Bush	a			23 48				
Kensington (Olympia) ⊖	a			23 51				
West Brompton ⊖	a			23 54				
Imperial Wharf	a			23 57				
Clapham Junction	d			00a02				
East Croydon	a							
London Euston [15] ⊖	a	23 27	23 30		00 17	00 20	00 42	00 46

A until 9 July, from 17 September
B from 16 July until 10 September
C from 29 October
D until 22 October

Table 66

Sundays

until 10 July

West Midlands, Northampton, Milton Keynes Central and Watford Junction - London

		LM	LM	LM	LM	LM	LM	LM	SN	LM		LM	VT	SN	LM	VT	VT	VT	LM	VT		VT	SN	LM	VT
		◇1	◇1	1		1	1	◇1	1	◇1		◇1	◇1	1	◇1	◇1	◇1	◇1	◇1	◇1		◇1	1	◇1	◇1
		A	A		🚌								☕			☕	☕	☕		☕		☕			☕
Wolverhampton 7 🚢	d												08 05							09 05					
Sandwell & Dudley	d												08 15							09 15					
Birmingham New Street 12	d												08 30							09 30					
Birmingham International ✈	d												08 40							09 40					
Coventry	d												08 51							09 51					
Nuneaton	d																					09 55			
Rugby	d												09 04							10 04					10 33
Northampton	d	22p55	23p30		06 20			07 53		08 23		08 53			09 30				10 07					10 37	
Wolverton	d	23p07	23p42		06 52			08 07		08 37		09 07			09 44				10 20					10 51	
Milton Keynes Central 10	a	23p10	23p45		07 00			08 10		08 40		09 10	09 37		09 47				10 24	10 37				10 54	11 06
	d	23p11	23p46	06 42		07 11	07 41	08 11		08 41		09 11	09 39		09 48			10 19	10 24	10 39				10 55	11 08
Bletchley	d	23p16	23p51	06 47		07 16	07 46	08 16		08 46		09 16			09 53				10 29					11 00	
Leighton Buzzard	d	23p22	23p57	06 53		07 22	07 52	08 22		08 52		09 22			09 59				10 36					11 06	
Cheddington	d	23p27				07 27		08 27				09 27							10 45						
Tring	d	23p36				07 36		08 36				09 36							10 50						
Berkhamsted	d	23p41		07 08		07 41	08 07	08 41		09 07		09 41			10 14				10 54					11 21	
Hemel Hempstead	d	23p45		07 13		07 45	08 12	08 45		09 12		09 45			10 19				10 59					11 26	
Apsley	d	23p49		07 16			08 15			09 15					10 22									11 29	
Kings Langley	d	23p52		07 19			08 18			09 18					10 25									11 32	
Watford Junction	a	23p56	00 19	07 23		07 52	08 23	08 52		09 23		09 52	10s07		10 30				11 06	11s11		11s16		11 37	11s43
	d	23p57	00 20	07 24		07 53	08 23	08 53	09 17	09 23		09 53		10 17	10 30				11 06				11 22	11 37	
Bushey	d																								
Harrow & Wealdstone ⊖	d	00 03		07 30		07 59	08 29	08 59	09 23	09 29		09 59		10 23	10 36				11 12				11 28	11 43	
Wembley Central ⊖	d																								
Shepherd's Bush	a								09 45					10 45									11 45		
Kensington (Olympia) ⊖	a								09 47					10 47									11 47		
West Brompton ⊖	a								09 50					10 50									11 50		
Imperial Wharf	a								09 53					10 53									11 53		
Clapham Junction	d								09a58					10a58									11a58		
East Croydon 🚢	a																								
London Euston 15 ⊖	a	00 20	00 46	07 47		08 13	08 43	09 13		09 43		10 13	10 28		10 50	10 57	11 02	11 06	11 26	11 31		11 37		11 57	12 05

		VT	LM	VT	LM	VT		VT	SN	LM	VT	VT	LM	VT	VT	VT		LM	VT	VT	VT	SN	LM	LM	LM
		◇1	◇1	◇1	◇1	◇1		◇1	1	1	◇1	◇1	1	◇1	◇1	◇1		◇1	◇1	◇1	◇1	1	◇1	1	1
		☕		☕		☕		☕			☕	☕		☕	☕	☕			☕	☕	☕				
Wolverhampton 7 🚢	d			10 05											11 05					11 45					
Sandwell & Dudley	d			10 15											11 15					11 57					
Birmingham New Street 12	d			10 30											11 30	11 50				12 10					
Birmingham International ✈	d			10 40											11 40	12 00				12 20					
Coventry	d			10 51											11 51	12 11				12 31					
Nuneaton	d					10 56						11 59									12 32				
Rugby	d			11 04				11 33						12 00	12 05	12 25							12 26		
Northampton	d		11 07		11 25													12 25					12 50		
Wolverton	d		11 21		11 37													12 37							
Milton Keynes Central 10	a		11 24	11 37	11 42	11 46		12 06						12 20	12 24			12 40			13 03		13 04		
	d	11 17	11 25	11 39	11 42	11 47		12 07					12 11	12 22	12 26			12 41	12 52		13 04		13 05		13 11
Bletchley	d		11 30		11 47					11 55			12 16					12 46							13 16
Leighton Buzzard	d		11 36		11 54					12 01			12 22					12 52					13 18		13 22
Cheddington	d		11 41							12 07			12 30												13 30
Tring	d		11 50							12 14			12 35											13 15	13 35
Berkhamsted	d		11 55		12 06					12 18			12 40					13 05						13 19	13 40
Hemel Hempstead	d		11 59		12 11					12 23			12 44					13 10						13 24	13 44
Apsley	d									12 26														13 27	
Kings Langley	d									12 29														13 30	
Watford Junction	a		12 06	12s07	12 18					12 34		12s50	12 51					13 17		13s18			13 33	13 35	13 51
	d		12 07		12 18				12 22	12 34			12 52					13 17				13 22	13 33	13 35	13 52
Bushey	d									12 37														13 38	
Harrow & Wealdstone ⊖	d		12 13		12 24				12 29	12 42			12 58					13 23				13 28		13 43	13 58
Wembley Central ⊖	d																								
Shepherd's Bush	a								12 45													13 45			
Kensington (Olympia) ⊖	a								12 47													13 47			
West Brompton ⊖	a								12 50													13 50			
Imperial Wharf	a								12 53													13 53			
Clapham Junction	d								12a58													13a58			
East Croydon 🚢	a																								
London Euston 15 ⊖	a	12 08	12 27	12 27	12 37	12 32		12 45		12 56	12 56	13 11	13 11	12 59	13 04	13 19		13 37	13 28	13 37	13 44		13 53	13 57	14 11

A not 22 May

Table 66

Sundays
until 10 July

West Midlands, Northampton, Milton Keynes Central and Watford Junction - London

		VT		VT	LM	VT	VT	SN	LM	VT	LM	LM		VT	VT	VT	LM	VT	VT	SN	LM	LM		LM	VT
		◇1		◇1	◇1	◇1	◇1	1	◇1	◇1	1	1		◇1	◇1	◇1	◇1	◇1	◇1	1	◇1	1		1	◇1
		☕		☕		☕	☕			☕				☕	☕	☕		☕	☕						☕
Wolverhampton 7	d			12 45												13 45									
Sandwell & Dudley	d			12 55												13 56									
Birmingham New Street 12	d	12 30		13 10						12 50				13 30	13 50	14 10									14 30
Birmingham International ✈	d	12 39		13 20						13 00				13 39	14 01	14 20									14 39
Coventry	d	12 51		13 31						13 11				13 51	14 11	14 31									14 51
Nuneaton	d								12 58										14 32						
Rugby	d								13 17	13 25					14 26						14 26				
Northampton	d				13 25				13 50								14 25				14 50				
Wolverton	d				13 37												14 37								
Milton Keynes Central 10	a	13 18			13 40				14 04					14 18			14 40		15 04		15 04				15 18
	d	13 19			13 41	13 51	14 03		14 05			14 11		14 19			14 41	14 51	15 05		15 05			15 11	15 19
Bletchley	d				13 46							14 16					14 46							15 16	
Leighton Buzzard	d				13 52				14 15			14 22					14 52				15 17			15 22	
Cheddington	d											14 30												15 30	
Tring	d										14 15	14 35										15 15		15 35	
Berkhamsted	d				14 05						14 19	14 40					15 05					15 19		15 40	
Hemel Hempstead	d				14 10						14 24	14 44					15 10					15 24		15 44	
Apsley	d										14 27											15 27			
Kings Langley	d										14 30											15 30			
Watford Junction	a			14s16	14 17				14 33		14 35	14 51				15s16	15 17				15 33	15 35		15 51	
	d				14 17			14 22	14 34		14 35	14 52					15 17			15 22	15 33	15 35		15 52	
Bushey	d										14 38											15 38			
Harrow & Wealdstone ⊖	d				14 23			14 28			14 43	14 58					15 23			15 28		15 43		15 58	
Wembley Central ⊖	d																								
Shepherd's Bush	a							14 45												15 45					
Kensington (Olympia) ⊖	a							14 47												15 47					
West Brompton ⊖	a							14 50												15 50					
Imperial Wharf	a							14 53												15 53					
Clapham Junction	d							14a58												15a58					
East Croydon	a																								
London Euston 15 ⊖	a	13 57		14 37	14 37	14 27	14 43		14 53	14 17	14 57	15 11		14 57	15 17	15 37	15 37	15 27	15 45		15 53	15 57		16 11	15 57

		VT	LM	VT	SN	LM	VT	VT		LM	LM	VT	VT	VT	LM	VT	VT	SN		LM	LM	LM	VT	VT	LM
		◇1	◇1	◇1	1	◇1	◇1	◇1		1	1	◇1	◇1	◇1	◇1	◇1	◇1	1		◇1	1	1	◇1	◇1	◇1
		☕		☕			☕	☕				☕	☕	☕		☕	☕						☕	☕	
Wolverhampton 7	d	14 45												15 45										16 45	
Sandwell & Dudley	d	14 56												15 56										16 56	
Birmingham New Street 12	d	15 10					14 50					15 30	15 50	16 10									16 30	17 10	
Birmingham International ✈	d	15 20					15 01					15 39	16 01	16 20									16 39	17 20	
Coventry	d	15 31					15 11					15 51	16 11	16 31									16 51	17 31	
Nuneaton	d					14 58																			
Rugby	d					15 17	15 26						16 24							16 25					
Northampton	d		15 25			15 50									16 25					16 50					17 25
Wolverton	d		15 37												16 37										17 37
Milton Keynes Central 10	a		15 40			16 04						16 18			16 40					17 04			17 18		17 40
	d		15 41	15 51		16 05		16 05			16 11	16 19			16 41	16 51	17 04			17 05		17 11	17 19		17 41
Bletchley	d		15 46								16 16				16 46							17 16			17 46
Leighton Buzzard	d		15 52			16 17					16 22				16 52					17 17		17 22			17 52
Cheddington	d										16 30											17 30			
Tring	d									16 15	16 35										17 15	17 35			
Berkhamsted	d		16 05							16 19	16 40				17 05						17 19	17 40			18 05
Hemel Hempstead	d		16 10							16 24	16 44				17 10						17 24	17 44			18 10
Apsley	d									16 27											17 27				
Kings Langley	d									16 30											17 30				
Watford Junction	a	16s16	16 17			16 33				16 35	16 51			17s16	17 17					17 33	17 35	17 51		18s16	18 17
	d		16 17		16 22	16 33				16 35	16 52				17 17			17 22		17 33	17 35	17 52			18 17
Bushey	d									16 38											17 38				
Harrow & Wealdstone ⊖	d		16 23		16 28					16 43	16 58				17 23			17 28			17 43	17 58			18 23
Wembley Central ⊖	d																								
Shepherd's Bush	a				16 45													17 45							
Kensington (Olympia) ⊖	a				16 47													17 47							
West Brompton ⊖	a				16 50													17 50							
Imperial Wharf	a				16 53													17 53							
Clapham Junction	d				16a58													17a58							
East Croydon	a																								
London Euston 15 ⊖	a	16 37	16 37	16 27		16 53	16 17	16 44		16 57	17 11	16 57	17 20	17 37	17 37	17 27	17 46			17 53	17 57	18 11	17 57	18 37	18 37

Table 66

Sundays
until 10 July

West Midlands, Northampton, Milton Keynes Central and Watford Junction - London

		VT ◇1 ⊡	SN 1	LM ◇1		VT ◇1 ⊡	VT ◇1 ⊡	LM 1	LM 1	VT ◇1 ⊡	VT ◇1 ⊡	LM ◇1	VT ◇1 ⊡	VT ◇1 ⊡		SN 1	LM ◇1	VT ◇1 ⊡	LM 1	LM 1	VT ◇1 ⊡	VT ◇1 ⊡	LM ◇1	VT ◇1 ⊡	
Wolverhampton 7 ⛴	d										17 45											18 45			
Sandwell & Dudley	d										17 56											18 56			
Birmingham New Street 12	d					16 50				17 30	18 10							17 50			18 30	19 10			
Birmingham International ✈	d					17 01				17 39	18 20							18 01			18 39	19 20			
Coventry	d					17 11				17 51	18 31							18 11			18 51	19 31			
Nuneaton	d			16 58																					
Rugby	d			17 18		17 26											18 24	18 26							
Northampton	d			17 50								18 25					18 50						19 25		
Wolverton	d											18 37											19 37		
Milton Keynes Central 10	a			18 04						18 18		18 40					19 04				19 18		19 40		
	d	17 51		18 05			18 05		18 11	18 19		18 41	18 51	19 03			19 05			19 11	19 19		19 41	19 51	
Bletchley	d								18 16			18 46								19 16			19 46		
Leighton Buzzard	d			18 17					18 22			18 52					19 17			19 22			19 52		
Cheddington	d								18 30											19 30					
Tring	d							18 15	18 35										19 15	19 35					
Berkhamsted	d							18 19	18 40			19 05							19 19	19 40			20 05		
Hemel Hempstead	d							18 24	18 44			19 10							19 24	19 44			20 10		
Apsley	d							18 27											19 27						
Kings Langley	d							18 30											19 30						
Watford Junction	a			18 35				18 35	18 51		19s16	19 17					19 33		19 35	19 51		20s16	20 17		
	d		18 22	18 35				18 35	18 52			19 17				19 22	19 33		19 35	19 52			20 17		
Bushey	d							18 38											19 38						
Harrow & Wealdstone ⊖	d		18 28					18 43	18 58			19 23				19 28			19 43	19 58			20 23		
Wembley Central ⊖	d																								
Shepherd's Bush	a		18 45													19 45									
Kensington (Olympia) ⊖	a		18 47													19 47									
West Brompton ⊖	a		18 50													19 50									
Imperial Wharf	a		18 53													19 53									
Clapham Junction	d		18a58													19a58									
East Croydon ⛴	a																								
London Euston 15 ⊖	a	18 27		18 53		18 17	18 44	18 57	19 11	18 57	19 37	19 37	19 27	19 43			19 53	19 17	19 57	20 11	19 57	20 37	20 37	20 27	

		VT ◇1 ⊡	SN 1	LM ◇1	VT ◇1 ⊡	LM 1	LM 1	VT ◇1 ⊡	SN 1	LM ◇1		VT ◇1 ⊡	VT ◇1 ⊡	LM ◇1	LM 1	VT ◇1 ⊡	VT ◇1 ⊡	SN 1	LM ◇1	VT ◇1 ⊡		VT ◇1 ⊡	LM ◇1	VT ◇1 ⊡	SN 1
Wolverhampton 7 ⛴	d												19 45											21 05	
Sandwell & Dudley	d												19 58											21 17	
Birmingham New Street 12	d				18 50			19 30					20 10			20 30								21 30	
Birmingham International ✈	d				19 01			19 39					20 20			20 40								21 40	
Coventry	d				19 11			19 51					20 31			20 51								21 51	
Nuneaton	d			18 58																			20 58		
Rugby	d			19 18	19 26									20 20		21 05							21 17	22 04	
Northampton	d			19 50						20 25				20 45					21 25				21 53		
Wolverton	d			20 02						20 37				21 02					21 39				22 07		
Milton Keynes Central 10	a			20 06				20 18		20 40				21 05		21 26			21 43				22 10	22 35	
	d	20 04		20 06			20 11	20 19		20 41		20 48		21 05	21 16	21 28	21 38		21 44	21 57		22 04	22 11	22 37	
Bletchley	d						20 16			20 46					21 21				21 49				22 16		
Leighton Buzzard	d			20 16			20 22			20 52				21 15	21 27				21 55				22 22		
Cheddington	d						20 27								21 32								22 27		
Tring	d					20 15	20 36								21 41								22 36		
Berkhamsted	d					20 19	20 41			21 08					21 46				22 08				22 41		
Hemel Hempstead	d					20 24	20 45			21 12					21 50				22 13				22 45		
Apsley	d					20 27				21 15									22 16						
Kings Langley	d					20 30				21 19									22 19						
Watford Junction	a			20 33		20 35	20 52			21 23			21s28	21 34	21 57	22s02			22 24	22s31			22 52	23s05	
	d		20 22	20 33		20 35	20 53		21 17	21 24				21 34	21 58			22 17	22 24				22 53		23 17
Bushey	d					20 38																			
Harrow & Wealdstone ⊖	d		20 28			20 43	20 59		21 23	21 30					22 04			22 23	22 30				22 59		23 23
Wembley Central ⊖	d																								
Shepherd's Bush	a		20 45						21 45									22 45							23 45
Kensington (Olympia) ⊖	a		20 47						21 47									22 47							23 47
West Brompton ⊖	a		20 50						21 50									22 50							23 50
Imperial Wharf	a		20 53						21 53									22 53							23 53
Clapham Junction	d		20a58						21a58									22a58							00 05
East Croydon ⛴	a																								00 22
London Euston 15 ⊖	a	20 44		20 53	20 17	20 58	21 15	20 57		21 44		21 31	21 48	21 55	22 18	22 23	22 28		22 44	22 53		22 56	23 14	23 25	

Table 66

West Midlands, Northampton, Milton Keynes Central and Watford Junction - London

Sundays
until 10 July

		LM	VT	VT	LM	VT	VT
		◇ 1	◇ 1	◇ 1	◇ 1	◇ 1	◇ 1
			☕	☕		☕	☕
Wolverhampton [7]	d					22 05	22 37
Sandwell & Dudley	d					22 15	22 47
Birmingham New Street [12]	d					22 30	23 00
Birmingham International ✈	d					22 40	23 10
Coventry	d					22 51	23 21
Nuneaton	d			22 18			
Rugby	d			22 32		23 04	23 34
Northampton	d	22 25			22 55		23s53
Wolverton	d	22 37			23 11		
Milton Keynes Central [10]	a	22 40		23 04	23 14	23 36	00s12
	d	22 41	22 47	23 05	23 15	23 37	
Bletchley	d	22 46			23 20		
Leighton Buzzard	d	22 52			23 26		
Cheddington	d				23 31		
Tring	d				23 40		
Berkhamsted	d	23 06			23 45		
Hemel Hempstead	d	23 11			23 49		
Apsley	d	23 14					
Kings Langley	d	23 17					
Watford Junction	a	23 22	23s26	23s34	23 56	00s06	00s42
	d	23 22			23 57		
Bushey	d						
Harrow & Wealdstone	d	23 28			00 03		
Wembley Central	d						
Shepherd's Bush	a						
Kensington (Olympia)	a						
West Brompton	a						
Imperial Wharf	a						
Clapham Junction	d						
East Croydon	a						
London Euston [15]	a	23 42	23 48	23 54	00 17	00 26	01 04

Sundays
17 July to 11 September

		LM	LM	LM	LM	LM	LM	LM	SN	LM	LM	VT	SN	LM	VT	VT	VT	LM	VT	VT	SN	LM	VT
		◇ 1	◇ 1	1		1	1	◇ 1	1	◇ 1	◇ 1	◇ 1	1	◇ 1	◇ 1	◇ 1	◇ 1	◇ 1	◇ 1	◇ 1	1	◇ 1	◇ 1
					🚌							☕			☕	☕	☕		☕	☕			☕
Wolverhampton [7]	d											08 05							09 05				
Sandwell & Dudley	d											08 15							09 15				
Birmingham New Street [12]	d											08 30							09 30				
Birmingham International ✈	d											08 40							09 40				
Coventry	d											08 51							09 51				
Nuneaton	d																			09 55			
Rugby	d											09 04							10 04				10 33
Northampton	d	22p55	23p30		06 20			07 53		08 23	08 53			09 30				10 07				10 37	
Wolverton	d	23p07	23p42		06 52			08 07		08 37	09 07			09 44				10 20				10 51	
Milton Keynes Central [10]	a	23p10	23p45		07 00			08 10		08 40	09 10	09 37		09 47				10 24	10 37			10 54	11 06
	d	23p11	23p46	06 42		07 11	07 41	08 11		08 41	09 11	09 39		09 48			10 19	10 24	10 39			10 55	11 08
Bletchley	d	23p16	23p51	06 47		07 16	07 46	08 16		08 46	09 16			09 53				10 29				11 00	
Leighton Buzzard	d	23p22	23p57	06 53		07 22	07 52	08 22		08 52	09 22			09 59				10 36				11 06	
Cheddington	d	23p27				07 27		08 27			09 27							10 45					
Tring	d	23p36				07 36		08 36			09 36							10 50					
Berkhamsted	d	23p41		07 08		07 41	08 07	08 41		09 07	09 41			10 14				10 54				11 21	
Hemel Hempstead	d	23p45		07 13		07 45	08 12	08 45		09 12	09 45			10 19				10 59				11 26	
Apsley	d	23p49		07 16			08 15			09 15				10 22								11 29	
Kings Langley	d	23p52		07 19			08 18			09 18				10 25								11 32	
Watford Junction	a	23p56	00 19	07 23		07 52	08 23	08 52		09 23	09 52	10s07		10 30				11 06	11s11	11s16		11 37	11s43
	d	23p57	00 20	07 24		07 53	08 23	08 53	09 17	09 23	09 53		10 17	10 30				11 06			11 22	11 37	
Bushey	d																						
Harrow & Wealdstone	d	00 03		07 30		07 59	08 29	08 59	09 23	09 29	09 59		10 23	10 36				11 12			11 28	11 43	
Wembley Central	d																						
Shepherd's Bush	a								09 45				10 45								11 45		
Kensington (Olympia)	a								09 47				10 47								11 47		
West Brompton	a								09 50				10 50								11 50		
Imperial Wharf	a								09 53				10 53								11 53		
Clapham Junction	d								09a58				10a58								11a58		
East Croydon	a																						
London Euston [15]	a	00 20	00 46	07 47		08 13	08 43	09 13		09 43	10 13	10 28		10 50	10 57	11 02	11 06	11 26	11 31	11 37		11 57	12 05

Table 66

Sundays

17 July to 11 September

West Midlands, Northampton, Milton Keynes Central and Watford Junction - London

		VT	LM	VT	LM	VT		VT	SN	LM	VT	VT	LM	VT	VT	VT		LM	VT	VT	VT	SN	LM	LM	LM
		◇1 ☕	◇1	◇1 ☕	◇1	◇1 ☕		◇1 ☕	1	1	◇1 ☕	◇1 ☕	1	◇1 ☕	◇1 ☕	◇1 ☕		◇1	◇1 ☕	◇1 ☕	◇1 ☕	1	◇1	1	1
Wolverhampton 7	d			10 05											11 05					11 45					
Sandwell & Dudley	d			10 15											11 15					11 57					
Birmingham New Street 12	d			10 30											11 30	11 50				12 10					
Birmingham International ✈	d			10 40											11 40	12 00				12 20					
Coventry	d			10 51											11 51	12 11				12 31					
Nuneaton	d					10 56						11 59									12 32				
Rugby	d			11 04				11 33						12 00	12 05	12 25							12 26		
Northampton	d		11 07		11 25													12 25					12 50		
Wolverton	d		11 21		11 37													12 37							
Milton Keynes Central 10	a		11 24	11 37	11 42	11 46		12 06						12 20	12 24			12 40			13 03		13 04		
	d	11 17	11 25	11 39	11 42	11 47		12 07					12 11	12 22	12 26			12 41	12 52		13 04		13 05		13 11
Bletchley	d		11 30		11 47					11 55			12 16					12 46							13 16
Leighton Buzzard	d		11 36		11 54					12 01			12 22					12 52					13 18		13 22
Cheddington	d		11 41							12 07			12 30												13 30
Tring	d		11 50							12 14			12 35											13 15	13 35
Berkhamsted	d		11 55		12 06					12 18			12 40					13 05						13 19	13 40
Hemel Hempstead	d		11 59		12 11					12 23			12 44					13 10						13 24	13 44
Apsley	d									12 26														13 27	
Kings Langley	d									12 29														13 30	
Watford Junction	a		12 06	12s07	12 18					12 34		12s50	12 51					13 17		13s18			13 33	13 35	13 51
	d		12 07		12 18				12 22	12 34			12 52					13 17				13 22	13 33	13 35	13 52
Bushey	d									12 37														13 38	
Harrow & Wealdstone ⊖	d		12 13		12 24				12 29	12 42			12 58					13 23				13 28		13 43	13 58
Wembley Central ⊖	d																								
Shepherd's Bush	a								12 45													13 45			
Kensington (Olympia) ⊖	a								12 47													13 47			
West Brompton ⊖	a								12 50													13 50			
Imperial Wharf	a								12 53													13 53			
Clapham Junction	d								12a58													13a58			
East Croydon	a																								
London Euston 15 ⊖	a	12 08	12 27	12 27	12 37	12 32		12 45		12 56	12 56	13 11	13 11	12 59	13 04	13 19		13 37	13 28	13 37	13 44		13 53	13 57	14 11

		VT		VT	LM	VT	VT	SN	LM	VT	LM	LM		VT	VT	VT	LM	VT	VT	SN	LM	LM		LM	VT
		◇1 ☕		◇1 ☕	◇1	◇1 ☕	◇1 ☕	1	◇1	◇1 ☕	1	1		◇1 ☕	◇1 ☕	◇1 ☕	◇1	◇1 ☕	◇1 ☕	1	◇1	1		1	◇1 ☕
Wolverhampton 7	d			12 45												13 45									
Sandwell & Dudley	d			12 55												13 56									
Birmingham New Street 12	d	12 30		13 10						12 50				13 30	13 50	14 10									14 30
Birmingham International ✈	d	12 39		13 20						13 00				13 39	14 01	14 20									14 39
Coventry	d	12 51		13 31						13 11				13 51	14 11	14 31									14 51
Nuneaton	d								12 58										14 32						
Rugby	d								13 17	13 25					14 26						14 26				
Northampton	d				13 25				13 50								14 25				14 50				
Wolverton	d				13 37												14 37								
Milton Keynes Central 10	a	13 18			13 40				14 04					14 18			14 40		15 04		15 04				15 18
	d	13 19			13 41	13 51	14 03		14 05			14 11		14 19			14 41	14 51	15 05		15 05			15 11	15 19
Bletchley	d				13 46							14 16					14 46							15 16	
Leighton Buzzard	d				13 52				14 15			14 22					14 52				15 17			15 22	
Cheddington	d											14 30												15 30	
Tring	d										14 15	14 35										15 15		15 35	
Berkhamsted	d				14 05						14 19	14 40					15 05					15 19		15 40	
Hemel Hempstead	d				14 10						14 24	14 44					15 10					15 24		15 44	
Apsley	d										14 27											15 27			
Kings Langley	d										14 30											15 30			
Watford Junction	a			14s16	14 17				14 33		14 35	14 51				15s16	15 17				15 33	15 35		15 51	
	d				14 17			14 22	14 34		14 35	14 52					15 17			15 22	15 33	15 35		15 52	
Bushey	d										14 38											15 38			
Harrow & Wealdstone ⊖	d				14 23			14 28			14 43	14 58					15 23			15 28		15 43		15 58	
Wembley Central ⊖	d																								
Shepherd's Bush	a							14 45												15 45					
Kensington (Olympia) ⊖	a							14 47												15 47					
West Brompton ⊖	a							14 50												15 50					
Imperial Wharf	a							14 53												15 53					
Clapham Junction	d							14a58												15a58					
East Croydon	a																								
London Euston 15 ⊖	a	13 57		14 37	14 37	14 27	14 43		14 53	14 18	14 57	15 11		14 57	15 17	15 37	15 37	15 27	15 45		15 53	15 57		16 11	15 57

Table 66

Sundays

17 July to 11 September

West Midlands, Northampton, Milton Keynes Central and Watford Junction - London

		VT	LM	VT	SN	LM	VT	VT		LM	LM	VT	VT	VT	LM	VT	VT	SN		LM	LM	LM	VT	VT	LM
		◇1	◇1	◇1	1	◇1	◇1	◇1		1	1	◇1	◇1	◇1	◇1	◇1	◇1	1		◇1	1	1	◇1	◇1	◇1
		☕		☕			☕	☕				☕	☕	☕		☕	☕						☕	☕	
Wolverhampton 7 🚌	d	14 45												15 45										16 45	
Sandwell & Dudley	d	14 56												15 56										16 56	
Birmingham New Street 12	d	15 10					14 50					15 30	15 50	16 10									16 30	17 10	
Birmingham International ✈	d	15 20					15 01					15 39	16 01	16 20									16 39	17 20	
Coventry	d	15 31					15 11					15 51	16 11	16 31									16 51	17 31	
Nuneaton	d					14 58																			
Rugby	d					15 17	15 26						16 24							16 25					
Northampton	d		15 25			15 50									16 25					16 50					17 25
Wolverton	d		15 37												16 37										17 37
Milton Keynes Central 10	a		15 40			16 04						16 18			16 40					17 04			17 18		17 40
	d		15 41	15 51		16 05		16 05			16 11	16 19			16 41	16 51	17 04			17 05		17 11	17 19		17 41
Bletchley	d		15 46								16 16				16 46							17 16			17 46
Leighton Buzzard	d		15 52			16 17					16 22				16 52					17 17		17 22			17 52
Cheddington	d										16 30											17 30			
Tring	d									16 15	16 35										17 15	17 35			
Berkhamsted	d		16 05							16 19	16 40				17 05						17 19	17 40			18 05
Hemel Hempstead	d		16 10							16 24	16 44				17 10						17 24	17 44			18 10
Apsley	d									16 27											17 27				
Kings Langley	d									16 30											17 30				
Watford Junction	a	16s16	16 17			16 33				16 35	16 51			17s16	17 17					17 33	17 35	17 51		18s16	18 17
	d		16 17		16 22	16 33				16 35	16 52				17 17			17 22		17 33	17 35	17 52			18 17
Bushey	d									16 38											17 38				
Harrow & Wealdstone ⊖	d		16 23		16 28					16 43	16 58				17 23			17 28			17 43	17 58			18 23
Wembley Central ⊖	d																								
Shepherd's Bush	a				16 45													17 45							
Kensington (Olympia) ⊖	a				16 47													17 47							
West Brompton ⊖	a				16 50													17 50							
Imperial Wharf	a				16 53													17 53							
Clapham Junction	d				16a58													17a58							
East Croydon 🚌	a																								
London Euston 15 ⊖	a	16 37	16 37	16 27		16 53	16 17	16 44		16 57	17 11	16 57	17 20	17 37	17 37	17 27	17 46			17 53	17 57	18 11	17 57	18 37	18 37

		VT	SN	LM		VT	VT	LM	LM	VT	VT	LM	VT	VT		SN	LM	VT	LM	LM	VT	VT	LM	VT	
		◇1	1	◇1		◇1	◇1	1	1	◇1	◇1	◇1	◇1	◇1		1	◇1	◇1	1	1	◇1	◇1	◇1	◇1	
		☕				☕	☕			☕	☕		☕	☕				☕			☕	☕		☕	
Wolverhampton 7 🚌	d										17 45											18 45			
Sandwell & Dudley	d										17 56											18 56			
Birmingham New Street 12	d					16 50				17 30	18 10							17 50			18 30	19 10			
Birmingham International ✈	d					17 01				17 39	18 20							18 01			18 39	19 20			
Coventry	d					17 11				17 51	18 31							18 11			18 51	19 31			
Nuneaton	d			16 58																					
Rugby	d			17 18		17 26											18 24	18 26							
Northampton	d			17 50								18 25					18 50						19 25		
Wolverton	d											18 37											19 37		
Milton Keynes Central 10	a			18 04						18 18		18 40					19 04				19 18		19 40		
	d	17 51		18 05			18 05		18 11	18 19		18 41	18 51	19 03			19 05			19 11	19 19		19 41	19 51	
Bletchley	d								18 16			18 46								19 16			19 46		
Leighton Buzzard	d			18 17					18 22			18 52					19 17			19 22			19 52		
Cheddington	d								18 30											19 30					
Tring	d							18 15	18 35										19 15	19 35					
Berkhamsted	d							18 19	18 40			19 05							19 19	19 40			20 05		
Hemel Hempstead	d							18 24	18 44			19 10							19 24	19 44			20 10		
Apsley	d							18 27											19 27						
Kings Langley	d							18 30											19 30						
Watford Junction	a			18 35				18 35	18 51		19s16	19 17					19 33		19 35	19 51		20s16	20 17		
	d		18 22	18 35				18 35	18 52			19 17				19 22	19 33		19 35	19 52			20 17		
Bushey	d							18 38											19 38						
Harrow & Wealdstone ⊖	d		18 28					18 43	18 58			19 23				19 28			19 43	19 58			20 23		
Wembley Central ⊖	d																								
Shepherd's Bush	a		18 45													19 45									
Kensington (Olympia) ⊖	a		18 47													19 47									
West Brompton ⊖	a		18 50													19 50									
Imperial Wharf	a		18 53													19 53									
Clapham Junction	d		18a58													19a58									
East Croydon 🚌	a																								
London Euston 15 ⊖	a	18 27		18 53		18 18	18 44	18 57	19 11	18 57	19 37	19 37	19 27	19 43			19 53	19 17	19 57	20 11	19 57	20 37	20 37	20 27	

Table 66

Sundays

17 July to 11 September

West Midlands, Northampton, Milton Keynes Central and Watford Junction - London

		VT	SN	LM	VT	LM	LM	VT	SN	LM		VT	VT	LM	LM	VT	VT	SN	LM	VT		VT	LM	VT	SN
		◇1	1	◇1	◇1	1	1	◇1	1	◇1		◇1	◇1	◇1	1	◇1	◇1	1	◇1	◇1		◇1	◇1	◇1	1
		☕			☕			☕				☕	☕			☕	☕			☕		☕		☕	
Wolverhampton 7 ⛴	d												19 45											21 05	
Sandwell & Dudley	d												19 58											21 17	
Birmingham New Street 12	d				18 50			19 30					20 10			20 30								21 30	
Birmingham International ✈	d				19 01			19 39					20 20			20 40								21 40	
Coventry	d				19 11			19 51					20 31			20 51								21 51	
Nuneaton	d			18 58																			20 58		
Rugby	d			19 18	19 26									20 20		21 05							21 17	22 04	
Northampton	d			19 50						20 25				20 45					21 25				21 53		
Wolverton	d			20 02						20 37				21 02					21 39				22 07		
Milton Keynes Central 10	a			20 06				20 18		20 40				21 05		21 26			21 43				22 10	22 35	
	d	20 04		20 06			20 11	20 19		20 41		20 48		21 05	21 16	21 28	21 38		21 44	21 57		22 04	22 11	22 37	
Bletchley	d						20 16			20 46					21 21				21 49				22 16		
Leighton Buzzard	d			20 16			20 22			20 52				21 15	21 27				21 55				22 22		
Cheddington	d						20 27								21 32								22 27		
Tring	d					20 15	20 36								21 41								22 36		
Berkhamsted	d					20 19	20 41			21 08					21 46				22 08				22 41		
Hemel Hempstead	d					20 24	20 45			21 12					21 50				22 13				22 45		
Apsley	d					20 27				21 15									22 16						
Kings Langley	d					20 30				21 19									22 19						
Watford Junction	a			20 33		20 35	20 52			21 23			21s28	21 34	21 57	22s02			22 24	22s31			22 52	23s05	
	d		20 22	20 33		20 35	20 53		21 17	21 24				21 34	21 58			22 17	22 24				22 53		23 17
Bushey	d					20 38																			
Harrow & Wealdstone ⊖	d		20 28			20 43	20 59		21 23	21 30					22 04			22 23	22 30				22 59		23 23
Wembley Central ⊖	d																								
Shepherd's Bush	a		20 45						21 45									22 45							23 45
Kensington (Olympia) ⊖	a		20 47						21 47									22 47							23 47
West Brompton ⊖	a		20 50						21 50									22 50							23 50
Imperial Wharf	a		20 53						21 53									22 53							23 53
Clapham Junction	d		20a58						21a58									22a58							00 05
East Croydon ⛴	a																								00 22
London Euston 15 ⊖	a	20 44		20 53	20 17	20 58	21 15	20 57		21 44		21 31	21 48	21 55	22 18	22 23	22 28		22 44	22 53		22 56	23 14	23 25	

		LM	VT	VT	LM	VT		VT
		◇1	◇1	◇1	◇1	◇1		◇1
			☕	☕		☕		☕
Wolverhampton 7 ⛴	d					22 05		22 37
Sandwell & Dudley	d					22 15		22 47
Birmingham New Street 12	d					22 30		23 00
Birmingham International ✈	d					22 40		23 10
Coventry	d					22 51		23 21
Nuneaton	d			22 18				
Rugby	d			22 32		23 04		23 34
Northampton	d	22 25			22 55			23s53
Wolverton	d	22 37			23 11			
Milton Keynes Central 10	a	22 40		23 04	23 14	23 36		00s12
	d	22 41	22 47	23 05	23 15	23 37		
Bletchley	d	22 46			23 20			
Leighton Buzzard	d	22 52			23 26			
Cheddington	d				23 31			
Tring	d				23 40			
Berkhamsted	d	23 06			23 45			
Hemel Hempstead	d	23 11			23 49			
Apsley	d	23 14						
Kings Langley	d	23 17						
Watford Junction	a	23 22	23s26	23s34	23 56	00s06		00s42
	d	23 22			23 57			
Bushey	d							
Harrow & Wealdstone ⊖	d	23 28			00 03			
Wembley Central ⊖	d							
Shepherd's Bush	a							
Kensington (Olympia) ⊖	a							
West Brompton ⊖	a							
Imperial Wharf	a							
Clapham Junction	d							
East Croydon ⛴	a							
London Euston 15 ⊖	a	23 42	23 48	23 54	00 17	00 26		01 04

Table 66

Sundays

18 September to 23 October

West Midlands, Northampton, Milton Keynes Central and Watford Junction - London

		LM	LM	LM	LM	LM	LM	LM	SN	LM		LM	VT	SN	LM	VT	VT	VT	LM	VT		VT	SN	LM	VT
		◇1	◇1	1	🚌	1	1	◇1	1	◇1		◇1	◇1 ☕	1	◇1	◇1 ☕	◇1 ☕	◇1 ☕	◇1	◇1 ☕		◇1 ☕	1	◇1	◇1 ☕
Wolverhampton 7	d												08 05							09 05					
Sandwell & Dudley	d												08 15							09 15					
Birmingham New Street 12	d												08 30							09 30					
Birmingham International ✈	d												08 40							09 40					
Coventry	d												08 51							09 51					
Nuneaton	d																					09 55			
Rugby	d												09 04							10 04					10 33
Northampton	d	22p55	23p30		06 20			07 53		08 23		08 53			09 30				10 07					10 37	
Wolverton	d	23p07	23p42		06 52			08 07		08 37		09 07			09 44				10 20					10 51	
Milton Keynes Central 10	a	23p10	23p45		07 00			08 10		08 40		09 10	09 37		09 47				10 24	10 37				10 54	11 06
	d	23p11	23p46	06 42		07 11	07 41	08 11		08 41		09 11	09 39		09 48			10 19	10 24	10 39				10 55	11 08
Bletchley	d	23p16	23p51	06 47		07 16	07 46	08 16		08 46		09 16			09 53				10 29					11 00	
Leighton Buzzard	d	23p22	23p57	06 53		07 22	07 52	08 22		08 52		09 22			09 59				10 36					11 06	
Cheddington	d	23p27				07 27		08 27				09 27							10 45						
Tring	d	23p36				07 36		08 36				09 36							10 50						
Berkhamsted	d	23p41		07 08		07 41	08 07	08 41		09 07		09 41			10 14				10 54					11 21	
Hemel Hempstead	d	23p45		07 13		07 45	08 12	08 45		09 12		09 45			10 19				10 59					11 26	
Apsley	d	23p49		07 16			08 15			09 15					10 22									11 29	
Kings Langley	d	23p52		07 19			08 18			09 18					10 25									11 32	
Watford Junction	a	23p56	00 19	07 23		07 52	08 23	08 52		09 23		09 52	10s07		10 30				11 06	11s11		11s16		11 37	11s43
	d	23p57	00 20	07 24		07 53	08 23	08 53	09 17	09 23		09 53		10 17	10 30				11 06				11 22	11 37	
Bushey	d																								
Harrow & Wealdstone ⊖	d	00 03		07 30		07 59	08 29	08 59	09 23	09 29		09 59		10 23	10 36				11 12				11 28	11 43	
Wembley Central ⊖	d																								
Shepherd's Bush	a								09 45					10 45									11 45		
Kensington (Olympia) ⊖	a								09 47					10 47									11 47		
West Brompton ⊖	a								09 50					10 50									11 50		
Imperial Wharf	a								09 53					10 53									11 53		
Clapham Junction	d								09a58					10a58									11a58		
East Croydon	a																								
London Euston 15 ⊖	a	00 20	00 46	07 47		08 13	08 43	09 13		09 43		10 13	10 28		10 50	10 57	11 02	11 06	11 26	11 31		11 37		11 57	12 05

		VT	LM	VT	LM	VT		VT	SN	LM	VT	VT	LM	VT	VT	VT		LM	VT	VT	VT	SN	LM	LM	LM
		◇1 ☕	◇1	◇1 ☕	◇1	◇1 ☕		◇1 ☕	1	1	◇1 ☕	◇1 ☕	1	◇1 ☕	◇1 ☕	◇1 ☕		◇1	◇1 ☕	◇1 ☕	◇1 ☕	1	◇1	1	1
Wolverhampton 7	d			10 05											11 05					11 45					
Sandwell & Dudley	d			10 15											11 15					11 57					
Birmingham New Street 12	d			10 30											11 30	11 50				12 10					
Birmingham International ✈	d			10 40											11 40	12 00				12 20					
Coventry	d			10 51											11 51	12 11				12 31					
Nuneaton	d					10 56						11 59									12 32				
Rugby	d			11 04				11 33						12 00	12 05	12 25							12 26		
Northampton	d		11 07		11 25													12 25					12 50		
Wolverton	d		11 21		11 37													12 37							
Milton Keynes Central 10	a		11 24	11 37	11 42	11 46		12 06						12 20	12 24			12 40			13 03		13 04		
	d	11 17	11 25	11 39	11 42	11 47		12 07					12 11	12 22	12 26			12 41	12 52		13 04		13 05		13 11
Bletchley	d		11 30		11 47					11 55			12 16					12 46							13 16
Leighton Buzzard	d		11 36		11 54					12 01			12 22					12 52					13 18		13 22
Cheddington	d		11 41							12 07			12 30												13 30
Tring	d		11 50							12 14			12 35											13 15	13 35
Berkhamsted	d		11 55		12 06					12 18			12 40					13 05						13 19	13 40
Hemel Hempstead	d		11 59		12 11					12 23			12 44					13 10						13 24	13 44
Apsley	d									12 26														13 27	
Kings Langley	d									12 29														13 30	
Watford Junction	a		12 06	12s07	12 18					12 34		12s50	12 51					13 17		13s18			13 33	13 35	13 51
	d		12 07		12 18				12 22	12 34			12 52					13 17				13 22	13 33	13 35	13 52
Bushey	d									12 37														13 38	
Harrow & Wealdstone ⊖	d		12 13		12 24				12 29	12 42			12 58					13 23				13 28		13 43	13 58
Wembley Central ⊖	d																								
Shepherd's Bush	a								12 45													13 45			
Kensington (Olympia) ⊖	a								12 47													13 47			
West Brompton ⊖	a								12 50													13 50			
Imperial Wharf	a								12 53													13 53			
Clapham Junction	d								12a58													13a58			
East Croydon	a																								
London Euston 15 ⊖	a	12 08	12 27	12 27	12 37	12 32		12 45		12 56	12 56	13 11	13 11	12 59	13 04	13 19		13 37	13 28	13 37	13 44		13 53	13 57	14 11

Table 66

Sundays

18 September to 23 October

West Midlands, Northampton, Milton Keynes Central and Watford Junction - London

		VT ◇1 ☕		VT ◇1 ☕	LM ◇1	VT ◇1 ☕	VT ◇1 ☕	SN 1	LM ◇1	VT ◇1 ☕	LM 1	LM 1		VT ◇1 ☕	VT ◇1 ☕	VT ◇1 ☕	LM ◇1	VT ◇1 ☕	VT ◇1 ☕	SN 1	LM ◇1	LM 1		LM 1	VT ◇1 ☕
Wolverhampton 7	d			12 45												13 45									
Sandwell & Dudley	d			12 55												13 56									
Birmingham New Street 12	d	12 30		13 10						12 50				13 30	13 50	14 10									14 30
Birmingham International	d	12 39		13 20						13 00				13 39	14 01	14 20									14 39
Coventry	d	12 51		13 31						13 11				13 51	14 11	14 31									14 51
Nuneaton	d								12 58										14 32						
Rugby	d								13 17	13 25					14 26						14 26				
Northampton	d				13 25				13 50								14 25				14 50				
Wolverton	d				13 37												14 37								
Milton Keynes Central 10	a	13 18			13 40				14 04					14 18			14 40		15 04		15 04				15 18
	d	13 19			13 41	13 51	14 03		14 05			14 11		14 19			14 41	14 51	15 05		15 05			15 11	15 19
Bletchley	d				13 46							14 16					14 46							15 16	
Leighton Buzzard	d				13 52				14 15			14 22					14 52				15 17			15 22	
Cheddington	d											14 30												15 30	
Tring	d										14 15	14 35										15 15		15 35	
Berkhamsted	d				14 05						14 19	14 40					15 05					15 19		15 40	
Hemel Hempstead	d				14 10						14 24	14 44					15 10					15 24		15 44	
Apsley	d										14 27											15 27			
Kings Langley	d										14 30											15 30			
Watford Junction	a			14s16	14 17				14 33		14 35	14 51				15s16	15 17				15 33	15 35		15 51	
	d				14 17			14 22	14 34		14 35	14 52					15 17			15 22	15 33	15 35		15 52	
Bushey	d										14 38											15 38			
Harrow & Wealdstone ⊖	d				14 23			14 28			14 43	14 58					15 23			15 28		15 43		15 58	
Wembley Central ⊖	d																								
Shepherd's Bush	a							14 45												15 45					
Kensington (Olympia) ⊖	a							14 47												15 47					
West Brompton ⊖	a							14 50												15 50					
Imperial Wharf	a							14 53												15 53					
Clapham Junction	d							14a58												15a58					
East Croydon	a																								
London Euston 15 ⊖	a	13 57		14 37	14 37	14 27	14 43		14 53	14 17	14 57	15 11		14 57	15 17	15 37	15 37	15 27	15 45		15 53	15 57		16 11	15 57

		VT ◇1 ☕	LM ◇1	VT ◇1 ☕	SN 1	LM ◇1	VT ◇1 ☕	VT ◇1 ☕		LM 1	LM 1	VT ◇1 ☕	VT ◇1 ☕	VT ◇1 ☕	LM ◇1	VT ◇1 ☕	VT ◇1 ☕	SN 1		LM ◇1	LM 1	LM 1	VT ◇1 ☕	VT ◇1 ☕	LM ◇1
Wolverhampton 7	d	14 45												15 45										16 45	
Sandwell & Dudley	d	14 56												15 56										16 56	
Birmingham New Street 12	d	15 10					14 50					15 30	15 50	16 10									16 30	17 10	
Birmingham International	d	15 20					15 01					15 39	16 01	16 20									16 39	17 20	
Coventry	d	15 31					15 11					15 51	16 11	16 31									16 51	17 31	
Nuneaton	d					14 58																			
Rugby	d					15 17	15 26						16 24							16 25					
Northampton	d		15 25			15 50									16 25					16 50					17 25
Wolverton	d		15 37												16 37										17 37
Milton Keynes Central 10	a		15 40			16 04						16 18			16 40					17 04			17 18		17 40
	d		15 41	15 51		16 05		16 05			16 11	16 19			16 41	16 51	17 04			17 05		17 11	17 19		17 41
Bletchley	d		15 46								16 16				16 46							17 16			17 46
Leighton Buzzard	d		15 52			16 17					16 22				16 52					17 17		17 22			17 52
Cheddington	d										16 30											17 30			
Tring	d									16 15	16 35										17 15	17 35			
Berkhamsted	d		16 05							16 19	16 40				17 05						17 19	17 40			18 05
Hemel Hempstead	d		16 10							16 24	16 44				17 10						17 24	17 44			18 10
Apsley	d									16 27											17 27				
Kings Langley	d									16 30											17 30				
Watford Junction	a	16s16	16 17			16 33				16 35	16 51			17s16	17 17					17 33	17 35	17 51		18s16	18 17
	d		16 17		16 22	16 33				16 35	16 52				17 17			17 22		17 33	17 35	17 52			18 17
Bushey	d									16 38											17 38				
Harrow & Wealdstone ⊖	d		16 23		16 28					16 43	16 58				17 23			17 28			17 43	17 58			18 23
Wembley Central ⊖	d																								
Shepherd's Bush	a				16 45													17 45							
Kensington (Olympia) ⊖	a				16 47													17 47							
West Brompton ⊖	a				16 50													17 50							
Imperial Wharf	a				16 53													17 53							
Clapham Junction	d				16a58													17a58							
East Croydon	a																								
London Euston 15 ⊖	a	16 37	16 37	16 27		16 53	16 17	16 44		16 57	17 11	16 57	17 20	17 37	17 37	17 27	17 46			17 53	17 57	18 11	17 57	18 37	18 37

Table 66

Sundays

18 September to 23 October

West Midlands, Northampton, Milton Keynes Central and Watford Junction - London

		VT	SN	LM		VT	VT	LM	LM	VT	VT	LM	VT	VT		SN	LM	VT	LM	LM	VT	VT	LM	VT	
		◇1	1	◇1		◇1	◇1	1	1	◇1	◇1	◇1	◇1	◇1		1	◇1	◇1	1	1	◇1	◇1	◇1	◇1	
		☕				☕	☕			☕	☕		☕	☕				☕			☕	☕		☕	
Wolverhampton 7	d										17 45											18 45			
Sandwell & Dudley	d										17 56											18 56			
Birmingham New Street 12	d					16 50				17 30	18 10							17 50			18 30	19 10			
Birmingham International	d					17 01				17 39	18 20							18 01			18 39	19 20			
Coventry	d					17 11				17 51	18 31							18 11			18 51	19 31			
Nuneaton	d			16 58																					
Rugby	d			17 18		17 26											18 24	18 26							
Northampton	d			17 50								18 25					18 50						19 25		
Wolverton	d											18 37											19 37		
Milton Keynes Central 10	a			18 04						18 18		18 40					19 04				19 18		19 40		
	d	17 51		18 05			18 05		18 11	18 19		18 41	18 51	19 03			19 05			19 11	19 19		19 41	19 51	
Bletchley	d								18 16			18 46								19 16			19 46		
Leighton Buzzard	d			18 17					18 22			18 52					19 17			19 22			19 52		
Cheddington	d								18 30											19 30					
Tring	d							18 15	18 35										19 15	19 35					
Berkhamsted	d							18 19	18 40			19 05							19 19	19 40			20 05		
Hemel Hempstead	d							18 24	18 44			19 10							19 24	19 44			20 10		
Apsley	d							18 27											19 27						
Kings Langley	d							18 30											19 30						
Watford Junction	a			18 35				18 35	18 51		19s16	19 17					19 33		19 35	19 51		20s16	20 17		
	d		18 22	18 35				18 35	18 52			19 17				19 22	19 33		19 35	19 52			20 17		
Bushey	d							18 38											19 38						
Harrow & Wealdstone ⊖	d		18 28					18 43	18 58			19 23				19 28			19 43	19 58			20 23		
Wembley Central ⊖	d																								
Shepherd's Bush	a		18 45													19 45									
Kensington (Olympia) ⊖	a		18 47													19 47									
West Brompton ⊖	a		18 50													19 50									
Imperial Wharf	a		18 53													19 53									
Clapham Junction	d		18a58													19a58									
East Croydon	a																								
London Euston 15 ⊖	a	18 27		18 53		18 17	18 44	18 57	19 11	18 57	19 37	19 37	19 27	19 43			19 53	19 17	19 57	20 11	19 57	20 37	20 37	20 27	

		VT	SN	LM	VT	LM	LM	VT	SN	LM		VT	VT	LM	LM	VT	VT	SN	LM	VT		VT	LM	VT	SN
		◇1	1	◇1	◇1	1	1	◇1	1	◇1		◇1	◇1	◇1	1	◇1	◇1	1	◇1	◇1		◇1	◇1	◇1	1
		☕			☕			☕				☕	☕			☕	☕			☕		☕		☕	
Wolverhampton 7	d												19 45											21 05	
Sandwell & Dudley	d												19 58											21 17	
Birmingham New Street 12	d				18 50			19 30					20 10			20 30								21 30	
Birmingham International	d				19 01			19 39					20 20			20 40								21 40	
Coventry	d				19 11			19 51					20 31			20 51								21 51	
Nuneaton	d			18 58																			20 58		
Rugby	d			19 18	19 26									20 20		21 05							21 17	22 04	
Northampton	d			19 50						20 25				20 45					21 25				21 53		
Wolverton	d			20 02						20 37				21 02					21 39				22 07		
Milton Keynes Central 10	a			20 06				20 18		20 40				21 05		21 26			21 43				22 10	22 35	
	d	20 04		20 06			20 11	20 19		20 41		20 48		21 05	21 16	21 28	21 38		21 44	21 57		22 04	22 11	22 37	
Bletchley	d						20 16			20 46					21 21				21 49				22 16		
Leighton Buzzard	d			20 16			20 22			20 52				21 15	21 27				21 55				22 22		
Cheddington	d						20 27								21 32								22 27		
Tring	d					20 15	20 36								21 41								22 36		
Berkhamsted	d					20 19	20 41			21 08					21 46				22 08				22 41		
Hemel Hempstead	d					20 24	20 45			21 12					21 50				22 13				22 45		
Apsley	d					20 27				21 15									22 16						
Kings Langley	d					20 30				21 19									22 19						
Watford Junction	a			20 33		20 35	20 52			21 23			21s28	21 34	21 57	22s02			22 24	22s31			22 52	23s05	
	d		20 22	20 33		20 35	20 53		21 17	21 24				21 34	21 58			22 17	22 24				22 53		23 17
Bushey	d					20 38																			
Harrow & Wealdstone ⊖	d		20 28			20 43	20 59		21 23	21 30					22 04			22 23	22 30				22 59		23 23
Wembley Central ⊖	d																								
Shepherd's Bush	a		20 45						21 45									22 45							23 45
Kensington (Olympia) ⊖	a		20 47						21 47									22 47							23 47
West Brompton ⊖	a		20 50						21 50									22 50							23 50
Imperial Wharf	a		20 53						21 53									22 53							23 53
Clapham Junction	d		20a58						21a58									22a58							00 05
East Croydon	a																								00 22
London Euston 15 ⊖	a	20 44		20 53	20 17	20 58	21 15	20 57		21 44		21 31	21 48	21 55	22 18	22 23	22 28		22 44	22 53		22 56	23 14	23 25	

Table 66

Sundays

18 September to 23 October

West Midlands, Northampton, Milton Keynes Central and Watford Junction - London

		LM	VT	VT	LM	VT		VT
		◇1	◇1	◇1	◇1	◇1		◇1
			🍴	🍴		🍴		🍴
Wolverhampton 7	d					22 05		22 37
Sandwell & Dudley	d					22 15		22 47
Birmingham New Street 12	d					22 30		23 00
Birmingham International	d					22 40		23 10
Coventry	d					22 51		23 21
Nuneaton	d			22 18				
Rugby	d			22 32		23 04		23 34
Northampton	d	22 25			22 55			23s53
Wolverton	d	22 37			23 11			
Milton Keynes Central 10	a	22 40		23 04	23 14	23 36		00s12
	d	22 41	22 47	23 05	23 15	23 37		
Bletchley	d	22 46			23 20			
Leighton Buzzard	d	22 52			23 26			
Cheddington	d				23 31			
Tring	d				23 40			
Berkhamsted	d	23 06			23 45			
Hemel Hempstead	d	23 11			23 49			
Apsley	d	23 14						
Kings Langley	d	23 17						
Watford Junction	a	23 22	23s26	23s34	23 56	00s06		00s42
	d	23 22			23 57			
Bushey	d							
Harrow & Wealdstone ⊖	d	23 28			00 03			
Wembley Central ⊖	d							
Shepherd's Bush	a							
Kensington (Olympia) ⊖	a							
West Brompton ⊖	a							
Imperial Wharf	a							
Clapham Junction	d							
East Croydon	a							
London Euston 15 ⊖	a	23 42	23 48	23 54	00 17	00 26		01 04

Sundays

from 30 October

		LM	LM	LM	LM	LM	LM	LM	SN	LM		LM	VT
		◇1	◇1	1	🚌	1	1	◇1	1	◇1		◇1	◇1 🍴
Wolverhampton 7	d												08 05
Sandwell & Dudley	d												08 15
Birmingham New Street 12	d												08 30
Birmingham International	d												08 40
Coventry	d												08 51
Nuneaton	d												
Rugby	d												09 04
Northampton	d	22p55	23p30		06 20			07 53		08 23		08 53	
Wolverton	d	23p07	23p42		06 52			08 07		08 37		09 07	
Milton Keynes Central 10	a	23p10	23p45		07 00			08 10		08 40		09 10	09 37
	d	23p11	23p46	06 42		07 11	07 41	08 11		08 41		09 11	09 39
Bletchley	d	23p16	23p51	06 47		07 16	07 46	08 16		08 46		09 16	
Leighton Buzzard	d	23p22	23p57	06 53		07 22	07 52	08 22		08 52		09 22	
Cheddington	d	23p27				07 27		08 27				09 27	
Tring	d	23p36				07 36		08 36				09 36	
Berkhamsted	d	23p41		07 08		07 41	08 07	08 41		09 07		09 41	
Hemel Hempstead	d	23p45		07 13		07 45	08 12	08 45		09 12		09 45	
Apsley	d	23p49		07 16			08 15			09 15			
Kings Langley	d	23p52		07 19			08 18			09 18			
Watford Junction	a	23p56	00 19	07 24		07 52	08 23	08 52		09 23		09 52	10s07
	d	23p57	00 20	07 24		07 53	08 23	08 53	09 17	09 23		09 53	
Bushey	d												
Harrow & Wealdstone ⊖	d	00 03		07 30		07 59	08 29	08 59	09 23	09 29		09 59	
Wembley Central ⊖	d												
Shepherd's Bush	a								09 45				
Kensington (Olympia) ⊖	a								09 47				
West Brompton ⊖	a								09 50				
Imperial Wharf	a								09 53				
Clapham Junction	d								09a58				
East Croydon	a												
London Euston 15 ⊖	a	00 17	00 42	07 44		08 13	08 43	09 13		09 43		10 13	10 28

		SN	LM	VT	VT	VT	LM	VT		VT	SN	LM	VT
		1	◇1	◇1 🍴	◇1 🍴	◇1 🍴	◇1	◇1 🍴		◇1 🍴	1	◇1	◇1 🍴
Wolverhampton 7	d							09 05					
Sandwell & Dudley	d							09 15					
Birmingham New Street 12	d							09 30					
Birmingham International	d							09 40					
Coventry	d							09 51					
Nuneaton	d									09 55			
Rugby	d							10 04					10 33
Northampton	d		09 30				10 07					10 37	
Wolverton	d		09 44				10 20					10 51	
Milton Keynes Central 10	a		09 47				10 24	10 37				10 54	11 06
	d		09 48			10 19	10 24	10 39				10 55	11 08
Bletchley	d		09 53				10 29					11 00	
Leighton Buzzard	d		09 59				10 36					11 06	
Cheddington	d						10 45						
Tring	d						10 50						
Berkhamsted	d		10 14				10 54					11 21	
Hemel Hempstead	d		10 19				10 59					11 26	
Apsley	d		10 22									11 29	
Kings Langley	d		10 25									11 32	
Watford Junction	a		10 30				11 06	11s11		11s16		11 37	11s43
	d	10 17	10 30				11 06				11 22	11 37	
Bushey	d												
Harrow & Wealdstone ⊖	d	10 23	10 36				11 12				11 28	11 43	
Wembley Central ⊖	d												
Shepherd's Bush	a	10 45									11 45		
Kensington (Olympia) ⊖	a	10 47									11 47		
West Brompton ⊖	a	10 50									11 50		
Imperial Wharf	a	10 53									11 53		
Clapham Junction	d	10a58									11a58		
East Croydon	a												
London Euston 15 ⊖	a		10 50	10 57	11 02	11 06	11 26	11 31		11 37		11 57	12 05

Table 66

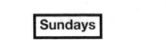

Sundays
from 30 October

West Midlands, Northampton, Milton Keynes Central and Watford Junction - London

		VT	LM	VT	LM	VT		VT	SN	LM	VT	VT	LM	VT	VT	VT		LM	VT	VT	VT	SN	LM	LM	LM
		◇1	◇1	◇1	◇1	◇1		◇1	1	1	◇1	◇1	1	◇1	◇1	◇1		◇1	◇1	◇1	◇1	1	◇1	1	1
		☕		☕		☕		☕			☕	☕		☕	☕	☕			☕	☕	☕				
Wolverhampton 7	d			10 05											11 05					11 45					
Sandwell & Dudley	d			10 15											11 15					11 57					
Birmingham New Street 12	d			10 30											11 30	11 50				12 10					
Birmingham International	d			10 40											11 40	12 00				12 20					
Coventry	d			10 51											11 51	12 11				12 31					
Nuneaton	d					10 56						11 59									12 32				
Rugby	d			11 04				11 33						12 00	12 05	12 25							12 26		
Northampton	d		11 07		11 25													12 25					12 50		
Wolverton	d		11 21		11 37													12 37							
Milton Keynes Central 10	a		11 24	11 37	11 42	11 46		12 06						12 20	12 24			12 40			13 03		13 04		
	d	11 17	11 25	11 39	11 42	11 47		12 07					12 11	12 22	12 26			12 41	12 52		13 04		13 05		13 11
Bletchley	d		11 30		11 47					11 55			12 16					12 46							13 16
Leighton Buzzard	d		11 36		11 54					12 01			12 22					12 52					13 18		13 22
Cheddington	d		11 41							12 07			12 30												13 30
Tring	d		11 50							12 14			12 35											13 15	13 35
Berkhamsted	d		11 55		12 06					12 18			12 40					13 05						13 19	13 40
Hemel Hempstead	d		11 59		12 11					12 23			12 44					13 10						13 24	13 44
Apsley	d									12 26														13 27	
Kings Langley	d									12 29														13 30	
Watford Junction	a		12 06	12s07	12 18					12 34		12s50	12 51					13 17		13s18			13 33	13 35	13 51
	d		12 07		12 18				12 22	12 34			12 52					13 17				13 22	13 33	13 35	13 52
Bushey	d									12 37														13 38	
Harrow & Wealdstone ⊖	d		12 13		12 24				12 29	12 42			12 58					13 23				13 28		13 43	13 58
Wembley Central ⊖	d																								
Shepherd's Bush	a								12 45													13 45			
Kensington (Olympia) ⊖	a								12 47													13 47			
West Brompton ⊖	a								12 50													13 50			
Imperial Wharf	a								12 53													13 53			
Clapham Junction	d								12a58													13a58			
East Croydon	a																								
London Euston 15 ⊖	a	12 08	12 27	12 27	12 37	12 32		12 45		12 56	12 56	13 11	13 11	12 59	13 04	13 19		13 37	13 28	13 37	13 44		13 53	13 57	14 11

		VT		VT	LM	VT	VT	SN	LM	VT	LM	LM		VT	VT	VT	LM	VT	VT	SN	LM	LM		LM	VT
		◇1		◇1	◇1	◇1	◇1	1	◇1	◇1	1	1		◇1	◇1	◇1	◇1	◇1	◇1	1	◇1	1		1	◇1
		☕		☕		☕	☕			☕				☕	☕	☕		☕	☕						☕
Wolverhampton 7	d			12 45												13 45									
Sandwell & Dudley	d			12 55												13 56									
Birmingham New Street 12	d	12 30		13 10						12 50				13 30	13 50	14 10									14 30
Birmingham International	d	12 39		13 20						13 00				13 39	14 01	14 20									14 39
Coventry	d	12 51		13 31						13 11				13 51	14 11	14 31									14 51
Nuneaton	d								12 58										14 32						
Rugby	d								13 17	13 25					14 26						14 26				
Northampton	d				13 25				13 50								14 25				14 50				
Wolverton	d				13 37												14 37								
Milton Keynes Central 10	a	13 18			13 40				14 04					14 18			14 40		15 04		15 04				15 18
	d	13 19			13 41	13 51	14 03		14 05			14 11		14 19			14 41	14 51	15 05		15 05			15 11	15 19
Bletchley	d				13 46							14 16					14 46							15 16	
Leighton Buzzard	d				13 52				14 15			14 22					14 52				15 17			15 22	
Cheddington	d											14 30												15 30	
Tring	d										14 15	14 35										15 15		15 35	
Berkhamsted	d				14 05						14 19	14 40					15 05					15 19		15 40	
Hemel Hempstead	d				14 10						14 24	14 44					15 10					15 24		15 44	
Apsley	d										14 27											15 27			
Kings Langley	d										14 30											15 30			
Watford Junction	a			14s16	14 17				14 33		14 35	14 51				15s16	15 17				15 33	15 35		15 51	
	d				14 17			14 22	14 34		14 35	14 52					15 17			15 22	15 33	15 35		15 52	
Bushey	d										14 38											15 38			
Harrow & Wealdstone ⊖	d				14 23			14 28			14 43	14 58					15 23			15 28		15 43		15 58	
Wembley Central ⊖	d																								
Shepherd's Bush	a							14 45												15 45					
Kensington (Olympia) ⊖	a							14 47												15 47					
West Brompton ⊖	a							14 50												15 50					
Imperial Wharf	a							14 53												15 53					
Clapham Junction	d							14a58												15a58					
East Croydon	a																								
London Euston 15 ⊖	a	13 57		14 37	14 37	14 27	14 43		14 53	14 17	14 57	15 11		14 57	15 17	15 37	15 37	15 27	15 45		15 53	15 57		16 11	15 57

Table 66

Sundays
from 30 October

West Midlands, Northampton, Milton Keynes Central and Watford Junction - London

		VT	LM	VT	SN	LM	VT	VT		LM	LM	VT	VT	VT	LM	VT	VT	SN		LM	LM	LM	VT	VT	LM
		◇1	◇1	◇1	1	◇1	◇1	◇1		1	1	◇1	◇1	◇1	◇1	◇1	◇1	1		◇1	1	1	◇1	◇1	◇1
		[trolley]		[trolley]			[trolley]	[trolley]				[trolley]	[trolley]	[trolley]		[trolley]	[trolley]						[trolley]	[trolley]	
Wolverhampton 7	d	14 45												15 45										16 45	
Sandwell & Dudley	d	14 56												15 56										16 56	
Birmingham New Street 12	d	15 10					14 50					15 30	15 50	16 10									16 30	17 10	
Birmingham International ✈	d	15 20					15 01					15 39	16 01	16 20									16 39	17 20	
Coventry	d	15 31					15 11					15 51	16 11	16 31									16 51	17 31	
Nuneaton	d					14 58																			
Rugby	d					15 17	15 26						16 24							16 25					
Northampton	d		15 25			15 50									16 25					16 50					17 25
Wolverton	d		15 37												16 37										17 37
Milton Keynes Central 10	a		15 40			16 04						16 18			16 40					17 04			17 18		17 40
	d		15 41	15 51		16 05		16 05			16 11	16 19			16 41	16 51	17 04			17 05		17 11	17 19		17 41
Bletchley	d		15 46								16 16				16 46							17 16			17 46
Leighton Buzzard	d		15 52			16 17					16 22				16 52					17 17		17 22			17 52
Cheddington	d										16 30											17 30			
Tring	d									16 15	16 35										17 15	17 35			
Berkhamsted	d		16 05							16 19	16 40				17 05						17 19	17 40			18 05
Hemel Hempstead	d		16 10							16 24	16 44				17 10						17 24	17 44			18 10
Apsley	d									16 27											17 27				
Kings Langley	d									16 30											17 30				
Watford Junction	a	16s16	16 17			16 33				16 35	16 51			17s16	17 17					17 33	17 35	17 51		18s16	18 17
	d		16 17		16 22	16 33				16 35	16 52				17 17			17 22		17 33	17 35	17 52			18 17
Bushey	d									16 38											17 38				
Harrow & Wealdstone ⊖	d		16 23		16 28					16 43	16 58				17 23			17 28			17 43	17 58			18 23
Wembley Central ⊖	d																								
Shepherd's Bush	a				16 45													17 45							
Kensington (Olympia) ⊖	a				16 47													17 47							
West Brompton ⊖	a				16 50													17 50							
Imperial Wharf	a				16 53													17 53							
Clapham Junction	d				16a58													17a58							
East Croydon	a																								
London Euston 15 ⊖	a	16 37	16 37	16 27		16 53	16 17	16 44		16 57	17 11	16 57	17 20	17 37	17 37	17 27	17 46			17 53	17 57	18 11	17 57	18 37	18 37

		VT	SN	LM		VT	VT	LM	LM	VT	VT	LM	VT	VT		SN	LM	VT	LM	LM	VT	VT	LM	VT	
		◇1	1	◇1		◇1	◇1	1	1	◇1	◇1	◇1	◇1	◇1		1	◇1	◇1	1	1	◇1	◇1	◇1	◇1	
		[trolley]				[trolley]	[trolley]			[trolley]	[trolley]		[trolley]	[trolley]				[trolley]			[trolley]	[trolley]		[trolley]	
Wolverhampton 7	d										17 45											18 45			
Sandwell & Dudley	d										17 56											18 56			
Birmingham New Street 12	d					16 50				17 30	18 10							17 50			18 30	19 10			
Birmingham International ✈	d					17 01				17 39	18 20							18 01			18 39	19 20			
Coventry	d					17 11				17 51	18 31							18 11			18 51	19 31			
Nuneaton	d			16 58																					
Rugby	d			17 18		17 26											18 24	18 26							
Northampton	d			17 50								18 25					18 50						19 25		
Wolverton	d											18 37											19 37		
Milton Keynes Central 10	a			18 04						18 18		18 40					19 04				19 18		19 40		
	d	17 51		18 05			18 05		18 11	18 19		18 41	18 51	19 03			19 05			19 11	19 19		19 41	19 51	
Bletchley	d								18 16			18 46								19 16			19 46		
Leighton Buzzard	d			18 17					18 22			18 52					19 17			19 22			19 52		
Cheddington	d								18 30											19 30					
Tring	d							18 15	18 35										19 15	19 35					
Berkhamsted	d							18 19	18 40			19 05							19 19	19 40			20 05		
Hemel Hempstead	d							18 24	18 44			19 10							19 24	19 44			20 10		
Apsley	d							18 27											19 27						
Kings Langley	d							18 30											19 30						
Watford Junction	a			18 35				18 35	18 51		19s16	19 17					19 33		19 35	19 51		20s16	20 17		
	d		18 22	18 35				18 35	18 52			19 17				19 22	19 33		19 35	19 52			20 17		
Bushey	d							18 38											19 38						
Harrow & Wealdstone ⊖	d		18 28					18 43	18 58			19 23				19 28			19 43	19 58			20 23		
Wembley Central ⊖	d																								
Shepherd's Bush	a		18 45													19 45									
Kensington (Olympia) ⊖	a		18 47													19 47									
West Brompton ⊖	a		18 50													19 50									
Imperial Wharf	a		18 53													19 53									
Clapham Junction	d		18a58													19a58									
East Croydon	a																								
London Euston 15 ⊖	a	18 27		18 53		18 17	18 44	18 57	19 11	18 57	19 37	19 37	19 27	19 43			19 53	19 17	19 57	20 11	19 57	20 37	20 37	20 27	

Table 66

Sundays
from 30 October

West Midlands, Northampton, Milton Keynes Central and Watford Junction - London

		VT	SN	LM	VT	LM	LM	VT	SN	LM		VT	VT	LM	LM	VT	VT	SN	LM	VT		VT	LM	VT	SN
		◇1 ☕	1	◇1	◇1 ☕	1	1	◇1 ☕	1	◇1		◇1 ☕	◇1 ☕	◇1	1	◇1 ☕	◇1 ☕	1	◇1	◇1 ☕		◇1 ☕	◇1	◇1 ☕	1
Wolverhampton 7	d												19 45											21 05	
Sandwell & Dudley	d												19 58											21 17	
Birmingham New Street 12	d				18 50			19 30					20 10			20 30								21 30	
Birmingham International	d				19 01			19 39					20 20			20 40								21 40	
Coventry	d				19 11			19 51					20 31			20 51								21 51	
Nuneaton	d			18 58																			20 58		
Rugby	d			19 18	19 26									20 20		21 05							21 17	22 04	
Northampton	d			19 50						20 25				20 45					21 25				21 53		
Wolverton	d			20 02						20 37				21 02					21 39				22 07		
Milton Keynes Central 10	a			20 06				20 18		20 40				21 05		21 26			21 43				22 10	22 35	
	d	20 04		20 06			20 11	20 19		20 41		20 48		21 05	21 16	21 28	21 38		21 44	21 57		22 04	22 11	22 37	
Bletchley	d						20 16			20 46					21 21				21 49				22 16		
Leighton Buzzard	d			20 16			20 22			20 52				21 15	21 27				21 55				22 22		
Cheddington	d						20 27								21 32								22 27		
Tring	d					20 15	20 36								21 41								22 36		
Berkhamsted	d					20 19	20 41			21 08					21 46				22 08				22 41		
Hemel Hempstead	d					20 24	20 45			21 12					21 50				22 13				22 45		
Apsley	d					20 27				21 15									22 16						
Kings Langley	d					20 30				21 19									22 19						
Watford Junction	a			20 33		20 35	20 52			21 23			21s28	21 34	21 57	22s02			22 24	22s31			22 52	23s05	
	d		20 22	20 33		20 35	20 53		21 17	21 24				21 34	21 58			22 17	22 24				22 53		23 17
Bushey	d					20 38																			
Harrow & Wealdstone ⊖	d		20 28			20 43	20 59		21 23	21 30					22 04			22 23	22 30				22 59		23 23
Wembley Central ⊖	d																								
Shepherd's Bush	a		20 45						21 45									22 45							23 45
Kensington (Olympia) ⊖	a		20 47						21 47									22 47							23 47
West Brompton ⊖	a		20 50						21 50									22 50							23 50
Imperial Wharf	a		20 53						21 53									22 53							23 53
Clapham Junction	d		20a58						21a58									22a58							00 05
East Croydon	a																								00 22
London Euston 15 ⊖	a	20 44		20 53	20 17	20 58	21 15	20 57		21 44		21 31	21 48	21 55	22 18	22 23	22 28		22 44	22 53		22 56	23 14	23 25	

		LM	VT	VT	LM	VT		VT
		◇1	◇1 ☕	◇1 ☕	◇1	◇1 ☕		◇1 ☕
Wolverhampton 7	d					22 05		22 37
Sandwell & Dudley	d					22 15		22 47
Birmingham New Street 12	d					22 30		23 00
Birmingham International	d					22 40		23 10
Coventry	d					22 51		23 21
Nuneaton	d			22 18				
Rugby	d			22 32		23 04		23 34
Northampton	d	22 25			22 55			23s53
Wolverton	d	22 37			23 11			
Milton Keynes Central 10	a	22 40		23 04	23 14	23 36		00s12
	d	22 41	22 47	23 05	23 15	23 37		
Bletchley	d	22 46			23 20			
Leighton Buzzard	d	22 52			23 26			
Cheddington	d				23 31			
Tring	d				23 40			
Berkhamsted	d	23 06			23 45			
Hemel Hempstead	d	23 11			23 49			
Apsley	d	23 14						
Kings Langley	d	23 17						
Watford Junction	a	23 22	23s26	23s34	23 56	00s06		00s42
	d	23 22			23 57			
Bushey	d							
Harrow & Wealdstone ⊖	d	23 28			00 03			
Wembley Central ⊖	d							
Shepherd's Bush	a							
Kensington (Olympia) ⊖	a							
West Brompton ⊖	a							
Imperial Wharf	a							
Clapham Junction	d							
East Croydon	a							
London Euston 15 ⊖	a	23 42	23 48	23 54	00 17	00 26		01 04

Network Diagram for Tables 67, 68, 69, 70

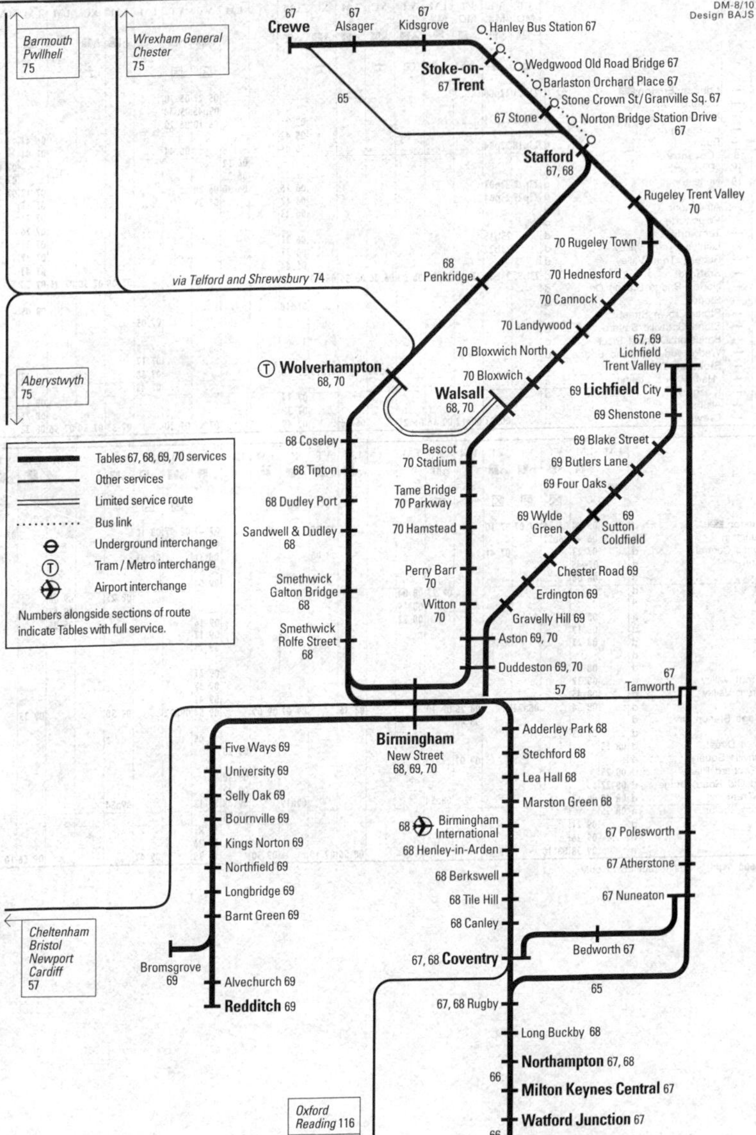

© 2010 Network Rail.
All rights reserved

London - Stoke-on-Trent and Crewe
Coventry - Nuneaton

Miles	Miles	Miles			VT	VT	VT	LM	VT	XC	LM	XC	LM		LM	VT	VT	LM	LM	XC	LM	LM	LM		LM
					MO	MX	MO	MX																	
					◇1	◇1	◇1	1	◇1	◇1	◇1	◇1	◇1			◇1	◇1		◇1	◇1	1	◇1			◇1
					(sleeper)	(sleeper)	(sleeper)		⊠	(trolley)		(trolley)				⊠	⊠	(bus)		(trolley)					
0	—	—	**London Euston** 15 ⊖	d	21p51	22p00										05 27	05 28								
17½	—	—	Watford Junction	d												05u45	05u44								
49¾	—	—	Milton Keynes Central	d	22p38	22p31							05 21			06 10	06 20								
65¾	—	—	Northampton	d									05 42									06 41			
84½	—	—	Rugby	d	23p18	22p54							06 05				06 44					07 01			
—	—	0	**Coventry**	d											06 12								07 06		
—	—	6¼	Bedworth	d											06 23								07 17		
99	—	10	Nuneaton	a	23p28	23p03							06 16		06 30	06 38						07 13	07 27		
—	—	—		d	23p29	23p04							06 17			06 39						07 15			
104	—	—	Atherstone	d									06 23									07 21			
108	—	—	Polesworth	d																		07 26			
111½	—	—	Tamworth	d		23b15							06 31									07 31			
117¾	—	—	Lichfield Trent Valley	d		23b22							06 37									07 37			
125¾	—	—	Rugeley Trent Valley	d			←						06 44									07 43			
135½	0	—	**Stafford**	d	23b53	23b38	23b53	23p53	06 02	06 30	06 36	06 55	06 58			07 03			07 08	07 30	07 36	07 54			08 09
—	—	—	Norton Bridge Station Drv	d	↔																				
144½	—	—	Stone	d									07c18									08 05			
—	—	—	Stone Crown Street	d														07 05							
—	—	—	Stone Granville Square	a																					
—	—	—	Barlaston Orchard Place	d														07 15							
—	—	—	Wedgwood Old Road Bridge	d														07 17							
151¾	—	—	**Stoke-on-Trent**	d						06a50		07a13	07 26					07 38				08 13			
—	—	—	Hanley Bus Station	a														07 45							
159	—	—	Kidsgrove	d									07 34									08 21			
161¼	—	—	Alsager	d									07 39									08 26			
167¾	24½	—	**Crewe**	a		00s03	00s12	00 16	06 21		06 56		07 49			07 22	07 30		07 33	07 50	07 56	08 38			08 30

		LM	LM	VT	VT	VT	LM	XC	LM		LM	VT	XC	LM	LM	LM	VT	VT	XC		LM	LM	VT	XC	LM
			◇1	◇1	◇1	◇1		◇1			◇1	◇1	◇1	1		◇1	◇1	◇1	◇1			1	◇1	◇1	1
		(bus)		⊠	⊠	⊠	(bus)	(trolley)				⊠	(trolley)		(bus)		⊠	⊠	(trolley)				⊠	(trolley)	
London Euston 15 ⊖	d		06 24	06 36	07 07	07 10						07 35				07 47	08 07	08 10					08 40		
Watford Junction	d		06 41	06u51												08 02									
Milton Keynes Central	d		07 23			07 41						08 06				08f31		08 41							
Northampton	d		07e45													08 45									
Rugby	d		08 04													09 04									
Coventry	d							07 27	08 04										08 27		09 06				
Bedworth	d								08 15												09 17				
Nuneaton	a		08 17						08 23							09 16					09 25				
	d		08 17													09 17									
Atherstone	d		08 23													09 23									
Polesworth	d																								
Tamworth	d		08 31													09 31									
Lichfield Trent Valley	d		08 37													09 37									
Rugeley Trent Valley	d		08 43													09 43									
Stafford	d		08 54		08a22		08 25	08 30			08 36		09 01	09 09		09 54	09a22		09 30			09 35		10 01	10 09
Norton Bridge Station Drv	d						08 40																		
Stone	d		09 05													10 05									
Stone Crown Street	d	08 15													09 20										
Stone Granville Square	a						09 02																		
Barlaston Orchard Place	d	08 25													09 30										
Wedgwood Old Road Bridge	d	08 27													09 32										
Stoke-on-Trent	d	08 48	09 13					08a54					09a19		09 48	10 13			09a54					10a19	
Hanley Bus Station	a	08 55													09 55										
Kidsgrove	d		09 21													10 21									
Alsager	d		09 26													10 26									
Crewe	a		09 38	08 10		08 47					08 56	09 10		09 30		10 38		09 47				09 56	10 10		10 30

b Previous night, stops to set down only

London - Stoke-on-Trent and Crewe
Coventry - Nuneaton

		VT	LM	LM	VT		VT	VT	LM	XC	LM	VT	LM	XC	LM		LM	LM	VT	VT	XC	LM	VT	LM	XC
		◇1		◇1	◇1		◇1	◇1		◇1	1	◇1		◇1	1			◇1	◇1	◇1	◇1	1	◇1		◇1
		A																							
		⊠	🚌		⊠		⊠	⊠	🚌	🛒		⊠		🛒			🚌		⊠	⊠	🛒		⊠		🛒
London Euston 15 ⊖	d	08 43		08 46	09 07		09 10	09 10				09 40						09 46	10 07	10 10			10 40		
Watford Junction	d			09 01														10 01							
Milton Keynes Central	d	09 13		09 25			09 40	09 41										10 25		10 41					
Northampton	d			09 45														10 45							
Rugby	d			10 04														11 04							
Coventry	d	09 42								09 27			10 42								10 27			11 42	
Bedworth	d												10 54											11 54	
Nuneaton	a			10 16									11 02					11 16						12 01	
	d			10 17														11 17							
Atherstone	d			10 23														11 23							
Polesworth	d																								
Tamworth	d			10 31														11 31							
Lichfield Trent Valley	d			10 37														11 37							
Rugeley Trent Valley	d			10 43														11 43							
Stafford	d			10 54	10a22				10 25	10 30	10 35			11 01	11 09			11 54	11a22		11 30	11 35			12 01
Norton Bridge Station Drv	d								10 40																
Stone	d			11 05														12 05							
Stone Crown Street	d		10 20														11 20								
Stone Granville Square	a								11 02																
Barlaston Orchard Place	d		10 30														11 30								
Wedgwood Old Road Bridge	d		10 32														11 32								
Stoke-on-Trent	d		10 48	11 13						10a54				11a19			11 48	12 13			11a54				12a19
Hanley Bus Station	a		10 55														11 55								
Kidsgrove	d			11 21														12 21							
Alsager	d			11 26														12 26							
Crewe	a	11 07		11 38			10 47	10 47			10 56	11 10			11 30			12 38		11 47		11 56	12 10		

			LM	LM	LM	VT	VT	XC	LM	VT	LM		LM	XC	LM	LM	LM	VT	VT	XC	LM		VT	LM	XC
			1		◇1	◇1	◇1	◇1	1	◇1				◇1	1		◇1	◇1	◇1	◇1	1		◇1		◇1
				🚌		☕	☕	🛒		☕	🚌			🛒		🚌		☕	☕	🛒			☕		🛒
London Euston 15 ⊖	d				10 46	11 07	11 10			11 40							11 46	12 07	12 10				12 40		
Watford Junction	d				11 01												12 01								
Milton Keynes Central	d				11 25		11 41										12 25		12 41						
Northampton	d				11 45												12 45								
Rugby	d				12 04												13 04								
Coventry	d							11 27					12 42							12 27				13 42	
Bedworth	d												12 53											13 53	
Nuneaton	a				12 16								13 00				13 16							14 00	
	d				12 17												13 17								
Atherstone	d				12 23												13 23								
Polesworth	d																								
Tamworth	d				12 31												13 31								
Lichfield Trent Valley	d				12 37												13 37								
Rugeley Trent Valley	d				12 43												13 43								
Stafford	d		12 09		12 54	12a22		12 30	12 35		12 35			13 01	13 09		13 54	13a22		13 30	13 35				14 01
Norton Bridge Station Drv	d										12 59														
Stone	d				13 05												14 05								
Stone Crown Street	d			12 20												13 20									
Stone Granville Square	a										13 39														
Barlaston Orchard Place	d			12 30												13 30									
Wedgwood Old Road Bridge	d			12 32												13 32									
Stoke-on-Trent	d			12 48	13 13			12a54						13a19		13 48	14 13			13a54					14a19
Hanley Bus Station	a			12 55												13 55									
Kidsgrove	d				13 21												14 21								
Alsager	d				13 26												14 26								
Crewe	a		12 30		13 38		12 47		12 56	13 10					13 30		14 38		13 47		13 56		14 10		

A from 18 July until 9 September

London - Stoke-on-Trent and Crewe
Coventry - Nuneaton

		LM	LM	LM	LM	VT	VT		XC	LM	VT	VT	LM	XC	LM	VT	LM		LM	VT	VT	XC	LM	VT	LM
											FO														
		1			◇1	◇1	◇1		◇1	1	◇	◇1		◇1	1	◇1			◇1	◇1	◇1	◇1	1	◇1	
																A									
			🚌	🚌													🚌								
						☕	☕		🛒		☕	☕		🛒		☕				☕	☕	🛒		☕	
London Euston 15 ⊖	d				12 46	13 07	13 10				13 33	13 40				13 43			13 46	14 07	14 10			14 40	
Watford Junction	d				13 01														14 01						
Milton Keynes Central	d				13 25		13 41									14 13			14 25		14 41				
Northampton	d				13 45														14 45						
Rugby	d				14 04														15 04						
Coventry	d								13 27				14 42			14 42						14 27			15 42
Bedworth	d												14 53												15 53
Nuneaton	a				14 16								15 00						15 16						16 00
	d				14 17														15 17						
Atherstone	d				14 23														15 23						
Polesworth	d																								
Tamworth	d				14 31														15 31						
Lichfield Trent Valley	d				14 37														15 37						
Rugeley Trent Valley	d				14 43														15 43						
Stafford	d	14 09	14 18		14 54	14a22			14 30	14 35				15 01	15 09				15 54	15a22		15 30	15 35		
Norton Bridge Station Drv	d		14 42																						
Stone	d				15 05														16 05						
Stone Crown Street	d			14 20													15 20								
Stone Granville Square	a		14 54																						
Barlaston Orchard Place	d			14 30													15 30								
Wedgwood Old Road Bridge	d			14 32													15 32								
Stoke-on-Trent	d			14 48	15 13				14a54					15a19			15 48		16 13			15a54			
Hanley Bus Station	a			14 55													15 55								
Kidsgrove	d				15 21														16 21						
Alsager	d				15 26														16 26						
Crewe	a	14 30			15 38		14 47			14 56	15 16	15 10			15 30	16 07			16 38		15 47		15 56	16 11	

		LM	LM		LM	LM	VT	VT	XC	LM	VT	LM	XC		LM	LM	LM	VT	VT	XC	LM	LM	VT		VT
		1				◇1	◇1	◇1	◇1	1	◇1		◇1		1		◇1	◇1	◇1	◇1	1		◇1		◇1
			🚌		🚌											🚌						🚌			
							☕	☕	🛒		☕		🛒					☕	☕	🛒			☕		☕
London Euston 15 ⊖	d					14 46	15 07	15 10			15 40						15 46	16 07	16 10				16 33		16 40
Watford Junction	d					15 01											16 01								
Milton Keynes Central	d					15 25		15 41									16 25		16u40						
Northampton	d					15 45											16 45								
Rugby	d					16 04											17 04						17 22		
Coventry	d								15 27			16 42								16 27					
Bedworth	d											16 53													
Nuneaton	a					16 16						17 00					17 16								
	d					16 17											17 17								
Atherstone	d					16 23											17 23								
Polesworth	d																								
Tamworth	d					16 31											17 31								
Lichfield Trent Valley	d					16 37											17 37								
Rugeley Trent Valley	d					16 43											17 43								
Stafford	d	16 09	16 18			16 54	16a22		16 30	16 35			17 01		17 09		18 20	17a22		17 30	17 36	17 40	17 56		
Norton Bridge Station Drv	d		16a42														↪					18a06			
Stone	d					17 05																			
Stone Crown Street	d				16 20											17 20									
Stone Granville Square	a																								
Barlaston Orchard Place	d				16 30											17 30									
Wedgwood Old Road Bridge	d				16 32											17 32									
Stoke-on-Trent	d				16 48	17 13			16a54				17a19			17 48				17a54					
Hanley Bus Station	a				16 55											17 55									
Kidsgrove	d					17 21																			
Alsager	d					17 26																			
Crewe	a	16 30				17 38		16 47		16 56	17 10				17 30				17 47		17 56		18 16		18 10

A from 18 July until 9 September

London - Stoke-on-Trent and Crewe
Coventry - Nuneaton

		XC	LM	LM	VT	LM	XC	LM	VT		LM	VT	VT	LM	XC	LM	VT	XC	LM		VT	LM	LM	LM	VT
		◇1	◇1	◇1	◇1		◇1		◇1		1	◇1	◇1		◇1	1	◇1	◇1			◇1	1		◇1	◇1
		⊥			⊠	🚌	⊥		⊠			⊠	⊠	🚌	⊥		⊠	⊥			⊠				⊠
London Euston 15 ⊖	d				17 07				17 10			17 33	17 40				18 07				18 10			18 29	18 33
Watford Junction	d																							18 47	
Milton Keynes Central	d								17u40												18u40			19 23	
Northampton	d																							19 45	
Rugby	d											18 23												20 04	19 23
Coventry	d						17 27	17 42										18 27	18 42				19 42		
Bedworth	d							17 54											18 53				19 54		
Nuneaton	a							18 01	18 11										19 00		19 12		20 01	20 16	
	d								18 12												19 13			20 17	
Atherstone	d																							20 23	
Polesworth	d																								
Tamworth	d																							20 31	
Lichfield Trent Valley	d																							→	
Rugeley Trent Valley	d			←																					
Stafford	d	18 01	18 09	18 20	18 24		18 30				18 35	18 55			19 01	19 09	19 24	19 29				19 36			19 56
Norton Bridge Station Drv	d																								
Stone	d			18 31																					
Stone Crown Street	d					18 20								18 45											
Stone Granville Square	a																								
Barlaston Orchard Place	d					18 30								18 53											
Wedgwood Old Road Bridge	d					18 32								18 55											
Stoke-on-Trent	d	18a19		18 41		18 48	18a54							19 06	19a19			19a54							
Hanley Bus Station	a					19 00								19 15											
Kidsgrove	d			18 49																					
Alsager	d			18 54																					
Crewe	a		18 30	19 05	18 42				18 53		19 00	19 14	19 10			19 30	19 42				19 53	20 01			20 15

		VT	XC	LM	VT		VT FO	VT	VT	XC	VT	LM	VT	LM	LM		VT	VT	XC	VT	VT	LM	XC	LM	VT
		◇1	◇1	1	◇1		◇	ℝ 1	ℝ 1	◇1	◇1	◇1	◇1		1		◇1	◇1	◇1	◇1	◇1 A	1	◇1		◇1
		⊠	⊥		⊠		☕	☕	☕		⊠		☕				☕	☕		☕	☕				☕
London Euston 15 ⊖	d	18 40			18 43		18 46	19 07	19 10				19 40				20 07	20 10		20 40					21 07
Watford Junction	d																								
Milton Keynes Central	d				19 13				19u40									20 40							21 38
Northampton	d																								
Rugby	d						19 39																		
Coventry	d				19 42					19 27				20 42					20 27				21 27	21 42	
Bedworth	d													20 53										21 53	
Nuneaton	a							20 02						21 00			21 02							22 00	22 07
	d							20 03									21 03								22 08
Atherstone	d																								
Polesworth	d											←													
Tamworth	d						19s59					20 31	20 43												
Lichfield Trent Valley	d						20s07					20 37	20 50												
Rugeley Trent Valley	d										←	20 43													
Stafford	d		20 01	20 09	20 52		20s35	20a26		20 30	20 52		21 04		21 09		21a27		21 32		21 55	22 09	22 30		
Norton Bridge Station Drv	d				→																				
Stone	d																								
Stone Crown Street	d																								
Stone Granville Square	a																								
Barlaston Orchard Place	d																								
Wedgwood Old Road Bridge	d																								
Stoke-on-Trent	d		20a19							20a54		21 05							21a54				22a53		
Hanley Bus Station	a																								
Kidsgrove	d											21 14													
Alsager	d											21 18													
Crewe	a	20 11		20 30			21s01		20 48		21 15	21 27	21 21		21 30			21 48		22 12	22 17	22 30			22 46

A until 9 September

London - Stoke-on-Trent and Crewe
Coventry - Nuneaton

Mondays to Fridays

		VT	SR	XC	LM	AW	VT	LM
		◇1		◇1	◇1	◇	◇1	1
		A						
London Euston 15 ⊖	d	21 10	21 15				22 00	
Watford Junction	d	21u25	21u33					
Milton Keynes Central	d						22 31	
Northampton	d							
Rugby	d	22 04					22 54	
Coventry	d							
Bedworth	d							
Nuneaton	a						23 03	
	d						23 04	
Atherstone	d							
Polesworth	d							
Tamworth	d						23s15	
Lichfield Trent Valley	d						23s22	
Rugeley Trent Valley	d							
Stafford	d	22 34		23 01	23 13	23 30	23s38	23 53
Norton Bridge Station Drv	d							
Stone	d							
Stone Crown Street	d							
Stone Granville Square	a							
Barlaston Orchard Place	d							
Wedgwood Old Road Bridge	d							
Stoke-on-Trent	d			23a20				
Hanley Bus Station	a							
Kidsgrove	d							
Alsager	d							
Crewe	a	22 53			23 43	23 55	00s03	00 16

Saturdays

		VT	LM	VT	XC	LM	LM	LM	XC	LM	LM	XC	VT	LM	LM	LM	XC	LM	LM	VT	LM	VT	LM
		◇1	1	◇1	◇1	◇1	◇1		◇1	◇1		◇1	◇1	◇1	◇1		◇1		◇1	◇1	◇1	◇1	
London Euston 15 ⊖	d	22p00											06 05						06 24	06 36		07 07	
Watford Junction	d												06u20						06 41	06u51			
Milton Keynes Central	d	22p31					05 21						06 41						07 23				
Northampton	d						05 42								06 38				07 45				
Rugby	d	22p54					06 05						07 03		06 58				08 04				
Coventry	d							06 16								07 16							
Bedworth	d							06 27								07 27							
Nuneaton	a	23p03					06 16	06 34							07 09	07 35			08 16				
	d	23p04					06 17								07 15				08 17				
Atherstone	d						06 23								07 21				08 23				
Polesworth	d														07 26								
Tamworth	d	23b15					06 31								07 31				08 31				
Lichfield Trent Valley	d	23b22					06 37								07 37				08 37				
Rugeley Trent Valley	d						06 44								07 43				08 43				
Stafford	d	23b38	23p53	06 01	06 30	06 36	06 54		07 01	07 08		07 31	07 34	07 38	07 54		08 01		08 54		08 09	08 23	08 25
Norton Bridge Station Drv	d																		↪				08 40
Stone	d						07 05								08 05								
Stone Crown Street	d										07 20							08 20					
Stone Granville Square	a																						09 02
Barlaston Orchard Place	d										07 28							08 28					
Wedgwood Old Road Bridge	d										07 30							08 30					
Stoke-on-Trent	d				06a50		07 13		07a18		07 41				08 13		08a19	08 41					
Hanley Bus Station	a										07 47							08 47					
Kidsgrove	d						07 21								08 21								
Alsager	d						07 26								08 26								
Crewe	a	00s03	00 16	06 20		06 56	07 36			07 33		07 50	07 53	07 58	08 37					08 10	08 30	08 41	

A until 9 September

b Previous night, stops to set down only

London - Stoke-on-Trent and Crewe
Coventry - Nuneaton

		XC	LM	VT	LM	LM		XC	LM	LM	LM	VT	VT	XC	LM	VT		LM	XC	LM	VT	LM	LM	VT	VT
		◇1	◇1	◇1	◇1			◇1	◇1		◇1	◇1	◇1	◇1	◇1	◇1			◇1	◇1	◇1		◇1	◇1	◇1
																					A				
		[trolley]		[buffet]				[buffet]		[bus]		[buffet]	[buffet]	[trolley]		[buffet]			[buffet]		[buffet]	[bus]		[buffet]	[buffet]
London Euston 15 ⊖	d			07 35							07 46	08 07	08 10			08 40					08 43		08 46	08 50	09 07
Watford Junction	d										08 01													09 05	
Milton Keynes Central	d			08 06							08 25		08 41								09 13		09 23	09 25	
Northampton	d										08 45												09b45		
Rugby	d										09 04												10 04		
Coventry	d	07 27				08 42								08 27				09 42			09 42				
Bedworth	d					08 53												09 53							
Nuneaton	a					09 00					09 16							10 00					10 16		
	d										09 17												10 17		
Atherstone	d										09 23												10 23		
Polesworth	d																								
Tamworth	d										09 31												10 31		
Lichfield Trent Valley	d										09 37												10 37		
Rugeley Trent Valley	d				←						09 43												10 43		
Stafford	d	08 30	08 36		08 54			09 01	09 09		09 54	09a22		09 30	09 35				10 01	10 09			10 54		10a22
Norton Bridge Station Drv	d																								
Stone	d				09 05						10 05												11 05		
Stone Crown Street	d									09 20												10 20			
Stone Granville Square	a																								
Barlaston Orchard Place	d									09 28												10 28			
Wedgwood Old Road Bridge	d									09 30												10 30			
Stoke-on-Trent	d	08a54			09 13			09a19		09 41	10 13			09a54					10a19			10 41	11 13		
Hanley Bus Station	a									09 47												10 47			
Kidsgrove	d				09 21						10 21												11 21		
Alsager	d				09 26						10 26												11 26		
Crewe	a		08 56	09 10	09 38				09 30		10 38		09 48		09 56	10 10				10 30	11 07		11 38	10 32	

		LM		XC	LM	VT	LM	XC	LM	LM	LM	VT		VT	XC	LM	VT	LM	XC	LM	LM	LM		VT	VT
				◇1	◇1	◇1		◇1	◇1		◇1	◇1		◇1	◇1	◇1	◇1		◇1	◇1		◇1		◇1	◇1
		[bus]		[trolley]		[buffet]		[buffet]		[bus]		[buffet]		[buffet]	[trolley]		[buffet]		[buffet]		[bus]			[buffet]	[buffet]
London Euston 15 ⊖	d					09 40					09 46	10 07		10 10			10 40					10 46		11 07	11 10
Watford Junction	d										10 01											11 01			
Milton Keynes Central	d										10 25			10 41								11 25			11 41
Northampton	d										10 45											11 45			
Rugby	d										11 04											12 04			
Coventry	d			09 27			10 42								10 27			11 45							
Bedworth	d						10 53											11 56							
Nuneaton	a						11 00				11 16							12 03				12 16			
	d										11 17											12 17			
Atherstone	d										11 23											12 23			
Polesworth	d																								
Tamworth	d										11 31											12 31			
Lichfield Trent Valley	d										11 37											12 37			
Rugeley Trent Valley	d										11 43											12 43			
Stafford	d	10 25		10 30	10 35			11 01	11 09		11 54	11a22			11 30	11 35			12 01	12 09		12 54		12a22	
Norton Bridge Station Drv	d	10 40																							
Stone	d										12 05											13 05			
Stone Crown Street	d									11 20											12 20				
Stone Granville Square	a	11 02																							
Barlaston Orchard Place	d									11 28											12 28				
Wedgwood Old Road Bridge	d									11 30											12 30				
Stoke-on-Trent	d			10a54				11a19		11 41	12 13				11a54				12a19		12 41	13 13			
Hanley Bus Station	a									11 47											12 47				
Kidsgrove	d										12 21											13 21			
Alsager	d										12 26											13 26			
Crewe	a				10 56	11 10			11 30		12 38			11 48		11 56	12 10			12 30		13 38			12 47

A from 16 July until 10 September

Table 67

Saturdays

London - Stoke-on-Trent and Crewe
Coventry - Nuneaton

		XC	LM	VT	LM	LM	XC	LM		LM	LM	VT	VT	XC	LM	VT	LM	XC		LM	LM	LM	LM	VT	VT
		◇1	◇1	◇1			◇1	◇1			◇1	◇1	◇1	◇1	◇1	◇1		◇1		◇1			◇1	◇1	◇1
					🚌					🚌											🚌	🚌			
		🛒		☕			☕					☕	☕	🛒		☕		☕						☕	☕
London Euston 15 ⊖	d			11 40							11 46	12 07	12 10			12 40							12 46	13 07	13 10
Watford Junction	d										12 01												13 01		
Milton Keynes Central	d										12 25		12 41										13 25		13 41
Northampton	d										12 45												13 45		
Rugby	d										13 04												14 04		
Coventry	d	11 27				12 45								12 27			13 45								
Bedworth	d					12 56											13 56								
Nuneaton	a					13 03					13 16						14 03						14 16		
	d										13 17												14 17		
Atherstone	d										13 23												14 23		
Polesworth	d																								
Tamworth	d										13 31												14 31		
Lichfield Trent Valley	d										13 37												14 37		
Rugeley Trent Valley	d										13 43												14 43		
Stafford	d	12 30	12 35		12 35		13 01	13 09			13 54	13a22		13 30	13 35			14 01		14 09	14 18		14 54	14a22	
Norton Bridge Station Drv	d				12 59																14 42				
Stone	d										14 05												15 05		
Stone Crown Street	d									13 20												14 20			
Stone Granville Square	a				13 39																14 54				
Barlaston Orchard Place	d									13 28												14 28			
Wedgwood Old Road Bridge	d									13 30												14 30			
Stoke-on-Trent	d	12a54					13a18			13 41	14 13			13a54				14a19				14 41	15 13		
Hanley Bus Station	a									13 47												14 47			
Kidsgrove	d										14 21												15 21		
Alsager	d										14 26												15 26		
Crewe	a		12 56	13 10				13 30			14 38		13 47		13 56	14 10				14 30			15 38		14 48

		XC	LM	VT		XC	LM	VT	LM	LM	LM	VT	VT	XC		LM	VT	LM	XC	LM	LM	LM	LM	VT	
		◇1	◇1	◇1		◇1	◇1	◇1			◇1	◇1	◇1	◇1		◇1	◇1		◇1	◇1			◇1	◇1	
								A																	
										🚌											🚌	🚌			
		🛒		☕		☕		☕				☕	☕	🛒			☕		☕					☕	
London Euston 15 ⊖	d			13 40				13 43			13 46	14 07	14 10				14 40						14 46	15 07	
Watford Junction	d										14 01												15 01		
Milton Keynes Central	d							14 13			14 25		14 41										15 25		
Northampton	d										14 45												15 45		
Rugby	d										15 04												16 04		
Coventry	d	13 27						14 42	14 45					14 27				15 45							
Bedworth	d								14 56									15 56							
Nuneaton	a								15 03		15 16							16 03					16 16		
	d										15 17												16 17		
Atherstone	d										15 23												16 23		
Polesworth	d																								
Tamworth	d										15 31												16 31		
Lichfield Trent Valley	d										15 37												16 37		
Rugeley Trent Valley	d										15 43												16 43		
Stafford	d	14 30	14 35			15 01	15 09				15 54	15a22		15 30		15 35			16 01	16 09	16 18		16 54	16a22	
Norton Bridge Station Drv	d																				16a42				
Stone	d										16 05												17 05		
Stone Crown Street	d									15 20												16 20			
Stone Granville Square	a																								
Barlaston Orchard Place	d									15 28												16 28			
Wedgwood Old Road Bridge	d									15 30												16 30			
Stoke-on-Trent	d	14a54				15a19				15 41	16 13			15a54					16a19			16 41	17 13		
Hanley Bus Station	a									15 47												16 47			
Kidsgrove	d										16 21												17 21		
Alsager	d										16 26												17 26		
Crewe	a		14 56	15 10			15 30	16 08			16 38		15 47			15 56	16 11			16 30			17 38		

A from 16 July until 10 September

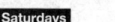

London - Stoke-on-Trent and Crewe
Coventry - Nuneaton

		VT	XC	LM	VT	LM	XC	LM	LM	LM		VT	VT	XC	LM	LM	VT	VT	LM	XC		LM	LM	VT	VT
		◇1	◇1	◇1	◇1		◇1	◇1		◇1		◇1	◇1	◇1	◇1		◇1	◇1		◇1		◇1	◇1	◇1	◇1
									🚌							🚌									
		☕	🛒		☕		☕					☕	☕	🛒			☕	☕		🛒				☕	☕
London Euston 15 ⊖	d	15 10			15 40					15 46		16 07	16 10				16 33	16 40					16 46	17 07	17 10
Watford Junction	d									16 01													17 01		
Milton Keynes Central	d	15 41								16 25			16 41										17 25		17 41
Northampton	d									16 45													17 45		
Rugby	d									17 04													18 04		
Coventry	d		15 27			16 45								16 27					17 45						
Bedworth	d					16 56													17 56						
Nuneaton	a					17 03				17 16									18 03				18 16	18 02	
	d									17 17													18 17	18 03	
Atherstone	d									17 23													18 23		
Polesworth	d																								
Tamworth	d									17 31							17 38						18 31		
Lichfield Trent Valley	d									17 37							17 45						18 37		
Rugeley Trent Valley	d									17 43													18 43		
Stafford	d		16 30	16 35			17 01	17 09		18b20		17a22		17 30	17 36	17 40	17a59			18 01		18 09	18 54	18a26	
Norton Bridge Station Drv	d															18a06									
Stone	d									18 31													19 05		
Stone Crown Street	d								17 20																
Stone Granville Square	a																								
Barlaston Orchard Place	d								17 28																
Wedgwood Old Road Bridge	d								17 30																
Stoke-on-Trent	d		16a54				17a19		17 41	18 41				17a54						18a19			19 13		
Hanley Bus Station	a								17 47																
Kidsgrove	d									18 49													19 21		
Alsager	d									18 54													19 26		
Crewe	a	16 47		16 56	17 10			17 30		19 05			17 47		17 56			18 10				18 30	19 36		18 48

		XC	LM	VT	LM	XC		LM	VT	LM	LM	VT	VT	XC	LM	VT		VT	XC	LM	VT	XC	LM	LM	VT
		◇1	◇1	◇1		◇1		◇1	◇1		1	◇1	◇1	◇1	◇1	◇1		◇1	◇1	1	◇1	◇1		◇1	◇1
									A																
					🚌																				
		🛒		☕		☕			☕			☕	☕	🛒		☕		☕	☕		☕				☕
London Euston 15 ⊖	d			17 40					17 43		17 46	18 07	18 10			18 33		18 40		18 46	19 07				19 30
Watford Junction	d										18 01									19 01					
Milton Keynes Central	d								18 13		18 25		18 41							19 27					
Northampton	d										18 45									19 45					
Rugby	d										19 04									20 04					
Coventry	d	17 27							18 42	18 45				18 27								19 27	20 15		
Bedworth	d									18 56													20 26		
Nuneaton	a									19 03	19 16									20 16	20 02		20 34		
	d										19 17									20 17	20 03				
Atherstone	d										19 23									20 23					
Polesworth	d																								
Tamworth	d										19 31					19 38				20 31					
Lichfield Trent Valley	d										19 37					19 46				20 37					
Rugeley Trent Valley	d										19 43									20 43					
Stafford	d	18 30	18 35			19 01		19 09			19 54	19a22		19 30	19 36	19a58			20 01	20 55	20 27	20 30		20 36	
Norton Bridge Station Drv	d																			↦					
Stone	d										20 05														
Stone Crown Street	d				18 45																				
Stone Granville Square	a																								
Barlaston Orchard Place	d				18 53																				
Wedgwood Old Road Bridge	d				18 55																				
Stoke-on-Trent	d	18a54			19 06	19a19					20 13			19a54					20a19			20a54			
Hanley Bus Station	a				19 12																				
Kidsgrove	d										20 21														
Alsager	d										20 26														
Crewe	a		18 56	19 10				19 30	20 07		20 36		19 48		19 58			20 10			20 45			20 57	21 01

A from 16 July until 10 September

Table 67

Saturdays

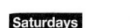

London - Stoke-on-Trent and Crewe
Coventry - Nuneaton

		VT		VT	LM	XC	LM	XC	XC	VT	VT	VT		LM	XC	VT	LM	XC	LM						
		◇1		◇1	1	◇1	◇1	◇1	◇1	◇1	◇1	◇1		◇1	◇1	◇1		◇1	◇1						
								A	B																
		☕		☕		☕		🛒		☕	☕	☕				☕									
London Euston 15 ⊖	d			19 40						20 11	20 20	20 31				21 00									
Watford Junction	d											20u46													
Milton Keynes Central	d										21 05					21 45									
Northampton	d																								
Rugby	d									21 15		21 36													
Coventry	d								20 27						21 27		21 45								
Bedworth	d																21 56								
Nuneaton	a										21 32						22 03								
	d										21 33														
Atherstone	d																								
Polesworth	d																								
Tamworth	d											21 53													
Lichfield Trent Valley	d											22 00													
Rugeley Trent Valley	d				←																				
Stafford	d	20 50			20 55	21 01	21 09	21 30	21 30	21 46				22 16	22 30	22 34		23 02	23 13						
Norton Bridge Station Drv	d																								
Stone	d				21 07																				
Stone Crown Street	d																								
Stone Granville Square	a																								
Barlaston Orchard Place	d																								
Wedgwood Old Road Bridge	d																								
Stoke-on-Trent	d				21 15	21a20		21a52	21a54		22a05				22a50			23a20							
Hanley Bus Station	a																								
Kidsgrove	d				21 23																				
Alsager	d				21 28																				
Crewe	a	21 09		21 18	21 38		21 30			22 05		22 35		22 40		22 58			23 37						

Sundays

until 10 July

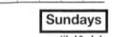

		VT	XC	VT	VT	LM	VT	XC	VT	LM		VT	XC	LM	VT	LM	VT	XC	VT	LM		LM	LM	VT	XC
		◇1	◇1	◇1	◇1	◇1	◇1	◇1	◇1	◇1		◇1	◇1	1	◇1	◇1	◇1	◇1	◇1	◇1			◇1	◇1	◇1
		☕	🛒	☕	☕		☕	🛒	☕			☕	🛒		☕		☕	🛒	☕					☕	🛒
London Euston 15 ⊖	d			08 10	08 15		08 45		09 15			09 45			10 15		10 45		11 15					12 02	
Watford Junction	d																								
Milton Keynes Central	d			08 56			09 32					10 33					11 33		12 03						
Northampton	d																			11 36					
Rugby	d						10 09					11 09					12 09			12 02					
Coventry	d												10 28					11 28				11 55			12 28
Bedworth	d																					12 06			
Nuneaton	a				09 43				10 44						11 46					12 13		12 13			
	d				09 44				10 45						11 47					12 16					
Atherstone	d																			12 21					
Polesworth	d																								
Tamworth	d																			12 30					
Lichfield Trent Valley	d																			12 36					
Rugeley Trent Valley	d																			12 42					
Stafford	d	09 17	09 33		10 08	10 16		10 33	11 09	11 16			11 32	11 44	12 13	12 17		12 33	12 53	13 00			13 09	13 25	13 34
Norton Bridge Station Drv	d																								
Stone	d													11 55						13 12					
Stone Crown Street	d																								
Stone Granville Square	a																								
Barlaston Orchard Place	d																								
Wedgwood Old Road Bridge	d																								
Stoke-on-Trent	d							10a51					11a51	12 03				12a52		13 20					13a56
Hanley Bus Station	a																								
Kidsgrove	d													12 11						13 28					
Alsager	d													12 15						13 32					
Crewe	a	09 35	09 54	10 17	10 28	10 37	10 55		11 30	11 37		11 55		12 26	12 33	12 37	12 56		13 13	13 43			13 30	13 43	

A until 10 September

B from 17 September

Table 67

London - Stoke-on-Trent and Crewe
Coventry - Nuneaton

Sundays
until 10 July

		VT ◇1 ⊡	LM	LM ◇1	LM ◇1	VT ◇1 ⊡		XC ◇1 ⫟	VT ◇1 ⊡	LM ◇1	LM ◇1	VT ◇1 ⊡	XC ◇1 ⫟	VT ◇1 ⊡	LM	LM		LM ◇1	LM ◇1	VT ◇1 ⊡	VT ◇1 ⊡	XC ◇1 ⫟	VT ◇1 ⊡	LM ◇1	VT ◇1 ⊡
London Euston [15] ⊖	d	12 35			12 50	13 02			13 35			14 02		14 35					14 50	15 02	15 05		15 35		16 02
Watford Junction	d				13 06														15 06						
Milton Keynes Central	d				13 36														15 36		15 39				
Northampton	d				13 56														15 56						
Rugby	d				14 17														16 17						
Coventry	d		13 46					13 26					14 26		14 46	15 46						15 26			
Bedworth	d		13 57												14 57	15 57									
Nuneaton	a		14 04		14 29										15 04	16 04			16 29						
	d				14 30														16 30						
Atherstone	d				14 37														16 37						
Polesworth	d																								
Tamworth	d				14 45														16 45						
Lichfield Trent Valley	d				14 51														16 51						
Rugeley Trent Valley	d				14 58						←								16 58						
Stafford	d			14 10	15 17	14 22		14 34		15 10	15 17	15 25	15 34					16 09	17 20	16a20		16 34		17 09	17a24
Norton Bridge Station Drv	d				→																				
Stone	d										15 32								17 30						
Stone Crown Street	d																								
Stone Granville Square	a																								
Barlaston Orchard Place	d																								
Wedgwood Old Road Bridge	d																								
Stoke-on-Trent	d							14a56			15 41		15a56						17 42			16a56			
Hanley Bus Station	a																								
Kidsgrove	d										15 52								17 50						
Alsager	d										15 58								17 54						
Crewe	a	14 12		14 30		14 43			15 12	15 30	16 07	15 43		16 12				16 30	18 06		16 50		17 12	17 30	

		VT ◇1 ⊡		XC ◇1 ⫟	VT ◇1 ⊡	LM	LM	LM ◇1	LM ◇1	VT ◇1 ⊡	VT ◇1 ⊡	XC ◇1 ⫟		VT ◇1 ⊡	LM ◇1	VT ◇1 ⊡	VT ◇1 ⊡	XC ◇1 ⫟	VT ◇1 ⊡	LM ◇1	LM ◇1	VT ◇1 ⊡		VT ◇1 ⊡	XC ◇1
London Euston [15] ⊖	d	16 05			16 35				16 50	17 02	17 05			17 35		18 02	18 05		18 35		18 50	19 02		19 05	
Watford Junction	d								17 06												19 06				
Milton Keynes Central	d	16 39							17 36		17 39						18 39				19 36			19 39	
Northampton	d								17 56												19 56				
Rugby	d								18 17												20 17				
Coventry	d			16 26		16 46	17 46					17 26						18 26							19 26
Bedworth	d					16 57	17 57																		
Nuneaton	a					17 04	18 04		18 29		18 09										20 29	20 00			
	d								18 30		18 10										20 30	20 01			
Atherstone	d								18 37												20 37				
Polesworth	d																								
Tamworth	d								18 45												20 45				
Lichfield Trent Valley	d								18 51												20 51				
Rugeley Trent Valley	d								18 58												20 58				
Stafford	d			17 36				18 09	19 17	18a24		18 36			19 10	19a24		19 38		20 09	21 16	20 30			20 37
Norton Bridge Station Drv	d																				→				
Stone	d								19 32																
Stone Crown Street	d																								
Stone Granville Square	a																								
Barlaston Orchard Place	d																								
Wedgwood Old Road Bridge	d																								
Stoke-on-Trent	d			17a56					19 41			18a56						19a56							20a56
Hanley Bus Station	a																								
Kidsgrove	d								19 52																
Alsager	d								19 57																
Crewe	a	17 50			18 12			18 30	20 06		18 53			19 12	19 30		19 50		20 12	20 30		20 48		20 53	

		LM	VT ◇1 ⊡	VT ◇1 ⊡	VT ◇1 ⊡	LM ◇1	VT ◇1 ⊡	VT ◇1 ⊡		XC ◇1	VT ◇1 ⊡	VT ◇1 ⊡	LM ◇1	VT ◇1 ⊡	SR [R] ⊡	XC ◇1	LM	VT ◇1 ⊡		AW ◇	VT ◇1 ⊡				
London Euston [15] ⊖	d			19 35	20 02		20 05	20 25				20 35		20 50	20 55			21 21			21 51				
Watford Junction	d														21u17										
Milton Keynes Central	d						20 38							21 37							22 38				
Northampton	d																								
Rugby	d													22 01							23 18				
Coventry	d	19 46								20 26						21 26	21 35								
Bedworth	d	19 57															21 46								
Nuneaton	a	20 04			21 00												21 53	22 51			23 28				
	d				21 01													22 52			23 29				
Atherstone	d																								
Polesworth	d																								
Tamworth	d							21 32																	
Lichfield Trent Valley	d							21 39																	
Rugeley Trent Valley	d					←																			
Stafford	d		20 52			21 16	21 33			21 37	21 57	22 00	22 16			22 37		23 17		23 31	23s53				
Norton Bridge Station Drv	d																								
Stone	d					21 32																			
Stone Crown Street	d																								
Stone Granville Square	a																								
Barlaston Orchard Place	d																								
Wedgwood Old Road Bridge	d																								
Stoke-on-Trent	d					21 43				21a56						22a55									
Hanley Bus Station	a																								
Kidsgrove	d					21 54																			
Alsager	d					22 01																			
Crewe	a		21 10	21 13	21 44	22 12	21 53	22 10			22 17	22 20	22 39	22 49				23 37		23 55	00s12				

Sundays

17 July to 11 September

London - Stoke-on-Trent and Crewe
Coventry - Nuneaton

		VT ◇1 🍴	XC ◇1 🛒	VT ◇1 🍴	VT ◇1 🍴	LM ◇1	VT ◇1 🍴	XC ◇1 🛒	VT ◇1 🍴	LM ◇1		VT ◇1 🍴	XC ◇1 🛒	LM 1	VT ◇1 🍴	LM ◇1	VT ◇1 🍴	XC ◇1 🛒	VT ◇1 🍴	LM ◇1		LM	LM ◇1	VT ◇1 🍴	XC ◇1 🛒
London Euston 15 ⊖	d			08 10	08 15		08 45		09 15			09 45			10 15		10 45		11 15					12 02	
Watford Junction	d																								
Milton Keynes Central	d			08 56			09 32					10 33					11 33		12 03						
Northampton	d																			11 36					
Rugby	d						10 09					11 09					12 09			12 02					
Coventry	d												10 28					11 28				11 55			12 28
Bedworth	d																					12 06			
Nuneaton	a				09 43				10 44						11 46					12 13		12 13			
	d				09 44				10 45						11 47					12 16					
Atherstone	d																			12 21					
Polesworth	d																								
Tamworth	d																			12 30					
Lichfield Trent Valley	d																			12 36					
Rugeley Trent Valley	d																			12 42					
Stafford	d	09 17	09 33		10 08	10 16		10 33	11 09	11 16			11 32	11 44	12 13	12 17		12 33	12 53	13 00			13 09	13 25	13 34
Norton Bridge Station Drv	d																								
Stone	d													11 55						13 12					
Stone Crown Street	d																								
Stone Granville Square	a																								
Barlaston Orchard Place	d																								
Wedgwood Old Road Bridge	d																								
Stoke-on-Trent	d							10a51					11a51	12 03				12a52		13 20					13a56
Hanley Bus Station	a																								
Kidsgrove	d													12 11						13 28					
Alsager	d													12 15						13 32					
Crewe	a	09 35	09 54	10 17	10 28	10 37	10 55		11 30	11 37		11 55		12 26	12 33	12 37	12 56		13 13	13 43			13 30	13 43	

		VT ◇1 🍴	LM	LM ◇1	LM ◇1	VT ◇1 🍴		XC ◇1 🛒	VT ◇1 🍴	LM ◇1	LM ◇1	VT ◇1 🍴	XC ◇1 🛒	VT ◇1 🍴	LM	LM		LM ◇1	LM ◇1	VT ◇1 🍴	VT ◇1 🍴	XC ◇1 🛒	VT ◇1 🍴	LM ◇1	VT ◇1 🍴
London Euston 15 ⊖	d	12 35			12 50	13 02			13 35			14 02		14 35					14 50	15 02	15 05		15 35		16 02
Watford Junction	d				13 06														15 06						
Milton Keynes Central	d				13 36														15 36		15 39				
Northampton	d				13 56														15 56						
Rugby	d				14 17														16 17						
Coventry	d		13 46					13 26					14 26		14 46	15 46						15 26			
Bedworth	d		13 57												14 57	15 57									
Nuneaton	a		14 04		14 29										15 04	16 04			16 29						
	d				14 30														16 30						
Atherstone	d				14 37														16 37						
Polesworth	d																								
Tamworth	d				14 45														16 45						
Lichfield Trent Valley	d				14 51														16 51						
Rugeley Trent Valley	d				14 58						←								16 58						
Stafford	d			14 10	15 17	14 22		14 34		15 10	15 17	15 25	15 34					16 09	17 20	16a21		16 34		17 09	17a24
Norton Bridge Station Drv	d				↦																				
Stone	d										15 32								17 30						
Stone Crown Street	d																								
Stone Granville Square	a																								
Barlaston Orchard Place	d																								
Wedgwood Old Road Bridge	d																								
Stoke-on-Trent	d							14a56			15 41		15a56						17 42			16a56			
Hanley Bus Station	a																								
Kidsgrove	d										15 52								17 50						
Alsager	d										15 58								17 54						
Crewe	a	14 12		14 30		14 43			15 12	15 30	16 07	15 43		16 12				16 30	18 06		16 50		17 12	17 30	

		VT ◇1 🍴		XC ◇1 🛒	VT ◇1 🍴	LM	LM	LM ◇1	LM ◇1	VT ◇1 🍴	VT ◇1 🍴	XC ◇1 🛒		VT ◇1 🍴	LM ◇1	VT ◇1 🍴	VT ◇1 🍴	XC ◇1 🛒	VT ◇1 🍴	LM ◇1	LM ◇1	VT ◇1 🍴		VT ◇1 🍴	XC ◇1
London Euston 15 ⊖	d	16 05			16 35				16 50	17 02	17 05			17 35		18 02	18 05		18 35		18 50	19 02		19 05	
Watford Junction	d								17 06												19 06				
Milton Keynes Central	d	16 39							17 36		17 39						18 39				19 36			19 39	
Northampton	d								17 56												19 56				
Rugby	d								18 17												20 17				
Coventry	d			16 26		16 46	17 46					17 26						18 26							19 26
Bedworth	d					16 57	17 57																		
Nuneaton	a					17 04	18 04		18 29		18 09										20 29	20 01			
	d								18 30		18 10										20 30	20 02			
Atherstone	d								18 37												20 37				
Polesworth	d																								
Tamworth	d								18 45												20 45				
Lichfield Trent Valley	d								18 51												20 51				
Rugeley Trent Valley	d								18 58												20 58				
Stafford	d			17 36				18 09	19 17	18a24		18 36			19 10	19a24		19 38		20 09	21 16	20 30			20 37
Norton Bridge Station Drv	d																				↦				
Stone	d								19 32																
Stone Crown Street	d																								
Stone Granville Square	a																								
Barlaston Orchard Place	d																								
Wedgwood Old Road Bridge	d																								
Stoke-on-Trent	d			17a56					19 41			18a56						19a56							20a56
Hanley Bus Station	a																								
Kidsgrove	d								19 52																
Alsager	d								19 57																
Crewe	a	17 50			18 12			18 30	20 06		18 53			19 12	19 30		19 50		20 12	20 30		20 48		20 53	

Table 67

Sundays

17 July to 11 September

London - Stoke-on-Trent and Crewe
Coventry - Nuneaton

		LM	VT	VT	VT	LM	VT	VT		XC	VT	VT	LM	VT	SR	XC	LM	VT		AW	VT				
															R										
			◇1	◇1	◇1	◇1	◇1	◇1		◇1	◇1	◇1	◇1	◇1	🛏	◇1		◇1		◇	◇1				
			☕	☕	☕		☕	☕			☕	☕		☕	☕			☕			☕				
London Euston 15 ⊖	d			19 35	20 02		20 05	20 25				20 35		20 50	20 55			21 21			21 51				
Watford Junction	d														21u17										
Milton Keynes Central	d						20 38							21 37							22 38				
Northampton	d																								
Rugby	d													22 01							23 18				
Coventry	d	19 46								20 26						21 26	21 35								
Bedworth	d	19 57															21 46								
Nuneaton	a	20 04			21 00												21 53	22 51			23 28				
	d				21 01													22 52			23 29				
Atherstone	d																								
Polesworth	d																								
Tamworth	d							21 32																	
Lichfield Trent Valley	d							21 39																	
Rugeley Trent Valley	d					←																			
Stafford	d		20 52			21 16	21 33			21 37	21 57	22 00	22 16			22 37		23 17		23 31	23s53				
Norton Bridge Station Drv	d																								
Stone	d					21 32																			
Stone Crown Street	d																								
Stone Granville Square	a																								
Barlaston Orchard Place	d																								
Wedgwood Old Road Bridge	d																								
Stoke-on-Trent	d					21 43				21a56						22a55									
Hanley Bus Station	a																								
Kidsgrove	d					21 54																			
Alsager	d					22 01																			
Crewe	a		21 10	21 13	21 44	22 12	21 53	22 10			22 17	22 20	22 39	22 49				23 37		23 55	00s12				

Sundays

18 September to 23 October

		VT	XC	VT	VT	LM	VT	XC	VT	LM		VT	XC	LM	VT	LM	VT	XC	VT	LM		LM	LM	VT	XC
		◇1	◇1	◇1	◇1	◇1	◇1	◇1	◇1	◇1		◇1	◇1	1	◇1	◇1	◇1	◇1	◇1	◇1			◇1	◇1	◇1
		☕	🍴	☕	☕		☕	🍴	☕			☕	🍴		☕		☕	🍴	☕					☕	🍴
London Euston 15 ⊖	d			08 10	08 15		08 45		09 15			09 45			10 15		10 45		11 15					12 02	
Watford Junction	d																								
Milton Keynes Central	d			08 56			09 32					10 33					11 33		12 03						
Northampton	d																			11 36					
Rugby	d						10 09					11 09					12 09			12 02					
Coventry	d												10 28					11 30				11 55			12 29
Bedworth	d																					12 06			
Nuneaton	a				09 43				10 44						11 46					12 13		12 13			
	d				09 44				10 45						11 47					12 16					
Atherstone	d																			12 21					
Polesworth	d																								
Tamworth	d																			12 30					
Lichfield Trent Valley	d																			12 36					
Rugeley Trent Valley	d																			12 42					
Stafford	d	09 17	09 33		10 08	10 16		10 33	11 09	11 16			11 32	11 44	12 13	12 17		12 33	12 53	13 00			13 09	13 25	13 34
Norton Bridge Station Drv	d																								
Stone	d													11 55						13 12					
Stone Crown Street	d																								
Stone Granville Square	a																								
Barlaston Orchard Place	d																								
Wedgwood Old Road Bridge	d																								
Stoke-on-Trent	d							10a51					11a51	12 03				12a52		13 20					13a56
Hanley Bus Station	a																								
Kidsgrove	d													12 11						13 28					
Alsager	d													12 15						13 32					
Crewe	a	09 35	09 54	10 17	10 28	10 37	10 55		11 30	11 37		11 55		12 26	12 33	12 37	12 56		13 13	13 43			13 30	13 43	

Table 67

Sundays

18 September to 23 October

London - Stoke-on-Trent and Crewe
Coventry - Nuneaton

		VT	LM	LM	LM	VT		XC	VT	LM	LM	VT	XC	VT	LM	LM		LM	LM	VT	VT	XC	VT	LM	VT
		◇1		◇1	◇1	◇1		◇1	◇1	◇1	◇1	◇1	◇1	◇1				◇1	◇1	◇1	◇1	◇1	◇1	◇1	◇1
		☕				☕		🛒	☕			☕	🛒	☕						☕	☕	🛒	☕		☕
London Euston 15 ⊖	d	12 35			12 50	13 02			13 35			14 02		14 35					14 50	15 02	15 05		15 35		16 02
Watford Junction	d				13 06														15 06						
Milton Keynes Central	d				13 36														15 36		15 39				
Northampton	d				13 56														15 56						
Rugby	d				14 17														16 17						
Coventry	d		13 46					13 26					14 26		14 46	15 46						15 26			
Bedworth	d		13 57												14 57	15 57									
Nuneaton	a		14 04		14 29										15 04	16 04			16 29						
	d				14 30														16 30						
Atherstone	d				14 37														16 37						
Polesworth	d																								
Tamworth	d				14 45														16 45						
Lichfield Trent Valley	d				14 51														16 51						
Rugeley Trent Valley	d				14 58						←								16 58						
Stafford	d			14 10	15 17	14 22		14 34		15 10	15 17	15 25	15 34					16 09	17 20	16a20		16 34		17 09	17a24
Norton Bridge Station Drv	d				↪																				
Stone	d										15 32								17 30						
Stone Crown Street	d																								
Stone Granville Square	a																								
Barlaston Orchard Place	d																								
Wedgwood Old Road Bridge	d																								
Stoke-on-Trent	d							14a56			15 41		15a56						17 42			16a56			
Hanley Bus Station	a																								
Kidsgrove	d										15 52								17 50						
Alsager	d										15 58								17 54						
Crewe	a	14 12		14 30		14 43			15 12	15 30	16 07	15 43		16 12				16 30	18 06		16 50		17 12	17 30	

		VT		XC	VT	LM	LM	LM	LM	VT	VT	XC		VT	LM	VT	VT	XC	VT	LM	LM	VT		VT	XC
		◇1		◇1	◇1			◇1	◇1	◇1	◇1	◇1		◇1	◇1	◇1	◇1	◇1	◇1	◇1	◇1	◇1		◇1	◇1
		☕		🛒	☕					☕	☕	🛒		☕		☕	☕	🛒	☕			☕		☕	
London Euston 15 ⊖	d	16 05			16 35				16 50	17 02	17 05			17 35		18 02	18 05		18 35		18 50	19 02		19 05	
Watford Junction	d								17 06												19 06				
Milton Keynes Central	d	16 39							17 36		17 39						18 39				19 36			19 39	
Northampton	d								17 56												19 56				
Rugby	d								18 17												20 17				
Coventry	d			16 26		16 46	17 46					17 26						18 26							19 26
Bedworth	d					16 57	17 57																		
Nuneaton	a					17 04	18 04		18 29		18 09										20 29	20 00			
	d								18 30		18 10										20 30	20 01			
Atherstone	d								18 37												20 37				
Polesworth	d																								
Tamworth	d								18 45												20 45				
Lichfield Trent Valley	d								18 51												20 51				
Rugeley Trent Valley	d								18 58												20 58				
Stafford	d			17 36				18 09	19 17	18a24		18 36			19 10	19a24		19 38		20 09	21 16	20 30			20 37
Norton Bridge Station Drv	d																				↪				
Stone	d								19 32																
Stone Crown Street	d																								
Stone Granville Square	a																								
Barlaston Orchard Place	d																								
Wedgwood Old Road Bridge	d																								
Stoke-on-Trent	d			17a56					19 41			18a56						19a56							20a56
Hanley Bus Station	a																								
Kidsgrove	d								19 52																
Alsager	d								19 57																
Crewe	a	17 50			18 12			18 30	20 06		18 53			19 12	19 30		19 50		20 12	20 30		20 48		20 53	

		LM	VT	VT	VT	LM	VT	VT		XC	VT	VT	LM	VT	SR	XC	LM	VT		AW	VT				
															R										
			◇1	◇1	◇1	◇1	◇1	◇1		◇1	◇1	◇1	◇1	◇1		◇1		◇1		◇	◇1				
															🛏										
			☕	☕	☕		☕	☕			☕	☕		☕	☕			☕			☕				
London Euston 15 ⊖	d			19 35	20 02		20 05	20 25				20 35		20 50	20 55			21 21			21 51				
Watford Junction	d														21u17										
Milton Keynes Central	d						20 38							21 37							22 38				
Northampton	d																								
Rugby	d													22 01							23 18				
Coventry	d	19 46								20 26						21 26	21 35								
Bedworth	d	19 57															21 46								
Nuneaton	a	20 04			21 00												21 53	22 51			23 28				
	d				21 01													22 52			23 29				
Atherstone	d																								
Polesworth	d																								
Tamworth	d							21 32																	
Lichfield Trent Valley	d							21 39																	
Rugeley Trent Valley	d					←																			
Stafford	d		20 52			21 16	21 33			21 37	21 57	22 00	22 16			22 37		23 17		23 31	23s53				
Norton Bridge Station Drv	d																								
Stone	d					21 32																			
Stone Crown Street	d																								
Stone Granville Square	a																								
Barlaston Orchard Place	d																								
Wedgwood Old Road Bridge	d																								
Stoke-on-Trent	d					21 43				21a56						22a55									
Hanley Bus Station	a																								
Kidsgrove	d					21 54																			
Alsager	d					22 01																			
Crewe	a		21 10	21 13	21 44	22 12	21 53	22 10			22 17	22 20	22 39	22 49				23 37		23 55	00s12				

Table 67

Sundays

from 30 October

London - Stoke-on-Trent and Crewe
Coventry - Nuneaton

		VT	XC	VT	VT	LM	VT	XC	VT	LM		VT	XC	LM	VT	LM	VT	XC	VT	LM		LM	LM	VT	XC
		◇1	◇1	◇1	◇1	◇1	◇1	◇1	◇1	◇1		◇1	◇1	1	◇1	◇1	◇1	◇1	◇1	◇1			◇1	◇1	◇1
		⊡	⊼	⊡	⊡		⊡	⊼	⊡			⊡	⊼		⊡		⊡	⊼	⊡					⊡	⊼
London Euston 15 ⊖	d			08 10	08 15		08 45		09 15			09 45			10 15		10 45		11 15					12 02	
Watford Junction	d																								
Milton Keynes Central	d			08 56			09 32					10 33					11 33		12 03						
Northampton	d																			11 36					
Rugby	d						10 09					11 09					12 09			12 02					
Coventry	d												10 28					11 29				11 55			12 28
Bedworth	d																					12 06			
Nuneaton	a				09 43				10 44						11 46					12 13		12 13			
	d				09 44				10 45						11 47					12 16					
Atherstone	d																			12 21					
Polesworth	d																								
Tamworth	d																			12 30					
Lichfield Trent Valley	d																			12 36					
Rugeley Trent Valley	d																			12 42					
Stafford	d	09 17	09 33		10 08	10 16		10 33	11 09	11 16			11 32	11 44	12 13	12 17		12 33	12 53	13 00			13 09	13 25	13 34
Norton Bridge Station Drv	d																								
Stone	d													11 55						13 12					
Stone Crown Street	d																								
Stone Granville Square	a																								
Barlaston Orchard Place	d																								
Wedgwood Old Road Bridge	d																								
Stoke-on-Trent	d							10a51					11a51	12 03				12a52		13 20					13a56
Hanley Bus Station	a																								
Kidsgrove	d													12 11						13 28					
Alsager	d													12 15						13 32					
Crewe	a	09 35	09 54	10 17	10 28	10 37	10 55		11 30	11 37		11 55		12 26	12 33	12 37	12 56		13 13	13 43			13 30	13 43	

		VT	LM	LM	LM	VT		XC	VT	LM	LM	VT	XC	VT	LM	LM		LM	LM	VT	VT	XC	VT	LM	VT
		◇1		◇1	◇1	◇1		◇1	◇1	◇1	◇1	◇1	◇1	◇1				◇1	◇1	◇1	◇1	◇1	◇1	◇1	◇1
		⊡				⊡		⊼	⊡			⊡	⊼	⊡						⊡	⊡	⊼	⊡		⊡
London Euston 15 ⊖	d	12 35			12 50	13 02			13 35			14 02		14 35					14 50	15 02	15 05		15 35		16 02
Watford Junction	d				13 06														15 06						
Milton Keynes Central	d				13 36														15 36		15 39				
Northampton	d				13 56														15 56						
Rugby	d				14 17														16 17						
Coventry	d		13 46					13 26					14 26		14 46	15 46						15 26			
Bedworth	d		13 57												14 57	15 57									
Nuneaton	a		14 04		14 29										15 04	16 04			16 29						
	d				14 30														16 30						
Atherstone	d				14 37														16 37						
Polesworth	d																								
Tamworth	d				14 45														16 45						
Lichfield Trent Valley	d				14 51														16 51						
Rugeley Trent Valley	d				14 58						←								16 58						
Stafford	d			14 10	15 17	14 22		14 34		15 10	15 17	15 25	15 34					16 09	17 20	16a20		16 34		17 09	17a24
Norton Bridge Station Drv	d				→																				
Stone	d										15 32								17 30						
Stone Crown Street	d																								
Stone Granville Square	a																								
Barlaston Orchard Place	d																								
Wedgwood Old Road Bridge	d																								
Stoke-on-Trent	d							14a56			15 41		15a56						17 42			16a56			
Hanley Bus Station	a																								
Kidsgrove	d										15 52								17 50						
Alsager	d										15 58								17 54						
Crewe	a	14 12		14 30		14 43			15 12	15 30	16 07	15 43		16 12				16 30	18 06		16 50		17 12	17 30	

		VT		XC	VT	LM	LM	LM	LM	VT	VT	XC		VT	LM	VT	VT	XC	VT	LM	LM	VT		VT	XC
		◇1		◇1	◇1			◇1	◇1	◇1	◇1	◇1		◇1	◇1	◇1	◇1	◇1	◇1	◇1	◇1	◇1		◇1	◇1
		⊡		⊼	⊡					⊡	⊡	⊼		⊡		⊡	⊡	⊼	⊡			⊡		⊡	
London Euston 15 ⊖	d	16 05			16 35				16 50	17 02	17 05			17 35		18 02	18 05		18 35		18 50	19 02		19 05	
Watford Junction	d								17 06												19 06				
Milton Keynes Central	d	16 39							17 36		17 39						18 39				19 36			19 39	
Northampton	d								17 56												19 56				
Rugby	d								18 17												20 17				
Coventry	d			16 26		16 46	17 46					17 26						18 26							19 26
Bedworth	d					16 57	17 57																		
Nuneaton	a					17 04	18 04		18 29		18 09										20 29	20 00			
	d								18 30		18 10										20 30	20 01			
Atherstone	d								18 37												20 37				
Polesworth	d																								
Tamworth	d								18 45												20 45				
Lichfield Trent Valley	d								18 51												20 51				
Rugeley Trent Valley	d								18 58												20 58				
Stafford	d			17 36				18 09	19 17	18a24		18 36			19 10	19a24		19 38		20 09	21 16	20 30			20 37
Norton Bridge Station Drv	d																				→				
Stone	d								19 32																
Stone Crown Street	d																								
Stone Granville Square	a																								
Barlaston Orchard Place	d																								
Wedgwood Old Road Bridge	d																								
Stoke-on-Trent	d			17a56					19 41			18a56						19a56							20a56
Hanley Bus Station	a																								
Kidsgrove	d								19 52																
Alsager	d								19 57																
Crewe	a	17 50			18 12			18 30	20 06		18 53			19 12	19 30		19 50		20 12	20 30		20 48		20 53	

Table 67

Sundays
from 30 October

London - Stoke-on-Trent and Crewe
Coventry - Nuneaton

		LM	VT	VT	VT	LM	VT	VT		XC	VT	VT	LM	VT	SR	XC	LM	VT		AW	VT
															R						
			◇ 1	◇ 1	◇ 1	◇ 1	◇ 1	◇ 1		◇ 1	◇ 1	◇ 1	◇ 1	◇ 1		◇ 1		◇ 1		◇	◇ 1
															🛏						
			☕	☕	☕		☕	☕			☕	☕		☕	☕			☕			☕
London Euston 15 ⊖	d			19 35	20 02		20 05	20 25				20 35		20 50	20 55			21 21			21 51
Watford Junction	d														21u17						
Milton Keynes Central	d						20 38							21 37							22 38
Northampton	d																				
Rugby	d													22 01							23 18
Coventry	d	19 46								20 26						21 26	21 35				
Bedworth	d	19 57															21 46				
Nuneaton	a	20 04			21 00												21 53	22 51			23 28
	d				21 01													22 52			23 29
Atherstone	d																				
Polesworth	d																				
Tamworth	d							21 32													
Lichfield Trent Valley	d							21 39													
Rugeley Trent Valley	d					⟵															
Stafford	d		20 52			21 16	21 33			21 37	21 57	22 00	22 16			22 37		23 17		23 31	23s53
Norton Bridge Station Drv	d																				
Stone	d					21 32															
Stone Crown Street	d																				
Stone Granville Square	a																				
Barlaston Orchard Place	d																				
Wedgwood Old Road Bridge	d																				
Stoke-on-Trent	d					21 43				21a56						22a55					
Hanley Bus Station	a																				
Kidsgrove	d					21 54															
Alsager	d					22 01															
Crewe	a		21 10	21 13	21 44	22 12	21 53	22 10			22 17	22 20	22 39	22 49				23 37		23 55	00s12

Crewe and Stoke-on-Trent - London
Nuneaton - Coventry

Miles	Miles	Miles			AW	LM	VT	LM	SR	XC	VT	XC	LM		VT	LM	VT	LM	XC	LM	VT	LM	VT		LM
						1	◇1 ⊠		R 🛏	◇1 🛒	◇1 ⊠	◇1 🛒	1		◇1 ⊠	🚌	◇1 ⊠	◇1	◇1 🛒	1	◇1 ⊠		◇1 ⊠		1
0	0	—	**Crewe**	d	04 59	05 18	05 36			05 47	06 02		06 20		06 29			06 35	06 38	06 47	06 53				07 16
6½	—	—	Alsager	d														06 44							
8¾	—	—	Kidsgrove	d														06 48							
—	—	—	Hanley Bus Station	d												06 50									
16	—	—	**Stoke-on-Trent**	d						06 07						06 56		06 58					07 06		
—	—	—	Wedgwood Old Road Bridge	d												07 08									
—	—	—	Barlaston Orchard Place	d												07 11									
—	—	—	Stone Granville Square	d												07a25									
23¼	—	—	Stone	d														07 06							
—	—	—	Norton Bridge Station Drv	d								←													
32¼	24½	—	**Stafford**	d	05a24		05 55			06 25	06 21	06 25	06a40				06 53	07 24	06a57	07a10			07 28		07a40
42	—	—	Rugeley Trent Valley	d		06 00				→								07 33							
50	—	—	Lichfield Trent Valley	d		06 07											07 08	07 40							
56¼	—	—	Tamworth	d		06 14											07 15	07 47							
59¾	—	—	Polesworth	d																					
63¾	—	—	Atherstone	d		06 23												07 56							
68¾	—	0	Nuneaton	a		06 29	06 17								07 06			08 02			07 32				
—	—	—		d		06 30	06 18	06 37							07 07			08 02			07 33	07 37			
—	—	3¾	Bedworth	d				06 44														07 44			
—	—	10	**Coventry**	a				06 56				07 24										07 57	08 30		
83¼	—	—	Rugby	a		06 47	06 30				06 52							08 18							
102	—	—	Northampton	a														08 41							
118	—	—	Milton Keynes Central	a			06 51				07 12							09 01							
150¼	—	—	Watford Junction	a														09 27					09s15		
167¾	—	—	**London Euston** 15 ⊖	a			07 28		07 47		07 50				08 07		08 22	09 44			08 33		09 34		

		VT	XC	LM	LM	LM	LM	LM	VT		XC	VT	VT	LM	VT	XC	LM	LM	LM		VT	LM	XC	LM	VT
		◇1 ⊠	◇1 🛒		◇1	1	🚌	🚌	◇1 ⊠		◇1 🛒	◇1 ⊠	◇1 ⊠	1	◇1 ⊠	◇1 🛒		◇1	1		◇1 ⊠	◇1	◇1 🛒	🚌	◇1 ⊠
Crewe	d	07 17			07 33	07 49			07 57					08 22	08 29			08 33	08 49		08 56				
Alsager	d				07 41													08 41							
Kidsgrove	d				07 46													08 46							
Hanley Bus Station	d						07 50																	09 00	
Stoke-on-Trent	d		07 44		07 54		08 01				08 07	08 12				08 44		08 54					09 07	09 11	
Wedgwood Old Road Bridge	d						08 10																	09 20	
Barlaston Orchard Place	d						08 11																	09 21	
Stone Granville Square	d						08a25																	09a30	
Stone	d				08 02													09 02							
Norton Bridge Station Drv	d							07 52																	
Stafford	d	07 35	08a01		08 21	08a10		08a22			08 25		08 36	08a42		09a02		09 21	09a09				09 25		09 36
Rugeley Trent Valley	d				08 33													09 33							
Lichfield Trent Valley	d				08 40													09 40							
Tamworth	d				08 47													09 47							
Polesworth	d																								
Atherstone	d				08 56													09 56							
Nuneaton	a				09 02							08 44						10 02							
	d			08 28	09 02							08 46					09 30	10 02							
Bedworth	d			08 35													09 37								
Coventry	a			08 47							09 24						09 56						10 24		
Rugby	a				09 18				08 45									10 18							
Northampton	a				09 41													10 42				←			
Milton Keynes Central	a				10 04													11 04			10 01	10 04			
Watford Junction	a				→							09s31						→				10 30			
London Euston 15 ⊖	a	08 52							09 38			09 52	09 56		10 04						10 38	10 49			10 56

		LM	VT	XC	LM		LM	LM	VT	LM	XC	LM	VT	LM	VT		XC	LM	LM	LM	VT	LM	XC	LM	VT
		1	◇1 ⊠	◇1 🛒	◇1		1	🚌	◇1 ⊠	◇1	◇1 🛒	🚌	◇1 ⊠	1	◇1 ⊠		◇1 🛒		◇1	1	◇1 ⊠	◇1	◇1 🛒	🚌	◇1 ⊠
Crewe	d	09 22	09 29		09 33		09 49		09 56					10 22	10 29				10 33	10 49	10 56				
Alsager	d				09 41														10 41						
Kidsgrove	d				09 46														10 46						
Hanley Bus Station	d											10 00												11 00	
Stoke-on-Trent	d			09 44	09 54						10 07	10 11					10 44		10 54				11 07	11 11	
Wedgwood Old Road Bridge	d											10 20												11 20	
Barlaston Orchard Place	d											10 21												11 21	
Stone Granville Square	d											10a30												11a30	
Stone	d				10 02														11 02						
Norton Bridge Station Drv	d							09 52																	
Stafford	d	09a42		10a02	10 21		10a09	10a22			10 25		10 36	10a42			11a01		11 21	11a09			11 25		11 34
Rugeley Trent Valley	d				10 33														11 33						
Lichfield Trent Valley	d				10 40														11 40						
Tamworth	d				10 47														11 47						
Polesworth	d																								
Atherstone	d				10 56														11 56						
Nuneaton	a				11 02														12 02						
	d				11 02													11 15	12 02						
Bedworth	d																	11 22							
Coventry	a										11 24							11 34					12 24		
Rugby	a				11 18														12 18						
Northampton	a				11 42					←									12 43			←			
Milton Keynes Central	a				12 04				11 01	11 04									13 04		12 01	12 04			
Watford Junction	a				→					11 31									→			12 30			
London Euston 15 ⊖	a		11 04						11 38	11 49			11 56		12 04						12 38	12 49			12 56

Crewe and Stoke-on-Trent - London
Nuneaton - Coventry

			LM	VT	XC	LM	LM	LM	VT	LM	XC		LM	LM	VT	LM	VT	LM	LM	LM	VT		LM	XC	LM
			1	◇1	◇1		◇1	1	◇1	◇1	◇1				◇1	1	◇1		◇1	1	◇1		◇1	◇1	
				☒	🚲				☕		🚲		🚌	🚌	☕		☕				☕			🚲	🚌
Crewe	d		11 22	11 29			11 33	11 49	11 56							12 22	12 29		12 33	12 49	12 56				
Alsager	d						11 41												12 41						
Kidsgrove	d						11 46												12 46						
Hanley Bus Station	d													12 00											13 00
Stoke-on-Trent	d				11 44		11 54				12 07			12 11					12 54					13 07	13 11
Wedgwood Old Road Bridge	d													12 20											13 20
Barlaston Orchard Place	d													12 21											13 21
Stone Granville Square	d												11 39	12a30											13a30
Stone	d						12 02												13 02						
Norton Bridge Station Drv	d												12 02												
Stafford	d		11a43		12a02		12 21	12a09			12 25		12a32		12 36	12a42			13 21	13a09				13 25	
Rugeley Trent Valley	d						12 33												13 33						
Lichfield Trent Valley	d						12 40												13 40						
Tamworth	d						12 47												13 47						
Polesworth	d																								
Atherstone	d						12 56												13 56						
Nuneaton	a						13 02												14 02						
	d					12 15	13 02											13 15	14 02						
Bedworth	d					12 22												13 22							
Coventry	a					12 34					13 24							13 38						14 24	
Rugby	a						13 18												14 18						
Northampton	a						13 48			←									14 42				←		
Milton Keynes Central	a						14 04		13 01	13 04									15 04		14 01		14 04		
Watford Junction	a						→			13 31									→				14 31		
London Euston 15 ⊖	a			13 03					13 38	13 49					13 56		14 04				14 38		14 49		

		LM	VT	XC	LM	LM	LM		LM	VT	LM	XC	LM	VT	VT	LM	VT		XC	LM	LM	LM	VT	LM	XC
		1	◇1	◇1		◇1	1			◇1	◇1	◇1		◇1	◇1	1	◇1		◇1		◇1	1	◇1	◇1	◇1
															A										
			☕	🚲					🚌	☕		🚲	🚌	☕	☒		☕		🚲				☕		🚲
Crewe	d	13 22	13 29			13 33	13 49			13 56					14 01	14 22	14 29				14 33	14 49	14 56		
Alsager	d					13 41															14 41				
Kidsgrove	d					13 46															14 46				
Hanley Bus Station	d												14 00												
Stoke-on-Trent	d			13 44		13 54						14 07	14 11						14 44		14 54				15 07
Wedgwood Old Road Bridge	d												14 20												
Barlaston Orchard Place	d												14 21												
Stone Granville Square	d								13 39				14a30												
Stone	d					14 02															15 02				
Norton Bridge Station Drv	d								13 54																
Stafford	d	13a42		14a01		14 21	14a09		14a15			14 25		14 36		14a46			15a02		15 21	15a09			15 25
Rugeley Trent Valley	d					14 33															15 33				
Lichfield Trent Valley	d					14 40															15 40				
Tamworth	d					14 47															15 47				
Polesworth	d																								
Atherstone	d					14 56															15 56				
Nuneaton	a					15 02															16 02				
	d				14 15	15 02														15 15	16 02				
Bedworth	d				14 22															15 22					
Coventry	a				14 34							15 24			15 30					15 34					16 24
Rugby	a					15 18															16 18				
Northampton	a					15 42					←										16 42			←	
Milton Keynes Central	a					16 04				15 01	15 04										17 04		16 01	16 04	
Watford Junction	a					→					15 30				16s15						→			16 30	
London Euston 15 ⊖	a		15 04							15 38	15 49			15 56	16 34		16 04						16 38	16 49	

A from 18 July until 9 September

Table 67

Mondays to Fridays

Crewe and Stoke-on-Trent - London
Nuneaton - Coventry

		LM	VT		LM	VT	XC	LM	LM	LM	LM	VT	VT		LM	XC	LM	VT	LM	VT	XC	LM	LM		LM
			◇1		1	◇1	◇1		◇1	1		◇1	◇1		◇1	◇1		◇1	1	◇1	◇1		◇1		1
		🚌	☕			☕	🛒				🚌	☕	☕			🛒	🚌	☕		☕	🛒				
Crewe	d				15 22	15 29			15 33	15 49		15 56	15 57						16 22	16 29			16 33		16 49
Alsager	d								15 41														16 41		
Kidsgrove	d								15 46														16 46		
Hanley Bus Station	d	15 00															16 00								
Stoke-on-Trent	d	15 11					15 44		15 54							16 07	16 11				16 44		16 54		
Wedgwood Old Road Bridge	d	15 20															16 20								
Barlaston Orchard Place	d	15 21															16 21								
Stone Granville Square	d	15a30									15 29						16a30								
Stone	d								16 02														17 02		
Norton Bridge Station Drv	d										15 52														
Stafford	d		15 36		15a42		16a02		16 21	16a09	16a13					16 25		16 36	16a46		17a02		17 21		17a10
Rugeley Trent Valley	d								16 33														17 33		
Lichfield Trent Valley	d								16 40														17 40		
Tamworth	d								16 47														17 47		
Polesworth	d																								
Atherstone	d								16 56														17 56		
Nuneaton	a								17 02														18 02		
	d							16 10	17 02													17 15	18 02		
Bedworth	d							16 17														17 22			
Coventry	a							16 34								17 24						17 36			
Rugby	a								17 18														18 18		
Northampton	a								17 42						←								18 42		
Milton Keynes Central	a								18 04			17s01	17 01		17 04								19 04		
Watford Junction	a								↪						17 30								↪		
London Euston 15 ⊖	a		16 56			17 04						17 38	17 38		17 49			17 56		18 03					

		VT	LM	XC	LM	VT	LM	VT	XC		LM	LM	LM	VT	LM	LM	VT	XC	VT		LM	VT	LM	XC	LM
		◇1	◇1	◇1		◇1	1	◇1	◇1			◇1	1	◇1	◇1		R 1 A	◇1	◇1		1	◇1	◇1	◇1	
		☕		🛒	🚌	☕		☕	🛒					⊠		🚌	☕	🛒	⊠			⊠		🛒	
Crewe	d	16 56					17 22	17 29				17 33	17 49	17 56			18 01	18 07			18 22	18 29			
Alsager	d											17 41													
Kidsgrove	d											17 46													
Hanley Bus Station	d				17 00											18 00									
Stoke-on-Trent	d			17 07	17 11				17 44			17 54				18 11								18 44	
Wedgwood Old Road Bridge	d				17 20											18 20									
Barlaston Orchard Place	d				17 21											18 21									
Stone Granville Square	d				17a30											18a30									
Stone	d											18 02													
Norton Bridge Station Drv	d																								
Stafford	d			17 25		17 36	17a42		18a03			18 21	18a09					18 28	18 36		18a42			19a01	
Rugeley Trent Valley	d											18 33													
Lichfield Trent Valley	d											18 40													
Tamworth	d											18 47													
Polesworth	d																								
Atherstone	d											18 56													
Nuneaton	a											19 02													
	d										18 10	19 02													19 15
Bedworth	d										18 17														19 22
Coventry	a			18 24							18 34						19 30	19 24							19 38
Rugby	a											19 18													
Northampton	a		←									19 45			←								←		
Milton Keynes Central	a	18 01	18 04			18 23						20 05		19 01	19 04							19 31	20 05		
Watford Junction	a		18 31					18s48				↪			19 31		20s15		19s42				20 31		
London Euston 15 ⊖	a	18 38	18 49			18 59		19 08						19 38	19 50		20 34		20 02			20 06	20 49		

A from 18 July until 9 September

Crewe and Stoke-on-Trent - London
Nuneaton - Coventry

		LM	LM	XC	LM		VT	VT	XC	LM	VT	LM	XC	LM	VT		VT	VT	XC	LM	VT	XC	LM	LM	VT
		◇1	1	◇1 A ⊼	1		◇1 ⊠	◇1 ⊠	◇1 ⊼	1	◇1 ☕		◇1 A ⊼	1	◇1 ☕		◇1 ☕	◇1 ☕	◇1	1	◇1 ☕	◇1		1	◇1 ☕
Crewe	d	18 33	18 49		19 18		19 23	19 29		19 55	19 56			20 18	20 23		20 29	20 41		20 47	20 53			21 18	21 24
Alsager	d	18 41																							
Kidsgrove	d	18 46																							
Hanley Bus Station	d																								
Stoke-on-Trent	d	18 54		19 07					19 44				20 07						20 44			21 07			
Wedgwood Old Road Bridge	d																								
Barlaston Orchard Place	d																								
Stone Granville Square	d																								
Stone	d	19 02																							
Norton Bridge Station Drv	d																								
Stafford	d	19b21	19a09	19 25	19a41		19 42		20a03	20a15			20 26	20a38			20 48		21a02	21a08	21a11	21a24		21a38	21 44
Rugeley Trent Valley	d	19 33																							
Lichfield Trent Valley	d	19 40																							21 58
Tamworth	d	19 47																							22 05
Polesworth	d																								
Atherstone	d	19 56																							
Nuneaton	a	20 02													21 02										22 16
	d	20 02										20 15			21 03								21 15		22 17
Bedworth	d											20 22											21 22		
Coventry	a			20 24								20 34	21 24										21 34		
Rugby	a	20 18																21 27							22 30
Northampton	a	20 43																							
Milton Keynes Central	a							20 32			21 03						21 35	21 47							22 58
Watford Junction	a						20s46								21s48										23s30
London Euston 15 ⊖	a						21 05	21 06			21 42				22 09		22 12	22 22							23 56

			XC	LM	LM	XC
			◇1	1		◇1
Crewe	d			22 20		
Alsager	d					
Kidsgrove	d					
Hanley Bus Station	d					
Stoke-on-Trent	d		22 08			22 47
Wedgwood Old Road Bridge	d					
Barlaston Orchard Place	d					
Stone Granville Square	d					
Stone	d					
Norton Bridge Station Drv	d					
Stafford	d		22a25	22a40		23a06
Rugeley Trent Valley	d					
Lichfield Trent Valley	d					
Tamworth	d					
Polesworth	d					
Atherstone	d					
Nuneaton	a					
	d				22 20	
Bedworth	d				22 27	
Coventry	a				22 39	
Rugby	a					
Northampton	a					
Milton Keynes Central	a					
Watford Junction	a					
London Euston 15 ⊖	a					

Saturdays

		AW	LM	SR	XC	VT	XC	VT	LM	VT		XC	LM	LM	LM	VT	VT	XC	LM	LM		LM	VT	LM	VT
				Ⓡ 🛏 ☕	◇1 ⊼	◇1 ☕	◇1 ⊼	◇1 ☕	◇1	◇1 ☕		◇1 ⊼	◇1	◇1	◇1	◇1 ☕	◇1 ☕	◇1 ⊼	🚌			◇1	◇1 ☕	◇1	◇1 ☕
Crewe	d	04 59			05 47	06 00			06 20	06 29			06 38	06 47	07 16	07 20	07 29					07 38	07 39	07 49	07 55
Alsager	d												06 47									07 47			
Kidsgrove	d												06 51									07 51			
Hanley Bus Station	d																		07 50						
Stoke-on-Trent	d				06 08							06 39	07 00					07 44	07 56			08 00			
Wedgwood Old Road Bridge	d																		08 05						
Barlaston Orchard Place	d																		08 06						
Stone Granville Square	d																		08a12						
Stone	d												07 08									08 08			
Norton Bridge Station Drv	d						←																		
Stafford	d	05a24			06 26	06 19	06 26	06 35	06a41			06a57	07 24	07a10	07a40	07 39		08a02				08 23		08a10	08 16
Rugeley Trent Valley	d				↦								07 33									↦			
Lichfield Trent Valley	d												07 40												08 31
Tamworth	d												07 47												08 37
Polesworth	d																								
Atherstone	d												07 56												
Nuneaton	a							06 57					08 02												
	d		06 47					06 59					08 02							08 14					
Bedworth	d		06 54																	08 21					
Coventry	a		07 06				07 24													08 33					
Rugby	a					06 49							08 18												
Northampton	a												08 40												
Milton Keynes Central	a					07 11				07 31			09 04												
Watford Junction	a					07s32		07s44					09 33												
London Euston 15 ⊖	a			07 47		07 52		08 05		08 09			09 50			08 59	09 04						09 30		09 46

A ⊼ to Stafford

Crewe and Stoke-on-Trent - London Nuneaton - Coventry

		LM	LM	XC	VT	LM		VT	XC	LM	LM	LM	LM	VT	LM	XC		VT	LM	VT	XC	LM	LM	LM	LM
		◇1		◇1	◇1	◇1		◇1	◇1		◇1	◇1		◇1	◇1	◇1		◇1	◇1	◇1	◇1		◇1	◇1	
			🚌										🚌												🚌
				trolley	☕			☕	trolley					☕		trolley		☕		☕	trolley				
Crewe	d					08 22		08 29			08 33	08 49		08 56					09 22	09 29			09 33	09 49	
Alsager	d										08 41												09 41		
Kidsgrove	d										08 46												09 46		
Hanley Bus Station	d												08 50												09 50
Stoke-on-Trent	d			08 07					08 44		08 54		08 56			09 07					09 44		09 54		09 56
Wedgwood Old Road Bridge	d												09 05												10 05
Barlaston Orchard Place	d												09 06												10 06
Stone Granville Square	d												09a12												10a12
Stone	d										09 02												10 02		
Norton Bridge Station Drv	d	←	07 52																						
Stafford	d	08 23	08a22	08 26	08 36	08a42			09a02		09 21	09a09				09 26		09 36	09a42		10a02		10 21	10a10	
Rugeley Trent Valley	d	08 33									09 33												10 33		
Lichfield Trent Valley	d	08 40									09 40												10 40		
Tamworth	d	08 47									09 47												10 47		
Polesworth	d																								
Atherstone	d	08 56									09 56												10 56		
Nuneaton	a	09 02			08 58						10 02							09 58					11 02		
	d	09 02			08 59					09 15	10 02							09 59				10 15	11 02		
Bedworth	d									09 22												10 22			
Coventry	a			09 24						09 34						10 24						10 34			
Rugby	a	09 18									10 18												11 18		
Northampton	a	09 39									10 39				←								11 39		
Milton Keynes Central	a	10 04									11 04			10 01	10 04								12 04		
Watford Junction	a	→									→				10 30								→		
London Euston 15 ⊖	a				10 00			10 04						10 37	10 49			11 01		11 04					

		LM		VT	LM	XC	VT	LM	VT	XC	LM	LM		LM	LM	VT	LM	XC	VT	LM	VT	XC		LM	LM
				◇1	◇1	◇1	◇1	◇1	◇1	◇1		◇1		◇1		◇1	◇1	◇1	◇1	◇1	◇1	◇1			◇1
		🚌													🚌										
				☕		trolley	☕		☕	trolley						☕		trolley	☕		☕	trolley			
Crewe	d			09 56				10 22	10 29			10 33		10 49		10 56				11 22	11 29				11 33
Alsager	d											10 41													11 41
Kidsgrove	d											10 46													11 46
Hanley Bus Station	d														10 50										
Stoke-on-Trent	d					10 07				10 44		10 54			10 56			11 07				11 44			11 54
Wedgwood Old Road Bridge	d														11 05										
Barlaston Orchard Place	d														11 06										
Stone Granville Square	d														11a12										
Stone	d											11 02													12 02
Norton Bridge Station Drv	d	09 52																							
Stafford	d	10a22				10 26	10 36	10a42		11a02		11 21		11a09				11 26	11 36	11a42		12a02			12 21
Rugeley Trent Valley	d											11 33													12 33
Lichfield Trent Valley	d											11 40													12 40
Tamworth	d											11 47													12 47
Polesworth	d																								
Atherstone	d											11 56													12 56
Nuneaton	a											12 02													13 02
	d										11 15	12 02												12 15	13 02
Bedworth	d										11 22													12 22	
Coventry	a					11 24					11 34							12 24						12 34	
Rugby	a											12 18													13 18
Northampton	a				←							12 39					←								13 39
Milton Keynes Central	a			11 01	11 04							13 04				12 01	12 04								14 04
Watford Junction	a				11 30							→					12 30								→
London Euston 15 ⊖	a			11 38	11 49		11 56		12 04							12 38	12 49		12 56		13 04				

		LM	LM	VT	LM	XC	LM	VT		LM	VT	XC	LM	LM	LM	LM	VT	LM		XC	VT	LM	VT	XC	LM
		◇1		◇1	◇1	◇1		◇1		◇1	◇1	◇1		◇1	◇1		◇1	◇1		◇1	◇1	◇1	◇1	◇1	
			🚌				🚌									🚌									
				☕		trolley		☕			☕	trolley					☕			trolley	☕		☕	trolley	
Crewe	d	11 49		11 56						12 22	12 29			12 33	12 49		12 57					13 22	13 29		
Alsager	d													12 41											
Kidsgrove	d													12 46											
Hanley Bus Station	d		11 50													12 50									
Stoke-on-Trent	d		11 56			12 07						12 44		12 54		12 56				13 07				13 44	
Wedgwood Old Road Bridge	d		12 05													13 05									
Barlaston Orchard Place	d		12 06													13 06									
Stone Granville Square	d		12a12				11 39									13a12									
Stone	d													13 02											
Norton Bridge Station Drv	d						12 02																		
Stafford	d	12a09				12 25	12a32	12 36		12a42		13a02		13 21	13a09					13 26	13 36	13a42		14a02	
Rugeley Trent Valley	d													13 33											
Lichfield Trent Valley	d													13 40											
Tamworth	d													13 47											
Polesworth	d																								
Atherstone	d													13 56											
Nuneaton	a													14 02											
	d												13 15	14 02											14 15
Bedworth	d												13 22												14 22
Coventry	a					13 24							13 34							14 24					14 34
Rugby	a													14 18											
Northampton	a				←									14 39				←							
Milton Keynes Central	a			13 01	13 04									15 04			14 01	14 04							
Watford Junction	a				13 30									→				14 30							
London Euston 15 ⊖	a			13 38	13 49			13 56			14 04						14 38	14 49			14 56		15 04		

Crewe and Stoke-on-Trent - London
Nuneaton - Coventry

		LM	LM	LM		LM	VT	LM	XC	VT	VT	LM	VT	XC		LM	LM	LM	LM	VT	LM	XC	VT	LM	
		◇1	◇1				◇1	◇1	◇1	◇1	◇1	◇1	◇1	◇1			◇1	◇1		◇1	◇1	◇1	◇1	◇1	
											A														
				🚌		🚌													🚌						
							☕		🛒	☕	☕		☕	🛒						☕		🛒	☕		
Crewe	d	13 33	13 49				13 56				14 01	14 22	14 29				14 33	14 49		14 56				15 22	
Alsager	d	13 41															14 41								
Kidsgrove	d	13 46															14 46								
Hanley Bus Station	d					13 50													14 50						
Stoke-on-Trent	d	13 54				13 56			14 07					14 44			14 54		14 56			15 07			
Wedgwood Old Road Bridge	d					14 05													15 05						
Barlaston Orchard Place	d					14 06													15 06						
Stone Granville Square	d			13 39		14a12													15a12						
Stone	d	14 02															15 02								
Norton Bridge Station Drv	d			13 54																					
Stafford	d	14 21	14a09	14a15					14 26	14 36		14a46		15a02			15 21	15a09				15 26	15 36	15a42	
Rugeley Trent Valley	d	14 33															15 33								
Lichfield Trent Valley	d	14 40															15 40								
Tamworth	d	14 47															15 47								
Polesworth	d																								
Atherstone	d	14 56															15 56								
Nuneaton	a	15 02															16 02								
	d	15 02														15 15	16 02								
Bedworth	d															15 22									
Coventry	a								15 24		15 30					15 34						16 24			
Rugby	a	15 18															16 18								
Northampton	a	15 39						←									16 39				←				
Milton Keynes Central	a	16 04					15 01	15 04									17 04			16 01	16 04				
Watford Junction	a	→						15 30			16s15						→				16 30				
London Euston 15 ⊖	a						15 38	15 49		15 56	16 34		16 04							16 38	16 49		16 56		

		VT	XC	LM	LM	LM	LM	LM	VT	LM		XC	VT	LM	VT	XC	LM	LM	LM	LM		VT	LM	XC	VT
		◇1	◇1		◇1	◇1			◇1	◇1		◇1	◇1	◇1	◇1	◇1		◇1	◇1			◇1	◇1	◇1	◇1
							🚌	🚌												🚌					
		☕	🛒						☕			🛒	☕		☕	🛒						☕		🛒	☕
Crewe	d	15 29			15 33	15 49			15 56					16 22	16 29			16 33	16 49			16 56			
Alsager	d				15 41													16 41							
Kidsgrove	d				15 46													16 46							
Hanley Bus Station	d							15 50												16 50					
Stoke-on-Trent	d		15 44		15 54			15 56				16 07				16 44		16 54		16 56				17 07	
Wedgwood Old Road Bridge	d							16 05												17 05					
Barlaston Orchard Place	d							16 06												17 06					
Stone Granville Square	d						15 29	16a12												17a12					
Stone	d				16 02													17 02							
Norton Bridge Station Drv	d						15 52																		
Stafford	d		16a02		16e21	16a09	16a13					16 25	16 36	16a46		17a02		17 21	17a09					17 26	17 36
Rugeley Trent Valley	d				16 33													17 33							
Lichfield Trent Valley	d				16 40													17 40							
Tamworth	d				16 47													17 47							
Polesworth	d																								
Atherstone	d				16 56													17 56							
Nuneaton	a				17 02													18 02							
	d			16 15	17 02												17 15	18 02							
Bedworth	d			16 22													17 22								
Coventry	a			16 34								17 24					17 34							18 24	
Rugby	a				17 18													18 18							
Northampton	a				17 39					←								18 39					←		
Milton Keynes Central	a				18 05				17 01	17 04								19 04				18 01	18 05		
Watford Junction	a				→					17 30								→					18 31		
London Euston 15 ⊖	a	17 04							17 38	17 49			17 55		18 04							18 38	18 49		18 56

A from 16 July until 10 September

Table 67

Saturdays

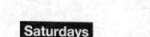

Crewe and Stoke-on-Trent - London
Nuneaton - Coventry

		LM	VT	LM	XC	LM		LM	LM	LM	XC	VT	VT	LM	VT	XC		LM	LM	LM	XC	VT	LM	VT	XC
		◇1	◇1	◇1	◇1			◇1	◇1		◇1	◇1	◇1	◇1	◇1	◇1			◇1	◇1	◇1	◇1	◇1	◇1	◇1
													A												
										[bus]															
			[catering]		[trolley]						[trolley]	[catering]	[catering]		[catering]	[trolley]					[trolley]	[catering]		[catering]	[trolley]
Crewe	d	17 22	17 29					17 33	17 49				18 01	18 22	18 29				18 33	18 49			19 22	19 29	
Alsager	d							17 41											18 41						
Kidsgrove	d							17 46											18 46						
Hanley Bus Station	d									17 50															
Stoke-on-Trent	d				17 44			17 54		17 56	18 08					18 44			18 54		19 07				19 44
Wedgwood Old Road Bridge	d									18 05															
Barlaston Orchard Place	d									18 06															
Stone Granville Square	d									18a12															
Stone	d							18 02											19 02						
Norton Bridge Station Drv	d																								
Stafford	d	17a42			18a03			18 21	18a09		18 27	18 36		18a42		19a02			19 21	19a09	19 25	19 36	19a42		20a02
Rugeley Trent Valley	d							18 33											19 33						
Lichfield Trent Valley	d							18 40											19 40						
Tamworth	d							18 47											19 47						
Polesworth	d																								
Atherstone	d							18 56											19 56						
Nuneaton	a							19 02											20 02						
	d					18 15		19 02										19 46	20 02						
Bedworth	d					18 22												19 53							
Coventry	a					18 34					19 24		19 30					20 05			20 24				
Rugby	a							19 18					19 42						20 18						
Northampton	a			←				19 41											20 39						
Milton Keynes Central	a			19 04									20 05												
Watford Junction	a			19 36									20s34												
London Euston 15 ⊖	a		19 04	19 53								19 56	20 56		20 04							21 15		21 18	

		LM		XC	VT	LM	VT	XC	VT	XC	LM	LM		XC	VT	VT	XC	LM	LM						
		◇1		◇1	◇1	◇1	◇1	◇1	◇1	◇1		◇1		◇1	◇1	◇1	◇1		◇1						
				B	C		D																		
				[trolley]	[catering]		[catering]		[catering]						[catering]	[catering]									
Crewe	d	19 51				20 22	20 23		20 47			21 17			21 43	22 04			22 23						
Alsager	d																								
Kidsgrove	d																								
Hanley Bus Station	d																								
Stoke-on-Trent	d			20 07				20 44		21 07				21 45			22 08								
Wedgwood Old Road Bridge	d																								
Barlaston Orchard Place	d																								
Stone Granville Square	d																								
Stone	d																								
Norton Bridge Station Drv	d																								
Stafford	d	20a11		20 26	20 36	20a42	20 42	21a02		21a26		21a42		22a02	22a07	22a23	22a32		22a47						
Rugeley Trent Valley	d																								
Lichfield Trent Valley	d																								
Tamworth	d																								
Polesworth	d																								
Atherstone	d																								
Nuneaton	a																								
	d										21 15							22 15							
Bedworth	d										21 22							22 22							
Coventry	a			21 24							21 34							22 34							
Rugby	a																								
Northampton	a																								
Milton Keynes Central	a								21 50																
Watford Junction	a																								
London Euston 15 ⊖	a				22 14		22 19		22 44																

A from 16 July until 10 September
B [trolley] to Stafford
C from 17 September
D until 10 September

Table 67

Sundays
until 10 July

Crewe and Stoke-on-Trent - London
Nuneaton - Coventry

		VT	VT	XC	VT	VT	XC	VT	LM	LM		VT	VT	XC	VT	LM	LM	VT	XC	VT		LM	VT	VT	LM
		◇1	◇1	◇1	◇1	◇1	◇1	◇1	◇1	1		◇1	◇1	◇1	◇1		◇1	◇1	◇1	◇1		1	◇1	◇1	◇1
																			A						
		⊥P	⊥P	⊥o	⊥P	⊥P	⊥o	⊥P				⊥P	⊥P	⊥o	⊥P			⊥P	⊥o	⊥P			⊥P	⊥P	
Crewe	d	08 43	08 53	09 05	09 13	09 43		10 14	10 20	10 37		10 43	10 55		11 14		11 38	11 49				12 22	12 30	12 56	
Alsager	d									10 46							11 46								
Kidsgrove	d									10 50							11 52								
Hanley Bus Station	d																								
Stoke-on-Trent	d						10 07			10 58				11 07			11 59		12 07						
Wedgwood Old Road Bridge	d																								
Barlaston Orchard Place	d																								
Stone Granville Square	d																								
Stone	d									11 06							12 08								
Norton Bridge Station Drv	d																								
Stafford	d	09 02		09 26	09 32		10 27	10 33	10a41	11a17				11 28	11 36		12 18		12 25	12 36		12a41			
Rugeley Trent Valley	d																12 28								
Lichfield Trent Valley	d																12 35								
Tamworth	d																12 42								
Polesworth	d																								
Atherstone	d																12 51								
Nuneaton	a				09 54			10 55							11 58		12 58	12 31							
	d				09 55			10 56							11 59	12 30	12 58	12 32							
Bedworth	d															12 36									
Coventry	a			10 24			11 24							12 24		12 54			13 24						
Rugby	a					10 31						11 31					13 17								
Northampton	a																13 39								←
Milton Keynes Central	a		10 17			11 06		11 46				12 06					14 04	13 03						14 02	14 04
Watford Junction	a	10s35			11s16	11s43							12s35		12s50		→								14 33
London Euston 15 ⊖	a	10 57	11 06		11 37	12 05		12 32				12 45	12 56		13 11			13 44		14 01			14 09	14 43	14 53

		XC	VT	LM	VT	LM		LM	VT	XC	VT	LM	VT	VT	LM	LM		XC	VT	LM	VT	LM	LM	VT	XC
		◇1	◇1	1	◇1			◇1	◇1	◇1	◇1	1	◇1	◇1	◇1			◇1	◇1	1	◇1		◇1	◇1	◇1
		⊥o	⊥P		⊥P				⊥P	⊥o	⊥P		⊥P	⊥P				⊥o	⊥P		⊥P			⊥P	⊥o
Crewe	d			13 22	13 30			13 38	13 51			14 22	14 29	14 54						15 22	15 29		15 38	15 54	
Alsager	d							13 46															15 46		
Kidsgrove	d							13 51															15 52		
Hanley Bus Station	d																								
Stoke-on-Trent	d	13 07						13 59		14 07								15 07					15 59		16 07
Wedgwood Old Road Bridge	d																								
Barlaston Orchard Place	d																								
Stone Granville Square	d																								
Stone	d							14 07															16 08		
Norton Bridge Station Drv	d																								
Stafford	d	13 25	13 36	13a42				14 18		14 25	14 36	14a42						15 25	15 36	15a42			16 18		16 25
Rugeley Trent Valley	d							14 28															16 28		
Lichfield Trent Valley	d							14 35															16 35		
Tamworth	d							14 42															16 42		
Polesworth	d																								
Atherstone	d							14 51															16 51		
Nuneaton	a							14 57	14 31														16 58		
	d					14 11		14 58	14 32							15 11						16 11	16 58		
Bedworth	d					14 17										15 17						16 17			
Coventry	a	14 24				14 34				15 24						15 34		16 24				16 34			17 24
Rugby	a							15 17															17 18		
Northampton	a							15 39							←								17 39		
Milton Keynes Central	a							16 04	15s04					16 04	16 04								18 04	17 03	
Watford Junction	a							→							16 33								→		
London Euston 15 ⊖	a		15 01		15 09				15 45		16 01		16 09	16 44	16 53				17 01		17 09			17 44	

		VT		LM	VT	VT	LM	LM	XC	VT	LM	VT		LM	LM	VT	XC	VT	LM	VT	VT	LM		XC	VT
		◇1		1	◇1	◇1	◇1		◇1	◇1	1	◇1			◇1	◇1	◇1	◇1	1	◇1	◇1	◇1		◇1	◇1
		⊥P			⊥P	⊥P			⊥o	⊥P		⊥P				⊥P	⊥o	⊥P		⊥P	⊥P			⊥o	⊥P
Crewe	d			16 22	16 29	16 54					17 22	17 29			17 38	17 55			18 22	18 29	18 55				
Alsager	d														17 46										
Kidsgrove	d														17 51										
Hanley Bus Station	d																								
Stoke-on-Trent	d								17 08						17 59		18 08							19 07	
Wedgwood Old Road Bridge	d																								
Barlaston Orchard Place	d																								
Stone Granville Square	d																								
Stone	d														18 07										
Norton Bridge Station Drv	d																								
Stafford	d	16 37		16a42					17 26	17 36	17a42				18 18		18 26	18 36	18a42					19 25	19 36
Rugeley Trent Valley	d														18 28										
Lichfield Trent Valley	d					17 27									18 35										
Tamworth	d														18 42										
Polesworth	d																								
Atherstone	d														18 51										
Nuneaton	a														18 58										
	d							17 11						18 11	18 58										
Bedworth	d							17 17						18 17											
Coventry	a							17 34	18 24					18 34			19 24							20 24	
Rugby	a														19 18										
Northampton	a						←								19 39							←			
Milton Keynes Central	a					18 04	18 04								20 06	19 02					20 03	20 06			
Watford Junction	a						18 35								→							20 33			
London Euston 15 ⊖	a	18 01			18 09	18 44	18 53			19 01		19 09				19 43		20 01		20 09	20 44	20 53			21 01

A ⊥o to Stafford

Table 67

Sundays
until 10 July

Crewe and Stoke-on-Trent - London
Nuneaton - Coventry

		LM	VT	LM	LM	XC	LM	VT		VT	LM	XC	AW	LM	LM	VT	VT	XC		LM	XC				
		1	◇1		◇1	◇1	1	◇1		◇1	◇1	◇1	◇	1		◇1	◇1	◇1		1	◇1				
						A																			
			🍴			🛒		🍴		🍴			🛒			🍴	🍴								
Crewe	d	19 22	19 29		19 36		20 18	20 24		20 47			20 52	21 17		21 23	21 40			22 22					
Alsager	d				19 44																				
Kidsgrove	d				19 50																				
Hanley Bus Station	d																								
Stoke-on-Trent	d				19 57	20 07						20 47						21 47			22 47				
Wedgwood Old Road Bridge	d																								
Barlaston Orchard Place	d																								
Stone Granville Square	d																								
Stone	d				20 06																				
Norton Bridge Station Drv	d																								
Stafford	d	19a42			20 16	20 27	20a38	20 43				21a08	21a16	21a37		21 43	22a01	22a06		22a42	23a04				
Rugeley Trent Valley	d				20 28																				
Lichfield Trent Valley	d				20 35											22 00									
Tamworth	d				20 42											22 06									
Polesworth	d																								
Atherstone	d				20 51																				
Nuneaton	a				20 58											22 17									
	d			20 11	20 58										22 00	22 18									
Bedworth	d			20 17											22 06										
Coventry	a			20 34		21 23									22 21										
Rugby	a				21 16											22 31									
Northampton	a				21 39						←														
Milton Keynes Central	a				22 10			21 36		21 55	22 10					23 04									
Watford Junction	a				→					22s31	22 52					23s34									
London Euston 15 ⊖	a		21 09					22 28		22 53	23 14					23 54									

Sundays
17 July to 11 September

		VT	VT	XC	XC	VT	VT	XC	XC	VT		LM	LM	VT	VT	XC	XC	VT	LM	LM		VT	XC	XC	VT
		◇1	◇1	◇1	◇1	◇1	◇1	◇1	◇1	◇1		◇1	1	◇1	◇1	◇1	◇1	◇1		◇1		◇1	◇1	◇1	◇1
				B	C			B	C							B	C						D	C	
		🍴	🍴	🛒	🛒	🍴	🍴	🛒	🛒	🍴				🍴	🍴	🛒	🛒	🍴				🍴	🛒	🛒	🍴
Crewe	d	08 43	08 53	09 05	09 05	09 13	09 43			10 14		10 20	10 37	10 43	10 55			11 14		11 38		11 49			
Alsager	d												10 46							11 46					
Kidsgrove	d												10 50							11 52					
Hanley Bus Station	d																								
Stoke-on-Trent	d							10 07	10 07				10 58			11 07	11 07			11 59			12 07	12 07	
Wedgwood Old Road Bridge	d																								
Barlaston Orchard Place	d																								
Stone Granville Square	d																								
Stone	d												11 06							12 08					
Norton Bridge Station Drv	d																								
Stafford	d	09 02		09 26	09 26	09 32		10 27	10 27	10 33		10a41	11a17			11 28	11 28	11 36		12 18			12 25	12 25	12 36
Rugeley Trent Valley	d																			12 28					
Lichfield Trent Valley	d																			12 35					
Tamworth	d																			12 42					
Polesworth	d																								
Atherstone	d																			12 51					
Nuneaton	a					09 54				10 55								11 58		12 58		12 31			
	d					09 55				10 56								11 59	12 30	12 58		12 32			
Bedworth	d																		12 36						
Coventry	a			10 24	10 33			11 24	11 28							12 24	12 27		12 54				13 24	13 27	
Rugby	a						10 31							11 31						13 17					
Northampton	a																			13 39					
Milton Keynes Central	a		10 17				11 06			11 46				12 06						14 04		13 03			
Watford Junction	a	10s35				11s16	11s43								12s35			12s50		→					
London Euston 15 ⊖	a	10 57	11 06			11 37	12 05			12 32				12 45	12 56			13 11				13 44			14 01

A 🛒 to Stafford
B 17 July, 24 July, 31 July
C from 7 August until 11 September. 🛒 to Stafford
D 17 July, 24 July, 31 July. 🛒 to Stafford

Table 67

17 July to 11 September

Crewe and Stoke-on-Trent - London
Nuneaton - Coventry

		LM	VT	VT	LM	XC		VT	LM	VT	LM	LM	VT	XC	VT	LM		VT	VT	LM	LM	XC	VT	LM	VT
		1	◇1	◇1	◇1	◇1		◇1	1	◇1		◇1	◇1	◇1	◇1	1		◇1	◇1	◇1		◇1	◇1	1	◇1
			🍴	🍴		🛒		🍴		🍴			🍴	🛒	🍴			🍴	🍴			🛒	🍴		🍴
Crewe	d	12 22	12 30	12 56					13 22	13 30		13 38	13 51			14 22		14 29	14 54					15 22	15 29
Alsager	d											13 46													
Kidsgrove	d											13 51													
Hanley Bus Station	d																								
Stoke-on-Trent	d					13 07						13 59		14 07								15 07			
Wedgwood Old Road Bridge	d																								
Barlaston Orchard Place	d																								
Stone Granville Square	d																								
Stone	d											14 07													
Norton Bridge Station Drv	d																								
Stafford	d	12a41				13 25		13 36	13a42			14 18		14 25	14 36	14a42						15 25	15 36	15a42	
Rugeley Trent Valley	d											14 28													
Lichfield Trent Valley	d											14 35													
Tamworth	d											14 42													
Polesworth	d																								
Atherstone	d											14 51													
Nuneaton	a											14 57	14 31												
	d										14 11	14 58	14 32								15 11				
Bedworth	d										14 17										15 17				
Coventry	a					14 24					14 34			15 24							15 34	16 24			
Rugby	a											15 17													
Northampton	a				←							15 39								←					
Milton Keynes Central	a			14 02	14 04							16 04	15s04						16 04	16 04					
Watford Junction	a				14 33							→								16 33					
London Euston 15 ⊖	a		14 09	14 43	14 53			15 01		15 09			15 45		16 01			16 09	16 44	16 53			17 01		17 09

		LM		LM	VT	XC	VT	LM	VT	VT	LM	LM		XC	VT	LM	VT	LM	LM	VT	XC	VT		LM	VT
				◇1	◇1	◇1	◇1	1	◇1	◇1	◇1			◇1	◇1	1	◇1		◇1	◇1	◇1	◇1		1	◇1
					🍴	🛒	🍴		🍴	🍴				🛒	🍴		🍴			🍴	🛒	🍴			🍴
Crewe	d			15 38	15 54			16 22	16 29	16 54						17 22	17 29		17 38	17 55				18 22	18 29
Alsager	d			15 46															17 46						
Kidsgrove	d			15 52															17 51						
Hanley Bus Station	d																								
Stoke-on-Trent	d			15 59		16 07								17 08					17 59		18 08				
Wedgwood Old Road Bridge	d																								
Barlaston Orchard Place	d																								
Stone Granville Square	d																								
Stone	d			16 08															18 07						
Norton Bridge Station Drv	d																								
Stafford	d			16 18		16 25	16 37	16a42						17 26	17 36	17a42			18 18		18 26	18 36		18a42	
Rugeley Trent Valley	d			16 28															18 28						
Lichfield Trent Valley	d			16 35						17 27									18 35						
Tamworth	d			16 42															18 42						
Polesworth	d																								
Atherstone	d			16 51															18 51						
Nuneaton	a			16 58															18 58						
	d	16 11		16 58								17 11						18 11	18 58						
Bedworth	d	16 17										17 17						18 17							
Coventry	a	16 34				17 24						17 34		18 24				18 34			19 24				
Rugby	a			17 18															19 18						
Northampton	a			17 39							←								19 39						
Milton Keynes Central	a			18 04	17 03					18 04	18 04								20 06	19 02					
Watford Junction	a			→							18 35								→						
London Euston 15 ⊖	a				17 44		18 01		18 09	18 44	18 53				19 01		19 09			19 43		20 01			20 09

		VT	LM	XC	VT	LM	VT	LM		LM	XC	LM	VT	VT	LM	XC	AW	LM		LM	VT	VT	XC	LM	XC
		◇1	◇1	◇1	◇1	1	◇1			◇1	◇1	1	◇1	◇1	◇1	◇1	◇	1			◇1	◇1	◇1	1	◇1
											A														
		🍴		🛒	🍴		🍴				🛒		🍴	🍴			🛒				🍴	🍴			
Crewe	d	18 55				19 22	19 29			19 36		20 18	20 24	20 47			20 52	21 17			21 23	21 40		22 22	
Alsager	d									19 44															
Kidsgrove	d									19 50															
Hanley Bus Station	d																								
Stoke-on-Trent	d			19 07						19 57	20 07					20 47							21 47		22 47
Wedgwood Old Road Bridge	d																								
Barlaston Orchard Place	d																								
Stone Granville Square	d																								
Stone	d									20 06															
Norton Bridge Station Drv	d																								
Stafford	d			19 25	19 36	19a42				20 16	20 27	20a38	20 43			21a08	21a16	21a37			21 43	22a01	22a06	22a42	23a04
Rugeley Trent Valley	d									20 28															
Lichfield Trent Valley	d									20 35											22 00				
Tamworth	d									20 42											22 06				
Polesworth	d																								
Atherstone	d									20 51															
Nuneaton	a									20 58											22 17				
	d							20 11		20 58										22 00	22 18				
Bedworth	d							20 17												22 06					
Coventry	a			20 24				20 34			21 23									22 21					
Rugby	a									21 16											22 31				
Northampton	a		←							21 39					←										
Milton Keynes Central	a	20 03	20 06							22 10			21 36	21 55	22 10						23 04				
Watford Junction	a		20 33							→				22s31	22 52						23s34				
London Euston 15 ⊖	a	20 44	20 53		21 01		21 09						22 28	22 53	23 14						23 54				

A 🛒 to Stafford

Table 67

Sundays

18 September to 23 October

Crewe and Stoke-on-Trent - London
Nuneaton - Coventry

		VT	VT	XC	VT	VT	XC	VT	LM	LM		VT	VT	XC	VT	LM	LM	VT	XC	VT		LM	VT	VT	LM
		◇1	◇1	◇1	◇1	◇1	◇1	◇1	◇1	1		◇1	◇1	◇1	◇1		◇1	◇1	◇1	◇1		1	◇1	◇1	◇1
				A			A							A					A						
		☕	☕	🛒	☕	☕	🛒	☕				☕	☕	🛒	☕			☕	🛒	☕			☕	☕	
Crewe	d	08 43	08 53	09 05	09 13	09 43		10 14	10 20	10 37		10 43	10 55		11 14		11 38	11 49				12 22	12 30	12 56	
Alsager	d									10 46							11 46								
Kidsgrove	d									10 50							11 52								
Hanley Bus Station	d																								
Stoke-on-Trent	d						10 07			10 58				11 07			11 59		12 07						
Wedgwood Old Road Bridge	d																								
Barlaston Orchard Place	d																								
Stone Granville Square	d																								
Stone	d									11 06							12 08								
Norton Bridge Station Drv	d																								
Stafford	d	09 02		09 26	09 32		10 27	10 33	10a41	11a17				11 28	11 36		12 18		12 25	12 36		12a41			
Rugeley Trent Valley	d																12 28								
Lichfield Trent Valley	d																12 35								
Tamworth	d																12 42								
Polesworth	d																								
Atherstone	d																12 51								
Nuneaton	a				09 54			10 55							11 58		12 58	12 31							
	d				09 55			10 56							11 59	12 30	12 58	12 32							
Bedworth	d															12 36									
Coventry	a			10 24			11 24							12 24		12 54			13 24						
Rugby	a					10 31						11 31					13 17								
Northampton	a																13 39								
Milton Keynes Central	a		10 17			11 06		11 46				12 06					14 04	13 03						14 02	← 14 04
Watford Junction	a	10s35			11s16	11s43							12s35		12s50		↪								14 33
London Euston 15 ⊖	a	10 57	11 06		11 37	12 05		12 32				12 45	12 56		13 11			13 44		14 01			14 09	14 43	14 53

		XC	VT	LM	VT	LM		LM	VT	XC	VT	LM	VT	VT	LM	LM		XC	VT	LM	VT	LM	LM	VT	XC
		◇1	◇1	1	◇1			◇1	◇1	◇1	◇1	1	◇1	◇1	◇1			◇1	◇1	1	◇1		◇1	◇1	◇1
		🛒	☕		☕				☕	🛒	☕		☕	☕				🛒	☕		☕			☕	🛒
Crewe	d			13 22	13 30			13 38	13 51			14 22	14 29	14 54						15 22	15 29		15 38	15 54	
Alsager	d							13 46															15 46		
Kidsgrove	d							13 51															15 52		
Hanley Bus Station	d																								
Stoke-on-Trent	d	13 07						13 59		14 07								15 07					15 59		16 07
Wedgwood Old Road Bridge	d																								
Barlaston Orchard Place	d																								
Stone Granville Square	d																								
Stone	d							14 07															16 08		
Norton Bridge Station Drv	d																								
Stafford	d	13 25	13 36	13a42				14 18		14 25	14 36	14a42						15 25	15 36	15a42			16 18		16 25
Rugeley Trent Valley	d							14 28															16 28		
Lichfield Trent Valley	d							14 35															16 35		
Tamworth	d							14 42															16 42		
Polesworth	d																								
Atherstone	d							14 51															16 51		
Nuneaton	a							14 57	14 31														16 58		
	d					14 11		14 58	14 32							15 11						16 11	16 58		
Bedworth	d					14 17										15 17						16 17			
Coventry	a	14 24				14 34				15 24						15 34		16 24				16 34			17 24
Rugby	a							15 17															17 18		
Northampton	a							15 39															17 39		
Milton Keynes Central	a							16 04	15s04					16 04	← 16 04								18 04	17 03	
Watford Junction	a							↪							16 33								↪		
London Euston 15 ⊖	a		15 01		15 09				15 45		16 01		16 09	16 44	16 53				17 01		17 09			17 44	

		VT		LM	VT	VT	LM	LM	XC	VT	LM	VT		LM	LM	VT	XC	VT	LM	VT	VT	LM		XC	VT
		◇1		1	◇1	◇1	◇1		◇1	◇1	1	◇1			◇1	◇1	◇1	◇1	1	◇1	◇1	◇1		◇1	◇1
		☕			☕	☕			🛒	☕		☕				☕	🛒	☕		☕	☕			🛒	☕
Crewe	d			16 22	16 29	16 54					17 22	17 29			17 38	17 55			18 22	18 29	18 55				
Alsager	d														17 46										
Kidsgrove	d														17 51										
Hanley Bus Station	d																								
Stoke-on-Trent	d								17 08						17 59		18 08							19 07	
Wedgwood Old Road Bridge	d																								
Barlaston Orchard Place	d																								
Stone Granville Square	d																								
Stone	d														18 07										
Norton Bridge Station Drv	d																								
Stafford	d	16 37		16a42					17 26	17 36	17a42				18 18		18 26	18 36	18a42					19 25	19 36
Rugeley Trent Valley	d														18 28										
Lichfield Trent Valley	d					17 27									18 35										
Tamworth	d														18 42										
Polesworth	d																								
Atherstone	d														18 51										
Nuneaton	a														18 58										
	d							17 11						18 11	18 58										
Bedworth	d							17 17						18 17											
Coventry	a							17 34	18 24					18 34			19 24							20 24	
Rugby	a														19 18										
Northampton	a														19 39										
Milton Keynes Central	a					18 04	← 18 04								20 06	19 02					20 03	← 20 06			
Watford Junction	a						18 35								↪							20 33			
London Euston 15 ⊖	a	18 01			18 09	18 44	18 53			19 01		19 09				19 43		20 01		20 09	20 44	20 53			21 01

A 🛒 to Stafford

Table 67

Sundays
18 September to 23 October

Crewe and Stoke-on-Trent - London
Nuneaton - Coventry

		LM	VT	LM	LM	XC	LM	VT		VT	LM	XC	AW	LM	LM	VT	VT	XC		LM	XC
		1	◇1		◇1	◇1	1	◇1		◇1	◇1	◇1	◇	1		◇1	◇1	◇1		1	◇1
						A															
			☕			🛒		☕		☕			🛒			☕	☕				
Crewe	d	19 22	19 29		19 36		20 18	20 24		20 47			20 52	21 17		21 23	21 40			22 22	
Alsager	d				19 44																
Kidsgrove	d				19 50																
Hanley Bus Station	d																				
Stoke-on-Trent	d				19 57	20 07						20 47						21 47			22 47
Wedgwood Old Road Bridge	d																				
Barlaston Orchard Place	d																				
Stone Granville Square	d																				
Stone	d				20 06																
Norton Bridge Station Drv	d																				
Stafford	d	19a42			20 16	20 27	20a38	20 43				21a08	21a16	21a37		21 43	22a01	22a06		22a42	23a04
Rugeley Trent Valley	d				20 28																
Lichfield Trent Valley	d				20 35											22 00					
Tamworth	d				20 42											22 06					
Polesworth	d																				
Atherstone	d				20 51																
Nuneaton	a				20 58											22 17					
	d			20 11	20 58										22 00	22 18					
Bedworth	d			20 17											22 06						
Coventry	a			20 34		21 23									22 21						
Rugby	a				21 16											22 31					
Northampton	a				21 39						←										
Milton Keynes Central	a				22 10			21 36		21 55	22 10					23 04					
Watford Junction	a				↦					22s31	22 52					23s34					
London Euston 15 ⊖	a		21 09					22 28		22 53	23 14					23 54					

Sundays
from 30 October

		VT	VT	XC	VT	VT	XC	VT	LM	LM		VT	VT	XC	VT	LM	LM	VT	XC	VT		LM	VT	VT	LM
		◇1	◇1	◇1	◇1	◇1	◇1	◇1	◇1	1		◇1	◇1	◇1	◇1		◇1	◇1	◇1	◇1		1	◇1	◇1	◇1
				A			A							A					A						
		☕	☕	🛒	☕	☕	🛒	☕				☕	☕	🛒	☕			☕	🛒	☕			☕	☕	
Crewe	d	08 43	08 53	09 05	09 13	09 43		10 14	10 20	10 37		10 43	10 55		11 14		11 38	11 49				12 22	12 30	12 56	
Alsager	d									10 46							11 46								
Kidsgrove	d									10 50							11 52								
Hanley Bus Station	d																								
Stoke-on-Trent	d						10 07			10 58				11 07			11 59		12 07						
Wedgwood Old Road Bridge	d																								
Barlaston Orchard Place	d																								
Stone Granville Square	d																								
Stone	d									11 06							12 08								
Norton Bridge Station Drv	d																								
Stafford	d	09 02		09 26	09 32		10 27	10 33	10a41	11a17				11 28	11 36		12 18		12 25	12 36		12a41			
Rugeley Trent Valley	d																12 28								
Lichfield Trent Valley	d																12 35								
Tamworth	d																12 42								
Polesworth	d																								
Atherstone	d																12 51								
Nuneaton	a				09 54			10 55							11 58		12 58	12 31							
	d				09 55			10 56							11 59	12 30	12 58	12 32							
Bedworth	d															12 36									
Coventry	a			10 24			11 24							12 24		12 54			13 24						
Rugby	a					10 31						11 31					13 17								
Northampton	a																13 39								←
Milton Keynes Central	a		10 17			11 06		11 46				12 06					14 04	13 03						14 02	14 04
Watford Junction	a	10s35			11s16	11s43							12s35		12s50		↦								14 33
London Euston 15 ⊖	a	10 57	11 06		11 37	12 05		12 32				12 45	12 56		13 11			13 44		14 01			14 09	14 43	14 53

		XC	VT	LM	VT	LM		LM	VT	XC	VT	LM	VT	VT	LM	LM		XC	VT	LM	VT	LM	LM	VT	XC
		◇1	◇1	1	◇1			◇1	◇1	◇1	◇1	1	◇1	◇1	◇1			◇1	◇1	1	◇1		◇1	◇1	◇1
		🛒	☕		☕				☕	🛒	☕		☕	☕				🛒	☕		☕			☕	🛒
Crewe	d			13 22	13 30			13 38	13 51			14 22	14 29	14 54						15 22	15 29		15 38	15 54	
Alsager	d							13 46															15 46		
Kidsgrove	d							13 51															15 52		
Hanley Bus Station	d																								
Stoke-on-Trent	d	13 07						13 59		14 07								15 07					15 59		16 07
Wedgwood Old Road Bridge	d																								
Barlaston Orchard Place	d																								
Stone Granville Square	d																								
Stone	d							14 07															16 08		
Norton Bridge Station Drv	d																								
Stafford	d	13 25	13 36	13a42				14 18		14 25	14 36	14a42						15 25	15 36	15a42			16 18		16 25
Rugeley Trent Valley	d							14 28															16 28		
Lichfield Trent Valley	d							14 35															16 35		
Tamworth	d							14 42															16 42		
Polesworth	d																								
Atherstone	d							14 51															16 51		
Nuneaton	a							14 57	14 31														16 58		
	d					14 11		14 58	14 32							15 11						16 11	16 58		
Bedworth	d					14 17										15 17						16 17			
Coventry	a	14 24				14 34				15 24						15 34		16 24				16 34			17 24
Rugby	a							15 17															17 18		
Northampton	a							15 39							←								17 39		
Milton Keynes Central	a							16 04	15s04					16 04	16 04								18 04	17 03	
Watford Junction	a							↦							16 33								↦		
London Euston 15 ⊖	a		15 01		15 09				15 45		16 01		16 09	16 44	16 53				17 01		17 09			17 44	

A 🛒 to Stafford

Table 67

Sundays

from 30 October

Crewe and Stoke-on-Trent - London
Nuneaton - Coventry

		VT		LM	VT	VT	LM	LM	XC	VT	LM	VT		LM	LM	VT	XC	VT	LM	VT	VT	LM		XC	VT
		◇1		1	◇1	◇1	◇1		◇1	◇1	1	◇1			◇1	◇1	◇1	◇1	1	◇1	◇1	◇1		◇1	◇1
		🍴			🍴	🍴			🛒	🍴		🍴				🍴	🛒	🍴		🍴	🍴			🛒	🍴
Crewe	d			16 22	16 29	16 54					17 22	17 29			17 38	17 55			18 22	18 29	18 55				
Alsager	d														17 46										
Kidsgrove	d														17 51										
Hanley Bus Station	d																								
Stoke-on-Trent	d								17 08						17 59		18 08							19 07	
Wedgwood Old Road Bridge	d																								
Barlaston Orchard Place	d																								
Stone Granville Square	d																								
Stone	d														18 07										
Norton Bridge Station Drv	d																								
Stafford	d	16 37		16a42					17 26	17 36	17a42				18 18		18 26	18 36	18a42					19 25	19 36
Rugeley Trent Valley	d														18 28										
Lichfield Trent Valley	d					17 27									18 35										
Tamworth	d														18 42										
Polesworth	d																								
Atherstone	d														18 51										
Nuneaton	a														18 58										
	d							17 11						18 11	18 58										
Bedworth	d							17 17						18 17											
Coventry	a							17 34	18 24					18 34			19 24							20 24	
Rugby	a														19 18										
Northampton	a						←								19 39							←			
Milton Keynes Central	a					18 04	18 04								20 06	19 02					20 03	20 06			
Watford Junction	a						18 35								→							20 33			
London Euston 15 ⊖	a	18 01			18 09	18 44	18 53			19 01		19 09				19 43		20 01		20 09	20 44	20 53			21 01

		LM	VT	LM	LM	XC	LM	VT		VT	LM	XC	AW	LM	LM	VT	VT	XC		LM	XC				
		1	◇1		◇1	◇1	1	◇1		◇1	◇1	◇1	◇	1		◇1	◇1	◇1		1	◇1				
						A																			
			🍴			🛒		🍴		🍴			🛒			🍴	🍴								
Crewe	d	19 22	19 29		19 36		20 18	20 24		20 47			20 52	21 17		21 23	21 40			22 22					
Alsager	d				19 44																				
Kidsgrove	d				19 50																				
Hanley Bus Station	d																								
Stoke-on-Trent	d				19 57	20 07						20 47						21 47			22 47				
Wedgwood Old Road Bridge	d																								
Barlaston Orchard Place	d																								
Stone Granville Square	d																								
Stone	d				20 06																				
Norton Bridge Station Drv	d																								
Stafford	d	19a42			20 16	20 27	20a38	20 43				21a08	21a16	21a37		21 43	22a01	22a06		22a42	23a04				
Rugeley Trent Valley	d				20 28																				
Lichfield Trent Valley	d				20 35											22 00									
Tamworth	d				20 42											22 06									
Polesworth	d																								
Atherstone	d				20 51																				
Nuneaton	a				20 58											22 17									
	d			20 11	20 58										22 00	22 18									
Bedworth	d			20 17											22 06										
Coventry	a			20 34		21 23									22 21										
Rugby	a				21 16											22 31									
Northampton	a				21 39						←														
Milton Keynes Central	a				22 10			21 36		21 55	22 10					23 04									
Watford Junction	a				→					22s31	22 52					23s34									
London Euston 15 ⊖	a		21 09					22 28		22 53	23 14					23 54									

A 🛒 to Stafford

Northampton - Coventry - Birmingham - Wolverhampton - Stafford

Miles			AW MX	LM MO	LM MX	VT MO	VT MO	LM MO	VT MX	VT MO	VT MX	VT	LM	XC	LM	LM	LM	VT	XC	LM	AW	LM	LM
				◇1	◇1	◇1 🛏	◇1 🛏	1	◇1 🛏	◇1 🛏	◇1 🛏	◇1 ☒		◇1 ⌶	◇1		◇1	◇1 ☒	◇1 ⌶	◇1	◇ ⌶		◇1
—	London Euston 15 ⊖	d			21p46	21p55	22p25		22p30	23p25	23p30												
0	**Northampton**	d		22p53	22b55			23p32									05 17			05 42			
9½	Long Buckby	d		23p03	23p06			23p42									05 27						
18¾	Rugby	d		23p13	23p17	23p21	23p48	23p52	00 01	00s46	01s00						05 38			06 05			
32¼	**Coventry**	a		23p25	23p29	23p31	23p57	00 06	00 10	00s57	01s13						05 49						
—		d		23p34	23p30	23p31	23p58		00 10								05 50						
34	Canley	d		23p37	23p33																		
36	Tile Hill	d		23p41	23p37												05 55						
38	Berkswell	d		23p44	23p40																		
41¼	Hampton-in-Arden	d		23p49	23p44												06 01						
43	**Birmingham International** ✈	a		23p52	23p47	23p42	00 08		00 21	01s08	01s24						06 04						
—		d		23p52	23p48	23p42	00 09		00 21								06 05					06 17	
45	Marston Green	d		23p55	23p51												06 08						
46½	Lea Hall	d			23p54																	06 22	
47¾	Stechford	d			23p57																	06 25	
49½	Adderley Park	d																				06 28	
51½	**Birmingham New Street** 12	a		00 04	00 04	23p54	00 21		00 32	01s21	01s36						06 16					06 33	
—		d	23p32			23p57	00 24		00 35			05 30	05 51	05 57	06 01	06 06		06 19	06 22		06 24		06 36
54¾	Smethwick Rolfe Street	d														06 12							
55½	Smethwick Galton Bridge 7	d													06 08	06 14					06 30		
56¾	Sandwell & Dudley	d											05 59			06 17							
57¾	Dudley Port	d														06 20							
58½	Tipton	d														06 22							
60	Coseley	d														06 25							
64¼	**Wolverhampton** 7	a	00 02			00 15	00 43		01 03	01 52	02 07	05 47	06 09	06 14	06 19	06 31		06 35	06 39		06 42		06 52
—		d										05 48		06 16	06 19				06 40				06 53
74¼	Penkridge	d													06 29								
79½	**Stafford**	a										06 01		06 29	06 35				06 53	06 58			07 08

		LM	LM	XC	LM	LM	LM	LM	VT	AW	VT	LM	LM	XC	LM	LM	VT	XC	LM	LM	LM	VT	LM
			1	◇1 ⌶	◇1	◇1		◇1	◇1 ☒	◇ ⌶	◇1 ☒	◇1		◇1 ⌶	◇1		◇1 ☒	◇1 ⌶	◇1	◇1		◇1 ☒	
London Euston 15 ⊖	d										06 03						06 23			05 30		06 43	
Northampton	d				05 55			06 16				06 41								06 55			
Long Buckby	d				06 06			06 27												07 06			
Rugby	d				06 17			06 38			06 51	07 01								07 17			
Coventry	a				06 29			06 49			07 02						07 22			07 29		07 42	
	d		06 10		06 30			06 50			07 02					07 07	07 22	07 27		07 30		07 42	
Canley	d		06 13		06 33											07 09				07 33			
Tile Hill	d		06 17		06 37			06 55								07 13				07 37			
Berkswell	d		06 20		06 40											07 16				07 40			
Hampton-in-Arden	d		06 24					07 01								07 20							
Birmingham International ✈	a		06 27		06 45			07 04			07 13					07 23	07 33	07 37		07 45		07 53	
	d		06 28		06 46			07 05		07 09	07 13				07 17	07 24	07 33	07 38		07 46		07 53	
Marston Green	d		06 31		06 49			07 08								07 27				07 49			
Lea Hall	d				06 52										07 22					07 52			
Stechford	d				06 55										07 25					07 55			
Adderley Park	d														07 28					07 58			
Birmingham New Street 12	a		06 39		07 01			07 16		07 20	07 27				07 32	07 36	07 45	07 48		08 03		08 08	
	d	06 38		06 57		07 01	07 08		07 20	07 24			07 27	07 31	07 36	07 38	07 49	07 57	08 01		08 05		08 08
Smethwick Rolfe Street	d	06 44					07 14									07 44							08 14
Smethwick Galton Bridge 7	d	06 46				07 08	07 16			07 30						07 46			08 08				08 16
Sandwell & Dudley	d	06 49					07 19									07 49	07 58				08 13		08 19
Dudley Port	d	06 52					07 22									07 52							08 22
Tipton	d	06 54					07 24									07 54							08 24
Coseley	d	06 57					07 27								07 46	07 57							08 27
Wolverhampton 7	a	07 03		07 14		07 19	07 33		07 36	07 42			07 45	07 48	07 53	08 03	08 11	08 14	08 19		08 24		08 33
	d			07 16		07 19									07 53			08 15	08 19				
Penkridge	d					07 30									08 03				08 29				
Stafford	a			07 29		07 36						07 53			08 09			08 29	08 35				

b Previous night, arr. 2249

Northampton - Coventry - Birmingham - Wolverhampton - Stafford

		LM	VT	AW	VT	LM	XC	LM	LM	LM	LM	VT	XC	LM	LM	LM	VT	LM	LM	VT	AW	VT
		◇1	◇1 ☒	◇ ⌶	◇1 ☒	◇1	◇1 ⌶		◇1		1	◇1 ☒	◇1 ⌶	◇1	◇1		◇1 ☒		◇1	◇1 ☒	◇ ⌶	◇1 ☒
London Euston 15 ⊖	d				07 03	06 24						07 23					07 43		06 53			08 03
Northampton	d	07 16				07 45								07 55					08 16			
Long Buckby	d	07 27												08 06					08 27			
Rugby	d	07 38			07 51	08 04								08 17					08 38			08 51
Coventry	a	07 49			08 02							08 22		08 29			08 42		08 49			09 02
	d	07 50			08 02						08 11	08 22	08 27	08 30			08 42		08 50			09 02
Canley	d										08 14			08 33								
Tile Hill	d	07 55									08 18			08 37					08 55			
Berkswell	d										08 21			08 40								
Hampton-in-Arden	d	08 01									08 25								09 01			
Birmingham International ✈	a	08 04			08 12						08 28	08 33	08 37	08 45			08 53		09 04			09 12
	d	08 05		08 09	08 13			08 17			08 29	08 33	08 38	08 46			08 53		09 05		09 09	09 13
Marston Green	d	08 08						08 20			08 32			08 49					09 08			
Lea Hall	d							08 23						08 52								
Stechford	d							08 26						08 55								
Adderley Park	d							08 29														
Birmingham New Street 12	a	08 16		08 20	08 27			08 33			08 42	08 45	08 48	09 01			09 08		09 16		09 20	09 27
	d		08 20	08 24			08 31		08 36	08 38		08 49	08 57		09 01	09 05		09 08		09 20	09 24	
Smethwick Rolfe Street	d									08 44								09 14				
Smethwick Galton Bridge 7	d			08 30						08 46					09 08			09 16			09 30	
Sandwell & Dudley	d									08 49		08 58				09 13		09 19				
Dudley Port	d									08 52								09 22				
Tipton	d									08 54								09 24				
Coseley	d								08 46	08 57								09 27				
Wolverhampton 7	a		08 37	08 42			08 48		08 53	09 03		09 11	09 14		09 19	09 24		09 33		09 37	09 43	
	d						08 49		08 53				09 15		09 19							
Penkridge	d								09 03													
Stafford	a					08 53	09 00		09 09				09 29		09 34							

		LM	XC	LM	LM	LM	LM	VT	XC	LM	LM	LM	VT	LM	VT	LM	VT	AW	VT	LM	XC	LM	LM
		◇1	◇1 ⌶		◇1		1	◇1 ☒	◇1 ⌶	◇1	◇1		◇1 A ☒		◇1 B ☒	◇1	◇1 A ☒	◇ ⌶	◇1 ☒	◇1	◇1 ⌶		◇1
London Euston 15 ⊖	d	07 47						08 23					08 43		08 43	07 54			09 03	08 46			
Northampton	d	08 45								08 55						09 16				09 45			
Long Buckby	d									09 06						09 27							
Rugby	d	09 04								09 17						09 38			09 51	10 04			
Coventry	a							09 22		09 29			09 42		09 42	09 49			10 02				
	d						09 11	09 22	09 27	09 30			09 42		09 42	09 50			10 02				
Canley	d						09 14			09 33													
Tile Hill	d						09 18			09 37						09 55							
Berkswell	d						09 21			09 40													
Hampton-in-Arden	d						09 25									10 01							
Birmingham International ✈	a						09 28	09 33	09 37	09 45			09 53		09 53	10 04			10 13				
	d			09 17			09 29	09 33	09 38	09 46			09 53		09 53	10 05		10 09	10 13			10 17	
Marston Green	d						09 32			09 49						10 08							
Lea Hall	d			09 22						09 52												10 21	
Stechford	d			09 25						09 55												10 24	
Adderley Park	d			09 28																		10 27	
Birmingham New Street 12	a			09 33			09 42	09 45	09 48	10 01			10 08		10 08	10 16		10 19	10 27			10 33	
	d		09 31		09 36	09 38		09 49	09 57		10 01	10 05		10 08	10 20		10 20	10 24			10 31		10 36
Smethwick Rolfe Street	d					09 44								10 14									
Smethwick Galton Bridge 7	d					09 46					10 08			10 16				10 30					
Sandwell & Dudley	d					09 49		09 58				10 13		10 19									
Dudley Port	d					09 52								10 22									
Tipton	d					09 54								10 24									
Coseley	d				09 46	09 57								10 27									10 46
Wolverhampton 7	a		09 48		09 53	10 03		10 11	10 14		10 19	10 24		10 33	10 37		10 37	10 42			10 48		10 53
	d		09 49		09 53				10 15		10 19										10 49		10 53
Penkridge	d				10 03																		11 03
Stafford	a	09 53	10 00		10 09				10 29		10 34									10 53	11 00		11 09

A until 15 July, from 12 September

B from 18 July until 9 September

Northampton - Coventry - Birmingham - Wolverhampton - Stafford

		LM	LM 1	VT ◇1 ⊠	XC ◇1 ⌶	LM ◇1	LM ◇1	LM	VT ◇1 ⊠	LM	LM ◇1	VT ◇1 Ꝑ	AW ◇ ⌶	VT ◇1 ⊠	LM ◇1	XC ◇1 ⌶	LM	LM ◇1	LM	LM 1	VT ◇1 ⊠	XC ◇1 ⌶	LM ◇1
London Euston 15 ⊖	d			09 23					09 43		08 54			10 03	09 46						10 23		
Northampton	d					09 55					10 16				10 45								10 55
Long Buckby	d					10 06					10 27												11 06
Rugby	d					10 17					10 38			10 51	11 04								11 17
Coventry	a			10 22		10 29			10 42		10 49			11 02							11 22		11 29
	d		10 11	10 22	10 27	10 30			10 42		10 50			11 02						11 11	11 22	11 27	11 30
Canley	d		10 14			10 33														11 14			11 33
Tile Hill	d		10 18			10 37					10 55									11 18			11 37
Berkswell	d		10 21			10 40														11 21			11 40
Hampton-in-Arden	d		10 25								11 01									11 25			
Birmingham International ✈	a		10 28	10 33	10 37	10 45			10 53		11 04			11 13						11 28	11 33	11 37	11 45
	d		10 29	10 33	10 38	10 46			10 53		11 05		11 09	11 13			11 17			11 29	11 33	11 38	11 46
Marston Green	d		10 32			10 49					11 08									11 32			11 49
Lea Hall	d					10 52											11 21						11 52
Stechford	d					10 55											11 24						11 55
Adderley Park	d																11 27						
Birmingham New Street 12	a		10 42	10 45	10 48	11 01			11 08		11 16		11 20	11 27			11 33			11 42	11 45	11 48	12 01
	d	10 38		10 49	10 57		11 01	11 05		11 08		11 20	11 24			11 31		11 36	11 38		11 49	11 57	
Smethwick Rolfe Street	d	10 44								11 14									11 44				
Smethwick Galton Bridge 7	d	10 46					11 08			11 16			11 30						11 46				
Sandwell & Dudley	d	10 49		10 58				11 13		11 19									11 49		11 58		
Dudley Port	d	10 52								11 22									11 52				
Tipton	d	10 54								11 24									11 54				
Coseley	d	10 57								11 27								11 46	11 57				
Wolverhampton 7 ⇌	a	11 03		11 11	11 14		11 19	11 24		11 33		11 37	11 42			11 48		11 53	12 03		12 11	12 14	
	d				11 15		11 19									11 49		11 53				12 15	
Penkridge	d																	12 03					
Stafford	a				11 28		11 34								11 53	12 00		12 09				12 29	

		LM ◇1	LM	VT ◇1 ⊠	LM	LM ◇1	VT ◇1 Ꝑ	AW ◇ ⌶	VT ◇1 Ꝑ	LM ◇1	XC ◇1 ⌶	LM	LM ◇1	LM	LM 1	VT ◇1 Ꝑ	XC ◇1 ⌶	LM ◇1	LM ◇1	LM	VT ◇1 Ꝑ	LM
London Euston 15 ⊖	d			10 43		09 54			11 03	10 46						11 23					11 43	
Northampton	d					11 16				11 45								11 55				
Long Buckby	d					11 27												12 06				
Rugby	d					11 38			11 51	12 04								12 17				
Coventry	a			11 42		11 49			12 02							12 22		12 29			12 42	
	d			11 42		11 50			12 02						12 11	12 22	12 27	12 30			12 42	
Canley	d														12 14			12 33				
Tile Hill	d					11 55									12 18			12 37				
Berkswell	d														12 21			12 40				
Hampton-in-Arden	d					12 01									12 25							
Birmingham International ✈	a			11 53		12 04			12 13						12 28	12 33	12 37	12 45			12 53	
	d			11 53		12 05		12 09	12 13			12 17			12 29	12 33	12 38	12 46			12 53	
Marston Green	d					12 08									12 32			12 49				
Lea Hall	d											12 21						12 52				
Stechford	d											12 24						12 55				
Adderley Park	d											12 27										
Birmingham New Street 12	a			12 08		12 16		12 20	12 27			12 33			12 42	12 45	12 48	13 01			13 08	
	d	12 01	12 05		12 08		12 20	12 24			12 31		12 36	12 38		12 49	12 57		13 01	13 05		13 08
Smethwick Rolfe Street	d				12 14									12 44								13 14
Smethwick Galton Bridge 7	d	12 08			12 16			12 30						12 46					13 08			13 16
Sandwell & Dudley	d		12 13		12 19									12 49		12 58				13 13		13 19
Dudley Port	d				12 22									12 52								13 22
Tipton	d				12 24									12 54								13 24
Coseley	d				12 27								12 46	12 57								13 27
Wolverhampton 7 ⇌	a	12 19	12 24		12 33		12 37	12 42			12 48		12 53	13 03		13 11	13 14		13 19	13 24		13 33
	d	12 19									12 49		12 53				13 15		13 19			
Penkridge	d												13 03									
Stafford	a	12 34								12 53	13 00		13 09				13 29		13 34			

Northampton - Coventry - Birmingham - Wolverhampton - Stafford

		LM ◇1	VT ◇1 Ꝑ	AW ◇ ⌶	VT ◇1 Ꝑ	LM ◇1	XC ◇1 ⌶	LM	LM ◇1	LM	LM 1	VT ◇1 Ꝑ	XC ◇1 ⌶	LM ◇1	LM ◇1	LM	VT ◇1 Ꝑ	LM	LM ◇1	VT ◇1 Ꝑ	AW ◇ ⌶	VT ◇1 Ꝑ	LM ◇1
London Euston 15 ⊖	d	10 54			12 03	11 46						12 23					12 43		11 54			13 03	12 46
Northampton	d	12 16				12 45								12 55					13 16				13 45
Long Buckby	d	12 27												13 06					13 27				
Rugby	d	12 38			12 51	13 04								13 17					13 38			13 51	14 04
Coventry	a	12 49			13 02							13 22		13 29			13 42		13 49			14 02	
	d	12 50			13 02						13 11	13 22	13 27	13 30			13 42		13 50			14 02	
Canley	d										13 14			13 33									
Tile Hill	d	12 55									13 18			13 37					13 55				
Berkswell	d										13 21			13 40									
Hampton-in-Arden	d	13 01									13 25								14 01				
Birmingham International ✈	a	13 04			13 13						13 28	13 33	13 37	13 45			13 53		14 04			14 13	
	d	13 05		13 09	13 13			13 17			13 29	13 33	13 38	13 46			13 53		14 05		14 09	14 13	
Marston Green	d	13 08									13 32			13 49					14 08				
Lea Hall	d							13 21						13 52									
Stechford	d							13 24						13 55									
Adderley Park	d							13 27															
Birmingham New Street 12	a	13 16		13 20	13 27			13 33			13 42	13 45	13 48	14 01			14 08		14 16		14 19	14 27	
	d		13 20	13 24			13 31		13 36	13 38		13 49	13 57		14 01	14 05		14 08		14 20	14 24		
Smethwick Rolfe Street	d									13 44								14 14					
Smethwick Galton Bridge 7	d			13 30						13 46					14 08			14 16			14 30		
Sandwell & Dudley	d									13 49		13 58				14 13		14 19					
Dudley Port	d									13 52								14 22					
Tipton	d									13 54								14 24					
Coseley	d								13 46	13 57								14 27					
Wolverhampton 7 ⇌	a		13 37	13 42			13 48		13 53	14 03		14 11	14 14		14 19	14 24		14 33		14 37	14 42		
	d						13 49		13 53				14 15		14 19								
Penkridge	d								14 03														
Stafford	a					13 53	14 00		14 09				14 29		14 34								14 53

		XC ◇1 ⌶	LM	LM ◇1	LM	LM 1	VT ◇1 Ꝑ	XC ◇1 ⌶	LM ◇1	LM ◇1	LM	VT ◇1 A Ꝑ	LM	VT ◇1 B Ꝑ	LM ◇1	VT ◇1 A Ꝑ	AW ◇ ⌶	VT ◇1 Ꝑ	LM ◇1	XC ◇1 ⌶	LM	LM ◇1
London Euston 15 ⊖	d						13 23					13 43		13 43	12 54			14 03	13 46			
Northampton	d								13 55						14 16				14 45			
Long Buckby	d								14 06						14 27							
Rugby	d								14 17						14 38			14 51	15 04			
Coventry	a						14 22		14 29			14 42		14 42	14 49			15 02				
	d					14 11	14 22	14 27	14 30			14 42		14 42	14 50			15 02				
Canley	d					14 14			14 33													
Tile Hill	d					14 18			14 37						14 55							
Berkswell	d					14 21			14 40													
Hampton-in-Arden	d					14 25									15 01							
Birmingham International ✈	a					14 28	14 33	14 37	14 45			14 53		14 53	15 04			15 13				
	d		14 17			14 29	14 33	14 38	14 46			14 53		14 53	15 05		15 09	15 13			15 17	
Marston Green	d					14 32			14 49						15 08							
Lea Hall	d		14 21						14 52												15 21	
Stechford	d		14 24						14 55												15 24	
Adderley Park	d		14 27																		15 27	
Birmingham New Street 12	a		14 33			14 42	14 45	14 48	15 01			15 08		15 08	15 16		15 19	15 27			15 33	
	d	14 31		14 36	14 38		14 49	14 57		15 01	15 05		15 08	15 20		15 20	15 26			15 31		15 36
Smethwick Rolfe Street	d				14 44								15 14									
Smethwick Galton Bridge 7	d				14 46					15 08			15 16				15 32					
Sandwell & Dudley	d				14 49		14 58				15 13		15 19									
Dudley Port	d				14 52								15 22									
Tipton	d				14 54								15 24									
Coseley	d			14 46	14 57								15 27									15 46
Wolverhampton 7 ⇌	a	14 48		14 53	15 03		15 11	15 14		15 19	15 24		15 33	15 37		15 37	15 44			15 49		15 53
	d	14 49		14 53				15 15		15 19												15 53
Penkridge	d			15 03																		16 03
Stafford	a	15 00		15 09				15 29		15 34									15 53			16 09

A until 15 July, from 12 September

B from 18 July until 9 September

Table 68

Mondays to Fridays

Northampton - Coventry - Birmingham - Wolverhampton - Stafford

		LM	LM	VT	XC	LM	LM	LM	VT	LM	LM	VT	AW	VT	LM	XC	LM	LM	LM	LM	VT	XC	LM
			1	◇1 ⊏	◇1 ╤	◇1	◇1		◇1 ⊏		◇1	▪ 1 ⊏	▪ ╤	◇1 ⊏	◇1	◇1 ╤		◇1		1	◇1 ⊏	◇1 ╤	◇1
London Euston 15 ⊖	d			14 23					14 43		13 54			15 03	14 46						15 23		
Northampton	d					14 55					15b16				15 45								
Long Buckby	d					15 06					15 27												
Rugby	d					15 17					15 38			15 51	16 04								
Coventry	a			15 22		15 29			15 42		15 49			16 02							16 22		
	d		15 11	15 22	15 27	15 30			15 42		15 50			16 02						16 11	16 22	16 27	
Canley	d		15 14			15 33														16 14			
Tile Hill	d		15 18			15 37					15 55									16 18			
Berkswell	d		15 21			15 40														16 21			
Hampton-in-Arden	d		15 25								16 01									16 25			
Birmingham International ✈	a		15 28	15 33	15 37	15 45			15 53		16 04			16 13						16 28	16 33	16 37	
	d		15 29	15 33	15 38	15 46			15 53		16 05		16 09	16 13			16 17			16 29	16 33	16 38	
Marston Green	d		15 32			15 49					16 08									16 32			
Lea Hall	d					15 52											16 21						
Stechford	d					15 55											16 24						
Adderley Park	d																16 27						
Birmingham New Street 12	a		15 42	15 45	15 48	16 01			16 08		16 16		16 20	16 27			16 33			16 42	16 45	16 48	
	d	15 38		15 49	15 57		16 01	16 05		16 08		16 20	16 24			16 31		16 36	16 38		16 49	16 57	17 01
Smethwick Rolfe Street	d	15 44								16 14									16 44				
Smethwick Galton Bridge 7	d	15 46					16 08			16 16			16 30						16 46				17 08
Sandwell & Dudley	d	15 49		15 58				16 13		16 19									16 49		16 58		
Dudley Port	d	15 52								16 22									16 53				
Tipton	d	15 54								16 24									16 55				
Coseley	d	15 57								16 27								16 46	16 58				
Wolverhampton 7	a	16 03		16 11	16 14		16 19	16 24		16 33		16 37	16 42			16 48		16 53	17 04		17 11	17 14	17 19
	d				16 15		16 19									16 49		16 53				17 15	17 19
Penkridge	d																	17 03					17 29
Stafford	a				16 29		16 34								16 53	17 00		17 09				17 29	17 35

		LM	LM	VT	LM	LM	VT	AW	VT	XC	LM	LM	LM	LM	LM	LM	VT	XC	LM	LM	LM	VT	LM
		◇1		◇1 ⊏		◇1	▪ 1 ⊏	◇ ╤	◇1 ⊏	◇1 ╤	◇1		◇1		1		◇1 ⊏	◇1 ╤	◇1	◇1		◇1 ⊏	
London Euston 15 ⊖	d			15 43		14 54			16 03		15 46						16 23					16 43	
Northampton	d	15 55				16c16					16 45								16 55				
Long Buckby	d	16 06				16 27													17 06				
Rugby	d	16 17				16 38			16 51		17 04								17 17				
Coventry	a	16 29		16 42		16 49			17 02								17 22		17 29			17 42	
	d	16 30		16 42		16 50			17 02						17 11		17 22	17 27	17 30			17 42	
Canley	d	16 33													17 14				17 33				
Tile Hill	d	16 37				16 55									17 18				17 37				
Berkswell	d	16 40													17 21				17 40				
Hampton-in-Arden	d					17 01									17 25								
Birmingham International ✈	a	16 45		16 53		17 04			17 13						17 28		17 33	17 37	17 45			17 53	
	d	16 46		16 53		17 05		17 09	17 13			17 17			17 29		17 33	17 38	17 46			17 53	
Marston Green	d	16 49				17 08									17 32				17 49				
Lea Hall	d	16 52										17 21							17 52				
Stechford	d	16 55										17 24							17 55				
Adderley Park	d											17 27											
Birmingham New Street 12	a	17 02		17 08		17 19		17 19	17 27			17 33			17 42		17 45	17 48	18 01			18 08	
	d		17 05		17 08		17 20	17 26		17 31			17 36	17 38		17 46	17 49	17 57		18 01	18 05		18 08
Smethwick Rolfe Street	d				17 14									17 44									18 14
Smethwick Galton Bridge 7	d				17 16			17 32						17 46						18 08			18 16
Sandwell & Dudley	d		17 13		17 19									17 49			17 58				18 13		18 19
Dudley Port	d				17 22									17 52		17 56							18 22
Tipton	d				17 24									17 54		17 58							18 24
Coseley	d				17 27								17 46	17 57									18 27
Wolverhampton 7	a		17 24		17 33		17 37	17 44		17 48			17 53	18 03		18 06	18 11	18 14		18 19	18 24		18 33
	d									17 49			17 53					18 15		18 19			
Penkridge	d												18 03							18 29			
Stafford	a									18 00	18 01		18 09					18 29		18 35			

b Arr. 1505

c Arr. 1605

Table 68

Mondays to Fridays

Northampton - Coventry - Birmingham - Wolverhampton - Stafford

		LM	VT	AW	VT	XC	LM	LM	LM	LM	VT	XC	LM	LM	LM	VT	LM	LM	VT	AW	VT	LM
		◇1	◇1 ⊏	◇ ╤	◇1 ⊠	◇1 ╤		◇1		1	◇1 ⊠	◇1 ╤	◇1	◇1		◇1 ⊠		◇1	◇1 ⊏	◇ ╤	◇1 ⊠	1
London Euston 15 ⊖	d	15 54			17 03						17 23					17 43		17 13			18 03	17 24
Northampton	d	17 16											17 55					18 16				18 41
Long Buckby	d	17 27											18 06					18 27				18 52
Rugby	d	17 38			17 51								18 17					18 38			18 51	19a04
Coventry	a	17 49			18 02						18 22		18 29			18 42		18 49			19 02	
	d	17 50			18 02					18 11	18 22	18 27	18 30			18 42		18 50			19 02	
Canley	d									18 14			18 33									
Tile Hill	d	17 55								18 18			18 37					18 55				
Berkswell	d									18 21			18 40									
Hampton-in-Arden	d	18 01								18 25								19 01				
Birmingham International ✈	a	18 04			18 13					18 28	18 33	18 37	18 45			18 53		19 04			19 13	
	d	18 05		18 09	18 13		18 17			18 29	18 33	18 38	18 46			18 53		19 05		19 09	19 13	
Marston Green	d	18 08								18 32			18 49					19 08				
Lea Hall	d						18 21						18 52									
Stechford	d						18 24						18 55									
Adderley Park	d						18 27															
Birmingham New Street 12	a	18 17		18 20	18 27		18 33			18 42	18 45	18 48	19 01			19 08		19 17		19 20	19 27	
	d		18 20	18 24		18 31		18 36	18 38		18 49	18 57		19 01	19 05		19 08		19 20	19 24		
Smethwick Rolfe Street	d								18 44								19 14					
Smethwick Galton Bridge 7	d			18 30					18 46					19 08			19 16			19 30		
Sandwell & Dudley	d								18 49		18 58				19 13		19 19					
Dudley Port	d								18 52								19 22					
Tipton	d								18 54								19 24					
Coseley	d							18 46	18 57								19 27					
Wolverhampton 7	a		18 37	18 42		18 48		18 53	19 03		19 11	19 14		19 19	19 24		19 33		19 37	19 42		
	d					18 49		18 53				19 15		19 19								
Penkridge	d							19 03						19 29								
Stafford	a					19 00		19 09				19 27		19 36								

		XC	LM	LM	LM	LM	VT	XC	LM	LM	LM	VT	LM	AW	VT	LM	XC	LM	LM	LM	LM	VT	XC
		◇1 ╤		◇1		1	◇1 ⊠	◇1 A ╤	◇1			◇1 ⊠	◇1	◇	▪ 1 ⊏	◇1	◇1		◇1		1	▪ 1 ⊏	◇1 A ╤
London Euston 15 ⊖	d						18 23		17 46			18 43	18 13		19 03	18 29						19 23	
Northampton	d								18 55				19 16			19 45							
Long Buckby	d								19 06				19 27										
Rugby	d								19 17				19 38		19 51	20a04							
Coventry	a						19 22		19 29			19 42	19 49		20 02							20 22	
	d					19 11	19 22	19 27	19 30			19 42	19 50		20 02						20 11	20 22	20 27
Canley	d					19 14			19 33												20 14		
Tile Hill	d					19 18			19 37				19 55								20 18		
Berkswell	d					19 21			19 40												20 21		
Hampton-in-Arden	d					19 25							20 01								20 25		
Birmingham International ✈	a					19 28	19 33	19 37	19 45			19 53	20 04		20 13						20 28	20 33	20 37
	d		19 17			19 29	19 33	19 38	19 46			19 53	20 05	20 09	20 13			20 17			20 29	20 33	20 38
Marston Green	d					19 32			19 49				20 08								20 32		
Lea Hall	d		19 21						19 52									20 21					
Stechford	d		19 24						19 55									20 24					
Adderley Park	d		19 27															20 27					
Birmingham New Street 12	a		19 33			19 42	19 45	19 48	20 03			20 06	20 16	20 20	20 27			20 33			20 42	20 45	20 48
	d	19 31		19 36	19 38		19 50	19 57		20 05	20 08	20 20		20 24			20 31		20 36	20 38		20 50	20 57
Smethwick Rolfe Street	d				19 44						20 14									20 44			
Smethwick Galton Bridge 7	d				19 46						20 16			20 30						20 46			
Sandwell & Dudley	d				19 49		19 59			20 13	20 19									20 49		20 59	
Dudley Port	d				19 52						20 22									20 52			
Tipton	d				19 54						20 24									20 54			
Coseley	d			19 46	19 57						20 27								20 46	20 57			
Wolverhampton 7	a	19 48		19 53	20 03		20 12	20 14		20 24	20 33	20 36		20 42			20 48		20 53	21 04		21 12	21 14
	d	19 49		19 53				20 16				20 36							20 53				21 16
Penkridge	d			20 03															21 03				
Stafford	a	20 00		20 09				20 29				20 49							21 09				21 31

A ╤ to Birmingham International

Table 68

Mondays to Fridays

Northampton - Coventry - Birmingham - Wolverhampton - Stafford

		LM	LM		LM	VT	LM	VT	AW	VT	LM	LM	LM		LM	VT	XC	LM	LM	VT	LM	LM	XC		VT
		◇1				◇1	◇1	◇1	◇	◇1		◇1			1	◇1	◇1	◇1		◇1	◇1		◇1		◇1
London Euston 15 ⊖	d	18 49				19 43				20 03						20 23				20 43	19 54				21 03
Northampton	d	19 55					20 16											20 55			21 16				
Long Buckby	d	20 06					20 27											21 06			21 27				
Rugby	d	20 17					20 38			20 51								21 17			21 38				21 57
Coventry	a	20 29				20 42	20 49			21 02						21 22		21 28		21 42	21 49				22 06
	d	20 30				20 42	20 50			21 02					21 11	21 22	21 27	21 29		21 42	21 50				22 07
Canley	d	20 33													21 14			21 32							
Tile Hill	d	20 37					20 55								21 18			21 36			21 55				
Berkswell	d	20 40													21 21			21 39							
Hampton-in-Arden	d						21 01								21 25						22 01				
Birmingham International ✈	a	20 45				20 53	21 04			21 13					21 28	21 33	21 37	21 44		21 53	22 04				22 18
	d	20 46				20 53	21 05		21 09	21 13	21 17				21 29	21 33	21 38	21 45		21 53	22 05				22 18
Marston Green	d	20 49					21 08								21 32			21 48			22 08				
Lea Hall	d	20 52									21 21							21 51							
Stechford	d	20 55									21 24							21 54							
Adderley Park	d										21 27														
Birmingham New Street 12	a	21 01				21 06	21 16		21 19	21 25	21 33				21 42	21 46	21 48	22 01		22 06	22 16				22 29
	d		21 05		21 08	21 13		21 20	21 24	21 28		21 36	21 38			21 50	21 57		22 08	22 13		22 21	22 30		22 33
Smethwick Rolfe Street	d				21 14								21 44						22 14						
Smethwick Galton Bridge 7	d				21 16				21 30				21 46						22 16						
Sandwell & Dudley	d		21 13		21 19	21 24							21 49			21 59			22 19	22 24		22 29			22 42
Dudley Port	d				21 22								21 52						22 22						
Tipton	d				21 24								21 54						22 24						
Coseley	d				21 27							21 46	21 57						22 27						
Wolverhampton 7	a		21 24		21 33	21 38		21 40	21 42	21 56		21 53	22 03			22 12	22 14		22 33	22 38		22 41	22 47		22 56
	d							21 41				21 53					22 16						22 48		
Penkridge	d											22 03													
Stafford	a							21 53				22 09					22 29						23 00		

		LM	LM	LM	LM	XC	AW	LM	LM		VT	LM	AW	XC	LM	VT	VT FX	VT FO
		◇1			1	◇1	◇	◇1	◇1		◇1	◇1		◇1	◇1	◇1	◇1	◇1
London Euston 15 ⊖	d							20 46			21 43	21 13			21 46	22 30	23 30	23 30
Northampton	d							21 55				22 18			22 55			
Long Buckby	d							22 06				22 29			23 06			
Rugby	d							22 17				22 40			23 17	00 01	01s00	01s05
Coventry	a							22 29			22 46	22 52			23 29	00 10	01s13	01s18
	d				22 11	22 24		22 30			22 46	22 53		23 27	23 30	00 10		
Canley	d				22 14			22 33							23 33			
Tile Hill	d				22 18			22 37				22 58			23 37			
Berkswell	d				22 21			22 40							23 40			
Hampton-in-Arden	d				22 25							23 04			23 44			
Birmingham International ✈	a				22 28	22 33		22 45			23 00	23 07		23 36	23 47	00 21	01s24	01s29
	d		22 22		22 29	22 34		22 46			23 01	23 08		23 37	23 48	00 21		
Marston Green	d				22 32			22 49				23 11			23 51			
Lea Hall	d		22 26					22 52							23 54			
Stechford	d		22 29					22 55							23 57			
Adderley Park	d		22 32															
Birmingham New Street 12	a		22 38		22 42	22 45		23 02			23 16	23 19		23 58	00 04	00 32	01s36	01s41
	d	22 36		22 38			22 55		23 09		23 20		23 32			00 35		
Smethwick Rolfe Street	d			22 44					23 15									
Smethwick Galton Bridge 7	d	22 43		22 46					23 17									
Sandwell & Dudley	d			22 49					23 20		23 34							
Dudley Port	d			22 52					23 24									
Tipton	d			22 54					23 26									
Coseley	d	22 50		22 57					23 29									
Wolverhampton 7	a	22 57		23 03			23 11		23 35		23 47		00 02			01 03	02 07	02 10
	d	22 57					23 13		23 36									
Penkridge	d	23 07							23 46									
Stafford	a	23 13					23 30		23 52									

Table 68

Saturdays

Northampton - Coventry - Birmingham - Wolverhampton - Stafford

		AW	LM	VT	VT	VT	XC	LM	LM	LM		VT	AW	XC	LM	LM	LM	LM	XC	LM		LM	LM	LM	LM
			◇1	◇1	◇1	◇1	◇1	◇1	◇1			◇1	◇	◇1		◇1		1	◇1	◇1		◇1			◇1
London Euston 15 ⊖	d		21p46	22p30	23p30																				
Northampton	d		22b55						05 42											05 55					06 16
Long Buckby	d		23p06																	06 06					06 27
Rugby	d		23p17	00 01	01s05				06 05											06 17					06 38
Coventry	a		23p29	00 10	01s18															06 29					06 49
	d		23p30	00 10														06 10		06 30					06 50
Canley	d		23p33															06 13		06 33					
Tile Hill	d		23p37															06 17		06 37					06 55
Berkswell	d		23p40															06 20		06 40					
Hampton-in-Arden	d		23p44															06 24							07 01
Birmingham International ✈	a		23p47	00 21	01s29													06 27		06 45					07 04
	d		23p48	00 21											06 17			06 28		06 46					07 05
Marston Green	d		23p51															06 31		06 49					07 08
Lea Hall	d		23p54												06 21					06 52					
Stechford	d		23p57												06 24					06 55					
Adderley Park	d														06 27										
Birmingham New Street 12	a		00 04	00 32	01s41										06 32			06 39		07 01					07 16
	d	23p32		00 35		05 30	05 57	06 01		06 08		06 20	06 24	06 31		06 36	06 38		06 57			07 01	07 05	07 08	
Smethwick Rolfe Street	d									06 14							06 44							07 14	
Smethwick Galton Bridge 7	d							06 07		06 16			06 30				06 46					07 07		07 16	
Sandwell & Dudley	d									06 19							06 49						07 13	07 19	
Dudley Port	d									06 22							06 52							07 22	
Tipton	d									06 24							06 54							07 24	
Coseley	d									06 27							06 57							07 27	
Wolverhampton 7	a	00 02		01 03	02 10	05 47	06 14	06 18		06 33		06 37	06 42	06 48		06 54	07 03		07 14			07 18	07 24	07 33	
	d					05 48	06 16	06 18						06 49		06 54			07 15			07 18			
Penkridge	d							06 29														07 30			
Stafford	a					06 00	06 29	06 35	06 54					07 00		07 08			07 29			07 36			

		LM	VT	AW	XC	LM		LM	LM	LM	VT	XC	LM	LM	LM	LM		LM	VT	AW	VT	LM	XC	LM	LM
		◇1	◇1	◇	◇1			◇1		1	◇1	◇1	◇1	◇1				◇1	◇1	◇	◇1	◇1	◇1		◇1
London Euston 15 ⊖	d										06 23										07 03	06 24			
Northampton	d	06 38											06 56					07 16				07 45			
Long Buckby	d												07 07					07 27							
Rugby	d	06 58											07 18					07 38			07 51	08 04			
Coventry	a										07 22		07 29					07 49			08 02				
	d									07 10	07 22	07 27	07 30					07 50			08 02				
Canley	d									07 13			07 33												
Tile Hill	d									07 17			07 37					07 55							
Berkswell	d									07 20			07 40												
Hampton-in-Arden	d									07 24								08 01							
Birmingham International ✈	a									07 27	07 33	07 37	07 45					08 04			08 13				
	d			07 09		07 17				07 28	07 33	07 38	07 46					08 05		08 09	08 13			08 17	
Marston Green	d									07 31			07 49					08 08							
Lea Hall	d					07 21							07 52											08 21	
Stechford	d					07 24							07 55											08 24	
Adderley Park	d					07 27																		08 27	
Birmingham New Street 12	a			07 20		07 32				07 42	07 45	07 48	08 01					08 16		08 20	08 27			08 32	
	d		07 20	07 24	07 31			07 36	07 38		07 49	07 57		08 01	08 05	08 08			08 20	08 24			08 31		08 36
Smethwick Rolfe Street	d								07 44							08 14									
Smethwick Galton Bridge 7	d			07 30					07 46					08 08		08 16				08 30					
Sandwell & Dudley	d								07 49		07 58				08 13	08 19									
Dudley Port	d								07 52							08 22									
Tipton	d								07 54							08 24									
Coseley	d							07 46	07 57							08 27									08 46
Wolverhampton 7	a		07 37	07 42	07 48			07 53	08 03		08 11	08 14		08 19	08 24	08 33			08 37	08 42			08 48		08 53
	d				07 49			07 53				08 15		08 19									08 49		08 53
Penkridge	d							08 03						08 29											09 03
Stafford	a	07 53			08 00			08 09				08 29		08 35								08 53	09 00		09 09

b Previous night, arr. 2249

Table 68

Saturdays

Northampton - Coventry - Birmingham - Wolverhampton - Stafford

		LM	LM	VT	XC	LM	LM	LM	VT	LM	LM	VT	AW	VT	LM	XC	LM	LM	LM	LM	VT	XC
			1	◇1 ⊡	◇1 ⌶	◇1	◇1		◇1 ⊡		◇1	◇1 ⊡	◇ ⌶	◇1 ⊡	◇1	◇1 ⌶		◇1		1	◇1 ⊡	◇1 ⌶
London Euston 15 ⊖	d			07 23					07 43					08 03	07 46						08 23	
Northampton	d					07 55					08 16				08 45							
Long Buckby	d					08 06					08 27											
Rugby	d					08 17					08 38			08 51	09 04							
Coventry	a			08 22		08 29			08 42		08 49			09 02							09 22	
	d		08 11	08 22	08 27	08 30			08 42		08 50			09 02						09 11	09 23	09 27
Canley	d		08 14			08 33														09 14		
Tile Hill	d		08 18			08 37					08 55									09 18		
Berkswell	d		08 21			08 40														09 21		
Hampton-in-Arden	d		08 25								09 01									09 25		
Birmingham International ✈	a		08 28	08 33	08 37	08 45			08 53		09 04			09 13						09 28	09 33	09 37
	d		08 29	08 33	08 38	08 46			08 53		09 05		09 09	09 13			09 17			09 29	09 34	09 38
Marston Green	d		08 32			08 49					09 08									09 32		
Lea Hall	d					08 52											09 21					
Stechford	d					08 55											09 24					
Adderley Park	d																09 27					
Birmingham New Street 12	a		08 42	08 45	08 48	09 01			09 08		09 16		09 20	09 27			09 32			09 42	09 45	09 48
	d	08 38		08 49	08 57		09 01	09 05		09 08		09 20	09 24			09 31		09 36	09 38		09 49	09 57
Smethwick Rolfe Street	d	08 44								09 14									09 44			
Smethwick Galton Bridge 7	d	08 46					09 08			09 16			09 30						09 46			
Sandwell & Dudley	d	08 49		08 58				09 13		09 19									09 49		09 58	
Dudley Port	d	08 52								09 22									09 52			
Tipton	d	08 54								09 24									09 54			
Coseley	d	08 57								09 27								09 46	09 57			
Wolverhampton 7	a	09 03		09 11	09 14		09 19	09 24		09 33		09 37	09 43			09 48		09 53	10 03		10 11	10 14
	d				09 15		09 19									09 49		09 53				10 15
Penkridge	d																	10 03				
Stafford	a				09 29		09 34								09 53	10 00		10 09				10 29

		LM	LM	LM	VT	LM	VT	LM	VT	AW	VT	XC	LM	LM	LM	LM	VT	XC	LM		LM	LM	VT
		◇1	◇1		◇1 A ⊡		◇1 B ⊡	◇1	◇1 A ⊡	◇ ⌶	◇1 ⊡	◇1 ⌶		◇1		1	◇1 ⊡	◇1 ⌶	◇1		◇1		◇1 ⊡
London Euston 15 ⊖	d				08 43		08 43				09 03						09 23		08 46				09 43
Northampton	d	08 55						09 16											09 45	09b55			
Long Buckby	d	09 06						09 27												10 06			
Rugby	d	09 17						09 38			09 52								10 04	10 17			
Coventry	a	09 29			09 42		09 42	09 49			10 03						10 22			10 29			10 42
	d	09 30			09 42		09 42	09 50			10 03					10 11	10 22	10 27		10 30			10 42
Canley	d	09 33														10 14				10 33			
Tile Hill	d	09 37						09 55								10 18				10 37			
Berkswell	d	09 40														10 21				10 40			
Hampton-in-Arden	d							10 01								10 25							
Birmingham International ✈	a	09 45			09 53		09 53	10 04			10 14					10 28	10 33	10 37		10 45			10 53
	d	09 46			09 53		09 53	10 05		10 09	10 14		10 17			10 29	10 33	10 38		10 46			10 53
Marston Green	d	09 49						10 08								10 32				10 49			
Lea Hall	d	09 52											10 21							10 52			
Stechford	d	09 55											10 24							10 55			
Adderley Park	d												10 27										
Birmingham New Street 12	a	10 01			10 08		10 08	10 16		10 19	10 27		10 32			10 42	10 45	10 48		11 01			11 08
	d		10 01	10 05		10 08	10 20		10 20	10 24		10 31		10 36	10 38		10 49	10 57			11 01	11 05	
Smethwick Rolfe Street	d					10 14									10 44								
Smethwick Galton Bridge 7	d		10 08			10 16				10 30					10 46						11 08		
Sandwell & Dudley	d			10 13		10 19									10 49		10 58					11 13	
Dudley Port	d					10 22									10 52								
Tipton	d					10 24									10 54								
Coseley	d					10 27								10 46	10 57								
Wolverhampton 7	a		10 19	10 24		10 33	10 37		10 37	10 42		10 48		10 53	11 03		11 11	11 14			11 19	11 24	
	d		10 19									10 49		10 53				11 15			11 19		
Penkridge	d													11 03									
Stafford	a		10 35									11 00		11 09				11 29	10 53		11 35		

A until 9 July, from 17 September

B from 16 July until 10 September

Table 68

Saturdays

Northampton - Coventry - Birmingham - Wolverhampton - Stafford

		LM	LM	VT	AW	VT	XC	LM	LM	LM	LM	VT	XC	LM		LM	LM	VT	LM	LM	VT	AW
			◇1	◇1 ⊡	◇ ⌶	◇1 ⊡	◇1 ⌶		◇1		1	◇1 ⊡	◇1 ⌶	◇1		◇1		◇1 ⊡		◇1	◇1 ⊡	◇ ⌶
London Euston 15 ⊖	d					10 03						10 23		09 46				10 43				
Northampton	d		10 16											10 45	10 55					11 16		
Long Buckby	d		10 27												11 06					11 27		
Rugby	d		10 38			10 51								11 04	11 17					11 38		
Coventry	a		10 49			11 02						11 22			11 29			11 42		11 49		
	d		10 50			11 02					11 11	11 22	11 27		11 30			11 42		11 50		
Canley	d										11 14				11 33							
Tile Hill	d		10 55								11 18				11 37					11 55		
Berkswell	d										11 21				11 40							
Hampton-in-Arden	d		11 01								11 25									12 01		
Birmingham International ✈	a		11 04			11 13					11 28	11 33	11 37		11 45			11 53		12 04		
	d		11 05		11 09	11 13		11 17			11 29	11 33	11 38		11 46			11 53		12 05		12 09
Marston Green	d		11 08								11 32				11 49					12 08		
Lea Hall	d							11 21							11 52							
Stechford	d							11 24							11 55							
Adderley Park	d							11 27														
Birmingham New Street 12	a		11 16		11 20	11 27		11 32			11 42	11 45	11 48		12 01			12 08		12 16		12 20
	d	11 08		11 20	11 24		11 31		11 36	11 38		11 49	11 57			12 01	12 05		12 08		12 20	12 24
Smethwick Rolfe Street	d	11 14								11 44									12 14			
Smethwick Galton Bridge 7	d	11 16			11 30					11 46						12 08			12 16			12 30
Sandwell & Dudley	d	11 19								11 49		11 58					12 13		12 19			
Dudley Port	d	11 22								11 52									12 22			
Tipton	d	11 24								11 54									12 24			
Coseley	d	11 27							11 46	11 57									12 27			
Wolverhampton 7	a	11 33		11 37	11 42		11 48		11 53	12 03		12 11	12 14			12 19	12 24		12 33		12 37	12 42
	d						11 49		11 53				12 15			12 19						
Penkridge	d								12 03													
Stafford	a						12 00		12 09				12 29	11 53		12 35						

		VT	XC	XC	LM	LM	LM	LM	VT	XC	LM		LM	LM	VT	LM	LM	VT	AW	VT	XC	LM	LM
		◇1 ⊡	◇1 A ⊡	◇1 B ⌶		◇1		1	◇1 ⊡	◇1 ⌶	◇1		◇1		◇1 ⊡		◇1	◇1 ⊡	◇ ⌶	◇1 ⊡	◇1 ⌶		◇1
London Euston 15 ⊖	d	11 03							11 23		10 46				11 43					12 03			
Northampton	d										11 45	11 55					12 16						
Long Buckby	d											12 06					12 27						
Rugby	d	11 51									12 04	12 17					12 38			12 51			
Coventry	a	12 02							12 22			12 29			12 42		12 49			13 02			
	d	12 02						12 11	12 22	12 27		12 30			12 42		12 50			13 02			
Canley	d							12 14				12 33											
Tile Hill	d							12 18				12 37					12 55						
Berkswell	d							12 21				12 40											
Hampton-in-Arden	d							12 25									13 01						
Birmingham International ✈	a	12 13						12 28	12 33	12 37		12 45			12 53		13 04			13 13			
	d	12 13			12 17			12 29	12 33	12 38		12 46			12 53		13 05		13 09	13 13		13 17	
Marston Green	d							12 32				12 49					13 08						
Lea Hall	d				12 21							12 52										13 21	
Stechford	d				12 24							12 55										13 24	
Adderley Park	d				12 27																	13 27	
Birmingham New Street 12	a	12 27			12 32			12 42	12 45	12 48		13 01			13 08		13 16		13 20	13 27		13 32	
	d		12 31	12 31		12 36	12 38		12 49	12 57			13 01	13 05		13 08		13 20	13 24		13 31		13 36
Smethwick Rolfe Street	d						12 44									13 14							
Smethwick Galton Bridge 7	d						12 46						13 08			13 16			13 30				
Sandwell & Dudley	d						12 49		12 58					13 13		13 19							
Dudley Port	d						12 52									13 22							
Tipton	d						12 54									13 24							
Coseley	d					12 46	12 57									13 27							13 46
Wolverhampton 7	a		12 48	12 48		12 53	13 03		13 11	13 14			13 19	13 24		13 33		13 37	13 42		13 48		13 53
	d		12 49	12 49		12 53				13 15			13 19								13 49		13 53
Penkridge	d					13 03																	14 03
Stafford	a		13 00	13 00		13 09				13 29	12 53		13 35								14 00		14 09

A until 10 September

B from 17 September

Northampton - Coventry - Birmingham - Wolverhampton - Stafford

		LM	LM	VT	XC	LM		LM	LM	VT	LM	LM	VT	AW	VT	XC	LM	LM	LM	LM	VT	XC
			1	◇1	◇1	◇1		◇1		◇1		◇1	◇1	◇	◇1	◇1		◇1		1	◇1	◇1
				☕	🛒					☕			☕	🛒	☕	🛒					☕	🛒
London Euston 15 ⊖	d			12 23		11 46				12 43					13 03						13 23	
Northampton	d					12 45	12 55					13 16										
Long Buckby	d						13 06					13 27										
Rugby	d					13 04	13 17					13 38			13 51							
Coventry	a			13 22			13 29			13 42		13 49			14 02						14 22	
	d		13 11	13 22	13 27		13 30			13 42		13 50			14 02					14 11	14 22	14 27
Canley	d		13 14				13 33													14 14		
Tile Hill	d		13 18				13 37					13 55								14 18		
Berkswell	d		13 21				13 40													14 21		
Hampton-in-Arden	d		13 25									14 01								14 25		
Birmingham International ✈	a		13 28	13 33	13 37		13 45			13 53		14 04			14 13					14 28	14 33	14 37
	d		13 29	13 33	13 38		13 46			13 53		14 05		14 09	14 13		14 17			14 29	14 33	14 38
Marston Green	d		13 32				13 49					14 08								14 32		
Lea Hall	d						13 52										14 21					
Stechford	d						13 55										14 24					
Adderley Park	d																14 27					
Birmingham New Street 12	a		13 42	13 45	13 48		14 01			14 08		14 16		14 19	14 27		14 32			14 42	14 45	14 48
	d	13 38		13 49	13 57			14 01	14 05		14 08		14 20	14 24		14 31		14 36	14 38		14 49	14 57
Smethwick Rolfe Street	d	13 44									14 14								14 44			
Smethwick Galton Bridge 7	d	13 46						14 08			14 16			14 30					14 46			
Sandwell & Dudley	d	13 49		13 58					14 13		14 19								14 49		14 58	
Dudley Port	d	13 52									14 22								14 52			
Tipton	d	13 54									14 24								14 54			
Coseley	d	13 57									14 27							14 46	14 57			
Wolverhampton 7	a	14 03		14 11	14 14			14 19	14 24		14 33		14 37	14 42		14 48		14 53	15 03		15 11	15 14
	d				14 15			14 19								14 49		14 53				15 15
Penkridge	d																	15 03				
Stafford	a				14 29	13 53		14 35								15 00		15 09				15 29

		LM		LM	LM	VT	LM	VT	LM	VT	AW	VT	XC	LM	LM	LM	LM	VT	XC	LM		LM
		◇1		◇1		◇1		◇1	◇1	◇1	◇	◇1	◇1		◇1		1	◇1	◇1	◇1		◇1
						A		B		A												
						☕		☕		☕	🛒	☕	🛒					☕	🛒			
London Euston 15 ⊖	d	12 46				13 43		13 43				14 03						14 23		13 46		
Northampton	d	13 45	13 55						14 16											14 45	14 55	
Long Buckby	d		14 06						14 27												15 06	
Rugby	d	14 04	14 17						14 38			14 51								15 04	15 17	
Coventry	a		14 29			14 42		14 42	14 49			15 02						15 22			15 29	
	d		14 30			14 42		14 42	14 50			15 02					15 11	15 22	15 27		15 30	
Canley	d		14 33														15 14				15 33	
Tile Hill	d		14 37						14 55								15 18				15 37	
Berkswell	d		14 40														15 21				15 40	
Hampton-in-Arden	d								15 01								15 25					
Birmingham International ✈	a		14 45			14 53		14 53	15 04			15 13					15 28	15 33	15 37		15 45	
	d		14 46			14 53		14 53	15 05		15 09	15 13		15 17			15 29	15 33	15 38		15 46	
Marston Green	d		14 49						15 08								15 32				15 49	
Lea Hall	d		14 52											15 21							15 52	
Stechford	d		14 55											15 24							15 55	
Adderley Park	d													15 27								
Birmingham New Street 12	a		15 01			15 08		15 08	15 16		15 20	15 27		15 32			15 42	15 45	15 48		16 01	
	d			15 01	15 05		15 08	15 20		15 20	15 24		15 31		15 36	15 38		15 49	15 57			16 01
Smethwick Rolfe Street	d						15 14									15 44						
Smethwick Galton Bridge 7	d			15 08			15 16				15 30					15 46						16 08
Sandwell & Dudley	d				15 13		15 19									15 49		15 58				
Dudley Port	d						15 22									15 52						
Tipton	d						15 24									15 54						
Coseley	d						15 27								15 46	15 57						
Wolverhampton 7	a			15 19	15 24		15 33	15 37		15 37	15 42		15 48		15 53	16 03		16 11	16 14			16 19
	d			15 19									15 49		15 53				16 15			16 19
Penkridge	d														16 03							
Stafford	a	14 53		15 35									16 00		16 09				16 29	15 53		16 35

A until 9 July, from 17 September

B from 16 July until 10 September

Northampton - Coventry - Birmingham - Wolverhampton - Stafford

		LM	VT	LM	LM	VT	AW	VT	XC	LM	LM	LM	LM	VT	XC	LM		LM	LM	VT	LM	LM	VT
			◇1		◇1	◇1	■	◇1	◇1		◇1		1	◇1	◇1	◇1		◇1		◇1		◇1	◇1
			☕			☕	🛒	☕	🛒					☕	🛒					☕			☕
London Euston 15 ⊖	d		14 43					15 03						15 23		14 46				15 43			
Northampton	d				15 16											15 45	15 55					16 16	
Long Buckby	d				15 27												16 06					16 27	
Rugby	d				15 38			15 51								16 04	16 17					16 38	
Coventry	a		15 42		15 49			16 02						16 22			16 29			16 42		16 49	
	d		15 42		15 50			16 02					16 11	16 22	16 27		16 30			16 42		16 50	
Canley	d												16 14				16 33						
Tile Hill	d				15 55								16 18				16 37					16 55	
Berkswell	d												16 21				16 40						
Hampton-in-Arden	d				16 01								16 25									17 01	
Birmingham International ✈	a		15 53		16 04			16 13					16 28	16 33	16 37		16 45			16 53		17 04	
	d		15 53		16 05		16 09	16 13		16 17			16 29	16 33	16 38		16 46			16 53		17 05	
Marston Green	d				16 08								16 32				16 49					17 08	
Lea Hall	d									16 21							16 52						
Stechford	d									16 24							16 55						
Adderley Park	d									16 27													
Birmingham New Street 12	a		16 08		16 16		16 20	16 27		16 32			16 42	16 45	16 48		17 01			17 08		17 16	
	d	16 05		16 08		16 20	16 24		16 31		16 36	16 38		16 49	16 57			17 01	17 05		17 08		17 20
Smethwick Rolfe Street	d			16 14								16 44									17 14		
Smethwick Galton Bridge 7	d			16 16			16 30					16 46						17 08			17 16		
Sandwell & Dudley	d	16 13		16 19								16 49		16 58					17 13		17 19		
Dudley Port	d			16 22								16 52									17 22		
Tipton	d			16 24								16 54									17 24		
Coseley	d			16 27							16 46	16 57									17 27		
Wolverhampton 7	a	16 24		16 33		16 37	16 42		16 48		16 53	17 04		17 11	17 14			17 19	17 24		17 33		17 37
	d								16 49		16 53				17 15			17 19					
Penkridge	d										17 03							17 29					
Stafford	a								17 00		17 09				17 29	16 53		17 35					

		AW	VT	XC	LM	LM	LM	LM	VT	XC	LM		LM	LM	VT	LM	LM	VT	AW	VT	XC	LM	LM
		◇	◇1	◇1		◇1		1	◇1	◇1	◇1		◇1		◇1		◇1	◇1	◇	◇1	◇1		◇1
		🛒	☕	🛒					☕	🛒					☕			☕	🛒	☕	🛒		
London Euston 15 ⊖	d		16 03						16 23		15 46				16 43					17 03			
Northampton	d										16 45	16 55					17 16						
Long Buckby	d											17 06					17 27						
Rugby	d		16 51								17 04	17 17					17 38			17 51			
Coventry	a		17 02						17 22			17 29			17 42		17 49			18 02			
	d		17 02					17 11	17 22	17 27		17 30			17 42		17 50			18 02			
Canley	d							17 14				17 33											
Tile Hill	d							17 18				17 37					17 55						
Berkswell	d							17 21				17 40											
Hampton-in-Arden	d							17 25									18 01						
Birmingham International ✈	a		17 13					17 28	17 33	17 37		17 45			17 53		18 04			18 13			
	d	17 09	17 13		17 17			17 29	17 33	17 38		17 46			17 53		18 05		18 09	18 13		18 17	
Marston Green	d							17 32				17 49					18 08						
Lea Hall	d				17 21							17 52										18 21	
Stechford	d				17 24							17 55										18 24	
Adderley Park	d				17 27																	18 27	
Birmingham New Street 12	a	17 20	17 27		17 32			17 42	17 45	17 48		18 01			18 08		18 16		18 20	18 27		18 32	
	d	17 24		17 31		17 36	17 38		17 49	17 57			18 01	18 05		18 08		18 20	18 24		18 31		18 36
Smethwick Rolfe Street	d						17 44									18 14							
Smethwick Galton Bridge 7	d	17 31					17 46						18 08			18 16			18 30				
Sandwell & Dudley	d						17 49		17 58					18 13		18 19							
Dudley Port	d						17 52									18 22							
Tipton	d						17 54									18 24							
Coseley	d					17 46	17 57									18 27							18 46
Wolverhampton 7	a	17 42		17 48		17 53	18 03		18 11	18 14			18 19	18 24		18 33		18 37	18 42		18 48		18 53
	d			17 49		17 53				18 15			18 19								18 49		18 53
Penkridge	d					18 03							18 29										19 03
Stafford	a			18 00		18 09				18 29	18 04		18 35								19 00		19 09

Northampton - Coventry - Birmingham - Wolverhampton - Stafford

		LM	LM	VT	XC	LM		LM	LM	VT	LM	VT	LM	VT	AW	XC	XC	VT	LM	LM	LM	VT
			1	◇1	◇1	◇1		◇1		◇1		◇1	◇1	◇1	◇	◇1	◇1	◇1			1	◇1
										A		B		A		C	D					
				☕	⌶					☕		☕		☕	⌶	☕	⌶	☕				☕
London Euston 15 ⊖	d			17 23		16 46				17 43		17 43						18 03				18 23
Northampton	d					17 45	17 55						18 16									
Long Buckby	d						18 06						18 27									
Rugby	d					18 04	18 17						18 38					18 51				
Coventry	a			18 22			18 29			18 42		18 42	18 49					19 02				19 22
	d		18 11	18 22	18 27		18 30			18 42		18 42	18 50					19 02			19 11	19 22
Canley	d		18 14				18 33														19 14	
Tile Hill	d		18 18				18 37						18 55								19 18	
Berkswell	d		18 21				18 40														19 21	
Hampton-in-Arden	d		18 25										19 01								19 25	
Birmingham International ✈	a		18 28	18 33	18 37		18 45			18 53		18 53	19 04					19 13			19 28	19 33
	d		18 29	18 33	18 38		18 46			18 53		18 53	19 05		19 09			19 13	19 17		19 29	19 33
Marston Green	d		18 32				18 49						19 08								19 32	
Lea Hall	d						18 52												19 21			
Stechford	d						18 55												19 24			
Adderley Park	d																		19 27			
Birmingham New Street 12	a		18 42	18 45	18 48		19 01			19 08		19 08	19 16		19 20			19 25	19 32		19 42	19 45
	d	18 38		18 49	18 57			19 01	19 05		19 08	19 20		19 20	19 24	19 31	19 31	19 42		19 38		19 50
Smethwick Rolfe Street	d	18 44									19 14									19 44		
Smethwick Galton Bridge 7	d	18 46						19 08			19 16				19 30					19 46		
Sandwell & Dudley	d	18 49		18 58					19 13		19 19							19 54		19 49		19 59
Dudley Port	d	18 52									19 22									19 52		
Tipton	d	18 54									19 24									19 54		
Coseley	d	18 57									19 27									19 57		
Wolverhampton 7	a	19 03		19 11	19 14			19 19	19 24		19 33	19 37		19 37	19 42	19 48	19 48	20 08		20 03		20 12
	d				19 15			19 19								19 49	19 49					
Penkridge	d							19 29														
Stafford	a				19 29	18 53		19 35								20 00	20 00					

		XC	LM		LM	LM	VT	LM	LM	VT	AW	XC	VT	LM	LM	LM	LM	VT	XC	XC	XC	LM	
		◇1	1		◇1		◇1		◇1	◇1	◇	◇1	◇1		◇1		1	◇1	◇1	◇1	◇1	1	
		E																	F	D	D		
		⌶					☕			☕			☕					☕	⌶	⌶	⌶		
London Euston 15 ⊖	d		17 46				18 43						19 03					19 23				18 46	
Northampton	d		18 45	18 55					19 16													19 45	19 55
Long Buckby	d			19 06					19 27														20 06
Rugby	d		19 04	19 17					19 38				19 51									20 04	20 17
Coventry	a			19 29			19 42		19 49				20 02					20 22					20 29
	d	19 27		19 30			19 42		19 50				20 02				20 11	20 22	20 27	20 27			20 30
Canley	d			19 33													20 14						20 33
Tile Hill	d			19 37					19 55								20 18						20 37
Berkswell	d			19 40													20 21						20 40
Hampton-in-Arden	d								20 01								20 25						
Birmingham International ✈	a	19 37		19 45			19 53		20 04				20 13				20 28	20 33	20 37	20 37			20 45
	d	19 38		19 46			19 53		20 05		20 09		20 13	20 17			20 29	20 33	20 39	20 39			20 46
Marston Green	d			19 49					20 08								20 32						20 49
Lea Hall	d			19 52										20 21									20 52
Stechford	d			19 55										20 24									20 55
Adderley Park	d													20 27									
Birmingham New Street 12	a	19 48		20 01			20 08		20 16		20 20		20 25	20 32			20 42	20 45	20 48	20 48			21 01
	d	19 57			20 01	20 05		20 08		20 20	20 24	20 31	20 42		20 36	20 38		20 50	20 57		20 57		
Smethwick Rolfe Street	d							20 14								20 44							
Smethwick Galton Bridge 7	d				20 08			20 16			20 30					20 46							
Sandwell & Dudley	d					20 13		20 19					20 54			20 49		20 59					
Dudley Port	d							20 22								20 52							
Tipton	d							20 24								20 54							
Coseley	d							20 27							20 46	20 57							
Wolverhampton 7	a	20 14			20 20	20 24		20 33		20 37	20 42	20 48	21 08		20 53	21 03		21 12	21 14		21 14		
	d	20 16			20 22					20 37		20 49			20 53				21 16		21 16		
Penkridge	d				20 31										21 03								
Stafford	a	20 29	19 53		20 37					20 49		21 00			21 09				21 29		21 29	20 54	

A until 9 July, from 17 September
B from 16 July until 10 September
C from 17 September
D until 10 September
E ⌶ to Birmingham International
F from 17 September. ⌶ to Birmingham International

Table 68

Saturdays

Northampton - Coventry - Birmingham - Wolverhampton - Stafford

		LM	LM	VT	AW	LM	LM	LM	LM	LM	XC	LM	LM	LM	VT	LM	XC	XC	LM	LM	LM	LM
				◇1	◇	◇1		◇1		1	◇1	◇1			◇1	◇1	◇1	◇1		◇1		1
				☕											☕		⌶					
London Euston 15 ⊖	d			19 43											20 25							
Northampton	d					20 16						20 55				21 16						
Long Buckby	d					20 27						21 06				21 27						
Rugby	d					20 44						21 17				21 38						
Coventry	a			20 49		20 55						21 29			21 36	21 49						
	d			20 49		20 55				21 11	21 27	21 30			21 36	21 50	21 56					22 11
Canley	d					20 58				21 14		21 33										22 14
Tile Hill	d					21 02				21 18		21 37				21 55						22 18
Berkswell	d					21 05				21 21		21 40										22 21
Hampton-in-Arden	d					21 10				21 25						22 01						22 25
Birmingham International ✈	a			21 00		21 13				21 28	21 37	21 45			21 50	22 04	22 10					22 28
	d			21 00	21 09	21 13	21 17			21 29	21 38	21 46			21 50	22 05	22 11		22 21			22 29
Marston Green	d					21 16				21 32		21 49				22 08						22 32
Lea Hall	d						21 21					21 52							22 25			
Stechford	d						21 24					21 55							22 28			
Adderley Park	d						21 27												22 31			
Birmingham New Street 12	a			21 12	21 19	21 25	21 32			21 42	21 48	22 01			22 04	22 16	22 22		22 36			22 42
	d	21 05	21 08	21 16	21 24			21 36	21 38		21 57		22 05	22 08	22 16			22 31		22 36	22 38	
Smethwick Rolfe Street	d		21 14						21 44					22 14							22 44	
Smethwick Galton Bridge 7	d		21 16		21 30				21 46					22 16						22 42	22 46	
Sandwell & Dudley	d	21 13	21 19						21 49				22 13	22 19	22 25						22 49	
Dudley Port	d		21 22						21 52					22 22							22 52	
Tipton	d		21 24						21 54					22 24							22 54	
Coseley	d		21 27					21 46	21 57					22 27						22 48	22 57	
Wolverhampton 7	a	21 24	21 33	21 38	21 42			21 53	22 03		22 14		22 24	22 33	22 38			22 48		22 55	23 03	
	d							21 59			22 16							22 49		22 56		
Penkridge	d							22 09												23 06		
Stafford	a							22 16			22 29							23 01		23 13		

		VT	XC	AW	LM	LM	LM	VT	AW	LM
		◇1	◇1		◇1		◇1	◇1		◇1
									A	
		☕	⌶					☕		
London Euston 15 ⊖	d	21 03						21 43		
Northampton	d				21 55		22 16			22 55
Long Buckby	d				22 06		22 27			23 06
Rugby	d	22 12			22 17		22 38	22 53		23 17
Coventry	a	22 22			22 29		22 49	23 02		23 29
	d	22 23	22 27		22 30		22 50	23 02		23 30
Canley	d				22 33					23 33
Tile Hill	d				22 37		22 55			23 37
Berkswell	d				22 40					23 40
Hampton-in-Arden	d						23 01			23 44
Birmingham International ✈	a	22 33	22 36		22 45		23 04	23 13		23 47
	d	22 34	22 38		22 46		23 05	23 13		23 48
Marston Green	d				22 49		23 08			23 51
Lea Hall	d				22 52					23 54
Stechford	d				22 55					23 57
Adderley Park	d									
Birmingham New Street 12	a	22 45	22 48		23 01		23 16	23 25		00 04
	d	22 48		22 55		23 08		23 28	23 35	
Smethwick Rolfe Street	d					23 14				
Smethwick Galton Bridge 7	d					23 16				
Sandwell & Dudley	d	22 57				23 19		23 37		
Dudley Port	d					23 22				
Tipton	d					23 24				
Coseley	d					23 27				
Wolverhampton 7	a	23 10		23 12		23 33		23 50	23 53	
	d									
Penkridge	d									
Stafford	a									

A until 18 June, from 6 August

Northampton - Coventry - Birmingham - Wolverhampton - Stafford

		LM	VT	XC	LM	LM	LM	VT	LM	LM	XC	AW	VT	LM	LM	LM	LM	VT	XC	AW	LM	LM	VT
		◇1 A	◇1 🍴	◇1 🛒	1		1	◇1 🍴	1	◇1	◇1 🛒		◇1 🍴		◇1	1	◇1	◇1 🍴	◇1 🛒	◇ 🛒	◇1		◇1 🍴
London Euston 15 ⊖	d																	08 50					
Northampton	d	22p55													09 30						10 00		
Long Buckby	d	23p06													09 40						10 10		
Rugby	d	23p17													09 50			10 14			10 20		
Coventry	a	23p29													10 03			10 23			10 32		
	d	23p30			08 37				09 07						10 04	10 08		10 24	10 28		10 34		
Canley	d	23p33			08 40				09 10							10 11					10 37		
Tile Hill	d	23p37			08 44				09 14							10 15					10 41		
Berkswell	d	23p40			08 47				09 17							10 18					10 44		
Hampton-in-Arden	d	23p44			08 51				09 21							10 22					10 48		
Birmingham International ✈	a	23p47			08 54				09 24						10 13	10 26		10 34	10 38		10 51		
	d	23p48			08 55		09 03		09 25			09 51			10 13	10 26		10 35	10 40	10 48	10 52		
Marston Green	d	23p51			08 58		09 06		09 28						10 16	10 29					10 55		
Lea Hall	d	23p54					09 09								10 20								
Stechford	d	23p57					09 12								10 22								
Adderley Park	d						09 15								10 26								
Birmingham New Street 12	a	00 04			09 06		09 20		09 36			10 02			10 30	10 38		10 47	10 50	10 58	11 03		
	d		08 45	09 01		09 09		09 20		09 42	10 01	10 05	10 20	10 23			10 42	10 51	11 01	11 05		11 09	11 20
Smethwick Rolfe Street	d					09 15								10 29								11 15	
Smethwick Galton Bridge 7	d					09 17								10 31								11 17	
Sandwell & Dudley	d					09 19								10 33				11 00				11 19	
Dudley Port	d					09 22								10 36								11 22	
Tipton	d					09 24								10 38								11 24	
Coseley	d					09 27								10 41								11 27	
Wolverhampton 7	a		09 02	09 18		09 32		09 37		09 59	10 18	10 21	10 37	10 46			10 59	11 13	11 18	11 26		11 32	11 37
	d		09 04	09 19						09 59	10 19						10 59		11 19				
Penkridge	d									10 10							11 10						
Stafford	a		09 16	09 32						10 16	10 32						11 16		11 31				

		LM	LM	VT	XC	LM	LM	LM	VT	AW	LM	LM	VT	XC	LM	LM	VT	VT	AW	XC	LM	LM	VT
		1	◇1	◇1 🍴	◇1 🛒	◇1	◇1		◇1 🍴	◇ 🛒	◇1	1	◇1 🍴	◇1 🛒	◇1		◇1 🍴	◇1 🍴	◇ 🛒	◇1 🛒	◇1	1	◇1 🍴
London Euston 15 ⊖	d			09 50									10 50					11 45					12 18
Northampton	d					11 00	11 36								12 00								
Long Buckby	d					11 10	11 46								12 10								
Rugby	d			11 15		11 20	12 02						12 14		12 21			12 48					
Coventry	a			11 25		11 32							12 24		12 32			12 56					13 20
	d	11 08		11 25	11 28	11 34						12 08	12 25	12 28	12 34			12 57				13 10	13 21
Canley	d					11 37									12 37								
Tile Hill	d					11 41									12 41							13 15	
Berkswell	d					11 44									12 44								
Hampton-in-Arden	d					11 48									12 48								
Birmingham International ✈	a	11 18		11 36	11 38	11 51						12 17	12 35	12 38	12 51			13 07				13 22	13 31
	d	11 18		11 36	11 40	11 52				12 08		12 18	12 36	12 40	12 52			13 08	13 12			13 22	13 32
Marston Green	d	11 21				11 55						12 21			12 55							13 25	
Lea Hall	d	11 24										12 24										13 29	
Stechford	d	11 27										12 27										13 31	
Adderley Park	d	11 30										12 30										13 35	
Birmingham New Street 12	a	11 36		11 49	11 50	12 03				12 18		12 36	12 48	12 50	13 03			13 22	13 21			13 40	13 44
	d		11 42	11 52	12 01			12 09	12 20	12 24	12 35		12 52	13 01		13 09	13 20		13 24	13 31	13 35		13 48
Smethwick Rolfe Street	d							12 15								13 15							
Smethwick Galton Bridge 7	d							12 17								13 17							
Sandwell & Dudley	d			12 02				12 19					13 01			13 19							13 57
Dudley Port	d							12 22								13 22							
Tipton	d							12 24								13 24							
Coseley	d							12 27								13 27							
Wolverhampton 7	a		11 59	12 15	12 19			12 32	12 37	12 42	12 52		13 14	13 18		13 32	13 37		13 41	13 48	13 52		14 10
	d		11 59		12 19						12 52			13 19							13 52		
Penkridge	d		12 10								13 03										14 03		
Stafford	a		12 16		12 32		12 54				13 09			13 33							14 10		

A not 22 May

Northampton - Coventry - Birmingham - Wolverhampton - Stafford

		XC	LM	VT	LM	VT	AW	VT	XC	LM	LM	VT	XC	LM	LM	VT	LM	VT	AW	VT	XC	LM
		◇1 🛒	◇1	◇1 🍴		◇1 🍴	◇ 🛒	◇1 🍴	◇1 🛒	◇1	1	◇1 🍴	◇1 🛒	◇1	◇1	◇1 🍴		◇1 🍴	◇ 🛒	◇1 🍴	◇1 🛒	◇1
London Euston 15 ⊖	d			12 38				12 58				13 18			12 50	13 38				13 58		
Northampton	d		12 53											13 51	13 56							
Long Buckby	d		13 03											14 01	14 06							
Rugby	d		13 15					13 49						14 15	14 17					14 49		
Coventry	a		13 28	13 40				14 00				14 20		14 28		14 40				15 00		
	d	13 26	13 29	13 40				14 00			14 10	14 20	14 26	14 29		14 40				15 00		
Canley	d		13 32											14 32								
Tile Hill	d		13 36								14 15			14 36								
Berkswell	d		13 39											14 39								
Hampton-in-Arden	d		13 43											14 43								
Birmingham International ✈	a	13 37	13 46	13 51				14 11			14 22	14 31	14 35	14 46		14 51				15 11		
	d	13 38	13 47	13 51			14 07	14 11			14 22	14 31	14 38	14 47		14 51			15 07	15 11		
Marston Green	d		13 50								14 25			14 50								
Lea Hall	d										14 29											
Stechford	d										14 31											
Adderley Park	d										14 35											
Birmingham New Street 12	a	13 48	13 58	14 05			14 18	14 25			14 40	14 44	14 48	14 58		15 05			15 18	15 25		
	d	14 01			14 09	14 20	14 24		14 31	14 35		14 48	15 01				15 09	15 20	15 24		15 31	15 35
Smethwick Rolfe Street	d				14 15												15 15					
Smethwick Galton Bridge 7	d				14 17												15 17					
Sandwell & Dudley	d				14 19							14 57					15 19					
Dudley Port	d				14 22												15 22					
Tipton	d				14 24												15 24					
Coseley	d				14 27												15 27					
Wolverhampton 7	a	14 18			14 32	14 37	14 42		14 48	14 52		15 10	15 18				15 32	15 37	15 42		15 48	15 52
	d	14 19								14 52			15 19									15 52
Penkridge	d									15 03												16 03
Stafford	a	14 33								15 10			15 33		15 14							16 09

		LM	VT	XC	LM	LM	VT	LM	VT	AW	VT	XC	LM	LM	VT	XC	LM	LM	VT	LM	VT	AW	VT
		1	◇1 🍴	◇1 🛒	◇1	◇1	◇1 🍴		◇1 🍴	◇ 🛒	◇1 🍴	◇1 🛒	◇1	1	◇1 🍴	◇1 🛒	◇1	◇1	◇1 🍴		◇1 🍴	◇ 🛒	◇1 🍴
London Euston 15 ⊖	d		14 18			13 50	14 38				14 58				15 18			14 50	15 38				15 58
Northampton	d				14 53	14 58											15 51	15 56					
Long Buckby	d				15 03	15 08											16 01	16 06					
Rugby	d				15 15	15a19					15 49						16 15	16 17					16 49
Coventry	a		15 20		15 28		15 40				16 00				16 20		16 28		16 40				17 00
	d	15 10	15 20	15 26	15 29		15 40				16 00			16 10	16 20	16 26	16 29		16 40				17 00
Canley	d				15 32												16 32						
Tile Hill	d	15 15			15 36									16 15			16 36						
Berkswell	d				15 39												16 39						
Hampton-in-Arden	d				15 43												16 43						
Birmingham International ✈	a	15 22	15 31	15 35	15 46		15 51				16 11			16 22	16 31	16 35	16 46		16 51				17 11
	d	15 22	15 31	15 38	15 47		15 51			16 07	16 11			16 22	16 31	16 38	16 47		16 51			17 07	17 11
Marston Green	d	15 25			15 50									16 25			16 50						
Lea Hall	d	15 29												16 29									
Stechford	d	15 31												16 31									
Adderley Park	d	15 35												16 35									
Birmingham New Street 12	a	15 40	15 44	15 48	15 58		16 05			16 18	16 25			16 41	16 44	16 48	16 58		17 05			17 18	17 25
	d		15 48	16 01				16 09	16 20	16 24		16 31	16 35		16 48	17 01				17 09	17 20	17 24	
Smethwick Rolfe Street	d							16 15												17 15			
Smethwick Galton Bridge 7	d							16 17												17 17			
Sandwell & Dudley	d		15 57					16 19							16 57					17 19			
Dudley Port	d							16 22												17 22			
Tipton	d							16 24												17 24			
Coseley	d							16 27												17 27			
Wolverhampton 7	a		16 10	16 18				16 32	16 37	16 42		16 48	16 52		17 10	17 18				17 32	17 37	17 42	
	d			16 19									16 52			17 19							
Penkridge	d												17 03										
Stafford	a			16 34									17 09			17 35		17 14					

Northampton - Coventry - Birmingham - Wolverhampton - Stafford

		XC	LM	LM	VT	XC	LM	LM	VT	LM	VT	AW	VT	XC	LM	LM	VT	XC	LM	LM	VT	LM
		◇1 ✕	◇1	1	◇1 ☕	◇1 ✕	◇1	◇1	◇1 ☕		◇1 ☕	◇ ✕	◇1 ☕	◇1	◇1	1	◇1 ☕	◇1 ✕	◇1	◇1	◇1 ☕	
London Euston 15 ⊖	d				16 18			15 50	16 38				16 58				17 18			16 50	17 38	
Northampton	d						16 53	16 58											17 51	17 56		
Long Buckby	d						17 03	17 08											18 01	18 06		
Rugby	d						17 15	17a19					17 49						18 15	18 17		
Coventry	a				17 20		17 28		17 40				18 00				18 20		18 28		18 40	
	d			17 10	17 20	17 26	17 29		17 40				18 00			18 10	18 20	18 26	18 29		18 40	
Canley	d						17 32												18 32			
Tile Hill	d			17 15			17 36									18 15			18 36			
Berkswell	d						17 39												18 39			
Hampton-in-Arden	d						17 43												18 43			
Birmingham International ✈	a			17 22	17 31	17 35	17 46		17 51				18 11			18 22	18 31	18 35	18 46		18 51	
	d			17 22	17 31	17 38	17 47		17 51			18 07	18 11			18 22	18 31	18 38	18 47		18 51	
Marston Green	d			17 25			17 50									18 25			18 50			
Lea Hall	d			17 29												18 29						
Stechford	d			17 31												18 31						
Adderley Park	d			17 35												18 35						
Birmingham New Street 12	a			17 41	17 44	17 48	17 58		18 05			18 18	18 25			18 41	18 44	18 48	18 58		19 05	
	d	17 31	17 35		17 48	18 01				18 09	18 20	18 24		18 31	18 35		18 48	19 01				19 09
Smethwick Rolfe Street	d									18 15												19 15
Smethwick Galton Bridge 7	d									18 17												19 17
Sandwell & Dudley	d				17 57					18 19							18 57					19 19
Dudley Port	d									18 22												19 22
Tipton	d									18 24												19 24
Coseley	d									18 27												19 27
Wolverhampton 7	a	17 48	17 52		18 10	18 18				18 32	18 37	18 42		18 48	18 52		19 10	19 18				19 32
	d		17 52			18 19									18 52			19 19				
Penkridge	d		18 03												19 03							
Stafford	a		18 09			18 35									19 10			19 37		19 14		

		VT	AW	XC	LM	VT	LM	VT	XC	LM	LM	VT	LM	XC	VT	AW	VT	XC	LM	VT	XC	LM	LM
		1 ☕	◇ ✕	◇1 ✕	◇1	◇1 ☕	1	◇1 ☕	◇1 A ✕	◇1	◇1	◇1 ☕		◇1 ✕	◇1 ☕	◇	◇1 ☕	◇1 ✕	1	◇1 ☕	◇1 A ✕	◇1	◇1
London Euston 15 ⊖	d					17 58		18 18			17 50	18 38					18 58			19 18			18 50
Northampton	d									18 53	18 58											19 51	19 56
Long Buckby	d									19 03	19 08											20 01	20 06
Rugby	d					18 49				19 15	19a19						19 49					20 15	20 17
Coventry	a					19 00		19 20		19 28		19 40					20 00			20 20		20 28	
	d					19 01	19 10	19 20	19 26	19 29		19 40		19 54			20 00		20 10	20 20	20 26	20 29	
Canley	d									19 32												20 32	
Tile Hill	d						19 15			19 36									20 15			20 36	
Berkswell	d									19 39												20 39	
Hampton-in-Arden	d									19 43												20 43	
Birmingham International ✈	a					19 11	19 22	19 31	19 35	19 46		19 51		20 03			20 11		20 22	20 31	20 35	20 46	
	d		19 07			19 12	19 22	19 31	19 38	19 47		19 51		20 04		20 07	20 11		20 22	20 31	20 38	20 47	
Marston Green	d						19 25			19 50									20 25			20 50	
Lea Hall	d						19 29												20 29				
Stechford	d						19 31												20 31				
Adderley Park	d						19 35												20 35				
Birmingham New Street 12	a		19 18			19 24	19 40	19 44	19 48	19 58		20 05		20 15		20 18	20 23		20 41	20 44	20 48	20 58	
	d	19 20	19 24	19 31	19 35	19 39		19 48	20 01				20 09		20 20	20 24	20 26	20 31		20 48	21 01		
Smethwick Rolfe Street	d												20 15										
Smethwick Galton Bridge 7	d												20 17										
Sandwell & Dudley	d					19 49		19 57					20 19				20 36			20 57			
Dudley Port	d												20 22										
Tipton	d												20 24										
Coseley	d												20 27										
Wolverhampton 7	a	19 37	19 42	19 48	19 52	20 02		20 10	20 18				20 32		20 36	20 42	20 46	20 50		21 10	21 18		
	d				19 52				20 19						20 38						21 19		
Penkridge	d				20 03																		
Stafford	a				20 09				20 36						20 51						21 36		21 14

A ✕ to Birmingham International

Table 68

Sundays
until 19 June

Northampton - Coventry - Birmingham - Wolverhampton - Stafford

		VT	LM	XC	VT	AW	VT	LM	LM	VT	XC	LM	LM	LM	VT	XC	AW	LM	VT	XC	AW	LM	LM
		◇1 ☕		◇1 ✕	◇1 ☕	◇	◇1 ☕	◇1	1	◇1 ☕	◇1	◇1	◇1		◇1 ☕	◇1		1	◇1 ☕	◇1	◇	◇1	
London Euston 15 ⊖	d	19 38					19 58			20 18			19 50		20 38				20 54				
Northampton	d											20 53	20 58									21 53	
Long Buckby	d											21 03	21 08									22 03	
Rugby	d						20 49					21 15	21a19						22 07			22 15	
Coventry	a	20 40					21 00			21 20		21 27			21 46				22 16			22 27	
	d	20 40		20 54			21 00		21 10	21 20	21 26	21 29			21 46	21 54		22 08	22 16	22 23		22 29	
Canley	d											21 32										22 32	
Tile Hill	d								21 15			21 36										22 36	
Berkswell	d											21 39										22 39	
Hampton-in-Arden	d											21 43										22 43	
Birmingham International ✈	a	20 51		21 03			21 11		21 22	21 31	21 35	21 46			21 57	22 03		22 17	22 27	22 32		22 46	
	d	20 51		21 04		21 07	21 11		21 22	21 31	21 38	21 47			21 57	22 04	22 11	22 18	22 27	22 33	22 40	22 47	
Marston Green	d								21 25			21 50						22 21				22 50	
Lea Hall	d								21 29									22 24					
Stechford	d								21 31									22 27					
Adderley Park	d								21 35									22 30					
Birmingham New Street 12	a	21 04		21 15		21 18	21 24		21 40	21 44	21 48	21 58			22 09	22 15	22 21	22 36	22 39	22 42	22 50	22 58	
	d	21 07	21 09		21 20	21 24	21 28	21 35		21 48	22 01			22 09	22 16		22 24		22 44		22 55		23 09
Smethwick Rolfe Street	d		21 15											22 15									23 15
Smethwick Galton Bridge 7	d		21 17											22 17									23 17
Sandwell & Dudley	d	21 16	21 19				21 37			21 57				22 19	22 25				22 53				23 19
Dudley Port	d		21 22											22 22									23 22
Tipton	d		21 24											22 24									23 24
Coseley	d		21 27											22 27									23 27
Wolverhampton 7	a	21 31	21 33		21 38	21 42	21 51	21 57		22 10	22 18			22 32	22 38		22 41		23 06		23 13		23 32
	d				21 38			21 58			22 19										23 15		
Penkridge	d							22 08															
Stafford	a				21 56			22 16			22 36										23 30		

		XC	AW	LM	LM	VT	VT	LM	VT
		◇1		1	◇1	◇1 ☕	◇1 ☕	1	◇1 ☕
London Euston 15 ⊖	d					21 55	22 25		23 25
Northampton	d				22 53			23 32	
Long Buckby	d				23 03			23 42	
Rugby	d				23 13	23 21	23 48	23 52	00s46
Coventry	a				23 25	23 31	23 57	00 06	00s57
	d	22 54		23 08	23 34	23 31	23 58		
Canley	d				23 37				
Tile Hill	d				23 41				
Berkswell	d				23 44				
Hampton-in-Arden	d				23 49				
Birmingham International ✈	a	23 03		23 17	23 52	23 42	00 08		01s08
	d	23 04	23 08	23 18	23 52	23 42	00 09		
Marston Green	d			23 21	23 55				
Lea Hall	d			23 24					
Stechford	d			23 27					
Adderley Park	d			23 30					
Birmingham New Street 12	a	23 14	23 19	23 36	00 04	23 54	00 21		01s21
	d		23 24			23 57	00 24		
Smethwick Rolfe Street	d								
Smethwick Galton Bridge 7	d								
Sandwell & Dudley	d								
Dudley Port	d								
Tipton	d								
Coseley	d								
Wolverhampton 7	a		23 40			00 15	00 43		01 52
	d								
Penkridge	d								
Stafford	a								

26 June to 31 July

Northampton - Coventry - Birmingham - Wolverhampton - Stafford

		LM ◇1	VT ◇1 ☕	XC ◇1 🛒	LM 1	LM	LM 1	VT ◇1 ☕	LM 1	LM ◇1	XC ◇1 🛒	AW	VT ◇1 ☕	LM	LM ◇1	LM 1	LM ◇1	VT ◇1 ☕	XC ◇1 🛒	AW ◇ 🛒	LM ◇1	LM	VT ◇1 ☕
London Euston 15 ⊖	d																	08 50					
Northampton	d	22p55													09 30						10 00		
Long Buckby	d	23p06													09 40						10 10		
Rugby	d	23p17													09 50			10 14			10 20		
Coventry	a	23p29													10 03			10 23			10 32		
	d	23p30			08 37				09 07						10 04	10 08		10 24	10 28		10 34		
Canley	d	23p33			08 40				09 10							10 11					10 37		
Tile Hill	d	23p37			08 44				09 14							10 15					10 41		
Berkswell	d	23p40			08 47				09 17							10 18					10 44		
Hampton-in-Arden	d	23p44			08 51				09 21							10 22					10 48		
Birmingham International ✈	a	23p47			08 54				09 24						10 13	10 26		10 34	10 38		10 51		
	d	23p48			08 55		09 03		09 25						10 13	10 26		10 35	10 40	10 48	10 52		
Marston Green	d	23p51			08 58		09 06		09 28						10 16	10 29					10 55		
Lea Hall	d	23p54					09 09								10 20								
Stechford	d	23p57					09 12								10 22								
Adderley Park	d						09 15								10 26								
Birmingham New Street 12	a	00 04			09 06		09 20		09 36						10 30	10 38		10 47	10 50	10 58	11 03		
	d		08 45	09 01		09 09		09 20		09 42	10 01	10 05	10 20	10 23			10 42	10 51	11 01	11 05		11 09	11 20
Smethwick Rolfe Street	d					09 15								10 29								11 15	
Smethwick Galton Bridge 7	d					09 17								10 31								11 17	
Sandwell & Dudley	d					09 19								10 33				11 00				11 19	
Dudley Port	d					09 22								10 36								11 22	
Tipton	d					09 24								10 38								11 24	
Coseley	d					09 27								10 41								11 27	
Wolverhampton 7 🚋	a		09 02	09 18		09 32		09 37		09 59	10 18	10 21	10 37	10 46			10 59	11 13	11 18	11 26		11 32	11 37
	d		09 04	09 19						09 59	10 19						10 59		11 19				
Penkridge	d									10 10							11 10						
Stafford	a		09 16	09 32						10 16	10 32						11 16		11 31				

		LM 1	LM ◇1	VT ◇1 ☕	XC ◇1 🛒	LM ◇1	LM ◇1	LM	VT ◇1 ☕	AW ◇ 🛒	LM ◇1	LM 1	VT ◇1 ☕	XC ◇1 🛒	LM ◇1	LM	VT ◇1 ☕	VT ◇1 ☕	AW ◇ 🛒	XC ◇1 🛒	LM ◇1	LM 1	VT ◇1 ☕
London Euston 15 ⊖	d			09 50									10 50					11 45					12 18
Northampton	d					11 00	11 36								12 00								
Long Buckby	d					11 10	11 46								12 10								
Rugby	d			11 15		11 20	12 02						12 14		12 21			12 48					
Coventry	a			11 25		11 32							12 24		12 32			12 56					13 20
	d	11 08		11 25	11 28	11 34						12 08	12 25	12 28	12 34			12 57				13 10	13 21
Canley	d					11 37									12 37								
Tile Hill	d					11 41									12 41							13 15	
Berkswell	d					11 44									12 44								
Hampton-in-Arden	d					11 48									12 48								
Birmingham International ✈	a	11 18		11 36	11 38	11 51						12 17	12 35	12 38	12 51			13 07				13 22	13 31
	d	11 18		11 36	11 40	11 52				12 08		12 18	12 36	12 40	12 52			13 08	13 12			13 22	13 32
Marston Green	d	11 21				11 55						12 21			12 55							13 25	
Lea Hall	d	11 24										12 24										13 29	
Stechford	d	11 27										12 27										13 31	
Adderley Park	d	11 30										12 30										13 35	
Birmingham New Street 12	a	11 36		11 49	11 50	12 03				12 18		12 36	12 48	12 50	13 03			13 22	13 21			13 40	13 44
	d		11 42	11 52	12 01			12 09	12 20	12 24	12 35		12 52	13 01		13 09	13 20		13 24	13 31	13 35		13 48
Smethwick Rolfe Street	d							12 15								13 15							
Smethwick Galton Bridge 7	d							12 17								13 17							
Sandwell & Dudley	d			12 02				12 19					13 01			13 19							13 57
Dudley Port	d							12 22								13 22							
Tipton	d							12 24								13 24							
Coseley	d							12 27								13 27							
Wolverhampton 7 🚋	a		11 59	12 15	12 19			12 32	12 37	12 42	12 52		13 14	13 18		13 32	13 37		13 41	13 48	13 52		14 10
	d		11 59		12 19						12 52			13 19							13 52		
Penkridge	d		12 10								13 03										14 03		
Stafford	a		12 16		12 32		12 54				13 09			13 33							14 10		

26 June to 31 July

Northampton - Coventry - Birmingham - Wolverhampton - Stafford

		XC ◇1 🛒	LM ◇1	VT ◇1 ☕	LM	VT ◇1 ☕	AW ◇ 🛒	VT ◇1 ☕	XC ◇1 🛒	LM ◇1	LM 1	VT ◇1 ☕	XC ◇1 🛒	LM ◇1	LM ◇1	VT ◇1 ☕	LM	VT ◇1 ☕	AW	VT ◇1 ☕	XC ◇1 🛒	LM ◇1
London Euston 15 ⊖	d			12 38				12 58				13 18			12 50	13 38				13 58		
Northampton	d		12 53											13 51	13 56							
Long Buckby	d		13 03											14 01	14 06							
Rugby	d		13 15					13 49						14 15	14 17					14 49		
Coventry	a		13 28	13 40				14 00				14 20		14 28		14 40				15 00		
	d	13 26	13 29	13 40				14 00			14 10	14 20	14 26	14 29		14 40				15 00		
Canley	d		13 32											14 32								
Tile Hill	d		13 36								14 15			14 36								
Berkswell	d		13 39											14 39								
Hampton-in-Arden	d		13 43											14 43								
Birmingham International ✈	a	13 37	13 46	13 51				14 11			14 22	14 31	14 35	14 46		14 51				15 11		
	d	13 38	13 47	13 51			14 07	14 11			14 22	14 31	14 38	14 47		14 51			15 07	15 11		
Marston Green	d		13 50								14 25			14 50								
Lea Hall	d										14 29											
Stechford	d										14 31											
Adderley Park	d										14 35											
Birmingham New Street 12	a	13 48	13 58	14 05			14 18	14 25			14 40	14 44	14 48	14 58		15 05			15 18	15 25		
	d	14 01			14 09	14 20	14 24		14 31	14 35		14 48	15 01				15 09	15 20	15 24		15 31	15 35
Smethwick Rolfe Street	d				14 15												15 15					
Smethwick Galton Bridge 7	d				14 17												15 17					
Sandwell & Dudley	d				14 19							14 57					15 19					
Dudley Port	d				14 22												15 22					
Tipton	d				14 24												15 24					
Coseley	d				14 27												15 27					
Wolverhampton 7 🚋	a	14 18			14 32	14 37	14 42		14 48	14 52		15 10	15 18				15 32	15 37	15 42		15 48	15 52
	d	14 19								14 52			15 19									15 52
Penkridge	d									15 03												16 03
Stafford	a	14 33								15 10			15 33		15 14							16 09

		LM 1	VT ◇1 ☕	XC ◇1 🛒	LM ◇1	LM ◇1	VT ◇1 ☕	LM	VT ◇1 ☕	AW ◇ 🛒	VT ◇1 A ☕	VT ◇1 B ☕	XC ◇1 🛒	LM ◇1	LM 1	VT ◇1 ☕	XC ◇1 🛒	LM ◇1	LM ◇1	VT ◇1 ☕	LM	VT ◇1 ☕	AW ◇ 🛒
London Euston 15 ⊖	d		14 18			13 50	14 38				14 58	14 58				15 18			14 50	15 38			
Northampton	d				14 53	14 58												15 51	15 56				
Long Buckby	d				15 03	15 08												16 01	16 06				
Rugby	d				15 15	15a19					15 49	15 49						16 15	16 17				
Coventry	a		15 20		15 28		15 40				15 59	16 00				16 20		16 28		16 40			
	d	15 10	15 20	15 26	15 29		15 40				15 59	16 00			16 10	16 20	16 26	16 29		16 40			
Canley	d				15 32													16 32					
Tile Hill	d	15 15			15 36										16 15			16 36					
Berkswell	d				15 39													16 39					
Hampton-in-Arden	d				15 43													16 43					
Birmingham International ✈	a	15 22	15 31	15 35	15 46		15 51				16 10	16 11			16 22	16 31	16 35	16 46		16 51			
	d	15 22	15 31	15 38	15 47		15 51			16 07	16 10	16 11			16 22	16 31	16 38	16 47		16 51			17 07
Marston Green	d	15 25			15 50										16 25			16 50					
Lea Hall	d	15 29													16 29								
Stechford	d	15 31													16 31								
Adderley Park	d	15 35													16 35								
Birmingham New Street 12	a	15 40	15 44	15 48	15 58		16 05			16 18	16 24	16 25			16 41	16 44	16 48	16 58		17 05			17 18
	d		15 48	16 01				16 09	16 20	16 24			16 31	16 35		16 48	17 01				17 09	17 20	17 24
Smethwick Rolfe Street	d							16 15													17 15		
Smethwick Galton Bridge 7	d							16 17													17 17		
Sandwell & Dudley	d		15 57					16 19								16 57					17 19		
Dudley Port	d							16 22													17 22		
Tipton	d							16 24													17 24		
Coseley	d							16 27													17 27		
Wolverhampton 7 🚋	a		16 10	16 18				16 32	16 37	16 42			16 48	16 52		17 10	17 18				17 32	17 37	17 42
	d			16 19										16 52			17 19						
Penkridge	d													17 03									
Stafford	a			16 34										17 09			17 35		17 14				

A 17 July, 24 July, 31 July

B 26 June, 3 July, 10 July

Table 68

Sundays
26 June to 31 July

Northampton - Coventry - Birmingham - Wolverhampton - Stafford

		VT	XC	LM	LM	VT	XC	LM	LM	VT	LM	VT	AW	VT	XC	LM	LM	VT	XC	LM	LM	VT
		◇1	◇1	◇1	1	◇1	◇1	◇1	◇1	◇1		◇1	◇	◇1	◇1	◇1	1	◇1	◇1	◇1	◇1	◇1
		⊡	⊥			⊡	⊥			⊡		⊡	⊥	⊡	⊥			⊡	⊥			⊡
London Euston 15 ⊖	d	15 58				16 18			15 50	16 38				16 58				17 18			16 50	17 38
Northampton	d							16 53	16 58											17 51	17 56	
Long Buckby	d							17 03	17 08											18 01	18 06	
Rugby	d	16 49						17 15	17a19					17 49						18 15	18 17	
Coventry	a	17 00				17 20		17 28		17 40				18 00				18 20		18 28		18 40
	d	17 00			17 10	17 20	17 26	17 29		17 40				18 00			18 10	18 20	18 26	18 29		18 40
Canley	d							17 32												18 32		
Tile Hill	d				17 15			17 36									18 15			18 36		
Berkswell	d							17 39												18 39		
Hampton-in-Arden	d							17 43												18 43		
Birmingham International ✈	a	17 11			17 22	17 31	17 35	17 46		17 51				18 11			18 22	18 31	18 35	18 46		18 51
	d	17 11			17 22	17 31	17 38	17 47		17 51			18 07	18 11			18 22	18 31	18 38	18 47		18 51
Marston Green	d				17 25			17 50									18 25			18 50		
Lea Hall	d				17 29												18 29					
Stechford	d				17 31												18 31					
Adderley Park	d				17 35												18 35					
Birmingham New Street 12	a	17 25			17 41	17 44	17 48	17 58		18 05			18 18	18 25			18 41	18 44	18 48	18 58		19 05
	d		17 31	17 35		17 48	18 01				18 09	18 20	18 24		18 31	18 35		18 48	19 01			
Smethwick Rolfe Street	d										18 15											
Smethwick Galton Bridge 7	d										18 17											
Sandwell & Dudley	d					17 57					18 19							18 57				
Dudley Port	d										18 22											
Tipton	d										18 24											
Coseley	d										18 27											
Wolverhampton 7 ⇌	a		17 48	17 52		18 10	18 18				18 32	18 37	18 42		18 48	18 52		19 10	19 18			
	d			17 52			18 19									18 52			19 19			
Penkridge	d			18 03												19 03						
Stafford	a			18 09			18 35									19 10			19 37		19 14	

		LM	VT	AW	XC	LM	VT	LM	VT	XC	LM	LM	VT	LM	XC	VT	AW	VT	VT	XC	LM	VT	XC
			R 1	◇	◇1	◇1	◇1	1	◇1	◇1	◇1	◇1	◇1		◇1	◇1	◇	◇1	◇1	◇1	1	◇1	◇1
										A								B	C				A
			⊡	⊥	⊥		⊡		⊡	⊥			⊡		⊥	⊡		⊡	⊡			⊡	⊥
London Euston 15 ⊖	d						17 58		18 18			17 50	18 38					18 58	18 58			19 18	
Northampton	d										18 53	18 58											
Long Buckby	d										19 03	19 08											
Rugby	d						18 49				19 15	19a19						19 49	19 49				
Coventry	a						19 00		19 20		19 28		19 40					19 59	20 00			20 20	
	d						19 01	19 10	19 20	19 26	19 29		19 40		19 54			19 59	20 00		20 10	20 20	20 26
Canley	d										19 32												
Tile Hill	d							19 15			19 36										20 15		
Berkswell	d										19 39												
Hampton-in-Arden	d										19 43												
Birmingham International ✈	a						19 11	19 22	19 31	19 35	19 46		19 51		20 03			20 10	20 11		20 22	20 31	20 35
	d			19 07			19 12	19 22	19 31	19 38	19 47		19 51		20 04		20 07	20 10	20 11		20 22	20 31	20 38
Marston Green	d							19 25			19 50										20 25		
Lea Hall	d							19 29													20 29		
Stechford	d							19 31													20 31		
Adderley Park	d							19 35													20 35		
Birmingham New Street 12	a			19 18			19 24	19 40	19 44	19 48	19 58		20 05		20 15		20 18	20 22	20 23		20 41	20 44	20 48
	d	19 09	19 20	19 24	19 31	19 35	19 39		19 48	20 01				20 09		20 20	20 24	20 26	20 26	20 31		20 48	21 01
Smethwick Rolfe Street	d	19 15												20 15									
Smethwick Galton Bridge 7	d	19 17												20 17									
Sandwell & Dudley	d	19 19					19 49		19 57					20 19				20 36	20 36			20 57	
Dudley Port	d	19 22												20 22									
Tipton	d	19 24												20 24									
Coseley	d	19 27												20 27									
Wolverhampton 7 ⇌	a	19 32	19 37	19 42	19 48	19 52	20 02		20 10	20 18				20 32		20 36	20 42	20 46	20 46	20 50		21 10	21 18
	d					19 52				20 19						20 38							21 19
Penkridge	d					20 03																	
Stafford	a					20 09				20 36						20 51							21 36

A ⊥ to Birmingham International

B 17 July, 24 July, 31 July

C 26 June, 3 July, 10 July

Table 68

Sundays
26 June to 31 July

Northampton - Coventry - Birmingham - Wolverhampton - Stafford

		LM	LM	VT	LM	XC	VT	AW	VT	LM	LM	VT	XC	LM	LM	LM	VT	XC	AW	LM	VT	XC	AW
		◇1	◇1	◇1		◇1	◇1	◇	◇1	◇1	1	◇1	◇1	◇1	◇1		◇1	◇1		1	◇1	◇1	◇
				⊡		⊥	⊡		⊡			⊡					⊡				⊡		
London Euston 15 ⊖	d		18 50	19 38					19 58			20 18			19 50		20 38				20 54		
Northampton	d	19 51	19 56											20 53	20 58								
Long Buckby	d	20 01	20 06											21 03	21 08								
Rugby	d	20 15	20 17						20 49					21 15	21a19						22 07		
Coventry	a	20 28		20 40					21 00			21 20		21 27			21 46				22 16		
	d	20 29		20 40		20 54			21 00		21 10	21 20	21 26	21 29			21 46	21 54		22 08	22 16	22 23	
Canley	d	20 32												21 32									
Tile Hill	d	20 36									21 15			21 36									
Berkswell	d	20 39												21 39									
Hampton-in-Arden	d	20 43												21 43									
Birmingham International ✈	a	20 46		20 51		21 03			21 11		21 22	21 31	21 35	21 46			21 57	22 03		22 17	22 27	22 32	
	d	20 47		20 51		21 04		21 07	21 11		21 22	21 31	21 38	21 47			21 57	22 04	22 11	22 18	22 27	22 33	22 40
Marston Green	d	20 50									21 25			21 50						22 21			
Lea Hall	d										21 29									22 24			
Stechford	d										21 31									22 27			
Adderley Park	d										21 35									22 30			
Birmingham New Street 12	a	20 58		21 04		21 15		21 18	21 24		21 40	21 44	21 48	21 58			22 09	22 15	22 21	22 36	22 39	22 42	22 50
	d			21 07	21 09		21 20	21 24	21 28	21 35		21 48	22 01			22 09	22 16		22 24		22 44		22 55
Smethwick Rolfe Street	d				21 15											22 15							
Smethwick Galton Bridge 7	d				21 17											22 17							
Sandwell & Dudley	d			21 16	21 19				21 37			21 57				22 19	22 25				22 53		
Dudley Port	d				21 22											22 22							
Tipton	d				21 24											22 24							
Coseley	d				21 27											22 27							
Wolverhampton 7 ⇌	a			21 31	21 33		21 38	21 42	21 51	21 57		22 10	22 18			22 32	22 38		22 41		23 06		23 13
	d						21 38			21 58			22 19										23 15
Penkridge	d									22 08													
Stafford	a		21 14				21 56			22 16			22 36										23 30

		LM	LM	XC	AW	LM	LM	VT	VT	LM	VT
		◇1		◇1		1	◇1	◇1	◇1	1	◇1
								⊡	⊡		⊡
London Euston 15 ⊖	d							21 55	22 25		23 25
Northampton	d	21 53					22 53			23 32	
Long Buckby	d	22 03					23 03			23 42	
Rugby	d	22 15					23 13	23 21	23 48	23 52	00s46
Coventry	a	22 27					23 25	23 31	23 57	00 06	00s57
	d	22 29		22 54		23 08	23 34	23 31	23 58		
Canley	d	22 32					23 37				
Tile Hill	d	22 36					23 41				
Berkswell	d	22 39					23 44				
Hampton-in-Arden	d	22 43					23 49				
Birmingham International ✈	a	22 46		23 03		23 17	23 52	23 42	00 08		01s08
	d	22 47		23 04	23 08	23 18	23 52	23 42	00 09		
Marston Green	d	22 50				23 21	23 55				
Lea Hall	d					23 24					
Stechford	d					23 27					
Adderley Park	d					23 30					
Birmingham New Street 12	a	22 58		23 14	23 19	23 36	00 04	23 54	00 21		01s21
	d		23 09		23 24			23 57	00 24		
Smethwick Rolfe Street	d		23 15								
Smethwick Galton Bridge 7	d		23 17								
Sandwell & Dudley	d		23 19								
Dudley Port	d		23 22								
Tipton	d		23 24								
Coseley	d		23 27								
Wolverhampton 7 ⇌	a		23 32		23 40			00 15	00 43		01 52
	d										
Penkridge	d										
Stafford	a										

Table 68

Sundays

7 August to 11 September

Northampton - Coventry - Birmingham - Wolverhampton - Stafford

		LM	VT	XC	LM	LM	LM	VT	LM	LM	XC	AW	VT	LM	LM	LM	LM	VT	XC	AW	LM	LM	VT
London Euston 15 ⊖	d																	08 50					
Northampton	d	22p55													09 30						10 00		
Long Buckby	d	23p06													09 40						10 10		
Rugby	d	23p17													09 50			10 14			10 20		
Coventry	a	23p29													10 03			10 23			10 32		
	d	23p30			08 37				09 07						10 04	10 08		10 24	10 28		10 34		
Canley	d	23p33			08 40				09 10							10 11					10 37		
Tile Hill	d	23p37			08 44				09 14							10 15					10 41		
Berkswell	d	23p40			08 47				09 17							10 18					10 44		
Hampton-in-Arden	d	23p44			08 51				09 21							10 22					10 48		
Birmingham International ✈	a	23p47			08 54				09 24						10 13	10 26		10 34	10 38		10 51		
	d	23p48			08 55		09 03		09 25			09 51			10 13	10 26		10 35	10 40	10 48	10 52		
Marston Green	d	23p51			08 58		09 06		09 28						10 16	10 29					10 55		
Lea Hall	d	23p54					09 09								10 20								
Stechford	d	23p57					09 12								10 22								
Adderley Park	d						09 15								10 26								
Birmingham New Street 12	a	00 04			09 06		09 20		09 36			10 02			10 30	10 38		10 47	10 50	10 58	11 03		
	d		08 45	09 01		09 09		09 20		09 42	10 01	10 05	10 20	10 23			10 42	10 51	11 01	11 05		11 09	11 20
Smethwick Rolfe Street	d					09 15								10 29								11 15	
Smethwick Galton Bridge 7	d					09 17								10 31								11 17	
Sandwell & Dudley	d					09 19								10 33				11 00				11 19	
Dudley Port	d					09 22								10 36								11 22	
Tipton	d					09 24								10 38								11 24	
Coseley	d					09 27								10 41								11 27	
Wolverhampton 7	a		09 02	09 18		09 32		09 37		09 59	10 18	10 21	10 37	10 46			10 59	11 13	11 18	11 26		11 32	11 37
	d		09 04	09 19						09 59	10 19						10 59		11 19				
Penkridge	d									10 10							11 10						
Stafford	a		09 16	09 32						10 16	10 32						11 16		11 31				

		LM	LM	VT	XC	LM	LM	LM	VT	AW	LM	LM	VT	XC	LM	LM	VT	VT	AW	XC	LM	LM	VT
London Euston 15 ⊖	d			09 50									10 50					11 45					12 18
Northampton	d					11 00	11 36								12 00								
Long Buckby	d					11 10	11 46								12 10								
Rugby	d			11 15		11 20	12 02						12 14		12 21			12 48					
Coventry	a			11 25		11 32							12 24		12 32			12 56					13 20
	d	11 08		11 25	11 28	11 34						12 08	12 25	12 28	12 34			12 57				13 10	13 21
Canley	d					11 37									12 37								
Tile Hill	d					11 41									12 41							13 15	
Berkswell	d					11 44									12 44								
Hampton-in-Arden	d					11 48									12 48								
Birmingham International ✈	a	11 18		11 36	11 38	11 51						12 17	12 35	12 38	12 51			13 07				13 22	13 31
	d	11 18		11 36	11 40	11 52				12 08		12 18	12 36	12 40	12 52			13 08	13 12			13 22	13 32
Marston Green	d	11 21				11 55						12 21			12 55							13 25	
Lea Hall	d	11 24										12 24										13 29	
Stechford	d	11 27										12 27										13 31	
Adderley Park	d	11 30										12 30										13 35	
Birmingham New Street 12	a	11 36		11 49	11 50	12 03				12 18		12 36	12 48	12 50	13 03			13 22	13 21			13 40	13 44
	d		11 42	11 52	12 01			12 09	12 20	12 24	12 35		12 52	13 01		13 09	13 20		13 24	13 31	13 35		13 48
Smethwick Rolfe Street	d							12 15								13 15							
Smethwick Galton Bridge 7	d							12 17								13 17							
Sandwell & Dudley	d			12 02				12 19					13 01			13 19							13 57
Dudley Port	d							12 22								13 22							
Tipton	d							12 24								13 24							
Coseley	d							12 27								13 27							
Wolverhampton 7	a		11 59	12 15	12 19			12 32	12 37	12 42	12 52		13 14	13 18		13 32	13 37		13 41	13 48	13 52		14 10
	d		11 59		12 19						12 52			13 19							13 52		
Penkridge	d		12 10								13 03										14 03		
Stafford	a		12 16		12 32		12 54				13 09			13 33							14 10		

Table 68

Sundays

7 August to 11 September

Northampton - Coventry - Birmingham - Wolverhampton - Stafford

		XC	LM	VT	LM	VT	AW	VT	XC	LM	LM	VT	XC	LM	LM	VT	LM	VT	AW	VT	XC	LM
London Euston 15 ⊖	d			12 38				12 58				13 18			12 50	13 38				13 58		
Northampton	d		12 53											13 51	13 56							
Long Buckby	d		13 03											14 01	14 06							
Rugby	d		13 15					13 49						14 15	14 17					14 49		
Coventry	a		13 28	13 49				14 00				14 20		14 28		14 40				15 00		
	d	13 26	13 29	13 40				14 00			14 10	14 20	14 26	14 29		14 40				15 00		
Canley	d		13 32											14 32								
Tile Hill	d		13 36								14 15			14 36								
Berkswell	d		13 39											14 39								
Hampton-in-Arden	d		13 43											14 43								
Birmingham International ✈	a	13 37	13 46	13 51				14 11			14 22	14 31	14 35	14 46		14 51				15 11		
	d	13 38	13 47	13 51			14 07	14 11			14 22	14 31	14 38	14 47		14 51			15 07	15 11		
Marston Green	d		13 50								14 25			14 50								
Lea Hall	d										14 29											
Stechford	d										14 31											
Adderley Park	d										14 35											
Birmingham New Street 12	a	13 48	13 58	14 05			14 18	14 25			14 40	14 44	14 48	14 58		15 05			15 18	15 25		
	d	14 01			14 09	14 20	14 24		14 31	14 35		14 48	15 01				15 09	15 20	15 24		15 31	15 35
Smethwick Rolfe Street	d				14 15												15 15					
Smethwick Galton Bridge 7	d				14 17												15 17					
Sandwell & Dudley	d				14 19							14 57					15 19					
Dudley Port	d				14 22												15 22					
Tipton	d				14 24												15 24					
Coseley	d				14 27												15 27					
Wolverhampton 7	a	14 18			14 32	14 37	14 42		14 48	14 52		15 10	15 18				15 32	15 37	15 42		15 48	15 52
	d	14 19								14 52			15 19									15 52
Penkridge	d									15 03												16 03
Stafford	a	14 33								15 10			15 33		15 14							16 09

		LM	VT	XC	LM	LM	VT	LM	VT	AW	VT	XC	LM	LM	VT	XC	LM	LM	VT	LM	VT	AW	VT
London Euston 15 ⊖	d		14 18			13 50	14 38				14 58				15 18			14 50	15 38				15 58
Northampton	d				14 53	14 58											15 51	15 56					
Long Buckby	d				15 03	15 08											16 01	16 06					
Rugby	d				15 15	15a19					15 49						16 15	16 17					16 49
Coventry	a		15 20		15 28		15 40				15 59				16 20		16 28		16 40				17 00
	d	15 10	15 20	15 26	15 29		15 40				15 59			16 10	16 20	16 26	16 29		16 40				17 00
Canley	d				15 32												16 32						
Tile Hill	d	15 15			15 36									16 15			16 36						
Berkswell	d				15 39												16 39						
Hampton-in-Arden	d				15 43												16 43						
Birmingham International ✈	a	15 22	15 31	15 35	15 46		15 51				16 10			16 22	16 31	16 35	16 46		16 51				17 11
	d	15 22	15 31	15 38	15 47		15 51			16 07	16 10			16 22	16 31	16 38	16 47		16 51			17 07	17 11
Marston Green	d	15 25			15 50									16 25			16 50						
Lea Hall	d	15 29												16 29									
Stechford	d	15 31												16 31									
Adderley Park	d	15 35												16 35									
Birmingham New Street 12	a	15 40	15 44	15 48	15 58		16 05			16 18	16 24			16 41	16 44	16 48	16 56		17 05			17 18	17 25
	d		15 48	16 01				16 09	16 20	16 24		16 31	16 35		16 48	17 01				17 09	17 20	17 24	
Smethwick Rolfe Street	d							16 15												17 15			
Smethwick Galton Bridge 7	d							16 17												17 17			
Sandwell & Dudley	d		15 57					16 19							16 57					17 19			
Dudley Port	d							16 22												17 22			
Tipton	d							16 24												17 24			
Coseley	d							16 27												17 27			
Wolverhampton 7	a		16 10	16 18				16 32	16 37	16 42		16 48	16 52		17 10	17 18				17 32	17 37	17 42	
	d			16 19									16 52			17 19							
Penkridge	d												17 03										
Stafford	a			16 34									17 09			17 35		17 14					

Northampton - Coventry - Birmingham - Wolverhampton - Stafford

		XC	LM	LM	VT	XC	LM	LM	VT	LM	VT	AW	VT	XC	LM	LM	VT	XC	LM	LM	VT	LM
		◇1	◇1	1	◇1	◇1	◇1	◇1	◇1		◇1	◇	◇1	◇1	◇1	1	◇1	◇1	◇1	◇1	◇1	
		🛒			☕	🛒			☕		☕	🛒	☕				☕	🛒			☕	
London Euston 15 ⊖	d				16 18			15 50	16 38				16 58				17 18			16 50	17 38	
Northampton	d						16 53	16 58											17 51	17 56		
Long Buckby	d						17 03	17 08											18 01	18 06		
Rugby	d						17 15	17a19					17 49						18 15	18 17		
Coventry	a				17 20		17 28		17 40				18 00				18 20		18 28		18 40	
	d			17 10	17 20	17 26	17 29		17 40				18 00			18 10	18 20	18 26	18 29		18 40	
Canley	d						17 32												18 32			
Tile Hill	d			17 15			17 36									18 15			18 36			
Berkswell	d						17 39												18 39			
Hampton-in-Arden	d						17 43												18 43			
Birmingham International ✈	a			17 22	17 31	17 35	17 46		17 51				18 11			18 22	18 31	18 35	18 46		18 51	
	d			17 22	17 31	17 38	17 47		17 51			18 07	18 11			18 22	18 31	18 38	18 47		18 51	
Marston Green	d			17 25			17 50									18 25			18 50			
Lea Hall	d			17 29												18 29						
Stechford	d			17 31												18 31						
Adderley Park	d			17 35												18 35						
Birmingham New Street 12	a			17 41	17 44	17 48	17 58		18 05			18 18	18 25			18 41	18 44	18 48	18 58		19 05	
	d	17 31	17 35		17 48	18 01				18 09	18 20	18 24		18 31	18 35		18 48	19 01				19 09
Smethwick Rolfe Street	d									18 15												19 15
Smethwick Galton Bridge 7	d									18 17												19 17
Sandwell & Dudley	d				17 57					18 19							18 57					19 19
Dudley Port	d									18 22												19 22
Tipton	d									18 24												19 24
Coseley	d									18 27												19 27
Wolverhampton 7 🚌	a	17 48	17 52		18 10	18 18				18 32	18 37	18 42		18 48	18 52		19 10	19 18				19 32
	d		17 52			18 19									18 52			19 19				
Penkridge	d		18 03												19 03							
Stafford	a		18 09			18 35									19 10			19 37		19 14		

		VT	AW	XC	LM	VT	LM	VT	XC	LM	LM	VT	LM	XC	VT	AW	VT	XC	LM	VT	XC	LM	LM
		1	◇	◇1	◇1	◇1	1	◇1	◇1	◇1	◇1	◇1		◇1	◇1	◇	◇1	◇1	1	◇1	◇1	◇1	◇1
									A												A		
		☕	🛒	🛒		☕		☕	🛒			☕		🛒	☕		☕	🛒		☕	🛒		
London Euston 15 ⊖	d					17 58		18 18			17 50	18 38					18 58			19 18			18 50
Northampton	d									18 53	18 58											19 51	19 56
Long Buckby	d									19 03	19 08											20 01	20 06
Rugby	d					18 49				19 15	19a19						19 49					20 15	20 17
Coventry	a					19 00		19 20		19 28		19 40					19 59			20 20		20 28	
	d					19 01	19 10	19 20	19 26	19 29		19 40		19 54			19 59		20 10	20 20	20 26	20 29	
Canley	d									19 32												20 32	
Tile Hill	d						19 15			19 36									20 15			20 36	
Berkswell	d									19 39												20 39	
Hampton-in-Arden	d									19 43												20 43	
Birmingham International ✈	a					19 11	19 22	19 31	19 35	19 46		19 51		20 03			20 10		20 22	20 31	20 35	20 46	
	d		19 07			19 12	19 22	19 31	19 38	19 47		19 51		20 04		20 07	20 10		20 22	20 31	20 38	20 47	
Marston Green	d						19 25			19 50									20 25			20 50	
Lea Hall	d						19 29												20 29				
Stechford	d						19 31												20 31				
Adderley Park	d						19 35												20 35				
Birmingham New Street 12	a		19 18			19 24	19 40	19 44	19 48	19 58		20 05		20 15		20 18	20 22		20 41	20 44	20 48	20 58	
	d	19 20	19 24	19 31	19 35	19 39		19 48	20 01				20 09		20 20	20 24	20 26	20 31		20 48	21 01		
Smethwick Rolfe Street	d												20 15										
Smethwick Galton Bridge 7	d												20 17										
Sandwell & Dudley	d					19 49		19 57					20 19				20 36			20 57			
Dudley Port	d												20 22										
Tipton	d												20 24										
Coseley	d												20 27										
Wolverhampton 7 🚌	a	19 37	19 42	19 48	19 52	20 02		20 10	20 18				20 32		20 36	20 42	20 46	20 50		21 10	21 18		
	d				19 52				20 19						20 38						21 19		
Penkridge	d				20 03																		
Stafford	a				20 09				20 36						20 51						21 36		21 14

A 🛒 to Birmingham International

Table 68

Sundays

7 August to 11 September

Northampton - Coventry - Birmingham - Wolverhampton - Stafford

		VT	LM	XC	VT	AW	VT	LM	LM	VT	XC	LM	LM	LM	VT	XC	AW	LM	VT	XC	AW	LM	LM
		◇1		◇1	◇1	◇	◇1	◇1	1	◇1	◇1	◇1	◇1		◇1	◇1		1	◇1	◇1	◇	◇1	
		☕		🛒	☕		☕			☕					☕				☕				
London Euston 15 ⊖	d	19 38					19 58			20 18			19 50		20 38				20 54				
Northampton	d											20 53	20 58									21 53	
Long Buckby	d											21 03	21 08									22 03	
Rugby	d						20 49					21 15	21a19						22 07			22 15	
Coventry	a	20 40					21 00			21 20		21 27			21 46				22 16			22 27	
	d	20 40		20 54			21 00		21 10	21 20	21 26	21 29			21 46	21 54		22 08	22 16	22 23		22 29	
Canley	d											21 32										22 32	
Tile Hill	d								21 15			21 36										22 36	
Berkswell	d											21 39										22 39	
Hampton-in-Arden	d											21 43										22 43	
Birmingham International ✈	a	20 51		21 03			21 11		21 22	21 31	21 35	21 46			21 57	22 03		22 17	22 27	22 32		22 46	
	d	20 51		21 04		21 07	21 11		21 22	21 31	21 38	21 47			21 57	22 04	22 11	22 18	22 27	22 33	22 40	22 47	
Marston Green	d								21 25			21 50						22 21				22 50	
Lea Hall	d								21 29									22 24					
Stechford	d								21 31									22 27					
Adderley Park	d								21 35									22 30					
Birmingham New Street 12	a	21 04		21 15		21 18	21 24		21 40	21 44	21 48	21 58			22 09	22 15	22 21	22 36	22 39	22 42	22 50	22 58	
	d	21 07	21 09		21 20	21 24	21 28	21 35		21 48	22 01			22 09	22 16		22 24		22 44		22 55		23 09
Smethwick Rolfe Street	d		21 15											22 15									23 15
Smethwick Galton Bridge 7	d		21 17											22 17									23 17
Sandwell & Dudley	d	21 16	21 19				21 37			21 57				22 19	22 25				22 53				23 19
Dudley Port	d		21 22											22 22									23 22
Tipton	d		21 24											22 24									23 24
Coseley	d		21 27											22 27									23 27
Wolverhampton 7 🚌	a	21 31	21 33		21 38	21 42	21 51	21 57		22 10	22 18			22 32	22 38		22 41		23 06		23 13		23 32
	d				21 38			21 58			22 19										23 15		
Penkridge	d							22 08															
Stafford	a				21 56			22 16			22 36										23 30		

		XC	AW	LM	LM	VT	VT	LM	VT
		◇1		1	◇1	◇1	◇1	1	◇1
						☕	☕		☕
London Euston 15 ⊖	d					21 55	22 25		23 25
Northampton	d				22 53			23 32	
Long Buckby	d				23 03			23 42	
Rugby	d				23 13	23 21	23 48	23 52	00s46
Coventry	a				23 25	23 31	23 57	00 06	00s57
	d	22 54		23 08	23 34	23 31	23 58		
Canley	d				23 37				
Tile Hill	d				23 41				
Berkswell	d				23 44				
Hampton-in-Arden	d				23 49				
Birmingham International ✈	a	23 03		23 17	23 52	23 42	00 08		01s08
	d	23 04	23 08	23 18	23 52	23 42	00 09		
Marston Green	d			23 21	23 55				
Lea Hall	d			23 24					
Stechford	d			23 27					
Adderley Park	d			23 30					
Birmingham New Street 12	a	23 14	23 19	23 36	00 04	23 54	00 21		01s21
	d		23 24			23 57	00 24		
Smethwick Rolfe Street	d								
Smethwick Galton Bridge 7	d								
Sandwell & Dudley	d								
Dudley Port	d								
Tipton	d								
Coseley	d								
Wolverhampton 7 🚌	a		23 40			00 15	00 43		01 52
	d								
Penkridge	d								
Stafford	a								

Table 68

Sundays

18 September to 23 October

Northampton - Coventry - Birmingham - Wolverhampton - Stafford

Station		LM ◇1	VT ◇1	XC ◇1	LM 1	LM	LM 1	VT ◇1	LM 1	LM ◇1		XC ◇1	AW	VT ◇1	LM	LM ◇1	LM 1	LM ◇1	VT ◇1	XC ◇1		AW ◇	LM ◇1	LM	VT ◇1
London Euston 15 ⊖	d																		08 50						
Northampton	d	22p55														09 30							10 00		
Long Buckby	d	23p06														09 40							10 10		
Rugby	d	23p17														09 50			10 14				10 20		
Coventry	a	23p29														10 03			10 23				10 32		
	d	23p30			08 37				09 07							10 04	10 08		10 24	10 28			10 34		
Canley	d	23p33			08 40				09 10								10 11						10 37		
Tile Hill	d	23p37			08 44				09 14								10 15						10 41		
Berkswell	d	23p40			08 47				09 17								10 18						10 44		
Hampton-in-Arden	d	23p44			08 51				09 21								10 22						10 48		
Birmingham International ✈	a	23p47			08 54				09 24							10 13	10 26		10 34	10 38			10 51		
	d	23p48			08 55		09 03		09 25				09 51			10 13	10 26		10 35	10 40		10 48	10 52		
Marston Green	d	23p51			08 58		09 06		09 28							10 16	10 29						10 55		
Lea Hall	d	23p54					09 09									10 20									
Stechford	d	23p57					09 12									10 22									
Adderley Park	d						09 15									10 26									
Birmingham New Street 12	a	00 04			09 06		09 20		09 36				10 02			10 30	10 38		10 47	10 50		10 58	11 03		
	d		08 45	09 01		09 09		09 20		09 42		10 01	10 05	10 20	10 23			10 42	10 51	11 01		11 05		11 09	11 20
Smethwick Rolfe Street	d					09 15									10 29									11 15	
Smethwick Galton Bridge 7	d					09 17									10 31									11 17	
Sandwell & Dudley	d					09 19									10 33				11 00					11 19	
Dudley Port	d					09 22									10 36									11 22	
Tipton	d					09 24									10 38									11 24	
Coseley	d					09 27									10 41									11 27	
Wolverhampton 7	a		09 02	09 18		09 32		09 37		09 59		10 18	10 21	10 37	10 46			10 59	11 13	11 18		11 26		11 32	11 37
	d		09 04	09 19						09 59		10 19						10 59		11 19					
Penkridge	d									10 10								11 10							
Stafford	a		09 16	09 32						10 16		10 32						11 16		11 31					

Station		LM 1	LM ◇1	VT ◇1	XC ◇1	LM ◇1		LM ◇1	LM	VT ◇1	AW ◇	LM ◇1	LM 1	VT ◇1	XC ◇1	LM ◇1		LM	VT ◇1	VT ◇1	AW ◇	XC ◇1	LM ◇1	LM 1	VT ◇1
London Euston 15 ⊖	d			09 50										10 50						11 45					12 18
Northampton	d					11 00		11 36								12 00									
Long Buckby	d					11 10		11 46								12 10									
Rugby	d			11 15		11 20		12 02						12 14		12 21				12 48					
Coventry	a			11 25		11 32								12 24		12 32				12 56					13 20
	d	11 08		11 25	11 30	11 34							12 08	12 25	12 29	12 34				12 57				13 10	13 21
Canley	d					11 37										12 37								13 15	
Tile Hill	d					11 41										12 41									
Berkswell	d					11 44										12 44									
Hampton-in-Arden	d					11 48										12 48									
Birmingham International ✈	a	11 18		11 36	11 41	11 51							12 17	12 35	12 41	12 51				13 07				13 22	13 31
	d	11 18		11 36	11 43	11 52					12 08		12 18	12 36	12 43	12 52				13 08	13 12			13 22	13 32
Marston Green	d	11 21				11 55							12 21			12 55								13 25	
Lea Hall	d	11 24											12 24											13 29	
Stechford	d	11 27											12 27											13 31	
Adderley Park	d	11 30											12 30											13 35	
Birmingham New Street 12	a	11 36		11 49	11 53	12 03					12 18		12 36	12 48	12 53	13 03				13 22	13 21			13 40	13 44
	d		11 42	11 52	12 01				12 09	12 20	12 24	12 35		12 52	13 01			13 09	13 20		13 24	13 31	13 35		13 48
Smethwick Rolfe Street	d								12 15									13 15							
Smethwick Galton Bridge 7	d								12 17									13 17							
Sandwell & Dudley	d			12 02					12 19					13 01				13 19							13 57
Dudley Port	d								12 22									13 22							
Tipton	d								12 24									13 24							
Coseley	d								12 27									13 27							
Wolverhampton 7	a		11 59	12 15	12 19				12 32	12 37	12 42	12 52		13 14	13 18			13 32	13 37		13 41	13 48	13 52		14 10
	d		11 59		12 19							12 52			13 19								13 52		
Penkridge	d		12 10									13 03											14 03		
Stafford	a		12 16		12 32			12 54				13 09			13 33								14 10		

Table 68

Sundays

18 September to 23 October

Northampton - Coventry - Birmingham - Wolverhampton - Stafford

Station		XC ◇1		LM ◇1	VT ◇1	LM	VT ◇1	AW ◇	VT ◇1	XC ◇1	LM ◇1	LM 1		VT ◇1	XC ◇1	LM ◇1	LM ◇1	VT ◇1	LM	VT ◇1	AW ◇	VT ◇1		XC ◇1	LM ◇1
London Euston 15 ⊖	d				12 38				12 58					13 18			12 50	13 38				13 58			
Northampton	d			12 53												13 51	13 56								
Long Buckby	d			13 03												14 01	14 06								
Rugby	d			13 15					13 49							14 15	14 17					14 49			
Coventry	a			13 28	13 40				14 00					14 20		14 28		14 40				15 00			
	d	13 26		13 29	13 40				14 00			14 10		14 20	14 26	14 29		14 40				15 00			
Canley	d			13 32												14 32									
Tile Hill	d			13 36								14 15				14 36									
Berkswell	d			13 39												14 39									
Hampton-in-Arden	d			13 43												14 43									
Birmingham International ✈	a	13 37		13 46	13 51				14 11			14 22		14 31	14 35	14 46		14 51				15 11			
	d	13 38		13 47	13 51			14 07	14 11			14 22		14 31	14 38	14 47		14 51			15 07	15 11			
Marston Green	d			13 50								14 25				14 50									
Lea Hall	d											14 29													
Stechford	d											14 31													
Adderley Park	d											14 35													
Birmingham New Street 12	a	13 48		13 58	14 05			14 18	14 25			14 40		14 44	14 48	14 58		15 05			15 18	15 25			
	d	14 01				14 09	14 20	14 24		14 31	14 35			14 48	15 01				15 09	15 20	15 24			15 31	15 35
Smethwick Rolfe Street	d					14 15													15 15						
Smethwick Galton Bridge 7	d					14 17													15 17						
Sandwell & Dudley	d					14 19								14 57					15 19						
Dudley Port	d					14 22													15 22						
Tipton	d					14 24													15 24						
Coseley	d					14 27													15 27						
Wolverhampton 7	a	14 18				14 32	14 37	14 42		14 48	14 52			15 10	15 18				15 32	15 37	15 42			15 48	15 52
	d	14 19									14 52				15 19										15 52
Penkridge	d										15 03														16 03
Stafford	a	14 33									15 10				15 33		15 14								16 09

Station		LM 1	VT ◇1	XC ◇1	LM ◇1	LM ◇1	VT ◇1	LM		VT ◇1	AW ◇	VT ◇1	XC ◇1	LM ◇1	LM 1	VT ◇1	XC ◇1	LM ◇1		LM ◇1	VT ◇1	LM	VT ◇1	AW ◇	VT ◇1
London Euston 15 ⊖	d		14 18			13 50	14 38					14 58				15 18				14 50	15 38				15 58
Northampton	d				14 53	14 58												15 51		15 56					
Long Buckby	d				15 03	15 08												16 01		16 06					
Rugby	d				15 15	15a19						15 49						16 15		16 17					16 49
Coventry	a		15 20		15 28		15 40					16 00				16 20		16 28			16 40				17 00
	d	15 10	15 20	15 26	15 29		15 40					16 00			16 10	16 20	16 26	16 29			16 40				17 00
Canley	d				15 32													16 32							
Tile Hill	d	15 15			15 36										16 15			16 36							
Berkswell	d				15 39													16 39							
Hampton-in-Arden	d				15 43													16 43							
Birmingham International ✈	a	15 22	15 31	15 35	15 46		15 51					16 11			16 22	16 31	16 35	16 46			16 51				17 11
	d	15 22	15 31	15 38	15 47		15 51				16 07	16 11			16 22	16 31	16 38	16 47			16 51			17 07	17 11
Marston Green	d	15 25			15 50										16 25			16 50							
Lea Hall	d	15 29													16 29										
Stechford	d	15 31													16 31										
Adderley Park	d	15 35													16 35										
Birmingham New Street 12	a	15 40	15 44	15 48	15 58		16 05				16 18	16 25			16 41	16 44	16 48	16 58			17 05			17 18	17 25
	d		15 48	16 01				16 09		16 20	16 24		16 31	16 35		16 48	17 01					17 09	17 20	17 24	
Smethwick Rolfe Street	d							16 15														17 15			
Smethwick Galton Bridge 7	d							16 17														17 17			
Sandwell & Dudley	d		15 57					16 19								16 57						17 19			
Dudley Port	d							16 22														17 22			
Tipton	d							16 24														17 24			
Coseley	d							16 27														17 27			
Wolverhampton 7	a		16 10	16 18				16 32		16 37	16 42		16 48	16 52		17 10	17 18					17 32	17 37	17 42	
	d			16 19										16 52			17 19								
Penkridge	d													17 03											
Stafford	a			16 34										17 09			17 35			17 14					

Table 68

Sundays

18 September to 23 October

Northampton - Coventry - Birmingham - Wolverhampton - Stafford

Station		XC	LM	LM	VT	XC	LM	LM	VT	LM	VT	AW	VT	XC	LM	LM	VT	XC	LM	LM	VT	LM
		◇1	◇1	1	◇1	◇1	◇1	◇1	◇1		◇1	◇	◇1	◇1	◇1	1	◇1	◇1	◇1	◇1	◇1	
		✠			⊡	✠			⊡		⊡	✠	⊡	✠			⊡	✠			⊡	
London Euston 15 ⊖	d				16 18			15 50	16 38				16 58				17 18			16 50	17 38	
Northampton	d						16 53	16 58											17 51	17 56		
Long Buckby	d						17 03	17 08											18 01	18 06		
Rugby	d						17 15	17a19					17 49						18 15	18 17		
Coventry	a				17 20		17 28		17 40				18 00				18 20		18 28		18 40	
	d			17 10	17 20	17 26	17 29		17 40				18 00			18 10	18 20	18 26	18 29		18 40	
Canley	d						17 32												18 32			
Tile Hill	d			17 15			17 36									18 15			18 36			
Berkswell	d						17 39												18 39			
Hampton-in-Arden	d						17 43												18 43			
Birmingham International ✈	a			17 22	17 31	17 35	17 46		17 51				18 11			18 22	18 31	18 35	18 46		18 51	
	d			17 22	17 31	17 38	17 47		17 51			18 07	18 11			18 22	18 31	18 38	18 47		18 51	
Marston Green	d			17 25			17 50									18 25			18 50			
Lea Hall	d			17 29												18 29						
Stechford	d			17 31												18 31						
Adderley Park	d			17 35												18 35						
Birmingham New Street 12	a			17 41	17 44	17 48	17 58		18 05			18 18	18 25			18 41	18 44	18 48	18 58		19 05	
	d	17 31	17 35		17 48	18 01				18 09	18 20	18 24		18 31	18 35		18 48	19 01				19 09
Smethwick Rolfe Street	d									18 15												19 15
Smethwick Galton Bridge 7	d									18 17												19 17
Sandwell & Dudley	d				17 57					18 19							18 57					19 19
Dudley Port	d									18 22												19 22
Tipton	d									18 24												19 24
Coseley	d									18 27												19 27
Wolverhampton 7	a	17 48	17 52		18 10	18 18				18 32	18 37	18 42		18 48	18 52		19 10	19 18				19 32
	d		17 52			18 19									18 52			19 19				
Penkridge	d		18 03												19 03							
Stafford	a		18 09			18 35									19 10			19 37		19 14		

Station		VT	AW	XC	LM	VT	LM	VT	XC	LM	LM	VT	LM	XC	VT	AW	VT	XC	LM	VT	XC	LM	LM
		1	◇	◇1	◇1	◇1	1	◇1	◇1	◇1	◇1	◇1		◇1	◇1	◇	◇1	◇1	1	◇1	◇1	◇1	◇1
									A												A		
		⊡	✠	✠		⊡		⊡	✠			⊡		✠	⊡		⊡	✠		⊡	✠		
London Euston 15 ⊖	d					17 58		18 18			17 50	18 38					18 58			19 18			18 50
Northampton	d									18 53	18 58											19 51	19 56
Long Buckby	d									19 03	19 08											20 01	20 06
Rugby	d					18 49				19 15	19a19						19 49					20 15	20 17
Coventry	a					19 00		19 20		19 28		19 40					20 00			20 20		20 28	
	d					19 01	19 10	19 20	19 26	19 29		19 40		19 54			20 00		20 10	20 20	20 26	20 29	
Canley	d									19 32												20 32	
Tile Hill	d						19 15			19 36									20 15			20 36	
Berkswell	d									19 39												20 39	
Hampton-in-Arden	d									19 43												20 43	
Birmingham International ✈	a					19 11	19 22	19 31	19 35	19 46		19 51		20 03			20 11		20 22	20 31	20 35	20 46	
	d		19 07			19 12	19 22	19 31	19 38	19 47		19 51		20 04		20 07	20 11		20 22	20 31	20 38	20 47	
Marston Green	d						19 25			19 50									20 25			20 50	
Lea Hall	d						19 29												20 29				
Stechford	d						19 31												20 31				
Adderley Park	d						19 35												20 35				
Birmingham New Street 12	a		19 18			19 24	19 40	19 44	19 48	19 58		20 05		20 15		20 18	20 23		20 41	20 44	20 48	20 58	
	d	19 20	19 24	19 31	19 35	19 39		19 48	20 01				20 09		20 20	20 24	20 26	20 31		20 48	21 01		
Smethwick Rolfe Street	d												20 15										
Smethwick Galton Bridge 7	d												20 17										
Sandwell & Dudley	d					19 49		19 57					20 19				20 36			20 57			
Dudley Port	d												20 22										
Tipton	d												20 24										
Coseley	d												20 27										
Wolverhampton 7	a	19 37	19 42	19 48	19 52	20 02		20 10	20 18				20 32		20 36	20 42	20 46	20 50		21 10	21 18		
	d				19 52				20 19						20 38						21 19		
Penkridge	d				20 03																		
Stafford	a				20 09				20 36						20 51						21 36		21 14

A ✠ to Birmingham International

Table 68

Sundays

18 September to 23 October

Northampton - Coventry - Birmingham - Wolverhampton - Stafford

Station		VT	LM	XC	VT	AW	VT	LM	LM	VT	XC	LM	LM	LM	VT	XC	AW	LM	VT	XC	AW	LM	LM
		◇1		◇1	◇1	◇	◇1	◇1	1	◇1	◇1	◇1	◇1		◇1	◇1		1	◇1	◇1	◇	◇1	
		⊡		✠	⊡		⊡			⊡					⊡				⊡				
London Euston 15 ⊖	d	19 38					19 58			20 18			19 50		20 38				20 54				
Northampton	d											20 53	20 58									21 53	
Long Buckby	d											21 03	21 08									22 03	
Rugby	d						20 49					21 15	21a19						22 07			22 15	
Coventry	a	20 40					21 00			21 20		21 27			21 46				22 16			22 27	
	d	20 40		20 54			21 00		21 10	21 20	21 26	21 29			21 46	21 54		22 08	22 16	22 23		22 29	
Canley	d											21 32										22 32	
Tile Hill	d								21 15			21 36										22 36	
Berkswell	d											21 39										22 39	
Hampton-in-Arden	d											21 43										22 43	
Birmingham International ✈	a	20 51		21 03			21 11		21 22	21 31	21 35	21 46			21 57	22 03		22 17	22 27	22 32		22 46	
	d	20 51		21 04		21 07	21 11		21 22	21 31	21 38	21 47			21 57	22 04	22 11	22 18	22 27	22 33	22 40	22 47	
Marston Green	d								21 25			21 50						22 21				22 50	
Lea Hall	d								21 29									22 24					
Stechford	d								21 31									22 27					
Adderley Park	d								21 35									22 30					
Birmingham New Street 12	a	21 04		21 15		21 18	21 24		21 40	21 44	21 48	21 58			22 09	22 15	22 21	22 36	22 39	22 42	22 50	22 58	
	d	21 07	21 09		21 20	21 24	21 28	21 35		21 48	22 01			22 09	22 16		22 24		22 44		22 55		23 09
Smethwick Rolfe Street	d		21 15											22 15									23 15
Smethwick Galton Bridge 7	d		21 17											22 17									23 17
Sandwell & Dudley	d	21 16	21 19				21 37			21 57				22 19	22 25				22 53				23 19
Dudley Port	d		21 22											22 22									23 22
Tipton	d		21 24											22 24									23 24
Coseley	d		21 27											22 27									23 27
Wolverhampton 7	a	21 31	21 33		21 38	21 42	21 51	21 57		22 10	22 18			22 32	22 38		22 41		23 06		23 13		23 32
	d				21 38			21 58			22 19										23 15		
Penkridge	d							22 08															
Stafford	a				21 56			22 16			22 36										23 30		

Station		XC	AW	LM	LM	VT	VT	LM	VT
		◇1		1	◇1	◇1	◇1	1	◇1
						⊡	⊡		⊡
London Euston 15 ⊖	d					21 55	22 25		23 25
Northampton	d				22 53			23 32	
Long Buckby	d				23 03			23 42	
Rugby	d				23 13	23 21	23 48	23 52	00s46
Coventry	a				23 25	23 31	23 57	00 06	00s57
	d	22 54		23 08	23 34	23 31	23 58		
Canley	d				23 37				
Tile Hill	d				23 41				
Berkswell	d				23 44				
Hampton-in-Arden	d				23 49				
Birmingham International ✈	a	23 03		23 17	23 52	23 42	00 08		01s08
	d	23 04	23 08	23 18	23 52	23 42	00 09		
Marston Green	d			23 21	23 55				
Lea Hall	d			23 24					
Stechford	d			23 27					
Adderley Park	d			23 30					
Birmingham New Street 12	a	23 14	23 19	23 36	00 04	23 54	00 21		01s21
	d		23 24			23 57	00 24		
Smethwick Rolfe Street	d								
Smethwick Galton Bridge 7	d								
Sandwell & Dudley	d								
Dudley Port	d								
Tipton	d								
Coseley	d								
Wolverhampton 7	a		23 40			00 15	00 43		01 52
	d								
Penkridge	d								
Stafford	a								

Northampton - Coventry - Birmingham - Wolverhampton - Stafford

		LM ◇1	VT ◇1	XC ◇1	LM 1	LM	LM 1	VT ◇1	LM 1	LM ◇1	XC ◇1	AW	VT ◇1	LM	LM ◇1	LM 1	LM ◇1	VT ◇1	XC ◇1	AW ◇	LM ◇1	LM	VT ◇1
London Euston 15 ⊖	d																	08 50					
Northampton	d	22p55													09 30						10 00		
Long Buckby	d	23p06													09 40						10 10		
Rugby	d	23p17													09 50			10 14			10 20		
Coventry	a	23p29													10 03			10 23			10 32		
	d	23p30			08 37				09 07						10 04	10 08		10 24	10 28		10 34		
Canley	d	23p33			08 40				09 10							10 11					10 37		
Tile Hill	d	23p37			08 44				09 14							10 15					10 41		
Berkswell	d	23p40			08 47				09 17							10 18					10 44		
Hampton-in-Arden	d	23p44			08 51				09 21							10 22					10 48		
Birmingham International ✈	a	23p47			08 54				09 24						10 13	10 26		10 34	10 38		10 51		
	d	23p48			08 55		09 03		09 25			09 51			10 13	10 26		10 35	10 40	10 48	10 52		
Marston Green	d	23p51			08 58		09 06		09 28						10 16	10 29					10 55		
Lea Hall	d	23p54					09 09								10 20								
Stechford	d	23p57					09 12								10 22								
Adderley Park	d						09 15								10 26								
Birmingham New Street 12	a	00 04			09 06		09 20		09 36			10 02			10 30	10 38		10 47	10 50	10 58	11 03		
	d		08 45	09 01		09 09		09 20		09 42	10 01	10 05	10 20	10 23			10 42	10 51	11 01	11 05		11 09	11 20
Smethwick Rolfe Street	d					09 15								10 29								11 15	
Smethwick Galton Bridge 7	d					09 17								10 31								11 17	
Sandwell & Dudley	d					09 19								10 33				11 00				11 19	
Dudley Port	d					09 22								10 36								11 22	
Tipton	d					09 24								10 38								11 24	
Coseley	d					09 27								10 41								11 27	
Wolverhampton 7 ⛴	a		09 02	09 18		09 32		09 37		09 59	10 18	10 21	10 37	10 46			10 59	11 13	11 18	11 26		11 32	11 37
	d		09 04	09 19						09 59	10 19						10 59		11 19				
Penkridge	d									10 10							11 10						
Stafford	a		09 16	09 32						10 16	10 32						11 16		11 31				

		LM 1	LM ◇1	VT ◇1	XC ◇1	LM ◇1	LM ◇1	LM	VT ◇1	AW ◇	LM ◇1	LM 1	VT ◇1	XC ◇1	LM ◇1	LM	VT ◇1	VT ◇1	AW ◇	XC ◇1	LM ◇1	LM 1	VT ◇1
London Euston 15 ⊖	d			09 50									10 50					11 45					12 18
Northampton	d					11 00	11 36								12 00								
Long Buckby	d					11 10	11 46								12 10								
Rugby	d			11 15		11 20	12 02						12 14		12 21			12 48					
Coventry	a			11 25		11 32							12 24		12 32			12 56					13 20
	d	11 08		11 25	11 29	11 34						12 08	12 25	12 28	12 34			12 57				13 10	13 21
Canley	d					11 37									12 37								
Tile Hill	d					11 41									12 41							13 15	
Berkswell	d					11 44									12 44								
Hampton-in-Arden	d					11 48									12 48								
Birmingham International ✈	a	11 18		11 36	11 41	11 51						12 17	12 35	12 38	12 51			13 07				13 22	13 31
	d	11 18		11 36	11 42	11 52				12 08		12 18	12 36	12 40	12 52			13 08	13 12			13 22	13 32
Marston Green	d	11 21				11 55						12 21			12 55							13 25	
Lea Hall	d	11 24										12 24										13 29	
Stechford	d	11 27										12 27										13 31	
Adderley Park	d	11 30										12 30										13 35	
Birmingham New Street 12	a	11 36		11 49	11 51	12 03				12 18		12 36	12 48	12 50	13 03			13 22	13 21			13 40	13 44
	d		11 42	11 52	12 01			12 09	12 20	12 24	12 35		12 52	13 01		13 09	13 20		13 24	13 31	13 35		13 48
Smethwick Rolfe Street	d							12 15								13 15							
Smethwick Galton Bridge 7	d							12 17								13 17							
Sandwell & Dudley	d			12 02				12 19					13 01			13 19							13 57
Dudley Port	d							12 22								13 22							
Tipton	d							12 24								13 24							
Coseley	d							12 27								13 27							
Wolverhampton 7 ⛴	a		11 59	12 15	12 19			12 32	12 37	12 42	12 52		13 14	13 18		13 32	13 37		13 41	13 48	13 52		14 10
	d		11 59		12 19						12 52			13 19							13 52		
Penkridge	d		12 10								13 03										14 03		
Stafford	a		12 16		12 32		12 54				13 09			13 33							14 10		

		XC ◇1	LM ◇1	VT ◇1	LM	VT ◇1	AW ◇	VT ◇1	XC ◇1	LM ◇1	LM 1	VT ◇1	XC ◇1	LM ◇1	LM ◇1	VT ◇1	LM	VT ◇1	AW ◇	VT ◇1	XC ◇1	LM ◇1
London Euston 15 ⊖	d			12 38				12 58				13 18			12 50	13 38				13 58		
Northampton	d		12 53											13 51	13 56							
Long Buckby	d		13 03											14 01	14 06							
Rugby	d		13 15					13 49						14 15	14 17					14 49		
Coventry	a		13 28	13 40				14 00				14 20		14 28		14 40				15 00		
	d	13 26	13 29	13 40				14 00			14 10	14 20	14 26	14 29		14 40				15 00		
Canley	d		13 32											14 32								
Tile Hill	d		13 36								14 15			14 36								
Berkswell	d		13 39											14 39								
Hampton-in-Arden	d		13 43											14 43								
Birmingham International ✈	a	13 37	13 46	13 51				14 11			14 22	14 31	14 35	14 46		14 51				15 11		
	d	13 38	13 47	13 51			14 07	14 11			14 22	14 31	14 38	14 47		14 51			15 07	15 11		
Marston Green	d		13 50								14 25			14 50								
Lea Hall	d										14 29											
Stechford	d										14 31											
Adderley Park	d										14 35											
Birmingham New Street 12	a	13 48	13 58	14 05			14 18	14 25			14 40	14 44	14 48	14 58		15 05			15 18	15 25		
	d	14 01			14 09	14 20	14 24		14 31	14 35		14 48	15 01				15 09	15 20	15 24		15 31	15 35
Smethwick Rolfe Street	d				14 15												15 15					
Smethwick Galton Bridge 7	d				14 17												15 17					
Sandwell & Dudley	d				14 19							14 57					15 19					
Dudley Port	d				14 22												15 22					
Tipton	d				14 24												15 24					
Coseley	d				14 27												15 27					
Wolverhampton 7 ⛴	a	14 18			14 32	14 37	14 42		14 48	14 52		15 10	15 18				15 32	15 37	15 42		15 48	15 52
	d	14 19								14 52			15 19									15 52
Penkridge	d									15 03												16 03
Stafford	a	14 33								15 10			15 33		15 14							16 09

		LM 1	VT ◇1	XC ◇1	LM ◇1	LM ◇1	VT ◇1	LM	VT ◇1	AW ◇	VT ◇1	XC ◇1	LM ◇1	LM 1	VT ◇1	XC ◇1	LM ◇1	LM ◇1	VT ◇1	LM	VT ◇1	AW ◇	VT ◇1
London Euston 15 ⊖	d		14 18			13 50	14 38				14 58				15 18			14 50	15 38				15 58
Northampton	d				14 53	14 58											15 51	15 56					
Long Buckby	d				15 03	15 08											16 01	16 06					
Rugby	d				15 15	15a19					15 49						16 15	16 17					16 49
Coventry	a		15 20		15 28		15 40				16 00				16 20		16 28		16 40				17 00
	d	15 10	15 20	15 26	15 29		15 40				16 00			16 10	16 20	16 26	16 29		16 40				17 00
Canley	d				15 32												16 32						
Tile Hill	d	15 15			15 36									16 15			16 36						
Berkswell	d				15 39												16 39						
Hampton-in-Arden	d				15 43												16 43						
Birmingham International ✈	a	15 22	15 31	15 35	15 46		15 51				16 11			16 22	16 31	16 35	16 46		16 51				17 11
	d	15 22	15 31	15 38	15 47		15 51			16 07	16 11			16 22	16 31	16 38	16 47		16 51			17 07	17 11
Marston Green	d	15 25			15 50									16 25			16 50						
Lea Hall	d	15 29												16 29									
Stechford	d	15 31												16 31									
Adderley Park	d	15 35												16 35									
Birmingham New Street 12	a	15 40	15 44	15 48	15 58		16 05			16 18	16 25			16 41	16 44	16 48	16 58		17 05			17 18	17 25
	d		15 48	16 01				16 09	16 20	16 24		16 31	16 35		16 48	17 01				17 09	17 20	17 24	
Smethwick Rolfe Street	d							16 15												17 15			
Smethwick Galton Bridge 7	d							16 17												17 17			
Sandwell & Dudley	d		15 57					16 19							16 57					17 19			
Dudley Port	d							16 22												17 22			
Tipton	d							16 24												17 24			
Coseley	d							16 27												17 27			
Wolverhampton 7 ⛴	a		16 10	16 18				16 32	16 37	16 42		16 48	16 52		17 10	17 18				17 32	17 37	17 42	
	d			16 19									16 52			17 19							
Penkridge	d												17 03										
Stafford	a			16 34									17 09			17 35		17 14					

Table 68

Sundays from 30 October

Northampton - Coventry - Birmingham - Wolverhampton - Stafford

		XC	LM	LM	VT	XC	LM	LM	VT	LM	VT	AW	VT	XC	LM	LM	VT	XC	LM	LM	VT	LM
		◇1 ⌶	◇1	1	◇1 ⊡	◇1 ⌶	◇1	◇1	◇1 ⊡		◇1 ⊡	◇ ⌶	◇1 ⊡	◇1	◇1	1	◇1 ⊡	◇1 ⌶	◇1	◇1	◇1 ⊡	
London Euston 15 ⊖	d				16 18			15 50	16 38				16 58				17 18			16 50	17 38	
Northampton	d						16 53	16 58											17 51	17 56		
Long Buckby	d						17 03	17 08											18 01	18 06		
Rugby	d						17 15	17a19					17 49						18 15	18 17		
Coventry	a				17 20		17 28		17 40				18 00				18 20		18 28		18 40	
	d			17 10	17 20	17 26	17 29		17 40				18 00			18 10	18 20	18 26	18 29		18 40	
Canley	d						17 32												18 32			
Tile Hill	d			17 15			17 36									18 15			18 36			
Berkswell	d						17 39												18 39			
Hampton-in-Arden	d						17 43												18 43			
Birmingham International ✈	a			17 22	17 31	17 35	17 46		17 51				18 11			18 22	18 31	18 35	18 46		18 51	
	d			17 22	17 31	17 38	17 47		17 51			18 07	18 11			18 22	18 31	18 38	18 47		18 51	
Marston Green	d			17 25			17 50									18 25			18 50			
Lea Hall	d			17 29												18 29						
Stechford	d			17 31												18 31						
Adderley Park	d			17 35												18 35						
Birmingham New Street 12	a			17 41	17 44	17 48	17 58		18 05			18 18	18 25			18 41	18 44	18 48	18 58		19 05	
	d	17 31	17 35		17 48	18 01				18 09	18 20	18 24		18 31	18 35		18 48	19 01				19 09
Smethwick Rolfe Street	d									18 15												19 15
Smethwick Galton Bridge 7	d									18 17												19 17
Sandwell & Dudley	d				17 57					18 19							18 57					19 19
Dudley Port	d									18 22												19 22
Tipton	d									18 24												19 24
Coseley	d									18 27												19 27
Wolverhampton 7	a	17 48	17 52		18 10	18 18				18 32	18 37	18 42		18 48	18 52		19 10	19 18				19 32
	d		17 52			18 19									18 52			19 19				
Penkridge	d		18 03												19 03							
Stafford	a		18 09			18 35									19 10			19 37		19 14		

		VT	AW	XC	LM	VT	LM	VT	XC	LM	LM	VT	LM	XC	VT	AW	VT	XC	LM	VT	XC	LM	LM
		1 ⊡	◇ ⌶	◇1 ⌶	◇1	◇1 ⊡	1	◇1 ⊡	◇1 A ⌶	◇1	◇1	◇1 ⊡		◇1 ⌶	◇1 ⊡	◇	◇1 ⊡	◇1 ⌶	1	◇1 ⊡	◇1 A ⌶	◇1	◇1
London Euston 15 ⊖	d					17 58		18 18			17 50	18 38					18 58			19 18			18 50
Northampton	d									18 53	18 58											19 51	19 56
Long Buckby	d									19 03	19 08											20 01	20 06
Rugby	d					18 49				19 15	19a19						19 49					20 15	20 17
Coventry	a					19 00		19 20		19 28		19 40					20 00			20 20		20 28	
	d					19 01	19 10	19 20	19 26	19 29		19 40		19 54			20 00		20 10	20 20	20 26	20 29	
Canley	d									19 32												20 32	
Tile Hill	d						19 15			19 36									20 15			20 36	
Berkswell	d									19 39												20 39	
Hampton-in-Arden	d									19 43												20 43	
Birmingham International ✈	a					19 11	19 22	19 31	19 35	19 46		19 51		20 03			20 11		20 22	20 31	20 35	20 46	
	d		19 07			19 12	19 22	19 31	19 38	19 47		19 51		20 04		20 07	20 11		20 22	20 31	20 38	20 47	
Marston Green	d						19 25			19 50									20 25			20 50	
Lea Hall	d						19 29												20 29				
Stechford	d						19 31												20 31				
Adderley Park	d						19 35												20 35				
Birmingham New Street 12	a		19 18			19 24	19 40	19 44	19 48	19 58		20 05		20 15		20 18	20 23		20 41	20 44	20 48	20 58	
	d	19 20	19 24	19 31	19 35	19 39		19 48	20 01				20 09		20 20	20 24	20 26	20 31		20 48	21 01		
Smethwick Rolfe Street	d												20 15										
Smethwick Galton Bridge 7	d												20 17										
Sandwell & Dudley	d					19 49		19 57					20 19				20 36			20 57			
Dudley Port	d												20 22										
Tipton	d												20 24										
Coseley	d												20 27										
Wolverhampton 7	a	19 37	19 42	19 48	19 52	20 02		20 10	20 18				20 32		20 36	20 42	20 46	20 50		21 10	21 18		
	d				19 52				20 19						20 38						21 19		
Penkridge	d				20 03																		
Stafford	a				20 09				20 36						20 51						21 36		21 14

A ⌶ to Birmingham International

Table 68

Sundays from 30 October

Northampton - Coventry - Birmingham - Wolverhampton - Stafford

		VT	LM	XC	VT	AW	VT	LM	LM	VT	XC	LM	LM	LM	VT	XC	AW	LM	VT	XC	AW	LM	LM
		◇1 ⊡		◇1 ⌶	◇1 ⊡	◇	◇1 ⊡	◇1	1	◇1 ⊡	◇1	◇1	◇1		◇1 ⊡	◇1		1	◇1 ⊡	◇1	◇	◇1	
London Euston 15 ⊖	d	19 38					19 58			20 18			19 50		20 38				20 54				
Northampton	d											20 53	20 58									21 53	
Long Buckby	d											21 03	21 08									22 03	
Rugby	d						20 49					21 15	21a19						22 07			22 15	
Coventry	a	20 40					21 00			21 20		21 27			21 46				22 16			22 27	
	d	20 40		20 54			21 00		21 10	21 20	21 26	21 29			21 46	21 54		22 08	22 16	22 23		22 29	
Canley	d											21 32										22 32	
Tile Hill	d								21 15			21 36										22 36	
Berkswell	d											21 39										22 39	
Hampton-in-Arden	d											21 43										22 43	
Birmingham International ✈	a	20 51		21 03			21 11		21 22	21 31	21 35	21 46			21 57	22 03		22 17	22 27	22 32		22 46	
	d	20 51		21 04		21 07	21 11		21 22	21 31	21 38	21 47			21 57	22 04	22 11	22 18	22 27	22 33	22 40	22 47	
Marston Green	d								21 25			21 50						22 21				22 50	
Lea Hall	d								21 29									22 24					
Stechford	d								21 31									22 27					
Adderley Park	d								21 35									22 30					
Birmingham New Street 12	a	21 04		21 15		21 18	21 24		21 40	21 44	21 48	21 58			22 09	22 15	22 21	22 36	22 39	22 42	22 50	22 58	
	d	21 07	21 09		21 20	21 24	21 28	21 35		21 48	22 01			22 09	22 16		22 24		22 44		22 55		23 09
Smethwick Rolfe Street	d		21 15											22 15									23 15
Smethwick Galton Bridge 7	d		21 17											22 17									23 17
Sandwell & Dudley	d	21 16	21 19				21 37			21 57				22 19	22 25				22 53				23 19
Dudley Port	d		21 22											22 22									23 22
Tipton	d		21 24											22 24									23 24
Coseley	d		21 27											22 27									23 27
Wolverhampton 7	a	21 31	21 33		21 38	21 42	21 51	21 57		22 10	22 18			22 32	22 38		22 41		23 06		23 13		23 32
	d				21 38			21 58			22 19										23 15		
Penkridge	d							22 08															
Stafford	a				21 56			22 16			22 36										23 30		

		XC	AW	LM	LM	VT	VT	LM	VT
		◇1		1	◇1	◇1 ⊡	◇1 ⊡	1	◇1 ⊡
London Euston 15 ⊖	d					21 55	22 25		23 25
Northampton	d				22 53			23 32	
Long Buckby	d				23 03			23 42	
Rugby	d				23 13	23 21	23 48	23 52	00s46
Coventry	a				23 25	23 31	23 57	00 06	00s57
	d	22 54		23 08	23 34	23 31	23 58		
Canley	d				23 37				
Tile Hill	d				23 41				
Berkswell	d				23 44				
Hampton-in-Arden	d				23 49				
Birmingham International ✈	a	23 03		23 17	23 52	23 42	00 08		01s08
	d	23 04	23 08	23 18	23 52	23 42	00 09		
Marston Green	d			23 21	23 55				
Lea Hall	d			23 24					
Stechford	d			23 27					
Adderley Park	d			23 30					
Birmingham New Street 12	a	23 14	23 19	23 36	[illegible]	23 54	00 21		01s21
	d		23 24			23 57	00 24		
Smethwick Rolfe Street	d								
Smethwick Galton Bridge 7	d								
Sandwell & Dudley	d								
Dudley Port	d								
Tipton	d								
Coseley	d								
Wolverhampton 7	a		23 40			00 15	00 43		01 52
	d								
Penkridge	d								
Stafford	a								

Stafford - Wolverhampton - Birmingham - Coventry - Northampton

Miles	Station		LM MX ◇1	VT MX ◇1 ⊐	VT MO ◇1 ⊐	VT MO ◇1 ⊐	VT MX ◇1 ⊐	LM MX 1	LM 1	VT ◇1 ⊠	VT ◇1 ⊠	LM ◇1	VT ◇1 ⊠	LM ◇1	AW	XC ◇1 ⊥	VT ◇1 ⊠	LM 1	AW	VT ◇1 ⊠	LM 1	LM 1	AW
—	**Stafford**	d													05 25								
0	Penkridge	d																					
9½	**Wolverhampton** 7 ⇌	a													05 39								
—		d		21p45	22p05	22p37	22p45			05 00	05 24				05 40		05 45		06 00	06 04			
18¾	Coseley	d																					
32¼	Tipton	d																					
34	Dudley Port	d																					
36	Sandwell & Dudley	d		21p56	22p15	22p47	22p55				05 34						05 56			06 15			
38	Smethwick Galton Bridge 7	d																	06 11				
41¼	Smethwick Rolfe Street	d																					
43	**Birmingham New Street** 12	a		22p05	22p24	22p56	23p04			05 26	05 43				06 01		06 05		06 16	06 24			← 06 16
—		d	21p33	22p10	22p30	23p00	23p10	23p53		05 29	05 50			05 53		06 03	06 10	06 13	06 36	06 30		06 33	06 36
45	Adderley Park	d																	→				
46½	Stechford	d																06 20					
47¾	Lea Hall	d																06 23					
49½	Marston Green	d	21p41					00 01						06 01				06 26				06 41	
51½	**Birmingham International** ✈	a	21p45	22p19	22p39	23p09	23p19	00 04		05 38	05 59			06 05		06 13	06 19	06 29		06 39		06 45	06 50
—		d	21p45	22p20	22p40	23p10	23p20	00 05		05 40	06 00			06 05		06 14	06 20	06 29		06 40		06 45	
54¾	Hampton-in-Arden	d	21p48															06 32				06 48	
55½	Berkswell	d												06 11				06 37					
56¾	Tile Hill	d	21p55											06 14				06 40				06 55	
57¾	Canley	d												06 17				06 44					
58½	**Coventry**	a	22p00	22p30	22p50	23p20	23p30	00 15		05 50	06 10			06 20		06 24	06 30	06 47		06 49		07 00	
—		d	22p01	22p31	22p51	23p21	23p31			05 51	06 11			06 21			06 31			06 51		07 01	
60	Rugby	d	22p12	22p43	23p04	23p34	23p44		05 20	06 03		06 13	06 20	06 32							07 02	07 12	
64¼	Long Buckby	d	22p21						05 30			06 23		06 41							07 12	07 21	
74¼	**Northampton**	a	22p33			23b53	00s05		05 42			06 35	06 39	06 53							07 24	07 34	
79½	London Euston 15 ⊖	a	00 21	00 04	00 26	01 04	01 14		06 50	07 02	07 13	07 40	07 30	08 02			07 34			07 53	08 49		

Station		LM	LM	VT ◇1 ⊠	LM ◇1	XC ◇1 ⊥	VT ◇1 ⊠	LM 1	LM	LM ◇1	VT ◇1 ⊠	VT ◇1 ⊠	AW	XC ◇1 ⊥	LM ◇1	LM	LM	LM ◇1	LM ◇1	VT ◇1 ⊠	LM ◇1	VT ◇1 ⊠	LM
Stafford	d					06 25				06 41				06 58				07 12	07 24				
Penkridge	d									06 47								07 18					
Wolverhampton 7 ⇌	a					06 39				06 57				07 12				07 28					
	d		06 17	06 27		06 41	06 45		06 49	06 58	07 04		07 10	07 15			07 19	07 28				07 32	07 36
Coseley	d		06 22						06 54	07 03							07 24						
Tipton	d		06 25						06 57								07 26						
Dudley Port	d		06 27						06 59								07 28						
Sandwell & Dudley	d		06 31	06 37			06 56		07 03		07 15						07 32						07 46
Smethwick Galton Bridge 7	d		06 34						07 06				07 21				07 34	07 40					
Smethwick Rolfe Street	d		06 36						07 09								07 36						
Birmingham New Street 12	a		06 43	06 46		06 58	07 05		07 14	07 18	07 24		07 26	07 31			07 44	07 48				07 55	07 55
	d	06 39		06 50	06 53	07 03	07 10	07 13			07 30		07 36		07 33	07 39				07 50	07 53		
Adderley Park	d	06 44														07 44							
Stechford	d	06 47						07 20								07 47							
Lea Hall	d	06 50						07 23								07 50							
Marston Green	d				07 01			07 26							07 41						08 01		
Birmingham International ✈	a	06 55		06 59	07 05	07 13	07 19	07 29					07 50		07 45	07 55				07 59	08 05		
	d			07 00	07 05	07 14	07 20	07 29				07 41			07 45					08 00	08 05		
Hampton-in-Arden	d				07 08										07 48								
Berkswell	d				07 13			07 35													08 11		
Tile Hill	d							07 38							07 55						08 14		
Canley	d				07 18										07 58						08 17		
Coventry	a			07 10	07 21	07 24	07 30	07 43				07 51			08 02					08 10	08 20		
	d			07 11	07 21		07 31					07 52			08 03					08 11	08 21		
Rugby	d				07 32										08 14				08 20	08 23	08 32		
Long Buckby	d				07 42										08 23						08 41		
Northampton	a				07 54										08 37				08 41		08 56		
London Euston 15 ⊖	a			08 14	09 10		08 30				08 42	08 49							09 44	09 13	10 18		

b Previous night, stops to set down only

Stafford - Wolverhampton - Birmingham - Coventry - Northampton

Station		LM	XC ◇1 ⊥	VT ◇1 ⊠	LM 1	LM	LM ◇1	LM	VT ◇1 ⊠	AW ◇ ⊥	XC ◇1 ⊥	LM ◇1	LM	LM	LM ◇1	LM ◇1	VT ◇1 ⊠	LM ◇1	VT ◇1 ⊠	LM	XC ◇1 ⊥	VT ◇1 ⊠
Stafford	d			07 28			07 41				08 02				08 10	08 21					08 25	
Penkridge	d						07 47								08 16							
Wolverhampton 7 ⇌	a			07 43			07 57				08 15				08 26						08 39	
	d	07 39		07 45		07 49	07 57	08 03		08 09	08 16			08 19	08 28				08 32	08 36	08 41	08 45
Coseley	d	07 44				07 54	08 03							08 24								
Tipton	d	07 47				07 57								08 26								
Dudley Port	d	07 49				07 59								08 28								
Sandwell & Dudley	d			07 56		08 02								08 32						08 46		08 56
Smethwick Galton Bridge 7	d	07 53				08 05				08 21				08 34	08 40							
Smethwick Rolfe Street	d	07 55				08 07								08 36								
Birmingham New Street 12	a	08 03		08 05		08 14	08 17	08 20		08 26	08 32			08 44	08 47				08 55	08 55	08 58	09 06
	d		08 03	08 10	08 13				08 30	08 36		08 33	08 39				08 50	08 53			09 03	09 10
Adderley Park	d												08 44									
Stechford	d				08 20								08 47									
Lea Hall	d				08 23								08 50									
Marston Green	d				08 26							08 41						09 01				
Birmingham International ✈	a		08 13	08 19	08 29				08 39	08 50		08 45	08 55				08 59	09 05			09 13	09 19
	d		08 14	08 20	08 29				08 40			08 45					09 00	09 05			09 14	09 20
Hampton-in-Arden	d				08 32							08 48										
Berkswell	d				08 37													09 11				
Tile Hill	d				08 40							08 55						09 14				
Canley	d				08 44													09 17				
Coventry	a		08 24	08 30	08 47				08 49			09 00					09 10	09 20			09 24	09 30
	d			08 31					08 51			09 01					09 11	09 21				09 31
Rugby	d											09 12				09 20	09 23	09 32				
Long Buckby	d											09 21						09 41				
Northampton	a											09 33				09 41		09 54				
London Euston 15 ⊖	a			09 34					09 54							10 49	10 14	11 17				10 34

Station		LM ◇1	LM	LM ◇1	VT ◇1 ⊠	LM ◇1	AW ◇ ⊥	XC ◇1 ⊥	LM	LM	LM ◇1	LM ◇1	VT ◇1 ⊠	LM ◇1	VT ◇1 ⊠	LM	XC ◇1 ⊥	VT ◇1 ⊠	LM ◇1	LM	LM ◇1	VT ◇1 ⊠	LM ◇1
Stafford	d			08 43				09 03			09 10	09 21					09 25				09 43		
Penkridge	d			08 48							09 16												
Wolverhampton 7 ⇌	a			08 58				09 15			09 27						09 39				09 56		
	d		08 49	08 58			09 10	09 16		09 19	09 28				09 32	09 36	09 41	09 45		09 49	09 57		
Coseley	d		08 54	09 04						09 24										09 54	10 03		
Tipton	d		08 56							09 26										09 56			
Dudley Port	d		08 58							09 28										09 58			
Sandwell & Dudley	d		09 02							09 32						09 46		09 56		10 02			
Smethwick Galton Bridge 7	d		09 04				09 21			09 34	09 40									10 04			
Smethwick Rolfe Street	d		09 06							09 36										10 06			
Birmingham New Street 12	a		09 14	09 18			09 26	09 39		09 44	09 47				09 55	09 56	09 58	10 05		10 14	10 17		
	d	09 13			09 30	09 33	09 36		09 39				09 50	09 53			10 03	10 10	10 13			10 30	10 33
Adderley Park	d								09 44														
Stechford	d	09 20							09 47										10 20				
Lea Hall	d	09 23							09 50										10 23				
Marston Green	d	09 25				09 41								10 01					10 25				10 41
Birmingham International ✈	a	09 29			09 39	09 45	09 50		09 55				09 59	10 05			10 13	10 19	10 29			10 39	10 45
	d	09 29			09 40	09 45							10 00	10 05			10 14	10 20	10 29			10 40	10 45
Hampton-in-Arden	d	09 32				09 48													10 32				10 48
Berkswell	d	09 37												10 11					10 37				
Tile Hill	d	09 40				09 55								10 14					10 40				10 55
Canley	d	09 43												10 17					10 43				
Coventry	a	09 47			09 49	10 00							10 10	10 20			10 24	10 30	10 47			10 49	11 00
	d				09 51	10 01							10 11	10 21				10 31				10 51	11 01
Rugby	d					10 12						10 20	10 24	10 32									11 12
Long Buckby	d					10 21								10 41									11 21
Northampton	a					10 33						10 42		10 54									11 33
London Euston 15 ⊖	a				10 54							11 49	11 14	12 17				11 34				11 54	

Table 68

Mondays to Fridays

Stafford - Wolverhampton - Birmingham - Coventry - Northampton

	AW	XC	LM	LM	LM	LM	VT	LM	VT	LM	XC	VT	LM	LM	LM	VT	AW	XC	LM	LM	LM	LM
	◇ ⊼	◇1 ⊼			◇1	◇1	◇1 ⊠	◇1	◇1 ⊠		◇1 ⊼	◇1 ⊠	◇1		◇1	◇1 ☕	◇ ⊼	◇1 ⊼	◇1			◇1
Stafford d		10 03			10 10	10 21					10 25				10 43			11 02				11 10
Penkridge d					10 16																	11 16
Wolverhampton [7] ⇌ a		10 15			10 27						10 39				10 56			11 15				11 27
d	10 09	10 17		10 19	10 28				10 32	10 36	10 41	10 45		10 49	10 57		11 09	11 16			11 19	11 28
Coseley d				10 24										10 54	11 03						11 24	
Tipton d				10 26										10 56							11 26	
Dudley Port d				10 28										10 58							11 28	
Sandwell & Dudley d				10 32						10 46		10 56		11 02							11 32	
Smethwick Galton Bridge [7] d	10 20			10 34	10 40									11 04			11 20				11 34	11 40
Smethwick Rolfe Street d				10 36										11 06							11 36	
Birmingham New Street [12] a	10 26	10 39		10 44	10 47				10 55	10 55	10 58	11 05		11 14	11 18		11 26	11 32			11 44	11 47
d	10 36		10 39				10 50	10 53			11 03	11 10	11 13			11 30	11 36		11 33	11 39		
Adderley Park d			10 44																	11 44		
Stechford d			10 47										11 20							11 47		
Lea Hall d			10 50										11 23							11 50		
Marston Green d								11 01					11 25						11 41			
Birmingham International ✈ a	10 50		10 55				10 59	11 05			11 13	11 19	11 29			11 39	11 50		11 45	11 55		
d							11 00	11 05			11 14	11 20	11 29			11 40			11 45			
Hampton-in-Arden d													11 32						11 48			
Berkswell d								11 11					11 37									
Tile Hill d								11 14					11 40						11 55			
Canley d								11 17					11 43									
Coventry a							11 10	11 20			11 24	11 30	11 47			11 49			12 00			
d							11 11	11 21				11 31				11 51			12 01			
Rugby d						11 20	11 24	11 32											12 12			
Long Buckby d								11 41											12 21			
Northampton a						11 42		11 54											12 33			
London Euston [15] ⊖ a						12 49	12 14	13 17				12 34				12 54						

	LM	VT	LM	VT	LM	XC	VT	LM	LM	LM	VT	LM	AW	XC	LM	LM	LM	VT	LM	LM	VT
	◇1	◇1 ☕	◇1	◇1 ⊠		◇1 ⊼	◇1 ☕	◇1		◇1	◇1 ☕	◇1	◇ ⊼	◇1 ⊼			◇1	◇1 ☕	◇1	◇1	◇1 ⊠
Stafford d	11 21					11 25				11 43				12 03			12 10		12 21		
Penkridge d																	12 16				
Wolverhampton [7] ⇌ a						11 39				11 57				12 15			12 27				
d				11 32	11 36	11 41	11 45		11 49	11 57			12 09	12 17		12 19	12 28				12 32
Coseley d									11 54	12 03						12 24					
Tipton d									11 56							12 26					
Dudley Port d									11 58							12 28					
Sandwell & Dudley d					11 46		11 56		12 02							12 32					
Smethwick Galton Bridge [7] d									12 04				12 20			12 34	12 40				
Smethwick Rolfe Street d									12 06							12 36					
Birmingham New Street [12] a				11 55	11 55	11 58	12 05		12 14	12 17			12 26	12 39		12 44	12 47				12 55
d		11 50	11 53			12 03	12 10	12 13			12 30	12 33	12 36		12 39			12 50		12 53	
Adderley Park d															12 44						
Stechford d								12 20							12 47						
Lea Hall d								12 23							12 50						
Marston Green d			12 01					12 25				12 41								13 01	
Birmingham International ✈ a		11 59	12 05			12 13	12 19	12 29			12 39	12 45	12 50		12 55			12 59		13 05	
d		12 00	12 05			12 14	12 20	12 29			12 40	12 45						13 00		13 05	
Hampton-in-Arden d								12 32				12 48									
Berkswell d			12 11					12 37												13 11	
Tile Hill d			12 14					12 40				12 55								13 14	
Canley d			12 17					12 43												13 17	
Coventry a		12 10	12 20			12 24	12 30	12 47			12 49	13 00						13 10		13 20	
d		12 11	12 21				12 31				12 51	13 01						13 11		13 21	
Rugby d	12 20	12 24	12 32									13 12						13 24	13 25	13 32	
Long Buckby d			12 41									13 22								13 41	
Northampton a	12 43		12 54									13 33							13 48	13 54	
London Euston [15] ⊖ a	13 49	13 14	14 17				13 34				13 55							14 14	14 49	15 17	

Table 68

Mondays to Fridays

Stafford - Wolverhampton - Birmingham - Coventry - Northampton

	LM	XC	VT	LM	LM	LM	VT	AW	XC	LM	LM	LM	LM	LM	VT	LM	VT	LM	XC	VT	LM	LM
		◇1 ⊼	◇1 ☕	◇1		◇1	◇1 ☕	◇ ⊼	◇1 ⊼	◇1			◇1	◇1	◇1 ☕	◇1	◇1 ☕		◇1 ⊼	◇1 ☕	◇1	
Stafford d		12 25				12 43							13 10	13 21					13 25			
Penkridge d													13 16									
Wolverhampton [7] ⇌ a		12 39				12 56							13 27						13 39			
d	12 36	12 41	12 45		12 49	12 57		13 09	13 14			13 19	13 28				13 32	13 36	13 41	13 45		13 49
Coseley d					12 54	13 03						13 24										13 54
Tipton d					12 56							13 26										13 56
Dudley Port d					12 58							13 28										13 58
Sandwell & Dudley d	12 46		12 56		13 02							13 32						13 46		13 56		14 02
Smethwick Galton Bridge [7] d					13 04			13 20				13 34	13 40									14 04
Smethwick Rolfe Street d					13 06							13 36										14 06
Birmingham New Street [12] a	12 55	12 58	13 05		13 14	13 17		13 26	13 31			13 44	13 47				13 55	13 55	13 58	14 05		14 14
d		13 03	13 10	13 13			13 30	13 36		13 33	13 39				13 50	13 53			14 03	14 10	14 13	
Adderley Park d											13 44											
Stechford d				13 20							13 47										14 20	
Lea Hall d				13 23							13 50										14 23	
Marston Green d				13 25						13 41						14 01					14 25	
Birmingham International ✈ a		13 13	13 19	13 29			13 39	13 50		13 45	13 55				13 59	14 05			14 13	14 19	14 29	
d		13 14	13 20	13 29			13 40			13 45					14 00	14 05			14 14	14 20	14 29	
Hampton-in-Arden d				13 32						13 48											14 32	
Berkswell d				13 37												14 11					14 37	
Tile Hill d				13 40						13 55						14 14					14 40	
Canley d				13 43												14 17					14 43	
Coventry a		13 24	13 30	13 47			13 49			14 00					14 10	14 20			14 24	14 30	14 47	
d			13 31				13 51			14 01					14 11	14 21				14 31		
Rugby d										14 12				14 20	14 24	14 32						
Long Buckby d										14 21						14 41						
Northampton a										14 33				14 42		14 54						
London Euston [15] ⊖ a			14 34				14 54							15 49	15 14	16 17				15 34		

	LM	VT	AW	XC	LM	LM	LM	LM	LM	VT	LM	VT	LM	XC	VT	VT	LM	LM	LM	VT	LM
	◇1	◇1 ☕	◇ ⊼	◇1 ⊼	◇1			◇1	◇1	◇1 ☕	◇1	◇1 A ⊠		◇1 ⊼	◇1 B ⊠	◇1 A ☕	◇1		◇1	◇1 ☕	◇1
Stafford d	13 43			14 02				14 10	14 21					14 25					14 46		
Penkridge d								14 16													
Wolverhampton [7] ⇌ a	13 56			14 15				14 27						14 39					14 59		
d	13 57		14 09	14 16			14 19	14 28				14 32	14 36	14 41	14 45	14 45		14 49	14 59		
Coseley d	14 03						14 24											14 54	15 05		
Tipton d							14 26											14 56			
Dudley Port d							14 28											14 58			
Sandwell & Dudley d							14 32						14 46		14 56	14 56		15 02			
Smethwick Galton Bridge [7] d			14 20				14 34	14 40										15 04			
Smethwick Rolfe Street d							14 36											15 06			
Birmingham New Street [12] a	14 17		14 26	14 32			14 44	14 47				14 55	14 55	14 58	15 05	15 05		15 14	15 20		
d		14 30	14 36		14 33	14 39				14 50	14 53			15 03	15 10	15 10	15 13			15 30	15 33
Adderley Park d						14 44															
Stechford d						14 47											15 20				
Lea Hall d						14 50											15 23				
Marston Green d					14 41						15 01						15 25				15 41
Birmingham International ✈ a		14 39	14 50		14 45	14 55				14 59	15 05			15 13	15 19	15 19	15 29			15 39	15 45
d		14 40			14 45					15 00	15 05			15 14	15 20	15 20	15 29			15 40	15 45
Hampton-in-Arden d					14 48												15 32				15 48
Berkswell d											15 11						15 37				
Tile Hill d					14 55						15 14						15 40				15 55
Canley d											15 17						15 43				
Coventry a		14 49			15 00					15 10	15 20			15 24	15 30	15 30	15 47			15 49	16 00
d		14 51			15 01					15 11	15 21				15 31	15 31				15 51	16 01
Rugby d					15 12				15 20	15 24	15 32										16 12
Long Buckby d					15 21						15 41										16 21
Northampton a					15 33				15 42		15 54										16 33
London Euston [15] ⊖ a		15 54							16 49	16 14	17 18				16 34	16 34				16 54	

A until 15 July, from 12 September

B from 18 July until 9 September

Stafford - Wolverhampton - Birmingham - Coventry - Northampton

		AW	XC	LM	LM	LM	LM	VT	LM	VT	LM	XC	VT	LM	LM	LM	VT	LM	AW	XC	LM	LM	LM
		◇ ⊼	◇1 ⊼			◇1	◇1	◇1 ☐	◇1	◇1 ☐		◇1 ⊼	◇1 ☐	1		◇1	◇1 ☐	◇1	◇ ⊼	◇1 ⊼			◇1
Stafford	d		15 03			15 10	15 21					15 25				15 43				16 03			16 10
Penkridge	d					15 16																	16 16
Wolverhampton 7	a		15 15			15 27						15 39				15 56				16 15			16 26
	d	15 09	15 17		15 19	15 28				15 32	15 36	15 41	15 45		15 49	15 57			16 09	16 17		16 19	16 28
Coseley	d				15 24										15 54	16 03						16 24	
Tipton	d				15 26										15 56							16 26	
Dudley Port	d				15 28										15 58							16 28	
Sandwell & Dudley	d				15 32						15 46		15 56		16 02							16 32	
Smethwick Galton Bridge 7	d	15 20			15 34	15 40									16 04				16 20			16 34	16 40
Smethwick Rolfe Street	d				15 36										16 06							16 36	
Birmingham New Street 12	a	15 26	15 39		15 44	15 47				15 55	15 55	15 58	16 05		16 14	16 17			16 26	16 39		16 44	16 47
	d	15 36		15 39				15 50	15 53			16 03	16 10	16 13			16 30	16 33	16 36		16 39		
Adderley Park	d			15 44																	16 44		
Stechford	d			15 47										16 20							16 47		
Lea Hall	d			15 50										16 23							16 50		
Marston Green	d								16 01					16 26				16 41					
Birmingham International ✈	a	15 50		15 55				15 59	16 05			16 13	16 19	16 29			16 39	16 45	16 50		16 55		
	d							16 00	16 05			16 14	16 20	16 29			16 40	16 45					
Hampton-in-Arden	d													16 32				16 48					
Berkswell	d								16 11					16 37									
Tile Hill	d								16 14					16 40				16 55					
Canley	d								16 17					16 44									
Coventry	a							16 10	16 20			16 24	16 30	16 47			16 49	17 00					
	d							16 11	16 21				16 31				16 51	17 01					
Rugby	d						16 20	16 24	16 32									17 12					
Long Buckby	d								16 41									17 21					
Northampton	a						16 42		16 54									17 33					
London Euston 15 ⊖	a						17 49	17 14	18 18				17 34				17 54						

		LM	VT	LM	VT	LM	XC	VT	LM	LM	LM	LM	VT	LM	AW	XC	LM	LM	LM	LM	VT	LM	VT
		◇1	◇1 ☐	◇1	◇1 ☐		◇1 ⊼	◇1 ☐	◇1		1	◇1	◇1 ⊠	◇1	◇ ⊼	◇1 ⊼			◇1	◇1	◇1 ⊠	◇1	◇1 ☐
Stafford	d	16 21					16 25					16 46				17 03			17 10	17 21			
Penkridge	d																		17 16				
Wolverhampton 7	a						16 39					16 59				17 15			17 27				
	d				16 32	16 36	16 41	16 45		16 49		16 59			17 10	17 16		17 19	17 28				17 32
Coseley	d									16 54		17 05						17 24					
Tipton	d									16 56								17 26					
Dudley Port	d									16 58								17 28					
Sandwell & Dudley	d					16 46		16 56		17 02								17 32					
Smethwick Galton Bridge 7	d									17 04					17 21			17 34	17 40				
Smethwick Rolfe Street	d									17 06								17 36					
Birmingham New Street 12	a				16 55	16 55	16 58	17 05		17 14		17 20			17 27	17 39		17 44	17 47				17 55
	d		16 50	16 53			17 03	17 10	17 13		17 16		17 30	17 33	17 36		17 39				17 50	17 53	
Adderley Park	d										17 21						17 44						
Stechford	d								17 20								17 47						
Lea Hall	d										17 25						17 50						
Marston Green	d			17 01							17 28			17 41								18 01	
Birmingham International ✈	a		16 59	17 05			17 13	17 19	17 25		17 32		17 39	17 45	17 50		17 55				17 59	18 05	
	d		17 00	17 05			17 14	17 20	17 26		17 33		17 40	17 45							18 00	18 05	
Hampton-in-Arden	d										17 36			17 48									
Berkswell	d			17 11							17 40											18 11	
Tile Hill	d			17 14					17 33					17 55								18 14	
Canley	d			17 17					17 36													18 17	
Coventry	a		17 10	17 20			17 24	17 30	17 40		17 47		17 49	18 00							18 10	18 20	
	d		17 11	17 21				17 31	17 41				17 51	18 01							18 11	18 21	
Rugby	d	17 20	17 24	17 32					17 52					18 12						18 20	18 24	18 32	
Long Buckby	d			17 41					18 01					18 21								18 41	
Northampton	a	17 42		17 54					18 16					18 33						18 42		18 54	
London Euston 15 ⊖	a	18 49	18 14	19 18				18 34	19 29				18 54							19 50	19 14	20 19	

Stafford - Wolverhampton - Birmingham - Coventry - Northampton

		LM	XC	VT	LM	LM	LM	VT	LM	AW	XC	LM	LM	LM	LM	VT	LM	VT	LM	XC	VT	VT
			◇1 ⊼	◇1 ⊠	1		◇1	◇1 ⊠	◇1	◇ ⊼	◇1 ⊼			◇1	◇1	◇1 ⊠	◇1	■ 1 A ☐		◇1 ⊼	■ 1 B ☐	◇1 A ⊠
Stafford	d		17 25				17 43				18 04			18 10	18 21					18 28		
Penkridge	d													18 16								
Wolverhampton 7	a		17 39				17 56				18 15			18 27						18 39		
	d	17 36	17 41	17 45		17 49	17 57			18 09	18 16		18 19	18 28				18 32	18 36	18 41	18 45	18 45
Coseley	d					17 54	18 03						18 24									
Tipton	d					17 56							18 26									
Dudley Port	d					17 58							18 28									
Sandwell & Dudley	d	17 46		17 56		18 02							18 32						18 46		18 56	18 56
Smethwick Galton Bridge 7	d					18 04				18 20			18 34	18 40								
Smethwick Rolfe Street	d					18 06							18 36									
Birmingham New Street 12	a	17 55	17 58	18 05		18 14	18 17			18 26	18 38		18 44	18 48				18 55	18 55	18 58	19 05	19 05
	d		18 03	18 10	18 13			18 30	18 33	18 36		18 39				18 50	18 53			19 03	19 10	19 10
Adderley Park	d											18 44										
Stechford	d				18 20							18 47										
Lea Hall	d				18 23							18 50										
Marston Green	d				18 26				18 41								19 01					
Birmingham International ✈	a		18 13	18 19	18 29			18 39	18 45	18 50		18 55				18 59	19 05			19 13	19 19	19 19
	d		18 14	18 20	18 29			18 40	18 45							19 00	19 05			19 14	19 20	19 20
Hampton-in-Arden	d				18 32				18 48													
Berkswell	d				18 37												19 11					
Tile Hill	d				18 40				18 55								19 14					
Canley	d				18 44												19 17					
Coventry	a		18 24	18 30	18 47			18 49	19 00							19 10	19 20			19 24	19 30	19 30
	d			18 31				18 51	19 01							19 11	19 21				19 31	19 31
Rugby	d								19 12						19 20	19 24	19 32					
Long Buckby	d								19 21								19 41					
Northampton	a								19 34						19 45		19 55					
London Euston 15 ⊖	a			19 34				19 54							20 49	20 14	21 17				20 34	20 34

		LM	LM	LM	VT	AW	XC	LM	LM	LM	LM	LM	VT	LM	VT	LM	XC	VT	LM	LM	LM	LM	AW
		1		◇1	◇1 ☐	◇ ⊼	◇1 ⊼	◇1			◇1	◇1	◇1 ☐	◇1	◇1 ☐		◇1 C ⊼	◇1 ☐	1		◇1	◇1	◇ ⊼
Stafford	d			18 43			19 02				19 10	19 21					19 25				19 42		
Penkridge	d										19 16										19 47		
Wolverhampton 7	a			18 56			19 15				19 27						19 39				19 57		
	d		18 49	18 57		19 09	19 16			19 19	19 28				19 32	19 36	19 41	19 45		19 49	19 57		20 10
Coseley	d		18 54	19 03						19 24										19 54	20 03		
Tipton	d		18 56							19 26										19 56			
Dudley Port	d		18 58							19 28										19 58			
Sandwell & Dudley	d		19 02							19 32						19 46		19 56		20 02			
Smethwick Galton Bridge 7	d		19 04			19 20				19 34	19 40									20 04			20 21
Smethwick Rolfe Street	d		19 06							19 36										20 06			
Birmingham New Street 12	a		19 14	19 17		19 26	19 32			19 44	19 47				19 55	19 55	19 58	20 05		20 14	20 18		20 26
	d	19 13			19 30	19 36		19 33	19 39				19 50	19 53			20 03	20 10	20 13			20 33	20 36
Adderley Park	d								19 44														
Stechford	d	19 20							19 47										20 20				
Lea Hall	d	19 23							19 50										20 23				
Marston Green	d	19 26						19 41						20 01					20 26			20 41	
Birmingham International ✈	a	19 29			19 39	19 50		19 45	19 55				19 59	20 05			20 13	20 19	20 29			20 45	20 50
	d	19 29			19 40			19 45					20 00	20 05			20 14	20 20	20 29			20 45	
Hampton-in-Arden	d	19 32						19 48											20 32			20 48	
Berkswell	d	19 37												20 11					20 37				
Tile Hill	d	19 40						19 55						20 14					20 40			20 55	
Canley	d	19 44												20 17					20 44				
Coventry	a	19 47			19 49			20 00					20 10	20 20			20 24	20 30	20 47			21 00	
	d				19 51			20 01					20 11	20 21				20 31				21 01	
Rugby	d							20 12				20 20	20 23	20 32								21 13	
Long Buckby	d							20 21						20 41								21 22	
Northampton	a							20 34				20 43		20 54								21 35	
London Euston 15 ⊖	a				20 54								21 14	22 20				21 38					

A until 15 July, from 12 September

B from 18 July until 9 September

C ⊼ to Wolverhampton

Table 68

Mondays to Fridays

Stafford - Wolverhampton - Birmingham - Coventry - Northampton

		XC	LM	LM	LM	VT	LM	VT	LM	XC	VT	LM	LM	LM	XC	LM	LM	LM	LM	VT	LM	LM
		◇1 A ⌶			◇1	◇1 ☕	◇1	■ 1 ☕		◇1 A ⌶	◇1 ☕	1		◇1	◇1	◇1			◇1	◇1 ☕	◇1	
Stafford	d	20 04			20 16					20 26				20 42	21 03				21 10	21 13		
Penkridge	d													20 47					21 16			
Wolverhampton 7	a	20 16			20 29					20 40				20 57	21 15				21 26	21 29		
	d	20 17		20 19	20 29			20 34	20 39	20 43	20 47		20 49	20 57	21 16			21 19	21 28	21 32		21 36
Coseley	d			20 24									20 54	21 03				21 24				
Tipton	d			20 26									20 56					21 26				
Dudley Port	d			20 28									20 58					21 28				
Sandwell & Dudley	d			20 32					20 48		20 57		21 02					21 32				21 46
Smethwick Galton Bridge 7	d			20 34	20 41								21 04					21 34	21 40			
Smethwick Rolfe Street	d			20 36									21 06					21 36				
Birmingham New Street 12	a	20 33		20 44	20 47			20 55	20 57	21 00	21 06		21 14	21 18	21 32			21 44	21 47	21 48		21 55
	d		20 39			20 50	20 53			21 03	21 10	21 13				21 33	21 39				21 53	
Adderley Park	d		20 44														21 44					
Stechford	d		20 47									21 20					21 47					
Lea Hall	d		20 50									21 23					21 50					
Marston Green	d						21 01					21 26				21 41					22 01	
Birmingham International ✈	a		20 55			20 59	21 05			21 13	21 19	21 29				21 45	21 55				22 05	
	d					21 00	21 05			21 14	21 20	21 29				21 45					22 05	
Hampton-in-Arden	d											21 32				21 48						
Berkswell	d						21 11					21 37									22 11	
Tile Hill	d						21 14					21 40				21 55					22 14	
Canley	d						21 17					21 44									22 17	
Coventry	a					21 10	21 20			21 24	21 30	21 53				22 00					22 20	
	d					21 11	21 21				21 31					22 01					22 21	
Rugby	d					21 23	21 32									22 12					22 37	
Long Buckby	d						21 41									22 21					22 46	
Northampton	a						21 54									22 33					22 58	
London Euston 15 ⊖	a					22 12	23 21				22 43					00 21						

		XC	XC	VT	LM	LM	LM	AW	LM	LM	VT	LM	VT	LM	XC	VT	LM	LM	AW	AW	LM	XC	LM
		◇1	◇1	◇1 ☕	1		◇1	◇	1		◇1 ☕	◇1	◇1 ☕		◇1	◇1 ☕	1		◇ B	◇ C	◇1	◇1	1
Stafford	d	21 25					21 41								22 26						22 41	23 07	
Penkridge	d						21 47														22 47		
Wolverhampton 7	a	21 39					21 57								22 39						22 57	23 19	
	d	21 41		21 45		21 49	21 57	22 09		22 19	22 28		22 32	22 36	22 41	22 45		22 49	22 55	22 55	22 57	23 21	
Coseley	d					21 54	22 03			22 24								22 54			23 03		
Tipton	d					21 56				22 26								22 56					
Dudley Port	d					21 58				22 28								22 58					
Sandwell & Dudley	d			21 56		22 02				22 32				22 46		22 55		23 02					
Smethwick Galton Bridge 7	d					22 04		22 20		22 34								23 04					
Smethwick Rolfe Street	d					22 06				22 36								23 06					
Birmingham New Street 12	a	22 00		22 05		22 14	22 17	22 32		22 44	22 50		22 55	22 55	22 58	23 04		23 14	23 27	23 29	23 18	23 39	
	d		22 03	22 10	22 13				22 33			22 53				23 10	23 13						23 53
Adderley Park	d																23 18						
Stechford	d				22 20												23 21						
Lea Hall	d				22 23												23 24						
Marston Green	d				22 26				22 41			23 01					23 27						00 01
Birmingham International ✈	a		22 13	22 19	22 29				22 45			23 05				23 19	23 30						00 04
	d		22 14	22 20	22 29				22 45			23 05				23 20	23 30						00 05
Hampton-in-Arden	d				22 32				22 48								23 33						
Berkswell	d				22 37							23 11					23 38						
Tile Hill	d				22 40				22 55			23 14					23 41						
Canley	d				22 44							23 17					23 45						
Coventry	a		22 24	22 30	22 47				23 00			23 20				23 30	23 48						00 15
	d			22 31								23 21				23 31							
Rugby	d			22 43								23 32				23 44							
Long Buckby	d											23 41											
Northampton	a											23 54				00s05							
London Euston 15 ⊖	a			00 04												01 14							

A ⌶ to Wolverhampton

B MWFO

C TThO

Table 68

Saturdays

Stafford - Wolverhampton - Birmingham - Coventry - Northampton

		LM	VT	VT	LM	VT	AW	XC	VT	LM	AW	VT	LM	AW	LM	LM	VT	LM	XC	VT	LM	LM	LM
		◇1	◇1 ☕	◇1 ☕	1	◇1 ☕		◇1 ⌶	◇1 ☕	1		◇1 ☕	◇1				◇1 ☕	◇1	◇1 ⌶	◇1 ☕	◇1		◇1
Stafford	d						05 25												06 26				06 41
Penkridge	d																						06 47
Wolverhampton 7	a						05 39												06 39				06 57
	d		21p45	22p45			05 40		05 45		06 03	06 06				06 19	06 27		06 41	06 45		06 49	06 57
Coseley	d															06 24						06 54	07 03
Tipton	d															06 26						06 56	
Dudley Port	d															06 28						06 58	
Sandwell & Dudley	d		21p56	22p55					05 56			06 17				06 32	06 37			06 56		07 02	
Smethwick Galton Bridge 7	d										06 14					06 34						07 04	
Smethwick Rolfe Street	d													←		06 36						07 06	
Birmingham New Street 12	a		22p05	23p04			05 58		06 05		06 20	06 26		06 20		06 44	06 47		06 57	07 05		07 14	07 17
	d	21p33	22p10	23p10	23p53	05 50		06 03	06 10	06 13	06 36	06 30	06 33	06 36	06 39		06 50	06 53	07 03	07 10	07 13		
Adderley Park	d										→				06 44								
Stechford	d									06 20					06 47						07 20		
Lea Hall	d									06 23					06 50						07 23		
Marston Green	d	21p41			00 01					06 26			06 41					07 01			07 25		
Birmingham International ✈	a	21p45	22p19	23p19	00 04	05 59		06 13	06 19	06 29		06 39	06 45	06 50	06 54		06 59	07 05	07 13	07 19	07 29		
	d	21p45	22p20	23p20	00 05	06 00		06 14	06 20	06 29		06 40	06 45				07 00	07 05	07 14	07 20	07 29		
Hampton-in-Arden	d	21p48								06 32			06 48								07 32		
Berkswell	d									06 37								07 11			07 37		
Tile Hill	d	21p55								06 40			06 55					07 14			07 40		
Canley	d									06 44								07 17			07 43		
Coventry	a	22p00	22p30	23p30	00 15	06 10		06 24	06 30	06 47		06 50	07 00				07 10	07 20	07 24	07 30	07 47		
	d	22p01	22p31	23p31		06 10			06 31			06 51	07 01				07 11	07 21		07 31			
Rugby	d	22p12	22p43	23p44		06 24							07 12				07 23	07 32					
Long Buckby	d	22p21											07 21					07 41					
Northampton	a	22p33		00s05									07 34					07 53					
London Euston 15 ⊖	a	00 21	00 04	01 14		07 16			07 38			07 55					08 14			08 34			

		VT	AW	XC	LM	LM	LM	LM	LM	VT	LM	VT	LM	XC	VT	LM	LM	LM	VT	LM	AW	XC	XC
		◇1 ☕		◇1 ⌶			◇1	◇1	◇1	◇1 ☕	◇1	◇1 ☕		◇1 ⌶	◇1 ☕	◇1		◇1	◇1 ☕	◇1	◇ ⌶	◇1 A ⌶	◇1 B ⌶
Stafford	d			06 58			07 12		07 24									07 41				08 03	08 03
Penkridge	d						07 18											07 47					
Wolverhampton 7	a			07 12			07 28											07 57				08 16	08 17
	d	07 04	07 10	07 15		07 19	07 28					07 32	07 36		07 44		07 49	07 57	08 06		08 09	08 18	08 18
Coseley	d					07 24											07 54	08 03					
Tipton	d					07 26											07 56						
Dudley Port	d					07 28											07 58						
Sandwell & Dudley	d	07 15				07 32							07 46		07 56		08 02						
Smethwick Galton Bridge 7	d		07 21			07 34	07 40										08 04				08 21		
Smethwick Rolfe Street	d					07 36											08 06						
Birmingham New Street 12	a	07 24	07 26	07 31		07 44	07 47					07 55	07 55		08 05		08 14	08 17	08 24		08 26	08 38	08 39
	d	07 30	07 36		07 39			07 33		07 50	07 53			08 03	08 10	08 13			08 30	08 33	08 36		
Adderley Park	d				07 44																		
Stechford	d				07 47											08 20							
Lea Hall	d				07 50											08 23							
Marston Green	d							07 41			08 01					08 25				08 41			
Birmingham International ✈	a	07 39	07 50		07 54			07 45		07 59	08 05			08 13	08 19	08 29			08 39	08 45	08 50		
	d	07 40						07 45		08 00	08 05			08 14	08 20	08 29			08 40	08 45			
Hampton-in-Arden	d							07 48								08 32				08 48			
Berkswell	d										08 11					08 37							
Tile Hill	d							07 55			08 14					08 40				08 55			
Canley	d										08 17					08 43							
Coventry	a	07 50						08 00		08 10	08 20			08 24	08 30	08 47			08 49	09 00			
	d	07 52						08 01		08 11	08 21				08 31				08 51	09 01			
Rugby	d							08 12	08 20	08 23	08 32									09 12			
Long Buckby	d							08 21			08 41									09 21			
Northampton	a							08 33	08 40		08 53									09 33			
London Euston 15 ⊖	a	08 54						09 50		09 14					09 35				09 55				

A from 17 September

B until 10 September

Table 68

Saturdays

Stafford - Wolverhampton - Birmingham - Coventry - Northampton

		LM		LM	LM	LM	VT	LM	VT	LM	XC	VT		LM	LM	LM	VT	LM	AW	XC	LM	LM		LM	LM
					◇■	◇■	◇■ 🍴	◇■	◇■ 🍴		◇■ ✠	◇■ 🍴		◇■		◇■	◇■ 🍴	◇■	◇ ✠	◇■ ✠				◇■	◇■
Stafford	d				08 10	08 23					08 26					08 43				09 03				09 10	09 21
Penkridge	d				08 16											08 48								09 16	
Wolverhampton ■	a				08 28						08 39					08 58				09 15				09 27	
	d			08 19	08 28				08 32	08 36	08 41	08 45			08 49	08 59			09 10	09 17		09 19		09 28	
Coseley	d			08 24											08 54	09 04						09 24			
Tipton	d			08 26											08 56							09 26			
Dudley Port	d			08 28											08 58							09 28			
Sandwell & Dudley	d			08 32						08 46		08 56			09 02							09 32			
Smethwick Galton Bridge ■	d			08 34	08 40										09 04				09 22			09 34		09 40	
Smethwick Rolfe Street	d			08 36											09 06							09 36			
Birmingham New Street ■	a			08 44	08 47				08 55	08 55	08 58	09 05			09 14	09 18			09 26	09 39		09 44		09 47	
	d	08 39					08 50	08 53			09 03	09 10		09 13			09 30	09 33	09 36		09 39				
Adderley Park	d	08 44																			09 44				
Stechford	d	08 47												09 20							09 47				
Lea Hall	d	08 50												09 23							09 50				
Marston Green	d							09 01						09 25				09 41							
Birmingham International ✈	a	08 54					08 59	09 05			09 13	09 19		09 29			09 39	09 45	09 50		09 54				
	d						09 00	09 05			09 14	09 20		09 29			09 40	09 45							
Hampton-in-Arden	d													09 32				09 48							
Berkswell	d							09 11						09 37											
Tile Hill	d							09 14						09 40				09 55							
Canley	d							09 17						09 43											
Coventry	a						09 10	09 20			09 24	09 30		09 47			09 49	10 00							
	d						09 11	09 21				09 31					09 51	10 01							
Rugby	d					09 20	09 23	09 32										10 12							10 20
Long Buckby	d							09 41										10 21							
Northampton	a					09 39		09 54										10 33							10 39
London Euston ■ ⊖	a					10 49	10 14					10 34					10 54								11 49

		VT	LM	VT	LM	XC	VT	LM		LM	LM	VT	AW	XC	LM	LM	LM	LM	LM		VT	LM	VT	LM	XC
		◇■ 🍴	◇■	◇■ 🍴		◇■ ✠	◇■ 🍴	◇■			◇■	◇■ 🍴	◇ ✠	◇■ ✠			◇■	◇■	◇■		◇■ 🍴	◇■	◇■ 🍴		◇■ ✠
Stafford	d					09 26					09 43			10 03			10 10		10 21						10 26
Penkridge	d																10 16								
Wolverhampton ■	a					09 39					09 56			10 15			10 27								10 39
	d			09 32	09 36	09 41	09 45			09 49	09 57		10 09	10 17		10 19	10 28						10 32	10 36	10 41
Coseley	d									09 54	10 03					10 24									
Tipton	d									09 56						10 26									
Dudley Port	d									09 58						10 28									
Sandwell & Dudley	d				09 46		09 56			10 02						10 32								10 46	
Smethwick Galton Bridge ■	d									10 04			10 20			10 34	10 40								
Smethwick Rolfe Street	d									10 06						10 36									
Birmingham New Street ■	a			09 55	09 55	09 58	10 05			10 14	10 17		10 26	10 39		10 44	10 47						10 55	10 55	10 58
	d	09 50	09 53			10 03	10 10	10 13				10 30	10 36		10 39			10 33			10 50	10 53			11 03
Adderley Park	d														10 44										
Stechford	d							10 20							10 47										
Lea Hall	d							10 23							10 50										
Marston Green	d		10 01					10 25										10 41				11 01			
Birmingham International ✈	a	09 59	10 05			10 13	10 19	10 29				10 39	10 50		10 54			10 45			10 59	11 05			11 13
	d	10 00	10 05			10 14	10 20	10 29				10 40						10 45			11 00	11 05			11 14
Hampton-in-Arden	d							10 32										10 48							
Berkswell	d		10 11					10 37														11 11			
Tile Hill	d		10 14					10 40										10 55				11 14			
Canley	d		10 17					10 43														11 17			
Coventry	a	10 10	10 20			10 24	10 30	10 47				10 49						11 00			11 10	11 20			11 24
	d	10 11	10 21				10 31					10 51						11 01			11 11	11 21			
Rugby	d	10 23	10 32															11 12	11 20		11 23	11 32			
Long Buckby	d		10 41															11 21				11 41			
Northampton	a		10 54															11 33	11 39			11 54			
London Euston ■ ⊖	a	11 14					11 34					11 54						12 49			12 14				

Table 68

Saturdays

Stafford - Wolverhampton - Birmingham - Coventry - Northampton

		VT	LM	LM	LM		VT	LM	AW	XC	LM	LM	LM	LM	VT		LM	VT	LM	XC	VT	LM	LM	LM	VT
		◇■ 🍴	◇■		◇■		◇■ 🍴	◇■	◇ ✠	◇■ ✠			◇■	◇■	◇■ 🍴		◇■	◇■ 🍴		◇■ ✠	◇■ 🍴	◇■		◇■	◇■ 🍴
Stafford	d				10 43					11 03			11 10	11 21						11 26				11 43	
Penkridge	d												11 16												
Wolverhampton ■	a				10 56					11 16			11 27							11 39				11 56	
	d	10 45		10 49	10 57				11 09	11 17		11 19	11 28					11 32	11 36	11 41	11 45		11 49	11 57	
Coseley	d			10 54	11 03							11 24											11 54	12 03	
Tipton	d			10 56								11 26											11 56		
Dudley Port	d			10 58								11 28											11 58		
Sandwell & Dudley	d	10 56		11 02								11 32							11 46		11 56		12 02		
Smethwick Galton Bridge ■	d			11 04					11 20			11 34	11 40										12 04		
Smethwick Rolfe Street	d			11 06								11 36											12 06		
Birmingham New Street ■	a	11 05		11 14	11 17				11 26	11 39		11 44	11 47					11 55	11 55	11 58	12 05		12 14	12 17	
	d	11 10	11 13				11 30	11 33	11 36		11 39				11 50		11 53			12 03	12 10	12 13			12 30
Adderley Park	d										11 44														
Stechford	d		11 20								11 47											12 20			
Lea Hall	d		11 23								11 50											12 23			
Marston Green	d		11 25					11 41									12 01					12 25			
Birmingham International ✈	a	11 19	11 29				11 39	11 45	11 50		11 54				11 59		12 05			12 13	12 19	12 29			12 39
	d	11 20	11 29				11 40	11 45							12 00		12 05			12 14	12 20	12 29			12 40
Hampton-in-Arden	d		11 32					11 48														12 32			
Berkswell	d		11 37														12 11					12 37			
Tile Hill	d		11 40					11 55									12 14					12 40			
Canley	d		11 43														12 17					12 43			
Coventry	a	11 30	11 47				11 49	12 00							12 10		12 20			12 24	12 30	12 47			12 49
	d	11 31					11 51	12 01							12 11		12 21				12 31				12 51
Rugby	d							12 12						12 20	12 23		12 32								
Long Buckby	d							12 21									12 41								
Northampton	a							12 33						12 39			12 54								
London Euston ■ ⊖	a	12 34					12 53							13 49	13 14						13 34				13 54

			LM	AW	XC	LM	LM	LM	LM	VT	LM		VT	LM	XC	VT	LM	LM	LM	VT	LM		AW	XC	LM
			◇■	◇ ✠	◇■ ✠			◇■	◇■	◇■ 🍴	◇■		◇■ 🍴		◇■ ✠	◇■ 🍴	◇■		◇■	◇■ 🍴	◇■		◇ ✠	◇■ ✠	
Stafford	d				12 03			12 10	12 21						12 25				12 43					13 03	
Penkridge	d							12 16																	
Wolverhampton ■	a				12 16			12 27							12 39				12 56					13 15	
	d			12 09	12 17		12 19	12 28					12 32	12 36	12 41	12 45		12 49	12 57				13 09	13 16	
Coseley	d						12 24											12 54	13 03						
Tipton	d						12 26											12 56							
Dudley Port	d						12 28											12 58							
Sandwell & Dudley	d						12 32							12 46		12 56		13 02							
Smethwick Galton Bridge ■	d			12 20			12 34	12 40										13 04					13 20		
Smethwick Rolfe Street	d						12 36											13 06							
Birmingham New Street ■	a			12 26	12 39		12 44	12 47					12 55	12 55	12 58	13 05		13 14	13 17				13 25	13 39	
	d		12 33	12 36		12 39				12 50	12 53				13 03	13 10	13 13			13 30	13 33		13 36		13 39
Adderley Park	d					12 44																			13 44
Stechford	d					12 47											13 20								13 47
Lea Hall	d					12 50											13 23								13 50
Marston Green	d		12 41								13 01						13 25				13 41				
Birmingham International ✈	a		12 45	12 50		12 54				12 59	13 05				13 13	13 19	13 29			13 39	13 45		13 50		13 54
	d		12 45							13 00	13 05				13 14	13 20	13 29			13 40	13 45				
Hampton-in-Arden	d		12 48														13 32				13 48				
Berkswell	d										13 11						13 37								
Tile Hill	d		12 55								13 14						13 40				13 55				
Canley	d										13 17						13 43								
Coventry	a		13 00							13 10	13 20				13 24	13 30	13 47			13 49	14 00				
	d		13 01							13 11	13 21					13 31				13 51	14 01				
Rugby	d		13 12						13 20	13 23	13 32										14 12				
Long Buckby	d		13 21								13 41										14 21				
Northampton	a		13 33						13 39		13 54										14 33				
London Euston ■ ⊖	a								14 49	14 14						14 34				14 54					

Stafford - Wolverhampton - Birmingham - Coventry - Northampton

		LM	LM ◇1	LM ◇1	VT ◇1 🍴	LM ◇1	VT ◇1 🍴	LM	XC ◇1 ⌶	VT ◇1 🍴	LM ◇1	LM	LM ◇1	VT ◇1 🍴	AW ◇ ⌶	XC ◇1 ⌶	LM	LM	LM ◇1	LM ◇1	LM ◇1	VT ◇1 🍴	LM ◇1
Stafford	d		13 10	13 21					13 26				13 43			14 03			14 10		14 21		
Penkridge	d		13 16																14 16				
Wolverhampton 7 ⇌	a		13 27						13 39				13 56			14 16			14 27				
	d	13 19	13 28				13 32	13 36	13 41	13 45		13 49	13 57		14 09	14 17		14 19	14 28				
Coseley	d	13 24										13 54	14 03					14 24					
Tipton	d	13 26										13 56						14 26					
Dudley Port	d	13 28										13 58						14 28					
Sandwell & Dudley	d	13 32						13 46		13 56		14 02						14 32					
Smethwick Galton Bridge 7	d	13 34	13 40									14 04			14 20			14 34	14 40				
Smethwick Rolfe Street	d	13 36										14 06						14 36					
Birmingham New Street 12	a	13 44	13 47				13 55	13 55	13 58	14 05		14 14	14 17		14 26	14 39		14 44	14 47				
	d				13 50	13 53			14 03	14 10	14 13			14 30	14 36		14 39			14 33		14 50	14 53
Adderley Park	d																14 44						
Stechford	d										14 20						14 47						
Lea Hall	d										14 23						14 50						
Marston Green	d					14 01					14 25									14 41			15 01
Birmingham International ✈	a				13 59	14 05			14 13	14 19	14 29			14 39	14 50		14 54			14 45		14 59	15 05
	d				14 00	14 05			14 14	14 20	14 29			14 40						14 45		15 00	15 05
Hampton-in-Arden	d										14 32									14 48			
Berkswell	d					14 11					14 37												15 11
Tile Hill	d					14 14					14 40									14 55			15 14
Canley	d					14 17					14 43												15 17
Coventry	a				14 10	14 20			14 24	14 30	14 47			14 49						15 00		15 10	15 20
	d				14 11	14 21				14 31				14 51						15 01		15 11	15 21
Rugby	d			14 20	14 23	14 32														15 12	15 20	15 23	15 32
Long Buckby	d					14 41														15 21			15 41
Northampton	a			14 39		14 54														15 33	15 39		15 54
London Euston 15 ⊖	a			15 49	15 14					15 34				15 54						16 49		16 14	

		VT ◇1 A 🍴	LM	XC ◇1 ⌶	VT ◇1 🍴	LM ◇1	LM	LM ◇1	VT ◇1 🍴	AW ◇ ⌶	XC ◇1 ⌶	LM	LM	LM ◇1	LM ◇1	LM ◇1	VT ◇1 🍴	LM ◇1	VT ◇1 🍴	LM	XC ◇1 ⌶	VT ◇1 🍴
Stafford	d			14 26				14 46			15 03			15 10		15 21					15 26	
Penkridge	d													15 16								
Wolverhampton 7 ⇌	a			14 39				14 59			15 16			15 27							15 39	
	d	14 32	14 36	14 41	14 45		14 49	14 59		15 09	15 17		15 19	15 28					15 32	15 36	15 41	15 45
Coseley	d						14 54	15 05					15 24									
Tipton	d						14 56						15 26									
Dudley Port	d						14 58						15 28									
Sandwell & Dudley	d		14 46		14 56		15 02						15 32							15 46		15 56
Smethwick Galton Bridge 7	d						15 04			15 20			15 34	15 40								
Smethwick Rolfe Street	d						15 06						15 36									
Birmingham New Street 12	a	14 55	14 55	14 58	15 05		15 14	15 18		15 26	15 39		15 44	15 47					15 55	15 55	15 58	16 05
	d			15 03	15 10	15 13			15 30	15 36		15 39			15 33		15 50	15 53			16 03	16 10
Adderley Park	d											15 44										
Stechford	d					15 20						15 47										
Lea Hall	d					15 23						15 50										
Marston Green	d					15 25									15 41			16 01				
Birmingham International ✈	a			15 13	15 19	15 29			15 39	15 50		15 54			15 45		15 59	16 05			16 13	16 19
	d			15 14	15 20	15 29			15 40						15 45		16 00	16 05			16 14	16 20
Hampton-in-Arden	d					15 32									15 48							
Berkswell	d					15 37												16 11				
Tile Hill	d					15 40									15 55			16 14				
Canley	d					15 43												16 17				
Coventry	a			15 24	15 30	15 47			15 49						16 00		16 10	16 20			16 24	16 30
	d				15 31				15 51						16 01		16 11	16 21				16 31
Rugby	d														16 12	16 20	16 23	16 32				
Long Buckby	d														16 21			16 41				
Northampton	a														16 33	16 39		16 54				
London Euston 15 ⊖	a				16 34				16 54						17 49		17 14					17 34

A until 9 July, from 17 September

Table 68

Saturdays

Stafford - Wolverhampton - Birmingham - Coventry - Northampton

		LM ◇1	LM	LM ◇1	VT ◇1 🍴	AW ◇ ⌶	XC ◇1 ⌶	LM	LM	LM ◇1	LM ◇1	LM ◇1	VT ◇1 🍴	LM ◇1	VT ◇1 🍴	LM	XC ◇1 ⌶	VT ◇1 🍴	LM ◇1	LM	LM ◇1	VT ◇1 🍴	AW ◇ ⌶
Stafford	d			15 43			16 03			16 10		16 21					16 25				16 46		
Penkridge	d									16 16													
Wolverhampton 7 ⇌	a			15 56			16 16			16 27							16 39				16 59		
	d		15 49	15 57		16 09	16 17		16 19	16 28					16 32	16 36	16 41	16 45		16 49	16 59		17 10
Coseley	d		15 54	16 03					16 24											16 54	17 05		
Tipton	d		15 56						16 26											16 56			
Dudley Port	d		15 58						16 28											16 58			
Sandwell & Dudley	d		16 02						16 32							16 46		16 56		17 02			
Smethwick Galton Bridge 7	d		16 04			16 20			16 34	16 40										17 04			17 21
Smethwick Rolfe Street	d		16 06						16 36											17 06			
Birmingham New Street 12	a		16 14	16 17		16 26	16 39		16 44	16 47					16 55	16 55	16 58	17 05		17 14	17 18		17 27
	d	16 13			16 30	16 36		16 39			16 33		16 50	16 53			17 03	17 10	17 13			17 30	17 36
Adderley Park	d							16 44											17 17				
Stechford	d	16 20						16 47											17 21				
Lea Hall	d	16 23						16 50											17 23				
Marston Green	d	16 25									16 41			17 01					17 25				
Birmingham International ✈	a	16 29			16 39	16 50		16 54			16 45		16 59	17 05			17 13	17 19	17 29			17 39	17 50
	d	16 29			16 40						16 45		17 00	17 05			17 14	17 20	17 30			17 40	
Hampton-in-Arden	d	16 32									16 48								17 33				
Berkswell	d	16 37												17 11					17 38				
Tile Hill	d	16 40									16 55			17 14					17 41				
Canley	d	16 43												17 17					17 44				
Coventry	a	16 47			16 49						17 00		17 10	17 20			17 24	17 30	17 47			17 49	
	d				16 51						17 01		17 11	17 21				17 31				17 51	
Rugby	d										17 12	17 20	17 23	17 32									
Long Buckby	d										17 21			17 41									
Northampton	a										17 33	17 39		17 54									
London Euston 15 ⊖	a				17 52						18 49		18 14					18 34				18 54	

		XC ◇1 ⌶	LM	LM	LM ◇1	LM ◇1	LM ◇1	VT ◇1 🍴	LM ◇1	VT ◇1 🍴	LM	XC ◇1 ⌶	VT ◇1 🍴	LM ◇1	LM	LM ◇1	VT ◇1 🍴	LM ◇1	AW ◇ ⌶	XC ◇1 ⌶	LM	LM	LM ◇1
Stafford	d	17 03			17 10		17 21					17 26				17 43				18 04			18 10
Penkridge	d				17 16																		18 16
Wolverhampton 7 ⇌	a	17 16			17 27							17 39				17 56				18 16			18 27
	d	17 17		17 19	17 28					17 32	17 36	17 41	17 45		17 49	17 57			18 09	18 17		18 19	18 28
Coseley	d			17 24											17 54	18 03						18 24	
Tipton	d			17 26											17 56							18 26	
Dudley Port	d			17 28											17 58							18 28	
Sandwell & Dudley	d			17 32							17 46		17 56		18 02							18 32	
Smethwick Galton Bridge 7	d			17 34	17 40										18 04				18 20			18 34	18 40
Smethwick Rolfe Street	d			17 36											18 06							18 36	
Birmingham New Street 12	a	17 39		17 44	17 47					17 55	17 55	17 58	18 05		18 14	18 17			18 26	18 38		18 44	18 47
	d		17 39			17 33		17 50	17 53			18 03	18 10	18 13			18 30	18 33	18 36		18 39		
Adderley Park	d		17 44																		18 44		
Stechford	d		17 47											18 20							18 47		
Lea Hall	d		17 50											18 23							18 50		
Marston Green	d					17 41			18 01					18 25				18 41					
Birmingham International ✈	a		17 54			17 45		17 59	18 05			18 13	18 19	18 29			18 39	18 45	18 50		18 54		
	d					17 45		18 00	18 05			18 14	18 20	18 29			18 40	18 45					
Hampton-in-Arden	d					17 48								18 32				18 48					
Berkswell	d								18 11					18 37									
Tile Hill	d					17 55			18 14					18 40				18 55					
Canley	d								18 17					18 43									
Coventry	a					18 00		18 10	18 20			18 24	18 30	18 47			18 49	19 00					
	d					18 01		18 11	18 21				18 31				18 51	19 01					
Rugby	d					18 12	18 20	18 23	18 32									19 12					
Long Buckby	d					18 21			18 41									19 21					
Northampton	a					18 33	18 39		18 54									19 33					
London Euston 15 ⊖	a					19 49		19 14					19 34				19 54						

Table 68

Saturdays

Stafford - Wolverhampton - Birmingham - Coventry - Northampton

		LM	VT	LM	VT	LM	XC	VT	VT	LM	LM	LM	LM	AW	XC	LM	LM	LM	LM	LM	VT	LM
		◇1	◇1	◇1	◇1		◇1	◇1	◇1	◇1		◇1	◇1	◇	◇1			◇1	◇1	◇1	◇1	
			⊡		A ⊡		⌶	A ⊡	B ⊡					⌶	⌶						⊡	
Stafford	d	18 21					18 27					18 43			19 03			19 10	19 21			
Penkridge	d																	19 16				
Wolverhampton 7	a						18 40					18 56			19 16			19 27				
	d				18 32	18 36	18 41	18 45	18 45		18 49	18 57		19 09	19 17		19 19	19 28			19 32	19 36
Coseley	d										18 54	19 03					19 24					
Tipton	d										18 56						19 26					
Dudley Port	d										18 58						19 28					
Sandwell & Dudley	d					18 46		18 56	18 56		19 02						19 32					19 46
Smethwick Galton Bridge 7	d										19 04			19 20			19 34	19 40				
Smethwick Rolfe Street	d										19 06						19 36					
Birmingham New Street 12	a				18 55	18 55	18 58	19 05	19 05		19 14	19 17		19 26	19 33		19 44	19 47			19 55	19 55
	d		18 50	18 53			19 03	19 10	19 10	19 13			19 33	19 36		19 39				19 53		
Adderley Park	d															19 44						
Stechford	d									19 20						19 47						
Lea Hall	d									19 23						19 50						
Marston Green	d			19 01						19 25			19 41							20 01		
Birmingham International ✈	a		18 59	19 05			19 13	19 19	19 19	19 29			19 45	19 50		19 54				20 05		
	d		19 00	19 05			19 14	19 20	19 20	19 29			19 45							20 05		
Hampton-in-Arden	d									19 32			19 48									
Berkswell	d			19 11						19 37										20 11		
Tile Hill	d			19 14						19 40			19 55							20 14		
Canley	d			19 17						19 43										20 17		
Coventry	a		19 10	19 20			19 24	19 30	19 30	19 47			20 00							20 20		
	d		19 11	19 21				19 31	19 31				20 01							20 21		
Rugby	d	19 20	19 23	19 32				19 44	19 44				20 12						20 20	20 32		
Long Buckby	d			19 41									20 21							20 41		
Northampton	a	19 41		19 53									20 34						20 39	20 53		
London Euston 15 ⊖	a		20 15					20 52	20 55													

		XC	VT	LM	LM	LM	LM	AW	XC	LM	LM	LM	LM	VT	LM	XC	VT	LM	LM	LM	VT	XC	LM
		◇1	◇1	1		◇1	◇1	◇	◇1			◇1	◇1	◇1		◇1	◇1	1		◇1	◇1	◇1	◇1
		⌶	⊡					⌶	⌶					⊡		C ⌶	⊡				⊡		
Stafford	d	19 25				19 43			20 03			20 12				20 26				20 43		21 03	
Penkridge	d					19 49														20 49			
Wolverhampton 7	a	19 39				19 59			20 16			20 28				20 39				20 57		21 15	
	d	19 41	19 45		19 49	19 59		20 10	20 17		20 19	20 28		20 32	20 36	20 41	20 45		20 49	20 57	21 07	21 16	
Coseley	d				19 54	20 04					20 24								20 54	21 03			
Tipton	d				19 56						20 26								20 56				
Dudley Port	d				19 58						20 28								20 58				
Sandwell & Dudley	d		19 56		20 02						20 32				20 46		20 56		21 02		21 17		
Smethwick Galton Bridge 7	d				20 04			20 21			20 34	20 40							21 04				
Smethwick Rolfe Street	d				20 06						20 36								21 06				
Birmingham New Street 12	a	19 58	20 05		20 14	20 17		20 26	20 33		20 44	20 47		20 55	20 57	20 58	21 05		21 14	21 17	21 26	21 32	
	d	20 03	20 10	20 13			20 33	20 36		20 39			20 53			21 03	21 10	21 13			21 30		21 33
Adderley Park	d									20 44													
Stechford	d			20 20						20 47								21 20					
Lea Hall	d			20 23						20 50								21 23					
Marston Green	d			20 26			20 41						21 01					21 26					21 41
Birmingham International ✈	a	20 13	20 19	20 29			20 45	20 50		20 54			21 05			21 13	21 19	21 29			21 39		21 45
	d	20 14	20 20	20 29			20 45						21 05			21 14	21 20	21 29			21 40		21 45
Hampton-in-Arden	d			20 32			20 48											21 32					21 48
Berkswell	d			20 37									21 11					21 37					
Tile Hill	d			20 40			20 55						21 14					21 40					21 55
Canley	d			20 44									21 17					21 44					
Coventry	a	20 24	20 30	20 47			21 00						21 20			21 24	21 30	21 47			21 50		22 00
	d		20 31				21 01						21 21				21 31				21 51		22 01
Rugby	d		20 43				21 12						21 32				21 43				22 03		22 12
Long Buckby	d						21 21						21 41										22 21
Northampton	a						21 34						21 53										22 34
London Euston 15 ⊖	a		21 56														22 55				23 30		

A until 9 July, from 17 September

B from 16 July until 10 September

C ⌶ to Wolverhampton

Table 68

Saturdays

Stafford - Wolverhampton - Birmingham - Coventry - Northampton

		LM	LM	LM	VT	LM	XC	LM	LM	LM	AW	XC	LM	LM	VT	LM	LM	VT	XC	LM	LM	LM
				◇1	◇1		◇1	1		◇1	◇	◇1	1		◇1	◇1		◇1	◇1	1		◇1
					⊡										⊡			⊡				
Stafford	d						21 27			21 42		22 03			22 08			22 24	22 33			22 47
Penkridge	d									21 48												22 53
Wolverhampton 7	a						21 39			21 58		22 14			22 22			22 38	22 45			23 03
	d		21 19		21 33	21 36	21 41		21 49	21 58	22 09	22 16		22 19	22 23		22 36	22 39	22 46		22 49	23 03
Coseley	d		21 24						21 54	22 04				22 24							22 54	23 09
Tipton	d		21 26						21 56					22 26							22 56	
Dudley Port	d		21 28						21 58					22 28							22 58	
Sandwell & Dudley	d		21 32			21 46			22 02					22 32			22 46				23 02	
Smethwick Galton Bridge 7	d		21 34						22 04		22 20			22 34							23 04	
Smethwick Rolfe Street	d		21 36						22 06					22 36							23 06	
Birmingham New Street 12	a		21 44		21 54	21 55	21 58		22 14	22 20	22 32	22 32		22 44	22 40		22 55	22 58	23 02		23 14	23 21
	d	21 39		21 53				22 13					22 33			22 53				23 13		
Adderley Park	d	21 44																		23 18		
Stechford	d	21 47						22 20												23 21		
Lea Hall	d	21 50						22 23												23 24		
Marston Green	d			22 01				22 26					22 41			23 01				23 27		
Birmingham International ✈	a	21 54		22 05				22 29					22 45			23 05				23 30		
	d			22 05				22 29					22 45			23 05				23 30		
Hampton-in-Arden	d							22 32					22 48							23 33		
Berkswell	d			22 11				22 37								23 11				23 38		
Tile Hill	d			22 14				22 40					22 55			23 14				23 41		
Canley	d			22 17				22 44								23 17				23 45		
Coventry	a			22 20				22 47					23 00			23 20				23 48		
	d			22 21												23 21						
Rugby	d			22 32												23 32						
Long Buckby	d			22 41												23 41						
Northampton	a			22 53												23 54						
London Euston 15 ⊖	a																					

		AW	AW
		◇	
		A	B
			🚌
Stafford	d		
Penkridge	d		
Wolverhampton 7	a		
	d	23 09	23 58
Coseley	d		
Tipton	d		
Dudley Port	d		
Sandwell & Dudley	d		
Smethwick Galton Bridge 7	d		
Smethwick Rolfe Street	d		
Birmingham New Street 12	a	23 29	00 48
	d		
Adderley Park	d		
Stechford	d		
Lea Hall	d		
Marston Green	d		
Birmingham International ✈	a		
	d		
Hampton-in-Arden	d		
Berkswell	d		
Tile Hill	d		
Canley	d		
Coventry	a		
	d		
Rugby	d		
Long Buckby	d		
Northampton	a		
London Euston 15 ⊖	a		

A until 18 June, from 6 August

B from 25 June until 30 July

Table 68

Sundays
until 19 June

Stafford - Wolverhampton - Birmingham - Coventry - Northampton

		VT	LM	LM	LM	XC	LM	AW	VT	LM	LM	XC	LM	AW	VT	LM	LM	XC	LM	AW	LM	VT	LM
		◇1 🛒	1	1		◇1 ☕	◇1		◇1 🛒	1		◇1 ☕	◇1		◇1 🛒	1		◇1 ☕	◇1	◇	◇1	◇1 🛒	1
Stafford	d											09 26						10 27			10 41		
Penkridge	d																				10 49		
Wolverhampton 7	a											09 40						10 42			11 00		
	d	08 05			08 22			09 00	09 05		09 22	09 41		09 59	10 05		10 22	10 43		10 58	11 01	11 05	
Coseley	d				08 27						09 27						10 27						
Tipton	d				08 29						09 29						10 29						
Dudley Port	d				08 31						09 31						10 31						
Sandwell & Dudley	d	08 15			08 35				09 15		09 35				10 15		10 35					11 15	
Smethwick Galton Bridge 7	d				08 37						09 37						10 37						
Smethwick Rolfe Street	d				08 39						09 39						10 39						
Birmingham New Street 12	a	08 24			08 46			09 15	09 24		09 46	09 58		10 14	10 24		10 46	10 59		11 14	11 17	11 26	
	d	08 30	08 34	08 38		09 03	09 14	09 20	09 30	09 34		10 03	10 14	10 20	10 30	10 34		11 03	11 14	11 20		11 30	11 34
Adderley Park	d			08 42						09 38						10 38							11 38
Stechford	d			08 46						09 42						10 42							11 42
Lea Hall	d			08 48						09 44						10 44							11 44
Marston Green	d		08 42	08 52			09 22			09 48			10 22			10 48			11 22				11 48
Birmingham International ✈	a	08 39	08 45	08 55		09 13	09 25	09 31	09 39	09 51		10 13	10 25	10 32	10 39	10 52		11 13	11 25	11 32		11 39	11 51
	d	08 40	08 45			09 14	09 25		09 40	09 51		10 14	10 25		10 40	10 52		11 14	11 25			11 40	11 51
Hampton-in-Arden	d						09 28						10 28						11 28				
Berkswell	d		08 51				09 33						10 33						11 33				
Tile Hill	d		08 54				09 36						10 36						11 36				
Canley	d		08 57				09 40						10 40						11 40				
Coventry	a	08 50	09 00			09 24	09 44		09 50	10 01		10 24	10 44		10 50	11 03		11 24	11 44			11 50	12 01
	d	08 51					09 44		09 51				10 44		10 51				11 44			11 51	
Rugby	d	09 04					09 56		10 04				10 56		11 04				11 56			12 05	
Long Buckby	d						10 06						11 06						12 06				
Northampton	a						10 17						11 17						12 17				
London Euston 15 ⊖	a	10 28							11 31						12 27							13 04	

		LM	VT	VT	XC	VT	LM	LM	VT	LM	LM	AW	LM	VT	VT	XC	VT	LM	LM	VT	LM	AW	LM
			◇1 🛒	◇1 🛒	◇1 ☕	◇1 🛒	◇1	◇1	◇1 🛒	◇1	1	◇ ☕		◇1 🛒	◇1 🛒	◇1 A 🛒☕	◇1 🛒	◇1	◇1	◇1 🛒	1	◇ ☕	
Stafford	d				11 28					12 18						12 25			12 42				
Penkridge	d																		12 49				
Wolverhampton 7	a				11 41											12 40			12 59				
	d	11 22		11 32	11 42	11 45						12 18	12 22		12 32	12 41	12 45		12 59			13 09	13 22
Coseley	d	11 27											12 27										13 27
Tipton	d	11 29											12 29										13 29
Dudley Port	d	11 31											12 31										13 31
Sandwell & Dudley	d	11 35				11 57							12 35				12 55						13 35
Smethwick Galton Bridge 7	d	11 37											12 37										13 37
Smethwick Rolfe Street	d	11 39											12 39										13 39
Birmingham New Street 12	a	11 48		11 55	12 00	12 06						12 33	12 46		12 55	12 58	13 06		13 16			13 24	13 46
	d		11 50		12 03	12 10		12 14	12 30		12 34	12 38		12 50		13 03	13 10	13 14		13 30	13 34	13 37	
Adderley Park	d										12 38										13 38		
Stechford	d										12 42										13 42		
Lea Hall	d										12 44										13 44		
Marston Green	d							12 22			12 48							13 22			13 48		
Birmingham International ✈	a		11 59		12 13	12 19		12 25	12 38		12 51	12 56		12 59		13 13	13 19	13 25		13 38	13 51	13 56	
	d		12 00		12 14	12 20		12 25	12 39		12 51			13 00		13 14	13 20	13 25		13 39	13 51		
Hampton-in-Arden	d							12 28										13 28					
Berkswell	d							12 33										13 33					
Tile Hill	d							12 36			12 58							13 36			13 58		
Canley	d							12 40										13 40					
Coventry	a		12 10		12 24	12 30		12 44	12 49		13 04			13 10		13 24	13 30	13 44		13 49	14 04		
	d		12 11			12 31		12 44	12 51					13 11			13 31	13 44		13 51			
Rugby	d		12 25				12 26	12 56		13 17				13 25				13 56					
Long Buckby	d						12 37	13 06		13 28								14 06					
Northampton	a						12 48	13 17		13 39								14 17					
London Euston 15 ⊖	a		13 19			13 37	13 53		13 57	14 53				14 17			14 37			14 57			

A 🛒 from Birmingham New Street
☕ to Wolverhampton

Table 68

Sundays
until 19 June

Stafford - Wolverhampton - Birmingham - Coventry - Northampton

		VT	VT	XC	VT	LM	LM	LM	VT	AW	XC	LM	LM	LM	VT	VT	XC	VT	LM	LM	VT	AW
		◇1 🛒	◇1 🛒	◇1 ☕	◇1 🛒	◇1	◇1	◇1	◇1 🛒	◇ ☕	◇1 ☕	◇1	1		◇1 🛒	◇1 🛒	◇1 ☕	◇1 🛒	◇1	◇1	◇1 🛒	◇ ☕
Stafford	d			13 25				13 43				14 18					14 25			14 43		
Penkridge	d							13 49												14 49		
Wolverhampton 7	a			13 40				13 58									14 40			14 58		
	d		13 32	13 41	13 45			13 58		14 09	14 15			14 22		14 33	14 41	14 45		14 58		15 09
Coseley	d													14 27								
Tipton	d													14 29								
Dudley Port	d													14 31								
Sandwell & Dudley	d				13 56									14 35				14 56				
Smethwick Galton Bridge 7	d													14 37								
Smethwick Rolfe Street	d													14 39								
Birmingham New Street 12	a		13 55	13 58	14 05			14 15		14 24	14 31			14 46		14 55	14 58	15 05		15 15		15 25
	d	13 50		14 03	14 10		14 14		14 30	14 37			14 34		14 50		15 03	15 10	15 14		15 30	15 37
Adderley Park	d												14 38									
Stechford	d												14 42									
Lea Hall	d												14 44									
Marston Green	d						14 22						14 48						15 22			
Birmingham International ✈	a	13 59		14 13	14 19		14 25		14 38	14 56			14 51		14 59		15 13	15 19	15 25		15 38	15 56
	d	14 01		14 14	14 20		14 25		14 39				14 51		15 01		15 14	15 20	15 25		15 39	
Hampton-in-Arden	d						14 28												15 28			
Berkswell	d						14 33												15 33			
Tile Hill	d						14 36						14 58						15 36			
Canley	d						14 40												15 40			
Coventry	a	14 11		14 24	14 30		14 44		14 49				15 04		15 11		15 24	15 30	15 44		15 49	
	d	14 11			14 31		14 44		14 51						15 11			15 31	15 44		15 51	
Rugby	d	14 26				14 26	14 56					15 17			15 26				15 56			
Long Buckby	d					14 37	15 06					15 28							16 06			
Northampton	a					14 48	15 17					15 39							16 17			
London Euston 15 ⊖	a	15 17			15 37	15 53			15 57			16 53			16 17			16 37			16 57	

		XC	LM	LM	VT	VT	XC	VT	LM	LM	LM	VT	AW	XC	LM	LM	LM	VT	VT	XC	VT	LM	LM
		◇1 ☕	1		◇1 🛒	◇1 🛒	◇1 ☕	◇1 🛒	◇1	◇1	◇1	◇1 🛒	◇ ☕	◇1 ☕	◇1	1		◇1 🛒	◇1 🛒	◇1 ☕	◇1 🛒	◇1	◇1
Stafford	d						15 25				15 43				16 18					16 25			16 43
Penkridge	d										15 49												16 49
Wolverhampton 7	a						15 40				15 58									16 40			16 58
	d	15 15		15 22		15 32	15 41	15 45			15 58		16 10	16 15			16 22		16 32	16 41	16 45		16 58
Coseley	d			15 27													16 27						
Tipton	d			15 29													16 29						
Dudley Port	d			15 31													16 31						
Sandwell & Dudley	d			15 35				15 56									16 35				16 56		
Smethwick Galton Bridge 7	d			15 37													16 37						
Smethwick Rolfe Street	d			15 39													16 39						
Birmingham New Street 12	a	15 31		15 46		15 55	15 58	16 05			16 15		16 26	16 31			16 46		16 55	16 58	17 05		17 15
	d		15 34		15 50		16 03	16 10		16 14		16 30	16 36			16 34		16 50		17 03	17 10	17 14	
Adderley Park	d		15 38													16 38							
Stechford	d		15 42													16 42							
Lea Hall	d		15 44													16 44							
Marston Green	d		15 48							16 22						16 48						17 22	
Birmingham International ✈	a		15 51		15 59		16 13	16 19		16 25		16 38	16 56			16 51		16 59		17 13	17 19	17 25	
	d		15 51		16 01		16 14	16 20		16 25		16 39				16 51		17 01		17 14	17 20	17 25	
Hampton-in-Arden	d									16 28												17 28	
Berkswell	d									16 33												17 33	
Tile Hill	d		15 58							16 36						16 58						17 36	
Canley	d									16 40												17 40	
Coventry	a		16 04		16 11		16 24	16 30		16 44		16 49				17 05		17 11		17 24	17 30	17 44	
	d				16 11			16 31		16 44		16 51						17 11			17 31	17 44	
Rugby	d				16 24				16 25	16 56					17 18			17 26				17 56	
Long Buckby	d								16 37	17 06					17 28							18 06	
Northampton	a								16 48	17 17					17 39							18 17	
London Euston 15 ⊖	a				17 20			17 37	17 53			17 57			18 53			18 17			18 37		

Table 68

Sundays until 19 June

Stafford - Wolverhampton - Birmingham - Coventry - Northampton

		VT	XC	LM	AW	LM	VT	VT	XC	VT	LM	LM	LM	VT	AW	XC	LM	LM	LM	VT	VT	XC
		◇1 ⊏	◇1 ⫪	1	◇ ⫪		◇1 ⊏	◇1 ⊏	◇1 ⫪	◇1 ⊏	◇1	◇1	◇1	◇1 ⊏	◇ ⫪	◇1 ⫪	◇1	1		◇1 ⊏	◇1 ⊏	◇1 ⫪
Stafford	d								17 26				17 43				18 18					18 26
Penkridge	d												17 49									
Wolverhampton 7	a								17 40				17 58									18 40
	d		17 15		17 19	17 22		17 32	17 41	17 45			17 58		18 10	18 15			18 22		18 33	18 41
Coseley	d					17 27													18 27			
Tipton	d					17 29													18 29			
Dudley Port	d					17 31													18 31			
Sandwell & Dudley	d					17 35				17 56									18 35			
Smethwick Galton Bridge 7	d					17 37													18 37			
Smethwick Rolfe Street	d					17 39													18 39			
Birmingham New Street 12	a		17 31		17 35	17 46		17 55	17 58	18 05			18 15		18 28	18 31			18 46		18 55	18 58
	d	17 30		17 34	17 38		17 50		18 03	18 10		18 14		18 30	18 37			18 34		18 50		19 03
Adderley Park	d			17 38														18 38				
Stechford	d			17 42														18 42				
Lea Hall	d			17 44														18 44				
Marston Green	d			17 48								18 22						18 48				
Birmingham International ✈	a	17 38		17 51	17 56		17 59		18 13	18 19		18 25		18 38	18 56			18 51		18 59		19 13
	d	17 39		17 51			18 01		18 14	18 20		18 25		18 39				18 51		19 01		19 14
Hampton-in-Arden	d											18 28										
Berkswell	d											18 33										
Tile Hill	d			17 58								18 36						18 58				
Canley	d											18 40										
Coventry	a	17 49		18 05			18 11		18 24	18 30		18 44		18 49				19 05		19 11		19 24
	d	17 51					18 11			18 31		18 44		18 51						19 11		
Rugby	d						18 26				18 24	18 56					19 18			19 26		
Long Buckby	d										18 37	19 06					19 28					
Northampton	a										18 48	19 17					19 39					
London Euston 15 ⊖	a	18 57					19 17			19 37	19 53			19 57			20 53			20 17		

		VT	LM	LM	VT	AW	XC	LM	LM	VT	XC	VT	LM	LM	LM	VT	AW	XC	LM	LM	LM	VT	XC
		◇1 ⊏	◇1	◇1	◇1 ⊏	◇	◇1 ⫪	1		◇1 ⊏	◇1 ⫪	◇1 ⊏	◇1	◇1	◇1	◇1 ⊏	◇ ⫪	◇1	◇1	1		◇1 ⊏	◇1 A ⫪
Stafford	d			18 43							19 25				19 43				20 16				20 27
Penkridge	d			18 49											19 49								
Wolverhampton 7	a			18 58							19 40				19 58								20 39
	d	18 45		18 58		19 09	19 15		19 22	19 32	19 41	19 45			19 58		20 09	20 15			20 22	20 33	20 41
Coseley	d								19 27												20 27		
Tipton	d								19 29												20 29		
Dudley Port	d								19 31												20 31		
Sandwell & Dudley	d	18 56							19 35			19 58									20 35		
Smethwick Galton Bridge 7	d								19 37												20 37		
Smethwick Rolfe Street	d								19 39												20 39		
Birmingham New Street 12	a	19 05		19 15		19 27	19 31		19 46	19 55	19 58	20 07			20 15		20 24	20 31			20 46	20 50	21 00
	d	19 10	19 14		19 30	19 37		19 34			20 03	20 10		20 14		20 30	20 37			20 34			21 03
Adderley Park	d							19 38												20 38			
Stechford	d							19 42												20 42			
Lea Hall	d							19 44												20 44			
Marston Green	d		19 22					19 48						20 22						20 48			
Birmingham International ✈	a	19 19	19 25		19 38	19 56		19 51			20 13	20 19		20 25		20 39	20 56			20 51			21 13
	d	19 20	19 25		19 39			19 51			20 14	20 20		20 25		20 40				20 51			21 14
Hampton-in-Arden	d		19 28											20 28									
Berkswell	d		19 33											20 33									
Tile Hill	d		19 36					19 58						20 36						20 58			
Canley	d		19 40											20 40									
Coventry	a	19 30	19 44		19 49			20 05			20 24	20 30		20 44		20 50				21 04			21 23
	d	19 31	19 44		19 51							20 31		20 44		20 51							
Rugby	d		19 56										20 20	20 56		21 05			21 17				
Long Buckby	d		20 06										20 32	21 06					21 28				
Northampton	a		20 17										20 43	21 17					21 39				
London Euston 15 ⊖	a	20 37			20 57							21 48	21 55			22 23			23 14				

A ⫪ to Wolverhampton

Table 68

Sundays until 19 June

Stafford - Wolverhampton - Birmingham - Coventry - Northampton

		LM	LM	VT	LM	AW	XC	LM	AW	LM	LM	VT	LM	AW	VT	XC	LM	VT	VT	LM	LM	XC
		◇1	◇1	◇1 ⊏	1	◇	◇1		◇ ⫪	◇1	◇1	◇1 ⊏	1	◇	◇1 ⊏	◇1		◇1 ⊏	◇1 ⊏	1	◇1	◇1
Stafford	d		20 39				21 09		21 16		21 38				22 02	22 06					22 45	23 05
Penkridge	d		20 45								21 45										22 51	
Wolverhampton 7	a		20 55				21 21		21 34		21 55				22 17	22 20					23 00	23 18
	d		20 58	21 05		21 12	21 22	21 25	21 35		21 58	22 05		22 09	22 18	22 22	22 25	22 32	22 37		23 00	23 19
Coseley	d							21 30									22 30					
Tipton	d							21 32									22 32					
Dudley Port	d							21 34									22 34					
Sandwell & Dudley	d			21 17				21 38				22 15					22 38		22 47			
Smethwick Galton Bridge 7	d							21 40									22 40					
Smethwick Rolfe Street	d							21 42									22 42					
Birmingham New Street 12	a		21 15	21 26		21 29	21 39	21 49	21 52		22 15	22 24		22 28	22 38	22 40	22 49	22 55	22 56		23 17	23 36
	d	21 14		21 30	21 34	21 37			21 55	22 14		22 30	22 34	22 41					23 00	23 14		
Adderley Park	d				21 38								22 38							23 19		
Stechford	d				21 42								22 42							23 22		
Lea Hall	d				21 44								22 45							23 25		
Marston Green	d	21 22			21 48					22 22			22 48							23 28		
Birmingham International ✈	a	21 25		21 39	21 51	21 56			22 09	22 25		22 39	22 51	22 56					23 09	23 31		
	d	21 25		21 40	21 51					22 25		22 40	22 52						23 10	23 32		
Hampton-in-Arden	d	21 28								22 28										23 35		
Berkswell	d	21 33								22 33										23 40		
Tile Hill	d	21 36								22 36										23 43		
Canley	d	21 40								22 40										23 46		
Coventry	a	21 44		21 50	22 01					22 44		22 50	23 01						23 20	23 50		
	d	21 44		21 51						22 44		22 51							23 21			
Rugby	d	21 56		22 04						22 56		23 04							23 34			
Long Buckby	d	22 06								23 06												
Northampton	a	22 17								23 17									23s53			
London Euston 15 ⊖	a			23 25								00 26							01 04			

Sundays 26 June to 31 July

		AW	VT	LM	LM	LM	XC	LM	VT	LM	LM	XC	LM	AW	VT	LM	LM	XC	LM	AW	LM	VT	LM
		🚌	◇1 ⊏	1	1		◇1 ⫪	◇1	◇1 ⊏	1		◇1 ⫪	◇1		◇1 ⊏	1		◇1 ⫪	◇1	◇	◇1	◇1 ⊏	1
Stafford	d											09 26						10 27			10 41		
Penkridge	d																				10 49		
Wolverhampton 7	a											09 40						10 42			11 00		
	d	23p58	08 05			08 22			09 05		09 22	09 41		09 59	10 05		10 22	10 43		10 58	11 01	11 05	
Coseley	d					08 27					09 27						10 27						
Tipton	d					08 29					09 29						10 29						
Dudley Port	d					08 31					09 31						10 31						
Sandwell & Dudley	d		08 15			08 35			09 15		09 35				10 15		10 35					11 15	
Smethwick Galton Bridge 7	d					08 37					09 37						10 37						
Smethwick Rolfe Street	d					08 39					09 39						10 39						
Birmingham New Street 12	a	00 48	08 24			08 46			09 24		09 46	09 58		10 14	10 24		10 46	10 59		11 14	11 17	11 26	
	d		08 30	08 34	08 38		09 03	09 14	09 30	09 34		10 03	10 14	10 20	10 30	10 34		11 03	11 14	11 20		11 30	11 34
Adderley Park	d				08 42					09 38						10 38							11 38
Stechford	d				08 46					09 42						10 42							11 42
Lea Hall	d				08 48					09 44						10 44							11 44
Marston Green	d			08 42	08 52			09 22		09 48			10 22			10 48			11 22				11 48
Birmingham International ✈	a		08 39	08 45	08 55		09 13	09 25	09 39	09 51		10 13	10 25	10 32	10 39	10 52		11 13	11 25	11 32		11 39	11 51
	d		08 40	08 45			09 14	09 25	09 40	09 51		10 14	10 25		10 40	10 52		11 14	11 25			11 40	11 51
Hampton-in-Arden	d							09 28					10 28						11 28				
Berkswell	d			08 51				09 33					10 33						11 33				
Tile Hill	d			08 54				09 36					10 36						11 36				
Canley	d			08 57				09 40					10 40						11 40				
Coventry	a		08 50	09 00			09 24	09 44	09 50	10 01		10 24	10 44		10 50	11 03		11 24	11 44			11 50	12 01
	d		08 51					09 44	09 51				10 44		10 51				11 44			11 51	
Rugby	d		09 04					09 56	10 04				10 56		11 04				11 56			12 05	
Long Buckby	d							10 06					11 06						12 06				
Northampton	a							10 17					11 17						12 17				
London Euston 15 ⊖	a		10 28						11 31						12 27							13 04	

Table 68

Sundays

26 June to 31 July

Stafford - Wolverhampton - Birmingham - Coventry - Northampton

Station		LM	VT	VT	XC	VT	LM	LM	VT	LM	LM	AW	LM	VT	VT	VT	XC	VT	LM	LM	VT	LM	AW
			◇1	◇1	◇1	◇1	◇1	◇1	◇1	◇1	1	◇		◇1 A	◇1 B	◇1	◇1	◇1	◇1	◇1	◇1	1	◇
Stafford	d				11 28					12 18							12 25			12 42			
Penkridge	d																			12 49			
Wolverhampton 7	a				11 41												12 40			12 59			
	d	11 22		11 32	11 42	11 45						12 18	12 22			12 32	12 41	12 45		12 59			13 09
Coseley	d	11 27											12 27										
Tipton	d	11 29											12 29										
Dudley Port	d	11 31											12 31										
Sandwell & Dudley	d	11 35				11 57							12 35					12 55					
Smethwick Galton Bridge 7	d	11 37											12 37										
Smethwick Rolfe Street	d	11 39											12 39										
Birmingham New Street 12	a	11 48		11 55	12 00	12 06						12 33	12 46			12 55	12 58	13 06		13 16			13 24
	d		11 50		12 03	12 10		12 14	12 30		12 34	12 38		12 50	12 50		13 03	13 10	13 14		13 30	13 34	13 37
Adderley Park	d										12 38											13 38	
Stechford	d										12 42											13 42	
Lea Hall	d										12 44											13 44	
Marston Green	d							12 22			12 48								13 22			13 48	
Birmingham International ✈	a		11 59		12 13	12 19		12 25	12 38		12 51	12 56		12 59	12 59		13 13	13 19	13 25		13 38	13 51	13 56
	d		12 00		12 14	12 20		12 25	12 39		12 51			13 00	13 00		13 14	13 20	13 25		13 39	13 51	
Hampton-in-Arden	d							12 28											13 28				
Berkswell	d							12 33											13 33				
Tile Hill	d							12 36			12 58								13 36			13 58	
Canley	d							12 40											13 40				
Coventry	a		12 10		12 24	12 30		12 44	12 49		13 04			13 10	13 10		13 24	13 30	13 44		13 49	14 04	
	d		12 11			12 31		12 44	12 51					13 11	13 11			13 31	13 44		13 51		
Rugby	d		12 25				12 26	12 56		13 17				13 25	13 25				13 56				
Long Buckby	d						12 37	13 06		13 28									14 06				
Northampton	a						12 48	13 17		13 39									14 17				
London Euston 15 ⊖	a		13 19			13 37	13 53		13 57	14 53				14 17	14 18			14 37			14 57		

Station		LM	VT	VT	XC	VT	LM	LM	LM	VT	AW	XC	LM	LM	LM	VT	VT	XC	VT	LM	LM	VT
			◇1	◇1	◇1	◇1	◇1	◇1	◇1	◇1	◇	◇1	◇1	1		◇1	◇1	◇1	◇1	◇1	◇1	◇1
Stafford	d				13 25				13 43				14 18					14 25			14 43	
Penkridge	d								13 49												14 49	
Wolverhampton 7	a				13 40				13 58									14 40			14 58	
	d	13 22		13 32	13 41	13 45			13 58		14 09	14 15			14 22		14 33	14 41	14 45		14 58	
Coseley	d	13 27													14 27							
Tipton	d	13 29													14 29							
Dudley Port	d	13 31													14 31							
Sandwell & Dudley	d	13 35				13 56									14 35				14 56			
Smethwick Galton Bridge 7	d	13 37													14 37							
Smethwick Rolfe Street	d	13 39													14 39							
Birmingham New Street 12	a	13 46		13 55	13 58	14 05			14 15		14 24	14 33			14 46		14 55	14 58	15 05		15 15	
	d		13 50		14 03	14 10		14 14		14 30	14 37			14 34		14 50		15 03	15 10	15 14		15 30
Adderley Park	d													14 38								
Stechford	d													14 42								
Lea Hall	d													14 44								
Marston Green	d							14 22						14 48						15 22		
Birmingham International ✈	a		13 59		14 13	14 19		14 25		14 38	14 56			14 51		14 59		15 13	15 19	15 25		15 38
	d		14 01		14 14	14 20		14 25		14 39				14 51		15 01		15 14	15 20	15 25		15 39
Hampton-in-Arden	d							14 28												15 28		
Berkswell	d							14 33												15 33		
Tile Hill	d							14 36						14 58						15 36		
Canley	d							14 40												15 40		
Coventry	a		14 11		14 24	14 30		14 44		14 49				15 04		15 11		15 24	15 30	15 44		15 49
	d		14 11			14 31		14 44		14 51						15 11			15 31	15 44		15 51
Rugby	d		14 26				14 26	14 56					15 17			15 26				15 56		
Long Buckby	d						14 37	15 06					15 28							16 06		
Northampton	a						14 48	15 17					15 39							16 17		
London Euston 15 ⊖	a		15 17			15 37	15 53			15 57			16 53			16 17			16 37			16 57

A 26 June, 3 July, 10 July

B 17 July, 24 July, 31 July

Table 68

Sundays

26 June to 31 July

Stafford - Wolverhampton - Birmingham - Coventry - Northampton

Station		AW	XC	LM	LM	VT	VT	XC	VT	LM	LM	LM	VT	AW	XC	LM	LM	LM	VT	VT	VT	XC	VT
		◇	◇1	1		◇1	◇1	◇1	◇1	◇1	◇1	◇1	◇1	◇	◇1	◇1	1		◇1 A	◇1 B	◇1	◇1	◇1
Stafford	d							15 25				15 43				16 18						16 25	
Penkridge	d											15 49											
Wolverhampton 7	a							15 40				15 58										16 40	
	d	15 09	15 15		15 22		15 32	15 41	15 45			15 58		16 10	16 15			16 22			16 32	16 41	16 45
Coseley	d				15 27													16 27					
Tipton	d				15 29													16 29					
Dudley Port	d				15 31													16 31					
Sandwell & Dudley	d				15 35				15 56									16 35					16 56
Smethwick Galton Bridge 7	d				15 37													16 37					
Smethwick Rolfe Street	d				15 39													16 39					
Birmingham New Street 12	a	15 25	15 30		15 46		15 55	15 58	16 05			16 15		16 26	16 31			16 46			16 55	16 58	17 05
	d	15 37		15 34		15 50		16 03	16 10		16 14		16 30	16 36			16 34		16 50	16 50		17 03	17 10
Adderley Park	d			15 38													16 38						
Stechford	d			15 42													16 42						
Lea Hall	d			15 44													16 44						
Marston Green	d			15 48							16 22						16 48						
Birmingham International ✈	a	15 56		15 51		15 59		16 13	16 19		16 25		16 38	16 56			16 51		16 59	16 59		17 13	17 19
	d			15 51		16 01		16 14	16 20		16 25		16 39				16 51		17 01	17 01		17 14	17 20
Hampton-in-Arden	d										16 28												
Berkswell	d										16 33												
Tile Hill	d			15 58							16 36						16 58						
Canley	d										16 40												
Coventry	a			16 04		16 11		16 24	16 30		16 44		16 49				17 05		17 11	17 11		17 24	17 30
	d					16 11			16 31		16 44		16 51						17 11	17 11			17 31
Rugby	d					16 24				16 25	16 56					17 18			17 26	17 26			
Long Buckby	d									16 37	17 06					17 28							
Northampton	a									16 48	17 17					17 39							
London Euston 15 ⊖	a					17 20			17 37	17 53			17 57			18 53			18 17	18 18			18 37

Station		LM	LM	VT	XC	LM	AW	LM	VT	VT	XC	VT	LM	LM	LM	VT	AW	XC	LM	LM	LM	VT
		◇1	◇1	◇1	◇1	1	◇		◇1	◇1	◇1	◇1	◇1	◇1	◇1	◇1	◇	◇1	◇1	1		◇1
Stafford	d		16 43								17 26				17 43				18 18			
Penkridge	d		16 49												17 49							
Wolverhampton 7	a		16 58								17 40				17 58							
	d		16 58		17 15		17 19	17 22		17 32	17 41	17 45			17 58		18 10	18 15			18 22	
Coseley	d							17 27													18 27	
Tipton	d							17 29													18 29	
Dudley Port	d							17 31													18 31	
Sandwell & Dudley	d							17 35				17 56									18 35	
Smethwick Galton Bridge 7	d							17 37													18 37	
Smethwick Rolfe Street	d							17 39													18 39	
Birmingham New Street 12	a		17 15		17 32		17 35	17 46		17 55	17 58	18 05			18 15		18 28	18 31			18 46	
	d	17 14		17 30		17 34	17 38		17 50		18 03	18 10		18 14		18 30	18 37			18 34		18 50
Adderley Park	d					17 38														18 38		
Stechford	d					17 42														18 42		
Lea Hall	d					17 44														18 44		
Marston Green	d	17 22				17 48								18 22						18 48		
Birmingham International ✈	a	17 25		17 38		17 51	17 55		17 59		18 13	18 19		18 25		18 38	18 56			18 51		18 59
	d	17 25		17 39		17 51			18 01		18 14	18 20		18 25		18 39				18 51		19 01
Hampton-in-Arden	d	17 28												18 28								
Berkswell	d	17 33												18 33								
Tile Hill	d	17 36				17 58								18 36						18 58		
Canley	d	17 40												18 40								
Coventry	a	17 44		17 49		18 05			18 11		18 24	18 30		18 44		18 49				19 05		19 11
	d	17 44		17 51					18 11			18 31		18 44		18 51						19 11
Rugby	d	17 56							18 26				18 24	18 56					19 18			19 26
Long Buckby	d	18 06											18 37	19 06					19 28			
Northampton	a	18 17											18 48	19 17					19 39			
London Euston 15 ⊖	a			18 57					19 17			19 37	19 53			19 57			20 53			20 17

A 26 June, 3 July, 10 July

B 17 July, 24 July, 31 July

Table 68

Sundays
26 June to 31 July

Stafford - Wolverhampton - Birmingham - Coventry - Northampton

Station		VT ◇1	XC ◇1	VT ◇1	LM ◇1	LM ◇1	VT ◇1	AW ◇	XC ◇1	LM 1		LM	VT ◇1	XC ◇1	VT ◇1	LM ◇1	LM ◇1	LM ◇1	VT ◇1	AW ◇		XC ◇1	LM ◇1	LM 1	LM
Stafford	d		18 26			18 43								19 25				19 43					20 16		
Penkridge	d					18 49												19 49							
Wolverhampton 7	a		18 40			18 58								19 40				19 58							
	d	18 33	18 41	18 45		18 58		19 09	19 15			19 22	19 32	19 41	19 45			19 58		20 09		20 15			20 22
Coseley	d											19 27													20 27
Tipton	d											19 29													20 29
Dudley Port	d											19 31													20 31
Sandwell & Dudley	d			18 56								19 35			19 58										20 35
Smethwick Galton Bridge 7	d											19 37													20 37
Smethwick Rolfe Street	d											19 39													20 39
Birmingham New Street 12	a	18 55	18 58	19 05		19 15		19 27	19 32			19 46	19 55	19 58	20 07			20 15		20 24		20 31			20 46
	d		19 03	19 10	19 14		19 30	19 37		19 34				20 03	20 10		20 14		20 30	20 37				20 34	
Adderley Park	d									19 38														20 38	
Stechford	d									19 42														20 42	
Lea Hall	d									19 44														20 44	
Marston Green	d				19 22					19 48							20 22							20 48	
Birmingham International	a		19 13	19 19	19 25		19 38	19 56		19 51				20 13	20 19		20 25		20 39	20 56				20 51	
	d		19 14	19 20	19 25		19 39			19 51				20 14	20 20		20 25		20 40					20 51	
Hampton-in-Arden	d				19 28												20 28								
Berkswell	d				19 33												20 33								
Tile Hill	d				19 36					19 58							20 36							20 58	
Canley	d				19 40												20 40								
Coventry	a		19 24	19 30	19 44		19 49			20 05				20 24	20 30		20 44		20 50					21 04	
	d			19 31	19 44		19 51								20 31		20 44		20 51						
Rugby	d				19 56											20 20	20 56		21 05				21 17		
Long Buckby	d				20 06											20 32	21 06						21 28		
Northampton	a				20 17											20 43	21 17						21 39		
London Euston 15 ⊖	a			20 37			20 57								21 48	21 55			22 23				23 14		

Station		VT ◇1	XC ◇1 A	LM ◇1	LM ◇1	VT ◇1		LM 1	AW ◇	XC ◇1	LM	AW ◇	LM ◇1	LM ◇1	VT ◇1	LM 1		AW ◇	VT ◇1	XC ◇1	LM	VT ◇1	VT ◇1	LM 1	LM ◇1
Stafford	d		20 27		20 39					21 09		21 16		21 38					22 02	22 06					22 45
Penkridge	d				20 45									21 45											22 51
Wolverhampton 7	a		20 39		20 55					21 21		21 34		21 55					22 17	22 20					23 00
	d	20 33	20 41		20 58	21 05			21 12	21 22	21 25	21 35		21 58	22 05			22 09	22 18	22 22	22 25	22 32	22 37		23 00
Coseley	d										21 30										22 30				
Tipton	d										21 32										22 32				
Dudley Port	d										21 34										22 34				
Sandwell & Dudley	d					21 17					21 38				22 15						22 38		22 47		
Smethwick Galton Bridge 7	d										21 40										22 40				
Smethwick Rolfe Street	d										21 42										22 42				
Birmingham New Street 12	a	20 50	21 00		21 15	21 26			21 29	21 39	21 49	21 52		22 15	22 24			22 28	22 38	22 40	22 49	22 55	22 56		23 17
	d		21 03	21 14		21 30		21 34	21 37			21 55	22 14		22 30	22 34		22 41					23 00	23 14	
Adderley Park	d							21 38								22 38								23 19	
Stechford	d							21 42								22 42								23 22	
Lea Hall	d							21 44								22 45								23 25	
Marston Green	d			21 22				21 48					22 22			22 48								23 28	
Birmingham International	a		21 13	21 25		21 39		21 51	21 56			22 09	22 25		22 39	22 51		22 56					23 09	23 31	
	d		21 14	21 25		21 40		21 51					22 25		22 40	22 52							23 10	23 32	
Hampton-in-Arden	d			21 28									22 28											23 35	
Berkswell	d			21 33									22 33											23 40	
Tile Hill	d			21 36									22 36											23 43	
Canley	d			21 40									22 40											23 46	
Coventry	a		21 23	21 44		21 50		22 01					22 44		22 50	23 01							23 20	23 50	
	d			21 44		21 51							22 44		22 51								23 21		
Rugby	d			21 56		22 04							22 56		23 04								23 34		
Long Buckby	d			22 06									23 06												
Northampton	a			22 17									23 17										23s53		
London Euston 15 ⊖	a					23 25									00 26								01 04		

A to Wolverhampton

Table 68

Sundays
26 June to 31 July

Stafford - Wolverhampton - Birmingham - Coventry - Northampton

Station		XC ◇1
Stafford	d	23 05
Penkridge	d	
Wolverhampton 7	a	23 18
	d	23 19
Coseley	d	
Tipton	d	
Dudley Port	d	
Sandwell & Dudley	d	
Smethwick Galton Bridge 7	d	
Smethwick Rolfe Street	d	
Birmingham New Street 12	a	23 36
	d	
Adderley Park	d	
Stechford	d	
Lea Hall	d	
Marston Green	d	
Birmingham International	a	
	d	
Hampton-in-Arden	d	
Berkswell	d	
Tile Hill	d	
Canley	d	
Coventry	a	
Rugby	d	
Long Buckby	d	
Northampton	a	
London Euston 15 ⊖	a	

Sundays
7 August to 11 September

Station		VT ◇1	LM 1	LM 1	LM	XC ◇1	LM ◇1	AW	VT ◇1	LM 1		LM	XC ◇1	LM ◇1	AW	VT ◇1	LM 1	LM	XC ◇1	LM ◇1		AW ◇	LM ◇1	VT ◇1	LM 1
Stafford	d												09 26						10 27				10 41		
Penkridge	d																						10 49		
Wolverhampton 7	a												09 40						10 42				11 00		
	d	08 05			08 22			09 00	09 05			09 22	09 41		09 59	10 05		10 22	10 43			10 58	11 01	11 05	
Coseley	d				08 27							09 27						10 27							
Tipton	d				08 29							09 29						10 29							
Dudley Port	d				08 31							09 31						10 31							
Sandwell & Dudley	d	08 15			08 35				09 15			09 35				10 15		10 35						11 15	
Smethwick Galton Bridge 7	d				08 37							09 37						10 37							
Smethwick Rolfe Street	d				08 39							09 39						10 39							
Birmingham New Street 12	a	08 24			08 46			09 15	09 24			09 46	09 58		10 14	10 24		10 46	10 59			11 14	11 17	11 26	
	d	08 30	08 34	08 38		09 03	09 14	09 20	09 30	09 34			10 03	10 14	10 20	10 30	10 34		11 03	11 14		11 20		11 30	11 34
Adderley Park	d			08 42						09 38							10 38								11 38
Stechford	d			08 46						09 42							10 42								11 42
Lea Hall	d			08 48						09 44							10 44								11 44
Marston Green	d		08 42	08 52			09 22			09 48				10 22			10 48			11 22					11 48
Birmingham International	a	08 39	08 45	08 55		09 13	09 25	09 31	09 39	09 51			10 13	10 25	10 32	10 39	10 52		11 13	11 25		11 32		11 39	11 51
	d	08 40	08 45			09 14	09 25		09 40	09 51			10 14	10 25		10 40	10 52		11 14	11 25				11 40	11 51
Hampton-in-Arden	d						09 28							10 28						11 28					
Berkswell	d		08 51				09 33							10 33						11 33					
Tile Hill	d		08 54				09 36							10 36						11 36					
Canley	d		08 57				09 40							10 40						11 40					
Coventry	a	08 50	09 00			09 33	09 44		09 50	10 01			10 33	10 44		10 50	11 03		11 28	11 44				11 50	12 01
	d	08 51					09 44		09 51					10 44		10 51				11 44				11 51	
Rugby	d	09 04					09 56		10 04					10 56		11 04				11 56				12 05	
Long Buckby	d						10 06							11 06						12 06					
Northampton	a						10 17							11 17						12 17					
London Euston 15 ⊖	a	10 28							11 31							12 27								13 04	

Table 68

Sundays
7 August to 11 September

Stafford - Wolverhampton - Birmingham - Coventry - Northampton

		LM	VT ◇1 ⊡	VT ◇1 ⊡	XC ◇1 ⌶	VT ◇1 ⊡	LM ◇1	LM ◇1	VT ◇1 ⊡	LM ◇1	LM 1	AW ◇ ⌶	LM	VT ◇1 ⊡	VT ◇1 ⊡	XC ◇1 ⌶	VT ◇1 ⊡	LM ◇1	LM ◇1	VT ◇1 ⊡	LM 1	AW ◇ ⌶	LM
Stafford	d				11 28					12 18						12 25			12 42				
Penkridge	d																		12 49				
Wolverhampton 7	a				11 41											12 40			12 59				
	d	11 22		11 32	11 42	11 45						12 18	12 22		12 32	12 41	12 45		12 59			13 09	13 22
Coseley	d	11 27											12 27										13 27
Tipton	d	11 29											12 29										13 29
Dudley Port	d	11 31											12 31										13 31
Sandwell & Dudley	d	11 35				11 57							12 35				12 55						13 35
Smethwick Galton Bridge 7	d	11 37											12 37										13 37
Smethwick Rolfe Street	d	11 39											12 39										13 39
Birmingham New Street 12	a	11 48		11 55	12 00	12 06						12 33	12 46		12 55	12 58	13 06		13 16			13 24	13 46
	d		11 50		12 03	12 10		12 14	12 30		12 34	12 38		12 50		13 03	13 10	13 14		13 30	13 34	13 37	
Adderley Park	d										12 38										13 38		
Stechford	d										12 42										13 42		
Lea Hall	d										12 44										13 44		
Marston Green	d							12 22			12 48							13 22			13 48		
Birmingham International ✈	a		11 59		12 13	12 19		12 25	12 38		12 51	12 56		12 59		13 13	13 19	13 25		13 38	13 51	13 56	
	d		12 00		12 14	12 20		12 25	12 39		12 51			13 00		13 14	13 20	13 25		13 39	13 51		
Hampton-in-Arden	d							12 28										13 28					
Berkswell	d							12 33										13 33					
Tile Hill	d							12 36			12 58							13 36			13 58		
Canley	d							12 40										13 40					
Coventry	a		12 10		12 27	12 30		12 44	12 49		13 04			13 10		13 27	13 30	13 44		13 49	14 04		
	d		12 11			12 31		12 44	12 51					13 11			13 31	13 44		13 51			
Rugby	d		12 25				12 26	12 56		13 17				13 25				13 56					
Long Buckby	d						12 37	13 06		13 28								14 06					
Northampton	a						12 48	13 17		13 39								14 17					
London Euston 15 ⊖	a		13 19			13 37	13 53		13 57	14 53				14 18			14 37			14 57			

		VT ◇1 ⊡	VT ◇1 ⊡	XC ◇1 ⌶	VT ◇1 ⊡	LM ◇1	LM ◇1	LM ◇1	VT ◇1 ⊡	AW ◇ ⌶	XC ◇1 ⌶	LM ◇1	LM 1	LM	VT ◇1 ⊡	VT ◇1 ⊡	XC ◇1 ⌶	VT ◇1 ⊡	LM ◇1	LM ◇1	VT ◇1 ⊡	AW ◇ ⌶
Stafford	d			13 25				13 43				14 18					14 25			14 43		
Penkridge	d							13 49												14 49		
Wolverhampton 7	a			13 40				13 58									14 40			14 58		
	d		13 32	13 41	13 45			13 58		14 09	14 15			14 22		14 33	14 41	14 45		14 58		15 09
Coseley	d													14 27								
Tipton	d													14 29								
Dudley Port	d													14 31								
Sandwell & Dudley	d				13 56									14 35				14 56				
Smethwick Galton Bridge 7	d													14 37								
Smethwick Rolfe Street	d													14 39								
Birmingham New Street 12	a		13 55	13 58	14 05			14 15		14 24	14 31			14 46		14 55	14 58	15 05		15 15		15 25
	d	13 50		14 03	14 10		14 14		14 30	14 37			14 34		14 50		15 03	15 10	15 14		15 30	15 37
Adderley Park	d												14 38									
Stechford	d												14 42									
Lea Hall	d												14 44									
Marston Green	d						14 22						14 48						15 22			
Birmingham International ✈	a	13 59		14 13	14 19		14 25		14 38	14 56			14 51		14 59		15 13	15 19	15 25		15 38	15 56
	d	14 01		14 14	14 20		14 25		14 39				14 51		15 01		15 14	15 20	15 25		15 39	
Hampton-in-Arden	d						14 28												15 28			
Berkswell	d						14 33												15 33			
Tile Hill	d						14 36						14 58						15 36			
Canley	d						14 40												15 40			
Coventry	a	14 11		14 24	14 30		14 44		14 49				15 04		15 11		15 24	15 30	15 44		15 49	
	d	14 11			14 31		14 44		14 51						15 11			15 31	15 44		15 51	
Rugby	d	14 26				14 26	14 56					15 17			15 26				15 56			
Long Buckby	d					14 37	15 06					15 28							16 06			
Northampton	a					14 48	15 17					15 39							16 17			
London Euston 15 ⊖	a	15 17			15 37	15 53			15 57			16 53			16 17			16 37			16 57	

Table 68

Sundays
7 August to 11 September

Stafford - Wolverhampton - Birmingham - Coventry - Northampton

		XC ◇1 ⌶	LM 1	LM	VT ◇1 ⊡	VT ◇1 ⊡	XC ◇1 ⌶	VT ◇1 ⊡	LM ◇1	LM ◇1	LM ◇1	VT ◇1 ⊡	AW ◇ ⌶	XC ◇1 ⌶	LM ◇1	LM 1	LM	VT ◇1 ⊡	VT ◇1 ⊡	XC ◇1 ⌶	VT ◇1 ⊡	LM ◇1	LM ◇1
Stafford	d						15 25				15 43				16 18					16 25			16 43
Penkridge	d										15 49												16 49
Wolverhampton 7	a						15 40				15 58									16 40			16 58
	d	15 15		15 22		15 32	15 41	15 45			15 58		16 10	16 15			16 22		16 32	16 41	16 45		16 58
Coseley	d			15 27													16 27						
Tipton	d			15 29													16 29						
Dudley Port	d			15 31													16 31						
Sandwell & Dudley	d			15 35				15 56									16 35				16 56		
Smethwick Galton Bridge 7	d			15 37													16 37						
Smethwick Rolfe Street	d			15 39													16 39						
Birmingham New Street 12	a	15 31		15 46		15 55	15 58	16 05			16 15		16 26	16 31			16 46		16 55	16 58	17 05		17 15
	d		15 34		15 50		16 03	16 10		16 14		16 30	16 36			16 34		16 50		17 03	17 10	17 14	
Adderley Park	d		15 38													16 38							
Stechford	d		15 42													16 42							
Lea Hall	d		15 44													16 44							
Marston Green	d		15 48							16 22						16 48						17 22	
Birmingham International ✈	a		15 51		15 59		16 13	16 19		16 25		16 38	16 56			16 51		16 59		17 13	17 19	17 25	
	d		15 51		16 01		16 14	16 20		16 25		16 39				16 51		17 01		17 14	17 20	17 25	
Hampton-in-Arden	d									16 28												17 28	
Berkswell	d									16 33												17 33	
Tile Hill	d		15 58							16 36						16 58						17 36	
Canley	d									16 40												17 40	
Coventry	a		16 04		16 11		16 24	16 30		16 44		16 49				17 05		17 11		17 24	17 30	17 44	
	d				16 11			16 31		16 44		16 51						17 11			17 31	17 44	
Rugby	d				16 24				16 25	16 56					17 18			17 26				17 56	
Long Buckby	d								16 37	17 06					17 28							18 06	
Northampton	a								16 48	17 17					17 39							18 17	
London Euston 15 ⊖	a				17 20			17 37	17 53			17 57			18 53			18 18			18 37		

		VT ◇1 ⊡	XC ◇1 ⌶	LM 1	AW ◇ ⌶	LM	VT ◇1 ⊡	VT ◇1 ⊡	XC ◇1 ⌶	VT ◇1 ⊡	LM ◇1	LM ◇1	LM ◇1	VT ◇1 ⊡	AW ◇ ⌶	XC ◇1 ⌶	LM ◇1	LM 1	LM	VT ◇1 ⊡	VT ◇1 ⊡	XC ◇1 ⌶
Stafford	d								17 26				17 43				18 18					18 26
Penkridge	d												17 49									
Wolverhampton 7	a								17 40				17 58									18 40
	d		17 15		17 19	17 22		17 32	17 41	17 45			17 58		18 10	18 15			18 22		18 33	18 41
Coseley	d					17 27													18 27			
Tipton	d					17 29													18 29			
Dudley Port	d					17 31													18 31			
Sandwell & Dudley	d					17 35				17 56									18 35			
Smethwick Galton Bridge 7	d					17 37													18 37			
Smethwick Rolfe Street	d					17 39													18 39			
Birmingham New Street 12	a		17 31		17 35	17 46		17 55	17 58	18 05			18 15		18 28	18 31			18 46		18 55	18 58
	d	17 30		17 34	17 38		17 50		18 03	18 10		18 14		18 30	18 37			18 34		18 50		19 03
Adderley Park	d			17 38														18 38				
Stechford	d			17 42														18 42				
Lea Hall	d			17 44														18 44				
Marston Green	d			17 48								18 22						18 48				
Birmingham International ✈	a	17 38		17 51	17 55		17 59		18 13	18 19		18 25		18 38	18 56			18 51		18 59		19 13
	d	17 39		17 51			18 01		18 14	18 20		18 25		18 39				18 51		19 01		19 14
Hampton-in-Arden	d											18 28										
Berkswell	d											18 33										
Tile Hill	d			17 58								18 36						18 58				
Canley	d											18 40										
Coventry	a	17 49		18 05			18 11		18 24	18 30		18 44		18 49				19 05		19 11		19 24
	d	17 51					18 11			18 31		18 44		18 51						19 11		
Rugby	d						18 26				18 24	18 56					19 18			19 26		
Long Buckby	d										18 37	19 06					19 28					
Northampton	a										18 48	19 17					19 39					
London Euston 15 ⊖	a	18 57					19 17			19 37	19 53			19 57			20 53			20 17		

Table 68

Sundays

7 August to 11 September

Stafford - Wolverhampton - Birmingham - Coventry - Northampton

		VT	LM	LM	VT	AW	XC	LM	LM	VT		XC	VT	LM	LM	LM	VT	AW	XC	LM		LM	LM	VT	XC
		◇1	◇1	◇1	◇1	◇	◇1	1		◇1		◇1	◇1	◇1	◇1	◇1	◇1	◇	◇1	◇1		1		◇1	◇1
																									A
		⊡			⊡		⊼			⊡		⊼	⊡				⊡	⊼						⊡	⊼
Stafford	d			18 43								19 25				19 43				20 16					20 27
Penkridge	d			18 49												19 49									
Wolverhampton 7	a			18 58								19 40				19 58									20 39
	d	18 45		18 58		19 09	19 15		19 22	19 32		19 41	19 45			19 58		20 09	20 15				20 22	20 33	20 41
Coseley	d								19 27														20 27		
Tipton	d								19 29														20 29		
Dudley Port	d								19 31														20 31		
Sandwell & Dudley	d	18 56							19 35				19 58										20 35		
Smethwick Galton Bridge 7	d								19 37														20 37		
Smethwick Rolfe Street	d								19 39														20 39		
Birmingham New Street 12	a	19 05		19 15		19 27	19 31		19 46	19 55		19 58	20 07			20 15		20 24	20 31				20 46	20 50	21 00
	d	19 10	19 14		19 30	19 37		19 34				20 03	20 10		20 14		20 30	20 37				20 34			21 03
Adderley Park	d							19 38														20 38			
Stechford	d							19 42														20 42			
Lea Hall	d							19 44														20 44			
Marston Green	d		19 22					19 48							20 22							20 48			
Birmingham International ✈	a	19 19	19 25		19 38	19 56		19 51				20 13	20 19		20 25		20 39	20 56				20 51			21 13
	d	19 20	19 25		19 39			19 51				20 14	20 20		20 25		20 40					20 51			21 14
Hampton-in-Arden	d		19 28												20 28										
Berkswell	d		19 33												20 33										
Tile Hill	d		19 36					19 58							20 36							20 58			
Canley	d		19 40												20 40										
Coventry	a	19 30	19 44		19 49			20 05				20 24	20 30		20 44		20 50					21 04			21 23
	d	19 31	19 44		19 51								20 31		20 44		20 51								
Rugby	d		19 56											20 20	20 56		21 05			21 17					
Long Buckby	d		20 06											20 32	21 06					21 28					
Northampton	a		20 17											20 43	21 17					21 39					
London Euston 15 ⊖	a	20 37			20 57								21 48	21 55			22 23			23 14					

		LM	LM	VT	LM	AW		XC	LM	AW	LM	LM	VT	LM	AW	VT		XC	LM	VT	VT	LM	LM	XC	
		◇1	◇1	◇1	1	◇		◇1		◇	◇1	◇1	◇1	1	◇	◇1		◇1		◇1	◇1	1	◇1	◇1	
				⊡						⊼			⊡			⊡				⊡	⊡				
Stafford	d		20 39					21 09		21 16		21 38				22 02		22 06					22 45	23 05	
Penkridge	d		20 45									21 45											22 51		
Wolverhampton 7	a		20 55					21 21		21 34		21 55				22 17		22 20					23 00	23 18	
	d		20 58	21 05		21 12		21 22	21 25	21 35		21 58	22 05		22 09	22 18		22 22	22 25	22 32	22 37		23 00	23 19	
Coseley	d								21 30										22 30						
Tipton	d								21 32										22 32						
Dudley Port	d								21 34										22 34						
Sandwell & Dudley	d			21 17					21 38				22 15						22 38		22 47				
Smethwick Galton Bridge 7	d								21 40										22 40						
Smethwick Rolfe Street	d								21 42										22 42						
Birmingham New Street 12	a		21 15	21 26		21 29		21 39	21 49	21 52		22 15	22 24		22 28	22 38		22 40	22 49	22 55	22 56		23 17	23 36	
	d	21 14		21 30	21 34	21 37				21 55	22 14		22 30	22 34	22 41						23 00	23 14			
Adderley Park	d				21 38									22 38								23 19			
Stechford	d				21 42									22 42								23 22			
Lea Hall	d				21 44									22 45								23 25			
Marston Green	d	21 22			21 48						22 22			22 48								23 28			
Birmingham International ✈	a	21 25		21 39	21 51	21 56				22 09	22 25		22 39	22 51	22 56						23 09	23 31			
	d	21 25		21 40	21 51						22 25		22 40	22 52							23 10	23 32			
Hampton-in-Arden	d	21 28									22 28											23 35			
Berkswell	d	21 33									22 33											23 40			
Tile Hill	d	21 36									22 36											23 43			
Canley	d	21 40									22 40											23 46			
Coventry	a	21 44		21 50	22 01						22 44		22 50	23 01							23 20	23 50			
	d	21 44		21 51							22 44		22 51								23 21				
Rugby	d	21 56		22 04							22 56		23 04								23 34				
Long Buckby	d	22 06									23 06														
Northampton	a	22 17									23 17										23s53				
London Euston 15 ⊖	a			23 25									00 26								01 04				

A ⊼ to Wolverhampton

Table 68

Sundays

18 September to 23 October

Stafford - Wolverhampton - Birmingham - Coventry - Northampton

		VT	LM	LM	LM	XC	LM	AW	VT	LM		LM	XC	LM	AW	VT	LM	LM	XC	LM		AW	LM	VT	LM
		◇1	1	1		◇1	◇1		◇1	1			◇1	◇1		◇1	1		◇1	◇1		◇	◇1	◇1	1
													A						A						
		⊡				⊼			⊡				⊡⊼			⊡			⊡⊼					⊡	
Stafford	d												09 26						10 27				10 41		
Penkridge	d																						10 49		
Wolverhampton 7	a												09 40						10 42				11 00		
	d	08 05			08 22			09 00	09 05			09 22	09 41		09 59	10 05		10 22	10 43			10 58	11 01	11 05	
Coseley	d				08 27							09 27						10 27							
Tipton	d				08 29							09 29						10 29							
Dudley Port	d				08 31							09 31						10 31							
Sandwell & Dudley	d	08 15			08 35				09 15			09 35				10 15		10 35						11 15	
Smethwick Galton Bridge 7	d				08 37							09 37						10 37							
Smethwick Rolfe Street	d				08 39							09 39						10 39							
Birmingham New Street 12	a	08 24			08 46			09 15	09 24			09 46	09 58		10 14	10 24		10 46	10 59			11 14	11 17	11 26	
	d	08 30	08 34	08 38		09 03	09 14	09 20	09 30	09 34			10 03	10 14	10 20	10 30	10 34		11 03	11 14		11 20		11 30	11 34
Adderley Park	d			08 42						09 38							10 38								11 38
Stechford	d			08 46						09 42							10 42								11 42
Lea Hall	d			08 48						09 44							10 44								11 44
Marston Green	d		08 42	08 52			09 22			09 48				10 22			10 48			11 22					11 48
Birmingham International ✈	a	08 39	08 45	08 55		09 13	09 25	09 32	09 39	09 51			10 13	10 25	10 32	10 39	10 52		11 13	11 25		11 32		11 39	11 51
	d	08 40	08 45			09 14	09 25		09 40	09 51			10 14	10 25		10 40	10 52		11 14	11 25				11 40	11 51
Hampton-in-Arden	d						09 28							10 28						11 28					
Berkswell	d		08 51				09 33							10 33						11 33					
Tile Hill	d		08 54				09 36							10 36						11 36					
Canley	d		08 57				09 40							10 40						11 40					
Coventry	a	08 50	09 00			09 24	09 44		09 50	10 01			10 24	10 44		10 50	11 03		11 24	11 44				11 50	12 01
	d	08 51					09 44		09 51					10 44		10 51				11 44				11 51	
Rugby	d	09 04					09 56		10 04					10 56		11 04				11 56				12 05	
Long Buckby	d						10 06							11 06						12 06					
Northampton	a						10 17							11 17						12 17					
London Euston 15 ⊖	a	10 28							11 31							12 27								13 04	

		LM	VT	VT	XC	VT		LM	LM	VT	LM	LM	AW	LM	VT	VT		XC	VT	LM	LM	VT	LM	AW	LM
			◇1	◇1	◇1	◇1		◇1	◇1	◇1	◇1	1	◇		◇1	◇1		◇1	◇1	◇1	◇1	◇1	1	◇	
			⊡	⊡	⊼	⊡				⊡			⊼		⊡	⊡		⊼	⊡			⊡		⊼	
Stafford	d				11 28						12 18							12 25			12 42				
Penkridge	d																				12 49				
Wolverhampton 7	a				11 41													12 40			12 59				
	d	11 22		11 32	11 42	11 45							12 18	12 22		12 32		12 41	12 45		12 59			13 10	13 22
Coseley	d	11 27												12 27											13 27
Tipton	d	11 29												12 29											13 29
Dudley Port	d	11 31												12 31											13 31
Sandwell & Dudley	d	11 35				11 57								12 35					12 55						13 35
Smethwick Galton Bridge 7	d	11 37												12 37											13 37
Smethwick Rolfe Street	d	11 39												12 39											13 39
Birmingham New Street 12	a	11 48		11 55	12 00	12 06							12 33	12 46		12 55		12 58	13 06		13 16			13 25	13 46
	d		11 50		12 03	12 10			12 14	12 30		12 34	12 38		12 50			13 03	13 10	13 14		13 30	13 34	13 37	
Adderley Park	d											12 38											13 38		
Stechford	d											12 42											13 42		
Lea Hall	d											12 44											13 44		
Marston Green	d								12 22			12 48								13 22			13 48		
Birmingham International ✈	a		11 59		12 13	12 19			12 25	12 38		12 51	12 57		12 59			13 13	13 19	13 25		13 38	13 51	13 55	
	d		12 00		12 14	12 20			12 25	12 39		12 51			13 00			13 14	13 20	13 25		13 39	13 51		
Hampton-in-Arden	d								12 28											13 28					
Berkswell	d								12 33											13 33					
Tile Hill	d								12 36			12 58								13 36			13 58		
Canley	d								12 40											13 40					
Coventry	a		12 10		12 24	12 30			12 44	12 49		13 04			13 10			13 24	13 30	13 44		13 49	14 04		
	d		12 11			12 31			12 44	12 51					13 11				13 31	13 44		13 51			
Rugby	d		12 25					12 26	12 56		13 17				13 25					13 56					
Long Buckby	d							12 37	13 06		13 28									14 06					
Northampton	a							12 48	13 17		13 39									14 17					
London Euston 15 ⊖	a		13 19			13 37		13 53		13 57	14 53				14 17				14 37			14 57			

A ⊡ from Birmingham New Street
⊼ to Wolverhampton

Table 68

Sundays

18 September to 23 October

Stafford - Wolverhampton - Birmingham - Coventry - Northampton

		VT		VT	XC	VT	LM	LM	LM	VT	AW	XC		LM	LM	LM	VT	VT	XC	VT	LM	LM		VT	AW
		◇1		◇1	◇1	◇1	◇1	◇1	◇1	◇1	◇	◇1		◇1	1		◇1	◇1	◇1	◇1	◇1	◇1		◇1	◇
		☕		☕	⊼	☕				☕	⊼	⊼					☕	☕	⊼	☕				☕	⊼
Stafford	d				13 25				13 43					14 18					14 25			14 43			
Penkridge	d								13 49													14 49			
Wolverhampton 7 ⇌	a				13 40				13 58										14 40			14 58			
	d			13 32	13 41	13 45			13 58		14 09	14 15				14 22		14 33	14 41	14 45		14 58			15 10
Coseley	d															14 27									
Tipton	d															14 29									
Dudley Port	d															14 31									
Sandwell & Dudley	d					13 56										14 35				14 56					
Smethwick Galton Bridge 7	d															14 37									
Smethwick Rolfe Street	d															14 39									
Birmingham New Street 12	a			13 55	13 58	14 05			14 15		14 24	14 31				14 46		14 55	14 58	15 05		15 15			15 26
	d	13 50			14 03	14 10		14 14		14 30	14 37				14 34		14 50		15 03	15 10	15 14			15 30	15 37
Adderley Park	d														14 38										
Stechford	d														14 42										
Lea Hall	d														14 44										
Marston Green	d							14 22							14 48						15 22				
Birmingham International ✈	a	13 59			14 13	14 19		14 25		14 38	14 56				14 51		14 59		15 13	15 19	15 25			15 38	15 55
	d	14 01			14 14	14 20		14 25		14 39					14 51		15 01		15 14	15 20	15 25			15 39	
Hampton-in-Arden	d							14 28													15 28				
Berkswell	d							14 33													15 33				
Tile Hill	d							14 36							14 58						15 36				
Canley	d							14 40													15 40				
Coventry	a	14 11			14 24	14 30		14 44		14 49					15 04		15 11		15 24	15 30	15 44			15 49	
	d	14 11				14 31		14 44		14 51							15 11			15 31	15 44			15 51	
Rugby	d	14 26					14 26	14 56						15 17			15 26				15 56				
Long Buckby	d						14 37	15 06						15 28							16 06				
Northampton	a						14 48	15 17						15 39							16 17				
London Euston 15 ⊖	a	15 17				15 37	15 53			15 57				16 53			16 17			16 37				16 57	

		XC	LM	LM	VT	VT	XC	VT		LM	LM	LM	VT	AW	XC	LM	LM	LM		VT	VT	XC	VT	LM	LM
		◇1	1		◇1	◇1	◇1	◇1		◇1	◇1	◇1	◇1	◇	◇1	◇1	1			◇1	◇1	◇1	◇1	◇1	◇1
		⊼			☕	☕	⊼	☕					☕	⊼	⊼					☕	☕	⊼	☕		
Stafford	d						15 25					15 43				16 18						16 25			16 43
Penkridge	d											15 49													16 49
Wolverhampton 7 ⇌	a						15 40					15 58										16 40			16 58
	d	15 15		15 22		15 32	15 41	15 45				15 58		16 10	16 15			16 22			16 32	16 41	16 45		16 58
Coseley	d			15 27														16 27							
Tipton	d			15 29														16 29							
Dudley Port	d			15 31														16 31							
Sandwell & Dudley	d			15 35				15 56										16 35					16 56		
Smethwick Galton Bridge 7	d			15 37														16 37							
Smethwick Rolfe Street	d			15 39														16 39							
Birmingham New Street 12	a	15 31		15 46		15 55	15 58	16 05				16 15		16 26	16 31			16 46			16 55	16 58	17 05		17 15
	d		15 34		15 50		16 03	16 10			16 14		16 30	16 36			16 34			16 50		17 03	17 10	17 14	
Adderley Park	d		15 38														16 38								
Stechford	d		15 42														16 42								
Lea Hall	d		15 44														16 44								
Marston Green	d		15 48								16 22						16 48							17 22	
Birmingham International ✈	a		15 51		15 59		16 13	16 19			16 25		16 38	16 56			16 51			16 59		17 13	17 19	17 25	
	d		15 51		16 01		16 14	16 20			16 25		16 39				16 51			17 01		17 14	17 20	17 25	
Hampton-in-Arden	d										16 28													17 28	
Berkswell	d										16 33													17 33	
Tile Hill	d		15 58								16 36						16 58							17 36	
Canley	d										16 40													17 40	
Coventry	a		16 04		16 11		16 24	16 30			16 44		16 49				17 05			17 11		17 24	17 30	17 44	
	d				16 11			16 31			16 44		16 51							17 11			17 31	17 44	
Rugby	d				16 24					16 25	16 56					17 18				17 26				17 56	
Long Buckby	d									16 37	17 06					17 28								18 06	
Northampton	a									16 48	17 17					17 39								18 17	
London Euston 15 ⊖	a				17 20			17 37		17 53			17 57			18 53				18 17			18 37		

Table 68

Sundays

18 September to 23 October

Stafford - Wolverhampton - Birmingham - Coventry - Northampton

		VT	XC	LM		AW	LM	VT	VT	XC	VT	LM	LM	LM		VT	AW	XC	LM	LM	LM	VT	VT	XC	
		◇1	◇1	1		◇		◇1	◇1	◇1	◇1	◇1	◇1	◇1		◇1	◇	◇1	◇1	1		◇1	◇1	◇1	
		☕	⊼			⊼		☕	☕	⊼	☕					☕	⊼	⊼				☕	☕	⊼	
Stafford	d									17 26				17 43					18 18					18 26	
Penkridge	d													17 49											
Wolverhampton 7 ⇌	a									17 40				17 58										18 40	
	d		17 15			17 19	17 22		17 32	17 41	17 45			17 58			18 10	18 15			18 22		18 33	18 41	
Coseley	d						17 27														18 27				
Tipton	d						17 29														18 29				
Dudley Port	d						17 31														18 31				
Sandwell & Dudley	d						17 35				17 56										18 35				
Smethwick Galton Bridge 7	d						17 37														18 37				
Smethwick Rolfe Street	d						17 39														18 39				
Birmingham New Street 12	a		17 31			17 35	17 46		17 55	17 58	18 05			18 15			18 28	18 31			18 46		18 55	18 58	
	d	17 30		17 34		17 38		17 50		18 03	18 10		18 14			18 30	18 37			18 34		18 50		19 03	
Adderley Park	d			17 38																18 38					
Stechford	d			17 42																18 42					
Lea Hall	d			17 44																18 44					
Marston Green	d			17 48									18 22							18 48					
Birmingham International ✈	a	17 38		17 51		17 55		17 59		18 13	18 19		18 25			18 38	18 56			18 51		18 59		19 13	
	d	17 39		17 51				18 01		18 14	18 20		18 25			18 39				18 51		19 01		19 14	
Hampton-in-Arden	d												18 28												
Berkswell	d												18 33												
Tile Hill	d			17 58									18 36							18 58					
Canley	d												18 40												
Coventry	a	17 49		18 05				18 11		18 24	18 30		18 44			18 49				19 05		19 11		19 24	
	d	17 51						18 11			18 31		18 44			18 51						19 11			
Rugby	d							18 26				18 24	18 56						19 18			19 26			
Long Buckby	d											18 37	19 06						19 28						
Northampton	a											18 48	19 17						19 39						
London Euston 15 ⊖	a	18 57						19 17			19 37	19 53				19 57			20 53			20 17			

		VT	LM	LM	VT	AW	XC	LM	LM	VT		XC	VT	LM	LM	LM	VT	AW	XC	LM		LM	LM	VT	XC
		◇1	◇1	◇1	◇1	◇	◇1	1		◇1		◇1	◇1	◇1	◇1	◇1	◇1	◇	◇1	◇1		1		◇1	◇1
																									A
		☕			☕		⊼			☕		⊼	☕				☕	⊼						☕	⊼
Stafford	d			18 43								19 25				19 43				20 16					20 27
Penkridge	d			18 49												19 49									
Wolverhampton 7 ⇌	a			18 58								19 40				19 58									20 39
	d	18 45		18 58		19 11	19 14		19 22	19 32		19 41	19 45			19 58		20 09	20 15				20 22	20 33	20 41
Coseley	d								19 27														20 27		
Tipton	d								19 29														20 29		
Dudley Port	d								19 31														20 31		
Sandwell & Dudley	d	18 56							19 35				19 58										20 35		
Smethwick Galton Bridge 7	d								19 37														20 37		
Smethwick Rolfe Street	d								19 39														20 39		
Birmingham New Street 12	a	19 05		19 15		19 28	19 31		19 46	19 55		19 58	20 07			20 15		20 24	20 31				20 46	20 50	21 00
	d	19 10	19 14		19 30	19 37		19 34				20 03	20 10		20 14		20 30	20 37				20 34			21 03
Adderley Park	d							19 38														20 38			
Stechford	d							19 42														20 42			
Lea Hall	d							19 44														20 44			
Marston Green	d		19 22					19 48							20 22							20 48			
Birmingham International ✈	a	19 19	19 25		19 38	19 55		19 51				20 13	20 19		20 25		20 39	20 56				20 51			21 13
	d	19 20	19 25		19 39			19 51				20 14	20 20		20 25		20 40					20 51			21 14
Hampton-in-Arden	d		19 28												20 28										
Berkswell	d		19 33												20 33										
Tile Hill	d		19 36					19 58							20 36							20 58			
Canley	d		19 40												20 40										
Coventry	a	19 30	19 44		19 49			20 05				20 24	20 30		20 44		20 50					21 04			21 23
	d	19 31	19 44		19 51								20 31		20 44		20 51								
Rugby	d		19 56											20 20	20 56		21 05			21 17					
Long Buckby	d		20 06											20 32	21 06					21 28					
Northampton	a		20 17											20 43	21 17					21 39					
London Euston 15 ⊖	a	20 37			20 57								21 48	21 55			22 23			23 14					

A ⊼ to Wolverhampton

Table 68

Sundays
18 September to 23 October

Stafford - Wolverhampton - Birmingham - Coventry - Northampton

		LM	LM	VT	LM	AW	XC	LM	AW	LM	LM	VT	LM	AW	VT	XC	LM	VT	VT	LM	LM	XC
		◇1	◇1	◇1 🍴	1	◇	◇1		◇ 🛒	◇1	◇1	◇1 🍴	1	◇	◇1 🍴	◇1		◇1 🍴	◇1 🍴	1	◇1	◇1
Stafford	d		20 39				21 09		21 16		21 38				22 02	22 06					22 45	23 05
Penkridge	d		20 45								21 45										22 51	
Wolverhampton 7 ⛴	a		20 55				21 21		21 34		21 55				22 17	22 20					23 00	23 18
	d		20 58	21 05		21 12	21 22	21 25	21 35		21 58	22 05		22 09	22 18	22 22	22 25	22 32	22 37		23 00	23 19
Coseley	d							21 30									22 30					
Tipton	d							21 32									22 32					
Dudley Port	d							21 34									22 34					
Sandwell & Dudley	d			21 17				21 38				22 15					22 38		22 47			
Smethwick Galton Bridge 7	d							21 40									22 40					
Smethwick Rolfe Street	d							21 42									22 42					
Birmingham New Street 12	a		21 15	21 26		21 29	21 39	21 49	21 52		22 15	22 24		22 28	22 38	22 40	22 49	22 55	22 56		23 17	23 36
	d	21 14		21 30	21 34	21 37			21 55	22 14		22 30	22 34	22 41					23 00	23 14		
Adderley Park	d				21 38								22 38							23 19		
Stechford	d				21 42								22 42							23 22		
Lea Hall	d				21 44								22 45							23 25		
Marston Green	d	21 22			21 48					22 22			22 48							23 28		
Birmingham International ✈	a	21 25		21 39	21 51	21 56			22 09	22 25		22 39	22 51	22 56					23 09	23 31		
	d	21 25		21 40	21 51					22 25		22 40	22 52						23 10	23 32		
Hampton-in-Arden	d	21 28								22 28										23 35		
Berkswell	d	21 33								22 33										23 40		
Tile Hill	d	21 36								22 36										23 43		
Canley	d	21 40								22 40										23 46		
Coventry	a	21 44		21 50	22 01					22 44		22 50	23 01						23 20	23 50		
	d	21 44		21 51						22 44		22 51							23 21			
Rugby	d	21 56		22 04						22 56		23 04							23 34			
Long Buckby	d	22 06								23 06												
Northampton	a	22 17								23 17									23s53			
London Euston 15 ⊖	a			23 25								00 26							01 04			

Sundays
from 30 October

		VT	LM	LM	LM	XC	LM	AW	VT	LM	LM	XC	LM	AW	VT	LM	LM	XC	LM	AW	LM	VT	LM
		◇1 🍴	1	1		◇1 🛒	◇1		◇1 🍴	1		◇1 🛒	◇1		◇1 🍴	1		◇1 🛒	◇1	◇	◇1	◇1 🍴	1
Stafford	d											09 26						10 27			10 41		
Penkridge	d																				10 49		
Wolverhampton 7 ⛴	a											09 40						10 42			11 00		
	d	08 05			08 22			09 00	09 05		09 22	09 41		09 59	10 05		10 22	10 43		10 58	11 01	11 05	
Coseley	d				08 27						09 27						10 27						
Tipton	d				08 29						09 29						10 29						
Dudley Port	d				08 31						09 31						10 31						
Sandwell & Dudley	d	08 15			08 35				09 15		09 35				10 15		10 35					11 15	
Smethwick Galton Bridge 7	d				08 37						09 37						10 37						
Smethwick Rolfe Street	d				08 39						09 39						10 39						
Birmingham New Street 12	a	08 24			08 46			09 15	09 24		09 46	09 58		10 14	10 24		10 46	10 59		11 14	11 17	11 26	
	d	08 30	08 34	08 38		09 03	09 14	09 20	09 30	09 34		10 03	10 14	10 20	10 30	10 34		11 03	11 14	11 20		11 30	11 34
Adderley Park	d			08 42						09 38						10 38							11 38
Stechford	d			08 46						09 42						10 42							11 42
Lea Hall	d			08 48						09 44						10 44							11 44
Marston Green	d		08 42	08 52			09 22			09 48			10 22			10 48			11 22				11 48
Birmingham International ✈	a	08 39	08 45	08 55		09 13	09 25	09 32	09 39	09 51		10 13	10 25	10 32	10 39	10 52		11 13	11 25	11 32		11 39	11 51
	d	08 40	08 45			09 14	09 25		09 40	09 51		10 14	10 25		10 40	10 52		11 14	11 25			11 40	11 51
Hampton-in-Arden	d						09 28						10 28						11 28				
Berkswell	d		08 51				09 33						10 33						11 33				
Tile Hill	d		08 54				09 36						10 36						11 36				
Canley	d		08 57				09 40						10 40						11 40				
Coventry	a	08 50	09 00			09 24	09 44		09 50	10 01		10 24	10 44		10 50	11 03		11 24	11 44			11 50	12 01
	d	08 51					09 44		09 51				10 44		10 51				11 44			11 51	
Rugby	d	09 04					09 56		10 04				10 56		11 04				11 56			12 05	
Long Buckby	d						10 06						11 06						12 06				
Northampton	a						10 17						11 17						12 17				
London Euston 15 ⊖	a	10 28							11 31						12 27							13 04	

Table 68

Sundays
from 30 October

Stafford - Wolverhampton - Birmingham - Coventry - Northampton

		LM	VT	VT	XC	VT	LM	LM	VT	LM	LM	AW	LM	VT	VT	XC	VT	LM	LM	VT	LM	AW	LM
			◇1 🍴	◇1 🍴	◇1 🛒	◇1 🍴	◇1	◇1	◇1 🍴	◇1	1	◇ 🛒		◇1 🍴	◇1 🍴	◇1 🛒	◇1 🍴	◇1	◇1	◇1 🍴	1	◇ 🛒	
Stafford	d				11 28					12 18						12 25			12 42				
Penkridge	d																		12 49				
Wolverhampton 7 ⛴	a				11 41											12 40			12 59				
	d	11 22		11 32	11 42	11 45						12 18	12 22		12 32	12 41	12 45		12 59			13 10	13 22
Coseley	d	11 27											12 27										13 27
Tipton	d	11 29											12 29										13 29
Dudley Port	d	11 31											12 31										13 31
Sandwell & Dudley	d	11 35				11 57							12 35				12 55						13 35
Smethwick Galton Bridge 7	d	11 37											12 37										13 37
Smethwick Rolfe Street	d	11 39											12 39										13 39
Birmingham New Street 12	a	11 48		11 55	12 00	12 06						12 33	12 46		12 55	12 58	13 06		13 16			13 25	13 46
	d		11 50		12 03	12 10		12 14	12 30		12 34	12 38		12 50		13 03	13 10	13 14		13 30	13 34	13 37	
Adderley Park	d										12 38										13 38		
Stechford	d										12 42										13 42		
Lea Hall	d										12 44										13 44		
Marston Green	d							12 22			12 48							13 22			13 48		
Birmingham International ✈	a		11 59		12 13	12 19		12 25	12 38		12 51	12 57		12 59		13 13	13 19	13 25		13 38	13 51	13 55	
	d		12 00		12 14	12 20		12 25	12 39		12 51			13 00		13 14	13 20	13 25		13 39	13 51		
Hampton-in-Arden	d							12 28										13 28					
Berkswell	d							12 33										13 33					
Tile Hill	d							12 36			12 58							13 36			13 58		
Canley	d							12 40										13 40					
Coventry	a		12 10		12 24	12 30		12 44	12 49		13 04			13 10		13 24	13 30	13 44		13 49	14 04		
	d		12 11			12 31		12 44	12 51					13 11			13 31	13 44		13 51			
Rugby	d		12 25				12 26	12 56		13 17				13 25				13 56					
Long Buckby	d						12 37	13 06		13 28								14 06					
Northampton	a						12 48	13 17		13 39								14 17					
London Euston 15 ⊖	a		13 19			13 37	13 53		13 57	14 53				14 17			14 37			14 57			

		VT	VT	XC	VT	LM	LM	LM	VT	AW	XC	LM	LM	LM	VT	VT	XC	VT	LM	LM	VT	AW
		◇1 🍴	◇1 🍴	◇1 🛒	◇1 🍴	◇1	◇1	◇1	◇1 🍴	◇ 🛒	◇1 🛒	◇1	1		◇1 🍴	◇1 🍴	◇1 🛒	◇1 🍴	◇1	◇1	◇1 🍴	◇ 🛒
Stafford	d			13 25				13 43				14 18					14 25			14 43		
Penkridge	d							13 49												14 49		
Wolverhampton 7 ⛴	a			13 40				13 58									14 40			14 58		
	d		13 32	13 41	13 45			13 58		14 09	14 15			14 22		14 33	14 41	14 45		14 58		15 10
Coseley	d													14 27								
Tipton	d													14 29								
Dudley Port	d													14 31								
Sandwell & Dudley	d				13 56									14 35				14 56				
Smethwick Galton Bridge 7	d													14 37								
Smethwick Rolfe Street	d													14 39								
Birmingham New Street 12	a		13 55	13 58	14 05			14 15		14 24	14 31			14 46		14 55	14 58	15 05		15 15		15 26
	d	13 50		14 03	14 10		14 14		14 30	14 37			14 34		14 50		15 03	15 10	15 14		15 30	15 37
Adderley Park	d												14 38									
Stechford	d												14 42									
Lea Hall	d												14 44									
Marston Green	d						14 22						14 48						15 22			
Birmingham International ✈	a	13 59		14 13	14 19		14 25		14 38	14 56			14 51		14 59		15 13	15 19	15 25		15 38	15 55
	d	14 01		14 14	14 20		14 25		14 39				14 51		15 01		15 14	15 20	15 25		15 39	
Hampton-in-Arden	d						14 28												15 28			
Berkswell	d						14 33												15 33			
Tile Hill	d						14 36						14 58						15 36			
Canley	d						14 40												15 40			
Coventry	a	14 11		14 24	14 30		14 44		14 49				15 04		15 11		15 24	15 30	15 44		15 49	
	d	14 11			14 31		14 44		14 51						15 11			15 31	15 44		15 51	
Rugby	d	14 26				14 26	14 56					15 17			15 26				15 56			
Long Buckby	d					14 37	15 06					15 28							16 06			
Northampton	a					14 48	15 17					15 39							16 17			
London Euston 15 ⊖	a	15 17			15 37	15 53			15 57			16 53			16 17			16 37			16 57	

Table 68

Sundays
from 30 October

Stafford - Wolverhampton - Birmingham - Coventry - Northampton

		XC	LM	LM	VT	VT	XC	VT	LM	LM	LM	VT	AW	XC	LM	LM	LM	VT	VT	XC	VT	LM	LM
		◇1	1		◇1	◇1	◇1	◇1	◇1	◇1	◇1	◇1	◇	◇1	◇1	1		◇1	◇1	◇1	◇1	◇1	◇1
		⊼			⊡	⊡	⊼	⊡				⊡	⊼	⊼				⊡	⊡	⊼	⊡		
Stafford	d						15 25				15 43				16 18					16 25			16 43
Penkridge	d										15 49												16 49
Wolverhampton 7	a						15 40				15 58									16 40			16 58
	d	15 15		15 22		15 32	15 41	15 45			15 58		16 10	16 15			16 22		16 32	16 41	16 45		16 58
Coseley	d			15 27													16 27						
Tipton	d			15 29													16 29						
Dudley Port	d			15 31													16 31						
Sandwell & Dudley	d			15 35				15 56									16 35				16 56		
Smethwick Galton Bridge 7	d			15 37													16 37						
Smethwick Rolfe Street	d			15 39													16 39						
Birmingham New Street 12	a	15 31		15 46		15 55	15 58	16 05			16 15		16 26	16 31			16 46		16 55	16 58	17 05		17 15
	d		15 34		15 50		16 03	16 10		16 14		16 30	16 36			16 34		16 50		17 03	17 10	17 14	
Adderley Park	d		15 38													16 38							
Stechford	d		15 42													16 42							
Lea Hall	d		15 44													16 44							
Marston Green	d		15 48							16 22						16 48						17 22	
Birmingham International ✈	a		15 51		15 59		16 13	16 19		16 25		16 38	16 56			16 51		16 59		17 13	17 19	17 25	
	d		15 51		16 01		16 14	16 20		16 25		16 39				16 51		17 01		17 14	17 20	17 25	
Hampton-in-Arden	d									16 28												17 28	
Berkswell	d									16 33												17 33	
Tile Hill	d		15 58							16 36						16 58						17 36	
Canley	d									16 40												17 40	
Coventry	a		16 04		16 11		16 24	16 30		16 44		16 49				17 05		17 11		17 24	17 30	17 44	
	d				16 11			16 31		16 44		16 51						17 11			17 31	17 44	
Rugby	d				16 24				16 25	16 56					17 18			17 26				17 56	
Long Buckby	d								16 37	17 06					17 28							18 06	
Northampton	a								16 48	17 17					17 39							18 17	
London Euston 15 ⊖	a				17 20			17 37	17 53			17 57			18 53			18 17			18 37		

		VT	XC	LM	AW	LM	VT	VT	XC	VT	LM	LM	LM	VT	LM	LM	AW	LM	VT	VT	XC	VT
		◇1	◇1	1	◇		◇1	◇1	◇1	◇1	◇1	◇1	◇1	◇1	◇1	1	◇		◇1	◇1	◇1	◇1
		⊡	⊼		⊼		⊡	⊡	⊼	⊡				⊡			⊼		⊡	⊡	⊼	⊡
Stafford	d								17 26				17 43		18 18						18 26	
Penkridge	d												17 49									
Wolverhampton 7	a								17 40				17 58								18 40	
	d		17 15		17 19	17 22		17 32	17 41	17 45			17 58				18 10	18 22		18 33	18 41	18 45
Coseley	d					17 27												18 27				
Tipton	d					17 29												18 29				
Dudley Port	d					17 31												18 31				
Sandwell & Dudley	d					17 35				17 56								18 35				18 56
Smethwick Galton Bridge 7	d					17 37												18 37				
Smethwick Rolfe Street	d					17 39												18 39				
Birmingham New Street 12	a		17 31		17 35	17 46		17 55	17 58	18 05			18 15				18 28	18 46		18 55	18 58	19 05
	d	17 30		17 34	17 38		17 50		18 03	18 10		18 14		18 30		18 34	18 37		18 50		19 03	19 10
Adderley Park	d			17 38												18 38						
Stechford	d			17 42												18 42						
Lea Hall	d			17 44												18 44						
Marston Green	d			17 48								18 22				18 48						
Birmingham International ✈	a	17 38		17 51	17 55		17 59		18 13	18 19		18 25		18 38		18 51	18 56		18 59		19 13	19 19
	d	17 39		17 51			18 01		18 14	18 20		18 25		18 39		18 51			19 01		19 14	19 20
Hampton-in-Arden	d											18 28										
Berkswell	d											18 33										
Tile Hill	d			17 58								18 36				18 58						
Canley	d											18 40										
Coventry	a	17 49		18 05			18 11		18 24	18 30		18 44		18 49		19 05			19 11		19 24	19 30
	d	17 51					18 11			18 31		18 44		18 51					19 11			19 31
Rugby	d						18 26				18 24	18 56			19 18				19 26			
Long Buckby	d										18 37	19 06			19 28							
Northampton	a										18 48	19 17			19 39							
London Euston 15 ⊖	a	18 57					19 17			19 37	19 53			19 57	20 53				20 17			20 37

Table 68

Sundays
from 30 October

Stafford - Wolverhampton - Birmingham - Coventry - Northampton

		LM	LM	VT	AW	XC	LM	LM	VT	XC	VT	LM	LM	LM	VT	AW	XC	LM	LM	LM	VT	XC	LM
		◇1	◇1	◇1	◇	◇1	1		◇1	◇1	◇1	◇1	◇1	◇1	◇1	◇	◇1	◇1	1		◇1	◇1	◇1
																						A	
				⊡		⊼			⊡	⊼	⊡				⊡	⊼					⊡	⊼	
Stafford	d		18 43							19 25				19 43				20 16				20 27	
Penkridge	d		18 49											19 49									
Wolverhampton 7	a		18 58							19 40				19 58								20 39	
	d		18 58		19 11	19 15		19 22	19 32	19 41	19 45			19 58		20 09	20 15			20 22	20 33	20 41	
Coseley	d							19 27												20 27			
Tipton	d							19 29												20 29			
Dudley Port	d							19 31												20 31			
Sandwell & Dudley	d							19 35			19 58									20 35			
Smethwick Galton Bridge 7	d							19 37												20 37			
Smethwick Rolfe Street	d							19 39												20 39			
Birmingham New Street 12	a		19 15		19 28	19 31		19 46	19 55	19 58	20 07			20 15		20 24	20 31			20 46	20 50	21 00	
	d	19 14		19 30	19 37		19 34			20 03	20 10		20 14		20 30	20 37			20 34			21 03	21 14
Adderley Park	d						19 38												20 38				
Stechford	d						19 42												20 42				
Lea Hall	d						19 44												20 44				
Marston Green	d	19 22					19 48						20 22						20 48				21 22
Birmingham International ✈	a	19 25		19 38	19 55		19 51			20 13	20 19		20 25		20 39	20 56			20 51			21 13	21 25
	d	19 25		19 39			19 51			20 14	20 20		20 25		20 40				20 51			21 14	21 25
Hampton-in-Arden	d	19 28											20 28										21 28
Berkswell	d	19 33											20 33										21 33
Tile Hill	d	19 36					19 58						20 36						20 58				21 36
Canley	d	19 40											20 40										21 40
Coventry	a	19 44		19 49			20 05			20 24	20 30		20 44		20 50				21 04			21 23	21 44
	d	19 44		19 51							20 31		20 44		20 51								21 44
Rugby	d	19 56										20 20	20 56		21 05			21 17					21 56
Long Buckby	d	20 06										20 32	21 06					21 28					22 06
Northampton	a	20 17										20 43	21 17					21 39					22 17
London Euston 15 ⊖	a			20 57							21 48	21 55			22 23			23 14					

		LM	VT	LM	AW	XC	LM	AW	LM	LM	VT	LM	AW	VT	XC	LM	VT	VT	LM	LM	XC
		◇1	◇1	1	◇	◇1		◇	◇1	◇1	◇1	1	◇	◇1	◇1		◇1	◇1	1	◇1	◇1
			⊡					⊼			⊡			⊡			⊡	⊡			
Stafford	d	20 39				21 09		21 16		21 38				22 02	22 06					22 45	23 05
Penkridge	d	20 45								21 45										22 51	
Wolverhampton 7	a	20 55				21 21		21 34		21 55				22 17	22 20					23 00	23 18
	d	20 58	21 05		21 12	21 22	21 25	21 35		21 58	22 05		22 09	22 18	22 22	22 25	22 32	22 37		23 00	23 19
Coseley	d						21 30									22 30					
Tipton	d						21 32									22 32					
Dudley Port	d						21 34									22 34					
Sandwell & Dudley	d		21 17				21 38				22 15					22 38		22 47			
Smethwick Galton Bridge 7	d						21 40									22 40					
Smethwick Rolfe Street	d						21 42									22 42					
Birmingham New Street 12	a	21 15	21 26		21 29	21 39	21 49	21 52		22 15	22 24		22 28	22 38	22 40	22 49	22 55	22 56		23 17	23 36
	d		21 30	21 34	21 37			21 55	22 14		22 30	22 34	22 41					23 00	23 14		
Adderley Park	d			21 38								22 38							23 19		
Stechford	d			21 42								22 42							23 22		
Lea Hall	d			21 44								22 45							23 25		
Marston Green	d			21 48					22 22			22 48							23 28		
Birmingham International ✈	a		21 39	21 51	21 56			22 09	22 25		22 39	22 51	22 56					23 09	23 31		
	d		21 40	21 51					22 25		22 40	22 52						23 10	23 32		
Hampton-in-Arden	d								22 28										23 35		
Berkswell	d								22 33										23 40		
Tile Hill	d								22 36										23 43		
Canley	d								22 40										23 46		
Coventry	a		21 50	22 01					22 44		22 50	23 01						23 20	23 50		
	d		21 51						22 44		22 51							23 21			
Rugby	d		22 04						22 56		23 04							23 34			
Long Buckby	d								23 06												
Northampton	a								23 17									23s53			
London Euston 15 ⊖	a		23 25								00 26							01 04			

A ⊼ to Wolverhampton

Table 69

Mondays to Fridays

until 21 October

Lichfield - Birmingham - Longbridge and Redditch

Miles	Miles			LM	LM	LM	LM	LM	LM	LM	LM	LM		LM	LM	LM	XC ◇1	LM	LM	LM	LM	LM		LM	LM
0	—	**Lichfield Trent Valley**	d							06 09		06 20						06 50		07 10		07 20			07 40
1¼	—	**Lichfield City**	d							06 12		06 24				06 44		06 54		07 13		07 24			07 43
4¼	—	Shenstone	d							06 17						06 49				07 18					07 48
6¾	—	Blake Street	d					06 03		06 21		06 32				06 53		07 02		07 22		07 32			07 52
8½	—	Butlers Lane	d					06 05		06 23		06 34				06 55		07 04		07 24		07 34			07 54
9½	—	Four Oaks	d					06 08	06 17	06 26		06 37		06 47		06 58		07 07	07 17	07 27		07 37		07 47	07 57
11	—	Sutton Coldfield	d					06 11	06 20	06 30		06 40		06 50		07 01		07 10	07 20	07 31		07 40		07 50	08 01
12	—	Wylde Green	d					06 14	06 23	06 32		06 43		06 53		07 04		07 13	07 23	07 33		07 43		07 53	08 03
12¾	—	Chester Road	d					06 16	06 25	06 35		06 45		06 55		07 06		07 15	07 25	07 36		07 45		07 55	08 06
13¾	—	Erdington	d					06 17	06 27	06 36		06 47		06 57		07 08		07 17	07 27	07 37		07 47		07 57	08 07
14½	—	Gravelly Hill	d					06 20	06 29	06 39		06 49		06 59		07 10		07 19	07 29	07 40		07 49		07 59	08 10
15¾	—	Aston	d					06 23	06 33	06 42		06 53		07 03		07 14		07 23	07 33	07 43		07 53		08 03	08 13
17	—	Duddeston	d					06 26	06 35	06 45				07 05					07 35	07 46				08 05	08 16
18½	0	**Birmingham New Street** 12	a					06 31	06 40	06 49		06 59		07 10		07 20		07 30	07 41	07 51		08 01		08 11	08 21
—	—		d	05 53	06 03	06 13	06 23	06 33	06 43	06 53	06 59	07 03		07 13	07 19	07 23	07 30	07 33	07 43	07 53	07 59	08 03		08 13	08 23
19½	—	Five Ways	d	05 56	06 06	06 16	06 26	06 36	06 46	06 56		07 06		07 16		07 26		07 36	07 46	07 56		08 06		08 16	08 26
20	1½	University	d	06 00	06 10	06 20	06 30	06 40	06 50	07 00	07 05	07 10		07 20	07 25	07 30	07a36	07 40	07 50	08 00	08 05	08 10		08 20	08 30
20¾	—	Selly Oak	d	06 03	06 13	06 23	06 33	06 43	06 53	07 03		07 13		07 23		07 33		07 43	07 53	08 03		08 13		08 23	08 33
21¾	—	Bournville	d	06 05	06 15	06 25	06 35	06 45	06 55	07 05		07 15		07 25		07 35		07 45	07 55	08 05		08 15		08 25	08 35
22¾	—	Kings Norton	d	06 07	06 17	06 27	06 37	06 47	06 57	07 07		07 17		07 27		07 37		07 47	07 57	08 07		08 17		08 27	08 37
24¼	—	Northfield	d	06 10	06 20	06 30	06 40	06 50	07 00	07 10		07 20		07 30		07 40		07 50	08 00	08 10		08 20		08 30	08 40
25¼	—	Longbridge	d	06a14	06a24	06 34	06a44	06a54	07 04	07a14		07a24		07 34		07a44		07a54	08 04	08a14		08a24		08 34	08a44
28	9½	Barnt Green	d			06 39			07 09					07 39	07 42				08 09		08 18			08 39	
29¾	—	Alvechurch	d			06 43			07 13					07 43					08 13					08 43	
33	—	**Redditch**	a			06 52			07 22					07 52					08 22					08 52	
—	13	Bromsgrove	a								07 21				07 46						08 22				

		XC ◇1	LM	LM	LM	LM	LM	LM		LM	LM	XC ◇1	LM	LM	LM	LM	LM	LM		LM	XC ◇1	LM	LM	LM	LM
Lichfield Trent Valley	d		07 52				08 10				08 41		08 50				09 20					09 50			
Lichfield City	d		07 56		08 10		08 13	08 26			08 44		08 54			09 13	09 24			09 43		09 54			10 13
Shenstone	d						08 18				08 49					09 18				09 48					10 18
Blake Street	d		08 04				08 22	08 33			08 53		09 02			09 22	09 32			09 52		10 02			10 22
Butlers Lane	d		08 06				08 24	08 35			08 55		09 04			09 24	09 34			09 54		10 04			10 24
Four Oaks	d		08 09	08 15	08 20		08 27	08 38		08 47	08 58		09 07	09 17		09 27	09 37	09 47		09 57		10 07	10 17		10 27
Sutton Coldfield	d		08 12	08 18	08 23		08 31	08 42		08 50	09 02		09 10	09 20		09 30	09 40	09 50		10 00		10 10	10 20		10 30
Wylde Green	d		08 15	08 21	08 26		08 33	08 44		08 53	09 04		09 13	09 23		09 33	09 43	09 53		10 03		10 13	10 23		10 33
Chester Road	d		08 17	08 23	08 28		08 36	08 47		08 55	09 07		09 15	09 25		09 35	09 45	09 55		10 05		10 15	10 25		10 35
Erdington	d		08 19	08 25	08 29		08 37	08 48		08 57	09 08		09 17	09 27		09 37	09 47	09 57		10 07		10 17	10 27		10 37
Gravelly Hill	d		08 21		08 32		08 40	08 51		08 59	09 11		09 19	09 29		09 39	09 49	09 59		10 09		10 19	10 29		10 39
Aston	d		08 24		08 35		08 43	08 54		09 03	09 14		09 23	09 33		09 43	09 53	10 03		10 13		10 23	10 33		10 43
Duddeston	d				08 37		08 46	08 57		09 05				09 35				10 05					10 35		
Birmingham New Street 12	a		08 30	08 36	08 42		08 51	09 01		09 12	09 20		09 30	09 41		09 50	10 00	10 11		10 21		10 30	10 41		10 50
	d	08 30	08 33		08 43	08 49	08 53	09 03		09 13	09 23	09 30	09 33	09 43	09 49	09 53	10 03	10 13		10 23	10 30	10 33	10 43	10 49	10 53
Five Ways	d		08 36		08 46		08 56	09 06		09 16	09 26		09 36	09 46		09 56	10 06	10 16		10 26		10 36	10 46		10 56
University	d	08a36	08 40		08 50	08 55	09 00	09 10		09 20	09 30	09a36	09 40	09 50	09 55	10 00	10 10	10 20		10 30	10a36	10 40	10 50	10 55	11 00
Selly Oak	d		08 43		08 53		09 03	09 13		09 23	09 33		09 43	09 53		10 03	10 13	10 23		10 33		10 43	10 53		11 03
Bournville	d		08 45		08 55		09 05	09 15		09 25	09 35		09 45	09 55		10 05	10 15	10 25		10 35		10 45	10 55		11 05
Kings Norton	d		08 47		08 57		09 07	09 17		09 27	09 37		09 47	09 57		10 07	10 17	10 27		10 37		10 47	10 57		11 07
Northfield	d		08 50		09 00		09 10	09 20		09 30	09 40		09 50	10 00		10 10	10 20	10 30		10 40		10 50	11 00		11 10
Longbridge	d		08a54		09 06		09a14	09a24		09 34	09a44		09a54	10 06		10a14	10a24	10 34		10a44		10a54	11 06		11a14
Barnt Green	d				09 10					09 39				10 10				10 39					11 10		
Alvechurch	d				09 15					09 43				10 15				10 43					11 15		
Redditch	a				09 22					09 52				10 22				10 52					11 22		
Bromsgrove	a					09 09									10 09									11 09	

		LM	LM	LM		XC ◇1	LM	LM	LM	LM	LM	LM	LM	XC ◇1		LM	LM	LM	LM	LM	LM	LM	XC ◇1	LM	
Lichfield Trent Valley	d	10 20					10 50				11 20					11 50				12 20				12 50	
Lichfield City	d	10 24		10 43			10 54			11 13	11 24		11 43			11 54			12 13	12 24		12 43		12 54	
Shenstone	d			10 48						11 18			11 48						12 18			12 48			
Blake Street	d	10 32		10 52			11 02			11 22	11 32		11 52			12 02			12 22	12 32		12 52		13 02	
Butlers Lane	d	10 34		10 54			11 04			11 24	11 34		11 54			12 04			12 24	12 34		12 54		13 04	
Four Oaks	d	10 37	10 47	10 57			11 07	11 17		11 27	11 37	11 47	11 57			12 07	12 17		12 27	12 37	12 47	12 57		13 07	
Sutton Coldfield	d	10 40	10 50	11 00			11 10	11 20		11 30	11 40	11 50	12 00			12 10	12 20		12 30	12 40	12 50	13 00		13 10	
Wylde Green	d	10 43	10 53	11 03			11 13	11 23		11 33	11 43	11 53	12 03			12 13	12 23		12 33	12 43	12 53	13 03		13 13	
Chester Road	d	10 45	10 55	11 05			11 15	11 25		11 35	11 45	11 55	12 05			12 15	12 25		12 35	12 45	12 55	13 05		13 15	
Erdington	d	10 47	10 57	11 07			11 17	11 27		11 37	11 47	11 57	12 07			12 17	12 27		12 37	12 47	12 57	13 07		13 17	
Gravelly Hill	d	10 49	10 59	11 09			11 19	11 29		11 39	11 49	11 59	12 09			12 19	12 29		12 39	12 49	12 59	13 09		13 19	
Aston	d	10 53	11 03	11 13			11 23	11 33		11 43	11 53	12 03	12 13			12 23	12 33		12 43	12 53	13 03	13 13		13 23	
Duddeston	d		11 05					11 35				12 05					12 35				13 05				
Birmingham New Street 12	a	11 00	11 11	11 21			11 30	11 41		11 50	12 00	12 11	12 21			12 30	12 41		12 50	13 00	13 11	13 21		13 31	
	d	11 03	11 13	11 23		11 30	11 33	11 43	11 49	11 53	12 03	12 13	12 23	12 30		12 33	12 43	12 49	12 53	13 03	13 13	13 23	13 30	13 33	
Five Ways	d	11 06	11 16	11 26			11 36	11 46		11 56	12 06	12 16	12 26			12 36	12 46		12 56	13 06	13 16	13 26		13 36	
University	d	11 10	11 20	11 30		11a36	11 40	11 50	11 55	12 00	12 10	12 20	12 30	12a36		12 40	12 50	12 55	13 00	13 10	13 20	13 30	13a36	13 40	
Selly Oak	d	11 13	11 23	11 33			11 43	11 53		12 03	12 13	12 23	12 33			12 43	12 53		13 03	13 13	13 23	13 33		13 43	
Bournville	d	11 15	11 25	11 35			11 45	11 55		12 05	12 15	12 25	12 35			12 45	12 55		13 05	13 15	13 25	13 35		13 45	
Kings Norton	d	11 17	11 27	11 37			11 47	11 57		12 07	12 17	12 27	12 37			12 47	12 57		13 07	13 17	13 27	13 37		13 47	
Northfield	d	11 20	11 30	11 40			11 50	12 00		12 10	12 20	12 30	12 40			12 50	13 00		13 10	13 20	13 30	13 40		13 50	
Longbridge	d	11a24	11 34	11a44			11a54	12 06		12a14	12a24	12 34	12a44			12a54	13 06		13a14	13a24	13 34	13a44		13a54	
Barnt Green	d		11 39					12 10				12 39					13 10				13 39				
Alvechurch	d		11 43					12 15				12 43					13 15				13 43				
Redditch	a		11 52					12 22				12 52					13 22				13 52				
Bromsgrove	a								12 09									13 09							

until 21 October

Lichfield - Birmingham - Longbridge and Redditch

		LM	LM	LM	LM	LM	LM	XC	LM	LM		LM	LM	LM	LM	LM	XC	LM	LM	LM		LM	LM	LM	LM
								◇1									◇1								
Lichfield Trent Valley	d				13 20				13 50					14 20				14 50					15 20		
Lichfield City	d			13 13	13 24		13 43		13 54				14 13	14 24		14 43		14 54				15 13	15 24		
Shenstone	d			13 18			13 48						14 18			14 48						15 18			
Blake Street	d			13 22	13 32		13 52		14 02				14 22	14 32		14 52		15 02				15 22	15 32		
Butlers Lane	d			13 24	13 34		13 54		14 04				14 24	14 34		14 54		15 04				15 24	15 34		
Four Oaks	d	13 17		13 27	13 37	13 47	13 57		14 07	14 17			14 27	14 37	14 47	14 57		15 07	15 17			15 27	15 37	15 47	
Sutton Coldfield	d	13 20		13 30	13 40	13 50	14 00		14 10	14 20			14 30	14 40	14 50	15 00		15 10	15 20			15 30	15 40	15 50	
Wylde Green	d	13 23		13 33	13 43	13 53	14 03		14 13	14 23			14 33	14 43	14 53	15 03		15 13	15 23			15 33	15 43	15 53	
Chester Road	d	13 25		13 35	13 45	13 55	14 05		14 15	14 25			14 35	14 45	14 55	15 05		15 15	15 25			15 35	15 45	15 55	
Erdington	d	13 27		13 37	13 47	13 57	14 07		14 17	14 27			14 37	14 47	14 57	15 07		15 17	15 27			15 37	15 47	15 57	
Gravelly Hill	d	13 29		13 39	13 49	13 59	14 09		14 19	14 29			14 39	14 49	14 59	15 09		15 19	15 29			15 39	15 49	15 59	
Aston	d	13 33		13 43	13 53	14 03	14 13		14 23	14 33			14 43	14 53	15 03	15 13		15 23	15 33			15 43	15 53	16 03	
Duddeston	d	13 35				14 05				14 35					15 05				15 35					16 05	
Birmingham New Street 12	a	13 41		13 50	14 00	14 11	14 21		14 30	14 41			14 50	15 00	15 11	15 21		15 30	15 40			15 50	16 01	16 11	
	d	13 43	13 49	13 53	14 03	14 13	14 23	14 30	14 33	14 43		14 49	14 53	15 03	15 13	15 23	15 30	15 33	15 43	15 49		15 53	16 03	16 13	16 19
Five Ways	d	13 46		13 56	14 06	14 16	14 26		14 36	14 46			14 56	15 06	15 16	15 26		15 36	15 46			15 56	16 06	16 16	
University	d	13 50	13 55	14 00	14 10	14 20	14 30	14a36	14 40	14 50		14 55	15 00	15 10	15 20	15 30	15a36	15 40	15 50	15 55		16 00	16 10	16 20	16 25
Selly Oak	d	13 53		14 03	14 13	14 23	14 33		14 43	14 53			15 03	15 13	15 23	15 33		15 43	15 53			16 03	16 13	16 23	
Bournville	d	13 55		14 05	14 15	14 25	14 35		14 45	14 55			15 05	15 15	15 25	15 35		15 45	15 55			16 05	16 15	16 25	
Kings Norton	d	13 57		14 07	14 17	14 27	14 37		14 47	14 57			15 07	15 17	15 27	15 37		15 47	15 57			16 07	16 17	16 27	
Northfield	d	14 00		14 10	14 20	14 30	14 40		14 50	15 00			15 10	15 20	15 30	15 40		15 50	16 00			16 10	16 20	16 30	
Longbridge	d	14 06		14a14	14a24	14 34	14a44		14a54	15 06			15a14	15a24	15 34	15a44		15a54	16 06			16a14	16a24	16 36	
Barnt Green	d	14 10				14 39				15 10					15 39				16 10					16 40	
Alvechurch	d	14 15				14 43				15 15					15 43				16 15					16 45	
Redditch	a	14 22				14 52				15 22					15 52				16 22					16 52	
Bromsgrove	a		14 09									15 09								16 09					16 40

		LM	XC	LM	LM	LM		LM	LM	LM	LM	LM	XC	LM	LM	LM		LM	LM	LM	LM	LM	LM	XC	LM
			◇1										◇1											◇1	
Lichfield Trent Valley	d			15 50					16 20					16 50						17 20			17 40		17 50
Lichfield City	d	15 43		15 54				16 13	16 24			16 43		16 54	17 05					17 24			17 44		17 54
Shenstone	d	15 48		15 59				16 18				16 48								17 29			17 49		
Blake Street	d	15 52		16 03				16 22	16 32			16 52		17 02	17 13					17 33			17 53		18 02
Butlers Lane	d	15 54		16 05				16 24	16 34			16 54		17 04	17 15					17 35			17 55		18 04
Four Oaks	d	15 57		16 08	16 17			16 27	16 37	16 47		16 57		17 07	17 18			17 28		17 38	17 47		17 58		18 07
Sutton Coldfield	d	16 00		16 11	16 20			16 30	16 40	16 50		17 00		17 10	17 21			17 31		17 41	17 50		18 01		18 10
Wylde Green	d	16 03		16 14	16 23			16 33	16 43	16 53		17 03		17 13	17 24			17 34		17 44	17 53		18 04		18 13
Chester Road	d	16 05		16 16	16 25			16 35	16 45	16 55		17 05		17 15	17 26			17 36		17 46	17 55		18 06		18 15
Erdington	d	16 07		16 18	16 27			16 37	16 47	16 57		17 07		17 17	17 28			17 38		17 48	17 57		18 08		18 17
Gravelly Hill	d	16 09		16 20	16 29			16 39	16 49	16 59		17 09		17 19	17 30			17 40		17 50	17 59		18 10		18 19
Aston	d	16 13		16 24	16 33			16 43	16 53	17 03		17 13		17 23	17 34			17 44		17 54	18 03		18 14		18 23
Duddeston	d				16 35					17 05					17 36						18 05				
Birmingham New Street 12	a	16 21		16 31	16 42			16 50	17 00	17 12		17 21		17 30	17 41			17 51		18 01	18 11		18 21		18 31
	d	16 23	16 30	16 33	16 43	16 49		16 53	17 03	17 13	17 19	17 23	17 30	17 33	17 43	17 49		17 53	17 59	18 03	18 13	18 19	18 23	18 30	18 33
Five Ways	d	16 26		16 36	16 46			16 56	17 06	17 16		17 26		17 36	17 46			17 56		18 06	18 16		18 26		18 36
University	d	16 30	16a36	16 40	16 50	16 55		17 00	17 10	17 20	17 25	17 30	17 36	17 40	17 50	17a55		18 00	18 05	18 10	18 20		18 30	18 36	18 40
Selly Oak	d	16 33		16 43	16 53			17 03	17 13	17 23		17 33		17 43	17 53			18 03		18 13	18 23		18 33		18 43
Bournville	d	16 35		16 45	16 55			17 05	17 15	17 25		17 35		17 45	17 55			18 05		18 15	18 25		18 35		18 45
Kings Norton	d	16 37		16 47	16 57			17 07	17 17	17 27		17 37		17 47	17 57			18 07		18 17	18 27		18 37		18 47
Northfield	d	16 40		16 52	17 00			17 10	17 20	17 30		17 40		17 50	18 00			18 10		18 20	18 30		18 40		18 50
Longbridge	d	16a44		16a56	17 06			17a14	17a24	17 36		17a44		17a54	18 06			18a14		18a24	18 34		18a44		18a54
Barnt Green	d				17 10					17 40					18 10						18 39				
Alvechurch	d				17 15					17 44					18 15						18 43				
Redditch	a				17 22					17 52					18 22						18 52				
Bromsgrove	a					17 09					17 40		17 51						18 21			18 44		18 49	

		LM		LM	LM	LM	LM	LM	XC	LM	LM	LM		LM	LM	LM	LM	XC	LM	LM	LM	LM		LM	LM
									◇1									◇1							
Lichfield Trent Valley	d			18 10	18 20					18 50					19 20				20 00			20 30			21 00
Lichfield City	d			18 14	18 24			18 43		18 54				19 13	19 24		19 43		20 04			20 34			21 04
Shenstone	d			18 19				18 48						19 18			19 48		20 09			20 39			21 09
Blake Street	d			18 23	18 32			18 52		19 02				19 22	19 32		19 52		20 13			20 43			21 13
Butlers Lane	d			18 25	18 34			18 54		19 04				19 24	19 34		19 54		20 15			20 45			21 15
Four Oaks	d	18 17		18 28	18 37	18 47		18 57		19 07	19 17			19 27	19 37	19 50	19 57		20 18			20 48			21 18
Sutton Coldfield	d	18 20		18 31	18 40	18 50		19 00		19 10	19 20			19 30	19 40	19 53	20 00		20 21			20 51			21 21
Wylde Green	d	18 23		18 34	18 43	18 53		19 03		19 13	19 23			19 33	19 43	19 56	20 03		20 24			20 54			21 24
Chester Road	d	18 25		18 36	18 45	18 55		19 05		19 15	19 25			19 35	19 45	19 58	20 05		20 26			20 56			21 26
Erdington	d	18 27		18 38	18 47	18 57		19 07		19 17	19 27			19 37	19 47	20 00	20 07		20 28			20 58			21 28
Gravelly Hill	d	18 29		18 40	18 49	18 59		19 09		19 19	19 29			19 39	19 49	20 02	20 09		20 30			21 00			21 30
Aston	d	18 33		18 44	18 53	19 03		19 13		19 23	19 33			19 43	19 53	20 06	20 13		20 33			21 03			21 33
Duddeston	d	18 35				19 05					19 35				19 55				20 36			21 06			21 36
Birmingham New Street 12	a	18 40		18 50	19 00	19 11		19 21		19 30	19 42			19 50	20 02	20 13	20 20		20 40			21 12			21 41
	d	18 43		18 53	19 03	19 13	19 19	19 23	19 30	19 33	19 43	19 49		19 53		20 13	20 23	20 30	20 43	20 53	20 59	21 13		21 23	21 43
Five Ways	d	18 46		18 56	19 06	19 16		19 26		19 36	19 46			19 56		20 16	20 26		20 46	20 56		21 16		21 26	21 46
University	d	18 50		19 00	19 10	19 20	19 25	19 30	19a36	19 40	19 50	19 55		20 00		20 20	20 30	20a36	20 50	21 00	21 05	21 20		21 30	21 50
Selly Oak	d	18 53		19 03	19 13	19 23		19 33		19 43	19 53			20 03		20 23	20 33		20 53	21 03		21 23		21 33	21 53
Bournville	d	18 55		19 05	19 15	19 25		19 35		19 45	19 55			20 05		20 25	20 35		20 55	21 05		21 25		21 35	21 55
Kings Norton	d	18 57		19 07	19 17	19 27		19 37		19 47	19 57			20 07		20 27	20 37		20 57	21 07		21 27		21 37	21 57
Northfield	d	19 00		19 10	19 20	19 30		19 40		19 50	20 00			20 10		20 30	20 40		21 00	21 10		21 30		21 40	22 00
Longbridge	d	19 04		19a14	19a24	19 36		19a44		19a54	20 06			20a14		20 34	20a44		21 04	21a14		21 34		21a44	22 04
Barnt Green	d	19 09				19 40					20 10					20 39			21 09			21 39			22 09
Alvechurch	d	19 13				19 45					20 15					20 43			21 13			21 43			22 13
Redditch	a	19 22				19 52					20 22					20 52			21 22			21 52			22 22
Bromsgrove	a						19 40					20 11									21 21				

Table 69

Mondays to Fridays

until 21 October

Lichfield - Birmingham - Longbridge and Redditch

		LM	LM	LM	LM	LM	LM	LM		LM	LM	LM
Lichfield Trent Valley	d			21 30		22 00				22 30	22 56	
Lichfield City	d			21 34		22 04				22 34	23 00	
Shenstone	d			21 39		22 09				22 39	23 05	
Blake Street	d			21 43		22 13				22 43	23 09	23 36
Butlers Lane	d			21 45		22 15				22 45	23 11	23 38
Four Oaks	d			21 48		22 18				22 48	23 14	23 41
Sutton Coldfield	d			21 51		22 21				22 51	23 17	23 44
Wylde Green	d			21 54		22 24				22 54	23 20	
Chester Road	d			21 56		22 26				22 56		
Erdington	d			21 58		22 28				22 58		
Gravelly Hill	d			22 00		22 30				23 00		
Aston	d			22 03		22 33				23 03		
Duddeston	d			22 06		22 36				23 06		
Birmingham New Street 12	a			22 11		22 41				23 11	23 31	23 59
	d	21 53	22 00	22 13	22 23	22 43	22 53	23 00		23 13	23 33	
Five Ways	d	21 56		22 16	22 26	22 46	22 56			23 16	23 36	
University	d	22 00	22 06	22 20	22 30	22 50	23 00	23 06		23 20	23 40	
Selly Oak	d	22 03		22 23	22 33	22 53	23 03			23 23	23 43	
Bournville	d	22 05		22 25	22 35	22 55	23 05			23 25	23 45	
Kings Norton	d	22 07		22 27	22 37	22 57	23 07			23 27	23 47	
Northfield	d	22 10		22 30	22 40	23 00	23 10			23 30	23 50	
Longbridge	d	22a14		22 34	22a44	23 04	23a14			23 34	23a54	
Barnt Green	d			22 39		23 09				23 39		
Alvechurch	d			22 43		23 13				23 43		
Redditch	a			22 52		23 22				23 52		
Bromsgrove	a		22 20					23 19				

Mondays to Fridays

from 24 October

		LM	LM	LM	LM	LM	LM	LM	LM	LM		XC ◇1 ⚲	LM	LM	LM	LM	LM	LM	LM	XC ◇1 ⚲		LM	LM	LM	LM
Lichfield Trent Valley	d							06 17					06 47				07 17					07 47			
Lichfield City	d					06 09		06 20					06 50	07 03			07 20	07 33				07 50	08 03		
Shenstone	d					06 14		06 26					06 56				07 26					07 56			
Blake Street	d				06 00	06 18		06 30					07 00	07 11			07 30	07 41				08 00	08 11		
Butlers Lane	d				06 02	06 21		06 32					07 02	07 13			07 32	07 43				08 02	08 13		
Four Oaks	d				06 05	06 24		06 35		06 54			07 05	07 16	07 24		07 35	07 46	07 54			08 05	08 16		08 24
Sutton Coldfield	d				06 09	06 27		06 39		06 57			07 09	07 20	07 27		07 39	07 50	07 57			08 09	08 20		08 27
Wylde Green	d				06 12	06 30		06 42		07 00			07 12	07 23	07 30		07 42	07 53	08 00			08 12	08 23		08 30
Chester Road	d				06 14	06 33		06 44		07 03			07 14	07 25	07 33		07 44	07 55	08 03			08 14	08 25		08 33
Erdington	d				06 16	06 35		06 46		07 05			07 16	07 27	07 35		07 46	07 57	08 05			08 16	08 27		08 35
Gravelly Hill	d				06 19	06 38		06 49		07 08			07 19	07 30	07 38		07 49	08 00	08 08			08 19	08 30		08 38
Aston	d				06 23	06 41		06 53		07 11			07 23	07 34	07 41		07 53	08 04	08 11			08 23	08 34		08 41
Duddeston	d				06 25	06 43				07 13				07 36	07 43			08 06	08 13				08 37		08 43
Birmingham New Street 12	a				06 30	06 49		07 00		07 20			07 30	07 41	07 51		08 01	08 12	08 21			08 31	08 41		08 51
	d	05 53	06 03	06 23	06 33	06 53	06 59	07 03	07 19	07 23		07 30	07 33	07 43	07 53	07 59	08 03	08 13	08 23	08 30		08 33	08 43	08 49	08 53
Five Ways	d	05 56	06 06	06 26	06 36	06 56		07 06		07 26			07 36	07 46	07 56		08 06	08 16	08 26			08 36	08 46		08 56
University	d	06 00	06 10	06 30	06 40	07 00	07 05	07 10	07 25	07 30		07a36	07 40	07 50	08 00	08 05	08 10	08 20	08 30	08a36		08 40	08 50	08 55	09 00
Selly Oak	d	06 03	06 13	06 33	06 43	07 03		07 13		07 33			07 43	07 53	08 03		08 13	08 23	08 33			08 43	08 53		09 03
Bournville	d	06 05	06 15	06 35	06 45	07 05		07 15		07 35			07 45	07 55	08 05		08 15	08 25	08 35			08 45	08 55		09 05
Kings Norton	d	06 08	06 18	06 38	06 48	07 08		07 18		07 38			07 48	07 58	08 08		08 18	08 28	08 38			08 48	08 58		09 08
Northfield	d	06 11	06 21	06 41	06 51	07 11		07 21		07 41			07 51	08 01	08 11		08 21	08 31	08 41			08 51	09 01		09 11
Longbridge	d	06a16	06 26	06a46	06 58	07a16		07 26		07a46			07 58	08a06	08a16		08 26	08a37	08a46			08 58	09a06		09a16
Barnt Green	d		06 39		07 09			07 39	07 42				08f09			08 18	08 39					09 09			
Alvechurch	d		06 43		07 13			07 43					08 13				08 43					09 13			
Redditch	a		06 52		07 22			07 52					08 22				08 52					09 22			
Bromsgrove	a						07 21		07 46							08 22								09 09	

Table 69

Mondays to Fridays

from 24 October

Lichfield - Birmingham - Longbridge and Redditch

		LM	LM	LM	XC ◇1	LM		LM	LM	LM	LM	LM	LM	XC ◇1	LM	LM		LM	LM	LM	XC ◇1	LM	LM	LM	LM
Lichfield Trent Valley	d	08 17				08 47		08 58			09 17	09 28			09 47				10 17			10 47			11 17
Lichfield City	d	08 20	08 32			08 50		09 01			09 20	09 31			09 50				10 20			10 50			11 20
Shenstone	d	08 26	08 37			08 56		09 07			09 26	09 37			09 56				10 26			10 56			11 26
Blake Street	d	08 30	08 41			09 00		09 11			09 30	09 41			10 00				10 30			11 00			11 30
Butlers Lane	d	08 32	08 44			09 02		09 13			09 32	09 43			10 02				10 32			11 02			11 32
Four Oaks	d	08 35	08 47	08 54		09 05		09 16		09 24	09 35	09 46	09 54		10 05			10 24	10 35	10 54		11 05		11 24	11 35
Sutton Coldfield	d	08 39	08 50	08 57		09 09		09 20		09 27	09 39	09 50	09 57		10 09			10 27	10 39	10 57		11 09		11 27	11 39
Wylde Green	d	08 42	08 53	09 00		09 12		09 23		09 30	09 42	09 53	10 00		10 12			10 30	10 42	11 00		11 12		11 30	11 42
Chester Road	d	08 44	08 56	09 03		09 14		09 25		09 33	09 44	09 55	10 03		10 14			10 33	10 44	11 03		11 14		11 33	11 44
Erdington	d	08 46	08 58	09 05		09 16		09 27		09 35	09 46	09 57	10 05		10 16			10 35	10 46	11 05		11 16		11 35	11 46
Gravelly Hill	d	08 49	09 01	09 08		09 19		09 30		09 38	09 49	10 00	10 08		10 19			10 38	10 49	11 08		11 19		11 38	11 49
Aston	d	08 53	09 04	09 11		09 23		09 34		09 41	09 53	10 04	10 11		10 23			10 41	10 53	11 11		11 23		11 41	11 53
Duddeston	d			09 13						09 43			10 13					10 43		11 13				11 43	
Birmingham New Street 12	a	09 01	09 11	09 19		09 31		09 42		09 51	10 01	10 11	10 21		10 31			10 51	11 01	11 21		11 31		11 51	12 01
	d	09 03	09 13	09 23	09 30	09 33			09 49	09 53	10 03	10 13	10 23	10 30	10 33	10 49		10 53	11 03	11 23	11 30	11 33	11 49	11 53	12 03
Five Ways	d	09 06	09 16	09 26		09 36				09 56	10 06	10 16	10 26		10 36			10 56	11 06	11 26		11 36		11 56	12 06
University	d	09 10	09 20	09 30	09a36	09 40			09 55	10 00	10 10	10 20	10 30	10a36	10 40	10 55		11 00	11 10	11 30	11a36	11 40	11 55	12 00	12 10
Selly Oak	d	09 13	09 23	09 33		09 43				10 03	10 13	10 23	10 33		10 43			11 03	11 13	11 33		11 43		12 03	12 13
Bournville	d	09 15	09 25	09 35		09 45				10 05	10 15	10 25	10 35		10 45			11 05	11 15	11 35		11 45		12 05	12 15
Kings Norton	d	09 18	09 28	09 38		09 48				10 08	10 18	10 28	10 38		10 48			11 08	11 18	11 38		11 48		12 08	12 18
Northfield	d	09 21	09 31	09 41		09 51				10 11	10 21	10 31	10 41		10 51			11 11	11 21	11 41		11 51		12 11	12 21
Longbridge	d	09 26	09a37	09a46		09 58				10a16	10 26	10a37	10a46		10 58			11a16	11 26	11a46		11 58		12a16	12 26
Barnt Green	d	09 39				10 09					10 39				11 09				11 39			12 09			12 39
Alvechurch	d	09 43				10 13					10 43				11 13				11 43			12 13			12 43
Redditch	a	09 52				10 22					10 52				11 22				11 52			12 22			12 52
Bromsgrove	a								10 09							11 09							12 09		

		LM		XC ◇1	LM	LM	LM	LM	LM	XC ◇1	LM	LM		LM	LM	LM	XC ◇1	LM	LM	LM	LM	LM		XC ◇1	LM
Lichfield Trent Valley	d				11 47			12 17			12 47				13 17			13 47			14 17				14 47
Lichfield City	d				11 50			12 20			12 50				13 20			13 50			14 20				14 50
Shenstone	d				11 56			12 26			12 56				13 26			13 56			14 26				14 56
Blake Street	d				12 00			12 30			13 00				13 30			14 00			14 30				15 00
Butlers Lane	d				12 02			12 32			13 02				13 32			14 02			14 32				15 02
Four Oaks	d	11 54			12 05		12 24	12 35	12 54		13 05			13 24	13 35	13 54		14 05		14 24	14 35	14 54			15 05
Sutton Coldfield	d	11 57			12 09		12 27	12 39	12 57		13 09			13 27	13 39	13 57		14 09		14 27	14 39	14 57			15 09
Wylde Green	d	12 00			12 12		12 30	12 42	13 00		13 12			13 30	13 42	14 00		14 12		14 30	14 42	15 00			15 12
Chester Road	d	12 03			12 14		12 33	12 44	13 03		13 14			13 33	13 44	14 03		14 14		14 33	14 44	15 03			15 14
Erdington	d	12 05			12 16		12 35	12 46	13 05		13 16			13 35	13 46	14 05		14 16		14 35	14 46	15 05			15 16
Gravelly Hill	d	12 08			12 19		12 38	12 49	13 08		13 19			13 38	13 49	14 08		14 19		14 38	14 49	15 08			15 19
Aston	d	12 11			12 23		12 41	12 53	13 11		13 23			13 41	13 53	14 11		14 23		14 41	14 53	15 11			15 23
Duddeston	d	12 13					12 43		13 13					13 43		14 13				14 43		15 13			
Birmingham New Street 12	a	12 21			12 31		12 51	13 01	13 21		13 31			13 51	14 01	14 21		14 31		14 51	15 01	15 21			15 31
	d	12 23		12 30	12 33	12 49	12 53	13 03	13 23	13 30	13 33	13 49		13 53	14 03	14 23	14 30	14 33	14 49	14 53	15 03	15 23		15 30	15 33
Five Ways	d	12 26			12 36		12 56	13 06	13 26		13 36			13 56	14 06	14 26		14 36		14 56	15 06	15 26			15 36
University	d	12 30		12a36	12 40	12 55	13 00	13 10	13 30	13a36	13 40	13 55		14 00	14 10	14 30	14a36	14 40	14 55	15 00	15 10	15 30		15a36	15 40
Selly Oak	d	12 33			12 43		13 03	13 13	13 33		13 43			14 03	14 13	14 33		14 43		15 03	15 13	15 33			15 43
Bournville	d	12 35			12 45		13 05	13 15	13 35		13 45			14 05	14 15	14 35		14 45		15 05	15 15	15 35			15 45
Kings Norton	d	12 38			12 48		13 08	13 18	13 38		13 48			14 08	14 18	14 38		14 48		15 08	15 18	15 38			15 48
Northfield	d	12 41			12 51		13 11	13 21	13 41		13 51			14 11	14 21	14 41		14 51		15 11	15 21	15 41			15 51
Longbridge	d	12a46			12 58		13a16	13 26	13a46		13 58			14a16	14 26	14a46		14 58		15a16	15 26	15a46			15 58
Barnt Green	d				13 09			13 39			14 09				14 39			15 09			15 39				16 09
Alvechurch	d				13 13			13 43			14 13				14 43			15 13			15 43				16 13
Redditch	a				13 22			13 52			14 22				14 52			15 22			15 52				16 22
Bromsgrove	a					13 09						14 09							15 09						

Table 69

Mondays to Fridays

from 24 October

Lichfield - Birmingham - Longbridge and Redditch

		LM	LM	LM	LM	LM	LM	LM		XC ◇1	LM	LM	LM	LM	LM	LM	LM	LM		XC ◇1	LM	LM	LM	LM	LM
Lichfield Trent Valley	d				15 17						15 47				16 17						16 47				
Lichfield City	d				15 20						15 50				16 20						16 50				
Shenstone	d				15 26						15 56				16 26						16 56				
Blake Street	d				15 30			15 49			16 00				16 30						17 00				
Butlers Lane	d				15 32			15 51			16 02				16 32						17 02				
Four Oaks	d			15 24	15 35	15 44		15 54			16 05			16 24	16 35			16 54			17 05			17 24	
Sutton Coldfield	d			15 27	15 39	15 47		15 57			16 09			16 27	16 39			16 57			17 09			17 27	
Wylde Green	d			15 30	15 42	15 50		16 00			16 12			16 30	16 42			17 00			17 12			17 30	
Chester Road	d			15 33	15 44	15 53		16 03			16 14			16 33	16 44			17 03			17 14			17 33	
Erdington	d			15 35	15 46	15 55		16 05			16 16			16 35	16 46			17 05			17 16			17 35	
Gravelly Hill	d			15 38	15 49	15 58		16 08			16 19			16 38	16 49			17 08			17 19			17 38	
Aston	d			15 41	15 53	16 01		16 11			16 23			16 41	16 53			17 11			17 23			17 41	
Duddeston	d			15 43		16 04		16 13						16 43				17 13						17 43	
Birmingham New Street 12	a			15 51	16 01	16 11		16 21			16 31			16 51	17 01			17 21			17 31			17 51	
	d	15 43	15 49	15 53	16 03	16 13	16 19	16 23		16 30	16 33	16 43	16 49	16 53	17 03	17 13	17 19	17 23		17 30	17 33	17 43	17 49	17 53	17 59
Five Ways	d	15 46		15 56	16 06	16 16		16 26			16 36	16 46		16 56	17 06	17 16		17 26			17 36	17 46		17 56	
University	d	15 50	15 55	16 00	16 10	16 20	16 25	16 30		16a36	16 40	16 50	16 55	17 00	17 10	17 20	17 25	17 30		17 36	17 40	17 50	17a55	18 00	18 05
Selly Oak	d	15 53		16 03	16 13	16 23		16 33			16 43	16 53		17 03	17 13	17 23		17 33			17 43	17 53		18 03	
Bournville	d	15 55		16 05	16 15	16 25		16 35			16 45	16 55		17 05	17 15	17 25		17 35			17 45	17 55		18 05	
Kings Norton	d	15 58		16 08	16 18	16 28		16 38			16 48	16 58		17 08	17 18	17 28		17 38			17 48	17 58		18 08	
Northfield	d	16 01		16 11	16 21	16 31		16 41			16 51	17 01		17 11	17 21	17 31		17 41			17 51	18 01		18 11	
Longbridge	d	16a06		16a16	16 26	16a36		16a46			16 58	17a06		17a16	17 26	17a37		17a46			17 58	18a06		18a16	
Barnt Green	d				16 39						17 09				17 39						18 09				
Alvechurch	d				16 43						17 13				17 43						18 13				
Redditch	a				16 52						17 22				17 52						18 22				
Bromsgrove	a		16 09				16 40						17 09				17 40			17 51					18 21

		LM	LM	LM		XC ◇1	LM	LM	LM	LM	LM	XC ◇1	LM	LM		LM	LM	LM	LM	XC ◇1	LM	LM	LM	LM
Lichfield Trent Valley	d	17 17					17 47		18 17				18 47					19 17			19 57			20 27
Lichfield City	d	17 20					17 50		18 20				18 50					19 20			20 00			20 30
Shenstone	d	17 26					17 56		18 26				18 56					19 26			20 06			20 36
Blake Street	d	17 30					18 00		18 30				19 00					19 30			20 10			20 40
Butlers Lane	d	17 32					18 02		18 32				19 02					19 32			20 12			20 42
Four Oaks	d	17 35		17 54			18 05	18 24	18 35		18 54		19 05	19 16				19 35	19 54		20 15			20 45
Sutton Coldfield	d	17 39		17 57			18 09	18 27	18 39		18 57		19 09	19 19				19 39	19 57		20 19			20 49
Wylde Green	d	17 42		18 00			18 12	18 30	18 42		19 00		19 12	19 22				19 42	20 00		20 22			20 52
Chester Road	d	17 44		18 03			18 14	18 33	18 44		19 03		19 14	19 25				19 44	20 03		20 24			20 54
Erdington	d	17 46		18 05			18 16	18 35	18 46		19 05		19 16	19 27				19 46	20 05		20 26			20 56
Gravelly Hill	d	17 49		18 08			18 19	18 38	18 49		19 08		19 19	19 30				19 49	20 08		20 29			20 59
Aston	d	17 53		18 11			18 23	18 41	18 53		19 11		19 23	19 33				19 53	20 11		20 33			21 03
Duddeston	d			18 13				18 43			19 13			19 35				19 55			20 35			21 05
Birmingham New Street 12	a	18 01		18 21			18 31	18 51	19 01		19 21		19 34	19 41				20 01	20 21		20 41			21 11
	d	18 04	18 19	18 23		18 30	18 33	18 53	19 03	19 19	19 23	19 30		19 43		19 49	19 53	20 13	20 23	20 30	20 43	20 53	20 59	21 13
Five Ways	d	18 07		18 26			18 36	18 56	19 06		19 26			19 46			19 56	20 16	20 26		20 46	20 56		21 16
University	d	18 11		18 30		18 36	18 40	19 00	19 10	19 25	19 30	19a36		19 50		19 55	20 00	20 20	20 30	20a36	20 50	21 00	21 05	21 20
Selly Oak	d	18 14		18 33			18 43	19 03	19 13		19 33			19 53			20 03	20 23	20 33		20 53	21 03		21 23
Bournville	d	18 16		18 35			18 45	19 05	19 15		19 35			19 55			20 05	20 25	20 35		20 55	21 05		21 25
Kings Norton	d	18 19		18 38			18 48	19 08	19 18		19 38			19 58			20 08	20 28	20 39		20 58	21 08		21 28
Northfield	d	18 22		18 41			18 51	19 11	19 21		19 41			20 01			20 11	20 31	20 42		21 01	21 11		21 31
Longbridge	d	18 27		18a46			18 58	19a16	19 26		19a46			20 05			20a16	20 35	20a46		21 05	21a16		21 35
Barnt Green	d	18 40					19 09		19 39					20 09				20 39			21 09			21 39
Alvechurch	d	18 44					19 13		19 43					20 14				20 44			21 14			21 44
Redditch	a	18 52					19 22		19 52					20 22				20 52			21 22			21 52
Bromsgrove	a		18 44			18 49				19 40						20 11							21 21	

		LM	LM	LM	LM	LM	LM	LM	LM	LM		LM	LM
Lichfield Trent Valley	d		20 57			21 27		21 57				22 27	22 55
Lichfield City	d		21 00			21 30		22 00				22 30	22 58
Shenstone	d		21 06			21 36		22 06				22 36	23 04
Blake Street	d		21 10			21 40		22 10				22 40	23 08
Butlers Lane	d		21 12			21 42		22 12				22 42	23 10
Four Oaks	d		21 15			21 45		22 15				22 45	23 13
Sutton Coldfield	d		21 19			21 49		22 19				22 49	23 17
Wylde Green	d		21 22			21 52		22 22				22 52	23 20
Chester Road	d		21 24			21 54		22 24				22 54	
Erdington	d		21 26			21 56		22 26				22 56	
Gravelly Hill	d		21 29			21 59		22 29				22 59	
Aston	d		21 33			22 03		22 33				23 03	
Duddeston	d		21 35			22 05		22 35				23 05	
Birmingham New Street 12	a		21 41			22 13		22 41				23 11	23 31
	d	21 23	21 43	21 53	22 00	22 13	22 23	22 43	22 53	23 00		23 13	23 33
Five Ways	d	21 26	21 46	21 56		22 16	22 26	22 46	22 56			23 16	23 36
University	d	21 30	21 50	22 00	22 06	22 20	22 30	22 50	23 00	23 06		23 20	23 40
Selly Oak	d	21 33	21 53	22 03		22 23	22 33	22 53	23 03			23 23	23 43
Bournville	d	21 35	21 55	22 05		22 25	22 35	22 55	23 05			23 25	23 45
Kings Norton	d	21 38	21 58	22 08		22 28	22 38	22 58	23 08			23 28	23 48
Northfield	d	21 41	22 01	22 11		22 31	22 41	23 01	23 11			23 31	23 51
Longbridge	d	21a46	22 05	22a16		22 35	22a46	23 05	23a16			23 35	23a56
Barnt Green	d		22 09			22 39		23 09				23 39	
Alvechurch	d		22 14			22 44		23 14				23 44	
Redditch	a		22 22			22 52		23 22				23 53	
Bromsgrove	a				22 20					23 19			

Table 69

Saturdays
until 22 October

Lichfield - Birmingham - Longbridge and Redditch

		XC ◇1	LM	LM	LM	LM	LM	LM	LM	LM		LM	LM	LM	XC ◇1 ⊥	LM	LM	LM	LM	LM		LM	LM	XC ◇1 ⊥	LM
Lichfield Trent Valley	d											06 20				06 50				07 20					07 50
Lichfield City	d											06 24	06 38			06 54	07 07			07 24			07 43		07 54
Shenstone	d											06 29				06 59				07 29			07 48		
Blake Street	d						06 03					06 33				07 03				07 33			07 52		08 02
Butlers Lane	d						06 05					06 35				07 05				07 35			07 54		08 04
Four Oaks	d						06 08					06 38	06 48			07 08	07 17			07 38		07 47	07 57		08 07
Sutton Coldfield	d						06 11					06 41	06 51			07 11	07 20			07 41		07 50	08 00		08 10
Wylde Green	d						06 14					06 44	06 54			07 14	07 23			07 44		07 53	08 03		08 13
Chester Road	d						06 16					06 46	06 56			07 16	07 25			07 46		07 55	08 05		08 15
Erdington	d						06 17					06 48	06 58			07 18	07 27			07 47		07 57	08 07		08 17
Gravelly Hill	d						06 20					06 50	07 00			07 20	07 29			07 50		07 59	08 09		08 19
Aston	d						06 23					06 53	07 04			07 23	07 33			07 53		08 03	08 13		08 23
Duddeston	d						06 26					06 56	07 06			07 26	07 35					08 05			
Birmingham New Street [12]	a						06 31					07 00	07 11			07 31	07 40			08 00		08 11	08 21		08 31
	d	05 42	05 53	06 03	06 13	06 23	06 33	06 43	06 49	06 53		07 03	07 13	07 23	07 30	07 33	07 43	07 49	07 53	08 03		08 13	08 23	08 30	08 33
Five Ways	d		05 56	06 06	06 16	06 26	06 36	06 46		06 56		07 06	07 16	07 26		07 36	07 46		07 56	08 06		08 16	08 26		08 36
University	d		06 00	06 10	06 20	06 30	06 40	06 50	06 55	07 00		07 10	07 20	07 30	07a36	07 40	07 50	07 55	08 00	08 10		08 20	08 30	08a36	08 40
Selly Oak	d		06 03	06 13	06 23	06 33	06 43	06 53		07 03		07 13	07 23	07 33		07 43	07 53		08 03	08 13		08 23	08 33		08 43
Bournville	d		06 05	06 15	06 25	06 35	06 45	06 55		07 05		07 15	07 25	07 35		07 45	07 55		08 05	08 15		08 25	08 35		08 45
Kings Norton	d		06 07	06 17	06 27	06 37	06 47	06 57		07 07		07 17	07 27	07 37		07 47	07 57		08 07	08 17		08 27	08 37		08 47
Northfield	d		06 10	06 20	06 30	06 40	06 50	07 00		07 10		07 20	07 30	07 40		07 50	08 00		08 10	08 20		08 30	08 40		08 50
Longbridge	d		06a14	06a24	06 34	06a44	06a54	07 06		07a14		07a24	07 34	07a44		07a54	08 06		08a14	08a24		08 34	08a44		08a54
Barnt Green	d				06 39			07 10					07 39				08 10					08 39			
Alvechurch	d				06 43			07 15					07 43				08 15					08 43			
Redditch	a				06 52			07 22					07 52				08 22					08 52			
Bromsgrove	a	06 03							07 09									08 09							

		LM	LM	LM	LM	LM		LM	XC ◇1 ⊥	LM	LM	LM	LM	LM	LM	LM		XC ◇1 ⊥	LM	LM	LM	LM	LM	LM	LM
Lichfield Trent Valley	d				08 20					08 50				09 20					09 50				10 20		
Lichfield City	d			08 13	08 24			08 43		08 54			09 13	09 24		09 43			09 54			10 13	10 24		10 43
Shenstone	d			08 18				08 48					09 18			09 48						10 18			10 48
Blake Street	d			08 22	08 32			08 52		09 02			09 22	09 32		09 52			10 02			10 22	10 32		10 52
Butlers Lane	d			08 24	08 34			08 54		09 04			09 24	09 34		09 54			10 04			10 24	10 34		10 54
Four Oaks	d	08 17		08 27	08 37	08 47		08 57		09 07	09 17		09 27	09 37	09 47	09 57			10 07	10 17		10 27	10 37	10 47	10 57
Sutton Coldfield	d	08 20		08 30	08 40	08 50		09 00		09 10	09 20		09 30	09 40	09 50	10 00			10 10	10 20		10 30	10 40	10 50	11 00
Wylde Green	d	08 23		08 33	08 43	08 53		09 03		09 13	09 23		09 33	09 43	09 53	10 03			10 13	10 23		10 33	10 43	10 53	11 03
Chester Road	d	08 25		08 35	08 45	08 55		09 05		09 15	09 25		09 35	09 45	09 55	10 05			10 15	10 25		10 35	10 45	10 55	11 05
Erdington	d	08 27		08 37	08 47	08 57		09 07		09 17	09 27		09 37	09 47	09 57	10 07			10 17	10 27		10 37	10 47	10 57	11 07
Gravelly Hill	d	08 29		08 39	08 49	08 59		09 09		09 19	09 29		09 39	09 49	09 59	10 09			10 19	10 29		10 39	10 49	10 59	11 09
Aston	d	08 33		08 43	08 53	09 03		09 13		09 23	09 33		09 43	09 53	10 03	10 13			10 23	10 33		10 43	10 53	11 03	11 13
Duddeston	d	08 35				09 05					09 35				10 05					10 35				11 05	
Birmingham New Street [12]	a	08 41		08 50	09 00	09 10		09 21		09 31	09 41		09 50	10 00	10 10	10 21			10 31	10 41		10 50	11 00	11 10	11 21
	d	08 43	08 49	08 53	09 03	09 13		09 23	09 30	09 33	09 43	09 49	09 53	10 03	10 13	10 23		10 30	10 33	10 43	10 49	10 53	11 03	11 13	11 23
Five Ways	d	08 46		08 56	09 06	09 16		09 26		09 36	09 46		09 56	10 06	10 16	10 26			10 36	10 46		10 56	11 06	11 16	11 26
University	d	08 50	08 55	09 00	09 10	09 20		09 30	09a36	09 40	09 50	09 55	10 00	10 10	10 20	10 30		10a36	10 40	10 50	10 55	11 00	11 10	11 20	11 30
Selly Oak	d	08 53		09 03	09 13	09 23		09 33		09 43	09 53		10 03	10 13	10 23	10 33			10 43	10 53		11 03	11 13	11 23	11 33
Bournville	d	08 55		09 05	09 15	09 25		09 35		09 45	09 55		10 05	10 15	10 25	10 35			10 45	10 55		11 05	11 15	11 25	11 35
Kings Norton	d	08 57		09 07	09 17	09 27		09 37		09 47	09 57		10 07	10 17	10 27	10 37			10 47	10 57		11 07	11 17	11 27	11 37
Northfield	d	09 00		09 10	09 20	09 30		09 40		09 50	10 00		10 10	10 20	10 30	10 40			10 50	11 00		11 10	11 20	11 30	11 40
Longbridge	d	09 06		09a14	09a24	09 34		09a44		09a54	10 06		10a14	10a24	10 34	10a44			10a54	11 06		11a14	11a24	11 34	11a44
Barnt Green	d	09 10				09 39					10 10				10 39					11 10				11 39	
Alvechurch	d	09 15				09 43					10 15				10 43					11 15				11 43	
Redditch	a	09 22				09 52					10 22				10 52					11 22				11 52	
Bromsgrove	a		09 09									10 09									11 09				

		XC ◇1 ⊥		LM	LM	LM	LM	LM	LM	LM	XC ◇1 ⊥	LM		LM	LM	LM	LM	LM	LM	XC ◇1 ⊥	LM	LM		LM	LM
Lichfield Trent Valley	d			10 50				11 20				11 50					12 20				12 50				
Lichfield City	d			10 54			11 13	11 24		11 43		11 54				12 13	12 24		12 43		12 54				13 13
Shenstone	d						11 18			11 48						12 18			12 48						13 18
Blake Street	d			11 02			11 22	11 32		11 52		12 02				12 22	12 32		12 52		13 02				13 22
Butlers Lane	d			11 04			11 24	11 34		11 54		12 04				12 24	12 34		12 54		13 04				13 24
Four Oaks	d			11 07	11 17		11 27	11 37	11 47	11 57		12 07		12 17		12 27	12 37	12 47	12 57		13 07	13 17			13 27
Sutton Coldfield	d			11 10	11 20		11 30	11 40	11 50	12 00		12 10		12 20		12 30	12 40	12 50	13 00		13 10	13 20			13 30
Wylde Green	d			11 13	11 23		11 33	11 43	11 53	12 03		12 13		12 23		12 33	12 43	12 53	13 03		13 13	13 23			13 33
Chester Road	d			11 15	11 25		11 35	11 45	11 55	12 05		12 15		12 25		12 35	12 45	12 55	13 05		13 15	13 25			13 35
Erdington	d			11 17	11 27		11 37	11 47	11 57	12 07		12 17		12 27		12 37	12 47	12 57	13 07		13 17	13 27			13 37
Gravelly Hill	d			11 19	11 29		11 39	11 49	11 59	12 09		12 19		12 29		12 39	12 49	12 59	13 09		13 19	13 29			13 39
Aston	d			11 23	11 33		11 43	11 53	12 03	12 13		12 23		12 33		12 43	12 53	13 03	13 13		13 23	13 33			13 43
Duddeston	d				11 35				12 05					12 35				13 05				13 35			
Birmingham New Street [12]	a			11 30	11 41		11 50	12 00	12 10	12 21		12 30		12 41		12 50	13 00	13 10	13 21		13 30	13 41			13 50
	d	11 30		11 33	11 43	11 49	11 53	12 03	12 13	12 23	12 30	12 33		12 43	12 49	12 53	13 03	13 13	13 23	13 30	13 33	13 43		13 49	13 53
Five Ways	d			11 36	11 46		11 56	12 06	12 16	12 26		12 36		12 46		12 56	13 06	13 16	13 26		13 36	13 46			13 56
University	d	11a36		11 40	11 50	11 55	12 00	12 10	12 20	12 30	12a36	12 40		12 50	12 55	13 00	13 10	13 20	13 30	13a36	13 40	13 50		13 55	14 00
Selly Oak	d			11 43	11 53		12 03	12 13	12 23	12 33		12 43		12 53		13 03	13 13	13 23	13 33		13 43	13 53			14 03
Bournville	d			11 45	11 55		12 05	12 15	12 25	12 35		12 45		12 55		13 05	13 15	13 25	13 35		13 45	13 55			14 05
Kings Norton	d			11 47	11 57		12 07	12 17	12 27	12 37		12 47		12 57		13 07	13 17	13 27	13 37		13 47	13 57			14 07
Northfield	d			11 50	12 00		12 10	12 20	12 30	12 40		12 50		13 00		13 10	13 20	13 30	13 40		13 50	14 00			14 10
Longbridge	d			11a54	12 06		12a14	12a24	12 34	12a44		12a54		13 06		13a14	13a24	13 34	13a44		13a54	14 06			14a14
Barnt Green	d				12 10				12 39					13 10				13 39				14 10			
Alvechurch	d				12 15				12 43					13 15				13 43				14 15			
Redditch	a				12 22				12 52					13 22				13 52				14 22			
Bromsgrove	a					12 09									13 09									14 10	

Table 69

Saturdays
until 22 October

Lichfield - Birmingham - Longbridge and Redditch

		LM	LM	LM	XC ◇1	LM	LM	LM		LM	LM	LM	LM	XC ◇1	LM	LM	LM	LM		LM	LM	LM	LM	XC ◇1	LM
Lichfield Trent Valley	d	13 20				13 50					14 20				14 50					15 20					15 50
Lichfield City	d	13 24		13 43		13 54				14 13	14 24		14 43		14 54			15 13		15 24			15 43		15 54
Shenstone	d			13 48						14 18			14 48					15 18					15 48		
Blake Street	d	13 32		13 52		14 02				14 22	14 32		14 52		15 02			15 22		15 32			15 52		16 02
Butlers Lane	d	13 34		13 54		14 04				14 24	14 34		14 54		15 04			15 24		15 34			15 54		16 04
Four Oaks	d	13 37	13 47	13 57		14 07	14 17			14 27	14 37	14 47	14 57		15 07	15 17		15 27		15 37	15 47		15 57		16 07
Sutton Coldfield	d	13 40	13 50	14 00		14 10	14 20			14 30	14 40	14 50	15 00		15 10	15 20		15 30		15 40	15 50		16 00		16 10
Wylde Green	d	13 43	13 53	14 03		14 13	14 23			14 33	14 43	14 53	15 03		15 13	15 23		15 33		15 43	15 53		16 03		16 13
Chester Road	d	13 45	13 55	14 05		14 15	14 25			14 35	14 45	14 55	15 05		15 15	15 25		15 35		15 45	15 55		16 05		16 15
Erdington	d	13 47	13 57	14 07		14 17	14 27			14 37	14 47	14 57	15 07		15 17	15 27		15 37		15 47	15 57		16 07		16 17
Gravelly Hill	d	13 49	13 59	14 09		14 19	14 29			14 39	14 49	14 59	15 09		15 19	15 29		15 39		15 49	15 59		16 09		16 19
Aston	d	13 53	14 03	14 13		14 23	14 33			14 43	14 53	15 03	15 13		15 23	15 33		15 43		15 53	16 03		16 13		16 23
Duddeston	d		14 05				14 35					15 05				15 35					16 05				
Birmingham New Street 12	a	14 00	14 10	14 21		14 30	14 41			14 50	15 00	15 10	15 20		15 30	15 41		15 50		16 00	16 10		16 21		16 30
	d	14 03	14 13	14 23	14 30	14 33	14 43	14 49		14 53	15 03	15 13	15 23	15 30	15 33	15 43	15 49	15 53		16 03	16 13	16 19	16 23	16 30	16 33
Five Ways	d	14 06	14 16	14 26		14 36	14 46			14 56	15 06	15 16	15 26		15 36	15 46		15 56		16 06	16 16		16 26		16 36
University	d	14 10	14 20	14 30	14a36	14 40	14 50	14 55		15 00	15 10	15 20	15 30	15a36	15 40	15 50	15 55	16 00		16 10	16 20		16 30	16a36	16 40
Selly Oak	d	14 13	14 23	14 33		14 43	14 53			15 03	15 13	15 23	15 33		15 43	15 53		16 03		16 13	16 23		16 33		16 43
Bournville	d	14 15	14 25	14 35		14 45	14 55			15 05	15 15	15 25	15 35		15 45	15 55		16 05		16 15	16 25		16 35		16 45
Kings Norton	d	14 17	14 27	14 37		14 47	14 57			15 07	15 17	15 27	15 37		15 47	15 57		16 07		16 17	16 27		16 37		16 47
Northfield	d	14 20	14 30	14 40		14 50	15 00			15 10	15 20	15 30	15 40		15 50	16 00		16 10		16 20	16 30		16 40		16 50
Longbridge	d	14a24	14 34	14a44		14a54	15 06			15a14	15a24	15 34	15a44		15a54	16 06		16a14		16a24	16 36		16a44		16a54
Barnt Green	d		14 39				15 10					15 39				16 10					16 40				
Alvechurch	d		14 43				15 15					15 43				16 15					16 45				
Redditch	a		14 52				15 22					15 52				16 22					16 52				
Bromsgrove	a							15 09									16 09					16 43			

		LM	LM	LM		LM	LM	LM	LM	XC ◇1	LM	LM	LM	LM		LM	LM	LM	XC ◇1	LM	LM	LM	LM	LM	
Lichfield Trent Valley	d					16 20					16 50					17 20				17 50				18 20	
Lichfield City	d			16 13		16 24			16 43		16 54			17 13		17 24		17 43		17 54			18 13	18 24	
Shenstone	d			16 18					16 48					17 18				17 48					18 18		
Blake Street	d			16 22		16 32			16 52		17 02			17 22		17 32		17 52		18 02			18 22	18 32	
Butlers Lane	d			16 24		16 34			16 54		17 04			17 24		17 34		17 54		18 04			18 24	18 34	
Four Oaks	d	16 17		16 27		16 37	16 47		16 57		17 07	17 17		17 27		17 37	17 47	17 57		18 07	18 17		18 27	18 37	
Sutton Coldfield	d	16 20		16 30		16 40	16 50		17 00		17 10	17 20		17 30		17 40	17 50	18 00		18 10	18 20		18 30	18 40	
Wylde Green	d	16 23		16 33		16 43	16 53		17 03		17 13	17 23		17 33		17 43	17 53	18 03		18 13	18 23		18 33	18 43	
Chester Road	d	16 25		16 35		16 45	16 55		17 05		17 15	17 25		17 35		17 45	17 55	18 05		18 15	18 25		18 35	18 45	
Erdington	d	16 27		16 37		16 47	16 57		17 07		17 17	17 27		17 37		17 47	17 57	18 07		18 17	18 27		18 37	18 47	
Gravelly Hill	d	16 29		16 39		16 49	16 59		17 09		17 19	17 29		17 39		17 49	17 59	18 09		18 19	18 29		18 39	18 49	
Aston	d	16 33		16 43		16 53	17 03		17 13		17 23	17 33		17 43		17 53	18 03	18 13		18 23	18 33		18 43	18 53	
Duddeston	d	16 35					17 05					17 35					18 05				18 35				
Birmingham New Street 12	a	16 41		16 50		17 00	17 10		17 21		17 30	17 41		17 50		18 00	18 10	18 21		18 30	18 41		18 50	19 00	
	d	16 43	16 49	16 53		17 03	17 13	17 19	17 23	17 30	17 33	17 43	17 49	17 53		18 03	18 13	18 23	18 30	18 33	18 43	18 49	18 53	19 03	
Five Ways	d	16 46		16 56		17 06	17 16		17 26		17 36	17 46		17 56		18 06	18 16	18 26		18 36	18 46		18 56	19 06	
University	d	16 50	16 55	17 00		17 10	17 20		17 30	17 36	17 40	17 50	17 55	18 00		18 10	18 20	18 30	18a36	18 40	18 50	18 55	19 00	19 10	
Selly Oak	d	16 53		17 03		17 13	17 23		17 33		17 43	17 53		18 03		18 13	18 23	18 33		18 43	18 53		19 03	19 13	
Bournville	d	16 55		17 05		17 15	17 25		17 35		17 45	17 55		18 05		18 15	18 25	18 35		18 45	18 55		19 05	19 15	
Kings Norton	d	16 57		17 07		17 17	17 27		17 37		17 47	17 57		18 07		18 17	18 27	18 37		18 47	18 57		19 07	19 17	
Northfield	d	17 00		17 10		17 20	17 30		17 40		17 50	18 00		18 10		18 20	18 30	18 40		18 50	19 00		19 10	19 20	
Longbridge	d	17 06		17a14		17a24	17 36		17a44		17a54	18 06		18a14		18a24	18 34	18a44		18a54	19 06		19a14	19a24	
Barnt Green	d	17 10					17 40					18 10					18 39				19 10				
Alvechurch	d	17 15					17 45					18 15					18 43				19 15				
Redditch	a	17 22					17 52					18 22					18 52				19 22				
Bromsgrove	a		17 10					17 40		17 49			18 09									19 09			

		LM	LM	LM	XC ◇1	LM	LM	LM	LM	LM		LM	XC ◇1	LM	LM	LM	LM	LM	LM	LM		LM	LM	LM	LM
Lichfield Trent Valley	d					18 50			19 20					20 00			20 30		21 00			21 30		22 00	
Lichfield City	d			18 43		18 54		19 13	19 24			19 43		20 04			20 34		21 04			21 34		22 04	
Shenstone	d			18 48				19 18				19 48		20 09			20 39		21 09			21 39		22 09	
Blake Street	d			18 52		19 02		19 22	19 32			19 52		20 13			20 43		21 13			21 43		22 13	
Butlers Lane	d			18 54		19 04		19 24	19 34			19 54		20 15			20 45		21 15			21 45		22 15	
Four Oaks	d	18 47		18 57		19 07	19 17	19 27	19 37	19 50		19 57		20 18			20 48		21 18			21 48		22 18	
Sutton Coldfield	d	18 50		19 00		19 10	19 20	19 30	19 40	19 53		20 00		20 21			20 51		21 21			21 51		22 21	
Wylde Green	d	18 53		19 03		19 13	19 23	19 33	19 43	19 56		20 03		20 24			20 54		21 24			21 54		22 24	
Chester Road	d	18 55		19 05		19 15	19 25	19 35	19 45	19 58		20 05		20 26			20 56		21 26			21 56		22 26	
Erdington	d	18 57		19 07		19 17	19 27	19 37	19 47	20 00		20 07		20 28			20 58		21 28			21 58		22 28	
Gravelly Hill	d	18 59		19 09		19 19	19 29	19 39	19 49	20 02		20 09		20 30			21 00		21 30			22 00		22 30	
Aston	d	19 03		19 13		19 23	19 33	19 43	19 53	20 06		20 13		20 33			21 03		21 33			22 03		22 33	
Duddeston	d	19 05					19 35		19 55					20 36			21 06		21 36			22 06		22 36	
Birmingham New Street 12	a	19 10		19 21		19 30	19 41	19 50	20 02	20 13		20 20		20 41			21 12		21 41			22 11		22 41	
	d	19 13	19 19	19 23	19 30	19 33	19 43	19 53		20 13		20 23	20 30	20 43	20 53	20 59	21 13	21 23	21 43	21 53		22 13	22 23	22 43	22 53
Five Ways	d	19 16		19 26		19 36	19 46	19 56		20 16		20 26		20 46	20 56		21 16	21 26	21 46	21 56		22 16	22 26	22 46	22 56
University	d	19 20	19 25	19 30	19a36	19 40	19 50	20 00		20 20		20 30	20a36	20 50	21 00	21 05	21 20	21 30	21 50	22 00		22 20	22 30	22 50	23 00
Selly Oak	d	19 23		19 33		19 43	19 53	20 03		20 23		20 33		20 53	21 03		21 23	21 33	21 53	22 03		22 23	22 33	22 53	23 03
Bournville	d	19 25		19 35		19 45	19 55	20 05		20 25		20 35		20 55	21 05		21 25	21 35	21 55	22 05		22 25	22 35	22 55	23 05
Kings Norton	d	19 27		19 37		19 47	19 57	20 07		20 27		20 37		20 57	21 07		21 27	21 37	21 57	22 07		22 27	22 37	22 57	23 07
Northfield	d	19 30		19 40		19 50	20 00	20 10		20 30		20 40		21 00	21 10		21 30	21 40	22 00	22 10		22 30	22 40	23 00	23 10
Longbridge	d	19 36		19a44		19a54	20 04	20a14		20 34		20a44		21 04	21a14		21 34	21a44	22 04	22a14		22 34	22a44	23 04	23a14
Barnt Green	d	19 40					20 09			20 39				21 09			21 39		22 09			22 39		23 09	
Alvechurch	d	19 45					20 13			20 43				21 13			21 43		22 13			22 43		23 13	
Redditch	a	19 52					20 22			20 52				21 22			21 51		22 22			22 52		23 22	
Bromsgrove	a		19 39													21 19									

Table 69

Saturdays
until 22 October

Lichfield - Birmingham - Longbridge and Redditch

		LM	LM	LM
Lichfield Trent Valley	d	22 30	22 56	
Lichfield City	d	22 34	23 00	
Shenstone	d	22 39	23 05	
Blake Street	d	22 43	23 09	23 36
Butlers Lane	d	22 45	23 11	23 38
Four Oaks	d	22 48	23 14	23 41
Sutton Coldfield	d	22 51	23 17	23 44
Wylde Green	d	22 54	23 20	
Chester Road	d	22 56		
Erdington	d	22 58		
Gravelly Hill	d	23 00		
Aston	d	23 03		
Duddeston	d	23 06		
Birmingham New Street 12	a	23 11	23 31	23 59
	d	23 13	23 33	
Five Ways	d	23 16	23 36	
University	d	23 20	23 40	
Selly Oak	d	23 23	23 43	
Bournville	d	23 25	23 45	
Kings Norton	d	23 27	23 47	
Northfield	d	23 30	23 50	
Longbridge	d	23 34	23a54	
Barnt Green	d	23 39		
Alvechurch	d	23 43		
Redditch	a	23 53		
Bromsgrove	a			

Saturdays
from 29 October

		XC ◇1	LM	LM	LM	LM	LM	LM	LM	LM	XC ◇1	LM	LM	LM	LM	LM	XC ◇1	LM	LM	LM	LM	LM	XC ◇1
Lichfield Trent Valley	d								06 17			06 47			07 17			07 47			08 17		
Lichfield City	d								06 20			06 50			07 20			07 50			08 20		
Shenstone	d								06 26			06 56			07 26			07 56			08 26		
Blake Street	d					06 00			06 30			07 00			07 30			08 00			08 30		
Butlers Lane	d					06 02			06 32			07 02			07 32			08 02			08 32		
Four Oaks	d					06 05		06 24	06 35	06 54		07 05		07 24	07 35	07 54		08 05		08 24	08 35	08 54	
Sutton Coldfield	d					06 09		06 27	06 39	06 57		07 09		07 27	07 39	07 57		08 09		08 27	08 39	08 57	
Wylde Green	d					06 12		06 30	06 42	07 00		07 12		07 30	07 42	08 00		08 12		08 30	08 42	09 00	
Chester Road	d					06 14		06 33	06 44	07 03		07 14		07 33	07 44	08 03		08 14		08 33	08 44	09 03	
Erdington	d					06 16		06 35	06 46	07 05		07 16		07 35	07 46	08 05		08 16		08 35	08 46	09 05	
Gravelly Hill	d					06 19		06 38	06 49	07 08		07 19		07 38	07 49	08 08		08 19		08 38	08 49	09 08	
Aston	d					06 23		06 41	06 53	07 11		07 23		07 41	07 53	08 11		08 23		08 41	08 53	09 11	
Duddeston	d					06 25		06 43		07 13				07 43		08 13				08 43		09 13	
Birmingham New Street 12	a					06 30		06 48	07 00	07 20		07 30		07 51	08 01	08 21		08 31		08 50	09 01	09 21	
	d	05 42	05 53	06 03	06 23	06 33	06 49	06 53	07 03	07 23	07 30	07 33	07 49	07 53	08 03	08 23	08 30	08 33	08 49	08 53	09 03	09 23	09 30
Five Ways	d		05 56	06 06	06 26	06 36		06 56	07 06	07 26		07 36		07 56	08 06	08 26		08 36		08 56	09 06	09 26	
University	d		06 00	06 10	06 30	06 40	06 55	07 00	07 10	07 30	07a36	07 40	07 55	08 00	08 10	08 30	08a36	08 40	08 55	09 00	09 10	09 30	09a36
Selly Oak	d		06 03	06 13	06 33	06 43		07 03	07 13	07 33		07 43		08 03	08 13	08 33		08 43		09 03	09 13	09 33	
Bournville	d		06 05	06 15	06 35	06 45		07 05	07 15	07 35		07 45		08 05	08 15	08 35		08 45		09 05	09 15	09 35	
Kings Norton	d		06 08	06 18	06 38	06 48		07 08	07 18	07 38		07 48		08 08	08 18	08 38		08 48		09 08	09 18	09 38	
Northfield	d		06 11	06 21	06 41	06 51		07 11	07 21	07 41		07 51		08 11	08 21	08 41		08 51		09 11	09 21	09 41	
Longbridge	d		06a16	06 26	06a46	06 58		07a16	07 26	07a46		07 58		08a16	08 26	08a46		08 58		09a16	09 26	09a46	
Barnt Green	d			06 39		07 09			07 39			08 09			08 39			09 09			09 39		
Alvechurch	d			06 43		07 13			07 43			08 13			08 43			09 13			09 43		
Redditch	a			06 52		07 22			07 52			08 22			08 52			09 22			09 52		
Bromsgrove	a	06 03					07 09						08 09						09 09				

Table 69

Saturdays
from 29 October

Lichfield - Birmingham - Longbridge and Redditch

		LM	LM	LM	LM	LM		XC ◇1	LM	LM	LM	LM	LM	XC ◇1	LM	LM		LM	LM	LM	XC ◇1	LM	LM	LM	LM
Lichfield Trent Valley	d	08 47			09 17				09 47			10 17			10 47				11 17			11 47			12 17
Lichfield City	d	08 50			09 20				09 50			10 20			10 50				11 20			11 50			12 20
Shenstone	d	08 56			09 26				09 56			10 26			10 56				11 26			11 56			12 26
Blake Street	d	09 00			09 30				10 00			10 30			11 00				11 30			12 00			12 30
Butlers Lane	d	09 02			09 32				10 02			10 32			11 02				11 32			12 02			12 32
Four Oaks	d	09 05		09 24	09 35	09 54			10 05		10 24	10 35	10 54		11 05			11 24	11 35	11 54		12 05		12 24	12 35
Sutton Coldfield	d	09 09		09 27	09 39	09 57			10 09		10 27	10 39	10 57		11 09			11 27	11 39	11 57		12 09		12 27	12 39
Wylde Green	d	09 12		09 30	09 42	10 00			10 12		10 30	10 42	11 00		11 12			11 30	11 42	12 00		12 12		12 30	12 42
Chester Road	d	09 14		09 33	09 44	10 03			10 14		10 33	10 44	11 03		11 14			11 33	11 44	12 03		12 14		12 33	12 44
Erdington	d	09 16		09 35	09 46	10 05			10 16		10 35	10 46	11 05		11 16			11 35	11 46	12 05		12 16		12 35	12 46
Gravelly Hill	d	09 19		09 38	09 49	10 08			10 19		10 38	10 49	11 08		11 19			11 38	11 49	12 08		12 19		12 38	12 49
Aston	d	09 23		09 41	09 53	10 11			10 23		10 41	10 53	11 11		11 23			11 41	11 53	12 11		12 23		12 41	12 53
Duddeston	d			09 43		10 13					10 43		11 13					11 43		12 13				12 43	
Birmingham New Street 12	a	09 31		09 50	10 01	10 21			10 31		10 50	11 01	11 21		11 31			11 50	12 01	12 21		12 31		12 50	13 01
	d	09 33	09 49	09 53	10 03	10 23		10 30	10 33	10 49	10 53	11 03	11 23	11 30	11 33	11 49		11 53	12 03	12 23	12 30	12 33	12 49	12 53	13 03
Five Ways	d	09 36		09 56	10 06	10 26			10 36		10 56	11 06	11 26		11 36			11 56	12 06	12 26		12 36		12 56	13 06
University	d	09 40	09 55	10 00	10 10	10 30		10a36	10 40	10 55	11 00	11 10	11 30	11a36	11 40	11 55		12 00	12 10	12 30	12a36	12 40	12 55	13 00	13 10
Selly Oak	d	09 43		10 03	10 13	10 33			10 43		11 03	11 13	11 33		11 43			12 03	12 13	12 33		12 43		13 03	13 13
Bournville	d	09 45		10 05	10 15	10 35			10 45		11 05	11 15	11 35		11 45			12 05	12 15	12 35		12 45		13 05	13 15
Kings Norton	d	09 48		10 08	10 18	10 38			10 48		11 08	11 18	11 38		11 48			12 08	12 18	12 38		12 48		13 08	13 18
Northfield	d	09 51		10 11	10 21	10 41			10 51		11 11	11 21	11 41		11 51			12 11	12 21	12 41		12 51		13 11	13 21
Longbridge	d	09 58		10a16	10 26	10a46			11 05		11a16	11 26	11a46		11 58			12a16	12 26	12a46		12 58		13a16	13 26
Barnt Green	d	10b09			10c39				11 09			11 39			12 09				12 39			13 09			13 39
Alvechurch	d	10 13			10 43				11 13			11 43			12 13				12 43			13 13			13 43
Redditch	a	10 22			10 52				11 22			11 52			12 22				12 52			13 22			13 52
Bromsgrove	a		10 09							11 09						12 09							13 09		

		LM		XC ◇1	LM	LM	LM	LM	LM	XC ◇1	LM	LM		LM	LM	LM	XC ◇1	LM	LM	LM	LM	LM		LM	XC ◇1
Lichfield Trent Valley	d				12 47			13 17			13 47				14 17			14 47			15 17				
Lichfield City	d				12 50			13 20			13 50				14 20			14 50			15 20				
Shenstone	d				12 56			13 26			13 56				14 26			14 56			15 26				
Blake Street	d				13 00			13 30			14 00				14 30			15 00			15 30				
Butlers Lane	d				13 02			13 32			14 02				14 32			15 02			15 32				
Four Oaks	d	12 54			13 05		13 24	13 35	13 54		14 05			14 24	14 35	14 54		15 05		15 24	15 35			15 54	
Sutton Coldfield	d	12 57			13 09		13 27	13 39	13 57		14 09			14 27	14 39	14 57		15 09		15 27	15 39			15 57	
Wylde Green	d	13 00			13 12		13 30	13 42	14 00		14 12			14 30	14 42	15 00		15 12		15 30	15 42			16 00	
Chester Road	d	13 03			13 14		13 33	13 44	14 03		14 14			14 33	14 44	15 03		15 14		15 33	15 44			16 03	
Erdington	d	13 05			13 16		13 35	13 46	14 05		14 16			14 35	14 46	15 05		15 16		15 35	15 46			16 05	
Gravelly Hill	d	13 08			13 19		13 38	13 49	14 08		14 19			14 38	14 49	15 08		15 19		15 38	15 49			16 08	
Aston	d	13 11			13 23		13 41	13 53	14 11		14 23			14 41	14 53	15 11		15 23		15 41	15 53			16 11	
Duddeston	d	13 13					13 43		14 13					14 43		15 13				15 43				16 13	
Birmingham New Street 12	a	13 21			13 31		13 50	14 01	14 21		14 31			14 50	15 01	15 21		15 31		15 50	16 01			16 20	
	d	13 23		13 30	13 33	13 49	13 53	14 03	14 23	14 30	14 33	14 49		14 53	15 03	15 23	15 30	15 33	15 49	15 53	16 03	16 19		16 23	16 30
Five Ways	d	13 26			13 36		13 56	14 06	14 26		14 36			14 56	15 06	15 26		15 36		15 56	16 06			16 26	
University	d	13 30		13a36	13 40	13 55	14 00	14 10	14 30	14a36	14 40	14 55		15 00	15 10	15 30	15a36	15 40	15 55	16 00	16 10			16 30	16a36
Selly Oak	d	13 33			13 43		14 03	14 13	14 33		14 43			15 03	15 13	15 33		15 43		16 03	16 13			16 33	
Bournville	d	13 35			13 45		14 05	14 15	14 35		14 45			15 05	15 15	15 35		15 45		16 05	16 15			16 35	
Kings Norton	d	13 38			13 48		14 08	14 18	14 38		14 48			15 08	15 18	15 38		15 48		16 08	16 18			16 38	
Northfield	d	13 41			13 51		14 11	14 21	14 41		14 51			15 11	15 21	15 41		15 51		16 11	16 21			16 41	
Longbridge	d	13a46			13 58		14a16	14 26	14a46		14 58			15a16	15 26	15a46		15 58		16a16	16 26			16a46	
Barnt Green	d				14 09			14 39			15 09				15 39			16 09			16 39				
Alvechurch	d				14 13			14 43			15 13				15 43			16 13			16 43				
Redditch	a				14 22			14 52			15 22				15 52			16 22			16 52				
Bromsgrove	a					14 10						15 09							16 09			16 43			

m Arr. 1502

Table 69

Saturdays
from 29 October

Lichfield - Birmingham - Longbridge and Redditch

		LM	LM	LM	LM	LM	LM	XC ◇1		LM	LM	LM	LM	LM	XC ◇1	LM	LM	LM		LM	LM	LM	XC ◇1	LM	LM
Lichfield Trent Valley	d	15 47			16 17					16 47			17 17			17 47				18 17				18 47	
Lichfield City	d	15 50			16 20					16 50			17 20			17 50				18 20				18 50	
Shenstone	d	15 56			16 26					16 56			17 26			17 56				18 26				18 56	
Blake Street	d	16 00			16 30					17 00			17 30			18 00				18 30				19 00	
Butlers Lane	d	16 02			16 32					17 02			17 32			18 02				18 32				19 02	
Four Oaks	d	16 05		16 24	16 35		16 54			17 05		17 24	17 35	17 54		18 05		18 24		18 35		18 54		19 05	19 16
Sutton Coldfield	d	16 09		16 27	16 39		16 57			17 09		17 27	17 39	17 57		18 09		18 27		18 39		18 57		19 09	19 19
Wylde Green	d	16 12		16 30	16 42		17 00			17 12		17 30	17 42	18 00		18 12		18 30		18 42		19 00		19 12	19 22
Chester Road	d	16 14		16 33	16 44		17 03			17 14		17 33	17 44	18 03		18 14		18 33		18 44		19 03		19 14	19 25
Erdington	d	16 16		16 35	16 46		17 05			17 16		17 35	17 46	18 05		18 16		18 35		18 46		19 05		19 16	19 27
Gravelly Hill	d	16 19		16 38	16 49		17 08			17 19		17 38	17 49	18 08		18 19		18 38		18 49		19 08		19 19	19 30
Aston	d	16 23		16 41	16 53		17 11			17 23		17 41	17 53	18 11		18 23		18 41		18 53		19 11		19 23	19 33
Duddeston	d			16 43			17 13					17 43		18 13				18 43				19 13			19 35
Birmingham New Street 12	a	16 31		16 50	17 01		17 21			17 31		17 50	18 01	18 21		18 31		18 51		19 01		19 21		19 34	19 41
	d	16 33	16 49	16 53	17 03	17 19	17 23	17 30		17 33	17 49	17 53	18 03	18 23	18 30	18 33	18 49	18 53		19 03	19 19	19 23	19 30		19 43
Five Ways	d	16 36		16 56	17 06		17 26			17 36		17 56	18 06	18 26		18 36		18 56		19 06		19 26			19 46
University	d	16 40	16 55	17 00	17 10		17 30	17 36		17 40	17 55	18 00	18 10	18 30	18a36	18 40	18 55	19 00		19 10	19 25	19 30	19a36		19 50
Selly Oak	d	16 43		17 03	17 13		17 33			17 43		18 03	18 13	18 33		18 43		19 03		19 13		19 33			19 53
Bournville	d	16 45		17 05	17 15		17 35			17 45		18 05	18 15	18 35		18 45		19 05		19 15		19 35			19 55
Kings Norton	d	16 48		17 08	17 18		17 38			17 48		18 08	18 18	18 38		18 48		19 08		19 18		19 38			19 58
Northfield	d	16 51		17 11	17 21		17 41			17 51		18 11	18 21	18 41		18 51		19 11		19 21		19 41			20 01
Longbridge	d	16 58		17a16	17 26		17a46			17 58		18a16	18 26	18a46		18 58		19a16		19 26		19a46			20 05
Barnt Green	d	17 09			17 39					18 09			18 39			19 09				19 39					20 09
Alvechurch	d	17 13			17 43					18 13			18 43			19 13				19 43					20 14
Redditch	a	17 22			17 52					18 22			18 52			19 22				19 52					20 22
Bromsgrove	a		17 10			17 40		17 49			18 09						19 09				19 39				

		LM	LM	LM		XC ◇1	LM	LM	LM	LM	LM	LM	LM	LM		LM	LM	LM	LM	LM					
Lichfield Trent Valley	d		19 17				19 57			20 27		20 57		21 27			21 57		22 27	22 55					
Lichfield City	d		19 20				20 00			20 30		21 00		21 30			22 00		22 30	22 58					
Shenstone	d		19 26				20 06			20 36		21 06		21 36			22 06		22 36	23 04					
Blake Street	d		19 30				20 10			20 40		21 10		21 40			22 10		22 40	23 08					
Butlers Lane	d		19 32				20 12			20 42		21 12		21 42			22 12		22 42	23 10					
Four Oaks	d		19 35	19 54			20 15			20 45		21 15		21 45			22 15		22 45	23 13					
Sutton Coldfield	d		19 39	19 57			20 19			20 49		21 19		21 49			22 19		22 49	23 17					
Wylde Green	d		19 42	20 00			20 22			20 52		21 22		21 52			22 22		22 52	23 20					
Chester Road	d		19 44	20 03			20 24			20 54		21 24		21 54			22 24		22 54						
Erdington	d		19 46	20 05			20 26			20 56		21 26		21 56			22 26		22 56						
Gravelly Hill	d		19 49	20 08			20 29			20 59		21 29		21 59			22 29		22 59						
Aston	d		19 53	20 11			20 33			21 03		21 33		22 03			22 33		23 03						
Duddeston	d		19 55				20 35			21 05		21 35		22 05			22 35		23 05						
Birmingham New Street 12	a		20 01	20 21			20 41			21 11		21 41		22 11			22 41		23 11	23 31					
	d	19 53	20 13	20 23		20 30	20 43	20 53	20 59	21 13	21 23	21 43	21 53	22 13		22 23	22 43	22 53	23 13	23 33					
Five Ways	d	19 56	20 16	20 26			20 46	20 56		21 16	21 26	21 46	21 56	22 16		22 26	22 46	22 56	23 16	23 36					
University	d	20 00	20 20	20 30		20a36	20 50	21 00	21 05	21 20	21 30	21 50	22 00	22 20		22 30	22 50	23 00	23 20	23 40					
Selly Oak	d	20 03	20 23	20 33			20 53	21 03		21 23	21 33	21 53	22 03	22 23		22 33	22 53	23 03	23 23	23 43					
Bournville	d	20 05	20 25	20 35			20 55	21 05		21 25	21 35	21 55	22 05	22 25		22 35	22 55	23 05	23 25	23 45					
Kings Norton	d	20 08	20 28	20 38			20 58	21 08		21 28	21 38	21 58	22 08	22 28		22 38	22 58	23 08	23 28	23 48					
Northfield	d	20 11	20 31	20 41			21 01	21 11		21 31	21 41	22 01	22 11	22 31		22 41	23 01	23 11	23 31	23 51					
Longbridge	d	20a16	20 35	20a46			21 05	21a16		21 35	21a46	22 05	22a16	22 35		22a46	23 05	23a16	23 35	23a56					
Barnt Green	d		20 39				21 09			21 39		22 09		22 39			23 09		23 39						
Alvechurch	d		20 44				21 14			21 44		22 14		22 44			23 14		23 44						
Redditch	a		20 52				21 22			21 52		22 22		22 52			23 22		23 53						
Bromsgrove	a								21 19																

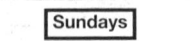

Sundays

		LM	LM	LM	LM	XC ◇1	LM	LM	XC ◇1	LM		LM	XC ◇1	LM	LM	LM	XC ◇1	LM	LM	XC ◇1		LM	LM	XC ◇1	LM
Lichfield Trent Valley	d				09 31		10 01	10 31		11 01		11 31		12 01	12 31			13 01	13 31			14 01	14 31		15 01
Lichfield City	d				09 35		10 05	10 35		11 05		11 35		12 05	12 35			13 05	13 35			14 05	14 35		15 05
Shenstone	d				09 40		10 10	10 40		11 10		11 40		12 10	12 40			13 10	13 40			14 10	14 40		15 10
Blake Street	d				09 44		10 14	10 44		11 14		11 44		12 14	12 44			13 14	13 44			14 14	14 44		15 14
Butlers Lane	d				09 46		10 16	10 46		11 16		11 46		12 16	12 46			13 16	13 46			14 16	14 46		15 16
Four Oaks	d			09 19	09 49		10 19	10 49		11 19		11 49		12 19	12 49			13 19	13 49			14 19	14 49		15 19
Sutton Coldfield	d			09 22	09 52		10 22	10 52		11 22		11 52		12 22	12 52			13 22	13 52			14 22	14 52		15 22
Wylde Green	d			09 25	09 55		10 25	10 55		11 25		11 55		12 25	12 55			13 25	13 55			14 25	14 55		15 25
Chester Road	d			09 27	09 57		10 27	10 57		11 27		11 57		12 27	12 57			13 27	13 57			14 27	14 57		15 27
Erdington	d			09 29	09 59		10 29	10 59		11 29		11 59		12 29	12 59			13 29	13 59			14 29	14 59		15 29
Gravelly Hill	d			09 31	10 01		10 31	11 01		11 31		12 01		12 31	13 01			13 31	14 01			14 31	15 01		15 31
Aston	d			09 35	10 05		10 35	11 05		11 35		12 05		12 35	13 05			13 35	14 05			14 35	15 05		15 35
Duddeston	d			09 37	10 07		10 37	11 07		11 37		12 07		12 38	13 07			13 37	14 07			14 37	15 07		15 37
Birmingham New Street 12	a			09 42	10 12		10 42	11 12		11 42		12 12		12 42	13 12			13 42	14 13			14 42	15 12		15 42
	d	08 55	09 15	09 45	10 15	10 30	10 45	11 15	11 30	11 45		12 15	12 30	12 45	13 15	13 24	13 30	13 45	14 15	14 30		14 45	15 15	15 30	15 45
Five Ways	d		09 19	09 49	10 19		10 49	11 19		11 49		12 19		12 49	13 19			13 49	14 19			14 49	15 19		15 49
University	d	09 01	09 23	09 53	10 23	10a36	10 53	11 23	11a36	11 53		12 23	12a36	12 53	13 23		13a36	13 53	14 23	14a36		14 53	15 23	15a36	15 53
Selly Oak	d		09 25	09 55	10 25		10 55	11 25		11 55		12 25		12 55	13 25			13 55	14 25			14 55	15 25		15 55
Bournville	d		09 27	09 57	10 27		10 57	11 27		11 57		12 27		12 57	13 27			13 57	14 27			14 57	15 27		15 57
Kings Norton	d		09 30	10 00	10 30		11 00	11 30		12 00		12 30		13 00	13 30			14 00	14 30			15 00	15 30		16 00
Northfield	d		09 33	10 03	10 33		11 03	11 33		12 03		12 33		13 03	13 33			14 03	14 33			15 03	15 33		16 03
Longbridge	d	09 09	09 36	10 06	10 36		11 06	11 36		12 06		12 36		13 06	13 36			14 06	14 36			15 06	15 36		16 06
Barnt Green	d		09 40	10 10	10 40		11 10	11 40		12 10		12 40		13 10	13 40			14 10	14 40			15 10	15 40		16 10
Alvechurch	d		09 45	10 15	10 45		11 15	11 45		12 15		12 45		13 15	13 45			14 15	14 45			15 15	15 45		16 15
Redditch	a	09 24	09 53	10 23	10 53		11 23	11 53		12 23		12 53		13 23	13 53			14 23	14 53			15 23	15 53		16 23
Bromsgrove	a															13 41									

Table 69

Sundays

Lichfield - Birmingham - Longbridge and Redditch

		LM	LM	XC	XC	LM		LM	XC	LM	LM	LM	XC	LM	LM	LM		XC	LM	LM	LM	LM	LM	LM	LM
				◇1	◇1				◇1				◇1					◇1							
				A	B																				
					🛒				🛒				🛒												
Lichfield Trent Valley	d		15 31			16 01		16 31		17 01		17 31		18 01		18 31			19 01	19 31	20 01		20 31	21 01	21 31
Lichfield City	d		15 35			16 05		16 35		17 05		17 35		18 05		18 35			19 05	19 35	20 05		20 35	21 05	21 35
Shenstone	d		15 40			16 10		16 40		17 10		17 40		18 10		18 40			19 10	19 40	20 10		20 40	21 10	21 40
Blake Street	d		15 44			16 14		16 44		17 14		17 44		18 14		18 44			19 14	19 44	20 14		20 44	21 14	21 44
Butlers Lane	d		15 46			16 16		16 46		17 16		17 46		18 16		18 46			19 16	19 46	20 16		20 46	21 16	21 46
Four Oaks	d		15 49			16 19		16 49		17 19		17 49		18 19		18 49			19 19	19 49	20 19		20 49	21 19	21 49
Sutton Coldfield	d		15 52			16 22		16 52		17 22		17 52		18 22		18 52			19 22	19 52	20 22		20 52	21 22	21 52
Wylde Green	d		15 55			16 25		16 55		17 25		17 55		18 25		18 55			19 25	19 55	20 25		20 55	21 25	21 55
Chester Road	d		15 57			16 27		16 57		17 27		17 57		18 27		18 57			19 27	19 57	20 27		20 57	21 27	21 57
Erdington	d		15 59			16 29		16 59		17 29		17 59		18 29		18 59			19 29	19 59	20 29		20 59	21 29	21 59
Gravelly Hill	d		16 01			16 31		17 01		17 31		18 01		18 31		19 01			19 31	20 01	20 31		21 01	21 31	22 01
Aston	d		16 05			16 35		17 05		17 35		18 05		18 35		19 05			19 35	20 05	20 35		21 05	21 35	22 05
Duddeston	d		16 07			16 37		17 07		17 37		18 07		18 37		19 07			19 37	20 07	20 37		21 07	21 37	22 07
Birmingham New Street 12	a		16 12			16 42		17 12		17 42		18 12		18 42		19 12			19 42	20 12	20 42		21 12	21 42	22 12
	d	16 00	16 15	16⟆30	16⟆30	16 45		17 15	17 30	17 45	18 00	18 15	18 30	18 45	19 00	19 15		19 30	19 45	20 15	20 45	21 00	21 15	21 45	22 15
Five Ways	d		16 19	⟆	⟆	16 49		17 19		17 49		18 19		18 49		19 19			19 49	20 19	20 49		21 19	21 49	22 19
University	d		16 23	16a36	16a36	16 53		17 23	17a36	17 53		18 23	18a36	18 53		19 23		19a36	19 53	20 23	20 53		21 23	21 53	22 23
Selly Oak	d		16 25			16 55		17 25		17 55		18 25		18 55		19 25			19 55	20 25	20 55		21 25	21 55	22 25
Bournville	d		16 27			16 57		17 27		17 57		18 27		18 57		19 27			19 57	20 27	20 57		21 27	21 57	22 27
Kings Norton	d		16 30			17 00		17 30		18 00		18 30		19 00		19 30			20 00	20 30	21 00		21 30	22 00	22 30
Northfield	d		16 33			17 03		17 33		18 03		18 33		19 03		19 33			20 03	20 33	21 03		21 33	22 03	22 33
Longbridge	d		16 36			17 06		17 36		18 06		18 36		19 06		19 36			20 06	20 36	21 06		21 36	22 06	22 36
Barnt Green	d		16 40			17 10		17 40		18 10		18 40		19 10		19 40			20 10	20 40	21 10		21 40	22 10	22 40
Alvechurch	d		16 45			17 15		17 45		18 15		18 45		19 15		19 45			20 15	20 45	21 15		21 45	22 15	22 45
Redditch	a		16 53			17 23		17 53		18 23		18 53		19 23		19 53			20 23	20 53	21 23		21 53	22 23	22 53
Bromsgrove	a	16 20									18 20				19 21							21 21			

		LM		LM	LM
Lichfield Trent Valley	d	22 01		22 31	23 01
Lichfield City	d	22 05		22 35	23 05
Shenstone	d	22 10		22 40	23 10
Blake Street	d	22 14		22 44	23 14
Butlers Lane	d	22 16		22 46	23 16
Four Oaks	d	22 19		22 49	23 19
Sutton Coldfield	d	22 22		22 52	23 22
Wylde Green	d	22 25		22 55	23 25
Chester Road	d	22 27		22 57	
Erdington	d	22 29		22 59	
Gravelly Hill	d	22 31		23 01	
Aston	d	22 35		23 05	
Duddeston	d	22 37		23 07	
Birmingham New Street 12	a	22 42		23 12	23 39
	d	22 45		23 15	
Five Ways	d	22 49		23 19	
University	d	22 53		23 23	
Selly Oak	d	22 55		23 25	
Bournville	d	22 57		23 27	
Kings Norton	d	23 00		23 30	
Northfield	d	23 03		23 33	
Longbridge	d	23 06		23 36	
Barnt Green	d	23 10		23 40	
Alvechurch	d	23 15		23 45	
Redditch	a	23 23		23 53	
Bromsgrove	a				

A until 23 October

B from 30 October

Redditch and Longbridge - Birmingham - Lichfield

Miles	Miles			LM	LM	LM	LM	LM	LM	LM	LM	LM		LM	LM	LM	LM	LM	LM	LM	LM	LM		XC ◇1	LM
—	0	Bromsgrove	d					06 22			06 44						07 24							07 49	
0	—	**Redditch**	d							06 27					06 57					07 27					
3¼	—	Alvechurch	d							06 32					07 02					07 32					
5	3½	Barnt Green	d							06 38					07 08					07 38					
7¾	—	Longbridge	d			06 12	06 22		06 32	06 42		06 52		07 02	07 12	07 22			07 32	07 42		07 52			08 02
8¾	—	Northfield	d			06 14	06 24		06 34	06 44		06 54		07 04	07 14	07 24			07 34	07 44		07 54			08 04
10¼	—	Kings Norton	d			06 17	06 27		06 37	06 47		06 57		07 07	07 17	07 27			07 37	07 47		07 57			08 07
11¼	—	Bournville	d			06 19	06 29		06 39	06 49		06 59		07 09	07 19	07 29			07 39	07 49		07 59			08 09
12¼	—	Selly Oak	d			06 22	06 32		06 42	06 52		07 02		07 12	07 22	07 32			07 42	07 52		08 02			08 12
13	11½	University	d			06 25	06 35	06 39	06 45	06 55	06 59	07 05		07 15	07 25	07 35			07 45	07 55	07 59	08 05		08 09	08 15
13½	—	Five Ways	d			06 29	06 39		06 49	06 59		07 09		07 19	07 29	07 39			07 49	07 59		08 09			08 19
14½	13	**Birmingham New Street** 12	a			06 33	06 42	06 45	06 52	07 02	07 07	07 13		07 22	07 33	07 42	07 45		07 52	08 03	08 09	08 12		08 16	08 22
—	—		d	06 02	06 25	06 35	06 45		06 55	07 05		07 15		07 25	07 35	07 45		07 55	07 57	08 05		08 15			08 25
16	—	Duddeston	d	06 06	06 29				06 59					07 29					08 01						08 29
17¼	—	Aston	d	06 09	06 32	06 41	06 51		07 02	07 11		07 21		07 32	07 41	07 51			08 04	08 11		08 21			08 32
18½	—	Gravelly Hill	d	06 12	06 35	06 45	06 54		07 05	07 14		07 24		07 35	07 44	07 54			08 07	08 14		08 24			08 35
19¼	—	Erdington	d	06 15	06 38	06 46	06 56		07 08	07 16		07 26		07 38	07 46	07 56			08 09	08 16		08 26			08 38
20¼	—	Chester Road	d	06 17	06 40	06 49	06 58		07 10	07 18		07 28		07 40	07 48	07 58			08 11	08 18		08 28			08 40
21	—	Wylde Green	d	06 19	06 42	06 50	07 00		07 12	07 21		07 30		07 42	07 50	08 00			08 13	08 20		08 30			08 42
22	—	Sutton Coldfield	d	06 22	06 45	06 54	07 04		07 15	07 24		07 34		07 45	07 53	08 03		08 08	08 16	08 24		08 34			08 45
23½	—	Four Oaks	d	06 25	06 48	06 58	07a11		07 18	07 28		07a41		07 48		08a09		08 11	08 19	08 28		08a41			08 48
24½	—	Butlers Lane	d	06 27	06 50	07 00			07 20	07 30				07 50					08 21	08 30					08 50
26¼	—	Blake Street	d	06 30	06 53	07 02			07 23	07 32				07 53					08 24	08 32					08 53
28¾	—	Shenstone	d	06 34	06 57				07 27					07 57					08 28	08 36					08 57
31¾	—	**Lichfield City**	d	06a40	07 02	07 11			07 32	07 42				08 02	08a08			08a22	08 33	08 41					09a02
33	—	**Lichfield Trent Valley**	a		07 06	07 16			07 36	07 46				08 06					08 36	08 46					

		LM	LM	LM	XC ◇1	LM	LM	LM		LM	LM	LM	LM	LM	XC ◇1	LM	LM	LM		LM	LM	LM	LM	XC ◇1	LM
Bromsgrove	d				08 24			08 42					09 11							09 54					
Redditch	d	07 57					08 27					08 57					09 27					09 57			
Alvechurch	d	08 02					08 32					09 02					09 32					10 02			
Barnt Green	d	08 08					08 38					09 08					09 38					10 08			
Longbridge	d	08 12		08 22		08 32	08 42			08 52	09 02	09 12		09 22		09 32	09 42	09 52			10 02	10 12	10 22		10 32
Northfield	d	08 14		08 24		08 34	08 44			08 54	09 04	09 14		09 24		09 34	09 44	09 54			10 04	10 14	10 24		10 34
Kings Norton	d	08 17		08 27		08 37	08 47			08 57	09 07	09 17		09 27		09 37	09 47	09 57			10 07	10 17	10 27		10 37
Bournville	d	08 19		08 29		08 39	08 49			08 59	09 09	09 19		09 29		09 39	09 49	09 59			10 09	10 19	10 29		10 39
Selly Oak	d	08 22		08 32		08 42	08 52			09 02	09 12	09 22		09 32		09 42	09 52	10 02			10 12	10 22	10 32		10 42
University	d	08 25	08 29	08 35	08 39	08 45	08 55	08 59		09 05	09 15	09 25	09 29	09 35	09 39	09 45	09 55	10 05		10 09	10 15	10 25	10 35	10 39	10 45
Five Ways	d	08 29		08 39		08 49	08 59			09 09	09 19	09 29		09 39		09 49	09 59	10 09			10 19	10 29	10 39		10 49
Birmingham New Street 12	a	08 33	08 37	08 42	08 45	08 53	09 03	09 07		09 13	09 22	09 33	09 42	09 42	09 45	09 52	10 03	10 12		10 24	10 22	10 33	10 42	10 45	10 53
	d	08 35		08 45		08 55	09 05			09 15	09 25	09 35		09 45		09 55	10 05	10 15			10 25	10 35	10 45		10 55
Duddeston	d					08 59					09 29					09 59					10 29				10 59
Aston	d	08 41		08 51		09 02	09 11			09 21	09 32	09 41		09 51		10 02	10 11	10 21			10 32	10 41	10 51		11 02
Gravelly Hill	d	08 44		08 54		09 05	09 14			09 24	09 35	09 44		09 54		10 05	10 14	10 24			10 35	10 44	10 54		11 05
Erdington	d	08 46		08 56		09 08	09 16			09 26	09 38	09 46		09 56		10 08	10 16	10 26			10 38	10 46	10 56		11 08
Chester Road	d	08 48		08 58		09 10	09 18			09 28	09 40	09 48		09 58		10 10	10 18	10 28			10 40	10 48	10 58		11 10
Wylde Green	d	08 50		09 00		09 12	09 20			09 30	09 42	09 50		10 00		10 12	10 20	10 30			10 42	10 50	11 00		11 12
Sutton Coldfield	d	08 54		09 04		09 15	09 24			09 34	09 45	09 54		10 04		10 15	10 24	10 34			10 45	10 54	11 04		11 15
Four Oaks	d	08 58		09a11		09 18	09 28			09a41	09 48	09 58		10a11		10 18	10 28	10a41			10 48	10 58	11a11		11 18
Butlers Lane	d	09 00				09 20	09 30				09 50	10 00				10 20	10 30				10 50	11 00			11 20
Blake Street	d	09 02				09 23	09 32				09 53	10 02				10 23	10 32				10 53	11 02			11 23
Shenstone	d					09 27					09 57					10 27					10 57				11 27
Lichfield City	d	09 11				09a34	09 41				10a02	10 11				10a32	10 41				11a02	11 11			11a32
Lichfield Trent Valley	a	09 15					09 45					10 15					10 45					11 15			

		LM	LM	LM		LM	LM	LM	XC ◇1	LM	LM	LM	LM	LM		LM	LM	XC ◇1	LM	LM	LM	LM	LM	LM	
Bromsgrove	d		10 42									11 42									12 42				
Redditch	d	10 27					10 57				11 27					11 57				12 27				12 57	
Alvechurch	d	10 32					11 02				11 32					12 02				12 32				13 02	
Barnt Green	d	10 38					11 08				11 38					12 08				12 38				13 08	
Longbridge	d	10 42		10 52		11 02	11 12	11 22		11 32	11 42		11 52	12 02		12 12	12 22		12 32	12 42		12 52	13 02	13 12	
Northfield	d	10 44		10 54		11 04	11 14	11 24		11 34	11 44		11 54	12 04		12 14	12 24		12 34	12 44		12 54	13 04	13 14	
Kings Norton	d	10 47		10 57		11 07	11 17	11 27		11 37	11 47		11 57	12 07		12 17	12 27		12 37	12 47		12 57	13 07	13 17	
Bournville	d	10 49		10 59		11 09	11 19	11 29		11 39	11 49		11 59	12 09		12 19	12 29		12 39	12 49		12 59	13 09	13 19	
Selly Oak	d	10 52		11 02		11 12	11 22	11 32		11 42	11 52		12 02	12 12		12 22	12 32		12 42	12 52		13 02	13 12	13 22	
University	d	10 55	10 59	11 05		11 15	11 25	11 35	11 39	11 45	11 55	11 59	12 05	12 15		12 25	12 35	12 39	12 45	12 55	12 59	13 05	13 15	13 25	
Five Ways	d	10 59		11 09		11 19	11 29	11 39		11 49	11 59		12 09	12 19		12 29	12 39		12 49	12 59		13 09	13 19	13 29	
Birmingham New Street 12	a	11 02	11 13	11 12		11 22	11 33	11 42	11 45	11 53	12 03	12 11	12 12	12 22		12 34	12 42	12 45	12 53	13 03	13 13	13 12	13 22	13 33	
	d	11 05		11 15		11 25	11 35	11 45		11 55	12 05		12 15	12 25		12 35	12 45		12 55	13 05		13 15	13 25	13 35	
Duddeston	d					11 29				11 59				12 29					12 59				13 29		
Aston	d	11 11		11 21		11 32	11 41	11 51		12 02	12 11		12 21	12 32		12 41	12 51		13 02	13 11		13 21	13 32	13 41	
Gravelly Hill	d	11 14		11 24		11 35	11 44	11 54		12 05	12 14		12 24	12 35		12 44	12 54		13 05	13 14		13 24	13 35	13 44	
Erdington	d	11 16		11 26		11 38	11 46	11 56		12 08	12 16		12 26	12 38		12 46	12 56		13 08	13 16		13 26	13 38	13 46	
Chester Road	d	11 18		11 28		11 40	11 48	11 58		12 10	12 18		12 28	12 40		12 48	12 58		13 10	13 18		13 28	13 40	13 48	
Wylde Green	d	11 20		11 30		11 42	11 50	12 00		12 12	12 20		12 30	12 42		12 50	13 00		13 12	13 20		13 30	13 42	13 50	
Sutton Coldfield	d	11 24		11 34		11 45	11 54	12 04		12 15	12 24		12 34	12 45		12 54	13 04		13 15	13 24		13 34	13 45	13 54	
Four Oaks	d	11 28		11a41		11 48	11 58	12a11		12 18	12 28		12a41	12 48		12 58	13a11		13 18	13 28		13a41	13 48	13 58	
Butlers Lane	d	11 30				11 50	12 00			12 20	12 30			12 50		13 00			13 20	13 30			13 50	14 00	
Blake Street	d	11 32				11 53	12 02			12 23	12 32			12 53		13 02			13 23	13 32			13 53	14 02	
Shenstone	d					11 57				12 27				12 57					13 27				13 57		
Lichfield City	d	11 41				12a02	12 11			12a32	12 41			13a02		13 11			13a32	13 41			14a02	14 11	
Lichfield Trent Valley	a	11 45					12 15				12 45					13 15				13 45				14 15	

Redditch and Longbridge - Birmingham - Lichfield

		LM	XC ◇1	LM	LM	LM	LM	LM	LM	LM		XC ◇1	LM	LM	LM	LM	LM	LM	LM	XC ◇1		LM	LM	LM	LM
Bromsgrove	d					13 42									14 42									15 42	
Redditch	d				13 27				13 57					14 27				14 57					15 27		
Alvechurch	d				13 32				14 02					14 32				15 02					15 32		
Barnt Green	d				13 38				14 08					14 38				15 08					15 38		
Longbridge	d	13 22		13 32	13 42		13 52	14 02	14 12	14 22			14 32	14 42		14 52	15 02	15 12	15 22			15 32	15 42		15 52
Northfield	d	13 24		13 34	13 44		13 54	14 04	14 14	14 24			14 34	14 44		14 54	15 04	15 14	15 24			15 34	15 44		15 54
Kings Norton	d	13 27		13 37	13 47		13 57	14 07	14 17	14 27			14 37	14 47		14 57	15 07	15 17	15 27			15 37	15 47		15 57
Bournville	d	13 29		13 39	13 49		13 59	14 09	14 19	14 29			14 39	14 49		14 59	15 09	15 19	15 29			15 39	15 49		15 59
Selly Oak	d	13 32		13 42	13 52		14 02	14 12	14 22	14 32			14 42	14 52		15 02	15 12	15 22	15 32			15 42	15 52		16 02
University	d	13 35	13 39	13 45	13 55	13 59	14 05	14 15	14 25	14 35		14 39	14 45	14 55	14 59	15 05	15 15	15 25	15 35	15 39		15 45	15 55	15 59	16 05
Five Ways	d	13 39		13 49	13 59		14 09	14 19	14 29	14 39			14 49	14 59		15 09	15 19	15 29	15 39			15 49	15 59		16 09
Birmingham New Street 12	a	13 42	13 45	13 53	14 03	14 12	14 12	14 22	14 33	14 42		14 45	14 53	15 03	15 13	15 12	15 22	15 33	15 42	15 45		15 53	16 03	16 13	16 12
	d	13 45		13 55	14 05		14 15	14 25	14 35	14 45			14 55	15 05		15 15	15 25	15 35	15 45			15 55	16 05		16 15
Duddeston	d			13 59				14 29					14 59				15 29					15 59			
Aston	d	13 51		14 02	14 11		14 21	14 32	14 41	14 51			15 02	15 11		15 21	15 32	15 41	15 51			16 02	16 11		16 21
Gravelly Hill	d	13 54		14 05	14 14		14 24	14 35	14 44	14 54			15 05	15 14		15 24	15 35	15 44	15 54			16 05	16 14		16 24
Erdington	d	13 56		14 08	14 16		14 26	14 38	14 46	14 56			15 08	15 16		15 26	15 38	15 46	15 56			16 08	16 16		16 26
Chester Road	d	13 58		14 10	14 18		14 28	14 40	14 48	14 58			15 10	15 18		15 28	15 40	15 48	15 58			16 10	16 18		16 28
Wylde Green	d	14 00		14 12	14 20		14 30	14 42	14 50	15 00			15 12	15 20		15 30	15 42	15 50	16 00			16 12	16 20		16 30
Sutton Coldfield	d	14 04		14 15	14 24		14 34	14 45	14 54	15 04			15 15	15 24		15 34	15 45	15 54	16 04			16 15	16 24		16 34
Four Oaks	d	14a11		14 18	14 28		14a41	14 48	14 58	15a11			15 18	15 28		15a41	15 48	15 58	16a11			16 18	16 28		16a41
Butlers Lane	d			14 20	14 30			14 50	15 00				15 20	15 30			15 50	16 00				16 20	16 30		
Blake Street	d			14 23	14 32			14 53	15 02				15 23	15 32			15 53	16 02				16 23	16 32		
Shenstone	d			14 27				14 57					15 27				15 57					16 27			
Lichfield City	d			14a32	14 41			15a02	15 11				15a32	15 41			16a02	16 11				16a32	16 41		
Lichfield Trent Valley	a				14 45				15 15					15 45				16 15					16 45		

		LM	LM	LM	XC ◇1	LM		LM	LM	LM	LM	LM	LM	XC ◇1	LM	LM		LM	LM	LM	LM	LM	XC ◇1	LM	LM
Bromsgrove	d								16 42									17 42							
Redditch	d		15 57					16 27				16 57				17 27					17 57				18 27
Alvechurch	d		16 02					16 32				17 02				17 32					18 02				18 32
Barnt Green	d		16 08					16 38	16 49			17 08				17 38					18 08				18 38
Longbridge	d	16 02	16 12	16 22		16 32		16 42		16 52	17 02	17 12	17 22		17 32	17 42			17 52	18 02	18 12	18 22		18 32	18 42
Northfield	d	16 04	16 14	16 24		16 34		16 44		16 54	17 04	17 14	17 24		17 34	17 44			17 54	18 04	18 14	18 24		18 34	18 44
Kings Norton	d	16 07	16 17	16 27		16 37		16 47		16 57	17 07	17 17	17 27		17 37	17 47			17 57	18 07	18 17	18 27		18 37	18 47
Bournville	d	16 09	16 19	16 29		16 39		16 49		16 59	17 09	17 19	17 29		17 39	17 49			17 59	18 09	18 19	18 29		18 39	18 49
Selly Oak	d	16 12	16 22	16 32		16 42		16 52		17 02	17 12	17 22	17 32		17 42	17 52			18 02	18 12	18 22	18 32		18 42	18 52
University	d	16 15	16 25	16 35	16 39	16 45		16 55	16 59	17 05	17 15	17 25	17 35	17 39	17 45	17 55		17 59	18 05	18 15	18 25	18 35	18 39	18 45	18 55
Five Ways	d	16 19	16 29	16 39		16 49		16 59		17 09	17 19	17 29	17 39		17 49	17 59			18 09	18 19	18 29	18 39		18 49	18 59
Birmingham New Street 12	a	16 22	16 34	16 42	16 45	16 53		17 03	17 13	17 12	17 23	17 33	17 42	17 45	17 53	18 03		18 13	18 12	18 23	18 33	18 42	18 45	18 53	19 03
	d	16 25	16 35	16 45		16 55		17 05		17 15	17 25	17 35	17 45		17 55	18 05			18 15	18 25	18 35	18 45		18 55	19 05
Duddeston	d	16 29				16 59					17 29				17 59					18 29				18 59	
Aston	d	16 32	16 41	16 51		17 02		17 11		17 21	17 32	17 41	17 51		18 02	18 11			18 21	18 32	18 41	18 51		19 02	19 11
Gravelly Hill	d	16 35	16 44	16 54		17 05		17 14		17 24	17 35	17 44	17 54		18 05	18 14			18 24	18 35	18 44	18 54		19 05	19 14
Erdington	d	16 38	16 46	16 56		17 08		17 16		17 26	17 38	17 46	17 56		18 08	18 16			18 26	18 38	18 46	18 56		19 08	19 16
Chester Road	d	16 39	16 48	16 58		17 10		17 18		17 28	17 40	17 48	17 58		18 10	18 18			18 28	18 40	18 48	18 58		19 10	19 18
Wylde Green	d	16 41	16 50	17 00		17 12		17 20		17 30	17 42	17 50	18 00		18 12	18 20			18 30	18 42	18 50	19 00		19 12	19 20
Sutton Coldfield	d	16 44	16 54	17 04		17 15		17 24		17 34	17 45	17 54	18 04		18 15	18 24			18 34	18 45	18 54	19 04		19 15	19 24
Four Oaks	d	16 48	16 58	17a11		17 18		17 28		17a41	17 48	17 58	18a11		18 18	18 28			18a41	18 48	18 58	19a11		19 18	19 28
Butlers Lane	d	16 50	17 00			17 20		17 30			17 50	18 00			18 20	18 30				18 50	19 00			19 20	19 30
Blake Street	d	16 52	17 02			17 23		17 32			17 53	18 02			18 23	18 32				18 53	19 02			19 23	19 32
Shenstone	d	16 56				17 27		17 36			17 57	18 06			18 27					18 57				19 27	
Lichfield City	d	17a02	17 11			17 32		17 41			18 02	18 11			18a32	18 41				19a02	19 11			19a32	19 41
Lichfield Trent Valley	a		17 15			17 36		17 46			18 06	18 16				18 45					19 15				19 45

		LM		LM	LM	LM	LM	XC ◇1	LM	LM	LM	LM		LM	LM	XC ◇1	LM	LM	LM	LM	LM	LM		XC ◇1	LM
Bromsgrove	d	18 43										19 46								21 00					
Redditch	d					18 57				19 27					19 57			20 27			20 57				21 27
Alvechurch	d					19 02				19 32					20 02			20 32			21 02				21 32
Barnt Green	d	18 50				19 08				19 38					20 08			20 38			21 08				21 38
Longbridge	d			18 52	19 02	19 12	19 22		19 32	19 42	19 52			20 02	20 12		20 30	20 42	20 57		21 12	21 27			21 42
Northfield	d			18 54	19 04	19 14	19 24		19 34	19 44	19 54			20 04	20 14		20 32	20 44	20 59		21 14	21 29			21 44
Kings Norton	d			18 57	19 07	19 17	19 27		19 37	19 47	19 57			20 07	20 17		20 35	20 47	21 02		21 17	21 32			21 47
Bournville	d			18 59	19 09	19 19	19 29		19 39	19 49	19 59			20 09	20 19		20 37	20 49	21 04		21 19	21 34			21 49
Selly Oak	d			19 02	19 12	19 22	19 32		19 42	19 52	20 02			20 12	20 22		20 40	20 52	21 07		21 22	21 37			21 52
University	d	19 00		19 05	19 15	19 25	19 35	19 39	19 45	19 55	20 05	20 09		20 15	20 25	20 39	20 42	20 55	21 10	21 17	21 25	21 40		21 46	21 55
Five Ways	d			19 09	19 19	19 29	19 39		19 49	19 59	20 09			20 19	20 29		20 46	20 59	21 14		21 29	21 44			21 59
Birmingham New Street 12	a	19 12		19 12	19 22	19 33	19 42	19 45	19 52	20 03	20 12	20 20		20 23	20 34	20 45	20 50	21 02	21 18	21 23	21 33	21 48		21 52	22 02
	d			19 15		19 35				20 05					20 35			21 05			21 35				22 05
Duddeston	d					19 39				20 09					20 39			21 09			21 39				22 09
Aston	d			19 21		19 42				20 12					20 42			21 12			21 42				22 12
Gravelly Hill	d			19 24		19 45				20 15					20 45			21 15			21 45				22 15
Erdington	d			19 26		19 48				20 18					20 48			21 18			21 48				22 18
Chester Road	d			19 28		19 50				20 20					20 50			21 20			21 50				22 20
Wylde Green	d			19 30		19 52				20 22					20 52			21 22			21 52				22 22
Sutton Coldfield	d			19 34		19 55				20 25					20 55			21 25			21 55				22 25
Four Oaks	d			19a41		19 58				20 28					20 58			21 28			21 58				22 28
Butlers Lane	d					20 00				20 30					21 00			21 30			22 00				22 30
Blake Street	d					20 03				20 33					21 03			21 33			22 03				22 33
Shenstone	d					20 07				20 37					21 07			21 37			22 07				22 37
Lichfield City	d					20 12				20 42					21 12			21 42			22 12				22 42
Lichfield Trent Valley	a					20 16				20 46					21 16			21 46			22 16				22 46

Table 69

Mondays to Fridays

until 21 October

Redditch and Longbridge - Birmingham - Lichfield

		LM	LM	LM	LM	LM	LM	LM	LM
Bromsgrove	d				22 28				
Redditch	d		21 57			22 27		22 57	
Alvechurch	d		22 02			22 32		23 02	
Barnt Green	d		22 08			22 38		23 08	
Longbridge	d	21 57	22 12	22 27		22 42	22 52	23 12	23 30
Northfield	d	21 59	22 14	22 29		22 44	22 54	23 14	23 32
Kings Norton	d	22 02	22 17	22 32		22 47	22 57	23 17	23 35
Bournville	d	22 04	22 19	22 34		22 49	22 59	23 19	23 37
Selly Oak	d	22 07	22 22	22 37		22 52	23 02	23 22	23 40
University	d	22 10	22 25	22 40	22 44	22 55	23 05	23 25	23 43
Five Ways	d	22 14	22 29	22 44		22 59	23 09	23 29	23 47
Birmingham New Street 12	a	22 17	22 33	22 47	22 50	23 03	23 12	23 34	23 50
	d		22 35	22 55			23 15		
Duddeston	d		22 39	22 59			23 19		
Aston	d		22 42	23 02			23 22		
Gravelly Hill	d		22 45	23 05			23 25		
Erdington	d		22 48	23 08			23 28		
Chester Road	d		22 50	23 10			23 30		
Wylde Green	d		22 52	23 12			23 32		
Sutton Coldfield	d		22 55	23 15			23 35		
Four Oaks	d		22 58	23 18			23 38		
Butlers Lane	d		23 00	23 20			23 40		
Blake Street	d		23 03	23a24			23 43		
Shenstone	d		23 07				23 47		
Lichfield City	d		23 12				23a52		
Lichfield Trent Valley	a		23 16						

Mondays to Fridays

from 24 October

		LM	LM	LM	LM	LM	LM	LM	LM	LM	LM	LM	LM	LM	LM	LM	XC ◇1	LM	LM	LM	LM	XC ◇1	LM
Bromsgrove	d				06 22		06 44				07 24						07 49					08 24	
Redditch	d			05 57				06 27		06 57						07 27					07 57		
Alvechurch	d			06 02				06 32		07 02						07 32					08 02		
Barnt Green	d			06 13				06 40		07 09						07 44					08 14		
Longbridge	d		06 02	06 22		06 32		06 52	07 02	07 22			07 32	07 42		07 52		08 02	08 12		08 22		08 32
Northfield	d		06 04	06 24		06 34		06 54	07 04	07 24			07 34	07 44		07 54		08 04	08 14		08 24		08 34
Kings Norton	d		06 07	06 27		06 37		06 57	07 07	07 27			07 37	07 47		07 57		08 07	08 17		08 27		08 37
Bournville	d		06 09	06 29		06 39		07 00	07 09	07 29			07 39	07 49		07 59		08 09	08 19		08 29		08 39
Selly Oak	d		06 12	06 32		06 42		07 02	07 12	07 32			07 42	07 52		08 02		08 12	08 22		08 32		08 42
University	d		06 15	06 35	06 39	06 45	06 59	07 05	07 15	07 35			07 45	07 55	07 59	08 05	08 09	08 15	08 25	08 29	08 35	08 39	08 45
Five Ways	d		06 19	06 39		06 49		07 09	07 19	07 39			07 49	07 59		08 09		08 19	08 29		08 39		08 49
Birmingham New Street 12	a		06 22	06 42	06 45	06 52	07 07	07 15	07 22	07 42	07 45		07 52	08 03	08 09	08 12	08 16	08 22	08 33	08 37	08 42	08 45	08 52
	d	06 01	06 25	06 45		06 55		07 15	07 25	07 45		07 55	07 57	08 05		08 15		08 25	08 35		08 45		08 55
Duddeston	d	06 05	06 29			06 59			07 29				08 01					08 29					08 59
Aston	d	06 08	06 32	06 51		07 02		07 22	07 32	07 51			08 04	08 11		08 21		08 32	08 41		08 51		09 02
Gravelly Hill	d	06 11	06 35	06 54		07 06		07 25	07 36	07 54			08 08	08 14		08 24		08 36	08 44		08 54		09 06
Erdington	d	06 14	06 38	06 57		07 09		07 28	07 39	07 57			08 11	08 17		08 27		08 39	08 47		08 57		09 09
Chester Road	d	06 16	06 40	06 59		07 11		07 30	07 41	07 59			08 13	08 19		08 29		08 41	08 49		08 59		09 11
Wylde Green	d	06 18	06 43	07 02		07 13		07 32	07 43	08 02			08 15	08 22		08 32		08 43	08 52		09 02		09 13
Sutton Coldfield	d	06 21	06 46	07 05		07 16		07 35	07 46	08 05		08 09	08 18	08 25		08 35		08 46	08 55		09 05		09 16
Four Oaks	d	06 24	06 49	07a13		07 20		07a43	07 50	08a13		08 13	08 22	08 28		08a43		08 50	08 58		09a13		09 20
Butlers Lane	d	06 26	06 52			07 22			07 52				08 24	08 31				08 52	09 01				09 22
Blake Street	d	06 29	06 54			07 25			07 55				08 27	08 33				08 55	09 03				09 25
Shenstone	d	06 33	06 59			07 29			07 59				08 31	08 38				08 59					09 29
Lichfield City	d	06 38	07 04			07 34			08 04			08a28	08 36	08 47				09 04	09 16				09 34
Lichfield Trent Valley	a	06 44	07 10			07 40			08 10				08 41	08 55				09 10	09 25				09 40

		LM	LM	LM	LM	LM	LM	LM	XC ◇1	LM	LM	LM	LM	LM	LM	XC ◇1	LM	LM	LM	LM	LM	XC ◇1	LM
Bromsgrove	d		08 42				09 11						09 54					10 42					
Redditch	d			08 27				08 57				09 27			09 57				10 27		10 57		
Alvechurch	d			08 32				09 02				09 32			10 02				10 32		11 02		
Barnt Green	d			08 39				09 09				09 47			10 09				10 39		11 09		
Longbridge	d	08 42		08 52	09 02	09 12		09 22		09 32	09 42	09 52		10 02	10 22		10 32		10 52	11 02	11 22		11 32
Northfield	d	08 44		08 54	09 04	09 14		09 24		09 34	09 44	09 54		10 04	10 24		10 34		10 54	11 04	11 24		11 34
Kings Norton	d	08 47		08 57	09 07	09 17		09 27		09 37	09 47	09 57		10 07	10 27		10 37		10 57	11 07	11 27		11 37
Bournville	d	08 49		08 59	09 09	09 19		09 29		09 39	09 49	09 59		10 09	10 29		10 39		10 59	11 09	11 29		11 39
Selly Oak	d	08 52		09 02	09 12	09 22		09 32		09 42	09 52	10 02		10 12	10 32		10 42		11 02	11 12	11 32		11 42
University	d	08 55	08 59	09 05	09 15	09 25	09 29	09 35	09 39	09 45	09 55	10 05	10 09	10 15	10 35	10 39	10 45	10 59	11 05	11 15	11 35	11 39	11 45
Five Ways	d	08 59		09 09	09 19	09 29		09 39		09 49	09 59	10 09		10 19	10 39		10 49		11 09	11 19	11 39		11 49
Birmingham New Street 12	a	09 03	09 07	09 12	09 22	09 32	09 42	09 42	09 45	09 52	10 03	10 12	10 24	10 22	10 42	10 45	10 52	11 13	11 12	11 22	11 42	11 45	11 52
	d	09 05		09 15	09 25	09 35		09 45		09 55	10 05	10 15		10 25	10 45		10 55		11 15	11 25	11 45		11 55
Duddeston	d				09 29					09 59				10 29			10 59			11 29			11 59
Aston	d	09 11		09 21	09 32	09 41		09 51		10 02	10 11	10 21		10 32	10 51		11 02		11 21	11 32	11 51		12 02
Gravelly Hill	d	09 14		09 24	09 36	09 44		09 54		10 06	10 14	10 24		10 36	10 54		11 06		11 24	11 36	11 54		12 06
Erdington	d	09 17		09 27	09 39	09 47		09 57		10 09	10 17	10 27		10 39	10 57		11 09		11 27	11 39	11 57		12 09
Chester Road	d	09 19		09 29	09 41	09 49		09 59		10 11	10 19	10 29		10 41	10 59		11 11		11 29	11 41	11 59		12 11
Wylde Green	d	09 22		09 32	09 43	09 52		10 02		10 13	10 22	10 32		10 43	11 02		11 13		11 32	11 43	12 02		12 13
Sutton Coldfield	d	09 25		09 35	09 46	09 55		10 05		10 16	10 25	10 35		10 46	11 05		11 16		11 35	11 46	12 05		12 16
Four Oaks	d	09 28		09a43	09 50	09 58		10a13		10 20	10 28	10 38		10a53	11a13		11 20		11a43	11 50	12a13		12 20
Butlers Lane	d	09 31			09 52	10 01				10 22	10 31	10 41					11 22			11 52			12 22
Blake Street	d	09 33			09 55	10 03				10 25	10 33	10 43					11 25			11 55			12 25
Shenstone	d				09 59					10 29		10 48					11 29			11 59			12 29
Lichfield City	d	09a45			10 04	10a15				10 34	10a45	10 57					11 34			12 04			12 34
Lichfield Trent Valley	a				10 10					10 40		11 02					11 40			12 10			12 40

Redditch and Longbridge - Birmingham - Lichfield

		LM	LM	LM	LM	XC ◇1 🛒	LM	LM	LM	LM	LM	XC ◇1 🛒	LM	LM	LM	LM	LM	XC ◇1 🛒	LM	LM	LM	LM
Bromsgrove	d	11 42						12 42						13 42						14 42		
Redditch	d		11 27		11 57				12 27		12 57				13 27		13 57				14 27	
Alvechurch	d		11 32		12 02				12 32		13 02				13 32		14 02				14 32	
Barnt Green	d		11 39		12 09				12 39		13 09				13 39		14 09				14 39	
Longbridge	d		11 52	12 02	12 22		12 32		12 52	13 02	13 22		13 32		13 52	14 02	14 22		14 32		1452	15 02
Northfield	d		11 54	12 04	12 24		12 34		12 54	13 04	13 24		13 34		13 54	14 04	14 24		14 34		14 54	15 04
Kings Norton	d		11 57	12 07	12 27		12 37		12 57	13 07	13 27		13 37		13 57	14 07	14 27		14 37		14 57	15 07
Bournville	d		11 59	12 09	12 29		12 39		12 59	13 09	13 29		13 39		13 59	14 09	14 29		14 39		14 59	15 09
Selly Oak	d		12 02	12 12	12 32		12 42		13 02	13 12	13 32		13 42		14 02	14 12	14 32		14 42		15 02	15 12
University	d	11 59	12 05	12 15	12 35	12 39	12 45	12 59	13 05	13 15	13 35	13 39	13 45	13 59	14 05	14 15	14 35	14 39	14 45	14 59	15 05	15 15
Five Ways	d		12 09	12 19	12 39		12 49		13 09	13 19	13 39		13 49		14 09	14 19	14 39		14 49		15 09	15 19
Birmingham New Street 12	a	12 11	12 12	12 22	12 42	12 45	12 52	13 13	13 12	13 22	13 42	13 45	13 52	14 12	14 12	14 22	14 42	14 45	14 52	15 13	15 12	15 22
	d		12 15	12 25	12 45		12 55		13 15	13 25	13 45		13 55		14 15	14 25	14 45		14 55		15 15	15 25
Duddeston	d			12 29			12 59			13 29			13 59			14 29			14 59			15 29
Aston	d		12 21	12 32	12 51		13 02		13 21	13 32	13 51		14 02		14 21	14 32	14 51		15 02		15 21	15 32
Gravelly Hill	d		12 24	12 36	12 54		13 06		13 24	13 36	13 54		14 06		14 24	14 36	14 54		15 06		15 24	15 36
Erdington	d		12 27	12 39	12 57		13 09		13 27	13 39	13 57		14 09		14 27	14 39	14 57		15 09		15 27	15 39
Chester Road	d		12 29	12 41	12 59		13 11		13 29	13 41	13 59		14 11		14 29	14 41	14 59		15 11		15 29	15 41
Wylde Green	d		12 32	12 43	13 02		13 13		13 32	13 43	14 02		14 13		14 32	14 43	15 02		15 13		15 32	15 43
Sutton Coldfield	d		12 35	12 46	13 05		13 16		13 35	13 46	14 05		14 16		14 35	14 46	15 05		15 16		15 35	15 46
Four Oaks	d		12a43	12 50	13a13		13 20		13a43	13 50	14a13		14 20		14a43	14 50	15a13		15 20		15 38	15 50
Butlers Lane	d			12 52			13 22			13 52			14 22			14 52			15 22		15 41	15 52
Blake Street	d			12 55			13 25			13 55			14 25			14 55			15 25		15a46	15 55
Shenstone	d			12 59			13 29			13 59			14 29			14 59			15 29			15 59
Lichfield City	d			13 04			13 34			14 04			14 34			15 04			15 34			16 04
Lichfield Trent Valley	a			13 10			13 40			14 10			14 40			15 10			15 40			16 10

		LM	LM	XC ◇1 🛒	LM	LM	LM	LM	LM	LM	XC ◇1 🛒	LM	LM	LM	LM	LM	LM	LM	XC ◇1	LM	LM	LM	LM
Bromsgrove	d					15 42									16 42							17 42	
Redditch	d		14 57				15 27			15 57				16 27				16 57					17 27
Alvechurch	d		15 02				15 32			16 02				16 32				17 02					17 32
Barnt Green	d		15 16				15 39			16 09				16 39	16 49			17 17					17 44
Longbridge	d	15 12	15 22		15 32		15 52	16 02	16 12	16 22		16 32		16 53		17 02		17 22		17 32			17 52
Northfield	d	15 14	15 24		15 34		15 54	16 04	16 14	16 24		16 34		16 55		17 04		17 24		17 34			17 54
Kings Norton	d	15 17	15 27		15 37		15 57	16 07	16 17	16 27		16 37		16 58		17 07		17 27		17 37			17 57
Bournville	d	15 19	15 29		15 39		15 59	16 09	16 19	16 29		16 39		17 00		17 09		17 29		17 39			17 59
Selly Oak	d	15 22	15 32		15 42		16 02	16 12	16 22	16 32		16 42		17 03		17 12		17 32		17 42			18 02
University	d	15 25	15 35	15 39	15 45	15 59	16 05	16 15	16 25	16 35	16 39	16 45	16 55	17 06	16 59	17 15	17 25	17 35	17 39	17 45	17 55	17 59	18 05
Five Ways	d	15 29	15 39		15 49		16 09	16 19	16 29	16 39		16 49	16 58	17 10		17 19	17 28	17 39		17 49	17 58		18 09
Birmingham New Street 12	a	15 32	15 42	15 45	15 52	16 13	16 12	16 22	16 33	16 42	16 45	16 52	17 02	17 13	17 13	17 22	17 32	17 42	17 45	17 52	18 02	18 13	18 12
	d	15 35	15 45		15 55		16 15	16 25	16 35	16 45		16 55	17 05	17 16		17 25	17 35	17 45		17 55	18 05		18 15
Duddeston	d				15 59			16 29				16 59				17 29				17 59			
Aston	d	15 41	15 51		16 02		16 21	16 32	16 41	16 51		17 02	17 11	17 22		17 32	17 41	17 51		18 02	18 11		18 21
Gravelly Hill	d	15 44	15 54		16 06		16 24	16 36	16 44	16 54		17 06	17 14	17 25		17 36	17 44	17 54		18 06	18 14		18 24
Erdington	d	15 47	15 57		16 09		16 27	16 39	16 47	16 57		17 09	17 17	17 28		17 39	17 47	17 57		18 09	18 17		18 27
Chester Road	d	15 49	15 59		16 11		16 29	16 41	16 49	16 59		17 11	17 19	17 30		17 41	17 49	17 59		18 11	18 19		18 29
Wylde Green	d	15 52	16 02		16 13		16 32	16 43	16 52	17 02		17 13	17 22	17 33		17 43	17 52	18 02		18 13	18 22		18 32
Sutton Coldfield	d	15 55	16 05		16 16		16 35	16 46	16 55	17 05		17 16	17 25	17 36		17 46	17 55	18 05		18 16	18 25		18 35
Four Oaks	d	15 58	16a13		16 20		16a43	16 50	16 58	17a13		17 20	17 28	17a43		17 50	17 58	18a13		18 20	18 28		18a43
Butlers Lane	d	16 01			16 22			16 52	17 01			17 22	17 31			17 52	18 01			18 22	18 31		
Blake Street	d	16 03			16 25			16 55	17a08			17 25	17 33			17 55	18 03			18 25	18 33		
Shenstone	d	16 08			16 29			16 59				17 29	17 38			17 59	18 08			18 29	18 38		
Lichfield City	d	16a15			16 34			17 04				17 34	17 49			18 04	18 19			18 34	18 49		
Lichfield Trent Valley	a				16 40			17 10				17 40	17 53			18 10	18 23			18 40	18 53		

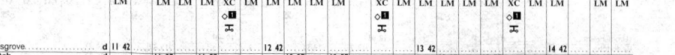

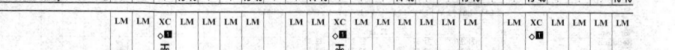

Table 69

Mondays to Fridays

from 24 October

Redditch and Longbridge - Birmingham - Lichfield

		LM	LM	XC	LM	LM	LM	LM	LM	XC	LM	LM	LM	LM	LM	XC	LM	LM	LM	LM	LM	XC
				◇1						◇1						◇1						◇1
Bromsgrove	d					18 43							19 46							21 00		
Redditch	d		17 57				18 27		18 57			19 27			19 57			20 27			20 57	
Alvechurch	d		18 02				18 32		19 02			19 32			20 02			20 32			21 02	
Barnt Green	d		18 09			18 50	18 39		19 08			19 38			20 08			20 38			21 08	
Longbridge	d	18 02	18 22		18 32		18 52	19 02	19 12		19 32	19 42		20 02	20 12		20 30	20 42	21 00		21 12	
Northfield	d	18 04	18 24		18 34		18 54	19 04	19 14		19 34	19 44		20 04	20 14		20 32	20 44	21 02		21 14	
Kings Norton	d	18 07	18 27		18 37		18 58	19 07	19 17		19 37	19 47		20 07	20 17		20 35	20 47	21 05		21 17	
Bournville	d	18 09	18 29		18 39		19 00	19 09	19 19		19 39	19 49		20 09	20 19		20 37	20 49	21 07		21 19	
Selly Oak	d	18 12	18 32		18 42		19 03	19 12	19 22		19 42	19 52		20 12	20 22		20 40	20 52	21 10		21 22	
University	d	18 15	18 35	18 39	18 45	19 00	19 06	19 15	19 25	19 39	19 45	19 55	20 09	20 15	20 25	20 39	20 43	20 55	21 13	21 17	21 25	21 46
Five Ways	d	18 19	18 39		18 49		19 10	19 19	19 29		19 49	19 59		20 19	20 29		20 47	20 59	21 17		21 29	
Birmingham New Street 12	a	18 22	18 42	18 45	18 52	19 12	19 13	19 22	19 32	19 45	19 55	20 03	20 20	20 25	20 33	20 45	20 53	21 02	21 23	21 23	21 33	21 52
	d	18 25	18 45		18 55		19 16	19 25	19 35			20 05			20 35			21 05			21 35	
Duddeston	d	18 29			18 59				19 39			20 09			20 39			21 09			21 39	
Aston	d	18 32	18 51		19 02		19 22	19 31	19 42			20 12			20 42			21 12			21 42	
Gravelly Hill	d	18 36	18 54		19 06		19 25	19 34	19 46			20 16			20 46			21 16			21 46	
Erdington	d	18 39	18 57		19 09		19 28	19 37	19 49			20 19			20 49			21 19			21 49	
Chester Road	d	18 41	18 59		19 11		19 30	19 39	19 51			20 21			20 51			21 21			21 51	
Wylde Green	d	18 43	19 02		19 13		19 33	19 42	19 53			20 23			20 53			21 23			21 53	
Sutton Coldfield	d	18 46	19 05		19 16		19 36	19 45	19 56			20 26			20 56			21 26			21 56	
Four Oaks	d	18 50	19a13		19 20		19a43	19 48	20 00			20 30			21 00			21 30			22 00	
Butlers Lane	d	18 52			19 22			19 51	20 02			20 32			21 02			21 32			22 02	
Blake Street	d	18 55			19 25			19 53	20 05			20 35			21 05			21 35			22 05	
Shenstone	d	18 59			19 29			19 58	20 09			20 39			21 09			21 39			22 09	
Lichfield City	d	19 04			19 34			20 03	20 14			20 44			21 14			21 44			22 14	
Lichfield Trent Valley	a	19 10			19 40			20 10	20 20			20 50			21 20			21 50			22 20	

		LM	LM	LM	LM	LM	LM	LM	LM	LM	LM
Bromsgrove	d						22 28				
Redditch	d		21 27		21 57			22 27		22 57	
Alvechurch	d		21 32		22 02			22 32		23 02	
Barnt Green	d		21 38		22 08			22 38		23 08	
Longbridge	d	21 30	21 42	22 00	22 12	22 27		22 45	22 53	23 12	23 30
Northfield	d	21 32	21 44	22 02	22 14	22 29		22 47	22 55	23 14	23 32
Kings Norton	d	21 35	21 47	22 05	22 17	22 32		22 50	22 58	23 17	23 35
Bournville	d	21 37	21 49	22 07	22 19	22 34		22 52	23 00	23 19	23 37
Selly Oak	d	21 40	21 52	22 10	22 22	22 37		22 55	23 03	23 22	23 40
University	d	21 43	21 55	22 13	22 25	22 40	22 44	22 58	23 06	23 25	23 43
Five Ways	d	21 47	21 59	22 17	22 29	22 44		23 02	23 10	23 29	23 47
Birmingham New Street 12	a	21 53	22 02	22 23	22 33	22 47	22 50	23 06	23 13	23 34	23 53
	d		22 05		22 35	22 55			23 15		
Duddeston	d		22 09		22 39	22 59			23 19		
Aston	d		22 12		22 42	23 02			23 22		
Gravelly Hill	d		22 16		22 46	23 06			23 26		
Erdington	d		22 19		22 49	23 09			23 29		
Chester Road	d		22 21		22 51	23 11			23 31		
Wylde Green	d		22 23		22 53	23 13			23 33		
Sutton Coldfield	d		22 26		22 56	23 16			23 36		
Four Oaks	d		22 30		23 00	23 20			23 40		
Butlers Lane	d		22 32		23 02	23 22			23 42		
Blake Street	d		22 35		23 05	23a28			23 45		
Shenstone	d		22 39		23 09				23 49		
Lichfield City	d		22 44		23 14				23a57		
Lichfield Trent Valley	a		22 50		23 20						

Saturdays

until 22 October

		LM	LM	LM	LM	LM	LM	LM	LM	LM	LM	LM	LM	LM	XC	LM	LM	LM	LM	LM	XC	LM	LM
															◇1						◇1		
Bromsgrove	d								06 51						07 44		07 52						
Redditch	d						06 27				06 57			07 27					07 57				08 27
Alvechurch	d						06 32				07 02			07 32					08 02				08 32
Barnt Green	d						06 38				07 08			07 38					08 08				08 38
Longbridge	d			06 12	06 22	06 32	06 42	06 52		07 02	07 12	07 22	07 32	07 42		07 52		08 02	08 12	08 22		08 32	08 42
Northfield	d			06 14	06 24	06 34	06 44	06 54		07 04	07 14	07 24	07 34	07 44		07 54		08 04	08 14	08 24		08 34	08 44
Kings Norton	d			06 17	06 27	06 37	06 47	06 57		07 07	07 17	07 27	07 37	07 47		07 57		08 07	08 17	08 27		08 37	08 47
Bournville	d			06 19	06 29	06 39	06 49	06 59		07 09	07 19	07 29	07 39	07 49		07 59		08 09	08 19	08 29		08 39	08 49
Selly Oak	d			06 22	06 32	06 42	06 52	07 02		07 12	07 22	07 32	07 42	07 52		08 02		08 12	08 22	08 32		08 42	08 52
University	d			06 25	06 35	06 45	06 55	07 05	07 09	07 15	07 25	07 35	07 45	07 55	08 00	08 05	08 09	08 15	08 25	08 35	08 39	08 45	08 55
Five Ways	d			06 29	06 39	06 49	06 59	07 09		07 19	07 29	07 39	07 49	07 59		08 09		08 19	08 29	08 39		08 49	08 59
Birmingham New Street 12	a			06 33	06 43	06 53	07 03	07 13	07 16	07 23	07 34	07 43	07 53	08 03	08 08	08 13	08 16	08 23	08 33	08 43	08 45	08 52	09 03
	d	05 57	06 25	06 35		06 55	07 05	07 15		07 25	07 35	07 45	07 55	08 05		08 15		08 25	08 35	08 45		08 55	09 05
Duddeston	d	06 01	06 29			06 59				07 29			07 59					08 29				08 59	
Aston	d	06 04	06 32			07 02	07 11	07 21		07 32	07 41	07 51	08 02	08 11		08 21		08 32	08 41	08 51		09 02	09 11
Gravelly Hill	d	06 07	06 35			07 05	07 14	07 24		07 35	07 44	07 54	08 05	08 14		08 24		08 35	08 44	08 54		09 05	09 14
Erdington	d	06 10	06 38	06 45		07 08	07 16	07 26		07 38	07 46	07 56	08 08	08 16		08 26		08 38	08 46	08 56		09 08	09 16
Chester Road	d	06 12	06 40	06 47		07 10	07 18	07 28		07 40	07 48	07 58	08 10	08 18		08 28		08 40	08 48	08 58		09 10	09 18
Wylde Green	d	06 14	06 42	06 49		07 12	07 20	07 30		07 42	07 50	08 00	08 12	08 20		08 30		08 42	08 50	09 00		09 12	09 20
Sutton Coldfield	d	06 17	06 45	06 52		07 15	07 24	07 34		07 45	07 54	08 04	08 15	08 24		08 34		08 45	08 54	09 04		09 15	09 24
Four Oaks	d	06 20	06 48	06 56		07 18	07 28	07a41		07 48	07 58	08a11	08 18	08 28		08a41		08 48	08 58	09a11		09 18	09 28
Butlers Lane	d	06 22	06 50	06 58		07 20	07 30			07 50	08 00		08 20	08 30				08 50	09 00			09 20	09 30
Blake Street	d	06 24	06 53	07 00		07 23	07 32			07 53	08 02		08 23	08 32				08 53	09 02			09 23	09 32
Shenstone	d	06 28	06 57			07 27				07 57			08 27	08 36				08 57				09 27	
Lichfield City	d	06a34	07a02	07 09		07a32	07 41			08a02	08 11		08a32	08 41				09a02	09 11			09a32	09 41
Lichfield Trent Valley	a			07 13			07 45				08 15			08 45					09 15				09 45

Table 69

Saturdays
until 22 October

Redditch and Longbridge - Birmingham - Lichfield

		LM	LM	LM	LM	LM		XC ◇1	LM	LM	LM	LM	LM	LM	LM	LM		XC ◇1	LM	LM	LM	LM	LM	LM	LM
Bromsgrove	d	08 42									09 42				10 13						10 42				11 15
Redditch	d				08 57					09 27				09 57						10 27				10 57	
Alvechurch	d				09 02					09 32				10 02						10 32				11 02	
Barnt Green	d				09 08					09 38				10 08						10 38				11 08	
Longbridge	d		08 52	09 02	09 12	09 22			09 32	09 42		09 52	10 02	10 12		10 22			10 32	10 42		10 52	11 02	11 12	
Northfield	d		08 54	09 04	09 14	09 24			09 34	09 44		09 54	10 04	10 14		10 24			10 34	10 44		10 54	11 04	11 14	
Kings Norton	d		08 57	09 07	09 17	09 27			09 37	09 47		09 57	10 07	10 17		10 27			10 37	10 47		10 57	11 07	11 17	
Bournville	d		08 59	09 09	09 19	09 29			09 39	09 49		09 59	10 09	10 19		10 29			10 39	10 49		10 59	11 09	11 19	
Selly Oak	d		09 02	09 12	09 22	09 32			09 42	09 52		10 02	10 12	10 22		10 32			10 42	10 52		11 02	11 12	11 22	
University	d	08 59	09 05	09 15	09 25	09 35		09 39	09 45	09 55	09 59	10 05	10 15	10 25		10 35		10 39	10 45	10 55	10 59	11 05	11 15	11 25	
Five Ways	d		09 09	09 19	09 29	09 39			09 49	09 59		10 09	10 19	10 29		10 39			10 49	10 59		11 09	11 19	11 29	
Birmingham New Street 12	a	09 11	09 13	09 23	09 33	09 43		09 45	09 53	10 03	10 11	10 13	10 23	10 33	10 41	10 43		10 45	10 53	11 03	11 11	11 13	11 23	11 33	11 38
	d		09 15	09 25	09 35	09 45			09 55	10 05		10 15	10 25	10 35		10 45			10 55	11 05		11 15	11 25	11 35	
Duddeston	d			09 29					09 59				10 29						10 59				11 29		
Aston	d		09 21	09 32	09 41	09 51			10 02	10 11		10 21	10 32	10 41		10 51			11 02	11 11		11 21	11 32	11 41	
Gravelly Hill	d		09 24	09 35	09 44	09 54			10 05	10 14		10 24	10 35	10 44		10 54			11 05	11 14		11 24	11 35	11 44	
Erdington	d		09 26	09 38	09 46	09 56			10 08	10 16		10 26	10 38	10 46		10 56			11 08	11 16		11 26	11 38	11 46	
Chester Road	d		09 28	09 40	09 48	09 58			10 10	10 18		10 28	10 40	10 48		10 58			11 10	11 18		11 28	11 40	11 48	
Wylde Green	d		09 30	09 42	09 50	10 00			10 12	10 20		10 30	10 42	10 50		11 00			11 12	11 20		11 30	11 42	11 50	
Sutton Coldfield	d		09 34	09 45	09 54	10 04			10 15	10 24		10 34	10 45	10 54		11 04			11 15	11 24		11 34	11 45	11 54	
Four Oaks	d		09a41	09 48	09 58	10a11			10 18	10 28		10a41	10 48	10 58		11a11			11 18	11 28		11a41	11 48	11 58	
Butlers Lane	d			09 50	10 00				10 20	10 30			10 50	11 00					11 20	11 30			11 50	12 00	
Blake Street	d			09 53	10 02				10 23	10 32			10 53	11 02					11 23	11 32			11 53	12 02	
Shenstone	d			09 57					10 27				10 57						11 27				11 57		
Lichfield City	d			10a02	10 11				10a32	10 41			11a02	11 11					11a32	11 41			12a02	12 11	
Lichfield Trent Valley	a				10 15					10 45				11 15						11 45				12 15	

		LM		XC ◇1	LM	LM	LM	LM	LM	LM	LM	XC ◇1		LM	LM	LM	LM	LM	LM	LM	XC ◇1	LM		LM	LM
Bromsgrove	d						11 42								12 42										13 42
Redditch	d					11 27				11 57					12 27				12 57					13 27	
Alvechurch	d					11 32				12 02					12 32				13 02					13 32	
Barnt Green	d					11 38				12 08					12 38				13 08					13 38	
Longbridge	d	11 22			11 32	11 42		11 52	12 02	12 12	12 22			12 32	12 42		12 52	13 02	13 12	13 22		13 32		13 42	
Northfield	d	11 24			11 34	11 44		11 54	12 04	12 14	12 24			12 34	12 44		12 54	13 04	13 14	13 24		13 34		13 44	
Kings Norton	d	11 27			11 37	11 47		11 57	12 07	12 17	12 27			12 37	12 47		12 57	13 07	13 17	13 27		13 37		13 47	
Bournville	d	11 29			11 39	11 49		11 59	12 09	12 19	12 29			12 39	12 49		12 59	13 09	13 19	13 29		13 39		13 49	
Selly Oak	d	11 32			11 42	11 52		12 02	12 12	12 22	12 32			12 42	12 52		13 02	13 12	13 22	13 32		13 42		13 52	
University	d	11 35		11 39	11 45	11 55	11 59	12 05	12 15	12 25	12 35	12 39		12 45	12 55	12 59	13 05	13 15	13 25	13 35	13 39	13 45		13 55	13 59
Five Ways	d	11 39			11 49	11 59		12 09	12 19	12 29	12 39			12 49	12 59		13 09	13 19	13 29	13 39		13 49		13 59	
Birmingham New Street 12	a	11 43		11 45	11 53	12 03	12 11	12 13	12 23	12 33	12 43	12 45		12 53	13 03	13 11	13 13	13 23	13 33	13 43	13 45	13 53		14 03	14 11
	d	11 45			11 55	12 05		12 15	12 25	12 35	12 45			12 55	13 05		13 15	13 25	13 35	13 45		13 55		14 05	
Duddeston	d				11 59				12 29					12 59				13 29				13 59			
Aston	d	11 51			12 02	12 11		12 21	12 32	12 41	12 51			13 02	13 11		13 21	13 32	13 41	13 51		14 02		14 11	
Gravelly Hill	d	11 54			12 05	12 14		12 24	12 35	12 44	12 54			13 05	13 14		13 24	13 35	13 44	13 54		14 05		14 14	
Erdington	d	11 56			12 08	12 16		12 26	12 38	12 46	12 56			13 08	13 16		13 26	13 38	13 46	13 56		14 08		14 16	
Chester Road	d	11 58			12 10	12 18		12 28	12 40	12 48	12 58			13 10	13 18		13 28	13 40	13 48	13 58		14 10		14 18	
Wylde Green	d	12 00			12 12	12 20		12 30	12 42	12 50	13 00			13 12	13 20		13 30	13 42	13 50	14 00		14 12		14 20	
Sutton Coldfield	d	12 04			12 15	12 24		12 34	12 45	12 54	13 04			13 15	13 24		13 34	13 45	13 54	14 04		14 15		14 24	
Four Oaks	d	12a11			12 18	12 28		12a41	12 48	12 58	13a11			13 18	13 28		13a41	13 48	13 58	14a11		14 18		14 28	
Butlers Lane	d				12 20	12 30			12 50	13 00				13 20	13 30			13 50	14 00			14 20		14 30	
Blake Street	d				12 23	12 32			12 53	13 02				13 23	13 32			13 53	14 02			14 23		14 32	
Shenstone	d				12 27				12 57					13 27				13 57				14 27			
Lichfield City	d				12a32	12 41			13a02	13 11				13a32	13 41			14a02	14 11			14a32		14 41	
Lichfield Trent Valley	a					12 45				13 15					13 45				14 15					14 45	

		LM	LM	LM	LM	XC ◇1	LM	LM		LM	LM	LM	LM	LM	XC ◇1	LM	LM	LM		LM	LM	LM	LM	LM	XC ◇1
Bromsgrove	d									14 42								15 42					16 12		
Redditch	d			13 57				14 27					14 57				15 27					15 57			
Alvechurch	d			14 02				14 32					15 02				15 32					16 02			
Barnt Green	d			14 08				14 38					15 08				15 38					16 08			
Longbridge	d	13 52	14 02	14 12	14 22		14 32	14 42			14 52	15 02	15 12	15 22		15 32	15 42			15 52	16 02	16 12		16 22	
Northfield	d	13 54	14 04	14 14	14 24		14 34	14 44			14 54	15 04	15 14	15 24		15 34	15 44			15 54	16 04	16 14		16 24	
Kings Norton	d	13 57	14 07	14 17	14 27		14 37	14 47			14 57	15 07	15 17	15 27		15 37	15 47			15 57	16 07	16 17		16 27	
Bournville	d	13 59	14 09	14 19	14 29		14 39	14 49			14 59	15 09	15 19	15 29		15 39	15 49			15 59	16 09	16 19		16 29	
Selly Oak	d	14 02	14 12	14 22	14 32		14 42	14 52			15 02	15 12	15 22	15 32		15 42	15 52			16 02	16 12	16 22		16 32	
University	d	14 05	14 15	14 25	14 35	14 39	14 45	14 55		14 59	15 05	15 15	15 25	15 35	15 39	15 45	15 55	15 59		16 05	16 15	16 25		16 35	16 39
Five Ways	d	14 09	14 19	14 29	14 39		14 49	14 59			15 09	15 19	15 29	15 39		15 49	15 59			16 09	16 19	16 29		16 39	
Birmingham New Street 12	a	14 13	14 23	14 33	14 43	14 45	14 53	15 03		15 11	15 13	15 23	15 33	15 43	15 45	15 53	16 03	16 11		16 13	16 23	16 33	16 45	16 43	16 45
	d	14 15	14 25	14 35	14 45		14 55	15 05			15 15	15 25	15 35	15 45		15 55	16 05			16 15	16 25	16 35		16 45	
Duddeston	d		14 29				14 59					15 29				15 59					16 29				
Aston	d	14 21	14 32	14 41	14 51		15 02	15 11			15 21	15 32	15 41	15 51		16 02	16 11			16 21	16 32	16 41		16 51	
Gravelly Hill	d	14 24	14 35	14 44	14 54		15 05	15 14			15 24	15 35	15 44	15 54		16 05	16 14			16 24	16 35	16 44		16 54	
Erdington	d	14 26	14 38	14 46	14 56		15 08	15 16			15 26	15 38	15 46	15 56		16 08	16 16			16 26	16 38	16 46		16 56	
Chester Road	d	14 28	14 40	14 48	14 58		15 10	15 18			15 28	15 40	15 48	15 58		16 10	16 18			16 28	16 40	16 48		16 58	
Wylde Green	d	14 30	14 42	14 50	15 00		15 12	15 20			15 30	15 42	15 50	16 00		16 12	16 20			16 30	16 42	16 50		17 00	
Sutton Coldfield	d	14 34	14 45	14 54	15 04		15 15	15 24			15 34	15 45	15 54	16 04		16 15	16 24			16 34	16 45	16 54		17 04	
Four Oaks	d	14a41	14 48	14 58	15a11		15 18	15 28			15a41	15 48	15 58	16a11		16 18	16 28			16a41	16 48	16 58		17a11	
Butlers Lane	d		14 50	15 00			15 20	15 30				15 50	16 00			16 20	16 30				16 50	17 00			
Blake Street	d		14 53	15 02			15 23	15 32				15 53	16 02			16 23	16 32				16 53	17 02			
Shenstone	d		14 57				15 27					15 57				16 27					16 57				
Lichfield City	d		15a02	15 11			15a32	15 41				16a02	16 11			16a32	16 41				17a02	17 11			
Lichfield Trent Valley	a			15 15				15 45					16 15				16 45					17 15			

Table 69

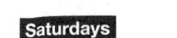

Saturdays
until 22 October

Redditch and Longbridge - Birmingham - Lichfield

		LM	LM	LM	LM	LM	LM	LM	XC ◇1	LM	LM	LM	LM	LM	LM	LM	XC ◇1	LM	LM	LM	LM	LM
Bromsgrove	d			16 42								17 44								18 44		
Redditch	d		16 27				16 57				17 27				17 57				18 27			
Alvechurch	d		16 32				17 02				17 32				18 02				18 32			
Barnt Green	d		16 38				17 08				17 38				18 08				18 38			
Longbridge	d	16 32	16 42		16 52	17 02	17 12	17 22		17 32	17 42		17 52	18 02	18 12	18 22		18 32	18 42		18 52	19 02
Northfield	d	16 34	16 44		16 54	17 04	17 14	17 24		17 34	17 44		17 54	18 04	18 14	18 24		18 34	18 44		18 54	19 04
Kings Norton	d	16 37	16 47		16 57	17 07	17 17	17 27		17 37	17 47		17 57	18 07	18 17	18 27		18 37	18 47		18 57	19 07
Bournville	d	16 39	16 49		16 59	17 09	17 19	17 29		17 39	17 49		17 59	18 09	18 19	18 29		18 39	18 49		18 59	19 09
Selly Oak	d	16 42	16 52		17 02	17 12	17 22	17 32		17 42	17 52		18 02	18 12	18 22	18 32		18 42	18 52		19 02	19 12
University	d	16 45	16 55	16 59	17 05	17 15	17 25	17 35	17 39	17 45	17 55	17 59	18 05	18 15	18 25	18 35	18 39	18 45	18 55	18 59	19 05	19 15
Five Ways	d	16 49	16 59		17 09	17 19	17 29	17 39		17 49	17 59		18 09	18 19	18 29	18 39		18 49	18 59		19 09	19 19
Birmingham New Street 12	a	16 53	17 03	17 11	17 13	17 23	17 33	17 43	17 45	17 53	18 03	18 11	18 13	18 23	18 33	18 43	18 45	18 53	19 03	19 11	19 13	19 23
	d	16 55	17 05		17 15	17 25	17 35	17 45		17 55	18 05		18 15	18 25	18 35	18 45		18 55	19 05		19 15	
Duddeston	d	16 59				17 29				17 59				18 29				18 59				
Aston	d	17 02	17 11		17 21	17 32	17 41	17 51		18 02	18 11		18 21	18 32	18 41	18 51		19 02	19 11		19 21	
Gravelly Hill	d	17 05	17 14		17 24	17 35	17 44	17 54		18 05	18 14		18 24	18 35	18 44	18 54		19 05	19 14		19 24	
Erdington	d	17 08	17 16		17 26	17 38	17 46	17 56		18 08	18 16		18 26	18 38	18 46	18 56		19 08	19 16		19 26	
Chester Road	d	17 10	17 18		17 28	17 40	17 48	17 58		18 10	18 18		18 28	18 40	18 48	18 58		19 10	19 18		19 28	
Wylde Green	d	17 12	17 20		17 30	17 42	17 50	18 00		18 12	18 20		18 30	18 42	18 50	19 00		19 12	19 20		19 30	
Sutton Coldfield	d	17 15	17 24		17 34	17 45	17 54	18 04		18 15	18 24		18 34	18 45	18 54	19 04		19 15	19 24		19 34	
Four Oaks	d	17 18	17 28		17a41	17 48	17 58	18a11		18 18	18 28		18a41	18 48	18 58	19a11		19 18	19 28		19a41	
Butlers Lane	d	17 20	17 30			17 50	18 00			18 20	18 30			18 50	19 00			19 20	19 30			
Blake Street	d	17 23	17 32			17 53	18 02			18 23	18 32			18 53	19 02			19 23	19 32			
Shenstone	d	17 27				17 57				18 27				18 57				19 27				
Lichfield City	d	17a32	17 41			18a02	18 11			18a32	18 41			19a02	19 11			19a32	19 40			
Lichfield Trent Valley	a		17 45				18 15				18 45				19 15				19 46			

		LM	LM	XC ◇1	LM	LM	LM	LM	LM	XC ◇1	LM	LM	LM	LM	LM	LM	LM	XC ◇1	LM	LM	XC ◇1	LM	LM
Bromsgrove	d													20 59				21 44					
Redditch	d	18 57				19 27			19 57			20 27			20 57		21 27			21 57			22 27
Alvechurch	d	19 02				19 32			20 02			20 32			21 02		21 32			22 02			22 32
Barnt Green	d	19 08				19 38			20 08			20 38			21 08		21 38			22 08			22 38
Longbridge	d	19 12	19 22		19 32	19 42	19 52	20 02	20 12		20 30	20 42	20 57		21 12	21 27	21 42		21 57	22 12		22 27	22 42
Northfield	d	19 14	19 24		19 34	19 44	19 54	20 04	20 14		20 32	20 44	20 59		21 14	21 29	21 44		21 59	22 14		22 29	22 44
Kings Norton	d	19 17	19 27		19 37	19 47	19 57	20 07	20 17		20 35	20 47	21 02		21 17	21 32	21 47		22 02	22 17		22 32	22 47
Bournville	d	19 19	19 29		19 39	19 49	19 59	20 09	20 19		20 37	20 49	21 04		21 19	21 34	21 49		22 04	22 19		22 34	22 49
Selly Oak	d	19 22	19 32		19 42	19 52	20 02	20 12	20 22		20 40	20 52	21 07		21 22	21 37	21 52		22 07	22 22		22 37	22 52
University	d	19 25	19 35	19 39	19 45	19 55	20 05	20 15	20 25	20 34	20 42	20 55	21 10	21 14	21 25	21 40	21 55	22 01	22 10	22 25	22 36	22 40	22 55
Five Ways	d	19 29	19 39		19 49	19 59	20 09	20 19	20 29		20 46	20 59	21 14		21 29	21 44	21 59		22 14	22 29		22 44	22 59
Birmingham New Street 12	a	19 33	19 43	19 45	19 53	20 03	20 13	20 23	20 33	20 40	20 51	21 03	21 18	21 21	21 33	21 48	22 03	22 07	22 18	22 33	22 42	22 48	23 03
	d	19 35				20 05			20 35			21 05			21 35		22 05			22 35		22 55	
Duddeston	d	19 39				20 09			20 39			21 09			21 39		22 09			22 39		22 59	
Aston	d	19 42				20 12			20 42			21 12			21 42		22 12			22 42		23 02	
Gravelly Hill	d	19 45				20 15			20 45			21 15			21 45		22 15			22 45		23 05	
Erdington	d	19 48				20 18			20 48			21 18			21 48		22 18			22 48		23 08	
Chester Road	d	19 50				20 20			20 50			21 20			21 50		22 20			22 50		23 10	
Wylde Green	d	19 52				20 22			20 52			21 22			21 52		22 22			22 52		23 12	
Sutton Coldfield	d	19 55				20 25			20 55			21 25			21 55		22 25			22 55		23 15	
Four Oaks	d	19 58				20 28			20 58			21 28			21 58		22 28			22 58		23 18	
Butlers Lane	d	20 00				20 30			21 00			21 30			22 00		22 30			23 00		23 20	
Blake Street	d	20 03				20 33			21 03			21 33			22 03		22 33			23 03		23a24	
Shenstone	d	20 07				20 37			21 07			21 37			22 07		22 37			23 07			
Lichfield City	d	20 12				20 42			21 12			21 42			22 12		22 42			23 12			
Lichfield Trent Valley	a	20 16				20 46			21 16			21 46			22 16		22 46			23 16			

		LM	LM	LM
Bromsgrove	d			
Redditch	d		22 57	
Alvechurch	d		23 02	
Barnt Green	d		23 08	
Longbridge	d	22 52	23 12	23 30
Northfield	d	22 54	23 14	23 32
Kings Norton	d	22 57	23 17	23 35
Bournville	d	22 59	23 19	23 37
Selly Oak	d	23 02	23 22	23 40
University	d	23 05	23 25	23 43
Five Ways	d	23 09	23 29	23 47
Birmingham New Street 12	a	23 13	23 33	23 51
	d	23 15		
Duddeston	d	23 19		
Aston	d	23 22		
Gravelly Hill	d	23 25		
Erdington	d	23 28		
Chester Road	d	23 30		
Wylde Green	d	23 32		
Sutton Coldfield	d	23 35		
Four Oaks	d	23 38		
Butlers Lane	d	23 40		
Blake Street	d	23 43		
Shenstone	d	23 47		
Lichfield City	d	23a52		
Lichfield Trent Valley	a			

Table 69

Saturdays
from 29 October

Redditch and Longbridge - Birmingham - Lichfield

		LM	LM	LM	LM	LM	LM	LM	LM	LM		XC	LM	LM	LM	LM	XC	LM	LM	LM		LM	LM	XC	LM
												◇1					◇1							◇1 🛒	
Bromsgrove	d						06 51					07 44		07 52					08 42						
Redditch	d			05 57		06 27			06 57				07 27			07 57				08 27			08 57		
Alvechurch	d			06 02		06 32			07 02				07 32			08 02				08 32			09 02		
Barnt Green	d			06 13		06 40			07 09				07 39			08 09				08 39			09 09		
Longbridge	d		06 02	06 22	06 32	06 52		07 02	07 22	07 32			07 52		08 02	08 22		08 32		08 52		09 02	09 22		09 32
Northfield	d		06 04	06 24	06 34	06 54		07 04	07 24	07 34			07 54		08 04	08 24		08 34		08 54		09 04	09 24		09 34
Kings Norton	d		06 07	06 27	06 37	06 57		07 07	07 27	07 37			07 57		08 07	08 27		08 37		08 57		09 07	09 27		09 37
Bournville	d		06 09	06 29	06 39	06 59		07 09	07 29	07 39			07 59		08 09	08 29		08 39		08 59		09 09	09 29		09 39
Selly Oak	d		06 12	06 32	06 42	07 02		07 12	07 32	07 42			08 02		08 12	08 32		08 42		09 02		09 12	09 32		09 42
University	d		06 15	06 35	06 45	07 05	07 09	07 15	07 35	07 45		08 00	08 05	08 09	08 15	08 35	08 39	08 45	08 59	09 05		09 15	09 35	09 39	09 45
Five Ways	d		06 19	06 39	06 49	07 09		07 19	07 39	07 49			08 09		08 19	08 39		08 49		09 09		09 19	09 39		09 49
Birmingham New Street 12	a		06 22	06 42	06 52	07 12	07 16	07 22	07 42	07 52		08 08	08 12	08 16	08 22	08 42	08 45	08 52	09 11	09 12		09 22	09 42	09 45	09 52
	d	05 57	06 25	06 45	06 55	07 15		07 25	07 45	07 55			08 15		08 25	08 45		08 55		09 15		09 25	09 45		09 55
Duddeston	d	06 01	06 29		06 59			07 29		07 59					08 29			08 59				09 29			09 59
Aston	d	06 04	06 32	06 51	07 02	07 21		07 32	07 51	08 02			08 21		08 32	08 51		09 02		09 21		09 32	09 51		10 02
Gravelly Hill	d	06 08	06 35	06 54	07 06	07 24		07 36	07 54	08 06			08 24		08 36	08 54		09 06		09 24		09 36	09 54		10 06
Erdington	d	06 11	06 38	06 57	07 09	07 27		07 39	07 57	08 09			08 27		08 39	08 57		09 09		09 27		09 39	09 57		10 09
Chester Road	d	06 13	06 40	06 59	07 11	07 29		07 41	07 59	08 11			08 29		08 41	08 59		09 11		09 29		09 41	09 59		10 11
Wylde Green	d	06 15	06 43	07 02	07 13	07 32		07 43	08 02	08 13			08 32		08 43	09 02		09 13		09 32		09 43	10 02		10 13
Sutton Coldfield	d	06 18	06 46	07 05	07 16	07 35		07 46	08 05	08 16			08 35		08 46	09 05		09 16		09 35		09 46	10 05		10 16
Four Oaks	d	06 22	06 49	07a13	07 20	07a43		07 50	08a13	08 20			08a43		08 50	09a13		09 20		09a43		09 50	10a13		10 20
Butlers Lane	d	06 24	06 52		07 22			07 52		08 22					08 52			09 22				09 52			10 22
Blake Street	d	06 27	06 54		07 25			07 55		08 25					08 55			09 25				09 55			10 25
Shenstone	d	06 31	06 59		07 29			07 59		08 29					08 59			09 29				09 59			10 29
Lichfield City	d	06 36	07 04		07 34			08 04		08 34					09 04			09 34				10 04			10 34
Lichfield Trent Valley	a	06 42	07 10		07 40			08 10		08 40					09 10			09 40				10 10			10 40

		LM	LM	LM	LM	LM		XC	LM	LM	LM	LM	LM	LM	XC	LM		LM	LM	LM	LM	XC	LM	LM	LM
								◇1 🛒							◇1 🛒							◇1 🛒			
Bromsgrove	d	09 42			10 13					10 42			11 15					11 42						12 42	
Redditch	d		09 27			09 57					10 27			10 57					11 27		11 57				12 27
Alvechurch	d		09 32			10 02					10 32			11 02					11 32		12 02				12 32
Barnt Green	d		09 39			10 09					10 39			11 09					11 39		12 09				12 39
Longbridge	d		09 52	10 02		10 22			10 32		10 52	11 02		11 22		11 32			11 52	12 02	12 22		12 32		12 52
Northfield	d		09 54	10 04		10 24			10 34		10 54	11 04		11 24		11 34			11 54	12 04	12 24		12 34		12 54
Kings Norton	d		09 57	10 07		10 27			10 37		10 57	11 07		11 27		11 37			11 57	12 07	12 27		12 37		12 57
Bournville	d		09 59	10 09		10 29			10 39		10 59	11 09		11 29		11 39			11 59	12 09	12 29		12 39		12 59
Selly Oak	d		10 02	10 12		10 32			10 42		11 02	11 12		11 32		11 42			12 02	12 12	12 32		12 42		13 02
University	d	09 59	10 05	10 15		10 35		10 39	10 45	10 59	11 05	11 15		11 35	11 39	11 45		11 59	12 05	12 15	12 35	12 39	12 45	12 59	13 05
Five Ways	d		10 09	10 19		10 39			10 49		11 09	11 19		11 39		11 49			12 09	12 19	12 39		12 49		13 09
Birmingham New Street 12	a	10 11	10 12	10 22	10 41	10 42		10 45	10 52	11 11	11 12	11 22	11 38	11 42	11 45	11 52		12 11	12 12	12 22	12 42	12 45	12 52	13 11	13 12
	d		10 15	10 25		10 45			10 55		11 15	11 25		11 45		11 55			12 15	12 25	12 45		12 55		13 15
Duddeston	d			10 29					10 59			11 29				11 59				12 29			12 59		
Aston	d		10 21	10 32		10 51			11 02		11 21	11 32		11 51		12 02			12 21	12 32	12 51		13 02		13 21
Gravelly Hill	d		10 24	10 36		10 54			11 06		11 24	11 36		11 54		12 06			12 24	12 36	12 54		13 06		13 24
Erdington	d		10 27	10 39		10 57			11 09		11 27	11 39		11 57		12 09			12 27	12 39	12 57		13 09		13 27
Chester Road	d		10 29	10 41		10 59			11 11		11 29	11 41		11 59		12 11			12 29	12 41	12 59		13 11		13 29
Wylde Green	d		10 32	10 43		11 02			11 13		11 32	11 43		12 02		12 13			12 32	12 43	13 02		13 13		13 32
Sutton Coldfield	d		10 35	10 46		11 05			11 16		11 35	11 46		12 05		12 16			12 35	12 46	13 05		13 16		13 35
Four Oaks	d		10a43	10 50		11a13			11 20		11a43	11 50		12a13		12 20			12a43	12 50	13a13		13 20		13a43
Butlers Lane	d			10 52					11 22			11 52				12 22				12 52			13 22		
Blake Street	d			10 55					11 25			11 55				12 25				12 55			13 25		
Shenstone	d			10 59					11 29			11 59				12 29				12 59			13 29		
Lichfield City	d			11 04					11 34			12 04				12 34				13 04			13 34		
Lichfield Trent Valley	a			11 10					11 40			12 10				12 40				13 10			13 40		

Table 69

Saturdays
from 29 October

Redditch and Longbridge - Birmingham - Lichfield

		LM		LM	XC ◇1 🛒	LM	LM	LM	LM	LM	XC ◇1 🛒	LM		LM	LM	LM	LM	XC ◇1 🛒	LM	LM	LM	LM		LM	LM
Bromsgrove	d						13 42							14 42						15 42					16 12
Redditch	d			12 57				13 27		13 57					14 27		14 57				15 27			15 57	
Alvechurch	d			13 02				13 32		14 02					14 32		15 02				15 32			16 02	
Barnt Green	d			13 09				13 39		14 09					14 39		15 09				15 39			16 09	
Longbridge	d	13 02		13 22		13 32		13 52	14 02	14 22		14 32			14 52	15 02	15 22		15 32		15 52	16 02		16 22	
Northfield	d	13 04		13 24		13 34		13 54	14 04	14 24		14 34			14 54	15 04	15 24		15 34		15 54	16 04		16 24	
Kings Norton	d	13 07		13 27		13 37		13 57	14 07	14 27		14 37			14 57	15 07	15 27		15 37		15 57	16 07		16 27	
Bournville	d	13 09		13 29		13 39		13 59	14 09	14 29		14 39			14 59	15 09	15 29		15 39		15 59	16 09		16 29	
Selly Oak	d	13 12		13 32		13 42		14 02	14 12	14 32		14 42			15 02	15 12	15 32		15 42		16 02	16 12		16 32	
University	d	13 15		13 35	13 39	13 45	13 59	14 05	14 15	14 35	14 39	14 45		14 59	15 05	15 15	15 35	15 39	15 45	15 59	16 05	16 15		16 35	
Five Ways	d	13 19		13 39		13 49		14 09	14 19	14 39		14 49			15 09	15 19	15 39		15 49		16 09	16 19		16 39	
Birmingham New Street 12	a	13 22		13 42	13 45	13 52	14 11	14 12	14 22	14 42	14 45	14 52		15 11	15 12	15 22	15 42	15 45	15 52	16 11	16 12	16 22		16 42	16 45
	d	13 25		13 45		13 55		14 15	14 25	14 45		14 55			15 15	15 25	15 45		15 55		16 15	16 25		16 45	
Duddeston	d	13 29				13 59			14 29			14 59				15 29			15 59			16 29			
Aston	d	13 32		13 51		14 02		14 21	14 32	14 51		15 02			15 21	15 32	15 51		16 02		16 21	16 32		16 51	
Gravelly Hill	d	13 36		13 54		14 06		14 24	14 36	14 54		15 06			15 24	15 36	15 54		16 06		16 24	16 36		16 54	
Erdington	d	13 39		13 57		14 09		14 27	14 39	14 57		15 09			15 27	15 39	15 57		16 09		16 27	16 39		16 57	
Chester Road	d	13 41		13 59		14 11		14 29	14 41	14 59		15 11			15 29	15 41	15 59		16 11		16 29	16 41		16 59	
Wylde Green	d	13 43		14 02		14 13		14 32	14 43	15 02		15 13			15 32	15 43	16 02		16 13		16 32	16 43		17 02	
Sutton Coldfield	d	13 46		14 05		14 16		14 35	14 46	15 05		15 16			15 35	15 46	16 05		16 16		16 35	16 46		17 05	
Four Oaks	d	13 50		14a13		14 20		14a43	14 50	15a13		15 20			15a43	15 50	16a13		16 20		16a43	16 50		17a13	
Butlers Lane	d	13 52				14 22			14 52			15 22				15 52			16 22			16 52			
Blake Street	d	13 55				14 25			14 55			15 25				15 55			16 25			16 55			
Shenstone	d	13 59				14 29			14 59			15 29				15 59			16 29			16 59			
Lichfield City	d	14 04				14 34			15 04			15 34				16 04			16 34			17 04			
Lichfield Trent Valley	a	14 10				14 40			15 10			15 40				16 10			16 40			17 10			

		XC ◇1 🛒	LM	LM	LM	LM	LM	XC ◇1		LM	LM	LM	LM	LM	XC ◇1	LM	LM	LM		LM	LM	XC ◇1	LM	LM	LM
Bromsgrove	d			16 42							17 44						18 44								
Redditch	d				16 27		16 57					17 27		17 57				18 27			18 57			19 27	
Alvechurch	d				16 32		17 02					17 32		18 02				18 32			19 02			19 32	
Barnt Green	d				16 39		17 09					17 39		18 09				18 39			19 08			19 38	
Longbridge	d		16 32		16 52	17 02	17 22			17 32		17 52	18 02	18 22		18 32		18 52		19 02	19 12		19 32	19 42	20 02
Northfield	d		16 34		16 54	17 04	17 24			17 34		17 54	18 04	18 24		18 34		18 54		19 04	19 14		19 34	19 44	20 04
Kings Norton	d		16 37		16 57	17 07	17 27			17 37		17 57	18 07	18 27		18 37		18 57		19 07	19 17		19 37	19 47	20 07
Bournville	d		16 39		16 59	17 09	17 29			17 39		17 59	18 09	18 29		18 39		18 59		19 09	19 19		19 39	19 49	20 09
Selly Oak	d		16 42		17 02	17 12	17 32			17 42		18 02	18 12	18 32		18 42		19 02		19 12	19 22		19 42	19 52	20 12
University	d	16 39	16 45	16 59	17 05	17 15	17 35	17 39		17 45	17 59	18 05	18 15	18 35	18 39	18 45	18 59	19 05		19 15	19 25	19 39	19 45	19 55	20 15
Five Ways	d		16 49		17 09	17 19	17 39			17 49		18 09	18 19	18 39		18 49		19 09		19 19	19 29		19 49	19 59	20 19
Birmingham New Street 12	a	16 45	16 52	17 11	17 12	17 22	17 42	17 45		17 52	18 11	18 12	18 22	18 42	18 45	18 52	19 11	19 12		19 22	19 32	19 45	19 55	20 03	20 25
	d		16 55		17 15	17 25	17 45			17 55		18 15	18 25	18 45		18 55		19 15		19 25	19 35			20 05	
Duddeston	d		16 59			17 29				17 59			18 29			18 59					19 39			20 09	
Aston	d		17 02		17 21	17 32	17 51			18 02		18 21	18 32	18 51		19 02		19 21		19 31	19 42			20 12	
Gravelly Hill	d		17 06		17 24	17 36	17 54			18 06		18 24	18 36	18 54		19 06		19 24		19 34	19 46			20 16	
Erdington	d		17 09		17 27	17 39	17 57			18 09		18 27	18 39	18 57		19 09		19 27		19 37	19 49			20 19	
Chester Road	d		17 11		17 29	17 41	17 59			18 11		18 29	18 41	18 59		19 11		19 29		19 39	19 51			20 21	
Wylde Green	d		17 13		17 32	17 43	18 02			18 13		18 32	18 43	19 02		19 13		19 32		19 42	19 53			20 23	
Sutton Coldfield	d		17 16		17 35	17 46	18 05			18 16		18 35	18 46	19 05		19 16		19 35		19 45	19 56			20 26	
Four Oaks	d		17 20		17a43	17 50	18a13			18 20		18a43	18 50	19a13		19 20		19a43		19 48	20 00			20 30	
Butlers Lane	d		17 22			17 52				18 22			18 52			19 22				19 51	20 02			20 32	
Blake Street	d		17 25			17 55				18 25			18 55			19 25				19 53	20 05			20 35	
Shenstone	d		17 29			17 59				18 29			18 59			19 29				19 58	20 09			20 39	
Lichfield City	d		17 34			18 04				18 34			19 04			19 34				20 03	20 14			20 44	
Lichfield Trent Valley	a		17 40			18 10				18 40			19 10			19 40				20 10	20 20			20 50	

		LM	XC ◇1	LM		LM	LM	LM	LM	LM	LM	XC ◇1	LM	LM		XC ◇1	LM	LM	LM	LM	LM
Bromsgrove	d							20 59				21 44									
Redditch	d	19 57				20 27			20 57		21 27			21 57				22 27		22 57	
Alvechurch	d	20 02				20 32			21 02		21 32			22 02				22 32		23 02	
Barnt Green	d	20 08				20 38			21 08		21 38			22 08				22 38		23 08	
Longbridge	d	20 12		20 30		20 42	20 57		21 12	21 30	21 42		22 00	22 12			22 30	22 45	22 53	23 12	23 30
Northfield	d	20 14		20 32		20 44	20 59		21 14	21 32	21 44		22 02	22 14			22 32	22 47	22 55	23 14	23 32
Kings Norton	d	20 17		20 35		20 47	21 02		21 17	21 35	21 47		22 05	22 17			22 35	22 50	22 58	23 17	23 35
Bournville	d	20 19		20 37		20 49	21 04		21 19	21 37	21 49		22 07	22 19			22 37	22 52	23 00	23 19	23 37
Selly Oak	d	20 22		20 40		20 52	21 07		21 22	21 40	21 52		22 10	22 22			22 40	22 55	23 03	23 22	23 40
University	d	20 25	20 34	20 43		20 55	21 10	21 14	21 25	21 43	21 55	22 01	22 13	22 25		22 36	22 43	22 58	23 06	23 25	23 43
Five Ways	d	20 29		20 47		20 59	21 14		21 29	21 47	21 59		22 17	22 29			22 47	23 02	23 10	23 29	23 47
Birmingham New Street 12	a	20 33	20 40	20 53		21 02	21 20	21 21	21 33	21 53	22 02	22 07	22 23	22 33		22 42	22 50	23 06	23 13	23 34	23 53
	d	20 35				21 04			21 35		22 05			22 35			22 55		23 15		
Duddeston	d	20 39				21 08			21 39		22 09			22 39			22 59		23 19		
Aston	d	20 42				21 11			21 42		22 12			22 42			23 02		23 22		
Gravelly Hill	d	20 46				21 15			21 46		22 16			22 46			23 06		23 26		
Erdington	d	20 49				21 18			21 49		22 19			22 49			23 09		23 29		
Chester Road	d	20 51				21 20			21 51		22 21			22 51			23 11		23 31		
Wylde Green	d	20 53				21 22			21 53		22 23			22 53			23 13		23 33		
Sutton Coldfield	d	20 56				21 25			21 56		22 26			22 56			23 16		23 36		
Four Oaks	d	21 00				21 29			22 00		22 30			23 00			23 20		23 40		
Butlers Lane	d	21 02				21 31			22 02		22 32			23 02			23 22		23 42		
Blake Street	d	21 05				21 34			22 05		22 35			23 05			23a28		23 45		
Shenstone	d	21 09				21 38			22 09		22 39			23 09					23 49		
Lichfield City	d	21 14				21 43			22 14		22 44			23 14					23a57		
Lichfield Trent Valley	a	21 20				21 49			22 20		22 50			23 20							

Table 69

Sundays

Redditch and Longbridge - Birmingham - Lichfield

		LM	LM	LM	LM	LM	LM	LM	LM	XC ◇1 A		XC ◇1 B 🚲	LM	LM	XC ◇1 C 🚲	XC ◇1 D	XC ◇1 E 🚲	LM	LM	XC ◇1 E		XC ◇1 B 🚲	XC ◇1 F	LM	LM
Bromsgrove	d																								
Redditch	d			09 27	09 57	10 27	10 57	11 27	11 57				12 27	12 57				13 27	13 57					14 27	14 57
Alvechurch	d			09 32	10 02	10 32	11 02	11 32	12 02				12 32	13 02				13 32	14 02					14 32	15 02
Barnt Green	d			09 38	10 08	10 38	11 08	11 38	12 08				12 38	13 08				13 38	14 08					14 38	15 08
Longbridge	d			09 43	10 13	10 43	11 13	11 43	12 13				12 43	13 13				13 43	14 13					14 43	15 13
Northfield	d			09 45	10 15	10 45	11 15	11 45	12 15				12 45	13 15				13 45	14 15					14 45	15 15
Kings Norton	d			09 48	10 18	10 48	11 18	11 48	12 18				12 48	13 18				13 48	14 18					14 48	15 18
Bournville	d			09 51	10 21	10 51	11 21	11 51	12 21				12 51	13 21				13 51	14 21					14 51	15 21
Selly Oak	d			09 53	10 23	10 53	11 23	11 53	12 23				12 53	13 23				13 53	14 23					14 53	15 23
University	d			09 56	10 26	10 56	11 26	11 56	12 26	12 39		12 39	12 56	13 26	13 35	13 35	13 35	13 56	14 26	14 38		14 38	14 38	14 56	15 26
Five Ways	d			10 00	10 30	11 00	11 30	12 00	12 30				13 00	13 30				14 00	14 30					15 00	15 30
Birmingham New Street 12	a			10 03	10 33	11 03	11 33	12 03	12 33	12 45		12 45	13 03	13 33	13 41	13 41	13 42	14 03	14 33	14 44		14 45	14 45	15 03	15 33
	d	09 06	09 36	10 06	10 36	11 06	11 36	12 06	12 36				13 06	13 36				14 06	14 36					15 06	15 36
Duddeston	d	09 10	09 40	10 10	10 40	11 10	11 40	12 10	12 40				13 10	13 40				14 10	14 40					15 10	15 40
Aston	d	09 13	09 43	10 13	10 43	11 13	11 43	12 13	12 43				13 13	13 43				14 13	14 43					15 13	15 43
Gravelly Hill	d	09 16	09 46	10 16	10 46	11 16	11 46	12 16	12 46				13 16	13 46				14 16	14 46					15 16	15 46
Erdington	d	09 19	09 49	10 19	10 49	11 19	11 49	12 19	12 49				13 19	13 49				14 19	14 49					15 19	15 49
Chester Road	d	09 21	09 51	10 21	10 51	11 21	11 51	12 21	12 51				13 21	13 51				14 21	14 51					15 21	15 51
Wylde Green	d	09 23	09 53	10 23	10 53	11 23	11 53	12 23	12 53				13 23	13 53				14 23	14 53					15 23	15 53
Sutton Coldfield	d	09 26	09 56	10 26	10 56	11 26	11 56	12 26	12 56				13 26	13 56				14 26	14 56					15 26	15 56
Four Oaks	d	09 29	09 59	10 29	10 59	11 29	11 59	12 29	12 59				13 29	13 59				14 29	14 59					15 29	15 59
Butlers Lane	d	09 31	10 01	10 31	11 01	11 31	12 01	12 31	13 01				13 31	14 01				14 31	15 01					15 31	16 01
Blake Street	d	09 34	10 04	10 34	11 04	11 34	12 04	12 34	13 04				13 34	14 04				14 34	15 04					15 34	16 04
Shenstone	d	09 38	10 08	10 38	11 08	11 38	12 08	12 38	13 08				13 38	14 08				14 38	15 08					15 38	16 08
Lichfield City	d	09 43	10 13	10 43	11 13	11 43	12 13	12 43	13 13				13 43	14 13				14 43	15 13					15 43	16 13
Lichfield Trent Valley	a	09 47	10 17	10 47	11 17	11 47	12 17	12 47	13 17				13 47	14 17				14 47	15 17					15 47	16 17

		LM	XC ◇1 B 🚲	XC ◇1 G	XC ◇1 E 🚲	XC ◇1 D 🚲		LM	LM	XC ◇1 H 🚲	XC ◇1 G	LM	LM	LM	XC ◇1 I 🚲	XC ◇1 C		LM	LM	LM	XC ◇1	LM	LM	XC ◇1 J	XC ◇1 E
Bromsgrove	d	15 10											16 51						17 52						
Redditch	d							15 27	15 57			16 27		16 57				17 27		17 57		18 27	18 57		
Alvechurch	d							15 32	16 02			16 32		17 02				17 32		18 02		18 32	19 02		
Barnt Green	d							15 38	16 08			16 38		17 08				17 38		18 08		18 38	19 08		
Longbridge	d							15 43	16 13			16 43		17 13				17 43		18 13		18 43	19 13		
Northfield	d							15 45	16 15			16 45		17 15				17 45		18 15		18 45	19 15		
Kings Norton	d							15 48	16 18			16 48		17 18				17 48		18 18		18 48	19 18		
Bournville	d							15 51	16 21			16 51		17 21				17 51		18 21		18 51	19 21		
Selly Oak	d							15 53	16 23			16 53		17 23				17 53		18 23		18 53	19 23		
University	d		15 35	15 35	15 35	15 36		15 56	16 26	16 35	16 35	16 56		17 26	17 35	17 35		17 56		18 26	18 35	18 56	19 26	19 35	19 35
Five Ways	d							16 00	16 30			17 00		17 30				18 00		18 30		19 00	19 30		
Birmingham New Street 12	a	15 37	15 41	15 41	15 42	15 43		16 03	16 33	16 41	16 41	17 03	17 17	17 33	17 41	17 41		18 03	18 14	18 33	18 41	19 03	19 33	19 41	19 42
	d							16 06	16 36			17 06		17 36				18 06		18 36		19 06	19 36		
Duddeston	d							16 10	16 40			17 10		17 40				18 10		18 40		19 10	19 40		
Aston	d							16 13	16 43			17 13		17 43				18 13		18 43		19 13	19 43		
Gravelly Hill	d							16 16	16 46			17 16		17 46				18 16		18 46		19 16	19 46		
Erdington	d							16 19	16 49			17 19		17 49				18 19		18 49		19 19	19 49		
Chester Road	d							16 21	16 51			17 21		17 51				18 21		18 51		19 21	19 51		
Wylde Green	d							16 23	16 53			17 23		17 53				18 23		18 53		19 23	19 53		
Sutton Coldfield	d							16 26	16 56			17 26		17 56				18 26		18 56		19 26	19 56		
Four Oaks	d							16 29	16 59			17 29		17 59				18 29		18 59		19 29	19 59		
Butlers Lane	d							16 31	17 01			17 31		18 01				18 31		19 01		19 31	20 01		
Blake Street	d							16 34	17 04			17 34		18 04				18 34		19 04		19 34	20 04		
Shenstone	d							16 38	17 08			17 38		18 08				18 38		19 08		19 38	20 08		
Lichfield City	d							16 43	17 13			17 43		18 13				18 43		19 13		19 43	20 13		
Lichfield Trent Valley	a							16 47	17 17			17 47		18 17				18 47		19 17		19 47	20 17		

A until 19 June, from 7 August until 23 October
B from 26 June until 31 July, from 30 October
C from 26 June until 11 September, from 30 October
D from 18 September until 23 October
E until 19 June
F from 7 August until 23 October
G from 7 August until 11 September
H until 31 July, from 18 September
I until 19 June, from 18 September until 23 October
J from 26 June

		LM		LM	LM	XC ◇1	LM	LM	LM	XC ◇1	LM	LM		XC ◇1	LM	LM
Bromsgrove	d				20 10				21 09							
Redditch	d	19 27		19 57			20 27	20 57			21 27	21 57			22 27	22 57
Alvechurch	d	19 32		20 02			20 32	21 02			21 32	22 02			22 32	23 02
Barnt Green	d	19 38		20 08			20 38	21 08			21 38	22 08			22 38	23 08
Longbridge	d	19 43		20 13			20 43	21 13			21 43	22 13			22 43	23 13
Northfield	d	19 45		20 15			20 45	21 15			21 45	22 15			22 45	23 15
Kings Norton	d	19 48		20 18			20 48	21 18			21 48	22 18			22 48	23 18
Bournville	d	19 51		20 21			20 51	21 21			21 51	22 21			22 51	23 21
Selly Oak	d	19 53		20 23			20 53	21 23			21 53	22 23			22 53	23 23
University	d	19 56		20 26		20 36	20 56	21 26		21 39	21 56	22 26		22 36	22 56	23 26
Five Ways	d	20 00		20 30			21 00	21 30			22 00	22 30			23 00	23 30
Birmingham New Street 12	a	20 03		20 33	20 36	20 42	21 03	21 33	21 42	21 45	22 03	22 33		22 42	23 03	23 33
	d	20 06		20 36			21 06	21 36			22 06	22 36			23 06	
Duddeston	d	20 10		20 40			21 10	21 40			22 10	22 40			23 10	
Aston	d	20 13		20 43			21 13	21 43			22 13	22 43			23 13	
Gravelly Hill	d	20 16		20 46			21 16	21 46			22 16	22 46			23 16	
Erdington	d	20 19		20 49			21 19	21 49			22 19	22 49			23 19	
Chester Road	d	20 21		20 51			21 21	21 51			22 21	22 51			23 21	
Wylde Green	d	20 23		20 53			21 23	21 53			22 23	22 53			23 23	
Sutton Coldfield	d	20 26		20 56			21 26	21 56			22 26	22 56			23 26	
Four Oaks	d	20 29		20 59			21 29	21 59			22 29	22 59			23 29	
Butlers Lane	d	20 31		21 01			21 31	22 01			22 31	23 01			23 31	
Blake Street	d	20 34		21 04			21 34	22 04			22 34	23 04			23 34	
Shenstone	d	20 38		21 08			21 38	22 08			22 38	23 08			23 38	
Lichfield City	d	20 43		21 13			21 43	22 13			22 43	23 13			23 43	
Lichfield Trent Valley	a	20 47		21 18			21 47	22 17			22 47	23 17			23 47	

Birmingham - Walsall and Rugeley

Miles			LM A 🚌	LM MX	LM A 🚌	LM	LM	LM	LM 1	LM	LM	LM	LM	LM	LM	LM	LM	LM	LM	LM	LM	LM	LM
—	Wolverhampton 7	d												07 49				08 49		09 19		09 49	
0	**Birmingham New Street 12**	d	22p34	23p18	22p55	05 33	05 56	06 27	06 47	07 17	07 39	07 47	08 07	08 17	08 39	08 47	09 07	09 17	09 39	09 47	10 07	10 17	10 39
1½	Duddeston	d	⌇	23p23	23p05		06 00	06 32	06 52	07 22		07 52		08 22		08 52		09 22		09 52		10 22	
2¾	Aston	d	⌇	23p26	23p10		06 03	06 35	06 55	07 25		07 55		08 25		08 55		09 25		09 55		10 25	
3½	Witton	d	⌇	23p28	23p17		06 05	06 37	06 57	07 27		07 57		08 27		08 57		09 27		09 57		10 27	
4¼	Perry Barr	d	⌇	23p31	23p25		06 07	06 39	06 59	07 29		07 59		08 29		08 59		09 29		09 59		10 29	
5¾	Hamstead	d	⌇	23p34	23p34	05 41	06 10	06 42	07 01	07 32		08 02		08 31		09 01		09 31		10 01		10 31	
8½	Tame Bridge Parkway	d	23p00	23p39	23p45	05 45	06 15	06 47	07 05	07 37	07 50	08 07	08 20	08 35	08 50	09 05	09 20	09 35	09 50	10 05	10 20	10 35	10 50
9½	Bescot Stadium	d	⌇	23p41	23p54	05 48	06 18	06 50	07 08	07 40		08 10		08 38		09 08		09 38		10 08		10 38	
10¾	**Walsall**	a	23p15	23p47	00⌇02	05 55	06 23	06 55	07 14	07 44	07 59	08 14	08 29	08 44	08 59	09 14	09 29	09 44	09 59	10 14	10 35	10 46	10 59
—		d	23p16	23p47			06 24	06 56		07 45	08 00		08 30		09 00		09 30		10 00				11 00
14	Bloxwich	d	23p25	23p54			06 31	07 03		07 52	08 07				09 07				10 07				11 07
14½	Bloxwich North	d	23p31	23p57			06 33	07 05		07 54	08 09				09 09				10 09				11 09
16¾	Landywood	d	23p42	00 02			06 37	07 09		07 58	08 13				09 13				10 13				11 13
18¾	Cannock	d	23p54	00 06			06 42	07 14		08 03	08 18		08 44		09 18		09 44		10 18				11 18
20¾	Hednesford	d	00⌇02	00a12			06 47	07 19		08a09	08 23		08 49		09 23		09 49		10 23				11 23
24¾	Rugeley Town	d	00⌇13				06 55	07 27			08 31		08 57		09 31		09 57		10 31				11 31
26¼	**Rugeley Trent Valley**	a	00⌇18				07 00	07 32			08 36		09 04		09 36		10 04		10 36				11 36

		LM	LM	LM	LM	LM	LM	LM	LM	LM	LM	LM	LM	LM	LM	LM	LM	LM	LM	LM	LM	LM	LM
Wolverhampton 7	d	10 19		10 49		11 19		11 49		12 19		12 49		13 19		13 49		14 19		14 49		15 19	
Birmingham New Street 12	d	10 47	11 07	11 17	11 39	11 47	12 07	12 17	12 39	12 47	13 07	13 17	13 39	13 47	14 07	14 17	14 39	14 47	15 07	15 17	15 39	15 47	16 07
Duddeston	d	10 52		11 22		11 52		12 22		12 52		13 22		13 52		14 22		14 52		15 22		15 52	
Aston	d	10 55		11 25		11 55		12 25		12 55		13 25		13 55		14 25		14 55		15 25		15 55	
Witton	d	10 57		11 27		11 57		12 27		12 57		13 27		13 57		14 27		14 57		15 27		15 57	
Perry Barr	d	10 59		11 29		11 59		12 29		12 59		13 29		13 59		14 29		14 59		15 29		15 59	
Hamstead	d	11 01		11 31		12 01		12 31		13 01		13 31		14 01		14 31		15 01		15 31		16 01	
Tame Bridge Parkway	d	11 05	11 20	11 35	11 50	12 05	12 20	12 35	12 50	13 05	13 20	13 35	13 50	14 05	14 20	14 35	14 50	15 05	15 20	15 35	15 50	16 05	16 20
Bescot Stadium	d	11 08		11 38		12 08		12 38		13 08		13 38		14 08		14 38		15 08		15 38		16 08	
Walsall	a	11 14	11 35	11 44	11 59	12 14	12 35	12 46	12 59	13 14	13 35	13 44	13 59	14 14	14 35	14 44	14 59	15 14	15 35	15 46	15 59	16 14	16 29
	d				12 00				13 00				14 00				15 00				16 00		16 31
Bloxwich	d				12 07				13 07				14 07				15 07				16 07		16 38
Bloxwich North	d				12 09				13 09				14 09				15 09				16 09		16 40
Landywood	d				12 13				13 13				14 13				15 13				16 13		16 45
Cannock	d				12 18				13 18				14 18				15 18				16 18		16 49
Hednesford	d				12 23				13 23				14 23				15 23				16 23		16 54
Rugeley Town	d				12 31				13 31				14 31				15 31				16 31		17 02
Rugeley Trent Valley	a				12 36				13 36				14 36				15 36				16 36		17 08

		LM	LM	LM	LM	LM	LM	LM	LM	LM	LM	LM	LM	LM	LM	LM	LM	LM	LM	LM	LM
Wolverhampton 7	d	15 49		16 19		16 49		17 19		17 49		18 19		19 19							
Birmingham New Street 12	d	16 17	16 39	16 47	17 07	17 17	17 42	17 47	18 12	18 17	18 39	18 47	19 17	19 47	20 17	20 47	21 17	21 47	22 17	22 47	23 18
Duddeston	d	16 22		16 52		17 22		17 52		18 22		18 52	19 22	19 52		20 52		21 52		22 52	23 23
Aston	d	16 25		16 55		17 25		17 55		18 25		18 55	19 25	19 55		20 55		21 55		22 55	23 26
Witton	d	16 27		16 57		17 27		17 57		18 27		18 57	19 27	19 57		20 57		21 57		22 57	23 28
Perry Barr	d	16 29		16 59		17 29		17 59		18 29		18 59	19 29	19 59		20 59		21 59		22 59	23 31
Hamstead	d	16 31		17 01		17 31		18 01		18 31		19 01	19 32	20 01		21 01		22 01		23 01	23 34
Tame Bridge Parkway	d	16 35	16 50	17 05	17 20	17 35	17 54	18 05	18 24	18 35	18 50	19 05	19 37	20 05	20 30	21 05	21 30	22 05	22 30	23 05	23 39
Bescot Stadium	d	16 38		17 08		17 38		18 08		18 38		19 08	19 40	20 08		21 08		22 08		23 08	23 41
Walsall	a	16 44	16 59	17 14	17 29	17 44	18 01	18 14	18 31	18 44	18 59	19 15	19 45	20 14	20 38	21 14	21 38	22 14	22 38	23 14	23 47
	d		17 00		17 30		18 02		18 31		19 00		19 46		20 39		21 39		22 39		23 47
Bloxwich	d		17 07		17 37		18 09		18 38		19 07		19 53		20 46		21 46		22 46		23 54
Bloxwich North	d		17 09		17 39		18 11		18 40		19 09		19 56		20 49		21 49		22 49		23 57
Landywood	d		17 13		17 43		18 15		18 44		19 13		20 00		20 53		21 53		22 53		00 02
Cannock	d		17 18		17 48		18 20		18 48		19 18		20 05		20 57		21 57		22 57		00 06
Hednesford	d		17 23		17 53		18 25		18 53		19 23		20 10		21 02		22 02		23 02		00a12
Rugeley Town	d		17 31		18 01		18 33		19 01		19 31		20 18		21 10		22 10		23 10		
Rugeley Trent Valley	a		17 36		18 06		18 38		19 08		19 36		20 22		21 15		22 15		23 15		

Saturdays

		LM	LM	LM	LM	LM	LM	LM	LM	LM	LM	LM	LM	LM	LM	LM	LM	LM	LM	LM	LM	LM	LM
Wolverhampton 7	d					06 49		07 19		07 49		08 19		08 49		09 19		09 49		10 19		10 49	
Birmingham New Street 12	d	23p18	06 02	06 27	07 00	07 17	07 39	07 47	08 07	08 17	08 39	08 47	09 07	09 17	09 39	09 47	10 07	10 17	10 39	10 47	11 07	11 17	11 39
Duddeston	d	23p23	06 06	06 32		07 22		07 52		08 22		08 52		09 22		09 52		10 22		10 52		11 22	
Aston	d	23p26	06 09	06 35	07 06	07 25		07 55		08 25		08 55		09 25		09 55		10 25		10 55		11 25	
Witton	d	23p28	06 11	06 37		07 27		07 57		08 27		08 57		09 27		09 57		10 27		10 57		11 27	
Perry Barr	d	23p31	06 13	06 40	07 09	07 29		07 59		08 29		08 59		09 29		09 59		10 29		10 59		11 29	
Hamstead	d	23p34	06 16	06 43	07 12	07 31		08 01		08 31		09 01		09 31		10 01		10 31		11 01		11 31	
Tame Bridge Parkway	d	23p39	06 21	06 48	07 17	07 35	07 50	08 05	08 20	08 35	08 50	09 05	09 20	09 35	09 50	10 05	10 20	10 35	10 50	11 05	11 20	11 35	11 50
Bescot Stadium	d	23p41	06 24	06 50		07 38		08 08		08 38		09 08		09 38		10 08		10 38		11 08		11 38	
Walsall	a	23p47	06 29	06 56	07 25	07 44	07 57	08 14	08 29	08 44	08 59	09 14	09 29	09 44	09 59	10 14	10 29	10 44	10 59	11 14	11 29	11 44	11 59
	d	23p47	06 30	06 57	07 26		07 57		08 30		09 00		09 30		10 00		10 30		11 00		11 30		12 00
Bloxwich	d	23p54	06 37	07 04	07 33		08 04				09 07				10 07				11 07				12 07
Bloxwich North	d	23p57	06 39	07 06	07 35		08 06				09 09				10 09				11 09				12 09
Landywood	d	00 02	06 43	07 10	07 39		08 10				09 13				10 13				11 13				12 13
Cannock	d	00 06	06 48	07 15	07 44		08 15		08 44		09 18		09 44		10 18		10 44		11 18		11 44		12 18
Hednesford	d	00a12	06a53	07 20	07 49		08 20		08 49		09 23		09 49		10 23		10 49		11 23		11 49		12 23
Rugeley Town	d			07 28	07 57		08 28		08 57		09 31		09 57		10 31		10 57		11 31		11 57		12 31
Rugeley Trent Valley	a			07 32	08 04		08 35		09 04		09 36		10 04		10 36		11 04		11 36		12 04		12 36

A MO from 27 June until 1 August

For connections to Stafford please refer to Table 67

Table 70

Saturdays

Birmingham - Walsall and Rugeley

Station		LM	LM	LM	LM	LM	LM	LM	LM	LM	LM	LM	LM	LM	LM	LM	LM	LM	LM	LM	LM	LM	LM
Wolverhampton 7 (bus)	d	11 19		11 49		12 19		12 49		13 19		13 49		14 19		14 49		15 19		15 49		16 19	
Birmingham New Street 12	d	11 47	12 07	12 17	12 39	12 47	13 07	13 17	13 39	13 47	14 07	14 17	14 39	14 47	15 07	15 17	15 39	15 47	16 07	16 17	16 39	16 47	17 07
Duddeston	d	11 52		12 22		12 52		13 22		13 52		14 22		14 52		15 22		15 52		16 22		16 52	
Aston	d	11 55		12 25		12 55		13 25		13 55		14 25		14 55		15 25		15 55		16 25		16 55	
Witton	d	11 57		12 27		12 57		13 27		13 57		14 27		14 57		15 27		15 57		16 27		16 57	
Perry Barr	d	11 59		12 29		12 59		13 29		13 59		14 29		14 59		15 29		15 59		16 29		16 59	
Hamstead	d	12 01		12 31		13 01		13 31		14 01		14 31		15 01		15 31		16 01		16 31		17 01	
Tame Bridge Parkway	d	12 05	12 20	12 35	12 50	13 05	13 20	13 35	13 50	14 05	14 20	14 35	14 50	15 05	15 20	15 35	15 50	16 05	16 20	16 35	16 50	17 05	17 20
Bescot Stadium	d	12 08		12 38		13 08		13 38		14 08		14 38		15 08		15 38		16 08		16 38		17 08	
Walsall	a	12 14	12 29	12 44	12 59	13 14	13 29	13 44	13 59	14 14	14 29	14 44	14 59	15 14	15 29	15 46	15 59	16 14	16 29	16 44	16 59	17 14	17 29
	d		12 30		13 00		13 30		14 00		14 30		15 00		15 30		16 00		16 30		17 00		17 30
Bloxwich	d				13 07				14 07				15 07				16 07				17 07		17 37
Bloxwich North	d				13 09				14 09				15 09				16 09				17 09		17 39
Landywood	d				13 13				14 13				15 13				16 13				17 13		17 43
Cannock	d		12 44		13 18		13 44		14 18		14 44		15 18		15 44		16 18		16 44		17 18		17 48
Hednesford	d		12 49		13 23		13 49		14 23		14 49		15 23		15 49		16 23		16 49		17 23		17 53
Rugeley Town	d		12 57		13 31		13 57		14 31		14 57		15 31		15 57		16 31		16 57		17 31		18 01
Rugeley Trent Valley	a		13 04		13 36		14 04		14 36		15 04		15 36		16 04		16 36		17 04		17 36		18 06

Station		LM	LM	LM	LM	LM	LM	LM	LM	LM	LM	LM	LM	LM	LM	LM	LM
Wolverhampton 7 (bus)	d	16 49		17 19		17 49		18 19		19 19							
Birmingham New Street 12	d	17 17	17 39	17 47	18 07	18 17	18 39	18 47	19 17	19 47	20 17	20 47	21 17	21 47	22 17	22 47	23 18
Duddeston	d	17 22		17 52		18 22		18 52	19 22	19 52		20 52		21 52		22 52	23 23
Aston	d	17 25		17 55		18 25		18 55	19 25	19 55		20 55		21 55		22 55	23 26
Witton	d	17 27		17 57		18 27		18 57	19 27	19 57		20 57		21 57		22 57	23 28
Perry Barr	d	17 29		17 59		18 29		18 59	19 29	19 59		20 59		21 59		22 59	23 31
Hamstead	d	17 31		18 01		18 31		19 01	19 32	20 01		21 01		22 01		23 01	23 34
Tame Bridge Parkway	d	17 35	17 50	18 05	18 20	18 35	18 50	19 05	19 37	20 05	20 31	21 05	21 31	22 05	22 31	23 05	23 39
Bescot Stadium	d	17 38		18 08		18 38		19 08	19 40	20 08		21 08		22 08		23 08	23 41
Walsall	a	17 44	17 59	18 14	18 29	18 44	18 59	19 14	19 45	20 14	20 38	21 14	21 38	22 14	22 38	23 14	23 47
	d		18 00		18 30		19 00		19 46		20 39		21 39		22 39		23 47
Bloxwich	d		18 07		18 37		19 07		19 53		20 46		21 46		22 46		23 54
Bloxwich North	d		18 09		18 39		19 09		19 56		20 49		21 49		22 49		23 57
Landywood	d		18 13		18 43		19 13		20 00		20 53		21 53		22 53		00 01
Cannock	d		18 18		18 48		19 18		20 05		20 57		21 57		22 57		00 06
Hednesford	d		18 23		18 53		19 23		20 10		21 02		22 02		23 02		00a12
Rugeley Town	d		18 31		19 01		19 31		20 18		21 10		22 10		23 10		
Rugeley Trent Valley	a		18 36		19 06		19 36		20 22		21 15		22 15		23 15		

Sundays

until 19 June

Station		LM A	LM	LM	LM	LM	LM	LM	LM	LM	LM	LM	LM	LM	LM	LM	LM	LM	LM	LM	LM	LM	LM
Wolverhampton 7 (bus)	d																						
Birmingham New Street 12	d	23p18	09 17	09 40	10 17	10 40	11 17	11 40	12 17	12 40	13 17	13 40	14 17	14 40	15 17	15 40	16 17	16 40	17 17	17 40	18 17	18 40	19 17
Duddeston	d	23p23	09 21		10 21		11 21		12 21		13 21		14 21		15 21		16 21		17 21		18 21		19 21
Aston	d	23p26	09 24		10 24		11 24		12 24		13 24		14 24		15 24		16 24		17 24		18 24		19 24
Witton	d	23p28	09 26		10 26		11 26		12 26		13 26		14 26		15 26		16 26		17 26		18 26		19 26
Perry Barr	d	23p31	09 29		10 29		11 29		12 29		13 29		14 29		15 29		16 29		17 29		18 29		19 29
Hamstead	d	23p34	09 32		10 32		11 32		12 32		13 32		14 32		15 32		16 32		17 32		18 32		19 32
Tame Bridge Parkway	d	23p39	09 37	09 52	10 37	10 52	11 37	11 52	12 37	12 52	13 37	13 52	14 37	14 52	15 37	15 52	16 37	16 52	17 37	17 52	18 37	18 52	19 37
Bescot Stadium	d	23p41	09 39		10 39		11 39		12 39		13 39		14 39		15 39		16 39		17 39		18 39		19 39
Walsall	a	23p47	09 44	10 00	10 44	11 00	11 44	12 00	12 44	13 00	13 44	14 00	14 44	15 00	15 44	16 00	16 44	17 00	17 44	18 00	18 46	19 00	19 44
	d	23p47		10 01		11 01		12 01		13 01		14 01		15 01		16 01		17 01		18 01		19 01	
Bloxwich	d	23p54		10 08		11 08		12 08		13 08		14 08		15 08		16 08		17 08		18 08		19 08	
Bloxwich North	d	23p57		10 10		11 10		12 10		13 10		14 10		15 10		16 10		17 10		18 10		19 10	
Landywood	d	00 01		10 15		11 15		12 15		13 15		14 15		15 15		16 15		17 15		18 15		19 15	
Cannock	d	00 06		10 19		11 19		12 19		13 19		14 19		15 19		16 19		17 19		18 19		19 19	
Hednesford	d	00a12		10 24		11 24		12 24		13 24		14 24		15 24		16 24		17 24		18 24		19 24	
Rugeley Town	d			10 32		11 32		12 32		13 32		14 32		15 32		16 32		17 32		18 32		19 32	
Rugeley Trent Valley	a			10 37		11 37		12 37		13 37		14 37		15 37		16 37		17 37		18 37		19 37	

Station		LM	LM	LM	LM	LM	LM	LM	LM
Wolverhampton 7 (bus)	d								
Birmingham New Street 12	d	19 40	20 17	20 40	21 17	21 40	22 17	22 40	23 17
Duddeston	d		20 21		21 21		22 21		23 21
Aston	d		20 24		21 24		22 24		23 24
Witton	d		20 26		21 26		22 26		23 26
Perry Barr	d		20 29		21 29		22 29		23 29
Hamstead	d		20 32		21 32		22 32		23 32
Tame Bridge Parkway	d	19 52	20 37	20 52	21 37	21 52	22 37	22 52	23 37
Bescot Stadium	d		20 39		21 39		22 39		23 39
Walsall	a	20 00	20 44	21 00	21 46	22 00	22 44	23 00	23 44
	d	20 01		21 01		22 01		23 01	
Bloxwich	d	20 08		21 08		22 08		23 08	
Bloxwich North	d	20 10		21 10		22 10		23 10	
Landywood	d	20 15		21 15		22 15		23 15	
Cannock	d	20 19		21 19		22 19		23 19	
Hednesford	d	20 24		21 24		22 24		23 24	
Rugeley Town	d	20 32		21 32		22 32		23 32	
Rugeley Trent Valley	a	20 37		21 37		22 37		23 37	

A not 22 May

For connections to Stafford please refer to Table 67

Table 70

Sundays
26 June to 31 July

Birmingham - Walsall and Rugeley

		LM	LM	LM	LM	LM	LM	LM	LM	LM
Wolverhampton 7	d									
Birmingham New Street 12	d	23p18	08 55	09 34	09 55	10 34	10 55	11 34	11 55	12 34
Duddeston	d	23p23	09 05		10 05		11 05		12 05	
Aston	d	23p26	09 10		10 10		11 10		12 10	
Witton	d	23p28	09 17		10 17		11 17		12 17	
Perry Barr	d	23p31	09 25		10 25		11 25		12 25	
Hamstead	d	23p34	09 34		10 34		11 34		12 34	
Tame Bridge Parkway	d	23p39	09 45	10 00	10 45	11 00	11 45	12 00	12 45	13 00
Bescot Stadium	d	23p41	09 54		10 54		11 54		12 54	
Walsall	a	23p47	10 02	10 15	11 02	11 15	12 02	12 15	13 02	13 15
	d	23p47		10 16		11 16		12 16		13 16
Bloxwich	d	23p54		10 25		11 25		12 25		13 25
Bloxwich North	d	23p57		10 31		11 31		12 31		13 31
Landywood	d	00 01		10 42		11 42		12 42		13 42
Cannock	d	00 06		10 54		11 54		12 54		13 54
Hednesford	d	00a12		11 02		12 02		13 02		14 02
Rugeley Town	d			11 13		12 13		13 13		14 13
Rugeley Trent Valley	a			11 18		12 18		13 18		14 18

		LM	LM	LM	LM	LM	LM	LM	LM	LM
Wolverhampton 7	d									
Birmingham New Street 12	d	12 55	13 34	13 55	14 34	14 55	15 34	15 55	16 34	16 55
Duddeston	d	13 05		14 05		15 05		16 05		17 05
Aston	d	13 10		14 10		15 10		16 10		17 10
Witton	d	13 17		14 17		15 17		16 17		17 17
Perry Barr	d	13 25		14 25		15 25		16 25		17 25
Hamstead	d	13 34		14 34		15 34		16 34		17 34
Tame Bridge Parkway	d	13 45	14 00	14 45	15 00	15 45	16 00	16 45	17 00	17 45
Bescot Stadium	d	13 54		14 54		15 54		16 54		17 54
Walsall	a	14 02	14 15	15 02	15 15	16 02	16 15	17 02	17 15	18 02
	d		14 16		15 16		16 16		17 16	
Bloxwich	d		14 25		15 25		16 25		17 25	
Bloxwich North	d		14 31		15 31		16 31		17 31	
Landywood	d		14 42		15 42		16 42		17 42	
Cannock	d		14 54		15 54		16 54		17 54	
Hednesford	d		15 02		16 02		17 02		18 02	
Rugeley Town	d		15 13		16 13		17 13		18 13	
Rugeley Trent Valley	a		15 18		16 18		17 18		18 18	

		LM	LM	LM	LM
Wolverhampton 7	d				
Birmingham New Street 12	d	17 34	17 55	18 34	18 55
Duddeston	d		18 05		19 05
Aston	d		18 10		19 10
Witton	d		18 17		19 17
Perry Barr	d		18 25		19 25
Hamstead	d		18 34		19 34
Tame Bridge Parkway	d	18 00	18 45	19 00	19 45
Bescot Stadium	d		18 54		19 54
Walsall	a	18 15	19 02	19 15	20 02
	d	18 16		19 16	
Bloxwich	d	18 25		19 25	
Bloxwich North	d	18 31		19 31	
Landywood	d	18 42		19 42	
Cannock	d	18 54		19 54	
Hednesford	d	19 02		20 02	
Rugeley Town	d	19 13		20 13	
Rugeley Trent Valley	a	19 18		20 18	

		LM	LM	LM	LM	LM		LM	LM	LM
Wolverhampton 7	d									
Birmingham New Street 12	d	19 34	19 55	20 34	20 55	21 34		21 55	22 34	22 55
Duddeston	d		20 05		21 05			22 05		23 05
Aston	d		20 10		21 10			22 10		23 10
Witton	d		20 17		21 17			22 17		23 17
Perry Barr	d		20 25		21 25			22 25		23 25
Hamstead	d		20 34		21 34			22 34		23 34
Tame Bridge Parkway	d	20 00	20 45	21 00	21 45	22 00		22 45	23 00	23 45
Bescot Stadium	d		20 54		21 54			22 54		23 54
Walsall	a	20 15	21 02	21 15	22 02	22 15		23 02	23 15	00 02
	d	20 16		21 16		22 16			23 16	
Bloxwich	d	20 25		21 25		22 25			23 25	
Bloxwich North	d	20 31		21 31		22 31			23 31	
Landywood	d	20 42		21 42		22 42			23 42	
Cannock	d	20 54		21 54		22 54			23 54	
Hednesford	d	21 02		22 02		23 02			00 02	
Rugeley Town	d	21 13		22 13		23 13			00 13	
Rugeley Trent Valley	a	21 18		22 18		23 18			00 18	

Sundays
from 7 August

		LM	LM	LM	LM	LM	LM	LM	LM	LM
Wolverhampton 7	d									
Birmingham New Street 12	d	23p18	09 17	09 40	10 17	10 40	11 17	11 40	12 17	12 40
Duddeston	d	23p23	09 21		10 21		11 21		12 21	
Aston	d	23p26	09 24		10 24		11 24		12 24	
Witton	d	23p28	09 26		10 26		11 26		12 26	
Perry Barr	d	23p31	09 29		10 29		11 29		12 29	
Hamstead	d	23p34	09 32		10 32		11 32		12 32	
Tame Bridge Parkway	d	23p39	09 37	09 52	10 37	10 52	11 37	11 52	12 37	12 52
Bescot Stadium	d	23p41	09 39		10 39		11 39		12 39	
Walsall	a	23p47	09 44	10 00	10 44	11 00	11 44	12 00	12 44	13 00
	d	23p47		10 01		11 01		12 01		13 01
Bloxwich	d	23p54		10 08		11 08		12 08		13 08
Bloxwich North	d	23p57		10 10		11 10		12 10		13 10
Landywood	d	00 01		10 15		11 15		12 15		13 15
Cannock	d	00 06		10 19		11 19		12 19		13 19
Hednesford	d	00a12		10 24		11 24		12 24		13 24
Rugeley Town	d			10 32		11 32		12 32		13 32
Rugeley Trent Valley	a			10 37		11 37		12 37		13 37

		LM	LM	LM	LM	LM	LM	LM	LM	LM
Wolverhampton 7	d									
Birmingham New Street 12	d	13 17	13 40	14 17	14 40	15 17	15 40	16 17	16 40	17 17
Duddeston	d	13 21		14 21		15 21		16 21		17 21
Aston	d	13 24		14 24		15 24		16 24		17 24
Witton	d	13 26		14 26		15 26		16 26		17 26
Perry Barr	d	13 29		14 29		15 29		16 29		17 29
Hamstead	d	13 32		14 32		15 32		16 32		17 32
Tame Bridge Parkway	d	13 37	13 52	14 37	14 52	15 37	15 52	16 37	16 52	17 37
Bescot Stadium	d	13 39		14 39		15 39		16 39		17 39
Walsall	a	13 44	14 00	14 44	15 00	15 44	16 00	16 44	17 00	17 44
	d		14 01		15 01		16 01		17 01	
Bloxwich	d		14 08		15 08		16 08		17 08	
Bloxwich North	d		14 10		15 10		16 10		17 10	
Landywood	d		14 15		15 15		16 15		17 15	
Cannock	d		14 19		15 19		16 19		17 19	
Hednesford	d		14 24		15 24		16 24		17 24	
Rugeley Town	d		14 32		15 32		16 32		17 32	
Rugeley Trent Valley	a		14 37		15 37		16 37		17 37	

		LM	LM	LM	LM
Wolverhampton 7	d				
Birmingham New Street 12	d	17 40	18 17	18 40	19 17
Duddeston	d		18 21		19 21
Aston	d		18 24		19 24
Witton	d		18 26		19 26
Perry Barr	d		18 29		19 29
Hamstead	d		18 32		19 32
Tame Bridge Parkway	d	17 52	18 37	18 52	19 37
Bescot Stadium	d		18 39		19 39
Walsall	a	18 00	18 46	19 00	19 44
	d	18 01		19 01	
Bloxwich	d	18 08		19 08	
Bloxwich North	d	18 10		19 10	
Landywood	d	18 15		19 15	
Cannock	d	18 19		19 19	
Hednesford	d	18 24		19 24	
Rugeley Town	d	18 32		19 32	
Rugeley Trent Valley	a	18 37		19 37	

		LM	LM	LM	LM	LM		LM	LM	LM
Wolverhampton 7	d									
Birmingham New Street 12	d	19 40	20 17	20 40	21 17	21 40		22 17	22 40	23 17
Duddeston	d		20 21		21 21			22 21		23 21
Aston	d		20 24		21 24			22 24		23 24
Witton	d		20 26		21 26			22 26		23 26
Perry Barr	d		20 29		21 29			22 29		23 29
Hamstead	d		20 32		21 32			22 32		23 32
Tame Bridge Parkway	d	19 52	20 37	20 52	21 37	21 52		22 37	22 52	23 37
Bescot Stadium	d		20 39		21 39			22 39		23 39
Walsall	a	20 00	20 44	21 00	21 46	22 00		22 44	23 00	23 44
	d	20 01		21 01		22 01			23 01	
Bloxwich	d	20 08		21 08		22 08			23 08	
Bloxwich North	d	20 10		21 10		22 10			23 10	
Landywood	d	20 15		21 15		22 15			23 15	
Cannock	d	20 19		21 19		22 19			23 19	
Hednesford	d	20 24		21 24		22 24			23 24	
Rugeley Town	d	20 32		21 32		22 32			23 32	
Rugeley Trent Valley	a	20 37		21 37		22 37			23 37	

For connections to Stafford please refer to Table 67

Table 70

Mondays to Fridays

Rugeley and Walsall - Birmingham

Miles			LM	LM	LM	LM	LM	LM	LM	LM	LM		LM	LM	LM	LM	LM	LM	LM	LM	LM		LM	LM	LM
			MX					◇1																	
0	**Rugeley Trent Valley**	d				06 21	06 39		07 04		07 39					08 42		09 06		09 42			10 06		
1½	Rugeley Town	d				06 25	06 43		07 08		07 43					08 46		09 10		09 46			10 10		
5½	Hednesford	d			06 07	06 33	06 51		07 16	07 39	07 51			08 17		08 54		09 18		09 54			10 18		
7½	Cannock	d			06 11	06 37	06 55		07 20	07 43	07 55			08 21		08 58		09 22		09 58			10 22		
9½	Landywood	d			06 14	06 40	06 58		07 23		07 58			08 24				09 25					10 25		
11¾	Bloxwich North	d			06 19	06 45	07 03		07 27		08 03			08 29				09 30					10 30		
12¼	Bloxwich	d			06 21	06 47	07 05		07 29		08 05			08 31				09 32					10 32		
15½	**Walsall**	a			06 28	06 54	07 12		07 37	07 57	08 13			08 38		09 12		09 39		10 12			10 39		
—		d	23p40	06 01	06 29	07 00	07 13	07 30	07 37	08 00	08 13		08 30	08 39	09 01	09 13	09 30	09 40	10 01	10 13	10 31		10 40	11 01	11 10
16¾	Bescot Stadium	d	23p44	06 04	06 34	07 04		07 34		08 04			08 34		09 04		09 34		10 04		10 34			11 04	
17¾	Tame Bridge Parkway	d	23p47	06 07	06 37	07 07	07 19	07 37	07 43	08 07	08 19		08 37	08 46	09 07	09 19	09 37	09 46	10 07	10 19	10 37		10 46	11 07	11 19
20½	Hamstead	d	23p51	06 11	06 41	07 12		07 41		08 11			08 41		09 11		09 41		10 11		10 41			11 11	
22	Perry Barr	d	23p55	06 14	06 44	07 15		07 44		08 14			08 44		09 14		09 44		10 14		10 44			11 14	
22¾	Witton	d	23p57	06 16	06 46	07 17		07 47		08 17			08 47		09 16		09 47		10 16		10 46			11 16	
23½	Aston	d	00 01	06 18	06 49	07 20		07 49		08 20			08 50		09 19		09 50		10 19		10 49			11 19	
24¾	Duddeston	d	00 04	06 21	06 52	07 23		07 52		08 23			08 53		09 21		09 53		10 21		10 51			11 21	
26¼	**Birmingham New Street** 12	a	00 09	06 28	06 57	07 28	07 36	07 57	08 00	08 29	08 36		08 57	09 02	09 28	09 36	09 57	10 03	10 28	10 36	10 58		11 03	11 28	11 36
—	Wolverhampton 7	a		07 03				08 19							10 03				11 03		11 33			12 03	

		LM	LM	LM	LM	LM	LM		LM	LM	LM	LM	LM	LM	LM	LM	LM		LM	LM	LM	LM	LM	LM	LM
Rugeley Trent Valley	d		11 06				12 06					13 06				14 06					15 06				16 06
Rugeley Town	d		11 10				12 10					13 10				14 10					15 10				16 10
Hednesford	d		11 18				12 18					13 18				14 18					15 18				16 18
Cannock	d		11 22				12 22					13 22				14 22					15 22				16 22
Landywood	d		11 25				12 25					13 25				14 25					15 25				16 25
Bloxwich North	d		11 30				12 30					13 30				14 30					15 30				16 30
Bloxwich	d		11 32				12 32					13 32				14 32					15 32				16 32
Walsall	a		11 39				12 39					13 39				14 39					15 39				16 39
	d	11 31	11 40	12 01	12 10	12 31	12 40		13 01	13 10	13 31	13 40	14 01	14 10	14 31	14 40	15 01		15 10	15 31	15 40	16 01	16 10	16 31	16 40
Bescot Stadium	d	11 34		12 04		12 34			13 04		13 34		14 04		14 34		15 04			15 34		16 04		16 34	
Tame Bridge Parkway	d	11 37	11 46	12 07	12 19	12 37	12 46		13 07	13 19	13 37	13 46	14 07	14 19	14 37	14 46	15 07		15 19	15 37	15 46	16 07	16 19	16 37	16 46
Hamstead	d	11 41		12 11		12 41			13 11		13 41		14 11		14 41		15 11			15 41		16 11		16 41	
Perry Barr	d	11 44		12 14		12 44			13 14		13 44		14 14		14 44		15 14			15 44		16 14		16 44	
Witton	d	11 46		12 16		12 46			13 16		13 46		14 16		14 46		15 16			15 46		16 16		16 46	
Aston	d	11 49		12 19		12 49			13 19		13 49		14 19		14 49		15 19			15 49		16 19		16 49	
Duddeston	d	11 51		12 21		12 51			13 21		13 51		14 21		14 51		15 21			15 51		16 21		16 51	
Birmingham New Street 12	a	11 58	12 03	12 28	12 36	12 58	13 03		13 28	13 36	13 58	14 03	14 28	14 36	14 58	15 03	15 28		15 36	15 58	16 03	16 30	16 36	16 59	17 03
Wolverhampton 7	a	12 33		13 03		13 33			14 03		14 33		15 03		15 33		16 03			16 33		17 04		17 33	

		LM	LM		LM	LM	LM	LM	LM	LM	LM	LM	LM		LM	LM	LM	LM	LM	LM	LM	LM	LM		
Rugeley Trent Valley	d		16 42			17 13		17 42		18 12		18 46			19 10	19 42		20 35		21 40		22 33			
Rugeley Town	d		16 46			17 17		17 46		18 16		18 50			19 14	19 46		20 39		21 44		22 37			
Hednesford	d		16 54			17 25		17 54		18 24		18 58			19 21	19 54		20 47		21 52		22 45			
Cannock	d		16 58			17 29		17 58		18 28		19 02			19 25	19 58		20 51		21 56		22 49			
Landywood	d					17 32				18 31					19 29	20 01		20 54		21 59		22 53			
Bloxwich North	d					17 37				18 36					19 33	20 06		20 59		22 04		22 58			
Bloxwich	d					17 39				18 38					19 35	20 08		21 01		22 06		23 00			
Walsall	a		17 12			17 46		18 12		18 45		19 16			19 43	20 15		21 08		22 16		23 07			
	d	17 01	17 13		17 31	17 47	18 01	18 13	18 31	18 46	19 01	19 18	19 36		19 43	20 16	20 40	21 10	21 40	22 17	22 40	23 10	23 40		
Bescot Stadium	d	17 04			17 34		18 04		18 34		19 04	19 23			19 48		20 44		21 44		22 44		23 44		
Tame Bridge Parkway	d	17 07	17 19		17 37	17 53	18 07	18 19	18 37	18 52	19 07	19 26			19 51	20 22	20 47	21 16	21 47	22 23	22 47	23 16	23 47		
Hamstead	d	17 11			17 41		18 11		18 41		19 11	19 30			19 55		20 51		21 51		22 51		23 51		
Perry Barr	d	17 14			17 44		18 14		18 44		19 14	19 33			19 58		20 55		21 55		22 55		23 55		
Witton	d	17 16			17 46		18 16		18 46		19 16	19 36			20 01		20 57		21 57		22 57		23 57		
Aston	d	17 19			17 49		18 19		18 49		19 19	19 39			20 03		21 00		22 00		23 00		00 01		
Duddeston	d	17 21			17 51		18 21		18 51		19 21	19 42			20 06		21 03		22 03		23 03		00 04		
Birmingham New Street 12	a	17 28	17 36		17 58	18 10	18 28	18 36	18 58	19 09	19 28	19 46			20 11	20 39	21 09	21 35	22 09	22 40	23 09	23 33	00 09		
Wolverhampton 7	a	18 03			18 33		19 03		19 33		20 03		19 50												

Saturdays

		LM	LM	LM	LM	LM	LM	LM	LM	LM		LM	LM	LM	LM	LM	LM	LM	LM	LM		LM	LM	LM	LM
Rugeley Trent Valley	d				06 26				07 39			08 06		08 42		09 06		09 42		10 06			10 42		11 06
Rugeley Town	d				06 30				07 43			08 10		08 46		09 10		09 46		10 10			10 46		11 10
Hednesford	d				06 38	06 58			07 51			08 18		08 54		09 18		09 54		10 18			10 54		11 18
Cannock	d				06 42	07 02			07 55			08 22		08 58		09 22		09 58		10 22			10 58		11 22
Landywood	d				06 45	07 05			07 58			08 25				09 25				10 25					11 25
Bloxwich North	d				06 50	07 10			08 03			08 30				09 30				10 30					11 30
Bloxwich	d				06 52	07 12			08 05			08 32				09 32				10 32					11 32
Walsall	a				06 59	07 19			08 12			08 39		09 12		09 39		10 12		10 39			11 12		11 39
	d	23p40	06 01	06 31	07 00	07 20	07 31	08 01	08 13	08 31		08 40	09 01	09 13	09 31	09 40	10 01	10 13	10 31	10 40		11 01	11 13	11 31	11 40
Bescot Stadium	d	23p44	06 04	06 34	07 04		07 34	08 04		08 34			09 04		09 34		10 04		10 34			11 04		11 34	
Tame Bridge Parkway	d	23p47	06 07	06 37	07 07	07 26	07 37	08 07	08 19	08 37		08 46	09 07	09 19	09 37	09 46	10 07	10 19	10 37	10 46		11 07	11 19	11 37	11 46
Hamstead	d	23p51	06 11	06 41	07 12		07 41	08 11		08 41			09 11		09 41		10 11		10 41			11 11		11 41	
Perry Barr	d	23p55	06 14	06 44	07 15		07 44	08 14		08 44			09 14		09 44		10 14		10 44			11 14		11 44	
Witton	d	23p57	06 16	06 46	07 17		07 46	08 16		08 46			09 16		09 46		10 16		10 46			11 16		11 46	
Aston	d	00 01	06 19	06 49	07 20		07 49	08 19		08 49			09 19		09 49		10 19		10 49			11 19		11 49	
Duddeston	d	00 04	06 21	06 51	07 23		07 51	08 21		08 51			09 21		09 51		10 21		10 51			11 21		11 51	
Birmingham New Street 12	a	00 09	06 28	06 58	07 28	07 48	07 58	08 28	08 36	08 58		09 03	09 29	09 36	09 58	10 03	10 29	10 36	10 58	11 03		11 28	11 36	11 58	12 03
Wolverhampton 7	a		07 03	07 33			08 33	09 03		09 33			10 03		10 33		11 03		11 33			12 03		12 33	

For connections from Stafford please refer to Table 67

Table 70

Saturdays

Rugeley and Walsall - Birmingham

		LM	LM	LM	LM	LM		LM	LM	LM	LM	LM	LM	LM	LM	LM		LM	LM	LM	LM	LM	LM	LM	LM
Rugeley Trent Valley	d		11 42		12 06			12 42		13 06		13 42		14 06		14 42			15 06		15 42		16 06		16 42
Rugeley Town	d		11 46		12 10			12 46		13 10		13 46		14 10		14 46			15 10		15 46		16 10		16 46
Hednesford	d		11 54		12 18			12 54		13 18		13 54		14 18		14 54			15 18		15 54		16 18		16 54
Cannock	d		11 58		12 22			12 58		13 22		13 58		14 22		14 58			15 22		15 58		16 22		16 58
Landywood	d				12 25					13 25				14 25					15 25				16 25		
Bloxwich North	d				12 30					13 30				14 30					15 30				16 30		
Bloxwich	d				12 32					13 32				14 32					15 32				16 32		
Walsall	a		12 12		12 39			13 12		13 39		14 12		14 39		15 12			15 39		16 12		16 39		17 12
	d	12 01	12 13	12 31	12 40	13 01		13 13	13 31	13 40	14 01	14 13	14 31	14 40	15 01	15 13		15 31	15 40	16 01	16 13	16 31	16 40	17 01	17 13
Bescot Stadium	d	12 04		12 34		13 04			13 34		14 04		14 34		15 04			15 34		16 04		16 34		17 04	
Tame Bridge Parkway	d	12 07	12 19	12 37	12 46	13 07		13 19	13 37	13 46	14 07	14 19	14 37	14 46	15 07	15 19		15 37	15 46	16 07	16 19	16 37	16 46	17 07	17 19
Hamstead	d	12 11		12 41		13 11			13 41		14 11		14 41		15 11			15 41		16 11		16 41		17 11	
Perry Barr	d	12 14		12 44		13 14			13 44		14 14		14 44		15 14			15 44		16 14		16 44		17 14	
Witton	d	12 16		12 46		13 16			13 46		14 16		14 46		15 16			15 46		16 16		16 46		17 16	
Aston	d	12 19		12 49		13 19			13 49		14 19		14 49		15 19			15 49		16 19		16 49		17 19	
Duddeston	d	12 21		12 51		13 21			13 51		14 21		14 51		15 21			15 51		16 21		16 51		17 21	
Birmingham New Street 12	a	12 28	12 36	12 58	13 03	13 28		13 36	13 58	14 03	14 28	14 36	14 58	15 03	15 28	15 36		15 58	16 03	16 28	16 36	16 58	17 03	17 28	17 36
Wolverhampton 7	a	13 03		13 33		14 03			14 33		15 03		15 33		16 03			16 33		17 04		17 33		18 03	

		LM		LM	LM	LM	LM	LM	LM	LM	LM	LM		LM	LM	LM	LM	LM	LM	LM
Rugeley Trent Valley	d			17 06		17 42		18 12		18 45	19 10	19 42			20 35		21 35		22 35	
Rugeley Town	d			17 10		17 46		18 16		18 49	19 14	19 46			20 39		21 39		22 39	
Hednesford	d			17 18		17 54		18 24		18 57	19 21	19 54			20 47		21 47		22 47	
Cannock	d			17 22		17 58		18 28		19 01	19 25	19 58			20 51		21 51		22 51	
Landywood	d			17 25				18 31			19 29	20 01			20 54		21 54		22 54	
Bloxwich North	d			17 30				18 36			19 33	20 06			20 59		21 59		22 59	
Bloxwich	d			17 32				18 38			19 35	20 08			21 01		22 01		23 01	
Walsall	a			17 39		18 12		18 45		19 15	19 43	20 15			21 08		22 08		23 08	
	d	17 31		17 40	18 01	18 13	18 31	18 46	19 01	19 18	19 43	20 16		20 40	21 10	21 40	22 10	22 40	23 10	23 40
Bescot Stadium	d	17 34			18 04		18 34		19 04	19 23	19 48			20 44		21 44		22 44		23 44
Tame Bridge Parkway	d	17 37		17 46	18 07	18 19	18 37	18 52	19 07	19 26	19 51	20 22		20 47	21 16	21 47	22 16	22 47	23 16	23 47
Hamstead	d	17 41			18 11		18 41		19 11	19 30	19 55			20 51		21 51		22 51		23 51
Perry Barr	d	17 44			18 14		18 44		19 14	19 33	19 58			20 55		21 55		22 55		23 55
Witton	d	17 46			18 16		18 46		19 16	19 36	20 01			20 57		21 57		22 57		23 57
Aston	d	17 49			18 19		18 49		19 19	19 39	20 03			21 00		22 00		23 00		00 01
Duddeston	d	17 51			18 21		18 51		19 21	19 42	20 06			21 03		22 03		23 03		00 04
Birmingham New Street 12	a	17 58		18 03	18 28	18 36	18 58	19 09	19 28	19 46	20 11	20 39		21 09	21 33	22 09	22 33	23 09	23 34	00 09
Wolverhampton 7	a	18 33			19 03		19 33		20 03											

Sundays

until 19 June

		LM A	LM	LM	LM	LM	LM	LM	LM	LM		LM	LM	LM	LM	LM	LM	LM	LM	LM		LM	LM	LM	LM
Rugeley Trent Valley	d			09 48		10 48		11 48		12 48			13 48		14 48		15 48		16 48			17 48		18 48	
Rugeley Town	d			09 52		10 52		11 52		12 52			13 52		14 52		15 52		16 52			17 52		18 52	
Hednesford	d			10 00		11 00		12 00		13 00			14 00		15 00		16 00		17 00			18 00		19 00	
Cannock	d			10 04		11 04		12 04		13 04			14 04		15 04		16 04		17 04			18 04		19 04	
Landywood	d			10 07		11 07		12 07		13 07			14 07		15 07		16 07		17 07			18 07		19 07	
Bloxwich North	d			10 12		11 12		12 12		13 12			14 12		15 12		16 12		17 12			18 12		19 12	
Bloxwich	d			10 14		11 14		12 14		13 14			14 14		15 14		16 14		17 14			18 14		19 14	
Walsall	a			10 21		11 21		12 21		13 21			14 21		15 21		16 21		17 21			18 21		19 21	
	d	23p40	10 00	10 23	11 00	11 23	12 00	12 23	13 00	13 23		14 00	14 23	15 00	15 23	16 00	16 23	17 00	17 23	18 00		18 23	19 00	19 23	20 00
Bescot Stadium	d	23p44	10 04		11 04		12 04		13 04			14 04		15 04		16 04		17 04		18 04			19 04		20 04
Tame Bridge Parkway	d	23p47	10 07	10 29	11 07	11 29	12 07	12 29	13 07	13 29		14 07	14 29	15 07	15 29	16 07	16 29	17 07	17 29	18 07		18 29	19 07	19 29	20 07
Hamstead	d	23p51	10 11		11 11		12 11		13 11			14 11		15 11		16 11		17 11		18 11			19 11		20 11
Perry Barr	d	23p55	10 14		11 14		12 14		13 14			14 14		15 14		16 14		17 14		18 14			19 14		20 14
Witton	d	23p57	10 17		11 17		12 17		13 17			14 17		15 17		16 17		17 17		18 17			19 17		20 17
Aston	d	00 01	10 20		11 20		12 20		13 20			14 20		15 20		16 20		17 20		18 20			19 20		20 20
Duddeston	d	00 04	10 23		11 23		12 23		13 23			14 23		15 23		16 23		17 23		18 23			19 23		20 23
Birmingham New Street 12	a	00 09	10 27	10 46	11 27	11 46	12 27	12 46	13 27	13 46		14 27	14 46	15 30	15 46	16 30	16 46	17 30	17 46	18 28		18 46	19 27	19 47	20 27
Wolverhampton 7	a																								

		LM	LM	LM	LM	LM		LM	LM
Rugeley Trent Valley	d	19 48		20 48		21 48			22 48
Rugeley Town	d	19 52		20 52		21 52			22 52
Hednesford	d	20 00		21 00		22 00			23 00
Cannock	d	20 04		21 04		22 04			23 04
Landywood	d	20 07		21 07		22 07			23 07
Bloxwich North	d	20 12		21 12		22 12			23 12
Bloxwich	d	20 14		21 14		22 14			23 14
Walsall	a	20 21		21 21		22 21			23 21
	d	20 23	21 00	21 23	22 00	22 23		23 00	23 23
Bescot Stadium	d		21 04		22 04			23 04	
Tame Bridge Parkway	d	20 29	21 07	21 29	22 07	22 29		23 07	23 29
Hamstead	d		21 11		22 11			23 11	
Perry Barr	d		21 14		22 14			23 14	
Witton	d		21 17		22 17			23 17	
Aston	d		21 20		22 20			23 20	
Duddeston	d		21 23		22 23			23 23	
Birmingham New Street 12	a	20 46	21 27	21 46	22 27	22 48		23 27	23 46
Wolverhampton 7	a								

A not 22 May

For connections from Stafford please refer to Table 67

Table 70

Rugeley and Walsall - Birmingham

Sundays

26 June to 31 July

		LM	LM 🚌	LM 🚌	LM 🚌	LM 🚌	LM 🚌	LM 🚌	LM 🚌	LM 🚌	LM 🚌	LM 🚌	LM 🚌	LM 🚌	LM 🚌	LM 🚌	LM 🚌	LM 🚌	LM 🚌	LM 🚌	LM 🚌	LM 🚌	LM 🚌
Rugeley Trent Valley	d			09 04		10 04		11 04		12 04		13 04		14 04		15 04		16 04		17 04		18 04	
Rugeley Town	d			09 10		10 10		11 10		12 10		13 10		14 10		15 10		16 10		17 10		18 10	
Hednesford	d			09 21		10 21		11 21		12 21		13 21		14 21		15 21		16 21		17 21		18 21	
Cannock	d			09 29		10 29		11 29		12 29		13 29		14 29		15 29		16 29		17 29		18 29	
Landywood	d			09 41		10 41		11 41		12 41		13 41		14 41		15 41		16 41		17 41		18 41	
Bloxwich North	d			09 52		10 52		11 52		12 52		13 52		14 52		15 52		16 52		17 52		18 52	
Bloxwich	d			09 58		10 58		11 58		12 58		13 58		14 58		15 58		16 58		17 58		18 58	
Walsall	a			10 06		11 06		12 06		13 06		14 06		15 06		16 06		17 06		18 06		19 06	
	d	23p40	09 43	10 07	10 43	11 07	11 43	12 07	12 43	13 07	13 43	14 07	14 43	15 07	15 43	16 07	16 43	17 07	17 43	18 07	18 43	19 07	19 43
Bescot Stadium	d	23p44	09 52		10 52		11 52		12 52		13 52		14 52		15 52		16 52		17 52		18 52		19 52
Tame Bridge Parkway	d	23p47	10 01	10 23	11 01	11 23	12 01	12 23	13 01	13 23	14 01	14 23	15 01	15 23	16 01	16 23	17 01	17 23	18 01	18 23	19 01	19 23	20 01
Hamstead	d	23p51	10 11		11 11		12 11		13 11		14 11		15 11		16 11		17 11		18 11		19 11		20 11
Perry Barr	d	23p55	10 21		11 21		12 21		13 21		14 21		15 21		16 21		17 21		18 21		19 21		20 21
Witton	d	23p57	10 28		11 28		12 28		13 28		14 28		15 28		16 28		17 28		18 28		19 28		20 28
Aston	d	00 01	10 32		11 32		12 32		13 32		14 32		15 32		16 32		17 32		18 32		19 32		20 32
Duddeston	d	00 04	10 37		11 37		12 37		13 37		14 37		15 37		16 37		17 37		18 37		19 37		20 37
Birmingham New Street 12	a	00 09	10 46	10 48	11 46	11 48	12 46	12 48	13 46	13 48	14 46	14 48	15 46	15 48	16 46	16 48	17 46	17 48	18 46	18 48	19 46	19 48	20 46
Wolverhampton 7	a																						

		LM 🚌	LM 🚌	LM 🚌	LM 🚌	LM 🚌	LM 🚌	LM 🚌
Rugeley Trent Valley	d	19 04		20 04		21 04		22 04
Rugeley Town	d	19 10		20 10		21 10		22 10
Hednesford	d	19 21		20 21		21 21		22 21
Cannock	d	19 29		20 29		21 29		22 29
Landywood	d	19 41		20 41		21 41		22 41
Bloxwich North	d	19 52		20 52		21 52		22 52
Bloxwich	d	19 58		20 58		21 58		22 58
Walsall	a	20 06		21 06		22 06		23 06
	d	20 07	20 43	21 07	21 43	22 07	22 43	23 07
Bescot Stadium	d		20 52		21 52		22 52	
Tame Bridge Parkway	d	20 23	21 01	21 23	22 01	22 23	23 01	23 23
Hamstead	d		21 11		22 11		23 11	
Perry Barr	d		21 21		22 21		23 21	
Witton	d		21 28		22 28		23 28	
Aston	d		21 32		22 32		23 32	
Duddeston	d		21 37		22 37		23 37	
Birmingham New Street 12	a	20 48	21 46	21 48	22 46	22 48	23 46	23 48
Wolverhampton 7	a							

Sundays

from 7 August

		LM	LM	LM	LM	LM	LM	LM	LM	LM	LM	LM	LM	LM	LM	LM	LM	LM	LM	LM	LM	LM	LM
Rugeley Trent Valley	d			09 48		10 48		11 48		12 48		13 48		14 48		15 48		16 48		17 48		18 48	
Rugeley Town	d			09 52		10 52		11 52		12 52		13 52		14 52		15 52		16 52		17 52		18 52	
Hednesford	d			10 00		11 00		12 00		13 00		14 00		15 00		16 00		17 00		18 00		19 00	
Cannock	d			10 04		11 04		12 04		13 04		14 04		15 04		16 04		17 04		18 04		19 04	
Landywood	d			10 07		11 07		12 07		13 07		14 07		15 07		16 07		17 07		18 07		19 07	
Bloxwich North	d			10 12		11 12		12 12		13 12		14 12		15 12		16 12		17 12		18 12		19 12	
Bloxwich	d			10 14		11 14		12 14		13 14		14 14		15 14		16 14		17 14		18 14		19 14	
Walsall	a			10 21		11 21		12 21		13 21		14 21		15 21		16 21		17 21		18 21		19 21	
	d	23p40	10 00	10 23	11 00	11 23	12 00	12 23	13 00	13 23	14 00	14 23	15 00	15 23	16 00	16 23	17 00	17 23	18 00	18 23	19 00	19 23	20 00
Bescot Stadium	d	23p44	10 04		11 04		12 04		13 04		14 04		15 04		16 04		17 04		18 04		19 04		20 04
Tame Bridge Parkway	d	23p47	10 07	10 29	11 07	11 29	12 07	12 29	13 07	13 29	14 07	14 29	15 07	15 29	16 07	16 29	17 07	17 29	18 07	18 29	19 07	19 29	20 07
Hamstead	d	23p51	10 11		11 11		12 11		13 11		14 11		15 11		16 11		17 11		18 11		19 11		20 11
Perry Barr	d	23p55	10 14		11 14		12 14		13 14		14 14		15 14		16 14		17 14		18 14		19 14		20 14
Witton	d	23p57	10 17		11 17		12 17		13 17		14 17		15 17		16 17		17 17		18 17		19 17		20 17
Aston	d	00 01	10 20		11 20		12 20		13 20		14 20		15 20		16 20		17 20		18 20		19 20		20 20
Duddeston	d	00 04	10 23		11 23		12 23		13 23		14 23		15 23		16 23		17 23		18 23		19 23		20 23
Birmingham New Street 12	a	00 09	10 27	10 46	11 27	11 46	12 27	12 46	13 27	13 46	14 27	14 46	15 30	15 46	16 30	16 46	17 30	17 46	18 28	18 46	19 27	19 47	20 27
Wolverhampton 7	a																						

		LM	LM	LM	LM	LM	LM	LM
Rugeley Trent Valley	d	19 48		20 48		21 48		22 48
Rugeley Town	d	19 52		20 52		21 52		22 52
Hednesford	d	20 00		21 00		22 00		23 00
Cannock	d	20 04		21 04		22 04		23 04
Landywood	d	20 07		21 07		22 07		23 07
Bloxwich North	d	20 12		21 12		22 12		23 12
Bloxwich	d	20 14		21 14		22 14		23 14
Walsall	a	20 21		21 21		22 21		23 21
	d	20 23	21 00	21 23	22 00	22 23	23 00	23 23
Bescot Stadium	d		21 04		22 04		23 04	
Tame Bridge Parkway	d	20 29	21 07	21 29	22 07	22 29	23 07	23 29
Hamstead	d		21 11		22 11		23 11	
Perry Barr	d		21 14		22 14		23 14	
Witton	d		21 17		22 17		23 17	
Aston	d		21 20		22 20		23 20	
Duddeston	d		21 23		22 23		23 23	
Birmingham New Street 12	a	20 46	21 27	21 46	22 27	22 48	23 27	23 46
Wolverhampton 7	a							

For connections from Stafford please refer to Table 67

Network Diagram for Tables 71, 72

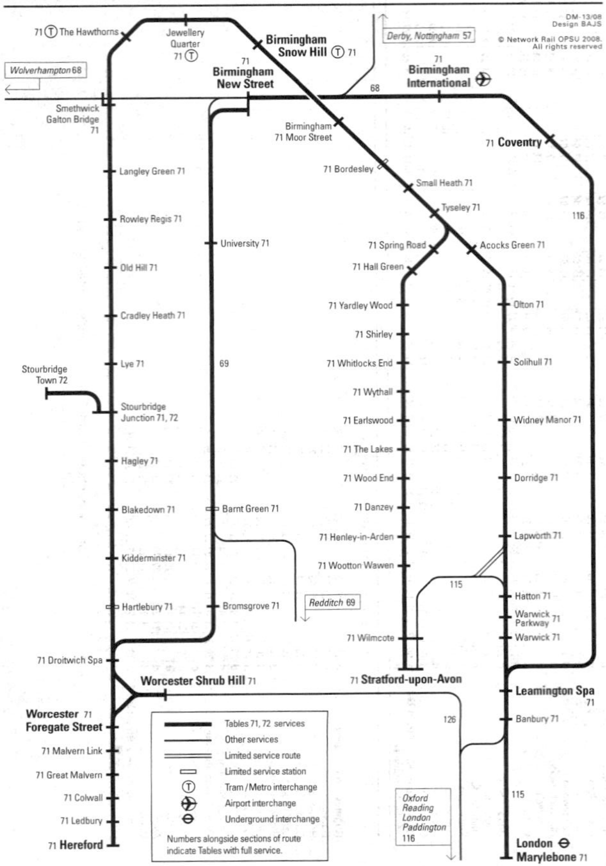

Hereford, Worcester and Stourbridge - Birmingham - Leamington Spa, Marylebone and Stratford-upon-Avon

Miles	Miles	Miles			LM	LM	GW	GW	XC	XC	LM	LM	LM		XC	LM	LM	LM	GW	LM	GW	XC	LM		LM
							◇1 A	◇1 B	◇1	◇1					◇1				◇1 A		◇1 B	◇1			
0	—	—	**Hereford** 7	d															05 34		05 35				
13¾	—	—	Ledbury	a															05 50		05 51				
—	—	—		d															05 50		05 52				
18	—	—	Colwall	d															05 58		05 59				
20¾	—	—	**Great Malvern**	a															06 03		06 04				
—	—	—		d			05 17	05 18			05 52								06 03		06 10				
22	—	—	Malvern Link	d			05 20	05 21			05 55								06 07		06 14				
28¾	0	—	**Worcester Foregate Street** 7	a			05 30	05 31			06 02								06 18		06 24				
—	—	—		d			05 31	05 32			06 04								06 18		06 25				
29½	—	—	**Worcester Shrub Hill** 7	a			05 35	05 36											06 21		06 29				
—	—	—		d		05 30												06 15		06 28					06 45
34¼	5½	—	Droitwich Spa	d		05 38					06 13							06 23		06 35					06 53
40½	—	—	Bromsgrove	d							06 22									06 44					
44	—	—	Barnt Green	d																					
52	—	—	University	d							06 39									06 59					
—	11	—	Hartlebury	d														06 30							07 01
—	14¾	—	**Kidderminster**	d		05 48												06 36							07 07
—	17¾	—	Blakedown	d														06 41							07 12
—	19½	—	Hagley	d														06 44							07 16
—	21½	—	**Stourbridge Junction** 2	d		05 57										06 24		06 49							07 21
—	22¾	—	Lye	d		06 01										06 28		06 53							
—	24	—	Cradley Heath	d		06 04										06 31		06 56							07 27
—	25½	—	Old Hill	d		06 08										06 35		07 00							
—	26¾	—	Rowley Regis	d		06 12										06 39		07 04							07 33
—	28½	0	Langley Green	d		06 15										06 42		07 07							
54½	—	6¼	**Birmingham New Street** 12	a							06 45									07 07					
—	—	—		d					06 03	06 33					07 03							07 33			
—	—	—	**Birmingham International** ✈	d					06 14						07 14										
—	—	—	**Coventry**	d					06 25						07 25										
—	29½	—	Smethwick Galton Bridge 7	d		06 18										06 46		07 11							07 38
—	30¼	—	The Hawthorns	d		06 21										06 48		07 13							07 41
—	32¾	—	Jewellery Quarter	d		06 25										06 52		07 17							07 45
—	33½	—	**Birmingham Snow Hill**	a		06 28										06 55		07 21							07 48
—	—	—		d	05 55	06 29						06 36	06 41			07 02	07 19	07 23					07 39		07 50
—	34	—	**Birmingham Moor Street**	d	05 58	06 32						06 39	06 44			07 05	07 22	07 26					07 42		07 53
—	34¾	—	Bordesley	d																					
—	35¾	9¼	Small Heath	d	06 02							06 43	06 48			07 09		07 30					07 46		
—	36¾	10¼	Tyseley	d	06 04	06 36						06 45	06 50			07 11		07 32					07 48		07 57
—	—	11¼	Acocks Green	d	06 07							06 48				07 14	07 27								08 00
—	—	12¼	Olton	d	06 10							06 51				07 17	07 30								08 03
—	—	14	Solihull	d	06 13							06 55				07 20	07 34								08 07
—	—	15½	Widney Manor	d	06 17							06 58				07 24	07 37								08 10
—	—	17½	Dorridge	d	06 21							07a03				07 28	07a42								08a16
—	—	20	Lapworth	d	06 25											07 32									
—	—	24¼	Hatton	d												07 38									
—	—	27	Warwick Parkway	d																					
—	—	28¼	Warwick	d												07 44									
—	—	30¼	**Leamington Spa** 5	a					06 36	06 58					07 37	07 49						08 04			
—	—	—		d					06 38	07 00					07 38							08 05			
—	—	—	Banbury	d					06a56	07a21					07a54							08a21			
—	—	—	**London Marylebone** 10 ⊖	a																					
—	37¾	—	Spring Road	d		06 39							06 53					07 35					07 51		
—	38¼	—	Hall Green	d		06 42							06 56					07 38					07 54		
—	39½	—	Yardley Wood	d		06 45							06 59					07 41					07 57		
—	40¾	—	Shirley	d		06 48							07 02					07 44					08 00		
—	41¾	—	Whitlocks End	d		06 51							07 05					07 47					08a02		
—	42¾	—	Wythall	d		06 53							07 07					07 50							
—	43¾	—	Earlswood (West Midlands)	d									07 10					07 52							
—	44½	—	The Lakes	d									07x12					07x55							
—	45¾	—	Wood End	d									07x14					07x57							
—	47½	—	Danzey	d									07x18					08x01							
—	50¼	—	Henley-in-Arden	d		07 04							07 23					08 07							
—	52¼	—	Wootton Wawen	d									07x25					08x10							
—	56	—	Wilmcote	d	06 42								07 31					08 15							
—	58¾	—	**Stratford-upon-Avon**	a	06 48	07 16							07 36					08 21							

A until 9 September

B from 12 September

Table 71

Hereford, Worcester and Stourbridge - Birmingham - Leamington Spa, Marylebone and Stratford-upon-Avon

		GW ■1 A	GW ■1 B	LM	LM	LM	LM	XC ◇1 🛒	LM	GW ◇1 B ∅	GW ◇1 A ∅	LM	LM	XC ◇1 🛒	LM	LM	LM	LM	LM	LM	XC ◇1 🛒	LM	GW ◇1 B 🛒
Hereford 7	d									06⌇43	06⌇43				07 08							07 34	
Ledbury	a									06⌇59	06⌇59				07 24							07 49	
	d									07⌇02	07⌇00				07 24							07 50	
Colwall	d									07⌇09	07⌇09				07 31							07 56	
Great Malvern	a									07⌇14	07⌇14				07 35							08 00	
	d			06 47					07 05	07⌇15	07⌇14				07 39							08 05	
Malvern Link	d			06 50					07 08	07⌇19	07⌇18				07 42							08 08	
Worcester Foregate Street 7	a			06 58					07 16	07⌇29	07⌇30				07 50							08 16	
	d	06⌇51	06⌇53	06 59					07 18	07⌇30	07⌇30	07 33			07 51		08 04					08 22	08⌇26
Worcester Shrub Hill 7	a	06⌇53	06⌇55	07 01					07 20	07⌇33	07⌇34				07 53								08⌇28
	d			07 06		07 15			07 25						07 57								
Droitwich Spa	d			07 14		07 23			07 33			07 42			08 05		08 13					08 32	
Bromsgrove	d			07 24																		08 42	
Barnt Green	d																						
University	d								07 59						08 29							08 59	
Hartlebury	d					07 30																	
Kidderminster	d				07 18	07 36						07 54					08 23			08 57			
Blakedown	d				07 24	07 41						08 00					08 28			09 02			
Hagley	d				07 28	07 45						08 04					08 32			09 05			
Stourbridge Junction 2	d				07 32	07 49	07 55					08 09	08 14				08 36	08 45	08 54	09 09			
Lye	d				07 36		07 59						08 18				08 40		08 58				
Cradley Heath	d				07 39	07 55	08 02					08 14	08 21				08 43	08 51	09 01	09 15			
Old Hill	d				07 43		08 06						08 25				08 47		09 05				
Rowley Regis	d				07 47	08 00	08 10					08 20	08 29				08 51	08 57	09 09	09 21			
Langley Green	d				07 50		08 13						08 32				08 54		09 12				
Birmingham New Street 12	a			07 45					08 09						08 37							09 07	
	d							08 03						08 33							09 03		
Birmingham International ✈	d							08 14													09 14		
Coventry	d							08 25													09 25		
Smethwick Galton Bridge 7	d				07 54	08 06	08 16					08 26	08 36				08 57	09 02	09 15	09 26			
The Hawthorns	d				07 56	08 08	08 19					08 28	08 38				08 59	09 05	09 17	09 29			
Jewellery Quarter	d				08 00	08 12	08 23					08 32	08 42				09 03	09 09	09 21	09 33			
Birmingham Snow Hill	a				08 03	08 15	08 26					08 35	08 45				09 06	09 15	09 25	09 36			
	d				08 05	08 17	08 27					08 37	08 47			08 57	09 07	09 17	09 27	09 37			
Birmingham Moor Street	d				08 08	08 20	08 30					08 40	08 50			09 00	09 10	09 20	09 30	09 40			
Bordesley	d																						
Small Heath	d				08 12							08 44					09 14			09 44			
Tyseley	d				08 14							08 46					09 16			09 46			
Acocks Green	d					08 25						08 49				09 05		09 25		09 49			
Olton	d					08 28						08 52				09 08		09 28		09 52			
Solihull	d					08 32						08 56				09 12		09 32		09 56			
Widney Manor	d					08 35						08 59				09 15		09 35		09 59			
Dorridge	d					08a41						09a04				09a21		09a41		10a04			
Lapworth	d																						
Hatton	d																						
Warwick Parkway	d																						
Warwick	d																						
Leamington Spa 8	a							08 36						08 59							09 36		
	d							08 38						09 00							09 38		
Banbury	d							08a54						09a18							09a54		
London Marylebone 10 ⊖	a																						
Spring Road	d				08 17		08 36						08 56				09 19		09 36				
Hall Green	d				08 20		08 39						08 59				09 22		09 39				
Yardley Wood	d				08 23		08 42						09 02				09 25		09 42				
Shirley	d				08 26		08 45						09 05				09 28		09 45				
Whitlocks End	d				08a28		08 48						09a07				09a30		09 48				
Wythall	d						08 50												09 50				
Earlswood (West Midlands)	d						08 53												09 53				
The Lakes	d						08x55												09x55				
Wood End	d						08x57												09x57				
Danzey	d						09x00												10x00				
Henley-in-Arden	d						09 05												10 05				
Wootton Wawen	d						09x08												10x08				
Wilmcote	d						09 13												10 13				
Stratford-upon-Avon	a						09 21												10 21				

A until 9 September **B** from 12 September

Table 71

Hereford, Worcester and Stourbridge - Birmingham - Leamington Spa, Marylebone and Stratford-upon-Avon

		LM	GW A	LM	XC ◇1 🛒	LM	GW B	LM	GW ◇1 A 🛒	LM	LM	LM	XC ◇1 🛒	LM	LM	GW ◇1 🛒	LM	LM	LM	XC ◇1 🛒	LM	LM	XC ◇1 🛒
Hereford 7	d													08 49									
Ledbury	a													09 05									
	d													09 08									
Colwall	d													09 14									
Great Malvern	a													09 18									
	d		08⌇26			08 38	08⌇51		08⌇58					09 19		09 54							
Malvern Link	d		08⌇29			08 41	08⌇53		09⌇00					09 22		09 56							
Worcester Foregate Street 7	a		08⌇42			08 49	09⌇03		09⌇09					09 30		10 05							
	d	08 38	08⌇54			08 52	09⌇03	09 06	09⌇09					09 31		10 05			10 16				
Worcester Shrub Hill 7	a	08 40	08⌇56				09⌇06		09⌇12					09 33		10 08							
	d	08 44												09 37	09 47								
Droitwich Spa	d	08 52				09 01		09 15						09 45	09 55				10 25				
Bromsgrove	d					09 11								09 54									
Barnt Green	d																						
University	d					09 29								10 09									
Hartlebury	d																						
Kidderminster	d	09 06						09 26		09 36		09 56			10 06			10 26	10 36			10 56	
Blakedown	d	09 11						09 31		09 41					10 11				10 41				
Hagley	d	09 15						09 35		09 45					10 15				10 44				
Stourbridge Junction 2	d	09 19		09 25				09 39		09 49	09 55	10 09			10 19		10 25	10 39	10 49		10 55	11 09	
Lye	d			09 29							09 59						10 29				10 59		
Cradley Heath	d	09 24		09 32				09 44		09 54	10 02	10 14			10 24		10 32	10 44	10 54		11 02	11 14	
Old Hill	d			09 36							10 06						10 36				11 06		
Rowley Regis	d	09 30		09 39				09 50		10 00	10 10	10 20			10 30		10 40	10 50	11 00		11 10	11 20	
Langley Green	d			09 42							10 13						10 43				11 13		
Birmingham New Street 12	a					09 42								10 24									
	d				09 33								10 03							10 33			11 03
Birmingham International ✈	d												10 14										11 14
Coventry	d												10 25										11 25
Smethwick Galton Bridge 7	d	09 36		09 46				09 56		10 06	10 16	10 26			10 36		10 46	10 56	11 06		11 16	11 26	
The Hawthorns	d	09 38		09 48				09 58		10 08	10 18	10 28			10 38		10 48	10 58	11 08		11 18	11 28	
Jewellery Quarter	d	09 42		09 52				10 02		10 12	10 22	10 32			10 42		10 52	11 02	11 12		11 22	11 32	
Birmingham Snow Hill	a	09 45		09 55				10 05		10 15	10 25	10 35			10 45		10 55	11 05	11 15		11 25	11 35	
	d	09 47		09 57				10 07		10 17	10 27	10 37			10 47		10 57	11 07	11 17		11 27	11 37	
Birmingham Moor Street	d	09 50		10 00				10 10		10 20	10 30	10 40			10 50		11 00	11 10	11 20		11 30	11 40	
Bordesley	d																						
Small Heath	d							10 14				10 44						11 14				11 44	
Tyseley	d							10 16				10 46						11 16				11 46	
Acocks Green	d			10 05						10 25		10 49					11 05		11 25			11 49	
Olton	d			10 08						10 28		10 52					11 08		11 28			11 52	
Solihull	d			10 12						10 32		10 56					11 12		11 32			11 56	
Widney Manor	d			10 15						10 35		10 59					11 15		11 35			11 59	
Dorridge	d			10a22						10a41		11a04					11a21		11a41			12a04	
Lapworth	d																						
Hatton	d																						
Warwick Parkway	d																						
Warwick	d																						
Leamington Spa 8	a				09 58								10 36							10 58			11 36
	d				10 00								10 38							11 00			11 38
Banbury	d				10a17								10a54							11a17			11a54
London Marylebone 10 ⊖	a																						
Spring Road	d	09 56						10 19			10 36				10 56			11 19			11 36		
Hall Green	d	09 59						10 22			10 39				10 59			11 22			11 39		
Yardley Wood	d	10 02						10 25			10 42				11 02			11 25			11 42		
Shirley	d	10 05						10 28			10 45				11 05			11 28			11 45		
Whitlocks End	d	10a07						10a30			10 48				11a07			11a30			11 48		
Wythall	d										10 50										11 50		
Earlswood (West Midlands)	d										10 53										11 53		
The Lakes	d										10x55										11x55		
Wood End	d										10x57										11x57		
Danzey	d										11x00										12x00		
Henley-in-Arden	d										11 05										12 05		
Wootton Wawen	d										11x08										12x08		
Wilmcote	d										11 13										12 13		
Stratford-upon-Avon	a										11 22										12 21		

A until 9 September **B** from 12 September

Hereford, Worcester and Stourbridge - Birmingham - Leamington Spa, Marylebone and Stratford-upon-Avon

		LM	LM	GW	LM	LM	LM	XC	LM	LM	XC	LM	LM	GW	LM	LM	LM	XC	LM	LM	XC	LM
				■				◇1 ⊼			◇1 ⊼			◇1 ⊼				◇1 ⊼			◇1 ⊼	
Hereford 7	d	09 40										10 40										11 40
Ledbury	a	09 56										10 56										11 56
	d	09 58										10 58										11 58
Colwall	d	10 04										11 04										12 04
Great Malvern	a	10 08										11 08										12 09
	d	10 10		10 51								11 10	11 34									12 10
Malvern Link	d	10 13		10 53								11 13	11 36									12 13
Worcester Foregate Street 7	a	10 21		11 02								11 21	11 45									12 22
	d	10 24		11 02			11 16					11 24	11 46	12 06			12 16					12 24
Worcester Shrub Hill 7	a			11 06										12 08								
	d		10 47																			
Droitwich Spa	d	10 33	10 55				11 25					11 33	11 55				12 25					12 33
Bromsgrove	d	10 42										11 42										12 42
Barnt Green	d																					
University	d	10 59										11 59										12 59
Hartlebury	d																					
Kidderminster	d		11 06			11 26	11 36			11 56			12 06			12 26	12 36			12 56		
Blakedown	d		11 11				11 41						12 11				12 41					
Hagley	d		11 14				11 44						12 14				12 44					
Stourbridge Junction 2	d		11 19		11 25	11 39	11 49		11 55	12 09			12 19		12 25	12 39	12 49		12 55	13 09		
Lye	d				11 29				11 59						12 29				12 59			
Cradley Heath	d		11 24		11 32	11 44	11 54		12 02	12 14			12 24		12 32	12 44	12 54		13 02	13 14		
Old Hill	d				11 36				12 06						12 36				13 06			
Rowley Regis	d		11 30		11 40	11 50	12 00		12 10	12 20			12 30		12 40	12 50	13 00		13 10	13 20		
Langley Green	d				11 43				12 13						12 43				13 13			
Birmingham New Street 12	a	11 13										12 11										13 13
	d							11 33			12 03							12 33			13 03	
Birmingham International ✈	d										12 14										13 14	
Coventry	d										12 25										13 25	
Smethwick Galton Bridge 7	d		11 36		11 46	11 56	12 06		12 16	12 26			12 36		12 46	12 56	13 06		13 16	13 26		
The Hawthorns	d		11 38		11 48	11 58	12 08		12 18	12 28			12 38		12 48	12 58	13 08		13 18	13 28		
Jewellery Quarter	d		11 42		11 52	12 02	12 12		12 22	12 32			12 42		12 52	13 02	13 12		13 22	13 32		
Birmingham Snow Hill	a		11 45		11 55	12 05	12 15		12 25	12 35			12 45		12 55	13 05	13 15		13 25	13 35		
	d		11 47		11 57	12 07	12 17		12 27	12 37			12 47		12 57	13 07	13 17		13 27	13 37		
Birmingham Moor Street	d		11 50		12 00	12 10	12 20		12 30	12 40			12 50		13 00	13 10	13 20		13 30	13 40		
Bordesley	d																					
Small Heath	d					12 14				12 44						13 14				13 44		
Tyseley	d					12 16				12 46						13 16				13 46		
Acocks Green	d				12 05		12 25			12 49					13 05		13 25			13 49		
Olton	d				12 08		12 28			12 52					13 08		13 28			13 52		
Solihull	d				12 12		12 32			12 56					13 12		13 32			13 56		
Widney Manor	d				12 15		12 35			12 59					13 15		13 35			13 59		
Dorridge	d				12a22		12a41			13a04					13a21		13a41			14a04		
Lapworth	d																					
Hatton	d																					
Warwick Parkway	d																					
Warwick	d																					
Leamington Spa 8	a							11 59			12 36							12 58			13 36	
	d							12 00			12 38							13 00			13 38	
Banbury	d							12a17			12a54							13a20			13a54	
London Marylebone 10 ⊖	a																					
Spring Road	d		11 56			12 19			12 36				12 56			13 19			13 36			
Hall Green	d		11 59			12 22			12 39				12 59			13 22			13 39			
Yardley Wood	d		12 02			12 25			12 42				13 02			13 25			13 42			
Shirley	d		12 05			12 28			12 45				13 05			13 28			13 45			
Whitlocks End	d		12a07			12a30			12 48				13a07			13a30			13 48			
Wythall	d								12 50										13 50			
Earlswood (West Midlands)	d								12 53										13 53			
The Lakes	d								12x55										13x55			
Wood End	d								12x57										13x57			
Danzey	d								13x00										14x00			
Henley-in-Arden	d								13 05										14 05			
Wootton Wawen	d								13x08										14x08			
Wilmcote	d								13 13										14 13			
Stratford-upon-Avon	a								13 21										14 21			

Hereford, Worcester and Stourbridge - Birmingham - Leamington Spa, Marylebone and Stratford-upon-Avon

		LM	GW	LM	XC	LM	LM	LM	LM	XC	LM	LM	GW	GW	LM	LM	LM	XC	LM	LM	XC	LM	GW
					◇1 ⊼					◇1 ⊼			◇1 A	◇1 B				◇1 ⊼			◇1 ⊼		1 A ⊼
Hereford 7	d										12 40		13 14	13 14								13 43	
Ledbury	a										12 56		13 30	13 30								14 00	
	d										12 58		13 31	13 31								14 00	
Colwall	d										13 04		13 39	13 38								14 06	
Great Malvern	a										13 09		13 44	13 44								14 11	
	d		12 51								13 10		13 44	13 47			14 00					14 11	14 26
Malvern Link	d		12 53								13 13		13 48	13 51			14 02					14 14	14 28
Worcester Foregate Street 7	a		13 02								13 21		13 58	14 01			14 10					14 23	14 38
	d	12 46	13 02								13 24		13 59	14 02			14 16					14 24	14 38
Worcester Shrub Hill 7	a		13 06										14 03	14 06									14 41
	d						13 17					13 47											
Droitwich Spa	d	12 55					13 25				13 33	13 55					14 25					14 33	
Bromsgrove	d										13 42											14 42	
Barnt Green	d																						
University	d										13 59											14 59	
Hartlebury	d																						
Kidderminster	d	13 06					13 36		13 56			14 06				14 26	14 36			14 56			
Blakedown	d	13 11					13 41					14 11					14 41						
Hagley	d	13 14					13 44					14 14					14 44						
Stourbridge Junction 2	d	13 19		13 25		13 39	13 49	13 55	14 09			14 19			14 25	14 39	14 49		14 55	15 09			
Lye	d			13 29				13 59							14 29				14 59				
Cradley Heath	d	13 24		13 32		13 44	13 54	14 02	14 14			14 24			14 32	14 44	14 54		15 02	15 14			
Old Hill	d			13 36				14 06							14 36				15 06				
Rowley Regis	d	13 30		13 40		13 50	14 00	14 10	14 20			14 30			14 40	14 50	15 00		15 10	15 20			
Langley Green	d			13 43				14 13							14 43				15 13				
Birmingham New Street 12	a										14 12											15 13	
	d				13 33					14 03								14 33			15 03		
Birmingham International ✈	d									14 14											15 14		
Coventry	d									14 25											15 25		
Smethwick Galton Bridge 7	d	13 36		13 46		13 56	14 06	14 16	14 26			14 36			14 46	14 56	15 06		15 16	15 26			
The Hawthorns	d	13 38		13 48		13 58	14 08	14 18	14 28			14 38			14 48	14 58	15 08		15 18	15 28			
Jewellery Quarter	d	13 42		13 52		14 02	14 12	14 22	14 32			14 42			14 52	15 02	15 12		15 22	15 32			
Birmingham Snow Hill	a	13 45		13 55		14 05	14 15	14 25	14 35			14 45			14 55	15 05	15 15		15 25	15 35			
	d	13 47		13 57		14 07	14 17	14 27	14 37			14 47			14 57	15 07	15 17		15 26	15 37			
Birmingham Moor Street	d	13 50		14 00		14 10	14 20	14 30	14 40			14 50			15 00	15 10	15 20		15 29	15 40			
Bordesley	d																						
Small Heath	d					14 14			14 44							15 14				15 44			
Tyseley	d					14 16			14 46							15 16				15 46			
Acocks Green	d			14 05			14 25		14 49						15 05		15 25			15 49			
Olton	d			14 08			14 28		14 52						15 08		15 28			15 52			
Solihull	d			14 12			14 32		14 56						15 12		15 32			15 56			
Widney Manor	d			14 15			14 35		14 59						15 15		15 35			15 59			
Dorridge	d			14a22			14a41		15a04						15a21		15a41			16a04			
Lapworth	d																						
Hatton	d																						
Warwick Parkway	d																						
Warwick	d																						
Leamington Spa 8	a				13 59					14 36								14 58			15 36		
	d				14 00					14 38								15 00			15 38		
Banbury	d				14a17					14a54								15a17			15a54		
London Marylebone 10 ⊖	a																						
Spring Road	d	13 56				14 19		14 36				14 56				15 19			15 35				
Hall Green	d	13 59				14 22		14 39				14 59				15 22			15 38				
Yardley Wood	d	14 02				14 25		14 42				15 02				15 25			15 41				
Shirley	d	14 05				14 28		14 45				15 05				15 28			15 44				
Whitlocks End	d	14a07				14a30		14 48				15a07				15a30			15 47				
Wythall	d							14 50											15 49				
Earlswood (West Midlands)	d							14 53											15 52				
The Lakes	d							14x55											15x54				
Wood End	d							14x57											15x56				
Danzey	d							15x00											15x59				
Henley-in-Arden	d							15 05											16 04				
Wootton Wawen	d							15x08											16x07				
Wilmcote	d							15 13											16 12				
Stratford-upon-Avon	a							15 21											16 21				

A from 12 September

B until 9 September

Hereford, Worcester and Stourbridge - Birmingham - Leamington Spa, Marylebone and Stratford-upon-Avon

		LM	GW	GW	LM	LM	LM	XC	LM	LM	XC	LM	GW	LM	GW	GW	LM	LM	LM	LM	XC	LM
			◇1					◇1			◇1		1		◇1	◇1					◇1	
			A										B		B	A						
			🍴					🍴			🍴				🍽	🍽					🍴	
Hereford 7	d											14 40			15 14	15 14						
Ledbury	a											14 56			15 30	15 30						
	d											14 58			15 31	15 30						
Colwall	d											15 04			15 38	15 38						
Great Malvern	a											15 09			15 43	15 43						
	d		14 35	14 51								15 10	15 22	15 30	15 44	15 43						
Malvern Link	d		14 37	14 53								15 13		15 32	15 48	15 47						
Worcester Foregate Street 7	a		14 52	15 02								15 21	15 30	15 40	15 58	15 58						
	d		14 52	15 02			15 16					15 24	15 34	15 41	15 59	16 02			16 07			
Worcester Shrub Hill 7	a		14 56	15 06									15 37	15 43	16 02	16 06						
	d	14 47												15 47						16 17		
Droitwich Spa	d	14 55					15 25					15 33		15 55					16 16	16 25		
Bromsgrove	d											15 42										
Barnt Green	d																					
University	d											15 59										
Hartlebury	d																		16 23			
Kidderminster	d	15 06				15 26	15 36			15 56				16 06				16 23	16 30	16 37		
Blakedown	d	15 11				15 31	15 41							16 11				16 28	16 35	16 43		
Hagley	d	15 14				15 34	15 44							16 14				16 31	16 39	16 47		
Stourbridge Junction 2	d	15 19			15 25	15 39	15 49		15 55	16 09				16 19			16 25	16 35	16 44	16 51		16 55
Lye	d				15 29				15 59								16 29					16 59
Cradley Heath	d	15 24			15 32	15 44	15 54		16 02	16 14				16 24			16 32	16 41	16 50	16 57		17 02
Old Hill	d				15 36				16 06								16 36					17 06
Rowley Regis	d	15 30			15 40	15 50	16 00		16 10	16 20				16 30			16 40	16 47	16 55	17 03		17 10
Langley Green	d				15 43				16 13								16 43					17 13
Birmingham New Street 12	a											16 13										
	d							15 33			16 03										16 33	
Birmingham International ✈	d										16 14											
Coventry	d										16 25											
Smethwick Galton Bridge 7	d	15 36			15 46	15 56	16 06		16 16	16 26				16 36			16 46	16 52	17 01	17 08		17 16
The Hawthorns 🚊	d	15 38			15 48	15 58	16 08		16 18	16 28				16 38			16 48	16 55	17 03	17 11		17 19
Jewellery Quarter 🚊	d	15 42			15 52	16 02	16 12		16 22	16 32				16 42			16 52	16 59	17 07	17 15		17 22
Birmingham Snow Hill 🚊	a	15 45			15 55	16 05	16 15		16 25	16 35				16 45			16 55	17 02	17 13	17 18		17 25
	d	15 47			15 57	16 07	16 17		16 26	16 37				16 47			16 57	17 03	17 14	17 22		17 27
Birmingham Moor Street	d	15 50			16 00	16 10	16 20		16 29	16 40				16 50			17 00	17 06	17 17	17 25		17 30
Bordesley	d																					
Small Heath	d					16 14				16 44				16 54					17 21			
Tyseley	d					16 16			16 33	16 46				16 56			17 04		17 23			17 34
Acocks Green	d				16 05		16 25			16 49							17 07			17 30		
Olton	d				16 08		16 28			16 52							17 10			17 33		
Solihull	d				16 12		16 32			16 56							17 14			17 37		
Widney Manor	d				16 15		16 35			16 59							17 17			17 40		
Dorridge	d				16a22		16a41			17a04							17a22			17a48		
Lapworth	d																					
Hatton	d																					
Warwick Parkway	d																					
Warwick	d																					
Leamington Spa 8	a							15 58			16 36										16 58	
	d							16 00			16 38										17 00	
Banbury	d							16a17			16a54										17a17	
London Marylebone 10 ⊖	a																					
Spring Road	d	15 56				16 19			16 36					16 59				17 12	17 26			17 37
Hall Green	d	15 59				16 22			16 39					17 02				17 15	17 29			17 40
Yardley Wood	d	16 02				16 25			16 42					17 05				17 18	17 32			17 43
Shirley	d	16 05				16 28			16 45					17 08				17 21	17 35			17 46
Whitlocks End	d	16a07				16a30			16 48					17a10				17 24	17a37			17 49
Wythall	d								16 50									17 26				17 51
Earlswood (West Midlands)	d								16 53													17 54
The Lakes	d								16x55													17x56
Wood End	d								16x57													17x58
Danzey	d								17x00													18x01
Henley-in-Arden	d								17 05									17 37				18 06
Wootton Wawen	d								17x08													18x09
Wilmcote	d								17 12													18 14
Stratford-upon-Avon	a								17 20									17 51				18 22

A until 9 September **B** from 12 September

Hereford, Worcester and Stourbridge - Birmingham - Leamington Spa, Marylebone and Stratford-upon-Avon

		XC	LM	XC	LM	LM	LM	GW	XC	LM	LM	LM	GW	LM	GW	LM	LM	XC	LM	LM	LM	XC	LM
		◇1		◇1					◇1				◇1		◇1			◇1				◇1	
													A		B								
		🍴		🍴					🍴				🍴		🍴			🍴				🍴	
Hereford 7	d		15 40											16 40									17 40
Ledbury	a		15 56											16 56									17 56
	d		15 58											16 58									18 01
Colwall	d		16 04											17 04									18 07
Great Malvern	a		16 09											17 09									18 12
	d		16 10					16 49					17 00	17 10		17 41							18 12
Malvern Link	d		16 13					16 51					17 02	17 13		17 44							18 15
Worcester Foregate Street 7	a		16 21					17 01					17 17	17 22		17 52							18 24
	d		16 24			16 34	16 47	17 02				17 16	17 20	17 24	17 28	17 53				17 56			18 25
Worcester Shrub Hill 7	a					16 36		17 04					17 23		17 30	17 55							
	d					16 40																	
Droitwich Spa	d		16 33			16 48	16 56					17 25		17 33						18 05			18 34
Bromsgrove	d		16 42											17 42									18 43
Barnt Green	d		16 49																				18 50
University	d		16 59											17 59									19 00
Hartlebury	d											17 32											
Kidderminster	d				16 53	16 59	17 06				17 27	17 38							18 00	18 16	18 38		
Blakedown	d					17 04	17 11				17 32	17 43							18 05		18 43		
Hagley	d					17 08	17 15				17 35	17 46							18 09		18 46		
Stourbridge Junction 2	d				17 06	17 13	17 19			17 25	17 39	17 50					17 55		18 13	18 25	18 50		
Lye	d									17 29							17 59			18 29	18 54		
Cradley Heath	d				17 12	17 19	17 24			17 32	17 45	17 56					18 02		18 19	18 32	18 57		
Old Hill	d									17 36							18 06			18 36	19 01		
Rowley Regis	d				17 17	17 24	17 30			17 40	17 51	18 02					18 10		18 25	18 40	19 05		
Langley Green	d									17 43							18 13			18 43	19 08		
Birmingham New Street 12	a		17 13											18 13									19 12
	d	17 03		17 33					18 03									18 33				19 03	
Birmingham International ✈	d	17 14							18 14													19 14	
Coventry	d	17 25							18 25													19 25	
Smethwick Galton Bridge 7	d				17 23	17 30	17 36			17 46	17 56	18 08					18 16		18 30	18 46	19 11		
The Hawthorns 🚊	d				17 25	17 32	17 38			17 48	17 58	18 10					18 19		18 33	18 48	19 14		
Jewellery Quarter 🚊	d				17 29	17 36	17 42			17 52	18 02	18 14					18 23		18 37	18 52	19 18		
Birmingham Snow Hill 🚊	a				17 32	17 39	17 45			17 55	18 05	18 17					18 26		18 41	18 55	19 21		
	d				17 35	17 42	17 47			17 57	18 07	18 22					18 27		18 45	18 57	19 22		
Birmingham Moor Street	d				17 38	17 45	17 50			18 00	18 10	18 25					18 30		18 48	19 00	19 25		
Bordesley	d																						
Small Heath	d				17 42	17 49	17 54			18 04	18 14						18 34		18 52	19 04			
Tyseley	d				17 45	17 51	17 56			18 06	18 16						18 36		18 54	19 06			
Acocks Green	d				17 48	17 54				18 09		18 30							18 57		19 30		
Olton	d				17 50	17 57				18 12		18 33							19 00		19 33		
Solihull	d				17 54	18 01				18 16		18 37							19 04		19 37		
Widney Manor	d				17 58	18 04				18 19		18 40							19 07		19 40		
Dorridge	d				18 02	18a09				18 23		18a45							19 11		19a47		
Lapworth	d				18 06					18 27									19 15				
Hatton	d				18 12					18 33									19 21				
Warwick Parkway	d				18 16					18 38													
Warwick	d				18 19					18 41									19 27				
Leamington Spa 8	a	17 36		17 59	18 24				18 36	18 47								18 58	19 32			19 37	
	d	17 38		18 00					18 38									19 00				19 38	
Banbury	d	17a54		18a18					18a54									19a17				19a54	
London Marylebone 10 ⊖	a																						
Spring Road	d						17 59				18 19						18 39			19 09			
Hall Green	d						18 02				18 22						18 42			19 12			
Yardley Wood	d						18 05				18 25						18 45			19 15			
Shirley	d						18 08				18 28						18 48			19 18			
Whitlocks End	d						18 11				18a30						18 51			19a20			
Wythall	d						18 13										18 53						
Earlswood (West Midlands)	d						18 16										18 56						
The Lakes	d						18x18										18x58						
Wood End	d						18x21										19x00						
Danzey	d						18x24										19x03						
Henley-in-Arden	d						18 29										19 08						
Wootton Wawen	d						18x32										19x10						
Wilmcote	d						18 38										19 16						
Stratford-upon-Avon	a						18 44										19 22						

A until 9 September **B** from 12 September

Hereford, Worcester and Stourbridge - Birmingham - Leamington Spa, Marylebone and Stratford-upon-Avon

		LM	LM	LM	GW	GW	GW	XC	LM	XC	LM	LM	GW	XC	LM	XC	LM	LM	GW	GW	GW	LM	LM
					◇1		1	◇1		◇1			◇1	◇1		◇1			◇1	◇1			
							A						B						B	A			C
Hereford 7	d										18 48						19 50					20 54	
Ledbury	a										19 03						20 06					21 10	
	d										19 04						20 17					21 14	
Colwall	d										19 10						20 23					21 20	
Great Malvern	a										19 15						20 27					21 24	
	d					18 51					19 15		19 44				20 28				21 15	21 25	
Malvern Link	d					18 53					19 18		19 46				20 31				21 18	21 28	
Worcester Foregate Street 7	a					19 03					19 27		19 54				20 39				21 27	21 36	
	d			18 46	18 49	19 03	19 27				19 28	19 46	19 54				20 42		20 59	20 59	21 28	21 37	
Worcester Shrub Hill 7	a				18 52	19 06	19 29						19 57						21 02	21 03	21 31	21 39	
	d		18 37															20 52					
Droitwich Spa	d		18 45	18 55							19 37	19 55					20 51	21 00					
Bromsgrove	d										19 46						21 00						
Barnt Green	d																						
University	d										20 09						21 17						
Hartlebury	d			19 02																			
Kidderminster	d		18 55	19 10								20 10						21 10					
Blakedown	d		19 00	19 15								20 15						21 15					
Hagley	d		19 04	19 19								20 19						21 19					
Stourbridge Junction 2	d		19 10	19 25					19 55			20 25			20 55			21 25					21 55
Lye	d			19 29					19 59			20 29			20 59			21 29					21 59
Cradley Heath	d		19 16	19 32					20 02			20 32			21 02			21 32					22 02
Old Hill	d			19 36					20 06			20 36			21 06			21 36					22 06
Rowley Regis	d		19 22	19 40					20 10			20 40			21 10			21 40					22 10
Langley Green	d			19 43					20 13			20 43			21 13			21 43					22 13
Birmingham New Street 12	a										20 20						21 23						
	d							19 33		20 03				20 33		21 03							
Birmingham International ✈	d									20 14						21 14							
Coventry	d									20 25						21 25							
Smethwick Galton Bridge 7	d		19 27	19 46					20 16			20 46			21 16			21 46					22 16
The Hawthorns	d		19 30	19 48					20 18			20 48			21 18			21 48					22 18
Jewellery Quarter	d		19 34	19 52					20 22			20 52			21 22			21 52					22 22
Birmingham Snow Hill	a		19 37	19 55					20 25			20 55			21 25			21 55					22 25
	d	19 27	19 38	19 57					20 27			20 57			21 27			21 57					22 27
Birmingham Moor Street	d	19 30	19a40	20 00					20 30			21 00			21 30			22 00					22 30
Bordesley	d																						
Small Heath	d	19 34		20 04					20 34			21 04			21 34			22 04					22 34
Tyseley	d	19 36		20 06					20 36			21 06			21 36			22 06					22 36
Acocks Green	d			20 09								21 09						22 09					
Olton	d			20 12								21 12						22 12					
Solihull	d			20 16								21 16						22 16					
Widney Manor	d			20 19								21 19						22 19					
Dorridge	d			20a24								21a24						22a24					
Lapworth	d																						
Hatton	d																						
Warwick Parkway	d																						
Warwick	d																						
Leamington Spa 8	a							20 04		20 36				20 58		21 36							
	d							20 05		20 38				21 00		21 38							
Banbury	d							20a22		20a54				21a17		21a54							
London Marylebone 10 ⊖	a																						
Spring Road	d	19 39							20 39						21 39								22 39
Hall Green	d	19 42							20 42						21 42								22 42
Yardley Wood	d	19 45							20 45						21 45								22 45
Shirley	d	19 48							20 48						21 48								22 48
Whitlocks End	d	19 51							20 51						21a50								22a50
Wythall	d	19 53							20 53														
Earlswood (West Midlands)	d	19 56							20 56														
The Lakes	d	19x58							20x58														
Wood End	d	20x00							21x00														
Danzey	d	20x03							21x03														
Henley-in-Arden	d	20 08							21 08														
Wootton Wawen	d	20x10							21x10														
Wilmcote	d	20 16							21 16														
Stratford-upon-Avon	a	20 23							21 23														

A until 9 September

B from 12 September

Hereford, Worcester and Stourbridge - Birmingham - Leamington Spa, Marylebone and Stratford-upon-Avon

		XC	LM	LM	LM	GW	GW	LM
		◇1				◇1	◇1	
						A	B	
Hereford 7	d			21 29		21 51	21 51	23 00
Ledbury	a			21 44		22 07	22 07	23 16
	d			21 45		22 09	22 09	23 17
Colwall	d			21 51		22 16	22 17	23 23
Great Malvern	a			21 55		22 22	22 22	23 27
	d			21 56		22 22	22 22	23 28
Malvern Link	d			21 59				23 31
Worcester Foregate Street 7	a			22 07		22 33	22 33	23 39
	d			22 10	22 17	22 34	22 34	23 40
Worcester Shrub Hill 7	a				22 19	22 38	22 38	23 45
	d		21 52		22 27			
Droitwich Spa	d		22 00	22 19	22 35			
Bromsgrove	d			22 28				
Barnt Green	d							
University	d			22 44				
Hartlebury	d							
Kidderminster	d		22 10		22 45			
Blakedown	d		22 15					
Hagley	d		22 19					
Stourbridge Junction 2	d		22 25		22 55			
Lye	d		22 29		22 59			
Cradley Heath	d		22 32		23 02			
Old Hill	d		22 36		23 06			
Rowley Regis	d		22 40		23 10			
Langley Green	d		22 43		23 13			
Birmingham New Street 12	a			22 50				
	d	22 03						
Birmingham International ✈	d	22 14						
Coventry	d	22 25						
Smethwick Galton Bridge 7	d		22 46		23 16			
The Hawthorns	d		22 48		23 18			
Jewellery Quarter	d		22 52		23 22			
Birmingham Snow Hill	a		22 55		23 24			
	d		22 57		23 25			
Birmingham Moor Street	d		23 00		23 28			
Bordesley	d							
Small Heath	d		23 04		23 32			
Tyseley	d		23 06		23 34			
Acocks Green	d		23 09					
Olton	d		23 12					
Solihull	d		23 16					
Widney Manor	d		23 19					
Dorridge	d		23 23					
Lapworth	d		23 27					
Hatton	d		23 33					
Warwick Parkway	d		23 38					
Warwick	d		23 41					
Leamington Spa 8	a	22 37	23 46					
	d	22 38						
Banbury	d	22a54						
London Marylebone 10 ⊖	a							
Spring Road	d				23 37			
Hall Green	d				23 40			
Yardley Wood	d				23 43			
Shirley	d				23 46			
Whitlocks End	d				23a48			
Wythall	d							
Earlswood (West Midlands)	d							
The Lakes	d							
Wood End	d							
Danzey	d							
Henley-in-Arden	d							
Wootton Wawen	d							
Wilmcote	d							
Stratford-upon-Avon	a							

A from 24 May until 9 September

B from 12 September

Table 71

Hereford, Worcester and Stourbridge - Birmingham - Leamington Spa, Marylebone and Stratford-upon-Avon

		LM	GW	XC	XC	LM	GW	XC	LM	LM	LM	GW	LM	GW	XC	XC	LM	LM	LM	LM	LM	GW	GW
			◇1 A	◇1	◇1		◇1 B	◇1				◇1 A		◇1 B	◇1	◇1						◇1 A	◇1 B
Hereford 7	d																					07 10	07 10
Ledbury	a																					07 28	07 28
	d																					07 30	07 30
Colwall	d																					07 38	07 37
Great Malvern	a																					07 42	07 42
	d		05 39				05 56				06 21	06 35		06 49							07 32	07 43	07 43
Malvern Link	d		05 42				05 59				06 24	06 39		06 53							07 35	07 46	07 46
Worcester Foregate Street 7	a		05 51				06 08				06 31	06 48		07 02							07 43	07 57	07 58
	d		05 52				06 09				06 33	06 50		07 04							07 46	07 57	07 59
Worcester Shrub Hill 7	a		05 55				06 11					06 53		07 07								08 01	08 02
	d	05 44				06 07				06 25			07 01				07 35						
Droitwich Spa	d	05 52				06 15				06 33	06 42		07 09				07 43				07 55		
Bromsgrove	d										06 51						07 52						
Barnt Green	d																						
University	d										07 09						08 09						
Hartlebury	d									06 40			07 16										
Kidderminster	d	06 02								06 46			07 22						07 46		08 06		
Blakedown	d	06 07								06 51			07 27						07 51		08 11		
Hagley	d	06 11								06 54			07 30						07 54		08 14		
Stourbridge Junction 2	d	06 15								07 02			07 35						07 59	08 05	08 19		
Lye	d	06 19								07 06			07 39							08 09			
Cradley Heath	d	06 22								07 09			07 42						08 04	08 12	08 24		
Old Hill	d	06 26								07 13			07 46							08 16			
Rowley Regis	d	06 30								07 17			07 50						08 10	08 20	08 30		
Langley Green	d	06 33								07 20			07 53							08 23			
Birmingham New Street 12	a					06 48					07 16						08 16						
	d			06 03	06 33			07 03							07 33	08 03							
Birmingham International ✈	d			06 14				07 14								08 14							
Coventry	d			06 25				07 25								08 25							
Smethwick Galton Bridge 7	d	06 36								07 23			07 56						08 16	08 26	08 36		
The Hawthorns	d	06 38								07 25			07 58						08 18	08 28	08 38		
Jewellery Quarter	d	06 42								07 29			08 02						08 22	08 32	08 42		
Birmingham Snow Hill	a	06 45								07 32			08 05						08 25	08 35	08 45		
	d	06 51							07 20	07 37			08 07					08 17	08 27	08 37	08 47		
Birmingham Moor Street	d	06 54							07 23	07 40			08 10					08 20	08 30	08 40	08 50		
Bordesley	d																						
Small Heath	d	06 58							07 27				08 14							08 44			
Tyseley	d	07 00							07 29				08 16							08 46			
Acocks Green	d	07 03								07 45								08 25		08 49			
Olton	d	07 06								07 48								08 28		08 52			
Solihull	d	07 10								07 52								08 32		08 56			
Widney Manor	d	07 13								07 55								08 35		08 59			
Dorridge	d	07a18								08a01								08a41		09a04			
Lapworth	d																						
Hatton	d																						
Warwick Parkway	d																						
Warwick	d																						
Leamington Spa 8	a			06 36	06 58			07 36							07 58	08 36							
	d			06 38	07 00			07 38							08 00	08 38							
Banbury	d			06a54	07a17			07a54							08a17	08a54							
London Marylebone 10 ⊖	a																						
Spring Road	d								07 32				08 19						08 36		08 56		
Hall Green	d								07 35				08 22						08 39		08 59		
Yardley Wood	d								07 38				08 25						08 42		09 02		
Shirley	d								07 41				08 28						08 45		09 05		
Whitlocks End	d								07 44				08a30						08 48		09a08		
Wythall	d								07 46										08 50				
Earlswood (West Midlands)	d								07 49										08 53				
The Lakes	d								07x51										08x55				
Wood End	d								07x53										08x57				
Danzey	d								07x56										09x00				
Henley-in-Arden	d								08 01										09 05				
Wootton Wawen	d								08x04										09x08				
Wilmcote	d								08 09										09 13				
Stratford-upon-Avon	a								08 17										09 21				

A until 10 September

B from 17 September

Table 71

Hereford, Worcester and Stourbridge - Birmingham - Leamington Spa, Marylebone and Stratford-upon-Avon

		XC	LM	LM	LM	LM	XC	LM	GW	LM	XC	LM	LM	GW	LM	LM	LM	LM	XC	LM	LM	LM	LM
		◇1					◇1		◇1 A		◇1			◇1 B					◇1				
Hereford 7	d							07 40												08 40			
Ledbury	a							07 56												08 56			
	d							07 58												08 58			
Colwall	d							08 04												09 04			
Great Malvern	a							08 08												09 09			
	d							08 10	08 43					08 43		09 00				09 10			
Malvern Link	d							08 13	08 47					08 46		09 03				09 13			
Worcester Foregate Street 7	a							08 21	08 56					08 57		09 11				09 22			
	d							08 24	08 58				08 56	08 57		09 16				09 24			
Worcester Shrub Hill 7	a								09 01					09 01									
	d				08 15																09 47		
Droitwich Spa	d				08 23			08 33					09 05			09 25				09 33	09 55		
Bromsgrove	d							08 42												09 42			
Barnt Green	d																						
University	d							08 59												09 59			
Hartlebury	d				08 30																		
Kidderminster	d				08 36								09 16		09 26	09 36		09 56			10 06		10 26
Blakedown	d				08 41										09 31	09 41					10 11		
Hagley	d				08 44										09 34	09 44					10 14		
Stourbridge Junction 2	d			08 35	08 49	08 55				09 09			09 25		09 39	09 49	09 55	10 09			10 19	10 25	10 39
Lye	d			08 39		08 59							09 29				09 59					10 29	
Cradley Heath	d			08 42	08 54	09 02				09 14			09 32		09 44	09 54	10 02	10 14			10 24	10 32	10 44
Old Hill	d			08 46		09 06							09 36				10 06					10 36	
Rowley Regis	d			08 50	09 00	09 10				09 20			09 40		09 50	10 00	10 10	10 20			10 30	10 40	10 50
Langley Green	d			08 53		09 13							09 43				10 13					10 43	
Birmingham New Street 12	a							09 11												10 11			
	d	08 33					09 03				09 33								10 03				
Birmingham International ✈	d						09 14												10 14				
Coventry	d						09 25												10 25				
Smethwick Galton Bridge 7	d			08 56	09 06	09 16				09 26			09 46		09 56	10 06	10 16	10 26			10 36	10 46	10 56
The Hawthorns	d			08 58	09 08	09 18				09 28			09 48		09 58	10 08	10 18	10 28			10 38	10 48	10 58
Jewellery Quarter	d			09 02	09 12	09 22				09 32			09 52		10 02	10 12	10 22	10 32			10 42	10 52	11 02
Birmingham Snow Hill	a			09 05	09 15	09 25				09 35			09 55		10 05	10 15	10 25	10 35			10 45	10 55	11 05
	d		08 57	09 07	09 17	09 27				09 37		09 47	09 57		10 07	10 17	10 27	10 37			10 47	10 57	11 07
Birmingham Moor Street	d		09 00	09 10	09 20	09 30				09 40		09 50	10 00		10 10	10 20	10 30	10 40			10 50	11 00	11 10
Bordesley	d																						
Small Heath	d			09 14						09 44					10 14			10 44					11 14
Tyseley	d			09 16						09 46					10 16			10 46					11 16
Acocks Green	d		09 05		09 25					09 49			10 05			10 25		10 49				11 05	
Olton	d		09 08		09 28					09 52			10 08			10 28		10 52				11 08	
Solihull	d		09 12		09 32					09 56			10 12			10 32		10 56				11 12	
Widney Manor	d		09 15		09 35					09 59			10 15			10 35		10 59				11 15	
Dorridge	d		09a21		09a41					10a04			10a22			10a41		11a04				11a22	
Lapworth	d																						
Hatton	d																						
Warwick Parkway	d																						
Warwick	d																						
Leamington Spa 8	a	08 58					09 36				09 58								10 36				
	d	09 00					09 38				10 00								10 38				
Banbury	d	09a17					09a54				10a17								10a54				
London Marylebone 10 ⊖	a																						
Spring Road	d			09 19		09 36						09 56			10 19		10 36				10 56		11 19
Hall Green	d			09 22		09 39						09 59			10 22		10 39				10 59		11 22
Yardley Wood	d			09 25		09 42						10 02			10 25		10 42				11 02		11 25
Shirley	d			09 28		09 45						10 05			10 28		10 45				11 05		11 28
Whitlocks End	d			09a30		09 48						10a08			10a30		10 48				11a08		11a30
Wythall	d					09 50											10 50						
Earlswood (West Midlands)	d					09 53											10 53						
The Lakes	d					09x55											10x55						
Wood End	d					09x57											10x57						
Danzey	d					10x00											11x00						
Henley-in-Arden	d					10 05											11 05						
Wootton Wawen	d					10x08											11x08						
Wilmcote	d					10 13											11 13						
Stratford-upon-Avon	a					10 21											11 21						

A from 17 September

B until 10 September

Table 71

Hereford, Worcester and Stourbridge - Birmingham - Leamington Spa, Marylebone and Stratford-upon-Avon

		XC	LM	GW	GW	LM	LM	LM	XC	LM	LM	GW	GW	GW	GW	LM	LM	LM	XC	LM	LM	XC
		◇1 工		◇1 A 工	◇1 B 工				◇1 工			◇1 A 工	■ B	■ A	◇1 B 工				◇1 工			◇1 工
Hereford 7	d									09 40												
Ledbury	a									09 56												
	d									09 58												
Colwall	d									10 04												
Great Malvern	a									10 08												
	d			09 43	09 51					10 10		10 32	10 46	10 51	10 58							
Malvern Link	d			09 46	09 54					10 13		10 35	10 48	10 53	11 01							
Worcester Foregate Street 7	a			09 55	10 02					10 21		10 56	10 56	11 02	11 09							
	d			09 57	10 04	10 16				10 24		10 57	10 57	11 02	11 11							
Worcester Shrub Hill 7	a			09 59	10 06							11 00	11 00	11 06	11 13							
	d		09 56								10 47							11 17				
Droitwich Spa	d		10 04			10 25				10 33	10 55							11 25				
Bromsgrove	d		10 13							10 42												
Barnt Green	d																					
University	d									10 59												
Hartlebury	d																					
Kidderminster	d					10 36		10 56			11 06						11 26	11 36			11 56	
Blakedown	d					10 41					11 11							11 41				
Hagley	d					10 44					11 14							11 44				
Stourbridge Junction 2	d					10 49	10 55	11 09			11 19					11 25	11 39	11 49		11 55	12 09	
Lye	d						10 59									11 29				11 59		
Cradley Heath	d					10 54	11 02	11 14			11 24					11 32	11 44	11 54		12 02	12 14	
Old Hill	d						11 06									11 36				12 06		
Rowley Regis	d					11 00	11 10	11 20			11 30					11 40	11 50	12 00		12 10	12 20	
Langley Green	d						11 13									11 43				12 13		
Birmingham New Street 12	a		10 41							11 11												
	d	10 33							11 03										11 33			12 03
Birmingham International ✈	d								11 14													12 14
Coventry	d								11 25													12 25
Smethwick Galton Bridge 7	d					11 06	11 16	11 26			11 36					11 46	11 56	12 06		12 16	12 26	
The Hawthorns ⇌	d					11 08	11 18	11 28			11 38					11 48	11 58	12 08		12 18	12 28	
Jewellery Quarter ⇌	d					11 12	11 22	11 32			11 42					11 52	12 02	12 12		12 22	12 32	
Birmingham Snow Hill ⇌	a					11 15	11 25	11 35			11 45					11 55	12 05	12 15		12 25	12 35	
	d					11 17	11 27	11 37			11 47					11 57	12 07	12 17		12 27	12 37	
Birmingham Moor Street	d					11 20	11 30	11 40			11 50					12 00	12 10	12 20		12 30	12 40	
Bordesley	d																					
Small Heath	d							11 44									12 14				12 44	
Tyseley	d							11 46									12 16				12 46	
Acocks Green	d					11 25		11 49								12 05		12 25			12 49	
Olton	d					11 28		11 52								12 08		12 28			12 52	
Solihull	d					11 32		11 56								12 12		12 32			12 56	
Widney Manor	d					11 35		11 59								12 15		12 35			12 59	
Dorridge	d					11a41		12a04								12a22		12a41			13a04	
Lapworth	d																					
Hatton	d																					
Warwick Parkway	d																					
Warwick	d																					
Leamington Spa 8	a	10 58							11 36										11 58			12 36
	d	11 00							11 38										12 00			12 38
Banbury	d	11a17							11a54										12a17			12a54
London Marylebone 10 ⊖	a																					
Spring Road	d						11 36				11 56						12 19			12 36		
Hall Green	d						11 39				11 59						12 22			12 39		
Yardley Wood	d						11 42				12 02						12 25			12 42		
Shirley	d						11 45				12 05						12 28			12 45		
Whitlocks End	d						11 48				12a08						12a30			12 48		
Wythall	d						11 50													12 50		
Earlswood (West Midlands)	d						11 53													12 53		
The Lakes	d						11x55													12x55		
Wood End	d						11x57													12x57		
Danzey	d						12x00													13x00		
Henley-in-Arden	d						12 05													13 05		
Wootton Wawen	d						12x08													13x08		
Wilmcote	d						12 13													13 13		
Stratford-upon-Avon	a						12 21													13 21		

A until 10 September **B** from 17 September

Table 71

Hereford, Worcester and Stourbridge - Birmingham - Leamington Spa, Marylebone and Stratford-upon-Avon

		LM	LM	LM	LM	LM	XC	LM	LM	XC	LM	GW	LM	GW	GW	LM	LM	LM	XC	LM	LM	XC	LM
							◇1 工			◇1 工				◇1 A ⊡	◇1 B ⊡				◇1 工			◇1 工	
Hereford 7	d	10 40									11 40			12 13	12 13								12 40
Ledbury	a	10 56									11 56			12 30	12 30								12 56
	d	10 58									11 58			12 31	12 31								12 58
Colwall	d	11 04									12 04			12 39	12 38								13 04
Great Malvern	a	11 08									12 08			12 43	12 43								13 08
	d	11 10	11 35								12 10			12 43	12 44								13 10
Malvern Link	d	11 13	11 37								12 13			12 46	12 48								13 13
Worcester Foregate Street 7	a	11 21	11 45								12 21			12 57	12 58								13 21
	d	11 24	11 46			12 16					12 24	12 40	12 46	12 57	12 59								13 24
Worcester Shrub Hill 7	a											12 42		13 02	13 02								
	d																	13 17					
Droitwich Spa	d	11 33	11 55			12 25					12 33		12 55					13 25					13 33
Bromsgrove	d	11 42									12 42												13 42
Barnt Green	d																						
University	d	11 59									12 59												13 59
Hartlebury	d																						
Kidderminster	d		12 06		12 26	12 36			12 56				13 06				13 26	13 36			13 56		
Blakedown	d		12 11			12 41							13 11					13 41					
Hagley	d		12 14			12 44							13 14					13 44					
Stourbridge Junction 2	d		12 19	12 25	12 39	12 49		12 55	13 09				13 19			13 25	13 39	13 49		13 55	14 09		
Lye	d			12 29				12 59								13 29				13 59			
Cradley Heath	d		12 24	12 32	12 44	12 54		13 02	13 14				13 24			13 32	13 44	13 54		14 02	14 14		
Old Hill	d			12 36				13 06								13 36				14 06			
Rowley Regis	d		12 30	12 40	12 50	13 00		13 10	13 20				13 30			13 40	13 50	14 00		14 10	14 20		
Langley Green	d			12 43				13 13								13 43				14 13			
Birmingham New Street 12	a	12 11									13 11												14 11
	d						12 33			13 03									13 33			14 03	
Birmingham International ✈	d									13 14												14 14	
Coventry	d									13 25												14 25	
Smethwick Galton Bridge 7	d		12 36	12 46	12 56	13 06		13 16	13 26				13 36			13 46	13 56	14 06		14 16	14 26		
The Hawthorns ⇌	d		12 38	12 48	12 58	13 08		13 18	13 28				13 38			13 48	13 58	14 08		14 18	14 28		
Jewellery Quarter ⇌	d		12 42	12 52	13 02	13 12		13 22	13 32				13 42			13 52	14 02	14 12		14 22	14 32		
Birmingham Snow Hill ⇌	a		12 45	12 55	13 05	13 15		13 25	13 35				13 45			13 55	14 05	14 15		14 25	14 35		
	d		12 47	12 57	13 07	13 17		13 27	13 37				13 47			13 57	14 07	14 17		14 27	14 37		
Birmingham Moor Street	d		12 50	13 00	13 10	13 20		13 30	13 40				13 50			14 00	14 10	14 20		14 30	14 40		
Bordesley	d																						
Small Heath	d				13 14				13 44								14 14				14 44		
Tyseley	d				13 16				13 46								14 16				14 46		
Acocks Green	d			13 05		13 25			13 49							14 05		14 25			14 49		
Olton	d			13 08		13 28			13 52							14 08		14 28			14 52		
Solihull	d			13 12		13 32			13 56							14 12		14 32			14 56		
Widney Manor	d			13 15		13 35			13 59							14 15		14 35			14 59		
Dorridge	d			13a21		13a41			14a04							14a22		14a41			15a04		
Lapworth	d																						
Hatton	d																						
Warwick Parkway	d																						
Warwick	d																						
Leamington Spa 8	a						13 00			13 36									13 58			14 36	
	d						13 02			13 38									14 00			14 38	
Banbury	d						13a19			13a54									14a17			14a54	
London Marylebone 10 ⊖	a																						
Spring Road	d		12 56		13 19			13 36					13 56				14 19			14 36			
Hall Green	d		12 59		13 22			13 39					13 59				14 22			14 39			
Yardley Wood	d		13 02		13 25			13 42					14 02				14 25			14 42			
Shirley	d		13 05		13 28			13 45					14 05				14 28			14 45			
Whitlocks End	d		13a08		13a30			13 48					14a08				14a30			14 48			
Wythall	d							13 50												14 50			
Earlswood (West Midlands)	d							13 53												14 53			
The Lakes	d							13x55												14x55			
Wood End	d							13x57												14x57			
Danzey	d							14x00												15x00			
Henley-in-Arden	d							14 05												15 05			
Wootton Wawen	d							14x08												15x08			
Wilmcote	d							14 13												15 13			
Stratford-upon-Avon	a							14 21												15 21			

A until 10 September **B** from 17 September

Hereford, Worcester and Stourbridge - Birmingham - Leamington Spa, Marylebone and Stratford-upon-Avon

		LM	LM	LM	LM	XC ◇1	LM	LM	XC ◇1	LM	LM	GW	LM	LM	LM	XC ◇1	LM	LM	XC ◇1	LM	LM	LM
Hereford 7	d									13 40										14 40		
Ledbury	a									13 56										14 56		
	d									13 58										14 58		
Colwall	d									14 04										15 04		
Great Malvern	a									14 08										15 08		
	d	13 35								14 10		14 51								15 10	15 30	
Malvern Link	d	13 37								14 13		14 53								15 13	15 32	
Worcester Foregate Street 7	a	13 45								14 21		15 02								15 21	15 40	
	d	13 46			14 16					14 24		15 02			15 16					15 24	15 46	
Worcester Shrub Hill 7	a											15 06										
	d										14 43											
Droitwich Spa	d	13 55			14 25					14 33	14 55				15 25					15 33	15 55	
Bromsgrove	d									14 42										15 42		
Barnt Green	d																					
University	d									14 59										15 59		
Hartlebury	d																					
Kidderminster	d	14 06		14 26	14 36			14 56			15 06			15 26	15 36			15 56			16 06	
Blakedown	d	14 11			14 41						15 11			15 31	15 41						16 11	
Hagley	d	14 14			14 44						15 14			15 34	15 44						16 14	
Stourbridge Junction 2	d	14 19	14 25	14 39	14 49		14 55	15 09			15 19		15 25	15 39	15 49		15 55	16 09			16 19	16 25
Lye	d		14 29				14 59						15 29				15 59					16 29
Cradley Heath	d	14 24	14 32	14 44	14 54		15 02	15 14			15 24		15 32	15 44	15 54		16 02	16 14			16 24	16 32
Old Hill	d		14 36				15 06						15 36				16 06					16 36
Rowley Regis	d	14 30	14 40	14 50	15 00		15 10	15 20			15 30		15 40	15 50	16 00		16 10	16 20			16 30	16 40
Langley Green	d		14 43				15 13						15 43				16 13					16 43
Birmingham New Street 12	a									15 11										16 11		
	d					14 33			15 03							15 33			16 03			
Birmingham International ✈	d								15 14										16 14			
Coventry	d								15 25										16 25			
Smethwick Galton Bridge 7	d	14 36	14 46	14 56	15 06		15 16	15 26			15 36		15 46	15 56	16 06		16 16	16 26			16 36	16 46
The Hawthorns 🚊	d	14 38	14 48	14 58	15 08		15 18	15 28			15 38		15 48	15 58	16 08		16 18	16 28			16 38	16 48
Jewellery Quarter 🚊	d	14 42	14 52	15 02	15 12		15 22	15 32			15 42		15 52	16 02	16 12		16 22	16 32			16 42	16 52
Birmingham Snow Hill 🚊	a	14 45	14 55	15 05	15 15		15 25	15 35			15 45		15 55	16 05	16 15		16 25	16 35			16 45	16 55
	d	14 47	14 57	15 07	15 17		15 27	15 37			15 47		15 57	16 07	16 17		16 27	16 37			16 47	16 57
Birmingham Moor Street	d	14 50	15 00	15 10	15 20		15 30	15 40			15 50		16 00	16 10	16 20		16 30	16 40			16 50	17 00
Bordesley	d																					
Small Heath	d			15 14				15 44						16 14				16 44			16 54	
Tyseley	d			15 16				15 46						16 16			16 34	16 46			16 56	17 04
Acocks Green	d		15 05		15 25			15 49					16 05		16 25			16 49				17 07
Olton	d		15 08		15 28			15 52					16 08		16 28			16 52				17 10
Solihull	d		15 12		15 32			15 56					16 12		16 32			16 56				17 14
Widney Manor	d		15 15		15 35			15 59					16 15		16 35			16 59				17 17
Dorridge	d		15a21		15a41			16a04					16a21		16a41			17a04				17a22
Lapworth	d																					
Hatton	d																					
Warwick Parkway	d																					
Warwick	d																					
Leamington Spa 8	a					14 58			15 36							16 00			16 36			
	d					15 00			15 38							16 02			16 38			
Banbury	d					15a19			15a54							16a18			16a54			
London Marylebone 10 ⊖	a																					
Spring Road	d	14 56		15 19			15 36				15 56			16 19			16 37				16 59	
Hall Green	d	14 59		15 22			15 39				15 59			16 22			16 40				17 02	
Yardley Wood	d	15 02		15 25			15 42				16 02			16 25			16 43				17 05	
Shirley	d	15 05		15 28			15 45				16 05			16 28			16 46				17 08	
Whitlocks End	d	15a08		15a30			15 48				16a08			16a30			16 49				17a11	
Wythall	d						15 50										16 51					
Earlswood (West Midlands)	d						15 53										16 54					
The Lakes	d						15x55										16x56					
Wood End	d						15x57										16x58					
Danzey	d						16x00										17x01					
Henley-in-Arden	d						16 05										17 06					
Wootton Wawen	d						16x08										17x09					
Wilmcote	d						16 13										17 14					
Stratford-upon-Avon	a						16 21										17 22					

Hereford, Worcester and Stourbridge - Birmingham - Leamington Spa, Marylebone and Stratford-upon-Avon

		LM	XC ◇1	LM	GW ◇1 A	GW ◇1 B	LM	LM	LM	XC ◇1	LM	LM	GW ◇1 A	GW ◇1 B	GW	LM	LM	LM	XC ◇1	LM	XC ◇1	LM	LM
Hereford 7	d				15 10	15 13					15 40											16 40	
Ledbury	a				15 27	15 30					15 56											16 56	
	d				15 29	15 31					15 58											16 58	
Colwall	d				15 36	15 38					16 04											17 04	
Great Malvern	a				15 41	15 43					16 08											17 08	
	d				15 42	15 44					16 10		16 32	16 34	16 51							17 10	
Malvern Link	d				15 45	15 48					16 13		16 35	16 37	16 53							17 13	
Worcester Foregate Street 7	a				15 56	15 58					16 21		16 56	16 52	17 04							17 21	
	d				15 57	15 59	16 15				16 24		16 57	16 54	17 04							17 24	17 48
Worcester Shrub Hill 7	a				16 00	16 02							17 00	16 56	17 07								
	d			15 54								16 47						17 15					
Droitwich Spa	d			16 03			16 24				16 33	16 55						17 23				17 35	17 57
Bromsgrove	d			16 12							16 42											17 44	
Barnt Green	d																						
University	d										16 59											17 59	
Hartlebury	d						16 31											17 30					
Kidderminster	d	16 26					16 37		16 56			17 06					17 26	17 36					18 07
Blakedown	d	16 31					16 42					17 11					17 31	17 41					18 12
Hagley	d	16 34					16 45					17 14					17 34	17 44					18 16
Stourbridge Junction 2	d	16 39					16 49	16 55	17 09			17 19				17 25	17 39	17 49		17 55			18 20
Lye	d							16 59								17 29				17 59			
Cradley Heath	d	16 44					16 54	17 02	17 14			17 24				17 32	17 44	17 54		18 02			18 25
Old Hill	d							17 06								17 36				18 06			
Rowley Regis	d	16 50					17 00	17 10	17 20			17 30				17 40	17 50	18 00		18 10			18 31
Langley Green	d							17 13								17 43				18 13			
Birmingham New Street 12	a			16 45							17 11											18 11	
	d		16 33							17 03									17 33		18 03		
Birmingham International ✈	d									17 14											18 14		
Coventry	d									17 25											18 25		
Smethwick Galton Bridge 7	d	16 56					17 06	17 16	17 26			17 36				17 46	17 56	18 06		18 16			18 37
The Hawthorns 🚊	d	16 58					17 08	17 18	17 28			17 38				17 48	17 58	18 08		18 18			18 39
Jewellery Quarter 🚊	d	17 02					17 12	17 22	17 32			17 42				17 52	18 02	18 12		18 22			18 43
Birmingham Snow Hill 🚊	a	17 05					17 16	17 25	17 35			17 45				17 55	18 05	18 15		18 25			18 46
	d	17 07					17 17	17 27	17 37			17 47				17 57	18 07	18 17		18 27			18 47
Birmingham Moor Street	d	17 10					17 20	17 30	17 40			17 50				18 00	18 10	18 20		18 30			18 50
Bordesley	d																						
Small Heath	d	17 14							17 44			17 54					18 14	18 24					18 54
Tyseley	d	17 16						17 34	17 46			17 56					18 16	18 26					18 56
Acocks Green	d						17 25		17 49							18 05		18 29					18 59
Olton	d						17 28		17 52							18 08		18 32					19 02
Solihull	d						17 32		17 56							18 12		18 36					19 06
Widney Manor	d						17 35		17 59							18 15		18 39					19 09
Dorridge	d						17a41		18a04							18a22		18a44					19a14
Lapworth	d																						
Hatton	d																						
Warwick Parkway	d																						
Warwick	d																						
Leamington Spa 8	a		16 59							17 36									18 00		18 36		
	d		17 00							17 38									18 02		18 38		
Banbury	d		17a17							17a54									18a18		18a54		
London Marylebone 10 ⊖	a																						
Spring Road	d	17 19						17 37				17 59					18 19			18 36			
Hall Green	d	17 22						17 40				18 02					18 22			18 39			
Yardley Wood	d	17 25						17 43				18 05					18 25			18 42			
Shirley	d	17 28						17 46				18 08					18 28			18 45			
Whitlocks End	d	17 31						17a49				18 11					18a30			18 48			
Wythall	d	17 33										18 13								18 50			
Earlswood (West Midlands)	d	17 36										18 16								18 53			
The Lakes	d	17x38										18x18								18x55			
Wood End	d	17x40										18x20								18x57			
Danzey	d	17x43										18x23								19x00			
Henley-in-Arden	d	17 48										18 28								19 05			
Wootton Wawen	d	17x51										18x30								19x07			
Wilmcote	d	17 56										18 36								19 13			
Stratford-upon-Avon	a	18 03										18 43								19 21			

A until 10 September

B from 17 September

Table 71

Saturdays

Hereford, Worcester and Stourbridge - Birmingham - Leamington Spa, Marylebone and Stratford-upon-Avon

		GW	GW	LM	LM	XC	LM	XC	LM	GW	GW	LM	GW	XC	LM	LM	GW	XC	XC	LM	XC	LM	LM
		◇1	◇1			◇1		◇1		◇1	◇1			◇1			◇1	◇1	◇1		◇1		
		A	B							A	B								B				
Hereford 7	d								17 40							19 11						20 00	
Ledbury	a								17 56							19 27						20 15	
	d								17 58							19 28						20 16	
Colwall	d								18 04							19 34						20 22	
Great Malvern	a								18 08							19 39						20 26	
	d	17 44	17 49		18 00				18 10	18 29	18 35		18 51			19 39						20 28	
Malvern Link	d	17 47	17 52		18 02				18 13	18 32	18 38		18 53			19 42						20 31	
Worcester Foregate Street 7	a	17 56	18 00		18 10				18 21	18 41	18 46		19 03			19 51						20 39	
	d	17 57	18 02		18 11				18 24	18 46	18 48	18 51	19 03			19 51	20 02					20 41	
Worcester Shrub Hill 7	a	18 00	18 04		18 13					18 45	18 50		19 06				20 05						
	d				18 17																		20 52
Droitwich Spa	d				18 25				18 35			19 00				20 00						20 50	21 00
Bromsgrove	d								18 44													20 59	
Barnt Green	d																						
University	d								18 59													21 14	
Hartlebury	d											19 07											
Kidderminster	d				18 36							19 13			19 40	20 10							21 10
Blakedown	d				18 41							19 18			19 45	20 15							21 15
Hagley	d				18 44							19 21			19 49	20 19							21 19
Stourbridge Junction 2	d			18 27	18 49		18 55					19 25			19 55	20 25				20 55			21 25
Lye	d			18 30			18 59					19 29			19 59	20 29				20 59			21 29
Cradley Heath	d			18 33	18 54		19 02					19 32			20 02	20 32				21 02			21 32
Old Hill	d			18 37			19 06					19 36			20 06	20 36				21 06			21 36
Rowley Regis	d			18 41	19 00		19 10					19 40			20 10	20 40				21 10			21 40
Langley Green	d			18 44			19 13					19 43			20 13	20 43				21 13			21 43
Birmingham New Street 12	a								19 11													21 21	
	d					18 33		19 03						19 33				20 03	20 33		21 03		
Birmingham International ✈	d							19 14										20 14			21 14		
Coventry	d							19 25										20 25			21 25		
Smethwick Galton Bridge 7	d			18 47	19 06		19 16					19 46			20 16	20 46				21 16			21 46
The Hawthorns	d			18 50	19 08		19 18					19 48			20 18	20 48				21 18			21 48
Jewellery Quarter	d			18 53	19 12		19 22					19 52			20 22	20 52				21 22			21 52
Birmingham Snow Hill	a			18 56	19 15		19 25					19 55			20 25	20 55				21 25			21 55
	d			18 57	19 17		19 27					19 57			20 27	20 57				21 27			21 57
Birmingham Moor Street	d			19 00	19 20		19 30					20 00			20 30	21 00				21 30			22 00
Bordesley	d																						
Small Heath	d			19 04	19 24		19 34					20 04			20 34	21 04				21 34			22 04
Tyseley	d			19 06	19 26		19 36					20 06			20 36	21 06				21 36			22 06
Acocks Green	d				19 29							20 09				21 09							22 09
Olton	d				19 32							20 12				21 12							22 12
Solihull	d				19 36							20 16				21 16							22 16
Widney Manor	d				19 39							20 19				21 19							22 19
Dorridge	d				19a44							20a24				21a24							22a24
Lapworth	d																						
Hatton	d																						
Warwick Parkway	d																						
Warwick	d																						
Leamington Spa 8	a					18 58		19 36						20 01				20 36	20 58		21 36		
	d					19 00		19 38						20 03				20 38	21 00		21 38		
Banbury	d					19a17		19a54						20a19				20a54	21a19		21a54		
London Marylebone 10 ⊖	a																						
Spring Road	d			19 09			19 39								20 39					21 39			
Hall Green	d			19 12			19 42								20 42					21 42			
Yardley Wood	d			19 15			19 45								20 45					21 45			
Shirley	d			19 18			19 48								20 48					21 48			
Whitlocks End	d			19a21			19 51								20 51					21a50			
Wythall	d						19 53								20 53								
Earlswood (West Midlands)	d						19 56								20 56								
The Lakes	d						19x58								20x58								
Wood End	d						20x00								21x00								
Danzey	d						20x03								21x03								
Henley-in-Arden	d						20 08								21 08								
Wootton Wawen	d						20x10								21x10								
Wilmcote	d						20 16								21 16								
Stratford-upon-Avon	a						20 23								21 23								

A until 10 September

B from 17 September

Table 71

Saturdays

Hereford, Worcester and Stourbridge - Birmingham - Leamington Spa, Marylebone and Stratford-upon-Avon

		GW	GW	GW	LM	LM	LM	LM	LM	GW	LM
		◇1	◇1							1	
		A	B								
Hereford 7	d	20 20	20 20				21 35				22 50
Ledbury	a	20 36	20 36				21 50				23 05
	d	20 40	20 40				21 51				23 06
Colwall	d	20 47	20 48				21 57				23 12
Great Malvern	a	20 52	20 52				22 02				23 16
	d	20 53	20 53	21 15		21 30	22 05			22 41	23 17
Malvern Link	d	20 57	20 57	21 17		21 32	22 08			22 44	23 20
Worcester Foregate Street 7	a	21 09	21 12	21 27		21 41	22 17			22 51	23 27
	d	21 11	21 12	21 27		21 42	22 18			22 53	23 28
Worcester Shrub Hill 7	a	21 14	21 18	21 30		21 44	22 20			22 55	23 34
	d					21 52			22 47		
Droitwich Spa	d					22 00			22 55		
Bromsgrove	d										
Barnt Green	d										
University	d										
Hartlebury	d										
Kidderminster	d					22 10			23 05		
Blakedown	d					22 15			23 10		
Hagley	d					22 19			23 14		
Stourbridge Junction 2	d				21 55	22 25		22 55	23 18		
Lye	d				21 59	22 29		22 59			
Cradley Heath	d				22 02	22 32		23 02			
Old Hill	d				22 06	22 36		23 06			
Rowley Regis	d				22 10	22 40		23 10			
Langley Green	d				22 13	22 43		23 13			
Birmingham New Street 12	a										
	d										
Birmingham International ✈	d										
Coventry	d										
Smethwick Galton Bridge 7	d				22 16	22 46		23 16			
The Hawthorns	d				22 18	22 48		23 18			
Jewellery Quarter	d				22 22	22 52		23 22			
Birmingham Snow Hill	a				22 25	22 55		23 25	23 36		
	d				22 27	22 57		23 27	23 37		
Birmingham Moor Street	d				22 30	23 00		23 30	23 40		
Bordesley	d										
Small Heath	d				22 34	23 04		23 34	23 44		
Tyseley	d				22 36	23 06		23 36	23 46		
Acocks Green	d					23 09			23 49		
Olton	d					23 12			23 52		
Solihull	d					23 16			23 56		
Widney Manor	d					23 19			23 59		
Dorridge	d					23a24			00 03		
Lapworth	d								00 07		
Hatton	d								00 13		
Warwick Parkway	d								00 18		
Warwick	d								00 21		
Leamington Spa 8	a								00 26		
	d										
Banbury	d										
London Marylebone 10 ⊖	a										
Spring Road	d				22 39			23 39			
Hall Green	d				22 42			23 42			
Yardley Wood	d				22 45			23 45			
Shirley	d				22 48			23 48			
Whitlocks End	d				22a50			23a50			
Wythall	d										
Earlswood (West Midlands)	d										
The Lakes	d										
Wood End	d										
Danzey	d										
Henley-in-Arden	d										
Wootton Wawen	d										
Wilmcote	d										
Stratford-upon-Avon	a										

A from 17 September

B until 10 September

Table 71

Sundays until 19 June

Hereford, Worcester and Stourbridge - Birmingham - Leamington Spa, Marylebone and Stratford-upon-Avon

		LM	GW	XC	LM	LM	XC	XC	LM	LM	XC	XC	LM	LM	GW	XC	XC	LM	LM	XC	XC	LM	LM
			◇1	◇1				◇1				◇1			◇1		◇1				◇1		
		A																					
			🛒	🛒			🚌	🛒			🚌	🛒			🛒	🚌	🛒			🚌	🍴		
Hereford 7	d																						
Ledbury	a																						
	d																						
Colwall	d																						
Great Malvern	a																						
	d		09 00							10 02				10 56	11 07				12 04				
Malvern Link	d		09 03							10 04				10 58	11 10				12 06				
Worcester Foregate Street 7	a		09 10							10 12				11 06	11 18				12 15				
	d		09 12							10 16				11 20	11 19				12 16				13 20
Worcester Shrub Hill 7	a		09 14							10 18					11 21				12 18				
	d	22p47				09 21				10 22									12 24				
Droitwich Spa	d	22p55				09 32				10 30				11 29					12 32				13 29
Bromsgrove	d	⌇																					
Barnt Green	d	⌇																					
University	d	⌇																					
Hartlebury	d	⌇																					
Kidderminster	d	23p05				09 42			10 08	10 40				11 39					12 42				13 39
Blakedown	d	23p10				09 47			10 13										12 47				
Hagley	d	23p14				09 51			10 17	10 47				11 46					12 51				13 46
Stourbridge Junction 2	d	23p18				09 55			10 22	10 52			11 22	11 52				12 22	12 55			13 22	13 52
Lye	d	⌇							10 25				11 25					12 25				13 25	
Cradley Heath	d	⌇				10 01			10 29	10 58			11 29	11 58				12 29	13 01			13 29	13 58
Old Hill	d	⌇							10 33				11 33					12 33				13 33	
Rowley Regis	d	⌇				10 06			10 36	11 03			11 36	12 03				12 36	13 06			13 36	14 03
Langley Green	d	⌇							10 39				11 39					12 39				13 39	
Birmingham New Street 12	a	⌇																					
	d	⌇		09 03				10 03				11 03					12 03				13 03		
Birmingham International ✈	d	⌇		09 14				10 14				11 14					12 14				13 14		
Coventry	d	⌇		09 25				10 25				11 25					12 25				13 25		
Smethwick Galton Bridge 7	d	⌇				10 12			10 43	11 09			11 43	12 08				12 43	13 11			13 43	14 08
The Hawthorns	d	⌇				10 15			10 45	11 12			11 45	12 11				12 45	13 14			13 45	14 11
Jewellery Quarter	d	⌇				10 18			10 49	11 15			11 49	12 14				12 49	13 17			13 49	14 14
Birmingham Snow Hill	a	23p36				10 20			10 52	11 17			11 52	12 17				12 52	13 20			13 52	14 17
	d	23p37			09 19	10 22			10 53	11 19			11 53	12 19				12 53	13 22			13 53	14 19
Birmingham Moor Street	d	23p40			09 22	10 25			10 56	11 22			11 56	12 22				12 56	13 25			13 56	14 22
Bordesley	d	⌇																					
Small Heath	d	23p44																					
Tyseley	d	23p46			09 26	10 29				11 26				12 26					13 29				14 26
Acocks Green	d	23p49							11 02				12 02					13 04				14 02	
Olton	d	23p52							11 04				12 04					13 06				14 04	
Solihull	d	23p56							11 08				12 08					13 10				14 08	
Widney Manor	d	23p59							11 11				12 11					13 13				14 11	
Dorridge	d	00 03							11a16				12a16					13a18				14a17	
Lapworth	d	00 07																					
Hatton	d	00 13																					
Warwick Parkway	d	00 18																					
Warwick	d	00 21																					
Leamington Spa 8	a	00 26		09 36				10 35				11 35					12 35				13 36		
	d						09 55				10 55					11 55				12 55			
Banbury	d						10a35				11a35					12a35				13a35			
London Marylebone 10 ⊖	a																						
Spring Road	d				09 29	10 32				11 29				12 29					13 32				14 29
Hall Green	d				09 32	10 35				11 32				12 32					13 35				14 32
Yardley Wood	d				09 35	10 38				11 35				12 35					13 38				14 35
Shirley	d				09 38	10 41				11 38				12 38					13 41				14 38
Whitlocks End	d				09 41	10 44				11 41				12 41					13 44				14 40
Wythall	d				09 43	10 46				11 43				12 43					13 46				14 43
Earlswood (West Midlands)	d																						
The Lakes	d				09x46	10x49				11x46				12x46					13x49				14x46
Wood End	d																						
Danzey	d																						
Henley-in-Arden	d				09 54	10 57				11 54				12 54					13 57				14 54
Wootton Wawen	d																						
Wilmcote	d				10 04	11 05				12 02				13 02					14 05				15 02
Stratford-upon-Avon	a				10 09	11 12				12 09				13 09					14 12				15 07

A not 22 May

Table 71

Sundays until 19 June

Hereford, Worcester and Stourbridge - Birmingham - Leamington Spa, Marylebone and Stratford-upon-Avon

		GW	GW	XC	XC	LM	LM	XC	XC	LM	XC	LM	GW	LM	LM	XC	LM	XC	XC	LM	LM	GW	LM
		◇1	◇1		◇1			◇1	◇1		◇1		◇1			◇1		◇1	◇1			◇1	
			🍴	🚌	🛒			🛒	🛒		🛒		🍴			🛒		🛒	🛒			🍴	
Hereford 7	d		13 28										14 30							15 30		16 33	
Ledbury	a		13 45										14 47							15 47		16 49	
	d		13 46										14 55							15 51		16 50	
Colwall	d		13 53										15 02							15 58		16 58	
Great Malvern	a		13 58										15 07							16 02		17 02	
	d	13 10	13 59									14 35	15 08							16 03		17 03	
Malvern Link	d	13 13	14 03									14 37	15 12							16 05		17 07	
Worcester Foregate Street 7	a	13 22	14 13									14 45	15 21							16 14		17 20	
	d	13 23	14 14				14 20					14 45	15 23	15 21						16 15	16 20	17 22	
Worcester Shrub Hill 7	a	13 27	14 17									14 48	15 26							16 18		17 27	
	d											14 53			15 46					16 33			
Droitwich Spa	d						14 29					15 01		15 30	15 54					16 41	16 29		
Bromsgrove	d											15 10								16 51			
Barnt Green	d																						
University	d																						
Hartlebury	d																						
Kidderminster	d						14 39							15 40	16 04						16 39		
Blakedown	d						14 44																
Hagley	d						14 48							15 47	16 11						16 46		
Stourbridge Junction 2	d					14 22	14 52			15 22				15 52	16 16		16 22				16 52		17 22
Lye	d					14 25				15 25							16 25						17 25
Cradley Heath	d					14 29	14 58			15 29				15 58			16 29				16 58		17 29
Old Hill	d					14 33				15 33							16 33						17 33
Rowley Regis	d					14 36	15 03			15 36				16 03			16 36				17 03		17 36
Langley Green	d					14 39				15 39							16 39						17 39
Birmingham New Street 12	a											15 37								17 17			
	d				14 03			14 33	15 03		15 33					16 03		16 33	17 03				
Birmingham International ✈	d				14 14				15 14							16 14			17 14				
Coventry	d				14 25				15 25							16 25			17 25				
Smethwick Galton Bridge 7	d					14 43	15 08			15 43				16 08	16 29		16 43				17 08		17 43
The Hawthorns	d					14 45	15 11			15 45				16 11			16 45				17 11		17 45
Jewellery Quarter	d					14 49	15 14			15 49				16 14			16 49				17 14		17 49
Birmingham Snow Hill	a					14 52	15 17			15 52				16 17	16 35		16 52				17 17		17 53
	d					14 53	15 19			15 53				16 19	16 45		16 53				17 19		17 53
Birmingham Moor Street	d					14 56	15 22			15 56				16 22	16a47		16 56				17 22		17 56
Bordesley	d																						
Small Heath	d																						
Tyseley	d						15 26							16 26							17 26		
Acocks Green	d					15 02				16 02							17 02						18 02
Olton	d					15 04				16 04							17 04						18 04
Solihull	d					15 08				16 08							17 08						18 08
Widney Manor	d					15 11				16 11							17 11						18 11
Dorridge	d					15a17				16a16							17a17						18a17
Lapworth	d																						
Hatton	d																						
Warwick Parkway	d																						
Warwick	d																						
Leamington Spa 8	a				14 36			14 59	15 36		15 59					16 36		16 59	17 36				
	d			13 45	14 38			15 00	15 38		16 00					16 38		17 00	17 38				
Banbury	d			14a25	14a54			15a18	15a54		16a17					16a54		17a17	17a54				
London Marylebone 10 ⊖	a																						
Spring Road	d						15 29							16 29							17 29		
Hall Green	d						15 32							16 32							17 32		
Yardley Wood	d						15 35							16 35							17 35		
Shirley	d						15 38							16 38							17 38		
Whitlocks End	d						15 41							16 41							17 41		
Wythall	d						15 43							16 43							17 43		
Earlswood (West Midlands)	d																						
The Lakes	d						15x46							16x46							17x46		
Wood End	d																						
Danzey	d																						
Henley-in-Arden	d						15 54							16 55							17 54		
Wootton Wawen	d																						
Wilmcote	d						16 02							17 03							18 02		
Stratford-upon-Avon	a						16 09							17 10							18 09		

Table 71

Sundays
until 19 June

Hereford, Worcester and Stourbridge - Birmingham - Leamington Spa, Marylebone and Stratford-upon-Avon

		LM	XC	XC	LM	LM	GW	GW	XC	XC	XC	LM	XC	XC	LM	GW	LM	XC	LM	GW	LM	LM	LM
			◇1 ⊼	◇1 ⊼			◇1 🍴	◇1 ⊼	◇1 ⊼	◇1 ⊼	◇1 ⊼		◇1 ⊼	◇1 ⊼		◇1		◇1		◇1			
Hereford 7	d							18 30											20 05				22 40
Ledbury	a							18 47											20 21				22 56
	d							18 48											20 22				22 56
Colwall	d							18 55											20 28				23 03
Great Malvern	a							19 00											20 33				23 07
	d				17 17			19 11								20 10			20 33	20 55		22 10	23 08
Malvern Link	d				17 20			19 14								20 11			20 36	20 59		22 13	23 10
Worcester Foregate Street 7	a				17 28			19 23								20 23			20 44	21 08		22 21	23 19
	d	17 20			17 28	18 20	18 25	19 25								20 24			20 45	21 10		22 22	23 22
Worcester Shrub Hill 7	a				17 31		18 26	19 26								20 26			20 47	21 12		22 24	23 24
	d				17 35							19 38			19 53		20 34		20 52		21 25	22 29	
Droitwich Spa	d	17 29			17 43	18 29						19 46			20 01		20 42		21 00		21 33	22 37	
Bromsgrove	d				17 52										20 10				21 09				
Barnt Green	d																						
University	d																						
Hartlebury	d																						
Kidderminster	d	17 39				18 39						19 56					20 52				21 43	22 47	
Blakedown	d	17 44																					
Hagley	d	17 48				18 46						20 03					20 59				21 50	22 54	
Stourbridge Junction 2	d	17 52				18 52						20 07					21 03				21 54	22 58	
Lye	d																						
Cradley Heath	d	17 58				18 58						20 13					21 08				21 59	23 04	
Old Hill	d																						
Rowley Regis	d	18 03				19 03						20 19					21 14				22 05	23 09	
Langley Green	d																						
Birmingham New Street 12	a				18 14										20 36				21 42				
	d		17 33	18 03					18 33	19 03	19 33		20 03	20 33				21 03					
Birmingham International ✈	d			18 14						19 14			20 14					21 14					
Coventry	d			18 25						19 25			20 25					21 24					
Smethwick Galton Bridge 7	d	18 08				19 08						20 24					21 19				22 10	23 14	
The Hawthorns 🚋	d	18 11				19 11						20 26					21 21				22 12	23 17	
Jewellery Quarter 🚋	d	18 14				19 14						20 30					21 25				22 16	23 20	
Birmingham Snow Hill 🚋	a	18 17				19 19						20 33					21 28				22 19	23 24	
	d	18 19				19 21						20 33					21 28				22 20		
Birmingham Moor Street	d	18 22				19a23						20a36					21a31				22a22		
Bordesley	d																						
Small Heath	d																						
Tyseley	d	18 26																					
Acocks Green	d																						
Olton	d																						
Solihull	d																						
Widney Manor	d																						
Dorridge	d																						
Lapworth	d																						
Hatton	d																						
Warwick Parkway	d																						
Warwick	d																						
Leamington Spa 8	a		18 00	18 36					18 59	19 36	19 59		20 36	20 58				21 34					
	d		18 01	18 38					19 00	19 38	20 00		20 38	21 00									
Banbury	d		18a19	18a54					19a17	19a54	20a18		20a54	21a17									
London Marylebone 10 ⊖	a																						
Spring Road	d	18 29																					
Hall Green	d	18 32																					
Yardley Wood	d	18 35																					
Shirley	d	18 38																					
Whitlocks End	d	18 41																					
Wythall	d	18 43																					
Earlswood (West Midlands)	d																						
The Lakes	d	18x46																					
Wood End	d																						
Danzey	d																						
Henley-in-Arden	d	18 54																					
Wootton Wawen	d																						
Wilmcote	d	19 02																					
Stratford-upon-Avon	a	19 09																					

Table 71

Sundays
26 June to 31 July

Hereford, Worcester and Stourbridge - Birmingham - Leamington Spa, Marylebone and Stratford-upon-Avon

		LM	XC	LM	LM	XC	LM	LM	LM	XC	LM	LM	GW	LM	XC	LM	LM	GW	XC	LM	LM	XC	LM
			◇1 ⊼		🚌	◇1 ⊼		🚌		◇1 ⊼		🚌	◇1 ⊼	🚌	◇1 ⊼		🚌	◇1 ⊼	◇1 ⊼		🚌	◇1 ⊼	
Hereford 7	d																						
Ledbury	a																						
	d																						
Colwall	d																						
Great Malvern	a																						
	d											08 20	09 00				09 20	11 07					
Malvern Link	d											08 31	09 03				09 31	11 10					
Worcester Foregate Street 7	a											08 51	09 10				09 51	11 18					
	d											08 52	09 12				09 52	11 19					
Worcester Shrub Hill 7	a											09 02	09 14				10 02	11 21					
	d	22p47			08 05							09 06					10 06						
Droitwich Spa	d	22p55			08 28							09 29					10 29						
Bromsgrove	d																						
Barnt Green	d																						
University	d																						
Hartlebury	d																						
Kidderminster	d	23p05			08 54			09 03				09 55					10 55						
Blakedown	d	23p10			09 03			09 11															
Hagley	d	23p14			09 11			09 19				10 11					11 11						
Stourbridge Junction 2	d	23p18			09 22			09 30				10 22		10 30			11 22				11 30		
Lye	d							09 36						10 36							11 36		
Cradley Heath	d				09 33			09 44				10 33		10 44			11 33				11 44		
Old Hill	d							09 52						10 52							11 52		
Rowley Regis	d				09 42			10 01				10 42		11 01			11 42				12 01		
Langley Green	d							10 11						11 11							12 11		
Birmingham New Street 12	a																						
	d		09 03			10 03				11 03					11 33				12 03			12 33	
Birmingham International ✈	d		09 14			10 14				11 14									12 14				
Coventry	d		09 25			10 25				11 25									12 25				
Smethwick Galton Bridge 7	d				09 55			10 20				10 55		11 20			11 55				12 20		
The Hawthorns 🚋	d				10 01			10 25				11 01		11 25			12 01				12 25		
Jewellery Quarter 🚋	d				10 11			10 34				11 11		11 34			12 11				12 34		
Birmingham Snow Hill 🚋	a	23p36			10 20			10 43				11 20		11 43			12 20				12 43		
	d	23p37		09 19			10 22		10 53		11 19					11 53				12 28			12 53
Birmingham Moor Street	d	23p40		09 22			10 25		10 56		11 22					11 56				12 31			12 56
Bordesley	d																						
Small Heath	d	23p44																					
Tyseley	d	23p46		09 26			10 29				11 26									12 35			
Acocks Green	d	23p49							11 02							12 02							13 04
Olton	d	23p52							11 04							12 04							13 06
Solihull	d	23p56							11 08							12 08							13 10
Widney Manor	d	23p59							11 11							12 11							13 13
Dorridge	d	00 03							11a16							12a16							13a18
Lapworth	d	00 07																					
Hatton	d	00 13																					
Warwick Parkway	d	00 18																					
Warwick	d	00 21																					
Leamington Spa 8	a	00 26	09 36			10 36				11 36					11 59				12 36			12 59	
	d		09 38			10 38				11 38					12 00				12 38			13 00	
Banbury	d		09a54			10a54				11a54					12a17				12a54			13a17	
London Marylebone 10 ⊖	a																						
Spring Road	d			09 29			10 32				11 29									12 38			
Hall Green	d			09 32			10 35				11 32									12 41			
Yardley Wood	d			09 35			10 38				11 35									12 44			
Shirley	d			09 38			10 41				11 38									12 47			
Whitlocks End	d			09 41			10 44				11 41									12 50			
Wythall	d			09 43			10 46				11 43									12 52			
Earlswood (West Midlands)	d																						
The Lakes	d			09x46			10x49				11x46									12x55			
Wood End	d																						
Danzey	d																						
Henley-in-Arden	d			09 54			10 57				11 54									13 03			
Wootton Wawen	d																						
Wilmcote	d			10 04			11 05				12 02									13 11			
Stratford-upon-Avon	a			10 09			11 12				12 09									13 18			

Table 71

Sundays
26 June to 31 July

Hereford, Worcester and Stourbridge - Birmingham - Leamington Spa, Marylebone and Stratford-upon-Avon

		LM	XC	LM	LM	LM		GW	XC	LM	LM	XC	LM	LM	LM	GW		XC	LM	LM	XC	LM	LM	XC	LM
			◇1					◇1	◇1			◇1				◇1		◇1			◇1			◇1	
Hereford 7	d															13 28									
Ledbury	a															13 45									
	d															13 46									
Colwall	d															13 53									
Great Malvern	a															13 58									
	d							13 10								13 59									14 35
Malvern Link	d							13 13								14 03									14 37
Worcester Foregate Street 7	a							13 22								14 13									14 45
	d					12 28		13 23							13 46	14 14									14 45
Worcester Shrub Hill 7	a							13 27								14 17									14 48
	d																								14 53
Droitwich Spa	d	11 33				12 37									13 55										15 01
Bromsgrove	d																								15 10
Barnt Green	d																								
University	d																								
Hartlebury	d																								
Kidderminster	d	11 59				12 47									14 05										
Blakedown	d	12 07				12 52									14 10										
Hagley	d	12 14				12 56									14 14										
Stourbridge Junction 2	d	12 25			12 30	13a00					13 20			13 30	14a17					14 22			14 30		
Lye	d				12 36									13 36									14 36		
Cradley Heath	d	12 36			12 44						13 31			13 44						14 33			14 44		
Old Hill	d				12 52									13 52									14 52		
Rowley Regis	d	12 45			13 01						13 40			14 01						14 42			15 01		
Langley Green	d				13 11									14 11									15 11		
Birmingham New Street 12	a																								15 37
	d		13 03						13 33			14 03						14 33			15 03			15 33	
Birmingham International ✈	d		13 14									14 14									15 14				
Coventry	d		13 25									14 25									15 25				
Smethwick Galton Bridge 7	d	12 58			13 20						13 53			14 20						14 55			15 20		
The Hawthorns	d	13 03			13 25						13 59			14 25						15 01			15 25		
Jewellery Quarter	d	13 12			13 34						14 09			14 34						15 11			15 34		
Birmingham Snow Hill	a	13 21			13 43						14 18			14 43						15 20			15 43		
	d			13 28						13 53			14 28						14 53			15 28			
Birmingham Moor Street	d			13 31						13 56			14 31						14 56			15 31			
Bordesley	d																								
Small Heath	d																								
Tyseley	d			13 35									14 35									15 35			
Acocks Green	d									14 02									15 02						
Olton	d									14 04									15 04						
Solihull	d									14 08									15 08						
Widney Manor	d									14 11									15 11						
Dorridge	d									14a17									15a17						
Lapworth	d																								
Hatton	d																								
Warwick Parkway	d																								
Warwick	d																								
Leamington Spa 8	a		13 36						13 59			14 36						14 59			15 36			15 59	
	d		13 38						14 00			14 38						15 00			15 38			16 00	
Banbury	d		13a54						14a17			14a54						15a18			15a54			16a17	
London Marylebone 10 ⊖	a																								
Spring Road	d			13 38									14 38									15 38			
Hall Green	d			13 41									14 41									15 41			
Yardley Wood	d			13 44									14 44									15 44			
Shirley	d			13 47									14 47									15 47			
Whitlocks End	d			13 50									14 49									15 50			
Wythall	d			13 52									14 52									15 52			
Earlswood (West Midlands)	d																								
The Lakes	d			13x55									14x55									15x55			
Wood End	d																								
Danzey	d																								
Henley-in-Arden	d			14 03									15 02									16 03			
Wootton Wawen	d																								
Wilmcote	d			14 11									15 10									16 11			
Stratford-upon-Avon	a			14 18									15 16									16 18			

Table 71

Sundays
26 June to 31 July

Hereford, Worcester and Stourbridge - Birmingham - Leamington Spa, Marylebone and Stratford-upon-Avon

		LM		LM	LM	LM	GW	LM	XC	LM	LM	XC		XC	LM	LM	GW	LM	LM	XC	XC	LM		LM	GW
							◇1		◇1			◇1		◇1			◇1			◇1	◇1				◇1
Hereford 7	d						14 30								15 30		16 33								
Ledbury	a						14 47								15 47		16 49								
	d						14 55								15 51		16 50								
Colwall	d						15 02								15 58		16 58								
Great Malvern	a						15 07								16 02		17 02								
	d						15 08								16 03		17 03					17 17			
Malvern Link	d						15 12								16 05		17 07					17 20			
Worcester Foregate Street 7	a						15 21								16 14		17 20					17 28			
	d					15 05	15 23								16 15	16 20	17 22		17 20			17 28		18 20	18 25
Worcester Shrub Hill 7	a						15 26								16 18		17 27					17 31			18 26
	d										16 00				16 33							17 35			
Droitwich Spa	d					15 14					16 08				16 41	16 29			17 29			17 43		18 29	
Bromsgrove	d														16 51							17 52			
Barnt Green	d																								
University	d																								
Hartlebury	d																								
Kidderminster	d					15 24					16 18					16 39			17 39					18 39	
Blakedown	d																		17 44						
Hagley	d					15 31					16 25					16 46			17 48					18 46	
Stourbridge Junction 2	d			15 15	15 30	15a34		15 39			16 31					16 52		17 22	17 52					18 52	
Lye	d																	17 25							
Cradley Heath	d			15 26	15 44						16 37					16 58		17 29	17 58					18 58	
Old Hill	d																	17 33							
Rowley Regis	d			15 35	16 01						16 42					17 03		17 36	18 03					19 03	
Langley Green	d																	17 39							
Birmingham New Street 12	a														17 17							18 14			
	d								16 03			16 33		17 03						17 33	18 03				
Birmingham International ✈	d								16 14					17 14							18 14				
Coventry	d								16 25					17 25							18 25				
Smethwick Galton Bridge 7	d			15 48							16 47					17 08		17 43	18 08					19 08	
The Hawthorns	d			15 54	16 25						16 50					17 11		17 45	18 11					19 11	
Jewellery Quarter	d			16 04	16 34						16 53					17 14		17 49	18 14					19 14	
Birmingham Snow Hill	a			16 13	16 43			16 14			16 55					17 17		17 53	18 17					19 19	
	d	15 53								16 19	16 57					17 19		17 53	18 19					19 21	
Birmingham Moor Street	d	15 56								16 22	17 00					17 22		17 56	18 22					19a23	
Bordesley	d																								
Small Heath	d																								
Tyseley	d									16 26						17 26			18 26						
Acocks Green	d	16 02									17 08							18 02							
Olton	d	16 04									17 10							18 04							
Solihull	d	16 08									17 14							18 08							
Widney Manor	d	16 11									17 17							18 11							
Dorridge	d	16a16									17a23							18a17							
Lapworth	d																								
Hatton	d																								
Warwick Parkway	d																								
Warwick	d																								
Leamington Spa 8	a								16 36			16 59		17 36						18 00	18 36				
	d								16 38			17 00		17 38						18 01	18 38				
Banbury	d								16a54			17a17		17a54						18a19	18a54				
London Marylebone 10 ⊖	a																								
Spring Road	d									16 29						17 29			18 29						
Hall Green	d									16 32						17 32			18 32						
Yardley Wood	d									16 35						17 35			18 35						
Shirley	d									16 38						17 38			18 38						
Whitlocks End	d									16 41						17 41			18 41						
Wythall	d									16 43						17 43			18 43						
Earlswood (West Midlands)	d																								
The Lakes	d									16x46						17x46			18x46						
Wood End	d																								
Danzey	d																								
Henley-in-Arden	d									16 55						17 54			18 54						
Wootton Wawen	d																								
Wilmcote	d									17 03						18 02			19 02						
Stratford-upon-Avon	a									17 10						18 09			19 09						

Table 71

Sundays
26 June to 31 July

Hereford, Worcester and Stourbridge - Birmingham - Leamington Spa, Marylebone and Stratford-upon-Avon

		GW	XC	XC	XC	LM	XC	XC		LM	GW	LM	XC	LM	GW	LM	LM	LM
		◇1 ⌶	◇1 ⌶	◇1 ⌶	◇1 ⌶		◇1 ⌶	◇1 ⌶			◇1		◇1		◇1			
Hereford 7	d	18 30												20 05				22 40
Ledbury	a	18 47												20 21				22 56
	d	18 48												20 22				22 56
Colwall	d	18 55												20 28				23 03
Great Malvern	a	19 00												20 33				23 07
	d	19 11									20 10			20 33	20 55		22 10	23 08
Malvern Link	d	19 14									20 11			20 36	20 59		22 13	23 10
Worcester Foregate Street 7	a	19 23									20 23			20 44	21 08		22 21	23 19
	d	19 25									20 24			20 45	21 10		22 22	23 22
Worcester Shrub Hill 7	a	19 26									20 26			20 47	21 12		22 24	23 24
	d					19 38				19 53		20 34		20 52		21 25	22 29	
Droitwich Spa	d					19 46				20 01		20 42		21 00		21 33	22 37	
Bromsgrove	d									20 10				21 09				
Barnt Green	d																	
University	d																	
Hartlebury	d																	
Kidderminster	d					19 56						20 52				21 43	22 47	
Blakedown	d																	
Hagley	d					20 03						20 59				21 50	22 54	
Stourbridge Junction 2	d					20 07						21 03				21 54	22 58	
Lye	d																	
Cradley Heath	d					20 13						21 08				21 59	23 04	
Old Hill	d																	
Rowley Regis	d					20 19						21 14				22 05	23 09	
Langley Green	d																	
Birmingham New Street 12	a									20 36				21 42				
	d		18 33	19 03	19 33		20 03	20 33					21 03					
Birmingham International ✈	d			19 14			20 14						21 14					
Coventry	d			19 25			20 25						21 24					
Smethwick Galton Bridge 7	d					20 24						21 19				22 10	23 14	
The Hawthorns 🚊	d					20 26						21 21				22 12	23 17	
Jewellery Quarter 🚊	d					20 30						21 25				22 16	23 20	
Birmingham Snow Hill 🚊	a					20 33						21 28				22 19	23 24	
	d					20 33						21 28				22 20		
Birmingham Moor Street	d					20a36						21a31				22a22		
Bordesley	d																	
Small Heath	d																	
Tyseley	d																	
Acocks Green	d																	
Olton	d																	
Solihull	d																	
Widney Manor	d																	
Dorridge	d																	
Lapworth	d																	
Hatton	d																	
Warwick Parkway	d																	
Warwick	d																	
Leamington Spa 8	a		18 59	19 36	19 59		20 36	20 58					21 34					
	d		19 00	19 38	20 00		20 38	21 00										
Banbury	d		19a17	19a54	20a18		20a54	21a17										
London Marylebone 10 ⊖	a																	
Spring Road	d																	
Hall Green	d																	
Yardley Wood	d																	
Shirley	d																	
Whitlocks End	d																	
Wythall	d																	
Earlswood (West Midlands)	d																	
The Lakes	d																	
Wood End	d																	
Danzey	d																	
Henley-in-Arden	d																	
Wootton Wawen	d																	
Wilmcote	d																	
Stratford-upon-Avon	a																	

Table 71

Sundays
7 August to 11 September

Hereford, Worcester and Stourbridge - Birmingham - Leamington Spa, Marylebone and Stratford-upon-Avon

		LM	GW	LM	LM	LM	LM	LM	LM	GW		LM	LM	LM	LM	GW	GW	XC	XC	XC		LM	LM	XC	XC
			◇1 ⌶							◇1 ⌶						◇1	◇1 ☕	🚌	🚌	◇1 ⌶				◇1 ⌶	◇1 ⌶
Hereford 7	d																13 28								
Ledbury	a																13 45								
	d																13 46								
Colwall	d																13 53								
Great Malvern	a																13 58								
	d		09 00				10 02		10 56	11 07			12 04			13 10	13 59								
Malvern Link	d		09 03				10 04		10 58	11 10			12 06			13 13	14 03								
Worcester Foregate Street 7	a		09 10				10 12		11 06	11 18			12 15			13 22	14 13								
	d		09 12				10 16		11 20	11 19			12 16		13 20	13 23	14 14						14 20		
Worcester Shrub Hill 7	a		09 14				10 18			11 21			12 18			13 27	14 17								
	d	22p47			09 21		10 22						12 24												
Droitwich Spa	d	22p55			09 32		10 30		11 29				12 32		13 29								14 29		
Bromsgrove	d																								
Barnt Green	d																								
University	d																								
Hartlebury	d																								
Kidderminster	d	23p05			09 42	10 08	10 40		11 39				12 42		13 39								14 39		
Blakedown	d	23p10			09 47	10 13							12 47										14 44		
Hagley	d	23p14			09 51	10 17	10 47		11 46				12 51		13 46								14 48		
Stourbridge Junction 2	d	23p18			09 55	10 22	10 52	11 22	11 52			12 22	12 55	13 22	13 52							14 22	14 52		
Lye	d					10 25		11 25				12 25		13 25								14 25			
Cradley Heath	d				10 01	10 29	10 58	11 29	11 58			12 29	13 01	13 29	13 58							14 29	14 58		
Old Hill	d					10 33		11 33				12 33		13 33								14 33			
Rowley Regis	d				10 06	10 36	11 03	11 36	12 03			12 36	13 06	13 36	14 03							14 36	15 03		
Langley Green	d					10 39		11 39				12 39		13 39								14 39			
Birmingham New Street 12	a																								
	d																			14 03				14 33	15 03
Birmingham International ✈	d																			14 14					15 14
Coventry	d																	13 35	13 35	14 25					15 25
Smethwick Galton Bridge 7	d				10 12	10 43	11 09	11 43	12 08			12 43	13 11	13 43	14 08							14 43	15 08		
The Hawthorns 🚊	d				10 15	10 45	11 12	11 45	12 11			12 45	13 14	13 45	14 11							14 45	15 11		
Jewellery Quarter 🚊	d				10 18	10 49	11 15	11 49	12 14			12 49	13 17	13 49	14 14							14 49	15 14		
Birmingham Snow Hill 🚊	a	23p36			10 20	10 52	11 17	11 52	12 17			12 52	13 20	13 52	14 17							14 52	15 17		
	d	23p37		09 19	10 22	10 53	11 19	11 53	12 19			12 53	13 22	13 53	14 19							14 53	15 19		
Birmingham Moor Street	d	23p40		09 22	10 25	10 56	11 22	11 56	12 22			12 56	13 25	13 56	14 22							14 56	15 22		
Bordesley	d																								
Small Heath	d	23p44																							
Tyseley	d	23p46		09 26	10 29		11 26		12 26				13 29		14 26								15 26		
Acocks Green	d	23p49				11 02		12 02				13 04		14 02								15 02			
Olton	d	23p52				11 04		12 04				13 06		14 04								15 04			
Solihull	d	23p56				11 08		12 08				13 10		14 08								15 08			
Widney Manor	d	23p59				11 11		12 11				13 13		14 11								15 11			
Dorridge	d	00 03				11a16		12a16				13a18		14a17								15a17			
Lapworth	d	00 07																							
Hatton	d	00 13																							
Warwick Parkway	d	00 18																							
Warwick	d	00 21																							
Leamington Spa 8	a	00 26																14 00	14 00	14 36				14 59	15 36
	d																		14 00	14 38				15 00	15 38
Banbury	d																		14a40	14a54				15a18	15a54
London Marylebone 10 ⊖	a																								
Spring Road	d			09 29	10 32		11 29		12 29				13 32		14 29								15 29		
Hall Green	d			09 32	10 35		11 32		12 32				13 35		14 32								15 32		
Yardley Wood	d			09 35	10 38		11 35		12 35				13 38		14 35								15 35		
Shirley	d			09 38	10 41		11 38		12 38				13 41		14 38								15 38		
Whitlocks End	d			09 41	10 44		11 41		12 41				13 44		14 40								15 41		
Wythall	d			09 43	10 46		11 43		12 43				13 46		14 43								15 43		
Earlswood (West Midlands)	d																								
The Lakes	d			09x46	10x49		11x46		12x46				13x49		14x46								15x46		
Wood End	d																								
Danzey	d																								
Henley-in-Arden	d			09 54	10 57		11 54		12 54				13 57		14 54								15 54		
Wootton Wawen	d																								
Wilmcote	d			10 04	11 05		12 02		13 02				14 05		15 02								16 02		
Stratford-upon-Avon	a			10 09	11 12		12 09		13 09				14 12		15 07								16 09		

Table 71

Hereford, Worcester and Stourbridge - Birmingham - Leamington Spa, Marylebone and Stratford-upon-Avon

		LM	XC	LM	GW	LM	LM	XC	LM	XC	XC	LM	LM	GW	LM	LM	XC	XC	LM	LM	GW	GW	XC
			◇1		◇1			◇1		◇1	◇1			◇1			◇1	◇1			◇1	◇1	◇1
Hereford 7	d				14 30							15 30		16 33								18 30	
Ledbury	a				14 47							15 47		16 49								18 47	
	d				14 55							15 51		16 50								18 48	
Colwall	d				15 02							15 58		16 58								18 55	
Great Malvern	a				15 07							16 02		17 02								19 00	
	d			14 35	15 08							16 03		17 03					17 17			19 11	
Malvern Link	d			14 37	15 12							16 05		17 07					17 20			19 14	
Worcester Foregate Street 7	a			14 45	15 21							16 14		17 20					17 28			19 23	
	d			14 45	15 23	15 21						16 15	16 20	17 22		17 20			17 28	18 20	18 25	19 25	
Worcester Shrub Hill 7	a			14 48	15 26							16 18		17 27					17 31		18 26	19 26	
	d			14 53			15 46					16 33							17 35				
Droitwich Spa	d			15 01		15 30	15 54					16 41	16 29			17 29			17 43	18 29			
Bromsgrove	d			15 10								16 51							17 52				
Barnt Green	d																						
University	d																						
Hartlebury	d																						
Kidderminster	d					15 40	16 04						16 39			17 39				18 39			
Blakedown	d															17 44							
Hagley	d					15 47	16 11						16 46			17 48				18 46			
Stourbridge Junction 2	d	15 22				15 52	16 16		16 22				16 52		17 22	17 52				18 52			
Lye	d	15 25							16 25						17 25								
Cradley Heath	d	15 29				15 58			16 29				16 58		17 29	17 58				18 58			
Old Hill	d	15 33							16 33						17 33								
Rowley Regis	d	15 36				16 03			16 36				17 03		17 36	18 03				19 03			
Langley Green	d	15 39							16 39						17 39								
Birmingham New Street 12	a			15 37								17 17							18 14				
	d		15 33					16 03		16 33	17 03						17 33	18 03					18 33
Birmingham International ✈	d							16 14			17 14							18 14					
Coventry	d							16 25			17 25							18 25					
Smethwick Galton Bridge 7	d	15 43				16 08	16 29		16 43				17 08		17 43	18 08				19 08			
The Hawthorns	d	15 45				16 11			16 45				17 11		17 45	18 11				19 11			
Jewellery Quarter	d	15 49				16 14			16 49				17 14		17 49	18 14				19 14			
Birmingham Snow Hill	a	15 52				16 17	16 35		16 52				17 17		17 53	18 17				19 19			
	d	15 53				16 19	16 45		16 53				17 19		17 53	18 19				19 21			
Birmingham Moor Street	d	15 56				16 22	16a47		16 56				17 22		17 56	18 22				19a23			
Bordesley	d																						
Small Heath	d																						
Tyseley	d					16 26							17 26			18 26							
Acocks Green	d	16 02							17 02						18 02								
Olton	d	16 04							17 04						18 04								
Solihull	d	16 08							17 08						18 08								
Widney Manor	d	16 11							17 11						18 11								
Dorridge	d	16a16							17a17						18a17								
Lapworth	d																						
Hatton	d																						
Warwick Parkway	d																						
Warwick	d																						
Leamington Spa 8	a		15 59					16 36		16 59	17 36						18 00	18 36					18 59
	d		16 00					16 38		17 00	17 38						18 01	18 38					19 00
Banbury	d		16a17					16a54		17a17	17a54						18a19	18a54					19a17
London Marylebone 10 ⊖	a																						
Spring Road	d					16 29							17 29			18 29							
Hall Green	d					16 32							17 32			18 32							
Yardley Wood	d					16 35							17 35			18 35							
Shirley	d					16 38							17 38			18 38							
Whitlocks End	d					16 41							17 41			18 41							
Wythall	d					16 43							17 43			18 43							
Earlswood (West Midlands)	d																						
The Lakes	d					16x46							17x46			18x46							
Wood End	d																						
Danzey	d																						
Henley-in-Arden	d					16 55							17 54			18 54							
Wootton Wawen	d																						
Wilmcote	d					17 03							18 02			19 02							
Stratford-upon-Avon	a					17 10							18 09			19 09							

Table 71

Hereford, Worcester and Stourbridge - Birmingham - Leamington Spa, Marylebone and Stratford-upon-Avon

		XC	XC	LM	XC	XC	LM	GW	LM	XC	LM	GW	LM	LM	LM
		◇1	◇1		◇1	◇1		◇1		◇1		◇1			
Hereford 7	d										20 05				22 40
Ledbury	a										20 21				22 56
	d										20 22				22 56
Colwall	d										20 28				23 03
Great Malvern	a										20 33				23 07
	d							20 10			20 33	20 55		22 10	23 08
Malvern Link	d							20 11			20 36	20 59		22 13	23 10
Worcester Foregate Street 7	a							20 23			20 44	21 08		22 21	23 19
	d							20 24			20 45	21 10		22 22	23 22
Worcester Shrub Hill 7	a							20 26			20 47	21 12		22 24	23 24
	d			19 38			19 53		20 34		20 52		21 25	22 29	
Droitwich Spa	d			19 46			20 01		20 42		21 00		21 33	22 37	
Bromsgrove	d						20 10				21 09				
Barnt Green	d														
University	d														
Hartlebury	d														
Kidderminster	d			19 56					20 52				21 43	22 47	
Blakedown	d														
Hagley	d			20 03					20 59				21 50	22 54	
Stourbridge Junction 2	d			20 07					21 03				21 54	22 58	
Lye	d														
Cradley Heath	d			20 13					21 08				21 59	23 04	
Old Hill	d														
Rowley Regis	d			20 19					21 14				22 05	23 09	
Langley Green	d														
Birmingham New Street 12	a						20 36				21 42				
	d	19 03	19 33		20 03	20 33				21 03					
Birmingham International ✈	d	19 14			20 14					21 14					
Coventry	d	19 25			20 25					21 24					
Smethwick Galton Bridge 7	d			20 24					21 19				22 10	23 14	
The Hawthorns	d			20 26					21 21				22 12	23 17	
Jewellery Quarter	d			20 30					21 25				22 16	23 20	
Birmingham Snow Hill	a			20 33					21 28				22 19	23 24	
	d			20 33					21 28				22 20		
Birmingham Moor Street	d			20a36					21a31				22a22		
Bordesley	d														
Small Heath	d														
Tyseley	d														
Acocks Green	d														
Olton	d														
Solihull	d														
Widney Manor	d														
Dorridge	d														
Lapworth	d														
Hatton	d														
Warwick Parkway	d														
Warwick	d														
Leamington Spa 8	a	19 36	19 59		20 36	20 58				21 34					
	d	19 38	20 00		20 38	21 00									
Banbury	d	19a54	20a18		20a54	21a17									
London Marylebone 10 ⊖	a														
Spring Road	d														
Hall Green	d														
Yardley Wood	d														
Shirley	d														
Whitlocks End	d														
Wythall	d														
Earlswood (West Midlands)	d														
The Lakes	d														
Wood End	d														
Danzey	d														
Henley-in-Arden	d														
Wootton Wawen	d														
Wilmcote	d														
Stratford-upon-Avon	a														

Table 71

Hereford, Worcester and Stourbridge - Birmingham - Leamington Spa, Marylebone and Stratford-upon-Avon

		LM	GW	XC	LM	LM	XC	XC	LM	LM	XC	XC	LM	LM	GW	XC	XC	LM	LM	XC	XC	LM	LM
			◇1	◇1			🚌	◇1			🚌	◇1			◇1	🚌	◇1			🚌	◇1		
			🍴	🍴				☕				☕			🍴		☕				☕		
Hereford 7	d																						
Ledbury	a																						
	d																						
Colwall	d																						
Great Malvern	a																						
	d		09 00							10 02				10 56	11 07				12 04				
Malvern Link	d		09 03							10 04				10 58	11 10				12 06				
Worcester Foregate Street 7	a		09 11							10 12				11 06	11 18				12 15				
	d		09 13							10 16				11 20	11 19				12 16				13 20
Worcester Shrub Hill 7	a		09 15							10 18					11 21				12 18				
	d	22p47				09 21				10 22									12 24				
Droitwich Spa	d	22p55				09 32				10 30				11 29					12 32				13 29
Bromsgrove	d																						
Barnt Green	d																						
University	d																						
Hartlebury	d																						
Kidderminster	d	23p05				09 42			10 08	10 40				11 39					12 42				13 39
Blakedown	d	23p10				09 47			10 13										12 47				
Hagley	d	23p14				09 51			10 17	10 47				11 46					12 51				13 46
Stourbridge Junction 2	d	23p18				09 55			10 22	10 52			11 22	11 52				12 22	12 55			13 22	13 52
Lye	d								10 25				11 25					12 25				13 25	
Cradley Heath	d					10 01			10 29	10 58			11 29	11 58				12 29	13 01			13 29	13 58
Old Hill	d								10 33				11 33					12 33				13 33	
Rowley Regis	d					10 06			10 36	11 03			11 36	12 03				12 36	13 06			13 36	14 03
Langley Green	d								10 39				11 39					12 39				13 39	
Birmingham New Street 12	a																						
	d			09 03				10 03				11 03					12 03				13 03		
Birmingham International ✈	d			09 14				10 14				11 14					12 14				13 14		
Coventry	d			09 25				10 25				11 25					12 25				13 25		
Smethwick Galton Bridge 7	d					10 12			10 43	11 09			11 43	12 08				12 43	13 11			13 43	14 08
The Hawthorns 🚋	d					10 15			10 45	11 12			11 45	12 11				12 45	13 14			13 45	14 11
Jewellery Quarter 🚋	d					10 18			10 49	11 15			11 49	12 14				12 49	13 17			13 49	14 14
Birmingham Snow Hill 🚋	a	23p36				10 20			10 52	11 17			11 52	12 17				12 52	13 20			13 52	14 17
	d	23p37			09 19	10 22			10 53	11 19			11 53	12 19				12 53	13 22			13 53	14 19
Birmingham Moor Street	d	23p40			09 22	10 25			10 56	11 22			11 56	12 22				12 56	13 25			13 56	14 22
Bordesley	d																						
Small Heath	d	23p44																					
Tyseley	d	23p46			09 26	10 29				11 26				12 26					13 29				14 26
Acocks Green	d	23p49							11 02				12 02					13 04				14 02	
Olton	d	23p52							11 04				12 04					13 06				14 04	
Solihull	d	23p56							11 08				12 08					13 10				14 08	
Widney Manor	d	23p59							11 11				12 11					13 13				14 11	
Dorridge	d	00 03							11a16				12a16					13a18				14a17	
Lapworth	d	00 07																					
Hatton	d	00 13																					
Warwick Parkway	d	00 18																					
Warwick	d	00 21																					
Leamington Spa 8	a	00 26		09 36				10 36				11 35					12 35				13 36		
	d						09 45				10 45					11 45				12 45			
Banbury	d						10a25				11a25					12a25				13a23			
London Marylebone 10 ⊖	a																						
Spring Road	d				09 29	10 32				11 29				12 29					13 32				14 29
Hall Green	d				09 32	10 35				11 32				12 32					13 35				14 32
Yardley Wood	d				09 35	10 38				11 35				12 35					13 38				14 35
Shirley	d				09 38	10 41				11 38				12 38					13 41				14 38
Whitlocks End	d				09 41	10 44				11 41				12 41					13 44				14 40
Wythall	d				09 43	10 46				11 43				12 43					13 46				14 43
Earlswood (West Midlands)	d																						
The Lakes	d				09x46	10x49				11x46				12x46					13x49				14x46
Wood End	d																						
Danzey	d																						
Henley-in-Arden	d				09 54	10 57				11 54				12 54					13 57				14 54
Wootton Wawen	d																						
Wilmcote	d				10 04	11 05				12 02				13 02					14 05				15 02
Stratford-upon-Avon	a				10 09	11 12				12 09				13 09					14 12				15 07

Table 71

Hereford, Worcester and Stourbridge - Birmingham - Leamington Spa, Marylebone and Stratford-upon-Avon

		GW	GW	XC	XC	XC	LM	LM	XC	XC	LM	XC	LM	GW	LM	LM	XC	LM	XC	XC	LM	LM	GW
		◇1	◇1	🚌	◇1	◇1			◇1	◇1		◇1		◇1			◇1		◇1	◇1			◇1
			☕		🍴	🍴			🍴	🍴		🍴		☕			🍴		🍴	🍴			☕
Hereford 7	d		13 28											14 30							15 30		16 33
Ledbury	a		13 45											14 47							15 47		16 49
	d		13 46											14 55							15 51		16 50
Colwall	d		13 53											15 02							15 58		16 58
Great Malvern	a		13 58											15 07							16 02		17 02
	d	13 10	13 59										14 35	15 08							16 03		17 03
Malvern Link	d	13 13	14 03										14 37	15 12							16 05		17 07
Worcester Foregate Street 7	a	13 22	14 13										14 45	15 21							16 14		17 20
	d	13 23	14 14					14 20					14 45	15 23	15 21						16 15	16 20	17 22
Worcester Shrub Hill 7	a	13 27	14 17										14 48	15 26							16 18		17 27
	d												14 53			15 46					16 33		
Droitwich Spa	d							14 29					15 01		15 30	15 54					16 41	16 29	
Bromsgrove	d												15 10								16 51		
Barnt Green	d																						
University	d																						
Hartlebury	d																						
Kidderminster	d							14 39							15 40	16 04						16 39	
Blakedown	d							14 44															
Hagley	d							14 48							15 47	16 11						16 46	
Stourbridge Junction 2	d						14 22	14 52			15 22				15 52	16 16		16 22				16 52	
Lye	d						14 25				15 25							16 25					
Cradley Heath	d						14 29	14 58			15 29				15 58			16 29				16 58	
Old Hill	d						14 33				15 33							16 33					
Rowley Regis	d						14 36	15 03			15 36				16 03			16 36				17 03	
Langley Green	d						14 39				15 39							16 39					
Birmingham New Street 12	a												15 37								17 17		
	d				13 33	14 03			14 33	15 03		15 33					16 03		16 33	17 03			
Birmingham International ✈	d					14 14				15 14							16 14			17 14			
Coventry	d					14 25				15 25							16 25			17 25			
Smethwick Galton Bridge 7	d						14 43	15 08			15 43				16 08	16 29		16 43				17 08	
The Hawthorns 🚋	d						14 45	15 11			15 45				16 11			16 45				17 11	
Jewellery Quarter 🚋	d						14 49	15 14			15 49				16 14			16 49				17 14	
Birmingham Snow Hill 🚋	a						14 52	15 17			15 52				16 17	16 35		16 52				17 17	
	d						14 53	15 19			15 53				16 19	16 45		16 53				17 19	
Birmingham Moor Street	d						14 56	15 22			15 56				16 22	16a47		16 56				17 22	
Bordesley	d																						
Small Heath	d																						
Tyseley	d							15 26							16 26							17 26	
Acocks Green	d						15 02				16 02							17 02					
Olton	d						15 04				16 04							17 04					
Solihull	d						15 08				16 08							17 08					
Widney Manor	d						15 11				16 11							17 11					
Dorridge	d						15a17				16a16							17a17					
Lapworth	d																						
Hatton	d																						
Warwick Parkway	d																						
Warwick	d																						
Leamington Spa 8	a				13 59	14 36			14 59	15 36		15 59					16 36		16 59	17 36			
	d			13 50	14 00	14 38			15 00	15 38		16 00					16 38		17 00	17 38			
Banbury	d			14a25	14a17	14a54			15a18	15a54		16a17					16a54		17a17	17a54			
London Marylebone 10 ⊖	a																						
Spring Road	d							15 29							16 29							17 29	
Hall Green	d							15 32							16 32							17 32	
Yardley Wood	d							15 35							16 35							17 35	
Shirley	d							15 38							16 38							17 38	
Whitlocks End	d							15 41							16 41							17 41	
Wythall	d							15 43							16 43							17 43	
Earlswood (West Midlands)	d																						
The Lakes	d							15x46							16x46							17x46	
Wood End	d																						
Danzey	d																						
Henley-in-Arden	d							15 54							16 55							17 54	
Wootton Wawen	d																						
Wilmcote	d							16 02							17 03							18 02	
Stratford-upon-Avon	a							16 09							17 10							18 09	

Table 71

Sundays
18 September to 23 October

Hereford, Worcester and Stourbridge - Birmingham - Leamington Spa, Marylebone and Stratford-upon-Avon

		LM		LM	XC ◇1	XC ◇1	LM	LM	GW ◇1	GW ◇1	XC ◇1	XC ◇1	XC ◇1	LM	XC ◇1	XC ◇1	LM	GW ◇1	LM	XC ◇1	LM	LM	GW ◇1	LM	LM
Hereford 7	d									18 30											20 05				22 40
Ledbury	a									18 47											20 21				22 56
	d									18 48											20 22				22 56
Colwall	d									18 55											20 28				23 03
Great Malvern	a									19 00											20 33				23 07
	d						17 17			19 11								20 10			20 33		21 15	22 10	23 08
Malvern Link	d						17 20			19 14								20 11			20 36		21 18	22 13	23 10
Worcester Foregate Street 7	a						17 28			19 23								20 23			20 44		21 31	22 21	23 19
	d			17 20			17 28	18 20	18 25	19 25								20 24			20 45		21 31	22 22	23 22
Worcester Shrub Hill 7	a						17 31		18 26	19 26								20 26			20 47		21 34	22 24	23 24
	d						17 35							19 38			19 53		20 34		20 52	21 25		22 29	
Droitwich Spa	d			17 29			17 43	18 29						19 46			20 01		20 42		21 00	21 33		22 37	
Bromsgrove	d						17 52										20 10				21 09				
Barnt Green	d																								
University	d																								
Hartlebury	d																								
Kidderminster	d			17 39				18 39						19 56					20 52			21 43		22 47	
Blakedown	d			17 44																					
Hagley	d			17 48				18 46						20 03					20 59			21 50		22 54	
Stourbridge Junction 2	d	17 22		17 52				18 52						20 07					21 03			21 54		22 58	
Lye	d	17 25																							
Cradley Heath	d	17 29		17 58				18 58						20 13					21 08			21 59		23 04	
Old Hill	d	17 33																							
Rowley Regis	d	17 36		18 03				19 03						20 19					21 14			22 05		23 09	
Langley Green	d	17 39																							
Birmingham New Street 12	a						18 14										20 36				21 42				
	d				17 33	18 03					18 33	19 03	19 33		20 03	20 33				21 03					
Birmingham International ✈	d					18 14						19 14			20 14					21 14					
Coventry	d					18 25						19 25			20 25					21 24					
Smethwick Galton Bridge 7	d	17 43		18 08				19 08						20 24					21 19			22 10		23 14	
The Hawthorns	d	17 45		18 11				19 11						20 26					21 21			22 12		23 17	
Jewellery Quarter	d	17 49		18 14				19 14						20 30					21 25			22 16		23 20	
Birmingham Snow Hill	a	17 53		18 17				19 19						20 33					21 28			22 19		23 24	
	d	17 53		18 19				19 21						20 33					21 28			22 20			
Birmingham Moor Street	d	17 56		18 22				19a23						20a36					21a31			22a22			
Bordesley	d																								
Small Heath	d																								
Tyseley	d			18 26																					
Acocks Green	d	18 02																							
Olton	d	18 04																							
Solihull	d	18 08																							
Widney Manor	d	18 11																							
Dorridge	d	18a17																							
Lapworth	d																								
Hatton	d																								
Warwick Parkway	d																								
Warwick	d																								
Leamington Spa 8	a				18 00	18 36					18 59	19 36	19 59		20 36	20 58				21 34					
	d				18 01	18 38					19 00	19 38	20 00		20 38	21 00									
Banbury	d				18a19	18a54					19a17	19a54	20a18		20a54	21a17									
London Marylebone 10 ⊖	a																								
Spring Road	d			18 29																					
Hall Green	d			18 32																					
Yardley Wood	d			18 35																					
Shirley	d			18 38																					
Whitlocks End	d			18 41																					
Wythall	d			18 43																					
Earlswood (West Midlands)	d																								
The Lakes	d			18x46																					
Wood End	d																								
Danzey	d																								
Henley-in-Arden	d			18 54																					
Wootton Wawen	d																								
Wilmcote	d			19 02																					
Stratford-upon-Avon	a			19 09																					

Table 71

Sundays
from 30 October

Hereford, Worcester and Stourbridge - Birmingham - Leamington Spa, Marylebone and Stratford-upon-Avon

		LM	XC ◇1	LM	LM	GW ◇1	XC	XC ◇1	LM	LM		XC	XC ◇1	LM	LM	GW ◇1	XC	XC ◇1	LM	LM		XC	XC ◇1	LM	LM
Hereford 7	d																								
Ledbury	a																								
	d																								
Colwall	d																								
Great Malvern	a																								
	d				09 03	09 15				10 02					10 56	11 15				12 04					
Malvern Link	d				09 06	09 18				10 04					10 58	11 18				12 06					
Worcester Foregate Street 7	a				09 15	09 26				10 12					11 06	11 26				12 15					
	d				09 15	09 28				10 16					11 20	11 27				12 16					13 20
Worcester Shrub Hill 7	a				09 18	09 30				10 18						11 29				12 18					
	d	22p47			09 23					10 22										12 24					
Droitwich Spa	d	22p55			09 32					10 30					11 29					12 32					13 29
Bromsgrove	d																								
Barnt Green	d																								
University	d																								
Hartlebury	d																								
Kidderminster	d	23p05			09 42				10 08	10 40					11 39					12 42					13 39
Blakedown	d	23p10			09 47				10 13											12 47					
Hagley	d	23p14			09 51				10 17	10 47					11 46					12 51					13 46
Stourbridge Junction 2	d	23p18			09 55				10 22	10 52				11 22	11 52				12 22	12 55				13 22	13 52
Lye	d								10 25					11 25					12 25					13 25	
Cradley Heath	d				10 01				10 29	10 58				11 29	11 58				12 29	13 01				13 29	13 58
Old Hill	d								10 33					11 33					12 33					13 33	
Rowley Regis	d				10 06				10 36	11 03				11 36	12 03				12 36	13 06				13 36	14 03
Langley Green	d								10 39					11 39					12 39					13 39	
Birmingham New Street 12	a																								
	d		09 03					10 03					11 03					12 03					13 03		
Birmingham International ✈	d		09 14					10 14					11 14					12 14					13 14		
Coventry	d		09 25					10 25					11 25					12 25					13 25		
Smethwick Galton Bridge 7	d				10 12				10 43	11 09				11 43	12 08				12 43	13 11				13 43	14 08
The Hawthorns	d				10 15				10 45	11 12				11 45	12 11				12 45	13 14				13 45	14 11
Jewellery Quarter	d				10 18				10 49	11 15				11 49	12 14				12 49	13 17				13 49	14 14
Birmingham Snow Hill	a	23p36			10 20				10 52	11 17				11 52	12 17				12 52	13 20				13 52	14 17
	d	23p37		09 19	10 22				10 53	11 19				11 53	12 19				12 53	13 22				13 53	14 19
Birmingham Moor Street	d	23p40		09 22	10 25				10 56	11 22				11 56	12 22				12 56	13 25				13 56	14 22
Bordesley	d																								
Small Heath	d	23p44																							
Tyseley	d	23p46		09 26	10 29					11 26					12 26					13 29					14 26
Acocks Green	d	23p49							11 02					12 02					13 04					14 02	
Olton	d	23p52							11 04					12 04					13 06					14 04	
Solihull	d	23p56							11 08					12 08					13 10					14 08	
Widney Manor	d	23p59							11 11					12 11					13 13					14 11	
Dorridge	d	00 03							11a16					12a16					13a18					14a17	
Lapworth	d	00 07																							
Hatton	d	00 13																							
Warwick Parkway	d	00 18																							
Warwick	d	00 21																							
Leamington Spa 8	a	00 26	09 36					10 44					11 45					12 35					13 36		
	d						09 45					10 45					11 45					12 45			
Banbury	d						10a25					11a25					12a25					13a23			
London Marylebone 10 ⊖	a																								
Spring Road	d			09 29	10 32					11 29					12 29					13 32					14 29
Hall Green	d			09 32	10 35					11 32					12 32					13 35					14 32
Yardley Wood	d			09 35	10 38					11 35					12 35					13 38					14 35
Shirley	d			09 38	10 41					11 38					12 38					13 41					14 38
Whitlocks End	d			09 41	10 44					11 41					12 41					13 44					14 40
Wythall	d			09 43	10 46					11 43					12 43					13 46					14 43
Earlswood (West Midlands)	d																								
The Lakes	d			09x46	10x49					11x46					12x46					13x49					14x46
Wood End	d																								
Danzey	d																								
Henley-in-Arden	d			09 54	10 57					11 54					12 54					13 57					14 54
Wootton Wawen	d																								
Wilmcote	d			10 04	11 05					12 02					13 02					14 05					15 02
Stratford-upon-Avon	a			10 09	11 12					12 09					13 09					14 12					15 07

Table 71

Sundays from 30 October

Hereford, Worcester and Stourbridge - Birmingham - Leamington Spa, Marylebone and Stratford-upon-Avon

		GW ◇1	GW ◇1 ⊏	XC 🚌	XC ◇1 ⊼	XC ◇1 ⊼	LM	LM	XC ◇1 ⊼	XC ◇1 ⊼	LM	XC ◇1 ⊼	LM	GW ◇1 ⊏	LM	LM	XC ◇1 ⊼	LM	XC ◇1 ⊼	XC ◇1 ⊼	LM	LM	GW ◇1 ⊏
Hereford 7	d		13 32											14 32							15 30		16 35
Ledbury	a		13 49											14 49							15 47		16 51
	d		13 50											14 55							15 51		16 52
Colwall	d		13 58											15 02							15 58		17 00
Great Malvern	a		14 02											15 07							16 02		17 04
	d	13 15	14 04									14 35	15 08							16 03		17 05
Malvern Link	d	13 18	14 08									14 37	15 12							16 05		17 09
Worcester Foregate Street 7	a	13 25	14 17									14 45	15 21							16 14		17 20
	d	13 26	14 19					14 20					14 45	15 23	15 21						16 15	16 20	17 22
Worcester Shrub Hill 7	a	13 32	14 22									14 48	15 26							16 18		17 27
	d												14 53			15 46					16 33		
Droitwich Spa	d							14 29					15 01		15 30	15 54					16 41	16 29	
Bromsgrove	d												15 10								16 51		
Barnt Green	d																						
University	d																						
Hartlebury	d																						
Kidderminster	d							14 39							15 40	16 04						16 39	
Blakedown	d							14 44															
Hagley	d							14 48							15 47	16 11						16 46	
Stourbridge Junction 2	d						14 22	14 52			15 22				15 52	16 16		16 22				16 52	
Lye	d						14 25				15 25							16 25					
Cradley Heath	d						14 29	14 58			15 29				15 58			16 29				16 58	
Old Hill	d						14 33				15 33							16 33					
Rowley Regis	d						14 36	15 03			15 36				16 03			16 36				17 03	
Langley Green	d						14 39				15 39							16 39					
Birmingham New Street 12	a												15 37								17 17		
	d				13 33	14 03			14 33	15 03		15 33					16 03		16 33	17 03			
Birmingham International ✈	d					14 14				15 14							16 14			17 14			
Coventry	d					14 25				15 25							16 25			17 25			
Smethwick Galton Bridge 7	d						14 43	15 08			15 43				16 08	16 29		16 43				17 08	
The Hawthorns 🚋	d						14 45	15 11			15 45				16 11			16 45				17 11	
Jewellery Quarter 🚋	d						14 49	15 14			15 49				16 14			16 49				17 14	
Birmingham Snow Hill 🚋	a						14 52	15 17			15 52				16 17	16 35		16 52				17 17	
	d						14 53	15 19			15 53				16 19	16 45		16 53				17 19	
Birmingham Moor Street	d						14 56	15 22			15 56				16 22	16a47		16 56				17 22	
Bordesley	d																						
Small Heath	d																						
Tyseley	d							15 26							16 26							17 26	
Acocks Green	d						15 02				16 02							17 02					
Olton	d						15 04				16 04							17 04					
Solihull	d						15 08				16 08							17 08					
Widney Manor	d						15 11				16 11							17 11					
Dorridge	d						15a17				16a16							17a17					
Lapworth	d																						
Hatton	d																						
Warwick Parkway	d																						
Warwick	d																						
Leamington Spa 8	a				13 59	14 36			14 59	15 36		15 59					16 36		16 59	17 36			
	d			13 50	14 00	14 38			15 00	15 38		16 00					16 38		17 00	17 38			
Banbury	d			14a25	14a17	14a54			15a18	15a54		16a17					16a54		17a17	17a54			
London Marylebone 10 ⊖	a																						
Spring Road	d							15 29							16 29							17 29	
Hall Green	d							15 32							16 32							17 32	
Yardley Wood	d							15 35							16 35							17 35	
Shirley	d							15 38							16 38							17 38	
Whitlocks End	d							15 41							16 41							17 41	
Wythall	d							15 43							16 43							17 43	
Earlswood (West Midlands)	d																						
The Lakes	d							15x46							16x46							17x46	
Wood End	d																						
Danzey	d																						
Henley-in-Arden	d							15 54							16 55							17 54	
Wootton Wawen	d																						
Wilmcote	d							16 02							17 03							18 02	
Stratford-upon-Avon	a							16 09							17 10							18 09	

Table 71

Sundays from 30 October

Hereford, Worcester and Stourbridge - Birmingham - Leamington Spa, Marylebone and Stratford-upon-Avon

		LM	LM	XC ◇1 ⊼	XC ◇1 ⊼	LM	LM	GW ◇1 ⊏	GW ◇1 ⊼	XC ◇1 ⊼	XC ◇1 ⊼	XC ◇1 ⊼	LM	XC ◇1 ⊼	XC ◇1 ⊼	LM	GW ◇1	LM	XC ◇1	LM	LM	GW ◇1	LM	LM
Hereford 7	d								18 30											20 05				22 40
Ledbury	a								18 47											20 21				22 56
	d								18 48											20 22				22 56
Colwall	d								18 55											20 28				23 03
Great Malvern	a								19 00											20 33				23 07
	d					17 17			19 15								20 15			20 33		21 15	22 10	23 08
Malvern Link	d					17 20			19 18								20 16			20 36		21 18	22 13	23 10
Worcester Foregate Street 7	a					17 28			19 27								20 27			20 44		21 31	22 21	23 19
	d		17 20			17 28	18 20	18 25	19 29								20 29			20 45		21 31	22 22	23 22
Worcester Shrub Hill 7	a					17 31		18 26	19 30								20 30			20 47		21 34	22 24	23 24
	d					17 35							19 38			19 53		20 34		20 52	21 25		22 29	
Droitwich Spa	d		17 29			17 43	18 29						19 46			20 01		20 42		21 00	21 33		22 37	
Bromsgrove	d					17 52										20 10				21 09				
Barnt Green	d																							
University	d																							
Hartlebury	d																							
Kidderminster	d		17 39				18 39						19 56					20 52			21 43		22 47	
Blakedown	d		17 44																					
Hagley	d		17 48				18 46						20 03					20 59			21 50		22 54	
Stourbridge Junction 2	d	17 22	17 52				18 52						20 07					21 03			21 54		22 58	
Lye	d	17 25																						
Cradley Heath	d	17 29	17 58				18 58						20 13					21 08			21 59		23 04	
Old Hill	d	17 33																						
Rowley Regis	d	17 36	18 03				19 03						20 19					21 14			22 05		23 09	
Langley Green	d	17 39																						
Birmingham New Street 12	a					18 14										20 36				21 42				
	d			17 33	18 03					18 33	19 03	19 33		20 03	20 33				21 03					
Birmingham International ✈	d				18 14						19 14			20 14					21 14					
Coventry	d				18 25						19 25			20 25					21 24					
Smethwick Galton Bridge 7	d	17 43	18 08				19 08						20 24					21 19			22 10		23 14	
The Hawthorns 🚋	d	17 45	18 11				19 11						20 26					21 21			22 12		23 17	
Jewellery Quarter 🚋	d	17 49	18 14				19 14						20 30					21 25			22 16		23 20	
Birmingham Snow Hill 🚋	a	17 53	18 17				19 19						20 33					21 28			22 19		23 24	
	d	17 53	18 19				19 21						20 33					21 28			22 20			
Birmingham Moor Street	d	17 56	18 22				19a23						20a36					21a31			22a22			
Bordesley	d																							
Small Heath	d																							
Tyseley	d		18 26																					
Acocks Green	d	18 02																						
Olton	d	18 04																						
Solihull	d	18 08																						
Widney Manor	d	18 11																						
Dorridge	d	18a17																						
Lapworth	d																							
Hatton	d																							
Warwick Parkway	d																							
Warwick	d																							
Leamington Spa 8	a			18 00	18 36					18 59	19 36	19 59		20 36	20 58				21 34					
	d			18 01	18 38					19 00	19 38	20 00		20 38	21 00									
Banbury	d			18a19	18a54					19a17	19a54	20a18		20a54	21a17									
London Marylebone 10 ⊖	a																							
Spring Road	d		18 29																					
Hall Green	d		18 32																					
Yardley Wood	d		18 35																					
Shirley	d		18 38																					
Whitlocks End	d		18 41																					
Wythall	d		18 43																					
Earlswood (West Midlands)	d																							
The Lakes	d		18x46																					
Wood End	d																							
Danzey	d																							
Henley-in-Arden	d		18 54																					
Wootton Wawen	d																							
Wilmcote	d		19 02																					
Stratford-upon-Avon	a		19 09																					

Stratford-upon-Avon, Marylebone and Leamington Spa - Birmingham - Stourbridge, Worcester and Hereford

Miles	Miles	Miles			LM MX	LM	GW	GW	LM	LM	LM	LM	LM		GW	LM	GW	GW	LM	LM	LM	LM	LM		LM
							1 A	1 B									◇1 B 🛒	◇1 A 🛒							
—	0	—	**Stratford-upon-Avon**	d																06 29			06 52		
—	2¾	—	Wilmcote	d																06 34			06 57		
—	6½	—	Wootton Wawen	d																06x39			07x02		
—	8¾	—	Henley-in-Arden	d																06 43			07 06		
—	11¼	—	Danzey	d																06x47			07x11		
—	13	—	Wood End	d																06x51			07x15		
—	14¼	—	The Lakes	d																06x53			07x18		
—	15	—	Earlswood (West Midlands)	d																06 55			07 20		
—	16	—	Wythall	d																06 58			07 23		
—	17	—	Whitlocks End	d								06 28	06 46							07 00			07 26		
—	18	—	Shirley	d								06 31	06 52							07 03			07 29		
—	19¼	—	Yardley Wood	d								06 34	06 55							07 06			07 32		
—	20½	—	Hall Green	d								06 37	06 58							07 09			07 36		
—	21	—	Spring Road	d								06 39	07 00							07 11			07 38		
—	—	—	**London Marylebone** 10 ⊖	d																					
—	—	—	Banbury	d																					
—	—	0	**Leamington Spa** 8	a																					
—	—	—		d						05 47									06 29						07 08
—	—	2	Warwick	d						05 51									06 33						07 12
—	—	3¼	Warwick Parkway	d						05 55									06 37						07 16
—	—	6	Hatton	d						06 00									06 42						07 21
—	—	10¼	Lapworth	d						06 06									06 48						07 28
—	—	12¼	Dorridge	d	22p33				05 54	06 11									06 53		07 09				07 34
—	—	14¾	Widney Manor	d	22p37				05 59	06 14									06 56		07 14				07 37
—	—	16¼	Solihull	d	22p41				06 02	06 18									07 00		07 17				07 41
—	—	18	Olton	d	22p44				06 06	06 21									07 03		07 21				07 44
—	—	19	Acocks Green	d	22p47				06 08	06 24									07 06		07 23				07 47
—	22	20	Tyseley	d	22p50				06 11	06 27		06 42	07 03						07 09	07 14	07 26		07 41		07 50
—	23	21	Small Heath	d	22p52				06 14	06 29		06 44	07 05						07 11	07 17	07 29		07 43		07 53
—	24	—	Bordesley	d																					
—	24¾	—	**Birmingham Moor Street**	d	22p56				06 18	06 33		06 48	07 09						07 15	07 22	07 33		07 47		07 57
—	25¼	—	**Birmingham Snow Hill** 🚊	a	22p59				06 20	06 37		06 51	07 12						07 19	07 24	07 35		07 52		07 59
—	—	—		d	23p00				06 22			06 53	07 13						07 23		07 37		07 53		08 03
—	26	—	Jewellery Quarter 🚊	d	23p02				06 24			06 55	07 15						07 25		07 39		07 55		08 05
—	28½	—	The Hawthorns 🚊	d	23p07				06 29			07 00	07 20						07 30		07 44		08 00		08 10
—	29¼	29	Smethwick Galton Bridge 7	d	23p10				06 31			07 03	07 23						07 33		07 47		08 03		08 13
—	—	—	**Coventry**	a																					
—	—	—	**Birmingham International** ✈	a																					
0	—	24	**Birmingham New Street** 12	a																					
—	—	—		d							06 59					07 19						07 59			
—	30½	30¼	Langley Green	d	23p13				06 34			07 06							07 36		07 50				08 16
—	32¼	—	Rowley Regis	d	23p16				06 38			07 09	07 28						07 39		07 53		08 08		08 19
—	33½	—	Old Hill	d	23p19				06 41			07 12							07 42		07 56				08 22
—	34¾	—	Cradley Heath	d	23p23				06 44			07 16	07 33						07 46		08 00		08 13		08 26
—	36¼	—	Lye	d	23p26				06 47			07 19							07 49		08 03				08 29
—	37¼	—	**Stourbridge Junction** 2	d	23p30				06 51			07 23	07a39						07 53		08a07		08 19		08 33
—	39¼	—	Hagley	d	23p33				06 54			07 26							07 56				08 23		08 36
—	41	—	Blakedown	d	23p36				06 57			07 29							07 59				08 26		08 39
—	44¼	—	**Kidderminster**	d	23p41				07 02			07 34							08 04				08 31		08a45
—	47¼	—	Hartlebury	d								07 39							08 09				08 36		
2½	—	—	University	d							07 05					07 25						08 05			
10½	—	—	Barnt Green	d												07 42						08 18			
13	—	—	Bromsgrove	d							07 22					07 47						08 23			
19¼	53½	—	Droitwich Spa	d	23p52				07 13		07 32	07 46				07 56			08 17			08 32	08 44		
25	—	—	**Worcester Shrub Hill** 7	a	00 01											08 03			08 25						
—	—	—		d		06 00	06 32	06 33							07 55	08 07	08 15	08 18	08 30						
25¾	58¾	—	**Worcester Foregate Street** 7	a		06 02	06 38	06 39	07 22		07 41	07 57			07 58	08 09	08 20	08 21	08 32			08 41	08 59		
—	—	—		d		06 03					07 43				07 58	08 11		08 22				08 42			
32½	—	—	Malvern Link	d		06 12					07 53				08 07	08 20		08 34				08 52			
33¾	—	—	**Great Malvern**	a		06 15					07 55				08 12	08 22		08 38				08 54			
—	—	—		d		06 15					08 01											08 55			
36½	—	—	Colwall	d		06 20					08 06											09 00			
40¾	—	—	Ledbury	a		06 27					08 13											09 07			
—	—	—		d		06 29					08 14											09 08			
54½	—	—	**Hereford** 7	a		06 50					08 34											09 26			

A until 9 September   B from 12 September

Stratford-upon-Avon, Marylebone and Leamington Spa - Birmingham - Stourbridge, Worcester and Hereford

		XC	LM	XC	LM	LM	LM	GW	GW		LM	LM	LM	XC	LM	LM	XC	LM	LM		XC	LM	GW	LM	LM
		◇1 🛒		◇1 🛒				1 A 🛒	1 B 🛒					◇1 🛒			◇1 🛒				◇1 🛒				
Stratford-upon-Avon	d		07 23								07 42								08 27						
Wilmcote	d										07 47								08 32						
Wootton Wawen	d										07x52								08x37						
Henley-in-Arden	d		07 34								07 57								08 41						
Danzey	d										08x02								08x45						
Wood End	d										08x06								08x49						
The Lakes	d										08x08								08x51						
Earlswood (West Midlands)	d		07 42								08 11								08 54						
Wythall	d		07 44								08 14								08 56						
Whitlocks End	d		07 47			08 07					08 16				08 35				08 59						09 19
Shirley	d		07 50			08 10					08 20				08 38				09 02						09 22
Yardley Wood	d		07 53			08 13					08 23				08 41				09 05						09 25
Hall Green	d		07 57			08 16					08 27				08 44				09 08						09 28
Spring Road	d		07 59			08 18					08 29				08 46				09 10						09 30
London Marylebone 10 ⊖	d																								
Banbury	d	06 54		07 26										07 54			08 27				08 54				
Leamington Spa 8	a	07 10		07 42										08 11			08 43				09 10				
	d	07 12		07 43			07 47						08 00	08 12			08 44				09 12				
Warwick	d						07 51						08 04												
Warwick Parkway	d						07 55						08 08												
Hatton	d						08 00						08 13												
Lapworth	d						08 06						08 19												
Dorridge	d				07 56		08 11					08 20	08 26					08 46				09 09			
Widney Manor	d				08 01		08 14					08 24	08 29					08 50				09 13			
Solihull	d				08 04		08 18					08 28	08 33					08 54				09 16			
Olton	d				08 08		08 21					08 32	08 37					08 57				09 20			
Acocks Green	d				08 11		08 24					08 35	08 39					09 00				09 22			
Tyseley	d				08 14	08 21	08 27				08 33	08 38	08 41		08 49			09 03							09 33
Small Heath	d					08 24	08 29				08 35		08 44		08 51			09 05							09 35
Bordesley	d																								
Birmingham Moor Street	d		08 06		08 19	08 28	08 33				08 39	08 42	08 48		08 55			09 09	09 17			09 29			09 39
Birmingham Snow Hill 🚊	a		08 10		08 21	08 30	08 37				08 42	08 47	08 51		08 58			09 12	09 20			09 31			09 42
	d		08 13		08 23	08 33					08 43		08 53		09 03			09 13	09 23			09 33			09 43
Jewellery Quarter 🚊	d		08 15		08 25	08 35					08 45		08 55		09 05			09 15	09 25			09 35			09 45
The Hawthorns 🚊	d		08 20		08 30	08 40					08 50		09 00		09 10			09 20	09 30			09 40			09 50
Smethwick Galton Bridge 7	d		08 23		08 33	08 43					08 53		09 03		09 13			09 23	09 33			09 43			09 53
Coventry	a	07 22												08 23							09 22				
Birmingham International ✈	a	07 37												08 37							09 37				
Birmingham New Street 12	a	07 48		08 15										08 48			09 18				09 48				
	d															08 49								09 49	
Langley Green	d					08 46									09 16							09 46			
Rowley Regis	d		08 28		08 38	08 49					08 58		09 08		09 19			09 28	09 38			09 49			09 58
Old Hill	d					08 52									09 22							09 52			
Cradley Heath	d		08 33		08 43	08 56					09 03		09 13		09 26			09 33	09 43			09 56			10 03
Lye	d					08 59									09 29							09 59			
Stourbridge Junction 2	d		08a39		08a49	09 03					09 09		09a19		09 33			09 39	09a49			10 03			10 09
Hagley	d										09 12							09 42							10 12
Blakedown	d										09 15							09 45							10 15
Kidderminster	d					09a12					09 20				09a42			09 50				10a13			10 20
Hartlebury	d																								
University	d															08 55								09 55	
Barnt Green	d																								
Bromsgrove	d															09 10								10 10	
Droitwich Spa	d										09 31					09 20		10 01						10 20	10 31
Worcester Shrub Hill 7	a										09 40														
	d							09 15	09 15														10 15		
Worcester Foregate Street 7	a							09 18	09 18							09 28		10 10					10 17	10 31	10 40
	d							09 18	09 18							09 32							10 18	10 32	10 42
Malvern Link	d							09 27	09 27							09 42							10 27	10 42	10 52
Great Malvern	a							09 32	09 33							09 44							10 32	10 44	10 55
	d															09 45								10 45	
Colwall	d															09 50								10 50	
Ledbury	a															09 57								10 57	
	d															09 59								10 59	
Hereford 7	a															10 17								11 19	

A from 12 September   B until 9 September

Table 71

Mondays to Fridays

Stratford-upon-Avon, Marylebone and Leamington Spa - Birmingham - Stourbridge, Worcester and Hereford

		XC	LM	LM	XC	GW	GW	LM	LM	LM	LM	XC	XC	GW	GW	LM	LM	LM	LM	LM	LM	GW	LM
		◇1			◇1	◇1	◇1					◇1	◇1	◇1	◇1							◇	
						A	B							A	B								
		⊼			⊼	⊡	⊡					⊼	⊼	⊼	⊼								
Stratford-upon-Avon	d								09 27											10 27			
Wilmcote	d								09 32											10 32			
Wootton Wawen	d								09x37											10x37			
Henley-in-Arden	d								09 41											10 41			
Danzey	d								09x45											10x45			
Wood End	d								09x49											10x49			
The Lakes	d								09x51											10x51			
Earlswood (West Midlands)	d								09 54											10 54			
Wythall	d								09 56											10 56			
Whitlocks End	d			09 39					09 59							10 19		10 39		10 59			
Shirley	d			09 42					10 02							10 22		10 42		11 02			
Yardley Wood	d			09 45					10 05							10 25		10 45		11 05			
Hall Green	d			09 48					10 08							10 28		10 48		11 08			
Spring Road	d			09 50					10 10							10 30		10 50		11 10			
London Marylebone 10 ⊖	d																						
Banbury	d	09 26			09 54							10 25	10 54										
Leamington Spa 8	a	09 42			10 10							10 42	11 10										
	d	09 43			10 12							10 43	11 12										
Warwick	d																						
Warwick Parkway	d																						
Hatton	d																						
Lapworth	d																						
Dorridge	d		09 28					09 46		10 09							10 28		10 46		11 09		
Widney Manor	d		09 32					09 50		10 13							10 32		10 50		11 13		
Solihull	d		09 36					09 54		10 17							10 36		10 54		11 17		
Olton	d		09 39					09 57		10 20							10 39		10 57		11 20		
Acocks Green	d		09 42					10 00		10 23							10 42		11 00		11 23		
Tyseley	d							10 03								10 33			11 03				
Small Heath	d							10 05								10 35			11 05				
Bordesley	d																						
Birmingham Moor Street	d		09 48	09 59				10 09	10 17	10 29						10 39	10 48	10 59	11 09	11 19	11 29		
Birmingham Snow Hill ⇌	a		09 51	10 02				10 12	10 20	10 32						10 42	10 51	11 02	11 12	11 22	11 32		
	d		09 53	10 03				10 13	10 23	10 33						10 43	10 53	11 03	11 13	11 23	11 33		
Jewellery Quarter ⇌	d		09 55	10 05				10 15	10 25	10 35						10 45	10 55	11 05	11 15	11 25	11 35		
The Hawthorns ⇌	d		10 00	10 10				10 20	10 30	10 40						10 50	11 00	11 10	11 20	11 30	11 40		
Smethwick Galton Bridge 7	d		10 03	10 13				10 23	10 33	10 43						10 53	11 03	11 13	11 23	11 33	11 43		
Coventry	a				10 22								11 22										
Birmingham International ✈	a				10 37								11 37										
Birmingham New Street 12	a	10 18			10 48							11 18	11 48										
	d										10 49												11 49
Langley Green	d			10 16						10 46								11 16			11 46		
Rowley Regis	d		10 08	10 19				10 28	10 38	10 49						10 58	11 08	11 19	11 28	11 38	11 49		
Old Hill	d			10 22						10 52								11 22			11 52		
Cradley Heath	d		10 13	10 26				10 33	10 43	10 56						11 03	11 13	11 26	11 33	11 43	11 56		
Lye	d			10 29						10 59								11 29			11 59		
Stourbridge Junction 2	d		10a19	10 33				10 39	10a49	11 03						11 09	11a19	11 33	11 39	11a49	12 03		
Hagley	d							10 42								11 12			11 42				
Blakedown	d							10 45								11 15			11 45				
Kidderminster	d			10a43				10 50		11a13						11 20		11a43	11 50		12a13		
Hartlebury	d																						
University	d										10 55												11 55
Barnt Green	d																						
Bromsgrove	d										11 10												12 10
Droitwich Spa	d							11 01			11 20					11 31			12 01				12 20
Worcester Shrub Hill 7	a															11 39							
	d					10 45	10 52							11 32	11 36							12 15	
Worcester Foregate Street 7	a					10 48	10 55	11 10			11 30			11 37	11 41				12 10			12 17	12 30
	d					10 49	10 56				11 32											12 18	12 32
Malvern Link	d					11 03	11 05				11 42											12 27	12 42
Great Malvern	a					11 06	11 09				11 44											12 34	12 44
	d					11 07	11 09				11 45												12 45
Colwall	d					11 14	11 15				11 50												12 50
Ledbury	a					11 22	11 23				11 57												12 57
	d					11 24	11 24				11 59												12 59
Hereford 7	a					11 42	11 43				12 19												13 19

A from 12 September

B until 9 September

Table 71

Mondays to Fridays

Stratford-upon-Avon, Marylebone and Leamington Spa - Birmingham - Stourbridge, Worcester and Hereford

		LM	LM	CH	XC	LM	XC	GW	GW	LM	LM	LM	LM	XC	XC	GW	GW	LM	LM	LM	LM	LM
				◇	◇1		◇1	◇1	◇1					◇1	◇1	◇1	◇1					
								A	B							A	B					
				⊼	⊼		⊼	⊡	⊡					⊼	⊼	⊼	⊼					
Stratford-upon-Avon	d										11 27											12 27
Wilmcote	d										11 32											12 32
Wootton Wawen	d										11x37											12x37
Henley-in-Arden	d										11 41											12 41
Danzey	d										11x45											12x45
Wood End	d										11x49											12x49
The Lakes	d										11x51											12x51
Earlswood (West Midlands)	d										11 54											12 54
Wythall	d										11 56											12 56
Whitlocks End	d	11 19				11 39					11 59							12 19		12 39		12 59
Shirley	d	11 22				11 42					12 02							12 22		12 42		13 02
Yardley Wood	d	11 25				11 45					12 05							12 25		12 45		13 05
Hall Green	d	11 28				11 48					12 08							12 28		12 48		13 08
Spring Road	d	11 30				11 50					12 10							12 30		12 50		13 10
London Marylebone 10 ⊖	d			10 07																		
Banbury	d			11 04	11 25		11 54							12 25	12 54							
Leamington Spa 8	a			11 21	11 41		12 11							12 42	13 10							
	d			11 21	11 43		12 12							12 43	13 12							
Warwick	d			11 24																		
Warwick Parkway	d			11 28																		
Hatton	d																					
Lapworth	d																					
Dorridge	d		11 28	11 38						11 46		12 09							12 28		12 46	
Widney Manor	d		11 32							11 50		12 13							12 32		12 50	
Solihull	d		11 36	11 43						11 54		12 17							12 36		12 54	
Olton	d		11 39							11 57		12 20							12 39		12 57	
Acocks Green	d		11 42							12 00		12 23							12 42		13 00	
Tyseley	d	11 33								12 03								12 33			13 03	
Small Heath	d	11 35								12 05								12 35			13 05	
Bordesley	d																					
Birmingham Moor Street	d	11 39	11 48	11 52		11 59				12 09	12 19	12 29						12 39	12 48	12 59	13 09	13 18
Birmingham Snow Hill ⇌	a	11 42	11 51	12 04		12 02				12 12	12 22	12 32						12 42	12 51	13 02	13 12	13 21
	d	11 43	11 53			12 03				12 13	12 23	12 33						12 43	12 53	13 03	13 13	13 23
Jewellery Quarter ⇌	d	11 45	11 55			12 05				12 15	12 25	12 35						12 45	12 55	13 05	13 15	13 25
The Hawthorns ⇌	d	11 50	12 00			12 10				12 20	12 30	12 40						12 50	13 00	13 10	13 20	13 30
Smethwick Galton Bridge 7	d	11 53	12 03			12 13				12 23	12 33	12 43						12 53	13 03	13 13	13 23	13 33
Coventry	a						12 24								13 22							
Birmingham International ✈	a						12 37								13 37							
Birmingham New Street 12	a				12 18		12 48							13 18	13 48							
	d												12 49									
Langley Green	d					12 16						12 46								13 16		
Rowley Regis	d	11 58	12 08			12 19				12 28	12 38	12 49						12 58	13 08	13 19	13 28	13 38
Old Hill	d					12 22						12 52								13 22		
Cradley Heath	d	12 03	12 13			12 26				12 33	12 43	12 56						13 03	13 13	13 26	13 33	13 43
Lye	d					12 29						12 59								13 29		
Stourbridge Junction 2	d	12 09	12a19			12 33				12 39	12a49	13 03						13 09	13a19	13a33	13 44	13a50
Hagley	d	12 12								12 42								13 12			13 47	
Blakedown	d	12 15								12 45								13 15			13 50	
Kidderminster	d	12 20				12a43				12 50		13a13						13 20			13 55	
Hartlebury	d																					
University	d												12 55									
Barnt Green	d																					
Bromsgrove	d												13 10									
Droitwich Spa	d	12 31								13 01			13 20					13 31			14 06	
Worcester Shrub Hill 7	a																	13 39			14 14	
	d							12 45	12 50							13 32	13 37					
Worcester Foregate Street 7	a	12 40						12 48	12 54	13 10			13 30			13 35	13 40					
	d							12 49	12 54	13 11			13 32			13 36	13 41					
Malvern Link	d							12 58	13 03	13 20			13 42			13 51	13 51					
Great Malvern	a							13 02	13 07	13 24			13 44			13 56	13 56					
	d							13 09	13 09				13 45									
Colwall	d							13 16	13 15				13 50									
Ledbury	a							13 24	13 23				13 58									
	d							13 31	13 31				14 01									
Hereford 7	a							13 50	13 50				14 19									

A from 12 September

B until 9 September

Stratford-upon-Avon, Marylebone and Leamington Spa - Birmingham - Stourbridge, Worcester and Hereford

		LM	GW	LM	LM	LM	CH	XC	LM	XC	GW	LM	LM	LM	LM	LM	LM	CH	XC	LM	XC	GW	LM
			◇				◇	◇1		◇1	◇1							◇	◇1		◇1	◇1	
											A											B	
							⊼	⊼		⊼	⊼								⊼		⊼	⊼	
Stratford-upon-Avon	d												13 27										
Wilmcote	d												13 32										
Wootton Wawen	d												13x37										
Henley-in-Arden	d												13 41										
Danzey	d												13x45										
Wood End	d												13x49										
The Lakes	d												13x51										
Earlswood (West Midlands)	d												13 54										
Wythall	d												13 56										
Whitlocks End	d				13 19				13 39				13 59			14 19				14 39			
Shirley	d				13 22				13 42				14 02			14 22				14 42			
Yardley Wood	d				13 25				13 45				14 05			14 25				14 45			
Hall Green	d				13 28				13 48				14 08			14 28				14 48			
Spring Road	d				13 30				13 50				14 10			14 30				14 50			
London Marylebone 10 ⊖	d						12 07											13 07					
Banbury	d						13 05	13 25		13 54								14 04	14 25		14 54		
Leamington Spa 8	a						13 21	13 42		14 10								14 20	14 40		15 11		
	d						13 21	13 43		14 12								14 20	14 41		15 12		
Warwick	d						13 24											14 24					
Warwick Parkway	d						13 28											14 27					
Hatton	d																						
Lapworth	d																						
Dorridge	d	13 09				13 28	13 38					13 46		14 09			14 28	14 37					14 46
Widney Manor	d	13 13				13 32						13 50		14 13			14 32						14 50
Solihull	d	13 17				13 36	13 43					13 54		14 17			14 36	14 43					14 54
Olton	d	13 20				13 39						13 57		14 20			14 39						14 57
Acocks Green	d	13 23				13 42						14 00		14 23			14 42						15 00
Tyseley	d				13 33							14 03				14 33							15 03
Small Heath	d				13 35							14 05				14 35							15 05
Bordesley	d																						
Birmingham Moor Street	d	13 29			13 39	13 48	13 52		13 58			14 09	14 17	14 29		14 39	14 48	14 52		14 59			15 09
Birmingham Snow Hill ⇌	a	13 32			13 42	13 51	14 04		14 02			14 12	14 20	14 32		14 42	14 51	15 04		15 02			15 12
	d	13 33			13 43	13 53			14 03			14 13	14 23	14 33		14 43	14 53			15 03			15 13
Jewellery Quarter ⇌	d	13 35			13 45	13 55			14 05			14 15	14 25	14 35		14 45	14 55			15 05			15 15
The Hawthorns ⇌	d	13 40			13 50	14 00			14 10			14 20	14 30	14 40		14 50	15 00			15 10			15 20
Smethwick Galton Bridge 7	d	13 43			13 53	14 03			14 13			14 23	14 33	14 43		14 53	15 03			15 13			15 23
Coventry	a									14 22											15 24		
Birmingham International ✈	a									14 37											15 37		
Birmingham New Street 12	a							14 18		14 48									15 18		15 48		
	d			13 49											14 49								
Langley Green	d	13 46							14 16					14 46						15 16			
Rowley Regis	d	13 49			13 58	14 08			14 19			14 28	14 38	14 49		14 58	15 08			15 19			15 28
Old Hill	d	13 52							14 22					14 52						15 22			
Cradley Heath	d	13 56			14 03	14 13			14 26			14 33	14 43	14 56		15 03	15 13			15 26			15 33
Lye	d	13 59							14 29					14 59						15 29			
Stourbridge Junction 2	d	14 03			14 09	14a19			14 33			14 39	14a49	15 03		15 09	15a19			15 33			15 39
Hagley	d				14 12							14 42				15 12				15 37			15 43
Blakedown	d				14 15							14 45				15 15							15 46
Kidderminster	d	14a13			14 20				14a43			14 50		15a13		15 20				15a44			15 51
Hartlebury	d																						
University	d			13 55											14 55								
Barnt Green	d																						
Bromsgrove	d			14 10											15 10								
Droitwich Spa	d			14 20	14 31							15 01			15 20	15 31							16 01
Worcester Shrub Hill 7	a				14 39																		16 11
	d		14 15		14 43						14 49											15 44	
Worcester Foregate Street 7	a		14 18	14 30	14 45						14 52	15 10			15 30	15 40						15 47	
	d		14 18	14 32	14 46						14 53				15 32							15 48	
Malvern Link	d		14 27	14 42	14 54						15 06				15 42							15 57	
Great Malvern	a		14 37	14 44	14 58						15 11				15 44							16 00	
	d			14 45											15 45								
Colwall	d			14 50											15 50								
Ledbury	a			14 57											15 57								
	d			14 59											15 59								
Hereford 7	a			15 19											16 19								

A from 12 September

B until 9 September

Stratford-upon-Avon, Marylebone and Leamington Spa - Birmingham - Stourbridge, Worcester and Hereford

		LM	LM	GW	LM	LM	LM	CH	XC	LM	GW	LM	LM	LM	XC	LM	LM	LM	XC	LM	LM	LM
				◇				◇	◇1		◇1				◇1				◇1			
											A											
									⊼						⊼				⊼			
Stratford-upon-Avon	d	14 27												15 27								
Wilmcote	d	14 32												15 32								
Wootton Wawen	d	14x37												15x37								
Henley-in-Arden	d	14 41												15 41								
Danzey	d	14x45												15x45								
Wood End	d	14x49												15x49								
The Lakes	d	14x51												15x51								
Earlswood (West Midlands)	d	14 54												15 54								
Wythall	d	14 56												15 56								
Whitlocks End	d	14 59				15 19				15 39				15 59				16 18			16 39	
Shirley	d	15 02				15 22				15 42				16 02				16 21			16 42	
Yardley Wood	d	15 05				15 25				15 45				16 05				16 24			16 45	
Hall Green	d	15 08				15 28				15 48				16 08				16 27			16 48	
Spring Road	d	15 10				15 30				15 50				16 10				16 29			16 50	
London Marylebone 10 ⊖	d							14 07														
Banbury	d							15 05	15 25						15 54				16 26			
Leamington Spa 8	a							15 22	15 42						16 10				16 43			
	d							15 22	15 43						16 12				16 44			
Warwick	d							15 25														
Warwick Parkway	d							15 29														
Hatton	d																					
Lapworth	d																					
Dorridge	d		15 09				15 28	15 38					15 46			16 09				16 27		
Widney Manor	d		15 13				15 32						15 50			16 13				16 31		
Solihull	d		15 17				15 36	15 43					15 54			16 17				16 35		
Olton	d		15 20				15 39						15 57			16 20				16 38		
Acocks Green	d		15 23				15 42						16 00			16 23				16 41		
Tyseley	d					15 33							16 03					16 32		16 44	16 53	
Small Heath	d					15 35							16 05					16 34				
Bordesley	d																					
Birmingham Moor Street	d	15 17	15 29			15 39	15 48	15 52		15 59			16 09	16 17		16 29		16 38		16 49	16 58	
Birmingham Snow Hill ⇌	a	15 20	15 32			15 42	15 51	16 04		16 02			16 12	16 21		16 32		16 41		16 51	17 02	
	d	15 23	15 33			15 43	15 53			16 03			16 13	16 23		16 33		16 43		16 53	17 03	
Jewellery Quarter ⇌	d	15 25	15 35			15 45	15 55			16 05			16 15	16 25		16 35		16 46		16 55	17 05	
The Hawthorns ⇌	d	15 30	15 40			15 50	16 00			16 10			16 20	16 30		16 40		16 51		17 00	17 10	
Smethwick Galton Bridge 7	d	15 33	15 43			15 53	16 03			16 13			16 23	16 33		16 43		16 54		17 03	17 13	
Coventry	a														16 22							
Birmingham International ✈	a														16 37							
Birmingham New Street 12	a								16 18						16 48				17 18			
	d				15 49							16 19					16 49					17 19
Langley Green	d		15 46							16 16						16 46					17 16	
Rowley Regis	d	15 38	15 49			15 58	16 08			16 19			16 28	16 38		16 49		16 59		17 08	17 19	
Old Hill	d		15 52							16 22						16 52					17 22	
Cradley Heath	d	15 43	15 56			16 03	16 13			16 26			16 33	16 43		16 56		17 05		17 13	17 26	
Lye	d		15 59							16 29						16 59					17 29	
Stourbridge Junction 2	d	15a49	16 03			16 09	16a19			16 33			16 39	16a49		17 03		17 11		17a19	17 33	
Hagley	d		16 06			16 12							16 42			17 06		17 15			17 37	
Blakedown	d					16 15							16 45			17 09		17 19			17 40	
Kidderminster	d		16a14			16 20				16a43			16 50			17a15		17 24			17a45	
Hartlebury	d																	17 29				
University	d				15 55							16 25					16 55					17 25
Barnt Green	d																					
Bromsgrove	d				16 10							16 41					17 10					17 41
Droitwich Spa	d				16 20	16 31						16 51	17 01				17 20	17 37				17 51
Worcester Shrub Hill 7	a											16 58					17 27					17 59
	d			16 15							16 40	17 06					17 32					18 04
Worcester Foregate Street 7	a			16 18	16 30	16 40					16 43	17 08	17 10				17 34	17 47				18 06
	d			16 18	16 32							17 09					17 35					18 07
Malvern Link	d			16 27	16 42							17 18					17 44					18 16
Great Malvern	a			16 33	16 44							17 21					17 46					18 18
	d				16 45												17 47					18 19
Colwall	d				16 50												17 52					18 24
Ledbury	a				16 57												17 59					18 31
	d				16 59												18 01					18 32
Hereford 7	a				17 19												18 21					18 52

A from 12 September

Table 71 | **Mondays to Fridays**

Stratford-upon-Avon, Marylebone and Leamington Spa - Birmingham - Stourbridge, Worcester and Hereford

		LM	CH	LM	XC	GW	LM	LM	CH	LM	LM	XC	LM	LM	LM	LM	GW	LM	XC	XC	GW	LM	LM
					◇1				◇			◇1					1		◇1	◇1	◇1		
																	C				C		
					✠				✠			✠							✠	✠	⊡		
Stratford-upon-Avon	d			16 23											17 23							17 55	
Wilmcote	d			16 28											17 28								
Wootton Wawen	d			16x33											17x33								
Henley-in-Arden	d			16 38											17 37							18 05	
Danzey	d			16x43											17x41								
Wood End	d			16x47											17x45								
The Lakes	d			16x49											17x47								
Earlswood (West Midlands)	d			16 52											17 50								
Wythall	d			16 55											17 52								
Whitlocks End	d			16 58						17 15				17 42	17 55							18 15	
Shirley	d			17 01						17 18				17 44	17 58							18 18	
Yardley Wood	d			17 04						17 21				17 47	18 01							18 21	
Hall Green	d			17 07						17 24				17 50	18 04							18 24	
Spring Road	d			17 09						17 26				17 52	18 06							18 26	
London Marylebone [10] ⊖	d		15 37						16 10														
Banbury	d		16 30		16 54							17 28							17 54	18 26			
Leamington Spa [8]	a		16 47		17 11							17 46							18 11	18 45			
	d		16 47		17 12							17 47							18 12	18 46			
Warwick	d																						
Warwick Parkway	d		16 53						17 16														
Hatton	d																						
Lapworth	d																						
Dorridge	d	16 46						17 09					17 28			18 02							18 23
Widney Manor	d	16 50						17 13					17 32			18 06							18 27
Solihull	d	16 54	17 04					17 17	17 27				17 36			18 10							18 31
Olton	d	16 57						17 20					17 39			18 13							18 34
Acocks Green	d	17 00						17 23					17 42			18 16							18 37
Tyseley	d	17 03								17 29			17 45			18 19						18 29	18 40
Small Heath	d	17 05								17 31			17 47			18 21						18 32	18 42
Bordesley	d																						
Birmingham Moor Street	d	17 09	17 12	17 16				17 29	17 35	17 35			17 51	17 59	18 13	18 25						18 36	18 46
Birmingham Snow Hill ⇌	a	17 12	17 21	17 19				17 32	17 48	17 38			17 54	18 02	18 16	18 29						18 39	18 49
	d	17 13		17 20				17 33		17 43			17 54	18 03	18 18	18 31						18 43	
Jewellery Quarter ⇌	d	17 16		17 23				17 36		17 45			17 57	18 05	18 20	18 33						18 45	
The Hawthorns ⇌	d	17 21		17 27				17 41		17 50			18 02	18 10	18 25	18 38						18 50	
Smethwick Galton Bridge [7]	d	17 24		17 30				17 44		17 53			18 05	18 13	18 28	18 41						18 53	
Coventry	a				17 23														18 22				
Birmingham International ✈	a				17 37														18 37				
Birmingham New Street [12]	a				17 48							18 18							18 48	19 18			
	d						17 49				17 59							18 19					
Langley Green	d			17 33						17 56				18 16		18 44							
Rowley Regis	d	17 30		17 37				17 50		17 59			18 10	18 19	18 33	18 47						18 58	
Old Hill	d			17 40						18 02				18 22		18 50							
Cradley Heath	d	17 35		17 43				17 55		18 06			18 15	18 26	18 38	18 54						19 04	
Lye	d			17 46						18 09				18 29		18 57							
Stourbridge Junction [2]	d	17 42		17a51				18 01		18 13			18 21	18 33	18 44	19a01						19 09	
Hagley	d	17 46						18 05		18 17			18 25	18 37	18 48							19 13	
Blakedown	d	17 49						18 08		18 20			18 28	18 40	18 51							19 16	
Kidderminster	d	17 54						18 13		18a26			18 33	18a45	18a56							19 21	
Hartlebury	d							18 18					18 38										
University	d						17 55				18 05												
Barnt Green	d																						
Bromsgrove	d										18 21							18 45					
Droitwich Spa	d	18 05					18 17	18 26			18 34		18 46					18 57				19 31	
Worcester Shrub Hill [7]	a	18 18					18 25				18 42		18 58					19 10					
	d					18 19	18 32				18 54						19 08				19 35		
Worcester Foregate Street [7]	a					18 22	18 34	18 36			18 56						19 11				19 38	19 41	
	d					18 22	18 35				18 57						19 11				19 39		
Malvern Link	d					18 30	18 44				19 06						19 20				19 48		
Great Malvern	a					18 37	18 46				19 09						19 24				19 52		
	d						18 48														19 52		
Colwall	d						18 53														19 58		
Ledbury	a						19 01														20 06		
	d						19 04														20 09		
Hereford [7]	a						19 24														20 27		

C from 12 September

Table 71 | **Mondays to Fridays**

Stratford-upon-Avon, Marylebone and Leamington Spa - Birmingham - Stourbridge, Worcester and Hereford

		LM	LM	GW	LM	XC	GW	LM	LM	LM	LM	XC	GW	GW	LM	LM	CH	XC	LM	XC	GW	GW	LM
				◇1		◇1						◇1	◇1	◇1				◇1		◇1	◇1	◇1	
				A		B						C	D	E				B			F	A	
				⊡		✠						✠	⊡	⊡				✠		✠	⊡	⊡	
Stratford-upon-Avon	d		18 25						18 50							19 26							
Wilmcote	d		18 30						18 55							19 31							
Wootton Wawen	d		18x35						19x00							19x36							
Henley-in-Arden	d		18 39						19 04							19 40							
Danzey	d		18x43													19x44							
Wood End	d		18x47													19x48							
The Lakes	d		18x49													19x50							
Earlswood (West Midlands)	d		18 52													19 53							
Wythall	d		18 54													19 55							
Whitlocks End	d	18 36	18 57						19 14	19 25						19 58							
Shirley	d	18 39	19 00						19 17	19 27						20 01							
Yardley Wood	d	18 42	19 03						19 20	19 30						20 04							
Hall Green	d	18 45	19 06						19 23	19 33						20 07							
Spring Road	d	18 47	19 08						19 25	19 35						20 09							
London Marylebone [10] ⊖	d																18 37						
Banbury	d					18 54						19 31					19 35	19 54		20 28			
Leamington Spa [8]	a					19 10						19 49					19 54	20 10		20 45			
	d					19 12						19 50					19 54	20 12		20 46			
Warwick	d																19 58						
Warwick Parkway	d																20 02						
Hatton	d																						
Lapworth	d																						
Dorridge	d							18 58							19 30		20 11						20 29
Widney Manor	d							19 02							19 34								20 33
Solihull	d							19 06							19 38		20 16						20 36
Olton	d							19 09							19 41								20 40
Acocks Green	d							19 12							19 44								20 42
Tyseley	d	18 50						19 15		19 38					19 47								20 45
Small Heath	d							19 17		19 40					19 49								20 48
Bordesley	d																						
Birmingham Moor Street	d	18 55	19 15					19 23	19 35	19 44					19 53	20 16	20 24						20 52
Birmingham Snow Hill ⇌	a	18 57	19 18					19 26	19 37	19 47					19 56	20 19	20 34						20 54
	d	18 59						19 27	19 38						19 58	20 20							20 55
Jewellery Quarter ⇌	d	19 01						19 29	19 41						20 00	20 22							20 58
The Hawthorns ⇌	d	19 06						19 34	19 45						20 05	20 27							21 02
Smethwick Galton Bridge [7]	d	19 09						19 37	19 48						20 08	20 30							21 05
Coventry	a					19 22												20 22					
Birmingham International ✈	a					19 37												20 37					
Birmingham New Street [12]	a					19 48						20 18						20 48		21 22			
	d				19 19						19 49								20 59				
Langley Green	d	19 12						19 40							20 11	20 33							21 08
Rowley Regis	d	19 15						19 43	19 54						20 14	20 36							21 11
Old Hill	d	19 18						19 46							20 17	20 39							21 14
Cradley Heath	d	19 22						19 50	19 59						20 21	20 43							21 17
Lye	d	19 25						19 53							20 24	20 46							21 20
Stourbridge Junction [2]	d	19a29						19 57	20a06						20 28	20a51							21 24
Hagley	d							20 00							20 31								21 28
Blakedown	d							20 03							20 34								21 31
Kidderminster	d							20 08							20 39								21 36
Hartlebury	d																						
University	d				19 25						19 55								21 05				
Barnt Green	d																						
Bromsgrove	d				19 41						20 12								21 22				
Droitwich Spa	d				19 52			20 19			20 26				20 50				21 32				21 47
Worcester Shrub Hill [7]	a				20 02			20 27			20 33				20 59								21 57
	d			19 45	20 10		20 20						20 41	20 42							21 47	21 49	22 03
Worcester Foregate Street [7]	a			19 48	20 12		20 22						20 45	20 45					21 40		21 50	21 52	22 05
	d			19 49	20 13		20 25						20 45	20 46					21 41		21 51	21 53	
Malvern Link	d			19 58	20 22		20 34						20 54	20 55					21 51		22 02	22 04	
Great Malvern	a			20 02	20 24		20 40						20 58	20 58					21 53		22 06	22 08	
	d			20 02	20 25								20 58	20 59					21 54		22 19	22 19	
Colwall	d			20 08	20 31								21 04	21 05					21 59		22 26	22 25	
Ledbury	a			20 16	20 38								21 12	21 12					22 06		22 33	22 33	
	d			20 17	20 41								21 14	21 14					22 09		22 35	22 35	
Hereford [7]	a			20 36	21 02								21 33	21 33					22 29		22 54	22 54	

A until 9 September
B ✠ to Birmingham International
C ✠ to Leamington Spa
D until 9 September. The Cathedrals Express
E from 12 September. The Cathedrals Express
F from 12 September

Table 71

Mondays to Fridays

Stratford-upon-Avon, Marylebone and Leamington Spa - Birmingham - Stourbridge, Worcester and Hereford

		LM	CH	XC	GW	GW	LM	LM	XC	XC	LM	LM	LM	XC	LM
				◇1	◇1	◇1			◇1	◇1				◇1	
					A	B									
Stratford-upon-Avon	d	20 26													
Wilmcote	d	20 31													
Wootton Wawen	d	20x36													
Henley-in-Arden	d	20 40													
Danzey	d	20x44													
Wood End	d	20x48													
The Lakes	d	20x50													
Earlswood (West Midlands)	d	20 53													
Wythall	d	20 55													
Whitlocks End	d	20 58									21 55				22 55
Shirley	d	21 01									21 57				22 57
Yardley Wood	d	21 04									22 00				23 00
Hall Green	d	21 07									22 03				23 03
Spring Road	d	21 09									22 05				23 05
London Marylebone 10 ⊖	d		19 37												
Banbury	d		20 37	20 54					21 41	21 54				22 54	
Leamington Spa 8	a		20 54	21 10					21 59	22 10				23 12	
	d		20 54	21 12					22 00	22 12				23 13	
Warwick	d		20 58												
Warwick Parkway	d		21 02												
Hatton	d														
Lapworth	d														
Dorridge	d		21 12					21 31					22 33		
Widney Manor	d							21 35					22 37		
Solihull	d		21 17					21 38					22 41		
Olton	d							21 42					22 44		
Acocks Green	d							21 44					22 47		
Tyseley	d							21 47			22 08		22 50		23 08
Small Heath	d							21 50			22 10		22 52		23 10
Bordesley	d														
Birmingham Moor Street	d	21 16	21 26					21 54			22 14		22 56		23 14
Birmingham Snow Hill	a	21 19	21 37					21 56			22 17		22 59		23 17
	d	21 20						21 57			22 20		23 00		
Jewellery Quarter	d	21 22						22 00			22 22		23 02		
The Hawthorns	d	21 27						22 04			22 27		23 07		
Smethwick Galton Bridge 7	d	21 30						22 07			22 30		23 10		
Coventry	a			21 22						22 22				23 25	
Birmingham International	a			21 37						22 33				23 36	
Birmingham New Street 12	a			21 48					22 30	22 45				23 49	
	d						22 00					23 00			
Langley Green	d	21 33						22 10			22 33		23 13		
Rowley Regis	d	21 36						22 13			22 36		23 16		
Old Hill	d	21 39						22 16			22 39		23 19		
Cradley Heath	d	21 43						22 19			22 43		23 23		
Lye	d	21 46						22 22			22 46		23 26		
Stourbridge Junction 2	d	21a50						22 26			22a50		23 30		
Hagley	d							22 30					23 33		
Blakedown	d							22 33					23 36		
Kidderminster	d							22 38					23 41		
Hartlebury	d														
University	d						22 06					23 06			
Barnt Green	d														
Bromsgrove	d						22 20					23 19			
Droitwich Spa	d						22 33	22 49				23 29	23 52		
Worcester Shrub Hill 7	a						22 47	22 57				23 37	00 01		
	d				22 40	22 40		23 05							
Worcester Foregate Street 7	a				22 43	22 44		23 07							
	d				22 44	22 44		23 08							
Malvern Link	d				22 52	22 53		23 16							
Great Malvern	a				22 58	22 59		23 19							
	d														
Colwall	d														
Ledbury	a														
	d														
Hereford 7	a														

A from 12 September

B until 9 September

Table 71

Saturdays

Stratford-upon-Avon, Marylebone and Leamington Spa - Birmingham - Stourbridge, Worcester and Hereford

		LM	LM	LM	LM	GW	GW	LM	LM	XC	LM	LM	XC	GW	GW	LM	LM	LM	LM	LM	GW	GW	LM
						◇1	◇1			◇1			◇1	◇1	◇1						◇1	◇1	
						A	B							B	A						B	A	
Stratford-upon-Avon	d																07 02		07 45				
Wilmcote	d																07 07		07 50				
Wootton Wawen	d																07x12		07x55				
Henley-in-Arden	d																07 16		07 59				
Danzey	d																07x20		08x04				
Wood End	d																07x24		08x08				
The Lakes	d																07x26		08x10				
Earlswood (West Midlands)	d																07 28		08 13				
Wythall	d																07 31		08 15				
Whitlocks End	d										07 03						07 33		08 18				
Shirley	d										07 05						07 36		08 21				
Yardley Wood	d										07 08						07 39		08 24				
Hall Green	d										07 11						07 42		08 27				
Spring Road	d										07 13						07 44		08 29				
London Marylebone 10 ⊖	d																						
Banbury	d									06 56			07 33										
Leamington Spa 8	a									07 12			07 50										
	d								06 26	07 14			07 51										07 56
Warwick	d								06 30														08 00
Warwick Parkway	d								06 34														08 04
Hatton	d								06 39														08 09
Lapworth	d								06 45														08 15
Dorridge	d	22p33							06 50							07 25		08 05					08 21
Widney Manor	d	22p37							06 53							07 29		08 09					08 24
Solihull	d	22p41							06 57							07 33		08 13					08 28
Olton	d	22p44							07 00							07 36		08 16					08 31
Acocks Green	d	22p47							07 03							07 39		08 19					08 34
Tyseley	d	22p50							07 06		07 16					07 42	07 47	08 22	08 32				08 37
Small Heath	d	22p52							07 08		07 19					07 44	07 50		08 34				08 39
Bordesley	d																						
Birmingham Moor Street	d	22p56			06 31			07 01	07 12		07 23					07 48	07 55	08 27	08 38				08 43
Birmingham Snow Hill	a	22p59			06 33			07 03	07 15		07 25					07 51	07 57	08 29	08 42				08 47
	d	23p00			06 35			07 05			07 28					07 53	08 03	08 30	08 43				08 53
Jewellery Quarter	d	23p02			06 37			07 07			07 30					07 55	08 05	08 33	08 45				08 55
The Hawthorns	d	23p07			06 42			07 12			07 35					08 00	08 10	08 37	08 50				09 00
Smethwick Galton Bridge 7	d	23p10			06 45			07 15			07 38					08 03	08 13	08 40	08 53				09 03
Coventry	a									07 24													
Birmingham International	a									07 37													
Birmingham New Street 12	a									07 48			08 17										
	d			06 49								07 49								08 49			
Langley Green	d	23p13			06 48			07 18			07 41						08 16	08 43					
Rowley Regis	d	23p16			06 51			07 21			07 44					08 08	08 19	08 47	08 58				09 08
Old Hill	d	23p19			06 54			07 24			07 47						08 22	08 50					
Cradley Heath	d	23p23			06 57			07 27			07 51					08 12	08 26	08 53	09 02				09 13
Lye	d	23p26			07 00			07 30			07 54						08 29	08 56					
Stourbridge Junction 2	d	23p30			07 04			07 35			07a58					08 18	08a33	09a00	09a08				09 19
Hagley	d	23p33			07 08			07 38								08 21							09 22
Blakedown	d	23p36			07 11			07 41								08 24							09 25
Kidderminster	d	23p41			07 16			07 46								08 29							09 30
Hartlebury	d				07 21																		
University	d			06 55								07 55								08 55			
Barnt Green	d																						
Bromsgrove	d			07 10								08 10								09 10			
Droitwich Spa	d	23p52		07 20	07 28			07 57				08 20				08 40				09 20			09 41
Worcester Shrub Hill 7	a	00 01			07 39			08 07															09 49
	d		06 30			07 44	07 46	08 11						08 41	08 45						09 41	09 44	
Worcester Foregate Street 7	a		06 32	07 30		07 46	07 48	08 13				08 30		08 44	08 47	08 49				09 30	09 44	09 46	
	d		06 33	07 32		07 48	07 50	08 14				08 32		08 45	08 48					09 32	09 45	09 48	
Malvern Link	d		06 42	07 42		07 57	07 59	08 23				08 42		08 54	08 57					09 42	09 54	09 57	
Great Malvern	a		06 44	07 44		08 01	08 03	08 26				08 44		09 00	09 04					09 44	10 00	10 04	
	d		06 45	07 45								08 45								09 45			
Colwall	d		06 50	07 50								08 50								09 50			
Ledbury	a		06 57	07 57								08 57								09 57			
	d		06 58	07 59								08 59								09 59			
Hereford 7	a		07 14	08 19								09 19								10 19			

A until 10 September

B from 17 September

Table 71

Saturdays

Stratford-upon-Avon, Marylebone and Leamington Spa - Birmingham - Stourbridge, Worcester and Hereford

		XC	XC	LM	LM	LM		XC	LM	GW	LM	LM	XC	LM	LM	XC		GW	GW	LM	LM	LM	LM	LM	XC
		◇1	◇1					◇1					◇1			◇1		◇1 A	◇1 B						◇1
Stratford-upon-Avon	d					08 27															09 27				
Wilmcote	d					08 32															09 32				
Wootton Wawen	d					08x37															09x37				
Henley-in-Arden	d					08 41															09 41				
Danzey	d					08x45															09x45				
Wood End	d					08x49															09x49				
The Lakes	d					08x51															09x51				
Earlswood (West Midlands)	d					08 54															09 54				
Wythall	d					08 56															09 56				
Whitlocks End	d			08 35		08 59						09 19			09 39						09 59			10 19	
Shirley	d			08 38		09 02						09 22			09 42						10 02			10 22	
Yardley Wood	d			08 41		09 05						09 25			09 45						10 05			10 25	
Hall Green	d			08 44		09 08						09 28			09 48						10 08			10 28	
Spring Road	d			08 46		09 10						09 30			09 50						10 10			10 30	
London Marylebone ⊖	d																								
Banbury	d	07 54	08 33					08 54					09 24			09 54									10 24
Leamington Spa	a	08 10	08 49					09 10					09 41			10 11									10 41
	d	08 12	08 50					09 12					09 42			10 12									10 42
Warwick	d																								
Warwick Parkway	d																								
Hatton	d																								
Lapworth	d																								
Dorridge	d				08 46				09 09					09 28						09 46		10 09			
Widney Manor	d				08 50				09 13					09 32						09 50		10 13			
Solihull	d				08 54				09 17					09 36						09 54		10 17			
Olton	d				08 57				09 20					09 39						09 57		10 20			
Acocks Green	d				09 00				09 23					09 42						10 00		10 23			
Tyseley	d			08 49	09 03							09 33								10 03				10 33	
Small Heath	d			08 51	09 05							09 35								10 05				10 35	
Bordesley	d																								
Birmingham Moor Street	d			08 55	09 09	09 17			09 29			09 39		09 48	09 58					10 09	10 17	10 29		10 39	
Birmingham Snow Hill	a			08 58	09 12	09 20			09 32			09 42		09 51	10 00					10 12	10 20	10 32		10 42	
	d			09 03	09 13	09 23			09 33			09 43		09 53	10 03					10 13	10 23	10 33		10 43	
Jewellery Quarter	d			09 05	09 15	09 25			09 35			09 45		09 55	10 05					10 15	10 25	10 35		10 45	
The Hawthorns	d			09 10	09 20	09 30			09 40			09 50		10 00	10 10					10 20	10 30	10 40		10 50	
Smethwick Galton Bridge	d			09 13	09 23	09 33			09 43			09 53		10 03	10 13					10 23	10 33	10 43		10 53	
Coventry	a	08 22						09 22								10 22									
Birmingham International ✈	a	08 37						09 37								10 37									
Birmingham New Street	a	08 48	09 19					09 48					10 17			10 48									11 18
	d										09 49												10 49		
Langley Green	d			09 16					09 46						10 16							10 46			
Rowley Regis	d			09 19	09 28	09 38			09 49			09 58		10 08	10 19					10 28	10 38	10 49		10 58	
Old Hill	d			09 22					09 52						10 22							10 52			
Cradley Heath	d			09 26	09 33	09 43			09 56			10 03		10 13	10 26					10 33	10 43	10 56		11 03	
Lye	d			09 29					09 59						10 29							10 59			
Stourbridge Junction	d			09 33	09 39	09a49			10 03			10 09		10a19	10 33					10 39	10a49	11 03		11 09	
Hagley	d				09 42							10 12								10 42				11 12	
Blakedown	d				09 45							10 15								10 45				11 15	
Kidderminster	d			09a42	09 50				10a12			10 20			10a42					10 50		11a12		11 20	
Hartlebury	d																								
University	d										09 55												10 55		
Barnt Green	d																								
Bromsgrove	d										10 10												11 10		
Droitwich Spa	d				10 01						10 20	10 31								11 01			11 20	11 31	
Worcester Shrub Hill	a											10 39												11 39	
	d									10 15								10 45	10 46						
Worcester Foregate Street	a				10 10					10 17	10 30							10 48	10 48	11 10			11 30		
	d									10 18	10 32							10 48	10 50	11 11			11 32		
Malvern Link	d									10 27	10 42							10 57	10 58	11 19			11 42		
Great Malvern	a									10 32	10 44							11 04	11 05	11 22			11 44		
	d										10 45							11 07	11 06				11 45		
Colwall	d										10 50							11 14	11 12				11 50		
Ledbury	a										10 57							11 21	11 20				11 57		
	d										10 59							11 23	11 22				11 59		
Hereford	a										11 19							11 41	11 41				12 19		

A until 10 September

B from 17 September

Table 71

Saturdays

Stratford-upon-Avon, Marylebone and Leamington Spa - Birmingham - Stourbridge, Worcester and Hereford

		LM		LM	LM	LM	XC	LM	GW	LM	LM	XC		LM	LM	XC	GW	GW	LM	LM	LM	LM		LM	XC
							◇1		◇			◇1				◇1	◇1 A	◇1 B							◇1
Stratford-upon-Avon	d					10 27														11 27					
Wilmcote	d					10 32														11 32					
Wootton Wawen	d					10x37														11x37					
Henley-in-Arden	d					10 41														11 41					
Danzey	d					10x45														11x45					
Wood End	d					10x49														11x49					
The Lakes	d					10x51														11x51					
Earlswood (West Midlands)	d					10 54														11 54					
Wythall	d					10 56														11 56					
Whitlocks End	d			10 39		10 59					11 19				11 39					11 59				12 19	
Shirley	d			10 42		11 02					11 22				11 42					12 02				12 22	
Yardley Wood	d			10 45		11 05					11 25				11 45					12 05				12 25	
Hall Green	d			10 48		11 08					11 28				11 48					12 08				12 28	
Spring Road	d			10 50		11 10					11 30				11 50					12 10				12 30	
London Marylebone ⊖	d																								
Banbury	d						10 54					11 24				11 54									12 24
Leamington Spa	a						11 10					11 41				12 10									12 41
	d						11 12					11 42				12 12									12 42
Warwick	d																								
Warwick Parkway	d																								
Hatton	d																								
Lapworth	d																								
Dorridge	d	10 28			10 46			11 09						11 28					11 46		12 09				
Widney Manor	d	10 32			10 50			11 13						11 32					11 50		12 13				
Solihull	d	10 36			10 54			11 17						11 36					11 54		12 17				
Olton	d	10 39			10 57			11 20						11 39					11 57		12 20				
Acocks Green	d	10 42			11 00			11 23						11 42					12 00		12 23				
Tyseley	d				11 03						11 33								12 03					12 33	
Small Heath	d				11 05						11 35								12 05					12 35	
Bordesley	d																								
Birmingham Moor Street	d	10 48		10 57	11 09	11 18		11 29			11 39			11 48	11 57				12 09	12 17	12 29			12 39	
Birmingham Snow Hill	a	10 51		11 01	11 12	11 20		11 32			11 42			11 51	12 01				12 12	12 20	12 32			12 42	
	d	10 53		11 03	11 13	11 23		11 33			11 43			11 53	12 03				12 13	12 23	12 33			12 43	
Jewellery Quarter	d	10 55		11 05	11 15	11 25		11 35			11 45			11 55	12 05				12 15	12 25	12 35			12 45	
The Hawthorns	d	11 00		11 10	11 20	11 30		11 40			11 50			12 00	12 10				12 20	12 30	12 40			12 50	
Smethwick Galton Bridge	d	11 03		11 13	11 23	11 33		11 43			11 53			12 03	12 13				12 23	12 33	12 43			12 53	
Coventry	a						11 22									12 22									
Birmingham International ✈	a						11 37									12 37									
Birmingham New Street	a						11 48					12 18				12 48									13 18
	d									11 49												12 49			
Langley Green	d			11 16				11 46							12 16						12 46				
Rowley Regis	d	11 08		11 19	11 28	11 38		11 49			11 58			12 08	12 19				12 28	12 38	12 49			12 58	
Old Hill	d			11 22				11 52							12 22						12 52				
Cradley Heath	d	11 13		11 26	11 33	11 43		11 56			12 03			12 13	12 26				12 33	12 43	12 56			13 03	
Lye	d			11 29				11 59							12 29						12 59				
Stourbridge Junction	d	11a19		11 33	11 39	11a49		12 03			12 09			12a19	12 33				12 39	12a49	13 03			13 09	
Hagley	d				11 42						12 12								12 42					13 12	
Blakedown	d				11 45						12 15								12 45					13 15	
Kidderminster	d			11a42	11 50			12a12			12 20				12a42				12 50		13a12			13 20	
Hartlebury	d																								
University	d									11 55												12 55			
Barnt Green	d																								
Bromsgrove	d									12 10												13 10			
Droitwich Spa	d				12 01					12 20	12 31								13 01			13 20		13 31	
Worcester Shrub Hill	a																							13 39	
	d								12 16								12 41	12 45							
Worcester Foregate Street	a				12 10				12 18	12 30	12 40						12 43	12 48	13 10			13 30			
	d									12 32							12 45	12 48	13 11			13 32			
Malvern Link	d									12 42							12 53	12 57	13 19			13 42			
Great Malvern	a									12 44							12 58	13 04	13 22			13 44			
	d									12 45							13 06	13 07				13 45			
Colwall	d									12 50							13 13	13 14				13 50			
Ledbury	a									12 57							13 21	13 21				13 57			
	d									12 59							13 23	13 23				13 59			
Hereford	a									13 19							13 40	13 40				14 19			

A from 17 September

B until 10 September

Table 71

Saturdays

Stratford-upon-Avon, Marylebone and Leamington Spa - Birmingham - Stourbridge, Worcester and Hereford

		LM	LM	XC	GW	GW	LM	LM	LM	GW	LM	LM	XC	LM	LM	LM	LM	XC	LM	LM	LM	XC	LM
				◇1	◇1 A	◇1 B				◇			◇1					◇1				◇1	
Stratford-upon-Avon	d							12 27									13 27						
Wilmcote	d							12 32									13 32						
Wootton Wawen	d							12x37									13x37						
Henley-in-Arden	d							12 41									13 41						
Danzey	d							12x45									13x45						
Wood End	d							12x49									13x49						
The Lakes	d							12x51									13x51						
Earlswood (West Midlands)	d							12 54									13 54						
Wythall	d							12 56									13 56						
Whitlocks End	d		12 39					12 59				13 19			13 39		13 59				14 19		
Shirley	d		12 42					13 02				13 22			13 42		14 02				14 22		
Yardley Wood	d		12 45					13 05				13 25			13 45		14 05				14 25		
Hall Green	d		12 48					13 08				13 28			13 48		14 08				14 28		
Spring Road	d		12 50					13 10				13 30			13 50		14 10				14 30		
London Marylebone 10 ⊖	d																						
Banbury	d			12 54									13 24					13 54				14 24	
Leamington Spa 8	a			13 10									13 41					14 10				14 41	
	d			13 12									13 42					14 12				14 42	
Warwick	d																						
Warwick Parkway	d																						
Hatton	d																						
Lapworth	d																						
Dorridge	d	12 28					12 46		13 09					13 28		13 46			14 09				14 28
Widney Manor	d	12 32					12 50		13 13					13 32		13 50			14 13				14 32
Solihull	d	12 36					12 54		13 17					13 36		13 54			14 17				14 36
Olton	d	12 39					12 57		13 20					13 39		13 57			14 20				14 39
Acocks Green	d	12 42					13 00		13 23					13 42		14 00			14 23				14 42
Tyseley	d						13 03					13 33				14 03					14 33		
Small Heath	d						13 05					13 35				14 05					14 35		
Bordesley	d											13 37											
Birmingham Moor Street	d	12 48	12 57				13 09	13 17	13 29			13 40		13 48	13 57	14 09	14 17		14 29		14 39		14 48
Birmingham Snow Hill ⇌	a	12 51	13 01				13 12	13 20	13 32			13 43		13 51	14 01	14 12	14 20		14 32		14 42		14 51
	d	12 53	13 03				13 13	13 23	13 33			13 43		13 53	14 03	14 13	14 23		14 33		14 43		14 53
Jewellery Quarter ⇌	d	12 55	13 05				13 15	13 25	13 35			13 45		13 55	14 05	14 15	14 25		14 35		14 45		14 55
The Hawthorns ⇌	d	13 00	13 10				13 20	13 30	13 40			13 50		14 00	14 10	14 20	14 30		14 40		14 50		15 00
Smethwick Galton Bridge 7	d	13 03	13 13				13 23	13 33	13 43			13 53		14 03	14 13	14 23	14 33		14 43		14 53		15 03
Coventry	a			13 22														14 22					
Birmingham International ✈	a			13 37														14 37					
Birmingham New Street 12	a			13 48									14 18					14 48				15 17	
	d										13 49									14 49			
Langley Green	d		13 16						13 46						14 16				14 46				
Rowley Regis	d	13 08	13 19				13 28	13 38	13 49			13 58		14 08	14 19	14 28	14 38		14 49		14 58		15 08
Old Hill	d		13 22						13 52						14 22				14 52				
Cradley Heath	d	13 13	13 26				13 33	13 43	13 56			14 03		14 13	14 26	14 33	14 43		14 56		15 03		15 13
Lye	d		13 29						13 59						14 29				14 59				
Stourbridge Junction 2	d	13a19	13 33				13 39	13a49	14 03			14 09		14a19	14 33	14 39	14a49		15 03		15 09		15a19
Hagley	d						13 42					14 12				14 42					15 12		
Blakedown	d						13 45					14 15				14 45					15 15		
Kidderminster	d		13a42				13 50		14a12			14 20			14a42	14 50			15a12		15 20		
Hartlebury	d																						
University	d										13 55									14 55			
Barnt Green	d																						
Bromsgrove	d										14 10									15 10			
Droitwich Spa	d						14 01				14 20	14 31				15 01				15 20	15 31		
Worcester Shrub Hill 7	a											14 40									15 39		
	d				13 41	13 45				14 15		14 46											
Worcester Foregate Street 7	a				13 44	13 47	14 10			14 18	14 30	14 48				15 10				15 30			
	d				13 45	13 48				14 18	14 32	14 49								15 32			
Malvern Link	d				13 54	13 57				14 27	14 42	14 57								15 42			
Great Malvern	a				14 00	14 04				14 31	14 44	15 00								15 44			
	d										14 45									15 45			
Colwall	d										14 50									15 50			
Ledbury	a										14 57									15 57			
	d										14 59									15 59			
Hereford 7	a										15 19									16 17			

A from 17 September

B until 10 September

Table 71

Saturdays

Stratford-upon-Avon, Marylebone and Leamington Spa - Birmingham - Stourbridge, Worcester and Hereford

		LM	GW	GW	LM	LM	CH	XC	LM	GW	LM	LM	XC	LM	LM	XC	GW	GW	LM	LM	LM	LM
			◇1 A	◇1 B			◇	◇1		◇			◇1			◇1	◇1 A	◇1 B				
Stratford-upon-Avon	d					14 27														15 27		
Wilmcote	d					14 32														15 32		
Wootton Wawen	d					14x37														15x37		
Henley-in-Arden	d					14 41														15 41		
Danzey	d					14x45														15x45		
Wood End	d					14x49														15x49		
The Lakes	d					14x51														15x51		
Earlswood (West Midlands)	d					14 54														15 54		
Wythall	d					14 56														15 56		
Whitlocks End	d	14 39				14 59						15 19			15 39					15 59		
Shirley	d	14 42				15 02						15 22			15 42					16 02		
Yardley Wood	d	14 45				15 05						15 25			15 45					16 05		
Hall Green	d	14 48				15 08						15 28			15 48					16 08		
Spring Road	d	14 50				15 10						15 30			15 50					16 10		
London Marylebone 10 ⊖	d																					
Banbury	d							14 54					15 24			15 54						
Leamington Spa 8	a							15 10					15 41			16 10						
	d						14 53	15 12					15 42			16 12						
Warwick	d						14 56															
Warwick Parkway	d						14 59															
Hatton	d						15 07															
Lapworth	d						15 13															
Dorridge	d				14 46		15 14		15 09					15 28					15 46		16 09	
Widney Manor	d				14 50				15 13					15 32					15 50		16 13	
Solihull	d				14 54		15 20		15 17					15 36					15 54		16 17	
Olton	d				14 57				15 20					15 39					15 57		16 20	
Acocks Green	d				15 00				15 23					15 42					16 00		16 23	
Tyseley	d				15 03							15 33							16 03			
Small Heath	d				15 05							15 35							16 05			
Bordesley	d																					
Birmingham Moor Street	d	14 57			15 09	15 17	15a28		15 29			15 39		15 48	15 57				16 09	16 17	16 29	
Birmingham Snow Hill ⇌	a	15 01			15 12	15 20			15 32			15 42		15 51	16 01				16 12	16 20	16 32	
	d	15 03			15 13	15 23			15 33			15 43		15 53	16 03				16 13	16 23	16 33	
Jewellery Quarter ⇌	d	15 05			15 15	15 25			15 35			15 45		15 55	16 05				16 15	16 25	16 35	
The Hawthorns ⇌	d	15 10			15 20	15 30			15 40			15 50		16 00	16 10				16 20	16 30	16 40	
Smethwick Galton Bridge 7	d	15 13			15 23	15 33			15 43			15 53		16 03	16 13				16 23	16 33	16 43	
Coventry	a							15 22								16 22						
Birmingham International ✈	a							15 37								16 37						
Birmingham New Street 12	a							15 48					16 17			16 48						
	d										15 49											16 49
Langley Green	d	15 16							15 46						16 16						16 46	
Rowley Regis	d	15 19			15 28	15 38			15 49			15 58		16 08	16 19				16 28	16 38	16 49	
Old Hill	d	15 22							15 52						16 22						16 52	
Cradley Heath	d	15 26			15 33	15 43			15 56			16 03		16 13	16 26				16 33	16 43	16 56	
Lye	d	15 29							15 59						16 29						16 59	
Stourbridge Junction 2	d	15 33			15 39	15a49			16 03			16 09		16a19	16 33				16 39	16a49	17 03	
Hagley	d				15 42							16 12							16 42		17 06	
Blakedown	d				15 45							16 15							16 45		17 09	
Kidderminster	d	15a42			15 50				16a12			16 20			16a42				16 50		17a15	
Hartlebury	d																					
University	d										15 55											16 55
Barnt Green	d																					
Bromsgrove	d										16 10											17 10
Droitwich Spa	d				16 01						16 20	16 31							17 01			17 20
Worcester Shrub Hill 7	a											16 39										
	d		15 41	15 45						16 15							16 41	16 45				
Worcester Foregate Street 7	a		15 44	15 47	16 10					16 17	16 30						16 44	16 48	17 10			17 30
	d		15 45	15 48						16 18	16 32						16 45	16 48	17 11			17 32
Malvern Link	d		15 54	15 57						16 26	16 42						16 54	16 57	17 20			17 42
Great Malvern	a		16 00	16 04						16 32	16 44						17 00	17 04	17 23			17 45
	d										16 45											17 45
Colwall	d										16 50											17 50
Ledbury	a										16 57											17 57
	d										16 59											17 59
Hereford 7	a										17 19											18 16

A from 17 September

B until 10 September

Table 71

Saturdays

Stratford-upon-Avon, Marylebone and Leamington Spa - Birmingham - Stourbridge, Worcester and Hereford

		LM	XC	LM	LM	GW	GW	LM	LM	LM	CH	XC	LM	GW	LM	LM	XC	LM	LM	XC	GW	GW	LM
			◇1			◇1	◇1				◇	◇1					◇1			◇1	◇1	◇1	
						A	B														B	A	
			🍴								🍴	🍴					🍴			🍴	☕	☕	
Stratford-upon-Avon	d									16 27													17 27
Wilmcote	d									16 32													17 32
Wootton Wawen	d									16x37													17x37
Henley-in-Arden	d									16 41													17 41
Danzey	d									16x45													17x45
Wood End	d									16x49													17x49
The Lakes	d									16x51													17x51
Earlswood (West Midlands)	d									16 54													17 54
Wythall	d									16 56													17 56
Whitlocks End	d	16 19			16 39					16 59						17 19							17 59
Shirley	d	16 22			16 42					17 02						17 22							18 02
Yardley Wood	d	16 25			16 45					17 05						17 25							18 05
Hall Green	d	16 28			16 48					17 08						17 28							18 08
Spring Road	d	16 30			16 50					17 10						17 30							18 10
London Marylebone 10 ⊖	d																						
Banbury	d		16 24									16 54					17 24			17 54			
Leamington Spa 8	a		16 41									17 10					17 41			18 10			
	d		16 42								16 53	17 12					17 42			18 12			
Warwick	d										16 56												
Warwick Parkway	d										16 59												
Hatton	d										17 07												
Lapworth	d										17 13												
Dorridge	d			16 27					16 46		17 14		17 09					17 28	17 46				
Widney Manor	d			16 31					16 50				17 13					17 32	17 50				
Solihull	d			16 35					16 54		17 20		17 17					17 36	17 54				
Olton	d			16 38					16 57				17 20					17 39	17 57				
Acocks Green	d			16 41					17 00				17 23					17 42	18 00				
Tyseley	d	16 33		16 44	16 53				17 03							17 33		17 45	18 03				
Small Heath	d	16 35							17 05							17 35			18 05				
Bordesley	d																						
Birmingham Moor Street	d	16 39		16 49	16 58				17 09	17 17	17a28		17 29			17 39		17 50	18 09				18 17
Birmingham Snow Hill ⇌	a	16 42		16 51	17 01				17 12	17 20			17 32			17 42		17 52	18 12				18 20
	d	16 43		16 53	17 03				17 13	17 23			17 33			17 43		17 53	18 13				18 23
Jewellery Quarter ⇌	d	16 45		16 55	17 05				17 15	17 25			17 35			17 45		17 55	18 15				18 25
The Hawthorns ⇌	d	16 50		17 00	17 10				17 20	17 30			17 40			17 50		18 00	18 20				18 30
Smethwick Galton Bridge 7	d	16 53		17 03	17 13				17 23	17 33			17 43			17 53		18 03	18 23				18 33
Coventry	a											17 22								18 22			
Birmingham International ✈	a											17 37								18 37			
Birmingham New Street 12	a		17 17									17 48					18 18			18 48			
	d							17 19							17 49								
Langley Green	d				17 16								17 46					18 06	18 26				
Rowley Regis	d	16 58		17 08	17 19				17 28	17 38			17 49			17 58		18 09	18 29				18 38
Old Hill	d				17 22								17 52					18 12	18 32				
Cradley Heath	d	17 03		17 13	17 26				17 33	17 43			17 56			18 03		18 16	18 36				18 43
Lye	d				17 29								17 59					18 19	18 39				
Stourbridge Junction 2	d	17 09		17a19	17 33				17 39	17a49			18 03			18 09		18a23	18a43				18 49
Hagley	d	17 12							17 42				18 06			18 12							18 52
Blakedown	d	17 15							17 45				18 09			18 15							18 55
Kidderminster	d	17 20			17a42				17 50				18a15			18 20							19 00
Hartlebury	d	17 25							17 55							18 25							19 05
University	d														17 55								
Barnt Green	d																						
Bromsgrove	d							17 40							18 10								
Droitwich Spa	d	17 33						17 50	18 03						18 20	18 33							19 13
Worcester Shrub Hill 7	a							17 58	18 12						18 27								
	d					17 41	17 45							18 19	18 31						18 51	18 52	
Worcester Foregate Street 7	a	17 43				17 44	17 47							18 21	18 33	18 43					18 54	18 54	19 22
	d					17 45	17 48							18 22	18 34						18 55	18 56	19 23
Malvern Link	d					17 54	17 57							18 30	18 44						19 04	19 04	19 32
Great Malvern	a					18 00	18 04							18 36	18 46						19 07	19 08	19 35
	d														18 47						19 08	19 08	
Colwall	d														18 52						19 14	19 14	
Ledbury	a														18 59						19 21	19 22	
	d														19 00						19 29	19 29	
Hereford 7	a														19 20						19 45	19 45	

A from 17 September

B until 10 September

Table 71

Saturdays

Stratford-upon-Avon, Marylebone and Leamington Spa - Birmingham - Stourbridge, Worcester and Hereford

		LM	LM	LM	XC	GW	GW	LM	LM	LM	XC	XC	XC	GW	LM	LM	GW	GW	LM	LM	LM	LM	LM
					◇1	◇1	◇1				◇1	◇1	◇1				◇1	◇1					
						A	B				C	D	C				A	B					
					🍴	☕	☕				🍴	🍴	🍴				☕	☕					
Stratford-upon-Avon	d								18 08							18 50				19 26			20 26
Wilmcote	d								18 13							18 55				19 31			20 31
Wootton Wawen	d								18x18							19x00				19x36			20x36
Henley-in-Arden	d								18 22							19 04				19 40			20 40
Danzey	d								18x26							19x08				19x44			20x44
Wood End	d								18x30							19x12				19x48			20x48
The Lakes	d								18x32							19x14				19x50			20x50
Earlswood (West Midlands)	d								18 35							19 16				19 53			20 53
Wythall	d								18 37							19 19				19 55			20 55
Whitlocks End	d		18 19						18 40							19 21				19 58			20 58
Shirley	d		18 22						18 43							19 25				20 01			21 01
Yardley Wood	d		18 25						18 46							19 28				20 04			21 04
Hall Green	d		18 28						18 49							19 31				20 07			21 07
Spring Road	d		18 30						18 51							19 33				20 09			21 09
London Marylebone 10 ⊖	d																						
Banbury	d				18 24						18 54	19 24	19 54										
Leamington Spa 8	a				18 41						19 10	19 41	20 10										
	d				18 42						19 12	19 42	20 12										
Warwick	d																						
Warwick Parkway	d																						
Hatton	d																						
Lapworth	d																						
Dorridge	d	18 09						18 28							19 01				19 28			20 28	
Widney Manor	d	18 13						18 32							19 05				19 32			20 32	
Solihull	d	18 17						18 36							19 09				19 36			20 36	
Olton	d	18 20						18 39							19 12				19 39			20 39	
Acocks Green	d	18 23						18 42							19 15				19 42			20 42	
Tyseley	d		18 33					18 45	18 54						19 18	19 36			19 45			20 45	
Small Heath	d		18 35					18 47	18 56						19 20	19 38			19 47			20 47	
Bordesley	d																						
Birmingham Moor Street	d	18 29	18 39					18 51	19 00						19 24	19 42			19 51	20 16		20 51	21 16
Birmingham Snow Hill ⇌	a	18 32	18 42					18 54	19 04						19 27	19 46			19 54	20 19		20 54	21 19
	d	18 33						18 58							19 28				19 55	20 20		20 55	21 20
Jewellery Quarter ⇌	d	18 35						19 00							19 30				19 57	20 22		20 57	21 22
The Hawthorns ⇌	d	18 40						19 05							19 35				20 02	20 27		21 02	21 27
Smethwick Galton Bridge 7	d	18 43						19 08							19 38				20 05	20 30		21 05	21 30
Coventry	a										19 22		20 22										
Birmingham International ✈	a										19 37		20 37										
Birmingham New Street 12	a				19 18						19 48	20 18	20 48										
	d			18 49						19 19											20 59		
Langley Green	d	18 46						19 11							19 41				20 08	20 33		21 08	21 33
Rowley Regis	d	18 49						19 14							19 44				20 11	20 36		21 11	21 36
Old Hill	d	18 52						19 17							19 47				20 14	20 39		21 14	21 39
Cradley Heath	d	18 56						19 21							19 51				20 18	20 43		21 18	21 43
Lye	d	18 59						19 24							19 54				20 21	20 46		21 21	21 46
Stourbridge Junction 2	d	19 03						19 28							19 58				20 25	20a50		21 25	21a50
Hagley	d	19 06						19 31							20 01				20 28			21 28	
Blakedown	d	19 09						19 34							20 04				20 31			21 31	
Kidderminster	d	19a15						19 39							20 09				20 36			21 36	
Hartlebury	d																						
University	d			18 55						19 25											21 05		
Barnt Green	d																						
Bromsgrove	d			19 10						19 40											21 20		
Droitwich Spa	d			19 20				19 50		19 57					20 20				20 47		21 30	21 47	
Worcester Shrub Hill 7	a			19 27				19 58							20 30				20 55		21 37	21 55	
	d			19 35		19 42	19 43							20 20			20 46	20 48	20 59		21 46		
Worcester Foregate Street 7	a			19 37		19 44	19 45			20 05				20 22			20 48	20 50	21 01		21 48		
	d			19 38						20 06				20 25			20 50	20 52	21 02		21 50		
Malvern Link	d			19 48						20 16				20 34			20 58	21 01	21 11		21 59		
Great Malvern	a			19 50						20 18				20 40			21 02	21 04	21 14		22 01		
	d									20 25							21 02	21 05			22 02		
Colwall	d									20 30							21 08	21 11			22 07		
Ledbury	a									20 38							21 16	21 18			22 14		
	d									20 39							21 18	21 20			22 15		
Hereford 7	a									21 02							21 34	21 36			22 35		

A from 17 September

B until 10 September

C 🍴 to Birmingham International

D 🍴 to Leamington Spa

Table 71

Saturdays

Stratford-upon-Avon, Marylebone and Leamington Spa - Birmingham - Stourbridge, Worcester and Hereford

		XC	XC	XC	XC	GW	GW	LM	LM	LM	LM
		◇1	◇1	◇1	◇1	◇1	◇1				
						A	B				
Stratford-upon-Avon	d										
Wilmcote	d										
Wootton Wawen	d										
Henley-in-Arden	d										
Danzey	d										
Wood End	d										
The Lakes	d										
Earlswood (West Midlands)	d										
Wythall	d										
Whitlocks End	d								21 54		22 57
Shirley	d								21 57		23 00
Yardley Wood	d								22 00		23 03
Hall Green	d								22 03		23 06
Spring Road	d								22 05		23 08
London Marylebone 10 ⊖	d										
Banbury	d	20 29	20 54	21 25	21 54						
Leamington Spa 8	a	20 45	21 10	21 44	22 10						
	d	20 46	21 12	21 45	22 12						
Warwick	d										
Warwick Parkway	d										
Hatton	d										
Lapworth	d										
Dorridge	d							21 28		22 33	
Widney Manor	d							21 32		22 37	
Solihull	d							21 36		22 41	
Olton	d							21 39		22 44	
Acocks Green	d							21 42		22 47	
Tyseley	d							21 45	22 08	22 50	23 11
Small Heath	d							21 47	22 10	22 52	23 13
Bordesley	d										
Birmingham Moor Street	d							21 51	22 14	22 56	23 17
Birmingham Snow Hill ⇌	a							21 54	22 17	22 59	23 20
	d							21 55	22 20	23 00	23 23
Jewellery Quarter ⇌	d							21 57	22 22	23 02	23 25
The Hawthorns ⇌	d							22 02	22 27	23 07	23 30
Smethwick Galton Bridge 7	d							22 05	22 30	23 10	23 33
Coventry	a		21 22	21 55	22 22						
Birmingham International ✈	a		21 37	22 10	22 36						
Birmingham New Street 12	a	21 18	21 48	22 22	22 48						
	d										
Langley Green	d							22 08	22 33	23 13	23 36
Rowley Regis	d							22 11	22 36	23 16	23 39
Old Hill	d							22 14	22 39	23 19	23 42
Cradley Heath	d							22 18	22 43	23 23	23 46
Lye	d							22 21	22 46	23 26	23 49
Stourbridge Junction 2	d							22 25	22a50	23 30	23a52
Hagley	d							22 28		23 33	
Blakedown	d							22 31		23 36	
Kidderminster	d							22 36		23 41	
Hartlebury	d										
University	d										
Barnt Green	d										
Bromsgrove	d										
Droitwich Spa	d							22 47		23 52	
Worcester Shrub Hill 7	a							22 55		00 01	
	d					22 04	22 08	22 59			
Worcester Foregate Street 7	a					22 06	22 11	23 01			
	d					22 08	22 11	23 02			
Malvern Link	d					22 17	22 20	23 10			
Great Malvern	a					22 22	22 27	23 13			
	d										
Colwall	d										
Ledbury	a										
	d										
Hereford 7	a										

A from 17 September

B until 10 September

Table 71

Sundays until 19 June

Stratford-upon-Avon, Marylebone and Leamington Spa - Birmingham - Stourbridge, Worcester and Hereford

		LM	LM	XC	XC	GW	LM	LM	XC	XC	GW	LM	LM	XC	XC	GW	LM	LM	LM	LM	XC	XC	LM
				◇1		◇1			◇1		◇1			◇1		◇1					◇1		
		A																					
Stratford-upon-Avon	d						09 30					10 30					11 30		12 30				
Wilmcote	d						09 35					10 35					11 35		12 35				
Wootton Wawen	d																						
Henley-in-Arden	d						09 42					10 42					11 42		12 42				
Danzey	d																						
Wood End	d																						
The Lakes	d						09x49					10x49					11x49		12x49				
Earlswood (West Midlands)	d																						
Wythall	d						09 53					10 53					11 53		12 53				
Whitlocks End	d						09 55					10 55					11 55		12 55				
Shirley	d						09 59					10 59					11 59		12 59				
Yardley Wood	d						10 02					11 02					12 02		13 02				
Hall Green	d						10 05					11 05					12 05		13 05				
Spring Road	d						10 07					11 07					12 07		13 07				
London Marylebone 10 ⊖	d																						
Banbury	d				10 00					11 00					12 00							13 00	
Leamington Spa 8	a				10 40					11 40					12 40							13 40	
	d			10 12					11 12					12 12							13 12		
Warwick	d																						
Warwick Parkway	d																						
Hatton	d																						
Lapworth	d																						
Dorridge	d	22p33						10 25					11 25					12 25					13 25
Widney Manor	d	22p37						10 29					11 29					12 29					13 29
Solihull	d	22p41						10 32					11 32					12 32					13 32
Olton	d	22p44						10 36					11 36					12 36					13 36
Acocks Green	d	22p47						10 38					11 38					12 38					13 38
Tyseley	d	22p50					10 10					11 10					12 10		13 10				
Small Heath	d	22p52																					
Bordesley	d																						
Birmingham Moor Street	d	22p56	09 26				10 17	10 45				11 17	11 45				12 17	12 45	13 17				13 45
Birmingham Snow Hill ⇌	a	22p59	09 28				10 19	10 47				11 19	11 47				12 19	12 47	13 19				13 48
	d	23p00	09 30				10 20	10 48				11 20	11 48				12 20	12 48	13 20				13 48
Jewellery Quarter ⇌	d	23p02	09 32				10 22	10 51				11 22	11 51				12 22	12 51	13 22				13 51
The Hawthorns ⇌	d	23p07	09 37				10 27	10 55				11 27	11 55				12 27	12 55	13 27				13 55
Smethwick Galton Bridge 7	d	23p10	09 39				10 29	10 58				11 29	11 58				12 29	12 58	13 29				13 58
Coventry	a			10 22					11 22					12 22							13 22		
Birmingham International ✈	a			10 38					11 38					12 38							13 37		
Birmingham New Street 12	a			10 50					11 50					12 50							13 48		
	d																			13 24			
Langley Green	d	23p13						11 01					12 01					13 01					14 01
Rowley Regis	d	23p16	09 44				10 34	11 04				11 34	12 04				12 34	13 04	13 34				14 04
Old Hill	d	23p19						11 07					12 07					13 07					14 07
Cradley Heath	d	23p23	09 49				10 39	11 10				11 39	12 10				12 39	13 10	13 39				14 10
Lye	d	23p26						11 13					12 13					13 13					14 13
Stourbridge Junction 2	d	23p30	09 54				10 45	11a17				11 45	12a17				12 45	13a17	13 45				14a18
Hagley	d	23p33	09 58				10 48					11 49					12 48		13 48				
Blakedown	d	23p36										11 52					12 51						
Kidderminster	d	23p41	10 04				10 55					11 57					12 56		13 55				
Hartlebury	d																						
University	d																						
Barnt Green	d																						
Bromsgrove	d																			13 42			
Droitwich Spa	d	23p52	10 15				11 06					12 08					13 08		14 06	13 52			
Worcester Shrub Hill 7	a	00 01	10 23				11 14					12 16					13 15			13 59			
	d		10 26			10 38	11 32				12 04					13 12	13 29			14 21			
Worcester Foregate Street 7	a		10 29			10 41	11 34				12 07					13 15	13 31		14 15	14 23			
	d		10 29			10 41	11 35				12 08					13 16	13 32			14 24			
Malvern Link	d		10 38			10 50	11 43				12 17					13 25	13 40			14 32			
Great Malvern	a		10 41			10 55	11 46				12 20					13 28	13 43			14 35			
	d										12 22					13 30				14 36			
Colwall	d										12 28					13 36				14 41			
Ledbury	a										12 35					13 43				14 48			
	d										12 37					13 49				14 49			
Hereford 7	a										12 54					14 06				15 10			

A not 22 May

Table 71

Sundays
until 19 June

Stratford-upon-Avon, Marylebone and Leamington Spa - Birmingham - Stourbridge, Worcester and Hereford

		XC	XC	XC	GW	LM	LM	LM	LM	LM	XC	XC	XC	XC	GW	LM	LM	LM	GW	LM	LM	LM	XC
		◇1 ⌶	🚌	◇1 ⌶	◇1						◇1 ⌶	◇1 ⌶	◇1 ⌶	◇1 ⌶	◇1 ⌶				◇1				◇1 ⌶
Stratford-upon-Avon	d					13 30		14 30								15 30				16 30			
Wilmcote	d					13 35		14 35								15 35				16 35			
Wootton Wawen	d																						
Henley-in-Arden	d					13 42		14 42								15 42				16 42			
Danzey	d																			16x47			
Wood End	d																						
The Lakes	d					13x49		14x49								15x49				16x51			
Earlswood (West Midlands)	d																						
Wythall	d					13 53		14 53								15 53				16 55			
Whitlocks End	d					13 55		14 55								15 55				16 57			
Shirley	d					13 59		14 59								15 59				17 01			
Yardley Wood	d					14 02		15 02								16 02				17 04			
Hall Green	d					14 05		15 05								16 05				17 07			
Spring Road	d					14 07		15 07								16 07				17 09			
London Marylebone [10] ⊖	d																						
Banbury	d		14 00	14 54							15 25	15 54	16 25	16 54									17 25
Leamington Spa [8]	a		14 40	15 11							15 41	16 11	16 41	17 11									17 41
	d	14 12		15 12							15 43	16 12	16 43	17 12									17 43
Warwick	d																						
Warwick Parkway	d																						
Hatton	d																						
Lapworth	d																						
Dorridge	d						14 25		15 25								16 25				17 25		
Widney Manor	d						14 29		15 29								16 29				17 29		
Solihull	d						14 32		15 32								16 32				17 32		
Olton	d						14 36		15 36								16 36				17 36		
Acocks Green	d						14 38		15 38								16 38				17 38		
Tyseley	d					14 10		15 10								16 10				17 12			
Small Heath	d																						
Bordesley	d																						
Birmingham Moor Street	d					14 17	14 45	15 17	15 45							16 17	16 45	17 02		17 17	17 45		
Birmingham Snow Hill ⇌	a					14 19	14 47	15 19	15 48							16 19	16 48	17 04		17 20	17 48		
	d					14 20	14 48	15 20	15 48							16 20	16 48	17 06		17 21	17 48		
Jewellery Quarter ⇌	d					14 22	14 51	15 22	15 51							16 22	16 51			17 24	17 51		
The Hawthorns ⇌	d					14 27	14 55	15 27	15 55							16 27	16 55			17 28	17 55		
Smethwick Galton Bridge [7]	d					14 29	14 58	15 29	15 58							16 29	16 58			17 31	17 58		
Coventry	a	14 22		15 22								16 22		17 22									
Birmingham International ✈	a	14 35		15 35								16 35		17 35									
Birmingham New Street [12]	a	14 48		15 48							16 12	16 48	17 12	17 48									18 11
	d									16 00												18 00	
Langley Green	d						15 01		16 01								17 01				18 01		
Rowley Regis	d					14 34	15 04	15 34	16 04							16 34	17 04			17 35	18 04		
Old Hill	d						15 07		16 07								17 07				18 07		
Cradley Heath	d					14 39	15 10	15 39	16 10							16 39	17 10			17 40	18 10		
Lye	d						15 13		16 13								17 13				18 13		
Stourbridge Junction [2]	d					14 45	15a17	15 45	16a18							16 45	17a18	17 27		17 46	18a19		
Hagley	d					14 48		15 48								16 48		17 30		17 50			
Blakedown	d					14 51																	
Kidderminster	d					14 56		15 54								16 54		17 36		17 56			
Hartlebury	d																						
University	d																						
Barnt Green	d																						
Bromsgrove	d									16 21												18 21	
Droitwich Spa	d					15 08		16 06		16 30						17 06		17 48		18 07		18 30	
Worcester Shrub Hill [7]	a									16 38										18 15		18 38	
	d				15 11					16 45					17 10				18 09			18 43	
Worcester Foregate Street [7]	a				15 13	15 16		16 14		16 47					17 13	17 14		18 01	18 11			18 45	
	d				15 14					16 48					17 13							18 46	
Malvern Link	d				15 24					16 57					17 23							18 55	
Great Malvern	a				15 27					17 01					17 26							18 58	
	d				15 28										17 27							18 58	
Colwall	d				15 34										17 33							19 03	
Ledbury	a				15 41										17 41							19 10	
	d				15 48										17 42							19 10	
Hereford [7]	a				16 07										18 01							19 31	

Table 71

Sundays
until 19 June

Stratford-upon-Avon, Marylebone and Leamington Spa - Birmingham - Stourbridge, Worcester and Hereford

		XC	GW	LM	LM	XC	XC	XC	XC	GW	LM	GW	LM	LM	XC	XC	GW	LM	LM	XC	XC	XC	LM
		◇1 ⌶	◇1 ⌶			◇1 ⌶	◇1 A ⌶	◇1 ⌶	◇1 A ⌶	◇1 ⌶		◇1			◇1 ⌶	◇1	◇1			◇1	◇1	◇1	
Stratford-upon-Avon	d			17 30							18 30		19 30										
Wilmcote	d			17 35							18 35		19 35										
Wootton Wawen	d																						
Henley-in-Arden	d			17 42							18 42		19 42										
Danzey	d																						
Wood End	d																						
The Lakes	d			17x49							18x49		19x49										
Earlswood (West Midlands)	d																						
Wythall	d			17 53							18 53		19 53										
Whitlocks End	d			17 55							18 55		19 55										
Shirley	d			17 59							18 59		19 59										
Yardley Wood	d			18 02							19 02		20 02										
Hall Green	d			18 05							19 05		20 05										
Spring Road	d			18 07							19 07		20 07										
London Marylebone [10] ⊖	d																						
Banbury	d	17 54				18 25	18 54	19 25	19 54						20 25	20 54				21 25	21 54	22 25	
Leamington Spa [8]	a	18 11				18 41	19 11	19 41	20 11						20 41	21 11				21 41	22 11	22 41	
	d	18 12				18 43	19 12	19 43	20 12						20 43	21 12				21 43	22 12	22 43	
Warwick	d																						
Warwick Parkway	d																						
Hatton	d																						
Lapworth	d																						
Dorridge	d																						
Widney Manor	d																						
Solihull	d																						
Olton	d																						
Acocks Green	d																						
Tyseley	d			18 10							19 10		20 10										
Small Heath	d																						
Bordesley	d																						
Birmingham Moor Street	d			18 17							19 15		20 15					21 35					22 52
Birmingham Snow Hill ⇌	a			18 19							19 18		20 18					21 37					22 54
	d			18 20							19 20		20 20					21 45					22 55
Jewellery Quarter ⇌	d			18 22							19 22		20 22					21 47					22 57
The Hawthorns ⇌	d			18 27							19 27		20 27					21 52					23 02
Smethwick Galton Bridge [7]	d			18 29							19 29		20 29					21 54					23 04
Coventry	a	18 22					19 22	19 53	20 22						20 53	21 22				21 53	22 22	22 53	
Birmingham International ✈	a	18 35					19 35	20 03	20 35						21 03	21 35				22 03	22 32	23 03	
Birmingham New Street [12]	a	18 48				19 11	19 48	20 15	20 48						21 15	21 48				22 15	22 42	23 14	
	d				19 00									21 00					22 05				
Langley Green	d																						
Rowley Regis	d			18 34							19 34		20 34					21 59					23 09
Old Hill	d																						
Cradley Heath	d			18 39							19 39		20 39					22 03					23 14
Lye	d																						
Stourbridge Junction [2]	d			18 45							19 45		20 45					22 09					23 19
Hagley	d			18 49							19 48		20 49					22 12					23 23
Blakedown	d			18 52																			
Kidderminster	d			18 57							19 55		20 57					22 18					23 29
Hartlebury	d																						
University	d																						
Barnt Green	d																						
Bromsgrove	d				19 21									21 21									
Droitwich Spa	d			19 08	19 31						20 08		21 09	21 31				22 30	22 38				23 40
Worcester Shrub Hill [7]	a			19 16	19 41						20 16		21 23	21 38				22 37	22 48				23 48
	d		19 13							20 07		21 16	21 28	21 42			22 12	22 41					
Worcester Foregate Street [7]	a		19 15							20 13		21 19	21 31	21 44			22 14	22 43					
	d		19 17							20 13		21 20	21 31	21 45			22 16	22 44					
Malvern Link	d		19 26							20 22		21 29	21 40	21 54			22 25	22 52					
Great Malvern	a		19 30							20 26		21 33	21 43	21 57			22 28	22 55					
	d											21 33		21 57									
Colwall	d											21 39		22 02									
Ledbury	a											21 46		22 09									
	d											21 48		22 10									
Hereford [7]	a											22 06		22 30									

A ⌶ to Birmingham International

Table 71

Sundays
26 June to 31 July

Stratford-upon-Avon, Marylebone and Leamington Spa - Birmingham - Stourbridge, Worcester and Hereford

		LM	LM	XC	LM	LM	LM	LM	GW	XC		XC	GW	LM	LM	LM	LM	GW	LM	LM		LM	LM	LM	LM
				◇1					◇1	◇1		◇1	◇1					◇1							
			🚌			🚌	🚌							🚌		🚌			🚌			🚌			
				✠					✠	✠		✠	⊏					⊏							
Stratford-upon-Avon	d							09 30									10 30						11 30		
Wilmcote	d							09 35									10 35						11 35		
Wootton Wawen	d																								
Henley-in-Arden	d							09 42									10 42						11 42		
Danzey	d																								
Wood End	d																								
The Lakes	d							09x49									10x49						11x49		
Earlswood (West Midlands)	d																								
Wythall	d							09 53									10 53						11 53		
Whitlocks End	d							09 55									10 55						11 55		
Shirley	d							09 59									10 59						11 59		
Yardley Wood	d							10 02									11 02						12 02		
Hall Green	d							10 05									11 05						12 05		
Spring Road	d							10 07									11 07						12 07		
London Marylebone 10 ⊖	d																								
Banbury	d			09 54						10 54		11 54													
Leamington Spa 8	a			10 11						11 11		12 11													
	d			10 12						11 12		12 12													
Warwick	d																								
Warwick Parkway	d																								
Hatton	d																								
Lapworth	d																								
Dorridge	d	22p33													10 25					11 25					
Widney Manor	d	22p37													10 29					11 29					
Solihull	d	22p41													10 32					11 32					
Olton	d	22p44													10 36					11 36					
Acocks Green	d	22p47													10 38					11 38					
Tyseley	d	22p50						10 10									11 10						12 10		
Small Heath	d	22p52																							
Bordesley	d																								
Birmingham Moor Street	d	22p56						10 17							10 45		11 17			11 45			12 17		
Birmingham Snow Hill 🚊	a	22p59						10 19							10 48		11 19			11 48			12 19		
	d	23p00	08 00			09 00	09 54							10 25		10 54			11 25			11 54			
Jewellery Quarter 🚊	d	23p02	08 10			09 10	10 03							10 35		11 03			11 35			12 03			
The Hawthorns 🚊	d	23p07	08 20			09 20	10 12							10 45		11 12			11 45			12 12			
Smethwick Galton Bridge 7	d	23p10	08 26			09 26	10 18							10 51		11 18			11 51			12 18			
Coventry	a			10 22						11 22		12 22													
Birmingham International ✈	a			10 38						11 38		12 38													
Birmingham New Street 12	a			10 50						11 50		12 50													
	d																								13 24
Langley Green	d	23p13					10 27									11 27						12 27			
Rowley Regis	d	23p16	08 39			09 39	10 38							11 04		11 38			12 04			12 38			
Old Hill	d	23p19					10 46									11 46						12 46			
Cradley Heath	d	23p23	08 48			09 48	10 54							11 13		11 54			12 13			12 54			
Lye	d	23p26					11 01									12 01						13 01			
Stourbridge Junction 2	d	23p30	08 59		09 54	09 59	11a07							11 24		12a07			12 24			13a06		13 11	
Hagley	d	23p33	09 10		09 58	10 10								11 35					12 35					13 14	
Blakedown	d	23p36																	12 42					13 17	
Kidderminster	d	23p41	09 26		10 04	10 26								11 51					12 51					13 22	
Hartlebury	d																								
University	d																								
Barnt Green	d																								
Bromsgrove	d																								13 42
Droitwich Spa	d	23p52	09 52		10 15	10a51								12 17					13 17					13 33	13 52
Worcester Shrub Hill 7	a	00 01	10 14		10 23									12 39					13 39						13 59
	d				10 26				10 38				12 04					13 12							14 21
Worcester Foregate Street 7	a				10 29				10 41				12 07					13 15						13 41	14 23
	d				10 29				10 41				12 08					13 16							14 24
Malvern Link	d				10 38				10 50				12 17					13 25							14 32
Great Malvern	a				10 41				10 55				12 20					13 28							14 35
	d												12 22					13 30							14 36
Colwall	d												12 28					13 36							14 41
Ledbury	a												12 35					13 43							14 48
	d												12 37					13 49							14 49
Hereford 7	a												12 54					14 06							15 10

Table 71

Sundays
26 June to 31 July

Stratford-upon-Avon, Marylebone and Leamington Spa - Birmingham - Stourbridge, Worcester and Hereford

		LM	LM	XC	LM	LM		LM	LM	XC	XC	XC	LM	LM	LM	LM		LM	XC	GW	LM	LM	LM	LM	LM
				◇1						◇1	◇1	◇1							◇1	◇1					
		🚌			🚌			🚌						🚌		🚌						🚌		🚌	
				✠						✠	✠	✠							✠	⊏					
Stratford-upon-Avon	d					12 30									13 30								14 30		
Wilmcote	d					12 35									13 35								14 35		
Wootton Wawen	d																								
Henley-in-Arden	d					12 42									13 42								14 42		
Danzey	d																								
Wood End	d																								
The Lakes	d					12x49									13x49								14x49		
Earlswood (West Midlands)	d																								
Wythall	d					12 53									13 53								14 53		
Whitlocks End	d					12 55									13 55								14 55		
Shirley	d					12 59									13 59								14 59		
Yardley Wood	d					13 02									14 02								15 02		
Hall Green	d					13 05									14 05								15 05		
Spring Road	d					13 07									14 07								15 07		
London Marylebone 10 ⊖	d																								
Banbury	d			12 54						13 35	13 54	14 25							14 54						
Leamington Spa 8	a			13 11						13 51	14 11	14 41							15 11						
	d			13 12						13 53	14 12	14 43							15 12						
Warwick	d																								
Warwick Parkway	d																								
Hatton	d																								
Lapworth	d																								
Dorridge	d		12 25						13 25									14 25							15 25
Widney Manor	d		12 29						13 29									14 29							15 29
Solihull	d		12 32						13 32									14 32							15 32
Olton	d		12 36						13 36									14 36							15 36
Acocks Green	d		12 38						13 38									14 38							15 38
Tyseley	d					13 10									14 10								15 10		
Small Heath	d																								
Bordesley	d																								
Birmingham Moor Street	d		12 45			13 17			13 45						14 17			14 45					15 17		15 45
Birmingham Snow Hill 🚊	a		12 48			13 19			13 49						14 19			14 48					15 19		15 49
	d	12 25			12 54			13 25						13 54		14 25						14 54		15 25	
Jewellery Quarter 🚊	d	12 35			13 03			13 35						14 03		14 35						15 03		15 35	
The Hawthorns 🚊	d	12 45			13 12			13 45						14 12		14 45						15 12		15 45	
Smethwick Galton Bridge 7	d	12 51			13 18			13 51						14 18		14 51						15 18		15 51	
Coventry	a			13 22							14 22								15 22						
Birmingham International ✈	a			13 37							14 35								15 35						
Birmingham New Street 12	a			13 48						14 19	14 48	15 13							15 48						
	d																								
Langley Green	d				13 27									14 27								15 27			
Rowley Regis	d	13 04			13 38			14 04						14 38		15 04						15 38		16 04	
Old Hill	d				13 46									14 46								15 46			
Cradley Heath	d	13 13			13 54			14 13						14 54		15 13						15 54		16 13	
Lye	d				14 01									15 01								16 01			
Stourbridge Junction 2	d	13 24			14a07			14a23					14 28	15a07		15a23					15 43	16a07		16a23	
Hagley	d	13 35											14 32								15 46				
Blakedown	d	13 42											14 35								15 49				
Kidderminster	d	13 51											14 40								15 54				
Hartlebury	d																								
University	d																								
Barnt Green	d																								
Bromsgrove	d																								
Droitwich Spa	d	14 17											14 51								16 06				
Worcester Shrub Hill 7	a	14 39																							
	d																			15 11					
Worcester Foregate Street 7	a												15 00							15 13	16 14				
	d																			15 14					
Malvern Link	d																			15 24					
Great Malvern	a																			15 27					
	d																			15 28					
Colwall	d																			15 34					
Ledbury	a																			15 41					
	d																			15 48					
Hereford 7	a																			16 07					

Table 71

Sundays
26 June to 31 July

Stratford-upon-Avon, Marylebone and Leamington Spa - Birmingham - Stourbridge, Worcester and Hereford

		LM	LM	XC	XC	XC	XC	GW	LM	LM	LM	GW	LM	LM	LM	XC	XC	GW	LM	LM	XC	XC
				◇1	◇1	◇1	◇1	◇1				◇1				◇1	◇1	◇1			◇1	◇1
																						A
				✠	✠	✠	✠	✠				☕				✠	✠	✠			✠	✠
Stratford-upon-Avon	d								15 30				16 30						17 30			
Wilmcote	d								15 35				16 35						17 35			
Wootton Wawen	d																					
Henley-in-Arden	d								15 42				16 42						17 42			
Danzey	d												16x47									
Wood End	d																					
The Lakes	d								15x49				16x51						17x49			
Earlswood (West Midlands)	d																					
Wythall	d								15 53				16 55						17 53			
Whitlocks End	d								15 55				16 57						17 55			
Shirley	d								15 59				17 01						17 59			
Yardley Wood	d								16 02				17 04						18 02			
Hall Green	d								16 05				17 07						18 05			
Spring Road	d								16 07				17 09						18 07			
London Marylebone 10 ⊖	d																					
Banbury	d			15 25	15 54	16 25	16 54									17 25	17 54				18 25	18 54
Leamington Spa 8	a			15 41	16 11	16 41	17 11									17 41	18 11				18 41	19 11
	d			15 43	16 12	16 43	17 12									17 43	18 12				18 43	19 12
Warwick	d																					
Warwick Parkway	d																					
Hatton	d																					
Lapworth	d																					
Dorridge	d									16 25				17 25								
Widney Manor	d									16 29				17 29								
Solihull	d									16 32				17 32								
Olton	d									16 36				17 36								
Acocks Green	d									16 38				17 38								
Tyseley	d								16 10				17 12						18 10			
Small Heath	d																					
Bordesley	d																					
Birmingham Moor Street	d								16 17	16 45	17 02		17 17	17 45					18 17			
Birmingham Snow Hill ⇌	a								16 19	16 48	17 04		17 20	17 48					18 19			
	d	15 54							16 20	16 48	17 06		17 21	17 48					18 20			
Jewellery Quarter ⇌	d	16 03							16 22	16 51			17 24	17 51					18 22			
The Hawthorns ⇌	d	16 12							16 27	16 55			17 28	17 55					18 27			
Smethwick Galton Bridge 7	d	16 18							16 29	16 58			17 31	17 58					18 29			
Coventry	a				16 22		17 22										18 22					19 22
Birmingham International ✈	a				16 35		17 35										18 35					19 35
Birmingham New Street 12	a			16 12	16 48	17 12	17 48									18 09	18 48				19 11	19 48
	d		16 00												18 00					19 00		
Langley Green	d	16 27								17 01				18 01								
Rowley Regis	d	16 38							16 34	17 04			17 35	18 04					18 34			
Old Hill	d	16 46								17 07				18 07								
Cradley Heath	d	16 54							16 39	17 10			17 40	18 10					18 39			
Lye	d	17 01								17 13				18 13								
Stourbridge Junction 2	d	17a07							16 45	17a18	17 27		17 46	18a19					18 45			
Hagley	d								16 48		17 30		17 50						18 49			
Blakedown	d																		18 52			
Kidderminster	d								16 54		17 36		17 56						18 57			
Hartlebury	d																					
University	d																					
Barnt Green	d																					
Bromsgrove	d		16 21												18 21					19 21		
Droitwich Spa	d		16 30						17 06		17 48		18 07		18 30				19 08	19 31		
Worcester Shrub Hill 7	a		16 38										18 15		18 38				19 16	19 41		
	d		16 45					17 10				18 09			18 43			19 13				
Worcester Foregate Street 7	a		16 47					17 13	17 14		18 01	18 11			18 45			19 15				
	d		16 48					17 13							18 46			19 17				
Malvern Link	d		16 57					17 23							18 55			19 26				
Great Malvern	a		17 01					17 26							18 58			19 30				
	d							17 27							18 58							
Colwall	d							17 33							19 03							
Ledbury	a							17 41							19 10							
	d							17 42							19 10							
Hereford 7	a							18 01							19 31							

A ✠ to Birmingham International

Table 71

Sundays
26 June to 31 July

Stratford-upon-Avon, Marylebone and Leamington Spa - Birmingham - Stourbridge, Worcester and Hereford

		XC	XC	GW	LM	GW	LM	LM	XC	XC	GW	LM	LM	XC	XC	XC	LM
		◇1	◇1	◇1		◇1			◇1	◇1	◇1			◇1	◇1	◇1	
			A														
		✠	✠	✠		☕			✠		☕						
Stratford-upon-Avon	d				18 30		19 30										
Wilmcote	d				18 35		19 35										
Wootton Wawen	d																
Henley-in-Arden	d				18 42		19 42										
Danzey	d																
Wood End	d																
The Lakes	d				18x49		19x49										
Earlswood (West Midlands)	d																
Wythall	d				18 53		19 53										
Whitlocks End	d				18 55		19 55										
Shirley	d				18 59		19 59										
Yardley Wood	d				19 02		20 02										
Hall Green	d				19 05		20 05										
Spring Road	d				19 07		20 07										
London Marylebone 10 ⊖	d																
Banbury	d	19 25	19 54						20 25	20 54				21 25	21 54	22 25	
Leamington Spa 8	a	19 41	20 11						20 41	21 11				21 41	22 11	22 41	
	d	19 43	20 12						20 43	21 12				21 43	22 12	22 43	
Warwick	d																
Warwick Parkway	d																
Hatton	d																
Lapworth	d																
Dorridge	d																
Widney Manor	d																
Solihull	d																
Olton	d																
Acocks Green	d																
Tyseley	d				19 10		20 10										
Small Heath	d																
Bordesley	d																
Birmingham Moor Street	d				19 15		20 15					21 35					22 52
Birmingham Snow Hill ⇌	a				19 18		20 18					21 37					22 54
	d				19 20		20 20					21 45					22 55
Jewellery Quarter ⇌	d				19 22		20 22					21 47					22 57
The Hawthorns ⇌	d				19 27		20 27					21 52					23 02
Smethwick Galton Bridge 7	d				19 29		20 29					21 54					23 04
Coventry	a	19 53	20 22						20 53	21 22				21 53	22 22	22 53	
Birmingham International ✈	a	20 03	20 35						21 03	21 35				22 03	22 32	23 03	
Birmingham New Street 12	a	20 15	20 48						21 15	21 48				22 15	22 42	23 14	
	d							21 00					22 05				
Langley Green	d																
Rowley Regis	d				19 34		20 34					21 59					23 09
Old Hill	d																
Cradley Heath	d				19 39		20 39					22 03					23 14
Lye	d																
Stourbridge Junction 2	d				19 45		20 45					22 09					23 19
Hagley	d				19 48		20 49					22 12					23 23
Blakedown	d																
Kidderminster	d				19 55		20 57					22 18					23 29
Hartlebury	d																
University	d																
Barnt Green	d																
Bromsgrove	d							21 21									
Droitwich Spa	d				20 08		21 09	21 31				22 30	22 38				23 40
Worcester Shrub Hill 7	a				20 16		21 23	21 38				22 37	22 48				23 48
	d			20 07		21 16	21 28	21 42			22 12	22 41					
Worcester Foregate Street 7	a			20 13		21 19	21 31	21 44			22 14	22 43					
	d			20 13		21 20	21 31	21 45			22 16	22 44					
Malvern Link	d			20 22		21 29	21 40	21 54			22 25	22 52					
Great Malvern	a			20 26		21 33	21 43	21 57			22 28	22 55					
	d					21 33		21 57									
Colwall	d					21 39		22 02									
Ledbury	a					21 46		22 09									
	d					21 48		22 10									
Hereford 7	a					22 06		22 30									

A ✠ to Birmingham International

Table 71

Sundays

7 August to 11 September

Stratford-upon-Avon, Marylebone and Leamington Spa - Birmingham - Stourbridge, Worcester and Hereford

		LM	LM	GW	LM	LM	GW	LM	LM	GW	LM	LM	LM	LM	LM	XC	XC	XC	GW	LM	LM	LM	LM
				◇1			◇1			◇1							◇1	◇1	◇1				
				⊼			⊡			⊡						🚌	⊼	⊼	⊡				
Stratford-upon-Avon	d				09 30			10 30			11 30		12 30							13 30		14 30	
Wilmcote	d				09 35			10 35			11 35		12 35							13 35		14 35	
Wootton Wawen	d																						
Henley-in-Arden	d				09 42			10 42			11 42		12 42							13 42		14 42	
Danzey	d																						
Wood End	d																						
The Lakes	d				09x49			10x49			11x49		12x49							13x49		14x49	
Earlswood (West Midlands)	d																						
Wythall	d				09 53			10 53			11 53		12 53							13 53		14 53	
Whitlocks End	d				09 55			10 55			11 55		12 55							13 55		14 55	
Shirley	d				09 59			10 59			11 59		12 59							13 59		14 59	
Yardley Wood	d				10 02			11 02			12 02		13 02							14 02		15 02	
Hall Green	d				10 05			11 05			12 05		13 05							14 05		15 05	
Spring Road	d				10 07			11 07			12 07		13 07							14 07		15 07	
London Marylebone 10 ⊖	d																						
Banbury	d															14 00	14 25	14 54					
Leamington Spa 8	a															14 40	14 41	15 11					
	d																14 43	15 12					
Warwick	d																						
Warwick Parkway	d																						
Hatton	d																						
Lapworth	d																						
Dorridge	d	22p33				10 25			11 25			12 25			13 25						14 25		15 25
Widney Manor	d	22p37				10 29			11 29			12 29			13 29						14 29		15 29
Solihull	d	22p41				10 32			11 32			12 32			13 32						14 32		15 32
Olton	d	22p44				10 36			11 36			12 36			13 36						14 36		15 36
Acocks Green	d	22p47				10 38			11 38			12 38			13 38						14 38		15 38
Tyseley	d	22p50			10 10			11 10			12 10		13 10							14 10		15 10	
Small Heath	d	22p52																					
Bordesley	d																						
Birmingham Moor Street	d	22p56	09 26		10 17	10 45		11 17	11 45		12 17	12 45	13 17		13 45					14 17	14 45	15 17	15 45
Birmingham Snow Hill 🚋	a	22p59	09 28		10 19	10 47		11 19	11 47		12 19	12 47	13 19		13 48					14 19	14 47	15 19	15 48
	d	23p00	09 30		10 20	10 48		11 20	11 48		12 20	12 48	13 20		13 48					14 20	14 48	15 20	15 48
Jewellery Quarter 🚋	d	23p02	09 32		10 22	10 51		11 22	11 51		12 22	12 51	13 22		13 51					14 22	14 51	15 22	15 51
The Hawthorns 🚋	d	23p07	09 37		10 27	10 55		11 27	11 55		12 27	12 55	13 27		13 55					14 27	14 55	15 27	15 55
Smethwick Galton Bridge 7	d	23p10	09 39		10 29	10 58		11 29	11 58		12 29	12 58	13 29		13 58					14 29	14 58	15 29	15 58
Coventry	a																	15 22					
Birmingham International ✈	a																	15 35					
Birmingham New Street 12	a																15 13	15 48					
	d													13 24									
Langley Green	d	23p13				11 01			12 01			13 01			14 01						15 01		16 01
Rowley Regis	d	23p16	09 44		10 34	11 04		11 34	12 04		12 34	13 04	13 34		14 04					14 34	15 04	15 34	16 04
Old Hill	d	23p19				11 07			12 07			13 07			14 07						15 07		16 07
Cradley Heath	d	23p23	09 49		10 39	11 10		11 39	12 10		12 39	13 10	13 39		14 10					14 39	15 10	15 39	16 10
Lye	d	23p26				11 13			12 13			13 13			14 13						15 13		16 13
Stourbridge Junction 2	d	23p30	09 54		10 45	11a17		11 45	12a17		12 45	13a17	13 45		14a18					14 45	15a17	15 45	16a18
Hagley	d	23p33	09 58		10 48			11 49			12 48		13 48							14 48		15 48	
Blakedown	d	23p36						11 52			12 51									14 51			
Kidderminster	d	23p41	10 04		10 55			11 57			12 56		13 55							14 56		15 54	
Hartlebury	d																						
University	d																						
Barnt Green	d																						
Bromsgrove	d													13 42									
Droitwich Spa	d	23p52	10 15		11 06			12 08			13 08		14 06	13 52						15 08		16 06	
Worcester Shrub Hill 7	a	00 01	10 23		11 14			12 16			13 15			13 59									
	d		10 26	10 38	11 32		12 07			13 12	13 29			14 21					15 11				
Worcester Foregate Street 7	a		10 29	10 41	11 34		12 10			13 15	13 31		14 15	14 23					15 13	15 16		16 14	
	d		10 29	10 42	11 35		12 11			13 16	13 32			14 24					15 14				
Malvern Link	d		10 38	10 51	11 43		12 20			13 25	13 40			14 32					15 24				
Great Malvern	a		10 41	10 56	11 46		12 23			13 28	13 43			14 35					15 27				
	d						12 24			13 30				14 36					15 28				
Colwall	d						12 30			13 36				14 41					15 34				
Ledbury	a						12 37			13 43				14 48					15 41				
	d						12 40			13 49				14 49					15 48				
Hereford 7	a						12 56			14 06				15 10					16 07				

Table 71

Sundays

7 August to 11 September

Stratford-upon-Avon, Marylebone and Leamington Spa - Birmingham - Stourbridge, Worcester and Hereford

		LM	XC	LM	XC	XC	LM	XC	GW	LM	GW	LM	LM	LM	XC	XC	GW	LM	LM	XC	XC	XC	XC
			◇1		◇1	◇1		◇1	◇1		◇1				◇1	◇1	◇1			◇1	◇1	◇1	◇1
																					A		A
			⊼		⊼	⊼		⊼	⊼		⊡				⊼	⊼	⊼			⊼	⊼	⊼	⊼
Stratford-upon-Avon	d			15 30								16 30						17 30					
Wilmcote	d			15 35								16 35						17 35					
Wootton Wawen	d																						
Henley-in-Arden	d			15 42								16 42						17 42					
Danzey	d											16x47											
Wood End	d																						
The Lakes	d			15x49								16x51						17x49					
Earlswood (West Midlands)	d																						
Wythall	d			15 53								16 55						17 53					
Whitlocks End	d			15 55								16 57						17 55					
Shirley	d			15 59								17 01						17 59					
Yardley Wood	d			16 02								17 04						18 02					
Hall Green	d			16 05								17 07						18 05					
Spring Road	d			16 07								17 09						18 07					
London Marylebone 10 ⊖	d																						
Banbury	d		15 25		15 54	16 25		16 54							17 25	17 54				18 25	18 54	19 25	19 54
Leamington Spa 8	a		15 41		16 11	16 41		17 11							17 41	18 11				18 41	19 11	19 41	20 11
	d		15 43		16 12	16 43		17 12							17 43	18 12				18 43	19 12	19 43	20 12
Warwick	d																						
Warwick Parkway	d																						
Hatton	d																						
Lapworth	d																						
Dorridge	d						16 25						17 25										
Widney Manor	d						16 29						17 29										
Solihull	d						16 32						17 32										
Olton	d						16 36						17 36										
Acocks Green	d						16 38						17 38										
Tyseley	d			16 10								17 12						18 10					
Small Heath	d																						
Bordesley	d																						
Birmingham Moor Street	d			16 17			16 45			17 02		17 17	17 45					18 17					
Birmingham Snow Hill 🚋	a			16 19			16 48			17 04		17 20	17 48					18 19					
	d			16 20			16 48			17 06		17 21	17 48					18 20					
Jewellery Quarter 🚋	d			16 22			16 51					17 24	17 51					18 22					
The Hawthorns 🚋	d			16 27			16 55					17 28	17 55					18 27					
Smethwick Galton Bridge 7	d			16 29			16 58					17 31	17 58					18 29					
Coventry	a				16 22			17 22								18 22					19 22	19 53	20 22
Birmingham International ✈	a				16 35			17 35								18 35					19 35	20 03	20 35
Birmingham New Street 12	a		16 12		16 48	17 12		17 48							18 09	18 48				19 11	19 48	20 15	20 48
	d	16 00												18 00					19 00				
Langley Green	d						17 01						18 01										
Rowley Regis	d			16 34			17 04					17 35	18 04					18 34					
Old Hill	d						17 07						18 07										
Cradley Heath	d			16 39			17 10					17 40	18 10					18 39					
Lye	d						17 13						18 13										
Stourbridge Junction 2	d			16 45			17a18			17 27		17 46	18a19					18 45					
Hagley	d			16 48						17 30		17 50						18 49					
Blakedown	d																	18 52					
Kidderminster	d			16 54						17 36		17 56						18 57					
Hartlebury	d																						
University	d																						
Barnt Green	d																						
Bromsgrove	d	16 21												18 21					19 21				
Droitwich Spa	d	16 30		17 06						17 48		18 07		18 30				19 08	19 31				
Worcester Shrub Hill 7	a	16 38										18 15		18 38				19 16	19 41				
	d	16 45							17 11		18 09			18 43			19 13						
Worcester Foregate Street 7	a	16 47		17 14					17 14	18 01	18 11			18 45			19 15						
	d	16 48							17 14					18 46			19 17						
Malvern Link	d	16 57							17 24					18 55			19 26						
Great Malvern	a	17 01							17 27					18 58			19 30						
	d								17 28					18 58									
Colwall	d								17 34					19 03									
Ledbury	a								17 42					19 10									
	d								17 43					19 10									
Hereford 7	a								18 02					19 31									

A ⊼ to Birmingham International

Table 71

Sundays
7 August to 11 September

Stratford-upon-Avon, Marylebone and Leamington Spa - Birmingham - Stourbridge, Worcester and Hereford

		GW	LM	GW	LM	LM	XC	XC	GW	LM	LM	XC	XC	XC	LM
		◇1		◇1			◇1	◇1	◇1			◇1	◇1	◇1	
		⊼		⊏			⊼		⊏						
Stratford-upon-Avon	d		18 30		19 30										
Wilmcote	d		18 35		19 35										
Wootton Wawen	d														
Henley-in-Arden	d		18 42		19 42										
Danzey	d														
Wood End	d														
The Lakes	d		18x49		19x49										
Earlswood (West Midlands)	d														
Wythall	d		18 53		19 53										
Whitlocks End	d		18 55		19 55										
Shirley	d		18 59		19 59										
Yardley Wood	d		19 02		20 02										
Hall Green	d		19 05		20 05										
Spring Road	d		19 07		20 07										
London Marylebone 10 ⊖	d														
Banbury	d						20 25	20 54				21 25	21 54	22 25	
Leamington Spa 8	a						20 41	21 11				21 41	22 11	22 41	
	d						20 43	21 12				21 43	22 12	22 43	
Warwick	d														
Warwick Parkway	d														
Hatton	d														
Lapworth	d														
Dorridge	d														
Widney Manor	d														
Solihull	d														
Olton	d														
Acocks Green	d														
Tyseley	d		19 10		20 10										
Small Heath	d														
Bordesley	d														
Birmingham Moor Street	d		19 15		20 15					21 35					22 52
Birmingham Snow Hill ⇌	a		19 18		20 18					21 37					22 54
	d		19 20		20 20					21 45					22 55
Jewellery Quarter ⇌	d		19 22		20 22					21 47					22 57
The Hawthorns ⇌	d		19 27		20 27					21 52					23 02
Smethwick Galton Bridge 7	d		19 29		20 29					21 54					23 04
Coventry	a						20 53	21 22				21 53	22 22	22 53	
Birmingham International ✈	a						21 03	21 35				22 03	22 32	23 03	
Birmingham New Street 12	a						21 15	21 48				22 15	22 42	23 14	
	d					21 00					22 05				
Langley Green	d														
Rowley Regis	d		19 34		20 34					21 59					23 09
Old Hill	d														
Cradley Heath	d		19 39		20 39					22 03					23 14
Lye	d														
Stourbridge Junction 2	d		19 45		20 45					22 09					23 19
Hagley	d		19 48		20 49					22 12					23 23
Blakedown	d														
Kidderminster	d		19 55		20 57					22 18					23 29
Hartlebury	d														
University	d														
Barnt Green	d														
Bromsgrove	d					21 21									
Droitwich Spa	d		20 08		21 09	21 31				22 30	22 38				23 40
Worcester Shrub Hill 7	a		20 16		21 23	21 38				22 37	22 48				23 48
	d	20 09		21 16	21 28	21 42			22 12	22 41					
Worcester Foregate Street 7	a	20 15		21 19	21 31	21 44			22 14	22 43					
	d	20 15		21 20	21 31	21 45			22 16	22 44					
Malvern Link	d	20 24		21 29	21 40	21 54			22 25	22 52					
Great Malvern	a	20 27		21 33	21 43	21 57			22 28	22 55					
	d			21 33		21 57									
Colwall	d			21 39		22 02									
Ledbury	a			21 46		22 09									
	d			21 48		22 10									
Hereford 7	a			22 06		22 30									

Table 71

Sundays
18 September to 23 October

Stratford-upon-Avon, Marylebone and Leamington Spa - Birmingham - Stourbridge, Worcester and Hereford

		LM	LM	XC	XC	GW	LM	LM	XC	XC	GW	LM	LM	XC	XC	GW	LM	LM	LM	LM	XC	XC	LM
				◇1		◇1			◇1		◇1			◇1		◇1					◇1		
				⊼	🚌	⊼			⊼	🚌	⊏			⊼	🚌	⊏					⊼	🚌	
Stratford-upon-Avon	d						09 30					10 30					11 30		12 30				
Wilmcote	d						09 35					10 35					11 35		12 35				
Wootton Wawen	d																						
Henley-in-Arden	d						09 42					10 42					11 42		12 42				
Danzey	d																						
Wood End	d																						
The Lakes	d						09x49					10x49					11x49		12x49				
Earlswood (West Midlands)	d																						
Wythall	d						09 53					10 53					11 53		12 53				
Whitlocks End	d						09 55					10 55					11 55		12 55				
Shirley	d						09 59					10 59					11 59		12 59				
Yardley Wood	d						10 02					11 02					12 02		13 02				
Hall Green	d						10 05					11 05					12 05		13 05				
Spring Road	d						10 07					11 07					12 07		13 07				
London Marylebone 10 ⊖	d																						
Banbury	d				10 30					11 25					12 25							13 25	
Leamington Spa 8	a				11 11					12 00					13 00							14 00	
	d			10 18					11 18					12 18							13 12		
Warwick	d																						
Warwick Parkway	d																						
Hatton	d																						
Lapworth	d																						
Dorridge	d	22p33						10 25					11 25					12 25					13 25
Widney Manor	d	22p37						10 29					11 29					12 29					13 29
Solihull	d	22p41						10 32					11 32					12 32					13 32
Olton	d	22p44						10 36					11 36					12 36					13 36
Acocks Green	d	22p47						10 38					11 38					12 38					13 38
Tyseley	d	22p50					10 10					11 10					12 10		13 10				
Small Heath	d	22p52																					
Bordesley	d																						
Birmingham Moor Street	d	22p56	09 26				10 17	10 45				11 17	11 45				12 17	12 45	13 17				13 45
Birmingham Snow Hill ⇌	a	22p59	09 28				10 19	10 47				11 19	11 47				12 19	12 47	13 19				13 48
	d	23p00	09 30				10 20	10 48				11 20	11 48				12 20	12 48	13 20				13 48
Jewellery Quarter ⇌	d	23p02	09 32				10 22	10 51				11 22	11 51				12 22	12 51	13 22				13 51
The Hawthorns ⇌	d	23p07	09 37				10 27	10 55				11 27	11 55				12 27	12 55	13 27				13 55
Smethwick Galton Bridge 7	d	23p10	09 39				10 29	10 58				11 29	11 58				12 29	12 58	13 29				13 58
Coventry	a			10 28					11 28					12 28							13 22		
Birmingham International ✈	a			10 38					11 41					12 41							13 37		
Birmingham New Street 12	a			10 50					11 53					12 53							13 48		
	d																			13 24			
Langley Green	d	23p13						11 01					12 01					13 01					14 01
Rowley Regis	d	23p16	09 44				10 34	11 04				11 34	12 04				12 34	13 04	13 34				14 04
Old Hill	d	23p19						11 07					12 07					13 07					14 07
Cradley Heath	d	23p23	09 49				10 39	11 10				11 39	12 10				12 39	13 10	13 39				14 10
Lye	d	23p26						11 13					12 13					13 13					14 13
Stourbridge Junction 2	d	23p30	09 54				10 45	11a17				11 45	12a17				12 45	13a17	13 45				14a18
Hagley	d	23p33	09 58				10 48					11 49					12 48		13 48				
Blakedown	d	23p36										11 52					12 51						
Kidderminster	d	23p41	10 04				10 55					11 57					12 56		13 55				
Hartlebury	d																						
University	d																						
Barnt Green	d																						
Bromsgrove	d																			13 42			
Droitwich Spa	d	23p52	10 15				11 06					12 08					13 08		14 06	13 52			
Worcester Shrub Hill 7	a	00 01	10 23				11 14					12 16					13 15			13 59			
	d		10 26			10 33	11 32				12 07					13 12	13 29			14 21			
Worcester Foregate Street 7	a		10 29			10 36	11 34				12 10					13 15	13 31		14 15	14 23			
	d		10 29			10 37	11 35				12 11					13 16	13 32			14 24			
Malvern Link	d		10 38			10 46	11 43				12 20					13 25	13 40			14 32			
Great Malvern	a		10 41			10 51	11 46				12 23					13 28	13 43			14 35			
	d										12 24					13 30				14 36			
Colwall	d										12 30					13 36				14 41			
Ledbury	a										12 37					13 43				14 48			
	d										12 40					13 49				14 49			
Hereford 7	a										12 56					14 06				15 10			

Table 71

Sundays from 30 October

Stratford-upon-Avon, Marylebone and Leamington Spa - Birmingham - Stourbridge, Worcester and Hereford

		LM	LM	XC	XC	GW	LM	LM	XC	XC	GW	LM	LM	XC	XC	GW	LM	LM	LM	LM	XC	XC	LM
				◇1 🛒	🚌	◇1 🛒			◇1 🛒	🚌	◇1 🍽			◇1 🛒	🚌	◇1 🍽					◇1 🛒	🚌	
Stratford-upon-Avon	d						09 30					10 30					11 30		12 30				
Wilmcote	d						09 35					10 35					11 35		12 35				
Wootton Wawen	d																						
Henley-in-Arden	d						09 42					10 42					11 42		12 42				
Danzey	d																						
Wood End	d																						
The Lakes	d						09x49					10x49					11x49		12x49				
Earlswood (West Midlands)	d																						
Wythall	d						09 53					10 53					11 53		12 53				
Whitlocks End	d						09 55					10 55					11 55		12 55				
Shirley	d						09 59					10 59					11 59		12 59				
Yardley Wood	d						10 02					11 02					12 02		13 02				
Hall Green	d						10 05					11 05					12 05		13 05				
Spring Road	d						10 07					11 07					12 07		13 07				
London Marylebone 10 ⊖	d																						
Banbury	d				10 30					11 25					12 25							13 25	
Leamington Spa 8	a				11 11					12 00					13 00							14 00	
	d			10 18					11 18					12 12							13 12		
Warwick	d																						
Warwick Parkway	d																						
Hatton	d																						
Lapworth	d																						
Dorridge	d	22p33						10 25					11 25					12 25					13 25
Widney Manor	d	22p37						10 29					11 29					12 29					13 29
Solihull	d	22p41						10 32					11 32					12 32					13 32
Olton	d	22p44						10 36					11 36					12 36					13 36
Acocks Green	d	22p47						10 38					11 38					12 38					13 38
Tyseley	d	22p50					10 10					11 10					12 10		13 10				
Small Heath	d	22p52																					
Bordesley	d																						
Birmingham Moor Street	d	22p56	09 26				10 17	10 45				11 17	11 45				12 17	12 45	13 17				13 45
Birmingham Snow Hill ⇌	a	22p59	09 28				10 19	10 47				11 19	11 47				12 19	12 47	13 19				13 48
	d	23p00	09 30				10 20	10 48				11 20	11 48				12 20	12 48	13 20				13 48
Jewellery Quarter ⇌	d	23p02	09 32				10 22	10 51				11 22	11 51				12 22	12 51	13 22				13 51
The Hawthorns ⇌	d	23p07	09 37				10 27	10 55				11 27	11 55				12 27	12 55	13 27				13 55
Smethwick Galton Bridge 7	d	23p10	09 39				10 29	10 58				11 29	11 58				12 29	12 58	13 29				13 58
Coventry	a			10 28					11 28					12 22							13 22		
Birmingham International ✈	a			10 38					11 41					12 38							13 37		
Birmingham New Street 12	a			10 50					11 51					12 50							13 48		
	d																			13 24			
Langley Green	d	23p13						11 01					12 01					13 01					14 01
Rowley Regis	d	23p16	09 44				10 34	11 04				11 34	12 04				12 34	13 04	13 34				14 04
Old Hill	d	23p19						11 07					12 07					13 07					14 07
Cradley Heath	d	23p23	09 49				10 39	11 10				11 39	12 10				12 39	13 10	13 39				14 10
Lye	d	23p26						11 13					12 13					13 13					14 13
Stourbridge Junction 2	d	23p30	09 54				10 45	11a17				11 45	12a17				12 45	13a17	13 45				14a18
Hagley	d	23p33	09 58				10 48					11 49					12 48		13 48				
Blakedown	d	23p36										11 52					12 51						
Kidderminster	d	23p41	10 04				10 55					11 57					12 56		13 55				
Hartlebury	d																						
University	d																						
Barnt Green	d																						
Bromsgrove	d																			13 42			
Droitwich Spa	d	23p52	10 15				11 06					12 08					13 08		14 06	13 52			
Worcester Shrub Hill 7	a	00 01	10 23				11 14					12 16					13 15			13 59			
	d		10 26			10 33	11 32				12 07					13 08	13 29			14 21			
Worcester Foregate Street 7	a		10 29			10 36	11 34				12 10					13 11	13 31		14 15	14 23			
	d		10 29			10 37	11 35				12 11					13 12	13 32			14 24			
Malvern Link	d		10 38			10 46	11 43				12 20					13 21	13 40			14 32			
Great Malvern	a		10 41			10 51	11 46				12 23					13 24	13 43			14 35			
	d										12 24					13 26				14 36			
Colwall	d										12 30					13 32				14 41			
Ledbury	a										12 37					13 39				14 48			
	d										12 40					13 51				14 49			
Hereford 7	a										12 56					14 08				15 10			

Table 71

Sundays from 30 October

Stratford-upon-Avon, Marylebone and Leamington Spa - Birmingham - Stourbridge, Worcester and Hereford

		XC	XC	GW	LM	LM	LM	LM	LM	XC	XC	XC	XC	GW	LM	LM	LM	GW	LM	LM	LM	XC	XC
		◇1 🛒	◇1 🛒	◇1 🍽						◇1 🛒	◇1 🛒	◇1 🛒	◇1 🛒	◇1 🛒				◇1 🍽				◇1 🛒	◇1 🛒
Stratford-upon-Avon	d				13 30		14 30								15 30				16 30				
Wilmcote	d				13 35		14 35								15 35				16 35				
Wootton Wawen	d																						
Henley-in-Arden	d				13 42		14 42								15 42				16 42				
Danzey	d																		16x47				
Wood End	d																						
The Lakes	d				13x49		14x49								15x49				16x51				
Earlswood (West Midlands)	d																						
Wythall	d				13 53		14 53								15 53				16 55				
Whitlocks End	d				13 55		14 55								15 55				16 57				
Shirley	d				13 59		14 59								15 59				17 01				
Yardley Wood	d				14 02		15 02								16 02				17 04				
Hall Green	d				14 05		15 05								16 05				17 07				
Spring Road	d				14 07		15 07								16 07				17 09				
London Marylebone 10 ⊖	d																						
Banbury	d		14 54							15 25	15 54	16 25	16 54									17 25	17 54
Leamington Spa 8	a		15 11							15 41	16 11	16 41	17 11									17 41	18 11
	d	14 12	15 12							15 43	16 12	16 43	17 12									17 43	18 12
Warwick	d																						
Warwick Parkway	d																						
Hatton	d																						
Lapworth	d																						
Dorridge	d					14 25		15 25								16 25				17 25			
Widney Manor	d					14 29		15 29								16 29				17 29			
Solihull	d					14 32		15 32								16 32				17 32			
Olton	d					14 36		15 36								16 36				17 36			
Acocks Green	d					14 38		15 38								16 38				17 38			
Tyseley	d				14 10		15 10								16 10				17 12				
Small Heath	d																						
Bordesley	d																						
Birmingham Moor Street	d				14 17	14 45	15 17	15 45							16 17	16 45	17 02		17 17	17 45			
Birmingham Snow Hill ⇌	a				14 19	14 47	15 19	15 48							16 19	16 48	17 04		17 20	17 48			
	d				14 20	14 48	15 20	15 48							16 20	16 48	17 06		17 21	17 48			
Jewellery Quarter ⇌	d				14 22	14 51	15 22	15 51							16 22	16 51			17 24	17 51			
The Hawthorns ⇌	d				14 27	14 55	15 27	15 55							16 27	16 55			17 28	17 55			
Smethwick Galton Bridge 7	d				14 29	14 58	15 29	15 58							16 29	16 58			17 31	17 58			
Coventry	a	14 22	15 22								16 22		17 22										18 22
Birmingham International ✈	a	14 35	15 35								16 35		17 35										18 35
Birmingham New Street 12	a	14 48	15 48							16 12	16 48	17 12	17 48									18 09	18 48
	d								16 00												18 00		
Langley Green	d					15 01		16 01								17 01				18 01			
Rowley Regis	d				14 34	15 04	15 34	16 04							16 34	17 04			17 35	18 04			
Old Hill	d					15 07		16 07								17 07				18 07			
Cradley Heath	d				14 39	15 10	15 39	16 10							16 39	17 10			17 40	18 10			
Lye	d					15 13		16 13								17 13				18 13			
Stourbridge Junction 2	d				14 45	15a17	15 45	16a18							16 45	17a18	17 27		17 46	18a19			
Hagley	d				14 48		15 48								16 48		17 30		17 50				
Blakedown	d				14 51																		
Kidderminster	d				14 56		15 54								16 54		17 36		17 56				
Hartlebury	d																						
University	d																						
Barnt Green	d																						
Bromsgrove	d								16 21												18 21		
Droitwich Spa	d				15 08		16 06		16 30						17 06		17 48		18 07		18 30		
Worcester Shrub Hill 7	a								16 38										18 15		18 38		
	d			15 11					16 45					17 09				18 05			18 43		
Worcester Foregate Street 7	a			15 13	15 16		16 14		16 47					17 12	17 14		18 01	18 08			18 45		
	d			15 14					16 48					17 12							18 46		
Malvern Link	d			15 24					16 57					17 22							18 55		
Great Malvern	a			15 27					17 01					17 25							18 58		
	d			15 28										17 26							18 58		
Colwall	d			15 34										17 32							19 03		
Ledbury	a			15 41										17 40							19 10		
	d			15 48										17 41							19 10		
Hereford 7	a			16 07										18 00							19 31		

Stratford-upon-Avon, Marylebone and Leamington Spa - Birmingham - Stourbridge, Worcester and Hereford

		XC	XC	GW	LM	LM	LM	LM	LM	XC	LM	XC	XC	LM	XC	GW	LM	GW	LM	LM	LM	XC	XC
		◇1	◇1	◇1						◇1		◇1	◇1		◇1	◇1		◇1				◇1	◇1
		⊤	⊤	⊡						⊤		⊤	⊤		⊤	⊤		⊡				⊤	⊤
Stratford-upon-Avon	d				13 30		14 30				15 30								16 30				
Wilmcote	d				13 35		14 35				15 35								16 35				
Wootton Wawen	d																						
Henley-in-Arden	d				13 42		14 42				15 42								16 42				
Danzey	d																		16x47				
Wood End	d																						
The Lakes	d				13x49		14x49				15x49								16x51				
Earlswood (West Midlands)	d																						
Wythall	d				13 53		14 53				15 53								16 55				
Whitlocks End	d				13 55		14 55				15 55								16 57				
Shirley	d				13 59		14 59				15 59								17 01				
Yardley Wood	d				14 02		15 02				16 02								17 04				
Hall Green	d				14 05		15 05				16 05								17 07				
Spring Road	d				14 07		15 07				16 07								17 09				
London Marylebone 10 ⊖	d																						
Banbury	d		14 54							15 25		15 54	16 25		16 54							17 25	17 54
Leamington Spa 8	a		15 11							15 41		16 11	16 41		17 11							17 41	18 11
	d	14 12	15 12							15 43		16 12	16 43		17 12							17 43	18 12
Warwick	d																						
Warwick Parkway	d																						
Hatton	d																						
Lapworth	d																						
Dorridge	d					14 25		15 25						16 25						17 25			
Widney Manor	d					14 29		15 29						16 29						17 29			
Solihull	d					14 32		15 32						16 32						17 32			
Olton	d					14 36		15 36						16 36						17 36			
Acocks Green	d					14 38		15 38						16 38						17 38			
Tyseley	d				14 10		15 10				16 10								17 12				
Small Heath	d																						
Bordesley	d																						
Birmingham Moor Street	d				14 17	14 45	15 17	15 45			16 17			16 45			17 02		17 17	17 45			
Birmingham Snow Hill ⇌	a				14 19	14 47	15 19	15 48			16 19			16 48			17 04		17 20	17 48			
	d				14 20	14 48	15 20	15 48			16 20			16 48			17 06		17 21	17 48			
Jewellery Quarter ⇌	d				14 22	14 51	15 22	15 51			16 22			16 51					17 24	17 51			
The Hawthorns ⇌	d				14 27	14 55	15 27	15 55			16 27			16 55					17 28	17 55			
Smethwick Galton Bridge 7	d				14 29	14 58	15 29	15 58			16 29			16 58					17 31	17 58			
Coventry	a	14 22	15 22									16 22			17 22								18 22
Birmingham International ✈	a	14 35	15 35									16 35			17 35								18 35
Birmingham New Street 12	a	14 48	15 48							16 12		16 48	17 12		17 48							18 09	18 48
	d								16 00												18 00		
Langley Green	d					15 01		16 01						17 01						18 01			
Rowley Regis	d				14 34	15 04	15 34	16 04			16 34			17 04					17 35	18 04			
Old Hill	d					15 07		16 07						17 07						18 07			
Cradley Heath	d				14 39	15 10	15 39	16 10			16 39			17 10					17 40	18 10			
Lye	d					15 13		16 13						17 13						18 13			
Stourbridge Junction 2	d				14 45	15a17	15 45	16a18			16 45			17a18			17 27		17 46	18a19			
Hagley	d				14 48		15 48				16 48						17 30		17 50				
Blakedown	d				14 51																		
Kidderminster	d				14 56		15 54				16 54						17 36		17 56				
Hartlebury	d																						
University	d																						
Barnt Green	d																						
Bromsgrove	d								16 21												18 21		
Droitwich Spa	d				15 08		16 06		16 30		17 06						17 48		18 07		18 30		
Worcester Shrub Hill 7	a								16 38										18 15		18 38		
	d			15 11					16 45							17 11		18 09			18 43		
Worcester Foregate Street 7	a			15 13	15 16		16 14		16 47		17 14					17 14	18 01	18 11			18 45		
	d			15 14					16 48							17 14					18 46		
Malvern Link	d			15 24					16 57							17 24					18 55		
Great Malvern	a			15 27					17 01							17 27					18 58		
	d			15 28												17 28					18 58		
Colwall	d			15 34												17 34					19 03		
Ledbury	a			15 41												17 42					19 10		
	d			15 48												17 43					19 10		
Hereford 7	a			16 07												18 02					19 31		

Stratford-upon-Avon, Marylebone and Leamington Spa - Birmingham - Stourbridge, Worcester and Hereford

		GW	LM	LM	XC	XC	XC	XC	GW	LM	GW	LM	LM	XC	XC	GW	LM	LM	XC	XC	XC	LM
		◇1			◇1	◇1	◇1	◇1	◇1		◇1			◇1	◇1	◇1			◇1	◇1	◇1	
						A		A														
		⊤			⊤	⊤	⊤	⊤	⊤		⊡			⊤		⊡						
Stratford-upon-Avon	d		17 30							18 30		19 30										
Wilmcote	d		17 35							18 35		19 35										
Wootton Wawen	d																					
Henley-in-Arden	d		17 42							18 42		19 42										
Danzey	d																					
Wood End	d																					
The Lakes	d		17x49							18x49		19x49										
Earlswood (West Midlands)	d																					
Wythall	d		17 53							18 53		19 53										
Whitlocks End	d		17 55							18 55		19 55										
Shirley	d		17 59							18 59		19 59										
Yardley Wood	d		18 02							19 02		20 02										
Hall Green	d		18 05							19 05		20 05										
Spring Road	d		18 07							19 07		20 07										
London Marylebone 10 ⊖	d																					
Banbury	d				18 25	18 54	19 25	19 54						20 25	20 54				21 25	21 54	22 25	
Leamington Spa 8	a				18 41	19 11	19 41	20 11						20 41	21 11				21 41	22 11	22 41	
	d				18 43	19 12	19 43	20 12						20 43	21 12				21 43	22 12	22 43	
Warwick	d																					
Warwick Parkway	d																					
Hatton	d																					
Lapworth	d																					
Dorridge	d																					
Widney Manor	d																					
Solihull	d																					
Olton	d																					
Acocks Green	d																					
Tyseley	d		18 10							19 10		20 10										
Small Heath	d																					
Bordesley	d																					
Birmingham Moor Street	d		18 17							19 15		20 15					21 35					22 52
Birmingham Snow Hill ⇌	a		18 19							19 18		20 18					21 37					22 54
	d		18 20							19 20		20 20					21 45					22 55
Jewellery Quarter ⇌	d		18 22							19 22		20 22					21 47					22 57
The Hawthorns ⇌	d		18 27							19 27		20 27					21 52					23 02
Smethwick Galton Bridge 7	d		18 29							19 29		20 29					21 54					23 04
Coventry	a					19 22	19 53	20 22						20 53	21 22				21 53	22 22	22 53	
Birmingham International ✈	a					19 35	20 03	20 35						21 03	21 35				22 03	22 32	23 03	
Birmingham New Street 12	a				19 11	19 48	20 15	20 48						21 15	21 48				22 15	22 42	23 14	
	d			19 00									21 00					22 05				
Langley Green	d																					
Rowley Regis	d		18 34							19 34		20 34					21 59					23 09
Old Hill	d																					
Cradley Heath	d		18 39							19 39		20 39					22 03					23 14
Lye	d																					
Stourbridge Junction 2	d		18 45							19 45		20 45					22 09					23 19
Hagley	d		18 49							19 48		20 49					22 12					23 23
Blakedown	d		18 52																			
Kidderminster	d		18 57							19 55		20 57					22 18					23 29
Hartlebury	d																					
University	d																					
Barnt Green	d																					
Bromsgrove	d			19 21									21 21									
Droitwich Spa	d		19 08	19 31						20 08		21 09	21 31				22 30	22 38				23 40
Worcester Shrub Hill 7	a		19 16	19 41						20 16		21 23	21 38				22 37	22 48				23 48
	d	19 13							20 09		21 16	21 28	21 42			22 10	22 41					
Worcester Foregate Street 7	a	19 15							20 15		21 19	21 31	21 44			22 12	22 43					
	d	19 17							20 15		21 20	21 31	21 45			22 14	22 44					
Malvern Link	d	19 26							20 24		21 29	21 40	21 54			22 23	22 52					
Great Malvern	a	19 30							20 27		21 33	21 43	21 57			22 26	22 55					
	d										21 33		21 57									
Colwall	d										21 39		22 02									
Ledbury	a										21 46		22 09									
	d										21 48		22 10									
Hereford 7	a										22 06		22 30									

A ⊤ to Birmingham International

Table 71

Stratford-upon-Avon, Marylebone and Leamington Spa - Birmingham - Stourbridge, Worcester and Hereford

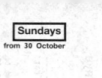

		GW		LM	LM	XC	XC	XC	XC	GW	LM	GW		LM	LM	XC	XC	GW	LM	LM	XC	XC		XC	LM
		◇1				◇1	◇1	◇1	◇1	◇1		◇1				◇1	◇1	◇1			◇1	◇1		◇1	
							A		A																
		🛒				🛒	🛒	🛒	🛒	🛒		🍽				🛒		🍽							
Stratford-upon-Avon	d			17 30							18 30			19 30											
Wilmcote	d			17 35							18 35			19 35											
Wootton Wawen	d																								
Henley-in-Arden	d			17 42							18 42			19 42											
Danzey	d																								
Wood End	d																								
The Lakes	d			17x49							18x49			19x49											
Earlswood (West Midlands)	d																								
Wythall	d			17 53							18 53			19 53											
Whitlocks End	d			17 55							18 55			19 55											
Shirley	d			17 59							18 59			19 59											
Yardley Wood	d			18 02							19 02			20 02											
Hall Green	d			18 05							19 05			20 05											
Spring Road	d			18 07							19 07			20 07											
London Marylebone 10 ⊖	d																								
Banbury	d					18 25	18 54	19 25	19 54							20 25	20 54				21 25	21 54		22 25	
Leamington Spa 8	a					18 41	19 11	19 41	20 11							20 41	21 11				21 41	22 11		22 41	
	d					18 43	19 12	19 43	20 12							20 43	21 12				21 43	22 12		22 43	
Warwick	d																								
Warwick Parkway	d																								
Hatton	d																								
Lapworth	d																								
Dorridge	d																								
Widney Manor	d																								
Solihull	d																								
Olton	d																								
Acocks Green	d																								
Tyseley	d			18 10							19 10			20 10											
Small Heath	d																								
Bordesley	d																								
Birmingham Moor Street	d			18 17							19 15			20 15					21 35						22 52
Birmingham Snow Hill 🚊	a			18 19							19 18			20 18					21 37						22 54
	d			18 20							19 20			20 20					21 45						22 55
Jewellery Quarter 🚊	d			18 22							19 22			20 22					21 47						22 57
The Hawthorns 🚊	d			18 27							19 27			20 27					21 52						23 02
Smethwick Galton Bridge 7	d			18 29							19 29			20 29					21 54						23 04
Coventry	a						19 22	19 53	20 22							20 53	21 22				21 53	22 22		22 53	
Birmingham International ✈	a						19 35	20 03	20 35							21 03	21 35				22 03	22 32		23 03	
Birmingham New Street 12	a					19 11	19 48	20 15	20 48							21 15	21 48				22 15	22 42		23 14	
	d				19 00										21 00					22 05					
Langley Green	d																								
Rowley Regis	d			18 34							19 34			20 34					21 59						23 09
Old Hill	d																								
Cradley Heath	d			18 39							19 39			20 39					22 03						23 14
Lye	d																								
Stourbridge Junction 2	d			18 45							19 45			20 45					22 09						23 19
Hagley	d			18 49							19 48			20 49					22 12						23 23
Blakedown	d			18 52																					
Kidderminster	d			18 57							19 55			20 57					22 18						23 29
Hartlebury	d																								
University	d																								
Barnt Green	d																								
Bromsgrove	d				19 21										21 21										
Droitwich Spa	d			19 08	19 31						20 08			21 09	21 31				22 30	22 38					23 40
Worcester Shrub Hill 7	a			19 16	19 41						20 16			21 16	21 38				22 37	22 48					23 48
	d	19 09								20 08		21 13		21 22	21 42			22 12	22 41						
Worcester Foregate Street 7	a	19 11								20 14		21 16		21 24	21 44			22 15	22 43						
	d	19 13								20 14		21 17		21 25	21 45			22 16	22 44						
Malvern Link	d	19 22								20 23		21 26		21 36	21 54			22 25	22 52						
Great Malvern	a	19 26								20 26		21 30		21 39	21 57			22 28	22 55						
	d											21 30			21 57										
Colwall	d											21 36			22 02										
Ledbury	a											21 43			22 09										
	d											21 45			22 10										
Hereford 7	a											22 02			22 30										

A 🛒 to Birmingham International

Table 72 — Mondays to Saturdays

Stourbridge Junction - Stourbridge Town

Miles			LM SX	LM	LM SX	LM	LM SX	LM SX		LM	LM SX	LM	LM	LM	LM		LM	LM	LM	LM	LM	LM		LM	LM
0	Stourbridge Junction ■	d	05 47	05 58	06 08	06 19	06 29	06 39	....	06 49	06 59	07 09	07 19	07 29	07 39	....	07 49	07 59	08 09	08 19	08 29	08 39	....	08 49	08 59
0¾	Stourbridge Town	a	05 50	06 01	06 11	06 22	06 32	06 42		06 52	07 02	07 12	07 22	07 32	07 42		07 52	08 02	08 12	08 22	08 32	08 42		08 52	09 02

		LM	LM	LM	LM		LM	LM	LM	LM	LM	LM		LM	LM	LM	LM	LM	LM		LM	LM	LM	LM	LM
Stourbridge Junction ■	d	09 09	09 19	09 29	09 39	....	09 49	09 59	10 09	10 19	10 29	10 39	....	10 49	10 59	11 09	11 19	11 29	11 39	....	11 49	11 59	12 09	12 19	12 29
Stourbridge Town	a	09 12	09 22	09 32	09 42		09 52	10 02	10 12	10 22	10 32	10 42		10 52	11 02	11 12	11 22	11 32	11 42		11 52	12 02	12 12	12 22	12 32

		LM		LM	LM	LM	LM	LM	LM		LM	LM	LM	LM	LM	LM		LM	LM	LM	LM	LM	LM		LM
Stourbridge Junction ■	d	12 39	....	12 49	12 59	13 09	13 19	13 29	13 39	....	13 49	13 59	14 09	14 19	14 29	14 39	....	14 49	14 59	15 09	15 19	15 29	15 39	....	15 49
Stourbridge Town	a	12 42		12 52	13 02	13 12	13 22	13 32	13 42		13 52	14 02	14 12	14 22	14 32	14 42		14 52	15 02	15 12	15 22	15 32	15 42		15 52

		LM	LM	LM	LM	LM		LM	LM	LM	LM	LM	LM		LM	LM	LM	LM	LM	LM		LM	LM	LM	LM
Stourbridge Junction ■	d	15 59	16 09	16 19	16 29	16 39	....	16 49	16 59	17 09	17 19	17 29	17 39	....	17 49	17 59	18 09	18 19	18 29	18 39	....	18 49	18 59	19 09	19 19
Stourbridge Town	a	16 02	16 12	16 22	16 32	16 42		16 52	17 02	17 12	17 22	17 32	17 42		17 52	18 02	18 12	18 22	18 32	18 42		18 52	19 02	19 12	19 22

		LM	LM		LM	LM	LM	LM	LM	LM		LM	LM	LM	LM	LM	LM		LM	LM	LM	LM	LM	LM	
Stourbridge Junction ■	d	19 29	19 39	....	19 49	19 59	20 09	20 19	20 29	20 39	....	20 49	20 59	21 09	21 19	21 29	21 39	....	21 49	21 59	22 09	22 19	22 29	22 39	....
Stourbridge Town	a	19 32	19 42		19 52	20 02	20 12	20 22	20 32	20 42		20 52	21 02	21 12	21 22	21 32	21 42		21 52	22 02	22 12	22 22	22 32	22 42	

		LM	LM	LM	LM	LM
Stourbridge Junction ■	d	22 50	23 00	23 15	23 30	23 54
Stourbridge Town	a	22 53	23 03	23 18	23 33	23 57

Sundays

		LM	LM	LM	LM	LM	LM		LM	LM	LM	LM	LM	LM		LM	LM	LM	LM	LM	LM		LM	LM	LM
Stourbridge Junction ■	d	09 43	10 00	10 11	10 21	10 41	10 54	....	11 11	11 21	11 41	11 54	12 11	12 21	....	12 41	12 54	13 11	13 21	13 41	13 54	....	14 11	14 21	14 41
Stourbridge Town	a	09 46	10 03	10 14	10 24	10 44	10 57		11 14	11 24	11 44	11 57	12 14	12 24		12 44	12 57	13 14	13 24	13 44	13 57		14 14	14 24	14 44

		LM	LM	LM		LM	LM	LM	LM	LM	LM		LM	LM	LM	LM	LM	LM		LM	LM	LM	LM	LM	
Stourbridge Junction ■	d	14 54	15 11	15 21	....	15 41	15 54	16 11	16 21	16 41	16 54	....	17 11	17 21	17 41	17 54	18 11	18 21	....	18 41	18 54	19 11	19 21	19 47	....
Stourbridge Town	a	14 57	15 14	15 24		15 44	15 57	16 14	16 24	16 44	16 57		17 14	17 24	17 44	17 57	18 14	18 24		18 44	18 57	19 14	19 24	19 50	

Table 72 — Mondays to Saturdays

Stourbridge Town - Stourbridge Junction

Miles			LM MX	LM SX	LM SX	LM SO	LM SX	LM SX		LM SX	LM SO	LM SX	LM	LM SX	LM		LM	LM	LM	LM	LM	LM		LM	LM
0	Stourbridge Town	d	23p59	05 52	06 03	06 10	06 13	06 24	....	06 34	06 40	06 44	06 54	07 04	07 14	....	07 24	07 34	07 44	07 54	08 04	08 14	....	08 24	08 34
0¾	Stourbridge Junction ■	a	00 02	05 55	06 06	06 13	06 16	06 27		06 37	06 43	06 47	06 57	07 07	07 17		07 27	07 37	07 47	07 57	08 07	08 17		08 27	08 37

		LM	LM	LM	LM		LM	LM	LM	LM	LM	LM		LM	LM	LM	LM	LM	LM		LM	LM	LM	LM	LM
Stourbridge Town	d	08 44	08 54	09 04	09 14	....	09 24	09 34	09 44	09 54	10 04	10 14	....	10 24	10 34	10 44	10 54	11 04	11 14	....	11 24	11 34	11 44	11 54	12 04
Stourbridge Junction ■	a	08 47	08 57	09 07	09 17		09 27	09 37	09 47	09 57	10 07	10 17		10 27	10 37	10 47	10 57	11 07	11 17		11 27	11 37	11 47	11 57	12 07

		LM		LM	LM	LM	LM	LM	LM		LM	LM	LM	LM	LM	LM		LM	LM	LM	LM	LM	LM		LM
Stourbridge Town	d	12 14	....	12 24	12 34	12 44	12 54	13 04	13 14	....	13 24	13 34	13 44	13 54	14 04	14 14	....	14 24	14 34	14 44	14 54	15 04	15 14	....	15 24
Stourbridge Junction ■	a	12 17		12 27	12 37	12 47	12 57	13 07	13 17		13 27	13 37	13 47	13 57	14 07	14 17		14 27	14 37	14 47	14 57	15 07	15 17		15 27

		LM	LM	LM	LM	LM		LM	LM	LM	LM	LM	LM		LM	LM	LM	LM	LM	LM		LM	LM	LM	LM
Stourbridge Town	d	15 34	15 44	15 54	16 04	16 14	....	16 24	16 34	16 44	16 54	17 04	17 14	....	17 24	17 34	17 44	17 54	18 04	18 14	....	18 24	18 34	18 44	18 54
Stourbridge Junction ■	a	15 37	15 47	15 57	16 07	16 17		16 27	16 37	16 47	16 57	17 07	17 17		17 27	17 37	17 47	17 57	18 07	18 17		18 27	18 37	18 47	18 57

		LM	LM		LM	LM	LM	LM	LM	LM		LM	LM	LM	LM	LM	LM		LM	LM	LM	LM	LM	LM	
Stourbridge Town	d	19 04	19 14	....	19 24	19 34	19 44	19 54	20 04	20 14	....	20 24	20 34	20 44	20 54	21 04	21 14	....	21 24	21 34	21 44	21 54	22 04	22 14	....
Stourbridge Junction ■	a	19 07	19 17		19 27	19 37	19 47	19 57	20 07	20 17		20 27	20 37	20 47	20 57	21 07	21 17		21 27	21 37	21 47	21 57	22 07	22 17	

		LM	LM	LM	LM	LM	LM		LM	LM
Stourbridge Town	d	22 24	22 34	22 44	22 55	23 05	23 20	....	23 35	23 59
Stourbridge Junction ■	a	22 27	22 37	22 47	22 58	23 08	23 23		23 38	00 02

Sundays

		LM A	LM	LM	LM	LM	LM		LM	LM	LM	LM	LM	LM		LM	LM	LM	LM	LM	LM		LM	LM	LM
Stourbridge Town	d	23p59	09 49	10 05	10 16	10 36	10 46	....	11 00	11 16	11 36	11 46	12 00	12 16	....	12 36	12 46	13 00	13 16	13 36	13 46	....	14 00	14 16	14 36
Stourbridge Junction ■	a	00 02	09 52	10 08	10 19	10 39	10 49		11 03	11 19	11 39	11 49	12 03	12 19		12 39	12 49	13 03	13 19	13 39	13 49		14 03	14 19	14 39

		LM	LM	LM		LM	LM	LM	LM	LM	LM		LM	LM	LM	LM	LM	LM		LM	LM	LM	LM	LM	LM
Stourbridge Town	d	14 46	15 00	15 16	....	15 36	15 46	16 00	16 16	16 36	16 46	....	17 00	17 16	17 36	17 46	18 00	18 16	....	18 36	18 46	19 00	19 16	19 36	19 55
Stourbridge Junction ■	a	14 49	15 03	15 19		15 39	15 49	16 03	16 19	16 39	16 49		17 03	17 19	17 39	17 49	18 03	18 19		18 39	18 49	19 03	19 19	19 39	19 58

A not 22 May

Network Diagram for Tables 74, 75

DM-23/10
Design BAJS
© Network Rail OPSU 2010.
All rights reserved

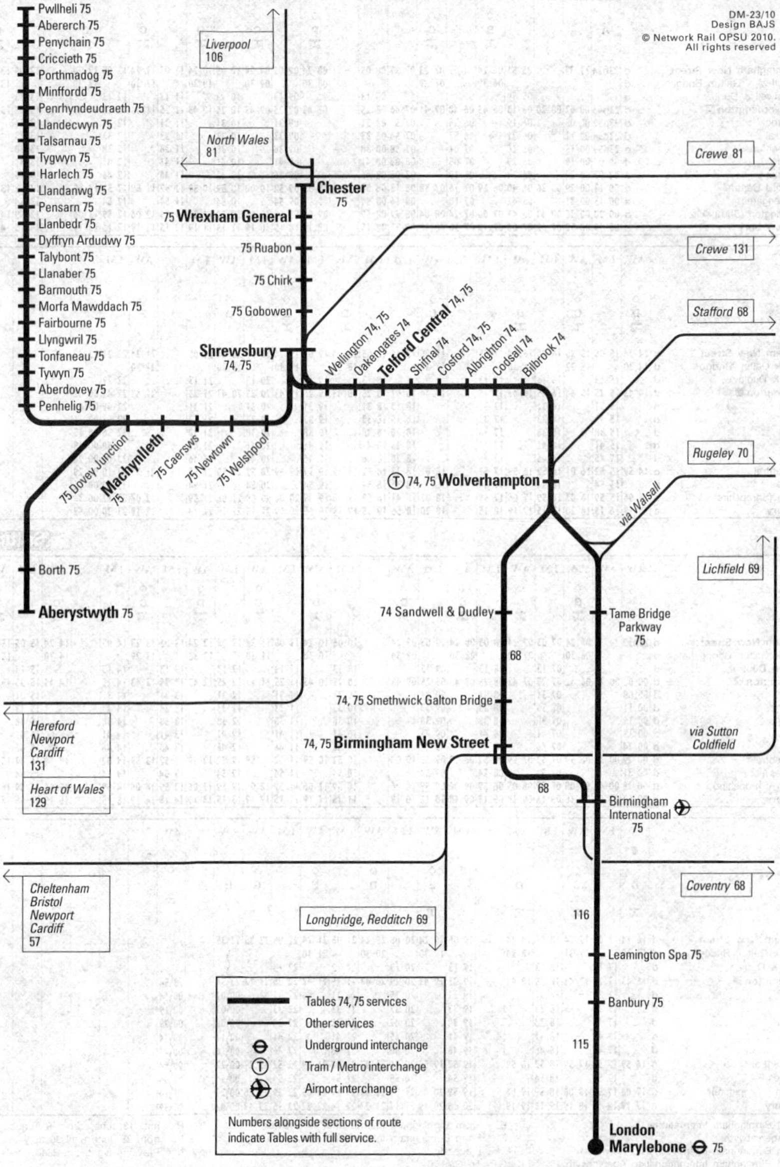

Table 74

Mondays to Fridays

Birmingham - Shrewsbury

Miles			AW MO A	AW MX	AW MX	LM	AW ◇ B	LM	AW ◇ C	LM	LM	AW ◇ D	LM	AW ◇ C	LM	AW ◇ D	LM	AW ◇ C	LM	AW ◇ D	LM	AW ◇ C	LM
0	**Birmingham New Street**	d	23p24	23p32		05 51	06 24		07 23	07 27	08 05	08 24	09 05	09 24	10 05	10 24	11 05	11 24	12 05	12 24	13 05	13 24	14 05
4	Smethwick Galton Bridge	d					06 30		07 29			08 30		09 30		10 30		11 30		12 30		13 30	
5¼	Sandwell & Dudley	d				05 59					08 13		09 13		10 13		11 13		12 13		13 13		14 13
13	**Wolverhampton 7**	d	23b46	00 02	00 20	06 13	06 43	06 48	07 41	07 46	08 25	08 43	09 25	09 43	10 25	10 43	11 25	11 43	12 25	12 43	13 25	13 43	14 25
17	Bilbrook	d	23p52	00 08		06 19		06 54		07 51	08 31		09 31		10 31		11 31		12 31		13 31		14 31
17½	Codsall	d	23p54	00 11		06 21		06 57		07 54	08 33		09 33		10 33		11 33		12 33		13 33		14 33
20¾	Albrighton	d	23p59	00 15		06 26		07 01		07 58	08 38		09 38		10 38		11 38		12 38		13 38		14 38
22¼	Cosford	d	00 02	00 19		06 29		07 05		08 02	08 41		09 41		10 41		11 41		12 41		13 41		14 41
25½	Shifnal	d	00 07	00 24		06 34		07 10		08 06	08 46		09 46		10 46		11 46		12 46		13 46		14 46
28½	Telford Central	d	00 13	00 29	00 36	06 40	06 59	07 16	07 58	08 13	08 52	08 59	09 52	10 00	10 52	10 59	11 52	11 59	12 52	12 59	13 52	13 59	14 52
29½	Oakengates	d	00 15	00 31		06 42		07 18		08 16	08 54		09 54		10 54		11 54		12 54		13 54		14 54
32½	Wellington (Shropshire)	d	00 20	00 36	00 43	06 47	07 06	07 24	08 04	08 22	08 59	09 06	09 59	10 06	10 59	11 06	11 59	12 06	12 59	13 06	13 59	14 06	14 59
43	**Shrewsbury**	a	00 35	00 52	01 02	07 00	07 18	07 38	08 18	08 37	09 15	09 19	10 15	10 19	11 15	11 19	12 15	12 19	13 15	13 19	14 15	14 19	15 15

		AW ◇ D	LM	AW ◇ C	LM	AW R D	LM	AW ◇ C	LM	LM	AW ◇ D	LM	AW ◇ E	LM	AW ◇ D	LM	AW ◇ F	LM	AW
Birmingham New Street	d	14 24	15 05	15 26	16 05	16 24	17 05	17 26	17 46	18 05	18 24	19 05	19 24	20 05	20 24	21 05	21 24	22 21	23 32
Smethwick Galton Bridge	d	14 30		15 32		16 30		17 32			18 30		19 30		20 30		21 30		
Sandwell & Dudley	d		15 13		16 13		17 13			18 13		19 13		20 13		21 13		22 29	
Wolverhampton 7	d	14 43	15 25	15 44	16 25	16 43	17 25	17 44	18 07	18 25	18 43	19 25	19 43	20 25	20 43	21 25	21 43	22 43	00 02
Bilbrook	d		15 31		16 31		17 31		18 13	18 31		19 31		20 31		21 31		22 49	00 08
Codsall	d		15 33		16 33		17 33		18 15	18 33		19 33		20 33		21 33		22 51	00 11
Albrighton	d		15 38		16 38		17 38		18 20	18 38		19 38		20 38		21 38		22 56	00 15
Cosford	d		15 41		16 41		17 41		18 23	18 41		19 41		20 41		21 41		22 59	00 19
Shifnal	d		15 46		16 46		17 46		18 28	18 46		19 46		20 46		21 46		23 04	00 24
Telford Central	d	14 59	15 52	16 01	16 52	16 59	17 52	18 01	18 33	18 52	18 59	19 52	19 59	20 52	20 59	21 52	21 59	23 10	00 29
Oakengates	d		15 54		16 54		17 54		18 35	18 54		19 54		20 54		21 54		23 12	00 31
Wellington (Shropshire)	d	15 06	15 59	16 07	16 59	17 06	17 59	18 07	18 41	18 59	19 06	19 59	20 06	20 59	21 06	21 59	22 07	23 17	00 36
Shrewsbury	a	15 19	16 15	16 20	17 15	17 19	18 15	18 20	18 56	19 15	19 19	20 15	20 19	21 15	21 19	22 14	22 19	23 30	00 52

Saturdays

		AW	AW	AW ◇ B	LM	AW ◇ C	LM	AW ◇ D	LM	AW ◇ C	LM	AW ◇ D	LM	AW ◇ C	LM	AW ◇ D	LM	AW ◇ C	LM	AW ◇ D	LM	AW ◇ C	LM
Birmingham New Street	d	23p32		06 24	07 05	07 24	08 05	08 24	09 05	09 24	10 05	10 24	11 05	11 24	12 05	12 24	13 05	13 23	14 05	14 24	15 05	15 24	16 05
Smethwick Galton Bridge	d			06 30		07 30		08 30		09 30		10 30		11 30		12 30		13 29		14 30		15 30	
Sandwell & Dudley	d				07 13		08 13		09 13		10 13		11 13		12 13		13 13		14 13		15 13		16 13
Wolverhampton 7	d	00 02	00 20	06 42	07 25	07 42	08 25	08 43	09 25	09 43	10 25	10 43	11 25	11 43	12 25	12 43	13 25	13 43	14 25	14 43	15 25	15 43	16 25
Bilbrook	d	00 08			07 31		08 31		09 31		10 31		11 31		12 31		13 31		14 31		15 31		16 31
Codsall	d	00 11			07 33		08 33		09 33		10 33		11 33		12 33		13 33		14 33		15 33		16 33
Albrighton	d	00 15			07 38		08 38		09 38		10 38		11 38		12 38		13 38		14 38		15 38		16 38
Cosford	d	00 19			07 41		08 41		09 41		10 41		11 41		12 41		13 41		14 41		15 41		16 41
Shifnal	d	00 24			07 46		08 46		09 46		10 46		11 46		12 46		13 46		14 46		15 46		16 46
Telford Central	d	00 29	00 36	06 59	07 52	07 59	08 52	08 59	09 52	10 00	10 52	10 59	11 52	11 59	12 52	12 59	13 52	13 59	14 52	14 59	15 52	15 59	16 52
Oakengates	d	00 31			07 54		08 54		09 54		10 54		11 54		12 54		13 54		14 54		15 54		16 54
Wellington (Shropshire)	d	00 36	00 43	07 05	07 59	08 05	08 59	09 06	09 59	10 06	10 59	11 06	11 59	12 06	12 59	13 06	13 59	14 06	14 59	15 06	15 59	16 06	16 59
Shrewsbury	a	00 52	00 59	07 18	08 15	08 18	09 15	09 19	10 15	10 19	11 15	11 19	12 15	12 19	13 15	13 19	14 15	14 19	15 15	15 19	16 15	16 19	17 15

		AW R D	LM	AW ◇ C	LM	AW ◇ D	LM	AW ◇ E	LM	AW ◇ D	LM	AW ◇ E	LM	AW G	AW H	AW I
Birmingham New Street	d	16 24	17 05	17 24	18 05	18 24	19 05	19 24	20 05	20 24	21 05	21 24	22 05	22 55	23 35	
Smethwick Galton Bridge	d	16 30		17 31		18 30		19 30		20 30		21 30				
Sandwell & Dudley	d		17 13		18 13		19 13		20 13		21 13		22 13			
Wolverhampton 7	d	16 43	17 25	17 43	18 25	18 43	19 25	19 43	20 29	20 43	21 25	21 42	22 25	23 13	23 54	23 54
Bilbrook	d		17 31		18 31		19 31		20 35		21 31		22 31		00 01	00 14
Codsall	d		17 33		18 33		19 33		20 37		21 33		22 33		00 03	00 19
Albrighton	d		17 38		18 38		19 38		20 42		21 38		22 38		00 08	00 29
Cosford	d		17 41		18 41		19 41		20 45		21 41		22 41		00 11	00 34
Shifnal	d		17 46		18 46		19 46		20 50		21 46		22 46		00 16	00 44
Telford Central	d	16 59	17 52	17 59	18 52	18 59	19 52	19 59	20 56	21 02	21 52	21 59	22 52	23 29	00 22	00 54
Oakengates	d		17 54		18 54		19 54		20 58		21 54		22 54		00 24	01 04
Wellington (Shropshire)	d	17 06	17 59	18 06	18 59	19 06	19 59	20 06	21 03	21 09	21 59	22 05	22 59	23 36	00 29	01 14
Shrewsbury	a	17 19	18 15	18 19	19 15	19 19	20 15	20 19	21 17	21 23	22 14	22 22	23 15	23 49	00 42	01 39

A From Birmingham International
B To Aberystwyth
C From Birmingham International to Holyhead
D From Birmingham International to Aberystwyth
E From Birmingham International to Chester
F From Birmingham International to Manchester Piccadilly
G To Crewe
H until 18 June, from 6 August
I from 25 June until 30 July
b Previous night, arr. 2340

Table 74

Birmingham - Shrewsbury

Sundays until 19 June

		AW	AW	AW	AW	AW	AW	AW	AW	AW	AW	AW	AW	AW	AW	AW	AW	AW	AW	AW	AW	AW
						◇	◇		◇	◇		◇	◇		◇	◇		◇	◇	◇		
		A		B		C	D		C	D		C	D		E	D		C	D	C	B	B
						🛒	🛒		🛒	🛒		🛒	🛒		🛒	🛒		🛒				
Birmingham New Street	d	23p35		10 05		11 05	12 24		13 24	14 24		15 24	16 24		17 24	18 24		19 24	20 24	21 24	22 24	23 24
Smethwick Galton Bridge	d																					
Sandwell & Dudley	d																					
Wolverhampton 7	d	23p54	00 20	10 22	11 06	11 27	12 42	13 06	13 42	14 43	15 06	15 43	16 43	17 06	17 43	18 43	19 06	19 43	20 43	21 43	22 42	23b46
Bilbrook	d	00 01		10 28	11 12	11 33		13 12			15 12			17 12			19 12			21 49	22 48	23 52
Codsall	d	00 03		10 31	11 15	11 35		13 15			15 15			17 15			19 15			21 51	22 50	23 54
Albrighton	d	00 08		10 35	11 19	11 40		13 19			15 19			17 19			19 19			21 56	22 55	23 59
Cosford	d	00 11		10 39	11 23	11 43		13 23			15 23			17 23			19 23			21 59	22 58	00 02
Shifnal	d	00 16		10 44	11 28	11 48		13 28			15 28			17 28			19 28			22 04	23 03	00 07
Telford Central	d	00 22	00 36	10 49	11 34	11 54	12 59	13 34	13 58	14 59	15 34	15 59	16 59	17 34	17 59	18 59	19 34	19 59	20 59	22 10	23 09	00 13
Oakengates	d	00 24		10 51	11 37	11 56		13 37			15 37			17 37			19 37			22 12	23 11	00 15
Wellington (Shropshire)	d	00 29	00 43	10 57	11 43	12 01	13 05	13 43	14 04	15 06	15 43	16 06	17 06	17 43	18 06	19 06	19 43	20 06	21 06	22 17	23 16	00 20
Shrewsbury	a	00 42	00 59	11 10	11 58	12 14	13 18	13 58	14 18	15 19	15 58	16 26	17 19	17 59	18 19	19 19	19 58	20 19	21 19	22 30	23 32	00 35

Sundays 26 June to 31 July

		AW	AW	AW	AW	AW	AW	AW	AW	AW	AW	AW	AW	AW	AW	AW	AW	AW	AW	AW	AW	AW
						◇	◇		◇	◇			◇		◇	◇		◇	◇	◇		
						B	D		B	D		B	D		B	D		B	D	C	B	B
		🚌	🚌			🛒	🛒		🛒	🛒			🛒		🛒	🛒		🛒				
Birmingham New Street	d			10 05		11 05	12 24		13 24	14 24		15 24	16 24		17 24	18 24		19 24	20 24	21 24	22 24	23 24
Smethwick Galton Bridge	d																					
Sandwell & Dudley	d																					
Wolverhampton 7	d	23p54	00 20	10 22	11 06	11 27	12 42	13 06	13 42	14 43	15 06	15 43	16 43	17 06	17 43	18 43	19 06	19 43	20 43	21 43	22 42	23 46
Bilbrook	d	00 14		10 28	11 12	11 33		13 12			15 12			17 12			19 12			21 49	22 48	23 52
Codsall	d	00 19		10 31	11 15	11 35		13 15			15 15			17 15			19 15			21 51	22 50	23 54
Albrighton	d	00 29		10 35	11 19	11 40		13 19			15 19			17 19			19 19			21 56	22 55	23 59
Cosford	d	00 34		10 39	11 23	11 43		13 23			15 23			17 23			19 23			21 59	22 58	00 02
Shifnal	d	00 44		10 44	11 28	11 48		13 28			15 28			17 28			19 28			22 04	23 03	00 07
Telford Central	d	00 54	01 05	10 49	11 34	11 54	12 59	13 34	13 58	14 59	15 34	15 59	16 59	17 34	17 59	18 59	19 34	19 59	20 59	22 10	23 09	00 13
Oakengates	d	01 04		10 51	11 37	11 56		13 37			15 37			17 37			19 37			22 12	23 11	00 15
Wellington (Shropshire)	d	01 14	01 20	10 57	11 43	12 01	13 05	13 43	14 04	15 06	15 43	16 06	17 06	17 43	18 05	19 06	19 43	20 06	21 06	22 17	23 16	00 20
Shrewsbury	a	01 39	01 45	11 10	11 58	12 14	13 18	13 58	14 18	15 19	15 58	16 26	17 19	17 59	18 19	19 19	19 58	20 18	21 19	22 30	23 32	00 35

Sundays 7 August to 11 September

		AW	AW	AW	AW	AW	AW	AW	AW	AW	AW	AW	AW	AW	AW	AW	AW	AW	AW	AW	AW	AW
						◇	◇		◇	◇		◇	◇		◇	◇		◇	◇	◇		
				B		C	D		C	D		C	D		E	D		C	D	C	B	B
						🛒	🛒		🛒	🛒		🛒	🛒		🛒	🛒		🛒				
Birmingham New Street	d	23p35		10 05		11 05	12 24		13 24	14 24		15 24	16 24		17 24	18 24		19 24	20 24	21 24	22 24	23 24
Smethwick Galton Bridge	d																					
Sandwell & Dudley	d																					
Wolverhampton 7	d	23p54	00 20	10 22	11 06	11 27	12 42	13 06	13 42	14 43	15 06	15 43	16 43	17 06	17 43	18 43	19 06	19 43	20 43	21 43	22 42	23b46
Bilbrook	d	00 01		10 28	11 12	11 33		13 12			15 12			17 12			19 12			21 49	22 48	23 52
Codsall	d	00 03		10 31	11 15	11 35		13 15			15 15			17 15			19 15			21 51	22 50	23 54
Albrighton	d	00 08		10 35	11 19	11 40		13 19			15 19			17 19			19 19			21 56	22 55	23 59
Cosford	d	00 11		10 39	11 23	11 43		13 23			15 23			17 23			19 23			21 59	22 58	00 02
Shifnal	d	00 16		10 44	11 28	11 48		13 28			15 28			17 28			19 28			22 04	23 03	00 07
Telford Central	d	00 22	00 36	10 49	11 34	11 54	12 59	13 34	13 58	14 59	15 34	15 59	16 59	17 34	17 59	18 59	19 34	19 59	20 59	22 10	23 09	00 13
Oakengates	d	00 24		10 51	11 37	11 56		13 37			15 37			17 37			19 37			22 12	23 11	00 15
Wellington (Shropshire)	d	00 29	00 43	10 57	11 43	12 01	13 05	13 43	14 04	15 06	15 43	16 06	17 06	17 43	18 05	19 06	19 43	20 06	21 06	22 17	23 16	00 20
Shrewsbury	a	00 42	00 59	11 10	11 58	12 14	13 18	13 58	14 18	15 19	15 58	16 26	17 19	17 59	18 19	19 19	19 58	20 19	21 19	22 30	23 32	00 35

Sundays from 18 September

		AW	AW	AW	AW	AW	AW	AW	AW	AW	AW	AW	AW	AW	AW	AW	AW	AW	AW	AW	AW	AW
						◇	◇		◇	◇		◇	◇		◇	◇		◇	◇	◇		
				B		C	D		C	D		C	D		E	D		C	D	C	B	B
						🛒	🛒		🛒	🛒		🛒	🛒		🛒	🛒		🛒				
Birmingham New Street	d	23p35		10 05		11 05	12 24		13 24	14 24		15 24	16 24		17 24	18 24		19 24	20 24	21 24	22 24	23 24
Smethwick Galton Bridge	d																					
Sandwell & Dudley	d																					
Wolverhampton 7	d	23p54	00 20	10 22	11 06	11 27	12 42	13 06	13 42	14 43	15 06	15 43	16 43	17 06	17 43	18 43	19 06	19 43	20 43	21 43	22 42	23b46
Bilbrook	d	00 01		10 28	11 12	11 33		13 12			15 12			17 12			19 12			21 49	22 48	23 52
Codsall	d	00 03		10 31	11 15	11 35		13 15			15 15			17 15			19 15			21 51	22 50	23 54
Albrighton	d	00 08		10 35	11 19	11 40		13 19			15 19			17 19			19 19			21 56	22 55	23 59
Cosford	d	00 11		10 39	11 23	11 43		13 23			15 23			17 23			19 23			21 59	22 58	00 02
Shifnal	d	00 16		10 44	11 28	11 48		13 28			15 28			17 28			19 28			22 04	23 03	00 07
Telford Central	d	00 22	00 36	10 49	11 34	11 54	12 59	13 34	13 58	14 59	15 34	15 59	16 59	17 34	17 59	18 59	19 34	19 59	20 59	22 10	23 09	00 13
Oakengates	d	00 24		10 51	11 37	11 56		13 37			15 37			17 37			19 37			22 12	23 11	00 15
Wellington (Shropshire)	d	00 29	00 43	10 57	11 43	12 01	13 05	13 43	14 04	15 06	15 43	16 06	17 06	17 43	18 06	19 06	19 43	20 06	21 06	22 17	23 16	00 20
Shrewsbury	a	00 42	00 59	11 10	11 58	12 14	13 18	13 58	14 18	15 19	15 58	16 26	17 19	17 59	18 19	19 19	19 58	20 18	21 19	22 30	23 32	00 35

A not 22 May
B From Birmingham International
C From Birmingham International to Chester
D From Birmingham International to Aberystwyth
E From Birmingham International to Holyhead

Shrewsbury - Birmingham

Miles			AW MO	AW MX	AW	LM	LM	AW	LM	LM	AW		LM	AW	LM	AW	LM	AW	LM	AW	LM		AW	LM	AW
				◇							◇			◇		◇		◇		◇			◇		◇
			A	B	C			C			D			E		D		E		D			E		D
			🚌								🛒			🛒		🛒		🛒		🛒			🛒		🛒
0	**Shrewsbury**	d	23p01	23p26	05 21	05 28	05 58	06 31	06 55	07 14	07 31		07 47	08 31	08 47	09 31	09 47	10 32	10 47	11 31	11 47		12 31	12 47	13 31
10½	Wellington (Shropshire)	d	23p26	23p40	05 35	05 41	06 12	06 45	07 09	07 28	07 45		08 01	08 45	09 01	09 45	10 01	10 46	11 01	11 45	12 01		12 45	13 01	13 45
13½	Oakengates	d	23p36	23p44		05 46	06 16			07 32			08 05		09 05		10 05		11 05		12 05			13 05	
14½	Telford Central	d	23p46	23p47	05 41	05 49	06 19	06 51	07 15	07 35	07 51		08 08	08 51	09 08	09 51	10 08	10 52	11 08	11 51	12 08		12 51	13 08	13 51
17½	Shifnal	d	23p56	23p52		05 54	06 24			07 40			08 13		09 13		10 13		11 13		12 13			13 13	
20¾	Cosford	d	00 06	23p57		05 59	06 29			07 45			08 18		09 18		10 18		11 18		12 18			13 18	
22¼	Albrighton	d	00 11	00 01		06 02	06 33			07 48			08 22		09 22		10 22		11 22		12 22			13 22	
25½	Codsall	d	00 21	00 06		06 07	06 38			07 54			08 27		09 27		10 27		11 27		12 27			13 27	
26	Bilbrook	d	00 26	00 08		06 09	06 40			07 56			08 29		09 29		10 29		11 29		12 29			13 29	
30	**Wolverhampton 7** ⇌	a	00 46	00 20	05 58	06 16	06 47	07 08	07 34	08 02	08 08		08 36	09 08	09 36	10 08	10 36	11 09	11 36	12 08	12 36		13 08	13 36	14 08
37¾	Sandwell & Dudley	a				06 31	07 03		07 46				08 46		09 46		10 46		11 46		12 46			13 46	
39	Smethwick Galton Bridge	a			06 11	06 34	07 06	07 21			08 20			09 21		10 20		11 20		12 20			13 20		14 20
43	**Birmingham New Street 12**	a			06 16	06 43	07 14	07 26	07 55	08 20	08 26		08 55	09 26	09 56	10 26	10 55	11 26	11 55	12 26	12 55		13 26	13 55	14 26

		LM	AW	LM	AW	LM	AW		LM	AW	LM	AW	LM	AW	LM	LM	AW		LM	AW	AW	AW
			◇		◇		◇			◇		◇		◇			◇			◇	◇	◇
			E		D		E			D		E		D			F			G	H	B
			🛒		🛒		🛒			🛒		🛒		🛒								
Shrewsbury	d	13 47	14 31	14 47	15 31	15 47	16 33		16 47	17 31	17 47	18 31	18 47	19 33	19 47	20 47	21 33		21 47	22 18	22 18	23 26
Wellington (Shropshire)	d	14 01	14 45	15 01	15 45	16 01	16 47		17 01	17 45	18 01	18 45	19 01	19 47	20 01	21 01	21 47		22 01	22 32	22 32	23 40
Oakengates	d	14 05		15 05		16 05			17 05		18 05		19 05		20 05	21 05			22 05			23 44
Telford Central	d	14 08	14 51	15 08	15 51	16 08	16 53		17 08	17 51	18 08	18 51	19 08	19 53	20 08	21 08	21 53		22 08	22 38	22 38	23 47
Shifnal	d	14 13		15 13		16 13			17 13		18 13		19 13		20 13	21 13			22 13			23 52
Cosford	d	14 18		15 18		16 18			17 18		18 18		19 18		20 18	21 18			22 18			23 57
Albrighton	d	14 22		15 22		16 22			17 22		18 22		19 22		20 22	21 22			22 22			00 01
Codsall	d	14 27		15 27		16 27			17 27		18 27		19 27		20 27	21 27			22 27			00 06
Bilbrook	d	14 29		15 29		16 29			17 29		18 29		19 29		20 29	21 29			22 29			00 08
Wolverhampton 7 ⇌	a	14 36	15 08	15 36	16 08	16 36	17 10		17 36	18 08	18 36	19 08	19 36	20 10	20 36	21 36	22 09		22 36	22 55	22 55	00 20
Sandwell & Dudley	a	14 46		15 46		16 46			17 46		18 46		19 46		20 48	21 46			22 46			
Smethwick Galton Bridge	a		15 20		16 20		17 21			18 20		19 20		20 21			22 20					
Birmingham New Street 12	a	14 55	15 26	15 55	16 26	16 55	17 27		17 55	18 26	18 55	19 26	19 55	20 26	20 57	21 55	22 32		22 55	23 27	23 29	

Saturdays

		AW	AW	AW	LM	AW	LM	AW	LM	AW		LM	AW	LM	AW	LM	AW	LM	AW	LM		AW	LM	AW	LM
		◇				◇		◇		◇			◇		◇		◇		◇			◇		◇	
		B	C	C		D		E		D			E		D		E		D			E		D	
						🛒		🛒		🛒			🛒		🛒		🛒		🛒			🛒		🛒	
Shrewsbury	d	23p26	05 24	06 31	06 47	07 31	07 47	08 31	08 47	09 31		09 47	10 32	10 47	11 31	11 47	12 31	12 47	13 31	13 47		14 31	14 47	15 31	15 47
Wellington (Shropshire)	d	23p40	05 38	06 45	07 01	07 45	08 01	08 45	09 01	09 45		10 01	10 46	11 01	11 45	12 01	12 45	13 01	13 45	14 01		14 45	15 01	15 45	16 01
Oakengates	d	23p44			07 05		08 05		09 05			10 05		11 05		12 05		13 05		14 05			15 05		16 05
Telford Central	d	23p47	05 44	06 51	07 08	07 51	08 08	08 51	09 08	09 51		10 08	10 52	11 08	11 51	12 08	12 51	13 08	13 51	14 08		14 51	15 08	15 51	16 08
Shifnal	d	23p52			07 13		08 13		09 13			10 13		11 13		12 13		13 13		14 13			15 13		16 13
Cosford	d	23p57			07 18		08 18		09 18			10 18		11 18		12 18		13 18		14 18			15 18		16 18
Albrighton	d	00 01			07 22		08 22		09 22			10 22		11 22		12 22		13 22		14 22			15 22		16 22
Codsall	d	00 06			07 27		08 27		09 27			10 27		11 27		12 27		13 27		14 27			15 27		16 27
Bilbrook	d	00 08			07 29		08 29		09 29			10 29		11 29		12 29		13 29		14 29			15 29		16 29
Wolverhampton 7 ⇌	a	00 20	06 01	07 08	07 36	08 08	08 36	09 08	09 36	10 08		10 36	11 09	11 36	12 08	12 36	13 08	13 36	14 08	14 36		15 08	15 36	16 08	16 36
Sandwell & Dudley	a				07 46		08 46		09 46			10 46		11 46		12 46		13 46		14 46			15 46		16 46
Smethwick Galton Bridge	a		06 14	07 21		08 20		09 22		10 20			11 20		12 20		13 20		14 20			15 20		16 20	
Birmingham New Street 12	a		06 20	07 26	07 55	08 26	08 55	09 26	09 55	10 26		10 55	11 26	11 55	12 26	12 55	13 25	13 55	14 26	14 55		15 26	15 55	16 26	16 55

		AW	LM	AW	LM	AW		LM	AW	LM	LM	AW	LM	AW	AW	AW		AW
		◇		◇		◇			◇			◇		◇		◇		
		E		D		E			D			F		I	J	K		J
		🛒		🛒		🛒			🛒						🚌			🚌
Shrewsbury	d	16 33	16 47	17 31	17 47	18 31		18 47	19 33	19 47	20 47	21 33	21 47	22 31	22 33	23 26		23 33
Wellington (Shropshire)	d	16 47	17 01	17 45	18 01	18 45		19 01	19 47	20 01	21 01	21 47	22 01	22 45	22 58	23 40		23 58
Oakengates	d		17 05		18 05			19 05		20 05	21 05		22 05			23 44		00 08
Telford Central	d	16 53	17 08	17 51	18 08	18 51		19 08	19 53	20 08	21 08	21 53	22 08	22 51	23 13	23 47		00 18
Shifnal	d		17 13		18 13			19 13		20 13	21 13		22 13			23 52		00 28
Cosford	d		17 18		18 18			19 18		20 18	21 18		22 18			23 57		00 38
Albrighton	d		17 22		18 22			19 22		20 22	21 22		22 22			00 01		00 43
Codsall	d		17 27		18 27			19 27		20 27	21 27		22 27			00 07		00 53
Bilbrook	d		17 29		18 29			19 29		20 29	21 29		22 29			00 09		00 58
Wolverhampton 7 ⇌	a	17 10	17 36	18 08	18 36	19 08		19 36	20 10	20 36	21 36	22 09	22 36	23 08	23 58	00 18		01 18
Sandwell & Dudley	a		17 46		18 46			19 46		20 46	21 46		22 45					
Smethwick Galton Bridge	a	17 21		18 20		19 20			20 21			22 20						
Birmingham New Street 12	a	17 27	17 55	18 26	18 55	19 26		19 55	20 26	20 57	21 55	22 32	22 55	23 29	00 48			

A From 27 June until 1 August. From Wrexham General
B From Chester
C To Birmingham International
D From Aberystwyth to Birmingham International
E From Holyhead to Birmingham International
F From Aberystwyth
G MWFO. From Holyhead
H TThO. From Holyhead
I until 18 June, from 6 August. From Holyhead
J from 25 June until 30 July
K until 18 June, from 6 August. From Chester

Table 74

Shrewsbury - Birmingham

Sundays

until 19 June

		AW	AW	AW	AW	AW	AW	AW	AW	AW	AW	AW	AW	AW	AW	AW	AW	AW	AW	AW	AW	AW
		◇ A	B	B		◇ C	◇ D (trolley)		◇ C (trolley)	◇ D (trolley)		◇ C (trolley)	◇ D (trolley)		◇ C (trolley)	◇ E (trolley)		◇ C	◇ D (trolley)	◇ C	◇ D	◇ F (trolley)
Shrewsbury	d	23p26	08 10	09 09	09 55	10 20	11 40	12 10	12 31	13 31	14 10	14 31	15 33	16 10	16 40	17 33	18 10	18 31	19 31	20 23	21 31	22 23
Wellington (Shropshire)	d	23p40	08 24	09 23	10 09	10 34	11 54	12 24	12 45	13 45	14 23	14 45	15 47	16 23	16 54	17 47	18 23	18 45	19 45	20 37	21 45	22 37
Oakengates	d	23p44	08 28	09 27	10 14			12 29			14 29			16 29			18 29			20 41		22 43
Telford Central	d	23p47	08 31	09 30	10 17	10 40	12 00	12 32	12 51	13 51	14 32	14 51	15 53	16 32	17 00	17 53	18 32	18 51	19 51	20 44	21 51	22 45
Shifnal	d	23p52	08 36	09 35	10 22			12 37			14 37			16 37			18 37			20 49		22 51
Cosford	d	23p57	08 41	09 40	10 28			12 43			14 43			16 43			18 43			20 54		22 56
Albrighton	d	00 01	08 44	09 43	10 31			12 46			14 46			16 46			18 46			20 57		22 59
Codsall	d	00 07	08 50	09 48	10 37			12 52			14 52			16 52			18 52			21 02		23 05
Bilbrook	d	00 09	08 52	09 50	10 39			12 54			14 54			16 54			18 54			21 04		23 07
Wolverhampton 7	a	00 18	08 59	09 57	10 50	10 57	12 17	13 05	13 08	14 08	15 03	15 08	16 10	17 03	17 15	18 10	19 03	19 08	20 08	21 11	22 08	23 13
Sandwell & Dudley	a																					
Smethwick Galton Bridge	a																					
Birmingham New Street 12	a		09 15	10 14		11 14	12 33		13 24	14 24		15 25	16 26		17 35	18 28		19 27	20 24	21 29	22 28	

Sundays

26 June to 31 July

		AW	AW	AW	AW	AW	AW	AW	AW	AW	AW	AW	AW	AW	AW	AW	AW	AW	AW	AW	AW	AW	AW
		(bus)	(bus)	B		◇ B	◇ D (trolley)		◇ B (trolley)	◇ D (trolley)		◇ B (trolley)	◇ D (trolley)		◇ B (trolley)	◇ E (trolley)		◇ B	◇ D (trolley)	◇ B	◇ D	◇	G (bus)
Shrewsbury	d	22p33	23p33	09 09	09 55	10 20	11 40	12 10	12 31	13 31	14 10	14 31	15 33	16 10	16 40	17 33	18 10	18 31	19 31	20 23	21 31	22 24	23 01
Wellington (Shropshire)	d	22p58	23p58	09 23	10 09	10 34	11 54	12 24	12 45	13 45	14 23	14 45	15 47	16 23	16 54	17 47	18 23	18 45	19 45	20 37	21 45	22 37	23 26
Oakengates	d		00 08	09 27	10 14			12 29			14 29			16 29			18 29			20 41		22 43	23 36
Telford Central	d	23p13	00 18	09 30	10 17	10 40	12 00	12 32	12 51	13 51	14 32	14 51	15 53	16 32	17 00	17 53	18 32	18 51	19 51	20 44	21 51	22 46	23 46
Shifnal	d		00 28	09 35	10 22			12 37			14 37			16 37			18 37			20 49		22 51	23 56
Cosford	d		00 38	09 40	10 28			12 43			14 43			16 43			18 43			20 54		22 56	00 06
Albrighton	d		00 43	09 43	10 31			12 46			14 46			16 46			18 46			20 57		22 59	00 11
Codsall	d		00 53	09 48	10 37			12 52			14 52			16 52			18 52			21 02		23 04	00 21
Bilbrook	d		00 58	09 50	10 39			12 54			14 54			16 54			18 54			21 04		23 06	00 26
Wolverhampton 7	a	23p58	01 18	09 57	10 50	10 57	12 17	13 05	13 08	14 08	15 03	15 08	16 10	17 03	17 15	18 10	19 03	19 08	20 08	21 11	22 08	23 16	00 46
Sandwell & Dudley	a																						
Smethwick Galton Bridge	a																						
Birmingham New Street 12	a	00 48		10 14		11 14	12 33		13 24	14 24		15 25	16 26		17 35	18 28		19 27	20 24	21 29	22 28		

Sundays

7 August to 11 September

		AW	AW	AW	AW	AW	AW	AW	AW	AW	AW	AW	AW	AW	AW	AW	AW	AW	AW	AW	AW	AW
		◇ H	B	B		◇ C	◇ D (trolley)		◇ C (trolley)	◇ D (trolley)		◇ C (trolley)	◇ D (trolley)		◇ C (trolley)	◇ E (trolley)		◇ C	◇ D (trolley)	◇ C	◇ D	◇ F (trolley)
Shrewsbury	d	23p26	08 10	09 09	09 55	10 20	11 40	12 10	12 31	13 31	14 10	14 31	15 33	16 10	16 40	17 33	18 10	18 31	19 31	20 23	21 31	22 23
Wellington (Shropshire)	d	23p40	08 24	09 23	10 09	10 34	11 54	12 24	12 45	13 45	14 23	14 45	15 47	16 23	16 54	17 47	18 23	18 45	19 45	20 37	21 45	22 37
Oakengates	d	23p44	08 28	09 27	10 14			12 29			14 29			16 29			18 29			20 41		22 43
Telford Central	d	23p47	08 31	09 30	10 17	10 40	12 00	12 32	12 51	13 51	14 32	14 51	15 53	16 32	17 00	17 53	18 32	18 51	19 51	20 44	21 51	22 45
Shifnal	d	23p52	08 36	09 35	10 22			12 37			14 37			16 37			18 37			20 49		22 51
Cosford	d	23p57	08 41	09 40	10 28			12 43			14 43			16 43			18 43			20 54		22 56
Albrighton	d	00 01	08 44	09 43	10 31			12 46			14 46			16 46			18 46			20 57		22 59
Codsall	d	00 07	08 50	09 48	10 37			12 52			14 52			16 52			18 52			21 02		23 05
Bilbrook	d	00 09	08 52	09 50	10 39			12 54			14 54			16 54			18 54			21 04		23 07
Wolverhampton 7	a	00 18	08 59	09 57	10 50	10 57	12 17	13 05	13 08	14 08	15 03	15 08	16 10	17 03	17 15	18 10	19 03	19 08	20 08	21 11	22 08	23 13
Sandwell & Dudley	a																					
Smethwick Galton Bridge	a																					
Birmingham New Street 12	a		09 15	10 14		11 14	12 33		13 24	14 24		15 25	16 26		17 35	18 28		19 27	20 24	21 29	22 28	

Sundays

from 18 September

		AW	AW	AW	AW	AW	AW	AW	AW	AW	AW	AW	AW	AW	AW	AW	AW	AW	AW	AW	AW	AW
		◇ H	B	B		◇ C	◇ D (trolley)		◇ C (trolley)	◇ D (trolley)		◇ C (trolley)	◇ D (trolley)		◇ C (trolley)	◇ E (trolley)		◇ C	◇ D (trolley)	◇ C	◇ D	◇ H
Shrewsbury	d	23p26	08 10	09 09	09 55	10 20	11 40	12 10	12 31	13 31	14 10	14 31	15 33	16 10	16 40	17 33	18 10	18 31	19 31	20 23	21 31	22 23
Wellington (Shropshire)	d	23p40	08 24	09 23	10 09	10 34	11 54	12 24	12 45	13 45	14 23	14 45	15 47	16 23	16 54	17 47	18 23	18 45	19 45	20 37	21 45	22 37
Oakengates	d	23p44	08 28	09 27	10 14			12 29			14 29			16 29			18 29			20 41		22 43
Telford Central	d	23p47	08 31	09 30	10 17	10 40	12 00	12 32	12 51	13 51	14 32	14 51	15 53	16 32	17 00	17 53	18 32	18 51	19 51	20 44	21 51	22 46
Shifnal	d	23p52	08 36	09 35	10 22			12 37			14 37			16 37			18 37			20 49		22 51
Cosford	d	23p57	08 41	09 40	10 28			12 43			14 43			16 43			18 43			20 54		22 56
Albrighton	d	00 01	08 44	09 43	10 31			12 46			14 46			16 46			18 46			20 57		22 59
Codsall	d	00 07	08 50	09 48	10 37			12 52			14 52			16 52			18 52			21 02		23 04
Bilbrook	d	00 09	08 52	09 50	10 39			12 54			14 54			16 54			18 54			21 04		23 06
Wolverhampton 7	a	00 18	08 59	09 57	10 50	10 57	12 17	13 05	13 08	14 08	15 03	15 10	16 10	17 03	17 15	18 10	19 03	19 10	20 08	21 11	22 08	23 16
Sandwell & Dudley	a																					
Smethwick Galton Bridge	a																					
Birmingham New Street 12	a		09 15	10 14		11 14	12 33		13 25	14 24		15 26	16 26		17 35	18 28		19 28	20 24	21 29	22 28	

A not 22 May. From Chester
B To Birmingham International
C From Chester to Birmingham International
D From Aberystwyth to Birmingham International
E From Pwllheli to Birmingham International
F From Holyhead
G From Wrexham General
H From Chester

Table 75

Mondays to Fridays

until 22 July

Birmingham and Shrewsbury - Chester, Aberystwyth, Barmouth and Pwllheli

Miles	Miles	Miles			AW MX	AW	AW	AW	AW	AW	AW	VT	AW	AW	AW	AW	AW	AW	AW	AW	AW	AW	AW
							◇				◇	◇ 1	◇ ⚲		◇ ⚲	◇ ⚲	◇ ⚲	◇	◇ ⚲	◇ ⚲	◇ ⚲	◇	◇ ⚲
—	—	—	London Marylebone 10 ⊖	d																			
—	—	—	Banbury	d																			
—	—	—	Leamington Spa 8	d																			
—	—	—	Birmingham International ✈	d												07 09			08 09	09 09			10 09
0	—	—	**Birmingham New Street 12**	d											06 24	07 23			08 24	09 24			10 24
—	—	—	Tame Bridge Parkway	d																			
—	—	—	Smethwick Galton Bridge 4	d											06 30	07 29			08 30	09 30			10 30
12¾	—	—	**Wolverhampton 7**	d											06 43	07 41			08 43	09 43			10 43
22	—	—	Cosford	d																			
28¼	—	—	Telford Central	d											06 59	07 58			08 59	10 00			10 59
32¼	—	—	Wellington (Shropshire)	d											07 06	08 04			09 06	10 06			11 06
42¾	—	—	**Shrewsbury**	a											07 18	08 18			09 19	10 19			11 19
—	—	—	Cardiff Central 7	d									05 10				07 21				09 21		
—	—	0	**Shrewsbury**	d	23p37			05 20	06 10				07 24		07 27	08 21	09 24		09 27	10 23	11 24		11 27
—	—	17¾	Gobowen	d	23p57			05 39	06 30				07 43			08 40	09 43			10 42	11 43		
—	—	20¾	Chirk	d	00 03			05 45	06 35				07 48			08 46	09 48			10 48	11 48		
—	—	25	Ruabon	d	00 09			05 51	06 42				07 54			08 52	09 54			10 54	11 54		
—	—	30	Wrexham General	a	00 14			05 57	06 49				08 01			08 59	10 01			11 00	12 01		
—	—	—		d	00 15			06 04				07 00	08 02			09 00	10 02			11 01	12 02		
—	—	42	**Chester**	a	00 35			06 24				07 16	08 19			09 17	10 19			11 19	12 19		
62½	—	—	Welshpool	d											07 49				09 49				11 49
76½	—	—	Newtown (Powys)	d											08 04				10 04				12 04
82	—	—	Caersws	d											08 13				10 13				12 13
103¾	0	—	**Machynlleth 4**	a											08 46				10 46				12 46
—	—	—		d		04 35	05 15			06 35	06 49			08 07	08 48			09 03	10 48			11 00	12 48
107¾	4	—	Dovey Junction 4	d		04 42	05 22			06 42	06 56			08 14	08 55			09 10	10 55			11 07	12 55
116	—	—	Borth	d		04 53				06 53				08 25	09 06				11 06				13 06
124¼	—	—	**Aberystwyth**	a		05 12				07 10				08 44	09 25				11 25				13 25
—	9	—	Penhelig	d			05x30				07x04							09x18				11x15	
—	10	—	Aberdovey	d			05 34				07 08							09 22				11 20	
—	13½	—	Tywyn	a			05 40				07 14							09 28				11 26	
—	—	—		d			05 41				07 15							09 29				11 26	
—	16	—	Tonfanau	d			05x44				07x19							09x32				11x30	
—	20	—	Llwyngwril	d			05x51				07x25							09x39				11x36	
—	22¾	—	Fairbourne	d			05 59				07 33							09 47				11 45	
—	23¾	—	Morfa Mawddach	d			06x00				07x35							09 48				11x46	
—	25½	—	**Barmouth**	a			06 07				07 41							09 55				11 53	
—	—	—		d			06 11				07 47							09 57				11 56	
—	26¾	—	Llanaber	d			06x14				07x50							10x00				11x59	
—	29¼	—	Talybont	d							07x54							10x04				12x03	
—	30¼	—	Dyffryn Ardudwy	d							07x57							10x07				12x06	
—	32½	—	Llanbedr	d							08x01							10x11				12x10	
—	33¼	—	Pensarn	d							08x03							10x13				12x12	
—	34	—	Llandanwg	d							08x05							10x15				12x14	
—	35¾	—	Harlech	a			06 31				08 09							10 21				12 20	
—	—	—		d			06 32				08 21							10 24				12 26	
—	38½	—	Tygwyn	d							08x24							10x27				12x29	
—	39¼	—	Talsarnau	d							08x27							10x30				12x32	
—	40½	—	Llandecwyn	d							08x30							10x33				12x35	
—	41¼	—	Penrhyndeudraeth	d							08 34							10 37				12 39	
—	42½	—	Minffordd	d							08 37							10 40				12 42	
—	44½	—	Porthmadog	a			06 48				08 43							10 45				12 47	
—	—	—		d			06 50				08 43							10 46				12 48	
—	49½	—	Criccieth	d							08 51							10 54				12 56	
—	54	—	Penychain	d			07x02				08x56							10x59				13x01	
—	55½	—	Abererch	d							08x59							11x02				13x04	
—	57½	—	**Pwllheli**	a			07 10				09 06							11 09				13 14	

For connections from London Euston please refer to Table 66

For connections from Manchester Piccadilly and Crewe please refer to Table 131

Table 75

Mondays to Fridays
until 22 July

Birmingham and Shrewsbury - Chester, Aberystwyth, Barmouth and Pwllheli

		AW	AW	AW	AW	AW	AW	AW	AW		AW	AW	AW	AW		AW	AW	AW	AW	AW	AW	AW	AW	AW	AW
		◇ ⊼	◇ ⊼	◇	◇ ⊼	◇ ⊼	◇ ⊼	◇	◇ ⊼		◇ ⊼	[R] ⊼	◇	[R] ⊼		◇ ⊼	[R] ⊼	◇ ⊼	◇	◇ ⊼	◇	◇	◇	◇	◇
London Marylebone [10] ⊖	d																								
Banbury	d																								
Leamington Spa [8]	d																								
Birmingham International ✈	d	11 09			12 09	13 09			14 09		15 09			16 09		17 09		18 09		19 09			20 09	21 09	
Birmingham New Street [12]	d	11 24			12 24	13 24			14 24		15 26			16 24		17 26		18 24		19 24			20 24	21 24	
Tame Bridge Parkway	d																								
Smethwick Galton Bridge [4]	d	11 30			12 30	13 30			14 30		15 32			16 30		17 32		18 30		19 30			20 30	21 30	
Wolverhampton [7] ⛴	d	11 43			12 43	13 43			14 43		15 44			16 43		17 44		18 43		19 43			20 43	21 43	
Cosford	d																								
Telford Central	d	11 59			12 59	13 59			14 59		16 01			16 59		18 01		18 59		19 59			20 59	21 59	
Wellington (Shropshire)	d	12 06			13 06	14 06			15 06		16 07			17 06		18 07		19 06		20 06			21 06	22 07	
Shrewsbury	a	12 19			13 19	14 19			15 19		16 20			17 19		18 20		19 19		20 19			21 19	22 19	
Cardiff Central [7]	d		11 21				13 21					15 21					17 21		18 18		19 34				
Shrewsbury	d	12 22	13 24		13 27	14 22	15 24		15 27		16 24	17 24		17 27		18 24	19 24	19 30	20 05	20 24	21 39		21 42	22 24	23 37
Gobowen	d	12 42	13 43			14 42	15 43				16 43	17 43				18 43	19 43			20 43	21 58			22 43	23 57
Chirk	d	12 47	13 48			14 47	15 48				16 49	17 48				18 49	19 48			20 49	22 03			22 49	00 03
Ruabon	d	12 54	13 54			14 54	15 54				16 55	17 54				18 55	19 54			20 55	22 09			22 55	00 09
Wrexham General	a	13 00	14 01			15 00	16 01				17 01	18 01				19 01	20 01		20 37	21 01	22 13			23 01	00 14
	d	13 00	14 02			15 00	16 02				17 02	18 02				19 02	20 02		20 41	21 02	22 14			23 01	00 15
Chester	a	13 19	14 19			15 19	16 20				17 22	18 20				19 20	20 20		20 57	21 19	22 34			23 19	00 35
Welshpool	d				13 49				15 49					17 49				19 52					22 04		
Newtown (Powys)	d				14 04				16 04					18 04				20 07					22 20		
Caersws	d				14 13				16 13					18 13				20 16					22 29		
Machynlleth [4]	a				14 46				16 46					18 46				20 47					23 00		
	d			12 56	14 48			14 56	16 48				17 00	18 48	19 00			20 49				21 17	23 07		
Dovey Junction [4]	d			13 03	14 55			15 03	16 55				17 07	18 55	19 07			20 56				21 24	23 14		
Borth	d				15 06				17 06					19 06				21 07					23 25		
Aberystwyth	a				15 25				17 25					19 25				21 25					23 44		
Penhelig	d			13x11				15x11					17x15		19x15							21x32			
Aberdovey	d			13 15				15 15					17 19		19 20							21 36			
Tywyn	a			13 21				15 21					17 25		19 26							21 42			
	d			13 23				15 26					17 27		19 26							21 43			
Tonfanau	d			13x26				15x29					17x30		19x30							21x46			
Llwyngwril	d			13x33				15x36					17x37		19x36							21x53			
Fairbourne	d			13 41				15 44					17 45		19 44							22 01			
Morfa Mawddach	d			13x42				15x45					17x46		19x46							22x02			
Barmouth	a			13 49				15 52					17 53		19 56							22 09			
	d			13 52				15 56					17 57									22 10			
Llanaber	d			13x55				15x59					18x00									22x13			
Talybont	d			13x59				16x02					18x03									22x17			
Dyffryn Ardudwy	d			14x02				16x05					18x06									22x20			
Llanbedr	d			14x06				16x09					18x10									22x24			
Pensarn	d			14x08				16x11					18x12									22x26			
Llandanwg	d			14x10				16x13					18x14									22x28			
Harlech	a			14 16				16 20					18 21									22 34			
	d			14 31				16 22					18 26									22 37			
Tygwyn	d			14x34				16x26					18x29									22x40			
Talsarnau	d			14x37				16x28					18x32									22x43			
Llandecwyn	d			14x40				16x31					18x35									22x46			
Penrhyndeudraeth	d			14 44				16 35					18 39									22 50			
Minffordd	d			14 47				16 39					18 42									22 53			
Porthmadog	a			14 52				16 44					18 47									22 59			
	d			14 53				16 44					18 48									22 59			
Criccieth	d			15 01				16 52					18 56									23 07			
Penychain	d			15x06				16x57					19x01									23x12			
Abererch	d			15x09				17x00					19x04									23x15			
Pwllheli	a			15 18				17 09					19 13									23 22			

For connections from London Euston please refer to Table 66

For connections from Manchester Piccadilly and Crewe please refer to Table 131

Table 75

Mondays to Fridays

25 July to 9 September

Birmingham and Shrewsbury - Chester, Aberystwyth, Barmouth and Pwllheli

		AW	AW	AW	AW	AW	AW	AW	VT	AW		AW	AW	AW	AW	AW	AW	AW	AW	AW		AW	AW	AW	AW
		MX																							
				◇				◇	◇ 1	◇ 🛒			◇ 🛒	◇ 🛒	◇ 🛒	◇	◇ 🛒	◇ 🛒	◇ 🛒	◇		◇ 🛒	◇ 🛒	◇ 🛒	◇
London Marylebone 10 ⊖	d																								
Banbury	d																								
Leamington Spa 8	d																								
Birmingham International ✈	d													07 09			08 09	09 09				10 09	11 09		
Birmingham New Street 12	d												06 24	07 23			08 24	09 24				10 24	11 24		
Tame Bridge Parkway	d																								
Smethwick Galton Bridge 4	d												06 30	07 29			08 30	09 30				10 30	11 30		
Wolverhampton 7 ⛴	d												06 43	07 41			08 43	09 43				10 43	11 43		
Cosford	d																								
Telford Central	d												06 59	07 58			08 59	10 00				10 59	11 59		
Wellington (Shropshire)	d												07 06	08 04			09 06	10 06				11 06	12 06		
Shrewsbury	a												07 18	08 18			09 19	10 19				11 19	12 19		
Cardiff Central 7	d									05 10					07 21				09 21					11 21	
Shrewsbury	d	23p37			05 20	06 10				07 24			07 27	08 21	09 24		09 27	10 23	11 24			11 27	12 22	13 24	
Gobowen	d	23p57			05 39	06 30				07 43				08 40	09 43			10 42	11 43				12 42	13 43	
Chirk	d	00 03			05 45	06 35				07 48				08 46	09 48			10 48	11 48				12 47	13 48	
Ruabon	d	00 09			05 51	06 42				07 54				08 52	09 54			10 54	11 54				12 54	13 54	
Wrexham General	a	00 14			05 57	06 49				08 01				08 59	10 01			11 00	12 01				13 00	14 01	
	d	00 15			06 04				07 00	08 02				09 00	10 02			11 01	12 02				13 00	14 02	
Chester	a	00 35			06 24				07 16	08 19				09 17	10 19			11 19	12 19				13 19	14 19	
Welshpool	d												07 49				09 49					11 49			
Newtown (Powys)	d												08 04				10 04					12 04			
Caersws	d												08 13				10 13					12 13			
Machynlleth 4	a												08 46				10 46					12 46			
	d		04 35	05 15			06 35	06 49				08 07	08 48			09 03	10 48			11 00		12 48			12 56
Dovey Junction 4	d		04 42	05 22			06 42	06 56				08 14	08 55			09 10	10 55			11 07		12 55			13 03
Borth	d		04 53				06 53					08 25	09 06				11 06					13 06			
Aberystwyth	a		05 12				07 10					08 44	09 25				11 25					13 25			
Penhelig	d			05x30				07x04								09x18				11x15					13x11
Aberdovey	d			05 34				07 08								09 22				11 20					13 15
Tywyn	a			05 40				07 14								09 28				11 26					13 21
	d			05 41				07 15								09 29				11 32					13 25
Tonfanau	d			05x44				07x19								09x32				11x36					13x28
Llwyngwril	d			05x51				07x25								09x39				11x42					13x35
Fairbourne	d			05 59				07 33								09 47				11 51					13 43
Morfa Mawddach	d			06x00				07x35								09 48				11x52					13x44
Barmouth	a			06 07				07 41								09 55				11 59					13 51
	d			06 11				07 47								09 57				12 01					13 53
Llanaber	d			06x14				07x50								10x00				12x04					13x56
Talybont	d							07x54								10x04				12x08					14x00
Dyffryn Ardudwy	d							07x57								10x07				12x11					14x03
Llanbedr	d							08x01								10x11				12x15					14x07
Pensarn	d							08x03								10x13				12x17					14x09
Llandanwg	d							08x05								10x15				12x19					14x11
Harlech	a			06 31				08 09								10 21				12 25					14 17
	d			06 32				08 21								10 24				12 28					14 31
Tygwyn	d							08x24								10x27				12x31					14x34
Talsarnau	d							08x27								10x30				12x34					14x37
Llandecwyn	d							08x30								10x33				12x37					14x40
Penrhyndeudraeth	d							08 34								10 37				12 41					14 44
Minffordd	d							08 37								10 40				12 44					14 47
Porthmadog	a			06 48				08 43								10 45				12 49					14 52
	d			06 50				08 43								10 46				12 50					14 53
Criccieth	d							08 51								10 54				12 58					15 01
Penychain	d			07x02				08x56								10x59				13x03					15x06
Abererch	d							08x59								11x02				13x06					15x09
Pwllheli	a			07 10				09 06								11 09				13 16					15 18

For connections from London Euston please refer to Table 66

For connections from Manchester Piccadilly and Crewe please refer to Table 131

Table 75

Mondays to Fridays

25 July to 9 September

Birmingham and Shrewsbury - Chester, Aberystwyth, Barmouth and Pwllheli

		AW	AW	AW	AW	AW		AW	AW	AW	AW		AW	AW	AW	AW		AW	AW	AW	AW	AW	AW		
									R		R			R											
		◇	◇	◇	◇	◇		◇		◇			◇		◇	◇		◇	◇	◇	◇	◇			
		🛒	🛒	🛒		🛒		🛒	🛒		🛒		🛒	🛒	🛒			🛒							
London Marylebone 10 ⊖	d																								
Banbury	d																								
Leamington Spa 8	d																								
Birmingham International ✈	d	12 09	13 09			14 09		15 09			16 09		17 09		18 09			19 09			20 09	21 09			
Birmingham New Street 12	d	12 24	13 24			14 24		15 26			16 24		17 26		18 24			19 24			20 24	21 24			
Tame Bridge Parkway	d																								
Smethwick Galton Bridge 4	d	12 30	13 30			14 30		15 32			16 30		17 32		18 30			19 30			20 30	21 30			
Wolverhampton 7 ⛴	d	12 43	13 43			14 43		15 44			16 43		17 44		18 43			19 43			20 43	21 43			
Cosford	d																								
Telford Central	d	12 59	13 59			14 59		16 01			16 59		18 01		18 59			19 59			20 59	21 59			
Wellington (Shropshire)	d	13 06	14 06			15 06		16 07			17 06		18 07		19 06			20 06			21 06	22 07			
Shrewsbury	a	13 19	14 19			15 19		16 20			17 19		18 20		19 19			20 19			21 19	22 19			
Cardiff Central 7	d			13 21					15 21					17 21		18 18			19 34						
Shrewsbury	d	13 27	14 22	15 24		15 27		16 24	17 24		17 27		18 24	19 24	19 30	20 05		20 24	21 39		21 42	22 24	23 37		
Gobowen	d		14 42	15 43				16 43	17 43				18 43	19 43				20 43	21 58			22 43	23 57		
Chirk	d		14 47	15 48				16 49	17 48				18 49	19 48				20 49	22 03			22 49	00 03		
Ruabon	d		14 54	15 54				16 55	17 54				18 55	19 54				20 55	22 09			22 55	00 09		
Wrexham General	a		15 00	16 01				17 01	18 01				19 01	20 01		20 37		21 01	22 13			23 01	00 14		
	d		15 00	16 02				17 02	18 02				19 02	20 02		20 41		21 02	22 14			23 01	00 15		
Chester	a		15 18	16 20				17 22	18 20				19 20	20 20		20 57		21 19	22 34			23 19	00 35		
Welshpool	d	13 49				15 49					17 49				19 52						22 04				
Newtown (Powys)	d	14 04				16 04					18 04				20 07						22 20				
Caersws	d	14 13				16 13					18 13				20 16						22 29				
Machynlleth 4	a	14 46				16 46					18 46				20 47						23 00				
	d	14 48			14 56	16 48				17 06	18 48	19 00			20 49					21 17	23 07				
Dovey Junction 4	d	14 55			15 03	16 55				17 12	18 55	19 07			20 56					21 24	23 14				
Borth	d	15 06				17 06					19 06				21 07						23 25				
Aberystwyth	a	15 25				17 25					19 25				21 25						23 44				
Penhelig	d				15x11					17x21		19x15								21x32					
Aberdovey	d				15 15					17 25		19 20								21 36					
Tywyn	a				15 21					17 31		19 26								21 42					
	d				15 26					17 31		19 26								21 43					
Tonfanau	d				15x29					17x35		19x30								21x46					
Llwyngwril	d				15x36					17x41		19x36								21x53					
Fairbourne	d				15 44					17 49		19 44								22 01					
Morfa Mawddach	d				15x45					17x51		19x46								22x02					
Barmouth	a				15 52					17 57		19 56								22 09					
	d				15 56					18 00										22 10					
Llanaber	d				15x59					18x03										22x13					
Talybont	d				16x02					18x06										22x17					
Dyffryn Ardudwy	d				16x05					18x09										22x20					
Llanbedr	d				16x09					18x13										22x24					
Pensarn	d				16x11					18x15										22x26					
Llandanwg	d				16x13					18x17										22x28					
Harlech	a				16 20					18 24										22 34					
	d				16 22					18 26										22 37					
Tygwyn	d				16x26					18x30										22x40					
Talsarnau	d				16x28					18x32										22x43					
Llandecwyn	d				16x31					18x35										22x46					
Penrhyndeudraeth	d				16 35					18 39										22 50					
Minffordd	d				16 39					18 42										22 53					
Porthmadog	a				16 44					18 47										22 59					
	d				16 44					18 48										22 59					
Criccieth	d				16 52					18 56										23 07					
Penychain	d				16x57					19x01										23x12					
Abererch	d				17x00					19x04										23x15					
Pwllheli	a				17 09					19 13										23 22					

For connections from London Euston please refer to Table 66

For connections from Manchester Piccadilly and Crewe please refer to Table 131

Birmingham and Shrewsbury - Chester, Aberystwyth, Barmouth and Pwllheli

		AW MX	AW	AW	AW	AW	AW	AW	VT	AW	AW	AW	AW	AW	AW	AW	AW	AW	AW	AW	AW	AW	AW
				◇				◇	◇[1]	◇ 🛒		◇ 🛒	◇ 🛒	◇ 🛒	◇	◇ 🛒	◇ 🛒	◇ 🛒	◇	◇ 🛒	◇ 🛒	◇ 🛒	◇
London Marylebone [10] ⊖	d																						
Banbury	d																						
Leamington Spa [8]	d																						
Birmingham International ✈	d												07 09			08 09	09 09			10 09	11 09		
Birmingham New Street [12]	d											06 24	07 23			08 24	09 24			10 24	11 24		
Tame Bridge Parkway	d																						
Smethwick Galton Bridge [4]	d											06 30	07 29			08 30	09 30			10 30	11 30		
Wolverhampton [7] ⛴	d											06 43	07 41			08 43	09 43			10 43	11 43		
Cosford	d																						
Telford Central	d											06 59	07 58			08 59	10 00			10 59	11 59		
Wellington (Shropshire)	d											07 06	08 04			09 06	10 06			11 06	12 06		
Shrewsbury	a											07 18	08 18			09 19	10 19			11 19	12 19		
Cardiff Central [7]	d									05 10				07 21				09 21				11 21	
Shrewsbury	d	23p37			05 20	06 10				07 24		07 27	08 21	09 24		09 27	10 23	11 24		11 27	12 22	13 24	
Gobowen	d	23p57			05 39	06 30				07 43			08 40	09 43			10 42	11 43			12 42	13 43	
Chirk	d	00 03			05 45	06 35				07 48			08 46	09 48			10 48	11 48			12 47	13 48	
Ruabon	d	00 09			05 51	06 42				07 54			08 52	09 54			10 54	11 54			12 54	13 54	
Wrexham General	a	00 14			05 57	06 49				08 01			08 59	10 01			11 00	12 01			13 00	14 01	
	d	00 15			06 04				07 00	08 02			09 00	10 02			11 01	12 02			13 00	14 02	
Chester	a	00 35			06 24				07 16	08 19			09 17	10 19			11 19	12 19			13 19	14 19	
Welshpool	d											07 49				09 49				11 49			
Newtown (Powys)	d											08 04				10 04				12 04			
Caersws	d											08 13				10 13				12 13			
Machynlleth [4]	a											08 46				10 46				12 46			
	d		04 35	05 15			06 35	06 49			08 07	08 48			09 03	10 48			11 00	12 48			12 56
Dovey Junction [4]	d		04 42	05 22			06 42	06 56			08 14	08 55			09 10	10 55			11 07	12 55			13 03
Borth	d		04 53				06 53				08 25	09 06				11 06				13 06			
Aberystwyth	a		05 12				07 10				08 44	09 25				11 25				13 25			
Penhelig	d			05x30				07x04							09x18				11x15				13x11
Aberdovey	d			05 34				07 08							09 22				11 20				13 15
Tywyn	a			05 40				07 14							09 28				11 26				13 21
	d			05 41				07 15							09 29				11 26				13 23
Tonfanau	d			05x44				07x19							09x32				11x30				13x26
Llwyngwril	d			05x51				07x25							09x39				11x36				13x33
Fairbourne	d			05 59				07 33							09 47				11 45				13 41
Morfa Mawddach	d			06x00				07x35							09 48				11x46				13x42
Barmouth	a			06 07				07 41							09 55				11 53				13 49
	d			06 11				07 47							09 57				11 56				13 52
Llanaber	d			06x14				07x50							10x00				11x59				13x55
Talybont	d							07x54							10x04				12x03				13x59
Dyffryn Ardudwy	d							07x57							10x07				12x06				14x02
Llanbedr	d							08x01							10x11				12x10				14x06
Pensarn	d							08x03							10x13				12x12				14x08
Llandanwg	d							08x05							10x15				12x14				14x10
Harlech	a			06 31				08 09							10 21				12 20				14 16
	d			06 32				08 21							10 24				12 26				14 31
Tygwyn	d							08x24							10x27				12x29				14x34
Talsarnau	d							08x27							10x30				12x32				14x37
Llandecwyn	d							08x30							10x33				12x35				14x40
Penrhyndeudraeth	d							08 34							10 37				12 39				14 44
Minffordd	d							08 37							10 40				12 42				14 47
Porthmadog	a			06 48				08 43							10 45				12 47				14 52
	d			06 50				08 43							10 46				12 48				14 53
Criccieth	d							08 51							10 54				12 56				15 01
Penychain	d			07x02				08x56							10x59				13x01				15x06
Abererch	d							08x59							11x02				13x04				15x09
Pwllheli	a			07 10				09 06							11 09				13 14				15 18

For connections from London Euston please refer to Table 66

For connections from Manchester Piccadilly and Crewe please refer to Table 131

Table 75

Mondays to Fridays

from 12 September

Birmingham and Shrewsbury - Chester, Aberystwyth, Barmouth and Pwllheli

		AW	AW	AW	AW	AW	AW	AW	AW	AW		AW	AW	AW	AW	AW	AW	AW	AW	AW	AW
								[R]		[R]			[R]								
		◇	◇	◇	◇	◇	◇		◇			◇		◇	◇	◇	◇	◇	◇	◇	
		🛒	🛒	🛒		🛒	🛒	🛒		🛒		🛒	🛒	🛒		🛒					
London Marylebone 10 ⊖	d																				
Banbury	d																				
Leamington Spa 8	d																				
Birmingham International ✈	d	12 09	13 09			14 09	15 09			16 09		17 09		18 09		19 09			20 09	21 09	
Birmingham New Street 12	d	12 24	13 24			14 24	15 26			16 24		17 26		18 24		19 24			20 24	21 24	
Tame Bridge Parkway	d																				
Smethwick Galton Bridge 4	d	12 30	13 30			14 30	15 32			16 30		17 32		18 30		19 30			20 30	21 30	
Wolverhampton 7 🚌	d	12 43	13 43			14 43	15 44			16 43		17 44		18 43		19 43			20 43	21 43	
Cosford	d																				
Telford Central	d	12 59	13 59			14 59	16 01			16 59		18 01		18 59		19 59			20 59	21 59	
Wellington (Shropshire)	d	13 06	14 06			15 06	16 07			17 06		18 07		19 06		20 06			21 06	22 07	
Shrewsbury	a	13 19	14 19			15 19	16 20			17 19		18 20		19 19		20 19			21 19	22 19	
Cardiff Central 7	d			13 21				15 21					17 21		18 18		19 34				
Shrewsbury	d	13 27	14 22	15 24		15 27	16 24	17 24		17 27		18 24	19 24	19 30	20 05	20 24	21 39		21 42	22 24	23 37
Gobowen	d		14 42	15 43			16 43	17 43				18 43	19 43			20 43	21 58			22 43	23 57
Chirk	d		14 47	15 48			16 49	17 48				18 49	19 48			20 49	22 03			22 49	00 03
Ruabon	d		14 54	15 54			16 55	17 54				18 55	19 54			20 55	22 09			22 55	00 09
Wrexham General	a		15 00	16 01			17 01	18 01				19 01	20 01		20 37	21 01	22 13			23 01	00 14
	d		15 00	16 02			17 02	18 02				19 02	20 02		20 41	21 02	22 14			23 01	00 15
Chester	a		15 18	16 20			17 22	18 20				19 20	20 20		20 57	21 19	22 34			23 19	00 35
Welshpool	d	13 49				15 49				17 49				19 52					22 04		
Newtown (Powys)	d	14 04				16 04				18 04				20 07					22 20		
Caersws	d	14 13				16 13				18 13				20 16					22 29		
Machynlleth 4	a	14 46				16 46				18 46				20 47					23 00		
	d	14 48			14 56	16 48			17 00	18 48	19 00			20 49				21 17	23 07		
Dovey Junction 4	d	14 55			15 03	16 55			17 07	18 55	19 07			20 56				21 24	23 14		
Borth	d	15 06				17 06				19 06				21 07					23 25		
Aberystwyth	a	15 25				17 25				19 25				21 25					23 44		
Penhelig	d				15x11				17x15		19x15							21x32			
Aberdovey	d				15 15				17 19		19 20							21 36			
Tywyn	a				15 21				17 25		19 26							21 42			
	d				15 26				17 27		19 26							21 43			
Tonfanau	d				15x29				17x30		19x30							21x46			
Llwyngwril	d				15x36				17x37		19x36							21x53			
Fairbourne	d				15 44				17 45		19 44							22 01			
Morfa Mawddach	d				15x45				17x46		19x46							22x02			
Barmouth	a				15 52				17 53		19 56							22 09			
	d				15 56				17 57									22 10			
Llanaber	d				15x59				18x00									22x13			
Talybont	d				16x02				18x03									22x17			
Dyffryn Ardudwy	d				16x05				18x06									22x20			
Llanbedr	d				16x09				18x10									22x24			
Pensarn	d				16x11				18x12									22x26			
Llandanwg	d				16x13				18x14									22x28			
Harlech	a				16 20				18 21									22 34			
	d				16 22				18 26									22 37			
Tygwyn	d				16x26				18x29									22x40			
Talsarnau	d				16x28				18x32									22x43			
Llandecwyn	d				16x31				18x35									22x46			
Penrhyndeudraeth	d				16 35				18 39									22 50			
Minffordd	d				16 39				18 42									22 53			
Porthmadog	a				16 44				18 47									22 59			
	d				16 44				18 48									22 59			
Criccieth	d				16 52				18 56									23 07			
Penychain	d				16x57				19x01									23x12			
Abererch	d				17x00				19x04									23x15			
Pwllheli	a				17 09				19 13									23 22			

For connections from London Euston please refer to Table 66

For connections from Manchester Piccadilly and Crewe please refer to Table 131

Table 75

Saturdays

Birmingham and Shrewsbury - Chester, Aberystwyth, Barmouth and Pwllheli

		AW	AW	AW	AW	AW	AW	AW	AW	AW	AW	AW	AW	AW	AW	AW	AW	AW	AW	AW	AW	AW	AW
				◇			◇		◇	◇	◇	◇	◇	◇	◇	◇	◇	◇	◇	◇	◇	◇	◇
						bike	bike			bike	bike	bike		bike	bike	bike		bike	bike	bike		bike	bike
London Marylebone 10 ⊖	d																						
Banbury	d																						
Leamington Spa 8	d																						
Birmingham International ✈	d										07 09			08 09	09 09			10 09	11 09			12 09	13 09
Birmingham New Street 12	d									06 24	07 23			08 24	09 24			10 24	11 24			12 24	13 23
Tame Bridge Parkway	d																						
Smethwick Galton Bridge 4	d									06 30	07 29			08 30	09 30			10 30	11 30			12 30	13 29
Wolverhampton 7 ⛴	d									06 42	07 41			08 43	09 43			10 43	11 43			12 43	13 43
Cosford	d																						
Telford Central	d									06 59	07 58			08 59	10 00			10 59	11 59			12 59	13 59
Wellington (Shropshire)	d									07 05	08 04			09 06	10 06			11 06	12 06			13 06	14 06
Shrewsbury	a									07 18	08 18			09 19	10 19			11 19	12 19			13 19	14 19
Cardiff Central 7	d						05 20					07 21				09 21				11 21			
Shrewsbury	d	23p37			05 20	06 10	07 24			07 27	08 21	09 24		09 27	10 23	11 24		11 27	12 22	13 24		13 27	14 22
Gobowen	d	23p57			05 39	06 30	07 43				08 40	09 43			10 42	11 43			12 42	13 43			14 42
Chirk	d	00 03			05 45	06 35	07 48				08 46	09 48			10 48	11 48			12 47	13 48			14 47
Ruabon	d	00 09			05 51	06 42	07 54				08 52	09 54			10 54	11 54			12 54	13 54			14 54
Wrexham General	a	00 14			05 57	06 48	08 00				08 59	10 01			11 00	12 01			13 00	14 01			15 00
	d	00 15			05 58	06 50	08 01				09 00	10 02			11 01	12 02			13 00	14 02			15 00
Chester	a	00 35			06 16	07 08	08 18				09 17	10 19			11 19	12 19			13 18	14 19			15 18
Welshpool	d									07 49				09 49				11 49				13 49	
Newtown (Powys)	d									08 04				10 04				12 04				14 04	
Caersws	d									08 13				10 13				12 13				14 13	
Machynlleth 4	a									08 46				10 46				12 46				14 46	
	d		04 35	05 15				06 35	06 49	08 48			09 03	10 48			11 00	12 48			12 56	14 48	
Dovey Junction 4	d		04 42	05 22				06 42	06 56	08 55			09 10	10 55			11 07	12 55			13 03	14 55	
Borth	d		04 53					06 53		09 06				11 06				13 06				15 06	
Aberystwyth	a		05 12					07 10		09 25				11 25				13 25				15 25	
Penhelig	d			05x30					07x04				09x18				11x15				13x11		
Aberdovey	d			05 34					07 08				09 22				11 20				13 15		
Tywyn	a			05 40					07 14				09 28				11 26				13 21		
	d			05 41					07 15				09 29				11 26				13 23		
Tonfanau	d			05x44					07x19				09x32				11x30				13x26		
Llwyngwril	d			05x51					07x25				09x39				11x36				13x33		
Fairbourne	d			05 59					07 33				09 47				11 45				13 41		
Morfa Mawddach	d			06x00					07x35				09 48				11x46				13x42		
Barmouth	a			06 09					07 41				09 55				11 53				13 49		
	d			06 11					07 47				09 57				11 56				13 52		
Llanaber	d			06x14					07x50				10x00				11x59				13x55		
Talybont	d								07x54				10x04				12x03				13x59		
Dyffryn Ardudwy	d								07x57				10x07				12x06				14x02		
Llanbedr	d								08x01				10x11				12x10				14x06		
Pensarn	d								08x03				10x13				12x12				14x08		
Llandanwg	d								08x05				10x15				12x14				14x10		
Harlech	a			06 32					08 09				10 21				12 20				14 16		
	d			06 32					08 21				10 24				12 26				14 31		
Tygwyn	d								08x24				10x27				12x29				14x34		
Talsarnau	d								08x27				10x30				12x32				14x37		
Llandecwyn	d								08x30				10x33				12x35				14x40		
Penrhyndeudraeth	d								08 34				10 37				12 39				14 44		
Minffordd	d								08 37				10 40				12 42				14 47		
Porthmadog	a			06 48					08 43				10 45				12 47				14 52		
	d			06 50					08 43				10 46				12 48				14 53		
Criccieth	d								08 51				10 54				12 56				15 01		
Penychain	d			07x02					08x56				10x59				13x01				15x06		
Abererch	d								08x59				11x02				13x04				15x09		
Pwllheli	a			07 10					09 06				11 09				13 14				15 18		

For connections from London Euston please refer to Table 66

For connections from Manchester Piccadilly and Crewe please refer to Table 131

Table 75

Saturdays

Birmingham and Shrewsbury - Chester, Aberystwyth, Barmouth and Pwllheli

		AW	AW	AW	AW	AW		AW	AW	AW	AW	AW	AW	AW	AW	AW		AW	AW	AW	AW
						R			R				R								
		◇	◇	◇	◇			◇		◇	◇			◇	◇	◇		◇	◇	◇	
										A	B										
		trolley		trolley	trolley	trolley			trolley	trolley	trolley		trolley	trolley	trolley						
London Marylebone 10 ⊖	d																				
Banbury	d																				
Leamington Spa 8	d																				
Birmingham International ✈	d			14 09	15 09				16 09	17 09	17 09			18 09	19 09				20 09	21 09	
Birmingham New Street 12	d			14 24	15 24				16 24	17 24	17 24			18 24	19 24				20 24	21 24	
Tame Bridge Parkway	d																				
Smethwick Galton Bridge 4	d			14 30	15 30				16 30	17 31	17 31			18 30	19 30				20 30	21 30	
Wolverhampton 7	d			14 43	15 43				16 43	17 43	17 43			18 43	19 43				20 43	21 42	
Cosford	d																				
Telford Central	d			14 59	15 59				16 59	17 59	17 59			18 59	19 59				21 02	21 59	
Wellington (Shropshire)	d			15 06	16 06				17 06	18 06	18 06			19 06	20 06				21 09	22 05	
Shrewsbury	a			15 19	16 19				17 19	18 19	18 19			19 19	20 19				21 23	22 22	
Cardiff Central 7	d	13 21				15 21							17 21			19 34					
Shrewsbury	d	15 24		15 27	16 22	17 24			17 27	18 22	18 22		19 24	19 30	20 24	21 37			21 42	22 24	23 33
Gobowen	d	15 43			16 42	17 43				18 42	18 42		19 43		20 43	21 56				22 43	23 52
Chirk	d	15 48			16 47	17 48				18 47	18 47		19 48		20 49	22 01				22 49	23 58
Ruabon	d	15 54			16 54	17 54				18 54	18 54		19 54		20 55	22 07				22 55	00 04
Wrexham General	a	16 01			17 00	18 01				19 01	19 01		20 01		21 01	22 13				23 01	00 10
	d	16 02			17 02	18 02				19 02	19 02	19 46	20 02		21 02	22 13				23 02	00 14
Chester	a	16 22			17 19	18 19				19 20	19 24	20 04	20 19		21 21	22 31				23 21	00 33
Welshpool	d			15 49					17 49					19 52					22 04		
Newtown (Powys)	d			16 04					18 04					20 07					22 20		
Caersws	d			16 13					18 13					20 16					22 29		
Machynlleth 4	a			16 46					18 46					20 47					22 59		
	d		14 56	16 48				17 00	18 48					20 49				21 17	23 04		
Dovey Junction 4	d		15 03	16 55				17 07	18 55					20 56				21 24	23 11		
Borth	d			17 06					19 06					21 07					23 22		
Aberystwyth	a			17 25					19 25					21 25					23 41		
Penhelig	d		15x11					17x15										21x32			
Aberdovey	d		15 15					17 19										21 36			
Tywyn	a		15 21					17 25										21 42			
	d		15 26					17 27										21 43			
Tonfanau	d		15x29					17x30										21x46			
Llwyngwril	d		15x36					17x37										21x53			
Fairbourne	d		15 44					17 45										22 01			
Morfa Mawddach	d		15x45					17x46										22x02			
Barmouth	a		15 52					17 53										22 09			
	d		15 56					17 57										22 10			
Llanaber	d		15x59					18x00										22x13			
Talybont	d		16x02					18x03										22x17			
Dyffryn Ardudwy	d		16x05					18x06										22x20			
Llanbedr	d		16x09					18x10										22x24			
Pensarn	d		16x11					18x12										22x26			
Llandanwg	d		16x13					18x14										22x28			
Harlech	a		16 20					18 21										22 34			
	d		16 22					18 26										22 37			
Tygwyn	d		16x26					18x29										22x40			
Talsarnau	d		16x28					18x32										22x43			
Llandecwyn	d		16x31					18x35										22x46			
Penrhyndeudraeth	d		16 35					18 39										22 50			
Minffordd	d		16 39					18 42										22 53			
Porthmadog	a		16 44					18 47										22 59			
	d		16 44					18 48										22 59			
Criccieth	d		16 52					18 56										23 07			
Penychain	d		16x57					19x01										23x12			
Abererch	d		17x00					19x04										23x15			
Pwllheli	a		17 09					19 13										23 22			

A from 17 September

B until 10 September

For connections from London Euston please refer to Table 66

For connections from Manchester Piccadilly and Crewe please refer to Table 131

Table 75

Sundays
until 19 June

Birmingham and Shrewsbury - Chester, Aberystwyth, Barmouth and Pwllheli

		AW	AW	AW	AW	AW	AW	AW	AW	AW	AW	AW	AW	AW	AW	AW		AW	AW	AW	AW	AW	AW	AW
												R						R			R		◇	
				◇	◇		◇			◇	◇		◇	◇	◇	◇			◇	◇		◇		
		A										B									D			
						🍴	🍴			🍴	🍴			🍴	🍴	🍴		🍴	🍴	🍴		🍴		
London Marylebone 10 ⊖	d																							
Banbury	d																							
Leamington Spa 8	d																							
Birmingham International ✈	d						10 48			12 08	13 12			14 07	15 07	16 07			17 07	18 07		19 07	20 07	
Birmingham New Street 12	d						11 05			12 24	13 24			14 24	15 24	16 24			17 24	18 24		19 24	20 24	
Tame Bridge Parkway	d																							
Smethwick Galton Bridge 4	d																							
Wolverhampton 7	d						11 27			12 42	13 42			14 43	15 43	16 43			17 43	18 43		19 43	20 43	
Cosford	d						11 43																	
Telford Central	d						11 54			12 59	13 58			14 59	15 59	16 59			17 59	18 59		19 59	20 59	
Wellington (Shropshire)	d						12 01			13 05	14 04			15 06	16 06	17 06			18 06	19 06		20 06	21 06	
Shrewsbury	a						12 14			13 18	14 18			15 19	16 26	17 19			18 19	19 19		20 19	21 19	
Cardiff Central 7	d											13 13						15 22			17 22			
Shrewsbury	d	23p33		08 45		10 16	12 17			13 27	14 20	15 20		15 27	16 27	17 27		17 30	18 20	19 27	19 32	20 22	21 30	
Gobowen	d	23p52				10 35	12 37				14 39	15 39			16 47			17 49	18 40		19 51	20 42		
Chirk	d	23p58				10 41	12 42				14 45	15 45			16 52			17 55	18 45		19 57	20 47		
Ruabon	d	00 04				10 47	12 49				14 51	15 51			16 59			18 01	18 51		20 03	20 54		
Wrexham General	a	00 10				10 53	12 55				14 57	15 57			17 06			18 07	18 57		20 09	21 00		
	d	00 14				10 54	12 56				14 58	16 08			17 07			18 08	18 58		20 12	21 01		22 35
Chester	a	00 33				11 12	13 20				15 18	16 25			17 27			18 25	19 16		20 29	21 20		22 53
Welshpool	d			09 07						13 49				15 49		17 49				19 49			21 52	
Newtown (Powys)	d			09 23						14 04				16 04		18 04				20 04			22 07	
Caersws	d			09 32						14 13				16 13		18 13				20 13			22 16	
Machynlleth 4	a			10 02						14 46				16 46		18 46				20 46			22 47	
																							22 49	
	d		08 50	10 05	10 10			10 50	12 35	14 48			15 00	16 48		18 48	18 55			20 48			22 56	
Dovey Junction 4	d		08 57	10 12	10 17			10 57	12 42	14 55			15 07	16 55		18 55	19 02			20 55			23 07	
Borth	d		09 08	10 22				11 08	12 53	15 06				17 06		19 06				21 06			23 26	
Aberystwyth	a		09 25	10 41				11 27	13 10	15 25				17 25		19 25				21 25				
Penhelig	d				10x25								15x15				19x10							
Aberdovey	d				10 30								15 20				19 14							
Tywyn	a				10 36								15 26				19 20							
	d				10 36								15 31				19 21							
Tonfanau	d				10x40								15x34				19x24							
Llwyngwril	d				10x47								15x41				19x31							
Fairbourne	d				10 55								15 49				19 39							
Morfa Mawddach	d				10x56								15x51				19x41							
Barmouth	a				11 03								15 58				19 48							
	d				11 05								15 59				19 49							
Llanaber	d				11x08								16x02				19x53							
Talybont	d				11x12								16x06				19x56							
Dyffryn Ardudwy	d				11x15								16x10				20x00							
Llanbedr	d				11x19								16x14				20x04							
Pensarn	d				11x22								16x16				20x07							
Llandanwg	d				11x24								16x18				20x09							
Harlech	a				11 30								16 25				20 15							
	d				11 33								16 25				20 18							
Tygwyn	d				11x36								16x29				20x21							
Talsarnau	d				11x39								16x32				20x24							
Llandecwyn	d				11x42								16x36				20x27							
Penrhyndeudraeth	d				11 46								16 39				20 31							
Minffordd	d				11 50								16 42				20 35							
Porthmadog	a				11 55								16 47				20 40							
	d				11 58								16 48				20 41							
Criccieth	d				12 05								16 55				20 48							
Penychain	d				12x11								17x01				20x54							
Abererch	d				12x14								17x04				20x57							
Pwllheli	a				12 24								17 14				21 07							

A not 22 May
B not until 29 May
D 22 May

For connections from London Euston please refer to Table 66

For connections from Manchester Piccadilly and Crewe please refer to Table 131

Table 75

Sundays
26 June to 31 July

Birmingham and Shrewsbury - Chester, Aberystwyth, Barmouth and Pwllheli

		AW	AW	AW ◇	AW 🚌	AW ◇	AW	AW 🛒	AW 🚌	AW	AW ◇ 🛒	AW	AW 🚌	AW ◇	AW ◇ 🛒	AW	AW 🚌	AW ◇ 🛒	AW 🚌	AW ◇ 🛒		AW 🚌	AW
London Marylebone 10 ⊖	d																						
Banbury	d																						
Leamington Spa 8	d																						
Birmingham International ✈	d										12 08				14 07					16 07			
Birmingham New Street 12	d										12 24				14 24					16 24			
Tame Bridge Parkway	d																						
Smethwick Galton Bridge 4	d																						
Wolverhampton 7 🚌	d										12 42				14 43					16 43			
Cosford	d																						
Telford Central	d										12 59				14 59					16 59			
Wellington (Shropshire)	d										13 05				15 06					17 06			
Shrewsbury	a										13 18				15 19					17 19			
Cardiff Central 7	d																						
Shrewsbury	d	23p33		08 45	09 34				12 23		13 27		14 28		15 27		15 50		16 36	17 27		17 35	
Gobowen	d	23p52			10 04				12 53				14 58				16 20		17 06			18 05	
Chirk	d	23p58			10 14				13 03				15 08				16 30		17 16			18 15	
Ruabon	d	00 04			10 29				13 18				15 23				16 45		17 31			18 30	
Wrexham General	a	00 10			10 44				13 33				15 38				17 00		17 46			18 45	
	d	00 14						11 03				13 43				15 48		17 10	17 46				18 58
Chester	a	00 33						11 21				14 06				16 11		17 30	18 11				19 16
Welshpool	d			09 07							13 49				15 49					17 49			
Newtown (Powys)	d			09 23							14 04				16 04					18 04			
Caersws	d			09 32							14 13				16 13					18 13			
Machynlleth 4	a			10 02							14 46				16 46					18 46			
	d		08 50	10 05		10 10	10 50			12 35	14 48			15 00	16 48					18 48	18 55		
Dovey Junction 4	d		08 57	10 12		10 17	10 57			12 42	14 55			15 07	16 55					18 55	19 02		
Borth	d		09 08	10 22			11 08			12 53	15 06				17 06					19 06			
Aberystwyth	a		09 25	10 41			11 27			13 10	15 25				17 25					19 25			
Penhelig	d					10x25								15x15							19x10		
Aberdovey	d					10 30								15 20							19 14		
Tywyn	a					10 36								15 26							19 20		
	d					10 36								15 31							19 21		
Tonfanau	d					10x40								15x34							19x24		
Llwyngwril	d					10x47								15x41							19x31		
Fairbourne	d					10 55								15 49							19 39		
Morfa Mawddach	d					10x56								15x51							19x41		
Barmouth	a					11 03								15 58							19 48		
	d					11 05								15 59							19 49		
Llanaber	d					11x08								16x02							19x53		
Talybont	d					11x12								16x06							19x56		
Dyffryn Ardudwy	d					11x15								16x10							20x00		
Llanbedr	d					11x19								16x14							20x04		
Pensarn	d					11x22								16x16							20x07		
Llandanwg	d					11x24								16x18							20x09		
Harlech	a					11 30								16 25							20 15		
	d					11 33								16 25							20 18		
Tygwyn	d					11x36								16x29							20x21		
Talsarnau	d					11x39								16x32							20x24		
Llandecwyn	d					11x42								16x36							20x27		
Penrhyndeudraeth	d					11 46								16 39							20 31		
Minffordd	d					11 50								16 42							20 35		
Porthmadog	a					11 55								16 47							20 40		
	d					11 58								16 48							20 41		
Criccieth	d					12 05								16 55							20 48		
Penychain	d					12x11								17x01							20x54		
Abererch	d					12x14								17x04							20x57		
Pwllheli	a					12 24								17 14							21 07		

For connections from London Euston please refer to Table 66

For connections from Manchester Piccadilly and Crewe please refer to Table 131

Table 75

Sundays
26 June to 31 July

Birmingham and Shrewsbury - Chester, Aberystwyth, Barmouth and Pwllheli

		AW	AW	AW	AW	AW		AW	AW	AW
					◇			◇		
		🚌	🚌	🚌	🛒	🚌				
London Marylebone 10 ⊖	d									
Banbury	d									
Leamington Spa 8	d									
Birmingham International ✈	d				18 07			20 07		
Birmingham New Street 12	d				18 24			20 24		
Tame Bridge Parkway	d									
Smethwick Galton Bridge 4	d									
Wolverhampton 7 ⛴	d				18 43			20 43		
Cosford	d									
Telford Central	d				18 59			20 59		
Wellington (Shropshire)	d				19 06			21 06		
Shrewsbury	a				19 19			21 19		
Cardiff Central 7	d									
Shrewsbury	d	18 29	18 51	19 23	19 27	20 28		21 30		
Gobowen	d	18 59	19 21	19 53		20 58				
Chirk	d	19 09	19 31	20 03		21 08				
Ruabon	d	19 24	19 46	20 18		21 23				
Wrexham General	a	19 39	20 01	20 33		21 38				
	d	19 39	20 01						21 49	22 35
Chester	a	20 04	20 26						22 12	22 53
Welshpool	d				19 49			21 52		
Newtown (Powys)	d				20 04			22 07		
Caersws	d				20 13			22 16		
Machynlleth 4	a				20 46			22 47		
	d				20 48			22 49		
Dovey Junction 4	d				20 55			22 56		
Borth	d				21 06			23 07		
Aberystwyth	a				21 25			23 26		
Penhelig	d									
Aberdovey	d									
Tywyn	a									
	d									
Tonfanau	d									
Llwyngwril	d									
Fairbourne	d									
Morfa Mawddach	d									
Barmouth	a									
	d									
Llanaber	d									
Talybont	d									
Dyffryn Ardudwy	d									
Llanbedr	d									
Pensarn	d									
Llandanwg	d									
Harlech	a									
	d									
Tygwyn	d									
Talsarnau	d									
Llandecwyn	d									
Penrhyndeudraeth	d									
Minffordd	d									
Porthmadog	a									
	d									
Criccieth	d									
Penychain	d									
Abererch	d									
Pwllheli	a									

For connections from London Euston please refer to Table 66

For connections from Manchester Piccadilly and Crewe please refer to Table 131

Table 75

Sundays

7 August to 11 September

Birmingham and Shrewsbury - Chester, Aberystwyth, Barmouth and Pwllheli

		AW	AW	AW	AW	AW	AW	AW	AW	AW		AW	AW	AW	AW	AW	AW		AW	AW		AW	AW	AW	AW
													R						R						
				◇	◇		◇			◇		◇		◇	◇	◇	◇			◇		◇	◇	◇	
						🛒	🛒			🛒		🛒			🛒	🛒	🛒		🛒	🛒		🛒	🛒		
London Marylebone 10 ⊖	d																								
Banbury	d																								
Leamington Spa 8	d																								
Birmingham International ✈	d						10 48			12 08		13 12			14 07	15 07	16 07			17 07		18 07	19 07	20 07	
Birmingham New Street 12	d						11 05			12 24		13 24			14 24	15 24	16 24			17 24		18 24	19 24	20 24	
Tame Bridge Parkway	d																								
Smethwick Galton Bridge 4	d																								
Wolverhampton 7 🚌	d						11 27			12 42		13 42			14 43	15 43	16 43			17 43		18 43	19 43	20 43	
Cosford	d						11 43																		
Telford Central	d						11 54			12 59		13 58			14 59	15 59	16 59			17 59		18 59	19 59	20 59	
Wellington (Shropshire)	d						12 01			13 05		14 04			15 06	16 06	17 06			18 05		19 06	20 06	21 06	
Shrewsbury	a						12 14			13 18		14 18			15 19	16 26	17 19			18 19		19 19	20 19	21 19	
Cardiff Central 7	d												13 13						15 22						
Shrewsbury	d	23p33		08 45		10 16	12 17			13 27		14 20	15 20		15 27	16 27	17 27		17 30	18 20		19 27	20 22	21 30	
Gobowen	d	23p52				10 35	12 37					14 39	15 39			16 47			17 49	18 40			20 42		
Chirk	d	23p58				10 41	12 42					14 45	15 45			16 52			17 55	18 45			20 47		
Ruabon	d	00 04				10 47	12 49					14 51	15 51			16 59			18 01	18 51			20 54		
Wrexham General	a	00 10				10 53	12 55					14 57	15 57			17 06			18 07	18 57			21 00		
	d	00 14				10 54	12 56					14 58	16 08			17 07			18 08	18 58			21 01		22 35
Chester	a	00 33				11 12	13 20					15 18	16 25			17 27			18 25	19 16			21 20		22 53
Welshpool	d			09 07						13 49					15 49		17 49					19 49		21 52	
Newtown (Powys)	d			09 23						14 04					16 04		18 04					20 04		22 07	
Caersws	d			09 32						14 13					16 13		18 13					20 13		22 16	
Machynlleth 4	a			10 02						14 46					16 46		18 46					20 46		22 47	
	d		08 50	10 05	10 10			10 50	12 35	14 48				15 00	16 48		18 48	18 55				20 48		22 49	
Dovey Junction 4	d		08 57	10 12	10 17			10 57	12 42	14 55				15 07	16 55		18 55	19 02				20 55		22 56	
Borth	d		09 08	10 22				11 08	12 53	15 06					17 06		19 06					21 06		23 07	
Aberystwyth	a		09 25	10 41				11 27	13 10	15 25					17 25		19 25					21 25		23 26	
Penhelig	d				10x25									15x15				19x10							
Aberdovey	d				10 30									15 20				19 14							
Tywyn	a				10 36									15 26				19 20							
	d				10 36									15 31				19 21							
Tonfanau	d				10x40									15x34				19x24							
Llwyngwril	d				10x47									15x41				19x31							
Fairbourne	d				10 55									15 49				19 39							
Morfa Mawddach	d				10x56									15x51				19x41							
Barmouth	a				11 03									15 58				19 48							
	d				11 05									15 59				19 49							
Llanaber	d				11x08									16x02				19x53							
Talybont	d				11x12									16x06				19x56							
Dyffryn Ardudwy	d				11x15									16x10				20x00							
Llanbedr	d				11x19									16x14				20x04							
Pensarn	d				11x22									16x16				20x07							
Llandanwg	d				11x24									16x18				20x09							
Harlech	a				11 30									16 25				20 15							
	d				11 33									16 25				20 18							
Tygwyn	d				11x36									16x29				20x21							
Talsarnau	d				11x39									16x32				20x24							
Llandecwyn	d				11x42									16x36				20x27							
Penrhyndeudraeth	d				11 46									16 39				20 31							
Minffordd	d				11 50									16 42				20 35							
Porthmadog	a				11 55									16 47				20 40							
	d				11 58									16 48				20 41							
Criccieth	d				12 05									16 55				20 48							
Penychain	d				12x11									17x01				20x54							
Abererch	d				12x14									17x04				20x57							
Pwllheli	a				12 24									17 14				21 07							

For connections from London Euston please refer to Table 66

For connections from Manchester Piccadilly and Crewe please refer to Table 131

Table 75

Sundays
from 18 September

Birmingham and Shrewsbury - Chester, Aberystwyth, Barmouth and Pwllheli

		AW	AW	AW	AW	AW	AW	AW	AW	AW		AW	AW	AW	AW	AW	AW	AW	AW	AW		AW			
										R					R										
						◇	◇	◇	◇			◇	◇	◇		◇	◇	◇	◇	◇					
				Trolley			Trolley	Trolley	Trolley			Trolley	Trolley	Trolley	Trolley	Trolley		Trolley	Trolley						
London Marylebone 10 ⊖	d																								
Banbury	d																								
Leamington Spa 8	d																								
Birmingham International ✈	d						10 48	12 08	13 12			14 07	15 07	16 07		17 07		18 07	19 07	20 07					
Birmingham New Street 12	d						11 05	12 24	13 24			14 24	15 24	16 24		17 24		18 24	19 24	20 24					
Tame Bridge Parkway	d																								
Smethwick Galton Bridge 4	d																								
Wolverhampton 7	d						11 27	12 42	13 42			14 43	15 43	16 43		17 43		18 43	19 43	20 43					
Cosford	d						11 43																		
Telford Central	d						11 54	12 59	13 58			14 59	15 59	16 59		17 59		18 59	19 59	20 59					
Wellington (Shropshire)	d						12 01	13 05	14 04			15 06	16 06	17 06		18 06		19 06	20 06	21 06					
Shrewsbury	a						12 14	13 18	14 18			15 19	16 26	17 19		18 19		19 19	20 18	21 19					
Cardiff Central 7	d									13 13					15 22										
Shrewsbury	d	23p33		10 16		11 27	12 17	13 27	14 20	15e20		15 27	16 27	17 27	17i30	18 20		19 27	20 21	21 30					
Gobowen	d	23p52		10 35			12 37		14 39	15 39			16 47		17 49	18 40			20 40						
Chirk	d	23p58		10 41			12 42		14 45	15 45			16 52		17 55	18 45			20 46						
Ruabon	d	00 04		10 47			12 49		14 51	15 51			16 59		18 01	18 51			20 52						
Wrexham General	a	00 10		10 53			12 55		14 57	15 57			17 06		18 07	18 57			21 00						
	d	00 14		10 54			12 56		14 58	16 08			17 07		18 08	18 58			21 01			22 35			
Chester	a	00 33		11 12			13 20		15 18	16 25			17 27		18 25	19 16			21 20			22 53			
Welshpool	d					11 49		13 49				15 49		17 49				19 49		21 52					
Newtown (Powys)	d					12 05		14 04				16 04		18 04				20 04		22 07					
Caersws	d					12 14		14 13				16 13		18 13				20 13		22 16					
Machynlleth 4	a					12 46		14 46				16 46		18 46				20 46		22 47					
	d		08 50		10 50	12 48		14 48				16 48		18 48			18 55	20 48		22 49					
Dovey Junction 4	d		08 57		10 57	12 55		14 55				16 55		18 55			19 02	20 55		22 56					
Borth	d		09 08		11 08	13 06		15 06				17 06		19 06				21 06		23 07					
Aberystwyth	a		09 25		11 27	13 23		15 25				17 25		19 25				21 25		23 26					
Penhelig	d																19x10								
Aberdovey	d																19 14								
Tywyn	a																19 20								
	d																19 21								
Tonfanau	d																19x24								
Llwyngwril	d																19x31								
Fairbourne	d																19 39								
Morfa Mawddach	d																19x41								
Barmouth	a																19 48								
	d																19 49								
Llanaber	d																19x53								
Talybont	d																19x56								
Dyffryn Ardudwy	d																20x00								
Llanbedr	d																20x04								
Pensarn	d																20x07								
Llandanwg	d																20x09								
Harlech	a																20 15								
	d																20 18								
Tygwyn	d																20x21								
Talsarnau	d																20x24								
Llandecwyn	d																20x27								
Penrhyndeudraeth	d																20 31								
Minffordd	d																20 35								
Porthmadog	a																20 40								
	d																20 41								
Criccieth	d																20 48								
Penychain	d																20x54								
Abererch	d																20x57								
Pwllheli	a																21 07								

For connections from London Euston please refer to Table 66

For connections from Manchester Piccadilly and Crewe please refer to Table 131

Table 75

Mondays to Fridays

until 22 July

Pwllheli, Barmouth, Aberystwyth and Chester - Shrewsbury and Birmingham

Miles	Miles	Miles			AW MO	AW MX	AW MO	AW MX	AW	AW	AW	AW	AW		AW	AW	AW	AW	AW	AW	AW	AW	AW		AW
						◇			◇	◇		◇	◇		◇	◇	◇	◇	◇		◇	◇	◇		◇
					A																				
					🚌																				
										🍴		🍴			🍴	🍴	🍴				🍴	🍴			🍴
—	0	—	**Pwllheli**	d														06 25	07 25				09 36		
—	1¾	—	Abererch	d														06x28	07x28				09x39		
—	3¼	—	Penychain	d														06x31	07 31				09 42		
—	7¾	—	Criccieth	d														06 39	07 39				09 50		
—	12¾	—	Porthmadog	a														06 47	07 47				09 58		
—	—	—		d														06 52	07 49				10 00		
—	15	—	Minffordd	d														06 56	07 53				10 04		
—	16¼	—	Penrhyndeudraeth	d														07 00	07 57				10 08		
—	17	—	Llandecwyn	d														07x02	07x59				10x10		
—	18¼	—	Talsarnau	d														07x04	08x02				10x12		
—	19	—	Tygwyn	d														07x07	08x04				10x15		
—	21½	—	Harlech	a														07 12	08 09				10 20		
—	—	—		d														07 16	08 30				10 25		
—	23½	—	Llandanwg	d														07x20	08x34				10x29		
—	24¼	—	Pensarn	d														07x21	08x35				10x32		
—	30½	—	Llanbedr	d														07x24	08x38				10x34		
—	27	—	Dyffryn Ardudwy	d														07x28	08x42				10x38		
—	28¼	—	Talybont	d														07x31	08x45				10x41		
—	25	—	Llanaber	d														07x35	08x49				10x46		
—	32	—	**Barmouth**	a														07 40	08 54				10 51		
—	—	—		d									06 46					07 49	09 00				10 53		
—	33¾	—	Morfa Mawddach	d									06x50					07x53	09x04				10x57		
—	34¾	—	Fairbourne	d									06 54					07 57	09 08				11 01		
—	37¼	—	Llwyngwril	d									07x00					08x03	09x14				11x07		
—	41½	—	Tonfanau	d									07x07					08x10	09x21				11x14		
—	44¼	—	Tywyn	a									07 11					08 14	09 25				11 19		
—	—	—		d									07 16					08 18	09 30				11 29		
—	47½	—	Aberdovey	d									07 22					08 24	09 36				11 35		
—	48½	—	Penhelig	d									07x25					08x26	09x38				11x37		
0	—	—	**Aberystwyth**	d			23p30	23p53		05 14							07 30					09 30			
8¼	—	—	Borth	d			23p43	00 06		05 27							07 43					09 43			
16½	53½	—	Dovey Junction 4	d			23p54	00 17		05 38			07 37				07 54	08 38	09 49			09 54	11 49		
20½	57½	—	**Machynlleth** 4	a			00 04	00 24		05 45			07 44				08 03	08 48	09 57			10 03	11 59		
—	—	—		d						05 47							08 07					10 07			
42¼	—	—	Caersws	d						06 15							08 37					10 37			
47¾	—	—	Newtown (Powys)	d						06 25							08 46					10 46			
61¾	—	—	Welshpool	d						06 41							09 01					11 01			
—	—	0	**Chester**	d		22p28			05 15		05 45	06 18			07 19	08 19				09 26	10 20				11 21
—	12	—	Wrexham General	a		22p44			05 31		06 03	06 35			07 35	08 34				09 42	10 35				11 36
—	—	—		d	21p51	22p44			05 31			06 38			07 44	08 34				09 42	10 36				11 36
—	—	17	Ruabon	d	22p06	22p51			05 38			06 45			07 51	08 41				09 49	10 42				11 44
—	—	21¼	Chirk	d	22p21	22p57			05 44			06 51			07 57	08 47				09 56	10 48				11 51
—	—	24¼	Gobowen	d	22p31	23p03			05 50			06 57			08 03	08 53				10 01	10 54				11 56
81½	—	42	**Shrewsbury**	a	23p01	23p23			06 10	07 11		07 17			08 23	09 13	09 25			10 22	11 14	11 25			12 27
—	—	—	Cardiff Central 7	a	⌇				08 17			09 18				11 15				12 08	13 22				
—	—	—	**Shrewsbury**	d	23p01	23p26				07 31					08 31		09 31					11 31			12 31
92	—	—	Wellington (Shropshire)	d	23p26	23p40				07 45					08 45		09 45					11 45			12 45
96	—	—	Telford Central	d	23p46	23p47				07 51					08 51		09 51					11 51			12 51
122¾	—	—	Cosford	d	00⌇06	23p57																			
111½	—	—	**Wolverhampton** 7	a	00⌇46	00 20				08 08					09 08		10 08					12 08			13 08
120¾	—	—	Smethwick Galton Bdg L.L.	a						08 20					09 21		10 20					12 20			13 20
—	—	—	Tame Bridge Parkway	d																					
124¾	—	—	**Birmingham New Street** 12	a						08 26					09 26		10 26					12 26			13 26
—	—	—	Birmingham International ✈	a						08 50					09 50		10 50					12 50			13 50
—	—	—	Leamington Spa 8	a																					
—	—	—	Banbury	a																					
—	—	—	London Marylebone 10 ⊖	a																					

A From 27 June until 18 July

For connections to Crewe and Manchester Piccadilly please refer to Table 131

For connections to London Euston please refer to Table 66

Table 75

Mondays to Fridays

until 22 July

Pwllheli, Barmouth, Aberystwyth and Chester - Shrewsbury and Birmingham

		AW	AW	AW	AW	AW	AW	AW	AW		AW	AW	AW	AW	AW	AW	AW	AW	AW		VT	AW	AW	AW	AW
		R																							
			◇	◇	◇	◇	◇	◇	◇		◇	◇	◇	◇	◇	◇	◇	◇	◇		◇1		◇	◇	
																							A	B	
		🛒	🛒		🛒	🛒	🛒		🛒		🛒	🛒		🛒	🛒	🛒		🛒							
Pwllheli	d			11 38				13 42					15 34				17 38								
Abererch	d			11x41				13x45					15x37				17x41								
Penychain	d			11 44				13x48					15 40				17 44								
Criccieth	d			11 52				13 56					15 48				17 52								
Porthmadog	a			12 00				14 04					15 56				18 00								
	d			12 02				14 06					15 58				18 02								
Minffordd	d			12 06				14 10					16 02				18 06								
Penrhyndeudraeth	d			12 10				14 14					16 06				18 10								
Llandecwyn	d			12x12				14x16					16x08				18x12								
Talsarnau	d			12x14				14x18					16x10				18x14								
Tygwyn	d			12x17				14x21					16x13				18x17								
Harlech	a			12 22				14 26					16 18				18 22								
	d			12 25				14 30					16 23				18 24								
Llandanwg	d			12x29				14x34					16x28				18x29								
Pensarn	d			12x30				14x35					16x29				18x31								
Llanbedr	d			12x33				14x38					16x31				18x32								
Dyffryn Ardudwy	d			12x37				14x42					16x35				18x36								
Talybont	d			12x40				14x45					16x38				18x39								
Llanaber	d			12x44				14x49					16x43				18x44								
Barmouth	a			12 49				14 54					16 48				18 49								
	d			12 53				14 57					16 53				18 51								
Morfa Mawddach	d			12x57				15x01					16x57				18x55								
Fairbourne	d			13 01				15 05					17 01				18 59								
Llwyngwril	d			13x07				15x11					17x07				19x05								
Tonfanau	d			13x14				15x18					17x14				19x12								
Tywyn	a			13 18				15 22					17 18				19 17								
	d			13 24				15 24					17 28				19 27								
Aberdovey	d			13 30				15 30					17 34				19 33								
Penhelig	d			13x32				15x32					17x36				19x36								
Aberystwyth	d		11 30				13 30					15 30				17 30			19 30						21 36
Borth	d		11 43				13 43					15 43				17 43			19 43						21 49
Dovey Junction 4	d		11 54	13 44			13 54	15 43				15 54	17 48			17 54	19 48		19 54						22 00
Machynlleth 4	a		12 03	13 54			14 03	15 51				16 03	17 58			18 03	19 57		20 03						22 07
	d		12 07				14 07					16 07				18 07			20 07						
Caersws	d		12 37				14 37					16 37				18 37			20 40						
Newtown (Powys)	d		12 46				14 46					16 46				18 46			20 49						
Welshpool	d		13 01				15 01					17 01				19 01			21 04						
Chester	d	12 19			13 19	14 19			15 18		16 19			17 19	18 18			19 28			20 22		21 21	21 21	
Wrexham General	a	12 34			13 35	14 34			15 36		16 35			17 37	18 35			19 44			20 38		21 37	21 37	
	d	12 34			13 35	14 34			15 36		16 35			17 37	18 35			19 44				20 49	21 37	21 37	
Ruabon	d	12 41			13 42	14 41			15 43		16 42			17 44	18 43			19 51				20 57	21 44	21 44	
Chirk	d	12 48			13 49	14 47			15 50		16 48			17 51	18 49			19 57				21 03	21 50	21 50	
Gobowen	d	12 53			13 54	14 53			15 55		16 54			17 56	18 55			20 03				21 08	21 56	21 56	
Shrewsbury	a	13 14	13 25		14 27	15 13	15 25		16 28		17 14	17 26		18 24	19 15	19 25		20 26	21 28			21 28	22 16	22 16	
Cardiff Central 7	a	15 21				17 15					19 21				21 20										
Shrewsbury	d		13 31		14 31		15 31		16 33			17 31		18 31		19 33			21 33				22 18	22 18	
Wellington (Shropshire)	d		13 45		14 45		15 45		16 47			17 45		18 45		19 47			21 47				22 32	22 32	
Telford Central	d		13 51		14 51		15 51		16 53			17 51		18 51		19 53			21 53				22 38	22 38	
Cosford	d																								
Wolverhampton 7 🚌	a		14 08		15 08		16 08		17 10			18 08		19 08		20 10			22 09				22 55	22 55	
Smethwick Galton Bdg L.L.	a		14 20		15 20		16 20		17 21			18 20		19 20		20 21			22 20						
Tame Bridge Parkway	d																								
Birmingham New Street 12	a		14 26		15 26		16 26		17 27			18 26		19 26		20 26			22 32				23 27	23 29	
Birmingham International ✈	a		14 50		15 50		16 50		17 50			18 50		19 50		20 50									
Leamington Spa 8	a																								
Banbury	a																								
London Marylebone 10 ⊖	a																								

A MWFO

B TThO

For connections to Crewe and Manchester Piccadilly please refer to Table 131

For connections to London Euston please refer to Table 66

Table 75

Mondays to Fridays

until 22 July

Pwllheli, Barmouth, Aberystwyth and Chester - Shrewsbury and Birmingham

		AW ◇	AW FO	AW ◇	AW
Pwllheli	d	20 00			
Abererch	d	20x03			
Penychain	d	20x06			
Criccieth	d	20 14			
Porthmadog	a	20 22			
	d	20 24			
Minffordd	d	20 28			
Penrhyndeudraeth	d	20 32			
Llandecwyn	d	20x34			
Talsarnau	d	20x36			
Tygwyn	d	20x39			
Harlech	a	20 44			
	d	20 46			
Llandanwg	d	20x50			
Pensarn	d	20x52			
Llanbedr	d	20x54			
Dyffryn Ardudwy	d	20x58			
Talybont	d	21x01			
Llanaber	d	21x06			
Barmouth	a	21 11			
	d	21 13	22 12		
Morfa Mawddach	d	21x17	22x16		
Fairbourne	d	21 21	22 20		
Llwyngwril	d	21x27	22x26		
Tonfanau	d	21x34	22x33		
Tywyn	a	21 39	22 37		
	d	21 46	22 39		
Aberdovey	d	21 52	22 45		
Penhelig	d	21x54	22x47		
Aberystwyth	d				23 53
Borth	d				00 06
Dovey Junction 4	d	22 06	22 59		00 17
Machynlleth 4	a	22 16	23 06		00 24
	d				
Caersws	d				
Newtown (Powys)	d				
Welshpool	d				
Chester	d			22 28	
Wrexham General	a			22 44	
	d			22 44	
Ruabon	d			22 51	
Chirk	d			22 57	
Gobowen	d			23 03	
Shrewsbury	a			23 23	
Cardiff Central 7	a				
Shrewsbury	d			23 26	
Wellington (Shropshire)	d			23 40	
Telford Central	d			23 47	
Cosford	d			23 57	
Wolverhampton 7	a			00 20	
Smethwick Galton Bdg L.L.	a				
Tame Bridge Parkway	d				
Birmingham New Street 12	a				
Birmingham International ✈	a				
Leamington Spa 8	a				
Banbury	a				
London Marylebone 10 ⊖	a				

For connections to Crewe and Manchester Piccadilly please refer to Table 131

For connections to London Euston please refer to Table 66

Table 75

Mondays to Fridays

25 July to 9 September

Pwllheli, Barmouth, Aberystwyth and Chester - Shrewsbury and Birmingham

		AW	AW MX	AW MO	AW MX	AW	AW	AW	AW	AW		AW	AW	AW	AW	AW	AW	AW	AW	AW		AW	AW	AW	AW
		A 🚌	◇			◇	◇ ⊤		◇ ⊤	◇		◇ ⊤	◇ ⊤	◇ ⊤	◇	◇		◇ ⊤	◇ ⊤	◇		◇ ⊤	Ⓡ ⊤	◇ ⊤	◇
Pwllheli	d														06 25	07 25				09 36					11 38
Abererch	d														06x28	07x28				09x39					11x41
Penychain	d														06x31	07 31				09 42					11 44
Criccieth	d														06 39	07 39				09 50					11 52
Porthmadog	a														06 47	07 47				09 58					12 00
	d														06 52	07 49				10 00					12 02
Minffordd	d														06 56	07 53				10 04					12 06
Penrhyndeudraeth	d														07 00	07 57				10 08					12 10
Llandecwyn	d														07x02	07x59				10x10					12x12
Talsarnau	d														07x04	08x02				10x12					12x14
Tygwyn	d														07x07	08x04				10x15					12x17
Harlech	a														07 12	08 09				10 20					12 22
	d														07 16	08 30				10 25					12 29
Llandanwg	d														07x20	08x34				10x29					12x33
Pensarn	d														07x21	08x35				10x30					12x34
Llanbedr	d														07x24	08x38				10x33					12x37
Dyffryn Ardudwy	d														07x28	08x42				10x37					12x41
Talybont	d														07x31	08x45				10x40					12x44
Llanaber	d														07x35	08x49				10x44					12x48
Barmouth	a														07 40	08 54				10 49					12 53
	d									06 46					07 49	09 00				11 04					12 56
Morfa Mawddach	d									06x50					07x53	09x04				11x08					13x00
Fairbourne	d									06 54					07 57	09 08				11 12					13 04
Llwyngwril	d									07x00					08x03	09x14				11x18					13x10
Tonfanau	d									07x07					08x10	09x21				11x25					13x17
Tywyn	a									07 11					08 14	09 25				11 30					13 21
	d									07 16					08 18	09 30				11 31					13 24
Aberdovey	d									07 22					08 24	09 36				11 37					13 30
Penhelig	d									07x25					08x26	09x38				11x40					13x32
Aberystwyth	d			23p30	23p53		05 14							07 30					09 30					11 30	
Borth	d			23p43	00 06		05 27							07 43					09 43					11 43	
Dovey Junction ④	d			23p54	00 17		05 38			07 37				07 54	08 38	09 49			09 54	11 52				11 54	13 44
Machynlleth ④	a			00 04	00 24		05 45			07 44				08 03	08 48	09 57			10 03	12 01				12 03	13 54
	d						05 47							08 07					10 07					12 07	
Caersws	d						06 15							08 37					10 37					12 37	
Newtown (Powys)	d						06 25							08 46					10 46					12 46	
Welshpool	d						06 41							09 01					11 01					13 01	
Chester	d		22p28			05 15		05 45	06 18			07 19	08 19				09 26	10 20				11 21	12 19		
Wrexham General	a		22p44			05 31		06 03	06 35			07 35	08 34				09 42	10 35				11 36	12 34		
	d	21p51	22p44			05 31			06 38			07 44	08 34				09 42	10 36				11 36	12 34		
Ruabon	d	22p06	22p51			05 38			06 45			07 51	08 41				09 49	10 42				11 44	12 41		
Chirk	d	22p21	22p57			05 44			06 51			07 57	08 47				09 56	10 48				11 51	12 48		
Gobowen	d	22p31	23p03			05 50			06 57			08 03	08 53				10 01	10 54				11 56	12 53		
Shrewsbury	a	23p01	23p23			06 10	07 11		07 17			08 23	09 13	09 25			10 22	11 14	11 25			12 27	13 14	13 25	
Cardiff Central ⑦	a					08 17			09 18				11 15				12 08	13 22					15 21		
Shrewsbury	d	23p01	23p26				07 31					08 31		09 31					11 31			12 31		13 31	
Wellington (Shropshire)	d	23p26	23p40				07 45					08 45		09 45					11 45			12 45		13 45	
Telford Central	d	23p46	23p47				07 51					08 51		09 51					11 51			12 51		13 51	
Cosford	d	00 06	23p57																						
Wolverhampton ⑦ 🚌	a	00 46	00 20				08 08					09 08		10 08					12 08			13 08		14 08	
Smethwick Galton Bdg L.L.	a						08 20					09 21		10 20					12 20			13 20		14 20	
Tame Bridge Parkway	d																								
Birmingham New Street ⑫	a						08 26					09 26		10 26					12 26			13 26		14 26	
Birmingham International ✈	a						08 50					09 50		10 50					12 50			13 50		14 50	
Leamington Spa ⑧	a																								
Banbury	a																								
London Marylebone ⑩ ⊖	a																								

A 25 July, 1 August

For connections to Crewe and Manchester Piccadilly please refer to Table 131

For connections to London Euston please refer to Table 66

Table 75

Mondays to Fridays

25 July to 9 September

Pwllheli, Barmouth, Aberystwyth and Chester - Shrewsbury and Birmingham

		AW	AW	AW	AW	AW		AW	AW	AW	AW	AW	AW	AW	AW	AW	VT	AW	AW	AW	AW	AW	AW	AW	AW
																							FO		
		◇	◇	◇	◇	◇		◇	◇	◇	◇	◇	◇	◇	◇	◇	◇1		◇	◇		◇		◇	
																			A	B					
		trolley	trolley	trolley		trolley		trolley	trolley		trolley	trolley	trolley		trolley										
Pwllheli	d				13 42					15 34				17 38								20 00			
Abererch	d				13x45					15x37				17x41								20x03			
Penychain	d				13x48					15 40				17 44								20x06			
Criccieth	d				13 56					15 48				17 52								20 14			
Porthmadog	a				14 04					15 56				18 00								20 22			
	d				14 06					15 58				18 02								20 24			
Minffordd	d				14 10					16 02				18 06								20 28			
Penrhyndeudraeth	d				14 14					16 06				18 10								20 32			
Llandecwyn	d				14x16					16x08				18x12								20x34			
Talsarnau	d				14x18					16x10				18x14								20x36			
Tygwyn	d				14x21					16x13				18x17								20x39			
Harlech	a				14 26					16 18				18 22								20 44			
	d				14 30					16 23				18 27								20 46			
Llandanwg	d				14x34					16x28				18x32								20x50			
Pensarn	d				14x35					16x29				18x34								20x52			
Llanbedr	d				14x38					16x31				18x35								20x54			
Dyffryn Ardudwy	d				14x42					16x35				18x39								20x58			
Talybont	d				14x45					16x38				18x42								21x01			
Llanaber	d				14x49					16x43				18x47								21x06			
Barmouth	a				14 54					16 48				18 52								21 11			
	d				14 57					16 53				18 54								21 13	22 12		
Morfa Mawddach	d				15x01					16x57				18x58								21x17	22x16		
Fairbourne	d				15 05					17 01				19 02								21 21	22 20		
Llwyngwril	d				15x11					17x07				19x08								21x27	22x26		
Tonfanau	d				15x18					17x14				19x15								21x34	22x33		
Tywyn	a				15 22					17 18				19 20								21 39	22 37		
	d				15 24					17 32				19 27								21 46	22 39		
Aberdovey	d				15 30					17 38				19 33								21 52	22 45		
Penhelig	d				15x32					17x41				19x36								21x54	22x47		
Aberystwyth	d			13 30					15 30				17 30			19 30					21 36				22 04
Borth	d			13 43					15 43				17 43			19 43					21 49				22 22
Dovey Junction 4	d			13 54	15 43				15 54	17 52			17 54	19 48		19 54					22 00	22 06	22 59		
Machynlleth 4	a			14 03	15 51				16 03	18 02			18 03	19 57		20 03					22 07	22 16	23 06		
	d			14 07					16 07				18 07			20 07									
Caersws	d			14 37					16 37				18 37			20 40									
Newtown (Powys)	d			14 46					16 46				18 46			20 49									
Welshpool	d			15 01					17 01				19 01			21 04									
Chester	d	13 19	14 19			15 18		16 19			17 19	18 18			19 28		20 22		21 21	21 21				22 28	
Wrexham General	a	13 35	14 34			15 36		16 35			17 37	18 35			19 44		20 38		21 37	21 37				22 44	
	d	13 35	14 34			15 36		16 35			17 37	18 35			19 44			20 49	21 37	21 37				22 44	
Ruabon	d	13 42	14 41			15 43		16 42			17 44	18 43			19 51			20 57	21 44	21 44				22 51	
Chirk	d	13 49	14 47			15 50		16 48			17 51	18 49			19 57			21 03	21 50	21 50				22 57	
Gobowen	d	13 54	14 53			15 55		16 54			17 56	18 55			20 03			21 08	21 56	21 56				23 03	
Shrewsbury	a	14 27	15 13	15 25		16 28		17 14	17 26		18 24	19 15	19 25		20 26	21 28		21 28	22 16	22 16				23 23	
Cardiff Central 7	a		17 15					19 21				21 20													
Shrewsbury	d	14 31		15 31		16 33			17 31		18 31		19 33			21 33			22 18	22 18				23 26	
Wellington (Shropshire)	d	14 45		15 45		16 47			17 45		18 45		19 47			21 47			22 32	22 32				23 40	
Telford Central	d	14 51		15 51		16 53			17 51		18 51		19 53			21 53			22 38	22 38				23 47	
Cosford	d																							23 57	
Wolverhampton 7	a	15 08		16 08		17 10			18 08		19 08		20 10			22 09			22 55	22 55				00 20	
Smethwick Galton Bdg L.L.	a	15 20		16 20		17 21			18 20		19 20		20 21			22 20									
Tame Bridge Parkway	d																								
Birmingham New Street 12	a	15 26		16 26		17 27			18 26		19 26		20 26			22 32			23 27	23 29					
Birmingham International ✈	a	15 50		16 50		17 50			18 50		19 50		20 50												
Leamington Spa 8	a																								
Banbury	a																								
London Marylebone 10 ⊖	a																								

A MWFO

B TThO

For connections to Crewe and Manchester Piccadilly please refer to Table 131

For connections to London Euston please refer to Table 66

Pwllheli, Barmouth, Aberystwyth and Chester - Shrewsbury and Birmingham

		AW MX	AW MO	AW MX	AW	AW	AW	AW	AW	AW		AW	AW	AW	AW	AW	AW	AW	AW	AW		AW	AW	AW	AW
																						■			
		◇			◇	◇		◇	◇	◇		◇	◇	◇	◇		◇	◇	◇	◇			◇	◇	◇
						🛒		🛒		🛒		🛒	🛒				🛒	🛒		🛒		🛒	🛒		🛒
Pwllheli	d													06 25	07 25				09 36					11 38	
Abererch	d													06x28	07x28				09x39					11x41	
Penychain	d													06x31	07 31				09 42					11 44	
Criccieth	d													06 39	07 39				09 50					11 52	
Porthmadog	a													06 47	07 47				09 58					12 00	
	d													06 52	07 49				10 00					12 02	
Minffordd	d													06 56	07 53				10 04					12 06	
Penrhyndeudraeth	d													07 00	07 57				10 08					12 10	
Llandecwyn	d													07x02	07x59				10x10					12x12	
Talsarnau	d													07x04	08x02				10x12					12x14	
Tygwyn	d													07x07	08x04				10x15					12x17	
Harlech	a													07 12	08 09				10 20					12 22	
	d													07 16	08 30				10 25					12 25	
Llandanwg	d													07x20	08x34				10x29					12x29	
Pensarn	d													07x21	08x35				10x32					12x30	
Llanbedr	d													07x24	08x38				10x34					12x33	
Dyffryn Ardudwy	d													07x28	08x42				10x38					12x37	
Talybont	d													07x31	08x45				10x41					12x40	
Llanaber	d													07x35	08x49				10x46					12x44	
Barmouth	a													07 40	08 54				10 51					12 49	
	d								06 46					07 49	09 00				10 53					12 53	
Morfa Mawddach	d								06x50					07x53	09x04				10x57					12x57	
Fairbourne	d								06 54					07 57	09 08				11 01					13 01	
Llwyngwril	d								07x00					08x03	09x14				11x07					13x07	
Tonfanau	d								07x07					08x10	09x21				11x14					13x14	
Tywyn	a								07 11					08 14	09 25				11 19					13 18	
	d								07 16					08 18	09 30				11 29					13 24	
Aberdovey	d								07 22					08 24	09 36				11 35					13 30	
Penhelig	d								07x25					08x26	09x38				11x37					13x32	
Aberystwyth	d		23p30	23p53		05 14							07 30					09 30					11 30		
Borth	d		23p43	00 06		05 27							07 43					09 43					11 43		
Dovey Junction ■4	d		23p54	00 17		05 38			07 37				07 54	08 38	09 49			09 54	11 49				11 54	13 44	
Machynlleth ■4	a		00 04	00 24		05 45			07 44				08 03	08 48	09 57			10 03	11 59				12 03	13 54	
	d					05 47							08 07					10 07					12 07		
Caersws	d					06 15							08 37					10 37					12 37		
Newtown (Powys)	d					06 25							08 46					10 46					12 46		
Welshpool	d					06 41							09 01					11 01					13 01		
Chester	d	22p28			05 15		05 45	06 18		07 19		08 19				09 26	10 20			11 21		12 19			13 19
Wrexham General	a	22p44			05 31		06 03	06 35		07 35		08 34				09 42	10 35			11 36		12 34			13 35
	d	22p44			05 31			06 38		07 44		08 34				09 42	10 36			11 36		12 34			13 35
Ruabon	d	22p51			05 38			06 45		07 51		08 41				09 49	10 42			11 44		12 41			13 42
Chirk	d	22p57			05 44			06 51		07 57		08 47				09 56	10 48			11 51		12 48			13 49
Gobowen	d	23p03			05 50			06 57		08 03		08 53				10 01	10 54			11 56		12 53			13 54
Shrewsbury	a	23p23			06 10	07 11		07 17		08 23		09 13	09 25			10 22	11 14	11 25		12 27		13 14	13 25		14 27
Cardiff Central ■7	a				08 17			09 18				11 15				12 08	13 22					15 21			
Shrewsbury	d	23p26				07 31				08 31			09 31					11 31		12 31			13 31		14 31
Wellington (Shropshire)	d	23p40				07 45				08 45			09 45					11 45		12 45			13 45		14 45
Telford Central	d	23p47				07 51				08 51			09 51					11 51		12 51			13 51		14 51
Cosford	d	23p57																							
Wolverhampton ■7 🚌	a	00 20				08 08				09 08			10 08					12 08		13 08			14 08		15 08
Smethwick Galton Bdg L.L.	a					08 20				09 21			10 20					12 20		13 20			14 20		15 20
Tame Bridge Parkway	d																								
Birmingham New Street ■12	a					08 26				09 26			10 26					12 26		13 26			14 26		15 26
Birmingham International ✈	a					08 50				09 50			10 50					12 50		13 50			14 50		15 50
Leamington Spa ■8	a																								
Banbury	a																								
London Marylebone ■10 ⊖	a																								

For connections to Crewe and Manchester Piccadilly please refer to Table 131

For connections to London Euston please refer to Table 66

Table 75

Mondays to Fridays

from 12 September

Pwllheli, Barmouth, Aberystwyth and Chester - Shrewsbury and Birmingham

		AW	AW	AW	AW	AW		AW	AW	AW	AW	AW	AW	AW	AW	VT		AW	AW	AW	AW	AW	AW FO	AW	AW
		◇	◇	◇	◇	◇		◇	◇	◇	◇	◇	◇	◇	◇	◇1			◇ A	◇ B		◇		◇	
		🛒	🛒		🛒	🛒		🛒		🛒	🛒	🛒		🛒											
Pwllheli	d			13 42					15 34				17 38									20 00			
Abererch	d			13x45					15x37				17x41									20x03			
Penychain	d			13x48					15 40				17 44									20x06			
Criccieth	d			13 56					15 48				17 52									20 14			
Porthmadog	a			14 04					15 56				18 00									20 22			
	d			14 06					15 58				18 02									20 24			
Minffordd	d			14 10					16 02				18 06									20 28			
Penrhyndeudraeth	d			14 14					16 06				18 10									20 32			
Llandecwyn	d			14x16					16x08				18x12									20x34			
Talsarnau	d			14x18					16x10				18x14									20x36			
Tygwyn	d			14x21					16x13				18x17									20x39			
Harlech	a			14 26					16 18				18 22									20 44			
	d			14 30					16 23				18 24									20 46			
Llandanwg	d			14x34					16x28				18x29									20x50			
Pensarn	d			14x35					16x29				18x31									20x52			
Llanbedr	d			14x38					16x31				18x32									20x54			
Dyffryn Ardudwy	d			14x42					16x35				18x36									20x58			
Talybont	d			14x45					16x38				18x39									21x01			
Llanaber	d			14x49					16x43				18x44									21x06			
Barmouth	a			14 54					16 48				18 49									21 11			
	d			14 57					16 53				18 51									21 13	22 12		
Morfa Mawddach	d			15x01					16x57				18x55									21x17	22x16		
Fairbourne	d			15 05					17 01				18 59									21 21	22 20		
Llwyngwril	d			15x11					17x07				19x05									21x27	22x26		
Tonfanau	d			15x18					17x14				19x12									21x34	22x33		
Tywyn	a			15 22					17 18				19 17									21 39	22 37		
	d			15 24					17 28				19 27									21 46	22 39		
Aberdovey	d			15 30					17 34				19 33									21 52	22 45		
Penhelig	d			15x32					17x36				19x36									21x54	22x47		
Aberystwyth	d		13 30					15 30				17 30			19 30						21 36				23 53
Borth	d		13 43					15 43				17 43			19 43						21 49				00 06
Dovey Junction 4	d		13 54	15 43				15 54	17 48			17 54	19 48		19 54						22 00	22 06	22 59		00 17
Machynlleth 4	a		14 03	15 51				16 03	17 58			18 03	19 57		20 03						22 07	22 16	23 06		00 24
	d		14 07					16 07				18 07			20 07										
Caersws	d		14 37					16 37				18 37			20 40										
Newtown (Powys)	d		14 46					16 46				18 46			20 49										
Welshpool	d		15 01					17 01				19 01			21 04										
Chester	d	14 19			15 18	16 19				17 19	18 18			19 28		20 22			21 21	21 21				22 28	
Wrexham General	a	14 34			15 36	16 35				17 37	18 35			19 44		20 38			21 37	21 37				22 44	
	d	14 34			15 36	16 35				17 37	18 35			19 44				20 49	21 37	21 37				22 44	
Ruabon	d	14 41			15 43	16 42				17 44	18 43			19 51				20 57	21 44	21 44				22 51	
Chirk	d	14 47			15 50	16 48				17 51	18 49			19 57				21 03	21 50	21 50				22 57	
Gobowen	d	14 53			15 55	16 54				17 56	18 55			20 03				21 08	21 56	21 56				23 03	
Shrewsbury	a	15 13	15 25		16 28	17 14		17 26		18 24	19 15	19 25		20 26	21 28			21 28	22 16	22 16				23 23	
Cardiff Central 7	a	17 15				19 21					21 20														
Shrewsbury	d		15 31		16 33			17 31		18 31		19 33			21 33				22 18	22 18				23 26	
Wellington (Shropshire)	d		15 45		16 47			17 45		18 45		19 47			21 47				22 32	22 32				23 40	
Telford Central	d		15 51		16 53			17 51		18 51		19 53			21 53				22 38	22 38				23 47	
Cosford	d																							23 57	
Wolverhampton 7 ⛴	a		16 08		17 10			18 08		19 08		20 10			22 09				22 55	22 55				00 20	
Smethwick Galton Bdg L.L.	a		16 20		17 21			18 20		19 20		20 21			22 20										
Tame Bridge Parkway	d																								
Birmingham New Street 12	a		16 26		17 27			18 26		19 26		20 26			22 32				23 27	23 29					
Birmingham International ✈	a		16 50		17 50			18 50		19 50		20 50													
Leamington Spa 8	a																								
Banbury	a																								
London Marylebone 10 ⊖	a																								

A MWFO

B TThO

For connections to Crewe and Manchester Piccadilly please refer to Table 131

For connections to London Euston please refer to Table 66

Table 75

Saturdays

Pwllheli, Barmouth, Aberystwyth and Chester - Shrewsbury and Birmingham

		AW	AW	AW	AW	AW	AW	AW	AW	AW	AW	AW	AW	AW	AW	AW	AW	AW	AW	AW	AW	AW	AW
																	■						
		◇		◇		◇	◇	◇	◇	◇	◇	◇	◇	◇	◇	◇		◇	◇	◇	◇	◇	◇
				🚲		🚲		🚲	🚲	🚲			🚲	🚲		🚲	🚲	🚲		🚲	🚲	🚲	
Pwllheli	d										06 25	07 25			09 36				11 38				13 42
Abererch	d										06x28	07x28			09x39				11x41				13x45
Penychain	d										06x31	07x31			09x42				11x44				13x48
Criccieth	d										06 39	07 39			09 50				11 52				13 56
Porthmadog	a										06 47	07 47			09 58				12 00				14 04
	d										06 52	07 49			10 00				12 02				14 06
Minffordd	d										06 56	07 53			10 04				12 06				14 10
Penrhyndeudraeth	d										07 00	07 57			10 08				12 10				14 14
Llandecwyn	d										07x02	07x59			10x10				12x12				14x16
Talsarnau	d										07x04	08x02			10x12				12x14				14x18
Tygwyn	d										07x07	08x04			10x15				12x17				14x21
Harlech	a										07 12	08 09			10 20				12 22				14 26
	d										07 16	08 30			10 25				12 25				14 30
Llandanwg	d										07x20	08x34			10x29				12x29				14x34
Pensarn	d										07x21	08x35			10x30				12x30				14x35
Llanbedr	d										07x24	08x38			10x33				12x33				14x38
Dyffryn Ardudwy	d										07x28	08x42			10x37				12x37				14x42
Talybont	d										07x31	08x45			10x40				12x40				14x45
Llanaber	d										07x35	08x49			10x44				12x44				14x49
Barmouth	a										07 40	08 54			10 49				12 49				14 54
	d						06 46				07 49	09 00			10 52				12 53				14 57
Morfa Mawddach	d						06x50				07x53	09x04			10x56				12x57				15x01
Fairbourne	d						06 54				07 57	09 08			11 00				13 01				15 05
Llwyngwril	d						07x00				08x03	09x14			11x06				13x07				15x11
Tonfanau	d						07x07				08x10	09x21			11x13				13x14				15x18
Tywyn	a						07 11				08 14	09 25			11 17				13 18				15 22
	d						07 16				08 18	09 30			11 27				13 24				15 24
Aberdovey	d						07 22				08 24	09 36			11 33				13 30				15 30
Penhelig	d						07x25				08x26	09x38			11x36				13x32				15x32
Aberystwyth	d		23p53	05 14						07 30				09 30				11 30				13 30	
Borth	d		00 06	05 27						07 43				09 43				11 43				13 43	
Dovey Junction ■	d		00 17	05 38			07 37			07 54	08 38	09 49		09 54	11 48			11 54	13 44			13 54	15 43
Machynlleth ■	a		00 24	05 45			07 44			08 03	08 48	09 57		10 03	11 57			12 03	13 53			14 03	15 51
	d			05 47						08 07				10 07				12 07				14 07	
Caersws	d			06 15						08 37				10 37				12 37				14 37	
Newtown (Powys)	d			06 25						08 46				10 46				12 46				14 46	
Welshpool	d			06 41						09 01				11 01				13 01				15 01	
Chester	d	22p28			05 37	06 12		07 21	08 19				09 19			11 21	12 19			13 19	14 19		
Wrexham General	a	22p44			05 55	06 35		07 37	08 34				09 35			11 36	12 34			13 35	14 35		
	d	22p44				06 38		07 37	08 34				09 35			11 37	12 34			13 35	14 35		
Ruabon	d	22p51				06 45		07 44	08 41				09 42			11 44	12 41			13 42	14 42		
Chirk	d	22p57				06 51		07 51	08 47				09 49			11 51	12 47			13 49	14 48		
Gobowen	d	23p03				06 57		07 56	08 53				09 54			11 56	12 53			13 54	14 54		
Shrewsbury	a	23p23		07 11		07 17		08 20	09 13	09 25			10 27	11 25		12 27	13 13	13 25		14 27	15 14	15 25	
Cardiff Central ■	a					09 22			11 15								15 26				17 12		
Shrewsbury	d	23p26		07 31				08 31		09 31			10 32	11 31		12 31		13 31		14 31		15 31	
Wellington (Shropshire)	d	23p40		07 45				08 45		09 45			10 46	11 45		12 45		13 45		14 45		15 45	
Telford Central	d	23p47		07 51				08 51		09 51			10 52	11 51		12 51		13 51		14 51		15 51	
Cosford	d	23p57																					
Wolverhampton ■ 🚌	a	00 20		08 08				09 08		10 08			11 09	12 08		13 08		14 08		15 08		16 08	
Smethwick Galton Bdg L.L.	a			08 20				09 22		10 20			11 20	12 20		13 20		14 20		15 20		16 20	
Tame Bridge Parkway	d																						
Birmingham New Street ■	a			08 26				09 26		10 26			11 26	12 26		13 25		14 26		15 26		16 26	
Birmingham International ✈	a			08 50				09 50		10 50			11 50	12 50		13 50		14 50		15 50		16 50	
Leamington Spa ■	a																						
Banbury	a																						
London Marylebone ■ ⊖	a																						

For connections to Crewe and Manchester Piccadilly please refer to Table 131

For connections to London Euston please refer to Table 66

Table 75

Saturdays

Pwllheli, Barmouth, Aberystwyth and Chester - Shrewsbury and Birmingham

		AW	AW	AW	AW	AW		AW	AW	AW	AW	AW	AW	AW	AW	AW		AW	AW	AW	AW				
		◇	◇	◇	◇	◇		◇	◇	◇	◇		◇	◇	◇			◇	◇	◇					
														A	B				B	A					
		🚲	🚲	🚲		🚲		🚲	🚲		🚲														
Pwllheli	d				15 34					17 38								20 00							
Abererch	d				15x37					17x41								20x03							
Penychain	d				15x40					17x44								20x06							
Criccieth	d				15 48					17 52								20 14							
Porthmadog	a				15 56					18 00								20 22							
	d				15 58					18 02								20 24							
Minffordd	d				16 02					18 06								20 28							
Penrhyndeudraeth	d				16 06					18 10								20 32							
Llandecwyn	d				16x08					18x12								20x34							
Talsarnau	d				16x10					18x14								20x36							
Tygwyn	d				16x13					18x17								20x39							
Harlech	a				16 18					18 22								20 44							
	d				16 23					18 24								20 46							
Llandanwg	d				16x28					18x29								20x50							
Pensarn	d				16x29					18x31								20x52							
Llanbedr	d				16x31					18x32								20x54							
Dyffryn Ardudwy	d				16x35					18x36								20x58							
Talybont	d				16x38					18x39								21x01							
Llanaber	d				16x43					18x44								21x06							
Barmouth	a				16 48					18 49								21 11							
	d				16 53					18 51								21 13							
Morfa Mawddach	d				16x57					18x55								21x17							
Fairbourne	d				17 01					18 59								21 21							
Llwyngwril	d				17x07					19x05								21x27							
Tonfanau	d				17x14					19x12								21x34							
Tywyn	a				17 18					19 17								21 39							
	d				17 28					19 27								21 46							
Aberdovey	d				17 34					19 33								21 52							
Penhelig	d				17x36					19x36								21x54							
Aberystwyth	d			15 30					17 30				19 30			21 36					23 46				
Borth	d			15 43					17 43				19 43			21 49					23 59				
Dovey Junction 4	d			15 54	17 48				17 54	19 48			19 54			22 00		22 06			00 10				
Machynlleth 4	a			16 03	17 58				18 03	19 57			20 03			22 07		22 16			00 17				
	d			16 07					18 07				20 07												
Caersws	d			16 37					18 37				20 38												
Newtown (Powys)	d			16 46					18 46				20 48												
Welshpool	d			17 01					19 01				21 04												
Chester	d	15 20	16 19			17 19		18 20			19 28	20 27		21 19	21 19				22 28	22 28					
Wrexham General	a	15 36	16 35			17 35		18 36			19 44	20 43		21 35	21 35				22 44	22 44					
	d	15 36	16 35			17 35		18 37			19 44	20 43		21 36	21 36				22 44	22 44					
Ruabon	d	15 43	16 42			17 42		18 43			19 51	20 51		21 44	21 44				22 51	22 51					
Chirk	d	15 50	16 48			17 49		18 50			19 57	20 57		21 51	21 51				22 57	22 57					
Gobowen	d	15 55	16 54			17 54		18 55			20 03	21 02		21 58	21 58				23 03	23 03					
Shrewsbury	a	16 28	17 14	17 25		18 23		19 16	19 25		20 26	21 22	21 28	22 20	22 20				23 23	23 23					
Cardiff Central 7	a		19 23					21 15																	
Shrewsbury	d	16 33		17 31		18 31			19 33				21 33		22 31				23 26						
Wellington (Shropshire)	d	16 47		17 45		18 45			19 47				21 47		22 45				23 40						
Telford Central	d	16 53		17 51		18 51			19 53				21 53		22 51				23 47						
Cosford	d																		23 57						
Wolverhampton 7	a	17 10		18 08		19 08			20 10				22 09		23 08				00 18						
Smethwick Galton Bdg L.L.	a	17 21		18 20		19 20			20 21				22 20												
Tame Bridge Parkway	d																								
Birmingham New Street 12	a	17 27		18 26		19 26			20 26				22 32		23 29										
Birmingham International ✈	a	17 50		18 50		19 50			20 50																
Leamington Spa 8	a																								
Banbury	a																								
London Marylebone 10 ⊖	a																								

A from 25 June until 30 July

B until 18 June, from 6 August

For connections to Crewe and Manchester Piccadilly please refer to Table 131

For connections to London Euston please refer to Table 66

Table 75

Sundays
until 19 June

Pwllheli, Barmouth, Aberystwyth and Chester - Shrewsbury and Birmingham

		AW	AW	AW	AW	AW	AW	AW	AW	AW	AW	AW	AW	AW	AW	AW	AW	AW	AW	AW	AW	AW	AW		
																	■								
		◇			◇	◇	◇	◇	◇	◇	◇	◇	◇	◇	◇	◇		◇	◇	◇	◇	◇			
		A	A											B											
						⊥	⊥		⊥		⊥	⊥	⊥	⊥	⊥		⊥	⊥				⊥			
Pwllheli	d									11 28				13 48					17 36						
Abererch	d									11x32				13x51					17x40						
Penychain	d									11x35				13x54					17x44						
Criccieth	d									11 41				14 02					17 50						
Porthmadog	a									11 51				14 10					17 59						
	d									11 57				14 12					18 00						
Minffordd	d									12 02				14 16					18 05						
Penrhyndeudraeth	d									12 06				14 20					18 09						
Llandecwyn	d									12x09				14x22					18x12						
Talsarnau	d									12x11				14x24					18x14						
Tygwyn	d									12x13				14x27					18x16						
Harlech	a									12 18				14 32					18 21						
	d									12 19				14 34					18 22						
Llandanwg	d									12x25				14x38					18x28						
Pensarn	d									12x28				14x40					18x30						
Llanbedr	d									12x30				14x42					18x32						
Dyffryn Ardudwy	d									12x34				14x46					18x36						
Talybont	d									12x37				14x49					18x39						
Llanaber	d									12x42				14x54					18x45						
Barmouth	a									12 46				14 59					18 48						
	d									12 48				15 01					18 50						
Morfa Mawddach	d									12x53				15x05					18x55						
Fairbourne	d									12 56				15 09					18 57						
Llwyngwril	d									13x04				15x15					19x05						
Tonfanau	d									13x11				15x22					19x12						
Tywyn	a									13 16				15 27					19 17						
	d									13 16				15 28					19 22						
Aberdovey	d									13 22				15 35					19 28						
Penhelig	d									13x26				15x37					19x32						
Aberystwyth	d		23p46			09 30			11 30			13 30			15 30			17 30			19 30		21 30		23 30
Borth	d		23p59			09 43			11 43			13 43			15 43			17 43			19 43		21 43		23 43
Dovey Junction ■	d		00⌇10			09 54			11 54	13 36		13 54		15 49	15 54			17 54	19 42		19 54		21 54		23 54
Machynlleth ■	a		00⌇17			10 03			12 03	13 45		14 03		15 59	16 03			18 03	19 52		20 03		22 04		00 04
	d					10 07			12 07			14 07		16 07				18 07			20 07				
Caersws	d					10 35			12 37			14 37		16 37				18 37			20 37				
Newtown (Powys)	d					10 45			12 46			14 46		16 46				18 46			20 46				
Welshpool	d					11 01			13 01			15 01		17 01				19 01			21 01				
Chester	d	22p28		08 08	09 22		11 31	12 21			13 31		15 31			17 31	18 24			19 26		21 26		22 04	
Wrexham General	a	22p44		08 26	09 38		11 47	12 38			13 47		15 47			17 47	18 40			19 42		21 42		22 22	
	d	22p44			09 38		11 48	12 38			13 48		15 48			17 48	18 41			19 42		21 44			
Ruabon	d	22p51			09 45		11 55	12 45			13 55		15 55			17 55	18 47			19 49		21 51			
Chirk	d	22p57			09 52		12 01	12 52			14 01		16 01			18 01	18 54			19 55		21 57			
Gobowen	d	23p03			09 57		12 07	12 57			14 07		16 07			18 07	18 59			20 01		22 02			
Shrewsbury	a	23p23			10 18	11 25	12 27	13 18	13 25		14 27	15 25	16 27	17 27		18 27	19 20	19 25		20 21	21 25	22 23			
Cardiff Central ■	a	⌇						15 31									21 36								
Shrewsbury	d	23p26			10 20	11 40	12 31		13 31		14 31	15 33	16 40	17 33		18 31		19 31		20 23	21 31	22 23			
Wellington (Shropshire)	d	23p40			10 34	11 54	12 45		13 45		14 45	15 47	16 54	17 47		18 45		19 45		20 37	21 45	22 37			
Telford Central	d	23p47			10 40	12 00	12 51		13 51		14 51	15 53	17 00	17 53		18 51		19 51		20 44	21 51	22 45			
Cosford	d	23p57																		20 54		22 56			
Wolverhampton ■	a	00⌇18			10 57	12 17	13 08		14 08		15 08	16 10	17 15	18 10		19 08		20 08		21 11	22 08	23 13			
Smethwick Galton Bdg L.L.	a																								
Tame Bridge Parkway	d																								
Birmingham New Street ■	a				11 14	12 33	13 24		14 24		15 25	16 26	17 35	18 28		19 27		20 24		21 29	22 28				
Birmingham International ✈	a				11 32	12 56	13 56		14 56		15 56	16 56	17 56	18 56		19 56		20 56		21 56	22 56				
Leamington Spa ■	a																								
Banbury	a																								
London Marylebone ■ ⊖	a																								

A not 22 May

B ⊥ from Machynlleth

For connections to Crewe and Manchester Piccadilly please refer to Table 131

For connections to London Euston please refer to Table 66

Table 75

Sundays

26 June to 31 July

Pwllheli, Barmouth, Aberystwyth and Chester - Shrewsbury and Birmingham

	AW	AW	AW	AW	AW	AW	AW	AW	AW		AW	AW	AW	AW	AW	AW	AW	AW	AW		AW	AW	AW	AW
					◇				◇		◇			◇			◇	◇					◇	◇
																	A							
				bus			bus	bus					bus			bus					bus	bus		
					trolley				trolley					trolley			trolley	trolley					trolley	
Pwllheli d											11 28						13 48							17 36
Abererch d											11x32						13x51							17x40
Penychain d											11x35						13x54							17x44
Criccieth d											11 41						14 02							17 50
Porthmadog a											11 51						14 10							17 59
d											11 57						14 12							18 00
Minffordd d											12 02						14 16							18 05
Penrhyndeudraeth d											12 06						14 20							18 09
Llandecwyn d											12x09						14x22							18x12
Talsarnau d											12x11						14x24							18x14
Tygwyn d											12x13						14x27							18x16
Harlech a											12 18						14 32							18 21
d											12 19						14 34							18 22
Llandanwg d											12x25						14x38							18x28
Pensarn d											12x28						14x40							18x30
Llanbedr d											12x30						14x42							18x32
Dyffryn Ardudwy d											12x34						14x46							18x36
Talybont d											12x37						14x49							18x39
Llanaber d											12x42						14x54							18x45
Barmouth a											12 46						14 59							18 48
d											12 48						15 01							18 50
Morfa Mawddach d											12x53						15x05							18x55
Fairbourne d											12 56						15 09							18 57
Llwyngwril d											13x04						15x15							19x05
Tonfanau d											13x11						15x22							19x12
Tywyn a											13 16						15 27							19 17
d											13 16						15 28							19 22
Aberdovey d											13 22						15 35							19 28
Penhelig d											13x26						15x37							19x32
Aberystwyth d	23p46				09 30				11 30					13 30				15 30					17 30	
Borth d	23p59				09 43				11 43					13 43				15 43					17 43	
Dovey Junction 4 d	00 10				09 54				11 54		13 36			13 54			15 49	15 54					17 54	19 42
Machynlleth 4 a	00 17				10 03				12 03		13 45			14 03			15 59	16 03					18 03	19 52
d					10 07				12 07					14 07			16 07						18 07	
Caersws d					10 35				12 37					14 37			16 37						18 37	
Newtown (Powys) d					10 45				12 46					14 46			16 46						18 46	
Welshpool d					11 01				13 01					15 01			17 01						19 01	
Chester d		08 08	08 34			10 45		11 35				12 45			14 54				16 45			17 37		
Wrexham General a		08 26	08 50			11 01		12 00				13 01			15 10				17 01			18 02		
d				09 00			11 11	12 00					13 11			15 20					17 11	18 02		
Ruabon d				09 15			11 26	12 15					13 26			15 35					17 26	18 17		
Chirk d				09 30			11 41	12 30					13 41			15 50					17 41	18 32		
Gobowen d				09 40			11 51	12 40					13 51			16 00					17 51	18 42		
Shrewsbury a				10 10	11 25		12 21	13 10	13 25				14 21	15 25		16 30	17 27				18 21	19 12	19 25	
Cardiff Central 7 a																								
Shrewsbury d					11 40				13 31					15 33			17 33						19 31	
Wellington (Shropshire) d					11 54				13 45					15 47			17 47						19 45	
Telford Central d					12 00				13 51					15 53			17 53						19 51	
Cosford d																								
Wolverhampton 7 a					12 17				14 08					16 10			18 10						20 08	
Smethwick Galton Bdg L.L. a																								
Tame Bridge Parkway d																								
Birmingham New Street 12 a					12 33				14 24					16 26			18 28						20 24	
Birmingham International a					12 56				14 56					16 56			18 56						20 56	
Leamington Spa 8 a																								
Banbury a																								
London Marylebone 10 ⊖ a																								

A trolley from Machynlleth

For connections to Crewe and Manchester Piccadilly please refer to Table 131

For connections to London Euston please refer to Table 66

Table 75

Sundays

26 June to 31 July

Pwllheli, Barmouth, Aberystwyth and Chester - Shrewsbury and Birmingham

		AW	AW	AW	AW	AW	AW	AW	AW	AW
				◇		◇				
			🚌		🚌			🚌		
						trolley				
Pwllheli	d									
Abererch	d									
Penychain	d									
Criccieth	d									
Porthmadog	a									
	d									
Minffordd	d									
Penrhyndeudraeth	d									
Llandecwyn	d									
Talsarnau	d									
Tygwyn	d									
Harlech	a									
	d									
Llandanwg	d									
Pensarn	d									
Llanbedr	d									
Dyffryn Ardudwy	d									
Talybont	d									
Llanaber	d									
Barmouth	a									
	d									
Morfa Mawddach	d									
Fairbourne	d									
Llwyngwril	d									
Tonfanau	d									
Tywyn	a									
	d									
Aberdovey	d									
Penhelig	d									
Aberystwyth	d			19 30			21 30			23 30
Borth	d			19 43			21 43			23 43
Dovey Junction 4	d			19 54			21 54			23 54
Machynlleth 4	a			20 03			22 04			00 04
	d			20 07						
Caersws	d			20 37						
Newtown (Powys)	d			20 46						
Welshpool	d			21 01						
Chester	d	18 37				21 26			22 04	
Wrexham General	a	18 53				21 42			22 22	
	d		19 03		21 04			21 51		
Ruabon	d		19 18		21 19			22 06		
Chirk	d		19 33		21 34			22 21		
Gobowen	d		19 43		21 44			22 31		
Shrewsbury	a		20 13	21 25	22 14			23 01		
Cardiff Central 7	a									
Shrewsbury	d			21 31				23 01		
Wellington (Shropshire)	d			21 45				23 26		
Telford Central	d			21 51				23 46		
Cosford	d							00 06		
Wolverhampton 7	a			22 08				00 46		
Smethwick Galton Bdg L.L.	a									
Tame Bridge Parkway	d									
Birmingham New Street 12	a			22 28						
Birmingham International	a			22 56						
Leamington Spa 8	a									
Banbury	a									
London Marylebone 10 ⊖	a									

For connections to Crewe and Manchester Piccadilly please refer to Table 131

For connections to London Euston please refer to Table 66

Table 75

Sundays

7 August to 11 September

Pwllheli, Barmouth, Aberystwyth and Chester - Shrewsbury and Birmingham

		AW	AW	AW	AW	AW	AW	AW	AW	AW	AW	AW	AW	AW	AW	AW	AW	AW	AW	AW	AW	AW	AW	AW	AW
																	R								
		◇			◇	◇	◇	◇	◇	◇	◇	◇	◇	◇	◇	◇		◇	◇	◇	◇	◇			
														A											
						🛒	🛒		🛒		🛒	🛒	🛒	🛒	🛒		🛒	🛒				🛒			
Pwllheli	d									11 28				13 48					17 36						
Abererch	d									11x32				13x51					17x40						
Penychain	d									11x35				13x54					17x44						
Criccieth	d									11 41				14 02					17 50						
Porthmadog	a									11 51				14 10					17 59						
	d									11 57				14 12					18 00						
Minffordd	d									12 02				14 16					18 05						
Penrhyndeudraeth	d									12 06				14 20					18 09						
Llandecwyn	d									12x09				14x22					18x12						
Talsarnau	d									12x11				14x24					18x14						
Tygwyn	d									12x13				14x27					18x16						
Harlech	a									12 18				14 32					18 21						
	d									12 19				14 34					18 22						
Llandanwg	d									12x25				14x38					18x28						
Pensarn	d									12x28				14x40					18x30						
Llanbedr	d									12x30				14x42					18x32						
Dyffryn Ardudwy	d									12x34				14x46					18x36						
Talybont	d									12x37				14x49					18x39						
Llanaber	d									12x42				14x54					18x45						
Barmouth	a									12 46				14 59					18 48						
	d									12 48				15 01					18 50						
Morfa Mawddach	d									12x53				15x05					18x55						
Fairbourne	d									12 56				15 09					18 57						
Llwyngwril	d									13x04				15x15					19x05						
Tonfanau	d									13x11				15x22					19x12						
Tywyn	a									13 16				15 27					19 17						
	d									13 16				15 28					19 22						
Aberdovey	d									13 22				15 35					19 28						
Penhelig	d									13x26				15x37					19x32						
Aberystwyth	d		23p46			09 30			11 30			13 30			15 30			17 30			19 30		21 30		23 30
Borth	d		23p59			09 43			11 43			13 43			15 43			17 43			19 43		21 43		23 43
Dovey Junction [4]	d		00 10			09 54			11 54	13 36		13 54		15 49	15 54			17 54	19 42		19 54		21 54		23 54
Machynlleth [4]	a		00 17			10 03			12 03	13 45		14 03		15 59	16 03			18 03	19 52		20 03		22 04		00 04
	d					10 07			12 07			14 07		16 07				18 07			20 07				
Caersws	d					10 35			12 37			14 37		16 37				18 37			20 37				
Newtown (Powys)	d					10 45			12 46			14 46		16 46				18 46			20 46				
Welshpool	d					11 01			13 01			15 01		17 01				19 01			21 01			22 04	
Chester	d	22p28		08 08	09 22		11 31	12 21			13 31		15 31			17 31	18 24			19 26		21 26		22 22	
Wrexham General	a	22p44		08 26	09 38		11 47	12 38			13 47		15 47			17 47	18 40			19 42		21 42			
	d	22p44			09 38		11 48	12 38			13 48		15 48			17 48	18 41			19 42		21 44			
Ruabon	d	22p51			09 45		11 55	12 45			13 55		15 55			17 55	18 47			19 49		21 51			
Chirk	d	22p57			09 52		12 01	12 52			14 01		16 01			18 01	18 54			19 55		21 57			
Gobowen	d	23p03			09 57		12 07	12 57			14 07		16 07			18 07	18 59			20 01		22 02			
Shrewsbury	a	23p23			10 18	11 25	12 27	13 18	13 25		14 27	15 25	16 27	17 27		18 27	19 20	19 25		20 21	21 25	22 23			
Cardiff Central [7]	a							15 31									21 36								
Shrewsbury	d	23p26			10 20	11 40	12 31		13 31		14 31	15 33	16 40	17 33		18 31		19 31		20 23	21 31	22 23			
Wellington (Shropshire)	d	23p40			10 34	11 54	12 45		13 45		14 45	15 47	16 54	17 47		18 45		19 45		20 37	21 45	22 37			
Telford Central	d	23p47			10 40	12 00	12 51		13 51		14 51	15 53	17 00	17 53		18 51		19 51		20 44	21 51	22 45			
Cosford	d	23p57																		20 54		22 56			
Wolverhampton [7]	a	00 18			10 57	12 17	13 08		14 08		15 08	16 10	17 15	18 10		19 08		20 08		21 11	22 08	23 13			
Smethwick Galton Bdg L.L.	a																								
Tame Bridge Parkway	d																								
Birmingham New Street [12]	a				11 14	12 33	13 24		14 24		15 25	16 26	17 35	18 28		19 27		20 24		21 29	22 28				
Birmingham International ✈	a				11 32	12 56	13 56		14 56		15 56	16 56	17 55	18 56		19 56		20 56		21 56	22 56				
Leamington Spa [8]	a																								
Banbury	a																								
London Marylebone [10] ⊖	a																								

A 🛒 from Machynlleth

For connections to Crewe and Manchester Piccadilly please refer to Table 131

For connections to London Euston please refer to Table 66

Table 75

Sundays

from 18 September

Pwllheli, Barmouth, Aberystwyth and Chester - Shrewsbury and Birmingham

		AW	AW	AW	AW	AW	AW	AW	AW	AW	AW	AW	AW	AW	AW	AW	AW	AW	AW	AW	AW	AW	AW
																■							
		◇			◇	◇	◇	◇	◇	◇	◇	◇	◇ A	◇	◇		◇	◇	◇	◇			
						🍴	🍴		🍴	🍴	🍴	🍴	🍴	🍴		🍴	🍴						
Pwllheli	d												13 48										
Abererch	d												13x51										
Penychain	d												13x54										
Criccieth	d												14 02										
Porthmadog	a												14 10										
	d												14 12										
Minffordd	d												14 16										
Penrhyndeudraeth	d												14 20										
Llandecwyn	d												14x22										
Talsarnau	d												14x24										
Tygwyn	d												14x27										
Harlech	a												14 32										
	d												14 34										
Llandanwg	d												14x38										
Pensarn	d												14x40										
Llanbedr	d												14x42										
Dyffryn Ardudwy	d												14x46										
Talybont	d												14x49										
Llanaber	d												14x54										
Barmouth	a												14 59										
	d												15 01										
Morfa Mawddach	d												15x05										
Fairbourne	d												15 09										
Llwyngwril	d												15x15										
Tonfanau	d												15x22										
Tywyn	a												15 27										
	d												15 28										
Aberdovey	d												15 35										
Penhelig	d												15x37										
Aberystwyth	d		23p46			09 30			11 30		13 30			15 30			17 30		19 30		21 30		23 30
Borth	d		23p59			09 43			11 43		13 43			15 43			17 43		19 43		21 43		23 43
Dovey Junction 4	d		00 10			09 54			11 54		13 54		15 49	15 54			17 54		19 54		21 54		23 54
Machynlleth 4	a		00 17			10 03			12 03		14 03		15 59	16 03			18 03		20 03		22 04		00 04
	d					10 07			12 07		14 07		16 07				18 07		20 07				
Caersws	d					10 35			12 37		14 37		16 37				18 37		20 37				
Newtown (Powys)	d					10 45			12 46		14 46		16 46				18 46		20 46				
Welshpool	d					11 01			13 01		15 01		17 01				19 01		21 01				
Chester	d	22p28		08 08	09 22		11 31	12 21		13 31		15 31			17 31	18 24		19 26		21 24		22 04	
Wrexham General	a	22p44		08 26	09 38		11 47	12 38		13 47		15 47			17 47	18 40		19 42		21 41		22 22	
	d	22p44			09 38		11 48	12 38		13 48		15 48			17 48	18 41		19 42		21 43			
Ruabon	d	22p51			09 45		11 55	12 45		13 55		15 55			17 55	18 47		19 49		21 50			
Chirk	d	22p57			09 52		12 01	12 52		14 01		16 01			18 01	18 54		19 55		21 56			
Gobowen	d	23p03			09 57		12 07	12 57		14 07		16 07			18 07	18 59		20 01		22 01			
Shrewsbury	a	23p23			10 18	11 25	12 27	13 18	13 25	14 27	15 25	16 27	17 27		18 27	19 20	19 25	20 21	21 25	22 22			
Cardiff Central 7	a							15 31								21 36							
Shrewsbury	d	23p26			10 20	11 40	12 31		13 31	14 31	15 33	16 40	17 33		18 31		19 31	20 23	21 31	22 23			
Wellington (Shropshire)	d	23p40			10 34	11 54	12 45		13 45	14 45	15 47	16 54	17 47		18 45		19 45	20 37	21 45	22 37			
Telford Central	d	23p47			10 40	12 00	12 51		13 51	14 51	15 53	17 00	17 53		18 51		19 51	20 44	21 51	22 46			
Cosford	d	23p57																20 54		22 56			
Wolverhampton 7 ⇌	a	00 18			10 57	12 17	13 08		14 08	15 10	16 10	17 15	18 10		19 10		20 08	21 11	22 08	23 16			
Smethwick Galton Bdg L.L.	a																						
Tame Bridge Parkway	d																						
Birmingham New Street 12	a				11 14	12 33	13 25		14 24	15 26	16 26	17 35	18 28		19 28		20 24	21 29	22 28				
Birmingham International ✈	a				11 32	12 57	13 55		14 56	15 55	16 56	17 55	18 56		19 55		20 56	21 56	22 56				
Leamington Spa 8	a																						
Banbury	a																						
London Marylebone 10 ⊖	a																						

A 🍴 from Machynlleth

For connections to Crewe and Manchester Piccadilly please refer to Table 131

For connections to London Euston please refer to Table 66

Network Diagram for Tables 78, 79, 84, 85, 86

DM-22/08
Design BAJS

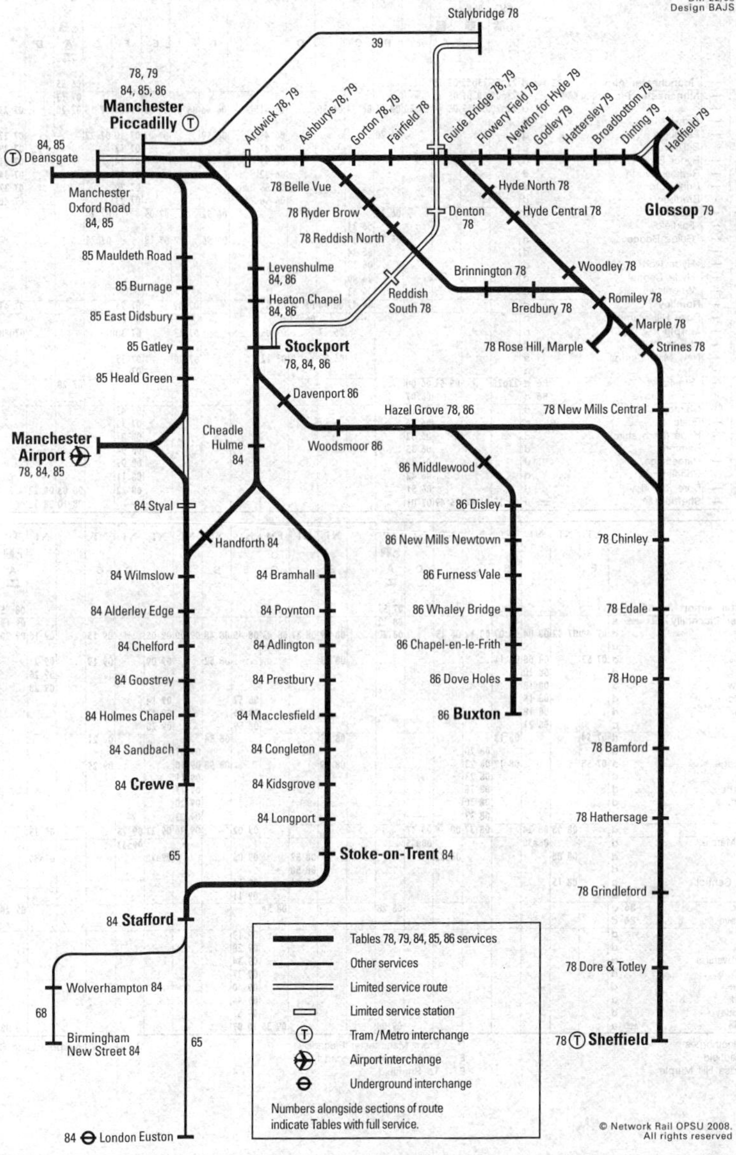

© Network Rail OPSU 2008.
All rights reserved

Table 78

Mondays to Fridays

until 30 September

Manchester Airport and Manchester Romiley, Marple, Chinley and Sheffield

Miles	Miles	Miles			TP MO ◇1	TP MX ◇1	TP ◇1 A	NT	NT B	NT C	NT	NT D	NT		NT E	NT	NT E	NT F	NT E	TP ◇1 A	NT D	NT	NT		EM ◇ G
—	—	—	**Manchester Airport** 85	d	22p55	23p52	05 15													06 55					
0	0	—	**Manchester Piccadilly 10**	a	23p09	00 09	05 33													07 13					
—	—	—		d	23p20	00 15	05 44	05 50	06 16	06 24	06 30		06 41		06 46	06 57	07 03	07 06	07 18	07 20		07 23	07 39		07 42
0½	0½	—	Ardwick	d																					
1½	1½	—	Ashburys	d					06 20				06 45		06 50		07 07	07 10	07 22			07 27			
2½	—	—	Belle Vue	d									06 47					07 12				07 29			
2¾	—	—	Ryder Brow	d									06 49					07 14				07 31			
3¾	—	—	Reddish North	d									06 52					07 17				07 34			
5½	—	—	Brinnington	d									06 55					07 20				07 37			
6½	—	—	Bredbury	d									06 58					07 23				07 40			
—	2½	—	Gorton	d					06 22						06 52		07 09		07 24						
—	3½	—	Fairfield	d						06 31													07 46		
—	4¾	—	Guide Bridge	a					06 26	06 34					06 56		07 13		07 28				07 49		
—	—	—		d						06 34													07 49		
—	6½	—	Hyde North	d						06 38													07 53		
—	7¾	—	Hyde Central	d						06 40													07 55		
—	9¼	—	Woodley	d						06 43		←											07 58		
7½	10½	—	**Romiley**	d						06 47	06 44	06 47	07 02			07 09		07 26				07 43	08 02		
—	12½	—	Rose Hill Marple	d						↪		06a53											08a08		
9	—	—	**Marple**	d							06 47		07 05			07 13		07 30				07a48			
11¼	—	—	Strines	d																					
12¾	—	—	New Mills Central	a							06 55		07 12			07 20		07 35							
—	—	—		d														07 39							
—	—	—	Stockport 86	d	23p28		05 52	06 00												07 28					07 54
—	—	0	Hazel Grove 86	d				06 07																	
16½	—	8½	**Chinley**	d				06 18										07 47							
22	—	—	Edale	d				06 26										07 55							
27¼	—	—	Hope (Derbyshire)	d				06 32										08 01							
29	—	—	Bamford	d				06 35										08 04							
30¾	—	—	Hathersage	d				06 39										08 09							
32¼	—	—	Grindleford	d				06 42										08 11			←				
37¾	—	—	Dore & Totley	d				06 51										08 22		08 03	08 22				08 28
42	—	—	**Sheffield 7**	a	00 15	01 06	06 49	07 01										↪		08 10	08 32				08 36

		NT E	NT	NT	NT E	NT C	NT	NT D	TP ◇1 A		NT E	NT	EM ◇ G	NT	NT B	NT C	NT	NT D	NT B		NT	TP ◇1 A	NT	EM ◇ G	NT
Manchester Airport 85	d								07 53													08 55			
Manchester Piccadilly 10	a								08 12													09 13			
	d	07 48	07 52	08 04	08 07	08 12	08 15		08 20		08 29	08 37	08 43	08 45	08 48	09 00	09 05		09 15		09 18	09 20	09 36	09 43	09 45
Ardwick	d																								
Ashburys	d	07 52		08 08	08 11						08 33				08 52		09 09		09 19		09 23				
Belle Vue	d			08 10																	09 26				
Ryder Brow	d			08 12																	09 28				
Reddish North	d			08 15										08 52			09 14								09 52
Brinnington	d			08 18										08 56			09 17								09 56
Bredbury	d			08 21										08 59			09 20								09 59
Gorton	d	07 54			08 13						08 35				08 54				09 21						
Fairfield	d					08 20										09 07							09 43		
Guide Bridge	a	07 58			08 17	08 23					08 39				08 58	09 10			09 25				09 46		
	d					08 23										09 11							09 46		
Hyde North	d					08 28										09 17							09 50		
Hyde Central	d					08 30										09 20							09 52		
Woodley	d					08 33		←								09 23		←					09 55		
Romiley	d		08 05	08 24		08 37	08 29	08 37						09 02		09 26	09 23	09 26			09 35		09 59		10 02
Rose Hill Marple	d			08a30		↪		08a45								↪		09a33					10a05		
Marple	d		08 08				08a33					08 52		09 06			09a28				09a40				10 06
Strines	d											08 56													10 10
New Mills Central	a		08 15									09 01		09 11											10 15
	d													09 11											
Stockport 86	d								08 28				08 54									09 28		09 54	
Hazel Grove 86	d																								
Chinley	d													09 19											
Edale	d													09 28											
Hope (Derbyshire)	d													09 34											
Bamford	d													09 37											
Hathersage	d													09 40											
Grindleford	d													09 44											
Dore & Totley	d													09 57											
Sheffield 7	a								09 08				09 35	10 07								10 08		10 35	

A To Cleethorpes
B To Hadfield
C To Rose Hill Marple
D From Manchester Piccadilly
E To Manchester Piccadilly
F To Sheffield
G From Liverpool Lime Street to Norwich

Manchester Airport and Manchester Romiley, Marple, Chinley and Sheffield

		NT A	NT	NT A	NT		TP ◇1 B	NT	EM ◇ C	NT	NT A	NT	NT A	TP ◇1 B	NT		NT	EM ◇ C	NT	NT A	NT	NT A	TP ◇1 B	NT	NT
Manchester Airport 85 ✈	d						09 55							10 55									11 55		
Manchester Piccadilly 10	a						10 13							11 13									12 13		
	d	09 48	10 03	10 15	10 18		10 20	10 36	10 43	10 45	10 48	11 03	11 18	11 20	11 23		11 36	11 43	11 45	11 48	12 03	12 18	12 20	12 23	12 36
Ardwick	d																								
Ashburys	d	09 52	10 07	10 19							10 52	11 07	11 22							11 52	12 07	12 22			
Belle Vue	d		10 09									11 09									12 09				
Ryder Brow	d		10 11									11 11									12 11				
Reddish North	d		10 14							10 52		11 14							11 52		12 14				
Brinnington	d		10 17							10 56		11 17							11 56		12 17				
Bredbury	d		10 20							10 59		11 20							11 59		12 20				
Gorton	d	09 54		10 21							10 54		11 24							11 54		12 24			
Fairfield	d							10 43									11 43								12 43
Guide Bridge	a	09 58		10 25				10 46			10 58		11 28				11 46			11 58		12 28			12 46
	d							10 46									11 46								12 46
Hyde North	d							10 50									11 50								12 50
Hyde Central	d							10 52									11 52								12 52
Woodley	d							10 55									11 55								12 55
Romiley	d		10 23		10b37			10 59		11 02		11 23			11 37		11 59		12 02		12 23			12 37	12 59
Rose Hill Marple	d				10a42			11a05							11a43		12a05							12a43	13a05
Marple	d		10 27							11 06		11 27							12 06		12 27				
Strines	d																		12 10						
New Mills Central	a		10 34							11 11		11 34							12 15		12 34				
	d									11 11															
Stockport 86	d						10 28		10 54					11 28				11 54					12 28		
Hazel Grove 86	d																								
Chinley	d									11 19															
Edale	d									11 28															
Hope (Derbyshire)	d									11 34															
Bamford	d									11 37															
Hathersage	d									11 40															
Grindleford	d									11 44															
Dore & Totley	d									11 53															
Sheffield 7	a						11 08		11 34	12 03				12 08				12 35					13 08		

			EM ◇ C	NT	NT A	NT	NT A	TP ◇1 B	NT	NT	EM ◇ C		NT	NT A	NT	NT A	TP ◇1 B	NT	NT	EM ◇ D	NT		NT A	NT	NT A
Manchester Airport 85 ✈	d							12 55									13 55								
Manchester Piccadilly 10	a							13 13									14 13								
	d		12 43	12 45	12 48	13 03	13 18	13 20	13 23	13 36	13 43		13 45	13 48	14 03	14 18	14 20	14 23	14 36	14 43	14 45		14 48	15 03	15 18
Ardwick	d																								
Ashburys	d				12 52	13 07	13 22							13 52	14 07	14 22							14 52	15 07	15 22
Belle Vue	d					13 09									14 09									15 09	
Ryder Brow	d					13 11									14 11									15 11	
Reddish North	d			12 52		13 14							13 52		14 14						14 52			15 14	
Brinnington	d			12 56		13 17							13 56		14 17						14 56			15 17	
Bredbury	d			12 59		13 20							13 59		14 20						14 59			15 20	
Gorton	d				12 54		13 24							13 54		14 24							14 54		15 24
Fairfield	d									13 43									14 43						
Guide Bridge	a				12 58		13 28			13 46				13 58		14 28			14 46				14 58		15 28
	d									13 46									14 46						
Hyde North	d									13 50									14 50						
Hyde Central	d									13 52									14 52						
Woodley	d									13 55									14 55						
Romiley	d			13 02		13 23			13 37	13 59			14 02		14 23			14 37	14 59		15 02			15 23	
Rose Hill Marple	d								13a43	14a05								14a43	15a05						
Marple	d			13 06		13 27							14 06		14 27						15 06			15 27	
Strines	d												14 10												
New Mills Central	a			13 11		13 34							14 15		14 34						15 11			15 34	
	d			13 11																	15 11				
Stockport 86	d		12 54					13 28			13 54						14 28			14 54					
Hazel Grove 86	d																								
Chinley	d			13 19																	15 19				
Edale	d			13 28																	15 28				
Hope (Derbyshire)	d			13 34																	15 34				
Bamford	d			13 37																	15 37				
Hathersage	d			13 40																	15 40				
Grindleford	d			13 44																	15 44				
Dore & Totley	d			13 57																	15 58				
Sheffield 7	a		13 35	14 04				14 08			14 35						15 08			15 35	16 04				

A To Hadfield
B To Cleethorpes
C From Liverpool Lime Street to Norwich
D From Liverpool Lime Street to Nottingham
b Arr. 1030

Table 78

Mondays to Fridays

until 30 September

Manchester Airport and Manchester Romiley, Marple, Chinley and Sheffield

		TP	NT	NT	EM	NT	NT		NT	NT	NT	TP	NT	NT	EM	NT	NT		NT	NT	NT	NT	TP	NT	NT
		◇1 A			◇ B		C				C	◇1 A		C	◇ B				C		C	D	◇1 A	E	
Manchester Airport 85	d	14 55										15 55											16 55		
Manchester Piccadilly 10	a	15 13										16 13											17 13		
	d	15 20	15 23	15 36	15 43	15 45	15 48		16 03	16 06	16 15	16 20	16 23	16 36	16 43	16 45	16 48		16 59	17 03	17 15	17 18	17 20		17 21
Ardwick	d																			17 07					
Ashburys	d						15 52		16 07		16 19			16 40		16 49	16 52		17 03	17 09	17 19				
Belle Vue	d								16 09							16 51				17 12					
Ryder Brow	d								16 11							16 53				17 14					
Reddish North	d					15 52			16 14				16 30			16 56				17 16					
Brinnington	d					15 56			16 17				16 34			16 59				17 20					
Bredbury	d					15 59			16 20				16 37			17 02				17 23		17 30			
Gorton	d						15 54				16 21			16 42					17 05		17 21				
Fairfield	d			15 43						16 13							16 56								
Guide Bridge	a			15 46			15 58			16 16	16 25			16 46			16 59		17 10		17 25				17 30
	d			15 46						16 16							16 59								17 30
Hyde North	d			15 50						16 20							17 03								17 34
Hyde Central	d			15 52						16 22							17 05								17 36
Woodley	d			15 55						16 25							17 08								17 39
Romiley	d		15 37	15 59		16 02			16 23	16 29			16 40			17 05	17 13			17 27		17 33			17 43
Rose Hill Marple	d		15a43	16a05						16a36							17a20								17a49
Marple	d					16 06			16 27				16a44			17 09				17a31		17 37			
Strines	d					16 10																17 41			
New Mills Central	a					16 13			16 34							17 16						17 45			
	d					16 13																17 45			
Stockport 86	d	15 28			15 54							16 28			16 54								17 28		
Hazel Grove 86	d																								
Chinley	d					16 21									17 09							17 51	17 43		
Edale	d					16 30																18 00			
Hope (Derbyshire)	d					16 36																18 06			
Bamford	d					16 39																18 09			
Hathersage	d					16 42																18 13			
Grindleford	d					16 46																18 16		←	
Dore & Totley	d					16 54									17 30							18 26	18 05	18 26	
Sheffield 7	a	16 08			16 34	17 03						17 08			17 37							→	18 15	18 37	

		NT	NT		EM	NT	NT	NT	NT	NT	TP	NT	NT		EM	NT	NT	NT	TP	NT	NT	EM	NT		NT
			C		◇ F		C			G	◇1 A				◇ B		G		◇1 A	G		◇ F			G
Manchester Airport 85	d										17 55								18 55						
Manchester Piccadilly 10	a										18 13								19 13						
	d	17 32	17 37		17 43	17 48	17 59	18 03	18 06	18 15	18 20	18 22	18 36		18 43	18 45	18 48	19 00	19 18	19 18	19 23	19 43	19 45		19 48
Ardwick	d								18 09																
Ashburys	d	17 36	17 41			17 52	18 03	18 07	18 11	18 19							18 52	19 04		19 22			19 49		19 52
Belle Vue	d	17 38						18 09										19 06					19 51		
Ryder Brow	d	17 40						18 11										19 08					19 53		
Reddish North	d	17 43				17 57		18 14								18 52		19 11					19 56		
Brinnington	d	17 46				18 00		18 17								18 56		19 14					19 59		
Bredbury	d	17 49				18 04		18 20								18 59		19 17					20 02		
Gorton	d		17 43				18 05			18 21							18 54			19 24					19 54
Fairfield	d								18 15				18 43												
Guide Bridge	a		17 47				18 09		18 18	18 25			18 46				18 58			19 28					19 58
	d								18 18				18 46												
Hyde North	d								18 22				18 50												
Hyde Central	d								18 25				18 52												
Woodley	d								18 28				18 55												
Romiley	d	17 53				18 07		18 23	18 31			18 35	18 59			19 02		19 20			19 38		20 05		
Rose Hill Marple	d								18a37				19a05												
Marple	d	17 57				18 11		18a28				18 39				19 06		19a25			19a43		20 09		
Strines	d	18 01				18 15						18 43											20 13		
New Mills Central	a	18 04				18 19						18 48				19 11							20 18		
	d					18 19										19 11									
Stockport 86	d				17 54						18 28				18 54				19 26			19 54			
Hazel Grove 86	d																								
Chinley	d				18 09	18a27										19 19									
Edale	d															19 28									
Hope (Derbyshire)	d															19 34									
Bamford	d															19 37									
Hathersage	d															19 40									
Grindleford	d															19 44									
Dore & Totley	d				18 34						19 03					19 53			20 01						
Sheffield 7	a				18 41						19 09				19 33	20 03			20 08			20 36			

A To Cleethorpes
B From Liverpool Lime Street to Norwich
C To Manchester Piccadilly
D To Sheffield
E From Manchester Piccadilly
F From Liverpool Lime Street to Nottingham
G To Hadfield

Manchester Airport and Manchester Romiley, Marple, Chinley and Sheffield

		TP FO ◇1 A	TP FX ◇1	NT	EM ◇ B	NT	NT C	TP ◇1 A	NT	NT C	TP ◇1	EM ◇ B	NT	NT C	NT	NT D	TP ◇1
Manchester Airport 85 ✈	d	19 55	19 55					20 47			21 47						23 52
Manchester Piccadilly 10	a	20 13	20 13					21 13			22 13						00 09
	d	20 20	20 20	20 36	20 43	20 45	20 48	21 20	21 45	21 48	22 20	22 28	22 45	22 48	23 24	23 27	00 15
Ardwick	d																
Ashburys	d						20 52		21 49	21 52			22 49	22 52	23 28	23 31	
Belle Vue	d								21 51				22 51		23 30		
Ryder Brow	d								21 53				22 53		23 32		
Reddish North	d					20 52			21 56				22 56		23 35		
Brinnington	d					20 56			21 59				22 59		23 38		
Bredbury	d					20 59			22 02				23 02		23 41		
Gorton	d						20 54			21 54				22 54		23 33	
Fairfield	d			20 43													
Guide Bridge	a			20 46			20 58			21 58				22 58		23 37	
	d			20 46													
Hyde North	d			20 50													
Hyde Central	d			20 52													
Woodley	d			20 55													
Romiley	d			20 59		21 02			22 05				23 05		23 44		
Rose Hill Marple	d			21a05													
Marple	d					21 06			22 09				23 09		23 48		
Strines	d								22 13				23 13		23 52		
New Mills Central	a					21 11			22 18				23 18		23 57		
	d					21 11											
Stockport 86	d	20 28	20 28		20 54			21 28			22 28	22 37					
Hazel Grove 86	d																
Chinley	d					21 19						22 53					
Edale	d					21 28						23 02					
Hope (Derbyshire)	d					21 34						23 08					
Bamford	d					21 37						23 11					
Hathersage	d					21 40						23 15					
Grindleford	d					21 44						23 19					
Dore & Totley	d	21 03	21 03			21 52						23 28					
Sheffield 7 ⇌	a	21 09	21 11		21 35	22 03		22 08			23 13	23 35					01 06

Mondays to Fridays
from 3 October

		TP MO ◇1	TP MX ◇1	TP ◇1 A	NT	NT E	NT F	NT	NT G	NT	NT E	NT	NT E	NT H	NT E	TP ◇1 A 🚲	NT G	NT	NT	EM ◇ I	NT E	NT	NT
Manchester Airport 85 ✈	d	22p55	23p52	05 15												06 55							
Manchester Piccadilly 10	a	23p09	00 09	05 33												07 13							
	d	23p20	00 15	05 44	05 50	06 13	06 24	06 30		06 41	06 46	06 57	07 03	07 06	07 18	07 20		07 23	07 39	07 42	07 47	07 52	08 04
Ardwick	d																						
Ashburys	d					06 17				06 45			07 07	07 10	07 22			07 27					08 08
Belle Vue	d									06 47				07 12				07 29					08 10
Ryder Brow	d									06 49				07 14				07 31					08 12
Reddish North	d									06 52				07 17				07 34					08 15
Brinnington	d									06 55				07 20				07 37					08 18
Bredbury	d									06 58				07 23				07 40					08 21
Gorton	d					06 19							07 09		07 24								
Fairfield	d						06 31												07 46				
Guide Bridge	a					06 23	06 34				06 54		07 13		07 28				07 49		07 55		
	d						06 34												07 49				
Hyde North	d						06 38												07 53				
Hyde Central	d						06 40												07 55				
Woodley	d						06 43		←										07 58				
Romiley	d						06 47	06 44	06 47	07 02		07 09		07 26				07 43	08 02			08 05	08 24
Rose Hill Marple	d						↦		06a53										08a08				08a30
Marple	d							06 47		07 05		07 13		07 30				07a48				08 08	
Strines	d																						
New Mills Central	a							06 55		07 12		07 20		07 35								08 15	
	d													07 39									
Stockport 86	d	23p28		05 52	06 00											07 28				07 54			
Hazel Grove 86	d				06 07																		
Chinley	d				06 18									07 47									
Edale	d				06 26									07 55									
Hope (Derbyshire)	d				06 32									08 01									
Bamford	d				06 35									08 04									
Hathersage	d				06 39									08 09									
Grindleford	d				06 42									08 11			←						
Dore & Totley	d				06 51									08 22		08 03	08 22			08 28			
Sheffield 7 ⇌	a	00 15	01 06	06 49	07 01									↦		08 10	08 32			08 36			

A To Cleethorpes
B From Liverpool Lime Street to Nottingham
C To Hadfield
D To Glossop
E To Manchester Piccadilly
F To Rose Hill Marple
G From Manchester Piccadilly
H To Sheffield
I From Liverpool Lime Street to Norwich

Manchester Airport and Manchester Romiley, Marple, Chinley and Sheffield

		NT	NT	NT	NT	TP	NT	NT	EM	NT	NT	NT	NT	NT	NT	NT	TP	NT	EM	NT	NT	NT	NT
						◇1			◇								◇1		◇				
		A	B		C	D	A		E		A	B		C	A		D		E		A		A
						🚲											🚲						
Manchester Airport 85 ✈	d					07 53											08 55						
Manchester Piccadilly 10	a					08 12											09 13						
	d	08 07	08 12	08 15		08 20	08 29	08 37	08 43	08 45	08 48	09 00	09 05		09 15	09 18	09 20	09 36	09 43	09 45	09 48	10 03	10 15
Ardwick	d																						
Ashburys	d	08 11									08 52		09 09		09 19	09 23					09 52	10 07	10 19
Belle Vue	d															09 26						10 09	
Ryder Brow	d															09 28						10 11	
Reddish North	d									08 52			09 14							09 52		10 14	
Brinnington	d									08 56			09 17							09 56		10 17	
Bredbury	d									08 59			09 20							09 59		10 20	
Gorton	d	08 13									08 54				09 21						09 54		10 21
Fairfield	d		08 20									09 07						09 43					
Guide Bridge	a	08 17	08 23				08 37				08 58	09 10			09 25			09 46			09 58		10 25
	d		08 23									09 11						09 46					
Hyde North	d		08 28									09 17						09 50					
Hyde Central	d		08 30									09 20						09 52					
Woodley	d		08 33		←							09 23		←				09 55					
Romiley	d		08 37	08 29	08 37					09 02		09 26	09 23	09 26		09 35		09 59		10 02		10 23	
Rose Hill Marple	d		→		08a45							→		09a33				10a05					
Marple	d			08a33				08 52		09 06			09a28			09a40				10 06		10 27	
Strines	d							08 56												10 10			
New Mills Central	a							09 01		09 11										10 15		10 34	
	d									09 11													
Stockport 86	d					08 28			08 54								09 28		09 54				
Hazel Grove 86	d																						
Chinley	d									09 19													
Edale	d									09 28													
Hope (Derbyshire)	d									09 34													
Bamford	d									09 37													
Hathersage	d									09 40													
Grindleford	d									09 44													
Dore & Totley	d									09 57													
Sheffield 7	a					09 08			09 35	10 07							10 08		10 35				

		NT	TP	NT	EM	NT	NT	NT	NT	TP	NT	NT	EM	NT	NT	NT	NT	TP	NT	NT	EM	NT
			◇1		◇					◇1			◇					◇1			◇	
			D		E		A		A	D			E		A		A	D			E	
			🚲							🚲								🚲				
Manchester Airport 85 ✈	d		09 55							10 55								11 55				
Manchester Piccadilly 10	a		10 13							11 13								12 13				
	d	10 18	10 20	10 36	10 43	10 45	10 48	11 03	11 18	11 20	11 23	11 36	11 43	11 45	11 48	12 03	12 18	12 20	12 23	12 36	12 43	12 45
Ardwick	d																					
Ashburys	d						10 52	11 07	11 22						11 52	12 07	12 22					
Belle Vue	d							11 09								12 09						
Ryder Brow	d							11 11								12 11						
Reddish North	d					10 52		11 14						11 52		12 14						12 52
Brinnington	d					10 56		11 17						11 56		12 17						12 56
Bredbury	d					10 59		11 20						11 59		12 20						12 59
Gorton	d						10 54		11 24						11 54		12 24					
Fairfield	d			10 43								11 43								12 43		
Guide Bridge	a			10 46			10 58		11 28			11 46			11 58		12 28			12 46		
	d			10 46								11 46								12 46		
Hyde North	d			10 50								11 50								12 50		
Hyde Central	d			10 52								11 52								12 52		
Woodley	d			10 55								11 55								12 55		
Romiley	d	10b37		10 59		11 02		11 23			11 37	11 59		12 02		12 23			12 37	12 59		13 02
Rose Hill Marple	d	10a42		11a05							11a43	12a05							12a43	13a05		
Marple	d					11 06		11 27						12 06		12 27						13 06
Strines	d													12 10								
New Mills Central	a					11 11		11 34						12 15		12 34						13 11
	d					11 11																13 11
Stockport 86	d		10 28		10 54					11 28			11 54					12 28			12 54	
Hazel Grove 86	d																					
Chinley	d					11 19																13 19
Edale	d					11 28																13 28
Hope (Derbyshire)	d					11 34																13 34
Bamford	d					11 37																13 37
Hathersage	d					11 40																13 40
Grindleford	d					11 44																13 44
Dore & Totley	d					11 53																13 57
Sheffield 7	a		11 08		11 34	12 03				12 08			12 35					13 08			13 35	14 04

A To Manchester Piccadilly
B To Rose Hill Marple
C From Manchester Piccadilly
D To Cleethorpes
E From Liverpool Lime Street to Norwich
b Arr. 1030

Table 78

Mondays to Fridays

from 3 October

Manchester Airport and Manchester Romiley, Marple, Chinley and Sheffield

		NT	NT	NT	TP	NT	NT	EM		NT	NT	NT	NT	TP	NT	NT	EM	NT		NT	NT	NT	TP	NT	NT
					◇1			◇						◇1			◇						◇1		
		A		A	B			C			A		A	B			C			A		A	B		
					🚲									🚲									🚲		
Manchester Airport 85 ✈	d				12 55									13 55									14 55		
Manchester Piccadilly 10 🚢	a				13 13									14 13									15 13		
	d	12 48	13 03	13 18	13 20	13 23	13 36	13 43		13 45	13 48	14 03	14 18	14 20	14 23	14 36	14 43	14 45		14 48	15 03	15 18	15 20	15 23	15 36
Ardwick	d																								
Ashburys	d	12 52	13 07	13 22							13 52	14 07	14 22							14 52	15 07	15 22			
Belle Vue	d		13 09									14 09									15 09				
Ryder Brow	d		13 11									14 11									15 11				
Reddish North	d		13 14							13 52		14 14						14 52			15 14				
Brinnington	d		13 17							13 56		14 17						14 56			15 17				
Bredbury	d		13 20							13 59		14 20						14 59			15 20				
Gorton	d	12 54		13 24							13 54		14 24							14 54		15 24			
Fairfield	d						13 43									14 43									15 43
Guide Bridge	a	12 58		13 28			13 46				13 58		14 28			14 46				14 58		15 28			15 46
	d						13 46									14 46									15 46
Hyde North	d						13 50									14 50									15 50
Hyde Central	d						13 52									14 52									15 52
Woodley	d						13 55									14 55									15 55
Romiley	d		13 23			13 37	13 59			14 02		14 23			14 37	14 59		15 02			15 23			15 37	15 59
Rose Hill Marple	d					13a43	14a05								14a43	15a05								15a43	16a05
Marple	d		13 27							14 06		14 27						15 06			15 27				
Strines	d									14 10															
New Mills Central	a		13 34							14 15		14 34						15 11			15 34				
	d																	15 11							
Stockport 86	d				13 28			13 54						14 28			14 54						15 28		
Hazel Grove 86	d																								
Chinley	d																	15 19							
Edale	d																	15 28							
Hope (Derbyshire)	d																	15 34							
Bamford	d																	15 37							
Hathersage	d																	15 40							
Grindleford	d																	15 44							
Dore & Totley	d																	15 58							
Sheffield 7 🚢	a				14 08			14 35						15 08			15 35	16 04					16 08		

		EM	NT	NT		NT	NT	NT	TP	NT	NT	EM	NT	NT		NT	NT	NT	NT	TP	NT	NT	NT	NT	
		◇							◇1			◇								◇1					
		C		A				A	B		A	C				A		A	D	B	E			A	
									🚲											🚲					
Manchester Airport 85 ✈	d								15 55											16 55					
Manchester Piccadilly 10 🚢	a								16 13											17 13					
	d	15 43	15 45	15 48		16 03	16 06	16 15	16 20	16 23	16 36	16 43	16 45	16 48		16 59	17 03	17 15	17 18	17 20		17 21	17 32	17 37	
Ardwick	d																17 07								
Ashburys	d			15 52		16 07		16 19			16 40		16 49	16 52		17 03	17 09	17 19					17 36	17 41	
Belle Vue	d					16 09							16 51				17 12						17 38		
Ryder Brow	d					16 11							16 53				17 14						17 40		
Reddish North	d		15 52			16 14				16 30			16 56				17 16						17 43		
Brinnington	d		15 56			16 17				16 34			16 59				17 20						17 46		
Bredbury	d		15 59			16 20				16 37			17 02				17 23		17 30				17 49		
Gorton	d			15 54				16 21			16 42					17 05		17 21						17 43	
Fairfield	d						16 13							16 56											
Guide Bridge	a			15 58			16 16	16 25			16 46			16 59		17 10		17 25				17 30		17 47	
	d						16 16							16 59								17 30			
Hyde North	d						16 20							17 03								17 34			
Hyde Central	d						16 22							17 05								17 36			
Woodley	d						16 25							17 08								17 39			
Romiley	d		16 02			16 23	16 29			16 40			17 05	17 13			17 27		17 33			17 43	17 53		
Rose Hill Marple	d						16a36							17a20								17a49			
Marple	d		16 06			16 27				16a44			17 09				17a31		17 37				17 57		
Strines	d		16 10																17 41				18 01		
New Mills Central	a		16 13			16 34							17 16						17 45				18 04		
	d		16 13																17 45						
Stockport 86	d	15 54							16 28			16 54								17 28					
Hazel Grove 86	d																								
Chinley	d		16 21									17 09							17 51	17 43					
Edale	d		16 30																18 00						
Hope (Derbyshire)	d		16 36																18 06						
Bamford	d		16 39																18 09						
Hathersage	d		16 42																18 13						
Grindleford	d		16 46																18 16		←				
Dore & Totley	d		16 54									17 30							18 26	18 05	18 26				
Sheffield 7 🚢	a	16 34	17 03						17 08			17 37							→	18 15	18 37				

A To Manchester Piccadilly
B To Cleethorpes
C From Liverpool Lime Street to Norwich
D To Sheffield
E From Manchester Piccadilly

Table 78

Mondays to Fridays

from 3 October

Manchester Airport and Manchester Romiley, Marple, Chinley and Sheffield

		EM	NT	NT	NT	NT	NT	TP	NT	NT	EM	NT	NT	NT	TP	NT	NT	EM	NT	NT	TP FO	TP FX	NT
		◇ A		B			C	◇1 D (bicycle symbol)			◇ E		C		◇1 D	C		◇ A		C	◇1 D	◇1	
Manchester Airport 85 ✈	d							17 55							18 55						19 55	19 55	
Manchester Piccadilly 10	a							18 13							19 13						20 13	20 13	
	d	17 43	17 48	17 59	18 03	18 06	18 15	18 20	18 22	18 36	18 43	18 45	18 48	19 00	19 18	19 18	19 23	19 43	19 45	19 48	20 20	20 20	20 36
Ardwick	d					18 09																	
Ashburys	d		17 52	18 03	18 07	18 11	18 19						18 52	19 04		19 22			19 49	19 52			
Belle Vue	d				18 09									19 06					19 51				
Ryder Brow	d				18 11									19 08					19 53				
Reddish North	d		17 57		18 14							18 52		19 11					19 56				
Brinnington	d		18 00		18 17							18 56		19 14					19 59				
Bredbury	d		18 04		18 20							18 59		19 17					20 02				
Gorton	d			18 05			18 21						18 54			19 24				19 54			
Fairfield	d					18 15				18 43													20 43
Guide Bridge	a			18 09		18 18	18 25			18 46			18 58			19 28				19 58			20 46
	d					18 18				18 46													20 46
Hyde North	d					18 22				18 50													20 50
Hyde Central	d					18 25				18 52													20 52
Woodley	d					18 28				18 55													20 55
Romiley	d		18 07		18 23	18 31			18 35	18 59		19 02		19 20			19 38		20 05				20 59
Rose Hill Marple	d					18a37				19a05													21a05
Marple	d		18 11		18a28				18 39			19 06		19a25			19a43		20 09				
Strines	d		18 15						18 43										20 13				
New Mills Central	a		18 19						18 48			19 11							20 18				
	d		18 19									19 11											
Stockport 86	d	17 54						18 28			18 54				19 26			19 54			20 28	20 28	
Hazel Grove 86	d																						
Chinley	d	18 09	18a27									19 19											
Edale	d											19 28											
Hope (Derbyshire)	d											19 34											
Bamford	d											19 37											
Hathersage	d											19 40											
Grindleford	d											19 44											
Dore & Totley	d	18 34						19 03				19 53			20 01						21 03	21 03	
Sheffield 7	a	18 41						19 09			19 33	20 03			20 08			20 36			21 09	21 11	

		EM	NT	NT	TP	NT	NT	TP	EM	NT	NT	NT	NT	TP
		◇ A		C	◇1 D		C	◇1	◇ A		C		F	◇1
Manchester Airport 85 ✈	d				20 47			21 47						23 52
Manchester Piccadilly 10	a				21 13			22 13						00 09
	d	20 43	20 45	20 48	21 20	21 45	21 48	22 20	22 28	22 45	22 48	23 24	23 27	00 15
Ardwick	d													
Ashburys	d			20 52		21 49	21 52			22 49	22 52	23 28	23 31	
Belle Vue	d					21 51				22 51		23 30		
Ryder Brow	d					21 53				22 53		23 32		
Reddish North	d		20 52			21 56				22 56		23 35		
Brinnington	d		20 56			21 59				22 59		23 38		
Bredbury	d		20 59			22 02				23 02		23 41		
Gorton	d			20 54			21 54				22 54		23 33	
Fairfield	d													
Guide Bridge	a			20 58			21 58				22 58		23 37	
	d													
Hyde North	d													
Hyde Central	d													
Woodley	d													
Romiley	d		21 02			22 05				23 05		23 44		
Rose Hill Marple	d													
Marple	d		21 06			22 09				23 09		23 48		
Strines	d					22 13				23 13		23 52		
New Mills Central	a		21 11			22 18				23 18		23 57		
	d		21 11											
Stockport 86	d	20 54			21 28			22 28	22 37					
Hazel Grove 86	d													
Chinley	d		21 19						22 53					
Edale	d		21 28						23 02					
Hope (Derbyshire)	d		21 34						23 08					
Bamford	d		21 37						23 11					
Hathersage	d		21 40						23 15					
Grindleford	d		21 44						23 19					
Dore & Totley	d		21 52						23 28					
Sheffield 7	a	21 35	22 03		22 08			23 13	23 35					01 06

A From Liverpool Lime Street to Nottingham
B To Manchester Piccadilly
C To Hadfield
D To Cleethorpes
E From Liverpool Lime Street to Norwich
F To Glossop

Table 78

Saturdays

Manchester Airport and Manchester Romiley, Marple, Chinley and Sheffield

		TP ◇1	TP ◇1 A	NT	NT B	NT	NT B	NT	NT B	TP ◇1 A ✠	NT	EM ◇ C	NT	NT B	NT	NT B	TP ◇1 A ✠	NT	NT	EM ◇ C	NT	NT B	NT
Manchester Airport 85 ✈	d	23p52	05 20							06 55							07 53						
Manchester Piccadilly 10	a	00 09	05 35							07 13							08 12						
	d	00 15	05 44	05 50	06 16	06 35	06 48	07 03	07 18	07 20	07 39	07 42	07 44	07 48	08 03	08 15	08 20	08 23	08 36	08 43	08 45	08 48	09 03
Ardwick	d																						
Ashburys	d				06 20	06 39	06 52	07 07	07 22					07 52	08 07	08 19						08 52	09 07
Belle Vue	d					06 41		07 09							08 09								09 09
Ryder Brow	d					06 43		07 11							08 11								09 11
Reddish North	d					06 46		07 14					07 52		08 14						08 52		09 14
Brinnington	d					06 49		07 17					07 56		08 17						08 56		09 17
Bredbury	d					06 52		07 20					07 59		08 20						08 59		09 20
Gorton	d				06 22		06 54		07 24					07 54		08 21						08 54	
Fairfield	d										07 46								08 43				
Guide Bridge	a				06 26		06 58		07 28		07 49			07 58		08 25			08 46			08 58	
	d										07 49								08 46				
Hyde North	d										07 53								08 50				
Hyde Central	d										07 55								08 52				
Woodley	d										07 58								08 55				
Romiley	d					06 55		07 23			08 02		08 02		08 23			08 37	08 59		09 02		09 23
Rose Hill Marple	d										08a10								09a05				
Marple	d					06 59		07a28					08 06		08a28			08a43			09 06		09a28
Strines	d																				09 10		
New Mills Central	a					07 04							08 11								09 13		
	d					07 04							08 11								09 13		
Stockport 86	d		05 52	06 00						07 28		07 54					08 28			08 54			
Hazel Grove 86	d			06 07																			
Chinley	d			06 18		07 12							08 19								09 21		
Edale	d			06 26		07 21							08 28								09 30		
Hope (Derbyshire)	d			06 32		07 27							08 34								09 36		
Bamford	d			06 35		07 30							08 37								09 39		
Hathersage	d			06 39		07 33							08 40								09 42		
Grindleford	d			06 42		07 37							08 44								09 46		
Dore & Totley	d			06 51		07 47				08 03		08 28	08 53								09 57		
Sheffield 7	a	01 06	06 49	07 01		07 57				08 10		08 36	09 03				09 08			09 35	10 06		

		NT B	TP ◇1 A ✠	NT	NT	EM ◇ C	NT	NT B	NT	NT B	TP ◇1 A ✠	NT	NT	EM ◇ C	NT	NT B	NT	NT B	TP ◇1 A ✠	NT	NT	EM ◇ C	NT
Manchester Airport 85 ✈	d		08 55								09 55								10 55				
Manchester Piccadilly 10	a		09 13								10 13								11 13				
	d	09 18	09 20	09 23	09 36	09 43	09 45	09 48	10 03	10 18	10 20	10 23	10 36	10 43	10 45	10 48	11 03	11 18	11 20	11 23	11 36	11 43	11 45
Ardwick	d																						
Ashburys	d	09 22						09 52	10 07	10 22						10 52	11 07	11 22					
Belle Vue	d								10 09								11 09						
Ryder Brow	d								10 11								11 11						
Reddish North	d						09 52		10 14						10 52		11 14						11 52
Brinnington	d						09 56		10 17						10 56		11 17						11 56
Bredbury	d						09 59		10 20						10 59		11 20						11 59
Gorton	d	09 24						09 54		10 24						10 54		11 24					
Fairfield	d				09 43								10 43								11 43		
Guide Bridge	a	09 28			09 46			09 58		10 28			10 46			10 58		11 28			11 46		
	d				09 46								10 46								11 46		
Hyde North	d				09 50								10 50								11 50		
Hyde Central	d				09 52								10 52								11 52		
Woodley	d				09 55								10 55								11 55		
Romiley	d			09 37	09 59		10 02		10 23			10 37	10 59		11 02		11 23			11 37	11 59		12 02
Rose Hill Marple	d				10a05							10a43	11a05							11a43	12a05		
Marple	d			09a43			10 06		10a28						11 06		11a28						12 06
Strines	d						10 10																12 10
New Mills Central	a						10 13								11 11								12 13
	d						10 13								11 11								12 13
Stockport 86	d		09 28			09 54					10 28			10 54					11 28			11 54	
Hazel Grove 86	d																						
Chinley	d						10 21								11 19								12 21
Edale	d						10 30								11 28								12 30
Hope (Derbyshire)	d						10 36								11 34								12 36
Bamford	d						10 39								11 37								12 39
Hathersage	d						10 42								11 40								12 42
Grindleford	d						10 46								11 44								12 46
Dore & Totley	d						10 57								11 57								12 54
Sheffield 7	a		10 08			10 35	11 04				11 08			11 35	12 04				12 08			12 35	13 03

A To Cleethorpes **B** To Hadfield **C** From Liverpool Lime Street to Norwich

Table 78

Saturdays

Manchester Airport and Manchester
Romiley, Marple, Chinley and Sheffield

Station		NT		NT	NT	TP	NT	NT	EM	NT	NT	NT		NT	TP	NT	NT	EM	NT	NT	NT	NT		TP	NT
						◇1			◇						◇1			◇						◇1	
		A			A	B			C		A			A	B			C		A		A		B	
						⚲									⚲									⚲	
Manchester Airport 85 ✈	d					11 55									12 55									13 55	
Manchester Piccadilly 10	a					12 13									13 13									14 13	
	d	11 48		12 03	12 18	12 20	12 23	12 36	12 43	12 45	12 48	13 03		13 18	13 20	13 23	13 36	13 43	13 45	13 48	14 03	14 18		14 20	14 23
Ardwick	d																								
Ashburys	d	11 52		12 07	12 22						12 52	13 07		13 22						13 52	14 07	14 22			
Belle Vue	d			12 09								13 09									14 09				
Ryder Brow	d			12 11								13 11									14 11				
Reddish North	d			12 14						12 52		13 14							13 52		14 14				
Brinnington	d			12 17						12 56		13 17							13 56		14 17				
Bredbury	d			12 20						12 59		13 20							13 59		14 20				
Gorton	d	11 54			12 24						12 54			13 24						13 54		14 24			
Fairfield	d							12 43									13 43								
Guide Bridge	a	11 58			12 28			12 46			12 58			13 28			13 46			13 58		14 28			
	d							12 46									13 46								
Hyde North	d							12 50									13 50								
Hyde Central	d							12 52									13 52								
Woodley	d							12 55									13 55								
Romiley	d			12 23			12 37	12 59		13 02		13 23				13 37	13 59		14 02		14 23				14 37
Rose Hill Marple	d						12a43	13a05								13a43	14a05								14a43
Marple	d			12a28						13 06		13a28							14 06		14a28				
Strines	d																		14 10						
New Mills Central	a									13 11									14 13						
	d									13 11									14 13						
Stockport 86	d					12 28			12 54						13 28			13 54						14 28	
Hazel Grove 86	d																								
Chinley	d									13 19									14 21						
Edale	d									13 28									14 30						
Hope (Derbyshire)	d									13 34									14 36						
Bamford	d									13 37									14 39						
Hathersage	d									13 40									14 42						
Grindleford	d									13 44									14 46						
Dore & Totley	d									13 57									14 57						
Sheffield 7	a					13 08			13 35	14 04					14 08			14 35	15 04					15 08	

Station		NT	EM	NT	NT	NT	NT	TP		NT	NT	EM	NT	NT	NT	NT	TP	NT		NT	EM	NT	NT	NT	NT
			◇					◇1				◇					◇1				◇				
			D		A		A	B				C		A		A	B				C		A		A
								⚲									⚲								
Manchester Airport 85 ✈	d							14 55									15 55								
Manchester Piccadilly 10	a							15 13									16 13								
	d	14 36	14 43	14 45	14 48	15 03	15 18	15 20		15 23	15 36	15 43	15 45	15 48	16 02	16 18	16 20	16 23		16 36	16 43	16 45	16 48	17 02	17 18
Ardwick	d																								
Ashburys	d				14 52	15 07	15 22							15 52	16 06	16 22							16 52	17 06	17 22
Belle Vue	d					15 09									16 08									17 08	
Ryder Brow	d					15 11									16 10									17 10	
Reddish North	d			14 52		15 14							15 52		16 13							16 52		17 13	
Brinnington	d			14 56		15 17							15 56		16 16							16 56		17 16	
Bredbury	d			14 59		15 20							15 59		16 19							16 59		17 19	
Gorton	d				14 54		15 24							15 54		16 24							16 54		17 24
Fairfield	d	14 43									15 43									16 43					
Guide Bridge	a	14 46			14 58		15 28				15 46			15 58		16 28				16 46			16 58		17 28
	d	14 46									15 46									16 46					
Hyde North	d	14 50									15 50									16 50					
Hyde Central	d	14 52									15 52									16 52					
Woodley	d	14 55									15 55									16 55					
Romiley	d	14 59		15 02		15 23				15 37	15 59		16 02		16 22			16 37		16 59		17 02		17 22	
Rose Hill Marple	d	15a05								15a43	16a05							16a43		17a05					
Marple	d			15 06		15a28							16 06		16a27							17 06		17a27	
Strines	d												16 10												
New Mills Central	a			15 11									16 13									17 11			
	d			15 11									16 13									17 11			
Stockport 86	d		14 54					15 28				15 54					16 28				16 54				
Hazel Grove 86	d																								
Chinley	d			15 19									16 21								17 09	17 19			
Edale	d			15 28									16 30									17 28			
Hope (Derbyshire)	d			15 34									16 36									17 34			
Bamford	d			15 37									16 39									17 37			
Hathersage	d			15 40									16 42									17 40			
Grindleford	d			15 44									16 46									17 44			
Dore & Totley	d			15 57									16 57								17 30	17 52			
Sheffield 7	a		15 36	16 04				16 08				16 35	17 04				17 08				17 37	18 01			

A To Hadfield
B To Cleethorpes
C From Liverpool Lime Street to Norwich
D From Liverpool Lime Street to Nottingham

Manchester Airport and Manchester Romiley, Marple, Chinley and Sheffield

		TP ◇1 A	NT	NT		EM ◇ B	NT	NT C	NT	NT C	TP ◇1 A	NT	NT	EM ◇ D		NT	NT C	TP ◇1 A	NT	EM ◇ B	NT	NT C	TP ◇1	NT
Manchester Airport 85 ✈	d	16 55									17 55							18 55					19 55	
Manchester Piccadilly 10	a	17 13									18 13							19 13					20 13	
	d	17 20	17 23	17 36		17 43	17 45	17 48	18 03	18 18	18 20	18 23	18 36	18 43		18 45	18 48	19 18	19 23	19 43	19 45	19 48	20 20	20 36
Ardwick	d																							
Ashburys	d							17 52	18 07	18 22							18 52		19 28		19 49	19 52		
Belle Vue	d								18 09										19 31		19 51			
Ryder Brow	d								18 11										19 33		19 53			
Reddish North	d						17 52		18 14							18 52			19 35		19 56			
Brinnington	d						17 56		18 17							18 56			19 39		19 59			
Bredbury	d						17 59		18 20							18 59			19 42		20 02			
Gorton	d							17 54		18 24							18 54					19 54		
Fairfield	d			17 43									18 43											20 43
Guide Bridge	a			17 46				17 58		18 28			18 46				18 58					19 58		20 46
	d			17 46									18 46											20 46
Hyde North	d			17 50									18 50											20 50
Hyde Central	d			17 52									18 52											20 52
Woodley	d			17 55									18 55											20 55
Romiley	d		17 37	17 59			18 02		18 23			18 37	18 59			19 02			19 45		20 05			20 59
Rose Hill Marple	d			18a05									19a05											21a05
Marple	d		17a43				18 06		18a28			18a43				19 06			19a49		20 09			
Strines	d						18 10														20 13			
New Mills Central	a						18 13									19 11					20 18			
	d						18 13									19 11								
Stockport 86	d	17 28				17 54					18 28			18 54				19 26		19 54			20 28	
Hazel Grove 86	d																							
Chinley	d	17 43				18 08	18 21									19 19								
Edale	d						18 30									19 28								
Hope (Derbyshire)	d						18 36									19 34								
Bamford	d						18 39									19 37								
Hathersage	d						18 42									19 40								
Grindleford	d						18 46									19 44								
Dore & Totley	d	18 05					18 54				19 03					19 57		20 01					21 03	
Sheffield 7	a	18 15				18 35	19 03				19 09			19 35		20 04		20 08		20 35			21 14	

		EM ◇ B	NT	NT C	TP ◇1 A	EM ◇ B	NT	NT C	TP ◇1	EM ◇ B		NT	NT C	NT	NT E
Manchester Airport 85 ✈	d				20 47				21 47						
Manchester Piccadilly 10	a				21 13				22 13						
	d	20 43	20 45	20 48	21 20	21 43	21 45	21 48	22 20	22 31		22 45	22 48	23 24	23 27
Ardwick	d														
Ashburys	d			20 52			21 49	21 52				22 49	22 52	23 28	23 31
Belle Vue	d						21 51					22 51		23 30	
Ryder Brow	d						21 53					22 53		23 32	
Reddish North	d		20 52				21 56					22 56		23 35	
Brinnington	d		20 56				21 59					22 59		23 38	
Bredbury	d		20 59				22 02					23 02		23 41	
Gorton	d			20 54				21 54					22 54		23 33
Fairfield	d														
Guide Bridge	a			20 58				21 58					22 58		23 37
	d														
Hyde North	d														
Hyde Central	d														
Woodley	d														
Romiley	d		21 02				22 05					23 05		23 44	
Rose Hill Marple	d														
Marple	d		21 06				22 09					23 09		23 48	
Strines	d						22 13					23 13		23 52	
New Mills Central	a		21 11				22 18					23 18		23 57	
	d		21 11												
Stockport 86	d	20 54			21 28	21 52			22 28	22 42					
Hazel Grove 86	d														
Chinley	d		21 19							22 57					
Edale	d		21 28							23 05					
Hope (Derbyshire)	d		21 34							23 11					
Bamford	d		21 37							23 15					
Hathersage	d		21 40							23 19					
Grindleford	d		21 44							23 23					
Dore & Totley	d		21 53							23 32					
Sheffield 7	a	21 34	22 03		22 08	22 31			23 16	23 39					

A To Cleethorpes
B From Liverpool Lime Street to Nottingham
C To Hadfield
D From Liverpool Lime Street to Norwich
E To Glossop

Table 78

Sundays
until 11 September

Manchester Airport and Manchester Romiley, Marple, Chinley and Sheffield

		NT	NT	TP ◇1	NT A	NT	NT A	NT A	NT	NT A	TP ◇1 B	NT A	NT	NT A	NT A	TP ◇1 C	EM ◇ D	NT A	NT A	TP ◇1 B	EM ◇ E	NT	NT A
Manchester Airport 85 ✈	d			08 40							10 44									12 55			
Manchester Piccadilly 10	a			08 54							10 58									13 09			
	d	07 45	08 22	08 58	09 18	09 22	09 30	10 18	10 45	10 48	11 18	11 18	11 45	11 48	12 18	12 18	12 44	12 48	13 18	13 20	13 44	13 45	13 48
Ardwick	d																						
Ashburys	d				09 22		09 34	10 22		10 52		11 22		11 52	12 22			12 52	13 22				13 52
Belle Vue	d																						
Ryder Brow	d																						
Reddish North	d	07 52	08 29			09 29			10 52				11 52									13 52	
Brinnington	d	07 56	08 33			09 33			10 56				11 56									13 56	
Bredbury	d	07 59	08 36			09 36			10 59				11 59									13 59	
Gorton	d				09 24		09 36	10 24		10 54		11 24		11 54	12 24			12 54	13 24				13 54
Fairfield	d																						
Guide Bridge	a				09 28		09 40	10 28		10 58		11 28		11 58	12 28			12 58	13 28				13 58
	d																						
Hyde North	d																						
Hyde Central	d																						
Woodley	d																						
Romiley	d	08 02	08 39			09 39			11 02				12 02									14 02	
Rose Hill Marple	d																						
Marple	d	08 06	08 43			09 43			11 06				12 06									14 06	
Strines	d	08 10	08 47			09 47			11 10				12 10									14 10	
New Mills Central	a	08 14	08 51			09 51			11 14				12 14									14 14	
	d	08 14	08 51			09 51			11 14				12 14									14 14	
Stockport 86	d			09 07							11 27					12 28	12 55			13 28	13 54		
Hazel Grove 86	d																						
Chinley	d	08 23	09 00			09 59			11 23				12 23									14 23	
Edale	d	08 32	09 09			10 08			11 32				12 32									14 32	
Hope (Derbyshire)	d	08 38	09 15			10 14			11 38				12 38									14 38	
Bamford	d	08 41	09 18			10 17			11 41				12 41									14 41	
Hathersage	d	08 45	09 22			10 20			11 45				12 45									14 45	
Grindleford	d	08 48	09 25			10 24			11 48				12 48									14 48	
Dore & Totley	d	08 57	09 34			10 34			11 57				12 57									14 57	
Sheffield 7	a	09 06	09 42	09 45		10 43			12 06		12 08		13 06			13 08	13 37			14 08	14 39	15 06	

		NT A	TP ◇1 B	EM ◇ E	NT	NT A	NT A	TP ◇1 B	EM ◇ E	NT	NT A	NT A	TP ◇1 B	EM ◇ E	NT	NT A	NT A	TP ◇1 B	EM ◇ F	NT	NT A	NT A	TP ◇1 B
Manchester Airport 85 ✈	d		13 55					14 55					15 55					16 55					17 55
Manchester Piccadilly 10	a		14 09					15 09					16 09					17 09					18 09
	d	14 18	14 20	14 44	14 45	14 48	15 18	15 20	15 44	15 45	15 48	16 18	16 20	16 44	16 45	16 48	17 18	17 20	17 44	17 45	17 48	18 18	18 20
Ardwick	d																						
Ashburys	d	14 22				14 52	15 22				15 52	16 22				16 52	17 22				17 52	18 22	
Belle Vue	d																						
Ryder Brow	d																						
Reddish North	d				14 52					15 52					16 52					17 52			
Brinnington	d				14 56					15 56					16 56					17 56			
Bredbury	d				14 59					15 59					16 59					17 59			
Gorton	d	14 24				14 54	15 24				15 54	16 24				16 54	17 24				17 54	18 24	
Fairfield	d																						
Guide Bridge	a	14 28				14 58	15 28				15 58	16 28				16 58	17 28				17 58	18 28	
	d																						
Hyde North	d																						
Hyde Central	d																						
Woodley	d																						
Romiley	d				15 02					16 02					17 02					18 02			
Rose Hill Marple	d																						
Marple	d				15 06					16 06					17 06					18 06			
Strines	d				15 10					16 10					17 10					18 10			
New Mills Central	a				15 14					16 14					17 14					18 14			
	d				15 14					16 14					17 14					18 14			
Stockport 86	d		14 28	14 54				15 28	15 54				16 28	16 54				17 28	17 54				18 28
Hazel Grove 86	d																						
Chinley	d				15 23					16 23					17 23					18 23			
Edale	d				15 32					16 32					17 32					18 32			
Hope (Derbyshire)	d				15 38					16 38					17 38					18 38			
Bamford	d				15 41					16 41					17 41					18 41			
Hathersage	d				15 45					16 45					17 45					18 45			
Grindleford	d				15 48					16 48					17 48					18 48			
Dore & Totley	d				15 57					16 57					17 57					18 57			
Sheffield 7	a		15 08	15 37	16 06			16 08	16 36	17 06			17 08	17 36	18 06			18 08	18 37	19 06			19 08

A To Hadfield
B To Cleethorpes
C To Doncaster
D To Norwich
E From Liverpool Lime Street to Norwich
F From Liverpool Lime Street to Nottingham

Table 78

Sundays until 11 September

Manchester Airport and Manchester Romiley, Marple, Chinley and Sheffield

		EM		NT	NT	TP	EM	NT	NT	TP	EM	NT		TP	EM	TP	NT	TP
		◇				◇1	◇			◇1	◇			◇1	◇	◇1		◇1
		A		B	B	C	D		B	C	D	B			D			
Manchester Airport 85 ✈	d					18 55				19 55				20 55		21 55		22 55
Manchester Piccadilly 10 ⛴	a					19 09				20 09				21 09		22 09		23 09
	d	18 44		18 48	19 18	19 20	19 44	19 45	19 48	20 18	20 44	20 48		21 20	22 11	22 15	22 20	23 20
Ardwick	d																	
Ashburys	d			18 52	19 22				19 52			20 52						
Belle Vue	d																	
Ryder Brow	d																	
Reddish North	d							19 52									22 27	
Brinnington	d							19 56									22 31	
Bredbury	d							19 59									22 34	
Gorton	d			18 54	19 24				19 54			20 54						
Fairfield	d																	
Guide Bridge	a			18 58	19 28				19 58			20 58						
	d																	
Hyde North	d																	
Hyde Central	d																	
Woodley	d																	
Romiley	d							20 02									22 37	
Rose Hill Marple	d																	
Marple	d							20 06									22 40	
Strines	d							20 10									22 44	
New Mills Central	a							20 14									22 49	
	d							20 14										
Stockport 86	d	18 54				19 28	19 54			20 27	20 54			21 28	22b28	22 23		23 28
Hazel Grove 86	d																	
Chinley	d							20 23							22 43			
Edale	d							20 32							22 51			
Hope (Derbyshire)	d							20 38							22 57			
Bamford	d							20 41							23 00			
Hathersage	d							20 45							23 03			
Grindleford	d							20 48							23 07			
Dore & Totley	d							20 57							23 17			
Sheffield 7 ⛴	a	19 34				20 08	20 34	21 06		21 08	21 36			22 12	23 25	23 04		00 15

Sundays 18 September to 23 October

		NT	TP	NT	NT	NT	NT	NT	NT	TP		NT	NT	NT	NT	TP	EM	NT	NT	TP		EM	NT	NT	NT
			◇1							◇1						◇1	◇			◇1		◇			
				B		B	B		B	C		B		B	B	E	F	B	B	C		A		B	B
Manchester Airport 85 ✈	d		08 40							10 44										12 55					
Manchester Piccadilly 10 ⛴	a		08 54							10 58										13 09					
	d	08 22	08 58	09 18	09 22	09 30	10 18	10 45	10 48	11 18		11 18	11 45	11 48	12 18	12 18	12 44	12 48	13 18	13 20		13 44	13 45	13 48	14 18
Ardwick	d																								
Ashburys	d			09 22		09 34	10 22		10 52			11 22		11 52	12 22			12 52	13 22					13 52	14 22
Belle Vue	d																								
Ryder Brow	d																								
Reddish North	d	08 29			09 29			10 52					11 52										13 52		
Brinnington	d	08 33			09 33			10 56					11 56										13 56		
Bredbury	d	08 36			09 36			10 59					11 59										13 59		
Gorton	d			09 24		09 36	10 24		10 54			11 24		11 54	12 24			12 54	13 24					13 54	14 24
Fairfield	d																								
Guide Bridge	a			09 28		09 40	10 28		10 58			11 28		11 58	12 28			12 58	13 28					13 58	14 28
	d																								
Hyde North	d																								
Hyde Central	d																								
Woodley	d																								
Romiley	d	08 39			09 39			11 02					12 02										14 02		
Rose Hill Marple	d																								
Marple	d	08 43			09 43			11 06					12 06										14 06		
Strines	d	08 47			09 47			11 10					12 10										14 10		
New Mills Central	a	08 51			09 51			11 14					12 14										14 14		
	d	08 51			09 51			11 14					12 14										14 14		
Stockport 86	d		09 07							11 27						12 28	12 55			13 28		13 54			
Hazel Grove 86	d																								
Chinley	d	09 00			09 59			11 23					12 23										14 23		
Edale	d	09 09			10 08			11 32					12 32										14 32		
Hope (Derbyshire)	d	09 15			10 14			11 38					12 38										14 38		
Bamford	d	09 18			10 17			11 41					12 41										14 41		
Hathersage	d	09 22			10 20			11 45					12 45										14 45		
Grindleford	d	09 25			10 24			11 48					12 48										14 48		
Dore & Totley	d	09 34			10 34			11 57					12 57										14 57		
Sheffield 7 ⛴	a	09 42	09 45		10 43			12 06		12 08			13 06			13 08	13 37			14 08		14 39	15 06		

A From Liverpool Lime Street to Norwich
B To Hadfield
C To Cleethorpes
D From Liverpool Lime Street to Nottingham
E To Doncaster
F To Norwich
b Arr. 2220

Table 78

Sundays

18 September to 23 October

Manchester Airport and Manchester Romiley, Marple, Chinley and Sheffield

		TP	EM	NT	NT	NT		TP	EM	NT	NT	NT	TP	EM	NT	NT		NT	TP	EM	NT	NT	NT	TP	EM
		◇1	◇					◇1	◇				◇1	◇					◇1	◇				◇1	◇
		A	B		C	C		A	B		C	C	A	B		C		C	A	D		C	C	A	B
Manchester Airport 85 ✈	d	13 55						14 55					15 55						16 55					17 55	
Manchester Piccadilly 10 ⇌	a	14 09						15 09					16 09						17 09					18 09	
	d	14 20	14 44	14 45	14 48	15 18		15 20	15 44	15 45	15 48	16 18	16 20	16 44	16 45	16 48		17 18	17 20	17 44	17 45	17 48	18 18	18 20	18 44
Ardwick	d																								
Ashburys	d				14 52	15 22					15 52	16 22				16 52		17 22				17 52	18 22		
Belle Vue	d																								
Ryder Brow	d																								
Reddish North	d			14 52						15 52					16 52						17 52				
Brinnington	d			14 56						15 56					16 56						17 56				
Bredbury	d			14 59						15 59					16 59						17 59				
Gorton	d				14 54	15 24					15 54	16 24				16 54		17 24				17 54	18 24		
Fairfield	d																								
Guide Bridge	a				14 58	15 28					15 58	16 28				16 58		17 28				17 58	18 28		
	d																								
Hyde North	d																								
Hyde Central	d																								
Woodley	d																								
Romiley	d			15 02						16 02					17 02						18 02				
Rose Hill Marple	d																								
Marple	d			15 06						16 06					17 06						18 06				
Strines	d			15 10						16 10					17 10						18 10				
New Mills Central	a			15 14						16 14					17 14						18 14				
	d			15 14						16 14					17 14						18 14				
Stockport 86	d	14 28	14 54					15 28	15 54				16 28	16 54					17 28	17 54				18 28	18 54
Hazel Grove 86	d																								
Chinley	d			15 23						16 23					17 23						18 23				
Edale	d			15 32						16 32					17 32						18 32				
Hope (Derbyshire)	d			15 38						16 38					17 38						18 38				
Bamford	d			15 41						16 41					17 41						18 41				
Hathersage	d			15 45						16 45					17 45						18 45				
Grindleford	d			15 48						16 48					17 48						18 48				
Dore & Totley	d			15 57						16 57					17 57						18 57				
Sheffield 7 ⇌	a	15 08	15 37	16 06				16 08	16 36	17 06			17 08	17 36	18 06				18 08	18 37	19 06			19 08	19 34

		NT		NT	TP	EM	NT	NT	TP	EM	NT	TP		EM	TP	NT	TP
					◇1	◇			◇1	◇		◇1		◇	◇1		◇1
		C		C	A	D		C	A	D	C			D			
Manchester Airport 85 ✈	d				18 55				19 55			20 55			21 55		22 55
Manchester Piccadilly 10 ⇌	a				19 09				20 09			21 09			22 09		23 09
	d	18 48		19 18	19 20	19 44	19 45	19 48	20 18	20 44	20 48	21 20		22 11	22 15	22 20	23 20
Ardwick	d																
Ashburys	d	18 52		19 22				19 52			20 52						
Belle Vue	d																
Ryder Brow	d																
Reddish North	d						19 52									22 27	
Brinnington	d						19 56									22 31	
Bredbury	d						19 59									22 34	
Gorton	d	18 54		19 24				19 54			20 54						
Fairfield	d																
Guide Bridge	a	18 58		19 28				19 58			20 58						
	d																
Hyde North	d																
Hyde Central	d																
Woodley	d																
Romiley	d						20 02									22 37	
Rose Hill Marple	d																
Marple	d						20 06									22 40	
Strines	d						20 10									22 44	
New Mills Central	a						20 14									22 49	
	d						20 14										
Stockport 86	d				19 28	19 54			20 27	20 54		21 28		22b28	22 23		23 28
Hazel Grove 86	d																
Chinley	d						20 23							22 43			
Edale	d						20 32							22 51			
Hope (Derbyshire)	d						20 38							22 57			
Bamford	d						20 41							23 00			
Hathersage	d						20 45							23 03			
Grindleford	d						20 48							23 07			
Dore & Totley	d						20 57							23 17			
Sheffield 7 ⇌	a				20 08	20 34	21 06		21 08	21 36		22 12		23 25	23 04		00 15

A To Cleethorpes
B From Liverpool Lime Street to Norwich
C To Hadfield
D From Liverpool Lime Street to Nottingham
b Arr. 2220

Table 78

Sundays
from 30 October

Manchester Airport and Manchester Romiley, Marple, Chinley and Sheffield

	NT	TP	NT	NT	NT	NT	NT	NT	TP		NT	NT	NT	NT	TP	EM	NT	NT	TP		EM	NT	NT	NT
		◇1							◇1						◇1	◇			◇1		◇			
			A		A	A		A	B		A		A	A	C	D	A	A	B		E		A	A
Manchester Airport 85 ✈ d		08 40							10 44										12 55					
Manchester Piccadilly 10 a		08 54							10 58										13 09					
d	08 22	08 58	09 18	09 22	09 30	10 18	10 45	10 48	11 18		11 18	11 45	11 48	12 18	12 18	12 44	12 48	13 18	13 20		13 44	13 45	13 48	14 18
Ardwick d																								
Ashburys d			09 22		09 34	10 22		10 52			11 22		11 52	12 22			12 52	13 22					13 52	14 22
Belle Vue d																								
Ryder Brow d																								
Reddish North d	08 29			09 29			10 52					11 52										13 52		
Brinnington d	08 33			09 33			10 56					11 56										13 56		
Bredbury d	08 36			09 36			10 59					11 59										13 59		
Gorton d			09 24		09 36	10 24		10 54			11 24		11 54	12 24			12 54	13 24					13 54	14 24
Fairfield d																								
Guide Bridge a			09 28		09 40	10 28		10 58			11 28		11 58	12 28			12 58	13 28					13 58	14 28
d																								
Hyde North d																								
Hyde Central d																								
Woodley d																								
Romiley d	08 39			09 39			11 02					12 02										14 02		
Rose Hill Marple d																								
Marple d	08 43			09 43			11 06					12 06										14 06		
Strines d	08 47			09 47			11 10					12 10										14 10		
New Mills Central a	08 51			09 51			11 14					12 14										14 14		
d	08 51			09 51			11 14					12 14										14 14		
Stockport 86 d		09 07							11 27						12 28	12 55			13 28		13 54			
Hazel Grove 86 d																								
Chinley d	09 00			09 59			11 23					12 23										14 23		
Edale d	09 09			10 08			11 32					12 32										14 32		
Hope (Derbyshire) d	09 15			10 14			11 38					12 38										14 38		
Bamford d	09 18			10 17			11 41					12 41										14 41		
Hathersage d	09 22			10 20			11 45					12 45										14 45		
Grindleford d	09 25			10 24			11 48					12 48										14 48		
Dore & Totley d	09 34			10 34			11 57					12 57										14 57		
Sheffield 7 a	09 42	09 45		10 43			12 06		12 08			13 06			13 08	13 37			14 08		14 39	15 06		

	TP	EM	NT	NT	NT		TP	EM	NT	NT	NT	TP	EM	NT	NT		NT	TP	EM	NT	NT	NT	TP	EM
	◇1	◇					◇1	◇				◇1	◇					◇1	◇				◇1	◇
	B	E		A	A		B	E		A	A	B	E		A		A	B	F		A	A	B	E
Manchester Airport 85 ✈ d	13 55						14 55					15 55						16 55					17 55	
Manchester Piccadilly 10 a	14 09						15 09					16 09						17 09					18 09	
d	14 20	14 44	14 45	14 48	15 18		15 20	15 44	15 45	15 48	16 18	16 20	16 44	16 45	16 48		17 18	17 20	17 44	17 45	17 48	18 18	18 20	18 44
Ardwick d																								
Ashburys d				14 52	15 22					15 52	16 22				16 52		17 22				17 52	18 22		
Belle Vue d																								
Ryder Brow d																								
Reddish North d			14 52						15 52					16 52						17 52				
Brinnington d			14 56						15 56					16 56						17 56				
Bredbury d			14 59						15 59					16 59						17 59				
Gorton d				14 54	15 24					15 54	16 24				16 54		17 24				17 54	18 24		
Fairfield d																								
Guide Bridge a				14 58	15 28					15 58	16 28				16 58		17 28				17 58	18 28		
d																								
Hyde North d																								
Hyde Central d																								
Woodley d																								
Romiley d			15 02						16 02					17 02						18 02				
Rose Hill Marple d																								
Marple d			15 06						16 06					17 06						18 06				
Strines d			15 10						16 10					17 10						18 10				
New Mills Central a			15 14						16 14					17 14						18 14				
d			15 14						16 14					17 14						18 14				
Stockport 86 d	14 28	14 54					15 28	15 54				16 28	16 54					17 28	17 54				18 28	18 54
Hazel Grove 86 d																								
Chinley d			15 23						16 23					17 23						18 23				
Edale d			15 32						16 32					17 32						18 32				
Hope (Derbyshire) d			15 38						16 38					17 38						18 38				
Bamford d			15 41						16 41					17 41						18 41				
Hathersage d			15 45						16 45					17 45						18 45				
Grindleford d			15 48						16 48					17 48						18 48				
Dore & Totley d			15 57						16 57					17 57						18 57				
Sheffield 7 a	15 08	15 37	16 06				16 08	16 36	17 06			17 08	17 36	18 06				18 08	18 37	19 06			19 08	19 34

A To Hadfield
B To Cleethorpes
C To Doncaster
D To Norwich
E From Liverpool Lime Street to Norwich
F From Liverpool Lime Street to Nottingham

Table 78

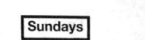

Sundays
from 30 October

Manchester Airport and Manchester Romiley, Marple, Chinley and Sheffield

		NT		NT	TP	EM	NT	NT	TP	EM	NT	TP		EM	TP	NT	TP
					◇1	◇			◇1	◇		◇1		◇	◇1		◇1
		A		A	B	C		A	B	C	A			C			
Manchester Airport 85 ✈	d				18 55				19 55			20 55			21 55		22 55
Manchester Piccadilly 10 ⇌	a				19 09				20 09			21 09			22 09		23 09
	d	18 48		19 18	19 20	19 44	19 45	19 48	20 18	20 44	20 48	21 20		22 11	22 15	22 20	23 20
Ardwick	d																
Ashburys	d	18 52		19 22				19 52			20 52						
Belle Vue	d																
Ryder Brow	d																
Reddish North	d						19 52									22 27	
Brinnington	d						19 56									22 31	
Bredbury	d						19 59									22 34	
Gorton	d	18 54		19 24				19 54			20 54						
Fairfield	d																
Guide Bridge	a	18 58		19 28				19 58			20 58						
	d																
Hyde North	d																
Hyde Central	d																
Woodley	d																
Romiley	d						20 02									22 37	
Rose Hill Marple	d																
Marple	d						20 06									22 40	
Strines	d						20 10									22 44	
New Mills Central	a						20 14									22 49	
	d						20 14										
Stockport 86	d				19 28	19 54			20 27	20 54		21 28		22b28	22 23		23 28
Hazel Grove 86	d																
Chinley	d						20 23							22 43			
Edale	d						20 32							22 51			
Hope (Derbyshire)	d						20 38							22 57			
Bamford	d						20 41							23 00			
Hathersage	d						20 45							23 03			
Grindleford	d						20 48							23 07			
Dore & Totley	d						20 57							23 17			
Sheffield 7 ⇌	a				20 08	20 34	21 06		21 08	21 36		22 12		23 25	23 04		00 15

A To Hadfield
B To Cleethorpes
C From Liverpool Lime Street to Nottingham
b Arr. 2220

Table 78

Mondays to Fridays

until 30 September

Sheffield, Chinley, Marple and Romiley Manchester and Manchester Airport

Miles	Miles	Miles	Station		NT MX	NT MX	TP ◇1	TP ◇1	NT A	NT	TP ◇1 B	NT	NT	NT A	EM ◇ C	NT	NT A	NT	NT	TP ◇1 D	NT E	NT	NT
0	—	—	**Sheffield 7**	d	22p47		03 45	05 11			06 11				06 20					07 09			
4¾	—	—	Dore & Totley	d	22p54										06 27					07 15			
9¾	—	—	Grindleford	d	23p01										06 35								
11¼	—	—	Hathersage	d	23p05										06 39								
13	—	—	Bamford	d	23p08										06 43								
14¾	—	—	Hope (Derbyshire)	d	23p12										06 47								
20	—	—	Edale	d	23p19										06 55								
25½	—	0	**Chinley**	d	23p27										07 03								
—	—	8½	Hazel Grove 86	a																			
—	—	—	Stockport 86	a	23p47			05 53			06 53				07 22					07 53			
29¼	—	—	New Mills Central	d		23p30				06 13			06 36			07 01			07 23				07 39
30¾	—	—	Strines	d		23p33				06 16			06 39			07 04			07 26				07 42
33	—	—	**Marple**	d		23p36				06 19			06 42			07 07			07 29				07 45
—	0	—	**Rose Hill Marple**	d								06 32						07 16				07 41	
34¼	2	—	**Romiley**	d		23p40				06 23		06 37	06 46			07 12		07 21	07 33			07 46	07 49
—	3¼	—	Woodley	d								06 40						07 24				07 49	
—	4¾	—	Hyde Central	d								06 43						07 27				07 52	
—	6	—	Hyde North	d								06 46						07 30				07 55	
—	7¾	—	Guide Bridge	d					06 27			06 50		06 57			07 27	07 34			07 47	07 59	
—	9	—	Fairfield	d								06 53						07 37				08 02	
—	10	—	Gorton	d					06 30					07 00			07 30				07 50		
35½	—	—	Bredbury	d		23p43				06 26			06 49			07 15			07 36				07 52
36½	—	—	Brinnington	d		23p45				06 28			06 52			07 17			07 39				07 55
38¼	—	—	Reddish North	d		23p48				06 31			06 55			07 20			07 43				07 58
39¼	—	—	Ryder Brow	d		23p51				06 34			06 58			07 24			07 45				
39½	—	—	Belle Vue	d		23p52				06 36			07 00			07 26			07 47				
40½	11	—	Ashburys	d		23p55			06 33	06 39			07 03	07 06		07 29	07 33		07 50		07 53		
41½	12	—	Ardwick	d													07 36						
42	12½	8¾	**Manchester Piccadilly 10**	a	00 02	00 03	04 40	06 05	06 42	06 47	07 02	07 03	07 12	07 15	07 34	07 36	07 43	07 47	07 56	08 02	08 03	08 12	08 09
—	—	—	**Manchester Airport** 85	a			05 00	06 29			07 29									08 26			

Station		NT E	NT	NT	EM ◇ C	NT E	NT	NT	NT	TP ◇1 D	NT E	NT	NT E	NT	NT	EM ◇ C	NT E	NT	TP ◇1 D	NT A	NT	NT	NT
Sheffield 7	d			07 12	07 35					08 05						08 42			09 11				09 14
Dore & Totley	d			07 19	07 42					08 11													09 21
Grindleford	d			07 29																			09 29
Hathersage	d			07 32																			09 32
Bamford	d			07 36																			09 36
Hope (Derbyshire)	d			07 39																			09 39
Edale	d			07 47																			09 47
Chinley	d			07 55	08 03					08 32													09 55
Hazel Grove 86	a				08 16																		
Stockport 86	a				08 24					08 53						09 25			09 53				
New Mills Central	d			08 02				08 22							09 04								10 01
Strines	d							08 25							09 07								10 04
Marple	d		07 59	08 09				08 29				08 48			09 10			09 35			09 52		10 07
Rose Hill Marple	d						08 15		08 35					08 59								09 55	
Romiley	d		08 03	08 13			08 20	08 33	08 40			08 51		09 04	09 14			09 38			09 56	10 00	10 11
Woodley	d						08 23							09 07								10 03	
Hyde Central	d						08 26							09 10								10 06	
Hyde North	d						08 29							09 13								10 09	
Guide Bridge	d	08 10				08 27	08 33				08 49		09 12	09 17			09 28			09 58		10 13	
Fairfield	d						08 36							09 20								10 16	
Gorton	d	08 13				08 31					08 52		09 15				09 31			10 01			
Bredbury	d		08 06					08 36	08 43			08 54			09 17			09 41					10 14
Brinnington	d		08 09					08 39	08 45			08 57			09 19			09 44					10 16
Reddish North	d		08 12					08 43	08 48			09 00			09 22			09 47					10 19
Ryder Brow	d		08 15									09 03									10 03		
Belle Vue	d		08 16									09 04									10 05		
Ashburys	d	08 16	08 20			08 34		08 48			08 56	09 07	09 18				09 34			10 04	10 07		
Ardwick	d		08 22						08 54														
Manchester Piccadilly 10	a	08 25	08 30	08 33	08 36	08 43	08 47	08 55	09 00	09 02	09 04	09 15	09 27	09 30	09 34	09 36	09 42	09 57	10 02	10 12	10 15	10 26	10 32
Manchester Airport 85	a									09 33									10 26				

A From Hadfield
B From Doncaster
C From Nottingham to Liverpool Lime Street
D From Cleethorpes
E From Manchester Piccadilly

Table 78

Mondays to Fridays

until 30 September

Sheffield, Chinley, Marple and Romiley Manchester and Manchester Airport

	EM ◇ A	NT B	NT	NT		TP ◇1 C ⚲	NT B	NT	NT	EM ◇ A	NT B	NT	NT	TP ◇1 C ⚲		NT B	NT	NT	EM ◇ A	NT B	NT	NT	TP ◇1 C ⚲	NT B
Sheffield 7 d	09 42					10 11			10 14	10 42				11 11					11 42				12 11	
Dore & Totley d									10 21															
Grindleford d									10 29															
Hathersage d									10 32															
Bamford d									10 36															
Hope (Derbyshire) d									10 39															
Edale d									10 47															
Chinley d									10 55															
Hazel Grove 86 a																								
Stockport 86 a	10 25					10 53				11 25				11 53					12 25				12 53	
New Mills Central d				10 30					11 01				11 30					12 01				12 30		
Strines d																		12 04						
Marple d				10 35					11 07				11 35					12 07				12 35		
Rose Hill Marple d			10 30					10 51				11 30					11 51				12 30			
Romiley d			10 35	10 38				10 56	11 11			11 35	11 38				11 56	12 11			12 35	12 38		
Woodley d			10 38									11 38									12 38			
Hyde Central d			10 41									11 41									12 41			
Hyde North d			10 44									11 44									12 44			
Guide Bridge d		10 28	10 48				10 58				11 28	11 48				11 58				12 28	12 48			12 58
Fairfield d			10 51									11 51									12 51			
Gorton d		10 31					11 01				11 31					12 01				12 31				13 01
Bredbury d				10 41					11 14				11 41					12 14				12 41		
Brinnington d				10 44					11 16				11 44					12 16				12 44		
Reddish North d				10 47					11 19				11 47					12 19				12 47		
Ryder Brow d								11 03									12 03							
Belle Vue d								11 05									12 05							
Ashburys d		10 34					11 04	11 07			11 34					12 04	12 07			12 34				13 04
Ardwick d																								
Manchester Piccadilly 10 a	10 36	10 42	11 02	10 57		11 02	11 12	11 15	11 32	11 36	11 42	12 02	11 57	12 02		12 12	12 15	12 32	12 36	12 42	13 02	12 57	13 02	13 12
Manchester Airport 85 a						11 26								12 26									13 26	

		NT	NT	EM ◇ A	NT B	NT	NT	TP ◇1 C ⚲	NT B	NT		NT	EM ◇ A	NT B	NT	NT	TP ◇1 C ⚲	NT B	NT	NT		EM ◇ A	NT B	NT
Sheffield 7 d			12 14	12 42				13 11					13 42				14 11			14 14		14 42		
Dore & Totley d			12 21																	14 21				
Grindleford d			12 29																	14 29				
Hathersage d			12 32																	14 32				
Bamford d			12 36																	14 36				
Hope (Derbyshire) d			12 39																	14 39				
Edale d			12 47																	14 47				
Chinley d			12 55																	14 55				
Hazel Grove 86 a																								
Stockport 86 a				13 25				13 53					14 25				14 53					15 25		
New Mills Central d			13 01				13 30					14 01				14 30				15 01				
Strines d												14 04												
Marple d			13 07				13 35					14 07				14 35				15 07				
Rose Hill Marple d		12 51				13 30				13 51					14 30				14 51					15 30
Romiley d		12 56	13 11			13 35	13 38			13 56		14 11			14 35	14 38			14 56	15 11				15 35
Woodley d						13 38									14 38									15 38
Hyde Central d						13 41									14 41									15 41
Hyde North d						13 44									14 44									15 44
Guide Bridge d					13 28	13 48			13 58					14 28	14 48			14 58					15 28	15 48
Fairfield d						13 51									14 51									15 51
Gorton d					13 31				14 01					14 31				15 01					15 31	
Bredbury d			13 14				13 41					14 14				14 41				15 14				
Brinnington d			13 16				13 44					14 16				14 44				15 16				
Reddish North d			13 19				13 47					14 19				14 47				15 19				
Ryder Brow d		13 03								14 03									15 03					
Belle Vue d		13 05								14 05									15 05					
Ashburys d		13 07			13 34				14 04	14 07				14 34				15 04	15 07				15 34	
Ardwick d																								
Manchester Piccadilly 10 a		13 15	13 32	13 36	13 42	14 02	13 57	14 02	14 12	14 15		14 32	14 36	14 42	15 02	14 57	15 02	15 12	15 15	15 32		15 36	15 42	16 02
Manchester Airport 85 a								14 26									15 26							

A From Norwich to Liverpool Lime Street

B From Hadfield

C From Cleethorpes

Table 78

Mondays to Fridays
until 30 September

Sheffield, Chinley, Marple and Romiley Manchester and Manchester Airport

		NT	TP	NT	NT	NT	EM		NT	NT	TP	NT	NT	NT	NT	NT	EM		NT	NT	NT	NT	TP	NT	NT
			◇1				◇				◇1						◇						◇1		
			A	B			C		B		A	D				D	C				D		A	D	
Sheffield 7	d		15 11				15 42				16 10				16 14		16 42						17 11		
Dore & Totley	d														16 21										
Grindleford	d														16 29										
Hathersage	d														16 32										
Bamford	d														16 36										
Hope (Derbyshire)	d														16 39										
Edale	d														16 47										
Chinley	d														16 55										
Hazel Grove 86	a																								
Stockport 86	a		15 53				16 25				16 53						17 25						17 53		
New Mills Central	d	15 30				16 01							16 37		17 01					17 23					
Strines	d					16 04																			
Marple	d	15 35				16 07							16 42	16 52	17 06					17 28					17 52
Rose Hill Marple	d				15 51					16 26									17 10			17 36			
Romiley	d	15 38			15 56	16 11				16 31			16 45	16 56	17 10				17 15	17 32		17 41			17 56
Woodley	d												16 49						17 18						
Hyde Central	d												16 52						17 21						
Hyde North	d												16 54						17 24						
Guide Bridge	d			15 58					16 28			16 49	16 58			17 15			17 28		17 42			17 58	
Fairfield	d																		17 31						
Gorton	d			16 01					16 31			16 52				17 18					17 45			18 01	
Bredbury	d	15 41				16 14				16 34					17 13							17 44			
Brinnington	d	15 44				16 16				16 37												17 46			
Reddish North	d	15 47				16 19				16 40												17 49			18 02
Ryder Brow	d				16 03					16 42				17 03											18 04
Belle Vue	d				16 05					16 44				17 05											18 06
Ashburys	d			16 04	16 07				16 34	16 47		16 55	17 03	17 07		17 24					17 48	17 55		18 04	18 08
Ardwick	d																								
Manchester Piccadilly 10	a	15 57	16 02	16 12	16 15	16 32	16 36		16 42	16 56	17 02	17 05	17 10	17 15	17 29	17 33	17 37		17 42	17 48	17 57	18 01	18 02	18 12	18 16
Manchester Airport 85	a		16 26								17 32												18 26		

		NT	NT		EM	NT	NT	TP	TP	NT	NT	NT	NT		EM	NT	TP	NT	NT	NT	NT	EM	NT		TP
					◇			◇1	◇1						◇		◇1					◇			◇1
			D		C			E	F	D		D			C	B	A			B		C	B		A
Sheffield 7	d	17 14			17 40			18 10	18 10						18 43		19 11				19 14	19 42			20 11
Dore & Totley	d	17 21																			19 21				
Grindleford	d	17 29																			19 29				
Hathersage	d	17 32																			19 32				
Bamford	d	17 36																			19 36				
Hope (Derbyshire)	d	17 39																			19 39				
Edale	d	17 47																			19 47				
Chinley	d	17 55						18 34	18 34				18 54								19 55				
Hazel Grove 86	a																								
Stockport 86	a				18 25			18 53	18 53						19 25		19 53					20 25			20 53
New Mills Central	d	18 01											19 01								20 01				
Strines	d	18 04											19 04												
Marple	d	18 07					18 35						19 07						19 37		20 07				
Rose Hill Marple	d					18 11					18 44							19 30							
Romiley	d	18 11				18 16	18 38				18 49		19 11					19 35	19 40		20 11				
Woodley	d					18 19												19 38							
Hyde Central	d					18 22												19 41							
Hyde North	d					18 25												19 44							
Guide Bridge	d		18 17			18 29				18 46		19 01				19 28		19 48		19 58			20 28		
Fairfield	d					18 32												19 51							
Gorton	d		18 20							18 49		19 04				19 31				20 01			20 31		
Bredbury	d	18 14					18 41				18 52		19 14						19 43		20 14				
Brinnington	d						18 44				18 54		19 16						19 46		20 16				
Reddish North	d						18 47				18 58		19 19						19 49		20 19				
Ryder Brow	d										19 00								19 51						
Belle Vue	d										19 02								19 53						
Ashburys	d		18 23							18 54	19 05	19 08				19 34			19 56	20 04			20 34		
Ardwick	d																								
Manchester Piccadilly 10	a	18 31	18 34		18 36	18 41	18 57	19 02	19 02	19 03	19 12	19 15	19 32		19 36	19 42	20 02	20 02	20 05	20 12	20 32	20 36	20 42		21 02
Manchester Airport 85	a							19 28	19 33								20 38								21 36

A From Cleethorpes
B From Hadfield
C From Norwich to Liverpool Lime Street
D From Manchester Piccadilly
E from 18 July until 30 September. From Cleethorpes
F until 15 July. From Cleethorpes

Table 78

Mondays to Fridays

until 30 September

Sheffield, Chinley, Marple and Romiley Manchester and Manchester Airport

		NT	NT	EM	NT	NT	NT	TP	NT	NT	NT	NT
				◇				◇1				
			A	B			A	C		A		
Sheffield 7	d			20 32		20 35		22 11			22 47	
Dore & Totley	d					20 43					22 54	
Grindleford	d					20 50					23 01	
Hathersage	d					20 53					23 05	
Bamford	d					20 57					23 08	
Hope (Derbyshire)	d					21 00					23 12	
Edale	d					21 08					23 19	
Chinley	d					21 16					23 27	
Hazel Grove 86	a											
Stockport 86	a			21 20				22 53			23 47	
New Mills Central	d	20 30				21b30			22 30			23 30
Strines	d	20 33							22 33			23 33
Marple	d	20 36				21 36			22 36			23 36
Rose Hill Marple	d				21 12							
Romiley	d	20 40			21 17	21 40			22 40			23 40
Woodley	d				21 20							
Hyde Central	d				21 23							
Hyde North	d				21 26							
Guide Bridge	d		20 58		21 30		21 58			22 58		
Fairfield	d				21 33							
Gorton	d		21 01				22 01			23 01		
Bredbury	d	20 43				21 43			22 43			23 43
Brinnington	d	20 45				21 45			22 45			23 45
Reddish North	d	20 48				21 48			22 48			23 48
Ryder Brow	d	20 51				21 51			22 51			23 51
Belle Vue	d	20 52				21 52			22 52			23 52
Ashburys	d	20 55	21 04			21 55	22 04		22 55	23 04		23 55
Ardwick	d											
Manchester Piccadilly 10	a	21 03	21 12	21 32	21 42	22 05	22 12	23 02	23 03	23 12	00 02	00 03
Manchester Airport 85 ✈	a							23 26				

Mondays to Fridays

from 3 October

		NT	NT	TP	TP	NT	NT	TP	NT	NT	NT	EM	NT	NT	NT	NT	TP	NT	NT	NT	NT	NT	NT
		MX	MX																				
				◇1	◇1			◇1				◇					◇1						
						A		D			A	E		F			C	F			F		
Sheffield 7	d	22p47		03 45	05 11			06 11				06 20					07 09						07 12
Dore & Totley	d	22p54										06 27					07 15						07 19
Grindleford	d	23p01										06 35											07 29
Hathersage	d	23p05										06 39											07 32
Bamford	d	23p08										06 43											07 36
Hope (Derbyshire)	d	23p12										06 47											07 39
Edale	d	23p19										06 55											07 47
Chinley	d	23p27										07 03											07 55
Hazel Grove 86	a																						
Stockport 86	a	23p47			05 53			06 53				07 22					07 53						
New Mills Central	d		23p30				06 10			06 33			06 58			07 20				07 36			08 02
Strines	d		23p33				06 13			06 36			07 01			07 23				07 39			
Marple	d		23p36				06 16			06 39			07 04			07 26				07 42		07 59	08 09
Rose Hill Marple	d								06 30						07 16				07 41				
Romiley	d		23p40				06 23		06 37	06 46			07 12		07 21	07 33			07 46	07 49		08 03	08 13
Woodley	d								06 40						07 24				07 49				
Hyde Central	d								06 43						07 27				07 52				
Hyde North	d								06 46						07 30				07 55				
Guide Bridge	d					06 27			06 50		06 57			07 28	07 34			07 47	07 59		08 10		
Fairfield	d								06 53						07 37				08 02				
Gorton	d					06 30					07 00			07 31				07 50			08 13		
Bredbury	d		23p43				06 26			06 49			07 15			07 36				07 52		08 06	
Brinnington	d		23p45				06 28			06 52			07 17			07 39				07 55		08 09	
Reddish North	d		23p48				06 31			06 55			07 20			07 43				07 58		08 12	
Ryder Brow	d		23p51				06 34			06 58			07 24			07 45						08 15	
Belle Vue	d		23p52				06 36			07 00			07 26			07 47						08 16	
Ashburys	d		23p55			06 33	06 39			07 03	07 06		07 29	07 34		07 50		07 53			08 16	08 20	
Ardwick	d													07 38								08 22	
Manchester Piccadilly 10	a	00 02	00 03	04 40	06 05	06 42	06 47	07 02	07 03	07 12	07 15	07 34	07 36	07 44	07 47	07 56	08 02	08 03	08 12	08 09	08 25	08 30	08 33
Manchester Airport 85 ✈	a			05 00	06 29			07 29									08 26						

A From Hadfield
B From Norwich
C From Cleethorpes
D From Doncaster
E From Nottingham to Liverpool Lime Street
F From Manchester Piccadilly
b Arr. 2122

Table 78

Mondays to Fridays

from 3 October

Sheffield, Chinley, Marple and Romiley Manchester and Manchester Airport

	EM ◇ A	NT B	NT	NT	NT		TP ◇1 C	NT B	NT	NT B	NT	NT	EM ◇ A	NT B	NT		TP ◇1 C	NT B	NT	NT	NT	EM ◇ D	NT B	NT
Sheffield 7 d	07 35						08 05						08 42				09 11				09 14	09 42		
Dore & Totley d	07 42						08 11														09 21			
Grindleford d																					09 29			
Hathersage d																					09 32			
Bamford d																					09 36			
Hope (Derbyshire) d																					09 39			
Edale d																					09 47			
Chinley d	08 03						08 32														09 55			
Hazel Grove 86 a	08 16																							
Stockport 86 a	08 24						08 53						09 25				09 53					10 25		
New Mills Central d				08 22								09 04									10 01			
Strines d				08 25								09 07									10 04			
Marple d				08 29					08 48			09 10			09 35				09 52		10 07			
Rose Hill Marple d			08 15		08 35						08 59									09 55				10 30
Romiley d			08 20	08 33	08 40				08 51		09 04	09 14			09 38				09 56	10 00	10 11			10 35
Woodley d			08 23								09 07									10 03				10 38
Hyde Central d			08 26								09 10									10 06				10 41
Hyde North d			08 29								09 13									10 09				10 44
Guide Bridge d		08 27	08 33					08 49		09 12	09 17			09 28				09 58		10 13			10 28	10 48
Fairfield d			08 36								09 20									10 16				10 51
Gorton d		08 31						08 52		09 15				09 31				10 01					10 31	
Bredbury d				08 36	08 43				08 54			09 17			09 41						10 14			
Brinnington d				08 39	08 45				08 57			09 19			09 44						10 16			
Reddish North d				08 43	08 48				09 00			09 22			09 47						10 19			
Ryder Brow d									09 03										10 03					
Belle Vue d									09 04										10 05					
Ashburys d		08 34		08 48				08 56	09 07	09 18				09 34				10 04	10 07				10 34	
Ardwick d					08 54																			
Manchester Piccadilly 10 a	08 36	08 43	08 47	08 55	09 00		09 02	09 04	09 15	09 27	09 30	09 34	09 36	09 42	09 57		10 02	10 11	10 15	10 26	10 32	10 36	10 41	11 02
Manchester Airport 85 a							09 33										10 26							

	NT		TP ◇1 C	NT B	NT	NT	EM ◇ D	NT B	NT	NT	TP ◇1 C		NT B	NT	NT	EM ◇ D	NT B	NT	NT	TP ◇1 C	NT B		NT	NT
Sheffield 7 d			10 11			10 14	10 42				11 11					11 42				12 11				12 14
Dore & Totley d						10 21																		12 21
Grindleford d						10 29																		12 29
Hathersage d						10 32																		12 32
Bamford d						10 36																		12 36
Hope (Derbyshire) d						10 39																		12 39
Edale d						10 47																		12 47
Chinley d						10 55																		12 55
Hazel Grove 86 a																								
Stockport 86 a			10 53				11 25				11 53					12 25				12 53				
New Mills Central d	10 30					11 01				11 30					12 01				12 30					13 01
Strines d															12 04									
Marple d	10 35					11 07				11 35					12 07				12 35					13 07
Rose Hill Marple d					10 51				11 30					11 51				12 30					12 51	
Romiley d	10 38				10 56	11 11			11 35	11 38				11 56	12 11			12 35	12 38				12 56	13 11
Woodley d									11 38									12 38						
Hyde Central d									11 41									12 41						
Hyde North d									11 44									12 44						
Guide Bridge d				10 58				11 28	11 48				11 58				12 28	12 48			12 58			
Fairfield d									11 51									12 51						
Gorton d				11 01				11 31					12 01				12 31				13 01			
Bredbury d	10 41					11 14				11 41					12 14				12 41					13 14
Brinnington d	10 44					11 16				11 44					12 16				12 44					13 16
Reddish North d	10 47					11 19				11 47					12 19				12 47					13 19
Ryder Brow d					11 03									12 03									13 03	
Belle Vue d					11 05									12 05									13 05	
Ashburys d				11 04	11 07			11 34					12 04	12 07			12 34				13 04		13 07	
Ardwick d																								
Manchester Piccadilly 10 a	10 57		11 02	11 11	11 15	11 32	11 36	11 41	12 02	11 57	12 02		12 11	12 15	12 32	12 36	12 41	13 02	12 57	13 02	13 11		13 15	13 32
Manchester Airport 85 a			11 26								12 26									13 26				

A From Nottingham to Liverpool Lime Street
B From Manchester Piccadilly
C From Cleethorpes
D From Norwich to Liverpool Lime Street

Table 78

Mondays to Fridays

from 3 October

Sheffield, Chinley, Marple and Romiley Manchester and Manchester Airport

		EM	NT	NT	NT	TP	NT	NT	NT	EM	NT	NT	NT	TP	NT	NT	NT	EM	NT	NT	NT	TP	NT
		◇				◇1				◇				◇1				◇				◇1	
		A	B			C	B			A	B			C	B			A	B			C	B
						🍴								🍴								🍴	
Sheffield 7	d	12 42				13 11				13 42				14 11			14 14	14 42				15 11	
Dore & Totley	d																14 21						
Grindleford	d																14 29						
Hathersage	d																14 32						
Bamford	d																14 36						
Hope (Derbyshire)	d																14 39						
Edale	d																14 47						
Chinley	d																14 55						
Hazel Grove 86	a																						
Stockport 86	a	13 25				13 53				14 25				14 53				15 25				15 53	
New Mills Central	d				13 30				14 01				14 30				15 01				15 30		
Strines	d								14 04														
Marple	d				13 35				14 07				14 35				15 07				15 35		
Rose Hill Marple	d			13 30				13 51				14 30				14 51				15 30			
Romiley	d			13 35	13 38			13 56	14 11			14 35	14 38			14 56	15 11			15 35	15 38		
Woodley	d			13 38								14 38								15 38			
Hyde Central	d			13 41								14 41								15 41			
Hyde North	d			13 44								14 44								15 44			
Guide Bridge	d		13 28	13 48			13 58				14 28	14 48			14 58				15 28	15 48			15 58
Fairfield	d			13 51								14 51								15 51			
Gorton	d		13 31				14 01				14 31				15 01				15 31				16 01
Bredbury	d				13 41				14 14				14 41				15 14				15 41		
Brinnington	d				13 44				14 16				14 44				15 16				15 44		
Reddish North	d				13 47				14 19				14 47				15 19				15 47		
Ryder Brow	d							14 03								15 03							
Belle Vue	d							14 05								15 05							
Ashburys	d		13 34				14 04	14 07			14 34				15 04	15 07			15 34				16 04
Ardwick	d																						
Manchester Piccadilly 10	a	13 36	13 41	14 02	13 57	14 02	14 11	14 15	14 32	14 36	14 41	15 02	14 57	15 02	15 11	15 15	15 32	15 36	15 41	16 02	15 57	16 02	16 11
Manchester Airport 85 ✈	a					14 26								15 26								16 26	

		NT	NT	EM	NT	NT	TP	NT	NT	NT	NT	NT	EM	NT	NT	NT	NT	TP	NT	NT	NT	NT
				◇			◇1						◇					◇1				
				A	B		C	B				B	A			B		C	B			B
							🍴											🍴				
Sheffield 7	d			15 42			16 10				16 14		16 42					17 11			17 14	
Dore & Totley	d										16 21										17 21	
Grindleford	d										16 29										17 29	
Hathersage	d										16 32										17 32	
Bamford	d										16 36										17 36	
Hope (Derbyshire)	d										16 39										17 39	
Edale	d										16 47										17 47	
Chinley	d										16 55										17 55	
Hazel Grove 86	a																					
Stockport 86	a			16 25			16 53						17 25					17 53				
New Mills Central	d		16 01						16 37		17 01				17 23						18 01	
Strines	d		16 04																		18 04	
Marple	d		16 07						16 42	16 52	17 06				17 28					17 52	18 07	
Rose Hill Marple	d	15 51				16 26								17 10			17 36					
Romiley	d	15 56	16 11			16 31			16 45	16 56	17 10			17 15	17 32		17 41			17 56	18 11	
Woodley	d								16 49					17 18								
Hyde Central	d								16 52					17 21								
Hyde North	d								16 54					17 24								
Guide Bridge	d				16 28			16 49	16 58			17 17		17 28		17 42			18 00			18 17
Fairfield	d													17 31								
Gorton	d				16 31			16 52				17 20				17 45						18 20
Bredbury	d		16 14			16 34					17 13						17 44				18 14	
Brinnington	d		16 16			16 37											17 46					
Reddish North	d		16 19			16 40											17 49			18 02		
Ryder Brow	d	16 03				16 42				17 03										18 04		
Belle Vue	d	16 05				16 44				17 05										18 06		
Ashburys	d	16 07			16 34	16 47		16 55	17 03	17 07		17 24				17 48	17 55			18 08		18 24
Ardwick	d																					
Manchester Piccadilly 10	a	16 15	16 32	16 36	16 41	16 56	17 02	17 05	17 10	17 15	17 29	17 33	17 37	17 42	17 48	17 57	18 01	18 02	18 12	18 16	18 31	18 34
Manchester Airport 85 ✈	a						17 32											18 26				

A From Norwich to Liverpool Lime Street

B From Manchester Piccadilly

C From Cleethorpes

Table 78

Mondays to Fridays

from 3 October

Sheffield, Chinley, Marple and Romiley Manchester and Manchester Airport

	EM	NT	NT	TP	NT	NT	NT	NT	EM		NT	TP	NT	NT	NT	NT	EM	NT	TP		NT	NT	EM	NT
	◇			◇1					◇			◇1					◇		◇1				◇	
	A			B	C		C		A		D	B			D		A	D	B			D	E	
				🚲								🚲												
Sheffield 7 d	17 40			18 10					18 43			19 11				19 14	19 42		20 11				20 32	
Dore & Totley d																19 21								
Grindleford d																19 29								
Hathersage d																19 32								
Bamford d																19 36								
Hope (Derbyshire) d																19 39								
Edale d																19 47								
Chinley d				18 34				18 54								19 55								
Hazel Grove 86 a																								
Stockport 86 a	18 25			18 53					19 25			19 53					20 25		20 53				21 20	
New Mills Central d								19 01								20 01					20 30			
Strines d								19 04													20 33			
Marple d			18 35					19 07						19 37		20 07					20 36			
Rose Hill Marple d		18 11				18 44							19 30											21 12
Romiley d		18 16	18 38			18 49		19 11					19 35	19 40		20 11					20 40			21 17
Woodley d		18 19											19 38											21 20
Hyde Central d		18 22											19 41											21 23
Hyde North d		18 25											19 44											21 26
Guide Bridge d		18 29			18 46		19 01				19 28		19 48		19 58			20 28				20 58		21 30
Fairfield d		18 32											19 51											21 33
Gorton d					18 49		19 04				19 31				20 01			20 31				21 01		
Bredbury d			18 41			18 52		19 14						19 43		20 14					20 43			
Brinnington d			18 44			18 54		19 16						19 46		20 16					20 45			
Reddish North d			18 47			18 58		19 19						19 49		20 19					20 48			
Ryder Brow d						19 00								19 51							20 51			
Belle Vue d						19 02								19 53							20 52			
Ashburys d					18 54	19 05	19 08				19 34			19 56	20 04			20 34			20 55	21 04		
Ardwick d																								
Manchester Piccadilly 10 a	18 36	18 41	18 57	19 02	19 03	19 12	19 15	19 32	19 36		19 42	20 02	20 02	20 05	20 12	20 32	20 36	20 42	21 02		21 03	21 12	21 32	21 42
Manchester Airport 85 ✈ a				19 28								20 38							21 36					

	NT	NT	TP	NT	NT		NT	NT
			◇1					
		D	B		D			
Sheffield 7 d	20 35		22 11				22 47	
Dore & Totley d	20 43						22 54	
Grindleford d	20 50						23 01	
Hathersage d	20 53						23 05	
Bamford d	20 57						23 08	
Hope (Derbyshire) d	21 00						23 12	
Edale d	21 08						23 19	
Chinley d	21 16						23 27	
Hazel Grove 86 a								
Stockport 86 a			22 53				23 47	
New Mills Central d	21b30			22 30				23 30
Strines d				22 33				23 33
Marple d	21 36			22 36				23 36
Rose Hill Marple d								
Romiley d	21 40			22 40				23 40
Woodley d								
Hyde Central d								
Hyde North d								
Guide Bridge d		21 58			22 58			
Fairfield d								
Gorton d		22 01			23 01			
Bredbury d	21 43			22 43				23 43
Brinnington d	21 45			22 45				23 45
Reddish North d	21 48			22 48				23 48
Ryder Brow d	21 51			22 51				23 51
Belle Vue d	21 52			22 52				23 52
Ashburys d	21 55	22 04		22 55	23 04			23 55
Ardwick d								
Manchester Piccadilly 10 a	22 05	22 12	23 02	23 03	23 12		00 02	00 03
Manchester Airport 85 ✈ a			23 26					

A From Norwich to Liverpool Lime Street
B From Cleethorpes
C From Manchester Piccadilly
D From Hadfield
E From Norwich
b Arr. 2122

Sheffield, Chinley, Marple and Romiley Manchester and Manchester Airport

		NT	NT	TP	TP	TP	NT	EM	NT	NT	NT	NT	NT	TP	NT	NT	EM	NT	NT	NT	TP	NT	NT
				◇1	◇1	◇1 A	B	◇ C	D	E	B			◇1 F	B		◇ C	B			◇1 F	B	
Sheffield [7]	d	22p47		03 45	05 11	06 11		06 20						07 09		07 12	07 35				08 05		
Dore & Totley	d	22p54						06 27						07 15		07 19	07 42				08 11		
Grindleford	d	23p01						06 35								07 29							
Hathersage	d	23p05						06 39								07 32							
Bamford	d	23p08						06 43								07 36							
Hope (Derbyshire)	d	23p12						06 47								07 39							
Edale	d	23p19						06 55								07 47							
Chinley	d	23p27						07 03								07 55	08 03				08 32		
Hazel Grove 86	a																08 16						
Stockport 86	a	23p47			05 53	06 53		07 22						07 53			08 24				08 53		
New Mills Central	d		23p30						06 58	07 01						08 01							
Strines	d		23p33						07 01	07 04						08 04							
Marple	d		23p36						07 04	07 07			07 35			08 07				08 35			08 52
Rose Hill Marple	d											07 30							08 30				
Romiley	d		23p40						07 12	07 12		07 35	07 38			08 12			08 35	08 38			08 56
Woodley	d											07 38							08 38				
Hyde Central	d											07 41							08 41				
Hyde North	d											07 44							08 44				
Guide Bridge	d						06 57				07 28	07 48			07 58			08 28	08 48			08 58	
Fairfield	d											07 51							08 51				
Gorton	d						07 00				07 31				08 01			08 31				09 01	
Bredbury	d		23p43						07 15	07 15			07 41			08 15				08 41			
Brinnington	d		23p45						07 17	07 17			07 44			08 16				08 44			
Reddish North	d		23p48						07 20	07 20			07 47			08 19				08 47			
Ryder Brow	d		23p51						07 24	07 24													09 03
Belle Vue	d		23p52						07 26	07 26													09 05
Ashburys	d		23p55				07 03		07 29	07 29	07 34				08 04			08 34				09 04	09 07
Ardwick	d																						
Manchester Piccadilly [10]	a	00 02	00 03	04 40	06 05	07 02	07 12	07 34	07 36	07 36	07 42	08 02	07 59	08 02	08 12	08 32	08 36	08 42	09 02	08 57	09 02	09 12	09 15
Manchester Airport 85	a			05 00	06 29	07 29								08 26							09 26		

		NT	EM	NT	NT	NT	TP	NT	NT	NT	EM	NT	NT	NT	TP	NT	NT	NT	EM	NT	NT	NT	TP
			◇ C	B			◇1 F	B			◇ G	B			◇1 F	B			◇ G	B			◇1 F
Sheffield [7]	d	08 14	08 42				09 11			09 14	09 42				10 11			10 14	10 42				11 11
Dore & Totley	d	08 21								09 21								10 21					
Grindleford	d	08 29								09 29								10 29					
Hathersage	d	08 32								09 32								10 32					
Bamford	d	08 36								09 36								10 36					
Hope (Derbyshire)	d	08 39								09 39								10 39					
Edale	d	08 47								09 47								10 47					
Chinley	d	08 55								09 55								10 55					
Hazel Grove 86	a																						
Stockport 86	a		09 25				09 53				10 25				10 53				11 25				11 53
New Mills Central	d	09 01								10 01								11 01					
Strines	d	09 04								10 04													
Marple	d	09 07				09 35			09 52	10 07				10 35				11 07				11 35	
Rose Hill Marple	d				09 30								10 30				10 51				11 30		
Romiley	d	09 11			09 35	09 38			09 56	10 11			10 35	10 38			10 56	11 11			11 35	11 38	
Woodley	d				09 38								10 38								11 38		
Hyde Central	d				09 41								10 41								11 41		
Hyde North	d				09 44								10 44								11 44		
Guide Bridge	d			09 28	09 48			09 58				10 28	10 48			10 58				11 28	11 48		
Fairfield	d				09 51								10 51								11 51		
Gorton	d			09 31				10 01				10 31				11 01				11 31			
Bredbury	d	09 14				09 41				10 14				10 41				11 14				11 41	
Brinnington	d	09 16				09 44				10 16				10 44				11 16				11 44	
Reddish North	d	09 19				09 47				10 19				10 47				11 19				11 47	
Ryder Brow	d								10 03								11 03						
Belle Vue	d								10 05								11 05						
Ashburys	d			09 34				10 04	10 07			10 34				11 04	11 07			11 34			
Ardwick	d																						
Manchester Piccadilly [10]	a	09 32	09 36	09 42	10 02	09 57	10 02	10 12	10 15	10 32	10 36	10 42	11 02	10 57	11 02	11 12	11 15	11 32	11 36	11 42	12 02	11 57	12 02
Manchester Airport 85	a						10 26								11 26								12 26

A From Doncaster
B From Hadfield
C From Nottingham to Liverpool Lime Street
D from 8 October
E until 1 October
F From Cleethorpes
G From Norwich to Liverpool Lime Street

Sheffield, Chinley, Marple and Romiley Manchester and Manchester Airport

		NT A	NT	NT	EM ◇ B	NT A	NT	NT	TP ◇1 C ✠	NT A	NT	NT	EM ◇ B	NT A	NT	NT	TP ◇1 C ✠	NT A	NT	NT	EM ◇ B	NT A
Sheffield 7 🚌	d			11 14	11 42				12 11			12 14	12 42				13 11			13 14	13 42	
Dore & Totley	d			11 21								12 21								13 21		
Grindleford	d			11 29								12 29								13 29		
Hathersage	d			11 32								12 32								13 32		
Bamford	d			11 36								12 36								13 36		
Hope (Derbyshire)	d			11 39								12 39								13 39		
Edale	d			11 47								12 47								13 47		
Chinley	d			11 55								12 55								13 55		
Hazel Grove 86	a																					
Stockport 86	a				12 25				12 53				13 25				13 53				14 25	
New Mills Central	d			12 01								13 01								14 01		
Strines	d			12 04																14 04		
Marple	d			12 07				12 35				13 07				13 35				14 07		
Rose Hill Marple	d		11 51				12 30				12 51				13 30				13 51			
Romiley	d		11 56	12 11			12 35	12 38			12 56	13 11			13 35	13 38			13 56	14 11		
Woodley	d						12 38								13 38							
Hyde Central	d						12 41								13 41							
Hyde North	d						12 44								13 44							
Guide Bridge	d	11 58				12 28	12 48			12 58				13 28	13 48			13 58				14 28
Fairfield	d						12 51								13 51							
Gorton	d	12 01				12 31				13 01				13 31				14 01				14 31
Bredbury	d			12 14				12 41				13 14				13 41				14 14		
Brinnington	d			12 16				12 44				13 16				13 44				14 16		
Reddish North	d			12 19				12 47				13 19				13 47				14 19		
Ryder Brow	d		12 03								13 03								14 03			
Belle Vue	d		12 05								13 05								14 05			
Ashburys	d	12 04	12 07			12 34				13 04	13 07			13 34				14 04	14 07			14 34
Ardwick	d																					
Manchester Piccadilly 10 🚌	a	12 12	12 15	12 32	12 36	12 42	13 02	12 57	13 02	13 12	13 15	13 32	13 36	13 42	14 02	13 57	14 02	14 12	14 15	14 32	14 36	14 42
Manchester Airport 85 ✈	a								13 26								14 26					

		NT	NT	TP ◇1 C ✠	NT A	NT	NT	EM ◇ B	NT A	NT	NT	TP ◇1 C ✠	NT A	NT	NT	EM ◇ B	NT A	NT	NT	TP ◇1 C ✠	NT A	NT	NT
Sheffield 7 🚌	d			14 11			14 14	14 42				15 11			15 14	15 42				16 10			16 14
Dore & Totley	d						14 21								15 21								16 21
Grindleford	d						14 29								15 29								16 29
Hathersage	d						14 32								15 32								16 32
Bamford	d						14 36								15 36								16 36
Hope (Derbyshire)	d						14 39								15 39								16 39
Edale	d						14 47								15 47								16 47
Chinley	d						14 55								15 55								16 55
Hazel Grove 86	a																						
Stockport 86	a			14 53				15 25				15 53				16 25				16 53			
New Mills Central	d						15 01								16 01								17 01
Strines	d														16 04								
Marple	d		14 35				15 07				15 35				16 07				16 34				17 07
Rose Hill Marple	d	14 30				14 51				15 30				15 51				16 30				16 51	
Romiley	d	14 35	14 38			14 56	15 11			15 35	15 38			15 56	16 11			16 35	16 38			16 56	17 11
Woodley	d	14 38								15 38								16 38					
Hyde Central	d	14 41								15 41								16 41					
Hyde North	d	14 44								15 44								16 44					
Guide Bridge	d	14 48			14 58				15 28	15 48			15 58				16 28	16 48			16 58		
Fairfield	d	14 51								15 51								16 51					
Gorton	d				15 01				15 31				16 01				16 31				17 01		
Bredbury	d		14 41				15 14				15 41				16 14				16 41				17 14
Brinnington	d		14 44				15 16				15 44				16 16				16 43				17 16
Reddish North	d		14 47				15 19				15 47				16 19				16 46				17 19
Ryder Brow	d					15 03								16 03								17 03	
Belle Vue	d					15 05								16 05								17 05	
Ashburys	d				15 04	15 07			15 34				16 04	16 07			16 34				17 04	17 07	
Ardwick	d																						
Manchester Piccadilly 10 🚌	a	15 02	14 57	15 02	15 12	15 15	15 32	15 36	15 42	16 02	15 57	16 02	16 12	16 15	16 33	16 36	16 42	17 02	16 56	17 02	17 12	17 15	17 32
Manchester Airport 85 ✈	a			15 26								16 26								17 32			

A From Hadfield
B From Norwich to Liverpool Lime Street
C From Cleethorpes

Table 78

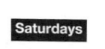

Sheffield, Chinley, Marple and Romiley Manchester and Manchester Airport

		EM	NT	NT	NT	TP	NT	NT	NT	EM	NT	NT	NT	TP	NT	NT	NT	EM	NT	TP	NT	NT
		◇				◇■				◇				◇■				◇		◇■		
		A	B			C	B			A	B			C	B			A	B	C		B
						⚲								⚲						⚲		
Sheffield ■ ⇌	d	16 42				17 11			17 14	17 40				18 10			18 14	18 42		19 11		
Dore & Totley	d								17 21								18 21					
Grindleford	d								17 29								18 28					
Hathersage	d								17 32								18 32					
Bamford	d								17 36								18 35					
Hope (Derbyshire)	d								17 39								18 39					
Edale	d								17 47								18 46					
Chinley	d								17 55					18 34			18 54					
Hazel Grove 86	a																					
Stockport 86	a	17 25				17 53				18 25				18 53				19 25		19 53		
New Mills Central	d								18 01								19 01					
Strines	d								18 04								19 04					
Marple	d				17 34			17 52	18 07				18 35			18 52	19 07					
Rose Hill Marple	d			17 30								18 30									19 30	
Romiley	d			17 35	17 38			17 56	18 11			18 35	18 38			18 56	19 11				19 35	
Woodley	d			17 38								18 38									19 38	
Hyde Central	d			17 41								18 41									19 41	
Hyde North	d			17 44								18 44									19 44	
Guide Bridge	d		17 28	17 48			17 58				18 28	18 48			18 58				19 28		19 48	19 58
Fairfield	d			17 51								18 51									19 51	
Gorton	d		17 31				18 01				18 31				19 01				19 31			20 01
Bredbury	d				17 41				18 14				18 41				19 14					
Brinnington	d				17 43				18 16				18 44				19 16					
Reddish North	d				17 46				18 19				18 47				19 19					
Ryder Brow	d							18 03								19 03						
Belle Vue	d							18 05								19 05						
Ashburys	d		17 34				18 04	18 07			18 34				19 04	19 07			19 34			20 04
Ardwick	d																					
Manchester Piccadilly ■ ⇌	a	17 37	17 42	18 02	17 56	18 02	18 12	18 15	18 32	18 36	18 42	19 02	18 57	19 02	19 12	19 15	19 32	19 36	19 42	20 02	20 02	20 12
Manchester Airport 85 ✈	a					18 26								19 28						20 36		

		NT	NT	EM	TP	NT	NT	EM	NT	NT	NT	NT	NT	NT	NT
				◇	◇■			◇							
				A	C		B	D			B		B		
Sheffield ■ ⇌	d		19 14	19 42	20 11			20 31		20 35				22 24	
Dore & Totley	d		19 21							20 42				22 31	
Grindleford	d		19 29							20 50				22 38	
Hathersage	d		19 32							20 53				22 41	
Bamford	d		19 36							20 57				22 45	
Hope (Derbyshire)	d		19 39							21 00				22 48	
Edale	d		19 47							21 08				22 56	
Chinley	d		19 55							21 16				23 04	
Hazel Grove 86	a														
Stockport 86	a			20 25	20 53			21 20						23 21	
New Mills Central	d		20 01			20 30				21b30		22 30			23 30
Strines	d					20 33						22 33			23 33
Marple	d	19 56	20 07			20 36				21 36		22 36			23 36
Rose Hill Marple	d								21 12						
Romiley	d	19 59	20 11			20 40			21 17	21 40		22 40			23 40
Woodley	d								21 20						
Hyde Central	d								21 23						
Hyde North	d								21 26						
Guide Bridge	d						20 58		21 30		21 58		22 58		
Fairfield	d								21 33						
Gorton	d						21 01				22 01		23 01		
Bredbury	d	20 02	20 14			20 43				21 43		22 43			23 43
Brinnington	d	20 05	20 16			20 45				21 45		22 45			23 45
Reddish North	d	20 08	20 19			20 48				21 48		22 48			23 48
Ryder Brow	d	20 10				20 51				21 51		22 51			23 51
Belle Vue	d	20 12				20 52				21 52		22 52			23 52
Ashburys	d	20 15				20 55	21 04			21 55	22 04	22 55	23 04		23 55
Ardwick	d														
Manchester Piccadilly ■ ⇌	a	20 22	20 32	20 36	21 02	21 03	21 12	21 32	21 42	22 05	22 12	23 03	23 12	23 43	00 03
Manchester Airport 85 ✈	a				21 36										

A From Norwich to Liverpool Lime Street
B From Hadfield
C From Cleethorpes
D From Norwich
b Arr. 2122

Table 78

Sundays
until 11 September

Sheffield, Chinley, Marple and Romiley Manchester and Manchester Airport

		NT A	TP ◇1	TP ◇1 B	NT	NT C	TP ◇1	NT C	NT	EM ◇ D		NT C	TP ◇1 E	NT C	NT	EM ◇ D	NT C	TP ◇1 E	NT C	NT		EM ◇ D	NT C	TP ◇1 E	NT C
Sheffield 7	d		07 50	09 10	09 20		10 10		10 20	10 41			11 10		11 14	11 38		12 10		12 13		12 41		13 10	
Dore & Totley	d				09 27				10 27	10 48					11 21					12 21					
Grindleford	d				09 34				10 34						11 29					12 28					
Hathersage	d				09 38				10 38						11 32					12 32					
Bamford	d				09 41				10 41						11 36					12 35					
Hope (Derbyshire)	d				09 45				10 45						11 39					12 39					
Edale	d				09 52				10 52						11 47					12 46					
Chinley	d				10 00				11 00						11 55					12 54					
Hazel Grove 86	a																								
Stockport 86	a		08 31	09 53			10 53			11 25			11 53			12 25		12 53				13 25		13 53	
New Mills Central	d	23p30			10 07				11 07						12 01					13 01					
Strines	d	23p33			10 10				11 10						12 04					13 04					
Marple	d	23p36			10 13				11 13						12 07					13 07					
Rose Hill Marple	d																								
Romiley	d	23p40			10 17				11 17						12 11					13 11					
Woodley	d																								
Hyde Central	d																								
Hyde North	d																								
Guide Bridge	d					10 28		10 58				11 28		11 58			12 28		12 58				13 28		13 58
Fairfield	d																								
Gorton	d					10 31		11 01				11 31		12 01			12 31		13 01				13 31		14 01
Bredbury	d	23p43			10 20				11 20						12 14					13 14					
Brinnington	d	23p45			10 22				11 22						12 16					13 16					
Reddish North	d	23p48			10 25				11 25						12 19					13 19					
Ryder Brow	d	23p51																							
Belle Vue	d	23p52																							
Ashburys	d	23p55				10 34		11 04				11 34		12 04			12 34		13 04				13 34		14 04
Ardwick	d																								
Manchester Piccadilly 10	a	00 03	08 42	10 04	10 37	10 42	11 06	11 12	11 38	11 37		11 42	12 06	12 12	12 31	12 37	12 42	13 06	13 12	13 31		13 37	13 42	14 06	14 12
Manchester Airport 85	a		09 07										12 29					13 29						14 29	

		NT	EM ◇ F	NT C	TP ◇1 G	NT C		EM ◇ F	NT C	TP ◇1 E	NT C	NT	EM ◇ D	NT C	TP ◇1 E	NT C		NT	EM ◇ D	NT C	TP ◇1 E	NT C	NT	EM ◇ F	NT C
Sheffield 7	d	13 13	13 38		14 11			14 39		15 11		15 14	15 38		16 11			16 15	16 44		17 11		17 14	17 44	
Dore & Totley	d	13 20										15 21						16 22					17 21		
Grindleford	d	13 28										15 29						16 30					17 29		
Hathersage	d	13 31										15 32						16 33					17 32		
Bamford	d	13 35										15 36						16 37					17 36		
Hope (Derbyshire)	d	13 38										15 39						16 40					17 39		
Edale	d	13 46										15 47						16 48					17 47		
Chinley	d	13 54										15 55						16 56					17 55		
Hazel Grove 86	a																								
Stockport 86	a		14 25		14 53			15 25		15 53			16 25		16 53				17 26		17 53			18 25	
New Mills Central	d	14 00										16 01						17 02					18 01		
Strines	d	14 03										16 04						17 05					18 04		
Marple	d	14 07										16 07						17 08					18 07		
Rose Hill Marple	d																								
Romiley	d	14 10										16 11						17 12					18 11		
Woodley	d																								
Hyde Central	d																								
Hyde North	d																								
Guide Bridge	d			14 28		14 58			15 28		15 58			16 28		16 58				17 28		17 58			18 28
Fairfield	d																								
Gorton	d			14 31		15 01			15 31		16 01			16 31		17 01				17 31		18 01			18 31
Bredbury	d	14 13										16 14						17 15					18 14		
Brinnington	d	14 16										16 16						17 17					18 16		
Reddish North	d	14 19										16 19						17 20					18 19		
Ryder Brow	d																								
Belle Vue	d																								
Ashburys	d			14 34		15 04			15 34		16 04			16 34		17 04				17 34		18 04			18 34
Ardwick	d																								
Manchester Piccadilly 10	a	14 31	14 37	14 42	15 06	15 12		15 37	15 42	16 06	16 12	16 31	16 37	16 42	17 06	17 12		17 32	17 37	17 42	18 06	18 12	18 31	18 37	18 42
Manchester Airport 85	a				15 29					16 34					17 29						18 29				

A not 22 May
B From Meadowhall
C From Hadfield
D From Nottingham to Liverpool Lime Street
E From Cleethorpes
F From Norwich to Liverpool Lime Street
G From Doncaster

Table 78

Sundays

until 11 September

Sheffield, Chinley, Marple and Romiley Manchester and Manchester Airport

		TP		NT	NT	EM	NT	TP	NT	NT	EM	NT		TP	NT	EM	TP	NT	NT	NT
		◇1				◇		◇1			◇			◇1		◇	◇1			
		A		B		C	B	A	B		D	B		A	B	D	A	B		
Sheffield 7	d	18 11			18 15	18 37		19 11		19 14	19 35			20 11		20 35	21 11		22 17	
Dore & Totley	d				18 22					19 21									22 24	
Grindleford	d				18 30					19 29									22 32	
Hathersage	d				18 33					19 32									22 35	
Bamford	d				18 37					19 36									22 39	
Hope (Derbyshire)	d				18 40					19 39									22 42	
Edale	d				18 48					19 47									22 50	
Chinley	d				18 56					19 55									22 58	
Hazel Grove 86	a																			
Stockport 86	a	18 53				19 25		19 55			20 25			20 53		21 24	21 53		23 16	
New Mills Central	d				19 02					20 01										23 01
Strines	d				19 05					20 04										23 04
Marple	d				19 08					20 07										23 07
Rose Hill Marple	d																			
Romiley	d				19 12					20 11										23 11
Woodley	d																			
Hyde Central	d																			
Hyde North	d																			
Guide Bridge	d			18 58			19 28		19 58			20 28			20 58			21 58		
Fairfield	d																			
Gorton	d			19 01			19 31		20 01			20 31			21 01			22 01		
Bredbury	d				19 15					20 14										23 14
Brinnington	d				19 17					20 16										23 16
Reddish North	d				19 20					20 19										23 19
Ryder Brow	d																			
Belle Vue	d																			
Ashburys	d			19 04			19 34		20 04			20 34			21 04			22 04		
Ardwick	d																			
Manchester Piccadilly 10	a	19 06		19 12	19 36	19 37	19 42	20 09	20 12	20 32	20 38	20 42		21 06	21 12	21 36	22 06	22 12	23 29	23 31
Manchester Airport 85 ✈	a	19 29						20 32						21 29			22 29			

Sundays

18 September to 23 October

		NT	TP	TP	NT	NT	TP	NT	EM	NT		TP	NT	NT	EM	NT	TP	NT	EM	NT		TP	NT	NT	EM
			◇1	◇1			◇1		◇			◇1			◇		◇1		◇			◇1			◇
				E		B		B	F	B		A	B		F	B	A	B	F	B		A	B		F
Sheffield 7	d		07 50	09 10	09 20		10 10		10 41			11 10		11 14	11 38		12 10		12 41			13 10		13 13	13 38
Dore & Totley	d				09 27				10 48					11 21										13 20	
Grindleford	d				09 34									11 29										13 28	
Hathersage	d				09 38									11 32										13 31	
Bamford	d				09 41									11 36										13 35	
Hope (Derbyshire)	d				09 45									11 39										13 38	
Edale	d				09 52									11 47										13 46	
Chinley	d				10 00									11 55										13 54	
Hazel Grove 86	a																								
Stockport 86	a		08 31	09 53					11 25			11 53			12 25		12 53		13 25			13 53			14 25
New Mills Central	d	23p30			10 07									12 01										14 00	
Strines	d	23p33			10 10									12 04										14 03	
Marple	d	23p36			10 13									12 07										14 07	
Rose Hill Marple	d																								
Romiley	d	23p40			10 17									12 11										14 10	
Woodley	d																								
Hyde Central	d																								
Hyde North	d																								
Guide Bridge	d					10 28		10 58		11 28			11 58			12 28		12 58		13 28			13 58		
Fairfield	d																								
Gorton	d					10 31		11 01		11 31			12 01			12 31		13 01		13 31			14 01		
Bredbury	d	23p43			10 20									12 14										14 13	
Brinnington	d	23p45			10 22									12 16										14 16	
Reddish North	d	23p48			10 25									12 19										14 19	
Ryder Brow	d	23p51																							
Belle Vue	d	23p52																							
Ashburys	d	23p55				10 34		11 04		11 34			12 04			12 34		13 04		13 34			14 04		
Ardwick	d																								
Manchester Piccadilly 10	a	00 03	08 42	10 06	10 37	10 42	11 04	11 12	11 37	11 42		12 06	12 12	12 31	12 37	12 42	13 06	13 12	13 37	13 42		14 06	14 12	14 31	14 37
Manchester Airport 85 ✈	a		09 07									12 34					13 29					14 34			

A From Cleethorpes
B From Hadfield
C From Norwich to Liverpool Lime Street
D From Norwich
E From Meadowhall
F From Nottingham to Liverpool Lime Street

Table 78

Sundays

18 September to 23 October

Sheffield, Chinley, Marple and Romiley Manchester and Manchester Airport

		NT	TP	NT	EM	NT		TP	NT	NT	EM	NT	TP	NT	EM	NT		TP	NT	NT	EM	NT	TP	NT	NT
			◇1		◇			◇1			◇		◇1		◇			◇1			◇		◇1		
		A	B	A	C	A		D	A		E	A	D	A	E	A		D	A		C	A	D	A	
Sheffield 7 ⛴	d		14 11		14 39			15 11		15 14	15 38		16 11		16 44			17 11		17 14	17 44		18 11		18 15
Dore & Totley	d									15 21										17 21					18 22
Grindleford	d									15 29										17 29					18 30
Hathersage	d									15 32										17 32					18 33
Bamford	d									15 36										17 36					18 37
Hope (Derbyshire)	d									15 39										17 39					18 40
Edale	d									15 47										17 47					18 48
Chinley	d									15 55										17 55					18 56
Hazel Grove 86	a																								
Stockport 86	a		14 53		15 25			15 53			16 25		16 53		17 26			17 53			18 25		18 53		
New Mills Central	d									16 01										18 01					19 02
Strines	d									16 04										18 04					19 05
Marple	d									16 07										18 07					19 08
Rose Hill Marple	d																								
Romiley	d									16 11										18 11					19 12
Woodley	d																								
Hyde Central	d																								
Hyde North	d																								
Guide Bridge	d	14 28		14 58		15 28			15 58			16 28		16 58		17 28			17 58			18 28		18 58	
Fairfield	d																								
Gorton	d	14 31		15 01		15 31			16 01			16 31		17 01		17 31			18 01			18 31		19 01	
Bredbury	d									16 14										18 14					19 15
Brinnington	d									16 16										18 16					19 17
Reddish North	d									16 19										18 19					19 20
Ryder Brow	d																								
Belle Vue	d																								
Ashburys	d	14 34		15 04		15 34			16 04			16 34		17 04		17 34			18 04			18 34		19 04	
Ardwick	d																								
Manchester Piccadilly 10 ⛴	a	14 42	15 06	15 12	15 37	15 42		16 06	16 12	16 31	16 37	16 42	17 06	17 12	17 37	17 42		18 06	18 12	18 31	18 37	18 42	19 06	19 12	19 36
Manchester Airport 85 ✈	a		15 34					16 34					17 29					18 29					19 29		

		EM		NT	TP	NT	NT	EM	NT	TP	NT	EM		TP	NT	NT	NT
		◇			◇1			◇		◇1		◇		◇1			
		C		A	D	A		F	A	D	A	F		D	A		
Sheffield 7 ⛴	d	18 37			19 11		19 14	19 35		20 11		20 35		21 11		22 17	
Dore & Totley	d						19 21									22 24	
Grindleford	d						19 29									22 32	
Hathersage	d						19 32									22 35	
Bamford	d						19 36									22 39	
Hope (Derbyshire)	d						19 39									22 42	
Edale	d						19 47									22 50	
Chinley	d						19 55									22 58	
Hazel Grove 86	a																
Stockport 86	a	19 25			19 55			20 25		20 53		21 24		21 53		23 16	
New Mills Central	d						20 01										23 01
Strines	d						20 04										23 04
Marple	d						20 07										23 07
Rose Hill Marple	d																
Romiley	d						20 11										23 11
Woodley	d																
Hyde Central	d																
Hyde North	d																
Guide Bridge	d			19 28		19 58			20 28		20 58				21 58		
Fairfield	d																
Gorton	d			19 31		20 01			20 31		21 01				22 01		
Bredbury	d						20 14										23 14
Brinnington	d						20 16										23 16
Reddish North	d						20 19										23 19
Ryder Brow	d																
Belle Vue	d																
Ashburys	d			19 34		20 04			20 34		21 04				22 04		
Ardwick	d																
Manchester Piccadilly 10 ⛴	a	19 37		19 42	20 09	20 12	20 32	20 38	20 42	21 06	21 12	21 36		22 06	22 12	23 29	23 31
Manchester Airport 85 ✈	a				20 32					21 29				22 29			

A From Hadfield
B From Doncaster
C From Norwich to Liverpool Lime Street
D From Cleethorpes
E From Nottingham to Liverpool Lime Street
F From Norwich

Table 78

Sundays
from 30 October

Sheffield, Chinley, Marple and Romiley Manchester and Manchester Airport

Station		NT	TP ◇1	TP ◇1 A	NT	NT B	TP ◇1	NT B	EM ◇ C	NT B		TP ◇1 D	NT B	NT	EM ◇ C	NT B	TP ◇1 D	NT B	EM ◇ C	NT B		TP ◇1 D	NT B	NT	EM ◇ C
Sheffield 7 ⇌	d		07 50	09 10	09 20		10 10		10 41			11 10		11 14	11 38		12 10		12 41			13 10		13 13	13 38
Dore & Totley	d				09 27				10 48					11 21										13 20	
Grindleford	d				09 34									11 29										13 28	
Hathersage	d				09 38									11 32										13 31	
Bamford	d				09 41									11 36										13 35	
Hope (Derbyshire)	d				09 45									11 39										13 38	
Edale	d				09 52									11 47										13 46	
Chinley	d				10 00									11 55										13 54	
Hazel Grove 86	a																								
Stockport 86	a		08 31	09 53					11 25			11 53			12 25		12 53		13 25			13 53			14 25
New Mills Central	d	23p30			10 07									12 01										14 00	
Strines	d	23p33			10 10									12 04										14 03	
Marple	d	23p36			10 13									12 07										14 07	
Rose Hill Marple	d																								
Romiley	d	23p40			10 17									12 11										14 10	
Woodley	d																								
Hyde Central	d																								
Hyde North	d																								
Guide Bridge	d					10 28		10 58		11 28			11 58			12 28		12 58		13 28			13 58		
Fairfield	d																								
Gorton	d					10 31		11 01		11 31			12 01			12 31		13 01		13 31			14 01		
Bredbury	d	23p43			10 20									12 14										14 13	
Brinnington	d	23p45			10 22									12 16										14 16	
Reddish North	d	23p48			10 25									12 19										14 19	
Ryder Brow	d	23p51																							
Belle Vue	d	23p52																							
Ashburys	d	23p55				10 34		11 04		11 34			12 04			12 34		13 04		13 34			14 04		
Ardwick	d																								
Manchester Piccadilly 10 ⇌	a	00 03	08 42	10 06	10 37	10 42	11 04	11 12	11 37	11 42		12 06	12 12	12 31	12 37	12 42	13 06	13 12	13 37	13 42		14 06	14 12	14 31	14 37
Manchester Airport 85 ✈	a		09 07									12 34					13 29					14 29			

Station		NT B	TP ◇1 E	NT B	EM ◇ F	NT B		TP ◇1 D	NT B	NT	EM ◇ C	NT B	TP ◇1 D	NT B	EM ◇ C	NT B		TP ◇1 D	NT B	NT	EM ◇ F	NT B	TP ◇1 D	NT B	NT
Sheffield 7 ⇌	d		14 11		14 39			15 11		15 14	15 38		16 11		16 44			17 11		17 14	17 44		18 11		18 15
Dore & Totley	d									15 21										17 21					18 22
Grindleford	d									15 29										17 29					18 30
Hathersage	d									15 32										17 32					18 33
Bamford	d									15 36										17 36					18 37
Hope (Derbyshire)	d									15 39										17 39					18 40
Edale	d									15 47										17 47					18 48
Chinley	d									15 55										17 55					18 56
Hazel Grove 86	a																								
Stockport 86	a		14 53		15 25			15 53			16 25		16 53		17 26			17 53			18 25		18 53		
New Mills Central	d									16 01										18 01					19 02
Strines	d									16 04										18 04					19 05
Marple	d									16 07										18 07					19 08
Rose Hill Marple	d																								
Romiley	d									16 11										18 11					19 12
Woodley	d																								
Hyde Central	d																								
Hyde North	d																								
Guide Bridge	d	14 28		14 58		15 28			15 58			16 28		16 58		17 28			17 58			18 28		18 58	
Fairfield	d																								
Gorton	d	14 31		15 01		15 31			16 01			16 31		17 01		17 31			18 01			18 31		19 01	
Bredbury	d									16 14										18 14					19 15
Brinnington	d									16 16										18 16					19 17
Reddish North	d									16 19										18 19					19 20
Ryder Brow	d																								
Belle Vue	d																								
Ashburys	d	14 34		15 04		15 34			16 04			16 34		17 04		17 34			18 04			18 34		19 04	
Ardwick	d																								
Manchester Piccadilly 10 ⇌	a	14 42	15 06	15 12	15 37	15 42		16 06	16 12	16 31	16 37	16 42	17 06	17 12	17 37	17 42		18 06	18 12	18 31	18 37	18 42	19 06	19 12	19 36
Manchester Airport 85 ✈	a		15 29					16 34					17 29					18 29					19 29		

A From Meadowhall
B From Hadfield
C From Nottingham to Liverpool Lime Street
D From Cleethorpes
E From Doncaster
F From Norwich to Liverpool Lime Street

Table 78

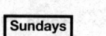

Sundays
from 30 October

Sheffield, Chinley, Marple and Romiley Manchester and Manchester Airport

		EM		NT	TP	NT	NT	EM	NT	TP	NT	EM		TP	NT	NT	NT
		◇			◇■			◇		◇■		◇		◇■			
		A		B	C	B		D	B	C	B	D		C	B		
Sheffield ■	d	18 37			19 11		19 14	19 35		20 11		20 35		21 11		22 17	
Dore & Totley	d						19 21									22 24	
Grindleford	d						19 29									22 32	
Hathersage	d						19 32									22 35	
Bamford	d						19 36									22 39	
Hope (Derbyshire)	d						19 39									22 42	
Edale	d						19 47									22 50	
Chinley	d						19 55									22 58	
Hazel Grove 86	a																
Stockport 86	a	19 25			19 55			20 25		20 53		21 24		21 53		23 16	
New Mills Central	d						20 01										23 01
Strines	d						20 04										23 04
Marple	d						20 07										23 07
Rose Hill Marple	d																
Romiley	d						20 11										23 11
Woodley	d																
Hyde Central	d																
Hyde North	d																
Guide Bridge	d			19 28		19 58			20 28		20 58				21 58		
Fairfield	d																
Gorton	d			19 31		20 01			20 31		21 01				22 01		
Bredbury	d						20 14										23 14
Brinnington	d						20 16										23 16
Reddish North	d						20 19										23 19
Ryder Brow	d																
Belle Vue	d																
Ashburys	d			19 34		20 04			20 34		21 04				22 04		
Ardwick	d																
Manchester Piccadilly ■	a	19 37		19 42	20 09	20 12	20 32	20 38	20 42	21 06	21 12	21 36		22 06	22 12	23 29	23 31
Manchester Airport 85	a				20 32					21 29				22 29			

A From Norwich to Liverpool Lime Street
B From Hadfield
C From Cleethorpes
D From Norwich

Table 79

Mondays to Fridays

until 30 September

Manchester - Glossop and Hadfield

Miles	Miles			NT	NT	NT	NT	NT	NT	NT	NT	NT	NT	NT	NT		NT	NT	NT	NT	NT	NT
0	—	**Manchester Piccadilly** 10 78 ⇌	d	06 16	06 46	07 03	07 18	07 48	08 07	08 29	08 48	09 15	09 48	10 15	10 48	and every 30 minutes until	15 48	16 15	16 36	16 59	17 15	17 37
0½	—	Ardwick 78	d																			
1½	—	Ashburys 78	d	06 20	06 50	07 07	07 22	07 52	08 11	08 33	08 52	09 19	09 52	10 19	10 52		15 52	16 19	16 40	17 03	17 19	17 41
2½	—	Gorton 78	d	06 22	06 52	07 09	07 24	07 54	08 13	08 35	08 54	09 21	09 54	10 21	10 54		15 54	16 21	16 42	17 05	17 21	17 43
4¾	—	Guide Bridge 78	d	06 26	06 56	07 13	07 28	07 58	08 17	08 39	08 58	09 25	09 58	10 25	10 58		15 58	16 25	16 46	17 10	17 25	17 47
6¾	—	Flowery Field	d	06 29	06 59	07 16	07 31	08 01	08 20	08 42	09 01	09 28	10 01	10 28	11 01		16 01	16 28	16 49	17 13	17 28	17 50
7½	—	Newton for Hyde	d	06 31	07 01	07 18	07 33	08 03	08 22	08 44	09 03	09 30	10 03	10 30	11 03		16 03	16 30	16 51	17 15	17 30	17 52
8½	—	Godley	d	06 33	07 03	07 20	07 35	08 05	08 24	08 46	09 05	09 32	10 05	10 32	11 05		16 05	16 32	16 53	17 17	17 32	17 54
9	—	Hattersley	d	06 35	07 05	07 22	07 37	08 07	08 26	08 48	09 07	09 34	10 07	10 34	11 07		16 07	16 34	16 55	17 19	17 34	17 56
10	—	Broadbottom	d	06 37	07 07	07 24	07 39	08 09	08 28	08 50	09 09	09 36	10 09	10 36	11 09		16 09	16 36	16 57	17 21	17 36	17 59
12¼	0	Dinting 3	d	06 45	07 15	07 35	07 45	08 14	08 34	08 56	09 16	09 46	10 16	10 46	11 16		16 16	16 42	17 03	17 27	17 42	18 05
13¼	—	**Glossop**	a	06 48	07b25	07b45	08b03	08b26	08b46	09b06	09 19	09 49	10 19	10 49	11 19		16 19	16 45	17 06	17 31	17 45	18 08
—	—		d	06 51							09 22	09 52	10 22	10 52	11 22		16 22	16 48	17 09	17 33	17 48	18 11
15	0¾	**Hadfield**	a	06 59	07 17	07 37	07 47	08 17	08 38	08 58	09 29	09 59	10 29	10 59	11 29		16 29	16 54	17 15	17 40	17 54	18 17

		NT	NT	NT	NT	NT		NT	NT
Manchester Piccadilly 10 78 ⇌	d	17 59	18 15	18 48	19 18	19 48	and hourly until	22 48	23 27
Ardwick 78	d								
Ashburys 78	d	18 03	18 19	18 52	19 22	19 52		22 52	23 31
Gorton 78	d	18 05	18 21	18 54	19 24	19 54		22 54	23 33
Guide Bridge 78	d	18 10	18 25	18 58	19 28	19 58		22 58	23 37
Flowery Field	d	18 13	18 28	19 01	19 31	20 01		23 01	23 40
Newton for Hyde	d	18 15	18 30	19 03	19 33	20 03		23 03	23 42
Godley	d	18 17	18 32	19 05	19 35	20 05		23 05	23 44
Hattersley	d	18 19	18 34	19 07	19 37	20 07		23 07	23 46
Broadbottom	d	18 21	18 36	19 09	19 39	20 09		23 09	23 48
Dinting 3	d	18 27	18 42	19 16	19 46	20 16		23 16	23 54
Glossop	a	18 30	18 45	19 19	19 49	20 19		23 19	
	d	18 33	18 48	19 22	19 52	20 22		23 22	
Hadfield	a	18 39	18 54	19 29	19 59	20 29		23 29	23 56

from 3 October

		NT	NT	NT	NT	NT	NT	NT	NT	NT	NT	NT	NT	NT	NT	NT		NT	NT	NT	NT	NT
Manchester Piccadilly 10 78 ⇌	d	06 13	06 46	07 03	07 18	07 47	08 07	08 29	08 48	09 15	09 48	10 15	10 48	11 18	11 48	12 18	and every 30 minutes until	15 18	15 48	16 15	16 36	16 59
Ardwick 78	d																					
Ashburys 78	d	06 17		07 07	07 22		08 11		08 52	09 19	09 52	10 19	10 52	11 22	11 52	12 22		15 22	15 52	16 19	16 40	17 03
Gorton 78	d	06 19		07 09	07 24		08 13		08 54	09 21	09 54	10 21	10 54	11 24	11 54	12 24		15 24	15 54	16 21	16 42	17 05
Guide Bridge 78	d	06 23	06 54	07 13	07 28	07 55	08 17	08 37	08 58	09 25	09 58	10 25	10 58	11 28	11 58	12 28		15 28	15 58	16 25	16 46	17 10
Flowery Field	d	06 26	06 57	07 16	07 31	07 58	08 20		09 01	09 28	10 01	10 28	11 01	11 31	12 01	12 31		15 31	16 01	16 28	16 49	17 13
Newton for Hyde	d	06 28	06 59	07 18	07 33	08 00	08 22		09 03	09 30	10 03	10 30	11 03	11 33	12 03	12 33		15 33	16 03	16 30	16 51	17 15
Godley	d	06 30		07 20	07 35	08 02	08 24		09 05	09 32	10 05	10 32	11 05	11 35	12 05	12 35		15 35	16 05	16 32	16 53	17 17
Hattersley	d	06 32	07 02	07 22	07 37	08 04	08 26		09 07	09 34	10 07	10 34	11 07	11 37	12 07	12 37		15 37	16 07	16 34	16 55	17 19
Broadbottom	d	06 34	07 04	07 24	07 39	08 06	08 28		09 09	09 36	10 09	10 36	11 09	11 39	12 09	12 39		15 39	16 09	16 36	16 57	17 20
Dinting 3	d	06 44	07 10	07 30	07 50	08 11	08 32	08 48	09 16	09 46	10 16	10 46	11 16	11 46	12 16	12 46		15 46	16 16	16 42	17 03	17 26
Glossop	a															12 49		15 49	16 19	16 45	17 06	17 30
	d															12 54		15 54	16 22	16 48	17 09	17 32
Hadfield	a	06 48	07 12	07 32	07 52	08 14	08 36	08 51	09 19	09 49	10 19	10 49	11 19	11 49	12 19	13 01		16 01	16 29	16 54	17 15	17 39

		NT	NT	NT	NT	NT	NT	NT		NT	NT
Manchester Piccadilly 10 78 ⇌	d	17 15	17 37	17 59	18 15	18 48	19 18	19 48	and hourly until	22 48	23 27
Ardwick 78	d										
Ashburys 78	d	17 19	17 41	18 03	18 19	18 52	19 22	19 52		22 52	23 31
Gorton 78	d	17 21	17 43	18 05	18 21	18 54	19 24	19 54		22 54	23 33
Guide Bridge 78	d	17 25	17 47	18 10	18 25	18 58	19 28	19 58		22 58	23 37
Flowery Field	d	17 28	17 50	18 13	18 28	19 01	19 31	20 01		23 01	23 40
Newton for Hyde	d	17 30	17 52	18 15	18 30	19 03	19 33	20 03		23 03	23 42
Godley	d	17 32	17 54	18 17	18 32	19 05	19 35	20 05		23 05	23 44
Hattersley	d	17 34	17 56	18 19	18 34	19 07	19 37	20 07		23 07	23 46
Broadbottom	d	17 36	17 58	18 21	18 36	19 09	19 39	20 09		23 09	23 48
Dinting 3	d	17 42	18 05	18 28	18 42	19 16	19 46	20 16		23 16	23 54
Glossop	a	17 45	18 08	18 31	18 45	19 19	19 49	20 19		23 19	
	d	17 48	18 12	18 34	18 48	19 22	19 52	20 22		23 22	
Hadfield	a	17 54	18 18	18 40	18 54	19 29	19 59	20 29		23 29	23 56

Saturdays

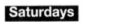

		NT	NT	NT	NT	NT	NT		NT	NT		NT	NT
Manchester Piccadilly 10 78 ⇌	d	06 16	06 48	07 18	07 48	08 15	08 48	and every 30 minutes until	18 48	19 48	and hourly until	22 48	23 27
Ardwick 78	d												
Ashburys 78	d	06 20	06 52	07 22	07 52	08 19	08 52		18 52	19 52		22 52	23 31
Gorton 78	d	06 22	06 54	07 24	07 54	08 21	08 54		18 54	19 54		22 54	23 33
Guide Bridge 78	d	06 26	06 58	07 28	07 58	08 25	08 58		18 58	19 58		22 58	23 37
Flowery Field	d	06 29	07 01	07 31	08 01	08 28	09 01		19 01	20 01		23 01	23 40
Newton for Hyde	d	06 31	07 03	07 33	08 03	08 30	09 03		19 03	20 03		23 03	23 42
Godley	d	06 33	07 05	07 35	08 05	08 32	09 05		19 05	20 05		23 05	23 44
Hattersley	d	06 35	07 07	07 37	08 07	08 34	09 07		19 07	20 07		23 07	23 46
Broadbottom	d	06 37	07 09	07 39	08 09	08 36	09 09		19 09	20 09		23 09	23 48
Dinting 3	d	06 45	07 16	07 46	08 16	08 46	09 16		19 16	20 16		23 16	23 54
Glossop	a	06 48	07 19	07 49	08 19	08 49	09 19		19 19	20 19		23 19	
	d	06 51	07 22	07 52	08 22	08 52	09 22		19 22	20 22		23 22	
Hadfield	a	06 59	07 29	07 59	08 29	08 59	09 29		19 29	20 29		23 29	23 56

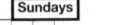

Sundays

		NT	NT	NT		NT	NT
Manchester Piccadilly 10 78 ⇌	d	09 18	09 30	10 18	and every 30 minutes until	19 48	20 48
Ardwick 78	d						
Ashburys 78	d	09 22	09 34	10 22		19 52	20 52
Gorton 78	d	09 24	09 36	10 24		19 54	20 54
Guide Bridge 78	d	09 28	09 58	10 28		19 58	20 58
Flowery Field	d	09 31	10 01	10 31		20 01	21 01
Newton for Hyde	d	09 33	10 03	10 33		20 03	21 03
Godley	d	09 35	10 05	10 35		20 05	21 05
Hattersley	d	09 37	10 07	10 37		20 07	21 07
Broadbottom	d	09 39	10 09	10 39		20 09	21 09
Dinting 3	d	09 46	10 16	10 46		20 16	21 16
Glossop	a	09 49	10 19	10 49		20 19	21 19
	d	09 52	10 22	10 52		20 22	21 22
Hadfield	a	09 58	10 28	10 58		20 28	21 28

Table 79

Mondays to Fridays

Hadfield and Glossop - Manchester

until 30 September

Miles	Miles				NT	NT	NT	NT	NT	NT	NT	NT	NT		NT		NT	NT	NT	NT	NT	NT	NT
0	0	**Hadfield**		d	06 00	06 30	07 00	07 20	07 40	07 58	08 21	08 41	09 01	and every 30 minutes until	16 01		16 31	16 57	17 22	17 44	17 59	18 28	18 43
1¾	—	**Glossop**		a	06 05	06 35	07 05	07 25	07 45	08 03	08 26	08 46	09 06		16 06								
—	—			d	06 08	06 38	07 08	07 28	07 48	08 06	08 29	08 49	09 09		16 09		16b22	16b48	17b09	17b33	17b48	18b11	18b33
2¾	0¾	Dinting 3		d	06 11	06 41	07 11	07 31	07 51	08 09	08 32	08 52	09 12		16 12		16 33	16 59	17 24	17 46	18 01	18 30	18 45
5	—	Broadbottom		d	06 15	06 45	07 15	07 35	07 56	08 13	08 37	08 57	09 16		16 16		16 37	17 03	17 28	17 50	18 05	18 34	18 49
6	—	Hattersley		d	06 18	06 48	07 18	07 38	07 59	08 16	08 40	08 59	09 19		16 19		16 40	17 06	17 31		18 08	18 37	18 52
6½	—	Godley		d	06 20	06 50	07 20	07 40	08 01	08 18	08 42	09 02	09 21		16 21		16 42	17 08	17 33		18 10	18 39	18 54
7½	—	Newton for Hyde		d	06 22	06 52	07 22	07 42	08 03	08 21	08 44	09 04	09 23		16 23		16 44	17 10	17 36	17 54	18 12	18 41	18 56
8¼	—	Flowery Field		d	06 24	06 54	07 24	07 44	08 06	08 23	08 46	09 07	09 25		16 25		16 46	17 12	17 38		18 14	18 43	18 58
10¼	—	Guide Bridge	78	a	06 27	06 57	07 27	07 47	08 10	08 26	08 49	09 11	09 28		16 28		16 49	17 15	17 42	17 58	18 17	18 46	19 01
12½	—	Gorton	78	a	06 30	07 00	07 30	07 50	08 13	08 30	08 52	09 15	09 31		16 31		16 52	17 18	17 45	18 01	18 20	18 49	19 04
13½	—	Ashburys	78	a	06 33	07 06	07 33	07 53	08 16	08 34	08 56	09 18	09 34		16 34		16 55	17 24	17 48	18 04	18 23	18 54	19 08
14½	—	Ardwick	78	a			07 35																
15	—	**Manchester Piccadilly** 10	78	a	06 42	07 15	07 43	08 03	08 25	08 43	09 04	09 27	09 42		16 42		17 05	17 33	17 57	18 12	18 34	19 03	19 15

			NT		NT		NT	NT
Hadfield		d	19 01	and every 30 minutes until	20 31		21 31	22 31
Glossop		a	19 06		20 36		21 36	22 36
		d	19 09		20 39		21 39	22 39
Dinting 3		d	19 12		20 42		21 42	22 42
Broadbottom		d	19 16		20 46		21 46	22 46
Hattersley		d	19 19		20 49		21 49	22 49
Godley		d	19 21		20 51		21 51	22 51
Newton for Hyde		d	19 23		20 53		21 53	22 53
Flowery Field		d	19 25		20 55		21 55	22 55
Guide Bridge	78	a	19 28		20 58		21 58	22 58
Gorton	78	a	19 31		21 01		22 01	23 01
Ashburys	78	a	19 34		21 04		22 04	23 04
Ardwick	78	a						
Manchester Piccadilly 10	78	a	19 42		21 12		22 12	23 12

from 3 October

			NT	NT	NT	NT	NT	NT	NT	NT	NT	NT		NT	NT		NT		NT	NT	NT	NT	NT	NT
Hadfield		d	05 55	06 25	06 55	07 15	07 35	07 55	08 17	08 39	08 55	09 24	and every 30 minutes until	12 24	13 05	and every 30 minutes until	16 05		16 31	16 57	17 18	17 44	17 56	18 22
Glossop		a	06 00	06 30	07 00	07 20	07 40	08 00	08 22	08 44	09 00	09 29		12 29										
		d	06 03	06 33	07 03	07 23	07 43	08 03	08 25	08 50	09 03	09 34		12 34					16b22	16b48	17b09	17b33	17b48	18b11
Dinting 3		d	06 06	06 36	07 06	07 26	07 46	08 06	08 28	08 54	09 07	09 37		12 37	13 07		16 07		16 33	16 59	17 20	17 46	17 59	18 24
Broadbottom		d	06 10	06 40	07 10	07 30	07 51	08 10	08 32	08 58	09 11	09 41		12 41	13 11		16 11		16 37	17 03	17 24	17 50	18 03	18 28
Hattersley		d	06 13	06 43	07 13	07 33	07 54	08 13	08 35	09 00	09 14	09 44		12 44	13 14		16 14		16 40	17 06	17 27		18 05	18 31
Godley		d	06 15	06 45	07 15	07 35	07 56	08 15	08 37	09 02	09 16	09 46		12 46	13 16		16 16		16 42	17 08	17 29		18 07	18 33
Newton for Hyde		d	06 17	06 47	07 17	07 37	07 58	08 18	08 39	09 04	09 19	09 48		12 48	13 18		16 18		16 44	17 10	17 32	17 54	18 09	18 35
Flowery Field		d	06 19	06 49	07 20	07 39	08 01	08 20	08 41	09 06	09 21	09 50		12 50	13 20		16 20		16 46	17 12	17 34		18 11	18 37
Guide Bridge	78	a	06 27	06 57	07 28	07 47	08 10	08 26	08 49	09 11	09 28	09 58		12 58	13 28		16 28		16 49	17 17	17 42	18 00	18 17	18 46
Gorton	78	a	06 30	07 00	07 30	07 50	08 13	08 30	08 52	09 15	09 31	10 01		13 01	13 31		16 31		16 52	17 20	17 45		18 20	18 49
Ashburys	78	a	06 33	07 06	07 34	07 53	08 16	08 34	08 56	09 18	09 34	10 04		13 04	13 34		16 34		16 55	17 24	17 48		18 23	18 54
Ardwick	78	a			07 36																			
Manchester Piccadilly 10	78	a	06 42	07 15	07 44	08 03	08 25	08 43	09 04	09 27	09 42	10 11		13 11	13 41		16 41		17 05	17 33	17 57	18 12	18 34	19 03

			NT	NT		NT		NT	NT
Hadfield		d	18 43	19 01	and every 30 minutes until	20 31		21 31	22 31
Glossop		a	18b33	19 06		20 36		21 36	22 36
		d		19 09		20 39		21 39	22 39
Dinting 3		d	18 45	19 12		20 42		21 42	22 42
Broadbottom		d	18 49	19 16		20 46		21 46	22 46
Hattersley		d	18 52	19 19		20 49		21 49	22 49
Godley		d	18 54	19 21		20 51		21 51	22 51
Newton for Hyde		d	18 56	19 23		20 53		21 53	22 53
Flowery Field		d	18 58	19 25		20 55		21 55	22 55
Guide Bridge	78	a	19 01	19 28		20 58		21 58	22 58
Gorton	78	a	19 04	19 31		21 01		22 01	23 01
Ashburys	78	a	19 08	19 34		21 04		22 04	23 04
Ardwick	78	a							
Manchester Piccadilly 10	78	a	19 15	19 42		21 12		22 12	23 12

Saturdays

			NT	NT		NT	NT	NT	NT
Hadfield		d	06 30	07 01	and every 30 minutes until	19 31	20 31	21 31	22 31
Glossop		a	06 35	07 06		19 36	20 36	21 36	22 36
		d	06 38	07 09		19 39	20 39	21 39	22 39
Dinting 3		d	06 41	07 12		19 42	20 42	21 42	22 42
Broadbottom		d	06 45	07 16		19 46	20 46	21 46	22 46
Hattersley		d	06 48	07 19		19 49	20 49	21 49	22 49
Godley		d	06 50	07 21		19 51	20 51	21 51	22 51
Newton for Hyde		d	06 52	07 23		19 53	20 53	21 53	22 53
Flowery Field		d	06 54	07 25		19 55	20 55	21 55	22 55
Guide Bridge	78	a	06 57	07 28		19 58	20 58	21 58	22 58
Gorton	78	a	07 00	07 31		20 01	21 01	22 01	23 01
Ashburys	78	a	07 03	07 34		20 04	21 04	22 04	23 04
Ardwick	78	a							
Manchester Piccadilly 10	78	a	07 12	07 42		20 12	21 12	22 12	23 12

Table 79

Sundays

			NT		NT	NT
Hadfield		d	10 01	and every 30 minutes until	20 31	21 31
Glossop		a	10 06		20 36	21 36
		d	10 09		20 39	21 39
Dinting 3		d	10 12		20 42	21 42
Broadbottom		d	10 16		20 46	21 46
Hattersley		d	10 19		20 49	21 49
Godley		d	10 21		20 51	21 51
Newton for Hyde		d	10 23		20 53	21 53
Flowery Field		d	10 25		20 55	21 55
Guide Bridge	78	a	10 28		20 58	21 58
Gorton	78	a	10 31		21 01	22 01
Ashburys	78	a	10 34		21 04	22 04
Ardwick	78	a				
Manchester Piccadilly 10	78	a	10 42		21 12	22 12

Network Diagram for Tables 81, 102

DM-35/08
Design BAJS

© Network Rail OPSU 2008. All rights reserved

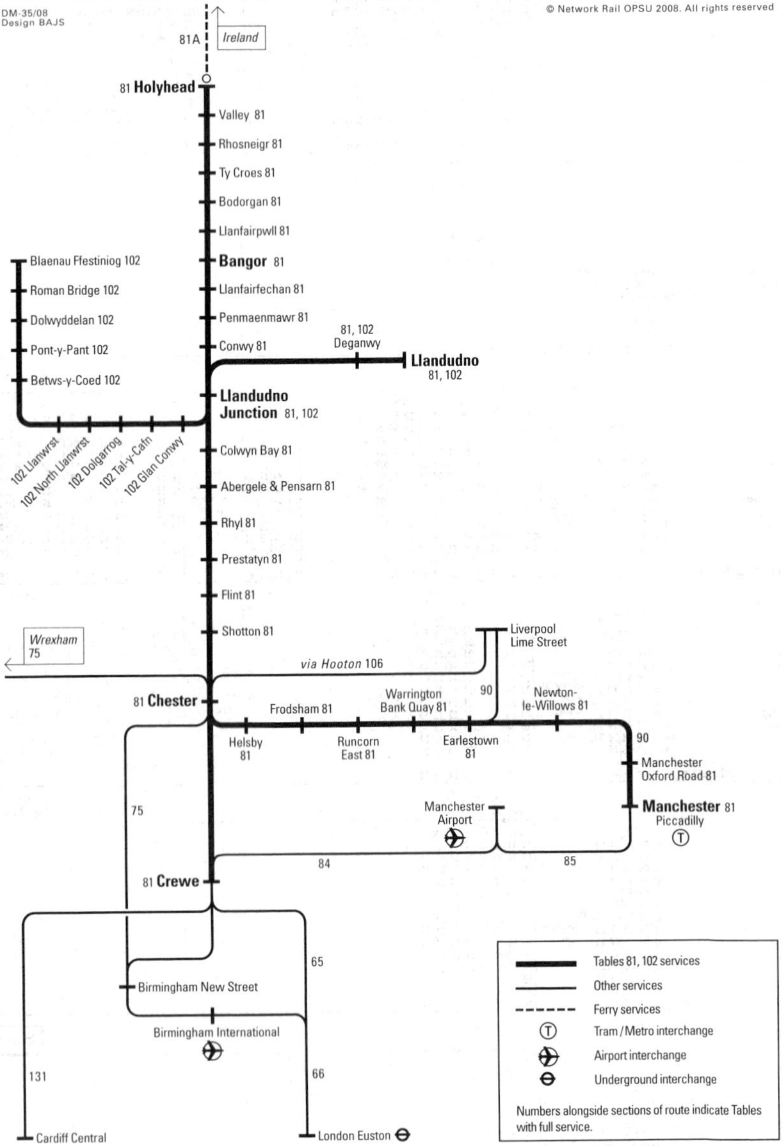

Table 81

Crewe and Manchester - Chester and North Wales

Mondays to Fridays

until 30 September

Miles	Miles			AW MX	AW MO	AW MX	AW MX	AW MO	AW MX	AW MO	AW MO	NT MX		AW MX	AW	AW	AW	VT	AW	AW	NT	AW		AW	AW
				◇	◇		◇		◇	◇	◇ A							◇[1] ⊠	◇ 🛒	◇ 🛒					◇ 🛒
—	—	London Euston [15] ⊖65	d																						
—	—	Birmingham New Street [12] 65	d				22p55				22p55							05 30							
—	—	Manchester Airport 84,85 ✈	d																05 33						
—	—	Cardiff Central [7] 131	d	19p34					20p55	21p04															
0	—	**Crewe [10]**	d		22p29		23p57		00 02	00 03	00 10							06 23		06 54		07 23			
—	0	**Manchester Pic'dilly [10] 90 ⛴**	d			23p14		23p25				23p17		00 25					05 50		06 17				06 50
—	0½	**Manchester Oxford Road 90**	d			23p17		23p28											05 53						06 53
—	16¼	Newton-le-Willows 90	d			23p36		23p46											06 12						07 12
—	18	Earlestown [8] 90	d			23p39		23p49											06 15						07 15
—	22	Warrington Bank Quay 90	d			23p48		23p56											06 26						07 22
—	27	Runcorn East	d			23p55		00 03											06 33						07 29
—	30¼	Frodsham	d			23p59		00 07											06 37						07 34
—	32¾	Helsby	d			00 03		00 11											06 41						07 38
—	—	Liverpool Lime Street [10] 106	d																						
21	40¼	**Chester**	a	22p34	22p50	00 15	00 18	00 24	00 27	00 25	00 31	00 43		01 29				06 43	06 53	07 14	07 45	07 46			07 50
—	—		d	22p56	23p00		00 40				00 35							06 44	06 55	07 23					07 55
29	—	Shotton	d	23p05	23p09														07 04						08 04
33½	—	Flint	d	23p11	23p15		00 53				00 48							06 57	07 10	07 36					08 10
47½	—	Prestatyn	d	23p24	23p28		01 06				01 01							07 10	07 23	07 49					08 23
51	—	Rhyl	d	23p30	23p34		01 12				01 07							07 16	07 29	07 55					08 29
55¼	—	Abergele & Pensarn	d	23p36															07 35						08 35
61½	—	Colwyn Bay	d	23p44	23p45		01 23				01 18							07 26	07 43	08 06					08 43
65½	0	**Llandudno Junction**	a	23p49	23p50		01 28				01 24							07 32	07 48	08 11					08 48
—	—		d	23p52	23p51		01 29				01 25				06 13	06 51	07 31	07 33	07 50	08 12				08 28	08 50
—	1¼	Deganwy	d												06x16	06x54	07x34		07x54					08x31	08x54
—	3	**Llandudno**	a												06 23	07 01	07 41		08 06					08 38	09 06
66½	—	Conwy	d	23b54	23b53															08x14					
70¾	—	Penmaenmawr	d	23b59	00x01															08x20					
73¼	—	Llanfairfechan	d	00x04	00x03															08x24					
80¾	—	**Bangor (Gwynedd)**	a	00 13	00 12		01 45				01 41							07 49		08 33					
—	—		d	00 14	00 14		01 45				01 41							07 49		08 37					
84½	—	Llanfairpwll	d	00x21																08x43					
93½	—	Bodorgan	d	00x31																08x53					
96¼	—	Ty Croes	d	00x35																08x57					
98	—	Rhosneigr	d	00x38																09x00					
102	—	Valley	d	00x43																09x06					
105½	—	**Holyhead**	a	00 58	00 49		02 15				02 17							08 23		09 20					

		AW	NT	AW	AW	AW	VT	AW		AW	NT	AW	AW	AW	VT	AW	NT	AW		AW	AW	VT	VT	AW	NT
		◇ 🛒				◇ 🛒	◇[1] ⊠	◇ B		◇ A 🛒				◇ 🛒	◇[1] ⊠	◇ 🛒					◇ 🛒	◇[1] ⊠	◇[1] ⊠	◇ A 🛒	
London Euston [15] ⊖65	d						07 10								08 10							09 10	09 10		
Birmingham New Street [12] 65	d									07 23														09 24	
Manchester Airport 84,85 ✈	d																								
Cardiff Central [7] 131	d	05 10														07 21									
Crewe [10]	d			08 23			08 49					09 23			09 49			10 23				10 49	10 49		
Manchester Pic'dilly [10] 90 ⛴	d		07 17			07 50					08 17			08 50			09 17				09 50				10 17
Manchester Oxford Road 90	d					07 53								08 53							09 53				
Newton-le-Willows 90	d					08 12								09 12							10 12				
Earlestown [8] 90	d					08 15								09 15							10 15				
Warrington Bank Quay 90	d					08 24								09 26							10 26				
Runcorn East	d					08 31								09 33							10 33				
Frodsham	d					08 35								09 37							10 37				
Helsby	d					08 39								09 41							10 41				
Liverpool Lime Street [10] 106	d																								
Chester	a	08 19	08 45	08 46		08 51	09 12			09 17	09 45	09 46		09 53	10 09	10 19	10 45	10 46			10 53	11 09	11 09	11 19	11 45
	d	08 22				08 55				09 22				09 55	10 16	10 24					10 55		11 16	11 22	
Shotton	d					09 04								10 04							11 04				
Flint	d	08 36				09 10				09 36				10 10	10 29	10 39					11 10			11 38	
Prestatyn	d	08 49				09 23				09 49				10 23	10 42	10 52					11 23			11 51	
Rhyl	d	08 55				09 29				09 55				10 29	10 48	10 58					11 29		11 43	11 57	
Abergele & Pensarn	d					09 35								10 35							11 35				
Colwyn Bay	d	09 06				09 43				10 06				10 43	10 59	11 09					11 43		11 54	12 08	
Llandudno Junction	a	09 11				09 48				10 11				10 48	11 04	11 14					11 48		12 00	12 13	
	d	09 12			09 28	09 50		10 00		10 12			10 28	10 50	11 06	11 15				11 26	11 50		12 01	12 14	
Deganwy	d				09x31	09x54		10x03					10x31	10x54						11x29	11x54				
Llandudno	a				09 38	10 06		10 13					10 38	11 06						11 36	12 06				
Conwy	d	09x14														11x17								12x16	
Penmaenmawr	d	09x20														11x23								12x22	
Llanfairfechan	d	09x24														11x27								12x26	
Bangor (Gwynedd)	a	09 33								10 28					11 27	11 38							12 16	12 35	
	d	09 35								10 29						11 40							12 17	12 37	
Llanfairpwll	d									10x35														12x43	
Bodorgan	d	09x49																						12x53	
Ty Croes	d	09x53																						12x57	
Rhosneigr	d	09x56																						13x00	
Valley	d									10x53														13x06	
Holyhead	a	10 14								11 07						12 14							12 50	13 18	

A From Birmingham International

B From Blaenau Ffestiniog

b Previous night, stops on request

Table 81

Mondays to Fridays

until 30 September

Crewe and Manchester - Chester and North Wales

	AW	AW	AW	VT	AW	AW	NT	AW	AW	AW	VT	AW	NT	AW	AW	AW	VT	AW	NT	AW	AW
			◇	◇1	◇ A	◇				◇	◇1	◇ B				◇	◇1	◇			◇
London Euston 15 ⊖65 d				10 10							11 10						12 10				
Birmingham New Street 12 65 d												11 24									
Manchester Airport 84,85 ✈ d																					
Cardiff Central 7 131 d						09 21												11 21			
Crewe 10 d	11 23			11 49				12 23			12 49			13 23			13 49			14 23	
Manchester Pic'dilly 10 90 ⛴ d			10 50				11 17			11 50			12 17			12 50			13 17		13 50
Manchester Oxford Road 90 d			10 53							11 53						12 53					13 53
Newton-le-Willows 90 d			11 12							12 12						13 12					14 12
Earlestown 8 90 d			11 15							12 15						13 15					14 15
Warrington Bank Quay 90 d			11 26							12 26						13 26					14 26
Runcorn East d			11 33							12 33						13 33					14 33
Frodsham d			11 37							12 37						13 37					14 37
Helsby d			11 41							12 41						13 41					14 41
Liverpool Lime Street 10 106 d																					
Chester a	11 46		11 53	12 12		12 19	12 45	12 46		12 53	13 12	13 19	13 45	13 46		13 53	14 12	14 19	14 45	14 46	14 53
d			11 55			12 23				12 55		13 22				13 55		14 23			14 55
Shotton d			12 04							13 04						14 04					15 04
Flint d			12 10			12 36				13 10		13 36				14 10		14 36			15 10
Prestatyn d			12 23			12 49				13 23		13 49				14 23		14 49			15 23
Rhyl d			12 29			12 55				13 29		13 55				14 29		14 55			15 29
Abergele & Pensarn d			12 35							13 35						14 35					15 35
Colwyn Bay d			12 43			13 06				13 43		14 06				14 43		15 06			15 43
Llandudno Junction a			12 48			13 11				13 48		14 11				14 48		15 11			15 48
d		12 28	12 50		13 00	13 12			13 28	13 50		14 12			14 28	14 50		15 12			15 50
Deganwy d		12x31	12x54		13x03				13x31	13x54					14x31	14x54					15x54
Llandudno a		12 38	13 06		13 13				13 38	14 06					14 38	15 06					16 06
Conwy d												14x14									
Penmaenmawr d												14x20									
Llanfairfechan d												14x24									
Bangor (Gwynedd) a						13 28						14 33						15 28			
d						13 29						14 35						15 30			
Llanfairpwll d						13x36												15x38			
Bodorgan d						13x46												15x48			
Ty Croes d						13x50												15x52			
Rhosneigr d						13x53												15x55			
Valley d						13x58												16x01			
Holyhead a						14 13						15 08						16 15			

	VT	AW	AW	NT	AW	AW	VT	AW	NT	AW	AW	VT	AW	NT	AW	AW	AW	AW	VT	AW	AW	NT
	◇1	◇ A	◇ B			◇	◇1	◇			◇	◇1	◇ B				◇ A	◇	◇1	■		
London Euston 15 ⊖65 d	13 10						14 10					15 10							16 10			
Birmingham New Street 12 65 d			13 24										15 26									
Manchester Airport 84,85 ✈ d																						
Cardiff Central 7 131 d								13 21												15 21		
Crewe 10 d	14 49				15 23		15 49			16 23		16 49			17 23				17 49			
Manchester Pic'dilly 10 90 ⛴ d				14 17		14 50			15 17		15 50			16 17				16 50			17 19	17 09
Manchester Oxford Road 90 d						14 53					15 53							16 53			17 22	
Newton-le-Willows 90 d						15 12					16 12							17 12			17 40	
Earlestown 8 90 d						15 15					16 15							17 15			17 44	
Warrington Bank Quay 90 d						15 26					16 26							17 26			17 53	
Runcorn East d						15 33					16 33							17 33			18 00	
Frodsham d						15 37					16 37							17 37			18 05	
Helsby d						15 41					16 41							17 41			18 09	
Liverpool Lime Street 10 106 d																						
Chester a	15 12		15 18	15 45	15 46	15 53	16 12	16 20	16 45	16 46	16 54	17 12	17 22	17 45	17 46			17 53	18 08	18 20	18 23	18 35
d			15 22			15 55		16 24			16 55		17 25					17 55	18 10	18 24		
Shotton d						16 04					17 04		17 35					18 04				
Flint d			15 37			16 10		16 37			17 10		17 41					18 10	18 23	18 37		
Prestatyn d			15 50			16 23		16 50			17 23		17 54					18 23	18 36	18 50		
Rhyl d			15 56			16 29		16 56			17 29		18 00					18 29	18 42	18 56		
Abergele & Pensarn d						16 35					17 35		18 06					18 35				
Colwyn Bay d			16 07			16 43		17 07			17 43		18 14					18 43	18 53	19 07		
Llandudno Junction a			16 12			16 48		17 12			17 49		18 19					18 48	18 58	19 12		
d		16 04	16 14			16 50		17 12			17 50		18 21			18 26	18 41	18 50	19 00	19 13		
Deganwy d		16x07				16x54					17x54					18x29	18x44	18x54				
Llandudno a		16 17				17 06					18 06					18 36	18 54	19 06				
Conwy d			16x16					17x14					18x23									
Penmaenmawr d			16x22					17x20					18x29									
Llanfairfechan d			16x26					17x24					18x33									
Bangor (Gwynedd) a			16 35					17 33					18 42						19 21	19 33		
d			16 36					17 35					18 43							19 35		
Llanfairpwll d								17x41												19 41		
Bodorgan d								17x51												19 51		
Ty Croes d								17x55												19 55		
Rhosneigr d								17x58												19 58		
Valley d								18x04												20 04		
Holyhead a			17 11					18 18					19 16							20 18		

A From Blaenau Ffestiniog

B From Birmingham International

until 30 September

Crewe and Manchester - Chester and North Wales

		AW	AW	AW ◇ 🚲	AW BHX R ⊠	VT ◇1 ⊠		VT ◇1 ⊠	AW ◇ A 🚲	NT	AW	AW 🚲	VT ◇1 B ⊠	AW	VT ◇1 ⊠	AW R 🚲		NT	AW	AW	AW ◇ C	AW R 🚲	VT R 1 ⊡	AW ◇ A 🚲	AW
London Euston 15 ⊖65	d					17 10		17 10					18 10		18 10								19 10		
Birmingham New Street 12 65	d								17 26															19 24	
Manchester Airport 84,85 ✈	d																								
Cardiff Central 7 131	d				16 15											17 21						18 18			
Crewe 10	d	18 23			18 43	18 56		18 56			19 23		19 56		19 56				20 23				20 50		21 00
Manchester Pic'dilly 10 90 ⛴	d			17 50						18 17		18 50						19 17		19 50					
Manchester Oxford Road 90	d			17 53								18 53								19 53					
Newton-le-Willows 90	d			18 12								19 12								20 12					
Earlestown 8 90	d			18 15								19 16								20 15					
Warrington Bank Quay 90	d			18 24								19 27								20 26					
Runcorn East	d			18 31								19 34								20 33					
Frodsham	d			18 36								19 38								20 37					
Helsby	d			18 40								19 42								20 41					
Liverpool Lime Street 10 106	d																								
Chester	a	18 46		18 53	19 06	19 15		19 15	19 20	19 45	19 46	19 54	20 15		20 15	20 20		20 45	20 46	20 53		20 57	21 10	21 19	21 23
	d			18 55	19 07			19 21	19 32						20 26	20 32						21 02	21 17		
Shotton	d			19 04					19 41							20 41									
Flint	d			19 10	19 21			19 35	19 47							20 47							21 30		
Prestatyn	d			19 23				19 48	20 00							21 02							21 43		
Rhyl	d			19 29	19 39			19 54	20 06						20 53	21 08						21 28	21 50		
Abergele & Pensarn	d			19 35					20 12																
Colwyn Bay	d			19 43				20 05	20 20						21 04	21 18						21 39	22 01		
Llandudno Junction	a			19 48	19 52			20 10	20 25						21 09	21 24						21 44	22 06		
	d		19 28	19 50	19 53			20 12	20 27					20 30	21 10	21 25					21 32	21 47	22 07		
Deganwy	d		19x31	19x54										20x33							21x35				
Llandudno	a		19 38	20 06										20 40							21 46				
Conwy	d								20x29																
Penmaenmawr	d								20x35																
Llanfairfechan	d								20x39																
Bangor (Gwynedd)	a				20 09			20 27	20 48						21 25	21 40						22 02	22 22		
	d				20 11			20 28	20 49						21 27	21 42						22 04	22 24		
Llanfairpwll	d								20x55							21x48									
Bodorgan	d								21x05							21x58									
Ty Croes	d								21x10							22x02									
Rhosneigr	d								21x13							22x05									
Valley	d								21x18							22x11									
Holyhead	a				20 49			20 59	21 31						21 59	22 25						22 34	22 56		

		NT		AW	AW	VT ◇1 ⊡	AW	AW ◇	NT	AW	AW D	AW E		AW ◇ F	AW D	AW E	AW	NT FX	NT FO	AW	AW ◇	AW ◇		NT	
London Euston 15 ⊖65	d					20 10																			
Birmingham New Street 12 65	d													21 24							22 55				
Manchester Airport 84,85 ✈	d				20 32						21 32	21 32													
Cardiff Central 7 131	d							19 34														20 55			
Crewe 10	d			21 23		21 50				22 23							23 23				23 57	00 02			
Manchester Pic'dilly 10 90 ⛴	d	20 17			20 50				21 17		21 50	21 50			22 12	22 12		22 17	22 17	23 14				23 17	
Manchester Oxford Road 90	d				20 53						21 53	21 53			22 29	22 29				23 17					
Newton-le-Willows 90	d				21 12						22 12	22 12			22 47	22 47				23 36					
Earlestown 8 90	d				21 15						22 15	22 15			22 50	22 50				23 39					
Warrington Bank Quay 90	d				21 24						22 24	22 26			22 59	23 01				23 48					
Runcorn East	d				21 33						22 31	22 33			23 06	23 08				23 55					
Frodsham	d				21 37						22 35	22 37			23 10	23 12				23 59					
Helsby	d				21 41						22 39	22 41			23 14	23 16				00 03					
Liverpool Lime Street 10 106	d																								
Chester	a	21 45		21 46	21 55	22 15		22 34	22 45	22 45	22 51	22 53		23 19	23 26	23 28	23 44	23 45	23 47	00 15	00 18	00 27		00 43	
	d						22 00	22 56													00 40				
Shotton	d						22 09	23 05																	
Flint	d						22 15	23 11													00 53				
Prestatyn	d						22 28	23 24													01 06				
Rhyl	d						22 34	23 30													01 12				
Abergele & Pensarn	d						22 40	23 36																	
Colwyn Bay	d						22 48	23 44													01 23				
Llandudno Junction	a						22 53	23 49													01 28				
	d						22 55	23 52													01 29				
Deganwy	d																								
Llandudno	a																								
Conwy	d						22x57	23x54																	
Penmaenmawr	d						23x03	23x59																	
Llanfairfechan	d						23x07	00x04																	
Bangor (Gwynedd)	a						23 16	00 13													01 45				
	d						23 17	00 14													01 45				
Llanfairpwll	d							00x21																	
Bodorgan	d							00x31																	
Ty Croes	d							00x35																	
Rhosneigr	d							00x38																	
Valley	d							00x43																	
Holyhead	a						23 50	00 58													02 15				

A From Birmingham International
B To Wrexham General
C From Blaenau Ffestiniog
D until 9 September
E from 12 September until 30 September
F From Birmingham International to Manchester Piccadilly

from 3 October

Crewe and Manchester - Chester and North Wales

		AW MX	AW MO	AW MX	AW MX	AW MO	AW MX	AW MO	AW MO	NT MX		AW MX	AW	AW	AW	VT	AW	AW	AW	NT		AW	AW	AW	AW
		◇	◇		◇		◇	◇	◇ A							◇1 ⊠	◇ 🛒	◇ 🛒					◇ 🛒	◇ 🛒	
London Euston 15 ⊖65	d																								
Birmingham New Street 12 65	d				22p55				22p55							05 30									
Manchester Airport 84,85 ✈	d																05 33								
Cardiff Central 7 131	d	19p34					20p55	21p04																05 10	
Crewe 10	d		22p29		23p57		00 02	00 03	00 10							06 23		06 54	07 23						08 23
Manchester Pic'dilly 10 90 ⛴	d			23p14		23p25				23p17		00 25					05 50			06 17			06 50		
Manchester Oxford Road 90	d			23p17		23p28											05 53						06 53		
Newton-le-Willows 90	d			23p36		23p46											06 12						07 12		
Earlestown 8 90	d			23p39		23p49											06 15						07 15		
Warrington Bank Quay 90	d			23p48		23p56											06 26						07 22		
Runcorn East	d			23p55		00 03											06 33						07 29		
Frodsham	d			23p59		00 07											06 37						07 34		
Helsby	d			00 03		00 11											06 41						07 38		
Liverpool Lime Street 10 106	d																								
Chester	a	22p34	22p50	00 15	00 18	00 24	00 27	00 25	00 31	00 45		01 29				06 43	06 53	07 14	07 46	07 47			07 50	08 19	08 46
	d	22p56	23p00		00 40				00 35							06 44	06 55	07 23					07 55	08 22	
Shotton	d	23p05	23p09														07 04						08 04		
Flint	d	23p11	23p15		00 53				00 48							06 57	07 10	07 36					08 10	08 36	
Prestatyn	d	23p24	23p28		01 06				01 01							07 10	07 23	07 49					08 23	08 49	
Rhyl	d	23p30	23p34		01 12				01 07							07 16	07 29	07 55					08 29	08 55	
Abergele & Pensarn	d	23p36															07 35						08 35		
Colwyn Bay	d	23p44	23p45		01 23				01 18							07 26	07 43	08 06					08 43	09 06	
Llandudno Junction	a	23p49	23p50		01 28				01 24							07 32	07 48	08 11					08 48	09 11	
	d	23p52	23p51		01 29				01 25				06 13	06 51	07 31	07 33	07 50	08 12				08 28	08 50	09 12	
Deganwy	d												06x16	06x54	07x34		07x54					08x31	08x54		
Llandudno	a												06 23	07 01	07 41		08 06					08 38	09 06		
Conwy	d	23b54	23b53															08x14						09x14	
Penmaenmawr	d	23b59	00x01															08x20						09x20	
Llanfairfechan	d	00x04	00x03															08x24						09x24	
Bangor (Gwynedd)	a	00 13	00 12		01 45				01 41							07 49		08 33						09 33	
	d	00 14	00 14		01 45				01 41							07 49		08 37						09 35	
Llanfairpwll	d	00x21																08x43							
Bodorgan	d	00x31																08x53						09x49	
Ty Croes	d	00x35																08x57						09x53	
Rhosneigr	d	00x38																09x00						09x56	
Valley	d	00x43																09x06							
Holyhead	a	00 58	00 49		02 15				02 17							08 23		09 20						10 14	

		NT	AW	AW	VT	AW		AW	AW	NT	AW	AW	VT	AW	AW	NT		AW	AW	VT	VT	AW	AW	NT	AW
				◇ 🛒	◇1 ⊠	◇ B		◇ A 🛒				◇ 🛒	◇1 ⊠	◇ 🛒					◇ 🛒	◇1 ⊠	◇1 ⊠	◇ A 🛒			
London Euston 15 ⊖65	d				07 10								08 10							09 10	09 10				
Birmingham New Street 12 65	d							07 23														09 24			
Manchester Airport 84,85 ✈	d																								
Cardiff Central 7 131	d													07 21											
Crewe 10	d				08 49				09 23				09 49		10 23					10 49	10 49		11 23		
Manchester Pic'dilly 10 90 ⛴	d	07 17		07 50						08 17		08 50				09 17			09 50					10 17	
Manchester Oxford Road 90	d			07 53								08 53							09 53						
Newton-le-Willows 90	d			08 12								09 12							10 12						
Earlestown 8 90	d			08 15								09 15							10 15						
Warrington Bank Quay 90	d			08 24								09 26							10 26						
Runcorn East	d			08 31								09 33							10 33						
Frodsham	d			08 35								09 37							10 37						
Helsby	d			08 39								09 41							10 41						
Liverpool Lime Street 10 106	d																								
Chester	a	08 47		08 51	09 12			09 17	09 46	09 47		09 53	10 09	10 19	10 46	10 47			10 53	11 09	11 09	11 19	11 46	11 47	
	d			08 55				09 22				09 55	10 16	10 24					10 55		11 16	11 22			
Shotton	d			09 04								10 04							11 04						
Flint	d			09 10				09 36				10 10	10 29	10 39					11 10			11 38			
Prestatyn	d			09 23				09 49				10 23	10 42	10 52					11 23			11 51			
Rhyl	d			09 29				09 55				10 29	10 48	10 58					11 29		11 43	11 57			
Abergele & Pensarn	d			09 35								10 35							11 35						
Colwyn Bay	d			09 43				10 06				10 43	10 59	11 09					11 43		11 54	12 08			
Llandudno Junction	a			09 48				10 11				10 48	11 04	11 14					11 48		12 00	12 13			
	d		09 28	09 50		10 00		10 12			10 28	10 50	11 06	11 15				11 26	11 50		12 01	12 14			12 28
Deganwy	d		09x31	09x54		10x03					10x31	10x54						11x29	11x54						12x31
Llandudno	a		09 38	10 06		10 13					10 38	11 06						11 36	12 06						12 38
Conwy	d													11x17								12x16			
Penmaenmawr	d													11x23								12x22			
Llanfairfechan	d													11x27								12x26			
Bangor (Gwynedd)	a							10 28					11 27	11 38							12 16	12 35			
	d							10 29						11 40							12 17	12 37			
Llanfairpwll	d							10x35														12x43			
Bodorgan	d																					12x53			
Ty Croes	d																					12x57			
Rhosneigr	d																					13x00			
Valley	d							10x53														13x06			
Holyhead	a							11 07						12 14							12 50	13 18			

A From Birmingham International
B From Blaenau Ffestiniog

b Previous night, stops on request

Crewe and Manchester - Chester and North Wales

		AW		VT	AW	AW	AW	NT	AW	AW	VT	AW		AW	NT	AW	AW	VT	AW	AW	NT	AW		VT	AW
		◇ 🛒		◇1 ⊠	◇ A	◇ 🛒				◇ 🛒	◇1 ☕	◇ B 🛒					◇ 🛒	◇1 ☕	◇ 🛒			◇ 🛒		◇1 ☕	◇ A
London Euston 15 ⊖65	d			10 10							11 10							12 10						13 10	
Birmingham New Street 12 65	d											11 24													
Manchester Airport 84,85 ✈	d																								
Cardiff Central 7 131	d					09 21													11 21						
Crewe 10	d			11 49			12 23				12 49			13 23				13 49		14 23				14 49	
Manchester Pic'dilly 10 90	d	10 50						11 17		11 50					12 17		12 50				13 17	13 50			
Manchester Oxford Road 90	d	10 53								11 53							12 53					13 53			
Newton-le-Willows 90	d	11 12								12 12							13 12					14 12			
Earlestown 8 90	d	11 15								12 15							13 15					14 15			
Warrington Bank Quay 90	d	11 26								12 26							13 26					14 26			
Runcorn East	d	11 33								12 33							13 33					14 33			
Frodsham	d	11 37								12 37							13 37					14 37			
Helsby	d	11 41								12 41							13 41					14 41			
Liverpool Lime Street 10 106	d																								
Chester	a	11 53		12 12		12 19	12 46	12 47		12 53	13 12	13 19		13 46	13 47		13 53	14 12	14 19	14 46	14 47	14 53		15 12	
	d	11 55				12 23				12 55		13 22					13 55		14 23			14 55			
Shotton	d	12 04								13 04							14 04					15 04			
Flint	d	12 10				12 36				13 10		13 36					14 10		14 36			15 10			
Prestatyn	d	12 23				12 49				13 23		13 49					14 23		14 49			15 23			
Rhyl	d	12 29				12 55				13 29		13 55					14 29		14 55			15 29			
Abergele & Pensarn	d	12 35								13 35							14 35					15 35			
Colwyn Bay	d	12 43				13 06				13 43		14 06					14 43		15 06			15 43			
Llandudno Junction	a	12 48				13 11				13 48		14 11					14 48		15 11			15 48			
	d	12 50			13 00	13 12			13 28	13 50		14 12				14 28	14 50		15 12			15 50			16 04
Deganwy	d	12x54			13x03				13x31	13x54						14x31	14x54					15x54			16x07
Llandudno	a	13 06			13 13				13 38	14 06						14 38	15 06					16 06			16 17
Conwy	d											14x14													
Penmaenmawr	d											14x20													
Llanfairfechan	d											14x24													
Bangor (Gwynedd)	a					13 28						14 33							15 28						
	d					13 29						14 35							15 30						
Llanfairpwll	d					13x36													15x38						
Bodorgan	d					13x46													15x48						
Ty Croes	d					13x50													15x52						
Rhosneigr	d					13x53													15x55						
Valley	d					13x58													16x01						
Holyhead	a					14 13						15 08							16 15						

		AW	AW	NT	AW	VT	AW	AW		NT	AW	VT	AW	AW	NT	AW	AW	AW		VT	AW	AW	NT	AW	AW
		◇ B 🛒			◇ 🛒	◇1 ☕	◇ 🛒				◇ 🛒	◇1 ☕	◇ B 🛒				◇ A	◇ 🛒		◇1 ☕	R 🛒	🛒			
London Euston 15 ⊖65	d					14 10						15 10								16 10					
Birmingham New Street 12 65	d	13 24											15 26												
Manchester Airport 84,85 ✈	d																								
Cardiff Central 7 131	d						13 21														15 21				
Crewe 10	d		15 23			15 49		16 23				16 49		17 23						17 49				18 23	
Manchester Pic'dilly 10 90	d			14 17	14 50					15 17	15 50				16 17			16 50				17 19	17 09		
Manchester Oxford Road 90	d				14 53						15 53							16 53				17 22			
Newton-le-Willows 90	d				15 12						16 12							17 12				17 40			
Earlestown 8 90	d				15 15						16 15							17 15				17 44			
Warrington Bank Quay 90	d				15 26						16 26							17 26				17 53			
Runcorn East	d				15 33						16 33							17 33				18 00			
Frodsham	d				15 37						16 37							17 37				18 05			
Helsby	d				15 41						16 41							17 41				18 09			
Liverpool Lime Street 10 106	d																								
Chester	a	15 18	15 46	15 47	15 53	16 12	16 20	16 46		16 47	16 54	17 12	17 22	17 46	17 47			17 53		18 08	18 20	18 23	18 35	18 46	
	d	15 22			15 55		16 24				16 55		17 25					17 55		18 10	18 24				
Shotton	d				16 04						17 04		17 35					18 04							
Flint	d	15 37			16 10		16 37				17 10		17 41					18 10		18 23	18 37				
Prestatyn	d	15 50			16 23		16 50				17 23		17 54					18 23		18 36	18 50				
Rhyl	d	15 56			16 29		16 56				17 29		18 00					18 29		18 42	18 56				
Abergele & Pensarn	d				16 35						17 35		18 06					18 35							
Colwyn Bay	d	16 07			16 43		17 07				17 43		18 14					18 43		18 53	19 07				
Llandudno Junction	a	16 12			16 48		17 12				17 49		18 19					18 48		18 58	19 12				
	d	16 14			16 50		17 12				17 50		18 21			18 26	18 41	18 50		19 00	19 13				19 28
Deganwy	d				16x54						17x54					18x29	18x44	18x54							19x31
Llandudno	a				17 06						18 06					18 36	18 54	19 06							19 38
Conwy	d	16x16					17x14						18x23												
Penmaenmawr	d	16x22					17x20						18x29												
Llanfairfechan	d	16x26					17x24						18x33												
Bangor (Gwynedd)	a	16 35					17 33						18 42							19 21	19 33				
	d	16 36					17 35						18 43								19 35				
Llanfairpwll	d						17x41														19 41				
Bodorgan	d						17x51														19 51				
Ty Croes	d						17x55														19 55				
Rhosneigr	d						17x58														19 58				
Valley	d						18x04														20 04				
Holyhead	a	17 11					18 18						19 16								20 18				

A From Blaenau Ffestiniog

B From Birmingham International

Crewe and Manchester - Chester and North Wales

	AW	AW BHX	VT		VT	AW	AW	NT	AW	VT	AW	VT	AW		AW	NT	AW	AW	AW	VT	AW	AW	AW
	◇	[R]	◇[1]		◇[1]	◇				◇[1]		◇[1]	[R]					◇	[R]	[R] [1]	◇		
						A				B								C			A		
	[trolley]	⊠	⊠		⊠	[trolley]			[trolley]	⊠		⊠	[trolley]						[trolley]	[buffet]	[trolley]		
London Euston [15] ⊖65 d			17 10		17 10					18 10		18 10								19 10			
Birmingham New Street [12] 65 d						17 26															19 24		
Manchester Airport 84,85 ✈ d																							
Cardiff Central [7] 131 d		16 15											17 21						18 18				
Crewe [10] d		18 43	18 56		18 56		19 23			19 56		19 56			20 23					20 50		21 00	21 23
Manchester Pic'dilly [10] 90 ⇌ d	17 50							18 17	18 50							19 17	19 50						
Manchester Oxford Road 90 d	17 53								18 53								19 53						
Newton-le-Willows 90 d	18 12								19 12								20 12						
Earlestown [8] 90 d	18 15								19 16								20 15						
Warrington Bank Quay 90 d	18 24								19 27								20 26						
Runcorn East d	18 31								19 34								20 33						
Frodsham d	18 36								19 38								20 37						
Helsby d	18 40								19 42								20 41						
Liverpool Lime Street [10] 106 d																							
Chester a	18 53	19 06	19 15		19 15	19 20	19 46	19 47	19 54	20 15		20 15	20 20		20 46	20 47	20 53		20 57	21 10	21 19	21 23	21 46
d	18 55	19 07			19 21	19 32						20 26	20 32						21 02	21 17			
Shotton d	19 04					19 41							20 41										
Flint d	19 10	19 21			19 35	19 47							20 47							21 30			
Prestatyn d	19 23				19 48	20 00							21 02							21 43			
Rhyl d	19 29	19 39			19 54	20 06						20 53	21 08						21 28	21 50			
Abergele & Pensarn d	19 35					20 12																	
Colwyn Bay d	19 43				20 05	20 20						21 04	21 18						21 39	22 01			
Llandudno Junction a	19 48	19 52			20 10	20 25						21 09	21 24						21 44	22 06			
d	19 50	19 53			20 12	20 27					20 30	21 10	21 25					21 32	21 47	22 07			
Deganwy d	19x54										20x33							21x35					
Llandudno a	20 06										20 40							21 46					
Conwy d						20x29																	
Penmaenmawr d						20x35																	
Llanfairfechan d						20x39																	
Bangor (Gwynedd) a		20 09			20 27	20 48						21 25	21 40						22 02	22 22			
d		20 11			20 28	20 49						21 27	21 42						22 04	22 24			
Llanfairpwll d						20x55							21x48										
Bodorgan d						21x05							21x58										
Ty Croes d						21x10							22x02										
Rhosneigr d						21x13							22x05										
Valley d						21x18							22x11										
Holyhead a		20 49			20 59	21 31						21 59	22 25						22 34	22 56			

	NT	AW	VT	AW	AW	AW	NT	AW	AW		AW	AW	AW	AW	NT FX	NT FO	AW	AW	AW		NT		
			◇[1]		◇						◇							◇	◇				
								D	E		F	D	E										
			[buffet]																				
London Euston [15] ⊖65 d			20 10																				
Birmingham New Street [12] 65 d											21 24							22 55					
Manchester Airport 84,85 ✈ d		20 32						21 32	21 32														
Cardiff Central [7] 131 d					19 34														20 55				
Crewe [10] d			21 50			22 23								23 23				23 57	00 02				
Manchester Pic'dilly [10] 90 ⇌ d	20 17	20 50					21 17	21 50	21 50			22 12	22 12		22 17	22 17	23 14				23 17		
Manchester Oxford Road 90 d		20 53						21 53	21 53			22 29	22 29				23 17						
Newton-le-Willows 90 d		21 12						22 12	22 12			22 47	22 47				23 36						
Earlestown [8] 90 d		21 15						22 15	22 15			22 50	22 50				23 39						
Warrington Bank Quay 90 d		21 24						22 24	22 26			22 59	23 01				23 48						
Runcorn East d		21 33						22 31	22 33			23 06	23 08				23 55						
Frodsham d		21 37						22 35	22 37			23 10	23 12				23 59						
Helsby d		21 41						22 39	22 41			23 14	23 16				00 03						
Liverpool Lime Street [10] 106 d																							
Chester a	21 47	21 55	22 15		22 34	22 45	22 47	22 51	22 53		23 19	23 26	23 28	23 44	23 47	23 49	00 15	00 18	00 27		00 45		
d				22 00	22 56													00 40					
Shotton d				22 09	23 05																		
Flint d				22 15	23 11													00 53					
Prestatyn d				22 28	23 24													01 06					
Rhyl d				22 34	23 30													01 12					
Abergele & Pensarn d				22 40	23 36																		
Colwyn Bay d				22 48	23 44													01 23					
Llandudno Junction a				22 53	23 49													01 28					
d				22 55	23 52													01 29					
Deganwy d																							
Llandudno a																							
Conwy d				22x57	23x54																		
Penmaenmawr d				23x03	23x59																		
Llanfairfechan d				23x07	00x04																		
Bangor (Gwynedd) a				23 16	00 13													01 45					
d				23 17	00 14													01 45					
Llanfairpwll d					00x21																		
Bodorgan d					00x31																		
Ty Croes d					00x35																		
Rhosneigr d					00x38																		
Valley d					00x43																		
Holyhead a				23 50	00 58													02 15					

A From Birmingham International
B To Wrexham General
C From Blaenau Ffestiniog
D from 24 October
E from 3 October until 21 October
F From Birmingham International to Manchester Piccadilly

Table 81

Saturdays

until 18 June

Crewe and Manchester - Chester and North Wales

		AW ◇	AW	AW ◇	AW ◇	NT	AW	AW	AW	AW		VT ◇1 ⊐	AW ◇ ⊥	AW ◇ ⊥	NT	AW	AW	AW ◇ ⊥	AW ◇ ⊥	NT		AW	AW	AW ◇ ⊥	AW ◇ A
London Euston [15] ⊖65	d																								
Birmingham New Street [12] 65	d			22p55								05 30													
Manchester Airport 84,85 ✈	d												05 33												
Cardiff Central [7] 131	d	19p34			20p55														05 20						
Crewe [10]	d			23p57	00 02							06 23		07 03		07 23						08 23			
Manchester Pic'dilly [10] 90	d		23p14			23p17	00 25						05 50		06 17			06 50		07 17				07 50	
Manchester Oxford Road 90	d		23p17										05 53					06 53						07 53	
Newton-le-Willows 90	d		23p36										06 12					07 12						08 12	
Earlestown [8] 90	d		23p39										06 15					07 15						08 15	
Warrington Bank Quay 90	d		23p48										06 26					07 22						08 24	
Runcorn East	d		23p55										06 33					07 29						08 31	
Frodsham	d		23p59										06 37					07 34						08 35	
Helsby	d		00 03										06 41					07 38						08 39	
Liverpool Lime Street [10] 106	d																								
Chester	a	22p34	00 15	00 18	00 27	00 43	01 29					06 43	06 53	07 23	07 45	07 46		07 51	08 18	08 45		08 46		08 51	
	d	22p56		00 40								06 44	06 55	07 25				07 55	08 22					08 55	
Shotton	d	23p05											07 04					08 04						09 04	
Flint	d	23p11		00 53								06 57	07 10	07 39				08 10	08 36					09 10	
Prestatyn	d	23p24		01 06								07 10	07 23	07 52				08 23	08 49					09 23	
Rhyl	d	23p30		01 12								07 16	07 29	07 58				08 29	08 55					09 29	
Abergele & Pensarn	d	23p36											07 35					08 35						09 35	
Colwyn Bay	d	23p44		01 23								07 27	07 43	08 09				08 43	09 06					09 43	
Llandudno Junction	a	23p49		01 28								07 33	07 48	08 14				08 48	09 11					09 48	
	d	23p52		01 29				06 13	06 51	07 31		07 33	07 50	08 15			08 28	08 50	09 12				09 28	09 50	10 00
Deganwy	d							06x16	06x54	07x34			07x54				08x31	08x54					09x31	09x54	10x03
Llandudno	a							06 23	07 01	07 41			08 06				08 38	09 06					09 38	10 06	10 13
Conwy	d	23b54												08x17					09x14						
Penmaenmawr	d	23b59												08x23					09x20						
Llanfairfechan	d	00x04												08x27					09x24						
Bangor (Gwynedd)	a	00 13		01 45								07 49		08 36					09 33						
	d	00 14		01 45								07 50		08 38					09 35						
Llanfairpwll	d	00x21												08x44											
Bodorgan	d	00x31												08x54					09x49						
Ty Croes	d	00x35												08x58					09x53						
Rhosneigr	d	00x38												09x01					09x56						
Valley	d	00x43												09x07											
Holyhead	a	00 58		02 15								08 23		09 21					10 14						

		AW ◇ B ⊥	NT	AW	AW	AW ◇ ⊥		VT ◇1 ⊐	AW ◇ ⊥	NT	AW	AW	AW ◇ ⊥	VT ◇1 ⊐	AW ◇ B ⊥	NT		AW	AW	AW ◇ ⊥	VT ◇1 ⊐	AW ◇ A	AW ◇ ⊥	NT	AW
London Euston [15] ⊖65	d							08 10						08 50							10 10				
Birmingham New Street [12] 65	d	07 23													09 24										
Manchester Airport 84,85 ✈	d																								
Cardiff Central [7] 131	d								07 21														09 21		
Crewe [10]	d			09 23				09 50			10 23			10 43				11 23			11 50				12 23
Manchester Pic'dilly [10] 90	d		08 17			08 50				09 17			09 50			10 17				10 50				11 17	
Manchester Oxford Road 90	d					08 53							09 53							10 53					
Newton-le-Willows 90	d					09 12							10 12							11 12					
Earlestown [8] 90	d					09 15							10 15							11 15					
Warrington Bank Quay 90	d					09 26							10 26							11 26					
Runcorn East	d					09 33							10 33							11 33					
Frodsham	d					09 37							10 37							11 37					
Helsby	d					09 41							10 41							11 41					
Liverpool Lime Street [10] 106	d																								
Chester	a	09 17	09 45	09 46		09 53		10 12	10 19	10 45	10 46		10 53	11 10	11 19	11 45		11 46		11 53	12 12		12 19	12 45	12 46
	d	09 22				09 55			10 22				10 55	11 12	11 22					11 55			12 23		
Shotton	d					10 04							11 04							12 04					
Flint	d	09 36				10 10			10 36				11 10		11 38					12 10			12 36		
Prestatyn	d	09 49				10 23			10 49				11 23		11 51					12 23			12 49		
Rhyl	d	09 55				10 29			10 55				11 29	11 41	11 57					12 29			12 55		
Abergele & Pensarn	d					10 35							11 35							12 35					
Colwyn Bay	d	10 06				10 43			11 06				11 43	11 54	12 08					12 43			13 06		
Llandudno Junction	a	10 11				10 48			11 11				11 48	12 00	12 13					12 48			13 11		
	d	10 12			10 28	10 50			11 12			11 26	11 50	12 01	12 14				12 28	12 50		13 00	13 12		
Deganwy	d				10x31	10x54						11x29	11x54						12x31	12x54		13x03			
Llandudno	a				10 38	11 06						11 36	12 06						12 38	13 06		13 13			
Conwy	d								11x14						12x16										
Penmaenmawr	d								11x20						12x22										
Llanfairfechan	d								11x24						12x26										
Bangor (Gwynedd)	a	10 28							11 33					12 19	12 34								13 28		
	d	10 29							11 35					12 20	12 37								13 29		
Llanfairpwll	d	10x35													12x43								13x36		
Bodorgan	d														12x53								13x46		
Ty Croes	d														12x57								13x50		
Rhosneigr	d														13x00								13x53		
Valley	d	10x53													13x06								13x58		
Holyhead	a	11 07							12 09					12 55	13 18								14 13		

A From Blaenau Ffestiniog
B From Birmingham International
b Previous night, stops on request

Crewe and Manchester - Chester and North Wales

	AW		AW	VT	AW	NT	AW	AW	AW	VT	AW		NT	AW	AW	AW	AW	VT	AW	AW	AW		NT	AW
			◇	◇[1]	◇ A				◇	◇[1]	◇			🚌			◇	◇[1]	◇ B	◇ A	🚌			
			🛒	🍽	🛒				🛒	🍽	🛒						🛒	🍽		🛒				
London Euston [15] ⊖65 d				11 10						12 10								13 10						
Birmingham New Street [12] 65 d					11 24															13 24				
Manchester Airport 84,85 ✈ d																								
Cardiff Central [7] 131 d											11 21													
Crewe [10] d				12 49			13 23			13 49					14 23			14 50						15 23
Manchester Pic'dilly [10] 90 ⇌ d			11 50			12 17			12 50				13 17				13 50				13 35		14 17	
Manchester Oxford Road 90 d			11 53						12 53												13 40			
Newton-le-Willows 90 d			12 12						13 12												14 10			
Earlestown [8] 90 d			12 15						13 15												14 20			
Warrington Bank Quay 90 d			12 26						13 26					13 45							14 45			
Runcorn East d			12 33						13 33					14 05							15 05			
Frodsham d			12 37						13 37					14 20							15 20			
Helsby d			12 41						13 41					14 25							15 25			
Liverpool Lime Street [10] 106 d																								
Chester a			12 53	13 12	13 18	13 45	13 46		13 53	14 12	14 19		14 45	14 45	14 46		14 53	15 12		15 19	15 45		15 45	15 46
d			12 55		13 22				13 55		14 23						14 55			15 24				
Shotton d			13 04						14 04								15 04							
Flint d			13 10		13 36				14 10		14 36						15 10			15 37				
Prestatyn d			13 23		13 49				14 23		14 49						15 23			15 50				
Rhyl d			13 29		13 55				14 29		14 55						15 29			15 56				
Abergele & Pensarn d			13 35						14 35								15 35							
Colwyn Bay d			13 43		14 06				14 43		15 06						15 43			16 07				
Llandudno Junction a			13 48		14 11				14 48		15 11						15 48			16 12				
d	13 28		13 50		14 12			14 28	14 50		15 12					15 30	15 50		16 00	16 14				
Deganwy d	13x31		13x54					14x31	14x54							15x33	15 54		16x03					
Llandudno a	13 38		14 06					14 38	15 06							15 40	16 06		16 13					
Conwy d					14x14															16x16				
Penmaenmawr d					14x20															16x22				
Llanfairfechan d					14x24															16x26				
Bangor (Gwynedd) a					14 33						15 28									16 35				
d					14 35						15 29									16 36				
Llanfairpwll d											15x36													
Bodorgan d											15x46													
Ty Croes d											15x50													
Rhosneigr d											15x53													
Valley d											15x58													
Holyhead a					15 08						16 13									17 11				

	AW	AW	VT	AW	AW	NT	AW		AW	AW	VT	AW	AW	NT	AW	AW	AW		AW	VT	AW	AW	NT	AW
		◇	◇[1]	◇	🚌					◇	◇[1]	◇ A	🚌				◇ B		◇	◇[1]	■	🚌		
		🛒	🍽	🛒						🛒	🍽	🛒							🛒	🍽	🛒			
London Euston [15] ⊖65 d			14 10								15 10									16 10				
Birmingham New Street [12] 65 d												15 24												
Manchester Airport 84,85 ✈ d																								
Cardiff Central [7] 131 d				13 21																	15 21			
Crewe [10] d			15 49				16 23				16 49				17 23					17 49				18 23
Manchester Pic'dilly [10] 90 ⇌ d		14 50			14 35	15 17				15 50			15 35	16 17					16 50			16 35	17 17	
Manchester Oxford Road 90 d					14 40								15 40									16 40		
Newton-le-Willows 90 d					15 10								16 10									17 10		
Earlestown [8] 90 d					15 20								16 20									17 20		
Warrington Bank Quay 90 d					15 45								16 45									17 45		
Runcorn East d					16 05								17 05									18 05		
Frodsham d					16 20								17 20									18 20		
Helsby d					16 25								17 25									18 25		
Liverpool Lime Street [10] 106 d																								
Chester a		15 53	16 10	16 22	16 45	16 45	16 46			16 53	17 12	17 19	17 45	17 45	17 46				17 53	18 09	18 19	18 45	18 45	18 46
d		15 55	16 12	16 26						16 55		17 22							17 55	18 16	18 24			
Shotton d		16 04								17 04		17 32							18 04					
Flint d		16 10	16 25	16 39						17 10		17 38							18 10	18 29	18 39			
Prestatyn d		16 23	16 38	16 52						17 23		17 51							18 23	18 42	18 52			
Rhyl d		16 29	16 45	16 58						17 29		17 57							18 29	18 49	18 58			
Abergele & Pensarn d		16 35								17 35		18 03							18 35					
Colwyn Bay d		16 43	16 56	17 09						17 43		18 11							18 43	19 00	19 09			
Llandudno Junction a		16 48	17 01	17 14						17 48		18 16							18 48	19 05	19 14			
d	16 26	16 50	17 02	17 14					17 28	17 50		18 18				18 26	18 41		18 50	19 06	19 15			
Deganwy d	16x29	16x54							17x31	17x54						18x29	18x44		18x54					
Llandudno a	16 36	17 06							17 38	18 06						18 36	18 54		19 06					
Conwy d				17x16								18x20												
Penmaenmawr d				17x22								18x26												
Llanfairfechan d				17x26								18x30												
Bangor (Gwynedd) a			17 17	17 35								18 39								19 21	19 32			
d			17 19	17 37								18 40								19 23	19 33			
Llanfairpwll d				17x43																	19 40			
Bodorgan d				17x53																	19 51			
Ty Croes d				17x57																	19 55			
Rhosneigr d				18x00																	19 58			
Valley d				18x06																	20 04			
Holyhead a			17 51	18 20								19 13								19 55	20 18			

A From Birmingham International

B From Blaenau Ffestiniog

Table 81

Saturdays
until 18 June

Crewe and Manchester - Chester and North Wales

		AW	AW	VT	AW	AW	NT	AW	AW	VT	AW	AW	AW	NT	AW	AW	AW	AW	AW	AW	NT	AW
			◇	◇ 1	◇					◇ 1		■					◇	◇	◇			
					A												A	B				
						(bus)							(bus)							(bus)		
			(trolley)	(buffet)	(trolley)				(trolley)	(buffet)		(trolley)					(trolley)					
London Euston 15 ⊖65	d			17 10						18 10												
Birmingham New Street 12 65	d				17 24												19 24					
Manchester Airport 84,85 ✈	d																					
Cardiff Central 7 131	d											17 21										
Crewe 10	d			18 50				19 23		19 50					20 23				21 00			21 23
Manchester Pic'dilly 10 90 ⛴	d		17 50			17 35	18 17		18 50				18 35	19 17		19 50				19 35	20 17	
Manchester Oxford Road 90	d					17 40							18 40							19 40		
Newton-le-Willows 90	d					18 10							19 10							20 10		
Earlestown 8 90	d					18 20							19 20							20 20		
Warrington Bank Quay 90	d					18 45							19 45							20 45		
Runcorn East	d					19 05							20 05							21 05		
Frodsham	d					19 20							20 20							21 20		
Helsby	d					19 25							20 25							21 25		
Liverpool Lime Street 10 106	d																					
Chester	a		18 53	19 10	19 24	19 45	19 45	19 46	19 54	20 12		20 19	20 45	20 45	20 46	20 57	21 21		21 21	21 45	21 45	21 46
	d		18 55	19 17	19 32							20 32							21 26			
Shotton	d		19 04		19 41							20 41							21 35			
Flint	d		19 10	19 30	19 47							20 47							21 41			
Prestatyn	d		19 23	19 43	20 00							21 00							21 54			
Rhyl	d		19 29	19 50	20 06							21 06							22 00			
Abergele & Pensarn	d		19 35		20 12														22 06			
Colwyn Bay	d		19 43	20 01	20 20							21 17							22 14			
Llandudno Junction	a		19 48	20 06	20 25							21 22							22 19			
	d	19 28	19 50	20 07	20 27						20 30	21 22						21 32	22 21			
Deganwy	d	19x31	19x54								20x33							21x35				
Llandudno	a	19 38	20 06								20 40							21 46				
Conwy	d				20x29														22 23			
Penmaenmawr	d				20x35														22 29			
Llanfairfechan	d				20x39														22 33			
Bangor (Gwynedd)	a			20 22	20 48							21 38							22 42			
	d			20 24	20 49							21 39							22 43			
Llanfairpwll	d				20x55							21x46										
Bodorgan	d				21x05							21x56										
Ty Croes	d				21x10							22x00										
Rhosneigr	d				21x13							22x03										
Valley	d				21x18							22x08										
Holyhead	a			20 56	21 31							22 23							23 18			

		AW	AW	AW	NT	AW	AW	AW	AW	NT	AW	AW	AW	NT	AW	AW	AW
			◇					◇				◇					
								A				C					
				(bus)									(bus)			(bus)	(bus)
London Euston 15 ⊖65	d																
Birmingham New Street 12 65	d							21 24									
Manchester Airport 84,85 ✈	d	20 32															
Cardiff Central 7 131	d		19 34									20 55					
Crewe 10	d					22 23			23 21			23 58					
Manchester Pic'dilly 10 90 ⛴	d	20 50		20 35	21 17		21 50			22 17	22 26		22 26	23 17	23 19	23 14	
Manchester Oxford Road 90	d			20 40									22 31			23 19	
Newton-le-Willows 90	d			21 10									23 01			23 49	
Earlestown 8 90	d			21 20									23 11			23 59	
Warrington Bank Quay 90	d			21 45									23 36			00 24	
Runcorn East	d			22 05									23 56			00 44	
Frodsham	d			22 20									00 11			00 59	
Helsby	d			22 25									00 16			01 04	
Liverpool Lime Street 10 106	d																
Chester	a	21 56	22 31	22 45	22 45	22 45	22 55	23 21	23 42	23 45	23 46	00 24	00 36	00 43	00 44	01 24	
	d		22 36														
Shotton	d		22 45														
Flint	d		22 51														
Prestatyn	d		23 05														
Rhyl	d		23 11														
Abergele & Pensarn	d		23 17														
Colwyn Bay	d		23 25														
Llandudno Junction	a		23 38														
	d																23 48
Deganwy	d																
Llandudno	a																
Conwy	d																23 56
Penmaenmawr	d																00 08
Llanfairfechan	d																00 23
Bangor (Gwynedd)	a																00 38
	d																00 38
Llanfairpwll	d																00 47
Bodorgan	d																00 57
Ty Croes	d																01 07
Rhosneigr	d																01 27
Valley	d																01 52
Holyhead	a																02 02

A From Birmingham International
B From Blaenau Ffestiniog
C From Carmarthen

Table 81

Saturdays

25 June to 10 September

Crewe and Manchester - Chester and North Wales

		AW	AW	AW	AW	NT	AW	AW	AW	AW		VT	AW	AW	NT	AW	AW	AW	AW	NT		AW	AW	AW	AW
		◇		◇	◇							◇1	◇	◇				◇	◇					◇	◇
																									A
												☕	🛒	🛒				🛒	🛒					🛒	
London Euston 15 ⊖65	d																								
Birmingham New Street 12 65	d			22p55								05 30													
Manchester Airport .. 84,85 ✈	d												05 33												
Cardiff Central 7 131	d	19p34			20p55														05 20						
Crewe 10	d			23p57	00 02							06 23		07 03		07 23						08 23			
Manchester Pic'dilly 10 90	d		23p14			23p17	00 25						05 50		06 17			06 50		07 17				07 50	
Manchester Oxford Road 90	d		23p17										05 53					06 53						07 53	
Newton-le-Willows 90	d		23p36										06 12					07 12						08 12	
Earlestown 8 90	d		23p39										06 15					07 15						08 15	
Warrington Bank Quay 90	d		23p48										06 26					07 22						08 24	
Runcorn East	d		23p55										06 33					07 29						08 31	
Frodsham	d		23p59										06 37					07 34						08 35	
Helsby	d		00 03										06 41					07 38						08 39	
Liverpool Lime Street 10 106	d																								
Chester	a	22p34	00 15	00 18	00 27	00 43	01 29					06 43	06 53	07 23	07 45	07 46		07 51	08 18	08 45		08 46		08 51	
	d	22p56		00 40								06 44	06 55	07 25				07 55	08 22					08 55	
Shotton	d	23p05											07 04					08 04						09 04	
Flint	d	23p11		00 53								06 57	07 10	07 39				08 10	08 36					09 10	
Prestatyn	d	23p24		01 06								07 10	07 23	07 52				08 23	08 49					09 23	
Rhyl	d	23p30		01 12								07 16	07 29	07 58				08 29	08 55					09 29	
Abergele & Pensarn	d	23p36											07 35					08 35						09 35	
Colwyn Bay	d	23p44		01 23								07 27	07 43	08 09				08 43	09 06					09 43	
Llandudno Junction	a	23p49		01 28								07 33	07 48	08 14				08 48	09 11					09 48	
	d	23p52		01 29				06 13	06 51	07 31		07 33	07 50	08 15			08 28	08 50	09 12				09 28	09 50	10 00
Deganwy	d							06x16	06x54	07x34			07x54				08x31	08x54					09x31	09x54	10x03
Llandudno	a							06 23	07 01	07 41			08 06				08 38	09 06					09 38	10 06	10 13
Conwy	d	23b54												08x17					09x14						
Penmaenmawr	d	23b59												08x23					09x20						
Llanfairfechan	d	00x04												08x27					09x24						
Bangor (Gwynedd)	a	00 13		01 45								07 49		08 36					09 33						
	d	00 14		01 45								07 50		08 38					09 35						
Llanfairpwll	d	00x21												08x44											
Bodorgan	d	00x31												08x54					09x49						
Ty Croes	d	00x35												08x58					09x53						
Rhosneigr	d	00x38												09x01					09x56						
Valley	d	00x43												09x07											
Holyhead	a	00 58		02 15								08 23		09 21					10 14						

		AW	NT	AW	AW	AW		VT	AW	NT	AW	AW	AW	VT	AW	NT		AW	AW	AW	VT	AW	AW	NT	AW
		◇				◇		◇1	◇				◇	◇1	◇					◇	◇1	◇	◇		
		B													B							A			
		🛒				🛒		☕	🛒				🛒	☕	🛒					🛒	☕		🛒		
London Euston 15 ⊖65	d							08 10						08 50							10 10				
Birmingham New Street 12 65	d	07 23													09 24										
Manchester Airport .. 84,85 ✈	d																								
Cardiff Central 7 131	d								07 21														09 21		
Crewe 10	d			09 23				09 50			10 23			10 43				11 23			11 50				12 23
Manchester Pic'dilly 10 90	d		08 17			08 50				09 17			09 50			10 17				10 50				11 17	
Manchester Oxford Road 90	d					08 53							09 53							10 53					
Newton-le-Willows 90	d					09 12							10 12							11 12					
Earlestown 8 90	d					09 15							10 15							11 15					
Warrington Bank Quay 90	d					09 26							10 26							11 26					
Runcorn East	d					09 33							10 33							11 33					
Frodsham	d					09 37							10 37							11 37					
Helsby	d					09 41							10 41							11 41					
Liverpool Lime Street 10 106	d																								
Chester	a	09 17	09 45	09 46		09 53		10 12	10 19	10 45	10 46		10 53	11 10	11 19	11 45		11 46		11 53	12 12		12 19	12 45	12 46
	d	09 22				09 55			10 22				10 55	11 12	11 22					11 55			12 23		
Shotton	d					10 04							11 04							12 04					
Flint	d	09 36				10 10			10 36				11 10		11 38					12 10			12 36		
Prestatyn	d	09 49				10 23			10 49				11 23		11 51					12 23			12 49		
Rhyl	d	09 55				10 29			10 55				11 29	11 41	11 57					12 29			12 55		
Abergele & Pensarn	d					10 35							11 35							12 35					
Colwyn Bay	d	10 06				10 43			11 06				11 43	11 54	12 08					12 43			13 06		
Llandudno Junction	a	10 11				10 48			11 11				11 48	12 00	12 13					12 48			13 11		
	d	10 12			10 28	10 50			11 12			11 26	11 50	12 01	12 14				12 28	12 50		13 00	13 12		
Deganwy	d				10x31	10x54						11x29	11x54						12x31	12x54		13x03			
Llandudno	a				10 38	11 06						11 36	12 06						12 38	13 06		13 13			
Conwy	d								11x14						12x16										
Penmaenmawr	d								11x20						12x22										
Llanfairfechan	d								11x24						12x26										
Bangor (Gwynedd)	a	10 28							11 33					12 19	12 34								13 28		
	d	10 29							11 35					12 20	12 37								13 29		
Llanfairpwll	d	10x35													12x43								13x36		
Bodorgan	d														12x53								13x46		
Ty Croes	d														12x57								13x50		
Rhosneigr	d														13x00								13x53		
Valley	d	10x53													13x06								13x58		
Holyhead	a	11 07							12 09					12 55	13 18								14 13		

A From Blaenau Ffestiniog
B From Birmingham International
b Previous night, stops on request

Table 81

Saturdays

25 June to 10 September

Crewe and Manchester - Chester and North Wales

	AW		AW	VT	AW	NT	AW	AW	AW	VT	AW		NT	AW	AW	AW	VT	AW	AW	NT	AW		AW	AW
			◇	◇ 1	◇				◇	◇ 1	◇					◇	◇ 1	◇	◇					◇
					A													B	A					
			🛒	☕	🛒				🛒	☕	🛒					🛒	☕		🛒					🛒
London Euston 15 ⊖65 d				11 10						12 10							13 10							
Birmingham New Street 12 65 d					11 24														13 24					
Manchester Airport 84,85 ✈ d																								
Cardiff Central 7 131 d											11 21													
Crewe 10 d				12 49			13 23			13 49				14 23			14 50				15 23			
Manchester Pic'dilly 10 90 d			11 50			12 17			12 50				13 17			13 50				14 17				14 50
Manchester Oxford Road 90 d			11 53						12 53							13 53								14 53
Newton-le-Willows 90 d			12 12						13 12							14 12								15 12
Earlestown 8 90 d			12 15						13 15							14 15								15 15
Warrington Bank Quay 90 d			12 26						13 26							14 26								15 26
Runcorn East d			12 33						13 33							14 33								15 33
Frodsham d			12 37						13 37							14 37								15 37
Helsby d			12 41						13 41							14 41								15 41
Liverpool Lime Street 10 106 d																								
Chester a			12 53	13 12	13 18	13 45	13 46		13 53	14 12	14 19		14 45	14 46		14 53	15 12		15 19	15 45	15 46			15 53
d			12 55		13 22				13 55		14 23					14 55			15 24					15 55
Shotton d			13 04						14 04							15 04								16 04
Flint d			13 10		13 36				14 10		14 36					15 10			15 37					16 10
Prestatyn d			13 23		13 49				14 23		14 49					15 23			15 50					16 23
Rhyl d			13 29		13 55				14 29		14 55					15 29			15 56					16 29
Abergele & Pensarn d			13 35						14 35							15 35								16 35
Colwyn Bay d			13 43		14 06				14 43		15 06					15 43			16 07					16 43
Llandudno Junction a			13 48		14 11				14 48		15 11					15 48			16 12					16 48
d	13 28		13 50		14 12			14 28	14 50		15 12				15 30	15 50		16 00	16 14				16 26	16 50
Deganwy d	13x31		13x54					14x31	14x54						15x33	15 54		16x03					16x29	16x54
Llandudno a	13 38		14 06					14 38	15 06						15 40	16 06		16 13					16 36	17 06
Conwy d					14x14														16x16					
Penmaenmawr d					14x20														16x22					
Llanfairfechan d					14x24														16x26					
Bangor (Gwynedd) a					14 33						15 28								16 35					
d					14 35						15 29								16 36					
Llanfairpwll d											15x36													
Bodorgan d											15x46													
Ty Croes d											15x50													
Rhosneigr d											15x53													
Valley d											15x58													
Holyhead a					15 08						16 13								17 11					

	VT	AW	NT	AW	AW	AW	VT		AW	NT	AW	AW	AW	AW	VT	AW	NT		AW	AW	AW	VT	AW	NT
																R								
	◇ 1	◇				◇	◇ 1		◇				◇	◇	◇ 1						◇	◇ 1	◇	
									A				B										A	
	☕	🛒				🛒	☕		🛒					🛒	☕	🛒					🛒	☕	🛒	
London Euston 15 ⊖65 d	14 10						15 10								16 10							17 10		
Birmingham New Street 12 65 d									15 24														17 24	
Manchester Airport 84,85 ✈ d																								
Cardiff Central 7 131 d		13 21														15 21								
Crewe 10 d	15 49			16 23			16 49				17 23				17 49				18 23			18 50		
Manchester Pic'dilly 10 90 d			15 17			15 50				16 17				16 50			17 17				17 50			18 17
Manchester Oxford Road 90 d						15 53								16 53							17 53			
Newton-le-Willows 90 d						16 12								17 12							18 12			
Earlestown 8 90 d						16 15								17 15							18 15			
Warrington Bank Quay 90 d						16 26								17 26							18 25			
Runcorn East d						16 33								17 33							18 32			
Frodsham d						16 37								17 37							18 36			
Helsby d						16 41								17 41							18 40			
Liverpool Lime Street 10 106 d																								
Chester a	16 10	16 22	16 45	16 46		16 53	17 12		17 19	17 45	17 46			17 53	18 09	18 19	18 45		18 46		18 52	19 10	19 24	19 45
d	16 12	16 26				16 55			17 22					17 55	18 16	18 24					18 55	19 17	19 32	
Shotton d						17 04			17 32					18 04							19 04		19 41	
Flint d	16 25	16 39				17 10			17 38					18 10	18 29	18 39					19 10	19 30	19 47	
Prestatyn d	16 38	16 52				17 23			17 51					18 23	18 42	18 52					19 23	19 43	20 00	
Rhyl d	16 45	16 58				17 29			17 57					18 29	18 49	18 58					19 29	19 50	20 06	
Abergele & Pensarn d						17 35			18 03					18 35							19 35		20 12	
Colwyn Bay d	16 56	17 09				17 43			18 11					18 43	19 00	19 09					19 43	20 01	20 20	
Llandudno Junction a	17 01	17 14				17 48			18 16					18 48	19 05	19 14					19 48	20 06	20 25	
d	17 02	17 14			17 28	17 50			18 18			18 26	18 41	18 50	19 06	19 15				19 28	19 50	20 07	20 27	
Deganwy d					17x31	17x54						18x29	18x44	18x54						19x31	19x54			
Llandudno a					17 38	18 06						18 36	18 54	19 06						19 38	20 06			
Conwy d		17x16							18x20														20x29	
Penmaenmawr d		17x22							18x26														20x35	
Llanfairfechan d		17x26							18x30														20x39	
Bangor (Gwynedd) a	17 17	17 35							18 39						19 21	19 32						20 22	20 48	
d	17 19	17 37							18 40						19 23	19 33						20 24	20 49	
Llanfairpwll d		17x43														19 40							20x55	
Bodorgan d		17x53														19 51							21x05	
Ty Croes d		17x57														19 55							21x10	
Rhosneigr d		18x00														19 58							21x13	
Valley d		18x06														20 04							21x18	
Holyhead a	17 51	18 20							19 13						19 55	20 18						20 56	21 31	

A From Birmingham International

B From Blaenau Ffestiniog

Table 81

Saturdays

25 June to 10 September

Crewe and Manchester - Chester and North Wales

		AW	AW	VT		AW	AW	NT	AW	AW	AW	AW	AW	NT		AW	AW	AW	NT	AW	AW	AW	AW	AW
			🚲	◇1 ☕			■ 🚲				◇ A 🚲	◇ B	◇					◇				◇ A		
London Euston 15 ⊖65	d			18 10																				
Birmingham New Street 12 65	d										19 24											21 24		
Manchester Airport 84,85 ✈	d																20 32							
Cardiff Central 7 131	d						17 21											19 34						
Crewe 10	d	19 23		19 50					20 23				21 00			21 23				22 23				23 21
Manchester Pic'dilly 10 90 ⇌	d		18 50					19 17		19 50				20 17			20 50		21 17		21 50		22 26	
Manchester Oxford Road 90	d		18 53							19 53							20 53				21 53		22 29	
Newton-le-Willows 90	d		19 12							20 12							21 12				22 12		22 47	
Earlestown 8 90	d		19 16							20 15							21 15				22 15		22 50	
Warrington Bank Quay 90	d		19 27							20 30							21 27				22 24		22 59	
Runcorn East	d		19 34							20 37							21 34				22 31		23 06	
Frodsham	d		19 38							20 41							21 38				22 35		23 10	
Helsby	d		19 42							20 45							21 42				22 39		23 14	
Liverpool Lime Street 10 106	d																							
Chester	a	19 46	19 54	20 12			20 19	20 45	20 46	20 57	21 21		21 21	21 45		21 46	21 57	22 31	22 45	22 45	22 53	23 21	23 26	23 42
	d						20 32						21 26					22 36						
Shotton	d						20 41						21 35					22 45						
Flint	d						20 47						21 41					22 51						
Prestatyn	d						21 00						21 54					23 05						
Rhyl	d						21 06						22 00					23 11						
Abergele & Pensarn	d												22 06					23 17						
Colwyn Bay	d						21 17						22 14					23 25						
Llandudno Junction	a						21 22						22 19					23 38						
	d					20 30	21 22					21 32	22 21											
Deganwy	d					20x33						21x35												
Llandudno	a					20 40						21 46												
Conwy	d												22 23											
Penmaenmawr	d												22 29											
Llanfairfechan	d												22 33											
Bangor (Gwynedd)	a						21 38						22 42											
	d						21 39						22 43											
Llanfairpwll	d						21x46																	
Bodorgan	d						21x56																	
Ty Croes	d						22x00																	
Rhosneigr	d						22x03																	
Valley	d						22x08																	
Holyhead	a						22 23						23 18											

		NT	AW	AW	NT	AW
				◇ C		🚌
London Euston 15 ⊖65	d					
Birmingham New Street 12 65	d					
Manchester Airport 84,85 ✈	d					
Cardiff Central 7 131	d			20 55		
Crewe 10	d			23 58		
Manchester Pic'dilly 10 90 ⇌	d	22 17	23 14		23 17	
Manchester Oxford Road 90	d		23 17			
Newton-le-Willows 90	d		23 36			
Earlestown 8 90	d		23 39			
Warrington Bank Quay 90	d		23 48			
Runcorn East	d		23 55			
Frodsham	d		23 59			
Helsby	d		00 03			
Liverpool Lime Street 10 106	d					
Chester	a	23 45	00 15	00 24	00 43	
	d					
Shotton	d					
Flint	d					
Prestatyn	d					
Rhyl	d					
Abergele & Pensarn	d					
Colwyn Bay	d					
Llandudno Junction	a					
	d					23 48
Deganwy	d					
Llandudno	a					
Conwy	d					23 56
Penmaenmawr	d					00 08
Llanfairfechan	d					00 23
Bangor (Gwynedd)	a					00 38
	d					00 38
Llanfairpwll	d					00 47
Bodorgan	d					00 57
Ty Croes	d					01 07
Rhosneigr	d					01 27
Valley	d					01 52
Holyhead	a					02 02

A From Birmingham International

B From Blaenau Ffestiniog

C from 25 June until 30 July. From Carmarthen

Table 81

Saturdays

17 September to 1 October

Crewe and Manchester - Chester and North Wales

	AW	AW	AW	AW	NT	AW	AW	AW	AW		VT	AW	AW	NT	AW	AW	AW	AW	NT		AW	AW	AW	AW
	◇		◇	◇							◇[1]	◇	◇				◇	◇					◇	◇
																								A
											☕	🛒	🛒				🛒	🛒					🛒	
London Euston [15] ⊖65 d																								
Birmingham New Street [12] 65 d			22p55								05 30													
Manchester Airport 84,85 ✈ d												05 33												
Cardiff Central [7] 131 d	19p34			20p55														05 20						
Crewe [10] d			23p57	00 02							06 23		07 03		07 23						08 23			
Manchester Pic'dilly [10] 90 ⛴ d		23p14			23p17	00 25						05 50		06 17			06 50		07 17				07 50	
Manchester Oxford Road 90 d		23p17										05 53					06 53						07 53	
Newton-le-Willows 90 d		23p36										06 12					07 12						08 12	
Earlestown [8] 90 d		23p39										06 15					07 15						08 15	
Warrington Bank Quay 90 d		23p48										06 26					07 22						08 24	
Runcorn East d		23p55										06 33					07 29						08 31	
Frodsham d		23p59										06 37					07 34						08 35	
Helsby d		00 03										06 41					07 38						08 39	
Liverpool Lime Street [10] 106 d																								
Chester a	22p34	00 15	00 18	00 27	00 43	01 29					06 43	06 53	07 23	07 45	07 46		07 51	08 18	08 45		08 46		08 51	
d	22p56		00 40								06 44	06 55	07 25				07 55	08 22					08 55	
Shotton d	23p05											07 04					08 04						09 04	
Flint d	23p11		00 53								06 57	07 10	07 39				08 10	08 36					09 10	
Prestatyn d	23p24		01 06								07 10	07 23	07 52				08 23	08 49					09 23	
Rhyl d	23p30		01 12								07 16	07 29	07 58				08 29	08 55					09 29	
Abergele & Pensarn d	23p36											07 35					08 35						09 35	
Colwyn Bay d	23p44		01 23								07 27	07 43	08 09				08 43	09 06					09 43	
Llandudno Junction a	23p49		01 28								07 33	07 48	08 14				08 48	09 11					09 48	
d	23p52		01 29				06 13	06 51	07 31		07 33	07 50	08 15			08 28	08 50	09 12				09 28	09 50	10 00
Deganwy d							06x16	06x54	07x34			07x54				08x31	08x54					09x31	09x54	10x03
Llandudno a							06 23	07 01	07 41			08 06				08 38	09 06					09 38	10 06	10 13
Conwy d	23b54												08x17					09x14						
Penmaenmawr d	23b59												08x23					09x20						
Llanfairfechan d	00x04												08x27					09x24						
Bangor (Gwynedd) a	00 13		01 45								07 49		08 36					09 33						
d	00 14		01 45								07 50		08 38					09 35						
Llanfairpwll d	00x21												08x44											
Bodorgan d	00x31												08x54					09x49						
Ty Croes d	00x35												08x58					09x53						
Rhosneigr d	00x38												09x01					09x56						
Valley d	00x43												09x07											
Holyhead a	00 58		02 15								08 23		09 21					10 14						

	AW	NT	AW	AW	AW		VT	AW	NT	AW	AW	AW	VT	AW	NT		AW	AW	AW	VT	AW	AW	NT	AW
	◇				◇		◇[1]	◇				◇	◇[1]	◇					◇	◇[1]	◇	◇		
	B													B							A			
	🛒				🛒		☕	🛒				🛒	☕	🛒					🛒	☕		🛒		
London Euston [15] ⊖65 d							08 10						08 50							10 10				
Birmingham New Street [12] 65 d	07 23													09 24										
Manchester Airport 84,85 ✈ d																								
Cardiff Central [7] 131 d								07 21														09 21		
Crewe [10] d			09 23				09 50			10 23			10 43				11 23			11 50				12 23
Manchester Pic'dilly [10] 90 ⛴ d		08 17			08 50				09 17			09 50			10 17				10 50				11 17	
Manchester Oxford Road 90 d					08 53							09 53							10 53					
Newton-le-Willows 90 d					09 12							10 12							11 12					
Earlestown [8] 90 d					09 15							10 15							11 15					
Warrington Bank Quay 90 d					09 26							10 26							11 26					
Runcorn East d					09 33							10 33							11 33					
Frodsham d					09 37							10 37							11 37					
Helsby d					09 41							10 41							11 41					
Liverpool Lime Street [10] 106 d																								
Chester a	09 17	09 45	09 46		09 53		10 12	10 19	10 45	10 46		10 53	11 10	11 19	11 45		11 46		11 53	12 12		12 19	12 45	12 46
d	09 22				09 55			10 22				10 55	11 12	11 22					11 55			12 23		
Shotton d					10 04							11 04							12 04					
Flint d	09 36				10 10			10 36				11 10		11 38					12 10			12 36		
Prestatyn d	09 49				10 23			10 49				11 23		11 51					12 23			12 49		
Rhyl d	09 55				10 29			10 55				11 29	11 41	11 57					12 29			12 55		
Abergele & Pensarn d					10 35							11 35							12 35					
Colwyn Bay d	10 06				10 43			11 06				11 43	11 54	12 08					12 43			13 06		
Llandudno Junction a	10 11				10 48			11 11				11 48	12 00	12 13					12 48			13 11		
d	10 12			10 28	10 50			11 12			11 26	11 50	12 01	12 14				12 28	12 50		13 00	13 12		
Deganwy d				10x31	10x54						11x29	11x54						12x31	12x54		13x03			
Llandudno a				10 38	11 06						11 36	12 06						12 38	13 06		13 13			
Conwy d								11x14						12x16										
Penmaenmawr d								11x20						12x22										
Llanfairfechan d								11x24						12x26										
Bangor (Gwynedd) a	10 28							11 33					12 19	12 34								13 28		
d	10 29							11 35					12 20	12 37								13 29		
Llanfairpwll d	10x35													12x43								13x36		
Bodorgan d														12x53								13x46		
Ty Croes d														12x57								13x50		
Rhosneigr d														13x00								13x53		
Valley d	10x53													13x06								13x58		
Holyhead a	11 07							12 09					12 55	13 18								14 13		

A From Blaenau Ffestiniog
B From Birmingham International
b Previous night, stops on request

Table 81

Saturdays

17 September to 1 October

Crewe and Manchester - Chester and North Wales

	AW		AW	VT	AW	NT	AW	AW	AW	VT	AW		NT	AW	AW	AW	VT	AW	AW	NT	AW		AW	AW
			◇	◇■1	◇				◇	◇■1	◇					◇	◇■1	◇	◇					◇
					A													B	A					
			🛒	🍽	🛒				🛒	🍽	🛒					🛒	🍽		🛒					🛒
London Euston ■15 ⊖65 d				11 10						12 10							13 10							
Birmingham New Street ■12 65 d					11 24														13 24					
Manchester Airport 84,85 ✈ d																								
Cardiff Central ■7 131 d											11 21													
Crewe ■10 d				12 49			13 23			13 49				14 23			14 50				15 23			
Manchester Pic'dilly ■10 90 ⛴ d			11 50			12 17			12 50				13 17			13 50				14 17				14 50
Manchester Oxford Road 90 d			11 53						12 53							13 53								14 53
Newton-le-Willows 90 d			12 12						13 12							14 12								15 12
Earlestown ■8 90 d			12 15						13 15							14 15								15 15
Warrington Bank Quay 90 d			12 26						13 26							14 26								15 26
Runcorn East d			12 33						13 33							14 33								15 33
Frodsham d			12 37						13 37							14 37								15 37
Helsby d			12 41						13 41							14 41								15 41
Liverpool Lime Street ■10 106 d																								
Chester a			12 53	13 12	13 18	13 45	13 46		13 53	14 12	14 19		14 45	14 46		14 53	15 12		15 19	15 45	15 46			15 53
d			12 55		13 22				13 55		14 23					14 55			15 24					15 55
Shotton d			13 04						14 04							15 04								16 04
Flint d			13 10		13 36				14 10		14 36					15 10			15 37					16 10
Prestatyn d			13 23		13 49				14 23		14 49					15 23			15 50					16 23
Rhyl d			13 29		13 55				14 29		14 55					15 29			15 56					16 29
Abergele & Pensarn d			13 35						14 35							15 35								16 35
Colwyn Bay d			13 43		14 06				14 43		15 06					15 43			16 07					16 43
Llandudno Junction a			13 48		14 11				14 48		15 11					15 48			16 12					16 48
d	13 28		13 50		14 12			14 28	14 50		15 12				15 30	15 50		16 00	16 14				16 26	16 50
Deganwy d	13x31		13x54					14x31	14x54						15x33	15 54		16x03					16x29	16x54
Llandudno a	13 38		14 06					14 38	15 06						15 40	16 06		16 13					16 36	17 06
Conwy d					14x14														16x16					
Penmaenmawr d					14x20														16x22					
Llanfairfechan d					14x24														16x26					
Bangor (Gwynedd) a					14 33						15 28								16 35					
d					14 35						15 29								16 36					
Llanfairpwll d											15x36													
Bodorgan d											15x46													
Ty Croes d											15x50													
Rhosneigr d											15x53													
Valley d											15x58													
Holyhead a					15 08						16 13								17 11					

	VT	AW	NT	AW	AW	AW	VT		AW	NT	AW	AW	AW	AW	VT	AW	NT		AW	AW	AW	VT	AW	NT
	◇■1	◇				◇	◇■1		◇				◇	◇	◇■1	■					◇	◇■1	◇	
									A				B										A	
	🍽	🛒				🛒	🍽		🛒					🛒	🍽	🛒					🛒	🍽	🛒	
London Euston ■15 ⊖65 d	14 10						15 10								16 10							17 10		
Birmingham New Street ■12 65 d									15 24														17 24	
Manchester Airport 84,85 ✈ d																								
Cardiff Central ■7 131 d		13 21														15 21								
Crewe ■10 d	15 49			16 23			16 49				17 23				17 49				18 23			18 50		
Manchester Pic'dilly ■10 90 ⛴ d			15 17			15 50				16 17				16 50			17 17				17 50			18 17
Manchester Oxford Road 90 d						15 53								16 53							17 53			
Newton-le-Willows 90 d						16 12								17 12							18 12			
Earlestown ■8 90 d						16 15								17 15							18 15			
Warrington Bank Quay 90 d						16 26								17 26							18 25			
Runcorn East d						16 33								17 33							18 32			
Frodsham d						16 37								17 37							18 36			
Helsby d						16 41								17 41							18 40			
Liverpool Lime Street ■10 106 d																								
Chester a	16 10	16 22	16 45	16 46		16 53	17 12		17 19	17 45	17 46			17 53	18 09	18 19	18 45		18 46		18 52	19 10	19 20	19 45
d	16 12	16 26				16 55			17 22					17 55	18 16	18 24					18 55	19 17	19 32	
Shotton d						17 04			17 32					18 04							19 04		19 41	
Flint d	16 25	16 39				17 10			17 38					18 10	18 29	18 39					19 10	19 30	19 47	
Prestatyn d	16 38	16 52				17 23			17 51					18 23	18 42	18 52					19 23	19 43	20 00	
Rhyl d	16 45	16 58				17 29			17 57					18 29	18 49	18 58					19 29	19 50	20 06	
Abergele & Pensarn d						17 35			18 03					18 35							19 35		20 12	
Colwyn Bay d	16 56	17 09				17 43			18 11					18 43	19 00	19 09					19 43	20 01	20 20	
Llandudno Junction a	17 01	17 14				17 48			18 16					18 48	19 05	19 14					19 48	20 06	20 25	
d	17 02	17 14			17 28	17 50			18 18			18 26	18 41	18 50	19 06	19 15				19 28	19 50	20 07	20 27	
Deganwy d					17x31	17x54						18x29	18x44	18x54						19x31	19x54			
Llandudno a					17 38	18 06						18 36	18 54	19 06						19 38	20 06			
Conwy d		17x16							18x20														20x29	
Penmaenmawr d		17x22							18x26														20x35	
Llanfairfechan d		17x26							18x30														20x39	
Bangor (Gwynedd) a	17 17	17 35							18 39						19 21	19 32						20 22	20 48	
d	17 19	17 37							18 40						19 23	19 33						20 24	20 49	
Llanfairpwll d		17x43														19 40							20x55	
Bodorgan d		17x53														19 51							21x05	
Ty Croes d		17x57														19 55							21x10	
Rhosneigr d		18x00														19 58							21x13	
Valley d		18x06														20 04							21x18	
Holyhead a	17 51	18 20							19 13						19 55	20 18						20 56	21 31	

A From Birmingham International

B From Blaenau Ffestiniog

Table 81

Saturdays

17 September to 1 October

Crewe and Manchester - Chester and North Wales

	AW	AW	VT	AW	AW	NT	AW	AW	AW	AW	AW	NT	AW	AW	AW	NT	AW	AW	AW	AW	NT
			◇1		B				◇ A	◇ B	◇				◇				◇ A		
		🍴	☕		🍴				🍴												
London Euston 15 ⊖65 d			18 10																		
Birmingham New Street 12 65 d									19 24										21 24		
Manchester Airport 84,85 ✈ d														20 32							
Cardiff Central 7 131 d					17 21										19 34						
Crewe 10 d	19 23		19 50				20 23				21 00		21 23				22 23			23 21	
Manchester Pic'dilly 10 90 ⛴ d		18 50				19 17		19 50				20 17		20 50		21 17		21 50			22 17
Manchester Oxford Road 90 d		18 53						19 53						20 53				21 53			
Newton-le-Willows 90 d		19 12						20 12						21 12				22 12			
Earlestown 8 90 d		19 16						20 15						21 15				22 15			
Warrington Bank Quay 90 d		19 27						20 30						21 27				22 24			
Runcorn East d		19 34						20 37						21 34				22 31			
Frodsham d		19 38						20 41						21 38				22 35			
Helsby d		19 42						20 45						21 42				22 39			
Liverpool Lime Street 10 106 d																					
Chester a	19 46	19 54	20 12		20 19	20 45	20 46	20 57	21 21		21 21	21 45	21 46	21 57	22 31	22 45	22 45	22 53	23 21	23 42	23 45
d					20 32						21 26				22 36						
Shotton d					20 41						21 35				22 45						
Flint d					20 47						21 41				22 51						
Prestatyn d					21 00						21 54				23 05						
Rhyl d					21 06						22 00				23 11						
Abergele & Pensarn d											22 06				23 17						
Colwyn Bay d					21 17						22 14				23 25						
Llandudno Junction a					21 22						22 19				23 38						
d				20 30	21 22					21 32	22 21										
Deganwy d				20x33						21x35											
Llandudno a				20 40						21 46											
Conwy d											22 23										
Penmaenmawr d											22 29										
Llanfairfechan d											22 33										
Bangor (Gwynedd) a					21 38						22 42										
d					21 39						22 43										
Llanfairpwll d					21x46																
Bodorgan d					21x56																
Ty Croes d					22x00																
Rhosneigr d					22x03																
Valley d					22x08																
Holyhead a					22 23						23 18										

	AW	AW	NT	AW	AW
		◇ C			🚌
London Euston 15 ⊖65 d					
Birmingham New Street 12 65 d					
Manchester Airport 84,85 ✈ d					
Cardiff Central 7 131 d		20 55			
Crewe 10 d		23 58			
Manchester Pic'dilly 10 90 ⛴ d	22 26		23 17	23 19	
Manchester Oxford Road 90 d					
Newton-le-Willows 90 d					
Earlestown 8 90 d					
Warrington Bank Quay 90 d					
Runcorn East d					
Frodsham d					
Helsby d					
Liverpool Lime Street 10 106 d					
Chester a	23 46	00 24	00 43	00 44	
d					
Shotton d					
Flint d					
Prestatyn d					
Rhyl d					
Abergele & Pensarn d					
Colwyn Bay d					
Llandudno Junction a					
d					23 48
Deganwy d					
Llandudno a					
Conwy d					23 56
Penmaenmawr d					00 08
Llanfairfechan d					00 23
Bangor (Gwynedd) a					00 38
d					00 38
Llanfairpwll d					00 47
Bodorgan d					00 57
Ty Croes d					01 07
Rhosneigr d					01 27
Valley d					01 52
Holyhead a					02 02

A From Birmingham International
B From Blaenau Ffestiniog
C From Carmarthen

Table 81

Crewe and Manchester - Chester and North Wales

		AW	AW	AW	AW	NT	AW	AW	AW	AW		VT	AW	AW	AW	NT	AW	AW	AW	AW		NT	AW	AW	AW
		◇		◇	◇							◇1	◇	◇				◇	◇					◇	◇ A
												🍽	🍴	🍴				🍴	🍴					🍴	
London Euston 15 ⊖65	d																								
Birmingham New Street 12 65	d			22p55								05 30													
Manchester Airport 84,85 ✈	d												05 33												
Cardiff Central 7 131	d	19p34			20p55														05 20						
Crewe 10	d			23p57	00 02							06 23		07 03	07 23					08 23					
Manchester Pic'dilly 10 90 ⛴	d		23p14			23p17	00 25						05 50			06 17		06 50				07 17		07 50	
Manchester Oxford Road 90	d		23p17										05 53					06 53						07 53	
Newton-le-Willows 90	d		23p36										06 12					07 12						08 12	
Earlestown 8 90	d		23p39										06 15					07 15						08 15	
Warrington Bank Quay 90	d		23p48										06 26					07 22						08 24	
Runcorn East	d		23p55										06 33					07 29						08 31	
Frodsham	d		23p59										06 37					07 34						08 35	
Helsby	d		00 03										06 41					07 38						08 39	
Liverpool Lime Street 10 106	d																								
Chester	a	22p34	00 15	00 18	00 27	00 45	01 29					06 43	06 53	07 23	07 46	07 47		07 51	08 18	08 46		08 47		08 51	
	d	22p56		00 40								06 44	06 55	07 25				07 55	08 22					08 55	
Shotton	d	23p05											07 04					08 04						09 04	
Flint	d	23p11		00 53								06 57	07 10	07 39				08 10	08 36					09 10	
Prestatyn	d	23p24		01 06								07 10	07 23	07 52				08 23	08 49					09 23	
Rhyl	d	23p30		01 12								07 16	07 29	07 58				08 29	08 55					09 29	
Abergele & Pensarn	d	23p36											07 35					08 35						09 35	
Colwyn Bay	d	23p44		01 23								07 27	07 43	08 09				08 43	09 06					09 43	
Llandudno Junction	a	23p49		01 28								07 33	07 48	08 14				08 48	09 11					09 48	
	d	23p52		01 29				06 13	06 51	07 31		07 33	07 50	08 15			08 28	08 50	09 12				09 28	09 50	10 00
Deganwy	d							06x16	06x54	07x34			07x54				08x31	08x54					09x31	09x54	10x03
Llandudno	a							06 23	07 01	07 41			08 06				08 38	09 06					09 38	10 06	10 13
Conwy	d	23b54												08x17					09x14						
Penmaenmawr	d	23b59												08x23					09x20						
Llanfairfechan	d	00x04												08x27					09x24						
Bangor (Gwynedd)	a	00 13		01 45								07 49		08 36					09 33						
	d	00 14		01 45								07 50		08 38					09 35						
Llanfairpwll	d	00x21												08x44											
Bodorgan	d	00x31												08x54					09x49						
Ty Croes	d	00x35												08x58					09x53						
Rhosneigr	d	00x38												09x01					09x56						
Valley	d	00x43												09x07											
Holyhead	a	00 58		02 15								08 23		09 21					10 14						

		AW	AW	NT	AW	AW		VT	AW	AW	NT	AW	AW	VT	AW	AW		NT	AW	AW	VT	AW	AW	AW	NT
		◇ B				◇		◇1	◇				◇	◇1	◇ B					◇	◇1	◇ A	◇		
		🍴				🍴		🍽	🍴				🍴	🍽	🍴					🍴	🍽		🍴		
London Euston 15 ⊖65	d							08 10						08 50							10 10				
Birmingham New Street 12 65	d	07 23													09 24										
Manchester Airport 84,85 ✈	d																								
Cardiff Central 7 131	d								07 21														09 21		
Crewe 10	d		09 23					09 50		10 23				10 43		11 23					11 50			12 23	
Manchester Pic'dilly 10 90 ⛴	d			08 17		08 50					09 17		09 50					10 17		10 50					11 17
Manchester Oxford Road 90	d					08 53							09 53							10 53					
Newton-le-Willows 90	d					09 12							10 12							11 12					
Earlestown 8 90	d					09 15							10 15							11 15					
Warrington Bank Quay 90	d					09 26							10 26							11 26					
Runcorn East	d					09 33							10 33							11 33					
Frodsham	d					09 37							10 37							11 37					
Helsby	d					09 41							10 41							11 41					
Liverpool Lime Street 10 106	d																								
Chester	a	09 17	09 46	09 47		09 53		10 12	10 19	10 46	10 47		10 53	11 10	11 19	11 46		11 47		11 53	12 12		12 19	12 46	12 47
	d	09 22				09 55			10 22				10 55	11 12	11 22					11 55			12 23		
Shotton	d					10 04							11 04							12 04					
Flint	d	09 36				10 10			10 36				11 10		11 38					12 10			12 36		
Prestatyn	d	09 49				10 23			10 49				11 23		11 51					12 23			12 49		
Rhyl	d	09 55				10 29			10 55				11 29	11 41	11 57					12 29			12 55		
Abergele & Pensarn	d					10 35							11 35							12 35					
Colwyn Bay	d	10 06				10 43			11 06				11 43	11 54	12 08					12 43			13 06		
Llandudno Junction	a	10 11				10 48			11 11				11 48	12 00	12 13					12 48			13 11		
	d	10 12			10 28	10 50			11 12			11 26	11 50	12 01	12 14				12 28	12 50		13 00	13 12		
Deganwy	d				10x31	10x54						11x29	11x54						12x31	12x54		13x03			
Llandudno	a				10 38	11 06						11 36	12 06						12 38	13 06		13 13			
Conwy	d								11x14						12x16										
Penmaenmawr	d								11x20						12x22										
Llanfairfechan	d								11x24						12x26										
Bangor (Gwynedd)	a	10 28							11 33					12 19	12 34								13 28		
	d	10 29							11 35					12 20	12 37								13 29		
Llanfairpwll	d	10x35													12x43								13x36		
Bodorgan	d														12x53								13x46		
Ty Croes	d														12x57								13x50		
Rhosneigr	d														13x00								13x53		
Valley	d	10x53													13x06								13x58		
Holyhead	a	11 07							12 09					12 55	13 18								14 13		

A From Blaenau Ffestiniog
B From Birmingham International
b Previous night, stops on request

Table 81

Saturdays
from 8 October

Crewe and Manchester - Chester and North Wales

	AW		AW	VT	AW	AW	NT	AW	AW	VT	AW		AW	NT	AW	AW	VT	AW	AW	AW	NT		AW	AW
			◇ 🚲	◇1 ☕	◇ A 🚲				◇ 🚲	◇1 ☕	◇ 🚲					◇ 🚲	◇1 ☕	◇ B	◇ A 🚲					◇ 🚲
London Euston 15 ⊖65 d				11 10						12 10							13 10							
Birmingham New Street 12 65 d					11 24														13 24					
Manchester Airport 84,85 ✈ d																								
Cardiff Central 7 131 d											11 21													
Crewe 10 d				12 49		13 23				13 49			14 23				14 50			15 23				
Manchester Pic'dilly 10 90 ⛴ d			11 50				12 17		12 50					13 17		13 50					14 17			14 50
Manchester Oxford Road 90 d			11 53						12 53							13 53								14 53
Newton-le-Willows 90 d			12 12						13 12							14 12								15 12
Earlestown 8 90 d			12 15						13 15							14 15								15 15
Warrington Bank Quay 90 d			12 26						13 26							14 26								15 26
Runcorn East d			12 33						13 33							14 33								15 33
Frodsham d			12 37						13 37							14 37								15 37
Helsby d			12 41						13 41							14 41								15 41
Liverpool Lime Street 10 106 d																								
Chester a			12 53	13 12	13 18	13 46	13 47		13 53	14 12	14 19		14 46	14 47		14 53	15 12		15 19	15 46	15 47			15 53
d			12 55		13 22				13 55		14 23					14 55			15 24					15 55
Shotton d			13 04						14 04							15 04								16 04
Flint d			13 10		13 36				14 10		14 36					15 10			15 37					16 10
Prestatyn d			13 23		13 49				14 23		14 49					15 23			15 50					16 23
Rhyl d			13 29		13 55				14 29		14 55					15 29			15 56					16 29
Abergele & Pensarn d			13 35						14 35							15 35								16 35
Colwyn Bay d			13 43		14 06				14 43		15 06					15 43			16 07					16 43
Llandudno Junction a			13 48		14 11				14 48		15 11					15 48			16 12					16 48
d	13 28		13 50		14 12			14 28	14 50		15 12				15 30	15 50		16 00	16 14				16 26	16 50
Deganwy d	13x31		13x54					14x31	14x54						15x33	15 54		16x03					16x29	16x54
Llandudno a	13 38		14 06					14 38	15 06						15 40	16 06		16 13					16 36	17 06
Conwy d					14x14														16x16					
Penmaenmawr d					14x20														16x22					
Llanfairfechan d					14x24														16x26					
Bangor (Gwynedd) a					14 33						15 28								16 35					
d					14 35						15 29								16 36					
Llanfairpwll d											15x36													
Bodorgan d											15x46													
Ty Croes d											15x50													
Rhosneigr d											15x53													
Valley d											15x58													
Holyhead a					15 08						16 13								17 11					

	VT	AW	AW	NT	AW	AW	VT		AW	AW	NT	AW	AW	AW	VT	AW	AW		NT	AW	AW	VT	AW	AW
	◇1 ☕	◇ 🚲				◇ 🚲	◇1 ☕		◇ A 🚲				◇ B	◇ 🚲	◇1 ☕	R 🚲					◇ 🚲	◇1 ☕	◇ A 🚲	
London Euston 15 ⊖65 d	14 10						15 10								16 10							17 10		
Birmingham New Street 12 65 d									15 24														17 24	
Manchester Airport 84,85 ✈ d																								
Cardiff Central 7 131 d		13 21														15 21								
Crewe 10 d	15 49		16 23				16 49			17 23					17 49		18 23					18 50		19 23
Manchester Pic'dilly 10 90 ⛴ d				15 17		15 50					16 17			16 50					17 17		17 50			
Manchester Oxford Road 90 d						15 53								16 53							17 53			
Newton-le-Willows 90 d						16 12								17 12							18 12			
Earlestown 8 90 d						16 15								17 15							18 15			
Warrington Bank Quay 90 d						16 26								17 26							18 25			
Runcorn East d						16 33								17 33							18 32			
Frodsham d						16 37								17 37							18 36			
Helsby d						16 41								17 41							18 40			
Liverpool Lime Street 10 106 d																								
Chester a	16 10	16 22	16 46	16 47		16 53	17 12		17 19	17 46	17 47			17 53	18 09	18 19	18 46		18 47		18 52	19 10	19 20	19 46
d	16 12	16 26				16 55			17 22					17 55	18 16	18 24					18 55	19 17	19 32	
Shotton d						17 04			17 32					18 04							19 04		19 41	
Flint d	16 25	16 39				17 10			17 38					18 10	18 29	18 39					19 10	19 30	19 47	
Prestatyn d	16 38	16 52				17 23			17 51					18 23	18 42	18 52					19 23	19 43	20 00	
Rhyl d	16 45	16 58				17 29			17 57					18 29	18 49	18 58					19 29	19 50	20 06	
Abergele & Pensarn d						17 35			18 03					18 35							19 35		20 12	
Colwyn Bay d	16 56	17 09				17 43			18 11					18 43	19 00	19 09					19 43	20 01	20 20	
Llandudno Junction a	17 01	17 14				17 48			18 16					18 48	19 05	19 14					19 48	20 06	20 25	
d	17 02	17 14			17 28	17 50			18 18			18 26	18 41	18 50	19 06	19 15				19 28	19 50	20 07	20 27	
Deganwy d					17x31	17x54						18x29	18x44	18x54						19x31	19x54			
Llandudno a					17 38	18 06						18 36	18 54	19 06						19 38	20 06			
Conwy d		17x16							18x20														20x29	
Penmaenmawr d		17x22							18x26														20x35	
Llanfairfechan d		17x26							18x30														20x39	
Bangor (Gwynedd) a	17 17	17 35							18 39						19 21	19 32						20 22	20 48	
d	17 19	17 37							18 40						19 23	19 33						20 24	20 49	
Llanfairpwll d		17x43														19 40							20x55	
Bodorgan d		17x53														19 51							21x05	
Ty Croes d		17x57														19 55							21x10	
Rhosneigr d		18x00														19 58							21x13	
Valley d		18x06														20 04							21x18	
Holyhead a	17 51	18 20							19 13						19 55	20 18						20 56	21 31	

A From Birmingham International

B From Blaenau Ffestiniog

Table 81

Saturdays
from 8 October

Crewe and Manchester - Chester and North Wales

		NT	AW	VT		AW	AW	AW	NT	AW	AW	AW	AW	AW		NT	AW	AW	AW	NT	AW	AW	AW	AW
				◇[1]			[B]				◇	◇	◇					◇				◇		
											A	B										A	C	
			╤	⊡			╤				╤													
London Euston [15] ⊖65	d			18 10																				
Birmingham New Street [12] 65	d										19 24											21 24		
Manchester Airport 84,85 ✈	d																20 32							
Cardiff Central [7] 131	d						17 21											19 34						
Crewe [10]	d			19 50				20 23					21 00	21 23					22 23					23 21
Manchester Pic'dilly [10] 90	d	18 17	18 50						19 17	19 50						20 17	20 50			21 17	21 50		22 26	
Manchester Oxford Road 90	d		18 53							19 53							20 53				21 53		22 29	
Newton-le-Willows 90	d		19 12							20 12							21 12				22 12		22 47	
Earlestown [8] 90	d		19 16							20 15							21 15				22 15		22 50	
Warrington Bank Quay 90	d		19 27							20 30							21 27				22 24		22 59	
Runcorn East	d		19 34							20 37							21 34				22 31		23 06	
Frodsham	d		19 38							20 41							21 38				22 35		23 10	
Helsby	d		19 42							20 45							21 42				22 39		23 14	
Liverpool Lime Street [10] 106	d																							
Chester	a	19 47	19 54	20 12			20 19	20 46	20 47	20 57	21 21		21 21	21 46		21 47	21 57	22 31	22 45	22 47	22 53	23 21	23 26	23 42
	d						20 32						21 26					22 36						
Shotton	d						20 41						21 35					22 45						
Flint	d						20 47						21 41					22 51						
Prestatyn	d						21 00						21 54					23 05						
Rhyl	d						21 06						22 00					23 11						
Abergele & Pensarn	d												22 06					23 17						
Colwyn Bay	d						21 17						22 14					23 25						
Llandudno Junction	a						21 22						22 19					23 38						
	d					20 30	21 22					21 32	22 21											
Deganwy	d					20x33						21x35												
Llandudno	a					20 40						21 46												
Conwy	d												22 23											
Penmaenmawr	d												22 29											
Llanfairfechan	d												22 33											
Bangor (Gwynedd)	a						21 38						22 42											
	d						21 39						22 43											
Llanfairpwll	d						21x46																	
Bodorgan	d						21x56																	
Ty Croes	d						22x00																	
Rhosneigr	d						22x03																	
Valley	d						22x08																	
Holyhead	a						22 23						23 18											

		AW	NT	AW	AW	AW	NT	AW
					◇			
		D		C	E	D		
								🚌
London Euston [15] ⊖65	d							
Birmingham New Street [12] 65	d							
Manchester Airport 84,85 ✈	d							
Cardiff Central [7] 131	d				20 55			
Crewe [10]	d				23 58			
Manchester Pic'dilly [10] 90	d	22 26	22 17	23 14		23 19	23 17	
Manchester Oxford Road 90	d			23 17				
Newton-le-Willows 90	d			23 36				
Earlestown [8] 90	d			23 39				
Warrington Bank Quay 90	d			23 48				
Runcorn East	d			23 55				
Frodsham	d			23 59				
Helsby	d			00 03				
Liverpool Lime Street [10] 106	d							
Chester	a	23 46	23 47	00 15	00 24	00 44	00 45	
	d							
Shotton	d							
Flint	d							
Prestatyn	d							
Rhyl	d							
Abergele & Pensarn	d							
Colwyn Bay	d							
Llandudno Junction	a							
	d							23 48
Deganwy	d							
Llandudno	a							
Conwy	d							23 56
Penmaenmawr	d							00 08
Llanfairfechan	d							00 23
Bangor (Gwynedd)	a							00 38
	d							00 38
Llanfairpwll	d							00 47
Bodorgan	d							00 57
Ty Croes	d							01 07
Rhosneigr	d							01 27
Valley	d							01 52
Holyhead	a							02 02

A From Birmingham International
B From Blaenau Ffestiniog
C from 29 October
D 8 October, 15 October, 22 October
E From Carmarthen

Table 81

Sundays
until 19 June

Crewe and Manchester - Chester and North Wales

	AW ◇ A	AW B 🚌	NT B	AW B	AW B 🚌	AW B 🚌	AW ◇	AW ◇	AW 🚌		AW	AW ◇	AW	NT C	AW	AW 🚌	AW	AW	VT ◇[1] 🍴		AW	AW	AW ◇ D	AW ◇
London Euston [15] ⊖65 d																								
Birmingham New Street [12] 65 d																								
Manchester Airport 84,85 ✈ d																								
Cardiff Central [7] 131 d	20p55																							
Crewe [10] d	23p58							08 27				09 27	09 57						10 42		10 57			11 27
Manchester Pic'dilly [10] 90 ⛴ d		22p26	23p17	23p19	23p14				07 28					09 22	09 54	08 49								
Manchester Oxford Road 90 d		22p31			23p19				07 33							08 54								
Newton-le-Willows 90 d		23p01			23p49				08 03							09 24								
Earlestown [8] 90 d		23p11			23p59				08 13							09 34								
Warrington Bank Quay 90 d		23p36			00 24				08 38							09 59								
Runcorn East d		23p56			00 44				08 58							10 19								
Frodsham d		00 11			00 59				09 13							10 34								
Helsby d		00 16			01 04				09 18							10 39								
Liverpool Lime Street [10] 106 d																								
Chester a	00 24	00 36	00 43	00 44	01 24			08 50	09 38			09 45	10 22	10 46	10 58	10 59			11 02		11 22			11 48
d							06 20	09 02				09 48							11 07					12 03
Shotton d												09 57												12 12
Flint d							06 33	09 15				10 03												12 18
Prestatyn d							06 46	09 28				10 16							11 30					12 31
Rhyl d							06 52	09 34				10 22							11 37					12 37
Abergele & Pensarn d												10 28												
Colwyn Bay d							07 03	09 45				10 36							11 48					12 48
Llandudno Junction a							07 08	09 49				10 41							11 53					12 53
d						23p48	07 09	09 54			10 00	10 43					10 50	11 25	11 54			12 00	12 42	12 54
Deganwy d											10x03						10x53	11x28				12x03	12x45	
Llandudno a											10 10						11 00	11 35				12 10	12 55	
Conwy d						23p56						10x45												
Penmaenmawr d						00 08						10x51												
Llanfairfechan d						00 23						10x55												
Bangor (Gwynedd) a						00 38	07 25	10 11				11 04							12 09					13 10
d						00 38	07 25	10 12				11 05							12 11					13 11
Llanfairpwll d						00 47						11x12												
Bodorgan d						00 57						11x22												
Ty Croes d						01 07						11x26												
Rhosneigr d						01 27						11x29												
Valley d						01 52						11x34												
Holyhead a						02 02	08 00	10 48				11 49							12 43					13 46

	AW 🚌	AW	AW	NT E	AW		AW	AW ◇ 🛒	AW 🚌	AW 🛒	AW	AW ◇ F 🛒	AW	AW ◇ 🛒	AW 🚌		AW 🛒	AW	NT E	AW	AW	AW ◇ 🛒	AW 🚌	AW 🛒
London Euston [15] ⊖65 d																								
Birmingham New Street [12] 65 d												11 05												
Manchester Airport 84,85 ✈ d																								
Cardiff Central [7] 131 d																								
Crewe [10] d			11 57					12 27			12 54			13 27				13 57				14 27		
Manchester Pic'dilly [10] 90 ⛴ d	09 47	10 55		11 22					10 45	11 58					11 45		12 58		13 22				12 45	13 53
Manchester Oxford Road 90 d	09 52								10 50						11 50								12 50	
Newton-le-Willows 90 d	10 22								11 20						12 20								13 20	
Earlestown [8] 90 d	10 32								11 30						12 30								13 30	
Warrington Bank Quay 90 d	10 57								11 55						12 55								13 55	
Runcorn East d	11 17								12 15						13 15								14 15	
Frodsham d	11 32								12 30						13 30								14 30	
Helsby d	11 37								12 35						13 35								14 35	
Liverpool Lime Street [10] 106 d																								
Chester a	11 57	11 57	12 20	12 46				12 48	12 55	13 02	13 15	13 20		13 47	13 55		14 01	14 20	14 46			14 47	14 55	14 55
d								13 02						14 02								15 02		
Shotton d								13 11						14 11								15 11		
Flint d								13 17						14 17								15 17		
Prestatyn d								13 30						14 30								15 30		
Rhyl d								13 36						14 36								15 36		
Abergele & Pensarn d								13 42						14 42								15 42		
Colwyn Bay d								13 50						14 50								15 50		
Llandudno Junction a								13 55						14 55								15 55		
d					12 58		13 39	13 57					14 02	14 57						15 00	15 30	15 57		
Deganwy d					13x01		13x42						14x05							15x03	15x33			
Llandudno a					13 08		13 49						14 12							15 10	15 40			
Conwy d								13x59														15x59		
Penmaenmawr d								14x05														16x05		
Llanfairfechan d								14x09														16x09		
Bangor (Gwynedd) a								14 18						15 12								16 18		
d								14 19						15 14								16 19		
Llanfairpwll d														15x20										
Bodorgan d														15x30										
Ty Croes d														15x34										
Rhosneigr d														15x37										
Valley d														15x43										
Holyhead a								14 53						15 57								16 53		

A not 22 May. From Carmarthen
B not 22 May
C From Wigan Wallgate
D From Blaenau Ffestiniog
E From Southport
F From Birmingham International

Table 81

Sundays
until 19 June

Crewe and Manchester - Chester and North Wales

	AW		AW	AW	AW	AW	AW	AW	AW	AW	AW		NT	AW	AW	AW	VT	AW	AW	AW	VT		AW	AW
	◇ A 🛒					◇ 🛒	🛒			■ B	■ C		D		◇ 🛒	🛒	◇1 🍴	◇ A 🛒	◇	🛒	◇1 🍴		◇ E	■ 🛒
London Euston 15 ⊖65 d																	15 05				16 05			
Birmingham New Street 12 65 d	13 24																	15 24						
Manchester Airport 84,85 ✈ d																								
Cardiff Central 7 131 d										13 13	13 18													15 22
Crewe 10 d			14 57			15 27		15 57							16 27		16 52		17 27		17 52			
Manchester Pic'dilly 10 90 ⇌ d							14 56						15 22			15 56				16 56				
Manchester Oxford Road 90 d							14 59									15 59				16 59				
Newton-le-Willows 90 d							15 18									16 18				17 18				
Earlestown 8 90 d							15 21									16 21				17 21				
Warrington Bank Quay 90 d							15 29									16 28				17 28				
Runcorn East d							15 36									16 35				17 35				
Frodsham d							15 40									16 39				17 39				
Helsby d							15 44									16 43				17 43				
Liverpool Lime Street 10 106 d																								
Chester a	15 18		15 20			15 47	15 56	16 20		16 25	16 24		16 46		16 47	16 55	17 14	17 27	17 48	17 55	18 14			18 25
d						16 02				16 35	16 36				17 02									18 29
Shotton d						16 11				16 44	16 45				17 11									18 38
Flint d						16 17				16 50	16 51				17 17									18 44
Prestatyn d						16 30				17 03	17 04				17 30									18 57
Rhyl d						16 36				17 09	17 10				17 36									19 03
Abergele & Pensarn d						16 42				17 15	17 16				17 42									19 09
Colwyn Bay d						16 50				17 23	17 24				17 50									19 17
Llandudno Junction a						16 55				17 28	17 29				17 55									19 22
d				16 04	16 39	16 57			17 05	17 30	17 31			17 40	17 57								18 31	19 24
Deganwy d				16x07	16x42				17x08					17x43									18x34	
Llandudno a				16 14	16 49				17 15					17 50									18 44	
Conwy d										17x32	17x33				17x59									19x26
Penmaenmawr d										17x38	17x39				18x05									19x32
Llanfairfechan d										17x42	17x43				18x09									19x36
Bangor (Gwynedd) a						17 12				17 51	17 52				18 18									19 45
d						17 14				17 57	17 54				18 19									19 45
Llanfairpwll d						17x20				18x03	18x00													
Bodorgan d						17x30				18x13	18x10													
Ty Croes d						17x34				18x17	18x14													
Rhosneigr d						17x37				18x20	18x17													
Valley d						17x43				18x26	18x23													
Holyhead a						17 57				18 40	18 37				18 54									20 20

	NT	AW	AW	VT	AW	AW	AW		VT	AW	NT	AW	AW	VT	AW	AW	AW		AW	NT	AW	AW	AW	AW
	D	◇	🛒	◇1 🍴	◇ A 🛒				◇1 🍴	■ F	D			◇1 🍴	◇ A 🛒	◇				D	◇		◇ A	
London Euston 15 ⊖65 d				17 05					18 05					19 05										
Birmingham New Street 12 65 d					17 24										19 24								21 24	
Manchester Airport 84,85 ✈ d																								
Cardiff Central 7 131 d										17 22														
Crewe 10 d		18 27		18 56		19 27			19 52			20 27		20 55		21 27			21 57		22 29		23 06	
Manchester Pic'dilly 10 90 ⇌ d	17 22		17 56				18 56				19 22		19 56				20 56			21 22		21 56		22 56
Manchester Oxford Road 90 d			17 59				18 59						19 59				20 59					21 59		22 59
Newton-le-Willows 90 d			18 18				19 18						20 18				21 18					22 18		23 18
Earlestown 8 90 d			18 21				19 21						20 21				21 21					22 21		23 21
Warrington Bank Quay 90 d			18 28				19 29						20 30				21 28					22 28		23 28
Runcorn East d			18 35				19 36						20 37				21 35					22 35		23 35
Frodsham d			18 39				19 40						20 41				21 39					22 39		23 39
Helsby d			18 43				19 44						20 45				21 43					22 43		23 43
Liverpool Lime Street 10 106 d																								
Chester a	18 46	18 47	18 55	19 14	19 16	19 48	19 56		20 11	20 29	20 46	20 48	20 57	21 14	21 20	21 46	21 55		22 18	22 46	22 50	22 55	23 31	23 55
d		18 52		19 22	19 38				20 18	20 36				21 17		22 00					23 00			
Shotton d		19 01			19 47					20 45						22 09					23 09			
Flint d		19 07		19 35	19 53				20 31	20 51				21 30		22 15					23 15			
Prestatyn d		19 21		19 48	20 06				20 44	21 04				21 43		22 28					23 28			
Rhyl d		19 27		19 55	20 12				20 51	21 10				21 50		22 34					23 34			
Abergele & Pensarn d		19 33			20 18					21 16						22 40								
Colwyn Bay d		19 41		20 06	20 26				21 02	21 24				22 01		22 48					23 45			
Llandudno Junction a		19 46		20 11	20 31				21 07	21 29				22 06		22 53					23 50			
d		19 47		20 12	20 33				21 08	21 31				22 07		22 55					23 51			
Deganwy d																								
Llandudno a																								
Conwy d		19x49			20x35					21x33											23x53			
Penmaenmawr d		19x55			20x41					21x39											00x01			
Llanfairfechan d		19x59			20x45					21x43											00x03			
Bangor (Gwynedd) a		20 08		20 27	20 54				21 23	21 52				22 22		23 10					00 12			
d		20 09		20 29	20 55				21 25	21 54				22 24		23 12					00 14			
Llanfairpwll d										22x00						23x18								
Bodorgan d										22x10						23x28								
Ty Croes d										22x14						23x32								
Rhosneigr d										22x17						23x35								
Valley d										22x23						23x41								
Holyhead a		20 44		20 59	21 30				21 57	22 37				22 56		23 55					00 49			

A From Birmingham International
B not until 29 May
C 29 May
D From Southport
E From Blaenau Ffestiniog
F 22 May

Table 81

Sundays until 19 June

Crewe and Manchester - Chester and North Wales

		AW	AW	AW ◇		AW ◇ A
London Euston 15 ⊖65	d					
Birmingham New Street 12 65	d					22 55
Manchester Airport 84,85 ✈	d					
Cardiff Central 7 131	d			21 04		
Crewe 10	d	23 38		00 03		00b10
Manchester Pic'dilly 10 90 ⛴	d		23 25			
Manchester Oxford Road 90	d		23 28			
Newton-le-Willows 90	d		23 46			
Earlestown 8 90	d		23 49			
Warrington Bank Quay 90	d		23 56			
Runcorn East	d		00 03			
Frodsham	d		00 07			
Helsby	d		00 11			
Liverpool Lime Street 10 106	d					
Chester	a	23 59	00 24	00 25		00 31
	d					00 35
Shotton	d					
Flint	d					00 48
Prestatyn	d					01 01
Rhyl	d					01 07
Abergele & Pensarn	d					
Colwyn Bay	d					01 18
Llandudno Junction	a					01 24
	d					01 25
Deganwy	d					
Llandudno	a					
Conwy	d					
Penmaenmawr	d					
Llanfairfechan	d					
Bangor (Gwynedd)	a					01 41
	d					01 41
Llanfairpwll	d					
Bodorgan	d					
Ty Croes	d					
Rhosneigr	d					
Valley	d					
Holyhead	a					02 17

Sundays 26 June to 31 July

		AW	AW ◇ B	NT	AW 🚌	AW ◇	AW ◇	AW 🚌	AW	AW ◇		AW	NT C	AW	AW	AW	VT ◇1 🍴	AW	AW	AW ◇ D		AW ◇	AW	AW	NT E
London Euston 15 ⊖65	d																								
Birmingham New Street 12 65	d																								
Manchester Airport 84,85 ✈	d																								
Cardiff Central 7 131	d		20p55																						
Crewe 10	d		23p58				08 27			09 27		09 57					10 42	10 57				11 27		11 57	
Manchester Pic'dilly 10 90 ⛴	d	23p14		23p17				07 28					09 22	09 56									10 55		11 22
Manchester Oxford Road 90	d	23p17						07 33						09 59									10 59		
Newton-le-Willows 90	d	23p36						08 03						10 18									11 20		
Earlestown 8 90	d	23p39						08 13						10 21									11 23		
Warrington Bank Quay 90	d	23p48						08 38						10 28									11 30		
Runcorn East	d	23p55						08 58						10 35									11 37		
Frodsham	d	23p59						09 13						10 40									11 41		
Helsby	d	00 03						09 18						10 44									11 45		
Liverpool Lime Street 10 106	d																								
Chester	a	00 15	00 24	00 43			08 50	09 38		09 45		10 22	10 46	10 59			11 02	11 22				11 48	11 57	12 20	12 46
	d					06 20	09 02			09 48							11 07					12 03			
Shotton	d									09 57												12 12			
Flint	d					06 33	09 15			10 03												12 18			
Prestatyn	d					06 46	09 28			10 16							11 30					12 31			
Rhyl	d					06 52	09 34			10 22							11 37					12 37			
Abergele & Pensarn	d									10 28															
Colwyn Bay	d					07 03	09 45			10 36							11 48					12 48			
Llandudno Junction	a					07 08	09 49			10 41							11 53					12 53			
	d				23p48	07 09	09 54		10 00	10 43					10 50	11 25	11 54		12 00	12 42		12 54			
Deganwy	d								10x03						10x53	11x28			12x03	12x45					
Llandudno	a								10 10						11 00	11 35			12 10	12 55					
Conwy	d				23p56					10x45															
Penmaenmawr	d				00 08					10x51															
Llanfairfechan	d				00 23					10x55															
Bangor (Gwynedd)	a				00 38	07 25	10 11			11 04							12 09					13 10			
	d				00 38	07 25	10 12			11 05							12 11					13 11			
Llanfairpwll	d				00 47					11x12															
Bodorgan	d				00 57					11x22															
Ty Croes	d				01 07					11x26															
Rhosneigr	d				01 27					11x29															
Valley	d				01 52					11x34															
Holyhead	a				02 02	08 00	10 48			11 49							12 43					13 46			

A From Birmingham International
B From Carmarthen
C From Wigan Wallgate
D From Blaenau Ffestiniog
E From Southport

Table 81

Sundays

26 June to 31 July

Crewe and Manchester - Chester and North Wales

	AW	AW	AW	AW	AW		AW	AW	AW	NT	AW	AW	AW	AW		AW	AW	AW	AW	AW	AW	NT	AW
			◇					◇						◇						◇				
											A												A	
			🍴	🍴				🍴	🍴					🍴	🍴					🍴	🍴			
London Euston [15] ⊖65 d																								
Birmingham New Street [12] 65 d																								
Manchester Airport 84,85 ✈ d																								
Cardiff Central [7] 131 d																								
Crewe [10] d			12 27		12 54			13 27		13 57				14 27			14 57			15 27		15 57		
Manchester Pic'dilly [10] 90 ⇌ d				11 56					12 56		13 22				13 56						14 56		15 22	
Manchester Oxford Road 90 d				11 59					12 59						13 59						14 59			
Newton-le-Willows 90 d				12 18					13 18						14 18						15 18			
Earlestown [8] 90 d				12 21					13 21						14 21						15 21			
Warrington Bank Quay 90 d				12 28					13 29						14 28						15 29			
Runcorn East d				12 35					13 36						14 35						15 36			
Frodsham d				12 39					13 40						14 39						15 40			
Helsby d				12 43					13 44						14 43						15 44			
Liverpool Lime Street [10] 106 d																								
Chester a			12 48	12 55	13 15			13 47	13 56	14 20	14 46			14 47	14 55		15 20			15 47	15 56	16 20	16 46	
d			13 02					14 02						15 02						16 02				
Shotton d			13 11					14 11						15 11						16 11				
Flint d			13 17					14 17						15 17						16 17				
Prestatyn d			13 30					14 30						15 30						16 30				
Rhyl d			13 36					14 36						15 36						16 36				
Abergele & Pensarn d			13 42					14 42						15 42						16 42				
Colwyn Bay d			13 50					14 50						15 50						16 50				
Llandudno Junction a			13 55					14 55						15 55						16 55				
d	12 58	13 39	13 57				14 02	14 57				15 00	15 30	15 57				16 04	16 39	16 57				17 05
Deganwy d	13x01	13x42					14x05					15x03	15x33					16x07	16x42					17x08
Llandudno a	13 08	13 49					14 12					15 10	15 40					16 14	16 49					17 15
Conwy d			13x59											15x59										
Penmaenmawr d			14x05											16x05										
Llanfairfechan d			14x09											16x09										
Bangor (Gwynedd) a			14 18					15 12						16 18						17 12				
d			14 19					15 14						16 19						17 14				
Llanfairpwll d								15x20												17x20				
Bodorgan d								15x30												17x30				
Ty Croes d								15x34												17x34				
Rhosneigr d								15x37												17x37				
Valley d								15x43												17x43				
Holyhead a			14 53					15 57						16 53						17 57				

	AW		AW	AW	VT	AW	AW	VT	AW	AW	AW		NT	AW	AW	VT	AW	AW	AW	VT	NT		AW	AW
											■													
			◇		◇[1]	◇		◇[1]	◇	◇				◇		◇[1]				◇[1]				
									B	C			A						B		A			
			🍴	🍴	☕		🍴	☕	🍴		🍴				🍴	☕				☕				
London Euston [15] ⊖65 d					15 05			16 05								17 05				18 05				
Birmingham New Street [12] 65 d																								
Manchester Airport 84,85 ✈ d																								
Cardiff Central [7] 131 d											15 22													
Crewe [10] d			16 27		16 52	17 27		17 52			18 02			18 27		18 56	19 27			19 52			20 27	
Manchester Pic'dilly [10] 90 ⇌ d				15 56			16 56						17 22		17 56			18 56			19 22			19 56
Manchester Oxford Road 90 d				15 59			16 59								17 59			18 59						19 59
Newton-le-Willows 90 d				16 18			17 18								18 18			19 18						20 18
Earlestown [8] 90 d				16 21			17 21								18 21			19 21						20 21
Warrington Bank Quay 90 d				16 28			17 28								18 28			19 29						20 30
Runcorn East d				16 35			17 35								18 35			19 36						20 37
Frodsham d				16 39			17 39								18 39			19 40						20 41
Helsby d				16 43			17 43								18 43			19 44						20 45
Liverpool Lime Street [10] 106 d																								
Chester a			16 47	16 55	17 14	17 48	17 55	18 14			18 22		18 46	18 47	18 55	19 14	19 48	19 56		20 11	20 46		20 48	20 57
d			17 02						17 32		18 29			18 52		19 22			19 38	20 18				
Shotton d			17 11						17 41		18 38			19 01					19 47					
Flint d			17 17						17 47		18 44			19 07		19 35			19 53	20 31				
Prestatyn d			17 30						18 00		18 57			19 21		19 48			20 06	20 44				
Rhyl d			17 36						18 06		19 03			19 27		19 55			20 12	20 51				
Abergele & Pensarn d			17 42						18 12		19 09			19 33					20 18					
Colwyn Bay d			17 50						18 20		19 17			19 41		20 06			20 26	21 02				
Llandudno Junction a			17 55						18 25		19 22			19 46		20 11			20 31	21 07				
d	17 40		17 57						18 27	18 31	19 24			19 47		20 12			20 33	21 08				
Deganwy d	17x43									18x34														
Llandudno a	17 50									18 44														
Conwy d			17x59								19x26			19x49					20x35					
Penmaenmawr d			18x05								19x32			19x55					20x41					
Llanfairfechan d			18x09								19x36			19x59					20x45					
Bangor (Gwynedd) a			18 18						18 42		19 45			20 08		20 27			20 54	21 23				
d			18 19						18 44		19 45			20 09		20 29			20 55	21 25				
Llanfairpwll d									18x50															
Bodorgan d									19x00															
Ty Croes d									19x04															
Rhosneigr d									19x07															
Valley d									19x13															
Holyhead a			18 54						19 27		20 20			20 44		20 59			21 25	21 57				

A From Southport

B From Wrexham General

C From Blaenau Ffestiniog

Table 81

Sundays
26 June to 31 July

Crewe and Manchester - Chester and North Wales

		VT	AW	AW	AW	NT	AW	AW		AW	AW	AW	AW	AW	AW
		◇1	◇				◇			◇				◇	◇
						A				B					B
		🍴													
London Euston 15 ⊖65	d	19 05													
Birmingham New Street 12 65	d									21 24					22 55
Manchester Airport 84,85 ✈	d														
Cardiff Central 7 131	d													21 04	
Crewe 10	d	20 55	21 27		21 57		22 29			23 06		23 38		00 03	00 10
Manchester Pic'dilly 10 90 ⇌	d			20 56		21 22		21 56			22 56		23 25		
Manchester Oxford Road 90	d			20 59				21 59			22 59		23 28		
Newton-le-Willows 90	d			21 18				22 18			23 18		23 46		
Earlestown 8 90	d			21 21				22 21			23 21		23 49		
Warrington Bank Quay 90	d			21 28				22 28			23 28		23 56		
Runcorn East	d			21 35				22 35			23 35		00 03		
Frodsham	d			21 39				22 39			23 39		00 07		
Helsby	d			21 43				22 43			23 43		00 11		
Liverpool Lime Street 10 106	d														
Chester	a	21 14	21 46	21 55	22 18	22 46	22 50	22 55		23 31	23 55	23 59	00 24	00 25	00 31
	d	21 17	22 00				23 00								00 35
Shotton	d		22 09				23 09								
Flint	d	21 30	22 15				23 15								00 48
Prestatyn	d	21 43	22 28				23 28								01 01
Rhyl	d	21 50	22 34				23 34								01 07
Abergele & Pensarn	d		22 40												
Colwyn Bay	d	22 01	22 48				23 45								01 18
Llandudno Junction	a	22 06	22 53				23 50								01 24
	d	22 07	22 55				23 51								01 25
Deganwy	d														
Llandudno	a														
Conwy	d						23x53								
Penmaenmawr	d						00x01								
Llanfairfechan	d						00x03								
Bangor (Gwynedd)	a	22 22	23 10				00 12								01 41
	d	22 24	23 12				00 14								01 41
Llanfairpwll	d		23x18												
Bodorgan	d		23x28												
Ty Croes	d		23x32												
Rhosneigr	d		23x35												
Valley	d		23x41												
Holyhead	a	22 56	23 55				00 49								02 17

Sundays
7 August to 11 September

		AW	NT	AW	AW	AW	AW	AW	AW	AW		NT	AW	AW	AW	VT	AW	AW	AW	AW		AW	AW	NT	AW
					◇	◇			◇							◇1			◇	◇					
												C							D					A	
				🚌			🚌									🍴									
London Euston 15 ⊖65	d																								
Birmingham New Street 12 65	d																								
Manchester Airport 84,85 ✈	d																								
Cardiff Central 7 131	d																								
Crewe 10	d					08 27			09 27	09 57						10 42	10 57			11 27			11 57		
Manchester Pic'dilly 10 90 ⇌	d	23p14	23p17				07 28					09 22	09 56									10 55		11 22	
Manchester Oxford Road 90	d	23p17					07 33						09 59									10 59			
Newton-le-Willows 90	d	23p36					08 03						10 18									11 20			
Earlestown 8 90	d	23p39					08 13						10 21									11 23			
Warrington Bank Quay 90	d	23p48					08 38						10 28									11 30			
Runcorn East	d	23p55					08 58						10 35									11 37			
Frodsham	d	23p59					09 13						10 40									11 41			
Helsby	d	00 03					09 18						10 44									11 45			
Liverpool Lime Street 10 106	d																								
Chester	a	00 15	00 43			08 50	09 38		09 45	10 22		10 46	10 59			11 02	11 22			11 48		11 57	12 20	12 46	
	d				06 20	09 02			09 48							11 07				12 03					
Shotton	d								09 57											12 12					
Flint	d				06 33	09 15			10 03											12 18					
Prestatyn	d				06 46	09 28			10 16							11 30				12 31					
Rhyl	d				06 52	09 34			10 22							11 37				12 37					
Abergele & Pensarn	d								10 28																
Colwyn Bay	d				07 03	09 45			10 36							11 48				12 48					
Llandudno Junction	a				07 08	09 49			10 41							11 53				12 53					
	d			23p48	07 09	09 54		10 00	10 43					10 50	11 25	11 54		12 00	12 42	12 54					12 58
Deganwy	d							10x03						10x53	11x28			12x03	12x45						13x01
Llandudno	a							10 10						11 00	11 35			12 10	12 55						13 08
Conwy	d			23p56					10x45																
Penmaenmawr	d			00 08					10x51																
Llanfairfechan	d			00 23					10x55																
Bangor (Gwynedd)	a			00 38	07 25	10 11			11 04							12 09				13 10					
	d			00 38	07 25	10 12			11 05							12 11				13 11					
Llanfairpwll	d			00 47					11x12																
Bodorgan	d			00 57					11x22																
Ty Croes	d			01 07					11x26																
Rhosneigr	d			01 27					11x29																
Valley	d			01 52					11x34																
Holyhead	a			02 02	08 00	10 48			11 49							12 43				13 46					

A From Southport
B From Birmingham International
C From Wigan Wallgate
D From Blaenau Ffestiniog

Table 81

Sundays

7 August to 11 September

Crewe and Manchester - Chester and North Wales

	AW	AW ◇ 🛒	AW 🛒	AW	AW ◇ A 🛒		AW	AW ◇ 🛒	AW 🛒	AW	NT B	AW	AW	AW ◇ 🛒	AW 🛒		AW ◇ A 🛒	AW	AW	AW	AW ◇ 🛒	AW 🛒	AW	AW
London Euston 15 ⊖65 d																								
Birmingham New Street 12 65 d					11 05												13 24							
Manchester Airport 84,85 ✈ d																								
Cardiff Central 7 131 d																								
Crewe 10 d		12 27		12 54				13 27		13 57				14 27				14 57			15 27		15 57	
Manchester Pic'dilly 10 90 ⛴ d			11 56						12 56		13 22				13 56							14 56		
Manchester Oxford Road 90 d			11 59						12 59						13 59							14 59		
Newton-le-Willows 90 d			12 18						13 18						14 18							15 18		
Earlestown 8 90 d			12 21						13 21						14 21							15 21		
Warrington Bank Quay 90 d			12 28						13 29						14 28							15 29		
Runcorn East d			12 35						13 36						14 35							15 36		
Frodsham d			12 39						13 40						14 39							15 40		
Helsby d			12 43						13 44						14 43							15 44		
Liverpool Lime Street 10 106 d																								
Chester a		12 48	12 55	13 15	13 20			13 47	13 56	14 20	14 46			14 47	14 55		15 18	15 20			15 47	15 56	16 20	
d		13 02						14 02						15 02							16 02			
Shotton d		13 11						14 11						15 11							16 11			
Flint d		13 17						14 17						15 17							16 17			
Prestatyn d		13 30						14 30						15 30							16 30			
Rhyl d		13 36						14 36						15 36							16 36			
Abergele & Pensarn d		13 42						14 42						15 42							16 42			
Colwyn Bay d		13 50						14 50						15 50							16 50			
Llandudno Junction a		13 55						14 55						15 55							16 55			
d	13 39	13 57					14 02	14 57				15 00	15 30	15 57					16 04	16 39	16 57			17 05
Deganwy d	13x42						14x05					15x03	15x33						16x07	16x42				17x08
Llandudno a	13 49						14 12					15 10	15 40						16 14	16 49				17 15
Conwy d		13x59												15x59										
Penmaenmawr d		14x05												16x05										
Llanfairfechan d		14x09												16x09										
Bangor (Gwynedd) a		14 18						15 12						16 18							17 12			
d		14 19						15 14						16 19							17 14			
Llanfairpwll d								15x20													17x20			
Bodorgan d								15x30													17x30			
Ty Croes d								15x34													17x34			
Rhosneigr d								15x37													17x37			
Valley d								15x43													17x43			
Holyhead a		14 53						15 57						16 53							17 57			

	AW ■		NT B	AW	AW ◇ 🛒	AW 🛒	VT ◇1 🍴	AW ◇ A 🛒	AW ◇	AW 🛒	VT ◇1 🍴		AW ◇ C	AW ■ 🛒	NT B	AW ◇	AW 🛒	VT ◇1 🍴	AW ◇ A 🛒	AW	AW		VT ◇1 🍴	NT B
London Euston 15 ⊖65 d							15 05				16 05							17 05					18 05	
Birmingham New Street 12 65 d								15 24											17 24					
Manchester Airport 84,85 ✈ d																								
Cardiff Central 7 131 d	13 13													15 22										
Crewe 10 d					16 27		16 52		17 27		17 52					18 27		18 56		19 27			19 52	
Manchester Pic'dilly 10 90 ⛴ d			15 22			15 56				16 56					17 22		17 56				18 56			19 22
Manchester Oxford Road 90 d						15 59				16 59							17 59				18 59			
Newton-le-Willows 90 d						16 18				17 18							18 18				19 18			
Earlestown 8 90 d						16 21				17 21							18 21				19 21			
Warrington Bank Quay 90 d						16 28				17 28							18 28				19 29			
Runcorn East d						16 35				17 35							18 35				19 36			
Frodsham d						16 39				17 39							18 39				19 40			
Helsby d						16 43				17 43							18 43				19 44			
Liverpool Lime Street 10 106 d																								
Chester a	16 25		16 46		16 47	16 55	17 14	17 27	17 48	17 55	18 14			18 25	18 46	18 47	18 55	19 14	19 16	19 48	19 56		20 11	20 46
d	16 35				17 02									18 29		18 52		19 22	19 38				20 18	
Shotton d	16 44				17 11									18 38		19 01			19 47					
Flint d	16 50				17 17									18 44		19 07		19 35	19 53				20 31	
Prestatyn d	17 03				17 30									18 57		19 21		19 48	20 06				20 44	
Rhyl d	17 09				17 36									19 03		19 27		19 55	20 12				20 51	
Abergele & Pensarn d	17 15				17 42									19 09		19 33			20 18					
Colwyn Bay d	17 23				17 50									19 17		19 41		20 06	20 26				21 02	
Llandudno Junction a	17 28				17 55									19 22		19 46		20 11	20 31				21 07	
d	17 30			17 40	17 57								18 31	19 24		19 47		20 12	20 33				21 08	
Deganwy d				17x43									18x34											
Llandudno a				17 50									18 44											
Conwy d	17x32				17x59									19x26		19x49			20x35					
Penmaenmawr d	17x38				18x05									19x32		19x55			20x41					
Llanfairfechan d	17x42				18x09									19x36		19x59			20x45					
Bangor (Gwynedd) a	17 51				18 18									19 45		20 08		20 27	20 54				21 23	
d	17 57				18 19									19 45		20 09		20 29	20 55				21 25	
Llanfairpwll d	18x03																							
Bodorgan d	18x13																							
Ty Croes d	18x17																							
Rhosneigr d	18x20																							
Valley d	18x26																							
Holyhead a	18 40				18 54									20 20		20 44		20 59	21 30				21 57	

A From Birmingham International

B From Southport

C From Blaenau Ffestiniog

Table 81

Sundays

7 August to 11 September

Crewe and Manchester - Chester and North Wales

		AW	AW	VT	AW	AW	AW	AW		NT	AW	AW	AW	AW	AW	AW	AW	AW
				◇[1]	◇	◇					◇		◇				◇	◇
					A					B			A					A
London Euston [15] ⊖65	d			19 05														
Birmingham New Street [12] 65	d				19 24								21 24					22 55
Manchester Airport 84,85 ✈	d																	
Cardiff Central [7] 131	d																21 04	
Crewe [10]	d	20 27		20 55		21 27		21 57			22 29		23 06		23 38		00 03	00 10
Manchester Pic'dilly [10] 90 ⛴	d		19 56				20 56			21 22		21 56		22 56		23 25		
Manchester Oxford Road 90	d		19 59				20 59					21 59		22 59		23 28		
Newton-le-Willows 90	d		20 18				21 18					22 18		23 18		23 46		
Earlestown [8] 90	d		20 21				21 21					22 21		23 21		23 49		
Warrington Bank Quay 90	d		20 30				21 28					22 28		23 28		23 56		
Runcorn East	d		20 37				21 35					22 35		23 35		00 03		
Frodsham	d		20 41				21 39					22 39		23 39		00 07		
Helsby	d		20 45				21 43					22 43		23 43		00 11		
Liverpool Lime Street [10] 106	d																	
Chester	a	20 48	20 57	21 14	21 20	21 46	21 55	22 18		22 46	22 50	22 55	23 31	23 55	23 59	00 24	00 25	00 31
	d			21 17		22 00					23 00							00 35
Shotton	d					22 09					23 09							
Flint	d			21 30		22 15					23 15							00 48
Prestatyn	d			21 43		22 28					23 28							01 01
Rhyl	d			21 50		22 34					23 34							01 07
Abergele & Pensarn	d					22 40												
Colwyn Bay	d			22 01		22 48					23 45							01 18
Llandudno Junction	a			22 06		22 53					23 50							01 24
	d			22 07		22 55					23 51							01 25
Deganwy	d																	
Llandudno	a																	
Conwy	d										23x53							
Penmaenmawr	d										00x01							
Llanfairfechan	d										00x03							
Bangor (Gwynedd)	a			22 22		23 10					00 12							01 41
	d			22 24		23 12					00 14							01 41
Llanfairpwll	d					23x18												
Bodorgan	d					23x28												
Ty Croes	d					23x32												
Rhosneigr	d					23x35												
Valley	d					23x41												
Holyhead	a			22 56		23 55					00 49							02 17

Sundays

18 September to 23 October

		AW	NT	AW	NT	AW	AW	AW	AW	NT		AW	VT	AW	AW	AW	AW	AW	AW	NT		NT	AW	AW	AW
		◇											◇[1]			◇							◇		
		C	D		E					F										G		H			
						🚌	🚌					🚌					🚌							🚌	
London Euston [15] ⊖65	d																								
Birmingham New Street [12] 65	d																								
Manchester Airport 84,85 ✈	d																								
Cardiff Central [7] 131	d	20p55																							
Crewe [10]	d	23p58						09 24	10 07				10 42		11 05	11 27			11 57				12 27		
Manchester Pic'dilly [10] 90 ⛴	d		23p17	23p19	23p17		07 28			09 22		08 49		09 56			09 47	10 55		11 22		11 22		10 45	11 58
Manchester Oxford Road 90	d						07 33					08 54					09 52							10 50	
Newton-le-Willows 90	d						08 03					09 24					10 22							11 20	
Earlestown [8] 90	d						08 13					09 34					10 32							11 30	
Warrington Bank Quay 90	d						08 38					09 59					10 57							11 55	
Runcorn East	d						08 58					10 19					11 17							12 15	
Frodsham	d						09 13					10 34					11 32							12 30	
Helsby	d						09 18					10 39					11 37							12 35	
Liverpool Lime Street [10] 106	d																								
Chester	a	00 24	00 43	00 44	00 45		09 38	09 42	10 32	10 46		10 59	11 02	11 04	11 30	11 48	11 57	11 57	12 20	12 46		12 48	12 48	12 55	13 01
	d							09 48					11 07			12 03							13 02		
Shotton	d							09 57								12 12							13 11		
Flint	d							10 03								12 18							13 17		
Prestatyn	d							10 16					11 30			12 31							13 30		
Rhyl	d							10 22					11 37			12 37							13 36		
Abergele & Pensarn	d							10 28															13 42		
Colwyn Bay	d							10 36					11 48			12 48							13 50		
Llandudno Junction	a							10 41					11 53			12 53							13 55		
	d					23p48		10 43					11 54			12 54							13 57		
Deganwy	d																								
Llandudno	a																								
Conwy	d					23p56		10x45															13x59		
Penmaenmawr	d					00 08		10x51															14x05		
Llanfairfechan	d					00 23		10x55															14x09		
Bangor (Gwynedd)	a					00 38		11 04					12 09			13 10							14 18		
	d					00 38		11 05					12 11			13 11							14 19		
Llanfairpwll	d					00 47		11x12																	
Bodorgan	d					00 57		11x22																	
Ty Croes	d					01 07		11x26																	
Rhosneigr	d					01 27		11x29																	
Valley	d					01 52		11x34																	
Holyhead	a					02 02		11 49					12 43			13 46							14 53		

A From Birmingham International
B From Southport
C From Carmarthen
D 18 September, 25 September, 2 October
E 9 October, 16 October, 23 October
F From Wigan Wallgate
G 18 September, 25 September, 2 October. From Southport
H 9 October, 16 October, 23 October. From Southport

Table 81

Sundays

18 September to 23 October

Crewe and Manchester - Chester and North Wales

	AW	AW	AW	AW	AW		AW	NT	AW	NT	AW	AW	AW	AW	AW		AW	AW	NT	AW	NT	AW	VT	AW
		◇ A ⊼	◇ ⊼	🚌	⊼			B	◇ ⊼	C	🚌	⊼	◇ A ⊼		◇ ⊼		⊼	R	B	◇ ⊼	C	⊼	◇1 ⊓	◇ A ⊼
London Euston 15 ⊖65 d																							15 05	
Birmingham New Street 12 65 d		11 05											13 24											15 24
Manchester Airport 84,85 ✈ d																								
Cardiff Central 7 131 d																		13 13						
Crewe 10 d	12 54		13 27				13 57		14 27					14 57	15 27					16 27			16 52	
Manchester Pic'dilly 10 90 ⇌ d				11 45	12 58			13 22		13 22	12 45	13 56					14 56		15 22		15 22	15 56		
Manchester Oxford Road 90 d				11 50							12 50						14 59					15 59		
Newton-le-Willows 90 d				12 20							13 20						15 18					16 18		
Earlestown 8 90 d				12 30							13 30						15 21					16 21		
Warrington Bank Quay 90 d				12 55							13 55						15 29					16 28		
Runcorn East d				13 15							14 15						15 36					16 35		
Frodsham d				13 30							14 30						15 40					16 39		
Helsby d				13 35							14 35						15 44					16 43		
Liverpool Lime Street 10 106 d																								
Chester a	13 15	13 20	13 47	13 55	14 00		14 20	14 46	14 47	14 48	14 55	14 58	15 18	15 20	15 47		15 56	16 25	16 46	16 47	16 48	16 55	17 14	17 27
d			14 02						15 02						16 02			16 35		17 02				
Shotton d			14 11						15 11						16 11			16 44		17 11				
Flint d			14 17						15 17						16 17			16 50		17 17				
Prestatyn d			14 30						15 30						16 30			17 03		17 30				
Rhyl d			14 36						15 36						16 36			17 09		17 36				
Abergele & Pensarn d			14 42						15 42						16 42			17 15		17 42				
Colwyn Bay d			14 50						15 50						16 50			17 23		17 50				
Llandudno Junction a			14 55						15 55						16 55			17 28		17 55				
d			14 57						15 57						16 57			17 30		17 57				
Deganwy d																								
Llandudno a																								
Conwy d									15x59									17x32		17x59				
Penmaenmawr d									16x05									17x38		18x05				
Llanfairfechan d									16x09									17x42		18x09				
Bangor (Gwynedd) a			15 12						16 18						17 12			17 51		18 18				
d			15 14						16 19						17 14			17 57		18 19				
Llanfairpwll d			15x20												17x20			18x03						
Bodorgan d			15x30												17x30			18x13						
Ty Croes d			15x34												17x34			18x17						
Rhosneigr d			15x37												17x37			18x20						
Valley d			15x43												17x43			18x26						
Holyhead a			15 57						16 53						17 57			18 40		18 54				

	AW		AW	VT	AW	NT	AW	NT	AW	VT	AW		AW	AW	VT	NT	NT	AW	AW	VT	AW		AW	AW
	◇		⊼	◇1 ⊓	R ⊼	B	◇	C	⊼	◇1 ⊓	◇ A ⊼				◇1 ⊓	B	C			◇1 ⊓	◇ A ⊼		◇	
London Euston 15 ⊖65 d				16 05						17 05					18 05					19 05				
Birmingham New Street 12 65 d											17 24										19 24			
Manchester Airport 84,85 ✈ d																								
Cardiff Central 7 131 d					15 22																			
Crewe 10 d	17 27			17 52			18 27			18 56			19 27		19 52			20 27		20 55			21 27	
Manchester Pic'dilly 10 90 ⇌ d			16 56			17 22		17 22	17 56					18 56		19 22	19 22		19 56					20 56
Manchester Oxford Road 90 d			16 59						17 59					18 59					19 59					20 59
Newton-le-Willows 90 d			17 18						18 18					19 18					20 18					21 18
Earlestown 8 90 d			17 21						18 21					19 21					20 21					21 21
Warrington Bank Quay 90 d			17 28						18 28					19 29					20 30					21 28
Runcorn East d			17 35						18 35					19 36					20 37					21 35
Frodsham d			17 39						18 39					19 40					20 41					21 39
Helsby d			17 43						18 43					19 44					20 45					21 43
Liverpool Lime Street 10 106 d																								
Chester a	17 46		17 55	18 14	18 25	18 46	18 47	18 48	18 55	19 14	19 16		19 48	19 56	20 11	20 46	20 48	20 48	20 57	21 14	21 20		21 46	21 55
d	18 02				18 29		18 52			19 22	19 38				20 18					21 17			22 00	
Shotton d	18 11				18 38		19 01				19 47												22 09	
Flint d	18 17				18 44		19 07			19 35	19 53				20 31					21 30			22 15	
Prestatyn d	18 30				18 57		19 21			19 48	20 06				20 44					21 43			22 28	
Rhyl d	18 36				19 03		19 27			19 55	20 12				20 51					21 50			22 34	
Abergele & Pensarn d	18 42				19 09		19 33				20 18												22 40	
Colwyn Bay d	18 50				19 17		19 41			20 06	20 26				21 02					22 01			22 48	
Llandudno Junction a	18 55				19 22		19 46			20 11	20 31				21 07					22 06			22 53	
d	18 57				19 24		19 47			20 12	20 33				21 08					22 07			22 55	
Deganwy d																								
Llandudno a																								
Conwy d					19x26		19x49				20x35													
Penmaenmawr d					19x32		19x55				20x41													
Llanfairfechan d					19x36		19x59				20x45													
Bangor (Gwynedd) a	19 12				19 45		20 08			20 27	20 54				21 23					22 22			23 10	
d	19 14				19 45		20 09			20 29	20 55				21 25					22 24			23 12	
Llanfairpwll d	19x20																						23x18	
Bodorgan d	19x30																						23x28	
Ty Croes d	19x34																						23x32	
Rhosneigr d	19x37																						23x35	
Valley d	19x43																						23x41	
Holyhead a	19 54				20 20		20 44			20 59	21 30				21 57					22 56			23 55	

A From Birmingham International

B 18 September, 25 September, 2 October. From Southport

C 9 October, 16 October, 23 October. From Southport

Table 81

Sundays
18 September to 23 October

Crewe and Manchester - Chester and North Wales

	AW	NT	NT	AW	AW	AW	AW		AW	AW	AW	AW
				◇		◇					◇	◇
		A	B			C						C
London Euston 15 ⊖65 d												
Birmingham New Street 12 65 d						21 24						22 55
Manchester Airport 84,85 ✈ d												
Cardiff Central 7 131 d											21 04	
Crewe 10 d	22 00			22 29		23 06			23 38		00 03	00 10
Manchester Pic'dilly 10 90 ⛴ d		21 20	21 22		21 56		22 56			23 25		
Manchester Oxford Road 90 d					21 59		22 59			23 28		
Newton-le-Willows 90 d					22 18		23 18			23 46		
Earlestown 8 90 d					22 21		23 21			23 49		
Warrington Bank Quay 90 d					22 28		23 28			23 56		
Runcorn East d					22 35		23 35			00 03		
Frodsham d					22 39		23 39			00 07		
Helsby d					22 43		23 43			00 11		
Liverpool Lime Street 10 106 d												
Chester a	22 21	22 46	22 46	22 50	22 55	23 31	23 55		23 59	00 24	00 25	00 31
d				23 00								00 35
Shotton d				23 09								
Flint d				23 15								00 48
Prestatyn d				23 28								01 01
Rhyl d				23 34								01 07
Abergele & Pensarn d												
Colwyn Bay d				23 45								01 18
Llandudno Junction a				23 50								01 24
d				23 51								01 25
Deganwy d												
Llandudno a												
Conwy d				23x53								
Penmaenmawr d				00x01								
Llanfairfechan d				00x03								
Bangor (Gwynedd) a				00 12								01 41
d				00 14								01 41
Llanfairpwll d												
Bodorgan d												
Ty Croes d												
Rhosneigr d												
Valley d												
Holyhead a				00 49								02 17

Sundays
from 30 October

	AW	AW	NT	AW	AW	AW	AW	NT	AW		VT	AW	AW	AW	AW	NT	AW	AW	AW		AW	AW	AW	AW
		◇									◇ 1		◇				◇				◇	◇		
		D						E								F					C			
				🚌	🚌						⊡						✠	✠			✠	✠	✠	
London Euston 15 ⊖65 d																								
Birmingham New Street 12 65 d																					11 05			
Manchester Airport 84,85 ✈ d																								
Cardiff Central 7 131 d		20p55																						
Crewe 10 d		23p58				09 24	10 07				10 42	11 05	11 27		11 57		12 27		12 54			13 27		13 57
Manchester Pic'dilly 10 90 ⛴ d	23p14		23p17		07 28			09 22	09 56					10 55		11 22		11 56					12 56	
Manchester Oxford Road 90 d	23p17				07 33				09 59					10 59				11 59					12 59	
Newton-le-Willows 90 d	23p36				08 03				10 18					11 20				12 18					13 18	
Earlestown 8 90 d	23p39				08 13				10 21					11 23				12 21					13 21	
Warrington Bank Quay 90 d	23p48				08 38				10 28					11 30				12 28					13 29	
Runcorn East d	23p55				08 58				10 35					11 37				12 35					13 36	
Frodsham d	23p59				09 13				10 40					11 41				12 39					13 40	
Helsby d	00 03				09 18				10 44					11 45				12 43					13 44	
Liverpool Lime Street 10 106 d																								
Chester a	00 15	00 24	00 45		09 38	09 42	10 32	10 46	10 59		11 02	11 30	11 48	11 57	12 20	12 48	12 48	12 55	13 15		13 20	13 47	13 56	14 20
d						09 48					11 07		12 03				13 02					14 02		
Shotton d						09 57							12 12				13 11					14 11		
Flint d						10 03							12 18				13 17					14 17		
Prestatyn d						10 16					11 30		12 31				13 30					14 30		
Rhyl d						10 22					11 37		12 37				13 36					14 36		
Abergele & Pensarn d						10 28											13 42					14 42		
Colwyn Bay d						10 36					11 48		12 48				13 50					14 50		
Llandudno Junction a						10 41					11 53		12 53				13 55					14 55		
d				23p48		10 43					11 54		12 54				13 57					14 57		
Deganwy d																								
Llandudno a																								
Conwy d				23p56		10x45											13x59							
Penmaenmawr d				00 08		10x51											14x05							
Llanfairfechan d				00 23		10x55											14x09							
Bangor (Gwynedd) a				00 38		11 04					12 09		13 10				14 18					15 12		
d				00 38		11 05					12 11		13 11				14 19					15 14		
Llanfairpwll d				00 47		11x12																15x20		
Bodorgan d				00 57		11x22																15x30		
Ty Croes d				01 07		11x26																15x34		
Rhosneigr d				01 27		11x29																15x37		
Valley d				01 52		11x34																15x43		
Holyhead a				02 02		11 49					12 43		13 46				14 53					15 57		

A 9 October, 16 October, 23 October. From Southport
B 18 September, 25 September, 2 October. From Southport
C From Birmingham International
D From Carmarthen
E From Wigan Wallgate
F From Southport

Table 81

Sundays from 30 October

Crewe and Manchester - Chester and North Wales

		AW	NT	AW	AW	AW		AW	AW	AW	AW	NT	AW	VT	AW	AW		AW	VT	AW	AW	NT	AW	VT	AW
		◇ 🚲	A	🚲	◇ B 🚲			◇ 🚲	🚲	R	◇ 🚲	A	🚲	◇1 ☕	◇ B 🚲	◇		🚲	◇1 ☕	R 🚲	◇	A	🚲	◇1 ☕	◇ B 🚲
London Euston [15] ⊖65	d													15 05					16 05					17 05	
Birmingham New Street [12] 65	d				13 24										15 24										17 24
Manchester Airport 84,85 ✈	d																								
Cardiff Central [7] 131	d									13 13										15 22					
Crewe [10]	d	14 27				14 57		15 27			16 27			16 52		17 27			17 52		18 27			18 56	
Manchester Pic'dilly [10] 90 ⇌	d		13 22	13 56					14 56			15 22	15 56					16 56				17 22	17 56		
Manchester Oxford Road 90	d			13 59					14 59				15 59					16 59					17 59		
Newton-le-Willows 90	d			14 18					15 18				16 18					17 18					18 18		
Earlestown [8] 90	d			14 21					15 21				16 21					17 21					18 21		
Warrington Bank Quay 90	d			14 28					15 29				16 28					17 28					18 28		
Runcorn East	d			14 35					15 36				16 35					17 35					18 35		
Frodsham	d			14 39					15 40				16 39					17 39					18 39		
Helsby	d			14 43					15 44				16 43					17 43					18 43		
Liverpool Lime Street [10] 106	d																								
Chester	a	14 47	14 48	14 55	15 18	15 20		15 47	15 56	16 25	16 47	16 48	16 55	17 14	17 27	17 46		17 55	18 14	18 25	18 47	18 48	18 55	19 14	19 16
	d	15 02						16 02		16 35	17 02					18 02				18 29	18 52			19 22	19 38
Shotton	d	15 11						16 11		16 44	17 11					18 11				18 38	19 01				19 47
Flint	d	15 17						16 17		16 50	17 17					18 17				18 44	19 07			19 35	19 53
Prestatyn	d	15 30						16 30		17 03	17 30					18 30				18 57	19 21			19 48	20 06
Rhyl	d	15 36						16 36		17 09	17 36					18 36				19 03	19 27			19 55	20 12
Abergele & Pensarn	d	15 42						16 42		17 15	17 42					18 42				19 09	19 33				20 18
Colwyn Bay	d	15 50						16 50		17 23	17 50					18 50				19 17	19 41			20 06	20 26
Llandudno Junction	a	15 55						16 55		17 28	17 55					18 55				19 22	19 46			20 11	20 31
	d	15 57						16 57		17 30	17 57					18 57				19 24	19 47			20 12	20 33
Deganwy	d																								
Llandudno	a																								
Conwy	d	15x59								17x32	17x59									19x26	19x49				20x35
Penmaenmawr	d	16x05								17x38	18x05									19x32	19x55				20x41
Llanfairfechan	d	16x09								17x42	18x09									19x36	19x59				20x45
Bangor (Gwynedd)	a	16 18						17 12		17 51	18 18					19 12				19 45	20 08			20 27	20 54
	d	16 19						17 14		17 57	18 19					19 14				19 45	20 09			20 29	20 55
Llanfairpwll	d							17x20		18x03						19x20									
Bodorgan	d							17x30		18x13						19x30									
Ty Croes	d							17x34		18x17						19x34									
Rhosneigr	d							17x37		18x20						19x37									
Valley	d							17x43		18x26						19x43									
Holyhead	a	16 53						17 57		18 40	18 54					19 54				20 20	20 44			20 59	21 30

		AW		AW	VT	NT	AW	AW	VT	AW	AW	AW		AW	NT	AW	AW	AW	AW	AW	AW	AW		AW	
					◇1 ☕	A			◇1 ☕	◇ B 🚲	◇				A	◇		◇ B				◇		◇ B	
London Euston [15] ⊖65	d				18 05				19 05																
Birmingham New Street [12] 65	d									19 24								21 24						22 55	
Manchester Airport 84,85 ✈	d																								
Cardiff Central [7] 131	d																					21 04			
Crewe [10]	d	19 27			19 52		20 27		20 55		21 27			22 00		22 29		23 06		23 38		00 03		00 10	
Manchester Pic'dilly [10] 90 ⇌	d			18 56		19 22		19 56				20 56			21 20		21 56		22 56		23 25				
Manchester Oxford Road 90	d			18 59				19 59				20 59					21 59		22 59		23 28				
Newton-le-Willows 90	d			19 18				20 18				21 18					22 18		23 18		23 46				
Earlestown [8] 90	d			19 21				20 21				21 21					22 21		23 21		23 49				
Warrington Bank Quay 90	d			19 29				20 30				21 28					22 28		23 28		23 56				
Runcorn East	d			19 36				20 37				21 35					22 35		23 35		00 03				
Frodsham	d			19 40				20 41				21 39					22 39		23 39		00 07				
Helsby	d			19 44				20 45				21 43					22 43		23 43		00 11				
Liverpool Lime Street [10] 106	d																								
Chester	a	19 48		19 56	20 11	20 48	20 48	20 57	21 14	21 20	21 46	21 55		22 21	22 46	22 50	22 55	23 31	23 55	23 59	00 24	00 25		00 31	
	d				20 18				21 17		22 00					23 00								00 35	
Shotton	d										22 09					23 09									
Flint	d				20 31				21 30		22 15					23 15								00 48	
Prestatyn	d				20 44				21 43		22 28					23 28								01 01	
Rhyl	d				20 51				21 50		22 34					23 34								01 07	
Abergele & Pensarn	d										22 40														
Colwyn Bay	d				21 02				22 01		22 48					23 45								01 18	
Llandudno Junction	a				21 07				22 06		22 53					23 50								01 24	
	d				21 08				22 07		22 55					23 51								01 25	
Deganwy	d																								
Llandudno	a																								
Conwy	d															23x53									
Penmaenmawr	d															00x01									
Llanfairfechan	d															00x03									
Bangor (Gwynedd)	a				21 23				22 22		23 10					00 12								01 41	
	d				21 25				22 24		23 12					00 14								01 41	
Llanfairpwll	d										23x18														
Bodorgan	d										23x28														
Ty Croes	d										23x32														
Rhosneigr	d										23x35														
Valley	d										23x41														
Holyhead	a				21 57				22 56		23 55					00 49								02 17	

A From Southport

B From Birmingham International

Table 81

Mondays to Fridays

until 30 September

North Wales and Chester - Manchester and Crewe

Miles	Miles	Station		NT	AW	AW	AW	AW	AW	AW	AW	NT	AW	VT	AW	AW	NT	AW	AW	AW	VT	VT	AW
				MX															BHX				
								◇					◇	◇1	◇			◇	◇		◇1	◇1	◇
								A					B					C				D	
													🛒	☒				🛒	☒	🛒	☒	☒	🛒
0	—	**Holyhead**	d										04 25	04 48				05 11	05 32		05 51		
3½	—	Valley	d										04x31										
7½	—	Rhosneigr	d																				
9¼	—	Ty Croes	d																				
12	—	Bodorgan	d																				
21	—	Llanfairpwll	d										04x48										
24¾	—	**Bangor (Gwynedd)**	a										04 55	05 14				05 38	06 00		06 17		
—	—		d										04 57	05 14				05 40	06 02		06 18		
32¼	—	Llanfairfechan	d															05x47					
34¾	—	Penmaenmawr	d															05x51					
39	—	Conwy	d															05x57					
—	0	**Llandudno**	d																				06 34
—	1¾	Deganwy	d																				06x38
40	3	**Llandudno Junction**	a										05 13	05 32				06 01	06 19		06 35		06 42
—	—		d						04 38				05 15	05 32	05 46			06 07	06 21		06 36		06 44
44	—	Colwyn Bay	d						04 44				05 21	05 38	05 52			06 13			06 42		06 50
50¼	—	Abergele & Pensarn	d						04 51														06 57
54½	—	Rhyl	d						04 57				05 31	05 49	06 02			06 23	06 36		06 53		07 03
58	—	Prestatyn	d						05 02				05 37		06 08			06 29			06 58		07 08
72	—	Flint	d						05 16				05 50		06 21			06 42	06 52		07 12		07 21
76¼	—	Shotton	d						05 22						06 27			06 48					07 27
84¼	0	**Chester**	a						05 33				06 05	06 17	06 38			07 00	07 07		07 26		07 38
—	—		d	22p48	03 36	04 22	04 55	05 15	05 37	05 38	05 51	06 05	06 18	06 26	06 40	06 43	07 03	07 19	07 08	07 12	07 35	07 35	07 40
—	—	Liverpool Lime Street 10 106	a																				
—	7½	Helsby	d							05 47					06 49					07 21			07 49
—	10	Frodsham	d							05 51					06 53					07 25			07 53
—	13¼	Runcorn East	d							05 56					06 59					07 31			07 59
—	18¼	Warrington Bank Quay 90	a							06 05					07 06					07 38			08 06
—	22¼	Earlestown 8 90	a							06 12					07 14					07 46			08 15
—	24	Newton-le-Willows 90	a							06 15					07 17					07 49			08 18
—	39¾	**Manchester Oxford Road** 90	a							06 35					07 41					08 09			08 41
—	40¼	**Manchester Pic'dilly** 10 90 ⛴	a	00 18	04 43					06 45		07 31			07 50		08 32			08 18			08 50
105½	—	**Crewe** 10	a			04 44	05 20		05 58		06 15			06 47		07 04			07 32		07 54	07 54	
—	—	Cardiff Central 7 131	a					08 17					09 18						09 58				
—	—	Manchester Airport 84,85 ✈	a		05 09																		
—	—	Birmingham New Street 12 65	a			06 01												09 26					
—	—	London Euston 15 ⊖65	a											08 33							09 38	09 38	

Station		AW	AW	NT	AW	VT	AW	AW	AW	NT	AW	AW	VT	AW	AW	AW	NT	AW	VT	AW	AW	AW	NT
												■											
					◇	◇1	◇				◇		◇1	◇				◇	◇1	◇			
											C												
					🛒	☒	🛒				🛒	🛒	☒	🛒				🛒	☒	🛒			
Holyhead	d				06 29	06 55					07 15	07 51						08 05	08 55				
Valley	d				06x35						07x21							08x11					
Rhosneigr	d				06x41						07x26							08x17					
Ty Croes	d				06x44						07x30							08x20					
Bodorgan	d				06x49						07x34							08x25					
Llanfairpwll	d				06x58						07x44							08x34					
Bangor (Gwynedd)	a				07 06	07 21					07 52	08 17						08 42	09 21				
	d				07 07	07 22					08 02	08 21						09 02	09 22				
Llanfairfechan	d										08x09							09x09					
Penmaenmawr	d										08x13							09x13					
Conwy	d										08x19							09x19					
Llandudno	d	07 08					07 45	08 08						08 45	09 08					09 45	10 10		
Deganwy	d	07x12					07x49	08x12						08x49	09x12					09x49	10x14		
Llandudno Junction	a	07 18			07 23	07 39	07 53	08 18			08 23	08 38		08 53	09 18			09 23	09 39	09 53	10 20		
	d				07 25	07 40	07 54				08 25	08 39		08 54				09 25	09 40	09 54			
Colwyn Bay	d				07 31	07 47	08 00				08 31	08 45		09 00				09 31	09 47	10 00			
Abergele & Pensarn	d						08 07							09 07						10 07			
Rhyl	d				07 41	07 58	08 13				08 41	08 56		09 13				09 41	09 58	10 13			
Prestatyn	d				07 47	08 04	08 19				08 47			09 19				09 47	10 04	10 19			
Flint	d				08 00	08 17	08 32				09 00			09 32				10 00	10 17	10 32			
Shotton	d						08 38							09 38						10 38			
Chester	a				08 15	08 31	08 50				09 15	09 23		09 50				10 15	10 31	10 50			
	d		07 55	08 07	08 19	08 35	08 52		08 55	09 07	09 19	09 26	09 35	09 52		09 55	10 07	10 20	10 35	10 52		10 55	11 07
Liverpool Lime Street 10 106	a																						
Helsby	d						09 01							10 01						11 01			
Frodsham	d						09 05							10 05						11 05			
Runcorn East	d						09 11							10 11						11 11			
Warrington Bank Quay 90	a						09 18							10 18						11 18			
Earlestown 8 90	a						09 26							10 26						11 26			
Newton-le-Willows 90	a						09 29							10 29						11 29			
Manchester Oxford Road 90	a						09 48							10 48						11 48			
Manchester Pic'dilly 10 90 ⛴	a			09 36			09 57			10 36				10 57			11 36			11 57			12 36
Crewe 10	a		08 18			08 54			09 18		09 40		09 54			10 18			10 54			11 18	
Cardiff Central 7 131	a				11 15							12 08						13 22					
Manchester Airport 84,85 ✈	a																						
Birmingham New Street 12 65	a										11 26												
London Euston 15 ⊖65	a					10 38							11 38						12 38				

A To Maesteg
B To Milford Haven
C To Birmingham International
D From Wrexham General

Table 81

Mondays to Fridays

until 30 September

North Wales and Chester - Manchester and Crewe

		AW	AW	VT		AW	AW	AW	NT	AW	VT	AW	AW	AW		NT	AW	VT	AW	AW	AW	NT	AW	AW	
		◇ A 🛒	◇ B	◇■1 ☕		◇ 🛒				■ 🛒	◇■1 ☕	◇ 🛒					◇ A 🛒	◇■1 ☕	◇ 🛒				◇ C 🛒	◇ B	
Holyhead	d	09 23								10 33							11 23						12 39		
Valley	d	09x29								10x39							11x29								
Rhosneigr	d	09x34															11x34								
Ty Croes	d	09x38															11x38								
Bodorgan	d	09x42															11x42								
Llanfairpwll	d	09x52								10x56							11x52								
Bangor (Gwynedd)	a	10 00								11 03							12 00						13 05		
	d	10 02								11 05							12 02	12 24					13 07		
Llanfairfechan	d	10x09															12x09								
Penmaenmawr	d	10x13															12x13								
Conwy	d	10x19															12x19								
Llandudno	d		10 22			10 44	11 08					11 44	12 08						12 44	13 10				13 22	
Deganwy	d		10x26			10x48	11x12					11x48	12x12						12x48	13x14				13x26	
Llandudno Junction	a	10 23	10 32			10 52	11 18			11 21		11 52	12 18				12 23	12 40	12 52	13 20			13 23	13 32	
	d	10 25				10 53				11 25		11 53					12 25	12 42	12 53				13 25		
Colwyn Bay	d	10 31				10 59				11 31		11 59					12 31	12 48	12 59				13 31		
Abergele & Pensarn	d					11 06						12 06							13 06						
Rhyl	d	10 41				11 12				11 41		12 12					12 41	12 59	13 12				13 41		
Prestatyn	d	10 47				11 18				11 47		12 18					12 47	13 05	13 18				13 47		
Flint	d	11 00				11 31				12 00		12 31					13 00	13 18	13 31				14 00		
Shotton	d					11 37						12 37							13 37						
Chester	a	11 15				11 49				12 14		12 49					13 14	13 32	13 49				14 15		
	d	11 21		11 35		11 50		11 55	12 07	12 19	12 35	12 50		12 55		13 07	13 19	13 35	13 50		13 55	14 07	14 19		
Liverpool Lime Street ■10 106	a																								
Helsby	d					12 00						13 00							14 00						
Frodsham	d					12 04						13 04							14 04						
Runcorn East	d					12 09						13 09							14 09						
Warrington Bank Quay 90	a					12 18						13 18							14 18						
Earlestown ■8 90	a					12 26						13 26							14 26						
Newton-le-Willows 90	a					12 29						13 29							14 29						
Manchester Oxford Road 90	a					12 48						13 48							14 48						
Manchester Pic'dilly ■10 90 ⛴	a					12 57			13 36			13 57				14 36			14 57			15 36			
Crewe ■10	a			11 54				12 18			12 54			13 18				13 54			14 18				
Cardiff Central ■7 131	a									15 21													17 15		
Manchester Airport 84,85 ✈	a																								
Birmingham New Street ■12 65	a	13 26															15 26								
London Euston ■15 ⊖65	a			13 38							14 38							15 38							

		VT	AW	AW	AW	NT	AW	VT	VT	AW		AW	NT	AW	AW	VT	AW	NT	AW	AW		AW	VT	AW	NT
		◇■1 ☕	◇ 🛒				◇ A 🛒	◇■1 ☕	◇■1 ☕	◇ 🛒				◇ 🛒	◇ 🛒	◇■1 ☕			◇ 🛒	◇ A 🛒		◇ B	◇■1 ⊠		
Holyhead	d						13 23	13 58							14 34					15 23					
Valley	d						13x29													15x29					
Rhosneigr	d						13x34													15x34					
Ty Croes	d						13x38													15x38					
Bodorgan	d						13x42													15x42					
Llanfairpwll	d						13x52													15x52					
Bangor (Gwynedd)	a						14 00	14 24							15 00					16 00					
	d						14 02	14 25							15 04					16 02					
Llanfairfechan	d						14x09								15x11					16x09					
Penmaenmawr	d						14x13								15x15					16x13					
Conwy	d						14x19								15x21					16x19					
Llandudno	d		13 44	14 08						14 40				15 08					16 06			16 20			
Deganwy	d		13x48	14x12						14x44				15x12					16x10			16x24			
Llandudno Junction	a		13 52	14 18			14 23	14 42		14 48				15 16	15 26				16 14	16 23		16 28			
	d		13 53				14 25	14 43		14 49				15 17	15 27				16 15	16 25					
Colwyn Bay	d		13 59				14 31	14 50		14 55				15 23	15 33				16 21	16 34					
Abergele & Pensarn	d		14 06							15 02				15 30					16 28						
Rhyl	d		14 12				14 41	15 00		15 08				15 36	15 44				16 34	16 44					
Prestatyn	d		14 18				14 47			15 14				15 42	15 49				16 39	16 50					
Flint	d		14 31				14 58			15 27				15 55	16 03				16 53	17 03					
Shotton	d		14 37							15 33				16 01					16 59						
Chester	a		14 49				15 13	15 27		15 44				16 13	16 15				17 10	17 15					
	d	14 35	14 50		14 55	15 07	15 18	15 35	15 35	15 46		15 55	16 07	16 22	16 19	16 35	16 55	17 07	17 19	17 19			17 35	17 55	18 07
Liverpool Lime Street ■10 106	a																								
Helsby	d		15 00							15 55				16 31					17 28						
Frodsham	d		15 04							15 59				16 35					17 33						
Runcorn East	d		15 09							16 04				16 41					17 38						
Warrington Bank Quay 90	a		15 18							16 12				16 51					17 49						
Earlestown ■8 90	a		15 26							16 26				16 59					17 57						
Newton-le-Willows 90	a		15 29							16 29				17 01					17 59						
Manchester Oxford Road 90	a		15 48							16 48				17 21					18 19						
Manchester Pic'dilly ■10 90 ⛴	a		15 57			16 36				16 57			17 36	17 30				18 36	18 28						19 35
Crewe ■10	a	14 54			15 18			15 54	15 54			16 18				16 54	17 18						17 54	18 18	
Cardiff Central ■7 131	a														19 21										
Manchester Airport 84,85 ✈	a																								
Birmingham New Street ■12 65	a						17 27													19 26					
London Euston ■15 ⊖65	a	16 38						17 38	17 38							18 38							19 38		

A To Birmingham International **B** To Blaenau Ffestiniog **C** To Maesteg

Table 81

Mondays to Fridays

until 30 September

North Wales and Chester - Manchester and Crewe

		AW	AW	AW	AW	AW		AW	NT	VT	AW	AW	AW	AW	NT	AW		AW	AW	AW	NT	AW	AW	VT	AW
		◇ 🛒	◇ 🛒		◇ A 🛒					◇■1 🍴	◇ 🛒	◇ B				◇ 🛒		◇				◇ C	◇ D	◇■1 🍴	
Holyhead	d		16 38		17 30											18 23						19 21	19 21		
Valley	d				17x36											18x29						19x27	19x27		
Rhosneigr	d				17x41											18x34						19x32	19x32		
Ty Croes	d				17x45											18x38						19x36	19x36		
Bodorgan	d				17x49											18x42						19x40	19x40		
Llanfairpwll	d				17x59											18x52						19x50	19x50		
Bangor (Gwynedd)	a		17 04		18 07											19 00						19 58	19 58		
	d		17 06		18 09											19 02						20 00	20 00	20 20	
Llanfairfechan	d				18x16											19x09						20x07	20x07		
Penmaenmawr	d				18x20											19x13						20x11	20x11		
Conwy	d				18x26											19x19						20x17	20x17		
Llandudno	d	17 06		18 08							18 44	19 03	19 08					19 42	20 08						20 42
Deganwy	d	17x10		18x12							18x48	19x07	19x12					19x46	20x12						20x46
Llandudno Junction	a	17 14	17 23	18 18	18 30						18 52	19 11	19 18			19 23		19 50	20 18			20 21	20 21	20 36	20 50
	d	17 14	17 25		18 32						18 53					19 25		19 51				20 23	20 23	20 38	20 51
Colwyn Bay	d	17 20	17 31		18 38						18 59					19 31		19 57				20 29	20 29	20 44	20 57
Abergele & Pensarn	d	17 27									19 06							20 04							21 04
Rhyl	d	17 33	17 41		18 48						19 12					19 41		20 10				20 39	20 39	20 55	21 11
Prestatyn	d	17 38	17 47		18 54						19 18					19 47		20 16				20 45	20 45	21 01	21 16
Flint	d	17 52	18 01		19 07						19 31					20 00		20 29				20 58	20 58	21 14	21 30
Shotton	d	17 58									19 37							20 35							21 36
Chester	a	18 11	18 15		19 24						19 49					20 15		20 47				21 15	21 15	21 28	21 47
	d	18 16	18 18			18 49		18 55	19 07	19 35	19 50			19 55	20 07	20 17		20 50		20 55	21 07	21 21	21 21	21 35	
Liverpool Lime Street ■10 106	a																								
Helsby	d	18 25				18 59					20 00							20 59							
Frodsham	d	18 30				19 03					20 04							21 03							
Runcorn East	d	18 35				19 08					20 09							21 09							
Warrington Bank Quay 90	a	18 45				19 18					20 18							21 18							
Earlestown ■8 90	a	18 57				19 26					20 26							21 26							
Newton-le-Willows 90	a	18 59				19 29					20 29							21 29							
Manchester Oxford Road 90	a	19 21				19 48					20 48							21 48							
Manchester Pic'dilly ■10 90 ⛴	a	19 29				19 52			20 35		20 52				21 35			21 57			22 35				
Crewe ■10	a							19 18		19 54				20 18		20 41				21 18				21 54	
Cardiff Central ■7 131	a		21 20																						
Manchester Airport 84,85 ✈	a					20 18					21 18														
Birmingham New Street ■12 65	a																					23 27	23 29	22 50	
London Euston ■15 ⊖65	a									21 42															

		AW		AW	AW	NT	AW
		E		F	◇		
Holyhead	d				20 37		
Valley	d						
Rhosneigr	d						
Ty Croes	d						
Bodorgan	d						
Llanfairpwll	d						
Bangor (Gwynedd)	a				21 04		
	d				21 06		
Llanfairfechan	d				21x13		
Penmaenmawr	d				21x17		
Conwy	d				21x23		
Llandudno	d						21 45
Deganwy	d						21x49
Llandudno Junction	a				21 27		21 53
	d				21 29		21 55
Colwyn Bay	d				21 35		22 01
Abergele & Pensarn	d				21 42		22 09
Rhyl	d				21 48		22 16
Prestatyn	d				21 53		22 22
Flint	d				22 07		22 37
Shotton	d				22 13		22 44
Chester	a				22 23		22 55
	d	21 49		21 52	22 26	22 48	23 01
Liverpool Lime Street ■10 106	a						
Helsby	d	21 58		22 01			
Frodsham	d	22 02		22 05			
Runcorn East	d	22 08		22 11			
Warrington Bank Quay 90	a	22 15		22 18			
Earlestown ■8 90	a	22 26		22 26			
Newton-le-Willows 90	a	22 29		22 29			
Manchester Oxford Road 90	a	22 50		22 50			
Manchester Pic'dilly ■10 90 ⛴	a	22 58		22 58		00 18	
Crewe ■10	a				22 50		23 26
Cardiff Central ■7 131	a						
Manchester Airport 84,85 ✈	a						
Birmingham New Street ■12 65	a						
London Euston ■15 ⊖65	a						

A To Shrewsbury
B To Blaenau Ffestiniog
C MWFO
D TThO
E from 12 September until 30 September
F until 9 September

North Wales and Chester - Manchester and Crewe

		NT MX	AW	AW	AW	AW ◇ A	AW	AW	AW	NT		AW ◇ B 🚲	VT ◇1 ⊠	AW ◇	AW	NT	AW ◇ C 🚲	AW BHX ◇ ⊠	AW 🚲	VT ◇1 ⊠		VT ◇1 D ⊠	AW ◇ 🚲	AW	AW
Holyhead	d											04 25	04 48				05 11	05 32		05 51					
Valley	d											04x31													
Rhosneigr	d																								
Ty Croes	d																								
Bodorgan	d																								
Llanfairpwll	d											04x48													
Bangor (Gwynedd)	a											04 55	05 14				05 38	06 00		06 17					
	d											04 57	05 14				05 40	06 02		06 18					
Llanfairfechan	d																05x47								
Penmaenmawr	d																05x51								
Conwy	d																05x57								
Llandudno	d																						06 34	07 08	
Deganwy	d																						06x38	07x12	
Llandudno Junction	a											05 13	05 32				06 01	06 19		06 35			06 42	07 18	
	d						04 38					05 15	05 32	05 46			06 07	06 21		06 36			06 44		
Colwyn Bay	d						04 44					05 21	05 38	05 52			06 13			06 42			06 50		
Abergele & Pensarn	d						04 51																06 57		
Rhyl	d						04 57					05 31	05 49	06 02			06 23	06 36		06 53			07 03		
Prestatyn	d						05 02					05 37		06 08			06 29			06 58			07 08		
Flint	d						05 16					05 50		06 21			06 42	06 52		07 12			07 21		
Shotton	d						05 22							06 27			06 48						07 27		
Chester	a						05 33					06 05	06 17	06 38			07 00	07 07		07 26			07 38		
	d	22p44	03 36	04 22	04 55	05 15	05 37	05 38	05 51	06 01		06 18	06 26	06 40	06 43	06 59	07 19	07 08	07 12	07 35		07 35	07 40		07 55
Liverpool Lime Street ■10 106	a																								
Helsby	d							05 47						06 49					07 21				07 49		
Frodsham	d							05 51						06 53					07 25				07 53		
Runcorn East	d							05 56						06 59					07 31				07 59		
Warrington Bank Quay 90	a							06 05						07 06					07 38				08 06		
Earlestown ■8 90	a							06 12						07 14					07 46				08 15		
Newton-le-Willows 90	a							06 15						07 17					07 49				08 18		
Manchester Oxford Road 90	a							06 35						07 41					08 09				08 41		
Manchester Pic'dilly ■10 90 ⇌	a	00 18	04 43					06 45		07 31				07 50		08 32			08 18				08 50		
Crewe ■10	a			04 44	05 20		05 58		06 15				06 47		07 04			07 32		07 54		07 54			08 18
Cardiff Central ■7 131	a					08 17						09 18						09 58							
Manchester Airport 84,85 ✈	a		05 09																						
Birmingham New Street ■12 65	a			06 01													09 26								
London Euston ■15 ⊖65	a												08 33							09 38		09 38			

		NT	AW ◇ 🚲	VT ◇1 ⊠	AW ◇ 🚲	AW		AW	NT	AW ◇ C 🚲	AW ■ 🚲	VT ◇1 ⊠	AW ◇ 🚲	AW	AW	NT		AW ◇ 🚲	VT ◇1 ⊠	AW ◇ 🚲	AW	AW	NT	AW ◇ C 🚲	AW ◇ E
Holyhead	d		06 29	06 55						07 15	07 51							08 05	08 55					09 23	
Valley	d		06x35							07x21								08x11						09x29	
Rhosneigr	d		06x41							07x26								08x17						09x34	
Ty Croes	d		06x44							07x30								08x20						09x38	
Bodorgan	d		06x49							07x34								08x25						09x42	
Llanfairpwll	d		06x58							07x44								08x34						09x52	
Bangor (Gwynedd)	a		07 06	07 21						07 52	08 17							08 42	09 21					10 00	
	d		07 07	07 22						08 02	08 21							09 02	09 22					10 02	
Llanfairfechan	d									08x09								09x09						10x09	
Penmaenmawr	d									08x13								09x13						10x13	
Conwy	d									08x19								09x19						10x19	
Llandudno	d				07 45	08 08							08 45	09 08						09 45	10 10				10 22
Deganwy	d				07x49	08x12							08x49	09x12						09x49	10x14				10x26
Llandudno Junction	a		07 23	07 39	07 53	08 18				08 23	08 38		08 53	09 18				09 23	09 39	09 53	10 20			10 23	10 32
	d		07 25	07 40	07 54					08 25	08 39		08 54					09 25	09 40	09 54				10 25	
Colwyn Bay	d		07 31	07 47	08 00					08 31	08 45		09 00					09 31	09 47	10 00				10 31	
Abergele & Pensarn	d				08 07								09 07							10 07					
Rhyl	d		07 41	07 58	08 13					08 41	08 56		09 13					09 41	09 58	10 13				10 41	
Prestatyn	d		07 47	08 04	08 19					08 47			09 19					09 47	10 04	10 19				10 47	
Flint	d		08 00	08 17	08 32					09 00			09 32					10 00	10 17	10 32				11 00	
Shotton	d				08 38								09 38							10 38					
Chester	a		08 15	08 31	08 50					09 15	09 23		09 50					10 15	10 31	10 50				11 15	
	d	08 03	08 19	08 35	08 52			08 55	09 03	09 19	09 26	09 35	09 52		09 55	10 03		10 20	10 35	10 52		10 55	11 03	11 21	
Liverpool Lime Street ■10 106	a																								
Helsby	d				09 01								10 01							11 01					
Frodsham	d				09 05								10 05							11 05					
Runcorn East	d				09 11								10 11							11 11					
Warrington Bank Quay 90	a				09 18								10 18							11 18					
Earlestown ■8 90	a				09 26								10 26							11 26					
Newton-le-Willows 90	a				09 29								10 29							11 29					
Manchester Oxford Road 90	a				09 48								10 48							11 48					
Manchester Pic'dilly ■10 90 ⇌	a	09 36			09 57				10 36				10 57			11 36				11 57			12 36		
Crewe ■10	a			08 54				09 18		09 40		09 54			10 18				10 54			11 18			
Cardiff Central ■7 131	a		11 15								12 08							13 22							
Manchester Airport 84,85 ✈	a																								
Birmingham New Street ■12 65	a									11 26														13 26	
London Euston ■15 ⊖65	a			10 38								11 38							12 38						

A To Maesteg
B To Milford Haven
C To Birmingham International
D From Wrexham General
E To Blaenau Ffestiniog

Table 81

Mondays to Fridays

from 3 October

North Wales and Chester - Manchester and Crewe

		VT		AW	AW	AW	NT	AW	VT	AW	AW	AW		NT	AW	VT	AW	AW	AW	NT	AW	AW		VT	AW
								R																	
		◇1		◇					◇1	◇					◇	◇1	◇				◇	◇		◇1	◇
															A						B	C			
		🍴		🛒				🛒	🍴	🛒					🛒	🍴	🛒				🛒			🍴	🛒
Holyhead	d							10 33							11 23						12 39				
Valley	d							10x39							11x29										
Rhosneigr	d														11x34										
Ty Croes	d														11x38										
Bodorgan	d														11x42										
Llanfairpwll	d							10x56							11x52										
Bangor (Gwynedd)	a							11 03							12 00						13 05				
	d							11 05							12 02	12 24					13 07				
Llanfairfechan	d														12x09										
Penmaenmawr	d														12x13										
Conwy	d														12x19										
Llandudno	d			10 44	11 08					11 44	12 08						12 44	13 10				13 22			13 44
Deganwy	d			10x48	11x12					11x48	12x12						12x48	13x14				13x26			13x48
Llandudno Junction	a			10 52	11 18			11 21		11 52	12 18				12 23	12 40	12 52	13 20			13 23	13 32			13 52
	d			10 53				11 25		11 53					12 25	12 42	12 53				13 25				13 53
Colwyn Bay	d			10 59				11 31		11 59					12 31	12 48	12 59				13 31				13 59
Abergele & Pensarn	d			11 06						12 06							13 06								14 06
Rhyl	d			11 12				11 41		12 12					12 41	12 59	13 12				13 41				14 12
Prestatyn	d			11 18				11 47		12 18					12 47	13 05	13 18				13 47				14 18
Flint	d			11 31				12 00		12 31					13 00	13 18	13 31				14 00				14 31
Shotton	d			11 37						12 37							13 37								14 37
Chester	a			11 49				12 14		12 49					13 14	13 32	13 49				14 15				14 49
	d	11 35		11 50		11 55	12 03	12 19	12 35	12 50		12 55		13 03	13 19	13 35	13 50		13 55	14 03	14 19			14 35	14 50
Liverpool Lime Street 10 106	a																								
Helsby	d			12 00						13 00							14 00								15 00
Frodsham	d			12 04						13 04							14 04								15 04
Runcorn East	d			12 09						13 09							14 09								15 09
Warrington Bank Quay 90	a			12 18						13 18							14 18								15 18
Earlestown 8 90	a			12 26						13 26							14 26								15 26
Newton-le-Willows 90	a			12 29						13 29							14 29								15 29
Manchester Oxford Road 90	a			12 48						13 48							14 48								15 48
Manchester Pic'dilly 10 90 ⛴	a			12 57			13 36			13 57				14 36			14 57			15 36					15 57
Crewe 10	a	11 54				12 18			12 54			13 18				13 54			14 18					14 54	
Cardiff Central 7 131	a							15 21													17 15				
Manchester Airport 84,85 ✈	a																								
Birmingham New Street 12 65	a														15 26										
London Euston 15 ⊖65	a	13 38							14 38							15 38								16 38	

		AW	AW	NT	AW	VT	VT	AW		AW	NT	AW	AW	VT	AW	NT	AW	AW		AW	VT	AW	NT	AW	AW
					◇	◇1	◇1	◇				◇	◇	◇1			◇	◇		◇	◇1			◇	◇
					A													A		C					
					🛒	🍴	🍴	🛒				🛒	🛒	🍴			🛒	🛒			⊠			🛒	🛒
Holyhead	d				13 23	13 58							14 34					15 23							16 38
Valley	d				13x29													15x29							
Rhosneigr	d				13x34													15x34							
Ty Croes	d				13x38													15x38							
Bodorgan	d				13x42													15x42							
Llanfairpwll	d				13x52													15x52							
Bangor (Gwynedd)	a				14 00	14 24							15 00					16 00							17 04
	d				14 02	14 25							15 04					16 02							17 06
Llanfairfechan	d				14x09								15x11					16x09							
Penmaenmawr	d				14x13								15x15					16x13							
Conwy	d				14x19								15x21					16x19							
Llandudno	d	14 08						14 40				15 08					16 06			16 20				17 06	
Deganwy	d	14x12						14x44				15x12					16x10			16x24				17x10	
Llandudno Junction	a	14 18			14 23	14 42		14 48				15 16	15 26				16 14	16 23		16 28				17 14	17 23
	d				14 25	14 43		14 49				15 17	15 27				16 15	16 25						17 14	17 25
Colwyn Bay	d				14 31	14 50		14 55				15 23	15 33				16 21	16 34						17 20	17 31
Abergele & Pensarn	d							15 02				15 30					16 28							17 27	
Rhyl	d				14 41	15 00		15 08				15 36	15 44				16 34	16 44						17 33	17 41
Prestatyn	d				14 47			15 14				15 42	15 49				16 39	16 50						17 38	17 47
Flint	d				14 58			15 27				15 55	16 03				16 53	17 03						17 52	18 01
Shotton	d							15 33				16 01					16 59							17 58	
Chester	a				15 13	15 27		15 44				16 13	16 15				17 10	17 15						18 11	18 15
	d		14 55	15 03	15 18	15 35	15 35	15 46		15 55	16 03	16 22	16 19	16 35	16 55	17 03	17 19	17 19			17 35	17 55	18 03	18 16	18 18
Liverpool Lime Street 10 106	a																								
Helsby	d							15 55				16 31					17 28							18 25	
Frodsham	d							15 59				16 35					17 33							18 30	
Runcorn East	d							16 04				16 41					17 38							18 35	
Warrington Bank Quay 90	a							16 12				16 51					17 49							18 45	
Earlestown 8 90	a							16 26				16 59					17 57							18 57	
Newton-le-Willows 90	a							16 29				17 01					17 59							18 59	
Manchester Oxford Road 90	a							16 48				17 21					18 19							19 21	
Manchester Pic'dilly 10 90 ⛴	a			16 36				16 57			17 36	17 30				18 36	18 28						19 35	19 29	
Crewe 10	a		15 18			15 54	15 54			16 18				16 54	17 18						17 54	18 18			
Cardiff Central 7 131	a												19 21												21 20
Manchester Airport 84,85 ✈	a																								
Birmingham New Street 12 65	a				17 27													19 26							
London Euston 15 ⊖65	a					17 38	17 38							18 38							19 38				

A To Birmingham International

B To Maesteg

C To Blaenau Ffestiniog

North Wales and Chester - Manchester and Crewe

		AW	AW	AW	AW	NT	VT	AW	AW	AW	AW	NT
			◇ A 🚲				◇1 ☕	◇ 🚲	◇ B			
Holyhead	d		17 30									
Valley	d		17x36									
Rhosneigr	d		17x41									
Ty Croes	d		17x45									
Bodorgan	d		17x49									
Llanfairpwll	d		17x59									
Bangor (Gwynedd)	a		18 07									
	d		18 09									
Llanfairfechan	d		18x16									
Penmaenmawr	d		18x20									
Conwy	d		18x26									
Llandudno	d	18 08						18 44	19 03	19 08		
Deganwy	d	18x12						18x48	19x07	19x12		
Llandudno Junction	a	18 18	18 30					18 52	19 11	19 18		
	d		18 32					18 53				
Colwyn Bay	d		18 38					18 59				
Abergele & Pensarn	d							19 06				
Rhyl	d		18 48					19 12				
Prestatyn	d		18 54					19 18				
Flint	d		19 07					19 31				
Shotton	d							19 37				
Chester	a		19 24					19 49				
	d			18 49	18 55	19 03	19 35	19 50			19 55	20 03
Liverpool Lime Street 10 106	a											
Helsby	d			18 59				20 00				
Frodsham	d			19 03				20 04				
Runcorn East	d			19 08				20 09				
Warrington Bank Quay 90	a			19 18				20 18				
Earlestown 8 90	a			19 26				20 26				
Newton-le-Willows 90	a			19 29				20 29				
Manchester Oxford Road 90	a			19 48				20 48				
Manchester Pic'dilly 10 90 ⛴	a			19 52		20 35		20 52				21 35
Crewe 10	a				19 18		19 54				20 18	
Cardiff Central 7 131	a											
Manchester Airport 84,85 ✈	a			20 18				21 18				
Birmingham New Street 12 65	a											
London Euston 15 ⊖65	a						21 42					

		AW	AW	AW	AW	NT	AW	AW	VT	AW	AW
		◇ 🚲	◇				◇ C	◇ D	◇1 ☕		E
Holyhead	d	18 23					19 21	19 21			
Valley	d	18x29					19x27	19x27			
Rhosneigr	d	18x34					19x32	19x32			
Ty Croes	d	18x38					19x36	19x36			
Bodorgan	d	18x42					19x40	19x40			
Llanfairpwll	d	18x52					19x50	19x50			
Bangor (Gwynedd)	a	19 00					19 58	19 58			
	d	19 02					20 00	20 00	20 20		
Llanfairfechan	d	19x09					20x07	20x07			
Penmaenmawr	d	19x13					20x11	20x11			
Conwy	d	19x19					20x17	20x17			
Llandudno	d		19 42	20 08						20 42	
Deganwy	d		19x46	20x12						20x46	
Llandudno Junction	a	19 23	19 50	20 18			20 21	20 21	20 36	20 50	
	d	19 25	19 51				20 23	20 23	20 38	20 51	
Colwyn Bay	d	19 31	19 57				20 29	20 29	20 44	20 57	
Abergele & Pensarn	d		20 04							21 04	
Rhyl	d	19 41	20 10				20 39	20 39	20 55	21 11	
Prestatyn	d	19 47	20 16				20 45	20 45	21 01	21 16	
Flint	d	20 00	20 29				20 58	20 58	21 14	21 30	
Shotton	d		20 35							21 36	
Chester	a	20 15	20 47				21 15	21 15	21 28	21 47	
	d	20 17	20 50		20 55	21 03	21 21	21 21	21 35		21 49
Liverpool Lime Street 10 106	a										
Helsby	d		20 59								21 58
Frodsham	d		21 03								22 02
Runcorn East	d		21 09								22 08
Warrington Bank Quay 90	a		21 18								22 15
Earlestown 8 90	a		21 26								22 26
Newton-le-Willows 90	a		21 29								22 29
Manchester Oxford Road 90	a		21 48								22 50
Manchester Pic'dilly 10 90 ⛴	a		21 57			22 35					22 58
Crewe 10	a	20 41			21 18				21 54		
Cardiff Central 7 131	a										
Manchester Airport 84,85 ✈	a										
Birmingham New Street 12 65	a						23 27	23 29	22 50		
London Euston 15 ⊖65	a										

		AW	AW	NT	AW
		F	◇		
Holyhead	d		20 37		
Valley	d				
Rhosneigr	d				
Ty Croes	d				
Bodorgan	d				
Llanfairpwll	d				
Bangor (Gwynedd)	a		21 04		
	d		21 06		
Llanfairfechan	d		21x13		
Penmaenmawr	d		21x17		
Conwy	d		21x23		
Llandudno	d				21 45
Deganwy	d				21x49
Llandudno Junction	a		21 27		21 53
	d		21 29		21 55
Colwyn Bay	d		21 35		22 01
Abergele & Pensarn	d		21 42		22 09
Rhyl	d		21 48		22 16
Prestatyn	d		21 53		22 22
Flint	d		22 07		22 37
Shotton	d		22 13		22 44
Chester	a		22 23		22 55
	d	21 52	22 26	22 44	23 01
Liverpool Lime Street 10 106	a				
Helsby	d	22 01			
Frodsham	d	22 05			
Runcorn East	d	22 11			
Warrington Bank Quay 90	a	22 18			
Earlestown 8 90	a	22 26			
Newton-le-Willows 90	a	22 29			
Manchester Oxford Road 90	a	22 50			
Manchester Pic'dilly 10 90 ⛴	a	22 58		00 18	
Crewe 10	a		22 50		23 26
Cardiff Central 7 131	a				
Manchester Airport 84,85 ✈	a				
Birmingham New Street 12 65	a				
London Euston 15 ⊖65	a				

A To Shrewsbury
B To Blaenau Ffestiniog
C MWFO
D TThO
E from 3 October until 21 October
F from 24 October

Saturdays

until 18 June

North Wales and Chester - Manchester and Crewe

		NT	AW	AW	AW	AW	AW	AW	NT	AW		AW	AW	NT	AW	VT	AW	AW	AW	AW		NT	AW	VT	AW
										◇		◇				◇1	◇	◇					◇	◇1	◇
															A		B								
Holyhead	d									04 25							05 22						06 35	06 52	
Valley	d									04x31							05x28						06x41		
Rhosneigr	d																05x33								
Ty Croes	d																05x37								
Bodorgan	d																05x41								
Llanfairpwll	d									04x48							05x51						06x58		
Bangor (Gwynedd)	a									04 55							05 59						07 05	07 18	
	d									04 57							06 01						07 07	07 20	
Llanfairfechan	d																06x08								
Penmaenmawr	d																06x12								
Conwy	d																06x18								
Llandudno	d																	06 34	07 08						07 45
Deganwy	d																	06x38	07x12						07x49
Llandudno Junction	a									05 13							06 22	06 42	07 18				07 23	07 36	07 53
	d					04 38				05 15			05 37				06 24	06 44					07 25	07 38	07 54
Colwyn Bay	d					04 44				05 21			05 43				06 30	06 50					07 31	07 44	08 00
Abergele & Pensarn	d					04 51							05 50					06 57							08 07
Rhyl	d					04 57				05 31			05 56				06 40	07 03					07 41	07 55	08 13
Prestatyn	d					05 02				05 37			06 01				06 46	07 08					07 47	08 01	08 19
Flint	d					05 16				05 50			06 15				06 59	07 21					08 00	08 15	08 32
Shotton	d					05 22							06 21					07 27							08 38
Chester	a					05 33				06 04			06 33				07 15	07 38					08 14	08 28	08 50
	d	22p48	03 36	04 22	04 55	05 37	05 38	05 51	06 05	06 12		06 13	06 35	07 03	07 12	07 17	07 21	07 40		07 55		08 07	08 19	08 35	08 52
Liverpool Lime Street 10 106	a																								
Helsby	d						05 47					06 22			07 21			07 49							09 01
Frodsham	d						05 51					06 26			07 25			07 53							09 05
Runcorn East	d						05 56					06 32			07 31			07 59							09 11
Warrington Bank Quay 90	a						06 05					06 39			07 38			08 06							09 18
Earlestown 8 90	a						06 12					06 47			07 46			08 15							09 26
Newton-le-Willows 90	a						06 15					06 50			07 49			08 18							09 29
Manchester Oxford Road 90	a						06 35					07 09			08 09			08 41							09 48
Manchester Pic'dilly 10 90	a	00 18	04 45				06 45		07 31			07 18		08 32	08 18			08 50				09 36			09 57
Crewe 10	a			04 44	05 20	05 58		06 15					06 59			07 36				08 18				08 54	
Cardiff Central 7 131	a									09 22													11 15		
Manchester Airport 84,85	a		05 17																						
Birmingham New Street 12 65	a			05 58													09 26								
London Euston 15 ⊖65	a															09 30								10 37	

		AW	AW	NT	AW	VT		AW	AW	AW	NT	AW	VT	AW	AW	AW		NT	AW	AW	VT	AW	AW	AW	NT
					◇	◇1		◇				◇	◇1	◇					◇	◇	◇1	◇			
					B														B	C					
Holyhead	d				07 15	07 55						08 20	08 55						09 23						
Valley	d				07x21							08x26							09x29						
Rhosneigr	d				07x26							08x32							09x34						
Ty Croes	d				07x30							08x35							09x38						
Bodorgan	d				07x34							08x40							09x42						
Llanfairpwll	d				07x44							08x49							09x52						
Bangor (Gwynedd)	a				07 52	08 21						08 57	09 21						10 00						
	d				08 02	08 22						09 02	09 22						10 02						
Llanfairfechan	d				08x09							09x09							10x09						
Penmaenmawr	d				08x13							09x13							10x13						
Conwy	d				08x19							09x19							10x19						
Llandudno	d	08 08						08 45	09 08					09 45	10 10					10 22		10 44	11 08		
Deganwy	d	08x12						08x49	09x12					09x49	10x14					10x26		10x48	11x12		
Llandudno Junction	a	08 18			08 23	08 39		08 53	09 18			09 23	09 39	09 53	10 20				10 23	10 32		10 52	11 18		
	d				08 25	08 40		08 54				09 25	09 40	09 54					10 25			10 53			
Colwyn Bay	d				08 31	08 47		09 00				09 31	09 47	10 00					10 31			10 59			
Abergele & Pensarn	d							09 07						10 07								11 06			
Rhyl	d				08 41	08 58		09 13				09 41	09 58	10 13					10 41			11 12			
Prestatyn	d				08 47	09 04		09 19				09 47	10 03	10 19					10 47			11 18			
Flint	d				09 00	09 17		09 32				10 00		10 32					11 00			11 31			
Shotton	d							09 38						10 38								11 37			
Chester	a				09 15	09 31		09 50				10 14	10 28	10 50					11 15			11 49			
	d		08 55	09 07	09 19	09 35		09 52		09 55	10 07	10 19	10 35	10 52		10 55		11 07	11 21		11 35	11 50		11 55	12 07
Liverpool Lime Street 10 106	a																								
Helsby	d							10 01						11 01								12 00			
Frodsham	d							10 05						11 05								12 04			
Runcorn East	d							10 11						11 11								12 09			
Warrington Bank Quay 90	a							10 18						11 18								12 18			
Earlestown 8 90	a							10 26						11 26								12 26			
Newton-le-Willows 90	a							10 29						11 29								12 29			
Manchester Oxford Road 90	a							10 48						11 48								12 48			
Manchester Pic'dilly 10 90	a			10 36				10 57			11 36			11 57				12 36				12 57			13 36
Crewe 10	a		09 18			09 54				10 18			10 54			11 18					11 54			12 18	
Cardiff Central 7 131	a											13 15													
Manchester Airport 84,85	a																								
Birmingham New Street 12 65	a				11 26														13 25						
London Euston 15 ⊖65	a					11 38							12 38								13 38				

A From Shrewsbury

B To Birmingham International

C To Blaenau Ffestiniog

Table 81

Saturdays until 18 June

North Wales and Chester - Manchester and Crewe

		AW		VT	AW	AW	AW	NT	AW	VT	VT	AW		AW	AW	AW	NT	AW	AW	VT	AW	AW		AW	AW
		■		◇■1	◇				◇	◇■1	◇■1	◇						◇	◇	◇■1	◇				
									A									B	C						
		🛒		🍴	🛒				🛒	🍴	🍴	🛒				🚌		🛒		🍴	🛒				🚌
Holyhead	d	10 33							11 23	11 55								12 38							
Valley	d	10x39							11x29																
Rhosneigr	d								11x34																
Ty Croes	d								11x38																
Bodorgan	d								11x42																
Llanfairpwll	d	10x56							11x52																
Bangor (Gwynedd)	a	11 03							12 00	12 20								13 05							
	d	11 05							12 02	12 21								13 07							
Llanfairfechan	d								12x09																
Penmaenmawr	d								12x13																
Conwy	d								12x19																
Llandudno	d				11 44	12 08						12 44		13 10					13 22		13 44	14 08			
Deganwy	d				11x48	12x12						12x48		13x14					13x26		13x48	14x12			
Llandudno Junction	a	11 21			11 52	12 18			12 23	12 38		12 52		13 20				13 23	13 32		13 52	14 18			
	d	11 25			11 53				12 25	12 39		12 53						13 25			13 53				
Colwyn Bay	d	11 31			11 59				12 31	12 46		12 59						13 31			13 59				
Abergele & Pensarn	d				12 06							13 06									14 06				
Rhyl	d	11 41			12 12				12 41	12 57		13 12						13 41			14 12				
Prestatyn	d	11 47			12 18				12 47			13 18						13 47			14 18				
Flint	d	12 00			12 31				13 00			13 31						14 00			14 31				
Shotton	d				12 37							13 37									14 37				
Chester	a	12 14			12 49				13 14	13 24		13 49						14 14			14 49				
	d	12 19		12 35	12 50		12 55	13 07	13 19	13 35	13 35	13 50			13 55	14 00	14 07	14 19		14 35	14 50			14 55	15 00
Liverpool Lime Street ■10 106	a																								
Helsby	d				13 00											14 20									15 20
Frodsham	d				13 04											14 25									15 25
Runcorn East	d				13 09											14 40									15 40
Warrington Bank Quay 90	a				13 18											15 00									16 00
Earlestown ■ 90	a				13 26											15 25									16 25
Newton-le-Willows 90	a				13 29											15 35									16 35
Manchester Oxford Road 90	a				13 48											16 05									17 05
Manchester Pic'dilly ■10 90 ⛴	a				13 57			14 36				14 57				16 10	15 36				15 57				17 10
Crewe ■10	a			12 54			13 18			13 54	13 54				14 18					14 54				15 18	
Cardiff Central ■7 131	a	15 26																17 15							
Manchester Airport 84,85 ✈	a																								
Birmingham New Street ■12 65	a								15 26																
London Euston ■15 ⊖65	a			14 38						15 38	15 38									16 38					

		NT	AW	VT	AW	AW	AW	AW		NT	AW	VT	AW	AW	AW	AW	NT	AW		AW	VT	AW	AW	AW	AW
			◇	◇■1	◇						◇	◇■1	◇					◇		◇	◇■1	◇			
			A															A		C					
			🛒	🍴	🛒			🚌			🛒	🍴	🛒			🚌		🛒			🍴	🛒			🚌
Holyhead	d		13 23								14 32	14 38						15 23							
Valley	d		13x29															15x29							
Rhosneigr	d		13x34															15x34							
Ty Croes	d		13x38															15x38							
Bodorgan	d		13x42															15x42							
Llanfairpwll	d		13x52															15x52							
Bangor (Gwynedd)	a		14 00								14 58	15 06						16 00							
	d		14 02								15 00	15 07						16 02							
Llanfairfechan	d		14x09								15x07							16x09							
Penmaenmawr	d		14x13								15x11							16x13							
Conwy	d		14x19								15x17							16x19							
Llandudno	d				14 42	15 08							15 44	16 10						16 20		16 44	17 08		
Deganwy	d				14x46	15x12							15x48	16x14						16x24		16x48	17x12		
Llandudno Junction	a		14 23		14 50	15 18					15 21	15 25	15 52	16 20				16 23		16 30		16 52	17 18		
	d		14 25		14 51						15 23	15 27	15 53					16 25				16 53			
Colwyn Bay	d		14 31		14 57						15 29	15 35	15 59					16 31				16 59			
Abergele & Pensarn	d				15 04								16 06									17 06			
Rhyl	d		14 41		15 10						15 39	15 48	16 12					16 41				17 12			
Prestatyn	d		14 47		15 16						15 45		16 18					16 47				17 18			
Flint	d		15 00		15 29						15 58		16 31					17 00				17 31			
Shotton	d				15 35								16 37									17 37			
Chester	a		15 17		15 46						16 12	16 18	16 49					17 15				17 49			
	d	15 07	15 20	15 35	15 48		15 55	16 00		16 07	16 19	16 24	16 50		16 55	17 00	17 07	17 19			17 35	17 50		17 55	18 00
Liverpool Lime Street ■10 106	a																								
Helsby	d							16 20								17 20									18 20
Frodsham	d							16 25								17 25									18 25
Runcorn East	d							16 40								17 40									18 40
Warrington Bank Quay 90	a							17 00								18 00									19 00
Earlestown ■ 90	a							17 25								18 25									19 25
Newton-le-Willows 90	a							17 35								18 35									19 35
Manchester Oxford Road 90	a							18 05								19 05									20 05
Manchester Pic'dilly ■10 90 ⛴	a	16 36			16 55			18 10		17 36			17 56			19 10	18 36					18 57			20 10
Crewe ■10	a			15 54			16 18					16 47			17 18						17 54			18 18	
Cardiff Central ■7 131	a										19 15														
Manchester Airport 84,85 ✈	a																								
Birmingham New Street ■12 65	a		17 27															19 26							
London Euston ■15 ⊖65	a			17 38								18 38													

A To Birmingham International **B** To Maesteg **C** To Blaenau Ffestiniog

Table 81

Saturdays

until 18 June

North Wales and Chester - Manchester and Crewe

		NT	AW	AW	AW	AW	AW	AW	NT	AW	AW	AW	AW	AW	NT	AW	VT	AW	AW	AW	AW	AW
			◇	◇		◇				◇	◇					◇	◇	◇				◇
						A					B											
								🚌						🚌							🚌	
			🚲	🚲		🚲				🚲						🚲	🛒					
Holyhead	d		16 37			17 30										18 23						19 21
Valley	d					17x36										18x29						19x27
Rhosneigr	d					17x41										18x34						19x32
Ty Croes	d					17x45										18x38						19x36
Bodorgan	d					17x49										18x42						19x40
Llanfairpwll	d					17x59										18x52						19x50
Bangor (Gwynedd)	a		17 04			18 07										19 00						19 58
	d		17 06			18 09										19 02						20 00
Llanfairfechan	d					18x16										19x09						20x07
Penmaenmawr	d					18x20										19x13						20x11
Conwy	d					18x26										19x19						20x17
Llandudno	d			17 44	18 08					18 44	19 03	19 08						19 42	20 08			
Deganwy	d			17x48	18x12					18x48	19x07	19x12						19x46	20x12			
Llandudno Junction	a		17 22	17 52	18 18	18 30				18 52	19 11	19 18				19 23		19 50	20 18			20 21
	d		17 24	17 53		18 32				18 53						19 25		19 51				20 23
Colwyn Bay	d		17 30	17 59		18 38				18 59						19 31		19 57				20 29
Abergele & Pensarn	d			18 06						19 06								20 04				
Rhyl	d		17 40	18 12		18 48				19 12						19 41		20 10				20 39
Prestatyn	d		17 46	18 18		18 54				19 18						19 47		20 16				20 45
Flint	d		17 59	18 31		19 07				19 31						20 00		20 29				20 58
Shotton	d			18 37						19 37								20 35				
Chester	a		18 15	18 49		19 20				19 49						20 15		20 47				21 15
	d	18 07	18 20	18 50			18 55	19 00	19 07	19 50			19 55	20 00	20 07	20 17	20 35	20 50		20 55	21 00	21 19
Liverpool Lime Street 10 106	a																					
Helsby	d							19 20						20 20							21 20	
Frodsham	d							19 25						20 25							21 25	
Runcorn East	d							19 40						20 40							21 40	
Warrington Bank Quay 90	a							20 00						21 00							22 00	
Earlestown 8 90	a							20 25						21 25							22 25	
Newton-le-Willows 90	a							20 35						21 35							22 35	
Manchester Oxford Road 90	a							21 05						22 05							23 05	
Manchester Pic'dilly 10 90 ⛴	a	19 35		19 51				21 10	20 35	20 57				22 10	21 35			21 57			23 10	
Crewe 10	a						19 18						20 18			20 41	20 54			21 18		
Cardiff Central 7 131	a		21 15																			
Manchester Airport 84,85 ✈	a			20 13																		
Birmingham New Street 12 65	a																					23 29
London Euston 15 ⊖65	a																					

		AW	NT	AW	AW	AW	NT	AW	AW	AW
						◇				
					🚌					🚌
Holyhead	d					20 37				
Valley	d									
Rhosneigr	d									
Ty Croes	d									
Bodorgan	d									
Llanfairpwll	d									
Bangor (Gwynedd)	a					21 05				
	d					21 06				
Llanfairfechan	d					21x13				
Penmaenmawr	d					21x17				
Conwy	d					21x23				
Llandudno	d	20 42						21 45		
Deganwy	d	20x46						21x49		
Llandudno Junction	a	20 50				21 28		21 53		
	d	20 51				21 29		21 55		
Colwyn Bay	d	20 57				21 35		22 01		
Abergele & Pensarn	d	21 04				21 42		22 09		
Rhyl	d	21 10				21 48		22 16		
Prestatyn	d	21 16				21 54		22 22		
Flint	d	21 29				22 07		22 37		
Shotton	d	21 35				22 13		22 44		
Chester	a	21 47				22 23		22 55		
	d		21 33	21 52	22 00	22 26	22 49	23 01	23 22	23 22
Liverpool Lime Street 10 106	a									
Helsby	d				22 20					23 42
Frodsham	d				22 25					23 47
Runcorn East	d				22 40					00 02
Warrington Bank Quay 90	a				23 00					00 22
Earlestown 8 90	a				23 25					00 47
Newton-le-Willows 90	a				23 35					00 57
Manchester Oxford Road 90	a				00 05					01 27
Manchester Pic'dilly 10 90 ⛴	a		23 00	23 08	00 10		00 15		00 31	01 32
Crewe 10	a					22 50		23 26		
Cardiff Central 7 131	a									
Manchester Airport 84,85 ✈	a									
Birmingham New Street 12 65	a									
London Euston 15 ⊖65	a									

A To Shrewsbury

B To Blaenau Ffestiniog

Table 81

Saturdays

25 June to 10 September

North Wales and Chester - Manchester and Crewe

		NT	AW	AW	AW	AW	AW	AW	NT	AW		AW	AW	NT	AW	VT	AW	AW	AW	AW		NT	AW	VT	AW
										◇		◇				◇1	◇	◇					◇	◇1	◇
															A		B								
										🛒					🛒	☕	🛒	🛒					🛒	☕	🛒
Holyhead	d									04 25							05 22						06 35	06 52	
Valley	d									04x31							05x28						06x41		
Rhosneigr	d																05x33								
Ty Croes	d																05x37								
Bodorgan	d																05x41								
Llanfairpwll	d									04x48							05x51						06x58		
Bangor (Gwynedd)	a									04 55							05 59						07 05	07 18	
	d									04 57							06 01						07 07	07 20	
Llanfairfechan	d																06x08								
Penmaenmawr	d																06x12								
Conwy	d																06x18								
Llandudno	d																	06 34	07 08						07 45
Deganwy	d																	06x38	07x12						07x49
Llandudno Junction	a									05 13							06 22	06 42	07 18				07 23	07 36	07 53
	d					04 38				05 15			05 37				06 24	06 44					07 25	07 38	07 54
Colwyn Bay	d					04 44				05 21			05 43				06 30	06 50					07 31	07 44	08 00
Abergele & Pensarn	d					04 51							05 50					06 57							08 07
Rhyl	d					04 57				05 31			05 56				06 40	07 03					07 41	07 55	08 13
Prestatyn	d					05 02				05 37			06 01				06 46	07 08					07 47	08 01	08 19
Flint	d					05 16				05 50			06 15				06 59	07 21					08 00	08 15	08 32
Shotton	d					05 22							06 21					07 27							08 38
Chester	a					05 33				06 04			06 33				07 15	07 38					08 14	08 28	08 50
	d	22p48	03 36	04 22	04 55	05 37	05 38	05 51	06 05	06 12		06 13	06 35	07 03	07 12	07 17	07 21	07 40		07 55		08 07	08 19	08 35	08 52
Liverpool Lime Street 10 106	a																								
Helsby	d						05 47					06 22			07 21			07 49							09 01
Frodsham	d						05 51					06 26			07 25			07 53							09 05
Runcorn East	d						05 56					06 32			07 31			07 59							09 11
Warrington Bank Quay 90	a						06 05					06 39			07 38			08 06							09 18
Earlestown 8 90	a						06 12					06 47			07 46			08 15							09 26
Newton-le-Willows 90	a						06 15					06 50			07 49			08 18							09 29
Manchester Oxford Road 90	a						06 35					07 09			08 09			08 41							09 48
Manchester Pic'dilly 10 90 🚊	a	00 18	04 45				06 45		07 31			07 18		08 32	08 18			08 50				09 36			09 57
Crewe 10	a			04 44	05 20	05 58		06 15					06 59			07 36				08 18				08 54	
Cardiff Central 7 131	a									09 22													11 15		
Manchester Airport 84,85 ✈	a		05 17																						
Birmingham New Street 12 65	a			05 58													09 26								
London Euston 15 ⊖65	a															09 30								10 37	

		AW	AW	NT	AW	VT		AW	AW	AW	NT	AW	VT	AW	AW	AW		NT	AW	AW	VT	AW	AW	AW	NT
					◇	◇1		◇				◇	◇1	◇					◇	◇	◇1	◇			
					B														B	C					
					🛒	☕		🛒				🛒	☕	🛒					🛒		☕	🛒			
Holyhead	d				07 15	07 55						08 20	08 55						09 23						
Valley	d				07x21							08x26							09x29						
Rhosneigr	d				07x26							08x32							09x34						
Ty Croes	d				07x30							08x35							09x38						
Bodorgan	d				07x34							08x40							09x42						
Llanfairpwll	d				07x44							08x49							09x52						
Bangor (Gwynedd)	a				07 52	08 21						08 57	09 21						10 00						
	d				08 02	08 22						09 02	09 22						10 02						
Llanfairfechan	d				08x09							09x09							10x09						
Penmaenmawr	d				08x13							09x13							10x13						
Conwy	d				08x19							09x19							10x19						
Llandudno	d	08 08						08 45	09 08					09 45	10 10					10 22		10 44	11 08		
Deganwy	d	08x12						08x49	09x12					09x49	10x14					10x26		10x48	11x12		
Llandudno Junction	a	08 18			08 23	08 39		08 53	09 18			09 23	09 39	09 53	10 20				10 23	10 32		10 52	11 18		
	d				08 25	08 40		08 54				09 25	09 40	09 54					10 25			10 53			
Colwyn Bay	d				08 31	08 47		09 00				09 31	09 47	10 00					10 31			10 59			
Abergele & Pensarn	d							09 07						10 07								11 06			
Rhyl	d				08 41	08 58		09 13				09 41	09 58	10 13					10 41			11 12			
Prestatyn	d				08 47	09 04		09 19				09 47	10 03	10 19					10 47			11 18			
Flint	d				09 00	09 17		09 32				10 00		10 32					11 00			11 31			
Shotton	d							09 38						10 38								11 37			
Chester	a				09 15	09 31		09 50				10 14	10 28	10 50					11 15			11 49			
	d		08 55	09 07	09 19	09 35		09 52		09 55	10 07	10 19	10 35	10 52		10 55		11 07	11 21		11 35	11 50		11 55	12 07
Liverpool Lime Street 10 106	a																								
Helsby	d							10 01						11 01								12 00			
Frodsham	d							10 05						11 05								12 04			
Runcorn East	d							10 11						11 11								12 09			
Warrington Bank Quay 90	a							10 18						11 18								12 18			
Earlestown 8 90	a							10 26						11 26								12 26			
Newton-le-Willows 90	a							10 29						11 29								12 29			
Manchester Oxford Road 90	a							10 48						11 48								12 48			
Manchester Pic'dilly 10 90 🚊	a			10 36				10 57			11 36			11 57				12 36				12 57			13 36
Crewe 10	a		09 18			09 54				10 18			10 54			11 18					11 54			12 18	
Cardiff Central 7 131	a											13 15													
Manchester Airport 84,85 ✈	a																								
Birmingham New Street 12 65	a				11 26														13 25						
London Euston 15 ⊖65	a					11 38							12 38								13 38				

A From Shrewsbury

B To Birmingham International

C To Blaenau Ffestiniog

Table 81

Saturdays

25 June to 10 September

North Wales and Chester - Manchester and Crewe

		AW		VT	AW	AW	AW	NT	AW	VT	VT	AW		AW	AW	NT	AW	AW	VT	AW	AW	AW		NT	AW
		[R]																							
				◇[1]	◇				◇	◇[1]	◇[1]	◇					◇	◇	◇[1]	◇					◇
									A								B	C							A
		[trolley]		[buffet]	[trolley]				[trolley]	[buffet]	[buffet]	[trolley]					[trolley]		[buffet]	[trolley]					[trolley]
Holyhead	d	10 33							11 23	11 55							12 38								13 23
Valley	d	10x39							11x29																13x29
Rhosneigr	d								11x34																13x34
Ty Croes	d								11x38																13x38
Bodorgan	d								11x42																13x42
Llanfairpwll	d	10x56							11x52																13x52
Bangor (Gwynedd)	a	11 03							12 00	12 20							13 05								14 00
	d	11 05							12 02	12 21							13 07								14 02
Llanfairfechan	d								12x09																14x09
Penmaenmawr	d								12x13																14x13
Conwy	d								12x19																14x19
Llandudno	d				11 44	12 08						12 44		13 10				13 22		13 44	14 08				
Deganwy	d				11x48	12x12						12x48		13x14				13x26		13x48	14x12				
Llandudno Junction	a	11 21			11 52	12 18			12 23	12 38		12 52		13 20			13 23	13 32		13 52	14 18				14 23
	d	11 25			11 53				12 25	12 39		12 53					13 25			13 53					14 25
Colwyn Bay	d	11 31			11 59				12 31	12 46		12 59					13 31			13 59					14 31
Abergele & Pensarn	d				12 06							13 06								14 06					
Rhyl	d	11 41			12 12				12 41	12 57		13 12					13 41			14 12					14 41
Prestatyn	d	11 47			12 18				12 47			13 18					13 47			14 18					14 47
Flint	d	12 00			12 31				13 00			13 31					14 00			14 31					15 00
Shotton	d				12 37							13 37								14 37					
Chester	a	12 14			12 49				13 14	13 24		13 49					14 14			14 49					15 17
	d	12 19		12 35	12 50		12 55	13 07	13 19	13 35	13 35	13 50			13 55	14 07	14 19		14 35	14 50		14 55		15 07	15 20
Liverpool Lime Street [10] 106	a																								
Helsby	d				13 00							14 00								15 00					
Frodsham	d				13 04							14 04								15 04					
Runcorn East	d				13 09							14 09								15 09					
Warrington Bank Quay 90	a				13 18							14 18								15 18					
Earlestown [8] 90	a				13 26							14 26								15 26					
Newton-le-Willows 90	a				13 29							14 29								15 29					
Manchester Oxford Road 90	a				13 48							14 48								15 48					
Manchester Pic'dilly [10] 90 ⛴	a				13 57			14 36				14 57				15 36				15 57				16 36	
Crewe [10]	a			12 54			13 18			13 54	13 54				14 18				14 54			15 18			
Cardiff Central [7] 131	a	15 26															17 15								
Manchester Airport 84,85 ✈	a																								
Birmingham New Street [12] 65	a								15 26																17 27
London Euston [15] ⊖65	a			14 38						15 38	15 38								16 38						

		VT	AW	AW	AW	NT	AW	VT		AW	AW	AW	NT	AW	AW	VT	AW	AW		AW	NT	AW	AW	AW	AW
		◇[1]	◇				◇	◇[1]		◇				◇	◇	◇[1]	◇					◇	◇		
														A	C										
		[buffet]	[trolley]				[trolley]	[buffet]		[trolley]				[trolley]		[buffet]	[trolley]					[trolley]	[trolley]		
Holyhead	d						14 32	14 38						15 23								16 37			
Valley	d													15x29											
Rhosneigr	d													15x34											
Ty Croes	d													15x38											
Bodorgan	d													15x42											
Llanfairpwll	d													15x52											
Bangor (Gwynedd)	a						14 58	15 06						16 00								17 04			
	d						15 00	15 07						16 02								17 06			
Llanfairfechan	d						15x07							16x09											
Penmaenmawr	d						15x11							16x13											
Conwy	d						15x17							16x19											
Llandudno	d		14 42	15 08						15 44	16 10				16 20		16 44	17 08					17 44	18 08	
Deganwy	d		14x46	15x12						15x48	16x14				16x24		16x48	17x12					17x48	18x12	
Llandudno Junction	a		14 50	15 18			15 21	15 25		15 52	16 20			16 23	16 30		16 52	17 18				17 22	17 52	18 18	
	d		14 51				15 23	15 27		15 53				16 25			16 53					17 24	17 53		
Colwyn Bay	d		14 57				15 29	15 35		15 59				16 31			16 59					17 30	17 59		
Abergele & Pensarn	d		15 04							16 06							17 06						18 06		
Rhyl	d		15 10				15 39	15 48		16 12				16 41			17 12					17 40	18 12		
Prestatyn	d		15 16				15 45			16 18				16 47			17 18					17 46	18 18		
Flint	d		15 29				15 58			16 31				17 00			17 31					17 59	18 31		
Shotton	d		15 35							16 37							17 37						18 37		
Chester	a		15 46				16 12	16 18		16 49				17 15			17 49					18 15	18 49		
	d	15 35	15 48		15 55	16 07	16 19	16 24		16 50		16 55	17 07	17 19		17 35	17 50			17 55	18 07	18 20	18 50		18 55
Liverpool Lime Street [10] 106	a																								
Helsby	d		15 57							17 00							18 00						19 00		
Frodsham	d		16 02							17 04							18 04						19 04		
Runcorn East	d		16 07							17 09							18 09						19 09		
Warrington Bank Quay 90	a		16 16							17 18							18 18						19 18		
Earlestown [8] 90	a		16 26							17 26							18 26						19 26		
Newton-le-Willows 90	a		16 29							17 29							18 29						19 29		
Manchester Oxford Road 90	a		16 48							17 48							18 48						19 48		
Manchester Pic'dilly [10] 90 ⛴	a		16 57			17 36				17 57			18 36				18 57				19 35		19 52		
Crewe [10]	a	15 54			16 18			16 47				17 18				17 54				18 18					19 18
Cardiff Central [7] 131	a						19 15															21 15			
Manchester Airport 84,85 ✈	a																						20 18		
Birmingham New Street [12] 65	a													19 26											
London Euston [15] ⊖65	a	17 38						18 38																	

A To Birmingham International

B To Maesteg

C To Blaenau Ffestiniog

Table 81

Saturdays

25 June to 10 September

North Wales and Chester - Manchester and Crewe

		NT	AW	19§35		AW	AW	AW	AW	NT	AW	VT	AW	AW		AW	AW	AW	AW	NT	AW	AW	NT	AW	AW
			◇			◇	◇				◇	◇	◇			◇		◇				◇			
			A				B									C		D							
			trolley			trolley					trolley	buffet													
Holyhead	d		17 30								18 23					19§21		19§21				20 37			
Valley	d		17x36								18x29					19x27		19x27							
Rhosneigr	d		17x41	20§00							18x34					19x32		19x32							
Ty Croes	d		17x45								18x38					19x36		19x36							
Bodorgan	d		17x49								18x42					19x40		19x40							
Llanfairpwll	d		17x59								18x52					19x50		19x50							
Bangor (Gwynedd)	a		18 07								19 00					19§58		19§58				21 05			
	d		18 09								19 02					20§00		20§00				21 06			
Llanfairfechan	d		18x16								19x09					20x07		20x07				21x13			
Penmaenmawr	d		18x20								19x13					20x11		20x11				21x17			
Conwy	d		18x26								19x19					20x17		20x17				21x23			
Llandudno	d					18 44	19 03	19 08					19 42	20 08					20 42					21 45	
Deganwy	d					18x48	19x07	19x12					19x46	20x12					20x46					21x49	
Llandudno Junction	a		18 30			18 52	19 11	19 18			19 23		19 50	20 18		20§21		20§21	20 50			21 28		21 53	
	d		18 32			18 53					19 25		19 51			20§23		20§23	20 51			21 29		21 55	
Colwyn Bay	d		18 38			18 59					19 31		19 57			20§29		20§29	20 57			21 35		22 01	
Abergele & Pensarn	d					19 06							20 04						21 04			21 42		22 09	
Rhyl	d		18 48			19 12					19 41		20 10			20§39		20§39	21 10			21 48		22 16	
Prestatyn	d		18 54			19 18					19 47		20 16			20§45		20§45	21 16			21 54		22 22	
Flint	d		19 07			19 31					20 00		20 29			20§58		20§58	21 29			22 07		22 37	
Shotton	d					19 37							20 35						21 35			22 13		22 44	
Chester	a		19 20			19 49					20 15		20 47			21§15		21§15	21 47			22 23		22 55	
	d	19 07				19 50			19 55	20 07	20 17	20 35	20 50				20 55	21§19		21 33	21 52	22 26	22 49	23 01	23 22
Liverpool Lime Street 10 106	a																								
Helsby	d					20 00							20 59								22 01				23 31
Frodsham	d					20 04							21 03								22 05				23 35
Runcorn East	d					20 09							21 09								22 11				23 41
Warrington Bank Quay 90	a					20 18							21 16								22 19				23 50
Earlestown 8 90	a					20 26							21 26								22 26				23 58
Newton-le-Willows 90	a					20 29							21 29								22 30				00 01
Manchester Oxford Road 90	a					20 48							21 48								22 50				
Manchester Pic'dilly 10 90 ⇌	a	20 35				20 57				21 35			21 57							23 00	22 58		00 15		00 26
Crewe 10	a								20 18		20 41	20 54					21 18					22 50		23 26	
Cardiff Central 7 131	a																								
Manchester Airport 84,85 ✈	a																								
Birmingham New Street 12 65	a																	23§29							
London Euston 15 ⊖65	a																								

A To Shrewsbury
B To Blaenau Ffestiniog
C from 25 June until 30 July. To Shrewsbury
D from 6 August until 10 September

Table 81

Saturdays

17 September to 1 October

North Wales and Chester - Manchester and Crewe

		NT	AW	AW	AW	AW	AW	AW	NT	AW		AW	AW	NT	AW	VT	AW	AW	AW	AW		NT	AW	VT	AW
										◇		◇				◇1	◇	◇					◇	◇1	◇
															A		B								
										🛒					🛒	🍴	🛒	🛒					🛒	🍴	🛒
Holyhead	d									04 25							05 22						06 35	06 52	
Valley	d									04x31							05x28						06x41		
Rhosneigr	d																05x33								
Ty Croes	d																05x37								
Bodorgan	d																05x41								
Llanfairpwll	d									04x48							05x51						06x58		
Bangor (Gwynedd)	a									04 55							05 59						07 05	07 18	
	d									04 57							06 01						07 07	07 20	
Llanfairfechan	d																06x08								
Penmaenmawr	d																06x12								
Conwy	d																06x18								
Llandudno	d																	06 34	07 08						07 45
Deganwy	d																	06x38	07x12						07x49
Llandudno Junction	a									05 13							06 22	06 42	07 18				07 23	07 36	07 53
	d					04 38				05 15			05 37				06 24	06 44					07 25	07 38	07 54
Colwyn Bay	d					04 44				05 21			05 43				06 30	06 50					07 31	07 44	08 00
Abergele & Pensarn	d					04 51							05 50					06 57							08 07
Rhyl	d					04 57				05 31			05 56				06 40	07 03					07 41	07 55	08 13
Prestatyn	d					05 02				05 37			06 01				06 46	07 08					07 47	08 01	08 19
Flint	d					05 16				05 50			06 15				06 59	07 21					08 00	08 15	08 32
Shotton	d					05 22							06 21					07 27							08 38
Chester	a					05 33				06 04			06 33				07 15	07 38					08 14	08 28	08 50
	d	22p48	03 36	04 22	04 55	05 37	05 38	05 51	06 05	06 12		06 13	06 35	07 03	07 12	07 17	07 21	07 40		07 55		08 07	08 19	08 35	08 52
Liverpool Lime Street 10 106	a																								
Helsby	d						05 47					06 22			07 21			07 49							09 01
Frodsham	d						05 51					06 26			07 25			07 53							09 05
Runcorn East	d						05 56					06 32			07 31			07 59							09 11
Warrington Bank Quay 90	a						06 05					06 39			07 38			08 06							09 18
Earlestown 8 90	a						06 12					06 47			07 46			08 15							09 26
Newton-le-Willows 90	a						06 15					06 50			07 49			08 18							09 29
Manchester Oxford Road 90	a						06 35					07 09			08 09			08 41							09 48
Manchester Pic'dilly 10 90 ⛴	a	00 18	04 45				06 45		07 31			07 18		08 32	08 18			08 50				09 36			09 57
Crewe 10	a			04 44	05 20	05 58		06 15					06 59			07 36				08 18				08 54	
Cardiff Central 7 131	a									09 22													11 15		
Manchester Airport 84,85 ✈	a		05 17																						
Birmingham New Street 12 65	a			05 58													09 26								
London Euston 15 ⊖65	a															09 30								10 37	

		AW	AW	NT	AW	VT		AW	AW	AW	NT	AW	VT	AW	AW	AW		NT	AW	AW	VT	AW	AW	AW	NT
					◇	◇1		◇				◇	◇1	◇					◇	◇	◇1	◇			
					B														B	C					
					🛒	🍴		🛒				🛒	🍴	🛒					🛒		🍴	🛒			
Holyhead	d				07 15	07 55						08 20	08 55						09 23						
Valley	d				07x21							08x26							09x29						
Rhosneigr	d				07x26							08x32							09x34						
Ty Croes	d				07x30							08x35							09x38						
Bodorgan	d				07x34							08x40							09x42						
Llanfairpwll	d				07x44							08x49							09x52						
Bangor (Gwynedd)	a				07 52	08 21						08 57	09 21						10 00						
	d				08 02	08 22						09 02	09 22						10 02						
Llanfairfechan	d				08x09							09x09							10x09						
Penmaenmawr	d				08x13							09x13							10x13						
Conwy	d				08x19							09x19							10x19						
Llandudno	d	08 08						08 45	09 08					09 45	10 10					10 22		10 44	11 08		
Deganwy	d	08x12						08x49	09x12					09x49	10x14					10x26		10x48	11x12		
Llandudno Junction	a	08 18			08 23	08 39		08 53	09 18			09 23	09 39	09 53	10 20				10 23	10 32		10 52	11 18		
	d				08 25	08 40		08 54				09 25	09 40	09 54					10 25			10 53			
Colwyn Bay	d				08 31	08 47		09 00				09 31	09 47	10 00					10 31			10 59			
Abergele & Pensarn	d							09 07						10 07								11 06			
Rhyl	d				08 41	08 58		09 13				09 41	09 58	10 13					10 41			11 12			
Prestatyn	d				08 47	09 04		09 19				09 47	10 03	10 19					10 47			11 18			
Flint	d				09 00	09 17		09 32				10 00		10 32					11 00			11 31			
Shotton	d							09 38						10 38								11 37			
Chester	a				09 15	09 31		09 50				10 14	10 28	10 50					11 15			11 49			
	d		08 55	09 07	09 19	09 35		09 52		09 55	10 07	10 19	10 35	10 52		10 55		11 07	11 21		11 35	11 50		11 55	12 07
Liverpool Lime Street 10 106	a																								
Helsby	d							10 01						11 01								12 00			
Frodsham	d							10 05						11 05								12 04			
Runcorn East	d							10 11						11 11								12 09			
Warrington Bank Quay 90	a							10 18						11 18								12 18			
Earlestown 8 90	a							10 26						11 26								12 26			
Newton-le-Willows 90	a							10 29						11 29								12 29			
Manchester Oxford Road 90	a							10 48						11 48								12 48			
Manchester Pic'dilly 10 90 ⛴	a			10 36				10 57			11 36			11 57				12 36				12 57			13 36
Crewe 10	a		09 18			09 54				10 18			10 54			11 18					11 54			12 18	
Cardiff Central 7 131	a											13 15													
Manchester Airport 84,85 ✈	a																								
Birmingham New Street 12 65	a				11 26														13 25						
London Euston 15 ⊖65	a					11 38							12 38								13 38				

A From Shrewsbury

B To Birmingham International

C To Blaenau Ffestiniog

Table 81

Saturdays

17 September to 1 October

North Wales and Chester - Manchester and Crewe

		AW		VT	AW	AW	AW	NT	AW	VT	AW	AW		AW	NT	AW	AW	VT	AW	AW	AW	NT		AW	VT
		R		◇■1	◇				◇ A	◇■1	◇					◇ B	◇ C	◇■1	◇					◇ A	◇■1
		🛒		🍽	🛒				🛒	🍽	🛒					🛒		🍽	🛒					🛒	🍽
Holyhead	d	10 33							11 23							12 38								13 23	
Valley	d	10x39							11x29															13x29	
Rhosneigr	d								11x34															13x34	
Ty Croes	d								11x38															13x38	
Bodorgan	d								11x42															13x42	
Llanfairpwll	d	10x56							11x52															13x52	
Bangor (Gwynedd)	a	11 03							12 00							13 05								14 00	
	d	11 05							12 02							13 07								14 02	
Llanfairfechan	d								12x09															14x09	
Penmaenmawr	d								12x13															14x13	
Conwy	d								12x19															14x19	
Llandudno	d				11 44	12 08					12 44	13 10					13 22		13 44	14 08					
Deganwy	d				11x48	12x12					12x48	13x14					13x26		13x48	14x12					
Llandudno Junction	a	11 21			11 52	12 18			12 23		12 52	13 20				13 23	13 32		13 52	14 18				14 23	
	d	11 25			11 53				12 25		12 53					13 25			13 53					14 25	
Colwyn Bay	d	11 31			11 59				12 31		12 59					13 31			13 59					14 31	
Abergele & Pensarn	d				12 06						13 06								14 06						
Rhyl	d	11 41			12 12				12 41		13 12					13 41			14 12					14 41	
Prestatyn	d	11 47			12 18				12 47		13 18					13 47			14 18					14 47	
Flint	d	12 00			12 31				13 00		13 31					14 00			14 31					15 00	
Shotton	d				12 37						13 37								14 37						
Chester	a	12 14			12 49				13 14		13 49					14 14			14 49					15 17	
	d	12 19		12 35	12 50		12 55	13 07	13 19	13 35	13 50			13 55	14 07	14 19		14 35	14 50		14 55	15 07		15 20	15 35
Liverpool Lime Street ■10 106	a																								
Helsby	d				13 00						14 00								15 00						
Frodsham	d				13 04						14 04								15 04						
Runcorn East	d				13 09						14 09								15 09						
Warrington Bank Quay 90	a				13 18						14 18								15 18						
Earlestown ■8 90	a				13 26						14 26								15 26						
Newton-le-Willows 90	a				13 29						14 29								15 29						
Manchester Oxford Road 90	a				13 48						14 48								15 48						
Manchester Pic'dilly ■10 90 ⛴	a				13 57			14 36			14 57				15 36				15 57			16 36			
Crewe ■10	a			12 54			13 18			13 54				14 18				14 54			15 18				15 54
Cardiff Central ■7 131	a	15 26														17 15									
Manchester Airport 84,85 ✈	a																								
Birmingham New Street ■12 65	a								15 26															17 27	
London Euston ■15 ⊖65	a			14 38						15 38								16 38							17 38

		AW	AW	AW	NT	AW	VT	AW		AW	AW	NT	AW	AW	VT	AW	AW	AW		NT	AW	AW	AW	AW	AW
		◇				◇	◇■1	◇					◇ A	◇ C	◇■1	◇					◇	◇		◇ D	
		🛒				🛒	🍽	🛒					🛒		🍽	🛒					🛒	🛒		🛒	
Holyhead	d					14 32	14 38						15 23								16 37			17 30	
Valley	d												15x29											17x36	
Rhosneigr	d												15x34											17x41	
Ty Croes	d												15x38											17x45	
Bodorgan	d												15x42											17x49	
Llanfairpwll	d												15x52											17x59	
Bangor (Gwynedd)	a					14 58	15 06						16 00								17 04			18 07	
	d					15 00	15 07						16 02								17 06			18 09	
Llanfairfechan	d					15x07							16x09											18x16	
Penmaenmawr	d					15x11							16x13											18x20	
Conwy	d					15x17							16x19											18x26	
Llandudno	d	14 42	15 08					15 44		16 10				16 20		16 44	17 08					17 44	18 08		
Deganwy	d	14x46	15x12					15x48		16x14				16x24		16x48	17x12					17x48	18x12		
Llandudno Junction	a	14 50	15 18			15 21	15 25	15 52		16 20			16 23	16 30		16 52	17 18				17 22	17 52	18 18	18 30	
	d	14 51				15 23	15 27	15 53					16 25			16 53					17 24	17 53		18 32	
Colwyn Bay	d	14 57				15 29	15 35	15 59					16 31			16 59					17 30	17 59		18 38	
Abergele & Pensarn	d	15 04						16 06								17 06						18 06			
Rhyl	d	15 10				15 39	15 48	16 12					16 41			17 12					17 40	18 12		18 48	
Prestatyn	d	15 16				15 45		16 18					16 47			17 18					17 46	18 18		18 54	
Flint	d	15 29				15 58		16 31					17 00			17 31					17 59	18 31		19 07	
Shotton	d	15 35						16 37								17 37						18 37			
Chester	a	15 46				16 12	16 18	16 49					17 15			17 49					18 15	18 49		19 24	
	d	15 48		15 55	16 07	16 19	16 24	16 50			16 55	17 07	17 19		17 35	17 50		17 55		18 07	18 20	18 50			18 55
Liverpool Lime Street ■10 106	a																								
Helsby	d	15 57						17 00								18 00						19 00			
Frodsham	d	16 02						17 04								18 04						19 04			
Runcorn East	d	16 07						17 09								18 09						19 09			
Warrington Bank Quay 90	a	16 16						17 18								18 18						19 18			
Earlestown ■8 90	a	16 26						17 26								18 26						19 26			
Newton-le-Willows 90	a	16 29						17 29								18 29						19 29			
Manchester Oxford Road 90	a	16 48						17 48								18 48						19 48			
Manchester Pic'dilly ■10 90 ⛴	a	16 57			17 36			17 57				18 36				18 57				19 35		19 52			
Crewe ■10	a			16 18			16 47				17 18				17 54			18 18							19 18
Cardiff Central ■7 131	a					19 15															21 15				
Manchester Airport 84,85 ✈	a																					20 18			
Birmingham New Street ■12 65	a												19 26												
London Euston ■15 ⊖65	a						18 38																		

A To Birmingham International
B To Maesteg
C To Blaenau Ffestiniog
D To Shrewsbury

Table 81

Saturdays

17 September to 1 October

North Wales and Chester - Manchester and Crewe

	NT	AW	AW		AW	AW	NT	AW	VT	AW	AW	AW	AW		AW	NT	AW	AW	NT	AW	AW			
		◇	◇					◇	◇	◇			◇					◇						
			A																					
		(trolley)						(trolley)	(buffet)															
Holyhead d								18 23					19 21					20 37						
Valley d								18x29					19x27											
Rhosneigr d								18x34					19x32											
Ty Croes d								18x38					19x36											
Bodorgan d								18x42					19x40											
Llanfairpwll d								18x52					19x50											
Bangor (Gwynedd) a								19 00					19 58					21 05						
d								19 02					20 00					21 06						
Llanfairfechan d								19x09					20x07					21x13						
Penmaenmawr d								19x13					20x11					21x17						
Conwy d								19x19					20x17					21x23						
Llandudno d		18 44	19 03		19 08					19 42	20 08				20 42					21 45				
Deganwy d		18x48	19x07		19x12					19x46	20x12				20x46					21x49				
Llandudno Junction a		18 52	19 11		19 18			19 23		19 50	20 18		20 21		20 50			21 28		21 53				
d		18 53						19 25		19 51			20 23		20 51			21 29		21 55				
Colwyn Bay d		18 59						19 31		19 57			20 29		20 57			21 35		22 01				
Abergele & Pensarn d		19 06								20 04					21 04			21 42		22 09				
Rhyl d		19 12						19 41		20 10			20 39		21 10			21 48		22 16				
Prestatyn d		19 18						19 47		20 16			20 45		21 16			21 54		22 22				
Flint d		19 31						20 00		20 29			20 58		21 29			22 07		22 37				
Shotton d		19 37								20 35					21 35			22 13		22 44				
Chester a		19 49						20 15		20 47			21 15		21 47			22 23		22 55				
d	19 07	19 50				19 55	20 07	20 17	20 35	20 50		20 55	21 19			21 33	21 52	22 26	22 49	23 01	23 22			
Liverpool Lime Street **10** 106 a																								
Helsby d		20 00								20 59							22 01							
Frodsham d		20 04								21 03							22 05							
Runcorn East d		20 09								21 09							22 11							
Warrington Bank Quay 90 a		20 18								21 16							22 19							
Earlestown **8** 90 a		20 26								21 26							22 26							
Newton-le-Willows 90 a		20 29								21 29							22 30							
Manchester Oxford Road 90 a		20 48								21 48							22 50							
Manchester Pic'dilly **10** 90 (ship) a	20 35	20 57					21 35			21 57						23 00	22 58		00 15		00 31			
Crewe **10** a						20 18		20 41	20 54			21 18						22 50		23 26				
Cardiff Central **7** 131 a																								
Manchester Airport 84,85 ✈ a																								
Birmingham New Street **12** 65 a													23 29											
London Euston **15** ⊖65 a																								

Saturdays

from 8 October

	NT	AW	AW	AW	AW	AW	AW	NT	AW		AW	AW	NT	AW	VT	AW	AW	AW	AW		NT	AW	VT	AW
									◇		◇				◇**1**	◇	◇					◇	◇**1**	◇
														B		C								
									(trolley)					(trolley)	(buffet)	(trolley)	(trolley)					(trolley)	(buffet)	(trolley)
Holyhead d									04 25							05 22						06 35	06 52	
Valley d									04x31							05x28						06x41		
Rhosneigr d																05x33								
Ty Croes d																05x37								
Bodorgan d																05x41								
Llanfairpwll d									04x48							05x51						06x58		
Bangor (Gwynedd) a									04 55							05 59						07 05	07 18	
d									04 57							06 01						07 07	07 20	
Llanfairfechan d																06x08								
Penmaenmawr d																06x12								
Conwy d																06x18								
Llandudno d																	06 34	07 08						07 45
Deganwy d																	06x38	07x12						07x49
Llandudno Junction a									05 13							06 22	06 42	07 18				07 23	07 36	07 53
d					04 38				05 15			05 37				06 24	06 44					07 25	07 38	07 54
Colwyn Bay d					04 44				05 21			05 43				06 30	06 50					07 31	07 44	08 00
Abergele & Pensarn d					04 51							05 50					06 57							08 07
Rhyl d					04 57				05 31			05 56				06 40	07 03					07 41	07 55	08 13
Prestatyn d					05 02				05 37			06 01				06 46	07 08					07 47	08 01	08 19
Flint d					05 16				05 50			06 15				06 59	07 21					08 00	08 15	08 32
Shotton d					05 22							06 21					07 27							08 38
Chester a					05 33				06 04			06 33				07 15	07 38					08 14	08 28	08 50
d	22p44	03 36	04 22	04 55	05 37	05 38	05 51	06 01	06 12		06 13	06 35	06 59	07 12	07 17	07 21	07 40		07 55		08 03	08 19	08 35	08 52
Liverpool Lime Street **10** 106 a																								
Helsby d						05 47					06 22			07 21			07 49							09 01
Frodsham d						05 51					06 26			07 25			07 53							09 05
Runcorn East d						05 56					06 32			07 31			07 59							09 11
Warrington Bank Quay 90 a						06 05					06 39			07 38			08 06							09 18
Earlestown **8** 90 a						06 12					06 47			07 46			08 15							09 26
Newton-le-Willows 90 a						06 15					06 50			07 49			08 18							09 29
Manchester Oxford Road 90 a						06 35					07 09			08 09			08 41							09 48
Manchester Pic'dilly **10** 90 (ship) a	00 18	04 45				06 45		07 31			07 18		08 32	08 18			08 50				09 36			09 57
Crewe **10** a			04 44	05 20	05 58		06 15					06 59			07 36				08 18				08 54	
Cardiff Central **7** 131 a									09 22													11 15		
Manchester Airport 84,85 ✈ a		05 17																						
Birmingham New Street **12** 65 a			05 58													09 26								
London Euston **15** ⊖65 a															09 30								10 37	

A To Blaenau Ffestiniog

B From Shrewsbury

C To Birmingham International

Table 81

Saturdays
from 8 October

North Wales and Chester - Manchester and Crewe

		AW	AW	NT	AW	VT		AW	AW	AW	NT	AW	VT	AW	AW	AW		NT	AW	AW	VT	AW	AW	AW	NT
					◇ A 🍴	◇■ ☕		◇ 🍴				◇ 🍴	◇■ ☕	◇ 🍴					◇ A 🍴	◇ B	◇■ ☕	◇ 🍴			
Holyhead	d				07 15	07 55						08 20	08 55						09 23						
Valley	d				07x21							08x26							09x29						
Rhosneigr	d				07x26							08x32							09x34						
Ty Croes	d				07x30							08x35							09x38						
Bodorgan	d				07x34							08x40							09x42						
Llanfairpwll	d				07x44							08x49							09x52						
Bangor (Gwynedd)	a				07 52	08 21						08 57	09 21						10 00						
	d				08 02	08 22						09 02	09 22						10 02						
Llanfairfechan	d				08x09							09x09							10x09						
Penmaenmawr	d				08x13							09x13							10x13						
Conwy	d				08x19							09x19							10x19						
Llandudno	d	08 08						08 45	09 08					09 45	10 10					10 22		10 44	11 08		
Deganwy	d	08x12						08x49	09x12					09x49	10x14					10x26		10x48	11x12		
Llandudno Junction	a	08 18			08 23	08 39		08 53	09 18			09 23	09 39	09 53	10 20				10 23	10 32		10 52	11 18		
	d				08 25	08 40		08 54				09 25	09 40	09 54					10 25			10 53			
Colwyn Bay	d				08 31	08 47		09 00				09 31	09 47	10 00					10 31			10 59			
Abergele & Pensarn	d							09 07						10 07								11 06			
Rhyl	d				08 41	08 58		09 13				09 41	09 58	10 13					10 41			11 12			
Prestatyn	d				08 47	09 04		09 19				09 47	10 03	10 19					10 47			11 18			
Flint	d				09 00	09 17		09 32				10 00		10 32					11 00			11 31			
Shotton	d							09 38						10 38								11 37			
Chester	a				09 15	09 31		09 50				10 14	10 28	10 50					11 15			11 49			
	d		08 55	09 03	09 19	09 35		09 52		09 55	10 03	10 19	10 35	10 52		10 55		11 03	11 21		11 35	11 50		11 55	12 03
Liverpool Lime Street ■ 106	a																								
Helsby	d							10 01						11 01								12 00			
Frodsham	d							10 05						11 05								12 04			
Runcorn East	d							10 11						11 11								12 09			
Warrington Bank Quay 90	a							10 18						11 18								12 18			
Earlestown ■ 90	a							10 26						11 26								12 26			
Newton-le-Willows 90	a							10 29						11 29								12 29			
Manchester Oxford Road 90	a							10 48						11 48								12 48			
Manchester Pic'dilly ■ 90 ⇌	a			10 36				10 57			11 36			11 57				12 36				12 57			13 36
Crewe ■	a		09 18			09 54				10 18			10 54			11 18					11 54			12 18	
Cardiff Central ■ 131	a											13 15													
Manchester Airport 84,85 ✈	a																								
Birmingham New Street ■ 65	a				11 26														13 25						
London Euston ■ ⊖65	a					11 38							12 38								13 38				

		AW		VT	AW	AW	AW	NT	AW	VT	AW	AW		AW	NT	AW	AW	VT	AW	AW	AW	NT		AW	VT
		■ 🍴		◇■ ☕	◇ 🍴				◇ A 🍴	◇■ ☕	◇ 🍴					◇ C 🍴	◇ B	◇■ ☕	◇ 🍴					◇ A 🍴	◇■ ☕
Holyhead	d	10 33							11 23							12 38								13 23	
Valley	d	10x39							11x29															13x29	
Rhosneigr	d								11x34															13x34	
Ty Croes	d								11x38															13x38	
Bodorgan	d								11x42															13x42	
Llanfairpwll	d	10x56							11x52															13x52	
Bangor (Gwynedd)	a	11 03							12 00							13 05								14 00	
	d	11 05							12 02							13 07								14 02	
Llanfairfechan	d								12x09															14x09	
Penmaenmawr	d								12x13															14x13	
Conwy	d								12x19															14x19	
Llandudno	d				11 44	12 08					12 44	13 10					13 22		13 44	14 08					
Deganwy	d				11x48	12x12					12x48	13x14					13x26		13x48	14x12					
Llandudno Junction	a	11 21			11 52	12 18			12 23		12 52	13 20				13 23	13 32		13 52	14 18				14 23	
	d	11 25			11 53				12 25		12 53					13 25			13 53					14 25	
Colwyn Bay	d	11 31			11 59				12 31		12 59					13 31			13 59					14 31	
Abergele & Pensarn	d				12 06						13 06								14 06						
Rhyl	d	11 41			12 12				12 41		13 12					13 41			14 12					14 41	
Prestatyn	d	11 47			12 18				12 47		13 18					13 47			14 18					14 47	
Flint	d	12 00			12 31				13 00		13 31					14 00			14 31					15 00	
Shotton	d				12 37						13 37								14 37						
Chester	a	12 14			12 49				13 14		13 49					14 14			14 49					15 17	
	d	12 19		12 35	12 50		12 55	13 03	13 19	13 35	13 50			13 55	14 03	14 19		14 35	14 50		14 55	15 03		15 20	15 35
Liverpool Lime Street ■ 106	a																								
Helsby	d				13 00						14 00								15 00						
Frodsham	d				13 04						14 04								15 04						
Runcorn East	d				13 09						14 09								15 09						
Warrington Bank Quay 90	a				13 18						14 18								15 18						
Earlestown ■ 90	a				13 26						14 26								15 26						
Newton-le-Willows 90	a				13 29						14 29								15 29						
Manchester Oxford Road 90	a				13 48						14 48								15 48						
Manchester Pic'dilly ■ 90 ⇌	a				13 57			14 36			14 57				15 36				15 57			16 36			
Crewe ■	a			12 54			13 18			13 54				14 18				14 54			15 18				15 54
Cardiff Central ■ 131	a	15 26														17 15									
Manchester Airport 84,85 ✈	a																								
Birmingham New Street ■ 65	a								15 26															17 27	
London Euston ■ ⊖65	a			14 38						15 38								16 38							17 38

A To Birmingham International **B** To Blaenau Ffestiniog **C** To Maesteg

Table 81

Saturdays
from 8 October

North Wales and Chester - Manchester and Crewe

		AW	AW	AW	NT	AW	VT	AW		AW	AW	NT	AW	AW	VT	AW	AW	AW		NT	AW	AW	AW	AW	AW
		◇				◇	◇1	◇					◇	◇	◇1	◇					◇	◇		◇	
													A	B										C	
		🚲				🚲	🛒	🚲					🚲		🛒	🚲					🚲	🚲		🚲	
Holyhead	d					14 32	14 38						15 23								16 37			17 30	
Valley	d												15x29											17x36	
Rhosneigr	d												15x34											17x41	
Ty Croes	d												15x38											17x45	
Bodorgan	d												15x42											17x49	
Llanfairpwll	d												15x52											17x59	
Bangor (Gwynedd)	a					14 58	15 06						16 00								17 04			18 07	
	d					15 00	15 07						16 02								17 06			18 09	
Llanfairfechan	d					15x07							16x09											18x16	
Penmaenmawr	d					15x11							16x13											18x20	
Conwy	d					15x17							16x19											18x26	
Llandudno	d	14 42	15 08					15 44		16 10				16 20		16 44	17 08					17 44	18 08		
Deganwy	d	14x46	15x12					15x48		16x14				16x24		16x48	17x12					17x48	18x12		
Llandudno Junction	a	14 50	15 18			15 21	15 25	15 52		16 20			16 23	16 30		16 52	17 18				17 22	17 52	18 18	18 30	
	d	14 51				15 23	15 27	15 53					16 25			16 53					17 24	17 53		18 32	
Colwyn Bay	d	14 57				15 29	15 35	15 59					16 31			16 59					17 30	17 59		18 38	
Abergele & Pensarn	d	15 04						16 06								17 06						18 06			
Rhyl	d	15 10				15 39	15 48	16 12					16 41			17 12					17 40	18 12		18 48	
Prestatyn	d	15 16				15 45		16 18					16 47			17 18					17 46	18 18		18 54	
Flint	d	15 29				15 58		16 31					17 00			17 31					17 59	18 31		19 07	
Shotton	d	15 35						16 37								17 37						18 37			
Chester	a	15 46				16 12	16 18	16 49					17 15			17 49					18 15	18 49		19 24	
	d	15 48		15 55	16 03	16 19	16 24	16 50			16 55	17 03	17 19		17 35	17 50		17 55		18 03	18 20	18 50			18 55
Liverpool Lime Street 10 106	a																								
Helsby	d	15 57						17 00								18 00						19 00			
Frodsham	d	16 02						17 04								18 04						19 04			
Runcorn East	d	16 07						17 09								18 09						19 09			
Warrington Bank Quay 90	a	16 16						17 18								18 18						19 18			
Earlestown 8 90	a	16 26						17 26								18 26						19 26			
Newton-le-Willows 90	a	16 29						17 29								18 29						19 29			
Manchester Oxford Road 90	a	16 48						17 48								18 48						19 48			
Manchester Pic'dilly 10 90 ⛴	a	16 57			17 36			17 57				18 36				18 57				19 35		19 52			
Crewe 10	a			16 18			16 47				17 18				17 54			18 18							19 18
Cardiff Central 7 131	a					19 15															21 15				
Manchester Airport 84,85 ✈	a																					20 18			
Birmingham New Street 12 65	a												19 26												
London Euston 15 ⊖65	a						18 38																		

		NT	AW	AW		AW	AW	NT	AW	VT	AW	AW	AW	AW		AW	NT	AW	AW	NT	AW	AW	AW		
			◇	◇					◇	◇	◇			◇					◇						
				B																		D	E		
			🚲						🚲	🛒															
Holyhead	d								18 23					19 21					20 37						
Valley	d								18x29					19x27											
Rhosneigr	d								18x34					19x32											
Ty Croes	d								18x38					19x36											
Bodorgan	d								18x42					19x40											
Llanfairpwll	d								18x52					19x50											
Bangor (Gwynedd)	a								19 00					19 58					21 05						
	d								19 02					20 00					21 06						
Llanfairfechan	d								19x09					20x07					21x13						
Penmaenmawr	d								19x13					20x11					21x17						
Conwy	d								19x19					20x17					21x23						
Llandudno	d		18 44	19 03		19 08					19 42	20 08				20 42					21 45				
Deganwy	d		18x48	19x07		19x12					19x46	20x12				20x46					21x49				
Llandudno Junction	a		18 52	19 11		19 18			19 23		19 50	20 18		20 21		20 50			21 28		21 53				
	d		18 53						19 25		19 51			20 23		20 51			21 29		21 55				
Colwyn Bay	d		18 59						19 31		19 57			20 29		20 57			21 35		22 01				
Abergele & Pensarn	d		19 06								20 04					21 04			21 42		22 09				
Rhyl	d		19 12						19 41		20 10			20 39		21 10			21 48		22 16				
Prestatyn	d		19 18						19 47		20 16			20 45		21 16			21 54		22 22				
Flint	d		19 31						20 00		20 29			20 58		21 29			22 07		22 37				
Shotton	d		19 37								20 35					21 35			22 13		22 44				
Chester	a		19 49						20 15		20 47			21 15		21 47			22 23		22 55				
	d	19 03	19 50				19 55	20 03	20 17	20 35	20 50		20 55	21 19			21 29	21 52	22 26	22 45	23 01	23 22	23 22		
Liverpool Lime Street 10 106	a																								
Helsby	d		20 00								20 59							22 01				23 31			
Frodsham	d		20 04								21 03							22 05				23 35			
Runcorn East	d		20 09								21 09							22 11				23 41			
Warrington Bank Quay 90	a		20 18								21 16							22 19				23 50			
Earlestown 8 90	a		20 26								21 26							22 26				23 58			
Newton-le-Willows 90	a		20 29								21 29							22 30				00 01			
Manchester Oxford Road 90	a		20 48								21 48							22 50							
Manchester Pic'dilly 10 90 ⛴	a	20 35	20 57					21 35			21 57						23 00	22 58		00 15		00 26	00 31		
Crewe 10	a						20 18		20 41	20 54			21 18						22 50		23 26				
Cardiff Central 7 131	a																								
Manchester Airport 84,85 ✈	a																								
Birmingham New Street 12 65	a													23 29											
London Euston 15 ⊖65	a																								

A To Birmingham International
B To Blaenau Ffestiniog
C To Shrewsbury
D from 29 October
E 8 October, 15 October, 22 October

Table 81

Sundays
until 19 June

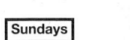

North Wales and Chester - Manchester and Crewe

	AW A 🚌	NT A	AW A	AW A 🚌	AW	AW	AW 🚌	AW ◇	NT B		AW ◇ C	AW	AW ◇	AW 🚌	AW	AW 🛒	AW ◇	AW ◇ D	AW 🚌		AW	AW	NT B	VT ◇1 ☕
Holyhead d								07 16					07 50				08 45							
Valley d													07x56											
Rhosneigr d													08x02											
Ty Croes d													08x05											
Bodorgan d													08x10											
Llanfairpwll d													08x19											
Bangor (Gwynedd) a								07 42					08 27				09 12							
d								07 43					08 28				09 13							
Llanfairfechan d													08x35											
Penmaenmawr d													08x39											
Conwy d													08x45											
Llandudno d																		10 22				11 07		
Deganwy d																		10x26				11x11		
Llandudno Junction a								07 59					08 50				09 29	10 30				11 17		
d								08 00					08 51				09 35							
Colwyn Bay d								08 07					08 57				09 41							
Abergele & Pensarn d								08 14									09 48							
Rhyl d								08 20					09 08				09 54							
Prestatyn d								08 25									09 59							
Flint d								08 39									10 13							
Shotton d								08 45					09 28				10 19							
Chester a								08 56					09 39				10 30							
d	22p00	22p49	23p22	23p22	07 56	08 27	08 41	08 57	08 58		09 22	09 27	09 42	09 49	09 57	10 36	10 39		10 40		10 57		11 07	11 28
Liverpool Lime Street 10 106 a																								
Helsby d	22p20			23p42			09 01							10 09					11 00					
Frodsham d	22p25			23p47			09 06							10 14					11 05					
Runcorn East d	22p40			00 02			09 21							10 29					11 20					
Warrington Bank Quay 90 a	23p00			00 22			09 41							10 49					11 40					
Earlestown 8 90 a	23p25			00 47			10 06							11 14					12 05					
Newton-le-Willows 90 a	23p35			00 57			10 16							11 24					12 15					
Manchester Oxford Road 90 a	00 05			01 27			10 46							11 54					12 45					
Manchester Pic'dilly 10 90 ⛴ a	00 10	00 15	00 31	01 32			10 51		10 23				10 51	11 59		11 44			12 50				12 32	
Crewe 10 a					08 22	08 52		09 22				09 52			10 22		11 01				11 22			11 47
Cardiff Central 7 131 a																								
Manchester Airport 84,85 ✈ a																								
Birmingham New Street 12 65 a											11 14													
London Euston 15 ⊖65 a																								13 44

	AW ◇ C 🛒	AW 🛒	AW 🚌	AW	AW ◇		AW	VT ◇1 ☕	AW	AW	AW 🛒	AW 🚌	AW	NT B	VT ◇1 ☕		AW	AW ◇ C 🛒	AW 🛒	AW 🚌	AW	VT ◇1 ☕	AW ◇ D	AW
Holyhead d					10 20			10 55							11 50							12 50		
Valley d					10x26																			
Rhosneigr d					10x31																			
Ty Croes d					10x35																			
Bodorgan d					10x39																			
Llanfairpwll d					10x49																			
Bangor (Gwynedd) a					10 57			11 21							12 16							13 16		
d					10 59			11 22							12 17							13 18		
Llanfairfechan d					11x06																			
Penmaenmawr d					11x10																			
Conwy d					11x16																			
Llandudno d									11 40	12 18							13 19						13 30	13 50
Deganwy d									11x44	12x22							13x23						13x34	13x54
Llandudno Junction a					11 20			11 39	11 50	12 28					12 34		13 29					13 34	13 38	14 00
d					11 22			11 40							12 35							13 36		
Colwyn Bay d					11 28			11 47							12 42							13 42		
Abergele & Pensarn d					11 35																			
Rhyl d					11 41			11 58							12 53							13 53		
Prestatyn d					11 46			12 03							12 59							13 59		
Flint d					12 00			12 17														14 13		
Shotton d					12 06																			
Chester a					12 18			12 30							13 24							14 26		
d	11 31	11 36	11 36	11 57	12 21		12 24	12 33			12 36	12 36	12 57	13 07	13 30			13 31	13 36	13 36	13 57	14 33		
Liverpool Lime Street 10 106 a																								
Helsby d			11 56									12 56								13 56				
Frodsham d			12 01									13 01								14 01				
Runcorn East d			12 16									13 16								14 16				
Warrington Bank Quay 90 a			12 36									13 36								14 36				
Earlestown 8 90 a			13 01									14 01								15 01				
Newton-le-Willows 90 a			13 11									14 11								15 11				
Manchester Oxford Road 90 a			13 41									14 41								15 41				
Manchester Pic'dilly 10 90 ⛴ a		12 48	13 46								13 43	14 46		14 33					14 44	15 46				
Crewe 10 a				12 22			12 45	12 52					13 18		13 50						14 18	14 52		
Cardiff Central 7 131 a					15 31																			
Manchester Airport 84,85 ✈ a																								
Birmingham New Street 12 65 a	13 24																	15 25						
London Euston 15 ⊖65 a								14 43							15 45							16 44		

A not 22 May
B To Southport
C To Birmingham International
D To Blaenau Ffestiniog

Table 81

Sundays
until 19 June

North Wales and Chester - Manchester and Crewe

		AW		AW	AW	NT	AW	VT	AW	AW	AW	AW		AW	AW	AW	AW	NT	AW	VT	AW	AW		AW	AW
							◇	◇■						◇					◇	◇■	◇				■
						A	B											A	B						
				🛒			🛒	🍴		🛒				🛒						🍴	🛒				🛒
Holyhead	d							13 55						14 30							15 40				16 25
Valley	d													14x36											16x31
Rhosneigr	d													14x42											16x36
Ty Croes	d													14x45											16x40
Bodorgan	d													14x50											16x44
Llanfairpwll	d													14x59											16x54
Bangor (Gwynedd)	a							14 21						15 07							16 06				17 02
	d							14 22						15 08							16 08				17 04
Llanfairfechan	d																				16x15				
Penmaenmawr	d																				16x19				
Conwy	d																				16x25				
Llandudno	d	14 20							15 11						15 45	16 16						16 52			
Deganwy	d	14x24							15x15						15x49	16x20						16x56			
Llandudno Junction	a	14 30						14 39	15 21					15 25	15 55	16 26					16 29	17 02			17 20
	d							14 40						15 26							16 35				17 25
Colwyn Bay	d							14 46						15 32							16 41				17 31
Abergele & Pensarn	d													15 39							16 48				17 38
Rhyl	d							14 57						15 45							16 54				17 44
Prestatyn	d							15 03						15 51							16 59				17 49
Flint	d													16 04							17 13				18 03
Shotton	d													16 10							17 19				18 11
Chester	a							15 31						16 21							17 31				18 21
	d			14 36	14 57	15 07	15 31	15 33		15 36	15 57	16 27		16 36			16 57	17 07	17 31	17 35	17 36			17 59	18 24
Liverpool Lime Street ■ 106	a																								
Helsby	d			14 45						15 45				16 45							17 45				
Frodsham	d			14 49						15 49				16 49							17 49				
Runcorn East	d			14 54						15 54				16 54							17 54				
Warrington Bank Quay 90	a			15 03						16 03				17 03							18 03				
Earlestown ■ 90	a			15 10						16 10				17 10							18 10				
Newton-le-Willows 90	a			15 13						16 13				17 13							18 13				
Manchester Oxford Road 90	a			15 32						16 32				17 32							18 32				
Manchester Pic'dilly ■ 90 ⛴	a			15 41		16 33				16 41				17 41				18 33			18 41				
Crewe ■	a				15 18			15 52			16 21	16 48					17 20			17 53				18 18	
Cardiff Central ■ 131	a																								21 36
Manchester Airport 84,85 ✈	a																								
Birmingham New Street ■ 65	a						17 35												19 27						
London Euston ■ ⊖65	a							17 44												19 43					

		AW	AW	VT	AW	AW	NT	AW		AW	AW	VT	AW	AW	AW	AW	AW	VT		AW	NT	AW	AW	AW	AW
				◇■				◇			◇	◇			◇	◇		◇							
							A				B				B	C					D				
				🍴				🛒				🍴			🛒	🛒		🍴							
Holyhead	d							17 30							18 25	19 15									
Valley	d														18x31	19x21									
Rhosneigr	d														18x36	19x26									
Ty Croes	d														18x40	19x30									
Bodorgan	d														18x44	19x34									
Llanfairpwll	d														18x54	19x44									
Bangor (Gwynedd)	a							17 57							19 02	19 52									
	d							17 59							19 04	19 54									
Llanfairfechan	d							18x06								20x01									
Penmaenmawr	d							18x10								20u05									
Conwy	d							18x16								20x11									
Llandudno	d	17 20	18 05							18 55															
Deganwy	d	17x24	18x09							18x59															
Llandudno Junction	a	17 30	18 15					18 20		19 05					19 20	20 15									
	d							18 24							19 24	20 21									
Colwyn Bay	d							18 30							19 30	20 27									
Abergele & Pensarn	d							18 37							19 37	20 34									
Rhyl	d							18 43							19 43	20 40									
Prestatyn	d							18 48							19 48	20 46									
Flint	d							19 02							20 02	21 00									
Shotton	d							19 10							20 10	21 06									
Chester	a							19 21							20 19	21 21									
	d			18 35	18 36	18 57	19 07	19 22			19 26	19 35	19 36	19 57	20 27		20 36	20 37		20 57	21 07	21 27	21 36	21 57	22 09
Liverpool Lime Street ■ 106	a																								
Helsby	d				18 45								19 45				20 45						21 45		22 18
Frodsham	d				18 49								19 49				20 49						21 49		22 22
Runcorn East	d				18 54								19 54				20 54						21 54		22 27
Warrington Bank Quay 90	a				19 03								20 03				21 03						22 03		22 36
Earlestown ■ 90	a				19 10								20 10				21 10						22 10		22 44
Newton-le-Willows 90	a				19 13								20 13				21 13						22 13		22 47
Manchester Oxford Road 90	a				19 32								20 32				21 32						22 32		23 06
Manchester Pic'dilly ■ 90 ⛴	a				19 41		20 33						20 41				21 41				22 33		22 41		23 15
Crewe ■	a			18 53		19 18		19 44				19 54		20 18	20 48			20 56		21 18		21 50		22 18	
Cardiff Central ■ 131	a																								
Manchester Airport 84,85 ✈	a																								
Birmingham New Street ■ 65	a										21 29				21 52										
London Euston ■ ⊖65	a			20 44																					

A To Southport
B To Birmingham International
C To Wolverhampton
D To Wigan Wallgate

Table 81

Sundays
until 19 June

North Wales and Chester - Manchester and Crewe

		AW ◇	AW ◇	AW A
Holyhead	d	20 35	21 40	
Valley	d	20x41		
Rhosneigr	d	20x46		
Ty Croes	d	20x50		
Bodorgan	d	20x54		
Llanfairpwll	d	21x04		
Bangor (Gwynedd)	a	21 12	22 09	
	d	21 14	22 11	
Llanfairfechan	d	21x21		
Penmaenmawr	d	21x25		
Conwy	d	21x31		
Llandudno	d			
Deganwy	d			
Llandudno Junction	a	21 35	22 27	
	d	21 37	22 29	
Colwyn Bay	d	21 43	22 35	
Abergele & Pensarn	d	21 50		
Rhyl	d	21 56	22 45	
Prestatyn	d	22 01	22 51	
Flint	d	22 15	23 04	
Shotton	d	22 21		
Chester	a	22 32	23 18	
	d	22 35		23 00
Liverpool Lime Street 10 106	a			
Helsby	d			
Frodsham	d			
Runcorn East	d			
Warrington Bank Quay 90	a			
Earlestown 8 90	a			
Newton-le-Willows 90	a			
Manchester Oxford Road 90	a			
Manchester Pic'dilly 10 90 ⇌	a			
Crewe 10	a	22 59		23 21
Cardiff Central 7 131	a			
Manchester Airport 84,85 ✈	a			
Birmingham New Street 12 65	a			
London Euston 15 ⊖65	a			

Sundays
26 June to 31 July

		NT	AW	AW	AW	AW	AW ◇	NT B	AW	AW ◇		AW	AW 🚲	AW ◇	AW ◇ C	AW	AW	NT B	VT ◇1 ☕	AW 🚲		AW	AW ◇	AW	VT ◇1 ☕
Holyhead	d						07 16			07 50				08 45									10 20		10 55
Valley	d									07x56													10x26		
Rhosneigr	d									08x02													10x31		
Ty Croes	d									08x05													10x35		
Bodorgan	d									08x10													10x39		
Llanfairpwll	d									08x19													10x49		
Bangor (Gwynedd)	a						07 42			08 27				09 12									10 57		11 21
	d						07 43			08 28				09 13									10 59		11 22
Llanfairfechan	d									08x35													11x06		
Penmaenmawr	d									08x39													11x10		
Conwy	d									08x45													11x16		
Llandudno	d														10 22		11 07								
Deganwy	d														10x26		11x11								
Llandudno Junction	a						07 59			08 50				09 29	10 30		11 17						11 20		11 39
	d						08 00			08 51				09 35									11 22		11 40
Colwyn Bay	d						08 07			08 57				09 41									11 28		11 47
Abergele & Pensarn	d						08 14							09 48									11 35		
Rhyl	d						08 20			09 08				09 54									11 41		11 58
Prestatyn	d						08 25							09 59									11 46		12 03
Flint	d						08 39							10 13									12 00		12 17
Shotton	d						08 45			09 28				10 19									12 06		
Chester	a						08 56			09 39				10 30									12 18		12 30
	d	22p49	23p22	07 56	08 27	08 41	08 57	08 58	09 27	09 42		09 57	10 36	10 39		10 57		11 07	11 28	11 36		11 57	12 18	12 24	12 33
Liverpool Lime Street 10 106	a																								
Helsby	d		23p31			08 50				09 51			10 45							11 45					
Frodsham	d		23p35			08 54				09 55			10 49							11 49					
Runcorn East	d		23p41			08 59				10 00			10 54							11 54					
Warrington Bank Quay 90	a		23p50			09 10				10 07			11 03							12 03					
Earlestown 8 90	a		23p58			09 16				10 19			11 10							12 10					
Newton-le-Willows 90	a		00 01			09 19				10 22			11 13							12 13					
Manchester Oxford Road 90	a					09 39				10 41			11 32							12 32					
Manchester Pic'dilly 10 90 ⇌	a	00 15	00 26			09 48		10 23		10 50			11 41					12 32		12 41					
Crewe 10	a			08 22	08 52		09 22		09 52			10 22		11 01		11 22			11 47			12 22	12 42	12 45	12 52
Cardiff Central 7 131	a																						15 31		
Manchester Airport 84,85 ✈	a																								
Birmingham New Street 12 65	a																								
London Euston 15 ⊖65	a																		13 44						14 43

A To Shrewsbury

B To Southport

C To Blaenau Ffestiniog

Table 81

Sundays

26 June to 31 July

North Wales and Chester - Manchester and Crewe

		AW	AW	AW	AW	NT		VT	AW	AW	AW	VT	AW	AW	AW	AW		AW	NT	VT	AW	AW	AW	AW	AW
								◇1				◇1	◇							◇1					◇
						A							B						A						
				🛒				☕		🛒		☕				🛒				☕		🛒			🛒
Holyhead	d							11 50				12 50								13 55					14 30
Valley	d																								14x36
Rhosneigr	d																								14x42
Ty Croes	d																								14x45
Bodorgan	d																								14x50
Llanfairpwll	d																								14x59
Bangor (Gwynedd)	a							12 16				13 16								14 21					15 07
	d							12 17				13 18								14 22					15 08
Llanfairfechan	d																								
Penmaenmawr	d																								
Conwy	d																								
Llandudno	d	11 40	12 18						13 19				13 30	13 50	14 20						15 11				
Deganwy	d	11x44	12x22						13x23				13x34	13x54	14x24						15x15				
Llandudno Junction	a	11 50	12 28					12 34	13 29			13 34	13 38	14 00	14 30					14 39	15 21				15 25
	d							12 35				13 36								14 40					15 26
Colwyn Bay	d							12 42				13 42								14 46					15 32
Abergele & Pensarn	d																								15 39
Rhyl	d							12 53				13 53								14 57					15 45
Prestatyn	d							12 59				13 59								15 03					15 51
Flint	d											14 13													16 04
Shotton	d																								16 10
Chester	a							13 24				14 26								15 31					16 21
	d			12 36	12 57	13 07		13 30		13 36	13 57	14 33				14 36		14 57	15 07	15 33		15 36	15 57	16 27	16 36
Liverpool Lime Street 10 106	a																								
Helsby	d			12 45						13 45						14 45						15 45			16 45
Frodsham	d			12 49						13 49						14 49						15 49			16 49
Runcorn East	d			12 54						13 54						14 54						15 54			16 54
Warrington Bank Quay 90	a			13 03						14 03						15 03						16 03			17 03
Earlestown 8 90	a			13 10						14 10						15 10						16 10			17 10
Newton-le-Willows 90	a			13 13						14 13						15 13						16 13			17 13
Manchester Oxford Road 90	a			13 32						14 32						15 32						16 32			17 32
Manchester Pic'dilly 10 90	a			13 41		14 33				14 41						15 41			16 33			16 41			17 41
Crewe 10	a				13 18			13 50			14 18	14 52						15 18		15 52			16 21	16 48	
Cardiff Central 7 131	a																								
Manchester Airport 84,85	a																								
Birmingham New Street 12 65	a																								
London Euston 15 ⊖65	a							15 45				16 44								17 44					

		AW		AW	AW	NT	VT	AW	AW	AW	AW	AW		AW	VT	AW	AW	NT	AW	AW	VT	AW		AW	AW
											R														
							◇1	◇							◇1				◇		◇				◇
						A												A							C
							☕	🛒			🛒				☕				🛒		☕				🛒
Holyhead	d							15 40			16 25								17 30						18 25
Valley	d										16x31														18x31
Rhosneigr	d										16x36														18x36
Ty Croes	d										16x40														18x40
Bodorgan	d										16x44														18x44
Llanfairpwll	d										16x54														18x54
Bangor (Gwynedd)	a							16 06			17 02								17 57						19 02
	d							16 08			17 04								17 59						19 04
Llanfairfechan	d							16x15											18x06						
Penmaenmawr	d							16x19											18x10						
Conwy	d							16x25											18x16						
Llandudno	d	15 45		16 16					16 52			17 20		18 05						18 55					
Deganwy	d	15x49		16x20					16x56			17x24		18x09						18x59					
Llandudno Junction	a	15 55		16 26				16 29	17 02		17 20	17 30		18 15					18 20	19 05					19 20
	d							16 35			17 25								18 24						19 24
Colwyn Bay	d							16 41			17 31								18 30						19 30
Abergele & Pensarn	d							16 48			17 38								18 37						19 37
Rhyl	d							16 54			17 44								18 43						19 43
Prestatyn	d							16 59			17 49								18 48						19 48
Flint	d							17 13			18 03								19 02						20 02
Shotton	d							17 19			18 11								19 10						20 10
Chester	a							17 31			18 21								19 21						20 19
	d				16 57	17 07	17 35	17 36		17 59	18 24				18 35	18 36	18 57	19 07	19 22		19 35	19 36		19 57	20 27
Liverpool Lime Street 10 106	a																								
Helsby	d							17 45								18 45						19 45			
Frodsham	d							17 49								18 49						19 49			
Runcorn East	d							17 54								18 54						19 54			
Warrington Bank Quay 90	a							18 03								19 03						20 03			
Earlestown 8 90	a							18 10								19 10						20 10			
Newton-le-Willows 90	a							18 13								19 13						20 13			
Manchester Oxford Road 90	a							18 32								19 32						20 32			
Manchester Pic'dilly 10 90	a					18 33		18 41								19 41		20 33				20 41			
Crewe 10	a				17 20		17 53			18 18	18 47				18 53		19 18		19 44		19 54			20 18	20 48
Cardiff Central 7 131	a										21 36														
Manchester Airport 84,85	a																								
Birmingham New Street 12 65	a																								21 52
London Euston 15 ⊖65	a						19 43								20 44										

A To Southport

B To Blaenau Ffestiniog

C To Birmingham International

Table 81

Sundays
26 June to 31 July

North Wales and Chester - Manchester and Crewe

	AW	AW	VT	AW	NT	AW	AW	AW	AW	AW	AW	AW
	◇		◇							◇	◇	
	A				B							C
	🛒		🍴									
Holyhead d	19 15									20 35	21 40	
Valley d	19x21									20x41		
Rhosneigr d	19x26									20x46		
Ty Croes d	19x30									20x50		
Bodorgan d	19x34									20x54		
Llanfairpwll d	19x44									21x04		
Bangor (Gwynedd) a	19 52									21 12	22 09	
d	19 54									21 14	22 11	
Llanfairfechan d	20x01									21x21		
Penmaenmawr d	20u05									21x25		
Conwy d	20x11									21x31		
Llandudno d												
Deganwy d												
Llandudno Junction a	20 15									21 35	22 27	
d	20 21									21 37	22 29	
Colwyn Bay d	20 27									21 43	22 35	
Abergele & Pensarn d	20 34									21 50		
Rhyl d	20 40									21 56	22 45	
Prestatyn d	20 46									22 01	22 51	
Flint d	21 00									22 15	23 04	
Shotton d	21 06									22 21		
Chester a	21 21									22 32	23 18	
d		20 36	20 37	20 57	21 07	21 27	21 36	21 57	22 09	22 35		23 00
Liverpool Lime Street 10 106 a												
Helsby d		20 45					21 45		22 18			
Frodsham d		20 49					21 49		22 22			
Runcorn East d		20 54					21 54		22 27			
Warrington Bank Quay 90 a		21 03					22 03		22 36			
Earlestown 8 90 a		21 10					22 10		22 44			
Newton-le-Willows 90 a		21 13					22 13		22 47			
Manchester Oxford Road 90 a		21 32					22 32		23 06			
Manchester Pic'dilly 10 90 🚌 a		21 41			22 33		22 41		23 15			
Crewe 10 a			20 56	21 18		21 50		22 18		22 59		23 21
Cardiff Central 7 131 a												
Manchester Airport 84,85 ✈ a												
Birmingham New Street 12 65 a												
London Euston 15 ⊖65 a												

Sundays
7 August to 11 September

	NT	AW	AW	AW	AW	AW	NT	AW	AW	AW	AW	AW	AW	AW	AW	AW	NT	VT	AW	AW	AW	AW
						◇		◇		◇			◇	◇				◇1	◇			◇
							D	E						F			D		E			
												🛒						🍴	🛒	🛒		
Holyhead d						07 16				07 50			08 45									10 20
Valley d										07x56												10x26
Rhosneigr d										08x02												10x31
Ty Croes d										08x05												10x35
Bodorgan d										08x10												10x39
Llanfairpwll d										08x19												10x49
Bangor (Gwynedd) a						07 42				08 27			09 12									10 57
d						07 43				08 28			09 13									10 59
Llanfairfechan d										08x35												11x06
Penmaenmawr d										08x39												11x10
Conwy d										08x45												11x16
Llandudno d														10 22		11 07						
Deganwy d														10x26		11x11						
Llandudno Junction a						07 59				08 50			09 29	10 30		11 17						11 20
d						08 00				08 51			09 35									11 22
Colwyn Bay d						08 07				08 57			09 41									11 28
Abergele & Pensarn d						08 14							09 48									11 35
Rhyl d						08 20				09 08			09 54									11 41
Prestatyn d						08 25							09 59									11 46
Flint d						08 39							10 13									12 00
Shotton d						08 45				09 28			10 19									12 06
Chester a						08 56				09 39			10 30									12 18
d	22p49	23p22	07 56	08 27	08 41	08 57	08 58	09 22	09 27	09 42	09 57	10 36	10 39		10 57		11 07	11 28	11 31	11 36	11 57	12 21
Liverpool Lime Street 10 106 a																						
Helsby d		23p31			08 50					09 51		10 45								11 45		
Frodsham d		23p35			08 54					09 55		10 49								11 49		
Runcorn East d		23p41			08 59					10 00		10 54								11 54		
Warrington Bank Quay 90 a		23p50			09 10					10 07		11 03								12 03		
Earlestown 8 90 a		23p58			09 16					10 19		11 10								12 10		
Newton-le-Willows 90 a		00 01			09 19					10 22		11 13								12 13		
Manchester Oxford Road 90 a					09 39					10 41		11 32								12 32		
Manchester Pic'dilly 10 90 🚌 a	00 15	00 26			09 48		10 23			10 50		11 41					12 32			12 41		
Crewe 10 a			08 22	08 52		09 22			09 52		10 22		11 01		11 22			11 47			12 22	
Cardiff Central 7 131 a																						15 31
Manchester Airport 84,85 ✈ a																						
Birmingham New Street 12 65 a								11 14											13 24			
London Euston 15 ⊖65 a																		13 44				

A To Wrexham General
B To Wigan Wallgate
C To Shrewsbury
D To Southport
E To Birmingham International
F To Blaenau Ffestiniog

Table 81

Sundays

7 August to 11 September

North Wales and Chester - Manchester and Crewe

		AW	VT	AW	AW	AW		AW	NT	VT	AW	AW	AW	AW	VT	AW		AW	AW	AW	AW	NT	AW	VT	AW
			◇1							◇1		◇			◇1	◇							◇	◇1	
									A			B				C						A	B		
			🍽			🛒				🍽		🛒	🛒		🍽					🛒			🛒	🍽	
Holyhead	d		10 55							11 50					12 50									13 55	
Valley	d																								
Rhosneigr	d																								
Ty Croes	d																								
Bodorgan	d																								
Llanfairpwll	d																								
Bangor (Gwynedd)	a		11 21							12 16					13 16									14 21	
	d		11 22							12 17					13 18									14 22	
Llanfairfechan	d																								
Penmaenmawr	d																								
Conwy	d																								
Llandudno	d			11 40	12 18						13 19					13 30		13 50	14 20						15 11
Deganwy	d			11x44	12x22						13x23					13x34		13x54	14x24						15x15
Llandudno Junction	a		11 39	11 50	12 28					12 34	13 29				13 34	13 38		14 00	14 30					14 39	15 21
	d		11 40							12 35					13 36									14 40	
Colwyn Bay	d		11 47							12 42					13 42									14 46	
Abergele & Pensarn	d																								
Rhyl	d		11 58							12 53					13 53									14 57	
Prestatyn	d		12 03							12 59					13 59									15 03	
Flint	d		12 17												14 13										
Shotton	d																								
Chester	a		12 30							13 24					14 26									15 31	
	d	12 24	12 33			12 36		12 57	13 07	13 30		13 31	13 36	13 57	14 33					14 36	14 57	15 07	15 31	15 33	
Liverpool Lime Street 10 106	a																								
Helsby	d					12 45							13 45							14 45					
Frodsham	d					12 49							13 49							14 49					
Runcorn East	d					12 54							13 54							14 54					
Warrington Bank Quay 90	a					13 03							14 03							15 03					
Earlestown 8 90	a					13 10							14 10							15 10					
Newton-le-Willows 90	a					13 13							14 13							15 13					
Manchester Oxford Road 90	a					13 32							14 32							15 32					
Manchester Pic'dilly 10 90 ⛴	a					13 41			14 33				14 41							15 41		16 33			
Crewe 10	a	12 45	12 52					13 18		13 50				14 18	14 52						15 18			15 52	
Cardiff Central 7 131	a																								
Manchester Airport 84,85 ✈	a																								
Birmingham New Street 12 65	a											15 25											17 35		
London Euston 15 ⊖65	a		14 43							15 45					16 44									17 44	

		AW		AW	AW	AW	AW	AW	AW	NT	AW	VT		AW	AW	AW	AW	AW	AW	VT	AW	AW		NT	AW
																	■								
						◇					◇	◇1		◇						◇1					◇
										A	B													A	
		🛒				🛒						🍽		🛒			🛒			🍽					🛒
Holyhead	d					14 30								15 40			16 25								17 30
Valley	d					14x36											16x31								
Rhosneigr	d					14x42											16x36								
Ty Croes	d					14x45											16x40								
Bodorgan	d					14x50											16x44								
Llanfairpwll	d					14x59											16x54								
Bangor (Gwynedd)	a					15 07								16 06			17 02								17 57
	d					15 08								16 08			17 04								17 59
Llanfairfechan	d													16x15											18x06
Penmaenmawr	d													16x19											18x10
Conwy	d													16x25											18x16
Llandudno	d						15 45	16 16							16 52			17 20	18 05						
Deganwy	d						15x49	16x20							16x56			17x24	18x09						
Llandudno Junction	a					15 25	15 55	16 26						16 29	17 02		17 20	17 30	18 15						18 20
	d					15 26								16 35			17 25								18 24
Colwyn Bay	d					15 32								16 41			17 31								18 30
Abergele & Pensarn	d					15 39								16 48			17 38								18 37
Rhyl	d					15 45								16 54			17 44								18 43
Prestatyn	d					15 51								16 59			17 49								18 48
Flint	d					16 04								17 13			18 03								19 02
Shotton	d					16 10								17 19			18 11								19 10
Chester	a					16 21								17 31			18 21								19 21
	d	15 36		15 57	16 27	16 36			16 57	17 07	17 31	17 35		17 36		17 59	18 24			18 35	18 36	18 57		19 07	19 22
Liverpool Lime Street 10 106	a																								
Helsby	d	15 45				16 45								17 45							18 45				
Frodsham	d	15 49				16 49								17 49							18 49				
Runcorn East	d	15 54				16 54								17 54							18 54				
Warrington Bank Quay 90	a	16 03				17 03								18 03							19 03				
Earlestown 8 90	a	16 10				17 10								18 10							19 10				
Newton-le-Willows 90	a	16 13				17 13								18 13							19 13				
Manchester Oxford Road 90	a	16 32				17 32								18 32							19 32				
Manchester Pic'dilly 10 90 ⛴	a	16 41				17 41				18 33				18 41							19 41			20 33	
Crewe 10	a			16 21	16 48				17 20			17 53				18 18				18 53		19 18			19 44
Cardiff Central 7 131	a																21 36								
Manchester Airport 84,85 ✈	a																								
Birmingham New Street 12 65	a										19 27														
London Euston 15 ⊖65	a											19 43								20 44					

A To Southport

B To Birmingham International

C To Blaenau Ffestiniog

Table 81

Sundays
7 August to 11 September

North Wales and Chester - Manchester and Crewe

	AW	AW	VT	AW	AW	AW	AW	AW	VT	AW	NT	AW	AW	AW	AW	AW	AW	AW
		◇	◇			◇	◇		◇							◇	◇	
		A				A	B				C							D
			🍴			🛒	🛒		🍴									
Holyhead d						18 25	19 15									20 35	21 40	
Valley d						18x31	19x21									20x41		
Rhosneigr d						18x36	19x26									20x46		
Ty Croes d						18x40	19x30									20x50		
Bodorgan d						18x44	19x34									20x54		
Llanfairpwll d						18x54	19x44									21x04		
Bangor (Gwynedd) a						19 02	19 52									21 12	22 09	
d						19 04	19 54									21 14	22 11	
Llanfairfechan d							20x01									21x21		
Penmaenmawr d							20u05									21x25		
Conwy d							20x11									21x31		
Llandudno d	18 55																	
Deganwy d	18x59																	
Llandudno Junction a	19 05					19 20	20 15									21 35	22 27	
d						19 24	20 21									21 37	22 29	
Colwyn Bay d						19 30	20 27									21 43	22 35	
Abergele & Pensarn d						19 37	20 34									21 50		
Rhyl d						19 43	20 40									21 56	22 45	
Prestatyn d						19 48	20 46									22 01	22 51	
Flint d						20 02	21 00									22 15	23 04	
Shotton d						20 10	21 06									22 21		
Chester a						20 19	21 21									22 32	23 18	
d		19 26	19 35	19 36	19 57	20 27		20 36	20 37	20 57	21 07	21 27	21 36	21 57	22 09	22 35		23 00
Liverpool Lime Street 10 106 a																		
Helsby d				19 45				20 45					21 45		22 18			
Frodsham d				19 49				20 49					21 49		22 22			
Runcorn East d				19 54				20 54					21 54		22 27			
Warrington Bank Quay 90 a				20 03				21 03					22 03		22 36			
Earlestown 8 90 a				20 10				21 10					22 10		22 44			
Newton-le-Willows 90 a				20 13				21 13					22 13		22 47			
Manchester Oxford Road 90 a				20 32				21 32					22 32		23 06			
Manchester Pic'dilly 10 90 ⇌ a				20 41				21 41			22 33		22 41		23 15			
Crewe 10 a			19 54		20 18	20 48			20 56	21 18		21 50		22 18		22 59		23 21
Cardiff Central 7 131 a																		
Manchester Airport 84,85 ✈ a																		
Birmingham New Street 12 65 a		21 29				21 52												
London Euston 15 ⊖65 a																		

Sundays
18 September to 23 October

	NT	NT	AW	AW	AW	AW	NT	NT	AW	AW	AW	AW	AW	AW	AW	NT	NT	VT	AW	AW	AW	AW
									◇		◇			◇				◇1	◇			◇
	E	F					G	H	A							G	H		A			
						🚌						🚌	🛒		🚌			🍴	🛒	🛒	🚌	
Holyhead d														08 45								10 20
Valley d																						10x26
Rhosneigr d																						10x31
Ty Croes d																						10x35
Bodorgan d																						10x39
Llanfairpwll d																						10x49
Bangor (Gwynedd) a														09 12								10 57
d														09 13								10 59
Llanfairfechan d																						11x06
Penmaenmawr d																						11x10
Conwy d																						11x16
Llandudno d																						
Deganwy d																						
Llandudno Junction a														09 29								11 20
d														09 35								11 22
Colwyn Bay d														09 41								11 28
Abergele & Pensarn d														09 48								11 35
Rhyl d														09 54								11 41
Prestatyn d														09 59								11 46
Flint d														10 13								12 00
Shotton d														10 19								12 06
Chester a														10 30								12 18
d	22p45	22p49	23p22	08 36	08 40	08 41	08 54	08 58	09 22	09 40	09 42	09 49	10 36	10 39	10 40	11 03	11 07	11 28	11 31	11 36	11 36	12 21
Liverpool Lime Street 10 106 a																						
Helsby d						09 01						10 09			11 00						11 56	
Frodsham d						09 06						10 14			11 05						12 01	
Runcorn East d						09 21						10 29			11 20						12 16	
Warrington Bank Quay 90 a						09 41						10 49			11 40						12 36	
Earlestown 8 90 a						10 06						11 14			12 05						13 01	
Newton-le-Willows 90 a						10 16						11 24			12 15						13 11	
Manchester Oxford Road 90 a						10 46						11 54			12 45						13 41	
Manchester Pic'dilly 10 90 ⇌ a	00 15	00 15	00 31	09 41		10 51	10 23	10 23			10 49	11 59	11 44		12 50	12 31	12 32			12 48	13 46	
Crewe 10 a					09 05					10 05				11 01				11 47				
Cardiff Central 7 131 a																						15 31
Manchester Airport 84,85 ✈ a																						
Birmingham New Street 12 65 a									11 14										13 25			
London Euston 15 ⊖65 a																		13 44				

A To Birmingham International
B To Wolverhampton
C To Wigan Wallgate
D To Shrewsbury
E 9 October, 16 October, 23 October
F 18 September, 25 September, 2 October
G 9 October, 16 October, 23 October. To Southport
H 18 September, 25 September, 2 October. To Southport

Table 81

Sundays

18 September to 23 October

North Wales and Chester - Manchester and Crewe

		AW	VT	AW	AW	NT		NT	AW	VT	AW	AW	AW	AW	VT	AW		NT	NT	AW	VT	AW	AW	AW	NT
			◇1							◇1	◇				◇1					◇	◇1			◇	
						A		B			C							A	B	C					A
			🍽	🛒	🚌					🍽	🛒	🛒	🚌		🍽	🛒				🛒	🍽	🛒		🛒	
Holyhead	d		10 55							11 50					12 50						13 55			14 30	
Valley	d																							14x36	
Rhosneigr	d																							14x42	
Ty Croes	d																							14x45	
Bodorgan	d																							14x50	
Llanfairpwll	d																							14x59	
Bangor (Gwynedd)	a		11 21							12 16					13 16						14 21			15 07	
	d		11 22							12 17					13 18						14 22			15 08	
Llanfairfechan	d																								
Penmaenmawr	d																								
Conwy	d																								
Llandudno	d																								
Deganwy	d																								
Llandudno Junction	a		11 39							12 34					13 34						14 39			15 25	
	d		11 40							12 35					13 36						14 40			15 26	
Colwyn Bay	d		11 47							12 42					13 42						14 46			15 32	
Abergele & Pensarn	d																							15 39	
Rhyl	d		11 58							12 53					13 53						14 57			15 45	
Prestatyn	d		12 03							12 59					13 59						15 03			15 51	
Flint	d		12 17												14 13									16 04	
Shotton	d																							16 10	
Chester	a		12 30							13 24					14 26						15 31			16 21	
	d	12 24	12 33	12 36	12 36	13 03		13 07	13 18	13 30	13 31	13 36	13 36	14 20	14 33	14 36		15 03	15 07	15 31	15 33	15 36	16 27	16 36	17 03
Liverpool Lime Street 10 106	a																								
Helsby	d				12 56							13 45	13 56			14 45						15 45		16 45	
Frodsham	d				13 01							13 49	14 01			14 49						15 49		16 49	
Runcorn East	d				13 16							13 54	14 16			14 54						15 54		16 54	
Warrington Bank Quay 90	a				13 36							14 03	14 36			15 03						16 03		17 03	
Earlestown 8 90	a				14 01							14 10				15 10						16 10		17 10	
Newton-le-Willows 90	a				14 11							14 13				15 13						16 13		17 13	
Manchester Oxford Road 90	a				14 41							14 32				15 32						16 32		17 32	
Manchester Pic'dilly 10 90 ⛴	a			13 43	14 46	14 33		14 33				14 41				15 41		16 33	16 33			16 41		17 41	18 33
Crewe 10	a	12 45	12 52						13 38	13 50				14 41	14 52						15 52		16 48		
Cardiff Central 7 131	a																								
Manchester Airport 84,85 ✈	a																								
Birmingham New Street 12 65	a										15 26									17 35					
London Euston 15 ⊖65	a		14 43							15 45					16 44						17 44				

		NT		AW	AW	VT	AW	AW	VT	AW	AW	NT		NT	AW	AW	VT	AW	AW	AW	AW	VT		AW	NT
								R																	
				◇	◇	◇1	◇		◇1						◇	◇	◇			◇		◇			
		B			C							A		B		C				C					D
						🍽		🛒	🍽						🛒		🍽			🛒		🍽			
Holyhead	d			15 30				16 25							17 30					18 25					
Valley	d							16x31												18x31					
Rhosneigr	d							16x36												18x36					
Ty Croes	d							16x40												18x40					
Bodorgan	d							16x44												18x44					
Llanfairpwll	d							16x54												18x54					
Bangor (Gwynedd)	a			15 56				17 02							17 57					19 02					
	d			15 58				17 04							17 59					19 04					
Llanfairfechan	d			16x05											18x06										
Penmaenmawr	d			16x09											18x10										
Conwy	d			16x15											18x16										
Llandudno	d																								
Deganwy	d																								
Llandudno Junction	a			16 19				17 20							18 20					19 20					
	d			16 25				17 25							18 24					19 24					
Colwyn Bay	d			16 31				17 31							18 30					19 30					
Abergele & Pensarn	d			16 38				17 38							18 37					19 37					
Rhyl	d			16 44				17 44							18 43					19 43					
Prestatyn	d			16 49				17 49							18 48					19 48					
Flint	d			17 03				18 03							19 02					20 02					
Shotton	d			17 09				18 11							19 10					20 10					
Chester	a			17 20				18 21							19 21					20 19					
	d	17 07		17 22	17 31	17 35	17 36	18 24	18 35	18 36	18 57	19 03		19 07	19 22	19 26	19 35	19 36	19 50	20 27	20 36	20 37		20 50	21 03
Liverpool Lime Street 10 106	a																								
Helsby	d						17 45			18 45								19 45			20 45				
Frodsham	d						17 49			18 49								19 49			20 49				
Runcorn East	d						17 54			18 54								19 54			20 54				
Warrington Bank Quay 90	a						18 03			19 03								20 03			21 03				
Earlestown 8 90	a						18 10			19 10								20 10			21 10				
Newton-le-Willows 90	a						18 13			19 13								20 13			21 13				
Manchester Oxford Road 90	a						18 32			19 32								20 32			21 32				
Manchester Pic'dilly 10 90 ⛴	a	18 33					18 41			19 41		20 33		20 33				20 41			21 41				22 33
Crewe 10	a			17 43		17 53			18 53		19 18				19 44		19 54		20 10	20 48		20 56		21 11	
Cardiff Central 7 131	a							21 36																	
Manchester Airport 84,85 ✈	a																								
Birmingham New Street 12 65	a				19 28											21 29				21 52					
London Euston 15 ⊖65	a					19 43			20 44																

A 9 October, 16 October, 23 October. To Southport
B 18 September, 25 September, 2 October. To Southport
C To Birmingham International
D 9 October, 16 October, 23 October. To Wigan Wallgate

Table 81

Sundays

18 September to 23 October

North Wales and Chester - Manchester and Crewe

		NT	AW	AW	AW	AW	AW	AW	AW
			◇				◇	◇	
		A							B
Holyhead	d		19 40				20 35	21 40	
Valley	d						20x41		
Rhosneigr	d						20x46		
Ty Croes	d						20x50		
Bodorgan	d						20x54		
Llanfairpwll	d						21x04		
Bangor (Gwynedd)	a		20 07				21 12	22 09	
	d		20 09				21 14	22 11	
Llanfairfechan	d		20x16				21x21		
Penmaenmawr	d		20x20				21x25		
Conwy	d		20x26				21x31		
Llandudno	d								
Deganwy	d								
Llandudno Junction	a		20 30				21 35	22 27	
	d		20 37				21 37	22 29	
Colwyn Bay	d		20 43				21 43	22 35	
Abergele & Pensarn	d		20 50				21 50		
Rhyl	d		20 56				21 56	22 45	
Prestatyn	d		21 01				22 01	22 51	
Flint	d		21 15				22 15	23 04	
Shotton	d		21 21				22 21		
Chester	a		21 34				22 32	23 18	
	d	21 07	21 35	21 36	21 50	22 09	22 35		23 00
Liverpool Lime Street [10] 106	a								
Helsby	d			21 45		22 18			
Frodsham	d			21 49		22 22			
Runcorn East	d			21 54		22 27			
Warrington Bank Quay 90	a			22 03		22 36			
Earlestown [8] 90	a			22 10		22 44			
Newton-le-Willows 90	a			22 13		22 47			
Manchester Oxford Road 90	a			22 32		23 06			
Manchester Pic'dilly [10] 90 ⛴	a	22 33		22 41		23 15			
Crewe [10]	a		21 59		22 11		22 59		23 21
Cardiff Central [7] 131	a								
Manchester Airport 84,85 ✈	a								
Birmingham New Street [12] 65	a								
London Euston [15] ⊖65	a								

Sundays

from 30 October

		NT	AW	AW	AW	NT	AW	AW	AW	AW	AW	NT	VT	AW	AW	AW	AW	VT	AW	NT	AW	VT	AW
							◇		◇		◇		◇[1]	◇		◇		◇[1]				◇[1]	◇
						C	D					C		D						C			D
										🚲			☕	🚲	🚲			☕	🚲			☕	🚲
Holyhead	d										08 45					10 20		10 55				11 50	
Valley	d															10x26							
Rhosneigr	d															10x31							
Ty Croes	d															10x35							
Bodorgan	d															10x39							
Llanfairpwll	d															10x49							
Bangor (Gwynedd)	a										09 12					10 57		11 21				12 16	
	d										09 13					10 59		11 22				12 17	
Llanfairfechan	d															11x06							
Penmaenmawr	d															11x10							
Conwy	d															11x16							
Llandudno	d																						
Deganwy	d																						
Llandudno Junction	a										09 29					11 20		11 39				12 34	
	d										09 35					11 22		11 40				12 35	
Colwyn Bay	d										09 41					11 28		11 47				12 42	
Abergele & Pensarn	d										09 48					11 35							
Rhyl	d										09 54					11 41		11 58				12 53	
Prestatyn	d										09 59					11 46		12 03				12 59	
Flint	d										10 13					12 00		12 17					
Shotton	d										10 19					12 06							
Chester	a										10 30					12 18		12 30				13 24	
	d	22p45	23p22	08 40	08 41	08 54	09 22	09 40	09 42	10 36	10 39	11 03	11 28	11 31	11 36	12 21	12 24	12 33	12 36	13 03	13 18	13 30	13 31
Liverpool Lime Street [10] 106	a																						
Helsby	d		23p31		08 50				09 51	10 45					11 45				12 45				
Frodsham	d		23p35		08 54				09 55	10 49					11 49				12 49				
Runcorn East	d		23p41		08 59				10 00	10 54					11 54				12 54				
Warrington Bank Quay 90	a		23p50		09 10				10 07	11 03					12 03				13 03				
Earlestown [8] 90	a		23p58		09 16				10 19	11 10					12 10				13 10				
Newton-le-Willows 90	a		00 01		09 19				10 22	11 13					12 13				13 13				
Manchester Oxford Road 90	a				09 39				10 41	11 32					12 32				13 32				
Manchester Pic'dilly [10] 90 ⛴	a	00 15	00 26		09 48	10 23			10 50	11 41		12 31			12 41				13 41	14 33			
Crewe [10]	a			09 05				10 05			11 01		11 47				12 45	12 52			13 38	13 50	
Cardiff Central [7] 131	a															15 31							
Manchester Airport 84,85 ✈	a																						
Birmingham New Street [12] 65	a						11 14							13 25									15 26
London Euston [15] ⊖65	a												13 44					14 43				15 45	

A 18 September, 25 September, 2 October. To Wigan Wallgate

B To Shrewsbury

C To Southport

D To Birmingham International

Table 81

Sundays
from 30 October

North Wales and Chester - Manchester and Crewe

		AW	AW	VT	AW	NT		AW	VT	AW	AW	AW	NT	AW	AW	VT		AW	AW	VT	AW	AW	NT	AW	AW
				◇1				◇	◇1			◇		◇	◇	◇1		◇	R	◇1				◇	◇
						A		B					A		B								A		B
Holyhead	d			12 50					13 55			14 30		15 30					16 25					17 30	
Valley	d											14x36							16x31						
Rhosneigr	d											14x42							16x36						
Ty Croes	d											14x45							16x40						
Bodorgan	d											14x50							16x44						
Llanfairpwll	d											14x59							16x54						
Bangor (Gwynedd)	a			13 16					14 21			15 07		15 56					17 02					17 57	
	d			13 18					14 22			15 08		15 58					17 04					17 59	
Llanfairfechan	d													16x05										18x06	
Penmaenmawr	d													16x09										18x10	
Conwy	d													16x15										18x16	
Llandudno	d																								
Deganwy	d																								
Llandudno Junction	a			13 34					14 39			15 25		16 19					17 20					18 20	
	d			13 36					14 40			15 26		16 25					17 25					18 24	
Colwyn Bay	d			13 42					14 46			15 32		16 31					17 31					18 30	
Abergele & Pensarn	d											15 39		16 38					17 38					18 37	
Rhyl	d			13 53					14 57			15 45		16 44					17 44					18 43	
Prestatyn	d			13 59					15 03			15 51		16 49					17 49					18 48	
Flint	d			14 13								16 04		17 03					18 03					19 02	
Shotton	d											16 10		17 09					18 11					19 10	
Chester	a			14 26					15 31			16 21		17 20					18 21					19 21	
	d	13 36	14 20	14 33	14 36	15 03		15 31	15 33	15 36	16 27	16 36	17 03	17 22	17 31	17 35		17 36	18 24	18 35	18 36	18 57	19 03	19 22	19 26
Liverpool Lime Street 10 106	a																								
Helsby	d	13 45			14 45					15 45		16 45						17 45			18 45				
Frodsham	d	13 49			14 49					15 49		16 49						17 49			18 49				
Runcorn East	d	13 54			14 54					15 54		16 54						17 54			18 54				
Warrington Bank Quay 90	a	14 03			15 03					16 03		17 03						18 03			19 03				
Earlestown 8 90	a	14 10			15 10					16 10		17 10						18 10			19 10				
Newton-le-Willows 90	a	14 13			15 13					16 13		17 13						18 13			19 13				
Manchester Oxford Road 90	a	14 32			15 32					16 32		17 32						18 32			19 32				
Manchester Pic'dilly 10 90	a	14 41			15 41	16 33				16 41		17 41	18 33					18 41			19 41		20 33		
Crewe 10	a		14 41	14 52					15 52		16 48			17 43		17 53				18 53		19 18		19 44	
Cardiff Central 7 131	a																		21 36						
Manchester Airport 84,85	a																								
Birmingham New Street 12 65	a							17 35							19 28										21 29
London Euston 15 ⊖65	a			16 44					17 44							19 43				20 44					

		VT		AW	AW	AW	AW	VT	AW	NT	AW	AW		AW	AW	AW	AW	AW
		◇				◇		◇			◇					◇	◇	
						B				C								D
Holyhead	d					18 25					19 40					20 35	21 40	
Valley	d					18x31										20x41		
Rhosneigr	d					18x36										20x46		
Ty Croes	d					18x40										20x50		
Bodorgan	d					18x44										20x54		
Llanfairpwll	d					18x54										21x04		
Bangor (Gwynedd)	a					19 02					20 07					21 12	22 09	
	d					19 04					20 09					21 14	22 11	
Llanfairfechan	d										20x16					21x21		
Penmaenmawr	d										20x20					21x25		
Conwy	d										20x26					21x31		
Llandudno	d																	
Deganwy	d																	
Llandudno Junction	a					19 20					20 30					21 35	22 27	
	d					19 24					20 37					21 37	22 29	
Colwyn Bay	d					19 30					20 43					21 43	22 35	
Abergele & Pensarn	d					19 37					20 50					21 50		
Rhyl	d					19 43					20 56					21 56	22 45	
Prestatyn	d					19 48					21 01					22 01	22 51	
Flint	d					20 02					21 15					22 15	23 04	
Shotton	d					20 10					21 21					22 21		
Chester	a					20 19					21 34					22 32	23 18	
	d	19 35		19 36	19 50	20 27	20 36	20 37	20 50	21 03	21 35	21 36		21 50	22 09	22 35		23 00
Liverpool Lime Street 10 106	a																	
Helsby	d			19 45			20 45					21 45			22 18			
Frodsham	d			19 49			20 49					21 49			22 22			
Runcorn East	d			19 54			20 54					21 54			22 27			
Warrington Bank Quay 90	a			20 03			21 03					22 03			22 36			
Earlestown 8 90	a			20 10			21 10					22 10			22 44			
Newton-le-Willows 90	a			20 13			21 13					22 13			22 47			
Manchester Oxford Road 90	a			20 32			21 32					22 32			23 06			
Manchester Pic'dilly 10 90	a			20 41			21 41			22 33		22 41			23 15			
Crewe 10	a	19 54			20 10	20 48		20 56	21 11		21 59			22 11		22 59		23 21
Cardiff Central 7 131	a																	
Manchester Airport 84,85	a																	
Birmingham New Street 12 65	a					21 52												
London Euston 15 ⊖65	a																	

A To Southport
B To Birmingham International
C To Wigan Wallgate
D To Shrewsbury

Table 81A

Holyhead - Dublin

		AW	AW	AW	AW	AW Sun	AW
		R	R	R	R	R	R
Holyhead	⛴ d	02 40	10 00	12 00	14 10	16 20	17 15
Dun Laoghaire	⛴ a	.	11 50	.	.	18 10	.
Dublin Ferryport §	⛴ a	05 55	.....	13 49	17 25	.....	19 15

Table 81A

Dublin - Holyhead

		AW	AW	AW	AW	AW	AW Sun	AW
		R A	R	R	R	R	R	R
Dublin Ferryport §	⛴ d	20p55	08 45	08 05	.....	14 30	.....	20 55
Dun Laoghaire	⛴ d		.	.	13 15	.	19 25	.
Holyhead	⛴ a	00 20	10 34	11 30	15 05	16 30	21 15	00 20

§ Bus connections to/from city centre and railway stations

A not 22 May

Manchester - Bolton - Wigan, Kirkby, Southport, Preston, Blackpool North and Barrow-in-Furness

Miles	Miles	Miles	Miles	Miles			TP	TP	NT	NT	TP	TP	TP	TP	TP	NT	TP	TP	NT	TP	TP	NT	NT	TP
							MO	MX	MX	MX		MX	MO											
							◇1	◇1			◇1	◇1	◇1	◇1	◇1		1	1		1	◇1			◇1
												A	A		B	C			D			E		F
0	0	0	—	—	Manchester Airport 85 ✈	d	22p30	22p29			00 01	00 38	00 48	04 00	04 12	04 34								05 45
1½	1½	1½	—	—	Heald Green 85	d		22p33																05 49
—	—	—	—	—	Buxton 86	d																		
—	—	—	—	—	Hazel Grove 86	d																		
—	—	—	—	—	Stockport 84	d																		
9¾	9¾	9¾	—	—	Manchester Piccadilly 10	d	22p46	22p46			00 16	00 53	01 03	04 15	04 30	04a47					05 46			06 03
10¼	10¼	10¼	—	—	Manchester Oxford Road	d	22p49	22p49																06 06
10½	10½	10½	—	—	Deansgate	d	22p51	22p51																
—	—	—	—	—	Rochdale 41	d																		
—	—	—	0	—	Manchester Victoria	d			23p20	23p23												05 55	06 00	
—	—	—	0¾	—	Salford Central	d																		
12	12	12	1¾	—	Salford Crescent	a	22p54	22p56	23p25	23p29		00 58	01 09		04 36						05 51	05 59	06 04	
—	—	—	—	—		d	22p55	22p56	23p26	23p30											05 52	06 00	06 05	
—	—	—	5¾	—	Swinton	d			23p33															
—	—	—	6½	—	Moorside	d			23p35															
—	—	—	8¼	—	Walkden	d			23p39															
—	—	—	11¾	—	Atherton	d			23p44															
—	—	—	13	—	Hag Fold	d			23p47															
—	—	—	13¾	—	Daisy Hill	d			23p50															
18	18	18	—	—	Kearsley	d																		
18¾	18	18¾	—	—	Farnworth	d																		
19¾	19¾	19¾	—	—	Moses Gate	d																		
21	21	21	—	—	Bolton	a	23p05	23p06		23p40	00s31			04s29								06 11	06 15	06 19
—	—	—	—	—		d	23p05	23p07		23p40													06 15	06 19
—	—	25½	—	—	Westhoughton	d																	06 23	
—	—	28	15¾	—	Hindley	d			23p54														06 27	
—	—	29½	17¼	0	Ince	d			23p57															
—	—	—	—	0¾	Wigan North Western	a								04 44							06 15			
—	—	30½	18¼	—	Wigan Wallgate	a			00 04														06 32	
—	—	—	—	—		d																	06 34	
—	—	—	20	—	Pemberton	d																	06 38	
—	—	—	22	—	Orrell	d																	06 42	
—	—	—	23¼	—	Upholland	d																	06 45	
—	—	—	25¼	—	Rainford	d																	06 49	
—	—	—	30½	—	Kirkby	a																	07 01	
—	—	33¼	—	—	Gathurst	d																		
—	—	35	—	—	Appley Bridge	d																		
—	—	37¼	—	—	Parbold	d																		
—	—	38¾	—	—	Hoscar	d																		
—	—	40¼	—	—	Burscough Bridge	d																		
—	—	41½	—	—	New Lane	d																		
—	—	43½	—	—	Bescar Lane	d																		
—	—	46¾	—	—	Meols Cop	d																		
—	—	48	—	—	Southport	a																		
24	24	—	—	—	Lostock	d	23p10			23p45														
26	26	—	—	—	Horwich Parkway	d	23p14	23p13		23p49														
27½	27½	—	—	—	Blackrod	d	23p17			23p52														
29½	29½	—	—	—	Adlington (Lancashire)	d	23p20			23p56														
33½	33½	—	—	—	Chorley	d	23p24	23p21		00 01														06 31
37	37	—	—	—	Leyland	d	23p34			00 12											06 27			
41	41	—	—	—	Preston 8 65,97	a	23p42	23p33		00 17	01s05			05s04							06 35			06 42
—	—	—	—	—		d	23p47	23p35		00 19							05 22			06 34	06 37			06 44
48¾	—	—	—	—	Kirkham & Wesham 97	a	23p56			00 28											06 46			
55¼	—	—	—	—	Poulton-le-Fylde 97	a	00 05	23p52		00 36											06 56			
57¼	—	—	—	—	Layton 97	a				00 43											06 59			
58½	—	—	—	—	Blackpool North 97	a	00 14	00 02		00 50	01 30			05 33							07 09			
—	62	—	—	—	Lancaster 6 65	a											05 39			06 50				06 59
—	—	—	—	—		d											05 43	05 46		06 50				07 00
—	81	—	—	—	Oxenholme Lake District 65	a												06 21						07 15
—	91	—	—	—	Windermere 83	a												06 41						
—	68	—	—	—	Carnforth	d											05a52			06a58				
—	71¾	—	—	—	Silverdale	d																		
—	74	—	—	—	Arnside	d																		
—	77¼	—	—	—	Grange-over-Sands	d													06 09					
—	79½	—	—	—	Kents Bank	d													06 12					
—	81½	—	—	—	Cark	d													06 17					
—	87½	—	—	—	Ulverston	d													06 25					
—	90¾	—	—	—	Dalton	d													06 33					
—	95	—	—	—	Roose	d													06 39					
—	96¾	—	—	—	Barrow-in-Furness	a													06 47					

A To York
B To Scarborough
C To Liverpool Lime Street
D To Carlisle
E To Clitheroe
F To Edinburgh

The Sunday service between Manchester Victoria and Wigan Wallgate via Atherton is funded by GMITA and will operate whilst funding exists

Manchester - Bolton - Wigan, Kirkby, Southport, Preston, Blackpool North and Barrow-in-Furness

		NT	TP	NT	NT	NT	TP	NT	TP	NT	NT	NT	NT	NT	NT	NT	NT	NT	NT	NT	NT	NT
			◇1				◇1		◇1													
			A			B	C	D			E			E	E	E	E	F				
Manchester Airport 85 ✈	d		06 18																			
Heald Green 85	d																					
Buxton 86	d					05 59																
Hazel Grove 86	d					06 33																
Stockport 84	d					06 41																
Manchester Piccadilly 10	d		06 33			06 54	07 07															
Manchester Oxford Road	d		06 36			06 57	07a09															
Deansgate	d					06 59																
Rochdale 41	d																					
Manchester Victoria	d	06 17		06 38	06 45																	
Salford Central	d			06 40	06 48																	
Salford Crescent	a	06 23		06 44	06 51	07 03																
	d	06 24		06 45	06 52	07 03																
Swinton	d				06 58																	
Moorside	d																					
Walkden	d				07 03																	
Atherton	d				07 08																	
Hag Fold	d																					
Daisy Hill	d				07 12																	
Kearsley	d			06 52																		
Farnworth	d			06 54																		
Moses Gate	d			06 57																		
Bolton	a	06 34	06 50	07 00		07 16																
	d	06 34	06 50	07 01																		
Westhoughton	d																					
Hindley	d				07 16																	
Ince	d																					
Wigan North Western	a			07 19																		
Wigan Wallgate	a				07 21																	
	d				07 23																	
Pemberton	d																					
Orrell	d																					
Upholland	d																					
Rainford	d																					
Kirkby	a																					
Gathurst	d				07 27																	
Appley Bridge	d				07 31																	
Parbold	d				07 35																	
Hoscar	d																					
Burscough Bridge	d				07 39																	
New Lane	d																					
Bescar Lane	d																					
Meols Cop	d				07 47																	
Southport	a				07 56																	
Lostock	d	06 39																				
Horwich Parkway	d	06 43																				
Blackrod	d	06 46																				
Adlington (Lancashire)	d	06 50																				
Chorley	d	06 55																				
Leyland	d	07 06																				
Preston 8 65,97	a	07 11	07 11																			
	d	07 13	07 14						07 20													
Kirkham & Wesham 97	a	07 22																				
Poulton-le-Fylde 97	a	07 30																				
Layton 97	a	07 34																				
Blackpool North 97	a	07 41																				
Lancaster 6 65	a		07 30						07 36													
	d							07 10	07 36													
Oxenholme Lake District 65	a																					
Windermere 83	a																					
Carnforth	d							07a19	07 45													
Silverdale	d								07 51													
Arnside	d								07a58													
Grange-over-Sands	d									08 00	09 34	10 07	11 10	11 52	13 02	14 14	16 03	17 18	18 10	19 10	21 50	22 50
Kents Bank	d									08 04		10 11	11 14	11 55		14 18	16 06	17 21	18 14	19 14	21 54	22 53
Cark	d									08 08	09 40	10 15	11 18	12 00		14 22	16 11	17 26	18 18	19 18	21 58	22 58
Ulverston	d									08 17	09 49	10 24	11 27	12 08	13 14	14 30	16 19	17 34	18 27	19 27	22 07	23 06
Dalton	d									08 25	09 57	10 32	11 35	12 16		14 39	16 27	17 43	18 35	19 35	22 15	23 14
Roose	d									08 31		10 38	11 41	12 22		14 45	16 33	17 49	18 41	19 41	22 21	23 20
Barrow-in-Furness	a									08 41	10 09	10 48	11 51	12 29	13 30	14 52	16 41	17 57	18 51	19 50	22 30	23 28

A To Glasgow Central
B To Clitheroe
C To Liverpool Lime Street
D To Leeds
E To Carlisle
F To Millom

The Sunday service between Manchester Victoria and Wigan Wallgate via Atherton is funded by GMITA and will operate whilst funding exists

Table 82

Mondays to Fridays
until 15 July

Manchester - Bolton - Wigan, Kirkby, Southport, Preston, Blackpool North and Barrow-in-Furness

		NT A	NT	NT B	TP FO ◇1 ⌶	TP FX ◇1 ⌶	TP	NT	NT C	NT	NT	TP ◇1 D ⌶	NT E	NT	NT F	TP ◇1 G ⌶	TP	NT A	NT	NT B	TP ◇1 ⌶	NT	NT
Manchester Airport	85 ✈ d				07 00	07 00						07 25									07 56		08 01
Heald Green	85 d											07 30											08 05
Buxton	86 d										06 23			06 50									
Hazel Grove	86 d										07 00			07 27									
Stockport	84 d										07 10			07 37									
Manchester Piccadilly 10	⇌ d				07 15	07 15					07 27	07 45		07 54		08 07					08 15		08 22
Manchester Oxford Road	d				07 18	07 18					07 30			07 57		08a09					08 19		08 26
Deansgate	⇌ d										07 32			07 59									08 28
Rochdale	41 d																						
Manchester Victoria	⇌ d	07 01	07 06					07 16	07 23	07 27			07 47		08 00			08 03	08 11			08 22	
Salford Central	d	07 04	07 09					07 19	07 26	07 30			07 50		08 03			08 08	08 13			08 25	
Salford Crescent	a	07 07	07 12					07 24	07 29	07 33	07 37		07 53	08 04	08 07			08 12	08 17			08 29	08 33
	d	07 08	07 13					07 25	07 30	07 33	07 37		07 53	08 04	08 08			08 13	08 17			08 30	08 34
Swinton	d	07 14											08 00					08 19					
Moorside	d	07 17											08 02					08 22					
Walkden	d	07 20								07 42			08 06					08 25					
Atherton	d	07 26								07 48			08 11					08 31					
Hag Fold	d	07 28											08 14					08 33					
Daisy Hill	d	07 31								07 51			08 17					08 36					
Kearsley	d										07 45												
Farnworth	d										07 47												
Moses Gate	d										07 49												
Bolton	a		07 23		07 31	07 31		07 35	07 41		07 53	07 59		08 14	08 19				08 27		08 32	08 40	08 44
	d		07 23		07 31	07 31		07 35			07 53	07 59		08 15					08 28		08 32	08 40	08 45
Westhoughton	d		07 31	←							08 01								08 35	←			08 53
Hindley	d	07 39	07 35	07 39									08 21					08 43	08 39	08 43			
Ince	d	→		07 42														→	08 42	08 46			
Wigan North Western	a										08 16												
Wigan Wallgate	a		07 40	07 45						08 03			08 26						08 45	08 49			09 00
	d		07 41	07 46									08 28						08 47	08 51			09 05
Pemberton	d			07 50																08 55			
Orrell	d			07 54																08 59			
Upholland	d			07 58																09 02			
Rainford	d			08 01																09 06			
Kirkby	a			08 13																09 18			
Gathurst	d		07 46										08 32						08 51				
Appley Bridge	d		07 49										08 36						08 55				09 11
Parbold	d		07 53																08 59				09 15
Hoscar	d		07 56																				
Burscough Bridge	d		07 59										08 42						09 03				09 20
New Lane	d		08 02																				
Bescar Lane	d		08 05																				
Meols Cop	d		08 10																09 11				
Southport	a		08 20										08 59						09 20				09 36
Lostock	d							07 42						08 20								08 45	
Horwich Parkway	d				07 38	07 38		07 46						08 24							08 39	08 49	
Blackrod	d							07 49														08 52	
Adlington (Lancashire)	d							07 53						08 29								08 56	
Chorley	d				07 46	07 46		07 58				08 11		08 34							08 47	09 01	
Leyland	d							08 08						08 43								09 12	
Preston 8	65,97 a				07 55	07 57		08 14				08 22		08 50							08 58	09 17	
	d				07 59	07 59	08 08	08 15				08 24		08 51							08 59	09 19	
Kirkham & Wesham	97 a				08 07	08 08		08 25														09 28	
Poulton-le-Fylde	97 a				08 18	08 18		08 33													09 16	09 36	
Layton	97 a				08 22	08 22		08 37														09 43	
Blackpool North	97 a				08 29	08 29		08 44						09 17							09 25	09 50	
Lancaster 6	65 a						08 25					08 39											
	d						08 25					08 40					09 31						
Oxenholme Lake District	65 a											08 54											
Windermere	83 a																						
Carnforth	d						08 34										09 39						
Silverdale	d						08 40										09 45						
Arnside	d						08a47										09a52						
Grange-over-Sands	d																						
Kents Bank	d																						
Cark	d																						
Ulverston	d																						
Dalton	d																						
Roose	d																						
Barrow-in-Furness	a																						

A To Kirkby
B From Manchester Victoria
C To Blackburn
D To Edinburgh
E From Huddersfield
F To Clitheroe
G From Hull to Liverpool Lime Street

The Sunday service between Manchester Victoria and Wigan Wallgate via Atherton is funded by GMITA and will operate whilst funding exists

Table 82

Mondays to Fridays
until 15 July

Manchester - Bolton - Wigan, Kirkby, Southport, Preston, Blackpool North and Barrow-in-Furness

		EM ◇ A	NT B	NT C	NT	TP ◇1 ⌶	NT	NT D	NT	TP ◇1 E ⌶		NT	NT	NT	NT	NT	NT F	TP ◇1 ⌶		NT	NT D	NT
Manchester Airport	85 ✈ d					08 25				09 00				09 03				09 29				
Heald Green	85 d					08 29												09 33				
Buxton	86 d																					
Hazel Grove	86 d	08 17					08 32													09 32		
Stockport	84 d	08 24					08 41													09 41		
Manchester Piccadilly 10	⇌ d	08 37				08 46	08 54			09 16				09 22				09 46		09 54		
Manchester Oxford Road	d	08a40				08 49	08 58			09 19				09 26				09 49		09 58		
Deansgate	⇌ d					08 51	09 00							09 28				09 51		10 00		
Rochdale	41 d			08 00											09 04							
Manchester Victoria	⇌ d		08 29	08 33	08 46			09 00	09 07			09 10	09 22		09 33	09 46					10 00	10 07
Salford Central	d		08 32	08 36	08 49			09 03	09 10			09 13	09 25		09 36	09 49					10 03	10 10
Salford Crescent	a		08 37	08 39	08 52	08 56	09 04	09 07	09 13			09 16	09 29	09 33	09 39	09 52		09 56		10 04	10 07	10 13
	d		08 37	08 40	08 53	08 56	09 04	09 08	09 13			09 17	09 30	09 34	09 40	09 53		09 56		10 04	10 08	10 13
Swinton	d				08 59							09 23				09 59						
Moorside	d											09 26										
Walkden	d				09 04							09 29				10 04						
Atherton	d				09 09							09 35				10 09						
Hag Fold	d											09 37										
Daisy Hill	d				09 13							09 40				10 13						
Kearsley	d			08 47											09 47							
Farnworth	d			08 49											09 49							
Moses Gate	d			08 52											09 52							
Bolton	a		08 49	08 55		09 06	09 14	09 19	09 23	09 32			09 40	09 45	09 55			10 06		10 14	10 19	10 23
	d			08 56		09 07	09 15		09 24	09 33			09 40	09 45	09 56			10 07		10 15		10 24
Westhoughton	d								09 31					09 53								10 31
Hindley	d				09 17				09 35			09 45		09 57		10 17						10 35
Ince	d											09 48										
Wigan North Western	a																					
Wigan Wallgate	a			09 14	09 22				09 44			09 51		10 02	10 13	10 22						10 44
	d				09 24							09 52		10 03		10 24						
Pemberton	d											09 56										
Orrell	d											10 00										
Upholland	d											10 04										
Rainford	d											10 07										
Kirkby	a											10 19										
Gathurst	d				09 28											10 28						
Appley Bridge	d				09 32									10 10		10 32						
Parbold	d				09 36									10 14		10 36						
Hoscar	d				09 39																	
Burscough Bridge	d				09 42									10 18		10 40						
New Lane	d				09 44																	
Bescar Lane	d				09 48																	
Meols Cop	d				09 53											10 48						
Southport	a				10 02									10 35		10 57						
Lostock	d						09 20						09 45							10 20		
Horwich Parkway	d					09 13	09 24						09 49					10 13		10 24		
Blackrod	d												09 52									
Adlington (Lancashire)	d												09 56									
Chorley	d					09 21	09 32			09 44			10 01					10 21		10 32		
Leyland	d						09 42						10 12							10 42		
Preston 8	65,97 a					09 33	09 50			09 55			10 17					10 33		10 51		
	d					09 38				09 58	10 07		10 19					10 38	10 45			
Kirkham & Wesham	97 a												10 28									
Poulton-le-Fylde	97 a					09 56							10 36					10 56				
Layton	97 a												10 43									
Blackpool North	97 a					10 05							10 51					11 05				
Lancaster 6	65 a									10 13	10 22								11 00			
	d										10 23						10 49		11 01			
Oxenholme Lake District	65 a																		11 17			
Windermere	83 a																		11 39			
Carnforth	d										10 32						10a58					
Silverdale	d																					
Arnside	d										10a44											
Grange-over-Sands	d																					
Kents Bank	d																					
Cark	d																					
Ulverston	d																					
Dalton	d																					
Roose	d																					
Barrow-in-Furness	a																					

A From Nottingham to Liverpool Lime Street
B To Blackburn
C From Todmorden
D To Clitheroe
E To Glasgow Central
F From Morecambe to Leeds

The Sunday service between Manchester Victoria and Wigan Wallgate via Atherton is funded by GMITA and will operate whilst funding exists

Manchester - Bolton - Wigan, Kirkby, Southport, Preston, Blackpool North and Barrow-in-Furness

	TP ◇1 A ✠	NT	NT	NT	NT	NT	TP ◇1 ✠	NT		NT B	NT	NT	TP	TP ◇1 C ✠	NT	NT	NT	NT		TP ◇1 ✠	NT	NT B	NT	TP ◇1 A ✠
Manchester Airport 85 ✈ d	10 00			10 03			10 29							11 00		11 03				11 29				12 00
Heald Green 85 d							10 33													11 33				
Buxton 86 d																								
Hazel Grove 86 d								10 33													11 33			
Stockport 84 d								10 41													11 41			
Manchester Piccadilly 10 ⇌ d	10 16			10 22			10 46	10 54						11 16		11 22				11 46	11 54			12 16
Manchester Oxford Road d	10 19			10 26			10 49	10 58						11 19		11 26				11 49	11 58			12 19
Deansgate ⇌ d				10 28			10 51	11 00								11 28				11 51	12 00			
Rochdale 41 d					10 05												11 04							
Manchester Victoria ⇌ d		10 10	10 22		10 33	10 46				11 00	11 07	11 10			11 22		11 33	11 46				12 00	12 07	
Salford Central d		10 13	10 25		10 36	10 49				11 03	11 10	11 13			11 25		11 36	11 49				12 03	12 10	
Salford Crescent a		10 16	10 29	10 33	10 39	10 52	10 56	11 04		11 07	11 13	11 16			11 29	11 33	11 39	11 52		11 56	12 04	12 07	12 13	
d		10 17	10 30	10 34	10 40	10 53	10 56	11 04		11 08	11 13	11 17			11 30	11 34	11 40	11 53		11 56	12 04	12 08	12 13	
Swinton d		10 23				10 59						11 23						11 59						
Moorside d		10 26										11 26												
Walkden d		10 29				11 04						11 29						12 04						
Atherton d		10 35				11 09						11 35						12 09						
Hag Fold d		10 37										11 37												
Daisy Hill d		10 40				11 13						11 40						12 13						
Kearsley d					10 47												11 47							
Farnworth d					10 49												11 49							
Moses Gate d					10 52												11 52							
Bolton a	10 32		10 40	10 45	10 55		11 06	11 14		11 19	11 23			11 32	11 40	11 45	11 55			12 06	12 14	12 19	12 23	12 32
d	10 33		10 40	10 45	10 56		11 07	11 15			11 24			11 33	11 40	11 45	11 56			12 07	12 15		12 24	12 33
Westhoughton d				10 53							11 31					11 53							12 31	
Hindley d		10 45		10 57		11 17					11 35	11 45				11 57		12 17					12 35	
Ince d		10 48										11 48												
Wigan North Western a																								
Wigan Wallgate a		10 51		11 02	11 13	11 22					11 44	11 51				12 02	12 13	12 22					12 44	
d		10 52		11 03		11 24						11 52				12 03		12 24						
Pemberton d		10 56										11 56												
Orrell d		11 00										12 00												
Upholland d		11 04										12 04												
Rainford d		11 07										12 07												
Kirkby a		11 19										12 19												
Gathurst d						11 28												12 28						
Appley Bridge d				11 10		11 32										12 10		12 32						
Parbold d				11 14		11 36										12 14		12 36						
Hoscar d						11 39																		
Burscough Bridge d				11 18		11 42										12 18		12 41						
New Lane d						11 44																		
Bescar Lane d						11 48																		
Meols Cop d						11 53												12 49						
Southport a				11 35		12 02										12 35		12 59						
Lostock d			10 45					11 20							11 45						12 20			
Horwich Parkway d			10 49				11 13	11 24							11 49					12 13	12 24			
Blackrod d			10 52												11 52									
Adlington (Lancashire) d			10 56												11 56									
Chorley d	10 44		11 01				11 21	11 32						11 44	12 01					12 21	12 32			12 44
Leyland d			11 12					11 42							12 12						12 42			
Preston 8 65,97 a	10 55		11 17				11 33	11 50						11 57	12 17					12 33	12 50			12 55
d	10 58		11 19				11 38							11 58	12 19					12 38				12 58
Kirkham & Wesham 97 a			11 28												12 28									
Poulton-le-Fylde 97 a			11 36				11 56								12 36					12 56				
Layton 97 a			11 43												12 43									
Blackpool North 97 a			11 50				12 05								12 50					13 05				
Lancaster 6 65 a	11 13													12 14										13 13
d	11 14												11 30	12 14										13 14
Oxenholme Lake District 65 a	11 28																							13 28
Windermere 83 a																								
Carnforth d													11 38	12 23										
Silverdale d													11 44	12 29										
Arnside d													11a51	12a36										
Grange-over-Sands d																								
Kents Bank d																								
Cark d																								
Ulverston d																								
Dalton d																								
Roose d																								
Barrow-in-Furness a																								

A To Edinburgh **B** To Clitheroe **C** ✠ to Chorley

The Sunday service between Manchester Victoria and Wigan Wallgate via Atherton is funded by GMITA and will operate whilst funding exists

Manchester - Bolton - Wigan, Kirkby, Southport, Preston, Blackpool North and Barrow-in-Furness

	NT	TP ◇1	NT	NT		NT	NT	TP ◇1 ✠	NT	NT A	NT	NT	NT B	TP ◇1 C ✠			NT	NT	NT	NT	TP ◇1 ✠	NT	NT A	NT
Manchester Airport 85 ✈ d				12 03				12 29						13 00				13 03			13 29			
Heald Green 85 d								12 33													13 33			
Buxton 86 d																								
Hazel Grove 86 d									12 33													13 33		
Stockport 84 d									12 41													13 41		
Manchester Piccadilly 10 ⇌ d				12 22				12 46	12 54					13 16				13 22			13 46	13 54		
Manchester Oxford Road d				12 26				12 49	12 58					13 19				13 26			13 49	13 58		
Deansgate ⇌ d				12 28				12 51	13 00									13 28			13 51	14 00		
Rochdale 41 d						12 04													13 04					
Manchester Victoria ⇌ d	12 10		12 22			12 33	12 46			13 00	13 07	13 10					13 22		13 33	13 46			14 00	14 07
Salford Central d	12 13		12 25			12 36	12 49			13 03	13 10	13 13					13 25		13 36	13 49			14 03	14 10
Salford Crescent a	12 16		12 29	12 33		12 39	12 52	12 56	13 04	13 07	13 13	13 16					13 29	13 33	13 39	13 52	13 56	14 04	14 07	14 13
d	12 17		12 30	12 34		12 40	12 53	12 56	13 04	13 08	13 13	13 17					13 30	13 34	13 40	13 53	13 56	14 04	14 08	14 13
Swinton d	12 23						12 59					13 23								13 59				
Moorside d	12 26											13 26												
Walkden d	12 29						13 04					13 29								14 04				
Atherton d	12 35						13 09					13 35								14 09				
Hag Fold d	12 37											13 37												
Daisy Hill d	12 40						13 13					13 40								14 13				
Kearsley d						12 47													13 47					
Farnworth d						12 49													13 49					
Moses Gate d						12 52													13 52					
Bolton a			12 40	12 45		12 55		13 06	13 14	13 19	13 23			13 32			13 40	13 45	13 55		14 06	14 14	14 19	14 23
d			12 40	12 45		12 56		13 07	13 15		13 24			13 33			13 40	13 45	13 56		14 07	14 15		14 24
Westhoughton d				12 53							13 31							13 53						14 31
Hindley d	12 45			12 57			13 17				13 35	13 45						13 57		14 17				14 35
Ince d	12 48											13 48												
Wigan North Western a																								
Wigan Wallgate a	12 51			13 02		13 13	13 22				13 44	13 51						14 02	14 13	14 22				14 44
d	12 52			13 03			13 24					13 52						14 03		14 24				
Pemberton d	12 56											13 56												
Orrell d	13 00											14 00												
Upholland d	13 04											14 04												
Rainford d	13 07											14 07												
Kirkby a	13 19											14 19												
Gathurst d							13 28													14 28				
Appley Bridge d				13 10			13 32											14 10		14 32				
Parbold d				13 14			13 36											14 14		14 36				
Hoscar d							13 39																	
Burscough Bridge d				13 18			13 42											14 18		14 41				
New Lane d							13 44																	
Bescar Lane d							13 48																	
Meols Cop d							13 53													14 49				
Southport a				13 35			14 02											14 35		14 59				
Lostock d			12 45						13 20								13 45					14 20		
Horwich Parkway d			12 49					13 13	13 24								13 49				14 13	14 24		
Blackrod d			12 52														13 52							
Adlington (Lancashire) d			12 56														13 56							
Chorley d			13 01					13 21	13 32					13 44			14 01				14 21	14 32		
Leyland d			13 12						13 42								14 12					14 42		
Preston 8 65,97 a			13 17					13 33	13 50					13 55			14 17				14 33	14 50		
d		13 04	13 19					13 38						13 58	14 04		14 19				14 38			
Kirkham & Wesham 97 a			13 28														14 28							
Poulton-le-Fylde 97 a			13 36					13 56									14 36				14 56			
Layton 97 a			13 43														14 43							
Blackpool North 97 a			13 50					14 05									14 51				15 05			
Lancaster 6 65 a		13 19												14 13	14 19									
d		13 20											13 48		14 20									
Oxenholme Lake District 65 a		13 36																						
Windermere 83 a		13 56																						
Carnforth d													13a58		14 28									
Silverdale d																								
Arnside d															14a40									
Grange-over-Sands d																								
Kents Bank d																								
Cark d																								
Ulverston d																								
Dalton d																								
Roose d																								
Barrow-in-Furness a																								

A To Clitheroe **B** From Heysham Port to Leeds **C** To Glasgow Central

The Sunday service between Manchester Victoria and Wigan Wallgate via Atherton is funded by GMITA and will operate whilst funding exists

Table 82

Manchester - Bolton - Wigan, Kirkby, Southport, Preston, Blackpool North and Barrow-in-Furness

Mondays to Fridays until 15 July

	TP ◇1 A ⌶	NT	NT	NT	NT	NT	TP ◇1 B ⌶	TP ◇1 C ⌶ FO	NT	NT D	NT	NT	TP	TP ◇1 E ⌶	NT	NT	NT	NT D	NT	TP ◇1 ⌶	NT
Manchester Airport 85 d	14 00			14 03			14 29	14 29						15 00		15 03				15 29	
Heald Green 85 d							14 33	14 33												15 33	
Buxton 86 d																					
Hazel Grove 86 d									14 33												15 33
Stockport 84 d									14 41												15 41
Manchester Piccadilly d	14 16			14 22			14 46	14 46	14 54					15 16		15 22				15 46	15 54
Manchester Oxford Road d	14 19			14 26			14 49	14 49	14 58					15 19		15 26				15 49	15 58
Deansgate d				14 28			14 51	14 51	15 00							15 28				15 51	16 00
Rochdale 41 d					14 04												15 04				
Manchester Victoria d		14 10	14 22		14 33	14 46				15 00	15 07	15 10			15 22		15 33	15 40	15 46		
Salford Central d		14 13	14 25		14 36	14 49				15 03	15 10	15 13			15 25		15 36	15 43	15 49		
Salford Crescent a		14 16	14 29	14 33	14 39	14 52	14 56	14 56	15 04	15 07	15 13	15 16			15 29	15 33	15 39	15 46	15 52	15 56	16 04
d		14 17	14 30	14 34	14 40	14 53	14 56	14 56	15 04	15 08	15 13	15 17			15 30	15 34	15 40	15 47	15 53	15 56	16 04
Swinton d		14 23				14 59						15 23							15 59		
Moorside d		14 26										15 26									
Walkden d		14 29				15 04						15 29							16 04		
Atherton d		14 35				15 09						15 35							16 09		
Hag Fold d		14 37										15 37									
Daisy Hill d		14 40				15 13						15 40							16 13		
Kearsley d					14 47												15 47				
Farnworth d					14 49												15 49				
Moses Gate d					14 52												15 52				
Bolton a	14 32		14 40	14 45	14 55		15 06	15 06	15 14	15 19	15 23			15 32	15 40	15 45	15 55	15 59		16 06	16 19
d	14 33		14 40	14 45	14 56		15 07	15 07	15 15		15 24			15 33	15 40	15 45	15 56			16 07	
Westhoughton d				14 53							15 31					15 53					
Hindley d		14 45		14 57		15 17					15 35	15 45				15 57			16 17		
Ince d		14 48										15 48									
Wigan North Western a																					
Wigan Wallgate a		14 51		15 02	15 13	15 22					15 44	15 51				16 02	16 13		16 22		
d		14 52		15 03		15 24						15 58				16 03			16 24		
Pemberton d		14 56										16 02									
Orrell d		15 00										16 06									
Upholland d		15 04										16 09									
Rainford d		15 07										16 13									
Kirkby a		15 19										16 25									
Gathurst d						15 28										16 08			16 28		
Appley Bridge d				15 10		15 32										16 11			16 32		
Parbold d				15 14		15 36										16 15			16 36		
Hoscar d																16 18					
Burscough Bridge d				15 18		15 40										16 21			16 40		
New Lane d																16 24					
Bescar Lane d																16 27					
Meols Cop d						15 48										16 32			16 48		
Southport a				15 35		15 57										16 42			16 57		
Lostock d			14 45						15 20						15 45					16 12	
Horwich Parkway d			14 49				15 13	15 13	15 24						15 49					16 15	
Blackrod d			14 52												15 52						
Adlington (Lancashire) d			14 56												15 56						
Chorley d	14 44		15 01				15 21	15 21	15 32					15 44	16 01					16 23	
Leyland d			15 12						15 42						16 12						
Preston 65,97 a	14 55		15 17				15 33	15 33	15 50					15 55	16 19					16 35	
d	14 58		15 19				15 38	15 38						15 58						16 38	
Kirkham & Wesham 97 a			15 28																	16 47	
Poulton-le-Fylde 97 a			15 36				15 56	15 58												16 57	
Layton 97 a			15 43																	17 00	
Blackpool North 97 a			15 50				16 05	16 07												17 07	
Lancaster 65 a	15 13													16 13							
d	15 14												15 20	16 14							
Oxenholme Lake District 65 a	15 28																				
Windermere 83 a																					
Carnforth d													15 28	16 23							
Silverdale d													15 34	16 29							
Arnside d													15a42	16a36							
Grange-over-Sands d																					
Kents Bank d																					
Cark d																					
Ulverston d																					
Dalton d																					
Roose d																					
Barrow-in-Furness a																					

A To Edinburgh
B until 23 June, FX from 27 June until 14 July
C From 24 June until 15 July
D To Clitheroe
E ⌶ to Chorley

The Sunday service between Manchester Victoria and Wigan Wallgate via Atherton is funded by GMITA and will operate whilst funding exists

Table 82

Manchester - Bolton - Wigan, Kirkby, Southport, Preston, Blackpool North and Barrow-in-Furness

Mondays to Fridays until 15 July

	NT	NT	TP	TP ◇1 A ⌶		TP ◇1	NT	NT	NT B	NT	NT	TP ◇1 ⌶	NT	NT	NT B	TP ◇1 C ⌶	NT D	NT	TP ◇1	NT	NT E	NT	NT
Manchester Airport 85 d				16 00						16 03		16 29				17 00						17 03	
Heald Green 85 d												16 33											
Buxton 86 d																							16 30
Hazel Grove 86 d														16 30									17 04
Stockport 84 d														16 41									17 12
Manchester Piccadilly d				16 16						16 22		16 46		16 54		17 15						17 22	17 27
Manchester Oxford Road d				16 19						16 26		16 49		16 58		17 18						17 26	17 30
Deansgate d										16 28				17 00									17 33
Rochdale 41 d											16 04										17 03		
Manchester Victoria d	16 07	16 10					16 20		16 23		16 36		16 46		17 00		17 06	17 10		17 19	17 23		
Salford Central d	16 10	16 13					16 23		16 26		16 39		16 49		17 03		17 09	17 12		17 22	17 27		
Salford Crescent a	16 13	16 16					16 26	16 38	16 30	16 34	16 42		16 52	17 04	17 07		17 13	17 16		17 25	17 29	17 34	17 38
d	16 13	16 17					16 27	16 38	16 31	16 34	16 43		16 53	17 04	17 08		17 14	17 17		17 27	17 30	17 34	17 38
Swinton d		16 23											16 59					17 23					
Moorside d		16 26											17 02					17 26					
Walkden d		16 29											17 05					17 31					
Atherton d		16 35											17 11				17 26	17 37					
Hag Fold d		16 37											17 14					17 39					
Daisy Hill d		16 40											17 17				17 30	17 43					
Kearsley d											16 50												
Farnworth d											16 52												
Moses Gate d	16 21										16 55												
Bolton a	16 25			16 32			16 37	16 48	16 42	16 45	16 58	17 05		17 14	17 19	17 31				17 37	17 42	17 45	17 48
d	16 25			16 33			16 37	16 49		16 45	16 59	17 06		17 15		17 32				17 37		17 45	17 49
Westhoughton d	16 33									16 53	17 06											17 53	
Hindley d	16 37	16 45								16 57	17 10		17 21					17 48					
Ince d		16 48											17 24					17 51					
Wigan North Western a																							
Wigan Wallgate a	16 46	16 51								17 02	17 19		17 31				17 38	17 54				18 01	
d		16 52								17 03							17 40	17 55				18 02	
Pemberton d		16 56																17 59					
Orrell d		17 00																18 03					
Upholland d		17 04																18 07					
Rainford d		17 07																18 10					
Kirkby a		17 19																18 22					
Gathurst d										17 08							17 44						
Appley Bridge d										17 11							17 48					18 09	
Parbold d										17 15							17 52					18 13	
Hoscar d																							
Burscough Bridge d										17 20							17 57					18 17	
New Lane d																							
Bescar Lane d																							
Meols Cop d										17 27							18 05					18 26	
Southport a										17 37							18 14					18 35	
Lostock d							16 43	16 54						17 20						17 43			17 54
Horwich Parkway d							16 47	16 58						17 24						17 47			17 58
Blackrod d							16 51	17 01												17 51			18 01
Adlington (Lancashire) d							16 55	17 05												17 55			18 05
Chorley d				16 44			17 00	17 10				17 19		17 32		17 44				18 00			18 10
Leyland d							17 11	17 21						17 42						18 11			
Preston 65,97 a				16 55			17 19	17 26				17 30		17 51		17 55				18 16			18 25
d				17 00	17 04	17 04	17 21	17 28				17 32				17 58			18 08	18 18			18 26
Kirkham & Wesham 97 a							17 30					17 41								18 27			
Poulton-le-Fylde 97 a							17 38					17 51								18 35			18 43
Layton 97 a							17 43					17 54								18 39			
Blackpool North 97 a							17 50					18 02								18 49			18 53
Lancaster 65 a				17 15	17 23	17 23		17 48								18 13			18 23				
d			17 19	17 16	17 25	17 25		17 48								18 14			18 24				
Oxenholme Lake District 65 a				17 30	17 43	17 43										18 28							
Windermere 83 a					18 08	18 08																	
Carnforth d			17 28					18 00											18 34				
Silverdale d			17 34					18 06											18 40				
Arnside d			17a41					18 13											18a47				
Grange-over-Sands d																							
Kents Bank d																							
Cark d																							
Ulverston d																							
Dalton d																							
Roose d																							
Barrow-in-Furness a																							

A To Edinburgh
B To Clitheroe
C To Glasgow Central
D From Stalybridge
E To Blackburn

The Sunday service between Manchester Victoria and Wigan Wallgate via Atherton is funded by GMITA and will operate whilst funding exists

Table 82

Manchester - Bolton - Wigan, Kirkby, Southport, Preston, Blackpool North and Barrow-in-Furness

Station		NT	NT	NT	TP	NT	NT	NT	TP	TP	TP	NT	NT	NT	NT	NT	TP	NT	NT	NT	NT	TP
					◇1 ⊼		A		◇1	◇1 B ⊼	◇1		C				◇1 ⊼		A		D	◇1 E ⊼
Manchester Airport 85 ✈	d				17 29					18 00				18 03			18 29					19 00
Heald Green 85	d				17 33												18 33					
Buxton 86	d					16 59												17 59				
Hazel Grove 86	d					17 33												18 33				
Stockport 84	d					17 41												18 41				
Manchester Piccadilly 10 ⇌	d				17 46	17 54				18 16				18 22			18 46	18 54				19 16
Manchester Oxford Road	d				17 49	17 58				18 19				18 26			18 49	18 58				19 19
Deansgate ⇌	d				17 51	18 00								18 28			18 51	19 00				
Rochdale 41	d												18 02									
Manchester Victoria ⇌	d	17 36	17 40	17 45			18 00	18 10				18 20	18 23		18 33	18 45			19 00	19 10		
Salford Central	d	17 39	17 43	17 48			18 03	18 13				18 23	18 26		18 36	18 48			19 03	19 13		
Salford Crescent	a	17 42	17 46	17 51	17 55	18 04	18 07	18 16				18 26	18 30	18 34	18 39	18 51	18 56	19 04	19 07	19 16		
	d	17 43	17 47	17 52	17 55	18 04	18 08	18 17				18 27	18 31	18 34	18 40	18 52	18 56	19 04	19 08	19 17		
Swinton	d			17 58				18 23								18 58				19 23		
Moorside	d			18 01				18 26								19 01				19 26		
Walkden	d			18 05				18 29								19 04				19 29		
Atherton	d		17 59	18 11				18 35								19 10				19 35		
Hag Fold	d			18 13				18 37								19 12				19 37		
Daisy Hill	d		18 03	18 17				18 40								19 15				19 40		
Kearsley	d	17 53													18 47							
Farnworth	d	17 55													18 49							
Moses Gate	d	17 57													18 52							
Bolton	a	18 01			18 06	18 14	18 19			18 32		18 37	18 42	18 45	18 55		19 06	19 19	19 20			19 32
	d	18 01			18 07	18 15				18 33		18 37		18 45	18 56		19 07					19 33
Westhoughton	d	18 09												18 53	19 03							
Hindley	d	18 13		18 22				18 45						18 57	19 09	19 20				19 45		
Ince	d			18 25				18 48								19 23				19 48		
Wigan North Western	a							18 56														
Wigan Wallgate	a	18 22	18 11	18 28										19 02	19 18	19 30				19 55		
	d		18 15	18 29										19 03								
Pemberton	d			18 33																		
Orrell	d			18 37																		
Upholland	d			18 41																		
Rainford	d			18 44																		
Kirkby	a			18 55																		
Gathurst	d		18 19											19 08								
Appley Bridge	d		18 23											19 11								
Parbold	d		18 28											19 15								
Hoscar	d		18 31																			
Burscough Bridge	d		18 34											19 19								
New Lane	d		18 37																			
Bescar Lane	d		18 40																			
Meols Cop	d		18 46											19 27								
Southport	a		18 55											19 37								
Lostock	d				18 12	18 20						18 42					19 12					
Horwich Parkway	d				18 15	18 24						18 46					19 15					
Blackrod	d				18 19							18 49										
Adlington (Lancashire)	d											18 53										
Chorley	d				18 26	18 32				18 44		18 58					19 23					19 44
Leyland	d					18 42						19 10										
Preston 8 65,97	a				18 38	18 48				18 55		19 18					19 33					19 55
	d				18 40	18 49				19 00	19 04	19 19					19 38					19 58
Kirkham & Wesham 97	a				18 49							19 28										
Poulton-le-Fylde 97	a				18 59							19 36					19 56					
Layton 97	a				19 02							19 43										
Blackpool North 97	a				19 09	19 16						19 50					20 05					
Lancaster 6 65	a									19 15	19 20											20 13
	d								18 29	19 16	19 20										19 24	20 14
Oxenholme Lake District 65	a								18 45	19 30												
Windermere 83	a								19 08													
Carnforth	d										19a28										19a34	20a22
Silverdale	d																					
Arnside	d																					
Grange-over-Sands	d																					
Kents Bank	d																					
Cark	d																					
Ulverston	d																					
Dalton	d																					
Roose	d																					
Barrow-in-Furness	a																					

A To Clitheroe
B To Edinburgh
C To Blackburn
D From Morecambe to Leeds
E ⊼ to Chorley

The Sunday service between Manchester Victoria and Wigan Wallgate via Atherton is funded by GMITA and will operate whilst funding exists

Table 82

Manchester - Bolton - Wigan, Kirkby, Southport, Preston, Blackpool North and Barrow-in-Furness

Station		NT	NT	TP	NT	TP	NT	NT	NT	NT	TP	NT	NT	NT	NT	NT	NT	TP	NT FO	NT FX	TP	NT	NT FO
				◇1	A	◇1				B	◇1	A				B	C	◇1	A	A	◇1	B	
Manchester Airport 85 ✈	d	19 03		19 29		20 00			20 03	20 09	20 29				21 03	21 09		21 29			22 00	22 08	
Heald Green 85	d			19 33						20 12	20 33					21 12		21 33				22 12	
Buxton 86	d																						
Hazel Grove 86	d																						
Stockport 84	d																						
Manchester Piccadilly 10 ⇌	d	19 20		19 46		20 16			20 20	20 32	20 46				21 20	21 32	21 38	21 46			22 16	22 32	
Manchester Oxford Road	d	19 24		19 49		20 19			20 24	20a36	20 49				21 24	21a36	21 44	21 49			22 19	22a36	
Deansgate ⇌	d	19 26		19 51					20 26		20 51				21 26		21a46	21 51					
Rochdale 41	d																						
Manchester Victoria ⇌	d		19 28		20 00		20 10	20 22				21 00	21 10	21 22					22 00	22 00			22 10
Salford Central	d		19 31		20 03		20 13	20 25				21 03	21 13	21 25					22 04				22 13
Salford Crescent	a	19 29	19 34	19 56	20 07		20 16	20 29	20 33		20 56	21 07	21 16	21 29	21 33			21 56	22 07	22 07			22 17
	d	19 30	19 35	19 56	20 08		20 17	20 30	20 34		20 56	21 08	21 17	21 30	21 34			21 56	22 08	22 08			22 17
Swinton	d						20 23						21 23										22 23
Moorside	d						20 26						21 26										22 26
Walkden	d						20 29						21 29										22 29
Atherton	d						20 35						21 35										22 35
Hag Fold	d						20 37						21 37										22 37
Daisy Hill	d						20 40						21 40										22 40
Kearsley	d																						
Farnworth	d																						
Moses Gate	d																						
Bolton	a	19 40	19 45	20 06	20 19	20 32		20 40	20 45		21 06	21 19		21 40	21 45			22 06	22 19	22 19	22 32		
	d	19 40	19 45	20 07		20 33		20 40	20 45		21 07			21 40	21 45			22 07			22 33		
Westhoughton	d	19 48							20 53						21 53								
Hindley	d	19 52					20 45		20 57				21 45		21 57								22 45
Ince	d						20 48						21 48										22 48
Wigan North Western	a																				22 48		
Wigan Wallgate	a	19 57					20 55		21 02				21 55		22 02								22 55
	d	19 59							21 03						22 03								
Pemberton	d																						
Orrell	d																						
Upholland	d																						
Rainford	d																						
Kirkby	a																						
Gathurst	d	20 03							21 08						22 08								
Appley Bridge	d	20 07							21 11						22 11								
Parbold	d	20 11							21 15						22 15								
Hoscar	d								21 18														
Burscough Bridge	d	20 15							21 21						22 20								
New Lane	d								21 24														
Bescar Lane	d								21 27														
Meols Cop	d	20 23							21 32						22 27								
Southport	a	20 32							21 42						22 37								
Lostock	d		19 50					20 45						21 45									
Horwich Parkway	d		19 54	20 13		20 39		20 49			21 13			21 49				22 13					
Blackrod	d		19 57					20 52						21 52									
Adlington (Lancashire)	d		20 01					20 56						21 56									
Chorley	d		20 06	20 21		20 46		21 01			21 21			22 01				22 21					
Leyland	d		20 18					21 12						22 12									
Preston 8 65,97	a		20 23	20 33		20 57		21 17			21 33			22 17				22 33			23 09		
	d		20 25	20 38		20 58		21 19			21 38			22 19				22 35			23 13		
Kirkham & Wesham 97	a		20 34					21 28						22 28									
Poulton-le-Fylde 97	a		20 42	20 56				21 36			21 56			22 36				22 52					
Layton 97	a		20 46					21 40						22 43									
Blackpool North 97	a		20 54	21 06				21 48			22 06			22 51				23 02					
Lancaster 6 65	a					21 13															23 28		
	d					21 14															23 29		
Oxenholme Lake District 65	a																						
Windermere 83	a																						
Carnforth	d					21a23															23a37		
Silverdale	d																						
Arnside	d																						
Grange-over-Sands	d																						
Kents Bank	d																						
Cark	d																						
Ulverston	d																						
Dalton	d																						
Roose	d																						
Barrow-in-Furness	a																						

A To Clitheroe
B From Wilmslow
C To Warrington Central

The Sunday service between Manchester Victoria and Wigan Wallgate via Atherton is funded by GMITA and will operate whilst funding exists

Table 82

Manchester - Bolton - Wigan, Kirkby, Southport, Preston, Blackpool North and Barrow-in-Furness

Station	NT FX	NT FO	NT FX	NT	TP ◇1	NT	NT FO A	NT FX A	NT FO	NT FX	NT FO	NT FX	TP FX ◇1 B
Manchester Airport 85 ✈ d				22 19	22 29								23 18
Heald Green 85 d					22 33								
Buxton 86 d													
Hazel Grove 86 d													
Stockport 84 d						22 34							
Manchester Piccadilly 10 ⇌ d				22 36	22 46	22 50							23 38
Manchester Oxford Road d				22 39	22 49	22 53							
Deansgate ⇌ d				22 41	22 51	22 55							
Rochdale 41 d													
Manchester Victoria ⇌ d	22 10	22 22	22 22				23 00	23 00	23 20	23 20	23 23	23 23	
Salford Central d		22 25					23 03		23 23		23 26		
Salford Crescent a	22 17	22 29	22 29	22 46	22 56	22 59	23 07	23 07	23 26	23 25	23 29	23 29	23 43
d	22 17	22 30	22 30	22 46	22 56	22 59	23 08	23 08	23 26	23 26	23 30	23 30	
Swinton d	22 23								23 33	23 33			
Moorside d	22 26								23 35	23 35			
Walkden d	22 29								23 39	23 39			
Atherton d	22 35								23 44	23 44			
Hag Fold d	22 37								23 47	23 47			
Daisy Hill d	22 40								23 50	23 50			
Kearsley d						23 07							
Farnworth d						23 09							
Moses Gate d						23 11							
Bolton a		22 40	22 40	22 56	23 06	23 15	23 19	23 19			23 40	23 40	
d		22 40	22 40	22 57	23 07	23 15					23 40	23 40	
Westhoughton d				23 04		23 23							
Hindley d	22 45			23 08		23 27			23 54	23 54			
Ince d	22 48								23 57	23 57			
Wigan North Western a													
Wigan Wallgate a	22 55			23 13		23 38			00 04	00 04			
d				23 15									
Pemberton d													
Orrell d													
Upholland d													
Rainford d													
Kirkby a													
Gathurst d				23 19									
Appley Bridge d				23 23									
Parbold d				23 27									
Hoscar d													
Burscough Bridge d				23 31									
New Lane d													
Bescar Lane d													
Meols Cop d				23 39									
Southport a				23 48									
Lostock d		22 45	22 45								23 45	23 45	
Horwich Parkway d		22 49	22 49		23 13						23 49	23 49	
Blackrod d		22 52	22 52								23 52	23 52	
Adlington (Lancashire) d		22 56	22 56								23 56	23 56	
Chorley d		23 01	23 01		23 21						00 01	00 01	
Leyland d		23 12	23 12								00 12	00 12	
Preston 8 65,97 a		23 17	23 17		23 33						00 17	00 17	
d		23 19	23 19		23 35						00 19	00 19	
Kirkham & Wesham 97 a		23 28	23 28								00 28	00 28	
Poulton-le-Fylde 97 a		23 36	23 36		23 52						00 36	00 36	
Layton 97 a		23 40	23 40								00 43	00 43	
Blackpool North 97 a		23 48	23 48		00 02						00 50	00 50	
Lancaster 6 65 a													
d													
Oxenholme Lake District 65 a													
Windermere 83 a													
Carnforth d													
Silverdale d													
Arnside d													
Grange-over-Sands d													
Kents Bank d													
Cark d													
Ulverston d													
Dalton d													
Roose d													
Barrow-in-Furness a													

A To Blackburn
B To York

The Sunday service between Manchester Victoria and Wigan Wallgate via Atherton is funded by GMITA and will operate whilst funding exists

Table 82

Manchester - Bolton - Wigan, Kirkby, Southport, Preston, Blackpool North and Barrow-in-Furness

Station	TP MX ◇1	TP MO ◇1	TP MX ◇1	NT MX	NT MX	TP ◇1	TP MX ◇1 A	TP MO ◇1 A	TP ◇1	TP ◇1 B	NT C	NT D	TP 1	TP MO ◇1 E	TP MX ◇1 F	NT G	NT	TP ◇1 H	NT	TP ◇1 I	NT	NT
Manchester Airport 85 ✈ d	22p00	22p30	22p29			00 01	00 38	00 48	04 00	04 12	04 34							05 45		06 18		
Heald Green 85 d			22p33															05 49				
Buxton 86 d																						
Hazel Grove 86 d																						
Stockport 84 d																						
Manchester Piccadilly 10 ⇌ d	22p16	22p46	22p46			00 16	00 53	01 03	04 15	04 30	04a47			05 46	05 46			06 03		06 33		
Manchester Oxford Road d	22p19	22p49	22p49															06 06		06 36		
Deansgate ⇌ d		22p51	22p51																			
Rochdale 41 d																						
Manchester Victoria ⇌ d				23p20	23p23											05 55	06 00		06 17		06 38	06 45
Salford Central d																					06 40	06 48
Salford Crescent a		22p54	22p56	23p25	23p29		00 58	01 09		04 36				05 51	05 51	05 59	06 04		06 23		06 44	06 51
d		22p55	22p56	23p26	23p30									05 52	05 52	06 00	06 05		06 24		06 45	06 52
Swinton d				23p33																		06 58
Moorside d				23p35																		
Walkden d				23p39																		07 03
Atherton d				23p44																		07 08
Hag Fold d				23p47																		
Daisy Hill d				23p50																		07 12
Kearsley d																					06 52	
Farnworth d																					06 54	
Moses Gate d																					06 57	
Bolton a	22p32	23p05	23p06		23p40	00s31			04s29							06 11	06 15	06 19	06 34	06 50	07 00	
d	22p33	23p05	23p07		23p40												06 15	06 19	06 34	06 50	07 01	
Westhoughton d																	06 23					
Hindley d				23p54													06 27					07 16
Ince d				23p57																		
Wigan North Western a	22p48								04 44					06 15	06 15						07 19	
Wigan Wallgate a				00 04													06 32					07 21
d																	06 34					07 23
Pemberton d																	06 38					
Orrell d																	06 42					
Upholland d																	06 45					
Rainford d																	06 49					
Kirkby a																	07 01					
Gathurst d																						07 27
Appley Bridge d																						07 31
Parbold d																						07 35
Hoscar d																						
Burscough Bridge d																						07 39
New Lane d																						
Bescar Lane d																						
Meols Cop d																						07 47
Southport a																						07 56
Lostock d		23p10			23p45														06 39			
Horwich Parkway d		23p14	23p13		23p49														06 43			
Blackrod d		23p17			23p52														06 46			
Adlington (Lancashire) d		23p20			23p56														06 50			
Chorley d		23p24	23p21		00 01													06 31	06 55			
Leyland d		23p34			00 12									06 27	06 27				07 06			
Preston 8 65,97 a	23p09	23p42	23p33		00 17	01s05			05s04					06 35	06 35			06 42	07 11	07 11		
d	23p13	23p47	23p35		00 19							05 22		06 37	06 37			06 44	07 13	07 14		
Kirkham & Wesham 97 a		23p56			00 28									06 46	06 46				07 22			
Poulton-le-Fylde 97 a		00 05	23p52		00 36									06 56	06 56				07 30			
Layton 97 a					00 43									06 59	06 59				07 34			
Blackpool North 97 a		00 14	00 02		00 50	01 30			05 33					07 05	07 06				07 41			
Lancaster 6 65 a	23p28											05 42						06 59		07 30		
d	23p29											05 42	05 46					07 00				
Oxenholme Lake District 65 a													06 21					07 15				
Windermere 83 a													06 41									
Carnforth d	23p37											05 52										
Silverdale d	23p43											05 58										
Arnside d	23p47											06 03										
Grange-over-Sands d	23p53											06 09										
Kents Bank d	23p56											06 12										
Cark d	00 01											06 17										
Ulverston d	00 09											06 25										
Dalton d	00 17											06 33										
Roose d	00 23											06 39										
Barrow-in-Furness a	00 32											06 47										

A To York
B To Scarborough
C To Liverpool Lime Street
D To Carlisle
E From 18 July until 5 September
F From 19 July until 2 September, from 6 September until 30 September
G To Clitheroe
H To Edinburgh
I To Glasgow Central

The Sunday service between Manchester Victoria and Wigan Wallgate via Atherton is funded by GMITA and will operate whilst funding exists

Table 82

Mondays to Fridays

18 July to 30 September

Manchester - Bolton - Wigan, Kirkby, Southport, Preston, Blackpool North and Barrow-in-Furness

		NT	TP	NT	TP	NT	NT	NT	TP	NT	NT	NT	NT	TP	NT	NT	NT	NT	TP	NT	NT	NT	NT
			◇1		◇1				◇1					◇1					◇1				
		A	B	C		D		E			F			G	H	I		A	J		D		E
									⊼					⊼					⊼				
Manchester Airport 85 ✈	d								07 00					07 25									
Heald Green 85	d													07 30									
Buxton 86	d	05 59											06 23				06 50						
Hazel Grove 86	d	06 33											07 00				07 27						
Stockport 84	d	06 41											07 10				07 37						
Manchester Piccadilly [10] ⇌	d	06 54	07 07						07 15				07 27	07 45			07 54		08 07				
Manchester Oxford Road	d	06 57	07a09						07 18				07 30				07 57		08a09				
Deansgate ⇌	d	06 59											07 32				07 59						
Rochdale 41	d																						
Manchester Victoria ⇌	d					07 01	07 06			07 16	07 23	07 27			07 47			08 00			08 03	08 11	
Salford Central	d					07 04	07 09			07 19	07 26	07 30			07 50			08 03			08 08	08 13	
Salford Crescent	a	07 03				07 07	07 12			07 24	07 29	07 33	07 37		07 53		08 04	08 07			08 12	08 17	
	d	07 03				07 08	07 13			07 25	07 30	07 33	07 37		07 53		08 04	08 08			08 13	08 17	
Swinton	d					07 14									08 00						08 19		
Moorside	d					07 17									08 02						08 22		
Walkden	d					07 20						07 42			08 06						08 25		
Atherton	d					07 26						07 48			08 11						08 31		
Hag Fold	d					07 28									08 14						08 33		
Daisy Hill	d					07 31						07 51			08 17						08 36		
Kearsley	d												07 45										
Farnworth	d												07 47										
Moses Gate	d												07 49										
Bolton	a	07 16					07 23		07 31	07 35	07 41		07 53	07 59			08 14	08 19				08 27	
	d						07 23		07 31	07 35			07 53	07 59			08 15					08 28	
Westhoughton	d						07 31	←					08 01									08 35	←
Hindley	d					07 39	07 35	07 39							08 21						08 43	08 39	08 43
Ince	d					↪		07 42													↪	08 42	08 46
Wigan North Western	a												08 16										
Wigan Wallgate	a						07 40	07 45				08 03			08 26							08 45	08 49
	d						07 41	07 46							08 28							08 47	08 51
Pemberton	d							07 50															08 55
Orrell	d							07 54															08 59
Upholland	d							07 58															09 02
Rainford	d							08 01															09 06
Kirkby	a							08 13															09 18
Gathurst	d						07 46								08 32							08 51	
Appley Bridge	d						07 49								08 36							08 55	
Parbold	d						07 53															08 59	
Hoscar	d						07 56																
Burscough Bridge	d						07 59								08 42							09 03	
New Lane	d						08 02																
Bescar Lane	d						08 05																
Meols Cop	d						08 10															09 11	
Southport	a						08 20								08 59							09 20	
Lostock	d									07 42							08 20						
Horwich Parkway	d								07 38	07 46							08 24						
Blackrod	d									07 49													
Adlington (Lancashire)	d									07 53							08 29						
Chorley	d								07 46	07 58				08 11			08 34						
Leyland	d									08 08							08 43						
Preston [8] 65,97	a								07 57	08 14				08 22			08 50						
	d				07 20				07 59	08 15				08 24		08 38	08 51						
Kirkham & Wesham 97	a								08 08	08 25													
Poulton-le-Fylde 97	a								08 18	08 33													
Layton 97	a								08 22	08 37													
Blackpool North 97	a								08 29	08 44							09 17						
Lancaster [6] 65	a				07 36									08 39		08 58							
	d			07 10	07 36									08 40		08 58				09 39			
Oxenholme Lake District 65	a													08 54									
Windermere 83	a																						
Carnforth	d			07a19	07 45											09 08				09 49			
Silverdale	d				07 51											09 14				09 56			
Arnside	d				07 55											09 19				10 00			
Grange-over-Sands	d				08 00											09 25				10 06			
Kents Bank	d				08 04											09 28				10 10			
Cark	d				08 08											09 33				10 14			
Ulverston	d				08 16											09 42				10 23			
Dalton	d				08 24											09 50				10 31			
Roose	d				08 30											09 56				10 37			
Barrow-in-Furness	a				08 40											10 04				10 47			

A To Clitheroe
B To Liverpool Lime Street
C To Leeds
D To Kirkby
E From Manchester Victoria
F To Blackburn
G To Edinburgh
H From Huddersfield
I To Carlisle
J From Hull to Liverpool Lime Street

The Sunday service between Manchester Victoria and Wigan Wallgate via Atherton is funded by GMITA and will operate whilst funding exists

Table 82

Mondays to Fridays

18 July to 30 September

Manchester - Bolton - Wigan, Kirkby, Southport, Preston, Blackpool North and Barrow-in-Furness

		TP	NT	NT	EM	NT	NT	NT	TP	NT	NT	NT	TP	NT	TP	TP	NT	NT	NT	NT	NT
		◇1			◇				◇1				◇1		◇1	1					
					A	B	C				D		E		F	G					H
		⊼							⊼				⊼								
Manchester Airport 85 ✈	d	07 56		08 01					08 25				09 00					09 03			
Heald Green 85	d			08 05					08 29												
Buxton 86	d																				
Hazel Grove 86	d				08 17					08 32											
Stockport 84	d				08 24					08 41											
Manchester Piccadilly [10] ⇌	d	08 15		08 22	08 37				08 46	08 54			09 16					09 22			
Manchester Oxford Road	d	08 19		08 26	08a40				08 49	08 58			09 19					09 26			
Deansgate ⇌	d			08 28					08 51	09 00								09 28			
Rochdale 41	d						08 00												09 04		
Manchester Victoria ⇌	d		08 22			08 29	08 33	08 46			09 00	09 07		09 10			09 22		09 33	09 46	
Salford Central	d		08 25			08 32	08 36	08 49			09 03	09 10		09 13			09 25		09 36	09 49	
Salford Crescent	a		08 29	08 33		08 37	08 39	08 52	08 56	09 04	09 07	09 13		09 16			09 29	09 33	09 39	09 52	
	d		08 30	08 34		08 37	08 40	08 53	08 56	09 04	09 08	09 13		09 17			09 30	09 34	09 40	09 53	
Swinton	d							08 59						09 23						09 59	
Moorside	d													09 26							
Walkden	d							09 04						09 29						10 04	
Atherton	d							09 09						09 35						10 09	
Hag Fold	d													09 37							
Daisy Hill	d							09 13						09 40						10 13	
Kearsley	d						08 47												09 47		
Farnworth	d						08 49												09 49		
Moses Gate	d						08 52												09 52		
Bolton	a	08 32	08 40	08 44		08 49	08 55		09 06	09 14	09 19	09 23	09 32				09 40	09 45	09 55		
	d	08 32	08 40	08 45			08 56		09 07	09 15		09 24	09 33				09 40	09 45	09 56		
Westhoughton	d			08 53								09 31						09 53			
Hindley	d							09 17				09 35		09 45				09 57		10 17	
Ince	d													09 48							
Wigan North Western	a																				
Wigan Wallgate	a			09 00			09 14	09 22				09 44		09 51				10 02	10 13	10 22	
	d			09 05				09 24						09 52				10 03		10 24	
Pemberton	d													09 56							
Orrell	d													10 00							
Upholland	d													10 04							
Rainford	d													10 07							
Kirkby	a													10 19							
Gathurst	d							09 28												10 28	
Appley Bridge	d			09 11				09 32										10 10		10 32	
Parbold	d			09 15				09 36										10 14		10 36	
Hoscar	d							09 39													
Burscough Bridge	d			09 20				09 42										10 18		10 40	
New Lane	d							09 44													
Bescar Lane	d							09 48													
Meols Cop	d							09 53												10 48	
Southport	a			09 36				10 02										10 35		10 57	
Lostock	d		08 45							09 20							09 45				
Horwich Parkway	d	08 39	08 49						09 13	09 24							09 49				
Blackrod	d		08 52														09 52				
Adlington (Lancashire)	d		08 56														09 56				
Chorley	d	08 47	09 01						09 21	09 32			09 44				10 01				
Leyland	d		09 12							09 42							10 12				
Preston [8] 65,97	a	08 58	09 17						09 33	09 50			09 55				10 17				
	d	08 59	09 19						09 38				09 58		10 07	10 07	10 19				
Kirkham & Wesham 97	a		09 28														10 28				
Poulton-le-Fylde 97	a	09 16	09 36						09 56								10 36				
Layton 97	a		09 43														10 43				
Blackpool North 97	a	09 25	09 50						10 05								10 51				
Lancaster [6] 65	a												10 13		10 22	10 22					
	d														10 23	10 23					10 49
Oxenholme Lake District 65	a																				
Windermere 83	a																				
Carnforth	d														10 32	10 32					10a58
Silverdale	d																				
Arnside	d														10 41	10 41					
Grange-over-Sands	d														10 46	10 46					
Kents Bank	d																				
Cark	d																				
Ulverston	d														10 59	10 59					
Dalton	d																				
Roose	d																				
Barrow-in-Furness	a														11 17	11 17					

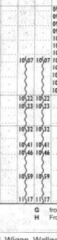

A From Nottingham to Liverpool Lime Street
B To Blackburn
C From Todmorden
D To Clitheroe
E To Glasgow Central
F from 12 September until 30 September
G from 18 July until 9 September
H From Morecambe to Leeds

The Sunday service between Manchester Victoria and Wigan Wallgate via Atherton is funded by GMITA and will operate whilst funding exists

Table 82

Mondays to Fridays

18 July to 30 September

Manchester - Bolton - Wigan, Kirkby, Southport, Preston, Blackpool North and Barrow-in-Furness

	TP ◇1 ✠		NT	NT A	NT	TP ◇1 B ✠	NT	NT	NT	NT	NT	TP ◇1 ✠	NT	NT A	NT	TP ◇1 C ✠	NT	NT	NT	NT	NT	TP ◇1 ✠
Manchester Airport 85 ✈ d	09 29					10 00			10 03			10 29				11 00			11 03			11 29
Heald Green 85 d	09 33											10 33										11 33
Buxton 86 d																						
Hazel Grove 86 d			09 32										10 33									
Stockport 84 d			09 41										10 41									
Manchester Piccadilly 10 d	09 46		09 54			10 16			10 22			10 46	10 54			11 16			11 22			11 46
Manchester Oxford Road d	09 49		09 58			10 19			10 26			10 49	10 58			11 19			11 26			11 49
Deansgate d	09 51		10 00						10 28			10 51	11 00						11 28			11 51
Rochdale 41 d										10 05										11 04		
Manchester Victoria d				10 00	10 07		10 10	10 22		10 33	10 46			11 00	11 07		11 10	11 22		11 33	11 46	
Salford Central d				10 03	10 10		10 13	10 25		10 36	10 49			11 03	11 10		11 13	11 25		11 36	11 49	
Salford Crescent a	09 56		10 04	10 07	10 13		10 16	10 29	10 33	10 39	10 52	10 56	11 04	11 07	11 13		11 16	11 29	11 33	11 39	11 52	11 56
d	09 56		10 04	10 08	10 13		10 17	10 30	10 34	10 40	10 53	10 56	11 04	11 08	11 13		11 17	11 30	11 34	11 40	11 53	11 56
Swinton d							10 23				10 59						11 23				11 59	
Moorside d							10 26										11 26					
Walkden d							10 29				11 04						11 29				12 04	
Atherton d							10 35				11 09						11 35				12 09	
Hag Fold d							10 37										11 37					
Daisy Hill d							10 40				11 13						11 40				12 13	
Kearsley d										10 47										11 47		
Farnworth d										10 49										11 49		
Moses Gate d										10 52										11 52		
Bolton a	10 06		10 14	10 19	10 23	10 32		10 40	10 45	10 55		11 06	11 14	11 19	11 23	11 32		11 40	11 45	11 55		12 06
d	10 07		10 15		10 24	10 33		10 40	10 45	10 56		11 07	11 15		11 24	11 33		11 40	11 45	11 56		12 07
Westhoughton d					10 31				10 53						11 31				11 53			
Hindley d					10 35		10 45		10 57		11 17				11 35		11 45		11 57		12 17	
Ince d							10 48										11 48					
Wigan North Western a																						
Wigan Wallgate a					10 44		10 51		11 02	11 13	11 22				11 44		11 51		12 02	12 13	12 22	
d							10 52		11 03		11 24						11 52		12 03		12 24	
Pemberton d							10 56										11 56					
Orrell d							11 00										12 00					
Upholland d							11 04										12 04					
Rainford d							11 07										12 07					
Kirkby a							11 19										12 19					
Gathurst d											11 28										12 28	
Appley Bridge d									11 10		11 32								12 10		12 32	
Parbold d									11 14		11 36								12 14		12 36	
Hoscar d											11 39											
Burscough Bridge d									11 18		11 42								12 18		12 41	
New Lane d											11 44											
Bescar Lane d											11 48											
Meols Cop d											11 53										12 49	
Southport a									11 35		12 02								12 35		12 59	
Lostock d			10 20					10 45					11 20					11 45				
Horwich Parkway d	10 13		10 24					10 49				11 13	11 24					11 49				12 13
Blackrod d								10 52										11 52				
Adlington (Lancashire) d								10 56										11 56				
Chorley d	10 21		10 32			10 44		11 01				11 21	11 32			11 44		12 01				12 21
Leyland d			10 42					11 12					11 42					12 12				
Preston 8 65,97 a	10 33		10 51			10 55		11 17				11 33	11 50			11 57		12 17				12 33
d	10 38	10 45				10 58		11 19				11 38				11 58		12 19				12 38
Kirkham & Wesham 97 a								11 28										12 28				
Poulton-le-Fylde 97 a	10 56							11 36				11 56						12 36				12 56
Layton 97 a								11 43										12 43				
Blackpool North 97 a	11 05							11 50				12 05						12 50				13 05
Lancaster 6 65 a		11 00				11 13										12 14						
d		11 01				11 14										12 14						
Oxenholme Lake District 65 a		11 17				11 28																
Windermere 83 a		11 39																				
Carnforth d																12 23						
Silverdale d																						
Arnside d																12 31						
Grange-over-Sands d																12 37						
Kents Bank d																						
Cark d																						
Ulverston d																12 50						
Dalton d																						
Roose d																						
Barrow-in-Furness a																13 10						

A To Clitheroe
B To Edinburgh
C ✠ to Chorley

The Sunday service between Manchester Victoria and Wigan Wallgate via Atherton is funded by GMITA and will operate whilst funding exists

Table 82

Mondays to Fridays

18 July to 30 September

Manchester - Bolton - Wigan, Kirkby, Southport, Preston, Blackpool North and Barrow-in-Furness

	NT	NT A	NT	TP ◇1 B ✠	NT	TP ◇1	NT	NT	NT	NT	TP ◇1 ✠	NT	NT A	NT	TP ◇1 C ✠	NT	NT	NT D	TP ◇1	NT	NT	NT
Manchester Airport 85 ✈ d				12 00				12 03			12 29				13 00						13 03	
Heald Green 85 d											12 33											
Buxton 86 d																						
Hazel Grove 86 d	11 33											12 33										
Stockport 84 d	11 41											12 41										
Manchester Piccadilly 10 d	11 54			12 16				12 22			12 46	12 54			13 16						13 22	
Manchester Oxford Road d	11 58			12 19				12 26			12 49	12 58			13 19						13 26	
Deansgate d	12 00							12 28			12 51	13 00									13 28	
Rochdale 41 d									12 04													13 04
Manchester Victoria d		12 00	12 07		12 10		12 22		12 33	12 46			13 00	13 07		13 10				13 22		13 33
Salford Central d		12 03	12 10		12 13		12 25		12 36	12 49			13 03	13 10		13 13				13 25		13 36
Salford Crescent a	12 04	12 07	12 13		12 16		12 29	12 33	12 39	12 52	12 56	13 04	13 07	13 13		13 16				13 29	13 33	13 39
d	12 04	12 08	12 13		12 17		12 30	12 34	12 40	12 53	12 56	13 04	13 08	13 13		13 17				13 30	13 34	13 40
Swinton d					12 23					12 59						13 23						
Moorside d					12 26											13 26						
Walkden d					12 29					13 04						13 29						
Atherton d					12 35					13 09						13 35						
Hag Fold d					12 37											13 37						
Daisy Hill d					12 40					13 13						13 40						
Kearsley d									12 47													13 47
Farnworth d									12 49													13 49
Moses Gate d									12 52													13 52
Bolton a	12 14	12 19	12 23	12 32			12 40	12 45	12 55		13 06	13 14	13 19	13 23	13 32					13 40	13 45	13 55
d	12 15		12 24	12 33			12 40	12 45	12 56		13 07	13 15		13 24	13 33					13 40	13 45	13 56
Westhoughton d			12 31					12 53						13 31							13 53	
Hindley d			12 35		12 45			12 57		13 17				13 35		13 45					13 57	
Ince d					12 48											13 48						
Wigan North Western a																						
Wigan Wallgate a			12 44		12 51			13 02	13 13	13 22				13 44		13 51					14 02	14 13
d					12 52			13 03		13 24						13 52					14 03	
Pemberton d					12 56											13 56						
Orrell d					13 00											14 00						
Upholland d					13 04											14 04						
Rainford d					13 07											14 07						
Kirkby a					13 19											14 19						
Gathurst d										13 28												
Appley Bridge d								13 10		13 32											14 10	
Parbold d								13 14		13 36											14 14	
Hoscar d										13 39												
Burscough Bridge d								13 18		13 42											14 18	
New Lane d										13 44												
Bescar Lane d										13 48												
Meols Cop d										13 53												
Southport a								13 35		14 02											14 35	
Lostock d	12 20						12 45					13 20								13 45		
Horwich Parkway d	12 24						12 49				13 13	13 24								13 49		
Blackrod d							12 52													13 52		
Adlington (Lancashire) d							12 56													13 56		
Chorley d	12 32			12 44			13 01				13 21	13 32			13 44					14 01		
Leyland d	12 42						13 12					13 42								14 12		
Preston 8 65,97 a	12 50			12 55			13 17				13 33	13 50			13 55					14 17		
d				12 58		13 04	13 19				13 38				13 58				14 04	14 19		
Kirkham & Wesham 97 a							13 28													14 28		
Poulton-le-Fylde 97 a							13 36				13 56									14 36		
Layton 97 a							13 43													14 43		
Blackpool North 97 a							13 50				14 05									14 51		
Lancaster 6 65 a				13 13		13 19									14 13				14 19			
d				13 14		13 20											13 32	13 48	14 20			
Oxenholme Lake District 65 a				13 28		13 36																
Windermere 83 a						13 56																
Carnforth d																	13 42	13a58	14 28			
Silverdale d																	13 48					
Arnside d																	13 52		14 37			
Grange-over-Sands d																	13 58		14 42			
Kents Bank d																	14 02					
Cark d																	14 06					
Ulverston d																	14 15		14 55			
Dalton d																	14 23					
Roose d																	14 29					
Barrow-in-Furness a																	14 39		15 16			

A To Clitheroe
B To Edinburgh
C To Glasgow Central
D From Heysham Port to Leeds

The Sunday service between Manchester Victoria and Wigan Wallgate via Atherton is funded by GMITA and will operate whilst funding exists

Table 82

Mondays to Fridays
18 July to 30 September

Manchester - Bolton - Wigan, Kirkby, Southport, Preston, Blackpool North and Barrow-in-Furness

		NT	TP ◇1 🍴	NT	NT A	NT	TP ◇1 B 🍴	NT	NT	NT	NT	NT	TP ◇1 C 🍴 FX	TP ◇1 D 🍴 FO	NT	NT A	NT	NT	NT E	TP ◇1 F 🍴	NT	NT
Manchester Airport 85 ✈	d		13 29				14 00			14 03			14 29	14 29						15 00		15 03
Heald Green 85	d		13 33										14 33	14 33								
Buxton 86	d																					
Hazel Grove 86	d			13 33											14 33							
Stockport 84	d			13 41											14 41							
Manchester Piccadilly 10 🚊	d		13 46	13 54			14 16			14 22			14 46	14 46	14 54					15 16		15 22
Manchester Oxford Road	d		13 49	13 58			14 19			14 26			14 49	14 49	14 58					15 19		15 26
Deansgate 🚊	d		13 51	14 00						14 28			14 51	14 51	15 00							15 28
Rochdale 41	d										14 04											
Manchester Victoria 🚊	d	13 46			14 00	14 07		14 10	14 22		14 33	14 46				15 00	15 07	15 10			15 22	
Salford Central	d	13 49			14 03	14 10		14 13	14 25		14 36	14 49				15 03	15 10	15 13			15 25	
Salford Crescent	a	13 52	13 56	14 04	14 07	14 13		14 16	14 29	14 33	14 39	14 52	14 56	14 56	15 04	15 07	15 13	15 16			15 29	15 33
	d	13 53	13 56	14 04	14 08	14 13		14 17	14 30	14 34	14 40	14 53	14 56	14 56	15 04	15 08	15 13	15 17			15 30	15 34
Swinton	d	13 59						14 23				14 59						15 23				
Moorside	d							14 26										15 26				
Walkden	d	14 04						14 29				15 04						15 29				
Atherton	d	14 09						14 35				15 09						15 35				
Hag Fold	d							14 37										15 37				
Daisy Hill	d	14 13						14 40				15 13						15 40				
Kearsley	d										14 47											
Farnworth	d										14 49											
Moses Gate	d										14 52											
Bolton	a		14 06	14 14	14 19	14 23	14 32		14 40	14 45	14 55		15 06	15 06	15 14	15 19	15 23			15 32	15 40	15 45
	d		14 07	14 15		14 24	14 33		14 40	14 45	14 56		15 07	15 07	15 15		15 24			15 33	15 40	15 45
Westhoughton	d					14 31				14 53							15 31					15 53
Hindley	d	14 17				14 35		14 45		14 57		15 17					15 35	15 45				15 57
Ince	d							14 48										15 48				
Wigan North Western	a																					
Wigan Wallgate	a	14 22				14 44		14 51		15 02	15 13	15 22					15 44	15 51				16 02
	d	14 24						14 52		15 03		15 24						15 58				16 03
Pemberton	d							14 56										16 02				
Orrell	d							15 00										16 06				
Upholland	d							15 04										16 09				
Rainford	d							15 07										16 13				
Kirkby	a							15 19										16 25				
Gathurst	d	14 28										15 28										16 08
Appley Bridge	d	14 32								15 10		15 32										16 11
Parbold	d	14 36								15 14		15 36										16 15
Hoscar	d																					16 18
Burscough Bridge	d	14 41								15 18		15 40										16 21
New Lane	d																					16 24
Bescar Lane	d																					16 27
Meols Cop	d	14 49										15 48										16 32
Southport	a	14 59								15 35		15 57										16 42
Lostock	d			14 20					14 45						15 20						15 45	
Horwich Parkway	d		14 13	14 24					14 49				15 13	15 13	15 24						15 49	
Blackrod	d								14 52												15 52	
Adlington (Lancashire)	d								14 56												15 56	
Chorley	d		14 21	14 32			14 44		15 01				15 21	15 21	15 32					15 44	16 01	
Leyland	d			14 42					15 12						15 42						16 12	
Preston 8 65,97	a		14 33	14 50			14 55		15 17				15 33	15 33	15 50					15 57	16 19	
	d		14 38				14 58		15 19				15 38	15 38						15 58		
Kirkham & Wesham 97	a								15 28													
Poulton-le-Fylde 97	a		14 56						15 36				15 56	15 58								
Layton 97	a								15 43													
Blackpool North 97	a		15 05						15 50				16 05	16 07								
Lancaster 6 65	a						15 13													16 14		
	d						15 14												15 34	16 15		
Oxenholme Lake District 65	a						15 28															
Windermere 83	a																					
Carnforth	d																		15 44	16 23		
Silverdale	d																		15 51	16 29		
Arnside	d																		15 55	16 33		
Grange-over-Sands	d																		16 01	16 39		
Kents Bank	d																		16 05	16 42		
Cark	d																		16 09	16 47		
Ulverston	d																		16 17	16 55		
Dalton	d																		16 26	17 03		
Roose	d																		16 32	17 09		
Barrow-in-Furness	a																		16 39	17 18		

A To Clitheroe
B To Edinburgh
C From 18 July until 8 September, from 12 September until 30 September
D From 22 July until 9 September
E To Carlisle
F 🍴 to Chorley

The Sunday service between Manchester Victoria and Wigan Wallgate via Atherton is funded by GMITA and will operate whilst funding exists

Table 82

Mondays to Fridays
18 July to 30 September

Manchester - Bolton - Wigan, Kirkby, Southport, Preston, Blackpool North and Barrow-in-Furness

		NT	NT A	NT	TP ◇1 🍴	NT	NT	NT	NT B	NT C	TP ◇1 D 🍴	TP ◇1 D 🍴	TP ◇1	NT	NT A	NT	NT	NT	TP ◇1 🍴	NT	NT	NT A
Manchester Airport 85 ✈	d				15 29						16 00					16 03			16 29			
Heald Green 85	d				15 33														16 33			
Buxton 86	d																15 27					
Hazel Grove 86	d					15 33											16 04				16 30	
Stockport 84	d					15 41											16 12				16 41	
Manchester Piccadilly 10 🚊	d				15 46	15 54					16 16					16 22	16 27		16 46		16 54	
Manchester Oxford Road	d				15 49	15 58					16 19					16 26	16 30		16 49		16 58	
Deansgate 🚊	d				15 51	16 00										16 28	16 33				17 00	
Rochdale 41	d	15 04																16 04				
Manchester Victoria 🚊	d	15 33	15 40	15 46			16 07	16 10						16 20	16 23			16 36		16 46		17 00
Salford Central	d	15 36	15 43	15 49			16 10	16 13						16 23	16 26			16 39		16 49		17 03
Salford Crescent	a	15 39	15 46	15 52	15 56	16 04	16 13	16 16						16 26	16 30	16 34	16 38	16 42		16 52	17 04	17 07
	d	15 40	15 47	15 53	15 56	16 04	16 13	16 17						16 27	16 31	16 34	16 38	16 43		16 53	17 04	17 08
Swinton	d			15 59				16 23												16 59		
Moorside	d							16 26												17 02		
Walkden	d			16 04				16 29												17 05		
Atherton	d			16 09				16 35												17 11		
Hag Fold	d							16 37												17 14		
Daisy Hill	d			16 13				16 40												17 17		
Kearsley	d	15 47																16 50				
Farnworth	d	15 49																16 52				
Moses Gate	d	15 52					16 21											16 55				
Bolton	a	15 55	15 59		16 06	16 19	16 25				16 32			16 37	16 42	16 45	16 48	16 58	17 05		17 14	17 19
	d	15 56			16 07		16 25				16 33			16 37		16 45	16 49	16 59	17 06		17 15	
Westhoughton	d						16 33									16 53		17 06				
Hindley	d			16 17			16 37	16 45								16 57		17 10		17 21		
Ince	d							16 48												17 24		
Wigan North Western	a																					
Wigan Wallgate	a	16 13		16 22			16 46	16 51								17 02		17 19		17 31		
	d			16 24				16 52								17 03						
Pemberton	d							16 56														
Orrell	d							17 00														
Upholland	d							17 04														
Rainford	d							17 07														
Kirkby	a							17 19														
Gathurst	d			16 28												17 08						
Appley Bridge	d			16 32												17 11						
Parbold	d			16 36												17 15						
Hoscar	d																					
Burscough Bridge	d			16 40												17 20						
New Lane	d																					
Bescar Lane	d																					
Meols Cop	d			16 48												17 27						
Southport	a			16 57												17 37						
Lostock	d				16 12									16 43			16 54				17 20	
Horwich Parkway	d				16 15									16 47			16 58				17 24	
Blackrod	d													16 51			17 01					
Adlington (Lancashire)	d													16 55			17 05					
Chorley	d				16 23						16 44			17 00			17 10		17 19		17 32	
Leyland	d													17 11			17 21				17 42	
Preston 8 65,97	a				16 35						16 55			17 19			17 26		17 30		17 51	
	d				16 38						17 00	17 04	17 04	17 21			17 28		17 32			
Kirkham & Wesham 97	a				16 47									17 30					17 41			
Poulton-le-Fylde 97	a				16 57									17 38					17 51			
Layton 97	a				17 00									17 43					17 54			
Blackpool North 97	a				17 07									17 50					18 02			
Lancaster 6 65	a										17 15	17 23	17 23				17 48					
	d								16 55	17 19	17 16	17 25	17 25				17 48					
Oxenholme Lake District 65	a										17 30	17 43	17 43									
Windermere 83	a											18 08	18 08									
Carnforth	d								17 05	17 28							18 00					
Silverdale	d								17 12	17 35							18 06					
Arnside	d								17 16	17 40							18 11					
Grange-over-Sands	d								17 22	17 46							18 19					
Kents Bank	d								17 26	17 49							18 23					
Cark	d								17 30	17 54							18 27					
Ulverston	d								17 39	18 02							18 36					
Dalton	d								17 48	18 10							18 44					
Roose	d								17 54	18 17							18 50					
Barrow-in-Furness	a								18 02	18 25							18 59					

A To Clitheroe
B To Millom
C From Morecambe
D To Edinburgh

The Sunday service between Manchester Victoria and Wigan Wallgate via Atherton is funded by GMITA and will operate whilst funding exists

Table 82

Mondays to Fridays
18 July to 30 September

Manchester - Bolton - Wigan, Kirkby, Southport, Preston, Blackpool North and Barrow-in-Furness

		TP ◇1 A	TP ◇1 A	NT B	NT	NT	NT C	NT	NT	NT	NT	NT	TP ◇1	NT	NT D	TP ◇1 E	TP ◇1 E	NT	NT	NT C	NT	NT
Manchester Airport 85 ✈	d	17 00						17 03					17 29			18 00					18 03	
Heald Green 85	d												17 33									
Buxton 86	d								16 30					16 59								
Hazel Grove 86	d								17 04					17 33								
Stockport 84	d								17 12					17 41								
Manchester Piccadilly 10	d	17 15						17 22	17 27				17 46	17 54		18 16					18 22	
Manchester Oxford Road	d	17 18						17 26	17 30				17 49	17 58		18 19					18 26	
Deansgate	d								17 33				17 51	18 00							18 28	
Rochdale 41	d						17 03													18 02		
Manchester Victoria	d			17 06	17 10	17 19	17 23			17 36	17 40	17 45			18 00			18 10	18 20	18 23		18 33
Salford Central	d			17 09	17 12	17 22	17 27			17 39	17 43	17 48			18 03			18 13	18 23	18 26		18 36
Salford Crescent	a			17 13	17 16	17 25	17 29	17 34	17 38	17 42	17 46	17 51	17 55	18 04	18 07			18 16	18 26	18 30	18 34	18 39
	d			17 14	17 17	17 27	17 30	17 34	17 38	17 43	17 47	17 52	17 55	18 04	18 08			18 17	18 27	18 31	18 34	18 40
Swinton	d				17 23							17 58						18 23				
Moorside	d				17 26							18 01						18 26				
Walkden	d				17 31							18 05						18 29				
Atherton	d			17 26	17 37						17 59	18 11						18 35				
Hag Fold	d				17 39							18 13						18 37				
Daisy Hill	d			17 30	17 43						18 03	18 17						18 40				
Kearsley	d									17 53												18 47
Farnworth	d									17 55												18 49
Moses Gate	d									17 57												18 52
Bolton	a	17 31				17 37	17 42	17 45	17 48	18 01			18 06	18 14	18 19	18 32			18 37	18 42	18 45	18 55
	d	17 32				17 37		17 45	17 49	18 01			18 07	18 15		18 33			18 37		18 45	18 56
Westhoughton	d							17 53		18 09											18 53	19 03
Hindley	d				17 48					18 13		18 22						18 45			18 57	19 09
Ince	d				17 51							18 25						18 48				
Wigan North Western	a																	18 56				
Wigan Wallgate	a			17 38	17 54			18 01		18 22	18 11	18 28									19 02	19 18
	d			17 40	17 55			18 02			18 15	18 29									19 03	
Pemberton	d				17 59							18 33										
Orrell	d				18 03							18 37										
Upholland	d				18 07							18 41										
Rainford	d				18 10							18 44										
Kirkby	a				18 22							18 55										
Gathurst	d			17 44							18 19										19 08	
Appley Bridge	d			17 48				18 09			18 23										19 11	
Parbold	d			17 52				18 13			18 28										19 15	
Hoscar	d										18 31											
Burscough Bridge	d			17 57				18 17			18 34										19 19	
New Lane	d										18 37											
Bescar Lane	d										18 40											
Meols Cop	d			18 05				18 26			18 46										19 27	
Southport	a			18 14				18 35			18 55										19 37	
Lostock	d					17 43			17 54				18 12	18 20					18 42			
Horwich Parkway	d					17 47			17 58				18 15	18 24					18 46			
Blackrod	d					17 51			18 01				18 19						18 49			
Adlington (Lancashire)	d					17 55			18 05										18 53			
Chorley	d	17 44				18 00			18 10				18 26	18 32		18 44			18 58			
Leyland	d					18 11								18 42					19 10			
Preston 8 65,97	a	17 55				18 16			18 25				18 38	18 48		18 55			19 18			
	d	17 58	18 08			18 18			18 26				18 40	18 49		19 00	19 04		19 19			
Kirkham & Wesham 97	a					18 27							18 49						19 28			
Poulton-le-Fylde 97	a					18 35			18 43				18 59						19 36			
Layton 97	a					18 39							19 02						19 43			
Blackpool North 97	a					18 49			18 53				19 09	19 16					19 50			
Lancaster 6 65	a	18 13	18 23													19 15	19 20					
	d	18 14	18 24													19 16	19 20					
Oxenholme Lake District 65	a	18 28														19 30						
Windermere 83	a																					
Carnforth	d		18 34														19 29					
Silverdale	d		18 40														19 35					
Arnside	d		18 44														19 39					
Grange-over-Sands	d		18 49														19 44					
Kents Bank	d		18 53														19 48					
Cark	d		18 57														19 52					
Ulverston	d		19 05														20 00					
Dalton	d		19 13														20 08					
Roose	d		19 19														20 14					
Barrow-in-Furness	a		19 30														20 24					

A To Glasgow Central
B From Stalybridge
C To Blackburn
D To Clitheroe
E To Edinburgh

The Sunday service between Manchester Victoria and Wigan Wallgate via Atherton is funded by GMITA and will operate whilst funding exists

Table 82

Mondays to Fridays
18 July to 30 September

Manchester - Bolton - Wigan, Kirkby, Southport, Preston, Blackpool North and Barrow-in-Furness

		NT	TP ◇1	NT	NT A	NT	NT B	TP ◇1	NT	NT	TP ◇1	NT A	TP ◇1	NT	NT	NT	NT C	TP ◇1	NT A	NT	NT	NT	NT
Manchester Airport 85 ✈	d		18 29					19 00	19 03		19 29		20 00			20 03	20 09	20 29					21 03
Heald Green 85	d		18 33								19 33						20 12	20 33					
Buxton 86	d			17 59																			
Hazel Grove 86	d			18 33																			
Stockport 84	d			18 41																			
Manchester Piccadilly 10	d		18 46	18 54				19 16	19 20		19 46		20 16			20 20	20 32	20 46					21 20
Manchester Oxford Road	d		18 49	18 58				19 19	19 24		19 49		20 19			20 24	20a36	20 49					21 24
Deansgate	d		18 51	19 00					19 26		19 51					20 26		20 51					21 26
Rochdale 41	d																						
Manchester Victoria	d	18 45			19 00	19 10				19 28		20 00		20 10	20 22				21 00	21 10		21 22	
Salford Central	d	18 48			19 03	19 13				19 31		20 03		20 13	20 25				21 03	21 13		21 25	
Salford Crescent	a	18 51	18 56	19 04	19 07	19 16			19 29	19 34	19 56	20 07		20 16	20 29	20 33		20 56	21 07	21 16		21 29	21 33
	d	18 52	18 56	19 04	19 08	19 17			19 30	19 35	19 56	20 08		20 17	20 30	20 34		20 56	21 08	21 17		21 30	21 34
Swinton	d	18 58				19 23								20 23						21 23			
Moorside	d	19 01				19 26								20 26						21 26			
Walkden	d	19 04				19 29								20 29						21 29			
Atherton	d	19 10				19 35								20 35						21 35			
Hag Fold	d	19 12				19 37								20 37						21 37			
Daisy Hill	d	19 15				19 40								20 40						21 40			
Kearsley	d																						
Farnworth	d																						
Moses Gate	d																						
Bolton	a		19 06	19 19	19 20			19 32	19 40	19 45	20 06	20 19	20 32		20 40	20 45		21 06	21 19			21 40	21 45
	d		19 07					19 33	19 40	19 45	20 07		20 33		20 40	20 45		21 07				21 40	21 45
Westhoughton	d								19 48							20 53							21 53
Hindley	d	19 20				19 45			19 52					20 45		20 57				21 45			21 57
Ince	d	19 23				19 48								20 48						21 48			
Wigan North Western	a																						
Wigan Wallgate	a	19 30				19 55			19 57					20 55		21 02				21 55			22 02
	d								19 59							21 03							22 03
Pemberton	d																						
Orrell	d																						
Upholland	d																						
Rainford	d																						
Kirkby	a																						
Gathurst	d								20 03							21 08							22 08
Appley Bridge	d								20 07							21 11							22 11
Parbold	d								20 11							21 15							22 15
Hoscar	d															21 18							
Burscough Bridge	d								20 15							21 21							22 20
New Lane	d															21 24							
Bescar Lane	d															21 27							
Meols Cop	d								20 23							21 32							22 27
Southport	a								20 32							21 42							22 37
Lostock	d		19 12							19 50					20 45							21 45	
Horwich Parkway	d		19 15							19 54	20 13		20 39		20 49			21 13				21 49	
Blackrod	d									19 57					20 52							21 52	
Adlington (Lancashire)	d									20 01					20 56							21 56	
Chorley	d		19 23					19 44		20 06	20 21		20 46		21 01			21 21				22 01	
Leyland	d									20 18					21 12							22 12	
Preston 8 65,97	a		19 33					19 55		20 23	20 33		20 57		21 17			21 33				22 17	
	d		19 38					19 58		20 25	20 38		20 58		21 19			21 38			21 51	22 19	
Kirkham & Wesham 97	a									20 34					21 28							22 28	
Poulton-le-Fylde 97	a		19 56							20 42	20 56				21 36			21 56				22 36	
Layton 97	a									20 46					21 40							22 43	
Blackpool North 97	a		20 05							20 54	21 06				21 48			22 06				22 51	
Lancaster 6 65	a							20 13					21 13								22 11		
	d						19 24	20 14					21 14								22 11		
Oxenholme Lake District 65	a																						
Windermere 83	a																						
Carnforth	d						19a34	20 22					21 23								22 21		
Silverdale	d							20 28					21 29								22 27		
Arnside	d							20 32					21 33								22 32		
Grange-over-Sands	d							20 38					21 39								22 38		
Kents Bank	d							20 41					21 42								22 41		
Cark	d							20 46					21 47								22 46		
Ulverston	d							20 54					21 55								22 54		
Dalton	d							21 02					22 03								23 02		
Roose	d							21 08					22 09								23 08		
Barrow-in-Furness	a							21 18					22 19								23 16		

A To Clitheroe
B From Morecambe to Leeds
C From Wilmslow

The Sunday service between Manchester Victoria and Wigan Wallgate via Atherton is funded by GMITA and will operate whilst funding exists

Table 82

Mondays to Fridays

18 July to 30 September

Manchester - Bolton - Wigan, Kirkby, Southport, Preston, Blackpool North and Barrow-in-Furness

			NT	NT	TP	NT	NT	TP	NT	NT	NT	NT	NT	NT	TP	NT	NT	NT	NT	NT	NT	NT	TP
						FO	FX			FO	FX	FO	FX				FO	FX	FO	FX	FO	FX	FX
					◇1			◇1							◇1								◇1
			A	B		C	C		A								D	D					E
Manchester Airport	85 ✈	d	21 09		21 29			22 00	22 08					22 19	22 29								23 18
Heald Green	85	d	21 12		21 33				22 12						22 33								
Buxton	86	d																					
Hazel Grove	86	d																					
Stockport	84	d														22 34							
Manchester Piccadilly 10		d	21 32	21 38	21 46			22 16	22 32					22 36	22 46	22 50							23 38
Manchester Oxford Road		d	21a36	21 44	21 49			22 19	22a36					22 39	22 49	22 53							
Deansgate		d		21a46	21 51									22 41	22 51	22 55							
Rochdale	41	d																					
Manchester Victoria		d				22 00	22 00			22 10	22 10	22 22	22 22				23 00	23 00	23 20	23 20	23 23	23 23	
Salford Central		d				22 04				22 13		22 25					23 03		23 23		23 26		
Salford Crescent		a			21 56	22 07	22 07			22 17	22 17	22 29	22 29	22 46	22 56	22 59	23 07	23 07	23 26	23 25	23 29	23 29	23 43
		d			21 56	22 08	22 08			22 17	22 17	22 30	22 30	22 46	22 56	22 59	23 08	23 08	23 26	23 26	23 30	23 30	
Swinton		d								22 23	22 23								23 33	23 33			
Moorside		d								22 26	22 26								23 35	23 35			
Walkden		d								22 29	22 29								23 39	23 39			
Atherton		d								22 35	22 35								23 44	23 44			
Hag Fold		d								22 37	22 37								23 47	23 47			
Daisy Hill		d								22 40	22 40								23 50	23 50			
Kearsley		d														23 07							
Farnworth		d														23 09							
Moses Gate		d														23 11							
Bolton		a			22 06	22 19	22 19	22 32				22 40	22 40	22 56	23 06	23 15	23 19	23 19			23 40	23 40	
		d			22 07			22 33				22 40	22 40	22 57	23 07	23 15					23 40	23 40	
Westhoughton		d												23 04		23 23							
Hindley		d								22 45	22 45			23 08		23 27			23 54	23 54			
Ince		d								22 48	22 48								23 57	23 57			
Wigan North Western		a						22 48															
Wigan Wallgate		a								22 55	22 55			23 13		23 38			00 04	00 04			
		d												23 15									
Pemberton		d																					
Orrell		d																					
Upholland		d																					
Rainford		d																					
Kirkby		a																					
Gathurst		d												23 19									
Appley Bridge		d												23 23									
Parbold		d												23 27									
Hoscar		d																					
Burscough Bridge		d												23 31									
New Lane		d																					
Bescar Lane		d																					
Meols Cop		d												23 39									
Southport		a												23 48									
Lostock		d										22 45	22 45								23 45	23 45	
Horwich Parkway		d			22 13							22 49	22 49		23 13						23 49	23 49	
Blackrod		d										22 52	22 52								23 52	23 52	
Adlington (Lancashire)		d										22 56	22 56								23 56	23 56	
Chorley		d			22 21							23 01	23 01		23 21						00 01	00 01	
Leyland		d										23 12	23 12								00 12	00 12	
Preston 8	65,97	a			22 33			23 09				23 17	23 17		23 33						00 17	00 17	
		d			22 35			23 13				23 19	23 19		23 35						00 19	00 19	
Kirkham & Wesham	97	a										23 28	23 28								00 28	00 28	
Poulton-le-Fylde	97	a			22 52							23 36	23 36		23 52						00 36	00 36	
Layton	97	a										23 40	23 40								00 43	00 43	
Blackpool North	97	a			23 02							23 48	23 48		00 02						00 50	00 50	
Lancaster 6	65	a						23 28															
		d						23 29															
Oxenholme Lake District	65	a																					
Windermere	83	a																					
Carnforth		d						23 37															
Silverdale		d						23 43															
Arnside		d						23 47															
Grange-over-Sands		d						23 53															
Kents Bank		d						23 56															
Cark		d						00 01															
Ulverston		d						00 09															
Dalton		d						00 17															
Roose		d						00 23															
Barrow-in-Furness		a						00 32															

A From Wilmslow
B To Warrington Central
C To Clitheroe
D To Blackburn
E To York

The Sunday service between Manchester Victoria and Wigan Wallgate via Atherton is funded by GMITA and will operate whilst funding exists

Table 82

Mondays to Fridays

from 3 October

Manchester - Bolton - Wigan, Kirkby, Southport, Preston, Blackpool North and Barrow-in-Furness

			TP	TP	TP	NT	NT	TP	TP	TP	TP	TP	NT	NT	TP	TP	NT	NT	TP	NT	TP	NT	NT	NT
			MX	MO	MX	MX	MX		MX	MO														
			◇1	◇1	◇1			◇1	◇1	◇1	◇1	◇1			1	◇1			◇1		◇1			
									A	A		B	C	D			E		F		G			E
Manchester Airport	85 ✈	d	22p00	22p30	22p29			00 01	00 38	00 48	04 00	04 12	04 34						05 45		06 18			
Heald Green	85	d			22p33														05 49					
Buxton	86	d																						05 59
Hazel Grove	86	d																						06 33
Stockport	84	d																						06 41
Manchester Piccadilly 10		d	22p16	22p46	22p46			00 16	00 53	01 03	04 15	04 30	04a47			05 46			06 03		06 33			06 54
Manchester Oxford Road		d	22p19	22p49	22p49														06 06		06 36			06 57
Deansgate		d		22p51	22p51																			06 59
Rochdale	41	d																						
Manchester Victoria		d				23p20	23p23										05 55	06 00		06 17		06 38	06 45	
Salford Central		d																				06 40	06 48	
Salford Crescent		a		22p54	22p56	23p25	23p29		00 58	01 09		04 36				05 51	05 59	06 04		06 23		06 44	06 51	07 03
		d		22p55	22p56	23p26	23p30									05 52	06 00	06 05		06 24		06 45	06 52	07 03
Swinton		d				23p33																	06 58	
Moorside		d				23p35																		
Walkden		d				23p39																	07 03	
Atherton		d				23p44																	07 08	
Hag Fold		d				23p47																		
Daisy Hill		d				23p50																	07 12	
Kearsley		d																				06 52		
Farnworth		d																				06 54		
Moses Gate		d																				06 57		
Bolton		a	22p32	23p05	23p06		23p40	00s31			04s29						06 11	06 15	06 19	06 34	06 50	07 00		07 16
		d	22p33	23p05	23p07		23p40											06 15	06 19	06 34	06 50	07 01		
Westhoughton		d																06 23						
Hindley		d				23p54												06 27					07 16	
Ince		d				23p57																		
Wigan North Western		a	22p48								04 44					06 15						07 19		
Wigan Wallgate		a				00 06												06 32					07 21	
		d																06 34					07 23	
Pemberton		d																06 38						
Orrell		d																06 42						
Upholland		d																06 45						
Rainford		d																06 49						
Kirkby		a																07 03						
Gathurst		d																					07 27	
Appley Bridge		d																					07 31	
Parbold		d																					07 35	
Hoscar		d																						
Burscough Bridge		d																					07 39	
New Lane		d																						
Bescar Lane		d																						
Meols Cop		d																					07 47	
Southport		a																					07 58	
Lostock		d		23p10			23p45													06 39				
Horwich Parkway		d		23p14	23p13		23p49													06 43				
Blackrod		d		23p17			23p52													06 46				
Adlington (Lancashire)		d		23p20			23p56													06 50				
Chorley		d		23p24	23p21		00 01												06 31	06 55				
Leyland		d		23p34			00 12									06 27				07 06				
Preston 8	65,97	a	23p09	23p42	23p33		00 17	01s05			05s04					06 35			06 42	07 11	07 11			
		d	23p13	23p47	23p35		00 19							05 22		06 37			06 44	07 13	07 14			
Kirkham & Wesham	97	a		23p56			00 28									06 46				07 22				
Poulton-le-Fylde	97	a		00 05	23p52		00 36									06 56				07 30				
Layton	97	a					00 43									06 59				07 34				
Blackpool North	97	a		00 14	00 02		00 52	01 30			05 33					07 06				07 43				
Lancaster 6	65	a	23p28											05 42					06 59		07 30			
		d	23p29											05 42	05 46				07 00					
Oxenholme Lake District	65	a													06 21				07 15					
Windermere	83	a													06 41									
Carnforth		d	23p37											05 52										
Silverdale		d	23p43											05 58										
Arnside		d	23p47											06 03										
Grange-over-Sands		d	23p53											06 09										
Kents Bank		d	23p56											06 12										
Cark		d	00 01											06 17										
Ulverston		d	00 09											06 25										
Dalton		d	00 17											06 33										
Roose		d	00 23											06 39										
Barrow-in-Furness		a	00 32											06 47										

A To York
B To Scarborough
C To Liverpool Lime Street
D To Carlisle
E To Clitheroe
F To Edinburgh
G To Glasgow Central

The Sunday service between Manchester Victoria and Wigan Wallgate via Atherton is funded by GMITA and will operate whilst funding exists

Table 82

Manchester - Bolton - Wigan, Kirkby, Southport, Preston, Blackpool North and Barrow-in-Furness

		TP ◇1 A	NT B	TP ◇1	NT C	NT	NT D	TP ◇1 🍴	NT	NT E	TP ◇1 F 🍴	NT	NT G	NT H	TP ◇1 I 🍴	NT J	NT	NT C	NT	NT D	TP ◇1 🍴	NT	NT
Manchester Airport 85 ✈	d							07 00			07 25										07 56		08 01
Heald Green 85	d										07 30												08 05
Buxton 86	d																						
Hazel Grove 86	d																						
Stockport 84	d																						
Manchester Piccadilly 10 ⇌	d	07 07						07 15			07 45				08 07						08 15		08 22
Manchester Oxford Road	d	07a09						07 18							08a09						08 19		08 26
Deansgate ⇌	d																						08 28
Rochdale 41	d																						
Manchester Victoria ⇌	d				07 01	07 06			07 16	07 23		07 27	07 47	08 00				08 03	08 11			08 22	
Salford Central	d				07 04	07 09			07 19	07 26		07 30	07 50	08 03				08 08	08 13			08 25	
Salford Crescent	a				07 07	07 12			07 24	07 29		07 33	07 53	08 07				08 12	08 17			08 29	08 33
	d				07 08	07 13			07 25	07 30		07 33	07 53	08 08				08 13	08 17			08 30	08 34
Swinton	d				07 14								08 00					08 19					
Moorside	d				07 17								08 02					08 22					
Walkden	d				07 20							07 42	08 06					08 25					
Atherton	d				07 26							07 48	08 11					08 31					
Hag Fold	d				07 28								08 14					08 33					
Daisy Hill	d				07 31							07 51	08 17					08 36					
Kearsley	d																						
Farnworth	d																						
Moses Gate	d																						
Bolton	a					07 23		07 31	07 35	07 41	07 59			08 19					08 27		08 32	08 40	08 44
	d					07 23		07 31	07 35		07 59								08 28		08 32	08 40	08 45
Westhoughton	d					07 31	←												08 35	←			08 53
Hindley	d				07 39	07 35	07 39						08 21					08 43	08 39	08 43			
Ince	d				→		07 42											→	08 42	08 46			
Wigan North Western	a																						
Wigan Wallgate	a					07 40	07 45					08 05	08 26						08 45	08 49			09 00
	d					07 41	07 46						08 28						08 47	08 51			09 05
Pemberton	d						07 50													08 55			
Orrell	d						07 54													08 59			
Upholland	d						07 58													09 02			
Rainford	d						08 01													09 06			
Kirkby	a						08 15													09 20			
Gathurst	d					07 46							08 32						08 51				
Appley Bridge	d					07 49							08 36						08 55				09 11
Parbold	d					07 53													08 59				09 15
Hoscar	d					07 56																	
Burscough Bridge	d					07 59							08 42						09 03				09 20
New Lane	d					08 02																	
Bescar Lane	d					08 05																	
Meols Cop	d					08 10													09 11				
Southport	a					08 22							09 01						09 22				09 38
Lostock	d								07 42													08 45	
Horwich Parkway	d							07 38	07 46												08 39	08 49	
Blackrod	d								07 49													08 52	
Adlington (Lancashire)	d								07 53													08 56	
Chorley	d							07 46	07 58		08 11										08 47	09 01	
Leyland	d								08 08													09 12	
Preston 8 65,97	a							07 57	08 14		08 22										08 58	09 17	
	d			07 20				07 59	08 15		08 24					08 38					08 59	09 19	
Kirkham & Wesham 97	a							08 08	08 25													09 28	
Poulton-le-Fylde 97	a							08 18	08 33												09 16	09 36	
Layton 97	a							08 22	08 37													09 43	
Blackpool North 97	a							08 29	08 46												09 25	09 52	
Lancaster 6 65	a			07 36							08 39					08 58							
	d		07 10	07 36							08 40					08 58	09 39						
Oxenholme Lake District 65	a										08 54												
Windermere 83	a																						
Carnforth	d		07a19	07 45												09 08	09 49						
Silverdale	d			07 51												09 14	09 56						
Arnside	d			07 55												09 19	10 00						
Grange-over-Sands	d			08 00												09 25	10 06						
Kents Bank	d			08 04												09 28	10 10						
Cark	d			08 08												09 33	10 14						
Ulverston	d			08 16												09 42	10 23						
Dalton	d			08 24												09 50	10 31						
Roose	d			08 30												09 56	10 37						
Barrow-in-Furness	a			08 40												10 04	10 47						

A To Liverpool Lime Street
B To Leeds
C To Kirkby
D From Manchester Victoria
E To Blackburn
F To Edinburgh
G From Huddersfield
H To Clitheroe
I From Hull to Liverpool Lime Street
J To Carlisle

The Sunday service between Manchester Victoria and Wigan Wallgate via Atherton is funded by GMITA and will operate whilst funding exists

Table 82

Manchester - Bolton - Wigan, Kirkby, Southport, Preston, Blackpool North and Barrow-in-Furness

		EM ◇ A	NT B	NT C	NT	TP ◇1 🍴	NT D	NT	TP ◇1 E 🍴	NT	TP ◇1	NT	NT	NT	NT F	TP ◇1 🍴		NT D	NT	TP ◇1 G 🍴	NT	NT
Manchester Airport 85 ✈	d					08 25			09 00				09 03			09 29				10 00		
Heald Green 85	d					08 29										09 33						
Buxton 86	d																					
Hazel Grove 86	d	08 17																				
Stockport 84	d	08 24																				
Manchester Piccadilly 10 ⇌	d	08 37				08 46			09 16				09 22			09 46				10 16		
Manchester Oxford Road	d	08a40				08 49			09 19				09 26			09 49				10 19		
Deansgate ⇌	d					08 51							09 28			09 51						
Rochdale 41	d			08 00																		
Manchester Victoria ⇌	d		08 29	08 33	08 46		09 00	09 07		09 10		09 22		09 46				10 00	10 07		10 10	10 22
Salford Central	d		08 32	08 36	08 49		09 03	09 10		09 13		09 25		09 49				10 03	10 10		10 13	10 25
Salford Crescent	a		08 37	08 39	08 52	08 56	09 07	09 13		09 16		09 29	09 33	09 52		09 56		10 07	10 13		10 16	10 29
	d		08 37	08 40	08 53	08 56	09 08	09 13		09 17		09 30	09 34	09 53		09 56		10 08	10 13		10 17	10 30
Swinton	d				08 59					09 23				09 59							10 23	
Moorside	d									09 26											10 26	
Walkden	d				09 04					09 29				10 04							10 29	
Atherton	d				09 09					09 35				10 09							10 35	
Hag Fold	d									09 37											10 37	
Daisy Hill	d				09 13					09 40				10 13							10 40	
Kearsley	d			08 47																		
Farnworth	d			08 49																		
Moses Gate	d			08 52																		
Bolton	a		08 49	08 55		09 06	09 19	09 23	09 32			09 40	09 45			10 06		10 19	10 23	10 32		10 40
	d			08 56		09 07		09 24	09 33			09 40	09 45			10 07			10 24	10 33		10 40
Westhoughton	d							09 31					09 53						10 31			
Hindley	d				09 17			09 35		09 45			09 57	10 17					10 35		10 45	
Ince	d									09 48											10 48	
Wigan North Western	a																					
Wigan Wallgate	a			09 14	09 22			09 46		09 51			10 02	10 22					10 46		10 51	
	d				09 24					09 52			10 03	10 24							10 52	
Pemberton	d									09 56											10 56	
Orrell	d									10 00											11 00	
Upholland	d									10 04											11 04	
Rainford	d									10 07											11 07	
Kirkby	a									10 21											11 21	
Gathurst	d				09 28									10 28								
Appley Bridge	d				09 32								10 10	10 32								
Parbold	d				09 36								10 14	10 36								
Hoscar	d				09 39																	
Burscough Bridge	d				09 42								10 18	10 40								
New Lane	d				09 44																	
Bescar Lane	d				09 48																	
Meols Cop	d				09 53									10 48								
Southport	a				10 04								10 37	10 59								
Lostock	d											09 45										10 45
Horwich Parkway	d					09 13						09 49				10 13						10 49
Blackrod	d											09 52										10 52
Adlington (Lancashire)	d											09 56										10 56
Chorley	d					09 21			09 44			10 01				10 21				10 44		11 01
Leyland	d											10 12										11 12
Preston 8 65,97	a					09 33			09 55			10 17				10 33				10 55		11 17
	d					09 38			09 58		10 07	10 19				10 38	10 45			10 58		11 19
Kirkham & Wesham 97	a											10 28										11 28
Poulton-le-Fylde 97	a					09 56						10 36				10 56						11 36
Layton 97	a											10 43										11 43
Blackpool North 97	a					10 05						10 53				11 05						11 52
Lancaster 6 65	a								10 13		10 22						11 00			11 13		
	d										10 23				10 49		11 01			11 14		
Oxenholme Lake District 65	a																11 17			11 28		
Windermere 83	a																11 39					
Carnforth	d										10 32				10a58							
Silverdale	d																					
Arnside	d										10 41											
Grange-over-Sands	d										10 46											
Kents Bank	d																					
Cark	d																					
Ulverston	d										10 59											
Dalton	d																					
Roose	d																					
Barrow-in-Furness	a										11 17											

A From Nottingham to Liverpool Lime Street
B To Blackburn
C From Todmorden
D To Clitheroe
E To Glasgow Central
F From Morecambe to Leeds
G To Edinburgh

The Sunday service between Manchester Victoria and Wigan Wallgate via Atherton is funded by GMITA and will operate whilst funding exists

Table 82

Mondays to Fridays
from 3 October

Manchester - Bolton - Wigan, Kirkby, Southport, Preston, Blackpool North and Barrow-in-Furness

	NT	NT	TP ◇1 ✠	NT A	NT	TP ◇1 B ✠	NT		NT	NT	NT	TP ◇1 ✠	NT A	NT	TP ◇1 C ✠	NT	TP ◇1		NT	NT	NT	TP ◇1 ✠	NT A	NT
Manchester Airport 85 ✈ d	10 03		10 29			11 00				11 03		11 29			12 00					12 03		12 29		
Heald Green 85 d			10 33									11 33										12 33		
Buxton 86 d																								
Hazel Grove 86 d																								
Stockport 84 d																								
Manchester Piccadilly 10 d	10 22		10 46			11 16				11 22		11 46			12 16					12 22		12 46		
Manchester Oxford Road d	10 26		10 49			11 19				11 26		11 49			12 19					12 26		12 49		
Deansgate d	10 28		10 51							11 28		11 51								12 28		12 51		
Rochdale 41 d																								
Manchester Victoria d		10 46		11 00	11 07		11 10		11 22		11 46		12 00	12 07		12 10			12 22		12 46		13 00	13 07
Salford Central d		10 49		11 03	11 10		11 13		11 25		11 49		12 03	12 10		12 13			12 25		12 49		13 03	13 10
Salford Crescent a	10 33	10 52	10 56	11 07	11 13		11 16		11 29	11 33	11 52	11 56	12 07	12 13		12 16			12 29	12 33	12 52	12 56	13 07	13 13
d	10 34	10 53	10 56	11 08	11 13		11 17		11 30	11 34	11 53	11 56	12 08	12 13		12 17			12 30	12 34	12 53	12 56	13 08	13 13
Swinton d		10 59					11 23				11 59					12 23					12 59			
Moorside d							11 26									12 26								
Walkden d		11 04					11 29				12 04					12 29					13 04			
Atherton d		11 09					11 35				12 09					12 35					13 09			
Hag Fold d							11 37									12 37								
Daisy Hill d		11 13					11 40				12 13					12 40					13 13			
Kearsley d																								
Farnworth d																								
Moses Gate d																								
Bolton a	10 45		11 06	11 19	11 23	11 32			11 40	11 45		12 06	12 19	12 23	12 32				12 40	12 45		13 06	13 19	13 23
d	10 45		11 07		11 24	11 33			11 40	11 45		12 07		12 24	12 33				12 40	12 45		13 07		13 24
Westhoughton d	10 53				11 31					11 53				12 31						12 53				13 31
Hindley d	10 57	11 17			11 35		11 45			11 57	12 17			12 35		12 45				12 57	13 17			13 35
Ince d							11 48									12 48								
Wigan North Western a																								
Wigan Wallgate a	11 02	11 22			11 46		11 51			12 02	12 22			12 46		12 51				13 02	13 22			13 46
d	11 03	11 24					11 52			12 03	12 24					12 52				13 03	13 24			
Pemberton d							11 56									12 56								
Orrell d							12 00									13 00								
Upholland d							12 04									13 04								
Rainford d							12 07									13 07								
Kirkby a							12 21									13 21								
Gathurst d		11 28									12 28										13 28			
Appley Bridge d	11 10	11 32								12 10	12 32									13 10	13 32			
Parbold d	11 14	11 36								12 14	12 36									13 14	13 36			
Hoscar d		11 39																			13 39			
Burscough Bridge d	11 18	11 42								12 18	12 41									13 18	13 42			
New Lane d		11 44																			13 44			
Bescar Lane d		11 48																			13 48			
Meols Cop d		11 53									12 49										13 53			
Southport a	11 37	12 04								12 37	13 01									13 37	14 04			
Lostock d									11 45										12 45					
Horwich Parkway d			11 13						11 49			12 13							12 49			13 13		
Blackrod d									11 52										12 52					
Adlington (Lancashire) d									11 56										12 56					
Chorley d			11 21			11 44			12 01			12 21			12 44				13 01			13 21		
Leyland d									12 12										13 12					
Preston 8 65,97 a			11 33			11 57			12 17			12 33			12 55				13 17			13 33		
d			11 38			11 58			12 19			12 38			12 58		13 04		13 19			13 38		
Kirkham & Wesham 97 a									12 28										13 28					
Poulton-le-Fylde 97 a			11 56						12 36			12 56							13 36			13 56		
Layton 97 a									12 43										13 43					
Blackpool North 97 a			12 05						12 52			13 05							13 52			14 05		
Lancaster 6 65 a						12 14									13 13		13 19							
d						12 14									13 14		13 20							
Oxenholme Lake District 65 a															13 28		13 36							
Windermere 83 a																	13 56							
Carnforth d						12 23																		
Silverdale d																								
Arnside d						12 31																		
Grange-over-Sands d						12 37																		
Kents Bank d																								
Cark d																								
Ulverston d						12 50																		
Dalton d																								
Roose d																								
Barrow-in-Furness a						13 10																		

A To Clitheroe
B ✠ to Chorley
C To Edinburgh

The Sunday service between Manchester Victoria and Wigan Wallgate via Atherton is funded by GMITA and will operate whilst funding exists

Table 82

Mondays to Fridays
from 3 October

Manchester - Bolton - Wigan, Kirkby, Southport, Preston, Blackpool North and Barrow-in-Furness

	TP ◇1 A ✠	NT	NT		NT B	TP ◇1	NT	NT	NT	TP ◇1 ✠	NT C	NT	TP ◇1 D ✠		NT	NT	NT	NT	TP ◇1 ✠	NT C	NT	NT	NT E	
Manchester Airport 85 ✈ d	13 00							13 03		13 29			14 00				14 03		14 29					
Heald Green 85 d										13 33									14 33					
Buxton 86 d																								
Hazel Grove 86 d																								
Stockport 84 d																								
Manchester Piccadilly 10 d	13 16							13 22		13 46			14 16				14 22		14 46					
Manchester Oxford Road d	13 19							13 26		13 49			14 19				14 26		14 49					
Deansgate d								13 28		13 51							14 28		14 51					
Rochdale 41 d																								
Manchester Victoria d		13 10					13 22		13 46		14 00	14 07			14 10	14 22		14 46		15 00	15 07	15 10		
Salford Central d		13 13					13 25		13 49		14 03	14 10			14 13	14 25		14 49		15 03	15 10	15 13		
Salford Crescent a		13 16					13 29	13 33	13 52	13 56	14 07	14 13			14 16	14 29	14 33	14 52	14 56	15 07	15 13	15 16		
d		13 17					13 30	13 34	13 53	13 56	14 08	14 13			14 17	14 30	14 34	14 53	14 56	15 08	15 13	15 17		
Swinton d		13 23							13 59						14 23			14 59				15 23		
Moorside d		13 26													14 26							15 26		
Walkden d		13 29							14 04						14 29			15 04				15 29		
Atherton d		13 35							14 09						14 35			15 09				15 35		
Hag Fold d		13 37													14 37							15 37		
Daisy Hill d		13 40							14 13						14 40			15 13				15 40		
Kearsley d																								
Farnworth d																								
Moses Gate d																								
Bolton a	13 32						13 40	13 45		14 06	14 19	14 23	14 32			14 40	14 45		15 06	15 19	15 23			
d	13 33						13 40	13 45		14 07		14 24	14 33			14 40	14 45		15 07		15 24			
Westhoughton d								13 53				14 31					14 53				15 31			
Hindley d		13 45						13 57	14 17			14 35			14 45		14 57	15 17			15 35	15 45		
Ince d		13 48													14 48							15 48		
Wigan North Western a																								
Wigan Wallgate a		13 51						14 02	14 22			14 46			14 51		15 02	15 22			15 46	15 51		
d		13 52						14 03	14 24						14 52		15 03	15 24				15 58		
Pemberton d		13 56													14 56							16 02		
Orrell d		14 00													15 00							16 06		
Upholland d		14 04													15 04							16 09		
Rainford d		14 07													15 07							16 13		
Kirkby a		14 21													15 21							16 27		
Gathurst d									14 28									15 28						
Appley Bridge d								14 10	14 32								15 10	15 32						
Parbold d								14 14	14 36								15 14	15 36						
Hoscar d																								
Burscough Bridge d								14 18	14 41								15 18	15 40						
New Lane d																								
Bescar Lane d																								
Meols Cop d									14 49									15 48						
Southport a								14 37	15 01								15 37	15 59						
Lostock d							13 45									14 45								
Horwich Parkway d							13 49			14 13						14 49			15 13					
Blackrod d							13 52									14 52								
Adlington (Lancashire) d							13 56									14 56								
Chorley d	13 44						14 01			14 21			14 44			15 01			15 21					
Leyland d							14 12									15 12								
Preston 8 65,97 a	13 55						14 17			14 33			14 55			15 17			15 33					
d	13 58					14 04	14 19			14 38			14 58			15 19			15 38					
Kirkham & Wesham 97 a							14 28									15 28								
Poulton-le-Fylde 97 a							14 36			14 56						15 36			15 56					
Layton 97 a							14 43									15 43								
Blackpool North 97 a							14 53			15 05						15 52			16 05					
Lancaster 6 65 a	14 13					14 19							15 13											
d			13 32		13 48	14 20							15 14										15 34	
Oxenholme Lake District 65 a													15 28											
Windermere 83 a																								
Carnforth d			13 42		13a58	14 28																	15 44	
Silverdale d			13 48																				15 51	
Arnside d			13 52			14 37																	15 55	
Grange-over-Sands d			13 58			14 42																	16 01	
Kents Bank d			14 02																				16 05	
Cark d			14 06																				16 09	
Ulverston d			14 15			14 55																	16 17	
Dalton d			14 23																				16 26	
Roose d			14 29																				16 32	
Barrow-in-Furness a			14 39			15 16																	16 39	

A To Glasgow Central
B From Heysham Port to Leeds
C To Clitheroe
D To Edinburgh
E To Carlisle

The Sunday service between Manchester Victoria and Wigan Wallgate via Atherton is funded by GMITA and will operate whilst funding exists

Manchester - Bolton - Wigan, Kirkby, Southport, Preston, Blackpool North and Barrow-in-Furness

Station	Table		TP ◇■ A ⌶	NT	NT	NT B	NT	TP ◇■ ⌶	NT	NT	NT	NT C	NT D	TP ◇■ E ⌶		TP ◇■	NT	NT B	NT	NT	TP ◇■ ⌶	NT	NT	NT B
Manchester Airport	85 ✈	d	15 00		15 03			15 29						16 00					16 03		16 29			
Heald Green	85	d						15 33													16 33			
Buxton	86	d																						
Hazel Grove	86	d							15 33														16 30	
Stockport	84	d							15 41														16 41	
Manchester Piccadilly ■	⇌	d	15 16		15 22			15 46	15 54					16 16					16 22		16 46		16 54	
Manchester Oxford Road		d	15 19		15 26			15 49	15 58					16 19					16 26		16 49		16 58	
Deansgate	⇌	d			15 28			15 51	16 00										16 28				17 00	
Rochdale	41	d																		16 04				
Manchester Victoria	⇌	d		15 22		15 40	15 46			16 07	16 10						16 20	16 23		16 36		16 46		17 00
Salford Central		d		15 25		15 43	15 49			16 10	16 13						16 23	16 26		16 39		16 49		17 03
Salford Crescent		a		15 29	15 33	15 46	15 52	15 56	16 04	16 13	16 16						16 26	16 30	16 34	16 42		16 52	17 04	17 07
		d		15 30	15 34	15 47	15 53	15 56	16 04	16 13	16 17						16 27	16 31	16 34	16 43		16 53	17 04	17 08
Swinton		d					15 59				16 23											16 59		
Moorside		d									16 26											17 02		
Walkden		d					16 04				16 29											17 05		
Atherton		d					16 09				16 35											17 11		
Hag Fold		d									16 37											17 14		
Daisy Hill		d					16 13				16 40											17 17		
Kearsley		d																		16 50				
Farnworth		d																		16 52				
Moses Gate		d								16 21										16 55				
Bolton		a	15 32	15 40	15 45	15 59		16 06	16 19	16 25				16 32			16 37	16 42	16 45	16 58	17 05		17 14	17 19
		d	15 33	15 40	15 45			16 07		16 25				16 33			16 37		16 45	16 59	17 06		17 15	
Westhoughton		d			15 53					16 33									16 53	17 06				
Hindley		d			15 57		16 17			16 37	16 45								16 57	17 10		17 21		
Ince		d									16 48											17 24		
Wigan North Western		a																						
Wigan Wallgate		a			16 02		16 22			16 48	16 51								17 02	17 19		17 33		
		d			16 03		16 24				16 52								17 03					
Pemberton		d									16 56													
Orrell		d									17 00													
Upholland		d									17 04													
Rainford		d									17 07													
Kirkby		a									17 21													
Gathurst		d			16 08		16 28												17 08					
Appley Bridge		d			16 11		16 32												17 11					
Parbold		d			16 15		16 36												17 15					
Hoscar		d			16 18																			
Burscough Bridge		d			16 21		16 40												17 20					
New Lane		d			16 24																			
Bescar Lane		d			16 27																			
Meols Cop		d			16 32		16 48												17 27					
Southport		a			16 44		16 59												17 39					
Lostock		d		15 45				16 12									16 43						17 20	
Horwich Parkway		d		15 49				16 15									16 47						17 24	
Blackrod		d		15 52													16 51							
Adlington (Lancashire)		d		15 56													16 55							
Chorley		d	15 44	16 01				16 23						16 44			17 00				17 19		17 32	
Leyland		d		16 12													17 11						17 42	
Preston ■	65,97	a	15 57	16 19				16 35						16 55			17 19				17 30		17 51	
		d	15 58					16 38						17 00	17 04	17 04	17 21				17 32			
Kirkham & Wesham	97	a						16 47									17 30				17 41			
Poulton-le-Fylde	97	a						16 57									17 38				17 51			
Layton	97	a						17 00									17 43				17 54			
Blackpool North	97	a						17 07									17 52				18 02			
Lancaster ■	65	a	16 14											17 15	17 23	17 23								
		d	16 15									16 55	17 19	17 16	17 25	17 25								
Oxenholme Lake District	65	a												17 30	17 43	17 43								
Windermere	83	a													18 08	18 08								
Carnforth		d	16 23									17 05	17 28											
Silverdale		d	16 29									17 12	17 35											
Arnside		d	16 33									17 16	17 40											
Grange-over-Sands		d	16 39									17 22	17 46											
Kents Bank		d	16 42									17 26	17 49											
Cark		d	16 47									17 30	17 54											
Ulverston		d	16 55									17 39	18 02											
Dalton		d	17 03									17 48	18 10											
Roose		d	17 09									17 54	18 17											
Barrow-in-Furness		a	17 18									18 02	18 25											

A ⌶ to Chorley
B To Clitheroe
C To Millom
D From Morecambe
E To Edinburgh

The Sunday service between Manchester Victoria and Wigan Wallgate via Atherton is funded by GMITA and will operate whilst funding exists

Manchester - Bolton - Wigan, Kirkby, Southport, Preston, Blackpool North and Barrow-in-Furness

Station	Table		TP ◇■ A ⌶		NT B	NT	NT	NT C	NT	NT	NT	NT	TP ◇■ ⌶	NT D	TP ◇■ E ⌶		NT	NT	NT C	NT	NT	NT	TP ◇■ ⌶	NT D
Manchester Airport	85 ✈	d	17 00						17 03				17 29		18 00					18 03			18 29	
Heald Green	85	d											17 33										18 33	
Buxton	86	d																						
Hazel Grove	86	d																						
Stockport	84	d																						
Manchester Piccadilly ■	⇌	d	17 15						17 22				17 46		18 16					18 22			18 46	
Manchester Oxford Road		d	17 18						17 26				17 49		18 19					18 26			18 49	
Deansgate	⇌	d											17 51							18 28			18 51	
Rochdale	41	d						17 03											18 02					
Manchester Victoria	⇌	d			17 06	17 10	17 19	17 23		17 36	17 40	17 45		18 00			18 10	18 20	18 23		18 33	18 45		19 00
Salford Central		d			17 09	17 12	17 22	17 27		17 39	17 43	17 48		18 03			18 13	18 23	18 26		18 36	18 48		19 03
Salford Crescent		a			17 13	17 16	17 25	17 29	17 34	17 42	17 46	17 51	17 55	18 07			18 16	18 26	18 30	18 34	18 39	18 51	18 56	19 07
		d			17 14	17 17	17 27	17 30	17 34	17 43	17 47	17 52	17 55	18 08			18 17	18 27	18 31	18 34	18 40	18 52	18 56	19 08
Swinton		d				17 23						17 58					18 23					18 58		
Moorside		d				17 26						18 01					18 26					19 01		
Walkden		d				17 31						18 05					18 29					19 04		
Atherton		d			17 26	17 37					17 59	18 11					18 35					19 10		
Hag Fold		d				17 39						18 13					18 37					19 12		
Daisy Hill		d			17 30	17 43					18 03	18 17					18 40					19 15		
Kearsley		d								17 53											18 47			
Farnworth		d								17 55											18 49			
Moses Gate		d								17 57											18 52			
Bolton		a	17 31				17 37	17 42	17 45	18 01			18 06	18 19	18 32			18 37	18 42	18 45	18 55		19 06	19 20
		d	17 32				17 37		17 45	18 01			18 07		18 33			18 37		18 45	18 56		19 07	
Westhoughton		d							17 53	18 09										18 53	19 03			
Hindley		d				17 48				18 13		18 22					18 45			18 57	19 09	19 20		
Ince		d				17 51						18 25					18 48					19 23		
Wigan North Western		a															18 56							
Wigan Wallgate		a			17 38	17 54			18 01	18 24	18 11	18 28								19 02	19 20	19 32		
		d			17 40	17 55			18 02		18 15	18 29								19 03				
Pemberton		d				17 59						18 33												
Orrell		d				18 03						18 37												
Upholland		d				18 07						18 41												
Rainford		d				18 10						18 44												
Kirkby		a				18 24						18 57												
Gathurst		d			17 44						18 19									19 08				
Appley Bridge		d			17 48				18 09		18 23									19 11				
Parbold		d			17 52				18 13		18 28									19 15				
Hoscar		d									18 31													
Burscough Bridge		d			17 57				18 17		18 34									19 19				
New Lane		d									18 37													
Bescar Lane		d									18 40													
Meols Cop		d			18 05						18 46									19 27				
Southport		a			18 16				18 37		18 57									19 39				
Lostock		d					17 43						18 12					18 42					19 12	
Horwich Parkway		d					17 47						18 15					18 46					19 15	
Blackrod		d					17 51						18 19					18 49						
Adlington (Lancashire)		d					17 55											18 53						
Chorley		d	17 44				18 00						18 26		18 44			18 58					19 23	
Leyland		d					18 11											19 10						
Preston ■	65,97	a	17 55				18 16						18 38		18 55			19 18					19 33	
		d	17 58	18 08			18 18						18 40		19 00	19 04		19 19					19 38	
Kirkham & Wesham	97	a					18 27						18 49					19 28						
Poulton-le-Fylde	97	a					18 35						18 59					19 36					19 56	
Layton	97	a					18 39						19 02					19 43						
Blackpool North	97	a					18 51						19 09					19 52					20 05	
Lancaster ■	65	a	18 13	18 23											19 15	19 20								
		d	18 14	18 24											19 16	19 20								
Oxenholme Lake District	65	a	18 28												19 30									
Windermere	83	a																						
Carnforth		d		18 34												19 29								
Silverdale		d		18 40												19 35								
Arnside		d		18 44												19 39								
Grange-over-Sands		d		18 49												19 44								
Kents Bank		d		18 53												19 48								
Cark		d		18 57												19 52								
Ulverston		d		19 05												20 00								
Dalton		d		19 13												20 08								
Roose		d		19 19												20 14								
Barrow-in-Furness		a		19 30												20 24								

A To Glasgow Central
B From Stalybridge
C To Blackburn
D To Clitheroe
E To Edinburgh

The Sunday service between Manchester Victoria and Wigan Wallgate via Atherton is funded by GMITA and will operate whilst funding exists

Table 82

Mondays to Fridays
from 3 October

Manchester - Bolton - Wigan, Kirkby, Southport, Preston, Blackpool North and Barrow-in-Furness

	NT	NT	TP	NT	NT	TP	NT	TP	NT	NT	NT	NT	TP	NT	NT	NT	NT	NT	NT	NT	TP
			◇1			◇1		◇1					◇1								◇1
		A					B					C		B					C	D	
Manchester Airport 85 ✈ d			19 00	19 03		19 29		20 00			20 03	20 09	20 29					21 03	21 09		21 29
Heald Green 85 d						19 33						20 12	20 33						21 12		21 33
Buxton 86 d																					
Hazel Grove 86 d																					
Stockport 84 d																					
Manchester Piccadilly 10 d			19 16	19 20		19 46		20 16			20 20	20 32	20 46					21 20	21 32	21 38	21 46
Manchester Oxford Road d			19 19	19 24		19 49		20 19			20 24	20a36	20 49					21 24	21a36	21 44	21 49
Deansgate d				19 26		19 51					20 26		20 51					21 26		21a46	21 51
Rochdale 41 d																					
Manchester Victoria d	19 10				19 28		20 00		20 10	20 22				21 00	21 10		21 22				
Salford Central d	19 13				19 31		20 03		20 13	20 25				21 03	21 13		21 25				
Salford Crescent a	19 16			19 29	19 34	19 56	20 07		20 16	20 29	20 33		20 56	21 07	21 16		21 29	21 33			21 56
d	19 17			19 30	19 35	19 56	20 08		20 17	20 30	20 34		20 56	21 08	21 17		21 30	21 34			21 56
Swinton d	19 23								20 23						21 23						
Moorside d	19 26								20 26						21 26						
Walkden d	19 29								20 29						21 29						
Atherton d	19 35								20 35						21 35						
Hag Fold d	19 37								20 37						21 37						
Daisy Hill d	19 40								20 40						21 40						
Kearsley d																					
Farnworth d																					
Moses Gate d																					
Bolton a			19 32	19 40	19 45	20 06	20 19	20 32		20 40	20 45		21 06	21 19			21 40	21 45			22 06
d			19 33	19 40	19 45	20 07		20 33		20 40	20 45		21 07				21 40	21 45			22 07
Westhoughton d				19 48							20 53							21 53			
Hindley d	19 45			19 52					20 45		20 57				21 45			21 57			
Ince d	19 48								20 48						21 48						
Wigan North Western a																					
Wigan Wallgate a	19 57			19 57					20 57		21 02				21 57			22 02			
d				19 59							21 03							22 03			
Pemberton d																					
Orrell d																					
Upholland d																					
Rainford d																					
Kirkby a																					
Gathurst d				20 03							21 08							22 08			
Appley Bridge d				20 07							21 11							22 11			
Parbold d				20 11							21 15							22 15			
Hoscar d											21 18										
Burscough Bridge d				20 15							21 21							22 20			
New Lane d											21 24										
Bescar Lane d											21 27										
Meols Cop d				20 23							21 32							22 27			
Southport a				20 34							21 42							22 39			
Lostock d					19 50					20 45							21 45				
Horwich Parkway d					19 54	20 13		20 39		20 49			21 13				21 49				22 13
Blackrod d					19 57					20 52							21 52				
Adlington (Lancashire) d					20 01					20 56							21 56				
Chorley d			19 44		20 06	20 21		20 46		21 01			21 21				22 01				22 21
Leyland d					20 18					21 12							22 12				
Preston 8 65,97 a			19 55		20 23	20 33		20 57		21 17			21 33				22 17				22 33
d			19 58		20 25	20 38		20 58		21 19			21 38			21 51	22 19				22 35
Kirkham & Wesham 97 a					20 34					21 28							22 28				
Poulton-le-Fylde 97 a					20 42	20 56				21 36			21 56				22 36				22 52
Layton 97 a					20 46					21 40							22 43				
Blackpool North 97 a					20 56	21 06				21 50			22 06				22 53				23 02
Lancaster 6 65 a			20 13					21 13								22 11					
d		19 24	20 14					21 14								22 11					
Oxenholme Lake District 65 a																					
Windermere 83 a																					
Carnforth d		19a34	20 22					21 23								22 21					
Silverdale d			20 28					21 29								22 27					
Arnside d			20 32					21 33								22 32					
Grange-over-Sands d			20 38					21 39								22 38					
Kents Bank d			20 41					21 42								22 41					
Cark d			20 46					21 47								22 46					
Ulverston d			20 54					21 55								22 54					
Dalton d			21 02					22 03								23 02					
Roose d			21 08					22 09								23 08					
Barrow-in-Furness a			21 18					22 19								23 16					

A From Morecambe to Leeds
B To Clitheroe
C From Wilmslow
D To Warrington Central

The Sunday service between Manchester Victoria and Wigan Wallgate via Atherton is funded by GMITA and will operate whilst funding exists

Table 82

Mondays to Fridays
from 3 October

Manchester - Bolton - Wigan, Kirkby, Southport, Preston, Blackpool North and Barrow-in-Furness

	NT	NT	TP	NT	NT	NT	NT	NT	NT	TP	NT	NT	NT	NT	NT	NT	NT	TP
	FO	FX			FO	FX	FO	FX				FO	FX	FO	FX	FO	FX	FX
			◇1							◇1								◇1
	A	A		B								C	C					D
Manchester Airport 85 ✈ d			22 00	22 08					22 19	22 29								23 18
Heald Green 85 d				22 12						22 33								
Buxton 86 d																		
Hazel Grove 86 d																		
Stockport 84 d											22 34							
Manchester Piccadilly 10 d			22 16	22 32					22 36	22 46	22 50							23 38
Manchester Oxford Road d			22 19	22a36					22 39	22 49	22 53							
Deansgate d									22 41	22 51	22 55							
Rochdale 41 d																		
Manchester Victoria d	22 00	22 00			22 10	22 10	22 22	22 22				23 00	23 00	23 20	23 20	23 23	23 23	
Salford Central d	22 04				22 13		22 25					23 03		23 23		23 26		
Salford Crescent a	22 07	22 07			22 17	22 17	22 29	22 29	22 46	22 56	22 59	23 07	23 07	23 26	23 25	23 29	23 29	23 43
d	22 08	22 08			22 17	22 17	22 30	22 30	22 46	22 56	22 59	23 08	23 08	23 26	23 26	23 30	23 30	
Swinton d					22 23	22 23								23 33	23 33			
Moorside d					22 26	22 26								23 35	23 35			
Walkden d					22 29	22 29								23 39	23 39			
Atherton d					22 35	22 35								23 44	23 44			
Hag Fold d					22 37	22 37								23 47	23 47			
Daisy Hill d					22 40	22 40								23 50	23 50			
Kearsley d											23 07							
Farnworth d											23 09							
Moses Gate d											23 11							
Bolton a	22 19	22 19	22 32				22 40	22 40	22 56	23 06	23 15	23 19	23 19			23 40	23 40	
d			22 33				22 40	22 40	22 57	23 07	23 15					23 40	23 40	
Westhoughton d									23 04		23 23							
Hindley d					22 45	22 45			23 08		23 27			23 54	23 54			
Ince d					22 48	22 48								23 57	23 57			
Wigan North Western a			22 48															
Wigan Wallgate a					22 57	22 57			23 13		23 38			00 06	00 06			
d									23 15									
Pemberton d																		
Orrell d																		
Upholland d																		
Rainford d																		
Kirkby a																		
Gathurst d									23 19									
Appley Bridge d									23 23									
Parbold d									23 27									
Hoscar d																		
Burscough Bridge d									23 31									
New Lane d																		
Bescar Lane d																		
Meols Cop d									23 39									
Southport a									23 50									
Lostock d							22 45	22 45								23 45	23 45	
Horwich Parkway d							22 49	22 49		23 13						23 49	23 49	
Blackrod d							22 52	22 52								23 52	23 52	
Adlington (Lancashire) d							22 56	22 56								23 56	23 56	
Chorley d							23 01	23 01		23 21						00 01	00 01	
Leyland d							23 12	23 12								00 12	00 12	
Preston 8 65,97 a			23 09				23 17	23 17		23 33						00 17	00 17	
d			23 13				23 19	23 19		23 35						00 19	00 19	
Kirkham & Wesham 97 a							23 28	23 28								00 28	00 28	
Poulton-le-Fylde 97 a							23 36	23 36		23 52						00 36	00 36	
Layton 97 a							23 40	23 40								00 43	00 43	
Blackpool North 97 a							23 50	23 50		00 02						00 52	00 52	
Lancaster 6 65 a			23 28															
d			23 29															
Oxenholme Lake District 65 a																		
Windermere 83 a																		
Carnforth d			23 37															
Silverdale d			23 43															
Arnside d			23 47															
Grange-over-Sands d			23 53															
Kents Bank d			23 56															
Cark d			00 01															
Ulverston d			00 09															
Dalton d			00 17															
Roose d			00 23															
Barrow-in-Furness a			00 32															

A To Clitheroe
B From Wilmslow
C To Blackburn
D To York

The Sunday service between Manchester Victoria and Wigan Wallgate via Atherton is funded by GMITA and will operate whilst funding exists

Table 82

Saturdays until 1 October

Manchester - Bolton - Wigan, Kirkby, Southport, Preston, Blackpool North and Barrow-in-Furness

Station		TP	TP	NT	NT	TP	TP	TP	TP	NT	TP	TP	TP	NT	NT	TP	NT	TP	NT	NT	NT	TP	TP
		◇■	◇■			◇■	◇■	◇■	◇■		■	■	◇■			◇■		◇■				◇■	◇■
		A					B		B	C		D		E		F		G			E	C	A
Manchester Airport 85 ✈	d	22p00	22p29			00 01	00 38	04 00	04 15	04 34						05 45		06 18					
Heald Green 85	d		22p33													05 49							
Buxton 86	d																				05 59		
Hazel Grove 86	d																				06 33		
Stockport 84	d																				06 41		
Manchester Piccadilly ■	d	22p16	22p46			00 16	00 53	04 15	04 30	04a47			05 43			06 03		06 33			06 54	07 07	
Manchester Oxford Road	d	22p19	22p49													06 06		06 36			06 57	07a09	
Deansgate	d		22p51																		06 59		
Rochdale 41	d																						
Manchester Victoria	d			23p20	23p23									05 55	06 00		06 17		06 38	06 45			
Salford Central	d			23p23	23p26														06 40	06 48			
Salford Crescent	a		22p56	23p26	23p29		00 58		04 36				05 48	05 59	06 04		06 23		06 44	06 51	07 03		
	d		22p56	23p26	23p30								05 49	06 00	06 05		06 24		06 45	06 52	07 03		
Swinton	d			23p33																06 58			
Moorside	d			23p35																			
Walkden	d			23p39																07 03			
Atherton	d			23p44																07 08			
Hag Fold	d			23p47																			
Daisy Hill	d			23p50																07 12			
Kearsley	d																		06 52				
Farnworth	d																		06 54				
Moses Gate	d																		06 57				
Bolton	a	22p32	23p06		23p40	00s31		04s29					05 59	06 11	06 15	06 19	06 34	06 50	07 00		07 16		
	d	22p33	23p07		23p40								05 59		06 15	06 19	06 34	06 50	07 01				
Westhoughton	d														06 23								
Hindley	d			23p54											06 27					07 16			
Ince	d			23p57																			
Wigan North Western	a	22p48																	07 19				
Wigan Wallgate	a			00 04											06 32					07 21			
	d														06 34					07 23			
Pemberton	d														06 38								
Orrell	d														06 42								
Upholland	d														06 45								
Rainford	d														06 49								
Kirkby	a														07 01								
Gathurst	d																			07 27			
Appley Bridge	d																			07 31			
Parbold	d																			07 35			
Hoscar	d																						
Burscough Bridge	d																			07 39			
New Lane	d																						
Bescar Lane	d																						
Meols Cop	d																			07 47			
Southport	a																			07 56			
Lostock	d				23p45												06 39						
Horwich Parkway	d		23p13		23p49								06 06				06 43						
Blackrod	d				23p52												06 46						
Adlington (Lancashire)	d				23p56												06 50						
Chorley	d		23p21		00 01								06 13			06 31	06 55						
Leyland	d				00 12								06 22				07 06						
Preston ■ 65,97	a	23p09	23p33		00 17	01s05		05s04					06 26			06 42	07 11	07 11					
	d	23p13	23p35		00 19							06 34	06 37			06 44	07 13	07 14					07 20
Kirkham & Wesham 97	a				00 28								06 46				07 22						
Poulton-le-Fylde 97	a		23p52		00 36								06 56				07 30						
Layton 97	a				00 43								06 59				07 34						
Blackpool North 97	a		00 02		00 50	01 30		05 33					07 06				07 41						
Lancaster ■ 65	a	23p28										06 50				06 59		07 30					07 36
	d	23p29									05 46	06 50				07 00							07 36
Oxenholme Lake District 65	a										06 21					07 15							
Windermere 83	a										06 41												
Carnforth	d	23p37										06a58											07 45
Silverdale	d	23p43																					07 51
Arnside	d	23p47																					07 55
Grange-over-Sands	d	23p53																					08 00
Kents Bank	d	23p56																					08 04
Cark	d	00 01																					08 08
Ulverston	d	00 09																					08 16
Dalton	d	00 17																					08 24
Roose	d	00 23																					08 30
Barrow-in-Furness	a	00 32																					08 40

A from 23 July until 1 October
B To York
C To Liverpool Lime Street
D until 16 July
E To Clitheroe
F To Edinburgh
G To Glasgow Central

The Sunday service between Manchester Victoria and Wigan Wallgate via Atherton is funded by GMITA and will operate whilst funding exists

Table 82

Saturdays until 1 October

Manchester - Bolton - Wigan, Kirkby, Southport, Preston, Blackpool North and Barrow-in-Furness

Station		TP	NT	NT	NT	NT	NT	TP	TP	NT	NT	TP	NT	NT	NT	TP	NT	NT	NT	TP	NT	NT	EM
		◇■						◇■	◇■			◇■				◇■				◇■			◇
		A	A	B	C		D	A	E		F	G			H	I			J				K
Manchester Airport 85 ✈	d							07 00	07 00			07 25								07 56		08 01	
Heald Green 85	d											07 30										08 05	
Buxton 86	d																						
Hazel Grove 86	d													07 32									08 17
Stockport 84	d													07 40									08 24
Manchester Piccadilly ■	d							07 15	07 15			07 45		07 54		08 07				08 15		08 22	08 37
Manchester Oxford Road	d							07 18	07 18					07 58		08a09				08 19		08 26	08a40
Deansgate	d													08 00								08 28	
Rochdale 41	d																						
Manchester Victoria	d				07 06	07 10				07 16	07 23		07 27		08 00		08 07	08 10			08 22		
Salford Central	d				07 09	07 13				07 19	07 26		07 30		08 03		08 10	08 13			08 25		
Salford Crescent	a				07 12	07 16				07 24	07 29		07 33	08 04	08 07		08 13	08 16			08 29	08 33	
	d				07 13	07 16				07 25	07 30		07 33	08 04	08 08		08 13	08 17			08 30	08 34	
Swinton	d				07 19													08 23					
Moorside	d				07 22													08 26					
Walkden	d				07 25								07 42					08 29					
Atherton	d				07 31								07 48					08 35					
Hag Fold	d				07 33													08 37					
Daisy Hill	d				07 36								07 51					08 40					
Kearsley	d																						
Farnworth	d																						
Moses Gate	d																						
Bolton	a					07 26		07 31	07 31	07 35	07 41	07 59		08 14	08 19		08 23			08 32	08 40	08 44	
	d					07 27		07 31	07 31	07 35		07 59		08 15			08 24			08 32	08 40	08 45	
Westhoughton	d					07 34	←										08 31					08 53	
Hindley	d				07 42	07 38	07 42										08 35	08 45					
Ince	d				→		07 45											08 48					
Wigan North Western	a																						
Wigan Wallgate	a					07 43	07 48						08 03				08 44	08 51				09 00	
	d					07 45	07 50											08 52				09 05	
Pemberton	d						07 54											08 56					
Orrell	d						07 58											09 00					
Upholland	d						08 01											09 04					
Rainford	d						08 05											09 07					
Kirkby	a						08 17											09 19					
Gathurst	d					07 49																	
Appley Bridge	d					07 53																09 11	
Parbold	d					07 57																09 15	
Hoscar	d					08 00																	
Burscough Bridge	d					08 03																09 20	
New Lane	d					08 05																	
Bescar Lane	d					08 09																	
Meols Cop	d					08 14																	
Southport	a					08 23																09 36	
Lostock	d									07 42				08 20							08 45		
Horwich Parkway	d							07 38	07 38	07 46				08 24						08 39	08 49		
Blackrod	d									07 49											08 52		
Adlington (Lancashire)	d									07 53				08 29							08 56		
Chorley	d							07 46	07 46	07 58		08 11		08 34						08 47	09 01		
Leyland	d									08 08				08 43							09 12		
Preston ■ 65,97	a							07 55	07 57	08 14		08 22		08 50						08 58	09 17		
	d	07 20						07 59	07 59	08 15		08 24							08 42	08 59	09 19		
Kirkham & Wesham 97	a							08 07	08 08	08 25											09 28		
Poulton-le-Fylde 97	a							08 18	08 18	08 33										09 16	09 36		
Layton 97	a							08 22	08 22	08 37											09 43		
Blackpool North 97	a							08 29	08 29	08 44										09 25	09 50		
Lancaster ■ 65	a	07 36										08 39							09 02				
	d	07 36		08 24															09 03				
Oxenholme Lake District 65	a																						
Windermere 83	a																						
Carnforth	d	07 45		08a33															09 13				
Silverdale	d	07 51																	09 18				
Arnside	d	07a58																	09 23				
Grange-over-Sands	d		08 00																09 29				
Kents Bank	d		08 04																09 32				
Cark	d		08 08																09 37				
Ulverston	d		08 17																09 45				
Dalton	d		08 25																09 53				
Roose	d		08 31																09 59				
Barrow-in-Furness	a		08 41																10 07				

A until 16 July
B To Leeds
C To Kirkby
D From Manchester Victoria
E from 23 July until 1 October
F To Blackburn
G To Edinburgh
H To Clitheroe
I From Hull to Liverpool Lime Street
J from 23 July until 1 October. To Carlisle
K From Nottingham to Liverpool Lime Street

The Sunday service between Manchester Victoria and Wigan Wallgate via Atherton is funded by GMITA and will operate whilst funding exists

Table 82

Saturdays until 1 October

Manchester - Bolton - Wigan, Kirkby, Southport, Preston, Blackpool North and Barrow-in-Furness

		NT	NT	NT	TP	TP	NT	NT	NT	NT	NT	TP	TP	TP		NT	NT	NT	NT	NT	TP	NT
						◇1						◇1	◇1	◇1							◇1	
		A	B		C	D		E			F	G	H	I				A				
						⊼								⊼							⊼	
Manchester Airport 85 ✈	d					08 25								09 00			09 03				09 29	
Heald Green 85	d					08 29															09 33	
Buxton 86	d						07 56															
Hazel Grove 86	d						08 33															09 33
Stockport 84	d						08 41															09 41
Manchester Piccadilly 10 ⇌	d					08 46	08 54							09 16			09 22				09 46	09 54
Manchester Oxford Road	d					08 49	08 58							09 19			09 26				09 49	09 58
Deansgate ⇌	d					08 51	09 00										09 28				09 51	10 00
Rochdale 41	d		08 00																09 04			
Manchester Victoria ⇌	d	08 29	08 33	08 46				09 00	09 07	09 10						09 22		09 29	09 32	09 46		
Salford Central	d	08 32	08 36	08 49				09 03	09 10	09 13						09 25		09 32	09 36	09 49		
Salford Crescent	a	08 37	08 39	08 52		08 56	09 04	09 07	09 13	09 16						09 29	09 33	09 37	09 39	09 52	09 56	10 04
	d	08 37	08 40	08 53		08 56	09 04	09 08	09 13	09 17						09 30	09 33	09 37	09 40	09 53	09 56	10 04
Swinton	d			08 59						09 23										09 59		
Moorside	d									09 26												
Walkden	d			09 04						09 29										10 04		
Atherton	d			09 09						09 35										10 09		
Hag Fold	d									09 37												
Daisy Hill	d			09 13						09 40										10 13		
Kearsley	d		08 47																09 47			
Farnworth	d		08 49																09 49			
Moses Gate	d		08 52																09 52			
Bolton	a	08 49	08 55			09 06	09 14	09 19	09 23					09 32		09 40	09 44	09 49	09 55		10 06	10 14
	d		08 56			09 07	09 15		09 24					09 33		09 40	09 45		09 56		10 07	10 15
Westhoughton	d								09 31								09 53					
Hindley	d			09 17					09 35	09 45							09 57			10 17		
Ince	d									09 48												
Wigan North Western	a																					
Wigan Wallgate	a		09 14	09 22					09 44	09 51							10 02		10 13	10 22		
	d			09 24						09 52							10 03			10 24		
Pemberton	d									09 56												
Orrell	d									10 00												
Upholland	d									10 04												
Rainford	d									10 07												
Kirkby	a									10 19												
Gathurst	d			09 28																10 28		
Appley Bridge	d			09 32													10 10			10 32		
Parbold	d			09 36													10 14			10 36		
Hoscar	d			09 39																		
Burscough Bridge	d			09 42													10 18			10 40		
New Lane	d			09 44																		
Bescar Lane	d			09 48																		
Meols Cop	d			09 53																10 48		
Southport	a			10 02													10 35			10 57		
Lostock	d						09 20									09 45						10 20
Horwich Parkway	d						09 24									09 49					10 13	10 24
Blackrod	d															09 52						
Adlington (Lancashire)	d															09 56						
Chorley	d					09 19	09 32							09 44		10 01					10 21	10 32
Leyland	d						09 42									10 12						10 42
Preston 8 65,97	a					09 30	09 50							09 55		10 17					10 33	10 50
	d					09 32						09 45	10 04	09 58	10 08	10 19					10 38	
Kirkham & Wesham 97	a															10 28						
Poulton-le-Fylde 97	a														10 26	10 36					10 56	
Layton 97	a															10 43						
Blackpool North 97	a														10 35	10 50					11 05	
Lancaster 6 65	a					09 47						10 00	10 19	10 13								
	d				09 26	09 48						10 01	10 20									
Oxenholme Lake District 65	a					10 04																
Windermere 83	a					10 26																
Carnforth	d				09 34							10 09	10 28									
Silverdale	d				09 40							10 15	10 34									
Arnside	d				09a47							10 19	10a41									
Grange-over-Sands	d										09 32	10 25										
Kents Bank	d										09 35	10 28										
Cark	d										09 40	10 33										
Ulverston	d										09 48	10 41										
Dalton	d										09 56	10 49										
Roose	d										10 02	10 55										
Barrow-in-Furness	a										10 10	11 04										

A To Blackburn
B From Hebden Bridge
C until 16 July
D ⊼ to Chorley
E To Clitheroe
F until 16 July. To Carlisle
G from 23 July until 1 October. From Blackpool North
H until 16 July. From Blackpool North
I To Glasgow Central

The Sunday service between Manchester Victoria and Wigan Wallgate via Atherton is funded by GMITA and will operate whilst funding exists

Table 82

Saturdays until 1 October

Manchester - Bolton - Wigan, Kirkby, Southport, Preston, Blackpool North and Barrow-in-Furness

		NT	NT	NT	NT	NT	TP	TP	NT	NT	NT	NT	TP	NT	NT	NT	NT	TP	NT	NT	TP	NT	TP
							◇1	◇1					◇1								◇1		◇1
		A			B	C		D							A			B	E	F	G	B	H
								⊼					⊼								⊼		⊼
Manchester Airport 85 ✈	d							10 00		10 03			10 29								11 00		11 00
Heald Green 85	d												10 33										
Buxton 86	d																						
Hazel Grove 86	d													10 33									
Stockport 84	d													10 41									
Manchester Piccadilly 10 ⇌	d							10 16		10 22			10 46	10 54							11 16		11 16
Manchester Oxford Road	d							10 19		10 26			10 49	10 58							11 19		11 19
Deansgate ⇌	d									10 28			10 51	11 00									
Rochdale 41	d										10 05												
Manchester Victoria ⇌	d	10 00	10 07	10 10					10 22		10 33	10 46			11 00	11 07	11 10						
Salford Central	d	10 03	10 10	10 13					10 25		10 36	10 49			11 03	11 10	11 13						
Salford Crescent	a	10 07	10 13	10 16					10 29	10 33	10 39	10 52	10 56	11 04	11 07	11 13	11 16						
	d	10 08	10 13	10 17					10 30	10 34	10 40	10 53	10 56	11 04	11 08	11 13	11 17						
Swinton	d			10 23								10 59					11 23						
Moorside	d			10 26													11 26						
Walkden	d			10 29								11 04					11 29						
Atherton	d			10 35								11 09					11 35						
Hag Fold	d			10 37													11 37						
Daisy Hill	d			10 40								11 13					11 40						
Kearsley	d										10 47												
Farnworth	d										10 49												
Moses Gate	d										10 52												
Bolton	a	10 19	10 23					10 32	10 40	10 45	10 55		11 06	11 14	11 19	11 23					11 32		11 32
	d		10 24					10 33	10 40	10 45	10 56		11 07	11 15		11 24					11 33		11 33
Westhoughton	d		10 31							10 53						11 31							
Hindley	d		10 35	10 45						10 57		11 17				11 35	11 45						
Ince	d			10 48													11 48						
Wigan North Western	a																						
Wigan Wallgate	a		10 44	10 51						11 02	11 13	11 22				11 44	11 51						
	d			10 52						11 03		11 24					11 52						
Pemberton	d			10 56													11 56						
Orrell	d			11 00													12 00						
Upholland	d			11 04													12 04						
Rainford	d			11 07													12 07						
Kirkby	a			11 19													12 19						
Gathurst	d											11 28											
Appley Bridge	d									11 10		11 32											
Parbold	d									11 14		11 36											
Hoscar	d											11 39											
Burscough Bridge	d									11 18		11 42											
New Lane	d											11 44											
Bescar Lane	d											11 48											
Meols Cop	d											11 53											
Southport	a									11 35		12 02											
Lostock	d								10 45					11 20									
Horwich Parkway	d								10 49				11 13	11 24									
Blackrod	d								10 52														
Adlington (Lancashire)	d								10 56														
Chorley	d							10 44	11 01				11 21	11 32							11 44		11 44
Leyland	d								11 12					11 42									
Preston 8 65,97	a							10 55	11 17				11 33	11 50							11 57		11 57
	d						10 45	10 58	11 19				11 38								11 58		11 58
Kirkham & Wesham 97	a								11 28														
Poulton-le-Fylde 97	a								11 36				11 56										
Layton 97	a								11 43														
Blackpool North 97	a								11 50				12 05										
Lancaster 6 65	a						11 00	11 13													12 14		12 14
	d					10 49	11 01	11 14										11 26		11 28	12 14		12 14
Oxenholme Lake District 65	a						11 17	11 28															
Windermere 83	a						11 39																
Carnforth	d					10a58												11 34		11 37	12 22		12 23
Silverdale	d																	11 40		11 43			
Arnside	d																	11a47		11 48	12a34		12 31
Grange-over-Sands	d				10 43														11 54	11 54		12 10	12 37
Kents Bank	d				10 47															11 57		12 13	
Cark	d				10 51															12 02		12 17	
Ulverston	d				11 00														12 06	12 10		12 26	12 50
Dalton	d				11 08															12 18		12 34	
Roose	d				11 14															12 24		12 40	
Barrow-in-Furness	a				11 22														12 25	12 32		12 49	13 10

A To Clitheroe
B until 16 July
C From Morecambe to Leeds
D To Edinburgh
E until 16 July. To Carlisle
F from 23 July until 1 October. To Carlisle
G until 16 July. ⊼ to Chorley
H from 23 July until 1 October. ⊼ to Chorley

The Sunday service between Manchester Victoria and Wigan Wallgate via Atherton is funded by GMITA and will operate whilst funding exists

Manchester - Bolton - Wigan, Kirkby, Southport, Preston, Blackpool North and Barrow-in-Furness

	NT	NT	NT	NT	TP ◇1 ✠	NT	NT A	NT	TP ◇1 B ✠	NT	TP ◇1	NT	NT	NT	NT	TP ◇1 ✠	NT	NT A	NT	NT	NT C
Manchester Airport 85 ✈ d		11 03			11 29				12 00				12 03			12 29					
Heald Green 85 d					11 33											12 33					
Buxton 86 d																					
Hazel Grove 86 d						11 33											12 33				
Stockport 84 d						11 41											12 41				
Manchester Piccadilly 10 ⇌ d		11 22			11 46	11 54			12 16				12 22			12 46	12 54				
Manchester Oxford Road d		11 26			11 49	11 58			12 19				12 26			12 49	12 58				
Deansgate ⇌ d		11 28			11 51	12 00							12 28			12 51	13 00				
Rochdale 41 d			11 04											12 04							
Manchester Victoria ⇌ d	11 22		11 33	11 46			12 00	12 07		12 10		12 22		12 33	12 46			13 00	13 07	13 10	
Salford Central d	11 25		11 36	11 49			12 03	12 10		12 13		12 25		12 36	12 49			13 03	13 10	13 13	
Salford Crescent a	11 29	11 33	11 39	11 52	11 56	12 04	12 07	12 13		12 16		12 29	12 33	12 39	12 52	12 56	13 04	13 07	13 13	13 16	
d	11 30	11 34	11 40	11 53	11 56	12 04	12 08	12 13		12 17		12 30	12 34	12 40	12 53	12 56	13 04	13 08	13 13	13 17	
Swinton d				11 59						12 23					12 59					13 23	
Moorside d										12 26										13 26	
Walkden d				12 04						12 29					13 04					13 29	
Atherton d				12 09						12 35					13 09					13 35	
Hag Fold d										12 37										13 37	
Daisy Hill d				12 13						12 40					13 13					13 40	
Kearsley d			11 47											12 47							
Farnworth d			11 49											12 49							
Moses Gate d			11 52											12 52							
Bolton a	11 40	11 45	11 55		12 06	12 14	12 19	12 23	12 32			12 40	12 45	12 55		13 06	13 14	13 19	13 23		
d	11 40	11 45	11 56		12 07	12 15		12 24	12 33			12 40	12 45	12 56		13 07	13 15		13 24		
Westhoughton d		11 53						12 31					12 53						13 31		
Hindley d		11 57		12 17				12 35		12 45			12 57		13 17				13 35	13 45	
Ince d										12 48										13 48	
Wigan North Western a																					
Wigan Wallgate a		12 02	12 13	12 22				12 44		12 51			13 02	13 13	13 22				13 44	13 51	
d		12 03		12 24						12 52			13 03		13 24					13 52	
Pemberton d										12 56										13 56	
Orrell d										13 00										14 00	
Upholland d										13 04										14 04	
Rainford d										13 07										14 07	
Kirkby a										13 19										14 19	
Gathurst d				12 28											13 28						
Appley Bridge d		12 10		12 32									13 10		13 32						
Parbold d		12 14		12 36									13 14		13 36						
Hoscar d															13 39						
Burscough Bridge d		12 18		12 41									13 18		13 42						
New Lane d															13 44						
Bescar Lane d															13 48						
Meols Cop d				12 49											13 53						
Southport a		12 35		12 59									13 35		14 02						
Lostock d	11 45					12 20						12 45					13 20				
Horwich Parkway d	11 49				12 13	12 24						12 49				13 13	13 24				
Blackrod d	11 52											12 52									
Adlington (Lancashire) d	11 56											12 56									
Chorley d	12 01				12 21	12 32			12 44			13 01				13 21	13 32				
Leyland d	12 12					12 42						13 12					13 42				
Preston 8 65,97 a	12 17				12 33	12 50			12 55			13 17				13 33	13 50				
d	12 19				12 38				12 58		13 04	13 19				13 38					
Kirkham & Wesham 97 a	12 28											13 28									
Poulton-le-Fylde 97 a	12 36				12 56							13 36				13 56					
Layton 97 a	12 43											13 43									
Blackpool North 97 a	12 50				13 05							13 50				14 05					
Lancaster 6 65 a									13 13		13 19										
d									13 14		13 20										
Oxenholme Lake District 65 a									13 28		13 36										
Windermere 83 a											13 56										
Carnforth d																					
Silverdale d																					
Arnside d																					
Grange-over-Sands d																					13 10
Kents Bank d																					13 13
Cark d																					13 18
Ulverston d																					13 26
Dalton d																					13 34
Roose d																					13 40
Barrow-in-Furness a																					13 46

A To Clitheroe
B To Edinburgh
C until 16 July. To Carlisle

The Sunday service between Manchester Victoria and Wigan Wallgate via Atherton is funded by GMITA and will operate whilst funding exists

Table 82

Saturdays
until 1 October

Manchester - Bolton - Wigan, Kirkby, Southport, Preston, Blackpool North and Barrow-in-Furness

	TP A	NT B	NT C	TP ◇1 D ✠	TP ◇1 E ✠	NT	NT	NT	NT	TP ◇1 ✠	NT	NT F	NT	NT	NT B	NT G	TP ◇1 H ✠		TP ◇1 A	NT	NT	NT
Manchester Airport 85 ✈ d				13 00	13 00		13 03			13 29							14 00				14 03	
Heald Green 85 d										13 33												
Buxton 86 d																						
Hazel Grove 86 d											13 33											
Stockport 84 d											13 41											
Manchester Piccadilly 10 ⇌ d				13 16	13 16		13 22			13 46	13 54						14 16				14 22	
Manchester Oxford Road d				13 19	13 19		13 26			13 49	13 58						14 19				14 26	
Deansgate ⇌ d							13 28			13 51	14 00										14 28	
Rochdale 41 d								13 04														14 04
Manchester Victoria ⇌ d						13 22		13 33	13 46			14 00	14 07	14 10						14 22		14 33
Salford Central d						13 25		13 36	13 49			14 03	14 10	14 13						14 25		14 36
Salford Crescent a						13 29	13 33	13 39	13 52	13 56	14 04	14 07	14 13	14 16						14 29	14 33	14 39
d						13 30	13 34	13 40	13 53	13 56	14 04	14 08	14 13	14 17						14 30	14 34	14 40
Swinton d									13 59					14 23								
Moorside d														14 26								
Walkden d									14 04					14 29								
Atherton d									14 09					14 35								
Hag Fold d														14 37								
Daisy Hill d									14 13					14 40								
Kearsley d								13 47														14 47
Farnworth d								13 49														14 49
Moses Gate d								13 52														14 52
Bolton a				13 32	13 32	13 40	13 45	13 55		14 06	14 14	14 19	14 23				14 32			14 40	14 45	14 55
d				13 33	13 33	13 40	13 45	13 56		14 07	14 15		14 24				14 33			14 40	14 45	14 56
Westhoughton d							13 53						14 31								14 53	
Hindley d							13 57		14 17				14 35	14 45							14 57	
Ince d														14 48								
Wigan North Western a																						
Wigan Wallgate a							14 02	14 13	14 22				14 44	14 51							15 02	15 13
d							14 03		14 24					14 52							15 03	
Pemberton d														14 56								
Orrell d														15 00								
Upholland d														15 04								
Rainford d														15 07								
Kirkby a														15 19								
Gathurst d									14 28													
Appley Bridge d							14 10		14 32												15 10	
Parbold d							14 14		14 36												15 14	
Hoscar d																						
Burscough Bridge d							14 18		14 41												15 18	
New Lane d																						
Bescar Lane d																						
Meols Cop d									14 49													
Southport a							14 35		14 59												15 35	
Lostock d						13 45					14 20									14 45		
Horwich Parkway d						13 49				14 13	14 24									14 49		
Blackrod d						13 52														14 52		
Adlington (Lancashire) d						13 56														14 56		
Chorley d				13 44	13 44	14 01				14 21	14 32						14 44			15 01		
Leyland d						14 12					14 42									15 12		
Preston 8 65,97 a				13 55	13 53	14 17				14 33	14 50						14 55			15 17		
d				13 58	14 00	14 19				14 38							14 58	15 04	15 04	15 19		
Kirkham & Wesham 97 a						14 28														15 28		
Poulton-le-Fylde 97 a						14 36				14 56										15 36		
Layton 97 a						14 43														15 43		
Blackpool North 97 a						14 48				15 05										15 50		
Lancaster 6 65 a				14 13	14 13												15 13	15 20	15 20			
d	13 32	13 32	13 48	14 14											14 22		15 14	15 20	15 20			
Oxenholme Lake District 65 a				14 28													15 28					
Windermere 83 a																						
Carnforth d	13 40	13 41	13a58												14 32			15 29	15 28			
Silverdale d	13 46	13 47													14 38				15 34			
Arnside d	13a53	13 52													14 42			15 37	15a42			
Grange-over-Sands d		13 58													14 48	15 15		15 43				
Kents Bank d		14 01													14 52	15 18						
Cark d		14 06													14 56	15 23						
Ulverston d		14 14													15 05	15 31		15 55				
Dalton d		14 22													15 13	15 39						
Roose d		14 28													15 19	15 45						
Barrow-in-Furness a		14 36													15 26	15 53		16 16				

A until 16 July
B from 23 July until 1 October. To Carlisle
C From Heysham Port to Leeds
D until 18 June, 17 September, 24 September, 1 October. To Glasgow Central
E from 25 June until 10 September. To Glasgow Central
F To Clitheroe
G until 16 July. To Carlisle
H To Edinburgh

The Sunday service between Manchester Victoria and Wigan Wallgate via Atherton is funded by GMITA and will operate whilst funding exists

Table 82

Saturdays until 1 October

Manchester - Bolton - Wigan, Kirkby, Southport, Preston, Blackpool North and Barrow-in-Furness

	NT	TP	NT	NT	NT	TP	NT	NT	TP	NT	NT	NT	NT	NT	TP	NT	NT	NT	NT	NT	TP	
		◇1				◇1			◇1						◇1						◇1	
				A		B		C	D				A						E	F	G	
		⚲				⚲			⚲						⚲						⚲	
Manchester Airport 85 d		14 29				15 00			15 00		15 03				15 29						16 00	
Heald Green 85 d		14 33													15 33							
Buxton 86 d																						
Hazel Grove 86 d			14 33													15 33						
Stockport 84 d			14 41													15 41						
Manchester Piccadilly 10 d		14 46	14 54			15 16			15 16		15 22				15 46	15 54					16 16	
Manchester Oxford Road d		14 49	14 58			15 19			15 19		15 26				15 49	15 58					16 19	
Deansgate d		14 51	15 00								15 28				15 51	16 00						
Rochdale 41 d												15 04										
Manchester Victoria d	14 46			15 00	15 07		15 10			15 22		15 33	15 40	15 46			16 07	16 10				
Salford Central d	14 49			15 03	15 10		15 13			15 25		15 36	15 43	15 49			16 10	16 13				
Salford Crescent a	14 52	14 56	15 04	15 07	15 13		15 16			15 29	15 33	15 39	15 46	15 52	15 56	16 04	16 13	16 16				
d	14 53	14 56	15 04	15 08	15 13		15 17			15 30	15 34	15 40	15 47	15 53	15 56	16 04	16 13	16 17				
Swinton d	14 59						15 23							15 59				16 23				
Moorside d							15 26											16 26				
Walkden d	15 04						15 29							16 04				16 29				
Atherton d	15 09						15 35							16 09				16 35				
Hag Fold d							15 37											16 37				
Daisy Hill d	15 13						15 40							16 13				16 40				
Kearsley d												15 47										
Farnworth d												15 49										
Moses Gate d												15 52										
Bolton a		15 06	15 14	15 19	15 23	15 32			15 32	15 40	15 45	15 55	15 59		16 06	16 14	16 23				16 32	
d		15 07	15 15		15 24	15 33			15 33	15 40	15 45	15 56			16 07	16 15	16 24				16 33	
Westhoughton d					15 31						15 53						16 31					
Hindley d	15 17				15 35		15 45				15 57			16 17			16 35	16 45				
Ince d							15 48											16 48				
Wigan North Western a																						
Wigan Wallgate a	15 22				15 44		15 51				16 02	16 13		16 22			16 44	16 51				
d	15 24						15 52				16 03			16 24				16 52				
Pemberton d							15 56											16 56				
Orrell d							16 00											17 00				
Upholland d							16 04											17 04				
Rainford d							16 07											17 07				
Kirkby a							16 19											17 19				
Gathurst d	15 28										16 08			16 28								
Appley Bridge d	15 32										16 11			16 32								
Parbold d	15 36										16 15			16 36								
Hoscar d											16 18											
Burscough Bridge d	15 40										16 21			16 40								
New Lane d											16 24											
Bescar Lane d											16 27											
Meols Cop d	15 48										16 32			16 48								
Southport a	15 57										16 42			16 57								
Lostock d			15 20							15 45						16 20						
Horwich Parkway d		15 13	15 24							15 49					16 13	16 24						
Blackrod d										15 52												
Adlington (Lancashire) d										15 56												
Chorley d		15 21	15 32			15 44			15 44	16 01					16 21	16 32					16 44	
Leyland d			15 42							16 12						16 42						
Preston 8 65,97 a		15 33	15 50			15 55			15 55	16 19					16 33	16 50					16 55	
d		15 38				15 58			15 58						16 38						17 00	17 04
Kirkham & Wesham 97 a															16 47							
Poulton-le-Fylde 97 a		15 56													16 57							
Layton 97 a															17 00							
Blackpool North 97 a		16 05													17 07							
Lancaster 8 65 a						16 13			16 14												17 15	17 20
d						16 14			16 15										16 40	17 00	17 16	17 21
Oxenholme Lake District 65 a																					17 30	17 37
Windermere 83 a																						18 00
Carnforth d						16 22			16 23										16a49	17 10		
Silverdale d						16 28			16 29											17 17		
Arnside d						16a36			16 33											17 21		
Grange-over-Sands d								16 33	16 39											17 27		
Kents Bank d								16 36	16 42											17 31		
Cark d								16 40	16 47											17 35		
Ulverston d								16 49	16 55											17 44		
Dalton d								16 57	17 03											17 53		
Roose d								17 03	17 09											17 59		
Barrow-in-Furness a								17 10	17 18											18 07		

A To Clitheroe
B until 16 July. ⚲ to Chorley
C until 16 July. To Carlisle
D from 23 July until 1 October. ⚲ to Chorley
E From Morecambe to Leeds
F from 23 July until 1 October. To Millom
G To Edinburgh

The Sunday service between Manchester Victoria and Wigan Wallgate via Atherton is funded by GMITA and will operate whilst funding exists

Table 82

Saturdays until 1 October

Manchester - Bolton - Wigan, Kirkby, Southport, Preston, Blackpool North and Barrow-in-Furness

	NT	NT	NT	NT	TP	NT	NT	NT	NT	NT	TP	NT	NT	TP	NT	TP	TP	NT	NT	NT	NT
					◇1									◇1		◇1	◇1				
		A						A			B	C	D	E	B	D	B		F		
					⚲									⚲							
Manchester Airport 85 d			16 03		16 29									17 00						17 03	
Heald Green 85 d					16 33																
Buxton 86 d																					
Hazel Grove 86 d							16 30														
Stockport 84 d							16 41														
Manchester Piccadilly 10 d			16 22		16 46		16 54							17 15						17 22	
Manchester Oxford Road d			16 26		16 49		16 58							17 18						17 26	
Deansgate d			16 28				17 00														
Rochdale 41 d				16 04															17 03		
Manchester Victoria d	16 20	16 23		16 36		16 46		17 00	17 07	17 10								17 19	17 23		17 36
Salford Central d	16 23	16 26		16 39		16 49		17 03	17 10	17 13								17 22	17 26		17 39
Salford Crescent a	16 26	16 30	16 34	16 42		16 52	17 04	17 07	17 13	17 17								17 25	17 30	17 34	17 42
d	16 27	16 31	16 34	16 43		16 53	17 04	17 08	17 13	17 17								17 27	17 31	17 34	17 43
Swinton d						16 59				17 23											
Moorside d						17 02				17 26											
Walkden d						17 05				17 29											
Atherton d						17 11				17 35											
Hag Fold d						17 14				17 37											
Daisy Hill d						17 17				17 40											
Kearsley d				16 50																	17 53
Farnworth d				16 52																	17 55
Moses Gate d				16 55																	17 57
Bolton a	16 37	16 42	16 45	16 58	17 05		17 14	17 19	17 23					17 31				17 37	17 42	17 45	18 01
d	16 37		16 45	16 59	17 06		17 15		17 24					17 32				17 37		17 45	18 01
Westhoughton d			16 53	17 06					17 31											17 53	18 09
Hindley d			16 57	17 10		17 21			17 35	17 45											18 13
Ince d						17 24				17 48											
Wigan North Western a																					
Wigan Wallgate a			17 02	17 19		17 27			17 44	17 51										18 01	18 22
d			17 03			17 29				17 52										18 02	
Pemberton d										17 56											
Orrell d										18 00											
Upholland d										18 04											
Rainford d										18 07											
Kirkby a										18 19											
Gathurst d			17 08			17 33															
Appley Bridge d			17 11			17 37														18 09	
Parbold d			17 15			17 41														18 13	
Hoscar d																					
Burscough Bridge d			17 20			17 45														18 17	
New Lane d																					
Bescar Lane d																					
Meols Cop d			17 27			17 53															
Southport a			17 37			18 02														18 35	
Lostock d	16 43						17 20											17 43			
Horwich Parkway d	16 47						17 24											17 47			
Blackrod d	16 51																	17 51			
Adlington (Lancashire) d	16 55																	17 55			
Chorley d	17 00				17 19		17 32							17 44				18 00			
Leyland d	17 11						17 42											18 11			
Preston 8 65,97 a	17 20				17 30		17 50							17 55				18 16			
d	17 21				17 32									17 58		18 02	18 02	18 18			
Kirkham & Wesham 97 a	17 30				17 41													18 27			
Poulton-le-Fylde 97 a	17 38				17 51													18 35			
Layton 97 a	17 43				17 54													18 39			
Blackpool North 97 a	17 50				18 02													18 46			
Lancaster 8 65 a														18 13		18 18	18 18				
d											17 26		17 32	18 14		18 18	18 18				
Oxenholme Lake District 65 a														18 28							
Windermere 83 a																					
Carnforth d											17 34		17 43			18 31	18 31				
Silverdale d											17 40		17 49			18 37	18 37				
Arnside d											17a47		17 53			18 41	18a44				
Grange-over-Sands d												17 28	17 59		18 10	18 46					
Kents Bank d												17 32	18 03		18 13	18 50					
Cark d												17 36	18 07		18 18	18 54					
Ulverston d												17 44	18 16		18 26	19 02					
Dalton d												17 53	18 24		18 34	19 10					
Roose d												17 59	18 30		18 40	19 16					
Barrow-in-Furness a												18 07	18 38		18 49	19 26					

A To Clitheroe
B until 16 July
C until 16 July. To Millom
D from 23 July until 1 October
E To Glasgow Central
F To Blackburn

The Sunday service between Manchester Victoria and Wigan Wallgate via Atherton is funded by GMITA and will operate whilst funding exists

Table 82

Saturdays until 1 October

Manchester - Bolton - Wigan, Kirkby, Southport, Preston, Blackpool North and Barrow-in-Furness

	NT	TP	NT	NT	NT	TP	NT	NT	TP	NT	NT	NT	NT	NT	TP	NT	NT	NT	NT	TP	NT	NT
		◇1				◇1			◇1						◇1					◇1		
		⌶			A	B ⌶		C	D ⌶		E				⌶		A		F	C	C	C
Manchester Airport 85 ✈ d		17 29				18 00			18 00			18 03			18 29					19 00		
Heald Green 85 d		17 33													18 33							
Buxton 86 d																						
Hazel Grove 86 d				17 33												18 33						
Stockport 84 d				17 41												18 41						
Manchester Piccadilly 10 ⇌ d		17 46		17 54		18 16			18 16			18 22			18 46	18 54				19 16		
Manchester Oxford Road d		17 49		17 58		18 19			18 19			18 26			18 49	18 58				19 19		
Deansgate ⇌ d		17 51		18 00								18 28			18 51	19 00						
Rochdale 41 d											18 02											
Manchester Victoria ⇌ d	17 40		17 50		18 00		18 08			18 20	18 23		18 33	18 45			19 00	19 10				
Salford Central d	17 43		17 53		18 03		18 12			18 23	18 26		18 36	18 48			19 03	19 13				
Salford Crescent a	17 46	17 55	17 58	18 04	18 07		18 16			18 26	18 30	18 34	18 39	18 51	18 56	19 04	19 07	19 16				
d	17 47	17 55	17 59	18 04	18 08		18 17			18 27	18 31	18 34	18 40	18 52	18 56	19 04	19 08	19 17				
Swinton d			18 05				18 23							18 58				19 23				
Moorside d			18 08				18 26							19 01				19 26				
Walkden d			18 11				18 29							19 04				19 29				
Atherton d	17 59		18 17				18 35							19 10				19 35				
Hag Fold d			18 19				18 37							19 12				19 37				
Daisy Hill d	18 03		18 22				18 40							19 15				19 40				
Kearsley d													18 47									
Farnworth d													18 49									
Moses Gate d													18 52									
Bolton a		18 06		18 14	18 19	18 32			18 32	18 37	18 42	18 45	18 55		19 06	19 19	19 20			19 32		
d		18 07		18 15		18 33			18 33	18 37		18 45	18 56		19 07					19 33		
Westhoughton d												18 53	19 03									
Hindley d			18 27				18 45					18 57	19 09	19 20				19 45				
Ince d							18 48							19 23				19 48				
Wigan North Western a							18 56															
Wigan Wallgate a	18 11		18 32									19 02	19 18	19 30				19 55				
d	18 15		18 33									19 03										
Pemberton d			18 37																			
Orrell d			18 41																			
Upholland d			18 45																			
Rainford d			18 48																			
Kirkby a			19 00																			
Gathurst d	18 19											19 07										
Appley Bridge d	18 23											19 11										
Parbold d	18 28											19 15										
Hoscar d	18 31																					
Burscough Bridge d	18 34											19 19										
New Lane d	18 37																					
Bescar Lane d	18 40																					
Meols Cop d	18 46											19 27										
Southport a	18 55											19 37										
Lostock d		18 12		18 20						18 42					19 12							
Horwich Parkway d		18 15		18 24						18 46					19 15							
Blackrod d		18 19								18 49												
Adlington (Lancashire) d										18 53												
Chorley d		18 26		18 32		18 44			18 44	18 58					19 23					19 44		
Leyland d				18 42						19 10												
Preston 8 65,97 a		18 38		18 48		18 55			18 55	19 18					19 33					19 58		
d		18 40		18 49		18 58			18 58	19 19					19 38					20 02		
Kirkham & Wesham 97 a		18 49								19 28												
Poulton-le-Fylde 97 a		18 59								19 36					19 56							
Layton 97 a		19 02								19 43												
Blackpool North 97 a		19 09		19 16						19 50					20 05							
Lancaster 6 65 a						19 13			19 13											20 17		
d						19 14			19 14										19 24	20 18		
Oxenholme Lake District 65 a																						
Windermere 83 a																						
Carnforth d						19a24			19 24										19a33	20a26		
Silverdale d									19 30													
Arnside d									19 34													
Grange-over-Sands d								19 17	19 40												19 45	20 15
Kents Bank d								19 21	19 43												19 49	20 19
Cark d								19 25	19 48												19 53	20 23
Ulverston d								19 34	19 56												20 02	20 32
Dalton d								19 42	20 04												20 10	20 40
Roose d								19 48	20 10												20 16	20 46
Barrow-in-Furness a								19 57	20 20												20 25	20 55

A To Clitheroe
B until 16 July. ⌶ to Chorley
C until 16 July
D from 23 July until 1 October. ⌶ to Chorley
E To Blackburn
F From Morecambe to Leeds

The Sunday service between Manchester Victoria and Wigan Wallgate via Atherton is funded by GMITA and will operate whilst funding exists

Table 82

Saturdays until 1 October

Manchester - Bolton - Wigan, Kirkby, Southport, Preston, Blackpool North and Barrow-in-Furness

	TP	NT	NT	TP	NT	TP	NT	NT	TP	NT	NT	NT	TP	AW	NT	NT	NT	NT	NT	NT	NT
	◇1			◇1		◇1			◇1				◇1								
	A				B	C		C	A			D		E	B		C	A			D
Manchester Airport 85 ✈ d	19 00	19 03		19 29		20 00			20 00		20 03	20 09	20 29	20 32						21 03	21 09
Heald Green 85 d				19 33								20 12	20 33								21 12
Buxton 86 d																					
Hazel Grove 86 d																					
Stockport 84 d																					
Manchester Piccadilly 10 ⇌ d	19 16	19 20		19 46		20 16			20 16		20 20	20 32	20 46	20a48						21 20	21 32
Manchester Oxford Road d	19 19	19 24		19 49		20 19			20 19		20 24	20a36	20 49							21 24	21a36
Deansgate ⇌ d		19 26		19 51							20 26		20 51							21 26	
Rochdale 41 d																					
Manchester Victoria ⇌ d			19 28		20 00		20 10			20 22					21 00	21 10			21 22		
Salford Central d			19 31		20 03		20 13			20 25					21 03	21 13			21 25		
Salford Crescent a		19 29	19 34	19 56	20 07		20 16			20 29	20 33		20 56		21 07	21 16			21 29	21 33	
d		19 30	19 35	19 56	20 08		20 17			20 30	20 34		20 56		21 08	21 17			21 30	21 34	
Swinton d							20 23									21 23					
Moorside d							20 26									21 26					
Walkden d							20 29									21 29					
Atherton d							20 35									21 35					
Hag Fold d							20 37									21 37					
Daisy Hill d							20 40									21 40					
Kearsley d																					
Farnworth d																					
Moses Gate d																					
Bolton a	19 32	19 40	19 45	20 06	20 19	20 32			20 32	20 40	20 45		21 06		21 19				21 40	21 45	
d	19 33	19 40	19 45	20 07		20 33			20 33	20 40	20 45		21 07						21 40	21 45	
Westhoughton d		19 48									20 53									21 53	
Hindley d		19 52					20 45				20 57					21 45				21 57	
Ince d							20 48									21 48					
Wigan North Western a																					
Wigan Wallgate a		19 57					20 55				21 02					21 55				22 02	
d		19 59									21 03									22 03	
Pemberton d																					
Orrell d																					
Upholland d																					
Rainford d																					
Kirkby a																					
Gathurst d		20 03									21 08									22 08	
Appley Bridge d		20 07									21 11									22 11	
Parbold d		20 11									21 15									22 15	
Hoscar d											21 18										
Burscough Bridge d		20 15									21 21									22 20	
New Lane d											21 24										
Bescar Lane d											21 27										
Meols Cop d		20 23									21 32									22 27	
Southport a		20 32									21 42									22 37	
Lostock d			19 50							20 45									21 45		
Horwich Parkway d			19 54	20 13		20 39			20 39	20 49			21 13						21 49		
Blackrod d			19 57							20 52									21 52		
Adlington (Lancashire) d			20 01							20 56									21 56		
Chorley d	19 44		20 06	20 21		20 46			20 46	21 01			21 21						22 01		
Leyland d			20 18							21 12									22 12		
Preston 8 65,97 a	19 58		20 24	20 33		20 57			20 57	21 17			21 33						22 18		
d	20 02		20 25	20 38		21 02			21 02	21 19			21 38					21 59	22 19		
Kirkham & Wesham 97 a			20 34							21 28									22 28		
Poulton-le-Fylde 97 a			20 42	20 56						21 36			21 56						22 36		
Layton 97 a			20 47							21 40									22 43		
Blackpool North 97 a			20 54	21 06						21 48			22 06						22 50		
Lancaster 6 65 a	20 17					21 17			21 17									22 19			
d	20 18					21 18			21 18									22 19			
Oxenholme Lake District 65 a																					
Windermere 83 a																					
Carnforth d	20 26					21a26			21 26									22 29			
Silverdale d	20 32								21 32									22 35			
Arnside d	20 36								21 36									22 40			
Grange-over-Sands d	20 42							21 30	21 42								22 30	22 46			
Kents Bank d	20 45							21 34	21 45								22 33	22 49			
Cark d	20 50							21 38	21 50								22 38	22 54			
Ulverston d	20 58							21 47	21 58								22 46	23 02			
Dalton d	21 06							21 55	22 06								22 54	23 10			
Roose d	21 12							22 01	22 12								23 00	23 16			
Barrow-in-Furness a	21 20							22 10	22 21								23 08	23 24			

A from 23 July until 1 October
B To Clitheroe
C until 16 July
D From Wilmslow
E until 18 June. To Chester

The Sunday service between Manchester Victoria and Wigan Wallgate via Atherton is funded by GMITA and will operate whilst funding exists

Table 82

Saturdays
until 1 October

Manchester - Bolton - Wigan, Kirkby, Southport, Preston, Blackpool North and Barrow-in-Furness

	NT	TP	NT	TP	TP	NT	NT	NT	NT	TP	NT	NT	NT	NT	TP
		◇1		◇1	◇1					◇1					◇1
	A		B	C	D	E						F			G
Manchester Airport 85 ✈ d		21 29		22 00	22 00	22 08		22 19		22 29					23 24
Heald Green 85 d		21 33				22 12				22 33					
Buxton 86 d															
Hazel Grove 86 d															
Stockport 84 d											22 40				
Manchester Piccadilly 10 d	21 38	21 46		22 16	22 16	22 32		22 36		22 46	22 54				23 41
Manchester Oxford Road d	21 44	21 49		22 19	22 19	22a36		22 39		22 49	22 58				
Deansgate d	21a46	21 51						22 41		22 51	23 00				
Rochdale 41 d															
Manchester Victoria d			22 00				22 22		22 45			23 05	23 16	23 20	
Salford Central d			22 03				22 25		22 48			23 08	23 19	23 23	
Salford Crescent a		21 56	22 07				22 29	22 46	22 51	22 56	23 02	23 11	23 22	23 26	23 46
d		21 56	22 08				22 30	22 46	22 52	22 56	23 04	23 12	23 22	23 26	
Swinton d									22 58					23 33	
Moorside d									23 01					23 35	
Walkden d									23 04					23 39	
Atherton d									23 10					23 44	
Hag Fold d									23 12					23 47	
Daisy Hill d									23 15					23 50	
Kearsley d											23 11				
Farnworth d											23 13				
Moses Gate d											23 16				
Bolton a		22 06	22 19	22 32	22 32		22 40	22 56		23 06	23 19	23 23	23 32		
d		22 07		22 33	22 33		22 40	22 57		23 07	23 20		23 33		
Westhoughton d								23 04			23 27				
Hindley d								23 08	23 20		23 31			23 54	
Ince d									23 23					23 57	
Wigan North Western a															
Wigan Wallgate a								23 13	23 30		23 41			00 04	
d								23 15							
Pemberton d															
Orrell d															
Upholland d															
Rainford d															
Kirkby a															
Gathurst d								23 19							
Appley Bridge d								23 23							
Parbold d								23 27							
Hoscar d															
Burscough Bridge d								23 31							
New Lane d															
Bescar Lane d															
Meols Cop d								23 39							
Southport a								23 48							
Lostock d							22 45						23 38		
Horwich Parkway d		22 13					22 49			23 13			23 42		
Blackrod d							22 52						23 45		
Adlington (Lancashire) d							22 56						23 49		
Chorley d		22 21					23 01			23 21			23 54		
Leyland d							23 12						00 04		
Preston 8 65,97 a		22 33		22 54	22 54		23 17			23 33			00 10		
d		22 35		22 55	22 55		23 19			23 35			00 11		
Kirkham & Wesham 97 a							23 28						00 21		
Poulton-le-Fylde 97 a		22 52					23 36			23 52			00 29		
Layton 97 a							23 40						00 33		
Blackpool North 97 a		23 02					23 48			00 02			00 40		
Lancaster 6 65 a				23 11	23 11										
d				23 11											
Oxenholme Lake District 65 a															
Windermere 83 a															
Carnforth d				23 20											
Silverdale d				23 26											
Arnside d				23 30											
Grange-over-Sands d				23 35											
Kents Bank d				23 39											
Cark d				23 43											
Ulverston d				23 51											
Dalton d				23 59											
Roose d				00 05											
Barrow-in-Furness a				00 15											

A To Warrington Central
B To Clitheroe
C from 23 July until 1 October
D until 16 July
E From Wilmslow
F To Blackburn
G until 10 September. To York

The Sunday service between Manchester Victoria and Wigan Wallgate via Atherton is funded by GMITA and will operate whilst funding exists

Table 82

Saturdays
from 8 October

Manchester - Bolton - Wigan, Kirkby, Southport, Preston, Blackpool North and Barrow-in-Furness

	TP	TP	NT	NT	TP	TP	TP	TP	NT	TP	TP	NT	NT	TP	NT	TP	NT	NT	NT	TP	TP	NT
	◇1	◇1			◇1	◇1	◇1	◇1		◇1	1			◇1		◇1				◇1	◇1	
						A		A	B			C		D		E			C	B		F
Manchester Airport 85 ✈ d	22p00	22p29			00 01	00 38	04 00	04 15	04 34					05 45		06 18						
Heald Green 85 d		22p33												05 49								
Buxton 86 d																			05 59			
Hazel Grove 86 d																			06 33			
Stockport 84 d																			06 41			
Manchester Piccadilly 10 d	22p16	22p46			00 16	00 53	04 15	04 30	04a47	05 43				06 03		06 33			06 54	07 07		
Manchester Oxford Road d	22p19	22p49												06 06		06 36			06 57	07a09		
Deansgate d		22p51																	06 59			
Rochdale 41 d																						
Manchester Victoria d			23p20	23p23								05 55	06 00		06 17		06 38	06 45				
Salford Central d			23p23	23p26													06 40	06 48				
Salford Crescent a		22p56	23p26	23p29		00 58		04 36		05 48		05 59	06 04		06 23		06 44	06 51	07 03			
d		22p56	23p26	23p30						05 49		06 00	06 05		06 24		06 45	06 52	07 03			
Swinton d			23p33															06 58				
Moorside d			23p35																			
Walkden d			23p39															07 03				
Atherton d			23p44															07 08				
Hag Fold d			23p47																			
Daisy Hill d			23p50															07 12				
Kearsley d																	06 52					
Farnworth d																	06 54					
Moses Gate d																	06 57					
Bolton a	22p32	23p06		23p40	00s31		04s29			05 59		06 11	06 15	06 19	06 34	06 50	07 00		07 16			
d	22p33	23p07		23p40						05 59			06 15	06 19	06 34	06 50	07 01					
Westhoughton d													06 23									
Hindley d			23p54										06 27					07 16				
Ince d			23p57																			
Wigan North Western a	22p48																07 19					
Wigan Wallgate a			00 06										06 32					07 21				
d													06 34					07 23				
Pemberton d													06 38									
Orrell d													06 42									
Upholland d													06 45									
Rainford d													06 49									
Kirkby a													07 03									
Gathurst d																		07 27				
Appley Bridge d																		07 31				
Parbold d																		07 35				
Hoscar d																						
Burscough Bridge d																		07 39				
New Lane d																						
Bescar Lane d																						
Meols Cop d																		07 47				
Southport a																		07 58				
Lostock d				23p45											06 39							
Horwich Parkway d		23p13		23p49						06 06					06 43							
Blackrod d				23p52											06 46							
Adlington (Lancashire) d				23p56											06 50							
Chorley d		23p21		00 01						06 13				06 31	06 55							
Leyland d				00 12						06 22					07 06							
Preston 8 65,97 a	23p09	23p33		00 17	01s05		05s04			06 26				06 42	07 11	07 11						
d	23p13	23p35		00 19						06 37				06 44	07 13	07 14					07 20	
Kirkham & Wesham 97 a				00 28						06 46					07 22							
Poulton-le-Fylde 97 a		23p52		00 36						06 56					07 30							
Layton 97 a				00 43						06 59					07 34							
Blackpool North 97 a		00 02		00 52	01 30		05 33			07 06					07 43							
Lancaster 6 65 a	23p28													06 59		07 30					07 36	
d	23p29										05 46			07 00							07 36	08 24
Oxenholme Lake District 65 a											06 21			07 15								
Windermere 83 a											06 41											
Carnforth d	23p37																				07 45	08a33
Silverdale d	23p43																				07 51	
Arnside d	23p47																				07 55	
Grange-over-Sands d	23p53																				08 00	
Kents Bank d	23p56																				08 04	
Cark d	00 01																				08 08	
Ulverston d	00 09																				08 16	
Dalton d	00 17																				08 24	
Roose d	00 23																				08 30	
Barrow-in-Furness a	00 32																				08 40	

A To York
B To Liverpool Lime Street
C To Clitheroe
D To Edinburgh
E To Glasgow Central
F To Leeds

The Sunday service between Manchester Victoria and Wigan Wallgate via Atherton is funded by GMITA and will operate whilst funding exists

Manchester - Bolton - Wigan, Kirkby, Southport, Preston, Blackpool North and Barrow-in-Furness

		NT A	NT	NT B	TP ◇1 ⌶	NT	NT C	TP ◇1 D ⌶	NT	NT	NT E	TP ◇1 F ⌶	NT	NT	NT G	TP ◇1 ⌶	NT	NT	EM ◇ H	NT C	NT I	NT	TP ◇1 J ⌶
Manchester Airport 85 ✈	d				07 00			07 25								07 56		08 01					08 25
Heald Green 85	d							07 30										08 05					08 29
Buxton 86	d																						
Hazel Grove 86	d									07 32									08 17				
Stockport 84	d									07 40									08 24				
Manchester Piccadilly 10	d				07 15			07 45		07 54		08 07				08 15		08 22	08 37				08 46
Manchester Oxford Road	d				07 18					07 58		08a09				08 19		08 26	08a40				08 49
Deansgate	d									08 00								08 28					08 51
Rochdale 41	d																				08 00		
Manchester Victoria	d	07 06	07 10			07 16	07 23		07 27		08 00		08 07	08 10			08 22			08 29	08 33	08 46	
Salford Central	d	07 09	07 13			07 19	07 26		07 30		08 03		08 10	08 13			08 25			08 32	08 36	08 49	
Salford Crescent	a	07 12	07 16			07 24	07 29		07 33	08 04	08 07		08 13	08 16			08 29	08 33		08 37	08 39	08 52	08 56
	d	07 13	07 16			07 25	07 30		07 33	08 04	08 08		08 13	08 17			08 30	08 34		08 37	08 40	08 53	08 56
Swinton	d	07 19												08 23								08 59	
Moorside	d	07 22												08 26									
Walkden	d	07 25							07 42					08 29								09 04	
Atherton	d	07 31							07 48					08 35								09 09	
Hag Fold	d	07 33												08 37									
Daisy Hill	d	07 36							07 51					08 40								09 13	
Kearsley	d																				08 47		
Farnworth	d																				08 49		
Moses Gate	d																				08 52		
Bolton	a		07 26		07 31	07 35	07 41	07 59		08 14	08 19		08 23			08 32	08 40	08 44		08 49	08 55		09 06
	d		07 27		07 31	07 35		07 59		08 15			08 24			08 32	08 40	08 45			08 56		09 07
Westhoughton	d		07 34	←									08 31					08 53					
Hindley	d	07 42	07 38	07 42									08 35	08 45								09 17	
Ince	d	→		07 45										08 48									
Wigan North Western	a																						
Wigan Wallgate	a		07 43	07 48					08 05				08 46	08 51				09 00			09 14	09 22	
	d		07 45	07 50										08 52				09 05				09 24	
Pemberton	d			07 54										08 56									
Orrell	d			07 58										09 00									
Upholland	d			08 01										09 04									
Rainford	d			08 05										09 07									
Kirkby	a			08 19										09 21									
Gathurst	d		07 49																			09 28	
Appley Bridge	d		07 53															09 11				09 32	
Parbold	d		07 57															09 15				09 36	
Hoscar	d		08 00																			09 39	
Burscough Bridge	d		08 03															09 20				09 42	
New Lane	d		08 05																			09 44	
Bescar Lane	d		08 09																			09 48	
Meols Cop	d		08 14																			09 53	
Southport	a		08 25															09 38				10 04	
Lostock	d					07 42				08 20							08 45						
Horwich Parkway	d				07 38	07 46				08 24						08 39	08 49						
Blackrod	d					07 49											08 52						
Adlington (Lancashire)	d					07 53				08 29							08 56						
Chorley	d				07 46	07 58		08 11		08 34						08 47	09 01						09 19
Leyland	d					08 08				08 43							09 12						
Preston 8 65,97	a				07 57	08 14		08 22		08 50						08 58	09 17						09 30
	d				07 59	08 15		08 24							08 42	08 59	09 19						09 32
Kirkham & Wesham 97	a				08 08	08 25											09 28						
Poulton-le-Fylde 97	a				08 18	08 33										09 16	09 36						
Layton 97	a				08 22	08 37											09 43						
Blackpool North 97	a				08 29	08 46										09 25	09 52						
Lancaster 8 65	a							08 39							09 02								09 47
	d														09 03								09 48
Oxenholme Lake District 65	a																						10 04
Windermere 83	a																						10 26
Carnforth	d														09 13								
Silverdale	d														09 18								
Arnside	d														09 23								
Grange-over-Sands	d														09 29								
Kents Bank	d														09 32								
Cark	d														09 37								
Ulverston	d														09 45								
Dalton	d														09 53								
Roose	d														09 59								
Barrow-in-Furness	a														10 07								

A To Kirkby
B From Manchester Victoria
C To Blackburn
D To Edinburgh
E To Clitheroe
F From Hull to Liverpool Lime Street
G To Carlisle
H From Nottingham to Liverpool Lime Street
I From Hebden Bridge
J ⌶ to Chorley

The Sunday service between Manchester Victoria and Wigan Wallgate via Atherton is funded by GMITA and will operate whilst funding exists

Manchester - Bolton - Wigan, Kirkby, Southport, Preston, Blackpool North and Barrow-in-Furness

		NT A	NT	NT	TP ◇1 B	TP ◇1 C ⌶		NT	NT	NT D	NT	TP ◇1 ⌶	NT A	NT	NT	NT E	TP ◇1	TP ◇1 F ⌶	NT	NT	NT	TP ◇1 ⌶
Manchester Airport 85 ✈	d					09 00			09 03			09 29						10 00		10 03		10 29
Heald Green 85	d											09 33										10 33
Buxton 86	d																					
Hazel Grove 86	d																					
Stockport 84	d																					
Manchester Piccadilly 10	d					09 16			09 22			09 46						10 16		10 22		10 46
Manchester Oxford Road	d					09 19			09 26			09 49						10 19		10 26		10 49
Deansgate	d								09 28			09 51								10 28		10 51
Rochdale 41	d																					
Manchester Victoria	d	09 00	09 07	09 10				09 22		09 29	09 46		10 00	10 07	10 10				10 22		10 46	
Salford Central	d	09 03	09 10	09 13				09 25		09 32	09 49		10 03	10 10	10 13				10 25		10 49	
Salford Crescent	a	09 07	09 13	09 16				09 29	09 33	09 37	09 52	09 56	10 07	10 13	10 16				10 29	10 33	10 52	10 56
	d	09 08	09 13	09 17				09 30	09 33	09 37	09 53	09 56	10 08	10 13	10 17				10 30	10 34	10 53	10 56
Swinton	d			09 23							09 59				10 23						10 59	
Moorside	d			09 26											10 26							
Walkden	d			09 29							10 04				10 29						11 04	
Atherton	d			09 35							10 09				10 35						11 09	
Hag Fold	d			09 37											10 37							
Daisy Hill	d			09 40							10 13				10 40						11 13	
Kearsley	d																					
Farnworth	d																					
Moses Gate	d																					
Bolton	a	09 19	09 23			09 32		09 40	09 44	09 49		10 06	10 19	10 23				10 32	10 40	10 45		11 06
	d		09 24			09 33		09 40	09 45			10 07		10 24				10 33	10 40	10 45		11 07
Westhoughton	d		09 31						09 53					10 31						10 53		
Hindley	d		09 35	09 45					09 57		10 17			10 35	10 45					10 57	11 17	
Ince	d			09 48											10 48							
Wigan North Western	a																					
Wigan Wallgate	a		09 46	09 51					10 02		10 22			10 46	10 51					11 02	11 22	
	d			09 52					10 03		10 24				10 52					11 03	11 24	
Pemberton	d			09 56											10 56							
Orrell	d			10 00											11 00							
Upholland	d			10 04											11 04							
Rainford	d			10 07											11 07							
Kirkby	a			10 21											11 21							
Gathurst	d										10 28										11 28	
Appley Bridge	d								10 10		10 32									11 10	11 32	
Parbold	d								10 14		10 36									11 14	11 36	
Hoscar	d																				11 39	
Burscough Bridge	d								10 18		10 40									11 18	11 42	
New Lane	d																				11 44	
Bescar Lane	d																				11 48	
Meols Cop	d										10 48										11 53	
Southport	a								10 37		10 59									11 37	12 04	
Lostock	d							09 45											10 45			
Horwich Parkway	d							09 49				10 13							10 49			11 13
Blackrod	d							09 52											10 52			
Adlington (Lancashire)	d							09 56											10 56			
Chorley	d					09 44		10 01				10 21						10 44	11 01			11 2
Leyland	d							10 12											11 12			
Preston 8 65,97	a					09 55		10 17				10 33						10 55	11 17			11 33
	d				09 45	09 58	10 08	10 19				10 38					10 45	10 58	11 19			11 38
Kirkham & Wesham 97	a							10 28											11 28			
Poulton-le-Fylde 97	a						10 26	10 36				10 56							11 36			11 56
Layton 97	a							10 43											11 43			
Blackpool North 97	a						10 35	10 52				11 05							11 52			12 05
Lancaster 8 65	a				10 00	10 13											11 00	11 13				
	d				10 01											10 49	11 01	11 14				
Oxenholme Lake District 65	a																11 17	11 28				
Windermere 83	a																11 39					
Carnforth	d				10 09											10a58						
Silverdale	d				10 15																	
Arnside	d				10 19																	
Grange-over-Sands	d				10 25																	
Kents Bank	d				10 28																	
Cark	d				10 33																	
Ulverston	d				10 41																	
Dalton	d				10 49																	
Roose	d				10 55																	
Barrow-in-Furness	a				11 04																	

A To Clitheroe
B From Blackpool North
C To Glasgow Central
D To Blackburn
E From Morecambe to Leeds
F To Edinburgh

The Sunday service between Manchester Victoria and Wigan Wallgate via Atherton is funded by GMITA and will operate whilst funding exists

Table 82

Saturdays from 8 October

Manchester - Bolton - Wigan, Kirkby, Southport, Preston, Blackpool North and Barrow-in-Furness

	NT A	NT	NT	NT B	TP ◇1 C ⌶	NT	NT	NT	TP ◇1 ⌶	NT A	NT	TP ◇1 D ⌶	NT	TP ◇1	NT	NT	NT	TP ◇1 ⌶	NT A	NT	NT	NT B
Manchester Airport 85 ✈ d					11 00		11 03		11 29			12 00				12 03		12 29				
Heald Green 85 d									11 33									12 33				
Buxton 86 d																						
Hazel Grove 86 d																						
Stockport 84 d																						
Manchester Piccadilly 10 ⇌ d					11 16		11 22		11 46			12 16				12 22		12 46				
Manchester Oxford Road d					11 19		11 26		11 49			12 19				12 26		12 49				
Deansgate ⇌ d							11 28		11 51							12 28		12 51				
Rochdale 41 d																						
Manchester Victoria ⇌ d	11 00	11 07	11 10			11 22		11 46		12 00	12 07		12 10		12 22		12 46		13 00	13 07	13 10	
Salford Central d	11 03	11 10	11 13			11 25		11 49		12 03	12 10		12 13		12 25		12 49		13 03	13 10	13 13	
Salford Crescent a	11 07	11 13	11 16			11 29	11 33	11 52	11 56	12 07	12 13		12 16		12 29	12 33	12 52	12 56	13 07	13 13	13 16	
d	11 08	11 13	11 17			11 30	11 34	11 53	11 56	12 08	12 13		12 17		12 30	12 34	12 53	12 56	13 08	13 13	13 17	
Swinton d			11 23					11 59					12 23				12 59				13 23	
Moorside d			11 26										12 26								13 26	
Walkden d			11 29					12 04					12 29				13 04				13 29	
Atherton d			11 35					12 09					12 35				13 09				13 35	
Hag Fold d			11 37										12 37								13 37	
Daisy Hill d			11 40					12 13					12 40				13 13				13 40	
Kearsley d																						
Farnworth d																						
Moses Gate d																						
Bolton a	11 19	11 23			11 32	11 40	11 45		12 06	12 19	12 23	12 32			12 40	12 45		13 06	13 19	13 23		
d		11 24			11 33	11 40	11 45		12 07		12 24	12 33			12 40	12 45		13 07		13 24		
Westhoughton d		11 31					11 53				12 31					12 53				13 31		
Hindley d		11 35	11 45				11 57	12 17			12 35		12 45			12 57	13 17			13 35	13 45	
Ince d			11 48										12 48								13 48	
Wigan North Western a																						
Wigan Wallgate a		11 46	11 51				12 02	12 22			12 46		12 51			13 02	13 22			13 46	13 51	
d			11 52				12 03	12 24					12 52			13 03	13 24				13 52	
Pemberton d			11 56										12 56								13 56	
Orrell d			12 00										13 00								14 00	
Upholland d			12 04										13 04								14 04	
Rainford d			12 07										13 07								14 07	
Kirkby a			12 21										13 21								14 21	
Gathurst d								12 28									13 28					
Appley Bridge d							12 10	12 32								13 10	13 32					
Parbold d							12 14	12 36								13 14	13 36					
Hoscar d																	13 39					
Burscough Bridge d							12 18	12 41								13 18	13 42					
New Lane d																	13 44					
Bescar Lane d																	13 48					
Meols Cop d								12 49									13 53					
Southport a							12 37	13 01								13 37	14 04					
Lostock d						11 45									12 45							
Horwich Parkway d						11 49			12 13						12 49			13 13				
Blackrod d						11 52									12 52							
Adlington (Lancashire) d						11 56									12 56							
Chorley d					11 44	12 01			12 21			12 44			13 01			13 21				
Leyland d						12 12									13 12							
Preston 8 65,97 a					11 57	12 17			12 33			12 55			13 17			13 33				
d					11 58	12 19			12 38			12 58		13 04	13 19			13 38				
Kirkham & Wesham 97 a						12 28									13 28							
Poulton-le-Fylde 97 a						12 36			12 56						13 36			13 56				
Layton 97 a						12 43									13 45							
Blackpool North 97 a						12 52			13 05						13 55			14 05				
Lancaster 6 65 a					12 14							13 13		13 19								
d				11 28	12 14							13 14		13 20								13 32
Oxenholme Lake District 65 a												13 28		13 36								
Windermere 83 a														13 56								
Carnforth d				11 37	12 23																	13 41
Silverdale d				11 43																		13 47
Arnside d				11 48	12 31																	13 52
Grange-over-Sands d				11 54	12 37																	13 58
Kents Bank d				11 57																		14 01
Cark d				12 02																		14 06
Ulverston d				12 10	12 50																	14 14
Dalton d				12 18																		14 22
Roose d				12 24																		14 28
Barrow-in-Furness a				12 32	13 10																	14 36

A To Clitheroe
B To Carlisle
C ⌶ to Chorley
D To Edinburgh

The Sunday service between Manchester Victoria and Wigan Wallgate via Atherton is funded by GMITA and will operate whilst funding exists

Table 82

Saturdays from 8 October

Manchester - Bolton - Wigan, Kirkby, Southport, Preston, Blackpool North and Barrow-in-Furness

	NT A	TP ◇1 B ⌶	NT	NT	NT	TP ◇1 ⌶	NT C	NT	NT	NT D	TP ◇1 E ⌶		NT	NT	NT	TP ◇1 ⌶	NT C	NT	TP ◇1 F ⌶	NT	NT
Manchester Airport 85 ✈ d		13 00		13 03		13 29					14 00			14 03		14 29			15 00		
Heald Green 85 d						13 33										14 33					
Buxton 86 d																					
Hazel Grove 86 d																					
Stockport 84 d																					
Manchester Piccadilly 10 ⇌ d		13 16		13 22		13 46					14 16			14 22		14 46			15 16		
Manchester Oxford Road d		13 19		13 26		13 49					14 19			14 26		14 49			15 19		
Deansgate ⇌ d				13 28		13 51								14 28		14 51					
Rochdale 41 d																					
Manchester Victoria ⇌ d			13 22		13 46		14 00	14 07	14 10				14 22		14 46		15 00	15 07		15 10	15 22
Salford Central d			13 25		13 49		14 03	14 10	14 13				14 25		14 49		15 03	15 10		15 13	15 25
Salford Crescent a			13 29	13 33	13 52	13 56	14 07	14 13	14 16				14 29	14 33	14 52	14 56	15 07	15 13		15 16	15 29
d			13 30	13 34	13 53	13 56	14 08	14 13	14 17				14 30	14 34	14 53	14 56	15 08	15 13		15 17	15 30
Swinton d					13 59				14 23						14 59					15 23	
Moorside d									14 26											15 26	
Walkden d					14 04				14 29						15 04					15 29	
Atherton d					14 09				14 35						15 09					15 35	
Hag Fold d									14 37											15 37	
Daisy Hill d					14 13				14 40						15 13					15 40	
Kearsley d																					
Farnworth d																					
Moses Gate d																					
Bolton a		13 32	13 40	13 45		14 06	14 19	14 23			14 32		14 40	14 45		15 06	15 19	15 23	15 32		15 40
d		13 33	13 40	13 45		14 07		14 24			14 33		14 40	14 45		15 07		15 24	15 33		15 40
Westhoughton d				13 53				14 31						14 53				15 31			
Hindley d				13 57	14 17			14 35	14 45					14 57	15 17			15 35		15 45	
Ince d									14 48											15 48	
Wigan North Western a																					
Wigan Wallgate a				14 02	14 22			14 46	14 51					15 02	15 22			15 46		15 51	
d				14 03	14 24				14 52					15 03	15 24					15 52	
Pemberton d									14 56											15 56	
Orrell d									15 00											16 00	
Upholland d									15 04											16 04	
Rainford d									15 07											16 07	
Kirkby a									15 21											16 21	
Gathurst d					14 28										15 28						
Appley Bridge d				14 10	14 32									15 10	15 32						
Parbold d				14 14	14 36									15 14	15 36						
Hoscar d																					
Burscough Bridge d				14 18	14 41									15 18	15 40						
New Lane d																					
Bescar Lane d																					
Meols Cop d					14 49										15 48						
Southport a				14 37	15 01									15 37	15 59						
Lostock d			13 45										14 45								15 45
Horwich Parkway d			13 49			14 13							14 49			15 13					15 49
Blackrod d			13 52										14 52								15 52
Adlington (Lancashire) d			13 56										14 56								15 56
Chorley d		13 44	14 01			14 21					14 44		15 01			15 21			15 44		16 01
Leyland d			14 12										15 12								16 12
Preston 8 65,97 a		13 55	14 17			14 33					14 55		15 17			15 33			15 55		16 19
d		13 58	14 19			14 38					14 58	15 04	15 19			15 38			15 58		
Kirkham & Wesham 97 a			14 28										15 28								
Poulton-le-Fylde 97 a			14 36			14 56							15 36			15 56					
Layton 97 a			14 43										15 43								
Blackpool North 97 a			14 50			15 05							15 52			16 05					
Lancaster 6 65 a		14 13									15 13	15 20							16 14		
d	13 48	14 14								14 22	15 14	15 20							16 15		
Oxenholme Lake District 65 a		14 28									15 28										
Windermere 83 a																					
Carnforth d	13a58									14 32		15 29							16 23		
Silverdale d										14 38									16 29		
Arnside d										14 42		15 37							16 33		
Grange-over-Sands d										14 48		15 43							16 39		
Kents Bank d										14 52									16 42		
Cark d										14 56									16 47		
Ulverston d										15 05		15 55							16 55		
Dalton d										15 13									17 03		
Roose d										15 19									17 09		
Barrow-in-Furness a										15 26		16 16							17 18		

A From Heysham Port to Leeds
B To Glasgow Central
C To Clitheroe
D To Carlisle
E To Edinburgh
F ⌶ to Chorley

The Sunday service between Manchester Victoria and Wigan Wallgate via Atherton is funded by GMITA and will operate whilst funding exists

Table 82

Saturdays
from 8 October

Manchester - Bolton - Wigan, Kirkby, Southport, Preston, Blackpool North and Barrow-in-Furness

Station		NT	NT A	NT	TP ◇1 ⌶	NT	NT	NT	NT B	NT C	TP ◇1 D ⌶	NT	NT A	NT	NT	TP ◇1 ⌶	NT	NT	NT A	NT	NT	NT
Manchester Airport	85 ✈ d	15 03			15 29						16 00			16 03		16 29						
Heald Green	85 d				15 33											16 33						
Buxton	86 d																					
Hazel Grove	86 d					15 33												16 30				
Stockport	84 d					15 41												16 41				
Manchester Piccadilly 10	⇌ d	15 22			15 46	15 54					16 16			16 22		16 46		16 54				
Manchester Oxford Road	d	15 26			15 49	15 58					16 19			16 26		16 49		16 58				
Deansgate	⇌ d	15 28			15 51	16 00								16 28				17 00				
Rochdale	41 d														16 04							
Manchester Victoria	⇌ d		15 40	15 46			16 07	16 10				16 20	16 23		16 36		16 46		17 00	17 07	17 10	
Salford Central	d		15 43	15 49			16 10	16 13				16 23	16 26		16 39		16 49		17 03	17 10	17 13	
Salford Crescent	a	15 33	15 46	15 52	15 56	16 04	16 13	16 16				16 26	16 30	16 34	16 42		16 52	17 04	17 07	17 13	17 17	
	d	15 34	15 47	15 53	15 56	16 04	16 13	16 17				16 27	16 31	16 34	16 43		16 53	17 04	17 08	17 13	17 17	
Swinton	d			15 59				16 23									16 59				17 23	
Moorside	d							16 26									17 02				17 26	
Walkden	d			16 04				16 29									17 05				17 29	
Atherton	d			16 09				16 35									17 11				17 35	
Hag Fold	d							16 37									17 14				17 37	
Daisy Hill	d			16 13				16 40									17 17				17 40	
Kearsley	d														16 50							
Farnworth	d														16 52							
Moses Gate	d														16 55							
Bolton	a	15 45	15 59		16 06	16 14	16 23				16 32	16 37	16 42	16 45	16 58	17 05		17 14	17 19	17 23		
	d	15 45			16 07	16 15	16 24				16 33	16 37		16 45	16 59	17 06		17 15		17 24		
Westhoughton	d	15 53					16 31							16 53	17 06					17 31		
Hindley	d	15 57		16 17			16 35	16 45						16 57	17 10		17 21			17 35	17 45	
Ince	d							16 48									17 24				17 48	
Wigan North Western	a																					
Wigan Wallgate	a	16 02		16 22			16 46	16 51						17 02	17 19		17 27			17 46	17 51	
	d	16 03		16 24				16 52						17 03			17 29				17 52	
Pemberton	d							16 56													17 56	
Orrell	d							17 00													18 00	
Upholland	d							17 04													18 04	
Rainford	d							17 07													18 07	
Kirkby	a							17 21													18 21	
Gathurst	d	16 08		16 28										17 08			17 33					
Appley Bridge	d	16 11		16 32										17 11			17 37					
Parbold	d	16 15		16 36										17 15			17 41					
Hoscar	d	16 18																				
Burscough Bridge	d	16 21		16 40										17 20			17 45					
New Lane	d	16 24																				
Bescar Lane	d	16 27																				
Meols Cop	d	16 32		16 48										17 27			17 53					
Southport	a	16 44		16 59										17 39			18 04					
Lostock	d					16 20						16 43						17 20				
Horwich Parkway	d				16 13	16 24						16 47						17 24				
Blackrod	d											16 51										
Adlington (Lancashire)	d											16 55										
Chorley	d				16 21	16 32					16 44	17 00				17 19		17 32				
Leyland	d					16 42						17 11						17 42				
Preston 8	65,97 a				16 33	16 50					16 55	17 20				17 30		17 50				
	d				16 38						17 00 / 17 04	17 21				17 32						
Kirkham & Wesham	97 a				16 47							17 30				17 41						
Poulton-le-Fylde	97 a				16 57							17 38				17 51						
Layton	97 a				17 00							17 43				17 54						
Blackpool North	97 a				17 07							17 52				18 02						
Lancaster 6	65 a										17 15 / 17 20											
	d								16 40	17 00	17 16 / 17 21											17 32
Oxenholme Lake District	65 a										17 30 / 17 37											
Windermere	83 a										18 00											
Carnforth	d								16a49	17 10												17 43
Silverdale	d									17 17												17 49
Arnside	d									17 21												17 53
Grange-over-Sands	d									17 27												17 59
Kents Bank	d									17 31												18 03
Cark	d									17 35												18 07
Ulverston	d									17 44												18 16
Dalton	d									17 53												18 24
Roose	d									17 59												18 30
Barrow-in-Furness	a									18 07												18 38

A To Clitheroe
B From Morecambe to Leeds
C To Millom
D To Edinburgh

The Sunday service between Manchester Victoria and Wigan Wallgate via Atherton is funded by GMITA and will operate whilst funding exists

Table 82

Saturdays
from 8 October

Manchester - Bolton - Wigan, Kirkby, Southport, Preston, Blackpool North and Barrow-in-Furness

Station		TP ◇1 A ⌶	TP ◇1	NT	NT B	NT	NT	NT	TP ◇1 ⌶	NT	NT C	TP ◇1 D ⌶	NT	NT	NT B	NT	NT	NT	TP ◇1 ⌶	NT C	NT	NT E	TP ◇1
Manchester Airport	85 ✈ d	17 00				17 03			17 29			18 00				18 03			18 29				19 00
Heald Green	85 d								17 33										18 33				
Buxton	86 d																						
Hazel Grove	86 d																						
Stockport	84 d																						
Manchester Piccadilly 10	⇌ d	17 15				17 22			17 46			18 16				18 22			18 46				19 16
Manchester Oxford Road	d	17 18				17 26			17 49			18 19				18 26			18 49				19 19
Deansgate	⇌ d								17 51							18 28			18 51				
Rochdale	41 d				17 03										18 02								
Manchester Victoria	⇌ d			17 19	17 23		17 36	17 40		17 50	18 00		18 08	18 20	18 23		18 33	18 45		19 00	19 10		
Salford Central	d			17 22	17 26		17 39	17 43		17 53	18 03		18 12	18 23	18 26		18 36	18 48		19 03	19 13		
Salford Crescent	a			17 25	17 30	17 34	17 42	17 46	17 55	17 58	18 07		18 16	18 26	18 30	18 34	18 39	18 51	18 56	19 07	19 16		
	d			17 27	17 31	17 34	17 43	17 47	17 55	17 59	18 08		18 17	18 27	18 31	18 34	18 40	18 52	18 56	19 08	19 17		
Swinton	d									18 05			18 23					18 58			19 23		
Moorside	d									18 08			18 26					19 01			19 26		
Walkden	d									18 11			18 29					19 04			19 29		
Atherton	d							17 59		18 17			18 35					19 10			19 35		
Hag Fold	d									18 19			18 37					19 12			19 37		
Daisy Hill	d							18 03		18 22			18 40					19 15			19 40		
Kearsley	d						17 53										18 47						
Farnworth	d						17 55										18 49						
Moses Gate	d						17 57										18 52						
Bolton	a	17 31		17 37	17 42	17 45	18 01		18 06		18 19	18 32		18 37	18 42	18 45	18 55		19 06	19 20			19 32
	d	17 32		17 37		17 45	18 01		18 07			18 33		18 37		18 45	18 56		19 07				19 33
Westhoughton	d					17 53	18 09									18 53	19 03						
Hindley	d						18 13			18 27			18 45			18 57	19 09	19 20			19 45		
Ince	d												18 48					19 23			19 48		
Wigan North Western	a												18 56										
Wigan Wallgate	a					18 01	18 24	18 11		18 32						19 02	19 20	19 32			19 57		
	d					18 02		18 15		18 33						19 03							
Pemberton	d									18 37													
Orrell	d									18 41													
Upholland	d									18 45													
Rainford	d									18 48													
Kirkby	a									19 02													
Gathurst	d							18 19								19 07							
Appley Bridge	d					18 09		18 23								19 11							
Parbold	d					18 13		18 28								19 15							
Hoscar	d							18 31															
Burscough Bridge	d					18 17		18 34								19 19							
New Lane	d							18 37															
Bescar Lane	d							18 40															
Meols Cop	d							18 46								19 27							
Southport	a					18 37		18 57								19 39							
Lostock	d			17 43					18 12					18 42					19 12				
Horwich Parkway	d			17 47					18 15					18 46					19 15				
Blackrod	d			17 51					18 19					18 49									
Adlington (Lancashire)	d			17 55										18 53									
Chorley	d	17 44		18 00					18 26			18 44		18 58					19 23				19 44
Leyland	d			18 11										19 10									
Preston 8	65,97 a	17 55		18 16					18 38			18 55		19 18					19 33				19 58
	d	17 58	18 02	18 18					18 40			18 58		19 19					19 38				20 02
Kirkham & Wesham	97 a			18 27					18 49					19 28									
Poulton-le-Fylde	97 a			18 35					18 59					19 36					19 56				
Layton	97 a			18 39					19 02					19 43									
Blackpool North	97 a			18 48					19 09					19 52					20 05				
Lancaster 6	65 a	18 13	18 18									19 13											20 17
	d	18 14	18 18									19 14										19 24	20 18
Oxenholme Lake District	65 a	18 28																					
Windermere	83 a																						
Carnforth	d		18 31									19 24										19a33	20 26
Silverdale	d		18 37									19 30											20 32
Arnside	d		18 41									19 34											20 36
Grange-over-Sands	d		18 46									19 40											20 42
Kents Bank	d		18 50									19 43											20 45
Cark	d		18 54									19 48											20 50
Ulverston	d		19 02									19 56											20 58
Dalton	d		19 10									20 04											21 06
Roose	d		19 16									20 10											21 12
Barrow-in-Furness	a		19 26									20 20											21 20

A To Glasgow Central
B To Blackburn
C To Clitheroe
D ⌶ to Chorley
E From Morecambe to Leeds

The Sunday service between Manchester Victoria and Wigan Wallgate via Atherton is funded by GMITA and will operate whilst funding exists

Table 82

Saturdays
from 8 October

Manchester - Bolton - Wigan, Kirkby, Southport, Preston, Blackpool North and Barrow-in-Furness

			NT	NT	TP	NT	TP	NT	NT	NT	NT	TP	NT	NT	NT	NT	NT	NT	NT	TP	NT	TP	NT
					◇1		◇1					◇1								◇1		◇1	
						A					B		A					B	C		A		B
Manchester Airport	85 ✈	d	19 03		19 29		20 00			20 03	20 09	20 29					21 03	21 09		21 29		22 00	22 08
Heald Green	85	d			19 33						20 12	20 33						21 12		21 33			22 12
Buxton	86	d																					
Hazel Grove	86	d																					
Stockport	84	d																					
Manchester Piccadilly 10	⇌	d	19 20		19 46		20 16			20 20	20 32	20 46					21 20	21 32	21 38	21 46		22 16	22 32
Manchester Oxford Road		d	19 24		19 49		20 19			20 24	20a36	20 49					21 24	21a36	21 44	21 49		22 19	22a36
Deansgate	⇌	d	19 26		19 51					20 26		20 51					21 26		21a46	21 51			
Rochdale	41	d																					
Manchester Victoria	⇌	d		19 28		20 00		20 10	20 22				21 00	21 10		21 22					22 00		
Salford Central		d		19 31		20 03		20 13	20 25				21 03	21 13		21 25					22 03		
Salford Crescent		a	19 29	19 34	19 56	20 07		20 16	20 29	20 33		20 56	21 07	21 16		21 29	21 33			21 56	22 07		
		d	19 30	19 35	19 56	20 08		20 17	20 30	20 34		20 56	21 08	21 17		21 30	21 34			21 56	22 08		
Swinton		d						20 23						21 23									
Moorside		d						20 26						21 26									
Walkden		d						20 29						21 29									
Atherton		d						20 35						21 35									
Hag Fold		d						20 37						21 37									
Daisy Hill		d						20 40						21 40									
Kearsley		d																					
Farnworth		d																					
Moses Gate		d																					
Bolton		a	19 40	19 45	20 06	20 19	20 32		20 40	20 45		21 06	21 19			21 40	21 45			22 06	22 19	22 32	
		d	19 40	19 45	20 07		20 33		20 40	20 45		21 07				21 40	21 45			22 07		22 33	
Westhoughton		d	19 48							20 53							21 53						
Hindley		d	19 52					20 45		20 57				21 45			21 57						
Ince		d						20 48						21 48									
Wigan North Western		a																					
Wigan Wallgate		a	19 57					20 57		21 02				21 57			22 02						
		d	19 59							21 03							22 03						
Pemberton		d																					
Orrell		d																					
Upholland		d																					
Rainford		d																					
Kirkby		a																					
Gathurst		d	20 03							21 08							22 08						
Appley Bridge		d	20 07							21 11							22 11						
Parbold		d	20 11							21 15							22 15						
Hoscar		d								21 18													
Burscough Bridge		d	20 15							21 21							22 20						
New Lane		d								21 24													
Bescar Lane		d								21 27													
Meols Cop		d	20 23							21 32							22 27						
Southport		a	20 34							21 44							22 39						
Lostock		d		19 50					20 45							21 45							
Horwich Parkway		d		19 54	20 13		20 39		20 49			21 13				21 49				22 13			
Blackrod		d		19 57					20 52							21 52							
Adlington (Lancashire)		d		20 01					20 56							21 56							
Chorley		d		20 06	20 21		20 46		21 01			21 21				22 01				22 21			
Leyland		d		20 18					21 12							22 12							
Preston 8	65,97	a		20 24	20 33		20 57		21 17			21 33				22 18				22 33		22 54	
		d		20 25	20 38		21 02		21 19			21 38			21 59	22 19				22 35		22 55	
Kirkham & Wesham	97	a		20 34					21 28							22 28							
Poulton-le-Fylde	97	a		20 42	20 56				21 36			21 56				22 36				22 52			
Layton	97	a		20 47					21 40							22 43							
Blackpool North	97	a		20 56	21 06				21 50			22 06				22 52				23 02			
Lancaster 6	65	a					21 17								22 19							23 11	
		d					21 18								22 19							23 11	
Oxenholme Lake District	65	a																					
Windermere	83	a																					
Carnforth		d					21 26								22 29							23 20	
Silverdale		d					21 32								22 35							23 26	
Arnside		d					21 36								22 40							23 30	
Grange-over-Sands		d					21 42								22 46							23 35	
Kents Bank		d					21 45								22 49							23 39	
Cark		d					21 50								22 54							23 43	
Ulverston		d					21 58								23 02							23 51	
Dalton		d					22 06								23 10							23 59	
Roose		d					22 12								23 16							00 05	
Barrow-in-Furness		a					22 21								23 24							00 15	

A To Clitheroe
B From Wilmslow
C To Warrington Central

The Sunday service between Manchester Victoria and Wigan Wallgate via Atherton is funded by GMITA and will operate whilst funding exists

Table 82

Saturdays
from 8 October

Manchester - Bolton - Wigan, Kirkby, Southport, Preston, Blackpool North and Barrow-in-Furness

			NT	NT	NT	TP	NT	NT	NT	NT
						◇1				
								A		
Manchester Airport	85 ✈	d		22 19		22 29				
Heald Green	85	d				22 33				
Buxton	86	d								
Hazel Grove	86	d								
Stockport	84	d					22 40			
Manchester Piccadilly 10	⇌	d		22 36		22 46	22 54			
Manchester Oxford Road		d		22 39		22 49	22 58			
Deansgate	⇌	d		22 41		22 51	23 00			
Rochdale	41	d								
Manchester Victoria	⇌	d	22 22		22 45			23 05	23 16	23 20
Salford Central		d	22 25		22 48			23 08	23 19	23 23
Salford Crescent		a	22 29	22 46	22 51	22 56	23 02	23 11	23 22	23 26
		d	22 30	22 46	22 52	22 56	23 04	23 12	23 22	23 26
Swinton		d			22 58					23 33
Moorside		d			23 01					23 35
Walkden		d			23 04					23 39
Atherton		d			23 10					23 44
Hag Fold		d			23 12					23 47
Daisy Hill		d			23 15					23 50
Kearsley		d					23 11			
Farnworth		d					23 13			
Moses Gate		d					23 16			
Bolton		a	22 40	22 56		23 06	23 19	23 23	23 32	
		d	22 40	22 57		23 07	23 20		23 33	
Westhoughton		d		23 04			23 27			
Hindley		d		23 08	23 20		23 31			23 54
Ince		d			23 23					23 57
Wigan North Western		a								
Wigan Wallgate		a		23 13	23 32		23 41			00 06
		d		23 15						
Pemberton		d								
Orrell		d								
Upholland		d								
Rainford		d								
Kirkby		a								
Gathurst		d		23 19						
Appley Bridge		d		23 23						
Parbold		d		23 27						
Hoscar		d								
Burscough Bridge		d		23 31						
New Lane		d								
Bescar Lane		d								
Meols Cop		d		23 39						
Southport		a		23 50						
Lostock		d	22 45						23 38	
Horwich Parkway		d	22 49			23 13			23 42	
Blackrod		d	22 52						23 45	
Adlington (Lancashire)		d	22 56						23 49	
Chorley		d	23 01			23 21			23 54	
Leyland		d	23 12						00 04	
Preston 8	65,97	a	23 17			23 33			00 10	
		d	23 19			23 35			00 11	
Kirkham & Wesham	97	a	23 28						00 21	
Poulton-le-Fylde	97	a	23 36			23 52			00 29	
Layton	97	a	23 40						00 33	
Blackpool North	97	a	23 50			00 02			00 42	
Lancaster 6	65	a								
		d								
Oxenholme Lake District	65	a								
Windermere	83	a								
Carnforth		d								
Silverdale		d								
Arnside		d								
Grange-over-Sands		d								
Kents Bank		d								
Cark		d								
Ulverston		d								
Dalton		d								
Roose		d								
Barrow-in-Furness		a								

A To Blackburn

The Sunday service between Manchester Victoria and Wigan Wallgate via Atherton is funded by GMITA and will operate whilst funding exists

Table 82

Sundays
until 19 June

Manchester - Bolton - Wigan, Kirkby, Southport, Preston, Blackpool North and Barrow-in-Furness

Station			TP	NT	NT	NT	TP	NT	NT	NT	TP	TP	TP	TP	TP	NT	NT	TP	NT	TP	NT	NT	NT	TP
			◇1				◇1				◇1	◇1	◇1	◇1	◇1			◇1		◇1				◇1
			A	A	A	B				B			C	D ⊼					B	E ⊼			F	
Manchester Airport	85 ✈	d	22p29				07 55				08 47			09 00				09 30		10 00				10 30
Heald Green	85	d	22p33																					
Buxton	86	d																						
Hazel Grove	86	d																						
Stockport	84	d															09 22						10 12	
Manchester Piccadilly 10	⇌	d	22p46				08 11				09 03		09 07	09 16			09 35	09 46		10 16			10 26	10 46
Manchester Oxford Road		d	22p49				08 14				09 06		09a09	09 19			09 38	09 49		10 19			10 38	10 49
Deansgate	⇌	d	22p51				08 16				09 08						09 40	09 51					10 40	10 51
Rochdale	41	d																						
Manchester Victoria	⇌	d		23p16	23p20	08 01		08 25	08 39	09 00						09 25			10 00		10 09	10 25		
Salford Central		d		23p19	23p23																			
Salford Crescent		a	22p56	23p22	23p26	08 07	08 19	08 29	08 44	09 06	09 11					09 29	09 44	09 54	10 06		10 15	10 29	10 44	10 54
		d	22p56	23p22	23p26	08 08	08 20	08 30	08 44	09 08	09 12					09 30	09 44	09 55	10 08		10 17	10 30	10 44	10 55
Swinton		d			23p33																10 23			
Moorside		d			23p35																10 26			
Walkden		d			23p39																10 29			
Atherton		d			23p44																10 35			
Hag Fold		d			23p47																10 37			
Daisy Hill		d			23p50																10 40			
Kearsley		d																						
Farnworth		d																						
Moses Gate		d																						
Bolton		a	23p06	23p32		08 19	08 30	08 40	08 54	09 19	09 22			09 32		09 40	09 54	10 05	10 19	10 32		10 40	10 54	11 05
		d	23p07	23p33			08 30	08 40	08 55		09 23			09 33		09 40	09 55	10 05		10 33		10 40	10 55	11 05
Westhoughton		d							09 02								10 02						11 02	
Hindley		d			23p54				09 06								10 06				10 45		11 06	
Ince		d			23p57																10 48			
Wigan North Western		a																						
Wigan Wallgate		a			00 04				09 11								10 11				10 55		11 11	
		d							09 13								10 13						11 13	
Pemberton		d																						
Orrell		d																						
Upholland		d																						
Rainford		d																						
Kirkby		a																						
Gathurst		d							09 17								10 17						11 17	
Appley Bridge		d							09 21								10 21						11 21	
Parbold		d							09 25								10 25						11 25	
Hoscar		d																						
Burscough Bridge		d							09 29								10 29						11 29	
New Lane		d																						
Bescar Lane		d																						
Meols Cop		d							09 37								10 37						11 37	
Southport		a							09 46								10 46						11 46	
Lostock		d		23p38				08 45								09 45						10 45		
Horwich Parkway		d	23p13	23p42			08 37	08 49			09 30					09 49		10 12				10 49		11 12
Blackrod		d		23p45				08 52								09 52						10 52		
Adlington (Lancashire)		d		23p49				08 56								09 56						10 56		
Chorley		d	23p21	23p54			08 45	09 01			09 37			09 44		10 01		10 20		10 44		11 01		11 20
Leyland		d		00 04				09 12								10 12						11 12		
Preston 8	65,97	a	23p33	00 10			08 56	09 18			09 49			09 57		10 18		10 32		10 57		11 18		11 32
		d	23p35	00 11			08 57	09 20			09 51	10 07		10 00	10 11	10 20		10 34		10 58		11 20		11 34
Kirkham & Wesham	97	a		00 21				09 29								10 29						11 29		
Poulton-le-Fylde	97	a	23p52	00 29			09 14	09 37			10 08					10 37		10 51				11 37		11 51
Layton	97	a		00 33				09 42								10 42						11 42		
Blackpool North	97	a	00 02	00 40			09 25	09 49			10 18					10 49		11 00				11 49		12 00
Lancaster 6	65	a										10 22		10 15	10 27					11 13				
		d										10 23		10 16	10 28					11 14				
Oxenholme Lake District	65	a										10 39		10 30						11 28				
Windermere	83	a										10 58												
Carnforth		d													10 36									
Silverdale		d													10 42									
Arnside		d													10a49									
Grange-over-Sands		d																						
Kents Bank		d																						
Cark		d																						
Ulverston		d																						
Dalton		d																						
Roose		d																						
Barrow-in-Furness		a																						

A not 22 May
B To Clitheroe
C To Liverpool Lime Street
D To Edinburgh
E To Glasgow Central
F From Chester

The Sunday service between Manchester Victoria and Wigan Wallgate via Atherton is funded by GMITA and will operate whilst funding exists

Table 82

Sundays
until 19 June

Manchester - Bolton - Wigan, Kirkby, Southport, Preston, Blackpool North and Barrow-in-Furness

Station			NT	TP	NT	TP	TP	NT	NT	NT	TP	NT	NT	NT	NT	TP	NT	NT	NT	TP	NT	NT	TP	TP
				◇1		◇1	◇1				◇1					◇1				◇1				◇1
			A	B				C				A			D	E ⊼			F		A			G ⊼
Manchester Airport	85 ✈	d					11 00	11 03			11 30					12 00	12 08			12 30				13 00
Heald Green	85	d						11 07									12 11							
Buxton	86	d																						
Hazel Grove	86	d																						
Stockport	84	d								11 15									12 22					
Manchester Piccadilly 10	⇌	d		11 07			11 16	11 26		11 33	11 46					12 16	12 29		12 36	12 46				13 16
Manchester Oxford Road		d		11a09			11 19	11a30		11 38	11 49					12 19	12a33		12 39	12 49				13 19
Deansgate	⇌	d								11 40	11 51								12 41	12 51				
Rochdale	41	d																						
Manchester Victoria	⇌	d	11 00		11 12				11 25			12 00	12 09					12 25			13 00	13 12		
Salford Central		d																						
Salford Crescent		a	11 06		11 16				11 29	11 44	11 54	12 06	12 13					12 29	12 45	12 54	13 06	13 16		
		d	11 08		11 17				11 30	11 44	11 55	12 08	12 17					12 30	12 45	12 55	13 08	13 17		
Swinton		d			11 23								12 23									13 23		
Moorside		d			11 26								12 26									13 26		
Walkden		d			11 29								12 29									13 29		
Atherton		d			11 35								12 35									13 35		
Hag Fold		d			11 37								12 37									13 37		
Daisy Hill		d			11 40								12 40									13 40		
Kearsley		d																						
Farnworth		d																						
Moses Gate		d																						
Bolton		a	11 19				11 32		11 40	11 54	12 05	12 19				12 32		12 40	12 55	13 05	13 19			13 32
		d					11 33		11 40	11 55	12 05					12 33		12 40	12 56	13 05				13 33
Westhoughton		d								12 02									13 03					
Hindley		d			11 45					12 06			12 45						13 07			13 45		
Ince		d			11 48								12 48									13 48		
Wigan North Western		a																						
Wigan Wallgate		a			11 55					12 11			12 55						13 12			13 55		
		d								12 13									13 14					
Pemberton		d																						
Orrell		d																						
Upholland		d																						
Rainford		d																						
Kirkby		a																						
Gathurst		d								12 17									13 18					
Appley Bridge		d								12 21									13 22					
Parbold		d								12 25									13 26					
Hoscar		d																						
Burscough Bridge		d								12 29									13 30					
New Lane		d																						
Bescar Lane		d																						
Meols Cop		d								12 37									13 38					
Southport		a								12 46									13 47					
Lostock		d							11 45									12 45						
Horwich Parkway		d							11 49		12 12							12 49		13 12				
Blackrod		d							11 52									12 52						
Adlington (Lancashire)		d							11 56									12 56						
Chorley		d					11 44		12 01		12 20					12 44		13 01		13 20				13 44
Leyland		d							12 12									13 12						
Preston 8	65,97	a					11 57		12 18		12 32					12 57		13 18		13 32				13 57
		d					11 58		12 20		12 34					12 58		13 20		13 34				14 00
Kirkham & Wesham	97	a							12 29									13 29						
Poulton-le-Fylde	97	a							12 37		12 51							13 37		13 51				
Layton	97	a							12 42									13 42						
Blackpool North	97	a							12 49		13 00							13 49		14 00				
Lancaster 6	65	a					12 13									13 13								14 15
		d				11 34	12 14								12 48	13 14							13 25	14 16
Oxenholme Lake District	65	a														13 28								14 30
Windermere	83	a																						
Carnforth		d				11 42	12 22								12a57								13 33	
Silverdale		d				11 48	12 28																13 39	
Arnside		d				11a55	12a35																13a46	
Grange-over-Sands		d												12 30										
Kents Bank		d												12 33										
Cark		d												12 37										
Ulverston		d												12 45										
Dalton		d												12 54										
Roose		d												13 00										
Barrow-in-Furness		a												13 07										

A To Clitheroe
B To Liverpool Lime Street
C From Alderley Edge
D From Morecambe to Leeds
E To Edinburgh
F From Chester
G To Glasgow Central

The Sunday service between Manchester Victoria and Wigan Wallgate via Atherton is funded by GMITA and will operate whilst funding exists

Table 82

Sundays
until 19 June

Manchester - Bolton - Wigan, Kirkby, Southport, Preston, Blackpool North and Barrow-in-Furness

	TP ◇1	NT	NT	TP ◇1	NT A	NT	NT	NT B	TP ◇1 C ✠	NT	NT D	TP ◇1	NT A	TP ◇1	NT	NT	NT	TP ◇1	NT A	TP ◇1 C ✠	NT
Manchester Airport 85 ✈ d				13 30					14 00			14 30		15 00				15 30		16 00	
Heald Green 85 d																					
Buxton 86 d																					
Hazel Grove 86 d																					
Stockport 84 d			13 22								14 21						15 22				
Manchester Piccadilly 10 ⇌ d			13 35	13 46					14 16		14 35	14 46		15 16			15 35	15 46		16 16	
Manchester Oxford Road d			13 38	13 49					14 19		14 38	14 49		15 19			15 38	15 49		16 19	
Deansgate ⇌ d			13 40	13 51							14 40	14 51					15 40	15 51			
Rochdale 41 d																					
Manchester Victoria ⇌ d		13 25			14 00		14 12			14 25			15 00		15 12	15 25			16 00		
Salford Central d																					
Salford Crescent a		13 29	13 44	13 54	14 06		14 16			14 29	14 44	14 54	15 06		15 16	15 29	15 44	15 54	16 06		
d		13 30	13 44	13 55	14 08		14 17			14 30	14 44	14 55	15 08		15 17	15 30	15 44	15 55	16 08		
Swinton d							14 23								15 23						
Moorside d							14 26								15 26						
Walkden d							14 29								15 29						
Atherton d							14 35								15 35						
Hag Fold d							14 37								15 37						
Daisy Hill d							14 40								15 40						
Kearsley d																					
Farnworth d																					
Moses Gate d																					
Bolton a		13 40	13 54	14 05	14 19				14 32	14 40	14 54	15 05	15 19	15 32		15 40	15 54	16 05	16 19	16 32	
d		13 40	13 55	14 05					14 33	14 40	14 55	15 05		15 33		15 40	15 55	16 05		16 33	
Westhoughton d			14 02								15 02						16 02				
Hindley d			14 06				14 45				15 06				15 45		16 06				
Ince d							14 48								15 48						
Wigan North Western a																					
Wigan Wallgate a			14 11				14 55				15 11				15 55		16 11				
d			14 13								15 13						16 13				
Pemberton d																					
Orrell d																					
Upholland d																					
Rainford d																					
Kirkby a																					
Gathurst d			14 17								15 17						16 17				
Appley Bridge d			14 21								15 21						16 21				
Parbold d			14 25								15 25						16 25				
Hoscar d																					
Burscough Bridge d			14 29								15 29						16 29				
New Lane d																					
Bescar Lane d																					
Meols Cop d			14 37								15 37						16 37				
Southport a			14 46								15 46						16 46				
Lostock d		13 45								14 45						15 45					
Horwich Parkway d		13 49		14 12						14 49		15 12				15 49		16 12			
Blackrod d		13 52								14 52						15 52					
Adlington (Lancashire) d		13 56								14 56						15 56					
Chorley d		14 01		14 20					14 44	15 01		15 20		15 44		16 01		16 20		16 44	
Leyland d		14 12								15 12						16 12					
Preston 8 65,97 a		14 18		14 32					14 57	15 18		15 32		15 57		16 18		16 32		16 57	
d	14 04	14 20		14 34					15 00	15 20		15 34		16 00		16 20		16 34		17 00	
Kirkham & Wesham 97 a		14 29								15 29						16 29					
Poulton-le-Fylde 97 a		14 37		14 51						15 37		15 51				16 37		16 51			
Layton 97 a		14 42								15 42						16 42					
Blackpool North 97 a		14 49		15 00						15 49		16 00				16 49		17 00			
Lancaster 6 65 a	14 20								15 15					16 15						17 15	
d	14 20							14 27	15 16					16 16						17 16	
Oxenholme Lake District 65 a									15 30											17 30	
Windermere 83 a																					
Carnforth d	14 29							14a59						16 24							
Silverdale d	14 35													16 30							
Arnside d	14a42													16a37							
Grange-over-Sands d						14 05															16 05
Kents Bank d						14 08															16 08
Cark d						14 12															16 12
Ulverston d						14 20															16 20
Dalton d						14 29															16 29
Roose d						14 35															16 35
Barrow-in-Furness a						14 42															16 42

A To Clitheroe
B To Leeds
C To Edinburgh
D From Chester

The Sunday service between Manchester Victoria and Wigan Wallgate via Atherton is funded by GMITA and will operate whilst funding exists

Table 82

Sundays
until 19 June

Manchester - Bolton - Wigan, Kirkby, Southport, Preston, Blackpool North and Barrow-in-Furness

	NT	TP ◇1	NT	NT A	TP ◇1	NT B	NT	NT C	TP ◇1 D ✠		NT	NT	NT	TP ◇1	NT B	TP ◇1 E ✠	NT	NT	NT A	TP ◇1	NT B	TP ◇1
Manchester Airport 85 ✈ d					16 30				17 00					17 30		18 00				18 30		19 00
Heald Green 85 d																						
Buxton 86 d																						
Hazel Grove 86 d																						
Stockport 84 d				16 21									17 22						18 21			
Manchester Piccadilly 10 ⇌ d				16 35	16 46				17 16				17 35	17 46		18 16			18 35	18 46		19 16
Manchester Oxford Road d				16 38	16 49				17 19				17 38	17 49		18 19			18 38	18 49		19 19
Deansgate ⇌ d				16 40	16 51								17 40	17 51					18 40	18 51		
Rochdale 41 d																						
Manchester Victoria ⇌ d	16 12		16 25			17 00	17 12					17 25			18 00		18 12	18 25			19 00	
Salford Central d																						
Salford Crescent a	16 16		16 29	16 44	16 54	17 06	17 16					17 29	17 44	17 54	18 06		18 16	18 29	18 44	18 54	19 06	
d	16 17		16 30	16 44	16 55	17 08	17 17					17 30	17 44	17 55	18 08		18 17	18 30	18 44	18 55	19 08	
Swinton d	16 23						17 23										18 23					
Moorside d	16 26						17 26										18 26					
Walkden d	16 29						17 29										18 29					
Atherton d	16 35						17 35										18 35					
Hag Fold d	16 37						17 37										18 37					
Daisy Hill d	16 40						17 40										18 40					
Kearsley d																						
Farnworth d																						
Moses Gate d																						
Bolton a			16 40	16 54	17 05	17 19			17 32			17 40	17 54	18 05	18 19	18 32		18 40	18 54	19 05	19 19	19 32
d			16 40	16 55	17 05				17 33			17 40	17 55	18 05		18 33		18 40	18 55	19 05		19 33
Westhoughton d				17 02									18 02						19 02			
Hindley d	16 45			17 06			17 45						18 06				18 45		19 06			
Ince d	16 48						17 48										18 48					
Wigan North Western a																						
Wigan Wallgate a	16 55			17 11			17 55						18 11				18 55		19 11			
d				17 13									18 13						19 13			
Pemberton d																						
Orrell d																						
Upholland d																						
Rainford d																						
Kirkby a																						
Gathurst d				17 17									18 17						19 17			
Appley Bridge d				17 21									18 21						19 21			
Parbold d				17 25									18 25						19 25			
Hoscar d																						
Burscough Bridge d				17 29									18 29						19 29			
New Lane d																						
Bescar Lane d																						
Meols Cop d				17 37									18 37						19 37			
Southport a				17 46									18 46						19 46			
Lostock d			16 45									17 45						18 45				
Horwich Parkway d			16 49		17 12							17 49		18 12				18 49		19 12		
Blackrod d			16 52									17 52						18 52				
Adlington (Lancashire) d			16 56									17 56						18 56				
Chorley d			17 01		17 20				17 44			18 01		18 20		18 44		19 01		19 20		19 44
Leyland d			17 12									18 12						19 12				
Preston 8 65,97 a			17 18		17 32				17 57			18 18		18 32		18 57		19 18		19 32		19 57
d		17 04	17 20		17 34				18 00	18 06		18 20		18 34		19 00		19 20		19 34		20 00
Kirkham & Wesham 97 a			17 29									18 29						19 29				
Poulton-le-Fylde 97 a			17 37		17 51							18 37		18 51				19 37		19 51		
Layton 97 a			17 42									18 42						19 42				
Blackpool North 97 a			17 49		18 00							18 49		19 00				19 49		20 00		
Lancaster 6 65 a		17 21							18 15	18 22						19 15						20 15
d		17 21						18 04	18 16	18 22						19 16						20 16
Oxenholme Lake District 65 a		17 39							18 30							19 30						
Windermere 83 a		17 58																				
Carnforth d								18a13		18 31												20a24
Silverdale d										18 37												
Arnside d										18a44												
Grange-over-Sands d											18 05											
Kents Bank d											18 08											
Cark d											18 12											
Ulverston d											18 20											
Dalton d											18 29											
Roose d											18 35											
Barrow-in-Furness a											18 42											

A From Chester
B To Clitheroe
C From Morecambe to Leeds
D To Glasgow Central
E To Edinburgh

The Sunday service between Manchester Victoria and Wigan Wallgate via Atherton is funded by GMITA and will operate whilst funding exists

Table 82

Sundays until 19 June

Manchester - Bolton - Wigan, Kirkby, Southport, Preston, Blackpool North and Barrow-in-Furness

	NT	NT	TP ◇1	NT A	NT	NT B	NT	NT C	TP ◇1	NT A	NT	NT	TP ◇1	NT D	NT	NT C	TP ◇1
Manchester Airport 85 ✈ d			19 30						20 30				21 30				22 30
Heald Green 85 d																	
Buxton 86 d																	
Hazel Grove 86 d																	
Stockport 84 d		19 22						20 21				21 22				22 21	
Manchester Piccadilly 10 d		19 35	19 46					20 35	20 46			21 35	21 46			22 35	22 46
Manchester Oxford Road d		19 38	19 49					20 38	20 49			21 38	21 49			22 38	22 49
Deansgate d		19 40	19 51					20 40	20 51			21 40	21 51			22 40	22 51
Rochdale 41 d																	
Manchester Victoria d	19 25			20 00			20 25			21 00	21 25			22 00			
Salford Central d																	
Salford Crescent a	19 29	19 44	19 54	20 06			20 29	20 44	20 54	21 06	21 29	21 44	21 54	22 06		22 44	22 54
d	19 30	19 44	19 55	20 08			20 30	20 44	20 55	21 08	21 30	21 44	21 55	22 08		22 44	22 55
Swinton d																	
Moorside d																	
Walkden d																	
Atherton d																	
Hag Fold d																	
Daisy Hill d																	
Kearsley d																	
Farnworth d																	
Moses Gate d																	
Bolton a	19 40	19 54	20 05	20 19			20 40	20 54	21 05	21 19	21 40	21 54	22 05	22 19		22 54	23 05
d	19 40	19 55	20 05				20 40	20 55	21 05		21 40	21 55	22 05			22 55	23 05
Westhoughton d		20 02						21 02				22 02				23 02	
Hindley d		20 06						21 06				22 06				23 06	
Ince d																	
Wigan North Western a																	
Wigan Wallgate a		20 11						21 11				22 15				23 15	
d		20 13						21 13									
Pemberton d																	
Orrell d																	
Upholland d																	
Rainford d																	
Kirkby a																	
Gathurst d		20 17						21 17									
Appley Bridge d		20 21						21 21									
Parbold d		20 25						21 25									
Hoscar d																	
Burscough Bridge d		20 29						21 29									
New Lane d																	
Bescar Lane d																	
Meols Cop d		20 37						21 37									
Southport a		20 46						21 46									
Lostock d	19 45						20 45				21 45						23 10
Horwich Parkway d	19 49		20 12				20 49		21 12		21 49						23 14
Blackrod d	19 52						20 52				21 52						23 17
Adlington (Lancashire) d	19 56						20 56				21 56						23 20
Chorley d	20 01		20 20				21 01		21 20		22 01		22 17				23 24
Leyland d	20 12						21 12				22 12						23 34
Preston 8 65,97 a	20 18		20 32				21 18		21 32		22 18		22 28				23 42
d	20 20		20 34				21 20		21 34		22 20		22 29				23 47
Kirkham & Wesham 97 a	20 29						21 29				22 29						23 56
Poulton-le-Fylde 97 a	20 37		20 51				21 37		21 51		22 37		22 46				00 05
Layton 97 a	20 42						21 42				22 42						
Blackpool North 97 a	20 49		21 00				21 49		22 00		22 49		22 55				00 14
Lancaster 8 65 a																	
d						20 20											
Oxenholme Lake District 65 a																	
Windermere 83 a																	
Carnforth d						20a29											
Silverdale d																	
Arnside d																	
Grange-over-Sands d					20 05										22 05		
Kents Bank d					20 08										22 08		
Cark d					20 12										22 12		
Ulverston d					20 20										22 20		
Dalton d					20 29										22 29		
Roose d					20 35										22 35		
Barrow-in-Furness a					20 42										22 42		

A To Clitheroe
B From Morecambe to Leeds
C From Chester
D To Blackburn

The Sunday service between Manchester Victoria and Wigan Wallgate via Atherton is funded by GMITA and will operate whilst funding exists

Table 82

Sundays 26 June to 31 July

Manchester - Bolton - Wigan, Kirkby, Southport, Preston, Blackpool North and Barrow-in-Furness

	TP ◇1 A	TP ◇1	NT	NT	NT B	TP ◇1	NT	NT	NT B		TP ◇1		TP ◇1 C	TP ◇1 D	TP ◇1 A	TP ◇1 E	NT E	NT F	NT		NT	NT G	TP ◇1	NT B
Manchester Airport 85 ✈ d	22p00	22p29				07 55					08 47			09 00									09 30	
Heald Green 85 d		22p33																						
Buxton 86 d																								
Hazel Grove 86 d																								
Stockport 84 d																					09 22			
Manchester Piccadilly 10 d	22p16	22p46				08 11					09 03		09 07	09 16							09 35		09 46	
Manchester Oxford Road d	22p19	22p49				08 14					09 06		09a09	09 19							09 38		09 49	
Deansgate d		22p51				08 16					09 08										09 40		09 51	
Rochdale 41 d																								
Manchester Victoria d			23p16	23p20	08 01		08 25	08 39	09 00									09 23	09 25					10 00
Salford Central d			23p19	23p23																				
Salford Crescent a		22p56	23p22	23p26	08 07	08 19	08 29	08 44	09 06		09 11							09 33	09 29		09 44		09 54	10 06
d		22p56	23p22	23p26	08 08	08 20	08 30	08 44	09 08		09 12							09 33	09 30		09 44		09 55	10 08
Swinton d				23p33														09 48						
Moorside d				23p35														09 52						
Walkden d				23p39														09 58						
Atherton d				23p44														10 12						
Hag Fold d				23p47														10 16						
Daisy Hill d				23p50														10 24						
Kearsley d																								
Farnworth d																								
Moses Gate d																								
Bolton a	22p32	23p06	23p32		08 19	08 30	08 40	08 54	09 19		09 22			09 32					09 40		09 54		10 05	10 19
d	22p33	23p07	23p33			08 30	08 40	08 55			09 23			09 33					09 40		09 55		10 05	
Westhoughton d								09 02													10 02	←		
Hindley d				23p54				09 06										10 34			10 06	10 34		
Ince d				23p57														→						
Wigan North Western a																								
Wigan Wallgate a				00 04				09 11													10 11	10 52		
d								09 13													10 13			
Pemberton d																								
Orrell d																								
Upholland d																								
Rainford d																								
Kirkby a																								
Gathurst d								09 17													10 17			
Appley Bridge d								09 21													10 21			
Parbold d								09 25													10 25			
Hoscar d																								
Burscough Bridge d								09 29													10 29			
New Lane d																								
Bescar Lane d																								
Meols Cop d								09 37													10 37			
Southport a								09 46													10 46			
Lostock d			23p38				08 45												09 45					
Horwich Parkway d		23p13	23p42			08 37	08 49				09 30								09 49				10 12	
Blackrod d			23p45				08 52												09 52					
Adlington (Lancashire) d			23p49				08 56												09 56					
Chorley d		23p21	23p54			08 45	09 01				09 37			09 44					10 01				10 20	
Leyland d			00 04				09 12												10 12					
Preston 8 65,97 a	22p54	23p33	00 10			08 56	09 18				09 49			09 57					10 18				10 32	
d	22p55	23p35	00 11			08 57	09 20				09 51	10 07		10 00		10 11			10 20				10 34	
Kirkham & Wesham 97 a			00 21				09 29												10 29					
Poulton-le-Fylde 97 a		23p52	00 29			09 14	09 37				10 08								10 37				10 51	
Layton 97 a			00 33				09 42												10 42					
Blackpool North 97 a		00 02	00 40			09 25	09 49				10 18								10 49				11 00	
Lancaster 8 65 a	23p11											10 22		10 15		10 27								
d	23p11											10 23		10 16	10 28	10 28								
Oxenholme Lake District 65 a												10 39		10 30										
Windermere 83 a												10 58												
Carnforth d	23p20														10 36	10 36								
Silverdale d	23p26														10 42	10 42								
Arnside d	23p30														10 46	10a49								
Grange-over-Sands d	23p35														10 52		12 30							
Kents Bank d	23p39														10 55		12 33							
Cark d	23p43														11 00		12 37							
Ulverston d	23p51														11 08		12 45							
Dalton d	23p59														11 16		12 54							
Roose d	00 05														11 22		13 00							
Barrow-in-Furness a	00 15														11 31		13 07							

A 24 July, 31 July
B To Clitheroe
C To Liverpool Lime Street
D To Edinburgh
E not from 24 July until 31 July
F To Wigan Wallgate
G From Manchester Victoria

The Sunday service between Manchester Victoria and Wigan Wallgate via Atherton is funded by GMITA and will operate whilst funding exists

Table 82

Sundays
26 June to 31 July

Manchester - Bolton - Wigan, Kirkby, Southport, Preston, Blackpool North and Barrow-in-Furness

		TP ◇■ A ✠	TP ◇■ B	NT C ⇌	NT	NT D	NT E ⇌	TP ◇■	NT F	TP ◇■ G	TP ◇■ H	TP ◇■ B	NT I	NT J	NT B	NT C ⇌	NT	NT	NT E ⇌	TP ◇■	NT F	TP ◇■ K ✠	NT
Manchester Airport 85 ✈	d	10 00						10 30			11 00	11 00	11 03							11 30		12 00	12 08
Heald Green 85	d												11 07										12 11
Buxton 86	d																						
Hazel Grove 86	d																						
Stockport 84	d					10 12												11 15					
Manchester Piccadilly 10 ⇌	d	10 16				10 26		10 46		11 07	11 16	11 16	11 26					11 33		11 46		12 16	12 29
Manchester Oxford Road	d	10 19				10 38		10 49		11a09	11 19	11 19	11a30					11 38		11 49		12 19	12a33
Deansgate ⇌	d					10 40		10 51										11 40		11 51			
Rochdale 41	d																						
Manchester Victoria ⇌	d			10 23	10 25				11 00							11 23	11 25				12 00		
Salford Central	d																						
Salford Crescent	a			10 33	10 29	10 44		10 54	11 06							11 33	11 29	11 44		11 54	12 06		
	d			10 33	10 30	10 44		10 55	11 08							11 33	11 30	11 44		11 55	12 08		
Swinton	d			10 48												11 48							
Moorside	d			10 52												11 52							
Walkden	d			10 58												11 58							
Atherton	d			11 12												12 12							
Hag Fold	d			11 16												12 16							
Daisy Hill	d			11 24												12 24							
Kearsley	d																						
Farnworth	d																						
Moses Gate	d																						
Bolton	a	10 32			10 40	10 54		11 05	11 19		11 32	11 32					11 40	11 54		12 05	12 19	12 32	
	d	10 33			10 40	10 55		11 05			11 33	11 33					11 40	11 55		12 05		12 33	
Westhoughton	d					11 02	←											12 02	←				
Hindley	d			11 34		11 06	11 34									12 34		12 06	12 34				
Ince	d			→												→							
Wigan North Western	a																						
Wigan Wallgate	a					11 11	11 52											12 11	12 52				
	d					11 13												12 13					
Pemberton	d																						
Orrell	d																						
Upholland	d																						
Rainford	d																						
Kirkby	a																						
Gathurst	d					11 17												12 17					
Appley Bridge	d					11 21												12 21					
Parbold	d					11 25												12 25					
Hoscar	d																						
Burscough Bridge	d					11 29												12 29					
New Lane	d																						
Bescar Lane	d																						
Meols Cop	d					11 37												12 37					
Southport	a					11 46												12 46					
Lostock	d				10 45												11 45						
Horwich Parkway	d				10 49			11 12									11 49			12 12			
Blackrod	d				10 52												11 52						
Adlington (Lancashire)	d				10 56												11 56						
Chorley	d	10 44			11 01			11 20			11 44	11 44					12 01			12 20		12 44	
Leyland	d				11 12												12 12						
Preston ■ 65,97	a	10 57			11 18			11 32			11 57	11 57					12 18			12 32		12 57	
	d	10 58			11 20			11 34			11 58	11 58					12 20			12 34		12 58	
Kirkham & Wesham 97	a				11 29												12 29						
Poulton-le-Fylde 97	a				11 37			11 51									12 37			12 51			
Layton 97	a				11 42												12 42						
Blackpool North 97	a				11 49			12 00									12 49			13 00			
Lancaster ■ 65	a	11 13									12 13	12 13										13 13	
	d	11 14	11 34								12 14	12 14		12 48								13 14	
Oxenholme Lake District 65	a	11 28																				13 28	
Windermere 83	a																						
Carnforth	d		11 42								12 22	12 22		12a57									
Silverdale	d		11 48								12 28	12 28											
Arnside	d		11a55								12 32	12a35											
Grange-over-Sands	d										12 38				14 05								
Kents Bank	d										12 41				14 08								
Cark	d										12 46				14 12								
Ulverston	d										12 54				14 20								
Dalton	d										13 02				14 29								
Roose	d										13 08				14 35								
Barrow-in-Furness	a										13 17				14 42								

A To Glasgow Central
B not from 24 July until 31 July
C To Wigan Wallgate
D From Chester
E From Manchester Victoria
F To Clitheroe
G To Liverpool Lime Street
H 24 July, 31 July
I From Alderley Edge
J From Morecambe to Leeds
K To Edinburgh

The Sunday service between Manchester Victoria and Wigan Wallgate via Atherton is funded by GMITA and will operate whilst funding exists

Table 82

Sundays
26 June to 31 July

Manchester - Bolton - Wigan, Kirkby, Southport, Preston, Blackpool North and Barrow-in-Furness

		TP A	NT B ⇌	NT	NT C	NT D ⇌	TP ◇■	NT E		TP ◇■ F ✠	TP ◇■ A	NT G	NT A	NT B ⇌	NT	NT	NT D ⇌	TP ◇■	NT E	TP ◇■ H ✠	NT B ⇌	NT
Manchester Airport 85 ✈	d						12 30			13 00								13 30		14 00		
Heald Green 85	d																					
Buxton 86	d																					
Hazel Grove 86	d																					
Stockport 84	d				12 22											13 22						
Manchester Piccadilly 10 ⇌	d				12 36		12 46			13 16						13 35		13 46		14 16		
Manchester Oxford Road	d				12 39		12 49			13 19						13 38		13 49		14 19		
Deansgate ⇌	d				12 41		12 51									13 40		13 51				
Rochdale 41	d																					
Manchester Victoria ⇌	d		12 23	12 25				13 00						13 23	13 25				14 00		14 23	14 25
Salford Central	d																					
Salford Crescent	a		12 33	12 29	12 45		12 54	13 06						13 33	13 29	13 44		13 54	14 06		14 33	14 29
	d		12 33	12 30	12 45		12 55	13 08						13 33	13 30	13 44		13 55	14 08		14 33	14 30
Swinton	d		12 48											13 48							14 48	
Moorside	d		12 52											13 52							14 52	
Walkden	d		12 58											13 58							14 58	
Atherton	d		13 12											14 12							15 12	
Hag Fold	d		13 16											14 16							15 16	
Daisy Hill	d		13 24											14 24							15 24	
Kearsley	d																					
Farnworth	d																					
Moses Gate	d																					
Bolton	a			12 40	12 55		13 05	13 19		13 32					13 40	13 54		14 05	14 19	14 32		14 40
	d			12 40	12 56		13 05			13 33					13 40	13 55		14 05		14 33		14 40
Westhoughton	d				13 03	←										14 02	←					
Hindley	d		13 34		13 07	13 34								14 34		14 06	14 34				15 34	
Ince	d		→											→							→	
Wigan North Western	a																					
Wigan Wallgate	a				13 12	13 52										14 11	14 52					
	d				13 14											14 13						
Pemberton	d																					
Orrell	d																					
Upholland	d																					
Rainford	d																					
Kirkby	a																					
Gathurst	d				13 18											14 17						
Appley Bridge	d				13 22											14 21						
Parbold	d				13 26											14 25						
Hoscar	d																					
Burscough Bridge	d				13 30											14 29						
New Lane	d																					
Bescar Lane	d																					
Meols Cop	d				13 38											14 37						
Southport	a				13 47											14 46						
Lostock	d			12 45											13 45							14 45
Horwich Parkway	d			12 49			13 12								13 49			14 12				14 49
Blackrod	d			12 52											13 52							14 52
Adlington (Lancashire)	d			12 56											13 56							14 56
Chorley	d			13 01			13 20			13 44					14 01			14 20		14 44		15 01
Leyland	d			13 12											14 12							15 12
Preston ■ 65,97	a			13 18			13 32			13 57					14 18			14 32		14 57		15 18
	d			13 20			13 34		14 00	14 04	14 04				14 20			14 34		15 00		15 20
Kirkham & Wesham 97	a			13 29											14 29							15 29
Poulton-le-Fylde 97	a			13 37			13 51								14 37			14 51				15 37
Layton 97	a			13 42											14 42							15 42
Blackpool North 97	a			13 49			14 00								14 49			15 30				15 49
Lancaster ■ 65	a								14 15	14 20	14 20									15 15		
	d	13 25							14 16	14 20	14 20	14 27								15 16		
Oxenholme Lake District 65	a								14 30											15 30		
Windermere 83	a																					
Carnforth	d	13 33								14 29	14 29	14a59										
Silverdale	d	13 39								14 35	14 35											
Arnside	d	13a46								14 39	14a42											
Grange-over-Sands	d									14 44			16 05									
Kents Bank	d									14 48			16 08									
Cark	d									14 52			16 12									
Ulverston	d									15 00			16 20									
Dalton	d									15 08			16 29									
Roose	d									15 14			16 35									
Barrow-in-Furness	a									15 24			16 42									

A not from 24 July until 31 July
B To Wigan Wallgate
C From Chester
D From Manchester Victoria
E To Clitheroe
F To Glasgow Central
G To Leeds
H To Edinburgh

The Sunday service between Manchester Victoria and Wigan Wallgate via Atherton is funded by GMITA and will operate whilst funding exists

Table 82

Sundays
26 June to 31 July

Manchester - Bolton - Wigan, Kirkby, Southport, Preston, Blackpool North and Barrow-in-Furness

		NT A	NT B	TP ◇1	NT C	TP ◇1 D	TP ◇1 E	NT D	NT E	NT F	NT	NT	NT B	TP ◇1	NT C	TP ◇1 G	TP ◇1	NT H	NT F	NT	NT A	NT B	TP ◇1
Manchester Airport 85	d			14 30		15 00	15 00							15 30		16 00							16 30
Heald Green 85	d																						
Buxton 86	d																						
Hazel Grove 86	d																						
Stockport 84	d	14 21										15 22									16 21		
Manchester Piccadilly 10	d	14 35		14 46		15 16	15 16					15 35		15 46		16 16					16 35		16 46
Manchester Oxford Road	d	14 38		14 49		15 19	15 19					15 38		15 49		16 19					16 38		16 49
Deansgate	d	14 40		14 51								15 40		15 51							16 40		16 51
Rochdale 41	d																						
Manchester Victoria	d				15 00					15 23	15 25				16 00				16 23	16 25			
Salford Central	d																						
Salford Crescent	a	14 44		14 54	15 06					15 33	15 29	15 44		15 54	16 06				16 33	16 29	16 44		16 54
	d	14 44		14 55	15 08					15 33	15 30	15 44		15 55	16 08				16 33	16 30	16 44		16 55
Swinton	d									15 48									16 48				
Moorside	d									15 52									16 52				
Walkden	d									15 58									16 58				
Atherton	d									16 12									17 12				
Hag Fold	d									16 16									17 16				
Daisy Hill	d									16 24									17 24				
Kearsley	d																						
Farnworth	d																						
Moses Gate	d																						
Bolton	a	14 54		15 05	15 19	15 32	15 32				15 40	15 54		16 05	16 19	16 32				16 40	16 54		17 05
	d	14 55		15 05		15 33	15 33				15 40	15 55		16 05		16 33				16 40	16 55		17 05
Westhoughton	d	15 02	←									16 02	←								17 02	←	
Hindley	d	15 06	15 34							16 34		16 06	16 34						17 34		17 06	17 34	
Ince	d									→									→				
Wigan North Western	a																						
Wigan Wallgate	a	15 11	15 52									16 11	16 52								17 11	17 52	
	d	15 13										16 13									17 13		
Pemberton	d																						
Orrell	d																						
Upholland	d																						
Rainford	d																						
Kirkby	a																						
Gathurst	d	15 17										16 17									17 17		
Appley Bridge	d	15 21										16 21									17 21		
Parbold	d	15 25										16 25									17 25		
Hoscar	d																						
Burscough Bridge	d	15 29										16 29									17 29		
New Lane	d																						
Bescar Lane	d																						
Meols Cop	d	15 37										16 37									17 37		
Southport	a	15 46										16 46									17 46		
Lostock	d										15 45									16 45			
Horwich Parkway	d			15 12							15 49			16 12						16 49			17 12
Blackrod	d										15 52									16 52			
Adlington (Lancashire)	d										15 56									16 56			
Chorley	d			15 20		15 44	15 44				16 01			16 20		16 44				17 01			17 20
Leyland	d										16 12									17 12			
Preston 8 65,97	a			15 32		15 57	15 57				16 18			16 32		16 57				17 18			17 32
	d			15 34		16 00	16 00				16 20			16 34		17 00	17 04			17 20			17 34
Kirkham & Wesham 97	a										16 29									17 29			
Poulton-le-Fylde 97	a			15 51							16 37			16 51						17 37			17 51
Layton 97	a										16 42									17 42			
Blackpool North 97	a			16 00							16 49			17 00						17 49			18 00
Lancaster 6 65	a					16 15	16 15									17 15	17 21						
	d					16 16	16 16	17 04								17 16	17 21	18 04					
Oxenholme Lake District 65	a															17 30	17 39						
Windermere 83	a																17 58						
Carnforth	d					16 24	16 24	17 14										18a13					
Silverdale	d					16 30	16 30	17 20															
Arnside	d					16 34	16a37	17 25															
Grange-over-Sands	d					16 40		17 31	18 05														
Kents Bank	d					16 43		17 34	18 08														
Cark	d					16 48		17 38	18 12														
Ulverston	d					16 55		17 46	18 20														
Dalton	d					17 03		17 55	18 29														
Roose	d					17 09		18 01	18 35														
Barrow-in-Furness	a					17 19		18 08	18 42														

A From Chester
B From Manchester Victoria
C To Clitheroe
D 24 July, 31 July
E not from 24 July until 31 July
F To Wigan Wallgate
G To Edinburgh
H From Morecambe to Leeds

The Sunday service between Manchester Victoria and Wigan Wallgate via Atherton is funded by GMITA and will operate whilst funding exists

Table 82

Sundays
26 June to 31 July

Manchester - Bolton - Wigan, Kirkby, Southport, Preston, Blackpool North and Barrow-in-Furness

		NT A	TP ◇1 B	TP ◇1 C	TP ◇1 D		NT E	NT F	NT	NT	NT G	TP ◇1	NT A	TP ◇1 H	NT F	NT	NT I	NT G	TP ◇1	NT A	TP ◇1 E	TP ◇1 C
Manchester Airport 85	d				17 00							17 30		18 00					18 30		19 00	19 00
Heald Green 85	d																					
Buxton 86	d																					
Hazel Grove 86	d																					
Stockport 84	d									17 22							18 21					
Manchester Piccadilly 10	d				17 16					17 35		17 46		18 16			18 35		18 46		19 16	19 16
Manchester Oxford Road	d				17 19					17 38		17 49		18 19			18 38		18 49		19 19	19 19
Deansgate	d									17 40		17 51					18 40		18 51			
Rochdale 41	d																					
Manchester Victoria	d	17 00						17 23	17 25				18 00		18 23	18 25				19 00		
Salford Central	d																					
Salford Crescent	a	17 06						17 33	17 29	17 44		17 54	18 06		18 33	18 29	18 44		18 54	19 06		
	d	17 08						17 33	17 30	17 44		17 55	18 08		18 33	18 30	18 44		18 55	19 08		
Swinton	d							17 48							18 48							
Moorside	d							17 52							18 52							
Walkden	d							17 58							18 58							
Atherton	d							18 12							19 12							
Hag Fold	d							18 16							19 16							
Daisy Hill	d							18 24							19 24							
Kearsley	d																					
Farnworth	d																					
Moses Gate	d																					
Bolton	a	17 19			17 32				17 40	17 54		18 05	18 19	18 32		18 40	18 54		19 05	19 19	19 32	19 32
	d				17 33				17 40	17 55		18 05		18 33		18 40	18 55		19 05		19 33	19 33
Westhoughton	d									18 02	←						19 02	←				
Hindley	d							18 34		18 06	18 34				19 34		19 06	19 34				
Ince	d							→							→							
Wigan North Western	a																					
Wigan Wallgate	a									18 11	18 52						19 11	19 52				
	d									18 13							19 13					
Pemberton	d																					
Orrell	d																					
Upholland	d																					
Rainford	d																					
Kirkby	a																					
Gathurst	d									18 17							19 17					
Appley Bridge	d									18 21							19 21					
Parbold	d									18 25							19 25					
Hoscar	d																					
Burscough Bridge	d									18 29							19 29					
New Lane	d																					
Bescar Lane	d																					
Meols Cop	d									18 37							19 37					
Southport	a									18 46							19 46					
Lostock	d								17 45							18 45						
Horwich Parkway	d								17 49			18 12				18 49			19 12			
Blackrod	d								17 52							18 52						
Adlington (Lancashire)	d								17 56							18 56						
Chorley	d				17 44				18 01			18 20		18 44		19 01			19 20		19 44	19 44
Leyland	d								18 12							19 12						
Preston 8 65,97	a				17 57				18 18			18 32		18 57		19 18			19 32		19 57	19 57
	d		18 08	18 12	18 08	18 12			18 20			18 34		19 00		19 20			19 34		20 00	20 00
Kirkham & Wesham 97	a								18 29							19 29						
Poulton-le-Fylde 97	a								18 37			18 51				19 37			19 51			
Layton 97	a								18 42							19 42						
Blackpool North 97	a								18 49			19 00				19 49			20 00			
Lancaster 6 65	a		18 23	18 28	18 23	18 28								19 15							20 15	20 15
	d		18 24	18 28	18 24	18 28								19 16							20 16	20 16
Oxenholme Lake District 65	a		18 38		18 38									19 30								
Windermere 83	a																					
Carnforth	d			18 37		18 37															20a24	20 24
Silverdale	d			18 43		18 43																20 30
Arnside	d			18 47		18a50																20 34
Grange-over-Sands	d			18 52			20 05															20 40
Kents Bank	d			18 56			20 08															20 43
Cark	d			19 00			20 12															20 48
Ulverston	d			19 08			20 20															20 56
Dalton	d			19 16			20 29															21 04
Roose	d			19 22			20 35															21 10
Barrow-in-Furness	a			19 32			20 42															21 20

A To Clitheroe
B From Blackpool North to Glasgow Central
C 24 July, 31 July
D To Glasgow Central
E not from 24 July until 31 July
F To Wigan Wallgate
G From Manchester Victoria
H To Edinburgh
I From Chester

The Sunday service between Manchester Victoria and Wigan Wallgate via Atherton is funded by GMITA and will operate whilst funding exists

Table 82

Sundays 26 June to 31 July

Manchester - Bolton - Wigan, Kirkby, Southport, Preston, Blackpool North and Barrow-in-Furness

	NT	NT	TP ◇1	NT A	NT B	NT	NT C	TP ◇1	NT A	TP ◇1 D	NT	NT	TP ◇1	NT E	NT F	NT G	NT C	TP ◇1
Manchester Airport 85 ✈ d			19 30					20 30					21 30					22 30
Heald Green 85 d																		
Buxton 86 d																		
Hazel Grove 86 d																		
Stockport 84 d		19 22					20 21					21 22					22 21	
Manchester Piccadilly 10 ⇌ d		19 35	19 46				20 35	20 46				21 35	21 46				22 35	22 46
Manchester Oxford Road d		19 38	19 49				20 38	20 49				21 38	21 49				22 38	22 49
Deansgate ⇌ d		19 40	19 51				20 40	20 51				21 40	21 51				22 40	22 51
Rochdale 41 d																		
Manchester Victoria ⇌ d	19 25			20 00		20 25			21 00		21 25			22 00				
Salford Central d																		
Salford Crescent a	19 29	19 44	19 54	20 06		20 29	20 44	20 54	21 06		21 29	21 44	21 54	22 06			22 44	22 54
d	19 30	19 44	19 55	20 08		20 30	20 44	20 55	21 08		21 30	21 44	21 55	22 08			22 44	22 55
Swinton d																		
Moorside d																		
Walkden d																		
Atherton d																		
Hag Fold d																		
Daisy Hill d																		
Kearsley d																		
Farnworth d																		
Moses Gate d																		
Bolton a	19 40	19 54	20 05	20 19		20 40	20 54	21 05	21 19		21 40	21 54	22 05	22 19			22 54	23 05
d	19 40	19 55	20 05			20 40	20 55	21 05			21 40	21 55	22 05				22 55	23 05
Westhoughton d		20 02					21 02					22 02					23 02	
Hindley d		20 06					21 06					22 06					23 06	
Ince d																		
Wigan North Western a																		
Wigan Wallgate a		20 11					21 11					22 15					23 15	
d		20 13					21 13											
Pemberton d																		
Orrell d																		
Upholland d																		
Rainford d																		
Kirkby a																		
Gathurst d		20 17					21 17											
Appley Bridge d		20 21					21 21											
Parbold d		20 25					21 25											
Hoscar d																		
Burscough Bridge d		20 29					21 29											
New Lane d																		
Bescar Lane d																		
Meols Cop d		20 37					21 37											
Southport a		20 46					21 46											
Lostock d	19 45					20 45					21 45							23 10
Horwich Parkway d	19 49		20 12			20 49		21 12			21 49							23 14
Blackrod d	19 52					20 52					21 52							23 17
Adlington (Lancashire) d	19 56					20 56					21 56							23 20
Chorley d	20 01		20 20			21 01		21 20			22 01		22 17					23 24
Leyland d	20 12					21 12					22 12							23 34
Preston 8 65,97 a	20 18		20 32			21 18		21 32			22 18		22 28					23 42
d	20 20		20 34			21 20		21 34			22 20		22 29					23 47
Kirkham & Wesham 97 a	20 29					21 29					22 29							23 56
Poulton-le-Fylde 97 a	20 37		20 51			21 37		21 51			22 37		22 46					00 05
Layton 97 a	20 42					21 42					22 42							
Blackpool North 97 a	20 49		21 00			21 49		22 00			22 49		22 55					00 14
Lancaster 8 65 a																		
d					20 20					21 23						22 05		
Oxenholme Lake District 65 a																		
Windermere 83 a																		
Carnforth d					20a29					21 31						22 15		
Silverdale d										21 37						22 21		
Arnside d										21 41						22 26		
Grange-over-Sands d										21 47					22 05	22 32		
Kents Bank d										21 50					22 08	22 35		
Cark d										21 55					22 12	22 39		
Ulverston d										22 02					22 20	22 47		
Dalton d										22 10					22 29	22 56		
Roose d										22 16					22 35	23 02		
Barrow-in-Furness a										22 26					22 42	23 09		

A To Clitheroe
B From Morecambe to Leeds
C From Chester
D 24 July, 31 July. From Windermere
E To Blackburn
F not from 24 July until 31 July
G 24 July, 31 July

The Sunday service between Manchester Victoria and Wigan Wallgate via Atherton is funded by GMITA and will operate whilst funding exists

Table 82

Sundays 7 August to 11 September

Manchester - Bolton - Wigan, Kirkby, Southport, Preston, Blackpool North and Barrow-in-Furness

	TP ◇1	TP ◇1	NT	NT	NT A	TP ◇1	NT	NT	NT A	TP ◇1		TP ◇1 B	TP ◇1 C ⊼	NT	NT	TP ◇1	NT A	NT	TP ◇1	TP ◇1 D ⊼	NT	NT E
Manchester Airport 85 ✈ d	22p00	22p29				07 55				08 47			09 00			09 30				10 00		
Heald Green 85 d		22p33																				
Buxton 86 d																						
Hazel Grove 86 d																						
Stockport 84 d															09 22							10 12
Manchester Piccadilly 10 ⇌ d	22p16	22p46				08 11				09 03		09 07	09 16		09 35	09 46				10 16		10 26
Manchester Oxford Road d	22p19	22p49				08 14				09 06		09a09	09 19		09 38	09 49				10 19		10 38
Deansgate ⇌ d		22p51				08 16				09 08					09 40	09 51						10 40
Rochdale 41 d																						
Manchester Victoria ⇌ d			23p16	23p20	08 01		08 25	08 39	09 00					09 25			10 00	10 09			10 25	
Salford Central d			23p19	23p23																		
Salford Crescent a		22p56	23p22	23p26	08 07	08 19	08 29	08 44	09 06	09 11				09 29	09 44	09 54	10 06	10 15			10 29	10 44
d		22p56	23p22	23p26	08 08	08 20	08 30	08 44	09 08	09 12				09 30	09 44	09 55	10 08	10 17			10 30	10 44
Swinton d				23p33														10 23				
Moorside d				23p35														10 26				
Walkden d				23p39														10 29				
Atherton d				23p44														10 35				
Hag Fold d				23p47														10 37				
Daisy Hill d				23p50														10 40				
Kearsley d																						
Farnworth d																						
Moses Gate d																						
Bolton a	22p32	23p06	23p32		08 19	08 30	08 40	08 54	09 19	09 22			09 32	09 40	09 54	10 05	10 19			10 32	10 40	10 54
d	22p33	23p07	23p33			08 30	08 40	08 55		09 23			09 33	09 40	09 55	10 05				10 33	10 40	10 55
Westhoughton d								09 02							10 02							11 02
Hindley d				23p54				09 06							10 06			10 45				11 06
Ince d				23p57														10 48				
Wigan North Western a																						
Wigan Wallgate a				00 04				09 11							10 11			10 55				11 11
d								09 13							10 13							11 13
Pemberton d																						
Orrell d																						
Upholland d																						
Rainford d																						
Kirkby a																						
Gathurst d								09 17							10 17							11 17
Appley Bridge d								09 21							10 21							11 21
Parbold d								09 25							10 25							11 25
Hoscar d																						
Burscough Bridge d								09 29							10 29							11 29
New Lane d																						
Bescar Lane d																						
Meols Cop d								09 37							10 37							11 37
Southport a								09 46							10 46							11 46
Lostock d			23p38				08 45							09 45							10 45	
Horwich Parkway d		23p13	23p42			08 37	08 49			09 30				09 49		10 12					10 49	
Blackrod d			23p45				08 52							09 52							10 52	
Adlington (Lancashire) d			23p49				08 56							09 56							10 56	
Chorley d		23p21	23p54			08 45	09 01			09 37			09 44	10 01		10 20				10 44	11 01	
Leyland d			00 04				09 12							10 12							11 12	
Preston 8 65,97 a	22p54	23p33	00 10			08 56	09 18			09 49			09 57	10 18		10 32				10 57	11 18	
d	22p55	23p35	00 11			08 57	09 20			09 51	10 07		10 00	10 20		10 34				10 58	11 20	
Kirkham & Wesham 97 a			00 21				09 29							10 29							11 29	
Poulton-le-Fylde 97 a		23p52	00 29			09 14	09 37			10 08				10 37		10 51					11 37	
Layton 97 a			00 33				09 42							10 42							11 42	
Blackpool North 97 a		00 02	00 40			09 25	09 49			10 18				10 49		11 00					11 49	
Lancaster 8 65 a	23p11										10 22		10 15							11 13		
d	23p11										10 23		10 16						10 28	11 14		
Oxenholme Lake District 65 a											10 39		10 30							11 28		
Windermere 83 a											10 58											
Carnforth d	23p20																		10 36			
Silverdale d	23p26																		10 42			
Arnside d	23p30																		10 46			
Grange-over-Sands d	23p35																		10 52			
Kents Bank d	23p39																		10 55			
Cark d	23p43																		11 00			
Ulverston d	23p51																		11 08			
Dalton d	23p59																		11 16			
Roose d	00 05																		11 22			
Barrow-in-Furness a	00 15																		11 31			

A To Clitheroe
B To Liverpool Lime Street
C To Edinburgh
D To Glasgow Central
E From Chester

The Sunday service between Manchester Victoria and Wigan Wallgate via Atherton is funded by GMITA and will operate whilst funding exists

Table 82

Manchester - Bolton - Wigan, Kirkby, Southport, Preston, Blackpool North and Barrow-in-Furness

		TP ◇■	NT A	TP ◇■ B	TP ◇■	NT C	NT	NT	NT	TP ◇■	NT A	NT	NT D	TP ◇■ E ✠	NT	NT	NT F	TP ◇■	NT A	TP ◇■ G ✠		NT	NT
Manchester Airport 85 ✈	d	10 30			11 00	11 03				11 30				12 00	12 08			12 30		13 00			
Heald Green 85	d					11 07									12 11								
Buxton 86	d																						
Hazel Grove 86	d																						
Stockport 84	d								11 15								12 22						
Manchester Piccadilly ■ ⇌	d	10 46		11 07	11 16	11 26			11 33	11 46				12 16	12 29		12 36	12 46		13 16			
Manchester Oxford Road	d	10 49		11a09	11 19	11a30			11 38	11 49				12 19	12a33		12 39	12 49		13 19			
Deansgate ⇌	d	10 51							11 40	11 51							12 41	12 51					
Rochdale 41	d																						
Manchester Victoria ⇌	d		11 00				11 12	11 25			12 00	12 09				12 25			13 00			13 12	13 25
Salford Central	d																						
Salford Crescent	a	10 54	11 06				11 16	11 29	11 44	11 54	12 06	12 13				12 29	12 45	12 54	13 06			13 16	13 29
	d	10 55	11 08				11 17	11 30	11 44	11 55	12 08	12 17				12 30	12 45	12 55	13 08			13 17	13 30
Swinton	d						11 23					12 23										13 23	
Moorside	d						11 26					12 26										13 26	
Walkden	d						11 29					12 29										13 29	
Atherton	d						11 35					12 35										13 35	
Hag Fold	d						11 37					12 37										13 37	
Daisy Hill	d						11 40					12 40										13 40	
Kearsley	d																						
Farnworth	d																						
Moses Gate	d																						
Bolton	a	11 05	11 19		11 32			11 40	11 54	12 05	12 19			12 32		12 40	12 55	13 05	13 19	13 32			13 40
	d	11 05			11 33			11 40	11 55	12 05				12 33		12 40	12 56	13 05		13 33			13 40
Westhoughton	d								12 02								13 03						
Hindley	d						11 45		12 06			12 45					13 07					13 45	
Ince	d						11 48					12 48										13 48	
Wigan North Western	a																						
Wigan Wallgate	a						11 55		12 11			12 55					13 12					13 55	
	d								12 13								13 14						
Pemberton	d																						
Orrell	d																						
Upholland	d																						
Rainford	d																						
Kirkby	a																						
Gathurst	d								12 17								13 18						
Appley Bridge	d								12 21								13 22						
Parbold	d								12 25								13 26						
Hoscar	d																						
Burscough Bridge	d								12 29								13 30						
New Lane	d																						
Bescar Lane	d																						
Meols Cop	d								12 37								13 38						
Southport	a								12 46								13 47						
Lostock	d							11 45								12 45							13 45
Horwich Parkway	d	11 12						11 49		12 12						12 49		13 12					13 49
Blackrod	d							11 52								12 52							13 52
Adlington (Lancashire)	d							11 56								12 56							13 56
Chorley	d	11 20			11 44			12 01		12 20				12 44		13 01		13 20		13 44			14 01
Leyland	d							12 12								13 12							14 12
Preston ■ 65,97	a	11 32			11 57			12 18		12 32				12 57		13 18		13 32		13 57			14 18
	d	11 34			11 58			12 20		12 34				12 58		13 20		13 34		14 00	14 04		14 20
Kirkham & Wesham 97	a							12 29								13 29							14 29
Poulton-le-Fylde 97	a	11 51						12 37		12 51						13 37		13 51					14 37
Layton 97	a							12 42								13 42							14 42
Blackpool North 97	a	12 00						12 49		13 00						13 49		14 00					14 49
Lancaster ■ 65	a				12 13									13 13						14 15	14 20		
	d				12 14								12 48	13 14						14 16	14 20		
Oxenholme Lake District 65	a													13 28						14 30			
Windermere 83	a																						
Carnforth	d				12 22								12a57								14 29		
Silverdale	d				12 28																14 35		
Arnside	d				12 32																14 39		
Grange-over-Sands	d				12 38																14 44		
Kents Bank	d				12 41																14 48		
Cark	d				12 46																14 52		
Ulverston	d				12 54																15 00		
Dalton	d				13 02																15 08		
Roose	d				13 08																15 14		
Barrow-in-Furness	a				13 17																15 24		

A To Clitheroe
B To Liverpool Lime Street
C From Alderley Edge
D From Morecambe to Leeds
E To Edinburgh
F From Chester
G To Glasgow Central

The Sunday service between Manchester Victoria and Wigan Wallgate via Atherton is funded by GMITA and will operate whilst funding exists

Table 82

Manchester - Bolton - Wigan, Kirkby, Southport, Preston, Blackpool North and Barrow-in-Furness

		NT	TP ◇■	NT A	NT	NT B	TP ◇■ C ✠	NT	NT D	TP ◇■	NT A	TP ◇■	NT	NT	NT	TP ◇■	NT A	NT	NT	TP ◇■ C ✠	TP ◇■	NT
Manchester Airport 85 ✈	d		13 30				14 00			14 30		15 00				15 30				16 00		
Heald Green 85	d																					
Buxton 86	d																					
Hazel Grove 86	d																					
Stockport 84	d	13 22							14 21						15 22							
Manchester Piccadilly ■ ⇌	d	13 35	13 46				14 16		14 35	14 46		15 16			15 35	15 46				16 16		
Manchester Oxford Road	d	13 38	13 49				14 19		14 38	14 49		15 19			15 38	15 49				16 19		
Deansgate ⇌	d	13 40	13 51						14 40	14 51					15 40	15 51						
Rochdale 41	d																					
Manchester Victoria ⇌	d			14 00	14 12			14 25			15 00		15 12	15 25			16 00	16 12				16 25
Salford Central	d																					
Salford Crescent	a	13 44	13 54	14 06	14 16			14 29	14 44	14 54	15 06		15 16	15 29	15 44	15 54	16 06	16 16				16 29
	d	13 44	13 55	14 08	14 17			14 30	14 44	14 55	15 08		15 17	15 30	15 44	15 55	16 08	16 17				16 30
Swinton	d				14 23								15 23					16 23				
Moorside	d				14 26								15 26					16 26				
Walkden	d				14 29								15 29					16 29				
Atherton	d				14 35								15 35					16 35				
Hag Fold	d				14 37								15 37					16 37				
Daisy Hill	d				14 40								15 40					16 40				
Kearsley	d																					
Farnworth	d																					
Moses Gate	d																					
Bolton	a	13 54	14 05	14 19			14 32	14 40	14 54	15 05	15 19	15 32		15 40	15 54	16 05	16 19			16 32		16 40
	d	13 55	14 05				14 33	14 40	14 55	15 05		15 33		15 40	15 55	16 05				16 33		16 40
Westhoughton	d	14 02							15 02						16 02							
Hindley	d	14 06			14 45				15 06				15 45		16 06			16 45				
Ince	d				14 48								15 48					16 48				
Wigan North Western	a																					
Wigan Wallgate	a	14 11			14 55				15 11				15 55		16 11			16 55				
	d	14 13							15 13						16 13							
Pemberton	d																					
Orrell	d																					
Upholland	d																					
Rainford	d																					
Kirkby	a																					
Gathurst	d	14 17							15 17						16 17							
Appley Bridge	d	14 21							15 21						16 21							
Parbold	d	14 25							15 25						16 25							
Hoscar	d																					
Burscough Bridge	d	14 29							15 29						16 29							
New Lane	d																					
Bescar Lane	d																					
Meols Cop	d	14 37							15 37						16 37							
Southport	a	14 46							15 46						16 46							
Lostock	d							14 45						15 45								16 45
Horwich Parkway	d		14 12					14 49		15 12				15 49		16 12						16 49
Blackrod	d							14 52						15 52								16 52
Adlington (Lancashire)	d							14 56						15 56								16 56
Chorley	d		14 20				14 44	15 01		15 20		15 44		16 01		16 20				16 44		17 01
Leyland	d							15 12						16 12								17 12
Preston ■ 65,97	a		14 32				14 57	15 18		15 32		15 57		16 18		16 32				16 57		17 18
	d		14 34				15 00	15 20		15 34		16 00		16 20		16 34				17 00	17 04	17 20
Kirkham & Wesham 97	a							15 29						16 29								17 29
Poulton-le-Fylde 97	a		14 51					15 37		15 51				16 37		16 51						17 37
Layton 97	a							15 42						16 42								17 42
Blackpool North 97	a		15 00					15 49		16 00				16 49		17 00						17 49
Lancaster ■ 65	a						15 15					16 15								17 15	17 21	
	d					14 27	15 16					16 16							17 04	17 16	17 21	
Oxenholme Lake District 65	a						15 30													17 30	17 39	
Windermere 83	a																				17 58	
Carnforth	d					14a59						16 24							17 14			
Silverdale	d											16 30							17 20			
Arnside	d											16 34							17 25			
Grange-over-Sands	d											16 40							17 31			
Kents Bank	d											16 43							17 34			
Cark	d											16 48							17 38			
Ulverston	d											16 55							17 46			
Dalton	d											17 03							17 55			
Roose	d											17 09							18 01			
Barrow-in-Furness	a											17 19							18 08			

A To Clitheroe
B To Leeds
C To Edinburgh
D From Chester

The Sunday service between Manchester Victoria and Wigan Wallgate via Atherton is funded by GMITA and will operate whilst funding exists

Manchester - Bolton - Wigan, Kirkby, Southport, Preston, Blackpool North and Barrow-in-Furness

	NT	TP	NT	NT	NT	TP	TP	TP	NT	NT	TP	NT	TP	NT	NT	NT	TP	NT	TP	NT	NT	TP
	A	◇1	B		C	◇1 D	◇1 E	◇1			◇1	B	◇1 F			A	◇1	B	◇1			◇1
Manchester Airport 85 ✈ d		16 30				17 00					17 30		18 00				18 30		19 00			19 30
Heald Green 85 d																						
Buxton 86 d																						
Hazel Grove 86 d																						
Stockport 84 d	16 21									17 22						18 21					19 22	
Manchester Piccadilly 10 ⇌ d	16 35	16 46				17 16				17 35	17 46		18 16			18 35	18 46		19 16		19 35	19 46
Manchester Oxford Road d	16 38	16 49				17 19				17 38	17 49		18 19			18 38	18 49		19 19		19 38	19 49
Deansgate ⇌ d	16 40	16 51								17 40	17 51					18 40	18 51				19 40	19 51
Rochdale 41 d																						
Manchester Victoria ⇌ d			17 00	17 12					17 25			18 00		18 12	18 25			19 00		19 25		
Salford Central d																						
Salford Crescent a	16 44	16 54	17 06	17 16					17 29	17 44	17 54	18 06		18 16	18 29	18 44	18 54	19 06		19 29	19 44	19 54
d	16 44	16 55	17 08	17 17					17 30	17 44	17 55	18 08		18 17	18 30	18 44	18 55	19 08		19 30	19 44	19 55
Swinton d				17 23										18 23								
Moorside d				17 26										18 26								
Walkden d				17 29										18 29								
Atherton d				17 35										18 35								
Hag Fold d				17 37										18 37								
Daisy Hill d				17 40										18 40								
Kearsley d																						
Farnworth d																						
Moses Gate d																						
Bolton a	16 54	17 05	17 19			17 32			17 40	17 54	18 05	18 19	18 32		18 40	18 54	19 05	19 19	19 32	19 40	19 54	20 05
d	16 55	17 05				17 33			17 40	17 55	18 05		18 33		18 40	18 55	19 05		19 33	19 40	19 55	20 05
Westhoughton d	17 02									18 02						19 02					20 02	
Hindley d	17 06			17 45						18 06				18 45		19 06					20 06	
Ince d				17 48										18 48								
Wigan North Western a																						
Wigan Wallgate a	17 11			17 55						18 11				18 55		19 11					20 11	
d	17 13									18 13						19 13					20 13	
Pemberton d																						
Orrell d																						
Upholland d																						
Rainford d																						
Kirkby a																						
Gathurst d	17 17									18 17						19 17					20 17	
Appley Bridge d	17 21									18 21						19 21					20 21	
Parbold d	17 25									18 25						19 25					20 25	
Hoscar d																						
Burscough Bridge d	17 29									18 29						19 29					20 29	
New Lane d																						
Bescar Lane d																						
Meols Cop d	17 37									18 37						19 37					20 37	
Southport a	17 46									18 46						19 46					20 46	
Lostock d									17 45						18 45					19 45		
Horwich Parkway d		17 12							17 49		18 12				18 49		19 12			19 49		20 12
Blackrod d									17 52						18 52					19 52		
Adlington (Lancashire) d									17 56						18 56					19 56		
Chorley d		17 20				17 44			18 01		18 20		18 44		19 01		19 20		19 44	20 01		20 20
Leyland d									18 12						19 12					20 12		
Preston 8 65,97 a		17 32				17 57			18 18		18 32		18 57		19 18		19 32		19 57	20 18		20 32
d		17 34				18 08	18 08	18 12	18 20		18 34		19 00		19 20		19 34		20 00	20 20		20 34
Kirkham & Wesham 97 a									18 29						19 29					20 29		
Poulton-le-Fylde 97 a		17 51							18 37		18 51				19 37		19 51			20 37		20 51
Layton 97 a									18 42						19 42					20 42		
Blackpool North 97 a		18 00							18 49		19 00				19 49		20 00			20 49		21 00
Lancaster 8 65 a						18 23	18 23	18 28					19 15						20 15			
d					18 04	18 24	18 24	18 28					19 16						20 16			
Oxenholme Lake District 65 a						18 38	18 38						19 30									
Windermere 83 a																						
Carnforth d					18a13			18 37											20 24			
Silverdale d								18 43											20 30			
Arnside d								18 47											20 34			
Grange-over-Sands d								18 52											20 40			
Kents Bank d								18 56											20 43			
Cark d								19 00											20 48			
Ulverston d								19 08											20 56			
Dalton d								19 16											21 04			
Roose d								19 22											21 10			
Barrow-in-Furness a								19 32											21 20			

A From Chester
B To Clitheroe
C From Morecambe to Leeds
D To Glasgow Central
E From Blackpool North to Glasgow Central
F To Edinburgh

The Sunday service between Manchester Victoria and Wigan Wallgate via Atherton is funded by GMITA and will operate whilst funding exists

Manchester - Bolton - Wigan, Kirkby, Southport, Preston, Blackpool North and Barrow-in-Furness

	NT	NT	NT	NT	TP	NT	TP	NT	NT	TP	NT	NT	NT	TP
	A	B		C	◇1	A	◇1 D			◇1	E		C	◇1
Manchester Airport 85 ✈ d					20 30					21 30				22 30
Heald Green 85 d														
Buxton 86 d														
Hazel Grove 86 d														
Stockport 84 d				20 21					21 22				22 21	
Manchester Piccadilly 10 ⇌ d				20 35	20 46				21 35	21 46			22 35	22 46
Manchester Oxford Road d				20 38	20 49				21 38	21 49			22 38	22 49
Deansgate ⇌ d				20 40	20 51				21 40	21 51			22 40	22 51
Rochdale 41 d														
Manchester Victoria ⇌ d	20 00		20 25			21 00		21 25			22 00			
Salford Central d														
Salford Crescent a	20 06		20 29	20 44	20 54	21 06		21 29	21 44	21 54	22 06		22 44	22 54
d	20 08		20 30	20 44	20 55	21 08		21 30	21 44	21 55	22 08		22 44	22 55
Swinton d														
Moorside d														
Walkden d														
Atherton d														
Hag Fold d														
Daisy Hill d														
Kearsley d														
Farnworth d														
Moses Gate d														
Bolton a	20 19		20 40	20 54	21 05	21 19		21 40	21 54	22 05	22 19		22 54	23 05
d			20 40	20 55	21 05			21 40	21 55	22 05			22 55	23 05
Westhoughton d				21 02					22 02				23 02	
Hindley d				21 06					22 06				23 06	
Ince d														
Wigan North Western a														
Wigan Wallgate a				21 11					22 15				23 15	
d				21 13										
Pemberton d														
Orrell d														
Upholland d														
Rainford d														
Kirkby a														
Gathurst d				21 17										
Appley Bridge d				21 21										
Parbold d				21 25										
Hoscar d														
Burscough Bridge d				21 29										
New Lane d														
Bescar Lane d														
Meols Cop d				21 37										
Southport a				21 46										
Lostock d			20 45					21 45						23 10
Horwich Parkway d			20 49		21 12			21 49						23 14
Blackrod d			20 52					21 52						23 17
Adlington (Lancashire) d			20 56					21 56						23 20
Chorley d			21 01		21 20			22 01		22 17				23 24
Leyland d			21 12					22 12						23 34
Preston 8 65,97 a			21 18		21 32			22 18		22 28				23 42
d			21 20		21 34			22 20		22 29				23 47
Kirkham & Wesham 97 a			21 29					22 29						23 56
Poulton-le-Fylde 97 a			21 37		21 51			22 37		22 46				00 05
Layton 97 a			21 42					22 42						
Blackpool North 97 a			21 49		22 00			22 49		22 55				00 14
Lancaster 8 65 a														
d		20 20					21 23					22 05		
Oxenholme Lake District 65 a														
Windermere 83 a														
Carnforth d		20a29					21 31					22 15		
Silverdale d							21 37					22 21		
Arnside d							21 41					22 26		
Grange-over-Sands d							21 47					22 32		
Kents Bank d							21 50					22 35		
Cark d							21 55					22 39		
Ulverston d							22 02					22 47		
Dalton d							22 10					22 56		
Roose d							22 16					23 02		
Barrow-in-Furness a							22 26					23 09		

A To Clitheroe
B From Morecambe to Leeds
C From Chester
D From Windermere
E To Blackburn

The Sunday service between Manchester Victoria and Wigan Wallgate via Atherton is funded by GMITA and will operate whilst funding exists

Table 82

Manchester - Bolton - Wigan, Kirkby, Southport, Preston, Blackpool North and Barrow-in-Furness

		TP	TP	NT	NT	TP	TP	NT	NT	NT	NT	TP	TP	TP	NT	NT	TP	NT	NT	TP	TP	TP	TP
		◇1	◇1			◇1	◇1					◇1	◇1	◇1			◇1			◇1	◇1	◇1	◇1
							A	B			B		C	A				B			D	A	
Manchester Airport 85 ✈	d	22p00	22p29			07 30	07 40					08 47	09 00	09 03			09 29				10 00	10 03	
Heald Green 85	d		22p33																				
Buxton 86	d																						
Hazel Grove 86	d																						
Stockport 84	d															09 22							
Manchester Piccadilly 10 ⇌	d	22p16	22p46			07 46	07 55					09 03	09 16	09 20		09 35	09 46				10 16	10 21	
Manchester Oxford Road	d	22p19	22p49			07 49						09 06	09 19			09 38	09 49				10 19		
Deansgate ⇌	d		22p51			07 51						09 08				09 40	09 51						
Rochdale 41	d																						
Manchester Victoria ⇌	d			23p16	23p20			08 01	08 25	08 39	09 00				09 25			10 00	10 09				
Salford Central	d			23p19	23p23																		
Salford Crescent	a		22p56	23p22	23p26	07 54	08 02	08 07	08 29	08 44	09 06	09 11		09 26	09 29	09 44	09 54	10 06	10 15			10 26	
	d		22p56	23p22	23p26	07 55		08 08	08 30	08 44	09 08	09 12			09 30	09 44	09 55	10 08	10 17				
Swinton	d				23p33														10 23				
Moorside	d				23p35														10 26				
Walkden	d				23p39														10 29				
Atherton	d				23p44														10 35				
Hag Fold	d				23p47														10 37				
Daisy Hill	d				23p50														10 40				
Kearsley	d																						
Farnworth	d																						
Moses Gate	d																						
Bolton	a	22p32	23p06	23p32		08 05		08 19	08 40	08 54	09 19	09 22	09 32		09 40	09 54	10 05	10 19			10 32		
	d	22p33	23p07	23p33		08 06			08 40	08 55		09 23	09 33		09 40	09 55	10 05				10 33		
Westhoughton	d									09 02						10 02							
Hindley	d				23p54					09 06						10 06			10 45				
Ince	d				23p57														10 48				
Wigan North Western	a																						
Wigan Wallgate	a				00 04					09 11						10 11			10 55				
	d									09 13						10 13							
Pemberton	d																						
Orrell	d																						
Upholland	d																						
Rainford	d																						
Kirkby	a																						
Gathurst	d									09 17						10 17							
Appley Bridge	d									09 21						10 21							
Parbold	d									09 25						10 25							
Hoscar	d																						
Burscough Bridge	d									09 29						10 29							
New Lane	d																						
Bescar Lane	d																						
Meols Cop	d									09 37						10 37							
Southport	a									09 46						10 46							
Lostock	d			23p38					08 45						09 45								
Horwich Parkway	d		23p13	23p42		08 12			08 49			09 30			09 49		10 12						
Blackrod	d			23p45					08 52						09 52								
Adlington (Lancashire)	d			23p49					08 56						09 56								
Chorley	d		23p21	23p54		08 20			09 01			09 37	09 44		10 01		10 20				10 44		
Leyland	d			00 04					09 12						10 12								
Preston 8 65,97	a	22p54	23p33	00 10		08 31			09 18			09 49	09 57		10 18		10 32				10 57		
	d	22p55	23p35	00 11		08 32			09 20			09 51	10 00		10 20		10 34				10 58		11 18
Kirkham & Wesham 97	a			00 21					09 29						10 29								
Poulton-le-Fylde 97	a		23p52	00 29		08 49			09 37			10 08			10 37		10 51						
Layton 97	a			00 33					09 42						10 42								
Blackpool North 97	a		00 02	00 40		08 58			09 49			10 18			10 49		11 00						
Lancaster 6 65	a	23p11											10 15								11 13		11 33
	d	23p11											10 16							10 23	11 14		11 34
Oxenholme Lake District 65	a												10 30							10 39	11 28		
Windermere 83	a																			10 58			
Carnforth	d	23p20																					11 42
Silverdale	d	23p26																					11 48
Arnside	d	23p30																					11 52
Grange-over-Sands	d	23p35																					11 58
Kents Bank	d	23p39																					12 01
Cark	d	23p43																					12 06
Ulverston	d	23p51																					12 13
Dalton	d	23p59																					12 21
Roose	d	00 05																					12 27
Barrow-in-Furness	a	00 15																					12 37

A To Newcastle
B To Clitheroe
C To Edinburgh
D To Glasgow Central

The Sunday service between Manchester Victoria and Wigan Wallgate via Atherton is funded by GMITA and will operate whilst funding exists

Table 82

Manchester - Bolton - Wigan, Kirkby, Southport, Preston, Blackpool North and Barrow-in-Furness

		NT	NT	TP	NT	NT	TP	NT	NT	NT	TP	NT	NT	NT	TP	TP	NT	NT	NT	TP	NT	TP	NT
				◇1			◇1				◇1				◇1	◇1				◇1		◇1	
			A		B		C	D				B		E	F	C			A		B	G	
Manchester Airport 85 ✈	d			10 30			11 03	11 03			11 30				12 00	12 03	12 08			12 30		12 58	
Heald Green 85	d							11 07									12 11						
Buxton 86	d																						
Hazel Grove 86	d																						
Stockport 84	d		10 12							11 15									12 22				
Manchester Piccadilly 10 ⇌	d		10 26	10 46			11 21	11 26		11 33	11 46				12 16	12 21	12 29		12 36	12 46		13 16	
Manchester Oxford Road	d		10 38	10 49				11a30		11 38	11 49				12 19		12a33		12 39	12 49		13 19	
Deansgate ⇌	d		10 40	10 51						11 40	11 51								12 41	12 51			
Rochdale 41	d																						
Manchester Victoria ⇌	d	10 25			11 00	11 12			11 25			12 00	12 09					12 25			13 00		13 12
Salford Central	d																						
Salford Crescent	a	10 29	10 44	10 54	11 06	11 16	11 26		11 29	11 44	11 54	12 06	12 13			12 26		12 29	12 45	12 54	13 06		13 16
	d	10 30	10 44	10 55	11 08	11 17			11 30	11 44	11 55	12 08	12 17					12 30	12 45	12 55	13 08		13 17
Swinton	d					11 23							12 23										13 23
Moorside	d					11 26							12 26										13 26
Walkden	d					11 29							12 29										13 29
Atherton	d					11 35							12 35										13 35
Hag Fold	d					11 37							12 37										13 37
Daisy Hill	d					11 40							12 40										13 40
Kearsley	d																						
Farnworth	d																						
Moses Gate	d																						
Bolton	a	10 40	10 54	11 05	11 19				11 40	11 54	12 05	12 19			12 32			12 40	12 55	13 05	13 19	13 32	
	d	10 40	10 55	11 05					11 40	11 55	12 05				12 33			12 40	12 56	13 05		13 33	
Westhoughton	d		11 02							12 02									13 03				
Hindley	d		11 06			11 45				12 06			12 45						13 07				13 45
Ince	d					11 48							12 48										13 48
Wigan North Western	a																						
Wigan Wallgate	a		11 11			11 55				12 11			12 55						13 12				13 55
	d		11 13							12 13									13 14				
Pemberton	d																						
Orrell	d																						
Upholland	d																						
Rainford	d																						
Kirkby	a																						
Gathurst	d		11 17							12 17									13 18				
Appley Bridge	d		11 21							12 21									13 22				
Parbold	d		11 25							12 25									13 26				
Hoscar	d																						
Burscough Bridge	d		11 29							12 29									13 30				
New Lane	d																						
Bescar Lane	d																						
Meols Cop	d		11 37							12 37									13 38				
Southport	a		11 46							12 46									13 47				
Lostock	d	10 45							11 45									12 45					
Horwich Parkway	d	10 49		11 12					11 49		12 12							12 49		13 12			
Blackrod	d	10 52							11 52									12 52					
Adlington (Lancashire)	d	10 56							11 56									12 56					
Chorley	d	11 01		11 20					12 01		12 20				12 44			13 01		13 20		13 44	
Leyland	d	11 12							12 12									13 12					
Preston 8 65,97	a	11 18		11 32					12 18		12 32				12 57			13 18		13 32		13 57	
	d	11 20		11 34					12 20		12 34				12 58			13 20		13 34		14 00	
Kirkham & Wesham 97	a	11 29							12 29									13 29					
Poulton-le-Fylde 97	a	11 37		11 51					12 37		12 51							13 37		13 51			
Layton 97	a	11 42							12 42									13 42					
Blackpool North 97	a	11 49		12 00					12 49		13 00							13 49		14 00			
Lancaster 6 65	a														13 13							14 15	
	d													12 48	13 14							14 16	
Oxenholme Lake District 65	a														13 28							14 30	
Windermere 83	a																						
Carnforth	d													12a57									
Silverdale	d																						
Arnside	d																						
Grange-over-Sands	d																						
Kents Bank	d																						
Cark	d																						
Ulverston	d																						
Dalton	d																						
Roose	d																						
Barrow-in-Furness	a																						

A From Chester
B To Clitheroe
C To Newcastle
D From Alderley Edge
E From Morecambe to Leeds
F To Edinburgh
G To Glasgow Central

The Sunday service between Manchester Victoria and Wigan Wallgate via Atherton is funded by GMITA and will operate whilst funding exists

Manchester - Bolton - Wigan, Kirkby, Southport, Preston, Blackpool North and Barrow-in-Furness

	TP ◇1 A	TP ◇1	NT	NT	TP ◇1	NT B	NT	NT C	TP ◇1 D ⊤	TP ◇1 A	NT	NT E	TP ◇1	NT B	TP ◇1	NT	TP ◇1 A	NT	NT	TP ◇1	NT B
Manchester Airport 85 ✈ d	13 03				13 30				13 58	14 03			14 30		14 58		15 03			15 30	
Heald Green 85 d																					
Buxton 86 d																					
Hazel Grove 86 d																					
Stockport 84 d				13 22								14 21							15 22		
Manchester Piccadilly 10 ⇌ d	13 21			13 35	13 46				14 16	14 21		14 35	14 46		15 16		15 21		15 35	15 46	
Manchester Oxford Road d				13 38	13 49				14 19			14 38	14 49		15 19				15 38	15 49	
Deansgate ⇌ d				13 40	13 51							14 40	14 51						15 40	15 51	
Rochdale 41 d																					
Manchester Victoria ⇌ d			13 25			14 00	14 12				14 25			15 00		15 12		15 25			16 00
Salford Central d																					
Salford Crescent a	13 26		13 29	13 44	13 54	14 06	14 16			14 26	14 29	14 44	14 54	15 06		15 16	15 26	15 29	15 44	15 54	16 06
d			13 30	13 44	13 55	14 08	14 17				14 30	14 44	14 55	15 08		15 17		15 30	15 44	15 55	16 08
Swinton d							14 23									15 23					
Moorside d							14 26									15 26					
Walkden d							14 29									15 29					
Atherton d							14 35									15 35					
Hag Fold d							14 37									15 37					
Daisy Hill d							14 40									15 40					
Kearsley d																					
Farnworth d																					
Moses Gate d																					
Bolton a			13 40	13 54	14 05	14 19			14 32		14 40	14 54	15 05	15 19	15 32			15 40	15 54	16 05	16 19
d			13 40	13 55	14 05				14 33		14 40	14 55	15 05		15 33			15 40	15 55	16 05	
Westhoughton d				14 02								15 02							16 02		
Hindley d				14 06			14 45					15 06				15 45			16 06		
Ince d							14 48									15 48					
Wigan North Western a																					
Wigan Wallgate a				14 11			14 55					15 11				15 55			16 11		
d				14 13								15 13							16 13		
Pemberton d																					
Orrell d																					
Upholland d																					
Rainford d																					
Kirkby a																					
Gathurst d				14 17								15 17							16 17		
Appley Bridge d				14 21								15 21							16 21		
Parbold d				14 25								15 25							16 25		
Hoscar d																					
Burscough Bridge d				14 29								15 29							16 29		
New Lane d																					
Bescar Lane d																					
Meols Cop d				14 37								15 37							16 37		
Southport a				14 46								15 46							16 46		
Lostock d			13 45								14 45							15 45			
Horwich Parkway d			13 49		14 12						14 49		15 12					15 49		16 12	
Blackrod d			13 52								14 52							15 52			
Adlington (Lancashire) d			13 56								14 56							15 56			
Chorley d			14 01		14 20				14 44		15 01		15 20		15 44			16 01		16 20	
Leyland d			14 12								15 12							16 12			
Preston 8 65,97 a			14 18		14 32				14 57		15 18		15 32		15 57			16 18		16 32	
d		14 04	14 20		14 34				15 00		15 20		15 34		16 00			16 20		16 34	
Kirkham & Wesham 97 a			14 29								15 29							16 29			
Poulton-le-Fylde 97 a			14 37		14 51						15 37		15 51					16 37		16 51	
Layton 97 a			14 42								15 42							16 42			
Blackpool North 97 a			14 49		15 00						15 49		16 00					16 49		17 00	
Lancaster 6 65 a		14 20							15 15						16 15						
d		14 20						14 27	15 16						16 16						
Oxenholme Lake District 65 a									15 30												
Windermere 83 a																					
Carnforth d		14 29						14a59							16 24						
Silverdale d															16 30						
Arnside d		14 37													16 34						
Grange-over-Sands d		14 43													16 40						
Kents Bank d															16 43						
Cark d															16 48						
Ulverston d		14 55													16 55						
Dalton d															17 03						
Roose d															17 09						
Barrow-in-Furness a		15 16													17 19						

A To Newcastle
B To Clitheroe
C To Leeds
D To Edinburgh
E From Chester

The Sunday service between Manchester Victoria and Wigan Wallgate via Atherton is funded by GMITA and will operate whilst funding exists

Manchester - Bolton - Wigan, Kirkby, Southport, Preston, Blackpool North and Barrow-in-Furness

	NT	NT	TP ◇1 A ⊤	TP ◇1 B	NT	NT C	TP ◇1	NT D	NT	NT E	TP ◇1 F ⊤		TP ◇1 B	NT	NT	TP ◇1	NT D	TP ◇1 A ⊤	NT	TP ◇1 G	NT	NT C
Manchester Airport 85 ✈ d			15 58	16 03			16 30				16 58		17 03			17 30		17 58		18 03		
Heald Green 85 d																						
Buxton 86 d																						
Hazel Grove 86 d																						
Stockport 84 d						16 21									17 22							18 21
Manchester Piccadilly 10 ⇌ d			16 16	16 21		16 35	16 46				17 16		17 21		17 35	17 46		18 16		18 21		18 35
Manchester Oxford Road d			16 19			16 38	16 49				17 19				17 38	17 49		18 19				18 38
Deansgate ⇌ d						16 40	16 51								17 40	17 51						18 40
Rochdale 41 d																						
Manchester Victoria ⇌ d	16 12				16 25			17 00	17 12					17 25			18 00		18 12		18 25	
Salford Central d																						
Salford Crescent a	16 16			16 26	16 29	16 44	16 54	17 06	17 16				17 26	17 29	17 44	17 54	18 06		18 16	18 26	18 29	18 44
d	16 17				16 30	16 44	16 55	17 08	17 17					17 30	17 44	17 55	18 08		18 17		18 30	18 44
Swinton d	16 23								17 23										18 23			
Moorside d	16 26								17 26										18 26			
Walkden d	16 29								17 29										18 29			
Atherton d	16 35								17 35										18 35			
Hag Fold d	16 37								17 37										18 37			
Daisy Hill d	16 40								17 40										18 40			
Kearsley d																						
Farnworth d																						
Moses Gate d																						
Bolton a			16 32		16 40	16 54	17 05	17 19			17 32			17 40	17 54	18 05	18 19	18 32			18 40	18 54
d			16 33		16 40	16 55	17 05				17 33			17 40	17 55	18 05		18 33			18 40	18 55
Westhoughton d						17 02									18 02							19 02
Hindley d	16 45					17 06			17 45						18 06				18 45			19 06
Ince d	16 48								17 48										18 48			
Wigan North Western a																						
Wigan Wallgate a	16 55					17 11			17 55						18 11				18 55			19 11
d						17 13									18 13							19 13
Pemberton d																						
Orrell d																						
Upholland d																						
Rainford d																						
Kirkby a																						
Gathurst d						17 17									18 17							19 17
Appley Bridge d						17 21									18 21							19 21
Parbold d						17 25									18 25							19 25
Hoscar d																						
Burscough Bridge d						17 29									18 29							19 29
New Lane d																						
Bescar Lane d																						
Meols Cop d						17 37									18 37							19 37
Southport a						17 46									18 46							19 46
Lostock d					16 45									17 45							18 45	
Horwich Parkway d					16 49		17 12							17 49		18 12					18 49	
Blackrod d					16 52									17 52							18 52	
Adlington (Lancashire) d					16 56									17 56							18 56	
Chorley d			16 44		17 01		17 20				17 44			18 01		18 20		18 44			19 01	
Leyland d					17 12									18 12							19 12	
Preston 8 65,97 a			16 57		17 18		17 32				17 57			18 18		18 32		18 57			19 18	
d			17 00		17 20		17 34				18 06	18 08		18 20		18 34		19 00			19 20	
Kirkham & Wesham 97 a					17 29									18 29							19 29	
Poulton-le-Fylde 97 a					17 37		17 51							18 37		18 51					19 37	
Layton 97 a					17 42									18 42							19 42	
Blackpool North 97 a					17 49		18 00							18 49		19 00					19 49	
Lancaster 6 65 a			17 15								18 22	18 23						19 15				
d		17 04	17 16							18 04	18 22	18 24						19 16				
Oxenholme Lake District 65 a			17 30									18 38						19 30				
Windermere 83 a																						
Carnforth d		17 14								18a13	18 31											
Silverdale d		17 20									18 37											
Arnside d		17 25									18 41											
Grange-over-Sands d		17 31									18 46											
Kents Bank d		17 34									18 50											
Cark d		17 38									18 54											
Ulverston d		17 46									19 02											
Dalton d		17 55									19 10											
Roose d		18 01									19 16											
Barrow-in-Furness a		18 08									19 26											

A To Edinburgh
B To Newcastle
C From Chester
D To Clitheroe
E From Morecambe to Leeds
F ⊤ to Preston
G To Middlesbrough

The Sunday service between Manchester Victoria and Wigan Wallgate via Atherton is funded by GMITA and will operate whilst funding exists

Table 82

Sundays

18 September to 2 October

Manchester - Bolton - Wigan, Kirkby, Southport, Preston, Blackpool North and Barrow-in-Furness

		TP	NT	TP	TP	NT	NT	TP	NT	TP	NT	NT	NT	TP	NT	TP	TP	NT	NT	TP	NT	TP
		◇1		◇1	◇1			◇1		◇1				◇1		◇1	◇1			◇1		◇1
			A		B				A	C	D		E		A	F	G				H	I
Manchester Airport 85 ✈	d	18 30		18 58	19 03			19 30		20 03				20 30		21 03				21 30		22 03
Heald Green 85	d																					
Buxton 86	d																					
Hazel Grove 86	d																					
Stockport 84	d						19 22						20 21						21 22			
Manchester Piccadilly 10 ⇌	d	18 46		19 16	19 21		19 35	19 46		20 21			20 35	20 46		21 21			21 35	21 46		22 18
Manchester Oxford Road	d	18 49		19 19			19 38	19 49					20 38	20 49					21 38	21 49		
Deansgate ⇌	d	18 51					19 40	19 51					20 40	20 51					21 40	21 51		
Rochdale 41	d																					
Manchester Victoria ⇌	d		19 00			19 25			20 00			20 25			21 00			21 25			22 00	
Salford Central	d																					
Salford Crescent	a	18 54	19 06		19 26	19 29	19 44	19 54	20 06	20 26		20 29	20 44	20 54	21 06	21 26		21 29	21 44	21 54	22 06	22 23
	d	18 55	19 08			19 30	19 44	19 55	20 08			20 30	20 44	20 55	21 08			21 30	21 44	21 55	22 08	
Swinton	d																					
Moorside	d																					
Walkden	d																					
Atherton	d																					
Hag Fold	d																					
Daisy Hill	d																					
Kearsley	d																					
Farnworth	d																					
Moses Gate	d																					
Bolton	a	19 05	19 19	19 32		19 40	19 54	20 05	20 19			20 40	20 54	21 05	21 19			21 40	21 54	22 05	22 19	
	d	19 05		19 33		19 40	19 55	20 05				20 40	20 55	21 05				21 40	21 55	22 05		
Westhoughton	d						20 02						21 02						22 02			
Hindley	d						20 06						21 06						22 06			
Ince	d																					
Wigan North Western	a																					
Wigan Wallgate	a						20 11						21 11						22 15			
	d						20 13						21 13									
Pemberton	d																					
Orrell	d																					
Upholland	d																					
Rainford	d																					
Kirkby	a																					
Gathurst	d						20 17						21 17									
Appley Bridge	d						20 21						21 21									
Parbold	d						20 25						21 25									
Hoscar	d																					
Burscough Bridge	d						20 29						21 29									
New Lane	d																					
Bescar Lane	d																					
Meols Cop	d						20 37						21 37									
Southport	a						20 46						21 46									
Lostock	d					19 45						20 45						21 45				
Horwich Parkway	d	19 12				19 49		20 12				20 49		21 12				21 49				
Blackrod	d					19 52						20 52						21 52				
Adlington (Lancashire)	d					19 56						20 56						21 56				
Chorley	d	19 20		19 44		20 01		20 20				21 01		21 20				22 01		22 17		
Leyland	d					20 12						21 12						22 12				
Preston 8 65,97	a	19 32		19 57		20 18		20 32				21 18		21 32				22 18		22 28		
	d	19 34		20 00		20 20		20 34				21 20		21 34				22 20		22 29		
Kirkham & Wesham 97	a					20 29						21 29						22 29				
Poulton-le-Fylde 97	a	19 51				20 37		20 51				21 37		21 51				22 37		22 46		
Layton 97	a					20 42						21 42						22 42				
Blackpool North 97	a	20 00				20 49		21 00				21 49		22 00				22 49		22 55		
Lancaster 6 65	a			20 15																		
	d			20 16							20 20						21 23					
Oxenholme Lake District 65	a																					
Windermere 83	a																					
Carnforth	d			20 24							20a29						21 31					
Silverdale	d			20 30													21 37					
Arnside	d			20 34													21 41					
Grange-over-Sands	d			20 40													21 47					
Kents Bank	d			20 43													21 50					
Cark	d			20 48													21 55					
Ulverston	d			20 56													22 02					
Dalton	d			21 04													22 10					
Roose	d			21 10													22 16					
Barrow-in-Furness	a			21 20													22 26					

A To Clitheroe
B To Newcastle
C To Scarborough
D From Morecambe to Leeds
E From Chester
F To York
G From Windermere
H To Blackburn
I To Manchester Victoria

The Sunday service between Manchester Victoria and Wigan Wallgate via Atherton is funded by GMITA and will operate whilst funding exists

Table 82

Sundays

18 September to 2 October

Manchester - Bolton - Wigan, Kirkby, Southport, Preston, Blackpool North and Barrow-in-Furness

		NT	NT	TP	TP
				◇1	◇1
			A		B
Manchester Airport 85 ✈	d			22 30	23 25
Heald Green 85	d				
Buxton 86	d				
Hazel Grove 86	d				
Stockport 84	d		22 21		
Manchester Piccadilly 10 ⇌	d		22 35	22 46	23 40
Manchester Oxford Road	d		22 38	22 49	
Deansgate ⇌	d		22 40	22 51	
Rochdale 41	d				
Manchester Victoria ⇌	d				
Salford Central	d				
Salford Crescent	a		22 44	22 54	23 45
	d		22 44	22 55	
Swinton	d				
Moorside	d				
Walkden	d				
Atherton	d				
Hag Fold	d				
Daisy Hill	d				
Kearsley	d				
Farnworth	d				
Moses Gate	d				
Bolton	a		22 54	23 05	
	d		22 55	23 05	
Westhoughton	d		23 02		
Hindley	d		23 06		
Ince	d				
Wigan North Western	a				
Wigan Wallgate	a		23 15		
	d				
Pemberton	d				
Orrell	d				
Upholland	d				
Rainford	d				
Kirkby	a				
Gathurst	d				
Appley Bridge	d				
Parbold	d				
Hoscar	d				
Burscough Bridge	d				
New Lane	d				
Bescar Lane	d				
Meols Cop	d				
Southport	a				
Lostock	d			23 10	
Horwich Parkway	d			23 14	
Blackrod	d			23 17	
Adlington (Lancashire)	d			23 20	
Chorley	d			23 24	
Leyland	d			23 34	
Preston 8 65,97	a			23 42	
	d			23 47	
Kirkham & Wesham 97	a			23 56	
Poulton-le-Fylde 97	a			00 05	
Layton 97	a				
Blackpool North 97	a			00 14	
Lancaster 6 65	a				
	d	22 05			
Oxenholme Lake District 65	a				
Windermere 83	a				
Carnforth	d	22 15			
Silverdale	d	22 21			
Arnside	d	22 26			
Grange-over-Sands	d	22 32			
Kents Bank	d	22 35			
Cark	d	22 39			
Ulverston	d	22 47			
Dalton	d	22 56			
Roose	d	23 02			
Barrow-in-Furness	a	23 09			

A From Chester
B To York

The Sunday service between Manchester Victoria and Wigan Wallgate via Atherton is funded by GMITA and will operate whilst funding exists

Table 82

Sundays from 9 October

Manchester - Bolton - Wigan, Kirkby, Southport, Preston, Blackpool North and Barrow-in-Furness

Station		TP	TP	NT	NT	TP	TP	NT	NT	NT	NT	TP	TP	TP	TP	NT	NT	TP	NT	NT	TP	TP	TP
		◇1	◇1			◇1	◇1					◇1	◇1	◇1	◇1			◇1			◇1	◇1	◇1
							A						B	C ✠	D							E ✠	D
Manchester Airport	85 ✈ d	22p00	22p29			07 30	07 40					08 47		09 00	09 03			09 29				10 00	10 03
Heald Green	85 d		22p33																				
Buxton	86 d																						
Hazel Grove	86 d																						
Stockport	84 d																09 22						
Manchester Piccadilly 10	⇌ d	22p16	22p46			07 46	07 55					09 03	09 07	09 16	09 20		09 35	09 46				10 16	10 21
Manchester Oxford Road	d	22p19	22p49			07 49						09 06	09a09	09 19			09 38	09 49				10 19	
Deansgate	⇌ d		22p51			07 51						09 08					09 40	09 51					
Rochdale	41 d																						
Manchester Victoria	⇌ d			23p16	23p20			08 01	08 25	08 39	09 00					09 25			10 00	10 09			
Salford Central	d			23p19	23p23																		
Salford Crescent	a		22p56	23p22	23p26	07 54	08 02	08 07	08 29	08 44	09 06	09 11			09 26	09 29	09 44	09 54	10 06	10 15			10 26
	d		22p56	23p22	23p26	07 55		08 08	08 30	08 44	09 08	09 12				09 30	09 44	09 55	10 08	10 17			
Swinton	d				23p33															10 23			
Moorside	d				23p35															10 26			
Walkden	d				23p39															10 29			
Atherton	d				23p44															10 35			
Hag Fold	d				23p47															10 37			
Daisy Hill	d				23p50															10 40			
Kearsley	d																						
Farnworth	d																						
Moses Gate	d																						
Bolton	a	22p32	23p06	23p32		08 05		08 20	08 40	08 54	09 20	09 22		09 32		09 40	09 54	10 05	10 20			10 32	
	d	22p33	23p07	23p33		08 06			08 40	08 55		09 23		09 33		09 40	09 55	10 05				10 33	
Westhoughton	d									09 02							10 02						
Hindley	d				23p54					09 06							10 06			10 45			
Ince	d				23p57															10 48			
Wigan North Western	a																						
Wigan Wallgate	a				00 06					09 11							10 11			10 57			
	d									09 13							10 13						
Pemberton	d																						
Orrell	d																						
Upholland	d																						
Rainford	d																						
Kirkby	a																						
Gathurst	d									09 17							10 17						
Appley Bridge	d									09 21							10 21						
Parbold	d									09 25							10 25						
Hoscar	d																						
Burscough Bridge	d									09 29							10 29						
New Lane	d																						
Bescar Lane	d																						
Meols Cop	d									09 37							10 37						
Southport	a									09 48							10 48						
Lostock	d			23p38					08 45							09 45							
Horwich Parkway	d		23p13	23p42		08 12			08 49			09 30				09 49		10 12					
Blackrod	d			23p45					08 52							09 52							
Adlington (Lancashire)	d			23p49					08 56							09 56							
Chorley	d		23p21	23p54		08 20			09 01			09 37		09 44		10 01		10 20				10 44	
Leyland	d			00 04					09 12							10 12							
Preston 8	65,97 a	22p54	23p33	00 10		08 31			09 18			09 49		09 57		10 18		10 32				10 57	
	d	22p55	23p35	00 11		08 32			09 20			09 51		10 00		10 20		10 34				10 58	
Kirkham & Wesham	97 a			00 21					09 29							10 29							
Poulton-le-Fylde	97 a		23p52	00 29		08 49			09 37			10 08				10 37		10 51					
Layton	97 a			00 33					09 42							10 42							
Blackpool North	97 a		00 02	00 42		08 58			09 51			10 18				10 51		11 00					
Lancaster 6	65 a	23p11												10 15								11 13	
	d	23p11												10 16							10 23	11 14	
Oxenholme Lake District	65 a													10 30							10 39	11 28	
Windermere	83 a																				10 58		
Carnforth	d	23p20																					
Silverdale	d	23p26																					
Arnside	d	23p30																					
Grange-over-Sands	d	23p35																					
Kents Bank	d	23p39																					
Cark	d	23p43																					
Ulverston	d	23p51																					
Dalton	d	23p59																					
Roose	d	00 05																					
Barrow-in-Furness	a	00 15																					

A To Newcastle
B from 30 October. To Liverpool Lime Street
C To Edinburgh
D 9 October, 16 October, 23 October. To Newcastle
E To Glasgow Central

The Sunday service between Manchester Victoria and Wigan Wallgate via Atherton is funded by GMITA and will operate whilst funding exists

Table 82

Sundays from 9 October

Manchester - Bolton - Wigan, Kirkby, Southport, Preston, Blackpool North and Barrow-in-Furness

Station		TP	NT	NT	TP	NT	TP	NT	TP	NT	NT	NT	TP	NT	NT	NT	TP	TP	NT	NT	NT	TP	NT
		◇1			◇1		◇1		◇1				◇1				◇1	◇1				◇1	
		A		B			C		D	E						F	G ✠	D			B		
Manchester Airport	85 ✈ d				10 30				11 03	11 03			11 30				12 00	12 03	12 08			12 30	
Heald Green	85 d									11 07									12 11				
Buxton	86 d																						
Hazel Grove	86 d																						
Stockport	84 d			10 12								11 15									12 21		
Manchester Piccadilly 10	⇌ d			10 26	10 46		11 07		11 21	11 26		11 33	11 46				12 16	12 21	12 29		12 35	12 46	
Manchester Oxford Road	d			10 38	10 49		11a09			11a30		11 38	11 49				12 19		12a33		12 38	12 49	
Deansgate	⇌ d			10 40	10 51							11 40	11 51								12 40	12 51	
Rochdale	41 d																						
Manchester Victoria	⇌ d		10 25			11 00		11 12			11 25			12 00	12 09					12 25			13 00
Salford Central	d																						
Salford Crescent	a		10 29	10 44	10 54	11 06		11 16	11 26		11 29	11 44	11 54	12 06	12 13			12 26		12 29	12 44	12 54	13 06
	d		10 30	10 44	10 55	11 08		11 17			11 30	11 44	11 55	12 08	12 17					12 30	12 44	12 55	13 08
Swinton	d							11 23							12 23								
Moorside	d							11 26							12 26								
Walkden	d							11 29							12 29								
Atherton	d							11 35							12 35								
Hag Fold	d							11 37							12 37								
Daisy Hill	d							11 40							12 40								
Kearsley	d																						
Farnworth	d																						
Moses Gate	d																						
Bolton	a		10 40	10 54	11 05	11 20					11 40	11 54	12 05	12 20			12 32			12 40	12 54	13 05	13 20
	d		10 40	10 55	11 05						11 40	11 55	12 05				12 33			12 40	12 55	13 05	
Westhoughton	d			11 02								12 02									13 02		
Hindley	d			11 06				11 45				12 06			12 45						13 06		
Ince	d							11 48							12 48								
Wigan North Western	a																						
Wigan Wallgate	a			11 11				11 57				12 11			12 57						13 11		
	d			11 13								12 13									13 13		
Pemberton	d																						
Orrell	d																						
Upholland	d																						
Rainford	d																						
Kirkby	a																						
Gathurst	d			11 17								12 17									13 17		
Appley Bridge	d			11 21								12 21									13 21		
Parbold	d			11 25								12 25									13 25		
Hoscar	d																						
Burscough Bridge	d			11 29								12 29									13 29		
New Lane	d																						
Bescar Lane	d																						
Meols Cop	d			11 37								12 37									13 37		
Southport	a			11 46								12 48									13 46		
Lostock	d		10 45								11 45									12 45			
Horwich Parkway	d		10 49		11 12						11 49		12 12							12 49		13 12	
Blackrod	d		10 52								11 52									12 52			
Adlington (Lancashire)	d		10 56								11 56									12 56			
Chorley	d		11 01		11 20						12 01		12 20				12 44			13 01		13 20	
Leyland	d		11 12								12 12									13 12			
Preston 8	65,97 a		11 18		11 32						12 18		12 32				12 57			13 18		13 32	
	d	11 18	11 20		11 34						12 20		12 34				12 58			13 20		13 34	
Kirkham & Wesham	97 a		11 29								12 29									13 29			
Poulton-le-Fylde	97 a		11 37		11 51						12 37		12 51							13 37		13 51	
Layton	97 a		11 42								12 42									13 42			
Blackpool North	97 a		11 51		12 00						12 51		13 00							13 51		14 00	
Lancaster 6	65 a	11 33															13 13						
	d	11 34														12 48	13 14						
Oxenholme Lake District	65 a																13 28						
Windermere	83 a																						
Carnforth	d	11 42														12a57							
Silverdale	d	11 48																					
Arnside	d	11 52																					
Grange-over-Sands	d	11 58																					
Kents Bank	d	12 01																					
Cark	d	12 06																					
Ulverston	d	12 13																					
Dalton	d	12 21																					
Roose	d	12 27																					
Barrow-in-Furness	a	12 37																					

A 9 October, 16 October, 23 October
B From Chester
C from 30 October. To Liverpool Lime Street
D 9 October, 16 October, 23 October. To Newcastle
E From Alderley Edge
F From Morecambe to Leeds
G To Edinburgh

The Sunday service between Manchester Victoria and Wigan Wallgate via Atherton is funded by GMITA and will operate whilst funding exists

Table 82

Sundays
from 9 October

Manchester - Bolton - Wigan, Kirkby, Southport, Preston, Blackpool North and Barrow-in-Furness

	TP ◇1 A ⊼	TP ◇1 B ⊼	NT	TP ◇1 C	TP ◇1	NT	NT	TP ◇1	NT	NT	NT D	TP ◇1 E ⊼	TP ◇1 F ⊼	TP ◇1 C	NT	NT G	TP ◇1	NT	TP ◇1 H	TP ◇1 I	NT
Manchester Airport 85 ✈ d	12 58	13 00		13 03				13 30				13 58	14 00	14 03			14 30		14 58	15 00	
Heald Green 85 d																					
Buxton 86 d																					
Hazel Grove 86 d																					
Stockport 84 d							13 22									14 21					
Manchester Piccadilly 10 ⇌ d	13 16	13 16		13 21			13 35	13 46				14 16	14 16	14 21		14 35	14 46		15 16	15 16	
Manchester Oxford Road d	13 19	13 19					13 38	13 49				14 19	14 19			14 38	14 49		15 19	15 19	
Deansgate ⇌ d							13 40	13 51								14 40	14 51				
Rochdale 41 d																					
Manchester Victoria ⇌ d			13 12			13 25			14 00	14 12					14 25			15 00			15 12
Salford Central d																					
Salford Crescent a			13 16	13 26		13 29	13 44	13 54	14 06	14 16				14 26	14 29	14 44	14 54	15 06			15 16
d			13 17			13 30	13 44	13 55	14 08	14 17					14 30	14 44	14 55	15 08			15 17
Swinton d			13 23							14 23											15 23
Moorside d			13 26							14 26											15 26
Walkden d			13 29							14 29											15 29
Atherton d			13 35							14 35											15 35
Hag Fold d			13 37							14 37											15 37
Daisy Hill d			13 40							14 40											15 40
Kearsley d																					
Farnworth d																					
Moses Gate d																					
Bolton a	13 32	13 32				13 40	13 54	14 05	14 20			14 32	14 32		14 40	14 54	15 05	15 20	15 32	15 32	
d	13 33	13 33				13 40	13 55	14 05				14 33	14 33		14 40	14 55	15 05		15 33	15 33	
Westhoughton d							14 02									15 02					
Hindley d			13 45				14 06			14 45						15 06					15 45
Ince d			13 48							14 48											15 48
Wigan North Western a																					
Wigan Wallgate a			13 57				14 11			14 57						15 11					15 57
d							14 13									15 13					
Pemberton d																					
Orrell d																					
Upholland d																					
Rainford d																					
Kirkby a																					
Gathurst d							14 17									15 17					
Appley Bridge d							14 21									15 21					
Parbold d							14 25									15 25					
Hoscar d																					
Burscough Bridge d							14 29									15 29					
New Lane d																					
Bescar Lane d																					
Meols Cop d							14 37									15 37					
Southport a							14 48									15 46					
Lostock d						13 45									14 45						
Horwich Parkway d						13 49		14 12							14 49		15 12				
Blackrod d						13 52									14 52						
Adlington (Lancashire) d						13 56									14 56						
Chorley d	13 44	13 44				14 01		14 20				14 44	14 44		15 01		15 20		15 44	15 44	
Leyland d						14 12									15 12						
Preston 8 65,97 a	13 57	13 57				14 18		14 32				14 57	14 57		15 18		15 32		15 57	15 57	
d	14 00	14 00			14 04	14 20		14 34				15 00	15 00		15 20		15 34		16 00	16 00	
Kirkham & Wesham 97 a						14 29									15 29						
Poulton-le-Fylde 97 a						14 37		14 51							15 37		15 51				
Layton 97 a						14 42									15 42						
Blackpool North 97 a						14 51		15 00							15 51		16 00				
Lancaster 6 65 a	14 15	14 15			14 20							15 15	15 15						16 15	16 15	
d	14 16	14 16			14 20						14 27	15 16	15 16						16 16	16 16	
Oxenholme Lake District 65 a	14 30	14 30										15 30	15 30								
Windermere 83 a																					
Carnforth d					14 29						14a59								16 24	16 24	
Silverdale d																			16 30	16 30	
Arnside d					14 37														16 34	16 34	
Grange-over-Sands d					14 43														16 40	16 40	
Kents Bank d																			16 43	16 43	
Cark d																			16 48	16 48	
Ulverston d					14 55														16 55	16 55	
Dalton d																			17 03	17 03	
Roose d																			17 09	17 09	
Barrow-in-Furness a					15 16														17 19	17 19	

A 9 October, 16 October, 23 October. To Glasgow Central
B from 30 October. To Glasgow Central
C 9 October, 16 October, 23 October. To Newcastle
D To Leeds
E 9 October, 16 October, 23 October. To Edinburgh
F from 30 October. To Edinburgh
G From Chester
H 9 October, 16 October, 23 October
I from 30 October

The Sunday service between Manchester Victoria and Wigan Wallgate via Atherton is funded by GMITA and will operate whilst funding exists

Table 82

Sundays
from 9 October

Manchester - Bolton - Wigan, Kirkby, Southport, Preston, Blackpool North and Barrow-in-Furness

	TP ◇1 A	NT	NT	TP ◇1	NT	NT	NT	TP ◇1 B ⊼	TP ◇1 C ⊼	TP ◇1 A	NT	NT D	TP ◇1	NT	NT	NT E	TP ◇1	TP ◇1 F ⊼		TP ◇1 G ⊼	TP ◇1 A	NT
Manchester Airport 85 ✈ d	15 03			15 30				15 58	16 00	16 03			16 30					16 58		17 00	17 03	
Heald Green 85 d																						
Buxton 86 d																						
Hazel Grove 86 d																						
Stockport 84 d			15 22									16 21										
Manchester Piccadilly 10 ⇌ d	15 21		15 35	15 46				16 16	16 16	16 21		16 35	16 46					17 16		17 16	17 21	
Manchester Oxford Road d			15 38	15 49				16 19	16 19			16 38	16 49					17 19		17 19		
Deansgate ⇌ d			15 40	15 51								16 40	16 51									
Rochdale 41 d																						
Manchester Victoria ⇌ d		15 25			16 00	16 12					16 25			17 00	17 12							17 25
Salford Central d																						
Salford Crescent a	15 26	15 29	15 44	15 54	16 06	16 16				16 26	16 29	16 44	16 54	17 06	17 16						17 26	17 29
d		15 30	15 44	15 55	16 08	16 17					16 30	16 44	16 55	17 08	17 17							17 30
Swinton d						16 23									17 23							
Moorside d						16 26									17 26							
Walkden d						16 29									17 29							
Atherton d						16 35									17 35							
Hag Fold d						16 37									17 37							
Daisy Hill d						16 40									17 40							
Kearsley d																						
Farnworth d																						
Moses Gate d																						
Bolton a		15 40	15 54	16 05	16 20			16 32	16 32		16 40	16 54	17 05	17 20				17 32		17 32		17 40
d		15 40	15 55	16 05				16 33	16 33		16 40	16 55	17 05					17 33		17 33		17 40
Westhoughton d			16 02									17 02										
Hindley d			16 06			16 45						17 06			17 45							
Ince d						16 48									17 48							
Wigan North Western a																						
Wigan Wallgate a			16 11			16 57						17 11			17 57							
d			16 13									17 13										
Pemberton d																						
Orrell d																						
Upholland d																						
Rainford d																						
Kirkby a																						
Gathurst d			16 17									17 17										
Appley Bridge d			16 21									17 21										
Parbold d			16 25									17 25										
Hoscar d																						
Burscough Bridge d			16 29									17 29										
New Lane d																						
Bescar Lane d																						
Meols Cop d			16 37									17 37										
Southport a			16 48									17 46										
Lostock d		15 45									16 45											17 45
Horwich Parkway d		15 49		16 12							16 49		17 12									17 49
Blackrod d		15 52									16 52											17 52
Adlington (Lancashire) d		15 56									16 56											17 56
Chorley d		16 01		16 20				16 44	16 44		17 01		17 20					17 44		17 44		18 01
Leyland d		16 12									17 12											18 12
Preston 8 65,97 a		16 18		16 32				16 57	16 57		17 18		17 32					17 57		17 57		18 18
d		16 20		16 34				17 00	17 00		17 20		17 34				18 06	18 06	18 08	18 08		18 20
Kirkham & Wesham 97 a		16 29									17 29											18 29
Poulton-le-Fylde 97 a		16 37		16 51							17 37		17 51									18 37
Layton 97 a		16 42									17 42											18 42
Blackpool North 97 a		16 51		17 00							17 51		18 00									18 51
Lancaster 6 65 a								17 15	17 15								18 22	18 22	18 23	18 23		
d							17 04	17 16	17 16							18 04	18 22	18 22	18 24	18 24		
Oxenholme Lake District 65 a								17 30	17 30										18 38	18 38		
Windermere 83 a																						
Carnforth d							17 14									18a13	18 31	18 31				
Silverdale d							17 20										18 37	18 37				
Arnside d							17 25										18 41	18 41				
Grange-over-Sands d							17 31										18 46	18 46				
Kents Bank d							17 34										18 50	18 50				
Cark d							17 38										18 54	18 54				
Ulverston d							17 46										19 02	19 02				
Dalton d							17 55										19 10	19 10				
Roose d							18 01										19 16	19 16				
Barrow-in-Furness a							18 08										19 26	19 26				

A 9 October, 16 October, 23 October. To Newcastle
B 9 October, 16 October, 23 October. To Edinburgh
C from 30 October. To Edinburgh
D From Chester
E From Morecambe to Leeds
F 9 October, 16 October, 23 October. ⊼ to Preston
G from 30 October. To Glasgow Central

The Sunday service between Manchester Victoria and Wigan Wallgate via Atherton is funded by GMITA and will operate whilst funding exists

Table 82

Sundays from 9 October

Manchester - Bolton - Wigan, Kirkby, Southport, Preston, Blackpool North and Barrow-in-Furness

	NT	TP	NT	TP	TP	NT	TP	NT	NT	TP	NT	TP	TP	TP	NT	NT	TP	NT	TP	NT	NT
		◇1		◇1	◇1		◇1			◇1		◇1	◇1	◇1			◇1		◇1		
				A	B		C		D			E	F	G					H	I	
Manchester Airport 85 ✈ d		17 30		17 58	18 00		18 03			18 30		18 58	19 00	19 03			19 30		20 03		
Heald Green 85 d																					
Buxton 86 d																					
Hazel Grove 86 d																					
Stockport 84 d	17 22								18 21							19 22					
Manchester Piccadilly 10 ⇌ d	17 35	17 46		18 16	18 16		18 21		18 35	18 46		19 16	19 16	19 21		19 35	19 46		20 21		
Manchester Oxford Road d	17 38	17 49		18 19	18 19				18 38	18 49		19 19	19 19			19 38	19 49				
Deansgate ⇌ d	17 40	17 51							18 40	18 51						19 40	19 51				
Rochdale 41 d																					
Manchester Victoria ⇌ d			18 00			18 12		18 25			19 00				19 25			20 00			20 25
Salford Central d																					
Salford Crescent a	17 44	17 54	18 06			18 16	18 26	18 29	18 44	18 54	19 06			19 26	19 29	19 44	19 54	20 06	20 26		20 29
d	17 44	17 55	18 08			18 17		18 30	18 44	18 55	19 08				19 30	19 44	19 55	20 08			20 30
Swinton d						18 23															
Moorside d						18 26															
Walkden d						18 29															
Atherton d						18 35															
Hag Fold d						18 37															
Daisy Hill d						18 40															
Kearsley d																					
Farnworth d																					
Moses Gate d																					
Bolton a	17 54	18 05	18 20	18 32	18 32			18 40	18 54	19 05	19 20	19 32	19 32		19 40	19 54	20 05	20 20			20 40
d	17 55	18 05		18 33	18 33			18 40	18 55	19 05		19 33	19 33		19 40	19 55	20 05				20 40
Westhoughton d	18 02								19 02							20 02					
Hindley d	18 06					18 45			19 06							20 06					
Ince d						18 48															
Wigan North Western a																					
Wigan Wallgate a	18 11					18 57			19 11							20 11					
d	18 13								19 13							20 13					
Pemberton d																					
Orrell d																					
Upholland d																					
Rainford d																					
Kirkby a																					
Gathurst d	18 17								19 17							20 17					
Appley Bridge d	18 21								19 21							20 21					
Parbold d	18 25								19 25							20 25					
Hoscar d																					
Burscough Bridge d	18 29								19 29							20 29					
New Lane d																					
Bescar Lane d																					
Meols Cop d	18 37								19 37							20 37					
Southport a	18 48								19 46							20 48					
Lostock d								18 45							19 45						20 45
Horwich Parkway d		18 12						18 49		19 12					19 49		20 12				20 49
Blackrod d								18 52							19 52						20 52
Adlington (Lancashire) d								18 56							19 56						20 56
Chorley d		18 20		18 44	18 44			19 01		19 20		19 44	19 44		20 01		20 20				21 01
Leyland d								19 12							20 12						21 12
Preston 8 65,97 a		18 32		18 57	18 57			19 18		19 32		19 57	19 57		20 18		20 32				21 18
d		18 34		19 00	19 00			19 20		19 34		20 00	20 00		20 20		20 34				21 20
Kirkham & Wesham 97 a								19 29							20 29						21 29
Poulton-le-Fylde 97 a		18 51						19 37		19 51					20 37		20 51				21 37
Layton 97 a								19 42							20 42						21 42
Blackpool North 97 a		19 00						19 51		20 00					20 51		21 00				21 51
Lancaster 6 65 a				19 15	19 15							20 15	20 15								
d				19 16	19 16							20 16	20 16							20 20	
Oxenholme Lake District 65 a				19 30	19 30																
Windermere 83 a																					
Carnforth d												20 24	20 24							20a29	
Silverdale d												20 30	20 30								
Arnside d												20 34	20 34								
Grange-over-Sands d												20 40	20 40								
Kents Bank d												20 43	20 43								
Cark d												20 48	20 48								
Ulverston d												20 56	20 56								
Dalton d												21 04	21 04								
Roose d												21 10	21 10								
Barrow-in-Furness a												21 20	21 20								

A 9 October, 16 October, 23 October. To Edinburgh
B from 30 October. To Edinburgh
C 9 October, 16 October, 23 October. To Middlesbrough
D From Chester
E 9 October, 16 October, 23 October
F from 30 October
G 9 October, 16 October, 23 October. To Newcastle
H 9 October, 16 October, 23 October. To Scarborough
I From Morecambe to Leeds

The Sunday service between Manchester Victoria and Wigan Wallgate via Atherton is funded by GMITA and will operate whilst funding exists

Table 82

Sundays from 9 October

Manchester - Bolton - Wigan, Kirkby, Southport, Preston, Blackpool North and Barrow-in-Furness

	NT	TP	NT	TP	TP	NT	NT	TP	NT	TP	NT	NT	TP	TP
		◇1		◇1	◇1			◇1		◇1			◇1	◇1
	A			B	C				D	E		A		B
Manchester Airport 85 ✈ d		20 30		21 03				21 30		22 03			22 30	23 25
Heald Green 85 d														
Buxton 86 d														
Hazel Grove 86 d														
Stockport 84 d	20 21						21 22					22 21		
Manchester Piccadilly 10 ⇌ d	20 35	20 46		21 21			21 35	21 46		22 18		22 35	22 46	23 40
Manchester Oxford Road d	20 38	20 49					21 38	21 49				22 38	22 49	
Deansgate ⇌ d	20 40	20 51					21 40	21 51				22 40	22 51	
Rochdale 41 d														
Manchester Victoria ⇌ d			21 00			21 25			22 00					
Salford Central d														
Salford Crescent a	20 44	20 54	21 06	21 26		21 29	21 44	21 54	22 06	22 23		22 44	22 54	23 45
d	20 44	20 55	21 08			21 30	21 44	21 55	22 08			22 44	22 55	
Swinton d														
Moorside d														
Walkden d														
Atherton d														
Hag Fold d														
Daisy Hill d														
Kearsley d														
Farnworth d														
Moses Gate d														
Bolton a	20 54	21 05	21 20			21 40	21 54	22 05	22 19			22 54	23 05	
d	20 55	21 05				21 40	21 55	22 05				22 55	23 05	
Westhoughton d	21 02						22 02					23 02		
Hindley d	21 06						22 06					23 06		
Ince d														
Wigan North Western a														
Wigan Wallgate a	21 11						22 15					23 15		
d	21 13													
Pemberton d														
Orrell d														
Upholland d														
Rainford d														
Kirkby a														
Gathurst d	21 17													
Appley Bridge d	21 21													
Parbold d	21 25													
Hoscar d														
Burscough Bridge d	21 29													
New Lane d														
Bescar Lane d														
Meols Cop d	21 37													
Southport a	21 46													
Lostock d						21 45							23 10	
Horwich Parkway d		21 12				21 49							23 14	
Blackrod d						21 52							23 17	
Adlington (Lancashire) d						21 56							23 20	
Chorley d		21 20				22 01		22 17					23 24	
Leyland d						22 12							23 34	
Preston 8 65,97 a		21 32				22 18		22 28					23 42	
d		21 34				22 20		22 29					23 47	
Kirkham & Wesham 97 a						22 29							23 56	
Poulton-le-Fylde 97 a		21 51				22 37		22 46					00 05	
Layton 97 a						22 42								
Blackpool North 97 a		22 00				22 51		22 55					00 14	
Lancaster 6 65 a														
d					21 23						22 05			
Oxenholme Lake District 65 a														
Windermere 83 a														
Carnforth d					21 31						22 15			
Silverdale d					21 37						22 21			
Arnside d					21 41						22 26			
Grange-over-Sands d					21 47						22 32			
Kents Bank d					21 50						22 35			
Cark d					21 55						22 39			
Ulverston d					22 02						22 47			
Dalton d					22 10						22 56			
Roose d					22 16						23 02			
Barrow-in-Furness a					22 26						23 09			

A From Chester
B 9 October, 16 October, 23 October. To York
C From Windermere
D To Blackburn
E 9 October, 16 October, 23 October. To Manchester Victoria

The Sunday service between Manchester Victoria and Wigan Wallgate via Atherton is funded by GMITA and will operate whilst funding exists

Barrow-in-Furness, Blackpool North, Preston, Southport, Kirkby and Wigan - Bolton - Manchester

Miles	Miles	Miles	Miles	Miles			TP	TP	NT	TP	TP	TP	TP	TP	NT	NT	TP	NT	TP	NT	NT	NT	NT	TP
							MX	MO	MX	MO	MX													
							◇1	◇1		◇1	◇1	◇1	◇1	◇1			◇1		◇1					◇1
										A	B	C		C	D							E	F	G
																			🍴					🍴
—	0	—	—	—	**Barrow-in-Furness**	d										05 12						06 56		
—	1¾	—	—	—	Roose	d																07 00		
—	6	—	—	—	Dalton	d																07 06		
—	9¼	—	—	—	Ulverston	d										05 28						07 15		
—	15¼	—	—	—	Cark	d																07 22		
—	17¼	—	—	—	Kents Bank	d																07 28		
—	19½	—	—	—	Grange-over-Sands	d										05a42						07a33		
—	22¾	—	—	—	Arnside	d																		
—	25	—	—	—	Silverdale	d																		
—	28¾	—	—	—	Carnforth	d																		06 15
—	—	—	—	—	Windermere	83 d																		
—	—	—	—	—	Oxenholme Lake District	65 d																		
—	34¾	—	—	—	**Lancaster** 6	65 a																		06 23
—	—	—	—	—		d																		06 23
0	—	—	—	—	**Blackpool North**	97 d	22p44	23p03	23p13				03 36		04 56				05 39					
1¼	—	—	—	—	Layton	97 d			23p16															
3¼	—	—	—	—	Poulton-le-Fylde	97 d	22p50	23p09	23p21						05 02				05 45					
9¼	—	—	—	—	Kirkham & Wesham	97 d		23p17	23p30															
—	55¾	—	—	—	**Preston** 8	65,97 a	23p08	23p28	23p40						05 20				06 03					06 42
—	—	—	—	—		d	23p10	23p28	23p42				04u01				05 16		06 05					06 44
21½	59¾	—	—	—	Leyland	d		23p34	23p48										06 10					
26	64¼	—	—	—	Chorley	d	23p21	23p41	23p55								05 26		06 16					06 53
29	67¼	—	—	—	Adlington (Lancashire)	d		23p45	00 01															
31	69¼	—	—	—	Blackrod	d		23p49	00 04										06 22					
32½	70¾	—	—	—	Horwich Parkway	d	23p28	23p52	00 08								05 33		06 26					07 00
34½	72¾	—	—	—	Lostock	d		23p56	00 13										06 30					
—	—	0	—	—	**Southport**	d																		
—	—	1¼	—	—	Meols Cop	d																		
—	—	4½	—	—	Bescar Lane	d																		
—	—	6½	—	—	New Lane	d																		
—	—	7¾	—	—	Burscough Bridge	d																		
—	—	9¼	—	—	Hoscar	d																		
—	—	10¾	—	—	Parbold	d																		
—	—	13	—	—	Appley Bridge	d																		
—	—	14¾	—	—	Gathurst	d																		
—	—	—	0	—	**Kirkby**	d																		
—	—	—	5¼	—	Rainford	d																		
—	—	—	7¼	—	Upholland	d																		
—	—	—	8½	—	Orrell	d																		
—	—	—	10½	—	Pemberton	d																		
—	—	17½	12¼	—	**Wigan Wallgate**	a																		
—	—	—	—	—		d												06 03		06 31	06 36			
—	—	—	—	0	Wigan North Western	d																		
—	—	18½	13¼	0¾	Ince	d												06 06			06 39			
—	—	20	14¾	—	Hindley	d												06 09		06 36	06 42			
—	—	22½	—	—	Westhoughton	d														06 41				
37½	75¾	27	—	—	**Bolton**	a	23p34	00 02	00 18								05 42		06 34	06 52				07 08
—	—	—	—	—		d	23p35	00 02	00 19				04u30				05 43		06 35	06 53			06 56	07 08
38¼	76½	27¾	—	—	Moses Gate	d																	06 59	
39¾	78	29¼	—	—	Farnworth	d																	07 01	
40½	78¾	30	—	—	Kearsley	d																	07 03	
—	—	—	17¼	—	Daisy Hill	d												06 13			06 46			
—	—	—	17½	—	Hag Fold	d												06 16			06 49			
—	—	—	18¾	—	Atherton	d												06 19			06 52			
—	—	—	22¼	—	Walkden	d												06 24			06 58			
—	—	—	24	—	Moorside	d												06 28			07 01			
—	—	—	24¾	—	Swinton	d												06 30			07 04			
46½	84¾	36	28¾	—	**Salford Crescent**	a	23p47										05 55	06 38	06 47	07 05	07 11		07 15	
—	—	—	—	—		d	23p47			00 37	00 49	03 40		04 53			05 55	06 38	06 47	07 08	07 11		07 15	
—	—	—	29¾	—	Salford Central	d												06 41			07 14		07 19	
—	—	—	30½	—	**Manchester Victoria**	⇌ a			00 36									06 46			07 20		07 26	
—	—	—	—	—	Rochdale	41 a																		
48	86¼	37½	—	—	Deansgate	⇌ a													06 51	07 11				
48¼	86½	37¾	—	—	**Manchester Oxford Road**	a													06 52	07 13				07 23
48¾	87	38¼	—	—	**Manchester Piccadilly** 10	⇌ a	23p53	00 18		00 43	00 53	03 44	04 48	04 58			06 01		06 56	07 17				07 27
—	—	—	—	—	Stockport	84 a														07 34				
—	—	—	—	—	Hazel Grove	86 a														07 45				
—	—	—	—	—	Buxton	86 a																		
57	95¼	46½	—	—	Heald Green	85 a	00 15												07 10					
58½	96¾	48	—	—	**Manchester Airport**	85 ✈ a	00 22	00 32		01 00	01 10	04 00	05 07	05 19			06 18		07 17					07 47

A From Middlesbrough
B From Newcastle
C From York
D To Colne
E From Millom
F From Blackburn
G 🍴 from Preston

The Sunday service between Manchester Victoria and Wigan Wallgate via Atherton is funded by GMITA and will operate whilst funding exists

Barrow-in-Furness, Blackpool North, Preston, Southport, Kirkby and Wigan - Bolton - Manchester

		NT	NT	NT	NT	TP	NT	NT	NT	NT	NT	NT	NT	NT	TP	TP	NT	NT	NT	NT	TP	TP
						◇1									◇1	◇1					◇1	◇1
				A	B		C				D		E	B		F				B		G
						🍴									🍴	🍴					🍴	🍴
Barrow-in-Furness	d												07 52									
Roose	d												07 56									
Dalton	d												08 02									
Ulverston	d												08 11									
Cark	d												08 19									
Kents Bank	d												08 24									
Grange-over-Sands	d												08a30									
Arnside	d																					
Silverdale	d																					
Carnforth	d			06 43												07 12						
Windermere	83 d																					
Oxenholme Lake District	65 d																					
Lancaster 6	65 a			06 52												07 21						
	d															07 22						07 47
Blackpool North	97 d		06 19			06 40				06 53	07 02				07 10				07 18		07 36	
Layton	97 d		06 22			06 43									07 13				07 21		07 39	
Poulton-le-Fylde	97 d		06 27			06 47					07 08				07 17				07 26		07 43	
Kirkham & Wesham	97 d		06 36			06 56									07 26				07 35		07 52	
Preston 8	65,97 a		06 46			07 07				07 15	07 28				07 37	07 41			07 46		08 03	08 07
	d		06 48			07 09				07 17	07 30				07 47				07 47		08 12	
Leyland	d		06 53							07 22	07 35								07 53			
Chorley	d		07 01			07 18				07 31					07 56				08 01		08 22	
Adlington (Lancashire)	d		07 06							07 36									08 06			
Blackrod	d		07 10							07 40									08 10			
Horwich Parkway	d		07 14			07 26				07 44									08 14			
Lostock	d		07 20			07 30				07 49									08 20			
Southport	d	06 23						06 53									07 21					
Meols Cop	d	06 28						06 58									07 26					
Bescar Lane	d							07 03														
New Lane	d							07 07														
Burscough Bridge	d	06 36						07 09									07 34					
Hoscar	d							07 13														
Parbold	d	06 41						07 16									07 39					
Appley Bridge	d	06 45						07 20									07 43					
Gathurst	d	06 49						07 23									07 47					
Kirkby	d											07 11										
Rainford	d											07 19										
Upholland	d											07 23										
Orrell	d											07 27										
Pemberton	d											07 30										
Wigan Wallgate	a	06 54						07 29				07 35					07 51					
	d	06 55					07 15	07 29				07 37					07 53	08 00				
Wigan North Western	d								07 22		07a50											
Ince	d						07 18		07 25			07 40										
Hindley	d						07 21		07 29			07 43					07 58					
Westhoughton	d	07 03							07 33								08 03					
Bolton	a	07 11	07 25			07 34			07 42	07 54					08 08		08 11		08 25		08 34	
	d	07 12	07 25		07 30	07 35			07 43	07 55				07 59	08 08		08 12		08 25	08 31	08 35	
Moses Gate	d								07 46					08 02								
Farnworth	d								07 48					08 04								
Kearsley	d								07 50					08 06								
Daisy Hill	d						07 26	07 39				07 47						08 07				
Hag Fold	d						07 29					07 50										
Atherton	d						07 32	07 43				07 53						08 12				
Walkden	d						07 38					07 59						08 18				
Moorside	d						07 41					08 03										
Swinton	d						07 44					08 06										
Salford Crescent	a	07 24	07 38		07 43	07 47	07 51	07 59	08 02	08 07		08 13		08 17			08 24	08 29	08 38	08 43	08 47	
	d	07 25	07 38		07 43	07 47	07 51	07 59	08 02	08 08		08 13		08 17			08 25	08 30	08 38	08 44	08 47	
Salford Central	d		07 41		07 46		07 55	08 02	08 05			08 16		08 20				08 32	08 41	08 46		
Manchester Victoria	⇌ a		07 47		07 53		08 00	08 08	08 12			08 20		08 25				08 38	08 48	08 52		
Rochdale	41 a											08 51										
Deansgate	⇌ a	07 28				07 51				08 11							08 28					
Manchester Oxford Road	a	07 30				07 52				08 14					08 23		08 31				08 52	
Manchester Piccadilly 10	⇌ a	07 34				07 56				08 18					08 27		08 35				08 56	
Stockport	84 a									08 34												
Hazel Grove	86 a									08 48												
Buxton	86 a																					
Heald Green	85 a					08 10											08 47				09 10	
Manchester Airport	85 ✈ a	07 53				08 17									08 47		08 53				09 19	

A From Skipton
B From Clitheroe
C To Stalybridge
D To Liverpool Lime Street
E From Maryport
F 🍴 from Preston
G From Edinburgh

The Sunday service between Manchester Victoria and Wigan Wallgate via Atherton is funded by GMITA and will operate whilst funding exists

Table 82

Mondays to Fridays
until 15 July

Barrow-in-Furness, Blackpool North, Preston, Southport, Kirkby and Wigan - Bolton - Manchester

			NT	NT	NT	NT	NT	TP		NT	NT	NT	TP	NT	NT	NT	TP	NT		NT	NT	NT	NT	TP	NT	NT
								◇1									◇1							◇1		
							A	B						C		D						A		E		
								trolley									trolley							trolley		
Barrow-in-Furness		d													09 20											
Roose		d													09 24											
Dalton		d													09 30											
Ulverston		d													09 39											
Cark		d													09 46											
Kents Bank		d													09 51											
Grange-over-Sands		d													09a57											
Arnside		d						08 03					08 55													
Silverdale		d						08 07					08 59													
Carnforth		d						08 16					09 08													
Windermere	83	d																								
Oxenholme Lake District	65	d																						09 11		
Lancaster 6	65	a						08 24					09 19											09 26		
		d						08 27																09 26		
Blackpool North	97	d										08 20					08 44									
Layton	97	d										08 23														
Poulton-le-Fylde	97	d										08 28					08 50									
Kirkham & Wesham	97	d										08 37														
Preston 8	65,97	a						08 45				08 47					09 08							09 45		
		d				08 17		08 47				08 49		09 04			09 10				09 23			09 47		
Leyland		d				08 23						08 54		09 09							09 29					
Chorley		d				08 33		08 56				09 02					09 21				09 36			09 56		
Adlington (Lancashire)		d				08 37						09 07														
Blackrod		d				08 41						09 10														
Horwich Parkway		d				08 45						09 14					09 28				09 45					
Lostock		d				08 50						09 20									09 50					
Southport		d			07 58					08 25										09 02					09 24	
Meols Cop		d			08 03					08 30										09 07						
Bescar Lane		d																								
New Lane		d																								
Burscough Bridge		d			08 11					08 38										09 15					09 36	
Hoscar		d																								
Parbold		d			08 16					08 43										09 20					09 41	
Appley Bridge		d			08 20					08 47										09 24					09 45	
Gathurst		d			08 23					08 50										09 27						
Kirkby		d									08 21															09 32
Rainford		d									08 29															09 40
Upholland		d									08 33															09 44
Orrell		d									08 36															09 47
Pemberton		d									08 39															09 50
Wigan Wallgate		a			08 28					08 55	08 45									09 32					09 51	09 56
		d	08 13		08 29					08 56	08 50							09 20		09 32			09 48		09 53	09 58
Wigan North Western		d		08 20										09a24												
Ince		d	08 16								08 53															10 01
Hindley		d	08 19	08 25	08 34						08 57							09 25		09 37					09 58	10 04
Westhoughton		d		08 29						09 04								09 29							10 02	
Bolton		a		08 38		08 55		09 08		09 12		09 25					09 34	09 38			09 55		10 02	10 08	10 12	
		d		08 39		08 56	09 02	09 08		09 13		09 25				09 31	09 35	09 39			09 56	10 00	10 03	10 08	10 13	
Moses Gate		d		08 42														09 42								
Farnworth		d		08 44														09 44								
Kearsley		d		08 46														09 46								
Daisy Hill		d	08 23		08 39						09 01									09 41						10 09
Hag Fold		d	08 26								09 04															10 12
Atherton		d	08 29		08 43						09 06									09 45						10 15
Walkden		d	08 35		08 49						09 12									09 50						10 20
Moorside		d	08 39								09 15															10 24
Swinton		d	08 42		08 54						09 18									09 55						10 26
Salford Crescent		a	08 50	08 56	09 02	09 08	09 15			09 25	09 27	09 38				09 43	09 47	09 56		10 03	10 08	10 13	10 15		10 25	10 34
		d	08 50	08 56	09 02	09 09	09 16			09 26	09 27	09 38				09 44	09 47	09 56		10 03	10 09	10 13	10 15		10 26	10 34
Salford Central		d	08 53	08 59	09 04		09 18				09 31	09 41				09 46		09 59		10 05		10 16	10 17			10 36
Manchester Victoria	⇌	a	08 59	09 06	09 11		09 26				09 38	09 47				09 52		10 06		10 12		10 21	10 25			10 43
Rochdale	41	a																					10 51			
Deansgate	⇌	a				09 12				09 29							09 51				10 12				10 29	
Manchester Oxford Road		a				09 14		09 23		09 31							09 52				10 14			10 23	10 31	
Manchester Piccadilly 10	⇌	a				09 18		09 27		09 35							09 56				10 18			10 27	10 35	
Stockport	84	a				09 34															10 34					
Hazel Grove	86	a				09 45															10 45					
Buxton	86	a																								
Heald Green	85	a															10 10									
Manchester Airport	85 ✈	a						09 47		09 53							10 17							10 47	10 53	

A From Blackburn
B trolley from Preston
C To L'pool Sth Pw Hl (Allertn)
D From Clitheroe
E From Glasgow Central

The Sunday service between Manchester Victoria and Wigan Wallgate via Atherton is funded by GMITA and will operate whilst funding exists

Table 82

Mondays to Fridays
until 15 July

Barrow-in-Furness, Blackpool North, Preston, Southport, Kirkby and Wigan - Bolton - Manchester

			NT	NT		NT	NT	NT	TP	TP	NT	NT	NT	NT	TP	NT	NT	NT	NT	NT	NT	TP	NT	NT		NT
									◇1	◇1					◇1							◇1				
				A		B	C	D		E					F				A		D					
									trolley	trolley					trolley							trolley				
Barrow-in-Furness		d					10 09													10 55						
Roose		d					10 13													10 59						
Dalton		d					10 19													11 05						
Ulverston		d					10 28													11 13						
Cark		d					10 35													11 21						
Kents Bank		d					10 40													11 25						
Grange-over-Sands		d					10a45													11a31						
Arnside		d													10 03											
Silverdale		d													10 07											
Carnforth		d				10 02									10 15											
Windermere	83	d																								
Oxenholme Lake District	65	d																								
Lancaster 6	65	a				10 12									10 24											
		d													10 26											
Blackpool North	97	d	09 20	09 37					09 43									10 20	10 37			10 44				
Layton	97	d	09 23															10 23								
Poulton-le-Fylde	97	d	09 28						09 49									10 28				10 50				
Kirkham & Wesham	97	d	09 37	09 52														10 37	10 52							
Preston 8	65,97	a	09 47	10 02					10 07					10 21	10 45			10 47	11 02			11 08				
		d	09 49	10 04						10 12				10 23	10 47			10 49	11 04			11 10				11 23
Leyland		d	09 54	10 09										10 29				10 54	11 09							11 29
Chorley		d	10 02							10 22				10 36	10 56			11 02				11 21				11 36
Adlington (Lancashire)		d	10 07															11 07								
Blackrod		d	10 10															11 10								
Horwich Parkway		d	10 14											10 45				11 14				11 28				11 45
Lostock		d	10 20											10 50				11 20								11 50
Southport		d										09 55				10 24								10 55		
Meols Cop		d										10 00												11 00		
Bescar Lane		d										10 05												11 05		
New Lane		d										10 09												11 09		
Burscough Bridge		d										10 11				10 36								11 11		
Hoscar		d										10 15												11 15		
Parbold		d										10 18				10 41								11 18		
Appley Bridge		d										10 22				10 45								11 22		
Gathurst		d										10 25												11 25		
Kirkby		d															10 32									
Rainford		d															10 40									
Upholland		d															10 44									
Orrell		d															10 47									
Pemberton		d															10 50									
Wigan Wallgate		a										10 30				10 51	10 56							11 30		
		d									10 20	10 32	10 48			10 53	10 58						11 20	11 32		
Wigan North Western		d		10a24															11a24							
Ince		d															11 01									
Hindley		d									10 25	10 37				10 58	11 04						11 25	11 37		
Westhoughton		d									10 29					11 02							11 29			
Bolton		a	10 25							10 35	10 38		11 02	10 55	11 08	11 12		11 25				11 34	11 38			11 55
		d	10 25					10 31		10 35	10 39		11 03	10 56	11 08	11 13		11 25			11 31	11 35	11 39			11 56
Moses Gate		d									10 42												11 42			
Farnworth		d									10 44												11 44			
Kearsley		d									10 46												11 46			
Daisy Hill		d										10 41					11 09							11 41		
Hag Fold		d															11 12									
Atherton		d										10 45					11 15							11 45		
Walkden		d										10 50					11 20							11 50		
Moorside		d															11 24									
Swinton		d										10 55					11 26							11 55		
Salford Crescent		a	10 38					10 43		10 47	10 56	11 02	11 15	11 08		11 25	11 34	11 38			11 43	11 47	11 56	12 02		12 08
		d	10 38					10 44		10 47	10 56	11 03	11 15	11 09		11 26	11 34	11 38			11 44	11 47	11 56	12 03		12 09
Salford Central		d	10 41					10 46			10 59	11 05	11 17				11 36	11 41			11 46		11 59	12 05		
Manchester Victoria	⇌	a	10 47					10 52			11 06	11 11	11 25				11 43	11 47			11 52		12 06	12 11		
Rochdale	41	a											11 51													
Deansgate	⇌	a								10 51						11 29						11 51				12 12
Manchester Oxford Road		a								10 52					11 23	11 31						11 52				12 14
Manchester Piccadilly 10	⇌	a								10 56					11 27	11 35						11 56				12 18
Stockport	84	a																								12 34
Hazel Grove	86	a																								12 45
Buxton	86	a																								
Heald Green	85	a								11 10												12 10				
Manchester Airport	85 ✈	a								11 17					11 50	11 53						12 17				

A To L'pool Sth Pw Hl (Allertn)
B From Leeds to Morecambe
C From Sellafield
D From Clitheroe
E From Edinburgh
F trolley from Preston

The Sunday service between Manchester Victoria and Wigan Wallgate via Atherton is funded by GMITA and will operate whilst funding exists

Table 82

Mondays to Fridays
until 15 July

Barrow-in-Furness, Blackpool North, Preston, Southport, Kirkby and Wigan - Bolton - Manchester

			NT	TP	NT	NT	NT	NT	NT	NT	TP	NT	TP	NT	NT	NT	NT	TP	NT	NT	NT	NT	NT	NT
				◇1 A ⊼				B		C	◇1	D	◇1 ⊼					◇1 E ⊼				B	F	D
Barrow-in-Furness		d							11 53														13 14	
Roose		d							11 57															
Dalton		d							12 03														13 23	
Ulverston		d							12 12														13 31	
Cark		d							12 19															
Kents Bank		d							12 24															
Grange-over-Sands		d							12a31														13a46	
Arnside		d									11 58													
Silverdale		d																						
Carnforth		d								12 02	12 09													
Windermere	83	d		10 49																				
Oxenholme Lake District	65	d		11 09														12 10						
Lancaster 6	65	a		11 26						12 11	12 17							12 26						
		d		11 26							12 18							12 26						
Blackpool North	97	d					11 20	11 37					11 44								12 20	12 37		
Layton	97	d					11 23														12 23			
Poulton-le-Fylde	97	d					11 28						11 50								12 28			
Kirkham & Wesham	97	d					11 37	11 52													12 37	12 52		
Preston 8	65,97	a		11 45			11 47	12 02			12 37		12 08					12 45			12 47	13 02		
		d		11 47			11 49	12 04					12 10			12 23		12 47			12 49	13 04		
Leyland		d					11 54	12 09								12 29					12 54	13 09		
Chorley		d		11 56			12 02						12 21			12 36		12 56			13 02			
Adlington (Lancashire)		d					12 07														13 07			
Blackrod		d					12 10														13 10			
Horwich Parkway		d					12 14						12 28			12 45					13 14			
Lostock		d					12 20									12 50					13 20			
Southport		d			11 24										12 00				12 24					
Meols Cop		d													12 05									
Bescar Lane		d																						
New Lane		d																						
Burscough Bridge		d			11 36										12 13				12 36					
Hoscar		d																						
Parbold		d			11 41										12 18				12 41					
Appley Bridge		d			11 45										12 22				12 45					
Gathurst		d													12 25									
Kirkby		d				11 32														12 32				
Rainford		d				11 40														12 40				
Upholland		d				11 44														12 44				
Orrell		d				11 47														12 47				
Pemberton		d				11 50														12 50				
Wigan Wallgate		a			11 51	11 56									12 30				12 51	12 56				
		d	11 48		11 53	11 58								12 20	12 32		12 48		12 53	12 58				
Wigan North Western		d						12a24														13a24		
Ince		d				12 01														13 01				
Hindley		d			11 58	12 04								12 25	12 37				12 58	13 04				
Westhoughton		d			12 02									12 29					13 02					
Bolton		a	12 02	12 08	12 12		12 25						12 34	12 38		12 55	13 02	13 08	13 12		13 25			
		d	12 03	12 08	12 13		12 25					12 31	12 35	12 39		12 56	13 03	13 08	13 13		13 25			13 31
Moses Gate		d												12 42										
Farnworth		d												12 44										
Kearsley		d												12 46										
Daisy Hill		d				12 09									12 41					13 09				
Hag Fold		d				12 12														13 12				
Atherton		d				12 15									12 45					13 15				
Walkden		d				12 20									12 50					13 20				
Moorside		d				12 24														13 24				
Swinton		d				12 26									12 55					13 26				
Salford Crescent		a	12 15		12 25	12 34	12 38					12 43	12 47	12 56	13 02	13 08	13 15		13 25	13 34	13 38			13 43
		d	12 15		12 26	12 34	12 38					12 44	12 47	12 56	13 03	13 09	13 15		13 26	13 34	13 38			13 44
Salford Central		d	12 17			12 36	12 41					12 46		12 59	13 05		13 17			13 36	13 41			13 46
Manchester Victoria	⇌	a	12 25			12 43	12 47					12 52		13 06	13 11		13 25			13 43	13 47			13 52
Rochdale	41	a	12 51														13 51							
Deansgate	⇌	a			12 29								12 51			13 12			13 29					
Manchester Oxford Road		a		12 23	12 31								12 52			13 14		13 23	13 31					
Manchester Piccadilly 10	⇌	a		12 27	12 35								12 56			13 18		13 27	13 35					
Stockport	84	a														13 34								
Hazel Grove	86	a														13 45								
Buxton	86	a																						
Heald Green	85	a											13 10											
Manchester Airport	85 ✈	a		12 47	12 53								13 17					13 47	13 53					

A ⊼ from Preston
B To L'pool Sth Pw Hl (Allertn)
C From Leeds to Heysham Port
D From Clitheroe
E From Edinburgh
F From Carlisle

The Sunday service between Manchester Victoria and Wigan Wallgate via Atherton is funded by GMITA and will operate whilst funding exists

Table 82

Mondays to Fridays
until 15 July

Barrow-in-Furness, Blackpool North, Preston, Southport, Kirkby and Wigan - Bolton - Manchester

			TP	NT	NT	NT	NT	TP	NT	NT	NT	NT	NT	TP	NT	NT	NT	NT	NT	TP	NT	NT	NT	NT
			◇1 ⊼					◇1 A ⊼				B	C	◇1 ⊼						◇1 D ⊼				B
Barrow-in-Furness		d																14 43						
Roose		d																14 47						
Dalton		d																14 53						
Ulverston		d																15 02						
Cark		d																15 09						
Kents Bank		d																15 14						
Grange-over-Sands		d																15a20						
Arnside		d																						
Silverdale		d																						
Carnforth		d																						
Windermere	83	d						12 51																
Oxenholme Lake District	65	d						13 09												14 09				
Lancaster 6	65	a						13 26												14 26				
		d						13 26												14 26				
Blackpool North	97	d	12 44								13 20	13 37		13 44									14 20	14 37
Layton	97	d									13 23												14 23	
Poulton-le-Fylde	97	d	12 50								13 28			13 50									14 28	
Kirkham & Wesham	97	d									13 37	13 52											14 37	14 52
Preston 8	65,97	a	13 08					13 45			13 47	14 02		14 08						14 45			14 47	15 02
		d	13 10			13 23		13 47			13 49	14 04		14 10			14 23			14 47			14 49	15 04
Leyland		d				13 29					13 54	14 09					14 29						14 54	15 09
Chorley		d	13 21			13 36		13 56			14 02			14 21			14 36			14 56			15 02	
Adlington (Lancashire)		d									14 07												15 07	
Blackrod		d									14 10												15 10	
Horwich Parkway		d	13 28			13 45					14 14			14 28			14 45						15 14	
Lostock		d				13 50					14 20						14 50						15 20	
Southport		d			12 54				13 24							14 00					14 24			
Meols Cop		d			12 59											14 05								
Bescar Lane		d			13 04																			
New Lane		d			13 08																			
Burscough Bridge		d			13 11				13 36							14 13					14 36			
Hoscar		d			13 15																			
Parbold		d			13 18				13 41							14 18					14 41			
Appley Bridge		d			13 22				13 45							14 22					14 45			
Gathurst		d			13 25											14 25								
Kirkby		d								13 32												14 32		
Rainford		d								13 40												14 40		
Upholland		d								13 44												14 44		
Orrell		d								13 47												14 47		
Pemberton		d								13 50												14 50		
Wigan Wallgate		a			13 30				13 51	13 56						14 30					14 51	14 56		
		d		13 20	13 32		13 48		13 53	13 58					14 20	14 32			14 48		14 53	14 58		
Wigan North Western		d										14a24												15a24
Ince		d								14 01												15 01		
Hindley		d		13 25	13 37				13 58	14 04					14 25	14 37					14 58	15 04		
Westhoughton		d		13 29					14 02						14 29						15 02			
Bolton		a	13 34	13 38		13 55	14 02	14 08	14 12		14 25			14 34	14 38		14 55		15 02	15 08	15 12		15 25	
		d	13 35	13 39		13 56	14 03	14 08	14 13		14 25		14 31	14 35	14 39		14 56		15 03	15 08	15 13		15 25	
Moses Gate		d		13 42											14 42									
Farnworth		d		13 44											14 44									
Kearsley		d		13 46											14 46									
Daisy Hill		d			13 41					14 09						14 41						15 09		
Hag Fold		d								14 12												15 12		
Atherton		d			13 45					14 15						14 45						15 15		
Walkden		d			13 50					14 20						14 50						15 20		
Moorside		d								14 24												15 24		
Swinton		d			13 55					14 26						14 55						15 26		
Salford Crescent		a	13 47	13 56	14 02	14 08	14 15		14 25	14 34	14 38		14 43	14 47	14 56	15 02	15 08		15 15		15 25	15 33	15 38	
		d	13 47	13 56	14 03	14 09	14 15		14 26	14 34	14 38		14 44	14 47	14 56	15 03	15 09		15 15		15 26	15 34	15 38	
Salford Central		d		13 59	14 05		14 17			14 36	14 41		14 46		14 59	15 05			15 17			15 36	15 41	
Manchester Victoria	⇌	a		14 06	14 11		14 25			14 43	14 47		14 52		15 06	15 11			15 25			15 43	15 47	
Rochdale	41	a					14 51												15 51					
Deansgate	⇌	a	13 51			14 12			14 29					14 51			15 12				15 29			
Manchester Oxford Road		a	13 52			14 14		14 23	14 31					14 52			15 14			15 23	15 31			
Manchester Piccadilly 10	⇌	a	13 56			14 18		14 27	14 35					14 56			15 18			15 27	15 35			
Stockport	84	a				14 34											15 34							
Hazel Grove	86	a				14 45											15 48							
Buxton	86	a																						
Heald Green	85	a	14 10											15 10										
Manchester Airport	85 ✈	a	14 17					14 47	14 53					15 17						15 47	15 53			

A ⊼ from Preston
B To L'pool Sth Pw Hl (Allertn)
C From Clitheroe
D From Edinburgh

The Sunday service between Manchester Victoria and Wigan Wallgate via Atherton is funded by GMITA and will operate whilst funding exists

Table 82

Mondays to Fridays until 15 July

Barrow-in-Furness, Blackpool North, Preston, Southport, Kirkby and Wigan - Bolton - Manchester

		TP ◇1	NT A	TP ◇1 ⊼	NT	NT	NT	NT	TP ◇1 B ⊼	NT	NT C	TP 1	NT	NT A	NT	NT	NT D	TP ◇1 ⊼	NT	NT E	NT	NT
Barrow-in-Furness	d												16 10									
Roose	d												16 14									
Dalton	d												16 20									
Ulverston	d												16 28									
Cark	d												16 36									
Kents Bank	d												16 40									
Grange-over-Sands	d												16a47									
Arnside	d	14 46										15 58										
Silverdale	d	14 50																				
Carnforth	d	14 59									15 38	16 09										
Windermere	83 d																					
Oxenholme Lake District	65 d								14 59													
Lancaster 6	65 a	15 07							15 13		15 47	16 18										
	d	15 08							15 14			16 18										
Blackpool North	97 d			14 44												15 20	15 37	15 44				
Layton	97 d															15 23						
Poulton-le-Fylde	97 d			14 50												15 28		15 50				
Kirkham & Wesham	97 d															15 37	15 52					
Preston 8	65,97 a	15 26		15 08					15 34			16 37				15 47	16 02	16 08				
	d			15 10			15 23		15 47							15 49	16 04	16 10			16 23	
Leyland	d						15 29									15 54	16 09				16 29	
Chorley	d			15 21			15 36		15 56							16 02		16 21			16 36	
Adlington (Lancashire)	d															16 07						
Blackrod	d															16 10						
Horwich Parkway	d			15 28			15 45									16 14		16 28			16 45	
Lostock	d						15 50									16 20					16 50	
Southport	d					14 54				15 24										15 58		
Meols Cop	d					14 59														16 03		
Bescar Lane	d					15 04																
New Lane	d					15 08																
Burscough Bridge	d					15 11				15 36										16 11		
Hoscar	d					15 15																
Parbold	d					15 18				15 41										16 16		
Appley Bridge	d					15 22				15 45										16 20		
Gathurst	d					15 25														16 24		
Kirkby	d														15 32							
Rainford	d														15 40							
Upholland	d														15 44							
Orrell	d														15 47							
Pemberton	d														15 50							
Wigan Wallgate	a					15 30				15 51					15 56					16 29		
	d				15 20	15 32		15 48		15 53					15 58				16 20	16 30		16 48
Wigan North Western	d																16a24					
Ince	d														16 01					16 33		
Hindley	d				15 25	15 37				15 58					16 04				16 25	16 37		
Westhoughton	d				15 29					16 02									16 29			
Bolton	a			15 34	15 38		15 55	16 02	16 08	16 12						16 25		16 34	16 38		16 55	17 02
	d		15 31	15 35	15 39		15 56	16 03	16 08	16 13				16 17		16 25		16 35	16 39		16 56	17 03
Moses Gate	d				15 42														16 42			
Farnworth	d				15 44														16 44			
Kearsley	d				15 46														16 46			
Daisy Hill	d					15 41									16 09					16 41		
Hag Fold	d														16 12							
Atherton	d					15 45									16 15					16 45		
Walkden	d					15 50									16 20					16 50		
Moorside	d														16 24							
Swinton	d					15 55									16 26					16 55		
Salford Crescent	a		15 43	15 47	15 56	16 02	16 08	16 15		16 25				16 30	16 34	16 38		16 47	16 56	17 02	17 08	17 15
	d		15 44	15 47	15 56	16 03	16 09	16 15		16 26				16 30	16 34	16 38		16 47	16 56	17 03	17 09	17 15
Salford Central	d		15 46		15 59	16 05		16 17						16 33	16 36	16 41			16 59	17 05		17 17
Manchester Victoria	⇌ a		15 54		16 06	16 11		16 23						16 41	16 43	16 47			17 06	17 13		17 23
Rochdale	41 a							16 51														17 51
Deansgate	⇌ a			15 51			16 12											16 51			17 15	
Manchester Oxford Road	a			15 52			16 14		16 23	16 31								16 52			17 17	
Manchester Piccadilly 10	⇌ a			15 56			16 18		16 27	16 35								16 56			17 21	
Stockport	84 a						16 34														17 32	
Hazel Grove	86 a						16 43														17 39	
Buxton	86 a						17 22														18 16	
Heald Green	85 a			16 10					16 40									17 10				
Manchester Airport	85 ✈ a			16 17					16 47	16 53								17 17				

A From Clitheroe
B From Glasgow Central
C From Leeds to Morecambe
D To Liverpool Lime Street
E To Huddersfield

The Sunday service between Manchester Victoria and Wigan Wallgate via Atherton is funded by GMITA and will operate whilst funding exists

Table 82

Mondays to Fridays until 15 July

Barrow-in-Furness, Blackpool North, Preston, Southport, Kirkby and Wigan - Bolton - Manchester

		TP FX ◇1 A ⊼	TP ◇1 B ⊼	NT	NT	NT	NT C	TP	NT	NT D	TP ◇1 ⊼	NT	NT	NT	NT D	TP ◇1 ⊼	NT	NT	NT	NT C	TP ◇1 E ⊼	TP	NT F
Barrow-in-Furness	d								17 20														18 03
Roose	d								17 24														18 07
Dalton	d								17 30														18 13
Ulverston	d								17 39														18 21
Cark	d								17 46														18 29
Kents Bank	d								17 51														18 33
Grange-over-Sands	d								17a58														18a40
Arnside	d	15 58						16 42														17 46	
Silverdale	d							16 46															
Carnforth	d	16 09						16 55														18 05	
Windermere	83 d																				17 06		
Oxenholme Lake District	65 d		16 08																		17 30		
Lancaster 6	65 a	16 18	16 23					17 05													17 47	18 14	
	d	16 18	16 23																		17 48		
Blackpool North	97 d					16 20	16 35				16 40					17 20				17 37			
Layton	97 d					16 23					16 43					17 23							
Poulton-le-Fylde	97 d					16 28					16 48					17 27							
Kirkham & Wesham	97 d					16 37	16 52				16 57									17 52			
Preston 8	65,97 a	16 37	16 42			16 47	17 02				17 08					17 45				18 02	18 06		
	d	16 47				16 49	17 04				17 10					17 47			17 56	18 04	18 08		
Leyland	d					16 54	17 09												18 01	18 09			
Chorley	d	16 56				17 02					17 21					17 56			18 08		18 19		
Adlington (Lancashire)	d					17 07													18 13				
Blackrod	d					17 10													18 17				
Horwich Parkway	d					17 14					17 28								18 20		18 26		
Lostock	d					17 20															18 30		
Southport	d			16 24									16 54				17 24						
Meols Cop	d												16 59				17 29						
Bescar Lane	d												17 04										
New Lane	d												17 08										
Burscough Bridge	d			16 36									17 11				17 37						
Hoscar	d												17 15										
Parbold	d			16 41									17 18				17 42						
Appley Bridge	d			16 45									17 22				17 46						
Gathurst	d												17 25										
Kirkby	d				16 32													17 32					
Rainford	d				16 40													17 40					
Upholland	d				16 44													17 44					
Orrell	d				16 47													17 47					
Pemberton	d				16 50													17 50					
Wigan Wallgate	a			16 51	16 56								17 30				17 52	17 57					
	d			16 53	16 58							17 20	17 32	17 39			17 54	17 59					
Wigan North Western	d						17a24													18a24			
Ince	d				17 01													18 02					
Hindley	d			16 58	17 04							17 25	17 37					18 05					
Westhoughton	d			17 02								17 29		17 47			18 02						
Bolton	a	17 08		17 12		17 25					17 34	17 38		17 55		18 08	18 12		18 30		18 34		
	d	17 08		17 13		17 25				17 31	17 35	17 39		17 56	18 02	18 08	18 13		18 30		18 35		
Moses Gate	d											17 42											
Farnworth	d											17 44											
Kearsley	d											17 46											
Daisy Hill	d				17 08								17 41					18 09					
Hag Fold	d				17 11													18 12					
Atherton	d				17 14								17 45					18 15					
Walkden	d				17 19								17 50					18 20					
Moorside	d				17 23													18 24					
Swinton	d				17 25								17 55					18 26					
Salford Crescent	a			17 25	17 33	17 38				17 43	17 47	17 56	18 02	18 08	18 15		18 25	18 33	18 43		18 47		
	d			17 26	17 33	17 38				17 44	17 48	17 56	18 03	18 09	18 15		18 26	18 33	18 43		18 47		
Salford Central	d				17 36	17 41				17 46		17 59	18 05		18 17			18 36	18 46				
Manchester Victoria	⇌ a				17 43	17 47				17 53		18 06	18 11		18 24			18 43	18 52				
Rochdale	41 a														18 47								
Deansgate	⇌ a										17 51			18 12							18 51		
Manchester Oxford Road	a	17 26		17 30							17 53			18 14		18 23	18 31				18 52		
Manchester Piccadilly 10	⇌ a	17 29		17 35							17 57			18 18		18 27	18 35				18 56		
Stockport	84 a													18 34									
Hazel Grove	86 a													18 43									
Buxton	86 a													19 22									
Heald Green	85 a	17 41									18 10					18 40					19 10		
Manchester Airport	85 ✈ a	17 48		17 53							18 16					18 47	18 53				19 17		

A ⊼ from Preston ◇ from Preston
B From Edinburgh
C To Liverpool Lime Street
D From Clitheroe
E ⊼ from Preston
F From Carlisle

The Sunday service between Manchester Victoria and Wigan Wallgate via Atherton is funded by GMITA and will operate whilst funding exists

Barrow-in-Furness, Blackpool North, Preston, Southport, Kirkby and Wigan - Bolton - Manchester

		NT	NT	NT	TP	NT	NT	NT	NT	NT	NT	TP	TP	TP	NT	NT	TP	TP	NT	NT	NT	TP	NT
				A	◇■ B ⌶		C			D	A	◇■ ⌶	◇■	◇■		E	◇■ F ⌶	◇■ G ⌶			D	◇■	
Barrow-in-Furness	d																						20 07
Roose	d																						20 11
Dalton	d																						20 17
Ulverston	d																						20 26
Cark	d																						20 33
Kents Bank	d																						20 38
Grange-over-Sands	d																						20a44
Arnside	d												18 17					18 50						
Silverdale	d																	18 54						
Carnforth	d						18 29						18 29					19 03					19 54	
Windermere 83	d													18 15										
Oxenholme Lake District 65	d													18 36					19 09					
Lancaster ■ 65	a						18 42						18 40	18 52				19 12					20 01	
	d				18 26								18 54	18 52				19 13					20 02	
Blackpool North 97	d								18 20	18 37		18 44									19 20	19 37		
Layton 97	d								18 23												19 23			
Poulton-le-Fylde 97	d								18 28			18 50									19 28			
Kirkham & Wesham 97	d								18 37	18 52											19 37			
Preston ■ 65,97	a				18 45				18 47	19 02		19 07		19 11			19 37	19 41		19 47	20 02	20 20	
	d				18 47				18 49	19 04		19 10		19 16				19 47		19 49	20 04		
Leyland	d								18 54	19 09										19 54	20 09		
Chorley	d				18 56				19 02			19 21		19 29				19 56		20 02			
Adlington (Lancashire)	d								19 07											20 07			
Blackrod	d								19 10											20 10			
Horwich Parkway	d								19 14			19 28		19 36						20 14			
Lostock	d								19 20											20 20			
Southport	d					18 17									19 00				19 23				
Meols Cop	d					18 22									19 05				19 28				
Bescar Lane	d					18 27																	
New Lane	d					18 31																	
Burscough Bridge	d					18 33									19 13				19 36				
Hoscar	d					18 37																	
Parbold	d					18 40									19 18				19 41				
Appley Bridge	d					18 44									19 22				19 45				
Gathurst	d					18 47									19 25				19 48				
Kirkby	d							18 32															
Rainford	d							18 40															
Upholland	d							18 44															
Orrell	d							18 47															
Pemberton	d							18 50															
Wigan Wallgate	a					18 52		18 56							19 30				19 53				
	d	18 20	18 32			18 53		18 58							19 32				19 55				
Wigan North Western	d									19a24											20a24		
Ince	d							19 01															
Hindley	d	18 25	18 37			18 58		19 04							19 37				20 00				
Westhoughton	d	18 29				19 02													20 04				
Bolton	a	18 38			19 08	19 12			19 25			19 34		19 42				20 08	20 12	20 25			
	d	18 39		19 02	19 08	19 13			19 25		19 31	19 35		19 43		20 02		20 08	20 13	20 25			
Moses Gate	d	18 42																					
Farnworth	d	18 44																					
Kearsley	d	18 46																					
Daisy Hill	d		18 41					19 08							19 41								
Hag Fold	d							19 11															
Atherton	d		18 45					19 14							19 45								
Walkden	d		18 50					19 19							19 50								
Moorside	d							19 23															
Swinton	d		18 55					19 25							19 55								
Salford Crescent	a	18 56	19 02	19 14		19 25		19 33	19 38		19 44	19 47			20 02	20 15			20 25	20 38			
	d	18 56	19 03	19 15		19 26		19 33	19 38		19 44	19 47			20 03	20 15			20 26	20 38			
Salford Central	d	18 59	19 05	19 17				19 36	19 41		19 46				20 05	20 17				20 41			
Manchester Victoria ⇌	a	19 06	19 11	19 23				19 43	19 47		19 53				20 11	20 24				20 47			
Rochdale 41	a																						
Deansgate ⇌	a					19 29						19 51							20 29				
Manchester Oxford Road	a				19 23	19 31						19 52		19 57				20 23	20 31				
Manchester Piccadilly ■ ⇌	a				19 27	19 35						19 56		20 01				20 27	20 35				
Stockport 84	a																						
Hazel Grove 86	a																						
Buxton 86	a																						
Heald Green 85	a											20 08		20 15									
Manchester Airport 85 ✈	a				19 47	19 53						20 17		20 24				20 47	20 53				

A From Clitheroe
B From Edinburgh
C From Leeds to Morecambe
D To Liverpool Lime Street
E From Blackburn
F ■ from Preston ⌶ from Preston
◇ from Preston
G From Glasgow Central

The Sunday service between Manchester Victoria and Wigan Wallgate via Atherton is funded by GMITA and will operate whilst funding exists

Barrow-in-Furness, Blackpool North, Preston, Southport, Kirkby and Wigan - Bolton - Manchester

		NT	TP	TP	NT	NT	NT	NT	NT	TP	TP	NT	NT	NT	NT	NT	NT	NT	NT	NT	TP	NT	TP
												FO	FX	FO	FX	FX	FO		FX	FO			FO
		A	◇■	◇■ B ⌶				C	A	◇■	◇■								A	A	◇■	C	◇■ B ⌶
Barrow-in-Furness	d																	21 43					
Roose	d																	21 47					
Dalton	d																	21 53					
Ulverston	d																	22 01					
Cark	d																	22 09					
Kents Bank	d																	22 13					
Grange-over-Sands	d																	22a18					
Arnside	d																						
Silverdale	d																						
Carnforth	d										20 54												
Windermere 83	d																						
Oxenholme Lake District 65	d			20 13																			22 10
Lancaster ■ 65	a			20 26							21 03												22 26
	d			20 26							21 03												22 26
Blackpool North 97	d		19 44				20 20	20 37		20 45						21 20	21 20				21 44	22 14	
Layton 97	d						20 23									21 23	21 23						
Poulton-le-Fylde 97	d		19 50				20 28			20 51						21 28	21 28				21 50		
Kirkham & Wesham 97	d						20 37									21 37	21 37						
Preston ■ 65,97	a		20 08	20 45			20 47	21 01		21 09	21 22					21 47	21 47				22 08	22 41	22 45
	d		20 10	20 47			20 49	21 04		21 10	21 31					21 49	21 49				22 10	22 43	22 47
Leyland	d						20 54	21 09								21 54	21 54					22 48	
Chorley	d		20 21	20 56			21 02			21 20						22 02	22 02				22 21		
Adlington (Lancashire)	d						21 07									22 07	22 07						
Blackrod	d						21 10									22 10	22 10						
Horwich Parkway	d		20 28				21 14			21 27						22 14	22 14				22 28		
Lostock	d						21 20									22 20	22 20						
Southport	d					20 23								21 23	21 23								
Meols Cop	d					20 28								21 28	21 28								
Bescar Lane	d																						
New Lane	d																						
Burscough Bridge	d					20 36								21 36	21 36								
Hoscar	d																						
Parbold	d					20 41								21 41	21 41								
Appley Bridge	d					20 45								21 45	21 45								
Gathurst	d					20 48								21 48	21 48								
Kirkby	d																						
Rainford	d																						
Upholland	d																						
Orrell	d																						
Pemberton	d																						
Wigan Wallgate	a					20 53								21 53	21 53								
	d				20 27	20 55						21 27	21 27	21 55	21 55								
Wigan North Western	d							21a23			21 48											23a02	
Ince	d				20 30							21 30	21 30										
Hindley	d				20 33	21 00						21 33	21 33	22 00	22 00								
Westhoughton	d					21 04								22 04	22 04								
Bolton	a		20 34	21 08		21 12	21 25			21 34				22 12	22 12	22 25	22 25				22 34		23 06
	d	20 31	20 35	21 08		21 13	21 25		21 31	21 35				22 13	22 13	22 25	22 25		22 31	22 31	22 35		23 07
Moses Gate	d																						
Farnworth	d																						
Kearsley	d																						
Daisy Hill	d				20 37							21 37	21 37										
Hag Fold	d				20 40							21 40	21 40										
Atherton	d				20 43							21 43	21 43										
Walkden	d				20 49							21 49	21 49										
Moorside	d				20 52							21 52	21 52										
Swinton	d				20 55							21 55	21 55										
Salford Crescent	a	20 43	20 47		21 02	21 25	21 38		21 43	21 47		22 02	22 02	22 25	22 25	22 38	22 38		22 43	22 43	22 47		
	d	20 44	20 47		21 03	21 26	21 38		21 44	21 47		22 03	22 03	22 26	22 26	22 38	22 38		22 44	22 44	22 47		
Salford Central	d	20 46			21 05		21 41		21 46			22 05		22 28			22 41			22 46			
Manchester Victoria ⇌	a	20 52			21 11		21 47		21 52			22 11	22 11	22 34	22 34	22 47	22 47		22 52	22 52			
Rochdale 41	a																						
Deansgate ⇌	a		20 51			21 29				21 51											22 51		
Manchester Oxford Road	a		20 52	21 23		21 31				21 52	22 26										22 52		23s21
Manchester Piccadilly ■ ⇌	a		20 56	21 27		21 35				21 56	22 30										22 56		23 31
Stockport 84	a																						
Hazel Grove 86	a																						
Buxton 86	a																						
Heald Green 85	a		21 10							22 09											23 09		
Manchester Airport 85 ✈	a		21 17	21 47		21 53				22 17	22 47										23 17		

A From Clitheroe
B From Edinburgh
C To Liverpool Lime Street

The Sunday service between Manchester Victoria and Wigan Wallgate via Atherton is funded by GMITA and will operate whilst funding exists

Mondays to Fridays
until 15 July

Barrow-in-Furness, Blackpool North, Preston, Southport, Kirkby and Wigan - Bolton - Manchester

Station			NT FO	NT FX	NT	NT	TP 1	NT A	TP ◇1 B	NT	NT C	TP ◇1	NT
Barrow-in-Furness		d											
Roose		d											
Dalton		d											
Ulverston		d											
Cark		d											
Kents Bank		d											
Grange-over-Sands		d											
Arnside		d											
Silverdale		d											
Carnforth		d					22 33						
Windermere	83	d							22 45				
Oxenholme Lake District	65	d							23 06				
Lancaster 6	65	a					22 42		23 23				
		d					22 42	23 07	23 24				
Blackpool North	97	d				22 20						22 44	23 13
Layton	97	d				22 23							23 16
Poulton-le-Fylde	97	d				22 28						22 50	23 21
Kirkham & Wesham	97	d				22 37							23 30
Preston 8	65,97	a				22 47	23 02	23 28	23 45			23 08	23 40
		d				22 49						23 10	23 42
Leyland		d				22 54							23 48
Chorley		d				23 02						23 21	23 55
Adlington (Lancashire)		d				23 07							00 01
Blackrod		d				23 10							00 04
Horwich Parkway		d				23 14						23 28	00 08
Lostock		d				23 20							00 13
Southport		d			22 18					23 10			
Meols Cop		d			22 23					23 15			
Bescar Lane		d			22 28								
New Lane		d			22 32								
Burscough Bridge		d			22 34					23 23			
Hoscar		d			22 38								
Parbold		d			22 41					23 28			
Appley Bridge		d			22 45					23 32			
Gathurst		d			22 48					23 35			
Kirkby		d											
Rainford		d											
Upholland		d											
Orrell		d											
Pemberton		d											
Wigan Wallgate		a			22 53					23 44			
		d	22 27	22 27	22 55								
Wigan North Western		d											
Ince		d	22 30	22 30									
Hindley		d	22 33	22 33	23 00								
Westhoughton		d			23 04								
Bolton		a			23 12	23 25						23 34	00 18
		d			23 13	23 25					23 31	23 35	00 19
Moses Gate		d											
Farnworth		d											
Kearsley		d											
Daisy Hill		d	22 37	22 37									
Hag Fold		d	22 40	22 40									
Atherton		d	22 43	22 43									
Walkden		d	22 49	22 49									
Moorside		d	22 52	22 52									
Swinton		d	22 55	22 55									
Salford Crescent		a	23 02	23 02	23 25	23 38					23 43	23 47	
		d	23 03	23 03	23 26	23 38					23 44	23 47	
Salford Central		d	23 05										
Manchester Victoria	⇌	a	23 13	23 13		23 47					23 52		00 36
Rochdale	41	a											
Deansgate	⇌	a			23 29								
Manchester Oxford Road		a			23 31								
Manchester Piccadilly 10	⇌	a			23 39							23 53	
Stockport	84	a											
Hazel Grove	86	a											
Buxton	86	a											
Heald Green	85	a										00 15	
Manchester Airport	85 ✈	a										00 22	

A From Morecambe
B To Blackpool North
C From Clitheroe

The Sunday service between Manchester Victoria and Wigan Wallgate via Atherton is funded by GMITA and will operate whilst funding exists

Table 82

Mondays to Fridays
18 July to 30 September

Barrow-in-Furness, Blackpool North, Preston, Southport, Kirkby and Wigan - Bolton - Manchester

Station			TP MX ◇1	TP MO ◇1	NT MX	TP ◇1 A	TP MX ◇1 B	TP ◇1 C	TP ◇1 D	TP ◇1	TP ◇1	TP ◇1 D	NT E	TP ◇1	NT	TP ◇1 ⚲	NT	NT	NT F	TP ◇1 G ⚲	NT	NT	NT H	NT I
Barrow-in-Furness		d									04 35									05 31				
Roose		d																						
Dalton		d																						
Ulverston		d									04 51									05 47				
Cark		d																						
Kents Bank		d																						
Grange-over-Sands		d									05 03									05 59				
Arnside		d									05 10									06 05				
Silverdale		d																						
Carnforth		d									05 19									06 15			06 43	
Windermere	83	d																						
Oxenholme Lake District	65	d																						
Lancaster 6	65	a									05 28									06 23			06 52	
		d																		06 23				
Blackpool North	97	d	22p44	23p03	23p13					03 36			04 56			05 39						06 19		
Layton	97	d			23p16																	06 22		
Poulton-le-Fylde	97	d	22p50	23p09	23p21								05 02			05 45						06 27		
Kirkham & Wesham	97	d		23p17	23p30																	06 36		
Preston 8	65,97	a	23p08	23p28	23p40								05 20			06 03				06 42		06 46		
		d	23p10	23p28	23p42					04u01				05 16		06 05				06 44		06 48		
Leyland		d		23p34	23p48											06 10						06 53		
Chorley		d	23p21	23p41	23p55									05 26		06 16				06 53		07 01		
Adlington (Lancashire)		d		23p45	00 01																	07 06		
Blackrod		d		23p49	00 04											06 22						07 10		
Horwich Parkway		d	23p28	23p52	00 08									05 33		06 26				07 00		07 14		
Lostock		d		23p56	00 13											06 30						07 20		
Southport		d																			06 23			
Meols Cop		d																			06 28			
Bescar Lane		d																						
New Lane		d																						
Burscough Bridge		d																			06 36			
Hoscar		d																						
Parbold		d																			06 41			
Appley Bridge		d																			06 45			
Gathurst		d																			06 49			
Kirkby		d																						
Rainford		d																						
Upholland		d																						
Orrell		d																						
Pemberton		d																						
Wigan Wallgate		a																			06 54			
		d													06 03		06 31	06 36			06 55			
Wigan North Western		d																						
Ince		d													06 06			06 39						
Hindley		d													06 09		06 36	06 42						
Westhoughton		d															06 41				07 03			
Bolton		a	23p34	00 02	00 18									05 42		06 34	06 52			07 08	07 11	07 25		
		d	23p35	00 02	00 19					04u30				05 43		06 35	06 53		06 56	07 08	07 12	07 25		07 30
Moses Gate		d																	06 59					
Farnworth		d																	07 01					
Kearsley		d																	07 03					
Daisy Hill		d													06 13			06 46						
Hag Fold		d													06 16			06 49						
Atherton		d													06 19			06 52						
Walkden		d													06 24			06 58						
Moorside		d													06 28			07 01						
Swinton		d													06 30			07 04						
Salford Crescent		a	23p47											05 55	06 38	06 47	07 05	07 11	07 15		07 24	07 38		07 43
		d	23p47			00 37	00 49	01 03	03 40			04 53		05 55	06 38	06 47	07 08	07 11	07 15		07 25	07 38		07 43
Salford Central		d													06 41			07 14	07 19			07 41		07 46
Manchester Victoria	⇌	a			00 36										06 46			07 20	07 26			07 47		07 53
Rochdale	41	a																						
Deansgate	⇌	a														06 51	07 11				07 28			
Manchester Oxford Road		a														06 52	07 13			07 23	07 30			
Manchester Piccadilly 10	⇌	a	23p53	00 18		00 43	00 53	01 08	03 44	04 48		04 58		06 01		06 56	07 17			07 27	07 34			
Stockport	84	a															07 34							
Hazel Grove	86	a															07 45							
Buxton	86	a																						
Heald Green	85	a	00 15													07 10								
Manchester Airport	85 ✈	a	00 22	00 32		01 00	01 10	01 25	04 00	05 07		05 19		06 18		07 17				07 47	07 53			

A MO from 18 July until 12 September. From Middlesbrough
B From Newcastle
C 19 September, 26 September. From Middlesbrough
D From York
E To Colne
F From Blackburn
G ⚲ from Preston
H From Skipton
I From Clitheroe

The Sunday service between Manchester Victoria and Wigan Wallgate via Atherton is funded by GMITA and will operate whilst funding exists

Table 82

Mondays to Fridays
18 July to 30 September

Barrow-in-Furness, Blackpool North, Preston, Southport, Kirkby and Wigan - Bolton - Manchester

	TP	NT	NT	NT	NT	NT	NT	NT	TP	NT	NT	NT	NT	TP	TP	NT	NT	NT	NT	NT	NT	TP
	◇■								◇■					◇■	◇■							◇■
		A				B		C	D				C		E	F					G	D
	🛒								🛒					🛒	🛒							🛒
Barrow-in-Furness d									06 20							07 00						07 29
Roose d									06 24							07 04						
Dalton d									06 31							07 10						07 38
Ulverston d									06 39							07 19						07 46
Cark d									06 47							07 26						07 54
Kents Bank d									06 51							07 32						
Grange-over-Sands d									06 55							07 36						08 01
Arnside d									07 01							07 42						08 07
Silverdale d									07 05							07 47						08 11
Carnforth d									07 12							07 55						08 18
Windermere 83 d																						
Oxenholme Lake District 65 d																						
Lancaster ■ 65 a									07 21							08 04						08 26
d									07 22						07 47	08 05						08 27
Blackpool North 97 d	06 40				06 53	07 02						07 18		07 36								
Layton 97 d	06 43											07 21		07 39								
Poulton-le-Fylde 97 d	06 47					07 08						07 26		07 43								
Kirkham & Wesham 97 d	06 56											07 35		07 52								
Preston ■ 65,97 a	07 07				07 15	07 28			07 41			07 46		08 03	08 07	08 30						08 45
d	07 09				07 17	07 30			07 47			07 47		08 12						08 17		08 47
Leyland d					07 22	07 35						07 53								08 23		
Chorley d	07 18				07 31				07 56			08 01		08 22						08 33		08 56
Adlington (Lancashire) d					07 36							08 06								08 37		
Blackrod d					07 40							08 10								08 41		
Horwich Parkway d	07 26				07 44							08 14								08 45		
Lostock d	07 30				07 49							08 20								08 50		
Southport d			06 53							07 21									07 58			
Meols Cop d			06 58							07 26									08 03			
Bescar Lane d			07 03																			
New Lane d			07 07																			
Burscough Bridge d			07 09							07 34									08 11			
Hoscar d			07 13																			
Parbold d			07 16							07 39									08 16			
Appley Bridge d			07 20							07 43									08 20			
Gathurst d			07 23							07 47									08 23			
Kirkby d							07 11															
Rainford d							07 19															
Upholland d							07 23															
Orrell d							07 27															
Pemberton d							07 30															
Wigan Wallgate a			07 29				07 35			07 51									08 28			
d		07 15	07 29				07 37			07 53	08 00						08 13		08 29			
Wigan North Western d				07 22		07a50												08 20				
Ince d		07 18		07 25			07 40										08 16					
Hindley d		07 21		07 29			07 43			07 58							08 19	08 25	08 34			
Westhoughton d				07 33						08 03								08 29				
Bolton a	07 34			07 42	07 54				08 08	08 11		08 25		08 34				08 38		08 55		09 08
d	07 35			07 43	07 55			07 59	08 08	08 12		08 25	08 31	08 35				08 39		08 56	09 02	09 08
Moses Gate d				07 46				08 02										08 42				
Farnworth d				07 48				08 04										08 44				
Kearsley d				07 50				08 06										08 46				
Daisy Hill d		07 26	07 39				07 47				08 07						08 23		08 39			
Hag Fold d		07 29					07 50										08 26					
Atherton d		07 32	07 43				07 53				08 12						08 29		08 43			
Walkden d		07 38					07 59				08 18						08 35		08 49			
Moorside d		07 41					08 03										08 39					
Swinton d		07 44					08 06										08 42		08 54			
Salford Crescent a	07 47	07 51	07 59	08 02	08 07		08 13	08 17		08 24	08 29	08 38	08 43	08 47			08 50	08 56	09 02	09 08	09 15	
d	07 47	07 51	07 59	08 02	08 08		08 13	08 17		08 25	08 30	08 38	08 44	08 47			08 50	08 56	09 02	09 09	09 16	
Salford Central d		07 55	08 02	08 05			08 16	08 20			08 32	08 41	08 46				08 53	08 59	09 04		09 18	
Manchester Victoria ⇌ a		08 00	08 08	08 12			08 20	08 25			08 38	08 48	08 52				08 59	09 06	09 11		09 26	
Rochdale 41 a							08 51															
Deansgate ⇌ a	07 51				08 11					08 28										09 12		
Manchester Oxford Road a	07 52				08 14				08 23	08 31				08 52						09 14		09 23
Manchester Piccadilly ■ ⇌ a	07 56				08 18				08 27	08 35				08 56						09 18		09 27
Stockport 84 a					08 34															09 34		
Hazel Grove 86 a					08 48															09 45		
Buxton 86 a																						
Heald Green 85 a	08 10									08 47				09 10								
Manchester Airport 85 ✈ a	08 17								08 47	08 53				09 19								09 47

A To Stalybridge
B To Liverpool Lime Street
C From Clitheroe
D 🛒 from Preston
E From Edinburgh
F From Millom
G From Blackburn

The Sunday service between Manchester Victoria and Wigan Wallgate via Atherton is funded by GMITA and will operate whilst funding exists

Table 82

Mondays to Fridays
18 July to 30 September

Barrow-in-Furness, Blackpool North, Preston, Southport, Kirkby and Wigan - Bolton - Manchester

	NT	NT	NT	NT	NT	NT	TP	NT	NT	NT	NT	NT	TP	NT	NT	NT	NT	NT	NT	TP	TP	NT
							◇■						◇■							◇■	◇■	
	A				B	C					D		E				B	F	C		G	
							🛒						🛒							🛒	🛒	
Barrow-in-Furness d	08 00																					
Roose d	08 04																					
Dalton d	08 10																					
Ulverston d	08 19																					
Cark d	08 27																					
Kents Bank d	08 32																					
Grange-over-Sands d	08 36																					
Arnside d	08 42																					
Silverdale d	08 47																					
Carnforth d	08 54																	10 02				
Windermere 83 d																						
Oxenholme Lake District 65 d													09 11									
Lancaster ■ 65 a	09 07												09 26					10 12				
d													09 26									
Blackpool North 97 d				08 20			08 44									09 20	09 37			09 43		
Layton 97 d				08 23												09 23						
Poulton-le-Fylde 97 d				08 28			08 50									09 28				09 49		
Kirkham & Wesham 97 d				08 37												09 37	09 52					
Preston ■ 65,97 a				08 47			09 08						09 45			09 47	10 02			10 07		10 21
d				08 49	09 04		09 10			09 23			09 47			09 49	10 04			10 12		10 23
Leyland d				08 54	09 09					09 29						09 54	10 09					10 29
Chorley d				09 02			09 21			09 36			09 56			10 02				10 22		10 36
Adlington (Lancashire) d				09 07												10 07						
Blackrod d				09 10												10 10						
Horwich Parkway d				09 14			09 28			09 45						10 14						10 45
Lostock d				09 20						09 50						10 20						10 50
Southport d		08 25							09 02					09 24								
Meols Cop d		08 30							09 07													
Bescar Lane d																						
New Lane d																						
Burscough Bridge d		08 38							09 15					09 36								
Hoscar d																						
Parbold d		08 43							09 20					09 41								
Appley Bridge d		08 47							09 24					09 45								
Gathurst d		08 50							09 27													
Kirkby d			08 21												09 32							
Rainford d			08 29												09 40							
Upholland d			08 33												09 44							
Orrell d			08 36												09 47							
Pemberton d			08 39												09 50							
Wigan Wallgate a		08 55	08 45						09 32					09 51	09 56							
d		08 56	08 50					09 20	09 32			09 48		09 53	09 58							
Wigan North Western d					09a24												10a24					
Ince d			08 53												10 01							
Hindley d			08 57					09 25	09 37					09 58	10 04							
Westhoughton d		09 04						09 29						10 02								
Bolton a		09 12		09 25			09 34	09 38		09 55		10 02	10 08	10 12		10 25				10 35		10 55
d		09 13		09 25		09 31	09 35	09 39		09 56	10 00	10 03	10 08	10 13		10 25			10 31	10 35		10 56
Moses Gate d								09 42														
Farnworth d								09 44														
Kearsley d								09 46														
Daisy Hill d			09 01						09 41						10 09							
Hag Fold d			09 04												10 12							
Atherton d			09 06						09 45						10 15							
Walkden d			09 12						09 50						10 20							
Moorside d			09 15												10 24							
Swinton d			09 18						09 55						10 26							
Salford Crescent a		09 25	09 27	09 38		09 43	09 47	09 56	10 03	10 08	10 13	10 15		10 25	10 34	10 38			10 43	10 47		11 08
d		09 26	09 27	09 38		09 44	09 47	09 56	10 03	10 09	10 13	10 15		10 26	10 34	10 38			10 44	10 47		11 09
Salford Central d			09 31	09 41		09 46		09 59	10 05		10 16	10 17			10 36	10 41			10 46			
Manchester Victoria ⇌ a			09 38	09 47		09 52		10 06	10 12		10 21	10 25			10 43	10 47			10 52			
Rochdale 41 a												10 51										
Deansgate ⇌ a		09 29					09 51			10 12				10 29						10 51		
Manchester Oxford Road a		09 31					09 52			10 14			10 23	10 31						10 52		
Manchester Piccadilly ■ ⇌ a		09 35					09 56			10 18			10 27	10 35						10 56		
Stockport 84 a										10 34												
Hazel Grove 86 a										10 45												
Buxton 86 a																						
Heald Green 85 a							10 10													11 10		
Manchester Airport 85 ✈ a		09 53					10 17						10 47	10 53						11 17		

A From Maryport
B To L'pool Sth Pw Hl (Allertn)
C From Clitheroe
D From Blackburn
E From Glasgow Central
F From Leeds to Morecambe
G From Edinburgh

The Sunday service between Manchester Victoria and Wigan Wallgate via Atherton is funded by GMITA and will operate whilst funding exists

Table 82

Mondays to Fridays

18 July to 30 September

Barrow-in-Furness, Blackpool North, Preston, Southport, Kirkby and Wigan - Bolton - Manchester

	NT	NT	NT	TP ◇1 A ⊼	NT B	NT	NT	NT	NT C	NT D	TP ◇1 ⊼	NT	NT	NT	NT	TP ◇1 A ⊼	NT	NT	NT	NT C	NT E	TP ◇1
Barrow-in-Furness d				09 23	10 16																	11 25
Roose d				09 27	10 20																	
Dalton d				09 34	10 26																	
Ulverston d				09 42	10 35																	11 41
Cark d				09 50	10 42																	
Kents Bank d				09 54	10 47																	
Grange-over-Sands d				09 58	10 51																	11 53
Arnside d				10 04	10 57																	11 59
Silverdale d				10 08	11 01																	
Carnforth d				10 15	11 08																12 02	12 09
Windermere 83 d																10 49						
Oxenholme Lake District 65 d																11 09						
Lancaster 6 65 a				10 25	11 20											11 26					12 11	12 18
d				10 26												11 26						12 18
Blackpool North 97 d								10 20	10 37		10 44								11 20	11 37		
Layton 97 d								10 23											11 23			
Poulton-le-Fylde 97 d								10 28			10 50								11 28			
Kirkham & Wesham 97 d								10 37	10 52										11 37	11 52		
Preston 8 65,97 a				10 45				10 47	11 02		11 08					11 45			11 47	12 02		12 37
d				10 47				10 49	11 04		11 10			11 23		11 47			11 49	12 04		
Leyland d								10 54	11 09					11 29					11 54	12 09		
Chorley d				10 56				11 02			11 21			11 36		11 56			12 02			
Adlington (Lancashire) d								11 07											12 07			
Blackrod d								11 10											12 10			
Horwich Parkway d								11 14			11 28			11 45					12 14			
Lostock d								11 20						11 50					12 20			
Southport d		09 55				10 24							10 55				11 24					
Meols Cop d		10 00											11 00									
Bescar Lane d		10 05											11 05									
New Lane d		10 09											11 09									
Burscough Bridge d		10 11				10 36							11 11				11 36					
Hoscar d		10 15											11 15									
Parbold d		10 18				10 41							11 18				11 41					
Appley Bridge d		10 22				10 45							11 22				11 45					
Gathurst d		10 25											11 25									
Kirkby d							10 32											11 32				
Rainford d							10 40											11 40				
Upholland d							10 44											11 44				
Orrell d							10 47											11 47				
Pemberton d							10 50											11 50				
Wigan Wallgate a		10 30				10 51	10 56						11 30				11 51	11 56				
d	10 20	10 32	10 48			10 53	10 58					11 20	11 32		11 48		11 53	11 58				
Wigan North Western d									11a24											12a24		
Ince d							11 01											12 01				
Hindley d	10 25	10 37				10 58	11 04					11 25	11 37				11 58	12 04				
Westhoughton d	10 29					11 02						11 29					12 02					
Bolton a	10 38		11 02	11 08		11 12		11 25			11 34	11 38		11 55	12 02	12 08	12 12		12 25			
d	10 39		11 03	11 08		11 13		11 25		11 31	11 35	11 39		11 56	12 03	12 08	12 13		12 25			
Moses Gate d	10 42											11 42										
Farnworth d	10 44											11 44										
Kearsley d	10 46											11 46										
Daisy Hill d		10 41					11 09						11 41					12 09				
Hag Fold d							11 12											12 12				
Atherton d		10 45					11 15						11 45					12 15				
Walkden d		10 50					11 20						11 50					12 20				
Moorside d							11 24											12 24				
Swinton d		10 55					11 26						11 55					12 26				
Salford Crescent a	10 56	11 02	11 15			11 25	11 34	11 38		11 43	11 47	11 56	12 02	12 08	12 15		12 25	12 34	12 38			
d	10 56	11 03	11 15			11 26	11 34	11 38		11 44	11 47	11 56	12 03	12 09	12 15		12 26	12 34	12 38			
Salford Central d	10 59	11 05	11 17				11 36	11 41		11 46		11 59	12 05		12 17			12 36	12 41			
Manchester Victoria ⇌ a	11 06	11 11	11 25				11 43	11 47		11 52		12 06	12 11		12 25			12 43	12 47			
Rochdale 41 a			11 51												12 51							
Deansgate ⇌ a						11 29					11 51			12 12			12 29					
Manchester Oxford Road a				11 23		11 31					11 52			12 14		12 23	12 31					
Manchester Piccadilly 10 ⇌ a				11 27		11 35					11 56			12 18		12 27	12 35					
Stockport 84 a														12 34								
Hazel Grove 86 a														12 45								
Buxton 86 a																						
Heald Green 85 a											12 10											
Manchester Airport 85 ✈ a				11 50		11 53					12 17					12 47	12 53					

A ⊼ from Preston
B From Sellafield
C To L'pool Sth Pw Hl (Allertn)
D From Clitheroe
E From Leeds to Heysham Port

The Sunday service between Manchester Victoria and Wigan Wallgate via Atherton is funded by GMITA and will operate whilst funding exists

Table 82

Mondays to Fridays

18 July to 30 September

Barrow-in-Furness, Blackpool North, Preston, Southport, Kirkby and Wigan - Bolton - Manchester

	NT A	TP ◇1 ⊼	NT	NT	NT	NT	TP ◇1 B ⊼	NT C	NT	NT	NT	NT D	NT A	TP ◇1 ⊼	NT	NT	NT	NT	TP ◇1 E ⊼	NT	TP ◇1	NT
Barrow-in-Furness d								12 11													13 25	
Roose d								12 15														
Dalton d								12 21														
Ulverston d								12 29													13 41	
Cark d								12 37														
Kents Bank d								12 41														
Grange-over-Sands d								12 45													13 53	
Arnside d								12 51													13 59	
Silverdale d								12 55														
Carnforth d								13 03													14 09	
Windermere 83 d																			12 51			
Oxenholme Lake District 65 d							12 10												13 09			
Lancaster 6 65 a							12 26	13 16											13 26		14 18	
d							12 26												13 26		14 18	
Blackpool North 97 d		11 44									12 20	12 37		12 44								
Layton 97 d											12 23											
Poulton-le-Fylde 97 d		11 50									12 28			12 50								
Kirkham & Wesham 97 d											12 37	12 52										
Preston 8 65,97 a		12 08					12 45				12 47	13 02		13 08					13 45		14 37	
d		12 10			12 23		12 47				12 49	13 04		13 10			13 23		13 47			
Leyland d					12 29						12 54	13 09					13 29					
Chorley d		12 21			12 36		12 56				13 02			13 21			13 36		13 56			
Adlington (Lancashire) d											13 07											
Blackrod d											13 10											
Horwich Parkway d		12 28			12 45						13 14			13 28			13 45					
Lostock d					12 50						13 20						13 50					
Southport d				12 00					12 24							12 54				13 24		
Meols Cop d				12 05												12 59						
Bescar Lane d																13 04						
New Lane d																13 08						
Burscough Bridge d				12 13					12 36							13 11				13 36		
Hoscar d																13 15						
Parbold d				12 18					12 41							13 18				13 41		
Appley Bridge d				12 22					12 45							13 22				13 45		
Gathurst d				12 25												13 25						
Kirkby d										12 32												13 32
Rainford d										12 40												13 40
Upholland d										12 44												13 44
Orrell d										12 47												13 47
Pemberton d										12 50												13 50
Wigan Wallgate a				12 30					12 51	12 56						13 30				13 51		13 56
d			12 20	12 32		12 48			12 53	12 58					13 20	13 32		13 48		13 53		13 58
Wigan North Western d												13a24										
Ince d										13 01												14 01
Hindley d			12 25	12 37					12 58	13 04					13 25	13 37				13 58		14 04
Westhoughton d			12 29						13 02						13 29					14 02		
Bolton a		12 34	12 38		12 55	13 02	13 08		13 12		13 25			13 34	13 38		13 55	14 02	14 08	14 12		
d	12 31	12 35	12 39		12 56	13 03	13 08		13 13		13 25		13 31	13 35	13 39		13 56	14 03	14 08	14 13		
Moses Gate d			12 42												13 42							
Farnworth d			12 44												13 44							
Kearsley d			12 46												13 46							
Daisy Hill d				12 41						13 09						13 41						14 09
Hag Fold d										13 12												14 12
Atherton d				12 45						13 15						13 45						14 15
Walkden d				12 50						13 20						13 50						14 20
Moorside d										13 24												14 24
Swinton d				12 55						13 26						13 55						14 26
Salford Crescent a	12 43	12 47	12 56	13 02	13 08	13 15			13 25	13 34	13 38		13 43	13 47	13 56	14 02	14 08	14 15		14 25		14 34
d	12 44	12 47	12 56	13 03	13 09	13 15			13 26	13 34	13 38		13 44	13 47	13 56	14 03	14 09	14 15		14 26		14 34
Salford Central d	12 46		12 59	13 05		13 17				13 36	13 41		13 46		13 59	14 05		14 17				14 36
Manchester Victoria ⇌ a	12 52		13 06	13 11		13 25				13 43	13 47		13 52		14 06	14 11		14 25				14 43
Rochdale 41 a						13 51												14 51				
Deansgate ⇌ a		12 51			13 12				13 29					13 51			14 12			14 29		
Manchester Oxford Road a		12 52			13 14		13 23		13 31					13 52			14 14		14 23	14 31		
Manchester Piccadilly 10 ⇌ a		12 56			13 18		13 27		13 35					13 56			14 18		14 27	14 35		
Stockport 84 a					13 34												14 34					
Hazel Grove 86 a					13 45												14 45					
Buxton 86 a																						
Heald Green 85 a		13 10												14 10								
Manchester Airport 85 ✈ a		13 17					13 47		13 53					14 17					14 47	14 53		

A From Clitheroe
B From Edinburgh
C From Carlisle
D To L'pool Sth Pw Hl (Allertn)
E ⊼ from Preston

The Sunday service between Manchester Victoria and Wigan Wallgate via Atherton is funded by GMITA and will operate whilst funding exists

Table 82

Mondays to Fridays
18 July to 30 September

Barrow-in-Furness, Blackpool North, Preston, Southport, Kirkby and Wigan - Bolton - Manchester

		NT	NT A	NT B	TP ◇1	NT	NT	NT	NT	TP ◇1 C	NT	NT	NT	NT A	NT B	TP ◇1	NT	NT	NT	NT	TP ◇1 D	NT
Barrow-in-Furness	d																					14 16
Roose	d																					14 20
Dalton	d																					14 26
Ulverston	d																					14 35
Cark	d																					14 42
Kents Bank	d																					14 47
Grange-over-Sands	d																					14 51
Arnside	d																					14 57
Silverdale	d																					15 01
Carnforth	d																					15 07
Windermere 83	d																					
Oxenholme Lake District 65	d									14 09											14 59	
Lancaster 6 65	a									14 26											15 13	15 20
	d									14 26											15 14	
Blackpool North 97	d	13 20	13 37		13 44								14 20	14 37		14 44						
Layton 97	d	13 23											14 23									
Poulton-le-Fylde 97	d	13 28			13 50								14 28			14 50						
Kirkham & Wesham 97	d	13 37	13 52										14 37	14 52								
Preston 8 65,97	a	13 47	14 02		14 08					14 45			14 47	15 02		15 08					15 34	
	d	13 49	14 04		14 10			14 23		14 47			14 49	15 04		15 10			15 23		15 47	
Leyland	d	13 54	14 09					14 29					14 54	15 09					15 29			
Chorley	d	14 02			14 21			14 36		14 56			15 02			15 21			15 36		15 56	
Adlington (Lancashire)	d	14 07											15 07									
Blackrod	d	14 10											15 10									
Horwich Parkway	d	14 14			14 28			14 45					15 14			15 28			15 45			
Lostock	d	14 20						14 50					15 20						15 50			
Southport	d						14 00				14 24							14 54				
Meols Cop	d						14 05											14 59				
Bescar Lane	d																	15 04				
New Lane	d																	15 08				
Burscough Bridge	d						14 13				14 36							15 11				
Hoscar	d																	15 15				
Parbold	d						14 18				14 41							15 18				
Appley Bridge	d						14 22				14 45							15 22				
Gathurst	d						14 25											15 25				
Kirkby	d											14 32										
Rainford	d											14 40										
Upholland	d											14 44										
Orrell	d											14 47										
Pemberton	d											14 50										
Wigan Wallgate	a						14 30				14 51	14 56						15 30				
	d					14 20	14 32		14 48		14 53	14 58					15 20	15 32		15 48		
Wigan North Western	d		14a24											15a24								
Ince	d											15 01										
Hindley	d					14 25	14 37				14 58	15 04					15 25	15 37				
Westhoughton	d					14 29					15 02						15 29					
Bolton	a	14 25			14 34	14 38		14 55	15 02	15 08	15 12		15 25			15 34	15 38		15 55	16 02	16 08	
	d	14 25		14 31	14 35	14 39		14 56	15 03	15 08	15 13		15 25		15 31	15 35	15 39		15 56	16 03	16 08	
Moses Gate	d					14 42											15 42					
Farnworth	d					14 44											15 44					
Kearsley	d					14 46											15 46					
Daisy Hill	d						14 41					15 09						15 41				
Hag Fold	d											15 12										
Atherton	d						14 45					15 15						15 45				
Walkden	d						14 50					15 20						15 50				
Moorside	d											15 24										
Swinton	d						14 55					15 26						15 55				
Salford Crescent	a	14 38		14 43	14 47	14 56	15 02	15 08	15 15		15 25	15 33	15 38		15 43	15 47	15 56	16 02	16 08	16 15		
	d	14 38		14 44	14 47	14 56	15 03	15 09	15 15		15 26	15 34	15 38		15 44	15 47	15 56	16 03	16 09	16 15		
Salford Central	d	14 41		14 46		14 59	15 05		15 17			15 36	15 41		15 46		15 59	16 05		16 17		
Manchester Victoria	a	14 47		14 52		15 06	15 11		15 25			15 43	15 47		15 54		16 06	16 11		16 23		
Rochdale 41	a								15 51											16 51		
Deansgate	a				14 51			15 12			15 29					15 51			16 12			
Manchester Oxford Road	a				14 52			15 14		15 23	15 31					15 52			16 14		16 23	
Manchester Piccadilly 10	a				14 56			15 18		15 27	15 35					15 56			16 18		16 27	
Stockport 84	a							15 34											16 34			
Hazel Grove 86	a							15 48											16 43			
Buxton 86	a																		17 22			
Heald Green 85	a				15 10											16 10					16 40	
Manchester Airport 85	a				15 17					15 47	15 53					16 17					16 47	

A To L'pool Sth Pw Hl (Allertn)
B From Clitheroe
C From Edinburgh
D From Glasgow Central

The Sunday service between Manchester Victoria and Wigan Wallgate via Atherton is funded by GMITA and will operate whilst funding exists

Table 82

Mondays to Fridays
18 July to 30 September

Barrow-in-Furness, Blackpool North, Preston, Southport, Kirkby and Wigan - Bolton - Manchester

		NT	NT A	TP ◇1	NT B	NT	NT	NT C	TP ◇1	NT	NT D	NT	NT	TP ◇1 E	NT	NT	NT	NT	NT C	NT B	TP ◇1	NT	NT
Barrow-in-Furness	d			15 25											16 20								
Roose	d														16 24								
Dalton	d														16 30								
Ulverston	d			15 41											16 38								
Cark	d														16 46								
Kents Bank	d														16 50								
Grange-over-Sands	d			15 53											16 54								
Arnside	d			15 59											17 00								
Silverdale	d														17 04								
Carnforth	d		15 38	16 09											17 12								
Windermere 83	d																						
Oxenholme Lake District 65	d													16 08									
Lancaster 6 65	a		15 47	16 18										16 23	17 26								
	d			16 18										16 23									
Blackpool North 97	d						15 20	15 37	15 44									16 20	16 35		16 40		
Layton 97	d						15 23											16 23			16 43		
Poulton-le-Fylde 97	d						15 28		15 50									16 28			16 48		
Kirkham & Wesham 97	d						15 37	15 52										16 37	16 52		16 57		
Preston 8 65,97	a			16 37			15 47	16 02	16 08					16 42				16 47	17 02		17 08		
	d						15 49	16 04	16 10			16 23		16 47				16 49	17 04		17 10		
Leyland	d						15 54	16 09				16 29						16 54	17 09				
Chorley	d						16 02		16 21			16 36		16 56				17 02			17 21		
Adlington (Lancashire)	d						16 07											17 07					
Blackrod	d						16 10											17 10					
Horwich Parkway	d						16 14		16 28			16 45						17 14			17 28		
Lostock	d						16 20					16 50						17 20					
Southport	d	15 24									15 58					16 24							16 54
Meols Cop	d										16 03												16 59
Bescar Lane	d																						17 04
New Lane	d																						17 08
Burscough Bridge	d	15 36									16 11					16 36							17 11
Hoscar	d																						17 15
Parbold	d	15 41									16 16					16 41							17 18
Appley Bridge	d	15 45									16 20					16 45							17 22
Gathurst	d										16 24												17 25
Kirkby	d					15 32											16 32						
Rainford	d					15 40											16 40						
Upholland	d					15 44											16 44						
Orrell	d					15 47											16 47						
Pemberton	d					15 50											16 50						
Wigan Wallgate	a	15 51				15 56					16 29					16 51	16 56						17 30
	d	15 53				15 58				16 20	16 30		16 48			16 53	16 58					17 20	17 32
Wigan North Western	d							16a24											17a24				
Ince	d					16 01					16 33						17 01						
Hindley	d	15 58				16 04				16 25	16 37					16 58	17 04					17 25	17 37
Westhoughton	d	16 02								16 29						17 02						17 29	
Bolton	a	16 12					16 25		16 34	16 38		16 55	17 02	17 08		17 12		17 25			17 34	17 38	
	d	16 13			16 17		16 25		16 35	16 39		16 56	17 03	17 08		17 13		17 25		17 31	17 35	17 39	
Moses Gate	d									16 42												17 42	
Farnworth	d									16 44												17 44	
Kearsley	d									16 46												17 46	
Daisy Hill	d					16 09					16 41						17 08						17 41
Hag Fold	d					16 12											17 11						
Atherton	d					16 15					16 45						17 14						17 45
Walkden	d					16 20					16 50						17 19						17 50
Moorside	d					16 24											17 23						
Swinton	d					16 26					16 55						17 25						17 55
Salford Crescent	a	16 25			16 30	16 34	16 38		16 47	16 56	17 02	17 08	17 15			17 25	17 33	17 38		17 43	17 47	17 56	18 02
	d	16 26			16 30	16 34	16 38		16 47	16 56	17 03	17 09	17 15			17 26	17 33	17 38		17 44	17 48	17 56	18 03
Salford Central	d				16 33	16 36	16 41			16 59	17 05		17 17				17 36	17 41		17 46		17 59	18 05
Manchester Victoria	a				16 41	16 43	16 47			17 06	17 13		17 23				17 43	17 47		17 53		18 06	18 11
Rochdale 41	a												17 51										
Deansgate	a								16 51			17 15									17 51		
Manchester Oxford Road	a	16 31							16 52			17 17		17 26		17 30					17 53		
Manchester Piccadilly 10	a	16 35							16 56			17 21		17 29		17 35					17 57		
Stockport 84	a											17 32											
Hazel Grove 86	a											17 39											
Buxton 86	a											18 16											
Heald Green 85	a								17 10					17 41							18 10		
Manchester Airport 85	a	16 53							17 17					17 48		17 53					18 16		

A From Leeds to Morecambe
B From Clitheroe
C To Liverpool Lime Street
D To Huddersfield
E From Edinburgh

The Sunday service between Manchester Victoria and Wigan Wallgate via Atherton is funded by GMITA and will operate whilst funding exists

Table 82

Mondays to Fridays
18 July to 30 September

Barrow-in-Furness, Blackpool North, Preston, Southport, Kirkby and Wigan - Bolton - Manchester

			NT	NT	TP	NT	NT	NT	NT	TP	TP	NT	NT	NT	TP	NT	NT	NT	NT	NT	NT	NT	TP
					◇■					◇■	◇■				◇■								◇■
				A					B	C	D			A	E			F			B	A	
					⊼					⊼					⊼								⊼
Barrow-in-Furness		d									17 21					17 43							
Roose		d																					
Dalton		d									17 30												
Ulverston		d									17 38					17 59							
Cark		d									17 46												
Kents Bank		d																					
Grange-over-Sands		d									17 53												
Arnside		d									17 59												
Silverdale		d																					
Carnforth		d									18 09					18 25		18 29					
Windermere	83	d								17 06													
Oxenholme Lake District	65	d								17 30													
Lancaster ■	65	a								17 47	18 20					18 38		18 42					
		d								17 48					18 26								
Blackpool North	97	d			17 20				17 37											18 20	18 37		18 44
Layton	97	d			17 23															18 23			
Poulton-le-Fylde	97	d			17 27															18 28			18 50
Kirkham & Wesham	97	d							17 52											18 37	18 52		
Preston ■	65,97	a			17 45				18 02	18 06					18 45					18 47	19 02		19 07
		d			17 47			17 56	18 04	18 08					18 47					18 49	19 04		19 10
Leyland		d						18 01	18 09											18 54	19 09		
Chorley		d			17 56			18 08		18 19					18 56					19 02			19 21
Adlington (Lancashire)		d						18 13												19 07			
Blackrod		d						18 17												19 10			
Horwich Parkway		d						18 20		18 26										19 14			19 28
Lostock		d								18 30										19 20			
Southport		d				17 24											18 17						
Meols Cop		d				17 29											18 22						
Bescar Lane		d															18 27						
New Lane		d															18 31						
Burscough Bridge		d				17 37											18 33						
Hoscar		d															18 37						
Parbold		d				17 42											18 40						
Appley Bridge		d				17 46											18 44						
Gathurst		d															18 47						
Kirkby		d					17 32												18 32				
Rainford		d					17 40												18 40				
Upholland		d					17 44												18 44				
Orrell		d					17 47												18 47				
Pemberton		d					17 50												18 50				
Wigan Wallgate		a				17 52	17 57										18 52		18 56				
		d	17 39			17 54	17 59					18 20	18 32				18 53		18 58				
Wigan North Western		d							18a24												19a24		
Ince		d					18 02												19 01				
Hindley		d					18 05					18 25	18 37				18 58		19 04				
Westhoughton		d	17 47			18 02						18 29					19 02						
Bolton		a	17 55		18 08	18 12		18 30		18 34		18 38			19 08		19 12			19 25			19 34
		d	17 56	18 02	18 08	18 13		18 30		18 35		18 39		19 02	19 08		19 13			19 25		19 31	19 35
Moses Gate		d										18 42											
Farnworth		d										18 44											
Kearsley		d										18 46											
Daisy Hill		d					18 09						18 41						19 08				
Hag Fold		d					18 12												19 11				
Atherton		d					18 15						18 45						19 14				
Walkden		d					18 20						18 50						19 19				
Moorside		d					18 24												19 23				
Swinton		d					18 26						18 55						19 25				
Salford Crescent		a	18 08	18 15		18 25	18 33	18 43		18 47		18 56	19 02	19 14			19 25		19 33	19 38		19 44	19 47
		d	18 09	18 15		18 26	18 33	18 43		18 47		18 56	19 03	19 15			19 26		19 33	19 38		19 44	19 47
Salford Central		d		18 17			18 36	18 46				18 59	19 05	19 17					19 36	19 41		19 46	
Manchester Victoria	⇌	a		18 24			18 43	18 52				19 06	19 11	19 23					19 43	19 47		19 53	
Rochdale	41	a		18 47																			
Deansgate	⇌	a	18 12							18 51							19 29						19 51
Manchester Oxford Road		a	18 14		18 23	18 31				18 52					19 23		19 31						19 52
Manchester Piccadilly ■	⇌	a	18 18		18 27	18 35				18 56					19 27		19 35						19 56
Stockport	84	a	18 34																				
Hazel Grove	86	a	18 43																				
Buxton	86	a	19 22																				
Heald Green	85	a			18 40					19 10													20 08
Manchester Airport	85 ✈	a			18 47	18 53				19 17					19 47		19 53						20 17

A From Clitheroe
B To Liverpool Lime Street
C ⊼ from Preston
D To Windermere
E From Edinburgh
F From Leeds to Morecambe

The Sunday service between Manchester Victoria and Wigan Wallgate via Atherton is funded by GMITA and will operate whilst funding exists

Table 82

Mondays to Fridays
18 July to 30 September

Barrow-in-Furness, Blackpool North, Preston, Southport, Kirkby and Wigan - Bolton - Manchester

			TP	NT	NT	NT	TP	NT	NT	NT	NT	TP	TP	NT	NT	NT	NT	NT	TP	TP	NT	NT	NT	NT
																					FO	FX	FO	FX
			◇■				◇■					◇■	◇■						◇■	◇■				
				A		B	C			D	E		F				D	E						
							⊼						⊼											
Barrow-in-Furness		d		18 03																20 08				
Roose		d		18 07																20 12				
Dalton		d		18 13																20 19				
Ulverston		d		18 21																20 27				
Cark		d		18 29																20 35				
Kents Bank		d		18 33																20 39				
Grange-over-Sands		d		18 37																20 43				
Arnside		d		18 43																20 49				
Silverdale		d		18 47																20 53				
Carnforth		d		18 55																21 01				
Windermere	83	d	18 15																					
Oxenholme Lake District	65	d	18 36				19 09						20 13											
Lancaster ■	65	a	18 52	19 05			19 26						20 26							21 10				
		d	18 52	19 06			19 26						20 26							21 10				
Blackpool North	97	d							19 20	19 37		19 44				20 20	20 37		20 45					
Layton	97	d							19 23							20 23								
Poulton-le-Fylde	97	d							19 28			19 50				20 28			20 51					
Kirkham & Wesham	97	d							19 37							20 37								
Preston ■	65,97	a	19 11	19 31			19 45		19 47	20 02		20 08	20 45			20 47	21 01		21 09	21 29				
		d	19 16				19 47		19 49	20 04		20 10	20 47			20 49	21 04		21 10	21 31				
Leyland		d							19 54	20 09						20 54	21 09							
Chorley		d	19 29				19 56		20 02			20 21	20 56			21 02			21 20					
Adlington (Lancashire)		d							20 07							21 07								
Blackrod		d							20 10							21 10								
Horwich Parkway		d	19 36						20 14			20 28				21 14			21 27					
Lostock		d							20 20							21 20								
Southport		d			19 00			19 23							20 23								21 23	21 23
Meols Cop		d			19 05			19 28							20 28								21 28	21 28
Bescar Lane		d																						
New Lane		d																						
Burscough Bridge		d			19 13			19 36							20 36								21 36	21 36
Hoscar		d																						
Parbold		d			19 18			19 41							20 41								21 41	21 41
Appley Bridge		d			19 22			19 45							20 45								21 45	21 45
Gathurst		d			19 25			19 48							20 48								21 48	21 48
Kirkby		d																						
Rainford		d																						
Upholland		d																						
Orrell		d																						
Pemberton		d																						
Wigan Wallgate		a			19 30			19 53							20 53								21 53	21 53
		d			19 32			19 55						20 27	20 55						21 27	21 27	21 55	21 55
Wigan North Western		d								20a24							21a23			21 48				
Ince		d												20 30							21 30	21 30		
Hindley		d			19 37			20 00						20 33	21 00						21 33	21 33	22 00	22 00
Westhoughton		d						20 04							21 04								22 04	22 04
Bolton		a	19 42				20 08	20 12	20 25			20 34	21 08		21 12	21 25			21 34				22 12	22 12
		d	19 43			20 02	20 08	20 13	20 25		20 31	20 35	21 08		21 13	21 25		21 31	21 35				22 13	22 13
Moses Gate		d																						
Farnworth		d																						
Kearsley		d																						
Daisy Hill		d			19 41									20 37							21 37	21 37		
Hag Fold		d												20 40							21 40	21 40		
Atherton		d			19 45									20 43							21 43	21 43		
Walkden		d			19 50									20 49							21 49	21 49		
Moorside		d												20 52							21 52	21 52		
Swinton		d			19 55									20 55							21 55	21 55		
Salford Crescent		a			20 02	20 15		20 25	20 38		20 43	20 47		21 02	21 25	21 38		21 43	21 47		22 02	22 02	22 25	22 25
		d			20 03	20 15		20 26	20 38		20 44	20 47		21 03	21 26	21 38		21 44	21 47		22 03	22 03	22 26	22 26
Salford Central		d			20 05	20 17			20 41		20 46			21 05		21 41		21 46			22 05		22 28	
Manchester Victoria	⇌	a			20 11	20 24			20 47		20 52			21 11		21 47		21 52			22 11	22 11	22 34	22 34
Rochdale	41	a																						
Deansgate	⇌	a						20 29				20 51			21 29				21 51					
Manchester Oxford Road		a	19 57				20 23	20 31				20 52	21 23		21 31				21 52	22 26				
Manchester Piccadilly ■	⇌	a	20 01				20 27	20 35				20 56	21 27		21 35				21 56	22 30				
Stockport	84	a																						
Hazel Grove	86	a																						
Buxton	86	a																						
Heald Green	85	a	20 15									21 10							22 09					
Manchester Airport	85 ✈	a	20 24				20 47	20 53				21 17	21 47		21 53				22 17	22 47				

A From Carlisle
B From Blackburn
C From Glasgow Central
D To Liverpool Lime Street
E From Clitheroe
F From Edinburgh

The Sunday service between Manchester Victoria and Wigan Wallgate via Atherton is funded by GMITA and will operate whilst funding exists

18 July to 30 September

Barrow-in-Furness, Blackpool North, Preston, Southport, Kirkby and Wigan - Bolton - Manchester

	NT FX	NT FO	NT FX	NT FO	TP	NT	TP FO	NT	NT FO	NT FX	NT	NT	NT	TP	NT	NT	TP	NT
					◇1		◇1							◇1			◇1	
			A	A		B	C ✠						D	E		A		
Barrow-in-Furness d								21 43										
Roose d								21 47										
Dalton d								21 53										
Ulverston d								22 01										
Cark d								22 09										
Kents Bank d								22 13										
Grange-over-Sands d								22 17										
Arnside d								22 23										
Silverdale d								22 27										
Carnforth d								22 35										
Windermere 83 d														22 45				
Oxenholme Lake District 65 d							22 10							23 06				
Lancaster 6 65 a							22 26	22 45						23 23				
d							22 26	22 46					23 07	23 24				
Blackpool North 97 d	21 20	21 20			21 44	22 14						22 20					22 44	23 13
Layton 97 d	21 23	21 23										22 23						23 16
Poulton-le-Fylde 97 d	21 28	21 28			21 50							22 28					22 50	23 21
Kirkham & Wesham 97 d	21 37	21 37										22 37						23 30
Preston 8 65,97 a	21 47	21 47			22 08	22 41	22 45	23 11				22 47	23 28	23 45			23 08	23 40
d	21 49	21 49			22 10	22 43	22 47					22 49					23 10	23 42
Leyland d	21 54	21 54				22 48						22 54						23 48
Chorley d	22 02	22 02			22 21							23 02					23 21	23 55
Adlington (Lancashire) d	22 07	22 07										23 07						00 01
Blackrod d	22 10	22 10										23 10						00 04
Horwich Parkway d	22 14	22 14			22 28							23 14					23 28	00 08
Lostock d	22 20	22 20										23 20						00 13
Southport d											22 18				23 10			
Meols Cop d											22 23				23 15			
Bescar Lane d											22 28							
New Lane d											22 32							
Burscough Bridge d											22 34				23 23			
Hoscar d											22 38							
Parbold d											22 41				23 28			
Appley Bridge d											22 45				23 32			
Gathurst d											22 48				23 35			
Kirkby d																		
Rainford d																		
Upholland d																		
Orrell d																		
Pemberton d																		
Wigan Wallgate a											22 53				23 44			
d									22 27	22 27	22 55							
Wigan North Western d						23a02												
Ince d									22 30	22 30								
Hindley d									22 33	22 33	23 00							
Westhoughton d											23 04							
Bolton a	22 25	22 25			22 34		23 06				23 12	23 25					23 34	00 18
d	22 25	22 25	22 31	22 31	22 35		23 07				23 13	23 25				23 31	23 35	00 19
Moses Gate d																		
Farnworth d																		
Kearsley d																		
Daisy Hill d									22 37	22 37								
Hag Fold d									22 40	22 40								
Atherton d									22 43	22 43								
Walkden d									22 49	22 49								
Moorside d									22 52	22 52								
Swinton d									22 55	22 55								
Salford Crescent a	22 38	22 38	22 43	22 43	22 47				23 02	23 02	23 25	23 38				23 43	23 47	
d	22 38	22 38	22 44	22 44	22 47				23 03	23 03	23 26	23 38				23 44	23 47	
Salford Central d		22 41		22 46					23 05									
Manchester Victoria a	22 47	22 47	22 52	22 52					23 13	23 13		23 47				23 52		00 36
Rochdale 41 a																		
Deansgate a					22 51						23 29							
Manchester Oxford Road a					22 52		23s21				23 31							
Manchester Piccadilly 10 a					22 56		23 31				23 39						23 53	
Stockport 84 a																		
Hazel Grove 86 a																		
Buxton 86 a																		
Heald Green 85 a					23 09												00 15	
Manchester Airport 85 ✈ a					23 17												00 22	

A From Clitheroe
B To Liverpool Lime Street
C From Edinburgh
D From Morecambe
E To Blackpool North

The Sunday service between Manchester Victoria and Wigan Wallgate via Atherton is funded by GMITA and will operate whilst funding exists

from 3 October

Barrow-in-Furness, Blackpool North, Preston, Southport, Kirkby and Wigan - Bolton - Manchester

	TP MX	TP MO	NT	NT MX	TP	TP MX	TP	TP	TP	TP	TP	NT	TP	NT	TP	NT	NT	NT	TP	NT	NT	NT
	◇1	◇1			◇1	◇1	◇1	◇1	◇1	◇1	◇1		◇1		◇1				◇1			
			A 🚌		B	C	D	E			E	F			✠			G	H ✠			I
Barrow-in-Furness d										04 35									05 31			
Roose d																						
Dalton d																						
Ulverston d										04 51									05 47			
Cark d																						
Kents Bank d																						
Grange-over-Sands d										05 03									05 59			
Arnside d										05 10									06 05			
Silverdale d																						
Carnforth d										05 19									06 15			06 43
Windermere 83 d																						
Oxenholme Lake District 65 d																						
Lancaster 6 65 a										05 28									06 23			06 52
d																			06 23			
Blackpool North 97 d	22p44	23p03		23p13					03 36			04 56			05 39						06 19	
Layton 97 d				23p16																	06 22	
Poulton-le-Fylde 97 d	22p50	23p09		23p21								05 02			05 45						06 27	
Kirkham & Wesham 97 d		23p17		23p30																	06 36	
Preston 8 65,97 a	23p08	23p28		23p40								05 20			06 03				06 42		06 46	
d	23p10	23p28		23p42					04u01				05 16		06 05				06 44		06 48	
Leyland d		23p34		23p48											06 10						06 53	
Chorley d	23p21	23p41		23p55									05 26		06 16				06 53		07 01	
Adlington (Lancashire) d		23p45		00 01																	07 06	
Blackrod d		23p49		00 04											06 22						07 10	
Horwich Parkway d	23p28	23p52		00 08									05 33		06 26				07 00		07 14	
Lostock d		23p56		00 13											06 30						07 20	
Southport d																				06 19		
Meols Cop d																				06 24		
Bescar Lane d																						
New Lane d																						
Burscough Bridge d																				06 32		
Hoscar d																						
Parbold d																				06 37		
Appley Bridge d																				06 41		
Gathurst d																				06 45		
Kirkby d																						
Rainford d																						
Upholland d																						
Orrell d																						
Pemberton d																						
Wigan Wallgate a																				06 52		
d														06 01		06 31	06 34			06 53		
Wigan North Western d																						
Ince d														06 04			06 37					
Hindley d														06 07		06 36	06 40					
Westhoughton d																06 41				07 01		
Bolton a	23p34	00 02		00 18									05 42		06 34	06 52			07 08	07 11	07 25	
d	23p35	00 02	00 06	00 19					04u30				05 43		06 35	06 53		06 56	07 08	07 12	07 25	
Moses Gate d																		06 59				
Farnworth d																		07 01				
Kearsley d																		07 03				
Daisy Hill d														06 11			06 44					
Hag Fold d														06 14			06 47					
Atherton d														06 17			06 50					
Walkden d														06 22			06 56					
Moorside d														06 26			06 59					
Swinton d														06 28			07 02					
Salford Crescent a	23p47		00 30										05 55	06 38	06 47	07 05	07 11	07 15		07 24	07 38	
d	23p47		00 31		00 37	00 49	01 03	03 40			04 53		05 55	06 38	06 47	07 08	07 11	07 15		07 25	07 38	
Salford Central d														06 41			07 14	07 19			07 41	
Manchester Victoria a			00 41	00 36										06 46			07 20	07 27			07 47	
Rochdale 41 a																						
Deansgate a															06 51	07 11				07 28		
Manchester Oxford Road a															06 52	07 13			07 23	07 30		
Manchester Piccadilly 10 a	23p53	00 18			00 43	00 53	01 08	03 44	04 48		04 58		06 01		06 56	07 17			07 27	07 34		
Stockport 84 a																07 34						
Hazel Grove 86 a																07 47						
Buxton 86 a																						
Heald Green 85 a	00 15														07 10							
Manchester Airport 85 ✈ a	00 22	00 32			01 00	01 10	01 25	04 00	05 07		05 19		06 18		07 17				07 47	07 53		

A MO from 31 October. From Clitheroe
B MO from 31 October. From Middlesbrough
C From Newcastle
D MO from 3 October until 24 October. From Middlesbrough
E From York
F To Colne
G From Blackburn
H ✠ from Preston
I From Skipton

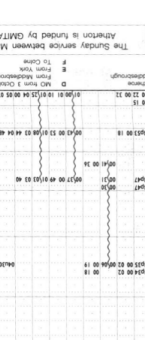

The Sunday service between Manchester Victoria and Wigan Wallgate via Atherton is funded by GMITA and will operate whilst funding exists

Table 82

Mondays to Fridays
from 3 October

Barrow-in-Furness, Blackpool North, Preston, Southport, Kirkby and Wigan - Bolton - Manchester

		NT A	TP ◇1 ⊤	NT B	NT	NT	NT	NT C	NT A	TP ◇1 D ⊤	NT	NT	NT A	TP ◇1 ⊤	TP ◇1 E ⊤	NT F	NT	NT	NT	NT	NT G	TP ◇1 D ⊤	NT H
Barrow-in-Furness	d									06 20						07 00						07 29	08 00
Roose	d									06 24						07 04							08 04
Dalton	d									06 31						07 10						07 38	08 10
Ulverston	d									06 39						07 19						07 46	08 19
Cark	d									06 47						07 26						07 54	08 27
Kents Bank	d									06 51						07 32							08 32
Grange-over-Sands	d									06 55						07 36						08 01	08 36
Arnside	d									07 01						07 42						08 07	08 42
Silverdale	d									07 05						07 47						08 11	08 47
Carnforth	d									07 12						07 55						08 18	08 54
Windermere 83	d																						
Oxenholme Lake District 65	d																						
Lancaster 8 65	a									07 21						08 04						08 26	09 07
	d									07 22					07 47	08 05						08 27	
Blackpool North 97	d		06 40				06 53	07 02				07 18		07 36									
Layton 97	d		06 43									07 21		07 39									
Poulton-le-Fylde 97	d		06 47					07 08				07 26		07 43									
Kirkham & Wesham 97	d		06 56									07 35		07 52									
Preston 8 65,97	a		07 07				07 15	07 28		07 41		07 46		08 03	08 07	08 30						08 45	
	d		07 09				07 17	07 30		07 47		07 47		08 12						08 17		08 47	
Leyland	d						07 22	07 35				07 53								08 23			
Chorley	d		07 18				07 31			07 56		08 01		08 22						08 33		08 56	
Adlington (Lancashire)	d						07 36					08 06								08 37			
Blackrod	d						07 40					08 10								08 41			
Horwich Parkway	d		07 26				07 44					08 14								08 45			
Lostock	d		07 30				07 49					08 20								08 50			
Southport	d				06 49														07 54				
Meols Cop	d				06 54														07 59				
Bescar Lane	d				06 59																		
New Lane	d				07 03																		
Burscough Bridge	d				07 05														08 07				
Hoscar	d				07 09																		
Parbold	d				07 12														08 12				
Appley Bridge	d				07 16														08 16				
Gathurst	d				07 19														08 19				
Kirkby	d																						
Rainford	d																						
Upholland	d																						
Orrell	d																						
Pemberton	d																						
Wigan Wallgate	a				07 27														08 26				
	d			07 15	07 27						07 58						08 13		08 27				
Wigan North Western	d					07 22		07a50										08 20					
Ince	d			07 18		07 25											08 16						
Hindley	d			07 21		07 29											08 19	08 25	08 32				
Westhoughton	d					07 33												08 29					
Bolton	a		07 34			07 42	07 54			08 08		08 25		08 34				08 38		08 55		09 08	
	d	07 30	07 35			07 43	07 55		07 59	08 08		08 25	08 31	08 35				08 39		08 56	09 02	09 08	
Moses Gate	d					07 46			08 02									08 42					
Farnworth	d					07 48			08 04									08 44					
Kearsley	d					07 50			08 06									08 46					
Daisy Hill	d			07 26	07 39						08 05						08 23		08 37				
Hag Fold	d			07 29													08 26						
Atherton	d			07 32	07 43						08 10						08 29		08 41				
Walkden	d			07 38							08 16						08 35		08 47				
Moorside	d			07 41													08 39						
Swinton	d			07 44													08 42		08 52				
Salford Crescent	a	07 43	07 47	07 51	07 59	08 02	08 07		08 17		08 29	08 38	08 43	08 47			08 52	08 56	09 02	09 08	09 15		
	d	07 43	07 47	07 51	07 59	08 02	08 08		08 17		08 30	08 38	08 44	08 47			08 52	08 56	09 02	09 09	09 16		
Salford Central	d	07 46		07 55	08 02	08 05			08 20		08 32	08 41	08 46				08 55	08 59	09 04		09 18		
Manchester Victoria 🚊	a	07 54		08 00	08 08	08 12			08 26		08 38	08 48	08 53				09 01	09 06	09 11		09 27		
Rochdale 41	a																						
Deansgate 🚊	a		07 51				08 11													09 12			
Manchester Oxford Road	a		07 52				08 14			08 23				08 52						09 14		09 23	
Manchester Piccadilly 10 🚊	a		07 56				08 18			08 27				08 56						09 18		09 27	
Stockport 84	a						08 34													09 34			
Hazel Grove 86	a						08 50													09 47			
Buxton 86	a																						
Heald Green 85	a		08 10											09 10									
Manchester Airport 85 ✈	a		08 17							08 47				09 19								09 47	

A From Clitheroe
B To Stalybridge
C To Liverpool Lime Street
D ⊤ from Preston
E From Edinburgh
F From Millom
G From Blackburn
H From Maryport

The Sunday service between Manchester Victoria and Wigan Wallgate via Atherton is funded by GMITA and will operate whilst funding exists

Table 82

Mondays to Fridays
from 3 October

Barrow-in-Furness, Blackpool North, Preston, Southport, Kirkby and Wigan - Bolton - Manchester

		NT	NT	NT A	NT B	TP ◇1 C ⊤	NT	NT	NT	NT D	TP ◇1 E ⊤	NT	NT	NT A	NT F	NT B	TP ◇1 ⊤	TP ◇1 G ⊤	NT	NT	TP ◇1 H ⊤	NT	NT I
Barrow-in-Furness	d																				09 23		10 16
Roose	d																				09 27		10 20
Dalton	d																				09 34		10 26
Ulverston	d																				09 42		10 35
Cark	d																				09 50		10 42
Kents Bank	d																				09 54		10 47
Grange-over-Sands	d																				09 58		10 51
Arnside	d																				10 04		10 57
Silverdale	d																				10 08		11 01
Carnforth	d														10 02						10 15		11 08
Windermere 83	d																						
Oxenholme Lake District 65	d										09 11												
Lancaster 8 65	a										09 26				10 12						10 25		11 20
	d										09 26										10 26		
Blackpool North 97	d		08 20			08 44							09 20	09 37			09 43						
Layton 97	d		08 23										09 23										
Poulton-le-Fylde 97	d		08 28			08 50							09 28				09 49						
Kirkham & Wesham 97	d		08 37										09 37	09 52									
Preston 8 65,97	a		08 47			09 08					09 45		09 47	10 02			10 07			10 21	10 45		
	d		08 49	09 04		09 10			09 23		09 47		09 49	10 04			10 12			10 23	10 47		
Leyland	d		08 54	09 09					09 29				09 54	10 09						10 29			
Chorley	d		09 02			09 21			09 36		09 56		10 02				10 22			10 36	10 56		
Adlington (Lancashire)	d		09 07										10 07										
Blackrod	d		09 10										10 10										
Horwich Parkway	d		09 14			09 28			09 45				10 14							10 45			
Lostock	d		09 20						09 50				10 20							10 50			
Southport	d							08 58														09 51	
Meols Cop	d							09 03														09 56	
Bescar Lane	d																					10 01	
New Lane	d																					10 05	
Burscough Bridge	d							09 11														10 07	
Hoscar	d																					10 11	
Parbold	d							09 16														10 14	
Appley Bridge	d							09 20														10 18	
Gathurst	d							09 23														10 21	
Kirkby	d	08 19										09 28											
Rainford	d	08 27										09 36											
Upholland	d	08 31										09 40											
Orrell	d	08 34										09 43											
Pemberton	d	08 37										09 46											
Wigan Wallgate	a	08 45						09 30				09 54										10 28	
	d	08 50					09 18	09 30				09 56							10 18			10 30	
Wigan North Western	d			09a24										10a24									
Ince	d	08 53										09 59											
Hindley	d	08 57					09 23	09 35				10 02							10 23			10 35	
Westhoughton	d						09 27												10 27				
Bolton	a		09 25			09 34	09 38		09 55		10 08		10 25				10 35		10 38	10 55	11 08		
	d		09 25		09 31	09 35	09 39		09 56	10 00	10 08		10 25			10 31	10 35		10 39	10 56	11 08		
Moses Gate	d						09 42												10 42				
Farnworth	d						09 44												10 44				
Kearsley	d						09 46												10 46				
Daisy Hill	d	09 01						09 39				10 07										10 39	
Hag Fold	d	09 04										10 10											
Atherton	d	09 06						09 43				10 13										10 43	
Walkden	d	09 12						09 48				10 18										10 48	
Moorside	d	09 15										10 22											
Swinton	d	09 18						09 53				10 24										10 53	
Salford Crescent	a	09 27	09 38		09 43	09 47	09 56	10 03	10 08	10 13		10 32	10 38			10 43	10 47		10 56	11 08		11 02	
	d	09 27	09 38		09 44	09 47	09 56	10 03	10 09	10 13		10 32	10 38			10 44	10 47		10 56	11 09		11 03	
Salford Central	d	09 31	09 41		09 46		09 59	10 05		10 16		10 36	10 41			10 46			10 59			11 05	
Manchester Victoria 🚊	a	09 38	09 47		09 53		10 06	10 12		10 22		10 43	10 47			10 53			11 06			11 11	
Rochdale 41	a																						
Deansgate 🚊	a					09 51			10 12								10 51						
Manchester Oxford Road	a					09 52			10 14		10 23						10 52				11 23		
Manchester Piccadilly 10 🚊	a					09 56			10 18		10 27						10 56				11 27		
Stockport 84	a								10 34														
Hazel Grove 86	a								10 47														
Buxton 86	a																						
Heald Green 85	a					10 10											11 10						
Manchester Airport 85 ✈	a					10 17					10 47						11 17				11 50		

A To L'pool Sth Pw Hl (Allertn)
B From Clitheroe
C not 9 December
D From Blackburn
E From Glasgow Central
F From Leeds to Morecambe
G From Edinburgh
H ⊤ from Preston
I From Sellafield

The Sunday service between Manchester Victoria and Wigan Wallgate via Atherton is funded by GMITA and will operate whilst funding exists

Table 82

Mondays to Fridays
from 3 October

Barrow-in-Furness, Blackpool North, Preston, Southport, Kirkby and Wigan - Bolton - Manchester

		NT	NT	NT	NT	TP	NT	NT	NT	TP	NT	NT	NT	NT	TP	NT	TP	NT	NT	NT	TP	NT	NT
						◇■				◇■					◇■		◇■				◇■		
				A	B					C			A	D		B					E	F	
						⊼				⊼							⊼				⊼		
Barrow-in-Furness	d														11 25							12 11	
Roose	d																					12 15	
Dalton	d																					12 21	
Ulverston	d														11 41							12 29	
Cark	d																					12 37	
Kents Bank	d																					12 41	
Grange-over-Sands	d														11 53							12 45	
Arnside	d														11 59							12 51	
Silverdale	d																					12 55	
Carnforth	d													12 02	12 09							13 03	
Windermere 83	d									10 49													
Oxenholme Lake District 65	d									11 09											12 10		
Lancaster ■ 65	a									11 26				12 11	12 18						12 26	13 16	
	d									11 26					12 18						12 26		
Blackpool North 97	d		10 20	10 37		10 44						11 20	11 37				11 44						
Layton 97	d		10 23									11 23											
Poulton-le-Fylde 97	d		10 28			10 50						11 28					11 50						
Kirkham & Wesham 97	d		10 37	10 52								11 37	11 52										
Preston ■ 65,97	a		10 47	11 02		11 08				11 45		11 47	12 02		12 37		12 08				12 45		
	d		10 49	11 04		11 10			11 23	11 47		11 49	12 04				12 10			12 23	12 47		
Leyland	d		10 54	11 09					11 29			11 54	12 09							12 29			
Chorley	d		11 02			11 21			11 36	11 56		12 02					12 21			12 36	12 56		
Adlington (Lancashire)	d		11 07									12 07											
Blackrod	d		11 10									12 10											
Horwich Parkway	d		11 14			11 28			11 45			12 14					12 28			12 45			
Lostock	d		11 20						11 50			12 20								12 50			
Southport	d							10 51											11 56				
Meols Cop	d							10 56											12 01				
Bescar Lane	d							11 01															
New Lane	d							11 05															
Burscough Bridge	d							11 07											12 09				
Hoscar	d							11 11															
Parbold	d							11 14											12 14				
Appley Bridge	d							11 18											12 18				
Gathurst	d							11 21											12 21				
Kirkby	d	10 28									11 28												12 28
Rainford	d	10 36									11 36												12 36
Upholland	d	10 40									11 40												12 40
Orrell	d	10 43									11 43												12 43
Pemberton	d	10 46									11 46												12 46
Wigan Wallgate	a	10 54						11 28			11 54								12 28				12 54
	d	10 56					11 18	11 30			11 56							12 18	12 30				12 56
Wigan North Western	d			11a24									12a24										
Ince	d	10 59									11 59												12 59
Hindley	d	11 02					11 23	11 35			12 02							12 23	12 35				13 02
Westhoughton	d						11 27											12 27					
Bolton	a		11 25			11 34	11 38		11 55	12 08		12 25					12 34	12 38		12 55	13 08		
	d		11 25		11 31	11 35	11 39		11 56	12 08		12 25				12 31	12 35	12 39		12 56	13 08		
Moses Gate	d						11 42											12 42					
Farnworth	d						11 44											12 44					
Kearsley	d						11 46											12 46					
Daisy Hill	d	11 07						11 39			12 07								12 39				13 07
Hag Fold	d	11 10									12 10												13 10
Atherton	d	11 13						11 43			12 13								12 43				13 13
Walkden	d	11 18						11 48			12 18								12 48				13 18
Moorside	d	11 22									12 22												13 22
Swinton	d	11 24						11 53			12 24								12 53				13 24
Salford Crescent	a	11 32	11 38		11 43	11 47	11 56	12 02	12 08		12 32	12 38				12 43	12 47	12 56	13 02	13 08			13 32
	d	11 32	11 38		11 44	11 47	11 56	12 03	12 09		12 32	12 38				12 44	12 47	12 56	13 03	13 09			13 32
Salford Central	d	11 36	11 41		11 46		11 59	12 05			12 36	12 41				12 46		12 59	13 05				13 36
Manchester Victoria ⇌	a	11 43	11 47		11 53		12 06	12 11			12 43	12 47				12 53		13 06	13 11				13 43
Rochdale 41	a																						
Deansgate ⇌	a					11 51			12 12								12 51			13 12			
Manchester Oxford Road	a					11 52			12 14	12 23							12 52			13 14	13 23		
Manchester Piccadilly ■ ⇌	a					11 56			12 18	12 27							12 56			13 18	13 27		
Stockport 84	a								12 34											13 34			
Hazel Grove 86	a								12 47											13 47			
Buxton 86	a																						
Heald Green 85	a					12 10											13 10						
Manchester Airport 85 ✈	a					12 17				12 47							13 17				13 47		

A To L'pool Sth Pw Hl (Allertn)
B From Clitheroe
C ⊼ from Preston
D From Leeds to Heysham Port
E From Edinburgh
F From Carlisle

The Sunday service between Manchester Victoria and Wigan Wallgate via Atherton is funded by GMITA and will operate whilst funding exists

Table 82

Mondays to Fridays
from 3 October

Barrow-in-Furness, Blackpool North, Preston, Southport, Kirkby and Wigan - Bolton - Manchester

		NT	NT	NT	TP	NT	NT	NT	TP	TP	NT	NT	NT	NT	TP	NT	NT	NT	TP	NT	NT	NT
					◇■				◇■	◇■					◇■				◇■			
			A	B					C				A	B					D			A
					⊼				⊼						⊼				⊼			
Barrow-in-Furness	d									13 25												
Roose	d																					
Dalton	d																					
Ulverston	d									13 41												
Cark	d																					
Kents Bank	d																					
Grange-over-Sands	d									13 53												
Arnside	d									13 59												
Silverdale	d																					
Carnforth	d									14 09												
Windermere 83	d								12 51													
Oxenholme Lake District 65	d								13 09										14 09			
Lancaster ■ 65	a								13 26	14 18									14 26			
	d								13 26	14 18									14 26			
Blackpool North 97	d	12 20	12 37		12 44							13 20	13 37		13 44						14 20	14 37
Layton 97	d	12 23										13 23									14 23	
Poulton-le-Fylde 97	d	12 28			12 50							13 28			13 50						14 28	
Kirkham & Wesham 97	d	12 37	12 52									13 37	13 52								14 37	14 52
Preston ■ 65,97	a	12 47	13 02		13 08				13 45	14 37		13 47	14 02		14 08				14 45		14 47	15 02
	d	12 49	13 04		13 10			13 23	13 47			13 49	14 04		14 10			14 23	14 47		14 49	15 04
Leyland	d	12 54	13 09					13 29				13 54	14 09					14 29			14 54	15 09
Chorley	d	13 02			13 21			13 36	13 56			14 02			14 21			14 36	14 56		15 02	
Adlington (Lancashire)	d	13 07										14 07									15 07	
Blackrod	d	13 10										14 10									15 10	
Horwich Parkway	d	13 14			13 28			13 45				14 14			14 28			14 45			15 14	
Lostock	d	13 20						13 50				14 20						14 50			15 20	
Southport	d						12 50										13 56					
Meols Cop	d						12 55										14 01					
Bescar Lane	d						13 00															
New Lane	d						13 04															
Burscough Bridge	d						13 07										14 09					
Hoscar	d						13 11															
Parbold	d						13 14										14 14					
Appley Bridge	d						13 18										14 18					
Gathurst	d						13 21										14 21					
Kirkby	d										13 28									14 28		
Rainford	d										13 36									14 36		
Upholland	d										13 40									14 40		
Orrell	d										13 43									14 43		
Pemberton	d										13 46									14 46		
Wigan Wallgate	a						13 28				13 54						14 28			14 54		
	d					13 18	13 30				13 56					14 18	14 30			14 56		
Wigan North Western	d		13a24										14a24									15a24
Ince	d										13 59									14 59		
Hindley	d					13 23	13 35				14 02					14 23	14 35			15 02		
Westhoughton	d					13 27										14 27						
Bolton	a	13 25			13 34	13 38		13 55	14 08			14 25			14 34	14 38		14 55	15 08		15 25	
	d	13 25		13 31	13 35	13 39		13 56	14 08			14 25		14 31	14 35	14 39		14 56	15 08		15 25	
Moses Gate	d					13 42										14 42						
Farnworth	d					13 44										14 44						
Kearsley	d					13 46										14 46						
Daisy Hill	d						13 39				14 07						14 39			15 07		
Hag Fold	d										14 10									15 10		
Atherton	d						13 43				14 13						14 43			15 13		
Walkden	d						13 48				14 18						14 48			15 18		
Moorside	d										14 22									15 22		
Swinton	d						13 53				14 24						14 53			15 24		
Salford Crescent	a	13 38		13 43	13 47	13 56	14 02	14 08			14 32	14 38		14 43	14 47	14 56	15 02	15 08		15 31	15 38	
	d	13 38		13 44	13 47	13 56	14 03	14 09			14 32	14 38		14 44	14 47	14 56	15 03	15 09		15 32	15 38	
Salford Central	d	13 41		13 46		13 59	14 05				14 36	14 41		14 46		14 59	15 05			15 36	15 41	
Manchester Victoria ⇌	a	13 47		13 53		14 06	14 11				14 43	14 47		14 53		15 06	15 11			15 43	15 47	
Rochdale 41	a																					
Deansgate ⇌	a				13 51			14 12							14 51			15 12				
Manchester Oxford Road	a				13 52			14 14	14 23						14 52			15 14	15 23			
Manchester Piccadilly ■ ⇌	a				13 56			14 18	14 27						14 56			15 18	15 27			
Stockport 84	a							14 34										15 34				
Hazel Grove 86	a							14 47										15 50				
Buxton 86	a																					
Heald Green 85	a				14 10										15 10							
Manchester Airport 85 ✈	a				14 17				14 47						15 17				15 47			

A To L'pool Sth Pw Hl (Allertn)
B From Clitheroe
C ⊼ from Preston
D From Edinburgh

The Sunday service between Manchester Victoria and Wigan Wallgate via Atherton is funded by GMITA and will operate whilst funding exists

Barrow-in-Furness, Blackpool North, Preston, Southport, Kirkby and Wigan - Bolton - Manchester

		NT A	TP ◇1 ⊼	NT	NT	NT	TP ◇1 B ⊼	NT	NT C	TP ◇1		NT A	NT	NT	NT D	TP ◇1 ⊼	NT	NT	TP ◇1 E ⊼	NT		NT	NT	NT D	NT A
Barrow-in-Furness	d							14 16		15 25										16 20					
Roose	d							14 20												16 24					
Dalton	d							14 26												16 30					
Ulverston	d							14 35		15 41										16 38					
Cark	d							14 42												16 46					
Kents Bank	d							14 47												16 50					
Grange-over-Sands	d							14 51		15 53										16 54					
Arnside	d							14 57		15 59										17 00					
Silverdale	d							15 01												17 04					
Carnforth	d							15 07	15 38	16 09										17 12					
Windermere 83	d																								
Oxenholme Lake District 65	d						14 59												16 08						
Lancaster 6 65	a						15 13	15 20	15 47	16 18									16 23	17 26					
	d						15 14			16 18									16 23						
Blackpool North 97	d		14 44											15 20	15 37	15 44							16 20	16 35	
Layton 97	d													15 23									16 23		
Poulton-le-Fylde 97	d		14 50											15 28		15 50							16 28		
Kirkham & Wesham 97	d													15 37	15 52								16 37	16 52	
Preston 8 65,97	a		15 08				15 34			16 37				15 47	16 02	16 08			16 42				16 47	17 02	
	d		15 10			15 23	15 47							15 49	16 04	16 10		16 23	16 47				16 49	17 04	
Leyland	d					15 29								15 54	16 09			16 29					16 54	17 09	
Chorley	d		15 21			15 36	15 56							16 02		16 21		16 36	16 56				17 02		
Adlington (Lancashire)	d													16 07									17 07		
Blackrod	d													16 10									17 10		
Horwich Parkway	d		15 28			15 45								16 14		16 28		16 45					17 14		
Lostock	d					15 50								16 20				16 50					17 20		
Southport	d				14 50																				
Meols Cop	d				14 55																				
Bescar Lane	d				15 00																				
New Lane	d				15 04																				
Burscough Bridge	d				15 07																				
Hoscar	d				15 11																				
Parbold	d				15 14																				
Appley Bridge	d				15 18																				
Gathurst	d				15 21																				
Kirkby	d												15 28									16 28			
Rainford	d												15 36									16 36			
Upholland	d												15 40									16 40			
Orrell	d												15 43									16 43			
Pemberton	d												15 46									16 46			
Wigan Wallgate	a				15 28								15 54									16 54			
	d			15 18	15 30								15 56				16 18					16 56			
Wigan North Western	d														16a24									17a24	
Ince	d												15 59									16 59			
Hindley	d			15 23	15 35								16 02				16 23					17 02			
Westhoughton	d			15 27													16 27								
Bolton	a		15 34	15 38		15 55	16 08							16 25		16 34	16 38	16 55	17 08				17 25		
	d	15 31	15 35	15 39		15 56	16 08					16 17		16 25		16 35	16 39	16 56	17 08				17 25		17 31
Moses Gate	d			15 42													16 42								
Farnworth	d			15 44													16 44								
Kearsley	d			15 46													16 46								
Daisy Hill	d				15 39								16 07									17 06			
Hag Fold	d												16 10									17 09			
Atherton	d				15 43								16 13									17 12			
Walkden	d				15 48								16 18									17 17			
Moorside	d												16 22									17 21			
Swinton	d				15 53								16 24									17 23			
Salford Crescent	a	15 43	15 47	15 56	16 02	16 08						16 30	16 34	16 38		16 47	16 56	17 08				17 31	17 38		17 43
	d	15 44	15 47	15 56	16 03	16 09						16 30	16 34	16 38		16 47	16 56	17 09				17 31	17 38		17 44
Salford Central	d	15 46		15 59	16 05							16 33	16 36	16 41			16 59					17 36	17 41		17 46
Manchester Victoria ⇌	a	15 55		16 06	16 11							16 42	16 43	16 47			17 06					17 43	17 47		17 54
Rochdale 41	a																								
Deansgate ⇌	a		15 51			16 12										16 51		17 15							
Manchester Oxford Road	a		15 52			16 14	16 23									16 52		17 17	17 26						
Manchester Piccadilly 10 ⇌	a		15 56			16 18	16 27									16 56		17 21	17 29						
Stockport 84	a					16 34												17 32							
Hazel Grove 86	a					16 43												17 39							
Buxton 86	a					17 24												18 19							
Heald Green 85	a		16 10				16 40									17 10			17 41						
Manchester Airport 85 ✈	a		16 17				16 47									17 17			17 48						

A From Clitheroe
B From Glasgow Central
C From Leeds to Morecambe
D To Liverpool Lime Street
E From Edinburgh

The Sunday service between Manchester Victoria and Wigan Wallgate via Atherton is funded by GMITA and will operate whilst funding exists

Barrow-in-Furness, Blackpool North, Preston, Southport, Kirkby and Wigan - Bolton - Manchester

		TP ◇1 ⊼	NT	NT	NT	NT A		TP ◇1 ⊼	NT	NT	NT B	TP ◇1 C ⊼	TP ◇1 D	NT	NT	NT A		TP ◇1 E ⊼	NT	NT F	NT	NT	NT B	NT A	TP ◇1 ⊼
Barrow-in-Furness	d												17 21						17 43						
Roose	d																								
Dalton	d												17 30												
Ulverston	d												17 38						17 59						
Cark	d												17 46												
Kents Bank	d																								
Grange-over-Sands	d												17 53												
Arnside	d												17 59												
Silverdale	d																								
Carnforth	d												18 09						18 25	18 29					
Windermere 83	d											17 06													
Oxenholme Lake District 65	d											17 30													
Lancaster 6 65	a											17 47	18 20						18 38	18 42					
	d											17 48						18 26							
Blackpool North 97	d	16 40						17 20			17 37											18 20	18 37		18 44
Layton 97	d	16 43						17 23														18 23			
Poulton-le-Fylde 97	d	16 48						17 27														18 28			18 50
Kirkham & Wesham 97	d	16 57									17 52											18 37	18 52		
Preston 8 65,97	a	17 08						17 45			18 02	18 06						18 45				18 47	19 02		19 07
	d	17 10						17 47		17 56	18 04	18 08						18 47				18 49	19 04		19 10
Leyland	d									18 01	18 09											18 54	19 09		
Chorley	d	17 21						17 56		18 08		18 19						18 56				19 02			19 21
Adlington (Lancashire)	d									18 13												19 07			
Blackrod	d									18 17												19 10			
Horwich Parkway	d	17 28								18 20		18 26										19 14			19 28
Lostock	d											18 30										19 20			
Southport	d			16 50																					
Meols Cop	d			16 55																					
Bescar Lane	d			17 00																					
New Lane	d			17 04																					
Burscough Bridge	d			17 07																					
Hoscar	d			17 11																					
Parbold	d			17 14																					
Appley Bridge	d			17 18																					
Gathurst	d			17 21																					
Kirkby	d								17 28												18 30				
Rainford	d								17 36												18 38				
Upholland	d								17 40												18 42				
Orrell	d								17 43												18 45				
Pemberton	d								17 46												18 48				
Wigan Wallgate	a			17 28					17 55												18 56				
	d		17 18	17 30	17 39				17 57					18 18	18 30						18 58				
Wigan North Western	d										18a24												19a24		
Ince	d								18 00												19 01				
Hindley	d		17 23	17 35					18 03					18 23	18 35						19 04				
Westhoughton	d		17 27		17 47									18 27											
Bolton	a	17 34	17 38		17 55			18 08		18 30		18 34		18 38				19 08				19 25			19 34
	d	17 35	17 39		17 56	18 02		18 08		18 30		18 35		18 39		19 02		19 08				19 25		19 31	19 35
Moses Gate	d		17 42											18 42											
Farnworth	d		17 44											18 44											
Kearsley	d		17 46											18 46											
Daisy Hill	d			17 39					18 07						18 39						19 08				
Hag Fold	d								18 10												19 11				
Atherton	d			17 43					18 13						18 43						19 14				
Walkden	d			17 48					18 18						18 48						19 19				
Moorside	d								18 22												19 23				
Swinton	d			17 53					18 24						18 53						19 25				
Salford Crescent	a	17 47	17 56	18 02	18 08	18 15			18 31	18 43		18 47		18 56	19 02	19 14					19 33	19 38		19 44	19 47
	d	17 48	17 56	18 03	18 09	18 15			18 31	18 43		18 47		18 56	19 03	19 15					19 33	19 38		19 44	19 47
Salford Central	d		17 59	18 05		18 17			18 36	18 46				18 59	19 05	19 17					19 36	19 41		19 46	
Manchester Victoria ⇌	a		18 06	18 11		18 24			18 43	18 52				19 06	19 11	19 24					19 43	19 47		19 54	
Rochdale 41	a					18 47																			
Deansgate ⇌	a	17 51			18 12							18 51													19 51
Manchester Oxford Road	a	17 53			18 14			18 23				18 52						19 23							19 52
Manchester Piccadilly 10 ⇌	a	17 57			18 18			18 27				18 56						19 27							19 56
Stockport 84	a				18 34																				
Hazel Grove 86	a				18 43																				
Buxton 86	a				19 24																				
Heald Green 85	a	18 10						18 40				19 10													20 08
Manchester Airport 85 ✈	a	18 16						18 47				19 17						19 47							20 17

A From Clitheroe
B To Liverpool Lime Street
C ⊼ from Preston
D To Windermere
E From Edinburgh
F From Leeds to Morecambe

The Sunday service between Manchester Victoria and Wigan Wallgate via Atherton is funded by GMITA and will operate whilst funding exists

Table 82

Mondays to Fridays
from 3 October

Barrow-in-Furness, Blackpool North, Preston, Southport, Kirkby and Wigan - Bolton - Manchester

Station	TP	NT	NT	NT	TP	NT	NT	NT	NT	TP	TP	NT	NT	NT	NT	TP	TP	NT FO	NT FX	NT FO	NT FX
	◇1				◇1					◇1	◇1					◇1	◇1				
		A		B	C			D	E		F			D	E						
Barrow-in-Furness d		18 03															20 08				
Roose d		18 07															20 12				
Dalton d		18 13															20 19				
Ulverston d		18 21															20 27				
Cark d		18 29															20 35				
Kents Bank d		18 33															20 39				
Grange-over-Sands d		18 37															20 43				
Arnside d		18 43															20 49				
Silverdale d		18 47															20 53				
Carnforth d		18 55															21 01				
Windermere 83 d	18 15																				
Oxenholme Lake District 65 d	18 36				19 09						20 13										
Lancaster 6 65 a	18 52	19 05			19 26						20 26						21 10				
d	18 52	19 06			19 26						20 26						21 10				
Blackpool North 97 d							19 20	19 37		19 44			20 20	20 37		20 45					
Layton 97 d							19 23						20 23								
Poulton-le-Fylde 97 d							19 28			19 50			20 28			20 51					
Kirkham & Wesham 97 d							19 37						20 37								
Preston 8 65,97 a	19 11	19 31			19 45		19 47	20 02		20 08	20 45		20 47	21 01		21 09	21 29				
d	19 16				19 47		19 49	20 04		20 10	20 47		20 49	21 04		21 10	21 31				
Leyland d							19 54	20 09					20 54	21 09							
Chorley d	19 29				19 56		20 02			20 21	20 56		21 02			21 20					
Adlington (Lancashire) d							20 07						21 07								
Blackrod d							20 10						21 10								
Horwich Parkway d	19 36						20 14			20 28			21 14			21 27					
Lostock d							20 20						21 20								
Southport d			18 56			19 23														21 19	21 19
Meols Cop d			19 01			19 28														21 24	21 24
Bescar Lane d																					
New Lane d																					
Burscough Bridge d			19 09			19 36														21 32	21 32
Hoscar d																					
Parbold d			19 14			19 41														21 37	21 37
Appley Bridge d			19 18			19 45														21 41	21 41
Gathurst d			19 21			19 48														21 44	21 44
Kirkby d																					
Rainford d																					
Upholland d																					
Orrell d																					
Pemberton d																					
Wigan Wallgate a			19 28			19 53														21 51	21 51
d			19 30			19 55						20 25						21 25	21 25	21 53	21 53
Wigan North Western d								20a24						21a23			21 48				
Ince d												20 28						21 28	21 28		
Hindley d			19 35			20 00						20 31						21 31	21 31	21 58	21 58
Westhoughton d						20 04														22 02	22 02
Bolton a	19 42				20 08	20 12	20 25			20 34	21 08		21 25			21 34				22 12	22 12
d	19 43			20 02	20 08	20 13	20 25		20 31	20 35	21 08		21 25		21 31	21 35				22 13	22 13
Moses Gate d																					
Farnworth d																					
Kearsley d																					
Daisy Hill d			19 39									20 35						21 35	21 35		
Hag Fold d												20 38						21 38	21 38		
Atherton d			19 43									20 41						21 41	21 41		
Walkden d			19 48									20 47						21 47	21 47		
Moorside d												20 50						21 50	21 50		
Swinton d			19 53									20 53						21 53	21 53		
Salford Crescent a			20 02	20 15		20 25	20 38		20 43	20 47		21 02	21 38		21 43	21 47		22 02	22 02	22 25	22 25
d			20 03	20 15		20 26	20 38		20 44	20 47		21 03	21 38		21 44	21 47		22 03	22 03	22 26	22 26
Salford Central d			20 05	20 17			20 41		20 46			21 05	21 41		21 46			22 05		22 28	
Manchester Victoria ⇌ a			20 11	20 25			20 47		20 53			21 11	21 47		21 53			22 11	22 11	22 34	22 34
Rochdale 41 a																					
Deansgate ⇌ a						20 29				20 51						21 51					
Manchester Oxford Road a	19 57				20 23	20 31				20 52	21 23					21 52	22 26				
Manchester Piccadilly 10 ⇌ a	20 01				20 27	20 35				20 56	21 27					21 56	22 30				
Stockport 84 a																					
Hazel Grove 86 a																					
Buxton 86 a																					
Heald Green 85 a	20 15									21 10						22 09					
Manchester Airport 85 ✈ a	20 24				20 47	20 53				21 17	21 47					22 17	22 47				

A From Carlisle
B From Blackburn
C From Glasgow Central
D To Liverpool Lime Street
E From Clitheroe
F From Edinburgh

The Sunday service between Manchester Victoria and Wigan Wallgate via Atherton is funded by GMITA and will operate whilst funding exists

Table 82

Mondays to Fridays
from 3 October

Barrow-in-Furness, Blackpool North, Preston, Southport, Kirkby and Wigan - Bolton - Manchester

Station	NT FX	NT FO	NT FX	NT FO	TP	NT	TP FO	NT	NT FO	NT FX	NT	NT	NT	TP	NT	NT	TP	NT
					◇1		◇1							◇1			◇1	
			A	A		B	C						D	E		A		
Barrow-in-Furness d								21 43										
Roose d								21 47										
Dalton d								21 53										
Ulverston d								22 01										
Cark d								22 09										
Kents Bank d								22 13										
Grange-over-Sands d								22 17										
Arnside d								22 23										
Silverdale d								22 27										
Carnforth d								22 35										
Windermere 83 d														22 45				
Oxenholme Lake District 65 d							22 10							23 06				
Lancaster 6 65 a							22 26	22 45						23 23				
d							22 26	22 46					23 07	23 24				
Blackpool North 97 d	21 20	21 20			21 44	22 14						22 20					22 44	23 13
Layton 97 d	21 23	21 23										22 23						23 16
Poulton-le-Fylde 97 d	21 28	21 28			21 50							22 28					22 50	23 21
Kirkham & Wesham 97 d	21 37	21 37										22 37						23 30
Preston 8 65,97 a	21 47	21 47			22 08	22 41	22 45	23 11				22 47	23 28	23 45			23 08	23 40
d	21 49	21 49			22 10	22 43	22 47					22 49					23 10	23 42
Leyland d	21 54	21 54				22 48						22 54						23 48
Chorley d	22 02	22 02			22 21							23 02					23 21	23 55
Adlington (Lancashire) d	22 07	22 07										23 07						00 01
Blackrod d	22 10	22 10										23 10						00 04
Horwich Parkway d	22 14	22 14			22 28							23 14					23 28	00 08
Lostock d	22 20	22 20										23 20						00 13
Southport d											22 18				23 10			
Meols Cop d											22 23				23 15			
Bescar Lane d											22 28							
New Lane d											22 32							
Burscough Bridge d											22 34				23 23			
Hoscar d											22 38							
Parbold d											22 41				23 28			
Appley Bridge d											22 45				23 32			
Gathurst d											22 48				23 35			
Kirkby d																		
Rainford d																		
Upholland d																		
Orrell d																		
Pemberton d																		
Wigan Wallgate a											22 53				23 44			
d									22 25	22 25	22 55							
Wigan North Western d						23a02												
Ince d									22 28	22 28								
Hindley d									22 31	22 31	23 00							
Westhoughton d											23 04							
Bolton a	22 25	22 25			22 34		23 06				23 12	23 25					23 34	00 18
d	22 25	22 25	22 31	22 31	22 35		23 07				23 13	23 25				23 31	23 35	00 19
Moses Gate d																		
Farnworth d																		
Kearsley d																		
Daisy Hill d									22 35	22 35								
Hag Fold d									22 38	22 38								
Atherton d									22 41	22 41								
Walkden d									22 47	22 47								
Moorside d									22 50	22 50								
Swinton d									22 53	22 53								
Salford Crescent a	22 38	22 38	22 43	22 43	22 47				23 02	23 02	23 25	23 38				23 43	23 47	
d	22 38	22 38	22 44	22 44	22 47				23 03	23 03	23 26	23 38				23 44	23 47	
Salford Central d		22 41		22 46					23 05									
Manchester Victoria ⇌ a	22 47	22 47	22 53	22 53					23 13	23 13		23 47				23 53		00 36
Rochdale 41 a																		
Deansgate ⇌ a					22 51						23 29							
Manchester Oxford Road a					22 52		23s21				23 31							
Manchester Piccadilly 10 ⇌ a					22 56		23 31				23 39						23 53	
Stockport 84 a																		
Hazel Grove 86 a																		
Buxton 86 a																		
Heald Green 85 a					23 09												00 15	
Manchester Airport 85 ✈ a					23 17												00 22	

A From Clitheroe
B To Liverpool Lime Street
C From Edinburgh
D From Morecambe
E To Blackpool North

The Sunday service between Manchester Victoria and Wigan Wallgate via Atherton is funded by GMITA and will operate whilst funding exists

Barrow-in-Furness, Blackpool North, Preston, Southport, Kirkby and Wigan - Bolton - Manchester

			TP	NT	TP	TP	TP	TP	TP	NT	TP		TP	NT	NT	NT	TP	NT	TP	NT	NT		TP	NT	NT	NT
			◇1		◇1	◇1	◇1	◇1	◇1		◇1		◇1				◇1		◇1				◇1			
					A	B		C	B	D						E	C	F	F							
																							⊼			
Barrow-in-Furness		d						04 35									05 31	06 03								
Roose		d																06 07								
Dalton		d																06 13								
Ulverston		d						04 51									05 47	06 21								
Cark		d																06 29								
Kents Bank		d																06 33								
Grange-over-Sands		d						05 03									05 59	06a40								
Arnside		d						05 10									06 05									
Silverdale		d																								
Carnforth		d						05 19									06 15		06 15							
Windermere	83	d																								
Oxenholme Lake District	65	d																								
Lancaster 6	65	a						05 28									06 23		06 23							
		d															06 23		06 23							
Blackpool North	97	d	22p44	23p13			03 36			04 56			05 39								06 19		06 40			06 53
Layton	97	d		23p16																	06 22		06 43			
Poulton-le-Fylde	97	d	22p50	23p21						05 02			05 45								06 27		06 47			
Kirkham & Wesham	97	d		23p30																	06 36		06 56			
Preston 8	65,97	a	23p08	23p40						05 20			06 03				06 42		06 42		06 46		07 07			07 15
		d	23p10	23p42			04u01				05 16		06 05				06 44		06 44		06 48		07 09			07 17
Leyland		d		23p48									06 10								06 53					07 22
Chorley		d	23p21	23p55							05 26		06 16				06 53		06 53		07 01		07 18			07 31
Adlington (Lancashire)		d		00 01																	07 06					07 36
Blackrod		d		00 04									06 22								07 10					07 40
Horwich Parkway		d	23p28	00 08							05 33		06 26				07 00		07 00		07 14		07 26			07 44
Lostock		d		00 13									06 30								07 20		07 30			07 49
Southport		d																		06 23						
Meols Cop		d																		06 28						
Bescar Lane		d																								
New Lane		d																								
Burscough Bridge		d																		06 36						
Hoscar		d																								
Parbold		d																		06 41						
Appley Bridge		d																		06 45						
Gathurst		d																		06 49						
Kirkby		d																								
Rainford		d																								
Upholland		d																								
Orrell		d																								
Pemberton		d																								
Wigan Wallgate		a																		06 54						
		d												06 31	06 36					06 55				07 15		
Wigan North Western		d																							07 22	
Ince		d													06 39									07 18	07 25	
Hindley		d												06 36	06 42									07 21	07 29	
Westhoughton		d												06 41						07 03					07 33	
Bolton		a	23p34	00 18							05 42		06 34	06 52			07 08		07 08	07 11	07 25		07 34		07 42	07 54
		d	23p35	00 19			04u30				05 43		06 35	06 53		06 56	07 08		07 08	07 12	07 25		07 35		07 43	07 55
Moses Gate		d														06 59									07 46	
Farnworth		d														07 01									07 48	
Kearsley		d														07 03									07 50	
Daisy Hill		d													06 46									07 26		
Hag Fold		d													06 49									07 29		
Atherton		d													06 52									07 32		
Walkden		d													06 58									07 38		
Moorside		d													07 01									07 41		
Swinton		d													07 04									07 44		
Salford Crescent		a	23p47								05 55		06 47	07 05	07 11	07 15				07 24	07 38		07 47	07 51	08 02	08 07
		d	23p47		00 49	03 37			04 46		05 55		06 47	07 08	07 11	07 15				07 25	07 38		07 47	07 51	08 02	08 08
Salford Central		d													07 14	07 19					07 41			07 55	08 05	
Manchester Victoria ⇌		a		00 36											07 20	07 24					07 47			08 01	08 12	
Rochdale	41	a																								
Deansgate ⇌		a											06 51	07 11						07 28			07 51			08 11
Manchester Oxford Road		a											06 52	07 13			07 23		07 23	07 30			07 52			08 14
Manchester Piccadilly 10 ⇌		a	23p53		00 53	03 44	04 48		04 52		06 01		06 56	07 17			07 27		07 27	07 34			07 56			08 18
Stockport	84	a												07 34												08 34
Hazel Grove	86	a												07 45												08 45
Buxton	86	a																								
Heald Green	85	a	00 15										07 10										08 10			
Manchester Airport ✈	85	a	00 22		01 10	04 00	05 07		05 10		06 18		07 17				07 47		07 47	07 53			08 17			

A From Newcastle
B From York
C from 23 July until 1 October
D To Colne
E From Blackburn
F until 16 July

The Sunday service between Manchester Victoria and Wigan Wallgate via Atherton is funded by GMITA and will operate whilst funding exists

Barrow-in-Furness, Blackpool North, Preston, Southport, Kirkby and Wigan - Bolton - Manchester

			NT	NT	NT	TP	NT		TP	NT	NT	NT	NT	TP	NT	NT	NT		NT	NT	TP	TP	NT	NT	NT	NT
						◇1			◇1					◇1							◇1	◇1				
			A		B	C	D		E			F	B							G	E	C	H			
						⊼			⊼					⊼							⊼	⊼				
Barrow-in-Furness		d				06 20	07 05															07 29	07 52			
Roose		d				06 24	07 09																07 56			
Dalton		d				06 31	07 15															07 38	08 02			
Ulverston		d				06 39	07 23															07 46	08 11			
Cark		d				06 47	07 31															07 54	08 19			
Kents Bank		d				06 51	07 35																08 24			
Grange-over-Sands		d				06 55	07a42															08 01	08a30			
Arnside		d				07 01															08 03	08 07				
Silverdale		d				07 05															08 07	08 11				
Carnforth		d				07 12			07 12			07 43									08 16	08 18				
Windermere	83	d																								
Oxenholme Lake District	65	d																								
Lancaster 6	65	a				07 21			07 21			07 52									08 24	08 26				
		d				07 22			07 22												08 27	08 27				
Blackpool North	97	d	07 02								07 18			07 44												08 20
Layton	97	d									07 21			07 47												08 23
Poulton-le-Fylde	97	d	07 08								07 26			07 51												08 28
Kirkham & Wesham	97	d									07 35			08 00												08 37
Preston 8	65,97	a	07 28			07 41			07 41		07 46			08 11							08 45	08 45				08 47
		d	07 30			07 47			07 47		07 47			08 12					08 17		08 47	08 47				08 49
Leyland		d	07 35								07 53								08 23							08 54
Chorley		d				07 56			07 56		08 01			08 22					08 33		08 56	08 56				09 02
Adlington (Lancashire)		d									08 06								08 37							09 07
Blackrod		d									08 10								08 41							09 10
Horwich Parkway		d									08 14								08 45							09 14
Lostock		d									08 20								08 50							09 20
Southport		d								07 21							07 53							08 25		
Meols Cop		d								07 26							07 58							08 30		
Bescar Lane		d															08 03									
New Lane		d															08 07									
Burscough Bridge		d								07 34							08 09							08 38		
Hoscar		d															08 13									
Parbold		d								07 39							08 16							08 43		
Appley Bridge		d								07 43							08 20							08 47		
Gathurst		d								07 47							08 23							08 50		
Kirkby		d		07 11																					08 21	
Rainford		d		07 19																					08 29	
Upholland		d		07 23																					08 33	
Orrell		d		07 27																					08 36	
Pemberton		d		07 30																					08 39	
Wigan Wallgate		a		07 35						07 51							08 28							08 55	08 45	
		d		07 37						07 53					08 13		08 29							08 56	08 50	
Wigan North Western		d	07a50													08 20										
Ince		d		07 40											08 16										08 53	
Hindley		d		07 43						07 58					08 19	08 25	08 34								08 57	
Westhoughton		d								08 03						08 29								09 04		
Bolton		a				08 08			08 08	08 11	08 25			08 34		08 38			08 55		09 08	09 08		09 12		09 25
		d			07 59	08 08			08 08	08 12	08 25		08 31	08 35		08 39			08 56	09 02	09 08	09 08		09 13		09 25
Moses Gate		d			08 02											08 42										
Farnworth		d			08 04											08 44										
Kearsley		d			08 06											08 46										
Daisy Hill		d		07 47											08 23		08 39								09 01	
Hag Fold		d		07 50											08 26										09 04	
Atherton		d		07 53											08 29		08 43								09 06	
Walkden		d		07 59											08 35		08 49								09 12	
Moorside		d		08 03											08 39										09 15	
Swinton		d		08 05											08 42		08 54								09 18	
Salford Crescent		a		08 13	08 17					08 24	08 38		08 43	08 47	08 50	08 56	09 03		09 08	09 15				09 25	09 27	09 38
		d		08 13	08 17					08 25	08 38		08 44	08 47	08 50	08 56	09 03		09 09	09 16				09 26	09 27	09 38
Salford Central		d		08 16	08 20						08 41		08 46		08 53	08 59	09 06			09 18					09 31	09 41
Manchester Victoria ⇌		a		08 20	08 25						08 47		08 52		08 59	09 06	09 11			09 26					09 38	09 47
Rochdale	41	a		08 51																09 54						
Deansgate ⇌		a								08 28									09 12					09 29		
Manchester Oxford Road		a				08 23			08 23	08 31				08 52					09 14		09 23	09 23		09 31		
Manchester Piccadilly 10 ⇌		a				08 27			08 27	08 35				08 56					09 18		09 27	09 27		09 35		
Stockport	84	a																	09 34							
Hazel Grove	86	a																	09 45							
Buxton	86	a																								
Heald Green	85	a								08 47				09 10												
Manchester Airport ✈	85	a				08 47			08 47	08 53				09 19							09 47	09 47		09 53		

A To Liverpool Lime Street
B From Clitheroe
C from 23 July until 1 October. ⊼ from Preston
D until 16 July
E until 16 July. ⊼ from Preston
F From Leeds
G From Blackburn
H until 16 July. From Maryport

The Sunday service between Manchester Victoria and Wigan Wallgate via Atherton is funded by GMITA and will operate whilst funding exists

Table 82

Saturdays until 1 October

Barrow-in-Furness, Blackpool North, Preston, Southport, Kirkby and Wigan - Bolton - Manchester

	NT A	NT B	TP ◇1 ⌶	NT	NT	NT	NT C	NT	TP ◇1 D ⌶	NT E	NT F	NT	NT	NT	NT A	NT	TP ◇1	NT B	TP ◇1 ⌶	TP ◇1 H ⌶	NT
Barrow-in-Furness d										08 25	09 20										
Roose d										08 29	09 24										
Dalton d										08 36	09 30										
Ulverston d										08 44	09 38										
Cark d										08 52	09 46										
Kents Bank d										08 57	09 50										
Grange-over-Sands d										09 01	09a57										
Arnside d										09 08											
Silverdale d										09 13											
Carnforth d										09 19						10 02					
Windermere 83 d																	09 38				
Oxenholme Lake District 65 d									09 12								09 58				
Lancaster 6 65 a									09 26	09 33						10 12	10 16				
d									09 27								10 16				
Blackpool North 97 d	08 38		08 44											09 20	09 37				09 43		
Layton 97 d														09 23							
Poulton-le-Fylde 97 d			08 50											09 28					09 49		
Kirkham & Wesham 97 d														09 37							
Preston 8 65,97 a	09 02		09 08						09 45					09 47	10 02		10 35		10 07		
d	09 04		09 10			09 23			09 47					09 49	10 04					10 12	
Leyland d	09 09					09 29								09 54	10 09						
Chorley d			09 21			09 36			09 56					10 02						10 22	
Adlington (Lancashire) d														10 07							
Blackrod d														10 10							
Horwich Parkway d			09 28			09 45								10 14							
Lostock d						09 50								10 20							
Southport d					09 02							09 24									
Meols Cop d					09 07																
Bescar Lane d																					
New Lane d																					
Burscough Bridge d					09 15							09 36									
Hoscar d																					
Parbold d					09 20							09 41									
Appley Bridge d					09 24							09 45									
Gathurst d					09 27																
Kirkby d													09 32								
Rainford d													09 40								
Upholland d													09 44								
Orrell d													09 47								
Pemberton d													09 50								
Wigan Wallgate a					09 32							09 51	09 56								
d				09 20	09 32			09 48				09 53	09 58								10 20
Wigan North Western d	09a24														10a24						
Ince d													10 01								
Hindley d				09 25	09 37							09 58	10 04								10 25
Westhoughton d				09 29								10 02									10 29
Bolton a			09 34	09 38		09 55		10 02	10 08			10 12		10 25						10 35	10 38
d		09 31	09 35	09 39		09 56	10 00	10 03	10 08			10 13		10 25				10 31		10 35	10 39
Moses Gate d				09 42																	10 42
Farnworth d				09 44																	10 44
Kearsley d				09 46																	10 46
Daisy Hill d					09 41								10 09								
Hag Fold d													10 12								
Atherton d					09 45								10 15								
Walkden d					09 50								10 20								
Moorside d													10 24								
Swinton d					09 55								10 26								
Salford Crescent a		09 43	09 47	09 56	10 03	10 08	10 13	10 15				10 25	10 34	10 38				10 44		10 47	10 56
d		09 44	09 47	09 56	10 03	10 09	10 13	10 15				10 26	10 34	10 38				10 44		10 47	10 56
Salford Central d		09 46		09 59	10 05		10 16	10 17					10 36	10 41				10 46			10 59
Manchester Victoria ⇌ a		09 52		10 06	10 12		10 21	10 25					10 43	10 47				10 51			11 06
Rochdale 41 a								10 51													
Deansgate ⇌ a			09 51			10 12						10 29								10 51	
Manchester Oxford Road a			09 52			10 14			10 23			10 31								10 52	
Manchester Piccadilly 10 ⇌ a			09 56			10 18			10 27			10 35								10 56	
Stockport 84 a						10 34															
Hazel Grove 86 a						10 45															
Buxton 86 a																					
Heald Green 85 a			10 10																	11 10	
Manchester Airport 85 ✈ a			10 17						10 47			10 53								11 17	

A To L'pool Sth Pw Hl (Allertn)
B From Clitheroe
C From Blackburn
D From Glasgow Central
E from 23 July until 1 October. From Maryport
F until 16 July
H From Edinburgh

The Sunday service between Manchester Victoria and Wigan Wallgate via Atherton is funded by GMITA and will operate whilst funding exists

Table 82

Saturdays until 1 October

Barrow-in-Furness, Blackpool North, Preston, Southport, Kirkby and Wigan - Bolton - Manchester

	NT	NT	NT A	NT	TP ◇1 B ⌶	TP ◇1 C ⌶	NT D	NT E	NT	NT	NT	NT F	NT G	TP ◇1 ⌶	NT	NT	NT	NT	TP ◇1 H ⌶	TP ◇1 I	NT J	NT
Barrow-in-Furness d						09 23	10 09	10 16												11 11	11 12	
Roose d						09 27	10 13	10 20														
Dalton d						09 34	10 19	10 26														
Ulverston d						09 42	10 27	10 34												11 27	11 28	
Cark d						09 50	10 35	10 42														
Kents Bank d						09 54	10 39	10 46														
Grange-over-Sands d						09 58	10a45	10 50												11 39	11a44	
Arnside d					10 03	10 04		10 56												11 45		
Silverdale d					10 07	10 08		11 01														
Carnforth d					10 15	10 15		11 09												11 55		
Windermere 83 d																			10 49			
Oxenholme Lake District 65 d																			11 09			
Lancaster 6 65 a					10 25	10 25		11 21											11 26	12 04		
d					10 26	10 26													11 26	12 04		
Blackpool North 97 d											10 20	10 37		10 44								
Layton 97 d											10 23											
Poulton-le-Fylde 97 d											10 28			10 50								
Kirkham & Wesham 97 d											10 37											
Preston 8 65,97 a					10 45	10 45					10 47	11 02		11 08					11 45	12 23		
d		10 23			10 47	10 47					10 49	11 04		11 10			11 23		11 47			
Leyland d		10 29									10 54	11 09					11 29					
Chorley d		10 36			10 56	10 56					11 02			11 21			11 36		11 56			
Adlington (Lancashire) d											11 07											
Blackrod d											11 10											
Horwich Parkway d		10 45									11 14			11 28			11 45					
Lostock d		10 50									11 20						11 50					
Southport d	09 55								10 24							10 55						11 24
Meols Cop d	10 00															11 00						
Bescar Lane d	10 05															11 05						
New Lane d	10 09															11 09						
Burscough Bridge d	10 11								10 36							11 11						11 36
Hoscar d	10 15															11 15						
Parbold d	10 18								10 41							11 18						11 41
Appley Bridge d	10 22								10 45							11 22						11 45
Gathurst d	10 25															11 25						
Kirkby d										10 32												
Rainford d										10 40												
Upholland d										10 44												
Orrell d										10 47												
Pemberton d										10 50												
Wigan Wallgate a	10 30								10 51	10 56						11 30						11 51
d	10 32			10 48					10 53	10 58					11 20	11 32		11 48				11 53
Wigan North Western d												11a24										
Ince d										11 01												
Hindley d	10 37								10 58	11 04					11 25	11 37						11 58
Westhoughton d									11 02						11 29							12 02
Bolton a		10 55		11 02	11 08	11 08			11 12		11 25			11 34	11 38		11 55	12 02	12 08			12 12
d		10 56	11 00	11 04	11 08	11 08			11 13		11 25		11 31	11 35	11 39		11 56	12 03	12 08			12 13
Moses Gate d															11 42							
Farnworth d															11 44							
Kearsley d															11 46							
Daisy Hill d	10 41									11 09						11 41						
Hag Fold d										11 12												
Atherton d	10 45									11 15						11 45						
Walkden d	10 50									11 20						11 50						
Moorside d										11 24												
Swinton d	10 55									11 26						11 55						
Salford Crescent a	11 02	11 08	11 12	11 16					11 25	11 34	11 38		11 43	11 47	11 56	12 02	12 08	12 15				12 25
d	11 03	11 09	11 13	11 16					11 26	11 34	11 38		11 44	11 47	11 56	12 03	12 09	12 15				12 26
Salford Central d	11 05		11 15	11 18						11 36	11 41		11 46		11 59	12 05		12 17				
Manchester Victoria ⇌ a	11 11		11 22	11 25						11 43	11 47		11 52		12 06	12 11		12 25				
Rochdale 41 a				11 51														12 51				
Deansgate ⇌ a		11 12							11 29					11 51			12 12					12 29
Manchester Oxford Road a		11 14			11 23	11 23			11 31					11 52			12 14		12 23			12 31
Manchester Piccadilly 10 ⇌ a		11 18			11 27	11 27			11 35					11 56			12 18		12 27			12 35
Stockport 84 a		11 34															12 34					
Hazel Grove 86 a		11 45															12 45					
Buxton 86 a																						
Heald Green 85 a														12 10								
Manchester Airport 85 ✈ a					11 47	11 47			11 53					12 17					12 47			12 53

A From Blackburn
B until 16 July. ⌶ from Preston
C from 23 July until 1 October. ⌶ from Preston
D until 16 July. From Sellafield
E from 23 July until 1 October. From Sellafield
F To L'pool Sth Pw Hl (Allertn)
G From Clitheroe
H ⌶ from Preston
I from 23 July until 10 September
J until 16 July

The Sunday service between Manchester Victoria and Wigan Wallgate via Atherton is funded by GMITA and will operate whilst funding exists

Table 82

Saturdays
until 1 October

Barrow-in-Furness, Blackpool North, Preston, Southport, Kirkby and Wigan - Bolton - Manchester

		NT	NT	NT	NT	TP	NT	TP	NT	NT	NT	NT	TP	TP	TP	TP	NT	TP	NT	NT	NT	NT	TP
						◇1		◇1					◇1	◇1	◇1	◇1		◇1					
				A	B	C	D						E	F	G	H	I	J				A	G
						✠		✠					✠	✠				✠					
Barrow-in-Furness	d															11 25	12 07						
Roose	d																						
Dalton	d																						
Ulverston	d															11 41	12 23						
Cark	d																						
Kents Bank	d																						
Grange-over-Sands	d															11 53	12a37						
Arnside	d														11 58	11 59							12 50
Silverdale	d																						12 54
Carnforth	d				12 02										12 09	12 09							13 03
Windermere	83 d																						
Oxenholme Lake District	65 d					12 05							12 05					12 10					
Lancaster 6	65 a				12 11										12 17	12 18		12 26					13 12
	d													12 14	12 18	12 18		12 26					
Blackpool North	97 d		11 15	11 37				11 44													12 20	12 37	
Layton	97 d		11 18																		12 23		
Poulton-le-Fylde	97 d		11 23					11 50													12 28		
Kirkham & Wesham	97 d		11 32																		12 37		
Preston 8	65,97 a		11 42	12 02		12 37		12 08					12 37	12 34	12 37	12 37		12 45			12 47	13 02	
	d		11 49	12 04				12 10			12 23		12 47					12 47			12 49	13 04	
Leyland	d		11 54	12 09							12 29										12 54	13 09	
Chorley	d		12 02					12 21			12 36		12 56					12 56			13 02		
Adlington (Lancashire)	d		12 07																		13 07		
Blackrod	d		12 10																		13 10		
Horwich Parkway	d		12 14					12 28			12 45										13 14		
Lostock	d		12 20								12 50										13 20		
Southport	d									12 00									12 24				
Meols Cop	d									12 05													
Bescar Lane	d																						
New Lane	d																						
Burscough Bridge	d									12 13									12 36				
Hoscar	d																						
Parbold	d									12 18									12 41				
Appley Bridge	d									12 22									12 45				
Gathurst	d									12 25													
Kirkby	d	11 32																		12 32			
Rainford	d	11 40																		12 40			
Upholland	d	11 44																		12 44			
Orrell	d	11 47																		12 47			
Pemberton	d	11 50																		12 50			
Wigan Wallgate	a	11 56								12 30									12 51	12 56			
	d	11 58							12 20	12 32		12 48							12 53	12 58			
Wigan North Western	d			12a24																		13a24	
Ince	d	12 01																		13 01			
Hindley	d	12 04							12 25	12 37									12 58	13 04			
Westhoughton	d								12 29										13 02				
Bolton	a		12 25					12 34	12 38		12 55	13 02	13 08					13 08	13 12		13 25		
	d		12 25				12 31	12 35	12 39		12 56	13 03	13 08					13 08	13 13		13 25		
Moses Gate	d								12 42														
Farnworth	d								12 44														
Kearsley	d								12 46														
Daisy Hill	d	12 09								12 41										13 09			
Hag Fold	d	12 12																		13 12			
Atherton	d	12 15								12 45										13 15			
Walkden	d	12 20								12 50										13 20			
Moorside	d	12 24																		13 24			
Swinton	d	12 26								12 55										13 26			
Salford Crescent	a	12 34	12 38				12 43	12 47	12 56	13 02	13 08	13 15							13 25	13 34	13 38		
	d	12 34	12 38				12 44	12 47	12 56	13 03	13 09	13 15							13 26	13 34	13 38		
Salford Central	d	12 36	12 41				12 46		12 59	13 05		13 17								13 36	13 41		
Manchester Victoria	⇌ a	12 43	12 47				12 52		13 06	13 11		13 25								13 43	13 47		
Rochdale	41 a											13 51											
Deansgate	⇌ a							12 51			13 12								13 29				
Manchester Oxford Road	a							12 52			13 14		13 23					13 23	13 31				
Manchester Piccadilly 10	⇌ a							12 56			13 18		13 27					13 27	13 35				
Stockport	84 a										13 34												
Hazel Grove	86 a										13 45												
Buxton	86 a																						
Heald Green	85 a							13 10															
Manchester Airport	85 ✈ a							13 17					13 47					13 47	13 53				

A To L'pool Sth Pw Hl (Allertn)
B From Leeds to Heysham Port
C from 25 June until 10 September. From Glasgow Central to Blackpool North
D From Clitheroe
E from 25 June until 10 September. From Glasgow Central
F from 25 June until 10 September. From Edinburgh
G until 16 July
H 17 September, 24 September, 1 October
I until 16 July. From Carlisle
J until 18 June, 17 September, 24 September, 1 October. From Edinburgh

The Sunday service between Manchester Victoria and Wigan Wallgate via Atherton is funded by GMITA and will operate whilst funding exists

Table 82

Saturdays
until 1 October

Barrow-in-Furness, Blackpool North, Preston, Southport, Kirkby and Wigan - Bolton - Manchester

		NT	NT	NT	TP	NT	NT	NT	NT	TP	NT	NT	NT	NT	TP	NT	TP	NT	NT	NT	NT	NT
					◇1					◇1					◇1		◇1					
		A	B	C						D				E	B	C						B
					✠					✠							✠					
Barrow-in-Furness	d	12 11	12 54																			13 47
Roose	d	12 15	12 58																			13 51
Dalton	d	12 21	13 04																			13 57
Ulverston	d	12 29	13 13																			14 06
Cark	d	12 37	13 20																			14 13
Kents Bank	d	12 41	13 25																			14 18
Grange-over-Sands	d	12 45	13a31																			14a25
Arnside	d	12 51													13 58							
Silverdale	d	12 55																				
Carnforth	d	13 03													14 09							
Windermere	83 d									12 51												
Oxenholme Lake District	65 d									13 09												
Lancaster 6	65 a	13 16								13 26					14 18							
	d									13 26					14 18							
Blackpool North	97 d				12 44								13 20	13 37			13 44					
Layton	97 d												13 23									
Poulton-le-Fylde	97 d				12 50								13 28				13 50					
Kirkham & Wesham	97 d												13 37									
Preston 8	65,97 a				13 08					13 45			13 47	14 02	14 37		14 08					
	d				13 10			13 23		13 47			13 49	14 04			14 10			14 23		
Leyland	d							13 29					13 54	14 09						14 29		
Chorley	d				13 21			13 36		13 56			14 02				14 21			14 36		
Adlington (Lancashire)	d												14 07									
Blackrod	d												14 10									
Horwich Parkway	d				13 28			13 45					14 14				14 28			14 45		
Lostock	d							13 50					14 20							14 50		
Southport	d						12 54				13 24								14 00			
Meols Cop	d						12 59												14 05			
Bescar Lane	d						13 04															
New Lane	d						13 08															
Burscough Bridge	d						13 11				13 36								14 13			
Hoscar	d						13 15															
Parbold	d						13 18				13 41								14 18			
Appley Bridge	d						13 22				13 45								14 22			
Gathurst	d						13 25												14 25			
Kirkby	d											13 32										
Rainford	d											13 40										
Upholland	d											13 44										
Orrell	d											13 47										
Pemberton	d											13 50										
Wigan Wallgate	a						13 30				13 51	13 56							14 30			
	d					13 20	13 32		13 48		13 53	13 58						14 20	14 32		14 48	
Wigan North Western	d													14a24								
Ince	d											14 01										
Hindley	d					13 25	13 37				13 58	14 04						14 25	14 37			
Westhoughton	d					13 29					14 02							14 29				
Bolton	a				13 34	13 38		13 55	14 02	14 08	14 12		14 25				14 34	14 38		14 55	15 02	
	d			13 31	13 35	13 39		13 56	14 03	14 08	14 13		14 25			14 31	14 35	14 39		14 56	15 03	
Moses Gate	d					13 42												14 42				
Farnworth	d					13 44												14 44				
Kearsley	d					13 46												14 46				
Daisy Hill	d						13 41					14 09							14 41			
Hag Fold	d											14 12										
Atherton	d						13 45					14 15							14 45			
Walkden	d						13 50					14 20							14 50			
Moorside	d											14 24										
Swinton	d						13 55					14 26							14 55			
Salford Crescent	a			13 43	13 47	13 56	14 02	14 08	14 15		14 25	14 34	14 38			14 43	14 47	14 56	15 02	15 08	15 15	
	d			13 44	13 47	13 56	14 03	14 09	14 15		14 26	14 34	14 38			14 44	14 47	14 56	15 03	15 09	15 15	
Salford Central	d			13 46		13 59	14 05		14 17			14 36	14 41			14 46		14 59	15 05		15 17	
Manchester Victoria	⇌ a			13 52		14 06	14 11		14 25			14 43	14 47			14 52		15 06	15 11		15 25	
Rochdale	41 a								14 51												15 51	
Deansgate	⇌ a				13 51			14 12			14 29						14 51			15 12		
Manchester Oxford Road	a				13 52			14 14		14 23	14 31						14 52			15 14		
Manchester Piccadilly 10	⇌ a				13 56			14 18		14 27	14 35						14 56			15 18		
Stockport	84 a							14 34												15 34		
Hazel Grove	86 a							14 45												15 45		
Buxton	86 a																					
Heald Green	85 a				14 10												15 10					
Manchester Airport	85 ✈ a				14 17					14 47	14 53						15 17					

A from 23 July until 1 October. From Carlisle
B until 16 July
C From Clitheroe
D ✠ from Preston
E To L'pool Sth Pw Hl (Allertn)

The Sunday service between Manchester Victoria and Wigan Wallgate via Atherton is funded by GMITA and will operate whilst funding exists

Barrow-in-Furness, Blackpool North, Preston, Southport, Kirkby and Wigan - Bolton - Manchester

		TP	TP	NT	NT	NT	NT	NT	NT	NT	TP	NT	NT	NT	NT	TP	NT	NT	TP	NT	NT	NT	NT
		◇1	◇1								◇1					◇1							
		A	B	C				D	E	F						G		H	E	I	E	F	
		🍴	🍴								🍴					🍴							
Barrow-in-Furness	d	13 25		14 16					14 50											15 18	16 15		
Roose	d			14 20					14 54											15 22	16 19		
Dalton	d			14 26					15 00											15 28	16 25		
Ulverston	d	13 41		14 35					15 08											15 36	16 33		
Cark	d			14 42					15 16											15 44	16 41		
Kents Bank	d			14 47					15 20											15 48	16 45		
Grange-over-Sands	d	13 53		14 51					15a27											15 52	16a52		
Arnside	d	13 59		14 57															15 56	15 58			
Silverdale	d			15 01															16 00	16 03			
Carnforth	d	14 09		15 08														15 36	16 09	16 11			
Windermere	83 d																						
Oxenholme Lake District	65 d		14 07													15 09							
Lancaster 8	65 a	14 18	14 22	15 20												15 26		15 45	16 19	16 24			
	d	14 18	14 22													15 26							
Blackpool North	97 d						14 20	14 37			14 44												
Layton	97 d						14 23																
Poulton-le-Fylde	97 d						14 28				14 50												
Kirkham & Wesham	97 d						14 37																
Preston 8	65,97 a	14 37	14 41				14 47	15 02			15 08					15 45							
	d	14 47					14 49	15 04			15 10			15 23		15 47							
Leyland	d						14 54	15 09						15 29									
Chorley	d	14 56					15 02				15 21			15 36		15 56							
Adlington (Lancashire)	d						15 07																
Blackrod	d						15 10																
Horwich Parkway	d						15 14				15 28			15 45									
Lostock	d						15 20							15 50									
Southport	d				14 24								14 54				15 24						
Meols Cop	d												14 59										
Bescar Lane	d												15 04										
New Lane	d												15 08										
Burscough Bridge	d				14 36								15 11				15 36						
Hoscar	d												15 15										
Parbold	d				14 41								15 18				15 41						
Appley Bridge	d				14 45								15 22				15 45						
Gathurst	d												15 25										
Kirkby	d					14 32																	15 32
Rainford	d					14 40																	15 40
Upholland	d					14 44																	15 44
Orrell	d					14 47																	15 47
Pemberton	d					14 50																	15 50
Wigan Wallgate	a				14 51	14 56							15 30				15 51						15 56
	d				14 53	14 58						15 20	15 32		15 48		15 53						15 58
Wigan North Western	d							15a24															
Ince	d					15 01																	16 01
Hindley	d				14 58	15 04						15 25	15 37				15 58						16 04
Westhoughton	d				15 02							15 29					16 02						
Bolton	a	15 08			15 12		15 25				15 34	15 38		15 55	16 02	16 08	16 12						
	d	15 08			15 13		15 25			15 31	15 35	15 39		15 56	16 03	16 08	16 13					16 17	
Moses Gate	d											15 42											
Farnworth	d											15 44											
Kearsley	d											15 46											
Daisy Hill	d					15 09							15 41										16 09
Hag Fold	d					15 12																	16 12
Atherton	d					15 15							15 45										16 15
Walkden	d					15 20							15 50										16 20
Moorside	d					15 24																	16 24
Swinton	d					15 26							15 55										16 26
Salford Crescent	a				15 25	15 34	15 38			15 43	15 47	15 56	16 02	16 08	16 15		16 25					16 30	16 33
	d				15 26	15 34	15 38			15 44	15 47	15 56	16 03	16 09	16 15		16 26					16 30	16 34
Salford Central	d					15 36	15 41			15 46		15 59	16 05		16 17							16 33	16 37
Manchester Victoria	⇌ a					15 43	15 47			15 54		16 06	16 11		16 23							16 41	16 43
Rochdale	41 a														16 51								
Deansgate	⇌ a				15 29						15 51			16 12									
Manchester Oxford Road	a	15 23			15 31						15 52			16 14		16 23	16 31						
Manchester Piccadilly 10	⇌ a	15 27			15 35						15 56			16 18		16 27	16 35						
Stockport	84 a													16 34									
Hazel Grove	86 a													16 45									
Buxton	86 a																						
Heald Green	85 a										16 10					16 40							
Manchester Airport	85 ✈ a	15 47			15 53						16 17					16 47	16 53						

A from 23 July until 1 October. 🍴 from Preston
B From Edinburgh
C from 23 July until 1 October. From Whitehaven
D To L'pool Sth Pw Hl (Allertn)
E until 16 July
F From Clitheroe
G From Glasgow Central
H From Leeds to Morecambe
I from 23 July until 1 October. From Carlisle

The Sunday service between Manchester Victoria and Wigan Wallgate via Atherton is funded by GMITA and will operate whilst funding exists

Barrow-in-Furness, Blackpool North, Preston, Southport, Kirkby and Wigan - Bolton - Manchester

		NT	NT	TP	NT	NT	NT	NT	TP	NT	NT	NT	NT	TP	TP	NT	NT	TP	NT	NT	NT	NT
				◇1					◇1					◇1	◇1			◇1				
			A						B				A	C	D	C	E					E
				🍴					🍴									🍴				
Barrow-in-Furness	d														16 22	16 55						
Roose	d															16 59						
Dalton	d														16 31	17 05						
Ulverston	d														16 39	17 13						
Cark	d														16 47	17 21						
Kents Bank	d															17 25						
Grange-over-Sands	d														16 54	17a32						
Arnside	d													16 58	17 00							
Silverdale	d													17 02	17 04							
Carnforth	d													17 11	17 11							
Windermere	83 d																					
Oxenholme Lake District	65 d								16 08													
Lancaster 8	65 a								16 26					17 19	17 19							
	d								16 26					17 20	17 20							
Blackpool North	97 d	15 20	15 37	15 44								16 20	16 35					16 40				
Layton	97 d	15 23										16 23						16 43				
Poulton-le-Fylde	97 d	15 28		15 50								16 28						16 48				
Kirkham & Wesham	97 d	15 37										16 37						16 57				
Preston 8	65,97 a	15 47	16 02	16 08					16 45			16 47	17 02	17 39	17 39			17 08				
	d	15 49	16 04	16 10			16 23		16 47			16 49	17 04					17 10			17 23	
Leyland	d	15 54	16 09				16 29					16 54	17 09								17 29	
Chorley	d	16 02		16 21			16 36		16 56			17 02						17 21			17 36	
Adlington (Lancashire)	d	16 07										17 07										
Blackrod	d	16 10										17 10										
Horwich Parkway	d	16 14		16 28			16 45					17 14						17 28			17 45	
Lostock	d	16 20					16 50					17 20									17 50	
Southport	d					16 00				16 24										16 54		
Meols Cop	d					16 05														16 59		
Bescar Lane	d																			17 04		
New Lane	d																			17 08		
Burscough Bridge	d					16 13				16 36										17 11		
Hoscar	d																			17 15		
Parbold	d					16 18				16 41										17 18		
Appley Bridge	d					16 22				16 45										17 22		
Gathurst	d					16 25														17 25		
Kirkby	d										16 32											
Rainford	d										16 40											
Upholland	d										16 44											
Orrell	d										16 47											
Pemberton	d										16 50											
Wigan Wallgate	a					16 30				16 51	16 56									17 30		
	d				16 20	16 32		16 48		16 53	16 58								17 20	17 32		
Wigan North Western	d		16a24										17a24									
Ince	d										17 01											
Hindley	d				16 25	16 37				16 58	17 04								17 25	17 37		
Westhoughton	d				16 29					17 02									17 29			
Bolton	a	16 25		16 34	16 38		16 55	17 02	17 08	17 12		17 25						17 34	17 38		17 55	
	d	16 25		16 35	16 39		16 56	17 03	17 08	17 13		17 25					17 31	17 35	17 39		17 56	18 02
Moses Gate	d				16 42														17 42			
Farnworth	d				16 44														17 44			
Kearsley	d				16 46														17 46			
Daisy Hill	d					16 41					17 08									17 41		
Hag Fold	d										17 11											
Atherton	d					16 45					17 14									17 45		
Walkden	d					16 50					17 19									17 50		
Moorside	d										17 23											
Swinton	d					16 55					17 25									17 55		
Salford Crescent	a	16 38		16 47	16 56	17 02	17 08	17 15		17 25	17 33	17 38					17 43	17 47	17 56	18 02	18 08	18 14
	d	16 38		16 47	16 56	17 03	17 09	17 15		17 26	17 33	17 38					17 44	17 47	17 56	18 03	18 09	18 15
Salford Central	d	16 41			16 59	17 05		17 17			17 36	17 41					17 46		17 59	18 05		18 17
Manchester Victoria	⇌ a	16 47			17 06	17 11		17 23			17 43	17 47					17 53		18 06	18 11		18 26
Rochdale	41 a							17 51														18 49
Deansgate	⇌ a			16 51			17 12			17 29								17 51			18 12	
Manchester Oxford Road	a			16 52			17 14		17 23	17 31								17 52			18 14	
Manchester Piccadilly 10	⇌ a			16 56			17 18		17 27	17 35								17 56			18 18	
Stockport	84 a						17 34														18 34	
Hazel Grove	86 a						17 43														18 45	
Buxton	86 a						18 25															
Heald Green	85 a			17 10					17 41									18 10				
Manchester Airport	85 ✈ a			17 17					17 48	17 53								18 17				

A To Liverpool Lime Street
B From Edinburgh
C until 16 July
D from 23 July until 1 October
E From Clitheroe

The Sunday service between Manchester Victoria and Wigan Wallgate via Atherton is funded by GMITA and will operate whilst funding exists

Barrow-in-Furness, Blackpool North, Preston, Southport, Kirkby and Wigan - Bolton - Manchester

			TP	NT	NT	NT	NT	TP	TP	TP	NT	NT	NT	NT	TP	NT	NT	NT	NT	NT	NT	TP	NT	NT
			◇1					◇1	◇1	◇1					◇1									
							A	B	C	D	E			F	G		H	I			A	C	E	C
			✠					✠							✠									
Barrow-in-Furness		d								17 21	17 57							18 03					19 02	19 30
Roose		d									18 01							18 07						19 34
Dalton		d								17 30	18 07							18 13						19 40
Ulverston		d								17 38	18 15							18 21					19 18	19 48
Cark		d								17 46	18 23							18 29						19 56
Kents Bank		d									18 27							18 33						20 00
Grange-over-Sands		d								17 53	18a32							18 37					19a34	20a07
Arnside		d							17 57	17 59								18 43				18 50		
Silverdale		d																18 47				18 54		
Carnforth		d							18 09	18 09							18 26	18 55				19 03		
Windermere	83	d						17 06																
Oxenholme Lake District	65	d						17b30																
Lancaster	65	a						17 47	18 16	18 16							18 38	19 05				19 12		
		d						17 48	18 17	18 17					18 26			19 06				19 13		
Blackpool North	97	d	17 20				17 37													18 20	18 37			
Layton	97	d	17 23																	18 23				
Poulton-le-Fylde	97	d	17 27																	18 28				
Kirkham & Wesham	97	d																		18 37				
Preston	65,97	a	17 45				18 02	18 06	18 37	18 35					18 45			19 31		18 47	19 00	19 33		
		d	17 47			17 56	18 04	18 08							18 47					18 49	19 04			
Leyland		d				18 01	18 09													18 54	19 09			
Chorley		d	17 56			18 08		18 19							18 56					19 02				
Adlington (Lancashire)		d				18 13														19 07				
Blackrod		d				18 17														19 10				
Horwich Parkway		d				18 20		18 26												19 14				
Lostock		d						18 30												19 20				
Southport		d		17 24									17 54			18 17								
Meols Cop		d		17 29									17 59			18 22								
Bescar Lane		d											18 04			18 27								
New Lane		d											18 08			18 31								
Burscough Bridge		d		17 37									18 11			18 33								
Hoscar		d											18 15			18 37								
Parbold		d		17 42									18 18			18 40								
Appley Bridge		d		17 46									18 22			18 44								
Gathurst		d											18 25			18 47								
Kirkby		d			17 32														18 32					
Rainford		d			17 40														18 40					
Upholland		d			17 44														18 44					
Orrell		d			17 47														18 47					
Pemberton		d			17 50														18 50					
Wigan Wallgate		a		17 52	17 57								18 30			18 52			18 56					
		d		17 54	17 59							18 20	18 32			18 53			18 58					
Wigan North Western		d					18a24														19a24			
Ince		d			18 02														19 01					
Hindley		d			18 05							18 25	18 37			18 58			19 04					
Westhoughton		d		18 02								18 29				19 02								
Bolton		a	18 08	18 12		18 30		18 34				18 38			19 08	19 12				19 25				
		d	18 08	18 13		18 30		18 35				18 39		19 02	19 08	19 13				19 25				
Moses Gate		d										18 42												
Farnworth		d										18 44												
Kearsley		d										18 46												
Daisy Hill		d			18 09								18 41						19 08					
Hag Fold		d			18 12														19 11					
Atherton		d			18 15								18 45						19 14					
Walkden		d			18 20								18 50						19 19					
Moorside		d			18 24														19 23					
Swinton		d			18 26								18 55						19 25					
Salford Crescent		a		18 25	18 33	18 43		18 47				18 56	19 02	19 14		19 25			19 33	19 38				
		d		18 26	18 33	18 43		18 47				18 56	19 03	19 15		19 26			19 33	19 38				
Salford Central		d			18 36	18 46						18 59	19 05	19 17					19 36	19 41				
Manchester Victoria		a			18 43	18 52						19 06	19 11	19 23					19 43	19 47				
Rochdale	41	a																						
Deansgate		a						18 51								19 29								
Manchester Oxford Road		a	18 23	18 31				18 52							19 23	19 31								
Manchester Piccadilly		a	18 27	18 35				18 56							19 27	19 35								
Stockport	84	a																						
Hazel Grove	86	a																						
Buxton	86	a																						
Heald Green	85	a	18 40					19 10																
Manchester Airport	85 ✈	a	18 47	18 53				19 17							19 51	19 53								

A To Liverpool Lime Street
B ✠ from Preston
C until 16 July
D from 23 July until 1 October
E until 16 July. From Carlisle
F From Clitheroe
G From Edinburgh
H From Leeds to Morecambe
I from 23 July until 1 October. From Carlisle
b Arr. 1725

The Sunday service between Manchester Victoria and Wigan Wallgate via Atherton is funded by GMITA and will operate whilst funding exists

Barrow-in-Furness, Blackpool North, Preston, Southport, Kirkby and Wigan - Bolton - Manchester

			NT	TP	NT	NT	TP	NT	NT	NT	NT	TP	TP	TP	NT	NT	NT	NT	NT	TP	TP	NT	NT	NT
				◇1			◇1					◇1	◇1	◇1						◇1	◇1			
			A			B	C			D	A		E	F				D	A	G		F		
							✠						✠											
Barrow-in-Furness		d																		19 33		20 45		
Roose		d																		19 37		20 49		
Dalton		d																		19 44		20 55		
Ulverston		d																		19 52		21 04		
Cark		d																		20 00		21 11		
Kents Bank		d																		20 04		21 16		
Grange-over-Sands		d																		20 08		21a23		
Arnside		d																		20 14				
Silverdale		d																		20 18				
Carnforth		d												20 25						20 25				
Windermere	83	d																						
Oxenholme Lake District	65	d					19 09						20 13											
Lancaster	65	a					19 26						20 26	20 34						20 34				
		d					19 26						20 26	20 35						20 35				
Blackpool North	97	d		18 42					19 20	19 37		19 43					20 20	20 37			20 42			
Layton	97	d							19 23								20 23							
Poulton-le-Fylde	97	d		18 48					19 28			19 49					20 28				20 48			
Kirkham & Wesham	97	d							19 37								20 37							
Preston	65,97	a		19 07			19 45		19 47	20 02		20 07	20 45	20 53			20 47	21 01		20 53	21 06			
		d		19 09			19 47		19 49	20 04		20 09	20 47				20 49	21 04		21 10				
Leyland		d							19 54	20 09							20 54	21 09						
Chorley		d		19 21			19 56		20 02			20 21	20 56				21 02			21 21				
Adlington (Lancashire)		d							20 07								21 07							
Blackrod		d							20 10								21 10							
Horwich Parkway		d		19 28					20 14			20 28					21 14			21 28				
Lostock		d							20 20								21 20							
Southport		d			19 00			19 23								20 23								21 23
Meols Cop		d			19 05			19 28								20 28								21 28
Bescar Lane		d																						
New Lane		d																						
Burscough Bridge		d			19 13			19 36								20 36								21 36
Hoscar		d																						
Parbold		d			19 18			19 41								20 41								21 41
Appley Bridge		d			19 22			19 45								20 45								21 45
Gathurst		d			19 25			19 48								20 48								21 48
Kirkby		d																						
Rainford		d																						
Upholland		d																						
Orrell		d																						
Pemberton		d																						
Wigan Wallgate		a			19 30			19 53								20 53								21 53
		d			19 32			19 55							20 27	20 55							21 27	21 55
Wigan North Western		d								20a24								21a23						
Ince		d													20 30								21 30	
Hindley		d			19 37			20 00							20 33	21 00							21 33	22 00
Westhoughton		d						20 04								21 04								22 04
Bolton		a		19 34			20 08	20 12	20 25			20 34	21 08			21 12	21 25			21 34				22 12
		d	19 31	19 35		20 02	20 08	20 13	20 25		20 31	20 35	21 08			21 13	21 25		21 31	21 35				22 13
Moses Gate		d																						
Farnworth		d																						
Kearsley		d																						
Daisy Hill		d			19 41										20 37								21 37	
Hag Fold		d													20 40								21 40	
Atherton		d			19 45										20 43								21 43	
Walkden		d			19 50										20 49								21 49	
Moorside		d													20 52								21 52	
Swinton		d			19 55										20 55								21 55	
Salford Crescent		a	19 44	19 47	20 02	20 15		20 25	20 38		20 43	20 47			21 02	21 25	21 38		21 43	21 47			22 02	22 25
		d	19 44	19 47	20 03	20 15		20 26	20 38		20 44	20 47			21 03	21 26	21 38		21 44	21 47			22 03	22 26
Salford Central		d	19 46		20 05	20 17			20 41		20 46				21 05		21 41		21 46				22 05	22 28
Manchester Victoria		a	19 53		20 11	20 24			20 47		20 52				21 11		21 47		21 52				22 11	22 34
Rochdale	41	a																						
Deansgate		a		19 51				20 29				20 51				21 29				21 51				
Manchester Oxford Road		a		19 52			20 23	20 31				20 52	21 23			21 31				21 52				
Manchester Piccadilly		a		19 56			20 27	20 35				20 56	21 27			21 35				21 56				
Stockport	84	a																						
Hazel Grove	86	a																						
Buxton	86	a																						
Heald Green	85	a		20 10								21 10								22 09				
Manchester Airport	85 ✈	a		20 17			20 47	20 53				21 17	21 47			21 53				22 17				

A From Clitheroe
B From Blackburn
C From Glasgow Central
D To Liverpool Lime Street
E From Edinburgh
F until 16 July
G from 23 July until 1 October

The Sunday service between Manchester Victoria and Wigan Wallgate via Atherton is funded by GMITA and will operate whilst funding exists

Table 82

Saturdays
until 1 October

Barrow-in-Furness, Blackpool North, Preston, Southport, Kirkby and Wigan - Bolton - Manchester

		NT	TP	NT	TP	NT	NT	NT	NT	TP		NT	NT	TP	NT	NT	NT
			◇1		◇1					1				◇1			
				A		B						C	D			A	
Barrow-in-Furness	d											21 43	21 43				
Roose	d											21 47	21 47				
Dalton	d											21 53	21 53				
Ulverston	d											22 01	22 01				
Cark	d											22 09	22 09				
Kents Bank	d											22 13	22 13				
Grange-over-Sands	d											22 17	22a20				
Arnside	d											22 23					
Silverdale	d											22 27					
Carnforth	d									22 33		22 35					
Windermere	83 d		21 40														
Oxenholme Lake District	65 d		22 01														
Lancaster 6	65 a		22 17							22 42		22 45					
	d		22 17							22 42		22 46					
Blackpool North	97 d	21 20			21 44	22 14			22 20					22 44			23 02
Layton	97 d	21 23							22 23								23 05
Poulton-le-Fylde	97 d	21 28			21 50				22 28					22 50			23 10
Kirkham & Wesham	97 d	21 37							22 37								23 19
Preston 8	65,97 a	21 47	22 38		22 08	22 41			22 47	23 02		23 11		23 08			23 29
	d	21 49			22 10	22 43			22 49					23 10			23 31
Leyland	d	21 54				22 48			22 54								23 36
Chorley	d	22 02			22 21				23 02					23 21			23 44
Adlington (Lancashire)	d	22 07							23 07								23 49
Blackrod	d	22 10							23 10								23 52
Horwich Parkway	d	22 14			22 28				23 14					23 28			23 56
Lostock	d	22 20							23 20								00 02
Southport	d							22 18							23 10		
Meols Cop	d							22 23							23 15		
Bescar Lane	d							22 28									
New Lane	d							22 32									
Burscough Bridge	d							22 34							23 23		
Hoscar	d							22 38									
Parbold	d							22 41							23 28		
Appley Bridge	d							22 45							23 32		
Gathurst	d							22 48							23 35		
Kirkby	d																
Rainford	d																
Upholland	d																
Orrell	d																
Pemberton	d																
Wigan Wallgate	a							22 53							23 44		
	d						22 27	22 55									
Wigan North Western	d					23a02											
Ince	d						22 30										
Hindley	d						22 33	23 00									
Westhoughton	d							23 04									
Bolton	a	22 25			22 34			23 12	23 25					23 34			00 07
	d	22 25		22 31	22 35			23 13	23 25					23 35		23 38	00 07
Moses Gate	d																
Farnworth	d																
Kearsley	d																
Daisy Hill	d						22 37										
Hag Fold	d						22 40										
Atherton	d						22 43										
Walkden	d						22 49										
Moorside	d						22 52										
Swinton	d						22 55										
Salford Crescent	a	22 38		22 43	22 47		23 02	23 25	23 38					23 47		23 48	
	d	22 38		22 44	22 47		23 03	23 26	23 38					23 47		23 51	
Salford Central	d	22 41		22 46			23 05										
Manchester Victoria	⇌ a	22 47		22 52			23 13		23 47							23 59	00 26
Rochdale	41 a																
Deansgate	⇌ a				22 51			23 29									
Manchester Oxford Road	a				22 52			23 31									
Manchester Piccadilly 10	⇌ a				22 56			23 39						23 53			
Stockport	84 a																
Hazel Grove	86 a																
Buxton	86 a																
Heald Green	85 a				23 09									00 15			
Manchester Airport	85 ✈ a				23 17									00 22			

A From Clitheroe
B To Liverpool Lime Street
C from 23 July until 1 October
D until 16 July

The Sunday service between Manchester Victoria and Wigan Wallgate via Atherton is funded by GMITA and will operate whilst funding exists

Table 82

Saturdays
from 8 October

Barrow-in-Furness, Blackpool North, Preston, Southport, Kirkby and Wigan - Bolton - Manchester

		TP	NT	TP	TP	TP	TP	TP	NT	TP		TP	NT	NT	NT	TP	NT	NT	TP	NT		NT	NT	NT	NT
		◇1		◇1	◇1	◇1	◇1	◇1		◇1		◇1				◇1			◇1						
				A	B			B	C						D									E	F
Barrow-in-Furness	d						04 35									05 31									
Roose	d																								
Dalton	d																								
Ulverston	d						04 51									05 47									
Cark	d																								
Kents Bank	d																								
Grange-over-Sands	d						05 03									05 59									
Arnside	d						05 10									06 05									
Silverdale	d																								
Carnforth	d						05 19									06 15									
Windermere	83 d																								
Oxenholme Lake District	65 d																								
Lancaster 6	65 a						05 28									06 23									
	d															06 23									
Blackpool North	97 d	22p44	23p13			03 36			04 56			05 39						06 19	06 40				06 53	07 02	
Layton	97 d		23p16															06 22	06 43						
Poulton-le-Fylde	97 d	22p50	23p21						05 02			05 45						06 27	06 47					07 08	
Kirkham & Wesham	97 d		23p30															06 36	06 56						
Preston 8	65,97 a	23p08	23p40						05 20			06 03				06 42		06 46	07 07				07 15	07 28	
	d	23p10	23p42			04u01				05 16		06 05				06 44		06 48	07 09				07 17	07 30	
Leyland	d		23p48									06 10						06 53					07 22	07 35	
Chorley	d	23p21	23p55							05 26		06 16				06 53		07 01	07 18				07 31		
Adlington (Lancashire)	d		00 01															07 06					07 36		
Blackrod	d		00 04									06 22						07 10					07 40		
Horwich Parkway	d	23p28	00 08							05 33		06 26				07 00		07 14	07 26				07 44		
Lostock	d		00 13									06 30						07 20	07 30				07 49		
Southport	d																06 19								
Meols Cop	d																06 24								
Bescar Lane	d																								
New Lane	d																								
Burscough Bridge	d																06 32								
Hoscar	d																								
Parbold	d																06 37								
Appley Bridge	d																06 41								
Gathurst	d																06 45								
Kirkby	d																								
Rainford	d																								
Upholland	d																								
Orrell	d																								
Pemberton	d																								
Wigan Wallgate	a																06 52								
	d												06 31	06 34			06 53			07 13					
Wigan North Western	d																					07 22		07a50	
Ince	d													06 37						07 16		07 25			
Hindley	d												06 36	06 40						07 19		07 29			
Westhoughton	d												06 41				07 01					07 33			
Bolton	a	23p34	00 18							05 42		06 34	06 52			07 08	07 11	07 25	07 34			07 42	07 54		
	d	23p35	00 19			04u30				05 43		06 35	06 53		06 56	07 08	07 12	07 25	07 35			07 43	07 55		07 59
Moses Gate	d														06 59							07 46			08 02
Farnworth	d														07 01							07 48			08 04
Kearsley	d														07 03							07 50			08 06
Daisy Hill	d													06 44						07 24					
Hag Fold	d													06 47						07 27					
Atherton	d													06 50						07 30					
Walkden	d													06 56						07 36					
Moorside	d													06 59						07 39					
Swinton	d													07 02						07 42					
Salford Crescent	a	23p47								05 55		06 47	07 05	07 11	07 15		07 24	07 38	07 47	07 51		08 02	08 07		08 17
	d	23p47		00 49	03 37			04 46		05 55		06 47	07 08	07 11	07 15		07 25	07 38	07 47	07 51		08 02	08 08		08 17
Salford Central	d													07 14	07 19			07 41		07 55		08 05			08 20
Manchester Victoria	⇌ a		00 36											07 20	07 25			07 47		08 01		08 12			08 26
Rochdale	41 a																								
Deansgate	⇌ a											06 51	07 11				07 28		07 51				08 11		
Manchester Oxford Road	a											06 52	07 13			07 23	07 30		07 52				08 14		
Manchester Piccadilly 10	⇌ a	23p53		00 53	03 44	04 48		04 52		06 01		06 56	07 17			07 27	07 34		07 56				08 18		
Stockport	84 a												07 34										08 34		
Hazel Grove	86 a												07 47										08 47		
Buxton	86 a																								
Heald Green	85 a	00 15										07 10							08 10						
Manchester Airport	85 ✈ a	00 22		01 10	04 00	05 07		05 10		06 18		07 17				07 47	07 53		08 17						

A From Newcastle
B From York
C To Colne
D From Blackburn
E To Liverpool Lime Street
F From Clitheroe

The Sunday service between Manchester Victoria and Wigan Wallgate via Atherton is funded by GMITA and will operate whilst funding exists

Table 82

Saturdays from 8 October

Barrow-in-Furness, Blackpool North, Preston, Southport, Kirkby and Wigan - Bolton - Manchester

			TP ◇1 A 🍴	NT	NT B	NT C	TP ◇1 🍴	NT	NT	NT	NT	NT D	TP ◇1 A 🍴	NT	NT	NT E	NT C	TP ◇1 🍴	NT	NT	NT	NT D	TP ◇1 F 🍴	NT G
Barrow-in-Furness		d	06 20										07 29											08 25
Roose		d	06 24																					08 29
Dalton		d	06 31										07 38											08 36
Ulverston		d	06 39										07 46											08 44
Cark		d	06 47										07 54											08 52
Kents Bank		d	06 51																					08 57
Grange-over-Sands		d	06 55										08 01											09 01
Arnside		d	07 01										08 07											09 08
Silverdale		d	07 05										08 11											09 13
Carnforth		d	07 12		07 43								08 18											09 19
Windermere	83	d																						
Oxenholme Lake District	65	d																					09 12	
Lancaster ■	65	a	07 21		07 52								08 26										09 26	09 33
		d	07 22										08 27										09 27	
Blackpool North	97	d		07 18			07 44								08 20	08 38		08 44						
Layton	97	d		07 21			07 47								08 23									
Poulton-le-Fylde	97	d		07 26			07 51								08 28			08 50						
Kirkham & Wesham	97	d		07 35			08 00								08 37									
Preston ■	65,97	a	07 41	07 46			08 11						08 45		08 47	09 02		09 08					09 45	
		d	07 47	07 47			08 12				08 17		08 47		08 49	09 04		09 10			09 23		09 47	
Leyland		d		07 53							08 23				08 54	09 09					09 29			
Chorley		d	07 56	08 01			08 22				08 33		08 56		09 02			09 21			09 36		09 56	
Adlington (Lancashire)		d		08 06							08 37				09 07									
Blackrod		d		08 10							08 41				09 10									
Horwich Parkway		d		08 14							08 45				09 14			09 28			09 45			
Lostock		d		08 20							08 50				09 20						09 50			
Southport		d								07 51										08 58				
Meols Cop		d								07 56										09 03				
Bescar Lane		d								08 01														
New Lane		d								08 05														
Burscough Bridge		d								08 07										09 11				
Hoscar		d								08 11														
Parbold		d								08 14										09 16				
Appley Bridge		d								08 18										09 20				
Gathurst		d								08 21										09 23				
Kirkby		d												08 19										
Rainford		d												08 27										
Upholland		d												08 31										
Orrell		d												08 34										
Pemberton		d												08 37										
Wigan Wallgate		a								08 28				08 45						09 30				
		d						08 11		08 29				08 50					09 18	09 30				
Wigan North Western		d							08 20							09a24								
Ince		d						08 14						08 53										
Hindley		d						08 17	08 25	08 34				08 57					09 23	09 35				
Westhoughton		d							08 29										09 27					
Bolton		a	08 08	08 25			08 34		08 38		08 55		09 08		09 25			09 34	09 38		09 55		10 08	
		d	08 08	08 25		08 31	08 35		08 39		08 56	09 02	09 08		09 25		09 31	09 35	09 39		09 56	10 00	10 08	
Moses Gate		d							08 42										09 42					
Farnworth		d							08 44										09 44					
Kearsley		d							08 46										09 46					
Daisy Hill		d						08 21		08 39				09 01						09 39				
Hag Fold		d						08 24						09 04										
Atherton		d						08 27		08 42				09 06						09 43				
Walkden		d						08 33		08 48				09 12						09 48				
Moorside		d						08 37						09 15										
Swinton		d						08 40		08 53				09 18						09 53				
Salford Crescent		a		08 38		08 43	08 47	08 50	08 56	09 03	09 08	09 15		09 27	09 38		09 43	09 47	09 56	10 03	10 08	10 13		
		d		08 38		08 44	08 47	08 50	08 56	09 03	09 09	09 16		09 27	09 38		09 44	09 47	09 56	10 03	10 09	10 13		
Salford Central		d		08 41		08 46		08 53	08 59	09 06		09 18		09 31	09 41		09 46		09 59	10 05		10 16		
Manchester Victoria 🚊		a		08 47		08 53		08 59	09 06	09 11		09 26		09 38	09 47		09 53		10 06	10 12		10 22		
Rochdale	41	a										09 54												
Deansgate 🚊		a									09 12							09 51			10 12			
Manchester Oxford Road		a	08 23				08 52				09 14		09 23					09 52			10 14		10 23	
Manchester Piccadilly ■10 🚊		a	08 27				08 56				09 18		09 27					09 56			10 18		10 27	
Stockport	84	a									09 34										10 34			
Hazel Grove	86	a									09 47										10 47			
Buxton	86	a																						
Heald Green	85	a					09 10											10 10						
Manchester Airport	85 ✈	a	08 47				09 19						09 47					10 17					10 47	

A 🍴 from Preston
B From Leeds
C From Clitheroe
D From Blackburn
E To L'pool Sth Pw Hl (Allertn)
F From Glasgow Central
G From Maryport

The Sunday service between Manchester Victoria and Wigan Wallgate via Atherton is funded by GMITA and will operate whilst funding exists

Table 82

Saturdays from 8 October

Barrow-in-Furness, Blackpool North, Preston, Southport, Kirkby and Wigan - Bolton - Manchester

			NT	NT	NT A	NT	TP ◇1	NT C	TP ◇1 🍴	TP ◇1 D 🍴	NT	NT	NT	NT E	TP ◇1 F 🍴	NT G	NT	NT	NT A	NT C	TP ◇1 🍴	NT	NT
Barrow-in-Furness		d													09 23	10 16							
Roose		d													09 27	10 20							
Dalton		d													09 34	10 26							
Ulverston		d													09 42	10 34							
Cark		d													09 50	10 42							
Kents Bank		d													09 54	10 46							
Grange-over-Sands		d													09 58	10 50							
Arnside		d													10 04	10 56							
Silverdale		d													10 08	11 01							
Carnforth		d				10 02									10 15	11 09							
Windermere	83	d					09 38																
Oxenholme Lake District	65	d					09 58																
Lancaster ■	65	a				10 12	10 16								10 25	11 21							
		d					10 16								10 26								
Blackpool North	97	d		09 20	09 37				09 43									10 20	10 37		10 44		
Layton	97	d		09 23														10 23					
Poulton-le-Fylde	97	d		09 28					09 49									10 28			10 50		
Kirkham & Wesham	97	d		09 37														10 37					
Preston ■	65,97	a		09 47	10 02		10 35		10 07						10 45			10 47	11 02		11 08		
		d		09 49	10 04				10 12				10 23		10 47			10 49	11 04		11 10		
Leyland		d		09 54	10 09								10 29					10 54	11 09				
Chorley		d		10 02					10 22				10 36		10 56			11 02			11 21		
Adlington (Lancashire)		d		10 07														11 07					
Blackrod		d		10 10														11 10					
Horwich Parkway		d		10 14									10 45					11 14			11 28		
Lostock		d		10 20									10 50					11 20					
Southport		d										09 51											10 51
Meols Cop		d										09 56											10 56
Bescar Lane		d										10 01											11 01
New Lane		d										10 05											11 05
Burscough Bridge		d										10 07											11 07
Hoscar		d										10 11											11 11
Parbold		d										10 14											11 14
Appley Bridge		d										10 18											11 18
Gathurst		d										10 21											11 21
Kirkby		d	09 28														10 28						
Rainford		d	09 36														10 36						
Upholland		d	09 40														10 40						
Orrell		d	09 43														10 43						
Pemberton		d	09 46														10 46						
Wigan Wallgate		a	09 54									10 28					10 54						11 28
		d	09 56								10 18	10 30					10 56					11 18	11 30
Wigan North Western		d			10a24														11a24				
Ince		d	09 59														10 59						
Hindley		d	10 02								10 23	10 35					11 02					11 23	11 35
Westhoughton		d									10 27											11 27	
Bolton		a		10 25					10 35		10 38		10 55		11 08			11 25			11 34	11 38	
		d		10 25				10 31	10 35		10 39		10 56	11 00	11 08			11 25		11 31	11 35	11 39	
Moses Gate		d									10 42											11 42	
Farnworth		d									10 44											11 44	
Kearsley		d									10 46											11 46	
Daisy Hill		d	10 07									10 39					11 07						11 39
Hag Fold		d	10 10														11 10						
Atherton		d	10 13									10 43					11 13						11 43
Walkden		d	10 18									10 48					11 18						11 48
Moorside		d	10 22														11 22						
Swinton		d	10 24									10 53					11 24						11 53
Salford Crescent		a	10 34	10 38				10 44	10 47		10 56	11 02	11 08	11 12			11 34	11 38		11 43	11 47	11 56	12 02
		d	10 34	10 38				10 44	10 47		10 56	11 03	11 09	11 13			11 34	11 38		11 44	11 47	11 56	12 03
Salford Central		d	10 36	10 41				10 46			10 59	11 05		11 15			11 36	11 41		11 46		11 59	12 05
Manchester Victoria 🚊		a	10 43	10 47				10 52			11 06	11 11		11 23			11 43	11 47		11 53		12 06	12 11
Rochdale	41	a																					
Deansgate 🚊		a							10 51				11 12								11 51		
Manchester Oxford Road		a							10 52				11 14		11 23						11 52		
Manchester Piccadilly ■10 🚊		a							10 56				11 18		11 27						11 56		
Stockport	84	a											11 34										
Hazel Grove	86	a											11 47										
Buxton	86	a																					
Heald Green	85	a							11 10												12 10		
Manchester Airport	85 ✈	a							11 17						11 47						12 17		

A To L'pool Sth Pw Hl (Allertn)
C From Clitheroe
D From Edinburgh
E From Blackburn
F 🍴 from Preston
G From Sellafield

The Sunday service between Manchester Victoria and Wigan Wallgate via Atherton is funded by GMITA and will operate whilst funding exists

Table 82

Saturdays from 8 October

Barrow-in-Furness, Blackpool North, Preston, Southport, Kirkby and Wigan - Bolton - Manchester

			NT	TP	NT	NT	NT	NT	TP	NT	TP	NT	NT	NT	TP	NT	NT	NT	NT	NT	TP	NT	NT	NT
				◇1 A ⊼			B	C	◇1	D	◇1 ⊼				◇1 E ⊼	F			B	D	◇1 ⊼			
Barrow-in-Furness		d							11 25							12 11								
Roose		d														12 15								
Dalton		d														12 21								
Ulverston		d							11 41							12 29								
Cark		d														12 37								
Kents Bank		d														12 41								
Grange-over-Sands		d							11 53							12 45								
Arnside		d							11 59							12 51								
Silverdale		d														12 55								
Carnforth		d						12 02	12 09							13 03								
Windermere	83	d		10 49																				
Oxenholme Lake District	65	d		11 09											12 10									
Lancaster 6	65	a		11 26				12 11	12 18						12 26	13 16								
		d		11 26					12 18						12 26									
Blackpool North	97	d				11 15	11 37				11 44							12 20	12 37		12 44			
Layton	97	d				11 18												12 23						
Poulton-le-Fylde	97	d				11 23					11 50							12 28			12 50			
Kirkham & Wesham	97	d				11 32												12 37						
Preston 8	65,97	a		11 45		11 42	12 02		12 37		12 08				12 45			12 47	13 02		13 08			
		d	11 23	11 47		11 49	12 04				12 10			12 23	12 47			12 49	13 04		13 10			13 23
Leyland		d	11 29			11 54	12 09							12 29				12 54	13 09					13 29
Chorley		d	11 36	11 56		12 02					12 21			12 36	12 56			13 02			13 21			13 36
Adlington (Lancashire)		d				12 07												13 07						
Blackrod		d				12 10												13 10						
Horwich Parkway		d	11 45			12 14					12 28			12 45				13 14			13 28			13 45
Lostock		d	11 50			12 20								12 50				13 20						13 50
Southport		d											11 56										12 50	
Meols Cop		d											12 01										12 55	
Bescar Lane		d																					13 00	
New Lane		d																					13 04	
Burscough Bridge		d											12 09										13 07	
Hoscar		d																					13 11	
Parbold		d											12 14										13 14	
Appley Bridge		d											12 18										13 18	
Gathurst		d											12 21										13 21	
Kirkby		d			11 28												12 28							
Rainford		d			11 36												12 36							
Upholland		d			11 40												12 40							
Orrell		d			11 43												12 43							
Pemberton		d			11 46												12 46							
Wigan Wallgate		a			11 54								12 28				12 54						13 28	
		d			11 56							12 18	12 30				12 56					13 18	13 30	
Wigan North Western		d					12a24												13a24					
Ince		d			11 59												12 59							
Hindley		d			12 02							12 23	12 35				13 02					13 23	13 35	
Westhoughton		d										12 27										13 27		
Bolton		a	11 55	12 08		12 25					12 34	12 38		12 55	13 08			13 25			13 34	13 38		13 55
		d	11 56	12 08		12 25				12 31	12 35	12 39		12 56	13 08			13 25		13 31	13 35	13 39		13 56
Moses Gate		d										12 42										13 42		
Farnworth		d										12 44										13 44		
Kearsley		d										12 46										13 46		
Daisy Hill		d			12 07								12 39				13 07						13 39	
Hag Fold		d			12 10												13 10							
Atherton		d			12 13								12 43				13 13						13 43	
Walkden		d			12 18								12 48				13 18						13 48	
Moorside		d			12 22												13 22							
Swinton		d			12 24								12 53				13 24						13 53	
Salford Crescent		a	12 08		12 34	12 38				12 43	12 47	12 56	13 00	13 08			13 34	13 38		13 43	13 47	13 56	14 02	14 08
		d	12 09		12 34	12 38				12 44	12 47	12 56	13 01	13 09			13 34	13 38		13 44	13 47	13 56	14 03	14 09
Salford Central		d			12 36	12 41				12 46		12 59	13 05				13 36	13 41		13 46		13 59	14 05	
Manchester Victoria	⇌	a			12 43	12 47				12 53		13 06	13 11				13 43	13 47		13 53		14 06	14 11	
Rochdale	41	a																						
Deansgate	⇌	a	12 12								12 51			13 12							13 51			14 12
Manchester Oxford Road		a	12 14	12 23							12 52			13 14	13 23						13 52			14 14
Manchester Piccadilly 10	⇌	a	12 18	12 27							12 56			13 18	13 27						13 56			14 18
Stockport	84	a	12 34											13 34										14 34
Hazel Grove	86	a	12 47											13 47										14 47
Buxton	86	a																						
Heald Green	85	a									13 10										14 10			
Manchester Airport	85 ✈	a		12 47							13 17				13 47						14 17			

A ⊼ from Preston
B To L'pool Sth Pw Hl (Allertn)
C From Leeds to Heysham Port
D From Clitheroe
E From Edinburgh
F From Carlisle

The Sunday service between Manchester Victoria and Wigan Wallgate via Atherton is funded by GMITA and will operate whilst funding exists

Table 82

Saturdays from 8 October

Barrow-in-Furness, Blackpool North, Preston, Southport, Kirkby and Wigan - Bolton - Manchester

			TP	NT	NT	NT	NT	TP	NT	NT	NT	TP	TP	NT	NT	NT	NT	NT	TP	NT	NT	NT	TP
			◇1 A ⊼			B	C	◇1 ⊼				◇1 A ⊼	◇1 D ⊼	E			B	C	◇1 ⊼				◇1 F ⊼
Barrow-in-Furness		d										13 25		14 16									
Roose		d												14 20									
Dalton		d												14 26									
Ulverston		d										13 41		14 35									
Cark		d												14 42									
Kents Bank		d												14 47									
Grange-over-Sands		d										13 53		14 51									
Arnside		d										13 59		14 57									
Silverdale		d												15 01									
Carnforth		d										14 09		15 08									
Windermere	83	d	12 51																				
Oxenholme Lake District	65	d	13 09										14 07										15 09
Lancaster 6	65	a	13 26									14 18	14 22	15 20									15 26
		d	13 26									14 18	14 22										15 26
Blackpool North	97	d			13 20	13 37		13 44								14 20	14 37		14 44				
Layton	97	d			13 23											14 23							
Poulton-le-Fylde	97	d			13 28			13 50								14 28			14 50				
Kirkham & Wesham	97	d			13 37											14 37							
Preston 8	65,97	a	13 45		13 47	14 02		14 08				14 37	14 41			14 47	15 02		15 08				15 45
		d	13 47		13 49	14 04		14 10			14 23	14 47				14 49	15 04		15 10			15 23	15 47
Leyland		d			13 54	14 09					14 29					14 54	15 09					15 29	
Chorley		d	13 56		14 02			14 21			14 36	14 56				15 02			15 21			15 36	15 56
Adlington (Lancashire)		d			14 07											15 07							
Blackrod		d			14 10											15 10							
Horwich Parkway		d			14 14			14 28			14 45					15 14			15 28			15 45	
Lostock		d			14 20						14 50					15 20						15 50	
Southport		d								13 56											14 50		
Meols Cop		d								14 01											14 55		
Bescar Lane		d																			15 00		
New Lane		d																			15 04		
Burscough Bridge		d								14 09											15 07		
Hoscar		d																			15 11		
Parbold		d								14 14											15 14		
Appley Bridge		d								14 18											15 18		
Gathurst		d								14 21											15 21		
Kirkby		d		13 28											14 28								
Rainford		d		13 36											14 36								
Upholland		d		13 40											14 40								
Orrell		d		13 43											14 43								
Pemberton		d		13 46											14 46								
Wigan Wallgate		a		13 54						14 28					14 54						15 28		
		d		13 56					14 18	14 30					14 56					15 18	15 30		
Wigan North Western		d				14a24											15a24						
Ince		d		13 59											14 59								
Hindley		d		14 02					14 23	14 35					15 02					15 23	15 35		
Westhoughton		d							14 27											15 27			
Bolton		a	14 08		14 25			14 34	14 38		14 55	15 08				15 25			15 34	15 38		15 55	16 08
		d	14 08		14 25		14 31	14 35	14 39		14 56	15 08				15 25		15 31	15 35	15 39		15 56	16 08
Moses Gate		d							14 42											15 42			
Farnworth		d							14 44											15 44			
Kearsley		d							14 46											15 46			
Daisy Hill		d		14 07						14 39					15 07						15 39		
Hag Fold		d		14 10											15 10								
Atherton		d		14 13						14 43					15 13						15 43		
Walkden		d		14 18						14 48					15 18						15 48		
Moorside		d		14 22											15 22								
Swinton		d		14 24						14 53					15 24						15 53		
Salford Crescent		a		14 34	14 38		14 43	14 47	14 56	15 02	15 08				15 34	15 38		15 43	15 47	15 56	16 02	16 08	
		d		14 34	14 38		14 44	14 47	14 56	15 03	15 09				15 34	15 38		15 44	15 47	15 56	16 03	16 09	
Salford Central		d		14 36	14 41		14 46		14 59	15 05					15 36	15 41		15 46		15 59	16 05		
Manchester Victoria	⇌	a		14 43	14 47		14 53		15 06	15 11					15 43	15 47		15 55		16 06	16 11		
Rochdale	41	a																					
Deansgate	⇌	a						14 51			15 12								15 51			16 12	
Manchester Oxford Road		a	14 23					14 52			15 14	15 23							15 52			16 14	16 23
Manchester Piccadilly 10	⇌	a	14 27					14 56			15 18	15 27							15 56			16 18	16 27
Stockport	84	a									15 34											16 34	
Hazel Grove	86	a									15 47											16 47	
Buxton	86	a																					
Heald Green	85	a						15 10											16 10				16 40
Manchester Airport	85 ✈	a	14 47					15 17				15 47							16 17				16 47

A ⊼ from Preston
B To L'pool Sth Pw Hl (Allertn)
C From Clitheroe
D From Edinburgh
E From Whitehaven
F From Glasgow Central

The Sunday service between Manchester Victoria and Wigan Wallgate via Atherton is funded by GMITA and will operate whilst funding exists

Table 82

Saturdays from 8 October

Barrow-in-Furness, Blackpool North, Preston, Southport, Kirkby and Wigan - Bolton - Manchester

		NT	NT	NT	NT	NT	NT	TP	NT	NT	NT	TP	TP	NT	NT	NT	NT	TP	NT	NT	NT	NT	TP
								◇1				◇1	◇1					◇1					◇1
		A	B	C			D					E				D	C					C	
								🛒				🛒						🛒					🛒
Barrow-in-Furness	d		15 18										16 22										
Roose	d		15 22																				
Dalton	d		15 28										16 31										
Ulverston	d		15 36										16 39										
Cark	d		15 44										16 47										
Kents Bank	d		15 48																				
Grange-over-Sands	d		15 52										16 54										
Arnside	d		15 58										17 00										
Silverdale	d		16 03										17 04										
Carnforth	d	15 36	16 11										17 11										
Windermere 83	d																						
Oxenholme Lake District 65	d											16 08											
Lancaster 6 65	a	15 45	16 24									16 26	17 19										
	d											16 26	17 20										
Blackpool North 97	d					15 20	15 37	15 44							16 20	16 35		16 40					17 20
Layton 97	d					15 23									16 23			16 43					17 23
Poulton-le-Fylde 97	d					15 28		15 50							16 28			16 48					17 27
Kirkham & Wesham 97	d					15 37									16 37			16 57					
Preston 8 65,97	a					15 47	16 02	16 08				16 45	17 39		16 47	17 02		17 08					17 45
	d					15 49	16 04	16 10			16 23	16 47			16 49	17 04		17 10			17 23		17 47
Leyland	d					15 54	16 09				16 29				16 54	17 09					17 29		
Chorley	d					16 02		16 21			16 36	16 56			17 02			17 21			17 36		17 56
Adlington (Lancashire)	d					16 07									17 07								
Blackrod	d					16 10									17 10								
Horwich Parkway	d					16 14		16 28			16 45				17 14			17 28			17 45		
Lostock	d					16 20					16 50				17 20						17 50		
Southport	d									15 56										16 50			
Meols Cop	d									16 01										16 55			
Bescar Lane	d																			17 00			
New Lane	d																			17 04			
Burscough Bridge	d									16 09										17 07			
Hoscar	d																			17 11			
Parbold	d									16 14										17 14			
Appley Bridge	d									16 18										17 18			
Gathurst	d									16 21										17 21			
Kirkby	d				15 28									16 28									
Rainford	d				15 36									16 36									
Upholland	d				15 40									16 40									
Orrell	d				15 43									16 43									
Pemberton	d				15 46									16 46									
Wigan Wallgate	a				15 54					16 28				16 54						17 28			
	d				15 56				16 18	16 30				16 56					17 18	17 30			
Wigan North Western	d						16a24									17a24							
Ince	d				15 59									16 59									
Hindley	d				16 02				16 23	16 35				17 02					17 23	17 35			
Westhoughton	d								16 27										17 27				
Bolton	a					16 25		16 34	16 38		16 55	17 08			17 25			17 34	17 38		17 55		18 08
	d			16 17		16 25		16 35	16 39		16 56	17 08			17 25		17 31	17 35	17 39		17 56	18 02	18 08
Moses Gate	d								16 42										17 42				
Farnworth	d								16 44										17 44				
Kearsley	d								16 46										17 46				
Daisy Hill	d				16 07					16 39				17 06						17 39			
Hag Fold	d				16 10									17 09									
Atherton	d				16 13					16 43				17 12						17 43			
Walkden	d				16 18					16 48				17 17						17 48			
Moorside	d				16 22									17 21									
Swinton	d				16 24					16 53				17 23						17 53			
Salford Crescent	a			16 30	16 33	16 38		16 47	16 56	17 02	17 08			17 33	17 38		17 43	17 47	17 56	18 02	18 08	18 14	
	d			16 30	16 34	16 38		16 47	16 56	17 03	17 09			17 33	17 38		17 44	17 47	17 56	18 03	18 09	18 15	
Salford Central	d			16 33	16 37	16 41			16 59	17 05				17 36	17 41		17 46		17 59	18 05		18 17	
Manchester Victoria ⇌	a			16 42	16 43	16 47			17 06	17 11				17 43	17 47		17 54		18 06	18 11		18 26	
Rochdale 41	a																					18 49	
Deansgate ⇌	a							16 51			17 12							17 51			18 12		
Manchester Oxford Road	a							16 52			17 14	17 23						17 52			18 14		18 23
Manchester Piccadilly 10 ⇌	a							16 56			17 18	17 27						17 56			18 18		18 27
Stockport 84	a										17 34										18 34		
Hazel Grove 86	a										17 43										18 47		
Buxton 86	a										18 27												
Heald Green 85	a							17 10				17 41						18 10					18 40
Manchester Airport 85 ✈	a							17 17				17 48						18 17					18 47

A From Leeds to Morecambe
B From Carlisle
C From Clitheroe
D To Liverpool Lime Street
E From Edinburgh

The Sunday service between Manchester Victoria and Wigan Wallgate via Atherton is funded by GMITA and will operate whilst funding exists

Table 82

Saturdays from 8 October

Barrow-in-Furness, Blackpool North, Preston, Southport, Kirkby and Wigan - Bolton - Manchester

		NT	NT	NT	TP	TP	NT	NT	NT	TP	NT	NT	NT	NT	NT	NT	TP	NT	NT	TP	NT	NT	NT
					◇1	◇1				◇1							◇1			◇1			
				A	B				C	D	E	F			A	C			G	H		A	C
					🛒					🛒										🛒			
Barrow-in-Furness	d					17 21						18 03											
Roose	d											18 07											
Dalton	d					17 30						18 13											
Ulverston	d					17 38						18 21											
Cark	d					17 46						18 29											
Kents Bank	d											18 33											
Grange-over-Sands	d					17 53						18 37											
Arnside	d					17 59						18 43											
Silverdale	d											18 47											
Carnforth	d					18 09					18 26	18 55											
Windermere 83	d				17 06																		
Oxenholme Lake District 65	d				17 30															19 09			
Lancaster 6 65	a				17 47	18 16					18 38	19 05								19 26			
	d				17 48	18 17				18 26		19 06								19 26			
Blackpool North 97	d			17 37										18 20	18 37		18 42				19 20	19 37	
Layton 97	d													18 23							19 23		
Poulton-le-Fylde 97	d													18 28			18 48				19 28		
Kirkham & Wesham 97	d													18 37							19 37		
Preston 8 65,97	a			18 02	18 06	18 35				18 45		19 31		18 47	19 00		19 07			19 45	19 47	20 02	
	d		17 56	18 04	18 08					18 47				18 49	19 04		19 09			19 47	19 49	20 04	
Leyland	d		18 01	18 09										18 54	19 09						19 54	20 09	
Chorley	d		18 08		18 19					18 56				19 02			19 21			19 56	20 02		
Adlington (Lancashire)	d		18 13											19 07							20 07		
Blackrod	d		18 17											19 10							20 10		
Horwich Parkway	d		18 20		18 26									19 14			19 28				20 14		
Lostock	d				18 30									19 20							20 20		
Southport	d							17 50										18 56					
Meols Cop	d							17 55										19 01					
Bescar Lane	d							18 00															
New Lane	d							18 04															
Burscough Bridge	d							18 07										19 09					
Hoscar	d							18 11															
Parbold	d							18 14										19 14					
Appley Bridge	d							18 18										19 18					
Gathurst	d							18 21										19 21					
Kirkby	d	17 28											18 30										
Rainford	d	17 36											18 38										
Upholland	d	17 40											18 42										
Orrell	d	17 43											18 45										
Pemberton	d	17 46											18 48										
Wigan Wallgate	a	17 55						18 28					18 56					19 28					
	d	17 57					18 18	18 30					18 57					19 30					
Wigan North Western	d			18a24											19a24							20a24	
Ince	d	18 00											19 00										
Hindley	d	18 03					18 23	18 35					19 04					19 35					
Westhoughton	d						18 27																
Bolton	a		18 30		18 34		18 38			19 08				19 25			19 34			20 08	20 25		
	d		18 30		18 35		18 39		19 02	19 08				19 25		19 31	19 35		20 02	20 08	20 25		20 31
Moses Gate	d						18 42																
Farnworth	d						18 44																
Kearsley	d						18 46																
Daisy Hill	d	18 07						18 39					19 08					19 39					
Hag Fold	d	18 10											19 11										
Atherton	d	18 13						18 43					19 13					19 43					
Walkden	d	18 18						18 48					19 19					19 48					
Moorside	d	18 22											19 22										
Swinton	d	18 24						18 53					19 25					19 53					
Salford Crescent	a	18 33	18 43		18 47		18 56	19 02	19 14				19 33	19 38		19 44	19 47	20 02	20 15		20 38		20 43
	d	18 33	18 43		18 47		18 56	19 03	19 15				19 33	19 38		19 44	19 47	20 03	20 15		20 38		20 44
Salford Central	d	18 36	18 46				18 59	19 05	19 17				19 36	19 41		19 46		20 05	20 17		20 41		20 46
Manchester Victoria ⇌	a	18 43	18 52				19 06	19 11	19 24				19 43	19 47		19 54		20 11	20 25		20 47		20 53
Rochdale 41	a																						
Deansgate ⇌	a				18 51												19 51						
Manchester Oxford Road	a				18 52					19 23							19 52			20 23			
Manchester Piccadilly 10 ⇌	a				18 56					19 27							19 56			20 27			
Stockport 84	a																						
Hazel Grove 86	a																						
Buxton 86	a																						
Heald Green 85	a				19 10												20 10						
Manchester Airport 85 ✈	a				19 17					19 51							20 17			20 47			

A To Liverpool Lime Street
B 🛒 from Preston
C From Clitheroe
D From Edinburgh
E From Leeds to Morecambe
F From Carlisle
G From Blackburn
H From Glasgow Central

The Sunday service between Manchester Victoria and Wigan Wallgate via Atherton is funded by GMITA and will operate whilst funding exists

Table 82

Saturdays from 8 October

Barrow-in-Furness, Blackpool North, Preston, Southport, Kirkby and Wigan - Bolton - Manchester

			TP ◇1	TP ◇1 A	NT	NT	NT B	NT C	TP ◇1	TP ◇1	NT	NT	NT	TP ◇1	NT C	TP ◇1	NT B	NT	NT	NT	TP 1	NT	TP ◇1
Barrow-in-Furness		d							19 33													21 43	
Roose		d							19 37													21 47	
Dalton		d							19 44													21 53	
Ulverston		d							19 52													22 01	
Cark		d							20 00													22 09	
Kents Bank		d							20 04													22 13	
Grange-over-Sands		d							20 08													22 17	
Arnside		d							20 14													22 23	
Silverdale		d							20 18													22 27	
Carnforth		d							20 25												22 33	22 35	
Windermere	83	d												21 40									
Oxenholme Lake District	65	d		20 13										22 01									
Lancaster 8	65	a		20 26					20 34					22 17							22 42	22 45	
		d		20 26					20 35					22 17							22 42	22 46	
Blackpool North	97	d	19 43			20 20	20 37			20 42			21 20			21 44	22 14			22 20			22 44
Layton	97	d				20 23							21 23							22 23			
Poulton-le-Fylde	97	d	19 49			20 28				20 48			21 28			21 50				22 28			22 50
Kirkham & Wesham	97	d				20 37							21 37							22 37			
Preston 8	65,97	a	20 07	20 45		20 47	21 01		20 53	21 06			21 47	22 38		22 08	22 41			22 47	23 02	23 11	23 08
		d	20 09	20 47		20 49	21 04		21 10				21 49			22 10	22 43			22 49			23 10
Leyland		d				20 54	21 09						21 54				22 48			22 54			
Chorley		d	20 21	20 56		21 02			21 21				22 02			22 21				23 02			23 21
Adlington (Lancashire)		d				21 07							22 07							23 07			
Blackrod		d				21 10							22 10							23 10			
Horwich Parkway		d	20 28			21 14			21 28				22 14			22 28				23 14			23 28
Lostock		d				21 20							22 20							23 20			
Southport		d										21 19							22 18				
Meols Cop		d										21 24							22 23				
Bescar Lane		d																	22 28				
New Lane		d																	22 32				
Burscough Bridge		d										21 32							22 34				
Hoscar		d																	22 38				
Parbold		d										21 37							22 41				
Appley Bridge		d										21 41							22 45				
Gathurst		d										21 44							22 48				
Kirkby		d																					
Rainford		d																					
Upholland		d																					
Orrell		d																					
Pemberton		d																					
Wigan Wallgate		a										21 51							22 53				
		d			20 25						21 25	21 53						22 25	22 55				
Wigan North Western		d					21a23										23a02						
Ince		d			20 28						21 28							22 28					
Hindley		d			20 31						21 31	21 58						22 31	23 00				
Westhoughton		d										22 02							23 04				
Bolton		a	20 34	21 08		21 25			21 34			22 10	22 25			22 34			23 12	23 25			23 34
		d	20 35	21 08		21 25		21 31	21 35			22 11	22 25		22 31	22 35			23 13	23 25			23 35
Moses Gate		d																					
Farnworth		d																					
Kearsley		d																					
Daisy Hill		d			20 35						21 35							22 35					
Hag Fold		d			20 38						21 38							22 38					
Atherton		d			20 41						21 41							22 41					
Walkden		d			20 47						21 47							22 47					
Moorside		d			20 50						21 50							22 50					
Swinton		d			20 53						21 53							22 53					
Salford Crescent		a	20 47		21 02	21 38		21 43	21 47		22 02	22 25	22 38		22 43	22 47		23 02	23 25	23 38			23 47
		d	20 47		21 03	21 38		21 44	21 47		22 03	22 26	22 38		22 44	22 47		23 03	23 26	23 38			23 47
Salford Central		d			21 05	21 41		21 46			22 05	22 28	22 41		22 46			23 05					
Manchester Victoria	⇌	a			21 11	21 47		21 53			22 11	22 34	22 47		22 53			23 13		23 47			
Rochdale	41	a																					
Deansgate	⇌	a	20 51						21 51							22 51			23 29				
Manchester Oxford Road		a	20 52	21 23					21 52							22 52			23 31				
Manchester Piccadilly 10	⇌	a	20 56	21 27					21 56							22 56			23 39				23 53
Stockport	84	a																					
Hazel Grove	86	a																					
Buxton	86	a																					
Heald Green	85	a	21 10						22 09							23 09							00 15
Manchester Airport	85 ✈	a	21 17	21 47					22 17							23 17							00 22

A From Edinburgh **B** To Liverpool Lime Street **C** From Clitheroe

The Sunday service between Manchester Victoria and Wigan Wallgate via Atherton is funded by GMITA and will operate whilst funding exists

Table 82

Saturdays from 8 October

Barrow-in-Furness, Blackpool North, Preston, Southport, Kirkby and Wigan - Bolton - Manchester

			NT	NT A	NT
Barrow-in-Furness		d			
Roose		d			
Dalton		d			
Ulverston		d			
Cark		d			
Kents Bank		d			
Grange-over-Sands		d			
Arnside		d			
Silverdale		d			
Carnforth		d			
Windermere	83	d			
Oxenholme Lake District	65	d			
Lancaster 8	65	a			
		d			
Blackpool North	97	d			23 02
Layton	97	d			23 05
Poulton-le-Fylde	97	d			23 10
Kirkham & Wesham	97	d			23 19
Preston 8	65,97	a			23 29
		d			23 31
Leyland		d			23 36
Chorley		d			23 44
Adlington (Lancashire)		d			23 49
Blackrod		d			23 52
Horwich Parkway		d			23 56
Lostock		d			00 02
Southport		d	23 10		
Meols Cop		d	23 15		
Bescar Lane		d			
New Lane		d			
Burscough Bridge		d	23 23		
Hoscar		d			
Parbold		d	23 28		
Appley Bridge		d	23 32		
Gathurst		d	23 35		
Kirkby		d			
Rainford		d			
Upholland		d			
Orrell		d			
Pemberton		d			
Wigan Wallgate		a	23 44		
		d			
Wigan North Western		d			
Ince		d			
Hindley		d			
Westhoughton		d			
Bolton		a			00 07
		d		23 38	00 07
Moses Gate		d			
Farnworth		d			
Kearsley		d			
Daisy Hill		d			
Hag Fold		d			
Atherton		d			
Walkden		d			
Moorside		d			
Swinton		d			
Salford Crescent		a		23 48	
		d		23 51	
Salford Central		d			
Manchester Victoria	⇌	a		00 01	00 26
Rochdale	41	a			
Deansgate	⇌	a			
Manchester Oxford Road		a			
Manchester Piccadilly 10	⇌	a			
Stockport	84	a			
Hazel Grove	86	a			
Buxton	86	a			
Heald Green	85	a			
Manchester Airport	85 ✈	a			

A From Clitheroe

The Sunday service between Manchester Victoria and Wigan Wallgate via Atherton is funded by GMITA and will operate whilst funding exists

Barrow-in-Furness, Blackpool North, Preston, Southport, Kirkby and Wigan - Bolton - Manchester

		TP	NT	TP	NT	NT	NT	NT	TP	NT	NT	NT	NT	NT	TP	NT	NT	NT	TP	NT	NT	NT	TP
		◇1		◇1					◇1						◇1				◇1				
		A	A		B		C	D		E				F		E		B			G		
Barrow-in-Furness	d																					10 45	
Roose	d																					10 49	
Dalton	d																					10 55	
Ulverston	d																					11 04	
Cark	d																					11 11	
Kents Bank	d																					11 16	
Grange-over-Sands	d																					11a21	
Arnside	d																						10 55
Silverdale	d																						10 59
Carnforth	d																				10 31		11 07
Windermere	83 d																						
Oxenholme Lake District	65 d																						
Lancaster 6	65 a																				10 40		11 18
	d																		10 21				
Blackpool North	97 d	22p44	23p02	07 48		08 20	08 36		08 44	08 50			09 20		09 44	09 50				10 20			
Layton	97 d		23p05			08 23							09 23							10 23			
Poulton-le-Fylde	97 d	22p50	23p10	07 54		08 28	08 42		08 50	08 56			09 28		09 50	09 56				10 28			
Kirkham & Wesham	97 d		23p19			08 37	08 51						09 37							10 37			
Preston 8	65,97 a	23p08	23p29	08 12		08 47	09 02		09 08	09 14			09 47		10 08	10 14			10 40	10 47			
	d	23p10	23p31	08 14		08 49			09 10	09 15			09 49		10 10	10 15			10 47	10 49			
Leyland	d		23p36			08 54				09 21			09 54			10 21				10 54			
Chorley	d	23p21	23p44	08 23		09 02			09 20				10 02		10 20				10 56	11 02			
Adlington (Lancashire)	d		23p49			09 07							10 07							11 07			
Blackrod	d		23p52			09 10							10 10							11 10			
Horwich Parkway	d	23p28	23p56	08 30		09 14			09 27				10 14		10 27					11 14			
Lostock	d		00 02			09 20							10 20							11 20			
Southport	d											09 10						10 05					
Meols Cop	d											09 15						10 10					
Bescar Lane	d																						
New Lane	d																						
Burscough Bridge	d											09 23						10 18					
Hoscar	d																						
Parbold	d											09 28						10 23					
Appley Bridge	d											09 32						10 27					
Gathurst	d											09 35						10 30					
Kirkby	d																						
Rainford	d																						
Upholland	d																						
Orrell	d																						
Pemberton	d																						
Wigan Wallgate	a											09 40						10 35					
	d				08 40						09 15	09 41					10 15	10 36					
Wigan North Western	d									09a35						10a36							
Ince	d										09 18						10 18						
Hindley	d				08 45						09 22	09 46					10 22	10 41					
Westhoughton	d				08 49							09 51						10 46					
Bolton	a	23p34	00 07	08 37	08 57	09 25			09 34			09 59	10 25		10 34			10 54	11 08	11 25			
	d	23p35	00 07	08 37	08 58	09 25		09 31	09 35			09 59	10 25	10 31	10 35			10 54	11 08	11 25			
Moses Gate	d																						
Farnworth	d																						
Kearsley	d																						
Daisy Hill	d										09 26						10 26						
Hag Fold	d										09 29						10 29						
Atherton	d										09 31						10 31						
Walkden	d										09 37						10 37						
Moorside	d										09 40						10 40						
Swinton	d										09 43						10 43						
Salford Crescent	a	23p47		08 49	09 10	09 38		09 43	09 47		09 50	10 12	10 38	10 43	10 47		10 50	11 07		11 38			
	d	23p47		08 50	09 11	09 38		09 44	09 47		09 51	10 12	10 38	10 44	10 47		10 51	11 07		11 38			
Salford Central	d																						
Manchester Victoria	⇌ a		00 26			09 45		09 52			09 57		10 45	10 52			10 57			11 45			
Rochdale	41 a																						
Deansgate	⇌ a			08 53	09 14				09 51			10 16			10 51			11 11					
Manchester Oxford Road	a			08 55	09 17				09 52			10 18			10 52			11 13	11 23				
Manchester Piccadilly 10	⇌ a	23p53		08 59	09 21				09 56			10 22			10 56			11 19	11 27				
Stockport	84 a				09 31							10 33						11 30					
Hazel Grove	86 a																						
Buxton	86 a																						
Heald Green	85 a	00 15																					
Manchester Airport	85 ✈ a	00 22		09 19					10 17						11 17				11 47				

A not 22 May
B To Chester
C To Carlisle
D From Blackburn
E To Liverpool Lime Street
F From Clitheroe
G From Leeds to Morecambe

The Sunday service between Manchester Victoria and Wigan Wallgate via Atherton is funded by GMITA and will operate whilst funding exists

Barrow-in-Furness, Blackpool North, Preston, Southport, Kirkby and Wigan - Bolton - Manchester

		NT	TP	NT	NT	NT	NT	NT	TP	NT	NT	NT	TP	NT	NT	TP	NT	NT	TP	NT	NT	NT	TP
			◇1						◇1				◇1						◇1				◇1
		A		B				A		B		C			D			A		B			E
Barrow-in-Furness	d																13 15						
Roose	d																13 19						
Dalton	d																13 24						
Ulverston	d																13 34						
Cark	d																13 41						
Kents Bank	d																13 46						
Grange-over-Sands	d																13a52						
Arnside	d												12 03			12 55							
Silverdale	d												12 07			12 59							
Carnforth	d												12 17		12 35	13 07							
Windermere	83 d																						
Oxenholme Lake District	65 d																						13 11
Lancaster 6	65 a												12 26		12 44	13 18							13 26
	d												12 26										13 26
Blackpool North	97 d		10 44	10 50			11 20		11 44	11 50				12 20					12 44	12 50			
Layton	97 d						11 23							12 23									
Poulton-le-Fylde	97 d		10 50	10 56			11 28		11 50	11 56				12 28					12 50	12 56			
Kirkham & Wesham	97 d						11 37							12 37									
Preston 8	65,97 a		11 08	11 14			11 47		12 08	12 14			12 45	12 47					13 08	13 14			13 45
	d		11 10	11 15			11 49		12 10	12 15			12 47	12 49					13 10	13 15			13 47
Leyland	d			11 21			11 54			12 21				12 54						13 21			
Chorley	d		11 20				12 02		12 20				12 56	13 02					13 20				13 56
Adlington (Lancashire)	d						12 07							13 07									
Blackrod	d						12 10							13 10									
Horwich Parkway	d		11 27				12 14		12 27					13 14					13 27				
Lostock	d						12 20							13 20									
Southport	d					11 05						12 05										13 01	
Meols Cop	d					11 10						12 10										13 06	
Bescar Lane	d																						
New Lane	d																						
Burscough Bridge	d					11 18						12 18										13 14	
Hoscar	d																						
Parbold	d					11 23						12 23										13 19	
Appley Bridge	d					11 27						12 27										13 23	
Gathurst	d					11 30						12 30										13 26	
Kirkby	d																						
Rainford	d																						
Upholland	d																						
Orrell	d																						
Pemberton	d																						
Wigan Wallgate	a					11 35						12 35										13 33	
	d				11 15	11 36					12 15	12 36									13 15	13 34	
Wigan North Western	d			11a35						12a35										13a35			
Ince	d				11 18						12 18										13 18		
Hindley	d				11 22	11 41					12 22	12 41									13 22	13 39	
Westhoughton	d					11 46						12 46										13 44	
Bolton	a		11 34			11 54	12 25		12 34			12 54	13 08	13 25					13 34			13 54	14 08
	d	11 31	11 35			11 54	12 25	12 31	12 35			12 54	13 08	13 25				13 31	13 35			13 54	14 08
Moses Gate	d																						
Farnworth	d																						
Kearsley	d																						
Daisy Hill	d				11 26						12 26										13 26		
Hag Fold	d				11 29						12 29										13 29		
Atherton	d				11 31						12 31										13 31		
Walkden	d				11 37						12 37										13 37		
Moorside	d				11 40						12 40										13 40		
Swinton	d				11 43						12 43										13 43		
Salford Crescent	a	11 43	11 47		11 50	12 07	12 38	12 43	12 47		12 50	13 07		13 38				13 43	13 47		13 50	14 07	
	d	11 44	11 47		11 51	12 07	12 38	12 44	12 47		12 51	13 07		13 38				13 44	13 47		13 51	14 07	
Salford Central	d																						
Manchester Victoria	⇌ a	11 52			11 57		12 45	12 52			12 57			13 45				13 52			13 57		
Rochdale	41 a																						
Deansgate	⇌ a		11 51			12 11			12 51			13 11							13 51			14 11	
Manchester Oxford Road	a		11 52			12 13			12 52			13 13	13 23						13 52			14 13	14 23
Manchester Piccadilly 10	⇌ a		11 56			12 19			12 56			13 19	13 27						13 56			14 19	14 27
Stockport	84 a					12 33						13 30										14 33	
Hazel Grove	86 a																						
Buxton	86 a																						
Heald Green	85 a																						
Manchester Airport	85 ✈ a		12 17						13 17				13 47						14 17				14 47

A From Clitheroe
B To Liverpool Lime Street
C To Chester
D From Leeds to Morecambe
E From Edinburgh

The Sunday service between Manchester Victoria and Wigan Wallgate via Atherton is funded by GMITA and will operate whilst funding exists

Table 82

Barrow-in-Furness, Blackpool North, Preston, Southport, Kirkby and Wigan - Bolton - Manchester

		NT	NT A	TP ◇1	NT B	NT	NT C	TP ◇1	NT	NT	NT A	TP ◇1	NT B	NT	NT	TP ◇1 D ⌶	NT	NT A	TP ◇1	NT B	NT	NT C
Barrow-in-Furness	d									14 50												
Roose	d									14 54												
Dalton	d									15 00												
Ulverston	d									15 09												
Cark	d									15 26												
Kents Bank	d									15 21												
Grange-over-Sands	d									15a26												
Arnside	d							14 03														
Silverdale	d							14 07														
Carnforth	d							14 17														
Windermere 83	d																					
Oxenholme Lake District 65	d															15 11						
Lancaster 8 65	a							14 26								15 26						
	d							14 26								15 26						
Blackpool North 97	d	13 20		13 44	13 50				14 20			14 44	14 50				15 20		15 44	15 50		
Layton 97	d	13 23							14 23								15 23					
Poulton-le-Fylde 97	d	13 28		13 50	13 56				14 28			14 50	14 56				15 28		15 50	15 56		
Kirkham & Wesham 97	d	13 37							14 37								15 37					
Preston 8 65,97	a	13 47		14 08	14 14			14 46	14 47			15 08	15 14			15 45	15 47		16 08	16 14		
	d	13 49		14 10	14 15			14 47	14 49			15 10	15 15			15 47	15 49		16 10	16 15		
Leyland	d	13 54			14 21				14 54				15 21				15 54			16 21		
Chorley	d	14 02		14 20				14 56	15 02			15 20				15 56	16 02		16 20			
Adlington (Lancashire)	d	14 07							15 07								16 07					
Blackrod	d	14 10							15 10								16 10					
Horwich Parkway	d	14 14		14 27					15 14			15 27					16 14		16 27			
Lostock	d	14 20							15 20								16 20					
Southport	d						14 05								15 05							16 05
Meols Cop	d						14 10								15 10							16 10
Bescar Lane	d																					
New Lane	d																					
Burscough Bridge	d						14 18								15 18							16 18
Hoscar	d																					
Parbold	d						14 23								15 23							16 23
Appley Bridge	d						14 27								15 27							16 27
Gathurst	d						14 30								15 30							16 30
Kirkby	d																					
Rainford	d																					
Upholland	d																					
Orrell	d																					
Pemberton	d																					
Wigan Wallgate	a						14 35								15 35							16 35
	d					14 15	14 36							15 15	15 36						16 15	16 36
Wigan North Western	d				14a35								15a35							16a35		
Ince	d					14 18								15 18							16 18	
Hindley	d					14 22	14 41							15 22	15 41						16 22	16 41
Westhoughton	d						14 46								15 46							16 46
Bolton	a	14 25		14 34			14 54	15 08	15 25			15 34			15 54	16 08	16 25		16 34			16 54
	d	14 25	14 31	14 35			14 54	15 08	15 25		15 31	15 35			15 54	16 08	16 25	16 31	16 35			16 54
Moses Gate	d																					
Farnworth	d																					
Kearsley	d																					
Daisy Hill	d					14 26								15 26							16 26	
Hag Fold	d					14 29								15 29							16 29	
Atherton	d					14 31								15 31							16 31	
Walkden	d					14 37								15 37							16 37	
Moorside	d					14 40								15 40							16 40	
Swinton	d					14 43								15 43							16 43	
Salford Crescent	a	14 38	14 43	14 47		14 50	15 07		15 38		15 43	15 47		15 50	16 07		16 38	16 43	16 47		16 50	17 07
	d	14 38	14 44	14 47		14 51	15 07		15 38		15 44	15 47		15 51	16 07		16 38	16 44	16 47		16 51	17 07
Salford Central	d																					
Manchester Victoria ⇌	a	14 45	14 52			14 57			15 45		15 52			15 57			16 45	16 52			16 57	
Rochdale 41	a																					
Deansgate ⇌	a			14 51			15 11					15 51			16 11				16 51			17 11
Manchester Oxford Road	a			14 52			15 13	15 23				15 52			16 13	16 23			16 52			17 13
Manchester Piccadilly 10 ⇌	a			14 56			15 19	15 27				15 56			16 19	16 27			16 56			17 19
Stockport 84	a						15 30								16 33							17 30
Hazel Grove 86	a																					
Buxton 86	a																					
Heald Green 85	a																					
Manchester Airport 85 ✈	a			15 17				15 47				16 17				16 47			17 17			

A From Clitheroe
B To Liverpool Lime Street
C To Chester
D From Edinburgh

The Sunday service between Manchester Victoria and Wigan Wallgate via Atherton is funded by GMITA and will operate whilst funding exists

Table 82

Barrow-in-Furness, Blackpool North, Preston, Southport, Kirkby and Wigan - Bolton - Manchester

		TP ◇1	NT	NT A	NT	NT B	TP ◇1	NT C	NT	NT	TP ◇1 D ⌶	TP ◇1 E ⌶	NT	NT B	TP ◇1	TP ◇1	NT C	NT F	TP ◇1 G ⌶	NT	NT	NT A	NT B
Barrow-in-Furness	d				17 13																18 55		
Roose	d				17 17																18 59		
Dalton	d				17 23																19 05		
Ulverston	d				17 32																19 14		
Cark	d				17 39																19 21		
Kents Bank	d				17 44																19 26		
Grange-over-Sands	d				17a49																19a31		
Arnside	d	16 05									16 56												
Silverdale	d										17 00												
Carnforth	d	16 18		16 37							17 08											19 04	
Windermere 83	d														16 58								
Oxenholme Lake District 65	d											17 09			17 16				18 10				
Lancaster 8 65	a	16 26		16 46							17 17	17 23			17 31				18 26			19 13	
	d	16 27									17 17	17 24			17 32				18 26				
Blackpool North 97	d		16 20				16 44	16 50					17 20			17 40	17 50			18 20			
Layton 97	d		16 23										17 23							18 23			
Poulton-le-Fylde 97	d		16 28				16 50	16 56					17 28			17 46	17 56			18 28			
Kirkham & Wesham 97	d		16 37										17 37							18 37			
Preston 8 65,97	a	16 45	16 47				17 08	17 14			17 37	17 42	17 47		17 51	18 04	18 14		18 45	18 47			
	d	16 47	16 49				17 10	17 15			17 47		17 49		18 10		18 15		18 47	18 49			
Leyland	d		16 54					17 21					17 54				18 21			18 54			
Chorley	d	16 56	17 02				17 20				17 56		18 02		18 20				18 56	19 02			
Adlington (Lancashire)	d		17 07										18 07							19 07			
Blackrod	d		17 10										18 10							19 10			
Horwich Parkway	d		17 14				17 27						18 14		18 27					19 14			
Lostock	d		17 20										18 20							19 20			
Southport	d									17 05								18 05					
Meols Cop	d									17 10								18 10					
Bescar Lane	d																						
New Lane	d																						
Burscough Bridge	d									17 18								18 18					
Hoscar	d																						
Parbold	d									17 23								18 23					
Appley Bridge	d									17 27								18 27					
Gathurst	d									17 30								18 30					
Kirkby	d																						
Rainford	d																						
Upholland	d																						
Orrell	d																						
Pemberton	d																						
Wigan Wallgate	a									17 35								18 35					
	d								17 15	17 36								18 36					
Wigan North Western	d							17a35									18a35						
Ince	d								17 18														
Hindley	d								17 22	17 41								18 41					
Westhoughton	d									17 46								18 46					
Bolton	a	17 08	17 25				17 34			17 54	18 08		18 25		18 34			18 54	19 08	19 25			
	d	17 08	17 25			17 31	17 35			17 54	18 08		18 25	18 31	18 35			18 54	19 08	19 25			19 31
Moses Gate	d																						
Farnworth	d																						
Kearsley	d																						
Daisy Hill	d								17 26														
Hag Fold	d								17 29														
Atherton	d								17 31														
Walkden	d								17 37														
Moorside	d								17 40														
Swinton	d								17 43														
Salford Crescent	a		17 38			17 43	17 47		17 50	18 07			18 38	18 43	18 47			19 07		19 38			19 43
	d		17 38			17 44	17 47		17 51	18 07			18 38	18 44	18 47			19 07		19 38			19 44
Salford Central	d																						
Manchester Victoria ⇌	a		17 45			17 52			17 57				18 45	18 52						19 45			19 52
Rochdale 41	a																						
Deansgate ⇌	a						17 51			18 11					18 51			19 11					
Manchester Oxford Road	a	17 23					17 52			18 13	18 23				18 52			19 13	19 23				
Manchester Piccadilly 10 ⇌	a	17 27					17 56			18 19	18 27				18 56			19 19	19 27				
Stockport 84	a									18 33								19 30					
Hazel Grove 86	a																						
Buxton 86	a																						
Heald Green 85	a																						
Manchester Airport 85 ✈	a	17 47					18 17				18 47				19 17				19 47				

A From Leeds to Morecambe
B From Clitheroe
C To Liverpool Lime Street
D ⌶ from Preston
E From Glasgow Central
F To Chester
G From Edinburgh

The Sunday service between Manchester Victoria and Wigan Wallgate via Atherton is funded by GMITA and will operate whilst funding exists

Table 82

Sundays
until 19 June

Barrow-in-Furness, Blackpool North, Preston, Southport, Kirkby and Wigan - Bolton - Manchester

			TP	NT	NT	TP	TP	NT	NT	TP	NT	NT	TP	NT	NT	NT	TP	TP	NT	TP	NT	NT	NT
			◇1			◇1	◇1			◇1			◇1				1	◇1		◇1			
				A		B ⌶	C ⌶		D		A	E	F ⌶	G					D		A		G
Barrow-in-Furness		d														20 48							
Roose		d														20 52							
Dalton		d														20 58							
Ulverston		d														21 07							
Cark		d														21 14							
Kents Bank		d														21 19							
Grange-over-Sands		d														21a24							
Arnside		d				18 55																	
Silverdale		d				18 59																	
Carnforth		d				19 08											21 05						
Windermere	83	d																20 40					
Oxenholme Lake District	65	d					19 07						20 10					21 01					
Lancaster 6	65	a				19 17	19 22						20 26				21 13	21 17					
		d				19 17	19 22						20 26					21 23					
Blackpool North	97	d	18 44	18 50				19 20		19 44	19 50			20 11	20 20					20 44	20 50		21 13
Layton	97	d						19 23							20 23								
Poulton-le-Fylde	97	d	18 50	18 56				19 28		19 50	19 56			20 17	20 28					20 50	20 56		21 19
Kirkham & Wesham	97	d						19 37							20 37								
Preston 8	65,97	a	19 08	19 14		19 37	19 42	19 47		20 08	20 14		20 45	20 34	20 47			21 41		21 08	21 14		21 36
		d	19 10	19 15		19 47		19 49		20 10	20 15		20 47		20 49					21 10	21 15		
Leyland		d		19 21				19 54			20 21				20 54						21 21		
Chorley		d	19 20			19 56		20 02		20 20			20 56		21 02					21 20			
Adlington (Lancashire)		d						20 07							21 07								
Blackrod		d						20 10							21 10								
Horwich Parkway		d	19 27					20 14		20 27					21 14					21 27			
Lostock		d						20 20							21 20								
Southport		d			19 05							20 05										21 05	
Meols Cop		d			19 10							20 10										21 10	
Bescar Lane		d																					
New Lane		d																					
Burscough Bridge		d			19 18							20 18										21 18	
Hoscar		d																					
Parbold		d			19 23							20 23										21 23	
Appley Bridge		d			19 27							20 27										21 27	
Gathurst		d			19 30							20 30										21 30	
Kirkby		d																					
Rainford		d																					
Upholland		d																					
Orrell		d																					
Pemberton		d																					
Wigan Wallgate		a			19 35							20 35										21 35	
		d			19 36							20 36										21 36	
Wigan North Western		d		19a35							20a35										21a35		
Ince		d																					
Hindley		d			19 41							20 41										21 41	
Westhoughton		d			19 46							20 46										21 46	
Bolton		a	19 34		19 54	20 08		20 25		20 34		20 54	21 08		21 25					21 34		21 54	
		d	19 35		19 54	20 08		20 25	20 31	20 35		20 54	21 08		21 25				21 31	21 35		21 54	
Moses Gate		d																					
Farnworth		d																					
Kearsley		d																					
Daisy Hill		d																					
Hag Fold		d																					
Atherton		d																					
Walkden		d																					
Moorside		d																					
Swinton		d																					
Salford Crescent		a	19 47		20 07			20 38	20 43	20 47		21 07			21 38				21 43	21 47		22 07	
		d	19 47		20 07			20 38	20 44	20 47		21 07			21 38				21 44	21 47		22 07	
Salford Central		d																					
Manchester Victoria	⇌	a						20 45	20 52						21 45				21 52				
Rochdale	41	a																					
Deansgate	⇌	a	19 51		20 11					20 51		21 11								21 51		22 11	
Manchester Oxford Road		a	19 52		20 13	20 23				20 52		21 13	21 23							21 52		22 13	
Manchester Piccadilly 10	⇌	a	19 56		20 19	20 27				20 56		21 19	21 27							21 56		22 19	
Stockport	84	a			20 33							21 30										22 33	
Hazel Grove	86	a																					
Buxton	86	a																					
Heald Green	85	a																					
Manchester Airport	85 ✈	a	20 17			20 47				21 17			21 47							22 17			

A To Liverpool Lime Street
B ⌶ from Preston
C From Glasgow Central
D From Clitheroe
E To Chester
F From Edinburgh
G To Leeds

The Sunday service between Manchester Victoria and Wigan Wallgate via Atherton is funded by GMITA and will operate whilst funding exists

Table 82

Sundays
until 19 June

Barrow-in-Furness, Blackpool North, Preston, Southport, Kirkby and Wigan - Bolton - Manchester

			NT	NT	NT	TP	TP	NT	NT	NT	TP
						◇1	◇1				◇1
				A	B	C ⌶	D ⌶		A	B	
Barrow-in-Furness		d									
Roose		d									
Dalton		d									
Ulverston		d									
Cark		d									
Kents Bank		d									
Grange-over-Sands		d									
Arnside		d									
Silverdale		d									
Carnforth		d									
Windermere	83	d									
Oxenholme Lake District	65	d									
Lancaster 6	65	a									
		d					22 04				
Blackpool North	97	d	21 20	21 50		21 56			22 44		23 03
Layton	97	d	21 23								
Poulton-le-Fylde	97	d	21 28	21 56		22 02			22 50		23 09
Kirkham & Wesham	97	d	21 37								23 17
Preston 8	65,97	a	21 47	22 14		22 20	22 24		23 08		23 28
		d	21 49	22 15		22 29			23 09		23 28
Leyland		d	21 54	22 21					23 15		23 34
Chorley		d	22 02			22 39					23 41
Adlington (Lancashire)		d	22 07								23 45
Blackrod		d	22 10								23 49
Horwich Parkway		d	22 14								23 52
Lostock		d	22 20								23 56
Southport		d						22 05			
Meols Cop		d						22 10			
Bescar Lane		d									
New Lane		d									
Burscough Bridge		d						22 18			
Hoscar		d									
Parbold		d						22 23			
Appley Bridge		d						22 27			
Gathurst		d						22 30			
Kirkby		d									
Rainford		d									
Upholland		d									
Orrell		d									
Pemberton		d									
Wigan Wallgate		a						22 35			
		d						22 36			
Wigan North Western		d		22a35					23a29		
Ince		d									
Hindley		d						22 41			
Westhoughton		d						22 46			
Bolton		a	22 25			22 50		22 54			00 02
		d	22 25		22 31	22 51		22 54		23 31	00 02
Moses Gate		d									
Farnworth		d									
Kearsley		d									
Daisy Hill		d									
Hag Fold		d									
Atherton		d									
Walkden		d									
Moorside		d									
Swinton		d									
Salford Crescent		a	22 38		22 43	23 03		23 07		23 43	
		d	22 38		22 44	23 04		23 07		23 44	
Salford Central		d									
Manchester Victoria	⇌	a	22 45		22 52					23 52	
Rochdale	41	a									
Deansgate	⇌	a				23 09		23 11			
Manchester Oxford Road		a				23 11		23 14			
Manchester Piccadilly 10	⇌	a				23 15		23 19			00 18
Stockport	84	a						23 33			
Hazel Grove	86	a									
Buxton	86	a									
Heald Green	85	a									
Manchester Airport	85 ✈	a				23 31					00 32

A To Liverpool Lime Street
B From Clitheroe
C ⌶ from Preston
D From Edinburgh

The Sunday service between Manchester Victoria and Wigan Wallgate via Atherton is funded by GMITA and will operate whilst funding exists

Table 82

Sundays
26 June to 31 July

Barrow-in-Furness, Blackpool North, Preston, Southport, Kirkby and Wigan - Bolton - Manchester

		TP ◇1	NT	TP ◇1	NT A	NT	NT B	NT C	NT (bus)	TP ◇1	NT D	NT	NT	NT E	NT (bus)	TP ◇1	NT D	NT A	TP ◇1 F	TP ◇1 G	NT	NT H	NT G
Barrow-in-Furness	d																		09 17				10 45
Roose	d																		09 21				10 49
Dalton	d																		09 28				10 55
Ulverston	d																		09 36				11 04
Cark	d																		09 44				11 11
Kents Bank	d																		09 48				11 16
Grange-over-Sands	d																		09 52				11a21
Arnside	d																		09 58				
Silverdale	d																		10 02				
Carnforth	d																		10 09			10 31	
Windermere 83	d																						
Oxenholme Lake District 65	d																						
Lancaster 6 65	a																		10 17			10 40	
	d																		10 21	10 21			
Blackpool North 97	d	22p44	23p02	07 48		08 20	08 36			08 44	08 50		09 20			09 44	09 50				10 20		
Layton 97	d		23p05			08 23							09 23								10 23		
Poulton-le-Fylde 97	d	22p50	23p10	07 54		08 28	08 42			08 50	08 56		09 28			09 50	09 56				10 28		
Kirkham & Wesham 97	d		23p19			08 37	08 51						09 37								10 37		
Preston 8 65,97	a	23p08	23p29	08 12		08 47	09 02			09 08	09 14		09 47			10 08	10 14		10 40	10 40	10 47		
	d	23p10	23p31	08 14		08 49				09 10	09 15		09 49			10 10	10 15		10 47	10 47	10 49		
Leyland	d		23p36			08 54					09 21		09 54				10 21				10 54		
Chorley	d	23p21	23p44	08 23		09 02				09 20			10 02			10 20			10 56	10 56	11 02		
Adlington (Lancashire)	d		23p49			09 07							10 07								11 07		
Blackrod	d		23p52			09 10							10 10								11 10		
Horwich Parkway	d	23p28	23p56	08 30		09 14				09 27			10 14			10 27					11 14		
Lostock	d		00 02			09 20							10 20								11 20		
Southport	d											09 10						10 05					
Meols Cop	d											09 15						10 10					
Bescar Lane	d																						
New Lane	d																						
Burscough Bridge	d											09 23						10 18					
Hoscar	d																						
Parbold	d											09 28						10 23					
Appley Bridge	d											09 32						10 27					
Gathurst	d											09 35						10 30					
Kirkby	d																						
Rainford	d																						
Upholland	d																						
Orrell	d																						
Pemberton	d																						
Wigan Wallgate	a											09 40						10 35					
	d				08 40				08 26			09 41			09 26			10 36					
Wigan North Western	d										09a35						10a36						
Ince	d																						
Hindley	d				08 45				08 44			09 46			09 44			10 41					
Westhoughton	d				08 49							09 51						10 46					
Bolton	a	23p34	00 07	08 37	08 57	09 25				09 34		09 59	10 25			10 34		10 54	11 08	11 08	11 25		
	d	23p35	00 07	08 37	08 58	09 25		09 31		09 35		09 59	10 25	10 31		10 35		10 54	11 08	11 08	11 25		
Moses Gate	d																						
Farnworth	d																						
Kearsley	d																						
Daisy Hill	d								08 54						09 54								
Hag Fold	d								09 02						10 02								
Atherton	d								09 06						10 06								
Walkden	d								09 20						10 20								
Moorside	d								09 26						10 26								
Swinton	d								09 30						10 30								
Salford Crescent	a	23p47		08 49	09 10	09 38		09 43	09 45	09 47		10 12	10 38	10 43	10 45	10 47		11 07			11 38		
	d	23p47		08 50	09 11	09 38		09 44	09 45	09 47		10 12	10 38	10 44	10 45	10 47		11 07			11 38		
Salford Central	d																						
Manchester Victoria ⇌	a		00 26			09 45		09 52	09 55				10 45	10 52	10 55						11 45		
Rochdale 41	a																						
Deansgate ⇌	a			08 53	09 14					09 51		10 16				10 51		11 11					
Manchester Oxford Road	a			08 55	09 17					09 52		10 18				10 52		11 13	11 23	11 23			
Manchester Piccadilly 10 ⇌	a	23p53		08 59	09 21					09 56		10 22				10 56		11 19	11 27	11 27			
Stockport 84	a				09 31							10 33						11 30					
Hazel Grove 86	a																						
Buxton 86	a																						
Heald Green 85	a	00 15																					
Manchester Airport 85 ✈	a	00 22		09 19						10 17						11 17			11 47	11 47			

A To Chester
B To Carlisle
C From Blackburn
D To Liverpool Lime Street
E From Clitheroe
F 24 July, 31 July
G not from 24 July until 31 July
H From Leeds to Morecambe

The Sunday service between Manchester Victoria and Wigan Wallgate via Atherton is funded by GMITA and will operate whilst funding exists

Table 82

Sundays
26 June to 31 July

Barrow-in-Furness, Blackpool North, Preston, Southport, Kirkby and Wigan - Bolton - Manchester

		TP A	NT B	NT (bus)	TP ◇1	NT C	NT	NT	NT B	NT (bus)	TP ◇1	NT C	NT D	TP ◇1 A	TP ◇1 E	NT	NT F	TP A	NT B	NT (bus)	TP ◇1	NT C	NT
Barrow-in-Furness	d														11 25								
Roose	d														11 29								
Dalton	d														11 35								
Ulverston	d														11 44								
Cark	d														11 51								
Kents Bank	d														11 55								
Grange-over-Sands	d														11 59								
Arnside	d	10 55												12 03	12 05			12 55					
Silverdale	d	10 59												12 07	12 10			12 59					
Carnforth	d	11 07												12 17	12 17		12 35	13 07					
Windermere 83	d																						
Oxenholme Lake District 65	d																						
Lancaster 6 65	a	11 18												12 26	12 26		12 44	13 18					
	d													12 26	12 26								
Blackpool North 97	d				10 44	10 50		11 20			11 44	11 50				12 20					12 44	12 50	
Layton 97	d							11 23								12 23							
Poulton-le-Fylde 97	d				10 50	10 56		11 28			11 50	11 56				12 28					12 50	12 56	
Kirkham & Wesham 97	d							11 37								12 37							
Preston 8 65,97	a				11 08	11 14		11 47			12 08	12 14		12 45	12 45	12 47					13 08	13 14	
	d				11 10	11 15		11 49			12 10	12 15		12 47	12 47	12 49					13 10	13 15	
Leyland	d					11 21		11 54				12 21				12 54						13 21	
Chorley	d				11 20			12 02			12 20			12 56	12 56	13 02					13 20		
Adlington (Lancashire)	d							12 07								13 07							
Blackrod	d							12 10								13 10							
Horwich Parkway	d				11 27			12 14			12 27					13 14					13 27		
Lostock	d							12 20								13 20							
Southport	d						11 05						12 05										13 01
Meols Cop	d						11 10						12 10										13 06
Bescar Lane	d																						
New Lane	d																						
Burscough Bridge	d						11 18						12 18										13 14
Hoscar	d																						
Parbold	d						11 23						12 23										13 19
Appley Bridge	d						11 27						12 27										13 23
Gathurst	d						11 30						12 30										13 26
Kirkby	d																						
Rainford	d																						
Upholland	d																						
Orrell	d																						
Pemberton	d																						
Wigan Wallgate	a						11 35						12 35										13 33
	d			10 26			11 36			11 26			12 36							12 26			13 34
Wigan North Western	d					11a35						12a35										13a35	
Ince	d																						
Hindley	d			10 44			11 41			11 44			12 41							12 44			13 39
Westhoughton	d						11 46						12 46										13 44
Bolton	a				11 34		11 54	12 25			12 34		12 54	13 08	13 08	13 25					13 34		13 54
	d		11 31		11 35		11 54	12 25	12 31		12 35		12 54	13 08	13 08	13 25			13 31		13 35		13 54
Moses Gate	d																						
Farnworth	d																						
Kearsley	d																						
Daisy Hill	d			10 54						11 54										12 54			
Hag Fold	d			11 02						12 02										13 02			
Atherton	d			11 06						12 06										13 06			
Walkden	d			11 20						12 20										13 20			
Moorside	d			11 26						12 26										13 26			
Swinton	d			11 30						12 30										13 30			
Salford Crescent	a		11 43	11 45	11 47		12 07	12 38	12 43	12 45	12 47		13 07			13 38			13 43	13 45	13 47		14 07
	d		11 44	11 45	11 47		12 07	12 38	12 44	12 45	12 47		13 07			13 38			13 44	13 45	13 47		14 07
Salford Central	d																						
Manchester Victoria ⇌	a		11 52	11 55				12 45	12 52	12 55						13 45			13 52	13 55			
Rochdale 41	a																						
Deansgate ⇌	a				11 51		12 11				12 51		13 11								13 51		14 11
Manchester Oxford Road	a				11 52		12 13				12 52		13 13	13 23	13 23						13 52		14 13
Manchester Piccadilly 10 ⇌	a				11 56		12 19				12 56		13 19	13 27	13 27						13 56		14 19
Stockport 84	a						12 33						13 30										14 33
Hazel Grove 86	a																						
Buxton 86	a																						
Heald Green 85	a																						
Manchester Airport 85 ✈	a				12 17						13 17			13 47	13 47						14 17		

A not from 24 July until 31 July
B From Clitheroe
C To Liverpool Lime Street
D To Chester
E 24 July, 31 July
F From Leeds to Morecambe

The Sunday service between Manchester Victoria and Wigan Wallgate via Atherton is funded by GMITA and will operate whilst funding exists

Sundays
26 June to 31 July

Barrow-in-Furness, Blackpool North, Preston, Southport, Kirkby and Wigan - Bolton - Manchester

		TP	NT	NT	NT	NT	NT	TP	NT	NT	TP	TP	NT	NT	NT	NT	TP	NT	NT	TP	NT	NT
		◇1						◇1			◇1	◇1					◇1			◇1		
		A	B	C		D			E	F	C	B		C	D			E		A		D
		🍴					🚌									🚌				🍴		
Barrow-in-Furness	d		12 45	13 15								13 25		14 50								
Roose	d		12 49	13 19								13 29		14 54								
Dalton	d		12 55	13 24								13 35		15 00								
Ulverston	d		13 04	13 34								13 44		15 09								
Cark	d		13 11	13 41								13 51		15 16								
Kents Bank	d		13 16	13 46								13 55		15 21								
Grange-over-Sands	d		13 20	13a52								13 59		15a26								
Arnside	d		13 26								14 03	14 05										
Silverdale	d		13 30								14 07	14 10										
Carnforth	d		13 37								14 17	14 17										
Windermere 83	d																					
Oxenholme Lake District 65	d	13 11																		15 11		
Lancaster 6 65	a	13 26	13 50								14 26	14 26								15 26		
	d	13 26									14 26	14 26								15 26		
Blackpool North 97	d				13 20			13 44	13 50				14 20				14 44	14 50			15 20	
Layton 97	d				13 23								14 23								15 23	
Poulton-le-Fylde 97	d				13 28			13 50	13 56				14 28				14 50	14 56			15 28	
Kirkham & Wesham 97	d				13 37								14 37								15 37	
Preston 8 65,97	a	13 45			13 47			14 08	14 14		14 46	14 45	14 47				15 08	15 14		15 45	15 47	
	d	13 47			13 49			14 10	14 15		14 47	14 47	14 49				15 10	15 15		15 47	15 49	
Leyland	d				13 54				14 21				14 54					15 21			15 54	
Chorley	d	13 56			14 02			14 20			14 56	14 56	15 02				15 20			15 56	16 02	
Adlington (Lancashire)	d				14 07								15 07								16 07	
Blackrod	d				14 10								15 10								16 10	
Horwich Parkway	d				14 14			14 27					15 14				15 27				16 14	
Lostock	d				14 20								15 20								16 20	
Southport	d									14 05									15 05			
Meols Cop	d									14 10									15 10			
Bescar Lane	d																					
New Lane	d																					
Burscough Bridge	d									14 18									15 18			
Hoscar	d																					
Parbold	d									14 23									15 23			
Appley Bridge	d									14 27									15 27			
Gathurst	d									14 30									15 30			
Kirkby	d																					
Rainford	d																					
Upholland	d																					
Orrell	d																					
Pemberton	d																					
Wigan Wallgate	a									14 35									15 35			
	d						13 26			14 36						14 26			15 36			
Wigan North Western	d								14a35									15a35				
Ince	d																					
Hindley	d						13 44			14 41						14 44			15 41			
Westhoughton	d									14 46									15 46			
Bolton	a	14 08			14 25			14 34		14 54	15 08	15 08	15 25				15 34		15 54	16 08	16 25	
	d	14 08			14 25	14 31		14 35		14 54	15 08	15 08	15 25		15 31		15 35		15 54	16 08	16 25	16 31
Moses Gate	d																					
Farnworth	d																					
Kearsley	d																					
Daisy Hill	d						13 54									14 54						
Hag Fold	d						14 02									15 02						
Atherton	d						14 06									15 06						
Walkden	d						14 20									15 20						
Moorside	d						14 26									15 26						
Swinton	d						14 30									15 30						
Salford Crescent	a				14 38	14 43	14 45	14 47		15 07			15 38		15 43	15 45	15 47		16 07		16 38	16 43
	d				14 38	14 44	14 45	14 47		15 07			15 38		15 44	15 45	15 47		16 07		16 38	16 44
Salford Central	d																					
Manchester Victoria ⇌	a				14 45	14 52	14 55						15 45		15 52	15 55					16 45	16 52
Rochdale 41	a																					
Deansgate ⇌	a							14 51		15 11							15 51		16 11			
Manchester Oxford Road	a	14 23						14 52		15 13	15 23	15 23					15 52		16 13	16 23		
Manchester Piccadilly 10 ⇌	a	14 27						14 56		15 19	15 27	15 27					15 56		16 19	16 27		
Stockport 84	a									15 30									16 33			
Hazel Grove 86	a																					
Buxton 86	a																					
Heald Green 85	a																					
Manchester Airport 85 ✈	a	14 47						15 17			15 47	15 47					16 17			16 47		

A From Edinburgh
B 24 July, 31 July
C not from 24 July until 31 July
D From Clitheroe
E To Liverpool Lime Street
F To Chester

The Sunday service between Manchester Victoria and Wigan Wallgate via Atherton is funded by GMITA and will operate whilst funding exists

Sundays
26 June to 31 July

Barrow-in-Furness, Blackpool North, Preston, Southport, Kirkby and Wigan - Bolton - Manchester

		NT	TP	NT	NT	TP	TP	NT	NT	NT	NT	TP	NT	NT	TP	TP	TP	TP	NT	NT	NT	NT
			◇1			◇1	◇1					◇1			◇1	◇1	◇1	◇1				
				A	B	C	D		E	F			A		C	G	H	I	D		F	
		🚌									🚌					🍴	🍴	🍴				🚌
Barrow-in-Furness	d					15 32									16 17		16 17		17 13			
Roose	d														16 21		16 21		17 17			
Dalton	d														16 28		16 28		17 23			
Ulverston	d					15 47									16 36		16 36		17 32			
Cark	d														16 44		16 44		17 39			
Kents Bank	d														16 48		16 48		17 44			
Grange-over-Sands	d					16 00									16 52		16 52		17a49			
Arnside	d					16 06	16 05								16 58	16 56	16 58					
Silverdale	d														17 02	17 00	17 02					
Carnforth	d					16 15	16 18		16 37						17 08	17 08	17 08					
Windermere 83	d																					
Oxenholme Lake District 65	d																	17 09				
Lancaster 6 65	a					16 23	16 26		16 46						17 17	17 17	17 17	17 23				
	d					16 24	16 27								17 17	17 17	17 17	17 24				
Blackpool North 97	d		15 44	15 50				16 20				16 44	16 50							17 20		
Layton 97	d							16 23												17 23		
Poulton-le-Fylde 97	d		15 50	15 56				16 28				16 50	16 56							17 28		
Kirkham & Wesham 97	d							16 37												17 37		
Preston 8 65,97	a		16 08	16 14		16 42	16 45	16 47				17 08	17 14		17 37	17 37	17 37	17 42		17 47		
	d		16 10	16 15		16 47	16 47	16 49				17 10	17 15			17 47		17 47		17 49		
Leyland	d			16 21				16 54					17 21							17 54		
Chorley	d		16 20			16 56	16 56	17 02				17 20				17 56		17 56		18 02		
Adlington (Lancashire)	d							17 07												18 07		
Blackrod	d							17 10												18 10		
Horwich Parkway	d		16 27					17 14				17 27								18 14		
Lostock	d							17 20												18 20		
Southport	d				16 05									17 05								
Meols Cop	d				16 10									17 10								
Bescar Lane	d																					
New Lane	d																					
Burscough Bridge	d				16 18									17 18								
Hoscar	d																					
Parbold	d				16 23									17 23								
Appley Bridge	d				16 27									17 27								
Gathurst	d				16 30									17 30								
Kirkby	d																					
Rainford	d																					
Upholland	d																					
Orrell	d																					
Pemberton	d																					
Wigan Wallgate	a				16 35									17 35								
	d	15 26			16 36						16 26			17 36								17 26
Wigan North Western	d			16a35									17a35									
Ince	d																					
Hindley	d	15 44			16 41						16 44			17 41								17 44
Westhoughton	d				16 46									17 46								
Bolton	a		16 34		16 54	17 08	17 08	17 25				17 34		17 54		18 08		18 08		18 25		
	d		16 35		16 54	17 08	17 08	17 25		17 31		17 35		17 54		18 08		18 08		18 25	18 31	
Moses Gate	d																					
Farnworth	d																					
Kearsley	d																					
Daisy Hill	d	15 54									16 54											17 54
Hag Fold	d	16 02									17 02											18 02
Atherton	d	16 06									17 06											18 06
Walkden	d	16 20									17 20											18 20
Moorside	d	16 26									17 26											18 26
Swinton	d	16 30									17 30											18 30
Salford Crescent	a	16 45	16 47		17 07			17 38		17 43	17 45	17 47		18 07						18 38	18 43	18 45
	d	16 45	16 47		17 07			17 38		17 44	17 45	17 47		18 07						18 38	18 44	18 45
Salford Central	d																					
Manchester Victoria ⇌	a	16 55						17 45		17 52	17 55									18 45	18 52	18 55
Rochdale 41	a																					
Deansgate ⇌	a		16 51		17 11							17 51		18 11								
Manchester Oxford Road	a		16 52		17 13	17 23	17 23					17 52		18 13		18 23		18 23				
Manchester Piccadilly 10 ⇌	a		16 56		17 19	17 27	17 27					17 56		18 19		18 27		18 27				
Stockport 84	a				17 30									18 33								
Hazel Grove 86	a																					
Buxton 86	a																					
Heald Green 85	a																					
Manchester Airport 85 ✈	a		17 17			17 47	17 47					18 17				18 47		18 47				

A To Liverpool Lime Street
B To Chester
C 24 July, 31 July
D not from 24 July until 31 July
E From Leeds to Morecambe
F From Clitheroe
G not from 24 July until 31 July. 🍴 from Preston
H 24 July, 31 July. 🍴 from Preston
I From Glasgow Central

The Sunday service between Manchester Victoria and Wigan Wallgate via Atherton is funded by GMITA and will operate whilst funding exists

Table 82

Sundays
26 June to 31 July

Barrow-in-Furness, Blackpool North, Preston, Southport, Kirkby and Wigan - Bolton - Manchester

			TP	TP	NT	NT	TP	NT	NT	NT	TP	NT	NT	TP	TP	TP	NT	TP	NT	NT	TP	NT	NT	TP
			◇1	◇1			◇1				◇1			◇1	◇1	◇1		◇1			◇1			◇1
					A	B	C		D	E		A		F	G	H	I	J		E		A	B	C
							✠								✠	✠		✠						✠
Barrow-in-Furness		d												18 17		18 17	18 55							
Roose		d												18 21		18 21	18 59							
Dalton		d												18 28		18 28	19 05							
Ulverston		d												18 36		18 36	19 14							
Cark		d												18 44		18 44	19 21							
Kents Bank		d												18 48		18 48	19 26							
Grange-over-Sands		d												18 52		18 52	19a31							
Arnside		d												18 58	18 55	18 58								
Silverdale		d												19 02	18 59	19 02								
Carnforth		d							19 04					19 08	19 08	19 08								
Windermere	83	d	16 58																					
Oxenholme Lake District	65	d	17 16				18 10											19 07						20 10
Lancaster 8	65	a	17 31				18 26		19 13					19 17	19 17	19 17		19 22						20 26
		d	17 32				18 26							19 17	19 17	19 17		19 22						20 26
Blackpool North	97	d		17 40	17 50			18 20			18 44	18 50							19 20		19 44	19 50		
Layton	97	d						18 23											19 23					
Poulton-le-Fylde	97	d		17 46	17 56			18 28			18 50	18 56							19 28		19 50	19 56		
Kirkham & Wesham	97	d						18 37											19 37					
Preston 8	65,97	a	17 51	18 04	18 14		18 45	18 47			19 08	19 14		19 37	19 37	19 37		19 42	19 47		20 08	20 14		20 45
		d		18 10	18 15		18 47	18 49			19 10	19 15			19 47			19 47	19 49		20 10	20 15		20 47
Leyland		d			18 21			18 54				19 21							19 54			20 21		
Chorley		d		18 20			18 56	19 02			19 20				19 56			19 56	20 02		20 20			20 56
Adlington (Lancashire)		d						19 07											20 07					
Blackrod		d						19 10											20 10					
Horwich Parkway		d		18 27				19 14			19 27								20 14		20 27			
Lostock		d						19 20											20 20					
Southport		d				18 05							19 05										20 05	
Meols Cop		d				18 10							19 10										20 10	
Bescar Lane		d																						
New Lane		d																						
Burscough Bridge		d				18 18							19 18										20 18	
Hoscar		d																						
Parbold		d				18 23							19 23										20 23	
Appley Bridge		d				18 27							19 27										20 27	
Gathurst		d				18 30							19 30										20 30	
Kirkby		d																						
Rainford		d																						
Upholland		d																						
Orrell		d																						
Pemberton		d																						
Wigan Wallgate		a				18 35							19 35										20 35	
		d				18 36							19 36										20 36	
Wigan North Western		d			18a35							19a35										20a35		
Ince		d																						
Hindley		d				18 41							19 41										20 41	
Westhoughton		d				18 46							19 46										20 46	
Bolton		a		18 34		18 54	19 08	19 25			19 34		19 54		20 08			20 08	20 25		20 34		20 54	21 08
		d		18 35		18 54	19 08	19 25		19 31	19 35		19 54		20 08			20 08	20 25	20 31	20 35		20 54	21 08
Moses Gate		d																						
Farnworth		d																						
Kearsley		d																						
Daisy Hill		d																						
Hag Fold		d																						
Atherton		d																						
Walkden		d																						
Moorside		d																						
Swinton		d																						
Salford Crescent		a		18 47		19 07		19 38		19 43	19 47		20 07						20 38	20 43	20 47		21 07	
		d		18 47		19 07		19 38		19 44	19 47		20 07						20 38	20 44	20 47		21 07	
Salford Central		d																						
Manchester Victoria	⇌	a						19 45		19 52									20 45	20 52				
Rochdale	41	a																						
Deansgate	⇌	a		18 51		19 11					19 51		20 11								20 51		21 11	
Manchester Oxford Road		a		18 52		19 13	19 23				19 52		20 13		20 23			20 23			20 52		21 13	21 23
Manchester Piccadilly 10	⇌	a		18 56		19 19	19 27				19 56		20 19		20 27			20 27			20 56		21 19	21 27
Stockport	84	a				19 30							20 33										21 30	
Hazel Grove	86	a																						
Buxton	86	a																						
Heald Green	85	a																						
Manchester Airport	85 ✈	a		19 17			19 47				20 17				20 47			20 47			21 17			21 47

A To Liverpool Lime Street
B To Chester
C From Edinburgh
D From Leeds to Morecambe
E From Clitheroe
F 24 July, 31 July
G not from 24 July until 31 July. ✠ from Preston
H 24 July, 31 July. ✠ from Preston
I not from 24 July until 31 July
J From Glasgow Central

The Sunday service between Manchester Victoria and Wigan Wallgate via Atherton is funded by GMITA and will operate whilst funding exists

Table 82

Sundays
26 June to 31 July

Barrow-in-Furness, Blackpool North, Preston, Southport, Kirkby and Wigan - Bolton - Manchester

			NT	NT	NT	NT	TP	TP	NT	TP	NT	NT	NT	NT	NT	NT	NT	TP	NT	NT	TP
							1	◇1		◇1								◇1			◇1
			A	B		C	C	C	D		E		B		E	D		F	E	D	
																		✠			
Barrow-in-Furness		d	20 02			20 48															
Roose		d	20 06			20 52															
Dalton		d	20 12			20 58															
Ulverston		d	20 21			21 07															
Cark		d	20 28			21 14															
Kents Bank		d	20 33			21 19															
Grange-over-Sands		d	20 37			21a24															
Arnside		d	20 43																		
Silverdale		d	20 47																		
Carnforth		d	20 54				21 05														
Windermere	83	d						20 40													
Oxenholme Lake District	65	d						21 01													
Lancaster 8	65	a	21 07				21 13	21 17													
		d						21 23										22 04			
Blackpool North	97	d		20 11	20 20					20 44	20 50		21 13	21 20	21 50				22 44		23 03
Layton	97	d			20 23									21 23							
Poulton-le-Fylde	97	d		20 17	20 28					20 50	20 56		21 19	21 28	21 56				22 50		23 09
Kirkham & Wesham	97	d			20 37									21 37							23 17
Preston 8	65,97	a		20 34	20 47			21 41		21 08	21 14		21 36	21 47	22 14			22 24	23 08		23 28
		d			20 49					21 10	21 15			21 49	22 15			22 34	23 09		23 28
Leyland		d			20 54						21 21			21 54	22 21				23 15		23 34
Chorley		d			21 02					21 20				22 02				22 44			23 41
Adlington (Lancashire)		d			21 07									22 07							23 45
Blackrod		d			21 10									22 10							23 49
Horwich Parkway		d			21 14					21 27				22 14							23 52
Lostock		d			21 20									22 20							23 56
Southport		d										21 05					22 05				
Meols Cop		d										21 10					22 10				
Bescar Lane		d																			
New Lane		d																			
Burscough Bridge		d										21 18					22 18				
Hoscar		d																			
Parbold		d										21 23					22 23				
Appley Bridge		d										21 27					22 27				
Gathurst		d										21 30					22 30				
Kirkby		d																			
Rainford		d																			
Upholland		d																			
Orrell		d																			
Pemberton		d																			
Wigan Wallgate		a										21 35					22 35				
		d										21 36					22 36				
Wigan North Western		d									21a35				22a35				23a29		
Ince		d																			
Hindley		d										21 41					22 41				
Westhoughton		d										21 46					22 46				
Bolton		a			21 25					21 34		21 54		22 25			22 54	22 59			00 02
		d			21 25				21 31	21 35		21 54		22 25		22 31	22 54	23 00		23 31	00 02
Moses Gate		d																			
Farnworth		d																			
Kearsley		d																			
Daisy Hill		d																			
Hag Fold		d																			
Atherton		d																			
Walkden		d																			
Moorside		d																			
Swinton		d																			
Salford Crescent		a			21 38				21 43	21 47		22 07		22 38		22 43	23 07	23 12		23 43	
		d			21 38				21 44	21 47		22 07		22 38		22 44	23 07	23 12		23 44	
Salford Central		d																			
Manchester Victoria	⇌	a			21 45				21 52					22 45		22 52				23 52	
Rochdale	41	a																			
Deansgate	⇌	a								21 51		22 11					23 11	23 17			
Manchester Oxford Road		a								21 52		22 13					23 14	23 19			
Manchester Piccadilly 10	⇌	a								21 56		22 19					23 19	23 23			00 18
Stockport	84	a										22 33					23 33				
Hazel Grove	86	a																			
Buxton	86	a																			
Heald Green	85	a																			
Manchester Airport	85 ✈	a								22 17								23 39			00 32

A 24 July, 31 July
B To Leeds
C not from 24 July until 31 July
D From Clitheroe
E To Liverpool Lime Street
F From Edinburgh

The Sunday service between Manchester Victoria and Wigan Wallgate via Atherton is funded by GMITA and will operate whilst funding exists

Table 82

Sundays
7 August to 11 September

Barrow-in-Furness, Blackpool North, Preston, Southport, Kirkby and Wigan - Bolton - Manchester

	TP	NT	TP	NT	NT	NT	NT	TP	NT		NT	NT	NT	NT	TP	NT	NT	NT	TP		NT	NT	NT	TP
	◇1		◇1	A		B	C	◇1	D					E	◇1	D		A	◇1			F	E	◇1
Barrow-in-Furness d																			09 17					
Roose d																			09 21					
Dalton d																			09 28					
Ulverston d																			09 36					
Cark d																			09 44					
Kents Bank d																			09 48					
Grange-over-Sands d																			09 52					
Arnside d																			09 58					
Silverdale d																			10 02					
Carnforth d																			10 09			10 31		
Windermere 83 d																								
Oxenholme Lake District 65 d																								
Lancaster 65 a																			10 17			10 40		
d																			10 21					
Blackpool North 97 d	22p44	23p02	07 48		08 20	08 36		08 44	08 50				09 20		09 44	09 50					10 20			10 44
Layton 97 d		23p05			08 23								09 23								10 23			
Poulton-le-Fylde 97 d	22p50	23p10	07 54		08 28	08 42		08 50	08 56				09 28		09 50	09 56					10 28			10 50
Kirkham & Wesham 97 d		23p19			08 37	08 51							09 37								10 37			
Preston 65,97 a	23p08	23p29	08 12		08 47	09 02		09 08	09 14				09 47		10 08	10 14			10 40		10 47			11 08
d	23p10	23p31	08 14		08 49			09 10	09 15				09 49		10 10	10 15			10 47		10 49			11 10
Leyland d		23p36			08 54				09 21				09 54			10 21					10 54			
Chorley d	23p21	23p44	08 23		09 02			09 20					10 02		10 20				10 56		11 02			11 20
Adlington (Lancashire) d		23p49			09 07								10 07								11 07			
Blackrod d		23p52			09 10								10 10								11 10			
Horwich Parkway d	23p28	23p56	08 30		09 14			09 27					10 14		10 27						11 14			11 27
Lostock d		00 02			09 20								10 20								11 20			
Southport d												09 10						10 05						
Meols Cop d												09 15						10 10						
Bescar Lane d																								
New Lane d																								
Burscough Bridge d												09 23						10 18						
Hoscar d																								
Parbold d												09 28						10 23						
Appley Bridge d												09 32						10 27						
Gathurst d												09 35						10 30						
Kirkby d																								
Rainford d																								
Upholland d																								
Orrell d																								
Pemberton d																								
Wigan Wallgate a												09 40						10 35						
d				08 40							09 15	09 41					10 15	10 36						
Wigan North Western d									09a35							10a36								
Ince d											09 18						10 18							
Hindley d				08 45							09 22	09 46					10 22	10 41						
Westhoughton d				08 49								09 51						10 46						
Bolton a	23p34	00 07	08 37	08 57	09 25			09 34				09 59	10 25		10 34			10 54	11 08		11 25			11 34
d	23p35	00 07	08 37	08 58	09 25		09 31	09 35				09 59	10 25	10 31	10 35			10 54	11 08		11 25		11 31	11 35
Moses Gate d																								
Farnworth d																								
Kearsley d																								
Daisy Hill d											09 26						10 26							
Hag Fold d											09 29						10 29							
Atherton d											09 31						10 31							
Walkden d											09 37						10 37							
Moorside d											09 40						10 40							
Swinton d											09 43						10 43							
Salford Crescent a	23p47		08 49	09 10	09 38		09 43	09 47			09 50	10 12	10 38	10 43	10 47		10 50	11 07			11 38		11 43	11 47
d	23p47		08 50	09 11	09 38		09 44	09 47			09 51	10 12	10 38	10 44	10 47		10 51	11 07			11 38		11 44	11 47
Salford Central d																								
Manchester Victoria ⇌ a		00 26			09 45		09 52				09 57		10 45	10 52			10 57				11 45		11 52	
Rochdale 41 a																								
Deansgate ⇌ a			08 53	09 14				09 51				10 16			10 51			11 11						11 51
Manchester Oxford Road a			08 55	09 17				09 52				10 18			10 52			11 13	11 23					11 52
Manchester Piccadilly 10 ⇌ a	23p53		08 59	09 21				09 56				10 22			10 56			11 19	11 27					11 56
Stockport 84 a				09 31								10 33						11 30						
Hazel Grove 86 a																								
Buxton 86 a																								
Heald Green 85 a	00 15																							
Manchester Airport 85 ✈ a	00 22		09 19					10 17							11 17				11 47					12 17

A To Chester
B To Carlisle
C From Blackburn
D To Liverpool Lime Street
E From Clitheroe
F From Leeds to Morecambe

The Sunday service between Manchester Victoria and Wigan Wallgate via Atherton is funded by GMITA and will operate whilst funding exists

Table 82

Sundays
7 August to 11 September

Barrow-in-Furness, Blackpool North, Preston, Southport, Kirkby and Wigan - Bolton - Manchester

	NT	NT	NT	NT	NT		TP	NT	NT	NT	TP	NT	NT	NT	TP		NT	NT	NT	TP	NT	NT	NT	TP
	A				B		◇1	A		C	◇1		D	B	◇1		A			◇1 E			B	◇1
Barrow-in-Furness d											11 25										12 45			
Roose d											11 29										12 49			
Dalton d											11 35										12 55			
Ulverston d											11 44										13 04			
Cark d											11 51										13 11			
Kents Bank d											11 55										13 16			
Grange-over-Sands d											11 59										13 20			
Arnside d											12 05										13 26			
Silverdale d											12 10										13 30			
Carnforth d											12 17		12 35								13 37			
Windermere 83 d																								
Oxenholme Lake District 65 d																				13 11				
Lancaster 65 a											12 26		12 44							13 26	13 50			
d											12 26									13 26				
Blackpool North 97 d	10 50			11 20			11 44	11 50				12 20			12 44		12 50					13 20		13 44
Layton 97 d				11 23								12 23										13 23		
Poulton-le-Fylde 97 d	10 56			11 28			11 50	11 56				12 28			12 50		12 56					13 28		13 50
Kirkham & Wesham 97 d				11 37								12 37										13 37		
Preston 65,97 a	11 14			11 47			12 08	12 14			12 45	12 47			13 08		13 14			13 45		13 47		14 08
d	11 15			11 49			12 10	12 15			12 47	12 49			13 10		13 15			13 47		13 49		14 10
Leyland d	11 21			11 54				12 21				12 54					13 21					13 54		
Chorley d				12 02			12 20				12 56	13 02			13 20					13 56		14 02		14 20
Adlington (Lancashire) d				12 07								13 07										14 07		
Blackrod d				12 10								13 10										14 10		
Horwich Parkway d				12 14			12 27					13 14			13 27							14 14		14 27
Lostock d				12 20								13 20										14 20		
Southport d			11 05							12 05									13 01					
Meols Cop d			11 10							12 10									13 06					
Bescar Lane d																								
New Lane d																								
Burscough Bridge d			11 18							12 18									13 14					
Hoscar d																								
Parbold d			11 23							12 23									13 19					
Appley Bridge d			11 27							12 27									13 23					
Gathurst d			11 30							12 30									13 26					
Kirkby d																								
Rainford d																								
Upholland d																								
Orrell d																								
Pemberton d																								
Wigan Wallgate a			11 35							12 35									13 33					
d		11 15	11 36						12 15	12 36								13 15	13 34					
Wigan North Western d	11a35							12a35									13a35							
Ince d		11 18							12 18									13 18						
Hindley d		11 22	11 41						12 22	12 41								13 22	13 39					
Westhoughton d			11 46							12 46									13 44					
Bolton a			11 54	12 25			12 34			12 54	13 08	13 25			13 34				13 54	14 08		14 25		14 34
d			11 54	12 25	12 31		12 35			12 54	13 08	13 25		13 31	13 35				13 54	14 08		14 25	14 31	14 35
Moses Gate d																								
Farnworth d																								
Kearsley d																								
Daisy Hill d		11 26							12 26									13 26						
Hag Fold d		11 29							12 29									13 29						
Atherton d		11 31							12 31									13 31						
Walkden d		11 37							12 37									13 37						
Moorside d		11 40							12 40									13 40						
Swinton d		11 43							12 43									13 43						
Salford Crescent a		11 50	12 07	12 38	12 43		12 47		12 50	13 07		13 38		13 43	13 47			13 50	14 07			14 38	14 43	14 47
d		11 51	12 07	12 38	12 44		12 47		12 51	13 07		13 38		13 44	13 47			13 51	14 07			14 38	14 44	14 47
Salford Central d																								
Manchester Victoria ⇌ a		11 57		12 45	12 52				12 57			13 45		13 52				13 57				14 45	14 52	
Rochdale 41 a																								
Deansgate ⇌ a			12 11				12 51			13 11					13 51				14 11					14 51
Manchester Oxford Road a			12 13				12 52			13 13	13 23				13 52				14 13	14 23				14 52
Manchester Piccadilly 10 ⇌ a			12 19				12 56			13 19	13 27				13 56				14 19	14 27				14 56
Stockport 84 a			12 33							13 30									14 33					
Hazel Grove 86 a																								
Buxton 86 a																								
Heald Green 85 a																								
Manchester Airport 85 ✈ a							13 17				13 47				14 17					14 47				15 17

A To Liverpool Lime Street
B From Clitheroe
C To Chester
D From Leeds to Morecambe
E From Edinburgh

The Sunday service between Manchester Victoria and Wigan Wallgate via Atherton is funded by GMITA and will operate whilst funding exists

Table 82

Sundays

7 August to 11 September

Barrow-in-Furness, Blackpool North, Preston, Southport, Kirkby and Wigan - Bolton - Manchester

	NT	NT	NT	TP	NT	NT	TP	NT	NT	NT	TP	NT	NT	TP	NT	NT	NT	TP	NT	NT	NT
	A		B	◇1		C	◇1	A			◇1 D ⌘		C	◇1	A		B	◇1		E	C
Barrow-in-Furness d				13 25														15 32			
Roose d				13 29																	
Dalton d				13 35																	
Ulverston d				13 44														15 47			
Cark d				13 51																	
Kents Bank d				13 55																	
Grange-over-Sands d				13 59														16 00			
Arnside d				14 05														16 06			
Silverdale d				14 10																	
Carnforth d				14 17														16 15		16 37	
Windermere 83 d																					
Oxenholme Lake District 65 d											15 11										
Lancaster 6 65 a				14 26							15 26							16 23		16 46	
d				14 26							15 26							16 24			
Blackpool North 97 d	13 50				14 20		14 44	14 50				15 20		15 44	15 50				16 20		
Layton 97 d					14 23							15 23							16 23		
Poulton-le-Fylde 97 d	13 56				14 28		14 50	14 56				15 28		15 50	15 56				16 28		
Kirkham & Wesham 97 d					14 37							15 37							16 37		
Preston 8 65,97 a	14 14			14 45	14 47		15 08	15 14			15 45	15 47		16 08	16 14			16 42	16 47		
d	14 15			14 47	14 49		15 10	15 15			15 47	15 49		16 10	16 15			16 47	16 49		
Leyland d	14 21				14 54			15 21				15 54			16 21				16 54		
Chorley d				14 56	15 02		15 20				15 56	16 02		16 20				16 56	17 02		
Adlington (Lancashire) d					15 07							16 07							17 07		
Blackrod d					15 10							16 10							17 10		
Horwich Parkway d					15 14		15 27					16 14		16 27					17 14		
Lostock d					15 20							16 20							17 20		
Southport d			14 05							15 05							16 05				
Meols Cop d			14 10							15 10							16 10				
Bescar Lane d																					
New Lane d																					
Burscough Bridge d			14 18							15 18							16 18				
Hoscar d																					
Parbold d			14 23							15 23							16 23				
Appley Bridge d			14 27							15 27							16 27				
Gathurst d			14 30							15 30							16 30				
Kirkby d																					
Rainford d																					
Upholland d																					
Orrell d																					
Pemberton d																					
Wigan Wallgate a			14 35							15 35							16 35				
d		14 15	14 36						15 15	15 36						16 15	16 36				
Wigan North Western d	14a35							15a35							16a35						
Ince d		14 18							15 18							16 18					
Hindley d		14 22	14 41						15 22	15 41						16 22	16 41				
Westhoughton d			14 46							15 46							16 46				
Bolton a			14 54	15 08	15 25		15 34			15 54	16 08	16 25		16 34			16 54	17 08	17 25		
d			14 54	15 08	15 25	15 31	15 35			15 54	16 08	16 25	16 31	16 35			16 54	17 08	17 25		17 31
Moses Gate d																					
Farnworth d																					
Kearsley d																					
Daisy Hill d		14 26							15 26							16 26					
Hag Fold d		14 29							15 29							16 29					
Atherton d		14 31							15 31							16 31					
Walkden d		14 37							15 37							16 37					
Moorside d		14 40							15 40							16 40					
Swinton d		14 43							15 43							16 43					
Salford Crescent a		14 50	15 07		15 38	15 43	15 47		15 50	16 07		16 38	16 43	16 47		16 50	17 07		17 38		17 43
d		14 51	15 07		15 38	15 44	15 47		15 51	16 07		16 38	16 44	16 47		16 51	17 07		17 38		17 44
Salford Central d																					
Manchester Victoria ⇌ a		14 57			15 45	15 52			15 57			16 45	16 52			16 57			17 45		17 52
Rochdale 41 a																					
Deansgate ⇌ a			15 11				15 51			16 11				16 51			17 11				
Manchester Oxford Road a			15 13	15 23			15 52			16 13	16 23			16 52			17 13	17 23			
Manchester Piccadilly 10 ⇌ a			15 19	15 27			15 56			16 19	16 27			16 56			17 19	17 27			
Stockport 84 a			15 30							16 33							17 30				
Hazel Grove 86 a																					
Buxton 86 a																					
Heald Green 85 a																					
Manchester Airport 85 ✈ a				15 47			16 17				16 47			17 17				17 47			

A To Liverpool Lime Street
B To Chester
C From Clitheroe
D From Edinburgh
E From Leeds to Morecambe

The Sunday service between Manchester Victoria and Wigan Wallgate via Atherton is funded by GMITA and will operate whilst funding exists

Table 82

Sundays

7 August to 11 September

Barrow-in-Furness, Blackpool North, Preston, Southport, Kirkby and Wigan - Bolton - Manchester

	TP	NT	NT	NT	TP	TP	NT	NT	TP	TP	NT	NT	TP	NT	NT	NT	TP	NT	NT	TP	TP	NT
	◇1	A			◇1 B ⌘	◇1 C ⌘		D	◇1	◇1	A	E	◇1 F ⌘		G	D	◇1	A		◇1 B ⌘	◇1 C ⌘	
Barrow-in-Furness d					16 17															18 17		
Roose d					16 21															18 21		
Dalton d					16 28															18 28		
Ulverston d					16 36															18 36		
Cark d					16 44															18 44		
Kents Bank d					16 48															18 48		
Grange-over-Sands d					16 52															18 52		
Arnside d					16 58															18 58		
Silverdale d					17 02															19 02		
Carnforth d					17 08										19 04					19 08		
Windermere 83 d									16 58													
Oxenholme Lake District 65 d						17 09			17 16				18 10								19 07	
Lancaster 6 65 a					17 17	17 23			17 31				18 26		19 13					19 17	19 22	
d					17 17	17 24			17 32				18 26							19 17	19 22	
Blackpool North 97 d	16 44	16 50					17 20			17 40	17 50			18 20			18 44	18 50				19 20
Layton 97 d							17 23							18 23								19 23
Poulton-le-Fylde 97 d	16 50	16 56					17 28			17 46	17 56			18 28			18 50	18 56				19 28
Kirkham & Wesham 97 d							17 37							18 37								19 37
Preston 8 65,97 a	17 08	17 14			17 37	17 42	17 47		17 51	18 04	18 14		18 45	18 47			19 08	19 14		19 37	19 42	19 47
d	17 10	17 15			17 47		17 49		18 10		18 15		18 47	18 49			19 10	19 15		19 47		19 49
Leyland d		17 21					17 54				18 21			18 54				19 21				19 54
Chorley d	17 20				17 56		18 02		18 20				18 56	19 02			19 20			19 56		20 02
Adlington (Lancashire) d							18 07							19 07								20 07
Blackrod d							18 10							19 10								20 10
Horwich Parkway d	17 27						18 14		18 27					19 14			19 27					20 14
Lostock d							18 20							19 20								20 20
Southport d				17 05								18 05							19 05			
Meols Cop d				17 10								18 10							19 10			
Bescar Lane d																						
New Lane d																						
Burscough Bridge d				17 18								18 18							19 18			
Hoscar d																						
Parbold d				17 23								18 23							19 23			
Appley Bridge d				17 27								18 27							19 27			
Gathurst d				17 30								18 30							19 30			
Kirkby d																						
Rainford d																						
Upholland d																						
Orrell d																						
Pemberton d																						
Wigan Wallgate a				17 35								18 35							19 35			
d			17 15	17 36								18 36							19 36			
Wigan North Western d		17a35									18a35							19a35				
Ince d			17 18																			
Hindley d			17 22	17 41								18 41							19 41			
Westhoughton d				17 46								18 46							19 46			
Bolton a	17 34			17 54	18 08		18 25		18 34			18 54	19 08	19 25			19 34		19 54	20 08		20 25
d	17 35			17 54	18 08		18 25	18 31	18 35			18 54	19 08	19 25		19 31	19 35		19 54	20 08		20 25
Moses Gate d																						
Farnworth d																						
Kearsley d																						
Daisy Hill d			17 26																			
Hag Fold d			17 29																			
Atherton d			17 31																			
Walkden d			17 37																			
Moorside d			17 40																			
Swinton d			17 43																			
Salford Crescent a	17 47		17 50	18 07			18 38	18 43	18 47			19 07		19 38		19 43	19 47		20 07			20 38
d	17 47		17 51	18 07			18 38	18 44	18 47			19 07		19 38		19 44	19 47		20 07			20 38
Salford Central d																						
Manchester Victoria ⇌ a			17 57				18 45	18 52						19 45		19 52						20 45
Rochdale 41 a																						
Deansgate ⇌ a	17 51			18 11					18 51			19 11					19 51		20 11			
Manchester Oxford Road a	17 52			18 13	18 23				18 52			19 13	19 23				19 52		20 13	20 23		
Manchester Piccadilly 10 ⇌ a	17 56			18 19	18 27				18 56			19 19	19 27				19 56		20 19	20 27		
Stockport 84 a				18 33								19 30							20 33			
Hazel Grove 86 a																						
Buxton 86 a																						
Heald Green 85 a																						
Manchester Airport 85 ✈ a	18 17				18 47				19 17				19 47				20 17			20 47		

A To Liverpool Lime Street
B ⌘ from Preston
C From Glasgow Central
D From Clitheroe
E To Chester
F From Edinburgh
G From Leeds to Morecambe

The Sunday service between Manchester Victoria and Wigan Wallgate via Atherton is funded by GMITA and will operate whilst funding exists

Table 82

Sundays
7 August to 11 September

Barrow-in-Furness, Blackpool North, Preston, Southport, Kirkby and Wigan - Bolton - Manchester

	NT A	TP ◇1	NT B	NT C	TP ◇1 D	NT	NT E	NT	NT A	TP ◇1	NT B	NT	NT E	NT	NT B	NT A	NT	TP ◇1 D	NT B	NT A	TP ◇1
Barrow-in-Furness d						20 02															
Roose d						20 06															
Dalton d						20 12															
Ulverston d						20 21															
Cark d						20 28															
Kents Bank d						20 33															
Grange-over-Sands d						20 37															
Arnside d						20 43															
Silverdale d						20 47															
Carnforth d						20 54															
Windermere 83 d																					
Oxenholme Lake District 65 d					20 10																
Lancaster ■ 65 a					20 26	21 07															
d					20 26													22 04			
Blackpool North 97 d		19 44	19 50				20 11	20 20		20 44	20 50		21 13	21 20	21 50				22 44		23 03
Layton 97 d								20 23						21 23							
Poulton-le-Fylde 97 d		19 50	19 56				20 17	20 28		20 50	20 56		21 19	21 28	21 56				22 50		23 09
Kirkham & Wesham 97 d								20 37						21 37							23 17
Preston ■ 65,97 a		20 08	20 14		20 45		20 34	20 47		21 08	21 14		21 36	21 47	22 14			22 24	23 08		23 28
d		20 10	20 15		20 47			20 49		21 10	21 15			21 49	22 15			22 34	23 09		23 28
Leyland d			20 21					20 54			21 21			21 54	22 21				23 15		23 34
Chorley d		20 20			20 56			21 02		21 20				22 02				22 44			23 41
Adlington (Lancashire) d								21 07						22 07							23 45
Blackrod d								21 10						22 10							23 49
Horwich Parkway d		20 27						21 14		21 27				22 14							23 52
Lostock d								21 20						22 20							23 56
Southport d				20 05								21 05					22 05				
Meols Cop d				20 10								21 10					22 10				
Bescar Lane d																					
New Lane d																					
Burscough Bridge d				20 18								21 18					22 18				
Hoscar d																					
Parbold d				20 23								21 23					22 23				
Appley Bridge d				20 27								21 27					22 27				
Gathurst d				20 30								21 30					22 30				
Kirkby d																					
Rainford d																					
Upholland d																					
Orrell d																					
Pemberton d																					
Wigan Wallgate a				20 35								21 35					22 35				
d				20 36								21 36					22 36				
Wigan North Western d			20a35								21a35				22a35				23a29		
Ince d																					
Hindley d				20 41								21 41					22 41				
Westhoughton d				20 46								21 46					22 46				
Bolton a		20 34		20 54	21 08			21 25		21 34		21 54		22 25			22 54	22 59			00 02
d	20 31	20 35		20 54	21 08			21 25	21 31	21 35		21 54		22 25		22 31	22 54	23 00		23 31	00 02
Moses Gate d																					
Farnworth d																					
Kearsley d																					
Daisy Hill d																					
Hag Fold d																					
Atherton d																					
Walkden d																					
Moorside d																					
Swinton d																					
Salford Crescent a	20 43	20 47		21 07				21 38	21 43	21 47		22 07		22 38		22 43	23 07	23 12		23 43	
d	20 44	20 47		21 07				21 38	21 44	21 47		22 07		22 38		22 44	23 07	23 12		23 44	
Salford Central d																					
Manchester Victoria ⇌ a	20 52							21 45	21 52					22 45		22 52				23 52	
Rochdale 41 a																					
Deansgate ⇌ a		20 51		21 11						21 51		22 11					23 11	23 17			
Manchester Oxford Road a		20 52		21 13	21 23					21 52		22 13					23 14	23 19			
Manchester Piccadilly ■ ⇌ a		20 56		21 19	21 27					21 56		22 19					23 19	23 23			00 18
Stockport 84 a				21 30								22 33					23 33				
Hazel Grove 86 a																					
Buxton 86 a																					
Heald Green 85 a																					
Manchester Airport 85 ✈ a		21 17			21 47					22 17								23 39			00 32

A From Clitheroe
B To Liverpool Lime Street
C To Chester
D From Edinburgh
E To Leeds

The Sunday service between Manchester Victoria and Wigan Wallgate via Atherton is funded by GMITA and will operate whilst funding exists

Table 82

Sundays
18 September to 2 October

Barrow-in-Furness, Blackpool North, Preston, Southport, Kirkby and Wigan - Bolton - Manchester

	TP ◇1	NT	NT A	TP ◇1	NT	NT B	TP ◇1	NT C	TP ◇1	NT D	NT	NT	TP ◇1 E	NT	NT F	NT G	TP ◇1	NT D	NT	TP ◇1 H	NT A	NT
Barrow-in-Furness d							09 17															
Roose d							09 21															
Dalton d							09 28															
Ulverston d							09 36															
Cark d							09 44															
Kents Bank d							09 48															
Grange-over-Sands d							09 52															
Arnside d							09 58															
Silverdale d							10 02															
Carnforth d							10 09								10 31							
Windermere 83 d																						
Oxenholme Lake District 65 d																						
Lancaster ■ 65 a							10 17								10 40							
d							10 21															
Blackpool North 97 d	22p44	23p02		08 14	08 20	08 36			08 44	08 50				09 20			09 44	09 50				10 20
Layton 97 d		23p05			08 23									09 23								10 23
Poulton-le-Fylde 97 d	22p50	23p10		08 20	08 28	08 42			08 50	08 56				09 28			09 50	09 56				10 28
Kirkham & Wesham 97 d		23p19			08 37	08 51								09 37								10 37
Preston ■ 65,97 a	23p08	23p29		08 38	08 47	09 02	10 40		09 08	09 14				09 47			10 08	10 14				10 47
d	23p10	23p31		08 42	08 49				09 10	09 15				09 49			10 10	10 15				10 49
Leyland d		23p36			08 54					09 21				09 54				10 21				10 54
Chorley d	23p21	23p44		08 51	09 02				09 20					10 02			10 20					11 02
Adlington (Lancashire) d		23p49			09 07									10 07								11 07
Blackrod d		23p52			09 10									10 10								11 10
Horwich Parkway d	23p28	23p56		08 59	09 14				09 27					10 14			10 27					11 14
Lostock d		00 02			09 20									10 20								11 20
Southport d												09 10									10 05	
Meols Cop d												09 15									10 10	
Bescar Lane d																						
New Lane d																						
Burscough Bridge d												09 23									10 18	
Hoscar d																						
Parbold d												09 28									10 23	
Appley Bridge d												09 32									10 27	
Gathurst d												09 35									10 30	
Kirkby d																						
Rainford d																						
Upholland d																						
Orrell d																						
Pemberton d																						
Wigan Wallgate a												09 40									10 35	
d			08 40								09 15	09 41							10 15		10 36	
Wigan North Western d										09a35								10a36				
Ince d											09 18								10 18			
Hindley d			08 45								09 22	09 46							10 22		10 41	
Westhoughton d			08 49									09 51									10 46	
Bolton a	23p34	00 07	08 57	09 05	09 25				09 34			09 59		10 25			10 34				10 54	11 25
d	23p35	00 07	08 58	09 06	09 25			09 31	09 35			09 59		10 25		10 31	10 35				10 54	11 25
Moses Gate d																						
Farnworth d																						
Kearsley d																						
Daisy Hill d											09 26								10 26			
Hag Fold d											09 29								10 29			
Atherton d											09 31								10 31			
Walkden d											09 37								10 37			
Moorside d											09 40								10 40			
Swinton d											09 43								10 43			
Salford Crescent a	23p47		09 10	09 18	09 38			09 43	09 47		09 50	10 12		10 38		10 43	10 47		10 50		11 07	11 38
d	23p47		09 11	09 18	09 38			09 44	09 47		09 51	10 12	10 27	10 38		10 44	10 47		10 51	11 03	11 07	11 38
Salford Central d																						
Manchester Victoria ⇌ a		00 26			09 45			09 52			09 57			10 45		10 52			10 57			11 45
Rochdale 41 a																						
Deansgate ⇌ a			09 14	09 23					09 51			10 16					10 51				11 11	
Manchester Oxford Road a			09 17	09 24					09 52			10 18					10 52				11 13	
Manchester Piccadilly ■ ⇌ a	23p53		09 21	09 28					09 56			10 22	10 33				10 56			11 08	11 19	
Stockport 84 a			09 31									10 33									11 30	
Hazel Grove 86 a																						
Buxton 86 a																						
Heald Green 85 a	00 15																					
Manchester Airport 85 ✈ a	00 22			09 50					10 17				10 55				11 17			11 25		

A To Chester
B To Carlisle
C From Blackburn
D To Liverpool Lime Street
E From York
F From Leeds to Morecambe
G From Clitheroe
H From Newcastle

The Sunday service between Manchester Victoria and Wigan Wallgate via Atherton is funded by GMITA and will operate whilst funding exists

Table 82

Sundays

18 September to 2 October

Barrow-in-Furness, Blackpool North, Preston, Southport, Kirkby and Wigan - Bolton - Manchester

		NT	TP	NT	NT	TP	NT	NT	NT	TP	NT	NT	TP	NT	TP	NT	NT	NT	TP	NT	NT	TP	NT
			◇1			◇1				◇1			◇1		◇1				◇1			◇1	
		A		B		C			A		B		D	E			F	A		B		G	
Barrow-in-Furness	d														11 25								
Roose	d														11 29								
Dalton	d														11 35								
Ulverston	d														11 44								
Cark	d														11 51								
Kents Bank	d														11 55								
Grange-over-Sands	d														11 59								
Arnside	d														12 05								
Silverdale	d														12 10								
Carnforth	d														12 17		12 35						
Windermere	83 d																						
Oxenholme Lake District	65 d																						
Lancaster 6	65 a														12 26		12 44						
	d														12 26								
Blackpool North	97 d		10 44	10 50				11 20		11 44	11 50					12 20			12 44	12 50			
Layton	97 d							11 23								12 23							
Poulton-le-Fylde	97 d		10 50	10 56				11 28		11 50	11 56					12 28			12 50	12 56			
Kirkham & Wesham	97 d							11 37								12 37							
Preston 8	65,97 a		11 08	11 14				11 47		12 08	12 14				12 45	12 47			13 08	13 14			
	d		11 10	11 15				11 49		12 10	12 15				12 47	12 49			13 10	13 15			
Leyland	d			11 21				11 54			12 21					12 54				13 21			
Chorley	d		11 20					12 02		12 20					12 56	13 02			13 20				
Adlington (Lancashire)	d							12 07								13 07							
Blackrod	d							12 10								13 10							
Horwich Parkway	d		11 27					12 14		12 27						13 14			13 27				
Lostock	d							12 20								13 20							
Southport	d						11 05							12 05									13 01
Meols Cop	d						11 10							12 10									13 06
Bescar Lane	d																						
New Lane	d																						
Burscough Bridge	d						11 18							12 18									13 14
Hoscar	d																						
Parbold	d						11 23							12 23									13 19
Appley Bridge	d						11 27							12 27									13 23
Gathurst	d						11 30							12 30									13 26
Kirkby	d																						
Rainford	d																						
Upholland	d																						
Orrell	d																						
Pemberton	d																						
Wigan Wallgate	a						11 35							12 35									13 33
	d				11 15		11 36					12 15		12 36							13 15		13 34
Wigan North Western	d			11a35							12a35									13a35			
Ince	d				11 18							12 18									13 18		
Hindley	d				11 22		11 41					12 22		12 41							13 22		13 39
Westhoughton	d						11 46							12 46									13 44
Bolton	a		11 34				11 54	12 25		12 34				12 54	13 08	13 25			13 34				13 54
	d	11 31	11 35				11 54	12 25	12 31	12 35				12 54	13 08	13 25		13 31	13 35				13 54
Moses Gate	d																						
Farnworth	d																						
Kearsley	d																						
Daisy Hill	d				11 26							12 26									13 26		
Hag Fold	d				11 29							12 29									13 29		
Atherton	d				11 31							12 31									13 31		
Walkden	d				11 37							12 37									13 37		
Moorside	d				11 40							12 40									13 40		
Swinton	d				11 43							12 43									13 43		
Salford Crescent	a	11 43	11 47		11 50		12 07	12 38	12 43	12 47		12 50		13 07		13 38		13 43	13 47		13 50		14 07
	d	11 44	11 47		11 51	12 03	12 07	12 38	12 44	12 47		12 51	13 03	13 07		13 38		13 44	13 47		13 51	14 03	14 07
Salford Central	d																						
Manchester Victoria	⇌ a	11 52			11 57			12 45	12 52			12 57				13 45		13 52			13 57		
Rochdale	41 a																						
Deansgate	⇌ a		11 51				12 11			12 51				13 11					13 51				14 11
Manchester Oxford Road	a		11 52				12 13			12 52				13 13	13 23				13 52				14 13
Manchester Piccadilly 10	⇌ a		11 56			12 08	12 19			12 56			13 08	13 19	13 27				13 56			14 08	14 19
Stockport	84 a						12 33							13 30									14 33
Hazel Grove	86 a																						
Buxton	86 a																						
Heald Green	85 a																						
Manchester Airport	85 ✈ a		12 17			12 25				13 17			13 25		13 47				14 17			14 25	

A From Clitheroe
B To Liverpool Lime Street
C From Scarborough
D From Middlesbrough
E To Chester
F From Leeds to Morecambe
G From Newcastle

The Sunday service between Manchester Victoria and Wigan Wallgate via Atherton is funded by GMITA and will operate whilst funding exists

Table 82

Sundays

18 September to 2 October

Barrow-in-Furness, Blackpool North, Preston, Southport, Kirkby and Wigan - Bolton - Manchester

		TP	NT	NT	NT	TP	NT	NT	TP	NT	TP	NT	NT	TP	NT	NT	TP	NT	TP	NT	NT	TP
		◇1				◇1			◇1		◇1			◇1			◇1		◇1			◇1
		A			B		C		D	E			B		C		D		A		B	
Barrow-in-Furness	d		12 45								13 25											
Roose	d		12 49								13 29											
Dalton	d		12 55								13 35											
Ulverston	d		13 04								13 44											
Cark	d		13 11								13 51											
Kents Bank	d		13 16								13 55											
Grange-over-Sands	d		13 20								13 59											
Arnside	d		13 26								14 05											
Silverdale	d		13 30								14 10											
Carnforth	d		13 37								14 17											
Windermere	83 d																					
Oxenholme Lake District	65 d	13 11																	15 11			
Lancaster 6	65 a	13 26	13 50								14 26								15 26			
	d	13 26									14 26								15 26			
Blackpool North	97 d			13 20		13 44	13 50					14 20		14 44	14 50					15 20		15 44
Layton	97 d			13 23								14 23								15 23		
Poulton-le-Fylde	97 d			13 28		13 50	13 56					14 28		14 50	14 56					15 28		15 50
Kirkham & Wesham	97 d			13 37								14 37								15 37		
Preston 8	65,97 a	13 45		13 47		14 08	14 14				14 45	14 47		15 08	15 14				15 45	15 47		16 08
	d	13 47		13 49		14 10	14 15				14 47	14 49		15 10	15 15				15 47	15 49		16 10
Leyland	d			13 54			14 21					14 54			15 21					15 54		
Chorley	d	13 56		14 02		14 20					14 56	15 02		15 20					15 56	16 02		16 20
Adlington (Lancashire)	d			14 07								15 07								16 07		
Blackrod	d			14 10								15 10								16 10		
Horwich Parkway	d			14 14		14 27						15 14		15 27						16 14		16 27
Lostock	d			14 20								15 20								16 20		
Southport	d									14 05								15 05				
Meols Cop	d									14 10								15 10				
Bescar Lane	d																					
New Lane	d																					
Burscough Bridge	d									14 18								15 18				
Hoscar	d																					
Parbold	d									14 23								15 23				
Appley Bridge	d									14 27								15 27				
Gathurst	d									14 30								15 30				
Kirkby	d																					
Rainford	d																					
Upholland	d																					
Orrell	d																					
Pemberton	d																					
Wigan Wallgate	a									14 35								15 35				
	d							14 15		14 36						15 15		15 36				
Wigan North Western	d						14a35								15a35							
Ince	d							14 18								15 18						
Hindley	d							14 22		14 41						15 22		15 41				
Westhoughton	d									14 46								15 46				
Bolton	a	14 08		14 25		14 34				14 54	15 08	15 25		15 34				15 54	16 08	16 25		16 34
	d	14 08		14 25	14 31	14 35				14 54	15 08	15 25	15 31	15 35				15 54	16 08	16 25	16 31	16 35
Moses Gate	d																					
Farnworth	d																					
Kearsley	d																					
Daisy Hill	d							14 26								15 26						
Hag Fold	d							14 29								15 29						
Atherton	d							14 31								15 31						
Walkden	d							14 37								15 37						
Moorside	d							14 40								15 40						
Swinton	d							14 43								15 43						
Salford Crescent	a			14 38	14 43	14 47		14 50		15 07		15 38	15 43	15 47		15 50		16 07		16 38	16 43	16 47
	d			14 38	14 44	14 47		14 51	15 03	15 07		15 38	15 44	15 47		15 51	16 03	16 07		16 38	16 44	16 47
Salford Central	d																					
Manchester Victoria	⇌ a			14 45	14 52			14 57				15 45	15 52			15 57				16 45	16 52	
Rochdale	41 a																					
Deansgate	⇌ a					14 51				15 11				15 51				16 11				16 51
Manchester Oxford Road	a	14 23				14 52				15 13	15 23			15 52				16 13	16 23			16 52
Manchester Piccadilly 10	⇌ a	14 27				14 56			15 08	15 19	15 27			15 56			16 08	16 19	16 27			16 56
Stockport	84 a									15 30								16 33				
Hazel Grove	86 a																					
Buxton	86 a																					
Heald Green	85 a																					
Manchester Airport	85 ✈ a	14 47				15 17			15 25		15 47			16 17			16 25		16 47			17 17

A From Edinburgh
B From Clitheroe
C To Liverpool Lime Street
D From Newcastle
E To Chester

The Sunday service between Manchester Victoria and Wigan Wallgate via Atherton is funded by GMITA and will operate whilst funding exists

Table 82

Sundays
18 September to 2 October

Barrow-in-Furness, Blackpool North, Preston, Southport, Kirkby and Wigan - Bolton - Manchester

	NT	NT	TP	NT	TP	NT	NT		NT	TP	NT	NT	TP	NT	TP	NT	NT		TP	NT	TP	NT	TP	NT
			◇1		◇1					◇1			◇1		◇1				◇1		◇1		◇1	
	A		B	C			D		E		A		B		F 🍴		E			A	B	C	G 🍴	
Barrow-in-Furness d					15 34																			
Roose d																								
Dalton d																								
Ulverston d					15 50																			
Cark d																								
Kents Bank d																								
Grange-over-Sands d					16 02																			
Arnside d					16 08																			
Silverdale d																								
Carnforth d					16 17		16 37																	
Windermere 83 d																								
Oxenholme Lake District 65 d															17 09								18 10	
Lancaster 65 a					16 26		16 46								17 23								18 26	
d					16 26										17 24								18 26	
Blackpool North 97 d	15 50					16 20				16 44	16 50					17 20			17 44	17 50				18 20
Layton 97 d						16 23										17 23								18 23
Poulton-le-Fylde 97 d	15 56					16 28				16 50	16 56					17 28			17 50	17 56				18 28
Kirkham & Wesham 97 d						16 37										17 37								18 37
Preston 65,97 a	16 14				16 45	16 47				17 08	17 14				17 42	17 47			18 08	18 14			18 45	18 47
d	16 15				16 47	16 49				17 10	17 15				17 47	17 49			18 10	18 15			18 47	18 49
Leyland d	16 21					16 54					17 21					17 54				18 21				18 54
Chorley d					16 56	17 02				17 20					17 56	18 02			18 20				18 56	19 02
Adlington (Lancashire) d						17 07										18 07								19 07
Blackrod d						17 10										18 10								19 10
Horwich Parkway d						17 14				17 27						18 14			18 27					19 14
Lostock d						17 20										18 20								19 20
Southport d				16 05										17 05								18 05		
Meols Cop d				16 10										17 10								18 10		
Bescar Lane d																								
New Lane d																								
Burscough Bridge d				16 18										17 18								18 18		
Hoscar d																								
Parbold d				16 23										17 23								18 23		
Appley Bridge d				16 27										17 27								18 27		
Gathurst d				16 30										17 30								18 30		
Kirkby d																								
Rainford d																								
Upholland d																								
Orrell d																								
Pemberton d																								
Wigan Wallgate a				16 35										17 35								18 35		
d		16 15		16 36								17 15		17 36								18 36		
Wigan North Western d	16a35										17a35									18a35				
Ince d		16 18										17 18												
Hindley d		16 22		16 41								17 22		17 41								18 41		
Westhoughton d				16 46										17 46								18 46		
Bolton a				16 54	17 08	17 25				17 34				17 54	18 08	18 25			18 34			18 54	19 08	19 25
d				16 54	17 08	17 25			17 31	17 35				17 54	18 08	18 25	18 31		18 35			18 54	19 08	19 25
Moses Gate d																								
Farnworth d																								
Kearsley d																								
Daisy Hill d		16 26										17 26												
Hag Fold d		16 29										17 29												
Atherton d		16 31										17 31												
Walkden d		16 37										17 37												
Moorside d		16 40										17 40												
Swinton d		16 43										17 43												
Salford Crescent a		16 50		17 07		17 38			17 43	17 47		17 50		18 07		18 38	18 43		18 47			19 07		19 38
d		16 51	17 03	17 07		17 38			17 44	17 47		17 51	18 03	18 07		18 38	18 44		18 47		19 03	19 07		19 38
Salford Central d																								
Manchester Victoria ⇌ a		16 57				17 45			17 52			17 57				18 45	18 52							19 45
Rochdale 41 a																								
Deansgate ⇌ a				17 11						17 51				18 11					18 51			19 11		
Manchester Oxford Road a				17 13	17 23					17 52				18 13	18 23				18 52			19 13	19 23	
Manchester Piccadilly 10 ⇌ a			17 08	17 19	17 27					17 56			18 08	18 19	18 27				18 56		19 08	19 19	19 27	
Stockport 84 a				17 30										18 33								19 30		
Hazel Grove 86 a																								
Buxton 86 a																								
Heald Green 85 a																								
Manchester Airport 85 ✈ a			17 25		17 47					18 17			18 25		18 47				19 17		19 25		19 47	

A To Liverpool Lime Street
B From Newcastle
C To Chester
D From Leeds to Morecambe
E From Clitheroe
F From Glasgow Central
G From Edinburgh

The Sunday service between Manchester Victoria and Wigan Wallgate via Atherton is funded by GMITA and will operate whilst funding exists

Table 82

Sundays
18 September to 2 October

Barrow-in-Furness, Blackpool North, Preston, Southport, Kirkby and Wigan - Bolton - Manchester

	NT	TP	NT		TP	NT	TP	NT	TP	NT	NT	TP	NT		NT	TP	NT	TP	NT	NT	NT	TP	NT	
		◇1			◇1		◇1		◇1			◇1				◇1		◇1				◇1		
	A		B			C	D		E 🍴		B		C		F	D	G	H 🍴			B		C	
Barrow-in-Furness d		18 17																	20 02					
Roose d		18 21																	20 06					
Dalton d		18 28																	20 12					
Ulverston d		18 36																	20 21					
Cark d		18 44																	20 28					
Kents Bank d		18 48																	20 33					
Grange-over-Sands d		18 52																	20 37					
Arnside d		18 58																	20 43					
Silverdale d		19 02																	20 47					
Carnforth d	19 04	19 08																	20 54					
Windermere 83 d																								
Oxenholme Lake District 65 d									19 07									20 10						
Lancaster 65 a	19 13	19 17							19 22									20 26	21 07					
d		19 17							19 22									20 26						
Blackpool North 97 d					18 44	18 50				19 20		19 44	19 50		20 11					20 20		20 44	20 50	
Layton 97 d										19 23										20 23				
Poulton-le-Fylde 97 d					18 50	18 56				19 28		19 50	19 56		20 17					20 28		20 50	20 56	
Kirkham & Wesham 97 d										19 37										20 37				
Preston 65,97 a		19 37			19 08	19 14			19 42	19 47		20 08	20 14		20 34			20 45		20 47		21 08	21 14	
d					19 10	19 15			19 47	19 49		20 10	20 15					20 47		20 49		21 10	21 15	
Leyland d						19 21				19 54			20 21							20 54			21 21	
Chorley d					19 20				19 56	20 02		20 20						20 56		21 02		21 20		
Adlington (Lancashire) d										20 07										21 07				
Blackrod d										20 10										21 10				
Horwich Parkway d					19 27					20 14		20 27								21 14		21 27		
Lostock d										20 20										21 20				
Southport d								19 05									20 05							
Meols Cop d								19 10									20 10							
Bescar Lane d																								
New Lane d																								
Burscough Bridge d								19 18									20 18							
Hoscar d																								
Parbold d								19 23									20 23							
Appley Bridge d								19 27									20 27							
Gathurst d								19 30									20 30							
Kirkby d																								
Rainford d																								
Upholland d																								
Orrell d																								
Pemberton d																								
Wigan Wallgate a								19 35									20 35							
d								19 36									20 36							
Wigan North Western d						19a35							20a35										21a35	
Ince d																								
Hindley d								19 41									20 41							
Westhoughton d								19 46									20 46							
Bolton a					19 34			19 54	20 08	20 25		20 34					20 54	21 08		21 25		21 34		
d			19 31		19 35			19 54	20 08	20 25	20 31	20 35					20 54	21 08		21 25	21 31	21 35		
Moses Gate d																								
Farnworth d																								
Kearsley d																								
Daisy Hill d																								
Hag Fold d																								
Atherton d																								
Walkden d																								
Moorside d																								
Swinton d																								
Salford Crescent a			19 43		19 47			20 07		20 38	20 43	20 47					21 07			21 38	21 43	21 47		
d			19 44		19 47		20 03	20 07		20 38	20 44	20 47				21 03	21 07			21 38	21 44	21 47		
Salford Central d																								
Manchester Victoria ⇌ a			19 52							20 45	20 52									21 45	21 52			
Rochdale 41 a																								
Deansgate ⇌ a					19 51			20 11				20 51					21 11					21 51		
Manchester Oxford Road a					19 52			20 13	20 23			20 52					21 13	21 23				21 52		
Manchester Piccadilly 10 ⇌ a					19 56		20 08	20 19	20 27			20 56				21 08	21 19	21 27				21 56		
Stockport 84 a								20 33									21 30							
Hazel Grove 86 a																								
Buxton 86 a																								
Heald Green 85 a																								
Manchester Airport 85 ✈ a					20 17		20 25		20 47			21 17				21 25		21 47				22 17		

A From Leeds to Morecambe
B From Clitheroe
C To Liverpool Lime Street
D From Newcastle
E From Glasgow Central
F To Leeds
G To Chester
H From Edinburgh

The Sunday service between Manchester Victoria and Wigan Wallgate via Atherton is funded by GMITA and will operate whilst funding exists

Table 82

Sundays
18 September to 2 October

Barrow-in-Furness, Blackpool North, Preston, Southport, Kirkby and Wigan - Bolton - Manchester

		NT	NT	NT	NT	NT	TP	TP	TP	NT		NT	NT	TP
							◇■	◇■	◇■					◇■
			A		B	C	D	E	F			B	C	
								✠	✠					
Barrow-in-Furness	d													
Roose	d													
Dalton	d													
Ulverston	d													
Cark	d													
Kents Bank	d													
Grange-over-Sands	d													
Arnside	d													
Silverdale	d													
Carnforth	d													
Windermere	83 d													
Oxenholme Lake District	65 d													
Lancaster ■	65 a													
	d								22 04					
Blackpool North	97 d		21 13	21 20	21 50			21 56				22 44		23 03
Layton	97 d			21 23										
Poulton-le-Fylde	97 d		21 19	21 28	21 56			22 02				22 50		23 09
Kirkham & Wesham	97 d			21 37										23 17
Preston ■	65,97 a		21 36	21 47	22 14			22 20	22 24			23 08		23 28
	d			21 49	22 15			22 29				23 09		23 28
Leyland	d			21 54	22 21							23 15		23 34
Chorley	d			22 02				22 39						23 41
Adlington (Lancashire)	d			22 07										23 45
Blackrod	d			22 10										23 49
Horwich Parkway	d			22 14										23 52
Lostock	d			22 20										23 56
Southport	d	21 05								22 05				
Meols Cop	d	21 10								22 10				
Bescar Lane	d													
New Lane	d													
Burscough Bridge	d	21 18								22 18				
Hoscar	d													
Parbold	d	21 23								22 23				
Appley Bridge	d	21 27								22 27				
Gathurst	d	21 30								22 30				
Kirkby	d													
Rainford	d													
Upholland	d													
Orrell	d													
Pemberton	d													
Wigan Wallgate	a	21 35								22 35				
	d	21 36								22 36				
Wigan North Western	d				22a35							23a29		
Ince	d													
Hindley	d	21 41								22 41				
Westhoughton	d	21 46								22 46				
Bolton	a	21 54		22 25				22 50		22 54				00 02
	d	21 54		22 25		22 31		22 51		22 54			23 31	00 02
Moses Gate	d													
Farnworth	d													
Kearsley	d													
Daisy Hill	d													
Hag Fold	d													
Atherton	d													
Walkden	d													
Moorside	d													
Swinton	d													
Salford Crescent	a	22 07		22 38		22 43		23 03		23 07			23 43	
	d	22 07		22 38		22 44	23 03	23 04		23 07			23 44	
Salford Central	d													
Manchester Victoria	⇌ a			22 45		22 52							23 52	
Rochdale	41 a													
Deansgate	⇌ a	22 11						23 09		23 11				
Manchester Oxford Road	a	22 13						23 11		23 14				
Manchester Piccadilly ■	⇌ a	22 19					23 08	23 15		23 19				00 18
Stockport	84 a	22 33								23 33				
Hazel Grove	86 a													
Buxton	86 a													
Heald Green	85 a													
Manchester Airport	85 ✈ a						23 25	23 31						00 32

A To Leeds
B To Liverpool Lime Street
C From Clitheroe
D From Newcastle
E ✠ from Preston
F From Edinburgh

The Sunday service between Manchester Victoria and Wigan Wallgate via Atherton is funded by GMITA and will operate whilst funding exists

Table 82

Sundays
from 9 October

Barrow-in-Furness, Blackpool North, Preston, Southport, Kirkby and Wigan - Bolton - Manchester

		TP	NT	NT	NT	NT	TP	NT	NT	TP		NT	TP	NT	NT	NT	TP	NT	NT	NT		TP	NT	NT	NT
		◇■					◇■			◇■			◇■				◇■					◇■			
			A		B	C			D			B		E			F		G	B			E	H	
									✠															🚌	
Barrow-in-Furness	d									09 17															
Roose	d									09 21															
Dalton	d									09 28															
Ulverston	d									09 36															
Cark	d									09 44															
Kents Bank	d									09 48															
Grange-over-Sands	d									09 52															
Arnside	d									09 58															
Silverdale	d									10 02															
Carnforth	d									10 09									10 31						
Windermere	83 d																								
Oxenholme Lake District	65 d																								
Lancaster ■	65 a									10 17									10 40						
	d									10 21															
Blackpool North	97 d	22p44		23p02			08 14	08 20	08 36				08 44	08 50				09 20				09 44	09 50	10 05	
Layton	97 d			23p05				08 23										09 23							
Poulton-le-Fylde	97 d	22p50		23p10			08 20	08 28	08 42				08 50	08 56				09 28				09 50	09 56		
Kirkham & Wesham	97 d			23p19				08 37	08 51									09 37							
Preston ■	65,97 a	23p08		23p29			08 38	08 47	09 02	10 40			09 08	09 14				09 47				10 08	10 14	10 44	
	d	23p10		23p31			08 42	08 49					09 10	09 15				09 49				10 10	10 15		
Leyland	d			23p36				08 54						09 21				09 54					10 21		
Chorley	d	23p21		23p44			08 51	09 02					09 20					10 02				10 20			
Adlington (Lancashire)	d			23p49				09 07										10 07							
Blackrod	d			23p52				09 10										10 10							
Horwich Parkway	d	23p28		23p56			08 59	09 14					09 27					10 14				10 27			
Lostock	d			00 02				09 20										10 20							
Southport	d															09 06									
Meols Cop	d															09 11									
Bescar Lane	d																								
New Lane	d																								
Burscough Bridge	d															09 19									
Hoscar	d																								
Parbold	d															09 24									
Appley Bridge	d															09 28									
Gathurst	d															09 31									
Kirkby	d																								
Rainford	d																								
Upholland	d																								
Orrell	d																								
Pemberton	d																								
Wigan Wallgate	a															09 38									
	d					08 40									09 13	09 39									10 13
Wigan North Western	d													09a35									10a36		
Ince	d														09 16										10 16
Hindley	d					08 45									09 20	09 44									10 20
Westhoughton	d					08 49										09 49									
Bolton	a	23p34		00 07		08 57	09 05	09 25					09 34			09 59		10 25				10 34			
	d	23p35	23p38	00 07	08 31	08 58	09 06	09 25				09 31	09 35			09 59		10 25		10 31		10 35			
Moses Gate	d																								
Farnworth	d																								
Kearsley	d																								
Daisy Hill	d														09 24										10 24
Hag Fold	d														09 27										10 27
Atherton	d														09 29										10 29
Walkden	d														09 35										10 35
Moorside	d														09 38										10 38
Swinton	d														09 41										10 41
Salford Crescent	a	23p47	23p48		08 43	09 10	09 18	09 38				09 43	09 47		09 50	10 12		10 38		10 43		10 47			10 50
	d	23p47	23p51		08 44	09 11	09 18	09 38				09 44	09 47		09 51	10 12	10 27	10 38		10 44		10 47			10 51
Salford Central	d																								
Manchester Victoria	⇌ a		00 01	00 26	08 53			09 45				09 53			09 57			10 45		10 53					10 57
Rochdale	41 a																								
Deansgate	⇌ a					09 14	09 23						09 51			10 16						10 51			
Manchester Oxford Road	a					09 17	09 24						09 52			10 18						10 52			
Manchester Piccadilly ■	⇌ a	23p53				09 21	09 28						09 56			10 22	10 33					10 56			
Stockport	84 a					09 31										10 33									
Hazel Grove	86 a																								
Buxton	86 a																								
Heald Green	85 a	00 15																							
Manchester Airport	85 ✈ a	00 22					09 50						10 17				10 55					11 17			

A From Clitheroe
B from 30 October
C To Chester
D 9 October, 16 October, 23 October. To Carlisle
E To Liverpool Lime Street
F 9 October, 16 October, 23 October. From York
G From Leeds to Morecambe
H from 30 October. To Hebden Bridge

The Sunday service between Manchester Victoria and Wigan Wallgate via Atherton is funded by GMITA and will operate whilst funding exists

Table 82

Sundays
from 9 October

Barrow-in-Furness, Blackpool North, Preston, Southport, Kirkby and Wigan - Bolton - Manchester

Station		TP	NT	NT	NT	TP	NT	NT	TP	NT	NT	NT	TP	NT	NT	NT	TP	NT	TP	NT	NT	NT	TP
		◇1				◇1			◇1				◇1				◇1		◇1				◇1
		A	B		C		D		E			C		D	F		G	B			H	C	
Barrow-in-Furness	d																		11 25				
Roose	d																		11 29				
Dalton	d																		11 35				
Ulverston	d																		11 44				
Cark	d																		11 51				
Kents Bank	d																		11 55				
Grange-over-Sands	d																		11 59				
Arnside	d																		12 05				
Silverdale	d																		12 10				
Carnforth	d																		12 17		12 35		
Windermere 83	d																						
Oxenholme Lake District 65	d																						
Lancaster 6 65	a																		12 26		12 44		
	d																		12 26				
Blackpool North 97	d			10 20		10 44	10 50				11 20		11 44	11 50	12 05					12 20			12 44
Layton 97	d			10 23							11 23									12 23			
Poulton-le-Fylde 97	d			10 28		10 50	10 56				11 28		11 50	11 56						12 28			12 50
Kirkham & Wesham 97	d			10 37							11 37									12 37			
Preston 8 65,97	a			10 47		11 08	11 14				11 47		12 08	12 14	12 44				12 45	12 47			13 08
	d			10 49		11 10	11 15				11 49		12 10	12 15					12 47	12 49			13 10
Leyland	d			10 54			11 21				11 54			12 21						12 54			
Chorley	d			11 02		11 20					12 02		12 20						12 56	13 02			13 20
Adlington (Lancashire)	d			11 07							12 07									13 07			
Blackrod	d			11 10							12 10									13 10			
Horwich Parkway	d			11 14		11 27					12 14		12 27							13 14			13 27
Lostock	d			11 20							12 20									13 20			
Southport	d		10 05							11 01								12 05					
Meols Cop	d		10 10							11 06								12 10					
Bescar Lane	d																						
New Lane	d																						
Burscough Bridge	d		10 18							11 14								12 18					
Hoscar	d																						
Parbold	d		10 23							11 19								12 23					
Appley Bridge	d		10 27							11 23								12 27					
Gathurst	d		10 30							11 26								12 30					
Kirkby	d																						
Rainford	d																						
Upholland	d																						
Orrell	d																						
Pemberton	d																						
Wigan Wallgate	a		10 35							11 33								12 35					
	d		10 36					11 13		11 34						12 13		12 36					
Wigan North Western	d						11a35							12a35									
Ince	d							11 16								12 16							
Hindley	d		10 41					11 20		11 39						12 20		12 41					
Westhoughton	d		10 46							11 44								12 46					
Bolton	a		10 54	11 25		11 34				11 54	12 25		12 34					12 54	13 08	13 25			13 34
	d		10 54	11 25	11 31	11 35				11 54	12 25	12 31	12 35					12 54	13 08	13 25		13 31	13 35
Moses Gate	d																						
Farnworth	d																						
Kearsley	d																						
Daisy Hill	d							11 24								12 24							
Hag Fold	d							11 27								12 27							
Atherton	d							11 29								12 29							
Walkden	d							11 35								12 35							
Moorside	d							11 38								12 38							
Swinton	d							11 41								12 41							
Salford Crescent	a		11 07	11 38	11 43	11 47		11 50		12 07	12 38	12 43	12 47			12 50		13 07		13 38		13 43	13 47
	d	11 03	11 07	11 38	11 44	11 47		11 51	12 03	12 07	12 38	12 44	12 47			12 51	13 03	13 07		13 38		13 44	13 47
Salford Central	d																						
Manchester Victoria ⇌	a			11 45	11 53			11 57			12 45	12 53				12 57				13 45		13 53	
Rochdale 41	a																						
Deansgate ⇌	a		11 11			11 51				12 11			12 51					13 11					13 51
Manchester Oxford Road	a		11 13			11 52				12 13			12 52					13 13	13 23				13 52
Manchester Piccadilly 10 ⇌	a	11 08	11 19			11 56			12 08	12 19			12 56				13 08	13 19	13 27				13 56
Stockport 84	a		11 30							12 33								13 30					
Hazel Grove 86	a																						
Buxton 86	a																						
Heald Green 85	a																						
Manchester Airport 85 ✈	a	11 25				12 17			12 25				13 17				13 25		13 47				14 17

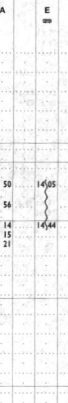

A 9 October, 16 October, 23 October. From Newcastle
B To Chester
C from 30 October
D To Liverpool Lime Street
E 9 October, 16 October, 23 October. From Scarborough
F from 30 October. To Hebden Bridge
G 9 October, 16 October, 23 October. From Middlesbrough
H From Leeds to Morecambe

The Sunday service between Manchester Victoria and Wigan Wallgate via Atherton is funded by GMITA and will operate whilst funding exists

Table 82

Sundays
from 9 October

Barrow-in-Furness, Blackpool North, Preston, Southport, Kirkby and Wigan - Bolton - Manchester

Station		NT	NT	TP	NT	TP	NT	NT	NT	TP	NT	NT	NT	TP	NT	TP	NT	NT	TP	NT	NT	TP
				◇1		◇1				◇1				◇1		◇1			◇1			◇1
		A		B		C			D		A	E		B	F			D		A		B
Barrow-in-Furness	d						12 45									13 25						
Roose	d						12 49									13 29						
Dalton	d						12 55									13 35						
Ulverston	d						13 04									13 44						
Cark	d						13 11									13 51						
Kents Bank	d						13 16									13 55						
Grange-over-Sands	d						13 20									13 59						
Arnside	d						13 26									14 05						
Silverdale	d						13 30									14 10						
Carnforth	d						13 37									14 17						
Windermere 83	d																					
Oxenholme Lake District 65	d					13 11																
Lancaster 6 65	a					13 26	13 50									14 26						
	d					13 26										14 26						
Blackpool North 97	d	12 50						13 20		13 44	13 50	14 05					14 20		14 44	14 50		
Layton 97	d							13 23									14 23					
Poulton-le-Fylde 97	d	12 56						13 28		13 50	13 56						14 28		14 50	14 56		
Kirkham & Wesham 97	d							13 37									14 37					
Preston 8 65,97	a	13 14				13 45		13 47		14 08	14 14	14 44				14 45	14 47		15 08	15 14		
	d	13 15				13 47		13 49		14 10	14 15					14 47	14 49		15 10	15 15		
Leyland	d	13 21						13 54			14 21						14 54			15 21		
Chorley	d					13 56		14 02		14 20						14 56	15 02		15 20			
Adlington (Lancashire)	d							14 07									15 07					
Blackrod	d							14 10									15 10					
Horwich Parkway	d							14 14		14 27							15 14		15 27			
Lostock	d							14 20									15 20					
Southport	d				12 57										14 05							
Meols Cop	d				13 02										14 10							
Bescar Lane	d																					
New Lane	d																					
Burscough Bridge	d				13 10										14 18							
Hoscar	d																					
Parbold	d				13 15										14 23							
Appley Bridge	d				13 19										14 27							
Gathurst	d				13 22										14 30							
Kirkby	d																					
Rainford	d																					
Upholland	d																					
Orrell	d																					
Pemberton	d																					
Wigan Wallgate	a				13 29										14 35							
	d		13 13		13 30								14 13		14 36						15 13	
Wigan North Western	d	13a35									14a35									15a35		
Ince	d		13 16										14 16								15 16	
Hindley	d		13 20		13 35								14 20		14 41						15 20	
Westhoughton	d				13 40										14 46							
Bolton	a				13 50	14 08		14 25		14 34					14 54	15 08	15 25		15 34			
	d				13 50	14 08		14 25	14 31	14 35					14 54	15 08	15 25	15 31	15 35			
Moses Gate	d																					
Farnworth	d																					
Kearsley	d																					
Daisy Hill	d		13 24										14 24								15 24	
Hag Fold	d		13 27										14 27								15 27	
Atherton	d		13 29										14 29								15 29	
Walkden	d		13 35										14 35								15 35	
Moorside	d		13 38										14 38								15 38	
Swinton	d		13 41										14 41								15 41	
Salford Crescent	a		13 50		14 03			14 38	14 43	14 47			14 50		15 07		15 38	15 43	15 47		15 50	
	d		13 51	14 03	14 03			14 38	14 44	14 47			14 51	15 03	15 07		15 38	15 44	15 47		15 51	16 03
Salford Central	d																					
Manchester Victoria ⇌	a		13 57					14 45	14 53				14 57				15 45	15 53			15 57	
Rochdale 41	a																					
Deansgate ⇌	a				14 07					14 51					15 11				15 51			
Manchester Oxford Road	a				14 09	14 23				14 52					15 13	15 23			15 52			
Manchester Piccadilly 10 ⇌	a			14 08	14 15	14 27				14 56				15 08	15 19	15 27			15 56			16 08
Stockport 84	a				14 29										15 30							
Hazel Grove 86	a																					
Buxton 86	a																					
Heald Green 85	a																					
Manchester Airport 85 ✈	a			14 25		14 47				15 17				15 25		15 47			16 17			16 25

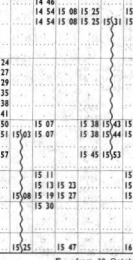

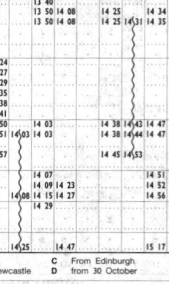

A To Liverpool Lime Street
B 9 October, 16 October, 23 October. From Newcastle
C From Edinburgh
D from 30 October
E from 30 October. To Hebden Bridge
F To Chester

The Sunday service between Manchester Victoria and Wigan Wallgate via Atherton is funded by GMITA and will operate whilst funding exists

Barrow-in-Furness, Blackpool North, Preston, Southport, Kirkby and Wigan - Bolton - Manchester

		NT	TP	NT	NT	TP	NT	NT	NT	TP	NT	TP	NT	NT	NT	TP	NT	NT	NT	TP	NT	TP	NT
			◇1 A		B	◇1	C	D		◇1 E	F	◇1		G	B	◇1	C	D		◇1 E		◇1 H	
Barrow-in-Furness	d											15 34											
Roose	d																						
Dalton	d																						
Ulverston	d											15 50											
Cark	d																						
Kents Bank	d																						
Grange-over-Sands	d											16 02											
Arnside	d											16 08											
Silverdale	d																						
Carnforth	d											16 17		16 37									
Windermere	83 d																					17 09	
Oxenholme Lake District	65 d		15 11																			17 23	
Lancaster	65 a		15 26									16 26		16 46								17 24	
	d		15 26									16 26											
Blackpool North	97 d			15 20		15 44	15 50	16 05					16 20			16 44	16 50	17 05					17 20
Layton	97 d			15 23									16 23										17 23
Poulton-le-Fylde	97 d			15 28		15 50	15 56						16 28			16 50	16 56						17 28
Kirkham & Wesham	97 d			15 37									16 37										17 37
Preston	65,97 a		15 45	15 47		16 08	16 14	16 44				16 45	16 47			17 08	17 14	17 44				17 42	17 47
	d		15 47	15 49		16 10	16 15					16 47	16 49			17 10	17 15					17 47	17 49
Leyland	d			15 54			16 21						16 54				17 21						17 54
Chorley	d		15 56	16 02		16 20						16 56	17 02			17 20						17 56	18 02
Adlington (Lancashire)	d			16 07									17 07										18 07
Blackrod	d			16 10									17 10										18 10
Horwich Parkway	d			16 14		16 27							17 14			17 27							18 14
Lostock	d			16 20									17 20										18 20
Southport	d	15 01									16 05										17 01		
Meols Cop	d	15 06									16 10										17 06		
Bescar Lane	d																						
New Lane	d																						
Burscough Bridge	d	15 14									16 18										17 14		
Hoscar	d																						
Parbold	d	15 19									16 23										17 19		
Appley Bridge	d	15 23									16 27										17 23		
Gathurst	d	15 26									16 30										17 26		
Kirkby	d																						
Rainford	d																						
Upholland	d																						
Orrell	d																						
Pemberton	d																						
Wigan Wallgate	a	15 33									16 35										17 33		
	d	15 34							16 13		16 36								17 13		17 34		
Wigan North Western	d						16a35										17a35						
Ince	d								16 16										17 16				
Hindley	d	15 39							16 20		16 41								17 20		17 39		
Westhoughton	d	15 44									16 46										17 44		
Bolton	a	15 54	16 08	16 25		16 34					16 54	17 08	17 25			17 34					17 54	18 08	18 25
	d	15 54	16 08	16 25	16 31	16 35					16 54	17 08	17 25		17 31	17 35					17 54	18 08	18 25
Moses Gate	d																						
Farnworth	d																						
Kearsley	d																						
Daisy Hill	d								16 24										17 24				
Hag Fold	d								16 27										17 27				
Atherton	d								16 29										17 29				
Walkden	d								16 35										17 35				
Moorside	d								16 38										17 38				
Swinton	d								16 41										17 41				
Salford Crescent	a	16 07		16 38	16 43	16 47			16 50		17 07		17 38		17 43	17 47			17 50		18 07		18 38
	d	16 07		16 38	16 44	16 47			16 51	17 03	17 07		17 38		17 44	17 47			17 51	18 03	18 07		18 38
Salford Central	d																						
Manchester Victoria	⇌ a			16 45	16 53				16 57				17 45		17 53				17 57				18 45
Rochdale	41 a																						
Deansgate	⇌ a	16 11				16 51					17 11					17 51					18 11		
Manchester Oxford Road	a	16 13	16 23			16 52					17 13	17 23				17 52					18 13	18 23	
Manchester Piccadilly 10	⇌ a	16 19	16 27			16 56				17 08	17 19	17 27				17 56				18 08	18 19	18 27	
Stockport	84 a	16 33									17 30										18 33		
Hazel Grove	86 a																						
Buxton	86 a																						
Heald Green	85 a																						
Manchester Airport	85 ✈ a		16 47			17 17				17 25		17 47				18 17				18 25		18 47	

A From Edinburgh
B from 30 October
C To Liverpool Lime Street
D from 30 October. To Hebden Bridge
E 9 October, 16 October, 23 October. From Newcastle
F To Chester
G From Leeds to Morecambe
H From Glasgow Central

The Sunday service between Manchester Victoria and Wigan Wallgate via Atherton is funded by GMITA and will operate whilst funding exists

Table 82

Sundays
from 9 October

Barrow-in-Furness, Blackpool North, Preston, Southport, Kirkby and Wigan - Bolton - Manchester

		NT	TP	NT	NT	TP	NT	TP	NT	NT	TP	NT	TP	NT	TP	NT	TP	TP	NT	NT	TP	NT
		A	◇1	B	C	◇1 D	E	◇1 F		G	◇1	A	◇1	B	◇1 D		◇1 H	◇1 I		A	◇1	B
Barrow-in-Furness	d										18 17						18 17					
Roose	d										18 21						18 21					
Dalton	d										18 28						18 28					
Ulverston	d										18 36						18 36					
Cark	d										18 44						18 44					
Kents Bank	d										18 48						18 48					
Grange-over-Sands	d										18 52						18 52					
Arnside	d										18 58						18 58					
Silverdale	d										19 02						19 02					
Carnforth	d									19 04	19 08						19 08					
Windermere	83 d																					
Oxenholme Lake District	65 d							18 10										19 07				
Lancaster	65 a							18 26		19 13	19 17						19 17	19 22				
	d							18 26			19 17						19 17	19 22				
Blackpool North	97 d		17 44	17 50	18 05				18 20				18 44	18 50					19 20		19 44	19 50
Layton	97 d								18 23										19 23			
Poulton-le-Fylde	97 d		17 50	17 56					18 28				18 50	18 56					19 28		19 50	19 56
Kirkham & Wesham	97 d								18 37										19 37			
Preston	65,97 a		18 08	18 14	18 44			18 45	18 47		19 37		19 08	19 14			19 37	19 42	19 47		20 08	20 14
	d		18 10	18 15				18 47	18 49				19 10	19 15				19 47	19 49		20 10	20 15
Leyland	d			18 21					18 54					19 21					19 54			20 21
Chorley	d		18 20					18 56	19 02				19 20					19 56	20 02		20 20	
Adlington (Lancashire)	d								19 07										20 07			
Blackrod	d								19 10										20 10			
Horwich Parkway	d		18 27						19 14				19 27						20 14		20 27	
Lostock	d								19 20										20 20			
Southport	d						18 05									19 01						
Meols Cop	d						18 10									19 06						
Bescar Lane	d																					
New Lane	d																					
Burscough Bridge	d						18 18									19 14						
Hoscar	d																					
Parbold	d						18 23									19 19						
Appley Bridge	d						18 27									19 23						
Gathurst	d						18 30									19 26						
Kirkby	d																					
Rainford	d																					
Upholland	d																					
Orrell	d																					
Pemberton	d																					
Wigan Wallgate	a						18 35									19 33						
	d						18 36									19 34						
Wigan North Western	d			18a35										19a35								20a35
Ince	d																					
Hindley	d						18 41									19 39						
Westhoughton	d						18 46									19 44						
Bolton	a		18 34				18 54	19 08	19 25				19 34			19 54		20 08	20 25		20 34	
	d	18 31	18 35				18 54	19 08	19 25			19 31	19 35			19 54		20 08	20 25	20 31	20 35	
Moses Gate	d																					
Farnworth	d																					
Kearsley	d																					
Daisy Hill	d																					
Hag Fold	d																					
Atherton	d																					
Walkden	d																					
Moorside	d																					
Swinton	d																					
Salford Crescent	a	18 43	18 47				19 07		19 38			19 43	19 47			20 07			20 38	20 43	20 47	
	d	18 44	18 47			19 03	19 07		19 38			19 44	19 47		20 03	20 07			20 38	20 44	20 47	
Salford Central	d																					
Manchester Victoria	⇌ a	18 53							19 45			19 53							20 45	20 53		
Rochdale	41 a																					
Deansgate	⇌ a		18 51				19 11						19 51			20 11					20 51	
Manchester Oxford Road	a		18 52				19 13	19 23					19 52			20 13		20 23			20 52	
Manchester Piccadilly 10	⇌ a		18 56			19 08	19 19	19 27					19 56		20 08	20 19		20 27			20 56	
Stockport	84 a						19 30									20 33						
Hazel Grove	86 a																					
Buxton	86 a																					
Heald Green	85 a																					
Manchester Airport	85 ✈ a		19 17			19 25		19 47					20 17		20 25			20 47			21 17	

A from 30 October
B To Liverpool Lime Street
C from 30 October. To Hebden Bridge
D 9 October, 16 October, 23 October. From Newcastle
E To Chester
F From Edinburgh
G From Leeds to Morecambe
H from 30 October. Bus from Preston
I From Glasgow Central

The Sunday service between Manchester Victoria and Wigan Wallgate via Atherton is funded by GMITA and will operate whilst funding exists

Table 82

Sundays from 9 October

Barrow-in-Furness, Blackpool North, Preston, Southport, Kirkby and Wigan - Bolton - Manchester

		NT	NT	TP	NT	TP	NT	NT	NT	NT		TP	NT	NT	NT	NT	NT	NT	TP	TP	TP	NT	NT	NT	TP
				◇■		◇■						◇■							◇■	◇■	◇■				◇■
		A	B	C	D	E			F	G			H		B		H	G	C	I	E		H	J	
		bus				trolley			bus											trolley	trolley			bus	
Barrow-in-Furness	d						20 02																		
Roose	d						20 06																		
Dalton	d						20 12																		
Ulverston	d						20 21																		
Cark	d						20 28																		
Kents Bank	d						20 33																		
Grange-over-Sands	d						20 37																		
Arnside	d						20 43																		
Silverdale	d						20 47																		
Carnforth	d						20 54																		
Windermere	83 d																								
Oxenholme Lake District	65 d					20 10																			
Lancaster ■	65 a					20 26	21 07																		
	d					20 26															22 04				
Blackpool North	97 d	20 05	20 11					20 20	20 40			20 44	20 50		21 13	21 20	21 50			21 56			22 44		23 03
Layton	97 d							20 23								21 23									
Poulton-le-Fylde	97 d		20 17					20 28	20 55			20 50	20 56		21 19	21 28	21 56			22 02			22 50		23 09
Kirkham & Wesham	97 d							20 37								21 37									23 17
Preston ■	65,97 a	20 44	20 34			20 45		20 47	21 35			21 08	21 14		21 36	21 47	22 14			22 20	22 24		23 08		23 28
	d					20 47		20 49				21 10	21 15			21 49	22 15			22 29			23 09		23 28
Leyland	d							20 54					21 21			21 54	22 21						23 15		23 34
Chorley	d					20 56		21 02				21 20				22 02				22 39					23 41
Adlington (Lancashire)	d							21 07								22 07									23 45
Blackrod	d							21 10								22 10									23 49
Horwich Parkway	d							21 14				21 27				22 14									23 52
Lostock	d							21 20								22 20									23 56
Southport	d				20 05									21 01								22 01			
Meols Cop	d				20 10									21 06								22 06			
Bescar Lane	d																								
New Lane	d																								
Burscough Bridge	d				20 18									21 14								22 14			
Hoscar	d																								
Parbold	d				20 23									21 19								22 19			
Appley Bridge	d				20 27									21 23								22 23			
Gathurst	d				20 30									21 26								22 26			
Kirkby	d																								
Rainford	d																								
Upholland	d																								
Orrell	d																								
Pemberton	d																								
Wigan Wallgate	a				20 35									21 33								22 33			
	d				20 36									21 34								22 34			
Wigan North Western	d												21a35				22a35						23a29		
Ince	d																								
Hindley	d				20 41									21 39								22 39			
Westhoughton	d				20 46									21 44								22 44			
Bolton	a				20 54	21 08		21 25				21 34		21 54		22 25				22 50		22 54			00 02
	d				20 54	21 08		21 25		21 31		21 35		21 54		22 25		22 31		22 51		22 54		23 06	00 02
Moses Gate	d																								
Farnworth	d																								
Kearsley	d																								
Daisy Hill	d																								
Hag Fold	d																								
Atherton	d																								
Walkden	d																								
Moorside	d																								
Swinton	d																								
Salford Crescent	a				21 07			21 38		21 43		21 47		22 07		22 38		22 43		23 03		23 07		23 30	
	d			21 03	21 07			21 38		21 44		21 47		22 07		22 38		22 44	23 03	23 04		23 07		23 31	
Salford Central	d																								
Manchester Victoria	⇌ a							21 45		21 53						22 45		22 53						23 41	
Rochdale	41 a																								
Deansgate	⇌ a				21 11							21 51		22 11						23 09		23 11			
Manchester Oxford Road	a				21 13	21 23						21 52		22 13						23 11		23 14			
Manchester Piccadilly ■	⇌ a			21 08	21 19	21 27						21 56		22 19					23 08	23 15		23 19			00 18
Stockport	84 a				21 30									22 33								23 33			
Hazel Grove	86 a																								
Buxton	86 a																								
Heald Green	85 a																								
Manchester Airport	85 ✈ a			21 25		21 47						22 17							23 25	23 31					00 32

A from 30 October. To Hebden Bridge
B 9 October, 16 October, 23 October. To Leeds
C 9 October, 16 October, 23 October. From Newcastle
D To Chester
E From Edinburgh
F from 30 October. To Leeds
G from 30 October
H To Liverpool Lime Street
I trolley from Preston
J from 30 October. From Clitheroe

The Sunday service between Manchester Victoria and Wigan Wallgate via Atherton is funded by GMITA and will operate whilst funding exists

Oxenholme - Lake District - Windermere

Mondays to Fridays

Miles			TP 1 A	TP 1	TP 1	TP 1	TP 1	TP ◇1 B	TP 1	TP ◇1 C	TP 1	TP 1	TP 1	TP ◇1 B	TP ◇1 D	TP 1	TP 1	TP 1	TP 1
0	**Oxenholme Lake District**	d	06 21	07 21	08 27	09 14	10 27	11 18	12 28	13 37	14 27	15 38	16 28	17 49	18 46	19 35	20 27	21 15	22 20
2¼	Kendal	d	06 26	07 25	08 31	09 18	10 31	11 22	12 32	13 41	14 31	15 43	16 32	17 53	18 50	19 39	20 31	21 19	22 24
4	Burneside	d		07x29	08x35	09x22		11 26	12x36		14x35	15x46	16x36	17x57	18x54	19x43	20x35	21x23	22x28
6½	Staveley	d		07x34	08x40	09x27		11 31	12x41		14x40	15x51	16x41	18x02	18x59	19x48	20x40	21x28	22x33
10	**Windermere**	a	06 41	07 40	08 46	09 33	10 44	11 39	12 47	13 56	14 46	15 59	16 48	18 08	19 08	19 54	20 46	21 34	22 39

Saturdays

		TP 1 A	TP 1	TP 1	TP 1	TP ◇1 B	TP ◇1 C	TP 1	TP ◇1 C	TP 1	TP 1	TP 1	TP ◇1 B	TP 1	TP 1	TP 1	TP 1
Oxenholme Lake District	d	06 21	07 21	08 27	09 11	10 05	11 18	12 28	13 37	14 33	15 38	16 28	17 38	18 37	19 35	20 23	21 15
Kendal	d	06 26	07 25	08 31	09 15	10 09	11 22	12 32	13 41	14 37	15 43	16 32	17 42	18 41	19 39	20 27	21 19
Burneside	d		07x29	08x35	09x19	10x13	11x26	12x36		14x41	15x46	16x36	17x46	18x45	19x43	20x31	21x23
Staveley	d		07x34	08x40	09x24	10x18	11x31	12x41		14x46	15x51	16x41	17x51	18x50	19x48	20x36	21x28
Windermere	a	06 41	07 40	08 46	09 30	10 26	11 39	12 47	13 56	14 52	15 59	16 48	18 00	18 56	19 54	20 42	21 34

Sundays

until 11 September

		TP ◇1 B	TP 1	TP 1	TP 1	TP 1	TP 1	TP 1	TP ◇1 C	TP 1	TP 1	TP 1
Oxenholme Lake District	d	10 40	11 35	12 29	13 35	14 37	15 35	16 29	17 39	18 37	19 29	20 16
Kendal	d	10 44	11 39	12 33	13 39	14 41	15 39	16 33	17 44	18 41	19 33	20 20
Burneside	d		11x43	12x37	13x43	14x45	15x43	16x37		18x45		20x24
Staveley	d		11x48	12x42	13x48	14x50	15x48	16x42		18x50		20x29
Windermere	a	10 58	11 54	12 48	13 54	14 56	15 54	16 48	17 58	18 56	19 45	20 35

from 18 September

		TP ◇1 A	TP 1	TP 1	TP 1	TP 1	TP 1	TP 1	TP 1	TP 1	TP 1	TP 1
Oxenholme Lake District	d	10 40	11 35	12 29	13 35	14 37	15 35	16 29	17 37	18 37	19 29	20 16
Kendal	d	10 44	11 39	12 33	13 39	14 41	15 39	16 33	17 41	18 41	19 33	20 20
Burneside	d		11x43	12x37	13x43	14x45	15x43	16x37	17x45	18x45		20x24
Staveley	d		11x48	12x42	13x48	14x50	15x48	16x42	17x50	18x50		20x29
Windermere	a	10 58	11 54	12 48	13 54	14 56	15 54	16 48	17 56	18 56	19 45	20 35

A From Lancaster
B From Manchester Airport
C From Preston
D From Barrow-in-Furness

Windermere - Oxenholme - Lake District

Mondays to Fridays

Miles			TP 1	TP 1	TP 1	TP 1	TP ◇1 A	TP 1	TP ◇1 A	TP 1	TP 1	TP 1	TP ◇1 A	TP ◇1 A	TP 1	TP 1	TP 1	TP 1	TP ◇1 B
0	**Windermere**	d	06 50	07 55	08 50	09 59	10 49	11 59	12 51	14 00	14 59	16 02	17 06	18 15	19 10	20 00	20 50	21 40	22 45
3½	Staveley	d	06x55	08x01		10x04	10x54	12x04		14x05	15x04		17x11	18x20		20x05	20x55	21x45	22x50
6	Burneside	d	07x00	08x06		10x09	10x59	12x09		14x10	15x09		17x16	18x25		20x10	21x00	21x50	22x55
7¾	Kendal	d	07 04	08 11	09 01	10 13	11 03	12 13	13 02	14 14	15 13	16 14	17 20	18 29	19 21	20 14	21 04	21 54	22 59
10	**Oxenholme Lake District**	a	07 09	08 16	09 06	10 18	11 08	12 18	13 07	14 19	15 18	16 19	17 25	18 34	19 27	20 19	21 09	21 59	23 04

Saturdays

		TP 1	TP 1	TP 1	TP ◇1	TP ◇1	TP 1	TP ◇1	TP 1	TP 1	TP 1	TP ◇1	TP 1	TP 1	TP 1	TP 1	TP ◇1
Windermere	d	06 50	07 55	08 50	09 38	10 49	11 59	12 51	14 00	14 59	16 02	17 06	18 02	19 00	20 00	20 47	21 40
Staveley	d	06x55	08x01		09x43	10x54	12x04		14x05	15x04		17x11	18x07	19x05	20x05		21x45
Burneside	d	07x00	08x06		09x48	10x59	12x09		14x10	15x09		17x16	18x12	19x10	20x10		21x50
Kendal	d	07 04	08 11	09 01	09 52	11 03	12 13	13 02	14 14	15 13	16 14	17 20	18 16	19 14	20 14	20 58	21 54
Oxenholme Lake District	a	07 09	08 16	09 06	09 57	11 08	12 18	13 07	14 19	15 18	16 19	17 25	18 21	19 19	20 19	21 04	21 59

Sundays

until 11 September

		TP 1	TP 1	TP 1	TP 1	TP 1	TP 1	TP ◇1	TP 1	TP 1	TP 1	TP ◇1
Windermere	d	11 01	11 58	12 58	13 58	15 00	15 58	16 58	18 04	19 00	19 49	20 40
Staveley	d		12x03	13x03	14x03		16x03		18x09	19x05		20x45
Burneside	d		12x08	13x08	14x08		16x08		18x14	19x10		20x50
Kendal	d	11 13	12 12	13 12	14 12	15 12	16 12	17 10	18 18	19 14	20 00	20 54
Oxenholme Lake District	a	11 18	12 18	13 17	14 17	15 17	16 17	17 15	18 23	19 19	20 05	20 59

from 18 September

		TP 1	TP 1	TP 1	TP 1	TP 1	TP 1	TP 1	TP 1	TP 1	TP 1	TP ◇1 D
Windermere	d	11 01	11 58	12 58	13 58	15 00	15 58	16 58	18 04	19 00	19 49	20 40
Staveley	d		12x03	13x03	14x03		16x03	17x03	18x09	19x05		20x45
Burneside	d		12x08	13x08	14x08		16x08	17x08	18x14	19x10		20x50
Kendal	d	11 13	12 12	13 12	14 12	15 12	16 12	17 12	18 18	19 14	20 00	20 54
Oxenholme Lake District	a	11 18	12 18	13 17	14 17	15 17	16 17	17 17	18 23	19 19	20 05	20 59

A To Manchester Airport
B To Blackpool North
C To Preston
D To Barrow-in-Furness

Stoke-on-Trent and Crewe - Manchester Airport, Stockport and Manchester

Miles	Miles	Miles	Station		NT MX A	NT MX	XC ◇1 B	VT MO ◇1 🛏	NT MX C	AW MX ◇ D	XC ◇1 E	XC ◇1 F	VT MX ◇1 🛏	VT MO ◇1 🛏	NT MX	TP ◇1 G	NT	NT	VT ◇1	NT H	NT	TP ◇1 I	AW
—	—	—	London Euston [15] ⊖65	d				21p25					22p00	21p51									
—	—	—	Birmingham New Street [12] 68	d			22p30			21p24	22p30	22p30											
—	—	—	Wolverhampton [7] 68 ⇌	d			22p48			21p43	22p48	22p48											
—	—	—	Stafford 65,68	d			23p01				23p01	23p01	23b38	23b53									
0	—	—	**Stoke-on-Trent** 50,68	d			23p21	23p29			23p21	23p21											
3	—	—	Longport 50	d																			
6¼	—	—	Kidsgrove 50	d																			
—	0	—	**Crewe [10]** 65	d		23p12							00s03	00s12	00 44			05 48	06 11				06 27
—	4¾	—	Sandbach	d		23p19												05 55					
—	8½	—	Holmes Chapel	d		23p24												06 00					
—	10½	—	Goostrey	d		23p27												06 03					
—	14¼	—	Chelford	d		23p31												06 07					
—	17¼	—	Alderley Edge	d		23p35												06 11					
—	19	0	**Wilmslow**	d		23p39											05 46	06 15	06 27				06 45
—	—	2	Styal	d																			
—	—	4¼	**Manchester Airport** ✈	a											01 16		05 53						
—	20½	—	Handforth	d		23p42												06 18					
11¼	—	—	Congleton	d																			
19¼	—	—	**Macclesfield**	a				23p45															
—	—	—		d				23p46													06 22		
22½	—	—	Prestbury	d																	06 26		
24½	—	—	Adlington (Cheshire)	d																	06 29		
26½	—	—	Poynton	d																	06 33		
28	—	—	Bramhall	d																	06 35		
29½	22¾	—	Cheadle Hulme	d		23p46												06 22			06 38		
31¾	25	—	**Stockport**	a		23p51		23p59					00s26	00s41				06 27	06 36		06 43		06 55
—	—	—		d	23p48	23p51		00 01	00 02							05 53		06 27	06 37	06 41	06 43	06 53	06 55
31¾	26½	—	Heaton Chapel	d		23p55												06 31			06 46		
34¾	28	—	Levenshulme	d		23p58												06 34			06 49		
37¾	31	—	**Manchester Piccadilly [10]** ⇌	a	00 02	00 07	00 12	00 12	00 18	00 28	00 32	00 33	00 35	00 53	01 36	06 05	06 25	06 42	06 49	06 52	06 58	07 02	07 07
—	—	—		d																06 54			
38¼	31½	—	**Manchester Oxford Road**	a																06 56			
38¾	32	—	Deansgate ⇌	a																06 59			

Station		NT J	NT K	NT	NT L	NT	NT C	EM ◇ M	XC ◇1 🍴	NT	NT	NT K	NT	XC ◇1 🍴	NT	TP ◇1 N 🍴	NT K	AW ◇ O	NT	NT J	TP ◇1 P 🍴	NT Q	NT R
London Euston [15] ⊖65	d																						
Birmingham New Street [12] 68	d								05 57					06 22									
Wolverhampton [7] 68 ⇌	d								06 16					06 40									
Stafford 65,68	d								06 30					06 55									
Stoke-on-Trent 50,68	d					06 30			06 51					07 14					07 17				
Longport 50	d					06 34													07 21				
Kidsgrove 50	d					06 38													07 25				
Crewe [10] 65	d									06 33	06 49							07 27					
Sandbach	d									06 40	06 56												
Holmes Chapel	d									06 44	07 00												
Goostrey	d										07 03												
Chelford	d										07 08												
Alderley Edge	d			06 49						06 53	07 12				07 30								
Wilmslow	d			06 52						06 57	07 16				07 33			07 44					
Styal	d																						
Manchester Airport ✈	a									07 04													
Handforth	d			06 55							07 19				07 37								
Congleton	d					06 45			07 03										07 32				
Macclesfield	a					06 52			07 11					07 30					07 39				
	d					06 53			07 12				07 15	07 31					07 40				
Prestbury	d					06 57							07 21						07 44				
Adlington (Cheshire)	d					07 00							07 24						07 47				
Poynton	d					07 04							07 27						07 51				
Bramhall	d					07 07							07 31						07 54				
Cheadle Hulme	d			06 59		07 11					07 24		07 34		07 42				07 59				
Stockport	a			07 04		07 15			07 27		07 29		07 41	07 45	07 47			07 54	08 03				
	d		06 58	07 04	07 10	07 16	07 19	07 22	07 28		07 29	07 31	07 42	07 50	07 48	07 53	07 57	07 54	08 04			08 10	
Heaton Chapel	d			07 08	07 15						07 33								08 07				
Levenshulme	d			07 11	07 18						07 36								08 10				
Manchester Piccadilly [10] ⇌	a		07 10	07 21	07 26	07 27	07 31	07 34	07 37	07 42	07 44	07 45	07 56	07 59	07 59	08 02	08 09	08 10	08 21			08 25	
	d	06 58			07 27			07 34												07 59	08 07		08 22
Manchester Oxford Road	a	07 00			07 29			07 37												08 01	08 09		08 24
Deansgate ⇌	a				07 32																		08 28

A From Sheffield
B ThFO
C From Chester
D From Birmingham International
E TWO until 15 June, TWO from 13 September
F TWO from 21 June until 7 September
G From Sheffield to Manchester Airport
H From Buxton to Clitheroe
I From Doncaster to Manchester Airport
J From Manchester Airport to Liverpool Lime Street
K From Hazel Grove
L until 30 September. From Buxton to Wigan North Western
M From Nottingham to Liverpool Lime Street
N From Cleethorpes to Manchester Airport
O From Cardiff Central
P From Hull to Liverpool Lime Street
Q From Buxton
R From Manchester Airport to Southport
b Previous night, stops to set down only

Stoke-on-Trent and Crewe - Manchester Airport, Stockport and Manchester

Station		NT	VT ◇1 ⊠	NT A	XC ◇1 🍴	EM ◇ B	NT	NT	NT	VT ◇1 ⊠	NT C	NT	XC ◇1 🍴	TP ◇1 D 🍴	VT ◇1 ⊠	AW ◇ E 🍴	NT	NT F	TP ◇1 G 🍴	NT H	VT ◇1 ⊠	TP ◇1 I 🍴	NT A
London Euston [15] ⊖65	d		06 17							06 36					06 55						07 20		
Birmingham New Street [12] 68	d				06 57								07 31										
Wolverhampton [7] 68 ⇌	d				07 16								07 49										
Stafford 65,68	d				07 30																		
Stoke-on-Trent 50,68	d		07 45									07 57	08 19		08 25						08 48		
Longport 50	d																						
Kidsgrove 50	d											08 04											
Crewe [10] 65	d	07 22			07 52				07 55	08 11						08 28							
Sandbach	d	07 35							08 02														
Holmes Chapel	d	07 41							08 07														
Goostrey	d	07 45																					
Chelford	d	07 51																					
Alderley Edge	d	07 56					07 53		08 15								08 49						
Wilmslow	d	08 00			08 09		07 56		08 19	08 27						08 45	08 52						
Styal	d						07 59																
Manchester Airport ✈	a						08 04																
Handforth	d	08 03							08 22								08 55						
Congleton	d											08 11											
Macclesfield	a		08 01									08 18	08 35		08 41								
	d		08 02					08 06				08 19	08 37		08 41								
Prestbury	d							08 10				08 23											
Adlington (Cheshire)	d											08 26											
Poynton	d							08 15				08 30											
Bramhall	d							08 17				08 33											
Cheadle Hulme	d	08 09						08 20	08 26			08 37					08 59						
Stockport	a	08 14	08 16		08 20			08 27	08 31	08 37		08 41	08 49		08 55	08 55	09 04				09 16		
	d	08 14	08 17	08 19	08 21	08 24		08 28	08 31	08 38	08 41	08 42	08 50	08 53	08 56	08 55	09 04			09 12	09 17		09 21
Heaton Chapel	d	08 18							08 35			08 45					09 08			09 16			
Levenshulme	d	08 21						08 32				08 48					09 11			09 19			
Manchester Piccadilly [10] ⇌	a	08 27	08 28	08 32	08 34	08 36	08 42	08 42	08 45	08 49	08 52	08 56	08 59	09 02	09 07	09 11	09 20			09 28	09 28		09 36
	d	08 29				08 37					08 54							09 01	09 07			09 16	
Manchester Oxford Road	a	08 33				08 40					08 56							09 03	09 09			09 18	
Deansgate ⇌	a										09 00												

Station		NT J	EM ◇ B	XC ◇1 K 🍴	NT	NT	VT ◇1 ⊠	TP ◇1 L 🍴	NT C	NT	XC ◇1 M 🍴	TP ◇1 D 🍴	VT ◇1 ⊠	AW ◇ N 🍴	NT	NT F	TP ◇1 O 🍴	NT H	VT ◇1 ⊠	NT A	NT J	EM ◇ P
London Euston [15] ⊖65	d						07 35						08 00						08 20			
Birmingham New Street [12] 68	d			07 57							08 31											
Wolverhampton [7] 68 ⇌	d			08 15							08 49											
Stafford 65,68	d			08 30							09 01											
Stoke-on-Trent 50,68	d			08 55						08 58	09 20		09 26						09 48			
Longport 50	d																					
Kidsgrove 50	d									09 05												
Crewe [10] 65	d				08 31	08 50	09 11							09 31								
Sandbach	d				08 38	08 57																
Holmes Chapel	d				08 42	09 02																
Goostrey	d				08 45	09 05																
Chelford	d				08 50	09 09																
Alderley Edge	d				08 54	09 13									09 48							
Wilmslow	d				08 57	09 17	09 27							09 48	09 51							
Styal	d																					
Manchester Airport ✈	a				09 04																	
Handforth	d					09 20									09 54							
Congleton	d									09 12												
Macclesfield	a			09 11						09 19			09 42									
	d			09 12						09 20			09 42									
Prestbury	d									09 24												
Adlington (Cheshire)	d									09 27												
Poynton	d									09 30												
Bramhall	d									09 33												
Cheadle Hulme	d					09 24				09 37					09 59							
Stockport	a			09 27		09 29	09 36			09 41	09 49		09 56	09 58	10 04				10 16			
	d		09 25	09 28		09 29	09 37		09 41	09 42	09 50	09 53	09 57	09 58	10 04			10 12	10 17	10 21		10 26
Heaton Chapel	d					09 33				09 45					10 08			10 16				
Levenshulme	d					09 36				09 48					10 11			10 19				
Manchester Piccadilly [10] ⇌	a		09 36	09 39	09 42	09 44	09 49		09 52	09 56	09 59	10 02	10 09	10 15	10 20			10 28	10 28	10 36		10 36
	d	09 22	09 37					09 46	09 54							10 01	10 07				10 22	10 37
Manchester Oxford Road	a	09 24	09 40					09 48	09 56							10 03	10 09				10 24	10 40
Deansgate ⇌	a	09 28						09 51	10 00												10 28	

A From Chester
B From Nottingham to Liverpool Lime Street
C until 30 September. From Hazel Grove to Preston
D From Cleethorpes to Manchester Airport
E From Cardiff Central
F From Manchester Airport to Liverpool Lime Street
G From Newcastle to Liverpool Lime Street
H From Buxton
I until 15 July. From Manchester Airport to Arnside
J From Manchester Airport to Southport
K From Southampton Central
L From Manchester Airport to Windermere
M From Bristol Temple Meads
N From Carmarthen
O From Scarborough to Liverpool Lime Street
P From Norwich to Liverpool Lime Street

Stoke-on-Trent and Crewe - Manchester Airport, Stockport and Manchester

		XC	NT	NT	VT	NT	NT	XC	TP	VT	AW	NT	NT	TP	NT	VT	TP	NT	NT	EM	XC	NT	NT
		◇1			◇1			◇1	◇1	◇1	◇			◇1		◇1	◇1			◇	◇1		
		A				B		C	D		E		F	G	H		I	J	K	L	M		
		✠			⊠			✠	✠	⊠	✠			✠		⊠	✠				✠		
London Euston 15 ⊖65	d				08 40					09 00						09 20							
Birmingham New Street 12 68	d	08 57						09 31													09 57		
Wolverhampton 7 68	d	09 15						09 49													10 15		
Stafford 65,68	d	09 30						10 01													10 30		
Stoke-on-Trent 50,68	d	09 55					09 58	10 20		10 25						10 48					10 55		
Longport 50	d																						
Kidsgrove 50	d						10 05																
Crewe 10 65	d		09 33	09 50	10 11						10 31											10 34	10 50
Sandbach	d		09 40	09 57																		10 41	10 57
Holmes Chapel	d		09 44	10 02																		10 45	11 02
Goostrey	d			10 05																			11 05
Chelford	d			10 09																			11 09
Alderley Edge	d		09 53	10 13								10 49										10 54	11 13
Wilmslow	d		09 57	10 17	10 27						10 49	10 52										10 57	11 17
Styal	d																						
Manchester Airport ✈	a		10 04																			11 04	
Handforth	d			10 20								10 55											11 20
Congleton	d						10 12																
Macclesfield	a	10 11					10 19			10 41											11 11		
	d	10 12					10 20			10 41											11 12		
Prestbury	d						10 24																
Adlington (Cheshire)	d						10 27																
Poynton	d						10 30																
Bramhall	d						10 33																
Cheadle Hulme	d			10 24			10 37					10 59											11 24
Stockport	a	10 27		10 29	10 36		10 41	10 49		10 55	10 58	11 04				11 16					11 27		11 29
	d	10 28		10 29	10 37	10 41	10 42	10 50	10 53	10 56	10 58	11 04			11 12	11 17		11 21		11 26	11 28		11 29
Heaton Chapel	d			10 33			10 45					11 08			11 16								11 33
Levenshulme	d			10 36			10 48					11 11			11 19								11 36
Manchester Piccadilly 10	a	10 39	10 42	10 44	10 49	10 52	10 56	10 59	11 02	11 07	11 15	11 20			11 28	11 28		11 36		11 36	11 39	11 42	11 44
	d					10 54							11 01	11 07			11 16		11 22	11 37			
Manchester Oxford Road	a					10 56							11 03	11 09			11 18		11 24	11 40			
Deansgate	a					11 00													11 28				

		VT	NT	NT	XC	TP	VT	AW	NT	NT	TP	NT	VT	NT	NT	EM	XC	NT	NT	VT	NT	NT
		◇1			◇1	◇1	◇1	◇			◇1		◇1			◇	◇1			◇1		
			B		N	D		O		F	G	H		J	K	L	M				B	
		⊠			✠	✠	⊠	✠			✠		⊠				✠			⊠		
London Euston 15 ⊖65	d	09 40					10 00						10 20							10 40		
Birmingham New Street 12 68	d				10 31												10 57					
Wolverhampton 7 68	d				10 49												11 15					
Stafford 65,68	d				11 01												11 30					
Stoke-on-Trent 50,68	d			10 58	11 20		11 25						11 48				11 55					11 58
Longport 50	d																					
Kidsgrove 50	d			11 05																		12 05
Crewe 10 65	d	11 11						11 31										11 34	11 50	12 11		
Sandbach	d																	11 41	11 57			
Holmes Chapel	d																	11 45	12 02			
Goostrey	d																		12 05			
Chelford	d																		12 09			
Alderley Edge	d								11 48									11 54	12 13			
Wilmslow	d	11 27						11 48	11 51									11 57	12 17	12 27		
Styal	d																					
Manchester Airport ✈	a																	12 04				
Handforth	d								11 54										12 20			
Congleton	d			11 12																		12 12
Macclesfield	a			11 19			11 41										12 11					12 19
	d			11 20			11 41										12 12					12 20
Prestbury	d			11 24																		12 24
Adlington (Cheshire)	d			11 27																		12 27
Poynton	d			11 30																		12 30
Bramhall	d			11 33																		12 33
Cheadle Hulme	d			11 37					11 59										12 24			12 37
Stockport	a	11 36		11 41	11 49		11 55	11 58	12 04				12 16				12 27		12 29	12 36		12 41
	d	11 37	11 41	11 42	11 50	11 53	11 56	11 58	12 04			12 12	12 17	12 21		12 26	12 28		12 29	12 37	12 41	12 42
Heaton Chapel	d			11 45					12 08			12 16							12 33			12 45
Levenshulme	d			11 48					12 11			12 19							12 36			12 48
Manchester Piccadilly 10	a	11 49	11 52	11 56	11 59	12 02	12 07	12 15	12 20			12 28	12 28	12 36		12 36	12 39	12 42	12 44	12 49	12 52	12 56
	d		11 54							12 01	12 07				12 22	12 37					12 54	
Manchester Oxford Road	a		11 56							12 03	12 09				12 24	12 40					12 56	
Deansgate	a		12 00												12 28						13 00	

A From Southampton Central
B until 30 September. From Hazel Grove to Preston
C From Cardiff Central
D From Cleethorpes to Manchester Airport
E From Carmarthen
F From Manchester Airport to Liverpool Lime Street
G From Scarborough to Liverpool Lime Street
H From Buxton
I From Manchester Airport to Arnside
J From Chester
K From Manchester Airport to Southport
L From Norwich to Liverpool Lime Street
M From Bournemouth
N From Paignton
O From Milford Haven

Stoke-on-Trent and Crewe - Manchester Airport, Stockport and Manchester

		XC	TP	VT	AW	NT	NT	TP	NT	VT	TP	NT	NT	EM	XC	NT	NT	VT	NT	NT	XC	TP	VT
		◇1	◇1	◇1	◇			◇1		◇1	◇1			◇	◇1			◇1			◇1	◇1	◇1
		A	B		C		D	E	F		G	H	I	J	K				L		A	B	
		✠	✠	⊓	✠			✠		⊓	✠				✠			⊓			✠	✠	⊓
London Euston 15 ⊖65	d			11 00						11 20								11 40					12 00
Birmingham New Street 12 68	d	11 31													11 57						12 31		
Wolverhampton 7 68	d	11 49													12 15						12 49		
Stafford 65,68	d	12 01													12 30						13 01		
Stoke-on-Trent 50,68	d	12 20		12 25						12 48					12 55					12 58	13 20		13 25
Longport 50	d																						
Kidsgrove 50	d																			13 05			
Crewe 10 65	d				12 31											12 34	12 50	13 11					
Sandbach	d															12 41	12 57						
Holmes Chapel	d															12 45	13 02						
Goostrey	d																13 05						
Chelford	d																13 09						
Alderley Edge	d					12 49										12 54	13 13						
Wilmslow	d				12 49	12 52										12 57	13 17	13 27					
Styal	d																						
Manchester Airport ✈	a															13 04							
Handforth	d					12 55											13 20						
Congleton	d																			13 12			
Macclesfield	a			12 41											13 11					13 19			13 41
	d			12 41											13 12					13 20			13 41
Prestbury	d																			13 24			
Adlington (Cheshire)	d																			13 27			
Poynton	d																			13 30			
Bramhall	d																			13 33			
Cheadle Hulme	d					12 59											13 24			13 37			
Stockport	a	12 49		12 55	12 58	13 04				13 16					13 27		13 29	13 36		13 41	13 49		13 55
	d	12 50	12 53	12 56	12 58	13 04			13 12	13 17		13 21		13 26	13 28		13 29	13 37	13 41	13 42	13 50	13 53	13 56
Heaton Chapel	d					13 08			13 16								13 33			13 45			
Levenshulme	d					13 11			13 19								13 36			13 48			
Manchester Piccadilly 10	a	12 59	13 02	13 07	13 15	13 20			13 28	13 28		13 36		13 36	13 39	13 42	13 44	13 49	13 52	13 56	13 59	14 02	14 07
	d						13 01	13 07			13 16		13 22	13 37					13 54				
Manchester Oxford Road	a						13 03	13 09			13 18		13 24	13 40					13 56				
Deansgate	a												13 28						14 00				

		AW	NT	NT	TP	NT	VT	NT	NT	EM	XC	NT	NT	VT	NT	NT	XC	TP	VT	AW	NT	NT	TP
		◇			◇1		◇1			◇	◇1			◇1			◇1	◇1	◇1	◇			◇1
		M		D	E	F		H	I	J	K				L		N	B		C		D	E
		✠			✠		⊓				✠			⊓			✠	✠	⊓	✠			✠
London Euston 15 ⊖65	d						12 20							12 40					13 00				
Birmingham New Street 12 68	d										12 57						13 31						
Wolverhampton 7 68	d										13 15						13 49						
Stafford 65,68	d										13 30						14 01						
Stoke-on-Trent 50,68	d						13 48				13 55					13 58	14 20		14 25				
Longport 50	d																						
Kidsgrove 50	d															14 05							
Crewe 10 65	d	13 31										13 34	13 50	14 11						14 31			
Sandbach	d											13 41	13 57										
Holmes Chapel	d											13 45	14 02										
Goostrey	d												14 05										
Chelford	d												14 09										
Alderley Edge	d		13 48									13 54	14 13								14 49		
Wilmslow	d	13 48	13 51									13 57	14 17	14 27						14 49	14 52		
Styal	d																						
Manchester Airport ✈	a											14 04											
Handforth	d		13 54										14 20								14 55		
Congleton	d															14 12							
Macclesfield	a										14 11					14 19			14 41				
	d										14 12					14 20			14 41				
Prestbury	d															14 24							
Adlington (Cheshire)	d															14 27							
Poynton	d															14 30							
Bramhall	d															14 33							
Cheadle Hulme	d		13 59										14 24			14 37					14 59		
Stockport	a	13 58	14 04				14 16				14 27		14 29	14 36		14 41	14 49		14 55	14 58	15 04		
	d	13 58	14 04			14 12	14 17	14 21		14 26	14 28		14 29	14 37	14 41	14 42	14 50	14 53	14 56	14 58	15 04		
Heaton Chapel	d		14 08			14 16							14 33			14 45					15 08		
Levenshulme	d		14 11			14 19							14 36			14 48					15 11		
Manchester Piccadilly 10	a	14 15	14 20			14 28	14 28	14 36		14 36	14 39	14 42	14 44	14 49	14 52	14 56	14 59	15 02	15 07	15 15	15 20		
	d			14 01	14 07				14 22	14 37					14 54							15 01	15 07
Manchester Oxford Road	a			14 03	14 09				14 24	14 40					14 56							15 03	15 09
Deansgate	a								14 28						15 00								

A From Bristol Temple Meads
B From Cleethorpes to Manchester Airport
C From Milford Haven
D From Manchester Airport to Liverpool Lime Street
E From Scarborough to Liverpool Lime Street
F From Buxton
G until 15 July. From Manchester Airport to Arnside
H From Chester
I From Manchester Airport to Southport
J From Norwich to Liverpool Lime Street
K From Bournemouth
L until 30 September. From Hazel Grove to Preston
M From Pembroke Dock
N From Paignton

Table 84

Mondays to Fridays

Stoke-on-Trent and Crewe - Manchester Airport, Stockport and Manchester

		NT	VT	TP	NT	NT	EM	XC	NT	NT		VT	NT	NT	XC	TP	VT	AW	NT	NT		TP	TP FX	NT
		A	◇1 ⊏	◇1 B ⊼	C	D	◇ E	◇1 F ⊼				◇1 ⊏	G		◇1 H ⊼	◇1 I ⊼	◇1 ⊏	◇ J ⊼		K		◇1 L ⊼	◇1 M ⊼	D
London Euston 15 ⊖65	d		13 20									13 40					14 00							
Birmingham New Street 12 68	d							13 57							14 31									
Wolverhampton 7 68	d							14 15							14 49									
Stafford 65,68	d							14 30							15 01									
Stoke-on-Trent 50,68	d		14 48					14 55						14 58	15 20		15 25							
Longport 50	d																							
Kidsgrove 50	d													15 05										
Crewe 10 65	d								14 34	14 50		15 11						15 29						
Sandbach	d								14 41	14 57														
Holmes Chapel	d								14 45	15 02														
Goostrey	d									15 05														
Chelford	d									15 09														
Alderley Edge	d								14 54	15 13									15 48					
Wilmslow	d								14 57	15 17		15 27						15 47	15 51					
Styal	d																							
Manchester Airport ✈	a								15 04															
Handforth	d									15 20									15 54					
Congleton	d													15 12										
Macclesfield	a							15 11						15 19			15 41							
	d							15 12						15 20			15 41							
Prestbury	d													15 24										
Adlington (Cheshire)	d													15 27										
Poynton	d													15 30										
Bramhall	d													15 33										
Cheadle Hulme	d									15 24				15 37					15 59					
Stockport	a		15 16					15 27		15 29		15 36		15 41	15 49		15 55	15 58	16 04					
	d	15 12	15 17		15 21		15 26	15 28		15 29		15 37	15 41	15 42	15 50	15 53	15 56	15 58	16 04					
Heaton Chapel	d	15 16								15 33				15 45					16 08					
Levenshulme	d	15 19								15 36				15 48					16 11					
Manchester Piccadilly 10	a	15 28	15 28		15 36		15 36	15 39	15 41	15 44		15 49	15 52	15 56	15 59	16 02	16 07	16 15	16 20					
	d			15 16		15 22	15 37		15 42				15 54							16 01		16 07	16 16	16 22
Manchester Oxford Road	a			15 18		15 24	15 40		15 46				15 56							16 03		16 09	16 18	16 24
Deansgate	a					15 28							16 00											16 28

		NT	VT	NT	EM	XC	NT		NT	VT	NT	NT	XC	TP	VT	AW	NT		VT	NT	TP	TP	NT	NT	EM
		N	◇1 ⊏	C	◇ E	◇1 F ⊼				◇1 ⊏	O		◇1 P ⊼	◇1 I ⊼	◇1 ⊏	◇ Q ⊼			◇1 ⊏	K	◇1 L ⊼	◇1 R ⊼	C	D	◇ E
London Euston 15 ⊖65	d		14 20							14 40					15 00				15 20						
Birmingham New Street 12 68	d					14 57							15 31												
Wolverhampton 7 68	d					15 15							15 50												
Stafford 65,68	d					15 30																			
Stoke-on-Trent 50,68	d		15 48			15 55						15 58	16 19		16 25				16 48						
Longport 50	d																								
Kidsgrove 50	d											16 05													
Crewe 10 65	d						15 33		15 50	16 12						16 31									
Sandbach	d						15 40		15 57																
Holmes Chapel	d						15 44		16 02																
Goostrey	d								16 05																
Chelford	d								16 09																
Alderley Edge	d						15 53		16 13								16 49								
Wilmslow	d						15 56		16 17	16 27						16 48	16 52								
Styal	d						15 59																		
Manchester Airport ✈	a						16 04																		
Handforth	d								16 20								16 55								
Congleton	d											16 12													
Macclesfield	a					16 11						16 19			16 41										
	d					16 12						16 20			16 41										
Prestbury	d											16 24													
Adlington (Cheshire)	d											16 27													
Poynton	d											16 30													
Bramhall	d											16 33													
Cheadle Hulme	d								16 24			16 37					16 59								
Stockport	a		16 16			16 27			16 29	16 36		16 41	16 47		16 54	16 58	17 04		17 16						
	d	16 12	16 17	16 21	16 26	16 28			16 29	16 37	16 41	16 42	16 50	16 53	16 55	16 58	17 04		17 17				17 21		17 26
Heaton Chapel	d	16 16							16 33			16 45					17 08								
Levenshulme	d	16 19							16 36			16 48					17 11								
Manchester Piccadilly 10	a	16 25	16 28	16 36	16 36	16 39	16 42		16 44	16 49	16 52	16 56	16 59	17 02	17 07	17 14	17 20		17 28				17 36		17 37
	d	16 27			16 37						16 54									17 01	17 07	17 15		17 22	17 37
Manchester Oxford Road	a	16 29			16 40						16 56									17 03	17 09	17 17		17 25	17 40
Deansgate	a	16 32									17 00														

A From Buxton
B From Manchester Airport to Arnside
C From Chester
D From Manchester Airport to Southport
E From Norwich to Liverpool Lime Street
F From Bournemouth
G From Hazel Grove to Bolton
H From Bristol Temple Meads
I From Cleethorpes to Manchester Airport
J From Carmarthen
K From Manchester Airport to Liverpool Lime Street
L From Scarborough to Liverpool Lime Street
M From Manchester Airport to Windermere
N from 18 July until 30 September. From Buxton to Barrow-in-Furness
O From Hazel Grove to Preston
P From Penzance
Q From Milford Haven
R from 18 July. From Manchester Airport to Barrow-in-Furness

Table 84

Mondays to Fridays

Stoke-on-Trent and Crewe - Manchester Airport, Stockport and Manchester

		XC	NT		NT	VT	NT	XC	TP	VT	AW	NT	NT		TP	NT	VT	TP	NT	NT	EM	XC	NT		NT
		◇1 A ⊼				◇1 ⊏		◇1 B ⊼	◇1 C ⊼	◇1 ⊏	◇ D ⊼		E		◇1 F ⊼	G	◇1 ⊏	◇1 H ⊼	I	J	◇ K	◇1 A ⊼			
London Euston 15 ⊖65	d					15 40				16 00							16 20								
Birmingham New Street 12 68	d	15 57						16 31														16 57			
Wolverhampton 7 68	d	16 15						16 49														17 15			
Stafford 65,68	d	16 30						17 01														17 30			
Stoke-on-Trent 50,68	d	16 55					16 58	17 20		17 25							17 48					17 55			
Longport 50	d																								
Kidsgrove 50	d						17 05																		
Crewe 10 65	d		16 34		16 50	17 11					17 30												17 33		17 50
Sandbach	d		16 41		16 57																		17 40		17 57
Holmes Chapel	d		16 45		17 02																		17 44		18 02
Goostrey	d				17 05																				18 05
Chelford	d				17 09																				18 09
Alderley Edge	d		16 54		17 13							17 48											17 53		18 13
Wilmslow	d		16 57		17 17	17 27					17 47	17 51											17 56		18 17
Styal	d																						17 59		
Manchester Airport ✈	a		17 04																				18 04		
Handforth	d				17 20							17 54													18 20
Congleton	d						17 12																		
Macclesfield	a	17 11					17 19			17 41												18 11			
	d	17 12					17 20			17 41												18 12			
Prestbury	d						17 24																		
Adlington (Cheshire)	d						17 27																		
Poynton	d						17 30																		
Bramhall	d						17 33																		
Cheadle Hulme	d				17 24		17 36					17 59													18 24
Stockport	a	17 27			17 29	17 36	17 41	17 49		17 55	17 57	18 04					18 16					18 27			18 29
	d	17 28			17 29	17 37	17 42	17 50	17 53	17 56	17 58	18 04				18 12	18 17		18 21		18 26	18 28			18 29
Heaton Chapel	d				17 33		17 45					18 08				18 16									18 33
Levenshulme	d				17 36		17 48					18 11				18 19									18 36
Manchester Piccadilly 10	a	17 39	17 42		17 44	17 49	17 56	17 59	18 02	18 07	18 13	18 20				18 28	18 28		18 36		18 36	18 39	18 42		18 44
	d												18 01		18 07			18 16		18 22	18 37				
Manchester Oxford Road	a												18 03		18 09			18 18		18 24	18 40				
Deansgate	a																			18 28					

		VT	NT	NT	XC	TP	VT	AW	NT		TP	NT	VT	TP	TP	NT	NT	NT	EM		XC	NT	VT	NT	XC
		◇1 ⊏	L		◇1 M ⊼	◇1 C ⊼	◇1 ⌧	■ N ⊼	E		◇1 F ⊼	G	◇1 ⌧	◇1 O ⊼	◇1 H	J		I	◇ K		◇1 A ⊼		◇1 ⌧		◇1 B ⊼
London Euston 15 ⊖65	d	16 40					17 00						17 20										17 40		
Birmingham New Street 12 68	d				17 31																17 57				18 31
Wolverhampton 7 68	d				17 49																18 15				18 49
Stafford 65,68	d				18 01																18 30				19 01
Stoke-on-Trent 50,68	d			17 58	18 20		18 25						18 49								18 55			18 58	19 20
Longport 50	d																								
Kidsgrove 50	d			18 05																				19 05	
Crewe 10 65	d	18 11						18 31									18 34					18 50	19 11		
Sandbach	d																18 41					18 57			
Holmes Chapel	d																18 45					19 02			
Goostrey	d																					19 05			
Chelford	d																					19 09			
Alderley Edge	d																18 54					19 13			
Wilmslow	d	18 27						18 48									18 57					19 17	19 27		
Styal	d																								
Manchester Airport ✈	a																19 05								
Handforth	d																					19 20			
Congleton	d			18 12																				19 12	
Macclesfield	a			18 19			18 41														19 11			19 19	
	d			18 20			18 41														19 12			19 20	
Prestbury	d			18 24																				19 24	
Adlington (Cheshire)	d			18 27																				19 27	
Poynton	d			18 30																				19 30	
Bramhall	d			18 33																				19 33	
Cheadle Hulme	d			18 37																		19 24		19 37	
Stockport	a	18 37		18 41	18 49		18 55	18 58					19 16								19 27	19 29	19 36	19 41	19 48
	d	18 38	18 41	18 42	18 50	18 53	18 56	18 58				19 12	19 17					19 21	19 26		19 28	19 29	19 37	19 42	19 50
Heaton Chapel	d			18 45								19 16												19 45	
Levenshulme	d			18 48								19 19												19 48	
Manchester Piccadilly 10	a	18 49	18 52	18 56	18 59	19 02	19 07	19 15				19 28	19 28				19 31	19 35	19 36		19 39	19 43	19 49	19 56	20 00
	d		18 54						19 01		19 07			19 16	19 16	19 20	19 32		19 37						
Manchester Oxford Road	a		18 56						19 03		19 09			19 18	19 18	19 22	19 36		19 40						
Deansgate	a		19 00													19 26									

A From Bournemouth
B From Bristol Temple Meads
C From Cleethorpes to Manchester Airport
D From Carmarthen
E From Manchester Airport to Liverpool Lime Street
F From Scarborough to Liverpool Lime Street
G From Buxton
H from 18 July. From Manchester Airport to Barrow-in-Furness
I From Chester
J From Manchester Airport to Southport
K From Norwich to Liverpool Lime Street
L until 30 September. From Buxton to Bolton
M From Paignton
N From Milford Haven
O until 15 July. From Manchester Airport to Carnforth

Stoke-on-Trent and Crewe - Manchester Airport, Stockport and Manchester

		TP	VT	AW	NT	TP	NT	VT	TP	NT	NT	NT	EM	XC	NT	VT	NT	XC	AW	TP	AW	VT	TP
		◇1	◇1			◇1		◇1	◇1				◇	◇1		◇1		◇1		◇1		1	◇1
		A		B	C	D	E		F	G		H	I	J				K	L	A	M		D
London Euston ⊖65	d		18 00					18 20								18 40						19 00	
Birmingham New Street 68	d													18 57				19 31					
Wolverhampton 68	d													19 15				19 49					
Stafford 65,68	d													19 29				20 01					
Stoke-on-Trent 50,68	d		19 25					19 48						19 55			19 58	20 20				20 25	
Longport 50	d																						
Kidsgrove 50	d																20 05						
Crewe 65	d			19 31											19 50	20 12					20 23		
Sandbach	d														19 57								
Holmes Chapel	d														20 02								
Goostrey	d														20 05								
Chelford	d														20 09								
Alderley Edge	d														20 13								
Wilmslow	d			19 48							19 56				20 17	20 27					20 40		
Styal	d																						
Manchester Airport	a										20 04												
Handforth	d														20 20								
Congleton	d																20 12						
Macclesfield	a		19 41											20 11			20 19					20 41	
	d		19 41											20 12			20 20					20 41	
Prestbury	d																20 24						
Adlington (Cheshire)	d																20 27						
Poynton	d																20 30						
Bramhall	d																20 33						
Cheadle Hulme	d														20 24		20 37						
Stockport	a		19 55	19 58				20 16						20 27	20 29	20 36	20 41	20 48			20 50	20 55	
	d	19 53	19 56	19 58			20 12	20 17				20 21	20 26	20 28	20 29	20 37	20 42	20 50		20 53	20 50	20 56	
Heaton Chapel	d						20 16										20 45						
Levenshulme	d						20 19										20 48						
Manchester Piccadilly	a	20 02	20 07	20 15			20 28	20 28			20 32	20 35	20 36	20 39	20 43	20 49	20 56	20 58		21 02	21 05	21 07	
	d				20 01	20 07			20 16	20 20	20 32		20 37						20 50				21 07
Manchester Oxford Road	a				20 03	20 09			20 18	20 22	20 36		20 40						20 52				21 09
Deansgate	a									20 26													

		NT	VT	EM	NT	NT	NT	XC	NT	VT	NT	XC	VT	AW	AW	NT	TP	NT	TP	NT	NT	XC
			1	◇				◇1		◇1		◇1	◇1	◇			◇1		◇1			◇1
		E		N	G		H	J				O		B	L	C	D	E	P		H	J
London Euston ⊖65	d		19 20							19 40			20 00									
Birmingham New Street 68	d							19 57				20 31										20 57
Wolverhampton 68	d							20 16				20 49										21 16
Stafford 65,68	d							20 30		21 04												21 32
Stoke-on-Trent 50,68	d		20 48					20 55			20 58	21 18	21 24									21 55
Longport 50	d																					
Kidsgrove 50	d										21 05											
Crewe 65	d								20 50	21 23				21 31								
Sandbach	d								20 57													
Holmes Chapel	d								21 02													
Goostrey	d								21 05													
Chelford	d								21 09													
Alderley Edge	d								21 13													
Wilmslow	d					20 56			21 17	21 38				21 48						21 55		
Styal	d																					
Manchester Airport	a					21 04														22 04		
Handforth	d								21 20													
Congleton	d										21 12											
Macclesfield	a							21 11			21 19		21 40									22 11
	d							21 12			21 20		21 40									22 12
Prestbury	d										21 24											
Adlington (Cheshire)	d										21 27											
Poynton	d										21 30											
Bramhall	d										21 33											
Cheadle Hulme	d								21 24		21 37											
Stockport	a		21 16					21 27	21 29		21 41	21 46	21 55	21 58								22 25
	d	21 12	21 17	21 20			21 21	21 28	21 29		21 42	21 49	21 56	21 59				22 12			22 21	22 26
Heaton Chapel	d	21 16									21 45							22 16				
Levenshulme	d	21 19									21 48							22 19				
Manchester Piccadilly	a	21 28	21 28	21 32		21 32	21 35	21 40	21 43	21 57	21 57	21 59	22 07	22 13				22 28		22 31	22 35	22 35
	d				21 20	21 32									21 50	22 01	22 07		22 16	22 32		
Manchester Oxford Road	a				21 22	21 36									21 52	22 03	22 09		22 18	22 36		
Deansgate	a				21 26																	

A From Cleethorpes to Manchester Airport
B From Carmarthen
C From Manchester Airport to Liverpool Lime Street
D From Scarborough to Liverpool Lime Street
E From Buxton
F From Manchester Airport to Carnforth
G From Manchester Airport to Southport
H From Chester
I From Norwich to Liverpool Lime Street
J From Bournemouth
K From Exeter St Davids
L From Manchester Airport to Chester
M From Milford Haven
N From Norwich
O From Bristol Temple Meads
P From Manchester Airport to Barrow-in-Furness

Stoke-on-Trent and Crewe - Manchester Airport, Stockport and Manchester

		NT	NT	NT	VT	TP	VT	NT	NT	XC	VT	AW	NT	NT	NT	XC	AW	XC	XC	VT
					◇1	◇1	◇1			◇1	◇1	◇				◇1	◇	◇1	◇1	◇1
			A	B		C				D		E	F	G		H	I	J	K	
London Euston ⊖65	d				20 40		21 00				21 40									22 00
Birmingham New Street 68	d									21 57						22 30	21 24	22 30	22 30	
Wolverhampton 68	d									22 16						22 48	21 43	22 48	22 48	
Stafford 65,68	d									22 30						23 01		23 01	23 01	23s38
Stoke-on-Trent 50,68	d						22 28	22 18		22 55	23 07					23 21		23 21	23 21	
Longport 50	d																			
Kidsgrove 50	d							22 25												
Crewe 65	d	21 45			22 13							23 07			23 12					00s03
Sandbach	d	21 52													23 19					
Holmes Chapel	d	21 58													23 24					
Goostrey	d	22 01													23 27					
Chelford	d	22 07													23 31					
Alderley Edge	d	22 12													23 35					
Wilmslow	d	22 15			22 29				22 56			23 25			23 39					
Styal	d																			
Manchester Airport	a								23 04											
Handforth	d	22 19													23 42					
Congleton	d							22 32												
Macclesfield	a						22 44	22 40		23 11	23 23									
	d						22 44	22 48		23 12	23 23									
Prestbury	d							22 53												
Adlington (Cheshire)	d							22 56												
Poynton	d							22 59												
Bramhall	d							23 02												
Cheadle Hulme	d	22 24						23 05							23 46					
Stockport	a	22 29			22 38		22 58	23 10		23 25	23 37	23 35			23 51					00s26
	d	22 29		22 34	22 39	22 53	22 59	23 10		23 26	23 38	23 35	23 41	23 48	23 51					
Heaton Chapel	d			22 38				23 14							23 55					
Levenshulme	d			22 41				23 17							23 58					
Manchester Piccadilly	a	22 43		22 48	22 48	23 02	23 11	23 25	23 33	23 37	23 46	23 53	23 54	00 02	00 07	00 12	00 28	00 32	00 33	00 35
	d		22 36	22 50																
Manchester Oxford Road	a		22 38	22 52																
Deansgate	a		22 41	22 55																

Saturdays

		NT	NT	XC	NT	NT	AW	VT	NT	TP	NT	NT	TP	AW	NT	NT	NT	NT	EM	XC	NT	NT	NT
				◇1			◇	◇1		◇1			◇1						◇	◇1			
		G			L	M	I			N		O	P			Q	F	R	S				T
London Euston ⊖65	d							22p00															
Birmingham New Street 68	d			22p30			21p24													05 57			
Wolverhampton 68	d			22p48			21p43													06 16			
Stafford 65,68	d			23p01				23b38												06 30			
Stoke-on-Trent 50,68	d			23p21																06 51			
Longport 50	d																						
Kidsgrove 50	d																						
Crewe 65	d		23p12					00s03	00 44					06 27							06 33	06 49	
Sandbach	d		23p19																		06 40	06 56	
Holmes Chapel	d		23p24																		06 44	07 00	
Goostrey	d		23p27																			07 03	
Chelford	d		23p31																			07 08	
Alderley Edge	d		23p35												06 49						06 53	07 12	
Wilmslow	d		23p39								05 46			06 45	06 52						06 57	07 16	
Styal	d																						
Manchester Airport	a								01 16		05 53										07 04		
Handforth	d		23p42												06 55							07 19	
Congleton	d																			07 03			
Macclesfield	a																			07 11			
	d																			07 12			
Prestbury	d																						
Adlington (Cheshire)	d																						
Poynton	d																						
Bramhall	d																						
Cheadle Hulme	d		23p46												06 59							07 24	
Stockport	a		23p51					00s26						06 55	07 04					07 27		07 29	
	d	23p48	23p51		00 02	00 03				05 53		06 41	06 53	06 55	07 04		07 12	07 19	07 22	07 28		07 29	07 40
Heaton Chapel	d		23p55												07 08		07 16					07 33	
Levenshulme	d		23p58												07 11		07 19					07 36	
Manchester Piccadilly	a	00 02	00 07	00 12	00 18	00 18	00 28	00 35	01 36	06 05	06 25	06 52	07 02	07 07	07 21		07 28	07 31	07 34	07 38	07 42	07 44	07 52
	d											06 54				06 58			07 34				07 54
Manchester Oxford Road	a											06 56				07 00			07 37				07 56
Deansgate	a											06 59											08 00

A From Manchester Airport to Southport
B To Wigan Wallgate
C From Cleethorpes to Manchester Airport
D From Bournemouth
E From Cardiff Central
F From Buxton
G From Sheffield
H WThFO
I From Birmingham International
J MTO until 14 June, MTO from 12 September
K MTO from 20 June until 6 September
L until 1 October. From Chester
M from 8 October. From Chester
N From Sheffield to Manchester Airport
O From Buxton to Clitheroe
P From Doncaster to Manchester Airport
Q From Manchester Airport to Liverpool Lime Street
R From Chester
S From Nottingham to Liverpool Lime Street
T From Hazel Grove to Preston
b Previous night, stops to set down only

Table 84

Stoke-on-Trent and Crewe - Manchester Airport, Stockport and Manchester

		NT	XC	TP	NT	AW	NT	NT	TP	NT	NT	XC	NT	EM	NT	NT	VT	TP	NT	NT	XC	TP	VT
			◇1 ✠	◇1 A ✠	B	◇ C		D	◇1 E ✠	F	G	◇1 ✠	H	◇ I			◇1 ⊡	◇1 J ✠	K		◇1 ✠	◇1 A ✠	◇1 ⊡
London Euston 15 ⊖65	d																06 36						06 55
Birmingham New Street 12 68	d		06 31									06 57									07 31		
Wolverhampton 7 68	d		06 49									07 15									07 49		
Stafford 65,68	d		07 01									07 31									08 01		
Stoke-on-Trent 50,68	d	06 57	07 19																	07 57	08 20		08 25
Longport 50	d																						
Kidsgrove 50	d	07 04																		08 04			
Crewe 10 65	d					07 27						07 54			07 30	07 55	08 11						
Sandbach	d														07 37	08 02							
Holmes Chapel	d														07 41	08 07							
Goostrey	d														07 44								
Chelford	d														07 49								
Alderley Edge	d						07 49								07 53	08 15							
Wilmslow	d					07 44	07 52					08 10			07 56	08 19	08 27						
Styal	d														07 59								
Manchester Airport ✈	a														08 05								
Handforth	d						07 55									08 22							
Congleton	d	07 11																		08 11			
Macclesfield	a	07 18	07 36																	08 18	08 36		08 41
	d	07 19	07 37																	08 19	08 37		08 41
Prestbury	d	07 23																		08 23			
Adlington (Cheshire)	d	07 26																		08 26			
Poynton	d	07 29																		08 30			
Bramhall	d	07 32																		08 33			
Cheadle Hulme	d	07 36					07 59									08 26				08 37			
Stockport	a	07 40	07 49			08 01	08 04					08 21				08 31	08 37			08 41	08 49		08 55
	d	07 41	07 50	07 53	07 57	08 01	08 04			08 12	08 19	08 21		08 24		08 31	08 38		08 41	08 42	08 50	08 53	08 56
Heaton Chapel	d	07 44					08 08			08 16						08 35				08 45			
Levenshulme	d	07 47					08 11			08 19										08 48			
Manchester Piccadilly 10	a	07 56	07 59	08 02	08 09	08 20	08 20			08 28	08 32	08 36		08 36	08 42	08 45	08 49		08 52	08 56	08 59	09 02	09 07
	d							07 59	08 07				08 22	08 37				08 46	08 54				
Manchester Oxford Road	a							08 01	08 09				08 24	08 40				08 48	08 56				
Deansgate	a												08 28					08 51	09 00				

		AW	NT	NT	TP	NT	VT	NT	NT	EM	XC	NT	NT	VT	NT	NT	XC	TP	VT	AW	NT	NT
		◇ C ✠		D	◇1 L ✠	F	◇1 ⊡	G	H	◇ I	◇1 M ✠			◇1 ⊡	N		◇1 O ⊡	◇1 A ✠	◇1 ⊡	◇ P ✠		D
London Euston 15 ⊖65	d						07 20							07 35					08 00			
Birmingham New Street 12 68	d										07 57						08 31					
Wolverhampton 7 68	d										08 15						08 49					
Stafford 65,68	d										08 30						09 01					
Stoke-on-Trent 50,68	d						08 48				08 55					08 58	09 20		09 25			
Longport 50	d																					
Kidsgrove 50	d															09 05						
Crewe 10 65	d	08 28										08 31	08 50	09 11						09 30		
Sandbach	d											08 38	08 57									
Holmes Chapel	d											08 42	09 02									
Goostrey	d											08 45	09 05									
Chelford	d											08 50	09 09									
Alderley Edge	d		08 49									08 54	09 13								09 49	
Wilmslow	d	08 45	08 52									08 57	09 17	09 27						09 47	09 52	
Styal	d																					
Manchester Airport ✈	a											09 04										
Handforth	d		08 55										09 20								09 55	
Congleton	d															09 12						
Macclesfield	a										09 11					09 19			09 41			
	d										09 12					09 20			09 41			
Prestbury	d															09 24						
Adlington (Cheshire)	d															09 27						
Poynton	d															09 30						
Bramhall	d															09 33						
Cheadle Hulme	d		08 59										09 24			09 37					09 59	
Stockport	a	08 58	09 04				09 16				09 27		09 29	09 36		09 41	09 49		09 55	09 57	10 04	
	d	08 59	09 04			09 12	09 17	09 21		09 25	09 28		09 29	09 37	09 41	09 42	09 50	09 53	09 56	09 58	10 04	
Heaton Chapel	d		09 08			09 16							09 33			09 45					10 08	
Levenshulme	d		09 11			09 19							09 36			09 48					10 11	
Manchester Piccadilly 10	a	09 15	09 20			09 28	09 28	09 36		09 36	09 39	09 42	09 44	09 49	09 52	09 56	09 59	10 02	10 07	10 14	10 20	
	d			09 01	09 07				09 22	09 37					09 54							10 01
Manchester Oxford Road	a			09 03	09 09				09 24	09 40					09 56							10 03
Deansgate	a								09 28						10 00							

A From Cleethorpes to Manchester Airport
B From Hazel Grove
C From Cardiff Central
D From Manchester Airport to Liverpool Lime Street
E From Hull to Liverpool Lime Street
F From Buxton
G From Chester
H From Manchester Airport to Southport
I From Nottingham to Liverpool Lime Street
J From Manchester Airport to Windermere
K until 1 October. From Buxton to Preston
L From Newcastle to Liverpool Lime Street
M From Southampton Central
N until 1 October. From Hazel Grove to Preston
O From Bristol Temple Meads
P From Carmarthen

Table 84

Stoke-on-Trent and Crewe - Manchester Airport, Stockport and Manchester

		TP	NT	VT	NT	NT	EM	XC	NT	NT	VT	NT	NT	XC	TP	VT	AW	NT	NT	TP	NT	VT	TP
		◇1 A ✠	B	◇1 ⊡	C	D	◇ E	◇1 F ✠			◇1 ⊡	G		◇1 H ⊡	◇1 I ✠	◇1 ⊡	◇ J ✠		K	◇1 A	B	◇1 ⊡	◇1 L ✠
London Euston 15 ⊖65	d			08 20							08 40					09 00						09 20	
Birmingham New Street 12 68	d							08 57						09 31									
Wolverhampton 7 68	d							09 15						09 49									
Stafford 65,68	d							09 30						10 01									
Stoke-on-Trent 50,68	d			09 48				09 55					09 58	10 20		10 25						10 48	
Longport 50	d																						
Kidsgrove 50	d												10 05										
Crewe 10 65	d								09 33	09 50	10 11						10 31						
Sandbach	d								09 40	09 57													
Holmes Chapel	d								09 44	10 02													
Goostrey	d									10 05													
Chelford	d									10 09													
Alderley Edge	d								09 53	10 13								10 49					
Wilmslow	d								09 57	10 17	10 27						10 49	10 52					
Styal	d																						
Manchester Airport ✈	a								10 04														
Handforth	d									10 20								10 55					
Congleton	d												10 12										
Macclesfield	a							10 11					10 19			10 41							
	d							10 12					10 20			10 41							
Prestbury	d												10 24										
Adlington (Cheshire)	d												10 27										
Poynton	d												10 30										
Bramhall	d												10 33										
Cheadle Hulme	d									10 24			10 37					10 59					
Stockport	a			10 16				10 27		10 29	10 36		10 41	10 49		10 55	10 58	11 04				11 16	
	d		10 12	10 17	10 21		10 26	10 28		10 29	10 37	10 41	10 42	10 50	10 53	10 56	10 58	11 04			11 12	11 17	
Heaton Chapel	d		10 16							10 33			10 45					11 08			11 16		
Levenshulme	d		10 19							10 36			10 48					11 11			11 19		
Manchester Piccadilly 10	a		10 28	10 28	10 36		10 36	10 39	10 42	10 44	10 49	10 52	10 56	10 59	11 02	11 07	11 15	11 20			11 28	11 28	
	d	10 07				10 22	10 37					10 54							11 01	11 07			11 16
Manchester Oxford Road	a	10 09				10 24	10 40					10 56							11 03	11 09			11 18
Deansgate	a					10 28						11 00											

		NT	NT	EM	XC	NT	NT	VT	NT	NT	XC	TP	VT	AW	NT	NT	TP	NT	VT	NT	NT	EM
		C	D	◇ E	◇1 M ✠			◇1 ⊡	G		◇1 N ⊡	◇1 I ✠	◇1 ⊡	◇ O ✠		K	◇1 A ✠	B	◇1 ⊡	C	D	◇ E
London Euston 15 ⊖65	d							09 40					10 00						10 20			
Birmingham New Street 12 68	d				09 57						10 31											
Wolverhampton 7 68	d				10 15						10 49											
Stafford 65,68	d				10 30						11 01											
Stoke-on-Trent 50,68	d				10 55					10 58	11 20		11 25						11 48			
Longport 50	d																					
Kidsgrove 50	d									11 05												
Crewe 10 65	d					10 34	10 50	11 11						11 31								
Sandbach	d					10 41	10 57															
Holmes Chapel	d					10 45	11 02															
Goostrey	d						11 05															
Chelford	d						11 09															
Alderley Edge	d					10 54	11 13								11 49							
Wilmslow	d					10 57	11 17	11 27						11 48	11 52							
Styal	d																					
Manchester Airport ✈	a					11 04																
Handforth	d						11 20								11 55							
Congleton	d									11 12												
Macclesfield	a				11 11					11 19			11 41									
	d				11 12					11 20			11 41									
Prestbury	d									11 24												
Adlington (Cheshire)	d									11 27												
Poynton	d									11 30												
Bramhall	d									11 33												
Cheadle Hulme	d						11 24			11 37					11 59							
Stockport	a				11 27		11 29	11 36		11 41	11 49		11 55	11 58	12 04				12 16			
	d	11 21		11 26	11 28		11 29	11 37	11 41	11 42	11 50	11 53	11 56	11 58	12 04			12 12	12 17	12 21		12 26
Heaton Chapel	d						11 33			11 45					12 08			12 16				
Levenshulme	d						11 36			11 48					12 11			12 19				
Manchester Piccadilly 10	a	11 36		11 36	11 39	11 42	11 44	11 49	11 52	11 56	11 59	12 02	12 07	12 15	12 20			12 28	12 28	12 36		12 36
	d		11 22	11 37					11 54							12 01	12 07				12 22	12 37
Manchester Oxford Road	a		11 24	11 40					11 56							12 03	12 09				12 24	12 40
Deansgate	a		11 28						12 00												12 28	

A From Scarborough to Liverpool Lime Street
B From Buxton
C From Chester
D From Manchester Airport to Southport
E From Norwich to Liverpool Lime Street
F From Southampton Central
G until 1 October. From Hazel Grove to Preston
H From Cardiff Central
I From Cleethorpes to Manchester Airport
J From Carmarthen
K From Manchester Airport to Liverpool Lime Street
L From Manchester Airport to Arnside
M From Bournemouth
N From Paignton
O From Milford Haven

Table 84

Saturdays

Stoke-on-Trent and Crewe - Manchester Airport, Stockport and Manchester

	XC ◇1 A	NT	NT	VT ◇1	NT B	NT	XC ◇1 C	TP ◇1 D	VT ◇1	AW ◇ E	NT	NT F	TP ◇1 G	NT H	VT ◇1	NT I	NT J	EM ◇ K	XC ◇1 A	NT	NT	VT ◇1
London Euston ⊖65 d				10 40					11 00						11 20							11 40
Birmingham New Street 68 d	10 57						11 31												11 57			
Wolverhampton 68 d	11 15						11 49												12 15			
Stafford 65,68 d	11 30						12 01												12 30			
Stoke-on-Trent 50,68 d	11 55					11 58	12 20		12 25						12 48				12 55			
Longport 50 d																						
Kidsgrove 50 d						12 05																
Crewe 65 d		11 34	11 50	12 11						12 31										12 34	12 50	13 11
Sandbach d		11 41	11 57																	12 41	12 57	
Holmes Chapel d		11 45	12 02																	12 45	13 02	
Goostrey d			12 05																		13 05	
Chelford d			12 09																		13 09	
Alderley Edge d		11 54	12 13								12 49									12 54	13 13	
Wilmslow d		11 57	12 17	12 27						12 49	12 52									12 57	13 17	13 27
Styal d																						
Manchester Airport ✈ a		12 04																		13 04		
Handforth d			12 20								12 55										13 20	
Congleton d						12 12																
Macclesfield a	12 11					12 19			12 41										13 11			
d	12 12					12 20			12 41										13 12			
Prestbury d						12 24																
Adlington (Cheshire) d						12 27																
Poynton d						12 30																
Bramhall d						12 33																
Cheadle Hulme d			12 24			12 37					12 59										13 24	
Stockport a	12 27		12 29	12 36		12 41	12 49		12 55	12 58	13 04				13 16				13 27		13 29	13 36
d	12 28		12 29	12 37	12 41	12 42	12 50	12 53	12 56	12 58	13 04			13 12	13 17	13 21		13 26	13 28		13 29	13 37
Heaton Chapel d			12 33			12 45					13 08			13 16							13 33	
Levenshulme d			12 36			12 48					13 11			13 19							13 36	
Manchester Piccadilly a	12 39	12 42	12 44	12 49	12 52	12 56	12 59	13 02	13 07	13 15	13 20			13 28	13 28	13 36		13 36	13 39	13 42	13 44	13 49
d					12 54							13 01	13 07				13 22	13 37				
Manchester Oxford Road a					12 56							13 03	13 09				13 24	13 40				
Deansgate a					13 00												13 28					

	NT B	NT	XC ◇1 L	XC ◇1 M	TP ◇1 D	VT ◇1	AW ◇ N	NT	NT F	TP ◇1 G	NT H	VT ◇1	TP ◇1 O	NT I	NT J	EM ◇ K	XC ◇1 A	NT	NT	VT ◇1	NT B	NT
London Euston ⊖65 d						12 00						12 20								12 40		
Birmingham New Street 68 d			12 31	12 31													12 57					
Wolverhampton 68 d			12 49	12 49													13 15					
Stafford 65,68 d			13 01	13 01													13 30					
Stoke-on-Trent 50,68 d		12 58	13 19	13 20		13 25						13 48					13 55					13 58
Longport 50 d																						
Kidsgrove 50 d		13 05																				14 05
Crewe 65 d							13 31											13 34	13 50	14 11		
Sandbach d																		13 41	13 57			
Holmes Chapel d																		13 45	14 02			
Goostrey d																			14 05			
Chelford d																			14 09			
Alderley Edge d								13 49										13 54	14 13			
Wilmslow d							13 48	13 52										13 57	14 17	14 27		
Styal d																						
Manchester Airport ✈ a																		14 04				
Handforth d								13 55											14 20			
Congleton d		13 12																				14 12
Macclesfield a		13 19				13 41											14 11					14 19
d		13 20				13 42											14 12					14 20
Prestbury d		13 24																				14 24
Adlington (Cheshire) d		13 27																				14 27
Poynton d		13 30																				14 30
Bramhall d		13 33																				14 33
Cheadle Hulme d		13 37						13 59											14 24			14 37
Stockport a		13 41	13 49	13 49		13 55	13 58	14 04				14 16					14 27		14 29	14 36		14 41
d	13 41	13 42	13 50	13 50	13 53	13 56	13 58	14 04			14 12	14 17		14 21		14 26	14 28		14 29	14 37	14 41	14 42
Heaton Chapel d		13 45						14 08			14 16								14 33			14 45
Levenshulme d		13 48						14 11			14 19								14 36			14 48
Manchester Piccadilly a	13 52	13 56	13 59	13 59	14 02	14 07	14 15	14 20			14 28	14 28		14 36		14 36	14 39	14 42	14 44	14 49	14 52	14 56
d	13 54								14 01	14 07			14 16		14 22	14 37					14 54	
Manchester Oxford Road a	13 56								14 03	14 09			14 18		14 24	14 40					14 56	
Deansgate a	14 00														14 28						15 00	

A From Bournemouth
B until 1 October. From Hazel Grove to Preston
C From Bristol Temple Meads
D From Cleethorpes to Manchester Airport
E From Milford Haven
F From Manchester Airport to Liverpool Lime Street
G From Scarborough to Liverpool Lime Street
H From Buxton
I From Chester
J From Manchester Airport to Southport
K From Norwich to Liverpool Lime Street
L until 10 September. From Plymouth
M from 17 September. From Bristol Temple Meads
N From Pembroke Dock
O from 23 July. From Manchester Airport to Barrow-in-Furness

Table 84

Saturdays

Stoke-on-Trent and Crewe - Manchester Airport, Stockport and Manchester

	XC ◇1 A	TP ◇1 B	VT ◇1	AW ◇ C	NT	NT D	TP ◇1 E	NT F	VT ◇1	TP ◇1 G	NT H	NT I	EM ◇ J	XC ◇1 K	NT	NT	VT ◇1	NT L	NT	XC ◇1 M	TP ◇1 B
London Euston ⊖65 d			13 00						13 20								13 40				
Birmingham New Street 68 d	13 31													13 57						14 31	
Wolverhampton 68 d	13 49													14 15						14 49	
Stafford 65,68 d	14 01													14 30						15 01	
Stoke-on-Trent 50,68 d	14 20		14 25						14 48					14 55					14 58	15 20	
Longport 50 d																					
Kidsgrove 50 d																			15 05		
Crewe 65 d				14 31											14 34	14 50	15 11				
Sandbach d															14 41	14 57					
Holmes Chapel d															14 45	15 02					
Goostrey d																15 05					
Chelford d																15 09					
Alderley Edge d					14 49										14 54	15 13					
Wilmslow d				14 49	14 52										14 57	15 17	15 27				
Styal d																					
Manchester Airport ✈ a															15 04						
Handforth d					14 55											15 20					
Congleton d																			15 12		
Macclesfield a			14 41											15 11					15 19		
d			14 41											15 12					15 20		
Prestbury d																			15 24		
Adlington (Cheshire) d																			15 27		
Poynton d																			15 30		
Bramhall d																			15 33		
Cheadle Hulme d					14 59											15 24			15 37		
Stockport a	14 49		14 55	14 58	15 04				15 16					15 27		15 29	15 36		15 41	15 49	
d	14 50	14 53	14 56	14 58	15 04			15 12	15 17		15 21		15 26	15 28		15 29	15 37	15 41	15 42	15 50	15 53
Heaton Chapel d					15 08			15 16								15 33			15 45		
Levenshulme d					15 11			15 19								15 36			15 48		
Manchester Piccadilly a	14 59	15 02	15 07	15 15	15 20			15 28	15 28		15 36		15 36	15 39	15 42	15 44	15 49	15 52	15 56	15 59	16 02
d						15 01	15 07			15 16		15 22	15 37					15 54			
Manchester Oxford Road a						15 03	15 09			15 18		15 24	15 40					15 56			
Deansgate a												15 28						16 00			

	VT ◇1	AW ◇ N	NT	NT D	TP ◇1 E	NT F	VT ◇1	TP ◇1 O	NT H	NT I	EM ◇ J	XC ◇1 K	NT	NT	VT ◇1	NT L	NT	XC ◇1 P	TP ◇1 B	VT ◇1	AW ◇ C	NT
London Euston ⊖65 d	14 00						14 20								14 40					15 00		
Birmingham New Street 68 d												14 57						15 31				
Wolverhampton 68 d												15 15						15 49				
Stafford 65,68 d												15 30						16 01				
Stoke-on-Trent 50,68 d	15 25						15 48					15 55					15 58	16 20		16 25		
Longport 50 d																						
Kidsgrove 50 d																	16 05					
Crewe 65 d		15 28											15 33	15 50	16 12						16 31	
Sandbach d													15 40	15 57								
Holmes Chapel d													15 44	16 02								
Goostrey d														16 05								
Chelford d														16 09								
Alderley Edge d			15 49										15 53	16 13								16 49
Wilmslow d		15 45	15 52										15 56	16 17	16 27						16 48	16 52
Styal d													15 59									
Manchester Airport ✈ a													16 04									
Handforth d			15 55											16 20								16 55
Congleton d																	16 12					
Macclesfield a	15 41											16 11					16 19			16 41		
d	15 41											16 12					16 20			16 41		
Prestbury d																	16 24					
Adlington (Cheshire) d																	16 27					
Poynton d																	16 30					
Bramhall d																	16 33					
Cheadle Hulme d			15 59											16 24			16 37					16 59
Stockport a	15 55	15 58	16 04				16 16					16 27		16 29	16 36		16 41	16 49		16 54	16 58	17 04
d	15 56	15 58	16 04			16 12	16 17		16 21		16 26	16 28		16 29	16 37	16 41	16 42	16 50	16 53	16 55	16 58	17 04
Heaton Chapel d			16 08			16 16								16 33			16 45					17 08
Levenshulme d			16 11			16 19								16 36			16 48					17 11
Manchester Piccadilly a	16 07	16 15	16 20			16 28	16 28		16 36		16 36	16 39	16 42	16 44	16 49	16 52	16 56	16 59	17 02	17 07	17 14	17 20
d				16 01	16 07			16 16		16 22	16 37					16 54						
Manchester Oxford Road a				16 03	16 09			16 18		16 24	16 40					16 56						
Deansgate a										16 28						17 00						

A From Paignton
B From Cleethorpes to Manchester Airport
C From Milford Haven
D From Manchester Airport to Liverpool Lime Street
E From Scarborough to Liverpool Lime Street
F From Buxton
G From Manchester Airport to Arnside
H From Chester
I From Manchester Airport to Southport
J From Norwich to Liverpool Lime Street
K From Bournemouth
L From Hazel Grove to Preston
M From Bristol Temple Meads
N From Carmarthen
O From Manchester Airport to Windermere
P From Penzance

Stoke-on-Trent and Crewe - Manchester Airport, Stockport and Manchester

	NT A	TP ◇1 B	NT C	VT ◇1	NT D	NT E	EM ◇ F	XC ◇1 G	NT	NT	VT ◇1	NT	XC ◇1 H	TP ◇1 I	VT ◇1	AW ◇ J	NT	NT A	TP ◇1 B	NT C	VT ◇1
London Euston ⊖65 d				15 20							15 40				16 00						16 20
Birmingham New Street 68 d								15 57					16 31								
Wolverhampton 68 d								16 15					16 49								
Stafford 65,68 d								16 30					17 01								
Stoke-on-Trent 50,68 d				16 48				16 55				16 58	17 20		17 25						17 48
Longport 50 d																					
Kidsgrove 50 d												17 05									
Crewe 65 d									16 34	16 50	17 11					17 28					
Sandbach d									16 41	16 57											
Holmes Chapel d									16 45	17 02											
Goostrey d										17 05											
Chelford d										17 09											
Alderley Edge d									16 54	17 13							17 49				
Wilmslow d									16 57	17 17	17 27					17 45	17 52				
Styal d																					
Manchester Airport a									17 04												
Handforth d										17 20							17 55				
Congleton d												17 12									
Macclesfield a								17 11				17 19			17 41						
d								17 12				17 20			17 41						
Prestbury d												17 24									
Adlington (Cheshire) d												17 27									
Poynton d												17 30									
Bramhall d												17 33									
Cheadle Hulme d										17 24		17 37					17 59				
Stockport a				17 16				17 27		17 29	17 36	17 41	17 49		17 55	17 58	18 04				18 16
d			17 12	17 17	17 21		17 26	17 28		17 29	17 37	17 42	17 50	17 53	17 56	17 58	18 04			18 12	18 17
Heaton Chapel d			17 16							17 33		17 45					18 08			18 16	
Levenshulme d			17 19							17 36		17 48					18 11			18 19	
Manchester Piccadilly a			17 28	17 28	17 36		17 37	17 39	17 42	17 44	17 49	17 56	17 59	18 02	18 07	18 15	18 20			18 28	18 28
d	17 01	17 07				17 22	17 37											18 01	18 07		
Manchester Oxford Road a	17 03	17 09				17 25	17 40											18 03	18 09		
Deansgate a																					

	TP ◇1 K	NT D	NT E	EM ◇ F	XC ◇1 G	NT	NT	VT ◇1	NT L	NT	XC ◇1 M	TP ◇1 I	VT ◇1	AW ■ N	NT A	TP ◇1 B	NT C	VT ◇1	TP ◇1 K	NT E	NT	NT D
London Euston ⊖65 d								16 40					17 00					17 20				
Birmingham New Street 68 d					16 57						17 31											
Wolverhampton 68 d					17 15						17 49											
Stafford 65,68 d					17 30						18 01											
Stoke-on-Trent 50,68 d					17 55					17 58	18 20		18 25					18 48				
Longport 50 d																						
Kidsgrove 50 d										18 05												
Crewe 65 d						17 33	17 50	18 11						18 31							18 34	
Sandbach d						17 40	17 57														18 41	
Holmes Chapel d						17 44	18 02														18 45	
Goostrey d							18 05															
Chelford d							18 09															
Alderley Edge d						17 53	18 13														18 54	
Wilmslow d						17 56	18 17	18 27						18 48							18 57	
Styal d						17 59																
Manchester Airport a						18 04															19 05	
Handforth d							18 20															
Congleton d										18 12												
Macclesfield a					18 11					18 19			18 41									
d					18 12					18 20			18 41									
Prestbury d										18 24												
Adlington (Cheshire) d										18 27												
Poynton d										18 30												
Bramhall d										18 33												
Cheadle Hulme d							18 24			18 37												
Stockport a					18 27		18 29	18 36		18 41	18 49		18 55	18 58				19 16				
d		18 21		18 26	18 28		18 29	18 37	18 41	18 42	18 50	18 53	18 56	18 58			19 12	19 17				19 21
Heaton Chapel d							18 33			18 45							19 16					
Levenshulme d							18 36			18 48							19 19					
Manchester Piccadilly a		18 36		18 36	18 39	18 42	18 44	18 49	18 52	18 56	18 59	19 02	19 07	19 15			19 28	19 28			19 31	19 35
d	18 16		18 22	18 37					18 54						19 01	19 07			19 16	19 20	19 32	
Manchester Oxford Road a	18 18		18 24	18 40					18 56						19 03	19 09			19 18	19 22	19 36	
Deansgate a			18 28						19 00											19 26		

A From Manchester Airport to Liverpool Lime Street
B From Scarborough to Liverpool Lime Street
C From Buxton
D From Chester
E From Manchester Airport to Southport
F From Norwich to Liverpool Lime Street
G From Bournemouth
H From Bristol Temple Meads
I From Cleethorpes to Manchester Airport
J From Carmarthen
K From Manchester Airport to Carnforth
L until 1 October. From Hazel Grove to Bolton
M From Paignton
N From Milford Haven

Stoke-on-Trent and Crewe - Manchester Airport, Stockport and Manchester

	EM ◇ A	XC ◇1 B	NT	VT ◇1	NT	XC ◇1 C	TP ◇1 D	VT ◇1	AW ■ E	NT F	TP ◇1 G	NT H	VT ◇1	TP ◇1 I	NT J	NT	NT K	EM ◇ A	XC ◇1 B	NT	VT ◇1	NT
London Euston ⊖65 d				17 40				18 00					18 20								18 40	
Birmingham New Street 68 d		17 57				18 31													18 57			
Wolverhampton 68 d		18 15				18 49													19 15			
Stafford 65,68 d		18 30				19 01													19 30			
Stoke-on-Trent 50,68 d		18 55			18 58	19 20		19 25					19 48						19 55			19 58
Longport 50 d																						
Kidsgrove 50 d					19 05																	20 05
Crewe 65 d			18 50	19 11					19 31											19 50	20 11	
Sandbach d			18 57																	19 57		
Holmes Chapel d			19 02																	20 02		
Goostrey d			19 05																	20 05		
Chelford d			19 09																	20 09		
Alderley Edge d			19 13																	20 13		
Wilmslow d			19 17	19 27					19 48							19 56				20 17	20 27	
Styal d																						
Manchester Airport a																20 04						
Handforth d			19 20																	20 20		
Congleton d					19 12																	20 12
Macclesfield a		19 11			19 19			19 41											20 11			20 19
d		19 12			19 20			19 41											20 12			20 20
Prestbury d					19 24																	20 24
Adlington (Cheshire) d					19 27																	20 27
Poynton d					19 30																	20 30
Bramhall d					19 33																	20 33
Cheadle Hulme d			19 24		19 37															20 24		20 37
Stockport a		19 27	19 29	19 36	19 41	19 49		19 55	19 58				20 16						20 27	20 29	20 36	20 41
d	19 26	19 28	19 29	19 37	19 42	19 50	19 53	19 56	19 58			20 12	20 17				20 21	20 26	20 28	20 29	20 37	20 42
Heaton Chapel d					19 45							20 16										20 45
Levenshulme d					19 48							20 19										20 48
Manchester Piccadilly a	19 36	19 39	19 43	19 49	19 56	19 59	20 02	20 07	20 15			20 28	20 28			20 31	20 35	20 36	20 39	20 43	20 49	20 56
d	19 37									20 01	20 07			20 16	20 20	20 32		20 37				
Manchester Oxford Road a	19 40									20 03	20 09			20 18	20 22	20 36		20 40				
Deansgate a															20 26							

	XC ◇1 L	AW M	TP ◇1 D	VT ◇1	AW ■ N	TP ◇1 G	NT H	VT ◇1	NT J	NT	EM ◇ O	NT K	XC ◇1 B	NT	VT ◇1	NT	XC ◇1 C	NT F	TP ◇1 G	NT H	TP ◇1 P
London Euston ⊖65 d				19 00				19 20							19 40						
Birmingham New Street 68 d	19 31												19 57				20 31				
Wolverhampton 68 d	19 49												20 16				20 49				
Stafford 65,68 d	20 01												20 30				21 01				
Stoke-on-Trent 50,68 d	20 20			20 25				20 48					20 55			20 58	21 21				
Longport 50 d																					
Kidsgrove 50 d																21 05					
Crewe 65 d					20 28									20 50	21 19						
Sandbach d														20 57							
Holmes Chapel d														21 02							
Goostrey d														21 05							
Chelford d														21 09							
Alderley Edge d														21 13							
Wilmslow d					20 45					20 56				21 17	21 34						
Styal d																					
Manchester Airport a										21 05											
Handforth d														21 20							
Congleton d																21 12					
Macclesfield a	20 36			20 41									21 11			21 19	21 38				
d	20 37			20 41									21 12			21 20	21 39				
Prestbury d																21 24					
Adlington (Cheshire) d																21 27					
Poynton d																21 30					
Bramhall d																21 33					
Cheadle Hulme d														21 24		21 37					
Stockport a	20 49			20 55	20 55			21 16					21 27	21 29	21 44	21 41	21 53				
d	20 50		20 53	20 56	20 55		21 12	21 17			21 20	21 21	21 28	21 29	21 45	21 42	21 54			22 12	
Heaton Chapel d							21 16									21 45				22 16	
Levenshulme d							21 19									21 48				22 19	
Manchester Piccadilly a	20 59		21 02	21 07	21 10		21 28	21 28		21 31	21 32	21 35	21 39	21 43	21 53	21 57	22 04			22 28	
d		20 50				21 07			21 20	21 32								22 01	22 07		22 16
Manchester Oxford Road a		20 52				21 09			21 22	21 36								22 03	22 09		22 18
Deansgate a									21 26												

A From Norwich to Liverpool Lime Street
B From Bournemouth
C From Bristol Temple Meads
D From Cleethorpes to Manchester Airport
E From Carmarthen
F From Manchester Airport to Liverpool Lime Street
G From Scarborough to Liverpool Lime Street
H From Buxton
I From Manchester Airport to Carnforth
J From Manchester Airport to Southport
K From Chester
L From Exeter St Davids
M from 25 June. From Manchester Airport to Chester
N From Milford Haven
O From Norwich
P From Manchester Airport to Barrow-in-Furness

Stoke-on-Trent and Crewe - Manchester Airport, Stockport and Manchester

		NT	XC	XC	NT	VT	NT	NT	NT	NT	XC	VT	NT	AW	NT	NT	NT	XC
			◇1	◇1		◇1					◇1	◇1		◇				◇1
			A	B			C	D	E		F		G	H		I		
			✕			☐						☐						
London Euston 15 ⊖65	d					20 20						21 00						
Birmingham New Street 12 68	d		20 57	20 57							21 57							22 31
Wolverhampton 7 68	d		21 16	21 16							22 16							22 49
Stafford 65,68	d		21 30	21 30							22 30	22 34						23 02
Stoke-on-Trent 50,68	d		21 53	21 55		22 05				22 18	22 51							23 21
Longport 50	d																	
Kidsgrove 50	d									22 25								
Crewe 10 65	d				21 50							22 59		23 06			23 12	
Sandbach	d				21 57												23 19	
Holmes Chapel	d				22 02												23 24	
Goostrey	d				22 05												23 27	
Chelford	d				22 09												23 31	
Alderley Edge	d				22 13												23 35	
Wilmslow	d	21 55			22 17							23 15		23 24	23 15		23 39	
Styal	d																	
Manchester Airport ✈	a	22 04													23 23			
Handforth	d				22 20												23 42	
Congleton	d									22 32								
Macclesfield	a		22 10	22 11		22 21				22 39	23 07							23 38
	d		22 11	22 12		22 21				22 40	23 08							23 39
Prestbury	d									22 44								
Adlington (Cheshire)	d									22 47								
Poynton	d									22 50								
Bramhall	d									22 53								
Cheadle Hulme	d				22 24					22 56							23 46	
Stockport	a		22 26	22 27	22 29	22 35				23 01	23 21	23 23		23 32			23 51	23 53
	d		22 27	22 28	22 29	22 36		22 40	22 48	23 01	23 22	23 24	23 22	23 33		23 41	23 51	23 54
Heaton Chapel	d							22 44		23 05							23 55	
Levenshulme	d							22 47		23 08							23 58	
Manchester Piccadilly 10	a	22 31	22 39	22 39	22 43	22 51		22 53	23 00	23 16	23 32	23 35	23 43	23 50	23 51	23 54	00 07	00 10
	d	22 32					22 36	22 54										
Manchester Oxford Road	a	22 36					22 38	22 56										
Deansgate	a						22 41	23 00										

		NT	XC	NT	TP	AW	NT	TP	NT	NT	NT	NT	TP	TP	AW	NT	TP	TP	NT	XC	VT	NT	VT
			◇1		◇1			◇1					◇1	◇1			◇1	◇1		◇1	◇1		◇1
		J	J	K	L		M	N	I	O	P	Q	R	S		I	T	U	V				
																				✕	☐		☐
London Euston 15 ⊖65	d																				08 10		08 20
Birmingham New Street 12 68	d		22p31																	09 01			
Wolverhampton 7 68	d		22p49																	09 19			
Stafford 65,68	d		23p02																	09 33			
Stoke-on-Trent 50,68	d		23p21																				10 21
Longport 50	d																						
Kidsgrove 50	d																						
Crewe 10 65	d	23p12				08 29									09 28					09 56	10 19		
Sandbach	d	23p19																					
Holmes Chapel	d	23p24																					
Goostrey	d	23p27																					
Chelford	d	23p31																					
Alderley Edge	d	23p35									09 19											10 19	
Wilmslow	d	23p39				08 48					09 23				09 48					10 13	10 34	10 23	
Styal	d																						
Manchester Airport ✈	a																						
Handforth	d	23p42									09 26											10 26	
Congleton	d																						
Macclesfield	a		23p38																				10 36
	d		23p39																				10 38
Prestbury	d																						
Adlington (Cheshire)	d																						
Poynton	d																						
Bramhall	d																						
Cheadle Hulme	d	23p46									09 30											10 30	
Stockport	a	23p51	23p53								09 38									10 21	10 43	10 35	10 51
	d	23p51	23p54	00 02	08 31				09 08	09 22	09 40		09 53	09 53		10 04			10 12	10 22	10 44	10 39	10 52
Heaton Chapel	d	23p55							09 12		09 44					10 08						10 43	
Levenshulme	d	23p58							09 15		09 47					10 11						10 46	
Manchester Piccadilly 10	a	00 07	00 10	00 15	08 42	09 06			09 23	09 33	09 54		10 04	10 06	10 12	10 20			10 23	10 37	10 55	10 56	11 04
	d						08 50	09 03		09 35		09 50					10 07	10 12	10 26				
Manchester Oxford Road	a						08 52	09 05		09 37		09 52					10 09	10 14	10 28				
Deansgate	a							09 08		09 40									10 40				

- **A** until 10 September. From Newquay
- **B** from 17 September. From Bournemouth
- **C** From Manchester Airport to Southport
- **D** To Wigan Wallgate
- **E** From Chester
- **F** From Bournemouth
- **G** From Sheffield
- **H** until 30 July, from 17 September. From Maesteg
- **I** From Buxton
- **J** not 22 May
- **K** not 22 May. From Chester
- **L** From Sheffield to Manchester Airport
- **M** until 11 September. From Manchester Airport to Liverpool Lime Street
- **N** until 11 September. From Manchester Airport to Windermere
- **O** To Southport
- **P** until 11 September
- **Q** From Manchester Airport to Liverpool Lime Street
- **R** until 11 September. From Meadowhall
- **S** from 18 September. From Meadowhall
- **T** until 11 September. From York to Liverpool Lime Street
- **U** from 30 October. From York to Liverpool Lime Street
- **V** From Chester to Southport

Stoke-on-Trent and Crewe - Manchester Airport, Stockport and Manchester

		NT	TP	AW	NT	TP	NT	NT	XC	EM	NT	AW	VT	NT	TP	TP	NT	NT	NT	NT	EM	XC	NT
			◇1	◇		◇1			◇1	◇		◇	◇1		◇1	◇1					◇	◇1	
		A	B	C	D	E		F		G		H		A	I	J	D	K	L	M	G	N	
									✕			✕	☐									✕	
London Euston 15 ⊖65	d												09 20										
Birmingham New Street 12 68	d								10 01													11 01	
Wolverhampton 7 68	d								10 19													11 19	
Stafford 65,68	d								10 33													11 32	
Stoke-on-Trent 50,68	d								10 52				11 22									11 52	
Longport 50	d																						
Kidsgrove 50	d																						
Crewe 10 65	d			10 28							10 56	11 23											
Sandbach	d										11 03												
Holmes Chapel	d										11 08												
Goostrey	d										11 11												
Chelford	d										11 15												
Alderley Edge	d						10 40				11 19												12 19
Wilmslow	d			10 47			10 43				11 23	11 42											12 23
Styal	d						10 47																
Manchester Airport ✈	a						10 56																
Handforth	d										11 26												12 26
Congleton	d																						
Macclesfield	a								11 08				11 37									12 09	
	d								11 09				11 38									12 10	
Prestbury	d																						
Adlington (Cheshire)	d																						
Poynton	d																						
Bramhall	d																						
Cheadle Hulme	d										11 30												12 30
Stockport	a			10 58					11 22		11 37		11 51									12 22	12 37
	d		10 53	10 58	11 11			11 15	11 23	11 26	11 37		11 53		11 53		12 11		12 21	12 22	12 26	12 27	12 37
Heaton Chapel	d							11 19			11 41						12 15						12 41
Levenshulme	d							11 22			11 44						12 18						12 44
Manchester Piccadilly 10	a		11 06	11 15	11 23		11 25	11 28	11 31	11 37	11 53	12 02	12 04		12 06		12 25		12 31	12 32	12 37	12 40	12 57
	d	10 50				11 16	11 26	11 33		11 38				11 50		12 07		12 29	12 35	12 36	12 38		
Manchester Oxford Road	a	10 52				11 18	11 30	11 35		11 41				11 52		12 09		12 33	12 37	12 38	12 41		
Deansgate	a							11 40											12 40	12 41			

		NT	TP	VT	AW	TP	NT	NT	TP	NT	EM	XC	VT	NT	NT	TP	AW	TP	NT	VT	NT	EM
			◇1	◇1	◇	◇1			◇1		◇	◇1	◇1			◇1	◇	◇1		◇1		◇
		A	I		H	O	D		P	F	G	Q			A	I	R	O	D		S	T
				☐	✕				✕			✕	☐				✕			☐		
London Euston 15 ⊖65	d			10 20									11 20							12 15		
Birmingham New Street 12 68	d											12 01										
Wolverhampton 7 68	d											12 19										
Stafford 65,68	d											12 33										
Stoke-on-Trent 50,68	d			12 25								12 54	13 11							13 50		
Longport 50	d																					
Kidsgrove 50	d																					
Crewe 10 65	d				12 28									12 56			13 29					
Sandbach	d													13 03								
Holmes Chapel	d													13 08								
Goostrey	d													13 11								
Chelford	d													13 15								
Alderley Edge	d							12 51						13 19								
Wilmslow	d				12 47			12 54						13 23			13 49					
Styal	d							12 58														
Manchester Airport ✈	a							13 05														
Handforth	d													13 26								
Congleton	d																					
Macclesfield	a			12 40								13 10	13 26									
	d			12 42								13 11	13 28									
Prestbury	d																					
Adlington (Cheshire)	d																					
Poynton	d																					
Bramhall	d																					
Cheadle Hulme	d													13 30								
Stockport	a			12 55	12 58							13 28	13 41	13 37			14 00			14 18		
	d		12 53	12 56	12 58		13 12			13 22	13 26	13 29	13 42	13 37		13 53	14 00		14 12	14 19	14 21	14 26
Heaton Chapel	d						13 16							13 41					14 16			
Levenshulme	d						13 19							13 44					14 19			
Manchester Piccadilly 10	a		13 06	13 08	13 15		13 27	13 31		13 33	13 37	13 40	13 53	13 55		14 06	14 19		14 27	14 29	14 33	14 37
	d	12 50				13 07			13 16	13 35	13 38				13 50			14 07			14 35	14 38
Manchester Oxford Road	a	12 52				13 09			13 18	13 37	13 41				13 52			14 09			14 37	14 41
Deansgate	a									13 40											14 40	

- **A** From Manchester Airport to Liverpool Lime Street
- **B** until 11 September. From Sheffield
- **C** From Shrewsbury
- **D** From Buxton
- **E** until 11 September. From Manchester Airport to Arnside
- **F** To Southport
- **G** From Nottingham to Liverpool Lime Street
- **H** From Cardiff Central
- **I** From Cleethorpes to Manchester Airport
- **J** until 11 September, from 30 October. From Newcastle to Liverpool Lime Street
- **K** From Manchester Airport
- **L** from 9 October. From Chester to Southport
- **M** until 2 October. From Chester to Southport
- **N** From Reading
- **O** until 11 September, from 30 October. From Scarborough to Liverpool Lime Street
- **P** from 24 July until 11 September. From Manchester Airport to Barrow-in-Furness
- **Q** From Southampton Central
- **R** From Carmarthen
- **S** From Chester to Southport
- **T** From Norwich to Liverpool Lime Street

Table 84

Sundays

Stoke-on-Trent and Crewe - Manchester Airport, Stockport and Manchester

	XC	VT	NT	XC	NT	TP	VT	AW	TP	NT	VT	NT	TP	NT	EM	XC	VT	NT	XC	NT	TP	VT
	◇1	◇1		◇1		◇1	◇1	◇	◇1		◇1		◇1		◇	◇1	◇1		◇1		◇1	◇1
	A				B	C		D	E	F			G	H	I	A			J	B	K	
London Euston ⊖65 d		12 35					12 55				13 15						13 35					13 55
Birmingham New Street 68 d	13 01			13 31												14 01			14 31			
Wolverhampton 68 d	13 19			13 49												14 19			14 49			
Stafford 65,68 d	13 34															14 34						
Stoke-on-Trent 50,68 d	13 57			14 21			14 26				14 50					14 57			15 21			15 26
Longport 50 d																						
Kidsgrove 50 d																						
Crewe 65 d		14 13						14 28									15 13	14 56				
Sandbach d																		15 03				
Holmes Chapel d																		15 08				
Goostrey d																		15 11				
Chelford d																		15 15				
Alderley Edge d			14 19									14 51						15 19				
Wilmslow d		14 29	14 23					14 47				14 54					15 29	15 23				
Styal d												14 58										
Manchester Airport a												15 05										
Handforth d			14 26															15 26				
Congleton d																						
Macclesfield a	14 14						14 42									15 14						15 42
d	14 15						14 42									15 15						15 42
Prestbury d																						
Adlington (Cheshire) d																						
Poynton d																						
Bramhall d																						
Cheadle Hulme d			14 30															15 30				
Stockport a	14 28	14 38	14 37				14 56	14 58			15 18					15 28	15 38	15 37				15 56
d	14 29	14 39	14 37			14 53	14 57	14 58		15 12	15 19			15 22	15 26	15 29	15 39	15 37			15 53	15 57
Heaton Chapel d			14 41							15 16								15 41				
Levenshulme d			14 44							15 19								15 44				
Manchester Piccadilly a	14 40	14 50	14 53	14 57		15 06	15 09	15 15		15 27	15 29	15 32		15 33	15 37	15 40	15 50	15 53	16 00		16 06	16 09
d					14 50				15 07				15 16	15 35	15 38					15 50		
Manchester Oxford Road a					14 52				15 09				15 18	15 37	15 41					15 52		
Deansgate a														15 40								

	AW	TP	NT	VT	NT	EM	XC	VT	NT	NT	XC	XC	NT	TP	VT	AW	TP	NT	VT	NT	TP
	◇	◇1		◇1		◇	◇1	◇1			◇1	◇1		◇1	◇1	■	◇1		◇1		◇1
	L	M	F		N	O	A				P	Q	B	K		D	E	F			R
London Euston ⊖65 d				14 15				14 35							14 55				15 15		
Birmingham New Street 68 d							15 01				15 31	15 31									
Wolverhampton 68 d							15 19				15 49	15 49									
Stafford 65,68 d							15 34														
Stoke-on-Trent 50,68 d				15 50			15 57			16 01	16 21	16 21			16 25				16 50		
Longport 50 d																					
Kidsgrove 50 d										16 08											
Crewe 65 d	15 28							16 13								16 28					
Sandbach d																					
Holmes Chapel d																					
Goostrey d																					
Chelford d																					
Alderley Edge d									16 19											16 51	
Wilmslow d	15 47							16 29	16 23							16 47				16 54	
Styal d																				16 58	
Manchester Airport a																				17 05	
Handforth d									16 26												
Congleton d										16 15											
Macclesfield a							16 14			16 22					16 42						
d							16 15			16 23					16 42						
Prestbury d										16 27											
Adlington (Cheshire) d										16 30											
Poynton d										16 33											
Bramhall d										16 36											
Cheadle Hulme d									16 30	16 39											
Stockport a	15 58			16 18			16 28	16 38	16 37	16 44					16 56	16 58			17 18		
d	15 58		16 12	16 19	16 21	16 26	16 29	16 39	16 37	16 44				16 53	16 57	16 58		17 12	17 19		
Heaton Chapel d			16 16						16 41									17 16			
Levenshulme d			16 19						16 44									17 19			
Manchester Piccadilly a	16 17		16 27	16 29	16 33	16 37	16 40	16 50	16 53	16 58	16 59	17 00		17 06	17 09	17 15		17 27	17 29	17 31	
d		16 07			16 35	16 38							16 50				17 07				17 16
Manchester Oxford Road a		16 09			16 37	16 41							16 52				17 09				17 18
Deansgate a					16 40																

A From Bournemouth
B From Manchester Airport to Liverpool Lime Street
C From Doncaster to Manchester Airport
D From Cardiff Central
E until 11 September, from 30 October. From Middlesbrough to Liverpool Lime Street
F From Buxton
G From Manchester Airport to Barrow-in-Furness
H To Southport
I From Norwich to Liverpool Lime Street
J From Paignton
K From Cleethorpes to Manchester Airport
L From Milford Haven
M until 11 September, from 30 October. From Scarborough to Liverpool Lime Street
N From Chester to Southport
O From Nottingham to Liverpool Lime Street
P from 26 June. From Plymouth
Q until 19 June. From Paignton
R until 17 July, from 18 September until 23 October. From Manchester Airport to Barrow-in-Furness

Table 84

Sundays

Stoke-on-Trent and Crewe - Manchester Airport, Stockport and Manchester

	NT	EM	XC	VT	NT	XC	NT	TP	VT	AW	TP	NT	VT	NT	EM	XC	VT	NT	XC	NT	TP	VT
		◇	◇1	◇1		◇1		◇1	◇1	■	◇1		◇1		◇	◇1	◇1		◇1		◇1	◇1
	A	B	C			D	E	F		G	H	I		J	K	C			L	E	F	
London Euston ⊖65 d				15 35					15 55				16 15				16 35					16 55
Birmingham New Street 68 d			16 01			16 31										17 01			17 31			
Wolverhampton 68 d			16 19			16 49										17 19			17 49			
Stafford 65,68 d			16 34													17 36						
Stoke-on-Trent 50,68 d			16 57			17 21			17 26				17 50			17 57			18 21			18 26
Longport 50 d																						
Kidsgrove 50 d																						
Crewe 65 d				17 13	16 56					17 28							18 13					
Sandbach d					17 03																	
Holmes Chapel d					17 08																	
Goostrey d					17 11																	
Chelford d					17 15																	
Alderley Edge d					17 19													18 19				
Wilmslow d				17 29	17 23					17 45							18 29	18 23				
Styal d																						
Manchester Airport a																						
Handforth d					17 26													18 26				
Congleton d																						
Macclesfield a			17 14						17 42							18 14						18 42
d			17 15						17 42							18 15						18 42
Prestbury d																						
Adlington (Cheshire) d																						
Poynton d																						
Bramhall d																						
Cheadle Hulme d					17 30													18 30				
Stockport a			17 28	17 38	17 37				17 56	17 58			18 18			18 28	18 38	18 37				18 56
d	17 22	17 27	17 29	17 39	17 37			17 53	17 57	17 58		18 12	18 19	18 21	18 26	18 29	18 39	18 37			18 53	18 57
Heaton Chapel d					17 41							18 16						18 41				
Levenshulme d					17 44							18 19						18 44				
Manchester Piccadilly a	17 33	17 37	17 40	17 50	17 53	17 56		18 06	18 09	18 17		18 27	18 29	18 33	18 37	18 40	18 50	18 53	18 56		19 06	19 09
d	17 35	17 38					17 50				18 07			18 35	18 38					18 50		
Manchester Oxford Road a	17 37	17 41					17 52				18 09			18 37	18 41					18 52		
Deansgate a	17 40													18 40								

	AW	TP	NT	VT	NT	TP	NT	EM	XC	VT	NT	XC	NT	TP	VT	AW	TP	NT	VT	NT	EM	XC
	■	◇1		◇1		◇1		◇	◇1	◇1		◇1		◇1	◇1	■	◇1		◇1		◇	◇1
	M	N	I			O	A	K	C			P	E	F		G	H	I		J	Q	C
London Euston ⊖65 d				17 15						17 35					17 55				18 15			
Birmingham New Street 68 d									18 01			18 31										19 01
Wolverhampton 68 d									18 19			18 49										19 19
Stafford 65,68 d									18 36													19 38
Stoke-on-Trent 50,68 d				18 50					18 57			19 21			19 26				19 50			19 57
Longport 50 d																						
Kidsgrove 50 d																						
Crewe 65 d	18 28									19 13	18 56					19 28						
Sandbach d											19 03											
Holmes Chapel d											19 08											
Goostrey d											19 11											
Chelford d											19 15											
Alderley Edge d					18 51						19 19											
Wilmslow d	18 47				18 54					19 29	19 23					19 47						
Styal d					18 58																	
Manchester Airport a					19 05																	
Handforth d											19 26											
Congleton d																						
Macclesfield a									19 15						19 42							20 14
d									19 15						19 42							20 15
Prestbury d																						
Adlington (Cheshire) d																						
Poynton d																						
Bramhall d																						
Cheadle Hulme d											19 30											
Stockport a	18 58			19 18					19 28	19 38	19 37				19 56	19 58			20 18			20 28
d	18 58		19 12	19 19			19 22	19 26	19 29	19 39	19 37			19 55	19 57	19 58		20 12	20 19	20 21	20 26	20 29
Heaton Chapel d			19 16								19 41							20 16				
Levenshulme d			19 19								19 44							20 19				
Manchester Piccadilly a	19 15		19 27	19 29	19 31		19 33	19 37	19 40	19 50	19 53	19 58		20 09	20 09	20 17		20 27	20 29	20 33	20 38	20 40
d		19 07				19 16	19 35	19 38					19 50				20 07			20 35		
Manchester Oxford Road a		19 09				19 18	19 37	19 41					19 52				20 09			20 37		
Deansgate a							19 40													20 40		

A To Southport
B From Nottingham to Liverpool Lime Street
C From Bournemouth
D From Plymouth
E From Manchester Airport to Liverpool Lime Street
F From Cleethorpes to Manchester Airport
G From Milford Haven
H until 11 September, from 30 October. From Scarborough to Liverpool Lime Street
I From Buxton
J From Chester to Southport
K From Norwich to Liverpool Lime Street
L From Bristol Temple Meads
M From Cardiff Central
N until 11 September, from 30 October. From Middlesbrough to Liverpool Lime Street
O From Manchester Airport to Barrow-in-Furness
P From Penzance
Q From Norwich

Stoke-on-Trent and Crewe - Manchester Airport, Stockport and Manchester

Station		VT	NT	NT	XC	NT	TP	VT	AW	TP	NT	VT	NT	NT	EM	XC	VT	NT	XC	XC	NT	TP
					A	B	C		D	E	F			G	H	I			J	K	B	C
London Euston ⊖65	d	18 35						18 55				19 15					19 35					
Birmingham New Street 68	d				19 31											20 01			20 31	20 31		
Wolverhampton 68	d				19 49											20 19			20 52	20 52		
Stafford 65,68	d															20 37						
Stoke-on-Trent 50,68	d			20 01	20 21			20 26				20 50				20 57			21 21	21 21		
Longport 50	d																					
Kidsgrove 50	d			20 08																		
Crewe 65	d	20 13							20 28								21 14	20 56				
Sandbach	d																	21 03				
Holmes Chapel	d																	21 08				
Goostrey	d																	21 11				
Chelford	d																	21 15				
Alderley Edge	d		20 19										20 51					21 19				
Wilmslow	d	20 29	20 23						20 46				20 54				21 30	21 23				
Styal	d												20 58									
Manchester Airport	a												21 05									
Handforth	d		20 26															21 26				
Congleton	d			20 15																		
Macclesfield	a			20 22				20 42								21 15						
	d			20 23				20 42								21 15						
Prestbury	d			20 27																		
Adlington (Cheshire)	d			20 30																		
Poynton	d			20 33																		
Bramhall	d			20 36																		
Cheadle Hulme	d		20 30	20 39														21 30				
Stockport	a	20 38	20 37	20 44				20 56	20 58			21 18				21 28	21 39	21 37				
	d	20 39	20 37	20 44			20 53	20 57	20 58		21 12	21 19		21 22	21 24	21 29	21 40	21 37				21 53
Heaton Chapel	d		20 41								21 16							21 41				
Levenshulme	d		20 44								21 19							21 44				
Manchester Piccadilly	a	20 50	20 53	20 58	21 00		21 06	21 09	21 14		21 27	21 29	21 31	21 33	21 36	21 40	21 50	21 53	21 56	21 56		22 06
	d					20 50				21 07				21 35							21 50	
Manchester Oxford Road	a					20 52				21 09				21 37							21 52	
Deansgate	a													21 40								

Station		VT	AW	TP	NT	VT	NT	XC	NT	VT	NT	NT	NT	NT	NT	XC	NT	VT	VT
			L	M	F		N	I			B	F	O			I			
London Euston ⊖65	d	19 55				20 15				20 35								21 25	21 51
Birmingham New Street 68	d							21 01								22 01			
Wolverhampton 68	d							21 19								22 19			
Stafford 65,68	d							21 37		22 00						22 37			23s53
Stoke-on-Trent 50,68	d	21 26				21 50		21 57							22 39	22 57		23 29	
Longport 50	d																		
Kidsgrove 50	d														22 46				
Crewe 65	d		21 28							22 21							22 56		00s12
Sandbach	d																23 03		
Holmes Chapel	d																23 08		
Goostrey	d																23 11		
Chelford	d																23 15		
Alderley Edge	d								22 19					22 51			23 19		
Wilmslow	d		21 45						22 23	22 36				22 54			23 23		
Styal	d													22 58					
Manchester Airport	a													23 05					
Handforth	d								22 26								23 26		
Congleton	d														22 53				
Macclesfield	a	21 42						22 14							23 00	23 12		23 45	
	d	21 42						22 15							23 01	23 13		23 46	
Prestbury	d														23 05				
Adlington (Cheshire)	d														23 08				
Poynton	d														23 11				
Bramhall	d														23 14				
Cheadle Hulme	d								22 30						23 17		23 30		
Stockport	a	21 56	21 58			22 18		22 28	22 37	22 45					23 22	23 27	23 35	23 59	00s41
	d	21 57	21 58		22 12	22 19	22 21	22 29	22 37	22 46		23 12	23 16		23 23	23 28	23 37	00 01	
Heaton Chapel	d				22 16				22 41			23 16					23 41		
Levenshulme	d				22 19				22 44			23 19					23 44		
Manchester Piccadilly	a	22 09	22 19		22 27	22 29	22 33	22 40	22 53	22 57		23 27	23 29	23 32	23 37	23 41	23 53	00 12	00 53
	d			22 07			22 35				22 50								
Manchester Oxford Road	a			22 09			22 37				22 52								
Deansgate	a						22 40												

A From Bristol Temple Meads
B From Manchester Airport to Liverpool Lime Street
C From Cleethorpes to Manchester Airport
D From Cardiff Central
E until 11 September, from 30 October. From Middlesbrough to Liverpool Lime Street
F From Buxton
G To Wigan Wallgate
H From Norwich
I From Bournemouth
J until 19 June, from 7 August. From Bristol Temple Meads
K from 26 June until 31 July
L From Milford Haven
M until 11 September, from 30 October. From Scarborough to Liverpool Lime Street
N From Chester to Wigan Wallgate
O From Sheffield

Manchester, Stockport and Manchester Airport - Crewe and Stoke-on-Trent

Miles	Miles	Miles	Station		NT MX	NT MO	NT	TP	AW	XC MTO	XC	VT	NT	TP	NT	VT	NT	XC	NT	NT	VT	TP	NT
						A	A	B	C	D	E			F	G		A	H				B	
0	0	—	Deansgate	d																			
0½	0½	—	**Manchester Oxford Road**	d		23p59																	
1	1	—	**Manchester Piccadilly**	a		00 02																	
—	—	—		d	23p38	00 04	04 15	04 44	04 49	05 00	05 00	05 05	05 35	05 44	05 50	05 55	05 58	06 00		06 06	06 10	06 12	06 15
4	4	—	Levenshulme	d	23p43															06 11			
5½	5½	—	Heaton Chapel	d	23p46															06 14			
7	7	—	**Stockport**	a	23p50							05 12		05 52	05 59	06 02		06 07		06 18	06 17		
—	—	—		d	23p50							05 13				06 03		06 08		06 19	06 18		
9¼	9¼	—	Cheadle Hulme	d	23p54															06 26			
9¾	—	—	Bramhall	d																			
12¼	—	—	Poynton	d																			
14¼	—	—	Adlington (Cheshire)	d																			
16¼	—	—	Prestbury	d																			
19	—	—	**Macclesfield**	a																	06 30		
—	—	—		d															06 03		06 31		
27	—	—	Congleton	d															06 10				
—	11½	—	Handforth	d	23p58															06 30			
—	—	0	**Manchester Airport**	d		00a19	04a30	05a00	05a09				06 05				06a14					06a29	06a39
—	—	2¼	Styal	d																			
—	13	4	**Wilmslow**	d	00 01								06 17			06 11				06 34			
—	14¾	—	Alderley Edge	d	00 04								06 20							06 37			
—	17¾	—	Chelford	d	00 08								06 24										
—	21½	—	Goostrey	d	00 12								06 29										
—	23½	—	Holmes Chapel	d	00 15								06 32							06 47			
—	27¼	—	Sandbach	d	00 20								06 36							06 53			
—	32	—	**Crewe** 65	a	00 30					05 43	05 44	05 34	06 46			06 27		06 32		07 04			
32½	—	—	Kidsgrove 50	a															06 16				
35¼	—	—	Longport 50	a																			
38¾	—	—	**Stoke-on-Trent** 50,68	a						06 06	06 06								06 26		06 46		
—	—	—	Stafford 68	a						06 24	06 24	05 53						06 57					
—	—	—	Wolverhampton 68	a						06 39	06 39							07 12					
—	—	—	Birmingham New Street 68	a						06 58	06 58							07 31					
—	—	—	London Euston ⊖65	a								07 28				08 07					08 22		

Station		NT	NT	VT	AW	NT	VT	VT	NT	NT	VT	NT	NT	TP	XC	NT	VT	NT	TP	NT	XC	AW	VT
		I	J		K					L		A		M	H			I	F	N	D	O	
Deansgate	d																			07 11			
Manchester Oxford Road	d											06 58								07 15			
Manchester Piccadilly	a											07 01								07 17			
	d	06 17	06 21	06 27	06 30	06 32	06 35	06 43	06 46	06 49	07 00	07 03	07 03	07 06	07 06	07 14	07 15	07 17	07 20	07 21	07 26	07 30	07 35
Levenshulme	d		06 28			06 37				06 55			07 09							07 28			
Heaton Chapel	d		06 31			06 40				06 58			07 12							07 31			
Stockport	a	06 27	06 34	06 34	06 38	06 44	06 43	06 50		07 01			07 16		07 15		07 22	07 26	07 28	07 34	07 34	07 38	07 43
	d			06 35	06 39	06 45	06 43	06 51			07u07		07 18		07 16		07 23				07 35	07 39	07 43
Cheadle Hulme	d					06 51							07 24										
Bramhall	d					06 54																	
Poynton	d					06 57																	
Adlington (Cheshire)	d					07 01																	
Prestbury	d					07 04																	
Macclesfield	a			06 47		07 07	06 55														07 47		07 56
	d			06 48		07 08	06 56														07 49		07 56
Congleton	d					07 15																	
Handforth	d												07 28										
Manchester Airport	d								07 11			07a22		07a29		07a38							
Styal	d																						
Wilmslow	d				06 46			06 59	07 21				07 31									07 46	
Alderley Edge	d								07 24				07 34										
Chelford	d												07 38										
Goostrey	d												07 43										
Holmes Chapel	d								07 32				07 46										
Sandbach	d								07 36				07 51										
Crewe 65	a				07 05			07 15	07 46				08 01									08 05	
Kidsgrove 50	a																						
Longport 50	a																						
Stoke-on-Trent 50,68	a			07 04		07 30	07 11								07 43		07 48				08 06		08 12
Stafford 68	a			07 27				07 34							08 01						08 24		
Wolverhampton 68	a			07 43											08 15						08 39		
Birmingham New Street 68	a			08 05											08 32						08 58		
London Euston ⊖65	a			09 34			08 45	08 52			08 58						09 23						09 52

A From Liverpool Lime Street
B From Sheffield
C From Chester
D To Bournemouth
E WThFO. To Bournemouth
F From Manchester Airport to Cleethorpes
G To Sheffield
H To Bristol Temple Meads
I To Chester
J To Hazel Grove
K To Cardiff Central
L To Buxton
M From Doncaster
N From Wigan Wallgate to Hazel Grove
O To Carmarthen

Table 84

Mondays to Fridays

Manchester, Stockport and Manchester Airport - Crewe and Stoke-on-Trent

Station		NT A	NT	EM ◇ B	NT [1]	NT [1]	NT C	VT ◇[1] ⊠	NT D	NT	TP ◇[1] E 🍴	XC ◇[1] F 🍴	NT [1]	VT ◇[1] ⊠	NT G	TP ◇[1] H 🍴	XC ◇[1] I 🍴	AW ◇ J 🍴	VT ◇[1] ⊠	NT K	NT	EM ◇ B	NT [1]
Deansgate 🚊	d	07 28																		08 29			
Manchester Oxford Road	d	07 32		07 38					07 58											08 33		08 39	
Manchester Piccadilly [10] 🚊	a	07 34		07 41					08 01											08 35		08 41	
	d	07 36	07 38	07 42	07 46	07 48	07 52	07 55	08 03	08 04	08 06	08 07	08 14	08 15	08 17	08 20	08 27	08 30	08 35	08 37	08 38	08 43	08 46
Levenshulme	d		07 43							08 09											08 43		
Heaton Chapel	d		07 46							08 12											08 46		
Stockport	a		07 50	07 53		07 57	08 01	08 03		08 16		08 15		08 22	08 27	08 28	08 34	08 38	08 42		08 50	08 53	
	d		07 51			07 58		08 04		08 17		08 16		08 23			08 35	08 39	08 43		08 51		
Cheadle Hulme	d		07 55			08 02				08 24											08 55		
Bramhall	d					08 05																	
Poynton	d					08 08																	
Adlington (Cheshire)	d					08 11																	
Prestbury	d					08 14																	
Macclesfield	a					08 18											08 47		08 55				
	d					08 18											08 49		08 56				
Congleton	d					08 26																	
Handforth	d		07 59							08 28											08 59		
Manchester Airport ✈	d	07a53			08 11				08a22		08a26		08a38							08a53			09 11
Styal	d				08 18																		
Wilmslow	d		08 02		08 22			08 11		08 31								08 46			09 02		09 21
Alderley Edge	d		08a08		08 25					08 34											09 05		09 24
Chelford	d									08 38													
Goostrey	d									08 43													
Holmes Chapel	d				08 33					08 46													09 32
Sandbach	d				08 37					08 52													09 36
Crewe [10] 65	a				08 47			08 27		09 04								09 05			09 23		09 46
Kidsgrove 50	a					08 32																	
Longport 50	a																						
Stoke-on-Trent 50,68	a					08 42						08 43		08 48			09 06		09 11				
Stafford 68	a											09 02					09 24						
Wolverhampton [7] 68 🚊	a											09 15					09 39						
Birmingham New Street [12] 68	a											09 39					09 58						
London Euston [15] ⊖65	a							10 04						10 23					10 42				

Station		NT [1]	NT C	VT ◇[1] ⊠	NT D	NT	TP ◇[1] E 🍴	XC ◇[1] L 🍴	NT [1]	VT ◇[1] ⊠	NT G	TP ◇[1] H 🍴	XC ◇[1] I 🍴	AW ◇ M 🍴	VT ◇[1] ⊠	NT K	NT	EM ◇ B	NT [1]	NT [1]	NT C	VT ◇[1] ⊠
Deansgate 🚊	d															09 29						
Manchester Oxford Road	d				08 58											09 33		09 39				
Manchester Piccadilly [10] 🚊	a				09 01											09 35		09 41				
	d	08 48	08 52	08 55	09 03	09 04	09 06	09 07	09 14	09 15	09 17	09 20	09 27	09 30	09 35	09 37	09 38	09 43	09 46	09 48	09 52	09 55
Levenshulme	d		08 58			09 09											09 43				09 58	
Heaton Chapel	d		09 01			09 12											09 46				10 01	
Stockport	a	08 57	09 04	09 03		09 16		09 15		09 22	09 27	09 28	09 34	09 38	09 42		09 50	09 53		09 57	10 04	10 03
	d	08 58		09 04		09 17		09 16		09 23			09 35	09 39	09 43		09 51			09 58		10 04
Cheadle Hulme	d	09 02				09 24											09 55			10 02		
Bramhall	d	09 05																		10 05		
Poynton	d	09 08																		10 08		
Adlington (Cheshire)	d	09 11																		10 11		
Prestbury	d	09 14																		10 14		
Macclesfield	a	09 18											09 47		09 55					10 18		
	d	09 18											09 49		09 56					10 18		
Congleton	d	09 26																		10 26		
Handforth	d					09 28											09 59					
Manchester Airport ✈	d				09a22		09a33		09a38							09a53			10 11			
Styal	d																					
Wilmslow	d			09 11		09 31								09 46			10 02		10 21			10 11
Alderley Edge	d					09 34											10a08		10 24			
Chelford	d					09 38																
Goostrey	d					09 43																
Holmes Chapel	d					09 46													10 32			
Sandbach	d					09 51													10 36			
Crewe [10] 65	a			09 27		10 01								10 05					10 46			10 27
Kidsgrove 50	a	09 32																		10 32		
Longport 50	a																					
Stoke-on-Trent 50,68	a	09 42						09 43		09 48			10 06		10 11					10 42		
Stafford 68	a							10 02					10 24									
Wolverhampton [7] 68 🚊	a							10 15					10 39									
Birmingham New Street [12] 68	a							10 39					10 58									
London Euston [15] ⊖65	a			11 04						11 23					11 42							12 04

A From Southport
B From Liverpool Lime Street to Norwich
C To Buxton
D From Liverpool Lime Street
E From Cleethorpes
F To Paignton
G To Chester
H From Manchester Airport to Cleethorpes
I To Bournemouth
J To Milford Haven
K until 30 September. From Southport
L To Bristol Temple Meads
M To Carmarthen

Table 84

Mondays to Fridays

Manchester, Stockport and Manchester Airport - Crewe and Stoke-on-Trent

Station		NT A	NT	TP ◇[1] B 🍴	XC ◇[1] C 🍴	NT [1]	VT ◇[1] ⊠	NT D	TP ◇[1] E 🍴	XC ◇[1] F 🍴	AW ◇ G 🍴	VT ◇[1] ⊠	NT H	NT	EM ◇ I	NT [1]	NT [1]	NT J	VT ◇[1] ⊠	NT A	NT	TP ◇[1] B 🍴	XC ◇[1] C 🍴
Deansgate 🚊	d												10 29										
Manchester Oxford Road	d	09 58											10 33		10 39					10 58			
Manchester Piccadilly [10] 🚊	a	10 01											10 35		10 41					11 01			
	d	10 03	10 04	10 06	10 07	10 14	10 15	10 17	10 20	10 27	10 30	10 35	10 37	10 38	10 43	10 46	10 48	10 52	10 55	11 03	11 04	11 06	11 07
Levenshulme	d		10 09											10 43				10 58			11 09		
Heaton Chapel	d		10 12											10 46				11 01			11 12		
Stockport	a		10 16		10 15		10 22	10 27	10 28	10 34	10 38	10 42		10 50	10 53		10 57	11 04	11 03		11 16		11 15
	d		10 17		10 16		10 23			10 35	10 39	10 43		10 51			10 58		11 04		11 17		11 16
Cheadle Hulme	d		10 24											10 55			11 02				11 24		
Bramhall	d																11 05						
Poynton	d																11 08						
Adlington (Cheshire)	d																11 11						
Prestbury	d																11 14						
Macclesfield	a									10 47		10 55					11 18						
	d									10 49		10 56					11 18						
Congleton	d																11 26						
Handforth	d		10 28											10 59							11 28		
Manchester Airport ✈	d	10a22		10a26		10a38							10a53			11 11				11a22		11a26	
Styal	d																						
Wilmslow	d		10 31								10 46			11 02		11 21			11 11		11 31		
Alderley Edge	d		10 34											11a08		11 24					11 34		
Chelford	d		10 38																		11 38		
Goostrey	d		10 43																		11 43		
Holmes Chapel	d		10 46													11 32					11 46		
Sandbach	d		10 51													11 36					11 51		
Crewe [10] 65	a		11 01								11 05					11 46			11 27		12 01		
Kidsgrove 50	a																11 32						
Longport 50	a																						
Stoke-on-Trent 50,68	a				10 43		10 48			11 06		11 11					11 42						11 43
Stafford 68	a				11 01					11 24													12 02
Wolverhampton [7] 68 🚊	a				11 15					11 39													12 15
Birmingham New Street [12] 68	a				11 32					11 58													12 39
London Euston [15] ⊖65	a						12 23					12 42							13 03				

Station		NT [1]	VT ◇[1] ⊡	NT D	TP ◇[1] E 🍴	XC ◇[1] F 🍴	AW ◇ K 🍴	VT ◇[1] ⊡	NT H	NT	EM ◇ I	NT [1]	NT [1]	NT J	VT ◇[1] ⊡	NT A	NT	TP ◇[1] B 🍴	XC ◇[1] L 🍴	NT [1]	VT ◇[1] ⊡	NT D
Deansgate 🚊	d								11 29													
Manchester Oxford Road	d								11 33		11 39					11 58						
Manchester Piccadilly [10] 🚊	a								11 35		11 41					12 01						
	d	11 14	11 15	11 17	11 20	11 27	11 30	11 35	11 37	11 38	11 43	11 46	11 48	11 52	11 55	12 03	12 04	12 06	12 07	12 14	12 15	12 17
Levenshulme	d									11 43				11 58			12 09					
Heaton Chapel	d									11 46				12 01			12 12					
Stockport	a		11 22	11 27	11 28	11 34	11 38	11 42		11 50	11 53		11 57	12 04	12 03		12 16		12 15		12 22	12 27
	d		11 23			11 35	11 39	11 43		11 51			11 58		12 04		12 17		12 16		12 23	
Cheadle Hulme	d									11 55			12 02				12 24					
Bramhall	d												12 05									
Poynton	d												12 08									
Adlington (Cheshire)	d												12 11									
Prestbury	d												12 14									
Macclesfield	a					11 47		11 55					12 18									
	d					11 49		11 56					12 18									
Congleton	d												12 26									
Handforth	d									11 59							12 28					
Manchester Airport ✈	d	11a38							11a53			12 11				12a22		12a26		12a38		
Styal	d																					
Wilmslow	d						11 46			12 02		12 21			12 11		12 31					
Alderley Edge	d									12a08		12 24					12 34					
Chelford	d																12 38					
Goostrey	d																12 43					
Holmes Chapel	d											12 32					12 46					
Sandbach	d											12 36					12 51					
Crewe [10] 65	a						12 05					12 46			12 27		13 01					
Kidsgrove 50	a												12 32									
Longport 50	a																					
Stoke-on-Trent 50,68	a		11 48			12 06		12 11					12 42						12 43		12 48	
Stafford 68	a					12 24																
Wolverhampton [7] 68 🚊	a					12 39													13 13			
Birmingham New Street [12] 68	a					12 58													13 31			
London Euston [15] ⊖65	a		13 23					13 42							14 04						14 23	

A From Liverpool Lime Street
B From Cleethorpes
C To Bristol Temple Meads
D To Chester
E From Manchester Airport to Cleethorpes
F To Bournemouth
G To Milford Haven
H until 30 September. From Southport
I From Liverpool Lime Street to Norwich
J To Buxton
K To Carmarthen
L To Exeter St Davids

Manchester, Stockport and Manchester Airport - Crewe and Stoke-on-Trent

	TP	XC	AW	VT	NT	NT	EM	NT	NT	NT	VT	NT	NT	TP	XC	NT	VT	NT	TP	XC	AW	VT
	◇1 A ✕	◇1 B ✕	■ C ✕	◇1 ☐	D		◇ E	1	1	F	◇1 ☐	G		◇1 H ✕	◇1 I ✕	1	◇1 ☐	J	◇1 A ✕	◇1 B ✕	■ K ✕	◇1 ☐
Deansgate d					12 29																	
Manchester Oxford Road d					12 33		12 39					12 58										
Manchester Piccadilly 10 a					12 35		12 41					13 01										
d	12 20	12 27	12 30	12 35	12 37	12 38	12 43	12 46	12 48	12 52	12 55	13 03	13 04	13 06	13 07	13 14	13 15	13 17	13 20	13 27	13 30	13 35
Levenshulme d						12 43				12 58			13 09									
Heaton Chapel d						12 46				13 01			13 12									
Stockport a	12 28	12 34	12 38	12 42		12 50	12 53		12 57	13 04	13 03		13 16		13 15		13 22	13 27	13 28	13 34	13 38	13 42
d		12 35	12 39	12 43		12 51			12 58		13 04		13 17		13 16		13 23			13 35	13 39	13 43
Cheadle Hulme d						12 55			13 02				13 24									
Bramhall d									13 05													
Poynton d									13 08													
Adlington (Cheshire) d									13 11													
Prestbury d									13 14													
Macclesfield a		12 47		12 55					13 18											13 47		13 55
d		12 49		12 56					13 18											13 49		13 56
Congleton d									13 26													
Handforth d						12 59							13 28									
Manchester Airport d					12a53			13 11				13a22		13a26		13a38						
Styal d								13 18														
Wilmslow d			12 46			13 02		13 22			13 11		13 31								13 46	
Alderley Edge d						13a08		13 25					13 34									
Chelford d													13 38									
Goostrey d													13 43									
Holmes Chapel d								13 33					13 46									
Sandbach d								13 37					13 51									
Crewe 10 65 a			13 05					13 47			13 27		14 01								14 05	
Kidsgrove 50 a									13 32													
Longport 50 a																						
Stoke-on-Trent 50,68 a		13 06		13 11					13 42						13 43		13 48			14 06		14 11
Stafford 68 a		13 24													14 01					14 24		
Wolverhampton 7 68 a		13 39													14 15					14 39		
Birmingham New Street 12 68 a		13 58													14 32					14 58		
London Euston 15 ⊖65 a				14 42							15 04						15 23					15 42

	NT	NT	EM	NT	NT	NT	VT	NT	NT	TP	XC	NT	VT	NT	TP	XC	AW	VT	NT	NT	EM	NT
	D		◇ E	1	1	F	◇1 ☐	G		◇1 H ✕	◇1 L ✕	1	◇1 ☐	J	◇1 A ✕	◇1 B ✕	■ C ✕	◇1 ☐	D		◇ M	1
Deansgate d	13 29																		14 29			
Manchester Oxford Road d	13 33		13 39					13 58											14 33		14 39	
Manchester Piccadilly 10 a	13 35		13 41					14 01											14 35		14 41	
d	13 37	13 38	13 43	13 46	13 48	13 52	13 55	14 03	14 04	14 06	14 07	14 14	14 15	14 17	14 20	14 27	14 30	14 35	14 37	14 38	14 43	14 46
Levenshulme d		13 43				13 58			14 09											14 43		
Heaton Chapel d		13 46				14 01			14 12											14 46		
Stockport a		13 50	13 53		13 57	14 04	14 03		14 16		14 15		14 22	14 27	14 28	14 34	14 38	14 42		14 50	14 53	
d		13 51			13 58		14 04		14 17		14 16		14 23			14 35	14 39	14 43		14 51		
Cheadle Hulme d		13 55			14 02				14 24											14 55		
Bramhall d					14 05																	
Poynton d					14 08																	
Adlington (Cheshire) d					14 11																	
Prestbury d					14 14																	
Macclesfield a					14 18											14 47		14 55				
d					14 18											14 49		14 56				
Congleton d					14 26																	
Handforth d		13 59							14 28											14 59		
Manchester Airport d	13a53			14 11				14a22		14a26		14a38							14a53			15 11
Styal d																						
Wilmslow d		14 02		14 21			14 11		14 31								14 46			15 02		15 21
Alderley Edge d		14a08		14 24					14 34											15a08		15 24
Chelford d									14 38													
Goostrey d									14 43													
Holmes Chapel d				14 32					14 46													15 32
Sandbach d				14 36					14 51													15 36
Crewe 10 65 a				14 46			14 27		15 01								15 05					15 46
Kidsgrove 50 a					14 32																	
Longport 50 a																						
Stoke-on-Trent 50,68 a					14 42						14 43		14 48			15 06		15 11				
Stafford 68 a											15 02					15 24						
Wolverhampton 7 68 a											15 15					15 39						
Birmingham New Street 12 68 a											15 39					15 58						
London Euston 15 ⊖65 a							16 04						16 23					16 42				

A From Manchester Airport to Cleethorpes
B To Bournemouth
C To Milford Haven
D until 30 September. From Southport
E From Liverpool Lime Street to Norwich
F To Buxton
G From Liverpool Lime Street
H From Cleethorpes
I To Bristol Temple Meads
J To Chester
K To Tenby
L To Paignton
M From Liverpool Lime Street to Nottingham

Manchester, Stockport and Manchester Airport - Crewe and Stoke-on-Trent

	NT	NT	VT	NT	NT	TP	XC	NT	VT	NT	TP	XC	AW	VT	NT	NT	EM	NT	NT	NT	VT
	1	A	◇1 ☐	B		◇1 C ✕	◇1 D ✕	1	◇1 ☐	E	◇1 F ✕	◇1 G ✕	■ H ✕	◇1 ☐	I		◇ J	1	1	A	◇1 ☐
Deansgate d															15 29						
Manchester Oxford Road d				14 58											15 33		15 39				
Manchester Piccadilly 10 a				15 01											15 35		15 41				
d	14 48	14 52	14 55	15 03	15 04	15 06	15 07	15 14	15 15	15 17	15 20	15 27	15 30	15 35	15 37	15 38	15 43	15 46	15 48	15 52	15 55
Levenshulme d		14 58			15 09											15 43				15 58	
Heaton Chapel d		15 01			15 12											15 46				16 01	
Stockport a	14 57	15 04	15 03		15 16		15 15		15 22	15 27	15 28	15 34	15 38	15 42		15 50	15 53		15 57	16 04	16 03
d	14 58		15 04		15 17		15 16		15 23			15 35	15 39	15 43		15 51			15 58		16 04
Cheadle Hulme d	15 02				15 24											15 55			16 02		
Bramhall d	15 05																		16 05		
Poynton d	15 08																		16 08		
Adlington (Cheshire) d	15 11																		16 11		
Prestbury d	15 14																		16 14		
Macclesfield a	15 18											15 47		15 55					16 18		
d	15 18											15 49		15 56					16 18		
Congleton d	15 26																		16 26		
Handforth d					15 28											15 59					
Manchester Airport d				15a22		15a26		15a38							15a53			16 11			
Styal d																					
Wilmslow d			15 11		15 31								15 46			16 02		16 21			16 11
Alderley Edge d					15 34											16a08		16 24			
Chelford d					15 38																
Goostrey d					15 43																
Holmes Chapel d					15 46													16 32			
Sandbach d					15 51													16 36			
Crewe 10 65 a			15 27		16 01								16 05					16 46			16 27
Kidsgrove 50 a	15 32																		16 32		
Longport 50 a																					
Stoke-on-Trent 50,68 a	15 42						15 43		15 48			16 06		16 11					16 42		
Stafford 68 a							16 02					16 24									
Wolverhampton 7 68 a							16 15					16 39									
Birmingham New Street 12 68 a							16 39					16 58									
London Euston 15 ⊖65 a			17 04						17 23					17 42							18 03

	NT	NT	TP	XC	NT	VT	NT	TP	XC	AW	VT	NT	NT	EM	NT	NT	VT	NT	NT	NT	TP	XC
	B		◇1 C ✕	◇1 D ✕	1	◇1 ☐	E	◇1 F ✕	◇1 G ✕	■ K ✕	◇1 ☐	I		◇ J	1	A	◇1 ☐	L	B		◇1 C ✕	◇1 M ✕
Deansgate d																						
Manchester Oxford Road d	15 58											16 33		16 39					16 58			
Manchester Piccadilly 10 a	16 01											16 35		16 41					17 01			
d	16 03	16 04	16 06	16 07	16 14	16 15	16 17	16 20	16 27	16 30	16 35	16 37	16 38	16 43	16 46	16 51	16 55	16 58	17 03	17 03	17 06	17 06
Levenshulme d		16 09											16 43					17 03		17 08		
Heaton Chapel d		16 12											16 46					17 06		17 11		
Stockport a		16 16		16 15		16 22	16 27	16 28	16 34	16 38	16 42		16 50	16 53		17 02	17 03	17 10		17 15		
d		16 17		16 16		16 23			16 35	16 39	16 43		16 51				17 04			17 16		
Cheadle Hulme d		16 24											16 55							17 24		
Bramhall d																						
Poynton d																						
Adlington (Cheshire) d																						
Prestbury d																						
Macclesfield a									16 47		16 55											17 26
d									16 49		16 56											17 27
Congleton d																						
Handforth d		16 28											16 59							17 28		
Manchester Airport d	16a22		16a26		16a38							16a53			17 11				17a22		17a32	
Styal d																						
Wilmslow d		16 31								16 46			17 03		17 21		17 11			17 31		
Alderley Edge d		16 34											17a09		17 24					17 34		
Chelford d		16 38																		17 38		
Goostrey d		16 43																		17 43		
Holmes Chapel d		16 46													17 32					17 46		
Sandbach d		16 51													17 36					17 51		
Crewe 10 65 a		17 01								17 05					17 46		17 27			18 01		
Kidsgrove 50 a																						
Longport 50 a																						
Stoke-on-Trent 50,68 a				16 43		16 49			17 06		17 11											17 43
Stafford 68 a				17 02					17 24													18 03
Wolverhampton 7 68 a				17 15					17 39													18 15
Birmingham New Street 12 68 a				17 39					17 58													18 38
London Euston 15 ⊖65 a						18 23					18 42						19 08					

A To Buxton
B From Liverpool Lime Street
C From Cleethorpes
D To Bristol Temple Meads
E To Chester
F From Manchester Airport to Cleethorpes
G To Bournemouth
H To Pembroke Dock
I until 30 September. From Southport
J From Liverpool Lime Street to Norwich
K To Milford Haven
L To Hazel Grove
M To Cardiff Central

Manchester, Stockport and Manchester Airport - Crewe and Stoke-on-Trent

		NT A	NT 1	VT ◇1 ⊠	NT 1	TP ◇1 B ⌶	NT C	XC ◇1 D ⌶	AW ■ E ⌶	VT ◇1 ⊠	NT F	NT	EM ◇ G	NT 1	NT H	VT ◇1 ⊠	NT I	XC ◇1 J ⌶	TP ◇1 K ⌶	NT	NT 1	VT ◇1 ⊠
Deansgate	d				17 10																	
Manchester Oxford Road	d				17 13						17 33		17 39				17 58					
Manchester Piccadilly 10	a				17 15						17 35		17 41				18 01					
	d	17 09	17 14	17 15	17 17	17 20	17 23	17 27	17 30	17 35	17 37	17 38	17 43	17 46	17 52	17 55	18 03	18 05	18 06	18 08	18 14	18 15
Levenshulme	d						17 28					17 43			17 58					18 13		
Heaton Chapel	d						17 31					17 46			18 01					18 16		
Stockport	a	17 17		17 22	17 27	17 28	17 35	17 35	17 38	17 42		17 50	17 53		18 04	18 03		18 12		18 20		18 22
	d			17 23	17 28			17 35	17 39	17 43		17 51				18 04		18 13		18 22		18 23
Cheadle Hulme	d				17 32							17 55								18 30		
Bramhall	d				17 35																	
Poynton	d				17 38																	
Adlington (Cheshire)	d				17 41																	
Prestbury	d				17 44																	
Macclesfield	a				17 48					17 55								18 25				
	d				17 48					17 56								18 26				
Congleton	d				17 56																	
Handforth	d											17 59								18 34		
Manchester Airport	d		17a39								17a53			18 11			18a22		18a26		18a38	
Styal	d													18 18								
Wilmslow	d							17 44	17 46			18 02		18 22		18 11				18 37		
Alderley Edge	d											18 05		18 25						18 40		
Chelford	d																			18 44		
Goostrey	d																			18 48		
Holmes Chapel	d													18 33						18 51		
Sandbach	d											18 16		18 37						18 56		
Crewe 10 65	a							18 05	18 05			18 26		18 47		18 27				19 06		
Kidsgrove 50	a																					
Longport 50	a																					
Stoke-on-Trent 50,68	a			17 49	18 10					18 11								18 43				18 48
Stafford 68	a							18 27										19 01				
Wolverhampton 7 68	a							18 39										19 15				
Birmingham New Street 12 68	a							18 58										19 32				
London Euston 15 ⊖65	a			19 23						19 42						20 06						20 23

		NT A	TP ◇1 B ⌶	NT L	XC ◇1 M ⌶	AW ◇ N ⌶	VT ◇1 ⊠	NT F	NT	EM ◇ O	NT 1	NT 1	NT H	VT ◇1 ⊠	NT I	NT	TP ◇1 K ⌶	XC ◇1 P ⌶	NT 1	VT ◇1	NT A	TP ◇1 B	NT C
Deansgate	d			18 12																			
Manchester Oxford Road	d			18 16				18 33		18 39					18 58								
Manchester Piccadilly 10	a			18 18				18 35		18 41					19 01								
	d	18 17	18 20	18 21	18 27	18 30	18 35	18 37	18 38	18 43	18 46	18 48	18 52	18 55	19 03	19 04	19 06	19 07	19 14	19 15	19 17	19 18	19 22
Levenshulme	d			18 28					18 43				18 58			19 09							19 28
Heaton Chapel	d			18 31					18 46				19 01			19 12							19 31
Stockport	a	18 27	18 28	18 34	18 34	18 38	18 42		18 50	18 53		18 57	19 04	19 03		19 16		19 15		19 22	19 27	19 26	19 34
	d				18 35	18 39	18 43		18 51			18 58		19 04		19 17		19 16		19 23			
Cheadle Hulme	d								18 55			19 02				19 24							
Bramhall	d											19 05											
Poynton	d											19 08											
Adlington (Cheshire)	d											19 11											
Prestbury	d											19 14											
Macclesfield	a						18 55					19 18								19 35			
	d						18 56					19 18								19 36			
Congleton	d				18 54							19 26											
Handforth	d								18 59							19 28							
Manchester Airport	d							18a53			19 14				19a24		19a28		19a38				
Styal	d																						
Wilmslow	d					18 46			19 02		19 26			19 11		19 31							
Alderley Edge	d								19a08		19a32					19 34							
Chelford	d															19 38							
Goostrey	d															19 43							
Holmes Chapel	d															19 46							
Sandbach	d															19 51							
Crewe 10 65	a					19 05								19 27		20 01							
Kidsgrove 50	a											19 32											
Longport 50	a																						
Stoke-on-Trent 50,68	a				19 06		19 11					19 42						19 43		19 51			
Stafford 68	a				19 24													20 03					
Wolverhampton 7 68	a				19 39													20 16					
Birmingham New Street 12 68	a				19 58													20 33					
London Euston 15 ⊖65	a						20 42							21 06						21 26			

A To Chester
B From Manchester Airport to Cleethorpes
C To Hazel Grove
D To Bournemouth
E To Cardiff Central
F until 30 September. From Southport
G From Liverpool Lime Street to Nottingham
H To Buxton
I From Liverpool Lime Street
J To Plymouth
K From Cleethorpes
L From Wigan Wallgate to Buxton
M To Bournemouth. ⌶ to Wolverhampton
N To Carmarthen
O From Liverpool Lime Street to Norwich
P To Bristol Temple Meads. ⌶ to Wolverhampton

Manchester, Stockport and Manchester Airport - Crewe and Stoke-on-Trent

		XC ◇1 A ⌶	AW ◇ B	NT C	EM ◇ D	NT 1	NT 1	NT E	AW F	VT ◇1	NT	TP ◇1 G	XC ◇1	TP ◇1 H ⌶	VT ◇1	NT I	TP ◇1 J	XC ◇1	AW ◇ B	NT K	EM ◇ D	NT 1	NT 1
Deansgate	d			19 29																20 29			
Manchester Oxford Road	d			19 33	19 39	19 43			19 49			20 07								20 33	20 39	20 43	
Manchester Piccadilly 10	a			19 35	19 41	19 45			19 52			20 09								20 35	20 41	20 45	
	d	19 27	19 30	19 37	19 43	19 46	19 48	19 51	19 54	19 55	20 04		20 07	20 14	20 15	20 17	20 20	20 27	20 30	20 37	20 43	20 46	20 48
Levenshulme	d							19 58			20 09												
Heaton Chapel	d							20 01			20 12												
Stockport	a	19 34	19 38		19 53		19 57	20 04		20 03	20 15		20 15		20 22	20 27	20 28	20 34	20 38		20 53		20 58
	d	19 35	19 39				19 58			20 04	20 17		20 16		20 23			20 35	20 39				20 58
Cheadle Hulme	d						20 02				20 24												21 02
Bramhall	d						20 05																21 05
Poynton	d						20 08																21 08
Adlington (Cheshire)	d						20 11																21 11
Prestbury	d						20 14																21 14
Macclesfield	a	19 47					20 18								20 35			20 47					21 18
	d	19 49					20 18								20 36			20 49					21 18
Congleton	d						20 26																21 26
Handforth	d										20 28												
Manchester Airport	d			19a53		20 14			20a18					20a38						20a53		21 14	
Styal	d																						
Wilmslow	d		19 46			20a24				20 11	20 31								20 46			21a24	
Alderley Edge	d										20 34												
Chelford	d										20 38												
Goostrey	d										20 43												
Holmes Chapel	d										20 46												
Sandbach	d										20 52												
Crewe 10 65	a		20 05							20 27	21 04								21 05				
Kidsgrove 50	a						20 32																21 32
Longport 50	a																						
Stoke-on-Trent 50,68	a	20 06					20 42						20 43		20 51			21 06					21 42
Stafford 68	a	20 25								20 47			21 02					21 24					
Wolverhampton 7 68	a	20 40											21 15					21 39					
Birmingham New Street 12 68	a	21 00											21 32					22 00					
London Euston 15 ⊖65	a									22 12					22 33								

		NT E	AW ◇ L ⌶	NT M	NT	TP ◇1 H	TP ◇1 N	VT ◇1	NT I	TP ◇1 O	XC ◇1	AW P	NT C	NT 1	NT 1	NT E	NT	XC ◇1	NT I	TP ◇1 J	EM ◇ D	AW ◇ P
Deansgate	d												21 29									
Manchester Oxford Road	d		20 49	20 58			21 07						21 33	21 43							22 24	
Manchester Piccadilly 10	a		20 52	21 01			21 09						21 35	21 45							22 26	
	d	20 51	20 54	21 03	21 04	21 06		21 15	21 17	21 20	21 27	21 35	21 37	21 46	21 48	21 52	22 04	22 07	22 17	22 20	22 28	22 35
Levenshulme	d	20 58			21 09											21 58	22 09					
Heaton Chapel	d	21 01			21 12											22 01	22 12					
Stockport	a	21 04			21 16			21 22	21 27	21 28	21 34	21 43			21 57	22 04	22 16	22 15	22 27	22 28	22 37	22 43
	d				21 17			21 23			21 35	21 44			21 58		22 17	22 16				22 44
Cheadle Hulme	d				21 24										22 02		22 24					
Bramhall	d														22 05							
Poynton	d														22 08							
Adlington (Cheshire)	d														22 11							
Prestbury	d														22 14							
Macclesfield	a							21 35			21 47				22 18			22 28				
	d							21 36			21 49				22 18			22 29				
Congleton	d														22 26							
Handforth	d				21 28												22 28					
Manchester Airport	d		21a18	21a24		21a36							21a53	22 14								
Styal	d																					
Wilmslow	d				21 31							21 51		22a22			22 31					22 52
Alderley Edge	d				21 34												22 34					
Chelford	d				21 38												22 38					
Goostrey	d				21 43												22 43					
Holmes Chapel	d				21 46												22 46					
Sandbach	d				21 51												22 51					
Crewe 10 65	a				22 01							22 11					23 01					23 10
Kidsgrove 50	a														22 32							
Longport 50	a																					
Stoke-on-Trent 50,68	a							21 51			22 07				22 42			22 46				
Stafford 68	a										22 25							23 06				
Wolverhampton 7 68	a										22 39							23 19				
Birmingham New Street 12 68	a										22 58							23 39				
London Euston 15 ⊖65	a							23 48														

A To Southampton Central. ⌶ to Wolverhampton
B To Cardiff Central
C until 30 September. From Southport
D From Liverpool Lime Street to Nottingham
E To Buxton
F From Chester
G From Liverpool Lime Street to Hull
H From Cleethorpes
I To Chester
J From Manchester Airport to Sheffield
K From Southport
L From Llandudno
M From Liverpool Lime Street
N From Liverpool Lime Street to York
O From Manchester Airport to Cleethorpes
P To Shrewsbury

Manchester, Stockport and Manchester Airport - Crewe and Stoke-on-Trent

Station		TP FO ◇1 A	NT 1	NT 1	NT	TP ◇1 B	NT C	NT 1	TP ◇1 D	NT E	NT
Deansgate	d										
Manchester Oxford Road	d		22 43						23 17		
Manchester Piccadilly 10	a		22 45						23 19		
	d	22 40	22 46	22 48	23 04	23 06	23 10	23 14		23 17	23 38
Levenshulme	d				23 09						23 43
Heaton Chapel	d				23 12						23 46
Stockport	a			22 57	23 16		23 19	23 23		23 26	23 50
	d			22 58	23 16			23 23			23 50
Cheadle Hulme	d			23 02	23 23			23 27			23 54
Bramhall	d			23 05				23 30			
Poynton	d			23 08				23 33			
Adlington (Cheshire)	d			23 11				23 37			
Prestbury	d			23 14				23 40			
Macclesfield	a			23 20				23 46			
	d										
Congleton	d										
Handforth	d				23 27						23 58
Manchester Airport	d	22a57	23 14			23a26					
Styal	d										
Wilmslow	d		23a22		23 31						00 01
Alderley Edge	d				23a37						00 04
Chelford	d										00 08
Goostrey	d										00 12
Holmes Chapel	d										00 15
Sandbach	d										00 20
Crewe 10 65	a										00 30
Kidsgrove 50	a										
Longport 50	a										
Stoke-on-Trent 50,68	a										
Stafford 68	a										
Wolverhampton 7 68	a										
Birmingham New Street 12 68	a										
London Euston 15 ⊖65	a										

Saturdays

Station		NT	NT F	TP ◇1 G	AW H	XC ◇1 I	VT ◇1	NT 1	TP ◇1 J	NT K	VT ◇1	NT F	NT 1	XC ◇1 L	NT	VT ◇1	TP ◇1 G	NT 1	NT E	AW ◇ M	VT ◇1	NT 1	NT 1
Deansgate	d																						
Manchester Oxford Road	d																						
Manchester Piccadilly 10	a																						
	d	23p38	04 15	04 44	04 58	05 11	05 25	05 35	05 44	05 50	05 55	05 58		06 00	06 06	06 10	06 12	06 15	06 17	06 30	06 35	06 44	06 46
Levenshulme	d	23p43													06 11								
Heaton Chapel	d	23p46													06 14								
Stockport	a	23p50					05 33		05 52	05 59	06 02			06 07	06 18	06 17			06 27	06 38	06 43	06 52	
	d	23p50					05 34				06 03			06 08	06 19	06 18				06 39	06 43	06 53	
Cheadle Hulme	d	23p54													06 26							06 57	
Bramhall	d																					07 00	
Poynton	d																					07 03	
Adlington (Cheshire)	d																					07 06	
Prestbury	d																					07 09	
Macclesfield	a													06 20		06 30					06 55	07 13	
	d												06 03	06 21		06 31					06 56	07 13	
Congleton	d												06 10									07 21	
Handforth	d	23p58													06 30								
Manchester Airport	d		04a30	05a00	05a17			06 05				06a14					06a29	06a39					07 11
Styal	d																						
Wilmslow	d	00 01					05 41	06 14			06 11				06 33					06 46			07 21
Alderley Edge	d	00 04						06 17							06 36								07 24
Chelford	d	00 08						06 21															
Goostrey	d	00 12						06 25															
Holmes Chapel	d	00 15						06 28							06 44								07 32
Sandbach	d	00 20						06 33							06 49								07 36
Crewe 10 65	a	00 30				05 41	05 57	06 43			06 27				06 59					07 05			07 46
Kidsgrove 50	a												06 16									07 28	
Longport 50	a																						
Stoke-on-Trent 50,68	a					06 07							06 26	06 38		06 46					07 11	07 40	
Stafford 68	a					06 25	06 17							06 57									
Wolverhampton 7 68	a					06 39								07 12									
Birmingham New Street 12 68	a					06 57								07 31									
London Euston 15 ⊖65	a						07 52				08 09					08 27					08 46		

A From Hull
B From Cleethorpes
C To Buxton
D From Liverpool Lime Street to York
E To Chester
F From Liverpool Lime Street
G From Sheffield
H From Chester
I To Bournemouth
J From Manchester Airport to Cleethorpes
K To Sheffield
L To Bristol Temple Meads
M To Milford Haven

Manchester, Stockport and Manchester Airport - Crewe and Stoke-on-Trent

Station		NT A	VT ◇1	NT B	NT	TP ◇1 C	XC ◇1 D	XC ◇1 E	NT 1	VT ◇1	NT F	TP ◇1 G	NT H	XC ◇1 I	AW ◇ J	VT ◇1	NT K	NT	EM ◇ L	NT 1	NT 1	NT A	VT ◇1
Deansgate	d												07 11				07 28						
Manchester Oxford Road	d			06 58									07 15				07 32		07 38				
Manchester Piccadilly 10	a			07 01									07 17				07 34		07 41				
	d	06 49	06 55	07 03	07 03	07 06	07 07	07 07	07 14	07 15	07 17	07 20	07 21	07 27	07 30	07 35	07 36	07 38	07 42	07 46	07 48	07 52	07 55
Levenshulme	d	06 55			07 09								07 28					07 43				07 57	
Heaton Chapel	d	06 58			07 12								07 31					07 46					
Stockport	a	07 01	07 03		07 16		07 15	07 14		07 22	07 27	07 28	07 34	07 34	07 38	07 43		07 50	07 53		07 57	08 02	08 03
	d		07 04		07 18		07 16	07 16		07 23				07 35	07 39	07 43		07 51			07 58		08 04
Cheadle Hulme	d				07 24													07 55			08 02		
Bramhall	d																				08 05		
Poynton	d																				08 08		
Adlington (Cheshire)	d																				08 11		
Prestbury	d																				08 14		
Macclesfield	a													07 47		07 56					08 18		
	d													07 49		07 56					08 18		
Congleton	d																				08 26		
Handforth	d				07 28													07 59					
Manchester Airport	d			07a22		07a29			07a38								07a53			08 11			
Styal	d																			08 18			
Wilmslow	d		07 11		07 31										07 46			08 01		08 22			08 11
Alderley Edge	d				07 34													08a07		08 25			
Chelford	d				07 38																		
Goostrey	d				07 43																		
Holmes Chapel	d				07 46															08 33			
Sandbach	d				07 51															08 37			
Crewe 10 65	a		07 27		08 01										08 05					08 47			08 27
Kidsgrove 50	a																				08 32		
Longport 50	a																						
Stoke-on-Trent 50,68	a						07 43	07 43		07 48				08 06		08 12					08 42		
Stafford 68	a						08 02	08 02						08 25									
Wolverhampton 7 68	a						08 16	08 17						08 39									
Birmingham New Street 12 68	a						08 38	08 39						08 58									
London Euston 15 ⊖65	a		09 04							09 23						09 42							10 04

Station		NT B	NT	TP ◇1 M	XC ◇1 N	NT 1	VT ◇1	NT F	TP ◇1 G	XC ◇1 I	AW ◇ O	VT ◇1	NT P	NT	EM ◇ L	NT 1	NT 1	NT A	VT ◇1	NT B	NT	TP ◇1 M
Deansgate	d												08 29									
Manchester Oxford Road	d	07 58											08 33		08 39					08 58		
Manchester Piccadilly 10	a	08 01											08 35		08 41					09 01		
	d	08 03	08 04	08 06	08 07	08 14	08 15	08 17	08 20	08 27	08 30	08 35	08 37	08 38	08 43	08 46	08 48	08 52	08 55	09 03	09 04	09 06
Levenshulme	d		08 09											08 43				08 58			09 09	
Heaton Chapel	d		08 12											08 46				09 01			09 12	
Stockport	a		08 16		08 15		08 22	08 27	08 28	08 34	08 38	08 43		08 50	08 53		08 57	09 04	09 03		09 16	
	d		08 17		08 16		08 23			08 35	08 39	08 43		08 51			08 58		09 04		09 17	
Cheadle Hulme	d		08 24											08 55			09 02				09 24	
Bramhall	d																09 05					
Poynton	d																09 08					
Adlington (Cheshire)	d																09 11					
Prestbury	d																09 14					
Macclesfield	a									08 47		08 55					09 18					
	d									08 49		08 56					09 18					
Congleton	d																09 26					
Handforth	d		08 28											08 59							09 28	
Manchester Airport	d	08a22		08a26		08a38							08a53			09 11				09a22		09a26
Styal	d																					
Wilmslow	d		08 31								08 46			09 02		09 21			09 11		09 31	
Alderley Edge	d		08 34											09a08		09 24					09 34	
Chelford	d		08 38																		09 38	
Goostrey	d		08 43																		09 43	
Holmes Chapel	d		08 46													09 32					09 46	
Sandbach	d		08 51													09 36					09 51	
Crewe 10 65	a		09 01								09 05					09 46			09 27		10 01	
Kidsgrove 50	a																09 32					
Longport 50	a																					
Stoke-on-Trent 50,68	a				08 43		08 48			09 06		09 11					09 42					
Stafford 68	a				09 02					09 25												
Wolverhampton 7 68	a				09 15					09 39												
Birmingham New Street 12 68	a				09 39					09 58												
London Euston 15 ⊖65	a						10 23					10 42							11 04			

A To Buxton
B From Liverpool Lime Street
C From Doncaster
D from 17 September. To Bristol Temple Meads
E until 10 September. To Newquay
F To Chester
G From Manchester Airport to Cleethorpes
H From Wigan Wallgate to Hazel Grove
I To Bournemouth
J To Carmarthen
K From Southport
L From Liverpool Lime Street to Norwich
M From Cleethorpes
N To Paignton
O To Milford Haven
P until 1 October. From Southport

Table 84

Manchester, Stockport and Manchester Airport - Crewe and Stoke-on-Trent

	XC	NT	VT	NT	TP	XC	AW	VT	NT	NT	EM	NT	NT	NT	VT	NT	NT	TP	XC	NT	VT	NT
	◇1	1	◇1		◇1	◇1	◇	◇1			◇	1	1		◇1			◇1	◇1	1	◇1	
	A ⌶		☕	B	C ⌶	D ⌶	E ⌶	☕	F		G			H	☕	I		J ⌶	A ⌶		☕	B
Deansgate d									09 29													
Manchester Oxford Road d									09 33		09 39					09 58						
Manchester Piccadilly a									09 35		09 41					10 01						
Manchester Piccadilly d	09 07	09 14	09 15	09 17	09 20	09 27	09 30	09 35	09 37	09 38	09 43	09 46	09 48	09 52	09 55	10 03	10 04	10 06	10 07	10 14	10 15	10 17
Levenshulme d										09 43				09 58			10 09					
Heaton Chapel d										09 46				10 01			10 12					
Stockport a	09 15		09 22	09 27	09 28	09 34	09 38	09 42		09 50	09 53		09 57	10 04	10 03		10 16		10 15		10 22	10 27
Stockport d	09 16		09 23			09 35	09 39	09 43		09 51			09 58		10 04		10 17		10 16		10 23	
Cheadle Hulme d										09 55			10 02				10 24					
Bramhall d													10 05									
Poynton d													10 08									
Adlington (Cheshire) d													10 11									
Prestbury d													10 14									
Macclesfield a						09 47		09 55					10 18									
Macclesfield d						09 49		09 56					10 18									
Congleton d													10 26									
Handforth d										09 59							10 28					
Manchester Airport ✈ d		09a38							09a53			10 11				10a22		10a26		10a38		
Styal d																						
Wilmslow d							09 46			10 02		10 21			10 11		10 31					
Alderley Edge d										10a08		10 24					10 34					
Chelford d																	10 38					
Goostrey d																	10 43					
Holmes Chapel d												10 32					10 46					
Sandbach d												10 36					10 51					
Crewe 65 a							10 05					10 46			10 27		11 01					
Kidsgrove 50 a													10 32									
Longport 50 a																						
Stoke-on-Trent 50,68 a	09 43		09 48			10 06		10 11					10 42						10 43		10 48	
Stafford 68 a	10 02					10 25													11 02			
Wolverhampton 68 a	10 15					10 39													11 16			
Birmingham New Street 68 a	10 39					10 58													11 39			
London Euston ⊖65 a			11 23					11 42							12 04						12 23	

	TP	XC	AW	VT	NT	NT	EM	NT	NT	NT	VT	NT	NT	TP	XC	NT	VT	NT	TP	XC	AW
	◇1	◇1	◇	◇1			◇	1	1		◇1			◇1	◇1	1	◇1		◇1	◇1	◇
	C ⌶	D ⌶	K ⌶	☕	F		G			H	☕	I		J ⌶	A ⌶		☕	B	C ⌶	D ⌶	E ⌶
Deansgate d					10 29																
Manchester Oxford Road d					10 33		10 39					10 58									
Manchester Piccadilly a					10 35		10 41					11 01									
Manchester Piccadilly d	10 20	10 27	10 30	10 35	10 37	10 38	10 43	10 46	10 48	10 52	10 55	11 03	11 04	11 06	11 07	11 14	11 15	11 17	11 20	11 27	11 30
Levenshulme d						10 43				10 58			11 09								
Heaton Chapel d						10 46				11 01			11 12								
Stockport a	10 28	10 34	10 38	10 42		10 50	10 53		10 57	11 04	11 03		11 16		11 15		11 22	11 27	11 28	11 34	11 38
Stockport d		10 35	10 39	10 43		10 51			10 58		11 04		11 17		11 16		11 23			11 35	11 39
Cheadle Hulme d						10 55			11 02				11 24								
Bramhall d									11 05												
Poynton d									11 08												
Adlington (Cheshire) d									11 11												
Prestbury d									11 14												
Macclesfield a		10 47		10 55					11 18											11 47	
Macclesfield d		10 49		10 56					11 18											11 49	
Congleton d									11 26												
Handforth d						10 59							11 28								
Manchester Airport ✈ d					10a53			11 11				11a22		11a26		11a38					
Styal d																					
Wilmslow d			10 46			11 02		11 21			11 11		11 31								11 46
Alderley Edge d						11a08		11 24					11 34								
Chelford d													11 38								
Goostrey d													11 43								
Holmes Chapel d								11 32					11 46								
Sandbach d								11 36					11 51								
Crewe 65 a			11 05					11 46			11 27		12 01								12 05
Kidsgrove 50 a									11 32												
Longport 50 a																					
Stoke-on-Trent 50,68 a		11 06		11 11					11 42						11 43		11 48			12 06	
Stafford 68 a		11 25													12 02					12 24	
Wolverhampton 68 a		11 39													12 16					12 39	
Birmingham New Street 68 a		11 58													12 39					12 58	
London Euston ⊖65 a				12 42							13 04						13 23				

A To Bristol Temple Meads
B To Chester
C From Manchester Airport to Cleethorpes
D To Bournemouth
E To Carmarthen
F until 1 October. From Southport
G From Liverpool Lime Street to Norwich
H To Buxton
I From Liverpool Lime Street
J From Cleethorpes
K To Milford Haven

Table 84

Manchester, Stockport and Manchester Airport - Crewe and Stoke-on-Trent

	VT	NT	NT	EM	NT	NT	NT	VT	NT	NT	TP	XC	NT	VT	NT	TP	XC	AW	VT	NT	NT	EM
	◇1			◇	1	1		◇1			◇1	◇1	1	◇1		◇1	◇1	■	◇1			◇
	☕	A		B			C	☕	D		E ⌶	F ⌶		☕	G	H ⌶	I ⌶	J ⌶	☕	A		B
Deansgate d		11 29																		12 29		
Manchester Oxford Road d		11 33		11 39					11 58											12 33		12 39
Manchester Piccadilly a		11 35		11 41					12 01											12 35		12 41
Manchester Piccadilly d	11 35	11 37	11 38	11 43	11 46	11 48	11 52	11 55	12 03	12 04	12 06	12 07	12 14	12 15	12 17	12 20	12 27	12 30	12 35	12 37	12 38	12 43
Levenshulme d			11 43				11 58			12 09											12 43	
Heaton Chapel d			11 46				12 01			12 12											12 46	
Stockport a	11 42		11 50	11 53		11 57	12 04	12 03		12 16		12 15		12 22	12 27	12 28	12 34	12 38	12 42		12 50	12 53
Stockport d	11 43		11 51			11 58		12 04		12 17		12 16		12 23			12 35	12 39	12 43		12 51	
Cheadle Hulme d			11 55			12 02				12 24											12 55	
Bramhall d						12 05																
Poynton d						12 08																
Adlington (Cheshire) d						12 11																
Prestbury d						12 14																
Macclesfield a	11 55					12 18											12 47		12 55			
Macclesfield d	11 56					12 18											12 49		12 56			
Congleton d						12 26																
Handforth d			11 59							12 28											12 59	
Manchester Airport ✈ d		11a53			12 11				12a22		12a26		12a38							12a53		
Styal d																						
Wilmslow d			12 02		12 21			12 11		12 31								12 46			13 02	
Alderley Edge d			12a08		12 24					12 34											13a08	
Chelford d										12 38												
Goostrey d										12 43												
Holmes Chapel d					12 32					12 46												
Sandbach d					12 36					12 51												
Crewe 65 a					12 46			12 27		13 01								13 05				
Kidsgrove 50 a						12 32																
Longport 50 a																						
Stoke-on-Trent 50,68 a	12 11					12 42						12 43		12 48			13 06		13 11			
Stafford 68 a												13 02					13 25					
Wolverhampton 68 a												13 15					13 39					
Birmingham New Street 68 a												13 39					13 58					
London Euston ⊖65 a	13 42							14 04						14 23					14 42			

	NT	NT	NT	VT	NT	NT	TP	XC	NT	VT	NT	TP	XC	AW	VT	NT	NT	EM	NT	NT	NT	VT
	1	1		◇1			◇1	◇1	1	◇1		◇1	◇1	■	◇1			◇	1	1		◇1
			C	☕	D		E ⌶	K ⌶		☕	G	H ⌶	I ⌶	L ⌶	☕	A		B			C	☕
Deansgate d																13 29						
Manchester Oxford Road d					12 58											13 33		13 39				
Manchester Piccadilly a					13 01											13 35		13 41				
Manchester Piccadilly d	12 46	12 48	12 52	12 55	13 03	13 04	13 06	13 07	13 14	13 15	13 17	13 20	13 27	13 30	13 35	13 37	13 38	13 43	13 46	13 48	13 52	13 55
Levenshulme d			12 58			13 09											13 43				13 58	
Heaton Chapel d			13 01			13 12											13 46				14 01	
Stockport a		12 57	13 04	13 03		13 16		13 15		13 22	13 27	13 28	13 34	13 38	13 42		13 50	13 53		13 57	14 04	14 03
Stockport d		12 58		13 04		13 17		13 16		13 23			13 35	13 39	13 43		13 51			13 58		14 04
Cheadle Hulme d		13 02				13 24											13 55			14 02		
Bramhall d		13 05																		14 05		
Poynton d		13 08																		14 08		
Adlington (Cheshire) d		13 11																		14 11		
Prestbury d		13 14																		14 14		
Macclesfield a		13 18											13 47		13 55					14 18		
Macclesfield d		13 18											13 49		13 56					14 18		
Congleton d		13 26																		14 26		
Handforth d						13 28											13 59					
Manchester Airport ✈ d	13 11				13a22		13a26		13a38							13a53			14 11			
Styal d	13 18																					
Wilmslow d	13 22			13 11		13 31								13 46			14 02		14 21			14 11
Alderley Edge d	13 25					13 34											14a08		14 24			
Chelford d						13 38																
Goostrey d						13 43																
Holmes Chapel d	13 33					13 46													14 32			
Sandbach d	13 37					13 51													14 36			
Crewe 65 a	13 47			13 27		14 01								14 05					14 46			14 27
Kidsgrove 50 a		13 32																		14 32		
Longport 50 a																						
Stoke-on-Trent 50,68 a		13 42						13 43		13 48			14 06		14 11					14 42		
Stafford 68 a								14 02					14 25									
Wolverhampton 68 a								14 16					14 39									
Birmingham New Street 68 a								14 39					14 58									
London Euston ⊖65 a				15 04						15 23					15 42							16 04

A until 1 October. From Southport
B From Liverpool Lime Street to Norwich
C To Buxton
D From Liverpool Lime Street
E From Cleethorpes
F To Exeter St Davids
G To Chester
H From Manchester Airport to Cleethorpes
I To Bournemouth
J To Milford Haven
K To Bristol Temple Meads
L To Pembroke Dock

Manchester, Stockport and Manchester Airport - Crewe and Stoke-on-Trent

	NT	NT	TP	XC	NT	VT	NT	TP	XC	AW	VT	NT	NT	EM	NT	NT	NT	VT	NT	NT	TP
	A		◇■ B ✕	◇■ C ✕	■	◇■	D	◇■ E ✕	◇■ F ✕	■ G ✕	◇■	H		◇ I	■	■	J	◇■	A		◇■ B ✕
Deansgate d												14 29									
Manchester Oxford Road d	13 58											14 33		14 39					14 58		
Manchester Piccadilly a	14 01											14 35		14 41					15 01		
Manchester Piccadilly d	14 03	14 04	14 06	14 07	14 14	14 15	14 17	14 20	14 27	14 30	14 35	14 37	14 38	14 43	14 46	14 48	14 52	14 55	15 03	15 04	15 06
Levenshulme d		14 09											14 43				14 58			15 09	
Heaton Chapel d		14 12											14 46				15 01			15 12	
Stockport a		14 16		14 15		14 22	14 27	14 28	14 34	14 38	14 42		14 50	14 53		14 57	15 04	15 03		15 16	
Stockport d		14 17		14 16		14 23			14 35	14 39	14 43		14 51			14 58		15 04		15 17	
Cheadle Hulme d		14 24											14 55			15 02				15 24	
Bramhall d																15 05					
Poynton d																15 08					
Adlington (Cheshire) d																15 11					
Prestbury d																15 14					
Macclesfield a									14 47		14 55					15 18					
Macclesfield d									14 49		14 56					15 18					
Congleton d																15 26					
Handforth d		14 28											14 59							15 28	
Manchester Airport d	14a22		14a26		14a38							14a53			15 11				15a22		15a26
Styal d																					
Wilmslow d		14 31								14 46			15 02		15 21			15 11		15 31	
Alderley Edge d		14 34											15a08		15 24					15 34	
Chelford d		14 38																		15 38	
Goostrey d		14 43																		15 43	
Holmes Chapel d		14 46													15 32					15 46	
Sandbach d		14 51													15 36					15 51	
Crewe 65 a		15 01								15 05					15 46			15 27		16 01	
Kidsgrove 50 a																15 32					
Longport 50 a																					
Stoke-on-Trent 50,68 a				14 43		14 48			15 06		15 11					15 42					
Stafford 68 a				15 02					15 25												
Wolverhampton 68 a				15 16					15 39												
Birmingham New Street 68 a				15 39					15 58												
London Euston 65 a						16 23					16 42							17 04			

	XC	NT	VT	NT	TP	XC	AW	VT	NT	NT	EM	NT	NT	NT	VT	NT	NT	TP	XC	NT	VT	NT
	◇■ C ✕	■	◇■	D	◇■ E ✕	◇■ F ✕	■ K ✕	◇■	H		◇ L	■	■	J	◇■	A		◇■ B ✕	◇■ C ✕	■	◇■	D
Deansgate d									15 29													
Manchester Oxford Road d									15 33		15 39					15 58						
Manchester Piccadilly a									15 35		15 41					16 01						
Manchester Piccadilly d	15 07	15 14	15 15	15 17	15 20	15 27	15 30	15 35	15 37	15 38	15 43	15 46	15 48	15 52	15 55	16 03	16 04	16 06	16 07	16 14	16 15	16 17
Levenshulme d										15 43				15 58			16 09					
Heaton Chapel d										15 46				16 01			16 12					
Stockport a	15 15		15 22	15 27	15 28	15 34	15 38	15 42		15 50	15 53		15 57	16 04	16 03		16 16		16 15		16 22	16 27
Stockport d	15 16		15 23			15 35	15 39	15 43		15 51			15 58		16 04		16 17		16 16		16 23	
Cheadle Hulme d										15 55			16 02				16 24					
Bramhall d													16 05									
Poynton d													16 08									
Adlington (Cheshire) d													16 11									
Prestbury d													16 14									
Macclesfield a						15 47		15 55					16 18									
Macclesfield d						15 49		15 56					16 18									
Congleton d													16 26									
Handforth d										15 59							16 28					
Manchester Airport d		15a38							15a53			16 11				16a22		16a26		16a38		
Styal d																						
Wilmslow d							15 46			16 02		16 21			16 11		16 31					
Alderley Edge d										16a08		16 24					16 34					
Chelford d																	16 38					
Goostrey d																	16 43					
Holmes Chapel d												16 32					16 46					
Sandbach d												16 36					16 51					
Crewe 65 a							16 05					16 46			16 27		17 01					
Kidsgrove 50 a													16 32									
Longport 50 a																						
Stoke-on-Trent 50,68 a	15 43		15 48			16 06		16 11					16 42						16 43		16 48	
Stafford 68 a	16 02					16 24													17 02			
Wolverhampton 68 a	16 16					16 39													17 16			
Birmingham New Street 68 a	16 39					16 58													17 39			
London Euston 65 a			17 23					17 42							18 04						18 23	

A From Liverpool Lime Street
B From Cleethorpes
C To Bristol Temple Meads
D To Chester
E From Manchester Airport to Cleethorpes
F To Bournemouth
G To Milford Haven
H until 1 October. From Southport
I From Liverpool Lime Street to Nottingham
J To Buxton
K To Pembroke Dock
L From Liverpool Lime Street to Norwich

Table 84

Saturdays

Manchester, Stockport and Manchester Airport - Crewe and Stoke-on-Trent

	TP	XC	AW	VT	NT	NT	EM	NT	NT	VT	NT	NT	TP	XC	NT	NT	VT	NT	TP	XC	AW
	◇■ A ✕	◇■ B ✕	■ C ✕	◇■	D		◇ E	■	F	◇■	G		◇■ H ✕	◇■ I ✕	J	■	◇■	K	◇■ A ✕	◇■ B ✕	■ I ✕
Deansgate d																					
Manchester Oxford Road d					16 33		16 39				16 58										
Manchester Piccadilly a					16 35		16 41				17 01										
Manchester Piccadilly d	16 20	16 27	16 30	16 35	16 37	16 38	16 43	16 46	16 51	16 55	17 03	17 03	17 06	17 06	17 09	17 14	17 15	17 17	17 20	17 27	17 30
Levenshulme d						16 43			16 58			17 08			17 14						
Heaton Chapel d						16 46			17 01			17 11			17 17						
Stockport a	16 28	16 34	16 38	16 42		16 50	16 53		17 04	17 03		17 15			17 21		17 22	17 27	17 28	17 35	17 38
Stockport d		16 35	16 39	16 43		16 51				17 04		17 16					17 23			17 36	17 39
Cheadle Hulme d						16 55						17 24									
Bramhall d																					
Poynton d																					
Adlington (Cheshire) d																					
Prestbury d																					
Macclesfield a		16 47		16 55										17 25							
Macclesfield d		16 49		16 56										17 26							
Congleton d																				17 54	
Handforth d						16 59						17 28									
Manchester Airport d					16a53			17 11			17a22		17a32			17a38					
Styal d																					
Wilmslow d			16 46			17 02		17 21		17 11		17 31									17 46
Alderley Edge d						17a08		17 24				17 34									
Chelford d												17 38									
Goostrey d												17 43									
Holmes Chapel d								17 32				17 46									
Sandbach d								17 36				17 51									
Crewe 65 a			17 05					17 46		17 27		18 01									18 05
Kidsgrove 50 a																					
Longport 50 a																					
Stoke-on-Trent 50,68 a		17 06		17 11										17 43			17 49			18 07	
Stafford 68 a		17 25												18 03						18 26	
Wolverhampton 68 a		17 39												18 16						18 40	
Birmingham New Street 68 a		17 58												18 38						18 58	
London Euston 65 a				18 42						19 04							19 23				

	VT	NT	NT	EM	NT	NT	VT	NT	XC	TP	NT	NT	VT	NT	TP	XC	AW	VT	NT	NT	EM	NT
	◇■	D		◇ L	■	F	◇■	G	◇■ M ✕	◇■ H ✕		■	◇■	K	◇■ A ✕	◇■ B ✕	◇ N ✕	◇■	D		◇ E	■
Deansgate d		17 29																				
Manchester Oxford Road d		17 33		17 39				17 58											18 33		18 39	
Manchester Piccadilly a		17 35		17 41				18 01											18 35		18 41	
Manchester Piccadilly d	17 35	17 37	17 38	17 43	17 46	17 52	17 55	18 03	18 05	18 06	18 08	18 14	18 15	18 17	18 20	18 27	18 30	18 35	18 37	18 38	18 43	18 46
Levenshulme d			17 43			17 58					18 13									18 43		
Heaton Chapel d			17 46			18 01					18 16									18 46		
Stockport a	17 42		17 50	17 53		18 04	18 03		18 12		18 20		18 22	18 27	18 28	18 34	18 38	18 42		18 50	18 53	
Stockport d	17 43		17 51				18 04		18 13		18 22		18 23			18 35	18 39	18 43		18 51		
Cheadle Hulme d			17 55								18 30									18 55		
Bramhall d																						
Poynton d																						
Adlington (Cheshire) d																						
Prestbury d																						
Macclesfield a	17 55								18 25									18 55				
Macclesfield d	17 56								18 26									18 56				
Congleton d																18 54						
Handforth d			17 59								18 34									18 59		
Manchester Airport d		17a53			18 11			18a22		18a26		18a38							18a53			19 14
Styal d					18 18																	
Wilmslow d			18 02		18 22		18 11				18 37						18 46			19 02		19 26
Alderley Edge d			18a08		18 25						18 40									19a08		19a32
Chelford d											18 44											
Goostrey d											18 48											
Holmes Chapel d					18 33						18 51											
Sandbach d					18 37						18 56											
Crewe 65 a					18 47		18 27				19 06						19 05					
Kidsgrove 50 a																						
Longport 50 a																						
Stoke-on-Trent 50,68 a	18 11								18 43				18 48			19 06		19 11				
Stafford 68 a									19 02							19 25						
Wolverhampton 68 a									19 16							19 39						
Birmingham New Street 68 a									19 33							19 58						
London Euston 65 a	19 42						20 04						20 25					20 57				

A From Manchester Airport to Cleethorpes
B To Bournemouth
C To Milford Haven
D until 1 October. From Southport
E From Liverpool Lime Street to Norwich
F To Buxton
G From Liverpool Lime Street
H From Cleethorpes
I To Cardiff Central
J To Hazel Grove
K To Chester
L From Liverpool Lime Street to Nottingham
M To Bristol Temple Meads
N To Carmarthen

Table 84

Sundays

Manchester, Stockport and Manchester Airport - Crewe and Stoke-on-Trent

	NT	NT	NT	NT	TP	VT	NT	XC	AW	VT	NT	NT	NT	NT	VT	TP	NT	AW	XC	VT	NT	NT
	1				◇1	◇1		◇1	■	◇1	1				◇1	◇1		■	◇1	◇1	1	
		A	B	C			D	E	F			G		C		H	I	J	E			G
						⊏		⊤	⊤	⊏					⊏			⊤	⊤	⊏		
Deansgate ⇌ d							10 16										11 11					
Manchester Oxford Road d				10 00			10 19							11 00			11 17				11 37	
Manchester Piccadilly [10] ⇌ a				10 03			10 22							11 03			11 19				11 40	
d	09 41	09 51	10 03	10 07	10 16	10 20	10 22	10 27	10 30	10 35	10 41	10 52	11 04	11 07	11 15	11 18	11 22	11 24	11 27	11 35	11 41	11 52
Levenshulme d		09 58	10 09									10 58	11 10									11 58
Heaton Chapel d		10 01	10 12									11 01	11 13									12 01
Stockport a		10 04	10 15			10 28	10 33	10 34	10 39	10 42		11 04	11 17		11 23	11 27	11 30	11 34	11 34	11 43		12 04
d			10 17			10 29		10 36	10 39	10 42			11 17		11 23			11 40	11 36	11 43		
Cheadle Hulme d			10 23										11 22									
Bramhall d																						
Poynton d																						
Adlington (Cheshire) d																						
Prestbury d																						
Macclesfield a								10 48		10 55									11 49	11 56		
d								10 49		10 55									11 49	11 56		
Congleton d																						
Handforth d			10 27										11 26									
Manchester Airport ✈ d	10a03			10a21	10a30						11 08			11a21							12a04	
Styal d											11 12											
Wilmslow d			10 30			10 36			10 48		11 16		11 29					11 47				
Alderley Edge d			10a36								11a21		11 32									
Chelford d													11 36									
Goostrey d													11 41									
Holmes Chapel d													11 44									
Sandbach d													11 49									
Crewe [10] 65 a						10 53			11 07				11 59					12 07				
Kidsgrove 50 a																						
Longport 50 a																						
Stoke-on-Trent 50,68 a								11 06		11 12					11 50				12 06	12 13		
Stafford 68 a								11 27											12 24			
Wolverhampton [7] 68 ⇌ a								11 41											12 40			
Birmingham New Street [12] 68 a								12 00											12 58			
London Euston [15] ⊖65 a						12 56				12 59					13 28					13 47		

	VT	NT	NT	TP	VT	TP	NT	XC	AW	VT	EM	NT	NT	VT	NT	NT	XC	XC	TP	VT	TP
	◇1			◇1	◇1	◇1		◇1	■	◇1	◇	1		◇1			◇1	◇1	◇1	◇1	◇1
			C	K		L	D	M	F		N		G		C		O	P	K		H
	⊏				⊏			⊤	⊤	⊏				⊏			⊤	⊤		⊏	
Deansgate ⇌ d							12 11														
Manchester Oxford Road d			12 00				12 17					12 43			13 00						
Manchester Piccadilly [10] ⇌ a			12 03				12 19					12 45			13 02						
d	11 55	12 04	12 07	12 13	12 15	12 18	12 22	12 26	12 30	12 35	12 44	12 47	12 52	12 55	13 04	13 04	13 07	13 07	13 13	13 15	13 20
Levenshulme d		12 09											12 58			13 09					
Heaton Chapel d		12 12											13 01			13 12					
Stockport a	12 04	12 16			12 23	12 28	12 33	12 35	12 39	12 44	12 53		13 04	13 04		13 16				13 22	13 28
d	12 05	12 16			12 23			12 35	12 40	12 44				13 05		13 17				13 22	
Cheadle Hulme d		12 22														13 21					
Bramhall d																					
Poynton d																					
Adlington (Cheshire) d																					
Prestbury d																					
Macclesfield a								12 48		12 57											
d								12 49		12 57											
Congleton d																					
Handforth d		12 26														13 25					
Manchester Airport ✈ d			12a21	12a29								13 12			13a24				13a29		
Styal d												13 16									
Wilmslow d	12 12	12 29							12 48			13 23		13 12		13 28					
Alderley Edge d		12a35										13a29				13 31					
Chelford d																13 35					
Goostrey d																13 40					
Holmes Chapel d																13 43					
Sandbach d																13 48					
Crewe [10] 65 a	12 28								13 07					13 28		13 58					
Kidsgrove 50 a																					
Longport 50 a																					
Stoke-on-Trent 50,68 a					12 50			13 06		13 14							13 42	13 42		13 49	
Stafford 68 a								13 24													
Wolverhampton [7] 68 ⇌ a								13 40									14 13	14 13			
Birmingham New Street [12] 68 a								13 58									14 31	14 33			
London Euston [15] ⊖65 a	14 09				14 27					14 47				15 09						15 27	

- **A** until 11 September, from 9 October. To Buxton
- **B** until 11 September
- **C** From Liverpool Lime Street
- **D** From Southport
- **E** To Coventry, ⊤ to Wolverhampton
- **F** To Milford Haven
- **G** To Buxton
- **H** From Manchester Airport to Cleethorpes
- **I** From Southport to Chester
- **J** To Cardiff Central
- **K** From Cleethorpes
- **L** To Doncaster
- **M** To Bournemouth
- **N** To Norwich
- **O** until 19 June, from 7 August
- **P** from 26 June until 31 July

Table 84

Sundays

Manchester, Stockport and Manchester Airport - Crewe and Stoke-on-Trent

	NT	XC	AW	VT	NT	EM	NT	VT	NT	NT	XC	XC	TP	VT	NT	TP	NT	XC	AW	VT	NT	NT
		◇1	■	◇1	1	◇		◇1			◇1	◇1	◇1	◇1		◇1		◇1	■	◇1	1	1
	A	B	C			D	E		F		G	H	I		J	K	L	B	M			
		⊤	⊤	⊏				⊏			⊤	⊤		⊏				⊤	⊤	⊏		
Deansgate ⇌ d	13 11														14 07		14 11					
Manchester Oxford Road d	13 17					13 39			14 00						14 13		14 17					
Manchester Piccadilly [10] ⇌ a	13 19					13 41			14 02						14 15		14 19					
d	13 22	13 27	13 30	13 35	13 41	13 44	13 52	13 55	14 04	14 04	14 07	14 07	14 13	14 15	14 18	14 20	14 22	14 27	14 30	14 35	14 41	14 41
Levenshulme d							13 58			14 09												
Heaton Chapel d							14 01			14 12												
Stockport a	13 30	13 35	13 39	13 42		13 53	14 04	14 03		14 16				14 22	14 29	14 28	14 33	14 34	14 38	14 42		14 49
d		13 36	13 40	13 42				14 04		14 17				14 22				14 36	14 39	14 42		14 51
Cheadle Hulme d										14 22												14 56
Bramhall d																						14 59
Poynton d																						15 02
Adlington (Cheshire) d																						15 04
Prestbury d																						15 07
Macclesfield a		13 48		13 55														14 48		14 55		15 11
d		13 49		13 55														14 49		14 55		15 11
Congleton d																						15 19
Handforth d										14 26												
Manchester Airport ✈ d					14a03				14a21				14a29								15 06	
Styal d																					15 10	
Wilmslow d			13 47					14 11		14 29									14 47		15 15	
Alderley Edge d										14a35											15a21	
Chelford d																						
Goostrey d																						
Holmes Chapel d																						
Sandbach d																						
Crewe [10] 65 a			14 07					14 27											15 07			
Kidsgrove 50 a																						15 25
Longport 50 a																						
Stoke-on-Trent 50,68 a		14 06		14 12							14 42	14 42		14 49				15 06		15 12		15 37
Stafford 68 a		14 24																15 24				
Wolverhampton [7] 68 ⇌ a		14 40									15 13	15 13						15 40				
Birmingham New Street [12] 68 a		14 58									15 30	15 31						15 58				
London Euston [15] ⊖65 a				15 47				16 09						16 27						16 47		

	EM	NT	VT	NT	NT	XC	TP	VT	TP	NT	XC	AW	VT	NT	EM	NT	VT	NT	NT	XC	XC
	◇		◇1			◇1	◇1	◇1	◇1		◇1	■	◇1	1	◇		◇1			◇1	◇1
	D	E		F			N		K	A	B	C			D	E		F		H	G
			⊏			⊤		⊏			⊤	⊤	⊏				⊏			⊤	⊤
Deansgate ⇌ d										15 11											
Manchester Oxford Road d	14 39			15 00						15 17					15 39			16 00			
Manchester Piccadilly [10] ⇌ a	14 41			15 02						15 19					15 41			16 02			
d	14 44	14 52	14 55	15 04	15 04	15 07	15 13	15 15	15 20	15 22	15 27	15 30	15 35	15 41	15 44	15 52	15 55	16 04	16 04	16 07	16 07
Levenshulme d		14 58			15 09											15 58			16 09		
Heaton Chapel d		15 01			15 12											16 01			16 12		
Stockport a	14 53	15 04	15 03		15 16			15 22	15 28	15 30	15 35	15 39	15 42		15 53	16 04	16 03		16 16		
d			15 04		15 17			15 22			15 36	15 39	15 42				16 04		16 17		
Cheadle Hulme d					15 22														16 22		
Bramhall d																					
Poynton d																					
Adlington (Cheshire) d																					
Prestbury d																					
Macclesfield a											15 48		15 55								
d											15 49		15 55								
Congleton d																					
Handforth d					15 26														16 26		
Manchester Airport ✈ d				15a21			15a29							16a03				16a21			
Styal d																					
Wilmslow d			15 11		15 29							15 47					16 11		16 29		
Alderley Edge d					15 32														16a35		
Chelford d					15 36																
Goostrey d					15 40																
Holmes Chapel d					15 43																
Sandbach d					15 48																
Crewe [10] 65 a			15 27		15 58							16 06					16 27				
Kidsgrove 50 a																					
Longport 50 a																					
Stoke-on-Trent 50,68 a						15 42		15 49			16 06		16 12							16 42	16 42
Stafford 68 a											16 24										
Wolverhampton [7] 68 ⇌ a						16 13					16 40									17 13	17 13
Birmingham New Street [12] 68 a						16 31					16 58									17 31	17 32
London Euston [15] ⊖65 a			17 09					17 27					17 47				18 09				

- **A** From Southport to Chester
- **B** To Bournemouth
- **C** To Cardiff Central
- **D** From Liverpool Lime Street to Norwich
- **E** To Buxton
- **F** From Liverpool Lime Street
- **G** from 26 June until 31 July
- **H** until 19 June, from 7 August
- **I** From Cleethorpes
- **J** from 9 October. From Southport
- **K** From Manchester Airport to Cleethorpes
- **L** until 2 October. From Southport
- **M** To Milford Haven
- **N** From Doncaster

Manchester, Stockport and Manchester Airport - Crewe and Stoke-on-Trent

	NT ■	NT A	VT ◇■	NT B	NT	TP ◇■ C	XC ◇■ D	NT ■	NT E	TP ◇■ F	NT G	XC ◇■ H	AW I	VT ◇■	NT J	EM ◇ K	NT ■	NT ■	NT A	AW ◇ L	AW ◇ M	NT
Deansgate d															19 29							
Manchester Oxford Road d				18 58											19 33	19 39	19 43			19 49		
Manchester Piccadilly a				19 01											19 35	19 41	19 45			19 52		
d	18 48	18 52	18 55	19 03	19 04	19 06	19 07	19 14	19 17	19 18	19 22	19 27	19 30	19 35	19 37	19 43	19 46	19 48	19 51	19 54	19 55	20 04
Levenshulme d		18 58			19 09						19 28								19 58			20 09
Heaton Chapel d		19 01			19 12						19 31								20 01			20 12
Stockport a	18 57	19 04	19 03		19 16		19 15		19 27	19 26	19 34	19 34	19 38	19 42		19 53		19 57	20 04			20 16
d	18 58		19 04		19 17		19 16					19 35	19 39	19 43				19 58				20 17
Cheadle Hulme d	19 02				19 24													20 02				20 24
Bramhall d	19 05																	20 05				
Poynton d	19 08																	20 08				
Adlington (Cheshire) d	19 11																	20 11				
Prestbury d	19 14																	20 14				
Macclesfield a	19 18											19 47		19 55				20 18				
d	19 18											19 49		19 56				20 18				
Congleton d	19 26																	20 26				
Handforth d					19 28																	20 28
Manchester Airport d				19a24		19a28		19a38							19a53		20 14			20a18	20a13	
Styal d																						
Wilmslow d			19 11		19 31								19 46				20a24					20 31
Alderley Edge d					19 34																	20 34
Chelford d					19 38																	20 38
Goostrey d					19 43																	20 43
Holmes Chapel d					19 46																	20 46
Sandbach d					19 51																	20 51
Crewe 65 a			19 27		20 01								20 05									21 01
Kidsgrove 50 a	19 32																	20 32				
Longport 50 a																						
Stoke-on-Trent 50,68 a	19 42						19 43					20 06		20 11				20 42				
Stafford 68 a							20 02					20 25										
Wolverhampton 68 a							20 16					20 39										
Birmingham New Street 68 a							20 33					20 58										
London Euston ⊖65 a			21 18											22 00								

	TP ◇■ C	TP ◇■ N	XC ◇■	NT E	TP ◇■ O	XC ◇■	AW I	VT ◇■	NT J	EM ◇ K	NT ■	NT ■	NT A	NT B	NT	TP ◇■ C	TP ◇■ N	XC ◇■	NT E	TP ◇■ F	XC ◇■
Deansgate d									20 29												
Manchester Oxford Road d		20 07							20 33	20 39	20 43			20 58			21 07				
Manchester Piccadilly a		20 09							20 35	20 41	20 45			21 01			21 09				
d	20 06		20 07	20 17	20 20	20 27	20 30	20 35	20 37	20 43	20 46	20 48	20 52	21 03	21 04	21 06		21 07	21 17	21 20	21 28
Levenshulme d													20 58		21 09						
Heaton Chapel d													21 01		21 12						
Stockport a			20 15	20 27	20 28	20 34	20 38	20 42		20 53		20 57	21 04		21 16				21 27	21 28	21 35
d			20 16			20 35	20 39	20 43				20 58			21 17						21 36
Cheadle Hulme d												21 02			21 24						
Bramhall d												21 05									
Poynton d												21 08									
Adlington (Cheshire) d												21 11									
Prestbury d												21 14									
Macclesfield a						20 47		20 55				21 18									21 48
d						20 49		20 56				21 18									21 50
Congleton d												21 26									
Handforth d															21 28						
Manchester Airport d	20a36								20a53		21 14			21a24		21a36					
Styal d																					
Wilmslow d							20 46				21a24				21 31						
Alderley Edge d															21 34						
Chelford d															21 38						
Goostrey d															21 43						
Holmes Chapel d															21 46						
Sandbach d															21 51						
Crewe 65 a							21 05								22 01						
Kidsgrove 50 a												21 32									
Longport 50 a																					
Stoke-on-Trent 50,68 a			20 43			21 06		21 11				21 42						21 43			22 07
Stafford 68 a			21 02			21 26												22 02			22 32
Wolverhampton 68 a			21 15			21 39												22 14			22 45
Birmingham New Street 68 a			21 32			21 58												22 32			23 02
London Euston ⊖65 a								23 04													

A To Buxton
B From Liverpool Lime Street
C From Cleethorpes
D To Bristol Temple Meads
E To Chester
F From Manchester Airport to Cleethorpes
G To Hazel Grove
H To Southampton Central. ✕ to Wolverhampton
I To Cardiff Central
J until 1 October. From Southport
K From Liverpool Lime Street to Nottingham
L from 25 June. From Llandudno
M until 18 June. From Llandudno
N From Liverpool Lime Street to York
O From Manchester Airport to Sheffield

Manchester, Stockport and Manchester Airport - Crewe and Stoke-on-Trent

	AW A	NT B	EM ◇ C	NT ■	NT ■	NT D	NT	NT E	TP ◇■ F	EM ◇ C	AW A	NT ■	NT ■	NT	NT D	NT ■	TP ◇■ G	NT E	NT
Deansgate d		21 29																	
Manchester Oxford Road d		21 33	21 39	21 43						22 27		22 43					23 17		
Manchester Piccadilly a		21 35	21 41	21 45						22 29		22 45					23 19		
d	21 35	21 37	21 43	21 46	21 48	21 52	22 04	22 17	22 20	22 31	22 35	22 46	22 48	23 04	23 10	23 14		23 17	23 37
Levenshulme d						21 58	22 09							23 09					23 42
Heaton Chapel d						22 01	22 12							23 12					23 45
Stockport a	21 43		21 52		21 58	22 04	22 16	22 27	22 28	22 41	22 43		22 57	23 16	23 19	23 23		23 26	23 49
d	21 44				21 58		22 17				22 44		22 58	23 16		23 23			23 50
Cheadle Hulme d					22 02		22 24						23 02	23 21		23 27			23 54
Bramhall d					22 05								23 05			23 30			
Poynton d					22 08								23 08			23 33			
Adlington (Cheshire) d					22 11								23 11			23 37			
Prestbury d					22 14								23 14			23 40			
Macclesfield a					22 18								23 20			23 46			
d					22 18														
Congleton d					22 26														
Handforth d							22 28							23 25					23 58
Manchester Airport d		21a53		22 14								23 14							
Styal d																			
Wilmslow d	21 51			22a22			22 31				22 52	23a22		23 28					00 01
Alderley Edge d							22 34							23 31					00a07
Chelford d							22 38							23 35					
Goostrey d							22 43							23 40					
Holmes Chapel d							22 46							23 43					
Sandbach d							22 51							23 48					
Crewe 65 a	22 11						23 01				23 10			23 58					
Kidsgrove 50 a					22 32														
Longport 50 a																			
Stoke-on-Trent 50,68 a					22 42														
Stafford 68 a																			
Wolverhampton 68 a																			
Birmingham New Street 68 a																			
London Euston ⊖65 a																			

Sundays

	NT H	NT ■	NT ■	TP ◇■ I	NT ■	TP ◇■ I	VT ◇■	TP ◇■ J	VT ◇■	XC ◇■ K	TP ◇■ I	NT ■	TP ◇■ L	NT D	TP ◇■ F	NT	NT M	TP ◇■ N	VT ◇■	NT O	XC ◇■ K	AW ◇ P
Deansgate d																				09 15		
Manchester Oxford Road d																	09 03	09 07		09 18		
Manchester Piccadilly a																	09 05	09 09		09 21		
d	23p37	05 41	06 41	07 08	07 41	07 50	08 05	08 13	08 20	08 27	08 38	08 41	08 47	08 55	08 58	09 04	09 07		09 20	09 22	09 27	09 30
Levenshulme d	23p42													09 00		09 09						
Heaton Chapel d	23p45													09 03		09 12						
Stockport a	23p49						08 13		08 28	08 34				09 07	09 06	09 17			09 27	09 31	09 35	09 39
d	23p50						08 14		08 28	08 36						09 17			09 27		09 36	09 39
Cheadle Hulme d	23p54															09 21						
Bramhall d																						
Poynton d																						
Adlington (Cheshire) d																						
Prestbury d																						
Macclesfield a									08 41										09 40		09 48	
d									08 42										09 40		09 49	
Congleton d																						
Handforth d	23p58															09 25						
Manchester Airport d		06a03	07a05	07a23	08a02	08a06		08a34			08a55	09 06	09a07				09a21					
Styal d												09 10										
Wilmslow d	00 01						08 22			08 43		09 15				09 28						09 47
Alderley Edge d	00a07											09a22				09 31						
Chelford d																09 35						
Goostrey d																09 40						
Holmes Chapel d																09 43						
Sandbach d																09 48						
Crewe 65 a							08 39			09 01						09 58						10 06
Kidsgrove 50 a																						
Longport 50 a																						
Stoke-on-Trent 50,68 a									08 59										09 57		10 05	
Stafford 68 a							09 01			09 25											10 26	
Wolverhampton 68 a										09 40											10 42	
Birmingham New Street 68 a										09 58											10 59	
London Euston ⊖65 a							10 57		11 02										12 08			

A To Shrewsbury
B until 1 October. From Southport
C From Liverpool Lime Street to Nottingham
D To Buxton
E To Chester
F From Manchester Airport to Sheffield
G From Liverpool Lime Street to York
H not 22 May
I from 18 September
J until 11 September
K To Coventry. ✕ to Wolverhampton
L From Sheffield
M until 11 September. From Liverpool Lime Street
N until 11 September, from 30 October. From Liverpool Lime Street to Hull
O From Wigan Wallgate to Chester
P To Cardiff Central

Manchester, Stockport and Manchester Airport - Crewe and Stoke-on-Trent

	TP	VT	TP	NT	XC	AW	VT	NT	EM	NT	VT	NT	NT	XC	TP	VT	TP	NT	XC	AW	VT	NT
	◇1	◇1	◇1		◇1	■	◇1	1	◇		◇1			◇1	◇1	◇1	◇1		◇1	■	◇1	1
	A		B	C	D	E			F	G		H			A		B	I	D	E		
		⊡			⊼	⊼	⊡				⊡			⊼		⊡			⊼	⊼	⊡	
Deansgate ⇌ d				16 11														17 11				
Manchester Oxford Road d				16 17					16 39			17 00						17 17				
Manchester Piccadilly 10 ⇌ a				16 19					16 41			17 02						17 19				
d	16 13	16 15	16 20	16 22	16 27	16 30	16 35	16 41	16 44	16 52	16 55	17 04	17 04	17 07	17 13	17 15	17 20	17 22	17 27	17 30	17 35	17 41
Levenshulme d										16 58			17 09									
Heaton Chapel d										17 01			17 12									
Stockport a		16 22	16 28	16 33	16 34	16 39	16 42		16 53	17 04	17 03		17 16			17 22	17 28	17 30	17 34	17 39	17 42	
d		16 23			16 36	16 39	16 42				17 04		17 17			17 22			17 36	17 39	17 42	
Cheadle Hulme d													17 22									
Bramhall d																						
Poynton d																						
Adlington (Cheshire) d																						
Prestbury d																						
Macclesfield a					16 48		16 55												17 48		17 55	
d					16 49		16 55												17 49		17 55	
Congleton d																						
Handforth d													17 26									
Manchester Airport ✈ d	16a34							17 06				17a21			17a29							18a03
Styal d								17 10														
Wilmslow d						16 47		17 15			17 11		17 29							17 47		
Alderley Edge d								17a21					17 32									
Chelford d													17 36									
Goostrey d													17 40									
Holmes Chapel d													17 43									
Sandbach d													17 48									
Crewe 10 65 a						17 06					17 27		17 58							18 07		
Kidsgrove 50 a																						
Longport 50 a																						
Stoke-on-Trent 50,68 a		16 48			17 06		17 12							17 42		17 49			18 06		18 12	
Stafford 68 a					17 25														18 25			
Wolverhampton 7 68 ⇌ a					17 40									18 13					18 40			
Birmingham New Street 12 68 a					17 58									18 31					18 58			
London Euston 15 ⊖65 a		18 27					18 47				19 09					19 27					19 47	

	EM	NT	VT	NT	NT	XC	XC	TP	VT	TP	NT	XC	AW	VT	NT	NT	EM	NT	VT	NT	NT	XC
	◇		◇1			◇1	◇1	◇1	◇1	◇1		◇1	■	◇1	1	1	◇		◇1			◇1
	J	G		H		K	L	A		B	C	M	E				F	G		H		
			⊡			⊼	⊼		⊡			⊼	⊼	⊡					⊡			⊼
Deansgate ⇌ d											18 11											
Manchester Oxford Road d	17 39			18 00							18 17						18 39			19 00		
Manchester Piccadilly 10 ⇌ a	17 41			18 02							18 19						18 41			19 02		
d	17 44	17 52	17 55	18 04	18 04	18 07	18 07	18 13	18 15	18 20	18 22	18 27	18 30	18 35	18 41	18 42	18 44	18 52	18 55	19 04	19 04	19 07
Levenshulme d		17 58			18 09													18 58			19 09	
Heaton Chapel d		18 01			18 12													19 01			19 12	
Stockport a	17 53	18 04	18 03		18 16				18 22	18 28	18 33	18 34	18 39	18 42		18 50	18 53	19 04	19 03		19 16	
d			18 04		18 17				18 22			18 36	18 39	18 42		18 52			19 04		19 17	
Cheadle Hulme d					18 22											18 57					19 22	
Bramhall d																19 00						
Poynton d																19 03						
Adlington (Cheshire) d																19 06						
Prestbury d																19 09						
Macclesfield a												18 48		18 55		19 13						
d												18 49		18 55		19 13						
Congleton d																19 21						
Handforth d					18 26																19 26	
Manchester Airport ✈ d				18a21				18a29							19 06					19a21		
Styal d															19 10							
Wilmslow d			18 11		18 29								18 47		19 15				19 11		19 29	
Alderley Edge d					18a35										19a21						19 32	
Chelford d																					19 36	
Goostrey d																					19 40	
Holmes Chapel d																					19 43	
Sandbach d																					19 48	
Crewe 10 65 a			18 27										19 06						19 27		19 58	
Kidsgrove 50 a																19 28						
Longport 50 a																						
Stoke-on-Trent 50,68 a						18 42	18 42		18 49			19 06		19 12		19 40						19 42
Stafford 68 a												19 24										
Wolverhampton 7 68 ⇌ a						19 13	19 13					19 40										20 13
Birmingham New Street 12 68 a						19 31	19 32					19 58										20 31
London Euston 15 ⊖65 a			20 09						20 27					20 47					21 09			

A From Cleethorpes
B From Manchester Airport to Cleethorpes
C From Southport
D To Bournemouth
E To Cardiff Central
F From Liverpool Lime Street to Norwich
G To Buxton
H From Liverpool Lime Street
I From Southport to Chester
J From Liverpool Lime Street to Nottingham
K until 19 June, from 7 August
L from 26 June until 31 July
M To Southampton Central

Manchester, Stockport and Manchester Airport - Crewe and Stoke-on-Trent

	TP	VT	TP	NT	XC	AW	VT	NT	EM	NT	NT	NT	TP	XC	TP	TP	VT	NT	AW	NT	EM
	◇1	◇1	◇1		◇1	◇	◇1	1	◇				◇1	◇1	◇1	◇1	◇1		◇	1	◇
	A		B	C	D	E			F	G	H		I		A	B		J	E		F
		⊡			⊼		⊡										⊡				
Deansgate ⇌ d				19 11														20 11			
Manchester Oxford Road d				19 17					19 39		20 00		20 07					20 17			20 39
Manchester Piccadilly 10 ⇌ a				19 19					19 41		20 02		20 09					20 19			20 41
d	19 13	19 15	19 20	19 22	19 27	19 30	19 35	19 41	19 44	19 52	20 04	20 04		20 07	20 16	20 18	20 20	20 22	20 30	20 41	20 44
Levenshulme d										19 58		20 09									
Heaton Chapel d										20 01		20 12									
Stockport a		19 22	19 28	19 30	19 34	19 39	19 41		19 53	20 04		20 16		20 15		20 26	20 27	20 33	20 38		20 53
d		19 22			19 36	19 39	19 41					20 17		20 16			20 27		20 39		
Cheadle Hulme d												20 22									
Bramhall d																					
Poynton d																					
Adlington (Cheshire) d																					
Prestbury d																					
Macclesfield a					19 48		19 54							20 28			20 40				
d					19 49		19 54							20 29			20 40				
Congleton d																					
Handforth d												20 26									
Manchester Airport ✈ d	19a29							20a03			20a21				20a32					21 06	
Styal d																				21 10	
Wilmslow d						19 47						20 29							20 47	21 15	
Alderley Edge d												20a37								21a21	
Chelford d																					
Goostrey d																					
Holmes Chapel d																					
Sandbach d																					
Crewe 10 65 a						20 07													21 07		
Kidsgrove 50 a																					
Longport 50 a																					
Stoke-on-Trent 50,68 a		19 49			20 06		20 11							20 46			20 57				
Stafford 68 a					20 26									21 08							
Wolverhampton 7 68 ⇌ a					20 39									21 21							
Birmingham New Street 12 68 a					21 00									21 39							
London Euston 15 ⊖65 a		21 31					21 58										22 56				

	NT	VT	NT	NT	XC	TP	TP	NT	AW	NT	NT	NT	NT	NT	XC	EM	TP	TP	NT	AW	TP	NT
		◇1			◇1	◇1	◇1			1	1				◇1	◇	◇1	◇1			◇1	1
	G		H			A	K	C				G	H			F	A	K	J		I	
		⊡																				
Deansgate ⇌ d								21 11											22 11			
Manchester Oxford Road d			21 00					21 17					22 00			22 07			22 17		22 37	
Manchester Piccadilly 10 ⇌ a			21 02					21 19					22 02			22 09			22 19		22 39	
d	20 52	20 55	21 04	21 04	21 07	21 13	21 20	21 22	21 34	21 41	21 41	21 52	22 04	22 04	22 07	22 11	22 13	22 15	22 22	22 35		22 46
Levenshulme d	20 58			21 09								21 58		22 09								
Heaton Chapel d	21 01			21 12								22 01		22 12								
Stockport a	21 04	21 03		21 16	21 15		21 28	21 30	21 42		21 49	22 04		22 16	22 15	22 20		22 23	22 33			
d		21 03		21 17	21 16				21 43		21 52			22 17	22 16							
Cheadle Hulme d				21 22							21 56			22 22								
Bramhall d											21 59											
Poynton d											22 02											
Adlington (Cheshire) d											22 05											
Prestbury d											22 08											
Macclesfield a		21 15			21 28						22 12				22 28							
d		21 15			21 29						22 13				22 29							
Congleton d											22 20											
Handforth d				21 26										22 26								
Manchester Airport ✈ d			21a21			21a29				22a03			22a21				22a29					23a09
Styal d																						
Wilmslow d				21 29					21 50					22 29						22 50		
Alderley Edge d				21 32										22a35								
Chelford d				21 36																		
Goostrey d				21 40																		
Holmes Chapel d				21 43																		
Sandbach d				21 48																		
Crewe 10 65 a				21 58					22 09											23 10		
Kidsgrove 50 a											22 26											
Longport 50 a																						
Stoke-on-Trent 50,68 a		21 32			21 46						22 36				22 46							
Stafford 68 a					22 06										23 04							
Wolverhampton 7 68 ⇌ a					22 20										23 18							
Birmingham New Street 12 68 a					22 40										23 36							
London Euston 15 ⊖65 a		23 48																				

A From Cleethorpes
B From Manchester Airport to Cleethorpes
C From Southport to Chester
D To Reading. ⊼ to Wolverhampton
E To Cardiff Central
F From Liverpool Lime Street to Nottingham
G To Buxton
H From Liverpool Lime Street
I until 11 September, from 30 October. From Liverpool Lime Street to York
J From Southport
K From Manchester Airport to Sheffield

Table 84

Sundays

Manchester, Stockport and Manchester Airport - Crewe and Stoke-on-Trent

		NT	NT	NT	TP	NT	NT
					◇1		
		A	B		C	D	B
Deansgate ⇌	d					23 11	
Manchester Oxford Road	d		23 00			23 17	23 59
Manchester Piccadilly 10 ⇌	a		23 02			23 19	00 02
	d	22 52	23 04	23 04	23 20	23 22	00 04
Levenshulme	d	22 58		23 09			
Heaton Chapel	d	23 01		23 12			
Stockport	a	23 04		23 16	23 28	23 33	
	d			23 17			
Cheadle Hulme	d			23 21			
Bramhall	d						
Poynton	d						
Adlington (Cheshire)	d						
Prestbury	d						
Macclesfield	a						
	d						
Congleton	d						
Handforth	d			23 25			
Manchester Airport ✈	d		23a21				00a19
Styal	d						
Wilmslow	d			23 28			
Alderley Edge	d			23a35			
Chelford	d						
Goostrey	d						
Holmes Chapel	d						
Sandbach	d						
Crewe 10 65	a						
Kidsgrove 50	a						
Longport 50	a						
Stoke-on-Trent 50,68	a						
Stafford 68	a						
Wolverhampton 7 68 ⇌	a						
Birmingham New Street 12 68	a						
London Euston 15 ⊖65	a						

A To Buxton
B From Liverpool Lime Street
C From Manchester Airport to Sheffield
D From Southport

Table 85

Manchester - Manchester Airport

Mondays to Fridays

until 15 July

Miles			TP	NT	TP	TP	TP	NT	TP	AW	TP		TP	NT	NT	TP	TP	TP	NT	NT	TP		NT	TP	NT
			MX	MO	MO	MX																			
			◇1		◇1	◇1	◇1		◇1		◇1		◇1	1		◇1	◇1	◇1	1	1	◇1			◇1	
—	Deansgate 🚊	d																							07 11
—	**Manchester Oxford Road**	d		23p59																			06 58		07 15
0	**Manchester Piccadilly** 10 🚊	a		00 02																			07 01		07 17
—		d	23p55	00 04	00 44	00 54	03 44	04 15	04 44	04 49	04 50		05 00	05 35	05 58	06 03	06 08	06 12	06 15	06 46	06 54		07 03	07 06	
3½	Mauldeth Road	d	00 04											05 42					06 22	06 53					
4½	Burnage	d	00 06											05 44					06 24	06 55					
5½	East Didsbury	d	00 09											05 46					06 26	06 57					
6¾	Gatley	d	00 12											05 49					06 29	06 59					
8¼	Heald Green	d	00 15											05 52					06 32	07 02					
9¾	**Manchester Airport** ✈	a	00 22	00 19	01 00	01 10	04 00	04 30	05 00	05 09	05 07		05 19	05 57	06 14	06 18	06 24	06 29	06 39	07 07	07 12		07 22	07 29	
—	Wilmslow 84	a												06 11						07 20					
—	Crewe 10 84	a												06 46						07 46					

		NT	TP	TP	NT	NT	TP		NT	TP	NT	TP	TP	NT	NT	TP	TP		NT	TP	NT	TP	TP	NT	NT
		1	◇1	◇1		1	◇1			◇1	1	◇1	◇1		1	◇1	◇1			◇1	1	◇1	◇1		1
				🛒			🛒			🛒		🛒	🛒			🛒	🛒			🛒		🛒	🛒		
Deansgate 🚊	d				07 28									08 29										09 29	
Manchester Oxford Road	d			07 24	07 32				07 58				08 24	08 33			08 54		08 58				09 24	09 33	
Manchester Piccadilly 10 🚊	a			07 27	07 34				08 01				08 27	08 35			08 56		09 01				09 27	09 35	
	d	07 14	07 23	07 29	07 36	07 46	07 54		08 03	08 06	08 14	08 24	08 29	08 37	08 46	08 54	08 58		09 03	09 06	09 14	09 24	09 29	09 37	09 46
Mauldeth Road	d	07 21				07 53					08 21				08 53						09 21				09 53
Burnage	d	07 23				07 55					08 23				08 55						09 23				09 55
East Didsbury	d	07 25				07 57					08 25				08 57					09 16	09 25				09 57
Gatley	d	07 27				07 59					08 27				08 59						09 27				09 59
Heald Green	d	07 30				08 02					08 30			08 47	09 02		09 10				09 30				10 02
Manchester Airport ✈	a	07 38	07 42	07 47	07 53	08 07	08 12		08 22	08 26	08 38	08 42	08 47	08 53	09 07	09 12	09 19		09 22	09 33	09 38	09 42	09 47	09 53	10 07
Wilmslow 84	a					08 21									09 20										10 20
Crewe 10 84	a					08 47									09 46										10 46

		TP	TP		NT	TP	NT	TP	TP	NT	NT	TP	TP		NT	TP	NT	TP	TP	NT	NT	TP	TP		NT
		◇1	◇1			◇1	1	◇1	◇1		1	◇1	◇1			◇1	1	◇1	◇1		1	◇1	◇1		
		🛒	🛒			🛒		🛒	🛒			🛒	🛒			🛒		🛒	🛒			🛒	🛒		
Deansgate 🚊	d		09 51							10 29			10 51							11 29			11 51		
Manchester Oxford Road	d		09 54		09 58				10 24	10 33			10 54		10 58				11 24	11 33			11 54		11 58
Manchester Piccadilly 10 🚊	a		09 56		10 01				10 27	10 35			10 56		11 01				11 27	11 35			11 56		12 01
	d	09 54	09 58		10 03	10 06	10 14	10 24	10 29	10 37	10 46	10 54	10 58		11 03	11 06	11 14	11 24	11 29	11 37	11 46	11 54	11 58		12 03
Mauldeth Road	d						10 21				10 53						11 21				11 53				
Burnage	d						10 23				10 55						11 23				11 55				
East Didsbury	d						10 25				10 57						11 25				11 57				
Gatley	d						10 27				10 59						11 27				11 59				
Heald Green	d		10 10				10 30				11 02		11 10				11 30				12 02		12 10		
Manchester Airport ✈	a	10 12	10 17		10 22	10 26	10 38	10 42	10 47	10 53	11 08	11 12	11 17		11 22	11 26	11 38	11 45	11 50	11 53	12 07	12 12	12 17		12 22
Wilmslow 84	a										11 20										12 20				
Crewe 10 84	a										11 46										12 46				

		TP	NT	TP	TP	NT	NT	TP	TP		NT	TP	NT	TP	TP	NT	NT	TP	TP		NT	TP	NT	TP	TP
		◇1	1	◇1	◇1		1	◇1	◇1			◇1	1	◇1	◇1		1	◇1	◇1			◇1	1	◇1	◇1
		🛒		🛒	🛒			🛒	🛒			🛒		🛒	🛒			🛒	🛒			🛒		🛒	🛒
Deansgate 🚊	d					12 29			12 51							13 29			13 51						
Manchester Oxford Road	d				12 24	12 33			12 54		12 58				13 24	13 33			13 54		13 58				14 24
Manchester Piccadilly 10 🚊	a				12 27	12 35			12 56		13 01				13 27	13 35			13 56		14 01				14 27
	d	12 06	12 14	12 24	12 29	12 37	12 46	12 54	12 58		13 03	13 06	13 14	13 24	13 29	13 37	13 46	13 54	13 58		14 03	14 06	14 14	14 24	14 29
Mauldeth Road	d		12 21				12 53						13 21				13 53						14 21		
Burnage	d		12 23				12 55						13 23				13 55						14 23		
East Didsbury	d		12 25				12 57						13 25				13 57						14 25		
Gatley	d		12 27				12 59						13 27				13 59						14 27		
Heald Green	d		12 30				13 02		13 10				13 30				14 02		14 10				14 30		
Manchester Airport ✈	a	12 26	12 38	12 42	12 47	12 53	13 07	13 12	13 17		13 22	13 26	13 38	13 42	13 47	13 53	14 07	14 12	14 17		14 22	14 26	14 38	14 42	14 47
Wilmslow 84	a						13 21										14 20								
Crewe 10 84	a						13 47										14 46								

		NT	NT	TP	TP		NT	TP	NT	TP	TP	NT	NT	TP	TP		NT	TP	NT	TP	TP	NT	NT	TP	TP
			1	◇1	◇1			◇1	1	◇1	◇1		1	◇1	◇1			◇1	1	◇1	◇1		1	◇1	◇1
				🛒	🛒			🛒		🛒	🛒			🛒	🛒			🛒		🛒	🛒			🛒	🛒
Deansgate 🚊	d	14 29			14 51							15 29			15 51										16 51
Manchester Oxford Road	d	14 33			14 54		14 58				15 24	15 33			15 54		15 58				16 24	16 33			16 54
Manchester Piccadilly 10 🚊	a	14 35			14 56		15 01				15 27	15 35			15 56		16 01				16 27	16 35			16 56
	d	14 37	14 46	14 54	14 58		15 03	15 06	15 14	15 24	15 29	15 37	15 46	15 54	15 58		16 03	16 06	16 14	16 24	16 29	16 37	16 46	16 54	16 58
Mauldeth Road	d		14 53						15 21				15 53						16 21				16 53		
Burnage	d		14 55						15 23				15 55						16 23				16 55		
East Didsbury	d		14 57						15 25				15 57						16 25				16 57		
Gatley	d		14 59						15 27				15 59						16 27				16 59		
Heald Green	d		15 02		15 10				15 30				16 02		16 10				16 30		16 40		17 02		17 10
Manchester Airport ✈	a	14 53	15 07	15 12	15 17		15 22	15 26	15 38	15 42	15 47	15 53	16 07	16 12	16 17		16 22	16 26	16 38	16 42	16 47	16 53	17 07	17 12	17 17
Wilmslow 84	a		15 20										16 20										17 20		
Crewe 10 84	a		15 46										16 46										17 46		

Table 85

Mondays to Fridays

until 15 July

Manchester - Manchester Airport

		NT	TP ◇1 ⚲	NT 1	TP ◇1 ⚲	NT	NT 1	TP ◇1 ⚲	TP ◇1 ⚲	NT		TP ◇1 ⚲	NT	NT 1	TP ◇1 ⚲	TP ◇1 ⚲	NT	NT 1	TP ◇1 ⚲	NT		TP ◇1 ⚲	NT 1	TP ◇1 ⚲
Deansgate 🚊	d								17 51				18 12											
Manchester Oxford Road	d		16 58			17 27	17 33			17 54	17 58			18 16			18 24	18 33			18 58				19 24
Manchester Piccadilly 10 🚊	a		17 01			17 29	17 35			17 57	18 01			18 18			18 27	18 35			19 01				19 27
	d		17 03	17 06	17 14	17 31	17 37	17 46	17 54	17 58	18 03		18 06		18 14	18 24	18 29	18 37	18 46	18 54	19 03		19 06	19 14	19 29
Mauldeth Road	d				17 21			17 53							18 21				18 53					19 21	
Burnage	d				17 23			17 55							18 23				18 55					19 23	
East Didsbury	d			17 19	17 25			17 57							18 25				18 57					19 25	
Gatley	d			17 22	17 27			17 59							18 27				18 59					19 27	
Heald Green	d			17 25	17 30	17 41		18 02		18 10					18 30		18 40		19 02					19 30	
Manchester Airport ✈	a		17 22	17 32	17 39	17 48	17 53	18 07	18 12	18 16	18 22		18 26		18 38	18 42	18 47	18 53	19 08	19 13	19 24		19 33	19 38	19 47
Wilmslow 84	a							18 21											19 23						
Crewe 10 84	a							18 47																	

		NT	TP ◇1 ⚲	NT 1	AW	TP ◇1 ⚲	TP ◇1		TP ◇1 ⚲	TP ◇1 ⚲	NT	TP ◇1	NT 1	AW ◇ ⚲	TP ◇1	NT	TP ◇1		TP ◇1 ⚲	NT	TP ◇1	NT 1	TP ◇1	TP ◇1	TP ◇1
Deansgate 🚊	d	19 29				19 51					20 29				20 51					21 29			21 51		
Manchester Oxford Road	d	19 33		19 43	19 49	19 54	19 59			20 24	20 33		20 43	20 49	20 54	20 58			21 24	21 33		21 43	21 54	22 27	
Manchester Piccadilly 10 🚊	a	19 35		19 45	19 52	19 56	20 01			20 27	20 35		20 45	20 52	20 56	21 01			21 27	21 35		21 45	21 56	22 30	
	d	19 37	19 40	19 46	19 54	19 58	20 03		20 14	20 29	20 37	20 40	20 46	20 54	20 58	21 03	21 06		21 29	21 37	21 40	21 46	21 58	22 32	22 40
Mauldeth Road	d			19 53					20 22				20 53				21 15					21 53			
Burnage	d			19 55					20 24				20 55				21 17					21 55			
East Didsbury	d			19 57					20 27				20 57				21 20					21 57			
Gatley	d			19 59					20 30				20 59				21 23					21 59			
Heald Green	d			20 02		20 10	20 15		20 33				21 02		21 10		21 26					22 02	22 09		
Manchester Airport ✈	a	19 53	19 59	20 07	20 18	20 17	20 24		20 38	20 47	20 53	20 57	21 07	21 18	21 17	21 24	21 36		21 47	21 53	21 57	22 10	22 17	22 47	22 57
Wilmslow 84	a			20 24									21 24									22 22			
Crewe 10 84	a																								

		NT 1	TP ◇1		TP ◇1	TP ◇1
Deansgate 🚊	d		22 51			
Manchester Oxford Road	d	22 43	22 54			
Manchester Piccadilly 10 🚊	a	22 45	22 56			
	d	22 46	22 58		23 06	23 55
Mauldeth Road	d	22 53				00 04
Burnage	d	22 55				00 06
East Didsbury	d	22 57				00 09
Gatley	d	22 59				00 12
Heald Green	d	23 02	23 09			00 15
Manchester Airport ✈	a	23 08	23 17		23 26	00 22
Wilmslow 84	a	23 22				
Crewe 10 84	a					

Mondays to Fridays

18 July to 30 September

		TP MX ◇1	NT MO	TP ◇1 A MO	TP MX ◇1	TP ◇1 B	TP ◇1	NT	TP ◇1	AW		TP ◇1	TP ◇1	NT 1	NT	TP ◇1	TP ◇1	TP ◇1	NT 1	NT 1		TP ◇1	NT	TP ◇1	NT
Deansgate 🚊	d																								07 11
Manchester Oxford Road	d		23p59																				06 58		07 15
Manchester Piccadilly 10 🚊	a		00 02																				07 01		07 17
	d	23p55	00 04	00 44	00 54	01 10	03 44	04 15	04 44	04 49		04 50	05 00	05 35	05 58	06 03	06 08	06 12	06 15	06 46		06 54	07 03	07 06	
Mauldeth Road	d	00 04												05 42					06 22	06 53					
Burnage	d	00 06												05 44					06 24	06 55					
East Didsbury	d	00 09												05 46					06 26	06 57					
Gatley	d	00 12												05 49					06 29	06 59					
Heald Green	d	00 15												05 52					06 32	07 02					
Manchester Airport ✈	a	00 22	00 19	01 00	01 10	01 25	04 00	04 30	05 00	05 09		05 07	05 19	05 57	06 14	06 18	06 24	06 29	06 39	07 07		07 12	07 22	07 29	
Wilmslow 84	a													06 11						07 20					
Crewe 10 84	a													06 46						07 46					

		NT 1	TP ◇1	TP ◇1 ⚲	NT	NT 1		TP ◇1 ⚲	NT	TP ◇1 ⚲	NT 1	TP ◇1 ⚲	TP ◇1 ⚲	NT	NT 1	TP ◇1 ⚲		TP ◇1 ⚲	NT	TP ◇1 ⚲	NT 1	TP ◇1 ⚲	TP ◇1 ⚲	NT	NT 1
Deansgate 🚊	d				07 28									08 29										09 29	
Manchester Oxford Road	d			07 24	07 32				07 58				08 24	08 33				08 54	08 58				09 24	09 33	
Manchester Piccadilly 10 🚊	a			07 27	07 34				08 01				08 27	08 35				08 56	09 01				09 27	09 35	
	d	07 14	07 23	07 29	07 36	07 46		07 54	08 03	08 06	08 14	08 24	08 29	08 37	08 46	08 54		08 58	09 03	09 06	09 14	09 24	09 29	09 37	09 46
Mauldeth Road	d	07 21				07 53					08 21				08 53						09 21				09 53
Burnage	d	07 23				07 55					08 23				08 55						09 23				09 55
East Didsbury	d	07 25				07 57					08 25				08 57					09 16	09 25				09 57
Gatley	d	07 27				07 59					08 27				08 59						09 27				09 59
Heald Green	d	07 30				08 02					08 30			08 47	09 02			09 10			09 30				10 02
Manchester Airport ✈	a	07 38	07 42	07 47	07 53	08 07		08 12	08 22	08 26	08 38	08 42	08 47	08 53	09 07	09 12		09 19	09 22	09 33	09 38	09 42	09 47	09 53	10 07
Wilmslow 84	a					08 21									09 20										10 20
Crewe 10 84	a					08 47									09 46										10 46

A From 18 July until 12 September

B 19 September, 26 September

Table 85

Mondays to Fridays

18 July to 30 September

Manchester - Manchester Airport

		TP ◇1 🛒		TP ◇1 🛒	NT	TP ◇1 🛒	NT 1	TP ◇1 🛒	TP ◇1 🛒	NT	NT 1	TP ◇1 🛒		TP ◇1 🛒	NT	TP ◇1 🛒	NT 1	TP ◇1 🛒	TP ◇1 🛒	NT	NT 1	TP ◇1 🛒		TP ◇1 🛒	NT
Deansgate	d			09 51						10 29				10 51						11 29				11 51	
Manchester Oxford Road	d			09 54	09 58				10 24	10 33				10 54	10 58				11 24	11 33				11 54	11 58
Manchester Piccadilly 10	a			09 56	10 01				10 27	10 35				10 56	11 01				11 27	11 35				11 56	12 01
	d	09 54		09 58	10 03	10 06	10 14	10 24	10 29	10 37	10 46	10 54		10 58	11 03	11 06	11 14	11 24	11 29	11 37	11 46	11 54		11 58	12 03
Mauldeth Road	d						10 21				10 53						11 21				11 53				
Burnage	d						10 23				10 55						11 23				11 55				
East Didsbury	d						10 25				10 57						11 25				11 57				
Gatley	d						10 27				10 59						11 27				11 59				
Heald Green	d			10 10			10 30				11 02			11 10			11 30				12 02			12 10	
Manchester Airport ✈	a	10 12		10 17	10 22	10 26	10 38	10 42	10 47	10 53	11 08	11 12		11 17	11 22	11 26	11 38	11 45	11 50	11 53	12 07	12 12		12 17	12 22
Wilmslow 84	a										11 20										12 20				
Crewe 10 84	a										11 46										12 46				

		TP ◇1 🛒	NT 1	TP ◇1 🛒	TP ◇1 🛒	NT	NT 1	TP ◇1 🛒		TP ◇1 🛒	NT	TP ◇1 🛒	NT 1	TP ◇1 🛒	TP ◇1 🛒	NT	NT 1	TP ◇1 🛒		TP ◇1 🛒	NT	TP ◇1 🛒	NT 1	TP ◇1 🛒	TP ◇1 🛒
Deansgate	d					12 29				12 51						13 29				13 51					
Manchester Oxford Road	d				12 24	12 33				12 54	12 58				13 24	13 33				13 54	13 58				14 24
Manchester Piccadilly 10	a				12 27	12 35				12 56	13 01				13 27	13 35				13 56	14 01				14 27
	d	12 06	12 14	12 24	12 29	12 37	12 46	12 54		12 58	13 03	13 06	13 14	13 24	13 29	13 37	13 46	13 54		13 58	14 03	14 06	14 14	14 24	14 29
Mauldeth Road	d		12 21				12 53						13 21				13 53						14 21		
Burnage	d		12 23				12 55						13 23				13 55						14 23		
East Didsbury	d		12 25				12 57						13 25				13 57						14 25		
Gatley	d		12 27				12 59						13 27				13 59						14 27		
Heald Green	d		12 30				13 02			13 10			13 30				14 02			14 10			14 30		
Manchester Airport ✈	a	12 26	12 38	12 42	12 47	12 53	13 07	13 12		13 17	13 22	13 26	13 38	13 42	13 47	13 53	14 07	14 12		14 17	14 22	14 26	14 38	14 42	14 47
Wilmslow 84	a						13 21										14 20								
Crewe 10 84	a						13 47										14 46								

		NT	NT 1	TP ◇1 🛒		TP ◇1 🛒	NT	TP ◇1 🛒	NT 1	TP ◇1 🛒	TP ◇1 🛒	NT	NT 1	TP ◇1 🛒		TP ◇1 🛒	NT	TP ◇1 🛒	NT 1	TP ◇1 🛒	TP ◇1 🛒	NT	NT 1	TP ◇1 🛒	
Deansgate	d	14 29				14 51						15 29				15 51									
Manchester Oxford Road	d	14 33				14 54	14 58				15 24	15 33				15 54	15 58				16 24	16 33			
Manchester Piccadilly 10	a	14 35				14 56	15 01				15 27	15 35				15 56	16 01				16 27	16 35			
	d	14 37	14 46	14 54		14 58	15 03	15 06	15 14	15 24	15 29	15 37	15 46	15 54		15 58	16 03	16 06	16 14	16 24	16 29	16 37	16 46	16 54	
Mauldeth Road	d		14 53						15 21				15 53						16 21				16 53		
Burnage	d		14 55						15 23				15 55						16 23				16 55		
East Didsbury	d		14 57						15 25				15 57						16 25				16 57		
Gatley	d		14 59						15 27				15 59						16 27				16 59		
Heald Green	d		15 02			15 10			15 30				16 02			16 10			16 30		16 40		17 02		
Manchester Airport ✈	a	14 53	15 07	15 12		15 17	15 22	15 26	15 38	15 42	15 47	15 53	16 07	16 12		16 17	16 22	16 26	16 38	16 42	16 47	16 53	17 07	17 12	
Wilmslow 84	a		15 20										16 20										17 20		
Crewe 10 84	a		15 46										16 46										17 46		

		TP ◇1 🛒	NT	TP ◇1 🛒	NT 1	TP ◇1 🛒	NT	NT 1	TP ◇1 🛒	TP ◇1 🛒		NT	TP ◇1 🛒	NT	NT 1	TP ◇1 🛒	TP ◇1 🛒	NT	NT 1	TP ◇1 🛒		NT	TP ◇1 🛒	NT 1	TP ◇1 🛒
Deansgate	d	16 51								17 51				18 12											
Manchester Oxford Road	d	16 54	16 58			17 27	17 33			17 54		17 58		18 16			18 24	18 33				18 58			19 24
Manchester Piccadilly 10	a	16 56	17 01			17 29	17 35			17 57		18 01		18 18			18 27	18 35				19 01			19 27
	d	16 58	17 03	17 06	17 14	17 31	17 37	17 46	17 54	17 58		18 03	18 06		18 14	18 24	18 29	18 37	18 46	18 54		19 03	19 06	19 14	19 29
Mauldeth Road	d				17 21			17 53							18 21				18 53					19 21	
Burnage	d				17 23			17 55							18 23				18 55					19 23	
East Didsbury	d			17 19	17 25			17 57							18 25				18 57					19 25	
Gatley	d			17 22	17 27			17 59							18 27				18 59					19 27	
Heald Green	d	17 10		17 25	17 30	17 41		18 02		18 10					18 30		18 40		19 02					19 30	
Manchester Airport ✈	a	17 17	17 22	17 32	17 39	17 48	17 53	18 07	18 12	18 16		18 22	18 26		18 38	18 42	18 47	18 53	19 08	19 13		19 24	19 28	19 38	19 47
Wilmslow 84	a							18 21											19 23						
Crewe 10 84	a							18 47																	

		NT	TP ◇1 🛒	NT 1	AW	TP ◇1 🛒		TP ◇1	TP ◇1 🛒	TP ◇1 🛒	NT	TP ◇1	NT 1	AW ◇ 🛒	TP ◇1	NT		TP ◇1	TP ◇1 🛒	NT	TP ◇1	NT 1	TP ◇1	TP ◇1	TP ◇1
Deansgate	d	19 29				19 51					20 29				20 51					21 29			21 51		
Manchester Oxford Road	d	19 33		19 43	19 49	19 54		19 59		20 24	20 33		20 43	20 49	20 54	20 58			21 24	21 33		21 43	21 54	22 27	
Manchester Piccadilly 10	a	19 35		19 45	19 52	19 56		20 01		20 27	20 35		20 45	20 52	20 56	21 01			21 27	21 35		21 45	21 56	22 30	
	d	19 37	19 40	19 46	19 54	19 58		20 03	20 14	20 29	20 37	20 40	20 46	20 54	20 58	21 03		21 06	21 29	21 37	21 40	21 46	21 58	22 32	22 40
Mauldeth Road	d			19 53					20 22				20 53					21 15				21 53			
Burnage	d			19 55					20 24				20 55					21 17				21 55			
East Didsbury	d			19 57					20 27				20 57					21 20				21 57			
Gatley	d			19 59					20 30				20 59					21 23				21 59			
Heald Green	d			20 02		20 10		20 15	20 33				21 02		21 10			21 26				22 02	22 09		
Manchester Airport ✈	a	19 53	19 59	20 07	20 18	20 17		20 24	20 38	20 47	20 53	20 57	21 07	21 18	21 17	21 24		21 36	21 47	21 53	21 57	22 10	22 17	22 47	22 57
Wilmslow 84	a			20 24									21 24									22 22			
Crewe 10 84	a																								

Table 85

Mondays to Fridays

18 July to 30 September

Manchester - Manchester Airport

	NT		TP	TP	TP
	1		◇1	◇1	◇1
Deansgate ⇌ d			22 51		
Manchester Oxford Road d	22 43		22 54		
Manchester Piccadilly 10 ⇌ a	22 45		22 56		
d	22 46		22 58	23 06	23 55
Mauldeth Road d	22 53				00 04
Burnage d	22 55				00 06
East Didsbury d	22 57				00 09
Gatley d	22 59				00 12
Heald Green d	23 02		23 09		00 15
Manchester Airport ✈ a	23 08		23 17	23 26	00 22
Wilmslow 84 a	23 22				
Crewe 10 84 a					

Mondays to Fridays

from 3 October

	TP	NT	TP	TP	TP	TP	NT	TP	AW		TP	TP	NT	NT	TP	TP	TP	NT	NT		TP	NT	TP	NT
	MX	MO	MO	MX	MO																			
	◇1		◇1	◇1	◇1	◇1		◇1			◇1	◇1	1		◇1	◇1	◇1	1	1		◇1		◇1	
			A		B																			
Deansgate ⇌ d																								07 11
Manchester Oxford Road d		23p59																				06 58		07 15
Manchester Piccadilly 10 ⇌ a		00 02																				07 01		07 17
d	23p55	00 04	00 44	00 54	01 10	03 44	04 15	04 44	04 49		04 50	05 00	05 35	05 58	06 03	06 08	06 12	06 15	06 46		06 54	07 03	07 06	
Mauldeth Road d	00 04												05 42					06 22	06 53					
Burnage d	00 06												05 44					06 24	06 55					
East Didsbury d	00 09												05 46					06 26	06 57					
Gatley d	00 12												05 49					06 29	06 59					
Heald Green d	00 15												05 52					06 32	07 02					
Manchester Airport ✈ a	00 22	00 19	01 00	01 10	01 25	04 00	04 30	05 00	05 09		05 07	05 19	05 57	06 14	06 18	06 24	06 29	06 39	07 07		07 12	07 22	07 29	
Wilmslow 84 a													06 11						07 20					
Crewe 10 84 a													06 46						07 46					

	NT	TP	TP	NT	NT		TP	NT	TP	NT	TP	TP	NT	NT	TP		TP	NT	TP	NT	TP	TP	NT	NT
	1	◇1	◇1		1		◇1		◇1	1	◇1	◇1		1	◇1		◇1		◇1	1	◇1	◇1		1
			⊥				⊥		⊥		⊥	⊥			⊥		⊥		⊥		⊥	⊥		
Deansgate ⇌ d				07 28									08 29										09 29	
Manchester Oxford Road d			07 24	07 32				07 58				08 24	08 33				08 54	08 58				09 24	09 33	
Manchester Piccadilly 10 ⇌ a			07 27	07 34				08 01				08 27	08 35				08 56	09 01				09 27	09 35	
d	07 14	07 23	07 29	07 36	07 46		07 54	08 03	08 06	08 14	08 24	08 29	08 37	08 46	08 54		08 58	09 03	09 06	09 14	09 24	09 29	09 37	09 46
Mauldeth Road d	07 21				07 53					08 21				08 53						09 21				09 53
Burnage d	07 23				07 55					08 23				08 55						09 23				09 55
East Didsbury d	07 25				07 57					08 25				08 57					09 16	09 25				09 57
Gatley d	07 27				07 59					08 27				08 59						09 27				09 59
Heald Green d	07 30				08 02					08 30			08 47	09 02			09 10			09 30				10 02
Manchester Airport ✈ a	07 38	07 42	07 47	07 53	08 07		08 12	08 22	08 26	08 38	08 42	08 47	08 53	09 07	09 12		09 19	09 22	09 33	09 38	09 42	09 47	09 53	10 07
Wilmslow 84 a					08 21									09 20										10 20
Crewe 10 84 a					08 47									09 46										10 46

	TP		TP	NT	TP	NT	TP	TP	NT	NT	TP		TP	NT	TP	NT	TP	TP	NT	NT	TP		TP	NT
	◇1		◇1		◇1	1	◇1	◇1		1	◇1		◇1		◇1	1	◇1	◇1		1	◇1		◇1	
			C																					
	⊥		⊥		⊥		⊥	⊥			⊥		⊥		⊥		⊥	⊥			⊥		⊥	
Deansgate ⇌ d			09 51						10 29				10 51						11 29				11 51	
Manchester Oxford Road d			09 54	09 58				10 24	10 33				10 54	10 58				11 24	11 33				11 54	11 58
Manchester Piccadilly 10 ⇌ a			09 56	10 01				10 27	10 35				10 56	11 01				11 27	11 35				11 56	12 01
d	09 54		09 58	10 03	10 06	10 14	10 24	10 29	10 37	10 46	10 54		10 58	11 03	11 06	11 14	11 24	11 29	11 37	11 46	11 54		11 58	12 03
Mauldeth Road d						10 21				10 53						11 21				11 53				
Burnage d						10 23				10 55						11 23				11 55				
East Didsbury d						10 25				10 57						11 25				11 57				
Gatley d						10 27				10 59						11 27				11 59				
Heald Green d			10 10			10 30				11 02			11 10			11 30				12 02			12 10	
Manchester Airport ✈ a	10 12		10 17	10 22	10 26	10 38	10 42	10 47	10 53	11 08	11 12		11 17	11 22	11 26	11 38	11 45	11 50	11 53	12 07	12 12		12 17	12 22
Wilmslow 84 a										11 20										12 20				
Crewe 10 84 a										11 46										12 46				

	TP	NT	TP	TP	NT	NT	TP		TP	NT	TP	NT	TP	TP	NT	NT	TP		TP	NT	TP	NT	TP	TP
	◇1	1	◇1	◇1		1	◇1		◇1		◇1	1	◇1	◇1		1	◇1		◇1		◇1	1	◇1	◇1
	⊥		⊥	⊥			⊥		⊥		⊥		⊥	⊥			⊥		⊥		⊥		⊥	⊥
Deansgate ⇌ d					12 29				12 51						13 29				13 51					
Manchester Oxford Road d				12 24	12 33				12 54	12 58				13 24	13 33				13 54	13 58				14 24
Manchester Piccadilly 10 ⇌ a				12 27	12 35				12 56	13 01				13 27	13 35				13 56	14 01				14 27
d	12 06	12 14	12 24	12 29	12 37	12 46	12 54		12 58	13 03	13 06	13 14	13 24	13 29	13 37	13 46	13 54		13 58	14 03	14 06	14 14	14 24	14 29
Mauldeth Road d		12 21				12 53						13 21				13 53						14 21		
Burnage d		12 23				12 55						13 23				13 55						14 23		
East Didsbury d		12 25				12 57						13 25				13 57						14 25		
Gatley d		12 27				12 59						13 27				13 59						14 27		
Heald Green d		12 30				13 02			13 10			13 30				14 02			14 10			14 30		
Manchester Airport ✈ a	12 26	12 38	12 42	12 47	12 53	13 07	13 12		13 17	13 22	13 26	13 38	13 42	13 47	13 53	14 07	14 12		14 17	14 22	14 26	14 38	14 42	14 47
Wilmslow 84 a						13 21										14 20								
Crewe 10 84 a						13 47										14 46								

A From 31 October

B From 3 October until 24 October

C not 9 December

Table 85

Mondays to Fridays

from 3 October

Manchester - Manchester Airport

		NT	NT	TP		TP	NT	TP	NT	TP	TP	NT	NT	TP		TP	NT	TP	NT	TP	TP	NT	NT	TP	
			1	◇1		◇1		◇1	1	◇1	◇1		1	◇1		◇1		◇1	1	◇1	◇1		1	◇1	
				🛒		🛒		🛒		🛒	🛒			🛒		🛒		🛒		🛒	🛒			🛒	
Deansgate 🚊	d	14 29				14 51						15 29				15 51									
Manchester Oxford Road	d	14 33				14 54	14 58				15 24	15 33				15 54	15 58				16 24	16 33			
Manchester Piccadilly 10 🚊	a	14 35				14 56	15 01				15 27	15 35				15 56	16 01				16 27	16 35			
	d	14 37	14 46	14 54		14 58	15 03	15 06	15 14	15 24	15 29	15 37	15 46	15 54		15 58	16 03	16 06	16 14	16 24	16 29	16 37	16 46	16 54	
Mauldeth Road	d		14 53						15 21				15 53						16 21				16 53		
Burnage	d		14 55						15 23				15 55						16 23				16 55		
East Didsbury	d		14 57						15 25				15 57						16 25				16 57		
Gatley	d		14 59						15 27				15 59						16 27				16 59		
Heald Green	d		15 02			15 10			15 30				16 02			16 10			16 30		16 40		17 02		
Manchester Airport ✈	a	14 53	15 07	15 12		15 17	15 22	15 26	15 38	15 42	15 47	15 53	16 07	16 12		16 17	16 22	16 26	16 38	16 42	16 47	16 53	17 07	17 12	
Wilmslow 84	a		15 20										16 20										17 20		
Crewe 10 84	a		15 46										16 46										17 46		

		TP	NT	TP	NT	TP	NT	NT	TP	TP		NT	TP	NT	NT	TP	TP	NT	NT	TP		NT	TP	NT	TP
		◇1		◇1	1	◇1		1	◇1	◇1			◇1		1	◇1	◇1		1	◇1			◇1	1	◇1
		🛒		🛒		🛒			🛒	🛒			🛒			🛒	🛒			🛒			🛒		🛒
Deansgate 🚊	d	16 51								17 51				18 12											
Manchester Oxford Road	d	16 54	16 58			17 27	17 33			17 54		17 58		18 16			18 24	18 33				18 58			19 24
Manchester Piccadilly 10 🚊	a	16 56	17 01			17 29	17 35			17 57		18 01		18 18			18 27	18 35				19 01			19 27
	d	16 58	17 03	17 06	17 14	17 31	17 37	17 46	17 54	17 58		18 03	18 06		18 14	18 24	18 29	18 37	18 46	18 54		19 03	19 06	19 14	19 29
Mauldeth Road	d				17 21			17 53							18 21				18 53					19 21	
Burnage	d				17 23			17 55							18 23				18 55					19 23	
East Didsbury	d			17 19	17 25			17 57							18 25				18 57					19 25	
Gatley	d			17 22	17 27			17 59							18 27				18 59					19 27	
Heald Green	d	17 10		17 25	17 30	17 41		18 02		18 10					18 30		18 40		19 02					19 30	
Manchester Airport ✈	a	17 17	17 22	17 32	17 39	17 48	17 53	18 07	18 12	18 16		18 22	18 26		18 38	18 42	18 47	18 53	19 08	19 13		19 24	19 28	19 38	19 47
Wilmslow 84	a							18 21											19 23						
Crewe 10 84	a							18 47																	

		NT	TP	NT	AW	TP		TP	TP	TP	NT	TP	NT	AW	TP	NT		TP	TP	NT	TP	NT	TP	TP	TP
			◇1	1		◇1		◇1	◇1	◇1		◇1	1	◇	◇1			◇1	◇1		◇1	1	◇1	◇1	◇1
			🛒			🛒			🛒	🛒				🛒					🛒						
Deansgate 🚊	d	19 29				19 51					20 29				20 51					21 29			21 51		
Manchester Oxford Road	d	19 33		19 43	19 49	19 54		19 59		20 24	20 33		20 43	20 49	20 54	20 58			21 24	21 33		21 43	21 54	22 27	
Manchester Piccadilly 10 🚊	a	19 35		19 45	19 52	19 56		20 01		20 27	20 35		20 45	20 52	20 56	21 01			21 27	21 35		21 45	21 56	22 30	
	d	19 37	19 40	19 46	19 54	19 58		20 03	20 14	20 29	20 37	20 40	20 46	20 54	20 58	21 03		21 06	21 29	21 37	21 40	21 46	21 58	22 32	22 40
Mauldeth Road	d			19 53					20 22				20 53					21 15				21 53			
Burnage	d			19 55					20 24				20 55					21 17				21 55			
East Didsbury	d			19 57					20 27				20 57					21 20				21 57			
Gatley	d			19 59					20 30				20 59					21 23				21 59			
Heald Green	d			20 02		20 10		20 15	20 33				21 02		21 10			21 26				22 02	22 09		
Manchester Airport ✈	a	19 53	19 59	20 07	20 18	20 17		20 24	20 38	20 47	20 53	20 57	21 07	21 18	21 17	21 24		21 36	21 47	21 53	21 57	22 10	22 17	22 47	22 57
Wilmslow 84	a			20 24									21 24									22 22			
Crewe 10 84	a																								

		NT		TP	TP	TP
		1		◇1	◇1	◇1
Deansgate 🚊	d			22 51		
Manchester Oxford Road	d	22 43		22 54		
Manchester Piccadilly 10 🚊	a	22 45		22 56		
	d	22 46		22 58	23 06	23 55
Mauldeth Road	d	22 53				00 04
Burnage	d	22 55				00 06
East Didsbury	d	22 57				00 09
Gatley	d	22 59				00 12
Heald Green	d	23 02		23 09		00 15
Manchester Airport ✈	a	23 08		23 17	23 26	00 22
Wilmslow 84	a	23 22				
Crewe 10 84	a					

Saturdays

until 18 June

		TP	TP	TP	NT	TP	TP	TP	AW	NT		NT	TP	TP	TP	NT	NT	TP	NT	TP		NT	NT	TP	TP
		◇1	◇1	◇1		◇1	◇1	◇1		1			◇1	◇1	◇1	1	1	◇1		◇1			1	◇1	◇1
Deansgate 🚊	d																					07 11			
Manchester Oxford Road	d																		06 58			07 15			07 24
Manchester Piccadilly 10 🚊	a																		07 01			07 17			07 27
	d	23p55	00 54	03 44	04 15	04 44	04 50	04 54	04 58	05 35		05 58	06 03	06 08	06 12	06 15	06 46	06 54	07 03	07 06			07 14	07 23	07 29
Mauldeth Road	d	00 04								05 42						06 22	06 53						07 21		
Burnage	d	00 06								05 44						06 24	06 55						07 23		
East Didsbury	d	00 09								05 46						06 26	06 57						07 25		
Gatley	d	00 12								05 49						06 29	06 59						07 27		
Heald Green	d	00 15								05 52						06 32	07 02						07 30		
Manchester Airport ✈	a	00 22	01 10	04 00	04 30	05 00	05 07	05 10	05 17	05 57		06 14	06 18	06 24	06 29	06 39	07 07	07 12	07 22	07 29			07 38	07 42	07 47
Wilmslow 84	a									06 11							07 20								
Crewe 10 84	a									06 43							07 46								

Table 85

Saturdays until 18 June

Manchester - Manchester Airport

		NT	NT 1	TP ◇1	NT	TP ◇1 🍴		NT 1	TP ◇1	TP ◇1 🍴	NT	NT 1	TP ◇1	TP ◇1 🍴	NT	TP ◇1 🍴		NT 1	TP ◇1 🍴	TP ◇1 🍴	NT	NT 1	TP ◇1 🍴	TP ◇1 🍴	NT
Deansgate ⇌	d	07 28									08 29										09 29			09 51	
Manchester Oxford Road	d	07 32			07 58					08 24	08 33			08 54	08 58					09 24	09 33			09 54	09 58
Manchester Piccadilly 10 ⇌	a	07 34			08 01					08 27	08 35			08 56	09 01					09 27	09 35			09 56	10 01
	d	07 36	07 46	07 54	08 03	08 06		08 14	08 24	08 29	08 37	08 46	08 54	08 58	09 03	09 06		09 14	09 24	09 29	09 37	09 46	09 54	09 58	10 03
Mauldeth Road	d		07 53					08 21				08 53						09 21				09 53			
Burnage	d		07 55					08 23				08 55						09 23				09 55			
East Didsbury	d		07 57					08 25				08 57				09 16		09 25				09 57			
Gatley	d		07 59					08 27				08 59						09 27				09 59			
Heald Green	d		08 02					08 30			08 47	09 02		09 10				09 30				10 02		10 10	
Manchester Airport ✈	a	07 53	08 07	08 12	08 22	08 26		08 38	08 42	08 47	08 53	09 08	09 12	09 19	09 22	09 26		09 38	09 42	09 47	09 53	10 07	10 12	10 17	10 22
Wilmslow 84	a		08 21									09 21										10 20			
Crewe 10 84	a		08 47									09 46										10 46			

		TP ◇1 🍴		NT 1	TP ◇1 🍴	TP ◇1 🍴	NT	NT 1	TP ◇1 🍴	TP ◇1 🍴	NT	TP ◇1 🍴		NT 1	TP ◇1 🍴	TP ◇1 🍴	NT	NT 1	TP ◇1 🍴	TP ◇1 🍴	NT	TP ◇1 🍴		NT 1	TP ◇1 🍴
Deansgate ⇌	d						10 29			10 51							11 29			11 51					
Manchester Oxford Road	d					10 24	10 33			10 54	10 58					11 24	11 33			11 54	11 58				
Manchester Piccadilly 10 ⇌	a					10 27	10 35			10 56	11 01					11 27	11 35			11 56	12 01				
	d	10 06		10 14	10 24	10 29	10 37	10 46	10 54	10 58	11 03	11 06		11 14	11 24	11 29	11 37	11 46	11 54	11 58	12 03	12 06		12 14	12 24
Mauldeth Road	d			10 21				10 53						11 21				11 53						12 21	
Burnage	d			10 23				10 55						11 23				11 55						12 23	
East Didsbury	d			10 25				10 57						11 25				11 57						12 25	
Gatley	d			10 27				10 59						11 27				11 59						12 27	
Heald Green	d			10 30				11 02		11 10				11 30				12 02		12 10				12 30	
Manchester Airport ✈	a	10 26		10 38	10 42	10 47	10 53	11 07	11 12	11 17	11 22	11 26		11 38	11 42	11 47	11 53	12 07	12 12	12 17	12 22	12 26		12 38	12 42
Wilmslow 84	a							11 20										12 20							
Crewe 10 84	a							11 46										12 46							

		TP ◇1 🍴	NT	NT 1	TP ◇1 🍴	TP ◇1 🍴	NT	TP ◇1 🍴		NT 1	TP ◇1 🍴	TP ◇1 🍴	NT	NT 1	TP ◇1 🍴	TP ◇1 🍴	NT	TP ◇1 🍴		NT 1	TP ◇1 🍴	TP ◇1 🍴	NT	NT 1	TP ◇1 🍴
Deansgate ⇌	d		12 29			12 51							13 29			13 51							14 29		
Manchester Oxford Road	d	12 24	12 33			12 54	12 58					13 24	13 33			13 54	13 58					14 24	14 33		
Manchester Piccadilly 10 ⇌	a	12 27	12 35			12 56	13 01					13 27	13 35			13 56	14 01					14 27	14 35		
	d	12 29	12 37	12 46	12 54	12 58	13 03	13 06		13 14	13 24	13 29	13 37	13 46	13 54	13 58	14 03	14 06		14 14	14 24	14 29	14 37	14 46	14 54
Mauldeth Road	d			12 53						13 21				13 53						14 21				14 53	
Burnage	d			12 55						13 23				13 55						14 23				14 55	
East Didsbury	d			12 57						13 25				13 57						14 25				14 57	
Gatley	d			12 59						13 27				13 59						14 27				14 59	
Heald Green	d			13 02		13 10				13 30				14 02		14 10				14 30				15 02	
Manchester Airport ✈	a	12 47	12 53	13 07	13 12	13 17	13 22	13 26		13 38	13 42	13 47	13 53	14 07	14 12	14 17	14 22	14 26		14 38	14 42	14 47	14 53	15 07	15 12
Wilmslow 84	a			13 21										14 20										15 20	
Crewe 10 84	a			13 47										14 46										15 46	

		TP ◇1 🍴	NT	TP ◇1 🍴		NT 1	TP ◇1 🍴	TP ◇1 🍴	NT	NT 1	TP ◇1 🍴	TP ◇1 🍴	NT	TP ◇1 🍴		NT 1	TP ◇1 🍴	TP ◇1 🍴	NT	NT 1	TP ◇1 🍴	TP ◇1 🍴	NT	TP ◇1 🍴	
Deansgate ⇌	d	14 51							15 29			15 51										16 51			
Manchester Oxford Road	d	14 54	14 58					15 24	15 33			15 54	15 58					16 24	16 33			16 54	16 58		
Manchester Piccadilly 10 ⇌	a	14 56	15 01					15 27	15 35			15 56	16 01					16 27	16 35			16 56	17 01		
	d	14 58	15 03	15 06		15 14	15 24	15 29	15 37	15 46	15 54	15 58	16 03	16 06		16 14	16 24	16 29	16 37	16 46	16 54	16 58	17 03	17 06	
Mauldeth Road	d					15 21				15 53						16 21				16 53					
Burnage	d					15 23				15 55						16 23				16 55					
East Didsbury	d					15 25				15 57						16 25				16 57				17 19	
Gatley	d					15 27				15 59						16 27				16 59				17 22	
Heald Green	d	15 10				15 30				16 02		16 10				16 30		16 40		17 02		17 10		17 25	
Manchester Airport ✈	a	15 17	15 22	15 26		15 38	15 42	15 47	15 53	16 07	16 12	16 17	16 22	16 26		16 38	16 42	16 47	16 53	17 07	17 12	17 17	17 22	17 32	
Wilmslow 84	a									16 20										17 20					
Crewe 10 84	a									16 46										17 46					

		NT 1	TP ◇1 🍴	NT	NT 1	TP ◇1 🍴	TP ◇1 🍴	NT	TP ◇1 🍴	NT 1		TP ◇1 🍴	TP ◇1 🍴	NT	NT 1	TP ◇1 🍴	NT	TP ◇1 🍴	NT 1	TP ◇1 🍴		NT	TP ◇1	NT 1	AW ◇ 🍴
Deansgate ⇌	d			17 29			17 51															19 29			
Manchester Oxford Road	d		17 24	17 33			17 54	17 58					18 24	18 33			18 58			19 24		19 33		19 43	
Manchester Piccadilly 10 ⇌	a		17 27	17 35			17 56	18 01					18 27	18 35			19 01			19 27		19 35		19 45	
	d	17 14	17 29	17 37	17 46	17 54	17 58	18 03	18 06	18 14		18 24	18 29	18 37	18 46	18 54	19 03	19 06	19 14	19 32		19 37	19 40	19 46	19 55
Mauldeth Road	d	17 21			17 53					18 21					18 53				19 21					19 53	
Burnage	d	17 23			17 55					18 23					18 55				19 23					19 55	
East Didsbury	d	17 25			17 57					18 25					18 57				19 25					19 57	
Gatley	d	17 27			17 59					18 27					18 59				19 27					19 59	
Heald Green	d	17 30	17 41		18 02		18 10			18 30			18 40		19 02				19 30					20 02	
Manchester Airport ✈	a	17 38	17 48	17 53	18 07	18 12	18 17	18 22	18 26	18 38		18 42	18 47	18 53	19 08	19 13	19 24	19 28	19 38	19 51		19 53	19 59	20 07	20 13
Wilmslow 84	a				18 21										19 23									20 24	
Crewe 10 84	a				18 47																				

Table 85

Saturdays
until 18 June

Manchester - Manchester Airport

		TP	TP	TP	NT	TP		NT	TP	NT	TP	TP	NT	TP	NT	TP		TP	NT	TP	TP
		◇1	◇1 🚲	◇1 🚲		◇1		1	◇1		◇1	◇1 🚲		◇1	1	◇1		◇1	1	◇1	◇1
Deansgate	🚊 d	19 51			20 29				20 51				21 29			21 51				22 51	
Manchester Oxford Road	d	19 54		20 24	20 33			20 43	20 54	20 58		21 24	21 33		21 43	21 54			22 43	22 54	
Manchester Piccadilly 10	🚊 a	19 56		20 27	20 35			20 45	20 56	21 01		21 27	21 35		21 45	21 56			22 45	22 56	
	d	19 58	20 06	20 32	20 37	20 40		20 46	20 58	21 03	21 06	21 29	21 37	21 40	21 46	21 58		22 40	22 46	22 58	23 55
Mauldeth Road	d		20 15					20 53			21 15				21 53				22 53		00 04
Burnage	d		20 17					20 55			21 17				21 55				22 55		00 06
East Didsbury	d		20 20					20 57			21 20				21 57				22 57		00 09
Gatley	d		20 23					20 59			21 23				21 59				22 59		00 12
Heald Green	d	20 10	20 26					21 02	21 10		21 26				22 02	22 09			23 02	23 09	00 15
Manchester Airport	✈ a	20 17	20 36	20 47	20 53	20 57		21 07	21 17	21 24	21 36	21 47	21 53	21 57	22 08	22 17		22 57	23 08	23 17	00 22
Wilmslow	84 a							21 24							22 22				23 22		
Crewe 10	84 a																				

Saturdays
25 June to 1 October

		TP	TP	TP	NT	TP	TP	TP	AW	NT		NT	TP	TP	TP	NT	NT	TP	NT	TP		NT	NT	TP	TP
		◇1	◇1	◇1		◇1	◇1	◇1		1			◇1	◇1	◇1	1	1	◇1		◇1			1	◇1	◇1
Deansgate	🚊 d																					07 11			
Manchester Oxford Road	d																		06 58			07 15			07 24
Manchester Piccadilly 10	🚊 a																		07 01			07 17			07 27
	d	23p55	00 54	03 44	04 15	04 44	04 50	04 54	04 58	05 35		05 58	06 03	06 08	06 12	06 15	06 46	06 54	07 03	07 06			07 14	07 23	07 29
Mauldeth Road	d	00 04								05 42						06 22	06 53						07 21		
Burnage	d	00 06								05 44						06 24	06 55						07 23		
East Didsbury	d	00 09								05 46						06 26	06 57						07 25		
Gatley	d	00 12								05 49						06 29	06 59						07 27		
Heald Green	d	00 15								05 52						06 32	07 02						07 30		
Manchester Airport	✈ a	00 22	01 10	04 00	04 30	05 00	05 07	05 10	05 17	05 57		06 14	06 18	06 24	06 29	06 39	07 07	07 12	07 22	07 29			07 38	07 42	07 47
Wilmslow	84 a									06 11							07 20								
Crewe 10	84 a									06 43							07 46								

		NT	NT	TP	NT	TP		NT	TP	TP	NT	NT	TP	TP	NT	TP		NT	TP	TP	NT	NT	TP	TP	NT
			1	◇1		◇1 🚲		1	◇1	◇1 🚲		1	◇1	◇1 🚲		◇1 🚲		1	◇1 🚲	◇1 🚲		1	◇1 🚲	◇1 🚲	
Deansgate	🚊 d	07 28									08 29										09 29			09 51	
Manchester Oxford Road	d	07 32			07 58					08 24	08 33			08 54	08 58					09 24	09 33			09 54	09 58
Manchester Piccadilly 10	🚊 a	07 34			08 01					08 27	08 35			08 56	09 01					09 27	09 35			09 56	10 01
	d	07 36	07 46	07 54	08 03	08 06		08 14	08 24	08 29	08 37	08 46	08 54	08 58	09 03	09 06		09 14	09 24	09 29	09 37	09 46	09 54	09 58	10 03
Mauldeth Road	d		07 53					08 21				08 53						09 21				09 53			
Burnage	d		07 55					08 23				08 55						09 23				09 55			
East Didsbury	d		07 57					08 25				08 57				09 16		09 25				09 57			
Gatley	d		07 59					08 27				08 59						09 27				09 59			
Heald Green	d		08 02					08 30			08 47	09 02		09 10				09 30				10 02		10 10	
Manchester Airport	✈ a	07 53	08 07	08 12	08 22	08 26		08 38	08 42	08 47	08 53	09 08	09 12	09 19	09 22	09 26		09 38	09 42	09 47	09 53	10 07	10 12	10 17	10 22
Wilmslow	84 a		08 21									09 21										10 20			
Crewe 10	84 a		08 47									09 46										10 46			

		TP		NT	TP	TP	NT	NT	TP	TP	NT	TP		NT	TP	TP	NT	NT	TP	TP	NT	TP		NT	TP
		◇1 🚲		1	◇1 🚲	◇1 🚲		1	◇1 🚲	◇1 🚲		◇1 🚲		1	◇1 🚲	◇1 🚲		1	◇1 🚲	◇1 🚲		◇1 🚲		1	◇1 🚲
Deansgate	🚊 d						10 29			10 51							11 29			11 51					
Manchester Oxford Road	d					10 24	10 33			10 54	10 58					11 24	11 33			11 54	11 58				
Manchester Piccadilly 10	🚊 a					10 27	10 35			10 56	11 01					11 27	11 35			11 56	12 01				
	d	10 06		10 14	10 24	10 29	10 37	10 46	10 54	10 58	11 03	11 06		11 14	11 24	11 29	11 37	11 46	11 54	11 58	12 03	12 06		12 14	12 24
Mauldeth Road	d			10 21				10 53						11 21				11 53						12 21	
Burnage	d			10 23				10 55						11 23				11 55						12 23	
East Didsbury	d			10 25				10 57						11 25				11 57						12 25	
Gatley	d			10 27				10 59						11 27				11 59						12 27	
Heald Green	d			10 30				11 02		11 10				11 30				12 02		12 10				12 30	
Manchester Airport	✈ a	10 26		10 38	10 42	10 47	10 53	11 07	11 12	11 17	11 22	11 26		11 38	11 42	11 47	11 53	12 07	12 12	12 17	12 22	12 26		12 38	12 42
Wilmslow	84 a							11 20										12 20							
Crewe 10	84 a							11 46										12 46							

		TP	NT	NT	TP	TP	NT	TP		NT	TP	TP	NT	NT	TP	TP	NT	TP		NT	TP	TP	NT	NT	TP
		◇1 🚲		1	◇1 🚲	◇1 🚲		◇1 🚲		1	◇1 🚲	◇1 🚲		1	◇1 🚲	◇1 🚲		◇1 🚲		1	◇1 🚲	◇1 🚲		1	◇1 🚲
Deansgate	🚊 d		12 29			12 51							13 29			13 51							14 29		
Manchester Oxford Road	d	12 24	12 33			12 54	12 58					13 24	13 33			13 54	13 58					14 24	14 33		
Manchester Piccadilly 10	🚊 a	12 27	12 35			12 56	13 01					13 27	13 35			13 56	14 01					14 27	14 35		
	d	12 29	12 37	12 46	12 54	12 58	13 03	13 06		13 14	13 24	13 29	13 37	13 46	13 54	13 58	14 03	14 06		14 14	14 24	14 29	14 37	14 46	14 54
Mauldeth Road	d			12 53						13 21				13 53						14 21				14 53	
Burnage	d			12 55						13 23				13 55						14 23				14 55	
East Didsbury	d			12 57						13 25				13 57						14 25				14 57	
Gatley	d			12 59						13 27				13 59						14 27				14 59	
Heald Green	d			13 02		13 10				13 30				14 02		14 10				14 30				15 02	
Manchester Airport	✈ a	12 47	12 53	13 07	13 12	13 17	13 22	13 26		13 38	13 42	13 47	13 53	14 07	14 12	14 17	14 22	14 26		14 38	14 42	14 47	14 53	15 07	15 12
Wilmslow	84 a			13 21										14 20										15 20	
Crewe 10	84 a			13 47										14 46										15 46	

Table 85

Saturdays

25 June to 1 October

Manchester - Manchester Airport

		TP	NT	TP		NT	TP	TP	NT	NT	TP	TP	NT	TP		NT	TP	TP	NT	NT	TP	TP	NT	TP	
		◇1 🛒		◇1 🛒		1	◇1 🛒	◇1 🛒		1	◇1 🛒	◇1 🛒		◇1 🛒		1	◇1 🛒	◇1 🛒		1	◇1 🛒	◇1 🛒		◇1 🛒	
Deansgate	d	14 51							15 29			15 51										16 51			
Manchester Oxford Road	d	14 54	14 58					15 24	15 33			15 54	15 58					16 24	16 33			16 54	16 58		
Manchester Piccadilly 10	a	14 56	15 01					15 27	15 35			15 56	16 01					16 27	16 35			16 56	17 01		
	d	14 58	15 03	15 06		15 14	15 24	15 29	15 37	15 46	15 54	15 58	16 03	16 06		16 14	16 24	16 29	16 37	16 46	16 54	16 58	17 03	17 06	
Mauldeth Road	d					15 21				15 53						16 21				16 53					
Burnage	d					15 23				15 55						16 23				16 55					
East Didsbury	d					15 25				15 57						16 25				16 57				17 19	
Gatley	d					15 27				15 59						16 27				16 59				17 22	
Heald Green	d	15 10				15 30				16 02		16 10				16 30		16 40		17 02		17 10		17 25	
Manchester Airport ✈	a	15 17	15 22	15 26		15 38	15 42	15 47	15 53	16 07	16 12	16 17	16 22	16 26		16 38	16 42	16 47	16 53	17 07	17 12	17 17	17 22	17 32	
Wilmslow 84	a									16 20										17 20					
Crewe 10 84	a									16 46										17 46					

		NT	TP	NT	NT	TP	TP	NT	TP	NT		TP	TP	NT	NT	TP	NT	TP	NT	TP		NT	TP	NT	AW
		1	◇1 🛒		1	◇1 🛒	◇1 🛒		◇1 🛒	1		◇1 🛒	◇1 🛒		1	◇1 🛒		◇1 🛒	1	◇1 🛒			◇1	1	◇ 🛒
Deansgate	d			17 29			17 51															19 29			
Manchester Oxford Road	d		17 24	17 33			17 54	17 58					18 24	18 33			18 58			19 24		19 33		19 43	19 49
Manchester Piccadilly 10	a		17 27	17 35			17 56	18 01					18 27	18 35			19 01			19 27		19 35		19 45	19 52
	d	17 14	17 29	17 37	17 46	17 54	17 58	18 03	18 06	18 14		18 24	18 29	18 37	18 46	18 54	19 03	19 06	19 14	19 32		19 37	19 40	19 46	19 54
Mauldeth Road	d	17 21			17 53					18 21					18 53				19 21					19 53	
Burnage	d	17 23			17 55					18 23					18 55				19 23					19 55	
East Didsbury	d	17 25			17 57					18 25					18 57				19 25					19 57	
Gatley	d	17 27			17 59					18 27					18 59				19 27					19 59	
Heald Green	d	17 30	17 41		18 02		18 10			18 30			18 40		19 02				19 30					20 02	
Manchester Airport ✈	a	17 38	17 48	17 53	18 07	18 12	18 17	18 22	18 26	18 38		18 42	18 47	18 53	19 08	19 13	19 24	19 28	19 38	19 51		19 53	19 59	20 07	20 18
Wilmslow 84	a				18 21										19 23									20 24	
Crewe 10 84	a				18 47																				

		TP	TP	TP	NT	TP		NT	TP	NT	TP	TP	NT	TP	NT	TP		TP	NT	TP	TP				
		◇1	◇1 🛒	◇1 🛒		◇1		1	◇1		◇1	◇1 🛒		◇1	1	◇1		◇1	1	◇1	◇1				
Deansgate	d	19 51			20 29				20 51				21 29			21 51				22 51					
Manchester Oxford Road	d	19 54		20 24	20 33			20 43	20 54	20 58		21 24	21 33		21 43	21 54			22 43	22 54					
Manchester Piccadilly 10	a	19 56		20 27	20 35			20 45	20 56	21 01		21 27	21 35		21 45	21 56			22 45	22 56					
	d	19 58	20 06	20 32	20 37	20 40		20 46	20 58	21 03	21 06	21 29	21 37	21 40	21 46	21 58		22 40	22 46	22 58	23 55				
Mauldeth Road	d		20 15					20 53			21 15				21 53				22 53		00 04				
Burnage	d		20 17					20 55			21 17				21 55				22 55		00 06				
East Didsbury	d		20 20					20 57			21 20				21 57				22 57		00 09				
Gatley	d		20 23					20 59			21 23				21 59				22 59		00 12				
Heald Green	d	20 10	20 26					21 02	21 10		21 26				22 02	22 09			23 02	23 09	00 15				
Manchester Airport ✈	a	20 17	20 36	20 47	20 53	20 57		21 07	21 17	21 24	21 36	21 47	21 53	21 57	22 08	22 17		22 57	23 08	23 17	00 22				
Wilmslow 84	a							21 24							22 22				23 22						
Crewe 10 84	a																								

Saturdays

from 8 October

		TP	TP	TP	NT	TP	TP	TP	AW	NT		NT	TP	TP	TP	NT	NT	TP	NT	TP		NT	NT	TP	TP
		◇1	◇1	◇1		◇1	◇1	◇1		1			◇1	◇1	◇1	1	1	◇1		◇1			1	◇1	◇1
Deansgate	d																					07 11			
Manchester Oxford Road	d																		06 58			07 15			07 24
Manchester Piccadilly 10	a																		07 01			07 17			07 27
	d	23p55	00 54	03 44	04 15	04 44	04 50	04 54	04 58	05 35		05 58	06 03	06 08	06 12	06 15	06 46	06 54	07 03	07 06			07 14	07 23	07 29
Mauldeth Road	d	00 04								05 42						06 22	06 53						07 21		
Burnage	d	00 06								05 44						06 24	06 55						07 23		
East Didsbury	d	00 09								05 46						06 26	06 57						07 25		
Gatley	d	00 12								05 49						06 29	06 59						07 27		
Heald Green	d	00 15								05 52						06 32	07 02						07 30		
Manchester Airport ✈	a	00 22	01 10	04 00	04 30	05 00	05 07	05 10	05 17	05 57		06 14	06 18	06 24	06 29	06 39	07 07	07 12	07 22	07 29			07 38	07 42	07 47
Wilmslow 84	a									06 11							07 20								
Crewe 10 84	a									06 43							07 46								

		NT	NT	TP	NT	TP		NT	TP	TP	NT	NT	TP	TP	NT	TP		NT	TP	TP	NT	NT	TP	TP	NT
			1	◇1		◇1 🛒		1	◇1	◇1 🛒		1	◇1	◇1 🛒		◇1 🛒		1	◇1 🛒	◇1 🛒		1	◇1 🛒	◇1 🛒	
Deansgate	d	07 28									08 29										09 29			09 51	
Manchester Oxford Road	d	07 32			07 58					08 24	08 33			08 54	08 58					09 24	09 33			09 54	09 58
Manchester Piccadilly 10	a	07 34			08 01					08 27	08 35			08 56	09 01					09 27	09 35			09 56	10 01
	d	07 36	07 46	07 54	08 03	08 06		08 14	08 24	08 29	08 37	08 46	08 54	08 58	09 03	09 06		09 14	09 24	09 29	09 37	09 46	09 54	09 58	10 03
Mauldeth Road	d		07 53					08 21				08 53						09 21				09 53			
Burnage	d		07 55					08 23				08 55						09 23				09 55			
East Didsbury	d		07 57					08 25				08 57				09 16		09 25				09 57			
Gatley	d		07 59					08 27				08 59						09 27				09 59			
Heald Green	d		08 02					08 30			08 47	09 02		09 10				09 30				10 02		10 10	
Manchester Airport ✈	a	07 53	08 07	08 12	08 22	08 26		08 38	08 42	08 47	08 53	09 08	09 12	09 19	09 22	09 26		09 38	09 42	09 47	09 53	10 07	10 12	10 17	10 22
Wilmslow 84	a		08 21									09 21										10 20			
Crewe 10 84	a		08 47									09 46										10 46			

Table 85

Saturdays
from 8 October

Manchester - Manchester Airport

	TP		NT	TP	TP	NT	NT	TP	TP	NT	TP		NT	TP	TP	NT	NT	TP	TP	NT	TP		NT	TP
	◇1		1	◇1	◇1		1	◇1	◇1		◇1		1	◇1	◇1		1	◇1	◇1		◇1		1	◇1
	🛒			🛒	🛒			🛒	🛒		🛒			🛒	🛒			🛒	🛒		🛒			🛒
Deansgate 🚊 d						10 29			10 51							11 29			11 51					
Manchester Oxford Road d					10 24	10 33			10 54	10 58					11 24	11 33			11 54	11 58				
Manchester Piccadilly 10 🚊 a					10 27	10 35			10 56	11 01					11 27	11 35			11 56	12 01				
d	10 06		10 14	10 24	10 29	10 37	10 46	10 54	10 58	11 03	11 06		11 14	11 24	11 29	11 37	11 46	11 54	11 58	12 03	12 06		12 14	12 24
Mauldeth Road d			10 21				10 53						11 21				11 53						12 21	
Burnage d			10 23				10 55						11 23				11 55						12 23	
East Didsbury d			10 25				10 57						11 25				11 57						12 25	
Gatley d			10 27				10 59						11 27				11 59						12 27	
Heald Green d			10 30				11 02		11 10				11 30				12 02		12 10				12 30	
Manchester Airport ✈ a	10 26		10 38	10 42	10 47	10 53	11 07	11 12	11 17	11 22	11 26		11 38	11 42	11 47	11 53	12 07	12 12	12 17	12 22	12 26		12 38	12 42
Wilmslow 84 a							11 20										12 20							
Crewe 10 84 a							11 46										12 46							

	TP	NT	NT	TP	TP	NT	TP		NT	TP	TP	NT	NT	TP	TP	NT	TP		NT	TP	TP	NT	NT	TP
	◇1		1	◇1	◇1		◇1		1	◇1	◇1		1	◇1	◇1		◇1		1	◇1	◇1		1	◇1
	🛒			🛒	🛒		🛒			🛒	🛒			🛒	🛒		🛒			🛒	🛒			🛒
Deansgate 🚊 d		12 29			12 51							13 29			13 51							14 29		
Manchester Oxford Road d	12 24	12 33			12 54	12 58					13 24	13 33			13 54	13 58					14 24	14 33		
Manchester Piccadilly 10 🚊 a	12 27	12 35			12 56	13 01					13 27	13 35			13 56	14 01					14 27	14 35		
d	12 29	12 37	12 46	12 54	12 58	13 03	13 06		13 14	13 24	13 29	13 37	13 46	13 54	13 58	14 03	14 06		14 14	14 24	14 29	14 37	14 46	14 54
Mauldeth Road d			12 53						13 21				13 53						14 21				14 53	
Burnage d			12 55						13 23				13 55						14 23				14 55	
East Didsbury d			12 57						13 25				13 57						14 25				14 57	
Gatley d			12 59						13 27				13 59						14 27				14 59	
Heald Green d			13 02		13 10				13 30				14 02		14 10				14 30				15 02	
Manchester Airport ✈ a	12 47	12 53	13 07	13 12	13 17	13 22	13 26		13 38	13 42	13 47	13 53	14 07	14 12	14 17	14 22	14 26		14 38	14 42	14 47	14 53	15 07	15 12
Wilmslow 84 a			13 21										14 20										15 20	
Crewe 10 84 a			13 47										14 46										15 46	

	TP	NT	TP		NT	TP	TP	NT	NT	TP	TP	NT	TP		NT	TP	TP	NT	NT	TP	TP	NT	TP	
	◇1		◇1		1	◇1	◇1		1	◇1	◇1		◇1		1	◇1	◇1		1	◇1	◇1		◇1	
	🛒		🛒			🛒	🛒			🛒	🛒		🛒			🛒	🛒			🛒	🛒		🛒	
Deansgate 🚊 d	14 51							15 29			15 51										16 51			
Manchester Oxford Road d	14 54	14 58					15 24	15 33			15 54	15 58					16 24	16 33			16 54	16 58		
Manchester Piccadilly 10 🚊 a	14 56	15 01					15 27	15 35			15 56	16 01					16 27	16 35			16 56	17 01		
d	14 58	15 03	15 06		15 14	15 24	15 29	15 37	15 46	15 54	15 58	16 03	16 06		16 14	16 24	16 29	16 37	16 46	16 54	16 58	17 03	17 06	
Mauldeth Road d					15 21				15 53						16 21				16 53					
Burnage d					15 23				15 55						16 23				16 55					
East Didsbury d					15 25				15 57						16 25				16 57				17 19	
Gatley d					15 27				15 59						16 27				16 59				17 22	
Heald Green d	15 10				15 30				16 02		16 10				16 30		16 40		17 02		17 10		17 25	
Manchester Airport ✈ a	15 17	15 22	15 26		15 38	15 42	15 47	15 53	16 07	16 12	16 17	16 22	16 26		16 38	16 42	16 47	16 53	17 07	17 12	17 17	17 22	17 32	
Wilmslow 84 a									16 20										17 20					
Crewe 10 84 a									16 46										17 46					

	NT	TP	NT	NT	TP	TP	NT	TP	NT		TP	TP	NT	NT	TP	NT	TP	NT	TP		NT	TP	NT	AW
	1	◇1		1	◇1	◇1		◇1	1		◇1	◇1		1	◇1		◇1	1	◇1			◇1	1	◇
		🛒			🛒	🛒		🛒			🛒	🛒			🛒		🛒		🛒					🛒
Deansgate 🚊 d			17 29			17 51															19 29			
Manchester Oxford Road d		17 24	17 33			17 54	17 58					18 24	18 33			18 58			19 24		19 33		19 43	19 49
Manchester Piccadilly 10 🚊 a		17 27	17 35			17 56	18 01					18 27	18 35			19 01			19 27		19 35		19 45	19 52
d	17 14	17 29	17 37	17 46	17 54	17 58	18 03	18 06	18 14		18 24	18 29	18 37	18 46	18 54	19 03	19 06	19 14	19 32		19 37	19 40	19 46	19 54
Mauldeth Road d	17 21			17 53					18 21					18 53				19 21					19 53	
Burnage d	17 23			17 55					18 23					18 55				19 23					19 55	
East Didsbury d	17 25			17 57					18 25					18 57				19 25					19 57	
Gatley d	17 27			17 59					18 27					18 59				19 27					19 59	
Heald Green d	17 30	17 41		18 02		18 10			18 30			18 40		19 02				19 30					20 02	
Manchester Airport ✈ a	17 38	17 48	17 53	18 07	18 12	18 17	18 22	18 26	18 38		18 42	18 47	18 53	19 08	19 13	19 24	19 28	19 38	19 51		19 53	19 59	20 07	20 18
Wilmslow 84 a				18 21										19 23									20 24	
Crewe 10 84 a				18 47																				

	TP	TP	TP	NT	TP		NT	TP	NT	TP	TP	NT	TP	NT	TP		TP	NT	TP	TP				
	◇1	◇1	◇1		◇1		1	◇1		◇1	◇1		◇1	1	◇1		◇1	1	◇1	◇1				
		🛒	🛒								🛒													
Deansgate 🚊 d	19 51			20 29				20 51				21 29			21 51				22 51					
Manchester Oxford Road d	19 54		20 24	20 33			20 43	20 54	20 58		21 24	21 33		21 43	21 54			22 43	22 54					
Manchester Piccadilly 10 🚊 a	19 56		20 27	20 35			20 45	20 56	21 01		21 27	21 35		21 45	21 56			22 45	22 56					
d	19 58	20 06	20 32	20 37	20 40		20 46	20 58	21 03	21 06	21 29	21 37	21 40	21 46	21 58		22 40	22 46	22 58	23 55				
Mauldeth Road d		20 15					20 53			21 15				21 53				22 53		00 04				
Burnage d		20 17					20 55			21 17				21 55				22 55		00 06				
East Didsbury d		20 20					20 57			21 20				21 57				22 57		00 09				
Gatley d		20 23					20 59			21 23				21 59				22 59		00 12				
Heald Green d	20 10	20 26					21 02	21 10		21 26				22 02	22 09			23 02	23 09	00 15				
Manchester Airport ✈ a	20 17	20 36	20 47	20 53	20 57		21 07	21 17	21 24	21 36	21 47	21 53	21 57	22 08	22 17		22 57	23 08	23 17	00 22				
Wilmslow 84 a							21 24							22 22				23 22						
Crewe 10 84 a																								

Table 85

Sundays

until 11 September

Manchester - Manchester Airport

	TP	TP	TP	TP	NT	TP	NT	TP	NT		TP	TP	NT	TP	TP	NT	NT	TP	NT		TP	NT	TP	TP
	◇1	◇1	◇1	◇1	1	◇1	1	◇1	1		◇1	◇1	1	◇1	◇1			◇1	1		◇1		◇1	◇1
	A	A																						
Deansgate d															08 53		09 15				09 51			
Manchester Oxford Road d															08 56	09 03	09 18				09 54	10 00		
Manchester Piccadilly a															08 59	09 05	09 21				09 56	10 03		
Manchester Piccadilly d	23p55	00 45	04 06	05 21	05 41	06 38	06 41	07 38	07 41		08 13	08 38	08 41	08 47	09 00	09 07		09 38	09 41		09 58	10 07	10 16	10 38
Mauldeth Road d	00 04				05 48		06 50		07 48				08 48						09 48					
Burnage d	00 06				05 50		06 52		07 50				08 50						09 50					
East Didsbury d	00 09				05 52		06 54		07 52				08 52						09 52					
Gatley d	00 12				05 54		06 56		07 54				08 54						09 54					
Heald Green d	00 15				05 57		06 59		07 57				08 57						09 57					
Manchester Airport a	00 22	01 00	04 23	05 38	06 03	06 55	07 05	07 55	08 02		08 26	08 55	09 04	09 07	09 19	09 21		09 55	10 03		10 17	10 21	10 30	10 55
Wilmslow 84 a													09 15											
Crewe 84 a																								

	NT	TP	NT	NT	TP		TP	NT	TP	NT	NT	TP	TP	NT	TP		NT	NT	TP	TP	TP	NT	TP	NT
	1	◇1			◇1		◇1	1	◇1			◇1	◇1	1	◇1				◇1	◇1	◇1	1	◇1	
Deansgate d		10 51		11 11					11 51		12 11				12 51			13 11					13 51	
Manchester Oxford Road d		10 54	11 00	11 17	11 24			11 37	11 54	12 00	12 17			12 43	12 54		13 00	13 17		13 24			13 54	14 00
Manchester Piccadilly a		10 56	11 03	11 19	11 27			11 40	11 56	12 03	12 19			12 45	12 56		13 02	13 19		13 27			13 56	14 02
Manchester Piccadilly d	10 41	10 58	11 07		11 29		11 38	11 41	11 58	12 07		12 13	12 38	12 47	12 58		13 04		13 13	13 29	13 38	13 41	13 58	14 04
Mauldeth Road d	10 48							11 48						12 54								13 48		
Burnage d	10 50							11 50						12 56								13 50		
East Didsbury d	10 52							11 52						12 58								13 52		
Gatley d	10 54							11 54						13 00								13 54		
Heald Green d	10 57							11 57						13 03								13 57		
Manchester Airport a	11 01	11 17	11 21		11 47		11 55	12 04	12 17	12 21		12 29	12 55	13 08	13 17		13 24		13 29	13 47	13 55	14 03	14 17	14 21
Wilmslow 84 a	11 16													13 19										
Crewe 84 a																								

	NT		TP	TP	TP	NT	TP	NT	NT	TP	TP		TP	NT	TP	NT	NT	TP	TP	TP	NT		TP	NT
			◇1	◇1	◇1	1	◇1			◇1	◇1		◇1	1	◇1			◇1	◇1	◇1	1		◇1	
																	B							
				trolley															trolley					
Deansgate d	14 11						14 51		15 11						15 51		16 11						16 51	
Manchester Oxford Road d	14 17			14 24			14 54	15 00	15 17		15 24				15 54	16 00	16 17		16 24				16 54	17 00
Manchester Piccadilly a	14 19			14 27			14 56	15 02	15 19		15 27				15 56	16 02	16 19		16 27				16 56	17 02
Manchester Piccadilly d			14 13	14 29	14 38	14 41	14 58	15 04		15 13	15 29		15 38	15 41	15 58	16 04		16 13	16 29	16 38	16 41		16 58	17 04
Mauldeth Road d						14 48								15 48							16 48			
Burnage d						14 50								15 50							16 50			
East Didsbury d						14 52								15 52							16 52			
Gatley d						14 54								15 54							16 54			
Heald Green d						14 57								15 57							16 57			
Manchester Airport a			14 29	14 47	14 55	15 02	15 17	15 21		15 29	15 47		15 55	16 03	16 17	16 21		16 34	16 47	16 55	17 02		17 17	17 21
Wilmslow 84 a						15 14															17 13			
Crewe 84 a																								

	NT	TP	TP	TP	NT	TP	NT		NT	TP	TP	TP	NT	TP	NT	NT	TP		TP	TP	NT	TP	NT	NT
		◇1	◇1	◇1	1	◇1				◇1	◇1	◇1	1	◇1			◇1		◇1	◇1	1	◇1		
											trolley								trolley					
Deansgate d	17 11					17 51			18 11					18 51		19 11						19 51		20 11
Manchester Oxford Road d	17 17		17 24			17 54	18 00		18 17		18 24			18 54	19 00	19 17			19 24			19 54	20 00	20 17
Manchester Piccadilly a	17 19		17 27			17 56	18 02		18 19		18 27			18 56	19 02	19 19			19 27			19 56	20 02	20 19
Manchester Piccadilly d		17 13	17 29	17 38	17 41	17 58	18 04			18 13	18 29	18 38	18 41	18 58	19 04		19 13		19 29	19 38	19 41	19 58	20 04	
Mauldeth Road d					17 48								18 48								19 48			
Burnage d					17 50								18 50								19 50			
East Didsbury d					17 52								18 52								19 52			
Gatley d					17 54								18 54								19 54			
Heald Green d					17 57								18 57								19 57			
Manchester Airport a		17 29	17 47	17 55	18 03	18 17	18 21			18 29	18 47	18 55	19 02	19 17	19 21		19 29		19 47	19 55	20 03	20 17	20 21	
Wilmslow 84 a													19 13											
Crewe 84 a																								

	TP	TP	TP	NT	TP	NT	NT	TP	TP	AW	NT	TP		NT	NT	TP	AW	TP	NT	NT	TP	NT	TP	NT
	◇1	◇1	◇1	1	◇1			◇1	◇1		1	◇1				◇1		◇1	1		◇1		◇1	
																					C		A	
		trolley							trolley												trolley		trolley	
Deansgate d					20 51		21 11					21 51			22 11						23 09	23 11	23 18	
Manchester Oxford Road d		20 24			20 54	21 00	21 17		21 24			21 54		22 00	22 17					23 00	23 12	23 17	23 21	23 59
Manchester Piccadilly a		20 27			20 56	21 02	21 19		21 27			21 56		22 02	22 19					23 02	23 15	23 19	23 23	00 02
Manchester Piccadilly d	20 16	20 29	20 38	20 41	20 58	21 04		21 13	21 29	21 34	21 41	21 58		22 04		22 13	22 35	22 38	22 46	23 04	23 15		23 24	00 04
Mauldeth Road d				20 48							21 48								22 53					
Burnage d				20 50							21 50								22 55					
East Didsbury d				20 52							21 52								22 57					
Gatley d				20 54							21 54								22 59					
Heald Green d				20 57							21 57								23 02					
Manchester Airport a	20 32	20 47	20 55	21 02	21 17	21 21		21 29	21 47		22 03	22 17		22 21		22 29		22 55	23 09	23 21	23 31		23 39	00 19
Wilmslow 84 a				21 13						21 50							22 50							
Crewe 84 a										22 09							23 10							

A not 22 May

B not 26 June

C until 19 June

Table 85

Sundays

18 September to 23 October

	TP	NT	NT	TP	NT	TP	TP	NT	TP	NT	NT	TP	NT	TP	NT	NT	TP	TP	NT		TP	NT	TP	NT
	◇1	1	1	◇1	1	◇1	◇1	1	◇1			◇1	1	◇1			◇1	◇1	1		◇1		◇1	
Deansgate d											09 15	09 23		09 51		10 16					10 51			11 11
Manchester Oxford Road d										09 42	09 18	09 26		09 54	10 00	10 19					10 54	11 00		11 17
Manchester Piccadilly 10 a										09 44	09 21	09 28		09 56	10 03	10 22					10 56	11 03		11 19
d	23p55	05 41	06 41	07 08	07 41	07 50	08 38	08 41	08 47	09 44		09 32	09 41	09 58	10 07		10 16	10 37	10 41		10 58	11 07	11 10	
Mauldeth Road d	00 04	05 48	06 50		07 48			08 48					09 48						10 48					
Burnage d	00 06	05 50	06 52		07 50			08 50					09 50						10 50					
East Didsbury d	00 09	05 52	06 54		07 52			08 52					09 52						10 52					
Gatley d	00 12	05 54	06 56		07 54			08 54					09 54						10 54					
Heald Green d	00 15	05 57	06 59		07 57			08 57					09 57						10 57					
Manchester Airport a	00 22	06 03	07 05	07 23	08 02	08 06	08 55	09 04	09 07			09 50	10 03	10 17	10 21		10 30	10 55	11 01		11 17	11 21	11 25	
Wilmslow 84 a								09 15											11 16					
Crewe 10 84 a																								

	NT	TP	NT	TP	NT		TP	NT	TP	NT	TP	NT	TP	TP	NT		TP	NT	NT	TP	NT	TP	TP	NT
	1	◇1		◇1			◇1	1	◇1		◇1		◇1	◇1	1		◇1		B	◇1	C	◇1	◇1 🛒	1
Deansgate d		11 51			12 11				12 51			13 11					13 51		14 07		14 11			
Manchester Oxford Road d	11 37	11 54	12 00		12 17			12 43	12 54	13 00		13 17		13 24			13 54	14 00	14 13		14 17		14 24	
Manchester Piccadilly 10 a	11 40	11 56	12 03		12 19			12 45	12 56	13 02		13 19		13 27			13 56	14 02	14 15		14 19		14 27	
d	11 41	11 58	12 07	12 10			12 13	12 47	12 58	13 04	13 10		13 13	13 29	13 41		13 58	14 04		14 10		14 13	14 29	14 41
Mauldeth Road d	11 48							12 54							13 48									14 48
Burnage d	11 50							12 56							13 50									14 50
East Didsbury d	11 52							12 58							13 52									14 52
Gatley d	11 54							13 00							13 54									14 54
Heald Green d	11 57							13 03							13 57									14 57
Manchester Airport a	12 04	12 17	12 21	12 25			12 34	13 08	13 17	13 24	13 25		13 29	13 47	14 03		14 17	14 21		14 25		14 34	14 47	15 02
Wilmslow 84 a								13 19																15 14
Crewe 10 84 a																								

	TP		NT	TP	NT	TP	TP	NT	TP	NT	TP		NT	TP	TP	NT	TP	NT	TP	NT	TP		TP	NT
	◇1			◇1		◇1	◇1	1	◇1		◇1			◇1	◇1 🛒	1	◇1		◇1		◇1		◇1	1
Deansgate d	14 51				15 11				15 51				16 11				16 51			17 11				
Manchester Oxford Road d	14 54		15 00		15 17		15 24		15 54	16 00			16 17		16 24		16 54	17 00		17 17			17 24	
Manchester Piccadilly 10 a	14 56		15 02		15 19		15 27		15 56	16 02			16 19		16 27		16 56	17 02		17 19			17 27	
d	14 58		15 04	15 10		15 13	15 29	15 41	15 58	16 04	16 10			16 13	16 29	16 41	16 58	17 04	17 10		17 13		17 29	17 41
Mauldeth Road d								15 48								16 48								17 48
Burnage d								15 50								16 50								17 50
East Didsbury d								15 52								16 52								17 52
Gatley d								15 54								16 54								17 54
Heald Green d								15 57								16 57								17 57
Manchester Airport a	15 17		15 21	15 25		15 34	15 47	16 03	16 17	16 21	16 25			16 34	16 47	17 02	17 17	17 21	17 25		17 29		17 47	18 03
Wilmslow 84 a																17 13								
Crewe 10 84 a																								

	TP	NT	TP	NT	TP	TP	NT		TP	NT	TP	NT	TP	TP	NT	TP	NT		TP	NT	TP	TP	NT	TP
	◇1		◇1		◇1	◇1 🛒	1		◇1		◇1		◇1	◇1 🛒	1	◇1			◇1		◇1	◇1 🛒	1	◇1
Deansgate d	17 51			18 11					18 51			19 11				19 51				20 11				20 51
Manchester Oxford Road d	17 54	18 00		18 17		18 24			18 54	19 00		19 17		19 24		19 54	20 00			20 17		20 24		20 54
Manchester Piccadilly 10 a	17 56	18 02		18 19		18 27			18 56	19 02		19 19		19 27		19 56	20 02			20 19		20 27		20 56
d	17 58	18 04	18 10		18 13	18 29	18 41		18 58	19 04	19 10		19 13	19 29	19 41	19 58	20 04		20 10		20 16	20 29	20 41	20 58
Mauldeth Road d							18 48								19 48								20 48	
Burnage d							18 50								19 50								20 50	
East Didsbury d							18 52								19 52								20 52	
Gatley d							18 54								19 54								20 54	
Heald Green d							18 57								19 57								20 57	
Manchester Airport a	18 17	18 21	18 25		18 29	18 47	19 02		19 17	19 21	19 25		19 29	19 47	20 03	20 17	20 21		20 25		20 32	20 47	21 02	21 17
Wilmslow 84 a							19 13																21 13	
Crewe 10 84 a																								

A from 26 June until 11 September

B 9 October, 16 October, 23 October

C 18 September, 25 September, 2 October

Table 85

Manchester - Manchester Airport

Sundays

18 September to 23 October

		NT	NT	TP		NT	TP	TP	AW	NT	TP	NT	NT	TP		AW	NT	NT	TP	TP	NT	NT			
				◇1			◇1	◇1		1	◇1			◇1			1		◇1	◇1					
			A			B		(trolley)												(trolley)					
Deansgate (tram)	d		21 09			21 11					21 51		22 11							23 09	23 11				
Manchester Oxford Road	d	21 00	21 15			21 17		21 24			21 54	22 00	22 17					23 00		23 12	23 17	23 59			
Manchester Piccadilly 10 (tram)	a	21 02	21 17			21 19		21 27			21 56	22 02	22 19					23 02		23 15	23 19	00 02			
	d	21 04		21 10			21 13	21 29	21 34	21 41	21 58	22 04		22 13		22 35	22 46	23 04	23 10	23 15		00 04			
Mauldeth Road	d									21 48							22 53								
Burnage	d									21 50							22 55								
East Didsbury	d									21 52							22 57								
Gatley	d									21 54							22 59								
Heald Green	d									21 57							23 02								
Manchester Airport (air)	a	21 21		21 25			21 29	21 47		22 03	22 17	22 21		22 29			23 09	23 21	23 25	23 31		00 19			
Wilmslow 84	a								21 50							22 50									
Crewe 10 84	a								22 09							23 10									

Sundays

from 30 October

		TP	NT	NT	TP	NT	TP	TP	NT	TP		NT	NT	TP	NT	TP	NT	NT	TP	TP		NT	TP	NT	NT
		◇1	1	1	◇1	1	◇1	◇1	1	◇1				◇1	1	◇1			◇1	◇1		1	◇1		
Deansgate (tram)	d												09 15	09 23		09 51		10 16					10 51		11 11
Manchester Oxford Road	d											09 06	09 18	09 26		09 54	10 00	10 19					10 54	11 00	11 17
Manchester Piccadilly 10 (tram)	a											09 09	09 21	09 28		09 56	10 03	10 22					10 56	11 03	11 19
	d	23p55	05 41	06 41	07 38	07 41	07 50	08 38	08 41	08 47		09 13		09 32	09 41	09 58	10 07		10 16	10 38		10 41	10 58	11 07	
Mauldeth Road	d	00 04	05 48	06 50		07 48			08 48						09 48							10 48			
Burnage	d	00 06	05 50	06 52		07 50			08 50						09 50							10 50			
East Didsbury	d	00 09	05 52	06 54		07 52			08 52						09 52							10 52			
Gatley	d	00 12	05 54	06 56		07 54			08 54						09 54							10 54			
Heald Green	d	00 15	05 57	06 59		07 57			08 57						09 57							10 57			
Manchester Airport (air)	a	00 22	06 03	07 05	07 55	08 02	08 06	08 55	09 04	09 07		09 27		09 50	10 03	10 17	10 21		10 30	10 55		11 01	11 17	11 21	
Wilmslow 84	a								09 15													11 16			
Crewe 10 84	a																								

		TP	NT	TP	NT	NT		TP	TP	NT	TP	NT	NT	TP	TP	TP		NT	TP	NT	NT	TP	TP	TP	NT
		◇1	1	◇1				◇1	◇1	1	◇1			◇1	◇1	◇1		1	◇1			◇1	◇1	◇1	1
																							(trolley)		
Deansgate (tram)	d			11 51		12 11					12 51		13 11						13 51		14 07				
Manchester Oxford Road	d		11 37	11 54	12 00	12 17				12 43	12 54	13 00	13 17		13 24				13 54	14 00	14 13		14 24		
Manchester Piccadilly 10 (tram)	a		11 40	11 56	12 03	12 19				12 45	12 56	13 02	13 19		13 27				13 56	14 02	14 15		14 27		
	d	11 38	11 41	11 58	12 07			12 13	12 38	12 47	12 58	13 04		13 13	13 29	13 38		13 41	13 58	14 04		14 13	14 29	14 38	14 41
Mauldeth Road	d		11 48							12 54								13 48							14 48
Burnage	d		11 50							12 56								13 50							14 50
East Didsbury	d		11 52							12 58								13 52							14 52
Gatley	d		11 54							13 00								13 54							14 54
Heald Green	d		11 57							13 03								13 57							14 57
Manchester Airport (air)	a	11 55	12 04	12 17	12 21			12 34	12 55	13 08	13 17	13 24		13 29	13 47	13 55		14 03	14 17	14 21		14 29	14 47	14 55	15 02
Wilmslow 84	a									13 19															15 14
Crewe 10 84	a																								

		TP		NT	NT	TP	TP	TP	NT	TP	NT	NT		TP	TP	TP	NT	TP	NT	NT	TP	TP		TP	NT
		◇1				◇1	◇1	◇1	1	◇1				◇1	◇1	◇1	1	◇1			◇1	◇1		◇1	1
															(trolley)										
Deansgate (tram)	d	14 51			15 11					15 51		16 11						16 51		17 11					
Manchester Oxford Road	d	14 54		15 00	15 17		15 24			15 54	16 00	16 17			16 24			16 54	17 00	17 17		17 24			
Manchester Piccadilly 10 (tram)	a	14 56		15 02	15 19		15 27			15 56	16 02	16 19			16 27			16 56	17 02	17 19		17 27			
	d	14 58		15 04		15 13	15 29	15 38	15 41	15 58	16 04			16 13	16 29	16 38	16 41	16 58	17 04		17 13	17 29		17 38	17 41
Mauldeth Road	d								15 48								16 48								17 48
Burnage	d								15 50								16 50								17 50
East Didsbury	d								15 52								16 52								17 52
Gatley	d								15 54								16 54								17 54
Heald Green	d								15 57								16 57								17 57
Manchester Airport (air)	a	15 17		15 21		15 29	15 47	15 55	16 03	16 17	16 21			16 34	16 47	16 55	17 02	17 17	17 21		17 29	17 47		17 55	18 03
Wilmslow 84	a																17 13								
Crewe 10 84	a																								

		TP	NT	NT	TP	TP	TP	NT		TP	NT	NT	TP	TP	TP	NT	TP	NT		NT	TP	TP	TP	NT	TP
		◇1			◇1	◇1	◇1	1		◇1			◇1	◇1	◇1	1	◇1				◇1	◇1	◇1	1	◇1
						(trolley)								(trolley)								(trolley)			
Deansgate (tram)	d	17 51		18 11						18 51		19 11					19 51			20 11					20 51
Manchester Oxford Road	d	17 54	18 00	18 17		18 24				18 54	19 00	19 17		19 24			19 54	20 00		20 17		20 24			20 54
Manchester Piccadilly 10 (tram)	a	17 56	18 02	18 19		18 27				18 56	19 02	19 19		19 27			19 56	20 02		20 19		20 27			20 56
	d	17 58	18 04		18 13	18 29	18 38	18 41		18 58	19 04		19 13	19 29	19 38	19 41	19 58	20 04			20 16	20 29	20 38	20 41	20 58
Mauldeth Road	d							18 48								19 48								20 48	
Burnage	d							18 50								19 50								20 50	
East Didsbury	d							18 52								19 52								20 52	
Gatley	d							18 54								19 54								20 54	
Heald Green	d							18 57								19 57								20 57	
Manchester Airport (air)	a	18 17	18 21		18 29	18 47	18 55	19 02		19 17	19 21		19 29	19 47	19 55	20 03	20 17	20 21			20 32	20 47	20 55	21 02	21 17
Wilmslow 84	a							19 13																21 13	
Crewe 10 84	a																								

A 9 October, 16 October, 23 October

B 18 September, 25 September, 2 October

Table 85

Sundays

from 30 October

Manchester - Manchester Airport

		NT	NT	TP		TP	AW	NT	TP	NT	NT	TP	AW	TP		NT	NT	TP	NT	NT
				◇1		◇1 (trolley)		1	◇1			◇1		◇1		1		◇1 (trolley)		
Deansgate	d		21 09						21 51		22 11							23 09	23 11	
Manchester Oxford Road	d	21 00	21 15			21 24			21 54	22 00	22 17						23 00	23 12	23 17	23 59
Manchester Piccadilly 10	a	21 02	21 17			21 27			21 56	22 02	22 19						23 02	23 15	23 19	00 02
	d	21 04		21 13		21 29	21 34	21 41	21 58	22 04		22 13	22 35	22 38		22 46	23 04	23 15		00 04
Mauldeth Road	d							21 48								22 53				
Burnage	d							21 50								22 55				
East Didsbury	d							21 52								22 57				
Gatley	d							21 54								22 59				
Heald Green	d							21 57								23 02				
Manchester Airport ✈	a	21 21		21 29		21 47		22 03	22 17	22 21		22 29		22 55		23 09	23 21	23 31		00 19
Wilmslow 84	a						21 50						22 50							
Crewe 10 84	a						22 09						23 10							

Table 85

Mondays to Fridays

until 15 July

Manchester Airport - Manchester

Miles				TP MX ◇1	TP ◇1	TP MX ◇1	TP MO ◇1	NT MX	TP ◇1	TP ◇1	NT	TP ◇1		AW ◇ ⌶	TP ◇1	TP ◇1 ⌶	NT	TP ◇1 ⌶	TP ◇1 ⌶	NT	NT	TP ◇1 ⌶		TP ◇1 ⌶	TP ◇1 ⌶	NT
—	Crewe 10	84	d					00 44																		06 33
—	Wilmslow	84	d														05 46									06 57
0	**Manchester Airport** ✈		d	23p52	00 01	00 38	00 48	01 20	04 00	04 12	04 34	05 15		05 33	05 37	05 45	06 01	06 18	06 23	06 41	06 46	06 55		07 00	07 05	07 17
1½	Heald Green		d													05 49	06 04				06 49					07 20
4	Gatley		d														06 07				06 52					07 23
5¼	East Didsbury		d														06 10				06 55					07 26
6¼	Burnage		d														06 12				06 57					07 28
7¼	Mauldeth Road		d														06 14				06 59					07 30
—	**Manchester Piccadilly 10**		a	00 09	00 15	00 51	01 01	01 36	04 14	04 27	04 47	05 33		05 48	05 51	06 00	06 25	06 31	06 39	06 56	07 11	07 13		07 14	07 22	07 42
—			d											05 50		06 03		06 33		06 58				07 15		
—	**Manchester Oxford Road**		a											05 52		06 05		06 35		07 00				07 17		
—	Deansgate		a																							

			TP ◇1 ⌶	TP ◇1 ⌶	NT	NT	TP ◇1 ⌶	TP ◇1 ⌶		NT	TP ◇1 ⌶	NT	TP ◇1 ⌶	TP ◇1 ⌶	NT	NT	TP ◇1 ⌶	TP ◇1 ⌶		NT	TP ◇1 ⌶	NT	TP ◇1 ⌶	TP ◇1 ⌶	NT	NT
Crewe 10	84	d																				08 31				
Wilmslow	84	d										07 56										08 57				
Manchester Airport ✈		d	07 25	07 35	07 38	07 46	07 53	07 56		08 01	08 05	08 17	08 25	08 35	08 41	08 46	08 55	09 00		09 03	09 05	09 17	09 29	09 35	09 41	09 46
Heald Green		d	07 30		07 42	07 49				08 05		08 20	08 29			08 49						09 20	09 33			09 49
Gatley		d			07 45	07 52		08 02				08 23	08 32			08 52						09 23				09 52
East Didsbury		d			07 48	07 55		08 05				08 26	08 35			08 55						09 26				09 55
Burnage		d				07 57						08 28				08 57						09 28				09 57
Mauldeth Road		d				07 59						08 30				08 59						09 30				09 59
Manchester Piccadilly 10		a	07 43	07 49	07 57	08 11	08 12	08 14		08 21	08 22	08 42	08 44	08 49	08 58	09 11	09 13	09 14		09 18	09 22	09 42	09 44	09 52	09 59	10 11
		d			07 59			08 15		08 22			08 46		09 01			09 16		09 22			09 46		10 01	
Manchester Oxford Road		a			08 01			08 17		08 24			08 48		09 03			09 18		09 24			09 48		10 03	
Deansgate		a								08 28			08 51							09 28			09 51			

			TP ◇1 ⌶	TP ◇1 ⌶		NT	TP ◇1 ⌶	NT	TP ◇1 ⌶	TP ◇1 ⌶	NT	NT	TP ◇1 ⌶	TP ◇1 ⌶		NT	TP ◇1 ⌶	NT	TP ◇1 ⌶	TP ◇1 ⌶	NT	NT	TP ◇1 ⌶	TP ◇1 ⌶		NT
Crewe 10	84	d						09 33										10 34								
Wilmslow	84	d						09 57										10 57								
Manchester Airport ✈		d	09 55	10 00		10 03	10 05	10 17	10 29	10 35	10 41	10 46	10 55	11 00		11 03	11 05	11 17	11 29	11 35	11 41	11 46	11 55	12 00		12 03
Heald Green		d						10 20	10 33			10 49						11 20	11 33			11 49				
Gatley		d						10 23				10 52						11 23				11 52				
East Didsbury		d						10 26				10 55						11 26				11 55				
Burnage		d						10 28				10 57						11 28				11 57				
Mauldeth Road		d						10 30				10 59						11 30				11 59				
Manchester Piccadilly 10		a	10 13	10 14		10 18	10 22	10 42	10 44	10 52	10 59	11 11	11 13	11 14		11 18	11 22	11 42	11 44	11 52	11 59	12 11	12 13	12 14		12 18
		d		10 16		10 22			10 46		11 01			11 16		11 22			11 46		12 01			12 16		12 22
Manchester Oxford Road		a		10 18		10 24			10 48		11 03			11 18		11 24			11 48		12 03			12 18		12 24
Deansgate		a				10 28			10 51							11 28			11 51							12 28

			TP ◇1 ⌶	NT	TP ◇1 ⌶	TP ◇1 ⌶	NT	NT	TP ◇1 ⌶	TP ◇1 ⌶		NT	TP ◇1 ⌶	NT	TP ◇1 ⌶	TP ◇1 ⌶	NT	NT	TP ◇1 ⌶	TP ◇1 ⌶		NT	TP ◇1 ⌶	NT	TP ◇1 ⌶	TP ◇1 ⌶
Crewe 10	84	d		11 34										12 34										13 34		
Wilmslow	84	d		11 57										12 57										13 57		
Manchester Airport ✈		d	12 05	12 17	12 29	12 35	12 41	12 46	12 55	13 00		13 03	13 05	13 17	13 29	13 35	13 41	13 46	13 55	14 00		14 03	14 05	14 17	14 29	14 35
Heald Green		d		12 20	12 33			12 49						13 20	13 33			13 49						14 20	14 33	
Gatley		d		12 23				12 52						13 23				13 52						14 23		
East Didsbury		d		12 26				12 55						13 26				13 55						14 26		
Burnage		d		12 28				12 57						13 28				13 57						14 28		
Mauldeth Road		d		12 30				12 59						13 30				13 59						14 30		
Manchester Piccadilly 10		a	12 22	12 42	12 44	12 52	12 59	13 11	13 13	13 14		13 18	13 22	13 42	13 44	13 52	13 59	14 11	14 13	14 14		14 18	14 22	14 42	14 44	14 52
		d			12 46		13 01			13 16		13 22			13 46		14 01			14 16		14 22			14 46	
Manchester Oxford Road		a			12 48		13 03			13 18		13 24			13 48		14 03			14 18		14 24			14 48	
Deansgate		a			12 51							13 28			13 51							14 28			14 51	

			NT	NT	TP ◇1 ⌶	TP ◇1 ⌶		NT	TP ◇1 ⌶	NT	TP ◇1 ⌶	NT	NT	TP ◇1 ⌶	TP ◇1 ⌶	NT		TP ◇1 ⌶	NT	TP ◇1 ⌶	TP ◇1 ⌶	NT	NT	TP ◇1 ⌶	TP ◇1 ⌶	NT
Crewe 10	84	d								14 34									15 33							
Wilmslow	84	d								14 57									15 56							
Manchester Airport ✈		d	14 41	14 46	14 55	15 00		15 03	15 05	15 17	15 35	15 41	15 46	15 55	16 00	16 03		16 05	1617	16 29	16 35	16 41	16 46	16 55	17 00	17 03
Heald Green		d		14 49						15 20			15 49						16 20	16 33			16 49			
Gatley		d		14 52						15 23			15 52						16 23				16 52			
East Didsbury		d		14 55						15 26			15 55						16 26				16 55			
Burnage		d		14 57						15 28			15 57						16 28				16 57			
Mauldeth Road		d		14 59						15 30			15 59						16 30				16 59			
Manchester Piccadilly 10		a	14 59	15 11	15 13	15 14		15 18	15 22	15 41	15 52	15 59	16 11	16 13	16 14	16 18		16 22	16 42	16 44	16 52	16 59	17 11	17 13	17 14	17 21
		d	15 01			15 16		15 22		15 42		16 01			16 16	16 22				16 46		17 01			17 15	17 22
Manchester Oxford Road		a	15 03			15 18		15 24		15 46		16 03			16 18	16 24				16 48		17 03			17 17	17 25
Deansgate		a						15 28								16 28										

Table 85

Manchester Airport - Manchester

Mondays to Fridays

until 15 July

		TP	NT	TP	NT	NT	TP	TP	NT	NT		TP	NT	NT	TP	TP	NT	NT	TP	TP		NT	NT	TP
		◇1 🛒		◇1 🛒			◇1 🛒	◇1 🛒				◇1			◇1	◇1 🛒			◇1	◇1				◇1
Crewe 10 84 d			16 34							17 33								18 34						
Wilmslow 84 d			16 57							17 56								18 57						
Manchester Airport ✈ d		17 05	17 17	17 35	17 41	17 46	17 55	18 00	18 03	18 17		18 35	18 41	18 46	18 55	19 00	19 03	19 09	19 19	19 29		19 41	19 46	19 55
Heald Green d			17 20			17 49				18 20				18 49				19 12		19 33			19 49	
Gatley d			17 23			17 52				18 23				18 52				19 15					19 52	
East Didsbury d			17 26			17 55				18 26				18 55				19 18					19 55	
Burnage d			17 28			17 57				18 28				18 57				19 20					19 57	
Mauldeth Road d			17 30			17 59				18 30				18 59				19 22					19 59	
Manchester Piccadilly 10 🚊 a		17 22	17 42	17 52	17 59	18 11	18 13	18 14	18 18	18 42		18 52	18 59	19 11	19 13	19 14	19 18	19 31	19 36	19 44		19 59	20 11	20 13
d					18 01			18 16	18 22				19 01			19 16	19 20	19 32		19 46		20 01		
Manchester Oxford Road a					18 03			18 18	18 24				19 03			19 18	19 22	19 36		19 48		20 03		
Deansgate 🚊 a									18 28								19 26			19 51				

	TP	NT	NT	TP	TP	AW		TP	NT	NT	TP	TP	AW	NT	TP	TP		NT	NT	TP	TP	NT	TP	TP
	◇1			◇1	◇1			◇1			◇1	◇1			◇1	◇1				◇1	◇1		◇1	◇1
Crewe 10 84 d																								
Wilmslow 84 d			19 56							20 56								21 55				22 56		
Manchester Airport ✈ d	20 00	20 03	20 09	20 20	20 29	20 32		20 47	21 03	21 09	21 20	21 29	21 32	21 41	21 47	22 00		22 08	22 19	22 22	22 29	23 09	23 18	23 52
Heald Green d			20 12		20 33			20 51		21 12		21 33			21 51			22 12			22 33	23 12		
Gatley d			20 15					20 54		21 15					21 54			22 15				23 15		
East Didsbury d			20 18					20 57		21 18					21 57			22 17				23 18		
Burnage d			20 20					20 59		21 20					21 59			22 19				23 20		
Mauldeth Road d			20 22					21 02		21 22					22 02			22 21				23 22		
Manchester Piccadilly 10 🚊 a	20 14	20 18	20 32	20 36	20 44	20 48		21 13	21 18	21 32	21 36	21 44	21 48	21 59	22 13	22 14		22 31	22 34	22 36	22 44	23 33	23 34	00 09
d	20 16	20 20	20 32		20 46	20 50			21 20	21 32		21 46	21 50	22 01		22 16		22 32	22 36		22 46			
Manchester Oxford Road a	20 18	20 22	20 36		20 48	20 52			21 22	21 36		21 48	21 52	22 03		22 18		22 36	22 38		22 48			
Deansgate 🚊 a		20 26			20 51				21 26			21 51							22 41		22 51			

Mondays to Fridays

18 July to 30 September

	TP	TP	TP	TP	NT	TP	TP	NT	TP		AW	TP	TP	NT	TP	TP	NT	NT	TP		TP	TP	NT	TP
	MX		MX	MO	MX																			
	◇1	◇1	◇1	◇1		◇1	◇1		◇1		◇ 🛒	◇1	◇1 🛒		◇1 🛒	◇1 🛒			◇1 🛒		◇1 🛒	◇1 🛒		◇1 🛒
Crewe 10 84 d					00 44																		06 33	
Wilmslow 84 d														05 46									06 57	
Manchester Airport ✈ d	23p52	00 01	00 38	00 48	01 20	04 00	04 12	04 34	05 15		05 33	05 37	05 45	06 01	06 18	06 23	06 41	06 46	06 55		07 00	07 05	07 17	07 25
Heald Green d													05 49	06 04				06 49					07 20	07 30
Gatley d														06 07				06 52					07 23	
East Didsbury d														06 10				06 55					07 26	
Burnage d														06 12				06 57					07 28	
Mauldeth Road d														06 14				06 59					07 30	
Manchester Piccadilly 10 🚊 a	00 09	00 15	00 51	01 01	01 36	04 14	04 27	04 47	05 33		05 48	05 51	06 00	06 25	06 31	06 39	06 56	07 11	07 13		07 14	07 22	07 42	07 43
d											05 50		06 03		06 33		06 58				07 15			
Manchester Oxford Road a											05 52		06 05		06 35		07 00				07 17			
Deansgate 🚊 a																								

	TP	NT	NT	TP	TP		NT	TP	NT	TP	TP	NT	NT	TP	TP		NT	TP	NT	TP	TP	NT	NT	TP
	◇1 🛒			◇1 🛒	◇1 🛒			◇1 🛒		◇1 🛒	◇1 🛒			◇1 🛒	◇1 🛒			◇1 🛒		◇1 🛒	◇1 🛒			◇1 🛒
Crewe 10 84 d																			08 31					
Wilmslow 84 d									07 56										08 57					
Manchester Airport ✈ d	07 35	07 38	07 46	07 53	07 56		08 01	08 05	08 17	08 25	08 35	08 41	08 46	08 55	09 00		09 03	09 05	09 17	09 29	09 35	09 41	09 46	09 55
Heald Green d		07 42	07 49				08 05		08 20	08 29			08 49						09 20	09 33			09 49	
Gatley d		07 45	07 52		08 02				08 23	08 32			08 52						09 23				09 52	
East Didsbury d		07 48	07 55		08 05				08 26	08 35			08 55						09 26				09 55	
Burnage d			07 57						08 28				08 57						09 28				09 57	
Mauldeth Road d			07 59						08 30				08 59						09 30				09 59	
Manchester Piccadilly 10 🚊 a	07 49	07 57	08 11	08 12	08 14		08 21	08 22	08 42	08 44	08 49	08 58	09 11	09 13	09 14		09 18	09 22	09 42	09 44	09 52	09 59	10 11	10 13
d		07 59			08 15		08 22			08 46		09 01			09 16		09 22			09 46		10 01		
Manchester Oxford Road a		08 01			08 17		08 24			08 48		09 03			09 18		09 24			09 48		10 03		
Deansgate 🚊 a							08 28			08 51							09 28			09 51				

	TP		NT	TP	NT	TP	TP	NT	NT	TP	TP		NT	TP	NT	TP	TP	NT	NT	TP	TP		NT	TP
	◇1 🛒			◇1 🛒		◇1 🛒	◇1 🛒			◇1 🛒	◇1 🛒			◇1 🛒		◇1 🛒	◇1 🛒			◇1 🛒	◇1 🛒			◇1 🛒
Crewe 10 84 d					09 33										10 34									
Wilmslow 84 d					09 57										10 57									
Manchester Airport ✈ d	10 00		10 03	10 05	10 17	10 29	10 35	10 41	10 46	10 55	11 00		11 03	11 05	11 17	11 29	11 35	11 41	11 46	11 55	12 00		12 03	12 05
Heald Green d					10 20	10 33			10 49						11 20	11 33			11 49					
Gatley d					10 23				10 52						11 23				11 52					
East Didsbury d					10 26				10 55						11 26				11 55					
Burnage d					10 28				10 57						11 28				11 57					
Mauldeth Road d					10 30				10 59						11 30				11 59					
Manchester Piccadilly 10 🚊 a	10 14		10 18	10 22	10 42	10 44	10 52	10 59	11 11	11 13	11 14		11 18	11 22	11 42	11 44	11 52	11 59	12 11	12 13	12 14		12 18	12 22
d	10 16		10 22			10 46		11 01			11 16		11 22			11 46		12 01			12 16		12 22	
Manchester Oxford Road a	10 18		10 24			10 48		11 03			11 18		11 24			11 48		12 03			12 18		12 24	
Deansgate 🚊 a			10 28			10 51							11 28			11 51							12 28	

Table 85

Manchester Airport - Manchester

Mondays to Fridays

18 July to 30 September

		NT	TP	TP	NT	NT	TP	TP		NT	TP	NT	TP	TP	NT	NT	TP	TP		NT	TP	NT	TP	TP	NT
			◇1	◇1			◇1	◇1			◇1		◇1	◇1			◇1	◇1			◇1		◇1	◇1	
			🛒	🛒			🛒	🛒			🛒		🛒	🛒			🛒	🛒			🛒		🛒	🛒	
Crewe 10	84 d	11 34										12 34										13 34			
Wilmslow	84 d	11 57										12 57										13 57			
Manchester Airport	✈ d	12 17	12 29	12 35	12 41	12 46	12 55	13 00		13 03	13 05	13 17	13 29	13 35	13 41	13 46	13 55	14 00		14 03	14 05	14 17	14 29	14 35	14 41
Heald Green	d	12 20	12 33			12 49						13 20	13 33			13 49						14 20	14 33		
Gatley	d	12 23				12 52						13 23				13 52						14 23			
East Didsbury	d	12 26				12 55						13 26				13 55						14 26			
Burnage	d	12 28				12 57						13 28				13 57						14 28			
Mauldeth Road	d	12 30				12 59						13 30				13 59						14 30			
Manchester Piccadilly 10	🚊 a	12 42	12 44	12 52	12 59	13 11	13 13	13 14		13 18	13 22	13 42	13 44	13 52	13 59	14 11	14 13	14 14		14 18	14 22	14 42	14 44	14 52	14 59
	d		12 46		13 01			13 16		13 22			13 46		14 01			14 16		14 22			14 46		15 01
Manchester Oxford Road	a		12 48		13 03			13 18		13 24			13 48		14 03			14 18		14 24			14 48		15 03
Deansgate	🚊 a		12 51							13 28			13 51							14 28			14 51		

		NT	TP	TP		NT	TP	NT	TP	NT	NT	TP	TP	NT		TP	NT	TP	TP	NT	NT	TP	TP	NT	
			◇1	◇1			◇1		◇1			◇1	◇1			◇1		◇1	◇1			◇1	◇1		
			🛒	🛒			🛒		🛒			🛒	🛒			🛒		🛒	🛒			🛒	🛒		
Crewe 10	84 d							14 34									15 33								
Wilmslow	84 d							14 57									15 56								
Manchester Airport	✈ d	14 46	14 55	15 00		15 03	15 05	15 17	15 35	15 41	15 46	15 55	16 00	16 03		16 05	16 17	16 29	16 35	16 41	16 46	16 55	17 00	17 03	
Heald Green	d	14 49						15 20			15 49						16 20	16 33			16 49				
Gatley	d	14 52						15 23			15 52						16 23				16 52				
East Didsbury	d	14 55						15 26			15 55						16 26				16 55				
Burnage	d	14 57						15 28			15 57						16 28				16 57				
Mauldeth Road	d	14 59						15 30			15 59						16 30				16 59				
Manchester Piccadilly 10	🚊 a	15 11	15 13	15 14		15 18	15 22	15 41	15 52	15 59	16 11	16 13	16 14	16 18		16 22	16 42	16 44	16 52	16 59	17 11	17 13	17 14	17 21	
	d			15 16		15 22		15 42		16 01			16 16	16 22				16 46		17 01			17 15	17 22	
Manchester Oxford Road	a			15 18		15 24		15 46		16 03			16 18	16 24				16 48		17 03			17 17	17 25	
Deansgate	🚊 a					15 28								16 28											

		TP	NT	TP	NT	NT	TP	TP	NT	NT		TP	NT	NT	TP	TP	NT	NT	TP	TP		NT	NT	TP	TP
		◇1		◇1			◇1	◇1				◇1			◇1	◇1			◇1	◇1				◇1	◇1
		🛒		🛒			🛒	🛒																	
Crewe 10	84 d		16 34							17 33								18 34							
Wilmslow	84 d		16 57							17 56								18 57							
Manchester Airport	✈ d	17 05	17 17	17 35	17 41	17 46	17 55	18 00	18 03	18 17		18 35	18 41	18 46	18 55	19 00	19 03	19 09	19 19	19 29		19 41	19 46	19 55	20 00
Heald Green	d		17 20			17 49				18 20				18 49				19 12		19 33			19 49		
Gatley	d		17 23			17 52				18 23				18 52				19 15					19 52		
East Didsbury	d		17 26			17 55				18 26				18 55				19 18					19 55		
Burnage	d		17 28			17 57				18 28				18 57				19 20					19 57		
Mauldeth Road	d		17 30			17 59				18 30				18 59				19 22					19 59		
Manchester Piccadilly 10	🚊 a	17 22	17 42	17 52	17 59	18 11	18 13	18 14	18 18	18 42		18 52	18 59	19 11	19 13	19 14	19 18	19 31	19 36	19 44		19 59	20 11	20 13	20 14
	d				18 01			18 16	18 22				19 01			19 16	19 20	19 32		19 46		20 01			20 16
Manchester Oxford Road	a				18 03			18 18	18 24				19 03			19 18	19 22	19 36		19 48		20 03			20 18
Deansgate	🚊 a								18 28								19 26			19 51					

		NT	NT	TP	TP	AW		TP	NT	NT	TP	TP	AW	NT	TP	TP		NT	NT	TP	TP	NT	TP	TP	
				◇1	◇1			◇1			◇1	◇1			◇1	◇1				◇1	◇1		◇1	◇1	
Crewe 10	84 d																								
Wilmslow	84 d		19 56							20 56								21 55				22 56			
Manchester Airport	✈ d	20 03	20 09	20 20	20 29	20 32		20 47	21 03	21 09	21 20	21 29	21 32	21 41	21 47	22 00		22 08	22 19	22 22	22 29	23 09	23 18	23 52	
Heald Green	d		20 12		20 33			20 51		21 12		21 33			21 51			22 12			22 33	23 12			
Gatley	d		20 15					20 54		21 15					21 54			22 15				23 15			
East Didsbury	d		20 18					20 57		21 18					21 57			22 17				23 18			
Burnage	d		20 20					20 59		21 20					21 59			22 19				23 20			
Mauldeth Road	d		20 22					21 02		21 22					22 02			22 21				23 22			
Manchester Piccadilly 10	🚊 a	20 18	20 32	20 36	20 44	20 48		21 13	21 18	21 32	21 36	21 44	21 48	21 59	22 13	22 14		22 31	22 34	22 36	22 44	23 33	23 34	00 09	
	d	20 20	20 32		20 46	20 50			21 20	21 32		21 46	21 50	22 01		22 16		22 32	22 36		22 46				
Manchester Oxford Road	a	20 22	20 36		20 48	20 52			21 22	21 36		21 48	21 52	22 03		22 18		22 36	22 38		22 48				
Deansgate	🚊 a	20 26			20 51				21 26			21 51							22 41		22 51				

Mondays to Fridays

from 3 October

		TP	TP	TP	TP	NT	TP	TP	NT	TP		AW	TP	TP	NT	TP	TP	NT	NT	TP		TP	TP	NT	TP
		MX		MX	MO	MX																			
		◇1	◇1	◇1	◇1		◇1	◇1		◇1		◇	◇1	◇1		◇1	◇1			◇1		◇1	◇1		◇1
												🛒		🛒		🛒	🛒			🛒		🛒	🛒		🛒
Crewe 10	84 d					00 44																		06 33	
Wilmslow	84 d														05 46									06 57	
Manchester Airport	✈ d	23p52	00 01	00 38	00 48	01 20	04 00	04 12	04 34	05 15		05 33	05 37	05 45	06 01	06 18	06 23	06 41	06 46	06 55		07 00	07 05	07 17	07 25
Heald Green	d													05 49	06 04				06 49					07 20	07 30
Gatley	d														06 07				06 52					07 23	
East Didsbury	d														06 10				06 55					07 26	
Burnage	d														06 12				06 57					07 28	
Mauldeth Road	d														06 14				06 59					07 30	
Manchester Piccadilly 10	🚊 a	00 09	00 15	00 51	01 01	01 36	04 14	04 27	04 47	05 33		05 48	05 51	06 00	06 25	06 31	06 39	06 56	07 11	07 13		07 14	07 22	07 42	07 43
	d											05 50		06 03		06 33		06 58				07 15			
Manchester Oxford Road	a											05 52		06 05		06 35		07 00				07 17			
Deansgate	🚊 a																								

Table 85

Mondays to Fridays

from 3 October

Manchester Airport - Manchester

		TP ◇1 🛒	NT	NT	TP ◇1 🛒	TP ◇1 🛒		NT	TP ◇1 🛒	NT	TP ◇1 🛒	TP ◇1 🛒	NT	NT	TP ◇1 🛒	TP ◇1 🛒		NT	TP ◇1 🛒	NT	TP ◇1 🛒	TP ◇1 🛒	NT	NT	TP ◇1 🛒
Crewe [10]	84 d																			08 31					
Wilmslow	84 d									07 56										08 57					
Manchester Airport ✈	d	07 35	07 38	07 46	07 53	07 56		08 01	08 05	08 17	08 25	08 35	08 41	08 46	08 55	09 00		09 03	09 05	09 17	09 29	09 35	09 41	09 46	09 55
Heald Green	d		07 42	07 49				08 05		08 20	08 29			08 49						09 20	09 33			09 49	
Gatley	d		07 45	07 52		08 02				08 23	08 32			08 52						09 23				09 52	
East Didsbury	d		07 48	07 55		08 05				08 26	08 35			08 55						09 26				09 55	
Burnage	d			07 57						08 28				08 57						09 28				09 57	
Mauldeth Road	d			07 59						08 30				08 59						09 30				09 59	
Manchester Piccadilly [10] 🚊	a	07 49	07 57	08 11	08 12	08 14		08 21	08 22	08 42	08 44	08 49	08 58	09 11	09 13	09 14		09 18	09 22	09 42	09 44	09 52	09 59	10 11	10 13
	d		07 59			08 15		08 22			08 46		09 01			09 16		09 22			09 46		10 01		
Manchester Oxford Road	a		08 01			08 17		08 24			08 48		09 03			09 18		09 24			09 48		10 03		
Deansgate 🚊	a							08 28			08 51							09 28			09 51				

		TP ◇1 🛒		NT	TP ◇1 🛒	NT	TP ◇1 🛒	TP ◇1 🛒	NT	NT	TP ◇1 🛒	TP ◇1 🛒		NT	TP ◇1 🛒	NT	TP ◇1 🛒	TP ◇1 🛒	NT	NT	TP ◇1 🛒	TP ◇1 🛒		NT	TP ◇1 🛒
Crewe [10]	84 d					09 33										10 34									
Wilmslow	84 d					09 57										10 57									
Manchester Airport ✈	d	10 00		10 03	10 05	10 17	10 29	10 35	10 41	10 46	10 55	11 00		11 03	11 05	11 17	11 29	11 35	11 41	11 46	11 55	12 00		12 03	12 05
Heald Green	d					10 20	10 33			10 49						11 20	11 33			11 49					
Gatley	d					10 23				10 52						11 23				11 52					
East Didsbury	d					10 26				10 55						11 26				11 55					
Burnage	d					10 28				10 57						11 28				11 57					
Mauldeth Road	d					10 30				10 59						11 30				11 59					
Manchester Piccadilly [10] 🚊	a	10 14		10 18	10 22	10 42	10 44	10 52	10 59	11 11	11 13	11 14		11 18	11 22	11 42	11 44	11 52	11 59	12 11	12 13	12 14		12 18	12 22
	d	10 16		10 22			10 46		11 01			11 16		11 22			11 46		12 01			12 16		12 22	
Manchester Oxford Road	a	10 18		10 24			10 48		11 03			11 18		11 24			11 48		12 03			12 18		12 24	
Deansgate 🚊	a			10 28			10 51							11 28			11 51							12 28	

		NT	TP ◇1 🛒	TP ◇1 🛒	NT	NT	TP ◇1 🛒	TP ◇1 🛒		NT	TP ◇1 🛒	NT	TP ◇1 🛒	TP ◇1 🛒	NT	NT	TP ◇1 🛒	TP ◇1 🛒		NT	TP ◇1 🛒	NT	TP ◇1 🛒	TP ◇1 🛒	NT
Crewe [10]	84 d	11 34										12 34										13 34			
Wilmslow	84 d	11 57										12 57										13 57			
Manchester Airport ✈	d	12 17	12 29	12 35	12 41	12 46	12 55	13 00		13 03	13 05	13 17	13 29	13 35	13 41	13 46	13 55	14 00		14 03	14 05	14 17	14 29	14 35	14 41
Heald Green	d	12 20	12 33			12 49						13 20	13 33			13 49						14 20	14 33		
Gatley	d	12 23				12 52						13 23				13 52						14 23			
East Didsbury	d	12 26				12 55						13 26				13 55						14 26			
Burnage	d	12 28				12 57						13 28				13 57						14 28			
Mauldeth Road	d	12 30				12 59						13 30				13 59						14 30			
Manchester Piccadilly [10] 🚊	a	12 42	12 44	12 52	12 59	13 11	13 13	13 14		13 18	13 22	13 42	13 44	13 52	13 59	14 11	14 13	14 14		14 18	14 22	14 42	14 44	14 52	14 59
	d		12 46		13 01			13 16		13 22			13 46		14 01			14 16		14 22			14 46		15 01
Manchester Oxford Road	a		12 48		13 03			13 18		13 24			13 48		14 03			14 18		14 24			14 48		15 03
Deansgate 🚊	a		12 51							13 28			13 51							14 28			14 51		

		NT	TP ◇1 🛒	TP ◇1 🛒		NT	TP ◇1 🛒	NT	TP ◇1 🛒	NT	NT	TP ◇1 🛒	TP ◇1 🛒	NT		TP ◇1 🛒	NT	TP ◇1 🛒	TP ◇1 🛒	NT	NT	TP ◇1 🛒	TP ◇1 🛒	NT	
Crewe [10]	84 d							14 34									15 33								
Wilmslow	84 d							14 57									15 56								
Manchester Airport ✈	d	14 46	14 55	15 00		15 03	15 05	15 17	15 35	15 41	15 46	15 55	16 00	16 03		16 05	16 17	16 29	16 35	16 41	16 46	16 55	17 00	17 03	
Heald Green	d	14 49						15 20			15 49						16 20	16 33			16 49				
Gatley	d	14 52						15 23			15 52						16 23				16 52				
East Didsbury	d	14 55						15 26			15 55						16 26				16 55				
Burnage	d	14 57						15 28			15 57						16 28				16 57				
Mauldeth Road	d	14 59						15 30			15 59						16 30				16 59				
Manchester Piccadilly [10] 🚊	a	15 11	15 13	15 14		15 18	15 22	15 41	15 52	15 59	16 11	16 13	16 14	16 18		16 22	16 42	16 44	16 52	16 59	17 11	17 13	17 14	17 21	
	d			15 16		15 22		15 42		16 01			16 16	16 22				16 46		17 01			17 15	17 22	
Manchester Oxford Road	a			15 18		15 24		15 46		16 03			16 18	16 24				16 48		17 03			17 17	17 25	
Deansgate 🚊	a					15 28								16 28											

		TP ◇1 🛒	NT	TP ◇1 🛒	NT	NT	TP ◇1 🛒	TP ◇1 🛒	NT	NT		TP ◇1	NT	NT	TP ◇1	TP ◇1	NT	NT	TP ◇1	TP ◇1		NT	NT	TP ◇1	TP ◇1
Crewe [10]	84 d		16 34							17 33								18 34							
Wilmslow	84 d		16 57							17 56								18 57							
Manchester Airport ✈	d	17 05	17 17	17 35	17 41	17 46	17 55	18 00	18 03	1817		18 35	18 41	18 46	18 55	19 00	19 03	19 09	19 19	19 29		19 41	19 46	19 55	20 00
Heald Green	d		17 20			17 49				18 20				18 49				19 12		19 33			19 49		
Gatley	d		17 23			17 52				18 23				18 52				19 15					19 52		
East Didsbury	d		17 26			17 55				18 26				18 55				19 18					19 55		
Burnage	d		17 28			17 57				18 28				18 57				19 20					19 57		
Mauldeth Road	d		17 30			17 59				18 30				18 59				19 22					19 59		
Manchester Piccadilly [10] 🚊	a	17 22	17 42	17 52	17 59	18 11	18 13	18 14	18 18	18 42		18 52	18 59	19 11	19 13	19 14	19 18	19 31	19 36	19 44		19 59	20 11	20 13	20 14
	d				18 01			18 16	18 22				19 01			19 16	19 20	19 32		19 46		20 01			20 16
Manchester Oxford Road	a				18 03			18 18	18 24				19 03			19 18	19 22	19 36		19 48		20 03			20 18
Deansgate 🚊	a								18 28								19 26			19 51					

Table 85

Mondays to Fridays

from 3 October

Manchester Airport - Manchester

	NT	NT	TP	TP	AW		TP	NT	NT	TP	TP	AW	NT	TP	TP		NT	NT	TP	TP	NT	TP	TP	
			◇1	◇1			◇1			◇1	◇1			◇1	◇1				◇1	◇1		◇1	◇1	
Crewe 10 84 d																								
Wilmslow 84 d		19 56							20 56								21 55				22 56			
Manchester Airport ✈ d	20 03	20 09	20 20	20 29	20 32		20 47	21 03	21 09	21 20	21 29	21 32	21 41	21 47	22 00		22 08	22 19	22 22	22 29	23 09	23 18	23 52	
Heald Green d		20 12		20 33			20 51		21 12		21 33			21 51			22 12			22 33	23 12			
Gatley d		20 15					20 54		21 15					21 54			22 15				23 15			
East Didsbury d		20 18					20 57		21 18					21 57			22 17				23 18			
Burnage d		20 20					20 59		21 20					21 59			22 19				23 20			
Mauldeth Road d		20 22					21 02		21 22					22 02			22 21				23 22			
Manchester Piccadilly 10 a	20 18	20 32	20 36	20 44	20 48		21 13	21 18	21 32	21 36	21 44	21 48	21 59	22 13	22 14		22 31	22 34	22 36	22 44	23 33	23 34	00 09	
d	20 20	20 32		20 46	20 50			21 20	21 32		21 46	21 50	22 01		22 16		22 32	22 36		22 46				
Manchester Oxford Road a	20 22	20 36		20 48	20 52			21 22	21 36		21 48	21 52	22 03		22 18		22 36	22 38		22 48				
Deansgate a	20 26			20 51				21 26			21 51							22 41		22 51				

Saturdays

until 18 June

	TP	TP	TP	NT	TP	TP	NT	TP	AW		TP	TP	NT	TP	TP	NT	NT	TP	TP		TP	NT	TP	TP
	◇1	◇1	◇1		◇1	◇1		◇1	◇ 🛒		◇1	◇1 🛒		◇1 🛒	◇1 🛒			◇1 🛒	◇1 🛒		◇1 🛒		◇1 🛒	◇1 🛒
Crewe 10 84 d				00 44																		06 33		
Wilmslow 84 d													05 46									06 57		
Manchester Airport ✈ d	23p52	00 01	00 38	01 20	04 00	04 15	04 34	05 20	05 33		05 37	05 45	06 01	06 18	06 23	06 41	06 46	06 55	07 00		07 05	07 17	07 25	07 33
Heald Green d												05 49	06 04				06 49					07 20	07 30	
Gatley d													06 07				06 52					07 23		
East Didsbury d													06 10				06 55					07 26		
Burnage d													06 12				06 57					07 28		
Mauldeth Road d													06 14				06 59					07 30		
Manchester Piccadilly 10 a	00 09	00 15	00 51	01 36	04 14	04 29	04 47	05 35	05 48		05 51	06 00	06 25	06 31	06 39	06 56	07 11	07 13	07 14		07 22	07 42	07 43	07 48
d									05 50			06 03		06 33		06 58			07 15					
Manchester Oxford Road a									05 52			06 05		06 35		07 00			07 17					
Deansgate a																								

	NT	NT	TP	TP	NT		TP	NT	TP	TP	NT	NT	TP	TP	NT		TP	NT	TP	TP	NT	NT	TP	TP
			◇1 🛒	◇1 🛒			◇1 🛒		◇1 🛒	◇1 🛒			◇1 🛒	◇1 🛒			◇1 🛒		◇1 🛒	◇1 🛒			◇1 🛒	◇1 🛒
Crewe 10 84 d								07 30										08 31						
Wilmslow 84 d								07 56										08 57						
Manchester Airport ✈ d	07 38	07 46	07 53	07 56	08 01		08 05	08 17	08 25	08 35	08 41	08 46	08 55	09 00	09 03		09 05	09 17	09 29	09 35	09 41	09 46	09 55	10 00
Heald Green d	07 42	07 49			08 05			08 20	08 29			08 49						09 20	09 33			09 49		
Gatley d	07 45	07 52		08 02				08 23	08 32			08 52						09 23				09 52		
East Didsbury d	07 48	07 55		08 05				08 26	08 35			08 55						09 26				09 55		
Burnage d		07 57						08 28				08 57						09 28				09 57		
Mauldeth Road d		07 59						08 30				08 59						09 30				09 59		
Manchester Piccadilly 10 a	07 57	08 11	08 12	08 14	08 21		08 22	08 42	08 44	08 49	08 59	09 11	09 13	09 14	09 18		09 22	09 42	09 44	09 52	09 59	10 11	10 13	10 14
d	07 59			08 15	08 22				08 46		09 01			09 16	09 22				09 46		10 01			10 16
Manchester Oxford Road a	08 01			08 17	08 24				08 48		09 03			09 18	09 24				09 48		10 03			10 18
Deansgate a					08 28				08 51						09 28				09 51					

	NT		TP	NT	TP	TP	NT	NT	TP	TP	NT		TP	NT	TP	TP	NT	NT	TP	TP	NT		TP	NT
			◇1		◇1 🛒	◇1 🛒			◇1 🛒	◇1 🛒			◇1 🛒		◇1 🛒	◇1 🛒			◇1 🛒	◇1 🛒			◇1 🛒	
Crewe 10 84 d				09 33										10 34										11 34
Wilmslow 84 d				09 57										10 57										11 57
Manchester Airport ✈ d	10 03		10 05	10 17	10 29	10 35	10 41	10 46	10 55	11 00	11 03		11 05	11 17	11 29	11 35	11 41	11 46	11 55	12 00	12 03		12 05	12 17
Heald Green d				10 20	10 33			10 49						11 20	11 33			11 49						12 20
Gatley d				10 23				10 52						11 23				11 52						12 23
East Didsbury d				10 26				10 55						11 26				11 55						12 26
Burnage d				10 28				10 57						11 28				11 57						12 28
Mauldeth Road d				10 30				10 59						11 30				11 59						12 30
Manchester Piccadilly 10 a	10 18		10 22	10 42	10 44	10 52	10 59	11 11	11 13	11 14	11 18		11 22	11 42	11 44	11 52	11 59	12 11	12 13	12 14	12 18		12 22	12 42
d	10 22				10 46		11 01			11 16	11 22				11 46		12 01			12 16	12 22			
Manchester Oxford Road a	10 24				10 48		11 03			11 18	11 24				11 48		12 03			12 18	12 24			
Deansgate a	10 28				10 51						11 28				11 51						12 28			

	TP	TP	NT	NT	TP	TP	NT		TP	NT	TP	TP	NT	NT	TP	TP	NT		TP	NT	TP	TP	NT	NT
	◇1 🛒	◇1 🛒			◇1 🛒	◇1 🛒			◇1 🛒		◇1 🛒	◇1 🛒			◇1 🛒	◇1 🛒			◇1 🛒		◇1 🛒	◇1		
Crewe 10 84 d										12 34										13 34				
Wilmslow 84 d										12 57										13 57				
Manchester Airport ✈ d	12 29	12 35	12 41	12 46	12 55	13 00	13 03		13 05	13 17	13 29	13 35	13 41	13 46	13 55	14 00	14 03		14 05	14 17	14 29	14 35	14 41	14 46
Heald Green d	12 33			12 49						13 20	13 33			13 49						14 20	14 33			14 49
Gatley d				12 52						13 23				13 52						14 23				14 52
East Didsbury d				12 55						13 26				13 55						14 26				14 55
Burnage d				12 57						13 28				13 57						14 28				14 57
Mauldeth Road d				12 59						13 30				13 59						14 30				14 59
Manchester Piccadilly 10 a	12 44	12 52	12 59	13 11	13 13	13 14	13 18		13 22	13 42	13 44	13 52	13 59	14 11	14 13	14 14	14 18		14 22	14 42	14 44	14 52	14 59	15 11
d	12 46		13 01			13 16	13 22				13 46		14 01			14 16	14 22				14 46		15 01	
Manchester Oxford Road a	12 48		13 03			13 18	13 24				13 48		14 03			14 18	14 24				14 48		15 03	
Deansgate a	12 51						13 28				13 51						14 28				14 51			

Table 85

Saturdays until 18 June

Manchester Airport - Manchester

	TP	TP	NT		TP	NT	TP	TP	NT	NT	TP	TP	NT		TP	NT	TP	TP	NT	NT	TP	TP	NT	
	◇1 🛒	◇1 🛒			◇1 🛒		◇1 🛒	◇1 🛒			◇1 🛒	◇1 🛒			◇1		◇1 🛒	◇1			◇1 🛒	◇1 🛒		
Crewe 10 84 d						14 34										15 33								
Wilmslow 84 d						14 57										15 56								
Manchester Airport ✈ d	14 55	15 00	15 03		15 05	15 17	15 29	15 35	15 41	15 46	15 55	16 00	16 03		16 05	16 17	16 29	16 35	16 41	16 46	16 55	17 00	17 03	
Heald Green d						15 20	15 33			15 49						16 20	16 33			16 49				
Gatley d						15 23				15 52						16 23				16 52				
East Didsbury d						15 26				15 55						16 26				16 55				
Burnage d						15 28				15 57						16 28				16 57				
Mauldeth Road d						15 30				15 59						16 30				16 59				
Manchester Piccadilly 10 ⛴ a	15 13	15 14	15 18		15 22	15 42	15 44	15 52	15 59	16 11	16 13	16 14	16 18		16 22	16 42	16 44	16 52	16 59	17 11	17 13	17 14	17 21	
d		15 16	15 22				15 46		16 01			16 16	16 22				16 46		17 01			17 15	17 22	
Manchester Oxford Road a		15 18	15 24				15 48		16 03			16 18	16 24				16 48		17 03			17 17	17 25	
Deansgate ⛴ a			15 28				15 51						16 28											

	TP	NT	TP	NT	NT	TP	TP	NT	NT		TP	NT	NT	TP	TP	NT	NT	TP	TP		NT	NT	TP	TP
	◇1		◇1			◇1 🛒	◇1 🛒				◇1			◇1	◇1			◇1	◇1				◇1	◇1
Crewe 10 84 d		16 34							17 33								18 34							
Wilmslow 84 d		16 57							17 56								18 57							
Manchester Airport ✈ d	17 05	17 17	17 35	17 41	17 46	17 55	18 00	18 03	18 17		18 35	18 41	18 46	18 55	19 00	19 03	19 09	19 19	19 29		19 41	19 46	19 55	20 00
Heald Green d		17 20			17 49				18 20				18 49				19 12		19 33			19 49		
Gatley d		17 23			17 52				18 23				18 52				19 15					19 52		
East Didsbury d		17 26			17 55				18 26				18 55				19 18					19 55		
Burnage d		17 28			17 57				18 28				18 57				19 20					19 57		
Mauldeth Road d		17 30			17 59				18 30				18 59				19 22					19 59		
Manchester Piccadilly 10 ⛴ a	17 22	17 42	17 52	17 59	18 11	18 13	18 14	18 18	18 42		18 52	18 59	19 11	19 13	19 14	19 18	19 31	19 36	19 44		19 59	20 11	20 13	20 14
d				18 01			18 16	18 22				19 01			19 16	19 20	19 32		19 46		20 01			20 16
Manchester Oxford Road a				18 03			18 18	18 24				19 03			19 18	19 22	19 36		19 48		20 03			20 18
Deansgate ⛴ a								18 28								19 26			19 51					

	NT	NT	TP	TP	AW		TP	NT	NT	TP	TP	NT	TP	TP	NT		NT	TP	TP	TP	NT			
			◇1	◇1			◇1			◇1	◇1		◇1	◇1				◇1	◇1	◇1				
Crewe 10 84 d																								
Wilmslow 84 d		19 56							20 56						21 55						23 15			
Manchester Airport ✈ d	20 03	20 09	20 20	20 29	20 32		20 47	21 03	21 09	21 20	21 29	21 41	21 47	22 00	22 08		22 19	22 22	22 29	23 24	23 27			
Heald Green d		20 12		20 33			20 51		21 12		21 33		21 51		22 12				22 33		23 30			
Gatley d		20 15					20 54		21 15				21 54		22 15						23 33			
East Didsbury d		20 18					20 57		21 18				21 57		22 17						23 36			
Burnage d		20 20					20 59		21 20				21 59		22 19						23 38			
Mauldeth Road d		20 22					21 02		21 22				22 02		22 21						23 40			
Manchester Piccadilly 10 ⛴ a	20 18	20 31	20 36	20 44	20 48		21 13	21 18	21 31	21 36	21 44	22 00	22 13	22 14	22 31		22 34	22 36	22 44	23 39	23 51			
d	20 20	20 32		20 46				21 20	21 32		21 46	22 01		22 16	22 32		22 36		22 46					
Manchester Oxford Road a	20 22	20 36		20 48				21 22	21 36		21 48	22 03		22 18	22 36		22 38		22 48					
Deansgate ⛴ a	20 26			20 51				21 26			21 51						22 41		22 51					

Saturdays 25 June to 1 October

	TP	TP	TP	NT	TP	TP	NT	TP	AW		TP	TP	NT	TP	TP	NT	NT	TP	TP		TP	NT	TP	TP
	◇1	◇1	◇1		◇1	◇1		◇1	◇ 🛒		◇1	◇1 🛒		◇1 🛒	◇1 🛒			◇1 🛒	◇1 🛒		◇1 🛒		◇1 🛒	◇1 🛒
Crewe 10 84 d				00 44																		06 33		
Wilmslow 84 d													05 46									06 57		
Manchester Airport ✈ d	23p52	00 01	00 38	01 20	04 00	04 15	04 34	05 20	05 33		05 37	05 45	06 01	06 18	06 23	06 41	06 46	06 55	07 00		07 05	07 17	07 25	07 33
Heald Green d												05 49	06 04				06 49					07 20	07 30	
Gatley d													06 07				06 52					07 23		
East Didsbury d													06 10				06 55					07 26		
Burnage d													06 12				06 57					07 28		
Mauldeth Road d													06 14				06 59					07 30		
Manchester Piccadilly 10 ⛴ a	00 09	00 15	00 51	01 36	04 14	04 29	04 47	05 35	05 48		05 51	06 00	06 25	06 31	06 39	06 56	07 11	07 13	07 14		07 22	07 42	07 43	07 48
d									05 50			06 03		06 33		06 58			07 15					
Manchester Oxford Road a									05 52			06 05		06 35		07 00			07 17					
Deansgate ⛴ a																								

	NT	NT	TP	TP	NT		TP	NT	TP	TP	NT	NT	TP	TP	NT		TP	NT	TP	TP	NT	NT	TP	TP
			◇1 🛒	◇1 🛒			◇1 🛒		◇1 🛒	◇1 🛒			◇1 🛒	◇1 🛒			◇1 🛒		◇1 🛒	◇1 🛒			◇1 🛒	◇1 🛒
Crewe 10 84 d								07 30										08 31						
Wilmslow 84 d								07 56										08 57						
Manchester Airport ✈ d	07 38	07 46	07 53	07 56	08 01		08 05	08 17	08 25	08 35	08 41	08 46	08 55	09 00	09 03		09 05	09 17	09 29	09 35	09 41	09 46	09 55	10 00
Heald Green d	07 42	07 49			08 05			08 20	08 29			08 49						09 20	09 33			09 49		
Gatley d	07 45	07 52		08 02				08 23	08 32			08 52						09 23				09 52		
East Didsbury d	07 48	07 55		08 05				08 26	08 35			08 55						09 26				09 55		
Burnage d		07 57						08 28				08 57						09 28				09 57		
Mauldeth Road d		07 59						08 30				08 59						09 30				09 59		
Manchester Piccadilly 10 ⛴ a	07 57	08 11	08 12	08 14	08 21		08 22	08 42	08 44	08 49	08 59	09 11	09 13	09 14	09 18		09 22	09 42	09 44	09 52	09 59	10 11	10 13	10 14
d	07 59			08 15	08 22				08 46		09 01			09 16	09 22				09 46		10 01			10 16
Manchester Oxford Road a	08 01			08 17	08 24				08 48		09 03			09 18	09 24				09 48		10 03			10 18
Deansgate ⛴ a					08 28				08 51						09 28				09 51					

Table 85

Saturdays

25 June to 1 October

Manchester Airport - Manchester

	NT		TP	NT	TP	TP	NT	NT	TP	TP	NT		TP	NT	TP	TP	NT	NT	TP	TP	NT		TP	NT
			◇1		◇1	◇1			◇1	◇1			◇1		◇1	◇1			◇1	◇1			◇1	
					trolley	trolley			trolley	trolley			trolley		trolley	trolley			trolley	trolley			trolley	
Crewe 10 84 d				09 33										10 34										11 34
Wilmslow 84 d				09 57										10 57										11 57
Manchester Airport ✈ d	10 03		10 05	10 17	10 29	10 35	10 41	10 46	10 55	11 00	11 03		11 05	11 17	11 29	11 35	11 41	11 46	11 55	12 00	12 03		12 05	12 17
Heald Green d				10 20	10 33			10 49						11 20	11 33			11 49						12 20
Gatley d				10 23				10 52						11 23				11 52						12 23
East Didsbury d				10 26				10 55						11 26				11 55						12 26
Burnage d				10 28				10 57						11 28				11 57						12 28
Mauldeth Road d				10 30				10 59						11 30				11 59						12 30
Manchester Piccadilly 10 a	10 18		10 22	10 42	10 44	10 52	10 59	11 11	11 13	11 14	11 18		11 22	11 42	11 44	11 52	11 59	12 11	12 13	12 14	12 18		12 22	12 42
d	10 22				10 46		11 01			11 16	11 22				11 46		12 01			12 16	12 22			
Manchester Oxford Road a	10 24				10 48		11 03			11 18	11 24				11 48		12 03			12 18	12 24			
Deansgate a	10 28				10 51						11 28				11 51						12 28			

	TP	TP	NT	NT	TP	TP	NT		TP	NT	TP	TP	NT	NT	TP	TP	NT		TP	NT	TP	TP	NT	NT
	◇1	◇1			◇1	◇1			◇1		◇1	◇1			◇1	◇1			◇1		◇1	◇1		
	trolley	trolley			trolley	trolley			trolley		trolley	trolley			trolley	trolley			trolley		trolley			
Crewe 10 84 d										12 34										13 34				
Wilmslow 84 d										12 57										13 57				
Manchester Airport ✈ d	12 29	12 35	12 41	12 46	12 55	13 00	13 03		13 05	13 17	13 29	13 35	13 41	13 46	13 55	14 00	14 03		14 05	14 17	14 29	14 35	14 41	14 46
Heald Green d	12 33			12 49						13 20	13 33			13 49						14 20	14 33			14 49
Gatley d				12 52						13 23				13 52						14 23				14 52
East Didsbury d				12 55						13 26				13 55						14 26				14 55
Burnage d				12 57						13 28				13 57						14 28				14 57
Mauldeth Road d				12 59						13 30				13 59						14 30				14 59
Manchester Piccadilly 10 a	12 44	12 52	12 59	13 11	13 13	13 14	13 18		13 22	13 42	13 44	13 52	13 59	14 11	14 13	14 14	14 18		14 22	14 42	14 44	14 52	14 59	15 11
d	12 46		13 01			13 16	13 22				13 46		14 01			14 16	14 22				14 46		15 01	
Manchester Oxford Road a	12 48		13 03			13 18	13 24				13 48		14 03			14 18	14 24				14 48		15 03	
Deansgate a	12 51						13 28				13 51						14 28				14 51			

	TP	TP	NT		TP	NT	TP	TP	NT	NT	TP	TP	NT		TP	NT	TP	TP	NT	NT	TP	TP	NT	
	◇1	◇1			◇1		◇1	◇1			◇1	◇1			◇1		◇1	◇1			◇1	◇1		
	trolley	trolley			trolley		trolley	trolley			trolley	trolley					trolley				trolley	trolley		
Crewe 10 84 d						14 34										15 33								
Wilmslow 84 d						14 57										15 56								
Manchester Airport ✈ d	14 55	15 00	15 03		15 05	15 17	15 29	15 35	15 41	15 46	15 55	16 00	16 03		16 05	16 17	16 29	16 35	16 41	16 46	16 55	17 00	17 03	
Heald Green d						15 20	15 33			15 49						16 20	16 33			16 49				
Gatley d						15 23				15 52						16 23				16 52				
East Didsbury d						15 26				15 55						16 26				16 55				
Burnage d						15 28				15 57						16 28				16 57				
Mauldeth Road d						15 30				15 59						16 30				16 59				
Manchester Piccadilly 10 a	15 13	15 14	15 18		15 22	15 42	15 44	15 52	15 59	16 11	16 13	16 14	16 18		16 22	16 42	16 44	16 52	16 59	17 11	17 13	17 14	17 21	
d		15 16	15 22				15 46		16 01			16 16	16 22				16 46		17 01			17 15	17 22	
Manchester Oxford Road a		15 18	15 24				15 48		16 03			16 18	16 24				16 48		17 03			17 17	17 25	
Deansgate a			15 28				15 51						16 28											

	TP	NT	TP	NT	NT	TP	TP	NT	NT		TP	NT	NT	TP	TP	NT	NT	TP	TP		NT	NT	TP	TP
	◇1		◇1			◇1	◇1				◇1			◇1	◇1			◇1	◇1				◇1	◇1
						trolley	trolley																	
Crewe 10 84 d		16 34							17 33								18 34							
Wilmslow 84 d		16 57							17 56								18 57							
Manchester Airport ✈ d	17 05	17 17	17 35	17 41	17 46	17 55	18 00	18 03	1817		18 35	18 41	18 46	18 55	19 00	19 03	19 09	19 19	19 29		19 41	19 46	19 55	20 00
Heald Green d		17 20			17 49				18 20				18 49				19 12		19 33			19 49		
Gatley d		17 23			17 52				18 23				18 52				19 15					19 52		
East Didsbury d		17 26			17 55				18 26				18 55				19 18					19 55		
Burnage d		17 28			17 57				18 28				18 57				19 20					19 57		
Mauldeth Road d		17 30			17 59				18 30				18 59				19 22					19 59		
Manchester Piccadilly 10 a	17 22	17 42	17 52	17 59	18 11	18 13	18 14	18 18	18 42		18 52	18 59	19 11	19 13	19 14	19 18	19 31	19 36	19 44		19 59	20 11	20 13	20 14
d				18 01			18 16	18 22				19 01			19 16	19 20	19 32		19 46		20 01			20 16
Manchester Oxford Road a				18 03			18 18	18 24				19 03			19 18	19 22	19 36		19 48		20 03			20 18
Deansgate a								18 28								19 26			19 51					

	NT	NT	TP	TP	AW		TP	NT	NT	TP	TP	NT	TP	TP	NT		NT	TP	TP	TP	NT			
			◇1	◇1			◇1			◇1	◇1		◇1	◇1				◇1	◇1	◇1				
Crewe 10 84 d																								
Wilmslow 84 d		19 56							20 56						21 55						23 15			
Manchester Airport ✈ d	20 03	20 09	20 20	20 29	20 32		20 47	21 03	21 09	21 20	21 29	21 41	21 47	22 00	22 08		22 19	22 22	22 29	23 24	23 27			
Heald Green d		20 12		20 33			20 51		21 12		21 33		21 51		22 12				22 33		23 30			
Gatley d		20 15					20 54		21 15				21 54		22 15						23 33			
East Didsbury d		20 18					20 57		21 18				21 57		22 17						23 36			
Burnage d		20 20					20 59		21 20				21 59		22 19						23 38			
Mauldeth Road d		20 22					21 02		21 22				22 02		22 21						23 40			
Manchester Piccadilly 10 a	20 18	20 31	20 36	20 44	20 48		21 13	21 18	21 31	21 36	21 44	22 00	22 13	22 14	22 31		22 34	22 36	22 44	23 39	23 51			
d	20 20	20 32		20 46	20 50			21 20	21 32		21 46	22 01		22 16	22 32		22 36		22 46					
Manchester Oxford Road a	20 22	20 36		20 48	20 52			21 22	21 36		21 48	22 03		22 18	22 36		22 38		22 48					
Deansgate a	20 26			20 51				21 26			21 51						22 41		22 51					

Table 85

Saturdays
from 8 October

Manchester Airport - Manchester

	TP	TP	TP	NT	TP	TP	NT	TP	AW		TP	TP	NT	TP	TP	NT	NT	TP	TP		TP	NT	TP	TP
	◇1	◇1	◇1		◇1	◇1		◇1	◇ 🚲		◇1	◇1 🚲		◇1 🚲	◇1 🚲			◇1 🚲	◇1 🚲		◇1 🚲		◇1 🚲	◇1 🚲
Crewe 10 84 d				00 44																		06 33		
Wilmslow 84 d													05 46									06 57		
Manchester Airport ✈ d	23p52	00 01	00 38	01 20	04 00	04 15	04 34	05 20	05 33		05 37	05 45	06 01	06 18	06 23	06 41	06 46	06 55	07 00		07 05	07 17	07 25	07 33
Heald Green d												05 49	06 04				06 49					07 20	07 30	
Gatley d													06 07				06 52					07 23		
East Didsbury d													06 10				06 55					07 26		
Burnage d													06 12				06 57					07 28		
Mauldeth Road d													06 14				06 59					07 30		
Manchester Piccadilly 10 a	00 09	00 15	00 51	01 36	04 14	04 29	04 47	05 35	05 48		05 51	06 00	06 25	06 31	06 39	06 56	07 11	07 13	07 14		07 22	07 42	07 43	07 48
d									05 50			06 03		06 33		06 58			07 15					
Manchester Oxford Road a									05 52			06 05		06 35		07 00			07 17					
Deansgate a																								

	NT	NT	TP	TP	NT		TP	NT	TP	TP	NT	NT	TP	TP	NT		TP	NT	TP	TP	NT	NT	TP	TP
			◇1 🚲	◇1 🚲			◇1 🚲		◇1 🚲	◇1 🚲			◇1 🚲	◇1 🚲			◇1 🚲		◇1 🚲	◇1 🚲			◇1 🚲	◇1 🚲
Crewe 10 84 d								07 30										08 31						
Wilmslow 84 d								07 56										08 57						
Manchester Airport ✈ d	07 38	07 46	07 53	07 56	08 01		08 05	08 17	08 25	08 35	08 41	08 46	08 55	09 00	09 03		09 05	09 17	09 29	09 35	09 41	09 46	09 55	10 00
Heald Green d	07 42	07 49			08 05			08 20	08 29			08 49						09 20	09 33			09 49		
Gatley d	07 45	07 52		08 02				08 23	08 32			08 52						09 23				09 52		
East Didsbury d	07 48	07 55		08 05				08 26	08 35			08 55						09 26				09 55		
Burnage d		07 57						08 28				08 57						09 28				09 57		
Mauldeth Road d		07 59						08 30				08 59						09 30				09 59		
Manchester Piccadilly 10 a	07 57	08 11	08 12	08 14	08 21		08 22	08 42	08 44	08 49	08 59	09 11	09 13	09 14	09 18		09 22	09 42	09 44	09 52	09 59	10 11	10 13	10 14
d	07 59			08 15	08 22				08 46		09 01			09 16	09 22				09 46		10 01			10 16
Manchester Oxford Road a	08 01			08 17	08 24				08 48		09 03			09 18	09 24				09 48		10 03			10 18
Deansgate a					08 28				08 51						09 28				09 51					

	NT		TP	NT	TP	TP	NT	NT	TP	TP	NT		TP	NT	TP	TP	NT	NT	TP	TP	NT		TP	NT
			◇1		◇1 🚲	◇1 🚲			◇1 🚲	◇1 🚲			◇1 🚲		◇1 🚲	◇1 🚲			◇1 🚲	◇1 🚲			◇1 🚲	
Crewe 10 84 d				09 33										10 34										11 34
Wilmslow 84 d				09 57										10 57										11 57
Manchester Airport ✈ d	10 03		10 05	10 17	10 29	10 35	10 41	10 46	10 55	11 00	11 03		11 05	11 17	11 29	11 35	11 41	11 46	11 55	12 00	12 03		12 05	12 17
Heald Green d				10 20	10 33			10 49						11 20	11 33			11 49						12 20
Gatley d				10 23				10 52						11 23				11 52						12 23
East Didsbury d				10 26				10 55						11 26				11 55						12 26
Burnage d				10 28				10 57						11 28				11 57						12 28
Mauldeth Road d				10 30				10 59						11 30				11 59						12 30
Manchester Piccadilly 10 a	10 18		10 22	10 42	10 44	10 52	10 59	11 11	11 13	11 14	11 18		11 22	11 42	11 44	11 52	11 59	12 11	12 13	12 14	12 18		12 22	12 42
d	10 22				10 46		11 01			11 16	11 22				11 46		12 01			12 16	12 22			
Manchester Oxford Road a	10 24				10 48		11 03			11 18	11 24				11 48		12 03			12 18	12 24			
Deansgate a	10 28				10 51						11 28				11 51						12 28			

	TP	TP	NT	NT	TP	TP	NT		TP	NT	TP	TP	NT	NT	TP	TP	NT		TP	NT	TP	TP	NT	NT
	◇1 🚲	◇1 🚲			◇1 🚲	◇1 🚲			◇1 🚲		◇1 🚲	◇1 🚲			◇1 🚲	◇1 🚲			◇1 🚲		◇1 🚲	◇1		
Crewe 10 84 d										12 34										13 34				
Wilmslow 84 d										12 57										13 57				
Manchester Airport ✈ d	12 29	12 35	12 41	12 46	12 55	13 00	13 03		13 05	13 17	13 29	13 35	13 41	13 46	13 55	14 00	14 03		14 05	14 17	14 29	14 35	14 41	14 46
Heald Green d	12 33			12 49						13 20	13 33			13 49						14 20	14 33			14 49
Gatley d				12 52						13 23				13 52						14 23				14 52
East Didsbury d				12 55						13 26				13 55						14 26				14 55
Burnage d				12 57						13 28				13 57						14 28				14 57
Mauldeth Road d				12 59						13 30				13 59						14 30				14 59
Manchester Piccadilly 10 a	12 44	12 52	12 59	13 11	13 13	13 14	13 18		13 22	13 42	13 44	13 52	13 59	14 11	14 13	14 14	14 18		14 22	14 42	14 44	14 52	14 59	15 11
d	12 46		13 01			13 16	13 22				13 46		14 01			14 16	14 22				14 46		15 01	
Manchester Oxford Road a	12 48		13 03			13 18	13 24				13 48		14 03			14 18	14 24				14 48		15 03	
Deansgate a	12 51						13 28				13 51						14 28				14 51			

	TP	TP	NT		TP	NT	TP	TP	NT	NT	TP	TP	NT		TP	NT	TP	TP	NT	NT	TP	TP	NT	
	◇1 🚲	◇1 🚲			◇1 🚲		◇1 🚲	◇1 🚲			◇1 🚲	◇1 🚲			◇1		◇1 🚲	◇1			◇1 🚲	◇1 🚲		
Crewe 10 84 d						14 34										15 33								
Wilmslow 84 d						14 57										15 56								
Manchester Airport ✈ d	14 55	15 00	15 03		15 05	15 17	15 29	15 35	15 41	15 46	15 55	16 00	16 03		16 05	1617	16 29	16 35	16 41	16 46	16 55	17 00	17 03	
Heald Green d						15 20	15 33			15 49						16 20	16 33			16 49				
Gatley d						15 23				15 52						16 23				16 52				
East Didsbury d						15 26				15 55						16 26				16 55				
Burnage d						15 28				15 57						16 28				16 57				
Mauldeth Road d						15 30				15 59						16 30				16 59				
Manchester Piccadilly 10 a	15 13	15 14	15 18		15 22	15 42	15 44	15 52	15 59	16 11	16 13	16 14	16 18		16 22	16 42	16 44	16 52	16 59	17 11	17 13	17 14	17 21	
d		15 16	15 22				15 46		16 01			16 16	16 22				16 46		17 01			17 15	17 22	
Manchester Oxford Road a		15 18	15 24				15 48		16 03			16 18	16 24				16 48		17 03			17 17	17 25	
Deansgate a			15 28				15 51						16 28											

Table 85

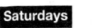

Saturdays
from 8 October

Manchester Airport - Manchester

		TP	NT	TP	NT	NT	TP	TP	NT	NT		TP	NT	NT	TP	TP	NT	NT	TP	TP		NT	NT	TP	TP
		◇1		◇1			◇1	◇1				◇1			◇1	◇1			◇1	◇1				◇1	◇1
							🛒	🛒																	
Crewe 10	84 d		16 34							17 33								18 34							
Wilmslow	84 d		16 57							17 56								18 57							
Manchester Airport ✈	d	17 05	17 17	17 35	17 41	17 46	17 55	18 00	18 03	18 17		18 35	18 41	18 46	18 55	19 00	19 03	19 09	19 19	19 29		19 41	19 46	19 55	20 00
Heald Green	d		17 20			17 49				18 20				18 49				19 12		19 33			19 49		
Gatley	d		17 23			17 52				18 23				18 52				19 15					19 52		
East Didsbury	d		17 26			17 55				18 26				18 55				19 18					19 55		
Burnage	d		17 28			17 57				18 28				18 57				19 20					19 57		
Mauldeth Road	d		17 30			17 59				18 30				18 59				19 22					19 59		
Manchester Piccadilly 10 🚊	a	17 22	17 42	17 52	17 59	18 11	18 13	18 14	18 18	18 42		18 52	18 59	19 11	19 13	19 14	19 18	19 31	19 36	19 44		19 59	20 11	20 13	20 14
	d				18 01			18 16	18 22				19 01			19 16	19 20	19 32		19 46		20 01			20 16
Manchester Oxford Road	a				18 03			18 18	18 24				19 03			19 18	19 22	19 36		19 48		20 03			20 18
Deansgate 🚊	a								18 28								19 26			19 51					

		NT	NT	TP	TP	AW		TP	NT	NT	TP	TP	NT	TP	TP	NT		NT	TP	TP	TP	NT			
				◇1	◇1			◇1			◇1	◇1		◇1	◇1				◇1	◇1	◇1				
Crewe 10	84 d																								
Wilmslow	84 d		19 56							20 56						21 55						23 15			
Manchester Airport ✈	d	20 03	20 09	20 20	20 29	20 32		20 47	21 03	21 09	21 20	21 29	21 41	21 47	22 00	22 08		22 19	22 22	22 29	23 24	23 27			
Heald Green	d		20 12		20 33			20 51		21 12		21 33		21 51		22 12				22 33		23 30			
Gatley	d		20 15					20 54		21 15				21 54		22 15						23 33			
East Didsbury	d		20 18					20 57		21 18				21 57		22 17						23 36			
Burnage	d		20 20					20 59		21 20				21 59		22 19						23 38			
Mauldeth Road	d		20 22					21 02		21 22				22 02		22 21						23 40			
Manchester Piccadilly 10 🚊	a	20 18	20 31	20 36	20 44	20 48		21 13	21 18	21 31	21 36	21 44	22 00	22 13	22 14	22 31		22 34	22 36	22 44	23 39	23 51			
	d	20 20	20 32		20 46	20 50			21 20	21 32		21 46	22 01		22 16	22 32		22 36		22 46					
Manchester Oxford Road	a	20 22	20 36		20 48	20 52			21 22	21 36		21 48	22 03		22 18	22 36		22 38		22 48					
Deansgate 🚊	a	20 26			20 51				21 26			21 51						22 41		22 51					

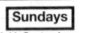

Sundays
until 11 September

		TP	TP	NT	TP	TP	NT	TP	TP	NT		NT	TP	TP	TP	NT	TP	TP	NT	TP		NT	TP	TP	NT
		◇1	◇1		◇1	◇1		◇1	◇1				◇1	◇1	◇1		◇1	◇1		◇1			◇1	◇1	
															🛒					🛒					
Crewe 10	84 d																								
Wilmslow	84 d																								
Manchester Airport ✈	d	01 22	04 43	06 09	06 24	07 24	07 30	07 55	08 06	08 09		08 35	08 40	08 47	09 00	09 06	09 20	09 30	09 35	10 00		10 08	10 20	10 30	10 35
Heald Green	d			06 12			07 33			08 12						09 09						10 11			
Gatley	d			06 15			07 36			08 15						09 12						10 14			
East Didsbury	d			06 18			07 39			08 18						09 15						10 17			
Burnage	d			06 20			07 41			08 20						09 17						10 19			
Mauldeth Road	d			06 22			07 43			08 22						09 19						10 21			
Manchester Piccadilly 10 🚊	a	01 36	04 57	06 31	06 38	07 37	07 54	08 08	08 24	08 30	08 00	08 48	08 54	09 01	09 14	09 29	09 37	09 44	09 48	10 14		10 29	10 37	10 44	10 48
	d							08 11			08 02	08 50		09 03	09 16			09 46	09 50	10 16				10 46	10 50
Manchester Oxford Road	a							08 13			08 04	08 52		09 05	09 18			09 48	09 52	10 18				10 48	10 52
Deansgate 🚊	a							08 16			08 05			09 08				09 51						10 51	

		TP	TP	NT	TP	TP		NT	TP	NT	TP	TP	NT	TP	TP	NT		TP	TP	NT	TP	TP	NT	TP	TP
		◇1	◇1		◇1	◇1			◇1		◇1	◇1		◇1	◇1			◇1	◇1		◇1	◇1		◇1	◇1
									🛒						🛒							🛒			
Crewe 10	84 d																								
Wilmslow	84 d			10 43												12 54									
Manchester Airport ✈	d	10 44	11 00	11 03	11 20	11 30		11 33	12 00	12 08	12 20	12 30	12 35	12 55	13 00	13 09		13 20	13 30	13 35	13 55	14 00	14 09	14 20	14 30
Heald Green	d			11 07						12 11						13 12							14 12		
Gatley	d			11 10						12 14						13 15							14 15		
East Didsbury	d			11 12						12 17						13 18							14 18		
Burnage	d			11 14						12 19						13 20							14 20		
Mauldeth Road	d			11 16						12 21						13 22							14 22		
Manchester Piccadilly 10 🚊	a	10 58	11 14	11 25	11 35	11 44		11 48	12 14	12 29	12 37	12 44	12 49	13 09	13 14	13 31		13 37	13 44	13 48	14 09	14 14	14 31	14 37	14 44
	d		11 16	11 26		11 46		11 50	12 16	12 29		12 46	12 50		13 16				13 46	13 50		14 16			14 46
Manchester Oxford Road	a		11 18	11 30		11 48		11 52	12 18	12 33		12 48	12 52		13 18				13 48	13 52		14 18			14 48
Deansgate 🚊	a					11 51						12 51							13 51						14 51

		NT		TP	TP	NT	TP	TP	NT	TP	TP	NT		TP	TP	NT	TP	TP	NT	TP	TP	NT		TP	TP
				◇1	◇1		◇1	◇1		◇1	◇1			◇1	◇1		◇1	◇1		◇1	◇1			◇1	◇1
											🛒							🛒							🛒
Crewe 10	84 d																								
Wilmslow	84 d					14 54													16 54						
Manchester Airport ✈	d	14 35		14 55	15 00	15 09	15 20	15 30	15 35	15 55	16 00	16 09		16 20	16 30	16 35	16 55	17 00	17 09	17 20	17 30	17 35		17 55	18 00
Heald Green	d					15 12						16 12							17 12						
Gatley	d					15 15						16 15							17 15						
East Didsbury	d					15 18						16 18							17 18						
Burnage	d					15 20						16 20							17 20						
Mauldeth Road	d					15 22						16 22							17 22						
Manchester Piccadilly 10 🚊	a	14 48		15 09	15 14	15 32	15 37	15 44	15 48	16 09	16 14	16 31		16 37	16 44	16 48	17 09	17 14	17 31	17 37	17 44	17 48		18 09	18 14
	d	14 50			15 16			15 46	15 50		16 16				16 46	16 50		17 16			17 46	17 50			18 16
Manchester Oxford Road	a	14 52			15 18			15 48	15 52		16 18				16 48	16 52		17 18			17 48	17 52			18 18
Deansgate 🚊	a							15 51							16 51						17 51				

Table 85

Manchester Airport - Manchester

Sundays
until 11 September

	NT	TP	TP	NT	TP	TP	NT		TP	TP	NT	TP	NT	TP	TP	NT	TP		NT	TP	TP	NT	TP	NT
		◇1	◇1		◇1	◇1			◇1	◇1		◇1		◇1	◇1		◇1			◇1	◇1		◇1	
Crewe 10 84 d																								
Wilmslow 84 d							18 54												20 54					
Manchester Airport d	18 09	18 20	18 30	18 35	18 55	19 00	19 09		19 20	19 30	19 35	19 55	20 09	20 20	20 30	20 35	20 55		21 09	21 20	21 30	21 35	21 55	22 09
Heald Green d	18 12						19 12						20 12						21 12					22 12
Gatley d	18 15						19 15						20 15						21 15					22 15
East Didsbury d	18 18						19 18						20 18						21 18					22 18
Burnage d	18 20						19 20						20 20						21 20					22 20
Mauldeth Road d	18 22						19 22						20 22						21 22					22 22
Manchester Piccadilly 10 a	18 31	18 37	18 44	18 48	19 09	19 14	19 31		19 37	19 44	19 48	20 09	20 31	20 37	20 44	20 48	21 09		21 31	21 37	21 44	21 48	22 09	22 31
d			18 46	18 50		19 16				19 46	19 50				20 46	20 50					21 46	21 50		
Manchester Oxford Road a			18 48	18 52		19 18				19 48	19 52				20 48	20 52					21 48	21 52		
Deansgate a			18 51							19 51					20 51						21 51			

	NT	TP	NT		TP
		◇1			◇1
Crewe 10 84 d					
Wilmslow 84 d			22 54		
Manchester Airport d	22 35	22 55	23 09		23 20
Heald Green d			23 12		
Gatley d			23 15		
East Didsbury d			23 18		
Burnage d			23 20		
Mauldeth Road d			23 22		
Manchester Piccadilly 10 a	22 48	23 09	23 32		23 37
d	22 50				
Manchester Oxford Road a	22 52				
Deansgate a					

Sundays
18 September to 23 October

	TP	NT	NT	TP	TP	NT	TP	TP	TP		TP	NT	TP	TP	TP	NT	TP	NT	TP		TP	NT	TP	NT
	◇1			◇1	◇1		◇1	◇1	◇1 🚲		◇1		◇1	◇1 🚲	◇1		◇1		◇1		◇1		◇1	
Crewe 10 84 d																								
Wilmslow 84 d																						10 43		
Manchester Airport d	01 22	06 09	07 09	07 30	07 40	08 24	08 40	08 47	09 00		09 03	09 06	09 29	10 00	10 03	10 08	10 30	10 35	10 44		11 03	11 03	11 30	11 33
Heald Green d		06 12	07 12			08 27						09 09				10 11						11 07		
Gatley d		06 15	07 15			08 30						09 12				10 14						11 10		
East Didsbury d		06 18	07 18			08 33						09 15				10 17						11 12		
Burnage d		06 20	07 20			08 35						09 17				10 19						11 14		
Mauldeth Road d		06 22	07 22			08 37						09 19				10 21						11 16		
Manchester Piccadilly 10 a	01 36	06 31	07 31	07 44	07 53	08 47	08 54	09 01	09 14		09 19	09 29	09 42	10 14	10 18	10 29	10 44	10 48	10 58		11 18	11 25	11 44	11 48
d				07 46				09 03	09 16				09 46	10 16			10 46	10 50				11 26	11 46	11 50
Manchester Oxford Road a				07 48				09 05	09 18				09 48	10 18			10 48	10 52				11 30	11 48	11 52
Deansgate a				07 51				09 08					09 51				10 51						11 51	

	TP	TP	NT	TP	NT		TP	TP	TP	NT	TP	NT	TP	TP	TP		NT	TP	NT	TP	TP	TP	NT	TP
	◇1 🚲	◇1		◇1			◇1	◇1 🚲	◇1		◇1		◇1	◇1 🚲	◇1			◇1		◇1	◇1	◇1		◇1
Crewe 10 84 d																								
Wilmslow 84 d										12 54													14 54	
Manchester Airport d	12 00	12 03	12 08	12 30	12 35		12 55	12 58	13 03	13 09	13 30	13 35	13 55	13 58	14 03		14 09	14 30	14 35	14 55	14 58	15 03	15 09	15 30
Heald Green d			12 11							13 12							14 12						15 12	
Gatley d			12 14							13 15							14 15						15 15	
East Didsbury d			12 17							13 18							14 18						15 18	
Burnage d			12 19							13 20							14 20						15 20	
Mauldeth Road d			12 21							13 22							14 22						15 22	
Manchester Piccadilly 10 a	12 14	12 18	12 29	12 44	12 49		13 09	13 14	13 18	13 31	13 44	13 48	14 09	14 14	14 18		14 31	14 44	14 48	15 09	15 14	15 18	15 32	15 44
d	12 16		12 29	12 46	12 50			13 16			13 46	13 50		14 16				14 46	14 50		15 16			15 46
Manchester Oxford Road a	12 18		12 33	12 48	12 52			13 18			13 48	13 52		14 18				14 48	14 52		15 18			15 48
Deansgate a				12 51							13 51							14 51						15 51

	NT		TP	TP	TP	NT	TP	NT	TP	TP	TP		NT	TP	NT	TP	TP	TP	NT	TP	NT		TP	TP
			◇1	◇1 🚲	◇1		◇1		◇1	◇1 🚲	◇1			◇1		◇1	◇1 🚲	◇1		◇1			◇1	◇1
Crewe 10 84 d																								
Wilmslow 84 d													16 54											
Manchester Airport d	15 35		15 55	15 58	16 03	16 09	16 30	16 35	16 55	16 58	17 03		17 09	17 30	17 35	17 55	17 58	18 03	18 09	18 30	18 35		18 55	18 58
Heald Green d						16 12							17 12						18 12					
Gatley d						16 15							17 15						18 15					
East Didsbury d						16 18							17 18						18 18					
Burnage d						16 20							17 20						18 20					
Mauldeth Road d						16 22							17 22						18 22					
Manchester Piccadilly 10 a	15 48		16 09	16 14	16 18	16 31	16 44	16 48	17 09	17 14	17 18		17 31	17 44	17 48	18 09	18 14	18 18	18 31	18 44	18 48		19 09	19 14
d	15 50			16 16			16 46	16 50		17 16				17 46	17 50		18 16			18 46	18 50			19 16
Manchester Oxford Road a	15 52			16 18			16 48	16 52		17 18				17 48	17 52		18 18			18 48	18 52			19 18
Deansgate a							16 51							17 51						18 51				

Table 85

Sundays

18 September to 23 October

Manchester Airport - Manchester

		TP	NT	TP	NT	TP	TP	NT		TP	NT	TP	TP	NT	TP	NT	TP	TP		NT	NT	TP	NT	TP	
		◇1		◇1		◇1	◇1			◇1		◇1	◇1		◇1		◇1	◇1				◇1		◇1	
Crewe 10 84	d																								
Wilmslow 84	d		18 54											20 54									22 54		
Manchester Airport	d	19 03	19 09	19 30	19 35	19 55	20 03	20 09		20 30	20 35	20 55	21 03	21 09	21 30	21 35	21 55	22 03		22 09	22 35	22 55	23 09	23 25	
Heald Green	d		19 12					20 12						21 12						22 12			23 12		
Gatley	d		19 15					20 15						21 15						22 15			23 15		
East Didsbury	d		19 18					20 18						21 18						22 18			23 18		
Burnage	d		19 20					20 20						21 20						22 20			23 20		
Mauldeth Road	d		19 22					20 22						21 22						22 22			23 22		
Manchester Piccadilly 10	a	19 18	19 31	19 44	19 48	20 09	20 18	20 31		20 44	20 48	21 09	21 18	21 31	21 44	21 48	22 09	22 16		22 31	22 48	23 09	23 32	23 38	
	d			19 46	19 50					20 46	20 50				21 46	21 50					22 50				
Manchester Oxford Road	a			19 48	19 52					20 48	20 52				21 48	21 52					22 52				
Deansgate	a			19 51						20 51					21 51										

Sundays

from 30 October

		TP	NT	NT	TP	TP	NT	TP	TP	TP		TP	NT	TP	NT	TP	NT	TP	TP	NT		TP	NT	TP	TP
		◇1			◇1	◇1		◇1	◇1	◇1 trolley		◇1		◇1		◇1 trolley		◇1	◇1			◇1		◇1	◇1
Crewe 10 84	d																								
Wilmslow 84	d																						10 43		
Manchester Airport	d	01 22	06 09	07 09	07 30	07 40	08 24	08 40	08 47	09 00		09 03	09 06	09 29	09 35	10 00	10 08	10 20	10 30	10 35		10 44	11 03	11 20	11 30
Heald Green	d		06 12	07 12			08 27						09 09				10 11						11 07		
Gatley	d		06 15	07 15			08 30						09 12				10 14						11 10		
East Didsbury	d		06 18	07 18			08 33						09 15				10 17						11 12		
Burnage	d		06 20	07 20			08 35						09 17				10 19						11 14		
Mauldeth Road	d		06 22	07 22			08 37						09 19				10 21						11 16		
Manchester Piccadilly 10	a	01 36	06 31	07 31	07 44	07 53	08 47	08 54	09 01	09 14		09 19	09 29	09 43	09 48	10 14	10 29	10 37	10 44	10 48		10 58	11 25	11 37	11 44
	d				07 46				09 03	09 16				09 46	09 50	10 16			10 46	10 50			11 26		11 46
Manchester Oxford Road	a				07 48				09 05	09 18				09 48	09 52	10 18			10 48	10 52			11 30		11 48
Deansgate	a				07 51				09 08					09 51					10 51						11 51

		NT	TP	NT	TP	TP		NT	TP	TP	NT	TP	TP	NT	TP	TP		NT	TP	TP	NT	TP	TP	NT	TP
			◇1 trolley		◇1	◇1			◇1	◇1 trolley		◇1	◇1		◇1	◇1 trolley			◇1	◇1		◇1	◇1		◇1
Crewe 10 84	d																								
Wilmslow 84	d										12 54													14 54	
Manchester Airport	d	11 33	12 00	12 08	12 20	12 30		12 35	12 55	13 00	13 09	13 20	13 30	13 35	13 55	14 00		14 09	14 20	14 30	14 35	14 55	15 00	15 09	15 20
Heald Green	d			12 11							13 12							14 12						15 12	
Gatley	d			12 14							13 15							14 15						15 15	
East Didsbury	d			12 17							13 18							14 18						15 18	
Burnage	d			12 19							13 20							14 20						15 20	
Mauldeth Road	d			12 21							13 22							14 22						15 22	
Manchester Piccadilly 10	a	11 48	12 14	12 29	12 34	12 44		12 49	13 09	13 14	13 31	13 37	13 44	13 48	14 09	14 14		14 31	14 37	14 44	14 48	15 09	15 14	15 32	15 37
	d	11 50	12 16	12 29		12 46		12 50		13 16			13 46	13 50		14 16				14 46	14 50		15 16		
Manchester Oxford Road	a	11 52	12 18	12 33		12 48		12 52		13 18			13 48	13 52		14 18				14 48	14 52		15 18		
Deansgate	a					12 51							13 51							14 51					

		TP		NT	TP	TP	NT	TP	TP	NT	TP	TP		NT	TP	TP	NT	TP	TP	NT	TP	TP		NT	TP
		◇1			◇1	◇1 trolley		◇1	◇1		◇1	◇1 trolley			◇1	◇1		◇1	◇1 trolley		◇1	◇1			◇1
Crewe 10 84	d																								
Wilmslow 84	d													16 54											
Manchester Airport	d	15 30		15 35	15 55	16 00	16 09	16 20	16 30	16 35	16 55	17 00		17 09	17 20	17 30	17 35	17 55	18 00	18 09	18 20	18 30		18 35	18 55
Heald Green	d						16 12							17 12						18 12					
Gatley	d						16 15							17 15						18 15					
East Didsbury	d						16 18							17 18						18 18					
Burnage	d						16 20							17 20						18 20					
Mauldeth Road	d						16 22							17 22						18 22					
Manchester Piccadilly 10	a	15 44		15 48	16 09	16 14	16 31	16 37	16 44	16 48	17 09	17 14		17 31	17 37	17 44	17 48	18 09	18 14	18 31	18 37	18 44		18 48	19 09
	d	15 46		15 50		16 16			16 46	16 50		17 16				17 46	17 50		18 16			18 46		18 50	
Manchester Oxford Road	a	15 48		15 52		16 18			16 48	16 52		17 18				17 48	17 52		18 18			18 48		18 52	
Deansgate	a	15 51							16 51							17 51						18 51			

		TP	NT	TP	TP	NT	TP	NT		TP	TP	NT	TP	NT	TP	TP	NT	TP		NT	NT	TP	NT	TP	
		◇1		◇1	◇1		◇1			◇1	◇1		◇1		◇1	◇1		◇1				◇1		◇1	
Crewe 10 84	d																								
Wilmslow 84	d		18 54											20 54									22 54		
Manchester Airport	d	19 00	19 09	19 20	19 30	19 35	19 55	20 09		20 20	20 30	20 35	20 55	21 09	21 20	21 30	21 35	21 55		22 09	22 35	22 55	23 09	23 20	
Heald Green	d		19 12					20 12						21 12						22 12			23 12		
Gatley	d		19 15					20 15						21 15						22 15			23 15		
East Didsbury	d		19 18					20 18						21 18						22 18			23 18		
Burnage	d		19 20					20 20						21 20						22 20			23 20		
Mauldeth Road	d		19 22					20 22						21 22						22 22			23 22		
Manchester Piccadilly 10	a	19 14	19 31	19 37	19 44	19 48	20 09	20 31		20 37	20 44	20 48	21 09	21 31	21 37	21 44	21 48	22 09		22 31	22 48	23 09	23 32	23 37	
	d	19 16			19 46	19 50					20 46	20 50				21 46	21 50				22 50				
Manchester Oxford Road	a	19 18			19 48	19 52					20 48	20 52				21 48	21 52				22 52				
Deansgate	a				19 51						20 51					21 51									

Table 86

Manchester - Hazel Grove and Buxton

Mondays to Fridays

until 30 September

Miles	Station		NT MX	NT A	NT	NT	NT B	NT	NT C	NT	NT D		NT	NT D	NT	NT D	NT	NT D	NT	NT D	NT		NT D	NT	NT D
—	Deansgate	d					07 11		08 12		09 12			10 12		11 12		12 12		13 12			14 12		15 12
—	Manchester Oxford Road	d					07 15		08 15		09 16			10 16		11 16		12 16		13 16			14 16		15 16
0	**Manchester Piccadilly** 10 84	d	23p10	05 50	06 21	06 49	07 21	07 52	08 20	08 52	09 21		09 52	10 21	10 52	11 21	11 52	12 21	12 52	13 21	13 52		14 21	14 52	15 21
3	Levenshulme 84	d			06 28	06 55	07 28		08 28	08 58	09 28		09 58	10 28	10 58	11 28	11 58	12 28	12 58	13 28	13 58		14 28	14 58	15 28
4½	Heaton Chapel 84	d			06 31	06 58	07 31		08 31	09 01	09 31		10 01	10 31	11 01	11 31	12 01	12 31	13 01	13 31	14 01		14 31	15 01	15 31
6	**Stockport** 84	d	23p20	06 00	06 35	07 02	07 35	08 01	08 35	09 05	09 35		10 05	10 35	11 05	11 35	12 05	12 35	13 05	13 35	14 05		14 35	15 05	15 35
7	Davenport	d	23p23		06 39	07 06	07 39	08 05	08 39	09 09	09 39		10 09	10 39	11 09	11 39	12 09	12 39	13 09	13 39	14 09		14 39	15 09	15 39
7¾	Woodsmoor	d	23p25		06 41	07 08	07 41	08 07	08 41	09 11	09 41		10 11	10 41	11 11	11 41	12 11	12 41	13 11	13 41	14 11		14 41	15 11	15 41
8¾	**Hazel Grove**	a	23p27	06 06	06 45	07 10	07 45	08 09	08 48	09 13	09 45		10 13	10 45	11 13	11 45	12 13	12 45	13 13	13 45	14 13		14 45	15 13	15 48
—		d	23p28			07 10		08 10		09 13			10 13		11 13		12 13		13 13		14 13			15 13	
11	Middlewood	d	23p32			07 15				09 18			10 18				12 18				14 18				
12½	Disley	d	23p36			07 19		08 17		09 22			10 22		11 20		12 22		13 20		14 22			15 20	
14¼	New Mills Newtown	d	23p40			07 22		08 20		09 25			10 25		11 24		12 25		13 24		14 25			15 24	
15¼	Furness Vale	d	23p42			07 25		08 23		09 28			10 28		11 26		12 28		13 26		14 28			15 26	
16¼	Whaley Bridge	d	23p45			07 28		08 26		09 31			10 31		11 29		12 31		13 29		14 31			15 29	
20½	Chapel-en-le-Frith	d	23p52			07 35		08 33		09 38			10 38		11 36		12 38		13 36		14 38			15 36	
22¾	Dove Holes	d	23p57			07 40				09 43			10 43				12 43				14 43				
25¾	**Buxton**	a	00 07			07 50		08 44		09 53			10 53		11 50		12 53		13 50		14 53			15 50	

Station		NT	NT D	NT	NT	NT D	NT		NT	NT B	NT	NT	NT	NT	NT	NT
Deansgate	d		16 12			17 15				18 12						
Manchester Oxford Road	d		16 16			17 19				18 16						
Manchester Piccadilly 10 84	d	15 52	16 21	16 51	16 58	17 23	17 23		17 52	18 21	18 52	19 22	19 51	20 51	21 52	23 10
Levenshulme 84	d	15 58	16 28		17 03		17 28		17 58	18 28	18 58	19 28	19 58	20 58	21 58	
Heaton Chapel 84	d	16 01	16 31		17 06		17 31		18 01	18 31	19 01	19 31	20 01	21 01	22 01	
Stockport 84	d	16 05	16 35	17 03	17 10	17 32	17 35		18 05	18 35	19 05	19 35	20 05	21 05	22 05	23 20
Davenport	d	16 09	16 39	17 06	17 14		17 39		18 09	18 39	19 09	19 39	20 09	21 09	22 09	23 23
Woodsmoor	d	16 11	16 41	17 08	17 16		17 41		18 11	18 41	19 11	19 41	20 11	21 11	22 11	23 25
Hazel Grove	a	16 13	16 43	17 10	17 20	17 39	17 45		18 13	18 43	19 13	19 45	20 13	21 13	22 13	23 27
	d	16 13	16 46	17 11		17 39			18 13	18 46	19 13		20 13	21 13	22 13	23 28
Middlewood	d	16 18		17 15					18 18		19 18		20 18	21 18	22 18	23 32
Disley	d	16 22	16 53	17 19		17 46			18 22	18 53	19 22		20 22	21 22	22 22	23 36
New Mills Newtown	d	16 25	16 56	17 23		17 50			18 25	18 56	19 25		20 25	21 25	22 25	23 40
Furness Vale	d	16 28	16 59	17 26		17 52			18 28	18 59	19 28		20 28	21 28	22 28	23 42
Whaley Bridge	d	16 31	17 02	17 29		17 55			18 31	19 02	19 31		20 31	21 31	22 31	23 45
Chapel-en-le-Frith	d	16 38	17 09	17 36		18 03			18 38	19 09	19 38		20 38	21 38	22 38	23 52
Dove Holes	d	16 43		17 41					18 43		19 43		20 43	21 43	22 43	23 57
Buxton	a	16 53	17 22	17 51		18 16			18 54	19 22	19 53		20 53	21 53	22 53	00 07

from 3 October

Station		NT MX	NT A	NT	NT	NT B	NT	NT C	NT	NT D		NT	NT D	NT	NT D	NT	NT D	NT	NT D	NT		NT D	NT	NT D	NT
Deansgate	d					07 11		08 12		09 12			10 12		11 12		12 12		13 12			14 12		15 12	
Manchester Oxford Road	d					07 15		08 15		09 16			10 16		11 16		12 16		13 16			14 16		15 16	
Manchester Piccadilly 10 84	d	23p10	05 50	06 21	06 49	07 21	07 52	08 20	08 52	09 21		09 52	10 21	10 52	11 21	11 52	12 21	12 52	13 21	13 52		14 21	14 52	15 21	15 52
Levenshulme 84	d			06 28	06 55	07 28		08 28	08 58	09 28		09 58	10 28	10 58	11 28	11 58	12 28	12 58	13 28	13 58		14 28	14 58	15 28	15 58
Heaton Chapel 84	d			06 31	06 58	07 31		08 31	09 01	09 31		10 01	10 31	11 01	11 31	12 01	12 31	13 01	13 31	14 01		14 31	15 01	15 31	16 01
Stockport 84	d	23p20	06 00	06 35	07 02	07 35	08 01	08 35	09 05	09 35		10 05	10 35	11 05	11 35	12 05	12 35	13 05	13 35	14 05		14 35	15 05	15 35	16 05
Davenport	d	23p23		06 39	07 06	07 39	08 05	08 39	09 09	09 39		10 09	10 39	11 09	11 39	12 09	12 39	13 09	13 39	14 09		14 39	15 09	15 39	16 09
Woodsmoor	d	23p25		06 41	07 08	07 41	08 07	08 41	09 11	09 41		10 11	10 41	11 11	11 41	12 11	12 41	13 11	13 41	14 11		14 41	15 11	15 41	16 11
Hazel Grove	a	23p27	06 06	06 47	07 10	07 47	08 09	08 50	09 13	09 47		10 13	10 47	11 13	11 45	12 13	12 47	13 13	13 47	14 13		14 47	15 13	15 50	16 13
	d	23p28			07 10		08 10		09 13			10 13		11 13		12 13		13 13		14 13			15 13		16 13
Middlewood	d	23p32			07 15				09 18			10 18				12 18				14 18					16 18
Disley	d	23p36			07 19		08 17		09 22			10 22		11 20		12 22		13 20		14 22			15 20		16 22
New Mills Newtown	d	23p40			07 22		08 20		09 25			10 25		11 24		12 25		13 24		14 25			15 24		16 25
Furness Vale	d	23p42			07 25		08 23		09 28			10 28		11 26		12 28		13 26		14 28			15 26		16 28
Whaley Bridge	d	23p45			07 28		08 26		09 31			10 31		11 29		12 31		13 29		14 31			15 29		16 31
Chapel-en-le-Frith	d	23p52			07 35		08 33		09 38			10 38		11 36		12 38		13 36		14 38			15 36		16 38
Dove Holes	d	23p57			07 40				09 43			10 43				12 43				14 43					16 43
Buxton	a	00 09			07 52		08 44		09 55			10 55		11 52		12 55		13 52		14 55			15 52		16 55

Station		NT D	NT	NT	NT D	NT		NT	NT B	NT	NT	NT	NT	NT	NT
Deansgate	d	16 12			17 15				18 12						
Manchester Oxford Road	d	16 16			17 19				18 16						
Manchester Piccadilly 10 84	d	16 21	16 51	16 58	17 23	17 23		17 52	18 21	18 52	19 22	19 51	20 51	21 52	23 10
Levenshulme 84	d	16 28		17 03		17 28		17 58	18 28	18 58	19 28	19 58	20 58	21 58	
Heaton Chapel 84	d	16 31		17 06		17 31		18 01	18 31	19 01	19 31	20 01	21 01	22 01	
Stockport 84	d	16 35	17 03	17 10	17 32	17 35		18 05	18 35	19 05	19 35	20 05	21 05	22 05	23 20
Davenport	d	16 39	17 06	17 14		17 39		18 09	18 39	19 09	19 39	20 09	21 09	22 09	23 23
Woodsmoor	d	16 41	17 08	17 16		17 41		18 11	18 41	19 11	19 41	20 11	21 11	22 11	23 25
Hazel Grove	a	16 43	17 10	17 22	17 39	17 47		18 13	18 43	19 13	19 47	20 13	21 13	22 13	23 27
	d	16 46	17 11		17 39			18 13	18 46	19 13		20 13	21 13	22 13	23 28
Middlewood	d		17 15					18 18		19 18		20 18	21 18	22 18	23 32
Disley	d	16 53	17 19		17 46			18 22	18 53	19 22		20 22	21 22	22 22	23 36
New Mills Newtown	d	16 56	17 23		17 50			18 25	18 56	19 25		20 25	21 25	22 25	23 40
Furness Vale	d	16 59	17 26		17 52			18 28	18 59	19 28		20 28	21 28	22 28	23 42
Whaley Bridge	d	17 02	17 29		17 55			18 31	19 02	19 31		20 31	21 31	22 31	23 45
Chapel-en-le-Frith	d	17 09	17 36		18 03			18 38	19 09	19 38		20 38	21 38	22 38	23 52
Dove Holes	d		17 41					18 43		19 43		20 43	21 43	22 43	23 57
Buxton	a	17 24	17 53		18 19			18 56	19 24	19 55		20 55	21 55	22 55	00 09

A To Sheffield
B From Wigan Wallgate
C From Blackpool North
D From Preston

Table 86

Saturdays

until 1 October

Manchester - Hazel Grove and Buxton

	NT	NT A	NT	NT B	NT	NT C	NT	NT D	NT	NT D	NT	NT D	NT	NT D	NT	NT D	NT	NT D	NT	NT D	NT	NT D
Deansgate ⛴ d				07 11		08 12		09 12		10 12		11 12		12 12		13 12		14 12		15 12		16 12
Manchester Oxford Road d				07 15		08 15		09 16		10 16		11 16		12 16		13 16		14 16		15 16		16 16
Manchester Piccadilly 10 84 ⛴ d	23p10	05 50	06 49	07 21	07 52	08 20	08 52	09 21	09 52	10 21	10 52	11 21	11 52	12 21	12 52	13 21	13 52	14 21	14 52	15 21	15 52	16 21
Levenshulme 84 d			06 55	07 28	07 57	08 28	08 58	09 28	09 58	10 28	10 58	11 28	11 58	12 28	12 58	13 28	13 58	14 28	14 58	15 28	15 58	16 28
Heaton Chapel 84 d			06 58	07 31		08 31	09 01	09 31	10 01	10 31	11 01	11 31	12 01	12 31	13 01	13 31	14 01	14 31	15 01	15 31	16 01	16 31
Stockport 84 d	23p20	06 00	07 02	07 35	08 02	08 35	09 05	09 35	10 05	10 35	11 05	11 35	12 05	12 35	13 05	13 35	14 05	14 35	15 05	15 35	16 05	16 35
Davenport d	23p23		07 06	07 39	08 06	08 39	09 09	09 39	10 09	10 39	11 09	11 39	12 09	12 39	13 09	13 39	14 09	14 39	15 09	15 39	16 09	16 39
Woodsmoor d	23p25		07 08	07 41	08 08	08 41	09 11	09 41	10 11	10 41	11 11	11 41	12 11	12 41	13 11	13 41	14 11	14 41	15 11	15 41	16 11	16 41
Hazel Grove a	23p27	06 06	07 10	07 45	08 11	08 45	09 13	09 45	10 13	10 45	11 13	11 45	12 13	12 45	13 13	13 45	14 13	14 45	15 13	15 45	16 13	16 45
d	23p28		07 10		08 11		09 13		10 13		11 13		12 13		13 13		14 13		15 13		16 13	
Middlewood d	23p32		07 15				09 18		10 18				12 18				14 18				16 18	
Disley d	23p36		07 19		08 18		09 22		10 22		11 20		12 22		13 20		14 22		15 20		16 22	
New Mills Newtown d	23p40		07 22		08 21		09 25		10 25		11 24		12 25		13 24		14 25		15 24		16 25	
Furness Vale d	23p42		07 25		08 24		09 28		10 28		11 26		12 28		13 26		14 28		15 26		16 28	
Whaley Bridge d	23p45		07 28		08 27		09 31		10 31		11 29		12 31		13 29		14 31		15 29		16 31	
Chapel-en-le-Frith d	23p52		07 35		08 34		09 38		10 38		11 36		12 38		13 36		14 38		15 36		16 38	
Dove Holes d	23p57		07 40				09 43		10 43				12 43				14 43				16 43	
Buxton a	00 07		07 50		08 48		09 53		10 53		11 50		12 53		13 50		14 53		15 50		16 53	

	NT	NT	NT D	NT	NT D	NT	NT	NT	NT	NT	NT
Deansgate ⛴ d			17 12		18 12						
Manchester Oxford Road d			17 16		18 16						
Manchester Piccadilly 10 84 ⛴ d	16 51	17 09	17 21	17 52	18 21	18 52	19 22	19 51	20 52	21 52	23 10
Levenshulme 84 d	16 58	17 14	17 28	17 58	18 28	18 58	19 28	19 58	20 58	21 58	
Heaton Chapel 84 d	17 01	17 17	17 31	18 01	18 31	19 01	19 31	20 01	21 01	22 01	
Stockport 84 d	17 05	17 32	17 35	18 05	18 35	19 05	19 35	20 05	21 05	22 05	23 20
Davenport d	17 09		17 39	18 09	18 39	19 09	19 39	20 09	21 09	22 09	23 23
Woodsmoor d	17 11		17 41	18 11	18 41	19 11	19 41	20 11	21 11	22 11	23 25
Hazel Grove a	17 13	17 39	17 43	18 13	18 45	19 13	19 45	20 13	21 13	22 13	23 27
d	17 13		17 46	18 13		19 13		20 13	21 13	22 13	23 28
Middlewood d			17 50			19 18		20 18	21 18	22 18	23 32
Disley d	17 20		17 54	18 20		19 22		20 22	21 22	22 22	23 36
New Mills Newtown d	17 24		17 58	18 24		19 25		20 25	21 25	22 25	23 40
Furness Vale d	17 26		18 00	18 26		19 28		20 28	21 28	22 28	23 42
Whaley Bridge d	17 29		18 03	18 29		19 31		20 31	21 31	22 31	23 45
Chapel-en-le-Frith d	17 36		18 10	18 36		19 38		20 38	21 38	22 38	23 52
Dove Holes d			18 15			19 43		20 43	21 43	22 43	23 57
Buxton a	17 50		18 25	18 50		19 53		20 53	21 53	22 53	00 07

from 8 October

	NT	NT A	NT	NT B	NT	NT C	NT	NT D	NT	NT D	NT	NT D	NT	NT D	NT	NT D	NT	NT D	NT	NT D	NT	NT D
Deansgate ⛴ d				07 11		08 12		09 12		10 12		11 12		12 12		13 12		14 12		15 12		16 12
Manchester Oxford Road d				07 15		08 15		09 16		10 16		11 16		12 16		13 16		14 16		15 16		16 16
Manchester Piccadilly 10 84 ⛴ d	23p10	05 50	06 49	07 21	07 52	08 20	08 52	09 21	09 52	10 21	10 52	11 21	11 52	12 21	12 52	13 21	13 52	14 21	14 52	15 21	15 52	16 21
Levenshulme 84 d			06 55	07 28	07 57	08 28	08 58	09 28	09 58	10 28	10 58	11 28	11 58	12 28	12 58	13 28	13 58	14 28	14 58	15 28	15 58	16 28
Heaton Chapel 84 d			06 58	07 31		08 31	09 01	09 31	10 01	10 31	11 01	11 31	12 01	12 31	13 01	13 31	14 01	14 31	15 01	15 31	16 01	16 31
Stockport 84 d	23p20	06 00	07 02	07 35	08 02	08 35	09 05	09 35	10 05	10 35	11 05	11 35	12 05	12 35	13 05	13 35	14 05	14 35	15 05	15 35	16 05	16 35
Davenport d	23p23		07 06	07 39	08 06	08 39	09 09	09 39	10 09	10 39	11 09	11 39	12 09	12 39	13 09	13 39	14 09	14 39	15 09	15 39	16 09	16 39
Woodsmoor d	23p25		07 08	07 41	08 08	08 41	09 11	09 41	10 11	10 41	11 11	11 41	12 11	12 41	13 11	13 41	14 11	14 41	15 11	15 41	16 11	16 41
Hazel Grove a	23p27	06 06	07 10	07 47	08 11	08 47	09 13	09 47	10 13	10 47	11 13	11 47	12 13	12 47	13 13	13 47	14 13	14 47	15 13	15 47	16 13	16 47
d	23p28		07 10		08 11		09 13		10 13		11 13		12 13		13 13		14 13		15 13		16 13	
Middlewood d	23p32		07 15				09 18		10 18				12 18				14 18				16 18	
Disley d	23p36		07 19		08 18		09 22		10 22		11 20		12 22		13 20		14 22		15 20		16 22	
New Mills Newtown d	23p40		07 22		08 21		09 25		10 25		11 24		12 25		13 24		14 25		15 24		16 25	
Furness Vale d	23p42		07 25		08 24		09 28		10 28		11 26		12 28		13 26		14 28		15 26		16 28	
Whaley Bridge d	23p45		07 28		08 27		09 31		10 31		11 29		12 31		13 29		14 31		15 29		16 31	
Chapel-en-le-Frith d	23p52		07 35		08 34		09 38		10 38		11 36		12 38		13 36		14 38		15 36		16 38	
Dove Holes d	23p57		07 40				09 43		10 43				12 43				14 43				16 43	
Buxton a	00 09		07 52		08 50		09 55		10 55		11 52		12 55		13 52		14 55		15 52		16 55	

	NT	NT	NT D	NT	NT D	NT	NT	NT	NT	NT	NT
Deansgate ⛴ d			17 12		18 12						
Manchester Oxford Road d			17 16		18 16						
Manchester Piccadilly 10 84 ⛴ d	16 51	17 09	17 21	17 52	18 21	18 52	19 22	19 51	20 52	21 52	23 10
Levenshulme 84 d	16 58	17 14	17 28	17 58	18 28	18 58	19 28	19 58	20 58	21 58	
Heaton Chapel 84 d	17 01	17 17	17 31	18 01	18 31	19 01	19 31	20 01	21 01	22 01	
Stockport 84 d	17 05	17 32	17 35	18 05	18 35	19 05	19 35	20 05	21 05	22 05	23 20
Davenport d	17 09		17 39	18 09	18 39	19 09	19 39	20 09	21 09	22 09	23 23
Woodsmoor d	17 11		17 41	18 11	18 41	19 11	19 41	20 11	21 11	22 11	23 25
Hazel Grove a	17 13	17 41	17 43	18 13	18 47	19 13	19 47	20 13	21 13	22 13	23 27
d	17 13		17 46	18 13		19 13		20 13	21 13	22 13	23 28
Middlewood d			17 50			19 18		20 18	21 18	22 18	23 32
Disley d	17 20		17 54	18 20		19 22		20 22	21 22	22 22	23 36
New Mills Newtown d	17 24		17 58	18 24		19 25		20 25	21 25	22 25	23 40
Furness Vale d	17 26		18 00	18 26		19 28		20 28	21 28	22 28	23 42
Whaley Bridge d	17 29		18 03	18 29		19 31		20 31	21 31	22 31	23 45
Chapel-en-le-Frith d	17 36		18 10	18 36		19 38		20 38	21 38	22 38	23 52
Dove Holes d			18 15			19 43		20 43	21 43	22 43	23 57
Buxton a	17 52		18 27	18 52		19 55		20 55	21 55	22 55	00 09

A To Sheffield
B From Wigan Wallgate
C From Blackpool North
D From Preston

Table 86

Manchester - Hazel Grove and Buxton

Sundays

until 11 September

	NT A	NT	NT	NT	NT	NT	NT	NT	NT	NT	NT	NT	NT	NT	NT	NT
Deansgate d																
Manchester Oxford Road d																
Manchester Piccadilly 84 d	23p10	08 55	09 51	10 52	11 52	12 52	13 52	14 52	15 52	16 52	17 52	18 52	19 52	20 52	21 52	22 52
Levenshulme 84 d		09 00	09 58	10 58	11 58	12 58	13 58	14 58	15 58	16 58	17 58	18 58	19 58	20 58	21 58	22 58
Heaton Chapel 84 d		09 03	10 01	11 01	12 01	13 01	14 01	15 01	16 01	17 01	18 01	19 01	20 01	21 01	22 01	23 01
Stockport 84 d	23p20	09 10	10 05	11 05	12 05	13 05	14 05	15 05	16 05	17 05	18 05	19 05	20 05	21 05	22 05	23 05
Davenport d	23p23	09 13	10 09	11 09	12 09	13 09	14 09	15 09	16 09	17 09	18 09	19 09	20 09	21 09	22 09	23 09
Woodsmoor d	23p25	09 15	10 11	11 11	12 11	13 11	14 11	15 11	16 11	17 11	18 11	19 11	20 11	21 11	22 11	23 11
Hazel Grove a	23p27	09 17	10 13	11 13	12 13	13 13	14 13	15 13	16 13	17 13	18 13	19 13	20 13	21 13	22 13	23 13
d	23p28	09 18	10 13	11 13	12 13	13 13	14 13	15 13	16 13	17 13	18 13	19 13	20 13	21 13	22 13	23 13
Middlewood d	23p32	09 22	10 18	11 18	12 18	13 18	14 18	15 18	16 18	17 18	18 18	19 18	20 18	21 18	22 18	23 18
Disley d	23p36	09 26	10 22	11 22	12 22	13 22	14 22	15 22	16 22	17 22	18 22	19 22	20 22	21 22	22 22	23 22
New Mills Newtown d	23p40	09 30	10 25	11 25	12 25	13 25	14 25	15 25	16 25	17 25	18 25	19 25	20 25	21 25	22 25	23 25
Furness Vale d	23p42	09 32	10 28	11 28	12 28	13 28	14 28	15 28	16 28	17 28	18 28	19 28	20 28	21 28	22 28	23 28
Whaley Bridge d	23p45	09 35	10 31	11 31	12 31	13 31	14 31	15 31	16 31	17 31	18 31	19 31	20 31	21 31	22 31	23 31
Chapel-en-le-Frith d	23p52	09 42	10 38	11 38	12 38	13 38	14 38	15 38	16 38	17 38	18 38	19 38	20 38	21 38	22 38	23 38
Dove Holes d	23p57	09 47	10 43	11 43	12 43	13 43	14 43	15 43	16 43	17 43	18 43	19 43	20 43	21 43	22 43	23 43
Buxton a	00 07	09 57	10 53	11 53	12 53	13 53	14 53	15 53	16 53	17 53	18 53	19 53	20 53	21 53	22 53	23 53

18 September to 2 October

	NT	NT	NT	NT	NT	NT	NT	NT	NT	NT	NT	NT	NT	NT	NT	NT
Deansgate d																
Manchester Oxford Road d																
Manchester Piccadilly 84 d	23p10	08 55	09 51	10 52	11 52	12 52	13 52	14 52	15 52	16 52	17 52	18 52	19 52	20 52	21 52	22 52
Levenshulme 84 d		09 00	09 58	10 58	11 58	12 58	13 58	14 58	15 58	16 58	17 58	18 58	19 58	20 58	21 58	22 58
Heaton Chapel 84 d		09 03	10 01	11 01	12 01	13 01	14 01	15 01	16 01	17 01	18 01	19 01	20 01	21 01	22 01	23 01
Stockport 84 d	23p20	09 10	10 05	11 05	12 05	13 05	14 05	15 05	16 05	17 05	18 05	19 05	20 05	21 05	22 05	23 05
Davenport d	23p23	09 13	10 09	11 09	12 09	13 09	14 09	15 09	16 09	17 09	18 09	19 09	20 09	21 09	22 09	23 09
Woodsmoor d	23p25	09 15	10 11	11 11	12 11	13 11	14 11	15 11	16 11	17 11	18 11	19 11	20 11	21 11	22 11	23 11
Hazel Grove a	23p27	09 17	10 13	11 13	12 13	13 13	14 13	15 13	16 13	17 13	18 13	19 13	20 13	21 13	22 13	23 13
d	23p28	09 18	10 13	11 13	12 13	13 13	14 13	15 13	16 13	17 13	18 13	19 13	20 13	21 13	22 13	23 13
Middlewood d	23p32	09 22	10 18	11 18	12 18	13 18	14 18	15 18	16 18	17 18	18 18	19 18	20 18	21 18	22 18	23 18
Disley d	23p36	09 26	10 22	11 22	12 22	13 22	14 22	15 22	16 22	17 22	18 22	19 22	20 22	21 22	22 22	23 22
New Mills Newtown d	23p40	09 30	10 25	11 25	12 25	13 25	14 25	15 25	16 25	17 25	18 25	19 25	20 25	21 25	22 25	23 25
Furness Vale d	23p42	09 32	10 28	11 28	12 28	13 28	14 28	15 28	16 28	17 28	18 28	19 28	20 28	21 28	22 28	23 28
Whaley Bridge d	23p45	09 35	10 31	11 31	12 31	13 31	14 31	15 31	16 31	17 31	18 31	19 31	20 31	21 31	22 31	23 31
Chapel-en-le-Frith d	23p52	09 42	10 38	11 38	12 38	13 38	14 38	15 38	16 38	17 38	18 38	19 38	20 38	21 38	22 38	23 38
Dove Holes d	23p57	09 47	10 43	11 43	12 43	13 43	14 43	15 43	16 43	17 43	18 43	19 43	20 43	21 43	22 43	23 43
Buxton a	00 07	09 57	10 53	11 53	12 53	13 53	14 53	15 53	16 53	17 53	18 53	19 53	20 53	21 53	22 53	23 53

from 9 October

	NT	NT	NT	NT	NT	NT	NT	NT	NT	NT	NT	NT	NT	NT	NT	NT
Deansgate d																
Manchester Oxford Road d																
Manchester Piccadilly 84 d	23p10	08 55	09 51	10 52	11 52	12 52	13 52	14 52	15 52	16 52	17 52	18 52	19 52	20 52	21 52	22 52
Levenshulme 84 d		09 00	09 58	10 58	11 58	12 58	13 58	14 58	15 58	16 58	17 58	18 58	19 58	20 58	21 58	22 58
Heaton Chapel 84 d		09 03	10 01	11 01	12 01	13 01	14 01	15 01	16 01	17 01	18 01	19 01	20 01	21 01	22 01	23 01
Stockport 84 d	23p20	09 10	10 05	11 05	12 05	13 05	14 05	15 05	16 05	17 05	18 05	19 05	20 05	21 05	22 05	23 05
Davenport d	23p23	09 13	10 09	11 09	12 09	13 09	14 09	15 09	16 09	17 09	18 09	19 09	20 09	21 09	22 09	23 09
Woodsmoor d	23p25	09 15	10 11	11 11	12 11	13 11	14 11	15 11	16 11	17 11	18 11	19 11	20 11	21 11	22 11	23 11
Hazel Grove a	23p27	09 17	10 13	11 13	12 13	13 13	14 13	15 13	16 13	17 13	18 13	19 13	20 13	21 13	22 13	23 13
d	23p28	09 18	10 13	11 13	12 13	13 13	14 13	15 13	16 13	17 13	18 13	19 13	20 13	21 13	22 13	23 13
Middlewood d	23p32	09 22	10 18	11 18	12 18	13 18	14 18	15 18	16 18	17 18	18 18	19 18	20 18	21 18	22 18	23 18
Disley d	23p36	09 26	10 22	11 22	12 22	13 22	14 22	15 22	16 22	17 22	18 22	19 22	20 22	21 22	22 22	23 22
New Mills Newtown d	23p40	09 30	10 25	11 25	12 25	13 25	14 25	15 25	16 25	17 25	18 25	19 25	20 25	21 25	22 25	23 25
Furness Vale d	23p42	09 32	10 28	11 28	12 28	13 28	14 28	15 28	16 28	17 28	18 28	19 28	20 28	21 28	22 28	23 28
Whaley Bridge d	23p45	09 35	10 31	11 31	12 31	13 31	14 31	15 31	16 31	17 31	18 31	19 31	20 31	21 31	22 31	23 31
Chapel-en-le-Frith d	23p52	09 42	10 38	11 38	12 38	13 38	14 38	15 38	16 38	17 38	18 38	19 38	20 38	21 38	22 38	23 38
Dove Holes d	23p57	09 47	10 43	11 43	12 43	13 43	14 43	15 43	16 43	17 43	18 43	19 43	20 43	21 43	22 43	23 43
Buxton a	00 09	09 59	10 55	11 55	12 55	13 55	14 55	15 55	16 55	17 55	18 55	19 55	20 55	21 55	22 55	23 55

A not 22 May

Table 86

Mondays to Fridays

until 30 September

Buxton and Hazel Grove - Manchester

Miles			NT A	NT	NT B	NT	NT C	NT	NT	EM ◇ D	NT	NT E	NT	NT E	NT	NT E	NT	NT E	NT	NT E	NT	NT E	NT
0	**Buxton**	d	05 59		06 23		06 50		07 24		07 48		08 27		09 27		10 30		11 27		12 30		13 25
3	Dove Holes	d			06 29		06 56		07 30				08 33		09 33				11 33				13 31
5¼	Chapel-en-le-Frith	d	06 08		06 34		07 01		07 35		07 57		08 38		09 38		10 39		11 38		12 39		13 36
9½	Whaley Bridge	d	06 14		06 40		07 07		07 41		08 03		08 44		09 44		10 45		11 44		12 45		13 42
10½	Furness Vale	d	06 17		06 43		07 10		07 44		08 06		08 47		09 47		10 48		11 47		12 48		13 45
11½	New Mills Newtown	d	06 20		06 46		07 13		07 47		08 10		08 50		09 50		10 51		11 50		12 51		13 48
13¼	Disley	d	06 24		06 49		07 17		07 51		08 14		08 53		09 53		10 55		11 53		12 55		13 51
14¾	Middlewood	d			06 53		07 21		07 55				08 57		09 57				11 57				13 55
17	**Hazel Grove**	a	06 32		06 59		07 27		08 00		08 22		09 03		10 03		11 03		12 03		13 03		14 01
—		d	06 33	06 50	07 00	07 22	07 27	07 48	08 01	08 17	08 22	08 32	09 04	09 32	10 04	10 33	11 04	11 33	12 04	12 33	13 04	13 33	14 01
18	Woodsmoor	d	06 35	06 52	07 02	07 24	07 30	07 50	08 03			08 34	09 06	09 34	10 06	10 35	11 06	11 35	12 06	12 35	13 06	13 35	14 03
18¾	Davenport	d	06 37	06 54	07 04	07 27	07 32	07 53	08 06			08 37	09 08	09 37	10 08	10 37	11 08	11 37	12 08	12 37	13 08	13 37	14 05
19¾	**Stockport**	84 a	06 41	06 58	07 08	07 31	07 37	07 57	08 10	08 24		08 41	09 12	09 41	10 12	10 41	11 12	11 41	12 12	12 41	13 12	13 41	14 09
21¼	Heaton Chapel	84 a			07 15		07 41						09 16		10 16		11 16		12 16		13 16		14 16
22¾	Levenshulme	84 a			07 18		07 44						09 19		10 19		11 19		12 19		13 19		14 19
25¾	**Manchester Piccadilly** 10	84 a	06 52	07 10	07 26	07 45	07 52	08 09	08 25	08 36	08 39	08 52	09 28	09 52	10 28	10 52	11 28	11 52	12 28	12 52	13 28	13 52	14 28
—	Manchester Oxford Road	a	06 56		07 29		07 56			08 40		08 56		09 56		10 56		11 56		12 56		13 56	
—	Deansgate	a	06 59		07 32		07 59					09 00		10 00		11 00		12 00		13 00		14 00	

		NT E	NT	NT F	NT G	NT E	NT C	NT C	NT	NT F	NT	NT	NT	NT	NT
Buxton	d		14 30		15 27		16 30	16 59	17 27	17 59	18 27	19 27	20 27	21 27	22 56
Dove Holes	d				15 33				17 33		18 33	19 33	20 33	21 33	23 02
Chapel-en-le-Frith	d		14 39		15 38		16 39	17 08	17 38	18 08	18 38	19 38	20 38	21 38	23 07
Whaley Bridge	d		14 45		15 44		16 45	17 14	17 44	18 14	18 44	19 44	20 44	21 44	23 13
Furness Vale	d		14 48		15 47		16 48	17 17	17 47	18 17	18 47	19 47	20 47	21 47	23 16
New Mills Newtown	d		14 51		15 50		16 51	17 20	17 50	18 20	18 50	19 50	20 50	21 50	23 19
Disley	d		14 55		15 53		16 55	17 24	17 53	18 24	18 53	19 53	20 53	21 53	23 22
Middlewood	d				15 57				17 57		18 57	19 57	20 57	21 57	23 26
Hazel Grove	a		15 03		16 03		17 03	17 32	18 03	18 32	19 03	20 03	21 03	22 03	23 31
	d	14 33	15 04	15 33	16 04	16 30	17 04	17 33	18 04	18 33	19 04	20 04	21 04	22 04	23 32
Woodsmoor	d	14 35	15 06	15 35	16 06	16 32	17 06	17 35	18 06	18 35	19 06	20 06	21 06	22 06	23 34
Davenport	d	14 37	15 08	15 37	16 08	16 35	17 08	17 37	18 08	18 37	19 08	20 08	21 08	22 08	23 36
Stockport	84 a	14 41	15 12	15 41	16 12	16 40	17 12	17 41	18 12	18 41	19 12	20 12	21 12	22 12	23 40
Heaton Chapel	84 a		15 16		16 16		17 16		18 16		19 16	20 16	21 16	22 16	
Levenshulme	84 a		15 19		16 19		17 19		18 19		19 19	20 19	21 19	22 19	
Manchester Piccadilly 10 84	a	14 52	15 28	15 52	16 25	16 52	17 25	17 52	18 28	18 52	19 28	20 28	21 28	22 28	23 54
Manchester Oxford Road	a	14 56		15 56	16 29	16 56	17 29	17 56		18 56					
Deansgate	a	15 00		16 00	16 32	17 00	17 32	18 00		19 00					

from 3 October

		NT A	NT	NT B	NT	NT C	NT	NT	EM ◇ D	NT	NT E	NT	NT E	NT	NT E	NT	NT E	NT	NT E	NT	NT E	NT	NT E
Buxton	d	05 54		06 18		06 45		07 19		07 43		08 22		09 22		10 25		11 22		12 25		13 20	
Dove Holes	d			06 24		06 51		07 25				08 28		09 28				11 28				13 26	
Chapel-en-le-Frith	d	06 03		06 29		06 56		07 30		07 52		08 33		09 33		10 34		11 33		12 34		13 31	
Whaley Bridge	d	06 09		06 35		07 02		07 36		07 58		08 39		09 39		10 40		11 39		12 40		13 37	
Furness Vale	d	06 12		06 38		07 05		07 39		08 01		08 42		09 42		10 43		11 42		12 43		13 40	
New Mills Newtown	d	06 15		06 41		07 08		07 42		08 05		08 45		09 45		10 46		11 45		12 46		13 43	
Disley	d	06 19		06 44		07 12		07 46		08 09		08 48		09 48		10 50		11 48		12 50		13 46	
Middlewood	d			06 48		07 16		07 50				08 52		09 52				11 52				13 50	
Hazel Grove	a	06 30		06 57		07 25		07 58		08 20		09 01		10 01		11 01		12 01		13 01		13 59	
	d	06 31	06 48	06 58	07 20	07 25	07 48	07 59	08 17	08 20	08 30	09 02	09 30	10 02	10 31	11 02	11 31	12 02	12 31	13 02	13 31	13 59	14 31
Woodsmoor	d	06 33	06 50	07 00	07 22	07 28	07 50	08 01			08 32	09 04	09 32	10 04	10 33	11 04	11 33	12 04	12 33	13 04	13 33	14 01	14 33
Davenport	d	06 35	06 52	07 02	07 25	07 30	07 53	08 04			08 35	09 06	09 35	10 06	10 35	11 06	11 35	12 06	12 35	13 06	13 35	14 03	14 35
Stockport	84 a	06 41	06 58	07 08	07 31	07 37	07 57	08 10	08 24		08 41	09 12	09 41	10 12	10 41	11 12	11 41	12 12	12 41	13 12	13 41	14 09	14 41
Heaton Chapel	84 a			07 15		07 41						09 16		10 16		11 16		12 16		13 16		14 16	
Levenshulme	84 a			07 18		07 44						09 19		10 19		11 19		12 19		13 19		14 19	
Manchester Piccadilly 10 84	a	06 52	07 10	07 26	07 45	07 52	08 09	08 25	08 36	08 39	08 52	09 28	09 52	10 28	10 52	11 28	11 52	12 28	12 52	13 28	13 52	14 28	14 52
Manchester Oxford Road	a	06 56		07 29		07 56			08 40		08 56		09 56		10 56		11 56		12 56		13 56		14 56
Deansgate	a	06 59		07 32		07 59					09 00		10 00		11 00		12 00		13 00		14 00		15 00

A To Clitheroe
B To Wigan North Western
C To Blackpool North
D From Nottingham to Liverpool Lime Street
E To Preston
F To Bolton
G To Arnside

		NT	NT A	NT B	NT C	NT D	NT D	NT	NT A	NT	NT	NT	NT	NT
Buxton	d	14 25		15 22		16 25	16 56	17 22	17 55	18 22	19 22	20 22	21 22	22 51
Dove Holes	d			15 28				17 28		18 28	19 28	20 28	21 28	22 57
Chapel-en-le-Frith	d	14 34		15 33		16 34	17 05	17 33	18 04	18 33	19 33	20 33	21 33	23 02
Whaley Bridge	d	14 40		15 39		16 40	17 11	17 39	18 10	18 39	19 39	20 39	21 39	23 08
Furness Vale	d	14 43		15 42		16 43	17 14	17 42	18 13	18 42	19 42	20 42	21 42	23 11
New Mills Newtown	d	14 46		15 45		16 46	17 17	17 45	18 16	18 45	19 45	20 45	21 45	23 14
Disley	d	14 50		15 48		16 50	17 21	17 48	18 20	18 48	19 48	20 48	21 48	23 17
Middlewood	d			15 52				17 52		18 52	19 52	20 52	21 52	23 21
Hazel Grove	a	15 01		16 01		17 01	17 32	18 01	18 32	19 01	20 01	21 01	22 01	23 29
	d	15 02	15 33	16 02	16 30	17 02	17 33	18 02	18 33	19 02	20 02	21 02	22 02	23 30
Woodsmoor	d	15 04	15 35	16 04	16 32	17 04	17 35	18 04	18 35	19 04	20 04	21 04	22 04	23 32
Davenport	d	15 06	15 37	16 06	16 35	17 06	17 37	18 06	18 37	19 06	20 06	21 06	22 06	23 34
Stockport	84 a	15 12	15 41	16 12	16 40	17 12	17 41	18 12	18 41	19 12	20 12	21 12	22 12	23 40
Heaton Chapel	84 a	15 16		16 16		17 16		18 16		19 16	20 16	21 16	22 16	
Levenshulme	84 a	15 19		16 19		17 19		18 19		19 19	20 19	21 19	22 19	
Manchester Piccadilly 10 84	a	15 28	15 52	16 25	16 52	17 25	17 52	18 28	18 52	19 28	20 28	21 28	22 28	23 54
Manchester Oxford Road	a		15 56	16 29	16 56	17 29	17 56		18 56					
Deansgate	a		16 00	16 32	17 00	17 32	18 00		19 00					

Table 86

Buxton and Hazel Grove - Manchester

Saturdays

until 1 October

		NT	NT	NT	NT	NT	EM	NT	NT	NT	NT	NT	NT	NT	NT	NT	NT	NT	NT	NT	NT	NT	NT
							◇																
		E		C			F	C		C		C		C		C		C		C		C	
Buxton	d	05 59	06 27	—	—	07 27	—	07 56	08 27	—	09 27	—	10 30	—	11 27	—	12 30	—	13 27	—	14 30	—	15 27
Dove Holes	d	—	06 33	—	—	07 33	—	08 02	08 33	—	09 33	—	—	—	11 33	—	—	—	13 33	—	—	—	15 33
Chapel-en-le-Frith	d	06 08	06 38	—	—	07 38	—	08 07	08 38	—	09 38	—	10 39	—	11 38	—	12 39	—	13 38	—	14 39	—	15 38
Whaley Bridge	d	06 14	06 44	—	—	07 44	—	08 13	08 44	—	09 44	—	10 45	—	11 44	—	12 45	—	13 44	—	14 45	—	15 44
Furness Vale	d	06 17	06 47	—	—	07 47	—	08 16	08 47	—	09 47	—	10 48	—	11 47	—	12 48	—	13 47	—	14 48	—	15 47
New Mills Newtown	d	06 20	06 50	—	—	07 50	—	08 19	08 50	—	09 50	—	10 51	—	11 50	—	12 51	—	13 50	—	14 51	—	15 50
Disley	d	06 24	06 53	—	—	07 53	—	08 22	08 53	—	09 53	—	10 55	—	11 53	—	12 55	—	13 53	—	14 55	—	15 53
Middlewood	d	—	06 57	—	—	07 57	—	08 26	08 57	—	09 57	—	—	—	11 57	—	—	—	13 57	—	—	—	15 57
Hazel Grove	a	06 32	07 03	—	—	08 03	—	08 32	09 03	—	10 03	—	11 03	—	12 03	—	13 03	—	14 03	—	15 03	—	16 03
	d	06 33	07 03	07 32	07 48	08 03	08 17	08 33	09 04	09 33	10 04	10 33	11 04	11 33	12 04	12 33	13 04	13 33	14 04	14 33	15 04	15 33	16 04
Woodsmoor	d	06 35	07 05	07 34	07 50	08 05	—	08 35	09 06	09 35	10 06	10 35	11 06	11 35	12 06	12 35	13 06	13 35	14 06	14 35	15 06	15 35	16 06
Davenport	d	06 37	07 07	07 36	07 53	08 07	—	08 37	09 08	09 37	10 08	10 37	11 08	11 37	12 08	12 37	13 08	13 37	14 08	14 37	15 08	15 37	16 08
Stockport 84	a	06 41	07 12	07 40	07 57	08 12	08 24	08 41	09 12	09 41	10 12	10 41	11 12	11 41	12 12	12 41	13 12	13 41	14 12	14 41	15 12	15 41	16 12
Heaton Chapel 84	a	—	07 16	—	—	08 16	—	—	09 16	—	10 16	—	11 16	—	12 16	—	13 16	—	14 16	—	15 16	—	16 16
Levenshulme 84	a	—	07 19	—	—	08 19	—	—	09 19	—	10 19	—	11 19	—	12 19	—	13 19	—	14 19	—	15 19	—	16 19
Manchester Piccadilly 10 84 ⛴	a	06 52	07 28	07 52	08 09	08 28	08 36	08 52	09 28	09 52	10 28	10 52	11 28	11 52	12 28	12 52	13 28	13 52	14 28	14 52	15 28	15 52	16 28
Manchester Oxford Road	a	06 56	—	07 56	—	—	08 40	08 56	—	09 56	—	10 56	—	11 56	—	12 56	—	13 56	—	14 56	—	15 56	—
Deansgate ⛴	a	06 59	—	08 00	—	—	—	09 00	—	10 00	—	11 00	—	12 00	—	13 00	—	14 00	—	15 00	—	16 00	—

		NT	NT	NT	NT	NT	NT	NT	NT	NT	NT
		C		D		A					
Buxton	d	—	16 30	—	17 27	—	18 27	19 27	20 27	21 27	22 56
Dove Holes	d	—	—	—	17 33	—	18 33	19 33	20 33	21 33	23 02
Chapel-en-le-Frith	d	—	16 39	—	17 38	—	18 38	19 38	20 38	21 38	23 07
Whaley Bridge	d	—	16 45	—	17 44	—	18 44	19 44	20 44	21 44	23 13
Furness Vale	d	—	16 48	—	17 47	—	18 47	19 47	20 47	21 47	23 16
New Mills Newtown	d	—	16 51	—	17 50	—	18 50	19 50	20 50	21 50	23 19
Disley	d	—	16 55	—	17 53	—	18 53	19 53	20 53	21 53	23 22
Middlewood	d	—	—	—	17 57	—	18 57	19 57	20 57	21 57	23 26
Hazel Grove	a	—	17 03	—	18 03	—	19 03	20 03	21 03	22 03	23 31
	d	16 30	17 04	17 33	18 04	18 33	19 04	20 04	21 04	22 04	23 32
Woodsmoor	d	16 32	17 06	17 35	18 06	18 35	19 06	20 06	21 06	22 06	23 34
Davenport	d	16 34	17 08	17 37	18 08	18 37	19 08	20 08	21 08	22 08	23 36
Stockport 84	a	16 40	17 12	17 41	18 12	18 41	19 12	20 12	21 12	22 12	23 40
Heaton Chapel 84	a	—	17 16	—	18 16	—	19 16	20 16	21 16	22 16	—
Levenshulme 84	a	—	17 19	—	18 19	—	19 19	20 19	21 19	22 19	—
Manchester Piccadilly 10 84 ⛴	a	16 52	17 28	17 52	18 28	18 52	19 28	20 28	21 28	22 28	23 54
Manchester Oxford Road	a	16 56	—	17 56	—	18 56	—	—	—	—	—
Deansgate ⛴	a	17 00	—	18 00	—	19 00	—	—	—	—	—

A To Bolton
B To Barrow-in-Furness
C To Preston
D To Blackpool North
E To Clitheroe
F From Nottingham to Liverpool Lime Street

from 8 October

		NT	NT	NT	NT	NT	EM	NT	NT	NT	NT	NT	NT	NT	NT	NT	NT	NT	NT	NT	NT	NT	NT
							◇																
		A		B			C	B		B		B		B		B		B		B		B	
Buxton	d	05 54	06 22	—	—	07 22	—	07 51	08 22	—	09 22	—	10 25	—	11 22	—	12 25	—	13 22	—	14 25	—	15 22
Dove Holes	d	—	06 28	—	—	07 28	—	07 57	08 28	—	09 28	—	—	—	11 28	—	—	—	13 28	—	—	—	15 28
Chapel-en-le-Frith	d	06 03	06 33	—	—	07 33	—	08 02	08 33	—	09 33	—	10 34	—	11 33	—	12 34	—	13 33	—	14 34	—	15 33
Whaley Bridge	d	06 09	06 39	—	—	07 39	—	08 08	08 39	—	09 39	—	10 40	—	11 39	—	12 40	—	13 39	—	14 40	—	15 39
Furness Vale	d	06 12	06 42	—	—	07 42	—	08 11	08 42	—	09 42	—	10 43	—	11 42	—	12 43	—	13 42	—	14 43	—	15 42
New Mills Newtown	d	06 15	06 45	—	—	07 45	—	08 14	08 45	—	09 45	—	10 46	—	11 45	—	12 46	—	13 45	—	14 46	—	15 45
Disley	d	06 19	06 48	—	—	07 48	—	08 17	08 48	—	09 48	—	10 50	—	11 48	—	12 50	—	13 48	—	14 50	—	15 48
Middlewood	d	—	06 52	—	—	07 52	—	08 21	08 52	—	09 52	—	—	—	11 52	—	—	—	13 52	—	—	—	15 52
Hazel Grove	a	06 30	07 01	—	—	08 01	—	08 30	09 01	—	10 01	—	11 01	—	12 01	—	13 01	—	14 01	—	15 01	—	16 01
	d	06 31	07 01	07 32	07 48	08 01	08 17	08 31	09 02	09 31	10 02	10 31	11 02	11 31	12 02	12 31	13 02	13 31	14 02	14 31	15 02	15 33	16 02
Woodsmoor	d	06 33	07 03	07 34	07 50	08 03	—	08 33	09 04	09 33	10 04	10 33	11 04	11 33	12 04	12 33	13 04	13 33	14 04	14 33	15 04	15 35	16 04
Davenport	d	06 35	07 05	07 36	07 53	08 05	—	08 35	09 06	09 35	10 06	10 35	11 06	11 35	12 06	12 35	13 06	13 35	14 06	14 35	15 06	15 37	16 06
Stockport 84	a	06 41	07 12	07 40	07 57	08 12	08 24	08 41	09 12	09 41	10 12	10 41	11 12	11 41	12 12	12 41	13 12	13 41	14 12	14 41	15 12	15 41	16 12
Heaton Chapel 84	a	—	07 16	—	—	08 16	—	—	09 16	—	10 16	—	11 16	—	12 16	—	13 16	—	14 16	—	15 16	—	16 16
Levenshulme 84	a	—	07 19	—	—	08 19	—	—	09 19	—	10 19	—	11 19	—	12 19	—	13 19	—	14 19	—	15 19	—	16 19
Manchester Piccadilly 10 84 ⛴	a	06 52	07 28	07 52	08 09	08 28	08 36	08 52	09 28	09 52	10 28	10 52	11 28	11 52	12 28	12 52	13 28	13 52	14 28	14 52	15 28	15 52	16 28
Manchester Oxford Road	a	06 56	—	07 56	—	—	08 40	08 56	—	09 56	—	10 56	—	11 56	—	12 56	—	13 56	—	14 56	—	15 56	—
Deansgate ⛴	a	06 59	—	08 00	—	—	—	09 00	—	10 00	—	11 00	—	12 00	—	13 00	—	14 00	—	15 00	—	16 00	—

		NT	NT	NT	NT	NT	NT	NT	NT	NT	NT
		B		D		E					
Buxton	d	—	16 25	—	17 22	—	18 22	19 22	20 22	21 22	22 51
Dove Holes	d	—	—	—	17 28	—	18 28	19 28	20 28	21 28	22 57
Chapel-en-le-Frith	d	—	16 34	—	17 33	—	18 33	19 33	20 33	21 33	23 02
Whaley Bridge	d	—	16 40	—	17 39	—	18 39	19 39	20 39	21 39	23 08
Furness Vale	d	—	16 43	—	17 42	—	18 42	19 42	20 42	21 42	23 11
New Mills Newtown	d	—	16 46	—	17 45	—	18 45	19 45	20 45	21 45	23 14
Disley	d	—	16 50	—	17 48	—	18 48	19 48	20 48	21 48	23 17
Middlewood	d	—	—	—	17 52	—	18 52	19 52	20 52	21 52	23 21
Hazel Grove	a	—	17 01	—	18 01	—	19 01	20 01	21 01	22 01	23 29
	d	16 30	17 02	17 31	18 02	18 31	19 02	20 02	21 02	22 02	23 30
Woodsmoor	d	16 32	17 04	17 33	18 04	18 33	19 04	20 04	21 04	22 04	23 32
Davenport	d	16 34	17 06	17 35	18 06	18 35	19 06	20 06	21 06	22 06	23 34
Stockport 84	a	16 40	17 12	17 41	18 12	18 41	19 12	20 12	21 12	22 12	23 40
Heaton Chapel 84	a	—	17 16	—	18 16	—	19 16	20 16	21 16	22 16	—
Levenshulme 84	a	—	17 19	—	18 19	—	19 19	20 19	21 19	22 19	—
Manchester Piccadilly 10 84 ⛴	a	16 52	17 28	17 52	18 28	18 52	19 28	20 28	21 28	22 28	23 54
Manchester Oxford Road	a	16 56	—	17 56	—	18 56	—	—	—	—	—
Deansgate ⛴	a	17 00	—	18 00	—	19 00	—	—	—	—	—

Table 86

Sundays

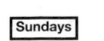

until 11 September

Buxton and Hazel Grove - Manchester

		NT	NT	NT	NT	NT	NT	NT	NT	NT		NT	NT	NT	NT	NT	NT
Buxton	d	08 23	09 19	10 27	11 26	12 27	13 27	14 27	15 27	16 27		17 27	18 27	19 27	20 27	21 27	22 27
Dove Holes	d	08 29	09 25	10 33	11 32	12 33	13 33	14 33	15 33	16 33		17 33	18 33	19 33	20 33	21 33	22 33
Chapel-en-le-Frith	d	08 34	09 30	10 38	11 37	12 38	13 38	14 38	15 38	16 38		17 38	18 38	19 38	20 38	21 38	22 38
Whaley Bridge	d	08 40	09 36	10 44	11 43	12 44	13 44	14 44	15 44	16 44		17 44	18 44	19 44	20 44	21 44	22 44
Furness Vale	d	08 43	09 39	10 47	11 46	12 47	13 47	14 47	15 47	16 47		17 47	18 47	19 47	20 47	21 47	22 47
New Mills Newtown	d	08 46	09 42	10 50	11 49	12 50	13 50	14 50	15 50	16 50		17 50	18 50	19 50	20 50	21 50	22 50
Disley	d	08 49	09 45	10 53	11 52	12 53	13 53	14 53	15 53	16 53		17 53	18 53	19 53	20 53	21 53	22 53
Middlewood	d	08 53	09 49	10 57	11 56	12 57	13 57	14 57	15 57	16 57		17 57	18 57	19 57	20 57	21 57	22 57
Hazel Grove	a	08 59	09 55	11 02	12 02	13 03	14 03	15 03	16 03	17 03		18 03	19 03	20 03	21 03	22 03	23 03
	d	09 00	09 55	11 03	12 02	13 04	14 04	15 04	16 04	17 04		18 04	19 04	20 04	21 04	22 04	23 04
Woodsmoor	d	09 02	09 57	11 05	12 04	13 06	14 06	15 06	16 06	17 06		18 06	19 06	20 06	21 06	22 06	23 06
Davenport	d	09 04	09 59	11 07	12 06	13 08	14 08	15 08	16 08	17 08		18 08	19 08	20 08	21 08	22 08	23 08
Stockport 84	a	09 08	10 04	11 11	12 11	13 12	14 12	15 12	16 12	17 12		18 12	19 12	20 12	21 12	22 12	23 12
Heaton Chapel 84	a	09 12	10 08		12 15	13 16	14 16	15 16	16 16	17 16		18 16	19 16	20 16	21 16	22 16	23 16
Levenshulme 84	a	09 15	10 11		12 18	13 19	14 19	15 19	16 19	17 19		18 19	19 19	20 19	21 19	22 19	23 19
Manchester Piccadilly 10 84	a	09 23	10 20	11 23	12 25	13 27	14 27	15 27	16 27	17 27		18 27	19 27	20 27	21 27	22 27	23 27
Manchester Oxford Road	a																
Deansgate	a																

A To Clitheroe
B To Preston
C From Nottingham to Liverpool Lime Street
D To Blackpool North
E To Bolton

Buxton and Hazel Grove - Manchester

18 September to 2 October

		NT	NT	NT	NT	NT	NT	NT	NT	NT		NT	NT	NT	NT	NT	NT
Buxton	d	08 23	09 19	10 27	11 26	12 27	13 27	14 27	15 27	16 27		17 27	18 27	19 27	20 27	21 27	22 27
Dove Holes	d	08 29	09 25	10 33	11 32	12 33	13 33	14 33	15 33	16 33		17 33	18 33	19 33	20 33	21 33	22 33
Chapel-en-le-Frith	d	08 34	09 30	10 38	11 37	12 38	13 38	14 38	15 38	16 38		17 38	18 38	19 38	20 38	21 38	22 38
Whaley Bridge	d	08 40	09 36	10 44	11 43	12 44	13 44	14 44	15 44	16 44		17 44	18 44	19 44	20 44	21 44	22 44
Furness Vale	d	08 43	09 39	10 47	11 46	12 47	13 47	14 47	15 47	16 47		17 47	18 47	19 47	20 47	21 47	22 47
New Mills Newtown	d	08 46	09 42	10 50	11 49	12 50	13 50	14 50	15 50	16 50		17 50	18 50	19 50	20 50	21 50	22 50
Disley	d	08 49	09 45	10 53	11 52	12 53	13 53	14 53	15 53	16 53		17 53	18 53	19 53	20 53	21 53	22 53
Middlewood	d	08 53	09 49	10 57	11 56	12 57	13 57	14 57	15 57	16 57		17 57	18 57	19 57	20 57	21 57	22 57
Hazel Grove	a	08 59	09 55	11 02	12 02	13 03	14 03	15 03	16 03	17 03		18 03	19 03	20 03	21 03	22 03	23 03
	d	09 00	09 55	11 03	12 02	13 04	14 04	15 04	16 04	17 04		18 04	19 04	20 04	21 04	22 04	23 04
Woodsmoor	d	09 02	09 57	11 05	12 04	13 06	14 06	15 06	16 06	17 06		18 06	19 06	20 06	21 06	22 06	23 06
Davenport	d	09 04	09 59	11 07	12 06	13 08	14 08	15 08	16 08	17 08		18 08	19 08	20 08	21 08	22 08	23 08
Stockport 84	a	09 08	10 04	11 11	12 11	13 12	14 12	15 12	16 12	17 12		18 12	19 12	20 12	21 12	22 12	23 12
Heaton Chapel 84	a	09 12	10 08		12 15	13 16	14 16	15 16	16 16	17 16		18 16	19 16	20 16	21 16	22 16	23 16
Levenshulme 84	a	09 15	10 11		12 18	13 19	14 19	15 19	16 19	17 19		18 19	19 19	20 19	21 19	22 19	23 19
Manchester Piccadilly 10 84	a	09 23	10 20	11 23	12 25	13 27	14 27	15 27	16 27	17 27		18 27	19 27	20 27	21 27	22 27	23 27
Manchester Oxford Road	a																
Deansgate	a																

from 9 October

		NT	NT	NT	NT	NT	NT	NT	NT	NT		NT	NT	NT	NT	NT	NT
Buxton	d	08 18	09 14	10 22	11 21	12 22	13 22	14 22	15 22	16 22		17 22	18 22	19 22	20 22	21 22	22 22
Dove Holes	d	08 24	09 20	10 28	11 27	12 28	13 28	14 28	15 28	16 28		17 28	18 28	19 28	20 28	21 28	22 28
Chapel-en-le-Frith	d	08 29	09 25	10 33	11 32	12 33	13 33	14 33	15 33	16 33		17 33	18 33	19 33	20 33	21 33	22 33
Whaley Bridge	d	08 35	09 31	10 39	11 38	12 39	13 39	14 39	15 39	16 39		17 39	18 39	19 39	20 39	21 39	22 39
Furness Vale	d	08 38	09 34	10 42	11 41	12 42	13 42	14 42	15 42	16 42		17 42	18 42	19 42	20 42	21 42	22 42
New Mills Newtown	d	08 41	09 37	10 45	11 44	12 45	13 45	14 45	15 45	16 45		17 45	18 45	19 45	20 45	21 45	22 45
Disley	d	08 44	09 40	10 48	11 47	12 48	13 48	14 48	15 48	16 48		17 48	18 48	19 48	20 48	21 48	22 48
Middlewood	d	08 48	09 44	10 52	11 51	12 52	13 52	14 52	15 52	16 52		17 52	18 52	19 52	20 52	21 52	22 52
Hazel Grove	a	08 57	09 53	11 00	12 00	13 01	14 01	15 01	16 01	17 01		18 01	19 01	20 01	21 01	22 01	23 01
	d	08 58	09 53	11 01	12 00	13 02	14 02	15 02	16 02	17 02		18 02	19 02	20 02	21 02	22 02	23 02
Woodsmoor	d	09 00	09 55	11 03	12 02	13 04	14 04	15 04	16 04	17 04		18 04	19 04	20 04	21 04	22 04	23 04
Davenport	d	09 02	09 57	11 05	12 04	13 06	14 06	15 06	16 06	17 06		18 06	19 06	20 06	21 06	22 06	23 06
Stockport 84	a	09 08	10 04	11 11	12 11	13 12	14 12	15 12	16 12	17 12		18 12	19 12	20 12	21 12	22 12	23 12
Heaton Chapel 84	a	09 12	10 08		12 15	13 16	14 16	15 16	16 16	17 16		18 16	19 16	20 16	21 16	22 16	23 16
Levenshulme 84	a	09 15	10 11		12 18	13 19	14 19	15 19	16 19	17 19		18 19	19 19	20 19	21 19	22 19	23 19
Manchester Piccadilly 10 84	a	09 23	10 20	11 23	12 25	13 27	14 27	15 27	16 27	17 27		18 27	19 27	20 27	21 27	22 27	23 27
Manchester Oxford Road	a																
Deansgate	a																

Network Diagram for Tables 88, 89, 90, 91

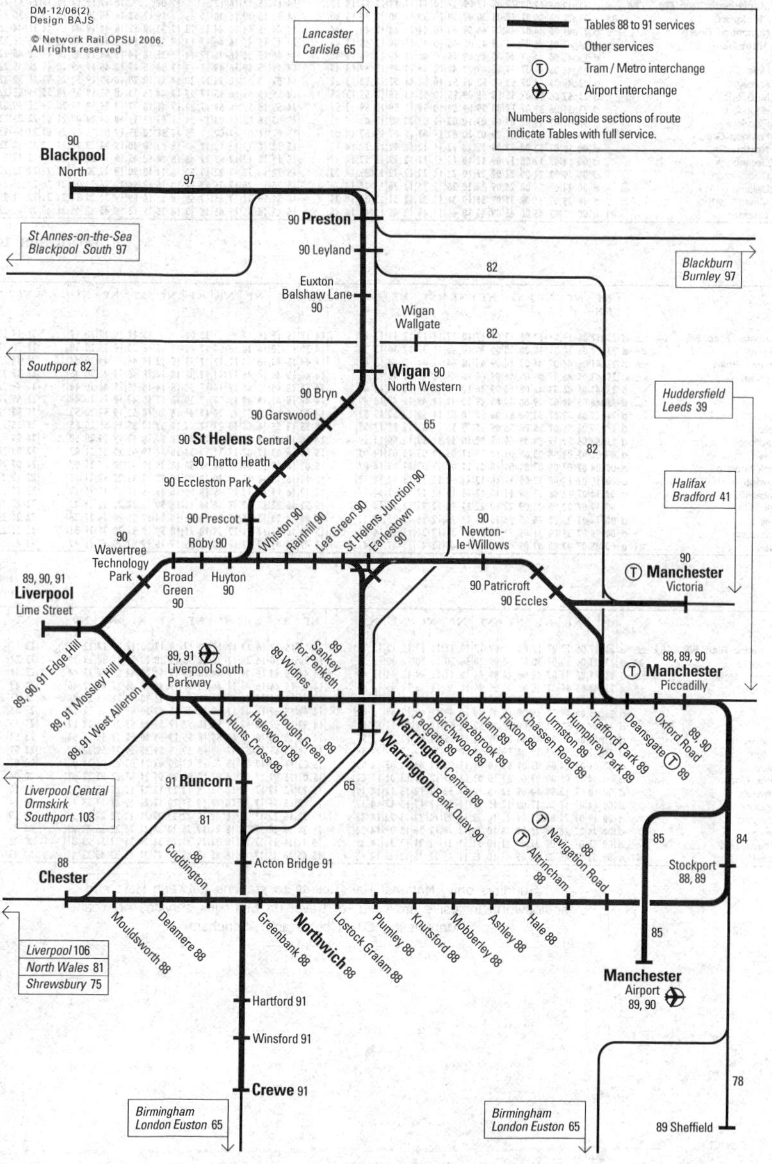

Table 88

Mondays to Fridays

until 30 September

Manchester - Northwich and Chester

Miles				NT MX	NT	NT	NT	NT	NT	NT	NT	NT	NT	NT	NT	NT	NT	NT	NT	NT	NT	NT	NT FX	NT FO	NT
0	**Manchester Picc.** 10	84	d	23p17	06 17	07 17	08 17	09 17	10 17	11 17	12 17	13 17	14 17	15 17	16 17		17 09		18 17	19 17	20 17	21 17	22 17	22 17	23 17
6½	**Stockport**	84	d	23p27	06 30	07 30	08 30	09 30	10 30	11 30	12 30	13 30	14 30	15 30	16 30	16 58	17 19	17 58	18 30	19 30	20 30	21 30	22 30	22 30	23 27
14¾	Navigation Road		d	23p41	06 44	07 44	08 44	09 44	10 44	11 44	12 44	13 44	14 44	15 44	16 44	17 12	17 33	18 12	18 44	19 44	20 44	21 44	22 44	22 44	23 41
15¼	**Altrincham**		a	23p43	06 46	07 46	08 46	09 46	10 46	11 46	12 46	13 46	14 46	15 46	16 46	17 14	17 35	18 14	18 46	19 46	20 46	21 46	22 46	22 46	23 43
—			d	23p43	06 46	07 46	08 46	09 46	10 46	11 46	12 46	13 46	14 46	15 46	16 46	17 14	17 35	18 14	18 46	19 46	20 46	21 46	22 46	22 46	23 43
16	Hale		d	23p46	06 49	07 49	08 49	09 49	10 49	11 49	12 49	13 49	14 49	15 49	16 49	17 17	17 38	18 17	18 49	19 49	20 49	21 49	22 49	22 49	23 46
17¾	Ashley		d	23p49	06 52	07 52	08 52	09 52	10 52	11 52	12 52	13 52	14 52	15 52	16 52	17 20	17 41	18 20	18 52	19 52	20 52	21 52	22 52	22 52	23 49
18½	Mobberley		d	23p52	06 55	07 55	08 55	09 55	10 55	11 55	12 55	13 55	14 55	15 55	16 55	17 23	17 44	18 23	18 55	19 55	20 55	21 55	22 55	22 55	23 52
22¼	Knutsford		d	23p57	06 59	07 59	08 59	09 59	10 59	11 59	12 59	13 59	14 59	15 59	16 59	17 27	17 49	18 27	18 59	19 59	20 59	21 59	22 59	22 59	23 57
24¾	Plumley		d	00 01	07 03	08 03	09 03	10 03	11 03	12 03	13 03	14 03	15 03	16 03	17 03	17 31	17 53	18 31	19 03	20 03	21 03	22 03	23 03	23 03	00 01
26¾	Lostock Gralam		d	00 04	07 07	08 07	09 07	10 07	11 07	12 07	13 07	14 07	15 07	16 07	17 07	17 35	17 56	18 35	19 07	20 07	21 07	22 07	23 07	23 07	00 04
28¼	**Northwich**		d	00 10	07 12	08 12	09 12	10 12	11 12	12 12	13 12	14 12	15 12	16 12	17 12	17 40	18 02	18 40	19 12	20 12	21 12	22 12	23 12	23 12	00 10
30	Greenbank		d	00 14	07 17	08 17	09 17	10 17	11 17	12 17	13 17	14 17	15 17	16 17	17 17	17 45	18 06	18 45	19 17	20 17	21 17	22 17	23 17	23 17	00 14
32¾	Cuddington		d	00 19	07 22	08 22	09 22	10 22	11 22	12 22	13 22	14 22	15 22	16 22	17 22	17 50	18 11	18 50	19 22	20 22	21 22	22 22	23 22	23 22	00 19
35¾	Delamere		d	00 24	07 26	08 26	09 26	10 26	11 26	12 26	13 26	14 26	15 26	16 26	17 26	17 54	18 16	18 54	19 26	20 26	21 26	22 26	23 26	23 26	00 24
38¾	Mouldsworth		d	00 28	07 31	08 31	09 31	10 31	11 31	12 31	13 31	14 31	15 31	16 31	17 31	17 59	18 21	18 59	19 31	20 31	21 31	22 31	23 31	23 31	00 28
45¼	**Chester**	81	a	00 43	07 45	08 45	09 45	10 45	11 45	12 45	13 45	14 45	15 45	16 45	17 45	18 13	18 35	19 13	19 45	20 45	21 45	22 45	23 45	23 47	00 43

Mondays to Fridays

from 3 October

			NT MX	NT	NT	NT	NT	NT	NT	NT	NT	NT	NT	NT	NT	NT	NT	NT	NT	NT	NT	NT FX	NT FO	NT
Manchester Picc. 10	84	d	23p17	06 17	07 17	08 17	09 17	10 17	11 17	12 17	13 17	14 17	15 17	16 17		17 09		18 17	19 17	20 17	21 17	22 17	22 17	23 17
Stockport	84	d	23p27	06 30	07 30	08 30	09 30	10 30	11 30	12 30	13 30	14 30	15 30	16 30	16 58	17 19	17 58	18 30	19 30	20 30	21 30	22 30	22 30	23 27
Navigation Road		d	23p41	06 44	07 44	08 44	09 44	10 44	11 44	12 44	13 44	14 44	15 44	16 44	17 12	17 33	18 12	18 44	19 44	20 44	21 44	22 44	22 44	23 41
Altrincham		a	23p43	06 46	07 46	08 46	09 46	10 46	11 46	12 46	13 46	14 46	15 46	16 46	17 14	17 35	18 14	18 46	19 46	20 46	21 46	22 46	22 46	23 43
		d	23p43	06 46	07 46	08 46	09 46	10 46	11 46	12 46	13 46	14 46	15 46	16 46	17 14	17 35	18 14	18 46	19 46	20 46	21 46	22 46	22 46	23 43
Hale		d	23p46	06 49	07 49	08 49	09 49	10 49	11 49	12 49	13 49	14 49	15 49	16 49	17 17	17 38	18 17	18 49	19 49	20 49	21 49	22 49	22 49	23 46
Ashley		d	23p49	06 52	07 52	08 52	09 52	10 52	11 52	12 52	13 52	14 52	15 52	16 52	17 20	17 41	18 20	18 52	19 52	20 52	21 52	22 52	22 52	23 49
Mobberley		d	23p52	06 55	07 55	08 55	09 55	10 55	11 55	12 55	13 55	14 55	15 55	16 55	17 23	17 44	18 23	18 55	19 55	20 55	21 55	22 55	22 55	23 52
Knutsford		d	23p57	06 59	07 59	08 59	09 59	10 59	11 59	12 59	13 59	14 59	15 59	16 59	17 27	17 49	18 27	18 59	19 59	20 59	21 59	22 59	22 59	23 57
Plumley		d	00 01	07 03	08 03	09 03	10 03	11 03	12 03	13 03	14 03	15 03	16 03	17 03	17 31	17 53	18 31	19 03	20 03	21 03	22 03	23 03	23 03	00 01
Lostock Gralam		d	00 04	07 07	08 07	09 07	10 07	11 07	12 07	13 07	14 07	15 07	16 07	17 07	17 35	17 56	18 35	19 07	20 07	21 07	22 07	23 07	23 07	00 04
Northwich		d	00 10	07 12	08 12	09 12	10 12	11 12	12 12	13 12	14 12	15 12	16 12	17 12	17 40	18 02	18 40	19 12	20 12	21 12	22 12	23 12	23 12	00 10
Greenbank		d	00 14	07 17	08 17	09 17	10 17	11 17	12 17	13 17	14 17	15 17	16 17	17 17	17 45	18 06	18 45	19 17	20 17	21 17	22 17	23 17	23 17	00 14
Cuddington		d	00 19	07 22	08 22	09 22	10 22	11 22	12 22	13 22	14 22	15 22	16 22	17 22	17 50	18 11	18 50	19 22	20 22	21 22	22 22	23 22	23 22	00 19
Delamere		d	00 24	07 26	08 26	09 26	10 26	11 26	12 26	13 26	14 26	15 26	16 26	17 26	17 54	18 16	18 54	19 26	20 26	21 26	22 26	23 26	23 26	00 24
Mouldsworth		d	00 28	07 31	08 31	09 31	10 31	11 31	12 31	13 31	14 31	15 31	16 31	17 31	17 59	18 21	18 59	19 31	20 31	21 31	22 31	23 31	23 31	00 28
Chester	81	a	00 45	07 47	08 47	09 47	10 47	11 47	12 47	13 47	14 47	15 47	16 47	17 47	18 12	18 35	19 15	19 47	20 47	21 47	22 47	23 47	23 49	00 45

Saturdays

until 1 October

			NT	NT	NT	NT	NT	NT	NT	NT	NT	NT	NT	NT	NT	NT	NT	NT	NT	NT	NT
Manchester Picc. 10	84	d	23p17	06 17	07 17	08 17	09 17	10 17	11 17	12 17	13 17	14 17	15 17	16 17	17 17	18 17	19 17	20 17	21 17	22 17	23 17
Stockport	84	d	23p27	06 30	07 30	08 30	09 30	10 30	11 30	12 30	13 30	14 30	15 30	16 30	17 30	18 30	19 30	20 30	21 30	22 30	23 27
Navigation Road		d	23p41	06 44	07 44	08 44	09 44	10 44	11 44	12 44	13 44	14 44	15 44	16 44	17 44	18 44	19 44	20 44	21 44	22 44	23 41
Altrincham		a	23p43	06 46	07 46	08 46	09 46	10 46	11 46	12 46	13 46	14 46	15 46	16 46	17 46	18 46	19 46	20 46	21 46	22 46	23 43
		d	23p43	06 46	07 46	08 46	09 46	10 46	11 46	12 46	13 46	14 46	15 46	16 46	17 46	18 46	19 46	20 46	21 46	22 46	23 43
Hale		d	23p46	06 49	07 49	08 49	09 49	10 49	11 49	12 49	13 49	14 49	15 49	16 49	17 49	18 49	19 49	20 49	21 49	22 49	23 46
Ashley		d	23p49	06 52	07 52	08 52	09 52	10 52	11 52	12 52	13 52	14 52	15 52	16 52	17 52	18 52	19 52	20 52	21 52	22 52	23 49
Mobberley		d	23p52	06 55	07 55	08 55	09 55	10 55	11 55	12 55	13 55	14 55	15 55	16 55	17 55	18 55	19 55	20 55	21 55	22 55	23 52
Knutsford		d	23p57	06 59	07 59	08 59	09 59	10 59	11 59	12 59	13 59	14 59	15 59	16 59	17 59	18 59	19 59	20 59	21 59	22 59	23 57
Plumley		d	00 01	07 03	08 03	09 03	10 03	11 03	12 03	13 03	14 03	15 03	16 03	17 03	18 03	19 03	20 03	21 03	22 03	23 03	00 01
Lostock Gralam		d	00 04	07 07	08 07	09 07	10 07	11 07	12 07	13 07	14 07	15 07	16 07	17 07	18 07	19 07	20 07	21 07	22 07	23 07	00 04
Northwich		d	00 10	07 12	08 12	09 12	10 12	11 12	12 12	13 12	14 12	15 12	16 12	17 12	18 12	19 12	20 12	21 12	22 12	23 12	00 10
Greenbank		d	00 14	07 17	08 17	09 17	10 17	11 17	12 17	13 17	14 17	15 17	16 17	17 17	18 17	19 17	20 17	21 17	22 17	23 17	00 14
Cuddington		d	00 19	07 22	08 22	09 22	10 22	11 22	12 22	13 22	14 22	15 22	16 22	17 22	18 22	19 22	20 22	21 22	22 22	23 22	00 19
Delamere		d	00 24	07 26	08 26	09 26	10 26	11 26	12 26	13 26	14 26	15 26	16 26	17 26	18 26	19 26	20 26	21 26	22 26	23 26	00 24
Mouldsworth		d	00 28	07 31	08 31	09 31	10 31	11 31	12 31	13 31	14 31	15 31	16 31	17 31	18 31	19 31	20 31	21 31	22 31	23 31	00 28
Chester	81	a	00 43	07 45	08 45	09 45	10 45	11 45	12 45	13 45	14 45	15 45	16 45	17 45	18 45	19 45	20 45	21 45	22 45	23 45	00 43

On Sundays only, National Rail Tickets to stations between Hale and Mouldsworth inclusive are valid for travel on Metrolink services between Manchester City Centre and Altrincham

Table 88

Saturdays
from 8 October

Manchester - Northwich and Chester

			NT	NT	NT	NT	NT	NT	NT	NT	NT	NT	NT	NT	NT	NT	NT	NT	NT	NT	NT
Manchester Picc. 10	84	d	23p17	06 17	07 17	08 17	09 17	10 17	11 17	12 17	13 17	14 17	15 17	16 17	17 17	18 17	19 17	20 17	21 17	22 17	23 17
Stockport	84	d	23p27	06 30	07 30	08 30	09 30	10 30	11 30	12 30	13 30	14 30	15 30	16 30	17 30	18 30	19 30	20 30	21 30	22 30	23 27
Navigation Road		d	23p41	06 44	07 44	08 44	09 44	10 44	11 44	12 44	13 44	14 44	15 44	16 44	17 44	18 44	19 44	20 44	21 44	22 44	23 41
Altrincham		a	23p43	06 46	07 46	08 46	09 46	10 46	11 46	12 46	13 46	14 46	15 46	16 46	17 46	18 46	19 46	20 46	21 46	22 46	23 43
		d	23p43	06 46	07 46	08 46	09 46	10 46	11 46	12 46	13 46	14 46	15 46	16 46	17 46	18 46	19 46	20 46	21 46	22 46	23 43
Hale		d	23p46	06 49	07 49	08 49	09 49	10 49	11 49	12 49	13 49	14 49	15 49	16 49	17 49	18 49	19 49	20 49	21 49	22 49	23 46
Ashley		d	23p49	06 52	07 52	08 52	09 52	10 52	11 52	12 52	13 52	14 52	15 52	16 52	17 52	18 52	19 52	20 52	21 52	22 52	23 49
Mobberley		d	23p52	06 55	07 55	08 55	09 55	10 55	11 55	12 55	13 55	14 55	15 55	16 55	17 55	18 55	19 55	20 55	21 55	22 55	23 52
Knutsford		d	23p57	06 59	07 59	08 59	09 59	10 59	11 59	12 59	13 59	14 59	15 59	16 59	17 59	18 59	19 59	20 59	21 59	22 59	23 57
Plumley		d	00 01	07 03	08 03	09 03	10 03	11 03	12 03	13 03	14 03	15 03	16 03	17 03	18 03	19 03	20 03	21 03	22 03	23 03	00 01
Lostock Gralam		d	00 04	07 07	08 07	09 07	10 07	11 07	12 07	13 07	14 07	15 07	16 07	17 07	18 07	19 07	20 07	21 07	22 07	23 07	00 04
Northwich		d	00 10	07 12	08 12	09 12	10 12	11 12	12 12	13 12	14 12	15 12	16 12	17 12	18 12	19 12	20 12	21 12	22 12	23 12	00 10
Greenbank		d	00 14	07 17	08 17	09 17	10 17	11 17	12 17	13 17	14 17	15 17	16 17	17 17	18 17	19 17	20 17	21 17	22 17	23 17	00 14
Cuddington		d	00 19	07 22	08 22	09 22	10 22	11 22	12 22	13 22	14 22	15 22	16 22	17 22	18 22	19 22	20 22	21 22	22 22	23 22	00 19
Delamere		d	00 24	07 26	08 26	09 26	10 26	11 26	12 26	13 26	14 26	15 26	16 26	17 26	18 26	19 26	20 26	21 26	22 26	23 26	00 24
Mouldsworth		d	00 28	07 31	08 31	09 31	10 31	11 31	12 31	13 31	14 31	15 31	16 31	17 31	18 31	19 31	20 31	21 31	22 31	23 31	00 28
Chester	81	a	00 45	07 47	08 47	09 47	10 47	11 47	12 47	13 47	14 47	15 47	16 47	17 47	18 47	19 47	20 47	21 47	22 47	23 47	00 45

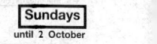

Sundays
until 2 October

			NT A	NT	NT	NT	NT	NT	NT	NT
Manchester Picc. 10	84	d	23p17	09 22	11 22	13 22	15 22	17 22	19 22	21 22
Stockport	84	d	23p27	09 31	11 31	13 31	15 31	17 31	19 31	21 31
Navigation Road		d	23p41	09 45	11 45	13 45	15 45	17 45	19 45	21 45
Altrincham		a	23p43	09 47	11 47	13 47	15 47	17 47	19 47	21 47
		d	23p43	09 47	11 47	13 47	15 47	17 47	19 47	21 47
Hale		d	23p46	09 50	11 50	13 50	15 50	17 50	19 50	21 50
Ashley		d	23p49	09 53	11 53	13 53	15 53	17 53	19 53	21 53
Mobberley		d	23p52	09 56	11 56	13 56	15 56	17 56	19 56	21 56
Knutsford		d	23p57	10 00	12 00	14 00	16 00	18 00	20 00	22 00
Plumley		d	00 01	10 05	12 04	14 04	16 04	18 04	20 04	22 04
Lostock Gralam		d	00 04	10 08	12 08	14 08	16 08	18 08	20 08	22 08
Northwich		d	00 10	10 13	12 13	14 13	16 13	18 13	20 13	22 13
Greenbank		d	00 14	10 18	12 18	14 18	16 18	18 18	20 18	22 18
Cuddington		d	00 19	10 23	12 23	14 23	16 23	18 23	20 23	22 23
Delamere		d	00 24	10 27	12 27	14 27	16 27	18 27	20 27	22 27
Mouldsworth		d	00 28	10 32	12 32	14 32	16 32	18 32	20 32	22 32
Chester	81	a	00 43	10 46	12 46	14 46	16 46	18 46	20 46	22 46

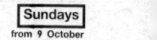

Sundays
from 9 October

			NT	NT	NT	NT	NT	NT	NT	NT
Manchester Picc. 10	84	d	23p17	09 22	11 22	13 22	15 22	17 22	19 22	21 22
Stockport	84	d	23p27	09 31	11 31	13 31	15 31	17 31	19 31	21 31
Navigation Road		d	23p41	09 45	11 45	13 45	15 45	17 45	19 45	21 45
Altrincham		a	23p43	09 47	11 47	13 47	15 47	17 47	19 47	21 47
		d	23p43	09 47	11 47	13 47	15 47	17 47	19 47	21 47
Hale		d	23p46	09 50	11 50	13 50	15 50	17 50	19 50	21 50
Ashley		d	23p49	09 53	11 53	13 53	15 53	17 53	19 53	21 53
Mobberley		d	23p52	09 56	11 56	13 56	15 56	17 56	19 56	21 56
Knutsford		d	23p57	10 00	12 00	14 00	16 00	18 00	20 00	22 00
Plumley		d	00 01	10 05	12 04	14 04	16 04	18 04	20 04	22 04
Lostock Gralam		d	00 04	10 08	12 08	14 08	16 08	18 08	20 08	22 08
Northwich		d	00 10	10 13	12 13	14 13	16 13	18 13	20 13	22 13
Greenbank		d	00 14	10 18	12 18	14 18	16 18	18 18	20 18	22 18
Cuddington		d	00 19	10 23	12 23	14 23	16 23	18 23	20 23	22 23
Delamere		d	00 24	10 27	12 27	14 27	16 27	18 27	20 27	22 27
Mouldsworth		d	00 28	10 32	12 32	14 32	16 32	18 32	20 32	22 32
Chester	81	a	00 45	10 46	12 48	14 48	16 48	18 48	20 48	22 48

A not 22 May

On Sundays only, National Rail Tickets to stations between Hale and Mouldsworth inclusive are valid for travel on Metrolink services between Manchester City Centre and Altrincham

Table 88

Chester and Northwich - Manchester

Mondays to Fridays
until 30 September

Miles				NT MX	NT	NT	NT	NT	NT	NT	NT	NT	NT	NT	NT	NT	NT	NT	NT	NT	NT	NT	NT
0	**Chester**	81	d	22p48	06 05	06 35	07 03	07 35	08 07	09 07	10 07	11 07	12 07	13 07	14 07	15 07	16 07	17 07	18 07	19 07	20 07	21 07	22 48
6½	Mouldsworth		d	22p59	06 16	06 46	07 14	07 46	08 18	09 18	10 18	11 18	12 18	13 18	14 18	15 18	16 18	17 18	18 18	19 18	20 18	21 18	22 59
9½	Delamere		d	23p04	06 21	06 51	07 19	07 51	08 23	09 23	10 23	11 23	12 23	13 23	14 23	15 23	16 23	17 23	18 23	19 23	20 23	21 23	23 04
12½	Cuddington		d	23p08	06 25	06 55	07 23	07 55	08 27	09 27	10 27	11 27	12 27	13 27	14 27	15 27	16 27	17 27	18 27	19 27	20 27	21 27	23 08
15¼	Greenbank		d	23p13	06 30	07 00	07 28	08 00	08 32	09 32	10 32	11 32	12 32	13 32	14 32	15 32	16 32	17 32	18 32	19 32	20 32	21 32	23 13
17	**Northwich**		d	23p17	06 35	07 05	07 33	08 05	08 37	09 37	10 37	11 37	12 37	13 37	14 37	15 37	16 37	17 37	18 37	19 37	20 37	21 37	23 17
18½	Lostock Gralam		d	23p20	06 38	07 08	07 36	08 08	08 40	09 40	10 40	11 40	12 40	13 40	14 40	15 40	16 40	17 40	18 40	19 40	20 40	21 40	23 20
20½	Plumley		d	23p24	06 41	07 11	07 40	08 11	08 43	09 43	10 43	11 43	12 43	13 43	14 43	15 43	16 43	17 43	18 43	19 43	20 43	21 43	23 24
23	Knutsford		d	23p29	06 46	07 17	07 45	08 17	08 49	09 49	10 49	11 49	12 49	13 49	14 49	15 49	16 49	17 49	18 49	19 49	20 49	21 49	23 29
26¾	Mobberley		d	23p33	06 50	07 21	07 49	08 21	08 53	09 53	10 53	11 53	12 53	13 53	14 53	15 53	16 53	17 53	18 53	19 53	20 53	21 53	23 33
27½	Ashley		d	23p36	06 54	07 24	07 53	08 24	08 56	09 56	10 56	11 56	12 56	13 56	14 56	15 56	16 56	17 56	18 56	19 56	20 56	21 56	23 36
29¼	Hale		d	23p39	06 57	07 28	07 57	08 28	08 59	09 59	10 59	11 59	12 59	13 59	14 59	15 59	16 59	17 59	18 59	19 59	20 59	21 59	23 39
30	**Altrincham**		a	23p44	07 01	07 32	08 01	08 32	09 04	10 04	11 04	12 04	13 04	14 04	15 04	16 04	17 04	18 04	19 04	20 04	21 04	22 04	23 44
—			d	23p44	07 02	07 33	08 02	08 33	09 04	10 04	11 04	12 04	13 04	14 04	15 04	16 04	17 04	18 04	19 04	20 04	21 04	22 04	23 44
30½	Navigation Road		d	23p46	07 04	07 35	08 04	08 35	09 06	10 06	11 06	12 06	13 06	14 06	15 06	16 06	17 06	18 06	19 06	20 06	21 06	22 06	23 46
38¾	**Stockport**	84	a	00 02	07 18	07 56	08 19	08 56	09 21	10 21	11 21	12 21	13 21	14 21	15 21	16 21	17 21	18 21	19 21	20 21	21 21	22 21	00 02
44¾	**Manchester Picc.** 10	81	a	00 18	07 31		08 32		09 36	10 36	11 36	12 36	13 36	14 36	15 36	16 36	17 36	18 36	19 35	20 35	21 35	22 35	00 18

Mondays to Fridays
from 3 October

			NT MX	NT	NT	NT	NT	NT	NT	NT	NT	NT	NT	NT	NT	NT	NT	NT	NT	NT	NT	NT
Chester	81	d	22p44	06 01	06 35	06 59	07 35	08 03	09 03	10 03	11 03	12 03	13 03	14 03	15 03	16 03	17 03	18 03	19 03	20 03	21 03	22 44
Mouldsworth		d	22p55	06 12	06 46	07 10	07 46	08 14	09 14	10 14	11 14	12 14	13 14	14 14	15 14	16 14	17 14	18 14	19 14	20 14	21 14	22 55
Delamere		d	23p00	06 17	06 51	07 15	07 51	08 19	09 19	10 19	11 19	12 19	13 19	14 19	15 19	16 19	17 19	18 19	19 19	20 19	21 19	23 00
Cuddington		d	23p04	06 21	06 55	07 19	07 55	08 23	09 23	10 23	11 23	12 23	13 23	14 23	15 23	16 23	17 23	18 23	19 23	20 23	21 23	23 04
Greenbank		d	23p09	06 26	07 00	07 24	08 00	08 28	09 28	10 28	11 28	12 28	13 28	14 28	15 28	16 28	17 28	18 28	19 28	20 28	21 28	23 09
Northwich		d	23p13	06 31	07 05	07 29	08 05	08 33	09 33	10 33	11 33	12 33	13 33	14 33	15 33	16 33	17 33	18 33	19 33	20 33	21 33	23 13
Lostock Gralam		d	23p16	06 34	07 08	07 32	08 08	08 36	09 36	10 36	11 36	12 36	13 36	14 36	15 36	16 36	17 36	18 36	19 36	20 36	21 36	23 16
Plumley		d	23p20	06 37	07 11	07 36	08 11	08 39	09 39	10 39	11 39	12 39	13 39	14 39	15 39	16 39	17 39	18 39	19 39	20 39	21 39	23 20
Knutsford		d	23p25	06 42	07 17	07 41	08 17	08 45	09 45	10 45	11 45	12 45	13 45	14 45	15 45	16 45	17 45	18 45	19 45	20 45	21 45	23 25
Mobberley		d	23p29	06 46	07 21	07 45	08 21	08 49	09 49	10 49	11 49	12 49	13 49	14 49	15 49	16 49	17 49	18 49	19 49	20 49	21 49	23 29
Ashley		d	23p32	06 50	07 24	07 49	08 24	08 52	09 52	10 52	11 52	12 52	13 52	14 52	15 52	16 52	17 52	18 52	19 52	20 52	21 52	23 32
Hale		d	23p35	06 53	07 28	07 53	08 28	08 55	09 55	10 55	11 55	12 55	13 55	14 55	15 55	16 55	17 55	18 55	19 55	20 55	21 55	23 35
Altrincham		a	23p40	06 57	07 32	07 57	08 32	09 00	10 00	11 00	12 00	13 00	14 00	15 00	16 00	17 00	18 00	19 00	20 00	21 00	22 00	23 40
		d	23p40	06 58	07 33	07 58	08 33	09 00	10 00	11 00	12 00	13 00	14 00	15 00	16 00	17 00	18 00	19 00	20 00	21 00	22 00	23 40
Navigation Road		d	23p42	07 00	07 35	08 00	08 35	09 02	10 02	11 02	12 02	13 02	14 02	15 02	16 02	17 02	18 02	19 02	20 02	21 02	22 02	23 42
Stockport	84	a	00 02	07 18	07 56	08 19	08 56	09 21	10 21	11 21	12 21	13 21	14 21	15 21	16 21	17 21	18 21	19 21	20 21	21 21	22 21	00 02
Manchester Picc. 10	81	a	00 18	07 31		08 32		09 36	10 36	11 36	12 36	13 36	14 36	15 36	16 36	17 36	18 36	19 35	20 35	21 35	22 35	00 18

Saturdays
until 1 October

			NT	NT	NT	NT	NT	NT	NT	NT	NT	NT	NT	NT	NT	NT	NT	NT	NT	NT
Chester	81	d	22p48	06 05	07 03	08 07	09 07	10 07	11 07	12 07	13 07	14 07	15 07	16 07	17 07	18 07	19 07	20 07	21 33	22 49
Mouldsworth		d	22p59	06 16	07 14	08 18	09 18	10 18	11 18	12 18	13 18	14 18	15 18	16 18	17 18	18 18	19 18	20 18	21 45	23 00
Delamere		d	23p04	06 21	07 19	08 23	09 23	10 23	11 23	12 23	13 23	14 23	15 23	16 23	17 23	18 23	19 23	20 23	21 49	23 05
Cuddington		d	23p08	06 25	07 23	08 27	09 27	10 27	11 27	12 27	13 27	14 27	15 27	16 27	17 27	18 27	19 27	20 27	21 54	23 09
Greenbank		d	23p13	06 30	07 28	08 32	09 32	10 32	11 32	12 32	13 32	14 32	15 32	16 32	17 32	18 32	19 32	20 32	21 58	23 14
Northwich		d	23p17	06 35	07 33	08 37	09 37	10 37	11 37	12 37	13 37	14 37	15 37	16 37	17 37	18 37	19 37	20 37	22 03	23 18
Lostock Gralam		d	23p20	06 38	07 36	08 40	09 40	10 40	11 40	12 40	13 40	14 40	15 40	16 40	17 40	18 40	19 40	20 40	22 06	23 21
Plumley		d	23p24	06 41	07 40	08 43	09 43	10 43	11 43	12 43	13 43	14 43	15 43	16 43	17 43	18 43	19 43	20 43	22 10	23 25
Knutsford		d	23p29	06 46	07 45	08 49	09 49	10 49	11 49	12 49	13 49	14 49	15 49	16 49	17 49	18 49	19 49	20 49	22 15	23 30
Mobberley		d	23p33	06 50	07 49	08 53	09 53	10 53	11 53	12 53	13 53	14 53	15 53	16 53	17 53	18 53	19 53	20 53	22 19	23 34
Ashley		d	23p36	06 54	07 53	08 56	09 56	10 56	11 56	12 56	13 56	14 56	15 56	16 56	17 56	18 56	19 56	20 56	22 23	23 37
Hale		d	23p39	06 57	07 57	08 59	09 59	10 59	11 59	12 59	13 59	14 59	15 59	16 59	17 59	18 59	19 59	20 59	22 26	23 40
Altrincham		a	23p44	07 01	08 01	09 04	10 04	11 04	12 04	13 04	14 04	15 04	16 04	17 04	18 04	19 04	20 04	21 04	22 30	23 45
		d	23p44	07 02	08 02	09 04	10 04	11 04	12 04	13 04	14 04	15 04	16 04	17 04	18 04	19 04	20 04	21 04	22 31	23 45
Navigation Road		d	23p46	07 04	08 04	09 06	10 06	11 06	12 06	13 06	14 06	15 06	16 06	17 06	18 06	19 06	20 06	21 06	22 33	23 47
Stockport	84	a	00 02	07 18	08 19	09 21	10 21	11 21	12 21	13 21	14 21	15 21	16 21	17 21	18 21	19 21	20 21	21 21	22 47	00 02
Manchester Picc. 10	81	a	00 18	07 31	08 32	09 36	10 36	11 36	12 36	13 36	14 36	15 36	16 36	17 36	18 36	19 35	20 35	21 35	23 00	00 15

Saturdays
from 8 October

			NT	NT	NT	NT	NT	NT	NT	NT	NT	NT	NT	NT	NT	NT	NT	NT	NT	NT
Chester	81	d	22p44	06 01	06 59	08 03	09 03	10 03	11 03	12 03	13 03	14 03	15 03	16 03	17 03	18 03	19 03	20 03	21 29	22 45
Mouldsworth		d	22p55	06 12	07 10	08 14	09 14	10 14	11 14	12 14	13 14	14 14	15 14	16 14	17 14	18 14	19 14	20 14	21 41	22 56
Delamere		d	23p00	06 17	07 15	08 19	09 19	10 19	11 19	12 19	13 19	14 19	15 19	16 19	17 19	18 19	19 19	20 19	21 45	23 01
Cuddington		d	23p04	06 21	07 19	08 23	09 23	10 23	11 23	12 23	13 23	14 23	15 23	16 23	17 23	18 23	19 23	20 23	21 50	23 05
Greenbank		d	23p09	06 26	07 24	08 28	09 28	10 28	11 28	12 28	13 28	14 28	15 28	16 28	17 28	18 28	19 28	20 28	21 54	23 10
Northwich		d	23p13	06 31	07 29	08 33	09 33	10 33	11 33	12 33	13 33	14 33	15 33	16 33	17 33	18 33	19 33	20 33	21 59	23 14
Lostock Gralam		d	23p16	06 34	07 32	08 36	09 36	10 36	11 36	12 36	13 36	14 36	15 36	16 36	17 36	18 36	19 36	20 36	22 02	23 17
Plumley		d	23p20	06 37	07 36	08 39	09 39	10 39	11 39	12 39	13 39	14 39	15 39	16 39	17 39	18 39	19 39	20 39	22 06	23 21
Knutsford		d	23p25	06 42	07 41	08 45	09 45	10 45	11 45	12 45	13 45	14 45	15 45	16 45	17 45	18 45	19 45	20 45	22 11	23 26
Mobberley		d	23p29	06 46	07 45	08 49	09 49	10 49	11 49	12 49	13 49	14 49	15 49	16 49	17 49	18 49	19 49	20 49	22 15	23 30
Ashley		d	23p32	06 50	07 49	08 52	09 52	10 52	11 52	12 52	13 52	14 52	15 52	16 52	17 52	18 52	19 52	20 52	22 19	23 33
Hale		d	23p35	06 53	07 53	08 55	09 55	10 55	11 55	12 55	13 55	14 55	15 55	16 55	17 55	18 55	19 55	20 55	22 22	23 36
Altrincham		a	23p40	06 57	07 57	09 00	10 00	11 00	12 00	13 00	14 00	15 00	16 00	17 00	18 00	19 00	20 00	21 00	22 26	23 41
		d	23p40	06 58	07 58	09 00	10 00	11 00	12 00	13 00	14 00	15 00	16 00	17 00	18 00	19 00	20 00	21 00	22 27	23 41
Navigation Road		d	23p42	07 00	08 00	09 02	10 02	11 02	12 02	13 02	14 02	15 02	16 02	17 02	18 02	19 02	20 02	21 02	22 29	23 43
Stockport	84	a	00 02	07 18	08 19	09 21	10 21	11 21	12 21	13 21	14 21	15 21	16 21	17 21	18 21	19 21	20 21	21 21	22 47	00 02
Manchester Picc. 10	81	a	00 18	07 31	08 32	09 36	10 36	11 36	12 36	13 36	14 36	15 36	16 36	17 36	18 36	19 35	20 35	21 35	23 00	00 15

On Sundays only, National Rail Tickets from stations between Mouldsworth and Hale inclusive are valid for travel on Metrolink services between Altrincham and Manchester City Centre

Table 88

Sundays
until 2 October

Chester and Northwich - Manchester

			NT A	NT	NT	NT	NT	NT	NT	NT
Chester	81	d	22p49	08 58	11 07	13 07	15 07	17 07	19 07	21 07
Mouldsworth		d	23p00	09 09	11 18	13 18	15 18	17 18	19 18	21 18
Delamere		d	23p05	09 14	11 23	13 23	15 23	17 23	19 23	21 23
Cuddington		d	23p09	09 18	11 27	13 27	15 27	17 27	19 27	21 27
Greenbank		d	23p14	09 23	11 32	13 32	15 32	17 32	19 32	21 32
Northwich		d	23p18	09 28	11 37	13 37	15 37	17 37	19 37	21 37
Lostock Gralam		d	23p21	09 31	11 40	13 40	15 40	17 40	19 40	21 40
Plumley		d	23p25	09 34	11 43	13 43	15 43	17 43	19 43	21 43
Knutsford		d	23p30	09 40	11 49	13 49	15 49	17 49	19 49	21 49
Mobberley		d	23p34	09 44	11 53	13 53	15 53	17 53	19 53	21 53
Ashley		d	23p37	09 47	11 56	13 56	15 56	17 56	19 56	21 56
Hale		d	23p40	09 50	11 59	13 59	15 59	17 59	19 59	21 59
Altrincham	🚊	a	23p45	09 55	12 04	14 04	16 04	18 04	20 04	22 04
		d	23p45	09 55	12 04	14 04	16 04	18 04	20 04	22 04
Navigation Road	🚊	d	23p47	09 57	12 06	14 06	16 06	18 06	20 06	22 06
Stockport	84	a	00 02	10 12	12 22	14 21	16 21	18 21	20 21	22 21
Manchester Picc. 10	81 🚊	a	00 15	10 23	12 32	14 33	16 33	18 33	20 33	22 33

Sundays
from 9 October

			NT	NT	NT	NT	NT	NT	NT	NT
Chester	81	d	22p45	08 54	11 03	13 03	15 03	17 03	19 03	21 03
Mouldsworth		d	22p56	09 05	11 14	13 14	15 14	17 14	19 14	21 14
Delamere		d	23p01	09 10	11 19	13 19	15 19	17 19	19 19	21 19
Cuddington		d	23p05	09 14	11 23	13 23	15 23	17 23	19 23	21 23
Greenbank		d	23p10	09 19	11 28	13 28	15 28	17 28	19 28	21 28
Northwich		d	23p14	09 24	11 33	13 33	15 33	17 33	19 33	21 33
Lostock Gralam		d	23p17	09 27	11 36	13 36	15 36	17 36	19 36	21 36
Plumley		d	23p21	09 30	11 39	13 39	15 39	17 39	19 39	21 39
Knutsford		d	23p26	09 36	11 45	13 45	15 45	17 45	19 45	21 45
Mobberley		d	23p30	09 40	11 49	13 49	15 49	17 49	19 49	21 49
Ashley		d	23p33	09 43	11 52	13 52	15 52	17 52	19 52	21 52
Hale		d	23p36	09 46	11 55	13 55	15 55	17 55	19 55	21 55
Altrincham	🚊	a	23p41	09 51	12 00	14 00	16 00	18 00	20 00	22 00
		d	23p41	09 51	12 00	14 00	16 00	18 00	20 00	22 00
Navigation Road	🚊	d	23p43	09 53	12 02	14 02	16 02	18 02	20 02	22 02
Stockport	84	a	00 02	10 12	12 21	14 21	16 21	18 21	20 21	22 21
Manchester Picc. 10	81 🚊	a	00 15	10 23	12 31	14 33	16 33	18 33	20 33	22 33

A not 22 May

On Sundays only, National Rail Tickets from stations between Mouldsworth and Hale inclusive are valid for travel on Metrolink services between Altrincham and Manchester City Centre

Liverpool - Warrington Central - Manchester and Manchester Airport

Miles	Station		NT MO	NT MX	NT	NT	NT	NT	NT	TP	NT		EM	NT	NT	NT	TP	NT	EM	NT	NT		TP	NT	EM
										◇1 A			◇ B				◇1 A		◇ B				◇1 A		◇ B
0	**Liverpool Lime Street** 10 90,91	d	23p01	23p38	03 38	05 13	05 49		06 13	06 15	06 21		06 47	06 50	07 13		07 15	07 26	07 43	07 51	08 13		08 22	08 26	08 52
1¾	Edge Hill 90,91	d		23p42			05 53							06 54				07 30						08 30	
3¾	Mossley Hill 91	d		23p47			05 58				06 29			06 59				07 35		07 59				08 35	
4½	West Allerton 91	d		23p50			06 00				06 31			07 01				07 37		08 01				08 37	
—	Liverpool Central 10 103	d																							
5½	L'pool Sth Parkway 7 91,103 ✈	d		23p53			06 03			06 25	06 34		06 57	07 04			07 25	07 40	07 53	08 04			08 32	08 40	09 03
7¼	Hunts Cross 103	d		23p56			06 07							07 08					07 59	08 08					
8¼	Halewood	d		23p59			06 09							07 10						08 10					
10½	Hough Green	d		00 03			06 13				06 41			07 14				07 47		08 14				08 47	
12¼	Widnes	d		00 06			06 17				06 44		07 07	07 18			07 33		08 05	08 18				08 50	09 11
16	Sankey for Penketh	d		00 11			06 22							07 23						08 23					
18½	**Warrington Central**	a		00 16			06 28			06 37	06 52		07 15	07 29			07 39	07 56	08 13	08 28			08 44	08 58	09 18
—		d		00 17				06 02		06 38	06 53		07 15			07 22	07 40	07 57	08 13	08 28			08 45	08 59	09 19
20¼	Padgate	d						06 05			06 56					07 25		08 00						09 02	
21¾	Birchwood	d						06 08		06 43	06 59		07 20			07 28	07 45	08 03	08 18	08 33			08 50	09 05	
24½	Glazebrook	d						06 13			07 04					07 33		08 08							
25¾	Irlam	d						06 16			07 07					07 36	07 50	08 11		08 39				09 11	
28	Flixton	d						06 20			07 11					07 40		08 15		08 43				09 15	
28½	Chassen Road	d						06 22			07 13					07 42		08 17		08 45					
29	Urmston	d						06 24			07 15					07 44		08 19		08 47				09 18	
30¼	Humphrey Park	d						06 26			07 17					07 46		08 21		08 49				09 20	
31	Trafford Park	d						06 29			07 20					07 49		08 24		08 52				09 23	
34	Deansgate 84,85	a						06 36			07 29					07 58		08 32		09 00				09 31	
34½	**Manchester Oxford Road** 84,85	a	23p59					06 41	06 57	07 00	07 36		07 38		07 57	08 03	08 04	08 36	08 38	09 04	08 57		09 05	09 36	09 39
35	**Manchester Piccadilly** 10 78,84,85	a	00 02	00 40	04 14	05 57			07 01	07 09			07 41		08 01		08 08		08 41		09 01		09 09		09 41
—	Stockport 84	a											07 53						08 53						09 53
—	Sheffield 7 78	a											08 36						09 35						10 35
44¾	**Manchester Airport** 85 ✈	a	00 19		04 30	06 14			07 22						08 22						09 22				

Station		NT	NT	TP	NT	EM	NT		NT	NT	TP	NT	EM	NT	NT	NT	TP		NT	EM	NT	NT	NT	TP	NT
				◇1 A		◇ B				C	◇1 A		◇ B			D	◇1 A			◇ B			D	◇1 A	
Liverpool Lime Street 10 90,91	d	08 55	09 13	09 22	09 27	09 52	09 55		10 13	10 16	10 22	10 27	10 52	10 55	11 13	11 16	11 22		11 27	11 52	11 55	12 13	12 16	12 22	12 27
Edge Hill 90,91	d	08 59					09 59							10 59							11 59				
Mossley Hill 91	d	09 04			09 35		10 04					10 35		11 04					11 35		12 04				12 35
West Allerton 91	d	09 06			09 37		10 06					10 37		11 06					11 37		12 06				12 37
Liverpool Central 10 103	d																								
L'pool Sth Parkway 7 91,103 ✈	d	09 09		09 32	09 40	10 03	10 09			10a27	10 32	10 40	11 03	11 09		11a27	11 32		11 40	12 03	12 09		12a27	12 32	12 40
Hunts Cross 103	d	09 13					10 13							11 13							12 13				
Halewood	d	09 16					10 16							11 16							12 16				
Hough Green	d	09 20			09 47		10 20					10 47		11 20					11 47		12 20				12 47
Widnes	d	09 23			09 50	10 11	10 23					10 50	11 11	11 23					11 50	12 11	12 23				12 50
Sankey for Penketh	d	09 28					10 28							11 28							12 28				
Warrington Central	a	09 33		09 44	09 58	10 18	10 33				10 44	10 58	11 18	11 33			11 44		11 58	12 18	12 33			12 44	12 58
	d	09 34		09 45	09 59	10 19	10 34				10 45	10 59	11 19	11 34			11 45		11 59	12 19	12 34			12 45	12 59
Padgate	d				10 02							11 02							12 02						13 02
Birchwood	d	09 38		09 50	10 05		10 38				10 50	11 05		11 38			11 50		12 05		12 38			12 50	13 05
Glazebrook	d				10 10														12 10						
Irlam	d	09 44			10 13		10 44					11 11		11 44					12 13		12 44				13 11
Flixton	d				10 17							11 15							12 17						13 15
Chassen Road	d				10 19														12 19						
Urmston	d	09 49			10 21		10 49					11 18		11 49					12 21		12 49				13 18
Humphrey Park	d											11 20													13 20
Trafford Park	d											11 23													13 23
Deansgate 84,85	a	09 59			10 31		10 59					11 31		11 59					12 31		12 59				13 31
Manchester Oxford Road 84,85	a	10 04	09 57	10 05	10 36	10 39	11 04		10 57		11 05	11 36	11 39	12 04	11 57		12 05		12 36	12 39	13 04	12 57		13 05	13 36
Manchester Piccadilly 10 78,84,85	a		10 01	10 09		10 41			11 01		11 09		11 41		12 01		12 09			12 41		13 01		13 09	
Stockport 84	a					10 53							11 53							12 53					
Sheffield 7 78	a					11 34							12 35							13 35					
Manchester Airport 85 ✈	a		10 22						11 22						12 22							13 22			

A To Scarborough
B To Norwich
C From Preston
D From Blackpool North

Liverpool - Warrington Central - Manchester and Manchester Airport

	EM ◇ A	NT		NT	NT B	TP ◇[1] C	NT	EM ◇ D	NT	NT	NT B	TP ◇[1] C		NT	EM ◇ A	NT	NT	NT B	TP ◇[1] E	NT	EM ◇ A	NT		NT
Liverpool Lime Street [10] 90,91 d	12 52	12 55		13 13	13 16	13 22	13 27	13 52	13 55	14 13	14 16	14 22		14 27	14 52	14 55	15 13	15 16	15 22	15 27	15 52	15 55		16 13
Edge Hill 90,91 d		12 59							13 59							14 59						15 59		
Mossley Hill 91 d		13 04					13 35		14 04					14 35		15 04				15 35		16 04		
West Allerton 91 d		13 06					13 37		14 06					14 37		15 06				15 37		16 06		
Liverpool Central [10] 103 d																								
L'pool Sth Parkway [7] 91,103 ✈ d	13 03	13 09			13a27	13 32	13 40	14 03	14 09		14a27	14 32		14 40	15 03	15 09		15a27	15 32	15 40	16 03	16 09		
Hunts Cross 103 d		13 13							14 13							15 13						16 13		
Halewood d		13 16							14 16							15 16						16 16		
Hough Green d		13 20					13 47		14 20					14 47		15 20				15 47		16 20		
Widnes d	13 11	13 23					13 50	14 11	14 23					14 50	15 11	15 23				15 50	16 11	16 23		
Sankey for Penketh d		13 28							14 28							15 28						16 28		
Warrington Central a	13 18	13 33				13 44	13 58	14 18	14 33			14 44		14 58	15 18	15 33			15 44	15 58	16 18	16 33		
d	13 19	13 34				13 45	13 59	14 19	14 34			14 45		14 59	15 19	15 34			15 45	15 59	16 19	16 34		
Padgate d							14 02							15 02						16 02				
Birchwood d		13 38				13 50	14 05		14 38			14 50		15 05		15 38			15 50	16 05		16 38		
Glazebrook d							14 10													16 10				
Irlam d		13 44					14 13		14 44					15 11		15 44				16 13		16 44		
Flixton d							14 17							15 15						16 17				
Chassen Road d							14 19													16 19				
Urmston d		13 49					14 21		14 49					15 18		15 49				16 21		16 49		
Humphrey Park d														15 20										
Trafford Park d														15 23										
Deansgate 84,85 ⛴ a		13 59					14 31		14 59					15 31		15 59				16 30		16 59		
Manchester Oxford Road 84,85 a	13 39	14 04		13 57		14 05	14 36	14 39	15 04	14 57		15 05		15 36	15 39	16 04	15 57		16 05	16 36	16 38	17 04		16 57
Manchester Piccadilly [10] 78,84,85 ⛴ a	13 41			14 01		14 09		14 41		15 01		15 09			15 41		16 01		16 09		16 41			17 01
Stockport 84 a	13 53							14 53							15 53						16 53			
Sheffield [7] 78 ⛴ a	14 35							15 35							16 34						17 37			
Manchester Airport 85 ✈ a				14 22						15 22							16 22							17 22

	NT B	TP ◇[1] C	NT	EM ◇ D	NT	NT	TP ◇[1] C	NT		EM ◇ A	NT	NT	TP ◇[1] C	NT	EM ◇ D	NT	TP ◇[1] F	NT		EM ◇ D	NT	NT	TP ◇[1] G	NT
Liverpool Lime Street [10] 90,91 d	16 16	16 22	16 27	16 52	16 55	17 06	17 22	17 25		17 52	17 55	18 13	18 22	18 25	18 52	18 55	19 22			19 52	19 55	20 09	20 22	20 55
Edge Hill 90,91 d					16 59			17 29			17 59			18 29		18 59					19 59			20 59
Mossley Hill 91 d			16 35		17 04			17 34			18 04			18 34		19 04					20 04			21 04
West Allerton 91 d			16 37		17 06			17 36			18 06			18 36		19 06					20 06			21 06
Liverpool Central [10] 103 d																								
L'pool Sth Parkway [7] 91,103 ✈ d	16a27	16 32	16 40	17 03	17 09		17 32	17 39		18 03	18 09		18 32	18 39	19 03	19 09	19 32			20 03	20 09		20 32	21 09
Hunts Cross 103 d					17 13			17 43			18 13			18 43		19 13					20 13			21 13
Halewood d					17 16			17 46			18 16			18 46		19 16					20 16			21 16
Hough Green d			16 47		17 20			17 50			18 20			18 50		19 20					20 20			21 20
Widnes d			16 50	17 11	17 23			17 53		18 11	18 23			18 53	19 11	19 23				20 11	20 23			21 23
Sankey for Penketh d					17 28			17 58			18 28			18 58		19 28					20 28			21 28
Warrington Central a		16 44	16 58	17 18	17 33		17 44	18 03		18 18	18 33		18 44	19 03	19 18	19 34	19 44			20 18	20 34		20 44	21 33
d		16 45	16 59	17 19	17 34		17 45	18 04		18 19	18 34		18 45	19 04	19 19		19 45	19 56		20 19			20 45	21 34
Padgate d			17 02					18 07						19 07				19 59						21 37
Birchwood d		16 50	17 05		17 38		17 50	18 10			18 38		18 50	19 10			19 50	20 02					20 50	21 40
Glazebrook d														19 15				20 07						21 45
Irlam d			17 11		17 44			18 16			18 44			19 18				20 10						21 48
Flixton d			17 15					18 20										20 14						21 52
Chassen Road d																		20 16						21 54
Urmston d			17 18		17 49			18 23			18 49			19 23				20 18						21 56
Humphrey Park d			17 20															20 20						21 58
Trafford Park d			17 23															20 23						22 01
Deansgate 84,85 ⛴ a			17 31		17 59			18 31			18 59			19 31				20 31						22 08
Manchester Oxford Road 84,85 a		17 05	17 36	17 38	18 04	17 57	18 05	18 36		18 39	19 04	18 57	19 05	19 36	19 39		20 05	20 36		20 39		20 57	21 06	22 13
Manchester Piccadilly [10] 78,84,85 ⛴ a		17 09		17 41		18 01	18 09			18 41		19 01	19 09		19 41		20 09			20 41		21 01	21 09	
Stockport 84 a				17 53						18 53					19 53					20 53				
Sheffield [7] 78 ⛴ a				18 41						19 33					20 36					21 35				
Manchester Airport 85 ✈ a						18 22						19 24										21 24		

A To Norwich
B From Blackpool North
C To Scarborough
D To Nottingham
E To Middlesbrough
F To Hull
G To York

Liverpool - Warrington Central - Manchester and Manchester Airport

	EM ◇ A	NT	TP ◇[1] B	LM [1] C	LM [1] D	LM [1] E	NT
Liverpool Lime Street [10] 90,91 d	21 37	21 55	22 30	22 31	22 34	23 34	23 38
Edge Hill 90,91 d		21 59					23 42
Mossley Hill 91 d		22 04					23 47
West Allerton 91 d		22 06					23 50
Liverpool Central [10] 103 d							
L'pool Sth Parkway [7] 91,103 ✈ d	21 47	22 09	22 40	22a41	22a44	23a44	23 53
Hunts Cross 103 d		22 13					23 56
Halewood d		22 16					23 59
Hough Green d		22 20					00 03
Widnes d	21 55	22 23					00 06
Sankey for Penketh d		22 28					00 11
Warrington Central a	22 03	22 33	22 52				00 16
d	22 03	22 34	22 53				00 17
Padgate d		22 37					
Birchwood d		22 40	22 58				
Glazebrook d		22 45					
Irlam d		22 48					
Flixton d		22 52					
Chassen Road d		22 54					
Urmston d		22 56					
Humphrey Park d		22 58					
Trafford Park d		23 01					
Deansgate 84,85 🚋 a		23 08					
Manchester Oxford Road 84,85 a	22 23	23 13	23 14				
Manchester Piccadilly [10] 78,84,85 🚋 a	22 26		23 19				00 40
Stockport 84 a	22 37						
Sheffield [7] 78 🚋 a	23 35						
Manchester Airport 85 ✈ a							

Saturdays

	NT	NT	NT	NT	NT	TP ◇[1] F 🍴	NT	EM ◇ G	NT	NT	TP ◇[1] F 🍴	NT
Liverpool Lime Street [10] 90,91 d	23p38	03 38	05 13	05 49	06 13	06 15	06 25	06 49	06 55	07 13	07 15	07 26
Edge Hill 90,91 d	23p42			05 53					06 59			07 30
Mossley Hill 91 d	23p47			05 58			06 33		07 04			07 35
West Allerton 91 d	23p50			06 00			06 35		07 06			07 37
Liverpool Central [10] 103 d												
L'pool Sth Parkway [7] 91,103 ✈ d	23p53			06 03		06 25	06 38	06 59	07 09		07 25	07 40
Hunts Cross 103 d	23p56			06 07					07 13			
Halewood d	23p59			06 09					07 16			
Hough Green d	00 03			06 13			06 46		07 20			07 47
Widnes d	00 06			06 17			06 49	07 07	07 23		07 33	
Sankey for Penketh d	00 11			06 22					07 28			
Warrington Central a	00 16			06 28		06 37	06 57	07 15	07 34		07 39	07 56
d	00 17					06 38	06 58	07 15			07 40	07 57
Padgate d							07 01					08 00
Birchwood d						06 43	07 04	07 20			07 45	08 03
Glazebrook d							07 09					08 08
Irlam d							07 12				07 50	08 11
Flixton d							07 16					08 15
Chassen Road d							07 18					08 17
Urmston d							07 20					08 19
Humphrey Park d							07 22					08 21
Trafford Park d							07 25					08 24
Deansgate 84,85 🚋 a							07 32					08 32
Manchester Oxford Road 84,85 a					06 57	07 00	07 37	07 38		07 57	08 04	08 36
Manchester Piccadilly [10] 78,84,85 🚋 a	00 40	04 14	05 57		07 01	07 09		07 41		08 01	08 08	
Stockport 84 a								07 53				
Sheffield [7] 78 🚋 a								08 36				
Manchester Airport 85 ✈ a		04 30	06 14		07 22					08 22		

	EM ◇ G	NT	NT	TP ◇[1] F 🍴	NT	EM ◇ G	NT	NT	TP ◇[1] F 🍴	NT
Liverpool Lime Street [10] 90,91 d	07 42	07 51	08 13	08 22	08 26	08 52	08 55	09 13	09 22	09 27
Edge Hill 90,91 d					08 30		08 59			
Mossley Hill 91 d		07 59			08 35		09 04			09 35
West Allerton 91 d		08 01			08 37		09 06			09 37
Liverpool Central [10] 103 d										
L'pool Sth Parkway [7] 91,103 ✈ d	07 52	08 04		08 32	08 40	09 03	09 09		09 32	09 40
Hunts Cross 103 d	07 59	08 08					09 13			
Halewood d		08 10					09 16			
Hough Green d		08 14			08 47		09 20			09 47
Widnes d	08 05	08 18			08 50	09 11	09 23			09 50
Sankey for Penketh d		08 23					09 28			
Warrington Central a	08 13	08 28		08 44	08 58	09 18	09 33		09 44	09 58
d	08 13	08 28		08 45	08 59	09 19	09 34		09 45	09 59
Padgate d					09 02					10 02
Birchwood d	08 18	08 33		08 50	09 05		09 38		09 50	10 05
Glazebrook d										10 10
Irlam d		08 39			09 11		09 44			10 13
Flixton d		08 43			09 15					10 17
Chassen Road d		08 45								10 19
Urmston d		08 47			09 18		09 49			10 21
Humphrey Park d		08 49			09 20					
Trafford Park d		08 52			09 23					
Deansgate 84,85 🚋 a		09 00			09 31		09 59			10 31
Manchester Oxford Road 84,85 a	08 38	09 04	08 57	09 05	09 36	09 39	10 04	09 57	10 05	10 36
Manchester Piccadilly [10] 78,84,85 🚋 a	08 41		09 01	09 09		09 41		10 01	10 09	
Stockport 84 a	08 53					09 53				
Sheffield [7] 78 🚋 a	09 35					10 35				
Manchester Airport 85 ✈ a			09 22					10 22		

A To Nottingham
B To York
C from 20 June until 9 September. To Crewe
D until 17 June, from 12 September. To Crewe
E To Crewe
F To Scarborough
G To Norwich

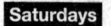

Liverpool - Warrington Central - Manchester and Manchester Airport

	EM ◇ A	NT	NT	NT B	TP ◇1 C	NT	EM ◇ A	NT	NT	NT B	TP ◇1 C	NT	EM ◇ A	NT	NT	NT B	TP ◇1 C	NT	EM ◇ A	NT	NT	NT B
Liverpool Lime Street 10 90,91 d	09 52	09 55	10 13	10 16	10 22	10 27	10 52	10 55	11 13	11 16	11 22	11 27	11 52	11 55	12 13	12 16	12 22	12 27	12 52	12 55	13 13	13 16
Edge Hill 90,91 d		09 59						10 59						11 59						12 59		
Mossley Hill 91 d		10 04				10 35		11 04				11 35		12 04				12 35		13 04		
West Allerton 91 d		10 06				10 37		11 06				11 37		12 06				12 37		13 06		
Liverpool Central 10 103 d																						
L'pool Sth Parkway 7 91,103 d	10 03	10 09		10a27	10 32	10 40	11 03	11 09		11a27	11 32	11 40	12 03	12 09		12a27	12 32	12 40	13 03	13 09		13a27
Hunts Cross 103 d		10 13						11 13						12 13						13 13		
Halewood d		10 16						11 16						12 16						13 16		
Hough Green d		10 20				10 47		11 20				11 47		12 20				12 47		13 20		
Widnes d	10 11	10 23				10 50	11 11	11 23				11 50	12 11	12 23				12 50	13 11	13 23		
Sankey for Penketh d		10 28						11 28						12 28						13 28		
Warrington Central a	10 18	10 33			10 44	10 58	11 18	11 33			11 44	11 58	12 18	12 33			12 44	12 58	13 18	13 33		
d	10 19	10 34			10 45	10 59	11 19	11 34			11 45	11 59	12 19	12 34			12 45	12 59	13 19	13 34		
Padgate d						11 02						12 02						13 02				
Birchwood d		10 38			10 50	11 05		11 38			11 50	12 05		12 38			12 50	13 05		13 38		
Glazebrook d												12 10										
Irlam d		10 44				11 11		11 44				12 13		12 44				13 11		13 44		
Flixton d						11 15						12 17						13 15				
Chassen Road d												12 19										
Urmston d		10 49				11 18		11 49				12 21		12 49				13 18		13 49		
Humphrey Park d						11 20												13 20				
Trafford Park d						11 23												13 23				
Deansgate 84,85 a		10 59				11 31		11 59				12 31		12 59				13 31		13 59		
Manchester Oxford Road 84,85 a	10 39	11 04	10 57		11 05	11 36	11 39	12 04	11 57		12 05	12 36	12 39	13 04	12 57		13 05	13 36	13 39	14 04	13 57	
Manchester Piccadilly 10 78,84,85 a	10 41		11 01		11 09		11 41		12 01		12 09		12 41		13 01		13 09		13 41		14 01	
Stockport 84 a	10 53						11 53						12 53						13 53			
Sheffield 7 78 a	11 35						12 35						13 35						14 35			
Manchester Airport 85 a			11 22						12 22						13 22						14 22	

	TP ◇1 C	NT	EM ◇ D	NT	NT	NT B	TP ◇1 C	NT	EM ◇ A	NT	NT	NT B	TP ◇1 C	NT	EM ◇ A	NT	NT	NT B	TP ◇1 C	NT	EM ◇ D
Liverpool Lime Street 10 90,91 d	13 22	13 27	13 52	13 55	14 13	14 16	14 22	14 27	14 52	14 55	15 13	15 16	15 22	15 27	15 52	15 55	16 13	16 16	16 22	16 27	16 52
Edge Hill 90,91 d				13 59						14 59						15 59					
Mossley Hill 91 d		13 35		14 04				14 35		15 04				15 35		16 04				16 35	
West Allerton 91 d		13 37		14 06				14 37		15 06				15 37		16 06				16 37	
Liverpool Central 10 103 d																					
L'pool Sth Parkway 7 91,103 d	13 32	13 40	14 03	14 09		14a27	14 32	14 40	15 03	15 09		15a27	15 32	15 40	16 03	16 09		16a27	16 32	16 40	17 03
Hunts Cross 103 d				14 13						15 13						16 13					
Halewood d				14 16						15 16						16 16					
Hough Green d		13 47		14 20				14 47		15 20				15 47		16 20				16 47	
Widnes d		13 50	14 11	14 23				14 50	15 11	15 23				15 50	16 11	16 23				16 50	17 11
Sankey for Penketh d				14 28						15 28						16 28					
Warrington Central a	13 44	13 58	14 18	14 33			14 44	14 58	15 18	15 33			15 44	15 58	16 18	16 33			16 44	16 58	17 18
d	13 45	13 59	14 19	14 34			14 45	14 59	15 19	15 34			15 45	15 59	16 19	16 34			16 45	16 59	17 19
Padgate d		14 02						15 02						16 02						17 02	
Birchwood d	13 50	14 05		14 38			14 50	15 05		15 38			15 50	16 05		16 38			16 50	17 05	
Glazebrook d		14 10												16 10							
Irlam d		14 13		14 44				15 11		15 44				16 13		16 44				17 11	
Flixton d		14 17						15 15						16 17						17 15	
Chassen Road d		14 19												16 19							
Urmston d		14 21		14 49				15 18		15 49				16 21		16 49				17 18	
Humphrey Park d								15 20												17 20	
Trafford Park d								15 23												17 23	
Deansgate 84,85 a		14 31		14 59				15 31		15 59				16 30		16 59				17 31	
Manchester Oxford Road 84,85 a	14 05	14 36	14 39	15 04	14 57		15 05	15 36	15 39	16 04	15 57		16 05	16 36	16 38	17 04	16 57		17 05	17 36	17 38
Manchester Piccadilly 10 78,84,85 a	14 09		14 41		15 01		15 09		15 41		16 01		16 09		16 41		17 01		17 09		17 41
Stockport 84 a			14 53						15 53						16 53						17 53
Sheffield 7 78 a			15 36						16 35						17 37						18 35
Manchester Airport 85 a					15 22						16 22						17 22				

A To Norwich
B From Blackpool North
C To Scarborough
D To Nottingham

Liverpool - Warrington Central - Manchester and Manchester Airport

	NT	NT	TP ◇1 A	NT	EM ◇ B	NT	NT		TP ◇1 A	NT	EM ◇ C	NT	TP ◇1 D	NT	EM ◇ C	NT	NT		TP ◇1 D	EM ◇ C	NT	EM ◇ C	NT	LM 1 E
Liverpool Lime Street 10 90,91 d	16 55	17 06	17 22	17 25	17 52	17 55	18 13		18 22	18 25	18 52	18 55	19 22		19 52	19 55	20 09		20 22	20 52	20 55	21 37	21 55	22 04
Edge Hill 90,91 d	16 59			17 29		17 59				18 29		18 59				19 59					20 59		21 59	
Mossley Hill 91 d	17 04			17 34		18 04				18 34		19 04				20 04					21 04		22 04	
West Allerton 91 d	17 06			17 36		18 06				18 36		19 06				20 06					21 06		22 06	
Liverpool Central 10 103 d																								
L'pool Sth Parkway 7 91,103 ✈ d	17 09		17 32	17 39	18 03	18 09			18 32	18 39	19 03	19 09	19 32		20 03	20 09			20 32	21 03	21 09	21 47	22 09	22a14
Hunts Cross 103 d	17 13			17 43		18 13				18 43		19 13				20 13					21 13		22 13	
Halewood d	17 16			17 46		18 16				18 46		19 16				20 16					21 16		22 16	
Hough Green d	17 20			17 50		18 20				18 50		19 20				20 20					21 20		22 20	
Widnes d	17 23			17 54	18 11	18 23				18 53	19 11	19 23			20 11	20 23				21 11	21 23	21 55	22 23	
Sankey for Penketh d	17 28			17 58		18 28				18 58		19 28				20 28					21 28		22 28	
Warrington Central a	17 33		17 44	18 03	18 18	18 33			18 44	19 03	19 18	19 34	19 44		20 18	20 34			20 44	21 18	21 33	22 03	22 33	
d	17 34		17 45	18 04	18 19	18 34			18 45	19 04	19 19		19 45	19 56	20 19				20 45	21 19	21 34	22 03	22 34	
Padgate d				18 07						19 07				19 59							21 37		22 37	
Birchwood d	17 38		17 50	18 10		18 38			18 50	19 10			19 50	20 02					20 50		21 40		22 40	
Glazebrook d										19 15				20 07							21 45		22 45	
Irlam d	17 44			18 16		18 44				19 18				20 10							21 48		22 48	
Flixton d				18 20										20 14							21 52		22 52	
Chassen Road d														20 16							21 54		22 54	
Urmston d	17 49			18 23		18 49				19 23				20 18							21 56		22 56	
Humphrey Park d														20 20							21 58		22 58	
Trafford Park d														20 23							22 01		23 01	
Deansgate 84,85 ⛴ a	17 59			18 31		18 59				19 31				20 31							22 08		23 08	
Manchester Oxford Road 84,85 a	18 04	17 57	18 05	18 36	18 39	19 04	18 57		19 05	19 36	19 39		20 05	20 36	20 39		20 57		21 06	21 38	22 13	22 26	23 13	
Manchester Piccadilly 10 78,84,85 ⛴ a		18 01	18 09		18 41		19 01		19 09		19 41		20 09		20 41		21 01		21 09	21 41		22 29		
Stockport 84 a					18 53						19 53				20 53					21 52		22 41		
Sheffield 7 78 ⛴ a					19 35						20 35				21 34					22 31		23 39		
Manchester Airport 85 ✈ a		18 22					19 24										21 24							

	TP ◇1 D	NT
Liverpool Lime Street 10 90,91 d	22 30	23 38
Edge Hill 90,91 d		23 42
Mossley Hill 91 d		23 47
West Allerton 91 d		23 49
Liverpool Central 10 103 d		
L'pool Sth Parkway 7 91,103 ✈ d	22 40	23 52
Hunts Cross 103 d		23 56
Halewood d		23 59
Hough Green d		00 03
Widnes d		00 06
Sankey for Penketh d		00 11
Warrington Central a	22 52	00 16
d	22 53	00 17
Padgate d		
Birchwood d	22 58	
Glazebrook d		
Irlam d		
Flixton d		
Chassen Road d		
Urmston d		
Humphrey Park d		
Trafford Park d		
Deansgate 84,85 ⛴ a		
Manchester Oxford Road 84,85 a	23 14	
Manchester Piccadilly 10 78,84,85 ⛴ a	23 19	00 39
Stockport 84 a		
Sheffield 7 78 ⛴ a		
Manchester Airport 85 ✈ a		

A To Scarborough
B To Norwich
C To Nottingham
D To York
E To Crewe

Table 89

Sundays

until 11 September

Liverpool - Warrington Central - Manchester and Manchester Airport

	NT	NT	TP	NT	NT	TP	NT	NT	TP		NT	NT	TP	NT	NT	TP	NT	EM	NT		TP	NT	EM	NT
			◇1			◇1			◇1				◇1			◇1		◇			◇1		◇	
	A		B			C			D				C			D		E			F		E	
Liverpool Lime Street [10] 90,91 d	23p38	08 05	08 22	08 26	09 01	09 22	09 26	10 01	10 22		10 26	11 01	11 22	11 26	12 01	12 22	12 26	12 52	13 01		13 22	13 26	13 52	14 01
Edge Hill 90,91 d	23p42																							
Mossley Hill 91 d	23p47			08 34			09 34				10 34			11 34			12 34					13 34		
West Allerton 91 d	23p49			08 36			09 36				10 36			11 36			12 36					13 36		
Liverpool Central [10] 103 d																								
L'pool Sth Parkway [7] 91,103 ✈ d	23p52		08 32	08 39		09 32	09 39		10 32		10 39		11 32	11 39		12 32	12 39	13 03			13 32	13 39	14 03	
Hunts Cross 103 d	23p56			08 43			09 43				10 43			11 43			12 43					13 43		
Halewood d	23p59			08 46			09 46				10 46			11 46			12 46					13 46		
Hough Green d	00 03			08 50			09 50				10 50			11 50			12 50					13 50		
Widnes d	00 06			08 53			09 53				10 53			11 53			12 53	13 11				13 53	14 11	
Sankey for Penketh d	00 11																							
Warrington Central a	00 16		08 44	09 01		09 44	10 01		10 44		11 01		11 44	12 01		12 44	13 01	13 18			13 44	14 01	14 18	
d	00 17		08 45	09 02		09 45	10 02		10 45		11 02		11 45	12 02		12 45	13 02	13 19			13 45	14 02	14 19	
Padgate d																								
Birchwood d			08 50	09 06		09 50	10 06		10 50		11 06		11 50	12 06		12 50	13 06				13 50	14 06		
Glazebrook d																								
Irlam d				09 12			10 12				11 12			12 12			13 12					14 12		
Flixton d																								
Chassen Road d																								
Urmston d				09 17			10 17				11 17			12 17			13 17					14 17		
Humphrey Park d																								
Trafford Park d																								
Deansgate 84,85 ⛴ a				09 27			10 27				11 27			12 27			13 27					14 27		
Manchester Oxford Road 84,85 a		09 01	09 05	09 31	09 59	10 06	10 31	10 59	11 05		11 31	11 59	12 05	12 31	12 59	13 05	13 31	13 39	13 59		14 05	14 31	14 39	14 59
Manchester Piccadilly [10] 78,84,85 ⛴ a	00 39	09 05	09 09		10 03	10 09		11 03	11 09			12 03	12 09		13 02	13 09		13 41	14 02		14 09		14 41	15 02
Stockport 84 a																		13 53					14 53	
Sheffield [7] 78 ⛴ a																		14 39					15 37	
Manchester Airport 85 ✈ a		09 21			10 21			11 21				12 21			13 24				14 21					15 21

	TP	NT	EM	NT	TP		NT	EM	NT	TP	NT	EM	NT	TP	NT		EM	NT	TP	NT	EM	NT	TP	NT
	◇1		◇		◇1			◇		◇1		◇		◇1			◇		◇1		◇		◇1	
	D		E		C			E		D		G		C			E		C		G		H	
Liverpool Lime Street [10] 90,91 d	14 22	14 26	14 52	15 01	15 22		15 26	15 52	16 01	16 22	16 26	16 52	17 01	17 22	17 26		17 52	18 01	18 22	18 26	18 52	19 01	19 22	19 26
Edge Hill 90,91 d																								
Mossley Hill 91 d		14 34					15 34				16 34				17 34					18 34				19 34
West Allerton 91 d		14 36					15 36				16 36				17 36					18 36				19 36
Liverpool Central [10] 103 d																								
L'pool Sth Parkway [7] 91,103 ✈ d	14 32	14 39	15 03		15 32		15 39	16 03		16 32	16 39	17 03		17 32	17 39		18 03		18 32	18 39	19 03		19 32	19 39
Hunts Cross 103 d		14 43					15 43				16 43				17 43					18 43				19 43
Halewood d		14 46					15 46				16 46				17 46					18 46				19 46
Hough Green d		14 50					15 50				16 50				17 50					18 50				19 50
Widnes d		14 53	15 11				15 53	16 11			16 53	17 11			17 53		18 11			18 53	19 11			19 53
Sankey for Penketh d																								
Warrington Central a	14 44	15 01	15 18		15 44		16 01	16 18		16 44	17 01	17 18		17 44	18 01		18 18		18 44	19 01	19 18		19 44	20 01
d	14 45	15 02	15 19		15 45		16 02	16 19		16 45	17 02	17 19		17 45	18 02		18 19		18 45	19 02	19 19		19 45	20 02
Padgate d																								
Birchwood d	14 50	15 06			15 50		16 06			16 50	17 06			17 50	18 06				18 50	19 06			19 50	20 06
Glazebrook d																								
Irlam d		15 12					16 12				17 12				18 12					19 12				20 12
Flixton d																								
Chassen Road d																								
Urmston d		15 17					16 17				17 17				18 17					19 17				20 17
Humphrey Park d																								
Trafford Park d																								
Deansgate 84,85 ⛴ a		15 27					16 27				17 27				18 27					19 27				20 27
Manchester Oxford Road 84,85 a	15 05	15 31	15 39	15 59	16 05		16 31	16 38	16 59	17 05	17 31	17 38	17 59	18 05	18 31		18 39	18 59	19 05	19 31	19 39	19 59	20 05	20 31
Manchester Piccadilly [10] 78,84,85 ⛴ a	15 09		15 41	16 02	16 09			16 41	17 02	17 09		17 41	18 02	18 09			18 41	19 02	19 09		19 41	20 02	20 09	
Stockport 84 a			15 53					16 53				17 53					18 53				19 53			
Sheffield [7] 78 ⛴ a			16 36					17 36				18 37					19 34				20 34			
Manchester Airport 85 ✈ a				16 21					17 21				18 21					19 21				20 21		

A not 22 May
B To Hull
C To Scarborough
D To Middlesbrough
E To Norwich
F until 31 July. To Scarborough
G To Nottingham
H To York

Table 89

Sundays until 11 September

Liverpool - Warrington Central - Manchester and Manchester Airport

	EM ◇ A		NT	TP ◇[1] B	NT	NT	EM ◇ A	NT	TP ◇[1] C	NT	NT		NT
Liverpool Lime Street [10] 90,91 d	19 52		20 01	20 22	20 26	21 01	21 22	21 26	21 52	22 01	22 26		23 01
Edge Hill 90,91 d													
Mossley Hill 91 d					20 34			21 34			22 34		
West Allerton 91 d					20 36			21 36			22 36		
Liverpool Central [10] 103 d													
L'pool Sth Parkway [7] 91,103 ✈ d	20 03			20 32	20 39			21 39	22 02		22 39		
Hunts Cross 103 d					20 43			21 43			22 43		
Halewood d					20 46			21 46			22 46		
Hough Green d					20 50			21 50			22 50		
Widnes d	20 11				20 53		21 39	21 53			22 53		
Sankey for Penketh d													
Warrington Central a	20 18			20 44	21 01		21 47	22 01	22 14		23 01		
d	20 19			20 45	21 02		21 47	22 02	22 15		23 02		
Padgate d													
Birchwood d				20 50	21 06			22 06	22 20		23 06		
Glazebrook d													
Irlam d					21 12			22 12			23 12		
Flixton d													
Chassen Road d													
Urmston d					21 17			22 17			23 17		
Humphrey Park d													
Trafford Park d													
Deansgate 84,85 🚌 a					21 27			22 27			23 27		
Manchester Oxford Road 84,85 a	20 39		20 59	21 05	21 31	21 59	22 06	22 31	22 35	22 59	23 31		23 59
Manchester Piccadilly [10] 78,84,85 🚌 a	20 41		21 02	21 09		22 02	22 09		22 39	23 02			00 02
Stockport 84 a	20 53						22 20						
Sheffield [7] 78 🚌 a	21 36						23 25						
Manchester Airport 85 ✈ a			21 21			22 21				23 21			00 19

Sundays 18 September to 23 October

	NT	NT	NT	NT	NT	NT	NT	NT	NT		NT	NT	EM ◇ D	NT	NT	EM ◇ D	NT	NT	EM ◇ D		NT	NT	EM ◇ D	NT
Liverpool Lime Street [10] 90,91 d	23p38	08 22	08 26	09 01	09 26	10 01	10 26	11 01	11 26		12 01	12 26	12 52	13 01	13 26	13 52	14 01	14 26	14 52		15 01	15 26	15 52	16 01
Edge Hill 90,91 d	23p42																							
Mossley Hill 91 d	23p47		08 34		09 34		10 34		11 34			12 34			13 34			14 34				15 34		
West Allerton 91 d	23p49		08 36		09 36		10 36		11 36			12 36			13 36			14 36				15 36		
Liverpool Central [10] 103 d																								
L'pool Sth Parkway [7] 91,103 ✈ d	23p52		08 39		09 39		10 39		11 39			12 39	13 03		13 39	14 03		14 39	15 03			15 39	16 03	
Hunts Cross 103 d	23p56		08 43		09 43		10 43		11 43			12 43			13 43			14 43				15 43		
Halewood d	23p59		08 46		09 46		10 46		11 46			12 46			13 46			14 46				15 46		
Hough Green d	00 03		08 50		09 50		10 50		11 50			12 50			13 50			14 50				15 50		
Widnes d	00 06		08 53		09 53		10 53		11 53			12 53	13 11		13 53	14 11		14 53	15 11			15 53	16 11	
Sankey for Penketh d	00 11																							
Warrington Central a	00 16		09 01		10 01		11 01		12 01			13 01	13 18		14 01	14 18		15 01	15 18			16 01	16 18	
d	00 17		09 02		10 02		11 02		12 02			13 02	13 19		14 02	14 19		15 02	15 19			16 02	16 19	
Padgate d																								
Birchwood d			09 06		10 06		11 06		12 06			13 06			14 06			15 06				16 06		
Glazebrook d																								
Irlam d			09 12		10 12		11 12		12 12			13 12			14 12			15 12				16 12		
Flixton d																								
Chassen Road d																								
Urmston d			09 17		10 17		11 17		12 17			13 17			14 17			15 17				16 17		
Humphrey Park d																								
Trafford Park d																								
Deansgate 84,85 🚌 a			09 27		10 27		11 27		12 27			13 27			14 27			15 27				16 27		
Manchester Oxford Road 84,85 a		09 19	09 31	09 59	10 31	10 59	11 31	11 59	12 31		12 59	13 31	13 39	13 59	14 31	14 39	14 59	15 31	15 39		15 59	16 31	16 38	16 59
Manchester Piccadilly [10] 78,84,85 🚌 a	00 39			10 03		11 03		12 03			13 02		13 41	14 02		14 41	15 02		15 41		16 02		16 41	17 02
Stockport 84 a													13 53			14 53			15 53				16 53	
Sheffield [7] 78 🚌 a													14 39			15 37			16 36				17 36	
Manchester Airport 85 ✈ a				10 21		11 21		12 21			13 24			14 21			15 21				16 21			17 21

A To Nottingham
B To Newcastle
C To York
D To Norwich

Table 89

Sundays

18 September to 23 October

Liverpool - Warrington Central - Manchester and Manchester Airport

	NT	EM ◇ A	NT	NT	EM ◇ B		NT	NT	EM ◇ A	NT	NT	EM ◇ A	NT	NT	NT		EM ◇ A	NT	NT	NT	NT			
Liverpool Lime Street 10 90,91 d	16 26	16 52	17 01	17 26	17 52		18 01	18 26	18 52	19 01	19 26	19 52	20 01	20 26	21 01		21 22	21 26	22 01	22 26	23 01			
Edge Hill 90,91 d																								
Mossley Hill 91 d	16 34			17 34				18 34			19 34			20 34				21 34		22 34				
West Allerton 91 d	16 36			17 36				18 36			19 36			20 36				21 36		22 36				
Liverpool Central 10 103 d																								
L'pool Sth Parkway 7 91,103 ✈ d	16 39	17 03		17 39	18 03			18 39	19 03		19 39	20 03		20 39				21 39		22 39				
Hunts Cross 103 d	16 43			17 43				18 43			19 43			20 43				21 43		22 43				
Halewood d	16 46			17 46				18 46			19 46			20 46				21 46		22 46				
Hough Green d	16 50			17 50				18 50			19 50			20 50				21 50		22 50				
Widnes d	16 53	17 11		17 53	18 11			18 53	19 11		19 53	20 11		20 53			21 39	21 53		22 53				
Sankey for Penketh d																								
Warrington Central a	17 01	17 18		18 01	18 18			19 01	19 18		20 01	20 18		21 01			21 47	22 01		23 01				
d	17 02	17 19		18 02	18 19			19 02	19 19		20 02	20 19		21 02			21 47	22 02		23 02				
Padgate d																								
Birchwood d	17 06			18 06				19 06			20 06			21 06				22 06		23 06				
Glazebrook d																								
Irlam d	17 12			18 12				19 12			20 12			21 12				22 12		23 12				
Flixton d																								
Chassen Road d																								
Urmston d	17 17			18 17				19 17			20 17			21 17				22 17		23 17				
Humphrey Park d																								
Trafford Park d																								
Deansgate 84,85 ⛴ a	17 27			18 27				19 27			20 27			21 27				22 27		23 27				
Manchester Oxford Road 84,85 a	17 31	17 38	17 59	18 31	18 39		18 59	19 31	19 39	19 59	20 31	20 39	20 59	21 31	21 59		22 06	22 31	22 59	23 31	23 59			
Manchester Piccadilly 10 78,84,85 ⛴ a		17 41	18 02		18 41		19 02		19 41	20 02		20 41	21 02		22 02		22 09		23 02		00 02			
Stockport 84 a		17 53			18 53				19 53			20 53					22 20							
Sheffield 7 78 ⛴ a		18 37			19 34				20 34			21 36					23 25							
Manchester Airport 85 ✈ a			18 21				19 21			20 21			21 21		22 21				23 21		00 19			

Sundays

from 30 October

	NT	TP ◇1 C	NT	NT	TP ◇1 D	NT	NT	TP ◇1 E	NT		NT	TP ◇1 D	NT	NT	TP ◇1 E	NT	EM ◇ B	NT	NT		EM ◇ B	NT	TP ◇1 E	NT
Liverpool Lime Street 10 90,91 d	23p38	08 22	08 26	09 01	09 22	09 26	10 01	10 22	10 26		11 01	11 22	11 26	12 01	12 22	12 26	12 52	13 01	13 26		13 52	14 01	14 22	14 26
Edge Hill 90,91 d	23p42																							
Mossley Hill 91 d	23p47		08 34			09 34			10 34				11 34			12 34			13 34					14 34
West Allerton 91 d	23p49		08 36			09 36			10 36				11 36			12 36			13 36					14 36
Liverpool Central 10 103 d																								
L'pool Sth Parkway 7 91,103 ✈ d	23p52	08 32	08 39		09 32	09 39		10 32	10 39			11 32	11 39		12 32	12 39	13 03		13 39		14 03		14 32	14 39
Hunts Cross 103 d	23p56		08 43			09 43			10 43				11 43			12 43			13 43					14 43
Halewood d	23p59		08 46			09 46			10 46				11 46			12 46			13 46					14 46
Hough Green d	00 03		08 50			09 50			10 50				11 50			12 50			13 50					14 50
Widnes d	00 06		08 53			09 53			10 53				11 53			12 53	13 11		13 53		14 11			14 53
Sankey for Penketh d	00 11																							
Warrington Central a	00 16	08 44	09 01		09 44	10 01		10 44	11 01			11 44	12 01		12 44	13 01	13 18		14 01		14 18		14 44	15 01
d	00 17	08 45	09 02		09 45	10 02		10 45	11 02			11 45	12 02		12 45	13 02	13 19		14 02		14 19		14 45	15 02
Padgate d																								
Birchwood d		08 50	09 06		09 50	10 06		10 50	11 06			11 50	12 06		12 50	13 06			14 06				14 50	15 06
Glazebrook d																								
Irlam d			09 12			10 12			11 12				12 12			13 12			14 12					15 12
Flixton d																								
Chassen Road d																								
Urmston d			09 17			10 17			11 17				12 17			13 17			14 17					15 17
Humphrey Park d																								
Trafford Park d																								
Deansgate 84,85 ⛴ a			09 27			10 27			11 27				12 27			13 27			14 27					15 27
Manchester Oxford Road 84,85 a		09 05	09 31	09 59	10 05	10 31	10 59	11 05	11 31		11 59	12 05	12 31	12 59	13 05	13 31	13 39	13 59	14 31		14 39	14 59	15 05	15 31
Manchester Piccadilly 10 78,84,85 ⛴ a	00 39	09 09		10 03	10 09		11 03	11 09			12 03	12 09		13 02	13 09		13 41	14 02			14 41	15 02	15 09	
Stockport 84 a																	13 53				14 53			
Sheffield 7 78 ⛴ a																	14 39				15 37			
Manchester Airport 85 ✈ a				10 21			11 21				12 21			13 24				14 21				15 21		

A To Nottingham
B To Norwich
C To Hull
D To Scarborough
E To Middlesbrough

Table 89

Sundays
from 30 October

Liverpool - Warrington Central - Manchester and Manchester Airport

	EM	NT	TP	NT	EM	NT	TP	NT	EM	NT	TP	NT	EM	NT	TP	NT	EM	NT	TP	NT	EM	NT
	◇		◇[1]		◇		◇[1]		◇		◇[1]		◇		◇[1]		◇		◇[1]		◇	
	A		B		A		C		D		B		A		B		D		E		D	
Liverpool Lime Street [10] 90,91 d	14 52	15 01	15 22	15 26	15 52	16 01	16 22	16 26	16 52	17 01	17 22	17 26	17 52	18 01	18 22	18 26	18 52	19 01	19 22	19 26	19 52	20 01
Edge Hill 90,91 d																						
Mossley Hill 91 d				15 34				16 34				17 34				18 34				19 34		
West Allerton 91 d				15 36				16 36				17 36				18 36				19 36		
Liverpool Central [10] 103 d																						
L'pool Sth Parkway [7] 91,103 ✈ d	15 03		15 32	15 39	16 03		16 32	16 39	17 03		17 32	17 39	18 03		18 32	18 39	19 03		19 32	19 39	20 03	
Hunts Cross 103 d				15 43				16 43				17 43				18 43				19 43		
Halewood d				15 46				16 46				17 46				18 46				19 46		
Hough Green d				15 50				16 50				17 50				18 50				19 50		
Widnes d	15 11			15 53	16 11			16 53	17 11			17 53	18 11			18 53	19 11			19 53	20 11	
Sankey for Penketh d																						
Warrington Central a	15 18		15 44	16 01	16 18		16 44	17 01	17 18		17 44	18 01	18 18		18 44	19 01	19 18		19 44	20 01	20 18	
d	15 19		15 45	16 02	16 19		16 45	17 02	17 19		17 45	18 02	18 19		18 45	19 02	19 19		19 45	20 02	20 19	
Padgate d																						
Birchwood d			15 50	16 06			16 50	17 06			17 50	18 06			18 50	19 06			19 50	20 06		
Glazebrook d																						
Irlam d				16 12				17 12				18 12				19 12				20 12		
Flixton d																						
Chassen Road d																						
Urmston d				16 17				17 17				18 17				19 17				20 17		
Humphrey Park d																						
Trafford Park d																						
Deansgate 84,85 ⛴ a				16 27				17 27				18 27				19 27				20 27		
Manchester Oxford Road 84,85 a	15 39	15 59	16 05	16 31	16 38	16 59	17 05	17 31	17 38	17 59	18 05	18 31	18 39	18 59	19 05	19 31	19 39	19 59	20 05	20 31	20 39	20 59
Manchester Piccadilly [10] 78,84,85 ⛴ a	15 41	16 02	16 09		16 41	17 02	17 09		17 41	18 02	18 09		18 41	19 02	19 09		19 41	20 02	20 09		20 41	21 02
Stockport 84 a	15 53				16 53				17 53				18 53				19 53				20 53	
Sheffield [7] 78 ⛴ a	16 36				17 36				18 37				19 34				20 34				21 36	
Manchester Airport 85 ✈ a		16 21				17 21				18 21				19 21				20 21				21 21

	TP	NT	NT	EM	NT	TP	NT	NT	NT
	◇[1]			◇		◇[1]			
	F			D		E			
Liverpool Lime Street [10] 90,91 d	20 22	20 26	21 01	21 22	21 26	21 52	22 01	22 26	23 01
Edge Hill 90,91 d									
Mossley Hill 91 d		20 34			21 34			22 34	
West Allerton 91 d		20 36			21 36			22 36	
Liverpool Central [10] 103 d									
L'pool Sth Parkway [7] 91,103 ✈ d	20 32	20 39			21 39	22 02		22 39	
Hunts Cross 103 d		20 43			21 43			22 43	
Halewood d		20 46			21 46			22 46	
Hough Green d		20 50			21 50			22 50	
Widnes d		20 53		21 39	21 53			22 53	
Sankey for Penketh d									
Warrington Central a	20 44	21 01		21 47	22 01	22 14		23 01	
d	20 45	21 02		21 47	22 02	22 15		23 02	
Padgate d									
Birchwood d	20 50	21 06			22 06	22 20		23 06	
Glazebrook d									
Irlam d		21 12			22 12			23 12	
Flixton d									
Chassen Road d									
Urmston d		21 17			22 17			23 17	
Humphrey Park d									
Trafford Park d									
Deansgate 84,85 ⛴ a		21 27			22 27			23 27	
Manchester Oxford Road 84,85 a	21 05	21 31	21 59	22 06	22 31	22 35	22 59	23 31	23 59
Manchester Piccadilly [10] 78,84,85 ⛴ a	21 09		22 02	22 09		22 39	23 02		00 02
Stockport 84 a				22 20					
Sheffield [7] 78 ⛴ a				23 25					
Manchester Airport 85 ✈ a			22 21				23 21		00 19

A To Norwich
B To Scarborough
C To Middlesbrough
D To Nottingham
E To York
F To Newcastle

Manchester Airport and Manchester - Warrington Central - Liverpool

Miles		NT MX	NT	LM 1 A	NT	LM 1 A	NT	LM 1 A	LM ◇1 B	NT		NT	NT	TP ◇1	NT	LM ◇1 B	EM ◇ C	LM 1 B	NT	NT		TP ◇1 D 🍴	LM ◇1 E	NT
0	**Manchester Airport** 85 ✈ d		04 34										06 41							07 38				
—	Sheffield 7 78 🚌 d																06 20							
—	Stockport 84 d																07 22							
9¾	**Manchester Piccadilly** 10 78,84,85 🚌 d		04 49										06 58	07 07			07 34			07 59		08 07		
10¼	**Manchester Oxford Road** 84,85 d	23p27								06 27		06 46	07 01	07 12			07 37		07 39	08 03		08 12		08 15
10¾	Deansgate 84,85 🚌 d	23p29								06 29									07 41					08 17
13¾	Trafford Park d	23p34								06 34									07 46					
14½	Humphrey Park d	23p36								06 36														
15¾	Urmston d	23p38								06 38		06 53							07 49					08 24
16¼	Chassen Road d	23p40								06 40														08 26
16¾	Flixton d	23p43								06 43									07 52					08 28
19	Irlam d	23p47								06 47		06 58							07 56					08 32
20¼	Glazebrook d	23p50								06 50									07 59					08 35
23	Birchwood d	23p54								06 54		07 04		07 25					08 04			08 25		08 40
24½	Padgate d	23p57								06 57									08 07					
26¼	**Warrington Central** a	00 01								07 01		07 12		07 30			07 53		08 10			08 30		08 45
—	d	00 02			06 03		06 37			07 01				07 30	07 35		07 53		08 11			08 30		08 45
28¾	Sankey for Penketh d	00 05			06 07		06 41			07 05					07 39				08 15					
32½	Widnes d	00 11			06 12		06 46			07 11					07 44		08 01		08 20					08 53
34¼	Hough Green d	00 13			06 15		06 49			07 14					07 47		08 05		08 24					08 56
36½	Halewood d	00 18			06 20		06 54			07 18					07 52				08 28					
37½	Hunts Cross 89 d	00 21			06 23		06 57			07 22					07 55		08s10		08 32					
39¼	L'pool Sth Parkway 7 91,103 ✈ d	00 27		06 10	06 27	06 37	07 01	07 08	07 32	07 27					07 59	08 10	08 18	08 32	08 37			08 47	08 59	09 06
—	Liverpool Central 10 103 a																							
40¼	West Allerton 91 a				06 31		07 05			07 30					08 03				08 40					09 09
41	Mossley Hill 91 a				06 33		07 07			07 33					08 06				08 43					09 12
43	Edge Hill 90,91 a				06 39		07 13			07 40					08 11				08 48					
44¾	**Liverpool Lime Street** 10 90,91 a	00 41	05 32	06 22	06 45	06 49	07 19	07 22	07 43	07 48			07 49	07 56	08 18	08 21	08 31	08 44	08 55	08 59		08 58	09 10	09 24

	EM ◇ C	LM ◇1 F	NT	NT	TP ◇1 G 🍴	LM 1 B		NT	EM ◇ C	LM 1 B	NT	NT	NT H	TP ◇1 I 🍴	LM 1 B	NT		EM ◇ J	LM 1 B	NT	NT	NT H	TP ◇1 I 🍴	LM 1 B
Manchester Airport 85 ✈ d				08 41								09 41									10 41			
Sheffield 7 78 🚌 d	07 35								08 42									09 42						
Stockport 84 d	08 24								09 25									10 26						
Manchester Piccadilly 10 78,84,85 🚌 d	08 37			09 01	09 07				09 37			10 01		10 07				10 37			11 01		11 07	
Manchester Oxford Road 84,85 d	08 41		08 44	09 04	09 12			09 15	09 41		09 44	10 04		10 12		10 16		10 41		10 44	11 04		11 12	
Deansgate 84,85 🚌 d			08 46					09 17			09 46					10 18				10 46				
Trafford Park d								09 22																
Humphrey Park d								09 24																
Urmston d			08 52					09 27			09 52					10 24				10 52				
Chassen Road d																10 26								
Flixton d								09 30								10 29								
Irlam d			08 57					09 34			09 57					10 33				10 57				
Glazebrook d																10 36								
Birchwood d			09 03		09 25			09 40			10 03			10 25		10 40				11 03			11 25	
Padgate d			09 06								10 06									11 06				
Warrington Central a	08 57		09 09		09 30			09 45	09 57		10 09			10 30		10 45		10 57		11 09			11 30	
d	08 57		09 10		09 30			09 45	09 57		10 10			10 30		10 46		10 57		11 10			11 30	
Sankey for Penketh d			09 14								10 14									11 14				
Widnes d	09 05		09 19					09 53	10 05		10 19					10 54		11 05		11 19				
Hough Green d			09 23					09 56			10 23					10 57				11 23				
Halewood d			09 27								10 27									11 27				
Hunts Cross 89 d			09 30								10 30									11 30				
L'pool Sth Parkway 7 91,103 ✈ d	09 15	09 31	09 36		09 47	09 59		10 06	10 15	10 32	10 36		10 36	10 47	10 59	11 06		11 15	11 31	11 36		11 36	11 47	11 59
Liverpool Central 10 103 a																								
West Allerton 91 a			09 39					10 10			10 39					11 10				11 39				
Mossley Hill 91 a			09 41					10 12			10 41					11 13				11 41				
Edge Hill 90,91 a			09 47								10 47									11 47				
Liverpool Lime Street 10 90,91 a	09 31	09 43	09 53	09 48	09 58	10 10		10 24	10 31	10 44	10 53	10 48	10 49	10 58	11 10	11 24		11 31	11 43	11 53	11 48	11 49	11 58	12 10

A From Crewe
B From Birmingham New Street
C From Nottingham
D From Hull
E From Birmingham International
F From Walsall
G From Newcastle
H To Blackpool North
I From Scarborough
J From Norwich

Manchester Airport and Manchester - Warrington Central - Liverpool

	NT	EM		LM	NT	NT	NT	TP	LM	NT	EM	LM		NT	NT	NT	TP	LM	NT	EM	LM	NT		NT
		◇		1				◇1	1		◇	1					◇1	1		◇	1			
		A		B			C	D	B		A	B				C	D	B		A	B			
								⊥									⊥							
Manchester Airport 85 d						11 41									12 41									13 41
Sheffield 7 78 d		10 42									11 42									12 42				
Stockport 84 d		11 26									12 26									13 26				
Manchester Piccadilly 10 78,84,85 d		11 37				12 01		12 07			12 37				13 01		13 07			13 37				14 01
Manchester Oxford Road 84,85 d	11 16	11 41			11 44	12 04		12 12		12 16	12 41			12 44	13 04		13 12		13 16	13 41		13 44		14 04
Deansgate 84,85 d	11 18				11 46					12 18				12 46					13 18			13 46		
Trafford Park d	11 23																		13 23					
Humphrey Park d	11 25																		13 25					
Urmston d	11 27				11 52					12 24				12 52					13 27			13 52		
Chassen Road d										12 26														
Flixton d	11 30									12 29									13 30					
Irlam d	11 34				11 57					12 33				12 57					13 34			13 57		
Glazebrook d										12 36														
Birchwood d	11 40				12 03			12 25		12 40				13 03			13 25		13 40			14 03		
Padgate d					12 06									13 06								14 06		
Warrington Central a	11 45	11 57			12 09			12 30		12 45	12 57			13 09			13 30		13 45	13 57		14 09		
d	11 46	11 57			12 10			12 30		12 46	12 57			13 10			13 30		13 46	13 57		14 10		
Sankey for Penketh d					12 14									13 14								14 14		
Widnes d	11 54	12 05			12 19					12 54	13 05			13 19					13 54	14 05		14 19		
Hough Green d	11 57				12 23					12 57				13 23					13 57			14 23		
Halewood d					12 27									13 27								14 27		
Hunts Cross 89 d					12 30									13 30								14 30		
L'pool Sth Parkway 7 91,103 d	12 06	12 15		12 32	12 36		12 36	12 47	12 59	13 06	13 15	13 31		13 36		13 36	13 47	13 59	14 06	14 15	14 31	14 36		
Liverpool Central 10 103 a																								
West Allerton 91 a	12 10				12 39					13 10				13 39					14 10			14 39		
Mossley Hill 91 a	12 13				12 41					13 13				13 41					14 13			14 41		
Edge Hill 90,91 a					12 47									13 47								14 47		
Liverpool Lime Street 10 90,91 a	12 24	12 31		12 44	12 53	12 48	12 49	12 58	13 10	13 24	13 31	13 43		13 53	13 48	13 49	13 58	14 10	14 24	14 31	14 43	14 53		14 48

	NT	TP	LM	NT	EM	LM	NT	NT		NT	TP	LM	NT	EM	LM	NT	NT	NT		TP	LM	NT	EM	LM
		◇1	1		◇	1					◇1	1		◇	1					◇1	1		◇	1
	C	D	B		A	B				C	D	B		A	B			C		D	B		A	B
		⊥									⊥									⊥				
Manchester Airport 85 d								14 41									15 41							
Sheffield 7 78 d					13 42									14 42									15 42	
Stockport 84 d					14 26									15 26									16 26	
Manchester Piccadilly 10 78,84,85 d		14 07			14 37			15 01			15 07			15 37			16 01			16 07			16 37	
Manchester Oxford Road 84,85 d		14 12		14 16	14 41		14 44	15 04			15 12		15 16	15 41		15 44	16 04			16 12		16 16	16 41	
Deansgate 84,85 d				14 18			14 46						15 18			15 46						16 18		
Trafford Park d													15 23											
Humphrey Park d													15 25											
Urmston d				14 24			14 52						15 27			15 52						16 24		
Chassen Road d				14 26																		16 26		
Flixton d				14 29									15 30									16 29		
Irlam d				14 33			14 57						15 34			15 57						16 33		
Glazebrook d				14 36																		16 36		
Birchwood d		14 25		14 40			15 03				15 25		15 40			16 03				16 25		16 40		
Padgate d							15 06									16 06						16 43		
Warrington Central a		14 30		14 45	14 57		15 09				15 30		15 45	15 57		16 09				16 30		16 47	16 57	
d		14 30		14 46	14 57		15 10				15 30		15 45	15 57		16 10				16 30		16 47	16 57	
Sankey for Penketh d							15 14									16 14								
Widnes d				14 54	15 05		15 19						15 53	16 05		16 19						16 55	17 05	
Hough Green d				14 57			15 23						15 56			16 23						16 58		
Halewood d							15 27						16 01			16 27								
Hunts Cross 89 d							15 30									16 30								
L'pool Sth Parkway 7 91,103 d	14 36	14 47	14 59	15 06	15 15	15 31	15 36			15 36	15 47	15 59	16 07	16 15	16 31	16 36		16 36		16 47	16 59	17 07	17 15	17 31
Liverpool Central 10 103 a																								
West Allerton 91 a				15 10			15 39						16 11			16 39						17 11		
Mossley Hill 91 a				15 13			15 41						16 13			16 42						17 13		
Edge Hill 90,91 a							15 47									16 47								
Liverpool Lime Street 10 90,91 a	14 49	14 58	15 10	15 24	15 31	15 43	15 53	15 48		15 49	15 58	16 10	16 25	16 31	16 45	16 54	16 48	16 49		16 58	17 10	17 25	17 31	17 43

A From Norwich
B From Birmingham New Street
C To Blackpool North
D From Scarborough

Manchester Airport and Manchester - Warrington Central - Liverpool

		NT	NT	TP ◇1 A 🍴	LM 1 B		NT	EM ◇ C	LM 1 B	NT	NT	TP ◇1 A 🍴	LM ◇1 B	NT	EM ◇ C		NT	LM 1 B	NT	TP ◇1 A 🍴	LM 1 B	NT FO	NT FX	EM ◇ C	NT
Manchester Airport 85 ✈	d		16 41								17 41								18 41						
Sheffield 7 78 🚌	d							16 42							17 40									18 43	
Stockport 84	d							17 26							18 26									19 26	
Manchester Piccadilly 10 78,84,85 🚌	d		17 01	17 07				17 37			18 01	18 07			18 37				19 01	19 07				19 37	
Manchester Oxford Road 84,85	d	16 43	17 04	17 11			17 13	17 42		17 44	18 04	18 12		18 16	18 41		18 44		19 04	19 12				19 41	19 44
Deansgate 84,85 🚌	d	16 45					17 15			17 46				18 18			18 46								19 46
Trafford Park	d	16 51					17 20			17 51				18 23			18 51								19 51
Humphrey Park	d						17 22			17 53				18 25			18 53								19 53
Urmston	d	16 54					17 25			17 55				18 27			18 55								19 55
Chassen Road	d						17 27			17 57				18 29			18 57								19 57
Flixton	d	16 57					17 29			18 00				18 32			19 00								20 00
Irlam	d	17 01					17 33	17 52		18 04				18 36			19 04								20 04
Glazebrook	d						17 36			18 07							19 07								20 07
Birchwood	d	17 07		17 25			17 41	17 58		18 11		18 25		18 41			19 11			19 25					20 11
Padgate	d	17 10					17 44			18 14							19 14								20 14
Warrington Central	a	17 13		17 30			17 48	18 03		18 18		18 30		18 46	18 57		19 20			19 30				19 57	20 18
	d	17 14		17 30			17 48	18 03		18 18		18 30		18 47	18 57					19 30		19 49	19 49	19 57	20 18
Sankey for Penketh	d	17 18					17 52							18 51								19 53	19 53		
Widnes	d	17 23					17 58	18 11						18 56	19 05							19 58	19 58	20 05	
Hough Green	d	17 27					18 01			18 28				18 59								20 01	20 02		20 28
Halewood	d	17 31					18 06							19 04								20 06	20 06		
Hunts Cross 89	d	17 34					18 09			18 33				19 07	19 12							20 09	20 09		20 33
L'pool Sth Parkway 7 91,103 ✈	d	17 39		17 47	17 59		18 14	18 22	18 33	18 38		18 47	19 06	19 13	19 18			19 32		19 47	20 06	20 12	20 13	20 16	20 38
Liverpool Central 10 103	a																								
West Allerton 91	a	17 42					18 18			18 41				19 16								20 16	20 16		20 41
Mossley Hill 91	a	17 45					18 20			18 44				19 18								20 18	20 18		20 44
Edge Hill 90,91	a	17 50					18 30			18 49				19 26								20 24	20 24		
Liverpool Lime Street 10 90,91	a	17 58	17 48	18 00	18 10		18 38	18 35	18 44	18 57	19 00	18 59	19 17	19 35	19 35			19 44	19 48	19 59	20 18	20 30	20 30	20 35	20 56

			NT	TP ◇1 A	LM 1 B	NT	EM ◇ C	NT	TP ◇1 A	NT	LM 1 B		NT	NT	TP ◇1 A	LM 1 D	LM 1 E	NT	NT
Manchester Airport 85 ✈	d		19 41											21 41					
Sheffield 7 78 🚌	d						19 42												
Stockport 84	d						20 26												
Manchester Piccadilly 10 78,84,85 🚌	d		20 01	20 07			20 37		21 07	21 38				22 01	22 07				
Manchester Oxford Road 84,85	d		20 04	20 12			20 41	20 44	21 12	21 44				22 04	22 12				23 27
Deansgate 84,85 🚌	d							20 46		21 46									23 29
Trafford Park	d							20 51		21 51									23 34
Humphrey Park	d							20 53		21 53									23 36
Urmston	d							20 55		21 55									23 38
Chassen Road	d							20 57		21 57									23 40
Flixton	d							21 00		22 00									23 43
Irlam	d							21 04		22 04									23 47
Glazebrook	d							21 07		22 07									23 50
Birchwood	d			20 25				21 11	21 25	22 11					22 25				23 54
Padgate	d							21 14		22 14									23 57
Warrington Central	a			20 30			20 57	21 20	21 30	22 20					22 30				00 01
	d			20 30		20 49	20 57		21 30				21 49		22 30			22 58	00 02
Sankey for Penketh	d					20 53							21 53					23 02	00 05
Widnes	d					20 58	21 05						21 58					23 07	00 11
Hough Green	d					21 01							22 01					23 10	00 13
Halewood	d					21 06							22 06					23 15	00 18
Hunts Cross 89	d					21 09							22 09					23 18	00 21
L'pool Sth Parkway 7 91,103 ✈	d			20 47	21 05	21 12	21 20		21 47		22 05		22 12		22 47	23 08	23 12	23 22	00 27
Liverpool Central 10 103	a																		
West Allerton 91	a					21 15							22 15					23 25	
Mossley Hill 91	a					21 18							22 18					23 27	
Edge Hill 90,91	a					21 23							22 23					23 32	
Liverpool Lime Street 10 90,91	a		20 48	20 59	21 16	21 30	21 35		21 58		22 15		22 30	22 48	23 00	23 23	23 26	23 39	00 41

A From Scarborough
B From Birmingham New Street
C From Norwich
D until 17 June, from 12 September. From Birmingham New Street
E from 20 June until 9 September. From Birmingham New Street

Table 89

Saturdays

Manchester Airport and Manchester - Warrington Central - Liverpool

	NT	NT	LM	NT	LM	NT	LM	NT	LM		NT	TP	NT	LM	EM	LM	NT	NT	TP		LM	NT	EM	LM
			1		1		◇1		◇1			◇1		◇1	◇	◇1			◇1		◇1		◇	◇1
			A		A		A		B					B	C	B			D		B		C	B
Manchester Airport 85 ✈ d		04 34									06 41							07 38						
Sheffield 7 78 🚌 d															06 20								07 35	
Stockport 84 d															07 22								08 24	
Manchester Piccadilly 10 78,84,85 🚌 d		04 49									06 58	07 07			07 34			07 59	08 07				08 37	
Manchester Oxford Road 84,85 d	23p27							06 22			07 01	07 12			07 37		07 39	08 03	08 12			08 15	08 41	
Deansgate 84,85 🚌 d	23p29							06 24									07 41					08 17		
Trafford Park d	23p34							06 29									07 46							
Humphrey Park d	23p36							06 31																
Urmston d	23p38							06 33									07 49					08 24		
Chassen Road d	23p40							06 35														08 26		
Flixton d	23p43							06 38									07 52					08 28		
Irlam d	23p47							06 42									07 56					08 32		
Glazebrook d	23p50							06 45									07 59					08 35		
Birchwood d	23p54							06 49				07 25					08 04		08 25			08 40		
Padgate d	23p57							06 52									08 07							
Warrington Central a	00 01							06 56				07 30			07 53		08 10		08 30			08 45	08 57	
d	00 02			06 03		06 37		06 56				07 30	07 40		07 53		08 11		08 30			08 45	08 57	
Sankey for Penketh d	00 05			06 07		06 41		07 00					07 44				08 15							
Widnes d	00 11			06 12		06 46		07 06					07 49		08 01		08 20					08 53	09 05	
Hough Green d	00 13			06 15		06 49		07 09					07 52		08 05		08 24					08 56		
Halewood d	00 18			06 20		06 54		07 13					07 57				08 28							
Hunts Cross 89 d	00 21			06 23		06 57		07 17					08 00		08s10		08 32							
L'pool Sth Parkway 7 91,103 ✈ d	00 27		06 15	06 27	06 39	07 01	07 08	07 22	07 30				08 03	08 12	08 18	08 34	08 37		08 47		08 59	09 06	09 15	09 31
Liverpool Central 10 103 a																								
West Allerton 91 a				06 31		07 05		07 25					08 06				08 40					09 09		
Mossley Hill 91 a				06 33		07 07		07 28					08 09				08 43					09 12		
Edge Hill 90,91 a				06 39		07 13		07 34					08 14				08 48							
Liverpool Lime Street 10 90,91 a	00 41	05 32	06 26	06 45	06 53	07 20	07 22	07 40	07 42		07 49	07 56	08 21	08 24	08 31	08 46	08 55	08 59	08 58		09 12	09 24	09 31	09 43

	NT	NT	TP	LM	NT		EM	LM	NT	NT	NT	TP	LM	NT	EM		LM	NT	NT	NT	TP	LM	NT	EM
			◇1	◇1			◇	◇1				◇1	◇1		◇		◇1				◇1	◇1		◇
			E	B			C	B			F	G	B		H		B			F	G	B		H
Manchester Airport 85 ✈ d		08 41								09 41									10 41					
Sheffield 7 78 🚌 d							08 42								09 42									10 42
Stockport 84 d							09 25								10 26									11 26
Manchester Piccadilly 10 78,84,85 🚌 d		09 01	09 07				09 37			10 01		10 07			10 37				11 01		11 07			11 37
Manchester Oxford Road 84,85 d	08 44	09 04	09 12		09 16		09 41		09 44	10 04		10 12		10 16	10 41			10 44	11 04		11 12		11 16	11 41
Deansgate 84,85 🚌 d	08 46				09 18				09 46					10 18				10 46					11 18	
Trafford Park d					09 23																		11 23	
Humphrey Park d					09 25																		11 25	
Urmston d	08 52				09 27				09 52					10 24				10 52					11 27	
Chassen Road d														10 26										
Flixton d					09 30									10 29									11 30	
Irlam d	08 57				09 34				09 57					10 33				10 57					11 34	
Glazebrook d														10 36										
Birchwood d	09 03		09 25		09 40				10 03			10 25		10 40				11 03			11 25		11 40	
Padgate d	09 06								10 06									11 06						
Warrington Central a	09 09		09 30		09 45		09 57		10 09			10 30		10 45	10 57			11 09			11 30		11 45	11 57
d	09 10		09 30		09 46		09 57		10 10			10 30		10 46	10 57			11 10			11 30		11 46	11 57
Sankey for Penketh d	09 14								10 14									11 14						
Widnes d	09 19				09 54		10 05		10 19					10 54	11 05			11 19					11 54	12 05
Hough Green d	09 23				09 57				10 23					10 57				11 23					11 57	
Halewood d	09 27								10 27									11 27						
Hunts Cross 89 d	09 30								10 30									11 30						
L'pool Sth Parkway 7 91,103 ✈ d	09 36		09 47	09 59	10 06		10 15	10 32	10 36		10 36	10 47	10 59	11 06	11 15		11 31	11 36		11 36	11 47	11 59	12 06	12 15
Liverpool Central 10 103 a																								
West Allerton 91 a	09 39				10 10				10 39					11 10				11 39					12 10	
Mossley Hill 91 a	09 41				10 12				10 41					11 13				11 41					12 13	
Edge Hill 90,91 a	09 47								10 47									11 47						
Liverpool Lime Street 10 90,91 a	09 53	09 48	09 58	10 10	10 23		10 31	10 44	10 53	10 48	10 49	10 58	11 10	11 24	11 31		11 43	11 53	11 48	11 49	11 58	12 10	12 24	12 31

A From Crewe
B From Birmingham New Street
C From Nottingham
D From Hull
E From Newcastle
F To Blackpool North
G From Scarborough
H From Norwich

Table 89

Saturdays

Manchester Airport and Manchester - Warrington Central - Liverpool

	LM ◇1 A		NT	NT	NT B	TP ◇1 C ⚲	LM ◇1 A	NT	EM ◇ D	LM ◇1 A	NT		NT	NT B	TP ◇1 C ⚲	LM ◇1 A	NT	EM ◇ D	LM ◇1 A	NT	NT		NT B	TP ◇1 C
Manchester Airport 85 ✈ d				11 41									12 41								13 41			
Sheffield 7 78 🚌 d									11 42									12 42						
Stockport 84 d									12 26									13 26						
Manchester Piccadilly 10 78,84,85 🚌 d				12 01		12 07			12 37				13 01		13 07			13 37			14 01			14 07
Manchester Oxford Road 84,85 d			11 44	12 04		12 12		12 16	12 41		12 44		13 04		13 12		13 16	13 41		13 44	14 04			14 12
Deansgate 84,85 🚌 d			11 46					12 18			12 46						13 18			13 46				
Trafford Park d																	13 23							
Humphrey Park d																	13 25							
Urmston d			11 52					12 24			12 52						13 27			13 52				
Chassen Road d								12 26																
Flixton d								12 29									13 30							
Irlam d			11 57					12 33			12 57						13 34			13 57				
Glazebrook d								12 36																
Birchwood d			12 03			12 25		12 40			13 03				13 25		13 40			14 03				14 25
Padgate d			12 06								13 06									14 06				
Warrington Central a			12 09			12 30		12 45	12 57		13 09				13 30		13 45	13 57		14 09				14 30
d			12 10			12 30		12 46	12 57		13 10				13 30		13 46	13 57		14 10				14 30
Sankey for Penketh d			12 14								13 14									14 14				
Widnes d			12 19					12 54	13 05		13 19						13 54	14 05		14 19				
Hough Green d			12 23					12 57			13 23						13 57			14 23				
Halewood d			12 27								13 27									14 27				
Hunts Cross 89 d			12 30								13 30									14 30				
L'pool Sth Parkway 7 91,103 ✈ d	12 32		12 36		12 36	12 47	12 59	13 06	13 15	13 31	13 36			13 36	13 47	13 59	14 06	14 15	14 31	14 36			14 36	14 47
Liverpool Central 10 103 a																								
West Allerton 91 a			12 39					13 10			13 39						14 10			14 39				
Mossley Hill 91 a			12 41					13 13			13 41						14 13			14 41				
Edge Hill 90,91 a			12 47								13 47									14 47				
Liverpool Lime Street 10 90,91 a	12 44		12 53	12 48	12 49	12 58	13 10	13 24	13 31	13 43	13 53		13 48	13 49	13 58	14 10	14 24	14 31	14 43	14 53	14 48		14 49	14 58

	LM ◇1 A	NT	EM ◇ D	LM ◇1 A	NT	NT	NT B		TP ◇1 C ⚲	LM ◇1 A	NT	EM ◇ D	LM ◇1 A	NT	NT	NT B	TP ◇1 C ⚲		LM ◇1 A	NT	EM ◇ D	LM ◇1 A	NT	NT
Manchester Airport 85 ✈ d						14 41									15 41									16 41
Sheffield 7 78 🚌 d			13 42									14 42									15 42			
Stockport 84 d			14 26									15 26									16 26			
Manchester Piccadilly 10 78,84,85 🚌 d			14 37			15 01			15 07			15 37			16 01		16 07				16 37			17 01
Manchester Oxford Road 84,85 d		14 16	14 41		14 44	15 04			15 12		15 16	15 41		15 44	16 04		16 12			16 16	16 41		16 43	17 04
Deansgate 84,85 🚌 d		14 18			14 46						15 18			15 46						16 18			16 45	
Trafford Park d											15 23												16 51	
Humphrey Park d											15 25													
Urmston d		14 24			14 52						15 27			15 52						16 24			16 54	
Chassen Road d		14 26																		16 26				
Flixton d		14 29									15 30									16 29			16 57	
Irlam d		14 33			14 57						15 34			15 57						16 33			17 01	
Glazebrook d		14 36																		16 36				
Birchwood d		14 40			15 03				15 25		15 40			16 03			16 25			16 40			17 07	
Padgate d					15 06									16 06						16 43			17 10	
Warrington Central a		14 45	14 57		15 09				15 30		15 45	15 57		16 09			16 30			16 47	16 57		17 13	
d		14 46	14 57		15 10				15 30		15 45	15 57		16 10			16 30			16 47	16 57		17 14	
Sankey for Penketh d					15 14									16 14									17 18	
Widnes d		14 54	15 05		15 19						15 53	16 05		16 19						16 55	17 05		17 23	
Hough Green d		14 57			15 23						15 56			16 23						16 58			17 27	
Halewood d					15 27						16 01			16 27									17 31	
Hunts Cross 89 d					15 30									16 30									17 34	
L'pool Sth Parkway 7 91,103 ✈ d	14 59	15 06	15 15	15 31	15 36		15 36		15 47	15 59	16 07	16 15	16 33	16 36		16 36	16 47		16 59	17 07	17 15	17 31	17 39	
Liverpool Central 10 103 a																								
West Allerton 91 a		15 10			15 39						16 11			16 39						17 11			17 42	
Mossley Hill 91 a		15 13			15 41						16 13			16 41						17 13			17 45	
Edge Hill 90,91 a					15 47									16 47									17 50	
Liverpool Lime Street 10 90,91 a	15 10	15 24	15 31	15 43	15 53	15 48	15 49		15 58	16 10	16 25	16 31	16 44	16 54	16 48	16 49	16 58		17 10	17 25	17 31	17 43	17 58	17 48

A From Birmingham New Street
B To Blackpool North
C From Scarborough
D From Norwich

Table 89

Saturdays

Manchester Airport and Manchester - Warrington Central - Liverpool

		TP	LM	NT		EM	LM	NT	NT	TP	LM	NT	EM	NT		LM	NT	TP	NT	EM	LM	NT	NT	TP
		◇1	◇1			◇	◇1			◇1	◇1		◇			◇1		◇1		◇	◇1			◇1
		A	B			C	B			A	B		C			B		A		C	B			A
		🚲								🚲														
Manchester Airport 85 ✈	d								17 41								18 41						19 41	
Sheffield 7 78 🚌	d					16 42							17 40							18 42				
Stockport 84	d					17 26							18 26							19 26				
Manchester Piccadilly 10 78,84,85 🚌	d	17 07				17 37			18 01	18 07			18 37				19 01	19 07		19 37			20 01	20 07
Manchester Oxford Road 84,85	d	17 11		17 13		17 42		17 44	18 04	18 12		18 16	18 41	18 44			19 04	19 12		19 41		19 44	20 04	20 12
Deansgate 84,85 🚌	d			17 15				17 46				18 18		18 46								19 46		
Trafford Park	d			17 20				17 51				18 23		18 51								19 51		
Humphrey Park	d			17 22				17 53				18 25		18 53								19 53		
Urmston	d			17 25				17 55				18 27		18 55								19 55		
Chassen Road	d			17 27				17 57				18 29		18 57								19 57		
Flixton	d			17 29				18 00				18 32		19 00								20 00		
Irlam	d			17 33		17 52		18 04				18 36		19 04								20 04		
Glazebrook	d			17 36				18 07						19 07								20 07		
Birchwood	d	17 25		17 41		17 58		18 11		18 25		18 41		19 11				19 25				20 11		20 25
Padgate	d			17 44				18 14						19 14								20 14		
Warrington Central	a	17 30		17 48		18 03		18 18		18 30		18 46	18 57	19 20				19 30		19 57		20 18		20 30
	d	17 30		17 48		18 03		18 18		18 30		18 47	18 57					19 30	19 34	19 57		20 18		20 30
Sankey for Penketh	d			17 52								18 51							19 38					
Widnes	d			17 58		18 11						18 56	19 05						19 43	20 05				
Hough Green	d			18 01				18 28				18 59							19 46			20 28		
Halewood	d			18 06								19 04							19 51					
Hunts Cross 89	d			18 09				18 33				19 07	19 12						19 54			20 33		
L'pool Sth Parkway 7 91,103 ✈	d	17 47	17 59	18 14		18 22	18 32	18 38		18 47	19 02	19 11	19 18			19 32		19 47	19 59	20 15	20 34	20 38		20 47
Liverpool Central 10 103	a																							
West Allerton 91	a			18 18				18 41				19 15							20 03			20 41		
Mossley Hill 91	a			18 20				18 44				19 18							20 05			20 44		
Edge Hill 90,91	a			18 30				18 50				19 26							20 11					
Liverpool Lime Street 10 90,91	a	18 00	18 10	18 38		18 35	18 44	18 57	19 00	18 59	19 14	19 35	19 35			19 44	19 48	19 59	20 18	20 30	20 46	20 55	20 48	20 59

		NT	EM	NT	LM	TP	NT	NT	NT	TP		NT	NT
			◇		◇1	◇1				◇1			
			C		B	A				A			
Manchester Airport 85 ✈	d								21 41				
Sheffield 7 78 🚌	d		19 42										
Stockport 84	d		20 26										
Manchester Piccadilly 10 78,84,85 🚌	d		20 37			21 07	21 38		22 01	22 07			
Manchester Oxford Road 84,85	d		20 41	20 44		21 12	21 44		22 04	22 12			23 20
Deansgate 84,85 🚌	d			20 46			21 46						23 22
Trafford Park	d			20 51			21 51						23 27
Humphrey Park	d			20 53			21 53						23 29
Urmston	d			20 55			21 55						23 31
Chassen Road	d			20 57			21 57						23 33
Flixton	d			21 00			22 00						23 36
Irlam	d			21 04			22 04						23 40
Glazebrook	d			21 07			22 07						23 43
Birchwood	d			21 11		21 25	22 11			22 25			23 47
Padgate	d			21 14			22 14						23 50
Warrington Central	a		20 57	21 20		21 30	22 20			22 30			23 54
	d	20 49	20 57			21 30		21 49		22 30		22 49	23 54
Sankey for Penketh	d	20 53						21 53				22 53	23 58
Widnes	d	20 58	21 05					21 58				22 58	00 04
Hough Green	d	21 01						22 01				23 01	00 06
Halewood	d	21 06						22 06				23 06	00 11
Hunts Cross 89	d	21 09						22 09				23 09	00 14
L'pool Sth Parkway 7 91,103 ✈	d	21 15	21 20		21 38	21 47		22 12		22 47		23 12	00 20
Liverpool Central 10 103	a												
West Allerton 91	a	21 19						22 15				23 15	
Mossley Hill 91	a	21 21						22 18				23 18	
Edge Hill 90,91	a	21 27						22 23				23 23	
Liverpool Lime Street 10 90,91	a	21 34	21 35		21 50	21 58		22 30	22 48	23 00		23 30	00 34

A From Scarborough

B From Birmingham New Street

C From Norwich

Table 89

Sundays

until 11 September

Manchester Airport and Manchester - Warrington Central - Liverpool

		NT	NT	NT	TP	NT	NT	NT	TP	LM		NT	NT	TP	LM	EM	NT	NT	TP	LM		EM	NT	NT	TP
					◇1				◇1	◇1				◇1	◇1	◇			◇1	◇1		◇			◇1
		A							B	C					C	D			E	C		D			F
Manchester Airport 85 ✈	d			08 35				09 35					10 35					11 33						12 35	
Sheffield 7 78 🚌	d															10 41						11 38			
Stockport 84	d															11 26						12 26			
Manchester Piccadilly 10 78,84,85 🚌	d			08 50	09 07			09 50	10 07				10 50	11 07		11 38		11 50	12 07			12 38		12 50	13 07
Manchester Oxford Road 84,85	d	23p20	08 06	08 53	09 12	09 15	09 45	09 53	10 12			10 45	10 53	11 12		11 42	11 45	11 53	12 12			12 42	12 45	12 53	13 12
Deansgate 84,85 🚌	d	23p22	08 08			09 17	09 47					10 47					11 47						12 47		
Trafford Park	d	23p27																							
Humphrey Park	d	23p29																							
Urmston	d	23p31	08 14			09 23	09 53					10 53					11 53						12 53		
Chassen Road	d	23p33																							
Flixton	d	23p36																							
Irlam	d	23p40	08 19			09 28	09 58					10 58					11 58						12 58		
Glazebrook	d	23p43																							
Birchwood	d	23p47	08 25		09 25	09 34	10 04		10 25			11 04		11 25			12 04		12 25				13 04		13 25
Padgate	d	23p50																							
Warrington Central	a	23p54	08 30		09 30	09 39	10 09		10 30			11 09		11 30		11 58	12 09		12 30			12 58	13 09		13 30
	d	23p54	08 30		09 30	09 39	10 09		10 30			11 09		11 30		11 59	12 09		12 30			12 58	13 09		13 30
Sankey for Penketh	d	23p58																							
Widnes	d	00 04	08 38			09 47	10 17					11 17				12 06	12 17					13 06	13 17		
Hough Green	d	00 06	08 42			09 51	10 21					11 21					12 21						13 21		
Halewood	d	00 11	08 46			09 55	10 25					11 25					12 25						13 25		
Hunts Cross 89	d	00 14	08 49			09 58	10 28					11 28					12 28						13 28		
L'pool Sth Parkway 7 91,103 ✈	d	00 20	08 54		09 47	10 03	10 33		10 47	11 09		11 33		11 47	12 10	12 17	12 33		12 47	13 10		13 17	13 33		13 47
Liverpool Central 10 103	a																								
West Allerton 91	a		08 57			10 06	10 36					11 36					12 36						13 36		
Mossley Hill 91	a		09 00			10 09	10 39					11 39					12 39						13 39		
Edge Hill 90,91	a																								
Liverpool Lime Street 10 90,91	a	00 34	09 11	09 52	10 00	10 20	10 50	10 54	10 59	11 20		11 50	11 54	11 59	12 21	12 30	12 50	12 54	12 58	13 21		13 30	13 50	13 54	13 58

		LM	EM	NT	NT	TP		LM	EM	NT	NT	TP	LM	EM	NT	NT		TP	LM	EM	NT	NT	TP	LM	EM
		◇1	◇			◇1		◇1	◇			◇1	◇1	◇				◇1	◇1	◇			◇1	◇1	◇
		C	D			F		C	G			H	C	G				F	C	D			H	C	D
Manchester Airport 85 ✈	d				13 35						14 35					15 35						16 35			
Sheffield 7 78 🚌	d		12 41						13 38					14 39						15 38					16 44
Stockport 84	d		13 26						14 26					15 26						16 26					17 27
Manchester Piccadilly 10 78,84,85 🚌	d		13 38		13 50	14 07			14 38		14 50	15 07		15 38		15 50		16 07		16 38		16 50	17 07		17 38
Manchester Oxford Road 84,85	d		13 42	13 45	13 53	14 12			14 42	14 45	14 53	15 12		15 42	15 45	15 53		16 12		16 42	16 45	16 53	17 12		17 42
Deansgate 84,85 🚌	d			13 47						14 47					15 47						16 47				
Trafford Park	d																								
Humphrey Park	d																								
Urmston	d			13 53						14 53					15 53						16 53				
Chassen Road	d																								
Flixton	d																								
Irlam	d			13 58						14 58					15 58						16 58				
Glazebrook	d																								
Birchwood	d			14 04		14 25				15 04		15 25			16 04			16 25			17 04		17 25		
Padgate	d																								
Warrington Central	a		13 58	14 09		14 30			14 58	15 09		15 30		15 58	16 09			16 30		16 58	17 09		17 30		17 58
	d		13 58	14 09		14 30			14 58	15 09		15 30		15 58	16 09			16 30		16 58	17 09		17 30		17 58
Sankey for Penketh	d																								
Widnes	d		14 06	14 17					15 06	15 17				16 06	16 17					17 06	17 17				18 06
Hough Green	d			14 21						15 21					16 21						17 21				
Halewood	d			14 25						15 25					16 25						17 25				
Hunts Cross 89	d			14 28						15 28					16 28						17 28				
L'pool Sth Parkway 7 91,103 ✈	d	14 03	14 16	14 33		14 47		15 03	15 16	15 33		15 47	16 03	16 16	16 33			16 47	17 03	17 16	17 33		17 47	18 03	18 16
Liverpool Central 10 103	a																								
West Allerton 91	a			14 36						15 36					16 36						17 36				
Mossley Hill 91	a			14 39						15 39					16 39						17 39				
Edge Hill 90,91	a																								
Liverpool Lime Street 10 90,91	a	14 14	14 30	14 50	14 54	14 58		15 14	15 30	15 50	15 54	15 58	16 14	16 30	16 50	16 54		16 58	17 14	17 30	17 50	17 54	17 58	18 14	18 30

A not 22 May
B From York
C From Birmingham New Street
D From Nottingham
E From Newcastle
F From Scarborough
G From Norwich
H From Middlesbrough

Table 89

Sundays

until 11 September

Manchester Airport and Manchester - Warrington Central - Liverpool

	NT		NT	TP ◇1 A	LM ◇1 B	EM ◇ C	NT	NT	TP ◇1 D	LM ◇1 B	EM ◇ C		NT	NT	TP ◇1 A	LM ◇1 B	NT	NT	TP ◇1 D	NT	NT	TP ◇1 A	NT	NT
Manchester Airport 85 ✈ d			17 35					18 35						19 35				20 35			21 35			22 35
Sheffield 7 78 ⇌ d						17 44					18 37													
Stockport 84 d						18 26					19 26													
Manchester Piccadilly 10 78,84,85 ⇌ d			17 50	18 07		18 38		18 50	19 07		19 38			19 50	20 07			20 50	21 07		21 50	22 07		22 50
Manchester Oxford Road 84,85 d	17 45		17 53	18 12		18 42	18 45	18 53	19 12		19 42		19 45	19 53	20 12		20 45	20 53	21 12	21 45	21 53	22 12	22 45	22 53
Deansgate 84,85 ⇌ d	17 47						18 47						19 47				20 47			21 47			22 47	
Trafford Park d																								
Humphrey Park d																								
Urmston d	17 53						18 53						19 53				20 53			21 53			22 53	
Chassen Road d																								
Flixton d																								
Irlam d	17 58						18 58						19 58				20 58			21 58			22 58	
Glazebrook d																								
Birchwood d	18 04			18 25			19 04		19 25				20 04		20 25		21 04		21 25	22 04		22 25	23 04	
Padgate d																								
Warrington Central a	18 09			18 30		18 58	19 09		19 30		19 58		20 09		20 30		21 09		21 30	22 09		22 30	23 09	
d	18 09			18 30		18 58	19 09		19 30		19 58		20 09		20 30		21 09		21 30	22 09		22 30	23 09	
Sankey for Penketh d																								
Widnes d	18 17					19 06	19 17				20 06		20 17				21 17			22 17			23 17	
Hough Green d	18 21						19 21						20 21				21 21			22 21			23 21	
Halewood d	18 25						19 25						20 25				21 25			22 25			23 25	
Hunts Cross 89 d	18 28						19 28						20 28				21 28			22 28			23 28	
L'pool Sth Parkway 7 91,103 ✈ d	18 33			18 47	19 03	19 17	19 33		19 47	20 03	20 16		20 33		20 47	21 03	21 33		21 47	22 33		22 47	23 33	
Liverpool Central 10 103 a																								
West Allerton 91 a	18 36						19 36						20 36				21 36			22 36			23 36	
Mossley Hill 91 a	18 39						19 39						20 39				21 39			22 39			23 39	
Edge Hill 90,91 a																								
Liverpool Lime Street 10 90,91 a	18 50		18 54	18 58	19 14	19 30	19 50	19 54	19 58	20 14	20 30		20 50	20 54	20 58	21 14	21 50	21 54	21 58	22 50	22 54	23 00	23 50	23 54

A From Scarborough
B From Birmingham New Street
C From Norwich
D From Middlesbrough

Table 89

Sundays

18 September to 23 October

Manchester Airport and Manchester - Warrington Central - Liverpool

	NT	NT	NT	NT	NT	LM	NT	NT	LM		EM	NT	NT	LM	EM	NT	NT	LM	EM		NT	NT	LM	EM
						◇1			◇1		◇			◇1	◇			◇1	◇				◇1	◇
						A			A		B			A	B			A	B				A	B
Manchester Airport 85 ✈ d					09 35			10 35					11 33				12 35					13 35		
Sheffield 7 78 🚌 d											10 41				11 38				12 41					13 38
Stockport 84 d											11 26				12 26				13 26					14 26
Manchester Piccadilly 10 78,84,85 🚌 d					09 50			10 50			11 38		11 50		12 38		12 50		13 38			13 50		14 38
Manchester Oxford Road 84,85 d	23p20	07 45	09 15	09 45	09 53		10 45	10 53			11 42	11 45	11 53		12 42	12 45	12 53		13 42		13 45	13 53		14 42
Deansgate 84,85 🚌 d	23p22	07 47	09 17	09 47			10 47					11 47				12 47					13 47			
Trafford Park d	23p27																							
Humphrey Park d	23p29																							
Urmston d	23p31	07 53	09 23	09 53			10 53					11 53				12 53					13 53			
Chassen Road d	23p33																							
Flixton d	23p36																							
Irlam d	23p40	07 58	09 28	09 58			10 58					11 58				12 58					13 58			
Glazebrook d	23p43																							
Birchwood d	23p47	08 04	09 34	10 04			11 04					12 04				13 04					14 04			
Padgate d	23p50																							
Warrington Central a	23p54	08 09	09 39	10 09			11 09				11 58	12 09			12 58	13 09			13 58		14 09			14 58
d	23p54	08 30	09 39	10 09			11 09				11 59	12 09			12 58	13 09			13 58		14 09			14 58
Sankey for Penketh d	23p58																							
Widnes d	00 04	08 38	09 47	10 17			11 17				12 06	12 17			13 06	13 17			14 06		14 17			15 06
Hough Green d	00 06	08 42	09 51	10 21			11 21					12 21				13 21					14 21			
Halewood d	00 11	08 46	09 55	10 25			11 25					12 25				13 25					14 25			
Hunts Cross 89 d	00 14	08 49	09 58	10 28			11 28					12 28				13 28					14 28			
L'pool Sth Parkway 7 91,103 ✈ d	00 20	08 54	10 03	10 33		11 09	11 33		12 10		12 17	12 33		13 10	13 17	13 33		14 03	14 16		14 33		15 03	15 16
Liverpool Central 10 103 a																								
West Allerton 91 a		08 57	10 06	10 36			11 36					12 36				13 36					14 36			
Mossley Hill 91 a		09 00	10 09	10 39			11 39					12 39				13 39					14 39			
Edge Hill 90,91 a																								
Liverpool Lime Street 10 90,91 a	00 34	09 11	10 20	10 50	10 54	11 20	11 50	11 54	12 21		12 30	12 50	12 54	13 21	13 30	13 50	13 54	14 14	14 30		14 50	14 54	15 14	15 30

	NT	NT	LM	EM	NT		NT	LM	EM	NT	NT	LM	EM	NT	NT		LM	EM	NT	NT	LM	EM	NT	NT
			◇1	◇				◇1	◇			◇1	◇				◇1	◇			◇1	◇		
			A	C				A	B			A	B				A	C			A	C		
Manchester Airport 85 ✈ d		14 35					15 35				16 35				17 35					18 35				19 35
Sheffield 7 78 🚌 d				14 39					15 38				16 44					17 44				18 37		
Stockport 84 d				15 26					16 26				17 27					18 26				19 26		
Manchester Piccadilly 10 78,84,85 🚌 d		14 50		15 38			15 50		16 38		16 50		17 38		17 50			18 38		18 50		19 38		19 50
Manchester Oxford Road 84,85 d	14 45	14 53		15 42	15 45		15 53		16 42	16 45	16 53		17 42	17 45	17 53			18 42	18 45	18 53		19 42	19 45	19 53
Deansgate 84,85 🚌 d	14 47				15 47					16 47				17 47					18 47				19 47	
Trafford Park d																								
Humphrey Park d																								
Urmston d	14 53				15 53					16 53				17 53					18 53				19 53	
Chassen Road d																								
Flixton d																								
Irlam d	14 58				15 58					16 58				17 58					18 58				19 58	
Glazebrook d																								
Birchwood d	15 04				16 04					17 04				18 04					19 04				20 04	
Padgate d																								
Warrington Central a	15 09			15 58	16 09				16 58	17 09			17 58	18 09				18 58	19 09			19 58	20 09	
d	15 09			15 58	16 09				16 58	17 09			17 58	18 09				18 58	19 09			19 58	20 09	
Sankey for Penketh d																								
Widnes d	15 17			16 06	16 17				17 06	17 17			18 06	18 17				19 06	19 17			20 06	20 17	
Hough Green d	15 21				16 21					17 21				18 21					19 21				20 21	
Halewood d	15 25				16 25					17 25				18 25					19 25				20 25	
Hunts Cross 89 d	15 28				16 28					17 28				18 28					19 28				20 28	
L'pool Sth Parkway 7 91,103 ✈ d	15 33		16 03	16 16	16 33			17 03	17 16	17 33		18 03	18 16	18 33			19 03	19 17	19 33		20 03	20 16	20 33	
Liverpool Central 10 103 a																								
West Allerton 91 a	15 36				16 36					17 36				18 36					19 36				20 36	
Mossley Hill 91 a	15 39				16 39					17 39				18 39					19 39				20 39	
Edge Hill 90,91 a																								
Liverpool Lime Street 10 90,91 a	15 50	15 54	16 14	16 30	16 50		16 54	17 14	17 30	17 50	17 54	18 14	18 30	18 50	18 54		19 14	19 30	19 50	19 54	20 14	20 30	20 50	20 54

A From Birmingham New Street

B From Nottingham

C From Norwich

Table 89

Sundays

18 September to 23 October

Manchester Airport and Manchester - Warrington Central - Liverpool

	LM ◇1 A	NT	NT	NT	NT	NT	NT
Manchester Airport 85 ✈ d			20 35		21 35		22 35
Sheffield 7 78 ⇌ d							
Stockport 84 d							
Manchester Piccadilly 10 78,84,85 ⇌ d			20 50		21 50		22 50
Manchester Oxford Road 84,85 d		20 45	20 53	21 45	21 53	22 45	22 53
Deansgate 84,85 ⇌ d		20 47		21 47		22 47	
Trafford Park d							
Humphrey Park d							
Urmston d		20 53		21 53		22 53	
Chassen Road d							
Flixton d							
Irlam d		20 58		21 58		22 58	
Glazebrook d							
Birchwood d		21 04		22 04		23 04	
Padgate d							
Warrington Central a		21 09		22 09		23 09	
d		21 09		22 09		23 09	
Sankey for Penketh d							
Widnes d		21 17		22 17		23 17	
Hough Green d		21 21		22 21		23 21	
Halewood d		21 25		22 25		23 25	
Hunts Cross 89 d		21 28		22 28		23 28	
L'pool Sth Parkway 7 91,103 ✈ d	21 03	21 33		22 33		23 33	
Liverpool Central 10 103 a							
West Allerton 91 a		21 36		22 36		23 36	
Mossley Hill 91 a		21 39		22 39		23 39	
Edge Hill 90,91 a							
Liverpool Lime Street 10 90,91 a	21 14	21 50	21 54	22 50	22 54	23 50	23 54

Sundays

from 30 October

	NT	NT	TP ◇1	NT	NT	NT	TP ◇1 B	LM ◇1 A	NT
Manchester Airport 85 ✈ d						09 35			
Sheffield 7 78 ⇌ d									
Stockport 84 d									
Manchester Piccadilly 10 78,84,85 ⇌ d			09 07			09 50	10 12		
Manchester Oxford Road 84,85 d	23p20	07 45	09 12	09 15	09 45	09 53	10 15		10 45
Deansgate 84,85 ⇌ d	23p22	07 47		09 17	09 47				10 47
Trafford Park d	23p27								
Humphrey Park d	23p29								
Urmston d	23p31	07 53		09 23	09 53				10 53
Chassen Road d	23p33								
Flixton d	23p36								
Irlam d	23p40	07 58		09 28	09 58				10 58
Glazebrook d	23p43								
Birchwood d	23p47	08 04	09 25	09 34	10 04		10 29		11 04
Padgate d	23p50								
Warrington Central a	23p54	08 09	09 30	09 39	10 09		10 33		11 09
d	23p54	08 30	09 30	09 39	10 09		10 34		11 09
Sankey for Penketh d	23p58								
Widnes d	00 04	08 38		09 47	10 17				11 17
Hough Green d	00 06	08 42		09 51	10 21				11 21
Halewood d	00 11	08 46		09 55	10 25				11 25
Hunts Cross 89 d	00 14	08 49		09 58	10 28				11 28
L'pool Sth Parkway 7 91,103 ✈ d	00 20	08 54	09 47	10 03	10 33		10 49	11 09	11 33
Liverpool Central 10 103 a									
West Allerton 91 a		08 57		10 06	10 36				11 36
Mossley Hill 91 a		09 00		10 09	10 39				11 39
Edge Hill 90,91 a									
Liverpool Lime Street 10 90,91 a	00 34	09 11	10 00	10 20	10 50	10 54	11 00	11 20	11 50

	NT	TP ◇1	LM ◇1 A	EM ◇ C	NT	NT	TP ◇1 D	LM ◇1 A	EM ◇ C	NT	NT	TP ◇1 E	LM ◇1 A
Manchester Airport 85 ✈ d	10 35					11 33					12 35		
Sheffield 7 78 ⇌ d				10 41					11 38				
Stockport 84 d				11 26					12 26				
Manchester Piccadilly 10 78,84,85 ⇌ d	10 50	11 07		11 38		11 50	12 07		12 38		12 50	13 07	
Manchester Oxford Road 84,85 d	10 53	11 12		11 42	11 45	11 53	12 12		12 42	12 45	12 53	13 12	
Deansgate 84,85 ⇌ d					11 47					12 47			
Trafford Park d													
Humphrey Park d													
Urmston d					11 53					12 53			
Chassen Road d													
Flixton d													
Irlam d					11 58					12 58			
Glazebrook d													
Birchwood d		11 25			12 04		12 25			13 04		13 25	
Padgate d													
Warrington Central a		11 30		11 58	12 09		12 30		12 58	13 09		13 30	
d		11 30		11 59	12 09		12 30		12 58	13 09		13 30	
Sankey for Penketh d													
Widnes d				12 06	12 17				13 06	13 17			
Hough Green d					12 21					13 21			
Halewood d					12 25					13 25			
Hunts Cross 89 d					12 28					13 28			
L'pool Sth Parkway 7 91,103 ✈ d		11 47	12 10	12 17	12 33		12 47	13 10	13 17	13 33		13 47	14 03
Liverpool Central 10 103 a													
West Allerton 91 a					12 36					13 36			
Mossley Hill 91 a					12 39					13 39			
Edge Hill 90,91 a													
Liverpool Lime Street 10 90,91 a	11 54	11 59	12 21	12 30	12 50	12 54	12 58	13 21	13 30	13 50	13 54	13 58	14 14

A From Birmingham New Street
B From York
C From Nottingham
D From Newcastle
E From Scarborough

Table 89

Sundays
from 30 October

Manchester Airport and Manchester - Warrington Central - Liverpool

	EM	NT	NT	TP	LM		EM	NT	NT	TP	LM	EM	NT	NT	TP		LM	EM	NT	NT	TP	LM	EM	NT
	◇			◇1	◇1		◇			◇1	◇1	◇			◇1		◇1	◇			◇1	◇1	◇	
	A			B	C		A			D	C	E			B		C	A			D	C	A	
Manchester Airport 85 ✈ d			13 35						14 35					15 35						16 35				
Sheffield 7 78 ⇌ d	12 41						13 38					14 39						15 38					16 44	
Stockport 84 d	13 26						14 26					15 26						16 26					17 27	
Manchester Piccadilly 10 78,84,85 ⇌ d	13 38		13 50	14 07			14 38		14 50	15 07		15 38		15 50	16 07			16 38		16 50	17 07		17 38	
Manchester Oxford Road 84,85 d	13 42	13 45	13 53	14 12			14 42	14 45	14 53	15 12		15 42	15 45	15 53	16 12			16 42	16 45	16 53	17 12		17 42	17 45
Deansgate 84,85 ⇌ d		13 47						14 47					15 47						16 47					17 47
Trafford Park d																								
Humphrey Park d																								
Urmston d		13 53						14 53					15 53						16 53					17 53
Chassen Road d																								
Flixton d																								
Irlam d		13 58						14 58					15 58						16 58					17 58
Glazebrook d																								
Birchwood d		14 04		14 25				15 04		15 25			16 04		16 25				17 04		17 25			18 04
Padgate d																								
Warrington Central a	13 58	14 09		14 30			14 58	15 09		15 30		15 58	16 09		16 30			16 58	17 09		17 30		17 58	18 09
d	13 58	14 09		14 30			14 58	15 09		15 30		15 58	16 09		16 30			16 58	17 09		17 30		17 58	18 09
Sankey for Penketh d																								
Widnes d	14 06	14 17					15 06	15 17				16 06	16 17					17 06	17 17				18 06	18 17
Hough Green d		14 21						15 21					16 21						17 21					18 21
Halewood d		14 25						15 25					16 25						17 25					18 25
Hunts Cross 89 d		14 28						15 28					16 28						17 28					18 28
L'pool Sth Parkway 7 91,103 ✈ d	14 16	14 33		14 47	15 03		15 16	15 33		15 47	16 03	16 16	16 33		16 47		17 03	17 16	17 33		17 47	18 03	18 16	18 33
Liverpool Central 10 103 a																								
West Allerton 91 a		14 36						15 36					16 36						17 36					18 36
Mossley Hill 91 a		14 39						15 39					16 39						17 39					18 39
Edge Hill 90,91 a																								
Liverpool Lime Street 10 90,91 a	14 30	14 50	14 54	14 58	15 14		15 30	15 50	15 54	15 58	16 14	16 30	16 50	16 54	16 58		17 14	17 30	17 50	17 54	17 58	18 14	18 30	18 50

	NT		TP	LM	EM	NT	NT	TP	LM	EM	NT		NT	TP	LM	NT	NT	TP	NT	NT	TP		NT	NT
			◇1	◇1	◇			◇1	◇1	◇				◇1	◇1			◇1			◇1			
			B	C	E			D	C	E				B	C			D			B			
Manchester Airport 85 ✈ d	17 35						18 35						19 35				20 35			21 35				22 35
Sheffield 7 78 ⇌ d					17 44					18 37														
Stockport 84 d					18 26					19 26														
Manchester Piccadilly 10 78,84,85 ⇌ d	17 50		18 07		18 38		18 50	19 07		19 38			19 50	20 07			20 50	21 07		21 50	22 07			22 50
Manchester Oxford Road 84,85 d	17 53		18 12		18 42	18 45	18 53	19 12		19 42	19 45		19 53	20 12		20 45	20 53	21 12	21 45	21 53	22 12		22 45	22 53
Deansgate 84,85 ⇌ d						18 47					19 47					20 47			21 47				22 47	
Trafford Park d																								
Humphrey Park d																								
Urmston d						18 53					19 53					20 53			21 53				22 53	
Chassen Road d																								
Flixton d																								
Irlam d						18 58					19 58					20 58			21 58				22 58	
Glazebrook d																								
Birchwood d			18 25			19 04		19 25			20 04			20 25		21 04		21 25	22 04		22 25		23 04	
Padgate d																								
Warrington Central a			18 30		18 58	19 09		19 30		19 58	20 09			20 30		21 09		21 30	22 09		22 30		23 09	
d			18 30		18 58	19 09		19 30		19 58	20 09			20 30		21 09		21 30	22 09		22 30		23 09	
Sankey for Penketh d																								
Widnes d					19 06	19 17				20 06	20 17					21 17			22 17				23 17	
Hough Green d						19 21					20 21					21 21			22 21				23 21	
Halewood d						19 25					20 25					21 25			22 25				23 25	
Hunts Cross 89 d						19 28					20 28					21 28			22 28				23 28	
L'pool Sth Parkway 7 91,103 ✈ d			18 47	19 03	19 17	19 33		19 47	20 03	20 16	20 33			20 47	21 03	21 33		21 47	22 33		22 47		23 33	
Liverpool Central 10 103 a																								
West Allerton 91 a						19 36					20 36					21 36			22 36				23 36	
Mossley Hill 91 a						19 39					20 39					21 39			22 39				23 39	
Edge Hill 90,91 a																								
Liverpool Lime Street 10 90,91 a	18 54		18 58	19 14	19 30	19 50	19 54	19 58	20 14	20 30	20 50		20 54	20 58	21 14	21 50	21 54	21 58	22 50	22 54	23 00		23 50	23 54

A From Nottingham
B From Scarborough
C From Birmingham New Street
D From Middlesbrough
E From Norwich

Table 90

Liverpool and St. Helens - Newton-le-Willows, Wigan, Preston and Manchester

Miles	Miles	Miles	Miles			NT MO	NT MO	NT MX	NT MX	NT	NT	NT	AW	NT	NT	NT	NT	NT	NT	AW	NT	NT	NT
													A							◇ B			
0	0	0	—	**Liverpool Lime Street** [10] 89,91	d	22p31	23p01	23p02	23p16	03 38	05 13	05 31		05 46	06 01	06 13	06 16	06 21	06 31		06 46	06 57	07 01
1¾	1¾	1¾	—	Edge Hill 89,91	d			23p06	23p20			05 35		05 50	06 05		06 20		06 35		06 50		07 05
2½	2½	2½	—	Wavertree Technology Park	d	22p37	23p07	23p08	23p22		05 19	05 37		05 52	06 07	06 19	06 22		06 37		06 52		07 07
3½	3½	3½	—	Broad Green	d	22p40	23p10	23p11	23p26			05 40		05 55	06 10		06 25		06 40		06 55		07 10
5	5	5	—	Roby	d	22p43	23p13	23p15	23p30			05 44		05 59	06 14		06 29		06 44		06 59		07 14
5½	5½	5½	—	Huyton	d	22p46	23p16	23p17	23p32			05 46		06 01	06 16		06 31		06 46		07 01	07 06	07 16
—	7¾	—	—	Prescot	d	22p50		23p22				05 51			06 21				06 51				07 21
—	8¾	—	—	Eccleston Park	d			23p24				05 53			06 23				06 53				07 23
—	9¾	—	—	Thatto Heath	d	22p54		23p27				05 56			06 26				06 56				07 26
—	11¼	—	—	**St Helens Central**	a	22p57		23p30				05 59			06 29				06 59			07 15	07 29
—	—	—	—		d	22p58		23p31				06 00			06 30				07 00			07 15	07 30
—	15	—	—	Garswood	d	23p05		23p38				06 07			06 37				07 07				07 37
—	16¼	—	—	Bryn	d			23p41				06 10			06 40				07 10				07 40
7½	—	7½	—	Whiston	d		23p19		23p36					06 05			06 35				07 05		
9	—	9	—	Rainhill	d		23p22		23p39					06 08			06 38				07 08		
10¾	—	10¾	—	Lea Green	d		23p26		23p42					06 11			06 41				07 11		
12	—	12	—	**St Helens Junction**	d		23p29		23p45		05 29			06 14		06 29	06 44				07 14		
—	—	—	—	Warrington Bank Quay	d								06 06							07 07			
14¾	—	14¾	—	Earlestown [8]	d		23p33		23p50				06 12	06 19			06 50			07 14	07 19		
—	—	—	—	Warrington Bank Quay	a												07 01						
16¼	—	16¼	0	**Newton-le-Willows**	d		23p36		23p53		05 35		06 15	06 22		06 35				07 17	07 22		
—	20	23¼	—	**Wigan North Western** 65	a	23p13		23p48				06 21			06 51				07 21			07 30	07 51
—	—	—	—		d	23p14		23p48														07 31	
—	28¼	31½	—	Euxton Balshaw Lane	d			23p59														07 41	
—	31	34¼	—	Leyland 82	a	23p27		00 04														07 46	
—	35	38¼	—	**Preston** [8] 65,82	a	23p35		00 13														07 56	
—	52½	—	—	Blackpool North 97	a	00 05																	
26¾	—	—	10½	Patricroft	d				00 05					06 34							07 34		
27¾	—	—	11½	Eccles	d		23p49		00 08					06 36							07 36		
31¾	—	—	—	**Manchester Victoria**	a				00 21					06 49							07 49		
—	—	—	15¾	**Manchester Oxford Road**	a		23p59						06 35			06 57		07 36		07 41			
—	—	—	16¼	**Manchester Piccadilly** [10]	a		00 02			04 14	05 57		06 45			07 01				07 50			
—	—	—	26	**Manchester Airport** 85	a		00 19			04 30	06 14					07 22							

		NT	AW	NT	NT	NT	AW	NT	NT	NT	NT	NT	NT	NT	NT	NT	NT	AW	NT	NT	NT	NT	NT
			A	C			◇ D								E			◇ D					E
Liverpool Lime Street [10] 89,91	d	07 13		07 16	07 26	07 31		07 46	07 57	08 01	08 13	08 16	08 26	08 31	08 44	08 57	09 01		09 13	09 16	09 27	09 31	09 46
Edge Hill 89,91	d			07 20	07 30	07 35		07 50		08 05		08 20	08 30	08 35	08 50		09 05			09 20		09 35	09 50
Wavertree Technology Park	d	07 19		07 22		07 37		07 52		08 07	08 19	08 22		08 37	08 52		09 07		09 19	09 22		09 37	09 52
Broad Green	d			07 25		07 40		07 55		08 10		08 25		08 40	08 55		09 10			09 25		09 40	09 55
Roby	d			07 29		07 44		07 59		08 14		08 29		08 44	08 59		09 14			09 29		09 44	09 59
Huyton	d			07 31		07 46		08 01	08 06	08 16		08 31		08 46	09 01	09 06	09 16			09 31		09 46	10 01
Prescot	d					07 51				08 21				08 51			09 21					09 51	
Eccleston Park	d					07 53				08 23				08 53			09 23					09 53	
Thatto Heath	d					07 56				08 26				08 56			09 26					09 56	
St Helens Central	a					07 59			08 15	08 29				08 59		09 15	09 29					09 59	
	d					08 00			08 15	08 30				09 00		09 15	09 30					10 00	
Garswood	d					08 07				08 37				09 07			09 37					10 07	
Bryn	d					08 10				08 40				09 10			09 40					10 10	
Whiston	d			07 35				08 05				08 35			09 05					09 35			10 05
Rainhill	d			07 38				08 08				08 38			09 08					09 38			10 08
Lea Green	d	07 28		07 41				08 11				08 41			09 11					09 41			10 11
St Helens Junction	d	07 31		07 44				08 14			08 29	08 44			09 14				09 29	09 44			10 14
Warrington Bank Quay	d		07 39				08 08											09 19					
Earlestown [8]	d		07 46	07 49			08 16	08 19				08 50			09 19			09 26		09 50			10 19
Warrington Bank Quay	a											09 01								10 01			
Newton-le-Willows	d	07 37	07 49	07 52			08 19	08 22			08 35				09 22			09 29	09 35				10 22
Wigan North Western 65	a					08 21			08 30	08 51				09 21		09 30	09 51					10 21	
	d								08 31							09 31							
Euxton Balshaw Lane	d								08 41							09 41							
Leyland 82	a								08 46							09 46							
Preston [8] 65,82	a								08 56							09 54							
Blackpool North 97	a															10 21							
Patricroft	d			08 04				08 34							09 34								10 34
Eccles	d			08 06				08 36							09 36								10 36
Manchester Victoria	a			08 19				08 50							09 47								10 49
Manchester Oxford Road	a	07 57	08 09		08 36		08 41				08 57		09 36					09 48	09 57		10 36		
Manchester Piccadilly [10]	a	08 01	08 18				08 50				09 01							09 57	10 01				
Manchester Airport 85	a	08 22									09 22								10 22				

A From Chester
B From Llandudno Junction
C To Huddersfield
D From Llandudno
E To Stalybridge

Liverpool and St. Helens - Newton-le-Willows, Wigan, Preston and Manchester

		NT	NT	AW	NT	NT		NT	NT	NT	NT	NT	AW	NT	NT	NT		NT	NT	NT	NT	AW	NT	NT	NT
				◇ A						B	C		◇ A						B	C		◇ A			
Liverpool Lime Street 10 89,91	d	09 57	10 01		10 13	10 16		10 27	10 31	10 46	10 57	11 01		11 13	11 16	11 27		11 31	11 46	11 57	12 01		12 13	12 16	12 27
Edge Hill 89,91	d		10 05			10 20			10 35	10 50		11 05			11 20			11 35	11 50		12 05			12 20	
Wavertree Technology Park	d		10 07		10 19	10 22			10 37	10 52		11 07		11 19	11 22			11 37	11 52		12 07		12 19	12 22	
Broad Green	d		10 10			10 25			10 40	10 55		11 10			11 25			11 40	11 55		12 10			12 25	
Roby	d		10 14			10 29			10 44	10 59		11 14			11 29			11 44	11 59		12 14			12 29	
Huyton	d	10 06	10 16			10 31			10 46	11 01	11 06	11 16			11 31			11 46	12 01	12 06	12 16			12 31	
Prescot	d		10 21						10 51			11 21						11 51			12 21				
Eccleston Park	d		10 23						10 53			11 23						11 53			12 23				
Thatto Heath	d		10 26						10 56			11 26						11 56			12 26				
St Helens Central	a	10 15	10 29						10 59		11 15	11 29						11 59		12 15	12 29				
	d	10 15	10 30						11 00		11 15	11 30						12 00		12 15	12 30				
Garswood	d		10 37						11 07			11 37						12 07			12 37				
Bryn	d		10 40						11 10			11 40						12 10			12 40				
Whiston	d					10 35				11 05					11 35				12 05					12 35	
Rainhill	d					10 38				11 08					11 38				12 08					12 38	
Lea Green	d					10 41				11 11					11 41				12 11					12 41	
St Helens Junction	d				10 29	10 44				11 14				11 29	11 44				12 14				12 29	12 44	
Warrington Bank Quay	d			10 19									11 19									12 19			
Earlestown 8	d			10 26		10 50				11 19			11 26		11 50				12 19			12 26		12 50	
Warrington Bank Quay	a					11 02									12 01									13 01	
Newton-le-Willows	d			10 29	10 35					11 22			11 29	11 35					12 22			12 29	12 35		
Wigan North Western 65	a	10 30	10 51						11 21		11 30	11 51						12 21		12 30	12 51				
	d	10 31									11 31									12 31					
Euxton Balshaw Lane	d	10 41									11 41									12 41					
Leyland 82	a	10 46									11 46									12 46					
Preston 8 65,82	a	10 54									11 54									12 54					
Blackpool North 97	a	11 21									12 21									13 21					
Patricroft	d									11 34									12 34						
Eccles	d									11 36									12 36						
Manchester Victoria	a									11 49									12 50						
Manchester Oxford Road	a			10 48	10 57			11 36					11 48	11 57		12 36						12 48	12 57		13 36
Manchester Piccadilly 10	a			10 57	11 01								11 57	12 01								12 57	13 01		
Manchester Airport 85	a				11 22									12 22									13 22		

		NT		NT	NT	NT	AW	NT	NT	NT	NT	NT		NT	NT	AW	NT	NT	NT	NT	NT	NT		NT	AW
				B	C		◇ A					B		C		◇ A					B	C			◇ A
Liverpool Lime Street 10 89,91	d	12 31		12 46	12 57	13 01		13 13	13 16	13 27	13 31	13 46		13 57	14 01		14 13	14 16	14 27	14 31	14 46	14 57		15 01	
Edge Hill 89,91	d	12 35		12 50		13 05			13 20		13 35	13 50			14 05			14 20		14 35	14 50			15 05	
Wavertree Technology Park	d	12 37		12 52		13 07		13 19	13 22		13 37	13 52			14 07		14 19	14 22		14 37	14 52			15 07	
Broad Green	d	12 40		12 55		13 10			13 25		13 40	13 55			14 10			14 25		14 40	14 55			15 10	
Roby	d	12 44		12 59		13 14			13 29		13 44	13 59			14 14			14 29		14 44	14 59			15 14	
Huyton	d	12 46		13 01	13 06	13 16			13 31		13 46	14 01		14 06	14 16			14 31		14 46	15 01	15 06		15 16	
Prescot	d	12 51				13 21					13 51				14 21					14 51				15 21	
Eccleston Park	d	12 53				13 23					13 53				14 23					14 53				15 23	
Thatto Heath	d	12 56				13 26					13 56				14 26					14 56				15 26	
St Helens Central	a	12 59			13 15	13 29					13 59			14 15	14 29					14 59		15 15		15 29	
	d	13 00			13 15	13 30					14 00			14 15	14 30					15 00		15 15		15 30	
Garswood	d	13 07				13 37					14 07				14 37					15 07				15 37	
Bryn	d	13 10				13 40					14 10				14 40					15 10				15 40	
Whiston	d			13 05					13 35			14 05						14 35			15 05				
Rainhill	d			13 08					13 38			14 08						14 38			15 08				
Lea Green	d			13 11					13 41			14 11						14 41			15 11				
St Helens Junction	d			13 14				13 29	13 44			14 14					14 29	14 44			15 14				
Warrington Bank Quay	d						13 19									14 19									15 19
Earlestown 8	d			13 19			13 26		13 50			14 19				14 26		14 50			15 19				15 26
Warrington Bank Quay	a								14 01									15 01							
Newton-le-Willows	d			13 22			13 29	13 35				14 22				14 29	14 35				15 22				15 29
Wigan North Western 65	a	13 21			13 30	13 51					14 21			14 30	14 51					15 21		15 30		15 51	
	d				13 31									14 31								15 31			
Euxton Balshaw Lane	d				13 41									14 41								15 41			
Leyland 82	a				13 46									14 46								15 46			
Preston 8 65,82	a				13 54									14 54								15 54			
Blackpool North 97	a				14 21									15 21								16 21			
Patricroft	d			13 34								14 34									15 34				
Eccles	d			13 36								14 36									15 36				
Manchester Victoria	a			13 47								14 50									15 49				
Manchester Oxford Road	a						13 48	13 57		14 36						14 48	14 57		15 36						15 48
Manchester Piccadilly 10	a						13 57	14 01								14 57	15 01								15 57
Manchester Airport 85	a							14 22									15 22								

A From Llandudno

B To Stalybridge

C From Liverpool South Parkway

Liverpool and St. Helens - Newton-le-Willows, Wigan, Preston and Manchester

		NT	NT	NT	NT	NT	NT	NT		AW	NT	NT	AW	NT	NT	NT	NT	NT		NT	NT	NT	NT	AW	NT
						A	B			◇ C 🍴			◇ C 🍴			A	B							◇ C 🍴	
Liverpool Lime Street [10] 89,91	d	15 13	15 16	15 27	15 31	15 46	15 57	16 01			16 13	16 16		16 27	16 31	16 46	16 57	17 01		17 06	17 10	17 19	17 27		17 35
Edge Hill 89,91	d		15 20		15 35	15 50		16 05				16 20			16 35	16 50		17 05			17 14		17 31		17 39
Wavertree Technology Park	d	15 19	15 22		15 37	15 52		16 07			16 19	16 22			16 37	16 52		17 07		17 12	17 16		17 33		17 41
Broad Green	d		15 25		15 40	15 55		16 10				16 25			16 40	16 55		17 10			17 19		17 36		17 44
Roby	d		15 29		15 44	15 59		16 14				16 29			16 44	16 59		17 14			17 23		17 40		17 48
Huyton	d		15 31		15 46	16 01	16 06	16 16				16 31			16 46	17 01	17 06	17 16		17 19	17 25	17 29	17 42		17 50
Prescot	d				15 51			16 21							16 51			17 21				17 33			
Eccleston Park	d				15 53			16 23							16 53			17 23				17 36			
Thatto Heath	d				15 56			16 26							16 56			17 26				17 38			
St Helens Central	a				15 59		16 15	16 29							16 59		17 15	17 29				17 42	17 51		
	d				16 00		16 15	16 30							17 00		17 15	17 30				17 42	17 51		
Garswood	d				16 07			16 37							17 07			17 37				17 49			
Bryn	d				16 10			16 40							17 10			17 40				17 52			
Whiston	d		15 35			16 05						16 35				17 05					17 28				17 54
Rainhill	d		15 38			16 08						16 38				17 08					17 32				17 57
Lea Green	d		15 41			16 11						16 41				17 11				17 26	17 35				18 00
St Helens Junction	d	15 29	15 44			16 14					16 29	16 44				17 14				17 29	17 39				18 03
Warrington Bank Quay	d									16 19			16 51											17 49	
Earlestown [8]	d		15 50			16 19				16 26		16 49	16 59			17 19					17 44			17 57	18 08
Warrington Bank Quay	a		16 01																						
Newton-le-Willows	d	15 35				16 22				16 29	16 35	16 52	17 02			17 22				17 35	17 47			18 00	18 11
Wigan North Western 65	a				16 21		16 30	16 51							17 21		17 30	17 52				18 04	18 04		
	d						16 30										17 31						18 05		
Euxton Balshaw Lane	d						16 40										17 41						18 16		
Leyland 82	a						16 45										17 46						18 21		
Preston [8] 65,82	a						16 54										17 54						18 31		
Blackpool North 97	a						17 21										18 24								
Patricroft	d					16 34						17 04				17 34					17 59				18 23
Eccles	d					16 36						17 06				17 36					18 01				18 25
Manchester Victoria	a					16 49						17 20				17 47					18 14				18 41
Manchester Oxford Road	a	15 57		16 36						16 48	16 57		17 21	17 36						17 57				18 19	
Manchester Piccadilly [10]	a	16 01								16 57	17 01		17 30							18 01				18 28	
Manchester Airport 85	a	16 22									17 22									18 22					

		NT	NT	NT		NT	NT	NT	AW	NT	NT	AW	NT	NT		NT	AW	NT	NT	NT	NT	AW	NT	NT	
									◇ C 🍴			D					◇ C 🍴					◇ C			
Liverpool Lime Street [10] 89,91	d	17 44	17 48	18 01		18 13	18 16	18 31		18 46	19 01		19 12	19 23		19 42		20 09	20 12	20 25	20 42		21 12	21 42	
Edge Hill 89,91	d		17 52	18 05			18 20	18 35		18 50	19 05		19 16			19 46			20 16		20 46		21 16	21 46	
Wavertree Technology Park	d	17 49	17 54	18 07		18 19	18 22	18 37		18 52	19 07		19 18			19 48		20 15	20 18		20 48		21 18	21 48	
Broad Green	d	17 52	17 57	18 10			18 25	18 40		18 55	19 10		19 21			19 51			20 21		20 51		21 21	21 51	
Roby	d		18 01	18 14			18 29	18 44		18 59	19 14		19 25			19 55			20 25		20 55		21 25	21 55	
Huyton	d	17 57	18 03	18 16			18 31	18 46		19 01	19 16		19 27	19 32		19 57			20 27	20 34	20 57		21 27	21 57	
Prescot	d	18 02		18 21				18 51			19 21					20 02					21 02			22 02	
Eccleston Park	d	18 05		18 23				18 53			19 23					20 04					21 04			22 04	
Thatto Heath	d	18 07		18 26				18 56			19 26					20 07					21 07			22 07	
St Helens Central	a	18 11		18 29				18 59			19 29			19 40		20 10				20 42	21 10			22 10	
	d	18 11		18 30				19 00			19 30			19 41		20 11				20 43	21 11			22 11	
Garswood	d	18 19		18 37				19 07			19 37					20 18					21 18			22 18	
Bryn	d	18 22		18 40				19 10			19 40					20 21					21 21			22 21	
Whiston	d		18 07				18 35			19 05			19 31						20 31				21 31		
Rainhill	d		18 10				18 38			19 08			19 34						20 34				21 34		
Lea Green	d		18 13				18 41			19 11			19 37						20 37				21 37		
St Helens Junction	d		18 16			18 29	18 44			19 14			19 40					20 25	20 40				21 40		
Warrington Bank Quay	d								18 46			19 19					20 19					21 19			
Earlestown [8]	d		18 21				18 50		18 57	19 19		19 26	19 45				20 26		20 45			21 26	21 45		
Warrington Bank Quay	a						19 01																		
Newton-le-Willows	d		18 24			18 35			19 00	19 22		19 29	19 48				20 29	20 35	20 48			21 29	21 48		
Wigan North Western 65	a	18 30		18 49				19 21			19 51			19 54		20 32				20 57	21 32			22 28	
	d	18 31		18 49										19 55						20 57				22 28	
Euxton Balshaw Lane	d	18 41		19 01										20 05						21 08				22 39	
Leyland 82	a	18 46		19 06										20 10						21 16				22 44	
Preston [8] 65,82	a	18 54		19 15										20 18						21 22				22 55	
Blackpool North 97	a	19 23												20 44						21 53				23 22	
Patricroft	d									19 34			20 00						21 00				22 00		
Eccles	d		18 36							19 36			20 02						21 02				22 02		
Manchester Victoria	a		18 49							19 49			20 16						21 15				22 15		
Manchester Oxford Road	a					18 57			19 21			19 48					20 48	20 57				21 48			
Manchester Piccadilly [10]	a					19 01			19 29			19 52					20 52	21 01				21 57			
Manchester Airport 85	a					19 24						20 18					21 18	21 24							

A To Huddersfield
B From Liverpool South Parkway
C From Llandudno
D From Chester

Liverpool and St. Helens - Newton-le-Willows, Wigan, Preston and Manchester

	TP ◇1 A	AW B	AW C	NT	NT	NT
Liverpool Lime Street 10 89,91 d				22 12	23 02	23 16
Edge Hill 89,91 d				22 16	23 06	23 20
Wavertree Technology Park d				22 18	23 08	23 22
Broad Green d				22 21	23 11	23 26
Roby d				22 25	23 15	23 30
Huyton d				22 27	23 17	23 32
Prescot d					23 22	
Eccleston Park d					23 24	
Thatto Heath d					23 27	
St Helens Central a					23 30	
d					23 31	
Garswood d					23 38	
Bryn d					23 41	
Whiston d				22 31		23 36
Rainhill d				22 34		23 39
Lea Green d				22 37		23 42
St Helens Junction d				22 40		23 45
Warrington Bank Quay d		22 16	22 19			
Earlestown 8 d		22 26	22 26	22 45		23 50
Warrington Bank Quay a						
Newton-le-Willows d		22 29	22 29	22 48		23 53
Wigan North Western 65 a					23 48	
d	21 48				23 48	
Euxton Balshaw Lane d					23 59	
Leyland 82 a					00 04	
Preston 8 65,82 a					00 13	
Blackpool North 97 a						
Patricroft d				23 00		00 05
Eccles d				23 02		00 08
Manchester Victoria ⛴ a				23 15		00 21
Manchester Oxford Road a	22 26	22 50	22 50			
Manchester Piccadilly 10 ⛴ a	22 30	22 58	22 58			
Manchester Airport 85 ✈ a	22 47					

Saturdays
until 18 June

	NT	NT	NT	NT	NT	AW D	NT	NT	NT	AW ◇ D	NT	NT	NT	NT E	NT	NT	NT	AW F	NT G	NT	NT	AW ◇ H
Liverpool Lime Street 10 89,91 d	23p02	23p16	03 38	05 13	05 31		05 46	06 01	06 13		06 16	06 25	06 31	06 46	06 57	07 01	07 13		07 16	07 26	07 31	
Edge Hill 89,91 d	23p06	23p20			05 35		05 50	06 05			06 20		06 35	06 50		07 05			07 20	07 30	07 35	
Wavertree Technology Park d	23p08	23p22		05 19	05 37		05 52	06 07	06 19		06 22		06 37	06 52		07 07	07 19		07 22		07 37	
Broad Green d	23p11	23p26			05 40		05 55	06 10			06 25		06 40	06 55		07 10			07 25		07 40	
Roby d	23p15	23p30			05 44		05 59	06 14			06 29		06 44	06 59		07 14			07 29		07 44	
Huyton d	23p17	23p32			05 46		06 01	06 16			06 31		06 46	07 01	07 06	07 16			07 31		07 46	
Prescot d	23p22				05 51			06 21					06 51			07 21					07 51	
Eccleston Park d	23p24				05 53			06 23					06 53			07 23					07 53	
Thatto Heath d	23p27				05 56			06 26					06 56			07 26					07 56	
St Helens Central a	23p30				05 59			06 29					06 59		07 15	07 29					07 59	
d	23p31				06 00			06 30					07 00		07 15	07 30					08 00	
Garswood d	23p38				06 07			06 37					07 07			07 37					08 07	
Bryn d	23p41				06 10			06 40					07 10			07 40					08 10	
Whiston d		23p36					06 05				06 35			07 05					07 35			
Rainhill d		23p39					06 08				06 38			07 08					07 38			
Lea Green d		23p42					06 11				06 41			07 11			07 28		07 41			
St Helens Junction d		23p45		05 29			06 14		06 29		06 44			07 14			07 31		07 44			
Warrington Bank Quay d						06 06				06 40								07 39				08 08
Earlestown 8 d		23p50				06 12	06 19			06 47	06 50			07 19				07 46	07 49			08 16
Warrington Bank Quay a											07 01											
Newton-le-Willows d		23p53		05 35		06 15	06 22		06 35	06 50				07 22			07 37	07 49	07 52			08 19
Wigan North Western 65 a	23p48				06 21			06 51					07 21		07 30	07 51					08 21	
d	23p48														07 31							
Euxton Balshaw Lane d	23p59														07 41							
Leyland 82 a	00 04														07 46							
Preston 8 65,82 a	00 13														07 54							
Blackpool North 97 a															08 21							
Patricroft d		00 05					06 34							07 34					08 04			
Eccles d		00 08					06 36							07 36					08 06			
Manchester Victoria ⛴ a		00 21					06 49							07 49					08 19			
Manchester Oxford Road a						06 35			06 57	07 09		07 37					07 57	08 09		08 36		08 41
Manchester Piccadilly 10 ⛴ a			04 14	05 57		06 45			07 01	07 18							08 01	08 18				08 50
Manchester Airport 85 ✈ a			04 30	06 14					07 22								08 22					

A From Barrow-in-Furness
B from 12 September until 21 October. From Chester
C until 9 September, from 24 October. From Chester
D From Chester
E To Stalybridge
F From Shrewsbury
G To Huddersfield
H From Llandudno

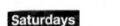

Liverpool and St. Helens - Newton-le-Willows, Wigan, Preston and Manchester

		NT	NT	NT	NT	NT		NT	NT	NT	NT	NT	AW	NT	NT	NT		NT	NT	NT	NT	AW	NT	NT	NT
										A			◇ B						A			◇ B			
Liverpool Lime Street [10] 89,91	d	07 46	07 57	08 01	08 13	08 16		08 26	08 31	08 44	08 57	09 01		09 13	09 16	09 27		09 31	09 46	09 57	10 01		10 13	10 16	10 27
Edge Hill 89,91	d	07 50		08 05		08 20		08 30	08 35	08 50		09 05			09 20			09 35	09 50		10 05			10 20	
Wavertree Technology Park	d	07 52		08 07	08 19	08 22			08 37	08 52		09 07		09 19	09 22			09 37	09 52		10 07		10 19	10 22	
Broad Green	d	07 55		08 10		08 25			08 40	08 55		09 10			09 25			09 40	09 55		10 10			10 25	
Roby	d	07 59		08 14		08 29			08 44	08 59		09 14			09 29			09 44	09 59		10 14			10 29	
Huyton	d	08 01	08 06	08 16		08 31			08 46	09 01	09 06	09 16			09 31			09 46	10 01	10 06	10 16			10 31	
Prescot	d			08 21					08 51			09 21						09 51			10 21				
Eccleston Park	d			08 23					08 53			09 23						09 53			10 23				
Thatto Heath	d			08 26					08 56			09 26						09 56			10 26				
St Helens Central	a		08 15	08 29					08 59		09 15	09 29						09 59		10 15	10 29				
	d		08 15	08 30					09 00		09 15	09 30						10 00		10 15	10 30				
Garswood	d			08 37					09 07			09 37						10 07			10 37				
Bryn	d			08 40					09 10			09 40						10 10			10 40				
Whiston	d	08 05				08 35				09 05					09 35				10 05					10 35	
Rainhill	d	08 08				08 38				09 08					09 38				10 08					10 38	
Lea Green	d	08 11				08 41				09 11					09 41				10 11					10 41	
St Helens Junction	d	08 14			08 29	08 44				09 14				09 29	09 44				10 14				10 29	10 44	
Warrington Bank Quay	d												09 19									10 19			
Earlestown [8]	d	08 19				08 50				09 19			09 26		09 50				10 19			10 26		10 50	
Warrington Bank Quay	a					09 01									10 01									11 01	
Newton-le-Willows	d	08 22			08 35					09 22			09 29	09 35					10 22			10 29	10 35		
Wigan North Western 65	a		08 30	08 51					09 21		09 30	09 51						10 21		10 30	10 51				
	d		08 31								09 31									10 31					
Euxton Balshaw Lane	d		08 41								09 41									10 41					
Leyland 82	a		08 46								09 46									10 46					
Preston [8] 65,82	a		08 54								09 54									10 54					
Blackpool North 97	a		09 21								10 21									11 21					
Patricroft	d	08 34								09 34									10 34						
Eccles	d	08 36								09 36									10 36						
Manchester Victoria	a	08 50								09 47									10 49						
Manchester Oxford Road	a				08 57			09 36					09 48	09 57		10 36						10 48	10 57		11 36
Manchester Piccadilly [10]	a				09 01								09 57	10 01								10 57	11 01		
Manchester Airport 85 ✈	a				09 22									10 22									11 22		

		NT		NT	NT	NT	AW	NT	NT	NT	NT	NT		NT	NT	AW	NT	NT	NT	NT	NT	NT		NT	AW
				A	C		◇ B					A		C		◇ B					A	C			◇ B
Liverpool Lime Street [10] 89,91	d	10 31		10 46	10 57	11 01		11 13	11 16	11 27	11 31	11 46		11 57	12 01		12 13	12 16	12 27	12 31	12 46	12 57		13 01	
Edge Hill 89,91	d	10 35		10 50		11 05			11 20		11 35	11 50			12 05			12 20		12 35	12 50			13 05	
Wavertree Technology Park	d	10 37		10 52		11 07		11 19	11 22		11 37	11 52			12 07		12 19	12 22		12 37	12 52			13 07	
Broad Green	d	10 40		10 55		11 10			11 25		11 40	11 55			12 10			12 25		12 40	12 55			13 10	
Roby	d	10 44		10 59		11 14			11 29		11 44	11 59			12 14			12 29		12 44	12 59			13 14	
Huyton	d	10 46		11 01	11 06	11 16			11 31		11 46	12 01		12 06	12 16			12 31		12 46	13 01	13 06		13 16	
Prescot	d	10 51				11 21					11 51				12 21					12 51				13 21	
Eccleston Park	d	10 53				11 23					11 53				12 23					12 53				13 23	
Thatto Heath	d	10 56				11 26					11 56				12 26					12 56				13 26	
St Helens Central	a	10 59			11 15	11 29					11 59			12 15	12 29					12 59		13 15		13 29	
	d	11 00			11 15	11 30					12 00			12 15	12 30					13 00		13 15		13 30	
Garswood	d	11 07				11 37					12 07				12 37					13 07				13 37	
Bryn	d	11 10				11 40					12 10				12 40					13 10				13 40	
Whiston	d			11 05					11 35			12 05						12 35			13 05				
Rainhill	d			11 08					11 38			12 08						12 38			13 08				
Lea Green	d			11 11					11 41			12 11						12 41			13 11				
St Helens Junction	d			11 14				11 29	11 44			12 14					12 29	12 44			13 14				
Warrington Bank Quay	d						11 19									12 19									13 19
Earlestown [8]	d			11 19			11 26		11 50			12 19				12 26		12 50			13 19				13 26
Warrington Bank Quay	a								12 01									13 01							
Newton-le-Willows	d			11 22			11 29	11 35				12 22				12 29	12 35				13 22				13 29
Wigan North Western 65	a	11 21			11 30	11 51					12 21			12 30	12 51					13 21		13 30		13 51	
	d				11 31									12 31								13 31			
Euxton Balshaw Lane	d				11 41									12 41								13 41			
Leyland 82	a				11 46									12 46								13 46			
Preston [8] 65,82	a				11 54									12 54								13 54			
Blackpool North 97	a				12 21									13 21								14 21			
Patricroft	d			11 34								12 34									13 34				
Eccles	d			11 36								12 36									13 36				
Manchester Victoria	a			11 49								12 49									13 49				
Manchester Oxford Road	a						11 48	11 57		12 36						12 48	12 57		13 36						13 48
Manchester Piccadilly [10]	a						11 57	12 01								12 57	13 01								13 57
Manchester Airport 85 ✈	a							12 22									13 22								

A To Stalybridge
B From Llandudno
C From Liverpool South Parkway

Table 90

Saturdays

until 18 June

Liverpool and St. Helens - Newton-le-Willows, Wigan, Preston and Manchester

		NT	NT	NT	NT	NT A	NT B	NT		NT	NT	NT	NT	NT A	NT B	NT	NT	AW C		NT	NT	NT	NT A	NT B	NT
Liverpool Lime Street 10 89,91	d	13 13	13 16	13 27	13 31	13 46	13 57	14 01		14 13	14 16	14 27	14 31	14 46	14 57	15 01	15 13			15 16	15 27	15 31	15 46	15 57	16 01
Edge Hill 89,91	d		13 20		13 35	13 50		14 05			14 20		14 35	14 50		15 05				15 20		15 35	15 50		16 05
Wavertree Technology Park	d	13 19	13 22		13 37	13 52		14 07		14 19	14 22		14 37	14 52		15 07	15 19			15 22		15 37	15 52		16 07
Broad Green	d		13 25		13 40	13 55		14 10			14 25		14 40	14 55		15 10				15 25		15 40	15 55		16 10
Roby	d		13 29		13 44	13 59		14 14			14 29		14 44	14 59		15 14				15 29		15 44	15 59		16 14
Huyton	d		13 31		13 46	14 01	14 06	14 16			14 31		14 46	15 01	15 06	15 16				15 31		15 46	16 01	16 06	16 16
Prescot	d				13 51			14 21					14 51			15 21						15 51			16 21
Eccleston Park	d				13 53			14 23					14 53			15 23						15 53			16 23
Thatto Heath	d				13 56			14 26					14 56			15 26						15 56			16 26
St Helens Central	a				13 59		14 15	14 29					14 59		15 15	15 29						15 59		16 15	16 29
	d				14 00		14 15	14 30					15 00		15 15	15 30						16 00		16 15	16 30
Garswood	d				14 07			14 37					15 07			15 37						16 07			16 37
Bryn	d				14 10			14 40					15 10			15 40						16 10			16 40
Whiston	d		13 35			14 05					14 35			15 05						15 35			16 05		
Rainhill	d		13 38			14 08					14 38			15 08						15 38			16 08		
Lea Green	d		13 41			14 11					14 41			15 11						15 41			16 11		
St Helens Junction	d	13 29	13 44			14 14				14 29	14 44			15 14			15 29			15 44			16 14		
Warrington Bank Quay	d																	15 00							
Earlestown 8	d		13 50			14 19					14 50			15 19				15 25		15 50			16 19		
Warrington Bank Quay	a		14 01								15 01									16 01					
Newton-le-Willows	d	13 35				14 22				14 35				15 22			15 35	15 35					16 22		
Wigan North Western 65	a				14 21		14 30	14 51					15 21		15 30	15 51						16 21		16 30	16 51
	d						14 31								15 31									16 31	
Euxton Balshaw Lane	d						14 41								15 41									16 41	
Leyland 82	a						14 46								15 46									16 46	
Preston 8 65,82	a						14 54								15 54									16 54	
Blackpool North 97	a						15 21								16 21									17 21	
Patricroft	d					14 34								15 34									16 34		
Eccles	d					14 36								15 36									16 36		
Manchester Victoria	a					14 50								15 49									16 49		
Manchester Oxford Road	a	13 57		14 36						14 57		15 36					15 57	16 05			16 36				
Manchester Piccadilly 10	a	14 01								15 01							16 01	16 10							
Manchester Airport 85 ✈	a	14 22								15 22							16 22								

		NT	AW C	NT		NT	NT	NT A	NT B	NT	NT	AW C	NT	NT		NT	NT	NT	NT	NT	NT	AW C	NT	NT	
Liverpool Lime Street 10 89,91	d	16 13		16 16		16 27	16 31	16 46	16 57	17 01	17 06		17 10	17 19		17 27	17 35	17 44	17 48	18 01	18 13		18 16	18 31	
Edge Hill 89,91	d			16 20			16 35	16 50		17 05			17 14			17 31	17 39		17 52	18 05			18 20	18 35	
Wavertree Technology Park	d	16 19		16 22			16 37	16 52		17 07	17 12		17 16			17 33	17 41	17 49	17 54	18 07	18 19		18 22	18 37	
Broad Green	d			16 25			16 40	16 55		17 10			17 19			17 36	17 44	17 52	17 57	18 10			18 25	18 40	
Roby	d			16 29			16 44	16 59		17 14			17 23			17 40	17 48		18 01	18 14			18 29	18 44	
Huyton	d			16 31			16 46	17 01	17 06	17 16	17 19		17 25	17 29		17 42	17 50	17 57	18 03	18 16			18 31	18 46	
Prescot	d						16 51			17 21				17 33				18 02		18 21				18 51	
Eccleston Park	d						16 53			17 23				17 36				18 05		18 23				18 53	
Thatto Heath	d						16 56			17 26				17 38				18 07		18 26				18 56	
St Helens Central	a						16 59		17 15	17 29				17 42		17 51		18 11		18 29				18 59	
	d						17 00		17 15	17 30				17 42		17 51		18 11		18 30				19 00	
Garswood	d						17 07			17 37				17 49				18 19		18 37				19 07	
Bryn	d						17 10			17 40				17 52				18 22		18 40				19 10	
Whiston	d			16 35				17 05					17 28				17 54		18 07				18 35		
Rainhill	d			16 38				17 08					17 32				17 57		18 10				18 38		
Lea Green	d			16 41				17 11			17 26		17 35				18 00		18 13				18 41		
St Helens Junction	d	16 29		16 44				17 14			17 29		17 39				18 03		18 16		18 29		18 44		
Warrington Bank Quay	d		16 00									17 00										18 00			
Earlestown 8	d		16 25	16 49				17 19				17 25	17 44				18 08		18 21			18 25	18 50		
Warrington Bank Quay	a																						19 01		
Newton-le-Willows	d	16 35	16 35	16 52				17 22			17 35	17 35	17 47				18 11		18 24		18 35	18 35			
Wigan North Western 65	a						17 21		17 30	17 52				18 04		18 05		18 30		18 49				19 21	
	d								17 31							18 05		18 31		18 49					
Euxton Balshaw Lane	d								17 41							18 16		18 41		19 01					
Leyland 82	a								17 46							18 21		18 46		19 06					
Preston 8 65,82	a								17 54							18 31		18 54		19 15					
Blackpool North 97	a								18 24									19 21							
Patricroft	d			17 04				17 34					17 59				18 23								
Eccles	d			17 06				17 36					18 01				18 25		18 36						
Manchester Victoria	a			17 20				17 47					18 15				18 41		18 49						
Manchester Oxford Road	a	16 57	17 05			17 36					17 57	18 05									18 57	19 05			
Manchester Piccadilly 10	a	17 01	17 10								18 01	18 10									19 01	19 10			
Manchester Airport 85 ✈	a	17 22									18 22										19 24				

A To Stalybridge

B From Liverpool South Parkway

C From Chester

Saturdays
until 18 June

Liverpool and St. Helens - Newton-le-Willows, Wigan, Preston and Manchester

		NT	AW	NT	NT	NT	NT	NT	AW	NT	NT	NT	AW	NT	NT	AW	NT	AW	NT	NT
			A						A				A			A		A		
Liverpool Lime Street 10 89,91	d	18 46		19 01	19 12	19 23	19 42	20 09		20 12	20 25	20 42		21 12	21 42		22 12		23 02	23 16
Edge Hill 89,91	d	18 50		19 05	19 16		19 46			20 16		20 46		21 16	21 46		22 16		23 06	23 20
Wavertree Technology Park	d	18 52		19 07	19 18		19 48	20 15		20 18		20 48		21 18	21 48		22 18		23 08	23 22
Broad Green	d	18 55		19 10	19 21		19 51			20 21		20 51		21 21	21 51		22 21		23 11	23 26
Roby	d	18 59		19 14	19 25		19 55			20 25		20 55		21 25	21 55		22 25		23 15	23 30
Huyton	d	19 01		19 16	19 27	19 32	19 57			20 27	20 34	20 57		21 27	21 57		22 27		23 17	23 32
Prescot	d			19 21			20 02					21 02			22 02				23 22	
Eccleston Park	d			19 23			20 04					21 04			22 04				23 24	
Thatto Heath	d			19 26			20 07					21 07			22 07				23 27	
St Helens Central	a			19 29		19 40	20 10				20 42	21 10			22 10				23 30	
	d			19 30		19 41	20 11				20 43	21 11			22 11				23 31	
Garswood	d			19 37			20 18					21 18			22 18				23 38	
Bryn	d			19 40			20 21					21 21			22 21				23 41	
Whiston	d	19 05			19 31					20 31				21 31			22 31			23 36
Rainhill	d	19 08			19 34					20 34				21 34			22 34			23 39
Lea Green	d	19 11			19 37					20 37				21 37			22 37			23 42
St Helens Junction	d	19 14			19 40			20 25		20 40				21 40			22 40			23 45
Warrington Bank Quay	d		19 00						20 00				21 00			22 00		23 00		
Earlestown 8	d	19 19	19 25		19 45				20 25	20 45			21 25	21 45		22 25	22 45	23 25		23 50
Warrington Bank Quay	a																			
Newton-le-Willows	d	19 22	19 35		19 48			20 35	20 35	20 48			21 35	21 48		22 35	22 48	23 35		23 53
Wigan North Western 65	a			19 51		19 54	20 32				20 57	21 32			22 28				23 48	
	d					19 55					20 57				22 28				23 48	
Euxton Balshaw Lane	d					20 05					21 08				22 39				23 59	
Leyland 82	a					20 10					21 16				22 44				00 04	
Preston 8 65,82	a					20 18					21 22				22 55				00 13	
Blackpool North 97	a					20 44					21 53				23 22					
Patricroft	d	19 34			20 00					21 00				22 00			23 00			00 05
Eccles	d	19 36			20 02					21 02				22 02			23 02			00 08
Manchester Victoria	a	19 49			20 15					21 15				22 15			23 15			00 21
Manchester Oxford Road	a		20 05					20 57	21 05				22 05			23 05		00 05		
Manchester Piccadilly 10	a		20 10					21 01	21 10				22 10			23 10		00 10		
Manchester Airport 85	a							21 24												

Saturdays
25 June to 10 September

		NT	NT	NT	NT	NT	AW	NT	NT	NT	AW	NT	NT	NT	NT	NT	NT	NT	AW	NT	NT	NT	AW
							A				◇ A				B				C	D			◇ E
Liverpool Lime Street 10 89,91	d	23p02	23p16	03 38	05 13	05 31		05 46	06 01	06 13		06 16	06 25	06 31	06 46	06 57	07 01	07 13		07 16	07 26	07 31	
Edge Hill 89,91	d	23p06	23p20			05 35		05 50	06 05			06 20		06 35	06 50		07 05			07 20	07 30	07 35	
Wavertree Technology Park	d	23p08	23p22		05 19	05 37		05 52	06 07	06 19		06 22		06 37	06 52		07 07	07 19		07 22		07 37	
Broad Green	d	23p11	23p26			05 40		05 55	06 10			06 25		06 40	06 55		07 10			07 25		07 40	
Roby	d	23p15	23p30			05 44		05 59	06 14			06 29		06 44	06 59		07 14			07 29		07 44	
Huyton	d	23p17	23p32			05 46		06 01	06 16			06 31		06 46	07 01	07 06	07 16			07 31		07 46	
Prescot	d	23p22				05 51			06 21					06 51			07 21					07 51	
Eccleston Park	d	23p24				05 53			06 23					06 53			07 23					07 53	
Thatto Heath	d	23p27				05 56			06 26					06 56			07 26					07 56	
St Helens Central	a	23p30				05 59			06 29					06 59		07 15	07 29					07 59	
	d	23p31				06 00			06 30					07 00		07 15	07 30					08 00	
Garswood	d	23p38				06 07			06 37					07 07			07 37					08 07	
Bryn	d	23p41				06 10			06 40					07 10			07 40					08 10	
Whiston	d		23p36					06 05				06 35			07 05					07 35			
Rainhill	d		23p39					06 08				06 38			07 08					07 38			
Lea Green	d		23p42					06 11				06 41			07 11			07 28		07 41			
St Helens Junction	d		23p45		05 29			06 14		06 29		06 44			07 14			07 31		07 44			
Warrington Bank Quay	d						06 06				06 40								07 39				08 08
Earlestown 8	d		23p50				06 12	06 19			06 47	06 50			07 19				07 46	07 49			08 16
Warrington Bank Quay	a											07 01											
Newton-le-Willows	d		23p53		05 35		06 15	06 22		06 35	06 50				07 22			07 37	07 49	07 52			08 19
Wigan North Western 65	a	23p48				06 21			06 51					07 21		07 30	07 51					08 21	
	d	23p48														07 31							
Euxton Balshaw Lane	d	23p59														07 41							
Leyland 82	a	00 04														07 46							
Preston 8 65,82	a	00 13														07 54							
Blackpool North 97	a															08 21							
Patricroft	d		00 05					06 34							07 34					08 04			
Eccles	d		00 08					06 36							07 36					08 06			
Manchester Victoria	a		00 21					06 49							07 49					08 19			
Manchester Oxford Road	a						06 35			06 57	07 09		07 37					07 57	08 09		08 36		08 41
Manchester Piccadilly 10	a			04 14	05 57		06 45			07 01	07 18							08 01	08 18				08 50
Manchester Airport 85	a			04 30	06 14					07 22								08 22					

A From Chester
B To Stalybridge
C From Shrewsbury
D To Huddersfield
E From Llandudno

Table 90

Saturdays

25 June to 10 September

Liverpool and St. Helens - Newton-le-Willows, Wigan, Preston and Manchester

		NT	NT	NT	NT	NT	NT	NT	NT	NT	NT	AW	NT	NT	NT	NT	NT	NT	NT	AW	NT	NT	NT
									A			◇ B ✠					A			◇ B ✠			
Liverpool Lime Street 10 89,91	d	07 46	07 57	08 01	08 13	08 16	08 26	08 31	08 44	08 57	09 01		09 13	09 16	09 27	09 31	09 46	09 57	10 01		10 13	10 16	10 27
Edge Hill 89,91	d	07 50		08 05		08 20	08 30	08 35	08 50		09 05			09 20		09 35	09 50		10 05			10 20	
Wavertree Technology Park	d	07 52		08 07	08 19	08 22		08 37	08 52		09 07		09 19	09 22		09 37	09 52		10 07		10 19	10 22	
Broad Green	d	07 55		08 10		08 25		08 40	08 55		09 10			09 25		09 40	09 55		10 10			10 25	
Roby	d	07 59		08 14		08 29		08 44	08 59		09 14			09 29		09 44	09 59		10 14			10 29	
Huyton	d	08 01	08 06	08 16		08 31		08 46	09 01	09 06	09 16			09 31		09 46	10 01	10 06	10 16			10 31	
Prescot	d			08 21				08 51			09 21					09 51			10 21				
Eccleston Park	d			08 23				08 53			09 23					09 53			10 23				
Thatto Heath	d			08 26				08 56			09 26					09 56			10 26				
St Helens Central	a		08 15	08 29				08 59		09 15	09 29					09 59		10 15	10 29				
	d		08 15	08 30				09 00		09 15	09 30					10 00		10 15	10 30				
Garswood	d			08 37				09 07			09 37					10 07			10 37				
Bryn	d			08 40				09 10			09 40					10 10			10 40				
Whiston	d	08 05				08 35			09 05					09 35			10 05					10 35	
Rainhill	d	08 08				08 38			09 08					09 38			10 08					10 38	
Lea Green	d	08 11				08 41			09 11					09 41			10 11					10 41	
St Helens Junction	d	08 14			08 29	08 44			09 14				09 29	09 44			10 14				10 29	10 44	
Warrington Bank Quay	d											09 19								10 19			
Earlestown 8	d	08 19				08 50			09 19			09 26		09 50			10 19			10 26		10 50	
Warrington Bank Quay	a					09 01								10 01								11 01	
Newton-le-Willows	d	08 22			08 35				09 22			09 29	09 35				10 22			10 29	10 35		
Wigan North Western 65	a		08 30	08 51				09 21		09 30	09 51					10 21		10 30	10 51				
	d		08 31							09 31								10 31					
Euxton Balshaw Lane	d		08 41							09 41								10 41					
Leyland 82	a		08 46							09 46								10 46					
Preston 8 65,82	a		08 54							09 54								10 54					
Blackpool North 97	a		09 21							10 21								11 21					
Patricroft	d	08 34							09 34								10 34						
Eccles	d	08 36							09 36								10 36						
Manchester Victoria ⇌	a	08 50							09 47								10 49						
Manchester Oxford Road	a				08 57		09 36					09 48	09 57		10 36					10 48	10 57		11 36
Manchester Piccadilly 10 ⇌	a				09 01							09 57	10 01							10 57	11 01		
Manchester Airport 85 ✈	a				09 22								10 22								11 22		

		NT	NT	NT	NT	AW	NT	NT	NT	NT	NT	NT	NT	AW	NT	NT	NT	NT	NT	NT	NT	AW
			A	C		◇ B ✠					A	C		◇ B ✠					A	C		◇ B ✠
Liverpool Lime Street 10 89,91	d	10 31	10 46	10 57	11 01		11 13	11 16	11 27	11 31	11 46	11 57	12 01		12 13	12 16	12 27	12 31	12 46	12 57	13 01	
Edge Hill 89,91	d	10 35	10 50		11 05			11 20		11 35	11 50		12 05			12 20		12 35	12 50		13 05	
Wavertree Technology Park	d	10 37	10 52		11 07		11 19	11 22		11 37	11 52		12 07		12 19	12 22		12 37	12 52		13 07	
Broad Green	d	10 40	10 55		11 10			11 25		11 40	11 55		12 10			12 25		12 40	12 55		13 10	
Roby	d	10 44	10 59		11 14			11 29		11 44	11 59		12 14			12 29		12 44	12 59		13 14	
Huyton	d	10 46	11 01	11 06	11 16			11 31		11 46	12 01	12 06	12 16			12 31		12 46	13 01	13 06	13 16	
Prescot	d	10 51			11 21					11 51			12 21					12 51			13 21	
Eccleston Park	d	10 53			11 23					11 53			12 23					12 53			13 23	
Thatto Heath	d	10 56			11 26					11 56			12 26					12 56			13 26	
St Helens Central	a	10 59		11 15	11 29					11 59		12 15	12 29					12 59		13 15	13 29	
	d	11 00		11 15	11 30					12 00		12 15	12 30					13 00		13 15	13 30	
Garswood	d	11 07			11 37					12 07			12 37					13 07			13 37	
Bryn	d	11 10			11 40					12 10			12 40					13 10			13 40	
Whiston	d		11 05					11 35			12 05					12 35			13 05			
Rainhill	d		11 08					11 38			12 08					12 38			13 08			
Lea Green	d		11 11					11 41			12 11					12 41			13 11			
St Helens Junction	d		11 14				11 29	11 44			12 14				12 29	12 44			13 14			
Warrington Bank Quay	d					11 19								12 19								13 19
Earlestown 8	d		11 19			11 26		11 50			12 19			12 26		12 50			13 19			13 26
Warrington Bank Quay	a							12 01								13 01						
Newton-le-Willows	d		11 22			11 29	11 35				12 22			12 29	12 35				13 22			13 29
Wigan North Western 65	a	11 21		11 30	11 51					12 21		12 30	12 51					13 21		13 30	13 51	
	d			11 31								12 31								13 31		
Euxton Balshaw Lane	d			11 41								12 41								13 41		
Leyland 82	a			11 46								12 46								13 46		
Preston 8 65,82	a			11 54								12 54								13 54		
Blackpool North 97	a			12 21								13 21								14 21		
Patricroft	d		11 34								12 34								13 34			
Eccles	d		11 36								12 36								13 36			
Manchester Victoria ⇌	a		11 49								12 49								13 49			
Manchester Oxford Road	a					11 48	11 57		12 36					12 48	12 57		13 36					13 48
Manchester Piccadilly 10 ⇌	a					11 57	12 01							12 57	13 01							13 57
Manchester Airport 85 ✈	a						12 22								13 22							

A To Stalybridge

B From Llandudno

C From Liverpool South Parkway

Table 90

Saturdays

25 June to 10 September

Liverpool and St. Helens - Newton-le-Willows, Wigan, Preston and Manchester

	NT	NT	NT	NT	NT	NT	NT		AW	NT	NT	NT	NT	NT	NT	NT	AW		NT	NT	NT	NT	NT	NT
					A	B			◇ C					A	B		◇ C						A	B
Liverpool Lime Street 10 89,91 d	13 13	13 16	13 27	13 31	13 46	13 57	14 01			14 13	14 16	14 27	14 31	14 46	14 57	15 01			15 13	15 16	15 27	15 31	15 46	15 57
Edge Hill 89,91 d		13 20		13 35	13 50		14 05				14 20		14 35	14 50		15 05				15 20		15 35	15 50	
Wavertree Technology Park d	13 19	13 22		13 37	13 52		14 07			14 19	14 22		14 37	14 52		15 07			15 19	15 22		15 37	15 52	
Broad Green d		13 25		13 40	13 55		14 10				14 25		14 40	14 55		15 10				15 25		15 40	15 55	
Roby d		13 29		13 44	13 59		14 14				14 29		14 44	14 59		15 14				15 29		15 44	15 59	
Huyton d		13 31		13 46	14 01	14 06	14 16				14 31		14 46	15 01	15 06	15 16				15 31		15 46	16 01	16 06
Prescot d				13 51			14 21						14 51			15 21						15 51		
Eccleston Park d				13 53			14 23						14 53			15 23						15 53		
Thatto Heath d				13 56			14 26						14 56			15 26						15 56		
St Helens Central a				13 59		14 15	14 29						14 59		15 15	15 29						15 59		16 15
d				14 00		14 15	14 30						15 00		15 15	15 30						16 00		16 15
Garswood d				14 07			14 37						15 07			15 37						16 07		
Bryn d				14 10			14 40						15 10			15 40						16 10		
Whiston d		13 35			14 05						14 35			15 05						15 35			16 05	
Rainhill d		13 38			14 08						14 38			15 08						15 38			16 08	
Lea Green d		13 41			14 11						14 41			15 11						15 41			16 11	
St Helens Junction d	13 29	13 44			14 14					14 29	14 44			15 14					15 29	15 44			16 14	
Warrington Bank Quay d									14 19								15 19							
Earlestown 8 d		13 50			14 19				14 26		14 50			15 19			15 26			15 50			16 19	
Warrington Bank Quay a		14 01									15 01									16 01				
Newton-le-Willows d	13 35				14 22				14 29	14 35				15 22			15 29		15 35				16 22	
Wigan North Western 65 a				14 21		14 30	14 51						15 21		15 30	15 51						16 21		16 30
d						14 31									15 31									16 31
Euxton Balshaw Lane d						14 41									15 41									16 41
Leyland 82 a						14 46									15 46									16 46
Preston 8 65,82 a						14 54									15 54									16 54
Blackpool North 97 a						15 21									16 21									17 21
Patricroft d					14 34									15 34									16 34	
Eccles d					14 36									15 36									16 36	
Manchester Victoria a					14 50									15 49									16 49	
Manchester Oxford Road a	13 57		14 36						14 48	14 57		15 36					15 48		15 57		16 36			
Manchester Piccadilly 10 a	14 01								14 57	15 01							15 57		16 01					
Manchester Airport 85 a	14 22									15 22									16 22					

	NT	AW	NT		NT	NT	NT	NT	NT	NT	AW	NT	NT		NT	NT	NT	NT	NT	NT	AW	NT	NT	
		◇ C						A	B		◇ C										◇ C			
Liverpool Lime Street 10 89,91 d	16 01		16 13		16 16	16 27	16 31	16 46	16 57	17 01		17 06	17 10		17 19	17 27	17 35	17 44	17 48	18 01		18 13	18 16	
Edge Hill 89,91 d	16 05				16 20		16 35	16 50		17 05			17 14			17 31	17 39		17 52	18 05			18 20	
Wavertree Technology Park d	16 07		16 19		16 22		16 37	16 52		17 07		17 12	17 16			17 33	17 41	17 49	17 54	18 07		18 19	18 22	
Broad Green d	16 10				16 25		16 40	16 55		17 10			17 19			17 36	17 44	17 52	17 57	18 10			18 25	
Roby d	16 14				16 29		16 44	16 59		17 14			17 23			17 40	17 48		18 01	18 14			18 29	
Huyton d	16 16				16 31		16 46	17 01	17 06	17 16		17 19	17 25		17 29	17 42	17 50	17 57	18 03	18 16			18 31	
Prescot d	16 21						16 51			17 21					17 33			18 02		18 21				
Eccleston Park d	16 23						16 53			17 23					17 36			18 05		18 23				
Thatto Heath d	16 26						16 56			17 26					17 38			18 07		18 26				
St Helens Central a	16 29						16 59		17 15	17 29					17 42	17 51		18 11		18 29				
d	16 30						17 00		17 15	17 30					17 42	17 51		18 11		18 30				
Garswood d	16 37						17 07			17 37					17 49			18 19		18 37				
Bryn d	16 40						17 10			17 40					17 52			18 22		18 40				
Whiston d					16 35			17 05					17 28				17 54		18 07				18 35	
Rainhill d					16 38			17 08					17 32				17 57		18 10				18 38	
Lea Green d					16 41			17 11				17 26	17 35				18 00		18 13				18 41	
St Helens Junction d			16 29		16 44			17 14				17 29	17 39				18 03		18 16			18 29	18 44	
Warrington Bank Quay d		16 19									17 19										18 19			
Earlestown 8 d		16 26			16 49			17 19			17 26		17 44				18 08		18 21		18 26		18 50	
Warrington Bank Quay a																							19 01	
Newton-le-Willows d		16 29	16 35		16 52			17 22			17 29	17 35	17 47				18 11		18 24		18 29	18 35		
Wigan North Western 65 a	16 51						17 21		17 30	17 52					18 04	18 05		18 30		18 49				
d									17 31							18 05		18 31		18 49				
Euxton Balshaw Lane d									17 41							18 16		18 41		19 01				
Leyland 82 a									17 46							18 21		18 46		19 06				
Preston 8 65,82 a									17 54							18 31		18 54		19 15				
Blackpool North 97 a									18 24									19 21						
Patricroft d					17 04			17 34					17 59				18 23							
Eccles d					17 06			17 36					18 01				18 25		18 36					
Manchester Victoria a					17 20			17 47					18 15				18 41		18 49					
Manchester Oxford Road a		16 48	16 57			17 36					17 48	17 57									18 48	18 57		
Manchester Piccadilly 10 a		16 57	17 01								17 57	18 01									18 57	19 01		
Manchester Airport 85 a			17 22									18 22										19 24		

A To Stalybridge

B From Liverpool South Parkway

C From Llandudno

Table 90

Saturdays

25 June to 10 September

Liverpool and St. Helens - Newton-le-Willows, Wigan, Preston and Manchester

		NT	NT	NT	AW ◇ A 🛒	NT	NT	NT	AW ◇ A 🛒	NT	NT	NT	NT	AW ◇ A	NT	NT	AW B	NT	NT	NT	AW B
Liverpool Lime Street [10] 89,91	d	18 31	18 46	19 01		19 12	19 23	19 42		20 09	20 12	20 25	20 42		21 12	21 42		22 12	23 02	23 16	
Edge Hill 89,91	d	18 35	18 50	19 05		19 16		19 46			20 16		20 46		21 16	21 46		22 16	23 06	23 20	
Wavertree Technology Park	d	18 37	18 52	19 07		19 18		19 48		20 15	20 18		20 48		21 18	21 48		22 18	23 08	23 22	
Broad Green	d	18 40	18 55	19 10		19 21		19 51			20 21		20 51		21 21	21 51		22 21	23 11	23 26	
Roby	d	18 44	18 59	19 14		19 25		19 55			20 25		20 55		21 25	21 55		22 25	23 15	23 30	
Huyton	d	18 46	19 01	19 16		19 27	19 32	19 57			20 27	20 34	20 57		21 27	21 57		22 27	23 17	23 32	
Prescot	d	18 51		19 21				20 02					21 02			22 02			23 22		
Eccleston Park	d	18 53		19 23				20 04					21 04			22 04			23 24		
Thatto Heath	d	18 56		19 26				20 07					21 07			22 07			23 27		
St Helens Central	a	18 59		19 29			19 40	20 10				20 42	21 10			22 10			23 30		
	d	19 00		19 30			19 41	20 11				20 43	21 11			22 11			23 31		
Garswood	d	19 07		19 37				20 18					21 18			22 18			23 38		
Bryn	d	19 10		19 40				20 21					21 21			22 21			23 41		
Whiston	d		19 05			19 31					20 31				21 31			22 31		23 36	
Rainhill	d		19 08			19 34					20 34				21 34			22 34		23 39	
Lea Green	d		19 11			19 37					20 37				21 37			22 37		23 42	
St Helens Junction	d		19 14			19 40				20 25	20 40				21 40			22 40		23 45	
Warrington Bank Quay	d				19 19				20 19					21 19			22 19				23 50
Earlestown [8]	d		19 19		19 26	19 45			20 26		20 45			21 26	21 45		22 27	22 45		23 50	23 58
Warrington Bank Quay	a																				
Newton-le-Willows	d		19 22		19 29	19 48			20 29	20 35	20 48			21 29	21 48		22 30	22 48		23 53	00 02
Wigan North Western 65	a	19 21		19 51			19 54	20 32				20 57	21 32			22 28			23 48		
	d						19 55					20 57				22 28			23 48		
Euxton Balshaw Lane	d						20 05					21 08				22 39			23 59		
Leyland 82	a						20 10					21 16				22 44			00 04		
Preston [8] 65,82	a						20 18					21 22				22 55			00 13		
Blackpool North 97	a						20 44					21 53				23 22					
Patricroft	d		19 34			20 00					21 00				22 00			23 00		00 05	
Eccles	d		19 36			20 02					21 02				22 02			23 02		00 08	
Manchester Victoria ⛴	a		19 49			20 15					21 15				22 15			23 15		00 21	
Manchester Oxford Road	a				19 48				20 48	20 57				21 48			22 50				
Manchester Piccadilly [10] ⛴	a				19 52				20 57	21 01				21 57			22 58				00 26
Manchester Airport 85 ✈	a				20 18					21 24											

Saturdays

from 17 September

		NT	NT	NT	NT	NT	AW B	NT	NT	NT	AW ◇ B	NT	NT	NT	NT C	NT	NT	NT	AW D 🛒	NT E	NT	NT	AW ◇ A 🛒
Liverpool Lime Street [10] 89,91	d	23p02	23p16	03 38	05 13	05 31		05 46	06 01	06 13		06 16	06 25	06 31	06 46	06 57	07 01	07 13		07 16	07 26	07 31	
Edge Hill 89,91	d	23p06	23p20			05 35		05 50	06 05			06 20		06 35	06 50		07 05			07 20	07 30	07 35	
Wavertree Technology Park	d	23p08	23p22		05 19	05 37		05 52	06 07	06 19		06 22		06 37	06 52		07 07	07 19		07 22		07 37	
Broad Green	d	23p11	23p26			05 40		05 55	06 10			06 25		06 40	06 55		07 10			07 25		07 40	
Roby	d	23p15	23p30			05 44		05 59	06 14			06 29		06 44	06 59		07 14			07 29		07 44	
Huyton	d	23p17	23p32			05 46		06 01	06 16			06 31		06 46	07 01	07 06	07 16			07 31		07 46	
Prescot	d	23p22				05 51			06 21					06 51			07 21					07 51	
Eccleston Park	d	23p24				05 53			06 23					06 53			07 23					07 53	
Thatto Heath	d	23p27				05 56			06 26					06 56			07 26					07 56	
St Helens Central	a	23p30				05 59			06 29					06 59		07 15	07 29					07 59	
	d	23p31				06 00			06 30					07 00		07 15	07 30					08 00	
Garswood	d	23p38				06 07			06 37					07 07			07 37					08 07	
Bryn	d	23p41				06 10			06 40					07 10			07 40					08 10	
Whiston	d		23p36					06 05				06 35			07 05					07 35			
Rainhill	d		23p39					06 08				06 38			07 08					07 38			
Lea Green	d		23p42					06 11				06 41			07 11			07 28		07 41			
St Helens Junction	d		23p45		05 29			06 14		06 29		06 44			07 14			07 31		07 44			
Warrington Bank Quay	d						06 06				06 40								07 39				08 08
Earlestown [8]	d		23p50				06 12	06 19			06 47	06 50			07 19				07 46	07 49			08 16
Warrington Bank Quay	a											07 01											
Newton-le-Willows	d		23p53		05 35		06 15	06 22		06 35	06 50				07 22			07 37	07 49	07 52			08 19
Wigan North Western 65	a	23p48				06 21			06 51					07 21		07 30	07 51					08 21	
	d	23p48														07 31							
Euxton Balshaw Lane	d	23p59														07 41							
Leyland 82	a	00 04														07 46							
Preston [8] 65,82	a	00 13														07 54							
Blackpool North 97	a															08 21							
Patricroft	d		00 05					06 34							07 34					08 04			
Eccles	d		00 08					06 36							07 36					08 06			
Manchester Victoria ⛴	a		00 21					06 49							07 49					08 19			
Manchester Oxford Road	a						06 35			06 57	07 09		07 37					07 57	08 09		08 36		08 41
Manchester Piccadilly [10] ⛴	a			04 14	05 57		06 45			07 01	07 18							08 01	08 18				08 50
Manchester Airport 85 ✈	a			04 30	06 14					07 22								08 22					

A From Llandudno
B From Chester
C To Stalybridge
D From Shrewsbury
E To Huddersfield

Table 90

Saturdays

from 17 September

Liverpool and St. Helens - Newton-le-Willows, Wigan, Preston and Manchester

		NT	NT	NT	NT	NT	NT	NT	NT	NT	NT	AW	NT	NT	NT	NT	NT	NT	NT	AW	NT	NT	NT
									A			◇ B					A			◇ B			
Liverpool Lime Street [10] 89,91	d	07 46	07 57	08 01	08 13	08 16	08 26	08 31	08 44	08 57	09 01		09 13	09 16	09 27	09 31	09 46	09 57	10 01		10 13	10 16	10 27
Edge Hill 89,91	d	07 50		08 05		08 20	08 30	08 35	08 50		09 05			09 20		09 35	09 50		10 05			10 20	
Wavertree Technology Park	d	07 52		08 07	08 19	08 22		08 37	08 52		09 07		09 19	09 22		09 37	09 52		10 07		10 19	10 22	
Broad Green	d	07 55		08 10		08 25		08 40	08 55		09 10			09 25		09 40	09 55		10 10			10 25	
Roby	d	07 59		08 14		08 29		08 44	08 59		09 14			09 29		09 44	09 59		10 14			10 29	
Huyton	d	08 01	08 06	08 16		08 31		08 46	09 01	09 06	09 16			09 31		09 46	10 01	10 06	10 16			10 31	
Prescot	d			08 21				08 51			09 21					09 51			10 21				
Eccleston Park	d			08 23				08 53			09 23					09 53			10 23				
Thatto Heath	d			08 26				08 56			09 26					09 56			10 26				
St Helens Central	a		08 15	08 29				08 59		09 15	09 29					09 59		10 15	10 29				
	d		08 15	08 30				09 00		09 15	09 30					10 00		10 15	10 30				
Garswood	d			08 37				09 07			09 37					10 07			10 37				
Bryn	d			08 40				09 10			09 40					10 10			10 40				
Whiston	d	08 05				08 35			09 05					09 35			10 05					10 35	
Rainhill	d	08 08				08 38			09 08					09 38			10 08					10 38	
Lea Green	d	08 11				08 41			09 11					09 41			10 11					10 41	
St Helens Junction	d	08 14			08 29	08 44			09 14				09 29	09 44			10 14				10 29	10 44	
Warrington Bank Quay	d											09 19								10 19			
Earlestown [8]	d	08 19				08 50			09 19			09 26		09 50			10 19			10 26		10 50	
Warrington Bank Quay	a					09 01								10 01								11 01	
Newton-le-Willows	d	08 22			08 35				09 22			09 29	09 35				10 22			10 29	10 35		
Wigan North Western 65	a		08 30	08 51				09 21		09 30	09 51					10 21		10 30	10 51				
	d		08 31							09 31								10 31					
Euxton Balshaw Lane	d		08 41							09 41								10 41					
Leyland 82	a		08 46							09 46								10 46					
Preston [8] 65,82	a		08 54							09 54								10 54					
Blackpool North 97	a		09 21							10 21								11 21					
Patricroft	d	08 34							09 34								10 34						
Eccles	d	08 36							09 36								10 36						
Manchester Victoria	a	08 50							09 47								10 49						
Manchester Oxford Road	a				08 57		09 36					09 48	09 57		10 36					10 48	10 57		11 36
Manchester Piccadilly [10]	a				09 01							09 57	10 01							10 57	11 01		
Manchester Airport 85	a				09 22								10 22								11 22		

		NT	NT	NT	NT	AW	NT	NT	NT	NT	NT	NT	NT	AW	NT	NT	NT	NT	NT	NT	NT	AW
			A	C		◇ B					A	C		◇ B					A	C		◇ B
Liverpool Lime Street [10] 89,91	d	10 31	10 46	10 57	11 01		11 13	11 16	11 27	11 31	11 46	11 57	12 01		12 13	12 16	12 27	12 31	12 46	12 57	13 01	
Edge Hill 89,91	d	10 35	10 50		11 05			11 20		11 35	11 50		12 05			12 20		12 35	12 50		13 05	
Wavertree Technology Park	d	10 37	10 52		11 07		11 19	11 22		11 37	11 52		12 07		12 19	12 22		12 37	12 52		13 07	
Broad Green	d	10 40	10 55		11 10			11 25		11 40	11 55		12 10			12 25		12 40	12 55		13 10	
Roby	d	10 44	10 59		11 14			11 29		11 44	11 59		12 14			12 29		12 44	12 59		13 14	
Huyton	d	10 46	11 01	11 06	11 16			11 31		11 46	12 01	12 06	12 16			12 31		12 46	13 01	13 06	13 16	
Prescot	d	10 51			11 21					11 51			12 21					12 51			13 21	
Eccleston Park	d	10 53			11 23					11 53			12 23					12 53			13 23	
Thatto Heath	d	10 56			11 26					11 56			12 26					12 56			13 26	
St Helens Central	a	10 59		11 15	11 29					11 59		12 15	12 29					12 59		13 15	13 29	
	d	11 00		11 15	11 30					12 00		12 15	12 30					13 00		13 15	13 30	
Garswood	d	11 07			11 37					12 07			12 37					13 07			13 37	
Bryn	d	11 10			11 40					12 10			12 40					13 10			13 40	
Whiston	d		11 05					11 35			12 05					12 35			13 05			
Rainhill	d		11 08					11 38			12 08					12 38			13 08			
Lea Green	d		11 11					11 41			12 11					12 41			13 11			
St Helens Junction	d		11 14				11 29	11 44			12 14				12 29	12 44			13 14			
Warrington Bank Quay	d					11 19								12 19								13 19
Earlestown [8]	d		11 19			11 26		11 50			12 19			12 26		12 50			13 19			13 26
Warrington Bank Quay	a							12 01								13 01						
Newton-le-Willows	d		11 22			11 29	11 35				12 22			12 29	12 35				13 22			13 29
Wigan North Western 65	a	11 21		11 30	11 51					12 21		12 30	12 51					13 21		13 30	13 51	
	d			11 31								12 31								13 31		
Euxton Balshaw Lane	d			11 41								12 41								13 41		
Leyland 82	a			11 46								12 46								13 46		
Preston [8] 65,82	a			11 54								12 54								13 54		
Blackpool North 97	a			12 21								13 21								14 21		
Patricroft	d		11 34								12 34								13 34			
Eccles	d		11 36								12 36								13 36			
Manchester Victoria	a		11 49								12 49								13 49			
Manchester Oxford Road	a					11 48	11 57		12 36					12 48	12 57		13 36					13 48
Manchester Piccadilly [10]	a					11 57	12 01							12 57	13 01							13 57
Manchester Airport 85	a						12 22								13 22							

A To Stalybridge
B From Llandudno
C From Liverpool South Parkway

Table 90

Saturdays
from 17 September

Liverpool and St. Helens - Newton-le-Willows, Wigan, Preston and Manchester

		NT	NT	NT	NT	NT A	NT B	NT		AW ◇ C	NT	NT	NT	NT	NT A	NT B	NT	AW ◇ C		NT	NT	NT	NT	NT A	NT B
Liverpool Lime Street 10 89,91	d	13 13	13 16	13 27	13 31	13 46	13 57	14 01			14 13	14 16	14 27	14 31	14 46	14 57	15 01			15 13	15 16	15 27	15 31	15 46	15 57
Edge Hill 89,91	d		13 20		13 35	13 50		14 05				14 20		14 35	14 50		15 05				15 20		15 35	15 50	
Wavertree Technology Park	d	13 19	13 22		13 37	13 52		14 07			14 19	14 22		14 37	14 52		15 07			15 19	15 22		15 37	15 52	
Broad Green	d		13 25		13 40	13 55		14 10				14 25		14 40	14 55		15 10				15 25		15 40	15 55	
Roby	d		13 29		13 44	13 59		14 14				14 29		14 44	14 59		15 14				15 29		15 44	15 59	
Huyton	d		13 31		13 46	14 01	14 06	14 16				14 31		14 46	15 01	15 06	15 16				15 31		15 46	16 01	16 06
Prescot	d				13 51			14 21						14 51			15 21						15 51		
Eccleston Park	d				13 53			14 23						14 53			15 23						15 53		
Thatto Heath	d				13 56			14 26						14 56			15 26						15 56		
St Helens Central	a				13 59		14 15	14 29						14 59		15 15	15 29						15 59		16 15
	d				14 00		14 15	14 30						15 00		15 15	15 30						16 00		16 15
Garswood	d				14 07			14 37						15 07			15 37						16 07		
Bryn	d				14 10			14 40						15 10			15 40						16 10		
Whiston	d		13 35			14 05						14 35			15 05						15 35			16 05	
Rainhill	d		13 38			14 08						14 38			15 08						15 38			16 08	
Lea Green	d		13 41			14 11						14 41			15 11						15 41			16 11	
St Helens Junction	d	13 29	13 44			14 14					14 29	14 44			15 14					15 29	15 44			16 14	
Warrington Bank Quay	d									14 19								15 19							
Earlestown 8	d		13 50			14 19				14 26		14 50			15 19			15 26			15 50			16 19	
Warrington Bank Quay	a		14 01									15 01									16 01				
Newton-le-Willows	d	13 35				14 22				14 29	14 35				15 22			15 29		15 35				16 22	
Wigan North Western 65	a				14 21		14 30	14 51						15 21		15 30	15 51						16 21		16 30
	d						14 31									15 31									16 31
Euxton Balshaw Lane	d						14 41									15 41									16 41
Leyland 82	a						14 46									15 46									16 46
Preston 8 65,82	a						14 54									15 54									16 54
Blackpool North 97	a						15 21									16 21									17 21
Patricroft	d					14 34									15 34									16 34	
Eccles	d					14 36									15 36									16 36	
Manchester Victoria	a					14 50									15 49									16 49	
Manchester Oxford Road	a	13 57		14 36						14 48	14 57		15 36					15 48		15 57		16 36			
Manchester Piccadilly 10	a	14 01								14 57	15 01							15 57		16 01					
Manchester Airport 85	a	14 22									15 22									16 22					

		NT	AW ◇ C	NT		NT	NT	NT	NT A	NT B	NT	AW ◇ C	NT	NT		NT	NT	NT	NT	NT	NT	AW ◇ C	NT	NT	
Liverpool Lime Street 10 89,91	d	16 01		16 13		16 16	16 27	16 31	16 46	16 57	17 01		17 06	17 10		17 19	17 27	17 35	17 44	17 48	18 01		18 13	18 16	
Edge Hill 89,91	d	16 05				16 20		16 35	16 50		17 05			17 14			17 31	17 39		17 52	18 05			18 20	
Wavertree Technology Park	d	16 07		16 19		16 22		16 37	16 52		17 07		17 12	17 16			17 33	17 41	17 49	17 54	18 07		18 19	18 22	
Broad Green	d	16 10				16 25		16 40	16 55		17 10			17 19			17 36	17 44	17 52	17 57	18 10			18 25	
Roby	d	16 14				16 29		16 44	16 59		17 14			17 23			17 40	17 48		18 01	18 14			18 29	
Huyton	d	16 16				16 31		16 46	17 01	17 06	17 16		17 19	17 25		17 29	17 42	17 50	17 57	18 03	18 16			18 31	
Prescot	d	16 21						16 51			17 21					17 33			18 02		18 21				
Eccleston Park	d	16 23						16 53			17 23					17 36			18 05		18 23				
Thatto Heath	d	16 26						16 56			17 26					17 38			18 07		18 26				
St Helens Central	a	16 29						16 59		17 15	17 29					17 42	17 51		18 11		18 29				
	d	16 30						17 00		17 15	17 30					17 42	17 51		18 11		18 30				
Garswood	d	16 37						17 07			17 37					17 49			18 19		18 37				
Bryn	d	16 40						17 10			17 40					17 52			18 22		18 40				
Whiston	d					16 35			17 05					17 28				17 54		18 07				18 35	
Rainhill	d					16 38			17 08					17 32				17 57		18 10				18 38	
Lea Green	d					16 41			17 11				17 26	17 35				18 00		18 13				18 41	
St Helens Junction	d			16 29		16 44			17 14				17 29	17 39				18 03		18 16			18 29	18 44	
Warrington Bank Quay	d		16 19									17 19										18 19			
Earlestown 8	d		16 26			16 49			17 19			17 26		17 44				18 08		18 21		18 26		18 50	
Warrington Bank Quay	a																							19 01	
Newton-le-Willows	d		16 29	16 35		16 52			17 22			17 29	17 35	17 47				18 11		18 24		18 29	18 35		
Wigan North Western 65	a	16 51						17 21		17 30	17 52					18 04	18 05		18 30		18 49				
	d									17 31							18 05		18 31		18 49				
Euxton Balshaw Lane	d									17 41							18 16		18 41		19 01				
Leyland 82	a									17 46							18 21		18 46		19 06				
Preston 8 65,82	a									17 54							18 31		18 54		19 15				
Blackpool North 97	a									18 24									19 21						
Patricroft	d					17 04			17 34					17 59				18 23							
Eccles	d					17 06			17 36					18 01				18 25		18 36					
Manchester Victoria	a					17 20			17 47					18 15				18 41		18 49					
Manchester Oxford Road	a		16 48	16 57			17 36					17 48	17 57									18 48	18 57		
Manchester Piccadilly 10	a		16 57	17 01								17 57	18 01									18 57	19 01		
Manchester Airport 85	a			17 22									18 22										19 24		

A To Stalybridge

B From Liverpool South Parkway

C From Llandudno

Table 90

Saturdays
from 17 September

Liverpool and St. Helens - Newton-le-Willows, Wigan, Preston and Manchester

	NT	NT	NT	AW ◇ A	NT	NT	NT	AW ◇ A	NT	NT	NT	NT	AW ◇ A	NT	NT	AW B	NT	TP ◇[1] C	NT	NT	AW D
Liverpool Lime Street [10] 89,91 d	18 31	18 46	19 01		19 12	19 23	19 42		20 09	20 12	20 25	20 42		21 12	21 42		22 12	22 30	23 02	23 16	
Edge Hill 89,91 d	18 35	18 50	19 05		19 16		19 46			20 16		20 46		21 16	21 46		22 16		23 06	23 20	
Wavertree Technology Park d	18 37	18 52	19 07		19 18		19 48		20 15	20 18		20 48		21 18	21 48		22 18		23 08	23 22	
Broad Green d	18 40	18 55	19 10		19 21		19 51			20 21		20 51		21 21	21 51		22 21		23 11	23 26	
Roby d	18 44	18 59	19 14		19 25		19 55			20 25		20 55		21 25	21 55		22 25		23 15	23 30	
Huyton d	18 46	19 01	19 16		19 27	19 32	19 57			20 27	20 34	20 57		21 27	21 57		22 27		23 17	23 32	
Prescot d	18 51		19 21				20 02					21 02			22 02				23 22		
Eccleston Park d	18 53		19 23				20 04					21 04			22 04				23 24		
Thatto Heath d	18 56		19 26				20 07					21 07			22 07				23 27		
St Helens Central a	18 59		19 29			19 40	20 10				20 42	21 10			22 10				23 30		
d	19 00		19 30			19 41	20 11				20 43	21 11			22 11				23 31		
Garswood d	19 07		19 37				20 18					21 18			22 18				23 38		
Bryn d	19 10		19 40				20 21					21 21			22 21				23 41		
Whiston d		19 05			19 31					20 31				21 31			22 31			23 36	
Rainhill d		19 08			19 34					20 34				21 34			22 34			23 39	
Lea Green d		19 11			19 37					20 37				21 37			22 37			23 42	
St Helens Junction d		19 14			19 40				20 25	20 40				21 40			22 40			23 45	
Warrington Bank Quay d				19 19				20 19					21 19			22 19					23 50
Earlestown [8] d		19 19		19 26	19 45			20 26		20 45			21 26	21 45		22 27	22 45			23 50	23 58
Warrington Bank Quay a																					
Newton-le-Willows d		19 22		19 29	19 48			20 29	20 35	20 48			21 29	21 48		22 30	22 48			23 53	00 02
Wigan North Western 65 a	19 21		19 51			19 54	20 32				20 57	21 32			22 28				23 48		
d						19 55					20 57				22 28				23 48		
Euxton Balshaw Lane d						20 05					21 08				22 39				23 59		
Leyland 82 a						20 10					21 16				22 44				00 04		
Preston [8] 65,82 a						20 18					21 22				22 55				00 13		
Blackpool North 97 a						20 44					21 53				23 22						
Patricroft d		19 34			20 00					21 00				22 00			23 00			00 05	
Eccles d		19 36			20 02					21 02				22 02			23 02			00 08	
Manchester Victoria 🚋 a		19 49			20 15					21 15				22 15			23 15			00 21	
Manchester Oxford Road a				19 48				20 48	20 57				21 48			22 50		23 14			
Manchester Piccadilly [10] 🚋 a				19 52				20 57	21 01				21 57			22 58		23 19			00 26
Manchester Airport 85 ✈ a				20 18					21 24												

Sundays
until 19 June

	AW E 🚌	NT F	NT F	AW E 🚌	NT	NT	NT	NT	AW B 🚌	NT	NT	AW B 🚌	NT	NT	AW B 🚌	NT	NT	AW B 🚌	NT	NT	AW B 🚌
Liverpool Lime Street [10] 89,91 d		23p02	23p16		08 05	08 31	09 01	09 31		10 01	10 31		11 01	11 31		12 01	12 31		13 01	13 31	
Edge Hill 89,91 d		23p06	23p20																		
Wavertree Technology Park d		23p08	23p22		08 11	08 37	09 07	09 37		10 07	10 37		11 07	11 37		12 07	12 37		13 07	13 37	
Broad Green d		23p11	23p26		08 14	08 40	09 10	09 40		10 10	10 40		11 10	11 40		12 10	12 40		13 10	13 40	
Roby d		23p15	23p30		08 17	08 43	09 13	09 43		10 13	10 43		11 13	11 43		12 13	12 43		13 13	13 43	
Huyton d		23p17	23p32		08 19	08 46	09 16	09 46		10 16	10 46		11 16	11 46		12 16	12 46		13 16	13 46	
Prescot d		23p22				08 50		09 50			10 50			11 50			12 50			13 50	
Eccleston Park d		23p24																			
Thatto Heath d		23p27				08 54		09 54			10 54			11 54			12 54			13 54	
St Helens Central a		23p30				08 57		09 57			10 57			11 57			12 57			13 57	
d		23p31				08 58		09 58			10 58			11 58			12 58			13 58	
Garswood d		23p38				09 05		10 05			11 05			12 05			13 05			14 05	
Bryn d		23p41																			
Whiston d			23p36		08 23		09 19			10 19			11 19			12 19			13 19		
Rainhill d			23p39		08 26		09 22			10 22			11 22			12 22			13 22		
Lea Green d			23p42		08 29		09 26			10 26			11 26			12 26			13 26		
St Helens Junction d			23p45		08 32		09 29			10 29			11 29			12 29			13 29		
Warrington Bank Quay d	23p00			00 22					09 41			10 49			11 40			12 36			13 36
Earlestown [8] d	23p25		23p50	00 47	08 37		09 33		10 06	10 33		11 14	11 33		12 05	12 33		13 01	13 33		14 01
Warrington Bank Quay a																					
Newton-le-Willows d	23p35		23p53	00 57	08 40		09 36		10 16	10 36		11 24	11 36		12 15	12 36		13 11	13 36		14 11
Wigan North Western 65 a		23p48				09 13		10 13			11 13			12 13			13 13			14 13	
d		23p48				09 14		10 14			11 14			12 14			13 14			14 14	
Euxton Balshaw Lane d		23p59				09 24		10 26			11 24			12 24			13 24			14 24	
Leyland 82 a		00 04				09 29		10 31			11 29			12 29			13 29			14 29	
Preston [8] 65,82 a		00 13				09 37		10 39			11 37			12 37			13 37			14 37	
Blackpool North 97 a						10 07		11 09			12 07			13 07			14 09			15 07	
Patricroft d			00 05																		
Eccles d			00 08		08 52		09 49			10 49			11 49			12 49			13 49		
Manchester Victoria 🚋 a			00 21																		
Manchester Oxford Road a	00 05			01 27	09 01		09 59		10 46	10 59		11 54	11 59		12 45	12 59		13 41	13 59		14 41
Manchester Piccadilly [10] 🚋 a	00 10			01 32	09 05		10 03		10 51	11 03		11 59	12 03		12 50	13 02		13 46	14 02		14 46
Manchester Airport 85 ✈ a					09 21		10 21			11 21			12 21			13 24			14 21		

A From Llandudno
B From Chester
C To Stalybridge
D from 29 October. From Chester
E not 22 May. From Chester
F not 22 May

Table 90

Sundays until 19 June

Liverpool and St. Helens - Newton-le-Willows, Wigan, Preston and Manchester

		NT	NT	AW	AW	NT		NT	AW	NT	NT	AW	NT	NT	AW	NT		NT	AW	NT	NT	AW	NT	NT	AW
												◇			◇										
				A	A				A			B			B				A			A			A
				▭	⊥				⊥			⊥			⊥										
Liverpool Lime Street 10 89,91	d	14 01	14 31			15 01		15 31		16 01	16 31		17 01	17 31		18 01		18 31		19 01	19 31		20 01	20 31	
Edge Hill 89,91	d																								
Wavertree Technology Park	d	14 07	14 37			15 07		15 37		16 07	16 37		17 07	17 37		18 07		18 37		19 07	19 37		20 07	20 37	
Broad Green	d	14 10	14 40			15 10		15 40		16 10	16 40		17 10	17 40		18 10		18 40		19 10	19 40		20 10	20 40	
Roby	d	14 13	14 43			15 13		15 43		16 13	16 43		17 13	17 43		18 13		18 43		19 13	19 43		20 13	20 43	
Huyton	d	14 16	14 46			15 16		15 46		16 16	16 46		17 16	17 46		18 16		18 46		19 16	19 46		20 16	20 46	
Prescot	d		14 50					15 50			16 50			17 50				18 50			19 50			20 50	
Eccleston Park	d																								
Thatto Heath	d		14 54					15 54			16 54			17 54				18 54			19 54			20 54	
St Helens Central	a		14 57					15 57			16 57			17 57				18 57			19 57			20 57	
	d		14 58					15 58			16 58			17 58				18 58			19 58			20 58	
Garswood	d		15 05					16 05			17 05			18 05				19 05			20 05			21 05	
Bryn	d																								
Whiston	d	14 19				15 19				16 19			17 19			18 19				19 19			20 19		
Rainhill	d	14 22				15 22				16 22			17 22			18 22				19 22			20 22		
Lea Green	d	14 26				15 26				16 26			17 26			18 26				19 26			20 26		
St Helens Junction	d	14 29				15 29				16 29			17 29			18 29				19 29			20 29		
Warrington Bank Quay	d			14 36	15 03				16 03			17 03			18 03				19 03			20 03			21 03
Earlestown 8	d	14 33		15 01	15 10	15 33			16 10	16 33		17 10	17 33		18 10	18 33			19 10	19 33		20 10	20 33		21 10
Warrington Bank Quay	a																								
Newton-le-Willows	d	14 36		15 11	15 13	15 36			16 13	16 36		17 13	17 36		18 13	18 36			19 13	19 36		20 13	20 36		21 13
Wigan North Western 65	a		15 13					16 13			17 13			18 13				19 13			20 13			21 13	
	d		15 14					16 14			17 14			18 14				19 14			20 14			21 14	
Euxton Balshaw Lane	d		15 24					16 24			17 24			18 24				19 24			20 24			21 24	
Leyland 82	a		15 29					16 29			17 29			18 29				19 29			20 29			21 29	
Preston 8 65,82	a		15 37					16 37			17 37			18 37				19 37			20 37			21 37	
Blackpool North 97	a		16 07					17 07			18 07			19 07				20 07			21 07			22 07	
Patricroft	d																								
Eccles	d	14 49				15 49				16 49			17 49			18 49				19 49			20 49		
Manchester Victoria	a																								
Manchester Oxford Road	a	14 59		15 41	15 32	15 59			16 32	16 59		17 32	17 59		18 32	18 59			19 32	19 59		20 32	20 59		21 32
Manchester Piccadilly 10	a	15 02		15 46	15 41	16 02			16 41	17 02		17 41	18 02		18 41	19 02			19 41	20 02		20 41	21 02		21 41
Manchester Airport 85 ✈	a	15 21				16 21				17 21			18 21			19 21				20 21			21 21		

		NT		NT	AW	NT	NT	AW	NT
					A			A	
Liverpool Lime Street 10 89,91	d	21 01		21 31		22 01	22 31		23 01
Edge Hill 89,91	d								
Wavertree Technology Park	d	21 07		21 37		22 07	22 37		23 07
Broad Green	d	21 10		21 40		22 10	22 40		23 10
Roby	d	21 13		21 43		22 13	22 43		23 13
Huyton	d	21 16		21 46		22 16	22 46		23 16
Prescot	d			21 50			22 50		
Eccleston Park	d								
Thatto Heath	d			21 54			22 54		
St Helens Central	a			21 57			22 57		
	d			21 58			22 58		
Garswood	d			22 05			23 05		
Bryn	d								
Whiston	d	21 19				22 19			23 19
Rainhill	d	21 22				22 22			23 22
Lea Green	d	21 26				22 26			23 26
St Helens Junction	d	21 29				22 29			23 29
Warrington Bank Quay	d				22 03			22 36	
Earlestown 8	d	21 33			22 10	22 33		22 44	23 33
Warrington Bank Quay	a								
Newton-le-Willows	d	21 36			22 13	22 36		22 47	23 36
Wigan North Western 65	a			22 13			23 13		
	d			22 14			23 14		
Euxton Balshaw Lane	d			22 24					
Leyland 82	a			22 29			23 27		
Preston 8 65,82	a			22 37			23 35		
Blackpool North 97	a			23 07			00 05		
Patricroft	d								
Eccles	d	21 49				22 49			23 49
Manchester Victoria	a								
Manchester Oxford Road	a	21 59			22 32	22 59		23 06	23 59
Manchester Piccadilly 10	a	22 02			22 41	23 02		23 15	00 02
Manchester Airport 85 ✈	a	22 21				23 21			00 19

A From Chester

B From Holyhead

Table 90

Sundays

26 June to 11 September

Liverpool and St. Helens - Newton-le-Willows, Wigan, Preston and Manchester

	NT	NT	AW	NT	NT	AW	NT	NT	AW	NT	NT	AW	NT	NT	AW	NT	NT	AW	NT	NT	AW
			A			A			◇ B			A			A			A			A
Liverpool Lime Street [10] 89,91 d	23p02	23p16		08 05	08 31		09 01	09 31		10 01	10 31		11 01	11 31		12 01	12 31		13 01	13 31	
Edge Hill 89,91 d	23p06	23p20																			
Wavertree Technology Park d	23p08	23p22		08 11	08 37		09 07	09 37		10 07	10 37		11 07	11 37		12 07	12 37		13 07	13 37	
Broad Green d	23p11	23p26		08 14	08 40		09 10	09 40		10 10	10 40		11 10	11 40		12 10	12 40		13 10	13 40	
Roby d	23p15	23p30		08 17	08 43		09 13	09 43		10 13	10 43		11 13	11 43		12 13	12 43		13 13	13 43	
Huyton d	23p17	23p32		08 19	08 46		09 16	09 46		10 16	10 46		11 16	11 46		12 16	12 46		13 16	13 46	
Prescot d	23p22				08 50			09 50			10 50			11 50			12 50			13 50	
Eccleston Park d	23p24																				
Thatto Heath d	23p27				08 54			09 54			10 54			11 54			12 54			13 54	
St Helens Central a	23p30				08 57			09 57			10 57			11 57			12 57			13 57	
d	23p31				08 58			09 58			10 58			11 58			12 58			13 58	
Garswood d	23p38				09 05			10 05			11 05			12 05			13 05			14 05	
Bryn d	23p41																				
Whiston d		23p36		08 23			09 19			10 19			11 19			12 19			13 19		
Rainhill d		23p39		08 26			09 22			10 22			11 22			12 22			13 22		
Lea Green d		23p42		08 29			09 26			10 26			11 26			12 26			13 26		
St Helens Junction d		23p45		08 32			09 29			10 29			11 29			12 29			13 29		
Warrington Bank Quay d			23p50			09 10			10 12			11 03			12 03			13 03			14 03
Earlestown [8] d		23p50	23p58	08 37		09 16	09 33		10 19	10 33		11 10	11 33		12 10	12 33		13 10	13 33		14 10
Warrington Bank Quay a																					
Newton-le-Willows d		23p53	00 02	08 40		09 19	09 36		10 22	10 36		11 13	11 36		12 13	12 36		13 13	13 36		14 13
Wigan North Western 65 a	23p48				09 13			10 13			11 13			12 13			13 13			14 13	
d	23p48				09 14			10 14			11 14			12 14			13 14			14 14	
Euxton Balshaw Lane d	23p59				09 24			10 26			11 24			12 24			13 24			14 24	
Leyland 82 a	00 04				09 29			10 31			11 29			12 29			13 29			14 29	
Preston [8] 65,82 a	00 13				09 37			10 39			11 37			12 37			13 37			14 37	
Blackpool North 97 a					10 07			11 09			12 07			13 07			14 09			15 07	
Patricroft d		00 05																			
Eccles d		00 08		08 52			09 49			10 49			11 49			12 49			13 49		
Manchester Victoria a		00 21																			
Manchester Oxford Road a				09 01		09 39	09 59		10 41	10 59		11 32	11 59		12 32	12 59		13 32	13 59		14 32
Manchester Piccadilly [10] a			00 26	09 05		09 48	10 03		10 50	11 03		11 41	12 03		12 41	13 02		13 41	14 02		14 41
Manchester Airport 85 ✈ a				09 21			10 21			11 21			12 21			13 24			14 21		

	NT	NT	AW	NT	NT	AW	NT	NT	AW	NT	NT	AW	NT	NT	AW	NT	NT	AW	NT	NT	AW	NT
			A			A			◇ B			◇ B			A			A			A	
Liverpool Lime Street [10] 89,91 d	14 01	14 31		15 01	15 31		16 01	16 31		17 01	17 31		18 01	18 31		19 01	19 31		20 01	20 31		21 01
Edge Hill 89,91 d																						
Wavertree Technology Park d	14 07	14 37		15 07	15 37		16 07	16 37		17 07	17 37		18 07	18 37		19 07	19 37		20 07	20 37		21 07
Broad Green d	14 10	14 40		15 10	15 40		16 10	16 40		17 10	17 40		18 10	18 40		19 10	19 40		20 10	20 40		21 10
Roby d	14 13	14 43		15 13	15 43		16 13	16 43		17 13	17 43		18 13	18 43		19 13	19 43		20 13	20 43		21 13
Huyton d	14 16	14 46		15 16	15 46		16 16	16 46		17 16	17 46		18 16	18 46		19 16	19 46		20 16	20 46		21 16
Prescot d		14 50			15 50			16 50			17 50			18 50			19 50			20 50		
Eccleston Park d																						
Thatto Heath d		14 54			15 54			16 54			17 54			18 54			19 54			20 54		
St Helens Central a		14 57			15 57			16 57			17 57			18 57			19 57			20 57		
d		14 58			15 58			16 58			17 58			18 58			19 58			20 58		
Garswood d		15 05			16 05			17 05			18 05			19 05			20 05			21 05		
Bryn d																						
Whiston d	14 19			15 19			16 19			17 19			18 19			19 19			20 19			21 19
Rainhill d	14 22			15 22			16 22			17 22			18 22			19 22			20 22			21 22
Lea Green d	14 26			15 26			16 26			17 26			18 26			19 26			20 26			21 26
St Helens Junction d	14 29			15 29			16 29			17 29			18 29			19 29			20 29			21 29
Warrington Bank Quay d			15 03			16 03			17 03			18 03			19 03			20 03			21 03	
Earlestown [8] d	14 33		15 10	15 33		16 10	16 33		17 10	17 33		18 10	18 33		19 10	19 33		20 10	20 33		21 10	21 33
Warrington Bank Quay a																						
Newton-le-Willows d	14 36		15 13	15 36		16 13	16 36		17 13	17 36		18 13	18 36		19 13	19 36		20 13	20 36		21 13	21 36
Wigan North Western 65 a		15 13			16 13			17 13			18 13			19 13			20 13			21 13		
d		15 14			16 14			17 14			18 14			19 14			20 14			21 14		
Euxton Balshaw Lane d		15 24			16 24			17 24			18 24			19 24			20 24			21 24		
Leyland 82 a		15 29			16 29			17 29			18 29			19 29			20 29			21 29		
Preston [8] 65,82 a		15 37			16 37			17 37			18 37			19 37			20 37			21 37		
Blackpool North 97 a		16 07			17 07			18 07			19 07			20 07			21 07			22 07		
Patricroft d																						
Eccles d	14 49			15 49			16 49			17 49			18 49			19 49			20 49			21 49
Manchester Victoria a																						
Manchester Oxford Road a	14 59		15 32	15 59		16 32	16 59		17 32	17 59		18 32	18 59		19 32	19 59		20 32	20 59		21 32	21 59
Manchester Piccadilly [10] a	15 02		15 41	16 02		16 41	17 02		17 41	18 02		18 41	19 02		19 41	20 02		20 41	21 02		21 41	22 02
Manchester Airport 85 ✈ a	15 21			16 21			17 21			18 21			19 21			20 21			21 21			22 21

A From Chester

B From Holyhead

Table 90

Sundays

26 June to 11 September

Liverpool and St. Helens - Newton-le-Willows, Wigan, Preston and Manchester

		NT	AW A	NT	NT	AW A	NT
Liverpool Lime Street [10] 89,91	d	21 31		22 01	22 31		23 01
Edge Hill 89,91	d						
Wavertree Technology Park	d	21 37		22 07	22 37		23 07
Broad Green	d	21 40		22 10	22 40		23 10
Roby	d	21 43		22 13	22 43		23 13
Huyton	d	21 46		22 16	22 46		23 16
Prescot	d	21 50			22 50		
Eccleston Park	d						
Thatto Heath	d	21 54			22 54		
St Helens Central	a	21 57			22 57		
	d	21 58			22 58		
Garswood	d	22 05			23 05		
Bryn	d						
Whiston	d			22 19			23 19
Rainhill	d			22 22			23 22
Lea Green	d			22 26			23 26
St Helens Junction	d			22 29			23 29
Warrington Bank Quay	d		22 03			22 36	
Earlestown [8]	d		22 10	22 33		22 44	23 33
Warrington Bank Quay	a						
Newton-le-Willows	d		22 13	22 36		22 47	23 36
Wigan North Western 65	a	22 13			23 13		
	d	22 14			23 14		
Euxton Balshaw Lane	d	22 24					
Leyland 82	a	22 29			23 27		
Preston [8] 65,82	a	22 37			23 35		
Blackpool North 97	a	23 07			00 05		
Patricroft	d						
Eccles	d			22 49			23 49
Manchester Victoria	a						
Manchester Oxford Road	a		22 32	22 59		23 06	23 59
Manchester Piccadilly [10]	a		22 41	23 02		23 15	00 02
Manchester Airport 85	a			23 21			00 19

Sundays

18 September to 23 October

		NT	NT	NT	NT	NT	NT	AW A	NT
Liverpool Lime Street [10] 89,91	d	23p02	23p16	08 22	08 31	09 01	09 31		10 01
Edge Hill 89,91	d	23p06	23p20						
Wavertree Technology Park	d	23p08	23p22	08 28	08 37	09 07	09 37		10 07
Broad Green	d	23p11	23p26	08 31	08 40	09 10	09 40		10 10
Roby	d	23p15	23p30	08 34	08 43	09 13	09 43		10 13
Huyton	d	23p17	23p32	08 36	08 46	09 16	09 46		10 16
Prescot	d	23p22			08 50		09 50		
Eccleston Park	d	23p24							
Thatto Heath	d	23p27			08 54		09 54		
St Helens Central	a	23p30			08 57		09 57		
	d	23p31			08 58		09 58		
Garswood	d	23p38			09 05		10 05		
Bryn	d	23p41							
Whiston	d		23p36	08 40		09 19			10 19
Rainhill	d		23p39	08 43		09 22			10 22
Lea Green	d		23p42	08 46		09 26			10 26
St Helens Junction	d		23p45	08 49		09 29			10 29
Warrington Bank Quay	d							09 41	
Earlestown [8]	d		23p50	08 54		09 33		10 06	10 33
Warrington Bank Quay	a								
Newton-le-Willows	d		23p53	08 57		09 36		10 16	10 36
Wigan North Western 65	a	23p48			09 13		10 13		
	d	23p48			09 14		10 14		
Euxton Balshaw Lane	d	23p59			09 24		10 26		
Leyland 82	a	00 04			09 29		10 31		
Preston [8] 65,82	a	00 13			09 37		10 39		
Blackpool North 97	a				10 07		11 09		
Patricroft	d		00 05						
Eccles	d		00 08	09 09		09 49			10 49
Manchester Victoria	a		00 21						
Manchester Oxford Road	a			09 19		09 59		10 46	10 59
Manchester Piccadilly [10]	a					10 03		10 51	11 03
Manchester Airport 85	a					10 21			11 21

		NT	AW A	NT	NT	AW A	NT	NT	AW A	NT	NT	AW A	AW A	NT
Liverpool Lime Street [10] 89,91	d	10 31		11 01	11 31		12 01	12 31		13 01	13 31			14 01
Edge Hill 89,91	d													
Wavertree Technology Park	d	10 37		11 07	11 37		12 07	12 37		13 07	13 37			14 07
Broad Green	d	10 40		11 10	11 40		12 10	12 40		13 10	13 40			14 10
Roby	d	10 43		11 13	11 43		12 13	12 43		13 13	13 43			14 13
Huyton	d	10 46		11 16	11 46		12 16	12 46		13 16	13 46			14 16
Prescot	d	10 50			11 50			12 50			13 50			
Eccleston Park	d													
Thatto Heath	d	10 54			11 54			12 54			13 54			
St Helens Central	a	10 57			11 57			12 57			13 57			
	d	10 58			11 58			12 58			13 58			
Garswood	d	11 05			12 05			13 05			14 05			
Bryn	d													
Whiston	d			11 19			12 19			13 19				14 19
Rainhill	d			11 22			12 22			13 22				14 22
Lea Green	d			11 26			12 26			13 26				14 26
St Helens Junction	d			11 29			12 29			13 29				14 29
Warrington Bank Quay	d		10 49			11 40			12 36			13 36	14 03	
Earlestown [8]	d		11 14	11 33		12 05	12 33		13 01	13 33		14 01	14 10	14 33
Warrington Bank Quay	a													
Newton-le-Willows	d		11 24	11 36		12 15	12 36		13 11	13 36		14 11	14 13	14 36
Wigan North Western 65	a	11 13			12 13			13 13			14 13			
	d	11 14			12 14			13 14			14 14			
Euxton Balshaw Lane	d	11 24			12 24			13 24			14 24			
Leyland 82	a	11 29			12 29			13 29			14 29			
Preston [8] 65,82	a	11 37			12 37			13 37			14 37			
Blackpool North 97	a	12 07			13 07			14 09			15 07			
Patricroft	d													
Eccles	d			11 49			12 49			13 49				14 49
Manchester Victoria	a													
Manchester Oxford Road	a		11 54	11 59		12 45	12 59		13 41	13 59		14 41	14 32	14 59
Manchester Piccadilly [10]	a		11 59	12 03		12 50	13 02		13 46	14 02		14 46	14 41	15 02
Manchester Airport 85	a			12 21			13 24			14 21				15 21

A From Chester

Table 90

Sundays

18 September to 23 October

Liverpool and St. Helens - Newton-le-Willows, Wigan, Preston and Manchester

		NT	AW	NT	NT	AW		NT	NT	AW	NT	NT	AW	NT	NT	AW		NT	NT	AW	NT	NT	AW	NT	NT
										◇			◇												
			A			A				B			A			A				A			A		
			🚲			🚲				🚲															
Liverpool Lime Street 10 89,91	d	14 31		15 01	15 31			16 01	16 31		17 01	17 31		18 01	18 31			19 01	19 31		20 01	20 31		21 01	21 31
Edge Hill 89,91	d																								
Wavertree Technology Park	d	14 37		15 07	15 37			16 07	16 37		17 07	17 37		18 07	18 37			19 07	19 37		20 07	20 37		21 07	21 37
Broad Green	d	14 40		15 10	15 40			16 10	16 40		17 10	17 40		18 10	18 40			19 10	19 40		20 10	20 40		21 10	21 40
Roby	d	14 43		15 13	15 43			16 13	16 43		17 13	17 43		18 13	18 43			19 13	19 43		20 13	20 43		21 13	21 43
Huyton	d	14 46		15 16	15 46			16 16	16 46		17 16	17 46		18 16	18 46			19 16	19 46		20 16	20 46		21 16	21 46
Prescot	d	14 50			15 50				16 50			17 50			18 50				19 50			20 50			21 50
Eccleston Park	d																								
Thatto Heath	d	14 54			15 54				16 54			17 54			18 54				19 54			20 54			21 54
St Helens Central	a	14 57			15 57				16 57			17 57			18 57				19 57			20 57			21 57
	d	14 58			15 58				16 58			17 58			18 58				19 58			20 58			21 58
Garswood	d	15 05			16 05				17 05			18 05			19 05				20 05			21 05			22 05
Bryn	d																								
Whiston	d			15 19				16 19			17 19			18 19				19 19			20 19			21 19	
Rainhill	d			15 22				16 22			17 22			18 22				19 22			20 22			21 22	
Lea Green	d			15 26				16 26			17 26			18 26				19 26			20 26			21 26	
St Helens Junction	d			15 29				16 29			17 29			18 29				19 29			20 29			21 29	
Warrington Bank Quay	d		15 03			16 03				17 03			18 03			19 03				20 03			21 03		
Earlestown 8	d		15 10	15 33		16 10		16 33		17 10	17 33		18 10	18 33		19 10		19 33		20 10	20 33		21 10	21 33	
Warrington Bank Quay	a																								
Newton-le-Willows	d		15 13	15 36		16 13		16 36		17 13	17 36		18 13	18 36		19 13		19 36		20 13	20 36		21 13	21 36	
Wigan North Western 65	a	15 13			16 13				17 13			18 13			19 13				20 13			21 13			22 13
	d	15 14			16 14				17 14			18 14			19 14				20 14			21 14			22 14
Euxton Balshaw Lane	d	15 24			16 24				17 24			18 24			19 24				20 24			21 24			22 24
Leyland 82	a	15 29			16 29				17 29			18 29			19 29				20 29			21 29			22 29
Preston 8 65,82	a	15 37			16 37				17 37			18 37			19 37				20 37			21 37			22 37
Blackpool North 97	a	16 07			17 07				18 07			19 07			20 07				21 07			22 07			23 07
Patricroft	d																								
Eccles	d			15 49				16 49			17 49			18 49				19 49			20 49			21 49	
Manchester Victoria ⇌	a																								
Manchester Oxford Road	a		15 32	15 59		16 32		16 59		17 32	17 59		18 32	18 59		19 32		19 59		20 32	20 59		21 32	21 59	
Manchester Piccadilly 10 ⇌	a		15 41	16 02		16 41		17 02		17 41	18 02		18 41	19 02		19 41		20 02		20 41	21 02		21 41	22 02	
Manchester Airport 85 ✈	a			16 21				17 21			18 21			19 21				20 21			21 21			22 21	

		AW		NT	NT	AW	NT
		A				A	
Liverpool Lime Street 10 89,91	d			22 01	22 31		23 01
Edge Hill 89,91	d						
Wavertree Technology Park	d			22 07	22 37		23 07
Broad Green	d			22 10	22 40		23 10
Roby	d			22 13	22 43		23 13
Huyton	d			22 16	22 46		23 16
Prescot	d				22 50		
Eccleston Park	d						
Thatto Heath	d				22 54		
St Helens Central	a				22 57		
	d				22 58		
Garswood	d				23 05		
Bryn	d						
Whiston	d			22 19			23 19
Rainhill	d			22 22			23 22
Lea Green	d			22 26			23 26
St Helens Junction	d			22 29			23 29
Warrington Bank Quay	d	22 03				22 36	
Earlestown 8	d	22 10		22 33		22 44	23 33
Warrington Bank Quay	a						
Newton-le-Willows	d	22 13		22 36		22 47	23 36
Wigan North Western 65	a				23 13		
	d				23 14		
Euxton Balshaw Lane	d						
Leyland 82	a				23 27		
Preston 8 65,82	a				23 35		
Blackpool North 97	a				00 05		
Patricroft	d						
Eccles	d			22 49			23 49
Manchester Victoria ⇌	a						
Manchester Oxford Road	a	22 32		22 59		23 06	23 59
Manchester Piccadilly 10 ⇌	a	22 41		23 02		23 15	00 02
Manchester Airport 85 ✈	a			23 21			00 19

A From Chester

B From Holyhead

Table 90

Sundays
from 30 October

Liverpool and St. Helens - Newton-le-Willows, Wigan, Preston and Manchester

		NT	NT	AW	NT	NT	AW	NT	NT	AW		NT		NT	AW	NT	NT	AW	NT	NT		AW	NT	NT	AW
				A			A			◇ A					A 🚲			A 🚲				A 🚲			A 🚲
Liverpool Lime Street [10] 89,91	d	23p02	23p16		08 05	08 31		09 01	09 31			10 01		10 31		11 01	11 31		12 01	12 31			13 01	13 31	
Edge Hill 89,91	d	23p06	23p20																						
Wavertree Technology Park	d	23p08	23p22		08 11	08 37		09 07	09 37			10 07		10 37		11 07	11 37		12 07	12 37			13 07	13 37	
Broad Green	d	23p11	23p26		08 14	08 40		09 10	09 40			10 10		10 40		11 10	11 40		12 10	12 40			13 10	13 40	
Roby	d	23p15	23p30		08 17	08 43		09 13	09 43			10 13		10 43		11 13	11 43		12 13	12 43			13 13	13 43	
Huyton	d	23p17	23p32		08 19	08 46		09 16	09 46			10 16		10 46		11 16	11 46		12 16	12 46			13 16	13 46	
Prescot	d	23p22				08 50			09 50					10 50			11 50			12 50				13 50	
Eccleston Park	d	23p24																							
Thatto Heath	d	23p27				08 54			09 54					10 54			11 54			12 54				13 54	
St Helens Central	a	23p30				08 57			09 57					10 57			11 57			12 57				13 57	
	d	23p31				08 58			09 58					10 58			11 58			12 58				13 58	
Garswood	d	23p38				09 05			10 05					11 05			12 05			13 05				14 05	
Bryn	d	23p41																							
Whiston	d		23p36		08 23			09 19				10 19				11 19			12 19				13 19		
Rainhill	d		23p39		08 26			09 22				10 22				11 22			12 22				13 22		
Lea Green	d		23p42		08 29			09 26				10 26				11 26			12 26				13 26		
St Helens Junction	d		23p45		08 32			09 29				10 29				11 29			12 29				13 29		
Warrington Bank Quay	d			23p50			09 10			10 12					11 03			12 03				13 03			14 03
Earlestown [8]	d		23p50	23p58	08 37		09 16	09 33		10 19		10 33			11 10	11 33		12 10	12 33			13 10	13 33		14 10
Warrington Bank Quay	a																								
Newton-le-Willows	d		23p53	00 02	08 40		09 19	09 36		10 22		10 36			11 13	11 36		12 13	12 36			13 13	13 36		14 13
Wigan North Western 65	a	23p48				09 13			10 13					11 13			12 13			13 13				14 13	
	d	23p48				09 14			10 14					11 14			12 14			13 14				14 14	
Euxton Balshaw Lane	d	23p59				09 24			10 26					11 24			12 24			13 24				14 24	
Leyland 82	a	00 04				09 29			10 31					11 29			12 29			13 29				14 29	
Preston [8] 65,82	a	00 13				09 37			10 39					11 37			12 37			13 37				14 37	
Blackpool North 97	a					10 07			11 09					12 07			13 07			14 09				15 07	
Patricroft	d		00 05																						
Eccles	d		00 08		08 52			09 49				10 49				11 49			12 49				13 49		
Manchester Victoria 🚊	a		00 21																						
Manchester Oxford Road	a				09 04		09 39	09 59		10 41		10 59			11 32	11 59		12 32	12 59			13 32	13 59		14 32
Manchester Piccadilly [10] 🚊	a			00 26	09 09		09 48	10 03		10 50		11 03			11 41	12 03		12 41	13 02			13 41	14 02		14 41
Manchester Airport 85 ✈	a				09 27			10 21				11 21				12 21			13 24				14 21		

		NT	NT	AW	NT	NT		AW	NT	NT	AW	NT	NT	AW	NT	NT		AW	NT	NT	AW	NT	NT	AW	NT
				A 🚲				A 🚲			◇ C 🚲			◇ A				A			A			A	
Liverpool Lime Street [10] 89,91	d	14 01	14 31		15 01	15 31			16 01	16 31		17 01	17 31		18 01	18 31			19 01	19 31		20 01	20 31		21 01
Edge Hill 89,91	d																								
Wavertree Technology Park	d	14 07	14 37		15 07	15 37			16 07	16 37		17 07	17 37		18 07	18 37			19 07	19 37		20 07	20 37		21 07
Broad Green	d	14 10	14 40		15 10	15 40			16 10	16 40		17 10	17 40		18 10	18 40			19 10	19 40		20 10	20 40		21 10
Roby	d	14 13	14 43		15 13	15 43			16 13	16 43		17 13	17 43		18 13	18 43			19 13	19 43		20 13	20 43		21 13
Huyton	d	14 16	14 46		15 16	15 46			16 16	16 46		17 16	17 46		18 16	18 46			19 16	19 46		20 16	20 46		21 16
Prescot	d		14 50			15 50				16 50			17 50			18 50				19 50			20 50		
Eccleston Park	d																								
Thatto Heath	d		14 54			15 54				16 54			17 54			18 54				19 54			20 54		
St Helens Central	a		14 57			15 57				16 57			17 57			18 57				19 57			20 57		
	d		14 58			15 58				16 58			17 58			18 58				19 58			20 58		
Garswood	d		15 05			16 05				17 05			18 05			19 05				20 05			21 05		
Bryn	d																								
Whiston	d	14 19			15 19				16 19			17 19			18 19				19 19			20 19			21 19
Rainhill	d	14 22			15 22				16 22			17 22			18 22				19 22			20 22			21 22
Lea Green	d	14 26			15 26				16 26			17 26			18 26				19 26			20 26			21 26
St Helens Junction	d	14 29			15 29				16 29			17 29			18 29				19 29			20 29			21 29
Warrington Bank Quay	d			15 03				16 03			17 03			18 03				19 03			20 03			21 03	
Earlestown [8]	d	14 33		15 10	15 33			16 10	16 33		17 10	17 33		18 10	18 33			19 10	19 33		20 10	20 33		21 10	21 33
Warrington Bank Quay	a																								
Newton-le-Willows	d	14 36		15 13	15 36			16 13	16 36		17 13	17 36		18 13	18 36			19 13	19 36		20 13	20 36		21 13	21 36
Wigan North Western 65	a		15 13			16 13				17 13			18 13			19 13				20 13			21 13		
	d		15 14			16 14				17 14			18 14			19 14				20 14			21 14		
Euxton Balshaw Lane	d		15 24			16 24				17 24			18 24			19 24				20 24			21 24		
Leyland 82	a		15 29			16 29				17 29			18 29			19 29				20 29			21 29		
Preston [8] 65,82	a		15 37			16 37				17 37			18 37			19 37				20 37			21 37		
Blackpool North 97	a		16 07			17 07				18 07			19 07			20 07				21 07			22 07		
Patricroft	d																								
Eccles	d	14 49			15 49				16 49			17 49			18 49				19 49			20 49			21 49
Manchester Victoria 🚊	a																								
Manchester Oxford Road	a	14 59		15 32	15 59			16 32	16 59		17 32	17 59		18 32	18 59			19 32	19 59		20 32	20 59		21 32	21 59
Manchester Piccadilly [10] 🚊	a	15 02		15 41	16 02			16 41	17 02		17 41	18 02		18 41	19 02			19 41	20 02		20 41	21 02		21 41	22 02
Manchester Airport 85 ✈	a	15 21			16 21				17 21			18 21			19 21				20 21			21 21			22 21

A From Chester

C From Holyhead

Table 90

Sundays
from 30 October

Liverpool and St. Helens - Newton-le-Willows, Wigan, Preston and Manchester

		NT	AW A	NT	NT	AW A	NT
Liverpool Lime Street 10 89,91	d	21 31		22 01	22 31		23 01
Edge Hill 89,91	d						
Wavertree Technology Park	d	21 37		22 07	22 37		23 07
Broad Green	d	21 40		22 10	22 40		23 10
Roby	d	21 43		22 13	22 43		23 13
Huyton	d	21 46		22 16	22 46		23 16
Prescot	d	21 50			22 50		
Eccleston Park	d						
Thatto Heath	d	21 54			22 54		
St Helens Central	a	21 57			22 57		
	d	21 58			22 58		
Garswood	d	22 05			23 05		
Bryn	d						
Whiston	d			22 19			23 19
Rainhill	d			22 22			23 22
Lea Green	d			22 26			23 26
St Helens Junction	d			22 29			23 29
Warrington Bank Quay	d		22 03			22 36	
Earlestown 8	d		22 10	22 33		22 44	23 33
Warrington Bank Quay	a						
Newton-le-Willows	d		22 13	22 36		22 47	23 36
Wigan North Western 65	a	22 13			23 13		
	d	22 14			23 14		
Euxton Balshaw Lane	d	22 24					
Leyland 82	a	22 29			23 27		
Preston 8 65,82	a	22 37			23 35		
Blackpool North 97	a	23 07			00 05		
Patricroft	d						
Eccles	d			22 49			23 49
Manchester Victoria ⇌	a						
Manchester Oxford Road	a		22 32	22 59		23 06	23 59
Manchester Piccadilly 10 ⇌	a		22 41	23 02		23 15	00 02
Manchester Airport 85 ✈	a			23 21			00 19

A From Chester

Manchester, Preston, Wigan and Newton-le-Willows - St. Helens and Liverpool

Miles	Miles	Miles	Miles			NT	NT	NT	NT	NT	AW	NT	NT	NT		NT	AW	NT	NT	NT	NT	NT	NT	AW
						MX	MO				◇ A						◇ A							◇ A
—	—	—	0	**Manchester Airport** 85	d			04 34			05 33							06 41						
—	—	—	9¾	**Manchester Piccadilly** [10]	d			04 49			05 50						06 50	06 58						07 50
—	—	—	10¼	**Manchester Oxford Road**	d						05 53						06 53	07 01						07 53
0	—	—	—	**Manchester Victoria**	d	23p09				05 39			06 09							07 09			07 39	
4	—	—	14½	Eccles	d	23p16				05 46			06 16							07 16			07 46	
5	—	—	15½	Patricroft	d	23p19				05 49			06 19							07 19			07 49	
—	—	—	—	Blackpool North 97	d		22p44															07 02		
—	0	0	—	**Preston** [8] 65,82	d		23p09															07 30		
—	4	4	—	Leyland 82	d		23p15															07 35		
—	6¾	6¾	—	Euxton Balshaw Lane	d		23p19															07 40		
—	15	15	—	**Wigan North Western** 65	a		23p29															07 50		
—	—	—	—		d		23p30					06 08		06 38		06 47			07 08		07 38	07 50		
15½	—	22	26	**Newton-le-Willows**	d	23p31				06 01	06 12		06 31			07 00	07 12	07 19		07 31			08 01	08 12
—	—	—	—	Warrington Bank Quay	d																			
17	—	23½	27½	Earlestown [8]	d	23p34				06 04	06 15		06 34			07 03	07 15			07 34			08 04	08 15
—	—	—	—	Warrington Bank Quay	a						06 25						07 22							08 23
19¾	—	26¼	30¼	**St Helens Junction**	d	23p39				06 09			06 39			07 09		07 24		07 39			08 09	
21	—	27½	31½	Lea Green	d	23p42				06 12			06 42			07 12				07 42			08 12	
22¾	—	29¼	33¼	Rainhill	d	23p46				06 16			06 46			07 16		07 29		07 46			08 16	
24¼	—	30¾	34¾	Whiston	d	23p49				06 19			06 49			07 19				07 49			08 19	
—	18¾	—	—	Bryn	d							06 15		06 45					07 15		07 45			
—	20	—	—	Garswood	d		23p40					06 19		06 49					07 19		07 49	07 59		
—	23¾	—	—	**St Helens Central**	a		23p46					06 25		06 55					07 25		07 55	08 06		
—	—	—	—		d		23p47		05 56			06 26		06 56					07 26		07 56	08 06		
—	25¼	—	—	Thatto Heath	d		23p50		05 59			06 29		06 59					07 29		07 59			
—	26¼	—	—	Eccleston Park	d				06 02			06 32		07 02					07 32		08 02			
—	27¼	—	—	Prescot	d		23p54		06 04			06 34		07 04					07 34		08 04	08 12		
26¼	29½	32¾	36¾	Huyton	d	23p53	23p59		06 08	06 23		06 38	06 53	07 08		07 23		07 34	07 38	07 53	08 08	08 16	08 23	
26¾	30	33¼	37¼	Roby	d	23p55	00 01		06 10	06 25		06 40	06 55	07 10		07 25			07 40	07 55	08 10		08 25	
28¼	31½	34¾	38¾	Broad Green	d	23p58	00 04		06 13	06 28		06 43	06 58	07 13		07 28			07 43	07 58	08 13	08 20	08 28	
29¼	32½	35¾	39¾	Wavertree Technology Park	d	00 01	00 07		06 16	06 31		06 46	07 01	07 16		07 31		07 39	07 46	08 01	08 16	08 24	08 31	
30	33¼	36½	40½	Edge Hill 89,91	d	00 04			06 19	06 34		06 49	07 04	07 19		07 34			07 49	08 04	08 19		08 34	
31¾	35	38¼	42¼	**Liverpool Lime Street** [10] 89,91	a	00 13	00 18	05 32	06 28	06 43		06 58	07 13	07 28		07 43		07 49	07 58	08 13	08 28	08 35	08 43	

		NT	NT	NT	NT	NT	AW	NT	NT	NT		NT	NT	NT	AW	NT	NT	NT	NT	NT		NT	AW	NT	NT
						B	◇ A			C				B	◇ A			C				B	◇ A		
Manchester Airport 85	d							08 41								09 41								10 41	
Manchester Piccadilly [10]	d						08 50	09 01							09 50	10 01							10 50	11 01	
Manchester Oxford Road	d						08 53	09 04							09 53	10 04							10 53	11 04	
Manchester Victoria	d		08 09			08 39								09 39								10 39			
Eccles	d		08 16			08 46								09 46								10 46			
Patricroft	d		08 19			08 49								09 49								10 49			
Blackpool North 97	d																	09 37							
Preston [8] 65,82	d									09 04								10 04							
Leyland 82	d									09 09								10 09							
Euxton Balshaw Lane	d									09 14								10 14							
Wigan North Western 65	a									09 24								10 24							
	d	07 58		08 28					09 08	09 24			09 38				10 08	10 24		10 38					11 08
Newton-le-Willows	d		08 31			09 01	09 12	09 22						10 01	10 12	10 22						11 01	11 12	11 22	
Warrington Bank Quay	d											09 22							10 22						
Earlestown [8]	d		08 34			09 04	09 15					09 34		10 04	10 15				10 34			11 04	11 15		
Warrington Bank Quay	a						09 25								10 25								11 25		
St Helens Junction	d		08 39			09 09		09 27				09 39		10 09		10 27			10 39			11 09		11 27	
Lea Green	d		08 42			09 12						09 42		10 12					10 42			11 12			
Rainhill	d		08 46			09 16						09 46		10 16					10 46			11 16			
Whiston	d		08 49			09 19						09 49		10 19					10 49			11 19			
Bryn	d	08 05		08 35					09 15				09 45				10 15			10 45					11 15
Garswood	d	08 09		08 39					09 19				09 49				10 19			10 49					11 19
St Helens Central	a	08 15		08 45					09 25	09 39			09 55				10 25	10 39		10 55					11 25
	d	08 16		08 46	08 56				09 26	09 39			09 56				10 26	10 39		10 56					11 26
Thatto Heath	d	08 19		08 49	08 59				09 29				09 59				10 29			10 59					11 29
Eccleston Park	d	08 22		08 52	09 02				09 32				10 02				10 32			11 02					11 32
Prescot	d	08 24		08 54	09 04				09 34				10 04				10 34			11 04					11 34
Huyton	d	08 28	08 53	08 58	09 08	09 23			09 38	09 48		09 53	10 08	10 23			10 38	10 48	10 53	11 08		11 23			11 38
Roby	d	08 30	08 55	09 00	09 10	09 25			09 40			09 55	10 10	10 25			10 40		10 55	11 10		11 25			11 40
Broad Green	d	08 33	08 58	09 03	09 13	09 28			09 43			09 58	10 13	10 28			10 43		10 58	11 13		11 28			11 43
Wavertree Technology Park	d	08 36	09 01	09 06	09 16	09 31		09 38	09 46			10 01	10 16	10 31		10 38	10 46		11 01	11 16		11 31		11 38	11 46
Edge Hill 89,91	d	08 39	09 04	09 09	09 19	09 34			09 49			10 04	10 19	10 34			10 49		11 04	11 19		11 34			11 49
Liverpool Lime Street [10] 89,91	a	08 50	09 13	09 18	09 28	09 43		09 48	09 58	10 02		10 13	10 28	10 43		10 48	10 58	11 02	11 13	11 28		11 43		11 48	11 58

A To Llandudno **B** From Stalybridge **C** To Liverpool South Parkway

Manchester, Preston, Wigan and Newton-le-Willows - St. Helens and Liverpool

		NT	NT	NT	NT	AW		NT	NT	NT	NT	NT	NT	AW	NT	NT		NT	NT	NT	NT	AW	NT	NT	NT
		A			B	◇ C				A			B	◇ C				A			B	◇ C			A
Manchester Airport 85 ✈	d							11 41							12 41								13 41		
Manchester Piccadilly 10	d					11 50		12 01						12 50	13 01							13 50	14 01		
Manchester Oxford Road	d					11 53		12 04						12 53	13 04							13 53	14 04		
Manchester Victoria	d				11 39								12 39								13 39				
Eccles	d				11 46								12 46								13 46				
Patricroft	d				11 49								12 49								13 49				
Blackpool North 97	d	10 37								11 37								12 37							13 37
Preston 8 65,82	d	11 04								12 04								13 04							14 04
Leyland 82	d	11 09								12 09								13 09							14 09
Euxton Balshaw Lane	d	11 14								12 14								13 14							14 14
Wigan North Western 65	a	11 24								12 24								13 24							14 24
	d	11 24		11 38					12 08	12 24		12 38				13 08		13 24		13 38				14 08	14 24
Newton-le-Willows	d				12 01	12 12		12 22					13 01	13 12	13 22						14 01	14 12	14 22		
Warrington Bank Quay	d		11 22								12 22								13 22						
Earlestown 8	d		11 34		12 04	12 15					12 34		13 04	13 15					13 34		14 04	14 15			
Warrington Bank Quay	a					12 25								13 25								14 25			
St Helens Junction	d		11 39		12 09			12 27			12 39		13 09		13 27				13 39		14 09		14 27		
Lea Green	d		11 42		12 12						12 42		13 12						13 42		14 12				
Rainhill	d		11 46		12 16						12 46		13 16						13 46		14 16				
Whiston	d		11 49		12 19						12 49		13 19						13 49		14 19				
Bryn	d			11 45					12 15			12 45				13 15				13 45				14 15	
Garswood	d			11 49					12 19			12 49				13 19				13 49				14 19	
St Helens Central	a	11 39		11 55					12 25	12 39		12 55				13 25		13 39		13 55				14 25	14 39
	d	11 39		11 56					12 26	12 39		12 56				13 26		13 39		13 56				14 26	14 39
Thatto Heath	d			11 59					12 29			12 59				13 29				13 59				14 29	
Eccleston Park	d			12 02					12 32			13 02				13 32				14 02				14 32	
Prescot	d			12 04					12 34			13 04				13 34				14 04				14 34	
Huyton	d	11 48	11 53	12 08	12 23				12 38	12 48	12 53	13 08	13 23			13 38		13 48	13 53	14 08	14 23			14 38	14 48
Roby	d		11 55	12 10	12 25				12 40		12 55	13 10	13 25			13 40			13 55	14 10	14 25			14 40	
Broad Green	d		11 58	12 13	12 28				12 43		12 58	13 13	13 28			13 43			13 58	14 13	14 28			14 43	
Wavertree Technology Park	d		12 01	12 16	12 31			12 38	12 46		13 01	13 16	13 31		13 38	13 46			14 01	14 16	14 31		14 38	14 46	
Edge Hill 89,91	d		12 04	12 19	12 34				12 49		13 04	13 19	13 34			13 49			14 04	14 19	14 34			14 49	
Liverpool Lime Street 10 89,91	a	12 02	12 13	12 28	12 43			12 48	12 58	13 02	13 13	13 28	13 43		13 48	13 58		14 02	14 13	14 28	14 43		14 48	14 58	15 02

		NT		NT	NT	AW	NT	NT	NT	NT	NT	NT		AW	NT	NT	NT	NT	NT	NT	AW	NT		NT	NT
					B	◇ C			A			B		◇ C						B	◇ C				
Manchester Airport 85 ✈	d						14 41								15 41							16 41			
Manchester Piccadilly 10	d					14 50	15 01							15 50	16 01						16 50	17 01			
Manchester Oxford Road	d					14 53	15 04							15 53	16 04						16 53	17 04			
Manchester Victoria	d				14 39							15 39								16 39					
Eccles	d				14 46							15 46								16 46					
Patricroft	d				14 49							15 49								16 49					
Blackpool North 97	d								14 37								15 37								16 35
Preston 8 65,82	d								15 04								16 04								17 04
Leyland 82	d								15 09								16 09								17 09
Euxton Balshaw Lane	d								15 14								16 14								17 14
Wigan North Western 65	a								15 24								16 24								17 24
	d			14 38				15 08	15 24		15 38					16 08	16 24		16 38					17 08	17 24
Newton-le-Willows	d				15 01	15 12	15 22					16 01		16 12	16 22					17 01	17 12	17 22			
Warrington Bank Quay	d	14 22								15 22								16 22							
Earlestown 8	d	14 34			15 04	15 15				15 34		16 04		16 15				16 34		17 04	17 15				
Warrington Bank Quay	a					15 25								16 26							17 25				
St Helens Junction	d	14 39			15 09		15 27			15 39		16 09			16 27			16 39		17 09		17 27			
Lea Green	d	14 42			15 12					15 42		16 12						16 42		17 12					
Rainhill	d	14 46			15 16					15 46		16 16						16 46		17 16					
Whiston	d	14 49			15 19					15 49		16 19						16 49		17 19					
Bryn	d			14 45				15 15			15 45					16 15			16 45					17 15	
Garswood	d			14 49				15 19			15 49					16 19			16 49					17 19	
St Helens Central	a			14 55				15 25	15 39		15 55					16 25	16 39		16 55					17 25	17 39
	d			14 56				15 26	15 39		15 56					16 26	16 39		16 56					17 26	17 39
Thatto Heath	d			14 59				15 29			15 59					16 29			16 59					17 29	
Eccleston Park	d			15 02				15 32			16 02					16 32			17 02					17 32	
Prescot	d			15 04				15 34			16 04					16 34			17 04					17 34	
Huyton	d	14 53		15 08	15 23			15 38	15 48	15 53	16 08	16 23				16 38	16 48	16 53	17 08	17 23				17 38	17 48
Roby	d	14 55		15 10	15 25			15 40		15 55	16 10	16 25				16 40		16 55	17 10	17 25				17 40	
Broad Green	d	14 58		15 13	15 28			15 43		15 58	16 13	16 28				16 43		16 58	17 13	17 28				17 43	
Wavertree Technology Park	d	15 01		15 16	15 31		15 38	15 46		16 01	16 16	16 31			16 38	16 46		17 01	17 16	17 31		17 38		17 46	
Edge Hill 89,91	d	15 04		15 19	15 34			15 49		16 04	16 19	16 34				16 49		17 04	17 19	17 34				17 49	
Liverpool Lime Street 10 89,91	a	15 13		15 28	15 43		15 48	15 58	16 02	16 13	16 28	16 43			16 48	16 58	17 05	17 13	17 28	17 43		17 48		17 58	18 02

A To Liverpool South Parkway **B** From Stalybridge **C** To Llandudno

Manchester, Preston, Wigan and Newton-le-Willows - St. Helens and Liverpool

		NT	AW	NT	NT	AW	NT	NT		NT	NT	NT	NT	AW	NT	NT	NT	NT		NT	AW	NT	NT	NT	NT
			A			◇ B								A							A				
Manchester Airport 85	d							17 41							18 41							19 41			
Manchester Piccadilly 10	d		17 19			17 50		18 01						18 50	19 01						19 50	20 01			
Manchester Oxford Road	d		17 22			17 53		18 04						18 53	19 04						19 53	20 04			
Manchester Victoria	d	17 09			17 37								18 39							19 39					
Eccles	d	17 16			17 46			18 11					18 46							19 46					
Patricroft	d	17 19			17 49								18 49							19 49					
Blackpool North 97	d										17 37						18 37							19 37	
Preston 8 65,82	d										18 04						19 04							20 04	
Leyland 82	d										18 09						19 09							20 09	
Euxton Balshaw Lane	d										18 14						19 14							20 14	
Wigan North Western 65	a										18 24						19 24							20 24	
	d			17 38			18 08			18 21	18 24	18 35				19 08	19 24						20 08	20 24	20 38
Newton-le-Willows	d	17 31	17 40		18 01	18 12		18 24		18 33			19 01	19 12	19 22					20 01	20 12	20 22			
Warrington Bank Quay	d																	19 22							
Earlestown 8	d	17 34	17 44		18 04	18 15				18 36			19 04	19 16				19 34		20 04	20 15				
Warrington Bank Quay	a		17 52			18 23								19 24							20 25				
St Helens Junction	d	17 39			18 09			18 29		18 41			19 09		19 27			19 39		20 09		20 27			
Lea Green	d	17 42			18 12			18 32		18 44			19 12					19 42		20 12					
Rainhill	d	17 46			18 16			18 36		18 48			19 16					19 46		20 16					
Whiston	d	17 49			18 19					18 51			19 19					19 49		20 19					
Bryn	d			17 45			18 15					18 45				19 15							20 15		20 45
Garswood	d			17 49			18 19					18 49				19 19							20 19		20 49
St Helens Central	a			17 55			18 25				18 39	18 55				19 25	19 39						20 25	20 39	20 55
	d			17 56			18 26				18 39	18 56				19 26	19 39						20 26	20 39	20 56
Thatto Heath	d			17 59			18 29					18 59				19 29							20 29		20 59
Eccleston Park	d			18 02			18 32					19 02				19 32							20 32		21 02
Prescot	d			18 04			18 34					19 04				19 34							20 34		21 04
Huyton	d	17 53		18 08	18 23		18 38	18 41		18 55	18 48	19 08	19 23			19 38	19 48	19 53		20 23			20 38	20 48	21 08
Roby	d	17 55		18 10	18 25			18 43		18 57		19 10	19 25			19 40		19 55		20 25			20 40		21 10
Broad Green	d	17 58		18 13	18 28			18 47		19 00		19 13	19 28			19 43		19 58		20 28			20 43		21 13
Wavertree Technology Park	d	18 01		18 16	18 31		18 43	18 50		19 03		19 16	19 31		19 38	19 46		20 01		20 31		20 38	20 46		21 16
Edge Hill 89,91	d	18 04		18 19	18 34		18 46			19 06		19 19	19 35			19 49		20 04		20 34			20 49		21 19
Liverpool Lime Street 10 89,91	a	18 13		18 28	18 43		18 54	19 00		19 15	19 03	19 28	19 43		19 48	19 58	20 02	20 13		20 43		20 48	20 58	21 02	21 28

		NT	AW	NT		NT	AW	AW	NT	AW	AW	NT	NT	NT		NT	AW
			A				C	D		C	D						A
Manchester Airport 85	d		20 32				21 32	21 32	21 41								
Manchester Piccadilly 10	d		20 50				21 50	21 50	22 01	22 12	22 12						23 14
Manchester Oxford Road	d		20 53				21 53	21 53	22 04	22 29	22 29						23 17
Manchester Victoria	d	20 39				21 39							22 39			23 09	
Eccles	d	20 46				21 46							22 46			23 16	
Patricroft	d	20 49				21 49							22 49			23 19	
Blackpool North 97	d			20 37										22 14			
Preston 8 65,82	d			21 04										22 43			
Leyland 82	d			21 09										22 48			
Euxton Balshaw Lane	d			21 14										22 53			
Wigan North Western 65	a			21 23										23 02			
	d			21 23								22 25		23 03			
Newton-le-Willows	d	21 01	21 12			22 01	22 12	22 12	22 22	22 47	22 47		23 01			23 31	23 36
Warrington Bank Quay	d																
Earlestown 8	d	21 04	21 15			22 04	22 15	22 15		22 50	22 50		23 04			23 34	23 39
Warrington Bank Quay	a		21 24				22 23	22 25		22 58	23 00						23 47
St Helens Junction	d	21 09				22 09			22 27				23 09			23 39	
Lea Green	d	21 12				22 12							23 12			23 42	
Rainhill	d	21 16				22 16							23 16			23 46	
Whiston	d	21 19				22 19							23 19			23 49	
Bryn	d			21 30								22 32		23 10			
Garswood	d			21 34								22 36		23 14			
St Helens Central	a			21 40								22 42		23 20			
	d			21 41								22 43		23 21			
Thatto Heath	d			21 44								22 46		23 24			
Eccleston Park	d			21 47								22 49		23 27			
Prescot	d			21 49								22 51		23 29			
Huyton	d	21 23		21 53		22 23						22 55	23 23	23 33		23 53	
Roby	d	21 25		21 55		22 25						22 57	23 25	23 35		23 55	
Broad Green	d	21 28		21 58		22 28						23 00	23 28	23 38		23 58	
Wavertree Technology Park	d	21 31		22 03		22 31			22 38			23 03	23 31	23 41		00 01	
Edge Hill 89,91	d	21 34		22 06		22 34						23 06	23 34	23 46		00 04	
Liverpool Lime Street 10 89,91	a	21 43		22 16		22 43			22 48			23 15	23 43	23 54		00 13	

A To Chester
B To Llandudno
C until 9 September, from 24 October. To Chester
D from 12 September until 21 October. To Chester

Table 90

Saturdays
until 18 June

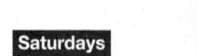

Manchester, Preston, Wigan and Newton-le-Willows - St. Helens and Liverpool

	NT	NT	NT	NT	AW	NT	NT	NT	NT		AW	NT	NT	NT	NT	NT	NT	AW	NT		NT	NT	NT	NT
					◇						◇							◇						
					A						A							A						B
Manchester Airport 85 ✈ d		04 34			05 33							06 41												
Manchester Piccadilly 10 d		04 49			05 50						06 50	06 58						07 50						
Manchester Oxford Road d					05 53						06 53	07 01						07 53						
Manchester Victoria d	23p09			05 39			06 09							07 09			07 39				08 09			08 39
Eccles d	23p16			05 46			06 16							07 16			07 46				08 16			08 46
Patricroft d	23p19			05 49			06 19							07 19			07 49				08 19			08 49
Blackpool North 97 d																07 02								
Preston 8 65,82 d																07 30								
Leyland 82 d																07 35								
Euxton Balshaw Lane d																07 40								
Wigan North Western 65 a																07 50								
d						06 08		06 38	06 47				07 08		07 38	07 50			07 58			08 28		
Newton-le-Willows d	23p31			06 01	06 12		06 31		07 00		07 12	07 19		07 31			08 01	08 12			08 31			09 01
Warrington Bank Quay d																								
Earlestown 8 d	23p34			06 04	06 15		06 34		07 03		07 15			07 34			08 04	08 15			08 34			09 04
Warrington Bank Quay a					06 25						07 22							08 23						
St Helens Junction d	23p39			06 09			06 39		07 09			07 24		07 39			08 09				08 39			09 09
Lea Green d	23p42			06 12			06 42		07 12					07 42			08 12				08 42			09 12
Rainhill d	23p46			06 16			06 46		07 16			07 29		07 46			08 16				08 46			09 16
Whiston d	23p49			06 19			06 49		07 19					07 49			08 19				08 49			09 19
Bryn d						06 15		06 45					07 15		07 45				08 05			08 35		
Garswood d						06 19		06 49					07 19		07 49	07 59			08 09			08 39		
St Helens Central a						06 25		06 55					07 25		07 55	08 06			08 15			08 45		
d			05 56			06 26		06 56					07 26		07 56	08 06			08 16			08 46	08 56	
Thatto Heath d			05 59			06 29		06 59					07 29		07 59				08 19			08 49	08 59	
Eccleston Park d			06 02			06 32		07 02					07 32		08 02				08 22			08 52	09 02	
Prescot d			06 04			06 34		07 04					07 34		08 04	08 12			08 24			08 54	09 04	
Huyton d	23p53		06 08	06 23		06 38	06 53	07 08	07 23			07 34	07 38	07 53	08 08	08 16	08 23		08 28		08 53	08 58	09 08	09 23
Roby d	23p55		06 10	06 25		06 40	06 55	07 10	07 25				07 40	07 55	08 10		08 25		08 30		08 55	09 00	09 10	09 25
Broad Green d	23p58		06 13	06 28		06 43	06 58	07 13	07 28				07 43	07 58	08 13	08 20	08 28		08 33		08 58	09 03	09 13	09 28
Wavertree Technology Park d	00 01		06 16	06 31		06 46	07 01	07 16	07 31			07 39	07 46	08 01	08 16	08 24	08 31		08 36		09 01	09 06	09 16	09 31
Edge Hill 89,91 d	00 04		06 19	06 34		06 49	07 04	07 19	07 34				07 49	08 04	08 19		08 34		08 39		09 04	09 09	09 19	09 34
Liverpool Lime Street 10 89,91 a	00 13	05 32	06 28	06 43		06 58	07 13	07 28	07 43			07 49	07 58	08 13	08 28	08 34	08 43		08 48		09 13	09 18	09 28	09 43

	AW	NT	NT	NT	NT		NT	NT	AW	NT	NT	NT	NT	NT	NT		AW	NT	NT	NT	NT	NT	NT	AW
	◇								◇								◇							◇
	A			C				B	A			C			B		A			C			B	A
Manchester Airport 85 ✈ d		08 41								09 41								10 41						
Manchester Piccadilly 10 d	08 50	09 01							09 50	10 01							10 50	11 01						11 50
Manchester Oxford Road d	08 53	09 04							09 53	10 04							10 53	11 04						11 53
Manchester Victoria d								09 39							10 39								11 39	
Eccles d								09 46							10 46								11 46	
Patricroft d								09 49							10 49								11 49	
Blackpool North 97 d				08 38								09 37								10 37				
Preston 8 65,82 d				09 04								10 04								11 04				
Leyland 82 d				09 09								10 09								11 09				
Euxton Balshaw Lane d				09 14								10 14								11 14				
Wigan North Western 65 a				09 24								10 24								11 24				
d			09 08	09 24			09 38				10 08	10 24		10 38					11 08	11 24		11 38		
Newton-le-Willows d	09 12	09 22						10 01	10 12	10 22					11 01		11 12	11 22					12 01	12 12
Warrington Bank Quay d					09 22								10 22								11 22			
Earlestown 8 d	09 15				09 34			10 04	10 15				10 34		11 04		11 15				11 34		12 04	12 15
Warrington Bank Quay a	09 25								10 25								11 25							12 25
St Helens Junction d		09 27			09 39			10 09		10 27			10 39		11 09			11 27			11 39		12 09	
Lea Green d					09 42			10 12					10 42		11 12						11 42		12 12	
Rainhill d					09 46			10 16					10 46		11 16						11 46		12 16	
Whiston d					09 49			10 19					10 49		11 19						11 49		12 19	
Bryn d			09 15				09 45				10 15			10 45					11 15			11 45		
Garswood d			09 19				09 49				10 19			10 49					11 19			11 49		
St Helens Central a			09 25	09 39			09 55				10 25	10 39		10 55					11 25	11 39		11 55		
d			09 26	09 39			09 56				10 26	10 39		10 56					11 26	11 39		11 56		
Thatto Heath d			09 29				09 59				10 29			10 59					11 29			11 59		
Eccleston Park d			09 32				10 02				10 32			11 02					11 32			12 02		
Prescot d			09 34				10 04				10 34			11 04					11 34			12 04		
Huyton d			09 38	09 48	09 53		10 08	10 23			10 38	10 48	10 53	11 08	11 23				11 38	11 48	11 53	12 08	12 23	
Roby d			09 40		09 55		10 10	10 25			10 40		10 55	11 10	11 25				11 40		11 55	12 10	12 25	
Broad Green d			09 43		09 58		10 13	10 28			10 43		10 58	11 13	11 28				11 43		11 58	12 13	12 28	
Wavertree Technology Park d		09 38	09 46		10 01		10 16	10 31		10 38	10 46		11 01	11 16	11 31			11 38	11 46		12 01	12 16	12 31	
Edge Hill 89,91 d			09 49		10 04		10 21	10 34			10 49		11 04	11 19	11 34				11 49		12 04	12 19	12 34	
Liverpool Lime Street 10 89,91 a		09 48	09 58	10 02	10 13		10 29	10 43		10 48	10 58	11 02	11 13	11 28	11 43			11 48	11 58	12 02	12 13	12 28	12 43	

A To Llandudno
B From Stalybridge
C To Liverpool South Parkway

Table 90

Saturdays
until 18 June

Manchester, Preston, Wigan and Newton-le-Willows - St. Helens and Liverpool

	NT	NT	NT A	NT	NT	NT B	AW ◇ C	NT	NT	NT A	NT	NT	NT B	AW D	NT	NT	NT A	NT	NT	NT B	AW D
Manchester Airport 85 ✈ d	11 41							12 41							13 41						
Manchester Piccadilly 10 d	12 01						12 50	13 01						13 35	14 01						14 35
Manchester Oxford Road d	12 04						12 53	13 04						13 40	14 04						14 40
Manchester Victoria d						12 39							13 39							14 39	
Eccles d						12 46							13 46							14 46	
Patricroft d						12 49							13 49							14 49	
Blackpool North 97 d			11 37							12 37							13 37				
Preston 8 65,82 d			12 04							13 04							14 04				
Leyland 82 d			12 09							13 09							14 09				
Euxton Balshaw Lane d			12 14							13 14							14 14				
Wigan North Western 65 a			12 24							13 24							14 24				
d		12 08	12 24		12 38				13 08	13 24		13 38				14 08	14 24		14 38		
Newton-le-Willows d	12 22					13 01	13 12	13 22					14 01	14 10	14 22					15 01	15 10
Warrington Bank Quay d				12 22							13 22							14 22			
Earlestown 8 d				12 34		13 04	13 15				13 34		14 04	14 20				14 34		15 04	15 20
Warrington Bank Quay a							13 25							14 45							15 45
St Helens Junction d	12 27			12 39		13 09		13 27			13 39		14 09		14 27			14 39		15 09	
Lea Green d				12 42		13 12					13 42		14 12					14 42		15 12	
Rainhill d				12 46		13 16					13 46		14 16					14 46		15 16	
Whiston d				12 49		13 19					13 49		14 19					14 49		15 19	
Bryn d		12 15			12 45				13 15			13 45				14 15			14 45		
Garswood d		12 19			12 49				13 19			13 49				14 19			14 49		
St Helens Central a		12 25	12 39		12 55				13 25	13 39		13 55				14 25	14 39		14 55		
d		12 26	12 39		12 56				13 26	13 39		13 56				14 26	14 39		14 56		
Thatto Heath d		12 29			12 59				13 29			13 59				14 29			14 59		
Eccleston Park d		12 32			13 02				13 32			14 02				14 32			15 02		
Prescot d		12 34			13 04				13 34			14 04				14 34			15 04		
Huyton d		12 38	12 48	12 53	13 08	13 23			13 38	13 48	13 53	14 08	14 23			14 38	14 48	14 53	15 08	15 23	
Roby d		12 40		12 55	13 10	13 25			13 40		13 55	14 10	14 25			14 40		14 55	15 10	15 25	
Broad Green d		12 43		12 58	13 13	13 28			13 43		13 58	14 13	14 28			14 43		14 58	15 13	15 28	
Wavertree Technology Park d	12 38	12 46		13 01	13 16	13 31		13 38	13 46		14 01	14 16	14 31		14 38	14 46		15 01	15 16	15 31	
Edge Hill 89,91 d		12 49		13 04	13 19	13 34			13 49		14 04	14 19	14 34			14 49		15 04	15 19	15 34	
Liverpool Lime Street 10 89,91 a	12 48	12 58	13 02	13 13	13 28	13 43		13 48	13 58	14 02	14 13	14 28	14 43		14 48	14 58	15 02	15 13	15 28	15 43	

	NT	NT	NT A	NT	NT	NT B	AW D	NT	NT	NT	NT	NT	NT B	AW D	NT	NT	NT	NT	NT	NT B	AW D	NT
Manchester Airport 85 ✈ d	14 41							15 41							16 41							
Manchester Piccadilly 10 d	15 01						15 35	16 01						16 35	17 01						17 35	
Manchester Oxford Road d	15 04						15 40	16 04						16 40	17 04						17 40	
Manchester Victoria d						15 39							16 39					17 09		17 39		
Eccles d						15 46							16 46					17 16		17 46		
Patricroft d						15 49							16 49					17 19		17 49		
Blackpool North 97 d			14 37							15 37							16 35					
Preston 8 65,82 d			15 04							16 04							17 04					
Leyland 82 d			15 09							16 09							17 09					
Euxton Balshaw Lane d			15 14							16 14							17 14					
Wigan North Western 65 a			15 24							16 24							17 24					
d		15 08	15 24		15 38				16 08	16 24		16 38				17 08	17 24		17 38			18 08
Newton-le-Willows d	15 22					16 01	16 10	16 22					17 01	17 10	17 22			17 31		18 01	18 10	
Warrington Bank Quay d				15 22							16 22											
Earlestown 8 d				15 34		16 04	16 20				16 34		17 04	17 20				17 34		18 04	18 20	
Warrington Bank Quay a							16 45							17 45							18 45	
St Helens Junction d	15 27			15 39		16 09		16 27			16 39		17 09		17 27			17 39		18 09		
Lea Green d				15 42		16 12					16 42		17 12					17 42		18 12		
Rainhill d				15 46		16 16					16 46		17 16					17 46		18 16		
Whiston d				15 49		16 19					16 49		17 19					17 49		18 19		
Bryn d		15 15			15 45				16 15			16 45				17 15			17 45			18 15
Garswood d		15 19			15 49				16 19			16 49				17 19			17 49			18 19
St Helens Central a		15 25	15 39		15 55				16 25	16 39		16 55				17 25	17 39		17 55			18 25
d		15 26	15 39		15 56				16 26	16 39		16 56				17 26	17 39		17 56			18 26
Thatto Heath d		15 29			15 59				16 29			16 59				17 29			17 59			18 29
Eccleston Park d		15 32			16 02				16 32			17 02				17 32			18 02			18 32
Prescot d		15 34			16 04				16 34			17 04				17 34			18 04			18 34
Huyton d		15 38	15 48	15 53	16 08	16 23			16 38	16 48	16 53	17 08	17 23			17 38	17 48	17 53	18 08	18 23		18 38
Roby d		15 40		15 55	16 10	16 25			16 40		16 55	17 10	17 25			17 40		17 55	18 10	18 25		
Broad Green d		15 43		15 58	16 13	16 28			16 43		16 58	17 13	17 28			17 43		17 58	18 13	18 28		
Wavertree Technology Park d	15 38	15 46		16 01	16 16	16 31		16 38	16 46		17 01	17 16	17 31		17 38	17 46		18 01	18 16	18 31		18 43
Edge Hill 89,91 d		15 49		16 04	16 19	16 34			16 49		17 04	17 19	17 34			17 49		18 04	18 19	18 34		18 46
Liverpool Lime Street 10 89,91 a	15 48	15 58	16 02	16 13	16 28	16 43		16 48	16 58	17 05	17 13	17 28	17 43		17 48	17 58	18 02	18 13	18 28	18 43		18 54

A To Liverpool South Parkway
B From Stalybridge
C To Llandudno
D To Chester

Table 90

Saturdays
until 18 June

Manchester, Preston, Wigan and Newton-le-Willows - St. Helens and Liverpool

		NT	NT	NT		NT	NT A	AW B	NT	NT	NT	NT	NT	AW B		NT	NT	NT	NT	NT	AW B	AW B	NT	NT	
Manchester Airport 85 ✈	d	17 41							18 41							19 41						20 32			
Manchester Piccadilly 10	d	18 01						18 35	19 01					19 35		20 01					20 35	20a48			
Manchester Oxford Road	d	18 04						18 40	19 04					19 40		20 04					20 40				
Manchester Victoria	d						18 39						19 39							20 39				21 39	
Eccles	d	18 11					18 46						19 46							20 46				21 46	
Patricroft	d						18 49						19 49							20 49				21 49	
Blackpool North 97	d			17 37							18 37							19 37					20 37		
Preston 8 65,82	d			18 04							19 04							20 04					21 04		
Leyland 82	d			18 09							19 09							20 09					21 09		
Euxton Balshaw Lane	d			18 14							19 14							20 14					21 14		
Wigan North Western 65	a			18 24							19 24							20 24					21 23		
	d		18 21	18 24		18 35				19 08	19 24						20 08	20 24	20 38				21 23		
Newton-le-Willows	d	18 24	18 33				19 01	19 10	19 22				20 01	20 10		20 22				21 01	21 10			22 01	
Warrington Bank Quay	d											19 22													
Earlestown 8	d		18 36				19 04	19 20				19 34	20 04	20 20						21 04	21 20			22 04	
Warrington Bank Quay	a							19 45						20 45							21 45				
St Helens Junction	d	18 29	18 41				19 09		19 27			19 39	20 09			20 27				21 09				22 09	
Lea Green	d	18 32	18 44				19 12					19 42	20 12							21 12				22 12	
Rainhill	d	18 36	18 48				19 16					19 46	20 16							21 16				22 16	
Whiston	d		18 51				19 19					19 49	20 19							21 19				22 19	
Bryn	d					18 45				19 15							20 15		20 45				21 30		
Garswood	d					18 49				19 19							20 19		20 49				21 34		
St Helens Central	a			18 39		18 55				19 25	19 39						20 25	20 39	20 55				21 40		
	d			18 39		18 56				19 26	19 39						20 26	20 39	20 56				21 41		
Thatto Heath	d					18 59				19 29							20 29		20 59				21 44		
Eccleston Park	d					19 02				19 32							20 32		21 02				21 47		
Prescot	d					19 04				19 34							20 34		21 04				21 49		
Huyton	d	18 41	18 55	18 48		19 08	19 23			19 38	19 48	19 53	20 23				20 38	20 48	21 08	21 23			21 53	22 23	
Roby	d	18 43	18 57			19 10	19 25			19 40		19 55	20 25				20 40		21 10	21 25			21 55	22 25	
Broad Green	d	18 47	19 00			19 13	19 28			19 43		19 58	20 28				20 43		21 13	21 28			21 58	22 28	
Wavertree Technology Park	d	18 50	19 03			19 16	19 31		19 38	19 46		20 01	20 31			20 38	20 46		21 16	21 31			22 03	22 31	
Edge Hill 89,91	d		19 06			19 19	19 34			19 49		20 04	20 34				20 49		21 19	21 34			22 06	22 34	
Liverpool Lime Street 10 89,91	a	19 00	19 15	19 02		19 28	19 43		19 48	19 58	20 02	20 13	20 43			20 48	20 58	21 02	21 28	21 43			22 14	22 43	

		NT	NT	NT	NT	AW B	NT	AW B
Manchester Airport 85 ✈	d	21 41						
Manchester Piccadilly 10	d	22 01				22 26		23 14
Manchester Oxford Road	d	22 04				22 31		23 19
Manchester Victoria	d			22 39			23 09	
Eccles	d			22 46			23 16	
Patricroft	d			22 49			23 19	
Blackpool North 97	d				22 14			
Preston 8 65,82	d				22 43			
Leyland 82	d				22 48			
Euxton Balshaw Lane	d				22 53			
Wigan North Western 65	a				23 02			
	d		22 25		23 03			
Newton-le-Willows	d	22 22		23 01		23 01	23 31	23 49
Warrington Bank Quay	d							
Earlestown 8	d			23 04		23 11	23 34	23 59
Warrington Bank Quay	a					23 36		00 24
St Helens Junction	d	22 27		23 09			23 39	
Lea Green	d			23 12			23 42	
Rainhill	d			23 16			23 46	
Whiston	d			23 19			23 49	
Bryn	d		22 32		23 10			
Garswood	d		22 36		23 14			
St Helens Central	a		22 42		23 20			
	d		22 43		23 21			
Thatto Heath	d		22 46		23 24			
Eccleston Park	d		22 49		23 27			
Prescot	d		22 51		23 29			
Huyton	d		22 55	23 23	23 33		23 53	
Roby	d		22 57	23 25	23 35		23 55	
Broad Green	d		23 00	23 28	23 38		23 57	
Wavertree Technology Park	d	22 38	23 03	23 31	23 41		00 01	
Edge Hill 89,91	d		23 06	23 34	23 46		00 04	
Liverpool Lime Street 10 89,91	a	22 48	23 15	23 43	23 54		00 13	

A From Stalybridge

B To Chester

Table 90

Saturdays

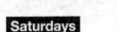

25 June to 10 September

Manchester, Preston, Wigan and Newton-le-Willows - St. Helens and Liverpool

	NT	NT	NT	NT	AW ◇ A	NT	NT	NT	NT		AW ◇ A	NT	NT	NT	NT	NT	NT	AW ◇ A	NT		NT	NT	NT	NT B
Manchester Airport 85 ✈ d		04 34			05 33							06 41												
Manchester Piccadilly 10 d		04 49			05 50						06 50	06 58						07 50						
Manchester Oxford Road d					05 53						06 53	07 01						07 53						
Manchester Victoria d	23p09			05 39			06 09							07 09			07 39				08 09			08 39
Eccles d	23p16			05 46			06 16							07 16			07 46				08 16			08 46
Patricroft d	23p19			05 49			06 19							07 19			07 49				08 19			08 49
Blackpool North 97 d																07 02								
Preston 8 65,82 d																07 30								
Leyland 82 d																07 35								
Euxton Balshaw Lane d																07 40								
Wigan North Western 65 a																07 50								
d						06 08		06 38	06 47				07 08		07 38	07 50			07 58			08 28		
Newton-le-Willows d	23p31			06 01	06 12		06 31		07 00		07 12	07 19		07 31			08 01	08 12			08 31			09 01
Warrington Bank Quay d																								
Earlestown 8 d	23p34			06 04	06 15		06 34		07 03		07 15			07 34			08 04	08 15			08 34			09 04
Warrington Bank Quay a					06 25						07 22							08 23						
St Helens Junction d	23p39			06 09			06 39		07 09			07 24		07 39			08 09				08 39			09 09
Lea Green d	23p42			06 12			06 42		07 12					07 42			08 12				08 42			09 12
Rainhill d	23p46			06 16			06 46		07 16			07 29		07 46			08 16				08 46			09 16
Whiston d	23p49			06 19			06 49		07 19					07 49			08 19				08 49			09 19
Bryn d						06 15		06 45					07 15		07 45				08 05			08 35		
Garswood d						06 19		06 49					07 19		07 49	07 59			08 09			08 39		
St Helens Central a						06 25		06 55					07 25		07 55	08 06			08 15			08 45		
d			05 56			06 26		06 56					07 26		07 56	08 06			08 16			08 46	08 56	
Thatto Heath d			05 59			06 29		06 59					07 29		07 59				08 19			08 49	08 59	
Eccleston Park d			06 02			06 32		07 02					07 32		08 02				08 22			08 52	09 02	
Prescot d			06 04			06 34		07 04					07 34		08 04	08 12			08 24			08 54	09 04	
Huyton d	23p53		06 08	06 23		06 38	06 53	07 08	07 23			07 34	07 38	07 53	08 08	08 16	08 23		08 28		08 53	08 58	09 08	09 23
Roby d	23p55		06 10	06 25		06 40	06 55	07 10	07 25				07 40	07 55	08 10		08 25		08 30		08 55	09 00	09 10	09 25
Broad Green d	23p58		06 13	06 28		06 43	06 58	07 13	07 28				07 43	07 58	08 13	08 20	08 28		08 33		08 58	09 03	09 13	09 28
Wavertree Technology Park d	00 01		06 16	06 31		06 46	07 01	07 16	07 31			07 39	07 46	08 01	08 16	08 24	08 31		08 36		09 01	09 06	09 16	09 31
Edge Hill 89,91 d	00 04		06 19	06 34		06 49	07 04	07 19	07 34				07 49	08 04	08 19		08 34		08 39		09 04	09 09	09 19	09 34
Liverpool Lime Street 10 89,91 a	00 13	05 32	06 28	06 43		06 58	07 13	07 28	07 43			07 49	07 58	08 13	08 28	08 34	08 43		08 48		09 13	09 18	09 28	09 43

	AW ◇ A	NT	NT	NT C	NT		NT	NT B	AW ◇ A	NT	NT	NT C	NT	NT	NT B		AW ◇ A	NT	NT	NT C	NT	NT	NT B	AW ◇ A
Manchester Airport 85 ✈ d		08 41								09 41								10 41						
Manchester Piccadilly 10 d	08 50	09 01							09 50	10 01							10 50	11 01						11 50
Manchester Oxford Road d	08 53	09 04							09 53	10 04							10 53	11 04						11 53
Manchester Victoria d								09 39							10 39								11 39	
Eccles d								09 46							10 46								11 46	
Patricroft d								09 49							10 49								11 49	
Blackpool North 97 d				08 38								09 37								10 37				
Preston 8 65,82 d				09 04								10 04								11 04				
Leyland 82 d				09 09								10 09								11 09				
Euxton Balshaw Lane d				09 14								10 14								11 14				
Wigan North Western 65 a				09 24								10 24								11 24				
d			09 08	09 24			09 38				10 08	10 24		10 38					11 08	11 24		11 38		
Newton-le-Willows d	09 12	09 22						10 01	10 12	10 22					11 01		11 12	11 22					12 01	12 12
Warrington Bank Quay d					09 22								10 22								11 22			
Earlestown 8 d	09 15				09 34			10 04	10 15				10 34		11 04		11 15				11 34		12 04	12 15
Warrington Bank Quay a	09 25								10 25								11 25							12 25
St Helens Junction d		09 27			09 39			10 09		10 27			10 39		11 09			11 27			11 39		12 09	
Lea Green d					09 42			10 12					10 42		11 12						11 42		12 12	
Rainhill d					09 46			10 16					10 46		11 16						11 46		12 16	
Whiston d					09 49			10 19					10 49		11 19						11 49		12 19	
Bryn d			09 15				09 45				10 15			10 45					11 15			11 45		
Garswood d			09 19				09 49				10 19			10 49					11 19			11 49		
St Helens Central a			09 25	09 39			09 55				10 25	10 39		10 55					11 25	11 39		11 55		
d			09 26	09 39			09 56				10 26	10 39		10 56					11 26	11 39		11 56		
Thatto Heath d			09 29				09 59				10 29			10 59					11 29			11 59		
Eccleston Park d			09 32				10 02				10 32			11 02					11 32			12 02		
Prescot d			09 34				10 04				10 34			11 04					11 34			12 04		
Huyton d			09 38	09 48	09 53		10 08	10 23			10 38	10 48	10 53	11 08	11 23				11 38	11 48	11 53	12 08	12 23	
Roby d			09 40		09 55		10 10	10 25			10 40		10 55	11 10	11 25				11 40		11 55	12 10	12 25	
Broad Green d			09 43		09 58		10 13	10 28			10 43		10 58	11 13	11 28				11 43		11 58	12 13	12 28	
Wavertree Technology Park d		09 38	09 46		10 01		10 16	10 31		10 38	10 46		11 01	11 16	11 31			11 38	11 46		12 01	12 16	12 31	
Edge Hill 89,91 d			09 49		10 04		10 21	10 34			10 49		11 04	11 19	11 34				11 49		12 04	12 19	12 34	
Liverpool Lime Street 10 89,91 a		09 48	09 58	10 02	10 13		10 29	10 43		10 48	10 58	11 02	11 13	11 28	11 43			11 48	11 58	12 02	12 13	12 28	12 43	

A To Llandudno

B From Stalybridge

C To Liverpool South Parkway

Table 90

Saturdays

25 June to 10 September

Manchester, Preston, Wigan and Newton-le-Willows - St. Helens and Liverpool

		NT		NT	NT A	NT	NT	NT B	AW ◇ C	NT	NT	NT A		NT	NT	NT B	AW ◇ C	NT	NT	NT A	NT	NT		NT B	AW ◇ C
Manchester Airport 85	d	11 41								12 41								13 41							
Manchester Piccadilly [10]	d	12 01							12 50	13 01							13 50	14 01							14 50
Manchester Oxford Road	d	12 04							12 53	13 04							13 53	14 04							14 53
Manchester Victoria	d							12 39								13 39								14 39	
Eccles	d							12 46								13 46								14 46	
Patricroft	d							12 49								13 49								14 49	
Blackpool North 97	d				11 37							12 37								13 37					
Preston [8] 65,82	d				12 04							13 04								14 04					
Leyland 82	d				12 09							13 09								14 09					
Euxton Balshaw Lane	d				12 14							13 14								14 14					
Wigan North Western 65	a				12 24							13 24								14 24					
	d			12 08	12 24		12 38				13 08	13 24			13 38				14 08	14 24		14 38			
Newton-le-Willows	d	12 22						13 01	13 12	13 22						14 01	14 12	14 22						15 01	15 12
Warrington Bank Quay	d					12 22								13 22							14 22				
Earlestown [8]	d					12 34		13 04	13 15					13 34		14 04	14 15				14 34			15 04	15 15
Warrington Bank Quay	a								13 25								14 25								15 25
St Helens Junction	d	12 27				12 39		13 09		13 27				13 39		14 09		14 27			14 39			15 09	
Lea Green	d					12 42		13 12						13 42		14 12					14 42			15 12	
Rainhill	d					12 46		13 16						13 46		14 16					14 46			15 16	
Whiston	d					12 49		13 19						13 49		14 19					14 49			15 19	
Bryn	d			12 15			12 45				13 15				13 45				14 15			14 45			
Garswood	d			12 19			12 49				13 19				13 49				14 19			14 49			
St Helens Central	a			12 25	12 39		12 55				13 25	13 39			13 55				14 25	14 39		14 55			
	d			12 26	12 39		12 56				13 26	13 39			13 56				14 26	14 39		14 56			
Thatto Heath	d			12 29			12 59				13 29				13 59				14 29			14 59			
Eccleston Park	d			12 32			13 02				13 32				14 02				14 32			15 02			
Prescot	d			12 34			13 04				13 34				14 04				14 34			15 04			
Huyton	d			12 38	12 48	12 53	13 08	13 23			13 38	13 48		13 53	14 08	14 23			14 38	14 48	14 53	15 08		15 23	
Roby	d			12 40		12 55	13 10	13 25			13 40			13 55	14 10	14 25			14 40		14 55	15 10		15 25	
Broad Green	d			12 43		12 58	13 13	13 28			13 43			13 58	14 13	14 28			14 43		14 58	15 13		15 28	
Wavertree Technology Park	d	12 38		12 46		13 01	13 16	13 31		13 38	13 46			14 01	14 16	14 31		14 38	14 46		15 01	15 16		15 31	
Edge Hill 89,91	d			12 49		13 04	13 19	13 34			13 49			14 04	14 19	14 34			14 49		15 04	15 19		15 34	
Liverpool Lime Street [10] 89,91	a	12 48		12 58	13 02	13 13	13 28	13 43		13 48	13 58	14 02		14 13	14 28	14 43		14 48	14 58	15 02	15 13	15 28		15 43	

		NT	NT	NT A	NT	NT	NT B	AW ◇ C		NT	NT	NT	NT	NT	NT B	AW ◇ C	NT	NT		NT	NT	NT	NT B	AW ◇ C	NT
Manchester Airport 85	d	14 41								15 41							16 41								
Manchester Piccadilly [10]	d	15 01						15 50		16 01						16 50	17 01							17 50	
Manchester Oxford Road	d	15 04						15 53		16 04						16 53	17 04							17 53	
Manchester Victoria	d						15 39								16 39						17 09		17 39		
Eccles	d						15 46								16 46						17 16		17 46		
Patricroft	d						15 49								16 49						17 19		17 49		
Blackpool North 97	d			14 37								15 37								16 35					
Preston [8] 65,82	d			15 04								16 04								17 04					
Leyland 82	d			15 09								16 09								17 09					
Euxton Balshaw Lane	d			15 14								16 14								17 14					
Wigan North Western 65	a			15 24								16 24								17 24					
	d		15 08	15 24		15 38					16 08	16 24		16 38				17 08		17 24		17 38			18 08
Newton-le-Willows	d	15 22					16 01	16 12		16 22					17 01	17 12	17 22				17 31		18 01	18 12	
Warrington Bank Quay	d				15 22								16 22												
Earlestown [8]	d				15 34		16 04	16 15					16 34		17 04	17 15					17 34		18 04	18 15	
Warrington Bank Quay	a							16 25								17 25								18 24	
St Helens Junction	d	15 27			15 39		16 09			16 27			16 39		17 09		17 27				17 39		18 09		
Lea Green	d				15 42		16 12						16 42		17 12						17 42		18 12		
Rainhill	d				15 46		16 16						16 46		17 16						17 46		18 16		
Whiston	d				15 49		16 19						16 49		17 19						17 49		18 19		
Bryn	d		15 15			15 45					16 15			16 45				17 15				17 45			18 15
Garswood	d		15 19			15 49					16 19			16 49				17 19				17 49			18 19
St Helens Central	a		15 25	15 39		15 55					16 25	16 39		16 55				17 25		17 39		17 55			18 25
	d		15 26	15 39		15 56					16 26	16 39		16 56				17 26		17 39		17 56			18 26
Thatto Heath	d		15 29			15 59					16 29			16 59				17 29				17 59			18 29
Eccleston Park	d		15 32			16 02					16 32			17 02				17 32				18 02			18 32
Prescot	d		15 34			16 04					16 34			17 04				17 34				18 04			18 34
Huyton	d		15 38	15 48	15 53	16 08	16 23				16 38	16 48	16 53	17 08	17 23			17 38		17 48	17 53	18 08	18 23		18 38
Roby	d		15 40		15 55	16 10	16 25				16 40		16 55	17 10	17 25			17 40			17 55	18 10	18 25		
Broad Green	d		15 43		15 58	16 13	16 28				16 43		16 58	17 13	17 28			17 43			17 58	18 13	18 28		
Wavertree Technology Park	d	15 38	15 46		16 01	16 16	16 31			16 38	16 46		17 01	17 16	17 31		17 38	17 46			18 01	18 16	18 31		18 43
Edge Hill 89,91	d		15 49		16 04	16 19	16 34				16 49		17 04	17 19	17 34			17 49			18 04	18 19	18 34		18 46
Liverpool Lime Street [10] 89,91	a	15 48	15 58	16 02	16 13	16 28	16 43			16 48	16 58	17 05	17 13	17 28	17 43		17 48	17 58		18 02	18 13	18 28	18 43		18 54

A To Liverpool South Parkway **B** From Stalybridge **C** To Llandudno

Table 90

Saturdays

25 June to 10 September

Manchester, Preston, Wigan and Newton-le-Willows - St. Helens and Liverpool

		NT	NT	NT		NT	NT A	AW B ⚲	NT	NT	NT	NT	NT	AW B		NT	NT	NT	NT	NT	AW B	NT	NT	AW B	
Manchester Airport 85 ✈	d	17 41							18 41							19 41					20 32				
Manchester Piccadilly 10 ⇌	d	18 01						18 50	19 01					19 50		20 01					20 50			21 50	
Manchester Oxford Road	d	18 04						18 53	19 04					19 53		20 04					20 53			21 53	
Manchester Victoria ⇌	d						18 39						19 39							20 39			21 39		
Eccles	d	18 11					18 46						19 46							20 46			21 46		
Patricroft	d						18 49						19 49							20 49			21 49		
Blackpool North 97	d			17 37							18 37							19 37				20 37			
Preston 8 65,82	d			18 04							19 04							20 04				21 04			
Leyland 82	d			18 09							19 09							20 09				21 09			
Euxton Balshaw Lane	d			18 14							19 14							20 14				21 14			
Wigan North Western 65	a			18 24							19 24							20 24				21 23			
	d		18 21	18 24		18 35				19 08	19 24						20 08	20 24	20 38			21 23			
Newton-le-Willows	d	18 24	18 33				19 01	19 12	19 22				20 01	20 12		20 22				21 01	21 12		22 01	22 12	
Warrington Bank Quay	d											19 22													
Earlestown 8	d		18 36				19 04	19 16				19 34	20 04	20 15						21 04	21 15		22 04	22 15	
Warrington Bank Quay	a							19 24						20 29							21 26			22 23	
St Helens Junction	d	18 29	18 41				19 09		19 27			19 39	20 09			20 27				21 09			22 09		
Lea Green	d	18 32	18 44				19 12					19 42	20 12							21 12			22 12		
Rainhill	d	18 36	18 48				19 16					19 46	20 16							21 16			22 16		
Whiston	d		18 51				19 19					19 49	20 19							21 19			22 19		
Bryn	d					18 45				19 15							20 15		20 45			21 30			
Garswood	d					18 49				19 19							20 19		20 49			21 34			
St Helens Central	a			18 39		18 55				19 25	19 39						20 25	20 39	20 55			21 40			
	d			18 39		18 56				19 26	19 39						20 26	20 39	20 56			21 41			
Thatto Heath	d					18 59				19 29							20 29		20 59			21 44			
Eccleston Park	d					19 02				19 32							20 32		21 02			21 47			
Prescot	d					19 04				19 34							20 34		21 04			21 49			
Huyton	d	18 41	18 55	18 48		19 08	19 23			19 38	19 48	19 53	20 23				20 38	20 48	21 08	21 23		21 53	22 23		
Roby	d	18 43	18 57			19 10	19 25			19 40		19 55	20 25				20 40		21 10	21 25		21 55	22 25		
Broad Green	d	18 47	19 00			19 13	19 28			19 43		19 58	20 28				20 43		21 13	21 28		21 58	22 28		
Wavertree Technology Park	d	18 50	19 03			19 16	19 31		19 38	19 46		20 01	20 31			20 38	20 46		21 16	21 31		22 03	22 31		
Edge Hill 89,91	d		19 06			19 19	19 34			19 49		20 04	20 34				20 49		21 19	21 34		22 06	22 34		
Liverpool Lime Street 10 89,91	a	19 00	19 15	19 02		19 28	19 43		19 48	19 58	20 02	20 13	20 43			20 48	20 58	21 02	21 28	21 43		22 14	22 43		

		NT	NT	AW B	NT	NT	NT	AW B
Manchester Airport 85 ✈	d	21 41						
Manchester Piccadilly 10 ⇌	d	22 01		22 26				23 14
Manchester Oxford Road	d	22 04		22 29				23 17
Manchester Victoria ⇌	d				22 39		23 09	
Eccles	d				22 46		23 16	
Patricroft	d				22 49		23 19	
Blackpool North 97	d					22 14		
Preston 8 65,82	d					22 43		
Leyland 82	d					22 48		
Euxton Balshaw Lane	d					22 53		
Wigan North Western 65	a					23 02		
	d		22 25			23 03		
Newton-le-Willows	d	22 22		22 47	23 01		23 31	23 36
Warrington Bank Quay	d							
Earlestown 8	d			22 50	23 04		23 34	23 39
Warrington Bank Quay	a			22 58				23 47
St Helens Junction	d	22 27			23 09		23 39	
Lea Green	d				23 12		23 42	
Rainhill	d				23 16		23 46	
Whiston	d				23 19		23 49	
Bryn	d		22 32			23 10		
Garswood	d		22 36			23 14		
St Helens Central	a		22 42			23 20		
	d		22 43			23 21		
Thatto Heath	d		22 46			23 24		
Eccleston Park	d		22 49			23 27		
Prescot	d		22 51			23 29		
Huyton	d		22 55		23 23	23 33	23 53	
Roby	d		22 57		23 25	23 35	23 55	
Broad Green	d		23 00		23 28	23 38	23 57	
Wavertree Technology Park	d	22 38	23 03		23 31	23 41	00 01	
Edge Hill 89,91	d		23 06		23 34	23 46	00 04	
Liverpool Lime Street 10 89,91	a	22 48	23 15		23 43	23 54	00 13	

A From Stalybridge

B To Chester

Table 90

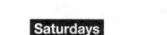

Saturdays
from 17 September

Manchester, Preston, Wigan and Newton-le-Willows - St. Helens and Liverpool

	NT	NT	NT	NT	AW	NT	NT	NT	NT		AW	NT	NT	NT	NT	NT	NT	AW	NT		NT	NT	NT	NT
					◇ A						◇ A							◇ A						B
Manchester Airport 85 ✈ d		04 34			05 33							06 41												
Manchester Piccadilly 10 d		04 49			05 50						06 50	06 58						07 50						
Manchester Oxford Road d					05 53						06 53	07 01						07 53						
Manchester Victoria d	23p09			05 39			06 09							07 09			07 39				08 09			08 39
Eccles d	23p16			05 46			06 16							07 16			07 46				08 16			08 46
Patricroft d	23p19			05 49			06 19							07 19			07 49				08 19			08 49
Blackpool North 97 d																07 02								
Preston 8 65,82 d																07 30								
Leyland 82 d																07 35								
Euxton Balshaw Lane d																07 40								
Wigan North Western 65 a																07 50								
d						06 08		06 38	06 47				07 08		07 38	07 50			07 58			08 28		
Newton-le-Willows d	23p31			06 01	06 12		06 31		07 00		07 12	07 19		07 31			08 01	08 12			08 31			09 01
Warrington Bank Quay d																								
Earlestown 8 d	23p34			06 04	06 15		06 34		07 03		07 15			07 34			08 04	08 15			08 34			09 04
Warrington Bank Quay a					06 25						07 22							08 23						
St Helens Junction d	23p39			06 09			06 39		07 09			07 24		07 39			08 09				08 39			09 09
Lea Green d	23p42			06 12			06 42		07 12					07 42			08 12				08 42			09 12
Rainhill d	23p46			06 16			06 46		07 16			07 29		07 46			08 16				08 46			09 16
Whiston d	23p49			06 19			06 49		07 19					07 49			08 19				08 49			09 19
Bryn d						06 15		06 45					07 15		07 45				08 05			08 35		
Garswood d						06 19		06 49					07 19		07 49	07 59			08 09			08 39		
St Helens Central a						06 25		06 55					07 25		07 55	08 06			08 15			08 45		
d			05 56			06 26		06 56					07 26		07 56	08 06			08 16			08 46	08 56	
Thatto Heath d			05 59			06 29		06 59					07 29		07 59				08 19			08 49	08 59	
Eccleston Park d			06 02			06 32		07 02					07 32		08 02				08 22			08 52	09 02	
Prescot d			06 04			06 34		07 04					07 34		08 04	08 12			08 24			08 54	09 04	
Huyton d	23p53		06 08	06 23		06 38	06 53	07 08	07 23			07 34	07 38	07 53	08 08	08 16	08 23		08 28		08 53	08 58	09 08	09 23
Roby d	23p55		06 10	06 25		06 40	06 55	07 10	07 25				07 40	07 55	08 10		08 25		08 30		08 55	09 00	09 10	09 25
Broad Green d	23p58		06 13	06 28		06 43	06 58	07 13	07 28				07 43	07 58	08 13	08 20	08 28		08 33		08 58	09 03	09 13	09 28
Wavertree Technology Park d	00 01		06 16	06 31		06 46	07 01	07 16	07 31			07 39	07 46	08 01	08 16	08 24	08 31		08 36		09 01	09 06	09 16	09 31
Edge Hill 89,91 d	00 04		06 19	06 34		06 49	07 04	07 19	07 34				07 49	08 04	08 19		08 34		08 39		09 04	09 09	09 19	09 34
Liverpool Lime Street 10 89,91 a	00 13	05 32	06 28	06 43		06 58	07 13	07 28	07 43			07 49	07 58	08 13	08 28	08 34	08 43		08 48		09 13	09 18	09 28	09 43

	AW	NT	NT	NT	NT		NT	NT	AW	NT	NT	NT	NT	NT	NT		AW	NT	NT	NT	NT	NT	NT	AW
	◇ A			C				B	◇ A			C			B		◇ A			C			B	◇ A
Manchester Airport 85 ✈ d		08 41								09 41								10 41						
Manchester Piccadilly 10 d	08 50	09 01							09 50	10 01							10 50	11 01						11 50
Manchester Oxford Road d	08 53	09 04							09 53	10 04							10 53	11 04						11 53
Manchester Victoria d								09 39							10 39								11 39	
Eccles d								09 46							10 46								11 46	
Patricroft d								09 49							10 49								11 49	
Blackpool North 97 d				08 38								09 37								10 37				
Preston 8 65,82 d				09 04								10 04								11 04				
Leyland 82 d				09 09								10 09								11 09				
Euxton Balshaw Lane d				09 14								10 14								11 14				
Wigan North Western 65 a				09 24								10 24								11 24				
d			09 08	09 24			09 38				10 08	10 24		10 38					11 08	11 24		11 38		
Newton-le-Willows d	09 12	09 22						10 01	10 12	10 22					11 01		11 12	11 22					12 01	12 12
Warrington Bank Quay d					09 22								10 22								11 22			
Earlestown 8 d	09 15				09 34			10 04	10 15				10 34		11 04		11 15				11 34		12 04	12 15
Warrington Bank Quay a	09 25								10 25								11 25							12 25
St Helens Junction d		09 27			09 39			10 09		10 27			10 39		11 09			11 27			11 39		12 09	
Lea Green d					09 42			10 12					10 42		11 12						11 42		12 12	
Rainhill d					09 46			10 16					10 46		11 16						11 46		12 16	
Whiston d					09 49			10 19					10 49		11 19						11 49		12 19	
Bryn d			09 15				09 45				10 15			10 45					11 15			11 45		
Garswood d			09 19				09 49				10 19			10 49					11 19			11 49		
St Helens Central a			09 25	09 39			09 55				10 25	10 39		10 55					11 25	11 39		11 55		
d			09 26	09 39			09 56				10 26	10 39		10 56					11 26	11 39		11 56		
Thatto Heath d			09 29				09 59				10 29			10 59					11 29			11 59		
Eccleston Park d			09 32				10 02				10 32			11 02					11 32			12 02		
Prescot d			09 34				10 04				10 34			11 04					11 34			12 04		
Huyton d			09 38	09 48	09 53		10 08	10 23			10 38	10 48	10 53	11 08	11 23				11 38	11 48	11 53	12 08	12 23	
Roby d			09 40		09 55		10 10	10 25			10 40		10 55	11 10	11 25				11 40		11 55	12 10	12 25	
Broad Green d			09 43		09 58		10 13	10 28			10 43		10 58	11 13	11 28				11 43		11 58	12 13	12 28	
Wavertree Technology Park d		09 38	09 46		10 01		10 16	10 31		10 38	10 46		11 01	11 16	11 31			11 38	11 46		12 01	12 16	12 31	
Edge Hill 89,91 d			09 49		10 04		10 21	10 34			10 49		11 04	11 19	11 34				11 49		12 04	12 19	12 34	
Liverpool Lime Street 10 89,91 a		09 48	09 58	10 02	10 13		10 29	10 43		10 48	10 58	11 02	11 13	11 28	11 43			11 48	11 58	12 02	12 13	12 28	12 43	

A To Llandudno
B From Stalybridge
C To Liverpool South Parkway

Table 90

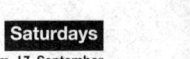

Saturdays
from 17 September

Manchester, Preston, Wigan and Newton-le-Willows - St. Helens and Liverpool

	NT	NT	NT	NT	NT	NT	AW	NT	NT	NT	NT	NT	NT	AW	NT	NT	NT	NT	NT	NT	AW
			A			B	◇ C			A			B	◇ C			A			B	◇ C
Manchester Airport 85 ✈ d	11 41							12 41							13 41						
Manchester Piccadilly 10 d	12 01						12 50	13 01						13 50	14 01						14 50
Manchester Oxford Road d	12 04						12 53	13 04						13 53	14 04						14 53
Manchester Victoria d						12 39							13 39							14 39	
Eccles d						12 46							13 46							14 46	
Patricroft d						12 49							13 49							14 49	
Blackpool North 97 d			11 37							12 37							13 37				
Preston 8 65,82 d			12 04							13 04							14 04				
Leyland 82 d			12 09							13 09							14 09				
Euxton Balshaw Lane d			12 14							13 14							14 14				
Wigan North Western 65 a			12 24							13 24							14 24				
d		12 08	12 24		12 38				13 08	13 24		13 38				14 08	14 24		14 38		
Newton-le-Willows d	12 22					13 01	13 12	13 22					14 01	14 12	14 22					15 01	15 12
Warrington Bank Quay d				12 22							13 22							14 22			
Earlestown 8 d				12 34		13 04	13 15				13 34		14 04	14 15				14 34		15 04	15 15
Warrington Bank Quay a							13 25							14 25							15 25
St Helens Junction d	12 27			12 39		13 09		13 27			13 39		14 09		14 27			14 39		15 09	
Lea Green d				12 42		13 12					13 42		14 12					14 42		15 12	
Rainhill d				12 46		13 16					13 46		14 16					14 46		15 16	
Whiston d				12 49		13 19					13 49		14 19					14 49		15 19	
Bryn d		12 15			12 45				13 15			13 45				14 15			14 45		
Garswood d		12 19			12 49				13 19			13 49				14 19			14 49		
St Helens Central a		12 25	12 39		12 55				13 25	13 39		13 55				14 25	14 39		14 55		
d		12 26	12 39		12 56				13 26	13 39		13 56				14 26	14 39		14 56		
Thatto Heath d		12 29			12 59				13 29			13 59				14 29			14 59		
Eccleston Park d		12 32			13 02				13 32			14 02				14 32			15 02		
Prescot d		12 34			13 04				13 34			14 04				14 34			15 04		
Huyton d		12 38	12 48	12 53	13 08	13 23			13 38	13 48	13 53	14 08	14 23			14 38	14 48	14 53	15 08	15 23	
Roby d		12 40		12 55	13 10	13 25			13 40		13 55	14 10	14 25			14 40		14 55	15 10	15 25	
Broad Green d		12 43		12 58	13 13	13 28			13 43		13 58	14 13	14 28			14 43		14 58	15 13	15 28	
Wavertree Technology Park d	12 38	12 46		13 01	13 16	13 31		13 38	13 46		14 01	14 16	14 31		14 38	14 46		15 01	15 16	15 31	
Edge Hill 89,91 d		12 49		13 04	13 19	13 34			13 49		14 04	14 19	14 34			14 49		15 04	15 19	15 34	
Liverpool Lime Street 10 89,91 a	12 48	12 58	13 02	13 13	13 28	13 43		13 48	13 58	14 02	14 13	14 28	14 43		14 48	14 58	15 02	15 13	15 28	15 43	

	NT	NT	NT	NT	NT	NT	AW	NT	NT	NT	NT	NT	NT	AW	NT	NT	NT	NT	NT	NT	AW	NT
			A			B	◇ C						B	◇ C						B	◇ C	
Manchester Airport 85 ✈ d	14 41							15 41							16 41							
Manchester Piccadilly 10 d	15 01						15 50	16 01						16 50	17 01						17 50	
Manchester Oxford Road d	15 04						15 53	16 04						16 53	17 04						17 53	
Manchester Victoria d						15 39							16 39					17 09		17 39		
Eccles d						15 46							16 46					17 16		17 46		
Patricroft d						15 49							16 49					17 19		17 49		
Blackpool North 97 d			14 37							15 37							16 35					
Preston 8 65,82 d			15 04							16 04							17 04					
Leyland 82 d			15 09							16 09							17 09					
Euxton Balshaw Lane d			15 14							16 14							17 14					
Wigan North Western 65 a			15 24							16 24							17 24					
d		15 08	15 24		15 38				16 08	16 24		16 38				17 08	17 24		17 38			18 08
Newton-le-Willows d	15 22					16 01	16 12	16 22					17 01	17 12	17 22			17 31		18 01	18 12	
Warrington Bank Quay d				15 22							16 22											
Earlestown 8 d				15 34		16 04	16 15				16 34		17 04	17 15				17 34		18 04	18 15	
Warrington Bank Quay a							16 25							17 25							18 24	
St Helens Junction d	15 27			15 39		16 09		16 27			16 39		17 09		17 27			17 39		18 09		
Lea Green d				15 42		16 12					16 42		17 12					17 42		18 12		
Rainhill d				15 46		16 16					16 46		17 16					17 46		18 16		
Whiston d				15 49		16 19					16 49		17 19					17 49		18 19		
Bryn d		15 15			15 45				16 15			16 45				17 15			17 45			18 15
Garswood d		15 19			15 49				16 19			16 49				17 19			17 49			18 19
St Helens Central a		15 25	15 39		15 55				16 25	16 39		16 55				17 25	17 39		17 55			18 25
d		15 26	15 39		15 56				16 26	16 39		16 56				17 26	17 39		17 56			18 26
Thatto Heath d		15 29			15 59				16 29			16 59				17 29			17 59			18 29
Eccleston Park d		15 32			16 02				16 32			17 02				17 32			18 02			18 32
Prescot d		15 34			16 04				16 34			17 04				17 34			18 04			18 34
Huyton d		15 38	15 48	15 53	16 08	16 23			16 38	16 48	16 53	17 08	17 23			17 38	17 48	17 53	18 08	18 23		18 38
Roby d		15 40		15 55	16 10	16 25			16 40		16 55	17 10	17 25			17 40		17 55	18 10	18 25		
Broad Green d		15 43		15 58	16 13	16 28			16 43		16 58	17 13	17 28			17 43		17 58	18 13	18 28		
Wavertree Technology Park d	15 38	15 46		16 01	16 16	16 31		16 38	16 46		17 01	17 16	17 31		17 38	17 46		18 01	18 16	18 31		18 43
Edge Hill 89,91 d		15 49		16 04	16 19	16 34			16 49		17 04	17 19	17 34			17 49		18 04	18 19	18 34		18 46
Liverpool Lime Street 10 89,91 a	15 48	15 58	16 02	16 13	16 28	16 43		16 48	16 58	17 05	17 13	17 28	17 43		17 48	17 58	18 02	18 13	18 28	18 43		18 54

A To Liverpool South Parkway
B From Stalybridge
C To Llandudno

Table 90

Saturdays
from 17 September

Manchester, Preston, Wigan and Newton-le-Willows - St. Helens and Liverpool

		NT	NT	NT		NT	NT A	AW B ⚲	NT	NT	NT	NT	NT	AW B		NT	NT	NT	NT	NT	AW B	NT	NT	AW B
Manchester Airport 85 ✈	d	17 41							18 41							19 41					20 32			
Manchester Piccadilly 10	d	18 01						18 50	19 01					19 50		20 01					20 50			21 50
Manchester Oxford Road	d	18 04						18 53	19 04					19 53		20 04					20 53			21 53
Manchester Victoria	d						18 39						19 39							20 39			21 39	
Eccles	d	18 11					18 46						19 46							20 46			21 46	
Patricroft	d						18 49						19 49							20 49			21 49	
Blackpool North 97	d			17 37							18 37							19 37				20 37		
Preston 8 65,82	d			18 04							19 04							20 04				21 04		
Leyland 82	d			18 09							19 09							20 09				21 09		
Euxton Balshaw Lane	d			18 14							19 14							20 14				21 14		
Wigan North Western 65	a			18 24							19 24							20 24				21 23		
	d		18 21	18 24		18 35				19 08	19 24						20 08	20 24	20 38			21 23		
Newton-le-Willows	d	18 24	18 33				19 01	19 12	19 22				20 01	20 12		20 22				21 01	21 12		22 01	22 12
Warrington Bank Quay	d											19 22												
Earlestown 8	d		18 36				19 04	19 16				19 34	20 04	20 15						21 04	21 15		22 04	22 15
Warrington Bank Quay	a							19 24						20 29							21 26			22 23
St Helens Junction	d	18 29	18 41				19 09		19 27			19 39	20 09			20 27				21 09			22 09	
Lea Green	d	18 32	18 44				19 12					19 42	20 12							21 12			22 12	
Rainhill	d	18 36	18 48				19 16					19 46	20 16							21 16			22 16	
Whiston	d		18 51				19 19					19 49	20 19							21 19			22 19	
Bryn	d					18 45				19 15							20 15		20 45			21 30		
Garswood	d					18 49				19 19							20 19		20 49			21 34		
St Helens Central	a			18 39		18 55				19 25	19 39						20 25	20 39	20 55			21 40		
	d			18 39		18 56				19 26	19 39						20 26	20 39	20 56			21 41		
Thatto Heath	d					18 59				19 29							20 29		20 59			21 44		
Eccleston Park	d					19 02				19 32							20 32		21 02			21 47		
Prescot	d					19 04				19 34							20 34		21 04			21 49		
Huyton	d	18 41	18 55	18 48		19 08	19 23			19 38	19 48	19 53	20 23				20 38	20 48	21 08	21 23		21 53	22 23	
Roby	d	18 43	18 57			19 10	19 25			19 40		19 55	20 25				20 40		21 10	21 25		21 55	22 25	
Broad Green	d	18 47	19 00			19 13	19 28			19 43		19 58	20 28				20 43		21 13	21 28		21 58	22 28	
Wavertree Technology Park	d	18 50	19 03			19 16	19 31		19 38	19 46		20 01	20 31			20 38	20 46		21 16	21 31		22 03	22 31	
Edge Hill 89,91	d		19 06			19 19	19 34			19 49		20 04	20 34				20 49		21 19	21 34		22 06	22 34	
Liverpool Lime Street 10 89,91	a	19 00	19 15	19 02		19 28	19 43		19 48	19 58	20 02	20 13	20 43			20 48	20 58	21 02	21 28	21 43		22 14	22 43	

		NT	NT	AW C	NT	NT	NT	AW C
Manchester Airport 85 ✈	d	21 41						
Manchester Piccadilly 10	d	22 01		22 26				23 14
Manchester Oxford Road	d	22 04		22 29				23 17
Manchester Victoria	d				22 39		23 09	
Eccles	d				22 46		23 16	
Patricroft	d				22 49		23 19	
Blackpool North 97	d					22 14		
Preston 8 65,82	d					22 43		
Leyland 82	d					22 48		
Euxton Balshaw Lane	d					22 53		
Wigan North Western 65	a					23 02		
	d		22 25			23 03		
Newton-le-Willows	d	22 22		22 47	23 01		23 31	23 36
Warrington Bank Quay	d							
Earlestown 8	d			22 50	23 04		23 34	23 39
Warrington Bank Quay	a			22 58				23 47
St Helens Junction	d	22 27			23 09		23 39	
Lea Green	d				23 12		23 42	
Rainhill	d				23 16		23 46	
Whiston	d				23 19		23 49	
Bryn	d		22 32			23 10		
Garswood	d		22 36			23 14		
St Helens Central	a		22 42			23 20		
	d		22 43			23 21		
Thatto Heath	d		22 46			23 24		
Eccleston Park	d		22 49			23 27		
Prescot	d		22 51			23 29		
Huyton	d		22 55		23 23	23 33	23 53	
Roby	d		22 57		23 25	23 35	23 55	
Broad Green	d		23 00		23 28	23 38	23 57	
Wavertree Technology Park	d	22 38	23 03		23 31	23 41	00 01	
Edge Hill 89,91	d		23 06		23 34	23 46	00 04	
Liverpool Lime Street 10 89,91	a	22 48	23 15		23 43	23 54	00 13	

A From Stalybridge

B To Chester

C from 29 October. To Chester

Table 90

Sundays
until 19 June

Manchester, Preston, Wigan and Newton-le-Willows - St. Helens and Liverpool

	NT A	AW B 🚌	AW C 🚌	NT	NT	AW C 🚌	NT	NT	AW C 🚌		NT	NT	AW C 🚌	NT	NT	AW C 🚌	NT	NT	AW C 🚌		NT	NT	NT	NT
Manchester Airport 85 ✈ d					08 35			09 35				10 35			11 33			12 35				13 35		14 35
Manchester Piccadilly [10] 🚇 d		23p14	07 28		08 50	08 49		09 50	09 47			10 50	10 45		11 50	11 45		12 50	12 45			13 50		14 50
Manchester Oxford Road d		23p19	07 33		08 53	08 54		09 53	09 52			10 53	10 50		11 53	11 50		12 53	12 50			13 53		14 53
Manchester Victoria 🚇 d	23p09																							
Eccles d	23p16				09 00			10 00				11 00			12 00			13 00				14 00		15 00
Patricroft d	23p19																							
Blackpool North 97 d							08 50				09 50			10 50			11 50				12 50		13 50	
Preston [8] 65,82 d							09 15				10 15			11 15			12 15				13 15		14 15	
Leyland 82 d							09 21				10 21			11 21			12 21				13 21		14 21	
Euxton Balshaw Lane d							09 25				10 25			11 25			12 25				13 25		14 25	
Wigan North Western 65 a							09 35				10 36			11 35			12 35				13 35		14 35	
d				08 36			09 36				10 36			11 36			12 36				13 36		14 36	
Newton-le-Willows d	23p31	23p49	08 03		09 13	09 24		10 13	10 22			11 13	11 20		12 13	12 20		13 13	13 20			14 13		15 13
Warrington Bank Quay d																								
Earlestown [8] d	23p34	23p59	08 13		09 16	09 34		10 16	10 32			11 16	11 30		12 16	12 30		13 16	13 30			14 16		15 16
Warrington Bank Quay a		00 24	08 38			09 59			10 57				11 55			12 55			13 55					
St Helens Junction d	23p39				09 21			10 21				11 21			12 21			13 21				14 21		15 21
Lea Green d	23p42				09 24			10 24				11 24			12 24			13 24				14 24		15 24
Rainhill d	23p46				09 28			10 28				11 28			12 28			13 28				14 28		15 28
Whiston d	23p49				09 31			10 31				11 31			12 31			13 31				14 31		15 31
Bryn d																								
Garswood d				08 46			09 46				10 46			11 46			12 46				13 46		14 46	
St Helens Central a				08 52			09 52				10 52			11 52			12 52				13 52		14 52	
d				08 53			09 53				10 53			11 53			12 53				13 53		14 53	
Thatto Heath d				08 56			09 56				10 56			11 56			12 56				13 56		14 56	
Eccleston Park d																								
Prescot d				09 00			10 00				11 00			12 00			13 00				14 00		15 00	
Huyton d	23p53			09 05	09 35		10 05	10 35			11 05	11 35		12 05	12 35		13 05	13 35			14 05	14 35	15 05	15 35
Roby d	23p55			09 07	09 37		10 07	10 37			11 07	11 37		12 07	12 37		13 07	13 37			14 07	14 37	15 07	15 37
Broad Green d	23p57			09 10	09 40		10 10	10 40			11 10	11 40		12 10	12 40		13 10	13 40			14 10	14 40	15 10	15 40
Wavertree Technology Park d	00 01			09 13	09 43		10 13	10 43			11 13	11 43		12 13	12 43		13 13	13 43			14 13	14 43	15 13	15 43
Edge Hill 89,91 d	00 04																							
Liverpool Lime Street [10] 89,91 a	00 13			09 26	09 52		10 24	10 54			11 24	11 54		12 24	12 54		13 24	13 54			14 24	14 54	15 24	15 54

	NT	AW C 🛒	NT	NT	AW C 🛒		NT	NT	AW C 🛒	NT	NT	AW C 🛒	NT	NT	AW C		NT	NT	AW C	NT	NT	AW C	NT	NT
Manchester Airport 85 ✈ d			15 35				16 35			17 35			18 35				19 35			20 35			21 35	
Manchester Piccadilly [10] 🚇 d		14 56	15 50		15 56		16 50		16 56	17 50		17 56	18 50		18 56		19 50		19 56	20 50		20 56	21 50	
Manchester Oxford Road d		14 59	15 53		15 59		16 53		16 59	17 53		17 59	18 53		18 59		19 53		19 59	20 53		20 59	21 53	
Manchester Victoria 🚇 d																								
Eccles d			16 00				17 00			18 00			19 00				20 00			21 00			22 00	
Patricroft d																								
Blackpool North 97 d	14 50			15 50				16 50			17 50			18 50				19 50			20 50			21 50
Preston [8] 65,82 d	15 15			16 15				17 15			18 15			19 15				20 15			21 15			22 15
Leyland 82 d	15 21			16 21				17 21			18 21			19 21				20 21			21 21			22 21
Euxton Balshaw Lane d	15 25			16 25				17 25			18 25			19 25				20 25			21 25			22 25
Wigan North Western 65 a	15 35			16 35				17 35			18 35			19 35				20 35			21 35			22 35
d	15 36			16 36				17 36			18 36			19 36				20 36			21 36			22 36
Newton-le-Willows d		15 18	16 13		16 18		17 13		17 18	18 13		18 18	19 13		19 18		20 13		20 18	21 13		21 18	22 13	
Warrington Bank Quay d																								
Earlestown [8] d		15 21	16 16		16 21		17 16		17 21	18 16		18 21	19 16		19 21		20 16		20 21	21 16		21 21	22 16	
Warrington Bank Quay a		15 28			16 27				17 27			18 27			19 28				20 29			21 27		
St Helens Junction d			16 21				17 21			18 21			19 21				20 21			21 21			22 21	
Lea Green d			16 24				17 24			18 24			19 24				20 24			21 24			22 24	
Rainhill d			16 28				17 28			18 28			19 28				20 28			21 28			22 28	
Whiston d			16 31				17 31			18 31			19 31				20 31			21 31			22 31	
Bryn d																								
Garswood d	15 46			16 46				17 46			18 46			19 46				20 46			21 46			22 46
St Helens Central a	15 52			16 52				17 52			18 52			19 52				20 52			21 52			22 53
d	15 53			16 53				17 53			18 53			19 53				20 53			21 53			22 53
Thatto Heath d	15 56			16 56				17 56			18 56			19 56				20 56			21 56			22 56
Eccleston Park d																								
Prescot d	16 00			17 00				18 00			19 00			20 00				21 00			22 00			23 00
Huyton d	16 05		16 35	17 05			17 35	18 05		18 35	19 05		19 35	20 05			20 35	21 05		21 35	22 05		22 35	23 05
Roby d	16 07		16 37	17 07			17 37	18 07		18 37	19 07		19 37	20 07			20 37	21 07		21 37	22 07		22 37	23 07
Broad Green d	16 10		16 40	17 10			17 40	18 10		18 40	19 10		19 40	20 10			20 40	21 10		21 40	22 10		22 40	23 10
Wavertree Technology Park d	16 13		16 43	17 13			17 43	18 13		18 43	19 13		19 43	20 13			20 43	21 13		21 43	22 13		22 43	23 13
Edge Hill 89,91 d																								
Liverpool Lime Street [10] 89,91 a	16 24		16 54	17 24			17 54	18 24		18 54	19 24		19 54	20 24			20 54	21 24		21 54	22 24		22 54	23 24

A not 22 May

B not 22 May. To Chester

C To Chester

Table 90

Sundays
until 19 June

Manchester, Preston, Wigan and Newton-le-Willows - St. Helens and Liverpool

		AW A		NT	NT	AW A	AW A
Manchester Airport 85 ✈	d			22 35			
Manchester Piccadilly [10]	d	21 56		22 50		22 56	23 25
Manchester Oxford Road	d	21 59		22 53		22 59	23 28
Manchester Victoria	d						
Eccles	d			23 00			
Patricroft	d						
Blackpool North 97	d				22 44		
Preston [8] 65,82	d				23 09		
Leyland 82	d				23 15		
Euxton Balshaw Lane	d				23 19		
Wigan North Western 65	a				23 29		
	d				23 30		
Newton-le-Willows	d	22 18		23 13		23 18	23 46
Warrington Bank Quay	d						
Earlestown [8]	d	22 21		23 16		23 21	23 49
Warrington Bank Quay	a	22 27				23 27	23 55
St Helens Junction	d			23 21			
Lea Green	d			23 24			
Rainhill	d			23 28			
Whiston	d			23 31			
Bryn	d						
Garswood	d				23 40		
St Helens Central	a				23 46		
	d				23 47		
Thatto Heath	d				23 50		
Eccleston Park	d						
Prescot	d				23 54		
Huyton	d			23 35	23 59		
Roby	d			23 37	00 01		
Broad Green	d			23 40	00 04		
Wavertree Technology Park	d			23 43	00 07		
Edge Hill 89,91	d						
Liverpool Lime Street [10] 89,91	a			23 54	00 18		

Sundays
26 June to 11 September

		NT	AW A 🚌	NT	NT	NT	NT	NT	AW A	NT		NT	AW A
Manchester Airport 85 ✈	d				08 35		09 35			10 35			
Manchester Piccadilly [10]	d		07 28		08 50		09 50		09 56	10 50			10 55
Manchester Oxford Road	d		07 33		08 53		09 53		09 59	10 53			10 59
Manchester Victoria	d	23p09											
Eccles	d	23p16			09 00		10 00			11 00			
Patricroft	d	23p19											
Blackpool North 97	d					08 50		09 50				10 50	
Preston [8] 65,82	d					09 15		10 15				11 15	
Leyland 82	d					09 21		10 21				11 21	
Euxton Balshaw Lane	d					09 25		10 25				11 25	
Wigan North Western 65	a					09 35		10 36				11 35	
	d			08 36		09 36		10 36				11 36	
Newton-le-Willows	d	23p31	08 03		09 13		10 13		10 18	11 13			11 20
Warrington Bank Quay	d												
Earlestown [8]	d	23p34	08 13		09 16		10 16		10 21	11 16			11 23
Warrington Bank Quay	a		08 38						10 27				11 29
St Helens Junction	d	23p39			09 21		10 21			11 21			
Lea Green	d	23p42			09 24		10 24			11 24			
Rainhill	d	23p46			09 28		10 28			11 28			
Whiston	d	23p49			09 31		10 31			11 31			
Bryn	d												
Garswood	d			08 46		09 46		10 46				11 46	
St Helens Central	a			08 52		09 52		10 52				11 52	
	d			08 53		09 53		10 53				11 53	
Thatto Heath	d			08 56		09 56		10 56				11 56	
Eccleston Park	d												
Prescot	d			09 00		10 00		11 00				12 00	
Huyton	d	23p53		09 05	09 35	10 05	10 35	11 05		11 35		12 05	
Roby	d	23p55		09 07	09 37	10 07	10 37	11 07		11 37		12 07	
Broad Green	d	23p57		09 10	09 40	10 10	10 40	11 10		11 40		12 10	
Wavertree Technology Park	d	00 01		09 13	09 43	10 13	10 43	11 13		11 43		12 13	
Edge Hill 89,91	d	00 04											
Liverpool Lime Street [10] 89,91	a	00 13		09 26	09 52	10 24	10 54	11 24		11 54		12 24	

		NT	NT	AW A 🛒	NT	NT	AW A 🛒	NT		NT	AW A 🛒	NT	NT
Manchester Airport 85 ✈	d	11 33			12 35			13 35				14 35	
Manchester Piccadilly [10]	d	11 50		11 56	12 50		12 56	13 50			13 56	14 50	
Manchester Oxford Road	d	11 53		11 59	12 53		12 59	13 53			13 59	14 53	
Manchester Victoria	d												
Eccles	d	12 00			13 00			14 00				15 00	
Patricroft	d												
Blackpool North 97	d		11 50			12 50				13 50			14 50
Preston [8] 65,82	d		12 15			13 15				14 15			15 15
Leyland 82	d		12 21			13 21				14 21			15 21
Euxton Balshaw Lane	d		12 25			13 25				14 25			15 25
Wigan North Western 65	a		12 35			13 35				14 35			15 35
	d		12 36			13 36				14 36			15 36
Newton-le-Willows	d	12 13		12 18	13 13		13 18	14 13			14 18	15 13	
Warrington Bank Quay	d												
Earlestown [8]	d	12 16		12 21	13 16		13 21	14 16			14 21	15 16	
Warrington Bank Quay	a			12 27			13 28				14 27		
St Helens Junction	d	12 21			13 21			14 21				15 21	
Lea Green	d	12 24			13 24			14 24				15 24	
Rainhill	d	12 28			13 28			14 28				15 28	
Whiston	d	12 31			13 31			14 31				15 31	
Bryn	d												
Garswood	d		12 46			13 46				14 46			15 46
St Helens Central	a		12 52			13 52				14 52			15 52
	d		12 53			13 53				14 53			15 53
Thatto Heath	d		12 56			13 56				14 56			15 56
Eccleston Park	d												
Prescot	d		13 00			14 00				15 00			16 00
Huyton	d	12 35	13 05		13 35	14 05		14 35		15 05		15 35	16 05
Roby	d	12 37	13 07		13 37	14 07		14 37		15 07		15 37	16 07
Broad Green	d	12 40	13 10		13 40	14 10		14 40		15 10		15 40	16 10
Wavertree Technology Park	d	12 43	13 13		13 43	14 13		14 43		15 13		15 43	16 13
Edge Hill 89,91	d												
Liverpool Lime Street [10] 89,91	a	12 54	13 24		13 54	14 24		14 54		15 24		15 54	16 24

A To Chester

Table 90

Sundays

26 June to 11 September

Manchester, Preston, Wigan and Newton-le-Willows - St. Helens and Liverpool

Station		AW A 🛒	NT	NT	AW A 🛒	NT		NT	AW A 🛒	NT	NT	AW A 🛒	NT
Manchester Airport 85 ✈	d		15 35			16 35				17 35			18 35
Manchester Piccadilly 10	d	14 56	15 50		15 56	16 50			16 56	17 50		17 56	18 50
Manchester Oxford Road	d	14 59	15 53		15 59	16 53			16 59	17 53		17 59	18 53
Manchester Victoria	d												
Eccles	d		16 00			17 00				18 00			19 00
Patricroft	d												
Blackpool North 97	d			15 50				16 50			17 50		
Preston 8 65,82	d			16 15				17 15			18 15		
Leyland 82	d			16 21				17 21			18 21		
Euxton Balshaw Lane	d			16 25				17 25			18 25		
Wigan North Western 65	a			16 35				17 35			18 35		
	d			16 36				17 36			18 36		
Newton-le-Willows	d	15 18	16 13		16 18	17 13			17 18	18 13		18 18	19 13
Warrington Bank Quay	d												
Earlestown 8	d	15 21	16 16		16 21	17 16			17 21	18 16		18 21	19 16
Warrington Bank Quay	a	15 28			16 27				17 27			18 27	
St Helens Junction	d		16 21			17 21				18 21			19 21
Lea Green	d		16 24			17 24				18 24			19 24
Rainhill	d		16 28			17 28				18 28			19 28
Whiston	d		16 31			17 31				18 31			19 31
Bryn	d												
Garswood	d			16 46				17 46			18 46		
St Helens Central	a			16 52				17 52			18 52		
	d			16 53				17 53			18 53		
Thatto Heath	d			16 56				17 56			18 56		
Eccleston Park	d												
Prescot	d			17 00				18 00			19 00		
Huyton	d		16 35	17 05		17 35		18 05		18 35	19 05		19 35
Roby	d		16 37	17 07		17 37		18 07		18 37	19 07		19 37
Broad Green	d		16 40	17 10		17 40		18 10		18 40	19 10		19 40
Wavertree Technology Park	d		16 43	17 13		17 43		18 13		18 43	19 13		19 43
Edge Hill 89,91	d												
Liverpool Lime Street 10 89,91	a		16 54	17 24		17 54		18 24		18 54	19 24		19 54

Station		NT	AW A	NT		NT	AW A	NT	NT	AW A	NT	NT	AW A
Manchester Airport 85 ✈	d			19 35				20 35			21 35		
Manchester Piccadilly 10	d		18 56	19 50			19 56	20 50		20 56	21 50		21 56
Manchester Oxford Road	d		18 59	19 53			19 59	20 53		20 59	21 53		21 59
Manchester Victoria	d												
Eccles	d			20 00				21 00			22 00		
Patricroft	d												
Blackpool North 97	d	18 50				19 50			20 50			21 50	
Preston 8 65,82	d	19 15				20 15			21 15			22 15	
Leyland 82	d	19 21				20 21			21 21			22 21	
Euxton Balshaw Lane	d	19 25				20 25			21 25			22 25	
Wigan North Western 65	a	19 35				20 35			21 35			22 35	
	d	19 36				20 36			21 36			22 36	
Newton-le-Willows	d		19 18	20 13			20 18	21 13		21 18	22 13		22 18
Warrington Bank Quay	d												
Earlestown 8	d		19 21	20 16			20 21	21 16		21 21	22 16		22 21
Warrington Bank Quay	a		19 28				20 29			21 27			22 27
St Helens Junction	d			20 21				21 21			22 21		
Lea Green	d			20 24				21 24			22 24		
Rainhill	d			20 28				21 28			22 28		
Whiston	d			20 31				21 31			22 31		
Bryn	d												
Garswood	d	19 46				20 46			21 46			22 46	
St Helens Central	a	19 52				20 52			21 52			22 53	
	d	19 53				20 53			21 53			22 53	
Thatto Heath	d	19 56				20 56			21 56			22 56	
Eccleston Park	d												
Prescot	d	20 00				21 00			22 00			23 00	
Huyton	d	20 05		20 35		21 05		21 35	22 05		22 35	23 05	
Roby	d	20 07		20 37		21 07		21 37	22 07		22 37	23 07	
Broad Green	d	20 10		20 40		21 10		21 40	22 10		22 40	23 10	
Wavertree Technology Park	d	20 13		20 43		21 13		21 43	22 13		22 43	23 13	
Edge Hill 89,91	d												
Liverpool Lime Street 10 89,91	a	20 24		20 54		21 24		21 54	22 24		22 54	23 24	

Station		NT		NT	AW A	AW A
Manchester Airport 85 ✈	d	22 35				
Manchester Piccadilly 10	d	22 50			22 56	23 25
Manchester Oxford Road	d	22 53			22 59	23 28
Manchester Victoria	d					
Eccles	d	23 00				
Patricroft	d					
Blackpool North 97	d			22 44		
Preston 8 65,82	d			23 09		
Leyland 82	d			23 15		
Euxton Balshaw Lane	d			23 19		
Wigan North Western 65	a			23 29		
	d			23 30		
Newton-le-Willows	d	23 13			23 18	23 46
Warrington Bank Quay	d					
Earlestown 8	d	23 16			23 21	23 49
Warrington Bank Quay	a				23 27	23 55
St Helens Junction	d	23 21				
Lea Green	d	23 24				
Rainhill	d	23 28				
Whiston	d	23 31				
Bryn	d					
Garswood	d			23 40		
St Helens Central	a			23 46		
	d			23 47		
Thatto Heath	d			23 50		
Eccleston Park	d					
Prescot	d			23 54		
Huyton	d	23 35		23 59		
Roby	d	23 37		00 01		
Broad Green	d	23 40		00 04		
Wavertree Technology Park	d	23 43		00 07		
Edge Hill 89,91	d					
Liverpool Lime Street 10 89,91	a	23 54		00 18		

A To Chester

Table 90

Sundays

18 September to 23 October

Manchester, Preston, Wigan and Newton-le-Willows - St. Helens and Liverpool

		NT		AW A 🚌	NT	NT	AW A 🚌	TP ◇1	NT	NT		AW A 🚌	NT	NT	AW A 🚌	NT	NT	AW A 🚌	NT	NT		AW A 🚌	NT	NT	NT
Manchester Airport 85 ✈	d													10 35			11 33			12 35				13 35	
Manchester Piccadilly 10	d			07 28			08 49			09 50		09 47		10 50	10 45		11 50	11 45		12 50		12 45		13 50	
Manchester Oxford Road	d			07 33			08 54			09 53		09 52		10 53	10 50		11 53	11 50		12 53		12 50		13 53	
Manchester Victoria	d	23p09				08 53		09 15																	
Eccles	d	23p16				09 00				10 00				11 00			12 00			13 00				14 00	
Patricroft	d	23p19																							
Blackpool North 97	d								08 50				09 50			10 50			11 50				12 50		13 50
Preston 8 65,82	d								09 15				10 15			11 15			12 15				13 15		14 15
Leyland 82	d								09 21				10 21			11 21			12 21				13 21		14 21
Euxton Balshaw Lane	d								09 25				10 25			11 25			12 25				13 25		14 25
Wigan North Western 65	a								09 35				10 36			11 35			12 35				13 35		14 35
	d				08 36				09 36				10 36			11 36			12 36				13 36		14 36
Newton-le-Willows	d	23p31		08 03		09 13	09 24	09 33		10 13		10 22		11 13	11 20		12 13	12 20		13 13		13 20		14 13	
Warrington Bank Quay	d																								
Earlestown 8	d	23p34		08 13		09 16	09 34			10 16		10 32		11 16	11 30		12 16	12 30		13 16		13 30		14 16	
Warrington Bank Quay	a			08 38			09 59					10 57			11 55			12 55				13 55			
St Helens Junction	d	23p39				09 21				10 21				11 21			12 21			13 21				14 21	
Lea Green	d	23p42				09 24				10 24				11 24			12 24			13 24				14 24	
Rainhill	d	23p46				09 28				10 28				11 28			12 28			13 28				14 28	
Whiston	d	23p49				09 31				10 31				11 31			12 31			13 31				14 31	
Bryn	d																								
Garswood	d				08 46				09 46				10 46			11 46			12 46				13 46		14 46
St Helens Central	a				08 52				09 52				10 52			11 52			12 52				13 52		14 52
	d				08 53				09 53				10 53			11 53			12 53				13 53		14 53
Thatto Heath	d				08 56				09 56				10 56			11 56			12 56				13 56		14 56
Eccleston Park	d																								
Prescot	d				09 00				10 00				11 00			12 00			13 00				14 00		15 00
Huyton	d	23p53			09 05	09 35			10 05	10 35			11 05	11 35		12 05	12 35		13 05	13 35			14 05	14 35	15 05
Roby	d	23p55			09 07	09 37			10 07	10 37			11 07	11 37		12 07	12 37		13 07	13 37			14 07	14 37	15 07
Broad Green	d	23p57			09 10	09 40			10 10	10 40			11 10	11 40		12 10	12 40		13 10	13 40			14 10	14 40	15 10
Wavertree Technology Park	d	00 01			09 13	09 43			10 13	10 43			11 13	11 43		12 13	12 43		13 13	13 43			14 13	14 43	15 13
Edge Hill 89,91	d	00 04																							
Liverpool Lime Street 10 89,91	a	00 13			09 26	09 52		09 58	10 24	10 54			11 24	11 54		12 24	12 54		13 24	13 54			14 24	14 54	15 24

		NT	NT	AW A 🚲	NT	NT		AW A 🚲	NT	NT	AW A 🚲	NT	NT	AW A 🚲	NT	NT		AW A	NT	NT	AW A	NT	NT	AW A	NT
Manchester Airport 85 ✈	d	14 35			15 35				16 35			17 35			18 35				19 35			20 35			21 35
Manchester Piccadilly 10	d	14 50		14 56	15 50			15 56	16 50		16 56	17 50		17 56	18 50			18 56	19 50		19 56	20 50		20 56	21 50
Manchester Oxford Road	d	14 53		14 59	15 53			15 59	16 53		16 59	17 53		17 59	18 53			18 59	19 53		19 59	20 53		20 59	21 53
Manchester Victoria	d																								
Eccles	d	15 00			16 00				17 00			18 00			19 00				20 00			21 00			22 00
Patricroft	d																								
Blackpool North 97	d		14 50			15 50				16 50			17 50			18 50				19 50			20 50		
Preston 8 65,82	d		15 15			16 15				17 15			18 15			19 15				20 15			21 15		
Leyland 82	d		15 21			16 21				17 21			18 21			19 21				20 21			21 21		
Euxton Balshaw Lane	d		15 25			16 25				17 25			18 25			19 25				20 25			21 25		
Wigan North Western 65	a		15 35			16 35				17 35			18 35			19 35				20 35			21 35		
	d		15 36			16 36				17 36			18 36			19 36				20 36			21 36		
Newton-le-Willows	d	15 13		15 18	16 13			16 18	17 13		17 18	18 13		18 18	19 13			19 18	20 13		20 18	21 13		21 18	22 13
Warrington Bank Quay	d																								
Earlestown 8	d	15 16		15 21	16 16			16 21	17 16		17 21	18 16		18 21	19 16			19 21	20 16		20 21	21 16		21 21	22 16
Warrington Bank Quay	a			15 28				16 27			17 27			18 27				19 28			20 29			21 27	
St Helens Junction	d	15 21			16 21				17 21			18 21			19 21				20 21			21 21			22 21
Lea Green	d	15 24			16 24				17 24			18 24			19 24				20 24			21 24			22 24
Rainhill	d	15 28			16 28				17 28			18 28			19 28				20 28			21 28			22 28
Whiston	d	15 31			16 31				17 31			18 31			19 31				20 31			21 31			22 31
Bryn	d																								
Garswood	d		15 46			16 46				17 46			18 46			19 46				20 46			21 46		
St Helens Central	a		15 52			16 52				17 52			18 52			19 52				20 52			21 52		
	d		15 53			16 53				17 53			18 53			19 53				20 53			21 53		
Thatto Heath	d		15 56			16 56				17 56			18 56			19 56				20 56			21 56		
Eccleston Park	d																								
Prescot	d		16 00			17 00				18 00			19 00			20 00				21 00			22 00		
Huyton	d	15 35	16 05		16 35	17 05			17 35	18 05		18 35	19 05		19 35	20 05			20 35	21 05		21 35	22 05		22 35
Roby	d	15 37	16 07		16 37	17 07			17 37	18 07		18 37	19 07		19 37	20 07			20 37	21 07		21 37	22 07		22 37
Broad Green	d	15 40	16 10		16 40	17 10			17 40	18 10		18 40	19 10		19 40	20 10			20 40	21 10		21 40	22 10		22 40
Wavertree Technology Park	d	15 43	16 13		16 43	17 13			17 43	18 13		18 43	19 13		19 43	20 13			20 43	21 13		21 43	22 13		22 43
Edge Hill 89,91	d																								
Liverpool Lime Street 10 89,91	a	15 54	16 24		16 54	17 24			17 54	18 24		18 54	19 24		19 54	20 24			20 54	21 24		21 54	22 24		22 54

A To Chester

Table 90

Sundays

18 September to 23 October

Manchester, Preston, Wigan and Newton-le-Willows - St. Helens and Liverpool

	NT		AW A	NT	NT	AW A	AW A
Manchester Airport 85 d				22 35			
Manchester Piccadilly 10 d			21 56	22 50		22 56	23 25
Manchester Oxford Road d			21 59	22 53		22 59	23 28
Manchester Victoria d							
Eccles d				23 00			
Patricroft d							
Blackpool North 97 d	21 50				22 44		
Preston 8 65,82 d	22 15				23 09		
Leyland 82 d	22 21				23 15		
Euxton Balshaw Lane d	22 25				23 19		
Wigan North Western 65 a	22 35				23 29		
d	22 36				23 30		
Newton-le-Willows d			22 18	23 13		23 18	23 46
Warrington Bank Quay d							
Earlestown 8 d			22 21	23 16		23 21	23 49
Warrington Bank Quay a			22 27			23 27	23 55
St Helens Junction d				23 21			
Lea Green d				23 24			
Rainhill d				23 28			
Whiston d				23 31			
Bryn d							
Garswood d	22 46				23 40		
St Helens Central a	22 53				23 46		
d	22 53				23 47		
Thatto Heath d	22 56				23 50		
Eccleston Park d							
Prescot d	23 00				23 54		
Huyton d	23 05			23 35	23 59		
Roby d	23 07			23 37	00 01		
Broad Green d	23 10			23 40	00 04		
Wavertree Technology Park d	23 13			23 43	00 07		
Edge Hill 89,91 d							
Liverpool Lime Street 10 89,91 a	23 24			23 54	00 18		

Sundays

from 30 October

	NT		AW A	NT	NT	NT	NT	NT	AW A		NT	NT	AW A	NT	NT	AW A	NT	NT	AW A		NT	NT	AW A	NT
Manchester Airport 85 d							09 35				10 35			11 33			12 35				13 35			14 35
Manchester Piccadilly 10 d			07 28				09 50		09 56		10 50		10 55	11 50		11 56	12 50		12 56		13 50		13 56	14 50
Manchester Oxford Road d			07 33				09 53		09 59		10 53		10 59	11 53		11 59	12 53		12 59		13 53		13 59	14 53
Manchester Victoria d	23p09				08 53																			
Eccles d	23p16				09 00		10 00				11 00			12 00			13 00				14 00			15 00
Patricroft d	23p19																							
Blackpool North 97 d						08 50		09 50				10 50			11 50			12 50				13 50		
Preston 8 65,82 d						09 15		10 15				11 15			12 15			13 15				14 15		
Leyland 82 d						09 21		10 21				11 21			12 21			13 21				14 21		
Euxton Balshaw Lane d						09 25		10 25				11 25			12 25			13 25				14 25		
Wigan North Western 65 a						09 35		10 36				11 35			12 35			13 35				14 35		
d				08 36		09 36		10 36				11 36			12 36			13 36				14 36		
Newton-le-Willows d	23p31		08 03		09 13		10 13		10 18		11 13		11 20	12 13		12 18	13 13		13 18		14 13		14 18	15 13
Warrington Bank Quay d																								
Earlestown 8 d	23p34		08 13		09 16		10 16		10 21		11 16		11 23	12 16		12 21	13 16		13 21		14 16		14 21	15 16
Warrington Bank Quay a			08 38						10 27				11 29			12 27			13 28				14 27	
St Helens Junction d	23p39				09 21		10 21				11 21			12 21			13 21				14 21			15 21
Lea Green d	23p42				09 24		10 24				11 24			12 24			13 24				14 24			15 24
Rainhill d	23p46				09 28		10 28				11 28			12 28			13 28				14 28			15 28
Whiston d	23p49				09 31		10 31				11 31			12 31			13 31				14 31			15 31
Bryn d																								
Garswood d				08 46		09 46		10 46				11 46			12 46			13 46				14 46		
St Helens Central a				08 52		09 52		10 52				11 52			12 52			13 52				14 52		
d				08 53		09 53		10 53				11 53			12 53			13 53				14 53		
Thatto Heath d				08 56		09 56		10 56				11 56			12 56			13 56				14 56		
Eccleston Park d																								
Prescot d				09 00		10 00		11 00				12 00			13 00			14 00				15 00		
Huyton d	23p53			09 05	09 35	10 05	10 35	11 05			11 35	12 05		12 35	13 05		13 35	14 05			14 35	15 05		15 35
Roby d	23p55			09 07	09 37	10 07	10 37	11 07			11 37	12 07		12 37	13 07		13 37	14 07			14 37	15 07		15 37
Broad Green d	23p57			09 10	09 40	10 10	10 40	11 10			11 40	12 10		12 40	13 10		13 40	14 10			14 40	15 10		15 40
Wavertree Technology Park d	00 01			09 13	09 43	10 13	10 43	11 13			11 43	12 13		12 43	13 13		13 43	14 13			14 43	15 13		15 43
Edge Hill 89,91 d	00 04																							
Liverpool Lime Street 10 89,91 a	00 13			09 26	09 52	10 24	10 54	11 24			11 54	12 24		12 54	13 24		13 54	14 24			14 54	15 24		15 54

A To Chester

Table 90

Sundays

from 30 October

Manchester, Preston, Wigan and Newton-le-Willows - St. Helens and Liverpool

		NT	AW A	NT	NT	AW A		NT	NT	AW A	NT	NT	AW A
Manchester Airport 85	d			15 35				16 35			17 35		
Manchester Piccadilly 10	d		14 56	15 50		15 56		16 50		16 56	17 50		17 56
Manchester Oxford Road	d		14 59	15 53		15 59		16 53		16 59	17 53		17 59
Manchester Victoria	d												
Eccles	d			16 00				17 00			18 00		
Patricroft	d												
Blackpool North 97	d	14 50			15 50				16 50			17 50	
Preston 8 65,82	d	15 15			16 15				17 15			18 15	
Leyland 82	d	15 21			16 21				17 21			18 21	
Euxton Balshaw Lane	d	15 25			16 25				17 25			18 25	
Wigan North Western 65	a	15 35			16 35				17 35			18 35	
	d	15 36			16 36				17 36			18 36	
Newton-le-Willows	d		15 18	16 13		16 18		17 13		17 18	18 13		18 18
Warrington Bank Quay	d												
Earlestown 8	d		15 21	16 16		16 21		17 16		17 21	18 16		18 21
Warrington Bank Quay	a		15 28			16 27				17 27			18 27
St Helens Junction	d			16 21				17 21			18 21		
Lea Green	d			16 24				17 24			18 24		
Rainhill	d			16 28				17 28			18 28		
Whiston	d			16 31				17 31			18 31		
Bryn	d												
Garswood	d	15 46			16 46				17 46			18 46	
St Helens Central	a	15 52			16 52				17 52			18 52	
	d	15 53			16 53				17 53			18 53	
Thatto Heath	d	15 56			16 56				17 56			18 56	
Eccleston Park	d												
Prescot	d	16 00			17 00				18 00			19 00	
Huyton	d	16 05		16 35	17 05			17 35	18 05		18 35	19 05	
Roby	d	16 07		16 37	17 07			17 37	18 07		18 37	19 07	
Broad Green	d	16 10		16 40	17 10			17 40	18 10		18 40	19 10	
Wavertree Technology Park	d	16 13		16 43	17 13			17 43	18 13		18 43	19 13	
Edge Hill 89,91	d												
Liverpool Lime Street 10 89,91	a	16 24		16 54	17 24			17 54	18 24		18 54	19 24	

		NT	NT	AW A		NT	NT	AW A	NT	NT	AW A	NT	NT
Manchester Airport 85	d	18 35				19 35			20 35			21 35	
Manchester Piccadilly 10	d	18 50		18 56		19 50		19 56	20 50		20 56	21 50	
Manchester Oxford Road	d	18 53		18 59		19 53		19 59	20 53		20 59	21 53	
Manchester Victoria	d												
Eccles	d	19 00				20 00			21 00			22 00	
Patricroft	d												
Blackpool North 97	d		18 50				19 50			20 50			21 50
Preston 8 65,82	d		19 15				20 15			21 15			22 15
Leyland 82	d		19 21				20 21			21 21			22 21
Euxton Balshaw Lane	d		19 25				20 25			21 25			22 25
Wigan North Western 65	a		19 35				20 35			21 35			22 35
	d		19 36				20 36			21 36			22 36
Newton-le-Willows	d	19 13		19 18		20 13		20 18	21 13		21 18	22 13	
Warrington Bank Quay	d												
Earlestown 8	d	19 16		19 21		20 16		20 21	21 16		21 21	22 16	
Warrington Bank Quay	a			19 28				20 29			21 27		
St Helens Junction	d	19 21				20 21			21 21			22 21	
Lea Green	d	19 24				20 24			21 24			22 24	
Rainhill	d	19 28				20 28			21 28			22 28	
Whiston	d	19 31				20 31			21 31			22 31	
Bryn	d												
Garswood	d		19 46				20 46			21 46			22 46
St Helens Central	a		19 52				20 52			21 52			22 53
	d		19 53				20 53			21 53			22 53
Thatto Heath	d		19 56				20 56			21 56			22 56
Eccleston Park	d												
Prescot	d		20 00				21 00			22 00			23 00
Huyton	d	19 35	20 05			20 35	21 05		21 35	22 05		22 35	23 05
Roby	d	19 37	20 07			20 37	21 07		21 37	22 07		22 37	23 07
Broad Green	d	19 40	20 10			20 40	21 10		21 40	22 10		22 40	23 10
Wavertree Technology Park	d	19 43	20 13			20 43	21 13		21 43	22 13		22 43	23 13
Edge Hill 89,91	d												
Liverpool Lime Street 10 89,91	a	19 54	20 24			20 54	21 24		21 54	22 24		22 54	23 24

		AW A		NT	NT	AW A	AW A
Manchester Airport 85	d			22 35			
Manchester Piccadilly 10	d	21 56		22 50		22 56	23 25
Manchester Oxford Road	d	21 59		22 53		22 59	23 28
Manchester Victoria	d						
Eccles	d			23 00			
Patricroft	d						
Blackpool North 97	d				22 44		
Preston 8 65,82	d				23 09		
Leyland 82	d				23 15		
Euxton Balshaw Lane	d				23 19		
Wigan North Western 65	a				23 29		
	d				23 30		
Newton-le-Willows	d	22 18		23 13		23 18	23 46
Warrington Bank Quay	d						
Earlestown 8	d	22 21		23 16		23 21	23 49
Warrington Bank Quay	a	22 27				23 27	23 55
St Helens Junction	d			23 21			
Lea Green	d			23 24			
Rainhill	d			23 28			
Whiston	d			23 31			
Bryn	d						
Garswood	d				23 40		
St Helens Central	a				23 46		
	d				23 47		
Thatto Heath	d				23 50		
Eccleston Park	d						
Prescot	d				23 54		
Huyton	d			23 35	23 59		
Roby	d			23 37	00 01		
Broad Green	d			23 40	00 04		
Wavertree Technology Park	d			23 43	00 07		
Edge Hill 89,91	d						
Liverpool Lime Street 10 89,91	a			23 54	00 18		

A To Chester

Liverpool - Runcorn and Crewe

Miles		LM 1 A MX	LM 1 B MX	VT ◇1 ⊠	NT C	VT ◇1 ⊠	TP ◇1 D 🛒	NT E	LM 1	EM ◇ F		NT C	VT ◇1 ⊠	LM 1	TP ◇1 D 🛒	NT E	LM 1	EM ◇ F	VT ◇1 ⊠	NT E		LM 1	TP ◇1 D 🛒	NT E
0	**Liverpool Lime Street** 10 90 d	23p34	23p34	05 27	05 49	06 05	06 15	06 21	06 30	06 47		06 50	07 00	07 04	07 15	07 26	07 34	07 43	07 48	07 51		08 04	08 22	08 26
1¾	Edge Hill 90 d				05 53							06 54				07 30								08 30
3¾	Mossley Hill d				05 58			06 29				06 59				07 35				07 59				08 35
4½	West Allerton d				06 00			06 31				07 01				07 37				08 01				08 37
5½	**Liverpool South Parkway** 7 ✈ a	23p44	23p44		06 03		06 25	06 34	06 39	06 57		07 04		07 13	07 25	07 40	07 43	07 53		08 04		08 15	08 32	08 40
—	d	23p45	23p45						06 40					07 14			07 44					08 15		
13	**Runcorn** a	23p55	23p55	05 42		06 20			06 47					07 21			07 51		08 03			08 24		
—	d	23p55	23p55	05 43		06 21			06 48				07u15	07 22			07 52		08 04			08 24		
21	Acton Bridge d	00 05	00 05						06 57					07 32								08 34		
23¾	Hartford d	00 10	00 10						07 02					07 36			08 04							
28	Winsford d	00 14	00 14						07 06								08 08							
35½	**Crewe** 10 65 a	00 25	00 28	06 00					07 14					07 48			08 19					08 47		
—	Birmingham New Street 12 65 a								08 17					08 47			09 18					09 47		
—	London Euston ⊖65 a			07 50		08 22							09 01						09 56					

	LM 1	VT ◇1 ⊠	EM ◇ F	NT E	LM 1	TP ◇1 D 🛒		NT E	LM 1	VT ◇1 ⊠	EM ◇ F	NT E	LM 1	NT G	TP ◇1 D 🛒	NT E		LM 1	VT ◇1 ⊠	EM ◇ F	NT E	LM 1	NT H	TP ◇1 D 🛒
Liverpool Lime Street 10 90 d	08 34	08 48	08 52	08 55	09 04	09 22		09 27	09 34	09 48	09 52	09 55	10 04	10 16	10 22	10 27		10 34	10 48	10 52	10 55	11 04	11 16	11 22
Edge Hill 90 d				08 59								09 59									10 59			
Mossley Hill d				09 04				09 35				10 04				10 35					11 04			
West Allerton d				09 06				09 37				10 06				10 37					11 06			
Liverpool South Parkway 7 ✈ a	08 43		09 02	09 09	09 15	09 32		09 40	09 43		10 02	10 09	10 15	10 27	10 32	10 40		10 43		11 02	11 09	11 15	11 27	11 32
d	08 44				09 15				09 44				10 15					10 44				11 15		
Runcorn a	08 51	09 03			09 24				09 51	10 03			10 24					10 51	11 03			11 24		
d	08 52	09 04			09 25				09 52	10 04			10 25					10 52	11 04			11 25		
Acton Bridge d	09 02																							
Hartford d	09 06								10 04									11 04						
Winsford d									10 08									11 08						
Crewe 10 65 a	09 20				09 44				10 19				10 45					11 19				11 45		
Birmingham New Street 12 65 a	10 17				10 47				11 18				11 47					12 17				12 47		
London Euston ⊖65 a		10 56								11 56									12 56					

	NT E	LM 1		VT ◇1 ▭	EM ◇ F	NT E	LM 1	NT H	TP ◇1 D 🛒	NT E	LM 1	EM ◇ F		NT E	LM 1	NT H	TP ◇1 D 🛒	NT E	LM 1	VT ◇1 ▭	EM ◇ I	NT E		LM 1
Liverpool Lime Street 10 90 d	11 27	11 34		11 48	11 52	11 55	12 04	12 16	12 22	12 27	12 34	12 52		12 55	13 04	13 16	13 22	13 27	13 34	13 48	13 52	13 55		14 04
Edge Hill 90 d						11 59								12 59								13 59		
Mossley Hill d	11 35					12 04				12 35				13 04				13 35				14 04		
West Allerton d	11 37					12 06				12 37				13 06				13 37				14 06		
Liverpool South Parkway 7 ✈ a	11 40	11 43			12 02	12 09	12 15	12 27	12 32	12 40	12 43	13 02		13 09	13 15	13 27	13 32	13 40	13 43		14 02	14 09		14 15
d		11 44					12 15				12 44				13 15				13 44					14 15
Runcorn a		11 51		12 03			12 24				12 51				13 24				13 51	14 03				14 24
d		11 52		12 04			12 25				12 52				13 25				13 52	14 04				14 25
Acton Bridge d											13 02													
Hartford d		12 04									13 06								14 04					
Winsford d		12 08																	14 08					
Crewe 10 65 a		12 19					12 45				13 20				13 45				14 19					14 45
Birmingham New Street 12 65 a		13 17					13 47				14 17				14 47				15 20					15 47
London Euston ⊖65 a				13 56																15 56				

	NT H	TP ◇1 D 🛒	NT E	LM 1	VT ◇1 ▭	EM ◇ F	NT E	LM 1		NT H	TP ◇1 J 🛒	NT E	LM 1	VT ◇1 ▭	EM ◇ F	NT E	LM 1	NT H		TP ◇1 D 🛒	NT E	LM 1	VT ◇1 ▭	EM ◇ I
Liverpool Lime Street 10 90 d	14 16	14 22	14 27	14 34	14 48	14 52	14 55	15 04		15 16	15 22	15 27	15 34	15 48	15 52	15 55	16 04	16 16		16 22	16 27	16 34	16 48	16 52
Edge Hill 90 d							14 59									15 59								
Mossley Hill d			14 35				15 04					15 35				16 04					16 35			
West Allerton d			14 37				15 06					15 37				16 06					16 37			
Liverpool South Parkway 7 ✈ a	14 27	14 32	14 40	14 43		15 02	15 09	15 15		15 27	15 32	15 40	15 43		16 02	16 09	16 15	16 27		16 32	16 40	16 43		17 02
d				14 44				15 15					15 44				16 15					16 44		
Runcorn a				14 51	15 03			15 24					15 51	16 03			16 24					16 52	17 03	
d				14 52	15 04			15 25					15 52	16 04			16 25					16 52	17 04	
Acton Bridge d																						17 01		
Hartford d				15 04									16 04									17 06		
Winsford d				15 08									16 08											
Crewe 10 65 a				15 19				15 45					16 19				16 45					17 19		
Birmingham New Street 12 65 a				16 17				16 47					17 20				17 47					18 17		
London Euston ⊖65 a					16 56									17 56									18 59	

A until 17 June, then from 13 September
B from 21 June until 9 September
C To Warrington Central
D To Scarborough
E To Manchester Oxford Road
F To Norwich
G From Preston
H From Blackpool North
I To Nottingham
J To Middlesbrough

Liverpool - Runcorn and Crewe

	NT	LM	TP	NT	LM	VT	EM	NT	LM	TP	NT	LM	VT	EM	NT	LM	TP	LM	VT	EM	NT	LM
		1	◇1		1	◇1	◇		1	◇1		1	◇1	◇		1	◇1	1	◇1	◇		1
	A		B	A			C	A		B	A			D	E		F			D	E	
			🛒			⊠							⊠						☕			
Liverpool Lime Street [10] 90 d	16 55	17 04	17 22	17 25	17 34	17 48	17 52	17 55	18 04	18 22	18 25	18 34	18 48	18 52	18 55	19 11	19 22	19 34	19 48	19 52	19 55	20 04
Edge Hill 90 d	16 59			17 29				17 59			18 29				18 59						19 59	
Mossley Hill d	17 04			17 34				18 04			18 34				19 04						20 04	
West Allerton d	17 06			17 36				18 06			18 36				19 06						20 06	
Liverpool South Parkway [7] ✈ a	17 09	17 15	17 32	17 39	17 43		18 02	18 09	18 14	18 32	18 39	18 43		19 02	19 09	19 20	19 32	19 43		20 02	20 09	20 15
d		17 15			17 44				18 15			18 44				19 21		19 44				20 15
Runcorn a		17 24			17 51	18 03			18 24			18 51	19 03			19 28		19 51	20 03			20 24
d		17 25			17 52	18 04			18 24			18 52	19 04			19 29		19 52	20 04			20 24
Acton Bridge d					18 01											19 40						
Hartford d					18 06							19 04						20 04				
Winsford d		17 39							18 38			19 08						20 08				
Crewe [10] 65 a		17 47			18 20				18 47			19 16	19 21			19 53		20 16	20 21			20 45
Birmingham New Street [12] 65 a		18 48			19 17				19 47			20 18				20 47		21 18				21 47
London Euston ⊖65 a						20 02							21 05						22 09			

	TP	LM	VT	NT	LM	EM	NT	TP	LM	LM	LM	LM	NT
	◇1	1	◇1		1	◇		◇1	1	1	1	1	
	G			A		D	A	G	H	I	I	H	J
			☕										
Liverpool Lime Street [10] 90 d	20 22	20 34	20 48	20 55	21 34	21 37	21 55	22 30	22 31	22 34	23 34	23 34	23 38
Edge Hill 90 d				20 59			21 59						23 42
Mossley Hill d				21 04			22 04						23 47
West Allerton d				21 06			22 06						23 50
Liverpool South Parkway [7] ✈ a	20 32	20 43		21 09	21 43	21 47	22 09	22 40	22 41	22 44	23 44	23 44	23 53
d		20 44			21 44				22 42	22 45	23 45	23 45	
Runcorn a		20 51	21 03		21 51				22 52	22 55	23 55	23 55	
d		20 52	21 04		21 52				22 52	22 55	23 55	23 55	
Acton Bridge d									23 01	23 04	00 05	00 05	
Hartford d		21 04			22 04				23 06	23 09	00 10	00 10	
Winsford d		21 08			22 08				23 10	23 13	00 14	00 14	
Crewe [10] 65 a		21 16	21 21		22 18				23 25	23 25	00 25	00 28	
Birmingham New Street [12] 65 a		22 17			23 18								
London Euston ⊖65 a			23 56										

Saturdays

until 18 June

	LM	VT	NT	TP	NT	LM	VT	EM	NT	LM	TP	VT	NT	LM	EM	VT	NT	LM	TP	NT	LM	VT
	1	◇1		◇1		◇1	◇1	◇		◇1	◇1	◇1		◇1	◇	◇1		◇1	◇1		◇1	◇1
			E	B	A			C	E		B		A		C		A		B	A		
		☕		🛒			☕				🛒	☕				☕			🛒			☕
Liverpool Lime Street [10] 90 d	23p34	05 47	05 49	06 15	06 25	06 32	06 45	06 49	06 55	07 04	07 15	07 19	07 26	07 34	07 42	07 48	07 51	08 04	08 22	08 26	08 34	08 48
Edge Hill 90 d			05 53						06 59				07 30							08 30		
Mossley Hill d			05 58		06 33				07 04				07 35				07 59			08 35		
West Allerton d			06 00		06 35				07 06				07 37				08 01			08 37		
Liverpool South Parkway [7] ✈ a	23p44		06 03	06 25	06 38	06 41		06 59	07 09	07 14	07 25		07 40	07 43	07 52		08 04	08 14	08 32	08 40	08 43	
d	23p45					06 42				07 14				07 44				08 15			08 44	
Runcorn a	23p55	06 02				06 49	07 00			07 22		07 35		07 51		08 03		08 24			08 51	09 03
d	23p55	06 03				06 50	07 01			07 22		07 36		07 52		08 04		08 24			08 52	09 04
Acton Bridge d	00 05									07 32								08 34			09 02	
Hartford d	00 10					07 02				07 36				08 04							09 06	
Winsford d	00 14					07 06								08 08								
Crewe [10] 65 a	00 25					07 14	07 18			07 47		07 52		08 19				08 47			09 20	
Birmingham New Street [12] 65 a						08 17				08 47				09 18				09 47			10 17	
London Euston ⊖65 a		08 05					08 59					09 46				10 00						11 01

	EM	NT	LM	TP	NT	LM	VT	EM	NT	LM	NT	TP	NT	LM	VT	EM	NT	LM	NT	TP	NT	LM
	◇		◇1	◇1		◇1	◇1	◇		◇1		◇1		◇1	◇1	◇		◇1		◇1		◇1
	C	A		B	A			C	A		K	B	A			C	A		K	B	A	
				🛒			☕					🛒			☕					🛒		
Liverpool Lime Street [10] 90 d	08 52	08 55	09 04	09 22	09 27	09 34	09 48	09 52	09 55	10 04	10 16	10 22	10 27	10 34	10 48	10 52	10 55	11 04	11 16	11 22	11 27	11 34
Edge Hill 90 d		08 59							09 59								10 59					
Mossley Hill d		09 04			09 35				10 04				10 35				11 04				11 35	
West Allerton d		09 06			09 37				10 06				10 37				11 06				11 37	
Liverpool South Parkway [7] ✈ a	09 02	09 09	09 15	09 32	09 40	09 43		10 02	10 09	10 15	10 27	10 32	10 40	10 43		11 02	11 09	11 15	11 27	11 32	11 40	11 43
d			09 15			09 44				10 15				10 44				11 15				11 44
Runcorn a			09 24			09 51	10 03			10 24				10 51	11 03			11 24				11 51
d			09 24			09 52	10 04			10 25				10 52	11 04			11 25				11 52
Acton Bridge d																						
Hartford d						10 04								11 04								12 04
Winsford d						10 08								11 08								12 08
Crewe [10] 65 a			09 44			10 19				10 45				11 19				11 45				12 19
Birmingham New Street [12] 65 a			10 47			11 17				11 47				12 17				12 47				13 17
London Euston ⊖65 a							11 56								12 56							

A To Manchester Oxford Road
B To Scarborough
C To Norwich
D To Nottingham
E To Warrington Central
F To Hull
G To York
H from 20 June until 9 September
I until 17 June, from 12 September
J To Manchester Piccadilly
K From Blackpool North

Table 91

Saturdays

until 18 June

Liverpool - Runcorn and Crewe

			VT		EM	NT	LM	NT	TP	NT	LM	VT	EM		NT	LM	NT	TP	NT	LM	VT	EM	NT		LM	NT
			◇1		◇		◇1		◇1		◇1	◇1	◇			◇1		◇1		◇1	◇1	◇			◇1	
					A	B		C	D	B			A		B		C	D	B			E	B			C
			☕						🛒			☕						🛒			☕					
Liverpool Lime Street 10	90	d	11 48		11 52	11 55	12 04	12 16	12 22	12 27	12 34	12 48	12 52		12 55	13 04	13 16	13 22	13 27	13 34	13 48	13 52	13 55		14 04	14 16
Edge Hill	90	d				11 59									12 59								13 59			
Mossley Hill		d				12 04				12 35					13 04				13 35				14 04			
West Allerton		d				12 06				12 37					13 06				13 37				14 06			
Liverpool South Parkway 7 ✈		a			12 02	12 09	12 15	12 27	12 32	12 40	12 43		13 02		13 09	13 15	13 27	13 32	13 40	13 43		14 02	14 09		14 15	14 27
		d					12 15				12 44					13 15				13 44					14 15	
Runcorn		a	12 03				12 24				12 51	13 03				13 24				13 51	14 03				14 24	
		d	12 04				12 25				12 52	13 04				13 25				13 52	14 04				14 25	
Acton Bridge		d									13 02															
Hartford		d									13 06									14 04						
Winsford		d																		14 08						
Crewe 10	65	a					12 45				13 20					13 45				14 19					14 45	
Birmingham New Street 12	65	a					13 47				14 17					14 47				15 18					15 47	
London Euston	⊖65	a	13 56									14 56									15 56					

			TP	NT	LM	VT	EM	NT	LM		NT	TP	NT	LM	VT	EM	NT	LM	NT		TP	NT	LM	VT	EM	NT
			◇1		◇1	◇1	◇		◇1			◇1		◇1	◇1	◇		◇1			◇1		◇1	◇1	◇	
			D	B			A	B			C	D	B			A	B		C		D	B			E	B
			🛒			☕									☕									☕		
Liverpool Lime Street 10	90	d	14 22	14 27	14 34	14 48	14 52	14 55	15 04		15 16	15 22	15 27	15 34	15 48	15 52	15 55	16 04	16 16		16 22	16 27	16 34	16 48	16 52	16 55
Edge Hill	90	d						14 59									15 59									16 59
Mossley Hill		d		14 35				15 04					15 35				16 04					16 35				17 04
West Allerton		d		14 37				15 06					15 37				16 06					16 37				17 06
Liverpool South Parkway 7 ✈		a	14 32	14 40	14 43		15 02	15 09	15 15		15 27	15 32	15 40	15 43		16 02	16 09	16 15	16 27		16 32	16 40	16 43		17 02	17 09
		d			14 44				15 15					15 44				16 15					16 44			
Runcorn		a			14 51	15 03			15 24					15 51	16 03			16 24					16 51	17 03		
		d			14 52	15 04			15 25					15 52	16 04			16 25					16 52	17 04		
Acton Bridge		d																					17 02			
Hartford		d			15 04									16 04									17 06			
Winsford		d			15 08									16 08												
Crewe 10	65	a			15 19				15 45					16 19				16 45					17 20			
Birmingham New Street 12	65	a			16 17				16 47					17 18				17 47					18 17			
London Euston	⊖65	a				16 56									17 55									18 56		

			LM	TP	NT		LM	VT	EM	NT	LM	TP	NT	LM	VT		EM	NT	LM	TP	LM	VT	EM	NT	TP	
			◇1	◇1			◇1	◇1	◇		◇1	◇1		◇1	◇1		◇		◇1	◇1	◇1	◇1	◇		◇1	
				D	B				A	B		D	B				E	F		G			E	F	G	
								☕							☕							☕				
Liverpool Lime Street 10	90	d	17 04	17 22	17 25		17 34	17 48	17 52	17 55	18 04	18 22	18 25	18 34	18 48		18 52	18 55	19 04	19 22	19 34	19 48	19 52	19 55	20 22	
Edge Hill	90	d			17 29					17 59			18 29					18 59						19 59		
Mossley Hill		d			17 34					18 04			18 34					19 04						20 04		
West Allerton		d			17 36					18 06			18 36					19 06						20 06		
Liverpool South Parkway 7 ✈		a	17 15	17 32	17 39		17 43		18 02	18 09	18 14	18 32	18 39	18 43			19 02	19 09	19 14	19 32	19 43		20 02	20 09	20 32	
		d	17 15				17 44				18 15			18 44					19 14		19 44					
Runcorn		a	17 24				17 51	18 03			18 24			18 51	19 03				19 23		19 51	20 03				
		d	17 25				17 52	18 04			18 24			18 52	19 04				19 23		19 52	20 04				
Acton Bridge		d					18 02												19 36							
Hartford		d					18 06							19 04							20 04					
Winsford		d	17 39								18 38			19 08							20 08					
Crewe 10	65	a	17 47				18 20				18 46			19 19					19 49		20 16	20 21				
Birmingham New Street 12	65	a	18 47				19 17				19 47			20 17					20 47		21 17					
London Euston	⊖65	a						19 56							21 15							22 19				

			LM	EM	NT	LM	EM	NT	LM	TP	NT
			◇1	◇		◇1	◇		1	◇1	
				E	B		E	B		G	H
Liverpool Lime Street 10	90	d	20 34	20 52	20 55	21 34	21 37	21 55	22 04	22 30	23 38
Edge Hill	90	d			20 59			21 59			23 42
Mossley Hill		d			21 04			22 04			23 47
West Allerton		d			21 06			22 06			23 49
Liverpool South Parkway 7 ✈		a	20 43	21 02	21 09	21 43	21 47	22 09	22 14	22 40	23 52
		d	20 44			21 44			22 14		
Runcorn		a	20 51			21 51			22 20		
		d	20 52			21 52			22 21		
Acton Bridge		d									
Hartford		d	21 03			22 04			22 33		
Winsford		d	21 08			22 08			22 37		
Crewe 10	65	a	21 16			22 21			22 48		
Birmingham New Street 12	65	a	22 20			23 21					
London Euston	⊖65	a									

A To Norwich
B To Manchester Oxford Road
C From Blackpool North
D To Scarborough
E To Nottingham
F To Warrington Central
G To York
H To Manchester Piccadilly

Table 91

Saturdays

25 June to 10 September

Liverpool - Runcorn and Crewe

			LM	VT	NT	TP	NT	LM	VT	EM	NT		LM	TP	VT	NT	LM	EM	VT	NT	LM		TP	NT	LM	VT
			1	◇1		◇1		◇1	◇1	◇			◇1	◇1	◇1		◇1	◇	◇1		◇1		◇1		◇1	◇1
					A	B	C			D	A			B		C		D		C			B	C		
				☕		🛒			☕					🛒	☕				☕				🛒			☕
Liverpool Lime Street 10	90	d	23p34	05 47	05 49	06 15	06 25	06 32	06 45	06 49	06 55		07 04	07 15	07 19	07 26	07 34	07 42	07 48	07 51	08 04		08 22	08 26	08 34	08 48
Edge Hill	90	d			05 53						06 59					07 30								08 30		
Mossley Hill		d			05 58		06 33				07 04					07 35				07 59				08 35		
West Allerton		d			06 00		06 35				07 06					07 37				08 01				08 37		
Liverpool South Parkway 7 ✈		a	23p44		06 03	06 25	06 38	06 41		06 59	07 09		07 14	07 25		07 40	07 43	07 52		08 04	08 14		08 32	08 40	08 43	
		d	23p45					06 42					07 14				07 44				08 15				08 44	
Runcorn		a	23p55	06 02				06 49	07 00				07 22		07 35		07 51		08 03		08 24				08 51	09 03
		d	23p55	06 03				06 50	07 01				07 22		07 36		07 52		08 04		08 24				08 52	09 04
Acton Bridge		d	00 05										07 32								08 34				09 02	
Hartford		d	00 10					07 02					07 36				08 04								09 06	
Winsford		d	00 14					07 06									08 08									
Crewe 10	65	a	00 28					07 14	07 18				07 47		07 52		08 19				08 47				09 20	
Birmingham New Street 12	65	a						08 17					08 47				09 18				09 47				10 17	
London Euston	⊖65	a		08 05					08 59						09 46				10 00							11 01

			EM	NT	LM	TP	NT		LM	VT	EM	NT	LM	NT	TP	NT	LM		VT	EM	NT	LM	NT	TP	NT	LM
			◇		◇1	◇1			◇1	◇1	◇		◇1		◇1		◇1		◇1	◇		◇1		◇1		◇1
			D	C		B	C				D	C		E	B	C				D	C		E	B	C	
						🛒				☕					🛒				☕					🛒		
Liverpool Lime Street 10	90	d	08 52	08 55	09 04	09 22	09 27		09 34	09 48	09 52	09 55	10 04	10 16	10 22	10 27	10 34		10 48	10 52	10 55	11 04	11 16	11 22	11 27	11 34
Edge Hill	90	d		08 59								09 59									10 59					
Mossley Hill		d		09 04			09 35					10 04				10 35					11 04				11 35	
West Allerton		d		09 06			09 37					10 06				10 37					11 06				11 37	
Liverpool South Parkway 7 ✈		a	09 02	09 09	09 15	09 32	09 40		09 43		10 02	10 09	10 15	10 27	10 32	10 40	10 43			11 02	11 09	11 15	11 27	11 32	11 40	11 43
		d			09 15				09 44				10 15				10 44					11 15				11 44
Runcorn		a			09 24				09 51	10 03			10 24				10 51		11 03			11 24				11 51
		d			09 24				09 52	10 04			10 25				10 52		11 04			11 25				11 52
Acton Bridge		d																								
Hartford		d							10 04								11 04									12 04
Winsford		d							10 08								11 08									12 08
Crewe 10	65	a			09 44				10 19				10 45				11 19					11 45				12 19
Birmingham New Street 12	65	a			10 47				11 17				11 47				12 17					12 47				13 17
London Euston	⊖65	a								11 56									12 56							

			VT		EM	NT	LM	NT	TP	NT	LM	VT	EM		NT	LM	NT	TP	NT	LM	VT	EM	NT		LM	NT
			◇1		◇		◇1		◇1		◇1	◇1	◇			◇1		◇1		◇1	◇1	◇			◇1	
					D	C		E	B	C			D		C		E	B	C			F	C			E
			☕						🛒			☕						🛒			☕					
Liverpool Lime Street 10	90	d	11 48		11 52	11 55	12 04	12 16	12 22	12 27	12 34	12 48	12 52		12 55	13 04	13 16	13 22	13 27	13 34	13 48	13 52	13 55		14 04	14 16
Edge Hill	90	d				11 59									12 59								13 59			
Mossley Hill		d				12 04				12 35					13 04				13 35				14 04			
West Allerton		d				12 06				12 37					13 06				13 37				14 06			
Liverpool South Parkway 7 ✈		a			12 02	12 09	12 15	12 27	12 32	12 40	12 43		13 02		13 09	13 15	13 27	13 32	13 40	13 43		14 02	14 09		14 15	14 27
		d					12 15				12 44					13 15				13 44					14 15	
Runcorn		a	12 03				12 24				12 51	13 03				13 24				13 51	14 03				14 24	
		d	12 04				12 25				12 52	13 04				13 25				13 52	14 04				14 25	
Acton Bridge		d									13 02															
Hartford		d									13 06									14 04						
Winsford		d																		14 08						
Crewe 10	65	a					12 45				13 20					13 45				14 19					14 45	
Birmingham New Street 12	65	a					13 47				14 17					14 47				15 18					15 47	
London Euston	⊖65	a	13 56									14 56									15 56					

			TP	NT	LM	VT	EM	NT	LM		NT	TP	NT	LM	VT	EM	NT	LM	NT		TP	NT	LM	VT	EM	NT
			◇1		◇1	◇1	◇		◇1			◇1		◇1	◇1	◇		◇1			◇1		◇1	◇1	◇	
			B	C			D	C			E	B	C			D	C		E		B	C			F	C
			🛒			☕									☕									☕		
Liverpool Lime Street 10	90	d	14 22	14 27	14 34	14 48	14 52	14 55	15 04		15 16	15 22	15 27	15 34	15 48	15 52	15 55	16 04	16 16		16 22	16 27	16 34	16 48	16 52	16 55
Edge Hill	90	d						14 59									15 59									16 59
Mossley Hill		d		14 35				15 04					15 35				16 04					16 35				17 04
West Allerton		d		14 37				15 06					15 37				16 06					16 37				17 06
Liverpool South Parkway 7 ✈		a	14 32	14 40	14 43		15 02	15 09	15 15		15 27	15 32	15 40	15 43		16 02	16 09	16 15	16 27		16 32	16 40	16 43		17 02	17 09
		d			14 44				15 15					15 44				16 15					16 44			
Runcorn		a			14 51	15 03			15 24					15 51	16 03			16 24					16 51	17 03		
		d			14 52	15 04			15 25					15 52	16 04			16 25					16 52	17 04		
Acton Bridge		d																					17 02			
Hartford		d			15 04									16 04									17 06			
Winsford		d			15 08									16 08												
Crewe 10	65	a			15 19				15 45					16 19				16 45					17 20			
Birmingham New Street 12	65	a			16 17				16 47					17 18				17 47					18 17			
London Euston	⊖65	a				16 56									17 55									18 56		

A To Warrington Central
B To Scarborough
C To Manchester Oxford Road
D To Norwich
E From Blackpool North
F To Nottingham

Table 91

Saturdays
25 June to 10 September

Liverpool - Runcorn and Crewe

			LM	TP	NT	LM	VT	EM	NT	LM	TP	NT	LM	VT	EM	NT	LM	TP	LM	VT	EM	NT	TP
			◇1	◇1		◇1	◇1	◇		◇1	◇1		◇1	◇1	◇		◇1	◇1	◇1	◇1	◇		◇1
				A	B			C	B		A	B			D	E		F			D	E	F
							☕							☕						☕			
Liverpool Lime Street 10	90	d	17 04	17 22	17 25	17 34	17 48	17 52	17 55	18 04	18 22	18 25	18 34	18 48	18 52	18 55	19 04	19 22	19 34	19 48	19 52	19 55	20 22
Edge Hill	90	d			17 29				17 59			18 29				18 59						19 59	
Mossley Hill		d			17 34				18 04			18 34				19 04						20 04	
West Allerton		d			17 36				18 06			18 36				19 06						20 06	
Liverpool South Parkway 7 ✈		a	17 15	17 32	17 39	17 43		18 02	18 09	18 14	18 32	18 39	18 43		19 02	19 09	19 14	19 32	19 43		20 02	20 09	20 32
		d	17 15			17 44				18 15			18 44				19 14		19 44				
Runcorn		a	17 24			17 51	18 03			18 24			18 51	19 03			19 23		19 51	20 03			
		d	17 25			17 52	18 04			18 24			18 52	19 04			19 23		19 52	20 04			
Acton Bridge		d				18 02											19 36						
Hartford		d				18 06							19 04						20 04				
Winsford		d	17 39							18 38			19 08						20 08				
Crewe 10	65	a	17 47			18 20				18 46			19 19				19 49		20 16	20 21			
Birmingham New Street 12	65	a	18 47			19 17				19 47			20 17				20 47		21 17				
London Euston ⊖	65	a					19 56							21 15						22 19			

			LM	EM	NT	LM	EM	NT	LM	TP	NT
			◇1	◇		◇1	◇		1	◇1	
				D	B		D	B		F	G
Liverpool Lime Street 10	90	d	20 34	20 52	20 55	21 34	21 37	21 55	22 04	22 30	23 38
Edge Hill	90	d			20 59			21 59			23 42
Mossley Hill		d			21 04			22 04			23 47
West Allerton		d			21 06			22 06			23 49
Liverpool South Parkway 7 ✈		a	20 43	21 02	21 09	21 43	21 47	22 09	22 14	22 40	23 52
		d	20 44			21 44			22 14		
Runcorn		a	20 51			21 51			22 20		
		d	20 52			21 52			22 21		
Acton Bridge		d									
Hartford		d	21 03			22 04			22 33		
Winsford		d	21 08			22 08			22 37		
Crewe 10	65	a	21 16			22 21			22 48		
Birmingham New Street 12	65	a	22 20			23 21					
London Euston ⊖	65	a									

Saturdays
from 17 September

			LM	VT	NT	TP	NT	LM	VT	EM	NT	LM	TP	VT	NT	LM	EM	VT	NT	LM	TP	NT	LM	VT
			1	◇1		◇1		◇1	◇1	◇		◇1	◇1	◇1		◇1	◇	◇1		◇1	◇1		◇1	◇1
					E	A	B			C	E		A		B		C		B		A	B		
				☕		🛒			☕				🛒	☕				☕			🛒			☕
Liverpool Lime Street 10	90	d	23p34	05 47	05 49	06 15	06 25	06 32	06 45	06 49	06 55	07 04	07 15	07 19	07 26	07 34	07 42	07 48	07 51	08 04	08 22	08 26	08 34	08 48
Edge Hill	90	d			05 53						06 59				07 30							08 30		
Mossley Hill		d			05 58		06 33				07 04				07 35				07 59			08 35		
West Allerton		d			06 00		06 35				07 06				07 37				08 01			08 37		
Liverpool South Parkway 7 ✈		a	23p44		06 03	06 25	06 38	06 41		06 59	07 09	07 14	07 25		07 40	07 43	07 52		08 04	08 14	08 32	08 40	08 43	
		d	23p45					06 42				07 14				07 44				08 15			08 44	
Runcorn		a	23p55	06 02				06 49	07 00			07 22		07 35		07 51		08 03		08 24			08 51	09 03
		d	23p55	06 03				06 50	07 01			07 22		07 36		07 52		08 04		08 24			08 52	09 04
Acton Bridge		d	00 05									07 32								08 34			09 02	
Hartford		d	00 10					07 02				07 36				08 04							09 06	
Winsford		d	00 14					07 06								08 08								
Crewe 10	65	a	00 25					07 14	07 18			07 47		07 52		08 19				08 47			09 20	
Birmingham New Street 12	65	a						08 17				08 47				09 18				09 47			10 17	
London Euston ⊖	65	a		08 05					08 59					09 46				10 00						11 01

			EM	NT	LM	TP	NT	LM	VT	EM	NT	LM	NT	TP	NT	LM	VT	EM	NT	LM	NT	TP	NT	LM
			◇		◇1	◇1		◇1	◇1	◇		◇1		◇1		◇1	◇1	◇		◇1		◇1		◇1
			C	B		A	B			C	B		H	A	B			C	B		H	A	B	
						🛒			☕					🛒			☕					🛒		
Liverpool Lime Street 10	90	d	08 52	08 55	09 04	09 22	09 27	09 34	09 48	09 52	09 55	10 04	10 16	10 22	10 27	10 34	10 48	10 52	10 55	11 04	11 16	11 22	11 27	11 34
Edge Hill	90	d		08 59							09 59								10 59					
Mossley Hill		d		09 04			09 35				10 04				10 35				11 04				11 35	
West Allerton		d		09 06			09 37				10 06				10 37				11 06				11 37	
Liverpool South Parkway 7 ✈		a	09 02	09 09	09 15	09 32	09 40	09 43		10 02	10 09	10 15	10 27	10 32	10 40	10 43		11 02	11 09	11 15	11 27	11 32	11 40	11 43
		d			09 15			09 44				10 15				10 44				11 15				11 44
Runcorn		a			09 24			09 51	10 03			10 24				10 51	11 03			11 24				11 51
		d			09 24			09 52	10 04			10 25				10 52	11 04			11 25				11 52
Acton Bridge		d																						
Hartford		d						10 04								11 04								12 04
Winsford		d						10 08								11 08								12 08
Crewe 10	65	a			09 44			10 19				10 45				11 19				11 45				12 19
Birmingham New Street 12	65	a			10 47			11 17				11 47				12 17				12 47				13 17
London Euston ⊖	65	a							11 56								12 56							

A To Scarborough
B To Manchester Oxford Road
C To Norwich
D To Nottingham
E To Warrington Central
F To York
G To Manchester Piccadilly
H From Blackpool North

Table 91

Saturdays

from 17 September

Liverpool - Runcorn and Crewe

	VT		EM	NT	LM	NT	TP	NT	LM	VT	EM		NT	LM	NT	TP	NT	LM	VT	EM	NT		LM	NT
	◇1		◇		◇1		◇1		◇1	◇1	◇			◇1		◇1		◇1	◇1	◇			◇1	
			A	B		C	D	B			A		B		C	D	B			A	B			C
Liverpool Lime Street 10 90 d	11 48		11 52	11 55	12 04	12 16	12 22	12 27	12 34	12 48	12 52		12 55	13 04	13 16	13 22	13 27	13 34	13 48	13 52	13 55		14 04	14 16
Edge Hill 90 d				11 59									12 59								13 59			
Mossley Hill d				12 04				12 35					13 04				13 35				14 04			
West Allerton d				12 06				12 37					13 06				13 37				14 06			
Liverpool South Parkway 7 a			12 02	12 09	12 15	12 27	12 32	12 40	12 43		13 02		13 09	13 15	13 27	13 32	13 40	13 43		14 02	14 09		14 15	14 27
d					12 15				12 44					13 15				13 44					14 15	
Runcorn a	12 03				12 24				12 51	13 03				13 24				13 51	14 03				14 24	
d	12 04				12 25				12 52	13 04				13 25				13 52	14 04				14 25	
Acton Bridge d									13 02															
Hartford d									13 06									14 04						
Winsford d																		14 08						
Crewe 10 65 a					12 45				13 20					13 45				14 19					14 45	
Birmingham New Street 12 65 a					13 47				14 17					14 47				15 18					15 47	
London Euston ⊖65 a	13 56									14 56									15 56					

	TP	NT	LM	VT	EM	NT	LM		NT	TP	NT	LM	VT	EM	NT	LM	NT		TP	NT	LM	VT	EM	NT
	◇1		◇1	◇1	◇		◇1			◇1		◇1	◇1	◇		◇1			◇1		◇1	◇1	◇	
	D	B			A	B			C	D	B			A	B		C		D	B			E	B
Liverpool Lime Street 10 90 d	14 22	14 27	14 34	14 48	14 52	14 55	15 04		15 16	15 22	15 27	15 34	15 48	15 52	15 55	16 04	16 16		16 22	16 27	16 34	16 48	16 52	16 55
Edge Hill 90 d						14 59									15 59									16 59
Mossley Hill d		14 35				15 04					15 35				16 04					16 35				17 04
West Allerton d		14 37				15 06					15 37				16 06					16 37				17 06
Liverpool South Parkway 7 a	14 32	14 40	14 43		15 02	15 09	15 15		15 27	15 32	15 40	15 43		16 02	16 09	16 15	16 27		16 32	16 40	16 43		17 02	17 09
d			14 44				15 15					15 44				16 15					16 44			
Runcorn a			14 51	15 03			15 24					15 51	16 03			16 24					16 51	17 03		
d			14 52	15 04			15 25					15 52	16 04			16 25					16 52	17 04		
Acton Bridge d																					17 02			
Hartford d			15 04									16 04									17 06			
Winsford d			15 08									16 08												
Crewe 10 65 a			15 19				15 45					16 19				16 45					17 20			
Birmingham New Street 12 65 a			16 17				16 47					17 18				17 47					18 17			
London Euston ⊖65 a				16 56									17 55									18 56		

	LM	TP	NT		LM	VT	EM	NT	LM	TP	NT	LM	VT		EM	NT	LM	TP	LM	VT	EM	NT	TP	
	◇1	◇1			◇1	◇1	◇		◇1	◇1		◇1	◇1		◇		◇1	◇1	◇1	◇1	◇		◇1	
		D	B				A	B		D	B				E	F		G			E	F	G	
Liverpool Lime Street 10 90 d	17 04	17 22	17 25		17 34	17 48	17 52	17 55	18 04	18 22	18 25	18 34	18 48		18 52	18 55	19 04	19 22	19 34	19 48	19 52	19 55	20 22	
Edge Hill 90 d			17 29					17 59			18 29					18 59						19 59		
Mossley Hill d			17 34					18 04			18 34					19 04						20 04		
West Allerton d			17 36					18 06			18 36					19 06						20 06		
Liverpool South Parkway 7 a	17 15	17 32	17 39		17 43		18 02	18 09	18 14	18 32	18 39	18 43			19 02	19 09	19 14	19 32	19 43		20 02	20 09	20 32	
d	17 15				17 44				18 15			18 44					19 14		19 44					
Runcorn a	17 24				17 51	18 03			18 24			18 51	19 03				19 23		19 51	20 03				
d	17 25				17 52	18 04			18 24			18 52	19 04				19 23		19 52	20 04				
Acton Bridge d					18 02												19 36							
Hartford d					18 06							19 04							20 04					
Winsford d	17 39								18 38			19 08							20 08					
Crewe 10 65 a	17 47				18 20				18 46			19 19					19 49		20 16					
Birmingham New Street 12 65 a	18 47				19 17				19 47			20 17					20 47		21 17					
London Euston ⊖65 a						19 56							21 15							22 14				

	LM	EM	NT	LM	EM	NT	LM	TP	NT
	◇1	◇		◇1	◇		1	◇1	
		E	B		E	B		H	I
Liverpool Lime Street 10 90 d	20 34	20 52	20 55	21 34	21 37	21 55	22 04	22 30	23 38
Edge Hill 90 d			20 59			21 59			23 42
Mossley Hill d			21 04			22 04			23 47
West Allerton d			21 06			22 06			23 49
Liverpool South Parkway 7 a	20 43	21 02	21 09	21 43	21 47	22 09	22 14	22 40	23 52
d	20 44			21 44			22 14		
Runcorn a	20 51			21 51			22 20		
d	20 52			21 52			22 21		
Acton Bridge d									
Hartford d	21 03			22 04			22 33		
Winsford d	21 08			22 08			22 37		
Crewe 10 65 a	21 16			22 21			22 48		
Birmingham New Street 12 65 a	22 20			23 21					
London Euston ⊖65 a									

A To Norwich
B To Manchester Oxford Road
C From Blackpool North
D To Scarborough
E To Nottingham
F To Warrington Central
G To York
H To Stalybridge
I To Manchester Piccadilly

Table 91

Sundays
until 11 September

Liverpool - Runcorn and Crewe

	VT	TP	NT	VT	TP	NT	VT	TP	NT		VT	TP	NT	LM	VT	TP	NT	LM	VT		EM	TP	NT	LM
	◇1	◇1		◇1	◇1		◇1	◇1			◇1	◇1		1	◇1	◇1		1	◇1		◇	◇1		1
		A	B		C	B		D	B			C	B			D	B				E	F	B	
	☕			☕			☕				☕				☕				☕					
Liverpool Lime Street 10 90 d	08 15	08 22	08 26	08 38	09 22	09 26	09 38	10 22	10 26		10 38	11 22	11 26	11 34	11 48	12 22	12 26	12 34	12 48		12 52	13 22	13 26	13 34
Edge Hill 90 d																								
Mossley Hill d			08 34			09 34			10 34				11 34				12 34						13 34	
West Allerton d			08 36			09 36			10 36				11 36				12 36						13 36	
Liverpool South Parkway 7 ✈ a		08 32	08 39		09 32	09 39		10 32	10 39			11 32	11 39	11 43		12 32	12 39	12 43			13 02	13 32	13 39	13 43
d														11 44				12 44						13 44
Runcorn a	08 34			08 53			09 53				10 53			11 51	12 03			12 51	13 03					13 51
d	08 35			08 54			09 54				10 54			11 52	12 04			12 52	13 04					13 52
Acton Bridge d																								
Hartford d														12 04				13 03						14 03
Winsford d														12 08				13 08						14 08
Crewe 10 65 a	08 52			09 11			10 12				11 12			12 20				13 19						14 18
Birmingham New Street 12 65 a														13 16				14 15						15 15
London Euston ⊖65 a	11 06			11 37			12 32				13 11				14 01				15 01					

	VT	EM	TP	NT	LM		VT	EM	TP	NT	LM	VT	EM	VT	TP		NT	LM	VT	EM	TP	NT	LM	VT
	◇1	◇	◇1		1		◇1	◇	◇1		1	◇1	◇	◇1	◇1			1	◇1	◇	◇1		1	◇1
		E	D	B				E	C	B			E		D		B			G	C	B		
	☕						☕					☕		☕					☕					☕
Liverpool Lime Street 10 90 d	13 48	13 52	14 22	14 26	14 34		14 48	14 52	15 22	15 26	15 34	15 48	15 52	16 18	16 22		16 26	16 34	16 48	16 52	17 22	17 26	17 34	17 48
Edge Hill 90 d																								
Mossley Hill d				14 34						15 34							16 34					17 34		
West Allerton d				14 36						15 36							16 36					17 36		
Liverpool South Parkway 7 ✈ a		14 02	14 32	14 39	14 43			15 02	15 32	15 39	15 43		16 02		16 32		16 39	16 43		17 02	17 32	17 39	17 43	
d					14 44						15 44							16 44					17 44	
Runcorn a	14 03				14 51		15 03				15 51	16 03		16 33				16 51	17 03				17 51	18 03
d	14 04				14 52		15 04				15 52	16 04		16 34				16 52	17 04				17 52	18 04
Acton Bridge d																								
Hartford d					15 03						16 03							17 03					18 03	
Winsford d					15 08						16 08							17 08					18 08	
Crewe 10 65 a					15 20						16 18			16 51				17 18					18 20	
Birmingham New Street 12 65 a					16 15						17 15							18 15					19 15	
London Euston ⊖65 a	16 01						17 01					18 01		18 44					19 01					20 01

	EM		TP	NT	LM	VT	EM	TP	NT	LM	VT		EM	TP	NT	LM	VT	NT	LM	TP	NT
	◇		◇1		1	◇1	◇	◇1		1	◇1		◇	◇1		1	◇1		1	◇1	
	E		C	B			G	H	B				G	I	B			B		H	B
						☕					☕						☕				
Liverpool Lime Street 10 90 d	17 52		18 22	18 26	18 34	18 48	18 52	19 22	19 26	19 34	19 48		19 52	20 22	20 26	20 34	20 48	21 26	21 34	21 52	22 26
Edge Hill 90 d																					
Mossley Hill d				18 34					19 34						20 34			21 34			22 34
West Allerton d				18 36					19 36						20 36			21 36			22 36
Liverpool South Parkway 7 ✈ a	18 02		18 32	18 39	18 43		19 02	19 32	19 39	19 43			20 02	20 32	20 39	20 43		21 39	21 43	22 02	22 39
d					18 44					19 44						20 44			21 44		
Runcorn a					18 51	19 03				19 51	20 03					20 51	21 03		21 51		
d					18 52	19 04				19 52	20 04					20 52	21 04		21 52		
Acton Bridge d																					
Hartford d					19 03					20 03						21 03			22 03		
Winsford d					19 08					20 08						21 08			22 08		
Crewe 10 65 a					19 20					20 16	20 22					21 16	21 21		22 18		
Birmingham New Street 12 65 a					20 15					21 15						22 15			23 17		
London Euston ⊖65 a						21 01					22 28						23 54				

Sundays
18 September to 23 October

	VT	NT	VT	NT	VT	NT	VT	NT	LM		VT	NT	LM	VT	EM	NT	LM	VT	EM		NT	LM	VT	EM
	◇1		◇1		◇1		◇1		1		◇1		1	◇1	◇		1	◇1	◇			1	◇1	◇
		B		B		B		B				B			E	B			E		B			E
	☕		☕		☕		☕				☕			☕				☕					☕	
Liverpool Lime Street 10 90 d	08 15	08 26	08 38	09 26	09 38	10 26	10 38	11 26	11 34		11 48	12 26	12 34	12 48	12 52	13 26	13 34	13 48	13 52		14 26	14 34	14 48	14 52
Edge Hill 90 d																								
Mossley Hill d		08 34		09 34		10 34		11 34				12 34				13 34					14 34			
West Allerton d		08 36		09 36		10 36		11 36				12 36				13 36					14 36			
Liverpool South Parkway 7 ✈ a		08 39		09 39		10 39		11 39	11 43			12 39	12 43		13 02	13 39	13 43		14 02		14 39	14 43		15 02
d									11 44				12 44				13 44					14 44		
Runcorn a	08 34		08 53		09 53		10 53		11 51		12 03		12 51	13 03			13 51	14 03				14 51	15 03	
d	08 35		08 54		09 54		10 54		11 52		12 04		12 52	13 04			13 52	14 04				14 52	15 04	
Acton Bridge d																								
Hartford d									12 04				13 03				14 03					15 03		
Winsford d									12 08				13 08				14 08					15 08		
Crewe 10 65 a	08 52		09 11		10 12		11 12		12 20				13 19				14 18					15 20		
Birmingham New Street 12 65 a									13 16				14 15				15 15					16 15		
London Euston ⊖65 a	11 06		11 37		12 32		13 11				14 01			15 01				16 01					17 01	

A To Hull
B To Manchester Oxford Road
C To Scarborough
D To Middlesbrough
E To Norwich
F until 31 July. To Scarborough
G To Nottingham
H To York
I To Newcastle

Table 91

Liverpool - Runcorn and Crewe

Sundays

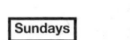

18 September to 23 October

	NT	LM	VT	EM	VT		NT	LM	VT	EM	NT	LM	VT	EM	NT		LM	VT	EM	NT	LM	VT	EM	NT
		1	◇1	◇	◇1			1	◇1	◇		1	◇1	◇			1	◇1	◇		1	◇1	◇	
	A			B			A			C	A			B	A				C	A			C	A
			☕		☕				☕				☕					☕				☕		
Liverpool Lime Street [10] 90 d	15 26	15 34	15 48	15 52	16 18		16 26	16 34	16 48	16 52	17 26	17 34	17 48	17 52	18 26		18 34	18 48	18 52	19 26	19 34	19 48	19 52	20 26
Edge Hill 90 d																								
Mossley Hill d	15 34						16 34				17 34				18 34					19 34				20 34
West Allerton d	15 36						16 36				17 36				18 36					19 36				20 36
Liverpool South Parkway [7] ✈ a	15 39	15 43		16 02			16 39	16 43		17 02	17 39	17 43		18 02	18 39		18 43		19 02	19 39	19 43		20 02	20 39
d		15 44						16 44				17 44					18 44				19 44			
Runcorn a		15 51	16 03		16 33			16 51	17 03			17 51	18 03				18 51	19 03			19 51	20 03		
d		15 52	16 04		16 34			16 52	17 04			17 52	18 04				18 52	19 04			19 52	20 04		
Acton Bridge d																								
Hartford d		16 03						17 03				18 03					19 03				20 03			
Winsford d		16 08						17 08				18 08					19 08				20 08			
Crewe [10] 65 a		16 18			16 51			17 18				18 20					19 20				20 16	20 22		
Birmingham New Street [12] 65 a		17 15						18 15				19 15					20 15				21 15			
London Euston ⊖65 a			18 01		18 44				19 01				20 01					21 01				22 28		

	LM		VT	NT	LM	NT
	1		◇1		1	
				A		A
			☕			
Liverpool Lime Street [10] 90 d	20 34		20 48	21 26	21 34	22 26
Edge Hill 90 d						
Mossley Hill d				21 34		22 34
West Allerton d				21 36		22 36
Liverpool South Parkway [7] ✈ a	20 43			21 39	21 43	22 39
d	20 44				21 44	
Runcorn a	20 51		21 03		21 51	
d	20 52		21 04		21 52	
Acton Bridge d						
Hartford d	21 03				22 03	
Winsford d	21 08				22 08	
Crewe [10] 65 a	21 16		21 21		22 18	
Birmingham New Street [12] 65 a	22 15				23 17	
London Euston ⊖65 a			23 54			

Sundays

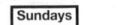

from 30 October

	VT	TP	NT	VT	TP	NT	VT	TP	NT		VT	TP	NT	LM	VT	TP	NT	LM	VT		EM	NT	LM	VT
	◇1	◇1		◇1	◇1		◇1	◇1			◇1	◇1		1	◇1	◇1		1	◇1		◇		1	◇1
		D	A		E	A		F	A			E	A			F	A				B	A		
	☕			☕			☕				☕				☕				☕					☕
Liverpool Lime Street [10] 90 d	08 15	08 22	08 26	08 38	09 22	09 26	09 38	10 22	10 26		10 38	11 22	11 26	11 34	11 48	12 22	12 26	12 34	12 48		12 52	13 26	13 34	13 48
Edge Hill 90 d																								
Mossley Hill d			08 34			09 34			10 34				11 34				12 34					13 34		
West Allerton d			08 36			09 36			10 36				11 36				12 36					13 36		
Liverpool South Parkway [7] ✈ a		08 32	08 39		09 32	09 39		10 32	10 39			11 32	11 39	11 43		12 32	12 39	12 43			13 02	13 39	13 43	
d														11 44				12 44					13 44	
Runcorn a	08 34			08 53			09 53				10 53			11 51	12 03			12 51	13 03				13 51	14 03
d	08 35			08 54			09 54				10 54			11 52	12 04			12 52	13 04				13 52	14 04
Acton Bridge d																								
Hartford d														12 04				13 03					14 03	
Winsford d														12 08				13 08					14 08	
Crewe [10] 65 a	08 52			09 11			10 12				11 12			12 20				13 19					14 18	
Birmingham New Street [12] 65 a														13 16				14 15					15 15	
London Euston ⊖65 a	11 06			11 37			12 32				13 11				14 01				15 01					16 01

	EM	TP	NT	LM	VT		EM	TP	NT	LM	VT	EM	VT	TP	NT		LM	VT	EM	TP	NT	LM	VT	EM
	◇	◇1		1	◇1		◇	◇1		1	◇1	◇	◇1	◇1			1	◇1	◇	◇1		1	◇1	◇
	B	F	A				B	E	A			B		F	A				C	E	A			B
					☕						☕		☕					☕					☕	
Liverpool Lime Street [10] 90 d	13 52	14 22	14 26	14 34	14 48		14 52	15 22	15 26	15 34	15 48	15 52	16 18	16 22	16 26		16 34	16 48	16 52	17 22	17 26	17 34	17 48	17 52
Edge Hill 90 d																								
Mossley Hill d			14 34						15 34						16 34						17 34			
West Allerton d			14 36						15 36						16 36						17 36			
Liverpool South Parkway [7] ✈ a	14 02	14 32	14 39	14 43			15 02	15 32	15 39	15 43		16 02		16 32	16 39		16 43		17 02	17 32	17 39	17 43		18 02
d				14 44						15 44							16 44					17 44		
Runcorn a				14 51	15 03					15 51	16 03		16 33				16 51	17 03				17 51	18 03	
d				14 52	15 04					15 52	16 04		16 34				16 52	17 04				17 52	18 04	
Acton Bridge d																								
Hartford d				15 03						16 03							17 03					18 03		
Winsford d				15 08						16 08							17 08					18 08		
Crewe [10] 65 a				15 20						16 18			16 51				17 18					18 20		
Birmingham New Street [12] 65 a				16 15						17 15							18 15					19 15		
London Euston ⊖65 a					17 01						18 01		18 44					19 01					20 01	

A To Manchester Oxford Road
B To Norwich
C To Nottingham
D To Hull
E To Scarborough
F To Middlesbrough

Table 91

Sundays
from 30 October

Liverpool - Runcorn and Crewe

	TP		NT	LM	VT	EM	TP	NT	LM	VT	EM		TP	NT	LM	VT	NT	LM	TP	NT				
	◇1			1	◇1	◇	◇1		1	◇1	◇		◇1		1	◇1		1	◇1					
	A		B			C	D	B			C		E	B			B		D	B				
					🍴					🍴						🍴								
Liverpool Lime Street 10 90 d	18 22		18 26	18 34	18 48	18 52	19 22	19 26	19 34	19 48	19 52		20 22	20 26	20 34	20 48	21 26	21 34	21 52	22 26				
Edge Hill 90 d																								
Mossley Hill d			18 34					19 34						20 34			21 34			22 34				
West Allerton d			18 36					19 36						20 36			21 36			22 36				
Liverpool South Parkway 7 ✈ a	18 32		18 39	18 43		19 02	19 32	19 39	19 43		20 02		20 32	20 39	20 43		21 39	21 43	22 02	22 39				
d				18 44					19 44						20 44			21 44						
Runcorn a				18 51	19 03				19 51	20 03					20 51	21 03		21 51						
d				18 52	19 04				19 52	20 04					20 52	21 04		21 52						
Acton Bridge d																								
Hartford d				19 03					20 03						21 03			22 03						
Winsford d				19 08					20 08						21 08			22 08						
Crewe 10 65 a				19 20					20 16	20 22					21 16	21 21		22 18						
Birmingham New Street 12 65 a				20 15					21 15						22 15			23 17						
London Euston ⊖65 a					21 01					22 28						23 54								

A To Scarborough
B To Manchester Oxford Road
C To Nottingham
D To York
E To Newcastle

Table 91

Mondays to Fridays

Crewe and Runcorn - Liverpool

Miles		VT	NT	LM	LM	NT	LM	NT	LM	NT		LM	VT	NT	LM	EM	LM	NT	TP	LM		VT	NT	EM
		MO	MX																					
		◇1		1	1		1		1			◇1	◇1		◇1	◇	1		◇1	◇1		◇1		◇
			A	B	C	D		D		A				D		E		A	F	G			A	E
		☕											☒						🛒			☒		
—	London Euston ⊖65 d	21p21											05 27									07 07		
—	Birmingham New Street 12 65 d											06 01			06 36		07 01			07 36				
0	**Crewe** 10 65 d	23p39		05 34	05 40		06 02		06 32			06 57	07 24		07 34		07 58			08 31				
7½	Winsford d						06 10		06 41			07 04			07 43		08 05							
11¾	Hartford d						06 15		06 46			07 09			07 48		08 10							
14½	Acton Bridge d						06 19		06 51			07 14			07 52		08 14							
22½	**Runcorn** a	23p56		05 58	05 58		06 27		06 59			07 23	07 41		08 00		08 22			08 50		08 55		
—	d	23p56		06 01	06 01		06 28		06 59			07 23	07 41		08 01		08 23			08 50		08 55		
30	**Liverpool South Parkway** 7 ✈ a			06 10	06 10		06 36		07 08			07 32			08 09		08 31			08 59				
—	d		00 27	06 10	06 10	06 27	06 37	07 01	07 08	07 27		07 32		07 59	08 10	08 18	08 32	08 37	08 47	08 59			09 06	09 15
31	West Allerton d					06 31		07 05		07 30				08 03				08 40					09 09	
31¾	Mossley Hill d					06 33		07 07		07 33				08 06				08 43					09 12	
33¾	Edge Hill 90 d					06 39		07 13		07 40				08 11				08 48						
35½	**Liverpool Lime Street** 10 90 a	00 23	00 41	06 22	06 22	06 45	06 49	07 19	07 22	07 48		07 43	08 01	08 18	08 21	08 31	08 44	08 55	08 58	09 10		09 15	09 24	09 31

	LM	NT	TP	LM	VT	NT		EM	LM	NT	NT	TP	LM	VT	NT	EM		LM	NT	NT	TP	LM	VT	NT
	◇1		◇1	1	◇1			◇	1			◇1	1	◇1		◇		1			◇1	1	◇1	
	H	A	I			A		E		J	A	K			A	L			J	A	K			A
			🛒		☒							🛒		☒							🛒		☒	
London Euston ⊖65 d					08 07									09 07									10 07	
Birmingham New Street 12 65 d	08 01			08 36					09 01				09 36					10 01				10 36		
Crewe 10 65 d	08 58			09 31					09 57				10 31					10 57				11 31		
Winsford d	09 07																	11 06						
Hartford d	09 12								10 10									11 11						
Acton Bridge d									10 14															
Runcorn a	09 22			09 50	09 55				10 22				10 50	10 55				11 21				11 50	11 55	
d	09 22			09 50	09 55				10 23				10 50	10 55				11 22				11 50	11 55	
Liverpool South Parkway 7 ✈ a	09 31			09 59					10 31				10 59					11 30				11 59		
d	09 31	09 36	09 47	09 59		10 06		10 15	10 32	10 36	10 36	10 47	10 59		11 06	11 15		11 31	11 36	11 36	11 47	11 59		12 06
West Allerton d		09 39				10 10					10 39				11 10					11 39				12 10
Mossley Hill d		09 41				10 12					10 41				11 13					11 41				12 13
Edge Hill 90 d		09 47									10 47									11 47				
Liverpool Lime Street 10 90 a	09 43	09 53	09 58	10 10	10 15	10 24		10 31	10 44	10 49	10 53	10 58	11 10	11 15	11 24	11 31		11 43	11 49	11 53	11 58	12 10	12 15	12 24

	EM	LM		NT	NT	TP	LM	VT	NT	EM	LM	NT		NT	TP	LM	VT	NT	EM	LM	NT	NT		TP
	◇	1				◇1	1	◇1		◇	1				◇1	1	◇1		◇	1				◇1
	L			J	A	K			A	L		J		A	K			A	L		J	A		K
						🛒		☕							🛒		☕							🛒
London Euston ⊖65 d								11 07									12 07							
Birmingham New Street 12 65 d		11 01					11 36				12 01					12 36				13 01				
Crewe 10 65 d		11 57					12 31				12 57					13 31				13 57				
Winsford d											13 06									14 06				
Hartford d		12 10									13 11									14 11				
Acton Bridge d		12 14																						
Runcorn a		12 23					12 50	12 55			13 21					13 50	13 55			14 21				
d		12 23					12 50	12 55			13 22					13 50	13 55			14 22				
Liverpool South Parkway 7 ✈ a		12 32					12 59				13 30					13 59				14 30				
d	12 15	12 32		12 36	12 36	12 47	12 59		13 06	13 15	13 31	13 36		13 36	13 47	13 59		14 06	14 15	14 31	14 36	14 36		14 47
West Allerton d					12 39				13 10					13 39				14 10				14 39		
Mossley Hill d					12 41				13 13					13 41				14 13				14 41		
Edge Hill 90 d					12 47									13 47								14 47		
Liverpool Lime Street 10 90 a	12 31	12 44		12 49	12 53	12 58	13 10	13 15	13 24	13 31	13 43	13 49		13 53	13 58	14 10	14 15	14 24	14 31	14 43	14 49	14 53		14 58

	LM	VT	NT	EM	LM	NT	NT	TP		LM	VT	NT	EM	LM	NT	NT	TP	LM		VT	NT	EM	LM	NT
	1	◇1		◇	1			◇1		1	◇1		◇	1			◇1	1		◇1		◇	1	
			A	L		J	A	K				A	L		J	A	K				A	L		A
		☕						🛒			☕						🛒			☕				
London Euston ⊖65 d		13 07									14 07									15 07				
Birmingham New Street 12 65 d	13 36				14 01					14 36				15 01				15 36					16 01	
Crewe 10 65 d	14 31				14 57					15 31				15 57				16 31					16 57	
Winsford d					15 06																		17 07	
Hartford d					15 11									16 10									17 12	
Acton Bridge d														16 14										
Runcorn a	14 50	14 55			15 21					15 50	15 55			16 22				16 50		16 55			17 21	
d	14 50	14 55			15 22					15 50	15 55			16 22				16 50		16 55			17 22	
Liverpool South Parkway 7 ✈ a	14 59				15 30					15 59				16 31				16 59					17 30	
d	14 59		15 06	15 15	15 31	15 36	15 36	15 47		15 59		16 07	16 15	16 31	16 36	16 36	16 47	16 59			17 07	17 15	17 31	17 39
West Allerton d			15 10				15 39					16 11				16 39					17 11			17 42
Mossley Hill d			15 13				15 41					16 13				16 42					17 13			17 45
Edge Hill 90 d							15 47									16 47								17 50
Liverpool Lime Street 10 90 a	15 10	15 15	15 24	15 31	15 43	15 49	15 53	15 58		16 10	16 15	16 25	16 31	16 45	16 49	16 54	16 58	17 10		17 15	17 25	17 31	17 43	17 58

A From Manchester Oxford Road
B from 20 June until 9 September
C until 17 June, from 12 September
D From Warrington Central
E From Nottingham
F From Hull
G From Birmingham International
H From Walsall
I From Newcastle
J To Blackpool North
K From Scarborough
L From Norwich

Table 91

Crewe and Runcorn - Liverpool

		TP	LM	VT	NT		EM	LM	NT	TP	LM	VT	NT	EM	LM		VT	TP	LM	VT	NT FO	NT FX	EM	VT	NT
		◇1	1	◇1			◇	1		◇1	◇1	◇1		◇	1		◇1	◇1	1	◇1			◇	◇1	
		A			B		C		B	A			B	C				A			D	D	C		B
		(trolley)		(buffet)						(trolley)		⊠					⊠	(trolley)		⊠				⊠	
London Euston ⊖65	d			16 07								17 07					17 33			18 07				18 33	
Birmingham New Street 12 65	d		16 36					17 01			17 36				18 01				18 36						
Crewe 10 65	d		17 31					18 01			18 31	18 44			19 02		19 16		19 31	19 44				20 17	
Winsford	d							18 09							19 10				19 42						
Hartford	d							18 14			18 44								19 47						
Acton Bridge	d										18 48														
Runcorn	a		17 50	17 55				18 23			18 56	19 02			19 22		19 33		19 57	20 01				20 34	
	d		17 50	17 55				18 24			18 57	19 02			19 23		19 33		19 57	20 01				20 34	
Liverpool South Parkway 7 ✈	a		17 59					18 32			19 05				19 31				20 06						
	d	17 47	17 59		18 14		18 22	18 33	18 38	18 47	19 06		19 13	19 18	19 32			19 47	20 06		20 12	20 13	20 16		20 38
West Allerton	d				18 18				18 41				19 16								20 16	20 16			20 41
Mossley Hill	d				18 20				18 44				19 18								20 18	20 18			20 44
Edge Hill 90	d				18 30				18 49				19 26								20 24	20 24			
Liverpool Lime Street 10 90	a	18 00	18 10	18 15	18 38		18 35	18 44	18 57	18 59	19 17	19 22	19 35	19 35	19 44		19 51	19 59	20 18	20 19	20 30	20 30	20 35	20 53	20 56

			TP	LM	VT	NT	EM	TP	LM	VT	NT		TP	LM	LM	VT	VT	NT
			◇1	1	1		◇	◇1	1	◇1			◇1	1	1	◇1	◇1	
			A			D	C	A			D		A	E	F	E	F	D
					(buffet)					(buffet)						(buffet)	(buffet)	
London Euston ⊖65	d				19 07					20 07						21 07	21 07	
Birmingham New Street 12 65	d			19 36					20 36					21 36	21 36			
Crewe 10 65	d			20 31					21 31					22 31	22 31	22 48	22 48	
Winsford	d			20 40					21 39					22 39	22 44			
Hartford	d			20 45					21 44					22 44	22 49			
Acton Bridge	d													22 48	22 54			
Runcorn	a			20 56	21 01				21 54	21 59				22 56	23 01	23 05	23 10	
	d			20 56	21 01				21 54	21 59				22 57	23 01	23 05	23 10	
Liverpool South Parkway 7 ✈	a			21 05					22 05					23 07	23 12			
	d		20 47	21 05		21 12	21 20	21 47	22 05		22 12		22 47	23 08	23 12			23 22
West Allerton	d					21 15					22 15							23 25
Mossley Hill	d					21 18					22 18							23 27
Edge Hill 90	d					21 23					22 23							23 32
Liverpool Lime Street 10 90	a		20 59	21 16	21 21	21 30	21 35	21 58	22 15	22 20	22 30		23 00	23 23	23 26	23 24	23 29	23 39

Saturdays

until 18 June

		NT	LM	NT	LM	NT	LM	NT	LM	NT		LM	EM	LM	NT	TP	LM	VT	NT	EM		LM	NT	TP	LM
			1		1		◇1		◇1			◇1	◇	◇1		◇1	◇1	◇1		◇		◇1		◇1	◇1
		B		D		D		B		D			G		B	H			B	G			B	I	
																(trolley)		(buffet)						(trolley)	
London Euston ⊖65	d																	07 07							
Birmingham New Street 12 65	d								06 01			06 36		07 01			07 36					08 01			08 36
Crewe 10 65	d		05 48		06 12		06 32		06 57			07 35		08 00			08 31	08 43				08 58			09 31
Winsford	d						06 41		07 05			07 44		08 07								09 07			
Hartford	d						06 46		07 10			07 49		08 12								09 12			
Acton Bridge	d						06 51					07 53		08 16											
Runcorn	a		06 07		06 31		06 59		07 20			08 02		08 24			08 50	09 00				09 21			09 50
	d		06 08		06 31		06 59		07 21			08 03		08 25			08 50	09 00				09 22			09 50
Liverpool South Parkway 7 ✈	a		06 15		06 39		07 08		07 30			08 11		08 33			08 59					09 30			09 59
	d	00 27	06 15	06 27	06 39	07 01	07 08	07 22	07 30	08 03		08 12	08 18	08 34	08 37	08 47	08 59		09 06	09 15		09 31	09 36	09 47	09 59
West Allerton	d			06 31		07 05		07 25		08 06					08 40				09 09				09 39		
Mossley Hill	d			06 33		07 07		07 28		08 09					08 43				09 12				09 41		
Edge Hill 90	d			06 39		07 13		07 34		08 14					08 48								09 47		
Liverpool Lime Street 10 90	a	00 41	06 26	06 45	06 53	07 20	07 22	07 40	07 42	08 21		08 24	08 31	08 46	08 55	08 58	09 12	09 21	09 24	09 31		09 43	09 53	09 58	10 10

		VT	NT	EM	LM	NT		NT	TP	LM	VT	NT	EM	LM	NT	NT		TP	LM	VT	NT	EM	LM	NT	NT
		◇1		◇	◇1				◇1	◇1	◇1		◇	◇1				◇1	◇1	◇1		◇	◇1		
			B	G		J		B	A			B	C		J	B		A			B	C		J	B
		(buffet)							(trolley)		(buffet)									(buffet)					
London Euston ⊖65	d	08 07									09 07									10 07					
Birmingham New Street 12 65	d				09 01					09 36				10 01					10 36				11 01		
Crewe 10 65	d				09 57					10 31				10 57					11 31				11 57		
Winsford	d													11 06											
Hartford	d				10 10									11 11									12 10		
Acton Bridge	d				10 14																		12 14		
Runcorn	a	09 55			10 22					10 50	10 55			11 21					11 50	11 55			12 22		
	d	09 55			10 23					10 50	10 55			11 22					11 50	11 55			12 23		
Liverpool South Parkway 7 ✈	a				10 31					10 59				11 30					11 59				12 31		
	d		10 06	10 15	10 32	10 36		10 36	10 47	10 59		11 06	11 15	11 31	11 36	11 36		11 47	11 59		12 06	12 15	12 32	12 36	12 36
West Allerton	d		10 10					10 39				11 10				11 39					12 10				12 39
Mossley Hill	d		10 12					10 41				11 13				11 41					12 13				12 41
Edge Hill 90	d							10 47								11 47									12 47
Liverpool Lime Street 10 90	a	10 15	10 23	10 31	10 44	10 49		10 53	10 58	11 10	11 15	11 24	11 31	11 43	11 49	11 53		11 58	12 10	12 15	12 24	12 31	12 44	12 49	12 53

A From Scarborough
B From Manchester Oxford Road
C From Norwich
D From Warrington Central
E until 17 June, from 12 September
F from 20 June until 9 September
G From Nottingham
H From Hull
I From Newcastle
J To Blackpool North

Table 91

Saturdays

until 18 June

Crewe and Runcorn - Liverpool

	TP		LM	VT	NT	EM	LM	NT	NT	TP	LM		VT	NT	EM	LM	NT	NT	TP	LM	VT		NT	EM
	◇1		◇1	◇1		◇	◇1			◇1	◇1		◇1		◇	◇1			◇1	◇1	◇1			◇
	A				B	C		D	B	A				B	C		D	B	A				B	C
	🛒			☕						🛒			☕								☕			
London Euston ⊖65 d				11 07									12 07								13 07			
Birmingham New Street 12 65 d			11 36				12 01				12 36					13 01				13 36				
Crewe 10 65 d			12 31				12 57				13 31					13 57				14 31				
Winsford d							13 06									14 06								
Hartford d							13 11									14 11								
Acton Bridge d																								
Runcorn a			12 50	12 55			13 21				13 50		13 55			14 21				14 50	14 55			
d			12 50	12 55			13 22				13 50		13 55			14 22				14 50	14 55			
Liverpool South Parkway 7 ✈ a			12 59				13 30				13 59					14 30				14 59				
d	12 47		12 59		13 06	13 15	13 31	13 36	13 36	13 47	13 59			14 06	14 15	14 31	14 36	14 36	14 47	14 59			15 06	15 15
West Allerton d					13 10				13 39					14 10				14 39					15 10	
Mossley Hill d					13 13				13 41					14 13				14 41					15 13	
Edge Hill 90 d									13 47									14 47						
Liverpool Lime Street 10 90 a	12 58		13 10	13 15	13 24	13 31	13 43	13 49	13 53	13 58	14 10		14 15	14 24	14 31	14 43	14 49	14 53	14 58	15 10	15 15		15 24	15 31

	LM	NT	NT	TP	LM	VT	NT		EM	LM	NT	NT	TP	LM	VT	NT	EM		LM	NT	TP	LM	VT	NT
	◇1			◇1	◇1	◇1			◇	◇1			◇1	◇1	◇1		◇		◇1		◇1	◇1	◇1	
		D	B	A			B		C		D	B	A			B	C			B	A			B
				🛒		☕							🛒		☕						🛒		☕	
London Euston ⊖65 d						14 07									15 07								16 07	
Birmingham New Street 12 65 d	14 01				14 36					15 01				15 36					16 01			16 36		
Crewe 10 65 d	14 57				15 31					15 57				16 31					16 57			17 31		
Winsford d	15 06																		17 06					
Hartford d	15 11									16 11									17 11					
Acton Bridge d										16 15														
Runcorn a	15 21				15 50	15 55				16 23				16 50	16 55				17 21			17 50	17 55	
d	15 22				15 50	15 55				16 24				16 50	16 55				17 22			17 50	17 55	
Liverpool South Parkway 7 ✈ a	15 30				15 59					16 32				16 59					17 30			17 59		
d	15 31	15 36	15 36	15 47	15 59		16 07		16 15	16 33	16 36	16 36	16 47	16 59		17 07	17 15		17 31	17 39	17 47	17 59		18 14
West Allerton d			15 39				16 11					16 39				17 11				17 42				18 18
Mossley Hill d			15 41				16 13					16 41				17 13				17 45				18 20
Edge Hill 90 d			15 47									16 47								17 50				18 30
Liverpool Lime Street 10 90 a	15 43	15 49	15 53	15 58	16 10	16 15	16 25		16 31	16 44	16 49	16 54	16 58	17 10	17 15	17 25	17 31		17 43	17 58	18 00	18 10	18 15	18 38

	EM	LM	VT		NT	TP	LM	VT	NT	EM	LM	TP	VT		NT	EM	LM	VT	NT	TP	VT	NT	EM	
	◇	◇1	◇1			◇1	◇1	◇1		◇	◇1	◇1	◇1			◇	◇1	◇1		◇1	◇1		◇	
	C				B	A			B	C		A			E	C			B	A		E	C	
			☕			🛒		☕					☕					☕			☕			
London Euston ⊖65 d			16 33					17 07					18 07					18 33			19 07			
Birmingham New Street 12 65 d		17 01					17 36				18 01						19 01							
Crewe 10 65 d		18 00					18 33				18 59						19 58				20 47			
Winsford d		18 08									19 08						20 07							
Hartford d		18 13					18 44				19 13						20 12							
Acton Bridge d																	20 16							
Runcorn a		18 23	18 31				18 52	18 59			19 22		19 55				20 24	20 32			21 05			
d		18 23	18 31				18 53	18 59			19 23		19 55				20 25	20 32			21 05			
Liverpool South Parkway 7 ✈ a		18 32					19 02				19 31						20 33							
d	18 22	18 32			18 38	18 47	19 02		19 11	19 18	19 32	19 47			19 59	20 15	20 34		20 38	20 47		21 15	21 20	
West Allerton d					18 41				19 15						20 03				20 41			21 19		
Mossley Hill d					18 44				19 18						20 05				20 44			21 21		
Edge Hill 90 d					18 50				19 26						20 11							21 27		
Liverpool Lime Street 10 90 a	18 35	18 44	18 51		18 57	18 59	19 14	19 17	19 35	19 35	19 44	19 59	20 15		20 18	20 30	20 46	20 52	20 55	20 59	21 25	21 34	21 35	

	LM	TP	NT	VT	TP	NT
	◇1	◇1		◇1	◇1	
		A	E		A	E
				☕		
London Euston ⊖65 d				20 11		
Birmingham New Street 12 65 d	20 01					
Crewe 10 65 d	21 05			22 06		
Winsford d	21 14					
Hartford d	21 19					
Acton Bridge d						
Runcorn a	21 29			22 24		
d	21 29			22 24		
Liverpool South Parkway 7 ✈ a	21 38					
d	21 38	21 47	22 12		22 47	23 12
West Allerton d			22 15			23 15
Mossley Hill d			22 18			23 18
Edge Hill 90 d			22 23			23 23
Liverpool Lime Street 10 90 a	21 50	21 58	22 30	22 46	23 00	23 30

A From Scarborough
B From Manchester Oxford Road
C From Norwich
D To Blackpool North
E From Warrington Central

Table 91

Saturdays

25 June to 10 September

Crewe and Runcorn - Liverpool

	NT	LM	NT	LM	NT	LM	NT	LM	NT		LM	EM	LM	NT	TP	LM	VT	NT	EM		LM	NT	TP	LM
		1		1		◇1		◇1			◇1	◇	◇1		◇1	◇1	◇1		◇		◇1		◇1	◇1
	A		B		B		A		B			C		A	D			A	C			A	E	
															🛒		🍴						🛒	
London Euston ⊖65 d																	07 07							
Birmingham New Street 12 65 d								06 01			06 36		07 01			07 36					08 01			08 36
Crewe 10 65 d		05 48		06 12		06 32		06 57			07 35		08 00			08 31	08 43				08 58			09 31
Winsford d						06 41		07 05			07 44		08 07								09 07			
Hartford d						06 46		07 10			07 49		08 12								09 12			
Acton Bridge d						06 51					07 53		08 16											
Runcorn a		06 07		06 31		06 59		07 20			08 02		08 24			08 50	09 00				09 21			09 50
d		06 08		06 31		06 59		07 21			08 03		08 25			08 50	09 00				09 22			09 50
Liverpool South Parkway 7 ✈ a		06 15		06 39		07 08		07 30			08 11		08 33			08 59					09 30			09 59
d	00 27	06 15	06 27	06 39	07 01	07 08	07 22	07 30	08 03		08 12	08 18	08 34	08 37	08 47	08 59		09 06	09 15		09 31	09 36	09 47	09 59
West Allerton d			06 31		07 05		07 25		08 06					08 40				09 09				09 39		
Mossley Hill d			06 33		07 07		07 28		08 09					08 43				09 12				09 41		
Edge Hill 90 d			06 39		07 13		07 34		08 14					08 48								09 47		
Liverpool Lime Street 10 90 a	00 41	06 26	06 45	06 53	07 20	07 22	07 40	07 42	08 21		08 24	08 31	08 46	08 55	08 58	09 12	09 21	09 24	09 31		09 43	09 53	09 58	10 10

	VT	NT	EM	LM	NT		NT	TP	LM	VT	NT	EM	LM	NT	NT		TP	LM	VT	NT	EM	LM	NT	NT
	◇1		◇	◇1				◇1	◇1	◇1		◇	◇1				◇1	◇1	◇1		◇	◇1		
		A	C		F		A	G			A	H		F	A		G			A	H		F	A
	🍴							🛒		🍴									🍴					
London Euston ⊖65 d	08 07									09 07									10 07					
Birmingham New Street 12 65 d				09 01					09 36				10 01					10 36				11 01		
Crewe 10 65 d				09 57					10 31				10 57					11 31				11 57		
Winsford d													11 06											
Hartford d				10 10									11 11									12 10		
Acton Bridge d				10 14																		12 14		
Runcorn a	09 55			10 22					10 50	10 55			11 21					11 50	11 55			12 22		
d	09 55			10 23					10 50	10 55			11 22					11 50	11 55			12 23		
Liverpool South Parkway 7 ✈ a				10 31					10 59				11 30					11 59				12 31		
d		10 06	10 15	10 32	10 36		10 36	10 47	10 59		11 06	11 15	11 31	11 36	11 36		11 47	11 59		12 06	12 15	12 32	12 36	12 36
West Allerton d		10 10					10 39				11 10				11 39					12 10				12 39
Mossley Hill d		10 12					10 41				11 13				11 41					12 13				12 41
Edge Hill 90 d							10 47								11 47									12 47
Liverpool Lime Street 10 90 a	10 15	10 23	10 31	10 44	10 49		10 53	10 58	11 10	11 15	11 24	11 31	11 43	11 49	11 53		11 58	12 10	12 15	12 24	12 31	12 44	12 49	12 53

	TP		LM	VT	NT	EM	LM	NT	NT	TP	LM		VT	NT	EM	LM	NT	NT	TP	LM	VT		NT	EM
	◇1		◇1	◇1		◇	◇1			◇1	◇1		◇1		◇	◇1			◇1	◇1	◇1			◇
	G				A	H		F	A	G				A	H		F	A	G				A	H
	🛒			🍴						🛒			🍴								🍴			
London Euston ⊖65 d				11 07									12 07								13 07			
Birmingham New Street 12 65 d			11 36				12 01				12 36					13 01				13 36				
Crewe 10 65 d			12 31				12 57				13 31					13 57				14 31				
Winsford d							13 06									14 06								
Hartford d							13 11									14 11								
Acton Bridge d																								
Runcorn a			12 50	12 55			13 21				13 50		13 55			14 21				14 50	14 55			
d			12 50	12 55			13 22				13 50		13 55			14 22				14 50	14 55			
Liverpool South Parkway 7 ✈ a			12 59				13 30				13 59					14 30				14 59				
d	12 47		12 59		13 06	13 15	13 31	13 36	13 36	13 47	13 59			14 06	14 15	14 31	14 36	14 36	14 47	14 59			15 06	15 15
West Allerton d					13 10				13 39					14 10				14 39					15 10	
Mossley Hill d					13 13				13 41					14 13				14 41					15 13	
Edge Hill 90 d									13 47									14 47						
Liverpool Lime Street 10 90 a	12 58		13 10	13 15	13 24	13 31	13 43	13 49	13 53	13 58	14 10		14 15	14 24	14 31	14 43	14 49	14 53	14 58	15 10	15 15		15 24	15 31

	LM	NT	NT	TP	LM	VT	NT		EM	LM	NT	NT	TP	LM	VT	NT	EM		LM	NT	TP	LM	VT	NT
	◇1			◇1	◇1	◇1			◇	◇1			◇1	◇1	◇1		◇		◇1		◇1	◇1	◇1	
		F	A	G			A		H		F	A	G			A	H			A	G			A
				🛒		🍴							🛒		🍴						🛒		🍴	
London Euston ⊖65 d						14 07									15 07								16 07	
Birmingham New Street 12 65 d	14 01				14 36					15 01				15 36					16 01			16 36		
Crewe 10 65 d	14 57				15 31					15 57				16 31					16 57			17 31		
Winsford d	15 06																		17 06					
Hartford d	15 11									16 11									17 11					
Acton Bridge d										16 15														
Runcorn a	15 21				15 50	15 55				16 23				16 50	16 55				17 21			17 50	17 55	
d	15 22				15 50	15 55				16 24				16 50	16 55				17 22			17 50	17 55	
Liverpool South Parkway 7 ✈ a	15 30				15 59					16 32				16 59					17 30			17 59		
d	15 31	15 36	15 36	15 47	15 59		16 07		16 15	16 33	16 36	16 36	16 47	16 59		17 07	17 15		17 31	17 39	17 47	17 59		18 14
West Allerton d			15 39				16 11					16 39				17 11				17 42				18 18
Mossley Hill d			15 41				16 13					16 41				17 13				17 45				18 20
Edge Hill 90 d			15 47									16 47								17 50				18 30
Liverpool Lime Street 10 90 a	15 43	15 49	15 53	15 58	16 10	16 15	16 25		16 31	16 44	16 49	16 54	16 58	17 10	17 15	17 25	17 31		17 43	17 58	18 00	18 10	18 15	18 38

A From Manchester Oxford Road
B From Warrington Central
C From Nottingham
D From Hull
E From Newcastle
F To Blackpool North
G From Scarborough
H From Norwich

Table 91

Crewe and Runcorn - Liverpool

Saturdays

25 June to 10 September

		EM	LM	VT	NT	TP	LM	VT	NT	EM	LM	TP	VT	NT	EM	LM	VT	NT	TP	VT	NT	EM
		◇	◇1	◇1		◇1	◇1	◇1		◇	◇1	◇1	◇1		◇	◇1	◇1		◇1	◇1		◇
		A			B	C			B	A		C		D	A			B	C		D	A
				☕		🛒		☕					☕				☕			☕		
London Euston ⊖65	d			16 33				17 07					18 07				18 33			19 07		
Birmingham New Street 12 65	d		17 01				17 36				18 01					19 01						
Crewe 10 65	d		18 00				18 33				18 59					19 58				20 47		
Winsford	d		18 08								19 08					20 07						
Hartford	d		18 13				18 44				19 13					20 12						
Acton Bridge	d															20 16						
Runcorn	a		18 23	18 31			18 52	18 59			19 22		19 55			20 24	20 32			21 05		
	d		18 23	18 31			18 53	18 59			19 23		19 55			20 25	20 32			21 05		
Liverpool South Parkway 7 ✈	a		18 32				19 02				19 31					20 33						
	d	18 22	18 32		18 38	18 47	19 02		19 11	19 18	19 32	19 47		19 59	20 15	20 34		20 38	20 47		21 15	21 20
West Allerton	d				18 41				19 15					20 03				20 41			21 19	
Mossley Hill	d				18 44				19 18					20 05				20 44			21 21	
Edge Hill 90	d				18 50				19 26					20 11							21 27	
Liverpool Lime Street 10 90	a	18 35	18 44	18 51	18 57	18 59	19 14	19 17	19 35	19 35	19 44	19 59	20 15	20 18	20 30	20 46	20 52	20 55	20 59	21 25	21 34	21 35

		LM	TP	NT	VT	TP	NT
		◇1	◇1		◇1	◇1	
			C	D		C	D
					☕		
London Euston ⊖65	d				20 11		
Birmingham New Street 12 65	d	20 01					
Crewe 10 65	d	2105			22 06		
Winsford	d	21 14					
Hartford	d	21 19					
Acton Bridge	d						
Runcorn	a	21 29			22 24		
	d	21 29			22 24		
Liverpool South Parkway 7 ✈	a	21 38					
	d	21 38	21 47	22 12		22 47	23 12
West Allerton	d			22 15			23 15
Mossley Hill	d			22 18			23 18
Edge Hill 90	d			22 23			23 23
Liverpool Lime Street 10 90	a	21 50	21 58	22 30	22 46	23 00	23 30

Saturdays

from 17 September

		NT	LM	NT	LM	NT	LM	NT	LM	NT	LM	EM	LM	NT	TP	LM	VT	NT	EM	LM	NT	TP	LM
			1		1		◇1		◇1		◇1	◇	◇1		◇1	◇1	◇1		◇	◇1		◇1	◇1
		B		D		D		B		D		E		B	F			B	E		B	G	
															🛒		☕					🛒	
London Euston ⊖65	d																07 07						
Birmingham New Street 12 65	d								06 01		06 36		07 01			07 36				08 01			08 36
Crewe 10 65	d		05 48		06 12		06 32		06 57		07 35		08 00			08 31	08 43			08 58			09 31
Winsford	d						06 41		07 05		07 44		08 07							09 07			
Hartford	d						06 46		07 10		07 49		08 12							09 12			
Acton Bridge	d						06 51				07 53		08 16										
Runcorn	a		06 07		06 31		06 59		07 20		08 02		08 24			08 50	09 00			09 21			09 50
	d		06 08		06 31		06 59		07 21		08 03		08 25			08 50	09 00			09 22			09 50
Liverpool South Parkway 7 ✈	a		06 15		06 39		07 08		07 30		08 11		08 33			08 59				09 30			09 59
	d	00 27	06 15	06 27	06 39	07 01	07 08	07 22	07 30	08 03	08 12	08 18	08 34	08 37	08 47	08 59		09 06	09 15	09 31	09 36	09 47	09 59
West Allerton	d			06 31		07 05		07 25		08 06				08 40				09 09			09 39		
Mossley Hill	d			06 33		07 07		07 28		08 09				08 43				09 12			09 41		
Edge Hill 90	d			06 39		07 13		07 34		08 14				08 48							09 47		
Liverpool Lime Street 10 90	a	00 41	06 26	06 45	06 53	07 20	07 22	07 40	07 42	08 21	08 24	08 31	08 46	08 55	08 58	09 12	09 21	09 24	09 31	09 43	09 53	09 58	10 10

		VT	NT	EM	LM	NT	NT	TP	LM	VT	NT	EM	LM	NT	NT	TP	LM	VT	NT	EM	LM	NT	NT
		◇1		◇	◇1			◇1	◇1	◇1		◇	◇1			◇1	◇1	◇1		◇	◇1		
			B	E		H	B	C			B	A		H	B	C			B	A		H	B
		☕						🛒		☕								☕					
London Euston ⊖65	d	08 07								09 07								10 07					
Birmingham New Street 12 65	d				09 01				09 36				10 01				10 36				11 01		
Crewe 10 65	d				09 57				10 31				10 57				11 31				11 57		
Winsford	d												11 06										
Hartford	d				10 10								11 11								12 10		
Acton Bridge	d				10 14																12 14		
Runcorn	a	09 55			10 22				10 50	10 55			11 21				11 50	11 55			12 22		
	d	09 55			10 23				10 50	10 55			11 22				11 50	11 55			12 23		
Liverpool South Parkway 7 ✈	a				10 31				10 59				11 30				11 59				12 31		
	d		10 06	10 15	10 32	10 36	10 36	10 47	10 59		11 06	11 15	11 31	11 36	11 36	11 47	11 59		12 06	12 15	12 32	12 36	12 36
West Allerton	d		10 10				10 39				11 10				11 39				12 10				12 39
Mossley Hill	d		10 12				10 41				11 13				11 41				12 13				12 41
Edge Hill 90	d						10 47								11 47								12 47
Liverpool Lime Street 10 90	a	10 15	10 23	10 31	10 44	10 49	10 53	10 58	11 10	11 15	11 24	11 31	11 43	11 49	11 53	11 58	12 10	12 15	12 24	12 31	12 44	12 49	12 53

A From Norwich
B From Manchester Oxford Road
C From Scarborough
D From Warrington Central
E From Nottingham
F From Hull
G From Newcastle
H To Blackpool North

Table 91

Saturdays
from 17 September

Crewe and Runcorn - Liverpool

	TP		LM	VT	NT	EM	LM	NT	NT	TP	LM		VT	NT	EM	LM	NT	NT	TP	LM	VT		NT	EM
	◇1		◇1	◇1		◇	◇1			◇1	◇1		◇1		◇	◇1			◇1	◇1	◇1			◇
	A				B	C		D	B	A				B	C		D	B	A				B	C
	🛒			☕						🛒			☕								☕			
London Euston ⊖65 d				11 07									12 07								13 07			
Birmingham New Street 12 65 d			11 36				12 01				12 36					13 01				13 36				
Crewe 10 65 d			12 31				12 57				13 31					13 57				14 31				
Winsford d							13 06									14 06								
Hartford d							13 11									14 11								
Acton Bridge d																								
Runcorn a			12 50	12 55			13 21				13 50		13 55			14 21				14 50	14 55			
d			12 50	12 55			13 22				13 50		13 55			14 22				14 50	14 55			
Liverpool South Parkway 7 ✈ a			12 59				13 30				13 59					14 30				14 59				
d	12 47		12 59		13 06	13 15	13 31	13 36	13 36	13 47	13 59			14 06	14 15	14 31	14 36	14 36	14 47	14 59			15 06	15 15
West Allerton d					13 10				13 39					14 10				14 39					15 10	
Mossley Hill d					13 13				13 41					14 13				14 41					15 13	
Edge Hill 90 d									13 47									14 47						
Liverpool Lime Street 10 90 a	12 58		13 10	13 15	13 24	13 31	13 43	13 49	13 53	13 58	14 10		14 15	14 24	14 31	14 43	14 49	14 53	14 58	15 10	15 15		15 24	15 31

	LM	NT	NT	TP	LM	VT	NT		EM	LM	NT	NT	TP	LM	VT	NT	EM		LM	NT	TP	LM	VT	NT
	◇1			◇1	◇1	◇1			◇	◇1			◇1	◇1	◇1		◇		◇1		◇1	◇1	◇1	
		D	B	A			B		C		D	B	A			B	C			B	A			B
				🛒		☕							🛒		☕						🛒		☕	
London Euston ⊖65 d						14 07									15 07								16 07	
Birmingham New Street 12 65 d	14 01				14 36					15 01				15 36					16 01			16 36		
Crewe 10 65 d	14 57				15 31					15 57				16 31					16 57			17 31		
Winsford d	15 06																		17 06					
Hartford d	15 11									16 11									17 11					
Acton Bridge d										16 15														
Runcorn a	15 21				15 50	15 55				16 23				16 50	16 55				17 21			17 50	17 55	
d	15 22				15 50	15 55				16 24				16 50	16 55				17 22			17 50	17 55	
Liverpool South Parkway 7 ✈ a	15 30				15 59					16 32				16 59					17 30			17 59		
d	15 31	15 36	15 36	15 47	15 59		16 07		16 15	16 33	16 36	16 36	16 47	16 59		17 07	17 15		17 31	17 39	17 47	17 59		18 14
West Allerton d			15 39				16 11					16 39				17 11				17 42				18 18
Mossley Hill d			15 41				16 13					16 41				17 13				17 45				18 20
Edge Hill 90 d			15 47									16 47								17 50				18 30
Liverpool Lime Street 10 90 a	15 43	15 49	15 53	15 58	16 10	16 15	16 25		16 31	16 44	16 49	16 54	16 58	17 10	17 15	17 25	17 31		17 43	17 58	18 00	18 10	18 15	18 38

	EM	LM	VT		NT	TP	LM	VT	NT	EM	LM	TP	VT		NT	EM	LM	VT	NT	TP	VT	NT	EM	
	◇	◇1	◇1			◇1	◇1	◇1		◇	◇1	◇1	◇1			◇	◇1	◇1		◇1	◇1		◇	
	C				B	A			B	C		A			E	C			B	A		E	C	
			☕			🛒		☕					☕					☕			☕			
London Euston ⊖65 d			16 33					17 07					18 07					18 33			19 07			
Birmingham New Street 12 65 d		17 01					17 36				18 01						19 01							
Crewe 10 65 d		18 00					18 33				18 59						19 58				20 47			
Winsford d		18 08									19 08						20 07							
Hartford d		18 13					18 44				19 13						20 12							
Acton Bridge d																	20 16							
Runcorn a		18 23	18 31				18 52	18 59			19 22		19 55				20 24	20 32			21 05			
d		18 23	18 31				18 53	18 59			19 23		19 55				20 25	20 32			21 05			
Liverpool South Parkway 7 ✈ a		18 32					19 02				19 31						20 33							
d	18 22	18 32			18 38	18 47	19 02		19 11	19 18	19 32	19 47			19 59	20 15	20 34		20 38	20 47		21 15	21 20	
West Allerton d					18 41				19 15						20 03				20 41			21 19		
Mossley Hill d					18 44				19 18						20 05				20 44			21 21		
Edge Hill 90 d					18 50				19 26						20 11							21 27		
Liverpool Lime Street 10 90 a	18 35	18 44	18 51		18 57	18 59	19 14	19 17	19 35	19 35	19 44	19 59	20 15		20 18	20 30	20 46	20 52	20 55	20 59	21 25	21 34	21 35	

	LM	TP	NT	VT	TP	NT
	◇1	◇1		◇1	◇1	
		A	E		A	E
				☕		
London Euston ⊖65 d				20 11		
Birmingham New Street 12 65 d	20 01					
Crewe 10 65 d	21 05			22 06		
Winsford d	21 14					
Hartford d	21 19					
Acton Bridge d						
Runcorn a	21 29			22 24		
d	21 29			22 24		
Liverpool South Parkway 7 ✈ a	21 38					
d	21 38	21 47	22 12		22 47	23 12
West Allerton d			22 15			23 15
Mossley Hill d			22 18			23 18
Edge Hill 90 d			22 23			23 23
Liverpool Lime Street 10 90 a	21 50	21 58	22 30	22 46	23 00	23 30

A From Scarborough
B From Manchester Oxford Road
C From Norwich
D To Blackpool North
E From Warrington Central

Table 91

Sundays
until 11 September

Crewe and Runcorn - Liverpool

	NT	NT	TP	NT	NT	TP	VT	LM	NT		TP	VT	LM	EM	NT	TP	VT	LM	EM		NT	VT	TP	LM
			◇1			◇1	◇1	◇1			◇1	◇1	◇1	◇		◇1	◇1	◇1	◇			◇1	◇1	◇1
	A	B	C	B	B	D			B		C			E	B	F			E		B		G	
							☕					☕					☕					☕		
London Euston ⊖65 d							08 15					09 15					10 15					11 15		
Birmingham New Street 12 65 d								09 42					10 42					11 42						12 35
Crewe 10 65 d							10 30	10 38				11 32	11 38				12 35	12 38				13 15		13 31
Winsford d								10 45					11 45					12 45						13 38
Hartford d								10 50					11 50					12 50						13 43
Acton Bridge d																								
Runcorn a							10 47	11 00				11 49	12 01				12 52	13 01				13 32		13 54
d							10 47	11 00				11 49	12 01				12 52	13 01				13 32		13 54
Liverpool South Parkway 7 ✈ a								11 09					12 10					13 10						14 03
d	00 20	08 54	09 47	10 03	10 33	10 47		11 09	11 33		11 47		12 10	12 17	12 33	12 47		13 10	13 17		13 33		13 47	14 03
West Allerton d		08 57		10 06	10 36				11 36						12 36						13 36			
Mossley Hill d		09 00		10 09	10 39				11 39						12 39						13 39			
Edge Hill 90 d																								
Liverpool Lime Street 10 90 a	00 34	09 11	10 00	10 20	10 50	10 59	11 09	11 20	11 50		11 59	12 10	12 21	12 30	12 50	12 58	13 14	13 21	13 30		13 50	13 54	13 58	14 14

	VT	EM	NT	TP	LM		VT	EM	NT	TP	LM	VT	EM	NT	TP		LM	VT	EM	NT	TP	LM	VT	EM
	◇1	◇		◇1	◇1		◇1	◇		◇1	◇1	◇1	◇		◇1		◇1	◇1	◇		◇1	◇1	◇1	◇
		E	B	G				H	B	I			H	B	G				E	B	I			E
	☕						☕					☕						☕					☕	
London Euston ⊖65 d	12 02						13 02					14 02						15 02					16 02	
Birmingham New Street 12 65 d					13 35						14 35						15 35					16 35		
Crewe 10 65 d	13 45				14 31		14 45				15 31	15 45					16 31					17 31		
Winsford d					14 38						15 38						16 38					17 38		
Hartford d					14 43						15 43						16 43					17 43		
Acton Bridge d																								
Runcorn a	14 02				14 54		15 02				15 54	16 02					16 54	16 57				17 54	17 57	
d	14 02				14 54		15 02				15 54	16 02					16 54	16 57				17 54	17 57	
Liverpool South Parkway 7 ✈ a					15 03						16 03						17 03					18 03		
d		14 16	14 33	14 47	15 03			15 16	15 33	15 47	16 03		16 16	16 33	16 47		17 03		17 16	17 33	17 47	18 03		18 16
West Allerton d			14 36						15 36					16 36						17 36				
Mossley Hill d			14 39						15 39					16 39						17 39				
Edge Hill 90 d																								
Liverpool Lime Street 10 90 a	14 24	14 30	14 50	14 58	15 14		15 24	15 30	15 50	15 58	16 14	16 24	16 30	16 50	16 58		17 14	17 16	17 30	17 50	17 58	18 14	18 16	18 30

	NT		TP	LM	VT	EM	NT	TP	LM	VT	EM		NT	TP	LM	VT	NT	TP	VT	VT	NT	TP	NT	VT
			◇1	◇1	◇1	◇		◇1	◇1	◇1	◇			◇1	◇1	◇1		◇1	◇1	◇1		◇1		◇1
	B		G			H	B	I			H		B	G			B	I			B	G	B	
					☕					☕						☕			☕	☕				☕
London Euston ⊖65 d					17 02					18 02						19 02			20 02	20 05				21 21
Birmingham New Street 12 65 d				17 35					18 35						19 35									
Crewe 10 65 d				18 31					19 31						20 31	20 50			21 46	21 55				23 39
Winsford d				18 38					19 38						20 38									
Hartford d				18 43					19 43						20 43									
Acton Bridge d																								
Runcorn a				18 54	18 57				19 54	19 58					20 54	21 07			22 03	22 12				23 56
d				18 54	18 57				19 54	19 58					20 54	21 07			22 03	22 12				23 56
Liverpool South Parkway 7 ✈ a				19 03					20 03						21 03									
d	18 33		18 47	19 03		19 17	19 33	19 47	20 03		20 16		20 33	20 47	21 03		21 33	21 47			22 33	22 47	23 33	
West Allerton d	18 36						19 36						20 36				21 36				22 36		23 36	
Mossley Hill d	18 39						19 39						20 39				21 39				22 39		23 39	
Edge Hill 90 d																								
Liverpool Lime Street 10 90 a	18 50		18 58	19 14	19 19	19 30	19 50	19 58	20 14	20 16	20 30		20 50	20 58	21 14	21 28	21 50	21 58	22 23	22 33	22 50	23 00	23 50	00 23

A not 22 May. From Manchester Oxford Road
B From Manchester Oxford Road
C From Manchester Piccadilly
D From York
E From Nottingham
F From Newcastle
G From Scarborough
H From Norwich
I From Middlesbrough

Table 91

Sundays

18 September to 23 October

Crewe and Runcorn - Liverpool

	NT	NT	NT	NT	VT	LM	NT	VT	LM		EM	NT	VT	LM	EM	NT	VT	LM	VT		EM	NT	LM	VT
					◇1	◇1		◇1	◇1		◇		◇1	◇1	◇		◇1	◇1	◇1		◇		◇1	◇1
	A	A	A	A			A				B	A			B	A					B	A		
					☕			☕					☕				☕		☕					☕
London Euston ⊖65 d					08 15			09 15					10 15				11 15		12 02					13 02
Birmingham New Street 12 65 d						09 42			10 42					11 42				12 35					13 35	
Crewe 10 65 d					10 30	10 38		11 32	11 38				12 35	12 38			13 15	13 31	13 45				14 31	14 45
Winsford d						10 45			11 45					12 45				13 38					14 38	
Hartford d						10 50			11 50					12 50				13 43					14 43	
Acton Bridge d																								
Runcorn a					10 47	11 00		11 49	12 01				12 52	13 01			13 32	13 54	14 02				14 54	15 02
d					10 47	11 00		11 49	12 01				12 52	13 01			13 32	13 54	14 02				14 54	15 02
Liverpool South Parkway 7 ✈ a						11 09			12 10					13 10				14 03					15 03	
d	00 20	08 54	10 03	10 33		11 09	11 33		12 10		12 17	12 33		13 10	13 17	13 33		14 03			14 16	14 33	15 03	
West Allerton d		08 57	10 06	10 36			11 36					12 36				13 36						14 36		
Mossley Hill d		09 00	10 09	10 39			11 39					12 39				13 39						14 39		
Edge Hill 90 d																								
Liverpool Lime Street 10 90 a	00 34	09 11	10 20	10 50	11 09	11 20	11 50	12 10	12 21		12 30	12 50	13 14	13 21	13 30	13 50	13 54	14 14	14 24		14 30	14 50	15 14	15 24

	EM	NT	LM	VT	EM		NT	LM	VT	EM	NT	LM	VT	EM	NT		LM	VT	EM	NT	LM	VT	EM	NT
	◇		◇1	◇1	◇			◇1	◇1	◇		◇1	◇1	◇			◇1	◇1	◇		◇1	◇1	◇	
	B	A			C		A			B	A			B	A				C	A			C	A
				☕					☕				☕					☕				☕		
London Euston ⊖65 d				14 02					15 02				16 02					17 02				18 02		
Birmingham New Street 12 65 d			14 35					15 35				16 35					17 35				18 35			
Crewe 10 65 d			15 31	15 45				16 31				17 31					18 31				19 31			
Winsford d			15 38					16 38				17 38					18 38				19 38			
Hartford d			15 43					16 43				17 43					18 43				19 43			
Acton Bridge d																								
Runcorn a			15 54	16 02				16 54	16 57			17 54	17 57				18 54	18 57			19 54	19 58		
d			15 54	16 02				16 54	16 57			17 54	17 57				18 54	18 57			19 54	19 58		
Liverpool South Parkway 7 ✈ a			16 03					17 03				18 03					19 03				20 03			
d	15 16	15 33	16 03		16 16		16 33	17 03		17 16	17 33	18 03		18 16	18 33		19 03		19 17	19 33	20 03		20 16	20 33
West Allerton d		15 36					16 36				17 36				18 36					19 36				20 36
Mossley Hill d		15 39					16 39				17 39				18 39					19 39				20 39
Edge Hill 90 d																								
Liverpool Lime Street 10 90 a	15 30	15 50	16 14	16 24	16 30		16 50	17 14	17 16	17 30	17 50	18 14	18 16	18 30	18 50		19 14	19 19	19 30	19 50	20 14	20 16	20 30	20 50

	LM		VT	NT	VT	VT	NT	NT	VT
	◇1		◇1		◇1	◇1			◇1
				A			A	A	
			☕		☕	☕			☕
London Euston ⊖65 d			19 02		20 02	20 05			21 21
Birmingham New Street 12 65 d	19 35								
Crewe 10 65 d	20 31		20 50		21 46	21 55			23 39
Winsford d	20 38								
Hartford d	20 43								
Acton Bridge d									
Runcorn a	20 54		21 07		22 03	22 12			23 56
d	20 54		21 07		22 03	22 12			23 56
Liverpool South Parkway 7 ✈ a	21 03								
d	21 03			21 33			22 33	23 33	
West Allerton d				21 36			22 36	23 36	
Mossley Hill d				21 39			22 39	23 39	
Edge Hill 90 d									
Liverpool Lime Street 10 90 a	21 14		21 28	21 50	22 23	22 33	22 50	23 50	00 23

Sundays

from 30 October

	NT	NT	TP	NT	NT	TP	VT	LM	NT		TP	VT	LM	EM	NT	TP	VT	LM	EM		NT	VT	TP	LM
			◇1			◇1	◇1	◇1			◇1	◇1	◇1	◇		◇1	◇1	◇1	◇			◇1	◇1	◇1
	A	A	D	A	A	E			A		D			B	A	F			B		A		G	
							☕					☕					☕					☕		
London Euston ⊖65 d							08 15					09 15					10 15					11 15		
Birmingham New Street 12 65 d								09 42					10 42					11 42						12 35
Crewe 10 65 d							10 30	10 38				11 32	11 38				12 35	12 38				13 15		13 31
Winsford d								10 45					11 45					12 45						13 38
Hartford d								10 50					11 50					12 50						13 43
Acton Bridge d																								
Runcorn a							10 47	11 00				11 49	12 01				12 52	13 01				13 32		13 54
d							10 47	11 00				11 49	12 01				12 52	13 01				13 32		13 54
Liverpool South Parkway 7 ✈ a								11 09					12 10					13 10						14 03
d	00 20	08 54	09 47	10 03	10 33	10 49		11 09	11 33		11 47		12 10	12 17	12 33	12 47		13 10	13 17		13 33		13 47	14 03
West Allerton d		08 57		10 06	10 36				11 36						12 36						13 36			
Mossley Hill d		09 00		10 09	10 39				11 39						12 39						13 39			
Edge Hill 90 d																								
Liverpool Lime Street 10 90 a	00 34	09 11	10 00	10 20	10 50	11 00	11 09	11 20	11 50		11 59	12 10	12 21	12 30	12 50	12 58	13 14	13 21	13 30		13 50	13 54	13 58	14 14

A From Manchester Oxford Road
B From Nottingham
C From Norwich
D From Manchester Piccadilly
E From York
F From Newcastle
G From Scarborough

Table 91

Sundays
from 30 October

Crewe and Runcorn - Liverpool

	VT	EM	NT	TP	LM		VT	EM	NT	TP	LM	VT	EM	NT	TP		LM	VT	EM	NT	TP	LM	VT	EM
	◇1	◇		◇1	◇1		◇1	◇		◇1	◇1	◇1	◇		◇1		◇1	◇1	◇		◇1	◇1	◇1	◇
		A	B	C				A	B	D			E	B	C				A	B	D			A
	☕						☕					☕						☕					☕	
London Euston ⊖65 d	12 02						13 02					14 02						15 02					16 02	
Birmingham New Street 12 65 d					13 35						14 35						15 35					16 35		
Crewe 10 65 d	13 45				14 31		14 45				15 31	15 45					16 31					17 31		
Winsford d					14 38						15 38						16 38					17 38		
Hartford d					14 43						15 43						16 43					17 43		
Acton Bridge d																								
Runcorn a	14 02				14 54		15 02				15 54	16 02					16 54	16 57				17 54	17 57	
d	14 02				14 54		15 02				15 54	16 02					16 54	16 57				17 54	17 57	
Liverpool South Parkway 7 ✈ a					15 03						16 03						17 03					18 03		
d		14 16	14 33	14 47	15 03			15 16	15 33	15 47	16 03		16 16	16 33	16 47		17 03		17 16	17 33	17 47	18 03		18 16
West Allerton d			14 36						15 36					16 36						17 36				
Mossley Hill d			14 39						15 39					16 39						17 39				
Edge Hill 90 d																								
Liverpool Lime Street 10 90 a	14 24	14 30	14 50	14 58	15 14		15 24	15 30	15 50	15 58	16 14	16 24	16 30	16 50	16 58		17 14	17 16	17 30	17 50	17 58	18 14	18 16	18 30

	NT		TP	LM	VT	EM	NT	TP	LM	VT	EM		NT	TP	LM	VT	NT	TP	VT	VT	NT	TP	NT	VT
			◇1	◇1	◇1	◇		◇1	◇1	◇1	◇			◇1	◇1	◇1		◇1	◇1	◇1		◇1		◇1
	B		C			E	B	D			E		B	C			B	D			B	C	B	☕
					☕					☕						☕			☕	☕				
London Euston ⊖65 d					17 02					18 02						19 02			20 02	20 05				21 21
Birmingham New Street 12 65 d				17 35					18 35						19 35									
Crewe 10 65 d				18 31					19 31						20 31	20 50			21 46	21 55				23 39
Winsford d				18 38					19 38						20 38									
Hartford d				18 43					19 43						20 43									
Acton Bridge d																								
Runcorn a				18 54	18 57				19 54	19 58					20 54	21 07			22 03	22 12				23 56
d				18 54	18 57				19 54	19 58					20 54	21 07			22 03	22 12				23 56
Liverpool South Parkway 7 ✈ a				19 03					20 03						21 03									
d	18 33		18 47	19 03		19 17	19 33	19 47	20 03		20 16		20 33	20 47	21 03		21 33	21 47			22 33	22 47	23 33	
West Allerton d	18 36						19 36						20 36				21 36				22 36		23 36	
Mossley Hill d	18 39						19 39						20 39				21 39				22 39		23 39	
Edge Hill 90 d																								
Liverpool Lime Street 10 90 a	18 50		18 58	19 14	19 19	19 30	19 50	19 58	20 14	20 16	20 30		20 50	20 58	21 14	21 28	21 50	21 58	22 23	22 33	22 50	23 00	23 50	00 23

A From Nottingham
B From Manchester Oxford Road
C From Scarborough
D From Middlesbrough
E From Norwich

Table 94

Mondays to Fridays

until 30 September

Manchester and Bolton - Blackburn - Clitheroe

Miles		NT	NT	NT	NT	NT	NT	NT	NT	NT	NT	NT	NT	NT	NT	NT	NT	NT	NT	NT	NT	NT
0	**Manchester Victoria** 82 ⛴ d		05 55		07 23	08 00	08 29	09 00	10 00	11 00	12 00	13 00	14 00	15 00	15 40	16 23	17 00	17 23	18 00	18 23	19 00	20 00
0¾	Salford Central 82 d				07 26	08 03	08 32	09 03	10 03	11 03	12 03	13 03	14 03	15 03	15 43	16 26	17 03	17 27	18 03	18 26	19 03	20 03
—	Manchester Piccadilly [10] 82 ⛴ d			06 54																		
1¾	Salford Crescent 82 d		06 00	07 03	07 30	08 08	08 37	09 08	10 08	11 08	12 08	13 08	14 08	15 08	15 47	16 31	17 08	17 30	18 08	18 31	19 08	20 08
10¾	**Bolton** 82 d		06 12	07 19	07 42	08 20	08 49	09 20	10 20	11 20	12 20	13 20	14 20	15 20	16 00	16 43	17 20	17 43	18 20	18 43	19 20	20 20
12½	Hall I' Th' Wood d		06 17	07 24	07 47	08 25	08 54	09 25	10 25	11 25	12 25	13 25	14 25	15 25	16 05	16 48	17 25	17 48	18 25	18 48	19 25	20 25
13½	Bromley Cross d		06 20	07 27	07 53	08 28	08 57	09 28	10 28	11 28	12 28	13 28	14 28	15 28	16 10	16 51	17 28	17 55	18 28	18 54	19 28	20 28
16½	Entwistle d				07x59	08x34		09x34	10x34	11x34	12x34	13x34	14x34	15x34	16x16	16x57	17x34		18x34		19x34	20x34
20¼	Darwen a		06 31	07 39	08 06	08 41	09 09	09 41	10 41	11 41	12 41	13 41	14 41	15 41	16 23	17 04	17 41	18 07	18 41	19 06	19 41	20 41
—	d		06 42	07 39	08 11	08 41	09 11	09 41	10 41	11 41	12 41	13 41	14 41	15 41	16 23	17 11	17 41	18 07	18 41	19 11	19 41	20 41
—	Blackpool North 97 d																					
—	Preston [8] 97 d																					
24½	**Blackburn** a		06 49	07 46	08 20	08 51	09 20	09 50	10 50	11 50	12 50	13 50	14 50	15 49	16 30	17 19	17 51	18 16	18 48	19 21	19 51	20 50
—	d	06 25	06 52	07 47		08 52		09 52	10 52	11 52	12 52	13 52	14 52	15 52	16 31	17 19	17 53		18 49		19 52	20 52
27¼	Ramsgreave & Wilpshire d	06 31	06 58	07 53		08 58		09 58	10 58	11 58	12 58	13 58	14 58	15 58	16 37	17 25	17 59		18 55		19 58	20 58
29¾	Langho d	06 35	07 02	07 57		09 02		10 02	11 02	12 02	13 02	14 02	15 02	16 02	16 41	17 30	18 03		18 59		20 02	21 02
31¾	Whalley d	06 39	07 06	08 01		09 06		10 06	11 06	12 06	13 06	14 06	15 06	16 06	16 45	17 34	18 07		19 03		20 06	21 06
34¼	**Clitheroe** a	06 50	07 17	08 12		09 17		10 17	11 17	12 17	13 17	14 17	15 17	16 17	16 56	17 44	18 18		19 14		20 17	21 17

	NT	NT FX	NT FO	NT FX	NT FO
Manchester Victoria 82 ⛴ d	21 00	22 00	22 00	23 00	23 00
Salford Central 82 d	21 03		22 04		23 03
Manchester Piccadilly [10] 82 ⛴ d					
Salford Crescent 82 d	21 08	22 08	22 08	23 08	23 08
Bolton 82 d	21 20	22 20	22 20	23 20	23 20
Hall I' Th' Wood d	21 25	22 25	22 25	23 25	23 25
Bromley Cross d	21 28	22 28	22 28	23 28	23 28
Entwistle d	21x34	22x34	22x34	23x34	23x34
Darwen a	21 41	22 41	22 41	23 41	23 41
d	21 41	22 41	22 41	23 41	23 41
Blackpool North 97 d					
Preston [8] 97 d					
Blackburn a	21 50	22 50	22 50	23 51	23 51
d	21 52	22 51	22 51		
Ramsgreave & Wilpshire d	21 58	22 57	22 57		
Langho d	22 02	23 01	23 01		
Whalley d	22 06	23 05	23 05		
Clitheroe a	22 17	23 16	23 16		

Mondays to Fridays

from 3 October

	NT	NT	NT	NT	NT	NT	NT	NT	NT	NT	NT	NT	NT	NT	NT	NT	NT	NT	NT	NT	NT	NT
Manchester Victoria 82 ⛴ d		05 55		07 23	08 00	08 29	09 00	10 00	11 00	12 00	13 00	14 00	15 00	15 40	16 23	17 00	17 23	18 00	18 23	19 00	20 00	21 00
Salford Central 82 d				07 26	08 03	08 32	09 03	10 03	11 03	12 03	13 03	14 03	15 03	15 43	16 26	17 03	17 27	18 03	18 26	19 03	20 03	21 03
Manchester Piccadilly [10] 82 ⛴ d			06 54																			
Salford Crescent 82 d		06 00	07 03	07 30	08 08	08 37	09 08	10 08	11 08	12 08	13 08	14 08	15 08	15 47	16 31	17 08	17 30	18 08	18 31	19 08	20 08	21 08
Bolton 82 d		06 12	07 19	07 42	08 20	08 49	09 20	10 20	11 20	12 20	13 20	14 20	15 20	16 00	16 43	17 20	17 43	18 20	18 43	19 20	20 20	21 20
Hall I' Th' Wood d		06 17	07 24	07 47	08 25	08 54	09 25	10 25	11 25	12 25	13 25	14 25	15 25	16 05	16 48	17 25	17 48	18 25	18 48	19 25	20 25	21 25
Bromley Cross d		06 20	07 27	07 53	08 28	08 57	09 28	10 28	11 28	12 28	13 28	14 28	15 28	16 10	16 51	17 28	17 55	18 28	18 54	19 28	20 28	21 28
Entwistle d				07x59	08x34		09x34	10x34	11x34	12x34	13x34	14x34	15x34	16x16	16x57	17x34		18x34		19x34	20x34	21x34
Darwen a		06 31	07 39	08 06	08 41	09 09	09 41	10 41	11 41	12 41	13 41	14 41	15 41	16 23	17 04	17 41	18 07	18 41	19 06	19 41	20 41	21 41
d		06 42	07 39	08 11	08 41	09 11	09 41	10 41	11 41	12 41	13 41	14 41	15 41	16 23	17 11	17 41	18 07	18 41	19 11	19 41	20 41	21 41
Blackpool North 97 d																						
Preston [8] 97 d																						
Blackburn a		06 49	07 46	08 20	08 51	09 20	09 50	10 50	11 50	12 50	13 50	14 50	15 49	16 30	17 19	17 51	18 16	18 48	19 21	19 51	20 50	21 50
d	06 25	06 52	07 47		08 52		09 52	10 52	11 52	12 52	13 52	14 52	15 52	16 31	17 19	17 53		18 49		19 52	20 52	21 52
Ramsgreave & Wilpshire d	06 31	06 58	07 53		08 58		09 58	10 58	11 58	12 58	13 58	14 58	15 58	16 37	17 25	17 59		18 55		19 58	20 58	21 58
Langho d	06 35	07 02	07 57		09 02		10 02	11 02	12 02	13 02	14 02	15 02	16 02	16 41	17 30	18 03		18 59		20 02	21 02	22 02
Whalley d	06 39	07 06	08 01		09 06		10 06	11 06	12 06	13 06	14 06	15 06	16 06	16 45	17 34	18 07		19 03		20 06	21 06	22 06
Clitheroe a	06 52	07 19	08 14		09 19		10 19	11 19	12 19	13 19	14 19	15 19	16 19	16 58	17 46	18 20		19 16		20 19	21 19	22 19

	NT FO	NT A FX	NT B FX	NT FX	NT FO
Manchester Victoria 82 ⛴ d	22 00	22 00	22 01	23 00	23 00
Salford Central 82 d	22 04				23 03
Manchester Piccadilly [10] 82 ⛴ d					
Salford Crescent 82 d	22 08	22 08	22 08	23 08	23 08
Bolton 82 d	22 20	22 20	22 20	23 20	23 20
Hall I' Th' Wood d	22 25	22 25	22 25	23 25	23 25
Bromley Cross d	22 28	22 28	22 28	23 28	23 28
Entwistle d	22x34	22x34	22x34	23x34	23x34
Darwen a	22 41	22 41	22 41	23 41	23 41
d	22 41	22 41	22 41	23 41	23 41
Blackpool North 97 d					
Preston [8] 97 d					
Blackburn a	22 50	22 50	22 52	23 51	23 51
d	22 51	22 51			
Ramsgreave & Wilpshire d	22 57	22 57			
Langho d	23 01	23 01			
Whalley d	23 05	23 05			
Clitheroe a	23 18				

A From 3 October until 20 October

B From 24 October

Table 94

Saturdays until 1 October

Manchester and Bolton - Blackburn - Clitheroe

		NT	NT	NT	NT	NT	NT	NT	NT	NT	NT	NT	NT	NT	NT	NT	NT	NT	NT	NT	NT	NT	NT
Manchester Victoria 82 ⛴	d		05 55		07 23	08 00	08 29	09 00	09 29	10 00	11 00	12 00	13 00	14 00	15 00	15 40	16 23	17 00	17 23	18 00	18 23	19 00	20 00
Salford Central 82	d				07 26	08 03	08 32	09 03	09 32	10 03	11 03	12 03	13 03	14 03	15 03	15 43	16 26	17 03	17 26	18 03	18 26	19 03	20 03
Manchester Piccadilly 10 82 ⛴	d			06 54																			
Salford Crescent 82	d		06 00	07 03	07 30	08 08	08 37	09 08	09 37	10 08	11 08	12 08	13 08	14 08	15 08	15 47	16 31	17 08	17 31	18 08	18 31	19 08	20 08
Bolton 82	d		06 12	07 19	07 42	08 20	08 49	09 20	09 49	10 20	11 20	12 20	13 20	14 20	15 20	16 00	16 43	17 20	17 43	18 20	18 43	19 20	20 20
Hall I' Th' Wood	d		06 17	07 24	07 47	08 25	08 54	09 25	09 54	10 25	11 25	12 25	13 25	14 25	15 25	16 05	16 48	17 25	17 48	18 25	18 48	19 25	20 25
Bromley Cross	d		06 20	07 27	07 53	08 28	08 57	09 28	09 57	10 28	11 28	12 28	13 28	14 28	15 28	16 10	16 51	17 28	17 55	18 28	18 54	19 28	20 28
Entwistle	d				07x59	08x34		09x34		10x34	11x34	12x34	13x34	14x34	15x34	16x16	16x57	17x34		18x34		19x34	20x34
Darwen	a		06 31	07 39	08 06	08 41	09 09	09 41	10 09	10 41	11 41	12 41	13 41	14 41	15 41	16 23	17 04	17 41	18 07	18 41	19 06	19 41	20 41
	d		06 42	07 39	08 11	08 41	09 11	09 41	10 11	10 41	11 41	12 41	13 41	14 41	15 41	16 23	17 11	17 41	18 07	18 41	19 11	19 41	20 41
Blackpool North 97	d																						
Preston 8 97	d																						
Blackburn	a		06 49	07 46	08 20	08 51	09 20	09 50	10 20	10 50	11 50	12 50	13 50	14 50	15 49	16 30	17 19	17 51	18 21	18 48	19 21	19 51	20 50
	d	06 25	06 52	07 47		08 52		09 52		10 52	11 52	12 52	13 52	14 52	15 52	16 31	17 19	17 53		18 49		19 52	20 52
Ramsgreave & Wilpshire	d	06 31	06 58	07 53		08 58		09 58		10 58	11 58	12 58	13 58	14 58	15 58	16 37	17 25	17 59		18 55		19 58	20 58
Langho	d	06 35	07 02	07 57		09 02		10 02		11 02	12 02	13 02	14 02	15 02	16 02	16 41	17 30	18 03		18 59		20 02	21 02
Whalley	d	06 39	07 06	08 01		09 06		10 06		11 06	12 06	13 06	14 06	15 06	16 06	16 45	17 34	18 07		19 03		20 06	21 06
Clitheroe	a	06 50	07 17	08 12		09 17		10 17		11 17	12 17	13 17	14 17	15 17	16 17	16 56	17 44	18 18		19 14		20 17	21 17

		NT	NT	NT
Manchester Victoria 82 ⛴	d	21 00	22 00	23 05
Salford Central 82	d	21 03	22 03	23 08
Manchester Piccadilly 10 82 ⛴	d			
Salford Crescent 82	d	21 08	22 08	23 12
Bolton 82	d	21 20	22 20	23 24
Hall I' Th' Wood	d	21 25	22 25	23 29
Bromley Cross	d	21 28	22 28	23 32
Entwistle	d	21x34	22x34	23x38
Darwen	a	21 41	22 41	23 45
	d	21 41	22 41	23 45
Blackpool North 97	d			
Preston 8 97	d			
Blackburn	a	21 50	22 50	23 54
	d	21 52	22 51	
Ramsgreave & Wilpshire	d	21 58	22 57	
Langho	d	22 02	23 01	
Whalley	d	22 06	23 05	
Clitheroe	a	22 17	23 16	

Saturdays from 8 October

		NT	NT	NT	NT	NT	NT	NT	NT	NT	NT	NT	NT	NT	NT	NT	NT	NT	NT	NT	NT	NT	NT
Manchester Victoria 82 ⛴	d		05 55		07 23	08 00	08 29	09 00	09 29	10 00	11 00	12 00	13 00	14 00	15 00	15 40	16 23	17 00	17 23	18 00	18 23	19 00	20 00
Salford Central 82	d				07 26	08 03	08 32	09 03	09 32	10 03	11 03	12 03	13 03	14 03	15 03	15 43	16 26	17 03	17 26	18 03	18 26	19 03	20 03
Manchester Piccadilly 10 82 ⛴	d			06 54																			
Salford Crescent 82	d		06 00	07 03	07 30	08 08	08 37	09 08	09 37	10 08	11 08	12 08	13 08	14 08	15 08	15 47	16 31	17 08	17 31	18 08	18 31	19 08	20 08
Bolton 82	d		06 12	07 19	07 42	08 20	08 49	09 20	09 49	10 20	11 20	12 20	13 20	14 20	15 20	16 00	16 43	17 20	17 43	18 20	18 43	19 20	20 20
Hall I' Th' Wood	d		06 17	07 24	07 47	08 25	08 54	09 25	09 54	10 25	11 25	12 25	13 25	14 25	15 25	16 05	16 48	17 25	17 48	18 25	18 48	19 25	20 25
Bromley Cross	d		06 20	07 27	07 53	08 28	08 57	09 28	09 57	10 28	11 28	12 28	13 28	14 28	15 28	16 10	16 51	17 28	17 55	18 28	18 54	19 28	20 28
Entwistle	d				07x59	08x34		09x34		10x34	11x34	12x34	13x34	14x34	15x34	16x16	16x57	17x34		18x34		19x34	20x34
Darwen	a		06 31	07 39	08 06	08 41	09 09	09 41	10 09	10 41	11 41	12 41	13 41	14 41	15 41	16 23	17 04	17 41	18 07	18 41	19 06	19 41	20 41
	d		06 42	07 39	08 11	08 41	09 11	09 41	10 11	10 41	11 41	12 41	13 41	14 41	15 41	16 23	17 11	17 41	18 07	18 41	19 11	19 41	20 41
Blackpool North 97	d																						
Preston 8 97	d																						
Blackburn	a		06 49	07 46	08 20	08 51	09 20	09 50	10 20	10 50	11 50	12 50	13 50	14 50	15 49	16 30	17 19	17 51	18 21	18 48	19 21	19 51	20 50
	d	06 25	06 52	07 47		08 52		09 52		10 52	11 52	12 52	13 52	14 52	15 52	16 31	17 19	17 53		18 49		19 52	20 52
Ramsgreave & Wilpshire	d	06 31	06 58	07 53		08 58		09 58		10 58	11 58	12 58	13 58	14 58	15 58	16 37	17 25	17 59		18 55		19 58	20 58
Langho	d	06 35	07 02	07 57		09 02		10 02		11 02	12 02	13 02	14 02	15 02	16 02	16 41	17 30	18 03		18 59		20 02	21 02
Whalley	d	06 39	07 06	08 01		09 06		10 06		11 06	12 06	13 06	14 06	15 06	16 06	16 45	17 34	18 07		19 03		20 06	21 06
Clitheroe	a	06 52	07 19	08 14		09 19		10 19		11 19	12 19	13 19	14 19	15 19	16 19	16 58	17 46	18 20		19 16		20 19	21 19

		NT	NT	NT
Manchester Victoria 82 ⛴	d	21 00	22 00	23 05
Salford Central 82	d	21 03	22 03	23 08
Manchester Piccadilly 10 82 ⛴	d			
Salford Crescent 82	d	21 08	22 08	23 12
Bolton 82	d	21 20	22 20	23 24
Hall I' Th' Wood	d	21 25	22 25	23 29
Bromley Cross	d	21 28	22 28	23 32
Entwistle	d	21x34	22x34	23x38
Darwen	a	21 41	22 41	23 45
	d	21 41	22 41	23 45
Blackpool North 97	d			
Preston 8 97	d			
Blackburn	a	21 50	22 50	23 54
	d	21 52	22 51	
Ramsgreave & Wilpshire	d	21 58	22 57	
Langho	d	22 02	23 01	
Whalley	d	22 06	23 05	
Clitheroe	a	22 19	23 18	

Table 94

Manchester and Bolton - Blackburn - Clitheroe

Sundays

until 11 September

	NT	NT 🛒	NT	NT 🛒	NT	NT	NT	NT	NT	NT	NT	NT	NT	NT	NT	NT	NT
Manchester Victoria 82 🚊 d	08 01		09 00		10 00	11 00	12 00	13 00	14 00	15 00	16 00	17 00	18 00	19 00	20 00	21 00	22 00
Salford Central 82 d																	
Manchester Piccadilly **10** 82 🚊 d																	
Salford Crescent 82 d	08 08		09 08		10 08	11 08	12 08	13 08	14 08	15 08	16 08	17 08	18 08	19 08	20 08	21 08	22 08
Bolton 82 d	08 20		09 20		10 20	11 20	12 20	13 20	14 20	15 20	16 20	17 20	18 20	19 20	20 20	21 20	22 20
Hall I' Th' Wood d	08 25		09 25		10 25	11 25	12 25	13 25	14 25	15 25	16 25	17 25	18 25	19 25	20 25	21 25	22 25
Bromley Cross d	08 28		09 28		10 28	11 28	12 28	13 28	14 28	15 28	16 28	17 28	18 28	19 28	20 28	21 28	22 28
Entwistle d	08x34		09x34		10x34	11x34	12x34	13x34	14x34	15x34	16x34	17x34	18x34	19x34	20x34	21x34	22x34
Darwen a	08 41		09 41		10 41	11 41	12 41	13 41	14 41	15 41	16 41	17 41	18 41	19 41	20 41	21 41	22 41
d	08 41		09 41		10 41	11 41	12 41	13 41	14 41	15 41	16 41	17 41	18 41	19 41	20 41	21 41	22 41
Blackpool North 97 d		08 36															
Preston **8** 97 d		09 05		10 00													
Blackburn a	08 48	09 25	09 48	10 19	10 48	11 48	12 48	13 48	14 48	15 48	16 48	17 48	18 48	19 48	20 48	21 48	22 50
d	08 57	09 27	09 50	10 22	10 50	11 50	12 50	13 50	14 50	15 50	16 50	17 50	18 50	19 50	20 50	21 50	
Ramsgreave & Wilpshire d	09 03	09 34	09 56	10 28	10 56	11 56	12 56	13 56	14 56	15 56	16 56	17 56	18 56	19 56	20 56	21 56	
Langho d	09 07	09 39	10 00	10 33	11 00	12 00	13 00	14 00	15 00	16 00	17 00	18 00	19 00	20 00	21 00	22 00	
Whalley d	09 11	09 43	10 04	10 38	11 04	12 04	13 04	14 04	15 04	16 04	17 04	18 04	19 04	20 04	21 04	22 04	
Clitheroe a	09 22	09 50	10 15	10 44	11 15	12 15	13 15	14 15	15 15	16 15	17 15	18 15	19 15	20 15	21 15	22 15	

Sundays

18 September to 2 October

	NT	NT 🛒	NT	NT	NT	NT	NT	NT	NT	NT	NT	NT	NT	NT	NT	NT
Manchester Victoria 82 🚊 d	08 01		09 00	10 00	11 00	12 00	13 00	14 00	15 00	16 00	17 00	18 00	19 00	20 00	21 00	22 00
Salford Central 82 d																
Manchester Piccadilly **10** 82 🚊 d																
Salford Crescent 82 d	08 08		09 08	10 08	11 08	12 08	13 08	14 08	15 08	16 08	17 08	18 08	19 08	20 08	21 08	22 08
Bolton 82 d	08 20		09 20	10 20	11 20	12 20	13 20	14 20	15 20	16 20	17 20	18 20	19 20	20 20	21 20	22 20
Hall I' Th' Wood d	08 25		09 25	10 25	11 25	12 25	13 25	14 25	15 25	16 25	17 25	18 25	19 25	20 25	21 25	22 25
Bromley Cross d	08 28		09 28	10 28	11 28	12 28	13 28	14 28	15 28	16 28	17 28	18 28	19 28	20 28	21 28	22 28
Entwistle d	08x34		09x34	10x34	11x34	12x34	13x34	14x34	15x34	16x34	17x34	18x34	19x34	20x34	21x34	22x34
Darwen a	08 41		09 41	10 41	11 41	12 41	13 41	14 41	15 41	16 41	17 41	18 41	19 41	20 41	21 41	22 41
d	08 41		09 41	10 41	11 41	12 41	13 41	14 41	15 41	16 41	17 41	18 41	19 41	20 41	21 41	22 41
Blackpool North 97 d		08 36														
Preston **8** 97 d		09 05														
Blackburn a	08 48	09 25	09 48	10 48	11 48	12 48	13 48	14 48	15 48	16 48	17 48	18 48	19 48	20 48	21 48	22 50
d	08 57	09 27	09 50	10 50	11 50	12 50	13 50	14 50	15 50	16 50	17 50	18 50	19 50	20 50	21 50	
Ramsgreave & Wilpshire d	09 03	09 34	09 56	10 56	11 56	12 56	13 56	14 56	15 56	16 56	17 56	18 56	19 56	20 56	21 56	
Langho d	09 07	09 39	10 00	11 00	12 00	13 00	14 00	15 00	16 00	17 00	18 00	19 00	20 00	21 00	22 00	
Whalley d	09 11	09 43	10 04	11 04	12 04	13 04	14 04	15 04	16 04	17 04	18 04	19 04	20 04	21 04	22 04	
Clitheroe a	09 22	09 50	10 15	11 15	12 15	13 15	14 15	15 15	16 15	17 15	18 15	19 15	20 15	21 15	22 15	

Sundays

9 October to 23 October

	NT 🛒	NT
Manchester Victoria 82 🚊 d		22 00
Salford Central 82 d		
Manchester Piccadilly **10** 82 🚊 d		
Salford Crescent 82 d		22 08
Bolton 82 d		22 20
Hall I' Th' Wood d		22 25
Bromley Cross d		22 28
Entwistle d		22x34
Darwen a		22 41
d		22 41
Blackpool North 97 d	08 36	
Preston **8** 97 d	09 05	
Blackburn a	09 25	22 50
d	09 27	
Ramsgreave & Wilpshire d	09 34	
Langho d	09 39	
Whalley d	09 43	
Clitheroe a	09 50	

Sundays

from 30 October

	NT 🚌	NT 🚌	NT 🚌	NT 🚌	NT 🚌	NT 🚌	NT 🚌	NT 🚌	NT 🚌	NT 🚌	NT 🚌	NT 🚌	NT 🚌	NT 🚌	NT 🚌	NT	NT 🚌
Manchester Victoria 82 🚊 d																22 00	
Salford Central 82 d																	
Manchester Piccadilly **10** 82 🚊 d																	
Salford Crescent 82 d																22 08	
Bolton 82 d	08 00	08 30	09 30	10 30	11 30	12 30	13 30	14 30	15 30	16 30	17 30	18 30	19 30	20 30	21 30	22 20	22 30
Hall I' Th' Wood d	08 08	08 38	09 38	10 38	11 38	12 38	13 38	14 38	15 38	16 38	17 38	18 38	19 38	20 38	21 38	22 25	22 38
Bromley Cross d	08 15	08 45	09 45	10 45	11 45	12 45	13 45	14 45	15 45	16 45	17 45	18 45	19 45	20 45	21 45	22 28	22 45
Entwistle d																22x34	
Darwen a	08 35	09 05	10 05	11 05	12 05	13 05	14 05	15 05	16 05	17 05	18 05	19 05	20 05	21 05	22 05	22 41	23 05
d	08 35	09 05	10 05	11 05	12 05	13 05	14 05	15 05	16 05	17 05	18 05	19 05	20 05	21 05	22 05	22 41	23 05
Blackpool North 97 d																	
Preston **8** 97 d																	
Blackburn a	08 50	09 20	10 20	11 20	12 20	13 20	14 20	15 20	16 20	17 20	18 20	19 20	20 20	21 20	22 20	22 50	23 20
d	08 50	09 20	10 20	11 20	12 20	13 20	14 20	15 20	16 20	17 20	18 20	19 20	20 20	21 20	22 20		
Ramsgreave & Wilpshire d	08 58	09 28	10 28	11 28	12 28	13 28	14 28	15 28	16 28	17 28	18 28	19 28	20 28	21 28	22 28		
Langho d	09 03	09 33	10 33	11 33	12 33	13 33	14 33	15 33	16 33	17 33	18 33	19 33	20 33	21 33	22 33		
Whalley d	09 14	09 44	10 44	11 44	12 44	13 44	14 44	15 44	16 44	17 44	18 44	19 44	20 44	21 44	22 44		
Clitheroe a	09 26	09 56	10 56	11 56	12 56	13 56	14 56	15 56	16 56	17 56	18 56	19 56	20 56	21 56	22 56		

Table 94

Mondays to Fridays

until 30 September

Clitheroe - Blackburn - Bolton and Manchester

Miles			NT	NT	NT	NT	NT	NT	NT	NT	NT	NT	NT	NT	NT	NT	NT	NT	NT	NT	NT	NT	NT
0	**Clitheroe**	d		06 40	07 07	07 40		08 26		09 40	10 40	11 40	12 40	13 40	14 40	15 26	16 40	17 09	18 09	18 40		19 40	20 40
2½	Whalley	d		06 46	07 13	07 46		08 32		09 46	10 46	11 46	12 46	13 46	14 46	15 32	16 46	17 15	18 15	18 46		19 46	20 46
4½	Langho	d		06 50	07 17	07 50		08 36		09 50	10 50	11 50	12 50	13 50	14 50	15 36	16 50	17 19	18 19	18 50		19 50	20 50
7	Ramsgreave & Wilpshire	d		06 55	07 22	07 55		08 41		09 55	10 55	11 55	12 55	13 55	14 55	15 41	16 55	17 24	18 24	18 55		19 55	20 55
9¾	**Blackburn**	a		07 01	07 29	08 02		08 47		10 01	11 01	12 01	13 01	14 01	15 01	15 47	17 01	17 30	18 30	19 01		20 01	21 01
—		d	06 28	07 01	07 29	08 03	08 32	09 03	09 31	10 03	11 03	12 03	13 03	14 03	15 03	15 51	17 03	17 31	18 31	19 03	19 31	20 03	21 03
—	Preston 8 97	a																					
—	Blackpool North 97	a																					
14	Darwen	a	06 35	07 09	07 37	08 10	08 39	09 11	09 38	10 10	11 10	12 10	13 10	14 10	15 10	15 58	17 10	17 38	18 38	19 10	19 38	20 10	21 10
—		d	06 35	07 09	07 40	08 10	08 42	09 11	09 41	10 10	11 10	12 10	13 10	14 10	15 10	15 58	17 10	17 41	18 41	19 10	19 42	20 10	21 10
17¾	Entwistle	d	06x42	07x16		08x17				10x17	11x17	12x17	13x17	14x17	15x17		17x17	17x48	18x48	19x17	19x49	20x17	21x17
20¾	Bromley Cross	d	06 48	07 21	07 51	08 23	08 52	09 22	09 52	10 23	11 23	12 23	13 23	14 23	15 23	16 09	17 23	17 54	18 54	19 23	19 54	20 23	21 23
21¾	Hall I' Th' Wood	d	06 50	07 24	07 53	08 25	08 55	09 25	09 55	10 25	11 25	12 25	13 25	14 25	15 25	16 12	17 25	17 56	18 56	19 25	19 57	20 25	21 25
23½	**Bolton** 82	a	06 55	07 30	07 58	08 30	09 02	09 30	10 00	10 30	11 30	12 30	13 30	14 30	15 30	16 17	17 30	18 01	19 01	19 31	20 02	20 30	21 30
32½	Salford Crescent 82	a	07 15	07 43	08 17	08 43	09 15	09 43	10 13	10 43	11 43	12 43	13 43	14 43	15 43	16 30	17 43	18 15	19 14	19 44	20 15	20 43	21 43
—	Manchester Piccadilly 10 82	a																					
33½	Salford Central 82	a	07 18	07 46	08 20	08 46	09 18	09 46	10 16	10 46	11 46	12 46	13 46	14 46	15 46	16 33	17 46	18 17	19 17	19 46	20 17	20 46	21 46
34¼	**Manchester Victoria** 82	a	07 26	07 53	08 25	08 52	09 26	09 52	10 21	10 52	11 52	12 52	13 52	14 52	15 54	16 41	17 53	18 24	19 23	19 53	20 24	20 52	21 52

		NT FX	NT FO	NT
Clitheroe	d	21 40	21 40	22 40
Whalley	d	21 46	21 46	22 46
Langho	d	21 50	21 50	22 50
Ramsgreave & Wilpshire	d	21 55	21 55	22 55
Blackburn	a	22 01	22 01	23 01
	d	22 03	22 03	23 03
Preston 8 97	a			
Blackpool North 97	a			
Darwen	a	22 10	22 10	23 10
	d	22 10	22 10	23 10
Entwistle	d	22x17	22x17	23x17
Bromley Cross	d	22 23	22 23	23 23
Hall I' Th' Wood	d	22 25	22 25	23 25
Bolton 82	a	22 30	22 30	23 30
Salford Crescent 82	a	22 43	22 43	23 43
Manchester Piccadilly 10 82	a			
Salford Central 82	a		22 46	
Manchester Victoria 82	a	22 52	22 52	23 52

Mondays to Fridays

from 3 October

		NT A MO	NT	NT	NT	NT	NT	NT	NT	NT	NT	NT	NT	NT	NT	NT	NT	NT	NT	NT	NT	NT	NT
Clitheroe	d	22p40		06 40	07 07	07 40		08 26		09 40	10 40	11 40	12 40	13 40	14 40	15 26	16 40	17 09	18 09	18 40		19 40	20 40
Whalley	d	22p52		06 46	07 13	07 46		08 32		09 46	10 46	11 46	12 46	13 46	14 46	15 32	16 46	17 15	18 15	18 46		19 46	20 46
Langho	d	23p03		06 50	07 17	07 50		08 36		09 50	10 50	11 50	12 50	13 50	14 50	15 36	16 50	17 19	18 19	18 50		19 50	20 50
Ramsgreave & Wilpshire	d	23p08		06 55	07 22	07 55		08 41		09 55	10 55	11 55	12 55	13 55	14 55	15 41	16 55	17 24	18 24	18 55		19 55	20 55
Blackburn	a	23p15		07 01	07 29	08 02		08 47		10 01	11 01	12 01	13 01	14 01	15 01	15 47	17 01	17 30	18 30	19 01		20 01	21 01
	d	23p16	06 28	07 01	07 29	08 03	08 32	09 03	09 31	10 03	11 03	12 03	13 03	14 03	15 03	15 51	17 03	17 31	18 31	19 03	19 31	20 03	21 03
Preston 8 97	a																						
Blackpool North 97	a																						
Darwen	a	23p31	06 35	07 09	07 37	08 10	08 39	09 11	09 38	10 10	11 10	12 10	13 10	14 10	15 10	15 58	17 10	17 38	18 38	19 10	19 38	20 10	21 10
	d	23p31	06 35	07 09	07 40	08 10	08 42	09 11	09 41	10 10	11 10	12 10	13 10	14 10	15 10	15 58	17 10	17 41	18 41	19 10	19 42	20 10	21 10
Entwistle	d		06x42	07x16		08x17				10x17	11x17	12x17	13x17	14x17	15x17		17x17	17x48	18x48	19x17	19x49	20x17	21x17
Bromley Cross	d	23p51	06 48	07 21	07 51	08 23	08 52	09 22	09 52	10 23	11 23	12 23	13 23	14 23	15 23	16 09	17 23	17 54	18 54	19 23	19 54	20 23	21 23
Hall I' Th' Wood	d	23p58	06 50	07 24	07 53	08 25	08 55	09 25	09 55	10 25	11 25	12 25	13 25	14 25	15 25	16 12	17 25	17 56	18 56	19 25	19 57	20 25	21 25
Bolton 82	a	00 06	06 55	07 30	07 58	08 30	09 02	09 30	10 00	10 30	11 30	12 30	13 30	14 30	15 30	16 17	17 30	18 01	19 01	19 31	20 02	20 30	21 30
Salford Crescent 82	a	00 30	07 15	07 43	08 17	08 43	09 15	09 43	10 13	10 43	11 43	12 43	13 43	14 43	15 43	16 30	17 43	18 15	19 14	19 44	20 15	20 43	21 43
Manchester Piccadilly 10 82	a																						
Salford Central 82	a		07 18	07 46	08 20	08 46	09 18	09 46	10 16	10 46	11 46	12 46	13 46	14 46	15 46	16 33	17 46	18 17	19 17	19 46	20 17	20 46	21 46
Manchester Victoria 82	a	00 41	07 27	07 54	08 26	08 53	09 27	09 53	10 22	10 53	11 53	12 53	13 53	14 53	15 55	16 42	17 54	18 24	19 24	19 54	20 25	20 53	21 53

		NT FX	NT FO	NT
Clitheroe	d	21 40	21 40	22 40
Whalley	d	21 46	21 46	22 46
Langho	d	21 50	21 50	22 50
Ramsgreave & Wilpshire	d	21 55	21 55	22 55
Blackburn	a	22 01	22 01	23 01
	d	22 03	22 03	23 03
Preston 8 97	a			
Blackpool North 97	a			
Darwen	a	22 10	22 10	23 10
	d	22 10	22 10	23 10
Entwistle	d	22x17	22x17	23x17
Bromley Cross	d	22 23	22 23	23 23
Hall I' Th' Wood	d	22 25	22 25	23 25
Bolton 82	a	22 30	22 30	23 30
Salford Crescent 82	a	22 43	22 43	23 43
Manchester Piccadilly 10 82	a			
Salford Central 82	a		22 46	
Manchester Victoria 82	a	22 53	22 53	23 53

A From 31 October

Table 94

Saturdays

until 1 October

Clitheroe - Blackburn - Bolton and Manchester

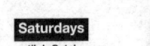

			NT	NT	NT	NT	NT	NT	NT	NT	NT	NT	NT	NT	NT	NT	NT	NT	NT	NT		NT	NT	NT	NT	NT
Clitheroe		d		07 07	07 40		08 26		09 40		10 40	11 40	12 40	13 40	14 40	15 26	16 40	17 09	18 09	18 40			19 40	20 40	21 40	22 46
Whalley		d		07 13	07 46		08 32		09 46		10 46	11 46	12 46	13 46	14 46	15 32	16 46	17 15	18 15	18 46			19 46	20 46	21 46	22 52
Langho		d		07 17	07 50		08 36		09 50		10 50	11 50	12 50	13 50	14 50	15 36	16 50	17 19	18 19	18 50			19 50	20 50	21 50	22 56
Ramsgreave & Wilpshire		d		07 22	07 55		08 41		09 55		10 55	11 55	12 55	13 55	14 55	15 41	16 55	17 24	18 24	18 55			19 55	20 55	21 55	23 01
Blackburn		a		07 28	08 02		08 47		10 01		11 01	12 01	13 01	14 01	15 01	15 47	17 01	17 30	18 30	19 01			20 01	21 01	22 01	23 07
		d	06 28	07 29	08 03	08 32	09 03	09 31	10 03	10 31	11 03	12 03	13 03	14 03	15 03	15 51	17 03	17 31	18 31	19 03		19 31	20 03	21 03	22 03	23 09
Preston 8	97	a																								
Blackpool North	97	a																								
Darwen		a	06 35	07 37	08 10	08 39	09 11	09 38	10 10	10 38	11 10	12 10	13 10	14 10	15 10	15 58	17 10	17 38	18 38	19 10		19 38	20 10	21 10	22 10	23 16
		d	06 35	07 40	08 10	08 42	09 11	09 41	10 10	10 39	11 10	12 10	13 10	14 10	15 10	15 58	17 10	17 41	18 41	19 10		19 42	20 10	21 10	22 10	23 16
Entwistle		d	06x42		08x17				10x17	10x46	11x17	12x17	13x17	14x17	15x17		17x17	17x48	18x48	19x17		19x49	20x17	21x17	22x17	23x23
Bromley Cross		d	06 48	07 51	08 23	08 52	09 22	09 52	10 23	10 51	11 23	12 23	13 23	14 23	15 23	16 09	17 23	17 54	18 54	19 23		19 54	20 23	21 23	22 23	23 29
Hall I' Th' Wood		d	06 50	07 53	08 25	08 55	09 25	09 55	10 25	10 54	11 25	12 25	13 25	14 25	15 25	16 12	17 25	17 56	18 56	19 25		19 57	20 25	21 25	22 25	23 31
Bolton	82	a	06 55	07 58	08 30	09 02	09 30	10 00	10 31	10 59	11 30	12 30	13 30	14 30	15 30	16 17	17 30	18 01	19 01	19 31		20 02	20 30	21 30	22 30	23 36
Salford Crescent	82	a	07 15	08 17	08 43	09 15	09 43	10 13	10 44	11 12	11 43	12 43	13 43	14 43	15 43	16 30	17 43	18 14	19 14	19 44		20 15	20 43	21 43	22 43	23 48
Manchester Piccadilly 10	82	a																								
Salford Central	82	a	07 19	08 20	08 46	09 18	09 46	10 16	10 46	11 15	11 46	12 46	13 46	14 46	15 46	16 33	17 46	18 17	19 17	19 46		20 17	20 46	21 46	22 46	
Manchester Victoria	82	a	07 24	08 25	08 52	09 26	09 52	10 21	10 51	11 22	11 52	12 52	13 52	14 52	15 54	16 41	17 53	18 26	19 23	19 53		20 24	20 52	21 52	22 52	23 59

Saturdays

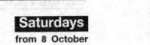

from 8 October

			NT	NT	NT	NT	NT	NT	NT	NT	NT		NT	NT	NT	NT	NT	NT	NT	NT	NT	NT	NT	NT	NT	NT
Clitheroe		d		07 07	07 40		08 26		09 40		10 40		11 40	12 40	13 40	14 40	15 26	16 40	17 09	18 09	18 40		19 40	20 40	21 40	22 46
Whalley		d		07 13	07 46		08 32		09 46		10 46		11 46	12 46	13 46	14 46	15 32	16 46	17 15	18 15	18 46		19 46	20 46	21 46	22 52
Langho		d		07 17	07 50		08 36		09 50		10 50		11 50	12 50	13 50	14 50	15 36	16 50	17 19	18 19	18 50		19 50	20 50	21 50	22 56
Ramsgreave & Wilpshire		d		07 22	07 55		08 41		09 55		10 55		11 55	12 55	13 55	14 55	15 41	16 55	17 24	18 24	18 55		19 55	20 55	21 55	23 01
Blackburn		a		07 28	08 02		08 47		10 01		11 01		12 01	13 01	14 01	15 01	15 47	17 01	17 30	18 30	19 01		20 01	21 01	22 01	23 07
		d	06 28	07 29	08 03	08 32	09 03	09 31	10 03	10 31	11 03		12 03	13 03	14 03	15 03	15 51	17 03	17 31	18 31	19 03	19 31	20 03	21 03	22 03	23 09
Preston 8	97	a																								
Blackpool North	97	a																								
Darwen		a	06 35	07 37	08 10	08 39	09 11	09 38	10 10	10 38	11 10		12 10	13 10	14 10	15 10	15 58	17 10	17 38	18 38	19 10	19 38	20 10	21 10	22 10	23 16
		d	06 35	07 40	08 10	08 42	09 11	09 41	10 10	10 39	11 10		12 10	13 10	14 10	15 10	15 58	17 10	17 41	18 41	19 10	19 42	20 10	21 10	22 10	23 16
Entwistle		d	06x42		08x17				10x17	10x46	11x17		12x17	13x17	14x17	15x17		17x17	17x48	18x48	19x17	19x49	20x17	21x17	22x17	23x23
Bromley Cross		d	06 48	07 51	08 23	08 52	09 22	09 52	10 23	10 51	11 23		12 23	13 23	14 23	15 23	16 09	17 23	17 54	18 54	19 23	19 54	20 23	21 23	22 23	23 29
Hall I' Th' Wood		d	06 50	07 53	08 25	08 55	09 25	09 55	10 25	10 54	11 25		12 25	13 25	14 25	15 25	16 12	17 25	17 56	18 56	19 25	19 57	20 25	21 25	22 25	23 31
Bolton	82	a	06 55	07 58	08 30	09 02	09 30	10 00	10 31	10 59	11 30		12 30	13 30	14 30	15 30	16 17	17 30	18 01	19 01	19 31	20 02	20 30	21 30	22 30	23 36
Salford Crescent	82	a	07 15	08 17	08 43	09 15	09 43	10 13	10 44	11 12	11 43		12 43	13 43	14 43	15 43	16 30	17 43	18 14	19 14	19 44	20 15	20 43	21 43	22 43	23 48
Manchester Piccadilly 10	82	a																								
Salford Central	82	a	07 19	08 20	08 46	09 18	09 46	10 16	10 46	11 15	11 46		12 46	13 46	14 46	15 46	16 33	17 46	18 17	19 17	19 46	20 17	20 46	21 46	22 46	
Manchester Victoria	82	a	07 25	08 26	08 53	09 26	09 53	10 22	10 52	11 23	11 53		12 53	13 53	14 53	15 55	16 42	17 54	18 26	19 24	19 54	20 25	20 53	21 53	22 53	00 01

Sundays

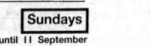

until 11 September

			NT	NT	NT	NT	NT	NT	NT	NT	NT		NT	NT	NT	NT 🚌	NT	NT	NT
Clitheroe		d		09 40	10 40	11 40	12 40	13 40	14 40	15 40	16 40		17 40	18 40	19 40	19 57	20 40	21 40	22 40
Whalley		d		09 46	10 46	11 46	12 46	13 46	14 46	15 46	16 46		17 46	18 46	19 46	20 04	20 46	21 46	22 46
Langho		d		09 50	10 50	11 50	12 50	13 50	14 50	15 50	16 50		17 50	18 50	19 50	20 09	20 50	21 50	22 50
Ramsgreave & Wilpshire		d		09 55	10 55	11 55	12 55	13 55	14 55	15 55	16 55		17 55	18 55	19 55	20 14	20 55	21 55	22 55
Blackburn		a		10 01	11 02	12 01	13 01	14 01	15 01	16 01	17 01		18 01	19 01	20 01	20 22	21 01	22 01	23 01
		d	09 03	10 03	11 03	12 03	13 03	14 03	15 03	16 03	17 03		18 03	19 03	20 03	20 25	21 03	22 03	23 03
Preston 8	97	a														20 47			
Blackpool North	97	a														21 16			
Darwen		a	09 10	10 10	11 10	12 10	13 10	14 10	15 10	16 10	17 10		18 10	19 10	20 10		21 10	22 10	23 10
		d	09 10	10 10	11 10	12 10	13 10	14 10	15 10	16 10	17 10		18 10	19 10	20 10		21 10	22 10	23 10
Entwistle		d	09x17	10x17	11x17	12x17	13x17	14x17	15x17	16x17	17x17		18x17	19x17	20x17		21x17	22x17	23x17
Bromley Cross		d	09 23	10 23	11 23	12 23	13 23	14 23	15 23	16 23	17 23		18 23	19 23	20 23		21 23	22 23	23 23
Hall I' Th' Wood		d	09 25	10 25	11 25	12 25	13 25	14 25	15 25	16 25	17 25		18 25	19 25	20 25		21 25	22 25	23 25
Bolton	82	a	09 30	10 30	11 30	12 30	13 30	14 30	15 30	16 30	17 30		18 30	19 30	20 30		21 30	22 30	23 30
Salford Crescent	82	a	09 43	10 43	11 43	12 43	13 43	14 43	15 43	16 43	17 43		18 43	19 43	20 43		21 43	22 43	23 43
Manchester Piccadilly 10	82	a																	
Salford Central	82	a																	
Manchester Victoria	82	a	09 52	10 52	11 52	12 52	13 52	14 52	15 52	16 52	17 52		18 52	19 52	20 52		21 52	22 52	23 52

Sundays

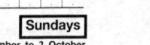

18 September to 2 October

			NT	NT	NT	NT	NT	NT	NT	NT	NT		NT	NT	NT	NT 🚌	NT	NT	NT
Clitheroe		d		09 40	10 40	11 40	12 40	13 40	14 40	15 40	16 40		17 40	18 40	19 40	19 57	20 40	21 40	22 40
Whalley		d		09 46	10 46	11 46	12 46	13 46	14 46	15 46	16 46		17 46	18 46	19 46	20 04	20 46	21 46	22 46
Langho		d		09 50	10 50	11 50	12 50	13 50	14 50	15 50	16 50		17 50	18 50	19 50	20 09	20 50	21 50	22 50
Ramsgreave & Wilpshire		d		09 55	10 55	11 55	12 55	13 55	14 55	15 55	16 55		17 55	18 55	19 55	20 14	20 55	21 55	22 55
Blackburn		a		10 01	11 02	12 01	13 01	14 01	15 01	16 01	17 01		18 01	19 01	20 01	20 22	21 01	22 01	23 01
		d	09 03	10 03	11 03	12 03	13 03	14 03	15 03	16 03	17 03		18 03	19 03	20 03	20 25	21 03	22 03	23 03
Preston 8	97	a														20 47			
Blackpool North	97	a														21 16			
Darwen		a	09 10	10 10	11 10	12 10	13 10	14 10	15 10	16 10	17 10		18 10	19 10	20 10		21 10	22 10	23 10
		d	09 10	10 10	11 10	12 10	13 10	14 10	15 10	16 10	17 10		18 10	19 10	20 10		21 10	22 10	23 10
Entwistle		d	09x17	10x17	11x17	12x17	13x17	14x17	15x17	16x17	17x17		18x17	19x17	20x17		21x17	22x17	23x17
Bromley Cross		d	09 23	10 23	11 23	12 23	13 23	14 23	15 23	16 23	17 23		18 23	19 23	20 23		21 23	22 23	23 23
Hall I' Th' Wood		d	09 25	10 25	11 25	12 25	13 25	14 25	15 25	16 25	17 25		18 25	19 25	20 25		21 25	22 25	23 25
Bolton	82	a	09 30	10 30	11 30	12 30	13 30	14 30	15 30	16 30	17 30		18 30	19 30	20 30		21 30	22 30	23 30
Salford Crescent	82	a	09 43	10 43	11 43	12 43	13 43	14 43	15 43	16 43	17 43		18 43	19 43	20 43		21 43	22 43	23 43
Manchester Piccadilly 10	82	a																	
Salford Central	82	a																	
Manchester Victoria	82	a	09 52	10 52	11 52	12 52	13 52	14 52	15 52	16 52	17 52		18 52	19 52	20 52		21 52	22 52	23 52

Table 94

Sundays

9 October to 23 October

Clitheroe - Blackburn - Bolton and Manchester

		NT	NT
Clitheroe	d	22p46	19 57
Whalley	d	22p52	20 04
Langho	d	22p56	20 09
Ramsgreave & Wilpshire	d	23p01	20 14
Blackburn	a	23p07	20 22
	d	23p09	20 25
Preston 8 97	a		20 47
Blackpool North 97	a		21 16
Darwen	a	23p16	
	d	23p16	
Entwistle	d	23b23	
Bromley Cross	d	23p29	
Hall I' Th' Wood	d	23p31	
Bolton 82	a	23p36	
Salford Crescent 82	a	23p48	
Manchester Piccadilly 10 82	a		
Salford Central 82	a		
Manchester Victoria 82	a	00 01	

Sundays

from 30 October

		NT	NT	NT	NT	NT	NT	NT	NT	NT	NT	NT	NT	NT	NT	NT	NT
Clitheroe	d	22p46	08 50	09 50	10 50	11 50	12 50	13 50	14 50	15 50	16 50	17 50	18 50	19 50	20 50	21 40	22 40
Whalley	d	22p52	09 02	10 02	11 02	12 02	13 02	14 02	15 02	16 02	17 02	18 02	19 02	20 02	21 02	21 52	22 52
Langho	d	22p56	09 13	10 13	11 13	12 13	13 13	14 13	15 13	16 13	17 13	18 13	19 13	20 13	21 13	22 03	23 03
Ramsgreave & Wilpshire	d	23p01	09 18	10 18	11 18	12 18	13 18	14 18	15 18	16 18	17 18	18 18	19 18	20 18	21 18	22 08	23 08
Blackburn	a	23p07	09 25	10 25	11 25	12 25	13 25	14 25	15 25	16 25	17 25	18 25	19 25	20 25	21 25	22 15	23 15
	d	23p09	09 26	10 26	11 26	12 26	13 26	14 26	15 26	16 26	17 26	18 26	19 26	20 26	21 26	22 16	23 16
Preston 8 97	a																
Blackpool North 97	a																
Darwen	a	23p16	09 41	10 41	11 41	12 41	13 41	14 41	15 41	16 41	17 41	18 41	19 41	20 41	21 41	22 31	23 31
	d	23p16	09 41	10 41	11 41	12 41	13 41	14 41	15 41	16 41	17 41	18 41	19 41	20 41	21 41	22 31	23 31
Entwistle	d	23b23															
Bromley Cross	d	23p29	10 01	11 01	12 01	13 01	14 01	15 01	16 01	17 01	18 01	19 01	20 01	21 01	22 01	22 51	23 51
Hall I' Th' Wood	d	23p31	10 08	11 08	12 08	13 08	14 08	15 08	16 08	17 08	18 08	19 08	20 08	21 08	22 08	22 58	23 58
Bolton 82	a	23p36	10 16	11 16	12 16	13 16	14 16	15 16	16 16	17 16	18 16	19 16	20 16	21 16	22 16	23 06	00 06
Salford Crescent 82	a	23p48														23 30	00 30
Manchester Piccadilly 10 82	a																
Salford Central 82	a																
Manchester Victoria 82	a	00 01														23 41	00 41

b Previous night, stops on request

Network Diagram for Tables 97, 98, 99, 100

DM-15/08
Design BAJS

© Network Rail OPSU 2008.
All rights reserved

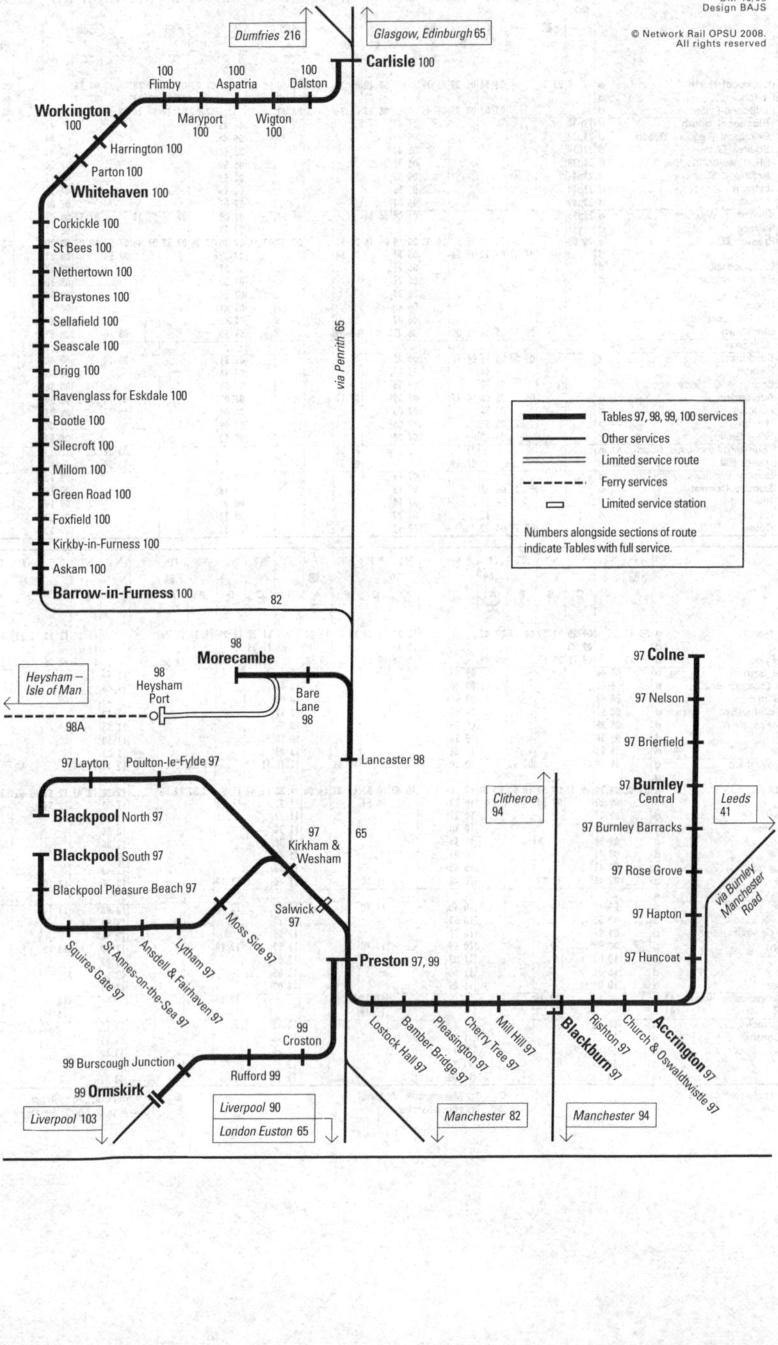

Table 97

Mondays to Fridays
until 15 July

Blackpool - Preston - Blackburn, Accrington, Burnley and Colne

Miles	Miles			NT MX	TP ◇1 A	NT	NT	NT B	TP ◇1 A 🚲	NT	NT C	NT B	TP ◇1 A 🚲	NT D	NT	NT E	TP ◇1 🚲	NT C	NT B	TP ◇1 🚲	NT	NT C	NT B
—	0	**Blackpool North**	d		03 31		04 56	05 29	05 39		06 19	06 28	06 40	06 53		07 02	07 10	07 18	07 29	07 36		08 20	08 29
—	1¼	Layton	d								06 22		06 43				07 13	07 21		07 39		08 23	
—	3¼	Poulton-le-Fylde	d				05 02	05 35	05 45		06 27	06 34	06 47			07 08	07 17	07 26	07 35	07 43		08 28	08 35
0	—	**Blackpool South**	d	23p30						05 42					06 42						07 42		
0½	—	Blackpool Pleasure Beach	d	23p32						05 44					06 44						07 44		
1¾	—	Squires Gate	d	23p34						05 46					06 46						07 46		
3¼	—	St Annes-on-the-Sea	d	23p38						05 50					06 50						07 50		
5¼	—	Ansdell & Fairhaven	d	23p41						05 53					06 53						07 53		
6½	—	Lytham	d	23p44						05 56					06 56						07 56		
9	—	Moss Side	d	23p49						06 01					07 01						08 01		
12¼	9¾	Kirkham & Wesham	d	23p56						06 08	06 36		06 56		07 09		07 26	07 35		07 52	08 09	08 37	
14¾	12¼	Salwick	d												07 13						08 13		
20	17½	**Preston** 8	a	00 08			05 20	05 52	06 03	06 19	06 46	06 52	07 07	07 15	07 20	07 28	07 37	07 46	07 52	08 03	08 20	08 47	08 52
—	—		d			04 47	05 22	05 54		06 21		06 54			07 22				07 54		08 22		08 54
22¾	—	Lostock Hall	d							06 26					07 27						08 27		
24	—	Bamber Bridge	d							06 29					07 30						08 30		
29	—	Pleasington	d							06 37					07 38						08 38		
30	—	Cherry Tree	d							06 40					07 41						08 41		
30¾	—	Mill Hill (Lancashire)	d							06 42					07 43						08 43		
32	—	**Blackburn**	a			05 03	05 38	06 09		06 45		07 09			07 50				08 10		08 47		09 10
—	—	Clitheroe 94	a																				
—	—	**Blackburn**	d			05 04	05 39	06 10		06 48		07 10			07 51				08 10		08 48		09 10
35¾	—	Rishton	d				05 44			06 53					07 56						08 53		
37½	—	Church & Oswaldtwistle	d				05 47			06 56					07 59						08 56		
38¼	—	**Accrington**	d			05 11	05 50	06 17		06 59		07 17			08 02				08 18		08 59		09 18
40	—	Huncoat	d				05 54			07 03					08 06						09 03		
41½	—	Hapton	d				05 57			07 06					08 09						09 06		
43	—	Rose Grove	d				06 00			07 09					08 12						09 09		
—	—	Burnley Manchester Road 41	a					06 26				07 26							08 26				09 26
—	—	Leeds 10 41	a					07 39				08 39							09 39				10 38
44	—	Burnley Barracks	d							07 12					08 15						09 12		
44½	—	**Burnley Central**	d			05 21	06 05			07 15					08 18						09 15		
46¾	—	Brierfield	d				06 09			07 19					08 22						09 19		
48	—	Nelson	d				06 12			07 22					08 25						09 22		
50	—	**Colne**	a			05 37	06 22			07 32					08 35						09 32		

		TP ◇1 A 🚲	NT	NT C	NT B	NT F	TP ◇1 A 🚲	NT	NT C	NT B	NT F	TP ◇1 A 🚲	NT	NT C	NT B	NT F	TP ◇1 A 🚲	NT	NT C	NT B	NT F	TP ◇1 A 🚲	NT
Blackpool North	d	08 44		09 20	09 29	09 37	09 43		10 20	10 29	10 37	10 44		11 20	11 29	11 37	11 44		12 20	12 29	12 37	12 44	
Layton	d			09 23					10 23					11 23					12 23				
Poulton-le-Fylde	d	08 50		09 28	09 35		09 49		10 28	10 35		10 50		11 28	11 35		11 50		12 28	12 35		12 50	
Blackpool South	d		08 44					09 44					10 44					11 44					12 44
Blackpool Pleasure Beach	d		08 46					09 46					10 46					11 46					12 46
Squires Gate	d		08 48					09 48					10 48					11 48					12 48
St Annes-on-the-Sea	d		08 52					09 52					10 52					11 52					12 52
Ansdell & Fairhaven	d		08 55					09 55					10 55					11 55					12 55
Lytham	d		08 58					09 58					10 58					11 58					12 58
Moss Side	d		09 03					10 03					11 03					12 03					13 03
Kirkham & Wesham	d		09 10	09 37		09 52		10 10	10 37		10 52		11 10	11 37		11 52		12 10	12 37		12 52		13 10
Salwick	d																						
Preston 8	a	09 08	09 20	09 47	09 52	10 02	10 07	10 20	10 47	10 52	11 02	11 08	11 20	11 47	11 52	12 02	12 08	12 20	12 47	12 52	13 02	13 08	13 20
	d		09 22		09 54			10 22		10 54			11 22		11 54			12 22		12 54			13 22
Lostock Hall	d		09 27					10 27					11 27					12 27					13 27
Bamber Bridge	d		09 30					10 30					11 30					12 30					13 30
Pleasington	d		09 38					10 38					11 38					12 38					13 38
Cherry Tree	d		09 41					10 41					11 41					12 41					13 41
Mill Hill (Lancashire)	d		09 43					10 43					11 43					12 43					13 43
Blackburn	a		09 46		10 09			10 46		11 10			11 46		12 10			12 46		13 10			13 46
Clitheroe 94	a																						
Blackburn	d		09 48		10 10			10 48		11 10			11 48		12 10			12 48		13 10			13 48
Rishton	d		09 53					10 53					11 53					12 53					13 53
Church & Oswaldtwistle	d		09 56					10 56					11 56					12 56					13 56
Accrington	d		09 59		10 17			10 59		11 18			11 59		12 18			12 59		13 18			13 59
Huncoat	d		10 03					11 03					12 03					13 03					14 03
Hapton	d		10 06					11 06					12 06					13 06					14 06
Rose Grove	d		10 09					11 09					12 09					13 09					14 09
Burnley Manchester Road 41	a				10 26					11 27					12 26					13 26			
Leeds 10 41	a				11 39					12 39					13 40					14 39			
Burnley Barracks	d		10 12					11 12					12 12					13 12					14 12
Burnley Central	d		10 15					11 15					12 15					13 15					14 15
Brierfield	d		10 19					11 19					12 19					13 19					14 19
Nelson	d		10 22					11 22					12 22					13 22					14 22
Colne	a		10 32					11 32					12 32					13 32					14 32

A To Manchester Airport
B To York
C To Manchester Victoria
D To Hazel Grove
E To Liverpool Lime Street
F To Liverpool South Parkway

Blackpool - Preston - Blackburn, Accrington, Burnley and Colne

		NT	NT	NT	TP	NT	NT	NT	NT	TP	NT	NT	NT	NT	TP	NT	NT	NT	NT	TP	NT	NT
					◇1					◇1					◇1					◇1		
		A	B	C	D		A	B	C	D		A	B	E	D		A	B	E	D		B
					trolley					trolley					trolley					trolley		
Blackpool North	d	13 20	13 29	13 37	13 44		14 20	14 29	14 37	14 44		15 20	15 29	15 37	15 44		16 20	16 29	16 35	16 40		17 14
Layton	d	13 23					14 23					15 23					16 23			16 43		
Poulton-le-Fylde	d	13 28	13 35		13 50		14 28	14 35		14 50		15 28	15 35		15 50		16 28	16 35		16 48		17 20
Blackpool South	d					13 44					14 44					15 44					16 44	
Blackpool Pleasure Beach	d					13 46					14 46					15 46					16 46	
Squires Gate	d					13 48					14 48					15 48					16 48	
St Annes-on-the-Sea	d					13 52					14 52					15 52					16 52	
Ansdell & Fairhaven	d					13 55					14 55					15 55					16 55	
Lytham	d					13 58					14 58					15 58					16 58	
Moss Side	d					14 03					15 03					16 02					17 03	
Kirkham & Wesham	d	13 37		13 52		14 10	14 37		14 52		15 10	15 37		15 52		16 10	16 37		16 52	16 57	17 10	17 29
Salwick	d															16 15						
Preston 8	a	13 47	13 52	14 02	14 08	14 20	14 47	14 52	15 02	15 08	15 20	15 47	15 52	16 02	16 08	16 22	16 47	16 52	17 02	17 08	17 20	17 44
	d		13 54			14 22		14 54			15 22		15 54			16 22		16 54			17 22	17 44
Lostock Hall	d					14 27					15 27					16 27					17 27	17 51
Bamber Bridge	d					14 30					15 30					16 30					17 30	17 54
Pleasington	d					14 38					15 38					16 38					17 38	18 01
Cherry Tree	d					14 41					15 41					16 41					17 41	18 05
Mill Hill (Lancashire)	d					14 43					15 43					16 43					17 43	18 07
Blackburn	a		14 10			14 46		15 10			15 47		16 09			16 48		17 10			17 48	18 11
Clitheroe 94	a																					
Blackburn	d		14 10			14 48		15 10			15 48		16 10			16 50		17 10			17 58	18 11
Rishton	d					14 53					15 53					16 55					18 03	
Church & Oswaldtwistle	d					14 56					15 56					16 58					18 06	
Accrington	d		14 18			14 59		15 18			15 59		16 17			17 01		17 18			18 09	18 19
Huncoat	d					15 03					16 03					17 05					18 13	
Hapton	d					15 06					16 06					17 08					18 16	
Rose Grove	d					15 09					16 09					17 11					18 19	
Burnley Manchester Road 41	a		14 26					15 26					16 26					17 26				18 27
Leeds 10 41	a		15 39					16 39					17 39					18 39				19 39
Burnley Barracks	d					15 12					16 12					17 14					18 22	
Burnley Central	d					15 15					16 15					17 18					18 25	
Brierfield	d					15 19					16 19					17 21					18 29	
Nelson	d					15 22					16 22					17 24					18 32	
Colne	a					15 32					16 32					17 34					18 42	

		TP	NT	NT	NT	NT	NT	TP	NT	NT	NT	TP	NT	NT	NT	NT	TP	NT	NT	TP	NT	NT	NT
		◇1						◇1				◇1					◇1			◇1			
		D	E		A	B	E	D		A	E	D		A	B	E	D		A	D		E	A
		trolley						trolley															
Blackpool North	d	17 20	17 37		18 20	18 29	18 37	18 44		19 20	19 37	19 44		20 20	20 29	20 37	20 45		21 20	21 37		22 14	22 20
Layton	d	17 23			18 23					19 23				20 23					21 23				22 23
Poulton-le-Fylde	d	17 27			18 28	18 35		18 50		19 28		19 50		20 28	20 35		20 51		21 28	21 43			22 28
Blackpool South	d			17 44					18 44				19 44					20 44			22 00		
Blackpool Pleasure Beach	d			17 46					18 46				19 46					20 46			22 02		
Squires Gate	d			17 48					18 48				19 48					20 48			22 04		
St Annes-on-the-Sea	d			17 52					18 52				19 52					20 52			22 08		
Ansdell & Fairhaven	d			17 55					18 55				19 55					20 55			22 11		
Lytham	d			17 58					18 58				19 58					20 58			22 14		
Moss Side	d			18 03					19 03				20 03					21 03			22 19		
Kirkham & Wesham	d		17 52	18 10	18 37		18 52		19 10	19 37			20 10	20 37				21 10	21 37		22 26		22 37
Salwick	d																						
Preston 8	a	17 45	18 02	18 20	18 47	18 52	19 02	19 07	19 20	19 47	20 02	20 08	20 20	20 47	20 53	21 01	21 09	21 20	21 47	22 01	22 36	22 41	22 47
	d			18 24		18 54			19 22				20 22		20 54			21 22			22 38		
Lostock Hall	d			18 30					19 27				20 27					21 27			22 43		
Bamber Bridge	d			18 33					19 30				20 30					21 30			22 46		
Pleasington	d			18 41					19 38				20 38					21 38			22 54		
Cherry Tree	d			18 44					19 41				20 41					21 41			22 57		
Mill Hill (Lancashire)	d			18 46					19 43				20 43					21 43			22 59		
Blackburn	a			18 52		19 10			19 46				20 46		21 09			21 46			23 04		
Clitheroe 94	a																						
Blackburn	d			18 53		19 10			19 48				20 48		21 10			21 48			23 05		
Rishton	d			18 58					19 53				20 53					21 53			23 10		
Church & Oswaldtwistle	d			19 01					19 56				20 56					21 56			23 13		
Accrington	d			19 04		19 18			19 59				20 59		21 17			21 59			23 16		
Huncoat	d			19 08					20 03				21 03					22 03			23 20		
Hapton	d			19 11					20 06				21 06					22 06			23 23		
Rose Grove	d			19 14					20 09				21 09					22 09			23 26		
Burnley Manchester Road 41	a					19 26									21 28								
Leeds 10 41	a					20 40									22 41								
Burnley Barracks	d			19 17					20 12				21 12					22 12			23 29		
Burnley Central	d			19 20					20 15				21 15					22 15			23 32		
Brierfield	d			19 24					20 19				21 19					22 19			23 36		
Nelson	d			19 27					20 22				21 22					22 22			23 39		
Colne	a			19 37					20 32				21 32					22 32			23 49		

A To Manchester Victoria
B To York
C To Liverpool South Parkway
D To Manchester Airport
E To Liverpool Lime Street

Table 97

Blackpool - Preston - Blackburn, Accrington, Burnley and Colne

Mondays to Fridays
until 15 July

		TP	NT	NT
		◇1		
		A	B	
Blackpool North	d	22 44	23 13	
Layton	d		23 16	
Poulton-le-Fylde	d	22 50	23 21	
Blackpool South	d			23 30
Blackpool Pleasure Beach	d			23 32
Squires Gate	d			23 34
St Annes-on-the-Sea	d			23 38
Ansdell & Fairhaven	d			23 41
Lytham	d			23 44
Moss Side	d			23 49
Kirkham & Wesham	d		23 30	23 56
Salwick	d			
Preston 8	a	23 08	23 40	00 08
	d			
Lostock Hall	d			
Bamber Bridge	d			
Pleasington	d			
Cherry Tree	d			
Mill Hill (Lancashire)	d			
Blackburn	a			
Clitheroe 94	a			
Blackburn	d			
Rishton	d			
Church & Oswaldtwistle	d			
Accrington	d			
Huncoat	d			
Hapton	d			
Rose Grove	d			
Burnley Manchester Road 41	a			
Leeds 10 41	a			
Burnley Barracks	d			
Burnley Central	d			
Brierfield	d			
Nelson	d			
Colne	a			

Mondays to Fridays
18 July to 30 September

		NT MX	TP	NT	NT	NT	TP	NT	NT	NT	TP	NT	NT	NT	TP	NT	NT	TP	NT	NT	NT	TP	NT
			◇1				◇1				◇1				◇1			◇1				◇1	
			A			C	A		B	C	A	D		E		B	C			B	C	A	
							🚲				🚲				🚲			🚲				🚲	
Blackpool North	d		03 31		04 56	05 29	05 39		06 19	06 28	06 40	06 53		07 02	07 10	07 18	07 29	07 36		08 20	08 29	08 44	
Layton	d								06 22		06 43				07 13	07 21		07 39		08 23			
Poulton-le-Fylde	d				05 02	05 35	05 45		06 27	06 34	06 47			07 08	07 17	07 26	07 35	07 43		08 28	08 35	08 50	
Blackpool South	d	23p30						05 42					06 42						07 42				08 44
Blackpool Pleasure Beach	d	23p32						05 44					06 44						07 44				08 46
Squires Gate	d	23p34						05 46					06 46						07 46				08 48
St Annes-on-the-Sea	d	23p38						05 50					06 50						07 50				08 52
Ansdell & Fairhaven	d	23p41						05 53					06 53						07 53				08 55
Lytham	d	23p44						05 56					06 56						07 56				08 58
Moss Side	d	23p49						06 01					07 01						08 01				09 03
Kirkham & Wesham	d	23p56						06 08	06 36		06 56		07 09		07 26	07 35		07 52	08 09	08 37			09 10
Salwick	d												07 13						08 13				
Preston 8	a	00 08			05 20	05 52	06 03	06 19	06 46	06 52	07 07	07 15	07 20	07 28	07 37	07 46	07 52	08 03	08 20	08 47	08 52	09 08	09 20
	d			04 47	05 22	05 54		06 21		06 54			07 22				07 54		08 22		08 54		09 22
Lostock Hall	d							06 26					07 27						08 27				09 27
Bamber Bridge	d							06 29					07 30						08 30				09 30
Pleasington	d							06 37					07 38						08 38				09 38
Cherry Tree	d							06 40					07 41						08 41				09 41
Mill Hill (Lancashire)	d							06 42					07 43						08 43				09 43
Blackburn	a			05 03	05 38	06 09		06 45		07 09			07 50				08 10		08 47		09 10		09 46
Clitheroe 94	a																						
Blackburn	d			05 04	05 39	06 10		06 48		07 10			07 51				08 10		08 48		09 10		09 48
Rishton	d				05 44			06 53					07 56						08 53				09 53
Church & Oswaldtwistle	d				05 47			06 56					07 59						08 56				09 56
Accrington	d			05 11	05 50	06 17		06 59		07 17			08 02				08 18		08 59		09 18		09 59
Huncoat	d				05 54			07 03					08 06						09 03				10 03
Hapton	d				05 57			07 06					08 09						09 06				10 06
Rose Grove	d				06 00			07 09					08 12						09 09				10 09
Burnley Manchester Road 41	a					06 26				07 26							08 26				09 26		
Leeds 10 41	a					07 39				08 39							09 39				10 38		
Burnley Barracks	d							07 12					08 15						09 12				10 12
Burnley Central	d			05 21	06 05			07 15					08 18						09 15				10 15
Brierfield	d				06 09			07 19					08 22						09 19				10 19
Nelson	d				06 12			07 22					08 25						09 22				10 22
Colne	a			05 37	06 22			07 32					08 35						09 32				10 32

A To Manchester Airport
B To Manchester Victoria
C To York
D To Hazel Grove
E To Liverpool Lime Street

18 July to 30 September

Blackpool - Preston - Blackburn, Accrington, Burnley and Colne

	NT	NT	NT	TP	NT	NT	NT	NT	TP	NT	NT	NT	NT	TP	NT	NT	NT	NT	TP	NT	NT	NT
				◇1					◇1					◇1					◇1			
	A	B	C	D		A	B	C	D		A	B	C	D		A	B	C	D		A	B
Blackpool North d	09 20	09 29	09 37	09 43		10 20	10 29	10 37	10 44		11 20	11 29	11 37	11 44		12 20	12 29	12 37	12 44		13 20	13 29
Layton d	09 23					10 23					11 23					12 23					13 23	
Poulton-le-Fylde d	09 28	09 35		09 49		10 28	10 35		10 50		11 28	11 35		11 50		12 28	12 35		12 50		13 28	13 35
Blackpool South d					09 44					10 44					11 44					12 44		
Blackpool Pleasure Beach d					09 46					10 46					11 46					12 46		
Squires Gate d					09 48					10 48					11 48					12 48		
St Annes-on-the-Sea d					09 52					10 52					11 52					12 52		
Ansdell & Fairhaven d					09 55					10 55					11 55					12 55		
Lytham d					09 58					10 58					11 58					12 58		
Moss Side d					10 03					11 03					12 03					13 03		
Kirkham & Wesham d	09 37		09 52		10 10	10 37		10 52		11 10	11 37		11 52		12 10	12 37		12 52		13 10	13 37	
Salwick d																						
Preston 8 a	09 47	09 52	10 02	10 07	10 20	10 47	10 52	11 02	11 08	11 20	11 47	11 52	12 02	12 08	12 20	12 47	12 52	13 02	13 08	13 20	13 47	13 52
d		09 54			10 22		10 54			11 22		11 54			12 22		12 54			13 22		13 54
Lostock Hall d					10 27					11 27					12 27					13 27		
Bamber Bridge d					10 30					11 30					12 30					13 30		
Pleasington d					10 38					11 38					12 38					13 38		
Cherry Tree d					10 41					11 41					12 41					13 41		
Mill Hill (Lancashire) d					10 43					11 43					12 43					13 43		
Blackburn a		10 09			10 46		11 10			11 46		12 10			12 46		13 10			13 46		14 10
Clitheroe 94 a																						
Blackburn d		10 10			10 48		11 10			11 48		12 10			12 48		13 10			13 48		14 10
Rishton d					10 53					11 53					12 53					13 53		
Church & Oswaldtwistle d					10 56					11 56					12 56					13 56		
Accrington d		10 17			10 59		11 18			11 59		12 18			12 59		13 18			13 59		14 18
Huncoat d					11 03					12 03					13 03					14 03		
Hapton d					11 06					12 06					13 06					14 06		
Rose Grove d					11 09					12 09					13 09					14 09		
Burnley Manchester Road 41 a		10 26					11 27					12 26					13 26					14 26
Leeds 10 41 a		11 39					12 39					13 40					14 39					15 39
Burnley Barracks d					11 12					12 12					13 12					14 12		
Burnley Central d					11 15					12 15					13 15					14 15		
Brierfield d					11 19					12 19					13 19					14 19		
Nelson d					11 22					12 22					13 22					14 22		
Colne a					11 32					12 32					13 32					14 32		

	NT	TP	NT	NT	NT	NT	TP	NT	NT	NT	NT	TP	NT	NT	NT	NT	TP	NT	NT	TP	NT
		◇1					◇1					◇1					◇1			◇1	
	C	D		A	B	C	D		A	B	E	D		A	B	E	D		B	D	E
Blackpool North d	13 37	13 44		14 20	14 29	14 37	14 44		15 20	15 29	15 37	15 44		16 20	16 29	16 35	16 40		17 14	17 20	17 37
Layton d				14 23					15 23					16 23			16 43			17 23	
Poulton-le-Fylde d		13 50		14 28	14 35		14 50		15 28	15 35		15 50		16 28	16 35		16 48		17 20	17 27	
Blackpool South d			13 44					14 44					15 44					16 44			
Blackpool Pleasure Beach d			13 46					14 46					15 46					16 46			
Squires Gate d			13 48					14 48					15 48					16 48			
St Annes-on-the-Sea d			13 52					14 52					15 52					16 52			
Ansdell & Fairhaven d			13 55					14 55					15 55					16 55			
Lytham d			13 58					14 58					15 58					16 58			
Moss Side d			14 03					15 03					16 02					17 03			
Kirkham & Wesham d	13 52		14 10	14 37		14 52		15 10	15 37		15 52		16 10	16 37		16 52	16 57	17 10	17 29		17 52
Salwick d													16 15								
Preston 8 a	14 02	14 08	14 20	14 47	14 52	15 02	15 08	15 20	15 47	15 52	16 02	16 08	16 22	16 47	16 52	17 02	17 08	17 20	17 44	17 45	18 02
d			14 22		14 54			15 22		15 54			16 22		16 54			17 22	17 44		
Lostock Hall d			14 27					15 27					16 27					17 27	17 51		
Bamber Bridge d			14 30					15 30					16 30					17 30	17 54		
Pleasington d			14 38					15 38					16 38					17 38	18 01		
Cherry Tree d			14 41					15 41					16 41					17 41	18 05		
Mill Hill (Lancashire) d			14 43					15 43					16 43					17 43	18 07		
Blackburn a			14 46		15 10			15 47		16 09			16 48		17 10			17 48	18 11		
Clitheroe 94 a																					
Blackburn d			14 48		15 10			15 48		16 10			16 50		17 10			17 58	18 11		
Rishton d			14 53					15 53					16 55					18 03			
Church & Oswaldtwistle d			14 56					15 56					16 58					18 06			
Accrington d			14 59		15 18			15 59		16 17			17 01		17 18			18 09	18 19		
Huncoat d			15 03					16 03					17 05					18 13			
Hapton d			15 06					16 06					17 08					18 16			
Rose Grove d			15 09					16 09					17 11					18 19			
Burnley Manchester Road 41 a					15 26					16 26					17 26				18 27		
Leeds 10 41 a					16 39					17 39					18 39				19 39		
Burnley Barracks d			15 12					16 12					17 14					18 22			
Burnley Central d			15 15					16 15					17 18					18 25			
Brierfield d			15 19					16 19					17 21					18 29			
Nelson d			15 22					16 22					17 24					18 32			
Colne a			15 32					16 32					17 34					18 42			

A To Manchester Victoria
B To York
C To Liverpool South Parkway
D To Manchester Airport
E To Liverpool Lime Street

Table 97

Mondays to Fridays

18 July to 30 September

Blackpool - Preston - Blackburn, Accrington, Burnley and Colne

		NT	NT	NT	NT	TP	NT	NT		NT	TP	NT	NT	NT	NT	TP	NT	NT		TP	NT	NT	NT	TP	NT
						◇1					◇1					◇1				◇1				◇1	
			A	B	C	D		A		C	D		A	B	C	D		A		D		C	A	D	A
						🛒																			
Blackpool North	d		18 20	18 29	18 37	18 44		19 20		19 37	19 44		20 20	20 29	20 37	20 45		21 20		21 37		22 14	22 20	22 44	23 13
Layton	d		18 23					19 23					20 23					21 23					22 23		23 16
Poulton-le-Fylde	d		18 28	18 35		18 50		19 28			19 50		20 28	20 35		20 51		21 28		21 43			22 28	22 50	23 21
Blackpool South	d	17 44					18 44					19 44					20 44				22 00				
Blackpool Pleasure Beach	d	17 46					18 46					19 46					20 46				22 02				
Squires Gate	d	17 48					18 48					19 48					20 48				22 04				
St Annes-on-the-Sea	d	17 52					18 52					19 52					20 52				22 08				
Ansdell & Fairhaven	d	17 55					18 55					19 55					20 55				22 11				
Lytham	d	17 58					18 58					19 58					20 58				22 14				
Moss Side	d	18 03					19 03					20 03					21 03				22 19				
Kirkham & Wesham	d	18 10	18 37		18 52		19 10	19 37				20 10	20 37				21 10	21 37			22 26		22 37		23 30
Salwick	d																								
Preston 8	a	18 20	18 47	18 52	19 02	19 07	19 20	19 47		20 02	20 08	20 20	20 47	20 53	21 01	21 09	21 20	21 47		22 01	22 36	22 41	22 47	23 08	23 40
	d	18 24		18 54			19 22					20 22		20 54			21 22				22 38				
Lostock Hall	d	18 30					19 27					20 27					21 27				22 43				
Bamber Bridge	d	18 33					19 30					20 30					21 30				22 46				
Pleasington	d	18 41					19 38					20 38					21 38				22 54				
Cherry Tree	d	18 44					19 41					20 41					21 41				22 57				
Mill Hill (Lancashire)	d	18 46					19 43					20 43					21 43				22 59				
Blackburn	a	18 52		19 10			19 46					20 46		21 09			21 46				23 04				
Clitheroe 94	a																								
Blackburn	d	18 53		19 10			19 48					20 48		21 10			21 48				23 05				
Rishton	d	18 58					19 53					20 53					21 53				23 10				
Church & Oswaldtwistle	d	19 01					19 56					20 56					21 56				23 13				
Accrington	d	19 04		19 18			19 59					20 59		21 17			21 59				23 16				
Huncoat	d	19 08					20 03					21 03					22 03				23 20				
Hapton	d	19 11					20 06					21 06					22 06				23 23				
Rose Grove	d	19 14					20 09					21 09					22 09				23 26				
Burnley Manchester Road 41	a			19 26										21 28											
Leeds 10 41	a			20 40										22 41											
Burnley Barracks	d	19 17					20 12					21 12					22 12				23 29				
Burnley Central	d	19 20					20 15					21 15					22 15				23 32				
Brierfield	d	19 24					20 19					21 19					22 19				23 36				
Nelson	d	19 27					20 22					21 22					22 22				23 39				
Colne	a	19 37					20 32					21 32					22 32				23 49				

		NT
Blackpool North	d	
Layton	d	
Poulton-le-Fylde	d	
Blackpool South	d	23 30
Blackpool Pleasure Beach	d	23 32
Squires Gate	d	23 34
St Annes-on-the-Sea	d	23 38
Ansdell & Fairhaven	d	23 41
Lytham	d	23 44
Moss Side	d	23 49
Kirkham & Wesham	d	23 56
Salwick	d	
Preston 8	a	00 08
	d	
Lostock Hall	d	
Bamber Bridge	d	
Pleasington	d	
Cherry Tree	d	
Mill Hill (Lancashire)	d	
Blackburn	a	
Clitheroe 94	a	
Blackburn	d	
Rishton	d	
Church & Oswaldtwistle	d	
Accrington	d	
Huncoat	d	
Hapton	d	
Rose Grove	d	
Burnley Manchester Road 41	a	
Leeds 10 41	a	
Burnley Barracks	d	
Burnley Central	d	
Brierfield	d	
Nelson	d	
Colne	a	

A To Manchester Victoria
B To York
C To Liverpool Lime Street
D To Manchester Airport

Table 97

Mondays to Fridays
from 3 October

Blackpool - Preston - Blackburn, Accrington, Burnley and Colne

		NT	NT	NT MX	TP	NT	NT	NT	TP	NT		NT	NT	TP	NT	NT	NT	TP	NT	NT		TP	NT	NT	NT
					◇1				◇1					◇1				◇1				◇1			
		A	A		B			C	B			D	C	B	E		F		D	C				D	C
		🚌	🚌						🍴					🍴				🍴				🍴			
Blackpool North	d	20p40			03 31		04 56	05 29	05 39			06 19	06 28	06 40	06 53		07 02	07 10	07 18	07 29		07 36		08 20	08 29
Layton	d											06 22		06 43				07 13	07 21			07 39		08 23	
Poulton-le-Fylde	d	20p55					05 02	05 35	05 45			06 27	06 34	06 47			07 08	07 17	07 26	07 35		07 43		08 28	08 35
Blackpool South	d			23p30						05 42						06 42							07 42		
Blackpool Pleasure Beach	d			23p32						05 44						06 44							07 44		
Squires Gate	d			23p34						05 46						06 46							07 46		
St Annes-on-the-Sea	d			23p38						05 50						06 50							07 50		
Ansdell & Fairhaven	d			23p41						05 53						06 53							07 53		
Lytham	d			23p44						05 56						06 56							07 56		
Moss Side	d			23p49						06 01						07 01							08 01		
Kirkham & Wesham	d			23p56						06 08		06 36		06 56		07 09		07 26	07 35			07 52	08 09	08 37	
Salwick	d															07 13							08 13		
Preston 8	a	21p35		00 08			05 20	05 52	06 03	06 19		06 46	06 52	07 07	07 15	07 20	07 28	07 37	07 46	07 52		08 03	08 20	08 47	08 52
	d	21p40	22p05			04 47	05 22	05 54		06 21			06 54			07 22				07 54			08 22		08 54
Lostock Hall	d		22p19							06 26						07 27							08 27		
Bamber Bridge	d		22p29							06 29						07 30							08 30		
Pleasington	d		22p47							06 37						07 38							08 38		
Cherry Tree	d		22p51							06 40						07 41							08 41		
Mill Hill (Lancashire)	d		22p57							06 42						07 43							08 43		
Blackburn	a	22p09	23p06			05 03	05 38	06 09		06 45			07 09			07 50				08 10			08 47		09 10
Clitheroe 94	a																								
Blackburn	d	22p10	23p07			05 04	05 39	06 10		06 48			07 10			07 51				08 10			08 48		09 10
Rishton	d		23p17				05 44			06 53						07 56							08 53		
Church & Oswaldtwistle	d		23p29				05 47			06 56						07 59							08 56		
Accrington	d	22p28	23p33			05 11	05 50	06 17		06 59			07 17			08 02				08 18			08 59		09 18
Huncoat	d		23p39				05 54			07 03						08 06							09 03		
Hapton	d		23p45				05 57			07 06						08 09							09 06		
Rose Grove	d		23p51				06 00			07 09						08 12							09 09		
Burnley Manchester Road 41	a	22p47						06 26					07 26							08 26					09 26
Leeds 10 41	a	01 03						07 39					08 39							09 39					10 38
Burnley Barracks	d		23p55							07 12						08 15							09 12		
Burnley Central	d		23p59			05 21	06 05			07 15						08 18							09 15		
Brierfield	d		00 07				06 09			07 19						08 22							09 19		
Nelson	d		00 12				06 12			07 22						08 25							09 22		
Colne	a		00 20			05 37	06 24			07 34						08 37							09 34		

		TP	NT	NT	NT	NT		TP	NT	NT	NT	NT	TP	NT	NT	NT		NT	TP	NT	NT	NT	NT	TP	NT
		◇1						◇1					◇1						◇1					◇1	
		G		D	C	H		B		D	C	H	B		D	C		H	B		D	C	H	B	
		🍴						🍴					🍴						🍴					🍴	
Blackpool North	d	08 44		09 20	09 29	09 37		09 43		10 20	10 29	10 37	10 44		11 20	11 29		11 37	11 44		12 20	12 29	12 37	12 44	
Layton	d			09 23						10 23					11 23						12 23				
Poulton-le-Fylde	d	08 50		09 28	09 35			09 49		10 28	10 35		10 50		11 28	11 35			11 50		12 28	12 35		12 50	
Blackpool South	d		08 44						09 44					10 44						11 44					12 44
Blackpool Pleasure Beach	d		08 46						09 46					10 46						11 46					12 46
Squires Gate	d		08 48						09 48					10 48						11 48					12 48
St Annes-on-the-Sea	d		08 52						09 52					10 52						11 52					12 52
Ansdell & Fairhaven	d		08 55						09 55					10 55						11 55					12 55
Lytham	d		08 58						09 58					10 58						11 58					12 58
Moss Side	d		09 03						10 03					11 03						12 03					13 03
Kirkham & Wesham	d		09 10	09 37		09 52			10 10	10 37		10 52		11 10	11 37			11 52		12 10	12 37		12 52		13 10
Salwick	d																								
Preston 8	a	09 08	09 20	09 47	09 52	10 02		10 07	10 20	10 47	10 52	11 02	11 08	11 20	11 47	11 52		12 02	12 08	12 20	12 47	12 52	13 02	13 08	13 20
	d		09 22		09 54				10 22		10 54			11 22		11 54				12 22		12 54			13 22
Lostock Hall	d		09 27						10 27					11 27						12 27					13 27
Bamber Bridge	d		09 30						10 30					11 30						12 30					13 30
Pleasington	d		09 38						10 38					11 38						12 38					13 38
Cherry Tree	d		09 41						10 41					11 41						12 41					13 41
Mill Hill (Lancashire)	d		09 43						10 43					11 43						12 43					13 43
Blackburn	a		09 46		10 09				10 46		11 10			11 46		12 10				12 46		13 10			13 46
Clitheroe 94	a																								
Blackburn	d		09 48		10 10				10 48		11 10			11 48		12 10				12 48		13 10			13 48
Rishton	d		09 53						10 53					11 53						12 53					13 53
Church & Oswaldtwistle	d		09 56						10 56					11 56						12 56					13 56
Accrington	d		09 59		10 17				10 59		11 18			11 59		12 18				12 59		13 18			13 59
Huncoat	d		10 03						11 03					12 03						13 03					14 03
Hapton	d		10 06						11 06					12 06						13 06					14 06
Rose Grove	d		10 09						11 09					12 09						13 09					14 09
Burnley Manchester Road 41	a				10 26						11 27					12 26						13 26			
Leeds 10 41	a				11 39						12 39					13 40						14 39			
Burnley Barracks	d		10 12						11 12					12 12						13 12					14 12
Burnley Central	d		10 15						11 15					12 15						13 15					14 15
Brierfield	d		10 19						11 19					12 19						13 19					14 19
Nelson	d		10 22						11 22					12 22						13 22					14 22
Colne	a		10 34						11 34					12 34						13 34					14 34

A MO from 31 October
B To Manchester Airport
C To York
D To Manchester Victoria
E To Hazel Grove
F To Liverpool Lime Street
G not 9 December. To Manchester Airport
H To Liverpool South Parkway

Table 97

Mondays to Fridays
from 3 October

Blackpool - Preston - Blackburn, Accrington, Burnley and Colne

		NT A		NT B	NT C	TP ◇1 D	NT	NT A	NT B	NT C	TP ◇1 D	NT		NT A	NT B	NT E	TP ◇1 D	NT	NT A	NT B	NT E	TP ◇1 D		NT	NT B
Blackpool North	d	13 20		13 29	13 37	13 44		14 20	14 29	14 37	14 44			15 20	15 29	15 37	15 44		16 20	16 29	16 35	16 40			17 14
Layton	d	13 23						14 23						15 23					16 23			16 43			
Poulton-le-Fylde	d	13 28		13 35		13 50		14 28	14 35		14 50			15 28	15 35		15 50		16 28	16 35		16 48			17 20
Blackpool South	d						13 44					14 44						15 44						16 44	
Blackpool Pleasure Beach	d						13 46					14 46						15 46						16 46	
Squires Gate	d						13 48					14 48						15 48						16 48	
St Annes-on-the-Sea	d						13 52					14 52						15 52						16 52	
Ansdell & Fairhaven	d						13 55					14 55						15 55						16 55	
Lytham	d						13 58					14 58						15 58						16 58	
Moss Side	d						14 03					15 03						16 02						17 03	
Kirkham & Wesham	d	13 37			13 52		14 10	14 37		14 52		15 10		15 37		15 52		16 10	16 37		16 52	16 57		17 10	17 29
Salwick	d																	16 15							
Preston 8	a	13 47		13 52	14 02	14 08	14 20	14 47	14 52	15 02	15 08	15 20		15 47	15 52	16 02	16 08	16 22	16 47	16 52	17 02	17 08		17 20	17 44
	d			13 54			14 22		14 54			15 22			15 54			16 22		16 54				17 22	17 44
Lostock Hall	d						14 27					15 27						16 27						17 27	17 51
Bamber Bridge	d						14 30					15 30						16 30						17 30	17 54
Pleasington	d						14 38					15 38						16 38						17 38	18 01
Cherry Tree	d						14 41					15 41						16 41						17 41	18 05
Mill Hill (Lancashire)	d						14 43					15 43						16 43						17 43	18 07
Blackburn	a			14 10			14 46		15 10			15 47			16 09			16 48		17 10				17 48	18 11
Clitheroe 94	a																								
Blackburn	d			14 10			14 48		15 10			15 48			16 10			16 50		17 10				17 58	18 11
Rishton	d						14 53					15 53						16 55						18 03	
Church & Oswaldtwistle	d						14 56					15 56						16 58						18 06	
Accrington	d			14 18			14 59		15 18			15 59			16 17			17 01		17 18				18 09	18 19
Huncoat	d						15 03					16 03						17 05						18 13	
Hapton	d						15 06					16 06						17 08						18 16	
Rose Grove	d						15 09					16 09						17 11						18 19	
Burnley Manchester Road 41	a			14 26					15 26						16 26					17 26					18 27
Leeds 10 41	a			15 39					16 39						17 39					18 39					19 39
Burnley Barracks	d						15 12					16 12						17 14						18 22	
Burnley Central	d						15 15					16 15						17 18						18 25	
Brierfield	d						15 19					16 19						17 21						18 29	
Nelson	d						15 22					16 22						17 24						18 32	
Colne	a						15 34					16 34						17 37						18 44	

		TP ◇1 D	NT E	NT	NT A	NT B	NT E	TP ◇1 D		NT	NT A	NT E	TP ◇1 D	NT	NT A	NT B	NT E	TP ◇1 D		NT	NT A	TP ◇1 D	NT	NT E	NT A
Blackpool North	d	17 20	17 37		18 20	18 29	18 37	18 44			19 20	19 37	19 44		20 20	20 29	20 37	20 45			21 20	21 37		22 14	22 20
Layton	d	17 23			18 23						19 23				20 23						21 23				22 23
Poulton-le-Fylde	d	17 27			18 28	18 35		18 50			19 28		19 50		20 28	20 35		20 51			21 28	21 43			22 28
Blackpool South	d			17 44						18 44				19 44						20 44			22 00		
Blackpool Pleasure Beach	d			17 46						18 46				19 46						20 46			22 02		
Squires Gate	d			17 48						18 48				19 48						20 48			22 04		
St Annes-on-the-Sea	d			17 52						18 52				19 52						20 52			22 08		
Ansdell & Fairhaven	d			17 55						18 55				19 55						20 55			22 11		
Lytham	d			17 58						18 58				19 58						20 58			22 14		
Moss Side	d			18 03						19 03				20 03						21 03			22 19		
Kirkham & Wesham	d		17 52	18 10	18 37		18 52			19 10	19 37			20 10	20 37					21 10	21 37		22 26		22 37
Salwick	d																								
Preston 8	a	17 45	18 02	18 20	18 47	18 52	19 02	19 07		19 20	19 47	20 02	20 08	20 20	20 47	20 53	21 01	21 09		21 20	21 47	22 01	22 36	22 41	22 47
	d			18 24		18 54				19 22				20 22		20 54				21 22			22 38		
Lostock Hall	d			18 30						19 27				20 27						21 27			22 43		
Bamber Bridge	d			18 33						19 30				20 30						21 30			22 46		
Pleasington	d			18 41						19 38				20 38						21 38			22 54		
Cherry Tree	d			18 44						19 41				20 41						21 41			22 57		
Mill Hill (Lancashire)	d			18 46						19 43				20 43						21 43			22 59		
Blackburn	a			18 52		19 10				19 46				20 46		21 09				21 46			23 04		
Clitheroe 94	a																								
Blackburn	d			18 53		19 10				19 48				20 48		21 10				21 48			23 05		
Rishton	d			18 58						19 53				20 53						21 53			23 10		
Church & Oswaldtwistle	d			19 01						19 56				20 56						21 56			23 13		
Accrington	d			19 04		19 18				19 59				20 59		21 17				21 59			23 16		
Huncoat	d			19 08						20 03				21 03						22 03			23 20		
Hapton	d			19 11						20 06				21 06						22 06			23 23		
Rose Grove	d			19 14						20 09				21 09						22 09			23 26		
Burnley Manchester Road 41	a					19 26										21 28									
Leeds 10 41	a					20 40										22 41									
Burnley Barracks	d			19 17						20 12				21 12						22 12			23 29		
Burnley Central	d			19 20						20 15				21 15						22 15			23 32		
Brierfield	d			19 24						20 19				21 19						22 19			23 36		
Nelson	d			19 27						20 22				21 22						22 22			23 39		
Colne	a			19 39						20 34				21 34						22 34			23 51		

A To Manchester Victoria
B To York
C To Liverpool South Parkway
D To Manchester Airport
E To Liverpool Lime Street

from 3 October

Blackpool - Preston - Blackburn, Accrington, Burnley and Colne

		TP ◇1 A	NT B	NT
Blackpool North	d	22 44	23 13	
Layton	d		23 16	
Poulton-le-Fylde	d	22 50	23 21	
Blackpool South	d			23 30
Blackpool Pleasure Beach	d			23 32
Squires Gate	d			23 34
St Annes-on-the-Sea	d			23 38
Ansdell & Fairhaven	d			23 41
Lytham	d			23 44
Moss Side	d			23 49
Kirkham & Wesham	d		23 30	23 56
Salwick	d			
Preston 8	a	23 08	23 40	00 08
	d			
Lostock Hall	d			
Bamber Bridge	d			
Pleasington	d			
Cherry Tree	d			
Mill Hill (Lancashire)	d			
Blackburn	a			
Clitheroe 94	a			
Blackburn	d			
Rishton	d			
Church & Oswaldtwistle	d			
Accrington	d			
Huncoat	d			
Hapton	d			
Rose Grove	d			
Burnley Manchester Road 41	a			
Leeds 10 41	a			
Burnley Barracks	d			
Burnley Central	d			
Brierfield	d			
Nelson	d			
Colne	a			

Saturdays

until 16 July

		NT	TP ◇1 A	NT	NT	NT C	TP ◇1 A	NT	NT B	NT C	TP ◇1 A ⚒	NT D	NT	NT E	NT B	NT C	TP ◇1 A ⚒	NT	NT B	NT C	NT F	TP ◇1 A ⚒	NT
Blackpool North	d		03 36		04 56	05 29	05 39		06 19	06 28	06 40	06 53		07 02	07 18	07 29	07 44		08 20	08 29	08 38	08 44	
Layton	d								06 22		06 43				07 21		07 47		08 23				
Poulton-le-Fylde	d				05 02	05 35	05 45		06 27	06 34	06 47			07 08	07 26	07 35	07 51		08 28	08 35		08 50	
Blackpool South	d	23p30						05 42					06 42					07 42					08 44
Blackpool Pleasure Beach	d	23p32						05 44					06 44					07 44					08 46
Squires Gate	d	23p34						05 46					06 46					07 46					08 48
St Annes-on-the-Sea	d	23p38						05 50					06 50					07 50					08 52
Ansdell & Fairhaven	d	23p41						05 53					06 53					07 53					08 55
Lytham	d	23p44						05 56					06 56					07 56					08 58
Moss Side	d	23p49						06 01					07 01					08 01					09 03
Kirkham & Wesham	d	23p56						06 08	06 36		06 56		07 09		07 35		08 00	08 09	08 37				09 10
Salwick	d												07 13					08 13					
Preston 8	a	00 08			05 20	05 52	06 03	06 19	06 46	06 52	07 07	07 15	07 20	07 28	07 46	07 52	08 11	08 20	08 47	08 52	09 02	09 08	09 20
	d			04 47	05 22	05 54		06 21		06 54			07 22			07 54		08 22		08 54			09 22
Lostock Hall	d							06 26					07 27					08 27					09 27
Bamber Bridge	d							06 29					07 30					08 30					09 30
Pleasington	d							06 37					07 38					08 38					09 38
Cherry Tree	d							06 40					07 41					08 41					09 41
Mill Hill (Lancashire)	d							06 42					07 43					08 43					09 43
Blackburn	a			05 03	05 38	06 09		06 45		07 09			07 50			08 09		08 46		09 09			09 46
Clitheroe 94	a																						
Blackburn	d			05 04	05 39	06 10		06 48		07 10			07 51			08 10		08 48		09 10			09 48
Rishton	d				05 44			06 53					07 56					08 53					09 53
Church & Oswaldtwistle	d				05 47			06 56					07 59					08 56					09 56
Accrington	d			05 11	05 50	06 17		06 59		07 17			08 02			08 17		08 59		09 17			09 59
Huncoat	d				05 54			07 03					08 06					09 03					10 03
Hapton	d				05 57			07 06					08 09					09 06					10 06
Rose Grove	d				06 00			07 09					08 12					09 09					10 09
Burnley Manchester Road 41	a					06 26				07 26						08 26				09 26			
Leeds 10 41	a					07 39				08 39						09 39				10 38			
Burnley Barracks	d							07 12					08 15					09 12					10 12
Burnley Central	d			05 21	06 05			07 15					08 18					09 15					10 15
Brierfield	d				06 09			07 19					08 22					09 19					10 19
Nelson	d				06 12			07 22					08 25					09 22					10 22
Colne	a			05 33	06 22			07 32					08 35					09 34					10 32

A To Manchester Airport
B To Manchester Victoria
C To York
D To Hazel Grove
E To Liverpool Lime Street
F Liverpool South Parkway

Table 97

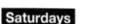

Blackpool - Preston - Blackburn, Accrington, Burnley and Colne

		TP ◇1 A	NT B	NT C	NT D	TP ◇1 E		NT	NT B	NT C	NT D	TP ◇1 E	NT	NT B	NT C	NT D		TP ◇1 E	NT	NT B	NT C	NT D	TP ◇1 E	NT	TP ◇1 F
Blackpool North	d	09 14	09 20	09 29	09 37	09 43			10 20	10 29	10 37	10 44		11 15	11 29	11 37		11 44		12 20	12 29	12 37	12 44		13 15
Layton	d		09 23						10 23					11 18						12 23					
Poulton-le-Fylde	d	09 20	09 28	09 35		09 49			10 28	10 35		10 50		11 23	11 35			11 50		12 28	12 35		12 50		
Blackpool South	d							09 44					10 44						11 44					12 44	
Blackpool Pleasure Beach	d							09 46					10 46						11 46					12 46	
Squires Gate	d							09 48					10 48						11 48					12 48	
St Annes-on-the-Sea	d							09 52					10 52						11 52					12 52	
Ansdell & Fairhaven	d							09 55					10 55						11 55					12 55	
Lytham	d							09 58					10 58						11 58					12 58	
Moss Side	d							10 03					11 03						12 03					13 03	
Kirkham & Wesham	d		09 37					10 10	10 37				11 10	11 32					12 10	12 37				13 10	
Salwick	d																								
Preston 8	a	09 41	09 47	09 52	10 02	10 07		10 20	10 47	10 52	11 02	11 08	11 20	11 42	11 52	12 02		12 08	12 20	12 47	12 51	13 02	13 08	13 20	13 38
	d			09 54				10 22		10 54			11 22		11 54				12 22		12 53			13 22	
Lostock Hall	d							10 27					11 27						12 27					13 27	
Bamber Bridge	d							10 30					11 30						12 30					13 30	
Pleasington	d							10 38					11 38						12 38					13 38	
Cherry Tree	d							10 41					11 41						12 41					13 41	
Mill Hill (Lancashire)	d							10 43					11 43						12 43					13 43	
Blackburn	a			10 09				10 46		11 09			11 46		12 09				12 46		13 08			13 46	
Clitheroe 94	a																								
Blackburn	d			10 10				10 48		11 10			11 48		12 10				12 48		13 09			13 48	
Rishton	d							10 53					11 53						12 53					13 53	
Church & Oswaldtwistle	d							10 56					11 56						12 56					13 56	
Accrington	d			10 18				10 59		11 17			11 59		12 17				12 59		13 16			13 59	
Huncoat	d							11 03					12 03						13 03					14 03	
Hapton	d							11 06					12 06						13 06					14 06	
Rose Grove	d							11 09					12 09						13 09					14 09	
Burnley Manchester Road 41	a			10 26						11 27					12 26						13 25				
Leeds 10 41	a			11 39						12 39					13 39						14 39				
Burnley Barracks	d							11 12					12 12						13 12					14 12	
Burnley Central	d							11 15					12 15						13 15					14 15	
Brierfield	d							11 19					12 19						13 19					14 19	
Nelson	d							11 22					12 22						13 22					14 22	
Colne	a							11 32					12 32						13 32					14 32	

		NT B		NT C	NT D	TP ◇1 E	NT	NT B	NT C	NT D	TP ◇1 E	NT		NT B	NT C	NT G	TP ◇1 E	NT	NT B	NT C	NT G	TP ◇1 E		NT	NT C
Blackpool North	d	13 20		13 29	13 37	13 44		14 20	14 29	14 37	14 44			15 20	15 29	15 37	15 44		16 20	16 29	16 35	16 40			17 14
Layton	d	13 23						14 23						15 23					16 23			16 43			
Poulton-le-Fylde	d	13 28		13 35		13 50		14 28	14 35		14 50			15 28	15 35		15 50		16 28	16 35		16 48			17 20
Blackpool South	d						13 44					14 44						15 44						16 44	
Blackpool Pleasure Beach	d						13 46					14 46						15 46						16 46	
Squires Gate	d						13 48					14 48						15 48						16 48	
St Annes-on-the-Sea	d						13 52					14 52						15 52						16 52	
Ansdell & Fairhaven	d						13 55					14 55						15 55						16 55	
Lytham	d						13 58					14 58						15 58						16 58	
Moss Side	d						14 03					15 03						16 03						17 03	
Kirkham & Wesham	d	13 37					14 10	14 37				15 10		15 37				16 10	16 37			16 57		17 10	17 29
Salwick	d																	16 15							
Preston 8	a	13 47		13 52	14 02	14 08	14 20	14 47	14 52	15 02	15 08	15 20		15 47	15 52	16 02	16 08	16 22	16 47	16 52	17 02	17 08		17 20	17 42
	d			13 54			14 22		14 54			15 22			15 54			16 22		16 54				17 22	17 44
Lostock Hall	d						14 27					15 27						16 27						17 27	17 51
Bamber Bridge	d						14 30					15 30						16 30						17 30	17 54
Pleasington	d						14 38					15 38						16 38						17 38	18 01
Cherry Tree	d						14 41					15 41						16 41						17 41	18 05
Mill Hill (Lancashire)	d						14 43					15 43						16 43						17 43	18 08
Blackburn	a			14 09			14 46		15 09			15 46			16 09			16 48		17 09				17 47	18 11
Clitheroe 94	a																								
Blackburn	d			14 10			14 48		15 10			15 48			16 10			16 50		17 10				17 48	18 11
Rishton	d						14 53					15 53						16 55						17 53	
Church & Oswaldtwistle	d						14 56					15 56						16 58						17 56	
Accrington	d			14 17			14 59		15 17			15 59			16 17			17 01		17 17				17 59	18 19
Huncoat	d						15 03					16 03						17 05						18 03	
Hapton	d						15 06					16 06						17 08						18 06	
Rose Grove	d						15 09					16 09						17 11						18 09	
Burnley Manchester Road 41	a			14 26					15 26						16 26					17 26					18 27
Leeds 10 41	a			15 39					16 39						17 39					18 39					19 39
Burnley Barracks	d						15 12					16 12						17 14						18 12	
Burnley Central	d						15 15					16 15						17 16						18 15	
Brierfield	d						15 19					16 19						17 21						18 19	
Nelson	d						15 22					16 22						17 24						18 22	
Colne	a						15 32					16 32						17 34						18 32	

A To Arnside
B To Manchester Victoria
C To York
D To Liverpool South Parkway
E To Manchester Airport
F from 25 June until 16 July
G To Liverpool Lime Street

Table 97

Saturdays

until 16 July

Blackpool - Preston - Blackburn, Accrington, Burnley and Colne

		TP ◇1 A	NT B	NT	NT C	NT D	NT B	TP ◇1 A	NT	NT C	NT B	TP ◇1 A	NT	NT C	NT D	NT B	TP ◇1 A	NT	NT C	TP ◇1 A	NT	NT B	NT C
Blackpool North	d	17 20	17 37		18 20	18 29	18 37	18 42		19 20	19 37	19 43		20 20	20 29	20 37	20 42		21 20	21 44		22 14	22 20
Layton	d	17 23			18 23					19 23				20 23					21 23				22 23
Poulton-le-Fylde	d	17 27			18 28	18 35		18 48		19 28		19 49		20 28	20 35		20 48		21 28	21 50			22 28
Blackpool South	d			17 44					18 44				19 44					20 44			22 00		
Blackpool Pleasure Beach	d			17 46					18 46				19 46					20 46			22 02		
Squires Gate	d			17 48					18 48				19 48					20 48			22 04		
St Annes-on-the-Sea	d			17 52					18 52				19 52					20 52			22 08		
Ansdell & Fairhaven	d			17 55					18 55				19 55					20 55			22 11		
Lytham	d			17 58					18 58				19 58					20 58			22 14		
Moss Side	d			18 03					19 03				20 03					21 03			22 19		
Kirkham & Wesham	d			18 10	18 37				19 10	19 37			20 10	20 37				21 10	21 37		22 26		22 37
Salwick	d																						
Preston 8	a	17 45	18 02	18 22	18 47	18 52	19 00	19 07	19 20	19 47	20 02	20 07	20 20	20 47	20 53	21 01	21 06	21 20	21 47	22 08	22 36	22 41	22 47
	d			18 24		18 54			19 22				20 22		20 54			21 22			22 38		
Lostock Hall	d			18 30					19 27				20 27					21 27			22 43		
Bamber Bridge	d			18 33					19 30				20 30					21 30			22 46		
Pleasington	d			18 41					19 38				20 38					21 38			22 54		
Cherry Tree	d			18 44					19 41				20 41					21 41			22 57		
Mill Hill (Lancashire)	d			18 46					19 43				20 43					21 43			22 59		
Blackburn	a			18 52		19 09			19 46				20 46		21 09			21 46			23 06		
Clitheroe 94	a																						
Blackburn	d			18 53		19 10			19 48				20 48		21 10			21 48					
Rishton	d			18 58					19 53				20 53					21 53					
Church & Oswaldtwistle	d			19 01					19 56				20 56					21 56					
Accrington	d			19 04		19 17			19 59				20 59		21 17			21 59					
Huncoat	d			19 08					20 03				21 03					22 03					
Hapton	d			19 11					20 06				21 06					22 06					
Rose Grove	d			19 14					20 09				21 09					22 09					
Burnley Manchester Road 41	a					19 26									21 28								
Leeds 10 41	a					20 39									22 37								
Burnley Barracks	d			19 17					20 12				21 12					22 12					
Burnley Central	d			19 20					20 15				21 15					22 15					
Brierfield	d			19 24					20 19				21 19					22 19					
Nelson	d			19 27					20 22				21 22					22 22					
Colne	a			19 37					20 32				21 32					22 32					

		TP ◇1 A	NT C	NT
Blackpool North	d	22 44	23 02	
Layton	d		23 05	
Poulton-le-Fylde	d	22 50	23 10	
Blackpool South	d			23 30
Blackpool Pleasure Beach	d			23 32
Squires Gate	d			23 34
St Annes-on-the-Sea	d			23 38
Ansdell & Fairhaven	d			23 41
Lytham	d			23 44
Moss Side	d			23 49
Kirkham & Wesham	d		23 19	23 56
Salwick	d			
Preston 8	a	23 08	23 29	00 08
	d			
Lostock Hall	d			
Bamber Bridge	d			
Pleasington	d			
Cherry Tree	d			
Mill Hill (Lancashire)	d			
Blackburn	a			
Clitheroe 94	a			
Blackburn	d			
Rishton	d			
Church & Oswaldtwistle	d			
Accrington	d			
Huncoat	d			
Hapton	d			
Rose Grove	d			
Burnley Manchester Road 41	a			
Leeds 10 41	a			
Burnley Barracks	d			
Burnley Central	d			
Brierfield	d			
Nelson	d			
Colne	a			

A To Manchester Airport
B To Liverpool Lime Street
C To Manchester Victoria
D To York

Saturdays

23 July to 1 October

Blackpool - Preston - Blackburn, Accrington, Burnley and Colne

	NT	TP	NT	NT	NT	TP	NT	NT	NT		TP	NT	NT	NT	NT	NT	TP	NT	NT		NT	NT	TP	NT
		◇1				◇1					◇1						◇1						◇1	
		A			B	A		C	B		A 🚲	D		E	C	B	A 🚲		C		B	F	A 🚲	
Blackpool North d		03 36		04 56	05 29	05 39		06 19	06 28		06 40	06 53		07 02	07 18	07 29	07 44		08 20		08 29	08 38	08 44	
Layton d								06 22			06 43				07 21		07 47		08 23					
Poulton-le-Fylde d				05 02	05 35	05 45		06 27	06 34		06 47			07 08	07 26	07 35	07 51		08 28		08 35		08 50	
Blackpool South d	23p30						05 42						06 42					07 42						08 44
Blackpool Pleasure Beach d	23p32						05 44						06 44					07 44						08 46
Squires Gate d	23p34						05 46						06 46					07 46						08 48
St Annes-on-the-Sea d	23p38						05 50						06 50					07 50						08 52
Ansdell & Fairhaven d	23p41						05 53						06 53					07 53						08 55
Lytham d	23p44						05 56						06 56					07 56						08 58
Moss Side d	23p49						06 01						07 01					08 01						09 03
Kirkham & Wesham d	23p56						06 08	06 36			06 56		07 09		07 35		08 00	08 09	08 37					09 10
Salwick d													07 13					08 13						
Preston 8 a	00 08			05 20	05 52	06 03	06 19	06 46	06 52		07 07	07 15	07 20	07 28	07 46	07 52	08 11	08 20	08 47		08 52	09 02	09 08	09 20
d			04 47	05 22	05 54		06 21		06 54				07 22			07 54		08 22			08 54			09 22
Lostock Hall d							06 26						07 27					08 27						09 27
Bamber Bridge d							06 29						07 30					08 30						09 30
Pleasington d							06 37						07 38					08 38						09 38
Cherry Tree d							06 40						07 41					08 41						09 41
Mill Hill (Lancashire) d							06 42						07 43					08 43						09 43
Blackburn a			05 03	05 38	06 09		06 45		07 09				07 50			08 09		08 46			09 09			09 46
Clitheroe 94 a																								
Blackburn d			05 04	05 39	06 10		06 48		07 10				07 51			08 10		08 48			09 10			09 48
Rishton d				05 44			06 53						07 56					08 53						09 53
Church & Oswaldtwistle d				05 47			06 56						07 59					08 56						09 56
Accrington d			05 11	05 50	06 17		06 59		07 17				08 02			08 17		08 59			09 17			09 59
Huncoat d				05 54			07 03						08 06					09 03						10 03
Hapton d				05 57			07 06						08 09					09 06						10 06
Rose Grove d				06 00			07 09						08 12					09 09						10 09
Burnley Manchester Road 41 a					06 26				07 26							08 26					09 26			
Leeds 10 41 a					07 39				08 39							09 39					10 38			
Burnley Barracks d							07 12						08 15					09 12						10 12
Burnley Central d			05 21	06 05			07 15						08 18					09 15						10 15
Brierfield d				06 09			07 19						08 22					09 19						10 19
Nelson d				06 12			07 22						08 25					09 22						10 22
Colne a			05 33	06 22			07 32						08 35					09 34						10 32

	TP	NT	NT	NT	TP		NT	NT	NT	NT	TP	NT	NT	NT	NT		TP	NT	NT	NT	NT	TP	NT	TP
	◇1				◇1						◇1						◇1					◇1		◇1
	G	C	B	F	A 🚲			C	B	F	A 🚲		C	B	F		A 🚲		C	B	F	A 🚲		H
Blackpool North d	09 14	09 20	09 29	09 37	09 43			10 20	10 29	10 37	10 44		11 15	11 29	11 37		11 44		12 20	12 29	12 37	12 44		13 15
Layton d		09 23						10 23					11 18						12 23					
Poulton-le-Fylde d	09 20	09 28	09 35		09 49			10 28	10 35		10 50		11 23	11 35			11 50		12 28	12 35		12 50		
Blackpool South d							09 44					10 44						11 44					12 44	
Blackpool Pleasure Beach d							09 46					10 46						11 46					12 46	
Squires Gate d							09 48					10 48						11 48					12 48	
St Annes-on-the-Sea d							09 52					10 52						11 52					12 52	
Ansdell & Fairhaven d							09 55					10 55						11 55					12 55	
Lytham d							09 58					10 58						11 58					12 58	
Moss Side d							10 03					11 03						12 03					13 03	
Kirkham & Wesham d		09 37					10 10	10 37				11 10	11 32					12 10	12 37				13 10	
Salwick d																								
Preston 8 a	09 41	09 47	09 52	10 02	10 07		10 20	10 47	10 52	11 02	11 08	11 20	11 42	11 52	12 02		12 08	12 20	12 47	12 51	13 02	13 08	13 20	13 38
d			09 54				10 22		10 54			11 22		11 54				12 22		12 53			13 22	
Lostock Hall d							10 27					11 27						12 27					13 27	
Bamber Bridge d							10 30					11 30						12 30					13 30	
Pleasington d							10 38					11 38						12 38					13 38	
Cherry Tree d							10 41					11 41						12 41					13 41	
Mill Hill (Lancashire) d							10 43					11 43						12 43					13 43	
Blackburn a			10 09				10 46		11 09			11 46		12 09				12 46		13 08			13 46	
Clitheroe 94 a																								
Blackburn d			10 10				10 48		11 10			11 48		12 10				12 48		13 09			13 48	
Rishton d							10 53					11 53						12 53					13 53	
Church & Oswaldtwistle d							10 56					11 56						12 56					13 56	
Accrington d			10 18				10 59		11 17			11 59		12 17				12 59		13 16			13 59	
Huncoat d							11 03					12 03						13 03					14 03	
Hapton d							11 06					12 06						13 06					14 06	
Rose Grove d							11 09					12 09						13 09					14 09	
Burnley Manchester Road 41 a			10 26						11 27					12 26						13 25				
Leeds 10 41 a			11 39						12 39					13 39						14 39				
Burnley Barracks d							11 12					12 12						13 12					14 12	
Burnley Central d							11 15					12 15						13 15					14 15	
Brierfield d							11 19					12 19						13 19					14 19	
Nelson d							11 22					12 22						13 22					14 22	
Colne a							11 32					12 32						13 32					14 32	

A To Manchester Airport
B To York
C To Manchester Victoria
D To Hazel Grove
E To Liverpool Lime Street
F To Liverpool South Parkway
G To Barrow-in-Furness
H from 23 July until 10 September

Table 97

Saturdays
23 July to 1 October

Blackpool - Preston - Blackburn, Accrington, Burnley and Colne

		NT		NT	NT	TP	NT	NT	NT	NT	TP	NT		NT	NT	NT	TP	NT	NT	NT	NT	TP		NT	NT
						◇1					◇1						◇1					◇1			
		A		B	C	D 🍴		A	B	C	D 🍴			A	B	E	D 🍴		A	B	E	D 🍴			B
Blackpool North	d	13 20		13 29	13 37	13 44		14 20	14 29	14 37	14 44			15 20	15 29	15 37	15 44		16 20	16 29	16 35	16 40			17 14
Layton	d	13 23						14 23						15 23					16 23			16 43			
Poulton-le-Fylde	d	13 28		13 35		13 50		14 28	14 35		14 50			15 28	15 35		15 50		16 28	16 35		16 48			17 20
Blackpool South	d						13 44					14 44						15 44						16 44	
Blackpool Pleasure Beach	d						13 46					14 46						15 46						16 46	
Squires Gate	d						13 48					14 48						15 48						16 48	
St Annes-on-the-Sea	d						13 52					14 52						15 52						16 52	
Ansdell & Fairhaven	d						13 55					14 55						15 55						16 55	
Lytham	d						13 58					14 58						15 58						16 58	
Moss Side	d						14 03					15 03						16 03						17 03	
Kirkham & Wesham	d	13 37					14 10	14 37				15 10		15 37				16 10	16 37			16 57		17 10	17 29
Salwick	d																	16 15							
Preston 8	a	13 47		13 52	14 02	14 08	14 20	14 47	14 52	15 02	15 08	15 20		15 47	15 52	16 02	16 08	16 22	16 47	16 52	17 02	17 08		17 20	17 42
	d			13 54			14 22		14 54			15 22			15 54			16 22		16 54				17 22	17 44
Lostock Hall	d						14 27					15 27						16 27						17 27	17 51
Bamber Bridge	d						14 30					15 30						16 30						17 30	17 54
Pleasington	d						14 38					15 38						16 38						17 38	18 01
Cherry Tree	d						14 41					15 41						16 41						17 41	18 05
Mill Hill (Lancashire)	d						14 43					15 43						16 43						17 43	18 08
Blackburn	a			14 09			14 46		15 09			15 46			16 09			16 48		17 09				17 47	18 11
Clitheroe 94	a																								
Blackburn	d			14 10			14 48		15 10			15 48			16 10			16 50		17 10				17 48	18 11
Rishton	d						14 53					15 53						16 55						17 53	
Church & Oswaldtwistle	d						14 56					15 56						16 58						17 56	
Accrington	d			14 17			14 59		15 17			15 59			16 17			17 01		17 17				17 59	18 19
Huncoat	d						15 03					16 03						17 05						18 03	
Hapton	d						15 06					16 06						17 08						18 06	
Rose Grove	d						15 09					16 09						17 11						18 09	
Burnley Manchester Road 41	a			14 26					15 26						16 26					17 26					18 27
Leeds 10 41	a			15 39					16 39						17 39					18 39					19 39
Burnley Barracks	d						15 12					16 12						17 14						18 12	
Burnley Central	d						15 15					16 15						17 16						18 15	
Brierfield	d						15 19					16 19						17 21						18 19	
Nelson	d						15 22					16 22						17 24						18 22	
Colne	a						15 32					16 32						17 34						18 32	

		TP	NT	NT	NT	NT	NT	TP		NT	NT	NT	TP	NT	NT	NT	NT	TP		NT	NT	TP	NT	NT	NT
		◇1						◇1					◇1					◇1				◇1			
		D 🍴	E		A	B	E	D			A	E	D		A	B	E	D			A	D		E	A
Blackpool North	d	17 20	17 37		18 20	18 29	18 37	18 42			19 20	19 37	19 43		20 20	20 29	20 37	20 42			21 20	21 44		22 14	22 20
Layton	d	17 23			18 23						19 23				20 23						21 23				22 23
Poulton-le-Fylde	d	17 27			18 28	18 35		18 48			19 28		19 49		20 28	20 35		20 48			21 28	21 50			22 28
Blackpool South	d			17 44						18 44				19 44						20 44			22 00		
Blackpool Pleasure Beach	d			17 46						18 46				19 46						20 46			22 02		
Squires Gate	d			17 48						18 48				19 48						20 48			22 04		
St Annes-on-the-Sea	d			17 52						18 52				19 52						20 52			22 08		
Ansdell & Fairhaven	d			17 55						18 55				19 55						20 55			22 11		
Lytham	d			17 58						18 58				19 58						20 58			22 14		
Moss Side	d			18 03						19 03				20 03						21 03			22 19		
Kirkham & Wesham	d			18 10	18 37					19 10	19 37			20 10	20 37					21 10	21 37		22 26		22 37
Salwick	d																								
Preston 8	a	17 45	18 02	18 22	18 47	18 52	19 00	19 07		19 20	19 47	20 02	20 07	20 20	20 47	20 53	21 01	21 06		21 20	21 47	22 08	22 36	22 41	22 47
	d			18 24		18 54				19 22				20 22		20 54				21 22			22 38		
Lostock Hall	d			18 30						19 27				20 27						21 27			22 43		
Bamber Bridge	d			18 33						19 30				20 30						21 30			22 46		
Pleasington	d			18 41						19 38				20 38						21 38			22 54		
Cherry Tree	d			18 44						19 41				20 41						21 41			22 57		
Mill Hill (Lancashire)	d			18 46						19 43				20 43						21 43			22 59		
Blackburn	a			18 52		19 09				19 46				20 46		21 09				21 46			23 06		
Clitheroe 94	a																								
Blackburn	d			18 53		19 10				19 48				20 48		21 10				21 48					
Rishton	d			18 58						19 53				20 53						21 53					
Church & Oswaldtwistle	d			19 01						19 56				20 56						21 56					
Accrington	d			19 04		19 17				19 59				20 59		21 17				21 59					
Huncoat	d			19 08						20 03				21 03						22 03					
Hapton	d			19 11						20 06				21 06						22 06					
Rose Grove	d			19 14						20 09				21 09						22 09					
Burnley Manchester Road 41	a					19 26										21 28									
Leeds 10 41	a					20 39										22 37									
Burnley Barracks	d			19 17						20 12				21 12						22 12					
Burnley Central	d			19 20						20 15				21 15						22 15					
Brierfield	d			19 24						20 19				21 19						22 19					
Nelson	d			19 27						20 22				21 22						22 22					
Colne	a			19 37						20 32				21 32						22 32					

A To Manchester Victoria
B To York
C To Liverpool South Parkway
D To Manchester Airport
E To Liverpool Lime Street

Table 97

Saturdays
23 July to 1 October

Blackpool - Preston - Blackburn, Accrington, Burnley and Colne

		TP ◇1 A	NT B	NT
Blackpool North	d	22 44	23 02	
Layton	d		23 05	
Poulton-le-Fylde	d	22 50	23 10	
Blackpool South	d			23 30
Blackpool Pleasure Beach	d			23 32
Squires Gate	d			23 34
St Annes-on-the-Sea	d			23 38
Ansdell & Fairhaven	d			23 41
Lytham	d			23 44
Moss Side	d			23 49
Kirkham & Wesham	d		23 19	23 56
Salwick	d			
Preston 8	a	23 08	23 29	00 08
	d			
Lostock Hall	d			
Bamber Bridge	d			
Pleasington	d			
Cherry Tree	d			
Mill Hill (Lancashire)	d			
Blackburn	a			
Clitheroe 94	a			
Blackburn	d			
Rishton	d			
Church & Oswaldtwistle	d			
Accrington	d			
Huncoat	d			
Hapton	d			
Rose Grove	d			
Burnley Manchester Road 41	a			
Leeds 10 41	a			
Burnley Barracks	d			
Burnley Central	d			
Brierfield	d			
Nelson	d			
Colne	a			

Saturdays
from 8 October

		NT	TP ◇1 A	NT	NT	NT C	TP ◇1 A	NT	NT B	NT C	TP ◇1 A	NT D	NT	NT E	NT B	NT C	TP ◇1 A	NT	NT B	NT C	NT F	TP ◇1 A	NT
Blackpool North	d		03 36		04 56	05 29	05 39		06 19	06 28	06 40	06 53		07 02	07 18	07 29	07 44		08 20	08 29	08 38	08 44	
Layton	d								06 22		06 43				07 21		07 47		08 23				
Poulton-le-Fylde	d				05 02	05 35	05 45		06 27	06 34	06 47			07 08	07 26	07 35	07 51		08 28	08 35		08 50	
Blackpool South	d	23p30						05 42					06 42					07 42					08 44
Blackpool Pleasure Beach	d	23p32						05 44					06 44					07 44					08 46
Squires Gate	d	23p34						05 46					06 46					07 46					08 48
St Annes-on-the-Sea	d	23p38						05 50					06 50					07 50					08 52
Ansdell & Fairhaven	d	23p41						05 53					06 53					07 53					08 55
Lytham	d	23p44						05 56					06 56					07 56					08 58
Moss Side	d	23p49						06 01					07 01					08 01					09 03
Kirkham & Wesham	d	23p56						06 08	06 36		06 56		07 09		07 35		08 00	08 09	08 37				09 10
Salwick	d												07 13					08 13					
Preston 8	a	00 08			05 20	05 52	06 03	06 19	06 46	06 52	07 07	07 15	07 20	07 28	07 46	07 52	08 11	08 20	08 47	08 52	09 02	09 08	09 20
	d			04 47	05 22	05 54		06 21		06 54			07 22			07 54		08 22		08 54			09 22
Lostock Hall	d							06 26					07 27					08 27					09 27
Bamber Bridge	d							06 29					07 30					08 30					09 30
Pleasington	d							06 37					07 38					08 38					09 38
Cherry Tree	d							06 40					07 41					08 41					09 41
Mill Hill (Lancashire)	d							06 42					07 43					08 43					09 43
Blackburn	a			05 03	05 38	06 09		06 45		07 09			07 50			08 09		08 46		09 09			09 46
Clitheroe 94	a																						
Blackburn	d			05 04	05 39	06 10		06 48		07 10			07 51			08 10		08 48		09 10			09 48
Rishton	d				05 44			06 53					07 56					08 53					09 53
Church & Oswaldtwistle	d				05 47			06 56					07 59					08 56					09 56
Accrington	d			05 11	05 50	06 17		06 59		07 17			08 02			08 17		08 59		09 17			09 59
Huncoat	d				05 54			07 03					08 06					09 03					10 03
Hapton	d				05 57			07 06					08 09					09 06					10 06
Rose Grove	d				06 00			07 09					08 12					09 09					10 09
Burnley Manchester Road 41	a					06 26				07 26						08 26				09 26			
Leeds 10 41	a					07 39				08 39						09 39				10 38			
Burnley Barracks	d							07 12					08 15					09 12					10 12
Burnley Central	d			05 21	06 05			07 15					08 18					09 15					10 15
Brierfield	d				06 09			07 19					08 22					09 19					10 19
Nelson	d				06 12			07 22					08 25					09 22					10 22
Colne	a			05 35	06 24			07 34					08 37					09 34					10 34

A To Manchester Airport
B To Manchester Victoria
C To York
D To Hazel Grove
E To Liverpool Lime Street
F To Liverpool South Parkway

Table 97

Saturdays

from 8 October

Blackpool - Preston - Blackburn, Accrington, Burnley and Colne

		TP	NT	NT	NT	TP	NT	NT	NT	NT	TP	NT	NT	NT	NT	TP	NT	NT	NT	NT	TP	NT	NT
		◇1				◇1					◇1					◇1					◇1		
		A	B	C	D	E 🛒		B	C	D	E 🛒		B	C	D	E 🛒		B	C	D	E 🛒		B
Blackpool North	d	09 14	09 20	09 29	09 37	09 43		10 20	10 29	10 37	10 44		11 15	11 29	11 37	11 44		12 20	12 29	12 37	12 44		13 20
Layton	d		09 23					10 23					11 18					12 23					13 23
Poulton-le-Fylde	d	09 20	09 28	09 35		09 49		10 28	10 35		10 50		11 23	11 35		11 50		12 28	12 35		12 50		13 28
Blackpool South	d						09 44					10 44					11 44					12 44	
Blackpool Pleasure Beach	d						09 46					10 46					11 46					12 46	
Squires Gate	d						09 48					10 48					11 48					12 48	
St Annes-on-the-Sea	d						09 52					10 52					11 52					12 52	
Ansdell & Fairhaven	d						09 55					10 55					11 55					12 55	
Lytham	d						09 58					10 58					11 58					12 58	
Moss Side	d						10 03					11 03					12 03					13 03	
Kirkham & Wesham	d		09 37				10 10	10 37				11 10	11 32				12 10	12 37				13 10	13 37
Salwick	d																						
Preston 8	a	09 41	09 47	09 52	10 02	10 07	10 20	10 47	10 52	11 02	11 08	11 20	11 42	11 52	12 02	12 08	12 20	12 47	12 51	13 02	13 08	13 20	13 47
	d			09 54			10 22		10 54			11 22		11 54			12 22		12 53			13 22	
Lostock Hall	d						10 27					11 27					12 27					13 27	
Bamber Bridge	d						10 30					11 30					12 30					13 30	
Pleasington	d						10 38					11 38					12 38					13 38	
Cherry Tree	d						10 41					11 41					12 41					13 41	
Mill Hill (Lancashire)	d						10 43					11 43					12 43					13 43	
Blackburn	a			10 09			10 46		11 09			11 46		12 09			12 46		13 08			13 46	
Clitheroe 94	a																						
Blackburn	d			10 10			10 48		11 10			11 48		12 10			12 48		13 09			13 48	
Rishton	d						10 53					11 53					12 53					13 53	
Church & Oswaldtwistle	d						10 56					11 56					12 56					13 56	
Accrington	d			10 18			10 59		11 17			11 59		12 17			12 59		13 16			13 59	
Huncoat	d						11 03					12 03					13 03					14 03	
Hapton	d						11 06					12 06					13 06					14 06	
Rose Grove	d						11 09					12 09					13 09					14 09	
Burnley Manchester Road 41	a			10 26					11 27					12 26					13 25				
Leeds 10 41	a			11 39					12 39					13 39					14 39				
Burnley Barracks	d						11 12					12 12					13 12					14 12	
Burnley Central	d						11 15					12 15					13 15					14 15	
Brierfield	d						11 19					12 19					13 19					14 19	
Nelson	d						11 22					12 22					13 22					14 22	
Colne	a						11 34					12 34					13 34					14 34	

		NT	NT	TP	NT	NT	NT	NT	TP	NT	NT	NT	NT	TP	NT	NT	NT	NT	TP	NT	NT	TP
				◇1					◇1					◇1					◇1			◇1
		C	D	E 🛒		B	C	D	E 🛒		B	C	F	E 🛒		B	C	F	E 🛒		C	E 🛒
Blackpool North	d	13 29	13 37	13 44		14 20	14 29	14 37	14 44		15 20	15 29	15 37	15 44		16 20	16 29	16 35	16 40		17 14	17 20
Layton	d					14 23					15 23					16 23			16 43			17 23
Poulton-le-Fylde	d	13 35		13 50		14 28	14 35		14 50		15 28	15 35		15 50		16 28	16 35		16 48		17 20	17 27
Blackpool South	d				13 44					14 44					15 44					16 44		
Blackpool Pleasure Beach	d				13 46					14 46					15 46					16 46		
Squires Gate	d				13 48					14 48					15 48					16 48		
St Annes-on-the-Sea	d				13 52					14 52					15 52					16 52		
Ansdell & Fairhaven	d				13 55					14 55					15 55					16 55		
Lytham	d				13 58					14 58					15 58					16 58		
Moss Side	d				14 03					15 03					16 03					17 03		
Kirkham & Wesham	d				14 10	14 37				15 10	15 37				16 10	16 37			16 57	17 10	17 29	
Salwick	d														16 15							
Preston 8	a	13 52	14 02	14 08	14 20	14 47	14 52	15 02	15 08	15 20	15 47	15 52	16 02	16 08	16 22	16 47	16 52	17 02	17 08	17 20	17 42	17 45
	d	13 54			14 22		14 54			15 22		15 54			16 22		16 54			17 22	17 44	
Lostock Hall	d				14 27					15 27					16 27					17 27	17 51	
Bamber Bridge	d				14 30					15 30					16 30					17 30	17 54	
Pleasington	d				14 38					15 38					16 38					17 38	18 01	
Cherry Tree	d				14 41					15 41					16 41					17 41	18 05	
Mill Hill (Lancashire)	d				14 43					15 43					16 43					17 43	18 08	
Blackburn	a	14 09			14 46		15 09			15 46		16 09			16 48		17 09			17 47	18 11	
Clitheroe 94	a																					
Blackburn	d	14 10			14 48		15 10			15 48		16 10			16 50		17 10			17 48	18 11	
Rishton	d				14 53					15 53					16 55					17 53		
Church & Oswaldtwistle	d				14 56					15 56					16 58					17 56		
Accrington	d	14 17			14 59		15 17			15 59		16 17			17 01		17 17			17 59	18 19	
Huncoat	d				15 03					16 03					17 05					18 03		
Hapton	d				15 06					16 06					17 08					18 06		
Rose Grove	d				15 09					16 09					17 11					18 09		
Burnley Manchester Road 41	a	14 26					15 26					16 26					17 26				18 27	
Leeds 10 41	a	15 39					16 39					17 39					18 39				19 39	
Burnley Barracks	d				15 12					16 12					17 14					18 12		
Burnley Central	d				15 15					16 15					17 16					18 15		
Brierfield	d				15 19					16 19					17 21					18 19		
Nelson	d				15 22					16 22					17 24					18 22		
Colne	a				15 34					16 34					17 36					18 34		

A To Barrow-in-Furness
B To Manchester Victoria
C To York
D To Liverpool South Parkway
E To Manchester Airport
F To Liverpool Lime Street

Table 97

Saturdays

from 8 October

Blackpool - Preston - Blackburn, Accrington, Burnley and Colne

		NT	NT	NT	NT	NT	TP	NT		NT	NT	TP	NT	NT	NT	NT	TP	NT		NT	TP	NT	NT	NT	TP
							◇1					◇1					◇1				◇1				◇1
		A		B	C	A	D			B	A	D		B	C	A	D			B	D		A	B	D
Blackpool North	d	17 37		18 20	18 29	18 37	18 42			19 20	19 37	19 43		20 20	20 29	20 37	20 42			21 20	21 44		22 14	22 20	22 44
Layton	d			18 23						19 23				20 23						21 23				22 23	
Poulton-le-Fylde	d			18 28	18 35		18 48			19 28		19 49		20 28	20 35		20 48			21 28	21 50			22 28	22 50
Blackpool South	d		17 44					18 44					19 44					20 44				22 00			
Blackpool Pleasure Beach	d		17 46					18 46					19 46					20 46				22 02			
Squires Gate	d		17 48					18 48					19 48					20 48				22 04			
St Annes-on-the-Sea	d		17 52					18 52					19 52					20 52				22 08			
Ansdell & Fairhaven	d		17 55					18 55					19 55					20 55				22 11			
Lytham	d		17 58					18 58					19 58					20 58				22 14			
Moss Side	d		18 03					19 03					20 03					21 03				22 19			
Kirkham & Wesham	d		18 10	18 37				19 10		19 37			20 10	20 37				21 10		21 37		22 26		22 37	
Salwick	d																								
Preston 8	a	18 02	18 22	18 47	18 52	19 00	19 07	19 20		19 47	20 02	20 07	20 20	20 47	20 53	21 01	21 06	21 20		21 47	22 08	22 36	22 41	22 47	23 08
	d		18 24		18 54			19 22					20 22		20 54			21 22				22 38			
Lostock Hall	d		18 30					19 27					20 27					21 27				22 43			
Bamber Bridge	d		18 33					19 30					20 30					21 30				22 46			
Pleasington	d		18 41					19 38					20 38					21 38				22 54			
Cherry Tree	d		18 44					19 41					20 41					21 41				22 57			
Mill Hill (Lancashire)	d		18 46					19 43					20 43					21 43				22 59			
Blackburn	a		18 52		19 09			19 46					20 46		21 09			21 46				23 06			
Clitheroe 94	a																								
Blackburn	d		18 53		19 10			19 48					20 48		21 10			21 48							
Rishton	d		18 58					19 53					20 53					21 53							
Church & Oswaldtwistle	d		19 01					19 56					20 56					21 56							
Accrington	d		19 04		19 17			19 59					20 59		21 17			21 59							
Huncoat	d		19 08					20 03					21 03					22 03							
Hapton	d		19 11					20 06					21 06					22 06							
Rose Grove	d		19 14					20 09					21 09					22 09							
Burnley Manchester Road 41	a				19 26										21 28										
Leeds 10 41	a				20 39										22 37										
Burnley Barracks	d		19 17					20 12					21 12					22 12							
Burnley Central	d		19 20					20 15					21 15					22 15							
Brierfield	d		19 24					20 19					21 19					22 19							
Nelson	d		19 27					20 22					21 22					22 22							
Colne	a		19 39					20 34					21 34					22 34							

		NT	NT
		B	
Blackpool North	d	23 02	
Layton	d	23 05	
Poulton-le-Fylde	d	23 10	
Blackpool South	d		23 30
Blackpool Pleasure Beach	d		23 32
Squires Gate	d		23 34
St Annes-on-the-Sea	d		23 38
Ansdell & Fairhaven	d		23 41
Lytham	d		23 44
Moss Side	d		23 49
Kirkham & Wesham	d	23 19	23 56
Salwick	d		
Preston 8	a	23 29	00 08
	d		
Lostock Hall	d		
Bamber Bridge	d		
Pleasington	d		
Cherry Tree	d		
Mill Hill (Lancashire)	d		
Blackburn	a		
Clitheroe 94	a		
Blackburn	d		
Rishton	d		
Church & Oswaldtwistle	d		
Accrington	d		
Huncoat	d		
Hapton	d		
Rose Grove	d		
Burnley Manchester Road 41	a		
Leeds 10 41	a		
Burnley Barracks	d		
Burnley Central	d		
Brierfield	d		
Nelson	d		
Colne	a		

A To Liverpool Lime Street
B To Manchester Victoria
C To York
D To Manchester Airport

Table 97

Sundays

until 11 September

Blackpool - Preston - Blackburn, Accrington, Burnley and Colne

Station		NT A	TP ◇1 B	NT	NT C	NT D	TP ◇1 B	NT E	NT F	NT C	NT D	NT	TP ◇1 B	NT E	NT F	NT C	TP ◇1 B	NT E	NT F	NT C	NT	TP ◇1 B	NT E
Blackpool North	d		07 48		08 20	08 36	08 44	08 50	09 11	09 20			09 44	09 50	10 11	10 20	10 44	10 50	11 13	11 20		11 44	11 50
Layton	d				08 23					09 23						10 23				11 23			
Poulton-le-Fylde	d		07 54		08 28	08 42	08 50	08 56	09 17	09 28			09 50	09 56	10 17	10 28	10 50	10 56	11 19	11 28		11 50	11 56
Blackpool South	d	23p30										09 28									11 24		
Blackpool Pleasure Beach	d	23p32										09 30									11 26		
Squires Gate	d	23p34										09 32									11 28		
St Annes-on-the-Sea	d	23p38										09 36									11 32		
Ansdell & Fairhaven	d	23p41										09 39									11 35		
Lytham	d	23p44										09 42									11 38		
Moss Side	d	23p49										09 47									11 43		
Kirkham & Wesham	d	23p56			08 37	08 51				09 37		09 54				10 37				11 37	11 50		
Salwick	d																						
Preston 8	a	00 08	08 12		08 47	09 02	09 08	09 14	09 34	09 47		10 04	10 08	10 14	10 34	10 47	11 08	11 14	11 36	11 47	12 00	12 08	12 14
	d			08 16		09 05			09 37		10 00	10 05			10 37				11 37		12 05		
Lostock Hall	d			08 21		09 11					10 05	10 11									12 11		
Bamber Bridge	d			08 24		09 14					10 08	10 14									12 14		
Pleasington	d											10 21									12 21		
Cherry Tree	d											10 24									12 24		
Mill Hill (Lancashire)	d											10 27									12 27		
Blackburn	a			08 35		09 25			09 53		10 19	10 30			10 53				11 54		12 30		
Clitheroe 94	a					09 50					10 44												
Blackburn	d			08 37					09 54			10 31			10 54				11 54		12 31		
Rishton	d											10 36									12 36		
Church & Oswaldtwistle	d											10 39									12 39		
Accrington	d			08 44					10 01			10 42			11 01				12 02		12 42		
Huncoat	d											10 47									12 47		
Hapton	d											10 50									12 50		
Rose Grove	d			08 51								10 53									12 53		
Burnley Manchester Road 41	a								10 10						11 10				12 10				
Leeds 10 41	a								11 21						12 22				13 22				
Burnley Barracks	d											10 56									12 56		
Burnley Central	d			08 56								10 58									12 58		
Brierfield	d			09 00								11 03									13 03		
Nelson	d			09 03								11 06									13 06		
Colne	a			09 15								11 15									13 15		

Station		NT F	NT C	NT	TP ◇1 B	NT E	NT F	NT C	NT	TP ◇1 B	NT E	NT F	NT C	NT	TP ◇1 B	NT E	NT F	NT C	NT	TP ◇1 B	NT E	NT F	NT C
Blackpool North	d	12 11	12 20		12 44	12 50	13 13	13 20		13 44	13 50	14 11	14 20		14 44	14 50	15 13	15 20		15 44	15 50	16 11	16 20
Layton	d		12 23					13 23					14 23					15 23					16 23
Poulton-le-Fylde	d	12 17	12 28		12 50	12 56	13 19	13 28		13 50	13 56	14 17	14 28		14 50	14 56	15 19	15 28		15 50	15 56	16 17	16 28
Blackpool South	d			12 24					13 24					14 27					15 27				
Blackpool Pleasure Beach	d			12 26					13 26					14 29					15 29				
Squires Gate	d			12 28					13 28					14 31					15 31				
St Annes-on-the-Sea	d			12 32					13 32					14 35					15 35				
Ansdell & Fairhaven	d			12 35					13 35					14 38					15 38				
Lytham	d			12 38					13 38					14 41					15 41				
Moss Side	d			12 43					13 43					14 46					15 46				
Kirkham & Wesham	d		12 37	12 50				13 37	13 50				14 37	14 53				15 37	15 53				16 37
Salwick	d																						
Preston 8	a	12 34	12 47	13 02	13 08	13 14	13 36	13 47	14 00	14 08	14 14	14 34	14 47	15 05	15 08	15 14	15 36	15 47	16 03	16 08	16 14	16 34	16 47
	d	12 37					13 37		14 05			14 37					15 37		16 05			16 37	
Lostock Hall	d								14 11										16 11				
Bamber Bridge	d								14 14										16 14				
Pleasington	d								14 21										16 21				
Cherry Tree	d								14 24										16 24				
Mill Hill (Lancashire)	d								14 27										16 27				
Blackburn	a	12 53					13 54		14 30			14 53					15 54		16 30			16 53	
Clitheroe 94	a																						
Blackburn	d	12 54					13 54		14 31			14 54					15 54		16 31			16 54	
Rishton	d								14 36										16 36				
Church & Oswaldtwistle	d								14 39										16 39				
Accrington	d	13 01					14 02		14 42			15 01					16 02		16 42			17 01	
Huncoat	d								14 47										16 47				
Hapton	d								14 50										16 50				
Rose Grove	d								14 53										16 53				
Burnley Manchester Road 41	a	13 10					14 10					15 10					16 10					17 10	
Leeds 10 41	a	14 22					15 22					16 22					17 20					18 21	
Burnley Barracks	d								14 56										16 56				
Burnley Central	d								14 58										16 58				
Brierfield	d								15 03										17 03				
Nelson	d								15 06										17 06				
Colne	a								15 15										17 15				

A not 22 May
B To Manchester Airport
C To Manchester Victoria
D To Carlisle
E To Liverpool Lime Street
F To York

Table 97

Sundays
until 11 September

Blackpool - Preston - Blackburn, Accrington, Burnley and Colne

		NT		TP ◇1 A	NT B	NT C	NT D	TP ◇1 E	NT	TP ◇1 A	NT	NT B		NT C	NT D	NT	TP ◇1 A	NT B	NT C	NT D	NT	TP ◇1 A		NT B	NT
Blackpool North	d			16 44	16 50	17 11	17 20	17 30		17 40		17 50		18 11	18 20		18 44	18 50	19 13	19 20		19 44		19 50	20 11
Layton	d						17 23								18 23					19 23					
Poulton-le-Fylde	d			16 50	16 56	17 17	17 28			17 46		17 56		18 17	18 28		18 50	18 56	19 19	19 28		19 50		19 56	20 17
Blackpool South	d	16 27							17 24							18 27					19 27				
Blackpool Pleasure Beach	d	16 29							17 26							18 29					19 29				
Squires Gate	d	16 31							17 28							18 31					19 31				
St Annes-on-the-Sea	d	16 35							17 32							18 35					19 35				
Ansdell & Fairhaven	d	16 38							17 35							18 38					19 38				
Lytham	d	16 41							17 38							18 41					19 41				
Moss Side	d	16 46							17 43							18 46					19 46				
Kirkham & Wesham	d	16 53					17 37		17 50						18 37	18 53				19 37	19 53				
Salwick	d																								
Preston 8	a	17 05		17 08	17 14	17 34	17 47	17 53	18 02	18 04		18 14		18 34	18 47	19 05	19 08	19 14	19 36	19 47	20 03	20 08		20 14	20 34
	d					17 37					18 05			18 37					19 37		20 05				20 37
Lostock Hall	d										18 11										20 11				
Bamber Bridge	d										18 14										20 14				
Pleasington	d										18 21										20 21				
Cherry Tree	d										18 24										20 24				
Mill Hill (Lancashire)	d										18 27										20 27				
Blackburn	a					17 53					18 30			18 53					19 54		20 30				20 53
Clitheroe 94	a																								
Blackburn	d					17 54					18 31			18 54					19 54		20 31				20 54
Rishton	d										18 36										20 36				
Church & Oswaldtwistle	d										18 39										20 39				
Accrington	d					18 01					18 42			19 01					20 02		20 42				21 01
Huncoat	d										18 47										20 47				
Hapton	d										18 50										20 50				
Rose Grove	d										18 53										20 53				
Burnley Manchester Road 41	a					18 10								19 10					20 10						21 10
Leeds 10 41	a					19 21								20 23					21 22						22 22
Burnley Barracks	d										18 56										20 56				
Burnley Central	d										18 58										20 58				
Brierfield	d										19 03										21 03				
Nelson	d										19 06										21 06				
Colne	a										19 15										21 15				

		NT D	NT	TP ◇1 A	NT B	NT	NT D	NT		NT B	TP ◇1	NT B	TP ◇1 A
Blackpool North	d	20 20		20 44	20 50	21 13	21 20			21 50	21 56	22 44	23 03
Layton	d	20 23					21 23						
Poulton-le-Fylde	d	20 28		20 50	20 56	21 19	21 28			21 56	22 02	22 50	23 09
Blackpool South	d		20 27					21 27					
Blackpool Pleasure Beach	d		20 29					21 29					
Squires Gate	d		20 31					21 31					
St Annes-on-the-Sea	d		20 35					21 35					
Ansdell & Fairhaven	d		20 38					21 38					
Lytham	d		20 41					21 41					
Moss Side	d		20 46					21 46					
Kirkham & Wesham	d	20 37	20 53				21 37	21 53					23 17
Salwick	d												
Preston 8	a	20 47	21 05	21 08	21 14	21 36	21 47	22 03		22 14	22 20	23 08	23 28
	d					21 39		22 05					
Lostock Hall	d							22 11					
Bamber Bridge	d							22 14					
Pleasington	d							22 21					
Cherry Tree	d							22 24					
Mill Hill (Lancashire)	d							22 27					
Blackburn	a					21 55		22 30					
Clitheroe 94	a												
Blackburn	d					21 55		22 31					
Rishton	d							22 36					
Church & Oswaldtwistle	d							22 39					
Accrington	d					22 03		22 42					
Huncoat	d							22 47					
Hapton	d							22 50					
Rose Grove	d							22 53					
Burnley Manchester Road 41	a					22 12							
Leeds 10 41	a					23 23							
Burnley Barracks	d							22 56					
Burnley Central	d							22 58					
Brierfield	d							23 03					
Nelson	d							23 06					
Colne	a							23 15					

A To Manchester Airport
B To Liverpool Lime Street
C To York
D To Manchester Victoria
E from 26 June until 11 September. To Glasgow Central

Sundays

18 September to 2 October

Blackpool - Preston - Blackburn, Accrington, Burnley and Colne

		NT	NT	TP ◇1 A	NT B	NT C	TP ◇1 A	NT D	NT E	NT B	NT	TP ◇1 A	NT D	NT E	NT B	TP ◇1 A	NT D	NT E	NT B	NT	TP ◇1 A	NT D	NT E
Blackpool North	d			08 14	08 20	08 36	08 44	08 50	09 01	09 20		09 44	09 50	10 11	10 20	10 44	10 50	11 13	11 20		11 44	11 50	12 11
Layton	d				08 23					09 23					10 23				11 23				
Poulton-le-Fylde	d			08 20	08 28	08 42	08 50	08 56	09 07	09 28		09 50	09 56	10 17	10 28	10 50	10 56	11 19	11 28		11 50	11 56	12 17
Blackpool South	d	23p30									09 28									11 24			
Blackpool Pleasure Beach	d	23p32									09 30									11 26			
Squires Gate	d	23p34									09 32									11 28			
St Annes-on-the-Sea	d	23p38									09 36									11 32			
Ansdell & Fairhaven	d	23p41									09 39									11 35			
Lytham	d	23p44									09 42									11 38			
Moss Side	d	23p49									09 47									11 43			
Kirkham & Wesham	d	23p56			08 37	08 51				09 37	09 54				10 37				11 37	11 50			
Salwick	d																						
Preston 8	a	00 08		08 38	08 47	09 02	09 08	09 14	09 24	09 47	10 04	10 08	10 14	10 34	10 47	11 08	11 14	11 36	11 47	12 00	12 08	12 14	12 34
	d		08 16			09 05			09 27		10 05			10 37				11 37		12 05			12 37
Lostock Hall	d		08 21			09 11					10 11									12 11			
Bamber Bridge	d		08 24			09 14					10 14									12 14			
Pleasington	d										10 21									12 21			
Cherry Tree	d										10 24									12 24			
Mill Hill (Lancashire)	d										10 27									12 27			
Blackburn	a		08 35			09 25			09 42		10 30			10 53				11 54		12 30			12 53
Clitheroe 94	a					09 50																	
Blackburn	d		08 37						09 44		10 31			10 54				11 54		12 31			12 54
Rishton	d										10 36									12 36			
Church & Oswaldtwistle	d										10 39									12 39			
Accrington	d		08 44						09 51		10 42			11 01				12 02		12 42			13 01
Huncoat	d										10 47									12 47			
Hapton	d										10 50									12 50			
Rose Grove	d		08 51								10 53									12 53			
Burnley Manchester Road 41	a								10 00					11 10				12 10					13 10
Leeds 10 41	a								11 21					12 22				13 22					14 22
Burnley Barracks	d										10 56									12 56			
Burnley Central	d		08 56								10 58									12 58			
Brierfield	d		09 00								11 03									13 03			
Nelson	d		09 03								11 06									13 06			
Colne	a		09 15								11 15									13 15			

		NT B	NT	TP ◇1 A	NT D	NT E	NT B	NT	TP ◇1 A	NT D	NT E	NT B	NT	TP ◇1 A	NT D	NT E	NT B	NT	TP ◇1 A	NT D	NT E	NT B	NT
Blackpool North	d	12 20		12 44	12 50	13 13	13 20		13 44	13 50	14 11	14 20		14 44	14 50	15 13	15 20		15 44	15 50	16 11	16 20	
Layton	d	12 23					13 23					14 23					15 23					16 23	
Poulton-le-Fylde	d	12 28		12 50	12 56	13 19	13 28		13 50	13 56	14 17	14 28		14 50	14 56	15 19	15 28		15 50	15 56	16 17	16 28	
Blackpool South	d		12 24					13 24					14 27					15 27					16 27
Blackpool Pleasure Beach	d		12 26					13 26					14 29					15 29					16 29
Squires Gate	d		12 28					13 28					14 31					15 31					16 31
St Annes-on-the-Sea	d		12 32					13 32					14 35					15 35					16 35
Ansdell & Fairhaven	d		12 35					13 35					14 38					15 38					16 38
Lytham	d		12 38					13 38					14 41					15 41					16 41
Moss Side	d		12 43					13 43					14 46					15 46					16 46
Kirkham & Wesham	d	12 37	12 50				13 37	13 50				14 37	14 53				15 37	15 53				16 37	16 53
Salwick	d																						
Preston 8	a	12 47	13 02	13 08	13 14	13 36	13 47	14 00	14 08	14 14	14 34	14 47	15 05	15 08	15 14	15 36	15 47	16 03	16 08	16 14	16 34	16 47	17 05
	d					13 37		14 05			14 37					15 37		16 05			16 37		
Lostock Hall	d							14 11										16 11					
Bamber Bridge	d							14 14										16 14					
Pleasington	d							14 21										16 21					
Cherry Tree	d							14 24										16 24					
Mill Hill (Lancashire)	d							14 27										16 27					
Blackburn	a					13 54		14 30			14 53					15 54		16 30			16 53		
Clitheroe 94	a																						
Blackburn	d					13 54		14 31			14 54					15 54		16 31			16 54		
Rishton	d							14 36										16 36					
Church & Oswaldtwistle	d							14 39										16 39					
Accrington	d					14 02		14 42			15 01					16 02		16 42			17 01		
Huncoat	d							14 47										16 47					
Hapton	d							14 50										16 50					
Rose Grove	d							14 53										16 53					
Burnley Manchester Road 41	a					14 10					15 10					16 10					17 10		
Leeds 10 41	a					15 22					16 22					17 20					18 21		
Burnley Barracks	d							14 56										16 56					
Burnley Central	d							14 58										16 58					
Brierfield	d							15 03										17 03					
Nelson	d							15 06										17 06					
Colne	a							15 15										17 15					

A To Manchester Airport
B To Manchester Victoria
C To Carlisle
D To Liverpool Lime Street
E To York

Table 97

Sundays

18 September to 2 October

Blackpool - Preston - Blackburn, Accrington, Burnley and Colne

		TP ◇1	NT	NT	NT	NT	NT	TP ◇1	NT	NT	NT	NT	TP ◇1	NT	NT	NT	NT	TP ◇1	NT	NT	NT	NT
		A	B	C	D			A	B	C	D		A	B	C	D		A	B		D	
Blackpool North	d	16 44	16 50	17 11	17 20			17 44	17 50	18 11	18 20		18 44	18 50	19 13	19 20		19 44	19 50	20 11	20 20	
Layton	d				17 23						18 23					19 23					20 23	
Poulton-le-Fylde	d	16 50	16 56	17 17	17 28			17 50	17 56	18 17	18 28		18 50	18 56	19 19	19 28		19 50	19 56	20 17	20 28	
Blackpool South	d					17 24						18 27					19 27					20 27
Blackpool Pleasure Beach	d					17 26						18 29					19 29					20 29
Squires Gate	d					17 28						18 31					19 31					20 31
St Annes-on-the-Sea	d					17 32						18 35					19 35					20 35
Ansdell & Fairhaven	d					17 35						18 38					19 38					20 38
Lytham	d					17 38						18 41					19 41					20 41
Moss Side	d					17 43						18 46					19 46					20 46
Kirkham & Wesham	d				17 37	17 50					18 37	18 53				19 37	19 53				20 37	20 53
Salwick	d																					
Preston 8	a	17 08	17 14	17 34	17 47	18 02		18 08	18 14	18 34	18 47	19 05	19 08	19 14	19 36	19 47	20 03	20 08	20 14	20 34	20 47	21 05
	d			17 37			18 05			18 37					19 37		20 05			20 37		
Lostock Hall	d						18 11										20 11					
Bamber Bridge	d						18 14										20 14					
Pleasington	d						18 21										20 21					
Cherry Tree	d						18 24										20 24					
Mill Hill (Lancashire)	d						18 27										20 27					
Blackburn	a			17 53			18 30			18 53					19 54		20 30			20 53		
Clitheroe 94	a																					
Blackburn	d			17 54			18 31			18 54					19 54		20 31			20 54		
Rishton	d						18 36										20 36					
Church & Oswaldtwistle	d						18 39										20 39					
Accrington	d			18 01			18 42			19 01					20 02		20 42			21 01		
Huncoat	d						18 47										20 47					
Hapton	d						18 50										20 50					
Rose Grove	d						18 53										20 53					
Burnley Manchester Road 41	a			18 10						19 10					20 10					21 10		
Leeds 10 41	a			19 21						20 23					21 22					22 22		
Burnley Barracks	d						18 56										20 56					
Burnley Central	d						18 58										20 58					
Brierfield	d						19 03										21 03					
Nelson	d						19 06										21 06					
Colne	a						19 15										21 15					

		TP ◇1	NT	NT	NT	NT	NT	TP ◇1	NT	TP ◇1
		A	B		D		B		B	A
Blackpool North	d	20 44	20 50	21 13	21 20		21 50	21 56	22 44	23 03
Layton	d				21 23					
Poulton-le-Fylde	d	20 50	20 56	21 19	21 28		21 56	22 02	22 50	23 09
Blackpool South	d					21 27				
Blackpool Pleasure Beach	d					21 29				
Squires Gate	d					21 31				
St Annes-on-the-Sea	d					21 35				
Ansdell & Fairhaven	d					21 38				
Lytham	d					21 41				
Moss Side	d					21 46				
Kirkham & Wesham	d				21 37	21 53				23 17
Salwick	d									
Preston 8	a	21 08	21 14	21 36	21 47	22 03	22 14	22 20	23 08	23 28
	d			21 39		22 05				
Lostock Hall	d					22 11				
Bamber Bridge	d					22 14				
Pleasington	d					22 21				
Cherry Tree	d					22 24				
Mill Hill (Lancashire)	d					22 27				
Blackburn	a			21 55		22 30				
Clitheroe 94	a									
Blackburn	d			21 55		22 31				
Rishton	d					22 36				
Church & Oswaldtwistle	d					22 39				
Accrington	d			22 03		22 42				
Huncoat	d					22 47				
Hapton	d					22 50				
Rose Grove	d					22 53				
Burnley Manchester Road 41	a			22 12						
Leeds 10 41	a			23 23						
Burnley Barracks	d					22 56				
Burnley Central	d					22 58				
Brierfield	d					23 03				
Nelson	d					23 06				
Colne	a					23 15				

A To Manchester Airport
B To Liverpool Lime Street
C To York
D To Manchester Victoria

Blackpool - Preston - Blackburn, Accrington, Burnley and Colne

		NT	NT	TP ◇1 A	NT B	NT C	TP ◇1 A	NT D	NT E	NT B	NT	TP ◇1 A	NT D	NT E	NT B	TP ◇1 A	NT D	NT E	NT B	NT	TP ◇1 A	NT D	NT E
Blackpool North	d			08 14	08 20	08 36	08 44	08 50	09 01	09 20		09 44	09 50	10 11	10 20	10 44	10 50	11 13	11 20		11 44	11 50	12 11
Layton	d				08 23					09 23					10 23				11 23				
Poulton-le-Fylde	d			08 20	08 28	08 42	08 50	08 56	09 07	09 28		09 50	09 56	10 17	10 28	10 50	10 56	11 19	11 28		11 50	11 56	12 17
Blackpool South	d	23p30									09 28									11 24			
Blackpool Pleasure Beach	d	23p32									09 30									11 26			
Squires Gate	d	23p34									09 32									11 28			
St Annes-on-the-Sea	d	23p38									09 36									11 32			
Ansdell & Fairhaven	d	23p41									09 39									11 35			
Lytham	d	23p44									09 42									11 38			
Moss Side	d	23p49									09 47									11 43			
Kirkham & Wesham	d	23p56			08 37	08 51				09 37	09 54				10 37				11 37	11 50			
Salwick	d																						
Preston 8	a	00 08		08 38	08 47	09 02	09 08	09 14	09 24	09 47	10 04	10 08	10 14	10 34	10 47	11 08	11 14	11 36	11 47	12 00	12 08	12 14	12 34
	d		08 16			09 05			09 27		10 05			10 37				11 37		12 05			12 37
Lostock Hall	d		08 21			09 11					10 11									12 11			
Bamber Bridge	d		08 24			09 14					10 14									12 14			
Pleasington	d										10 21									12 21			
Cherry Tree	d										10 24									12 24			
Mill Hill (Lancashire)	d										10 27									12 27			
Blackburn	a		08 35			09 25			09 42		10 30			10 53				11 54		12 30			12 53
Clitheroe 94	a					09 50																	
Blackburn	d		08 37						09 44		10 31			10 54				11 54		12 31			12 54
Rishton	d										10 36									12 36			
Church & Oswaldtwistle	d										10 39									12 39			
Accrington	d		08 44						09 51		10 42			11 01				12 02		12 42			13 01
Huncoat	d										10 47									12 47			
Hapton	d										10 50									12 50			
Rose Grove	d		08 51								10 53									12 53			
Burnley Manchester Road 41	a								10 00					11 10				12 10					13 10
Leeds 10 41	a								11 21					12 22				13 22					14 22
Burnley Barracks	d										10 56									12 56			
Burnley Central	d		08 56								10 58									12 58			
Brierfield	d		09 00								11 03									13 03			
Nelson	d		09 03								11 06									13 06			
Colne	a		09 13								11 13									13 17			

		NT B	NT	TP ◇1 A	NT D	NT E	NT B	NT	TP ◇1 A	NT D	NT E	NT B	NT	TP ◇1 A	NT D	NT E	NT B	NT	TP ◇1 A	NT D	NT E	NT B	NT
Blackpool North	d	12 20		12 44	12 50	13 13	13 20		13 44	13 50	14 11	14 20		14 44	14 50	15 13	15 20		15 44	15 50	16 11	16 20	
Layton	d	12 23					13 23					14 23					15 23					16 23	
Poulton-le-Fylde	d	12 28		12 50	12 56	13 19	13 28		13 50	13 56	14 17	14 28		14 50	14 56	15 19	15 28		15 50	15 56	16 17	16 28	
Blackpool South	d		12 24					13 24					14 27					15 27					16 27
Blackpool Pleasure Beach	d		12 26					13 26					14 29					15 29					16 29
Squires Gate	d		12 28					13 28					14 31					15 31					16 31
St Annes-on-the-Sea	d		12 32					13 32					14 35					15 35					16 35
Ansdell & Fairhaven	d		12 35					13 35					14 38					15 38					16 38
Lytham	d		12 38					13 38					14 41					15 41					16 41
Moss Side	d		12 43					13 43					14 46					15 46					16 46
Kirkham & Wesham	d	12 37	12 50				13 37	13 50				14 37	14 53				15 37	15 53				16 37	16 53
Salwick	d																						
Preston 8	a	12 47	13 02	13 08	13 14	13 36	13 47	14 00	14 08	14 14	14 34	14 47	15 05	15 08	15 14	15 36	15 47	16 03	16 08	16 14	16 34	16 47	17 05
	d					13 37		14 05			14 37					15 37		16 05			16 37		
Lostock Hall	d							14 11										16 11					
Bamber Bridge	d							14 14										16 14					
Pleasington	d							14 21										16 21					
Cherry Tree	d							14 24										16 24					
Mill Hill (Lancashire)	d							14 27										16 27					
Blackburn	a					13 54		14 30			14 53					15 54		16 30			16 53		
Clitheroe 94	a																						
Blackburn	d					13 54		14 31			14 54					15 54		16 31			16 54		
Rishton	d							14 36										16 36					
Church & Oswaldtwistle	d							14 39										16 39					
Accrington	d					14 02		14 42			15 01					16 02		16 42			17 01		
Huncoat	d							14 47										16 47					
Hapton	d							14 50										16 50					
Rose Grove	d							14 53										16 53					
Burnley Manchester Road 41	a					14 10					15 10					16 10					17 10		
Leeds 10 41	a					15 22					16 22					17 20					18 21		
Burnley Barracks	d							14 56										16 56					
Burnley Central	d							14 58										16 58					
Brierfield	d							15 03										17 03					
Nelson	d							15 06										17 06					
Colne	a							15 17										17 17					

A To Manchester Airport
B To Manchester Victoria
C To Carlisle
D To Liverpool Lime Street
E To York

Table 97

Sundays

9 October to 23 October

Blackpool - Preston - Blackburn, Accrington, Burnley and Colne

		TP ◇1 A		NT B	NT C	NT D	NT	NT	TP ◇1 A	NT B	NT C	NT D		NT	TP ◇1 A	NT B	NT C	NT D	NT	TP ◇1 A	NT B	NT		NT D	NT
Blackpool North	d	16 44		16 50	17 11	17 20			17 44	17 50	18 11	18 20			18 44	18 50	19 13	19 20		19 44	19 50	20 11		20 20	
Layton	d					17 23						18 23						19 23						20 23	
Poulton-le-Fylde	d	16 50		16 56	17 17	17 28			17 50	17 56	18 17	18 28			18 50	18 56	19 19	19 28		19 50	19 56	20 17		20 28	
Blackpool South	d						17 24	17 24						18 27					19 27						20 27
Blackpool Pleasure Beach	d						17 26	17 26						18 29					19 29						20 29
Squires Gate	d						17 28	17 28						18 31					19 31						20 31
St Annes-on-the-Sea	d						17 32	17 32						18 35					19 35						20 35
Ansdell & Fairhaven	d						17 35	17 35						18 38					19 38						20 38
Lytham	d						17 38	17 38						18 41					19 41						20 41
Moss Side	d						17 43	17 43						18 46					19 46						20 46
Kirkham & Wesham	d					17 37	17 50	17 50				18 37		18 53				19 37	19 53					20 37	20 53
Salwick	d																								
Preston 8	a	17 08		17 14	17 34	17 47	18 02	18 00	18 08	18 14	18 34	18 47		19 05	19 08	19 14	19 36	19 47	20 03	20 08	20 14	20 34		20 47	21 05
	d				17 37			18 05			18 37						19 37		20 05			20 37			
Lostock Hall	d							18 11											20 11						
Bamber Bridge	d							18 14											20 14						
Pleasington	d							18 21											20 21						
Cherry Tree	d							18 24											20 24						
Mill Hill (Lancashire)	d							18 27											20 27						
Blackburn	a				17 53			18 30			18 53						19 54		20 30			20 53			
Clitheroe 94	a																								
Blackburn	d				17 54			18 31			18 54						19 54		20 31			20 54			
Rishton	d							18 36											20 36						
Church & Oswaldtwistle	d							18 39											20 39						
Accrington	d				18 01			18 42			19 01						20 02		20 42			21 01			
Huncoat	d							18 47											20 47						
Hapton	d							18 50											20 50						
Rose Grove	d							18 53											20 53						
Burnley Manchester Road 41	a				18 10						19 10						20 10					21 10			
Leeds 10 41	a				19 21						20 23						21 22					22 22			
Burnley Barracks	d							18 56											20 56						
Burnley Central	d							18 58											20 58						
Brierfield	d							19 03											21 03						
Nelson	d							19 06											21 06						
Colne	a							19 17											21 17						

		TP ◇1 A	NT B	NT	NT D	NT	NT B	TP ◇1		NT B	TP ◇1 A
Blackpool North	d	20 44	20 50	21 13	21 20		21 50	21 56		22 44	23 03
Layton	d				21 23						
Poulton-le-Fylde	d	20 50	20 56	21 19	21 28		21 56	22 02		22 50	23 09
Blackpool South	d					21 27					
Blackpool Pleasure Beach	d					21 29					
Squires Gate	d					21 31					
St Annes-on-the-Sea	d					21 35					
Ansdell & Fairhaven	d					21 38					
Lytham	d					21 41					
Moss Side	d					21 46					
Kirkham & Wesham	d				21 37	21 53					23 17
Salwick	d										
Preston 8	a	21 08	21 14	21 36	21 47	22 03	22 14	22 20		23 08	23 28
	d			21 39		22 05					
Lostock Hall	d					22 11					
Bamber Bridge	d					22 14					
Pleasington	d					22 21					
Cherry Tree	d					22 24					
Mill Hill (Lancashire)	d					22 27					
Blackburn	a			21 55		22 30					
Clitheroe 94	a										
Blackburn	d			21 55		22 31					
Rishton	d					22 36					
Church & Oswaldtwistle	d					22 39					
Accrington	d			22 03		22 42					
Huncoat	d					22 47					
Hapton	d					22 50					
Rose Grove	d					22 53					
Burnley Manchester Road 41	a			22 12							
Leeds 10 41	a			23 23							
Burnley Barracks	d					22 56					
Burnley Central	d					22 58					
Brierfield	d					23 03					
Nelson	d					23 06					
Colne	a					23 17					

A To Manchester Airport
B To Liverpool Lime Street
C To York
D To Manchester Victoria

Table 97

Sundays

from 30 October

Blackpool - Preston - Blackburn, Accrington, Burnley and Colne

		NT	NT	NT	NT	TP	NT	TP	NT	NT	NT	NT	TP	NT	NT	NT	NT	TP	NT	NT	NT	NT	NT
						◇1		◇1					◇1					◇1					
						A	B	A	C	B	D		A	C	E	F	B	A	C	F	B	D	
			🚌		🚌							🚌			🚌								🚌
Blackpool North	d					08 14	08 20	08 44	08 50	09 20			09 44	09 50	10 05	10 11	10 20	10 44	10 50	11 13	11 20		
Layton	d						08 23			09 23							10 23				11 23		
Poulton-le-Fylde	d					08 20	08 28	08 50	08 56	09 28			09 50	09 56		10 17	10 28	10 50	10 56	11 19	11 28		
Blackpool South	d	23p30									09 28											11 24	
Blackpool Pleasure Beach	d	23p32									09 30											11 26	
Squires Gate	d	23p34									09 32											11 28	
St Annes-on-the-Sea	d	23p38									09 36											11 32	
Ansdell & Fairhaven	d	23p41									09 39											11 35	
Lytham	d	23p44									09 42											11 38	
Moss Side	d	23p49									09 47											11 43	
Kirkham & Wesham	d	23p56					08 37			09 37	09 54						10 37				11 37	11 50	
Salwick	d																						
Preston 8	a	00 08				08 38	08 47	09 08	09 14	09 47	10 04		10 08	10 14	10 44	10 34	10 47	11 08	11 14	11 36	11 47	12 00	
	d		07 32	08 16	08 16							10 05			10 45	10 37				11 37			12 05
Lostock Hall	d		07 46	08 21	08 30							10 19											12 19
Bamber Bridge	d		07 56	08 24	08 40							10 29											12 29
Pleasington	d											10 47											12 47
Cherry Tree	d											10 51											12 51
Mill Hill (Lancashire)	d											10 57											12 57
Blackburn	a		08 14	08 35	08 58							11 06			11 14	10 53				11 54			13 06
Clitheroe 94	a																						
Blackburn	d		08 15	08 37	08 59							11 07			11 15	10 54				11 54			13 07
Rishton	d											11 17											13 17
Church & Oswaldtwistle	d											11 29											13 29
Accrington	d		08 33	08 44	09 17							11 33			11 33	11 01				12 02			13 33
Huncoat	d											11 39											13 39
Hapton	d											11 45											13 45
Rose Grove	d		08 40	08 51	09 24							11 51											13 51
Burnley Manchester Road 41	a														11 52	11 10				12 10			
Leeds 10 41	a															12 22				13 22			
Burnley Barracks	d											11 55											13 55
Burnley Central	d		08 50	08 56	09 34							11 59											13 59
Brierfield	d		08 58	09 00	09 42							12 07											14 07
Nelson	d		09 03	09 03	09 47							12 12											14 12
Colne	a		09 11	09 13	09 55							12 20											14 20

		TP	NT	NT	NT	NT	NT	TP	NT	NT	NT	NT	NT	TP	NT	NT	NT	NT	NT	TP	NT	NT	NT
		◇1						◇1						◇1						◇1			
		A	C	E	F	B	D	A	C	F	B	D		A	C	E	F	B	D	A	C	F	B
				🚌									🚌			🚌							
Blackpool North	d	11 44	11 50	12 05	12 11	12 20		12 44	12 50	13 13	13 20			13 44	13 50	14 05	14 11	14 20		14 44	14 50	15 13	15 20
Layton	d					12 23					13 23							14 23					15 23
Poulton-le-Fylde	d	11 50	11 56		12 17	12 28		12 50	12 56	13 19	13 28			13 50	13 56		14 17	14 28		14 50	14 56	15 19	15 28
Blackpool South	d						12 24					13 24							14 27				
Blackpool Pleasure Beach	d						12 26					13 26							14 29				
Squires Gate	d						12 28					13 28							14 31				
St Annes-on-the-Sea	d						12 32					13 32							14 35				
Ansdell & Fairhaven	d						12 35					13 35							14 38				
Lytham	d						12 38					13 38							14 41				
Moss Side	d						12 43					13 43							14 46				
Kirkham & Wesham	d					12 37	12 50				13 37	13 50						14 37	14 53				15 37
Salwick	d																						
Preston 8	a	12 08	12 14	12 44	12 34	12 47	13 00	13 08	13 14	13 36	13 47	14 00		14 08	14 14	14 44	14 34	14 47	15 03	15 08	15 14	15 36	15 47
	d			12 45	12 37					13 37			14 05			14 45	14 37					15 37	
Lostock Hall	d												14 19										
Bamber Bridge	d												14 29										
Pleasington	d												14 47										
Cherry Tree	d												14 51										
Mill Hill (Lancashire)	d												14 57										
Blackburn	a			13 14	12 53					13 54			15 06			15 14	14 53					15 54	
Clitheroe 94	a																						
Blackburn	d			13 15	12 54					13 54			15 07			15 15	14 54					15 54	
Rishton	d												15 17										
Church & Oswaldtwistle	d												15 29										
Accrington	d			13 33	13 01					14 02			15 33			15 33	15 01					16 02	
Huncoat	d												15 39										
Hapton	d												15 45										
Rose Grove	d												15 51										
Burnley Manchester Road 41	a			13 52	13 10					14 10						15 52	15 10					16 10	
Leeds 10 41	a				14 22					15 22							16 22					17 20	
Burnley Barracks	d												15 55										
Burnley Central	d												15 59										
Brierfield	d												16 07										
Nelson	d												16 12										
Colne	a												16 20										

A To Manchester Airport
B To Manchester Victoria
C To Liverpool Lime Street
D 30 October, 6 November
E To Hebden Bridge
F To York

Table 97

Sundays
from 30 October

Blackpool - Preston - Blackburn, Accrington, Burnley and Colne

		NT		NT	TP	NT	NT	NT	NT	NT	TP	NT		NT	NT	NT	NT	NT	TP	NT	NT	NT		NT	NT
					◇1						◇1								◇1						
		A			B	C	D	E	F	A	B	C		D	E	F	A		B	C	D	E		F	A
				bus			bus							bus				bus			bus				
Blackpool North	d				15 44	15 50	16 05	16 11	16 20		16 44	16 50		17 05	17 11	17 20			17 44	17 50	18 05	18 11		18 20	
Layton	d								16 23							17 23								18 23	
Poulton-le-Fylde	d				15 50	15 56		16 17	16 28		16 50	16 56			17 17	17 28			17 50	17 56		18 17		18 28	
Blackpool South	d	15 27								16 27							17 24								18 27
Blackpool Pleasure Beach	d	15 29								16 29							17 26								18 29
Squires Gate	d	15 31								16 31							17 28								18 31
St Annes-on-the-Sea	d	15 35								16 35							17 32								18 35
Ansdell & Fairhaven	d	15 38								16 38							17 35								18 38
Lytham	d	15 41								16 41							17 38								18 41
Moss Side	d	15 46								16 46							17 43								18 46
Kirkham & Wesham	d	15 53							16 37	16 53						17 37	17 50							18 37	18 53
Salwick	d																								
Preston 8	a	16 03			16 08	16 14	16 44	16 34	16 47	17 03	17 08	17 14		17 44	17 34	17 47	18 00		18 08	18 14	18 44	18 34		18 47	19 03
	d			16 05			16 45	16 37						17 45	17 37			18 05			18 45	18 37			
Lostock Hall	d			16 19														18 19							
Bamber Bridge	d			16 29														18 29							
Pleasington	d			16 47														18 47							
Cherry Tree	d			16 51														18 51							
Mill Hill (Lancashire)	d			16 57														18 57							
Blackburn	a			17 06			17 14	16 53						18 14	17 53			19 06			19 14	18 53			
Clitheroe 94	a																								
Blackburn	d			17 07			17 15	16 54						18 15	17 54			19 07			19 15	18 54			
Rishton	d			17 17														19 17							
Church & Oswaldtwistle	d			17 29														19 29							
Accrington	d			17 33			17 33	17 01						18 33	18 01			19 33			19 33	19 01			
Huncoat	d			17 39														19 39							
Hapton	d			17 45														19 45							
Rose Grove	d			17 51														19 51							
Burnley Manchester Road 41	a						17 52	17 10						18 52	18 10						19 52	19 10			
Leeds 10 41	a							18 21							19 21							20 23			
Burnley Barracks	d			17 55														19 55							
Burnley Central	d			17 59														19 59							
Brierfield	d			18 07														20 07							
Nelson	d			18 12														20 12							
Colne	a			18 20														20 20							

		TP	NT	NT	NT	NT	NT	TP		NT	NT	NT	NT	NT	NT	TP	NT	NT	NT	NT	NT	NT	TP	NT	TP
		◇1						◇1								◇1							◇1		◇1
		B	C	E	F	A		B		C	D		F	A		B	C		F	A		C		C	B
							bus				bus				bus						bus				
Blackpool North	d	18 44	18 50	19 13	19 20			19 44		19 50	20 05	20 11	20 20		20 40	20 44	20 50	21 13	21 20			21 50	21 56	22 44	23 03
Layton	d				19 23								20 23						21 23						
Poulton-le-Fylde	d	18 50	18 56	19 19	19 28			19 50		19 56		20 17	20 28		20 55	20 50	20 56	21 19	21 28			21 56	22 02	22 50	23 09
Blackpool South	d					19 27								20 27						21 27					
Blackpool Pleasure Beach	d					19 29								20 29						21 29					
Squires Gate	d					19 31								20 31						21 31					
St Annes-on-the-Sea	d					19 35								20 35						21 35					
Ansdell & Fairhaven	d					19 38								20 38						21 38					
Lytham	d					19 41								20 41						21 41					
Moss Side	d					19 46								20 46						21 46					
Kirkham & Wesham	d				19 37	19 53							20 37	20 53					21 37	21 53					23 17
Salwick	d																								
Preston 8	a	19 08	19 14	19 36	19 47	20 03		20 08		20 14	20 44	20 34	20 47	21 03	21 35	21 08	21 14	21 36	21 47	22 03		22 14	22 20	23 08	23 28
	d			19 37			20 05				20 45	20 37			21 40			21 39			22 05				
Lostock Hall	d						20 19														22 19				
Bamber Bridge	d						20 29														22 29				
Pleasington	d						20 47														22 47				
Cherry Tree	d						20 51														22 51				
Mill Hill (Lancashire)	d						20 57														22 57				
Blackburn	a			19 54			21 06				21 14	20 53			22 09			21 55			23 06				
Clitheroe 94	a																								
Blackburn	d			19 54			21 07				21 15	20 54			22 10			21 55			23 07				
Rishton	d						21 17														23 17				
Church & Oswaldtwistle	d						21 29														23 29				
Accrington	d			20 02			21 33				21 33	21 01			22 28			22 03			23 33				
Huncoat	d						21 39														23 39				
Hapton	d						21 45														23 45				
Rose Grove	d						21 51														23 51				
Burnley Manchester Road 41	a			20 10							21 52	21 10			22 47			22 12							
Leeds 10 41	a			21 22								22 22			01 03			23 23							
Burnley Barracks	d						21 55														23 55				
Burnley Central	d						21 59														23 59				
Brierfield	d						22 07														00 07				
Nelson	d						22 12														00 12				
Colne	a						22 20														00 20				

A 30 October, 6 November
B To Manchester Airport
C To Liverpool Lime Street
D To Hebden Bridge
E To York
F To Manchester Victoria

Colne, Burnley, Accrington and Blackburn - Preston - Blackpool

Miles	Miles			TP MX ◇1 A	NT MO B	TP MO ◇1 A	TP MX ◇1 C	NT MX D	TP ◇1 A	TP ◇1 A	TP ◇1 E	NT		NT D	NT	TP FO ◇1 A 🛒	TP FX ◇1 A 🛒	NT	NT D	NT F	NT	NT G		TP ◇1 A 🛒	NT D
0	—	**Colne**	d									05 40						06 46			07 47				
2	—	Nelson	d									05 45						06 51			07 52				
3¼	—	Brierfield	d									05 48						06 54			07 55				
5½	—	**Burnley Central**	d									05 53						06 59			08 00				
—	—	Burnley Barracks	d									05 55						07 01			08 02				
—	—	Leeds ■10 41	d												05 51					06 51					
—	—	Burnley Manchester Road 41	d												06 57					07 57					
7	—	Rose Grove	d									05 58						07 05			08 05				
8½	—	Hapton	d									06 01									08 08				
10	—	Huncoat	d									06 04						07 09			08 11				
11¾	—	Accrington	d									06 09			07 07			07 14		08 06	08 16				
12½	—	Church & Oswaldtwistle	d									06 11						07 16			08 18				
14¼	—	Rishton	d									06 14						07 19			08 21				
18	—	**Blackburn**	a									06 24			07 16			07 24		08 15	08 27				
—	—	Clitheroe 94	d																						
—	—	**Blackburn**	d									06 25			07 16			07 35		08 15	08 35				
19¼	—	Mill Hill (Lancashire)	d									06 28						07 38		08 19	08 38				
20	—	Cherry Tree	d									06 30						07 40			08 40				
21	—	Pleasington	d									06 32						07 42			08 42				
26	—	Bamber Bridge	d									06 39			07 26			07 49		08 27	08 49				
27¼	—	Lostock Hall	d									06 42			07 28			07 52		08 30	08 52				
30	—	**Preston ■8**	a									06 50			07 36			08 00		08 38	09 00				
—	—		d	23p35	23p39	23p47	23p51	00 19			06 37	07 00		07 13	07 38	07 59	07 59	08 02	08 15	08 40	09 02	08 51		08 59	09 19
35¼	5¼	Salwick	d									07 07						08 09							
37¾	7¾	Kirkham & Wesham	d			23p56		00 28			06 46	07 11		07 22		08 08	08 09	08 13	08 25		09 11				09 28
41	—	Moss Side	d									07 17						08 19			09 17				
43½	—	Lytham	d									07 21						08 23			09 21				
44¾	—	Ansdell & Fairhaven	d									07 24						08 26			09 24				
46¾	—	St Annes-on-the-Sea	d									07 28						08 30			09 28				
48¼	—	Squires Gate	d									07 32						08 34			09 32				
49½	—	Blackpool Pleasure Beach	d									07 34						08 36			09 34				
50	—	**Blackpool South**	a									07 38						08 41			09 39				
—	14¼	Poulton-le-Fylde	d	23p52	23p56	00 05	00 08	00 36			06 56			07 30	07 54	08 18	08 18		08 33	08 56				09 16	09 36
—	16¼	Layton	d					00 43			06 59			07 34		08 22	08 22		08 37						09 43
—	17½	**Blackpool North**	a	00 02	00 05	00 14	00 16	00 50	01 30	05 33	07 09			07 41	08 05	08 29	08 29		08 44	09 05		09 17		09 25	09 50

		NT F	TP ◇1 A 🛒	NT B	NT	NT D	NT F	TP ◇1 A 🛒		NT B	NT	NT D	NT F	TP ◇1 A 🛒	NT H	NT	NT D	NT F		TP ◇1 A 🛒	NT H	NT	NT D	NT F	TP ◇1 A 🛒
Colne	d				08 50						09 50					10 50						11 50			
Nelson	d				08 55						09 55					10 55						11 55			
Brierfield	d				08 58						09 58					10 58						11 58			
Burnley Central	d				09 03						10 03					11 03						12 03			
Burnley Barracks	d				09 05						10 05					11 05						12 05			
Leeds ■10 41	d	07 51					08 51						09 53					10 53						11 53	
Burnley Manchester Road 41	d	08 57					09 57						10 57					11 57						12 57	
Rose Grove	d				09 08						10 08					11 08						12 08			
Hapton	d				09 11						10 11					11 11						12 11			
Huncoat	d				09 14						10 14					11 14						12 14			
Accrington	d	09 06			09 19		10 06				10 19		11 06			11 19		12 06				12 19		13 06	
Church & Oswaldtwistle	d				09 21						10 21					11 21						12 21			
Rishton	d				09 24						10 24					11 24						12 24			
Blackburn	a	09 15			09 34		10 15				10 34		11 15			11 34		12 15				12 34		13 15	
Clitheroe 94	d																								
Blackburn	d	09 15			09 35		10 15				10 35		11 15			11 35		12 15				12 35		13 15	
Mill Hill (Lancashire)	d				09 38						10 38					11 38						12 38			
Cherry Tree	d				09 40						10 40					11 40						12 40			
Pleasington	d				09 42						10 42					11 42						12 42			
Bamber Bridge	d				09 49						10 49					11 49						12 49			
Lostock Hall	d				09 52						10 52					11 52						12 52			
Preston ■8	a	09 32			10 00		10 33				11 00		11 32			12 00		12 33				13 00		13 33	
	d	09 34	09 38	09 55	10 02	10 19	10 34	10 38		10 55	11 02	11 19	11 34	11 38	11 55	12 02	12 19	12 34		12 38	12 55	13 02	13 19	13 34	13 38
Salwick	d															12 09									
Kirkham & Wesham	d			10 05	10 11	10 28				11 05	11 11	11 28			12 05	12 13	12 28				13 05	13 11	13 28		
Moss Side	d				10 17						11 17					12 19						13 17			
Lytham	d				10 21						11 21					12 23						13 21			
Ansdell & Fairhaven	d				10 24						11 24					12 26						13 24			
St Annes-on-the-Sea	d				10 28						11 28					12 30						13 28			
Squires Gate	d				10 32						11 32					12 34						13 32			
Blackpool Pleasure Beach	d				10 34						11 34					12 36						13 34			
Blackpool South	a				10 39						11 41					12 41						13 39			
Poulton-le-Fylde	d	09 51	09 56			10 36	10 51	10 56				11 36	11 51	11 56			12 36	12 51		12 56			13 36	13 51	13 56
Layton	d					10 43						11 43					12 43						13 43		
Blackpool North	a	10 01	10 05	10 21		10 51	11 01	11 05		11 21		11 50	12 00	12 05	12 21		12 50	13 00		13 05	13 21		13 50	14 00	14 05

A From Manchester Airport
B From Liverpool Lime Street
C From Windermere
D From Manchester Victoria
E From Manchester Piccadilly
F From York
G From Buxton
H From Liverpool South Parkway

Table 97

Mondays to Fridays

until 15 July

Colne, Burnley, Accrington and Blackburn - Preston - Blackpool

		NT A	NT	NT B		NT C	TP ◇1 D	NT A	NT	NT B	NT C	TP ◇1 E	TP ◇1 F FO	NT A		NT	NT C	TP ◇1 D	NT A	NT	NT B	TP ◇1 D	NT C	NT A	
Colne	d		12 50						13 50							14 50				15 50					
Nelson	d		12 55						13 55							14 55				15 55					
Brierfield	d		12 58						13 58							14 58				15 58					
Burnley Central	d		13 03						14 03							15 03				16 03					
Burnley Barracks	d		13 05						14 05							15 05				16 05					
Leeds 10 41	d					12 53					13 53						14 53						15 52		
Burnley Manchester Road 41	d					13 57					14 57						15 57						16 58		
Rose Grove	d		13 08						14 08							15 08				16 08					
Hapton	d		13 11						14 11							15 11				16 11					
Huncoat	d		13 14						14 14							15 14				16 14					
Accrington	d		13 19			14 06			14 19		15 06					15 19	16 06			16 19			17 06		
Church & Oswaldtwistle	d		13 21						14 21							15 21				16 21					
Rishton	d		13 24						14 24							15 24				16 24					
Blackburn	a		13 34			14 15			14 34		15 15					15 33	16 15			16 34			17 15		
Clitheroe 94	d																								
Blackburn	d		13 35			14 15			14 35		15 15					15 35	16 15			16 35			17 16		
Mill Hill (Lancashire)	d		13 38						14 38							15 38				16 38					
Cherry Tree	d		13 40						14 40							15 40				16 40					
Pleasington	d		13 42						14 42							15 42				16 42					
Bamber Bridge	d		13 49						14 49							15 49				16 49					
Lostock Hall	d		13 52						14 52							15 52				16 52					
Preston 8	a		14 00			14 33			15 00		15 33					16 00	16 33			17 00			17 33		
	d	13 55	14 02	14 19		14 34	14 38	14 55	15 02	15 19	15 34	15 38	15 38	15 55		16 02	16 34	16 38	16 56	17 02	17 21	17 32	17 35	17 55	
Salwick	d															16 09									
Kirkham & Wesham	d	14 05	14 11	14 28				15 05	15 11	15 28				16 05		16 13		16 47	17 05	17 11	17 30	17 41		18 05	
Moss Side	d		14 17						15 17							16 19				17 17					
Lytham	d		14 21						15 21							16 23				17 21					
Ansdell & Fairhaven	d		14 24						15 24							16 26				17 24					
St Annes-on-the-Sea	d		14 28						15 28							16 30				17 28					
Squires Gate	d		14 32						15 32							16 34				17 32					
Blackpool Pleasure Beach	d		14 34						15 34							16 36				17 34					
Blackpool South	a		14 39						15 39							16 41				17 39					
Poulton-le-Fylde	d			14 36		14 51	14 56			15 36	15 51	15 56	15 58				16 51	16 57	17 13		17 38	17 51	17 56	18 13	
Layton	d			14 43						15 43								17 00			17 43	17 54			
Blackpool North	a	14 21		14 51		15 00	15 05	15 21		15 50	16 00	16 05	16 07	16 21			17 00	17 07	17 21		17 50	18 02	18 06	18 24	

		NT	NT B	NT G	NT C	TP ◇1 D	NT G	NT H	NT	NT		NT B	NT C	NT	TP ◇1 D	NT H	NT B	NT C	NT	TP ◇1 D		NT	NT B	NT H	TP ◇1 D
Colne	d	16 50							17 50					18 54					19 50			20 50			
Nelson	d	16 55							17 55					18 59					19 55			20 55			
Brierfield	d	16 58							17 58					19 02					19 58			20 58			
Burnley Central	d	17 03							18 03					19 07					20 03			21 03			
Burnley Barracks	d	17 05							18 05					19 09					20 05			21 05			
Leeds 10 41	d				16 51								17 51					18 51							
Burnley Manchester Road 41	d				17 57								18 57					19 57							
Rose Grove	d	17 08							18 08					19 12					20 08			21 08			
Hapton	d	17 11							18 11					19 15					20 11			21 11			
Huncoat	d	17 14							18 14					19 18					20 14			21 14			
Accrington	d	17 19			18 06				18 19				19 06	19 23				20 06	20 19			21 19			
Church & Oswaldtwistle	d	17 21							18 21					19 25					20 21			21 21			
Rishton	d	17 24							18 24					19 28					20 24			21 24			
Blackburn	a	17 34			18 15				18 34				19 15	19 34				20 15	20 34			21 34			
Clitheroe 94	d																								
Blackburn	d	17 35			18 15				18 35	18 44			19 15	19 35				20 15	20 35			21 35			
Mill Hill (Lancashire)	d	17 38							18 38					19 38					20 38			21 38			
Cherry Tree	d	17 40							18 40					19 40					20 40			21 40			
Pleasington	d	17 42							18 42					19 42					20 42			21 42			
Bamber Bridge	d	17 49							18 49					19 49					20 49			21 49			
Lostock Hall	d	17 52							18 52					19 52					20 52			21 52			
Preston 8	a	18 00			18 33				19 00	19 05			19 32	20 00				20 32	21 00			22 02			
	d	18 02	18 18	18 26	18 34	18 40	18 49	18 55	19 02	19 08		19 19	19 34	20 02	19 38	20 19	20 25	20 34	21 02	20 38			21 19	21 24	21 38
Salwick	d																								
Kirkham & Wesham	d	18 11	18 27			18 49		19 05	19 11			19 28		20 11			20 34		21 11				21 28		
Moss Side	d	18 17							19 17					20 17					21 17						
Lytham	d	18 21							19 21					20 21					21 21						
Ansdell & Fairhaven	d	18 24							19 24					20 24					21 24						
St Annes-on-the-Sea	d	18 28							19 28					20 28					21 28						
Squires Gate	d	18 32							19 32					20 32					21 32						
Blackpool Pleasure Beach	d	18 34							19 34					20 34					21 34						
Blackpool South	a	18 39							19 39					20 39					21 41						
Poulton-le-Fylde	d		18 35	18 43	18 50	18 59						19 36	19 50		19 56		20 42	20 50		20 56			21 36		21 56
Layton	d		18 39			19 02						19 43					20 47						21 40		
Blackpool North	a		18 49	18 53	18 58	19 09	19 16	19 23		19 33		19 50	20 00		20 05	20 44	20 54	21 00		21 06			21 48	21 53	22 06

A From Liverpool South Parkway
B From Manchester Victoria
C From York
D From Manchester Airport
E until 23 June, FX from 27 June until 14 July. From Manchester Airport
F From 24 June until 15 July. From Manchester Airport
G From Buxton
H From Liverpool Lime Street

until 15 July

Colne, Burnley, Accrington and Blackburn - Preston - Blackpool

			NT	NT	NT	TP	NT	NT	NT	TP	TP
						◇1				◇1	◇1
			A	B		C		D	A	C	E
Colne		d			21 45		22 55				
Nelson		d			21 50		23 00				
Brierfield		d			21 53		23 03				
Burnley Central		d			21 58		23 08				
Burnley Barracks		d			22 00		23 10				
Leeds 10	41	d		20 51							
Burnley Manchester Road	41	d		21 56							
Rose Grove		d			22 03		23 13				
Hapton		d			22 06						
Huncoat		d			22 09						
Accrington		d		22 05	22 14		23 20				
Church & Oswaldtwistle		d			22 16						
Rishton		d			22 19						
Blackburn		a		22 13	22 25		23 29				
Clitheroe	94	d									
Blackburn		d		22 14	22 26		23 31				
Mill Hill (Lancashire)		d			22 29		23 34				
Cherry Tree		d			22 31						
Pleasington		d			22 33						
Bamber Bridge		d			22 40		23 42				
Lostock Hall		d			22 43		23 44				
Preston 8		a		22 31	22 51		23 53				
		d	22 19	22 32	22 52	22 35		22 57	23 19	23 35	23 51
Salwick		d									
Kirkham & Wesham		d	22 28		23 02				23 28		
Moss Side		d			23 08						
Lytham		d			23 12						
Ansdell & Fairhaven		d			23 15						
St Annes-on-the-Sea		d			23 19						
Squires Gate		d			23 22						
Blackpool Pleasure Beach		d			23 25						
Blackpool South		a			23 31						
Poulton-le-Fylde		d	22 36	22 49		22 52			23 36	23 52	00 08
Layton		d	22 43						23 40		
Blackpool North		a	22 51	22 59		23 02		23 22	23 48	00 02	00 16

Mondays to Fridays

18 July to 30 September

			TP	NT	TP	TP	NT	TP	TP	TP	TP	NT	NT	NT	TP	NT	NT	NT	NT	NT	TP	NT	NT	TP
			MX	MO	MO	MX	MX			MO	MX													
			◇1		◇1	◇1		◇1	◇1	◇1	◇1				◇1						◇1			◇1
			C	D	C	E	A	C	C	F	G		A		C 🍴		A	B		H	C 🍴	A	B	C 🍴
Colne		d										05 40				06 46			07 47					
Nelson		d										05 45				06 51			07 52					
Brierfield		d										05 48				06 54			07 55					
Burnley Central		d										05 53				06 59			08 00					
Burnley Barracks		d										05 55				07 01			08 02					
Leeds 10	41	d												05 51				06 51					07 51	
Burnley Manchester Road	41	d												06 57				07 57					08 57	
Rose Grove		d										05 58				07 05			08 05					
Hapton		d										06 01							08 08					
Huncoat		d										06 04				07 09			08 11					
Accrington		d										06 09		07 07		07 14		08 06	08 16				09 06	
Church & Oswaldtwistle		d										06 11				07 16			08 18					
Rishton		d										06 14				07 19			08 21					
Blackburn		a										06 24		07 16		07 24		08 15	08 27				09 15	
Clitheroe	94	d																						
Blackburn		d										06 25		07 16		07 35		08 15	08 35				09 15	
Mill Hill (Lancashire)		d										06 28				07 38		08 19	08 38					
Cherry Tree		d										06 30				07 40			08 40					
Pleasington		d										06 32				07 42			08 42					
Bamber Bridge		d										06 39		07 26		07 49		08 27	08 49					
Lostock Hall		d										06 42		07 28		07 52		08 30	08 52					
Preston 8		a										06 50		07 36		08 00		08 38	09 00				09 32	
		d	23p35	23p39	23p47	23p51	00 19			06 37	06 37	07 00	07 13	07 38	07 59	08 02	08 15	08 40	09 02	08 51	08 59	09 19	09 34	09 38
Salwick		d										07 07				08 09								
Kirkham & Wesham		d			23p56		00 28			06 46	06 46	07 11	07 22		08 09	08 13	08 25		09 11			09 28		
Moss Side		d										07 17				08 19			09 17					
Lytham		d										07 21				08 23			09 21					
Ansdell & Fairhaven		d										07 24				08 26			09 24					
St Annes-on-the-Sea		d										07 28				08 30			09 28					
Squires Gate		d										07 32				08 34			09 32					
Blackpool Pleasure Beach		d										07 34				08 36			09 34					
Blackpool South		a										07 38				08 41			09 39					
Poulton-le-Fylde		d	23p52	23p56	00 05	00 08	00 36			06 56	06 56		07 30	07 54	08 18		08 33	08 56			09 16	09 36	09 51	09 56
Layton		d					00 43			06 59	06 59		07 34		08 22		08 37					09 43		
Blackpool North		a	00 02	00 05	00 14	00 16	00 50	01 30	05 33	07 05	07 06		07 41	08 05	08 29		08 44	09 05		09 17	09 25	09 50	10 01	10 05

A From Manchester Victoria
B From York
C From Manchester Airport
D From Liverpool Lime Street
E From Windermere
F From 18 July until 5 September. From Manchester Piccadilly
G From 19 July until 2 September, from 6 September until 30 September. From Manchester Piccadilly
H From Buxton

Table 97

Mondays to Fridays

18 July to 30 September

Colne, Burnley, Accrington and Blackburn - Preston - Blackpool

		NT	NT	NT	NT	TP		NT	NT	NT	NT	TP	NT	NT	NT	NT		TP	NT	NT	NT	NT	TP	NT	NT
						◇1						◇1						◇1					◇1		
		A		B	C	D		A		B	C	D	E		B	C		D	E		B	C	D	E	
						🛒						🛒						🛒					🛒		
Colne	d		08 50						09 50					10 50						11 50					12 50
Nelson	d		08 55						09 55					10 55						11 55					12 55
Brierfield	d		08 58						09 58					10 58						11 58					12 58
Burnley Central	d		09 03						10 03					11 03						12 03					13 03
Burnley Barracks	d		09 05						10 05					11 05						12 05					13 05
Leeds 10 41	d				08 51						09 53					10 53						11 53			
Burnley Manchester Road 41	d				09 57						10 57					11 57						12 57			
Rose Grove	d		09 08						10 08					11 08						12 08					13 08
Hapton	d		09 11						10 11					11 11						12 11					13 11
Huncoat	d		09 14						10 14					11 14						12 14					13 14
Accrington	d		09 19		10 06				10 19		11 06			11 19		12 06				12 19		13 06			13 19
Church & Oswaldtwistle	d		09 21						10 21					11 21						12 21					13 21
Rishton	d		09 24						10 24					11 24						12 24					13 24
Blackburn	a		09 34		10 15				10 34		11 15			11 34		12 15				12 34		13 15			13 34
Clitheroe 94	d																								
Blackburn	d		09 35		10 15				10 35		11 15			11 35		12 15				12 35		13 15			13 35
Mill Hill (Lancashire)	d		09 38						10 38					11 38						12 38					13 38
Cherry Tree	d		09 40						10 40					11 40						12 40					13 40
Pleasington	d		09 42						10 42					11 42						12 42					13 42
Bamber Bridge	d		09 49						10 49					11 49						12 49					13 49
Lostock Hall	d		09 52						10 52					11 52						12 52					13 52
Preston 8	a		10 00		10 33				11 00		11 32			12 00		12 33				13 00		13 33			14 00
	d	09 55	10 02	10 19	10 34	10 38		10 55	11 02	11 19	11 34	11 38	11 55	12 02	12 19	12 34		12 38	12 55	13 02	13 19	13 34	13 38	13 55	14 02
Salwick	d													12 09											
Kirkham & Wesham	d	10 05	10 11	10 28				11 05	11 11	11 28			12 05	12 13	12 28				13 05	13 11	13 28			14 05	14 11
Moss Side	d		10 17						11 17					12 19						13 17					14 17
Lytham	d		10 21						11 21					12 23						13 21					14 21
Ansdell & Fairhaven	d		10 24						11 24					12 26						13 24					14 24
St Annes-on-the-Sea	d		10 28						11 28					12 30						13 28					14 28
Squires Gate	d		10 32						11 32					12 34						13 32					14 32
Blackpool Pleasure Beach	d		10 34						11 34					12 36						13 34					14 34
Blackpool South	a		10 39						11 41					12 41						13 39					14 39
Poulton-le-Fylde	d			10 36	10 51	10 56				11 36	11 51	11 56			12 36	12 51		12 56			13 36	13 51	13 56		
Layton	d			10 43						11 43					12 43						13 43				
Blackpool North	a	10 21		10 51	11 01	11 05		11 21		11 50	12 00	12 05	12 21		12 50	13 00		13 05	13 21		13 50	14 00	14 05	14 21	

		NT		NT	TP	NT	NT	NT	NT	TP	TP	NT		NT	NT	TP	NT	NT	NT	TP	NT	NT		NT	NT
					◇1					◇1	◇1					◇1				◇1					
		B		C	D	E		B	C	F	G	E			C	D	E		B	D	C	E			B
					🛒					🛒	🛒					🛒				🛒					
										FX	FO														
Colne	d						13 50							14 50				15 50						16 50	
Nelson	d						13 55							14 55				15 55						16 55	
Brierfield	d						13 58							14 58				15 58						16 58	
Burnley Central	d						14 03							15 03				16 03						17 03	
Burnley Barracks	d						14 05							15 05				16 05						17 05	
Leeds 10 41	d			12 53					13 53						14 53						15 52				
Burnley Manchester Road 41	d			13 57					14 57						15 57						16 58				
Rose Grove	d						14 08							15 08				16 08						17 08	
Hapton	d						14 11							15 11				16 11						17 11	
Huncoat	d						14 14							15 14				16 14						17 14	
Accrington	d			14 06			14 19		15 06					15 19	16 06			16 19			17 06			17 19	
Church & Oswaldtwistle	d						14 21							15 21				16 21						17 21	
Rishton	d						14 24							15 24				16 24						17 24	
Blackburn	a			14 15			14 34		15 15					15 33	16 15			16 34			17 15			17 34	
Clitheroe 94	d																								
Blackburn	d			14 15			14 35		15 15					15 35	16 15			16 35			17 16			17 35	
Mill Hill (Lancashire)	d						14 38							15 38				16 38						17 38	
Cherry Tree	d						14 40							15 40				16 40						17 40	
Pleasington	d						14 42							15 42				16 42						17 42	
Bamber Bridge	d						14 49							15 49				16 49						17 49	
Lostock Hall	d						14 52							15 52				16 52						17 52	
Preston 8	a			14 33			15 00		15 33					16 00	16 33			17 00			17 33			18 00	
	d	14 19		14 34	14 38	14 55	15 02	15 19	15 34	15 38	15 38	15 55		16 02	16 34	16 38	16 56	17 02	17 21	17 32	17 35	17 55		18 02	18 18
Salwick	d													16 09											
Kirkham & Wesham	d	14 28				15 05	15 11	15 28				16 05		16 13		16 47	17 05	17 11	17 30	17 41		18 05		18 11	18 27
Moss Side	d						15 17							16 19				17 17						18 17	
Lytham	d						15 21							16 23				17 21						18 21	
Ansdell & Fairhaven	d						15 24							16 26				17 24						18 24	
St Annes-on-the-Sea	d						15 28							16 30				17 28						18 28	
Squires Gate	d						15 32							16 34				17 32						18 32	
Blackpool Pleasure Beach	d						15 34							16 36				17 34						18 34	
Blackpool South	a						15 39							16 41				17 39						18 39	
Poulton-le-Fylde	d	14 36		14 51	14 56			15 36	15 51	15 56	15 58				16 51	16 57	17 13		17 38	17 51	17 56	18 13			18 35
Layton	d	14 43						15 43								17 00			17 43	17 54					18 39
Blackpool North	a	14 51		15 00	15 05	15 21		15 50	16 00	16 05	16 07	16 21			17 00	17 07	17 21		17 50	18 02	18 06	18 24			18 49

A From Liverpool Lime Street
B From Manchester Victoria
C From York
D From Manchester Airport
E From Liverpool South Parkway
F From 18 July until 8 September, from 12 September until 30 September. From Manchester Airport
G From 22 July until 9 September. From Manchester Airport

Table 97

Mondays to Fridays

18 July to 30 September

Colne, Burnley, Accrington and Blackburn - Preston - Blackpool

		NT	NT	TP	NT	NT	NT	NT		NT	NT	NT	TP	NT	NT	NT	NT	TP		NT	NT	NT	TP	NT	NT
				◇1									◇1					◇1					◇1		
		A	B	C	A	D				E	B		C	D	E	B		C			E	D	C	E	B
Colne	d						17 50					18 54					19 50			20 50					
Nelson	d						17 55					18 59					19 55			20 55					
Brierfield	d						17 58					19 02					19 58			20 58					
Burnley Central	d						18 03					19 07					20 03			21 03					
Burnley Barracks	d						18 05					19 09					20 05			21 05					
Leeds 10 41	d		16 51								17 51					18 51									20 51
Burnley Manchester Road 41	d		17 57								18 57					19 57									21 56
Rose Grove	d						18 08					19 12					20 08			21 08					
Hapton	d						18 11					19 15					20 11			21 11					
Huncoat	d						18 14					19 18					20 14			21 14					
Accrington	d		18 06				18 19				19 06	19 23				20 06	20 19			21 19					22 05
Church & Oswaldtwistle	d						18 21					19 25					20 21			21 21					
Rishton	d						18 24					19 28					20 24			21 24					
Blackburn	a		18 15				18 34				19 15	19 34				20 15	20 34			21 34					22 13
Clitheroe 94	d																								
Blackburn	d		18 15				18 35	18 44			19 15	19 35				20 15	20 35			21 35					22 14
Mill Hill (Lancashire)	d						18 38					19 38					20 38			21 38					
Cherry Tree	d						18 40					19 40					20 40			21 40					
Pleasington	d						18 42					19 42					20 42			21 42					
Bamber Bridge	d						18 49					19 49					20 49			21 49					
Lostock Hall	d						18 52					19 52					20 52			21 52					
Preston 8	a		18 33				19 00	19 05			19 32	20 00				20 32	21 00			22 02					22 31
	d	18 26	18 34	18 40	18 49	18 55	19 02	19 08		19 19	19 34	20 02	19 38	20 19	20 25	20 34	21 02	20 38			21 19	21 24	21 38	22 19	22 32
Salwick	d																								
Kirkham & Wesham	d			18 49		19 05	19 11			19 28		20 11			20 34		21 11				21 28			22 28	
Moss Side	d						19 17					20 17					21 17								
Lytham	d						19 21					20 21					21 21								
Ansdell & Fairhaven	d						19 24					20 24					21 24								
St Annes-on-the-Sea	d						19 28					20 28					21 28								
Squires Gate	d						19 32					20 32					21 32								
Blackpool Pleasure Beach	d						19 34					20 34					21 34								
Blackpool South	a						19 39					20 39					21 41								
Poulton-le-Fylde	d	18 43	18 50	18 59						19 36	19 50		19 56		20 42	20 50		20 56			21 36		21 56	22 36	22 49
Layton	d			19 02						19 43					20 47						21 40			22 43	
Blackpool North	a	18 53	18 58	19 09	19 16	19 23		19 33		19 50	20 00		20 05	20 44	20 54	21 00		21 06			21 48	21 53	22 06	22 51	22 59

		NT	TP	NT		NT	NT	TP	TP
			◇1					◇1	◇1
			C			D	E	C	F
Colne	d	21 45		22 55					
Nelson	d	21 50		23 00					
Brierfield	d	21 53		23 03					
Burnley Central	d	21 58		23 08					
Burnley Barracks	d	22 00		23 10					
Leeds 10 41	d								
Burnley Manchester Road 41	d								
Rose Grove	d	22 03		23 13					
Hapton	d	22 06							
Huncoat	d	22 09							
Accrington	d	22 14		23 20					
Church & Oswaldtwistle	d	22 16							
Rishton	d	22 19							
Blackburn	a	22 25		23 29					
Clitheroe 94	d								
Blackburn	d	22 26		23 31					
Mill Hill (Lancashire)	d	22 29		23 34					
Cherry Tree	d	22 31							
Pleasington	d	22 33							
Bamber Bridge	d	22 40		23 42					
Lostock Hall	d	22 43		23 44					
Preston 8	a	22 51		23 53					
	d	22 52	22 35			22 57	23 19	23 35	23 51
Salwick	d								
Kirkham & Wesham	d	23 02					23 28		
Moss Side	d	23 08							
Lytham	d	23 12							
Ansdell & Fairhaven	d	23 15							
St Annes-on-the-Sea	d	23 19							
Squires Gate	d	23 22							
Blackpool Pleasure Beach	d	23 25							
Blackpool South	a	23 31							
Poulton-le-Fylde	d		22 52				23 36	23 52	00 08
Layton	d						23 40		
Blackpool North	a		23 02			23 22	23 48	00 02	00 16

A From Buxton
B From York
C From Manchester Airport
D From Liverpool Lime Street
E From Manchester Victoria
F From Windermere

Table 97

Mondays to Fridays

from 3 October

Colne, Burnley, Accrington and Blackburn - Preston - Blackpool

		TP	NT	TP	TP	NT	TP	TP	TP	NT		NT	NT	TP	NT	NT	NT	NT	NT	TP		NT	NT	TP	NT
		MX	MO	MO	MX	MX																			
		◇1		◇1	◇1		◇1	◇1	◇1					◇1						◇1				◇1	
		A	B	A	C	D	A	A	E			D		A		D	F		G	A		D	F	A	B
														🚲						🚲				🚲	
Colne	d									05 40					06 46			07 47							
Nelson	d									05 45					06 51			07 52							
Brierfield	d									05 48					06 54			07 55							
Burnley Central	d									05 53					06 59			08 00							
Burnley Barracks	d									05 55					07 01			08 02							
Leeds [10] 41	d												05 51				06 51						07 51		
Burnley Manchester Road 41	d												06 57				07 57						08 57		
Rose Grove	d									05 58					07 05			08 05							
Hapton	d									06 01								08 08							
Huncoat	d									06 04					07 09			08 11							
Accrington	d									06 09			07 07		07 14		08 06	08 16					09 06		
Church & Oswaldtwistle	d									06 11					07 16			08 18							
Rishton	d									06 14					07 19			08 21							
Blackburn	a									06 24			07 16		07 24		08 15	08 27					09 15		
Clitheroe 94	d																								
Blackburn	d									06 25			07 16		07 35		08 15	08 35					09 15		
Mill Hill (Lancashire)	d									06 28					07 38		08 19	08 38							
Cherry Tree	d									06 30					07 40			08 40							
Pleasington	d									06 32					07 42			08 42							
Bamber Bridge	d									06 39			07 26		07 49		08 27	08 49							
Lostock Hall	d									06 42			07 28		07 52		08 30	08 52							
Preston [8]	a									06 50			07 36		08 00		08 38	09 00					09 32		
	d	23p35	23p39	23p47	23p51	00 19			06 37	07 00		07 13	07 38	07 59	08 02	08 15	08 40	09 02	08 51	08 59		09 19	09 34	09 38	09 55
Salwick	d									07 07					08 09										
Kirkham & Wesham	d			23p56		00 28			06 46	07 11		07 22		08 09	08 13	08 25		09 11				09 28			10 05
Moss Side	d									07 17					08 19			09 17							
Lytham	d									07 21					08 23			09 21							
Ansdell & Fairhaven	d									07 24					08 26			09 24							
St Annes-on-the-Sea	d									07 28					08 30			09 28							
Squires Gate	d									07 32					08 34			09 32							
Blackpool Pleasure Beach	d									07 34					08 36			09 34							
Blackpool South	a									07 40					08 43			09 41							
Poulton-le-Fylde	d	23p52	23p56	00 05	00 08	00 36			06 56			07 30	07 54	08 18		08 33	08 56			09 16		09 36	09 51	09 56	
Layton	d					00 43			06 59			07 34		08 22		08 37						09 43			
Blackpool North	a	00 02	00 05	00 14	00 16	00 50	01 30	05 33	07 06			07 43	08 05	08 29		08 46	09 05		09 17	09 25		09 52	10 01	10 05	10 21

		NT	NT	NT	TP	NT		NT	NT	NT	TP	NT	NT	NT	NT	TP		NT	NT	NT	NT	TP	NT	NT	NT
					◇1						◇1					◇1						◇1			
			D	F	A	B			D	F	A	H		D	F	A		H		D	F	A	H		D
					🚲						🚲					🚲						🚲			
Colne	d	08 50						09 50					10 50						11 50					12 50	
Nelson	d	08 55						09 55					10 55						11 55					12 55	
Brierfield	d	08 58						09 58					10 58						11 58					12 58	
Burnley Central	d	09 03						10 03					11 03						12 03					13 03	
Burnley Barracks	d	09 05						10 05					11 05						12 05					13 05	
Leeds [10] 41	d			08 51						09 53					10 53						11 53				
Burnley Manchester Road 41	d			09 57						10 57					11 57						12 57				
Rose Grove	d	09 08						10 08					11 08						12 08					13 08	
Hapton	d	09 11						10 11					11 11						12 11					13 11	
Huncoat	d	09 14						10 14					11 14						12 14					13 14	
Accrington	d	09 19		10 06				10 19		11 06			11 19		12 06				12 19		13 06			13 19	
Church & Oswaldtwistle	d	09 21						10 21					11 21						12 21					13 21	
Rishton	d	09 24						10 24					11 24						12 24					13 24	
Blackburn	a	09 34		10 15				10 34		11 15			11 34		12 15				12 34		13 15			13 34	
Clitheroe 94	d																								
Blackburn	d	09 35		10 15				10 35		11 15			11 35		12 15				12 35		13 15			13 35	
Mill Hill (Lancashire)	d	09 38						10 38					11 38						12 38					13 38	
Cherry Tree	d	09 40						10 40					11 40						12 40					13 40	
Pleasington	d	09 42						10 42					11 42						12 42					13 42	
Bamber Bridge	d	09 49						10 49					11 49						12 49					13 49	
Lostock Hall	d	09 52						10 52					11 52						12 52					13 52	
Preston [8]	a	10 00		10 33				11 00		11 32			12 00		12 33				13 00		13 33			14 00	
	d	10 02	10 19	10 34	10 38	10 55		11 02	11 19	11 34	11 38	11 55	12 02	12 19	12 34	12 38		12 55	13 02	13 19	13 34	13 38	13 55	14 02	14 19
Salwick	d												12 09												
Kirkham & Wesham	d	10 11	10 28			11 05		11 11	11 28			12 05	12 13	12 28				13 05	13 11	13 28			14 05	14 11	14 28
Moss Side	d	10 17						11 17					12 19						13 17					14 17	
Lytham	d	10 21						11 21					12 23						13 21					14 21	
Ansdell & Fairhaven	d	10 24						11 24					12 26						13 24					14 24	
St Annes-on-the-Sea	d	10 28						11 28					12 30						13 28					14 28	
Squires Gate	d	10 32						11 32					12 34						13 32					14 32	
Blackpool Pleasure Beach	d	10 34						11 34					12 36						13 34					14 34	
Blackpool South	a	10 41						11 39					12 43						13 41					14 41	
Poulton-le-Fylde	d		10 36	10 51	10 56				11 36	11 51	11 56			12 36	12 51	12 56				13 36	13 51	13 56			14 36
Layton	d		10 43						11 43					12 43						13 43					14 43
Blackpool North	a		10 53	11 01	11 05	11 21			11 52	12 00	12 05	12 21		12 52	13 00	13 05		13 21		13 52	14 00	14 05	14 21		14 53

A From Manchester Airport
B From Liverpool Lime Street
C From Windermere
D From Manchester Victoria
E From Manchester Piccadilly
F From York
G From Buxton
H From Liverpool South Parkway

Table 97

Mondays to Fridays

from 3 October

Colne, Burnley, Accrington and Blackburn - Preston - Blackpool

		NT		TP	NT	NT	NT	NT	TP	NT	NT	NT		TP	NT	NT	NT	TP	NT	NT	NT	NT		NT	NT
				◇1					◇1					◇1				◇1							
		A		B	C		D	A	B	C		A		B	C		D	B	A	C		D		E	A
				(trolley)					(trolley)					(trolley)				(trolley)							
Colne	d					13 50					14 50					15 50					16 50				
Nelson	d					13 55					14 55					15 55					16 55				
Brierfield	d					13 58					14 58					15 58					16 58				
Burnley Central	d					14 03					15 03					16 03					17 03				
Burnley Barracks	d					14 05					15 05					16 05					17 05				
Leeds 10 41	d	12 53						13 53				14 53							15 52						16 51
Burnley Manchester Road 41	d	13 57						14 57				15 57							16 58						17 57
Rose Grove	d					14 08					15 08					16 08					17 08				
Hapton	d					14 11					15 11					16 11					17 11				
Huncoat	d					14 14					15 14					16 14					17 14				
Accrington	d	14 06				14 19		15 06			15 19	16 06				16 19			17 06		17 19				18 06
Church & Oswaldtwistle	d					14 21					15 21					16 21					17 21				
Rishton	d					14 24					15 24					16 24					17 24				
Blackburn	a	14 15				14 34		15 15			15 33	16 15				16 34			17 15		17 34				18 15
Clitheroe 94	d																								
Blackburn	d	14 15				14 35		15 15			15 35	16 15				16 35			17 16		17 35				18 15
Mill Hill (Lancashire)	d					14 38					15 38					16 38					17 38				
Cherry Tree	d					14 40					15 40					16 40					17 40				
Pleasington	d					14 42					15 42					16 42					17 42				
Bamber Bridge	d					14 49					15 49					16 49					17 49				
Lostock Hall	d					14 52					15 52					16 52					17 52				
Preston 8	a	14 33				15 00		15 33			16 00	16 33				17 00			17 33		18 00				18 33
	d	14 34		14 38	14 55	15 02	15 19	15 34	15 38	15 55	16 02	16 34		16 38	16 56	17 02	17 21	17 32	17 35	17 55	18 02	18 18		18 26	18 34
Salwick	d										16 09														
Kirkham & Wesham	d				15 05	15 11	15 28			16 05	16 13			16 47	17 05	17 11	17 30	17 41		18 05	18 11	18 27			
Moss Side	d					15 17					16 19					17 17					18 17				
Lytham	d					15 21					16 23					17 21					18 21				
Ansdell & Fairhaven	d					15 24					16 26					17 24					18 24				
St Annes-on-the-Sea	d					15 28					16 30					17 28					18 28				
Squires Gate	d					15 32					16 34					17 32					18 32				
Blackpool Pleasure Beach	d					15 34					16 36					17 34					18 34				
Blackpool South	a					15 41					16 43					17 41					18 41				
Poulton-le-Fylde	d	14 51		14 56			15 36	15 51	15 56			16 51		16 57	17 13		17 38	17 51	17 56	18 13		18 35		18 43	18 50
Layton	d						15 43							17 00			17 43	17 54				18 39			
Blackpool North	a	15 00		15 05	15 21		15 52	16 00	16 05	16 21		17 00		17 07	17 21		17 52	18 02	18 06	18 24		18 51		18 55	18 58

		TP	NT	NT	NT	NT	NT	NT		NT	TP	NT	NT	NT	NT	TP	NT	NT		NT	TP	NT	NT	NT	TP
		◇1									◇1					◇1					◇1				◇1
		B	E	F			D	A			B	F	D	A		B		D		F	B	D	A		B
		(trolley)									(trolley)														
Colne	d				17 50					18 54					19 50		20 50							21 45	
Nelson	d				17 55					18 59					19 55		20 55							21 50	
Brierfield	d				17 58					19 02					19 58		20 58							21 53	
Burnley Central	d				18 03					19 07					20 03		21 03							21 58	
Burnley Barracks	d				18 05					19 09					20 05		21 05							22 00	
Leeds 10 41	d							17 51						18 51									20 51		
Burnley Manchester Road 41	d							18 57						19 57									21 56		
Rose Grove	d				18 08					19 12					20 08		21 08							22 03	
Hapton	d				18 11					19 15					20 11		21 11							22 06	
Huncoat	d				18 14					19 18					20 14		21 14							22 09	
Accrington	d				18 19			19 06		19 23				20 06	20 19		21 19						22 05	22 14	
Church & Oswaldtwistle	d				18 21					19 25					20 21		21 21							22 16	
Rishton	d				18 24					19 28					20 24		21 24							22 19	
Blackburn	a				18 34			19 15		19 34				20 15	20 34		21 34						22 13	22 25	
Clitheroe 94	d																								
Blackburn	d				18 35	18 44		19 15		19 35				20 15	20 35		21 35						22 14	22 26	
Mill Hill (Lancashire)	d				18 38					19 38					20 38		21 38							22 29	
Cherry Tree	d				18 40					19 40					20 40		21 40							22 31	
Pleasington	d				18 42					19 42					20 42		21 42							22 33	
Bamber Bridge	d				18 49					19 49					20 49		21 49							22 40	
Lostock Hall	d				18 52					19 52					20 52		21 52							22 43	
Preston 8	a				19 00	19 05		19 32		20 00				20 32	21 00		22 02						22 31	22 51	
	d	18 40	18 49	18 55	19 02	19 08	19 19	19 34		20 02	19 38	20 19	20 25	20 34	21 02	20 38		21 19		21 24	21 38	22 19	22 32	22 52	22 35
Salwick	d																								
Kirkham & Wesham	d	18 49		19 05	19 11		19 28			20 11			20 34		21 11			21 28				22 28		23 02	
Moss Side	d				19 17					20 17					21 17									23 08	
Lytham	d				19 21					20 21					21 21									23 12	
Ansdell & Fairhaven	d				19 24					20 24					21 24									23 15	
St Annes-on-the-Sea	d				19 28					20 28					21 28									23 19	
Squires Gate	d				19 32					20 32					21 32									23 22	
Blackpool Pleasure Beach	d				19 34					20 34					21 34									23 25	
Blackpool South	a				19 41					20 41					21 39									23 29	
Poulton-le-Fylde	d	18 59					19 36	19 50			19 56		20 42	20 50		20 56		21 36			21 56	22 36	22 49		22 52
Layton	d	19 02					19 43						20 47					21 40				22 43			
Blackpool North	a	19 09	19 16	19 23		19 33	19 52	20 00			20 05	20 44	20 56	21 00		21 06		21 50		21 53	22 06	22 53	22 59		23 02

A From York
B From Manchester Airport
C From Liverpool South Parkway
D From Manchester Victoria
E From Buxton
F From Liverpool Lime Street

Table 97

Mondays to Fridays
from 3 October

Colne, Burnley, Accrington and Blackburn - Preston - Blackpool

		NT	NT A	NT B		TP ◇1 C	TP ◇1 D
Colne	d	22 55					
Nelson	d	23 00					
Brierfield	d	23 03					
Burnley Central	d	23 08					
Burnley Barracks	d	23 10					
Leeds 10 41	d						
Burnley Manchester Road 41	d						
Rose Grove	d	23 13					
Hapton	d						
Huncoat	d						
Accrington	d	23 20					
Church & Oswaldtwistle	d						
Rishton	d						
Blackburn	a	23 29					
Clitheroe 94	d						
Blackburn	d	23 31					
Mill Hill (Lancashire)	d	23 34					
Cherry Tree	d						
Pleasington	d						
Bamber Bridge	d	23 42					
Lostock Hall	d	23 44					
Preston 8	a	23 53					
	d		22 57	23 19		23 35	23 51
Salwick	d						
Kirkham & Wesham	d			23 28			
Moss Side	d						
Lytham	d						
Ansdell & Fairhaven	d						
St Annes-on-the-Sea	d						
Squires Gate	d						
Blackpool Pleasure Beach	d						
Blackpool South	a						
Poulton-le-Fylde	d			23 36		23 52	00 08
Layton	d			23 40			
Blackpool North	a		23 22	23 50		00 02	00 16

Saturdays
until 16 July

		TP ◇1 C	TP ◇1 D	NT B	TP ◇1 C	TP ◇1 C	TP ◇1 E	NT	NT B	NT		NT A	TP ◇1 C 🚲	NT	NT B	NT F	NT	NT A	TP ◇1 C 🚲	NT B		NT F	NT	NT A	TP ◇1 C
Colne	d							05 40						06 50			07 50						08 50		
Nelson	d							05 45						06 55			07 55						08 55		
Brierfield	d							05 48						06 58			07 58						08 58		
Burnley Central	d							05 53						07 03			08 03						09 03		
Burnley Barracks	d							05 55						07 05			08 05						09 05		
Leeds 10 41	d									05 51						06 51						07 51			
Burnley Manchester Road 41	d									06 57						07 57						08 57			
Rose Grove	d							05 58						07 08			08 08						09 08		
Hapton	d							06 01						07 11			08 11						09 11		
Huncoat	d							06 04						07 14			08 14						09 14		
Accrington	d							06 09		07 06				07 19		08 06	08 19					09 06	09 19		
Church & Oswaldtwistle	d							06 11						07 21			08 21						09 21		
Rishton	d							06 14						07 24			08 24						09 24		
Blackburn	a							06 23		07 16				07 33		08 14	08 33					09 14	09 33		
Clitheroe 94	d																								
Blackburn	d							06 25		07 16				07 35		08 15	08 35					09 15	09 35		
Mill Hill (Lancashire)	d							06 28						07 38		08 18	08 38						09 38		
Cherry Tree	d							06 30						07 40			08 40						09 40		
Pleasington	d							06 32						07 42			08 42						09 42		
Bamber Bridge	d							06 39		07 26				07 49		08 27	08 49						09 49		
Lostock Hall	d							06 42		07 28				07 52		08 30	08 52						09 52		
Preston 8	a							06 50		07 36				08 00		08 38	09 00					09 32	10 00		
	d	23p35	23p51	00 19			06 37	07 00	07 13	07 38		07 55	07 59	08 02	08 15	08 40	09 02	08 55	08 59	09 19		09 34	10 02	09 55	10 08
Salwick	d							07 07						08 09											
Kirkham & Wesham	d			00 28			06 46	07 11	07 22				08 08	08 13	08 25		09 11			09 28			10 11		
Moss Side	d							07 17						08 19			09 17						10 17		
Lytham	d							07 21						08 23			09 21						10 21		
Ansdell & Fairhaven	d							07 24						08 26			09 24						10 24		
St Annes-on-the-Sea	d							07 28						08 30			09 28						10 28		
Squires Gate	d							07 32						08 34			09 32						10 32		
Blackpool Pleasure Beach	d							07 34						08 36			09 34						10 34		
Blackpool South	a							07 38						08 43			09 41						10 39		
Poulton-le-Fylde	d	23p52	00 08	00 36			06 56		07 30	07 54			08 18		08 33	08 56			09 16	09 36		09 51			10 26
Layton	d			00 43			06 59		07 34				08 22		08 37					09 43					
Blackpool North	a	00 02	00 16	00 50	01 30	05 33	07 06		07 41	08 05		08 21	08 29		08 44	09 05		09 21	09 25	09 50		10 01		10 21	10 35

A From Liverpool Lime Street
B From Manchester Victoria
C From Manchester Airport
D From Windermere
E From Manchester Piccadilly
F From York

Table 97

Saturdays
until 16 July

Colne, Burnley, Accrington and Blackburn - Preston - Blackpool

		NT	NT	NT	TP	NT		NT	NT	NT	TP	NT	NT	NT	NT	TP		TP	NT	NT	NT	NT	TP	NT	NT
					◇1						◇1					◇1		◇1					◇1		
		A	B		C	D		A	B		C	E	A	B		C		F	E	A	B		C	E	A
					🛒						🛒					🛒							🛒		
Colne	d			09 50						10 50					11 50							12 50			
Nelson	d			09 55						10 55					11 55							12 55			
Brierfield	d			09 58						10 58					11 58							12 58			
Burnley Central	d			10 03						11 03					12 03							13 03			
Burnley Barracks	d			10 05						11 05					12 05							13 05			
Leeds 10 41	d		08 51						09 53					10 53							11 53				
Burnley Manchester Road 41	d		09 57						10 57					11 57							12 57				
Rose Grove	d			10 08						11 08					12 08							13 08			
Hapton	d			10 11						11 11					12 11							13 11			
Huncoat	d			10 14						11 14					12 14							13 14			
Accrington	d		10 06	10 19					11 06	11 19				12 06	12 19						13 06	13 19			
Church & Oswaldtwistle	d			10 21						11 21					12 21							13 21			
Rishton	d			10 24						11 24					12 24							13 24			
Blackburn	a		10 14	10 33					11 14	11 33				12 14	12 33						13 14	13 33			
Clitheroe 94	d																								
Blackburn	d		10 15	10 35					11 15	11 35				12 15	12 35						13 15	13 35			
Mill Hill (Lancashire)	d			10 38						11 38					12 38							13 38			
Cherry Tree	d			10 40						11 40					12 40							13 40			
Pleasington	d			10 42						11 42					12 42							13 42			
Bamber Bridge	d			10 49						11 49					12 49							13 49			
Lostock Hall	d			10 52						11 52					12 52							13 52			
Preston 8	a		10 32	11 00					11 32	12 00				12 32	13 00						13 32	14 00			
	d	10 19	10 34	11 02	10 38	10 55		11 19	11 34	12 02	11 38	11 55	12 19	12 34	13 02	12 38		12 48	12 55	13 19	13 34	14 02	13 38	13 55	14 19
Salwick	d									12 09															
Kirkham & Wesham	d	10 28		11 11				11 28		12 13			12 28		13 11					13 28		14 11			14 28
Moss Side	d			11 17						12 19					13 17							14 17			
Lytham	d			11 21						12 23					13 21							14 21			
Ansdell & Fairhaven	d			11 24						12 26					13 24							14 24			
St Annes-on-the-Sea	d			11 28						12 30					13 28							14 28			
Squires Gate	d			11 32						12 34					13 32							14 32			
Blackpool Pleasure Beach	d			11 34						12 36					13 34							14 34			
Blackpool South	a			11 39						12 41					13 39							14 41			
Poulton-le-Fylde	d	10 36	10 51		10 56			11 36	11 50		11 56		12 36	12 50		12 56				13 36	13 50		13 56		14 36
Layton	d	10 43						11 43					12 43							13 43					14 43
Blackpool North	a	10 50	11 01		11 05	11 21		11 50	12 00		12 05	12 21	12 50	13 00		13 05		13 12	13 21	13 50	14 00		14 05	14 21	14 48

		NT		NT	TP	NT	NT	NT	NT	TP	NT	NT		TP	NT	NT	NT	TP	NT	NT	NT	NT		NT	TP
					◇1					◇1				◇1				◇1							◇1
		B			C	E	A	B		C	E	B		C		E	A	C	B		E	A		B	C
					🛒					🛒				🛒				🛒							🛒
Colne	d			13 50					14 50						15 50					16 50					
Nelson	d			13 55					14 55						15 55					16 55					
Brierfield	d			13 58					14 58						15 58					16 58					
Burnley Central	d			14 03					15 03						16 03					17 03					
Burnley Barracks	d			14 05					15 05						16 05					17 05					
Leeds 10 41	d	12 53						13 53				14 53							15 52					16 51	
Burnley Manchester Road 41	d	13 57						14 57				15 57							16 58					17 57	
Rose Grove	d			14 08					15 08						16 08					17 08					
Hapton	d			14 11					15 11						16 11					17 11					
Huncoat	d			14 14					15 14						16 14					17 14					
Accrington	d	14 06		14 19				15 06	15 19			16 06			16 19				17 06	17 19				18 06	
Church & Oswaldtwistle	d			14 21					15 21						16 21					17 21					
Rishton	d			14 24					15 24						16 24					17 24					
Blackburn	a	14 14		14 33				15 14	15 33			16 14			16 33				17 14	17 34				18 14	
Clitheroe 94	d																								
Blackburn	d	14 15		14 35				15 15	15 35			16 15			16 35				17 15	17 35				18 15	
Mill Hill (Lancashire)	d			14 38					15 38						16 38					17 38					
Cherry Tree	d			14 40					15 40						16 40					17 40					
Pleasington	d			14 42					15 42						16 42					17 42					
Bamber Bridge	d			14 49					15 49						16 49					17 49					
Lostock Hall	d			14 52					15 52						16 52					17 52					
Preston 8	a	14 32		15 00				15 32	16 00			16 32			17 00				17 32	18 00				18 33	
	d	14 34		15 02	14 38	14 55	15 19	15 34	16 02	15 38	15 55	16 34		16 38	17 02	16 55	17 21	17 32	17 35	18 02	17 55	18 18		18 34	18 40
Salwick	d								16 09																
Kirkham & Wesham	d			15 11			15 28		16 13					16 47	17 11		17 30	17 41		18 11		18 27			18 49
Moss Side	d			15 17					16 19						17 17					18 17					
Lytham	d			15 21					16 23						17 21					18 21					
Ansdell & Fairhaven	d			15 24					16 26						17 24					18 24					
St Annes-on-the-Sea	d			15 28					16 30						17 28					18 28					
Squires Gate	d			15 32					16 34						17 32					18 32					
Blackpool Pleasure Beach	d			15 34					16 36						17 34					18 34					
Blackpool South	a			15 39					16 41						17 39					18 39					
Poulton-le-Fylde	d	14 50			14 56		15 36	15 50		15 56		16 50		16 57		17 12	17 38	17 51	17 56			18 35		18 50	18 59
Layton	d						15 43							17 00			17 43	17 54				18 39			19 02
Blackpool North	a	15 00			15 05	15 21	15 50	16 00		16 05	16 21	17 00		17 07		17 21	17 50	18 02	18 06		18 24	18 46		19 00	19 09

A From Manchester Victoria
B From York
C From Manchester Airport
D From Liverpool Lime Street
E From Liverpool South Parkway
F from 25 June until 16 July. From Glasgow Central

Table 97

Saturdays
until 16 July

Colne, Burnley, Accrington and Blackburn - Preston - Blackpool

		NT	NT	NT	NT	NT	NT	TP	NT	NT	NT	NT	TP	NT	NT	NT	TP	NT	NT	NT	TP	NT	NT
								◇1					◇1				◇1				◇1		
			A	B	C	D		E	B	C	D		E		C	B	E	C	D		E		B
								(bicycle)															
Colne	d	17 50					18 50					19 50		20 50						21 45		22 55	
Nelson	d	17 55					18 55					19 55		20 55						21 50		23 00	
Brierfield	d	17 58					18 58					19 58		20 58						21 53		23 03	
Burnley Central	d	18 03					19 03					20 03		21 03						21 58		23 08	
Burnley Barracks	d	18 05					19 05					20 05		21 05						22 00		23 10	
Leeds 10 41	d					17 51					18 51								20 51				
Burnley Manchester Road 41	d					18 57					19 57								21 56				
Rose Grove	d	18 08					19 08					20 08		21 08						22 03		23 13	
Hapton	d	18 11					19 11					20 11		21 11						22 06			
Huncoat	d	18 14					19 14					20 14		21 14						22 09			
Accrington	d	18 19				19 06	19 19				20 06	20 19		21 19					22 05	22 14		23 20	
Church & Oswaldtwistle	d	18 21					19 21					20 21		21 21						22 16			
Rishton	d	18 24					19 24					20 24		21 24						22 19			
Blackburn	a	18 34				19 14	19 33				20 15	20 33		21 33					22 13	22 24		23 28	
Clitheroe 94	d																						
Blackburn	d	18 35				19 15	19 35				20 15	20 35		21 35					22 14	22 25		23 30	
Mill Hill (Lancashire)	d	18 38					19 38					20 38		21 38						22 28		23 33	
Cherry Tree	d	18 40					19 40					20 40		21 40						22 30			
Pleasington	d	18 42					19 42					20 42		21 42						22 32			
Bamber Bridge	d	18 49					19 49					20 49		21 49						22 39		23 41	
Lostock Hall	d	18 52					19 52					20 52		21 52						22 42		23 43	
Preston 8	a	19 00				19 32	20 00				20 32	21 00		22 02					22 31	22 50		23 54	
	d	19 02	18 49	18 55	19 19	19 34	20 02	19 38	20 19	20 25	20 34	21 02	20 38		21 19	21 24	21 38	22 19	22 32	22 51	22 35		22 57
Salwick	d																						
Kirkham & Wesham	d	19 11			19 28		20 11			20 34		21 11			21 28			22 28		23 01			
Moss Side	d	19 17					20 17					21 17								23 07			
Lytham	d	19 21					20 21					21 21								23 11			
Ansdell & Fairhaven	d	19 24					20 24					21 24								23 14			
St Annes-on-the-Sea	d	19 28					20 28					21 28								23 18			
Squires Gate	d	19 32					20 32					21 32								23 21			
Blackpool Pleasure Beach	d	19 34					20 34					21 34								23 24			
Blackpool South	a	19 39					20 39					21 39								23 28			
Poulton-le-Fylde	d				19 36	19 50		19 56		20 42	20 50		20 56		21 36		21 56	22 36	22 49		22 52		
Layton	d				19 43					20 47					21 40			22 43					
Blackpool North	a		19 16	19 21	19 50	20 00		20 05	20 44	20 54	21 00		21 06		21 48	21 53	22 06	22 50	22 59		23 02		23 22

		NT	TP
			◇1
		C	E
Colne	d		
Nelson	d		
Brierfield	d		
Burnley Central	d		
Burnley Barracks	d		
Leeds 10 41	d		
Burnley Manchester Road 41	d		
Rose Grove	d		
Hapton	d		
Huncoat	d		
Accrington	d		
Church & Oswaldtwistle	d		
Rishton	d		
Blackburn	a		
Clitheroe 94	d		
Blackburn	d		
Mill Hill (Lancashire)	d		
Cherry Tree	d		
Pleasington	d		
Bamber Bridge	d		
Lostock Hall	d		
Preston 8	a		
	d	23 19	23 35
Salwick	d		
Kirkham & Wesham	d	23 28	
Moss Side	d		
Lytham	d		
Ansdell & Fairhaven	d		
St Annes-on-the-Sea	d		
Squires Gate	d		
Blackpool Pleasure Beach	d		
Blackpool South	a		
Poulton-le-Fylde	d	23 36	23 52
Layton	d	23 40	
Blackpool North	a	23 48	00 02

A From Hazel Grove
B From Liverpool Lime Street
C From Manchester Victoria
D From York
E From Manchester Airport

Table 97

Saturdays

23 July to 1 October

Colne, Burnley, Accrington and Blackburn - Preston - Blackpool

		TP	TP	NT	TP	TP	TP	NT	NT	NT		NT	TP	NT	NT	NT	NT	NT	TP	NT		NT	NT	NT	TP
		◇1	◇1		◇1	◇1	◇1						◇1						◇1						◇1
		A	B	C	A	A	D		C			E	A 🚲		C	F		E	A 🚲	C		F		E	A
Colne	d							05 40						06 50			07 50						08 50		
Nelson	d							05 45						06 55			07 55						08 55		
Brierfield	d							05 48						06 58			07 58						08 58		
Burnley Central	d							05 53						07 03			08 03						09 03		
Burnley Barracks	d							05 55						07 05			08 05						09 05		
Leeds 10 41	d									05 51						06 51						07 51			
Burnley Manchester Road 41	d									06 57						07 57						08 57			
Rose Grove	d							05 58						07 08			08 08						09 08		
Hapton	d							06 01						07 11			08 11						09 11		
Huncoat	d							06 04						07 14			08 14						09 14		
Accrington	d							06 09		07 06				07 19		08 06	08 19					09 06	09 19		
Church & Oswaldtwistle	d							06 11						07 21			08 21						09 21		
Rishton	d							06 14						07 24			08 24						09 24		
Blackburn	a							06 23		07 16				07 33		08 14	08 33					09 14	09 33		
Clitheroe 94	d																								
Blackburn	d							06 25		07 16				07 35		08 15	08 35					09 15	09 35		
Mill Hill (Lancashire)	d							06 28						07 38		08 18	08 38						09 38		
Cherry Tree	d							06 30						07 40			08 40						09 40		
Pleasington	d							06 32						07 42			08 42						09 42		
Bamber Bridge	d							06 39		07 26				07 49		08 27	08 49						09 49		
Lostock Hall	d							06 42		07 28				07 52		08 30	08 52						09 52		
Preston 8	a							06 50		07 36				08 00		08 38	09 00					09 32	10 00		
	d	23p35	23p51	00 19			06 37	07 00	07 13	07 38		07 55	07 59	08 02	08 15	08 40	09 02	08 55	08 59	09 19		09 34	10 02	09 55	10 08
Salwick	d							07 07						08 09											
Kirkham & Wesham	d			00 28			06 46	07 11	07 22				08 09	08 13	08 25		09 11			09 28			10 11		
Moss Side	d							07 17						08 19			09 17						10 17		
Lytham	d							07 21						08 23			09 21						10 21		
Ansdell & Fairhaven	d							07 24						08 26			09 24						10 24		
St Annes-on-the-Sea	d							07 28						08 30			09 28						10 28		
Squires Gate	d							07 32						08 34			09 32						10 32		
Blackpool Pleasure Beach	d							07 34						08 36			09 34						10 34		
Blackpool South	a							07 38						08 43			09 41						10 39		
Poulton-le-Fylde	d	23p52	00 08	00 36			06 56		07 30	07 54			08 18		08 33	08 56			09 16	09 36		09 51			10 26
Layton	d			00 43			06 59		07 34				08 22		08 37					09 43					
Blackpool North	a	00 02	00 16	00 50	01 30	05 33	07 06		07 41	08 05		08 21	08 29		08 44	09 05		09 21	09 25	09 50		10 01		10 21	10 35

		NT	NT	NT	TP	NT		NT	NT	NT	TP	NT	NT	NT	NT	TP		TP	NT	NT	NT	NT	TP	NT	NT
					◇1						◇1					◇1		◇1					◇1		
		C	F		A 🚲	E		C	F		A 🚲	G	C	F		A 🚲		H	G	C	F		A 🚲	G	C
Colne	d			09 50						10 50					11 50							12 50			
Nelson	d			09 55						10 55					11 55							12 55			
Brierfield	d			09 58						10 58					11 58							12 58			
Burnley Central	d			10 03						11 03					12 03							13 03			
Burnley Barracks	d			10 05						11 05					12 05							13 05			
Leeds 10 41	d		08 51						09 53					10 53							11 53				
Burnley Manchester Road 41	d		09 57						10 57					11 57							12 57				
Rose Grove	d			10 08						11 08					12 08							13 08			
Hapton	d			10 11						11 11					12 11							13 11			
Huncoat	d			10 14						11 14					12 14							13 14			
Accrington	d		10 06	10 19					11 06	11 19				12 06	12 19						13 06	13 19			
Church & Oswaldtwistle	d			10 21						11 21					12 21							13 21			
Rishton	d			10 24						11 24					12 24							13 24			
Blackburn	a		10 14	10 33					11 14	11 33				12 14	12 33						13 14	13 33			
Clitheroe 94	d																								
Blackburn	d		10 15	10 35					11 15	11 35				12 15	12 35						13 15	13 35			
Mill Hill (Lancashire)	d			10 38						11 38					12 38							13 38			
Cherry Tree	d			10 40						11 40					12 40							13 40			
Pleasington	d			10 42						11 42					12 42							13 42			
Bamber Bridge	d			10 49						11 49					12 49							13 49			
Lostock Hall	d			10 52						11 52					12 52							13 52			
Preston 8	a		10 32	11 00					11 32	12 00				12 32	13 00						13 32	14 00			
	d	10 19	10 34	11 02	10 38	10 55		11 19	11 34	12 02	11 38	11 55	12 19	12 34	13 02	12 38		12 48	12 55	13 19	13 34	14 02	13 38	13 55	14 19
Salwick	d									12 09															
Kirkham & Wesham	d	10 28		11 11				11 28		12 13			12 28		13 11					13 28		14 11			14 28
Moss Side	d			11 17						12 19					13 17							14 17			
Lytham	d			11 21						12 23					13 21							14 21			
Ansdell & Fairhaven	d			11 24						12 26					13 24							14 24			
St Annes-on-the-Sea	d			11 28						12 30					13 28							14 28			
Squires Gate	d			11 32						12 34					13 32							14 32			
Blackpool Pleasure Beach	d			11 34						12 36					13 34							14 34			
Blackpool South	a			11 39						12 41					13 39							14 41			
Poulton-le-Fylde	d	10 36	10 51		10 56			11 36	11 50		11 56		12 36	12 50		12 56				13 36	13 50		13 56		14 36
Layton	d	10 43						11 43					12 43							13 43					14 43
Blackpool North	a	10 50	11 01		11 05	11 21		11 50	12 00		12 05	12 21	12 50	13 00		13 05		13 12	13 21	13 50	14 00		14 05	14 21	14 48

A From Manchester Airport
B From Windermere
C From Manchester Victoria
D From Manchester Piccadilly
E From Liverpool Lime Street
F From York
G From Liverpool South Parkway
H from 23 July until 10 September. From Glasgow Central

Table 97

Saturdays

23 July to 1 October

Colne, Burnley, Accrington and Blackburn - Preston - Blackpool

		NT		NT	TP	NT	NT	NT	NT	TP	NT	NT		TP	NT	NT	NT	TP	NT	NT	NT	NT		NT	TP
					◇1					◇1				◇1				◇1							◇1
		A			B	C	D	A		B	C	A		B		C	D	B	A		C	D		A	B
Colne	d			13 50					14 50						15 50					16 50					
Nelson	d			13 55					14 55						15 55					16 55					
Brierfield	d			13 58					14 58						15 58					16 58					
Burnley Central	d			14 03					15 03						16 03					17 03					
Burnley Barracks	d			14 05					15 05						16 05					17 05					
Leeds 10 41	d	12 53						13 53				14 53							15 52					16 51	
Burnley Manchester Road 41	d	13 57						14 57				15 57							16 58					17 57	
Rose Grove	d			14 08					15 08						16 08					17 08					
Hapton	d			14 11					15 11						16 11					17 11					
Huncoat	d			14 14					15 14						16 14					17 14					
Accrington	d	14 06		14 19				15 06	15 19			16 06			16 19				17 06	17 19				18 06	
Church & Oswaldtwistle	d			14 21					15 21						16 21					17 21					
Rishton	d			14 24					15 24						16 24					17 24					
Blackburn	a	14 14		14 33				15 14	15 33			16 14			16 33				17 14	17 34				18 14	
Clitheroe 94	d																								
Blackburn	d	14 15		14 35				15 15	15 35			16 15			16 35				17 15	17 35				18 15	
Mill Hill (Lancashire)	d			14 38					15 38						16 38					17 38					
Cherry Tree	d			14 40					15 40						16 40					17 40					
Pleasington	d			14 42					15 42						16 42					17 42					
Bamber Bridge	d			14 49					15 49						16 49					17 49					
Lostock Hall	d			14 52					15 52						16 52					17 52					
Preston 8	a	14 32		15 00				15 32	16 00			16 32			17 00				17 32	18 00				18 33	
	d	14 34		15 02	14 38	14 55	15 19	15 34	16 02	15 38	15 55	16 34		16 38	17 02	16 55	17 21	17 32	17 35	18 02	17 55	18 18		18 34	18 40
Salwick	d								16 09																
Kirkham & Wesham	d			15 11			15 28		16 13					16 47	17 11		17 30	17 41		18 11		18 27			18 49
Moss Side	d			15 17					16 19						17 17					18 17					
Lytham	d			15 21					16 23						17 21					18 21					
Ansdell & Fairhaven	d			15 24					16 26						17 24					18 24					
St Annes-on-the-Sea	d			15 28					16 30						17 28					18 28					
Squires Gate	d			15 32					16 34						17 32					18 32					
Blackpool Pleasure Beach	d			15 34					16 36						17 34					18 34					
Blackpool South	a			15 39					16 41						17 39					18 39					
Poulton-le-Fylde	d	14 50			14 56		15 36	15 50		15 56		16 50		16 57		17 12	17 38	17 51	17 56			18 35		18 50	18 59
Layton	d						15 43							17 00			17 43	17 54				18 39			19 02
Blackpool North	a	15 00			15 05	15 21	15 50	16 00		16 05	16 21	17 00		17 07		17 21	17 50	18 02	18 06		18 24	18 46		19 00	19 09

		NT	NT	NT	NT	NT	NT	TP		NT	NT	NT	NT	TP	NT	NT	NT	TP		NT	NT	NT	TP	NT	NT
								◇1						◇1				◇1					◇1		
			E	F	D	A		B		F	D	A		B		D	F	B		D	A		B		F
Colne	d	17 50					18 50						19 50		20 50							21 45		22 55	
Nelson	d	17 55					18 55						19 55		20 55							21 50		23 00	
Brierfield	d	17 58					18 58						19 58		20 58							21 53		23 03	
Burnley Central	d	18 03					19 03						20 03		21 03							21 58		23 08	
Burnley Barracks	d	18 05					19 05						20 05		21 05							22 00		23 10	
Leeds 10 41	d					17 51						18 51									20 51				
Burnley Manchester Road 41	d					18 57						19 57									21 56				
Rose Grove	d	18 08					19 08						20 08		21 08							22 03		23 13	
Hapton	d	18 11					19 11						20 11		21 11							22 06			
Huncoat	d	18 14					19 14						20 14		21 14							22 09			
Accrington	d	18 19				19 06	19 19					20 06	20 19		21 19						22 05	22 14		23 20	
Church & Oswaldtwistle	d	18 21					19 21						20 21		21 21							22 16			
Rishton	d	18 24					19 24						20 24		21 24							22 19			
Blackburn	a	18 34				19 14	19 33					20 15	20 33		21 33						22 13	22 24		23 28	
Clitheroe 94	d																								
Blackburn	d	18 35				19 15	19 35					20 15	20 35		21 35						22 14	22 25		23 30	
Mill Hill (Lancashire)	d	18 38					19 38						20 38		21 38							22 28		23 33	
Cherry Tree	d	18 40					19 40						20 40		21 40							22 30			
Pleasington	d	18 42					19 42						20 42		21 42							22 32			
Bamber Bridge	d	18 49					19 49						20 49		21 49							22 39		23 41	
Lostock Hall	d	18 52					19 52						20 52		21 52							22 42		23 43	
Preston 8	a	19 00				19 32	20 00					20 32	21 00		22 02						22 31	22 50		23 54	
	d	19 02	18 49	18 55	19 19	19 34	20 02	19 38		20 19	20 25	20 34	21 02	20 38		21 19	21 24	21 38		22 19	22 32	22 51	22 35		22 57
Salwick	d																								
Kirkham & Wesham	d	19 11			19 28		20 11				20 34		21 11			21 28				22 28		23 01			
Moss Side	d	19 17					20 17						21 17									23 07			
Lytham	d	19 21					20 21						21 21									23 11			
Ansdell & Fairhaven	d	19 24					20 24						21 24									23 14			
St Annes-on-the-Sea	d	19 28					20 28						21 28									23 18			
Squires Gate	d	19 32					20 32						21 32									23 21			
Blackpool Pleasure Beach	d	19 34					20 34						21 34									23 24			
Blackpool South	a	19 39					20 39						21 39									23 28			
Poulton-le-Fylde	d				19 36	19 50		19 56			20 42	20 50		20 56		21 36		21 56		22 36	22 49		22 52		
Layton	d				19 43						20 47					21 40				22 43					
Blackpool North	a		19 16	19 21	19 50	20 00		20 05		20 44	20 54	21 00		21 06		21 48	21 53	22 06		22 50	22 59		23 02		23 22

A From York
B From Manchester Airport
C From Liverpool South Parkway
D From Manchester Victoria
E From Hazel Grove
F From Liverpool Lime Street

Colne, Burnley, Accrington and Blackburn - Preston - Blackpool

Saturdays
23 July to 1 October

		NT ◇1 A	TP ◇1 B
Colne	d	.	.
Nelson	d	.	.
Brierfield	d	.	.
Burnley Central	d	.	.
Burnley Barracks	d	.	.
Leeds 10 41	d	.	.
Burnley Manchester Road 41	d	.	.
Rose Grove	d	.	.
Hapton	d	.	.
Huncoat	d	.	.
Accrington	d	.	.
Church & Oswaldtwistle	d	.	.
Rishton	d	.	.
Blackburn	a	.	.
Clitheroe 94	d	.	.
Blackburn	d	.	.
Mill Hill (Lancashire)	d	.	.
Cherry Tree	d	.	.
Pleasington	d	.	.
Bamber Bridge	d	.	.
Lostock Hall	d	.	.
Preston 8	a	.	.
	d	23 19	23 35
Salwick	d	.	.
Kirkham & Wesham	d	23 28	.
Moss Side	d	.	.
Lytham	d	.	.
Ansdell & Fairhaven	d	.	.
St Annes-on-the-Sea	d	.	.
Squires Gate	d	.	.
Blackpool Pleasure Beach	d	.	.
Blackpool South	a	.	.
Poulton-le-Fylde	d	23 36	23 52
Layton	d	23 40	.
Blackpool North	a	23 48	00 02

Saturdays
from 8 October

		TP ◇1 B	TP ◇1 C	NT A	TP ◇1 B	TP ◇1 B	TP ◇1 D	NT	NT A	NT		NT E	TP ◇1 B 🚲	NT	NT A	NT F	NT	NT E	TP ◇1 B 🚲	NT A		NT F	NT	NT E	TP ◇1 B
Colne	d	.	.	.	.	.	.	05 40	.	.	.	.	.	06 50	.	.	07 50	.	.	.	.	.	08 50	.	.
Nelson	d	.	.	.	.	.	.	05 45	.	.	.	.	.	06 55	.	.	07 55	.	.	.	.	.	08 55	.	.
Brierfield	d	.	.	.	.	.	.	05 48	.	.	.	.	.	06 58	.	.	07 58	.	.	.	.	.	08 58	.	.
Burnley Central	d	.	.	.	.	.	.	05 53	.	.	.	.	.	07 03	.	.	08 03	.	.	.	.	.	09 03	.	.
Burnley Barracks	d	.	.	.	.	.	.	05 55	.	.	.	.	.	07 05	.	.	08 05	.	.	.	.	.	09 05	.	.
Leeds 10 41	d	.	.	.	.	.	.	.	.	05 51	.	.	.	.	.	06 51	.	.	.	.	.	07 51	.	.	.
Burnley Manchester Road 41	d	.	.	.	.	.	.	.	.	06 57	.	.	.	.	.	07 57	.	.	.	.	.	08 57	.	.	.
Rose Grove	d	.	.	.	.	.	.	05 58	.	.	.	.	.	07 08	.	.	08 08	.	.	.	.	.	09 08	.	.
Hapton	d	.	.	.	.	.	.	06 01	.	.	.	.	.	07 11	.	.	08 11	.	.	.	.	.	09 11	.	.
Huncoat	d	.	.	.	.	.	.	06 04	.	.	.	.	.	07 14	.	.	08 14	.	.	.	.	.	09 14	.	.
Accrington	d	.	.	.	.	.	.	06 09	.	07 06	.	.	.	07 19	.	08 06	08 19	.	.	.	.	09 06	09 19	.	.
Church & Oswaldtwistle	d	.	.	.	.	.	.	06 11	.	.	.	.	.	07 21	.	.	08 21	.	.	.	.	.	09 21	.	.
Rishton	d	.	.	.	.	.	.	06 14	.	.	.	.	.	07 24	.	.	08 24	.	.	.	.	.	09 24	.	.
Blackburn	a	.	.	.	.	.	.	06 23	.	07 16	.	.	.	07 33	.	08 14	08 33	.	.	.	.	09 14	09 33	.	.
Clitheroe 94	d	.	.	.	.	.	.	.	.	.	.	.	.	.	.	.	.	.	.	.	.	.	.	.	.
Blackburn	d	.	.	.	.	.	.	06 25	.	07 16	.	.	.	07 35	.	08 15	08 35	.	.	.	.	09 15	09 35	.	.
Mill Hill (Lancashire)	d	.	.	.	.	.	.	06 28	.	.	.	.	.	07 38	.	08 18	08 38	.	.	.	.	.	09 38	.	.
Cherry Tree	d	.	.	.	.	.	.	06 30	.	.	.	.	.	07 40	.	.	08 40	.	.	.	.	.	09 40	.	.
Pleasington	d	.	.	.	.	.	.	06 32	.	.	.	.	.	07 42	.	.	08 42	.	.	.	.	.	09 42	.	.
Bamber Bridge	d	.	.	.	.	.	.	06 39	.	07 26	.	.	.	07 49	.	08 27	08 49	.	.	.	.	.	09 49	.	.
Lostock Hall	d	.	.	.	.	.	.	06 42	.	07 28	.	.	.	07 52	.	08 30	08 52	.	.	.	.	.	09 52	.	.
Preston 8	a	.	.	.	.	.	.	06 50	.	07 36	.	.	.	08 00	.	08 38	09 00	.	.	.	.	09 32	10 00	.	.
	d	23p35	23p51	00 19	.	.	06 37	07 00	07 13	07 38	.	07 55	07 59	08 02	08 15	08 40	09 02	08 55	08 59	09 19	.	09 34	10 02	09 55	10 08
Salwick	d	.	.	.	.	.	.	07 07	.	.	.	.	.	08 09	.	.	.	.	.	.	.	.	.	.	.
Kirkham & Wesham	d	.	.	00 28	.	.	06 46	07 11	07 22	.	.	.	08 09	08 13	08 25	.	09 11	.	.	09 28	.	.	10 11	.	.
Moss Side	d	.	.	.	.	.	.	07 17	.	.	.	.	.	08 19	.	.	09 17	.	.	.	.	.	10 17	.	.
Lytham	d	.	.	.	.	.	.	07 21	.	.	.	.	.	08 23	.	.	09 21	.	.	.	.	.	10 21	.	.
Ansdell & Fairhaven	d	.	.	.	.	.	.	07 24	.	.	.	.	.	08 26	.	.	09 24	.	.	.	.	.	10 24	.	.
St Annes-on-the-Sea	d	.	.	.	.	.	.	07 28	.	.	.	.	.	08 30	.	.	09 28	.	.	.	.	.	10 28	.	.
Squires Gate	d	.	.	.	.	.	.	07 32	.	.	.	.	.	08 34	.	.	09 32	.	.	.	.	.	10 32	.	.
Blackpool Pleasure Beach	d	.	.	.	.	.	.	07 34	.	.	.	.	.	08 36	.	.	09 34	.	.	.	.	.	10 34	.	.
Blackpool South	a	.	.	.	.	.	.	07 40	.	.	.	.	.	08 41	.	.	09 39	.	.	.	.	.	10 41	.	.
Poulton-le-Fylde	d	23p52	00 08	00 36	.	.	06 56	.	07 30	07 54	.	.	08 18	.	08 33	08 56	.	.	09 16	09 36	.	09 51	.	.	10 26
Layton	d	.	.	00 43	.	.	06 59	.	07 34	.	.	.	08 22	.	08 37	.	.	.	.	09 43	.	.	.	.	.
Blackpool North	a	00 02	00 16	00 52	01 30	05 33	07 06	.	07 43	08 05	.	08 21	08 29	.	08 46	09 05	.	09 21	09 25	09 52	.	10 01	.	10 21	10 35

A From Manchester Victoria
B From Manchester Airport
C From Windermere
D From Manchester Piccadilly
E From Liverpool Lime Street
F From York

Table 97

Saturdays
from 8 October

Colne, Burnley, Accrington and Blackburn - Preston - Blackpool

		NT A	NT B	NT	TP ◇1 C	NT D		NT A	NT B	NT	TP ◇1 C	NT E	NT A	NT B	NT	TP ◇1 C		NT E	NT A	NT B	NT	TP ◇1 C	NT E	NT A	NT B
Colne	d			09 50						10 50					11 50						12 50				
Nelson	d			09 55						10 55					11 55						12 55				
Brierfield	d			09 58						10 58					11 58						12 58				
Burnley Central	d			10 03						11 03					12 03						13 03				
Burnley Barracks	d			10 05						11 05					12 05						13 05				
Leeds 10 41	d		08 51						09 53					10 53						11 53					12 53
Burnley Manchester Road 41	d		09 57						10 57					11 57						12 57					13 57
Rose Grove	d			10 08						11 08					12 08						13 08				
Hapton	d			10 11						11 11					12 11						13 11				
Huncoat	d			10 14						11 14					12 14						13 14				
Accrington	d		10 06	10 19					11 06	11 19				12 06	12 19					13 06	13 19				14 06
Church & Oswaldtwistle	d			10 21						11 21					12 21						13 21				
Rishton	d			10 24						11 24					12 24						13 24				
Blackburn	a		10 14	10 33					11 14	11 33				12 14	12 33					13 14	13 33				14 14
Clitheroe 94	d																								
Blackburn	d		10 15	10 35					11 15	11 35				12 15	12 35					13 15	13 35				14 15
Mill Hill (Lancashire)	d			10 38						11 38					12 38						13 38				
Cherry Tree	d			10 40						11 40					12 40						13 40				
Pleasington	d			10 42						11 42					12 42						13 42				
Bamber Bridge	d			10 49						11 49					12 49						13 49				
Lostock Hall	d			10 52						11 52					12 52						13 52				
Preston 8	a		10 32	11 00					11 32	12 00				12 32	13 00					13 32	14 00				14 32
	d	10 19	10 34	11 02	10 38	10 55		11 19	11 34	12 02	11 38	11 55	12 19	12 34	13 02	12 38		12 55	13 19	13 34	14 02	13 38	13 55	14 19	14 34
Salwick	d									12 09															
Kirkham & Wesham	d	10 28		11 11				11 28		12 13			12 28		13 11				13 28		14 11			14 28	
Moss Side	d			11 17						12 19					13 17						14 17				
Lytham	d			11 21						12 23					13 21						14 21				
Ansdell & Fairhaven	d			11 24						12 26					13 24						14 24				
St Annes-on-the-Sea	d			11 28						12 30					13 28						14 28				
Squires Gate	d			11 32						12 34					13 32						14 32				
Blackpool Pleasure Beach	d			11 34						12 36					13 34						14 34				
Blackpool South	a			11 41						12 43					13 41						14 39				
Poulton-le-Fylde	d	10 36	10 51		10 56			11 36	11 50		11 56		12 36	12 50		12 56			13 36	13 50		13 56		14 36	14 50
Layton	d	10 43						11 43					12 43						13 45					14 43	
Blackpool North	a	10 52	11 01		11 05	11 21		11 52	12 00		12 05	12 21	12 52	13 00		13 05		13 21	13 55	14 00		14 05	14 21	14 50	15 00

		NT		TP ◇1 C	NT E	NT A	NT B	NT	TP ◇1 C	NT E	NT B	TP ◇1 C		NT	NT E	NT A	TP ◇1 C	NT B	NT	NT E	NT A	NT B		TP ◇1 C	NT
Colne	d	13 50						14 50						15 50					16 50						17 50
Nelson	d	13 55						14 55						15 55					16 55						17 55
Brierfield	d	13 58						14 58						15 58					16 58						17 58
Burnley Central	d	14 03						15 03						16 03					17 03						18 03
Burnley Barracks	d	14 05						15 05						16 05					17 05						18 05
Leeds 10 41	d						13 53				14 53							15 52				16 51			
Burnley Manchester Road 41	d						14 57				15 57							16 58				17 57			
Rose Grove	d	14 08						15 08						16 08					17 08						18 08
Hapton	d	14 11						15 11						16 11					17 11						18 11
Huncoat	d	14 14						15 14						16 14					17 14						18 14
Accrington	d	14 19					15 06	15 19			16 06			16 19				17 06	17 19			18 06			18 19
Church & Oswaldtwistle	d	14 21						15 21						16 21					17 21						18 21
Rishton	d	14 24						15 24						16 24					17 24						18 24
Blackburn	a	14 33					15 14	15 33			16 14			16 33				17 14	17 34			18 14			18 34
Clitheroe 94	d																								
Blackburn	d	14 35					15 15	15 35			16 15			16 35				17 15	17 35			18 15			18 35
Mill Hill (Lancashire)	d	14 38						15 38						16 38					17 38						18 38
Cherry Tree	d	14 40						15 40						16 40					17 40						18 40
Pleasington	d	14 42						15 42						16 42					17 42						18 42
Bamber Bridge	d	14 49						15 49						16 49					17 49						18 49
Lostock Hall	d	14 52						15 52						16 52					17 52						18 52
Preston 8	a	15 00					15 32	16 00			16 32			17 00				17 32	18 00			18 33			19 00
	d	15 02		14 38	14 55	15 19	15 34	16 02	15 38	15 55	16 34	16 38		17 02	16 55	17 21	17 32	17 35	18 02	17 55	18 18	18 34		18 40	19 02
Salwick	d							16 09																	
Kirkham & Wesham	d	15 11				15 28		16 13				16 47		17 11		17 30	17 41		18 11		18 27			18 49	19 11
Moss Side	d	15 17						16 19						17 17					18 17						19 17
Lytham	d	15 21						16 23						17 21					18 21						19 21
Ansdell & Fairhaven	d	15 24						16 26						17 24					18 24						19 24
St Annes-on-the-Sea	d	15 28						16 30						17 28					18 28						19 28
Squires Gate	d	15 32						16 34						17 32					18 32						19 32
Blackpool Pleasure Beach	d	15 34						16 36						17 34					18 34						19 34
Blackpool South	a	15 41						16 43						17 41					18 41						19 41
Poulton-le-Fylde	d			14 56		15 36	15 50		15 56		16 50	16 57			17 12	17 38	17 51	17 56			18 35	18 50		18 59	
Layton	d					15 43						17 00				17 43	17 54				18 39			19 02	
Blackpool North	a			15 05	15 21	15 52	16 00		16 05	16 21	17 00	17 07			17 21	17 52	18 02	18 06		18 24	18 48	19 00		19 09	

A From Manchester Victoria
B From York
C From Manchester Airport
D From Liverpool Lime Street
E From Liverpool South Parkway

Table 97

Saturdays
from 8 October

Colne, Burnley, Accrington and Blackburn - Preston - Blackpool

		NT A	NT B	NT C	NT D	NT	TP ◇1 E	NT B		NT C	NT D	NT	TP ◇1 E	NT	NT C	NT B	TP ◇1 E	NT C	NT D	NT	TP ◇1 E	NT	NT B	NT C	TP ◇1 E
Colne	d					18 50						19 50		20 50						21 45		22 55			
Nelson	d					18 55						19 55		20 55						21 50		23 00			
Brierfield	d					18 58						19 58		20 58						21 53		23 03			
Burnley Central	d					19 03						20 03		21 03						21 58		23 08			
Burnley Barracks	d					19 05						20 05		21 05						22 00		23 10			
Leeds 10 41	d				17 51						18 51								20 51						
Burnley Manchester Road 41	d				18 57						19 57								21 56						
Rose Grove	d					19 08						20 08		21 08						22 03		23 13			
Hapton	d					19 11						20 11		21 11						22 06					
Huncoat	d					19 14						20 14		21 14						22 09					
Accrington	d				19 06	19 19					20 06	20 19		21 19					22 05	22 14		23 20			
Church & Oswaldtwistle	d					19 21						20 21		21 21						22 16					
Rishton	d					19 24						20 24		21 24						22 19					
Blackburn	a				19 14	19 33					20 15	20 33		21 33					22 13	22 24		23 28			
Clitheroe 94	d																								
Blackburn	d				19 15	19 35					20 15	20 35		21 35					22 14	22 25		23 30			
Mill Hill (Lancashire)	d					19 38						20 38		21 38						22 28		23 33			
Cherry Tree	d					19 40						20 40		21 40						22 30					
Pleasington	d					19 42						20 42		21 42						22 32					
Bamber Bridge	d					19 49						20 49		21 49						22 39		23 41			
Lostock Hall	d					19 52						20 52		21 52						22 42		23 43			
Preston 8	a				19 32	20 00					20 32	21 00		22 02					22 31	22 50		23 54			
	d	18 49	18 55	19 19	19 34	20 02	19 38	20 19		20 25	20 34	21 02	20 38		21 19	21 24	21 38	22 19	22 32	22 51	22 35		22 57	23 19	23 35
Salwick	d																								
Kirkham & Wesham	d			19 28		20 11				20 34		21 11			21 28			22 28		23 01				23 28	
Moss Side	d					20 17						21 17								23 07					
Lytham	d					20 21						21 21								23 11					
Ansdell & Fairhaven	d					20 24						21 24								23 14					
St Annes-on-the-Sea	d					20 28						21 28								23 18					
Squires Gate	d					20 32						21 32								23 21					
Blackpool Pleasure Beach	d					20 34						21 34								23 24					
Blackpool South	a					20 41						21 41								23 30					
Poulton-le-Fylde	d			19 36	19 50		19 56			20 42	20 50		20 56		21 36		21 56	22 36	22 49		22 52			23 36	23 52
Layton	d			19 43						20 47					21 40			22 43						23 40	
Blackpool North	a	19 16	19 21	19 52	20 00		20 05	20 44		20 56	21 00		21 06		21 50	21 53	22 06	22 52	22 59		23 02		23 22	23 50	00 02

A From Hazel Grove
B From Liverpool Lime Street
C From Manchester Victoria
D From York
E From Manchester Airport

Sundays
until 11 September

		TP ◇1 A	NT B	TP ◇1 C	NT D	NT E	TP ◇1 C	NT D	NT	NT		TP ◇1 C	NT E	NT F	NT D	TP ◇1 C	NT E	NT F	NT D	NT		TP ◇1 C	NT E	NT F	NT D
Colne	d								09 15											11 34					
Nelson	d								09 20											11 39					
Brierfield	d								09 23											11 42					
Burnley Central	d								09 28											11 47					
Burnley Barracks	d								09 30											11 49					
Leeds 10 41	d									08 45				09 35				10 35						11 35	
Burnley Manchester Road 41	d									09 50				10 39				11 39						12 39	
Rose Grove	d								09 33											11 52					
Hapton	d								09 36											11 55					
Huncoat	d								09 39											11 58					
Accrington	d								09 44	09 59				10 48				11 47		12 03				12 47	
Church & Oswaldtwistle	d								09 46											12 05					
Rishton	d								09 49											12 08					
Blackburn	a								09 55	10 08				10 57				11 56		12 14				12 56	
Clitheroe 94	d																								
Blackburn	d								09 57	10 08				10 57				11 57		12 16				12 57	
Mill Hill (Lancashire)	d								10 00											12 19					
Cherry Tree	d								10 02											12 21					
Pleasington	d								10 04											12 23					
Bamber Bridge	d								10 11											12 30					
Lostock Hall	d								10 14											12 33					
Preston 8	a								10 22	10 27				11 14				12 14		12 42				13 14	
	d	23p35	00 11	08 57	09 20	09 39	09 51	10 20	10 24	10 29		10 34	10 40	11 16	11 20	11 34	11 39	12 15	12 20	12 43		12 34	12 39	13 15	13 20
Salwick	d																								
Kirkham & Wesham	d		00 21		09 29			10 29	10 33						11 29				12 29	12 51					13 29
Moss Side	d								10 39											12 57					
Lytham	d								10 43											13 01					
Ansdell & Fairhaven	d								10 46											13 04					
St Annes-on-the-Sea	d								10 50											13 08					
Squires Gate	d								10 54											13 12					
Blackpool Pleasure Beach	d								10 56											13 14					
Blackpool South	a								11 01											13 19					
Poulton-le-Fylde	d	23p52	00 29	09 14	09 37	09 57	10 08	10 37		10 46		10 51	10 57	11 33	11 37	11 51	11 57	12 32	12 37			12 51	12 57	13 32	13 37
Layton	d		00 33		09 42			10 42							11 42				12 42						13 42
Blackpool North	a	00 02	00 40	09 25	09 49	10 07	10 18	10 49		10 53		11 00	11 09	11 40	11 49	12 00	12 07	12 39	12 49			13 00	13 07	13 39	13 49

A not 22 May. From Manchester Airport
B not 22 May. From Manchester Victoria
C From Manchester Airport
D From Manchester Victoria
E From Liverpool Lime Street
F From York

Table 97

Sundays
until 11 September

Colne, Burnley, Accrington and Blackburn - Preston - Blackpool

		TP	NT	NT	NT	NT	TP	NT	NT	NT	TP	NT	NT	NT	NT	TP	NT	NT	NT	TP	NT	NT	NT
		◇1					◇1				◇1					◇1				◇1			
		C	E	F	D		C	E	F	D	C	E	F	D		C	E	F	D	C	E	F	D
Colne	d					13 34									15 34								
Nelson	d					13 39									15 39								
Brierfield	d					13 42									15 42								
Burnley Central	d					13 47									15 47								
Burnley Barracks	d					13 49									15 49								
Leeds 10 41	d			12 35					13 35				14 35					15 35				16 35	
Burnley Manchester Road 41	d			13 39					14 39				15 39					16 38				17 39	
Rose Grove	d					13 52									15 52								
Hapton	d					13 55									15 55								
Huncoat	d					13 58									15 58								
Accrington	d			13 47		14 03			14 47				15 47		16 03			16 47				17 47	
Church & Oswaldtwistle	d					14 05									16 05								
Rishton	d					14 08									16 08								
Blackburn	a			13 56		14 14			14 56				15 56		16 14			16 56				17 56	
Clitheroe 94	d																						
Blackburn	d			13 57		14 16			14 57				15 57		16 16			16 56				17 57	
Mill Hill (Lancashire)	d					14 19									16 19								
Cherry Tree	d					14 21									16 21								
Pleasington	d					14 23									16 23								
Bamber Bridge	d					14 30									16 30								
Lostock Hall	d					14 33									16 33								
Preston 8	a			14 14		14 42			15 14				16 14		16 42			17 13				18 14	
	d	13 34	13 39	14 15	14 20	14 43	14 34	14 39	15 15	15 20	15 34	15 39	16 15	16 20	16 43	16 34	16 39	17 15	17 20	17 34	17 39	18 15	18 20
Salwick	d																						
Kirkham & Wesham	d				14 29	14 51				15 29				16 29	16 52				17 29				18 29
Moss Side	d					14 57									16 58								
Lytham	d					15 01									17 02								
Ansdell & Fairhaven	d					15 04									17 05								
St Annes-on-the-Sea	d					15 08									17 09								
Squires Gate	d					15 12									17 12								
Blackpool Pleasure Beach	d					15 14									17 15								
Blackpool South	a					15 19									17 19								
Poulton-le-Fylde	d	13 51	13 57	14 31	14 37		14 51	14 57	15 32	15 37	15 51	15 57	16 32	16 37		16 51	16 57	17 31	17 37	17 51	17 57	18 32	18 37
Layton	d				14 42					15 42				16 42					17 42				18 42
Blackpool North	a	14 00	14 09	14 39	14 49		15 00	15 07	15 39	15 49	16 00	16 07	16 39	16 49		17 00	17 07	17 39	17 49	18 00	18 07	18 39	18 49

A not 22 May. From Manchester Airport
B not 22 May. From Manchester Victoria
C From Manchester Airport
D From Manchester Victoria
E From Liverpool Lime Street
F From York

		NT	NT	TP	NT	NT	NT	TP	NT	NT	NT	NT	TP	NT	NT	NT	NT	TP	NT	NT	NT	NT
				◇1				◇1					◇1					◇1				
				A	B	C	D	A	B	C	D		A	B	E	C	D	A	B	C		D
															⚲							
Colne	d	17 34	17 35									19 34									21 34	
Nelson	d	17 39	17 40									19 39									21 39	
Brierfield	d	17 42	17 43									19 42									21 42	
Burnley Central	d	17 47	17 48									19 47									21 47	
Burnley Barracks	d	17 49	17 50									19 49									21 49	
Leeds 10 41	d					17 35				18 35						19 35				20 35		
Burnley Manchester Road 41	d					18 39				19 39						20 39				21 39		
Rose Grove	d	17 52	17 53									19 52									21 52	
Hapton	d	17 55	17 56									19 55									21 55	
Huncoat	d	17 58	17 59									19 58									21 58	
Accrington	d	18 03	18 04			18 47				19 47		20 03				20 47				21 47	22 03	
Church & Oswaldtwistle	d	18 05	18 06									20 05									22 05	
Rishton	d	18 08	18 09									20 08									22 08	
Blackburn	a	18 14	18 14			18 56				19 57		20 14				20 56				21 56	22 14	
Clitheroe 94	d														19 57							
Blackburn	d	18 16	18 16			18 57				19 57		20 16			20 25	20 57				21 57	22 16	
Mill Hill (Lancashire)	d	18 19	18 19									20 19									22 19	
Cherry Tree	d	18 21	18 21									20 21									22 21	
Pleasington	d	18 23	18 23									20 23									22 23	
Bamber Bridge	d	18 30	18 30									20 30			20 34						22 30	
Lostock Hall	d	18 33	18 33									20 33			20 38						22 33	
Preston 8	a	18 42	18 42			19 14				20 14		20 42			20 47	21 14				22 14	22 44	
	d	18 43		18 34	18 39	19 15	19 20	19 34	19 39	20 16	20 20	20 43	20 34	20 39	20 49	21 15	21 20	21 34	21 39	22 15		22 20
Salwick	d																					
Kirkham & Wesham	d	18 51					19 29				20 29	20 51			20 59		21 29					22 29
Moss Side	d	18 57										20 57										
Lytham	d	19 01										21 01										
Ansdell & Fairhaven	d	19 04										21 04										
St Annes-on-the-Sea	d	19 08										21 08										
Squires Gate	d	19 12										21 12										
Blackpool Pleasure Beach	d	19 14										21 14										
Blackpool South	a	19 19										21 19										
Poulton-le-Fylde	d			18 51	18 57	19 32	19 37	19 51	19 57	20 32	20 37		20 51	20 57	21 07	21 32	21 37	21 51	21 57	22 32		22 37
Layton	d						19 42				20 42						21 42					22 42
Blackpool North	a			19 00	19 07	19 39	19 49	20 00	20 07	20 39	20 49		21 00	21 07	21 16	21 39	21 49	22 00	22 07	22 39		22 49

A From Manchester Airport
B From Liverpool Lime Street
C From York
D From Manchester Victoria
E From Carlisle

Table 97

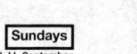

Sundays
until 11 September

Colne, Burnley, Accrington and Blackburn - Preston - Blackpool

		TP ◇1 A	NT B	NT B	TP ◇1 A
Colne	d				
Nelson	d				
Brierfield	d				
Burnley Central	d				
Burnley Barracks	d				
Leeds 10 41	d				
Burnley Manchester Road 41	d				
Rose Grove	d				
Hapton	d				
Huncoat	d				
Accrington	d				
Church & Oswaldtwistle	d				
Rishton	d				
Blackburn	a				
Clitheroe 94	d				
Blackburn	d				
Mill Hill (Lancashire)	d				
Cherry Tree	d				
Pleasington	d				
Bamber Bridge	d				
Lostock Hall	d				
Preston 8	a				
	d	22 29	22 39	23 39	23 47
Salwick	d				
Kirkham & Wesham	d				23 56
Moss Side	d				
Lytham	d				
Ansdell & Fairhaven	d				
St Annes-on-the-Sea	d				
Squires Gate	d				
Blackpool Pleasure Beach	d				
Blackpool South	a				
Poulton-le-Fylde	d	22 46	22 57	23 56	00 05
Layton	d				
Blackpool North	a	22 55	23 07	00 05	00 14

A From Manchester Airport
B From Liverpool Lime Street
C From York
D From Manchester Victoria
E From Carlisle

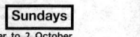

Sundays
18 September to 2 October

		TP ◇1 A	NT B	TP ◇1 A	NT B	NT C	TP ◇1 A	NT B	NT	NT		TP ◇1 A	NT C	NT D	NT B	TP ◇1 A	NT C	NT D	NT B	NT		TP ◇1 A	NT C	NT D	NT B
Colne	d								09 15											11 34					
Nelson	d								09 20											11 39					
Brierfield	d								09 23											11 42					
Burnley Central	d								09 28											11 47					
Burnley Barracks	d								09 30											11 49					
Leeds 10 41	d									08 45				09 35				10 35						11 35	
Burnley Manchester Road 41	d									09 50				10 39				11 39						12 39	
Rose Grove	d								09 33											11 52					
Hapton	d								09 36											11 55					
Huncoat	d								09 39											11 58					
Accrington	d								09 44	09 59				10 48				11 47		12 03				12 47	
Church & Oswaldtwistle	d								09 46											12 05					
Rishton	d								09 49											12 08					
Blackburn	a								09 55	10 08				10 57				11 56		12 14				12 56	
Clitheroe 94	d																								
Blackburn	d								09 57	10 08				10 57				11 57		12 16				12 57	
Mill Hill (Lancashire)	d								10 00											12 19					
Cherry Tree	d								10 02											12 21					
Pleasington	d								10 04											12 23					
Bamber Bridge	d								10 11											12 30					
Lostock Hall	d								10 14											12 33					
Preston 8	a								10 22	10 27				11 14				12 14		12 42				13 14	
	d	23p35	00 11	08 32	09 20	09 39	09 51	10 20	10 24	10 29		10 34	10 40	11 16	11 20	11 34	11 39	12 15	12 20	12 43		12 34	12 39	13 15	13 20
Salwick	d																								
Kirkham & Wesham	d		00 21		09 29			10 29	10 33						11 29				12 29	12 51					13 29
Moss Side	d								10 39											12 57					
Lytham	d								10 43											13 01					
Ansdell & Fairhaven	d								10 46											13 04					
St Annes-on-the-Sea	d								10 50											13 08					
Squires Gate	d								10 54											13 12					
Blackpool Pleasure Beach	d								10 56											13 14					
Blackpool South	a								11 01											13 19					
Poulton-le-Fylde	d	23p52	00 29	08 49	09 37	09 57	10 08	10 37		10 46		10 51	10 57	11 33	11 37	11 51	11 57	12 32	12 37			12 51	12 57	13 32	13 37
Layton	d		00 33		09 42			10 42							11 42				12 42						13 42
Blackpool North	a	00 02	00 40	08 58	09 49	10 07	10 18	10 49		10 53		11 00	11 09	11 40	11 49	12 00	12 07	12 39	12 49			13 00	13 07	13 39	13 49

A From Manchester Airport
B From Manchester Victoria
C From Liverpool Lime Street
D From York

Table 97

Sundays

18 September to 2 October

Colne, Burnley, Accrington and Blackburn - Preston - Blackpool

		TP ◇1 A	NT C	NT D	NT B	NT	TP ◇1 A	NT C	NT D	NT B	TP ◇1 A	NT C	NT D	NT B	NT	TP ◇1 A	NT C	NT D	NT B	TP ◇1 A	NT C	NT D	NT B
Colne	d					13 34									15 34								
Nelson	d					13 39									15 39								
Brierfield	d					13 42									15 42								
Burnley Central	d					13 47									15 47								
Burnley Barracks	d					13 49									15 49								
Leeds 10 41	d			12 35					13 35				14 35					15 35				16 35	
Burnley Manchester Road 41	d			13 39					14 39				15 39					16 38				17 39	
Rose Grove	d					13 52									15 52								
Hapton	d					13 55									15 55								
Huncoat	d					13 58									15 58								
Accrington	d			13 47		14 03			14 47				15 47		16 03			16 47				17 47	
Church & Oswaldtwistle	d					14 05									16 05								
Rishton	d					14 08									16 08								
Blackburn	a			13 56		14 14			14 56				15 56		16 14			16 56				17 56	
Clitheroe 94	d																						
Blackburn	d			13 57		14 16			14 57				15 57		16 16			16 56				17 57	
Mill Hill (Lancashire)	d					14 19									16 19								
Cherry Tree	d					14 21									16 21								
Pleasington	d					14 23									16 23								
Bamber Bridge	d					14 30									16 30								
Lostock Hall	d					14 33									16 33								
Preston 8	a			14 14		14 42			15 14				16 14		16 42			17 13				18 14	
	d	13 34	13 39	14 15	14 20	14 43	14 34	14 39	15 15	15 20	15 34	15 39	16 15	16 20	16 43	16 34	16 39	17 15	17 20	17 34	17 39	18 15	18 20
Salwick	d																						
Kirkham & Wesham	d				14 29	14 51				15 29				16 29	16 52				17 29				18 29
Moss Side	d					14 57									16 58								
Lytham	d					15 01									17 02								
Ansdell & Fairhaven	d					15 04									17 05								
St Annes-on-the-Sea	d					15 08									17 09								
Squires Gate	d					15 12									17 12								
Blackpool Pleasure Beach	d					15 14									17 15								
Blackpool South	a					15 19									17 19								
Poulton-le-Fylde	d	13 51	13 57	14 31	14 37		14 51	14 57	15 32	15 37	15 51	15 57	16 32	16 37		16 51	16 57	17 31	17 37	17 51	17 57	18 32	18 37
Layton	d				14 42					15 42				16 42					17 42				18 42
Blackpool North	a	14 00	14 09	14 39	14 49		15 00	15 07	15 39	15 49	16 00	16 07	16 39	16 49		17 00	17 07	17 39	17 49	18 00	18 07	18 39	18 49

A From Manchester Airport
B From Manchester Victoria
C From Liverpool Lime Street
D From York

		NT	NT	TP ◇1 A	NT B	NT C	NT D	TP ◇1 A	NT B	NT C	NT D	NT	TP ◇1 A	NT B	NT E 🚲	NT C	NT D	TP ◇1 A	NT B	NT C	NT	NT D
Colne	d	17 34	17 35									19 34									21 34	
Nelson	d	17 39	17 40									19 39									21 39	
Brierfield	d	17 42	17 43									19 42									21 42	
Burnley Central	d	17 47	17 48									19 47									21 47	
Burnley Barracks	d	17 49	17 50									19 49									21 49	
Leeds 10 41	d					17 35				18 35						19 35				20 35		
Burnley Manchester Road 41	d					18 39				19 39						20 39				21 39		
Rose Grove	d	17 52	17 53									19 52									21 52	
Hapton	d	17 55	17 56									19 55									21 55	
Huncoat	d	17 58	17 59									19 58									21 58	
Accrington	d	18 03	18 04			18 47				19 47		20 03				20 47				21 47	22 03	
Church & Oswaldtwistle	d	18 05	18 06									20 05									22 05	
Rishton	d	18 08	18 09									20 08									22 08	
Blackburn	a	18 14	18 14			18 56				19 57		20 14				20 56				21 56	22 14	
Clitheroe 94	d														19 57							
Blackburn	d	18 16	18 16			18 57				19 57		20 16			20 25	20 57				21 57	22 16	
Mill Hill (Lancashire)	d	18 19	18 19									20 19									22 19	
Cherry Tree	d	18 21	18 21									20 21									22 21	
Pleasington	d	18 23	18 23									20 23									22 23	
Bamber Bridge	d	18 30	18 30									20 30			20 34						22 30	
Lostock Hall	d	18 33	18 33									20 33			20 38						22 33	
Preston 8	a	18 42	18 42			19 14				20 14		20 42			20 47	21 14				22 14	22 44	
	d	18 43		18 34	18 39	19 15	19 20	19 34	19 39	20 16	20 20	20 43	20 34	20 39	20 49	21 15	21 20	21 34	21 39	22 15		22 20
Salwick	d																					
Kirkham & Wesham	d	18 51					19 29				20 29	20 51			20 59		21 29					22 29
Moss Side	d	18 57										20 57										
Lytham	d	19 01										21 01										
Ansdell & Fairhaven	d	19 04										21 04										
St Annes-on-the-Sea	d	19 08										21 08										
Squires Gate	d	19 12										21 12										
Blackpool Pleasure Beach	d	19 14										21 14										
Blackpool South	a	19 19										21 19										
Poulton-le-Fylde	d			18 51	18 57	19 32	19 37	19 51	19 57	20 32	20 37		20 51	20 57	21 07	21 32	21 37	21 51	21 57	22 32		22 37
Layton	d						19 42				20 42						21 42					22 42
Blackpool North	a			19 00	19 07	19 39	19 49	20 00	20 07	20 39	20 49		21 00	21 07	21 16	21 39	21 49	22 00	22 07	22 39		22 49

A From Manchester Airport
B From Liverpool Lime Street
C From York
D From Manchester Victoria
E From Carlisle

Table 97

Sundays

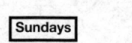

18 September to 2 October

Colne, Burnley, Accrington and Blackburn - Preston - Blackpool

		TP ◇1 A	NT B	NT B	TP ◇1 A
Colne	d				
Nelson	d				
Brierfield	d				
Burnley Central	d				
Burnley Barracks	d				
Leeds 10 41	d				
Burnley Manchester Road 41	d				
Rose Grove	d				
Hapton	d				
Huncoat	d				
Accrington	d				
Church & Oswaldtwistle	d				
Rishton	d				
Blackburn	a				
Clitheroe 94	d				
Blackburn	d				
Mill Hill (Lancashire)	d				
Cherry Tree	d				
Pleasington	d				
Bamber Bridge	d				
Lostock Hall	d				
Preston 8	a				
	d	22 29	22 39	23 39	23 47
Salwick	d				
Kirkham & Wesham	d				23 56
Moss Side	d				
Lytham	d				
Ansdell & Fairhaven	d				
St Annes-on-the-Sea	d				
Squires Gate	d				
Blackpool Pleasure Beach	d				
Blackpool South	a				
Poulton-le-Fylde	d	22 46	22 57	23 56	00 05
Layton	d				
Blackpool North	a	22 55	23 07	00 05	00 14

A From Manchester Airport
B From Liverpool Lime Street
C From York
D From Manchester Victoria
E From Carlisle

Sundays

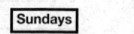

9 October to 23 October

		TP ◇1 A	NT B	TP ◇1 A	NT	NT B	NT C	TP ◇1 A	NT B	NT		NT	TP ◇1 A	NT C	NT D	NT B	TP ◇1 A	NT C	NT D	NT		NT B	NT	TP ◇1 A	NT C
Colne	d									09 15													11 34		
Nelson	d									09 20													11 39		
Brierfield	d									09 23													11 42		
Burnley Central	d									09 28													11 47		
Burnley Barracks	d									09 30													11 49		
Leeds 10 41	d											08 45			09 35				10 35						
Burnley Manchester Road 41	d											09 50			10 39				11 39						
Rose Grove	d									09 33													11 52		
Hapton	d									09 36													11 55		
Huncoat	d									09 39													11 58		
Accrington	d									09 44		09 59			10 48				11 47				12 03		
Church & Oswaldtwistle	d									09 46													12 05		
Rishton	d									09 49													12 08		
Blackburn	a									09 55		10 08			10 57				11 56				12 14		
Clitheroe 94	d																								
Blackburn	d									09 57		10 08			10 57				11 57				12 16		
Mill Hill (Lancashire)	d									10 00													12 19		
Cherry Tree	d									10 02													12 21		
Pleasington	d									10 04													12 23		
Bamber Bridge	d									10 11													12 30		
Lostock Hall	d									10 14													12 33		
Preston 8	a									10 22		10 27			11 14				12 14				12 42		
	d	23p35	00 11	08 32	08 48	09 20	09 39	09 51	10 20	10 24		10 29	10 34	10 40	11 16	11 20	11 34	11 39	12 15	11 43		12 20	12 43	12 34	12 39
Salwick	d																								
Kirkham & Wesham	d		00 21		08 56	09 29			10 29	10 33						11 29				11 51		12 29	12 51		
Moss Side	d				09 02					10 39										11 57			12 57		
Lytham	d				09 06					10 43										12 01			13 01		
Ansdell & Fairhaven	d				09 09					10 46										12 04			13 04		
St Annes-on-the-Sea	d				09 13					10 50										12 08			13 08		
Squires Gate	d				09 17					10 54										12 12			13 12		
Blackpool Pleasure Beach	d				09 19					10 56										12 14			13 14		
Blackpool South	a				09 28					11 03										12 23			13 21		
Poulton-le-Fylde	d	23p52	00 29	08 49		09 37	09 57	10 08	10 37			10 46	10 51	10 57	11 33	11 37	11 51	11 57	12 32			12 37		12 51	12 57
Layton	d		00 33			09 42			10 42							11 42						12 42			
Blackpool North	a	00 02	00 42	08 58		09 51	10 07	10 18	10 51			10 53	11 00	11 09	11 40	11 51	12 00	12 07	12 39			12 51		13 00	13 07

A From Manchester Airport
B From Manchester Victoria
C From Liverpool Lime Street
D From York

Sundays

9 October to 23 October

Colne, Burnley, Accrington and Blackburn - Preston - Blackpool

		NT D	NT B	TP ◇1 A	NT C	NT D		NT	NT B	NT	TP ◇1 A	NT C	NT D	NT B	TP ◇1 A	NT C		NT D	NT	NT B	NT	TP ◇1 A	NT C	NT D	NT B
Colne	d									13 34											15 34				
Nelson	d									13 39											15 39				
Brierfield	d									13 42											15 42				
Burnley Central	d									13 47											15 47				
Burnley Barracks	d									13 49											15 49				
Leeds 10 41	d	11 35				12 35							13 35					14 35						15 35	
Burnley Manchester Road 41	d	12 39				13 39							14 39					15 39						16 38	
Rose Grove	d									13 52											15 52				
Hapton	d									13 55											15 55				
Huncoat	d									13 58											15 58				
Accrington	d	12 47				13 47				14 03			14 47					15 47			16 03			16 47	
Church & Oswaldtwistle	d									14 05											16 05				
Rishton	d									14 08											16 08				
Blackburn	a	12 56				13 56				14 14			14 56					15 56			16 14			16 56	
Clitheroe 94	d																								
Blackburn	d	12 57				13 57				14 16			14 57					15 57			16 16			16 56	
Mill Hill (Lancashire)	d									14 19											16 19				
Cherry Tree	d									14 21											16 21				
Pleasington	d									14 23											16 23				
Bamber Bridge	d									14 30											16 30				
Lostock Hall	d									14 33											16 33				
Preston 8	a	13 14				14 14				14 42			15 14					16 14			16 42			17 13	
	d	13 15	13 20	13 34	13 39	14 15		13 43	14 20	14 43	14 34	14 39	15 15	15 20	15 34	15 39		16 15	15 43	16 20	16 43	16 34	16 39	17 15	17 20
Salwick	d																								
Kirkham & Wesham	d		13 29					13 51	14 29	14 51				15 29					15 51	16 29	16 52				17 29
Moss Side	d							13 57		14 57									15 57		16 58				
Lytham	d							14 01		15 01									16 01		17 02				
Ansdell & Fairhaven	d							14 04		15 04									16 04		17 05				
St Annes-on-the-Sea	d							14 08		15 08									16 08		17 09				
Squires Gate	d							14 12		15 12									16 12		17 12				
Blackpool Pleasure Beach	d							14 14		15 14									16 14		17 15				
Blackpool South	a							14 21		15 21									16 23		17 21				
Poulton-le-Fylde	d	13 32	13 37	13 51	13 57	14 31			14 37		14 51	14 57	15 32	15 37	15 51	15 57		16 32		16 37		16 51	16 57	17 31	17 37
Layton	d		13 42						14 42					15 42						16 42					17 42
Blackpool North	a	13 39	13 51	14 00	14 09	14 39			14 51		15 00	15 07	15 39	15 51	16 00	16 07		16 39		16 51		17 00	17 07	17 39	17 51

A From Manchester Airport
B From Manchester Victoria
C From Liverpool Lime Street
D From York

		TP ◇1 A		NT B	NT C	NT	NT D	NT	NT	TP ◇1 A	NT B	NT C		NT D	TP ◇1 A	NT B	NT C	NT	NT D	NT	TP ◇1 A	NT B		NT E	NT C
Colne	d							17 34	17 35											19 34					
Nelson	d							17 39	17 40											19 39					
Brierfield	d							17 42	17 43											19 42					
Burnley Central	d							17 47	17 48											19 47					
Burnley Barracks	d							17 49	17 50											19 49					
Leeds 10 41	d				16 35							17 35					18 35								19 35
Burnley Manchester Road 41	d				17 39							18 39					19 39								20 39
Rose Grove	d							17 52	17 53											19 52					
Hapton	d							17 55	17 56											19 55					
Huncoat	d							17 58	17 59											19 58					
Accrington	d				17 47			18 03	18 04			18 47					19 47			20 03					20 47
Church & Oswaldtwistle	d							18 05	18 06											20 05					
Rishton	d							18 08	18 09											20 08					
Blackburn	a				17 56			18 14	18 14			18 56					19 57			20 14					20 56
Clitheroe 94	d																							19 57	
Blackburn	d				17 57			18 16	18 16			18 57					19 57			20 16				20 25	20 57
Mill Hill (Lancashire)	d							18 19	18 19											20 19					
Cherry Tree	d							18 21	18 21											20 21					
Pleasington	d							18 23	18 23											20 23					
Bamber Bridge	d							18 30	18 30											20 30				20 34	
Lostock Hall	d							18 33	18 33											20 33				20 38	
Preston 8	a				18 14			18 42	18 42			19 14					20 14			20 42				20 47	21 14
	d	17 34		17 39	18 15	17 43	18 20	18 43		18 34	18 39	19 15		19 20	19 34	19 39	20 16	19 43	20 20	20 43	20 34	20 39		20 49	21 15
Salwick	d																								
Kirkham & Wesham	d					17 51	18 29	18 51						19 29				19 51	20 29	20 51				20 59	
Moss Side	d					17 57		18 57										19 57		20 57					
Lytham	d					18 01		19 01										20 01		21 01					
Ansdell & Fairhaven	d					18 04		19 04										20 04		21 04					
St Annes-on-the-Sea	d					18 08		19 08										20 08		21 08					
Squires Gate	d					18 12		19 12										20 12		21 12					
Blackpool Pleasure Beach	d					18 14		19 14										20 14		21 14					
Blackpool South	a					18 21		19 21										20 23		21 21					
Poulton-le-Fylde	d	17 51		17 57	18 32		18 37			18 51	18 57	19 32		19 37	19 51	19 57	20 32		20 37		20 51	20 57		21 07	21 32
Layton	d						18 42							19 42					20 42						
Blackpool North	a	18 00		18 07	18 39		18 51			19 00	19 07	19 39		19 51	20 00	20 07	20 39		20 51		21 00	21 07		21 16	21 39

A From Manchester Airport
B From Liverpool Lime Street
C From York
D From Manchester Victoria
E From Carlisle

Table 97

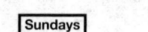

Sundays
9 October to 23 October

Colne, Burnley, Accrington and Blackburn - Preston - Blackpool

		NT	TP	NT	NT	NT	NT	TP	NT	NT	TP
			◇1					◇1			◇1
		D	A	B	C		D	A	B	B	A
Colne	d					21 34					
Nelson	d					21 39					
Brierfield	d					21 42					
Burnley Central	d					21 47					
Burnley Barracks	d					21 49					
Leeds 10 41	d				20 35						
Burnley Manchester Road 41	d				21 39						
Rose Grove	d					21 52					
Hapton	d					21 55					
Huncoat	d					21 58					
Accrington	d				21 47	22 03					
Church & Oswaldtwistle	d					22 05					
Rishton	d					22 08					
Blackburn	a				21 56	22 14					
Clitheroe 94	d										
Blackburn	d				21 57	22 16					
Mill Hill (Lancashire)	d					22 19					
Cherry Tree	d					22 21					
Pleasington	d					22 23					
Bamber Bridge	d					22 30					
Lostock Hall	d					22 33					
Preston 8	a				22 14	22 44					
	d	21 20	21 34	21 39	22 15		22 20	22 29	22 39	23 39	23 47
Salwick	d										
Kirkham & Wesham	d	21 29					22 29				23 56
Moss Side	d										
Lytham	d										
Ansdell & Fairhaven	d										
St Annes-on-the-Sea	d										
Squires Gate	d										
Blackpool Pleasure Beach	d										
Blackpool South	a										
Poulton-le-Fylde	d	21 37	21 51	21 57	22 32		22 37	22 46	22 57	23 56	00 05
Layton	d	21 42					22 42				
Blackpool North	a	21 51	22 00	22 07	22 39		22 51	22 55	23 07	00 05	00 14

A From Manchester Airport
B From Liverpool Lime Street
C From York
D From Manchester Victoria
E From Carlisle

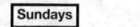

Sundays
from 30 October

		TP	NT	NT	TP	NT	NT	NT	TP	NT	NT	NT	TP	NT	NT	NT	NT	TP	NT	NT	NT	NT	NT
		◇1			◇1				◇1				◇1					◇1					
		A	B	(bus)	A	C	B	D	A	B		C	A	D	E	(bus)	B	A	D	F (bus)	E	C	B
Colne	d			08 04												09 16							
Nelson	d			08 12												09 24							
Brierfield	d			08 17												09 29							
Burnley Central	d			08 25												09 37							
Burnley Barracks	d			08 30												09 42							
Leeds 10 41	d										08 45				09 35						10 35		
Burnley Manchester Road 41	d										09 50				10 39					11 00	11 39		
Rose Grove	d			08 34												09 46							
Hapton	d			08 40												09 52							
Huncoat	d			08 48												10 00							
Accrington	d			08 54							09 59				10 48	10 06				11 20	11 47		
Church & Oswaldtwistle	d			08 58												10 10							
Rishton	d			09 10												10 22							
Blackburn	a			09 19							10 08				10 57	10 31				11 37	11 56		
Clitheroe 94	d																						
Blackburn	d			09 20							10 08				10 57	10 32				11 38	11 57		
Mill Hill (Lancashire)	d			09 30												10 42							
Cherry Tree	d			09 36												10 48							
Pleasington	d			09 40												10 52							
Bamber Bridge	d			09 58												11 10							
Lostock Hall	d			10 08												11 20							
Preston 8	a			10 22							10 27				11 14	11 34				12 08	12 14		
	d	23p35	00 11		08 32	08 48	09 20	09 39	09 51	10 20	10 29	10 23	10 34	10 40	11 16		11 20	11 34	11 39	12 10	12 15	11 43	12 20
Salwick	d																						
Kirkham & Wesham	d		00 21			08 56	09 29			10 29		10 31					11 29					11 51	12 29
Moss Side	d					09 02						10 37										11 57	
Lytham	d					09 06						10 41										12 01	
Ansdell & Fairhaven	d					09 09						10 44										12 04	
St Annes-on-the-Sea	d					09 13						10 48										12 08	
Squires Gate	d					09 17						10 52										12 12	
Blackpool Pleasure Beach	d					09 19						10 54										12 14	
Blackpool South	a					09 26						11 01										12 21	
Poulton-le-Fylde	d	23p52	00 29		08 49		09 37	09 57	10 08	10 37	10 46		10 51	10 57	11 33		11 37	11 51	11 57		12 32		12 37
Layton	d		00 33				09 42			10 42							11 42						12 42
Blackpool North	a	00 02	00 42		08 58		09 51	10 07	10 18	10 51	10 53		11 00	11 09	11 40		11 51	12 00	12 07	12 50	12 39		12 51

A From Manchester Airport
B From Manchester Victoria
C 30 October, 6 November
D From Liverpool Lime Street
E From York
F From Hebden Bridge

Table 97

Sundays
from 30 October

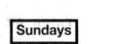

Colne, Burnley, Accrington and Blackburn - Preston - Blackpool

		TP ◇1 A	NT D	NT E	NT (bus)	NT C	NT B	TP ◇1 A	NT D	NT F (bus)	NT E	NT C	NT B	TP ◇1 A	NT D	NT E	NT (bus)	NT C	NT B	TP ◇1 A	NT D	NT F (bus)	NT E
Colne	d				11 35												13 35						
Nelson	d				11 43												13 43						
Brierfield	d				11 48												13 48						
Burnley Central	d				11 56												13 56						
Burnley Barracks	d				12 01												14 01						
Leeds 10 41	d			11 35							12 35					13 35							14 35
Burnley Manchester Road 41	d			12 39						13 00	13 39					14 39						15 00	15 39
Rose Grove	d				12 05												14 05						
Hapton	d				12 11												14 11						
Huncoat	d				12 19												14 19						
Accrington	d			12 47	12 25					13 20	13 47					14 47	14 25					15 20	15 47
Church & Oswaldtwistle	d				12 29												14 29						
Rishton	d				12 41												14 41						
Blackburn	a			12 56	12 50					13 37	13 56					14 56	14 50					15 37	15 56
Clitheroe 94	d																						
Blackburn	d			12 57	12 51					13 38	13 57					14 57	14 51					15 38	15 57
Mill Hill (Lancashire)	d				13 01												15 01						
Cherry Tree	d				13 07												15 07						
Pleasington	d				13 11												15 11						
Bamber Bridge	d				13 29												15 29						
Lostock Hall	d				13 39												15 39						
Preston 8	a			13 14	13 53					14 08	14 14					15 14	15 53					16 08	16 14
	d	12 34	12 39	13 15		12 43	13 20	13 34	13 39	14 10	14 15	13 43	14 20	14 34	14 39	15 15		14 43	15 20	15 34	15 39	16 10	16 15
Salwick	d																						
Kirkham & Wesham	d					12 51	13 29					13 51	14 29					14 51	15 29				
Moss Side	d					12 57						13 57						14 57					
Lytham	d					13 01						14 01						15 01					
Ansdell & Fairhaven	d					13 04						14 04						15 04					
St Annes-on-the-Sea	d					13 08						14 08						15 08					
Squires Gate	d					13 12						14 12						15 12					
Blackpool Pleasure Beach	d					13 14						14 14						15 14					
Blackpool South	a					13 19						14 23						15 21					
Poulton-le-Fylde	d	12 51	12 57	13 32			13 37	13 51	13 57		14 31		14 37	14 51	14 57	15 32			15 37	15 51	15 57		16 32
Layton	d						13 42						14 42						15 42				
Blackpool North	a	13 00	13 07	13 39			13 51	14 00	14 09	14 50	14 39		14 51	15 00	15 07	15 39			15 51	16 00	16 07	16 50	16 39

A From Manchester Airport
B From Manchester Victoria
C 30 October, 6 November
D From Liverpool Lime Street
E From York
F From Hebden Bridge

		NT A	NT B	TP ◇1 C	NT D	NT E	NT (bus)	NT A	NT B	TP ◇1 C	NT D	NT F (bus)	NT E	NT A	NT B	TP ◇1 C	NT D	NT F (bus)	NT E	NT (bus)	NT A	NT B
Colne	d						15 35													17 35		
Nelson	d						15 43													17 43		
Brierfield	d						15 48													17 48		
Burnley Central	d						15 56													17 56		
Burnley Barracks	d						16 01													18 01		
Leeds 10 41	d					15 35							16 35						17 35			
Burnley Manchester Road 41	d					16 38						17 00	17 39					18 00	18 39			
Rose Grove	d						16 05													18 05		
Hapton	d						16 11													18 11		
Huncoat	d						16 19													18 19		
Accrington	d					16 47	16 25					17 20	17 47					18 20	18 47	18 25		
Church & Oswaldtwistle	d						16 29													18 29		
Rishton	d						16 41													18 41		
Blackburn	a					16 56	16 50					17 37	17 56					18 37	18 56	18 50		
Clitheroe 94	d																					
Blackburn	d					16 56	16 51					17 38	17 57					18 38	18 57	18 51		
Mill Hill (Lancashire)	d						17 01													19 01		
Cherry Tree	d						17 07													19 07		
Pleasington	d						17 11													19 11		
Bamber Bridge	d						17 29													19 29		
Lostock Hall	d						17 39													19 39		
Preston 8	a					17 13	17 53					18 08	18 14					19 08	19 14	19 53		
	d	15 43	16 20	16 34	16 39	17 15		16 43	17 20	17 34	17 39	18 10	18 15	17 43	18 20	18 34	18 39	19 10	19 15		18 43	19 20
Salwick	d																					
Kirkham & Wesham	d	15 51	16 29					16 51	17 29					17 51	18 29						18 51	19 29
Moss Side	d	15 57						16 57						17 57							18 57	
Lytham	d	16 01						17 01						18 01							19 01	
Ansdell & Fairhaven	d	16 04						17 04						18 04							19 04	
St Annes-on-the-Sea	d	16 08						17 08						18 08							19 08	
Squires Gate	d	16 12						17 12						18 12							19 12	
Blackpool Pleasure Beach	d	16 14						17 14						18 14							19 14	
Blackpool South	a	16 21						17 21						18 23							19 21	
Poulton-le-Fylde	d		16 37	16 51	16 57	17 31			17 37	17 51	17 57		18 32		18 37	18 51	18 57		19 32			19 37
Layton	d		16 42						17 42						18 42							19 42
Blackpool North	a		16 51	17 00	17 07	17 39			17 51	18 00	18 07	18 50	18 39		18 51	19 00	19 07	19 50	19 39			19 51

A 30 October, 6 November
B From Manchester Victoria
C From Manchester Airport
D From Liverpool Lime Street
E From York
F From Hebden Bridge

Table 97

Sundays
from 30 October

Colne, Burnley, Accrington and Blackburn - Preston - Blackpool

		TP ◇1 C	NT D	NT F (bus)	NT E	NT A	NT B	TP ◇1 C		NT D	NT E	NT (bus)	NT A	NT B	TP ◇1 C	NT D	NT F (bus)	NT E		NT	NT (bus)	NT B	TP ◇1 C	NT D	NT D
Colne	d											19 35								21 34	21 35				
Nelson	d											19 43								21 39	21 43				
Brierfield	d											19 48								21 42	21 48				
Burnley Central	d											19 56								21 47	21 56				
Burnley Barracks	d											20 01								21 49	22 01				
Leeds 10	41 d				18 35						19 35							20 35							
Burnley Manchester Road	41 d			19 00	19 39						20 39						21 00	21 39							
Rose Grove	d											20 05								21 52	22 05				
Hapton	d											20 11								21 55	22 11				
Huncoat	d											20 19								21 58	22 19				
Accrington	d			19 20	19 47						20 47	20 25					21 20	21 47		22 03	22 25				
Church & Oswaldtwistle	d											20 29								22 05	22 29				
Rishton	d											20 41								22 08	22 41				
Blackburn	a			19 37	19 57						20 56	20 50					21 37	21 56		22 14	22 50				
Clitheroe	94 d																								
Blackburn	d			19 38	19 57						20 57	20 51					21 38	21 57		22 16	22 51				
Mill Hill (Lancashire)	d											21 01								22 19	23 01				
Cherry Tree	d											21 07								22 21	23 07				
Pleasington	d											21 11								22 23	23 11				
Bamber Bridge	d											21 29								22 30	23 29				
Lostock Hall	d											21 39								22 33	23 39				
Preston 8	a			20 08	20 14						21 14	21 53					22 08	22 14		22 44	23 53				
	d	19 34	19 39	20 10	20 16	19 43	20 20	20 34		20 39	21 15		20 43	21 20	21 34	21 39	22 10	22 15				22 20	22 29	22 39	23 39
Salwick	d																								
Kirkham & Wesham	d					19 51	20 29						20 51	21 29								22 29			
Moss Side	d					19 57							20 57												
Lytham	d					20 01							21 01												
Ansdell & Fairhaven	d					20 04							21 04												
St Annes-on-the-Sea	d					20 08							21 08												
Squires Gate	d					20 12							21 12												
Blackpool Pleasure Beach	d					20 14							21 14												
Blackpool South	a					20 21							21 21												
Poulton-le-Fylde	d	19 51	19 57		20 32		20 37	20 51		20 57	21 32			21 37	21 51	21 57		22 32				22 37	22 46	22 57	23 56
Layton	d						20 42							21 42								22 42			
Blackpool North	a	20 00	20 07	20 50	20 39		20 51	21 00		21 07	21 39			21 51	22 00	22 07	22 50	22 39				22 51	22 55	23 07	00 05

A 30 October, 6 November
B From Manchester Victoria
C From Manchester Airport
D From Liverpool Lime Street
E From York
F From Hebden Bridge

		TP ◇1 A
Colne	d	
Nelson	d	
Brierfield	d	
Burnley Central	d	
Burnley Barracks	d	
Leeds 10	41 d	
Burnley Manchester Road	41 d	
Rose Grove	d	
Hapton	d	
Huncoat	d	
Accrington	d	
Church & Oswaldtwistle	d	
Rishton	d	
Blackburn	a	
Clitheroe	94 d	
Blackburn	d	
Mill Hill (Lancashire)	d	
Cherry Tree	d	
Pleasington	d	
Bamber Bridge	d	
Lostock Hall	d	
Preston 8	a	
	d	23 47
Salwick	d	
Kirkham & Wesham	d	23 56
Moss Side	d	
Lytham	d	
Ansdell & Fairhaven	d	
St Annes-on-the-Sea	d	
Squires Gate	d	
Blackpool Pleasure Beach	d	
Blackpool South	a	
Poulton-le-Fylde	d	00 05
Layton	d	
Blackpool North	a	00 14

A From Manchester Airport

Table 98

Lancaster - Morecambe and Heysham

Mondays to Fridays

until 15 July

Miles			TP 1	NT	NT	NT	NT	NT	NT	NT	NT	NT	NT	NT	NT	NT	NT	NT	NT	NT	NT	NT	NT	NT	NT
0	Lancaster 6	82 d	05 46	06 38	07 25	07 58	08 35	09 50	10 20	11 22	12 02	12 28	13 44	14 27	15 25	16 03	16 49	17 38	18 33	18 49	19 40	20 22	21 03	22 06	22 35
2½	Bare Lane	d	05 52	06 44	07 31	08 04	08 41	09 56	10 27	11 28	12 08	12 34	13 50	14 33	15 31	16 09	16 55	17 44	18 39	18 55	19 46	20 28	21 09	22 12	22 41
4¼	Morecambe	a	05 56	06 49	07 36	08 09	08 46	10 01	10 33	11 33	12 13	12 39	13 55	14 38	15 36	16 13	17 00	17 49	18 44	19 01	19 50	20 32	21 13	22 16	22 45
—		d										12 42													
8½	Heysham Port	a										12 57													

Mondays to Fridays

from 18 July

		TP 1	NT	NT	NT	NT	NT	NT	NT	NT	NT	NT	NT	NT	NT	NT	NT	NT	NT	NT	NT	NT	NT	NT
Lancaster 6	82 d	05 46	06 38	07 25	08 35	09 15	10 20	11 22	12 02	12 28	13 44	14 27	15 25	16 03	16 19	16 49	17 38	18 33	18 49	19 40	20 22	21 03	22 06	22 35
Bare Lane	d	05 52	06 44	07 31	08 41	09 21	10 27	11 28	12 08	12 34	13 50	14 33	15 31	16 09	16 26	16 55	17 44	18 39	18 55	19 46	20 28	21 09	22 12	22 41
Morecambe	a	05 56	06 49	07 36	08 46	09 26	10 33	11 33	12 13	12 39	13 55	14 38	15 36	16 13	16 30	17 00	17 49	18 44	19 01	19 50	20 32	21 13	22 16	22 45
	d									12 42														
Heysham Port	a									12 57														

Saturdays

		TP 1	NT	NT	NT	NT	NT	NT	NT A	NT	NT	NT	NT	NT	NT	NT	NT	NT	NT	NT	NT	NT	NT
Lancaster 6	82 d	05 46	06 38	07 25	07 57	08 35	09 15	10 05	10 19	11 23	12 02	12 25	13 24	14 27	15 25	15 49	16 03	17 04	17 37	18 21	18 47	19 40	20 22
Bare Lane	d	05 52	06 44	07 31	08 03	08 41	09 21	10 11	10 26	11 29	12 08	12 31	13 30	14 33	15 31	15 56	16 09	17 10	17 43	18 27	18 53	19 46	20 28
Morecambe	a	05 56	06 49	07 36	08 08	08 46	09 26	10 16	10 32	11 34	12 13	12 36	13 35	14 38	15 36	16 02	16 14	17 15	17 48	18 32	18 59	19 50	20 32
	d											12 39											
Heysham Port	a											12 54											

		NT	NT	NT
Lancaster 6	82 d	21 03	22 06	22 35
Bare Lane	d	21 09	22 12	22 41
Morecambe	a	21 13	22 16	22 45
	d			
Heysham Port	a			

Sundays

until 17 July

		NT	NT	NT	NT	NT	NT	NT	NT	NT	NT	NT	NT	NT
Lancaster 6	82 d	10 45	11 05	12 00	12 05	13 01	13 20	14 27	15 05	15 45	16 26	16 51	19 23	21 18
Bare Lane	d	10 51	11 11	12 06	12 11	13 07	13 26	14 34	15 11	15 51	16 32	16 56	19 29	21 24
Morecambe	a	10 57	11 16	12 10	12 16	13 13	13 30	14 38	15 16	15 55	16 36	17 03	19 35	21 29
	d													
Heysham Port	a													

Sundays

24 July to 11 September

		NT	NT	NT	NT	NT	NT	NT	NT	NT	NT	NT	NT	NT
Lancaster 6	82 d	10 45	11 05	12 00	12 05	13 01	13 20	14 27	15 05	15 45	16 26	16 51	19 23	21 18
Bare Lane	d	10 51	11 11	12 06	12 11	13 07	13 27	14 34	15 11	15 51	16 32	16 56	19 29	21 24
Morecambe	a	10 57	11 16	12 11	12 16	13 13	13 31	14 38	15 16	15 55	16 36	17 03	19 35	21 29
	d			12 14			13 34							
Heysham Port	a			12 29			13 47							

Sundays

from 18 September

		NT	NT	NT	NT	NT	NT	NT
Lancaster 6	82 d	10 45	13 01	14 27	15 05	16 51	19 23	21 18
Bare Lane	d	10 51	13 07	14 34	15 11	16 56	19 29	21 24
Morecambe	a	10 57	13 13	14 38	15 16	17 03	19 35	21 29
	d							
Heysham Port	a							

Table 98

Heysham and Morecambe - Lancaster

Mondays to Fridays

until 15 July

Miles			TP ■1	NT	NT	NT	NT	NT	NT	NT	NT	NT	NT	NT	NT	NT	NT	NT	NT	NT	NT	NT	NT
0	**Heysham Port**	d											13 15										
4¼	**Morecambe**	a											13 25										
—		d	05 59	06 19	07 03	07 42	08 11	08 51	10 34	10 55	11 39	12 32	13 29	13 58	14 42	15 45	16 19	17 03	17 56	19 00	19 08	19 55	20 40
6	Bare Lane	d	06a03	06 23	07 07	07 46	08 15	08 55	10 38	10 59	11 43	12 36	13 36	14 02	14 46	15 49	16a23	17 07	18 00	19 04	19 12	19 59	20 44
8½	**Lancaster ■6** 82	a		06 30	07 14	07 53	08 21	09 03	10 45	11 06	11 50	12 43	13 42	14 09	14 53	15 56		17 16	18 07	19 11	19 19	20 06	20 51

		NT	NT	NT
Heysham Port	d			
Morecambe	a			
	d	21 36	22 20	22 55
Bare Lane	d	21 40	22 24	22 59
Lancaster ■6 82	a	21 47	22 31	23 05

Mondays to Fridays

from 18 July

		TP ■1	NT	NT	NT	NT	NT	NT	NT	NT	NT	NT	NT	NT	NT	NT	NT	NT	NT	NT	NT	NT	NT
Heysham Port	d												13 15										
Morecambe	a												13 25										
	d	05 59	06 19	07 03	07 42	08 11	08 51	09 32	10 34	10 55	11 39	12 32	13 29	13 58	14 42	15 45	16 19	16 34	17 03	17 56	19 00	19 08	19 55
Bare Lane	d	06a03	06 23	07 07	07 46	08 15	08 55	09 36	10 38	10 59	11 43	12 36	13 36	14 02	14 46	15 49	16a23	16 38	17 07	18 00	19 04	19 12	19 59
Lancaster ■6 82	a		06 30	07 14	07 53	08 21	09 03	09 43	10 45	11 06	11 50	12 43	13 42	14 09	14 53	15 56		16 45	17 14	18 07	19 11	19 19	20 06

		NT	NT	NT	NT
Heysham Port	d				
Morecambe	a				
	d	20 40	21 36	22 20	22 55
Bare Lane	d	20 44	21 40	22 24	22 59
Lancaster ■6 82	a	20 51	21 47	22 31	23 05

Saturdays

		TP ■1	NT	NT	NT	NT	NT	NT	NT	NT	NT	NT	NT	NT	NT	NT	NT	NT	NT	NT	NT	NT	NT
Heysham Port	d												13 15										
Morecambe	a												13 25										
	d	05 59	06 19	07 03	07 38	08 11	08 51	09 41	10 34	10 54	11 40	12 32	13 29	13 58	14 42	15 44	16 19	16 40	17 20	17 56	18 58	19 09	19 55
Bare Lane	d	06a03	06 23	07 07	07 42	08 15	08 55	09 45	10 38	10 58	11 44	12 36	13 36	14 02	14 46	15 48	16 24	16 44	17 24	18 00	19 02	19 13	19 59
Lancaster ■6 82	a		06 30	07 14	07 49	08 22	09 03	09 52	10 45	11 05	11 51	12 43	13 42	14 09	14 53	15 55	16 30	16 50	17 31	18 07	19 09	19 20	20 06

		NT	NT	NT
Heysham Port	d			
Morecambe	a			
	d	20 40	21 36	22 20
Bare Lane	d	20 44	21 40	22 24
Lancaster ■6 82	a	20 51	21 47	22 31

Sundays

until 17 July

		NT	NT	NT	NT	NT	NT	NT	NT	NT	NT	NT	NT	NT
Heysham Port	d													
Morecambe	a													
	d	11 20	11 35	12 20	12 56	13 23	13 39	14 46	15 21	16 02	16 42	17 45	20 00	21 41
Bare Lane	d	11 24	11 39	12 24	13 03	13 27	13 46	14a50	15 25	16 06	16 46	17 49	20 04	21 45
Lancaster ■6 82	a	11 30	11 46	12 30	13 10	13 33	13 53		15 32	16 13	16 53	17 55	20 11	21 51

Sundays

24 July to 11 September

		NT	NT	NT	NT	NT	NT	NT	NT	NT	NT	NT	NT	NT
Heysham Port	d				12 42		14 00							
Morecambe	a				12 52		14 10							
	d	11 20	11 35	12 20	12 56	13 23	14 17	14 46	15 21	16 02	16 42	17 45	20 00	21 41
Bare Lane	d	11 24	11 39	12 24	13 03	13 27	14 24	14a50	15 25	16 06	16 46	17 49	20 04	21 45
Lancaster ■6 82	a	11 30	11 46	12 30	13 10	13 33	14 31		15 32	16 13	16 53	17 55	20 11	21 51

Sundays

from 18 September

		NT	NT	NT	NT	NT	NT	NT
Heysham Port	d							
Morecambe	a							
	d	12 20	13 23	14 46	15 21	17 45	20 00	21 41
Bare Lane	d	12 24	13 27	14a50	15 25	17 49	20 04	21 45
Lancaster ■6 82	a	12 30	13 33		15 32	17 55	20 11	21 51

Table 98A

Mondays to Fridays

To and from The Isle of Man via Heysham and Liverpool

One Class only on ship

	VT	VT A	VT B	VT C	VT D	VT	VT E	VT F	VT D	VT G
Liverpool Landing Stage d	..	..	..	11 15	..	..	18 15	19 00	20 00	20 30
Heysham Port d	02 15	10 15	11 00	⌇	11 45	14 15	⌇	⌇	⌇	⌇
Douglas (Isle of Man) a	05 45	12 15	13 00	13 45	13 45	16 45	20 45	21 30	22 30	23 00

Saturdays

	VT	VT H	VT I	VT J	VT K	VT J	VT L	VT M
Liverpool Landing Stage d	..	11 15	..	..	..	18 15	19 00	20 30
Heysham Port d	02 15	⌇	12 15	13 45	14 15	⌇	⌇	⌇
Douglas (Isle of Man) a	05 45	13 45	14 15	17 15	17 45	20 45	21 30	23 00

Sundays

	VT N	VT O	VT N	VT P	VT Q	VT N	VT R	VT S	VT T
Liverpool Landing Stage d	..	..	..	..	..	18 15	19 00	20 30	21 00
Heysham Port d	01 15	02 15	10 30	12 00	14 15	⌇	⌇	⌇	⌇
Douglas (Isle of Man) a	04 45	05 45	12 30	15 30	17 45	20 45	21 30	23 00	23 30

Mondays to Fridays

	VT U	VT V	VT W	VT X	VT Y	VT Z	VT [	VT AA	VT BB	VT CC	VT
Douglas (Isle of Man) d	06 00	07 00	07 30	08 00	08 15	08 45	14 00	15 00	15 30	16 30	19 45
Heysham Port a	⌇	09 15	⌇	11 30	11 45	12 15	⌇	⌇	⌇	⌇	23 15
Liverpool Landing Stage a	08 30	..	10 00	..	..	..	16 45	17 30	18 00	19 00	..

Saturdays

	VT DD	VT J	VT EE	VT I	VT FF	VT GG	VT HH	VT J	VT II	VT JJ	VT KK	VT LL
Douglas (Isle of Man) d	06 30	07 00	07 30	07 45	08 15	08 45	10 00	14 30	15 00	15 30	16 30	20 00
Heysham Port a	⌇	09 00	⌇	09 45	11 45	12 15	⌇	⌇	⌇	⌇	⌇	22 30
Liverpool Landing Stage a	08 30	..	10 00	..	..	..	12 30	17 00	17 30	18 00	19 00	..

Sundays

	VT T	VT MM	VT N	VT R	VT NN	VT OO	VT T	VT
Douglas (Isle of Man) d	08 00	08 45	14 30	15 00	15 30	16 30	17 00	19 45
Heysham Port a	11 30	12 15	⌇	⌇	⌇	⌇	⌇	23 15
Liverpool Landing Stage a	..	..	17 00	17 30	18 00	19 00	19 30	..

A from 8 June until 10 June
B 2 June
C 23 May, 27 May, 30 May, MThFO from 13 June until 12 September, not 23 June, 4 July, 15 July, also MFO from 16 September until 30 September
D 3 June
E 31 May, 1 June, 6 June, from 8 June until 10 June
F until 28 October, not 31 May, 1 June, from 3 June until 10 June, from 25 August until 5 September
G from 25 August until 5 September
H until 1 October, not 4 June, 11 June
I 4 June
J 11 June
K until 29 October, not 11 June
L until 29 October, not 4 June, 11 June, 27 August, 3 September
M 4 June, 27 August, 3 September
N 12 June
O until 27 November, not 19 June, 3 July, 14 August, 11 September, 2 October, 6 November
P 2 October
Q until 30 October, not 2 October
R until 30 October, not 5 June, 12 June, 28 August, 4 September, 2 October
S 28 August, 4 September
T 5 June
U 26 August
V 2 June, 3 June
W 24 May, 25 May, 5 July, 13 September
X from 31 May until 3 June
Y 18 August, 19 August, 26 August
Z not 31 May, 3 June, 18 August, 19 August, 26 August
[from 31 May until 2 June
AA until 28 October, not from 31 May until 2 June, from 6 June until 10 June, from 25 August until 5 September
BB 25 August, 26 August
CC from 29 August until 5 September
DD 27 August
EE until 1 October, not 4 June, 11 June, 27 August
FF 20 August, 27 August
GG until 29 October, not 20 August, 27 August
HH from 8 October until 29 October
II until 1 October, not 4 June, 11 June, 27 August, 3 September
JJ 4 June, 27 August
KK 3 September
LL not 18 June, 2 July, 13 August, 10 September, 1 October, 5 November, 3 December
MM until 30 October, not 5 June
NN 28 August
OO 4 September

Table 99

Mondays to Saturdays

Ormskirk - Preston

Miles			NT	NT	NT	NT	NT	NT	NT	NT	NT		NT	NT	NT
0	**Ormskirk**	d	06 58	08 06	09 17	10 54	12 17	13 40	14 53	16 38	17 52	....	19 08	20 19	22 17
2½	Burscough Junction	d	07 02	08 10	09 21	10 58	12 21	13 44	14 57	16 42	17 56		19 12	20 23	22 21
5½	Rufford	d	07 07	08 15	09 25	11 03	12 25	13 49	15 01	16 46	18 01	....	19 17	20 27	22 25
8	Croston	d	07 11	08 19	09 30	11 07	12 30	13 54	15 06	16 51	18 06		19 21	20 32	22 30
15	**Preston** 8	a	07 29	08 36	09 47	11 24	12 47	14 12	15 23	17 07	18 23	....	19 39	20 49	22 46

Table 99

Mondays to Saturdays

Preston - Ormskirk

Miles			NT	NT	NT	NT	NT	NT	NT	NT	NT		NT	NT SX	NT SO	NT
0	**Preston** 8	d	06 25	07 33	08 41	10 07	11 32	12 59	14 17	15 39	17 10	....	18 34	19 42	19 44	21 37
7	Croston	d	06 36	07 45	08 52	10 19	11 43	13 11	14 28	15 51	17 22		18 47	19 53	19 55	21 49
9½	Rufford	d	06 41	07 50	08 57	10 24	11 48	13 16	14 33	15 56	17 27	....	18 51	19 58	20 00	21 53
12½	Burscough Junction	d	06 46	07 55	09 02	10 29	11 53	13 21	14 38	16 01	17 32		18 56	20 03	20 05	21 58
15	**Ormskirk**	a	06 55	08 04	09 11	10 38	12 00	13 30	14 45	16 10	17 41	....	19 05	20 12	20 14	22 07

For connections to Liverpool Central please refer to Table 103

No Sunday Service

Table 100

Mondays to Fridays

until 15 July

Barrow-in-Furness - Whitehaven and Carlisle

Miles			NT	NT	NT	NT	NT	NT	NT	NT	NT	NT	NT	NT	NT	NT	NT	NT	NT	NT	NT
—	Lancaster ■ 82	d																			
0	**Barrow-in-Furness**	d		06 00	06 50	08 01		09 10	10 11	11 22		12 31	13 32	14 54	16 42	17 28	18 05		19 35		21 25
6	Askam	d		06 10	07 00	08 11		09 20	10 21	11 32		12 41	13 42	15 04	16 52	17 40	18 15		19 45		21 35
9¼	Kirkby-in-Furness	d		06 14	07x04	08x15		09x24	10x25	11x36		12x45	13x46	15x08	16x56	17x44	18x19		19x49		21x39
11¼	Foxfield	d		06x18	07x08	08x18		09x27	10x28	11x39		12x48	13x50	15x11	16x59	17x48	18x22		19x52		21x42
13½	Green Road	d		06x22	07x12	08x22		09x31	10x32	11x43		12x52	13x53	15x15	17x03	17x51	18x26		19x56		21x46
16	Millom	a		06 29	07 19	08 28		09 37	10 38	11 49		12 58	14 00	15 21	17 09	17 58	18 35		20 05		21 55
—		d		06 29	07 19	08 29		09 38	10 39	11 49		12 59	14 00	15 22	17 10	17 58					
19	Silecroft	d		06x34	07x24			09x42	10x43	11x54		13x03	14x04	15x26	17x14	18x03					
24½	Bootle	d		06x41	07x31			09x49	10x50	12x00		13x10	14x11	15x33	17x21	18x09					
29¼	Ravenglass for Eskdale	d		06 47	07 37	08 44		09 55	10 56	12 06		13 16	14 17	15 39	17 27	18 15					
31	Drigg	d		06x51	07x41			09x58	10x59	12x09		13x19	14x20	15x42	17x30	18x18					
33¼	Seascale	d		06x54	07x44	08x49		10x01	11x02	12x12		13x22	14x23	15x45	17x33	18x21					
35	Sellafield	d		07 02	07 51	08a58		10 10	11 07	12 18		13 28	14 29	15 51	17 39	18 27					
37	Braystones	d		07x05	07x54							13x31				18x31					
38¼	Nethertown	d		07x08	07x57							13x34				18x33					
41¼	St Bees	d		07 12	08 01			10 20	11 20	12 27		13 40	14 38	16 00	17 49	18 45					
44¾	Corkickle	d		07x17	08x06			10x25	11x25	12x32		13x45	14x43	16x05	17x54	18x50					
45¾	**Whitehaven**	a		07 20	08 10			10 27	11 27	12 36		13 47	14 46	16 09	17 56	18 53					
—		d	06 30	07 25	08 11		09 02	10 28	11 29	12 37	13 05	13 49	14 48	16 11	17 58	18 55		19 31		20 30	
47	Parton	d	06x33	07x29	08x15		09x05	10x31	11x32	12x41		13x52	14x51	16x15	18x01	18x58		19x34		20x33	
50½	Harrington	d	06x41	07x37	08x23		09x13	10x40	11x40	12x49		14x00	14x59	16x23	18x09	19x06		19x42		20x41	
52¼	**Workington**	d	06 48	07 43	08 29		09 20	10 46	11 47	12 55	13 22	14 07	15 06	16 29	18 16	19 12		19 49		20 48	
56	Flimby	d	06x52	07x48	08x34		09x24	10x50	11x51	13x00		14x11	15x10	16x34	18x20	19x17		19x53		20x52	
58	Maryport	d	06 56	07 51	08 37		09 28	10 54	11 55	13 03	13 30	14 15	15 14	16 37	18 26	19 20		19 57		20 56	
65½	Aspatria	d	07x05	08x01	08x47		09x37	11x03	12x04	13x13		14x24	15x23	16x47	18x35	19x30		20x06		21x05	
71¾	Wigton	d	07 15	08 11	08 57		09 47	11 13	12 14	13 23	13 50	14 34	15 33	16 57	18 45	19 40		20 16		21 15	
81¼	Dalston	d	07x24	08x19	09x05		09x56	11x22	12x23	13x31		14x43	15x42	17x05	18x54	19x48		20x25		21x24	
85¼	**Carlisle ■**	a	07 38	08 35	09 22		10 13	11 37	12 39	13 47	14 11	14 59	15 58	17 21	19 08	20 04		20 41		21 39	

Mondays to Fridays

from 18 July

		NT	NT	NT	NT	NT	NT	NT	NT	NT	NT	NT	NT	NT	NT	NT	NT	NT	NT	NT
Lancaster ■ 82	d			05 42				08 58						15 34		16 55				
Barrow-in-Furness	d		06 00	06 50	08 01		09 10	10 11	11 22		12 31	13 31	14 54	16 41	17 28	18 05		19 35		21 25
Askam	d		06 10	07 00	08 11		09 20	10 21	11 32		12 41	13 41	15 04	16 51	17 40	18 15		19 45		21 35
Kirkby-in-Furness	d		06 14	07x04	08x15		09x24	10x25	11x36		12x45	13x45	15x08	16x55	17x44	18x19		19x49		21x39
Foxfield	d		06x18	07x08	08x18		09x27	10x29	11x39		12x48	13x48	15x11	16x58	17x48	18x22		19x52		21x42
Green Road	d		06x22	07x12	08x22		09x31	10x32	11x43		12x52	13x52	15x15	17x02	17x51	18x26		19x56		21x46
Millom	a		06 29	07 19	08 28		09 37	10 39	11 49		12 58	13 58	15 21	17 08	17 58	18 35		20 05		21 55
	d		06 29	07 19	08 29		09 38	10 39	11 49		12 59	13 58	15 22	17 09	17 58					
Silecroft	d		06x34	07x24			09x42	10x44	11x54		13x03	14x03	15x26	17x13	18x03					
Bootle	d		06x41	07x31			09x49	10x50	12x00		13x10	14x09	15x33	17x20	18x09					
Ravenglass for Eskdale	d		06 47	07 37	08 44		09 55	10 56	12 06		13 15	14 15	15 39	17 26	18 15					
Drigg	d		06x51	07x41			09x58	10x59	12x09		13x18	14x18	15x42	17x29	18x18					
Seascale	d		06x54	07x44	08x49		10x01	11x02	12x12		13x21	14x21	15x45	17x32	18x21					
Sellafield	d		07 02	07 51	08a58		10 10	11 07	12 18		13 28	14 27	15 51	17 39	18 27					
Braystones	d		07x05	07x54								14x31			18x31					
Nethertown	d		07x08	07x57								14x33			18x33					
St Bees	d		07 12	08 01			10 20	11 20	12 27		13 38	14 38	16 00	17 49	18 45					
Corkickle	d		07x17	08x06			10x25	11x25	12x32		13x43	14x43	16x05	17x54	18x50					
Whitehaven	a		07 20	08 10			10 27	11 27	12 36		13 45	14 46	16 09	17 57	18 53					
	d	06 30	07 25	08 11		09 02	10 28	11 29	12 37	13 05	13 47	14 48	16 11	17 58	18 55		19 31		20 30	
Parton	d	06x33	07x29	08x15		09x05	10x31	11x32	12x41		13x50	14x51	16x15	18x02	18x58		19x34		20x33	
Harrington	d	06x41	07x37	08x23		09x13	10x40	11x40	12x49		13x58	14x59	16x23	18x10	19x06		19x42		20x41	
Workington	d	06 48	07 43	08 29		09 20	10 46	11 47	12 55	13 22	14 05	15 06	16 29	18 16	19 12		19 49		20 48	
Flimby	d	06x52	07x48	08x34		09x24	10x50	11x51	13x00		14x09	15x10	16x34	18x21	19x17		19x53		20x52	
Maryport	d	06 56	07 51	08 37		09 28	10 54	11 55	13 03	13 30	14 13	15 14	16 37	18 26	19 20		19 57		20 56	
Aspatria	d	07x05	08x01	08x47		09x37	11x03	12x04	13x13		14x22	15x23	16x47	18x36	19x30		20x06		21x05	
Wigton	d	07 15	08 11	08 57		09 47	11 13	12 14	13 23	13 50	14 32	15 33	16 57	18 46	19 40		20 16		21 15	
Dalston	d	07x24	08x19	09x05		09x56	11x22	12x23	13x31		14x41	15x42	17x05	18x54	19x48		20x25		21x24	
Carlisle ■	a	07 38	08 35	09 22		10 13	11 37	12 39	13 47	14 11	14 57	15 58	17 21	19 08	20 04		20 41		21 39	

Table 100

Saturdays

until 16 July

Barrow-in-Furness - Whitehaven and Carlisle

		NT	NT	NT	NT	NT	NT	NT	NT	NT	NT	NT	NT	NT	NT	NT	NT	NT	NT
Lancaster ■ 82	d																		
Barrow-in-Furness	d		06 00	07 05	08 01		09 07	10 12	11 22		12 34	13 50	15 57	17 25	18 10		19 35		21 25
Askam	d		06 10	07 15	08 11		09 17	10 22	11 32		12 44	14 00	16 07	17 35	18 20		19 45		21 35
Kirkby-in-Furness	d		06x14	07x19	08x15		09x21	10x26	11x36		12x48	14x04	16x11	17x39	18x24		19x49		21x39
Foxfield	d		06x17	07x23	08x18		09x24	10x29	11x39		12x51	14x07	16x15	17x42	18x27		19x52		21x42
Green Road	d		06x21	07x27	08x22		09x28	10x33	11x43		12x55	14x11	16x18	17x46	18x31		19x56		21x46
Millom	a		06 25	07 34	08 28		09 34	10 39	11 49		13 01	14 17	16 25	17 52	18 40		20 05		21 55
	d		06 26	07 34	08 29		09 35	10 40	11 50		13 02	14 18	16 25	17 53					
Silecroft	d		06x30	07x39			09x39	10x44	11x54		13x06	14x22	16x30	17x57					
Bootle	d		06x37	07x46			09x46	10x51	12x01		13x13	14x29	16x36	18x04					
Ravenglass for Eskdale	d		06 42	07 52	08 44		09 52	10 57	12 07		13 19	14 35	16 42	18 10					
Drigg	d		06x45	07x56			09x55	11x00	12x10		13x22	14x38	16x45	18x13					
Seascale	d		06x50	07x59	08x49		09x58	11x05	12x13		13x25	14x41	16x48	18x16					
Sellafield	d		06 55	08 06	08a58		10 04	11 10	12 19		13 31	14 47	16 54	18 22					
Braystones	d		06x59	08x09									16x58	18x26					
Nethertown	d		07x01	08x12									17x00	18x28					
St Bees	d		07 06	08 16			10 14	11 19	12 29		13 40	14 56	17 06	18 33					
Corkickle	d		07x11	08x21			10x19	11x24	12x34		13x45	15x01	17x11	18x38					
Whitehaven	a		07 15	08 25			10 22	11 27	12 41		13 49	15 05	17 14	18 41					
	d	06 30	07 19	08 26		09 15	10 24	11 29		12 54	13 50	15 06	17 16	18 43		19 31		20 30	
Parton	d	06x33	07x23	08x30		09x18	10x27	11x32		12x57	13x54	15x10	17x19	18x46		19x34		20x33	
Harrington	d	06x41	07x31	08x38		09x26	10x35	11x40		13x05	14x02	15x18	17x27	18x54		19x42		20x41	
Workington	d	06 48	07 37	08 44		09 33	10 42	11 47		13 12	14 09	15 24	17 34	19 01		19 49		20 48	
Flimby	d	06x52	07x42	08x49		09x37	10x46	11x51		13x16	14x13	15x29	17x38	19x05		19x53		20x52	
Maryport	d	06 56	07 45	08 52		09 41	10 50	11 55		13 20	14 17	15 32	17 42	19 09		19 57		20 56	
Aspatria	d	07x05	07x55	09x02		09x50	10x59	12x04		13x29	14x26	15x42	17x51	19x18		20x06		21x05	
Wigton	d	07 15	08 05	09 12		10 00	11 09	12 14		13 39	14 36	15 52	18 01	19 28		20 16		21 15	
Dalston	d	07x24	08x13	09x20		10x08	11x18	12x23		13x48	14x45	16x00	18x10	19x37		20x25		21x24	
Carlisle ■	a	07 38	08 27	09 36		10 24	11 34	12 39		14 04	15 01	16 16	18 26	19 53		20 41		21 39	

Table 100

Saturdays

from 23 July

Barrow-in-Furness - Whitehaven and Carlisle

			NT	NT	NT	NT	NT	NT	NT	NT	NT		NT	NT	NT	NT	NT	NT	NT	NT	NT		NT
Lancaster 6	82	d							09 03				11 28		13 32	14 22		17 00					
Barrow-in-Furness		d		06 00	07 05	08 01		09 07	10 11	11 22			12 34	13 50	14 50	15 33	17 25	18 10		19 35			21 25
Askam		d		06 10	07 15	08 11		09 17	10 21	11 32			12 44	14 00	15 00	15 43	17 35	18 20		19 45			21 35
Kirkby-in-Furness		d		06x14	07x19	08x15		09x21	10x25	11x36			12x48	14x04	15x04	15x47	17x39	18x24		19x49			21x39
Foxfield		d		06x17	07x23	08x18		09x24	10x28	11x39			12x51	14x07	15x07	15x50	17x42	18x27		19x52			21x42
Green Road		d		06x21	07x27	08x22		09x28	10x32	11x43			12x55	14x11	15x11	15x54	17x46	18x31		19x56			21x46
Millom		a		06 25	07 34	08 28		09 34	10 38	11 49			13 01	14 17	15 17	16 00	17 52	18 40		20 05			21 55
		d		06 26	07 34	08 29		09 35	10 39	11 50			13 02	14 18	15 18	16 01	17 53						
Silecroft		d		06x30	07x39			09x39	10x43	11x54			13x06	14x22	15x22	16x05	17x57						
Bootle		d		06x37	07x46			09x46	10x50	12x01			13x13	14x29	15x29	16x12	18x04						
Ravenglass for Eskdale		d		06 42	07 52	08 44		09 52	10 56	12 07			13 19	14 35	15 35	16 18	18 10						
Drigg		d		06x45	07x56			09x55	10x59	12x10			13x22	14x38	15x38	16x21	18x13						
Seascale		d		06x50	07x59	08x49		09x58	11x04	12x13			13x25	14x41	15x41	16x24	18x16						
Sellafield		d		06 55	08 06	08a58		10 04	11 10	12 19			13 31	14 47	15 51	16 30	18 22						
Braystones		d		06x59	08x09											16x34	18x26						
Nethertown		d		07x01	08x12											16x36	18x28						
St Bees		d		07 06	08 16			10 14	11 19	12 29			13 40	14 56	16 01	16 46	18 33						
Corkickle		d		07x11	08x21			10x19	11x24	12x34			13x45	15x01	16x06	16x51	18x38						
Whitehaven		a		07 15	08 25			10 22	11 27	12 41			13 49	15 05	16 09	16 54	18 41						
		d	06 30	07 19	08 26		09 15	10 24	11 29		12 54		13 50	15 06	16 11	16 56	18 43		19 31		20 30		
Parton		d	06x33	07x23	08x30		09x18	10x27	11x32		12x57		13x54	15x10	16x15	17x00	18x46		19x34		20x33		
Harrington		d	06x41	07x31	08x38		09x26	10x35	11x40		13x05		14x02	15x18	16x23	17x08	18x54		19x42		20x41		
Workington		d	06 48	07 37	08 44		09 33	10 42	11 47		13 12		14 09	15 24	16 29	17 14	19 01		19 49		20 48		
Flimby		d	06x52	07x42	08x49		09x37	10x46	11x51		13x16		14x13	15x29	16x34	17x19	19x05		19x53		20x52		
Maryport		d	06 56	07 45	08 52		09 41	10 50	11 55		13 20		14 17	15 32	16 37	17 22	19 09		19 57		20 56		
Aspatria		d	07x05	07x55	09x02		09x50	10x59	12x04		13x29		14x26	15x42	16x47	17x32	19x18		20x06		21x05		
Wigton		d	07 15	08 05	09 12		10 00	11 09	12 14		13 39		14 36	15 52	16 57	17 42	19 28		20 16		21 15		
Dalston		d	07x24	08x13	09x20		10x08	11x18	12x23		13x48		14x45	16x00	17x05	17x50	19x37		20x25		21x24		
Carlisle 8		a	07 38	08 27	09 36		10 24	11 34	12 39		14 04		15 01	16 16	17 21	18 06	19 53		20 41		21 39		

Table 100

Sundays

Barrow-in-Furness - Whitehaven and Carlisle

			NT	NT	NT
Lancaster 6	82	d			
Barrow-in-Furness		d			
Askam		d			
Kirkby-in-Furness		d			
Foxfield		d			
Green Road		d			
Millom		a			
		d			
Silecroft		d			
Bootle		d			
Ravenglass for Eskdale		d			
Drigg		d			
Seascale		d			
Sellafield		d			
Braystones		d			
Nethertown		d			
St Bees		d			
Corkickle		d			
Whitehaven		a			
		d	12 57	16 28	20 28
Parton		d	13x00	16x31	20x31
Harrington		d	13x08	16x39	20x39
Workington		d	13 15	16 46	20 46
Flimby		d	13x19	16x50	20x50
Maryport		d	13 23	16 54	20 54
Aspatria		d	13x32	17x03	21x03
Wigton		d	13 42	17 13	21 13
Dalston		d	13x50	17x21	21x21
Carlisle 8		a	14 07	17 37	21 38

No Sunday Service Barrow-in-Furness to Whitehaven

Table 100

Mondays to Fridays

until 15 July

Carlisle and Whitehaven - Barrow-in-Furness

Miles			NT	NT	NT	NT	NT	NT	NT	NT	NT	NT	NT	NT	NT	NT	NT	NT	NT	NT	NT	NT
0	**Carlisle** 8	d				07 44		08 44	09 40	10 43	11 54	12 47	14 20	15 12	16 31	17 27	17 59	19 15		20 33	21 50	
4	Dalston	d				07x52		08x52	09x48	10x51	12x02	12x55	14x28	15x20	16x39	17x35	18x07	19x23		20x41	21x58	
11½	Wigton	d				08 01		09 01	09 57	11 00	12 11	13 04	14 37	15 29	16 48	17 44	18 16	19 32		20 50	22 07	
19¾	Aspatria	d				08x11		09x11	10x07	11x10	12x21	13x14	14x47	15x39	16x58	17x54	18x26	19x42		21x00	22x17	
27¼	Maryport	d		06 00		08 21		09 21	10 17	11 20	12 31	13 24	14 57	15 49	17 08	18 04	18 37	19 52		21 10	22 27	
29¼	Flimby	d		06x03		08x24		09x24	10x20	11x23	12x34	13x27	15x00	15x52	17x11	18x07	18x40	19x55		21x13	22x30	
33	**Workington**	d		06 09		08 33		09 33	10 29	11 32	12 43	13 36	15 09	16 01	17 20	18 16	18 48	20 04		21 22	22 39	
34¾	Harrington	d		06x13		08x36		09x36	10x32	11x35	12x46	13x39	15x12	16x04	17x23	18x19	18x52	20x07		21x25	22x42	
38¼	Parton	d		06x21		08x45		09x45	10x42	11x44	12x56	13x48	15x21	16x13	17x32	18x28	19x00	20x16		21x34	22x51	
39½	**Whitehaven**	a		06 26		08 54		09 49	10 47	11 50	13 04	13 54	15 27	16 19	17 38	18 34	19 10	20 25		21 43	23 00	
—		d		06 28	07 28			09 51	10 48	11 51		13 56	15 28	16 20	17 39	18 35						
40½	Corkickle	d		06x30	07x30			09x53	10x50	11x53		13x58	15x30	16x22	17x41	18x37						
44	St Bees	d		06 35	07 35			09 58	10 56	11 59		14 03	15 36	16 28	17 50	18 43						
47	Nethertown	d		06x39						12x03			15x40		17x54							
48¼	Braystones	d		06x42						12x05			15x42		17x57							
50¼	Sellafield	d		06 48	07 48		09 07	10 09	11 08	12 11		14 14	15b54	16 42	18 03	18 54						
52	Seascale	d		06x51	07x51		09x10	10x14	11x11	12x14		14x17	15x57	16x45	18x07	18x57						
54¼	Drigg	d		06x54	07x54		09x13	10x17	11x14	12x17		14x20	16x01	16x49	18x11	19x00						
56	Ravenglass for Eskdale	d		06 57	07 57		09 16	10 20	11 18	12 21		14 23	16 04	16 52	18 14	19 03						
60¾	Bootle	d		07x03	08x03		09x22	10x26	11x23	12x26		14x29	16x10	16x58	18x20	19x09						
66¼	Silecroft	d		07x09	08x09		09x28	10x32	11x30	12x33		14x35	16x17	17x05	18x27	19x15						
69¼	Millom	a		07 16	08 14		09 35	10 39	11 37	12 40		14 42	16 24	17 12	18 34	19 22						
—		d	06 10	07 17	08 15		09 36	10 40	11 37	12 40		14 43	16 25	17 13	18 34	19 23			20 12			22 02
71¾	Green Road	d	06x14	07x21	08x19		09x40	10x44	11x41	12x44		14x47	16x29	17x17	18x39	19x27			20x16			22x06
73¾	Foxfield	d	06x17	07x24	08x22		09x43	10x47	11x44	12x47		14x50	16x33	17x21	18x43	19x30			20x19			22x09
76	Kirkby-in-Furness	d	06x21	07x28	08x26		09x47	10x51	11x48	12x51		14x54	16x38	17x26	18x47	19x34			20x23			22x13
79¼	Askam	d	06 26	07 33	08 31		09 52	10 56	11 53	12 56		14 59	16 43	17 31	18 52	19 39			20 28			22 18
85¼	**Barrow-in-Furness**	a	06 42	07 49	08 49		10 07	11 14	12 09	13 12		15 17	17 01	17 47	19 10	19 57			20 45			22 35
—	Lancaster 6 82	a																				

Mondays to Fridays

from 18 July

		NT	NT	NT	NT	NT	NT	NT	NT	NT	NT	NT	NT	NT	NT	NT	NT	NT	NT	NT	NT
Carlisle 8	d				07 44		08 44	09 40	10 43	11 50	12 47	14 20	15 12	16 31	17 27	17 59	19 15		20 33	21 50	
Dalston	d				07x52		08x52	09x48	10x51	11x58	12x55	14x28	15x20	16x39	17x35	18x07	19x23		20x41	21x58	
Wigton	d				08 01		09 01	09 57	11 00	12 07	13 04	14 37	15 29	16 48	17 44	18 16	19 32		20 50	22 07	
Aspatria	d				08x11		09x11	10x07	11x10	12x17	13x14	14x47	15x39	16x58	17x54	18x26	19x42		21x00	22x17	
Maryport	d		06 00		08 21		09 21	10 17	11 20	12 27	13 24	14 57	15 49	17 08	18 04	18 37	19 52		21 10	22 27	
Flimby	d		06x03		08x24		09x24	10x20	11x23	12x30	13x27	15x00	15x52	17x11	18x07	18x40	19x55		21x13	22x30	
Workington	d		06 09		08 33		09 33	10 29	11 32	12 39	13 36	15 09	16 01	17 20	18 16	18 48	20 04		21 22	22 39	
Harrington	d		06x13		08x36		09x36	10x32	11x35	12x42	13x39	15x12	16x04	17x23	18x19	18x52	20x07		21x25	22x42	
Parton	d		06x21		08x45		09x45	10x42	11x44	12x52	13x48	15x21	16x13	17x32	18x28	19x00	20x16		21x34	22x51	
Whitehaven	a		06 26		08 54		09 49	10 47	11 50	13 00	13 54	15 27	16 19	17 38	18 34	19 10	20 25		21 43	23 00	
	d		06 28	07 28			09 51	10 48	11 51		13 56	15 28	16 20	17 39	18 35						
Corkickle	d		06x30	07x30			09x53	10x50	11x53		13x58	15x30	16x22	17x41	18x37						
St Bees	d		06 35	07 35			09 58	10 56	11 59		14 03	15 36	16 28	17 50	18 43						
Nethertown	d		06x39						12x03			15x40		17x54							
Braystones	d		06x42						12x05			15x42		17x57							
Sellafield	d		06 48	07 48		09 07	10 09	11 08	12 11		14 14	15 54	16 42	18 03	18 54						
Seascale	d		06x51	07x51		09x10	10x14	11x11	12x14		14x17	15x57	16x45	18x07	18x57						
Drigg	d		06x54	07x54		09x13	10x17	11x14	12x17		14x20	16x01	16x49	18x11	19x00						
Ravenglass for Eskdale	d		06 57	07 57		09 16	10 20	11 18	12 21		14 23	16 04	16 52	18 14	19 03						
Bootle	d		07x03	08x03		09x22	10x26	11x23	12x26		14x29	16x10	16x58	18x20	19x09						
Silecroft	d		07x09	08x09		09x28	10x32	11x30	12x33		14x35	16x17	17x05	18x27	19x15						
Millom	a		07 16	08 14		09 35	10 39	11 37	12 40		14 42	16 24	17 12	18 34	19 22						
	d	06 10	07 17	08 15		09 36	10 40	11 37	12 40		14 43	16 25	17 13	18 34	19 23			20 12			22 02
Green Road	d	06x14	07x21	08x19		09x40	10x44	11x41	12x44		14x47	16x29	17x17	18x39	19x27			20x16			22x06
Foxfield	d	06x17	07x24	08x22		09x43	10x47	11x44	12x47		14x50	16x33	17x21	18x43	19x30			20x19			22x09
Kirkby-in-Furness	d	06x21	07x28	08x26		09x47	10x51	11x48	12x51		14x54	16x38	17x26	18x47	19x34			20x23			22x13
Askam	d	06 26	07 33	08 31		09 52	10 56	11 53	12 56		14 59	16 43	17 31	18 52	19 39			20 28			22 18
Barrow-in-Furness	a	06 42	07 49	08 49		10 07	11 14	12 09	13 12		15 17	17 01	17 47	19 10	19 57			20 45			22 35
Lancaster 6 82	a	08 04	09 07			11 20		13 16					19 05								

Saturdays

until 16 July

		NT	NT	NT	NT	NT	NT	NT	NT	NT	NT	NT	NT	NT	NT	NT	NT	NT	NT	NT	NT
Carlisle 8	d			07 44		08 37	09 40	10 43	11 39		12 48	14 21	15 25	16 30	17 40	18 15	19 00	20 05		21 45	
Dalston	d			07x52		08x45	09x48	10x51	11x47		12x56	14x29	15x33	16x38	17x48	18 24	19x08	20x13		21x53	
Wigton	d			08 01		08 54	09 57	11 00	11 56		13 05	14 38	15 42	16 47	17 57	18 33	19 17	20 22		22 02	
Aspatria	d			08x11		09x04	10x07	11x10	12x06		13x15	14x48	15x52	16x57	18x07	18 43	19x27	20x32		22x12	
Maryport	d		06 00	08 21		09 14	10 17	11 20	12 16		13 25	14 58	16 02	17 07	18 17	18 54	19 37	20 42		22 22	
Flimby	d		06x03	08x24		09x17	10x20	11x23	12x19		13x28	15x01	16x05	17x10	18x20	18 57	19x40	20x45		22x25	
Workington	d		06 09	08 33		09 26	10 29	11 32	12 28		13 37	15 10	16 14	17 19	18 29	19 06	19 49	20 54		22 34	
Harrington	d		06x13	08x36		09x29	10x32	11x35	12x31		13x40	15x14	16x18	17x23	18x32	19 10	19x52	20x57		22x37	
Parton	d		06x21	08x45		09x38	10x40	11x44	12x40		13x49	15x22	16x26	17x31	18x41	19x19	20x01	21x06		22x46	
Whitehaven	a		06 26	08 54		09 44	10 47	11 50	12 49		13 55	15 28	16 32	17 37	18 47	19 28	20 10	21 15		22 55	
	d		06 28			09 45	10 48	11 51		12 54	13 57	15 30	16 34	17 39	18 48						
Corkickle	d		06x30			09x47	10x50	11x53		12x56	13x59	15x32	16x36	17x41	18x50						
St Bees	d		06 35			09 53	10 56	11 59		13 01	14 04	15 37	16 43	17 46	18 56						
Nethertown	d		06x39					12x03				15x41		17x50							
Braystones	d		06x42					12x05				15x44		17x53							
Sellafield	d		06 48		09 07	10 03	11 06	12 12		13 12	14 15	15 50	16 53	17 59	19 06						
Seascale	d		06x51		09x10	10x06	11x09	12x15		13x15	14x18	15x53	16x56	18x02	19x09						
Drigg	d		06x54		09x13	10x09	11x12	12x18		13x18	14x21	15x56	16x59	18x05	19x12						
Ravenglass for Eskdale	d		06 57		09 16	10 13	11 16	12 22		13 21	14 24	15 59	17 03	18 08	19 16						
Bootle	d		07x03		09x22	10x18	11x21	12x27		13x27	14x30	16x05	17x08	18x14	19x21						
Silecroft	d		07x09		09x28	10x25		12x34		13x33	14x36	16x11	17x15	18x20	19x28						
Millom	a		07 16		09 35	10 32	11 33	12 41		13 40	14 43	16 18	17 22	18 27	19 35						
	d	06 10	07 17		09 36	10 32	11 33	12 41		13 41	14 44	16 19	17 22	18 28	19 36				20 12		22 02
Green Road	d	06x14	07x21		09x40	10x36		12x45		13x45	14x48	16x23	17x26	18x32	19x40				20x16		22x06
Foxfield	d	06x17	07x24		09x43	10x40	11x40	12x49		13x48	14x51	16x26	17x30	18x35	19x43				20x19		22x09
Kirkby-in-Furness	d	06x21	07x28		09x47	10x44	11x44	12x53		13x52	14x55	16x30	17x34	18x39	19x47				20x23		22x13
Askam	d	06 26	07 33		09 52	10 49	11 49	12 58		13 57	15 00	16 35	17 39	18 44	19 52				20 28		22 18
Barrow-in-Furness	a	06 42	07 49		10 07	11 07	12 05	13 16		14 13	15 16	16 53	17 55	19 02	20 10				20 45		22 35
Lancaster 6 82	a																				

Table 100

Saturdays
from 23 July

Carlisle and Whitehaven - Barrow-in-Furness

		NT	NT	NT	NT	NT	NT	NT	NT	NT		NT	NT	NT	NT	NT	NT	NT	NT	NT		NT	NT		
Carlisle 8	d			07 44		08 37	09 40	10 43	11 39			12 48	14 21	15 25	16 30	17 40	18 15	19 00	20 05			21 45			
Dalston	d			07x52		08x45	09x48	10x51	11x47			12x56	14x29	15x33	16x38	17x48	18 24	19x08	20x13			21x53			
Wigton	d			08 01		08 54	09 57	11 00	11 56			13 05	14 38	15 42	16 47	17 57	18 33	19 17	20 22			22 02			
Aspatria	d			08x11		09x04	10x07	11x10	12x06			13x15	14x48	15x52	16x57	18x07	18 43	19x27	20x32			22x12			
Maryport	d		06 26	08 21		09 14	10 17	11 20	12 16			13 25	14 58	16 02	17 07	18 17	18 54	19 37	20 42			22 22			
Flimby	d		06x29	08x24		09x17	10x20	11x23	12x19			13x28	15x01	16x05	17x10	18x20	18 57	19x40	20x45			22x25			
Workington	d		06 37	08 33		09 26	10 29	11 32	12 28			13 37	15 10	16 14	17 19	18 29	19 06	19 49	20 54			22 34			
Harrington	d		06x41	08x36		09x29	10x32	11x35	12x31			13x40	15x14	16x18	17x23	18x32	19 10	19x52	20x57			22x37			
Parton	d		06x49	08x45		09x38	10x40	11x44	12x40			13x49	15x22	16x26	17x31	18x41	19x19	20x01	21x06			22x46			
Whitehaven	a		06 55	08 54		09 44	10 47	11 50	12 49			13 55	15 28	16 32	17 37	18 47	19 28	20 10	21 15			22 55			
	d		06 57			09 45	10 48	11 51		12 54		13 57	15 30	16 34	17 39	18 48									
Corkickle	d		06x59			09x47	10x50	11x53		12x56		13x59	15x32	16x36	17x41	18x50									
St Bees	d		07 10			09 53	10 56	11 59		13 01		14 04	15 37	16 43	17 46	18 56									
Nethertown	d		07x14				11x00						15x41		17x50										
Braystones	d		07x16				11x02						15x44		17x53										
Sellafield	d		07 22		09 07	10 03	11 08	12 10		13 12		14 15	15 50	16 53	17 59	19 06									
Seascale	d		07x25		09x10	10x06	11x11	12x13		13x15		14x18	15x53	16x56	18x02	19x09									
Drigg	d		07x28		09x13	10x09	11x14	12x16		13x18		14x21	15x56	16x59	18x05	19x12									
Ravenglass for Eskdale	d		07 32		09 16	10 13	11 18	12 20		13 21		14 24	15 59	17 03	18 08	19 16									
Bootle	d		07x37		09x22	10x18	11x23	12x25		13x27		14x30	16x05	17x08	18x14	19x21									
Silecroft	d		07x44		09x28	10x25	11x30	12x32		13x33		14x36	16x11	17x15	18x20	19x28									
Millom	a		07 51		09 35	10 32	11 37	12 39		13 40		14 43	16 18	17 22	18 27	19 35									
	d	06 10	07 51		09 36	10 32	11 37	12 39		13 41		14 44	16 19	17 22	18 28	19 36				20 12			22 02		
Green Road	d	06x14	07x55		09x40	10x36	11x41	12x43		13x45		14x48	16x23	17x26	18x32	19x40				20x16			22x06		
Foxfield	d	06x17	07x59		09x43	10x40	11x44	12x47		13x48		14x51	16x26	17x30	18x35	19x43				20x19			22x09		
Kirkby-in-Furness	d	06x21	08x03		09x47	10x44	11x48	12x51		13x52		14x55	16x30	17x34	18x39	19x47				20x23			22x13		
Askam	d	06 26	08 08		09 52	10 49	11 53	12 56		13 57		15 00	16 35	17 39	18 44	19 52				20 28			22 18		
Barrow-in-Furness	a	06 42	08 24		10 07	11 07	12 09	13 14		14 13		15 16	16 53	17 55	19 02	20 10				20 45			22 35		
Lancaster 6 82	a		09 33		11 21		13 16			15 20		16 24		19 05											

Sundays

		NT	NT	NT
Carlisle 8	d	15 00	19 00	21 50
Dalston	d	15x08	19x08	21x58
Wigton	d	15 17	19 17	22 07
Aspatria	d	15x27	19x27	22x17
Maryport	d	15 37	19 37	22 27
Flimby	d	15x40	19x40	22x30
Workington	d	15 49	19 49	22 39
Harrington	d	15x52	19x52	22x42
Parton	d	16x01	20x01	22x51
Whitehaven	a	16 10	20 10	23 00
	d			
Corkickle	d			
St Bees	d			
Nethertown	d			
Braystones	d			
Sellafield	d			
Seascale	d			
Drigg	d			
Ravenglass for Eskdale	d			
Bootle	d			
Silecroft	d			
Millom	a			
	d			
Green Road	d			
Foxfield	d			
Kirkby-in-Furness	d			
Askam	d			
Barrow-in-Furness	a			
Lancaster 6 82	a			

No Sunday Service Whitehaven to Barrow-in-Furness

Network Diagram for Tables 101, 103, 106, 109

DM-14/06(2)
Design BAJS

© Network Rail OPSU 2006.
All rights reserved

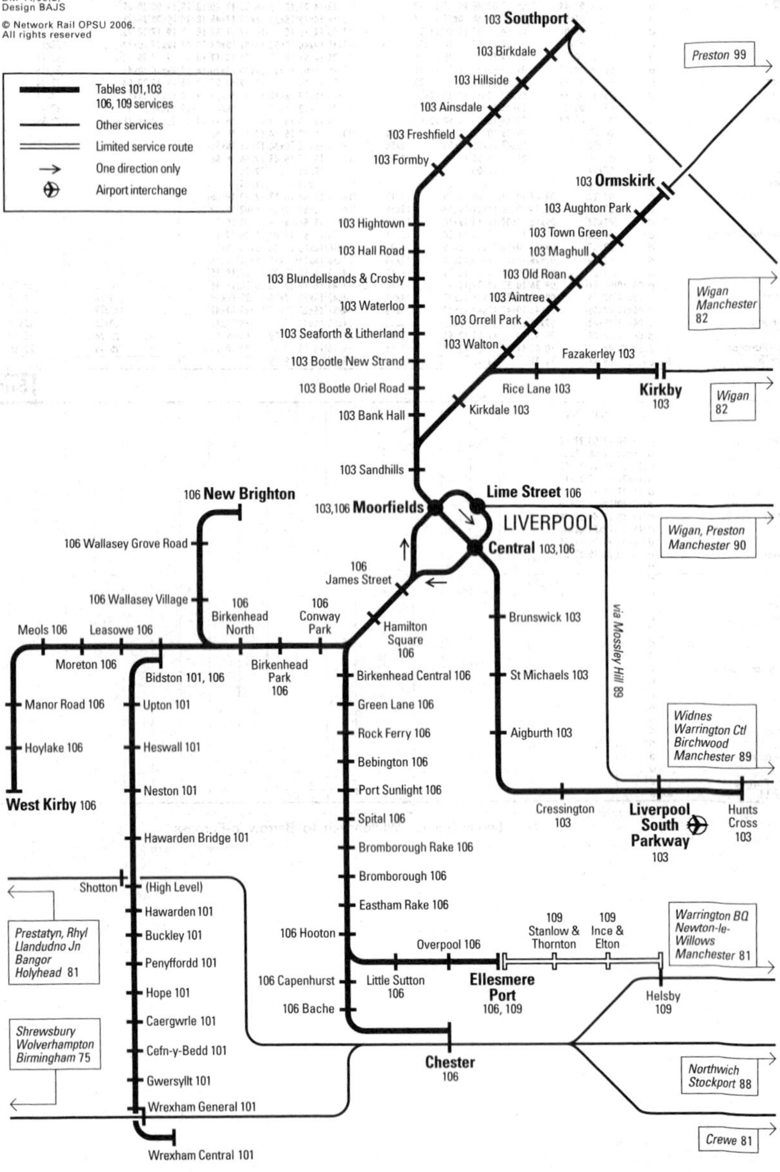

Table 101

Mondays to Fridays

Wrexham - Bidston

Miles			AW	AW BHX	AW	AW BHX	AW	AW BHX	AW	AW BHX	AW		AW BHX	AW	AW BHX	AW	AW
0	**Wrexham Central**	d		07 28	08 30	09 30	10 30	11 30	12 30	13 30	14 30		15 30	16 30	17 43	19 44	21 55
0½	**Wrexham General**	a		07 30	08 32	09 32	10 32	11 32	12 32	13 32	14 32		15 32	16 32	17 45	19 46	21 57
—		d	06 31	07 30	08 32	09 32	10 32	11 32	12 32	13 32	14 32		15 32	16 32	17 45	19 46	21 57
2¼	Gwersyllt	d	06 35	07 34	08 36	09 36	10 36	11 36	12 36	13 36	14 36		15 36	16 36	17 49	19 50	22 01
4	Cefn-y-Bedd	d	06 40	07 39	08 41	09 41	10 41	11 41	12 41	13 41	14 41		15 41	16 41	17 54	19 55	22 06
4¾	Caergwrle	d	06 42	07 41	08 43	09 43	10 43	11 43	12 43	13 43	14 43		15 43	16 43	17 56	19 57	22 08
5¼	Hope (Flintshire)	d	06 44	07 43	08 45	09 45	10 45	11 45	12 45	13 45	14 45		15 45	16 45	17 58	19 59	22 10
7¼	Penyffordd	d	06 48	07 47	08 49	09 49	10 49	11 49	12 49	13 49	14 49		15 49	16 49	18 02	20 03	22 14
8½	Buckley	d	06 51	07 50	08 52	09 52	10 52	11 52	12 52	13 52	14 52		15 52	16 52	18 05	20 06	22 17
10½	Hawarden	d	06 55	07 54	08 56	09 56	10 56	11 56	12 56	13 56	14 56		15 56	16 56	18 09	20 10	22 21
12¾	Shotton High Level	d	06 59	07 59	09 00	10 00	11 00	12 00	13 00	14 00	15 00		16 00	17 00	18 13	20 14	22 25
13¼	Hawarden Bridge	d	07x01	08x01										17x02			
18¾	Neston	d	07 10	08 10	09 10	10 10	11 10	12 10	13 10	14 10	15 10		16 10	17 11	18 23	20 24	22 35
21¼	Heswall	d	07 15	08 15	09 15	10 15	11 15	12 15	13 15	14 15	15 15		16 15	17 16	18 28	20 29	22 40
25½	Upton	d	07 21	08 21	09 21	10 21	11 21	12 21	13 21	14 21	15 21		16 21	17 22	18 34	20 35	22 46
27½	**Bidston**	a	07 30	08 30	09 31	10 30	11 30	12 30	13 30	14 30	15 30		16 30	17 31	18 45	20 44	22 55

Saturdays

		AW	AW	AW	AW	AW	AW	AW	AW	AW		AW	AW	AW	AW	AW
Wrexham Central	d		07 28	08 30	09 30	10 30	11 30	12 30	13 30	14 30		15 30	16 30	17 43	19 44	21 55
Wrexham General	a		07 30	08 32	09 32	10 32	11 32	12 32	13 32	14 32		15 32	16 32	17 45	19 46	21 57
	d	06 31	07 30	08 32	09 32	10 32	11 32	12 32	13 32	14 32		15 32	16 32	17 45	19 46	21 57
Gwersyllt	d	06 35	07 34	08 36	09 36	10 36	11 36	12 36	13 36	14 36		15 36	16 36	17 49	19 50	22 01
Cefn-y-Bedd	d	06 40	07 39	08 41	09 41	10 41	11 41	12 41	13 41	14 41		15 41	16 41	17 54	19 55	22 06
Caergwrle	d	06 42	07 41	08 43	09 43	10 43	11 43	12 43	13 43	14 43		15 43	16 43	17 56	19 57	22 08
Hope (Flintshire)	d	06 44	07 43	08 45	09 45	10 45	11 45	12 45	13 45	14 45		15 45	16 45	17 58	19 59	22 10
Penyffordd	d	06 48	07 47	08 49	09 49	10 49	11 49	12 49	13 49	14 49		15 49	16 49	18 02	20 03	22 14
Buckley	d	06 51	07 50	08 52	09 52	10 52	11 52	12 52	13 52	14 52		15 52	16 52	18 05	20 06	22 17
Hawarden	d	06 55	07 54	08 56	09 56	10 56	11 56	12 56	13 56	14 56		15 56	16 56	18 09	20 10	22 21
Shotton High Level	d	06 59	07 59	09 00	10 00	11 00	12 00	13 00	14 00	15 00		16 00	17 00	18 13	20 14	22 25
Hawarden Bridge	d	07x01	08x01										17x02			
Neston	d	07 10	08 10	09 10	10 10	11 10	12 10	13 10	14 10	15 10		16 10	17 11	18 23	20 24	22 35
Heswall	d	07 15	08 15	09 15	10 15	11 15	12 15	13 15	14 15	15 15		16 15	17 16	18 28	20 29	22 40
Upton	d	07 21	08 21	09 21	10 21	11 21	12 21	13 21	14 21	15 21		16 21	17 22	18 34	20 35	22 46
Bidston	a	07 30	08 30	09 31	10 30	11 30	12 30	13 30	14 30	15 30		16 30	17 31	18 45	20 44	22 55

Sundays

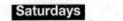

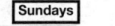

		AW	AW	AW	AW	AW	AW
Wrexham Central	d		11 11	13 41	16 11	18 41	21 11
Wrexham General	a		11 13	13 43	16 13	18 43	21 13
	d	08 44	11 14	13 44	16 14	18 44	21 14
Gwersyllt	d	08 48	11 18	13 48	16 18	18 48	21 18
Cefn-y-Bedd	d	08 53	11 23	13 53	16 23	18 53	21 23
Caergwrle	d	08 55	11 25	13 55	16 25	18 55	21 25
Hope (Flintshire)	d	08 57	11 27	13 57	16 27	18 57	21 27
Penyffordd	d	09 01	11 31	14 01	16 31	19 01	21 31
Buckley	d	09 04	11 34	14 04	16 34	19 04	21 34
Hawarden	d	09 08	11 38	14 08	16 38	19 08	21 38
Shotton High Level	d	09 12	11 42	14 12	16 42	19 12	21 42
Hawarden Bridge	d						
Neston	d	09 22	11 52	14 22	16 52	19 22	21 52
Heswall	d	09 27	11 57	14 27	16 57	19 27	21 57
Upton	d	09 33	12 03	14 33	17 03	19 33	22 03
Bidston	a	09 42	12 12	14 42	17 12	19 42	22 12

For connections to Liverpool Lime Street please refer to Table 106

Table 101

Mondays to Fridays

Bidston - Wrexham

Miles			AW BHX	AW	AW BHX	AW	AW BHX	AW	AW BHX	AW	AW BHX		AW	AW BHX	AW	AW BHX	AW	AW
0	**Bidston**	d		07 31	08 31	09 32	10 32	11 32	12 32	13 32	14 32		15 32	16 31	17 45	18 46	20 56	22 56
2	Upton	d		07 32	08 32	09 33	10 33	11 33	12 33	13 33	14 33		15 33	16 32	17 46	18 47	20 57	22 57
6¼	Heswall	d		07 39	08 39	09 40	10 40	11 40	12 40	13 40	14 40		15 40	16 39	17 53	18 54	21 04	23 04
8¾	Neston	d		07 44	08 44	09 45	10 45	11 45	12 45	13 45	14 45		15 45	16 44	17 58	18 59	21 09	23 09
14¼	Hawarden Bridge	d		07x53	08x53									16x53	18x07			
14¾	Shotton High Level	d		07 55	08 55	09 55	10 55	11 55	12 55	13 55	14 55		15 55	16 55	18 09	19 09	21 19	23 20
17½	Hawarden	d		08 00	09 00	10 00	11 00	12 00	13 00	14 00	15 00		16 00	17 00	18 14	19 14	21 24	23 25
19	Buckley	d		08 05	09 05	10 05	11 05	12 05	13 05	14 05	15 05		16 05	17 05	18 19	19 19	21 29	23 30
20¼	Penyffordd	d		08 08	09 08	10 08	11 08	12 08	13 08	14 08	15 08		16 08	17 08	18 22	19 22	21 32	23 33
22¼	Hope (Flintshire)	d		08 12	09 12	10 12	11 12	12 12	13 12	14 12	15 12		16 12	17 12	18 26	19 26	21 36	23 37
22¾	Caergwrle	d		08 14	09 14	10 14	11 14	12 14	13 14	14 14	15 14		16 14	17 14	18 28	19 28	21 38	23 39
23½	Cefn-y-Bedd	d		08 16	09 16	10 16	11 16	12 16	13 16	14 16	15 16		16 16	17 16	18 30	19 30	21 40	23 41
25¼	Gwersyllt	d		08 20	09 20	10 20	11 20	12 20	13 20	14 20	15 20		16 20	17 20	18 34	19 34	21 44	23 47
27	**Wrexham General**	a		08 27	09 27	10 27	11 27	12 27	13 27	14 27	15 27		16 27	17 27	18 41	19 41	21 51	23 54
—		d	07 10	08 27	09 27	10 27	11 27	12 27	13 27	14 27	15 27		16 27	17 27	18 41	19 41	21 51	
27½	**Wrexham Central**	a	07 13	08 32	09 32	10 32	11 32	12 32	13 32	14 32	15 32		16 32	17 32	18 46	19 46	21 56	

Saturdays

		AW	AW	AW	AW	AW	AW	AW	AW	AW		AW	AW	AW	AW	AW	AW
Bidston	d		07 31	08 31	09 32	10 32	11 32	12 32	13 32	14 32		15 32	16 31	17 45	18 46	20 56	22 56
Upton	d		07 32	08 32	09 33	10 33	11 33	12 33	13 33	14 33		15 33	16 32	17 46	18 47	20 57	22 57
Heswall	d		07 39	08 39	09 40	10 40	11 40	12 40	13 40	14 40		15 40	16 39	17 53	18 54	21 04	23 04
Neston	d		07 44	08 44	09 45	10 45	11 45	12 45	13 45	14 45		15 45	16 44	17 58	18 59	21 09	23 09
Hawarden Bridge	d		07x53	08x53									16x53	18x07			
Shotton High Level	d		07 55	08 55	09 55	10 55	11 55	12 55	13 55	14 55		15 55	16 55	18 09	19 09	21 19	23 20
Hawarden	d		08 00	09 00	10 00	11 00	12 00	13 00	14 00	15 00		16 00	17 00	18 14	19 14	21 24	23 25
Buckley	d		08 05	09 05	10 05	11 05	12 05	13 05	14 05	15 05		16 05	17 05	18 19	19 19	21 29	23 30
Penyffordd	d		08 08	09 08	10 08	11 08	12 08	13 08	14 08	15 08		16 08	17 08	18 22	19 22	21 32	23 33
Hope (Flintshire)	d		08 12	09 12	10 12	11 12	12 12	13 12	14 12	15 12		16 12	17 12	18 26	19 26	21 36	23 37
Caergwrle	d		08 14	09 14	10 14	11 14	12 14	13 14	14 14	15 14		16 14	17 14	18 28	19 28	21 38	23 39
Cefn-y-Bedd	d		08 16	09 16	10 16	11 16	12 16	13 16	14 16	15 16		16 16	17 16	18 30	19 30	21 40	23 41
Gwersyllt	d		08 20	09 20	10 20	11 20	12 20	13 20	14 20	15 20		16 20	17 20	18 34	19 34	21 44	23 47
Wrexham General	a		08 27	09 27	10 27	11 27	12 27	13 27	14 27	15 27		16 27	17 27	18 41	19 41	21 51	23 54
	d	07 10	08 27	09 27	10 27	11 27	12 27	13 27	14 27	15 27		16 27	17 27	18 41	19 41	21 51	
Wrexham Central	a	07 13	08 32	09 32	10 32	11 32	12 32	13 32	14 32	15 32		16 32	17 32	18 46	19 46	21 56	

Sundays

		AW	AW	AW	AW	AW	AW
Bidston	d	09 57	12 27	14 57	17 27	19 57	22 27
Upton	d	09 58	12 28	14 58	17 28	19 58	22 28
Heswall	d	10 05	12 35	15 05	17 35	20 05	22 35
Neston	d	10 10	12 40	15 10	17 40	20 10	22 40
Hawarden Bridge	d						
Shotton High Level	d	10 20	12 50	15 20	17 50	20 20	22 50
Hawarden	d	10 25	12 55	15 25	17 55	20 25	22 55
Buckley	d	10 30	13 00	15 30	18 00	20 30	23 00
Penyffordd	d	10 33	13 03	15 33	18 03	20 33	23 03
Hope (Flintshire)	d	10 37	13 07	15 37	18 07	20 37	23 07
Caergwrle	d	10 39	13 09	15 39	18 09	20 39	23 09
Cefn-y-Bedd	d	10 41	13 11	15 41	18 11	20 41	23 11
Gwersyllt	d	10 45	13 15	15 45	18 15	20 45	23 15
Wrexham General	a	10 52	13 22	15 52	18 22	20 52	23 25
	d	10 53	13 23	15 53	18 23	20 53	
Wrexham Central	a	10 58	13 28	15 58	18 28	20 58	

For connections from Liverpool Lime Street please refer to Table 106

Llandudno - Blaenau Ffestiniog

Miles				AW ◇	AW ◇	AW ◇	AW ◇	AW ◇	AW ◇
0	**Llandudno**	81	d			10 22	13 22	16 20	19 03
1¾	Deganwy	81	d			10x26	13x26	16x24	19x07
3	**Llandudno Junction**	81	d	05 35	07 39	10 34	13 34	16 33	19 20
5	Glan Conwy		d		07x42	10x37	13x37	16x36	19x23
8½	Tal-y-Cafn		d	05 43	07 48	10 43	13 43	16 42	19 29
11½	Dolgarrog		d		07x53	10x48	13x48	16x47	19x34
14½	North Llanrwst		d	05 52	08x00	10x54	13x54	16x53	19x40
15	Llanrwst		d	05 53	08 02	10 56	13 56	16 55	19 42
18½	Betws-y-Coed		d	05 59	08 08	11 02	14 02	17 01	19 48
22¾	Pont-y-Pant		d		08x16	11x10	14x10	17x09	19x56
24¼	Dolwyddelan		d		08x19	11x13	14x13	17x12	19x59
26	Roman Bridge		d		08x23	11x17	14x17	17x16	20x03
31	**Blaenau Ffestiniog**		a	06 29	08 42	11 36	14 36	17 35	20 20

Saturdays

			AW ◇	AW ◇	AW ◇	AW ◇	AW ◇	AW ◇
Llandudno	81	d			10 22	13 22	16 20	19 03
Deganwy	81	d			10x26	13x26	16x24	19x07
Llandudno Junction	81	d	05 35	07 39	10 34	13 34	16 33	19b20
Glan Conwy		d		07x42	10x37	13x37	16x36	19x23
Tal-y-Cafn		d	05 43	07 48	10 43	13 43	16 42	19 29
Dolgarrog		d		07x53	10x48	13x48	16x47	19x34
North Llanrwst		d	05 52	08x00	10x54	13x54	16x53	19x40
Llanrwst		d	05 53	08 02	10 56	13 56	16 55	19 42
Betws-y-Coed		d	05 59	08 08	11 02	14 02	17 01	19 48
Pont-y-Pant		d		08x16	11x10	14x10	17x09	19x56
Dolwyddelan		d		08x19	11x13	14x13	17x12	19x59
Roman Bridge		d		08x23	11x17	14x17	17x16	20x03
Blaenau Ffestiniog		a	06 29	08 42	11 36	14 36	17 35	20 20

Sundays

until 11 September

			AW ◇	AW ◇	AW ◇
Llandudno	81	d	10 22	13 30	
Deganwy	81	d	10x26	13x34	
Llandudno Junction	81	d	10 32	13 40	16 15
Glan Conwy		d	10x35	13x43	16x18
Tal-y-Cafn		d	10 41	13 49	16 24
Dolgarrog		d	10x46	13x54	16x29
North Llanrwst		d	10x52	14x00	16x35
Llanrwst		d	10 54	14 02	16 37
Betws-y-Coed		d	11 00	14 08	16 43
Pont-y-Pant		d	11x08	14x16	16x51
Dolwyddelan		d	11x11	14x19	16x54
Roman Bridge		d	11x15	14x23	16x58
Blaenau Ffestiniog		a	11 32	14 40	17 15

For connections from Crewe, Chester, Rhyl and Bangor (Gwynedd) please refer to Table 81

On Sundays from 18th September 2011 until 4th December 2011
A bus service is available at Llandudno Junction Station to various destinations between Blaenau Ffestiniog & Llandudno, please contact Traveline 0871 200 22 33 for further information on these services or contact a staff member at Llandudno Junction upon arrival

Table 102

Mondays to Fridays

Blaenau Ffestiniog - Llandudno

Miles				AW	AW		AW	AW		AW	AW
				◇	◇		◇	◇		◇	◇
—	**Blaenau Ffestiniog**		d	06 30	08 46		11 46	14 57		17 37	20 23
—	Roman Bridge		d	06x40	08x56		11x56	15x07		17x47	20x33
6¾	Dolwyddelan		d	06x43	09x00		12x00	15x11		17x51	20x37
8¼	Pont-y-Pant		d	06x46	09x03		12x03	15x14		17x54	20x40
12½	Betws-y-Coed		d	06 56	09 13		12 13	15 24		18 04	20 50
16	Llanrwst		d	07 02	09 19		12 19	15 30		18 10	20 56
16½	North Llanrwst		d	07x03	09x20		12x20	15x31		18x11	20x57
19½	Dolgarrog		d	07x09	09x27		12x27	15x38		18x18	21x04
22½	Tal-y-Cafn		d	07x15	09x33		12x33	15x44		18x24	21x10
26	Glan Conwy		d	07x21	09x39		12x39	15x50		18x30	21x16
28	**Llandudno Junction**	81	a	07 31	09 45		12 45	15 56		18 35	21 21
29¼	Deganwy	81	a		10x03		13x03	16x07		18x44	21x35
31	**Llandudno**	81	a		10 13		13 13	16 17		18 54	21 46

Saturdays

			AW	AW		AW	AW		AW	AW
			◇	◇		◇	◇		◇	◇
Blaenau Ffestiniog		d	06 30	08 46		11 46	14 57		17 37	20 23
Roman Bridge		d	06x40	08x56		11x56	15x07		17x47	20x33
Dolwyddelan		d	06x43	09x00		12x00	15x11		17x51	20x37
Pont-y-Pant		d	06x46	09x03		12x03	15x14		17x54	20x40
Betws-y-Coed		d	06 56	09 13		12 13	15 24		18 04	20 50
Llanrwst		d	07 02	09 19		12 19	15 30		18 10	20 56
North Llanrwst		d	07x03	09x20		12x20	15x31		18x11	20x57
Dolgarrog		d	07x09	09x27		12x27	15x38		18x18	21x04
Tal-y-Cafn		d	07x15	09x33		12x33	15x44		18x24	21x10
Glan Conwy		d	07x21	09x39		12x39	15x50		18x30	21x16
Llandudno Junction	81	a	07 31	09 45		12 45	15 56		18 35	21 21
Deganwy	81	a		10x03		13x03	16x03		18x44	21x35
Llandudno	81	a		10 13		13 13	16 13		18 54	21 46

Sundays

until 11 September

			AW	AW		AW
			◇	◇		◇
Blaenau Ffestiniog		d	11 45	15 03		17 30
Roman Bridge		d	11x55	15x13		17x40
Dolwyddelan		d	11x58	15x16		17x44
Pont-y-Pant		d	12x01	15x19		17x48
Betws-y-Coed		d	12 11	15 29		17 57
Llanrwst		d	12 17	15 35		18 03
North Llanrwst		d	12x18	15x36		18x05
Dolgarrog		d	12x24	15x42		18x11
Tal-y-Cafn		d	12x29	15x48		18x17
Glan Conwy		d	12x35	15x54		18x23
Llandudno Junction	81	a	12 40	15 59		18 29
Deganwy	81	a	12x45			18x34
Llandudno	81	a	12 55			18 44

For connections to Bangor (Gwynedd), Rhyl, Chester and Crewe please refer to Table 81

On Sundays from 18th September 2011 until 4th December 2011
A bus service is available at Llandudno Junction Station to various destinations between Blaenau Ffestiniog & Llandudno, please contact Traveline 0871 200 22 33 for further information on these services or contact a staff member at Llandudno Junction upon arrival

Hunts Cross and Liverpool - Kirkby, Ormskirk and Southport

Miles	Miles	Miles			ME	ME MX	ME MO	ME	ME	ME	ME	ME	ME		ME	ME	ME	ME	ME	ME	ME	ME	ME		ME
0	—	—	**Hunts Cross** 89	d	23p06	23p21									06 06		06 21			06 36		06 51			
1½	—	—	**Liverpool Sth Parkway** 7 89 ✈	d	23p09	23p24									06 09		06 24			06 39		06 54			
2½	—	—	Cressington	d	23p12	23p27									06 12		06 27			06 42		06 57			
3¼	—	—	Aigburth	d	23p14	23p29									06 14		06 29			06 44		06 59			
4½	—	—	St Michaels	d	23p16	23p31									06 16		06 31			06 46		07 01			
5¾	—	—	Brunswick	d	23p19	23p34									06 19		06 34			06 49		07 04			
7¼	0	0	**Liverpool Central** 10	a	23p23	23p38									06 23		06 38			06 53		07 08			
—	—	—		d	23p23	23p38	23p38	23p40	23p55		05 55	06 08	06 10		06 23	06 25	06 38	06 40	06 50	06 53	06 55	07 08	07 10		07 20
7¾	0½	0½	**Moorfields** 10	d	23p25	23p40	23p40	23p42	23p57		05 57	06 10	06 12		06 25	06 27	06 40	06 42	06 52	06 55	06 57	07 10	07 12		07 22
9¼	2	2	Sandhills	d	23p29	23p44	23p44	23p46	00 01	05 59	06 01	06 14	06 16		06 29	06 31	06 44	06 46	06 56	06 59	07 01	07 14	07 16		07 26
—	3	3	Kirkdale	d				23p49	00 04		06 04		06 19			06 34		06 49	06 59		07 04		07 19		07 29
—	—	4¼	Rice Lane	d					00 07		06 07					06 37			07 02						07 32
—	—	5¾	Fazakerley	d					00 10		06 10					06 40			07 03						07 34
—	—	7½	**Kirkby**	a					00 13		06 13					06 43			07 08						07 38
—	4¼	—	Walton (Merseyside)	d				23p52					06 22					06 52			07 07		07 22		
—	4½	—	Orrell Park	d				23p53					06 23					06 53			07 08		07 23		
—	5½	—	Aintree	d				23p56					06 26					06 56			07 11		07 26		
—	6¼	—	Old Roan	d				23p58					06 28					06 58			07 13		07 28		
—	8	—	Maghull	d				00 01					06 31					07 01			07 16		07 31		
—	10½	—	Town Green	d				00 05					06 35					07 05			07 20		07 35		
—	11½	—	Aughton Park	d				00 07					06 37					07 07			07 22		07 37		
—	12¾	—	**Ormskirk**	a				00 12					06 42					07 12			07 27		07 42		
10	—	—	Bank Hall	d	23p31	23p46	23p46			06 01		06 16			06 31		06 46			07 01		07 16			
10¾	—	—	Bootle Oriel Road	d	23p33	23p48	23p48			06 03		06 18			06 33		06 48			07 03		07 18			
11	—	—	Bootle New Strand	d	23p35	23p50	23p50			06 05		06 20			06 35		06 50			07 05		07 20			
12	—	—	Seaforth & Litherland	d	23p37	23p52	23p52			06 07		06 22			06 37		06 52			07 07		07 22			
13¼	—	—	Waterloo (Merseyside)	d	23p39	23p54	23p54			06 09		06 24			06 39		06 54			07 09		07 24			
14¼	—	—	Blundellsands & Crosby	d	23p42	23p57	23p57			06 12		06 27			06 42		06 57			07 12		07 27			
15	—	—	Hall Road	d	23p44	23p59	23p59			06 14		06 29			06 44		06 59			07 14		07 29			
17	—	—	Hightown	d	23p47	00 02	00 02			06 17		06 32			06 47		07 02			07 17		07 32			
19	—	—	Formby	d	23p51	00 06	00 06			06 21		06 36			06 51		07 06			07 21		07 36			
20	—	—	Freshfield	d	23p53	00 08	00 08			06 23		06 38			06 53		07 08			07 23		07 38			
22¾	—	—	Ainsdale	d	23p57	00 12	00 12			06 27		06 42			06 57		07 12			07 27		07 42			
24½	—	—	Hillside	d	23p59	00 15	00 15			06 30		06 45			07 00		07 15			07 30		07 45			
25¼	—	—	Birkdale	d	00 02	00 17	00 17			06 32		06 47			07 02		07 17			07 32		07 47			
26¼	—	—	**Southport**	a	00 07	00 22	00 22			06 37		06 52			07 07		07 22			07 37		07 52			

		ME	ME	ME	ME	ME	ME	ME	ME		ME	ME	ME	ME	ME	ME	ME	ME	ME SO		ME SX	ME	ME	ME SO	ME SX
Hunts Cross 89	d	07 06			07 21			07 36				07 51			08 06			08 21					08 36		
Liverpool Sth Parkway 7 89 ✈	d	07 09			07 24			07 39				07 54			08 09			08 24					08 39		
Cressington	d	07 12			07 27			07 42				07 57			08 12			08 27					08 42		
Aigburth	d	07 14			07 29			07 44				07 59			08 14			08 29					08 44		
St Michaels	d	07 16			07 31			07 46				08 01			08 16			08 31					08 46		
Brunswick	d	07 19			07 34			07 49				08 04			08 19			08 34					08 49		
Liverpool Central 10	a	07 23			07 38			07 53				08 08			08 23			08 38					08 53		
	d	07 23	07 25	07 35	07 38	07 40	07 50	07 53	07 55		08 05	08 08	08 10	08 20	08 23	08 25	08 35	08 38	08 40		08 40	08 50	08 53	08 55	08 55
Moorfields 10	d	07 25	07 27	07 37	07 40	07 42	07 52	07 55	07 57		08 07	08 10	08 12	08 22	08 25	08 27	08 37	08 40	08 42		08 42	08 52	08 55	08 57	08 57
Sandhills	d	07 29	07 31	07 41	07 44	07 46	07 56	07 59	08 01		08 11	08 14	08 16	08 26	08 29	08 31	08 41	08 44	08 46		08 46	08 56	08 59	09 01	09 01
Kirkdale	d		07 34	07 44		07 49	07 59		08 04		08 14		08 19	08 29		08 34	08 44		08 49		08 49	08 59		09 04	09 04
Rice Lane	d			07 47			08 02				08 17			08 32			08 47					09 02			
Fazakerley	d			07 49			08 04				08 19			08 34			08 49					09 05			
Kirkby	a			07 53			08 08				08 23			08 38			08 53					09 08			
Walton (Merseyside)	d		07 37			07 52			08 07				08 22			08 37			08 52		08 52			09 07	09 07
Orrell Park	d		07 38			07 53			08 08				08 23			08 38			08 53		08 53			09 08	09 08
Aintree	d		07 41			07 56			08 11				08 26			08 41			08 56		08 56			09 11	09 11
Old Roan	d		07 43			07 58			08 13				08 28			08 43			08 58		08 58			09 13	09 13
Maghull	d		07 46			08 01			08 16				08 31			08 46			09 01		09 01			09 16	09 16
Town Green	d		07 50			08 05			08 20				08 35			08 50			09 05		09 05			09 20	09 20
Aughton Park	d		07 52			08 07			08 22				08 37			08 52			09 07		09 07			09 22	09 22
Ormskirk	a		07 57			08 12			08 27				08 42			08 57			09 12		09 13			09 27	09 28
Bank Hall	d	07 31			07 46			08 01				08 16			08 31			08 46					09 01		
Bootle Oriel Road	d	07 33			07 48			08 03				08 18			08 33			08 48					09 03		
Bootle New Strand	d	07 35			07 50			08 05				08 20			08 35			08 50					09 05		
Seaforth & Litherland	d	07 37			07 52			08 07				08 22			08 37			08 52					09 07		
Waterloo (Merseyside)	d	07 39			07 54			08 09				08 24			08 39			08 54					09 09		
Blundellsands & Crosby	d	07 42			07 57			08 12				08 27			08 42			08 57					09 12		
Hall Road	d	07 44			07 59			08 14				08 29			08 44			08 59					09 14		
Hightown	d	07 47			08 02			08 17				08 32			08 47			09 02					09 17		
Formby	d	07 51			08 06			08 21				08 36			08 51			09 06					09 21		
Freshfield	d	07 53			08 08			08 23				08 38			08 53			09 08					09 23		
Ainsdale	d	07 57			08 12			08 27				08 42			08 57			09 12					09 27		
Hillside	d	08 00			08 15			08 30				08 45			09 00			09 15					09 30		
Birkdale	d	08 02			08 17			08 32				08 47			09 02			09 17					09 32		
Southport	a	08 07			08 22			08 37				08 52			09 07			09 22					09 37		

Table 103

Hunts Cross and Liverpool - Kirkby, Ormskirk and Southport

		ME	ME	ME	ME	ME	ME	ME	ME	ME SO	ME SX	ME	ME	ME	ME	ME	ME	ME	ME	ME	ME	ME	ME
Hunts Cross 89	d		08 51			09 06			09 21				09 36			09 51			10 06			10 21	
Liverpool Sth Parkway 7 89 ✈	d		08 54			09 09			09 24				09 39			09 54			10 09			10 24	
Cressington	d		08 57			09 12			09 27				09 42			09 57			10 12			10 27	
Aigburth	d		08 59			09 14			09 29				09 44			09 59			10 14			10 29	
St Michaels	d		09 01			09 16			09 31				09 46			10 01			10 16			10 31	
Brunswick	d		09 04			09 19			09 34				09 49			10 04			10 19			10 34	
Liverpool Central 10	a		09 08			09 23			09 38				09 53			10 08			10 23			10 38	
	d	09 05	09 08	09 10	09 20	09 23	09 25	09 35	09 38	09 40	09 40	09 50	09 53	09 55	10 05	10 08	10 10	10 20	10 23	10 25	10 35	10 38	10 40
Moorfields 10	d	09 07	09 10	09 12	09 22	09 25	09 27	09 37	09 40	09 42	09 42	09 52	09 55	09 57	10 07	10 10	10 12	10 22	10 25	10 27	10 37	10 40	10 42
Sandhills	d	09 11	09 14	09 16	09 26	09 29	09 31	09 41	09 44	09 46	09 46	09 56	09 59	10 01	10 11	10 14	10 16	10 26	10 29	10 31	10 41	10 44	10 46
Kirkdale	d	09 14		09 19	09 29		09 34	09 44		09 49	09 49	09 59		10 04	10 14		10 19	10 29		10 34	10 44		10 49
Rice Lane	d	09 17			09 32			09 47				10 02			10 17			10 32			10 47		
Fazakerley	d	09 19			09 34			09 49				10 04			10 19			10 34			10 49		
Kirkby	a	09 23			09 38			09 53				10 08			10 23			10 38			10 53		
Walton (Merseyside)	d			09 22			09 37			09 52	09 52			10 07			10 22			10 37			10 52
Orrell Park	d			09 23			09 38			09 53	09 53			10 08			10 23			10 38			10 53
Aintree	d			09 26			09 41			09 56	09 56			10 11			10 26			10 41			10 56
Old Roan	d			09 28			09 43			09 58	09 58			10 13			10 28			10 43			10 58
Maghull	d			09 31			09 46			10 01	10 01			10 16			10 31			10 46			11 01
Town Green	d			09 35			09 50			10 05	10 05			10 20			10 35			10 50			11 05
Aughton Park	d			09 37			09 52			10 07	10 07			10 22			10 37			10 52			11 07
Ormskirk	a			09 42			09 57			10 12	10 13			10 27			10 42			10 57			11 12
Bank Hall	d		09 16			09 31			09 46				10 01			10 16			10 31			10 46	
Bootle Oriel Road	d		09 18			09 33			09 48				10 03			10 18			10 33			10 48	
Bootle New Strand	d		09 20			09 35			09 50				10 05			10 20			10 35			10 50	
Seaforth & Litherland	d		09 22			09 37			09 52				10 07			10 22			10 37			10 52	
Waterloo (Merseyside)	d		09 24			09 39			09 54				10 09			10 24			10 39			10 54	
Blundellsands & Crosby	d		09 27			09 42			09 57				10 12			10 27			10 42			10 57	
Hall Road	d		09 29			09 44			09 59				10 14			10 29			10 44			10 59	
Hightown	d		09 32			09 47			10 02				10 17			10 32			10 47			11 02	
Formby	d		09 36			09 51			10 06				10 21			10 36			10 51			11 06	
Freshfield	d		09 38			09 53			10 08				10 23			10 38			10 53			11 08	
Ainsdale	d		09 42			09 57			10 12				10 27			10 42			10 57			11 12	
Hillside	d		09 45			10 00			10 15				10 30			10 45			11 00			11 15	
Birkdale	d		09 47			10 02			10 17				10 32			10 47			11 02			11 17	
Southport	a		09 52			10 07			10 22				10 37			10 52			11 07			11 22	

		ME	ME	ME	ME	ME	ME	ME	ME	ME	ME	ME	ME	ME	ME	ME	ME	ME	ME	ME	ME	ME
Hunts Cross 89	d		10 36			10 51			11 06			11 21			11 36			11 51			12 06	
Liverpool Sth Parkway 7 89 ✈	d		10 39			10 54			11 09			11 24			11 39			11 54			12 09	
Cressington	d		10 42			10 57			11 12			11 27			11 42			11 57			12 12	
Aigburth	d		10 44			10 59			11 14			11 29			11 44			11 59			12 14	
St Michaels	d		10 46			11 01			11 16			11 31			11 46			12 01			12 16	
Brunswick	d		10 49			11 04			11 19			11 34			11 49			12 04			12 19	
Liverpool Central 10	a		10 53			11 08			11 23			11 38			11 53			12 08			12 23	
	d	10 50	10 53	10 55	11 05	11 08	11 10	11 20	11 23	11 25	11 35	11 38	11 40	11 50	11 53	11 55	12 05	12 08	12 10	12 20	12 23	12 25
Moorfields 10	d	10 52	10 55	10 57	11 07	11 10	11 12	11 22	11 25	11 27	11 37	11 40	11 42	11 52	11 55	11 57	12 07	12 10	12 12	12 22	12 25	12 27
Sandhills	d	10 56	10 59	11 01	11 11	11 14	11 16	11 26	11 29	11 31	11 41	11 44	11 46	11 56	11 59	12 01	12 11	12 14	12 16	12 26	12 29	12 31
Kirkdale	d	10 59		11 04	11 14		11 19	11 29		11 34	11 44		11 49	11 59		12 04	12 14		12 19	12 29		12 34
Rice Lane	d	11 02			11 17			11 32			11 47			12 02			12 17			12 32		
Fazakerley	d	11 04			11 19			11 34			11 49			12 04			12 19			12 34		
Kirkby	a	11 08			11 23			11 38			11 53			12 08			12 23			12 38		
Walton (Merseyside)	d			11 07			11 22			11 37			11 52			12 07			12 22			12 37
Orrell Park	d			11 08			11 23			11 38			11 53			12 08			12 23			12 38
Aintree	d			11 11			11 26			11 41			11 56			12 11			12 26			12 41
Old Roan	d			11 13			11 28			11 43			11 58			12 13			12 28			12 43
Maghull	d			11 16			11 31			11 46			12 01			12 16			12 31			12 46
Town Green	d			11 20			11 35			11 50			12 05			12 20			12 35			12 50
Aughton Park	d			11 22			11 37			11 52			12 07			12 22			12 37			12 52
Ormskirk	a			11 27			11 42			11 57			12 12			12 27			12 42			12 57
Bank Hall	d		11 01			11 16			11 31			11 46			12 01			12 16			12 31	
Bootle Oriel Road	d		11 03			11 18			11 33			11 48			12 03			12 18			12 33	
Bootle New Strand	d		11 05			11 20			11 35			11 50			12 05			12 20			12 35	
Seaforth & Litherland	d		11 07			11 22			11 37			11 52			12 07			12 22			12 37	
Waterloo (Merseyside)	d		11 09			11 24			11 39			11 54			12 09			12 24			12 39	
Blundellsands & Crosby	d		11 12			11 27			11 42			11 57			12 12			12 27			12 42	
Hall Road	d		11 14			11 29			11 44			11 59			12 14			12 29			12 44	
Hightown	d		11 17			11 32			11 47			12 02			12 17			12 32			12 47	
Formby	d		11 21			11 36			11 51			12 06			12 21			12 36			12 51	
Freshfield	d		11 23			11 38			11 53			12 08			12 23			12 38			12 53	
Ainsdale	d		11 27			11 42			11 57			12 12			12 27			12 42			12 57	
Hillside	d		11 30			11 45			12 00			12 15			12 30			12 45			13 00	
Birkdale	d		11 32			11 47			12 02			12 17			12 32			12 47			13 02	
Southport	a		11 37			11 52			12 07			12 22			12 37			12 52			13 07	

Hunts Cross and Liverpool - Kirkby, Ormskirk and Southport

	ME	ME	ME	ME	ME	ME		ME	ME	ME	ME	ME	ME	ME	ME	ME		ME	ME	ME	ME	ME	ME	ME
Hunts Cross 89 d		12 21			12 36				12 51			13 06			13 21				13 36			13 51		
Liverpool Sth Parkway 7 89 ✈ d		12 24			12 39				12 54			13 09			13 24				13 39			13 54		
Cressington d		12 27			12 42				12 57			13 12			13 27				13 42			13 57		
Aigburth d		12 29			12 44				12 59			13 14			13 29				13 44			13 59		
St Michaels d		12 31			12 46				13 01			13 16			13 31				13 46			14 01		
Brunswick d		12 34			12 49				13 04			13 19			13 34				13 49			14 04		
Liverpool Central 10 a		12 38			12 53				13 08			13 23			13 38				13 53			14 08		
d	12 35	12 38	12 40	12 50	12 53	12 55		13 05	13 08	13 10	13 20	13 23	13 25	13 35	13 38	13 40		13 50	13 53	13 55	14 05	14 08	14 10	14 20
Moorfields 10 d	12 37	12 40	12 42	12 52	12 55	12 57		13 07	13 10	13 12	13 22	13 25	13 27	13 37	13 40	13 42		13 52	13 55	13 57	14 07	14 10	14 12	14 22
Sandhills d	12 41	12 44	12 46	12 56	12 59	13 01		13 11	13 14	13 16	13 26	13 29	13 31	13 41	13 44	13 46		13 56	13 59	14 01	14 11	14 14	14 16	14 26
Kirkdale d	12 44		12 49	12 59		13 04		13 14		13 19	13 29		13 34	13 44		13 49		13 59		14 04	14 14		14 19	14 29
Rice Lane d	12 47			13 02				13 17			13 32			13 47				14 02			14 17			14 32
Fazakerley d	12 49			13 04				13 19			13 34			13 49				14 04			14 19			14 34
Kirkby a	12 53			13 08				13 23			13 38			13 53				14 08			14 23			14 38
Walton (Merseyside) d			12 52			13 07				13 22			13 37			13 52				14 07			14 22	
Orrell Park d			12 53			13 08				13 23			13 38			13 53				14 08			14 23	
Aintree d			12 56			13 11				13 26			13 41			13 56				14 11			14 26	
Old Roan d			12 58			13 13				13 28			13 43			13 58				14 13			14 28	
Maghull d			13 01			13 16				13 31			13 46			14 01				14 16			14 31	
Town Green d			13 05			13 20				13 35			13 50			14 05				14 20			14 35	
Aughton Park d			13 07			13 22				13 37			13 52			14 07				14 22			14 37	
Ormskirk a			13 12			13 27				13 42			13 57			14 12				14 27			14 42	
Bank Hall d		12 46			13 01				13 16			13 31			13 46				14 01			14 16		
Bootle Oriel Road d		12 48			13 03				13 18			13 33			13 48				14 03			14 18		
Bootle New Strand d		12 50			13 05				13 20			13 35			13 50				14 05			14 20		
Seaforth & Litherland d		12 52			13 07				13 22			13 37			13 52				14 07			14 22		
Waterloo (Merseyside) d		12 54			13 09				13 24			13 39			13 54				14 09			14 24		
Blundellsands & Crosby d		12 57			13 12				13 27			13 42			13 57				14 12			14 27		
Hall Road d		12 59			13 14				13 29			13 44			13 59				14 14			14 29		
Hightown d		13 02			13 17				13 32			13 47			14 02				14 17			14 32		
Formby d		13 06			13 21				13 36			13 51			14 06				14 21			14 36		
Freshfield d		13 08			13 23				13 38			13 53			14 08				14 23			14 38		
Ainsdale d		13 12			13 27				13 42			13 57			14 12				14 27			14 42		
Hillside d		13 15			13 30				13 45			14 00			14 15				14 30			14 45		
Birkdale d		13 17			13 32				13 47			14 02			14 17				14 32			14 47		
Southport a		13 22			13 37				13 52			14 07			14 22				14 37			14 52		

	ME	ME		ME	ME	ME	ME	ME	ME	ME	ME	ME		ME	ME	ME	ME	ME	ME	ME	ME	ME		ME
Hunts Cross 89 d	14 06				14 21			14 36			14 51				15 06			15 21			15 36			
Liverpool Sth Parkway 7 89 ✈ d	14 09				14 24			14 39			14 54				15 09			15 24			15 39			
Cressington d	14 12				14 27			14 42			14 57				15 12			15 27			15 42			
Aigburth d	14 14				14 29			14 44			14 59				15 14			15 29			15 44			
St Michaels d	14 16				14 31			14 46			15 01				15 16			15 31			15 46			
Brunswick d	14 19				14 34			14 49			15 04				15 19			15 34			15 49			
Liverpool Central 10 a	14 23				14 38			14 53			15 08				15 23			15 38			15 53			
d	14 23	14 25		14 35	14 38	14 40	14 50	14 53	14 55	15 05	15 08	15 10		15 20	15 23	15 25	15 35	15 38	15 40	15 50	15 53	15 55		16 05
Moorfields 10 d	14 25	14 27		14 37	14 40	14 42	14 52	14 55	14 57	15 07	15 10	15 12		15 22	15 25	15 27	15 37	15 40	15 42	15 52	15 55	15 57		16 07
Sandhills d	14 29	14 31		14 41	14 44	14 46	14 56	14 59	15 01	15 11	15 14	15 16		15 26	15 29	15 31	15 41	15 44	15 46	15 56	15 59	16 01		16 11
Kirkdale d		14 34		14 44		14 49	14 59		15 04	15 14		15 19		15 29		15 34	15 44		15 49	15 59		16 04		16 14
Rice Lane d				14 47			15 02			15 17				15 32			15 47			16 02				16 17
Fazakerley d				14 49			15 04			15 19				15 34			15 49			16 04				16 19
Kirkby a				14 53			15 08			15 23				15 38			15 53			16 08				16 23
Walton (Merseyside) d		14 37				14 52			15 07			15 22				15 37			15 52			16 07		
Orrell Park d		14 38				14 53			15 08			15 23				15 38			15 53			16 08		
Aintree d		14 41				14 56			15 11			15 26				15 41			15 56			16 11		
Old Roan d		14 43				14 58			15 13			15 28				15 43			15 58			16 13		
Maghull d		14 46				15 01			15 16			15 31				15 46			16 01			16 16		
Town Green d		14 50				15 05			15 20			15 35				15 50			16 05			16 20		
Aughton Park d		14 52				15 07			15 22			15 37				15 52			16 07			16 22		
Ormskirk a		14 57				15 12			15 27			15 42				15 57			16 12			16 27		
Bank Hall d	14 31				14 46			15 01			15 16				15 31			15 46			16 01			
Bootle Oriel Road d	14 33				14 48			15 03			15 18				15 33			15 48			16 03			
Bootle New Strand d	14 35				14 50			15 05			15 20				15 35			15 50			16 05			
Seaforth & Litherland d	14 37				14 52			15 07			15 22				15 37			15 52			16 07			
Waterloo (Merseyside) d	14 39				14 54			15 09			15 24				15 39			15 54			16 09			
Blundellsands & Crosby d	14 42				14 57			15 12			15 27				15 42			15 57			16 12			
Hall Road d	14 44				14 59			15 14			15 29				15 44			15 59			16 14			
Hightown d	14 47				15 02			15 17			15 32				15 47			16 02			16 17			
Formby d	14 51				15 06			15 21			15 36				15 51			16 06			16 21			
Freshfield d	14 53				15 08			15 23			15 38				15 53			16 08			16 23			
Ainsdale d	14 57				15 12			15 27			15 42				15 57			16 12			16 27			
Hillside d	15 00				15 15			15 30			15 45				16 00			16 15			16 30			
Birkdale d	15 02				15 17			15 32			15 47				16 02			16 17			16 32			
Southport a	15 07				15 22			15 37			15 52				16 07			16 22			16 37			

Hunts Cross and Liverpool - Kirkby, Ormskirk and Southport

	ME	ME	ME	ME	ME	ME	ME	ME		ME	ME	ME	ME	ME	ME	ME SX	ME	ME		ME	ME	ME	ME	ME
Hunts Cross 89 d	15 51			16 06			16 21				16 36			16 51				17 06				17 21		
Liverpool Sth Parkway 7 89 ✈ d	15 54			16 09			16 24				16 39			16 54				17 09				17 24		
Cressington d	15 57			16 12			16 27				16 42			16 57				17 12				17 27		
Aigburth d	15 59			16 14			16 29				16 44			16 59				17 14				17 29		
St Michaels d	16 01			16 16			16 31				16 46			17 01				17 16				17 31		
Brunswick d	16 04			16 19			16 34				16 49			17 04				17 19				17 34		
Liverpool Central 10 a	16 08			16 23			16 38				16 53			17 08				17 23				17 38		
d	16 08	16 10	16 20	16 23	16 25	16 35	16 38	16 40		16 50	16 53	16 55	17 05	17 08	17 10	17 13	17 20	17 23		17 25	17 35	17 38	17 40	17 50
Moorfields 10 d	16 10	16 12	16 22	16 25	16 27	16 37	16 40	16 42		16 52	16 55	16 57	17 07	17 10	17 12	17 15	17 22	17 25		17 27	17 37	17 40	17 42	17 52
Sandhills d	16 14	16 16	16 26	16 29	16 31	16 41	16 44	16 46		16 56	16 59	17 01	17 11	17 14	17 16	17 19	17 26	17 29		17 31	17 41	17 44	17 46	17 56
Kirkdale d		16 19	16 29		16 34	16 44		16 49		16 59		17 04	17 14		17 19		17 29			17 34	17 44		17 49	17 59
Rice Lane d			16 32			16 47				17 02			17 17				17 32				17 47			18 02
Fazakerley d			16 34			16 49				17 04			17 19				17 34				17 49			18 04
Kirkby a			16 38			16 53				17 08			17 23				17 38				17 53			18 08
Walton (Merseyside) d		16 22			16 37			16 52				17 07			17 22					17 37			17 52	
Orrell Park d		16 23			16 38			16 53				17 08			17 23					17 38			17 53	
Aintree d		16 26			16 41			16 56				17 11			17 26					17 41			17 56	
Old Roan d		16 28			16 43			16 58				17 13			17 28					17 43			17 58	
Maghull d		16 31			16 46			17 01				17 16			17 31					17 46			18 01	
Town Green d		16 35			16 50			17 05				17 20			17 35					17 50			18 05	
Aughton Park d		16 37			16 52			17 07				17 22			17 37					17 52			18 07	
Ormskirk a		16 42			16 57			17 12				17 27			17 42					17 57			18 12	
Bank Hall d	16 16			16 31			16 46				17 01			17 16		17 21		17 31				17 46		
Bootle Oriel Road d	16 18			16 33			16 48				17 03			17 18		17 23		17 33				17 48		
Bootle New Strand d	16 20			16 35			16 50				17 05			17 20		17 25		17 35				17 50		
Seaforth & Litherland d	16 22			16 37			16 52				17 07			17 22		17 27		17 37				17 52		
Waterloo (Merseyside) d	16 24			16 39			16 54				17 09			17 24		17 29		17 39				17 54		
Blundellsands & Crosby d	16 27			16 42			16 57				17 12			17 27		17 32		17 42				17 57		
Hall Road d	16 29			16 44			16 59				17 14			17 29		17 34		17 44				17 59		
Hightown d	16 32			16 47			17 02				17 17			17 32		17 37		17 47				18 02		
Formby d	16 36			16 51			17 06				17 21			17 36		17 41		17 51				18 06		
Freshfield d	16 38			16 53			17 08				17 23			17 38		17 43		17 53				18 08		
Ainsdale d	16 42			16 57			17 12				17 27			17 42		17 47		17 57				18 12		
Hillside d	16 45			17 00			17 15				17 30			17 45		17 50		18 00				18 15		
Birkdale d	16 47			17 02			17 17				17 32			17 47		17 52		18 02				18 17		
Southport a	16 52			17 07			17 22				17 37			17 52		17 57		18 07				18 22		

	ME	ME	ME	ME		ME	ME	ME	ME	ME	ME	ME	ME	ME		ME	ME	ME	ME	ME	ME SO	ME SX	ME	ME
Hunts Cross 89 d	17 36			17 51				18 06			18 21			18 36				18 51		19 06			19 21	
Liverpool Sth Parkway 7 89 ✈ d	17 39			17 54				18 09			18 24			18 39				18 54		19 09			19 24	
Cressington d	17 42			17 57				18 12			18 27			18 42				18 57		19 12			19 27	
Aigburth d	17 44			17 59				18 14			18 29			18 44				18 59		19 14			19 29	
St Michaels d	17 46			18 01				18 16			18 31			18 46				19 01		19 16			19 31	
Brunswick d	17 49			18 04				18 19			18 34			18 49				19 04		19 19			19 34	
Liverpool Central 10 a	17 53			18 08				18 23			18 38			18 53				19 08		19 23			19 38	
d	17 53	17 55	18 05	18 08		18 10	18 20	18 23	18 25	18 35	18 38	18 40	18 50	18 53		18 55	19 05	19 08	19 10	19 23	19 25	19 25	19 38	19 40
Moorfields 10 d	17 55	17 57	18 07	18 10		18 12	18 22	18 25	18 27	18 37	18 40	18 42	18 52	18 55		18 57	19 07	19 10	19 12	19 25	19 27	19 27	19 40	19 42
Sandhills d	17 59	18 01	18 11	18 14		18 16	18 26	18 29	18 31	18 41	18 44	18 46	18 56	18 59		19 01	19 11	19 14	19 16	19 29	19 31	19 31	19 44	19 46
Kirkdale d		18 04	18 14			18 19	18 29		18 34	18 44		18 49	18 59			19 04	19 14		19 19		19 34	19 34		19 49
Rice Lane d			18 17				18 32			18 47			19 02				19 17				19 37	19 37		
Fazakerley d			18 19				18 34			18 49			19 04				19 19				19 40	19 40		
Kirkby a			18 23				18 38			18 53			19 08				19 23				19 43	19 45		
Walton (Merseyside) d		18 07				18 22			18 37			18 52				19 07			19 22					19 52
Orrell Park d		18 08				18 23			18 38			18 53				19 08			19 23					19 53
Aintree d		18 11				18 26			18 41			18 56				19 11			19 26					19 56
Old Roan d		18 13				18 28			18 43			18 58				19 13			19 28					19 58
Maghull d		18 16				18 31			18 46			19 01				19 16			19 31					20 01
Town Green d		18 20				18 35			18 50			19 05				19 20			19 35					20 05
Aughton Park d		18 22				18 37			18 52			19 07				19 22			19 37					20 07
Ormskirk a		18 27				18 42			18 57			19 12				19 27			19 42					20 13
Bank Hall d	18 01			18 16				18 31			18 46			19 01				19 16		19 31			19 46	
Bootle Oriel Road d	18 03			18 18				18 33			18 48			19 03				19 18		19 33			19 48	
Bootle New Strand d	18 05			18 20				18 35			18 50			19 05				19 20		19 35			19 50	
Seaforth & Litherland d	18 07			18 22				18 37			18 52			19 07				19 22		19 37			19 52	
Waterloo (Merseyside) d	18 09			18 24				18 39			18 54			19 09				19 24		19 39			19 54	
Blundellsands & Crosby d	18 12			18 27				18 42			18 57			19 12				19 27		19 42			19 57	
Hall Road d	18 14			18 29				18 44			18 59			19 14				19 29		19 44			19 59	
Hightown d	18 17			18 32				18 47			19 02			19 17				19 32		19 47			20 02	
Formby d	18 21			18 36				18 51			19 06			19 21				19 36		19 51			20 06	
Freshfield d	18 23			18 38				18 53			19 08			19 23				19 38		19 53			20 08	
Ainsdale d	18 27			18 42				18 57			19 12			19 27				19 42		19 57			20 12	
Hillside d	18 30			18 45				19 00			19 15			19 30				19 45		20 00			20 15	
Birkdale d	18 32			18 47				19 02			19 17			19 32				19 47		20 02			20 17	
Southport a	18 37			18 52				19 07			19 22			19 37				19 52		20 07			20 22	

Hunts Cross and Liverpool - Kirkby, Ormskirk and Southport

		ME	ME SO	ME SX	ME	ME	ME	ME	ME	ME		ME	ME	ME	ME	ME	ME	ME	ME	ME		ME	ME	ME
Hunts Cross 89	d	19 36			19 51		20 06		20 21			20 36		20 51		21 06		21 21		21 36			21 51	
Liverpool Sth Parkway 7 89 ✈	d	19 39			19 54		20 09		20 24			20 39		20 54		21 09		21 24		21 39			21 54	
Cressington	d	19 42			19 57		20 12		20 27			20 42		20 57		21 12		21 27		21 42			21 57	
Aigburth	d	19 44			19 59		20 14		20 29			20 44		20 59		21 14		21 29		21 44			21 59	
St Michaels	d	19 46			20 01		20 16		20 31			20 46		21 01		21 16		21 31		21 46			22 01	
Brunswick	d	19 49			20 04		20 19		20 34			20 49		21 04		21 19		21 34		21 49			22 04	
Liverpool Central 10	a	19 53			20 08		20 23		20 38			20 53		21 08		21 23		21 38		21 53			22 08	
	d	19 53	19 55	19 55	20 08	20 10	20 23	20 25	20 38	20 40		20 53	20 55	21 08	21 10	21 23	21 25	21 38	21 40	21 53		21 55	22 08	22 10
Moorfields 10	d	19 55	19 57	19 57	20 10	20 12	20 25	20 27	20 40	20 42		20 55	20 57	21 10	21 12	21 25	21 27	21 40	21 42	21 55		21 57	22 10	22 12
Sandhills	d	19 59	20 01	20 01	20 14	20 16	20 29	20 31	20 44	20 46		20 59	21 01	21 14	21 16	21 29	21 31	21 44	21 46	21 59		22 01	22 14	22 16
Kirkdale	d		20 04	20 04		20 19		20 34		20 49			21 04		21 19		21 34		21 49			22 04		22 19
Rice Lane	d		20 07	20 07				20 37					21 07				21 37					22 07		
Fazakerley	d		20 10	20 10				20 40					21 10				21 40					22 10		
Kirkby	a		20 13	20 15				20 43					21 13				21 43					22 13		
Walton (Merseyside)	d					20 22				20 52					21 22				21 52					22 22
Orrell Park	d					20 23				20 53					21 23				21 53					22 23
Aintree	d					20 26				20 56					21 26				21 56					22 26
Old Roan	d					20 28				20 58					21 28				21 58					22 28
Maghull	d					20 31				21 01					21 31				22 01					22 31
Town Green	d					20 35				21 05					21 35				22 05					22 35
Aughton Park	d					20 37				21 07					21 37				22 07					22 37
Ormskirk	a					20 42				21 12					21 42				22 12					22 42
Bank Hall	d	20 01			20 16		20 31		20 46			21 01		21 16		21 31		21 46		22 01			22 16	
Bootle Oriel Road	d	20 03			20 18		20 33		20 48			21 03		21 18		21 33		21 48		22 03			22 18	
Bootle New Strand	d	20 05			20 20		20 35		20 50			21 05		21 20		21 35		21 50		22 05			22 20	
Seaforth & Litherland	d	20 07			20 22		20 37		20 52			21 07		21 22		21 37		21 52		22 07			22 22	
Waterloo (Merseyside)	d	20 09			20 24		20 39		20 54			21 09		21 24		21 39		21 54		22 09			22 24	
Blundellsands & Crosby	d	20 12			20 27		20 42		20 57			21 12		21 27		21 42		21 57		22 12			22 27	
Hall Road	d	20 14			20 29		20 44		20 59			21 14		21 29		21 44		21 59		22 14			22 29	
Hightown	d	20 17			20 32		20 47		21 02			21 17		21 32		21 47		22 02		22 17			22 32	
Formby	d	20 21			20 36		20 51		21 06			21 21		21 36		21 51		22 06		22 21			22 36	
Freshfield	d	20 23			20 38		20 53		21 08			21 23		21 38		21 53		22 08		22 23			22 38	
Ainsdale	d	20 27			20 42		20 57		21 12			21 27		21 42		21 57		22 12		22 27			22 42	
Hillside	d	20 30			20 45		21 00		21 15			21 30		21 45		22 00		22 15		22 30			22 45	
Birkdale	d	20 32			20 47		21 02		21 17			21 32		21 47		22 02		22 17		22 32			22 47	
Southport	a	20 37			20 52		21 07		21 22			21 37		21 52		22 07		22 22		22 37			22 52	

		ME	ME	ME	ME	ME	ME		ME	ME	ME	ME	ME	ME	ME
Hunts Cross 89	d	22 06		22 21		22 36			22 51		23 06		23 21		
Liverpool Sth Parkway 7 89 ✈	d	22 09		22 24		22 39			22 54		23 09		23 24		
Cressington	d	22 12		22 27		22 42			22 57		23 12		23 27		
Aigburth	d	22 14		22 29		22 44			22 59		23 14		23 29		
St Michaels	d	22 16		22 31		22 46			23 01		23 16		23 31		
Brunswick	d	22 19		22 34		22 49			23 04		23 19		23 34		
Liverpool Central 10	a	22 23		22 38		22 53			23 08		23 23		23 38		
	d	22 23	22 25	22 38	22 40	22 53	22 55		23 08	23 10	23 23	23 25	23 38	23 40	23 55
Moorfields 10	d	22 25	22 27	22 40	22 42	22 55	22 57		23 10	23 12	23 25	23 27	23 40	23 42	23 57
Sandhills	d	22 29	22 31	22 44	22 46	22 59	23 01		23 14	23 16	23 29	23 31	23 44	23 46	00 01
Kirkdale	d		22 34		22 49		23 04			23 19		23 34		23 49	00 04
Rice Lane	d		22 37				23 07					23 37			00 07
Fazakerley	d		22 40				23 10					23 40			00 10
Kirkby	a		22 43				23 13					23 43			00 13
Walton (Merseyside)	d				22 52					23 22				23 52	
Orrell Park	d				22 53					23 23				23 53	
Aintree	d				22 56					23 26				23 56	
Old Roan	d				22 58					23 28				23 58	
Maghull	d				23 01					23 31				00 01	
Town Green	d				23 05					23 35				00 05	
Aughton Park	d				23 07					23 37				00 07	
Ormskirk	a				23 12					23 42				00 12	
Bank Hall	d	22 31		22 46		23 01			23 16		23 31		23 46		
Bootle Oriel Road	d	22 33		22 48		23 03			23 18		23 33		23 48		
Bootle New Strand	d	22 35		22 50		23 05			23 20		23 35		23 50		
Seaforth & Litherland	d	22 37		22 52		23 07			23 22		23 37		23 52		
Waterloo (Merseyside)	d	22 39		22 54		23 09			23 24		23 39		23 54		
Blundellsands & Crosby	d	22 42		22 57		23 12			23 27		23 42		23 57		
Hall Road	d	22 44		22 59		23 14			23 29		23 44		23 59		
Hightown	d	22 47		23 02		23 17			23 32		23 47		00 02		
Formby	d	22 51		23 06		23 21			23 36		23 51		00 06		
Freshfield	d	22 53		23 08		23 23			23 38		23 53		00 08		
Ainsdale	d	22 57		23 12		23 27			23 42		23 57		00 12		
Hillside	d	23 00		23 15		23 30			23 45		23 59		00 15		
Birkdale	d	23 02		23 17		23 32			23 47		00 02		00 17		
Southport	a	23 07		23 22		23 37			23 52		00 07		00 22		

Table 103

Sundays

Hunts Cross and Liverpool - Kirkby, Ormskirk and Southport

		ME A	ME A	ME A	ME A	ME	ME	ME	ME	ME		ME	ME	ME	ME	ME	ME	ME	ME	ME		ME	ME	ME	ME
Hunts Cross 89	d	23p06	23p21					08 06				08 36			09 06			09 36					10 06		
Liverpool Sth Parkway 7 89	d	23p09	23p24					08 09				08 39			09 09			09 39					10 09		
Cressington	d	23p12	23p27					08 12				08 42			09 12			09 42					10 12		
Aigburth	d	23p14	23p29					08 14				08 44			09 14			09 44					10 14		
St Michaels	d	23p16	23p31					08 16				08 46			09 16			09 46					10 16		
Brunswick	d	23p19	23p34					08 19				08 49			09 19			09 49					10 19		
Liverpool Central 10	a	23p23	23p38					08 23				08 53			09 23			09 53					10 23		
	d	23p23	23p38	23p40	23p55	08 08	08 10	08 23	08 25	08 40		08 53	08 55	09 10	09 23	09 25	09 40	09 53	09 55	10 08		10 10	10 23	10 25	10 38
Moorfields 10	d	23p25	23p40	23p42	23p57	08 10	08 12	08 25	08 27	08 42		08 55	08 57	09 12	09 25	09 27	09 42	09 55	09 57	10 10		10 12	10 25	10 27	10 40
Sandhills	d	23p29	23p44	23p46	00 01	08 14	08 16	08 29	08 31	08 46		08 59	09 01	09 16	09 29	09 31	09 46	09 59	10 01	10 14		10 16	10 29	10 31	10 44
Kirkdale	d			23p49	00 04		08 19		08 34	08 49			09 04	09 19		09 34	09 49		10 04			10 19		10 34	
Rice Lane	d				00 07				08 37				09 07			09 37			10 07					10 37	
Fazakerley	d				00 10				08 40				09 10			09 40			10 10					10 40	
Kirkby	a				00 13				08 43				09 13			09 43			10 13					10 43	
Walton (Merseyside)	d			23p52			08 22			08 52				09 22			09 52					10 22			
Orrell Park	d			23p53			08 23			08 53				09 23			09 53					10 23			
Aintree	d			23p56			08 26			08 56				09 26			09 56					10 26			
Old Roan	d			23p58			08 28			08 58				09 28			09 58					10 28			
Maghull	d			00 01			08 31			09 01				09 31			10 01					10 31			
Town Green	d			00 05			08 35			09 05				09 35			10 05					10 35			
Aughton Park	d			00 07			08 37			09 07				09 37			10 07					10 37			
Ormskirk	a			00 12			08 42			09 12				09 42			10 12					10 42			
Bank Hall	d	23p31	23p46			08 16		08 31				09 01			09 31			10 01		10 16			10 31		10 46
Bootle Oriel Road	d	23p33	23p48			08 18		08 33				09 03			09 33			10 03		10 18			10 33		10 48
Bootle New Strand	d	23p35	23p50			08 20		08 35				09 05			09 35			10 05		10 20			10 35		10 50
Seaforth & Litherland	d	23p37	23p52			08 22		08 37				09 07			09 37			10 07		10 22			10 37		10 52
Waterloo (Merseyside)	d	23p39	23p54			08 24		08 39				09 09			09 39			10 09		10 24			10 39		10 54
Blundellsands & Crosby	d	23p42	23p57			08 27		08 42				09 12			09 42			10 12		10 27			10 42		10 57
Hall Road	d	23p44	23p59			08 29		08 44				09 14			09 44			10 14		10 29			10 44		10 59
Hightown	d	23p47	00 02			08 32		08 47				09 17			09 47			10 17		10 32			10 47		11 02
Formby	d	23p51	00 06			08 36		08 51				09 21			09 51			10 21		10 36			10 51		11 06
Freshfield	d	23p53	00 08			08 38		08 53				09 23			09 53			10 23		10 38			10 53		11 08
Ainsdale	d	23p57	00 12			08 42		08 57				09 27			09 57			10 27		10 42			10 57		11 12
Hillside	d	23p59	00 15			08 45		09 00				09 30			10 00			10 30		10 45			11 00		11 15
Birkdale	d	00 02	00 17			08 47		09 02				09 32			10 02			10 32		10 47			11 02		11 17
Southport	a	00 07	00 22			08 52		09 07				09 37			10 07			10 37		10 52			11 07		11 22

		ME	ME	ME	ME	ME		ME	ME	ME	ME	ME	ME	ME	ME	ME		ME	ME	ME	ME	ME	ME	ME	ME
Hunts Cross 89	d		10 36					11 06				11 36				12 06					12 36				13 06
Liverpool Sth Parkway 7 89	d		10 39					11 09				11 39				12 09					12 39				13 09
Cressington	d		10 42					11 12				11 42				12 12					12 42				13 12
Aigburth	d		10 44					11 14				11 44				12 14					12 44				13 14
St Michaels	d		10 46					11 16				11 46				12 16					12 46				13 16
Brunswick	d		10 49					11 19				11 49				12 19					12 49				13 19
Liverpool Central 10	a		10 53					11 23				11 53				12 23					12 53				13 23
	d	10 40	10 53	10 55	11 08	11 10		11 23	11 25	11 38	11 40	11 53	11 55	12 08	12 10	12 23		12 25	12 38	12 40	12 53	12 55	13 08	13 10	13 23
Moorfields 10	d	10 42	10 55	10 57	11 10	11 12		11 25	11 27	11 40	11 42	11 55	11 57	12 10	12 12	12 25		12 27	12 40	12 42	12 55	12 57	13 10	13 12	13 25
Sandhills	d	10 46	10 59	11 01	11 14	11 16		11 29	11 31	11 44	11 46	11 59	12 01	12 14	12 16	12 29		12 31	12 44	12 46	12 59	13 01	13 14	13 16	13 29
Kirkdale	d	10 49		11 04		11 19			11 34		11 49		12 04		12 19			12 34		12 49		13 04		13 19	
Rice Lane	d			11 07					11 37				12 07					12 37				13 07			
Fazakerley	d			11 10					11 40				12 10					12 40				13 10			
Kirkby	a			11 13					11 43				12 13					12 43				13 13			
Walton (Merseyside)	d	10 52				11 22					11 52				12 22					12 52				13 22	
Orrell Park	d	10 53				11 23					11 53				12 23					12 53				13 23	
Aintree	d	10 56				11 26					11 56				12 26					12 56				13 26	
Old Roan	d	10 58				11 28					11 58				12 28					12 58				13 28	
Maghull	d	11 01				11 31					12 01				12 31					13 01				13 31	
Town Green	d	11 05				11 35					12 05				12 35					13 05				13 35	
Aughton Park	d	11 07				11 37					12 07				12 37					13 07				13 37	
Ormskirk	a	11 12				11 42					12 12				12 42					13 12				13 42	
Bank Hall	d		11 01		11 16			11 31		11 46		12 01		12 16		12 31			12 46		13 01		13 16		13 31
Bootle Oriel Road	d		11 03		11 18			11 33		11 48		12 03		12 18		12 33			12 48		13 03		13 18		13 33
Bootle New Strand	d		11 05		11 20			11 35		11 50		12 05		12 20		12 35			12 50		13 05		13 20		13 35
Seaforth & Litherland	d		11 07		11 22			11 37		11 52		12 07		12 22		12 37			12 52		13 07		13 22		13 37
Waterloo (Merseyside)	d		11 09		11 24			11 39		11 54		12 09		12 24		12 39			12 54		13 09		13 24		13 39
Blundellsands & Crosby	d		11 12		11 27			11 42		11 57		12 12		12 27		12 42			12 57		13 12		13 27		13 42
Hall Road	d		11 14		11 29			11 44		11 59		12 14		12 29		12 44			12 59		13 14		13 29		13 44
Hightown	d		11 17		11 32			11 47		12 02		12 17		12 32		12 47			13 02		13 17		13 32		13 47
Formby	d		11 21		11 36			11 51		12 06		12 21		12 36		12 51			13 06		13 21		13 36		13 51
Freshfield	d		11 23		11 38			11 53		12 08		12 23		12 38		12 53			13 08		13 23		13 38		13 53
Ainsdale	d		11 27		11 42			11 57		12 12		12 27		12 42		12 57			13 12		13 27		13 42		13 57
Hillside	d		11 30		11 45			12 00		12 15		12 30		12 45		13 00			13 15		13 30		13 45		14 00
Birkdale	d		11 32		11 47			12 02		12 17		12 32		12 47		13 02			13 17		13 32		13 47		14 02
Southport	a		11 37		11 52			12 07		12 22		12 37		12 52		13 07			13 22		13 37		13 52		14 07

A not 22 May

Table 103

Sundays

Hunts Cross and Liverpool - Kirkby, Ormskirk and Southport

		ME		ME	ME	ME	ME	ME	ME	ME	ME	ME		ME	ME	ME	ME	ME	ME	ME	ME	ME		ME	ME
Hunts Cross 89	d					13 36				14 06					14 36				15 06					15 36	
Liverpool Sth Parkway 7 89 ✈	d					13 39				14 09					14 39				15 09					15 39	
Cressington	d					13 42				14 12					14 42				15 12					15 42	
Aigburth	d					13 44				14 14					14 44				15 14					15 44	
St Michaels	d					13 46				14 16					14 46				15 16					15 46	
Brunswick	d					13 49				14 19					14 49				15 19					15 49	
Liverpool Central 10	a					13 53				14 23					14 53				15 23					15 53	
	d	13 25		13 38	13 40	13 53	13 55	14 08	14 10	14 23	14 25	14 38		14 40	14 53	14 55	15 08	15 10	15 23	15 25	15 38	15 40		15 53	15 55
Moorfields 10	d	13 27		13 40	13 42	13 55	13 57	14 10	14 12	14 25	14 27	14 40		14 42	14 55	14 57	15 10	15 12	15 25	15 27	15 40	15 42		15 55	15 57
Sandhills	d	13 31		13 44	13 46	13 59	14 01	14 14	14 16	14 29	14 31	14 44		14 46	14 59	15 01	15 14	15 16	15 29	15 31	15 44	15 46		15 59	16 01
Kirkdale	d	13 34			13 49		14 04		14 19		14 34			14 49		15 04		15 19		15 34		15 49			16 04
Rice Lane	d	13 37					14 07				14 37					15 07				15 37					16 07
Fazakerley	d	13 40					14 10				14 40					15 10				15 40					16 10
Kirkby	a	13 43					14 13				14 43					15 13				15 43					16 13
Walton (Merseyside)	d				13 52				14 22					14 52				15 22				15 52			
Orrell Park	d				13 53				14 23					14 53				15 23				15 53			
Aintree	d				13 56				14 26					14 56				15 26				15 56			
Old Roan	d				13 58				14 28					14 58				15 28				15 58			
Maghull	d				14 01				14 31					15 01				15 31				16 01			
Town Green	d				14 05				14 35					15 05				15 35				16 05			
Aughton Park	d				14 07				14 37					15 07				15 37				16 07			
Ormskirk	a				14 12				14 42					15 12				15 42				16 12			
Bank Hall	d			13 46		14 01		14 16		14 31		14 46			15 01		15 16		15 31		15 46			16 01	
Bootle Oriel Road	d			13 48		14 03		14 18		14 33		14 48			15 03		15 18		15 33		15 48			16 03	
Bootle New Strand	d			13 50		14 05		14 20		14 35		14 50			15 05		15 20		15 35		15 50			16 05	
Seaforth & Litherland	d			13 52		14 07		14 22		14 37		14 52			15 07		15 22		15 37		15 52			16 07	
Waterloo (Merseyside)	d			13 54		14 09		14 24		14 39		14 54			15 09		15 24		15 39		15 54			16 09	
Blundellsands & Crosby	d			13 57		14 12		14 27		14 42		14 57			15 12		15 27		15 42		15 57			16 12	
Hall Road	d			13 59		14 14		14 29		14 44		14 59			15 14		15 29		15 44		15 59			16 14	
Hightown	d			14 02		14 17		14 32		14 47		15 02			15 17		15 32		15 47		16 02			16 17	
Formby	d			14 06		14 21		14 36		14 51		15 06			15 21		15 36		15 51		16 06			16 21	
Freshfield	d			14 08		14 23		14 38		14 53		15 08			15 23		15 38		15 53		16 08			16 23	
Ainsdale	d			14 12		14 27		14 42		14 57		15 12			15 27		15 42		15 57		16 12			16 27	
Hillside	d			14 15		14 30		14 45		15 00		15 15			15 30		15 45		16 00		16 15			16 30	
Birkdale	d			14 17		14 32		14 47		15 02		15 17			15 32		15 47		16 02		16 17			16 32	
Southport	a			14 22		14 37		14 52		15 07		15 22			15 37		15 52		16 07		16 22			16 37	

		ME	ME	ME	ME	ME	ME	ME		ME	ME	ME	ME	ME	ME	ME	ME	ME		ME	ME	ME	ME	ME	ME
Hunts Cross 89	d			16 06				16 36					17 06				17 36					18 06			
Liverpool Sth Parkway 7 89 ✈	d			16 09				16 39					17 09				17 39					18 09			
Cressington	d			16 12				16 42					17 12				17 42					18 12			
Aigburth	d			16 14				16 44					17 14				17 44					18 14			
St Michaels	d			16 16				16 46					17 16				17 46					18 16			
Brunswick	d			16 19				16 49					17 19				17 49					18 19			
Liverpool Central 10	a			16 23				16 53					17 23				17 53					18 23			
	d	16 08	16 10	16 23	16 25	16 38	16 40	16 53		16 55	17 08	17 10	17 23	17 25	17 38	17 40	17 53	17 55		18 08	18 10	18 23	18 25	18 38	18 40
Moorfields 10	d	16 10	16 12	16 25	16 27	16 40	16 42	16 55		16 57	17 10	17 12	17 25	17 27	17 40	17 42	17 55	17 57		18 10	18 12	18 25	18 27	18 40	18 42
Sandhills	d	16 14	16 16	16 29	16 31	16 44	16 46	16 59		17 01	17 14	17 16	17 29	17 31	17 44	17 46	17 59	18 01		18 14	18 16	18 29	18 31	18 44	18 46
Kirkdale	d		16 19		16 34		16 49			17 04		17 19		17 34		17 49		18 04			18 19		18 34		18 49
Rice Lane	d				16 37					17 07				17 37				18 07					18 37		
Fazakerley	d				16 40					17 10				17 40				18 10					18 40		
Kirkby	a				16 43					17 13				17 43				18 13					18 43		
Walton (Merseyside)	d		16 22				16 52					17 22				17 52					18 22				18 52
Orrell Park	d		16 23				16 53					17 23				17 53					18 23				18 53
Aintree	d		16 26				16 56					17 26				17 56					18 26				18 56
Old Roan	d		16 28				16 58					17 28				17 58					18 28				18 58
Maghull	d		16 31				17 01					17 31				18 01					18 31				19 01
Town Green	d		16 35				17 05					17 35				18 05					18 35				19 05
Aughton Park	d		16 37				17 07					17 37				18 07					18 37				19 07
Ormskirk	a		16 42				17 12					17 42				18 12					18 42				19 12
Bank Hall	d	16 16		16 31		16 46		17 01			17 16		17 31		17 46		18 01			18 16		18 31		18 46	
Bootle Oriel Road	d	16 18		16 33		16 48		17 03			17 18		17 33		17 48		18 03			18 18		18 33		18 48	
Bootle New Strand	d	16 20		16 35		16 50		17 05			17 20		17 35		17 50		18 05			18 20		18 35		18 50	
Seaforth & Litherland	d	16 22		16 37		16 52		17 07			17 22		17 37		17 52		18 07			18 22		18 37		18 52	
Waterloo (Merseyside)	d	16 24		16 39		16 54		17 09			17 24		17 39		17 54		18 09			18 24		18 39		18 54	
Blundellsands & Crosby	d	16 27		16 42		16 57		17 12			17 27		17 42		17 57		18 12			18 27		18 42		18 57	
Hall Road	d	16 29		16 44		16 59		17 14			17 29		17 44		17 59		18 14			18 29		18 44		18 59	
Hightown	d	16 32		16 47		17 02		17 17			17 32		17 47		18 02		18 17			18 32		18 47		19 02	
Formby	d	16 36		16 51		17 06		17 21			17 36		17 51		18 06		18 21			18 36		18 51		19 06	
Freshfield	d	16 38		16 53		17 08		17 23			17 38		17 53		18 08		18 23			18 38		18 53		19 08	
Ainsdale	d	16 42		16 57		17 12		17 27			17 42		17 57		18 12		18 27			18 42		18 57		19 12	
Hillside	d	16 45		17 00		17 15		17 30			17 45		18 00		18 15		18 30			18 45		19 00		19 15	
Birkdale	d	16 47		17 02		17 17		17 32			17 47		18 02		18 17		18 32			18 47		19 02		19 17	
Southport	a	16 52		17 07		17 22		17 37			17 52		18 07		18 22		18 37			18 52		19 07		19 22	

Table 103

Sundays

Hunts Cross and Liverpool - Kirkby, Ormskirk and Southport

		ME	ME	ME		ME	ME	ME	ME	ME	ME	ME	ME	ME		ME	ME	ME	ME	ME	ME	ME	ME	ME
Hunts Cross 89	d	18 36					19 06				19 36					20 06				20 36				21 06
Liverpool Sth Parkway 7 89 ✈	d	18 39					19 09				19 39					20 09				20 39				21 09
Cressington	d	18 42					19 12				19 42					20 12				20 42				21 12
Aigburth	d	18 44					19 14				19 44					20 14				20 44				21 14
St Michaels	d	18 46					19 16				19 46					20 16				20 46				21 16
Brunswick	d	18 49					19 19				19 49					20 19				20 49				21 19
Liverpool Central 10	a	18 53					19 23				19 53					20 23				20 53				21 23
	d	18 53	18 55	19 08		19 10	19 23	19 25	19 38	19 40	19 53	19 55	20 08	20 10		20 23	20 25	20 38	20 40	20 53	20 55	21 08	21 10	21 23
Moorfields 10	d	18 55	18 57	19 10		19 12	19 25	19 27	19 40	19 42	19 55	19 57	20 10	20 12		20 25	20 27	20 40	20 42	20 55	20 57	21 10	21 12	21 25
Sandhills	d	18 59	19 01	19 14		19 16	19 29	19 31	19 44	19 46	19 59	20 01	20 14	20 16		20 29	20 31	20 44	20 46	20 59	21 01	21 14	21 16	21 29
Kirkdale	d		19 04			19 19		19 34		19 49		20 04		20 19			20 34		20 49		21 04		21 19	
Rice Lane	d		19 07					19 37				20 07					20 37				21 07			
Fazakerley	d		19 10					19 40				20 10					20 40				21 10			
Kirkby	a		19 13					19 43				20 13					20 43				21 13			
Walton (Merseyside)	d					19 22				19 52				20 22					20 52				21 22	
Orrell Park	d					19 23				19 53				20 23					20 53				21 23	
Aintree	d					19 26				19 56				20 26					20 56				21 26	
Old Roan	d					19 28				19 58				20 28					20 58				21 28	
Maghull	d					19 31				20 01				20 31					21 01				21 31	
Town Green	d					19 35				20 05				20 35					21 05				21 35	
Aughton Park	d					19 37				20 07				20 37					21 07				21 37	
Ormskirk	a					19 42				20 12				20 42					21 12				21 42	
Bank Hall	d	19 01		19 16			19 31		19 46		20 01		20 16			20 31		20 46		21 01		21 16		21 31
Bootle Oriel Road	d	19 03		19 18			19 33		19 48		20 03		20 18			20 33		20 48		21 03		21 18		21 33
Bootle New Strand	d	19 05		19 20			19 35		19 50		20 05		20 20			20 35		20 50		21 05		21 20		21 35
Seaforth & Litherland	d	19 07		19 22			19 37		19 52		20 07		20 22			20 37		20 52		21 07		21 22		21 37
Waterloo (Merseyside)	d	19 09		19 24			19 39		19 54		20 09		20 24			20 39		20 54		21 09		21 24		21 39
Blundellsands & Crosby	d	19 12		19 27			19 42		19 57		20 12		20 27			20 42		20 57		21 12		21 27		21 42
Hall Road	d	19 14		19 29			19 44		19 59		20 14		20 29			20 44		20 59		21 14		21 29		21 44
Hightown	d	19 17		19 32			19 47		20 02		20 17		20 32			20 47		21 02		21 17		21 32		21 47
Formby	d	19 21		19 36			19 51		20 06		20 21		20 36			20 51		21 06		21 21		21 36		21 51
Freshfield	d	19 23		19 38			19 53		20 08		20 23		20 38			20 53		21 08		21 23		21 38		21 53
Ainsdale	d	19 27		19 42			19 57		20 12		20 27		20 42			20 57		21 12		21 27		21 42		21 57
Hillside	d	19 30		19 45			20 00		20 15		20 30		20 45			21 00		21 15		21 30		21 45		22 00
Birkdale	d	19 32		19 47			20 02		20 17		20 32		20 47			21 02		21 17		21 32		21 47		22 02
Southport	a	19 37		19 52			20 07		20 22		20 37		20 52			21 07		21 22		21 37		21 52		22 07

		ME	ME	ME	ME	ME	ME	ME	ME	ME		ME	ME	ME	ME	ME	ME	ME	ME	ME		ME	ME	ME
Hunts Cross 89	d				21 36				22 06					22 36				23 06	23 06					
Liverpool Sth Parkway 7 89 ✈	d				21 39				22 09					22 39				23 09	23 09					
Cressington	d				21 42				22 12					22 42				23 12	23 12					
Aigburth	d				21 44				22 14					22 44				23 14	23 14					
St Michaels	d				21 46				22 16					22 46				23 16	23 16					
Brunswick	d				21 49				22 19					22 49				23 19	23 19					
Liverpool Central 10	a				21 53				22 23					22 53				23 23	23 23					
	d	21 25	21 38	21 40	21 53	21 55	22 08	22 10	22 23	22 25		22 38	22 40	22 53	22 55	23 08	23 10	23 23	23 23	23 25		23 38	23 40	23 55
Moorfields 10	d	21 27	21 40	21 42	21 55	21 57	22 10	22 12	22 25	22 27		22 40	22 42	22 55	22 57	23 10	23 12	23 25	23 25	23 27		23 40	23 42	23 57
Sandhills	d	21 31	21 44	21 46	21 59	22 01	22 14	22 16	22 29	22 31		22 44	22 46	22 59	23 01	23 14	23 16	23 29	23a29	23 31		23 44	23 46	00 01
Kirkdale	d	21 34		21 49		22 04		22 19		22 34			22 49		23 04		23 19			23 34			23 49	00 04
Rice Lane	d	21 37				22 07				22 37					23 07					23 37				00 07
Fazakerley	d	21 40				22 10				22 40					23 10					23 40				00 10
Kirkby	a	21 43				22 13				22 43					23 13					23 43				00 13
Walton (Merseyside)	d			21 52				22 22					22 52				23 22						23 52	
Orrell Park	d			21 53				22 23					22 53				23 23						23 53	
Aintree	d			21 56				22 26					22 56				23 26						23 56	
Old Roan	d			21 58				22 28					22 58				23 28						23 58	
Maghull	d			22 01				22 31					23 01				23 31						00 01	
Town Green	d			22 05				22 35					23 05				23 35						00 05	
Aughton Park	d			22 07				22 37					23 07				23 37						00 07	
Ormskirk	a			22 12				22 42					23 12				23 42						00 12	
Bank Hall	d		21 46		22 01		22 16		22 31			22 46		23 01		23 16		23 31				23 46		
Bootle Oriel Road	d		21 48		22 03		22 18		22 33			22 48		23 03		23 18		23 33				23 48		
Bootle New Strand	d		21 50		22 05		22 20		22 35			22 50		23 05		23 20		23 35				23 50		
Seaforth & Litherland	d		21 52		22 07		22 22		22 37			22 52		23 07		23 22		23 37				23 52		
Waterloo (Merseyside)	d		21 54		22 09		22 24		22 39			22 54		23 09		23 24		23 39				23 54		
Blundellsands & Crosby	d		21 57		22 12		22 27		22 42			22 57		23 12		23 27		23 42				23 57		
Hall Road	d		21 59		22 14		22 29		22 44			22 59		23 14		23 29		23 44				23 59		
Hightown	d		22 02		22 17		22 32		22 47			23 02		23 17		23 32		23 47				00 02		
Formby	d		22 06		22 21		22 36		22 51			23 06		23 21		23 36		23 51				00 06		
Freshfield	d		22 08		22 23		22 38		22 53			23 08		23 23		23 38		23 53				00 08		
Ainsdale	d		22 12		22 27		22 42		22 57			23 12		23 27		23 42		23 57				00 12		
Hillside	d		22 15		22 30		22 45		23 00			23 15		23 30		23 45		23 59				00 15		
Birkdale	d		22 17		22 32		22 47		23 02			23 17		23 32		23 47		00 02				00 17		
Southport	a		22 22		22 37		22 52		23 07			23 22		23 37		23 52		00 07				00 22		

Southport, Ormskirk and Kirby - Liverpool and Hunts Cross

Miles	Miles	Miles			ME	ME	ME	ME	ME	ME	ME	ME	ME		ME	ME	ME	ME	ME	ME	ME	ME	ME		ME
0	—	—	**Southport**	d	22p58	23p16				05 43		05 58			06 13		06 28		06 43			06 58			
1	—	—	Birkdale	d	23p02	23p20				05 47		06 02			06 17		06 32		06 47			07 02			
2	—	—	Hillside	d	23p04	23p22				05 49		06 04			06 19		06 34		06 49			07 04			
3½	—	—	Ainsdale	d	23p07	23p25				05 52		06 07			06 22		06 37		06 52			07 07			
6¼	—	—	Freshfield	d	23p11	23p29				05 56		06 11			06 26		06 41		06 56			07 11			
7¼	—	—	Formby	d	23p13	23p31				05 58		06 13			06 28		06 43		06 58			07 13			
9¼	—	—	Hightown	d	23p17	23p35				06 02		06 17			06 32		06 47		07 02			07 17			
11¼	—	—	Hall Road	d	23p20	23p38				06 05		06 20			06 35		06 50		07 05			07 20			
12	—	—	Blundellsands & Crosby	d	23p22	23p40				06 07		06 22			06 37		06 52		07 07			07 22			
13	—	—	Waterloo (Merseyside)	d	23p25	23p43				06 10		06 25			06 40		06 55		07 10			07 25			
14¼	—	—	Seaforth & Litherland	d	23p27	23p45				06 12		06 27			06 42		06 57		07 12			07 27			
15¼	—	—	Bootle New Strand	d	23p30	23p48				06 15		06 30			06 45		07 00		07 15			07 30			
15½	—	—	Bootle Oriel Road	d	23p31	23p49				06 16		06 31			06 46		07 01		07 16			07 31			
16¼	—	—	Bank Hall	d	23p33	23p51				06 18		06 33			06 48		07 03		07 18			07 33			
—	0	—	**Ormskirk**	d					05 50				06 20					06 50			07 05				07 20
—	1¼	—	Aughton Park	d					05 53				06 23					06 53			07 08				07 23
—	2¼	—	Town Green	d					05 55				06 25					06 55			07 10				07 25
—	4¾	—	Maghull	d					06 00				06 30					07 00			07 15				07 30
—	6½	—	Old Roan	d					06 03				06 33					07 03			07 18				07 33
—	7¼	—	Aintree	d					06 05				06 35					07 05			07 20				07 35
—	8¼	—	Orrell Park	d					06 07				06 37					07 07			07 22				07 37
—	8½	—	Walton (Merseyside)	d					06 09				06 39					07 09			07 24				07 39
—	—	0	**Kirkby**	d			05 48				06 18					06 48				07 13			07 28		
—	—	1¾	Fazakerley	d			05 51				06 21					06 51				07 16			07 31		
—	—	3¼	Rice Lane	d			05 54				06 24					06 54				07 19			07 34		
—	9¾	4½	Kirkdale	d			05 57		06 12		06 27		06 42			06 57		07 12		07 22	07 27		07 37		07 42
17	10¾	5½	Sandhills	d	23p36	23p55	06 00	06 06	06 14	06 21	06 30	06 36	06 44		06 51	07 00	07 06	07 14	07 21	07 25	07 29	07 36	07 40		07 44
18½	12¼	7	**Moorfields 10**	d	23p40	23p58	06 03	06 10	06 18	06 25	06 33	06 40	06 48		06 55	07 03	07 10	07 18	07 25	07 28	07 33	07 40	07 43		07 48
19	12¾	7½	**Liverpool Central 10**	a	23p43	00 01	06 06	06 13	06 20	06 28	06 36	06 43	06 50		06 58	07 06	07 13	07 20	07 28	07 31	07 35	07 43	07 46		07 50
—	—	—		d	23p44			06 14		06 29		06 43			06 59		07 14		07 29			07 44			
20½	—	—	Brunswick	d	23p47			06 17		06 32		06 47			07 02		07 17		07 32			07 47			
21¾	—	—	St Michaels	d	23p50			06 20		06 35		06 49			07 05		07 20		07 35			07 50			
23	—	—	Aigburth	d	23p52			06 22		06 37		06 52			07 07		07 22		07 37			07 52			
23¾	—	—	Cressington	d	23p54			06 24		06 39		06 54			07 09		07 24		07 39			07 54			
24¾	—	—	**Liverpool Sth Parkway 7 89 ✈**	d	23p57			06 27		06 42		06 56			07 12		07 27		07 42			07 57			
26¼	—	—	**Hunts Cross** 89	a	00 01			06 31		06 46		07 01			07 16		07 31		07 46			08 01			

		ME	ME	ME	ME	ME	ME	ME	ME		ME SX	ME	ME	ME	ME SX	ME	ME	ME	ME		ME	ME	ME	ME	ME
Southport	d	07 13			07 28			07 43			07 48		07 58		08 03		08 13				08 28			08 43	
Birkdale	d	07 17			07 32			07 47			07 52		08 02		08 07		08 17				08 32			08 47	
Hillside	d	07 19			07 34			07 49			07 54		08 04		08 09		08 19				08 34			08 49	
Ainsdale	d	07 22			07 37			07 52			07 57		08 07		08 12		08 22				08 37			08 52	
Freshfield	d	07 26			07 41			07 56			08 01		08 11		08 16		08 26				08 41			08 56	
Formby	d	07 28			07 43			07 58			08 03		08 13		08 18		08 28				08 43			08 58	
Hightown	d	07 32			07 47			08 02			08 07		08 17		08 22		08 32				08 47			09 02	
Hall Road	d	07 35			07 50			08 05			08 10		08 20		08 25		08 35				08 50			09 05	
Blundellsands & Crosby	d	07 37			07 52			08 07			08 12		08 22		08 27		08 37				08 52			09 07	
Waterloo (Merseyside)	d	07 40			07 55			08 10			08 15		08 25		08 30		08 40				08 55			09 10	
Seaforth & Litherland	d	07 42			07 57			08 12			08 17		08 27		08 32		08 42				08 57			09 12	
Bootle New Strand	d	07 45			08 00			08 15			08 20		08 30		08 35		08 45				09 00			09 15	
Bootle Oriel Road	d	07 46			08 01			08 16			08 21		08 31		08 36		08 46				09 01			09 16	
Bank Hall	d	07 48			08 03			08 18			08 23		08 33		08 38		08 48				09 03			09 18	
Ormskirk	d			07 35			07 50					08 05				08 20			08 35				08 50		
Aughton Park	d			07 38			07 53					08 08				08 23			08 38				08 53		
Town Green	d			07 40			07 55					08 10				08 25			08 40				08 55		
Maghull	d			07 45			08 00					08 15				08 30			08 45				09 00		
Old Roan	d			07 48			08 03					08 18				08 33			08 48				09 03		
Aintree	d			07 50			08 05					08 20				08 35			08 50				09 05		
Orrell Park	d			07 52			08 07					08 22				08 37			08 52				09 07		
Walton (Merseyside)	d			07 54			08 09					08 24				08 39			08 54				09 09		
Kirkby	d		07 43			07 58			08 13					08 28				08 43				08 58			09 13
Fazakerley	d		07 46			08 01			08 16					08 31				08 46				09 01			09 16
Rice Lane	d		07 49			08 04			08 19					08 34				08 49				09 04			09 19
Kirkdale	d		07 52	07 57		08 07	08 12		08 22			08 27		08 37		08 42		08 52	08 57			09 07	09 12		09 22
Sandhills	d	07 51	07 55	07 59	08 06	08 10	08 14	08 21	08 25		08 27	08 29	08 36	08 40	08 42	08 44	08 51	08 55	08 59		09 06	09 10	09 14	09 21	09 25
Moorfields 10	d	07 55	07 58	08 03	08 10	08 13	08 18	08 25	08 28		08 31	08 33	08 40	08 43	08 46	08 48	08 55	08 58	09 03		09 10	09 13	09 18	09 25	09 28
Liverpool Central 10	a	07 58	08 01	08 05	08 13	08 16	08 20	08 28	08 31		08 33	08 35	08 43	08 46	08 48	08 50	08 58	09 01	09 05		09 13	09 16	09 20	09 28	09 31
	d	07 59			08 14			08 29					08 44				08 59				09 14			09 29	
Brunswick	d	08 02			08 17			08 32					08 47				09 02				09 17			09 32	
St Michaels	d	08 05			08 20			08 35					08 50				09 05				09 20			09 35	
Aigburth	d	08 07			08 22			08 37					08 52				09 07				09 22			09 37	
Cressington	d	08 09			08 24			08 39					08 54				09 09				09 24			09 39	
Liverpool Sth Parkway 7 89 ✈	d	08 12			08 27			08 42					08 57				09 12				09 27			09 42	
Hunts Cross 89	a	08 16			08 31			08 46					09 01				09 16				09 31			09 46	

Table 103

Mondays to Saturdays

Southport, Ormskirk and Kirby - Liverpool and Hunts Cross

		ME	ME	ME	ME		ME	ME	ME	ME	ME	ME	ME	ME	ME		ME	ME	ME	ME	ME	ME	ME	ME	ME
Southport	d		08 58				09 13			09 28			09 43				09 58			10 13			10 28		
Birkdale	d		09 02				09 17			09 32			09 47				10 02			10 17			10 32		
Hillside	d		09 04				09 19			09 34			09 49				10 04			10 19			10 34		
Ainsdale	d		09 07				09 22			09 37			09 52				10 07			10 22			10 37		
Freshfield	d		09 11				09 26			09 41			09 56				10 11			10 26			10 41		
Formby	d		09 13				09 28			09 43			09 58				10 13			10 28			10 43		
Hightown	d		09 17				09 32			09 47			10 02				10 17			10 32			10 47		
Hall Road	d		09 20				09 35			09 50			10 05				10 20			10 35			10 50		
Blundellsands & Crosby	d		09 22				09 37			09 52			10 07				10 22			10 37			10 52		
Waterloo (Merseyside)	d		09 25				09 40			09 55			10 10				10 25			10 40			10 55		
Seaforth & Litherland	d		09 27				09 42			09 57			10 12				10 27			10 42			10 57		
Bootle New Strand	d		09 30				09 45			10 00			10 15				10 30			10 45			11 00		
Bootle Oriel Road	d		09 31				09 46			10 01			10 16				10 31			10 46			11 01		
Bank Hall	d		09 33				09 48			10 03			10 18				10 33			10 48			11 03		
Ormskirk	d	09 05			09 20				09 35			09 50			10 05				10 20			10 35			10 50
Aughton Park	d	09 08			09 23				09 38			09 53			10 08				10 23			10 38			10 53
Town Green	d	09 10			09 25				09 40			09 55			10 10				10 25			10 40			10 55
Maghull	d	09 15			09 30				09 45			10 00			10 15				10 30			10 45			11 00
Old Roan	d	09 18			09 33				09 48			10 03			10 18				10 33			10 48			11 03
Aintree	d	09 20			09 35				09 50			10 05			10 20				10 35			10 50			11 05
Orrell Park	d	09 22			09 37				09 52			10 07			10 22				10 37			10 52			11 07
Walton (Merseyside)	d	09 24			09 39				09 54			10 09			10 24				10 39			10 54			11 09
Kirkby	d			09 28				09 43			09 58			10 13				10 28			10 43			10 58	
Fazakerley	d			09 31				09 46			10 01			10 16				10 31			10 46			11 01	
Rice Lane	d			09 34				09 49			10 04			10 19				10 34			10 49			11 04	
Kirkdale	d	09 27		09 37	09 42			09 52	09 57		10 07	10 12		10 22	10 27			10 37	10 42		10 52	10 57		11 07	11 12
Sandhills	d	09 29	09 36	09 40	09 44		09 51	09 55	09 59	10 06	10 10	10 14	10 21	10 25	10 29		10 36	10 40	10 44	10 51	10 55	10 59	11 06	11 10	11 14
Moorfields 10	d	09 33	09 40	09 43	09 48		09 55	09 58	10 03	10 10	10 13	10 18	10 25	10 28	10 33		10 40	10 43	10 48	10 55	10 58	11 03	11 10	11 13	11 18
Liverpool Central 10	a	09 35	09 43	09 46	09 50		09 58	10 01	10 05	10 13	10 16	10 20	10 28	10 31	10 35		10 43	10 46	10 50	10 58	11 01	11 05	11 13	11 16	11 20
	d		09 44				09 59			10 14			10 29				10 44			10 59			11 14		
Brunswick	d		09 47				10 02			10 17			10 32				10 47			11 02			11 17		
St Michaels	d		09 50				10 05			10 20			10 35				10 50			11 05			11 20		
Aigburth	d		09 52				10 07			10 22			10 37				10 52			11 07			11 22		
Cressington	d		09 54				10 09			10 24			10 39				10 54			11 09			11 24		
Liverpool Sth Parkway 7 89 ✈	d		09 57				10 12			10 27			10 42				10 57			11 12			11 27		
Hunts Cross 89	a		10 01				10 16			10 31			10 46				11 01			11 16			11 31		

			ME	ME	ME	ME	ME	ME	ME	ME	ME		ME	ME	ME	ME	ME	ME	ME	ME	ME		ME	ME	ME
Southport	d		10 43			10 58			11 13				11 28			11 43			11 58				12 13		
Birkdale	d		10 47			11 02			11 17				11 32			11 47			12 02				12 17		
Hillside	d		10 49			11 04			11 19				11 34			11 49			12 04				12 19		
Ainsdale	d		10 52			11 07			11 22				11 37			11 52			12 07				12 22		
Freshfield	d		10 56			11 11			11 26				11 41			11 56			12 11				12 26		
Formby	d		10 58			11 13			11 28				11 43			11 58			12 13				12 28		
Hightown	d		11 02			11 17			11 32				11 47			12 02			12 17				12 32		
Hall Road	d		11 05			11 20			11 35				11 50			12 05			12 20				12 35		
Blundellsands & Crosby	d		11 07			11 22			11 37				11 52			12 07			12 22				12 37		
Waterloo (Merseyside)	d		11 10			11 25			11 40				11 55			12 10			12 25				12 40		
Seaforth & Litherland	d		11 12			11 27			11 42				11 57			12 12			12 27				12 42		
Bootle New Strand	d		11 15			11 30			11 45				12 00			12 15			12 30				12 45		
Bootle Oriel Road	d		11 16			11 31			11 46				12 01			12 16			12 31				12 46		
Bank Hall	d		11 18			11 33			11 48				12 03			12 18			12 33				12 48		
Ormskirk	d				11 05			11 20			11 35				11 50			12 05			12 20				12 35
Aughton Park	d				11 08			11 23			11 38				11 53			12 08			12 23				12 38
Town Green	d				11 10			11 25			11 40				11 55			12 10			12 25				12 40
Maghull	d				11 15			11 30			11 45				12 00			12 15			12 30				12 45
Old Roan	d				11 18			11 33			11 48				12 03			12 18			12 33				12 48
Aintree	d				11 20			11 35			11 50				12 05			12 20			12 35				12 50
Orrell Park	d				11 22			11 37			11 52				12 07			12 22			12 37				12 52
Walton (Merseyside)	d				11 24			11 39			11 54				12 09			12 24			12 39				12 54
Kirkby	d			11 13			11 28			11 43				11 58			12 13			12 28				12 43	
Fazakerley	d			11 16			11 31			11 46				12 01			12 16			12 31				12 46	
Rice Lane	d			11 19			11 34			11 49				12 04			12 19			12 34				12 49	
Kirkdale	d			11 22	11 27		11 37	11 42		11 52	11 57			12 07	12 12		12 22	12 27		12 37	12 42			12 52	12 57
Sandhills	d		11 21	11 25	11 29	11 36	11 40	11 44	11 51	11 55	11 59		12 06	12 10	12 14	12 21	12 25	12 29	12 36	12 40	12 44		12 51	12 55	12 59
Moorfields 10	d		11 25	11 28	11 33	11 40	11 43	11 48	11 55	11 58	12 03		12 10	12 13	12 18	12 25	12 28	12 33	12 40	12 43	12 48		12 55	12 58	13 03
Liverpool Central 10	a		11 28	11 31	11 35	11 43	11 46	11 50	11 58	12 01	12 05		12 13	12 16	12 20	12 28	12 31	12 35	12 43	12 46	12 50		12 58	13 01	13 05
	d		11 29			11 44			11 59				12 14			12 29			12 44				12 59		
Brunswick	d		11 32			11 47			12 02				12 17			12 32			12 47				13 02		
St Michaels	d		11 35			11 50			12 05				12 20			12 35			12 50				13 05		
Aigburth	d		11 37			11 52			12 07				12 22			12 37			12 52				13 07		
Cressington	d		11 39			11 54			12 09				12 24			12 39			12 54				13 09		
Liverpool Sth Parkway 7 89 ✈	d		11 42			11 57			12 12				12 27			12 42			12 57				13 12		
Hunts Cross 89	a		11 46			12 01			12 16				12 31			12 46			13 01				13 16		

Southport, Ormskirk and Kirby - Liverpool and Hunts Cross

	ME	ME	ME	ME	ME	ME		ME	ME	ME	ME	ME	ME	ME	ME	ME		ME	ME	ME	ME	ME	ME	ME
Southport d	12 28			12 43				12 58			13 13			13 28				13 43			13 58			14 13
Birkdale d	12 32			12 47				13 02			13 17			13 32				13 47			14 02			14 17
Hillside d	12 34			12 49				13 04			13 19			13 34				13 49			14 04			14 19
Ainsdale d	12 37			12 52				13 07			13 22			13 37				13 52			14 07			14 22
Freshfield d	12 41			12 56				13 11			13 26			13 41				13 56			14 11			14 26
Formby d	12 43			12 58				13 13			13 28			13 43				13 58			14 13			14 28
Hightown d	12 47			13 02				13 17			13 32			13 47				14 02			14 17			14 32
Hall Road d	12 50			13 05				13 20			13 35			13 50				14 05			14 20			14 35
Blundellsands & Crosby d	12 52			13 07				13 22			13 37			13 52				14 07			14 22			14 37
Waterloo (Merseyside) d	12 55			13 10				13 25			13 40			13 55				14 10			14 25			14 40
Seaforth & Litherland d	12 57			13 12				13 27			13 42			13 57				14 12			14 27			14 42
Bootle New Strand d	13 00			13 15				13 30			13 45			14 00				14 15			14 30			14 45
Bootle Oriel Road d	13 01			13 16				13 31			13 46			14 01				14 16			14 31			14 46
Bank Hall d	13 03			13 18				13 33			13 48			14 03				14 18			14 33			14 48
Ormskirk d			12 50			13 05				13 20			13 35			13 50				14 05			14 20	
Aughton Park d			12 53			13 08				13 23			13 38			13 53				14 08			14 23	
Town Green d			12 55			13 10				13 25			13 40			13 55				14 10			14 25	
Maghull d			13 00			13 15				13 30			13 45			14 00				14 15			14 30	
Old Roan d			13 03			13 18				13 33			13 48			14 03				14 18			14 33	
Aintree d			13 05			13 20				13 35			13 50			14 05				14 20			14 35	
Orrell Park d			13 07			13 22				13 37			13 52			14 07				14 22			14 37	
Walton (Merseyside) d			13 09			13 24				13 39			13 54			14 09				14 24			14 39	
Kirkby d		12 58			13 13				13 28			13 43			13 58				14 13			14 28		
Fazakerley d		13 01			13 16				13 31			13 46			14 01				14 16			14 31		
Rice Lane d		13 04			13 19				13 34			13 49			14 04				14 19			14 34		
Kirkdale d		13 07	13 12		13 22	13 27			13 37	13 42		13 52	13 57		14 07	14 12			14 22	14 27		14 37	14 42	
Sandhills d	13 06	13 10	13 14	13 21	13 25	13 29		13 36	13 40	13 44	13 51	13 55	13 59	14 06	14 10	14 14		14 21	14 25	14 29	14 36	14 40	14 44	14 51
Moorfields 10 d	13 10	13 13	13 18	13 25	13 28	13 33		13 40	13 43	13 48	13 55	13 58	14 03	14 10	14 13	14 18		14 25	14 28	14 33	14 40	14 43	14 48	14 55
Liverpool Central 10 a	13 13	13 16	13 20	13 28	13 31	13 35		13 43	13 46	13 50	13 58	14 01	14 05	14 13	14 16	14 20		14 28	14 31	14 35	14 43	14 46	14 50	14 58
d	13 14			13 29				13 44			13 59			14 14				14 29			14 44			14 59
Brunswick d	13 17			13 32				13 47			14 02			14 17				14 32			14 47			15 02
St Michaels d	13 20			13 35				13 50			14 05			14 20				14 35			14 50			15 05
Aigburth d	13 22			13 37				13 52			14 07			14 22				14 37			14 52			15 07
Cressington d	13 24			13 39				13 54			14 09			14 24				14 39			14 54			15 09
Liverpool Sth Parkway 7 89 ✈ d	13 27			13 42				13 57			14 12			14 27				14 42			14 57			15 12
Hunts Cross 89 a	13 31			13 46				14 01			14 16			14 31				14 46			15 01			15 16

	ME	ME		ME	ME	ME	ME	ME	ME	ME	ME	ME		ME	ME	ME	ME	ME	ME	ME	ME	ME		ME
Southport d				14 28			14 43			14 58				15 13			15 28			15 43				15 58
Birkdale d				14 32			14 47			15 02				15 17			15 32			15 47				16 02
Hillside d				14 34			14 49			15 04				15 19			15 34			15 49				16 04
Ainsdale d				14 37			14 52			15 07				15 22			15 37			15 52				16 07
Freshfield d				14 41			14 56			15 11				15 26			15 41			15 56				16 11
Formby d				14 43			14 58			15 13				15 28			15 43			15 58				16 13
Hightown d				14 47			15 02			15 17				15 32			15 47			16 02				16 17
Hall Road d				14 50			15 05			15 20				15 35			15 50			16 05				16 20
Blundellsands & Crosby d				14 52			15 07			15 22				15 37			15 52			16 07				16 22
Waterloo (Merseyside) d				14 55			15 10			15 25				15 40			15 55			16 10				16 25
Seaforth & Litherland d				14 57			15 12			15 27				15 42			15 57			16 12				16 27
Bootle New Strand d				15 00			15 15			15 30				15 45			16 00			16 15				16 30
Bootle Oriel Road d				15 01			15 16			15 31				15 46			16 01			16 16				16 31
Bank Hall d				15 03			15 18			15 33				15 48			16 03			16 18				16 33
Ormskirk d		14 35				14 50			15 05			15 20				15 35			15 50			16 05		
Aughton Park d		14 38				14 53			15 08			15 23				15 38			15 53			16 08		
Town Green d		14 40				14 55			15 10			15 25				15 40			15 55			16 10		
Maghull d		14 45				15 00			15 15			15 30				15 45			16 00			16 15		
Old Roan d		14 48				15 03			15 18			15 33				15 48			16 03			16 18		
Aintree d		14 50				15 05			15 20			15 35				15 50			16 05			16 20		
Orrell Park d		14 52				15 07			15 22			15 37				15 52			16 07			16 22		
Walton (Merseyside) d		14 54				15 09			15 24			15 39				15 54			16 09			16 24		
Kirkby d	14 43				14 58			15 13			15 28				15 43			15 58			16 13			
Fazakerley d	14 46				15 01			15 16			15 31				15 46			16 01			16 16			
Rice Lane d	14 49				15 04			15 19			15 34				15 49			16 04			16 19			
Kirkdale d	14 52	14 57			15 07	15 12		15 22	15 27		15 37	15 42			15 52	15 57		16 07	16 12		16 22	16 27		
Sandhills d	14 55	14 59		15 06	15 10	15 14	15 21	15 25	15 29	15 36	15 40	15 44		15 51	15 55	15 59	16 06	16 10	16 14	16 21	16 25	16 29		16 36
Moorfields 10 d	14 58	15 03		15 10	15 13	15 18	15 25	15 28	15 33	15 40	15 43	15 48		15 55	15 58	16 03	16 10	16 13	16 18	16 25	16 28	16 33		16 40
Liverpool Central 10 a	15 01	15 05		15 13	15 16	15 20	15 28	15 31	15 35	15 43	15 46	15 50		15 58	16 01	16 05	16 13	16 16	16 20	16 28	16 31	16 35		16 43
d				15 14			15 29			15 44				15 59			16 14			16 29				16 44
Brunswick d				15 17			15 32			15 47				16 02			16 17			16 32				16 47
St Michaels d				15 20			15 35			15 50				16 05			16 20			16 35				16 50
Aigburth d				15 22			15 37			15 52				16 07			16 22			16 37				16 52
Cressington d				15 24			15 39			15 54				16 09			16 24			16 39				16 54
Liverpool Sth Parkway 7 89 ✈ d				15 27			15 42			15 57				16 12			16 27			16 42				16 57
Hunts Cross 89 a				15 31			15 46			16 01				16 16			16 31			16 46				17 01

Southport, Ormskirk and Kirby - Liverpool and Hunts Cross

		ME	ME	ME	ME	ME	ME	ME	ME		ME	ME	ME	ME	ME	ME	ME	ME	ME		ME	ME	ME	ME	ME
Southport	d			16 13			16 28				16 43			16 58			17 13				17 28			17 43	
Birkdale	d			16 17			16 32				16 47			17 02			17 17				17 32			17 47	
Hillside	d			16 19			16 34				16 49			17 04			17 19				17 34			17 49	
Ainsdale	d			16 22			16 37				16 52			17 07			17 22				17 37			17 52	
Freshfield	d			16 26			16 41				16 56			17 11			17 26				17 41			17 56	
Formby	d			16 28			16 43				16 58			17 13			17 28				17 43			17 58	
Hightown	d			16 32			16 47				17 02			17 17			17 32				17 47			18 02	
Hall Road	d			16 35			16 50				17 05			17 20			17 35				17 50			18 05	
Blundellsands & Crosby	d			16 37			16 52				17 07			17 22			17 37				17 52			18 07	
Waterloo (Merseyside)	d			16 40			16 55				17 10			17 25			17 40				17 55			18 10	
Seaforth & Litherland	d			16 42			16 57				17 12			17 27			17 42				17 57			18 12	
Bootle New Strand	d			16 45			17 00				17 15			17 30			17 45				18 00			18 15	
Bootle Oriel Road	d			16 46			17 01				17 16			17 31			17 46				18 01			18 16	
Bank Hall	d			16 48			17 03				17 18			17 33			17 48				18 03			18 18	
Ormskirk	d		16 20			16 35			16 50				17 05			17 20			17 35				17 50		
Aughton Park	d		16 23			16 38			16 53				17 08			17 23			17 38				17 53		
Town Green	d		16 25			16 40			16 55				17 10			17 25			17 40				17 55		
Maghull	d		16 30			16 45			17 00				17 15			17 30			17 45				18 00		
Old Roan	d		16 33			16 48			17 03				17 18			17 33			17 48				18 03		
Aintree	d		16 35			16 50			17 05				17 20			17 35			17 50				18 05		
Orrell Park	d		16 37			16 52			17 07				17 22			17 37			17 52				18 07		
Walton (Merseyside)	d		16 39			16 54			17 09				17 24			17 39			17 54				18 09		
Kirkby	d	16 28			16 43			16 58				17 13			17 28			17 43				17 58			18 13
Fazakerley	d	16 31			16 46			17 01				17 16			17 31			17 46				18 01			18 16
Rice Lane	d	16 34			16 49			17 04				17 19			17 34			17 49				18 04			18 19
Kirkdale	d	16 37	16 42		16 52	16 57		17 07	17 12			17 22	17 27		17 37	17 42		17 52	17 57			18 07	18 12		18 22
Sandhills	d	16 40	16 44	16 51	16 55	16 59	17 06	17 10	17 14		17 21	17 25	17 29	17 36	17 40	17 44	17 51	17 55	17 59		18 06	18 10	18 14	18 21	18 25
Moorfields 10	d	16 43	16 48	16 55	16 58	17 03	17 10	17 13	17 18		17 25	17 28	17 33	17 40	17 43	17 48	17 55	17 58	18 03		18 10	18 13	18 18	18 25	18 28
Liverpool Central 10	a	16 46	16 50	16 58	17 01	17 05	17 13	17 16	17 20		17 28	17 31	17 35	17 43	17 46	17 50	17 58	18 01	18 05		18 13	18 16	18 20	18 28	18 31
	d			16 59			17 14				17 29			17 44			17 59				18 14			18 29	
Brunswick	d			17 02			17 17				17 32			17 47			18 02				18 17			18 32	
St Michaels	d			17 05			17 20				17 35			17 50			18 05				18 20			18 35	
Aigburth	d			17 07			17 22				17 37			17 52			18 07				18 22			18 37	
Cressington	d			17 09			17 24				17 39			17 54			18 09				18 24			18 39	
Liverpool Sth Parkway 7 89 ✈	d			17 12			17 27				17 42			17 57			18 12				18 27			18 42	
Hunts Cross 89	a			17 16			17 31				17 46			18 01			18 16				18 31			18 46	

		ME	ME	ME	ME		ME	ME	ME	ME	ME	ME	ME	ME	ME		ME	ME	ME	ME	ME	ME	ME	ME	ME
Southport	d		17 58				18 13			18 28			18 43				18 58			19 13		19 28		19 43	
Birkdale	d		18 02				18 17			18 32			18 47				19 02			19 17		19 32		19 47	
Hillside	d		18 04				18 19			18 34			18 49				19 04			19 19		19 34		19 49	
Ainsdale	d		18 07				18 22			18 37			18 52				19 07			19 22		19 37		19 52	
Freshfield	d		18 11				18 26			18 41			18 56				19 11			19 26		19 41		19 56	
Formby	d		18 13				18 28			18 43			18 58				19 13			19 28		19 43		19 58	
Hightown	d		18 17				18 32			18 47			19 02				19 17			19 32		19 47		20 02	
Hall Road	d		18 20				18 35			18 50			19 05				19 20			19 35		19 50		20 05	
Blundellsands & Crosby	d		18 22				18 37			18 52			19 07				19 22			19 37		19 52		20 07	
Waterloo (Merseyside)	d		18 25				18 40			18 55			19 10				19 25			19 40		19 55		20 10	
Seaforth & Litherland	d		18 27				18 42			18 57			19 12				19 27			19 42		19 57		20 12	
Bootle New Strand	d		18 30				18 45			19 00			19 15				19 30			19 45		20 00		20 15	
Bootle Oriel Road	d		18 31				18 46			19 01			19 16				19 31			19 46		20 01		20 16	
Bank Hall	d		18 33				18 48			19 03			19 18				19 33			19 48		20 03		20 18	
Ormskirk	d	18 05			18 20				18 35			18 50			19 05				19 20				19 50		
Aughton Park	d	18 08			18 23				18 38			18 53			19 08				19 23				19 53		
Town Green	d	18 10			18 25				18 40			18 55			19 10				19 25				19 55		
Maghull	d	18 15			18 30				18 45			19 00			19 15				19 30				20 00		
Old Roan	d	18 18			18 33				18 48			19 03			19 18				19 33				20 03		
Aintree	d	18 20			18 35				18 50			19 05			19 20				19 35				20 05		
Orrell Park	d	18 22			18 37				18 52			19 07			19 22				19 37				20 07		
Walton (Merseyside)	d	18 24			18 39				18 54			19 09			19 24				19 39				20 09		
Kirkby	d			18 28				18 43			18 58			19 13				19 28			19 48				20 18
Fazakerley	d			18 31				18 46			19 01			19 16				19 31			19 51				20 21
Rice Lane	d			18 34				18 49			19 04			19 19				19 34			19 54				20 24
Kirkdale	d	18 27		18 37	18 42			18 52	18 57		19 07	19 12		19 22	19 27			19 37	19 42		19 57		20 12		20 27
Sandhills	d	18 29	18 36	18 40	18 44		18 51	18 55	18 59	19 06	19 10	19 14	19 21	19 25	19 29		19 36	19 40	19 44	19 51	20 00	20 06	20 14	20 21	20 30
Moorfields 10	d	18 33	18 40	18 43	18 48		18 55	18 58	19 03	19 10	19 13	19 18	19 25	19 28	19 33		19 40	19 43	19 48	19 55	20 03	20 10	20 18	20 25	20 33
Liverpool Central 10	a	18 35	18 43	18 46	18 50		18 58	19 01	19 05	19 13	19 16	19 20	19 28	19 31	19 35		19 43	19 46	19 50	19 58	20 06	20 13	20 20	20 28	20 36
	d		18 44				18 59			19 14			19 29				19 44			19 59		20 14		20 29	
Brunswick	d		18 47				19 02			19 17			19 32				19 47			20 02		20 17		20 32	
St Michaels	d		18 50				19 05			19 20			19 35				19 50			20 05		20 20		20 35	
Aigburth	d		18 52				19 07			19 22			19 37				19 52			20 07		20 22		20 37	
Cressington	d		18 54				19 09			19 24			19 39				19 54			20 09		20 24		20 39	
Liverpool Sth Parkway 7 89 ✈	d		18 57				19 12			19 27			19 42				19 57			20 12		20 27		20 42	
Hunts Cross 89	a		19 01				19 16			19 31			19 46				20 01			20 16		20 31		20 46	

Table 103

Mondays to Saturdays

Southport, Ormskirk and Kirby - Liverpool and Hunts Cross

Station			ME	ME	ME	ME	ME	ME	ME	ME	ME		ME	ME	ME	ME	ME	ME	ME	ME	ME		ME	ME	ME
Southport	d		19 58		20 13		20 28		20 43		20 58			21 13		21 28		21 43		21 58			22 13		22 28
Birkdale	d		20 02		20 17		20 32		20 47		21 02			21 17		21 32		21 47		22 02			22 17		22 32
Hillside	d		20 04		20 19		20 34		20 49		21 04			21 19		21 34		21 49		22 04			22 19		22 34
Ainsdale	d		20 07		20 22		20 37		20 52		21 07			21 22		21 37		21 52		22 07			22 22		22 37
Freshfield	d		20 11		20 26		20 41		20 56		21 11			21 26		21 41		21 56		22 11			22 26		22 41
Formby	d		20 13		20 28		20 43		20 58		21 13			21 28		21 43		21 58		22 13			22 28		22 43
Hightown	d		20 17		20 32		20 47		21 02		21 17			21 32		21 47		22 02		22 17			22 32		22 47
Hall Road	d		20 20		20 35		20 50		21 05		21 20			21 35		21 50		22 05		22 20			22 35		22 50
Blundellsands & Crosby	d		20 22		20 37		20 52		21 07		21 22			21 37		21 52		22 07		22 22			22 37		22 52
Waterloo (Merseyside)	d		20 25		20 40		20 55		21 10		21 25			21 40		21 55		22 10		22 25			22 40		22 55
Seaforth & Litherland	d		20 27		20 42		20 57		21 12		21 27			21 42		21 57		22 12		22 27			22 42		22 57
Bootle New Strand	d		20 30		20 45		21 00		21 15		21 30			21 45		22 00		22 15		22 30			22 45		23 00
Bootle Oriel Road	d		20 31		20 46		21 01		21 16		21 31			21 46		22 01		22 16		22 31			22 46		23 01
Bank Hall	d		20 33		20 48		21 03		21 18		21 33			21 48		22 03		22 18		22 33			22 48		23 03
Ormskirk	d			20 20				20 50					21 20				21 50				22 20				
Aughton Park	d			20 23				20 53					21 23				21 53				22 23				
Town Green	d			20 25				20 55					21 25				21 55				22 25				
Maghull	d			20 30				21 00					21 30				22 00				22 30				
Old Roan	d			20 33				21 03					21 33				22 03				22 33				
Aintree	d			20 35				21 05					21 35				22 05				22 35				
Orrell Park	d			20 37				21 07					21 37				22 07				22 37				
Walton (Merseyside)	d			20 39				21 09					21 39				22 09				22 39				
Kirkby	d					20 48				21 18					21 48				22 18					22 48	
Fazakerley	d					20 51				21 21					21 51				22 21					22 51	
Rice Lane	d					20 54				21 24					21 54				22 24					22 54	
Kirkdale	d			20 42		20 57		21 12		21 27			21 42		21 57		22 12		22 27		22 42			22 57	
Sandhills	d		20 36	20 44	20 51	21 00	21 06	21 14	21 21	21 30	21 36		21 44	21 51	22 00	22 06	22 14	22 21	22 30	22 36	22 44		22 51	23 00	23 06
Moorfields 10	d		20 40	20 48	20 55	21 03	21 10	21 18	21 25	21 33	21 40		21 48	21 55	22 03	22 10	22 18	22 25	22 33	22 40	22 48		22 55	23 03	23 10
Liverpool Central 10	a		20 43	20 50	20 58	21 06	21 13	21 20	21 28	21 36	21 43		21 50	21 58	22 06	22 13	22 20	22 28	22 36	22 43	22 50		22 58	23 06	23 13
	d		20 44		20 59		21 14		21 29		21 44			21 59		22 14		22 29		22 44			22 59		23 14
Brunswick	d		20 47		21 02		21 17		21 32		21 47			22 02		22 17		22 32		22 47			23 02		23 17
St Michaels	d		20 50		21 05		21 20		21 35		21 50			22 05		22 20		22 35		22 50			23 05		23 20
Aigburth	d		20 52		21 07		21 22		21 37		21 52			22 07		22 22		22 37		22 52			23 07		23 22
Cressington	d		20 54		21 09		21 24		21 39		21 54			22 09		22 24		22 39		22 54			23 09		23 24
Liverpool Sth Parkway 7 89 ✈	d		20 57		21 12		21 27		21 42		21 57			22 12		22 27		22 42		22 57			23 12		23 27
Hunts Cross 89	a		21 01		21 16		21 31		21 46		22 01			22 16		22 31		22 46		23 01			23 18		23 32

Station		ME	ME	ME	ME	ME	ME
Southport	d		22 43		22 58		23 16
Birkdale	d		22 47		23 02		23 20
Hillside	d		22 49		23 04		23 22
Ainsdale	d		22 52		23 07		23 25
Freshfield	d		22 56		23 11		23 29
Formby	d		22 58		23 13		23 31
Hightown	d		23 02		23 17		23 35
Hall Road	d		23 05		23 20		23 38
Blundellsands & Crosby	d		23 07		23 22		23 40
Waterloo (Merseyside)	d		23 10		23 25		23 43
Seaforth & Litherland	d		23 12		23 27		23 45
Bootle New Strand	d		23 15		23 30		23 48
Bootle Oriel Road	d		23 16		23 31		23 49
Bank Hall	d		23 18		23 33		23 51
Ormskirk	d	22 50				23 20	
Aughton Park	d	22 53				23 23	
Town Green	d	22 55				23 25	
Maghull	d	23 00				23 30	
Old Roan	d	23 03				23 33	
Aintree	d	23 05				23 35	
Orrell Park	d	23 07				23 37	
Walton (Merseyside)	d	23 09				23 39	
Kirkby	d			23 18			
Fazakerley	d			23 21			
Rice Lane	d			23 24			
Kirkdale	d	23 12		23 27		23 42	
Sandhills	d	23 14	23 21	23 30	23 36	23 44	23 55
Moorfields 10	d	23 18	23 25	23 33	23 40	23 48	23 58
Liverpool Central 10	a	23 20	23 28	23 36	23 43	23 50	00 01
	d		23 29		23 44		
Brunswick	d		23 32		23 47		
St Michaels	d		23 35		23 50		
Aigburth	d		23 37		23 52		
Cressington	d		23 39		23 54		
Liverpool Sth Parkway 7 89 ✈	d		23 42		23 57		
Hunts Cross 89	a		23 46		00 01		

Table 103

Sundays

Southport, Ormskirk and Kirby - Liverpool and Hunts Cross

		ME A	ME A	ME	ME	ME	ME	ME	ME	ME		ME	ME	ME	ME	ME	ME	ME	ME	ME		ME	ME	ME	ME
Southport	d	22p58	23p16			07 58			08 28				08 58			09 28			09 58			10 13		10 28	
Birkdale	d	23p02	23p20			08 02			08 32				09 02			09 32			10 02			10 17		10 32	
Hillside	d	23p04	23p22			08 04			08 34				09 04			09 34			10 04			10 19		10 34	
Ainsdale	d	23p07	23p25			08 07			08 37				09 07			09 37			10 07			10 22		10 37	
Freshfield	d	23p11	23p29			08 11			08 41				09 11			09 41			10 11			10 26		10 41	
Formby	d	23p13	23p31			08 13			08 43				09 13			09 43			10 13			10 28		10 43	
Hightown	d	23p17	23p35			08 17			08 47				09 17			09 47			10 17			10 32		10 47	
Hall Road	d	23p20	23p38			08 20			08 50				09 20			09 50			10 20			10 35		10 50	
Blundellsands & Crosby	d	23p22	23p40			08 22			08 52				09 22			09 52			10 22			10 37		10 52	
Waterloo (Merseyside)	d	23p25	23p43			08 25			08 55				09 25			09 55			10 25			10 40		10 55	
Seaforth & Litherland	d	23p27	23p45			08 27			08 57				09 27			09 57			10 27			10 42		10 57	
Bootle New Strand	d	23p30	23p48			08 30			09 00				09 30			10 00			10 30			10 45		11 00	
Bootle Oriel Road	d	23p31	23p49			08 31			09 01				09 31			10 01			10 31			10 46		11 01	
Bank Hall	d	23p33	23p51			08 33			09 03				09 33			10 03			10 33			10 48		11 03	
Ormskirk	d						08 20			08 50				09 20			09 50			10 20					10 50
Aughton Park	d						08 23			08 53				09 23			09 53			10 23					10 53
Town Green	d						08 25			08 55				09 25			09 55			10 25					10 55
Maghull	d						08 30			09 00				09 30			10 00			10 30					11 00
Old Roan	d						08 33			09 03				09 33			10 03			10 33					11 03
Aintree	d						08 35			09 05				09 35			10 05			10 35					11 05
Orrell Park	d						08 37			09 07				09 37			10 07			10 37					11 07
Walton (Merseyside)	d						08 39			09 09				09 39			10 09			10 39					11 09
Kirkby	d				08 18			08 48				09 18			09 48			10 18					10 48		
Fazakerley	d				08 21			08 51				09 21			09 51			10 21					10 51		
Rice Lane	d				08 24			08 54				09 24			09 54			10 24					10 54		
Kirkdale	d				08 27		08 42	08 57		09 12		09 27		09 42	09 57		10 12	10 27		10 42			10 57		11 12
Sandhills	d	23p36	23p55		08 30	08 36	08 44	09 00	09 06	09 14		09 30	09 36	09 44	10 00	10 06	10 14	10 30	10 36	10 44		10 51	11 00	11 06	11 14
Moorfields 10	d	23p40	23p58		08 33	08 40	08 48	09 03	09 10	09 18		09 33	09 40	09 48	10 03	10 10	10 18	10 33	10 40	10 48		10 55	11 03	11 10	11 18
Liverpool Central 10	a	23p43	00 01		08 36	08 43	08 50	09 06	09 13	09 20		09 36	09 43	09 50	10 06	10 13	10 20	10 36	10 43	10 50		10 58	11 06	11 13	11 20
	d	23p44		08 14		08 44			09 14				09 44			10 14			10 44					11 14	
Brunswick	d	23p47		08 17		08 47			09 17				09 47			10 17			10 47					11 17	
St Michaels	d	23p50		08 20		08 50			09 20				09 50			10 20			10 50					11 20	
Aigburth	d	23p52		08 22		08 52			09 22				09 52			10 22			10 52					11 22	
Cressington	d	23p54		08 24		08 54			09 24				09 54			10 24			10 54					11 24	
Liverpool Sth Parkway 7 89 ⇚	d	23p57		08 27		08 57			09 27				09 57			10 27			10 57					11 27	
Hunts Cross 89	a	00 01		08 31		09 01			09 31				10 01			10 31			11 01					11 31	

		ME	ME	ME	ME	ME		ME	ME	ME	ME	ME	ME	ME	ME	ME		ME	ME	ME	ME	ME	ME	ME	ME
Southport	d	10 43		10 58		11 13			11 28		11 43		11 58		12 13			12 28		12 43		12 58		13 13	
Birkdale	d	10 47		11 02		11 17			11 32		11 47		12 02		12 17			12 32		12 47		13 02		13 17	
Hillside	d	10 49		11 04		11 19			11 34		11 49		12 04		12 19			12 34		12 49		13 04		13 19	
Ainsdale	d	10 52		11 07		11 22			11 37		11 52		12 07		12 22			12 37		12 52		13 07		13 22	
Freshfield	d	10 56		11 11		11 26			11 41		11 56		12 11		12 26			12 41		12 56		13 11		13 26	
Formby	d	10 58		11 13		11 28			11 43		11 58		12 13		12 28			12 43		12 58		13 13		13 28	
Hightown	d	11 02		11 17		11 32			11 47		12 02		12 17		12 32			12 47		13 02		13 17		13 32	
Hall Road	d	11 05		11 20		11 35			11 50		12 05		12 20		12 35			12 50		13 05		13 20		13 35	
Blundellsands & Crosby	d	11 07		11 22		11 37			11 52		12 07		12 22		12 37			12 52		13 07		13 22		13 37	
Waterloo (Merseyside)	d	11 10		11 25		11 40			11 55		12 10		12 25		12 40			12 55		13 10		13 25		13 40	
Seaforth & Litherland	d	11 12		11 27		11 42			11 57		12 12		12 27		12 42			12 57		13 12		13 27		13 42	
Bootle New Strand	d	11 15		11 30		11 45			12 00		12 15		12 30		12 45			13 00		13 15		13 30		13 45	
Bootle Oriel Road	d	11 16		11 31		11 46			12 01		12 16		12 31		12 46			13 01		13 16		13 31		13 46	
Bank Hall	d	11 18		11 33		11 48			12 03		12 18		12 33		12 48			13 03		13 18		13 33		13 48	
Ormskirk	d				11 20					11 50				12 20					12 50				13 20		
Aughton Park	d				11 23					11 53				12 23					12 53				13 23		
Town Green	d				11 25					11 55				12 25					12 55				13 25		
Maghull	d				11 30					12 00				12 30					13 00				13 30		
Old Roan	d				11 33					12 03				12 33					13 03				13 33		
Aintree	d				11 35					12 05				12 35					13 05				13 35		
Orrell Park	d				11 37					12 07				12 37					13 07				13 37		
Walton (Merseyside)	d				11 39					12 09				12 39					13 09				13 39		
Kirkby	d		11 18					11 48				12 18				12 48					13 18				13 48
Fazakerley	d		11 21					11 51				12 21				12 51					13 21				13 51
Rice Lane	d		11 24					11 54				12 24				12 54					13 24				13 54
Kirkdale	d		11 27		11 42			11 57		12 12		12 27		12 42		12 57			13 12		13 27		13 42		13 57
Sandhills	d	11 21	11 30	11 36	11 44	11 51		12 00	12 06	12 14	12 21	12 30	12 36	12 44	12 51	13 00		13 06	13 14	13 21	13 30	13 36	13 44	13 51	14 00
Moorfields 10	d	11 25	11 33	11 40	11 48	11 55		12 03	12 10	12 18	12 25	12 33	12 40	12 48	12 55	13 03		13 10	13 18	13 25	13 33	13 40	13 48	13 55	14 03
Liverpool Central 10	a	11 28	11 36	11 43	11 50	11 58		12 06	12 13	12 20	12 28	12 36	12 43	12 50	12 58	13 06		13 13	13 20	13 28	13 36	13 43	13 50	13 58	14 06
	d			11 44					12 14				12 44					13 14				13 44			
Brunswick	d			11 47					12 17				12 47					13 17				13 47			
St Michaels	d			11 50					12 20				12 50					13 20				13 50			
Aigburth	d			11 52					12 22				12 52					13 22				13 52			
Cressington	d			11 54					12 24				12 54					13 24				13 54			
Liverpool Sth Parkway 7 89 ⇚	d			11 57					12 27				12 57					13 27				13 57			
Hunts Cross 89	a			12 01					12 31				13 01					13 31				14 01			

A not 22 May

Table 103

Sundays

Southport, Ormskirk and Kirby - Liverpool and Hunts Cross

		ME		ME	ME	ME	ME	ME	ME	ME	ME	ME		ME	ME	ME	ME	ME	ME	ME	ME	ME		ME	ME
Southport	d	13 28			13 43		13 58		14 13		14 28			14 43		14 58		15 13		15 28		15 43			15 58
Birkdale	d	13 32			13 47		14 02		14 17		14 32			14 47		15 02		15 17		15 32		15 47			16 02
Hillside	d	13 34			13 49		14 04		14 19		14 34			14 49		15 04		15 19		15 34		15 49			16 04
Ainsdale	d	13 37			13 52		14 07		14 22		14 37			14 52		15 07		15 22		15 37		15 52			16 07
Freshfield	d	13 41			13 56		14 11		14 26		14 41			14 56		15 11		15 26		15 41		15 56			16 11
Formby	d	13 43			13 58		14 13		14 28		14 43			14 58		15 13		15 28		15 43		15 58			16 13
Hightown	d	13 47			14 02		14 17		14 32		14 47			15 02		15 17		15 32		15 47		16 02			16 17
Hall Road	d	13 50			14 05		14 20		14 35		14 50			15 05		15 20		15 35		15 50		16 05			16 20
Blundellsands & Crosby	d	13 52			14 07		14 22		14 37		14 52			15 07		15 22		15 37		15 52		16 07			16 22
Waterloo (Merseyside)	d	13 55			14 10		14 25		14 40		14 55			15 10		15 25		15 40		15 55		16 10			16 25
Seaforth & Litherland	d	13 57			14 12		14 27		14 42		14 57			15 12		15 27		15 42		15 57		16 12			16 27
Bootle New Strand	d	14 00			14 15		14 30		14 45		15 00			15 15		15 30		15 45		16 00		16 15			16 30
Bootle Oriel Road	d	14 01			14 16		14 31		14 46		15 01			15 16		15 31		15 46		16 01		16 16			16 31
Bank Hall	d	14 03			14 18		14 33		14 48		15 03			15 18		15 33		15 48		16 03		16 18			16 33
Ormskirk	d			13 50				14 20				14 50					15 20				15 50				
Aughton Park	d			13 53				14 23				14 53					15 23				15 53				
Town Green	d			13 55				14 25				14 55					15 25				15 55				
Maghull	d			14 00				14 30				15 00					15 30				16 00				
Old Roan	d			14 03				14 33				15 03					15 33				16 03				
Aintree	d			14 05				14 35				15 05					15 35				16 05				
Orrell Park	d			14 07				14 37				15 07					15 37				16 07				
Walton (Merseyside)	d			14 09				14 39				15 09					15 39				16 09				
Kirkby	d					14 18				14 48					15 18				15 48					16 18	
Fazakerley	d					14 21				14 51					15 21				15 51					16 21	
Rice Lane	d					14 24				14 54					15 24				15 54					16 24	
Kirkdale	d			14 12		14 27		14 42		14 57		15 12			15 27		15 42		15 57		16 12			16 27	
Sandhills	d	14 06		14 14	14 21	14 30	14 36	14 44	14 51	15 00	15 06	15 14		15 21	15 30	15 36	15 44	15 51	16 00	16 06	16 14	16 21		16 30	16 36
Moorfields 10	d	14 10		14 18	14 25	14 33	14 40	14 48	14 55	15 03	15 10	15 18		15 25	15 33	15 40	15 48	15 55	16 03	16 10	16 18	16 25		16 33	16 40
Liverpool Central 10	a	14 13		14 20	14 28	14 36	14 43	14 50	14 58	15 06	15 13	15 20		15 28	15 36	15 43	15 50	15 58	16 06	16 13	16 20	16 28		16 36	16 43
	d	14 14					14 44				15 14					15 44				16 14					16 44
Brunswick	d	14 17					14 47				15 17					15 47				16 17					16 47
St Michaels	d	14 20					14 50				15 20					15 50				16 20					16 50
Aigburth	d	14 22					14 52				15 22					15 52				16 22					16 52
Cressington	d	14 24					14 54				15 24					15 54				16 24					16 54
Liverpool Sth Parkway 7 89 ✈	d	14 27					14 57				15 27					15 57				16 27					16 57
Hunts Cross 89	a	14 31					15 01				15 31					16 01				16 31					17 01

		ME	ME	ME	ME	ME	ME	ME		ME	ME	ME	ME	ME	ME	ME	ME	ME		ME	ME	ME	ME	ME	ME
Southport	d		16 13		16 28		16 43			16 58		17 13		17 28		17 43		17 58			18 13		18 28		18 43
Birkdale	d		16 17		16 32		16 47			17 02		17 17		17 32		17 47		18 02			18 17		18 32		18 47
Hillside	d		16 19		16 34		16 49			17 04		17 19		17 34		17 49		18 04			18 19		18 34		18 49
Ainsdale	d		16 22		16 37		16 52			17 07		17 22		17 37		17 52		18 07			18 22		18 37		18 52
Freshfield	d		16 26		16 41		16 56			17 11		17 26		17 41		17 56		18 11			18 26		18 41		18 56
Formby	d		16 28		16 43		16 58			17 13		17 28		17 43		17 58		18 13			18 28		18 43		18 58
Hightown	d		16 32		16 47		17 02			17 17		17 32		17 47		18 02		18 17			18 32		18 47		19 02
Hall Road	d		16 35		16 50		17 05			17 20		17 35		17 50		18 05		18 20			18 35		18 50		19 05
Blundellsands & Crosby	d		16 37		16 52		17 07			17 22		17 37		17 52		18 07		18 22			18 37		18 52		19 07
Waterloo (Merseyside)	d		16 40		16 55		17 10			17 25		17 40		17 55		18 10		18 25			18 40		18 55		19 10
Seaforth & Litherland	d		16 42		16 57		17 12			17 27		17 42		17 57		18 12		18 27			18 42		18 57		19 12
Bootle New Strand	d		16 45		17 00		17 15			17 30		17 45		18 00		18 15		18 30			18 45		19 00		19 15
Bootle Oriel Road	d		16 46		17 01		17 16			17 31		17 46		18 01		18 16		18 31			18 46		19 01		19 16
Bank Hall	d		16 48		17 03		17 18			17 33		17 48		18 03		18 18		18 33			18 48		19 03		19 18
Ormskirk	d	16 20				16 50					17 20				17 50					18 20				18 50	
Aughton Park	d	16 23				16 53					17 23				17 53					18 23				18 53	
Town Green	d	16 25				16 55					17 25				17 55					18 25				18 55	
Maghull	d	16 30				17 00					17 30				18 00					18 30				19 00	
Old Roan	d	16 33				17 03					17 33				18 03					18 33				19 03	
Aintree	d	16 35				17 05					17 35				18 05					18 35				19 05	
Orrell Park	d	16 37				17 07					17 37				18 07					18 37				19 07	
Walton (Merseyside)	d	16 39				17 09					17 39				18 09					18 39				19 09	
Kirkby	d			16 48				17 18					17 48				18 18					18 48			
Fazakerley	d			16 51				17 21					17 51				18 21					18 51			
Rice Lane	d			16 54				17 24					17 54				18 24					18 54			
Kirkdale	d	16 42		16 57		17 12		17 27			17 42		17 57		18 12		18 27			18 42		18 57		19 12	
Sandhills	d	16 44	16 51	17 00	17 06	17 14	17 21	17 30		17 36	17 44	17 51	18 00	18 06	18 14	18 21	18 30	18 36		18 44	18 51	19 00	19 06	19 14	19 21
Moorfields 10	d	16 48	16 55	17 03	17 10	17 18	17 25	17 33		17 40	17 48	17 55	18 03	18 10	18 18	18 25	18 33	18 40		18 48	18 55	19 03	19 10	19 18	19 25
Liverpool Central 10	a	16 50	16 58	17 06	17 13	17 20	17 28	17 36		17 43	17 50	17 58	18 06	18 13	18 20	18 28	18 36	18 43		18 50	18 58	19 06	19 13	19 20	19 28
	d				17 14					17 44				18 14				18 44					19 14		
Brunswick	d				17 17					17 47				18 17				18 47					19 17		
St Michaels	d				17 20					17 50				18 20				18 50					19 20		
Aigburth	d				17 22					17 52				18 22				18 52					19 22		
Cressington	d				17 24					17 54				18 24				18 54					19 24		
Liverpool Sth Parkway 7 89 ✈	d				17 27					17 57				18 27				18 57					19 27		
Hunts Cross 89	a				17 31					18 01				18 31				19 01					19 31		

Table 103

Sundays

Southport, Ormskirk and Kirby - Liverpool and Hunts Cross

		ME	ME	ME		ME	ME	ME	ME	ME	ME	ME	ME	ME		ME	ME	ME	ME	ME	ME	ME	ME	ME
Southport	d		18 58			19 13		19 28		19 43		19 58		20 13			20 28		20 43		20 58		21 13	
Birkdale	d		19 02			19 17		19 32		19 47		20 02		20 17			20 32		20 47		21 02		21 17	
Hillside	d		19 04			19 19		19 34		19 49		20 04		20 19			20 34		20 49		21 04		21 19	
Ainsdale	d		19 07			19 22		19 37		19 52		20 07		20 22			20 37		20 52		21 07		21 22	
Freshfield	d		19 11			19 26		19 41		19 56		20 11		20 26			20 41		20 56		21 11		21 26	
Formby	d		19 13			19 28		19 43		19 58		20 13		20 28			20 43		20 58		21 13		21 28	
Hightown	d		19 17			19 32		19 47		20 02		20 17		20 32			20 47		21 02		21 17		21 32	
Hall Road	d		19 20			19 35		19 50		20 05		20 20		20 35			20 50		21 05		21 20		21 35	
Blundellsands & Crosby	d		19 22			19 37		19 52		20 07		20 22		20 37			20 52		21 07		21 22		21 37	
Waterloo (Merseyside)	d		19 25			19 40		19 55		20 10		20 25		20 40			20 55		21 10		21 25		21 40	
Seaforth & Litherland	d		19 27			19 42		19 57		20 12		20 27		20 42			20 57		21 12		21 27		21 42	
Bootle New Strand	d		19 30			19 45		20 00		20 15		20 30		20 45			21 00		21 15		21 30		21 45	
Bootle Oriel Road	d		19 31			19 46		20 01		20 16		20 31		20 46			21 01		21 16		21 31		21 46	
Bank Hall	d		19 33			19 48		20 03		20 18		20 33		20 48			21 03		21 18		21 33		21 48	
Ormskirk	d			19 20					19 50				20 20					20 50				21 20		
Aughton Park	d			19 23					19 53				20 23					20 53				21 23		
Town Green	d			19 25					19 55				20 25					20 55				21 25		
Maghull	d			19 30					20 00				20 30					21 00				21 30		
Old Roan	d			19 33					20 03				20 33					21 03				21 33		
Aintree	d			19 35					20 05				20 35					21 05				21 35		
Orrell Park	d			19 37					20 07				20 37					21 07				21 37		
Walton (Merseyside)	d			19 39					20 09				20 39					21 09				21 39		
Kirkby	d	19 18					19 48				20 18					20 48				21 18				21 48
Fazakerley	d	19 21					19 51				20 21					20 51				21 21				21 51
Rice Lane	d	19 24					19 54				20 24					20 54				21 24				21 54
Kirkdale	d	19 27		19 42			19 57		20 12		20 27		20 42			20 57		21 12		21 27		21 42		21 57
Sandhills	d	19 30	19 36	19 44		19 51	20 00	20 06	20 14	20 21	20 30	20 36	20 44	20 51		21 00	21 06	21 14	21 21	21 30	21 36	21 44	21 51	22 00
Moorfields 10	d	19 33	19 40	19 48		19 55	20 03	20 10	20 18	20 25	20 33	20 40	20 48	20 55		21 03	21 10	21 18	21 25	21 33	21 40	21 48	21 55	22 03
Liverpool Central 10	a	19 36	19 43	19 50		19 58	20 06	20 13	20 20	20 28	20 36	20 43	20 50	20 58		21 06	21 13	21 20	21 28	21 36	21 43	21 50	21 58	22 06
	d		19 44					20 14				20 44					21 14				21 44			
Brunswick	d		19 47					20 17				20 47					21 17				21 47			
St Michaels	d		19 50					20 20				20 50					21 20				21 50			
Aigburth	d		19 52					20 22				20 52					21 22				21 52			
Cressington	d		19 54					20 24				20 54					21 24				21 54			
Liverpool Sth Parkway 7 89 ✈	d		19 57					20 27				20 57					21 27				21 57			
Hunts Cross 89	a		20 01					20 31				21 01					21 31				22 01			

		ME	ME	ME	ME	ME	ME	ME	ME	ME		ME	ME	ME	ME	ME	ME
Southport	d	21 28		21 43		21 58		22 13		22 28			22 43		22 58		23 16
Birkdale	d	21 32		21 47		22 02		22 17		22 32			22 47		23 02		23 20
Hillside	d	21 34		21 49		22 04		22 19		22 34			22 49		23 04		23 22
Ainsdale	d	21 37		21 52		22 07		22 22		22 37			22 52		23 07		23 25
Freshfield	d	21 41		21 56		22 11		22 26		22 41			22 56		23 11		23 29
Formby	d	21 43		21 58		22 13		22 28		22 43			22 58		23 13		23 31
Hightown	d	21 47		22 02		22 17		22 32		22 47			23 02		23 17		23 35
Hall Road	d	21 50		22 05		22 20		22 35		22 50			23 05		23 20		23 38
Blundellsands & Crosby	d	21 52		22 07		22 22		22 37		22 52			23 07		23 22		23 40
Waterloo (Merseyside)	d	21 55		22 10		22 25		22 40		22 55			23 10		23 25		23 43
Seaforth & Litherland	d	21 57		22 12		22 27		22 42		22 57			23 12		23 27		23 45
Bootle New Strand	d	22 00		22 15		22 30		22 45		23 00			23 15		23 30		23 48
Bootle Oriel Road	d	22 01		22 16		22 31		22 46		23 01			23 16		23 31		23 49
Bank Hall	d	22 03		22 18		22 33		22 48		23 03			23 18		23 33		23 51
Ormskirk	d		21 50				22 20					22 50				23 20	
Aughton Park	d		21 53				22 23					22 53				23 23	
Town Green	d		21 55				22 25					22 55				23 25	
Maghull	d		22 00				22 30					23 00				23 30	
Old Roan	d		22 03				22 33					23 03				23 33	
Aintree	d		22 05				22 35					23 05				23 35	
Orrell Park	d		22 07				22 37					23 07				23 37	
Walton (Merseyside)	d		22 09				22 39					23 09				23 39	
Kirkby	d				22 18				22 48					23 18			
Fazakerley	d				22 21				22 51					23 21			
Rice Lane	d				22 24				22 54					23 24			
Kirkdale	d		22 12		22 27		22 42		22 57			23 12		23 27		23 42	
Sandhills	d	22 06	22 14	22 21	22 30	22 36	22 44	22 51	23 00	23 06		23 14	23 21	23 30	23 36	23 44	23 55
Moorfields 10	d	22 10	22 18	22 25	22 33	22 40	22 48	22 55	23 03	23 10		23 18	23 25	23 33	23 40	23 48	23 58
Liverpool Central 10	a	22 13	22 20	22 28	22 36	22 43	22 50	22 58	23 06	23 13		23 20	23 28	23 36	23 43	23 50	00 01
	d	22 14				22 44				23 14					23 44		
Brunswick	d	22 17				22 47				23 17					23 47		
St Michaels	d	22 20				22 50				23 20					23 50		
Aigburth	d	22 22				22 52				23 22					23 52		
Cressington	d	22 24				22 54				23 24					23 54		
Liverpool Sth Parkway 7 89 ✈	d	22 27				22 57				23 27					23 57		
Hunts Cross 89	a	22 31				23 01				23 31					00 01		

Liverpool and Birkenhead - New Brighton, West Kirby, Ellesmere Port and Chester

Miles	Miles	Miles	Miles			ME	ME	ME	ME	ME	ME	ME	ME	ME	ME	ME	ME	ME	ME	ME	ME	ME	ME
0	—	0	0	Moorfields 10	d	23p26	23p31	23p41	23p46	05 36	05 56	06 06	06 16	06 21	06 26	06 41	06 46	06 51	06 56	07 11	07 16	07 21	07 26
0½	—	0½	0½	Liverpool Lime Street 10	d	23p28	23p33	23p43	23p48	05 38	05 58	06 08	06 18	06 23	06 28	06 43	06 48	06 53	06 58	07 13	07 18	07 23	07 28
1	—	1	1	Liverpool Central 10	d	23p30	23p35	23p45	23p50	05 40	06 00	06 10	06 20	06 25	06 30	06 45	06 50	06 55	07 00	07 15	07 20	07 25	07 30
1½	—	1½	1½	James Street	d	23p32	23p37	23p47	23p52	05 42	06 02	06 12	06 22	06 27	06 32	06 47	06 52	06 57	07 02	07 17	07 22	07 27	07 32
2¾	—	2¾	2¾	Hamilton Square	d	23p35	23p40	23p50	23p55	05 45	06 05	06 15	06 25	06 30	06 35	06 50	06 55	07 00	07 05	07 20	07 25	07 30	07 35
—	—	3¼	3¼	Conway Park	d		23p42		23p57				06 27	06 32			06 57	07 02			07 27	07 32	
—	—	4	4	Birkenhead Park	d		23p44		23p59				06 29	06 34			06 59	07 04			07 29	07 34	
—	—	4¾	4¾	Birkenhead North	d		23p47		00 02				06 32	06 37			07 02	07 07			07 32	07 37	
—	—	—	6¼	Wallasey Village	d				00 07				06 37				07 07				07 37		
—	—	—	6½	Wallasey Grove Road	d				00 08				06 38				07 08				07 38		
—	—	—	7¾	**New Brighton**	a				00 13				06 43				07 13				07 43		
—	—	5¼	—	Bidston	d		23p50							06 40				07 10				07 40	
—	—	6½	—	Leasowe	d		23p52							06 42				07 12				07 42	
—	—	7	—	Moreton (Merseyside)	d		23p54							06 44				07 14				07 44	
—	—	8¼	—	Meols	d		23p58							06 48				07 18				07 48	
—	—	9½	—	Manor Road	d		23p59							06 50				07 20				07 50	
—	—	10	—	Hoylake	d		00 02							06 52				07 22				07 52	
—	—	11¼	—	**West Kirby**	a		00 07							06 57				07 27				07 57	
3	—	—	—	Birkenhead Central	d	23p37		23p52		05 47	06 07	06 17			06 37	06 52			07 07	07 22			07 37
3¾	—	—	—	Green Lane	d	23p39		23p54		05 49	06 09	06 19			06 39	06 54			07 09	07 24			07 39
4½	—	—	—	Rock Ferry	d	23p42		23p57		05 52	06 12	06 22			06 42	06 57			07 12	07 27			07 42
5½	—	—	—	Bebington	d	23p44		23p59		05 54	06 14	06 24			06 44	06 59			07 14	07 29			07 44
6½	—	—	—	Port Sunlight	d	23p46		00 01		05 56	06 16	06 26			06 46	07 01			07 16	07 31			07 46
7	—	—	—	Spital	d	23p48		00 03		05 58	06 18	06 28			06 48	07 03			07 18	07 33			07 48
7¾	—	—	—	Bromborough Rake	d	23p50		00 05		06 00	06 20	06 30			06 50	07 05			07 20	07 35			07 50
8½	—	—	—	Bromborough	d	23p52		00 07		06 02	06 22	06 32			06 52	07 07			07 22	07 37			07 52
9	—	—	—	Eastham Rake	d	23p55		00 10		06 05	06 25	06 35			06 55	07 10			07 25	07 40			07 55
10	0	—	—	Hooton	d	23p57		00 12		06 07	06 27	06 37			06 57	07 12			07 27	07 42			07 57
—	1½	—	—	Little Sutton	d	00 01					06 31				07 01				07 31				08 01
—	2½	—	—	Overpool	d	00 03					06 33				07 03				07 33				08 03
—	4	—	—	**Ellesmere Port**	a	00 07					06 37				07 07				07 37				08 07
13	—	—	—	Capenhurst	d			00 17		06 12		06 42				07 17				07 47			
16¾	—	—	—	Bache	d			00 22		06 17		06 47				07 22				07 52			
18¼	—	—	—	**Chester**	a			00 26		06 26		06 56				07 26				07 56			

		ME	ME	ME	ME	ME	ME SX	ME SO	ME	ME	ME	ME	ME	ME	ME	ME	ME	ME	ME SO	ME	ME SO	ME SX	ME
Moorfields 10	d	07 31	07 36	07 41	07 46	07 51	07 53	07 56	08 01	08 06	08 11	08 16	08 21	08 26	08 31	08 36	08 41	08 46	08 48	08 51	08 56	08 56	09 01
Liverpool Lime Street 10	d	07 33	07 38	07 43	07 48	07 53	07 55	07 58	08 03	08 08	08 13	08 18	08 23	08 28	08 33	08 38	08 43	08 48	08 50	08 53	08 58	08 58	09 03
Liverpool Central 10	d	07 35	07 40	07 45	07 50	07 55	07 57	08 00	08 05	08 10	08 15	08 20	08 25	08 30	08 35	08 40	08 45	08 50	08 52	08 55	09 00	09 00	09 05
James Street	d	07 37	07 42	07 47	07 52	07 57	07 59	08 02	08 07	08 12	08 17	08 22	08 27	08 32	08 37	08 42	08 47	08 52	08 54	08 57	09 02	09 02	09 07
Hamilton Square	d	07 40	07 45	07 50	07 55	08 00	08 02	08 05	08 10	08 15	08 20	08 25	08 30	08 35	08 40	08 45	08 50	08 55	08 57	09 00	09 05	09 05	09 10
Conway Park	d	07 42	07 47		07 57	08 02			08 12	08 17		08 27	08 32		08 42	08 47		08 57		09 02			09 12
Birkenhead Park	d	07 44	07 49		07 59	08 04			08 14	08 19		08 29	08 34		08 44	08 49		08 59		09 04			09 14
Birkenhead North	d	07 47	07 52		08 02	08 07			08 17	08 22		08 32	08 37		08 47	08 52		09 02		09 07			09 17
Wallasey Village	d	07 52			08 07				08 22			08 37			08 52			09 07					09 22
Wallasey Grove Road	d	07 53			08 08				08 23			08 38			08 53			09 08					09 23
New Brighton	a	07 58			08 13				08 28			08 43			08 58			09 13					09 28
Bidston	d		07 55			08 10				08 25			08 40			08 55				09 10			
Leasowe	d		07 57			08 12				08 27			08 42			08 57				09 12			
Moreton (Merseyside)	d		07 59			08 14				08 29			08 44			08 59				09 14			
Meols	d		08 03			08 18				08 33			08 48			09 03				09 18			
Manor Road	d		08 05			08 20				08 35			08 50			09 05				09 20			
Hoylake	d		08 07			08 22				08 37			08 52			09 07				09 22			
West Kirby	a		08 12			08 27				08 42			08 57			09 12				09 27			
Birkenhead Central	d			07 52			08 05	08 07			08 22			08 37			08 52		09 00		09 07	09 07	
Green Lane	d			07 54			08 07	08 09			08 24			08 39			08 54		09 02		09 09	09 09	
Rock Ferry	d			07 57			08 09	08 12			08 27			08 42			08 57		09 04		09 12	09 12	
Bebington	d			07 59			08 12	08 14			08 29			08 44			08 59		09 07		09 14	09 14	
Port Sunlight	d			08 01			08 14	08 16			08 31			08 46			09 01		09 09		09 16	09 16	
Spital	d			08 03			08 16	08 18			08 33			08 48			09 03		09 11		09 18	09 18	
Bromborough Rake	d			08 05			08 18	08 20			08 35			08 50			09 05		09 13		09 20	09 20	
Bromborough	d			08 07			08 20	08 22			08 37			08 52			09 07		09 15		09 22	09 22	
Eastham Rake	d			08 10			08 22	08 25			08 40			08 55			09 10		09 17		09 25	09 25	
Hooton	d			08 12			08 24	08 27			08 42			08 57			09 12		09 19		09 27	09 27	
Little Sutton	d						08 29	08 31						09 01					09 24			09 31	
Overpool	d						08 31	08 33						09 03					09 26			09 33	
Ellesmere Port	a						08 34	08 37						09 07					09 31			09 37	
Capenhurst	d			08 17							08 47						09 17						
Bache	d			08 22							08 52						09 22						
Chester	a			08 26							08 56						09 26				09 38		

Liverpool and Birkenhead - New Brighton, West Kirby, Ellesmere Port and Chester

		ME	ME	ME	ME	ME		ME	ME	ME	ME	ME	ME	ME	ME	ME		ME	ME	ME	ME	ME	ME	ME	ME
Moorfields 10	d	09 06	09 11	09 16	09 18	09 21		09 26	09 31	09 36	09 41	09 46	09 48	09 51	09 56	10 01		10 06	10 11	10 16	10 18	10 21	10 26	10 31	10 36
Liverpool Lime Street 10	d	09 08	09 13	09 18	09 20	09 23		09 28	09 33	09 38	09 43	09 48	09 50	09 53	09 58	10 03		10 08	10 13	10 18	10 20	10 23	10 28	10 33	10 38
Liverpool Central 10	d	09 10	09 15	09 20	09 22	09 25		09 30	09 35	09 40	09 45	09 50	09 52	09 55	10 00	10 05		10 10	10 15	10 20	10 22	10 25	10 30	10 35	10 40
James Street	d	09 12	09 17	09 22	09 24	09 27		09 32	09 37	09 42	09 47	09 52	09 54	09 57	10 02	10 07		10 12	10 17	10 22	10 24	10 27	10 32	10 37	10 42
Hamilton Square	d	09 15	09 20	09 25	09 27	09 30		09 35	09 40	09 45	09 50	09 55	09 57	10 00	10 05	10 10		10 15	10 20	10 25	10 27	10 30	10 35	10 40	10 45
Conway Park	d	09 17		09 27		09 32			09 42	09 47		09 57		10 02		10 12		10 17		10 27		10 32		10 42	10 47
Birkenhead Park	d	09 19		09 29		09 34			09 44	09 49		09 59		10 04		10 14		10 19		10 29		10 34		10 44	10 49
Birkenhead North	d	09 22		09 32		09 37			09 47	09 52		10 02		10 07		10 17		10 22		10 32		10 37		10 47	10 52
Wallasey Village	d			09 37					09 52			10 07				10 22				10 37				10 52	
Wallasey Grove Road	d			09 38					09 53			10 08				10 23				10 38				10 53	
New Brighton	a			09 43					09 58			10 13				10 28				10 43				10 58	
Bidston	d	09 25				09 40				09 55				10 10				10 25				10 40			10 55
Leasowe	d	09 27				09 42				09 57				10 12				10 27				10 42			10 57
Moreton (Merseyside)	d	09 29				09 44				09 59				10 14				10 29				10 44			10 59
Meols	d	09 33				09 48				10 03				10 18				10 33				10 48			11 03
Manor Road	d	09 35				09 50				10 05				10 20				10 35				10 50			11 05
Hoylake	d	09 37				09 52				10 07				10 22				10 37				10 52			11 07
West Kirby	a	09 42				09 57				10 12				10 27				10 42				10 57			11 12
Birkenhead Central	d		09 22		09 30			09 37			09 52		10 00		10 07				10 22		10 30		10 37		
Green Lane	d		09 24		09 32			09 39			09 54		10 02		10 09				10 24		10 32		10 39		
Rock Ferry	d		09 27		09 34			09 42			09 57		10 04		10 12				10 27		10 34		10 42		
Bebington	d		09 29		09 37			09 44			09 59		10 07		10 14				10 29		10 37		10 44		
Port Sunlight	d		09 31		09 39			09 46			10 01		10 09		10 16				10 31		10 39		10 46		
Spital	d		09 33		09 41			09 48			10 03		10 11		10 18				10 33		10 41		10 48		
Bromborough Rake	d		09 35		09 43			09 50			10 05		10 13		10 20				10 35		10 43		10 50		
Bromborough	d		09 37		09 45			09 52			10 07		10 15		10 22				10 37		10 45		10 52		
Eastham Rake	d		09 40		09 47			09 55			10 10		10 17		10 25				10 40		10 47		10 55		
Hooton	d		09 42		09 49			09 57			10 12		10 19		10 27				10 42		10 49		10 57		
Little Sutton	d				09 54								10 24								10 54				
Overpool	d				09 56								10 26								10 56				
Ellesmere Port	a				09 59								10 29								10 59				
Capenhurst	d		09 47								10 17								10 47						
Bache	d		09 52								10 22								10 52						
Chester	a		09 56					10 08			10 26				10 38				10 56				11 08		

		ME		ME	ME	ME	ME	ME	ME	ME	ME	ME		ME	ME	ME	ME	ME	ME	ME	ME	ME		ME	ME
Moorfields 10	d	10 41		10 46	10 48	10 51	10 56	11 01	11 06	11 11	11 16	11 18		11 21	11 26	11 31	11 36	11 41	11 46	11 48	11 51	11 56		12 01	12 06
Liverpool Lime Street 10	d	10 43		10 48	10 50	10 53	10 58	11 03	11 08	11 13	11 18	11 20		11 23	11 28	11 33	11 38	11 43	11 48	11 50	11 53	11 58		12 03	12 08
Liverpool Central 10	d	10 45		10 50	10 52	10 55	11 00	11 05	11 10	11 15	11 20	11 22		11 25	11 30	11 35	11 40	11 45	11 50	11 52	11 55	12 00		12 05	12 10
James Street	d	10 47		10 52	10 54	10 57	11 02	11 07	11 12	11 17	11 22	11 24		11 27	11 32	11 37	11 42	11 47	11 52	11 54	11 57	12 02		12 07	12 12
Hamilton Square	d	10 50		10 55	10 57	11 00	11 05	11 10	11 15	11 20	11 25	11 27		11 30	11 35	11 40	11 45	11 50	11 55	11 57	12 00	12 05		12 10	12 15
Conway Park	d			10 57		11 02		11 12	11 17		11 27			11 32		11 42	11 47		11 57		12 02			12 12	12 17
Birkenhead Park	d			10 59		11 04		11 14	11 19		11 29			11 34		11 44	11 49		11 59		12 04			12 14	12 19
Birkenhead North	d			11 02		11 07		11 17	11 22		11 32			11 37		11 47	11 52		12 02		12 07			12 17	12 22
Wallasey Village	d			11 07				11 22			11 37					11 52			12 07					12 22	
Wallasey Grove Road	d			11 08				11 23			11 38					11 53			12 08					12 23	
New Brighton	a			11 13				11 28			11 43					11 58			12 13					12 28	
Bidston	d					11 10			11 25					11 40			11 55				12 10				12 25
Leasowe	d					11 12			11 27					11 42			11 57				12 12				12 27
Moreton (Merseyside)	d					11 14			11 29					11 44			11 59				12 14				12 29
Meols	d					11 18			11 33					11 48			12 03				12 18				12 33
Manor Road	d					11 20			11 35					11 50			12 05				12 20				12 35
Hoylake	d					11 22			11 37					11 52			12 07				12 22				12 37
West Kirby	a					11 27			11 42					11 57			12 12				12 27				12 42
Birkenhead Central	d	10 52			11 00		11 07			11 22		11 30			11 37			11 52		12 00		12 07			
Green Lane	d	10 54			11 02		11 09			11 24		11 32			11 39			11 54		12 02		12 09			
Rock Ferry	d	10 57			11 04		11 12			11 27		11 34			11 42			11 57		12 04		12 12			
Bebington	d	10 59			11 07		11 14			11 29		11 37			11 44			11 59		12 07		12 14			
Port Sunlight	d	11 01			11 09		11 16			11 31		11 39			11 46			12 01		12 09		12 16			
Spital	d	11 03			11 11		11 18			11 33		11 41			11 48			12 03		12 11		12 18			
Bromborough Rake	d	11 05			11 13		11 20			11 35		11 43			11 50			12 05		12 13		12 20			
Bromborough	d	11 07			11 15		11 22			11 37		11 45			11 52			12 07		12 15		12 22			
Eastham Rake	d	11 10			11 17		11 25			11 40		11 47			11 55			12 10		12 17		12 25			
Hooton	d	11 12			11 19		11 27			11 42		11 49			11 57			12 12		12 19		12 27			
Little Sutton	d				11 24							11 54								12 24					
Overpool	d				11 26							11 56								12 26					
Ellesmere Port	a				11 29							11 59								12 30					
Capenhurst	d	11 17								11 47								12 17							
Bache	d	11 22								11 52								12 22							
Chester	a	11 26					11 38			11 56					12 08			12 26				12 38			

Liverpool and Birkenhead - New Brighton, West Kirby, Ellesmere Port and Chester

		ME	ME	ME	ME	ME	ME	ME		ME	ME	ME	ME	ME	ME	ME	ME	ME		ME	ME	ME	ME	ME	ME
Moorfields 10	d	12 11	12 16	12 18	12 21	12 26	12 31	12 36		12 41	12 46	12 48	12 51	12 56	13 01	13 06	13 11	13 16		13 18	13 21	13 26	13 31	13 36	13 41
Liverpool Lime Street 10	d	12 13	12 18	12 20	12 23	12 28	12 33	12 38		12 43	12 48	12 50	12 53	12 58	13 03	13 08	13 13	13 18		13 20	13 23	13 28	13 33	13 38	13 43
Liverpool Central 10	d	12 15	12 20	12 22	12 25	12 30	12 35	12 40		12 45	12 50	12 52	12 55	13 00	13 05	13 10	13 15	13 20		13 22	13 25	13 30	13 35	13 40	13 45
James Street	d	12 17	12 22	12 24	12 27	12 32	12 37	12 42		12 47	12 52	12 54	12 57	13 02	13 07	13 12	13 17	13 22		13 24	13 27	13 32	13 37	13 42	13 47
Hamilton Square	d	12 20	12 25	12 27	12 30	12 35	12 40	12 45		12 50	12 55	12 57	13 00	13 05	13 10	13 15	13 20	13 25		13 27	13 30	13 35	13 40	13 45	13 50
Conway Park	d		12 27		12 32		12 42	12 47			12 57		13 02		13 12	13 17		13 27			13 32		13 42	13 47	
Birkenhead Park	d		12 29		12 34		12 44	12 49			12 59		13 04		13 14	13 19		13 29			13 34		13 44	13 49	
Birkenhead North	d		12 32		12 37		12 47	12 52			13 02		13 07		13 17	13 22		13 32			13 37		13 47	13 52	
Wallasey Village	d		12 37				12 52				13 07				13 22			13 37					13 52		
Wallasey Grove Road	d		12 38				12 53				13 08				13 23			13 38					13 53		
New Brighton	a		12 43				12 58				13 13				13 28			13 43					13 58		
Bidston	d				12 40			12 55					13 10			13 25					13 40			13 55	
Leasowe	d				12 42			12 57					13 12			13 27					13 42			13 57	
Moreton (Merseyside)	d				12 44			12 59					13 14			13 29					13 44			13 59	
Meols	d				12 48			13 03					13 18			13 33					13 48			14 03	
Manor Road	d				12 50			13 05					13 20			13 35					13 50			14 05	
Hoylake	d				12 52			13 07					13 22			13 37					13 52			14 07	
West Kirby	a				12 57			13 12					13 27			13 42					13 57			14 12	
Birkenhead Central	d	12 22		12 30		12 37				12 52		13 00		13 07			13 22			13 30		13 37			13 52
Green Lane	d	12 24		12 32		12 39				12 54		13 02		13 09			13 24			13 32		13 39			13 54
Rock Ferry	d	12 27		12 34		12 42				12 57		13 04		13 12			13 27			13 34		13 42			13 57
Bebington	d	12 29		12 37		12 44				12 59		13 07		13 14			13 29			13 37		13 44			13 59
Port Sunlight	d	12 31		12 39		12 46				13 01		13 09		13 16			13 31			13 39		13 46			14 01
Spital	d	12 33		12 41		12 48				13 03		13 11		13 18			13 33			13 41		13 48			14 03
Bromborough Rake	d	12 35		12 43		12 50				13 05		13 13		13 20			13 35			13 43		13 50			14 05
Bromborough	d	12 37		12 45		12 52				13 07		13 15		13 22			13 37			13 45		13 52			14 07
Eastham Rake	d	12 40		12 47		12 55				13 10		13 17		13 25			13 40			13 47		13 55			14 10
Hooton	d	12 42		12 49		12 57				13 12		13 19		13 27			13 42			13 49		13 57			14 12
Little Sutton	d			12 54								13 24								13 54					
Overpool	d			12 56								13 26								13 56					
Ellesmere Port	a			12 59								13 29								13 59					
Capenhurst	d	12 47								13 17							13 47								14 17
Bache	d	12 52								13 22							13 52								14 22
Chester	a	12 56				13 08				13 26				13 38			13 56					14 08			14 26

		ME	ME	ME		ME	ME	ME	ME	ME	ME	ME	ME	ME		ME	ME	ME	ME	ME	ME	ME	ME	ME	
Moorfields 10	d	13 46	13 48	13 51		13 56	14 01	14 06	14 11	14 16	14 18	14 21	14 26	14 31		14 36	14 41	14 46	14 48	14 51	14 56	15 01	15 06	15 11	
Liverpool Lime Street 10	d	13 48	13 50	13 53		13 58	14 03	14 08	14 13	14 18	14 20	14 23	14 28	14 33		14 38	14 43	14 48	14 50	14 53	14 58	15 03	15 08	15 13	
Liverpool Central 10	d	13 50	13 52	13 55		14 00	14 05	14 10	14 15	14 20	14 22	14 25	14 30	14 35		14 40	14 45	14 50	14 52	14 55	15 00	15 05	15 10	15 15	
James Street	d	13 52	13 54	13 57		14 02	14 07	14 12	14 17	14 22	14 24	14 27	14 32	14 37		14 42	14 47	14 52	14 54	14 57	15 02	15 07	15 12	15 17	
Hamilton Square	d	13 55	13 57	14 00		14 05	14 10	14 15	14 20	14 25	14 27	14 30	14 35	14 40		14 45	14 50	14 55	14 57	15 00	15 05	15 10	15 15	15 20	
Conway Park	d	13 57		14 02			14 12	14 17		14 27		14 32		14 42		14 47		14 57		15 02		15 12	15 17		
Birkenhead Park	d	13 59		14 04			14 14	14 19		14 29		14 34		14 44		14 49		14 59		15 04		15 14	15 19		
Birkenhead North	d	14 02		14 07			14 17	14 22		14 32		14 37		14 47		14 52		15 02		15 07		15 17	15 22		
Wallasey Village	d	14 07					14 22			14 37				14 52				15 07				15 22			
Wallasey Grove Road	d	14 08					14 23			14 38				14 53				15 08				15 23			
New Brighton	a	14 13					14 28			14 43				14 58				15 13				15 28			
Bidston	d			14 10				14 25				14 40				14 55				15 10			15 25		
Leasowe	d			14 12				14 27				14 42				14 57				15 12			15 27		
Moreton (Merseyside)	d			14 14				14 29				14 44				14 59				15 14			15 29		
Meols	d			14 18				14 33				14 48				15 03				15 18			15 33		
Manor Road	d			14 20				14 35				14 50				15 05				15 20			15 35		
Hoylake	d			14 22				14 37				14 52				15 07				15 22			15 37		
West Kirby	a			14 27				14 42				14 57				15 12				15 27			15 42		
Birkenhead Central	d		14 00			14 07			14 22		14 30		14 37				14 52		15 00		15 07			15 22	
Green Lane	d		14 02			14 09			14 24		14 32		14 39				14 54		15 02		15 09			15 24	
Rock Ferry	d		14 04			14 12			14 27		14 34		14 42				14 57		15 04		15 12			15 27	
Bebington	d		14 07			14 14			14 29		14 37		14 44				14 59		15 07		15 14			15 29	
Port Sunlight	d		14 09			14 16			14 31		14 39		14 46				15 01		15 09		15 16			15 31	
Spital	d		14 11			14 18			14 33		14 41		14 48				15 03		15 11		15 18			15 33	
Bromborough Rake	d		14 13			14 20			14 35		14 43		14 50				15 05		15 13		15 20			15 35	
Bromborough	d		14 15			14 22			14 37		14 45		14 52				15 07		15 15		15 22			15 37	
Eastham Rake	d		14 17			14 25			14 40		14 47		14 55				15 10		15 17		15 25			15 40	
Hooton	d		14 19			14 27			14 42		14 49		14 57				15 12		15 19		15 27			15 42	
Little Sutton	d		14 24								14 54								15 24						
Overpool	d		14 26								14 56								15 26						
Ellesmere Port	a		14 29								14 59								15 29						
Capenhurst	d								14 47								15 17							15 47	
Bache	d								14 52								15 22							15 52	
Chester	a					14 38			14 56				15 08				15 26				15 38			15 56	

Liverpool and Birkenhead - New Brighton, West Kirby, Ellesmere Port and Chester

		ME	ME	ME	ME	ME	ME	ME	ME	ME	ME	ME	ME	ME	ME	ME	ME	ME	ME	ME	ME	ME	ME
														SX								SX	
Moorfields 10	d	15 16	15 18	15 21	15 26	15 31	15 36	15 41	15 46	15 48	15 51	15 56	16 01	16 03	16 06	16 11	16 16	16 18	16 21	16 26	16 31	16 33	16 36
Liverpool Lime Street 10	d	15 18	15 20	15 23	15 28	15 33	15 38	15 43	15 48	15 50	15 53	15 58	16 03	16 05	16 08	16 13	16 18	16 20	16 23	16 28	16 33	16 35	16 38
Liverpool Central 10	d	15 20	15 22	15 25	15 30	15 35	15 40	15 45	15 50	15 52	15 55	16 00	16 05	16 07	16 10	16 15	16 20	16 22	16 25	16 30	16 35	16 37	16 40
James Street	d	15 22	15 24	15 27	15 32	15 37	15 42	15 47	15 52	15 54	15 57	16 02	16 07	16 09	16 12	16 17	16 22	16 24	16 27	16 32	16 37	16 39	16 42
Hamilton Square	d	15 25	15 27	15 30	15 35	15 40	15 45	15 50	15 55	15 57	16 00	16 05	16 10	16a12	16 15	16 20	16 25	16a27	16 30	16 35	16 40	16 42	16 45
Conway Park	d	15 27		15 32		15 42	15 47		15 57		16 02		16 12		16 17		16 27		16 32		16 42		16 47
Birkenhead Park	d	15 29		15 34		15 44	15 49		15 59		16 04		16 14		16 19		16 29		16 34		16 44		16 49
Birkenhead North	d	15 32		15 37		15 47	15 52		16 02		16 07		16 17		16 22		16 32		16 37		16 47		16 52
Wallasey Village	d	15 37				15 52			16 07				16 22				16 37				16 52		
Wallasey Grove Road	d	15 38				15 53			16 08				16 23				16 38				16 53		
New Brighton	a	15 43				15 58			16 13				16 28				16 43				16 58		
Bidston	d			15 40			15 55				16 10				16 25				16 40				16 55
Leasowe	d			15 42			15 57				16 12				16 27				16 42				16 57
Moreton (Merseyside)	d			15 44			15 59				16 14				16 29				16 44				16 59
Meols	d			15 48			16 03				16 18				16 33				16 48				17 03
Manor Road	d			15 50			16 05				16 20				16 35				16 50				17 05
Hoylake	d			15 52			16 07				16 22				16 37				16 52				17 07
West Kirby	a			15 57			16 12				16 27				16 42				16 57				17 12
Birkenhead Central	d		15 30		15 37			15 52		16 00		16 07				16 22				16 37		16 45	
Green Lane	d		15 32		15 39			15 54		16 02		16 09				16 24				16 39		16 47	
Rock Ferry	d		15 34		15 42			15 57		16 04		16 12				16 27				16 42		16 49	
Bebington	d		15 37		15 44			15 59		16 07		16 14				16 29				16 44		16 52	
Port Sunlight	d		15 39		15 46			16 01		16 09		16 16				16 31				16 46		16 54	
Spital	d		15 41		15 48			16 03		16 11		16 18				16 33				16 48		16 56	
Bromborough Rake	d		15 43		15 50			16 05		16 13		16 20				16 35				16 50		16 58	
Bromborough	d		15 45		15 52			16 07		16 15		16 22				16 37				16 52		17 00	
Eastham Rake	d		15 47		15 55			16 10		16 17		16 25				16 40				16 55		17 02	
Hooton	d		15 49		15 57			16 12		16 19		16 27				16 42				16 57		17 04	
Little Sutton	d		15 54							16 24												17 09	
Overpool	d		15 56							16 26												17 11	
Ellesmere Port	a		15 59							16 29												17 15	
Capenhurst	d							16 17								16 47							
Bache	d							16 22								16 52							
Chester	a				16 08			16 26				16 38				16 56				17 08			

		ME	ME	ME	ME	ME	ME	ME	ME	ME	ME	ME	ME	ME	ME	ME	ME	ME	ME	ME	ME	ME	ME
						SO	SX		SX						SO	SX		SX					
Moorfields 10	d	16 41	16 46	16 48	16 51	16 56	16 56	17 01	17 03	17 06	17 11	17 16	17 18	17 21	17 26	17 26	17 31	17 33	17 36	17 41	17 46	17 48	17 51
Liverpool Lime Street 10	d	16 43	16 48	16 50	16 53	16 58	16 58	17 03	17 05	17 08	17 13	17 18	17 20	17 23	17 28	17 28	17 33	17 35	17 38	17 43	17 48	17 50	17 53
Liverpool Central 10	d	16 45	16 50	16 52	16 55	17 00	17 00	17 05	17 07	17 10	17 15	17 20	17 22	17 25	17 30	17 30	17 35	17 37	17 40	17 45	17 50	17 52	17 55
James Street	d	16 47	16 52	16 54	16 57	17 02	17 02	17 07	17 09	17 12	17 17	17 22	17 24	17 27	17 32	17 32	17 37	17 39	17 42	17 47	17 52	17 54	17 57
Hamilton Square	d	16 50	16 55	16 57	17 00	17 05	17 05	17 10	17 12	17 15	17 20	17 25	17 27	17 30	17 35	17 35	17 40	17 42	17 45	17 50	17 55	17 57	18 00
Conway Park	d		16 57		17 02			17 12		17 17		17 27		17 32			17 42		17 47		17 57		18 02
Birkenhead Park	d		16 59		17 04			17 14		17 19		17 29		17 34			17 44		17 49		17 59		18 04
Birkenhead North	d		17 02		17 07			17 17		17 22		17 32		17 37			17 47		17 52		18 02		18 07
Wallasey Village	d		17 07					17 22				17 37					17 52				18 07		
Wallasey Grove Road	d		17 08					17 23				17 38					17 53				18 08		
New Brighton	a		17 13					17 28				17 43					17 58				18 13		
Bidston	d				17 10					17 25				17 40					17 55				18 10
Leasowe	d				17 12					17 27				17 42					17 57				18 12
Moreton (Merseyside)	d				17 14					17 29				17 44					17 59				18 14
Meols	d				17 18					17 33				17 48					18 03				18 18
Manor Road	d				17 20					17 35				17 50					18 05				18 20
Hoylake	d				17 22					17 37				17 52					18 07				18 22
West Kirby	a				17 27					17 42				17 57					18 12				18 27
Birkenhead Central	d	16 52		17 00		17 07	17 07		17 15		17 22		17 30		17 37	17 37		17 45		17 52		18 00	
Green Lane	d	16 54		17 02		17 09	17 09		17 17		17 24		17 32		17 39	17 39		17 47		17 54		18 02	
Rock Ferry	d	16 57		17 04		17 12	17 12		17 19		17 27		17 34		17 42	17 42		17 49		17 57		18 04	
Bebington	d	16 59		17 07		17 14	17 14		17 22		17 29		17 37		17 44	17 44		17 52		17 59		18 07	
Port Sunlight	d	17 01		17 09		17 16	17 16		17 24		17 31		17 39		17 46	17 46		17 54		18 01		18 09	
Spital	d	17 03		17 11		17 18	17 18		17 26		17 33		17 41		17 48	17 48		17 56		18 03		18 11	
Bromborough Rake	d	17 05		17 13		17 20	17 20		17 28		17 35		17 43		17 50	17 50		17 58		18 05		18 13	
Bromborough	d	17 07		17 15		17 22	17 22		17 30		17 37		17 45		17 52	17 52		18 00		18 07		18 15	
Eastham Rake	d	17 10		17 17		17 25	17 25		17 32		17 40		17 47		17 55	17 55		18 02		18 10		18 17	
Hooton	d	17 12		17 19		17 27	17 27		17 34		17 42		17 49		17 57	17 57		18 04		18 12		18 19	
Little Sutton	d			17 24					17 39				17 54					18 09				18 24	
Overpool	d			17 26					17 41				17 56					18 11				18 26	
Ellesmere Port	a			17 29					17 45				17 59					18 15				18 29	
Capenhurst	d	17 17					17 32				17 47					18 02				18 17			
Bache	d	17 22					17 37				17 52					18 07				18 22			
Chester	a	17 26				17 38	17 41				17 56				18 08	18 11				18 26			

Liverpool and Birkenhead - New Brighton, West Kirby, Ellesmere Port and Chester

		ME		ME	ME	ME	ME	ME	ME	ME	ME	ME		ME	ME	ME	ME	ME	ME	ME	ME	ME		ME	ME
Moorfields 10	d	17 56		18 01	18 06	18 11	18 16	18 18	18 21	18 26	18 31	18 36		18 41	18 46	18 48	18 51	18 56	19 01	19 06	19 11	19 16		19 26	19 31
Liverpool Lime Street 10	d	17 58		18 03	18 08	18 13	18 18	18 20	18 23	18 28	18 33	18 38		18 43	18 48	18 50	18 53	18 58	19 03	19 08	19 13	19 18		19 28	19 33
Liverpool Central 10	d	18 00		18 05	18 10	18 15	18 20	18 22	18 25	18 30	18 35	18 40		18 45	18 50	18 52	18 55	19 00	19 05	19 10	19 15	19 20		19 30	19 35
James Street	d	18 02		18 07	18 12	18 17	18 22	18 24	18 27	18 32	18 37	18 42		18 47	18 52	18 54	18 57	19 02	19 07	19 12	19 17	19 22		19 32	19 37
Hamilton Square	d	18 05		18 10	18 15	18 20	18 25	18 27	18 30	18 35	18 40	18 45		18 50	18 55	18 57	19 00	19 05	19 10	19 15	19 20	19 25		19 35	19 40
Conway Park	d			18 12	18 17		18 27		18 32		18 42	18 47			18 57		19 02		19 12	19 17		19 27			19 42
Birkenhead Park	d			18 14	18 19		18 29		18 34		18 44	18 49			18 59		19 04		19 14	19 19		19 29			19 44
Birkenhead North	d			18 17	18 22		18 32		18 37		18 47	18 52			19 02		19 07		19 17	19 22		19 32			19 47
Wallasey Village	d			18 22			18 37				18 52				19 07				19 22			19 37			
Wallasey Grove Road	d			18 23			18 38				18 53				19 08				19 23			19 38			
New Brighton	a			18 28			18 43				18 58				19 13				19 28			19 43			
Bidston	d				18 25				18 40			18 55					19 10			19 25					19 50
Leasowe	d				18 27				18 42			18 57					19 12			19 27					19 52
Moreton (Merseyside)	d				18 29				18 44			18 59					19 14			19 29					19 54
Meols	d				18 33				18 48			19 03					19 18			19 33					19 58
Manor Road	d				18 35				18 50			19 05					19 20			19 35					20 00
Hoylake	d				18 37				18 52			19 07					19 22			19 37					20 02
West Kirby	a				18 42				18 57			19 12					19 27			19 42					20 07
Birkenhead Central	d	18 07				18 22		18 30		18 37				18 52		19 00		19 07			19 22			19 37	
Green Lane	d	18 09				18 24		18 32		18 39				18 54		19 02		19 09			19 24			19 39	
Rock Ferry	d	18 12				18 27		18 34		18 42				18 57		19 04		19 12			19 27			19 42	
Bebington	d	18 14				18 29		18 37		18 44				18 59		19 07		19 14			19 29			19 44	
Port Sunlight	d	18 16				18 31		18 39		18 46				19 01		19 09		19 16			19 31			19 46	
Spital	d	18 18				18 33		18 41		18 48				19 03		19 11		19 18			19 33			19 48	
Bromborough Rake	d	18 20				18 35		18 43		18 50				19 05		19 13		19 20			19 35			19 50	
Bromborough	d	18 22				18 37		18 45		18 52				19 07		19 15		19 22			19 37			19 52	
Eastham Rake	d	18 25				18 40		18 47		18 55				19 10		19 17		19 25			19 40			19 55	
Hooton	d	18 27				18 42		18 49		18 57				19 12		19 19		19 27			19 42			19 57	
Little Sutton	d							18 54								19 24								20 01	
Overpool	d							18 56								19 26								20 03	
Ellesmere Port	a							18 59								19 29								20 07	
Capenhurst	d					18 47								19 17							19 47				
Bache	d					18 52								19 22							19 52				
Chester	a	18 38				18 56				19 08				19 26				19 38			19 56				

		ME	ME	ME	ME		ME		ME	ME	ME	ME	ME	ME
Moorfields 10	d	19 41	19 46	19 56	20 01		23 01		23 11	23 16	23 26	23 31	23 41	23 46
Liverpool Lime Street 10	d	19 43	19 48	19 58	20 03		23 03		23 13	23 18	23 28	23 33	23 43	23 48
Liverpool Central 10	d	19 45	19 50	20 00	20 05		23 05		23 15	23 20	23 30	23 35	23 45	23 50
James Street	d	19 47	19 52	20 02	20 07		23 07		23 17	23 22	23 32	23 37	23 47	23 52
Hamilton Square	d	19 50	19 55	20 05	20 10		23 10		23 20	23 25	23 35	23 40	23 50	23 55
Conway Park	d		19 57		20 12		23 12			23 27		23 42		23 57
Birkenhead Park	d		19 59		20 14		23 14			23 29		23 44		23 59
Birkenhead North	d		20 02		20 17		23 17			23 32		23 47		00 02
Wallasey Village	d		[illegible]							23 37				00 07
Wallasey Grove Road	d		20 08							23 38				00 08
New Brighton	a		20 13							23 43				00 13
Bidston	d				20 20		23 20					23 50		
Leasowe	d				20 22		23 22					23 52		
Moreton (Merseyside)	d				20 24	and at the same minutes past each hour until	23 24					23 54		
Meols	d				20 28		23 28					23 58		
Manor Road	d				20 30		23 30					23 59		
Hoylake	d				20 32		23 32					00 02		
West Kirby	a				20 37		23 37					00 07		
Birkenhead Central	d	19 52		20 07					23 22		23 37		23 52	
Green Lane	d	19 54		20 09					23 24		23 39		23 54	
Rock Ferry	d	19 57		20 12					23 27		23 42		23 57	
Bebington	d	19 59		20 14					23 29		23 44		23 59	
Port Sunlight	d	20 01		20 16					23 31		23 46		00 01	
Spital	d	20 03		20 18					23 33		23 48		00 03	
Bromborough Rake	d	20 05		20 20					23 35		23 50		00 05	
Bromborough	d	20 07		20 22					23 37		23 52		00 07	
Eastham Rake	d	20 10		20 25					23 40		23 55		00 10	
Hooton	d	20 12		20 27					23 42		23 57		00 12	
Little Sutton	d			20 31							00 01			
Overpool	d			20 33							00 03			
Ellesmere Port	a			20 37							00 07			
Capenhurst	d	20 17							23 47				00 17	
Bache	d	20 22							23 52				00 22	
Chester	a	20 26							23 56				00 26	

Table 106

Sundays

Liverpool and Birkenhead - New Brighton, West Kirby, Ellesmere Port and Chester

		ME A	ME A	ME A	ME A	ME	ME	ME	ME	ME		ME	ME	ME	ME		ME	ME	ME		ME	ME	ME	ME
Moorfields 10	d	23p26	23p31	23p41	23p46	07 56	08 11	08 16	08 26	08 31		08 41	08 46	08 56	09 01		23 01	23 11	23 16		23 26	23 31	23 41	23 46
Liverpool Lime Street 10	d	23p28	23p33	23p43	23p48	07 58	08 13	08 18	08 28	08 33		08 43	08 48	08 58	09 03		23 03	23 13	23 18		23 28	23 33	23 43	23 48
Liverpool Central 10	d	23p30	23p35	23p45	23p50	08 00	08 15	08 20	08 30	08 35		08 45	08 50	09 00	09 05		23 05	23 15	23 20		23 30	23 35	23 45	23 50
James Street	d	23p32	23p37	23p47	23p52	08 02	08 17	08 22	08 32	08 37		08 47	08 52	09 02	09 07		23 07	23 17	23 22		23 32	23 37	23 47	23 52
Hamilton Square	d	23p35	23p40	23p50	23p55	08 05	08 20	08 25	08 35	08 40		08 50	08 55	09 05	09 10		23 10	23 20	23 25		23 35	23 40	23 50	23 55
Conway Park	d		23p42		23p57			08 27		08 42			08 57		09 12		23 12		23 27			23 42		23 57
Birkenhead Park	d		23p44		23p59			08 29		08 44			08 59		09 14		23 14		23 29			23 44		23 59
Birkenhead North	d		23p47		00 02			08 32		08 47			09 02		09 17		23 17		23 32			23 47		00 02
Wallasey Village	d				00 07			08 37					09 07						23 37					00 07
Wallasey Grove Road	d				00 08			08 38					09 08						23 38					00 08
New Brighton	a				00 13			08 43					09 13						23 43					00 13
Bidston	d		23p50							08 50					09 20		23 20					23 50		
Leasowe	d		23p52							08 52					09 22		23 22					23 52		
Moreton (Merseyside)	d		23p54							08 54					09 24	and at the same minutes past each hour until	23 24					23 54		
Meols	d		23p58							08 58					09 28		23 28					23 58		
Manor Road	d		23p59							09 00					09 30		23 30					23 59		
Hoylake	d		00 02							09 02					09 32		23 32					00 02		
West Kirby	a		00 07							09 07					09 37		23 37					00 07		
Birkenhead Central	d	23p37		23p52		08 07	08 22		08 37			08 52		09 07				23 22			23 37		23 52	
Green Lane	d	23p39		23p54		08 09	08 24		08 39			08 54		09 09				23 24			23 39		23 54	
Rock Ferry	d	23p42		23p57		08 12	08 27		08 42			08 57		09 12				23 27			23 42		23 57	
Bebington	d	23p44		23p59		08 14	08 29		08 44			08 59		09 14				23 29			23 44		23 59	
Port Sunlight	d	23p46		00 01		08 16	08 31		08 46			09 01		09 16				23 31			23 46		00 01	
Spital	d	23p48		00 03		08 18	08 33		08 48			09 03		09 18				23 33			23 48		00 03	
Bromborough Rake	d	23p50		00 05		08 20	08 35		08 50			09 05		09 20				23 35			23 50		00 05	
Bromborough	d	23p52		00 07		08 22	08 37		08 52			09 07		09 22				23 37			23 52		00 07	
Eastham Rake	d	23p55		00 10		08 25	08 40		08 55			09 10		09 25				23 40			23 55		00 10	
Hooton	d	23p57		00 12		08 27	08 42		08 57			09 12		09 27				23 42			23 57		00 12	
Little Sutton	d	00 01				08 31			09 01					09 31							00 01			
Overpool	d	00 03				08 33			09 03					09 33							00 03			
Ellesmere Port	a	00 07				08 37			09 07					09 37							00 07			
Capenhurst	d			00 17			08 47					09 17						23 47					00 17	
Bache	d			00 22			08 52					09 22						23 52					00 22	
Chester	a			00 26			08 56					09 26						23 56					00 26	

A not 22 May

Chester, Ellesmere Port, West Kirby and New Brighton - Birkenhead and Liverpool

Miles	Miles	Miles	Miles			ME	ME	ME	ME	ME	ME	ME	ME	ME	ME	ME	ME	ME	ME	ME	ME	ME	ME SX	ME SO	ME
0	—	—	—	**Chester**	d					06 00				06 30						07 00					
1½	—	—	—	Bache	d					06 03				06 33						07 03					
5¼	—	—	—	Capenhurst	d					06 09				06 39						07 09					
—	0	—	—	**Ellesmere Port**	d								06 19				06 49						07 17	07 19	
—	1½	—	—	Overpool	d								06 22				06 52						07 20	07 22	
—	2½	—	—	Little Sutton	d								06 24				06 54						07 22	07 24	
8¼	4	—	—	Hooton	d		05 44			06 14			06 29	06 44			06 59			07 14			07 26	07 29	
9¼	—	—	—	Eastham Rake	d		05 46			06 16			06 31	06 46			07 01			07 16			07 28	07 31	
9¾	—	—	—	Bromborough	d		05 48			06 18			06 33	06 48			07 03			07 18			07 31	07 33	
10½	—	—	—	Bromborough Rake	d		05 50			06 20			06 35	06 50			07 05			07 20			07 33	07 35	
11¼	—	—	—	Spital	d		05 52			06 22			06 37	06 52			07 07			07 22			07 35	07 37	
11¾	—	—	—	Port Sunlight	d		05 54			06 24			06 39	06 54			07 09			07 24			07 37	07 39	
12¾	—	—	—	Bebington	d		05 56			06 26			06 41	06 56			07 11			07 26			07 39	07 41	
13¾	—	—	—	Rock Ferry	d	05 44	05 59			06 29			06 44	06 59			07 14			07 29			07 42	07 44	
14½	—	—	—	Green Lane	d	05 47	06 02			06 32			06 47	07 02			07 17			07 32			07 44	07 47	
15	—	—	—	Birkenhead Central	d	05 49	06 04			06 34			06 49	07 04			07 19			07 34			07 47	07 49	
—	—	0	—	**West Kirby**	d				05 51			06 21				06 51			07 06			07 21			
—	—	1	—	Hoylake	d				05 54			06 24				06 54			07 09			07 24			
—	—	1¾	—	Manor Road	d				05 56			06 26				06 56			07 11			07 26			
—	—	3	—	Meols	d				05 58			06 28				06 58			07 13			07 28			
—	—	4¼	—	Moreton (Merseyside)	d				06 01			06 31				07 01			07 16			07 31			
—	—	4¾	—	Leasowe	d				06 03			06 33				07 03			07 18			07 33			
—	—	5¾	—	Bidston	d				06 06			06 36				07 06			07 21			07 36			
—	—	—	0	**New Brighton**	d			05 53			06 23				06 53			07 08			07 23				07 38
—	—	—	1¼	Wallasey Grove Road	d			05 57			06 27				06 57			07 12			07 27				07 42
—	—	—	1½	Wallasey Village	d			05 59			06 29				06 59			07 14			07 29				07 44
—	—	6½	3	Birkenhead North	d			06 04	06 09		06 34	06 39			07 04	07 09		07 19	07 24		07 34	07 39			07 49
—	—	7½	3¾	Birkenhead Park	d			06 06	06 11		06 36	06 41			07 06	07 11		07 21	07 26		07 36	07 41			07 51
—	—	8¼	4½	Conway Park	d			06 09	06 14		06 39	06 44			07 09	07 14		07 24	07 29		07 39	07 44			07 54
15½	—	8¾	5	Hamilton Square	d	05 51	06 06	06 11	06 16	06 36	06 41	06 46	06 51	07 06	07 11	07 16	07 21	07 26	07 31	07 36	07 41	07 46	07 49	07 51	07 56
16¾	—	8¾	6¼	James Street	d	05 54	06 09	06 14	06 19	06 39	06 44	06 49	06 54	07 09	07 14	07 19	07 24	07 29	07 34	07 39	07 44	07 49	07 52	07 54	07 59
17¼	—	10¼	7¾	Moorfields 10	a	05 56	06 11	06 16	06 21	06 41	06 46	06 51	06 56	07 11	07 16	07 21	07 26	07 31	07 36	07 41	07 46	07 51	07 53	07 56	08 01
17¾	—	10¾	8¼	Liverpool Lime Street 10	a	05 58	06 13	06 18	06 23	06 43	06 48	06 53	06 58	07 13	07 18	07 23	07 28	07 33	07 38	07 43	07 48	07 53	07 55	07 58	08 03
18½	—	11¼	8¾	**Liverpool Central 10**	a	06 01	06 15	06 20	06 25	06 45	06 50	06 55	07 00	07 15	07 20	07 25	07 30	07 35	07 40	07 45	07 50	07 55	07 57	08 00	08 05

		ME SX	ME	ME SO	ME	ME SX	ME	ME	ME	ME SX		ME	ME SO	ME	ME SX	ME SO	ME	ME SO	ME SX	ME		ME	ME	ME	ME
Chester	d	07 22		07 30		07 37				07 52			08 00		08 07			08 15					08 32		
Bache	d	07 26		07 33		07 41				07 56			08 03		08 11			08 18							
Capenhurst	d	07 32		07 39		07 47				08 02			08 09		08 17			08 24							
Ellesmere Port	d							07 49								08 12			08 17						08 42
Overpool	d							07 52								08 15			08 20						08 45
Little Sutton	d							07 54								08 17			08 22						08 47
Hooton	d	07 36		07 44		07 51		07 59		08 06			08 14		08 21	08 21		08 29	08 29				08 44		08 51
Eastham Rake	d	07 38		07 46		07 53		08 01		08 08			08 16		08 23	08 23		08 31	08 31				08 46		08 53
Bromborough	d	07 41		07 48		07 56		08 03		08 11			08 18		08 26	08 26		08 33	08 33				08 48		08 56
Bromborough Rake	d	07 43		07 50		07 58		08 05		08 13			08 20		08 28	08 28		08 35	08 35				08 50		08 58
Spital	d	07 45		07 52		08 00		08 07		08 15			08 22		08 30	08 30		08 37	08 37				08 52		09 00
Port Sunlight	d	07 47		07 54		08 02		08 09		08 17			08 24		08 32	08 32		08 39	08 39				08 54		09 02
Bebington	d	07 49		07 56		08 04		08 11		08 19			08 26		08 34	08 34		08 41	08 41				08 56		09 04
Rock Ferry	d	07 52		07 59		08 07		08 14		08 22			08 29		08 37	08 37		08 44	08 44				08 59		09 07
Green Lane	d	07 54		08 02		08 09		08 17		08 24			08 32		08 39	08 39		08 47	08 47				09 02		09 09
Birkenhead Central	d	07 57		08 04		08 12		08 19		08 27			08 34		08 42	08 42		08 49	08 49				09 04		09 12
West Kirby	d		07 36				07 51					08 06					08 21					08 36			
Hoylake	d		07 39				07 54					08 09					08 24					08 39			
Manor Road	d		07 41				07 56					08 11					08 26					08 41			
Meols	d		07 43				07 58					08 13					08 28					08 43			
Moreton (Merseyside)	d		07 46				08 01					08 16					08 31					08 46			
Leasowe	d		07 48				08 03					08 18					08 33					08 48			
Bidston	d		07 51				08 06					08 21					08 36					08 51			
New Brighton	d				07 53				08 08					08 23						08 38				08 53	
Wallasey Grove Road	d				07 57				08 12					08 27						08 42				08 57	
Wallasey Village	d				07 59				08 14					08 29						08 44				08 59	
Birkenhead North	d		07 54		08 04		08 09		08 19			08 24		08 34			08 39			08 49		08 54		09 04	
Birkenhead Park	d		07 56		08 06		08 11		08 21			08 26		08 36			08 41			08 51		08 56		09 06	
Conway Park	d		07 59		08 09		08 14		08 24			08 29		08 39			08 44			08 54		08 59		09 09	
Hamilton Square	d	07 59	08 01	08 06	08 11	08 14	08 16	08 21	08 26	08 29		08 31	08 36	08 41	08 44	08 44	08 46	08 51	08 51	08 56		09 01	09 06	09 11	09 14
James Street	d	08 02	08 04	08 09	08 14	08 17	08 19	08 24	08 29	08 32		08 34	08 39	08 44	08 47	08 47	08 49	08 54	08 54	08 59		09 04	09 09	09 14	09 17
Moorfields 10	a	08 03	08 06	08 11	08 16	08 18	08 21	08 26	08 31	08 33		08 36	08 41	08 46	08 48	08 48	08 51	08 56	08 56	09 01		09 06	09 11	09 16	09 18
Liverpool Lime Street 10	a	08 05	08 08	08 13	08 18	08 20	08 23	08 28	08 33	08 35		08 38	08 43	08 48	08 50	08 50	08 53	08 58	08 58	09 03		09 08	09 13	09 18	09 20
Liverpool Central 10	a	08 07	08 10	08 15	08 20	08 22	08 25	08 30	08 35	08 37		08 40	08 45	08 50	08 52	08 52	08 55	09 00	09 00	09 05		09 10	09 15	09 20	09 22

Chester, Ellesmere Port, West Kirby and New Brighton - Birkenhead and Liverpool

		ME	ME	ME	ME	ME		ME	ME	ME	ME	ME	ME	ME	ME	ME		ME	ME	ME	ME	ME	ME	ME	ME
Chester	d		08 45			09 02					09 15			09 32					09 45			10 02			
Bache	d		08 48								09 18								09 48						
Capenhurst	d		08 54								09 24								09 54						
Ellesmere Port	d								09 12							09 42								10 12	
Overpool	d								09 15							09 45								10 15	
Little Sutton	d								09 17							09 47								10 17	
Hooton	d		08 59			09 14			09 21		09 29			09 44		09 51			09 59			10 14		10 21	
Eastham Rake	d		09 01			09 16			09 23		09 31			09 46		09 53			10 01			10 16		10 23	
Bromborough	d		09 03			09 18			09 26		09 33			09 48		09 56			10 03			10 18		10 26	
Bromborough Rake	d		09 05			09 20			09 28		09 35			09 50		09 58			10 05			10 20		10 28	
Spital	d		09 07			09 22			09 30		09 37			09 52		10 00			10 07			10 22		10 30	
Port Sunlight	d		09 09			09 24			09 32		09 39			09 54		10 02			10 09			10 24		10 32	
Bebington	d		09 11			09 26			09 34		09 41			09 56		10 04			10 11			10 26		10 34	
Rock Ferry	d		09 14			09 29			09 37		09 44			09 59		10 07			10 14			10 29		10 37	
Green Lane	d		09 17			09 32			09 39		09 47			10 02		10 09			10 17			10 32		10 39	
Birkenhead Central	d		09 19			09 34			09 42		09 49			10 04		10 12			10 19			10 34		10 42	
West Kirby	d	08 51			09 06					09 21			09 36					09 51			10 06				10 21
Hoylake	d	08 54			09 09					09 24			09 39					09 54			10 09				10 24
Manor Road	d	08 56			09 11					09 26			09 41					09 56			10 11				10 26
Meols	d	08 58			09 13					09 28			09 43					09 58			10 13				10 28
Moreton (Merseyside)	d	09 01			09 16					09 31			09 46					10 01			10 16				10 31
Leasowe	d	09 03			09 18					09 33			09 48					10 03			10 18				10 33
Bidston	d	09 06			09 21					09 36			09 51					10 06			10 21				10 36
New Brighton	d			09 08				09 23				09 38			09 53					10 08			10 23		
Wallasey Grove Road	d			09 12				09 27				09 42			09 57					10 12			10 27		
Wallasey Village	d			09 14				09 29				09 44			09 59					10 14			10 29		
Birkenhead North	d	09 09		09 19	09 24			09 34		09 39		09 49	09 54		10 04			10 09		10 19	10 24		10 34		10 39
Birkenhead Park	d	09 11		09 21	09 26			09 36		09 41		09 51	09 56		10 06			10 11		10 21	10 26		10 36		10 41
Conway Park	d	09 14		09 24	09 29			09 39		09 44		09 54	09 59		10 09			10 14		10 24	10 29		10 39		10 44
Hamilton Square	d	09 16	09 21	09 26	09 31	09 36		09 41	09 44	09 46	09 51	09 56	10 01	10 06	10 11	10 14		10 16	10 21	10 26	10 31	10 36	10 41	10 44	10 46
James Street	d	09 19	09 24	09 29	09 34	09 39		09 44	09 47	09 49	09 54	09 59	10 04	10 09	10 14	10 17		10 19	10 24	10 29	10 34	10 39	10 44	10 47	10 49
Moorfields 10	a	09 21	09 26	09 31	09 36	09 41		09 46	09 48	09 51	09 56	10 01	10 06	10 11	10 16	10 18		10 21	10 26	10 31	10 36	10 41	10 46	10 48	10 51
Liverpool Lime Street 10	a	09 23	09 28	09 33	09 38	09 43		09 48	09 50	09 53	09 58	10 03	10 08	10 13	10 18	10 20		10 23	10 28	10 33	10 38	10 43	10 48	10 50	10 53
Liverpool Central 10	a	09 25	09 30	09 35	09 40	09 45		09 50	09 52	09 55	10 00	10 05	10 10	10 15	10 20	10 22		10 25	10 30	10 35	10 40	10 45	10 50	10 52	10 55

		ME		ME	ME	ME	ME	ME	ME	ME	ME	ME		ME	ME	ME	ME	ME	ME	ME	ME	ME		ME	ME
Chester	d	10 15				10 32				10 45				11 02				11 15			11 32				
Bache	d	10 18								10 48								11 18							
Capenhurst	d	10 24								10 54								11 24							
Ellesmere Port	d							10 42								11 12								11 42	
Overpool	d							10 45								11 15								11 45	
Little Sutton	d							10 47								11 17								11 47	
Hooton	d	10 29				10 44		10 51		10 59				11 14		11 21		11 29			11 44			11 51	
Eastham Rake	d	10 31				10 46		10 53		11 01				11 16		11 23		11 31			11 46			11 53	
Bromborough	d	10 33				10 48		10 56		11 03				11 18		11 26		11 33			11 48			11 56	
Bromborough Rake	d	10 35				10 50		10 58		11 05				11 20		11 28		11 35			11 50			11 58	
Spital	d	10 37				10 52		11 00		11 07				11 22		11 30		11 37			11 52			12 00	
Port Sunlight	d	10 39				10 54		11 02		11 09				11 24		11 32		11 39			11 54			12 02	
Bebington	d	10 41				10 56		11 04		11 11				11 26		11 34		11 41			11 56			12 04	
Rock Ferry	d	10 44				10 59		11 07		11 14				11 29		11 37		11 44			11 59			12 07	
Green Lane	d	10 47				11 02		11 09		11 17				11 32		11 39		11 47			12 02			12 09	
Birkenhead Central	d	10 49				11 04		11 12		11 19				11 34		11 42		11 49			12 04			12 12	
West Kirby	d				10 36				10 51			11 06					11 21			11 36					11 51
Hoylake	d				10 39				10 54			11 09					11 24			11 39					11 54
Manor Road	d				10 41				10 56			11 11					11 26			11 41					11 56
Meols	d				10 43				10 58			11 13					11 28			11 43					11 58
Moreton (Merseyside)	d				10 46				11 01			11 16					11 31			11 46					12 01
Leasowe	d				10 48				11 03			11 18					11 33			11 48					12 03
Bidston	d				10 51				11 06			11 21					11 36			11 51					12 06
New Brighton	d			10 38			10 53				11 08				11 23				11 38			11 53			
Wallasey Grove Road	d			10 42			10 57				11 12				11 27				11 42			11 57			
Wallasey Village	d			10 44			10 59				11 14				11 29				11 44			11 59			
Birkenhead North	d			10 49	10 54		11 04		11 09		11 19	11 24			11 34		11 39		11 49	11 54		12 04			12 09
Birkenhead Park	d			10 51	10 56		11 06		11 11		11 21	11 26			11 36		11 41		11 51	11 56		12 06			12 11
Conway Park	d			10 54	10 59		11 09		11 14		11 24	11 29			11 39		11 44		11 54	11 59		12 09			12 14
Hamilton Square	d	10 51		10 56	11 01	11 06	11 11	11 14	11 16	11 21	11 26	11 31		11 36	11 41	11 44	11 46	11 51	11 56	12 01	12 06	12 11		12 14	12 16
James Street	d	10 54		10 59	11 04	11 09	11 14	11 17	11 19	11 24	11 29	11 34		11 39	11 44	11 47	11 49	11 54	11 59	12 04	12 09	12 14		12 17	12 19
Moorfields 10	a	10 56		11 01	11 06	11 11	11 16	11 18	11 21	11 26	11 31	11 36		11 41	11 46	11 48	11 51	11 56	12 01	12 06	12 11	12 16		12 18	12 21
Liverpool Lime Street 10	a	10 58		11 03	11 08	11 13	11 18	11 20	11 23	11 28	11 33	11 38		11 43	11 48	11 50	11 53	11 58	12 03	12 08	12 13	12 18		12 20	12 23
Liverpool Central 10	a	11 00		11 05	11 10	11 15	11 20	11 22	11 25	11 30	11 35	11 40		11 45	11 50	11 52	11 55	12 00	12 05	12 10	12 15	12 20		12 22	12 25

Chester, Ellesmere Port, West Kirby and New Brighton - Birkenhead and Liverpool

		ME	ME	ME	ME	ME	ME	ME		ME	ME	ME	ME	ME	ME	ME	ME	ME		ME	ME	ME	ME	ME	ME
Chester	d	11 45			12 02					12 15			12 32				12 45				13 02				13 15
Bache	d	11 48								12 18							12 48								13 18
Capenhurst	d	11 54								12 24							12 54								13 24
Ellesmere Port	d						12 12								12 42								13 12		
Overpool	d						12 15								12 45								13 15		
Little Sutton	d						12 17								12 47								13 17		
Hooton	d	11 59			12 14		12 21			12 29			12 44		12 51		12 59				13 14		13 21		13 29
Eastham Rake	d	12 01			12 16		12 23			12 31			12 46		12 53		13 01				13 16		13 23		13 31
Bromborough	d	12 03			12 18		12 26			12 33			12 48		12 56		13 03				13 18		13 26		13 33
Bromborough Rake	d	12 05			12 20		12 28			12 35			12 50		12 58		13 05				13 20		13 28		13 35
Spital	d	12 07			12 22		12 30			12 37			12 52		13 00		13 07				13 22		13 30		13 37
Port Sunlight	d	12 09			12 24		12 32			12 39			12 54		13 02		13 09				13 24		13 32		13 39
Bebington	d	12 11			12 26		12 34			12 41			12 56		13 04		13 11				13 26		13 34		13 41
Rock Ferry	d	12 14			12 29		12 37			12 44			12 59		13 07		13 14				13 29		13 37		13 44
Green Lane	d	12 17			12 32		12 39			12 47			13 02		13 09		13 17				13 32		13 39		13 47
Birkenhead Central	d	12 19			12 34		12 42			12 49			13 04		13 12		13 19				13 34		13 42		13 49
West Kirby	d			12 06				12 21				12 36				12 51				13 06				13 21	
Hoylake	d			12 09				12 24				12 39				12 54				13 09				13 24	
Manor Road	d			12 11				12 26				12 41				12 56				13 11				13 26	
Meols	d			12 13				12 28				12 43				12 58				13 13				13 28	
Moreton (Merseyside)	d			12 16				12 31				12 46				13 01				13 16				13 31	
Leasowe	d			12 18				12 33				12 48				13 03				13 18				13 33	
Bidston	d			12 21				12 36				12 51				13 06				13 21				13 36	
New Brighton	d		12 08			12 23					12 38			12 53				13 08				13 23			
Wallasey Grove Road	d		12 12			12 27					12 42			12 57				13 12				13 27			
Wallasey Village	d		12 14			12 29					12 44			12 59				13 14				13 29			
Birkenhead North	d		12 19	12 24		12 34		12 39			12 49	12 54		13 04		13 09		13 19		13 24		13 34		13 39	
Birkenhead Park	d		12 21	12 26		12 36		12 41			12 51	12 56		13 06		13 11		13 21		13 26		13 36		13 41	
Conway Park	d		12 24	12 29		12 39		12 44			12 54	12 59		13 09		13 14		13 24		13 29		13 39		13 44	
Hamilton Square	d	12 21	12 26	12 31	12 36	12 41	12 44	12 46		12 51	12 56	13 01	13 06	13 11	13 14	13 16	13 21	13 26		13 31	13 36	13 41	13 44	13 46	13 51
James Street	d	12 24	12 29	12 34	12 39	12 44	12 47	12 49		12 54	12 59	13 04	13 09	13 14	13 17	13 19	13 24	13 29		13 34	13 39	13 44	13 47	13 49	13 54
Moorfields 10	a	12 26	12 31	12 36	12 41	12 46	12 48	12 51		12 56	13 01	13 06	13 11	13 16	13 18	13 21	13 26	13 31		13 36	13 41	13 46	13 48	13 51	13 56
Liverpool Lime Street 10	a	12 28	12 33	12 38	12 43	12 48	12 50	12 53		12 58	13 03	13 08	13 13	13 18	13 20	13 23	13 28	13 33		13 38	13 43	13 48	13 50	13 53	13 58
Liverpool Central 10	a	12 30	12 35	12 40	12 45	12 50	12 52	12 55		13 00	13 05	13 10	13 15	13 20	13 22	13 25	13 30	13 35		13 40	13 45	13 50	13 52	13 55	14 00

		ME	ME	ME		ME	ME	ME	ME	ME	ME	ME	ME	ME		ME	ME	ME	ME	ME	ME	ME	ME	ME	
Chester	d			13 32					13 45			14 02					14 15			14 32				14 45	
Bache	d								13 48								14 18							14 48	
Capenhurst	d								13 54								14 24							14 54	
Ellesmere Port	d						13 42							14 12								14 42			
Overpool	d						13 45							14 15								14 45			
Little Sutton	d						13 47							14 17								14 47			
Hooton	d			13 44			13 51		13 59			14 14		14 21			14 29			14 44		14 51		14 59	
Eastham Rake	d			13 46			13 53		14 01			14 16		14 23			14 31			14 46		14 53		15 01	
Bromborough	d			13 48			13 56		14 03			14 18		14 26			14 33			14 48		14 56		15 03	
Bromborough Rake	d			13 50			13 58		14 05			14 20		14 28			14 35			14 50		14 58		15 05	
Spital	d			13 52			14 00		14 07			14 22		14 30			14 37			14 52		15 00		15 07	
Port Sunlight	d			13 54			14 02		14 09			14 24		14 32			14 39			14 54		15 02		15 09	
Bebington	d			13 56			14 04		14 11			14 26		14 34			14 41			14 56		15 04		15 11	
Rock Ferry	d			13 59			14 07		14 14			14 29		14 37			14 44			14 59		15 07		15 14	
Green Lane	d			14 02			14 09		14 17			14 32		14 39			14 47			15 02		15 09		15 17	
Birkenhead Central	d			14 04			14 12		14 19			14 34		14 42			14 49			15 04		15 12		15 19	
West Kirby	d		13 36					13 51			14 06					14 21			14 36				14 51		
Hoylake	d		13 39					13 54			14 09					14 24			14 39				14 54		
Manor Road	d		13 41					13 56			14 11					14 26			14 41				14 56		
Meols	d		13 43					13 58			14 13					14 28			14 43				14 58		
Moreton (Merseyside)	d		13 46					14 01			14 16					14 31			14 46				15 01		
Leasowe	d		13 48					14 03			14 18					14 33			14 48				15 03		
Bidston	d		13 51					14 06			14 21					14 36			14 51				15 06		
New Brighton	d	13 38				13 53				14 08			14 23					14 38			14 53				
Wallasey Grove Road	d	13 42				13 57				14 12			14 27					14 42			14 57				
Wallasey Village	d	13 44				13 59				14 14			14 29					14 44			14 59				
Birkenhead North	d	13 49	13 54			14 04		14 09		14 19	14 24		14 34			14 39		14 49	14 54		15 04		15 09		
Birkenhead Park	d	13 51	13 56			14 06		14 11		14 21	14 26		14 36			14 41		14 51	14 56		15 06		15 11		
Conway Park	d	13 54	13 59			14 09		14 14		14 24	14 29		14 39			14 44		14 54	14 59		15 09		15 14		
Hamilton Square	d	13 56	14 01	14 06		14 11	14 14	14 16	14 21	14 26	14 31	14 36	14 41	14 44		14 46	14 51	14 56	15 01	15 06	15 11	15 14	15 16	15 21	
James Street	d	13 59	14 04	14 09		14 14	14 17	14 19	14 24	14 29	14 34	14 39	14 44	14 47		14 49	14 54	14 59	15 04	15 09	15 14	15 17	15 19	15 24	
Moorfields 10	a	14 01	14 06	14 11		14 16	14 18	14 21	14 26	14 31	14 36	14 41	14 46	14 48		14 51	14 56	15 01	15 06	15 11	15 16	15 18	15 21	15 26	
Liverpool Lime Street 10	a	14 03	14 08	14 13		14 18	14 20	14 23	14 28	14 33	14 38	14 43	14 48	14 50		14 53	14 58	15 03	15 08	15 13	15 18	15 20	15 23	15 28	
Liverpool Central 10	a	14 05	14 10	14 15		14 20	14 22	14 25	14 30	14 35	14 40	14 45	14 50	14 52		14 55	15 00	15 05	15 10	15 15	15 20	15 22	15 25	15 30	

Chester, Ellesmere Port, West Kirby and New Brighton - Birkenhead and Liverpool

		ME	ME	ME	ME	ME	ME	ME	ME	ME		ME	ME	ME	ME	ME	ME	ME	ME	ME		ME	ME	ME	ME
Chester	d			15 02				15 15				15 32				15 45			16 02					16 15	
Bache	d							15 18								15 48								16 18	
Capenhurst	d							15 24								15 54								16 24	
Ellesmere Port	d					15 12								15 42								16 12			
Overpool	d					15 15								15 45								16 15			
Little Sutton	d					15 17								15 47								16 17			
Hooton	d			15 14		15 21		15 29				15 44		15 51		15 59			16 14			16 21		16 29	
Eastham Rake	d			15 16		15 23		15 31				15 46		15 53		16 01			16 16			16 23		16 31	
Bromborough	d			15 18		15 26		15 33				15 48		15 56		16 03			16 18			16 26		16 33	
Bromborough Rake	d			15 20		15 28		15 35				15 50		15 58		16 05			16 20			16 28		16 35	
Spital	d			15 22		15 30		15 37				15 52		16 00		16 07			16 22			16 30		16 37	
Port Sunlight	d			15 24		15 32		15 39				15 54		16 02		16 09			16 24			16 32		16 39	
Bebington	d			15 26		15 34		15 41				15 56		16 04		16 11			16 26			16 34		16 41	
Rock Ferry	d			15 29		15 37		15 44				15 59		16 07		16 14			16 29			16 37		16 44	
Green Lane	d			15 32		15 39		15 47				16 02		16 09		16 17			16 32			16 39		16 47	
Birkenhead Central	d			15 34		15 42		15 49				16 04		16 12		16 19			16 34			16 42		16 49	
West Kirby	d		15 06				15 21			15 36					15 51			16 06					16 21		
Hoylake	d		15 09				15 24			15 39					15 54			16 09					16 24		
Manor Road	d		15 11				15 26			15 41					15 56			16 11					16 26		
Meols	d		15 13				15 28			15 43					15 58			16 13					16 28		
Moreton (Merseyside)	d		15 16				15 31			15 46					16 01			16 16					16 31		
Leasowe	d		15 18				15 33			15 48					16 03			16 18					16 33		
Bidston	d		15 21				15 36			15 51					16 06			16 21					16 36		
New Brighton	d	15 08			15 23				15 38				15 53				16 08			16 23					16 38
Wallasey Grove Road	d	15 12			15 27				15 42				15 57				16 12			16 27					16 42
Wallasey Village	d	15 14			15 29				15 44				15 59				16 14			16 29					16 44
Birkenhead North	d	15 19	15 24		15 34		15 39		15 49	15 54			16 04		16 09		16 19	16 24		16 34			16 39		16 49
Birkenhead Park	d	15 21	15 26		15 36		15 41		15 51	15 56			16 06		16 11		16 21	16 26		16 36			16 41		16 51
Conway Park	d	15 24	15 29		15 39		15 44		15 54	15 59			16 09		16 14		16 24	16 29		16 39			16 44		16 54
Hamilton Square	d	15 26	15 31	15 36	15 41	15 44	15 46	15 51	15 56	16 01		16 06	16 11	16 14	16 16	16 21	16 26	16 31	16 36	16 41		16 44	16 46	16 51	16 56
James Street	d	15 29	15 34	15 39	15 44	15 47	15 49	15 54	15 59	16 04		16 09	16 14	16 17	16 19	16 24	16 29	16 34	16 39	16 44		16 47	16 49	16 54	16 59
Moorfields 10	a	15 31	15 36	15 41	15 46	15 48	15 51	15 56	16 01	16 06		16 11	16 16	16 18	16 21	16 26	16 31	16 36	16 41	16 46		16 48	16 51	16 56	17 01
Liverpool Lime Street 10	a	15 33	15 38	15 43	15 48	15 50	15 53	15 58	16 03	16 08		16 13	16 18	16 20	16 23	16 28	16 33	16 38	16 43	16 48		16 50	16 53	16 58	17 03
Liverpool Central 10	a	15 35	15 40	15 45	15 50	15 52	15 55	16 00	16 05	16 10		16 15	16 20	16 22	16 25	16 30	16 35	16 40	16 45	16 50		16 52	16 55	17 00	17 05

		ME	ME	ME	ME	ME		ME	ME	ME	ME	ME	ME	ME	ME	ME		ME	ME	ME	ME	ME	ME	ME	ME
Chester	d		16 32					16 45			17 02				17 15				17 32				17 45		
Bache	d							16 48							17 18								17 48		
Capenhurst	d							16 54							17 24								17 54		
Ellesmere Port	d				16 42								17 12								17 42				
Overpool	d				16 45								17 15								17 45				
Little Sutton	d				16 47								17 17								17 47				
Hooton	d		16 44		16 51			16 59			17 14		17 21		17 29				17 44		17 51		17 59		
Eastham Rake	d		16 46		16 53			17 01			17 16		17 23		17 31				17 46		17 53		18 01		
Bromborough	d		16 48		16 56			17 03			17 18		17 26		17 33				17 48		17 56		18 03		
Bromborough Rake	d		16 50		16 58			17 05			17 20		17 28		17 35				17 50		17 58		18 05		
Spital	d		16 52		17 00			17 07			17 22		17 30		17 37				17 52		18 00		18 07		
Port Sunlight	d		16 54		17 02			17 09			17 24		17 32		17 39				17 54		18 02		18 09		
Bebington	d		16 56		17 04			17 11			17 26		17 34		17 41				17 56		18 04		18 11		
Rock Ferry	d		16 59		17 07			17 14			17 29		17 37		17 44				17 59		18 07		18 14		
Green Lane	d		17 02		17 09			17 17			17 32		17 39		17 47				18 02		18 09		18 17		
Birkenhead Central	d		17 04		17 12			17 19			17 34		17 42		17 49				18 04		18 12		18 19		
West Kirby	d	16 36				16 51				17 06				17 21				17 36				17 51			18 06
Hoylake	d	16 39				16 54				17 09				17 24				17 39				17 54			18 09
Manor Road	d	16 41				16 56				17 11				17 26				17 41				17 56			18 11
Meols	d	16 43				16 58				17 13				17 28				17 43				17 58			18 13
Moreton (Merseyside)	d	16 46				17 01				17 16				17 31				17 46				18 01			18 16
Leasowe	d	16 48				17 03				17 18				17 33				17 48				18 03			18 18
Bidston	d	16 51				17 06				17 21				17 36				17 51				18 06			18 21
New Brighton	d			16 53					17 08			17 23				17 38				17 53				18 08	
Wallasey Grove Road	d			16 57					17 12			17 27				17 42				17 57				18 12	
Wallasey Village	d			16 59					17 14			17 29				17 44				17 59				18 14	
Birkenhead North	d	16 54		17 04		17 09			17 19	17 24		17 34		17 39		17 49		17 54		18 04		18 09		18 19	18 24
Birkenhead Park	d	16 56		17 06		17 11			17 21	17 26		17 36		17 41		17 51		17 56		18 06		18 11		18 21	18 26
Conway Park	d	16 59		17 09		17 14			17 24	17 29		17 39		17 44		17 54		17 59		18 09		18 14		18 24	18 29
Hamilton Square	d	17 01	17 06	17 11	17 14	17 16		17 21	17 26	17 31	17 36	17 41	17 44	17 46	17 51	17 56		18 01	18 06	18 11	18 14	18 16	18 21	18 26	18 31
James Street	d	17 04	17 09	17 14	17 17	17 19		17 24	17 29	17 34	17 39	17 44	17 47	17 49	17 54	17 59		18 04	18 09	18 14	18 17	18 19	18 24	18 29	18 34
Moorfields 10	a	17 06	17 11	17 16	17 18	17 21		17 26	17 31	17 36	17 41	17 46	17 48	17 51	17 56	18 01		18 06	18 11	18 16	18 18	18 21	18 26	18 31	18 36
Liverpool Lime Street 10	a	17 08	17 13	17 18	17 20	17 23		17 28	17 33	17 38	17 43	17 48	17 50	17 53	17 58	18 03		18 08	18 13	18 18	18 20	18 23	18 28	18 33	18 38
Liverpool Central 10	a	17 10	17 15	17 20	17 22	17 25		17 30	17 35	17 40	17 45	17 50	17 52	17 55	18 00	18 05		18 10	18 15	18 20	18 22	18 25	18 30	18 35	18 40

Chester, Ellesmere Port, West Kirby and New Brighton - Birkenhead and Liverpool

		ME		ME	ME	ME	ME	ME	ME	ME	ME	ME		ME	ME	ME	ME	ME	ME	ME	ME	ME		ME	ME
Chester	d	18 02					18 15			18 30					19 00				19 30					20 00	
Bache	d						18 18			18 33					19 03				19 33					20 03	
Capenhurst	d						18 24			18 39					19 09				19 39					20 09	
Ellesmere Port	d				18 12							18 46					19 16				19 49				
Overpool	d				18 15							18 49					19 19				19 52				
Little Sutton	d				18 17							18 51					19 21				19 54				
Hooton	d	18 14			18 21		18 29			18 44		18 59			19 14		19 29		19 44		19 59			20 14	
Eastham Rake	d	18 16			18 23		18 31			18 46		19 01			19 16		19 31		19 46		20 01			20 16	
Bromborough	d	18 18			18 26		18 33			18 48		19 03			19 18		19 33		19 48		20 03			20 18	
Bromborough Rake	d	18 20			18 28		18 35			18 50		19 05			19 20		19 35		19 50		20 05			20 20	
Spital	d	18 22			18 30		18 37			18 52		19 07			19 22		19 37		19 52		20 07			20 22	
Port Sunlight	d	18 24			18 32		18 39			18 54		19 09			19 24		19 39		19 54		20 09			20 24	
Bebington	d	18 26			18 34		18 41			18 56		19 11			19 26		19 41		19 56		20 11			20 26	
Rock Ferry	d	18 29			18 37		18 44			18 59		19 14			19 29		19 44		19 59		20 14			20 29	
Green Lane	d	18 32			18 39		18 47			19 02		19 17			19 32		19 47		20 02		20 17			20 32	
Birkenhead Central	d	18 34			18 42		18 49			19 04		19 19			19 34		19 49		20 04		20 19			20 34	
West Kirby	d					18 21			18 36					19 01				19 31				20 01			
Hoylake	d					18 24			18 39					19 04				19 34				20 04			
Manor Road	d					18 26			18 41					19 06				19 36				20 06			
Meols	d					18 28			18 43					19 08				19 38				20 08			
Moreton (Merseyside)	d					18 31			18 46					19 11				19 41				20 11			
Leasowe	d					18 33			18 48					19 13				19 43				20 13			
Bidston	d					18 36			18 51					19 16				19 46				20 16			
New Brighton	d			18 23				18 38			18 53					19 23				19 53					20 23
Wallasey Grove Road	d			18 27				18 42			18 57					19 27				19 57					20 27
Wallasey Village	d			18 29				18 44			18 59					19 29				19 59					20 29
Birkenhead North	d			18 34		18 39		18 49	18 54		19 04			19 19		19 34		19 49		20 04		20 19			20 34
Birkenhead Park	d			18 36		18 41		18 51	18 56		19 06			19 21		19 36		19 51		20 06		20 21			20 36
Conway Park	d			18 39		18 44		18 54	18 59		19 09			19 24		19 39		19 54		20 09		20 24			20 39
Hamilton Square	d	18 36		18 41	18 44	18 46	18 51	18 56	19 01	19 06	19 11	19 21		19 26	19 36	19 41	19 51	19 56	20 06	20 11	20 21	20 26		20 36	20 41
James Street	d	18 39		18 44	18 47	18 49	18 54	18 59	19 04	19 09	19 14	19 24		19 29	19 39	19 44	19 54	19 59	20 09	20 14	20 24	20 29		20 39	20 44
Moorfields 10	a	18 41		18 46	18 48	18 51	18 56	19 01	19 06	19 11	19 16	19 26		19 31	19 41	19 46	19 56	20 01	20 11	20 16	20 26	20 31		20 41	20 46
Liverpool Lime Street 10	a	18 43		18 48	18 50	18 53	18 58	19 03	19 08	19 13	19 18	19 28		19 33	19 43	19 48	19 58	20 03	20 13	20 18	20 28	20 33		20 43	20 48
Liverpool Central 10	a	18 45		18 50	18 52	18 55	19 00	19 05	19 10	19 15	19 20	19 30		19 35	19 45	19 50	20 00	20 05	20 15	20 20	20 30	20 35		20 45	20 50

		ME	ME	ME	ME	ME	ME	ME		ME	ME	ME	ME	ME	ME	ME	ME	ME		ME	ME	ME	ME	ME	ME
Chester	d			20 30				21 00					21 30				22 00					22 30			
Bache	d			20 33				21 03					21 33				22 03					22 33			
Capenhurst	d			20 39				21 09					21 39				22 09					22 39			
Ellesmere Port	d	20 19				20 49					21 19				21 49					22 19				22 49	
Overpool	d	20 22				20 52					21 22				21 52					22 22				22 52	
Little Sutton	d	20 24				20 54					21 24				21 54					22 24				22 54	
Hooton	d	20 29		20 44		20 59		21 14			21 29		21 44		21 59		22 14			22 29		22 44		22 59	
Eastham Rake	d	20 31		20 46		21 01		21 16			21 31		21 46		22 01		22 16			22 31		22 46		23 01	
Bromborough	d	20 33		20 48		21 03		21 18			21 33		21 48		22 03		22 18			22 33		22 48		23 03	
Bromborough Rake	d	20 35		20 50		21 05		21 20			21 35		21 50		22 05		22 20			22 35		22 50		23 05	
Spital	d	20 37		20 52		21 07		21 22			21 37		21 52		22 07		22 22			22 37		22 52		23 07	
Port Sunlight	d	20 39		20 54		21 09		21 24			21 39		21 54		22 09		22 24			22 39		22 54		23 09	
Bebington	d	20 41		20 56		21 11		21 26			21 41		21 56		22 11		22 26			22 41		22 56		23 11	
Rock Ferry	d	20 44		20 59		21 14		21 29			21 44		21 59		22 14		22 29			22 44		22 59		23 14	
Green Lane	d	20 47		21 02		21 17		21 32			21 47		22 02		22 17		22 32			22 47		23 02		23 17	
Birkenhead Central	d	20 49		21 04		21 19		21 34			21 49		22 04		22 19		22 34			22 49		23 04		23 19	
West Kirby	d		20 31				21 01					21 31				22 01					22 31				23 01
Hoylake	d		20 34				21 04					21 34				22 04					22 34				23 04
Manor Road	d		20 36				21 06					21 36				22 06					22 36				23 06
Meols	d		20 38				21 08					21 38				22 08					22 38				23 08
Moreton (Merseyside)	d		20 41				21 11					21 41				22 11					22 41				23 11
Leasowe	d		20 43				21 13					21 43				22 13					22 43				23 13
Bidston	d		20 46				21 16					21 46				22 16					22 46				23 16
New Brighton	d				20 53					21 23				21 53				22 23					22 53		
Wallasey Grove Road	d				20 57					21 27				21 57				22 27					22 57		
Wallasey Village	d				20 59					21 29				21 59				22 29					22 59		
Birkenhead North	d		20 49		21 04		21 19			21 34		21 49		22 04		22 19		22 34			22 49		23 04		23 19
Birkenhead Park	d		20 51		21 06		21 21			21 36		21 51		22 06		22 21		22 36			22 51		23 06		23 21
Conway Park	d		20 54		21 09		21 24			21 39		21 54		22 09		22 24		22 39			22 54		23 09		23 24
Hamilton Square	d	20 51	20 56	21 06	21 11	21 21	21 26	21 36		21 41	21 51	21 56	22 06	22 11	22 21	22 26	22 36	22 41		22 51	22 56	23 06	23 11	23 21	23 26
James Street	d	20 54	20 59	21 09	21 14	21 24	21 29	21 39		21 44	21 54	21 59	22 09	22 14	22 24	22 29	22 39	22 44		22 54	22 59	23 09	23 14	23 24	23 29
Moorfields 10	a	20 56	21 01	21 11	21 16	21 26	21 31	21 41		21 46	21 56	22 01	22 11	22 16	22 26	22 31	22 41	22 46		22 56	23 01	23 11	23 16	23 26	23 31
Liverpool Lime Street 10	a	20 58	21 03	21 13	21 18	21 28	21 33	21 43		21 48	21 58	22 03	22 13	22 18	22 28	22 33	22 43	22 48		22 58	23 03	23 13	23 18	23 28	23 33
Liverpool Central 10	a	21 00	21 05	21 15	21 20	21 30	21 35	21 45		21 50	22 00	22 05	22 15	22 20	22 30	22 35	22 45	22 50		23 00	23 05	23 15	23 20	23 30	23 35

Chester, Ellesmere Port, West Kirby and New Brighton - Birkenhead and Liverpool

		ME	ME	ME
Chester	d	23 00		
Bache	d	23 03		
Capenhurst	d	23 09		
Ellesmere Port	d			23 19
Overpool	d			23 22
Little Sutton	d			23 24
Hooton	d	23 14		23 29
Eastham Rake	d	23 16		23 31
Bromborough	d	23 18		23 33
Bromborough Rake	d	23 20		23 35
Spital	d	23 22		23 37
Port Sunlight	d	23 24		23 39
Bebington	d	23 26		23 41
Rock Ferry	d	23 29		23 44
Green Lane	d	23 32		23 47
Birkenhead Central	d	23 34		23 49
West Kirby	d			
Hoylake	d			
Manor Road	d			
Meols	d			
Moreton (Merseyside)	d			
Leasowe	d			
Bidston	d			
New Brighton	d		23 23	
Wallasey Grove Road	d		23 27	
Wallasey Village	d		23 29	
Birkenhead North	d		23 34	
Birkenhead Park	d		23 36	
Conway Park	d		23 39	
Hamilton Square	d	23 36	23 41	23 51
James Street	d	23 39	23 44	23 54
Moorfields [10]	a	23 41	23 46	23 56
Liverpool Lime Street [10]	a	23 43	23 48	23 58
Liverpool Central [10]	a	23 45	23 50	23 59

Sundays

		ME	ME	ME	ME	ME	ME	ME	ME	ME		ME	ME	ME	ME	ME	ME	ME
Chester	d					08 00				08 30		22 30				23 00		
Bache	d					08 03				08 33		22 33				23 03		
Capenhurst	d					08 09				08 39		22 39				23 09		
Ellesmere Port	d			07 49				08 19						22 49				23 19
Overpool	d			07 52				08 22						22 52				23 22
Little Sutton	d			07 54				08 24						22 54				23 24
Hooton	d			07 59		08 14		08 29		08 44		22 44		22 59		23 14		23 29
Eastham Rake	d			08 01		08 16		08 31		08 46		22 46		23 01		23 16		23 31
Bromborough	d			08 03		08 18		08 33		08 48		22 48		23 03		23 18		23 33
Bromborough Rake	d			08 05		08 20		08 35		08 50		22 50		23 05		23 20		23 35
Spital	d			08 07		08 22		08 37		08 52		22 52		23 07		23 22		23 37
Port Sunlight	d			08 09		08 24		08 39		08 54		22 54		23 09		23 24		23 39
Bebington	d			08 11		08 26		08 41		08 56		22 56		23 11		23 26		23 41
Rock Ferry	d	07 49		08 14		08 29		08 44		08 59	and at the same minutes past each hour until	22 59		23 14		23 29		23 44
Green Lane	d	07 52		08 17		08 32		08 47		09 02		23 02		23 17		23 32		23 47
Birkenhead Central	d	07 54		08 19		08 34		08 49		09 04		23 04		23 19		23 34		23 49
West Kirby	d				08 01				08 31						23 01			
Hoylake	d				08 04				08 34						23 04			
Manor Road	d				08 06				08 36						23 06			
Meols	d				08 08				08 38						23 08			
Moreton (Merseyside)	d				08 11				08 41						23 11			
Leasowe	d				08 13				08 43						23 13			
Bidston	d				08 16				08 46						23 16			
New Brighton	d		07 53				08 23						22 53				23 23	
Wallasey Grove Road	d		07 57				08 27						22 57				23 27	
Wallasey Village	d		07 59				08 29						22 59				23 29	
Birkenhead North	d		08 04		08 19		08 34		08 49				23 04		23 19		23 34	
Birkenhead Park	d		08 06		08 21		08 36		08 51				23 06		23 21		23 36	
Conway Park	d		08 09		08 24		08 39		08 54				23 09		23 24		23 39	
Hamilton Square	d	07 56	08 11	08 21	08 26	08 36	08 41	08 51	08 56	09 06		23 06	23 11	23 21	23 26	23 36	23 41	23 51
James Street	d	07 59	08 14	08 24	08 29	08 39	08 44	08 54	08 59	09 09		23 09	23 14	23 24	23 29	23 39	23 44	23 54
Moorfields [10]	a	08 01	08 16	08 26	08 31	08 41	08 46	08 56	09 01	09 11		23 11	23 16	23 26	23 31	23 41	23 46	23 56
Liverpool Lime Street [10]	a	08 03	08 18	08 28	08 33	08 43	08 48	08 58	09 03	09 13		23 13	23 18	23 28	23 33	23 43	23 48	23 58
Liverpool Central [10]	a	08 05	08 20	08 30	08 35	08 45	08 50	09 00	09 05	09 15		23 15	23 20	23 30	23 35	23 45	23 50	23 59

Table 109

Mondays to Saturdays

Helsby - Ellesmere Port

Miles			NT	NT	AW A (bus) SO	NT	NT
—	Warrington Bank Quay	81 d	05 49		13∫45		
0	**Helsby**	d	06 03	06 33	14a25	15 17	15 48
2	Ince & Elton	d	06 06	06 36		15 20	15 51
2¾	Stanlow & Thornton	d	06 08	06 38		15 22	15 53
5¼	**Ellesmere Port**	a	06 15	06 45		15 28	15 59

A Until 18 June

Table 109

Mondays to Saturdays

Ellesmere Port - Helsby

Miles			NT	NT SX	NT SO	NT	NT
0	**Ellesmere Port**	d	06 19	06 56	06 56	15 34	16 04
2½	Stanlow & Thornton	d	06 23	07 00	07 00	15 38	16 08
3¼	Ince & Elton	d	06 26	07 03	07 03	15 41	16 11
5¼	**Helsby**	a	06 30	07 06	07 07	15 45	16 14
—	Warrington Bank Quay	81 a		07 23			16 34

No Sunday Service

Network Diagram for Tables 114, 115

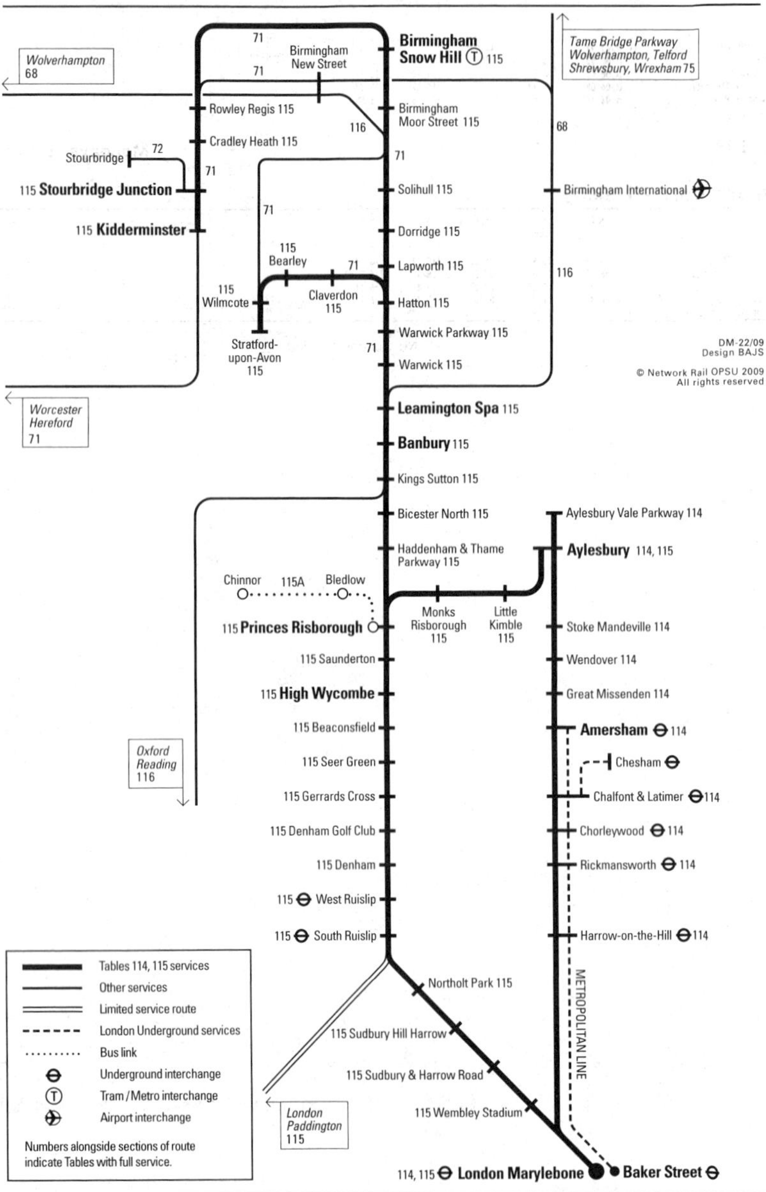

© Network Rail OPSU 2009
All rights reserved

Table 114

London - Amersham and Aylesbury

Miles				CH MX A	CH MO B ◇	CH MX A	CH MX A	CH C	CH C ◇	CH C	CH C	CH C	CH C	CH C ◇	CH C	CH C	CH C ◇	CH C	CH C	CH C	CH C	CH C ◇	CH C	CH C
0	**London Marylebone** 10	⊖	d	22p57	23p27	23p27	23p57	0632	0704	0726	0756	0827	0857	0927	0957	1027	1057	1127	1157	1227	1257	1327	1357	1427
9	Harrow-on-the-Hill 3 §	⊖	d	23p09	23p39	23p39	0009	0645	0716	0738	0808	0839	0909	0939	1009	1039	1109	1139	1209	1239	1309	1339	1409	1439
17	Rickmansworth §	⊖	d	23p19	23p49	23p49	0019	0655	0727	0748	0818	0849	0919	0949	1019	1049	1119	1149	1219	1249	1319	1349	1419	1449
19¼	Chorleywood §	⊖	d	23p24	23p54	23p54	0024	0700	0731	0753	0823	0854	0924	0954	1024	1054	1124	1154	1224	1254	1324	1354	1424	1454
21½	Chalfont & Latimer §	⊖	d	23p28	23p58	23p58	0028	0704	0735	0757	0827	0858	0928	0958	1028	1058	1128	1158	1228	1258	1328	1358	1428	1458
23½	**Amersham** §	⊖	d	23p32	0002	0002	0032	0708	0739	0801	0831	0902	0932	1002	1032	1102	1132	1202	1232	1302	1332	1402	1432	1502
28¾	Great Missenden		d	23p38	0008	0008	0038	0714	0746	0807	0837	0908	0938	1008	1038	1108	1138	1208	1238	1308	1338	1408	1438	1508
33¼	Wendover		d	23p44	0014	0014	0044	0720	0752	0813	0843	0914	0944	1014	1044	1114	1144	1214	1244	1314	1344	1414	1444	1514
35¼	Stoke Mandeville		d	23p48	0018	0018	0048	0724	0756	0817	0847	0918	0948	1018	1048	1118	1148	1218	1248	1318	1348	1418	1448	1518
37¾	**Aylesbury**		d	23p53	00a26	00a26	00a56	0730	0801	08a25	0852	09a26	0953	10a26	1053	11a26	1153	12a26	1253	13a26	1353	14a26	1453	15a26
40½	**Aylesbury Vale Parkway**		a	0001				0739	0808		0900		1001		1101		1201		1301		1401		1501	

			CH C ◇	CH C	CH C	CH C	CH C	CH C	CH C	CH C	CH C	CH C	CH C	CH C	CH C	CH C	CH C	CH C	CH C	CH C ◇	CH C	CH C	CH C	CH C
London Marylebone 10	⊖	d	1457	1527	1557	1627	1642	1657	1716	1727	1747	1803	1818	1836	1850	1909	1925	1957	2027	2057	2127	2157	2227	2257
Harrow-on-the-Hill 3 §	⊖	d	1509	1539	1609	1639		1709		1740		1815		1848	1903		1937	2009	2039	2109	2139	2209	2239	2309
Rickmansworth §	⊖	d	1519	1549	1619	1649		1719		1750							1947	2019	2049	2119	2149	2219	2249	2319
Chorleywood §	⊖	d	1524	1554	1624	1654		1724		1755		1829		1902	1917		1952	2024	2054	2124	2154	2224	2254	2324
Chalfont & Latimer §	⊖	d	1528	1558	1628	1658		1728		1759		1833		1906	1921		1956	2028	2058	2128	2158	2228	2258	2328
Amersham §	⊖	d	1532	1602	1632	1702	1715	1732		1803	1818	1838		1910	1925		2000	2032	2102	2132	2202	2232	2302	2332
Great Missenden		d	1538	1608	1638	1708	1722	1738	1751	1809	1825	1844	1856	1916	1931	1946	2006	2038	2108	2138	2208	2238	2308	2338
Wendover		d	1544	1614	1644	1714	1728	1744	1757	1815	1831	1850	1902	1922	1937	1952	2012	2044	2114	2144	2214	2244	2314	2344
Stoke Mandeville		d	1548	1618	1648	1718	1732	1748	1801	1819	1835	1854	1906	1926	1941	1957	2016	2048	2118	2148	2218	2248	2318	2348
Aylesbury		d	1553	16a26	1653	17a26	1737	17a56	1806	18a26	1840	19a02	1911	19a34	19a49	2009	20a24	2053	21a26	2153	22a26	2253	23a26	2353
Aylesbury Vale Parkway		a	1601		1702		1743		1815		1846		1918			2015		2101		2201		2301		0001

			CH C	CH C
London Marylebone 10	⊖	d	2327	2357
Harrow-on-the-Hill 3 §	⊖	d	2339	0009
Rickmansworth §	⊖	d	2349	0019
Chorleywood §	⊖	d	2354	0024
Chalfont & Latimer §	⊖	d	2358	0028
Amersham §	⊖	d	0002	0032
Great Missenden		d	0008	0038
Wendover		d	0014	0044
Stoke Mandeville		d	0018	0048
Aylesbury		d	00a26	00a56
Aylesbury Vale Parkway		a		

Saturdays

			CH D	CH D	CH D	CH D	CH D ◇	CH D	CH D	CH D ◇	CH D	CH D	CH D	CH D	CH D ◇	CH D	CH D	CH D	CH D	CH D	CH D ◇	CH D	CH D	CH D
London Marylebone 10	⊖	d	22p57	23p27	23p57		0727	0757	0827	0857	0927	0957	1027	1057	1127	1157	1227	1257	1357	1427	1457	1527	1557	1627
Harrow-on-the-Hill 3 §	⊖	d	23p09	23p39	0009		0739	0809	0839	0909	0939	1009	1039	1109	1139	1209	1239	1309	1409	1439	1509	1539	1609	1639
Rickmansworth §	⊖	d	23p19	23p49	0019		0749	0819	0849	0919	0949	1019	1049	1119	1149	1219	1249	1319	1419	1449	1519	1549	1619	1649
Chorleywood §	⊖	d	23p24	23p54	0024		0754	0824	0854	0924	0954	1024	1054	1124	1154	1224	1254	1324	1424	1454	1524	1554	1624	1654
Chalfont & Latimer §	⊖	d	23p28	23p58	0028		0758	0828	0858	0928	0958	1028	1058	1128	1158	1228	1258	1328	1428	1458	1528	1558	1628	1658
Amersham §	⊖	d	23p32	0002	0032	0705	0802	0832	0902	0932	1002	1032	1102	1132	1202	1232	1302	1332	1432	1502	1532	1602	1632	1702
Great Missenden		d	23p38	0008	0038	0711	0808	0838	0908	0938	1008	1038	1108	1138	1208	1238	1308	1338	1438	1508	1538	1608	1638	1708
Wendover		d	23p44	0014	0044	0717	0814	0844	0914	0944	1014	1044	1114	1144	1214	1244	1314	1344	1444	1514	1544	1614	1644	1714
Stoke Mandeville		d	23p48	0018	0048	0721	0818	0848	0918	0948	1018	1048	1118	1148	1218	1248	1318	1348	1448	1518	1548	1618	1648	1718
Aylesbury		d	23p53	00a26	00a56	07a29	08a26	0853	09a26	0953	10a26	1053	11a26	1153	12a26	1253	13a26	1353	1453	15a26	1553	16a26	1653	17a26
Aylesbury Vale Parkway		a	0001					0901		1001		1101		1201		1301		1401	1501		1601		1701	

			CH D	CH D	CH D	CH D	CH D	CH D	CH D	CH ◇ D	CH D	CH D	CH D
London Marylebone 10	⊖	d	1657	1727	1757	1827	1857	1927	1957	2057	2157	2257	2357
Harrow-on-the-Hill 3 §	⊖	d	1709	1739	1809	1839	1909	1939	2009	2109	2209	2309	0009
Rickmansworth §	⊖	d	1719	1749	1819	1849	1919	1949	2019	2119	2219	2319	0019
Chorleywood §	⊖	d	1724	1754	1824	1854	1924	1954	2024	2124	2224	2324	0024
Chalfont & Latimer §	⊖	d	1728	1758	1828	1858	1928	1958	2028	2128	2228	2328	0028
Amersham §	⊖	d	1732	1802	1832	1902	1932	2002	2032	2132	2232	2332	0032
Great Missenden		d	1738	1808	1838	1908	1938	2008	2038	2138	2238	2338	0038
Wendover		d	1744	1814	1844	1914	1944	2014	2044	2144	2244	2344	0044
Stoke Mandeville		d	1748	1818	1848	1918	1948	2018	2048	2148	2248	2348	0048
Aylesbury		d	1753	18a26	1853	19a26	1953	20a26	2053	2153	2253	2353	00a56
Aylesbury Vale Parkway		a	1801		1901		2001		2101	2201	2301	0001	

§ London Underground Limited (Metropolitan Line) services operate between Harrow-on-the-Hill, Rickmansworth, Chorleywood, Chalfont & Latimer and Amersham

A Until 2 September
B Until 5 September, 28 November
C until 2 September
D until 3 September

Table 114

Sundays

London - Amersham and Aylesbury

		CH	CH	CH	CH	CH	CH	CH	CH	CH
						◇				◇
		A	B	A	B	B	B	B	B	B
London Marylebone 10	⊖ d	22p57		23p57		0827	0927	1027	1127	1227
Harrow-on-the-Hill 3 §	⊖ d	23p09		0009		0839	0939	1039	1139	1239
Rickmansworth §	⊖ d	23p19		0019		0849	0949	1049	1149	1249
Chorleywood §	⊖ d	23p24		0024		0854	0954	1054	1154	1254
Chalfont & Latimer §	⊖ d	23p28		0028		0858	0958	1058	1158	1258
Amersham §	⊖ d	23p32	0002	0032	0832	0902	1002	1102	1202	1302
Great Missenden	d	23p38	0008	0038	0838	0908	1008	1108	1208	1308
Wendover	d	23p44	0014	0044	0844	0914	1014	1114	1214	1314
Stoke Mandeville	d	23p48	0018	0048	0848	0918	1018	1118	1218	1318
Aylesbury	d	23p53	00a26	00a56	08a56	0923	1023	1123	1223	1323
Aylesbury Vale Parkway	a	0001				0931	1031	1131	1231	1331

		CH	CH	CH	CH	CH	CH	CH	CH	CH	CH	CH	CH	CH
					◇									
		B	B	B	B	B	B	B	B	B	B	B	B	B
London Marylebone 10	⊖ d	1327	1427		1527		1627		1727		1827		1927	
Harrow-on-the-Hill 3 §	⊖ d	1339	1439		1539		1639		1739		1839		1939	
Rickmansworth §	⊖ d	1349	1449		1549		1649		1749		1849		1949	
Chorleywood §	⊖ d	1354	1454		1554		1654		1754		1854		1954	
Chalfont & Latimer §	⊖ d	1358	1458		1558		1658		1758		1858		1958	
Amersham §	⊖ d	1402	1502	1532	1602	1632	1702	1732	1802	1832	1902	1932	2002	2032
Great Missenden	d	1408	1508	1538	1608	1638	1708	1738	1808	1838	1908	1938	2008	2038
Wendover	d	1414	1514	1544	1614	1644	1714	1744	1814	1844	1914	1944	2014	2044
Stoke Mandeville	d	1418	1518	1548	1618	1648	1718	1748	1818	1848	1918	1948	2018	2048
Aylesbury	d	1423	1523	15a56	1623	16a56	1723	17a56	1823	18a56	1923	19a56	2023	20a56
Aylesbury Vale Parkway	a	1431	1531		1631		1731		1831		1931		2031	

		CH	CH	CH	CH	CH
						◇
		B	B	B	B	B
London Marylebone 10	⊖ d	2027		2127	2227	2327
Harrow-on-the-Hill 3 §	⊖ d	2039		2139	2239	2339
Rickmansworth §	⊖ d	2049		2149	2249	2349
Chorleywood §	⊖ d	2054		2154	2254	2354
Chalfont & Latimer §	⊖ d	2058		2158	2258	2358
Amersham §	⊖ d	2102	2132	2202	2302	0002
Great Missenden	d	2108	2138	2208	2308	0008
Wendover	d	2114	2144	2214	2314	0014
Stoke Mandeville	d	2118	2148	2218	2318	0018
Aylesbury	d	2123	21a56	2223	2323	00a26
Aylesbury Vale Parkway	a	2131		2231	2331	

§ London Underground Limited (Metropolitan Line) services operate between Harrow-on-the-Hill, Rickmansworth, Chorleywood, Chalfont & Latimer and Amersham

A from 29 May until 4 September
B until 4 September, 27 November

Aylesbury and Amersham - London

Mondays to Fridays

Miles			CH A	CH A	CH A	CH A	CH A	CH A	CH A	CH A	CH A	CH A	CH A	CH A	CH A	CH A	CH A	CH A	CH A	CH ◇ A	CH A	CH A	CH ◇ A
0	**Aylesbury Vale Parkway**	d	05 26	06 06		06 40		07 13		07 45		08 16		09 05	09 30		10 30		11 30		12 30		13 30
2¾	**Aylesbury**	d	05 31	06 11	06 26	06 45	07 00	07 18	07 32	07 50	08 05	08 21	08 35	09 10	09 35	10 05	10 35	11 05	11 35	12 05	12 35	13 05	13 35
5¼	Stoke Mandeville	d	05 35	06 15	06 30	06 49	07 04	07 22	07 36	07 54	08 09	08 25	08 39	09 14	09 39	10 09	10 39	11 09	11 39	12 09	12 39	13 09	13 39
7¼	Wendover	d	05 39	06 19	06 34	06 53	07 08	07 26	07 40	07 58	08 13	08 29	08 43	09 18	09 43	10 13	10 43	11 13	11 43	12 13	12 43	13 13	13 43
11¾	Great Missenden	d	05 45	06 25	06 40	07 00	07 14	07 32	07 46	08 04	08 19	08 35	08 49	09 24	09 49	10 19	10 49	11 19	11 49	12 19	12 49	13 19	13 49
17	**Amersham** §	⊖ d	05 52	06 32	06 47	07 07	07 21	07 39	07 53	08 11	08 26	08 42	08 56	09 31	09 56	10 26	10 56	11 26	11 56	12 26	12 56	13 26	13 56
19	Chalfont & Latimer §	⊖ d		06 36	06 51		07 25		07 57		08 30		09 00	09 35	10 00	10 30	11 00	11 30	12 00	12 30	13 00	13 30	14 00
21¼	Chorleywood §	⊖ d		06 39	06 54		07 28		08 00		08 33		09 03	09 38	10 03	10 33	11 03	11 33	12 03	12 33	13 03	13 33	14 03
23½	Rickmansworth §	⊖ d			06 59				08 05		08 38		09 08	09 43	10 08	10 38	11 08	11 38	12 08	12 38	13 08	13 38	14 08
31½	Harrow-on-the-Hill 3 §	⊖ d	06 11	06 54	07 10		07 43		08 16		08 49		09 19	09 54	10 19	10 49	11 19	11 49	12 19	12 49	13 19	13 49	14 19
40½	**London Marylebone** 10	⊖ a	06 25	07 10	07 25	07 42	07 58	08 15	08 32	08 44	09 05	09 16	09 35	10 10	10 35	11 05	11 35	12 05	12 35	13 05	13 35	14 05	14 35

		CH A	CH A	CH ◇ A	CH A	CH A	CH ◇ A	CH A	CH A	CH A	CH A	CH A	CH ◇ A	CH A	CH A	CH ◇ A	CH A	CH A	CH A
Aylesbury Vale Parkway	d		14 30		15 30		16 30		17 30		18 20			19 30		20 30		21 30	22 30
Aylesbury	d	14 05	14 35	15 05	15 35	16 05	16 35	17 05	17 35	17 55	18 25	18 45	19 15	19 35	20 05	20 35	21 05	21 35	22 35
Stoke Mandeville	d	14 09	14 39	15 09	15 39	16 09	16 39	17 09	17 39	17 59	18 29	18 49	19 19	19 39	20 09	20 39	21 09	21 39	22 39
Wendover	d	14 13	14 43	15 13	15 43	16 13	16 43	17 13	17 43	18 03	18 33	18 53	19 23	19 43	20 13	20 43	21 13	21 43	22 43
Great Missenden	d	14 19	14 49	15 19	15 49	16 19	16 49	17 19	17 49	18 09	18 39	18 59	19 29	19 49	20 19	20 49	21 19	21 49	22 49
Amersham §	⊖ d	14 26	14 56	15 26	15 56	16 26	16 56	17 26	17 56	18 16	18 46	19 06	19 36	19 56	20 26	20 56	21 26	21 56	22 56
Chalfont & Latimer §	⊖ d	14 30	15 00	15 30	16 00	16 30	17 00	17 30	18 00	18 20	18 50	19 10	19 40	20 00	20 30	21 00	21 30	22 00	23 00
Chorleywood §	⊖ d	14 33	15 03	15 33	16 03	16 33	17 03	17 33	18 03	18 23	18 53	19 13	19 43	20 03	20 33	21 03	21 33	22 03	23 03
Rickmansworth §	⊖ d	14 38	15 08	15 38	16 08	16 38	17 08	17 38	18 08	18 28	18 58	19 18	19 48	20 08	20 38	21 08	21 38	22 08	23 08
Harrow-on-the-Hill 3 §	⊖ d	14 49	15 19	15 49	16 19	16 49	17 19	17 49	18 19	18 39	19 09	19 29	19 59	20 19	20 49	21 19	21 49	22 19	23 19
London Marylebone 10	⊖ a	15 05	15 35	16 05	16 35	17 05	17 35	18 05	18 35	18 55	19 25	19 45	20 15	20 35	21 05	21 35	22 05	22 35	23 35

Saturdays

		CH ◇ B	CH B	CH B	CH B	CH B	CH B	CH B	CH B	CH B	CH B	CH B	CH B	CH B	CH B	CH ◇ B	CH B	CH ◇ B	CH B	CH B	CH ◇ B	CH B	CH B
Aylesbury Vale Parkway	d			07 00	07 30		08 30		09 30		10 30	11 30		12 30		13 30		14 30		15 30		16 30	
Aylesbury	d	06 05	06 35	07 05	07 35	08 05	08 35	09 05	09 35	10 05	10 35	11 35	12 05	12 35	13 05	13 35	14 05	14 35	15 05	15 35	16 05	16 35	17 05
Stoke Mandeville	d	06 09	06 39	07 09	07 39	08 09	08 39	09 09	09 39	10 09	10 39	11 39	12 09	12 39	13 09	13 39	14 09	14 39	15 09	15 39	16 09	16 39	17 09
Wendover	d	06 13	06 43	07 13	07 43	08 13	08 43	09 13	09 43	10 13	10 43	11 43	12 13	12 43	13 13	13 43	14 13	14 43	15 13	15 43	16 13	16 43	17 13
Great Missenden	d	06 19	06 49	07 19	07 49	08 19	08 49	09 19	09 49	10 19	10 49	11 49	12 19	12 49	13 19	13 49	14 19	14 49	15 19	15 49	16 19	16 49	17 19
Amersham §	⊖ d	06 26	06a58	07 26	07 56	08 26	08 56	09 26	09 56	10 26	10 56	11 56	12 26	12 56	13 26	13 56	14 26	14 56	15 26	15 56	16 26	16 56	17 26
Chalfont & Latimer §	⊖ d	06 30		07 30	08 00	08 30	09 00	09 30	10 00	10 30	11 00	12 00	12 30	13 00	13 30	14 00	14 30	15 00	15 30	16 00	16 30	17 00	17 30
Chorleywood §	⊖ d	06 33		07 33	08 03	08 33	09 03	09 33	10 03	10 33	11 03	12 03	12 33	13 03	13 33	14 03	14 33	15 03	15 33	16 03	16 33	17 03	17 33
Rickmansworth §	⊖ d	06 38		07 38	08 08	08 38	09 08	09 38	10 08	10 38	11 08	12 08	12 38	13 08	13 38	14 08	14 38	15 08	15 38	16 08	16 38	17 08	17 38
Harrow-on-the-Hill 3 §	⊖ d	06 49		07 49	08 19	08 49	09 19	09 49	10 19	10 49	11 19	12 19	12 49	13 19	13 49	14 19	14 49	15 19	15 49	16 19	16 49	17 19	17 49
London Marylebone 10	⊖ a	07 05		08 05	08 35	09 05	09 35	10 05	10 35	11 05	11 35	12 35	13 05	13 35	14 05	14 35	15 05	15 35	16 05	16 35	17 05	17 35	18 05

		CH B	CH ◇ B	CH B	CH B	CH B	CH ◇ B	CH B	CH B
Aylesbury Vale Parkway	d	17 30		18 30		19 46	20 46	21 46	
Aylesbury	d	17 35	18 05	18 35	19 05	20 05	21 05	22 05	23 20
Stoke Mandeville	d	17 39	18 09	18 39	19 09	20 09	21 09	22 09	23 24
Wendover	d	17 43	18 13	18 43	19 13	20 13	21 13	22 13	23 28
Great Missenden	d	17 49	18 19	18 49	19 19	20 19	21 19	22 19	23 34
Amersham §	⊖ d	17 56	18 26	18 56	19 26	20 26	21 26	22 26	23a43
Chalfont & Latimer §	⊖ d	18 00	18 30	19 00	19 30	20 30	21 30	22 30	
Chorleywood §	⊖ d	18 03	18 33	19 03	19 33	20 33	21 33	22 33	
Rickmansworth §	⊖ d	18 08	18 38	19 08	19 38	20 38	21 38	22 38	
Harrow-on-the-Hill 3 §	⊖ d	18 19	18 49	19 19	19 49	20 49	21 49	22 49	
London Marylebone 10	⊖ a	18 35	19 05	19 35	20 05	21 05	22 05	23 05	

Sundays

		CH ◇ C	CH ◇ D	CH C	CH D	CH C	CH D	CH C	CH D	CH C	CH D	CH C	CH D	CH C	CH D	CH ◇ C	CH ◇ D	CH C	CH D	CH E	CH C	CH D	CH E
Aylesbury Vale Parkway	d	07 30	07 30	08 30	08 30	09 00	09 00	10 00	10 00	11 00	11 00	12 00	12 00	13 00	13 00	14 00	14 00	15 00	15 00		16 00	16 00	
Aylesbury	d	07 35	07 35	08 35	08 35	09 05	09 05	10 05	10 05	11 05	11 05	12 05	12 05	13 05	13 05	14 05	14 05	15 05	15 05	15 35	16 05	16 05	16 35
Stoke Mandeville	d	07 39	07 39	08 39	08 39	09 09	09 09	10 09	10 09	11 09	11 09	12 09	12 09	13 09	13 09	14 09	14 09	15 09	15 09	15 39	16 09	16 09	16 39
Wendover	d	07 43	07 43	08 43	08 43	09 13	09 13	10 13	10 13	11 13	11 13	12 13	12 13	13 13	13 13	14 13	14 13	15 13	15 13	15 43	16 13	16 13	16 43
Great Missenden	d	07 49	07 49	08 49	08 49	09 19	09 19	10 19	10 19	11 19	11 19	12 19	12 19	13 19	13 19	14 19	14 19	15 19	15 19	15 49	16 19	16 19	16 49
Amersham §	⊖ d	07 56	07 56	08 56	08 56	09 26	09 26	10 26	10 26	11 26	11 26	12 26	12 26	13 26	13 26	14 26	14 26	15 26	15 26	15a58	16 26	16 26	16a58
Chalfont & Latimer §	⊖ d	08 00	08 00	09 00	09 00	09 30	09 30	10 30	10 30	11 30	11 30	12 30	12 30	13 30	13 30	14 30	14 30	15 30	15 30		16 30	16 30	
Chorleywood §	⊖ d	08 03	08 03	09 03	09 03	09 33	09 33	10 33	10 33	11 33	11 33	12 33	12 33	13 33	13 33	14 33	14 33	15 33	15 33		16 33	16 33	
Rickmansworth §	⊖ d	08 08	08 08	09 08	09 08	09 38	09 38	10 38	10 38	11 38	11 38	12 38	12 38	13 38	13 38	14 38	14 38	15 38	15 38		16 38	16 38	
Harrow-on-the-Hill 3 §	⊖ d	08 19	08 19	09 19	09 19	09 49	09 49	10 49	10 49	11 49	11 49	12 49	12 49	13 49	13 49	14 49	14 49	15 49	15 49		16 49	16 49	
London Marylebone 10	⊖ a	08 33	08 35	09 33	09 35	10 03	10 05	11 03	11 05	12 03	12 05	13 03	13 05	14 04	14 05	15 03	15 05	16 03	16 05		17 03	17 05	

§ London Underground Limited (Metropolitan Line) services operate between Harrow-on-the-Hill, Rickmansworth, Chorleywood, Chalfont & Latimer and Amersham

A until 2 September
B until 3 September
C 27 November
D until 4 September
E until 4 September, 27 November

Table 114

Sundays

Aylesbury and Amersham - London

			CH	CH	CH	CH	CH	CH	CH	CH	CH	CH	CH	CH	CH	CH	CH	CH	CH	CH	CH
									◇	◇									◇	◇
			A	B	C	A	B	C	A	B	C	A	B	C	A	B	C	C	A	B
Aylesbury Vale Parkway		d	17 00	17 00		18 00	18 00		19 00	19 00		20 00	20 00		21 00	21 00		22 00		
Aylesbury		d	17 05	17 05	17 35	18 05	18 05	18 35	19 05	19 05	19 35	20 05	20 05	20 35	21 05	21 05	21 35	22 05	22 35	22 35
Stoke Mandeville		d	17 09	17 09	17 39	18 09	18 09	18 39	19 09	19 09	19 39	20 09	20 09	20 39	21 09	21 09	21 39	22 09	22 39	22 39
Wendover		d	17 13	17 13	17 43	18 13	18 13	18 43	19 13	19 13	19 43	20 13	20 13	20 43	21 13	21 13	21 43	22 13	22 43	22 43
Great Missenden		d	17 19	17 19	17 49	18 19	18 19	18 49	19 19	19 19	19 49	20 19	20 19	20 49	21 19	21 19	21 49	22 19	22 49	22 49
Amersham §	⊖	d	17 26	17 26	17a58	18 26	18 26	18a58	19 26	19 26	19a58	20 26	20 26	20a58	21 26	21 26	21a58	22a28	22 56	22 56
Chalfont & Latimer §	⊖	d	17 30	17 30		18 30	18 30		19 30	19 30		20 30	20 30		21 30	21 30			23 00	23 00
Chorleywood §	⊖	d	17 33	17 33		18 33	18 33		19 33	19 33		20 33	20 33		21 33	21 33			23 03	23 03
Rickmansworth §	⊖	d	17 38	17 38		18 38	18 38		19 38	19 38		20 38	20 38		21 38	21 38			23 08	23 08
Harrow-on-the-Hill 3 §	⊖	d	17 49	17 49		18 49	18 49		19 49	19 49		20 49	20 49		21 49	21 49			23 19	23 19
London Marylebone 10	⊖	a	18 04	18 05		19 04	19 05		20 03	20 05		21 03	21 05		22 03	22 05			23 34	23 35

§ London Underground Limited (Metropolitan Line) services operate between Harrow-on-the-Hill, Rickmansworth, Chorleywood, Chalfont & Latimer and Amersham

A 27 November
B until 4 September
C until 4 September, 27 November

London - High Wycombe, Aylesbury, Banbury, Stratford-upon-Avon, Birmingham Snow Hill and Kidderminster

Miles	Miles	Miles			CH	CH	CH	CH	CH	CH	CH	CH	CH		CH	CH	CH	CH	CH	CH	CH	CH	CH		CH
					◇	◇																			
					MO	MX	MX		MO	MO	MX	MX	MX			MO	MO	MX							
					A	B	B	C	D	E	B	B	B		C	D	F	B	G	G	G	G	G		G
—	—	—	**London Marylebone** 10 ⊖	d	22p00	22p20	22p40	22p45	22p45		23p10	23p30	23p54		23p45	23p45		00ʃ10			06ʃ00	06ʃ10	06ʃ28		
—	—	0	**London Paddington** 15 ⊖	d	ʃ	ʃ	ʃ	ʃ	ʃ		ʃ	ʃ	ʃ		ʃ	ʃ		ʃ			ʃ	ʃ	ʃ		
6½	—	—	Wembley Stadium	d	ʃ	ʃ	22p49	22p53	22p54		23p19	23p39	ʃ		23p53	23p54		00ʃ19			06ʃ09	ʃ	06ʃ37		
8	—	—	Sudbury & Harrow Road	d	ʃ	ʃ	ʃ	ʃ	ʃ		ʃ	ʃ	ʃ		ʃ	ʃ		ʃ			ʃ	ʃ	ʃ		
8¾	—	—	Sudbury Hill Harrow	d	ʃ	ʃ	ʃ	ʃ	ʃ		ʃ	ʃ	ʃ		ʃ	ʃ		ʃ			ʃ	ʃ	ʃ		
9¾	—	—	Northolt Park	d	ʃ	ʃ	ʃ	22p58	22p59		ʃ	23p44	ʃ		23p58	23p59		00ʃ24			06ʃ14	ʃ	06ʃ42		
11½	—	—	South Ruislip § ⊖	d	ʃ	ʃ	22p56	23p02	23p03		ʃ	23p48	ʃ		00ʃ03	00ʃ03		00ʃ28			06ʃ18	ʃ	06ʃ46		
13¼	—	—	West Ruislip 3 § ⊖	d	ʃ	ʃ	ʃ	23p05	23p06		ʃ	23p51	ʃ		00ʃ06	00ʃ06		00ʃ31			ʃ	06ʃ27	06ʃ49		
16	—	—	Denham	d	ʃ	ʃ	23p02	23p10	23p11		ʃ	23p56	ʃ		00ʃ11	00ʃ11		00ʃ36			06ʃ24	06ʃ31	06ʃ54		
17	—	—	Denham Golf Club	d	ʃ	ʃ	ʃ	ʃ	23p13		ʃ	23p58	ʃ		00ʃ13	00ʃ13		00ʃ38			ʃ	06ʃ34	ʃ		
18¾	—	—	Gerrards Cross 1	d	ʃ	ʃ	23p07	23p13	23p16		23p33	00ʃ01	00ʃ15		00ʃ16	00ʃ16		00ʃ41			06ʃ28	06ʃ38	06ʃ58		
21¼	—	—	Seer Green	d	ʃ	ʃ	23p11	23p19	23p21		ʃ	00ʃ06	ʃ		00ʃ21	00ʃ21		00ʃ46			06ʃ33	ʃ	ʃ		
23	—	—	Beaconsfield	d	ʃ	ʃ	23p15	23p21	23p24		23p39	00ʃ09	00ʃ21		00ʃ23	00ʃ24		00ʃ49			06ʃ36	06ʃ44	07ʃ04		
27¾	—	—	**High Wycombe** 1	d	ʃ	ʃ	23p21	23p27	23p30		23p45	00ʃ15	00ʃ27		00ʃ29	00ʃ30		00ʃ55		06ʃ07	06a45	06ʃ51	07a14		
32¾	—	—	Saunderton	d	ʃ	ʃ	ʃ	23p33	23p37		ʃ	00ʃ22	00ʃ34		00ʃ36	00ʃ37		01ʃ02		06ʃ13		06ʃ57			
36	—	—	**Princes Risborough** 2	d	ʃ	ʃ	23p31	23p38	23p43	23p48	23p56	00ʃ27	00ʃ40		00ʃ42	00ʃ43	00ʃ48	01ʃ07		06ʃ19		07ʃ03			07ʃ10
—	1½	—	Monks Risborough	d	ʃ	ʃ	ʃ	ʃ	ʃ	23p51	ʃ	00ʃ31	ʃ		ʃ	ʃ	00ʃ51	01ʃ11		ʃ		ʃ			07ʃ13
—	3	—	Little Kimble	d	ʃ	ʃ	ʃ	ʃ	ʃ	23p55	ʃ	00ʃ34	ʃ		ʃ	ʃ	00ʃ55	01ʃ14		ʃ		ʃ			07ʃ17
—	7½	—	**Aylesbury**	a	ʃ	ʃ	ʃ	ʃ	ʃ	00ʃ06	ʃ	00ʃ49	ʃ		ʃ	ʃ	01ʃ06	01ʃ29		ʃ		ʃ			07ʃ28
4¾	—	—	Haddenham & Thame Parkway	d	ʃ	23p02	23p38	23p45	23p50		00ʃ03		00ʃ47		00ʃ48	00ʃ50				06ʃ26		07ʃ10			
54¾	—	—	**Bicester North** 3	d	22p51	23p13	23p52	00ʃ02	00ʃ04		00ʃ16		01ʃ00		01ʃ01	01ʃ04				06ʃ41		07ʃ22			
65¼	—	—	Kings Sutton	d	ʃ	ʃ	00ʃ04	00ʃ12	00ʃ16		ʃ		01ʃ12		ʃ	ʃ				06ʃ54		07ʃ33			
68¾	—	—	**Banbury**	d	23p06	23p30	00a14	00a22	00a25		00a40		01a21		01a21	01a24				07ʃ02		07a44			
88¾	—	—	**Leamington Spa** 8	d	23p23	23p46													06ʃ55	07ʃ22					
90¾	—	—	Warwick	d	23p27	23p50													06ʃ59	07ʃ26					
92	—	—	Warwick Parkway	d	23p31	23p54													07ʃ02	07ʃ30					
94¾	—	—	Hatton	d	ʃ	ʃ													07ʃ07	07ʃ34					
—	—	7¾	Claverdon	d	ʃ	ʃ													07ʃ12	ʃ					
—	—	10	Bearley	d	ʃ	ʃ													07ʃ17	ʃ					
—	—	11½	Wilmcote	d	ʃ	ʃ													07ʃ21	ʃ					
—	—	15¼	**Stratford-upon-Avon**	a	ʃ	ʃ													07ʃ30	ʃ					
99	—	—	Lapworth	a	ʃ	ʃ														ʃ					
101½	—	—	Dorridge	a	23p41	00ʃ03														07ʃ42					
104¾	—	—	Solihull	a	23p44	00ʃ08														07ʃ49					
111¼	—	—	**Birmingham Moor Street**	a	23p53	00ʃ20														08ʃ02					
112	—	—	**Birmingham Snow Hill** ⛴	a	00ʃ04															08ʃ10					
—	—	—	Rowley Regis	a																					
—	—	—	Cradley Heath	a																					
—	—	—	**Stourbridge Junction** 2	a																					
—	—	—	**Kidderminster**	a																					

§ London Underground Limited (Central Line) also operate services between South Ruislip and West Ruislip at frequent intervals

A until 5 September. ◇ from Banbury

B Until 2 September

C 28 November

D Until 5 September

E Until 5 September, 28 November

F Until 29 August

G until 2 September

London - High Wycombe, Aylesbury, Banbury, Stratford-upon-Avon, Birmingham Snow Hill and Kidderminster

		CH	CH	CH	CH	CH	CH	CH	CH	CH	CH	CH	CH	CH	CH	CH	CH	CH	CH	CH	CH	CH	CH
				◇	◇					◇			◇				◇			◇	◇		
		A	A	A	A	A	A	A	A	A	A	A	A	A	A	A	A	A	A	A	A	A	A
																	🛒	🛒		🛒	🛒		
London Marylebone [10] ⊖	d	0650	0653		0715	0718	0736	0739		0749	0753	0800	0820	0824	0830		0850	0854	0900	0920	0924		0930
London Paddington [15] ⊖	d																						
Wembley Stadium	d		0702			0728						0809			0839				0909				
Sudbury & Harrow Road	d																						
Sudbury Hill Harrow	d							0751				0813			0843								
Northolt Park	d							0753						0836					0914				0944
South Ruislip § ⊖	d							0757				0818							0918				
West Ruislip [3] § ⊖	d		0711			0737						0821			0850								
Denham	d		0716			0741						0826			0854				0924				
Denham Golf Club	d					0744									0857								
Gerrards Cross [1]	d		0721		0736	0748		08a09			0815	0830		0846	0900			0915	0928				0954
Seer Green	d		0726			0752					0820	0835		0850					0933				0959
Beaconsfield	d		0729		0742	0756					0823	0838		0854	0906			0921	0936				1003
High Wycombe [1]	d	0720	07a38		0750	08a05	0806			0820	0830	08a49		0900	09a15		0920	0928	09a47				1011
Saunderton	d						0812				0836			0907									1018
Princes Risborough [2]	d	0731			0800		0818		0823	0830	0842			0912		0918	0930	0937				1011	10a28
Monks Risborough	d								0826							0921						1014	
Little Kimble	d								0830							0925						1018	
Aylesbury	a								0841							0936						1029	
Haddenham & Thame Parkway	d	0738			0806		0824			0837	0849			0919			0936	0944			1009		
Bicester North [3]	d	0750			0817		08a42			0848	09a07		0913	09a38			0948	0958		1012	1022		
Kings Sutton	d				0829													1009					
Banbury	d	0805			0834					0903			0929				1004	10a18		1029	1038		
Leamington Spa [8]	d	0823		0827	0852					0921			0947				1021			1048	1058		
Warwick	d	0827		0832	0856					0925							1025			1052	1102		
Warwick Parkway	d	0831		0835	0859					0928			0952				1029			1056			
Hatton	d			0840	0906																1108		
Claverdon	d			0846																	1114		
Bearley	d			0851																	1119		
Wilmcote	d			0856																	1124		
Stratford-upon-Avon	a			0902																	1135		
Lapworth	a				0910																		
Dorridge	a	0842			0916					0938							1038						
Solihull	a	0847			0919					0942			1004				1043			1107			
Birmingham Moor Street	a	0859			0934					0951			1017				1051			1118			
Birmingham Snow Hill ⛴	a	0907								1001							1101						
Rowley Regis	a																						
Cradley Heath	a																						
Stourbridge Junction [2]	a																						
Kidderminster	a																						

§ London Underground Limited (Central Line) also operate services between South Ruislip and West Ruislip at frequent intervals

A until 2 September

Table 115

Mondays to Fridays

London - High Wycombe, Aylesbury, Banbury, Stratford-upon-Avon, Birmingham Snow Hill and Kidderminster

Station		CH	CH	CH	CH	CH	CH	CH	CH	CH	CH	CH
			◇			◇	◇			◇	◇	
		A	A	A	A	A	A	A	A	B	A	A
			🚲			🚲				🚲	🚲	
London Marylebone [10] ⊖	d	0934	0950	0954	1000	1020	1024	1030		1050	1054	1100
London Paddington [15] ⊖	d											
Wembley Stadium	d	0944			1009			1039				1109
Sudbury & Harrow Road	d											
Sudbury Hill Harrow	d	0948						1043				
Northolt Park	d				1014			1046				1114
South Ruislip § ⊖	d				1018							1118
West Ruislip [3] § ⊖	d	0954						1051				
Denham	d	0959			1024			1055				1124
Denham Golf Club	d	1001						1058				
Gerrards Cross [1]	d	1005		1015	1028		1045	1101			1115	1128
Seer Green	d				1033			1106				1133
Beaconsfield	d	1011		1021	1036		1051	1109			1121	1136
High Wycombe [1]	d	10a20	1022	1028	10a47		1057	11a18		1120	1128	11a45
Saunderton	d						1103					
Princes Risborough [2]	d		1032	1038			1109		1112	1130	1137	
Monks Risborough	d								1115			
Little Kimble	d								1119			
Aylesbury	a								1130			
Haddenham & Thame Parkway	d		1038	1045			1116			1136	1144	
Bicester North [3]	d		1050	11a01		1112	1130			1148	1158	
Kings Sutton	d										1209	
Banbury	d		1105			1129	1147			1205	12a18	
Leamington Spa [8]	d		1122			1148	1207			1222		
Warwick	d		1126				1211			1226		
Warwick Parkway	d		1130			1153				1230		
Hatton	d						1217					
Claverdon	d						1222					
Bearley	d						1227					
Wilmcote	d											
Stratford-upon-Avon	a						1240					
Lapworth	a											
Dorridge	a		1139							1240		
Solihull	a		1145			1211				1244		
Birmingham Moor Street	a		1152			1225				1252		
Birmingham Snow Hill ⛴	a		1202							1302		
Rowley Regis	a											
Cradley Heath	a											
Stourbridge Junction [2]	a											
Kidderminster	a											

Station		CH	CH	CH	CH	CH	CH	CH	CH	CH	CH	CH
						◇						
		A	A	A	A	B	A	A	A	A	A	A
		🚲				🚲						
London Marylebone [10] ⊖	d	1120		1130		1150	1154	1200	1220	1224	1230	
London Paddington [15] ⊖	d				1136							
Wembley Stadium	d			1139				1209			1239	
Sudbury & Harrow Road	d											
Sudbury Hill Harrow	d			1143							1243	
Northolt Park	d			1146				1214			1246	
South Ruislip § ⊖	d							1218				
West Ruislip [3] § ⊖	d			1151							1251	
Denham	d			1155				1224			1255	
Denham Golf Club	d										1258	
Gerrards Cross [1]	d			1200	1203		1215	1228		1245	1301	
Seer Green	d				1208			1233			1306	
Beaconsfield	d			1206	1211		1221	1236		1251	1309	
High Wycombe [1]	d			1212	12a19	1220	1228	12a45		1258	13a19	
Saunderton	d			1219						1304		
Princes Risborough [2]	d		1207	12a27		1230	1238			1310		1314
Monks Risborough	d		1210									1317
Little Kimble	d		1214									1321
Aylesbury	a		1225									1332
Haddenham & Thame Parkway	d					1236	1245			1317		
Bicester North [3]	d	1212				1248	13a01		1312	13a33		
Kings Sutton	d											
Banbury	d	1229				1305			1329			
Leamington Spa [8]	d	1247				1322			1347			
Warwick	d					1326						
Warwick Parkway	d	1252				1330			1352			
Hatton	d											
Claverdon	d											
Bearley	d											
Wilmcote	d											
Stratford-upon-Avon	a											
Lapworth	a											
Dorridge	a					1339						
Solihull	a	1305				1345			1404			
Birmingham Moor Street	a	1317				1352			1417			
Birmingham Snow Hill ⛴	a					1402						
Rowley Regis	a											
Cradley Heath	a											
Stourbridge Junction [2]	a											
Kidderminster	a											

§ London Underground Limited (Central Line) also operate services between South Ruislip and West Ruislip at frequent intervals

A until 2 September

B until 2 September. ◇ from Banbury

London - High Wycombe, Aylesbury, Banbury, Stratford-upon-Avon, Birmingham Snow Hill and Kidderminster

		CH	CH	CH	CH	CH	CH	CH	CH	CH	CH	CH	CH	CH	CH	CH	CH	CH	CH	CH	CH	CH
		◇			◇				◇							◇	◇					
		A	A	A	A	A	A	A	A	A	A	A	A	A	A	A	A	A	A	A	A	A
					⚲																	
London Marylebone 10 ⊖	d	12 50	12 54	13 00		13 20	13 24	13 30	13 50	13 54	14 00	14 20	14 24	14 30		14 50	14 54	15 00	15 20		15 23	15 30
London Paddington 15 ⊖	d																					
Wembley Stadium	d			13 09				13 39			14 09			14 39				15 09			15 33	15 39
Sudbury & Harrow Road	d																					
Sudbury Hill Harrow	d							13 43						14 43							15 37	
Northolt Park	d			13 14				13 46			14 14			14 46				15 14			15 39	
South Ruislip § ⊖	d			13 18							14 18							15 18				
West Ruislip 3 § ⊖	d							13 51						14 51							15 44	15 49
Denham	d			13 24				13 55			14 24			14 55				15 24				15 53
Denham Golf Club	d							13 58						14 58								15 56
Gerrards Cross 1	d		13 15	13 28			13 45	14 01		14 15	14 28		14 45	15 01			15 15	15 28			15 51	15 59
Seer Green	d			13 33				14 06			14 33			15 06				15 33			15 55	
Beaconsfield	d		13 21	13 36			13 51	14 09		14 21	14 36		14 51	15 09			15 21	15 36			15 59	16 05
High Wycombe 1	d	13 20	13 28	13a45			13 59	14a18	14 20	14 28	14a45		14 58	15a18		15 20	15 28	15a45	15 50		16 06	16a14
Saunderton	d						14 06						15 04								16 13	
Princes Risborough 2	d	13 30	13 38				14 12		14 30	14 38			15 10		15 14	15 30	15 38		16 01	16 07	16a21	
Monks Risborough	d						14 16								15 17					16 10		
Little Kimble	d						14 19								15 21					16 14		
Aylesbury	a						14 33								15 32					16 25		
Haddenham & Thame Parkway	d	13 36	13 45						14 36	14 45			15 17			15 36	15 45		16 07			
Bicester North 3	d	13 48	13 59			14 12			14 48	15a01		15 12	15a34			15 48	15 58		16 19			
Kings Sutton	d		14 11														16 09					
Banbury	d	14 04	14a20			14 29			15 05			15 29				16 05	16 16		16 34			
Leamington Spa 8	d	14 21			14 31	14 47			15 22			15 47				16 22	16 35		16 52			
Warwick	d	14 25			14 36				15 26							16 26	16 39					
Warwick Parkway	d	14 29				14 52			15 30			15 52				16 30			16 58			
Hatton	d				14 43												16 45					
Claverdon	d				14 48												16 51					
Bearley	d				14 53												16 56					
Wilmcote	d				14 57												17 01					
Stratford-upon-Avon	a				15 06												17 13					
Lapworth	a																					
Dorridge	a	14 38							15 39							16 39						
Solihull	a	14 43				15 05			15 44			16 05				16 44			17 09			
Birmingham Moor Street	a	14 52				15 17			15 52			16 13				16 52			17 19			
Birmingham Snow Hill ⛴	a	15 01							16 01			16 21				17 02			17 31			
Rowley Regis	a																					
Cradley Heath	a																					
Stourbridge Junction 2	a																					
Kidderminster	a																					

§ London Underground Limited (Central Line) also operate services between South Ruislip and West Ruislip at frequent intervals

A until 2 September

London - High Wycombe, Aylesbury, Banbury, Stratford-upon-Avon, Birmingham Snow Hill and Kidderminster

		CH	CH	CH	CH	CH	CH	CH	CH	CH	CH	CH	CH	CH	CH	CH	CH	CH	CH	CH	CH	CH	CH
												◇											
		A	A	A	A	A	A	A	A	A	A	B	A	A	A	A	A	A	A	A	A	A	A
			[trolley]				[trolley]	[trolley]				[trolley]											
London Marylebone [10] ⊖	d	15 42	16 00	16 03	16 06	16 09	16 30	16 34	16 38	16 42	16 45	17 00	17 04		17 07	17 10	17 16	17 19	17 30	17 33	17 37	17 44	17 47
London Paddington [15] ⊖	d																						
Wembley Stadium	d					16 19			16 47						17 17	17 21					17 48		
Sudbury & Harrow Road	d					16 22										17 24							
Sudbury Hill Harrow	d					16 24														17 45			
Northolt Park	d					16 27					16 58							17 32		17 47			
South Ruislip § ⊖	d				16 21						17 01					17 29						17 59	
West Ruislip [3] § ⊖	d					16 32			16 56						17 26						17 57		
Denham	d					16 36			17 01						17 30					17 55		18 05	
Denham Golf Club	d				16 28											17 36							
Gerrards Cross [1]	d	16 04		16 24	16 31	16 41			17 05		17 09				17 35			17 42			18 04	18 09	
Seer Green	d				16 36						17 14							17 47		18 01			
Beaconsfield	d	16 10		16 31	16 39	16 47			17 11		17 17					17 45		17 50		18 05		18 15	
High Wycombe [1]	d	16 16		16 37	16 46	16a56		17 04	17 18		17a27		17 34		17 46	17a55		17 57		18a14	18 15	18 21	
Saunderton	d				16 52										17 53							18 28	
Princes Risborough [2]	d	16 25		16 47	16 58			17 14	17a31				17 45	17 51	17 58			18a09			18 24	18 33	
Monks Risborough	d				17 01									17 54								18 37	
Little Kimble	d				17 05									17 58								18 40	
Aylesbury	a				17 18					17 36				18 09			18 06					18 56	18 40
Haddenham & Thame Parkway	d	16 32		16 54				17 21					17 52		18 05				18 15		18 31		
Bicester North [3]	d	16a49	16 52	17a11			17 23	17 33					18 08		18a23				18 27		18 45		
Kings Sutton	d							17 44													18 56		
Banbury	d		17 07				17 39	17 50				18 03	18 29						18 42		19a06		
Leamington Spa [8]	d		17 24				17 59	18 08				18 23	18 48						18 59				
Warwick	d							18 13					18 52						19 03				
Warwick Parkway	d		17 30				18 05	18 16				18 28							19 06				
Hatton	d							18 21					18 57										
Claverdon	d												19 02										
Bearley	d																						
Wilmcote	d												19 09										
Stratford-upon-Avon	a												19 21										
Lapworth	a							18 26															
Dorridge	a		17 39				18 16	18 31				18 38							19 15				
Solihull	a		17 44				18 22	18 35				18 42							19 20				
Birmingham Moor Street	a		17 52				18 35	18 48				18 57							19 28				
Birmingham Snow Hill	a		18 03					18 58				19 01							19 38				
Rowley Regis	a											19 24											
Cradley Heath	a											19 29											
Stourbridge Junction [2]	a											19 35											
Kidderminster	a											19 48											

§ London Underground Limited (Central Line) also operate services between South Ruislip and West Ruislip at frequent intervals

A until 2 September

B until 2 September. [trolley] to Birmingham Moor Street

London - High Wycombe, Aylesbury, Banbury, Stratford-upon-Avon, Birmingham Snow Hill and Kidderminster

		CH	CH	CH	CH	CH	CH	CH	CH	CH	CH	CH	CH	CH	CH	CH	CH	CH	CH	CH	CH	CH
			◇											◇						◇		
		A	B	A	A	A	A	A	A	A	A	A	A	B	A	A	A	A	A	A	A	A
			⚲											⚲								
London Marylebone 10 ⊖	d	17 52	18 00	18 06	18 09	18 12	18 15	18 18	18 21	18 30	18 33	18 40	18 44	19 00	19 03	19 06	19 09	19 12	19 30	19 33	19 36	19 40
London Paddington 15 ⊖	d																					
Wembley Stadium	d						18 25						18 54					19 22				19 50
Sudbury & Harrow Road	d								18 32									19 25				
Sudbury Hill Harrow	d								18 34									19 27				
Northolt Park	d	18 04							18 37			18 53						19 30				19 55
South Ruislip § ⊖	d						18 32						19 01			19 21						19 58
West Ruislip 3 § ⊖	d					18 29						18 58						19 35				20 02
Denham	d					18 33							19 07					19 39				20 06
Denham Golf Club	d						18 39											19 42				
Gerrards Cross 1	d				18 31	18 38	18 43		18a49			19 05	19 12			19 29		19 45			19 58	20 11
Seer Green	d	18 16				18 42						19 09				19 33						20 16
Beaconsfield	d	18 20				18 46	18 50				19 00	19 13	19 18			19 37					20 04	20 20
High Wycombe 1	d	18a29			18 42	18 53	18a59				19 06	19a23	19 25		19 33	19 43		19a59		20 03	20 21	20a29
Saunderton	d				18 48								19 31			19 50					20 27	
Princes Risborough 2	d			18 46	18 54	19 02					19 16		19 37		19 43	19a59				20 14	20 34	
Monks Risborough	d												19 40								20 37	
Little Kimble	d												19 44								20 41	
Aylesbury	a					19 22		19 10					19 58				20 08				20 55	
Haddenham & Thame Parkway	d			18 55	19 01						19 23				19 50				20 14	20 20		
Bicester North 3	d			19 08	19a17					19 23	19a40				20 03				20 25	20 32		
Kings Sutton	d														20 15							
Banbury	d		19 07	19a27						19 39				20 06	20a26				20 40	20 49		
Leamington Spa 8	d		19 24							19 57				20 23					20 59	21 06		
Warwick	d									20 02									21 03	21 11		
Warwick Parkway	d		19 30							20 07				20 28					21 06			
Hatton	d																			21 18		
Claverdon	d																			21 24		
Bearley	d																			21 29		
Wilmcote	d																			21 32		
Stratford-upon-Avon	a																			21 44		
Lapworth	a																					
Dorridge	a		19 39							20 17				20 38					21 15			
Solihull	a		19 44							20 23				20 42					21 20			
Birmingham Moor Street	a		19 56							20 37				20 54					21 28			
Birmingham Snow Hill ⛴	a		20 02											20 58					21 38			
Rowley Regis	a		20 24											21 19								
Cradley Heath	a		20 29											21 25								
Stourbridge Junction 2	a		20 35											21 32								
Kidderminster	a		20 50											21 49								

§ London Underground Limited (Central Line) also operate services between South Ruislip and West Ruislip at frequent intervals

A until 2 September

B until 2 September. ⚲ to Birmingham Moor Street

London - High Wycombe, Aylesbury, Banbury, Stratford-upon-Avon, Birmingham Snow Hill and Kidderminster

		CH	CH	CH	CH	CH	CH	CH	CH	CH	CH	CH	CH	CH	CH	CH	CH	CH	CH	CH	CH
					◇		◇				◇			◇							
		A	A	A	A	A	A	A	A	A	A	A	A	A	A	A	B	C	A	B	C
London Marylebone 10 ⊖	d	20 00	20 06	20 10	20 30	20 33	21 00	21 03	21 18		21 33	21 40	22 03	22 20	22 23	22 40	23 10	23 10	23 30	23 54	23 54
London Paddington 15 ⊖	d																				
Wembley Stadium	d			20 19		20 43		21 12				21 49			22 32	22 49	23 19	23 19	23 39		
Sudbury & Harrow Road	d					20 46															
Sudbury Hill Harrow	d					20 48															
Northolt Park	d			20 24		20 51		21 17				21 54			22 37				23 44		
South Ruislip § ⊖	d					20 54						21 58				22 56			23 48		
West Ruislip 3 § ⊖	d			20 29				21 22							22 42				23 51		
Denham	d			20 34		21 00		21 27				22 04			22 47	23 02			23 56		
Denham Golf Club	d			20 36		21 03						22 06			22 49				23 58		
Gerrards Cross 1	d		20 27	20 40		21 07		21 31	21 39			22 10	22 24		22 53	23 07	23 33	23 33	00 01	00 15	00 15
Seer Green	d			20 44		21 11		21 36				22 14			22 57	23 11			00 06		
Beaconsfield	d		20 33	20 47		21 15		21 39	21 46			22 18	22 30		23 01	23 15	23 39	23 39	00 09	00 21	00 21
High Wycombe 1	d		20 40	20 54	21 00	21a24		21 46	21 52			22 24	22 36		23 07	23 21	23 45	23 45	00 15	00 27	00 27
Saunderton	d			21 00				21 52				22 31			23 14				00 22	00 34	00 34
Princes Risborough 2	d		20 49	21 06	21 11			21 58	22 02			22 36	22 46		23 20	23 31	23 56	23 56	00 27	00 40	00 40
Monks Risborough	d			21 09				22 01							23 24				00 31		
Little Kimble	d			21 13				22 05							23 27				00 34		
Aylesbury	a			21 27				22 19				22 55			23 41				00 49		
Haddenham & Thame Parkway	d		20 56		21 17		21 42		22 09		22 16		22 53	23 02		23 38	00 03	00 03		00 47	00 47
Bicester North 3	d	20 52	21a13		21 28		21 56		22a25		22 28		23a09	23 13		23 52	00 16	00 16		01 00	01 00
Kings Sutton	d				21 41											00 04				01 12	01 12
Banbury	d	21 08			21 47		22 14				22 43			23 30		00a14	00 33	00a40		01 19	01a21
Leamington Spa 8	d	21 27			22 06		22 32			22 40	23 00			23 46			00 52			01a39	
Warwick	d				22 10					22 44	23 04			23 50			00 56				
Warwick Parkway	d	21 32			22 13		22 37				23 07			23 54			01a06				
Hatton	d																				
Claverdon	d																				
Bearley	d																				
Wilmcote	d																				
Stratford-upon-Avon	a									23 11											
Lapworth	a																				
Dorridge	a	21 43			22 23		22 47				23 16			00 03							
Solihull	a	21 48			22 27		22 52				23 21			00 08							
Birmingham Moor Street	a	21 58			22 36		23 01				23 35			00 20							
Birmingham Snow Hill ⛴	a	22 04			22 45		23 04														
Rowley Regis	a	22 24					23 38														
Cradley Heath	a	22 29					23 44														
Stourbridge Junction 2	a	22 35					23 52														
Kidderminster	a	22 50																			

§ London Underground Limited (Central Line) also operate services between South Ruislip and West Ruislip at frequent intervals

A until 2 September

B FO until 2 September

C FX until 1 September

Table 115

Saturdays

London - High Wycombe, Aylesbury, Banbury, Stratford-upon-Avon, Birmingham Snow Hill and Kidderminster

		CH ◇ A	CH A	CH A	CH A	CH A	CH A	CH A	CH A	CH A	CH A	CH ◇ B	CH A	CH A	CH A	CH A	CH A	CH ◇ A	CH ◇ C	CH ◇ C	CH A	CH A	CH ◇ C
London Marylebone [10] ⊖	d	22p20	22p40	23p10	23p30	23p54	0010		0624			0724		0818	0824	0845		0853	0912	0915	0924		0945
London Paddington [15] ⊖	d																						
Wembley Stadium	d		22p49	23p19	23p39		0019		0633			0733			0833						0933		
Sudbury & Harrow Road	d																						
Sudbury Hill Harrow	d																						
Northolt Park	d				23p44		0024		0638			0738			0838						0938		
South Ruislip § ⊖	d		22p56		23p48		0028		0642			0742			0842						0942		
West Ruislip [3] § ⊖	d				23p51		0031		0645			0745			0845						0945		
Denham	d		23p02		23p56		0036		0650			0750			0850						0950		
Denham Golf Club	d				23p58		0038		0652			0752			0852						0952		
Gerrards Cross [1]	d		23p07	23p33	0001	0015	0041		0655			0755		0839	0855			0914		0936	0955		
Seer Green	d		23p11		0006		0046		0700			0800			0900						1000		
Beaconsfield	d		23p15	23p39	0009	0021	0049		0703			0803		0845	0903			0920		0942	1003		
High Wycombe [1]	d		23p21	23p45	0015	0027	0055	0610	0710			0810		0851	09a13	0915		0927		0948	10a13		1015
Saunderton	d				0022	0034	0102	0616	0716			0816		0858						0955			
Princes Risborough [2]	d		23p31	23p56	0027	0040	0107	0622	0722	0730		0822	0830	0904		0925	0928	0937		1001		1011	1025
Monks Risborough	d				0031		0111			0733			0833				0931					1014	
Little Kimble	d				0034		0114			0737			0837				0935					1018	
Aylesbury	a				0049		0129			0747			0847				0945					1028	
Haddenham & Thame Parkway	d	23p02	23p38	0003		0047		0629	0729			0829		0911		0932		0943		1008			1031
Bicester North [3]	d	23p13	23p52	0016		0100		0642	0744			0842		0922		0945		0958	1005	1022			1043
Kings Sutton	d		0004			0112		0653				0853						1009					
Banbury	d	23p30	00a14	0033		0119		0702	0801			0858		0938		1001		10a18	1020	1038			1058
Leamington Spa [8]	d	23p46		0052		01a39		0721	0821		0830	0916		0958		1020			1037	1058			1116
Warwick	d	23p50		0056				0725	0824		0834	0920		1002		1024			1041	1102			1120
Warwick Parkway	d	23p54		01a06				0729	0828		0837	0924		1005		1028				1105			1124
Hatton	d								0833		0842			1010									
Claverdon	d										0848												
Bearley	d										0853												
Wilmcote	d										0857												
Stratford-upon-Avon	a										0910								1111				
Lapworth	a								0838					1015									
Dorridge	a	0003						0739	0842			0933		1020		1038				1115			1133
Solihull	a	0008						0744	0850			0938		1025		1044				1120			1138
Birmingham Moor Street	a	0020						0757	0859			0951		1033		1056				1134			1155
Birmingham Snow Hill	a							0808	0908			1002		1042						1142			
Rowley Regis	a																						
Cradley Heath	a																						
Stourbridge Junction [2]	a																						
Kidderminster	a																						

§ London Underground Limited (Central Line) also operate services between South Ruislip and West Ruislip at frequent intervals

A until 3 September

B until 3 September. ◇ from High Wycombe

C until 3 September. ◇ from Banbury

Table 115

Saturdays

London - High Wycombe, Aylesbury, Banbury, Stratford-upon-Avon, Birmingham Snow Hill and Kidderminster

		CH	CH	CH	CH	CH		CH	CH	CH	CH	CH	CH	CH	CH	CH		CH	CH	CH	CH	CH	CH	CH	CH
			◇		◇			◇				◇						◇					◇		
		A	B	A	B	A		B	A	A	A	B	A	A	A	A		B	A	A	A	A	B	A	A
London Marylebone 10 ⊖	d	10 00	10 18	10 24	10 50			10 53	11 00	11 20	11 24	11 50		11 53	12 20	12 30		12 50		12 53	13 20	13 24	13 50		13 53
London Paddington 15 ⊖	d																								
Wembley Stadium	d	10 09		10 33					11 09		11 33			12 02		12 39				13 02		13 33			14 02
Sudbury & Harrow Road	d																								
Sudbury Hill Harrow	d																								
Northolt Park	d	10 14		10 38					11 14		11 38					12 44						13 38			
South Ruislip § ⊖	d	10 18							11 18		11 42					12 48						13 42			
West Ruislip 3 § ⊖	d			10 43							11 45					12 51						13 45			
Denham	d	10 24		10 48					11 24		11 50					12 56						13 50			
Denham Golf Club	d			10 50							11 52					12 58						13 52			
Gerrards Cross 1	d	10 28		10 54				11 14	11 28		11 55			12 16		13 01				13 16		13 55			14 16
Seer Green	d	10 33		10 58					11 33		12 00					13 06						14 00			
Beaconsfield	d	10 36		11 01				11 20	11 36		12 03			12 22		13 09				13 22		14 03			14 22
High Wycombe 1	d	10a45	10 48	11a11				11 27	11a45	11 50	12a13			12 28	12 49	13a19				13 28	13 50	14a13			14 28
Saunderton	d		10 54					11 33						12 35						13 35					14 35
Princes Risborough 2	d		11 01			11 08		11 39		12 01			12 11	12 40	12 59				13 09	13 40	14 01			14 11	14 40
Monks Risborough	d					11 11							12 14						13 12					14 14	
Little Kimble	d					11 15							12 18						13 16					14 18	
Aylesbury	a					11 25							12 28						13 26					14 28	
Haddenham & Thame Parkway	d		11 07					11 45		12 07				12 47	13 05					13 47	14 07				14 47
Bicester North 3	d		11 19		11 42			12 00		12 19		12 42		13a03	13 17			13 42		14 01	14 19		14 42		14 59
Kings Sutton	d							12 11																	15 10
Banbury	d		11 35		11 58			12 18		12 35		12 58			13 32			13 58		14a21	14 35		14 58		15 16
Leamington Spa 8	d		11 54		12 16			12 37		12 54		13 16			13 50			14 16			14 54		15 16		15 34
Warwick	d		11 58		12 20			12 41		12 58		13 20			13 57			14 20			14 58		15 20		15 38
Warwick Parkway	d		12 01		12 24					13 01		13 24			14 01			14 24			15 01		15 24		
Hatton	d		12 06					12 48							14 05										15 44
Claverdon	d							12 54																	15 51
Bearley	d							12 59																	15 56
Wilmcote	d							13 04																	15 59
Stratford-upon-Avon	a							13 16																	16 13
Lapworth	a		12 11												14 11										
Dorridge	a		12 16		12 33					13 14		13 34			14 16			14 34			15 14		15 34		
Solihull	a		12 20		12 38					13 19		13 39			14 20			14 38			15 19		15 38		
Birmingham Moor Street	a		12 34		12 54					13 32		13 54			14 33			14 54			15 32		15 54		
Birmingham Snow Hill ⛴	a		12 42							13 41					14 42						15 41				
Rowley Regis	a																								
Cradley Heath	a																								
Stourbridge Junction 2	a																								
Kidderminster	a																								

§ London Underground Limited (Central Line) also operate services between South Ruislip and West Ruislip at frequent intervals

A until 3 September

B until 3 September. ◇ from Banbury

Table 115

Saturdays

London - High Wycombe, Aylesbury, Banbury, Stratford-upon-Avon, Birmingham Snow Hill and Kidderminster

		CH ◇ A		CH B	CH ◇ A	CH B	CH B	CH B	CH B	CH B	CH B	CH B		CH B	CH B	CH B	CH B	CH B	CH B	CH B	CH B	CH B		CH B	CH ◇ A
London Marylebone 10 ⊖	d	14 20		14 24	14 50		14 53	15 00	15 20	15 24	15 50			15 53	16 00	16 20	16 24	16 50		16 53	17 00	17 20		17 30	17 50
London Paddington 15 ⊖	d																								
Wembley Stadium	d			14 33				15 09		15 33					16 09		16 33				17 09			17 39	
Sudbury & Harrow Road	d																								
Sudbury Hill Harrow	d																								
Northolt Park	d			14 38				15 14		15 38					16 14		16 38				17 14			17 44	
South Ruislip § ⊖	d			14 42				15 18							16 18		16 42				17 18				
West Ruislip 3 § ⊖	d			14 45						15 43							16 45							17 49	
Denham	d			14 50				15 24		15 48					16 24		16 50				17 24			17 54	
Denham Golf Club	d			14 52						15 50							16 52							17 56	
Gerrards Cross 1	d			14 55			15 14	15 28		15 54				16 14	16 28		16 55			17 14	17 28			18 00	
Seer Green	d			15 00				15 33		15 58					16 33		17 00				17 33			18 04	
Beaconsfield	d			15 03			15 20	15 36		16 01				16 20	16 36		17 03			17 20	17 36			18 07	
High Wycombe 1	d	14 50		15a13			15 27	15a45	15 50	16a11				16 27	16a45	16 50	17a13			17 27	17a45	17 49		18a17	
Saunderton	d						15 33							16 33						17 33					
Princes Risborough 2	d	15 01				15 05	15 39		16 01			16 05		16 39		17 01			17 11	17 39		17 59			
Monks Risborough	d					15 08						16 08							17 14						
Little Kimble	d					15 12						16 12							17 18						
Aylesbury	a					15 22						16 22							17 28						
Haddenham & Thame Parkway	d	15 07					15 45		16 07					16 45		17 07				17 45		18 05			
Bicester North 3	d	15 19			15 42		16a03		16 19		16 42			17a02		17 19		17 42		18 00		18 17			18 45
Kings Sutton	d																			18 11					
Banbury	d	15 35			15 58				16 35		16 58					17 35		17 58		18 18		18 32			19 03
Leamington Spa 8	d	15 54			16 16				16 54		17 16					17 54		18 16		18 37		18 50			19 23
Warwick	d	15 58			16 20				16 58		17 20					17 58		18 20		18 41		18 57			19 27
Warwick Parkway	d	16 01			16 24				17 01		17 24					18 01		18 24				19 01			19 30
Hatton	d	16 06							17 06							18 06				18 48		19 06			
Claverdon	d																			18 54					
Bearley	d																			18 59					
Wilmcote	d																			19 04					
Stratford-upon-Avon	a																			19 16					
Lapworth	a	16 11							17 11							18 11						19 11			
Dorridge	a	16 16			16 33				17 16		17 33					18 16		18 34				19 16			19 40
Solihull	a	16 20			16 39				17 20		17 39					18 20		18 38				19 20			19 47
Birmingham Moor Street	a	16 33			16 55				17 33		17 56					18 33		18 58				19 30			19 58
Birmingham Snow Hill ⛴	a	16 41							17 41							18 41						19 38			
Rowley Regis	a																								
Cradley Heath	a																								
Stourbridge Junction 2	a																								
Kidderminster	a																								

§ London Underground Limited (Central Line) also operate services between South Ruislip and West Ruislip at frequent intervals

A until 3 September. ◇ from Banbury

B until 3 September

Table 115

Saturdays

London - High Wycombe, Aylesbury, Banbury, Stratford-upon-Avon, Birmingham Snow Hill and Kidderminster

Station		CH A	CH A	CH A	CH A	CH A	CH ◇ B	CH A		CH A	CH A	CH A	CH A
London Marylebone 10 ⊖	d		1753	1800	1820	1830	1850			1853	1900	1920	
London Paddington 15 ⊖	d												
Wembley Stadium	d			1809		1839					1909		
Sudbury & Harrow Road	d												
Sudbury Hill Harrow	d												
Northolt Park	d			1814		1844					1914		
South Ruislip § ⊖	d			1818							1918		
West Ruislip 3 § ⊖	d					1849							
Denham	d			1824		1854					1924		
Denham Golf Club	d					1856							
Gerrards Cross 1	d		1814	1828		1900				1914	1928		
Seer Green	d			1833		1904					1933		
Beaconsfield	d		1820	1836		1907				1920	1936		
High Wycombe 1	d		1827	18a45	1850	19a17				1927	1943	1949	
Saunderton	d		1833							1933			
Princes Risborough 2	d	1808	1839		1901			1908		1939	1954	1959	2005
Monks Risborough	d	1811						1911					2008
Little Kimble	d	1815						1915					2012
Aylesbury	a	1825						1925			2012		2022
Haddenham & Thame Parkway	d		1845		1907					1945		2005	
Bicester North 3	d		19a02		1919		1945			2000		2017	
Kings Sutton	d									2011			
Banbury	d				1935		2003			2019		2033	
Leamington Spa 8	d				1954		2023			2038		2051	
Warwick	d				1958		2027			2042		2057	
Warwick Parkway	d				2001		2030					2101	
Hatton	d				2006					2049		2106	
Claverdon	d									2054			
Bearley	d												
Wilmcote	d												
Stratford-upon-Avon	a									2110			
Lapworth	a				2011							2111	
Dorridge	a				2016		2040					2116	
Solihull	a				2020		2046					2120	
Birmingham Moor Street	a				2029		2058					2130	
Birmingham Snow Hill	a				2038							2138	
Rowley Regis	a												
Cradley Heath	a												
Stourbridge Junction 2	a												
Kidderminster	a												

Station		CH A	CH ◇ B	CH A	CH A	CH C		CH ◇ D	CH A	CH A	CH C	CH ◇ D	CH A
London Marylebone 10 ⊖	d	1930	2000	2005	2040	2049		2049	2115	2140	2200	2200	2210
London Paddington 15 ⊖	d												
Wembley Stadium	d	1939		2014					2124				2219
Sudbury & Harrow Road	d												
Sudbury Hill Harrow	d												
Northolt Park	d	1944		2019					2129				2224
South Ruislip § ⊖	d			2023					2133				2228
West Ruislip 3 § ⊖	d	1949		2026					2136				2231
Denham	d	1954		2031					2141				2236
Denham Golf Club	d	1956		2033					2143				2238
Gerrards Cross 1	d	2000		2036	2101				2146	2201			2241
Seer Green	d	2004		2041					2151				2246
Beaconsfield	d	2007		2044	2107				2154	2207			2249
High Wycombe 1	d	2013	2030	2050	2113	2120		2120	2200	2213			2255
Saunderton	d	2020			2120				2207				2302
Princes Risborough 2	d	2027	2041	2100	2127	2130		2130	2214	2224			2307
Monks Risborough	d	2030			2130				2217				2311
Little Kimble	d	2034			2134				2221				2314
Aylesbury	a	2047		2119	2147				2235				2329
Haddenham & Thame Parkway	d		2048			2137		2137		2231			
Bicester North 3	d		2100			2150		2150		22a47	2251	2251	
Kings Sutton	d												
Banbury	d		2119			22a06		2206			23a06	2306	
Leamington Spa 8	d		2138					2226				2323	
Warwick	d		2142					2230				2327	
Warwick Parkway	d		2146					2234				2331	
Hatton	d												
Claverdon	d												
Bearley	d												
Wilmcote	d												
Stratford-upon-Avon	a												
Lapworth	a												
Dorridge	a		2156					2244				2340	
Solihull	a		2202					2249				2347	
Birmingham Moor Street	a		2216					2258				0001	
Birmingham Snow Hill	a		2227					2307					
Rowley Regis	a												
Cradley Heath	a												
Stourbridge Junction 2	a												
Kidderminster	a												

Station		CH A	CH A	CH A		CH A
London Marylebone 10 ⊖	d	2245	2310	2314		2345
London Paddington 15 ⊖	d					
Wembley Stadium	d	2254	2319	2323		2354
Sudbury & Harrow Road	d					
Sudbury Hill Harrow	d					
Northolt Park	d			2328		
South Ruislip § ⊖	d			2332		
West Ruislip 3 § ⊖	d			2335		
Denham	d			2340		
Denham Golf Club	d			2342		
Gerrards Cross 1	d	2308	2333	2345		0008
Seer Green	d			2350		
Beaconsfield	d	2314	2339	2353		0014
High Wycombe 1	d	2320	2345	2359		0020
Saunderton	d			0006		
Princes Risborough 2	d	2332	2356	0012		0032
Monks Risborough	d			0016		
Little Kimble	d			0019		
Aylesbury	a			0034		
Haddenham & Thame Parkway	d	2338	0003			0038
Bicester North 3	d	2352	0016			0052
Kings Sutton	d	0003				0103
Banbury	d	00a14	00a36			01a14
Leamington Spa 8	d					
Warwick	d					
Warwick Parkway	d					
Hatton	d					
Claverdon	d					
Bearley	d					
Wilmcote	d					
Stratford-upon-Avon	a					
Lapworth	a					
Dorridge	a					
Solihull	a					
Birmingham Moor Street	a					
Birmingham Snow Hill	a					
Rowley Regis	a					
Cradley Heath	a					
Stourbridge Junction 2	a					
Kidderminster	a					

§ London Underground Limited (Central Line) also operate services between South Ruislip and West Ruislip at frequent intervals

A until 3 September

B until 3 September. ◇ from Banbury

C until 18 June, from 6 August until 3 September

D from 25 June until 30 July. ◇ from Banbury

London - High Wycombe, Aylesbury, Banbury, Stratford-upon-Avon, Birmingham Snow Hill and Kidderminster

		CH ◇ A	CH B	CH B	CH B	CH B	CH C	CH D	CH C	CH D	CH D	CH C	CH E	CH ◇ C	CH C	CH D	CH ◇ C	CH E	CH ◇ C	CH E	CH D	CH C	CH F
London Marylebone	d	22p00	22p45	23p10	23p14	23p45	0010	0010	0735	0735	0750	0754	0810	0825	0854	0854	0920	0915	0924	0945	0954	0954	
London Paddington	d																						
Wembley Stadium	d		22p54	23p19	23p23	23p54	0018	0019	0743	0744	0759	0802			0902	0903					1003	1002	
Sudbury & Harrow Road	d																						
Sudbury Hill Harrow	d																						
Northolt Park	d				23p28		0023	0024			0804	0807			0907	0908					1008	1007	
South Ruislip §	d				23p32		0027	0028	0750	0751	0808	0811			0911	0912					1012	1011	
West Ruislip §	d				23p35		0030	0031			0811	0814			0914	0915					1015	1014	
Denham	d				23p40		0035	0036	0755	0757	0816	0819			0919	0920					1020	1019	
Denham Golf Club	d				23p42		0037	0038			0818	0821				0922						1021	
Gerrards Cross	d		23p08	23p33	23p45	0008	0040	0041	0800	0802	0821	0824			0922	0925		0936	0942		1024	1025	
Seer Green	d				23p50		0045	0046			0826	0829			0928	0930					1028	1028	
Beaconsfield	d		23p14	23p39	23p53	0014	0047	0049	0806	0808	0829	0831			0930	0933		0942	0948		1032	1032	
High Wycombe	d		23p20	23p45	23p59	0020	0053	0055	0812	0814	0835	0837	0840	0849	0936	0939		0949	0954		1038	1037	
Saunderton	d				0006		0100	0102			0842	0844			0942	0946					1045	1045	
Princes Risborough	d		23p32	23p56	0012	0032	0105	0107	0822	0825	0847	0849	0851	0859	0947	0951		0959	1003		1050	1049	
Monks Risborough	d				0016		0108	0111			0851	0852			0951	0955					1054	1053	
Little Kimble	d				0019		0112	0114			0854	0856			0954	0958					1057	1056	
Aylesbury	a				0034		0126	0129			0909	0913			1009	1013					1111	1110	
Haddenham & Thame Parkway	d		23p38	0003		0038			0828	0832			0858	0905				1006	1010				
Bicester North	d	22p51	23p52	0016		0052			08a44	08a48			0909	0917			1003	1020	1024	1040			
Kings Sutton	d		0003			0103							0921						1038				
Banbury	d	23p06	00a14	00a36		01a14							0927	0931			1018	1036	1045	1100			
Leamington Spa	d	23p23											0946	0950			1037	1056	1105	1120			1120
Warwick	d	23p27											0950	0954			1041	1100	1109	1124			1124
Warwick Parkway	d	23p31											0953	0957			1045	1104					
Hatton	d												0958	1002					1116	1131			1131
Claverdon	d																						
Bearley	d																						
Wilmcote	d																		1127	1142			1142
Stratford-upon-Avon	a																		1143	1154			1154
Lapworth	a												1003	1007									
Dorridge	a	23p40											1008	1012			1054	1115					
Solihull	a	23p47											1012	1016			1100	1121					
Birmingham Moor Street	a	0001											1022	1028			1107	1130					
Birmingham Snow Hill	a												1037	1041			1117	1140					
Rowley Regis	a																						
Cradley Heath	a																						
Stourbridge Junction	a																						
Kidderminster	a																						

§ London Underground Limited (Central Line) also operate services between South Ruislip and West Ruislip at frequent intervals

A from 26 June until 31 July. ◇ from Banbury
B from 29 May until 4 September
C 27 November
D until 4 September
E from 26 June until 31 July
F until 19 June, from 7 August until 4 September

Table 115

Sundays

London - High Wycombe, Aylesbury, Banbury, Stratford-upon-Avon, Birmingham Snow Hill and Kidderminster

		CH	CH	CH	CH	CH	CH	CH	CH	CH	CH	CH	CH	CH	CH	CH	CH	CH	CH	CH	CH	CH	CH
		◇			◇	◇					◇	◇	◇	◇	◇	◇						◇	
		A	B	A	C	A	A	D	A	B	A	A	B	E	C	A	D	A	A	B	A	A	D
London Marylebone 10 ⊖	d	10 20	10 15	10 24	10 50	10 50	10 54	10 54	11 20	11 20	11 24	11 50	11 45		11 50	11 50	11 54	11 54	12 20	12 20	12 24	12 50	12 33
London Paddington 15 ⊖	d																						
Wembley Stadium	d			10 32			11 02	11 03			11 32						12 03	12 02			12 32		12 42
Sudbury & Harrow Road	d																						
Sudbury Hill Harrow	d																						
Northolt Park	d						11 07	11 08									12 08	12 07					
South Ruislip § ⊖	d						11 11	11 12									12 12	12 11					
West Ruislip 3 § ⊖	d						11 14	11 15									12 15	12 14					
Denham	d						11 19	11 20									12 20	12 19					
Denham Golf Club	d							11 22										12 21					
Gerrards Cross 1	d		10 36	10 45		11 07	11 22	11 25		11 41	11 45					12 07	12 24	12 25		12 41	12 45		12 56
Seer Green	d						11 28	11 30									12 28	12 28					
Beaconsfield	d		10 42	10 51		11 13	11 30	11 33		11 47	11 51					12 13	12 32	12 32		12 47	12 51		13 02
High Wycombe 1	d		10 49	10 57		11 19	11 36	11 39		11 54	11 57					12 19	12 38	12 37		12 54	12 57		13 08
Saunderton	d						11 42	11 46									12 45	12 45					
Princes Risborough 2	d		10 59	11 06		11 29	11 47	11 51		12 04	12 06					12 29	12 50	12 49		13 04	13 06		13 18
Monks Risborough	d						11 51	11 55									12 54	12 53					
Little Kimble	d						11 54	11 58									12 57	12 56					
Aylesbury	a						12 09	12 13									13 11	13 10					
Haddenham & Thame Parkway	d		11 06	11 12		11 35				12 11	12 12					12 35				13 11	13 12		13 25
Bicester North 3	d	11 03	11 20	11a28	11 45	11 47			12 03	12 25	12 26	12 39	12 40		12 45	12 46			13 05	13 25	13a28	13 39	13a41
Kings Sutton	d		11 33								12 41									13 36			
Banbury	d	11 17	11 38		12 02	12 01			12 17	12 41	12 47	12 59	13 00		13 05	13 05			13 17	13 41		13 56	
Leamington Spa 8	d	11 36	11 58		12 22	12 20			12 35	13 01	13 07	13 19	13 20	13 20	13 25	13 24			13 36	14 01		14 16	
Warwick	d	11 40	12 02			12 24				13 05	13 11		13 24	13 24		13 28				14 05			
Warwick Parkway	d	11 43	12 06		12 27	12 27			12 41	13 09		13 24			13 31	13 32			13 41	14 09		14 22	
Hatton	d		12 11			12 32					13 18		13 31	13 31									
Claverdon	d																						
Bearley	d																						
Wilmcote	d										13 30		13 42	13 42									
Stratford-upon-Avon	a										13 41		13 54	13 54									
Lapworth	a		12 16			12 37														14 17			
Dorridge	a	11 52	12 19		12 37	12 42			12 50	13 18		13 33			13 41	13 40			13 51	14 21		14 32	
Solihull	a	11 58	12 26		12 43	12 46			12 55	13 24		13 39			13 46	13 45			13 55	14 27		14 37	
Birmingham Moor Street	a	12 06	12 34		12 54	12 56			13 04	13 35		13 47			13 58	13 53			14 04	14 35		14 47	
Birmingham Snow Hill ⛴	a	12 15	12 43			12 59				13 44						13 57				14 46			
Rowley Regis	a																						
Cradley Heath	a																						
Stourbridge Junction 2	a																						
Kidderminster	a																						

§ London Underground Limited (Central Line) also operate services between South Ruislip and West Ruislip at frequent intervals

A 27 November

B from 26 June until 31 July

C from 26 June until 31 July. ◇ from Banbury

D until 4 September

E until 19 June, from 7 August until 4 September

Table 115

Sundays

London - High Wycombe, Aylesbury, Banbury, Stratford-upon-Avon, Birmingham Snow Hill and Kidderminster

		CH ◇ A		CH ◇ B	CH B	CH C	CH B	CH C	CH ◇ B	CH ◇ C	CH ◇ D	CH ◇ B	
London Marylebone 10 ⊖	d	12 50		12 50	12 54	12 54	13 20	13 20	13 24	13 33	13 50	13 50	
London Paddington 15 ⊖	d												
Wembley Stadium	d				13 02	13 03			13 32	13 42			
Sudbury & Harrow Road	d												
Sudbury Hill Harrow	d												
Northolt Park	d				13 07	13 08							
South Ruislip § ⊖	d				13 11	13 12							
West Ruislip 3 § ⊖	d				13 14	13 15							
Denham	d				13 19	13 20							
Denham Golf Club	d					13 22							
Gerrards Cross 1	d			13 07	13 22	13 25		13 41	13 45	13 56		14 07	
Seer Green	d				13 28	13 30							
Beaconsfield	d			13 13	13 30	13 33		13 47	13 51	14 02		14 13	
High Wycombe 1	d			13 19	13 36	13 39		13 54	13 57	14 08		14 19	
Saunderton	d				13 42	13 46							
Princes Risborough 2	d			13 29	13 47	13 51		14 04	14 06	14 18		14 29	
Monks Risborough	d				13 51	13 55							
Little Kimble	d				13 54	13 58							
Aylesbury	a				14 09	14 13							
Haddenham & Thame Parkway	d			13 35				14 11	14 12	14 25		14 35	
Bicester North 3	d	13 45		13 46			14 03	14 25	14 26	14 40	14 45	14 46	
Kings Sutton	d								14 36	14 53			
Banbury	d	14 02		14 05			14 17	14 41	14 43	15 00	15 05	15 05	
Leamington Spa 8	d	14 22		14 23			14 36	15 01	15 03	15 20	15 25	15 23	
Warwick	d			14 27				15 05	15 07	15 24		15 27	
Warwick Parkway	d	14 27		14 31			14 41	15 09			15 31	15 31	
Hatton	d			14 36					15 14	15 31			
Claverdon	d												
Bearley	d												
Wilmcote	d								15 25	15 42			
Stratford-upon-Avon	a								15 40	15 54			
Lapworth	a			14 42									
Dorridge	a	14 37		14 45			14 50	15 18			15 41	15 40	
Solihull	a	14 43		14 50			14 55	15 24			15 46	15 45	
Birmingham Moor Street	a	14 54		14 58			15 00	15 33			15 58	15 53	
Birmingham Snow Hill	a			15 02				15 42				15 57	
Rowley Regis	a												
Cradley Heath	a												
Stourbridge Junction 2	a												
Kidderminster	a												

		CH C	CH B	CH ◇ B	CH ◇ D	CH B	CH C	CH ◇ D	CH ◇ B	CH B		CH C	CH B
London Marylebone 10 ⊖	d	13 54	13 54	14 20	14 20	14 24	14 33	14 50	14 50	14 54		14 54	15 20
London Paddington 15 ⊖	d												
Wembley Stadium	d	14 03	14 02			14 32	14 42			15 02		15 03	
Sudbury & Harrow Road	d												
Sudbury Hill Harrow	d												
Northolt Park	d	14 08	14 07							15 07		15 08	
South Ruislip § ⊖	d	14 12	14 11							15 11		15 12	
West Ruislip 3 § ⊖	d	14 15	14 14							15 14		15 15	
Denham	d	14 20	14 19							15 19		15 20	
Denham Golf Club	d		14 21									15 22	
Gerrards Cross 1	d	14 24	14 25		14 41	14 45	14 56		15 07	15 22		15 25	
Seer Green	d	14 28	14 28							15 28		15 30	
Beaconsfield	d	14 32	14 32		14 47	14 51	15 02		15 13	15 30		15 33	
High Wycombe 1	d	14 38	14 37		14 54	14 57	15 08		15 19	15 36		15 39	
Saunderton	d	14 45	14 45							15 42		15 46	
Princes Risborough 2	d	14 50	14 49		15 04	15 06	15 18		15 29	15 47		15 51	
Monks Risborough	d	14 54	14 53							15 51		15 55	
Little Kimble	d	14 57	14 56							15 54		15 58	
Aylesbury	a	15 11	15 10							16 09		16 13	
Haddenham & Thame Parkway	d				15 11	15 12	15 25		15 35				
Bicester North 3	d			15 04	15 25	15a28	15a41	15 45	15 46				16 03
Kings Sutton	d												
Banbury	d			15 17	15 41			16 02	16 01				16 17
Leamington Spa 8	d			15 36	16 00			16 22	16 20				16 36
Warwick	d				16 04				16 24				
Warwick Parkway	d			15 40	16 07			16 27	16 27				16 41
Hatton	d			15 46	16 12								
Claverdon	d												
Bearley	d												
Wilmcote	d												
Stratford-upon-Avon	a												
Lapworth	a				16 17								
Dorridge	a				16 21			16 37	16 37				16 50
Solihull	a			15 53	16 27			16 43	16 41				16 55
Birmingham Moor Street	a			15 58	16 36			16 54	16 50				17 03
Birmingham Snow Hill	a				16 49				16 54				
Rowley Regis	a												
Cradley Heath	a												
Stourbridge Junction 2	a												
Kidderminster	a												

§ London Underground Limited (Central Line) also operate services between South Ruislip and West Ruislip at frequent intervals

A from 26 June until 31 July. ◇ from Banbury

B 27 November

C until 4 September

D until 4 September. ◇ from Banbury

Table 115

Sundays

London - High Wycombe, Aylesbury, Banbury, Stratford-upon-Avon, Birmingham Snow Hill and Kidderminster

		CH	CH	CH	CH	CH	CH	CH	CH	CH	CH	CH	CH	CH	CH	CH	CH	CH	CH	CH	CH	CH	CH
			◇	◇															◇	◇			
		A	B	A	B	B	A	A	B	A	B	A	B	B	A	A	B	A	B	A	B	B	A
London Marylebone 10 ⊖	d	15 20	15 24	15 33	15 50	15 54	15 57	16 00	16 20	16 22	16 24	16 36	16 50	16 54	16 57	17 00	17 20	17 20	17 24	17 36	17 50	17 54	17 57
London Paddington 15 ⊖	d																						
Wembley Stadium	d		15 32	15 42		16 02		16 09			16 32	16 45		17 02		17 09			17 32	17 45		18 02	
Sudbury & Harrow Road	d																						
Sudbury Hill Harrow	d																						
Northolt Park	d					16 07		16 14						17 07		17 14						18 07	
South Ruislip § ⊖	d					16 11		16 18						17 11		17 18						18 11	
West Ruislip 3 § ⊖	d					16 14		16 21						17 14		17 21						18 14	
Denham	d					16 19		16 26						17 19		17 26						18 19	
Denham Golf Club	d					16 21										17 28						18 21	
Gerrards Cross 1	d	15 41	15 45	15 56	16 07	16 25		16 30		16 43	16 45	16 59	17 07	17 22		17 31		17 41	17 45	17 59	18 07	18 25	
Seer Green	d					16 28		16 34						17 28		17 36						18 28	
Beaconsfield	d	15 47	15 51	16 02	16 13	16 32		16 38		16 49	16 51	17 05	17 13	17 30		17 39		17 47	17 51	18 05	18 13	18 32	
High Wycombe 1	d	15 54	15 57	16 08	16 19	16 37		16 44		16 56	16 57	17 11	17 19	17 36		17 45		17 54	17 57	18 11	18 19	18 37	
Saunderton	d					16 45		16 51						17 42		17 52						18 45	
Princes Risborough 2	d	16 04	16 06	16 18	16 29	16 49		16 56		17 07	17 06	17 21	17 29	17 47		17 57		18 04	18 06	18 21	18 29	18 49	
Monks Risborough	d					16 53		17 00						17 51		18 01						18 53	
Little Kimble	d					16 56		17 03						17 54		18 04						18 56	
Aylesbury	a					17 11		17 18						18 09		18 19						19 10	
Haddenham & Thame Parkway	d	16 11	16 12	16 25	16 35					17 14	17 12	17 28	17 35					18 11	18 12	18 28	18 35		
Bicester North 3	d	16 25	16 27	16 40	16 50		16 52		17 03	17 27	17a28	17a44	17 46		17 52		18 03	18 25	18 26	18 42	18 46		18 52
Kings Sutton	d		16 39	16 53															18 36	18 53			
Banbury	d	16 41	16 46	17 00	17 03		17 09		17 17	17 44			18 01		18 09		18 17	18 41	18 43	19 00	19 01		19 09
Leamington Spa 3	d	17 01	17 06	17 20	17 21		17 29		17 35	18 03			18 20		18 29		18 36	19 01	19 03	19 20	19 20		19 29
Warwick	d	17 05	17 10	17 24	17 26					18 08			18 24					19 05	19 07	19 24	19 24		
Warwick Parkway	d	17 09			17 29		17 34		17 41	18 11			18 27		18 34		18 41	19 09			19 27		19 34
Hatton	d		17 17	17 31						18 16									19 13	19 31			
Claverdon	d																						
Bearley	d																						
Wilmcote	d		17 28	17 42															19 26	19 42			
Stratford-upon-Avon	a		17 40	17 54															19 36	19 54			
Lapworth	a									18 21													
Dorridge	a	17 18			17 38		17 44			18 25			18 37		18 44		18 50	19 18			19 37		19 44
Solihull	a	17 24			17 44		17 50		17 52	18 32			18 41		18 50		18 55	19 26			19 41		19 50
Birmingham Moor Street	a	17 33			17 51		18 01		18 01	18 41			18 50		19 01		19 05	19 35			19 51		20 01
Birmingham Snow Hill ⛴	a	17 42			17 56					18 49			18 53					19 43			19 54		
Rowley Regis	a																						
Cradley Heath	a																						
Stourbridge Junction 2	a																						
Kidderminster	a																						

§ London Underground Limited (Central Line) also operate services between South Ruislip and West Ruislip at frequent intervals

A until 4 September
B 27 November

Table 115

Sundays

London - High Wycombe, Aylesbury, Banbury, Stratford-upon-Avon, Birmingham Snow Hill and Kidderminster

		CH	CH	CH	CH	CH	CH	CH	CH	CH	CH	CH	CH	CH	CH	CH	CH	CH	CH	CH	CH	CH
											◇	◇							◇		◇	◇
		A	B	A	B	A	B	B	A	A	B	C	B	A	B	B	A	A	B	A	B	C
London Marylebone 10 ⊖	d	1800	1820	1820	1824	1836	1850	1854	1857	1900	1920	1922	1924	1936	1950	1954	1957	2000	2020	2020	2050	2050
London Paddington 15 ⊖	d																					
Wembley Stadium	d	1809			1832	1845		1902		1909			1932	1945		2002		2009				
Sudbury & Harrow Road	d																					
Sudbury Hill Harrow	d																					
Northolt Park	d	1814						1907		1914						2007		2014				
South Ruislip § ⊖	d	1818						1911		1918						2011		2018				
West Ruislip 3 § ⊖	d	1821						1914		1921						2014		2021				
Denham	d	1826						1919		1926						2019		2026				
Denham Golf Club	d									1928						2021						
Gerrards Cross 1	d	1830		1841	1845	1859	1907	1922		1931		1943	1945	1959	2007	2025		2030	2037	2041	2107	2111
Seer Green	d	1834						1928		1936						2028		2034				
Beaconsfield	d	1838		1847	1851	1905	1913	1930		1939		1949	1951	2005	2013	2032		2038	2043	2047	2113	2117
High Wycombe 1	d	1844		1854	1857	1911	1919	1936		1945		1956	1957	2011	2019	2037		2044	2049	2054	2119	2124
Saunderton	d	1851						1942		1952						2045		2051				
Princes Risborough 2	d	1856		1904	1906	1921	1929	1947		1957		2007	2006	2021	2029	2049		2056	2059	2104	2129	2134
Monks Risborough	d	1900						1951		2001						2053		2100				
Little Kimble	d	1903						1954		2004						2056		2103				
Aylesbury	a	1917						2009		2019						2111		2118				
Haddenham & Thame Parkway	d			1911	1912	1928	1935					2014	2012	2028	2035				2105	2111	2135	2141
Bicester North 3	d		1903	1925	19a26	1942	1947		1952		2003	2027	2026	2042	2047		2052		2117	2125	2147	2155
Kings Sutton	d												2036	2053								
Banbury	d		1917	1941		20a02	2001		2009		2018	2044	20a49	21a04	2101		2109		2131	2141	2201	2211
Leamington Spa 8	d		1934	2001			2020		2029		2035	2103			2120		2129		2150	2201	2219	2231
Warwick	d			2005			2024					2108			2124				2154	2205	2223	2235
Warwick Parkway	d		1939	2009			2027		2034		2041	2111			2127		2134		2157	2209	2227	2239
Hatton	d																				2232	2243
Claverdon	d																					
Bearley	d																					
Wilmcote	d																					
Stratford-upon-Avon	a																					
Lapworth	a			2017																	2237	2249
Dorridge	a			2021			2037		2044			2121			2137		2144		2207	2219	2242	2253
Solihull	a		1950	2028			2041		2050		2053	2128			2141		2150		2211	2224	2249	2300
Birmingham Moor Street	a		1959	2038			2050		2101		2102	2138			2150		2201		2221	2235	2258	2309
Birmingham Snow Hill ⛴	a			2046			2053					2147			2153					2243		2317
Rowley Regis	a																					
Cradley Heath	a																					
Stourbridge Junction 2	a																					
Kidderminster	a																					

§ London Underground Limited (Central Line) also operate services between South Ruislip and West Ruislip at frequent intervals

A until 4 September

B 27 November

C until 4 September. ◇ from Banbury

London - High Wycombe, Aylesbury, Banbury, Stratford-upon-Avon, Birmingham Snow Hill and Kidderminster

			CH	CH	CH	CH	CH	CH	CH	CH	CH	CH	CH	CH	CH
							◇		◇						
			A	B	A	B	C	B	A	A	A	B	D	A	B
London Marylebone 10	⊖	d	21 10	21 10	21 35	21 40	22 00	22 10	22 10	22 15	22 45	22 45		23 45	23 45
London Paddington 15	⊖	d													
Wembley Stadium		d	21 18	21 19				22 19		22 23	22 53	22 54		23 53	23 54
Sudbury & Harrow Road		d													
Sudbury Hill Harrow		d													
Northolt Park		d	21 23	21 24				22 24		22 28	22 58	22 59		23 58	23 59
South Ruislip §	⊖	d	21 27	21 28				22 28		22 32	23 02	23 03		00 03	00 03
West Ruislip 3 §	⊖	d	21 30	21 31				22 31		22 35	23 05	23 06		00 06	00 06
Denham		d	21 35	21 36				22 36		22 40	23 10	23 11		00 11	00 11
Denham Golf Club		d		21 38						22 42		23 13		00 13	00 13
Gerrards Cross 1		d	21 38	21 41	21 53	22 01		22 40		22 46	23 13	23 16		00 16	00 16
Seer Green		d	21 44	21 46				22 44		22 49	23 19	23 21		00 21	00 21
Beaconsfield		d	21 46	21 49	21 59	22 07		22 48		22 53	23 21	23 24		00 23	00 24
High Wycombe 1		d	21 52	21 55	22 05	22 13		22 54		22 58	23 27	23 30		00 29	00 30
Saunderton		d	21 58	22 02				23 01		23 06	23 33	23 37		00 36	00 37
Princes Risborough 2		d	22 03	22 07	22 15	22 24		23 06		23 10	23 38	23 43	23 48	00 42	00 43
Monks Risborough		d	22 07	22 11				23 10		23 14			23 51		
Little Kimble		d	22 10	22 14				23 13		23 17			23 55		
Aylesbury		a	22 25	22 29				23 27		23 31			00 06		
Haddenham & Thame Parkway		d			22 22	22 31					23 45	23 50		00 48	00 50
Bicester North 3		d			22a38	22a47	22 51		22 52		00 02	00 04		01 01	01 04
Kings Sutton		d									00 12	00 16			
Banbury		d					23 06		23 05		00a22	00a25		01a21	01a24
Leamington Spa 8		d					23 23		23 23						
Warwick		d					23 27		23 26						
Warwick Parkway		d					23 31		23 31						
Hatton		d													
Claverdon		d													
Bearley		d													
Wilmcote		d													
Stratford-upon-Avon		a													
Lapworth		a													
Dorridge		a					23 41		23 40						
Solihull		a					23 44		23 44						
Birmingham Moor Street		a					23 53		23 52						
Birmingham Snow Hill	⛴	a					00 04								
Rowley Regis		a													
Cradley Heath		a													
Stourbridge Junction 2		a													
Kidderminster		a													

§ London Underground Limited (Central Line) also operate services between South Ruislip and West Ruislip at frequent intervals

A 27 November
B until 4 September
C until 4 September. ◇ from Banbury
D until 4 September, 27 November

Table 115

Kidderminster, Birmingham Snow Hill, Stratford-upon-Avon, Banbury, Aylesbury and High Wycombe - London

Miles	Miles	Miles			CH	CH	CH	CH	CH	CH	CH	CH	CH	CH	CH	CH	CH	CH	CH	CH	CH	CH	CH
					◇															◇			
					A	A	B	B	B	B	B	B	B	B	B	B	B	B	B	B	B	B	B
					MX	MX								[trolley]						[trolley]			
—	—	—	**Kidderminster**	d																			
—	—	—	**Stourbridge Junction** [2]	d																			
—	—	—	Cradley Heath	d																			
—	—	—	Rowley Regis	d																			
0	—	—	**Birmingham Snow Hill**	d																			
0¾	—	—	**Birmingham Moor Street**	d																0543			
7¼	—	—	Solihull	d																0552			
10½	—	—	Dorridge	d																0558			
13	—	—	Lapworth	d																			
—	—	0	**Stratford-upon-Avon**	d																	0611		
—	—	2¾	Wilmcote	d																	0616		
—	—	4¼	Bearley	d																	0620		
—	—	7¼	Claverdon	d																	0625		
17¼	—	9¼	Hatton	d																	0630		
20	—	12	Warwick Parkway	d										0540						0609			
21¼	—	13¼	Warwick	d																0613	0637		
23¼	—	15¼	**Leamington Spa** [8]	d										0545						0618	06a42		
43¼	—	—	**Banbury**	d					0524					0603					0623	0638			
46¾	—	—	Kings Sutton	d					0528										0627				
57¼	—	—	**Bicester North** [3]	d					0541		0554			0617					0641	0653			
70¼	—	—	Haddenham & Thame Parkway	d					0554		0607			0630					0654				
—	0	—	**Aylesbury**	d		23p01	0505	0535		0549			0619			0629	0645						
—	4½	—	Little Kimble	d		23p09	0513			0557						0637							
—	6	—	Monks Risborough	d		23p13	0517			0601						0641							
76	7½	—	**Princes Risborough** [2]	d		23p16	0520	0548	0601	0605	0614		0632	0636		0645			0703				
79¼	—	—	Saunderton	d			0525			0610						0650							
84¼	—	—	**High Wycombe** [1]	d	23p20	23p26	0532	0558	0612	0617	0624	0628	0650		0655	0702		0708	0713				0721
89	—	—	Beaconsfield	d	23p26	23p33	0538	0604	0618	0623		0634	0656		0701	0708			0720				0727
90¾	—	—	Seer Green	d	23p29		0541	0607				0637						0717					0730
93¼	—	—	Gerrards Cross [1]	d	23p33	23p39	0545	0612	0624	0628		0641	0701		0706	0714		0721					0734
95	—	—	Denham Golf Club	d	23p36		0549					0645			0710								
96	—	—	Denham	d	23p39		0551	0616				0647			0712								0738
98¾	—	—	West Ruislip [3] § ⊖	d	23p46		0556			0637		0652	0708									0736	
100½	—	—	South Ruislip § ⊖	d	23p49		0559		0632	0641					0718								0744
102¼	—	—	Northolt Park	d	23p53		0603			0644		0657	0713									0741	
103¼	—	—	Sudbury Hill Harrow	d								0659										0743	
104	—	—	Sudbury & Harrow Road	d						0648												0746	
105½	—	—	Wembley Stadium	d	23p58	23p53	0608		0639	0651		0703				0728							0751
—	—	12	**London Paddington** [15] ⊖	a																			
112	—	—	**London Marylebone** [10] ⊖	a	0017	0006	0620	0639	0651	0707	0656	0716	0731	0718	0737	0741	0742	0747	0750	0753		0801	0805

§ London Underground Limited (Central Line) also operate services between South Ruislip and West Ruislip at frequent intervals

A until 2 September
B until 2 September

Kidderminster, Birmingham Snow Hill, Stratford-upon-Avon, Banbury, Aylesbury and High Wycombe - London

		CH	CH	CH	CH	CH	CH	CH	CH		CH	CH	CH	CH	CH	CH	CH	CH	CH		CH	CH	CH	CH	CH
														◇							◇				
		A	A	A	A	A	A	A	A		A	A	A	A	A	A	A	A	A		A	A	A	A	A
					🛒									🛒							🛒				🛒
Kidderminster	d													06 10							06 30				
Stourbridge Junction 2	d													06 18							06 39				
Cradley Heath	d													06 24							06 44				
Rowley Regis	d													06 30							06 50				
Birmingham Snow Hill	d													06 51							07 14				
Birmingham Moor Street	d				06 14									06 55							07 17				
Solihull	d				06 23									07 03							07 28				
Dorridge	d				06 29									07 08							07 34				
Lapworth	d																								
Stratford-upon-Avon	d												06 47												
Wilmcote	d																								
Bearley	d																								
Claverdon	d																								
Hatton	d												07 03												
Warwick Parkway	d				06 40								07 09	07 19							07 47				
Warwick	d												07 13								07 50				
Leamington Spa 8	d				06 47				06 54				07 18	07 24							07 54				
Banbury	d		06 53		07 07				07 13				07 35	07 42					08 00		08 12				
Kings Sutton	d																								
Bicester North 3	d	06 58	07 08						07 33			07 40	07 51						08 14		08 26				08 47
Haddenham & Thame Parkway	d	07 11	07 22						07 46			07 53	08 03						08 25		08 37				09 00
Aylesbury	d			07 18				07 28			07 50				08 02			08 21						08 44	
Little Kimble	d							07 36							08 10									08 52	
Monks Risborough	d							07 40							08 14									08 56	
Princes Risborough 2	d	07 19	07 30					07 44	07 54			08 00			08a21				08 31				08 56	09a02	09 08
Saunderton	d	07 24										08 05							08 36				09 01		
High Wycombe 1	d	07 30				07 45	07 50	07 55				08 12					08 31		08 43			08 55	09 08		09 18
Beaconsfield	d	07 37					07 56	08 01				08 18					08 37		08 49			09 01	09 14		09 24
Seer Green	d							08 04									08 40						09 17		
Gerrards Cross 1	d	07 43				07 55	08 02					08 23				08 34	08 45		08 55			09 06	09 21		09 30
Denham Golf Club	d						08 05															09 10			
Denham	d						08 08									08 38	08 49					09 12			
West Ruislip 3 § ⊖	d							08 15								08 42						09 17			
South Ruislip § ⊖	d						08 14												09 04				09 29		
Northolt Park	d					08 05										08 47						09 22			
Sudbury Hill Harrow	d															08 50						09 24			
Sudbury & Harrow Road	d															08 52						09 27			
Wembley Stadium	d					08 10	08 21		08 27										09 11			09 30			
London Paddington 15 ⊖	a																								
London Marylebone 10 ⊖	a	08 08	08 11	08 15	08 17	08 25	08 35	08 38	08 42		08 44	08 49	08 52	08 54		09 10	09 14	09 16	09 25		09 27	09 44	09 48		09 55

§ London Underground Limited (Central Line) also operate services between South Ruislip and West Ruislip at frequent intervals

A until 2 September

Kidderminster, Birmingham Snow Hill, Stratford-upon-Avon, Banbury, Aylesbury and High Wycombe - London

		CH	CH	CH	CH	CH	CH	CH	CH	CH	CH	CH	CH	CH	CH	CH	CH	CH	CH	CH	CH	CH	CH
		◇				◇	◇							◇			◇	◇			◇		
		A	A	A	A	A	A	A	A	A	A	A	A	B	A	A	A	A	A	A	A	A	A
		🛒				🛒					🛒												
Kidderminster	d	0656				0730					0809												
Stourbridge Junction 2	d	0707				0740					0823												
Cradley Heath	d	0714				0745					0828												
Rowley Regis	d	0722				0753					0834												
Birmingham Snow Hill	d	0745				0812					0852			0912							1012		
Birmingham Moor Street	d	0748				0815					0855			0915				0955			1015		
Solihull	d	0757				0825					0905			0924				1003			1023		
Dorridge	d	0803				0830					0910			0929				1008			1028		
Lapworth	d													0933									
Stratford-upon-Avon	d		0801														0935						
Wilmcote	d		0806														0941						
Bearley	d		0810														0945						
Claverdon	d		0815														0951						
Hatton	d		0820											0939			0957						
Warwick Parkway	d	0814				0841					0921			0944				1019			1039		
Warwick	d	0818	0829			0844					0924			0947			1004	1022			1042		
Leamington Spa 8	d	0824	08a35			0849					0929			0953			1008	1026			1046		
Banbury	d	0845				0910	0915				0948			1011			1025	1045			1104		
Kings Sutton	d	0850					0919																
Bicester North 3	d	0900			0912		0931			0947	1004			1027			1040	1100		1111	1120		
Haddenham & Thame Parkway	d	0912			0925		0944			1000				1038			1053			1124	1131		
Aylesbury	d							0944							1038							1141	
Little Kimble	d							0952							1046							1149	
Monks Risborough	d							0956							1050							1153	
Princes Risborough 2	d				0932		0951	10a02		1006			1037	1046	10a56		1059			1131	1139	11a59	
Saunderton	d				0937								1042							1136			
High Wycombe 1	d			0932	0944	0951	1001		1006	1017		1034	1048	1056		1100	1110		1130	1143	1149		1200
Beaconsfield	d			0938	0950				1012	1023		1040	1054			1106	1116		1136	1149			1206
Seer Green	d			0941					1015			1043				1109			1139				1209
Gerrards Cross 1	d			0946	0955				1019	1029		1047	1100			1113	1121		1143	1154			1213
Denham Golf Club	d			0949								1050							1146				
Denham	d				0959				1023			1053				1117			1149				1217
West Ruislip 3 § ⊖	d			0955								1057							1153				
South Ruislip § ⊖	d				1005				1029							1123							1223
Northolt Park	d			1000					1032			1102				1126			1158				1226
Sudbury Hill Harrow	d								1035							1129							1229
Sudbury & Harrow Road	d																						
Wembley Stadium	d			1005					1039			1107				1133			1203				1233
London Paddington 15 ⊖	a																						
London Marylebone 10 ⊖	a	0959		1018	1025	1028	1038		1052	1055	1101	1121	1125	1131		1147	1150	1155	1217	1220	1225		1247

§ London Underground Limited (Central Line) also operate services between South Ruislip and West Ruislip at frequent intervals

A until 2 September

B until 2 September. ◇ from Banbury

Kidderminster, Birmingham Snow Hill, Stratford-upon-Avon, Banbury, Aylesbury and High Wycombe - London

		CH	CH	CH	CH	CH	CH	CH	CH	CH	CH	CH	CH	CH	CH	CH	CH	CH	CH	CH	CH	CH
			◇			◇							◇				◇				◇	
		A	A	A	A	B	A	A	A	A	A	A	A	A	A	A	A	A	A	A	A	A
Kidderminster	d																					
Stourbridge Junction 2	d																					
Cradley Heath	d																					
Rowley Regis	d																					
Birmingham Snow Hill	d					11 12							12 12								13 12	
Birmingham Moor Street	d		10 55			11 15				11 55			12 15				12 55				13 15	
Solihull	d		11 03			11 23				12 05			12 23				13 03				13 25	
Dorridge	d					11 28							12 27								13 31	
Lapworth	d																					
Stratford-upon-Avon	d								11 38									13 08				
Wilmcote	d																	13 13				
Bearley	d																	13 17				
Claverdon	d								11 47									13 22				
Hatton	d								11 54									13 28				
Warwick Parkway	d		11 14			11 39				12 19			12 38				13 14				13 41	
Warwick	d					11 42			12 01				12 42					13 36			13 45	
Leamington Spa 8	d		11 21			11 46			12 05	12 26			12 46				13 21	13a42			13 53	
Banbury	d	11 24	11 39			12 08			12 24	12 47			13 04				13 39				14 11	
Kings Sutton	d	11 28							12 28													
Bicester North 3	d	11 41	11 54			12 23			12 41	13 02		13 11	13 19			13 41	13 54				14 26	
Haddenham & Thame Parkway	d	11 54				12 35			12 54			13 24	13 30			13 54					14 38	
Aylesbury	d						12 41							13 41								14 41
Little Kimble	d						12 49							13 49								14 49
Monks Risborough	d						12 53							13 53								14 53
Princes Risborough 2	d	12 02			12 33	12 41	12a59		13 01			13 31	13 38	13a59		14 01				14 37	14 45	14a59
Saunderton	d				12 38							13 36								14 42		
High Wycombe 1	d	12 12		12 30	12 44	12 52		13 00	13 11		13 30	13 43	13 48		14 00	14 11			14 30	14 48	14 55	
Beaconsfield	d	12 18		12 36	12 50			13 06	13 17		13 36	13 49			14 06	14 17			14 36	14 54		
Seer Green	d			12 39				13 09			13 39				14 09				14 39			
Gerrards Cross 1	d	12 23		12 43	12 56			13 13	13 23		13 43	13 54			14 13	14 23			14 43	15 00		
Denham Golf Club	d			12 46							13 46								14 46			
Denham	d			12 49				13 17			13 49				14 17				14 49			
West Ruislip 3 § ⊖	d			12 53							13 53								14 53			
South Ruislip § ⊖	d							13 23							14 23							
Northolt Park	d			12 58				13 26			13 58				14 26				14 58			
Sudbury Hill Harrow	d							13 29							14 29							
Sudbury & Harrow Road	d																					
Wembley Stadium	d			13 03				13 33			14 03				14 33				15 03			
London Paddington 15 ⊖	a																					
London Marylebone 10 ⊖	a	12 50	12 55	13 17	13 21	13 25		13 47	13 51	13 57	14 17	14 20	14 25		14 47	14 50	14 55		15 18	15 25	15 28	

§ London Underground Limited (Central Line) also operate services between South Ruislip and West Ruislip at frequent intervals

A until 2 September

B until 2 September. ◇ from Banbury

Table 115

Mondays to Fridays

Kidderminster, Birmingham Snow Hill, Stratford-upon-Avon, Banbury, Aylesbury and High Wycombe - London

		CH	CH	CH	CH	CH	CH	CH	CH	CH	CH	CH	CH	CH	CH	CH	CH	CH	CH	CH	CH	CH	CH
				◇			◇				◇			◇		◇	◇						
		A	A	A	A	A	A	A	A	A	A	A	A	A	A	A	A	A	A	A	A	A	A
Kidderminster	d																						
Stourbridge Junction 2	d																						
Cradley Heath	d																						
Rowley Regis	d																						
Birmingham Snow Hill	d						14 12							15 12							16 12		
Birmingham Moor Street	d			13 55			14 15				14 55			15 15			15 55				16 15		
Solihull	d			14 03			14 25				15 03			15 23			16 05				16 25		
Dorridge	d						14 31							15 28							16 30		
Lapworth	d																				16 34		
Stratford-upon-Avon	d															15 37							
Wilmcote	d															15 42							
Bearley	d															15 46							
Claverdon	d															15 51							
Hatton	d															15 57					16 40		
Warwick Parkway	d			14 14			14 41				15 14			15 39			16 16				16 45		
Warwick	d						14 45				15 18			15 42		16 04					16 49		
Leamington Spa 8	d			14 21			14 53				15 23			15 46		16 08	16 23				16 54		
Banbury	d		14 24	14 38			15 12				15 40		15 48	16 05		16 27	16 42				17 12		
Kings Sutton	d		14 28										15 53										
Bicester North 3	d		14 41	14 55		15 11	15 27			15 41	15 55		16 11	16 20		16 42	16 57				17 26	17 33	
Haddenham & Thame Parkway	d		14 54			15 24	15 39			15 54			16 24	16 33		16 56	17 08				17 37		
Aylesbury	d							15 41							16 38					17 24			
Little Kimble	d							15 49							16 46					17 32			
Monks Risborough	d							15 53							16 50					17 36			
Princes Risborough 2	d		15 02			15 31	15 46	15a59		16 01			16 33	16 42	16 53	17 04			17 39	17a42	17 44	17 51	
Saunderton	d					15 36							16 38			17 09						17 56	
High Wycombe 1	d	15 00	15 12		15 30	15 43	15 56		16 00	16 11		16 30	16 46	16 52	17 03	17 17	17 24	17 30	17 49		17 54	18 03	18 08
Beaconsfield	d	15 06	15 18		15 36	15 49			16 06	16 17		16 36	16 52		17 09	17 23		17 36	17 55			18 09	18 14
Seer Green	d	15 09			15 39				16 09			16 39			17 12			17 40					18 17
Gerrards Cross 1	d	15 13	15 23		15 43	15 54			16 13	16 23		16 43	16 58		17 17	17 29		17 44	18 00			18 14	18 21
Denham Golf Club	d				15 46							16 46			17 20								18 24
Denham	d	15 17			15 49				16 17			16 49			17 23			17 49					18 27
West Ruislip 3 § ⊖	d				15 53							16 53						17 54				18 21	
South Ruislip § ⊖	d	15 23							16 23						17 29								18 33
Northolt Park	d	15 26			15 58				16 26			16 58			17 32			17 59					
Sudbury Hill Harrow	d	15 29							16 29						17 35								
Sudbury & Harrow Road	d																						
Wembley Stadium	d	15 33			16 03				16 33			17 03			17 39			18 05				18 29	
London Paddington 15 ⊖	a																						
London Marylebone 10 ⊖	a	15 47	15 50	15 53	16 17	16 20	16 29		16 47	16 53	16 56	17 18	17 25	17 28	17 53	17 57	18 00	18 20	18 26		18 29	18 45	18 52

§ London Underground Limited (Central Line) also operate services between South Ruislip and West Ruislip at frequent intervals

A until 2 September

Kidderminster, Birmingham Snow Hill, Stratford-upon-Avon, Banbury, Aylesbury and High Wycombe - London

		CH	CH	CH	CH	CH	CH	CH	CH	CH	CH	CH	CH	CH	CH	CH	CH	CH	CH	CH	CH	CH
															◇					◇		
		A	A	A	A	A	A	A	A	A	A	A	A	A	A	A	A	A	A	A	A	A
Kidderminster	d																					
Stourbridge Junction ■	d																					
Cradley Heath	d																					
Rowley Regis	d																					
Birmingham Snow Hill ⇌	d			16 52			17 10				17 52				18 12		18 40					19 48
Birmingham Moor Street	d			16 55			17 13				17 55				18 15		18 43					19 51
Solihull	d			17 05			17 22				18 05				18 25		18 51					20 01
Dorridge	d			17 10			17 29				18 13				18 30		18 56					20 06
Lapworth	d						17 33								18 34							
Stratford-upon-Avon	d							17 40												19 31		
Wilmcote	d																			19 36		
Bearley	d							17 48														
Claverdon	d							17 54												19 43		
Hatton	d						17 39								18 40							
Warwick Parkway	d			17 20			17 44				18 22				18 45		19 06					20 16
Warwick	d			17 23			17 48	18 05			18 26				18 49					19 53		20 19
Leamington Spa ■	d			17 28			17 52	18 09			18 31				18 54		19 12			19 57		20 24
Banbury	d			17 45			18 13	18 26			18 49				19 12		19 32			20 14		20 43
Kings Sutton	d			17 50											19 17					20 19		
Bicester North ■	d			18 02			18 28	18 41		18 48	19 03			19 25	19 31		19 47	19 58		20 34		20 58
Haddenham & Thame Parkway	d			18 14			18 40			19 01					19 44		20 00	20 11		20 47		21 11
Aylesbury	d				18 09							19 20							20 16			
Little Kimble	d				18 17														20 24			
Monks Risborough	d				18 21							19 31							20 28			
Princes Risborough ■	d		18 15		18 24		18 47			19 09		19a37		19 43	19 51			20 18	20 31	20 55		21 18
Saunderton	d				18 29					19 14				19 48					20 36			
High Wycombe ■	d	18 22	18 25	18 30	18 36	18 46	18 57		19 07	19 21	19 28		19 36	19 55	20 01	20 06	20 18	20 28	20 43	21 05	21 10	21 28
Beaconsfield	d		18 32		18 42	18 52			19 13	19 27			19 42	20 01		20 12		20 34	20 49	21 11	21 16	
Seer Green	d					18 55			19 16				19 45			20 15					21 19	
Gerrards Cross ■	d	18 32	18 37		18 48	18 59			19 20	19 33			19 49	20 06		20 19		20 40	20 54	21 16	21 23	
Denham Golf Club	d								19 23							20 22					21 26	
Denham	d				18 52	19 03			19 26				19 53			20 25			20 58		21 29	
West Ruislip ■ § ⊖	d					19 07							19 57						21 03		21 33	
South Ruislip § ⊖	d				18 58				19 32							20 31					21 37	
Northolt Park	d	18 42				19 12			19 35				20 02			20 34					21 40	
Sudbury Hill Harrow	d	18 44							19 38													
Sudbury & Harrow Road	d																					
Wembley Stadium	d				19 05	19 17			19 42				20 07			20 39		20 54	21 11		21 45	
London Paddington ■ ⊖	a																					
London Marylebone ■ ⊖	a	18 59	19 05	19 08	19 17	19 31	19 36	19 39	19 55	19 58	20 05		20 21	20 31	20 34	20 52	20 55	21 08	21 25	21 41	21 59	22 02

§ London Underground Limited (Central Line) also operate services between South Ruislip and West Ruislip at frequent intervals

A until 2 September

Kidderminster, Birmingham Snow Hill, Stratford-upon-Avon, Banbury, Aylesbury and High Wycombe - London

		CH	CH	CH	CH	CH	CH	CH
					◇		◇	
		A	A	A	A	A	A	A
Kidderminster	d							
Stourbridge Junction 2	d							
Cradley Heath	d							
Rowley Regis	d							
Birmingham Snow Hill	d			20 42	21 34			
Birmingham Moor Street	d			20 45	21 37			
Solihull	d			20 53	21 45			
Dorridge	d			20 58	21 50			
Lapworth	d							
Stratford-upon-Avon	d					23 15		
Wilmcote	d							
Bearley	d							
Claverdon	d							
Hatton	d							
Warwick Parkway	d			21 08	22 00			
Warwick	d			21 11	22 03	23 34		
Leamington Spa 8	d			21 15	22 08	23 38		
Banbury	d			21 34	22 30	23a55		
Kings Sutton	d				22 35			
Bicester North 3	d			21 51	22 46			
Haddenham & Thame Parkway	d			22 04	22 57			
Aylesbury	d		21 34					23 01
Little Kimble	d		21 42					23 09
Monks Risborough	d		21 46					23 13
Princes Risborough 2	d		21 49	22 11	23 04			23 16
Saunderton	d		21 54		23 09			
High Wycombe 1	d	21 36	22 01	22 21	23 15		23 20	23 26
Beaconsfield	d	21 42	22 07				23 26	23 33
Seer Green	d		22 10				23 29	
Gerrards Cross 1	d	21 47	22 14				23 33	23 39
Denham Golf Club	d		22 17				23 36	
Denham	d	21 51	22 20				23 39	
West Ruislip 3 § ⊖	d	21 56	22 24				23 46	
South Ruislip § ⊖	d		22 28				23 49	
Northolt Park	d		22 31				23 53	
Sudbury Hill Harrow	d							
Sudbury & Harrow Road	d							
Wembley Stadium	d	22 04	22 36		23 36		23 58	23 53
London Paddington 15 ⊖	a							
London Marylebone 10 ⊖	a	22 18	22 50	22 55	23 49		00 17	00 06

§ London Underground Limited (Central Line) also operate services between South Ruislip and West Ruislip at frequent intervals

A until 2 September

Table 115

Saturdays

Kidderminster, Birmingham Snow Hill, Stratford-upon-Avon, Banbury, Aylesbury and High Wycombe - London

		CH	CH	CH	CH	CH	CH	CH	CH	CH
		◇							◇	◇
		A	A	A	A	A	A	A	B	B
Kidderminster	d									
Stourbridge Junction 2	d									
Cradley Heath	d									
Rowley Regis	d									
Birmingham Snow Hill	d									
Birmingham Moor Street	d								06 15	06 40
Solihull	d								06 25	06 50
Dorridge	d								06 31	06 55
Lapworth	d									
Stratford-upon-Avon	d									
Wilmcote	d									
Bearley	d									
Claverdon	d									
Hatton	d									
Warwick Parkway	d								06 41	07 05
Warwick	d								06 45	07 08
Leamington Spa 8	d								06 49	07 13
Banbury	d					06 05	06 33		07 08	07 31
Kings Sutton	d					06 09				
Bicester North 3	d					06 22	06 48		07 24	07 46
Haddenham & Thame Parkway	d					06 35	07 01		07 35	07 59
Aylesbury	d		23p01	05 15	05 57			06 57		
Little Kimble	d		23p09	05 23	06 05			07 05		
Monks Risborough	d		23p13	05 27	06 09			07 09		
Princes Risborough 2	d		23p16	05 30	06 12	06 43		07 12	07 43	
Saunderton	d			05 35	06 17			07 17		
High Wycombe 1	d	23p20	23p26	05 42	06 24	06 53		07 24	07 53	
Beaconsfield	d	23p26	23p33	05 48	06 30	06 59		07 30	07 59	
Seer Green	d	23p29		05 51	06 33			07 33		
Gerrards Cross 1	d	23p33	23p39	05 55	06 37	07 04		07 37	08 04	
Denham Golf Club	d	23p36		05 58	06 40			07 40		
Denham	d	23p39		06 01	06 43			07 43		
West Ruislip 3 § ⊖	d	23p46		06 05	06 47			07 47		
South Ruislip § ⊖	d	23p49		06 09	06 51			07 51		
Northolt Park	d	23p53		06 12	06 54			07 54		
Sudbury Hill Harrow	d									
Sudbury & Harrow Road	d									
Wembley Stadium	d	23p58	23p53	06 17	06 59	07 17		07 59		
London Paddington 15 ⊖	a									
London Marylebone 10 ⊖	a	00 17	00 06	06 31	07 13	07 31	07 48	08 13	08 29	08 47

		CH	CH	CH	CH	CH	CH	CH	CH	CH	CH	CH	CH	CH
					◇			◇				◇		◇
		A	A	A	B	A	A	B	A	A	A	C	A	B
Kidderminster	d		06 37			07 14						08 13		
Stourbridge Junction 2	d		06 45			07 22						08 26		
Cradley Heath	d		06 50			07 27						08 32		
Rowley Regis	d		06 56			07 33						08 37		
Birmingham Snow Hill	d		07 12			07 52		08 12				08 52		09 12
Birmingham Moor Street	d		07 15			07 55		08 15				08 55		09 15
Solihull	d		07 25			08 05		08 25				09 05		09 25
Dorridge	d		07 30			08 10		08 32				09 10		09 30
Lapworth	d		07 34					08 36						09 34
Stratford-upon-Avon	d				07 36									
Wilmcote	d													
Bearley	d													
Claverdon	d				07 47									
Hatton	d		07 40		07 57			08 42						
Warwick Parkway	d		07 44			08 20		08 47				09 20		09 44
Warwick	d		07 47		08 04	08 24		08 50				09 24		09 47
Leamington Spa 8	d		07 52		08 09	08 28		08 53				09 28		09 53
Banbury	d		08 11		08 29	08 47		09 13			09 29	09 47		10 13
Kings Sutton	d				08 33						09 33			
Bicester North 3	d		08 27		08 46			09 28			09 46			10 28
Haddenham & Thame Parkway	d		08 38		08 59			09 40			09 59			10 40
Aylesbury	d	07 57					09 07		09 48					
Little Kimble	d	08 05					09 15		09 56					
Monks Risborough	d	08 09					09 19		10 00					
Princes Risborough 2	d	08 12	08 46		09 06		09 22	09 47	10a06		10 09			10 47
Saunderton	d	08 17					09 27				10 13			
High Wycombe 1	d	08 24	08 56	09 04	09 18		09 34	09 57		10 04	10 20		10 34	10 57
Beaconsfield	d	08 30		09 10	09 24		09 40			10 10	10 26		10 40	
Seer Green	d	08 33		09 13			09 43			10 13			10 43	
Gerrards Cross 1	d	08 37		09 17	09 30		09 47			10 17	10 32		10 47	
Denham Golf Club	d	08 40					09 50						10 50	
Denham	d	08 43		09 21			09 53			10 21			10 53	
West Ruislip 3 § ⊖	d	08 47					09 57						10 57	
South Ruislip § ⊖	d	08 51		09 27						10 27				
Northolt Park	d	08 54		09 30			10 02			10 30			11 02	
Sudbury Hill Harrow	d													
Sudbury & Harrow Road	d													
Wembley Stadium	d	08 59		09 35			10 07			10 35			11 07	
London Paddington 15 ⊖	a													
London Marylebone 10 ⊖	a	09 14	09 29	09 50	09 55	09 59	10 23	10 34		10 50	10 58	11 02	11 21	11 32

§ London Underground Limited (Central Line) also operate services between South Ruislip and West Ruislip at frequent intervals

A until 3 September

B until 3 September. ◇ from Banbury

C until 3 September. ◇ from Stourbridge Junction

Table 115

Saturdays

Kidderminster, Birmingham Snow Hill, Stratford-upon-Avon, Banbury, Aylesbury and High Wycombe - London

		CH	CH	CH	CH	CH	CH	CH	CH	CH	CH	CH
					◇		◇				◇	
		A	A	A	B	A	B	A	A	A	B	A
Kidderminster	d				09 03							
Stourbridge Junction 2	d				09 15							
Cradley Heath	d				09 21							
Rowley Regis	d				09 27							
Birmingham Snow Hill	d				09 52		10 12					
Birmingham Moor Street	d				09 55		10 15				10 55	
Solihull	d				10 05		10 24				11 05	
Dorridge	d				10 10		10 30				11 10	
Lapworth	d						10 34					
Stratford-upon-Avon	d			09 36								
Wilmcote	d			09 42								
Bearley	d			09 47								
Claverdon	d			09 52								
Hatton	d			09 57			10 40					
Warwick Parkway	d				10 20		10 45				11 20	
Warwick	d			10 04	10 24		10 48				11 24	
Leamington Spa 8	d			10 09	10 28		10 53				11 28	
Banbury	d			10 29	10 47		11 13			11 29	11 47	
Kings Sutton	d									11 33		
Bicester North 3	d			10 46	11 02		11 28			11 46	12 02	
Haddenham & Thame Parkway	d			10 59			11 40			11 59		
Aylesbury	d	10 41						11 38				
Little Kimble	d	10 46						11 46				
Monks Risborough	d	10 50						11 50				
Princes Risborough 2	d	10a59		11 06			11 47	11a56		12 06		
Saunderton	d			11 11						12 11		
High Wycombe 1	d		11 04	11 18		11 34	11 57		12 04	12 18		12 34
Beaconsfield	d		11 10	11 24		11 40			12 10	12 24		12 40
Seer Green	d		11 13			11 43			12 13			12 43
Gerrards Cross 1	d		11 17	11 30		11 47			12 17	12 30		12 47
Denham Golf Club	d					11 50						12 50
Denham	d		11 21			11 53			12 21			12 53
West Ruislip 3 § ⊖	d					11 57						12 57
South Ruislip § ⊖	d		11 27						12 27			13 01
Northolt Park	d		11 30			12 02			12 30			13 04
Sudbury Hill Harrow	d											
Sudbury & Harrow Road	d											
Wembley Stadium	d		11 35			12 07			12 35			13 09
London Paddington 15 ⊖	a											
London Marylebone 10 ⊖	a		11 50	11 56	11 59	12 21	12 31		12 48	12 58	13 01	13 23

		CH	CH	CH	CH	CH	CH	CH	CH	CH	CH	CH
		◇										◇
		B	A	A	A	A	A	A	A	A	A	B
Kidderminster	d											
Stourbridge Junction 2	d											
Cradley Heath	d											
Rowley Regis	d											
Birmingham Snow Hill	d	11 12					12 12					13 12
Birmingham Moor Street	d	11 15			11 55		12 15			12 55		13 15
Solihull	d	11 25			12 04		12 25			13 05		13 25
Dorridge	d	11 30			12 10		12 30			13 10		13 30
Lapworth	d						12 34					
Stratford-upon-Avon	d			11 36								
Wilmcote	d			11 42								
Bearley	d			11 47								
Claverdon	d			11 52								
Hatton	d			11 57			12 40					
Warwick Parkway	d	11 40			12 20		12 45			13 20		13 41
Warwick	d	11 43		12 04	12 24		12 48			13 24		13 45
Leamington Spa 8	d	11 48		12 09	12 28		12 53			13 28		13 53
Banbury	d	12 05		12 29	12 47		13 13			13 47		14 13
Kings Sutton	d			12 33								
Bicester North 3	d	12 22		12 46	13 02		13 28		13 46	14 02		14 28
Haddenham & Thame Parkway	d	12 35		12 59			13 40		13 59			14 40
Aylesbury	d		12 38					13 38				
Little Kimble	d		12 46					13 46				
Monks Risborough	d		12 50					13 50				
Princes Risborough 2	d	12 43	12a56	13 06			13 47	13a56	14 06			14 47
Saunderton	d			13 11					14 11			
High Wycombe 1	d	12 53		13 18		13 34	13 57		14 18		14 34	14 57
Beaconsfield	d			13 24		13 40			14 24		14 40	
Seer Green	d					13 43					14 43	
Gerrards Cross 1	d			13 30		13 47			14 30		14 47	
Denham Golf Club	d					13 50					14 50	
Denham	d					13 53					14 53	
West Ruislip 3 § ⊖	d					13 57					14 57	
South Ruislip § ⊖	d					14 01					15 01	
Northolt Park	d					14 04					15 04	
Sudbury Hill Harrow	d											
Sudbury & Harrow Road	d											
Wembley Stadium	d			13 43		14 09			14 43		15 09	
London Paddington 15 ⊖	a											
London Marylebone 10 ⊖	a	13 26		13 58	14 01	14 23	14 32		14 58	15 01	15 23	15 31

§ London Underground Limited (Central Line) also operate services between South Ruislip and West Ruislip at frequent intervals

A until 3 September

B until 3 September. ◇ from Banbury

Table 115

Saturdays

Kidderminster, Birmingham Snow Hill, Stratford-upon-Avon, Banbury, Aylesbury and High Wycombe - London

	CH		CH	CH	CH	CH	CH	CH	CH	CH	CH		CH	CH	CH	CH	CH	CH	CH	CH	CH		CH	CH
				◇						◇							◇							◇
	A		A	B	A	A	A	A	A	B	A		A	A	A	A	B	A	A	A	A		A	B
Kidderminster d																								
Stourbridge Junction 2 d																								
Cradley Heath d																								
Rowley Regis d																								
Birmingham Snow Hill d						14 12							15 12						16 12					
Birmingham Moor Street d				13 55		14 15				14 55			15 15				15 55		16 15					16 55
Solihull d				14 05		14 25				15 05			15 25				16 05		16 25					17 05
Dorridge d				14 10		14 30				15 10			15 30				16 10		16 30					17 10
Lapworth d						14 34													16 34					
Stratford-upon-Avon d									14 36															
Wilmcote d									14 42															
Bearley d									14 47															
Claverdon d									14 52															
Hatton d						14 40			14 57										16 40					
Warwick Parkway d				14 20		14 45				15 20			15 40				16 20		16 45					17 20
Warwick d				14 24		14 48			15 04	15 24			15 43				16 24		16 48					17 24
Leamington Spa 8 d				14 28		14 53			15 09	15 28			15 48				16 28		16 53					17 28
Banbury d				14 47		15 13			15 29	15 47			16 05				16 47		17 13					17 47
Kings Sutton d									15 33															
Bicester North 3 d			14 46	15 02		15 28			15 46	16 02			16 22			16 46	17 02		17 28				17 46	18 02
Haddenham & Thame Parkway d			14 59			15 40			15 59				16 35			16 59			17 40				17 59	
Aylesbury d	14 38						15 38							16 38						17 38				
Little Kimble d	14 46						15 46							16 46						17 46				
Monks Risborough d	14 50						15 50							16 50						17 50				
Princes Risborough 2 d	14a56		15 06			15 47	15a56		16 06				16 43	16a56		17 06			17 47	17a56			18 06	
Saunderton d			15 11						16 11							17 11							18 11	
High Wycombe 1 d			15 18		15 34	15 57		16 04	16 18		16 34		16 53		17 04	17 18		17 34	17 57		18 04		18 18	18 26
Beaconsfield d			15 24		15 40			16 10	16 24		16 40				17 10	17 24		17 40			18 10		18 24	
Seer Green d					15 43			16 13			16 43				17 13			17 43			18 13			
Gerrards Cross 1 d			15 30		15 47			16 17	16 30		16 47				17 17	17 30		17 47			18 17		18 30	
Denham Golf Club d					15 50						16 50							17 50						
Denham d					15 53			16 21			16 53				17 21			17 53			18 21			
West Ruislip 3 § ⊖ d					15 57						16 57							17 57						
South Ruislip § ⊖ d					16 01			16 27							17 27						18 27			
Northolt Park d					16 04			16 30			17 02				17 30			18 02			18 30			
Sudbury Hill Harrow d																								
Sudbury & Harrow Road d																								
Wembley Stadium d			15 43		16 09			16 35			17 07				17 35			18 07			18 35			
London Paddington 15 ⊖ a																								
London Marylebone 10 ⊖ a			15 58	16 01	16 23	16 37		16 50	16 56	16 59	17 21		17 29		17 49	17 58	18 01	18 21	18 32		18 48		18 58	19 01

§ London Underground Limited (Central Line) also operate services between South Ruislip and West Ruislip at frequent intervals

A until 3 September

B until 3 September. ◇ from Banbury

Table 115

Saturdays

Kidderminster, Birmingham Snow Hill, Stratford-upon-Avon, Banbury, Aylesbury and High Wycombe - London

	CH	CH	CH	CH	CH	CH	CH		CH	CH	CH	CH	CH	CH	CH	CH	CH		CH	CH
											◇		◇		◇				◇	
	A	A	A	A	A	A	A		A	A	B	A	B	A	B	A	A		B	A
Kidderminster d																				
Stourbridge Junction 2 d																				
Cradley Heath d																				
Rowley Regis d																				
Birmingham Snow Hill d		17 12									18 12		19 12		20 12				21 15	
Birmingham Moor Street d		17 15					17 55				18 15		19 15		20 15				21 18	
Solihull d		17 25					18 05				18 25		19 25		20 25				21 27	
Dorridge d		17 30					18 10				18 32		19 32		20 32				21 34	
Lapworth d		17 34									18 36		19 36		20 36				21 38	
Stratford-upon-Avon d			17 40											19 48		21 15				
Wilmcote d														19 54						
Bearley d														19 59						
Claverdon d														20 04						
Hatton d		17 40									18 42		19 42	20 10	20 42	21a33			21 43	
Warwick Parkway d		17 45					18 20				18 47		19 47	20 16	20 47				21 48	
Warwick d		17 48	18 02				18 24				18 50		19 50	20 19	20 50				21 51	
Leamington Spa 8 d		17 53	18 06				18 28				18 54		19 54	20 23	20 54				21 55	
Banbury d		18 13	18 23			18 32	18 47				19 13		20 15	20 42	21 15				22 15	
Kings Sutton d						18 36								20 47					22 20	
Bicester North 3 d		18 28	18 37			18 48	19 02				19 29	20 00	20 31	21 00	21 31				22 32	
Haddenham & Thame Parkway d		18 40				19 01					19 42	20 13	20 44	21 13	21 44				22 45	
Aylesbury d				18 38					19 30								21 55			22 45
Little Kimble d				18 46					19 38								22 03			22 53
Monks Risborough d				18 50					19 42								22 07			22 57
Princes Risborough 2 d		18 47		18a58		19 08			19a48		19 50	20 21	20 52	21 21	21 52		22 10		22 54	23 00
Saunderton d						19 13						20 26		21 26			22 15			23 05
High Wycombe 1 d	18 34	18 57			19 04	19 20	19 26			19 34	20 00	20 34	21 02	21 34	22 02		22 22		23 04	23 12
Beaconsfield d	18 40				19 10	19 26				19 40	20 06	20 40	21 08	21 40	22 08		22 28			23 18
Seer Green d	18 43				19 13					19 43		20 43		21 43			22 31			23 21
Gerrards Cross 1 d	18 47				19 17	19 31				19 47	20 11	20 47	21 13	21 47	22 13		22 36			23 26
Denham Golf Club d	18 50									19 50		20 50		21 50			22 39			23 29
Denham d	18 53				19 21					19 53		20 53		21 53			22 42			23 32
West Ruislip 3 § ⊖ d	18 57									19 57		20 57		21 57			22 46			23 36
South Ruislip § ⊖ d					19 27					20 01		21 01		22 01			22 50			23 40
Northolt Park d	19 02				19 30					20 04		21 04		22 04			22 53			23 43
Sudbury Hill Harrow d																				
Sudbury & Harrow Road d																				
Wembley Stadium d	19 07				19 35					20 09		21 09		22 09	22 27		22 59		23 27	23 49
London Paddington 15 ⊖ a																				
London Marylebone 10 ⊖ a	19 21	19 30	19 37		19 50	19 58	20 01			20 23	20 37	21 23	21 39	22 23	22 40		23 15		23 40	00 06

§ London Underground Limited (Central Line) also operate services between South Ruislip and West Ruislip at frequent intervals

A until 3 September

B until 3 September. ◇ from Banbury

Table 115

Sundays

Kidderminster, Birmingham Snow Hill, Stratford-upon-Avon, Banbury, Aylesbury and High Wycombe - London

		CH	CH	CH	CH	CH	CH	CH	CH	CH	CH	CH	CH	CH	CH	CH	CH	CH	CH	CH	CH	CH	CH
																◇		◇			◇		◇
		A	B	C	C	C	B	B	C	C	B	B	C	C	B	D	E	C	B	C	D	E	C
Kidderminster	d																						
Stourbridge Junction 2	d																						
Cradley Heath	d																						
Rowley Regis	d																						
Birmingham Snow Hill	d																						
Birmingham Moor Street	d															08 43		08 55			09 13		09 27
Solihull	d															08 52		09 04			09 22		09 36
Dorridge	d															08 57		09 09			09 27		09 41
Lapworth	d																						
Stratford-upon-Avon	d																						
Wilmcote	d																						
Bearley	d																						
Claverdon	d																						
Hatton	d																						
Warwick Parkway	d															09 08		09 19			09 37		09 50
Warwick	d															09 11		09 22			09 40		
Leamington Spa 8	d															09 16		09 27			09 45		09 57
Banbury	d											09 03	09 07			09 35	09 35	09 45	09 47	09 55	10 04	10 04	10 15
Kings Sutton	d											09 08	09 12										
Bicester North 3	d				08 17			08 24		09 02	09 02	09 20	09 24			09 50	09 50	10 00	10 02	10 09	10 20	10 20	10 29
Haddenham & Thame Parkway	d				08 28			08 35		09 14	09 15	09 33	09 35						10 15	10 21			
Aylesbury	d	22p45	07 26	07 26		08 20	08 20		08 30					09 30	09 30								
Little Kimble	d	22p53	07 34	07 34		08 28	08 28		08 38					09 38	09 38								
Monks Risborough	d	22p57	07 38	07 38		08 32	08 32		08 42					09 42	09 42								
Princes Risborough 2	d	23p00	07 41	07 41	08 35	08 35	08 35	08 43	08 45	09 21	09 22	09 41	09 42	09 45	09 45				10 22	10 26			
Saunderton	d	23p05	07 46	07 46				08 48	08 50					09 50	09 50								
High Wycombe 1	d	23p12	07 53	07 53	08 45	08 45	08 45	08 55	08 57	09 31	09 32	09 52	09 53	09 57	09 57				10 32	10 36			
Beaconsfield	d	23p18	07 59	07 59	08 51	08 51	08 51	09 01	09 03	09 37	09 38			10 03	10 03				10 38	10 42			
Seer Green	d	23p21	08 02	08 02				09 04	09 06					10 06	10 06								
Gerrards Cross 1	d	23p26	08 06	08 06	08 56	08 57	08 57	09 09	09 10	09 41	09 43			10 10	10 10				10 43	10 48			
Denham Golf Club	d	23p29	08 09	08 09										10 13	10 13								
Denham	d	23p32	08 12	08 12				09 13	09 15					10 16	10 16								
West Ruislip 3 § ⊖	d	23p36	08 16	08 17				09 17	09 19					10 20	10 20								
South Ruislip § ⊖	d	23p40	08 20	08 20				09 21	09 23					10 24	10 24								
Northolt Park	d	23p43	08 23	08 24				09 24	09 26					10 27	10 27								
Sudbury Hill Harrow	d																						
Sudbury & Harrow Road	d																						
Wembley Stadium	d	23p49	08 28	08 29				09 29	09 31					10 32	10 32								
London Paddington 15 ⊖	a																						
London Marylebone 10 ⊖	a	00 06	08 42	08 42	09 21	09 20	09 22	09 44	09 44	10 05	10 09	10 25	10 26	10 44	10 47	10 50	10 50	10 59	11 10	11 15	11 20	11 20	11 26

§ London Underground Limited (Central Line) also operate services between South Ruislip and West Ruislip at frequent intervals

A from 29 May until 4 September
B until 4 September
C 27 November
D from 26 June until 31 July
◇ from Banbury
E until 19 June, from 7 August until 4 September

Table 115

Sundays

Kidderminster, Birmingham Snow Hill, Stratford-upon-Avon, Banbury, Aylesbury and High Wycombe - London

		CH	CH	CH	CH	CH	CH	CH	CH	CH	CH	CH	CH	CH	CH	CH	CH	CH	CH	CH	CH	CH	CH
							◇	◇		◇		◇			◇		◇			◇		◇	
		A	B	C	D	B	B	E	D	E	D	B	B	A	E	D	B	B	A	E	D	B	A
Kidderminster	d																						
Stourbridge Junction 2	d																						
Cradley Heath	d																						
Rowley Regis	d																						
Birmingham Snow Hill	d			09 40		09 48									10 40		10 47						
Birmingham Moor Street	d			09 43		09 51				10 13		10 27			10 43		10 50			11 13		11 27	
Solihull	d			09 52		10 00				10 22		10 36			10 52		10 59			11 22		11 36	
Dorridge	d			09 57		10 05				10 27		10 41			10 57		11 04			11 27		11 41	
Lapworth	d														11 01		11 08						
Stratford-upon-Avon	d						10 00	10 00															
Wilmcote	d						10 04	10 05															
Bearley	d																						
Claverdon	d																						
Hatton	d						10 17	10 17							11 07		11 14						
Warwick Parkway	d			10 08		10 15				10 37		10 50			11 12		11 19			11 37		11 49	
Warwick	d					10 19	10 25	10 25		10 40							11 22			11 40			
Leamington Spa 8	d			10 16		10 25	10 29	10 29		10 45		10 57			11 18		11 27			11 45		11 56	
Banbury	d			10 35	10 35	10 41	10 48	10 48	10 48	11 04	11 04	11 15			11 37	11 37	11 45			12 04	12 04	12 13	
Kings Sutton	d						10 52	10 53	10 53														
Bicester North 3	d			10 50	10 50	10 56	11 04	11 06	11 06	11 20	11 20	11 29			11 53	11 53	12 00	12 06	12 06	12 20	12 20	12 26	
Haddenham & Thame Parkway	d			11 03	11 03	11 08	11 16	11 19	11 19						12 06	12 06	12 11	12 18	12 19				
Aylesbury	d	10 28	10 28										11 30	11 30									12 28
Little Kimble	d	10 36	10 36										11 38	11 38									12 36
Monks Risborough	d	10 40	10 40										11 42	11 42									12 40
Princes Risborough 2	d	10 43	10 43	11 11	11 11	11 15	11 23	11 26	11 26				11 45	11 45	12 15	12 15	12 19	12 25	12 26				12 43
Saunderton	d	10 48	10 48										11 50	11 50									12 48
High Wycombe 1	d	10 55	10 55	11 21	11 21	11 25	11 33	11 36	11 36				11 57	11 57	12 25	12 25	12 29	12 35	12 36				12 55
Beaconsfield	d	11 01	11 01	11 27	11 27	11 31	11 39	11 42	11 42				12 03	12 03	12 31	12 31	12 35	12 41	12 42				13 01
Seer Green	d	11 04	11 04										12 06	12 06									13 04
Gerrards Cross 1	d	11 08	11 08	11 33	11 33	11 37	11 44	11 48	11 48				12 10	12 10	12 36	12 36	12 40	12 46	12 48				13 08
Denham Golf Club	d												12 13	12 13									
Denham	d	11 12	11 13										12 16	12 16									13 12
West Ruislip 3 § ⊖	d	11 16	11 17										12 20	12 20									13 16
South Ruislip § ⊖	d	11 20	11 21										12 24	12 24									13 20
Northolt Park	d	11 23	11 24										12 27	12 27									13 23
Sudbury Hill Harrow	d																						
Sudbury & Harrow Road	d																						
Wembley Stadium	d	11 28	11 29				11 56	12 01	12 01				12 32	12 32				12 58	13 01				13 28
London Paddington 15 ⊖	a																						
London Marylebone 10 ⊖	a	11 42	11 42	11 57	11 57	12 02	12 11	12 16	12 16	12 20	12 20	12 26	12 46	12 47	13 01	13 01	13 05	13 11	13 14	13 20	13 20	13 13	13 42

§ London Underground Limited (Central Line) also operate services between South Ruislip and West Ruislip at frequent intervals

A until 4 September
B 27 November
C from 26 June until 31 July
D until 19 June, from 7 August until 4 September
E from 26 June until 31 July.
◇ from Banbury

Table 115

Sundays

Kidderminster, Birmingham Snow Hill, Stratford-upon-Avon, Banbury, Aylesbury and High Wycombe - London

		CH	CH	CH	CH	CH	CH	CH	CH	CH	CH
						◇	◇				
		A	B	C	A	A	D	C	B	C	A
Kidderminster	d										
Stourbridge Junction 2	d										
Cradley Heath	d										
Rowley Regis	d										
Birmingham Snow Hill	d		11 40		11 47						
Birmingham Moor Street	d		11 43		11 50				12 13		12 27
Solihull	d		11 52		11 59				12 22		12 36
Dorridge	d		11 57		12 04				12 27		12 41
Lapworth	d										
Stratford-upon-Avon	d					12 00	12 00				
Wilmcote	d					12 04	12 05				
Bearley	d										
Claverdon	d										
Hatton	d					12 17	12 17				
Warwick Parkway	d		12 08		12 14				12 37		12 49
Warwick	d				12 18	12 25	12 25		12 40		
Leamington Spa 8	d		12 16		12 24	12 29	12 29		12 45		12 56
Banbury	d		12 35	12 35	12 40	12 48	12 48	12 48	13 04	13 04	13 13
Kings Sutton	d					12 52	12 53	12 53			
Bicester North 3	d		12 50	12 50	12 55	13 04	13 06	13 06	13 20	13 20	13 28
Haddenham & Thame Parkway	d		13 03	13 03	13 07	13 16	13 19	13 19			
Aylesbury	d	12 28									
Little Kimble	d	12 36									
Monks Risborough	d	12 40									
Princes Risborough 2	d	12 43	13 11	13 11	13 14	13 23	13 26	13 26			
Saunderton	d	12 48									
High Wycombe 1	d	12 55	13 21	13 21	13 24	13 33	13 36	13 36			
Beaconsfield	d	13 01	13 27	13 27	13 30	13 39	13 42	13 42			
Seer Green	d	13 04									
Gerrards Cross 1	d	13 08	13 33	13 33	13 36	13 44	13 48	13 48			
Denham Golf Club	d										
Denham	d	13 13									
West Ruislip 3 § ⊖	d	13 17									
South Ruislip § ⊖	d	13 21									
Northolt Park	d	13 24									
Sudbury Hill Harrow	d										
Sudbury & Harrow Road	d										
Wembley Stadium	d	13 29				13 56	14 01	14 01			
London Paddington 15 ⊖	a										
London Marylebone 10 ⊖	a	13 42	13 58	13 58	14 02	14 11	14 16	14 16	14 20	14 20	14 25

		CH	CH	CH	CH	CH	CH	CH	CH	CH	CH	CH
										◇		◇
		A	E	A	B	C	A	A	E	D	C	A
Kidderminster	d											
Stourbridge Junction 2	d											
Cradley Heath	d											
Rowley Regis	d											
Birmingham Snow Hill	d				12 40		12 47					
Birmingham Moor Street	d				12 43		12 50			13 13		13 27
Solihull	d				12 52		12 59			13 22		13 35
Dorridge	d				12 58		13 05			13 27		13 40
Lapworth	d											
Stratford-upon-Avon	d											
Wilmcote	d											
Bearley	d											
Claverdon	d											
Hatton	d											
Warwick Parkway	d				13 08		13 14			13 37		13 49
Warwick	d						13 18			13 40		
Leamington Spa 8	d				13 16		13 23			13 45		13 56
Banbury	d				13 35	13 35	13 41			14 04	14 04	14 14
Kings Sutton	d											
Bicester North 3	d				13 50	13 50	13 56	14 06	14 06	14 20	14 20	14 28
Haddenham & Thame Parkway	d				14 03	14 03	14 07	14 18	14 19			
Aylesbury	d	13 28	13 30									
Little Kimble	d	13 36	13 38									
Monks Risborough	d	13 40	13 42									
Princes Risborough 2	d	13 43	13 45		14 11	14 11	14 14	14 25	14 26			
Saunderton	d	13 48	13 50									
High Wycombe 1	d	13 55	13 57		14 21	14 21	14 24	14 35	14 36			
Beaconsfield	d	14 01	14 03		14 27	14 27	14 30	14 41	14 42			
Seer Green	d	14 04	14 06									
Gerrards Cross 1	d	14 08	14 10		14 33	14 33	14 36	14 46	14 48			
Denham Golf Club	d	14 11	14 13									
Denham	d	14 14	14 16	←								
West Ruislip 3 § ⊖	d	14 21	14 20	14 21								
South Ruislip § ⊖	d	→	14 24	14 24								
Northolt Park	d		14 27	14 28								
Sudbury Hill Harrow	d											
Sudbury & Harrow Road	d											
Wembley Stadium	d		14 32	14 33				14 58	15 01			
London Paddington 15 ⊖	a											
London Marylebone 10 ⊖	a		14 47	14 48	15 00	15 00	15 02	15 11	15 14	15 20	15 20	15 25

§ London Underground Limited (Central Line) also operate services between South Ruislip and West Ruislip at frequent intervals

A 27 November
B from 26 June until 31 July
C until 19 June, from 7 August until 4 September
D from 26 June until 31 July.
◇ from Banbury
E until 4 September

Table 115

Sundays

Kidderminster, Birmingham Snow Hill, Stratford-upon-Avon, Banbury, Aylesbury and High Wycombe - London

		CH	CH	CH	CH	CH	CH	CH	CH	CH	CH	CH	CH	CH	CH	CH	CH	CH	CH	CH	CH	CH	CH
						◇	◇	◇	◇													◇	◇
		A	B	A	B	C	D	D	B	B	A	A	B	B	A	A	B	A	B	A	B	B	D
Kidderminster	d																						
Stourbridge Junction 2	d																						
Cradley Heath	d																						
Rowley Regis	d																						
Birmingham Snow Hill	d			13 40	13 45							14 40	14 47							15 40	15 47		
Birmingham Moor Street	d			13 43	13 48			14 13	14 27			14 43	14 50			15 13	15 30			15 43	15 50		
Solihull	d			13 52	13 57			14 22	14 36			14 52	14 59			15 22	15 39			15 52	15 59		
Dorridge	d			13 57	14 02			14 27	14 41			14 57	15 04			15 27				15 57	16 04		
Lapworth	d			14 01	14 06															16 01			
Stratford-upon-Avon	d					14 00	14 00															16 00	16 00
Wilmcote	d					14 04	14 05															16 04	16 05
Bearley	d																						
Claverdon	d																						
Hatton	d			14 07	14 11	14 17	14 17													16 07		16 17	16 17
Warwick Parkway	d			14 12	14 16			14 37	14 49			15 08	15 14			15 37	15 45			16 12	16 14		
Warwick	d				14 20	14 25	14 25	14 40					15 18			15 40					16 17	16 25	16 25
Leamington Spa 8	d			14 18	14 23	14 29	14 29	14 45	14 56			15 16	15 24			15 45	15 50			16 18	16 22	16 29	16 29
Banbury	d			14 37	14 40	14 48	14 48	15 04	15 13			15 35	15 40			16 04	16 10			16 37	16 40	16 48	16 48
Kings Sutton	d					14 52	14 53															16 52	16 53
Bicester North 3	d			14 53	14 55	15 04	15 06	15 20	15 28			15 50	15 55	16 06	16 06	16 20	16 26			16 53	16 54	17 04	17 06
Haddenham & Thame Parkway	d			15 06	15 07	15 16	15 19					16 03	16 07	16 18	16 19					17 06	17 06	17 16	17 19
Aylesbury	d	14 28	14 28							15 30	15 30							16 28	16 30				
Little Kimble	d	14 36	14 36							15 38	15 38							16 36	16 38				
Monks Risborough	d	14 40	14 40							15 42	15 42							16 40	16 42				
Princes Risborough 2	d	14 43	14 43	15 15	15 15	15 23	15 26			15 45	15 45	16 11	16 14	16 25	16 26			16 43	16 43	17 15	17 14	17 23	17 26
Saunderton	d	14 48	14 48							15 50	15 50							16 48	16 48				
High Wycombe 1	d	14 55	14 55	15 25	15 25	15 33	15 36			15 57	15 57	16 21	16 24	16 35	16 36			16 55	16 56	17 25	17 24	17 33	17 36
Beaconsfield	d	15 01	15 01	15 31	15 31	15 39	15 42			16 03	16 03	16 27	16 30	16 39	16 42			17 01	17 02	17 31	17 30	17 39	17 42
Seer Green	d	15 04	15 04							16 06	16 06							17 04	17 05				
Gerrards Cross 1	d	15 08	15 08	15 36	15 35	15 44	15 48			16 10	16 10	16 33	16 36	16 43	16 48			17 08	17 09	17 36	17 35	17 44	17 48
Denham Golf Club	d									16 13	16 13												
Denham	d	15 12	15 13							16 16	16 16							17 12	17 13				
West Ruislip 3 § ⊖	d	15 16	15 17							16 20	16 20							17 16	17 19				
South Ruislip § ⊖	d	15 20	15 21							16 24	16 24							17 20	17 23				
Northolt Park	d	15 23	15 24							16 27	16 27							17 23	17 26				
Sudbury Hill Harrow	d																						
Sudbury & Harrow Road	d																						
Wembley Stadium	d	15 28	15 29			15 56	16 01			16 32	16 32			16 55	17 01			17 28	17 31			17 56	18 01
London Paddington 15 ⊖	a																						
London Marylebone 10 ⊖	a	15 42	15 42	16 02	16 01	16 11	16 16	16 19	16 25	16 46	16 47	16 58	17 01	17 10	17 14	17 18	17 24	17 42	17 43	18 02	18 01	18 10	18 16

§ London Underground Limited (Central Line) also operate services between South Ruislip and West Ruislip at frequent intervals

A until 4 September
B 27 November
C 27 November. ◇ from Banbury
D until 4 September. ◇ from Banbury

Table 115

Sundays

Kidderminster, Birmingham Snow Hill, Stratford-upon-Avon, Banbury, Aylesbury and High Wycombe - London

		CH	CH	CH	CH	CH	CH	CH	CH	CH	CH	CH	CH	CH	CH	CH	CH	CH	CH	CH	CH	CH
																◇	◇	◇	◇			
		A	B	B	A	A	B	B	A	A	B	A	B	A	B	B	C	C	B	B	A	A
Kidderminster	d																					
Stourbridge Junction 2	d																					
Cradley Heath	d																					
Rowley Regis	d																					
Birmingham Snow Hill	d					16 40	16 47							17 40	17 47							18 40
Birmingham Moor Street	d	16 13	16 27			16 43	16 50			17 13	17 29			17 43	17 50			18 13	18 27			18 43
Solihull	d	16 22	16 36			16 52	16 59			17 22	17 38			17 52	17 59			18 22	18 36			18 52
Dorridge	d	16 27	16 41			16 57	17 04			17 27				17 57	18 04			18 27	18 41			18 57
Lapworth	d													18 01								
Stratford-upon-Avon	d															18 00	18 00					
Wilmcote	d															18 04	18 05					
Bearley	d																					
Claverdon	d																					
Hatton	d													18 07		18 17	18 17					
Warwick Parkway	d	16 37	16 50			17 08	17 14			17 37	17 48			18 12	18 14			18 37	18 49			19 08
Warwick	d	16 40					17 18			17 40					18 17	18 25	18 25	18 40				
Leamington Spa 8	d	16 45	16 56			17 16	17 24			17 45	17 55			18 18	18 22	18 29	18 29	18 45	18 56			19 16
Banbury	d	17 04	17 14			17 35	17 40			18 07	18 13			18 37	18 40	18 48	18 48	19 04	19 13			19 35
Kings Sutton	d															18 52	18 53					
Bicester North 3	d	17 20	17 29			17 50	17 55	18 06	18 06	18 23	18 28			18 53	18 54	19 04	19 06	19 20	19 28			19 50
Haddenham & Thame Parkway	d					18 03	18 07	18 18	18 19					19 06	19 06	19 16	19 19					20 03
Aylesbury	d			17 30	17 30							18 28	18 28							19 30	19 30	
Little Kimble	d			17 38	17 38							18 36	18 36							19 38	19 38	
Monks Risborough	d			17 42	17 42							18 40	18 40							19 42	19 42	
Princes Risborough 2	d			17 42	17 45	18 11	18 14	18 25	18 26			18 43	18 43	19 15	19 14	19 23	19 26			19 45	19 45	20 11
Saunderton	d			17 47	17 50							18 48	18 48							19 50	19 50	
High Wycombe 1	d			17 54	17 57	18 21	18 24	18 35	18 36			18 55	18 55	19 25	19 24	19 33	19 36			19 57	19 57	20 21
Beaconsfield	d			18 00	18 03	18 27	18 30	18 41	18 42			19 01	19 01	19 31	19 30	19 39	19 42			20 03	20 03	20 27
Seer Green	d			18 03	18 06							19 04	19 04							20 06	20 06	
Gerrards Cross 1	d			18 07	18 10	18 33	18 36	18 46	18 48			19 08	19 08	19 36	19 35	19 44	19 48			20 10	20 10	20 33
Denham Golf Club	d			18 10	18 13															20 13	20 13	
Denham	d			18 13	18 16							19 12	19 13							20 16	20 16	
West Ruislip 3 § ⊖	d			18 17	18 20							19 16	19 17							20 20	20 20	
South Ruislip § ⊖	d			18 21	18 24							19 20	19 21							20 24	20 24	
Northolt Park	d			18 24	18 27							19 23	19 24							20 27	20 27	
Sudbury Hill Harrow	d																					
Sudbury & Harrow Road	d																					
Wembley Stadium	d			18 29	18 32			18 58	19 01			19 28	19 29			19 56	20 01			20 32	20 32	
London Paddington 15 ⊖	a																					
London Marylebone 10 ⊖	a	18 20	18 24	18 44	18 47	18 58	19 01	19 11	19 14	19 21	19 22	19 42	19 42	20 02	20 00	20 10	20 16	20 19	20 23	20 45	20 48	20 58

§ London Underground Limited (Central Line) also operate services between South Ruislip and West Ruislip at frequent intervals

A until 4 September
B 27 November
C until 4 September. ◇ from Banbury

Table 115

Sundays

Kidderminster, Birmingham Snow Hill, Stratford-upon-Avon, Banbury, Aylesbury and High Wycombe - London

		CH	CH	CH	CH	CH	CH	CH	CH	CH		CH	CH	CH
					◇	◇	◇	◇	◇				◇	◇
		A	A	A	B	C	A	A	B	A		C	A	B
Kidderminster	d													
Stourbridge Junction 2	d													
Cradley Heath	d													
Rowley Regis	d													
Birmingham Snow Hill	d	18 47			19 15			20 15	20 15				21 15	21 15
Birmingham Moor Street	d	18 50		19 30	19 18			20 18	20 18				21 18	21 18
Solihull	d	18 59		19 39	19 28			20 28	20 28				21 28	21 28
Dorridge	d	19 04			19 35			20 35	20 35				21 35	21 35
Lapworth	d				19 39									
Stratford-upon-Avon	d					19 57	19 59							
Wilmcote	d					20 02	20 04							
Bearley	d													
Claverdon	d													
Hatton	d				19 44	20 14	20 17							
Warwick Parkway	d	19 12		19 49	19 49			20 45	20 45				21 45	21 45
Warwick	d	19 17			19 52	20 22	20 24	20 48	20 48				21 48	21 48
Leamington Spa 8	d	19 22		19 57	19 56	20 26	20a29	20 53	20 53				21 53	21 53
Banbury	d	19 39		20 14	20 15	20 46		21 12	21 12				22 14	22 15
Kings Sutton	d			20 19	20 20								22 19	22 20
Bicester North 3	d	19 54	20 21	20 32	20 33	21 02		21 28	21 29				22 31	22 33
Haddenham & Thame Parkway	d	20 05	20 33		20 46			21 40	21 42				22 43	22 46
Aylesbury	d									22 24		22 32		
Little Kimble	d									22 32		22 40		
Monks Risborough	d									22 36		22 44		
Princes Risborough 2	d	20 13	20 45		20 54			21 48	21 50	22a42		22a50	22 51	22 54
Saunderton	d		20 50		20 59			21 53	21 55				22 56	22 59
High Wycombe 1	d	20 23	20 56		21 06			21 59	22 02				23 03	23 06
Beaconsfield	d	20 29	21 02		21 12			22 05	22 08				23 09	23 12
Seer Green	d		21 05		21 15			22 08	22 11				23 12	23 15
Gerrards Cross 1	d	20 34	21 09		21 19			22 13	22 15				23 16	23 19
Denham Golf Club	d							22 16	22 18					
Denham	d		21 14		21 24			22 18	22 21				23 21	23 23
West Ruislip 3 § ⊖	d		21 19		21 28			22 23	22 25				23 25	23 27
South Ruislip § ⊖	d		21 22		21 32			22 26	22 29				23 29	23 31
Northolt Park	d		21 26		21 35			22 30	22 32				23 32	23 34
Sudbury Hill Harrow	d													
Sudbury & Harrow Road	d													
Wembley Stadium	d		21 31		21 40			22 34	22 37				23 37	23 39
London Paddington 15 ⊖	a													
London Marylebone 10 ⊖	a	20 59	21 43	21 26	21 53	22 01		22 48	22 51				23 50	23 53

§ London Underground Limited (Central Line) also operate services between South Ruislip and West Ruislip at frequent intervals

A 27 November

B until 4 September. ◇ from Banbury

C until 4 September

Table 115A

Mondays to Fridays

Chinnor - Princes Risborough

Bus Service

		CH	CH	CH	CH	CH	CH
Chinnor, Lower Road	d	06 08	06 41	07 30	08 03	09 09	09 40
Chinnor, Estover Way	d	06 10	06 43	07 32	08 05	09 11	09 42
Chinnor, The Wheatsheaf	d	06 11	06 44	07 33	08 06	09 12	09 43
Chinnor, The Red Lion	d	06 14	06 47	07 36	08 09	09 15	09 46
Bledlow, Village Hall	d	06 17	06 50	07 39	08 12	09 18	09 49
Princes Risborough	a	06 24	06 57	07 46	08 19	09 25	09 56

Table 115A

Mondays to Fridays

Princes Risborough - Chinnor

Bus Service

		CH	CH	CH	CH	CH	CH	CH
Princes Risborough	d	16 48	17 21	18 13	18 50	19 25	20 04	20 54
Bledlow, Village Hall	d	16 55	17 28	18 20	18 57	19 32	20 11	21 01
Chinnor, Lower Road	d	16 58	17 31	18 23	19 00	19 35	20 14	21 04
Chinnor, Estover Way	d	17 00	17 35	18 25	19 02	19 37	20 16	21 06
Chinnor, The Wheatsheaf	d	17 01	17 36	18 26	19 03	19 38	20 17	21 07
Chinnor, The Red Lion	a	17 04	17 39	18 29	19 06	19 41	20 20	21 10

No Saturday or Sunday service

Network Diagram for Tables 116, 117, 118, 119, 120, 121, 122, 126

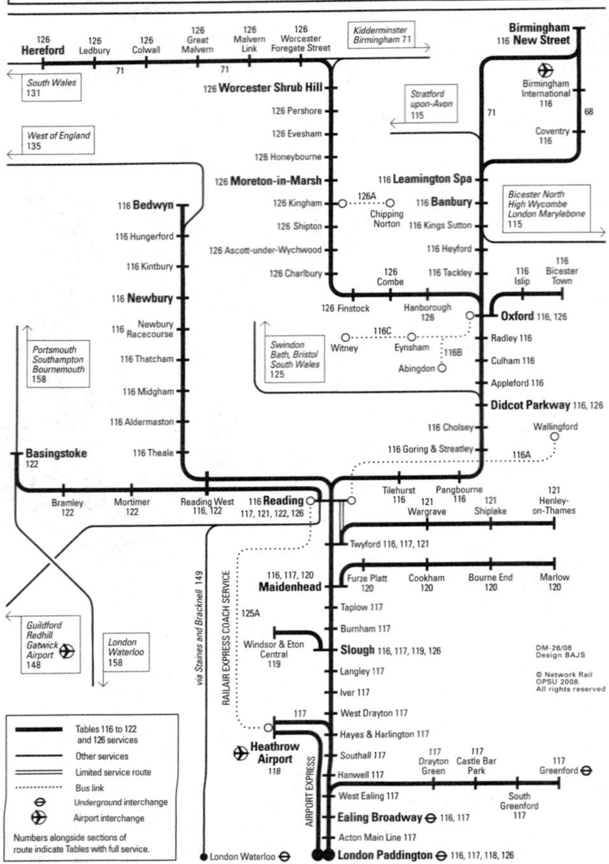

London and Reading - Bedwyn, Oxford, Bicester, Banbury and Birmingham

Miles	Miles			GW A	GW ■ B	GW ■ C	GW ■ D	GW MX ■	GW MX ◇■	GW MX ■	GW ◇■ E	GW ■ B	GW ■ C	GW ■ D	GW MX ◇■	CH F	GW A	GW MX ■	GW MX ◇■	GW ◇■ E	GW A	GW MX ■	GW MX ■
0	—	**London Paddington** ⊖	d		22p43	22p43	22p43	22p45	22p49		23p03				23p20			23p29	23p30	23p37			
5¾	—	Ealing Broadway ⊖	d		22p50	22p50	22p50	22p54										23p37					
18½	—	Slough	d		23p16	23p16	23p16	23p12	23p07						23p39			23p54					
24¼	—	Maidenhead	d		23p24	23p24	23p24	23p23										00 01					
31	—	Twyford	d		23p32	23p33	23p34	23p31		←		←	←	←				00 09				←	
36	0	**Reading**	d		23b53	23b53	23b53	23p40	23p34	23p40	23p47	23p53	23p53	23p53	00 04			00 19	00 08	00 15		00 19	00 20
—	1	Reading West	d		→	→	→	→										→					00s23
—	5¼	Theale	d																				00s29
—	8¾	Aldermaston	d																				00s34
—	10¾	Midgham	d																				00s37
—	13½	Thatcham	d																				00s42
—	16½	Newbury Racecourse	d																				00s47
—	17	**Newbury**	a																				00 52
—	—		d																				
—	22½	Kintbury	d																				
—	25½	Hungerford	d																				
—	30½	**Bedwyn**	a																				
38¾	—	Tilehurst	d							23p44		23p57	23p57	23p57								00 23	
41½	—	Pangbourne	d							23p49		00 01	00 01	00 01								00 28	
44¾	—	Goring & Streatley	d							23p52		00 07	00 07	00 07								00 32	
48½	—	Cholsey	d							23p57		00 12	00 12	00 12								00 37	
53¼	—	**Didcot Parkway**	a							00 06	00s02	00 18	00 18	00 18					00 25	00s32		00 45	
—	—		d	23p45						00 06							00 25				00 40	00 45	
55¼	—	Appleford	d																			00 50	
56¼	—	Culham	d																			00 52	
58½	—	Radley	d							00 14							00 40					00 56	
63½	0	**Oxford**	a	00 10					00 11	00 23					00 32		00 55				01 05	01 08	
—	—		d													00 38							
—	5¾	Islip	d																				
—	11¾	**Bicester Town**	a																				
72½	—	Tackley	d													00 48							
75¼	—	Heyford	d													00 53							
82¾	—	Kings Sutton	d													01 01							
86¼	—	**Banbury**	a													01 10							
106¼	—	Leamington Spa	a																				
115¾	—	Coventry	a																				
126½	—	Birmingham International	a																				
135	—	**Birmingham New Street**	a																				

		GW ◇■ G	GW MX ◇■	GW ■	GW ■	CH ■	GW ■	GW ■	GW ■	GW ◇■	XC ◇■	GW ■	GW ◇■	GW ■	XC ◇■	GW ■	GW ■	GW ■	CH ■	GW ■	GW ◇■	XC ◇■	GW ■
London Paddington ⊖	d	23p47	00 22				05 17		05 22	05 36			05 48			05 57	06 20				06 30		
Ealing Broadway ⊖	d	23p55							05 30							06 05							
Slough	d	00 09	00 39				05 33		05 54	05 52			06 05			06 29	06 35						
Maidenhead	d	00 17							06 02							06 37							
Twyford	d								06 10					←		06 45				←			
Reading	d	00 31	01 00	05 18			05 52	05 57	06 21	06 07	06 11	06 15	06 21	06 21	06 41	06 53	06 51	06 52		06 53	06 56	07 11	07 12
Reading West	d			05 20					→			06 17				→		06 54					07 14
Theale	d			05 26								06 23						07 00					07 20
Aldermaston	d			05 31								06 28						07 05					07 25
Midgham	d			05 35								06 32						07 09					07 29
Thatcham	d			05 40								06 37						07 14					07 34
Newbury Racecourse	d			05 44								06 41						07 18					07 38
Newbury	a			05 47								06 47						07 21					07 44
	d			05 47														07 21					
Kintbury	d			05 54														07 28					
Hungerford	d			05 58														07 32					
Bedwyn	a			06 08														07 42					
Tilehurst	d							06 01						06 25						06 57			
Pangbourne	d							06 05						06 29						07 01			
Goring & Streatley	d							06 10						06 34						07 06			
Cholsey	d							06 15						06 39						07 11			
Didcot Parkway	a	00 49	01 19				06 07	06 22		06 20			06 39	06 47			07 06			07 19	07 10		
	d	00 51	01 19				06 08	06 25					06 39	06 48			07 08			07 25			
Appleford	d																			07 30			
Culham	d							06 31												07 32			
Radley	d												06 48							07 36			
Oxford	a	01 02	01 33				06 22	06 41			06 34		06 56	07 03	07 05		07 21			07 47		07 35	
	d				05 45	05 51		06 41			06 36				07 07				07 27			07 36	
Islip	d					06 04													07 41				
Bicester Town	a					06 16													07 53				
Tackley	d				05 54			06 49															
Heyford	d				05 58			06 55															
Kings Sutton	d				06 07			07 02															
Banbury	a				06 14			07 10			06 52				07 24							07 53	
Leamington Spa	a										07 10				07 42							08 11	
Coventry	a										07 22											08 23	
Birmingham International	a										07 37											08 37	
Birmingham New Street	a										07 48				08 15							08 48	

A MO until 12 September, MO from 31 October
B MO from 31 October
C MO until 1 August
D MO from 8 August until 12 September
E MO until 24 October
F MX until 2 September
G MO from 19 September until 24 October
b Previous night, arr. 2343

London and Reading - Bedwyn, Oxford, Bicester, Banbury and Birmingham

		GW 1	GW 1	GW ◇1 🍴	GW ◇1 A 🍴	GW ◇1 🍴	XC ◇1 🛒	GW 1	GW 1	GW 1	CH 1	GW 1	XC ◇1 🛒	GW 1	GW 1	GW ◇1 🍴	GW 1	GW 1	GW 1	GW ◇1 🍴	GW 1	XC ◇1 🛒
London Paddington 15 ⊖	d	06 48	06 57	07 00	07 06	07 15			07 18	07 21					07 27	07 48	07 50		07 57	08 00		
Ealing Broadway ⊖	d		07 05												07 35				08 05			
Slough 3	d	07 04	07 29							07 36					07 59		08 06		08 29			
Maidenhead 3	d		07 37												08 07				08 38			
Twyford 3	d		07 45									←			08 15			←	08 46			
Reading 7	d	07 22	07 53	07 26	07 33	07 41	07 41	07 43	07 48	07 52		07 53	08 11	08 12	08 23	08 16	08 22	08 23	08 55	08 27	08 34	08 41
Reading West	d		→											08 14	→				→			
Theale	d								07 56					08 20							08 41	
Aldermaston	d								08 01					08 25							08 46	
Midgham	d													08 29								
Thatcham	d								08 08					08 34							08 53	
Newbury Racecourse	d													08 38								
Newbury	a				07 47				08 13					08 44							08 59	
	d								08 13												08 59	
Kintbury	d								08 20												09 05	
Hungerford	d								08 24												09 09	
Bedwyn	a								08 34												09 20	
Tilehurst	d	07 27										07 57						08 27				
Pangbourne	d	07 31										08 01						08 31				
Goring & Streatley	d	07 36										08 06						08 36				
Cholsey	d	07 41										08 11						08 41				
Didcot Parkway	a	07 49		07 40		07 55		08 02				08 20				08 32		08 50		08 40		
	d	07 50						08 08				08 25						08 55				
Appleford	d							08 13										09 00				
Culham	d							08 15										09 01				
Radley	d							08 19				08 33						09 06				
Oxford	a	08 02					08 05	08 29		08 19		08 43	08 34				08 49	09 15				09 05
	d						08 07				08 35		08 36				08 53					09 07
Islip	d										08 48											
Bicester Town	a										09 01											
Tackley	d																09 01					
Heyford	d																09 06					
Kings Sutton	d																09 15					
Banbury	a						08 26						08 52				09 21					09 25
Leamington Spa 8	a						08 43						09 10									09 42
Coventry	a												09 22									
Birmingham International	a												09 37									
Birmingham New Street 12	a						09 18						09 48									10 18

		GW 1	GW ◇1 🍴	GW 1	GW ◇1 🍴	GW 1	GW 1	GW 1	GW ◇1 🍴	XC ◇1 🛒	GW 1	GW 1	CH 1	GW 1	XC ◇1 🛒	GW 1	GW ◇1 🍴	GW 1	GW ◇1 🛒	GW 1	GW 1	GW ◇1 🍴	XC ◇1 🛒
London Paddington 15 ⊖	d	08 06	08 15	08 18	08 22			08 27	08 30			08 51				08 57	09 15	09 18	09 21		09 27	09 30	
Ealing Broadway ⊖	d							08 35								09 05					09 35		
Slough 3	d	08 26			08 36			08 59				09 06				09 27			09 36		09 57		
Maidenhead 3	d	08 34						09 06								09 34					10 04		
Twyford 3	d	08 43				←	←	09 16						←		09 42				←	10 12		
Reading 7	d	08 53	08 41	08 48	08 52	08 53	08 55	09 23	08 57	09 11	09 12	09 22		09 23	09 41	09 53	09 41	09 48	09 52	09 53	10 23	09 57	10 11
Reading West	d	→						→			09 14					→					→		
Theale	d			08 56							09 20							09 56					
Aldermaston	d										09 25												
Midgham	d										09 29												
Thatcham	d			09 04							09 34							10 04					
Newbury Racecourse	d										09 38												
Newbury	a			09 13							09 44							10 10					
	d																	10 10					
Kintbury	d																	10 17					
Hungerford	d																	10 21					
Bedwyn	a																	10 31					
Tilehurst	d						09 00							09 27						09 57			
Pangbourne	d						09 04							09 31						10 01			
Goring & Streatley	d						09 09							09 36						10 06			
Cholsey	d						09 14							09 41						10 11			
Didcot Parkway	a		08 55			09 11	09 22		09 11			09 37		09 50			09 55			10 18		10 11	
	d					09 12	09 25					09 38		09 55						10 25			
Appleford	d																						
Culham	d													10 01									
Radley	d						09 33							10 03									
Oxford	a				09 20	09 26	09 43			09 34		09 52		10 14	10 04				10 18	10 41			10 34
	d									09 36			10 00		10 07								10 36
Islip	d												10 13										
Bicester Town	a												10 25										
Tackley	d																						
Heyford	d																						
Kings Sutton	d																						
Banbury	a									09 52					10 24								10 52
Leamington Spa 8	a									10 10					10 42								11 10
Coventry	a									10 22													11 22
Birmingham International	a									10 37													11 37
Birmingham New Street 12	a									10 48					11 18								11 48

A The Devon Express

London and Reading - Bedwyn, Oxford, Bicester, Banbury and Birmingham

		GW 1	GW ◇1 🍴	GW ◇1 A	GW ◇1 B	CH 1	GW 1	XC ◇1 🛒	GW 1	GW ◇1 🍴	GW 1	GW ◇1 🍴	GW 1	GW 1	GW 1	GW ◇1 🍴	XC ◇1 🛒	GW 1	GW ◇1	GW 1	XC ◇1 🛒	GW 1	GW ◇1 🍴
London Paddington 15 ⊖	d		09 48	09 50	09 50				09 57	10 15	10 18	10 22			10 27	10 30			10 50			10 57	11 15
Ealing Broadway ⊖	d								10 05						10 35							11 05	
Slough 3	d			10 06	10 06				10 27			10 36			10 57				11 06			11 27	
Maidenhead 3	d								10 34						11 04							11 34	
Twyford 3	d						←		10 42					←	11 12					←		11 42	
Reading 7	d	10 12	10 16	10 22	10 22		10 23	10 41	10 53	10 41	10 48	10 52		10 53	11 23	10 57	11 11	11 12	11 21	11 23	11 41	11 53	11 41
Reading West	d	10 14							→						→			11 14				→	
Theale	d	10 20									10 56							11 20					
Aldermaston	d	10 25																11 25					
Midgham	d	10 29																11 29					
Thatcham	d	10 34									11 04							11 34					
Newbury Racecourse	d	10 38																11 38					
Newbury	a	10 44									11 10							11 44					
	d										11 10												
Kintbury	d										11 17												
Hungerford	d										11 21												
Bedwyn	a										11 31												
Tilehurst	d						10 27							10 57						11 27			
Pangbourne	d						10 31							11 01						11 31			
Goring & Streatley	d						10 36							11 06						11 36			
Cholsey	d						10 41							11 11						11 41			
Didcot Parkway	a		10 32				10 49			10 55				11 19		11 11			11 37	11 50			11 55
	d						10 55							11 25					11 38	11 55			
Appleford	d						11 00																
Culham	d																						
Radley	d						11 03													12 03			
Oxford	a			10 47	10 48		11 14	11 04				11 18		11 41			11 34		11 50	12 14	12 05		
	d					11 00		11 07					11 24				11 36				12 07		
Islip	d					11 13																	
Bicester Town	a					11 25																	
Tackley	d												11 33										
Heyford	d												11 37										
Kings Sutton	d												11 46										
Banbury	a							11 24					11 52				11 52				12 24		
Leamington Spa 8	a							11 41									12 11				12 42		
Coventry	a																12 24						
Birmingham International	a																12 37						
Birmingham New Street 12	a							12 18									12 48				13 18		

		GW 1	GW ◇1 🛒	GW 1	GW 1	GW ◇1 🍴	XC ◇1 🛒	GW 1	GW ◇1 C 🍴	GW ◇1 🛒	GW 1	XC ◇1 🛒	GW 1	GW ◇1 🍴	GW ◇1 🍴	GW ◇1 A 🛒	GW ◇1 B 🛒	CH 1	GW 1	GW 1	GW ◇1 🍴	XC ◇1 🛒
London Paddington 15 ⊖	d	11 18	11 20		11 27	11 30			11 48	11 50			11 57	12 15	12 18	12 21	12 21			12 27	12 30	
Ealing Broadway ⊖	d				11 35								12 05							12 35		
Slough 3	d		11 36		11 57					12 06			12 27			12 36	12 36			12 57		
Maidenhead 3	d				12 04								12 34							13 04		
Twyford 3	d			←	12 12						←		12 42						←	13 12		
Reading 7	d	11 48	11 52	11 53	12 23	11 57	12 11	12 12	12 16	12 22	12 23	12 41	12 53	12 41	12 48	12 52	12 52		12 53	13 23	12 57	13 11
Reading West	d				→			12 14					→							→		
Theale	d	11 56						12 20							12 56							
Aldermaston	d							12 25														
Midgham	d							12 29														
Thatcham	d	12 04						12 34							13 04							
Newbury Racecourse	d							12 38														
Newbury	a	12 10						12 44							13 12							
	d	12 10													13 12							
Kintbury	d	12 17																				
Hungerford	d	12 21													13 21							
Bedwyn	a	12 31													13 30							
Tilehurst	d			11 57							12 27								12 57			
Pangbourne	d			12 01							12 31								13 01			
Goring & Streatley	d			12 06							12 36								13 06			
Cholsey	d			12 11							12 41								13 11			
Didcot Parkway	a			12 20		12 11			12 32		12 49			12 55					13 19		13 11	
	d			12 25							12 55								13 25			
Appleford	d										13 00											
Culham	d																					
Radley	d										13 03											
Oxford	a		12 18	12 41			12 34			12 48	13 14	13 04				13 18	13 19		13 41			13 34
	d						12 36					13 07						13 30				13 36
Islip	d																	13 43				
Bicester Town	a																	13 55				
Tackley	d																					
Heyford	d																					
Kings Sutton	d																					
Banbury	a						12 52					13 24										13 52
Leamington Spa 8	a						13 10					13 42										14 10
Coventry	a						13 22															14 22
Birmingham International	a						13 37															14 37
Birmingham New Street 12	a						13 48					14 18										14 48

A from 12 September

B until 9 September

C The Cheltenham Spa Express

London and Reading - Bedwyn, Oxford, Bicester, Banbury and Birmingham

		GW 1	GW ◇1 🛒	GW 1	XC ◇1 🛒	GW 1	GW ◇1 ☕	GW 1	GW ◇1 🛒	GW 1	GW 1	GW 1	GW ◇1 ☕	XC ◇1 🛒	GW 1	GW ◇1 ☕	GW ◇1 🛒	CH 1	GW 1	XC ◇1 🛒	GW 1	GW ◇1 ☕	GW 1
London Paddington 15 ⊖	d		12 50			12 57	13 15	13 18	13 21			13 27	13 30			13 48	13 50				13 57	14 15	14 18
Ealing Broadway ⊖	d					13 05						13 35									14 05		
Slough 3	d		13 06			13 27			13 36			13 57					14 06				14 27		
Maidenhead 3	d					13 34						14 04									14 34		
Twyford 3	d			←		13 42					←	14 12							←		14 42		
Reading 7	d	13 12	13 22	13 23	13 41	13 53	13 41	13 48	13 52		13 53	14 23	13 57	14 11	14 12	14 16	14 22		14 23	14 41	14 53	14 41	14 48
Reading West	d	13 14				→						→			14 14						→		
Theale	d	13 20						13 56							14 20								14 56
Aldermaston	d	13 25													14 25								
Midgham	d	13 29													14 29								
Thatcham	d	13 34						14 04							14 34								15 04
Newbury Racecourse	d	13 38													14 38								
Newbury	a	13 44						14 10							14 44								15 10
	d							14 10															15 10
Kintbury	d							14 17															15 17
Hungerford	d							14 21															15 21
Bedwyn	a							14 31															15 31
Tilehurst	d			13 27							13 57								14 27				
Pangbourne	d			13 31							14 01								14 31				
Goring & Streatley	d			13 36							14 06								14 36				
Cholsey	d			13 41							14 11								14 41				
Didcot Parkway	a		13 37	13 49			13 55				14 20		14 11			14 32			14 49			14 55	
	d		13 38	13 55							14 25								14 55				
Appleford	d																		15 00				
Culham	d			14 01																			
Radley	d			14 03															15 03				
Oxford	a		13 50	14 14	14 04				14 18		14 42			14 34			14 48		15 14	15 05			
	d				14 07					14 24				14 36				15 00		15 07			
Islip	d																	15 13					
Bicester Town	a																	15 25					
Tackley	d									14 33													
Heyford	d									14 37													
Kings Sutton	d									14 46													
Banbury	a				14 24					14 52				14 53						15 24			
Leamington Spa 8	a				14 40									15 11						15 42			
Coventry	a													15 24									
Birmingham International	a													15 37									
Birmingham New Street 12	a				15 18									15 48						16 18			

		GW ◇1 A 🛒	GW 1	GW 1	GW ◇1 ☕	XC ◇1 🛒	GW 1	GW ◇1 🛒	GW 1	XC ◇1 🛒	GW 1	GW ◇1 ☕	GW 1	GW ◇1 🛒	GW 1	CH 1	GW 1	GW 1	GW ◇1 ☕	XC ◇1 🛒	GW 1	GW ◇1 ☕
London Paddington 15 ⊖	d	14 21		14 27	14 30			14 50			14 57	15 15	15 18	15 22				15 27	15 30			15 48
Ealing Broadway ⊖	d			14 35							15 05							15 35				
Slough 3	d	14 36		14 57				15 06			15 27			15 36				15 59				
Maidenhead 3	d			15 04							15 34							16 07				
Twyford 3	d		←	15 12					←		15 42						←	16 15				
Reading 7	d	14 52	14 53	15 23	14 57	15 11	15 12	15 22	15 23	15 41	15 53	15 41	15 48	15 52			15 53	16 24	15 57	16 11	16 12	16 16
Reading West	d			→			15 14				→							→			16 14	
Theale	d						15 20						15 56								16 20	
Aldermaston	d						15 25														16 25	
Midgham	d						15 29														16 29	
Thatcham	d						15 34						16 04								16 34	
Newbury Racecourse	d						15 38														16 38	
Newbury	a						15 44						16 10								16 44	
	d												16 10									
Kintbury	d												16 17									
Hungerford	d												16 21									
Bedwyn	a												16 31									
Tilehurst	d		14 57						15 27								15 57					
Pangbourne	d		15 01						15 31								16 01					
Goring & Streatley	d		15 06						15 36								16 06					
Cholsey	d		15 11						15 41								16 11					
Didcot Parkway	a		15 21		15 11			15 37	15 49			15 55					16 19		16 11			16 32
	d		15 25					15 38	15 55								16 25					
Appleford	d																					
Culham	d								16 01													
Radley	d								16 03								16 33					
Oxford	a	15 18	15 41			15 34		15 50	16 14	16 04				16 18			16 43			16 34		
	d					15 36				16 07					16 23	16 26				16 36		
Islip	d															16 39						
Bicester Town	a															16 51						
Tackley	d														16 32							
Heyford	d														16 36							
Kings Sutton	d														16 45							
Banbury	a					15 52				16 25					16 51					16 52		
Leamington Spa 8	a					16 10				16 43										17 11		
Coventry	a					16 22														17 23		
Birmingham International	a					16 37														17 37		
Birmingham New Street 12	a					16 48				17 18										17 48		

A 🛒 to Reading

London and Reading - Bedwyn, Oxford, Bicester, Banbury and Birmingham

		GW ◇1 ☕	GW 1	XC ◇1 🛒	GW 1	GW 1	GW ◇1 ☕	GW 1	GW ◇1 🛒	GW 1	GW 1	GW ◇1 ☕	GW ◇1 ☕	GW 1	XC ◇1 🛒	GW 1	CH 1	GW ◇1	GW 1	GW ◇1 ☕	GW ◇1 ☕	GW ◇1 ☕	GW ◇1 ☕
London Paddington 15 ⊖	d	15 51				15 57	16 15	16 18	16 22		16 27	16 30	16 36					16 49		17 00	17 03	17 06	17 15
Ealing Broadway ⊖	d					16 05					16 35												
Slough 3	d	16 06				16 27			16 36		16 57							17 04					
Maidenhead 3	d					16 34					17 04												
Twyford 3	d		←			16 42				←	17 12								←			17 28	
Reading 7	d	16 22	16 24	16 41		16 53	16 41	16 48	16 52	16 53	17 23	16 57	17 04		17 11	17 12		17 20	17 23	17 26	17 32	17 36	17 41
Reading West	d					→					→					17 14							
Theale	d							16 56								17 20						17 45	
Aldermaston	d							17 01								17 25							
Midgham	d															17 29							
Thatcham	d							17 08								17 34						17 55	
Newbury Racecourse	d													←		17 38							
Newbury	a							17 14					17 18	17 14		17 44					17 47	18 02	
	d				17 08			17 24					17 19	17 24								18 02	
Kintbury	d				17 14			→						17 31								18 10	
Hungerford	d				17 19								17a28	17 35								18 16	
Bedwyn	a				17 28									17 45								18 24	
Tilehurst	d		16 27							16 57									17 27				
Pangbourne	d		16 31							17 01									17 31				
Goring & Streatley	d		16 36							17 06									17 36				
Cholsey	d		16 41							17 11									17 41				
Didcot Parkway	a		16 50				16 54		17 08	17 20		17 11						17 35	17 49	17 40			17 55
	d		16 55						17 09	17 25								17 37	17 55				
Appleford	d		17 00							17 30													
Culham	d		17 01							17 32													
Radley	d		17 06							17 36									18 03				
Oxford	a	16 47	17 15	17 04					17 23	17 44					17 34			17 50	18 13				
	d			17 07						17 45					17 36		17 45						
Islip	d																17 58						
Bicester Town	a																18 10						
Tackley	d									17 54													
Heyford	d									17 58													
Kings Sutton	d									18 07													
Banbury	a			17 27						18 15					17 53								
Leamington Spa 8	a			17 46											18 11								
Coventry	a														18 22								
Birmingham International	a														18 37								
Birmingham New Street 12	a			18 18											18 48								

		XC ◇1 🛒	GW 1	GW ◇1 ☕	GW 1	GW ◇1 ☕	GW 1	GW ◇1	GW ◇1 ☕	XC ◇1 A 🛒	GW 1	GW 1	GW ◇1 ☕	GW ◇1	GW ◇1 ☕	GW ◇1 B ☕	GW 1	GW ◇1 ☕	GW ◇1 ☕	XC ◇1 C 🛒	GW 1	GW 1	GW ◇1 D ☕
London Paddington 15 ⊖	d		17 18	17 22	17 25	17 30		17 33	17 36				17 48		17 50	18 00		18 06	18 15		18 15	18 18	18 22
Ealing Broadway ⊖	d				17 33																18 23		
Slough 3	d				17 58																18 47		
Maidenhead 3	d		17 40		18 10			17 53							18 09						18 57	18 40	
Twyford 3	d		17 48		18 17		←	18 07						←			←	18 28			19 05	18 48	
Reading 7	d	17 41	17 57	17 50	18 28	17 56	17 57	18 18	18 04	18 11		18 12	18 16	18 18	18 22	18 27	18 28	18 37	18 41	18 41	19 18	18 57	18 50
Reading West	d		→		→			→				18 14									→	→	
Theale	d											18 20						18 45					
Aldermaston	d											18 25											
Midgham	d											18 29											
Thatcham	d											18 34						18 55					
Newbury Racecourse	d											18 38											
Newbury	a								18 18			18 44						19 02					
	d										18 26							19 02					
Kintbury	d										18 32							19 10					
Hungerford	d										18 37							19 16					
Bedwyn	a										18 46							19 24					
Tilehurst	d						18 01							18 24			18 33						
Pangbourne	d						18 06							18 30			18 38						
Goring & Streatley	d						18 11							18 36			18 43						
Cholsey	d						18 16							18 42			18 49						
Didcot Parkway	a					18 10	18 22						18 32	18 50		18 40	18 56		18 55				
	d						18 25							18 51			18 58						
Appleford	d																19 04						
Culham	d						18 31																
Radley	d						18 35										19 09						
Oxford	a	18 05		18 15			18 45			18 34				19 06	18 47		19 17			19 11			19 21
	d	18 07								18 36							19 18			19 12			
Islip	d																						
Bicester Town	a																						
Tackley	d																19 28						
Heyford	d																19 32						
Kings Sutton	d																19 41						
Banbury	a	18 25								18 53							19 47			19 30			
Leamington Spa 8	a	18 42								19 10										19 49			
Coventry	a									19 22													
Birmingham International	a									19 37													
Birmingham New Street 12	a	19 18								19 48										20 18			

A 🛒 to Birmingham International
B The Bristolian
C 🛒 to Leamington Spa
D The Cathedrals Express

London and Reading - Bedwyn, Oxford, Bicester, Banbury and Birmingham

		CH	GW FO	GW FX	GW	GW	GW	XC	GW	GW	GW	GW	GW	GW	GW FO	GW FX	GW FO	GW FX	XC	GW FO	GW FX	GW
		1	1	1	◇1 ⊏	1	◇1 ⊏	◇1 A ⊼	1	1	◇1 ⊏	1	◇1 ⊼	◇1 ⊏	1	1	1 B ✕	1 C ✕	◇1 ⊼	1	◇1 ⊏	1
London Paddington 15 ⊖	d		18 25	18 25	18 30		18 33				18 47		18 51	19 00			19 03	19 03		19 12	19 15	
Ealing Broadway ⊖	d		18 33	18 33																		
Slough 3	d		18 59	18 59									19 06									
Maidenhead 3	d		19 10	19 10																		
Twyford 3	d		19 18	19 18		←					19 09	←			←	←						
Reading 7	d		19 27	19 27	18 56	18 57	19 02	19 11		19 12	19 18	19 18	19 22	19 27	19 27	19 27	19u33	19 33	19 41	19 41	19 41	
Reading West	d		→	→						19 14												
Theale	d									19 20												
Aldermaston	d									19 25												
Midgham	d									19 29												
Thatcham	d									19 34												
Newbury Racecourse	d									19 38												
Newbury	a						19 16			19 44							19 49	19 49				
	d						19 17		19 27													19 57
Kintbury	d								19 33													20 03
Hungerford	d						19 27		19 38													20 08
Bedwyn	a						19 35		19 47													20 17
Tilehurst	d					19 01						19 24			19 31	19 31						
Pangbourne	d					19 06						19 28			19 35	19 35						
Goring & Streatley	d					19 11						19 33			19 40	19 40						
Cholsey	d					19 16						19 38			19 46	19 46						
Didcot Parkway	a				19 10	19 22					19 32	19 47		19 41	19 53	19 53				19 59	19 55	
	d					19 25						19 55			20 01	20 08				20 08		
Appleford	d															20 13				20 13		
Culham	d											20 03										
Radley	d					19 33										20 18				20 18		
Oxford	a					19 43		19 34				20 13	19 48		20 18	20 27			20 05	20 28		
	d	19 30						19 36											20 07			
Islip	d	19 43																				
Bicester Town	a	19 55																				
Tackley	d																					
Heyford	d																					
Kings Sutton	d																					
Banbury	a							19 52											20 27			
Leamington Spa 8	a							20 10											20 45			
Coventry	a							20 22														
Birmingham International	a							20 37														
Birmingham New Street 12	a							20 48											21 22			

		GW	GW	GW FX	GW FO	GW	GW	GW	GW	XC	GW	GW	CH	GW	GW	GW	GW	GW	XC	GW	GW	GW	GW
		1	1	◇1 ⊏	◇1 ⊏	1	◇1 ⊏	1	◇1 ⊏	◇1	◇1 ⊏	◇1 ⊼	1	1	1	◇1 ⊏	◇1 ⊏	1	◇1	◇1 ⊏	1	1	◇1 ⊏
London Paddington 15 ⊖	d		19 18	19 22	19 22	19 27	19 30		19 45		19 48	19 50			19 57	20 00	20 15			20 20		20 27	20 35
Ealing Broadway ⊖	d					19 35									20 05							20 35	
Slough 3	d			19 36	19 36	19 59						20 06			20 27					20 36		20 57	
Maidenhead 3	d		19 40			20 09					20 06				20 34							21 04	
Twyford 3	d		19 48			20 17		←						←	20 42						←	21 12	
Reading 7	d	19 42	19 57	19 52	19 52	20 23	19 57	19 57	20 12	20 11	20 18	20 22		20 23	20 53	20 27	20 41	20 41	20 41	20 52	20 53	21 27	21 02
Reading West	d	19 44	→			→									→			20 44				→	
Theale	d	19 50																20 50					
Aldermaston	d	19 55																20 55					
Midgham	d	19 59																20 58					
Thatcham	d	20 04																21 03					
Newbury Racecourse	d	20 08																21 08					
Newbury	a	20 17							20 27									21 11					21 17
	d	20 32																21 22					
Kintbury	d	20 38																21 29					
Hungerford	d	20 42																21 33					
Bedwyn	a	20 52																21 43					
Tilehurst	d							20 01						20 27							20 57		
Pangbourne	d							20 06						20 31							21 01		
Goring & Streatley	d							20 11						20 36							21 06		
Cholsey	d							20 16						20 41							21 11		
Didcot Parkway	a						20 11	20 22			20 32			20 51		20 41	20 55				21 19		
	d							20 25						20 55							21 25		
Appleford	d													20 59									
Culham	d							20 31															
Radley	d							20 35						21 04							21 33		
Oxford	a			20 18	20 21			20 46		20 34		20 47		21 13					21 21	21 16	21 43		
	d									20 36		20 55	21 00						21 23				
Islip	d												21 13										
Bicester Town	a												21 25										
Tackley	d											21 04											
Heyford	d											21 08											
Kings Sutton	d											21 17											
Banbury	a									20 52		21 23							21 39				
Leamington Spa 8	a									21 10									21 59				
Coventry	a									21 22													
Birmingham International	a									21 37													
Birmingham New Street 12	a									21 48									22 30				

A ⊼ to Birmingham International

London and Reading - Bedwyn, Oxford, Bicester, Banbury and Birmingham

		GW	XC	GW	GW	GW	GW	GW	XC	GW	GW	GW	GW	GW	GW FO	GW	GW	GW	CH FO	GW	GW	GW FO
		◇1 ⊏	◇1	1	◇1 ⊼	1	1	◇1 ⊏	◇1	◇1	1	1	1	◇1 A ⊏	◇1 ⊼	◇1 B ⊏	◇1 C	1	1	1	1	◇1 ⊏
London Paddington 15 ⊖	d	20 45			20 51		20 57	21 15		21 21			21 27	21 45	21 48	21 48	21 48				21 57	22 15
Ealing Broadway ⊖	d						21 05						21 35								22 05	
Slough 3	d				21 06		21 27			21 36			21 54		22 03	22 03	22 03				22 33	
Maidenhead 3	d						21 34						22 01								22 41	
Twyford 3	d					←	21 42				←		22 09							←	22 49	
Reading 7	d	21 11	21 11		21 22	21 27	21 57	21 41	21 46	21 52	21 57	22 01	22 27	22 11	22 22	22 22	22 22			22 27	22 58	22 41
Reading West	d						→					22 03	→								→	
Theale	d											22 10										
Aldermaston	d											22 15										
Midgham	d											22 18										
Thatcham	d											22 23										
Newbury Racecourse	d											22 28										
Newbury	a											22 31										
	d											22 31										
Kintbury	d											22 37										
Hungerford	d											22 42										
Bedwyn	a											22 52										
Tilehurst	d					21 32					22 02									22 32		
Pangbourne	d					21 36					22 07									22 37		
Goring & Streatley	d					21 40					22 10									22 40		
Cholsey	d					21 45					22 15									22 45		
Didcot Parkway	a	21 25				21 54		22 00			22 25			22 30						22 55		23 00
	d					21 55					22 25									22 55		
Appleford	d					21 59														23 00		
Culham	d					22 01														23 01		
Radley	d					22 05														23 04		
Oxford	a		21 34		21 53	22 16			22 28	22 24	22 40				22 47	22 47	22 47			23 17		
	d		21 36	21 41					22 30									23 06	23 12			
Islip	d																		23 25			
Bicester Town	a																		23 37			
Tackley	d			21 50														23 15				
Heyford	d			21 54														23 19				
Kings Sutton	d			22 03														23 28				
Banbury	a		21 52	22 09					22 53									23 35				
Leamington Spa 8	a		22 10						23 12													
Coventry	a		22 22						23 25													
Birmingham International	a		22 33						23 36													
Birmingham New Street 12	a		22 45						23 58													

		GW FX	GW FO	GW	GW	GW FX	GW FO	GW FX	GW	GW FO	GW FX	GW	GW FO	GW FX	GW FX	GW FO	GW FO	GW FX	GW FO	GW FX	GW FO
		◇1 ⊏	◇1	1	1	◇1	◇1 ⊏	◇1 ⊏	1	◇1	◇1	1	◇1	◇1	1	1	◇1 ⊏	◇1 ⊏	1	1	1
London Paddington 15 ⊖	d	22 15	22 21			22 21	22 45	22 45	22 45	22 49	22 49		23 20	23 20	23 29	23 29	23 30	23 30	23 42		
Ealing Broadway ⊖	d								22 54						23 37	23 37					
Slough 3	d		22 36			22 42			23 12	23 06	23 07		23 39	23 39	23 54	23 54			23 59		
Maidenhead 3	d								23 23						00 01	00 01			00 06		
Twyford 3	d			←					23 31			←			00 09	00 09				←	←
Reading 7	d	22 50	22 52	22 58	23 00	23 06	23 11	23 21	23 40	23 22	23 34	23 40	23 54	00 04	00 19	00 23	00 05	00 08	00 17	00 19	00 23
Reading West	d				23 02				→						→	→					
Theale	d				23 08																
Aldermaston	d				23 13																
Midgham	d				23 17																
Thatcham	d				23 22																
Newbury Racecourse	d				23 26																
Newbury	a				23 29																
	d				23 29																
Kintbury	d				23 36																
Hungerford	d				23 40																
Bedwyn	a				23 50																
Tilehurst	d			23 02								23 44								00 23	00 27
Pangbourne	d			23 06								23 49								00 28	00 32
Goring & Streatley	d			23 10								23 52								00 32	00 35
Cholsey	d			23 15								23 57								00 37	00 40
Didcot Parkway	a	23 07		23 25			23 29	23 38				00 06					00 23	00 25	00 43	00 45	00 49
	d			23 28								00 06							00 44	00 45	00 49
Appleford	d																			00 50	00 54
Culham	d																			00 52	00 56
Radley	d											00 14								00 56	01 00
Oxford	a		23 25	23 44		23 37				23 48	00 11	00 23	00 28	00 32					01 00	01 08	01 10
	d																				
Islip	d																				
Bicester Town	a																				
Tackley	d																				
Heyford	d																				
Kings Sutton	d																				
Banbury	a																				
Leamington Spa 8	a																				
Coventry	a																				
Birmingham International	a																				
Birmingham New Street 12	a																				

A not 23 May

B FX from 12 September

C FX until 8 September

London and Reading - Bedwyn, Oxford, Bicester, Banbury and Birmingham

		GW	GW	CH	GW	GW	GW	GW	GW	GW	GW	GW	GW	GW	GW	GW	XC	GW	GW	GW	CH	GW	XC
		■	◇■		■	◇■	■	■	■	◇■	■	■	■	■	◇■	■	◇■	■	■	◇■	■	■	◇■
				A		⊡											⊼						⊼
London Paddington ⊖	d	22p45	23p20		23p29	23p30	23p42			00 22					05 21				05 25	05 50			
Ealing Broadway ⊖	d	22p54			23p37														05 33				
Slough ■	d	23p12	23p39		23p54		23p59			00 39					05 38				05 51	06 06			
Maidenhead ■	d	23p23			00 01		00 06												06 02				
Twyford ■	d	23p31			00 09			←											06 10				
Reading ■	d	23p40	23p54		00 23	00 05	00 17	00 23	00 20	00 56	05 10	05 41		05 46	05 54		06 11	06 12	06 21	06 22			06 46
Reading West	d				→				00s23		05 13	05 44						06 14					
Theale	d								00s29		05 19	05 50						06 20					
Aldermaston	d								00s34		05 24	05 55						06 25					
Midgham	d								00s37		05 27	05 58						06 29					
Thatcham	d								00s42		05 32	06 03						06 34					
Newbury Racecourse	d								00s47		05 37	06 08						06 38					
Newbury	a								00 52		05 39	06 10						06 44					
	d										05 39	06 10											
Kintbury	d										05 46	06 17											
Hungerford	d										05 50	06 21											
Bedwyn	a										05 59	06 30											
Tilehurst	d	23p44						00 27						05 50					06 25				
Pangbourne	d	23p49						00 32						05 54					06 29				
Goring & Streatley	d	23p52						00 35						05 59					06 34				
Cholsey	d	23p57						00 40						06 04		←			06 39			←	
Didcot Parkway	a	00 06				00 23	00 43	00 49		01 13				06 12	06 07	06 12			06 46	06 37		06 46	
	d	00 06					00 44	00 49		01 14				06 13	06 08	06 13			06 47	06 38		06 47	
Appleford	d							00 54						→		06 17			→				
Culham	d							00 56								06 20							
Radley	d	00 14						01 00								06 24						06 54	
Oxford	a	00 23	00 28				01 00	01 10		01 27					06 22	06 32	06 36			06 52		07 04	07 10
	d			00 38									06 16				06 38				07 00		07 12
Islip	d																				07 13		
Bicester Town	a																				07 25		
Tackley	d			00 48									06 25										
Heyford	d			00 53									06 29										
Kings Sutton	d			01 01									06 38										
Banbury	a			01 10									06 46				06 54						07 32
Leamington Spa ■	a																07 12						07 50
Coventry	a																07 24						
Birmingham International	a																07 37						
Birmingham New Street ■	a																07 48						08 17

		GW	GW	GW	GW	GW	GW	XC	GW	GW	GW	CH	GW	GW	XC	GW	GW	GW	GW	XC	GW	GW	GW
		■	■	◇■	■	■	◇■	◇■	■	◇■	■	■	■	■	◇■	■	◇■	■	■ ■	◇■	■	◇■	■
							⊡	⊼							⊼				⊡	⊼			
London Paddington ⊖	d		05 57	06 21		06 27	06 30			06 50						06 57	07 21	07 27	07 30			07 50	
Ealing Broadway ⊖	d		06 05			06 35										07 05		07 35					
Slough ■	d		06 31	06 38		06 57				07 06						07 27	07 38	07 57				08 06	
Maidenhead ■	d		06 42			07 04										07 34		08 04					
Twyford ■	d		06 50		←	07 12							←			07 42		08 12					←
Reading ■	d	06 48	06 56	06 54	06 56	07 23	06 59	07 11	07 11	07 22			07 23	07 35	07 47	07 53	07 54	08 23	07 57	08 11	08 18	08 22	08 23
Reading West	d		→			→			07 14									→			08 20		
Theale	d	06 55							07 20					07 44							08 27		
Aldermaston	d								07 25												08 32		
Midgham	d								07 29												08 36		
Thatcham	d	07 04							07 34					07 52							08 41		
Newbury Racecourse	d								07 38												08 45		
Newbury	a	07 09							07 43					07 58							08 50		
	d	07 09												07 58									
Kintbury	d	07 16												08 04									
Hungerford	d	07 20												08 09									
Bedwyn	a	07 29												08 18									
Tilehurst	d				07 00								07 27			07 57							08 27
Pangbourne	d				07 04								07 31			08 01							08 31
Goring & Streatley	d				07 09								07 36			08 06							08 36
Cholsey	d				07 14								07 41			08 11							08 41
Didcot Parkway	a				07 30		07 12						07 49			08 19			08 12				08 48
	d				07 30								07 51			08 25							08 55
Appleford	d																						09 00
Culham	d												07 56										
Radley	d												08 00										09 03
Oxford	a			07 19	07 44			07 34		07 48			08 10		08 13	08 41	08 19			08 34		08 48	09 15
	d							07 36			07 53	08 07			08 15					08 36			
Islip	d											08 20											
Bicester Town	a											08 32											
Tackley	d										08 02												
Heyford	d										08 06												
Kings Sutton	d										08 15												
Banbury	a							07 52			08 23				08 32					08 52			
Leamington Spa ■	a							08 10							08 49					09 10			
Coventry	a							08 22												09 22			
Birmingham International	a							08 37												09 37			
Birmingham New Street ■	a							08 48							09 19					09 48			

A not 10 September

London and Reading - Bedwyn, Oxford, Bicester, Banbury and Birmingham

		XC	GW	GW	GW	GW	GW	GW	CH	GW	GW	GW	XC	GW	GW	GW	XC	GW	GW	GW	GW	GW
		◇■	■	■	◇■	■	■	◇■	■	■	◇■	■ ■	◇■	■	◇■	■	◇■	■	■	■	■	◇■
		⊼			⊡			⊡			⊡	A ⊡	⊼				⊼					
London Paddington ⊖	d			07 57	08 15	08 18		08 21		08 27	08 30	08 35			08 50				08 57	09 18		09 21
Ealing Broadway ⊖	d			08 05						08 35									09 05			
Slough ■	d			08 27				08 39		08 57					09 06				09 27			09 39
Maidenhead ■	d			08 34						09 04									09 34			
Twyford ■	d			08 42			←			09 12						←			09 42		←	
Reading ■	d	08 40		08 53	08 41	08 47	08 53	08 54		09 23	08 57	09u04	09 11	09 12	09 22	09 23	09 40		09 53	09 48	09 53	09 54
Reading West	d			→						→				09 14					→			
Theale	d					08 55								09 20						09 56		
Aldermaston	d													09 25								
Midgham	d													09 29								
Thatcham	d					09 03								09 34						10 04		
Newbury Racecourse	d													09 38								
Newbury	a					09 10						09 20		09 44						10 10		
	d		08 58			09 24														10 10		
Kintbury	d		09 04			09 31														10 17		
Hungerford	d		09 09			09 35														10 21		
Bedwyn	a		09 17			09 44														10 30		
Tilehurst	d						08 57									09 27					09 57	
Pangbourne	d						09 01									09 31					10 01	
Goring & Streatley	d						09 06									09 36					10 06	
Cholsey	d						09 11									09 41					10 11	
Didcot Parkway	a				08 54		09 19				09 12					09 48					10 18	
	d						09 25									09 55					10 25	
Appleford	d																					
Culham	d															10 01						
Radley	d															10 03						
Oxford	a	09 04					09 41	09 18					09 34		09 48	10 15	10 04				10 41	10 19
	d	09 07							09 27				09 36				10 07	10 16				
Islip	d								09 41													
Bicester Town	a								09 53													
Tackley	d																	10 25				
Heyford	d																	10 29				
Kings Sutton	d																	10 39				
Banbury	a	09 23											09 52				10 23	10 46				
Leamington Spa ■	a	09 41											10 11				10 41					
Coventry	a												10 22									
Birmingham International	a												10 37									
Birmingham New Street ■	a	10 17											10 48				11 18					

		GW	GW	XC	GW	GW	CH	GW	XC	GW	GW	GW	GW	GW	GW	GW	XC	GW	GW	GW	XC	GW	GW
		■	◇■	◇■	■	◇■	■	■	◇■	■	◇■	■	■	◇■	■	◇■	◇■	■	◇■	■	◇■	■	■
			⊡	⊼					⊼		⊡			⊡		⊡	⊼		⊼		⊼		
London Paddington ⊖	d	09 27	09 30			09 50				09 57	10 15	10 18		10 21	10 27	10 30			10 50				10 57
Ealing Broadway ⊖	d	09 35								10 05					10 35								11 05
Slough ■	d	09 57				10 06				10 27				10 39	10 57				11 06				11 27
Maidenhead ■	d	10 04								10 34					11 04								11 34
Twyford ■	d	10 12						←		10 42			←		11 12					←			11 42
Reading ■	d	10 23	09 57	10 11	10 12	10 22		10 23	10 40	10 53	10 41	10 48	10 53	10 54	11 23	10 57	11 11	11 12	11 22	11 23	11 40		11 53
Reading West	d	→			10 14					→					→			11 14					→
Theale	d				10 20							10 56						11 20					
Aldermaston	d				10 25													11 25					
Midgham	d				10 29													11 29					
Thatcham	d				10 34							11 04						11 34					
Newbury Racecourse	d				10 38													11 38					
Newbury	a				10 44							11 10						11 44					
	d											11 23											
Kintbury	d											11 30											
Hungerford	d											11 34											
Bedwyn	a											11 44											
Tilehurst	d							10 27					10 57							11 27			
Pangbourne	d							10 31					11 01							11 31			
Goring & Streatley	d							10 36					11 06							11 36			
Cholsey	d							10 41					11 11							11 41			
Didcot Parkway	a		10 12					10 48			10 54		11 19			11 12				11 49			
	d							10 55					11 25							11 55			
Appleford	d							11 00															
Culham	d																						
Radley	d							11 03												12 03			
Oxford	a			10 34		10 48		11 15	11 04				11 41	11 19			11 34		11 48	12 15	12 04		
	d			10 36			11 00		11 07								11 36				12 07	12 16	
Islip	d						11 13																
Bicester Town	a						11 25																
Tackley	d																					12 25	
Heyford	d																					12 29	
Kings Sutton	d																					12 39	
Banbury	a			10 52					11 23								11 52				12 23	12 46	
Leamington Spa ■	a			11 10					11 41								12 10				12 41		
Coventry	a			11 22													12 22						
Birmingham International	a			11 37													12 37						
Birmingham New Street ■	a			11 48					12 18								12 48				13 18		

A The Torbay Express

Table 116

Saturdays
until 10 September

London and Reading - Bedwyn, Oxford, Bicester, Banbury and Birmingham

		GW	GW	GW	CH	GW	GW	XC	GW	GW	GW	XC	GW	GW	GW	GW	GW	GW	GW	GW	XC	GW
		■	■	◇■ ⌶	■	■	◇■ Ø	◇■ ⌶	■	◇■	■	◇■ ⌶	■	◇■ 🛒	■	■	◇■	■	◇■ 🛒	■ 🛒	◇■ ⌶	■
London Paddington 15 ⊖	d	11 18		11 21		11 27	11 30			11 50			11 57	12 15	12 18		12 21	12 27	12 30	12 35		
Ealing Broadway ⊖	d					11 35							12 05					12 35				
Slough 3	d			11 39		11 57				12 06			12 27				12 39	12 57				
Maidenhead 3	d					12 04							12 34					13 04				
Twyford 3	d		←			12 12					←		12 42			←		13 12				
Reading 7	d	11 48	11 53	11 55		12 23	11 58	12 11	12 12	12 22	12 23	12 40	12 53	12 41	12 48	12 53	12 54	13 23	12 57	13u06	13 11	
Reading West	d					→			12 14				→					→				
Theale	d	11 56							12 20						12 56							
Aldermaston	d								12 25													
Midgham	d								12 29													
Thatcham	d	12 04							12 34						13 04							
Newbury Racecourse	d								12 38													
Newbury	a	12 10							12 44						13 16					13 21		
	d	12 25																				13 26
Kintbury	d	12 31																				13 32
Hungerford	d	12 36																				13 37
Bedwyn	a	12 45																				13 45
Tilehurst	d		11 57								12 27					12 57						
Pangbourne	d		12 01								12 31					13 01						
Goring & Streatley	d		12 06								12 36					13 06						
Cholsey	d		12 11								12 41					13 11						
Didcot Parkway	a		12 19				12 12				12 48			12 54		13 19			13 12			
	d		12 25								12 55					13 25						
Appleford	d										13 00											
Culham	d																					
Radley	d										13 03											
Oxford	a		12 41	12 20				12 34		12 48	13 15	13 04				13 41	13 19				13 34	
	d				12 30			12 36				13 07									13 36	
Islip	d				12 43																	
Bicester Town	a				12 55																	
Tackley	d																					
Heyford	d																					
Kings Sutton	d																					
Banbury	a							12 52				13 23									13 52	
Leamington Spa 8	a							13 10				13 41									14 10	
Coventry	a							13 22													14 22	
Birmingham International	a							13 37													14 37	
Birmingham New Street 12	a							13 48				14 18									14 48	

		GW	CH	GW	GW	XC	GW	GW	GW	GW	GW	GW	GW	XC	GW	GW	CH	GW	XC	GW	GW	GW	GW
		■	■	◇■ ⌶	■	◇■ ⌶	■	■	■	■	◇■ ⌶	■	◇■ 🛒	◇■ ⌶	■	◇■ ⌶	■	■	◇■ ⌶	■	◇■ 🛒	■	■
London Paddington 15 ⊖	d			12 50				12 57	13 18		13 21	13 27	13 30			13 50				13 57	14 15	14 18	
Ealing Broadway ⊖	d							13 05				13 35								14 05			
Slough 3	d			13 06				13 27			13 39	13 57				14 06				14 27			
Maidenhead 3	d							13 34				14 04								14 34			
Twyford 3	d				←			13 42		←		14 12						←		14 42			←
Reading 7	d	13 12		13 22	13 23	13 40		13 53	13 48	13 53	13 55	14 23	13 59	14 11	14 12	14 22		14 23	14 40	14 53	14 41	14 48	14 53
Reading West	d	13 14						→				→			14 14					→			
Theale	d	13 20							13 56						14 20							14 56	
Aldermaston	d	13 25													14 25								
Midgham	d	13 29													14 29								
Thatcham	d	13 34							14 04						14 34							15 04	
Newbury Racecourse	d	13 38													14 38								
Newbury	a	13 44							14 10						14 44							15 10	
	d								14 10													15 10	
Kintbury	d								14 17													15 17	
Hungerford	d								14 21													15 21	
Bedwyn	a								14 31													15 31	
Tilehurst	d				13 27					13 57								14 27					14 57
Pangbourne	d				13 31					14 01								14 31					15 01
Goring & Streatley	d				13 36					14 06								14 36					15 06
Cholsey	d				13 41					14 11								14 41					15 11
Didcot Parkway	a				13 48					14 19			14 12					14 48			14 54		15 19
	d				13 55					14 25								14 55					15 25
Appleford	d																	15 00					
Culham	d				14 01																		
Radley	d				14 03													15 03					
Oxford	a			13 48	14 15	14 04				14 41	14 19			14 34		14 48		15 15	15 04				15 41
	d		13 41			14 07	14 16							14 36			14 57		15 07				
Islip	d		13 54														15 10						
Bicester Town	a		14 06														15 22						
Tackley	d						14 25																
Heyford	d						14 29																
Kings Sutton	d						14 38																
Banbury	a					14 23	14 46							14 52					15 23				
Leamington Spa 8	a					14 41								15 10					15 41				
Coventry	a													15 22									
Birmingham International	a													15 37									
Birmingham New Street 12	a					15 17								15 48					16 17				

Table 116

Saturdays
until 10 September

London and Reading - Bedwyn, Oxford, Bicester, Banbury and Birmingham

		GW	GW	GW	XC	GW	GW	CH	GW	XC	GW	GW	GW	GW	GW	GW	GW	XC	GW	GW	GW	XC	CH
		◇■ ⌶	■	◇■ 🛒	◇■ ⌶	■	◇■	■	■	◇■ ⌶	■	■	■	■	◇■ A ⌶	■	◇■ 🛒	◇■ ⌶	■	◇■	■	◇■ ⌶	■
London Paddington 15 ⊖	d	14 21	14 27	14 30			14 50					14 57	15 18		15 21	15 27	15 30			15 50			
Ealing Broadway ⊖	d		14 35									15 05				15 35							
Slough 3	d	14 39	14 57				15 06					15 27			15 39	15 57				16 06			
Maidenhead 3	d		15 04									15 34				16 04							
Twyford 3	d		15 12						←			15 42		←		16 12					←		
Reading 7	d	14 54	15 23	14 57	15 11	15 12	15 22		15 23	15 40		15 53	15 48	15 53	15 55	16 23	15 59	16 11	16 12	16 22	16 23	16 40	
Reading West	d		→			15 14						→				→			16 14				
Theale	d					15 20							15 56						16 20				
Aldermaston	d					15 25													16 25				
Midgham	d					15 29													16 29				
Thatcham	d					15 34							16 04						16 34				
Newbury Racecourse	d					15 38													16 38				
Newbury	a					15 44							16 10						16 44				
	d												16 10										
Kintbury	d												16 17										
Hungerford	d												16 21										
Bedwyn	a												16 31										
Tilehurst	d								15 27					15 57							16 27		
Pangbourne	d								15 31					16 01							16 31		
Goring & Streatley	d								15 36					16 06							16 36		
Cholsey	d								15 41					16 11							16 41		
Didcot Parkway	a			15 12					15 48					16 19			16 12				16 48		
	d								15 55					16 25							16 55		
Appleford	d																				17 00		
Culham	d								16 01														
Radley	d								16 03												17 03		
Oxford	a	15 18			15 34		15 48		16 15	16 04				16 41	16 19			16 34		16 48	17 15	17 04	
	d				15 36			16 01		16 07	16 16							16 36				17 07	17 10
Islip	d							16 14															17 23
Bicester Town	a							16 26															17 35
Tackley	d										16 25												
Heyford	d										16 29												
Kings Sutton	d										16 39												
Banbury	a				15 52					16 23	16 46							16 52				17 23	
Leamington Spa 8	a				16 10					16 41								17 10				17 41	
Coventry	a				16 22													17 22					
Birmingham International	a				16 37													17 37					
Birmingham New Street 12	a				16 48					17 17								17 48				18 18	

		GW	GW	GW	GW	GW	GW	GW	XC	GW	GW	GW	XC	GW	GW	GW	GW	GW	GW	GW	XC	GW
		■	◇■ 🛒	■	■	◇■ 🛒	■	◇■ 🛒	◇■ ⌶	■	◇■ ⌶	■	◇■ ⌶	■	■	■	■	◇■ 🛒	■	◇■ 🛒	◇■ B ⌶	■
London Paddington 15 ⊖	d	15 57	16 15	16 18		16 21	16 27	16 30			16 50				16 57	17 18		17 21	17 27	17 30		
Ealing Broadway ⊖	d	16 05					16 35								17 05				17 35			
Slough 3	d	16 27				16 39	16 57				17 06				17 27			17 39	17 57			
Maidenhead 3	d	16 34					17 04								17 34				18 04			
Twyford 3	d	16 42			←		17 12					←			17 42		←		18 12			
Reading 7	d	16 53	16 41	16 48	16 53	16 54	17 23	16 57	17 11	17 12	17 22	17 23	17 40		17 54	17 48	17 54	17 55	18 23	17 57	18 11	18 12
Reading West	d	→					→			17 14					→				→			18 14
Theale	d			16 56						17 20						17 56						18 20
Aldermaston	d									17 25												18 25
Midgham	d									17 29												18 29
Thatcham	d			17 04						17 34						18 04						18 34
Newbury Racecourse	d									17 38												18 38
Newbury	a			17 10						17 44						18 10						18 44
	d			17 10												18 10						
Kintbury	d			17 17												18 17						
Hungerford	d			17 21												18 21						
Bedwyn	a			17 31												18 30						
Tilehurst	d				16 57							17 27					17 57					
Pangbourne	d				17 01							17 31					18 01					
Goring & Streatley	d				17 06							17 36					18 06					
Cholsey	d				17 11							17 41					18 11					
Didcot Parkway	a		16 54		17 19			17 12				17 48					18 19			18 12		
	d				17 25							17 55					18 25					
Appleford	d																					
Culham	d											18 01										
Radley	d											18 03										
Oxford	a				17 41	17 18			17 34		17 47	18 15	18 04				18 41	18 18			18 34	
	d								17 36				18 07	18 16							18 36	
Islip	d																					
Bicester Town	a																					
Tackley	d													18 25								
Heyford	d													18 29								
Kings Sutton	d													18 38								
Banbury	a								17 52				18 23	18 46							18 52	
Leamington Spa 8	a								18 10				18 41								19 10	
Coventry	a								18 22												19 22	
Birmingham International	a								18 37												19 37	
Birmingham New Street 12	a								18 48				19 18								19 48	

A ⌶ to Reading

B ⌶ to Birmingham International

London and Reading - Bedwyn, Oxford, Bicester, Banbury and Birmingham

		CH 1	GW ◇1 🍴	GW 1	XC ◇1 A 🍴	GW 1	GW ◇1 ☕	GW 1	GW 1	GW ◇1 ☕	GW 1	GW ◇1 ☕	XC ◇1 🍴	GW ◇1	CH 1	GW 1	GW 1	GW 1	GW ◇1 ☕	XC ◇1 🍴	GW 1	GW ◇1	GW 1
London Paddington 15 ⊖	d		17 50			17 57	18 15	18 18		18 21	18 27	18 30		18 50				18 57	19 06			19 21	
Ealing Broadway ⊖	d					18 05					18 35							19 05					
Slough 3	d		18 06			18 27				18 39	18 57			19 06				19 27				19 38	
Maidenhead 3	d					18 34					19 04							19 34					
Twyford 3	d			←		18 42			←		19 12						←	19 42					←
Reading 7	d		18 22	18 23	18 40	18 53	18 41	18 48	18 53	18 54	19 23	18 57	19 11	19 23			19 23	19 53	19 32	19 40	19 49	19 52	19 53
Reading West	d					→					→							→			19 52		
Theale	d							18 56													19 58		
Aldermaston	d																				20 03		
Midgham	d																				20 06		
Thatcham	d							19 04													20 11		
Newbury Racecourse	d																				20 16		
Newbury	a							19 10											19 48		20 18		
	d							19 10													20 18		
Kintbury	d							19 17													20 25		
Hungerford	d							19 21													20 29		
Bedwyn	a							19 30													20 38		
Tilehurst	d			18 27					18 57								19 27						19 57
Pangbourne	d			18 31					19 01								19 32						20 01
Goring & Streatley	d			18 36					19 06								19 37						20 06
Cholsey	d			18 41					19 11								19 42						20 11
Didcot Parkway	a			18 48			18 54		19 19			19 12					19 49						20 19
	d			18 55					19 25								19 55						20 25
Appleford	d			19 00																			
Culham	d																20 01						
Radley	d			19 03													20 03						
Oxford	a		18 48	19 15	19 04				19 41	19 18			19 34	19 48			20 15			20 04		20 20	20 41
	d	18 41			19 07								19 36		19 48	19 56				20 07			
Islip	d	18 54													20 01								
Bicester Town	a	19 06													20 13								
Tackley	d															20 05							
Heyford	d															20 09							
Kings Sutton	d															20 18							
Banbury	a				19 23								19 52			20 25				20 28			
Leamington Spa 8	a				19 41								20 10							20 45			
Coventry	a												20 22										
Birmingham International	a												20 37										
Birmingham New Street 12	a				20 18								20 48							21 18			

		GW 1	GW ◇1 ☕	XC ◇1	GW ◇1 B 🍴	CH 1	GW 1	GW 1	GW ◇1 ☕	GW ◇1 ☕	GW ◇1 ☕	XC ◇1 🍴	GW 1	GW ◇1	GW 1	GW 1	GW 1	GW ◇1 ☕	XC ◇1 🍴	GW ◇1 🍴	GW 1	GW 1
London Paddington 15 ⊖	d	19 27	19 30		19 50			19 57	20 00	20 06	20 15			20 20			20 27	20 30		20 50		20 57
Ealing Broadway ⊖	d	19 35						20 05									20 35					21 05
Slough 3	d	19 57			20 06			20 27						20 35			20 57			21 06		21 27
Maidenhead 3	d	20 04						20 34									21 04					21 34
Twyford 3	d	20 12					←	20 42								←	21 12				←	21 42
Reading 7	d	20 23	19 57	20 11	20 22		20 23	20 53	20 27	20 33	20 41	20 40	20 49	20 51		20 53	21 23	20 57	21 11	21 22	21 23	21 53
Reading West	d	→						→					20 52				→					→
Theale	d												20 58									
Aldermaston	d												21 03									
Midgham	d												21 06									
Thatcham	d												21 11									
Newbury Racecourse	d												21 16									
Newbury	a									20 47			21 18									
	d												21 32									
Kintbury	d												21 39									
Hungerford	d												21 43									
Bedwyn	a												21 52									
Tilehurst	d						20 27									20 57					21 27	
Pangbourne	d						20 32									21 01					21 31	
Goring & Streatley	d						20 37									21 06					21 36	
Cholsey	d						20 42									21 11					21 41	
Didcot Parkway	a		20 11				20 49		20 41		20 54					21 19		21 12		21 39	21 48	
	d						20 55									21 25				21 40	21 55	
Appleford	d						21 00															
Culham	d																				22 01	
Radley	d						21 03														22 03	
Oxford	a			20 34	20 47		21 15					21 04		21 19		21 41			21 34	21 53	22 15	
	d			20 36		21 00						21 07			21 20				21 36			
Islip	d					21 13																
Bicester Town	a					21 25																
Tackley	d														21 29							
Heyford	d														21 33							
Kings Sutton	d														21 42							
Banbury	a			20 52								21 23			21 49				21 52			
Leamington Spa 8	a			21 10								21 44							22 10			
Coventry	a			21 22								21 55							22 22			
Birmingham International	a			21 37								22 10							22 36			
Birmingham New Street 12	a			21 48								22 22							22 48			

A 🍴 to Leamington Spa

B 🍴 to Reading

Table 116

Saturdays
until 10 September

London and Reading - Bedwyn, Oxford, Bicester, Banbury and Birmingham

		GW ◇1	CH 1	GW 1	GW ◇1 ☕	GW 1	GW ◇1	GW 1	GW ◇1 ☕	GW ◇1	GW 1	GW ◇1 ☕	GW 1	GW 🚌	GW 1	GW ◇1	GW 1	GW 1	GW ◇1 ☕	GW ◇1	GW 1
London Paddington 15 ⊖	d	21 17			21 30		21 50	21 57	22 00	22 15		22 35			22 45	23 00		23 20	23 30	23 33	
Ealing Broadway ⊖	d							22 05							22 55			23 28			
Slough 3	d	21 35					22 06	22 27		22 32					23 21	23 17		23 54		23 50	
Maidenhead 3	d							22 34							23 32			00 05			
Twyford 3	d			←				22 42			←				23 39		←	00 13			←
Reading 7	d	21 52		21 53	21 57	22 03	22 22	22 53	22 27	22 51	22 53	23 02	23 12		23 49	23 34	23 49	00 20	23 59	00 08	00 20
Reading West	d					22 06		→					23 14		→			→			
Theale	d					22 12							23 20								
Aldermaston	d					22 17							23 25								
Midgham	d					22 20							23 29								
Thatcham	d					22 25							23 34								
Newbury Racecourse	d					22 30							23 38								
Newbury	a					22 32							23 41								
	d					22 32							23 41								
Kintbury	d					22 39							23 48								
Hungerford	d					22 43							23 52								
Bedwyn	a					22 51							00 01								
Tilehurst	d			21 57							22 57						23 53				00 24
Pangbourne	d			22 01							23 01						23 58				
Goring & Streatley	d			22 06							23 06						00 03				00 31
Cholsey	d			22 11							23 11						00 08				00 36
Didcot Parkway	a	22 07		22 19	22 12		22 37		22 41	23 06	23 19	23 21				23 51	00 14		00 18	00 22	00 44
	d	22 08		22 25			22 37			23 07	23 20					23 51	00 15			00 24	00 45
Appleford	d																				00s49
Culham	d																				00s51
Radley	d			22 34							23 27						00s22				00s55
Oxford	a	22 20		22 44			22 49			23 20	23 37					00 03	00 32			00 38	01 05
	d		22 25											23 47							
Islip	d		22 38																		
Bicester Town	a		22 50																		
Tackley	d													00s06							
Heyford	d													00s20							
Kings Sutton	d																				
Banbury	a													00 45							
Leamington Spa 8	a																				
Coventry	a																				
Birmingham International	a																				
Birmingham New Street 12	a																				

Saturdays
from 17 September

		GW 1	GW ◇1	GW 1	GW ◇1 ☕	GW 1	GW 1	GW 1	GW ◇1	GW 1	GW 1	GW 1	GW 1	GW ◇1	GW 1	XC ◇1 🍴	GW 1	GW 1	GW ◇1	CH 1	GW 1	XC ◇1 🍴	GW 1
London Paddington 15 ⊖	d	22p45	23p20	23p29	23p30	23p42			00 22					05 21				05 25	05 50				
Ealing Broadway ⊖	d	22p54		23p37														05 33					
Slough 3	d	23p12	23p39	23p54		23p59			00 39					05 38				05 51	06 06				
Maidenhead 3	d	23p23		00 01		00 06												06 02					
Twyford 3	d	23p31		00 09			←											06 10					
Reading 7	d	23p40	23p54	00 23	00 05	00 17	00 23	00 20	00 56	05 10	05 41		05 46	05 54		06 11	06 12	06 21	06 22			06 46	06 48
Reading West	d			→				00s23		05 13	05 44						06 14						
Theale	d							00s29		05 19	05 50						06 20						06 55
Aldermaston	d							00s34		05 24	05 55						06 25						
Midgham	d							00s37		05 27	05 58						06 29						
Thatcham	d							00s42		05 32	06 03						06 34						07 04
Newbury Racecourse	d							00s47		05 37	06 08						06 38						
Newbury	a							00 52		05 39	06 10						06 44						07 09
	d									05 39	06 10												07 09
Kintbury	d									05 46	06 17												07 16
Hungerford	d									05 50	06 21												07 20
Bedwyn	a									05 59	06 30												07 29
Tilehurst	d	23p44					00 27						05 50					06 25					
Pangbourne	d	23p49					00 32						05 54					06 29					
Goring & Streatley	d	23p52					00 35						05 59					06 34					
Cholsey	d	23p57					00 40						06 04		←			06 39			←		
Didcot Parkway	a	00 06			00 23	00 43	00 49		01 13				06 12	06 07	06 12			06 46	06 37		06 46		
	d	00 06				00 44	00 49		01 14				06 13	06 08	06 13			06 47	06 38		06 47		
Appleford	d						00 54						→		06 17			→					
Culham	d						00 56								06 20								
Radley	d	00 14					01 00								06 24						06 54		
Oxford	a	00 23	00 28			01 00	01 10		01 27					06 22	06 32	06 36			06 52		07 04	07 10	
	d											06 16				06 38				07 00		07 12	
Islip	d																			07 13			
Bicester Town	a																			07 25			
Tackley	d											06 25											
Heyford	d											06 29											
Kings Sutton	d											06 38											
Banbury	a											06 46				06 54						07 32	
Leamington Spa 8	a															07 12						07 50	
Coventry	a															07 24							
Birmingham International	a															07 37							
Birmingham New Street 12	a															07 48						08 17	

Table 116

London and Reading - Bedwyn, Oxford, Bicester, Banbury and Birmingham

Saturdays
from 17 September

		GW [1]	GW ◇[1]	GW [1]	GW [1]	GW ◇[1] ⊡	XC ◇[1] ⌶	GW [1]	GW ◇[1]	GW [1]	CH [1]	GW [1]	XC ◇[1] ⌶	GW [1]	GW [1]	GW ◇[1]	GW [1]	GW ■ [1] ⊡	XC ◇[1] ⌶	GW [1]	GW ◇[1]	GW [1]	XC ◇[1] ⌶
London Paddington [15] ⊖	d	05 57	06 21		06 27	06 30			06 50						06 57	07 21	07 27	07 30			07 50		
Ealing Broadway ⊖	d	06 05			06 35										07 05		07 35						
Slough [3]	d	06 31	06 38		06 57				07 06						07 27	07 38	07 57				08 06		
Maidenhead [3]	d	06 42			07 04										07 34		08 04						
Twyford [3]	d	06 50		←	07 12							←			07 42		08 12					←	
Reading [7]	d	06 56	06 54	06 56	07 23	06 59	07 11	07 11	07 22			07 23	07 47	07 48	07 53	07 53	08 23	07 57	08 11	08 18	08 22	08 23	08 40
Reading West	d	→			→			07 14									→			08 20			
Theale	d							07 20						07 57						08 27			
Aldermaston	d							07 25												08 32			
Midgham	d							07 29												08 36			
Thatcham	d							07 34						08 05						08 41			
Newbury Racecourse	d							07 38												08 45			
Newbury	a							07 43						08 11						08 50			
	d													08 11									
Kintbury	d													08 17									
Hungerford	d													08 22									
Bedwyn	a													08 31									
Tilehurst	d			07 00								07 27			07 57							08 27	
Pangbourne	d			07 04								07 31			08 01							08 31	
Goring & Streatley	d			07 09								07 36			08 06							08 36	
Cholsey	d			07 14								07 41			08 11							08 41	
Didcot Parkway	a			07 30		07 12						07 49			08 19			08 12				08 48	
	d			07 30								07 51			08 25							08 55	
Appleford	d																					09 00	
Culham	d											07 56											
Radley	d											08 00										09 03	
Oxford	a		07 18	07 44			07 34		07 48			08 10	08 13		08 41	08 19			08 34		08 48	09 15	09 04
	d						07 36			07 53	08 07		08 15						08 36				09 07
Islip	d										08 20												
Bicester Town	a										08 32												
Tackley	d									08 02													
Heyford	d									08 06													
Kings Sutton	d									08 15													
Banbury	a						07 52			08 23			08 32						08 52				09 23
Leamington Spa [8]	a						08 10						08 49						09 10				09 41
Coventry	a						08 22												09 22				
Birmingham International	a						08 37												09 37				
Birmingham New Street [12]	a						08 48						09 19						09 48				10 17

		GW [1]	GW [1]	GW ◇[1] ⊡	GW ◇[1] ⊡	GW [1]	GW ◇[1] ⊡	CH [1]	GW [1]	GW ◇[1] ⊡	XC ◇[1] ⌶	GW [1]	GW ◇[1]	GW [1]	XC ◇[1] ⌶	GW [1]	GW [1]	GW [1]	GW [1]	GW ◇[1]	GW [1]	GW ◇[1] ⊡
London Paddington [15] ⊖	d		07 57	08 15	08 18		08 21		08 27	08 30			08 50				08 57	09 18		09 21	09 27	09 30
Ealing Broadway ⊖	d		08 05						08 35								09 05				09 35	
Slough [3]	d		08 27				08 39		08 57				09 06				09 27			09 39	09 57	
Maidenhead [3]	d		08 34						09 04								09 34				10 04	
Twyford [3]	d		08 42			←			09 12					←			09 42		←		10 12	
Reading [7]	d		08 53	08 41	08 49	08 53	08 54		09 23	08 57	09 11	09 12	09 22	09 23	09 40		09 53	09 48	09 53	09 54	10 23	09 57
Reading West	d		→						→			09 14					→				→	
Theale	d				08 58							09 20						09 56				
Aldermaston	d											09 25										
Midgham	d											09 29										
Thatcham	d				09 07							09 34						10 04				
Newbury Racecourse	d											09 38										
Newbury	a				09 13							09 44						10 10				
	d	08 58			09 14													10 10				
Kintbury	d	09 04																10 17				
Hungerford	d	09 09			09 23													10 21				
Bedwyn	a	09 17			09 30													10 30				
Tilehurst	d					08 57								09 27					09 57			
Pangbourne	d					09 01								09 31					10 01			
Goring & Streatley	d					09 06								09 36					10 06			
Cholsey	d					09 11								09 41					10 11			
Didcot Parkway	a			08 54		09 19				09 12				09 48					10 18			10 12
	d					09 25								09 55					10 25			
Appleford	d																					
Culham	d													10 01								
Radley	d													10 03								
Oxford	a					09 41	09 18				09 34		09 48	10 15	10 04				10 41	10 19		
	d							09 27			09 36				10 07	10 16						
Islip	d							09 41														
Bicester Town	a							09 53														
Tackley	d															10 25						
Heyford	d															10 29						
Kings Sutton	d															10 39						
Banbury	a										09 52				10 23	10 46						
Leamington Spa [8]	a										10 11				10 41							
Coventry	a										10 22											
Birmingham International	a										10 37											
Birmingham New Street [12]	a										10 48				11 18							

Table 116

London and Reading - Bedwyn, Oxford, Bicester, Banbury and Birmingham

Saturdays
from 17 September

		XC ◇[1] ⌶	GW [1]	GW ◇[1]	CH [1]	GW [1]	XC ◇[1] ⌶	GW [1]	GW ◇[1] ⊡	GW [1]	GW [1]	GW ◇[1] ⊡	GW [1]	GW ◇[1] ⊡	XC ◇[1] ⌶	GW [1]	GW ◇[1] ⌶	GW [1]	XC ◇[1] ⌶	GW [1]	GW [1]	GW [1]	GW [1]
London Paddington [15] ⊖	d			09 50				09 57	10 15	10 18		10 21	10 27	10 30			10 50				10 57	11 18	
Ealing Broadway ⊖	d							10 05					10 35								11 05		
Slough [3]	d			10 06				10 27				10 39	10 57				11 06				11 27		
Maidenhead [3]	d							10 34					11 04								11 34		
Twyford [3]	d					←		10 42			←		11 12					←			11 42		←
Reading [7]	d	10 11	10 12	10 22		10 23	10 40	10 53	10 41	10 48	10 53	10 54	11 23	10 57	11 11	11 12	11 22	11 23	11 40		11 53	11 48	11 53
Reading West	d		10 14					→					→			11 14					→		
Theale	d		10 20							10 56						11 20						11 56	
Aldermaston	d		10 25													11 25							
Midgham	d		10 29													11 29							
Thatcham	d		10 34							11 04						11 34						12 04	
Newbury Racecourse	d		10 38													11 38							
Newbury	a		10 44							11 10						11 44						12 10	
	d									11 11												12 11	
Kintbury	d									11 17												12 17	
Hungerford	d									11 22												12 22	
Bedwyn	a									11 31												12 31	
Tilehurst	d					10 27					10 57							11 27					11 57
Pangbourne	d					10 31					11 01							11 31					12 01
Goring & Streatley	d					10 36					11 06							11 36					12 06
Cholsey	d					10 41					11 11							11 41					12 11
Didcot Parkway	a					10 48			10 54		11 19			11 12				11 49					12 19
	d					10 55					11 25							11 55					12 25
Appleford	d					11 00																	
Culham	d																						
Radley	d					11 03												12 03					
Oxford	a	10 34		10 48		11 15	11 04				11 41	11 19			11 34		11 48	12 15	12 04				12 41
	d	10 36			11 00		11 07								11 36				12 07	12 16			
Islip	d				11 13																		
Bicester Town	a				11 25																		
Tackley	d																			12 25			
Heyford	d																			12 29			
Kings Sutton	d																			12 39			
Banbury	a	10 52					11 23								11 52				12 23	12 46			
Leamington Spa [8]	a	11 10					11 41								12 10				12 41				
Coventry	a	11 22													12 22								
Birmingham International	a	11 37													12 37								
Birmingham New Street [12]	a	11 48					12 18								12 48				13 18				

		GW ◇[1] ⌶	CH [1]	GW [1]	GW ◇[1] ⊘	XC ◇[1] ⌶	GW [1]	GW ◇[1]	GW [1]	XC ◇[1] ⌶	GW [1]	GW ◇[1] ⊡	GW ◇[1] ⊡	GW [1]	GW ◇[1]	GW [1]	GW ◇[1] ⊡	XC ◇[1] ⌶	GW [1]	CH [1]	GW ◇[1] ⌶	GW [1]
London Paddington [15] ⊖	d	11 21		11 27	11 30			11 50			11 57	12 15	12 18		12 21	12 27	12 30				12 50	
Ealing Broadway ⊖	d			11 35							12 05					12 35						
Slough [3]	d	11 39		11 57				12 06			12 27				12 39	12 57					13 06	
Maidenhead [3]	d			12 04							12 34					13 04						
Twyford [3]	d			12 12					←		12 42			←		13 12						←
Reading [7]	d	11 55		12 23	11 58	12 11	12 12	12 22	12 23	12 40	12 53	12 41	12 49	12 53	12 54	13 23	12 57	13 11	13 12		13 22	13 23
Reading West	d			→			12 14				→					→			13 14			
Theale	d						12 20						12 57						13 20			
Aldermaston	d						12 25												13 25			
Midgham	d						12 29												13 29			
Thatcham	d						12 34						13 05						13 34			
Newbury Racecourse	d						12 38												13 38			
Newbury	a						12 44						13 12						13 44			
	d												13 13									
Kintbury	d																					
Hungerford	d												13 21									
Bedwyn	a												13 29									
Tilehurst	d								12 27					12 57								13 27
Pangbourne	d								12 31					13 01								13 31
Goring & Streatley	d								12 36					13 06								13 36
Cholsey	d								12 41					13 11								13 41
Didcot Parkway	a				12 12				12 48			12 54		13 19			13 12					13 48
	d								12 55					13 25								13 55
Appleford	d								13 00													
Culham	d																					14 01
Radley	d								13 03													14 03
Oxford	a	12 20				12 34		12 48	13 15	13 04				13 41	13 19			13 34			13 48	14 15
	d		12 30			12 36				13 07								13 36		13 41		
Islip	d		12 43																	13 54		
Bicester Town	a		12 55																	14 06		
Tackley	d																					
Heyford	d																					
Kings Sutton	d																					
Banbury	a					12 52				13 23								13 52				
Leamington Spa [8]	a					13 10				13 41								14 10				
Coventry	a					13 22												14 22				
Birmingham International	a					13 37												14 37				
Birmingham New Street [12]	a					13 48				14 18								14 48				

London and Reading - Bedwyn, Oxford, Bicester, Banbury and Birmingham

		XC	GW	GW	GW	GW	GW	GW	GW	XC	GW	GW	CH	GW	XC	GW	GW	GW	GW	GW	GW	GW	XC
		◇1	1	1	1	1	◇1	1	◇1	◇1	1	◇1	1	1	◇1	1	◇1	1	1	◇1	1	◇1	◇1
		⌶					⌶		⊏	⌶		⌶			⌶		⊏			⌶		⊏	⌶
London Paddington 15 ⊖	d			12 57	13 18		13 21	13 27	13 30			13 50				13 57	14 15	14 18		14 21	14 27	14 30	
Ealing Broadway ⊖	d			13 05				13 35								14 05					14 35		
Slough 3	d			13 27			13 39	13 57				14 06				14 27				14 39	14 57		
Maidenhead 3	d			13 34				14 04								14 34					15 04		
Twyford 3	d			13 42		←		14 12						←		14 42			←		15 12		
Reading 7	d	13 40		13 53	13 48	13 53	13 55	14 23	13 59	14 11	14 12	14 22		14 23	14 40	14 53	14 41	14 48	14 53	14 54	15 23	14 57	15 11
Reading West	d			→				→			14 14					→					→		
Theale	d				13 56						14 20							14 56					
Aldermaston	d										14 25												
Midgham	d										14 29												
Thatcham	d				14 04						14 34							15 04					
Newbury Racecourse	d										14 38												
Newbury	a				14 10						14 44							15 10					
	d				14 10													15 10					
Kintbury	d				14 17													15 17					
Hungerford	d				14 21													15 21					
Bedwyn	a				14 31													15 31					
Tilehurst	d					13 57								14 27					14 57				
Pangbourne	d					14 01								14 31					15 01				
Goring & Streatley	d					14 06								14 36					15 06				
Cholsey	d					14 11								14 41					15 11				
Didcot Parkway	a					14 19			14 12					14 48			14 54		15 19			15 12	
	d					14 25								14 55					15 25				
Appleford	d													15 00									
Culham	d																						
Radley	d													15 03									
Oxford	a	14 04				14 41	14 19			14 34		14 48		15 15	15 04				15 41	15 18			15 34
	d	14 07	14 16							14 36			14 57		15 07								15 36
Islip	d												15 10										
Bicester Town	a												15 22										
Tackley	d		14 25																				
Heyford	d		14 29																				
Kings Sutton	d		14 38																				
Banbury	a	14 23	14 46							14 52					15 23								15 52
Leamington Spa 3	a	14 41								15 10					15 41								16 10
Coventry	a									15 22													16 22
Birmingham International	a									15 37													16 37
Birmingham New Street 12	a	15 17								15 48					16 17								16 48

		GW	GW	CH	GW	XC	GW	GW	GW	GW	GW	GW	GW	XC	GW	GW	GW	XC	CH	GW	GW	GW	GW
		1	◇1	1	1	◇1	1	1	1	1	◇1	1	◇1	◇1	1	◇1	1	◇1	1	1	◇1	1	1
						⌶					A ⌶		⊏	⌶				⌶			⊏		
London Paddington 15 ⊖	d		14 50					14 57	15 18		15 21	15 27	15 30			15 50				15 57	16 15	16 18	
Ealing Broadway ⊖	d							15 05				15 35								16 05			
Slough 3	d		15 06					15 27			15 39	15 57				16 06				16 27			
Maidenhead 3	d							15 34				16 04								16 34			
Twyford 3	d				←			15 42		←		16 12					←			16 42			←
Reading 7	d	15 12	15 22		15 23	15 40		15 53	15 48	15 53	15 55	16 23	15 59	16 11	16 12	16 22	16 23	16 40		16 53	16 41	16 48	16 53
Reading West	d	15 14						→				→			16 14					→			
Theale	d	15 20							15 56						16 20							16 56	
Aldermaston	d	15 25													16 25								
Midgham	d	15 29													16 29								
Thatcham	d	15 34							16 04						16 34							17 04	
Newbury Racecourse	d	15 38													16 38								
Newbury	a	15 44							16 10						16 44							17 10	
	d								16 10													17 10	
Kintbury	d								16 17													17 17	
Hungerford	d								16 21													17 21	
Bedwyn	a								16 31													17 31	
Tilehurst	d				15 27					15 57							16 27						16 57
Pangbourne	d				15 31					16 01							16 31						17 01
Goring & Streatley	d				15 36					16 06							16 36						17 06
Cholsey	d				15 41					16 11							16 41						17 11
Didcot Parkway	a				15 48					16 19			16 12				16 48				16 54		17 19
	d				15 55					16 25							16 55						17 25
Appleford	d																17 00						
Culham	d				16 01																		
Radley	d				16 03												17 03						
Oxford	a		15 48		16 15	16 04				16 41	16 19			16 34		16 48	17 15	17 04					17 41
	d			16 01		16 07	16 16							16 36				17 07	17 10				
Islip	d			16 14															17 23				
Bicester Town	a			16 26															17 35				
Tackley	d						16 25																
Heyford	d						16 29																
Kings Sutton	d						16 39																
Banbury	a					16 23	16 46							16 52				17 23					
Leamington Spa 3	a					16 41								17 10				17 41					
Coventry	a													17 22									
Birmingham International	a													17 37									
Birmingham New Street 12	a					17 17								17 48				18 18					

A ⌶ to Reading

London and Reading - Bedwyn, Oxford, Bicester, Banbury and Birmingham

		GW	GW	GW	XC	GW	GW	GW	XC	GW	GW	GW	GW	GW	GW	GW	XC	GW	CH	GW	GW	XC
		◇1	1	◇1	◇1	1	◇1	1	◇1	1	1	1	1	◇1	1	◇1	◇1	1	1	◇1	1	◇1
		⊏		⊏	⌶		⌶		⌶					⊏		⊏	A ⌶			⌶		B ⌶
London Paddington 15 ⊖	d	16 21	16 27	16 30			16 50				16 57	17 18		17 21	17 27	17 30				17 50		
Ealing Broadway ⊖	d		16 35								17 05				17 35							
Slough 3	d	16 39	16 57				17 06				17 27			17 39	17 57					18 06		
Maidenhead 3	d		17 04								17 34				18 04							
Twyford 3	d		17 12					←			17 42		←		18 12						←	
Reading 7	d	16 54	17 23	16 57	17 11	17 12	17 22	17 23	17 40		17 54	17 48	17 54	17 55	18 23	17 57	18 11	18 12		18 22	18 23	18 40
Reading West	d		→			17 14					→				→			18 14				
Theale	d					17 20						17 56						18 20				
Aldermaston	d					17 25												18 25				
Midgham	d					17 29												18 29				
Thatcham	d					17 34						18 04						18 34				
Newbury Racecourse	d					17 38												18 38				
Newbury	a					17 44						18 10						18 44				
	d											18 10										
Kintbury	d											18 17										
Hungerford	d											18 21										
Bedwyn	a											18 30										
Tilehurst	d							17 27					17 57								18 27	
Pangbourne	d							17 31					18 01								18 31	
Goring & Streatley	d							17 36					18 06								18 36	
Cholsey	d							17 41					18 11								18 41	
Didcot Parkway	a			17 12				17 48					18 19			18 12					18 48	
	d							17 55					18 25								18 55	
Appleford	d																				19 00	
Culham	d							18 01														
Radley	d							18 03													19 03	
Oxford	a	17 18			17 34		17 47	18 15	18 04				18 41	18 18			18 34			18 48	19 15	19 04
	d				17 36				18 07	18 16							18 36		18 41			19 07
Islip	d																		18 54			
Bicester Town	a																		19 06			
Tackley	d									18 25												
Heyford	d									18 29												
Kings Sutton	d									18 38												
Banbury	a				17 52				18 23	18 46							18 52					19 23
Leamington Spa 3	a				18 10				18 41								19 10					19 41
Coventry	a				18 22												19 22					
Birmingham International	a				18 37												19 37					
Birmingham New Street 12	a				18 48				19 18								19 48					20 18

		GW	GW	GW	GW	GW	GW	GW	XC	GW	CH	GW	GW	GW	GW	GW	XC	GW	GW	GW	GW	GW	XC
		1	◇1	1	1	◇1	1	◇1	◇1	◇1	1	1	1	1	◇1	◇1	◇1	1	◇1	1	1	◇1	◇1
			⊏			⊏		⊏	A ⌶						⊏	⊏	⌶					⊏	
London Paddington 15 ⊖	d	17 57	18 15	18 18		18 21	18 27	18 30		18 50				18 57	19 06	19 15			19 21		19 27	19 30	
Ealing Broadway ⊖	d	18 05					18 35							19 05							19 35		
Slough 3	d	18 27				18 39	18 57			19 06				19 27					19 38		19 57		
Maidenhead 3	d	18 34					19 04							19 34							20 04		
Twyford 3	d	18 42			←		19 12						←	19 42						←	20 12		
Reading 7	d	18 53	18 41	18 48	18 53	18 54	19 23	18 57	19 11	19 23			19 23	19 53	19 32	19 41	19 40	19 49	19 52	19 53	20 23	19 57	20 11
Reading West	d	→					→							→				19 52			→		
Theale	d			18 56														19 58					
Aldermaston	d																	20 03					
Midgham	d																	20 06					
Thatcham	d			19 04														20 11					
Newbury Racecourse	d																	20 16					
Newbury	a			19 10											19 48			20 18					
	d			19 10														20 18					
Kintbury	d			19 17														20 25					
Hungerford	d			19 21														20 29					
Bedwyn	a			19 30														20 38					
Tilehurst	d				18 57								19 27							19 57			
Pangbourne	d				19 01								19 31							20 01			
Goring & Streatley	d				19 06								19 36							20 06			
Cholsey	d				19 11								19 41							20 11			
Didcot Parkway	a		18 54		19 19			19 12					19 48			19 54				20 19		20 11	
	d				19 25								19 55							20 25			
Appleford	d																						
Culham	d												20 01										
Radley	d												20 03										
Oxford	a				19 41	19 18			19 34	19 48			20 14				20 04		20 20	20 41			20 34
	d								19 36		19 48	19 56					20 07						20 36
Islip	d										20 01												
Bicester Town	a										20 13												
Tackley	d											20 05											
Heyford	d											20 09											
Kings Sutton	d											20 18											
Banbury	a								19 52			20 25					20 28						20 52
Leamington Spa 3	a								20 10								20 45						21 10
Coventry	a								20 22														21 22
Birmingham International	a								20 37														21 37
Birmingham New Street 12	a								20 48								21 18						21 48

A ⌶ to Birmingham International

B ⌶ to Leamington Spa

Table 116

Saturdays from 17 September

London and Reading - Bedwyn, Oxford, Bicester, Banbury and Birmingham

		GW	CH	GW	GW	GW	GW	GW	XC	GW	GW	GW	GW	GW	GW	XC	GW	GW	GW	GW	CH	GW
		◇1	1	1	1	◇1	◇1	◇1	◇1	1	◇1	1	1	1	◇1	◇1	◇1	1	1	◇1	1	1
		A																				
		⌶				⊐	⊐	⊐	⌶						⊐	⌶	⌶					
London Paddington 15 ⊖	d	19 50			19 57	20 00	20 06	20 15			20 20			20 27	20 30		20 50		20 57	21 17		
Ealing Broadway ⊖	d				20 05									20 35					21 05			
Slough 3	d	20 06			20 27						20 35			20 57			21 06		21 27	21 35		
Maidenhead 3	d				20 34									21 04					21 34			
Twyford 3	d			←	20 42								←	21 12				←	21 42			←
Reading 7	d	20 22		20 23	20 53	20 27	20 33	20 41	20 40	20 49	20 51		20 53	21 23	20 57	21 11	21 22	21 23	21 53	21 52		21 53
Reading West	d				→					20 52				→					→			
Theale	d									20 58												
Aldermaston	d									21 03												
Midgham	d									21 06												
Thatcham	d									21 11												
Newbury Racecourse	d									21 16												
Newbury	a						20 47			21 18												
	d									21 32												
Kintbury	d									21 39												
Hungerford	d									21 43												
Bedwyn	a									21 52												
Tilehurst	d			20 27									20 57					21 27				21 57
Pangbourne	d			20 32									21 01					21 31				22 01
Goring & Streatley	d			20 37									21 06					21 36				22 06
Cholsey	d			20 42									21 11					21 41				22 11
Didcot Parkway	a			20 49		20 41		20 54					21 19		21 12		21 39	21 48		22 07		22 19
	d			20 55									21 25				21 40	21 55		22 08		22 25
Appleford	d			21 00																		
Culham	d																	22 01				
Radley	d			21 03														22 03				22 34
Oxford	a	20 47		21 14					21 04		21 19		21 41			21 34	21 53	22 15		22 20		22 44
	d		21 00						21 07			21 20				21 36					22 25	
Islip	d		21 13																		22 38	
Bicester Town	a		21 25																		22 50	
Tackley	d											21 29										
Heyford	d											21 33										
Kings Sutton	d											21 42										
Banbury	a								21 23			21 49				21 52						
Leamington Spa 8	a								21 44							22 10						
Coventry	a								21 55							22 22						
Birmingham International	a								22 10							22 36						
Birmingham New Street 12	a								22 22							22 48						

		GW	GW	GW	GW	GW	GW	GW	GW	GW	GW	GW	GW	GW	GW	GW	GW
		◇1	1	◇1	1	◇1	◇1	1	◇1	1		1	◇1	1	1	◇1	1
											🚌						
		⊐				⊐			⊐							⊐	
London Paddington 15 ⊖	d	21 30		21 50	21 57	22 00	22 15		22 35			22 45	23 00		23 20	23 30	
Ealing Broadway ⊖	d				22 05							22 55			23 28		
Slough 3	d			22 06	22 27		22 32					23 21	23 17		23 54		
Maidenhead 3	d				22 34							23 32			00 05		
Twyford 3	d				22 42			←				23 39		←	00 13		←
Reading 7	d	21 57	22 03	22 22	22 53	22 27	22 51	22 53	23 02	23 12		23 49	23 34	23 49	00 20	23 59	00 20
Reading West	d		22 06		→					23 14		→			→		
Theale	d		22 12							23 20							
Aldermaston	d		22 17							23 25							
Midgham	d		22 20							23 29							
Thatcham	d		22 25							23 34							
Newbury Racecourse	d		22 30							23 38							
Newbury	a		22 32							23 41							
	d		22 32							23 41							
Kintbury	d		22 39							23 48							
Hungerford	d		22 43							23 52							
Bedwyn	a		22 51							00 01							
Tilehurst	d							22 57						23 53			00 24
Pangbourne	d							23 01						23 58			
Goring & Streatley	d							23 06						00 03			00 31
Cholsey	d							23 11						00 08			00 36
Didcot Parkway	a	22 12		22 37		22 41	23 06	23 19	23 21				23 51	00 17		00 18	00 47
	d			22 37			23 07	23 20									
Appleford	d																
Culham	d																
Radley	d							23 27									
Oxford	a			22 49			23 20	23 37									
	d										23 47						
Islip	d																
Bicester Town	a																
Tackley	d										00s06						
Heyford	d										00s20						
Kings Sutton	d																
Banbury	a										00 45						
Leamington Spa 8	a																
Coventry	a																
Birmingham International	a																
Birmingham New Street 12	a																

A ⌶ to Reading

Table 116

Sundays until 19 June

London and Reading - Bedwyn, Oxford, Bicester, Banbury and Birmingham

		GW	GW	GW	GW	GW	GW	GW	GW	GW	GW	GW	GW	GW	GW	GW	CH	GW	GW	XC	GW	GW	GW
		1		1	◇1	1	1	◇1	◇1	1	1		1	◇1		◇1	1	1	◇1	◇1	◇1	1	1
		A	A	A	A	A	A	A	A		A												
			🚌					⊐						⊐		⌶			⊐	⌶			
London Paddington 15 ⊖	d			22p45	23p00		23p20	23p30	23p33				07 28	08 00		08 03			08 30		08 42		08 43
Ealing Broadway ⊖	d			22p55			23p28						07 36										08 50
Slough 3	d			23p21	23p17		23p54		23p50				07 58			08 25					09 01		09 21
Maidenhead 3	d			23p32			00 05						08 08			08 33							09 31
Twyford 3	d			23p39		←	00 13				←		08 16					←					09 39
Reading 7	d	23p12		23p49	23p34	23p49	00 20	23p59	00 08	00 15	00 20	08 14	08 51	08 38	08 44	08 47		08 51	09 11	09 11	09 23		09 47
Reading West	d	23p14		→			→			00s18		08 17	→										→
Theale	d	23p20								00s24		08 23			08 51								
Aldermaston	d	23p25								00s29		08 28											
Midgham	d	23p29								00s32		08 31											
Thatcham	d	23p34								00s37		08 36			09 00								
Newbury Racecourse	d	23p38								00s42													
Newbury	a	23p41								00 45		08 43			09 05								
	d	23p41													09 06								
Kintbury	d	23p48													09 12								
Hungerford	d	23p52													09 17								
Bedwyn	a	00 01													09 24								
Tilehurst	d					23p53					00 24							08 55					
Pangbourne	d					23p58												09 00					
Goring & Streatley	d					00 03					00 31							09 05					
Cholsey	d					00 08					00 36							09 11					
Didcot Parkway	a				23p51	00 14		00 18	00 22		00 44			08 52		09 02		09 16	09 26		09 38		
	d				23p51	00 15			00 24		00 45					09 04		09 27			09 39		
Appleford	d										00s49												
Culham	d										00s51												
Radley	d					00s22					00s55							09 34					
Oxford	a				00 03	00 32			00 38		01 05					09 15		09 43		09 34	09 53		
	d		23p47														09 36			09 37		10 00	
Islip	d																09 49						
Bicester Town	a																10 01						
Tackley	d		00s06																			10 09	
Heyford	d		00s20																			10 13	
Kings Sutton	d																					10 22	
Banbury	a		00 45																	09 53		10 30	
Leamington Spa 8	a																						
Coventry	a																						
Birmingham International	a																						
Birmingham New Street 12	a																						

		GW	GW	GW	GW	GW	XC	GW	CH	GW	GW	GW	GW	GW	XC	GW	GW	GW	GW	GW	GW	CH	XC
		◇1	◇1	1	1	◇1	◇1	◇1	1	1	◇1	1	1	◇1	◇1	◇1	1	◇1	1	1	◇1	1	◇1
		⊐	⊐			⊐	⌶	⊐			⊐			⊐	⌶	⊐		⊐			⊐		⌶
London Paddington 15 ⊖	d	08 57	09 00		09 04	09 30		09 35		09 43	10 00		10 04	10 30		10 42	10 43	11 00		11 04	11 30		
Ealing Broadway ⊖	d									09 50							10 50						
Slough 3	d				09 26			09 55		10 22			10 26			10 59	11 22			11 26			
Maidenhead 3	d				09 35					10 32			10 34				11 31			11 35			
Twyford 3	d			←						10 40		←					11 39		←				
Reading 7	d	09 34	09 38	09 47	09 49	10 06	10 11	10 15		10 47	10 38	10 47	10 51	11 05	11 11	11 22	11 47	11 38	11 47	11 50	12 06		12 11
Reading West	d				09 52					→			10 54				→						
Theale	d				09 58								11 00							11 57			
Aldermaston	d				10 03								11 05										
Midgham	d				10 06								11 08										
Thatcham	d				10 11								11 13							12 06			
Newbury Racecourse	d												11 18										
Newbury	a	09 50			10 17								11 22							12 11			
	d				10 17															12 12			
Kintbury	d				10 23															12 18			
Hungerford	d				10 28															12 23			
Bedwyn	a				10 37															12 32			
Tilehurst	d			09 51								10 51							11 51				
Pangbourne	d			09 56								10 57							11 56				
Goring & Streatley	d			10 01								11 02							12 01				
Cholsey	d			10 06								11 07							12 06				
Didcot Parkway	a		09 52	10 13		10 21		10 29			10 52	11 14		11 19		11 36		11 52	12 13		12 19		
	d			10 14				10 29				11 14				11 37			12 14				
Appleford	d			10 18																			
Culham	d																						
Radley	d			10 23								11 21							12 21				
Oxford	a			10 31			10 35	10 43				11 31			11 35	11 50			12 32				12 35
	d						10 37		10 56						11 37							12 33	12 37
Islip	d								11 09													12 46	
Bicester Town	a								11 21													12 58	
Tackley	d																						
Heyford	d																						
Kings Sutton	d																						
Banbury	a						10 53								11 53								12 53
Leamington Spa 8	a																						
Coventry	a																						
Birmingham International	a																						
Birmingham New Street 12	a																						

A not 22 May

London and Reading - Bedwyn, Oxford, Bicester, Banbury and Birmingham

		GW	GW	GW	GW	GW	GW	GW	XC	GW	CH	GW	GW	GW	GW	GW	GW	XC	GW	GW	GW	GW
		◇[1]	[1]	◇[1] ☕	◇[1] ☕	[1]	[1]	◇[1] ☕	◇[1] 🛒	◇[1] ☕	[1]	[1]	[1]	◇[1] ☕	[1]	[1]	◇[1] ☕	◇[1] 🛒	◇[1] ☕	[1]	◇[1] ☕	◇[1] ☕
London Paddington [15] ⊖	d	11 42	11 43	11 57	12 00		12 04	12 30		12 42			12 43	13 00		13 04	13 37		13 42	13 43	13 57	14 00
Ealing Broadway ⊖	d		11 50										12 50							13 50		
Slough [3]	d	12 01	12 22				12 26			12 59			13 22			13 26			14 01	14 22		
Maidenhead [3]	d		12 31				12 36						13 31			13 34				14 32		
Twyford [3]	d		12 39			←							13 39		←					14 40		
Reading [7]	d	12 24	12 47	12 34	12 38	12 47	12 51	13 05	13 11	13 22			13 47	13 38	13 47	13 50	14 12	14 11	14 23	14 47	14 34	14 38
Reading West	d		→				12 54						→							→		
Theale	d						13 00									13 57						
Aldermaston	d						13 05															
Midgham	d						13 09															
Thatcham	d						13 14									14 06						
Newbury Racecourse	d						13 18															
Newbury	a			12 49			13 22									14 11					14 49	
	d															14 12						
Kintbury	d															14 18						
Hungerford	d															14 23						
Bedwyn	a															14 32						
Tilehurst	d					12 50									13 50							
Pangbourne	d					12 56									13 55							
Goring & Streatley	d					13 01									14 00							
Cholsey	d					13 06									14 05							
Didcot Parkway	a	12 39			12 52	13 12		13 19		13 36				13 52	14 12		14 26		14 38			14 52
	d	12 40				13 13				13 37					14 13				14 39			
Appleford	d					13 18																
Culham	d																					
Radley	d					13 22									14 20							
Oxford	a	12 52				13 31			13 35	13 51					14 30			14 35	14 53			
	d								13 37		13 56	14 20						14 37				
Islip	d										14 09											
Bicester Town	a										14 21											
Tackley	d											14 29										
Heyford	d											14 33										
Kings Sutton	d											14 42										
Banbury	a								13 53			14 50						14 53				
Leamington Spa [8]	a																	15 11				
Coventry	a																	15 22				
Birmingham International	a																	15 35				
Birmingham New Street [12]	a																	15 48				

		XC	GW	GW	CH	XC	GW	GW	GW	GW	XC	GW	GW	XC	GW	GW	CH	GW	GW	GW	XC	GW	GW
		◇[1] 🛒	[1]	[1]	[1]	◇[1] 🛒	◇[1] ☕	◇[1] 🛒	[1]	◇[1] ☕	◇[1] 🛒	[1]	[1]	◇[1] 🛒	◇[1] ☕	◇[1] ☕	[1]	[1]	◇[1] ☕	◇[1] ☕	◇[1] 🛒	[1]	[1]
London Paddington [15] ⊖	d			14 02			14 37	14 42	14 43	15 00			15 04		15 37	15 42		15 43	15 57	16 00			
Ealing Broadway ⊖	d								14 50									15 50					
Slough [3]	d			14 26				15 02	15 21				15 25			16 01		16 21					
Maidenhead [3]	d			14 35					15 31				15 35					16 31					
Twyford [3]	d		←						15 39			←						16 39					←
Reading [7]	d	14 40	14 47	14 50		15 11	15 17	15 22	15 46	15 38	15 40	15 46	15 50	16 11	16 18	16 21		16 46	16 34	16 38	16 40		16 46
Reading West	d			14 53					→									→					
Theale	d			14 59									15 57										
Aldermaston	d			15 04																			
Midgham	d			15 08																			
Thatcham	d			15 13									16 06										
Newbury Racecourse	d			15 17																			
Newbury	a			15 21									16 11						16 49				
	d												16 12										
Kintbury	d												16 18										
Hungerford	d												16 23										
Bedwyn	a												16 32										
Tilehurst	d		14 51									15 50											16 50
Pangbourne	d		14 56									15 55											16 55
Goring & Streatley	d		15 01									16 00											17 00
Cholsey	d		15 06									16 05											17 05
Didcot Parkway	a		15 13				15 30	15 36		15 52		16 12			16 31	16 37				16 52			17 12
	d		15 14					15 37				16 13				16 37							17 13
Appleford	d		15 18																				
Culham	d																						
Radley	d		15 23									16 20											17 20
Oxford	a	15 03	15 31			15 35		15 51			16 03	16 28		16 35		16 51					17 03		17 28
	d	15 06			15 33	15 37					16 06			16 37			16 56				17 06	17 19	
Islip	d				15 46												17 09						
Bicester Town	a				15 58												17 21						
Tackley	d																					17 28	
Heyford	d																					17 32	
Kings Sutton	d																					17 41	
Banbury	a	15 23				15 53					16 23			16 53							17 23	17 47	
Leamington Spa [8]	a	15 41				16 11					16 41			17 11							17 41		
Coventry	a					16 22								17 22									
Birmingham International	a					16 35								17 35									
Birmingham New Street [12]	a	16 12				16 48					17 12			17 48							18 11		

London and Reading - Bedwyn, Oxford, Bicester, Banbury and Birmingham

		GW	XC	GW	GW	XC	GW	GW	GW	GW	XC	GW	CH	GW	GW	GW	GW	XC	GW	GW	XC	GW
		[1]	◇[1] 🛒	◇[1] ☕	◇[1] 🛒	◇[1] 🛒	[1]	◇[1] ☕	[1]	[1]	◇[1] A 🛒	◇[1] ☕	[1]	◇[1] 🛒	[1]	◇[1] ☕	◇[1] ☕	◇[1] 🛒	[1]	[1]	◇[1] A 🛒	◇[1] ☕
London Paddington [15] ⊖	d	16 02		16 37	16 42		16 43	17 00		17 04		17 37		17 42	17 43	17 57	18 00			18 12		18 37
Ealing Broadway ⊖	d						16 50								17 50							
Slough [3]	d	16 25			17 01		17 21			17 25				18 01	18 22					18 30		
Maidenhead [3]	d	16 34					17 31			17 34					18 31					18 42		
Twyford [3]	d						17 39		←						18 39				←			
Reading [7]	d	16 49	17 11	17 14	17 22	17 40	17 46	17 40	17 46	17 51	18 11	18 17		18 21	18 47	18 34	18 38	18 40	18 47	18 57	19 11	19 15
Reading West	d	16 52					→								→					19 00		
Theale	d	16 58								17 58										19 06		
Aldermaston	d	17 03																		19 11		
Midgham	d	17 07																		19 15		
Thatcham	d	17 12								18 07										19 20		
Newbury Racecourse	d	17 16																		19 24		
Newbury	a	17 20								18 12						18 49				19 29		
	d									18 13												
Kintbury	d									18 19												
Hungerford	d									18 24												
Bedwyn	a									18 33												
Tilehurst	d								17 50										18 51			
Pangbourne	d								17 55										18 56			
Goring & Streatley	d								18 00										19 01			
Cholsey	d								18 05										19 06			
Didcot Parkway	a			17 28	17 37			17 52	18 12			18 30		18 36			18 52		19 13			19 29
	d				17 37				18 13					18 36					19 14			
Appleford	d								18 17													
Culham	d																					
Radley	d								18 22										19 21			
Oxford	a		17 35		17 51	18 03			18 30		18 35			18 51				19 03	19 29		19 35	
	d		17 37			18 06					18 37		18 35					19 06			19 37	
Islip	d												18 48									
Bicester Town	a												19 00									
Tackley	d																					
Heyford	d																					
Kings Sutton	d																					
Banbury	a		17 53			18 23					18 53							19 23			19 53	
Leamington Spa [8]	a		18 11			18 41					19 11							19 41			20 11	
Coventry	a		18 22								19 22							19 53			20 22	
Birmingham International	a		18 35								19 35							20 03			20 35	
Birmingham New Street [12]	a		18 48			19 11					19 48							20 15			20 48	

		GW	CH	GW	GW	XC	GW	GW	XC	GW	GW	GW	GW	GW	XC	GW	GW	CH	XC	GW	GW	GW	GW
		◇[1] ☕	[1]	[1]	◇[1] ☕	◇[1] 🛒	[1]	[1]	◇[1]	◇[1] ☕	◇[1] ☕	[1]	◇[1] ☕	◇[1] ☕	◇[1]	[1]	[1]	[1]	◇[1]	◇[1] ☕	◇[1]	[1]	◇[1] ☕
London Paddington [15] ⊖	d	18 42		18 43	19 00			19 04		19 37	19 42	19 43	19 57	20 00						20 37	20 42	20 43	21 00
Ealing Broadway ⊖	d			18 50								19 50										20 50	
Slough [3]	d	19 01		19 22				19 25			19 59	20 22									21 03	21 22	
Maidenhead [3]	d			19 31				19 35				20 31										21 32	
Twyford [3]	d			19 39			←					20 40					←					21 40	
Reading [7]	d	19 24		19 47	19 38	19 40	19 47	19 51	20 11	20 17	20 22	20 47	20 34	20 38	20 40	20 44	20 47		21 11	21 16	21 23	21 49	21 38
Reading West	d			→								→				20 47						→	
Theale	d							19 59								20 53							
Aldermaston	d															20 58							
Midgham	d															21 01							
Thatcham	d							20 07								21 06							
Newbury Racecourse	d															21 11							
Newbury	a							20 13					20 49			21 15							
	d							20 13															
Kintbury	d							20 20															
Hungerford	d							20 24															
Bedwyn	a							20 34															
Tilehurst	d						19 51										20 51						
Pangbourne	d						19 56										20 56						
Goring & Streatley	d						20 01										21 01						
Cholsey	d						20 06										21 06						
Didcot Parkway	a	19 37			19 52		20 13			20 31	20 36			20 52			21 13			21 29	21 38		21 52
	d	19 38					20 14				20 37						21 14				21 39		
Appleford	d																						
Culham	d																						
Radley	d						20 21										21 21						
Oxford	a	19 52				20 03	20 30		20 35		20 51				21 03		21 32		21 35		21 51		
	d		19 56			20 06			20 37						21 06			21 33	21 37				
Islip	d		20 09															21 46					
Bicester Town	a		20 21															21 58					
Tackley	d																						
Heyford	d																						
Kings Sutton	d																						
Banbury	a					20 24			20 53						21 23				21 53				
Leamington Spa [8]	a					20 41			21 11						21 41				22 11				
Coventry	a					20 53			21 22						21 53				22 22				
Birmingham International	a					21 03			21 35						22 03				22 32				
Birmingham New Street [12]	a					21 15			21 48						22 15				22 42				

A 🛒 to Birmingham International

Table 116

London and Reading - Bedwyn, Oxford, Bicester, Banbury and Birmingham

Sundays until 19 June

Station		XC ◇1	GW 1	GW 1	GW ◇1 🍴	GW ◇1	GW 1	GW ◇1 🍴	GW 1	GW 1	GW 1 A	GW 🚌	GW ◇1	GW 🚌	GW 1	GW ◇1 🍴	GW ◇1 🍴
London Paddington 15 ⊖	d				21 37	21 42	21 43	22 03			22 15		22 42		22 43	23 03	23 37
Ealing Broadway ⊖	d						21 50				22 24				22 50		
Slough 3	d					22 00	22 23				22 46		23 01		23 16		
Maidenhead 3	d						22 33				22 56				23 24		
Twyford 3	d			←			22 41			←	23 04				23 33		
Reading 7	d	21 40	21 44	21 49	22 15	22 24	22 49	22 42	22 44	22 49	23 12		23 21		23 53	23 47	00 15
Reading West	d						→		22 47		23 15						
Theale	d		21 51						22 53		23 21						
Aldermaston	d								22 58								
Midgham	d								23 01								
Thatcham	d		22 00						23 06		23 30						
Newbury Racecourse	d								23 11								
Newbury	a		22 05						23 15		23 37						
	d		22 06														
Kintbury	d		22 12														
Hungerford	d		22 17														
Bedwyn	a		22 25														
Tilehurst	d			21 53						22 53					23 57		
Pangbourne	d			21 57						22 59					00 01		
Goring & Streatley	d			22 02						23 03					00 07		
Cholsey	d			22 07						23 08					00 12		
Didcot Parkway	a			22 14	22 30	22 40		22 57		23 18			23 36		00 18	00s02	00s32
	d			22 15		22 40						23 27		23 45			
Appleford	d																
Culham	d																
Radley	d			22 22								23 42					
Oxford	a	22 03		22 30		22 52						23 57		00 10			
	d	22 06															
Islip	d																
Bicester Town	a																
Tackley	d																
Heyford	d																
Kings Sutton	d																
Banbury	a	22 23															
Leamington Spa 8	a	22 41															
Coventry	a	22 53															
Birmingham International	a	23 03															
Birmingham New Street 12	a	23 14															

Sundays 26 June to 31 July

Station		GW 1	GW 🚌	GW 1	GW ◇1	GW 1	GW 1	GW ◇1 🍴	GW ◇1	GW 1	GW 1	GW	GW 1	GW ◇1 🍴	GW ◇1 🍴	GW	GW ◇1 🛒	CH 1	GW 1	XC ◇1 🛒	GW ◇1	GW 1	GW 1
London Paddington 15 ⊖	d			22p45	23p00		23p20	23p30	23p33				07 28	07 57	08 00		08 03				08 42		08 43
Ealing Broadway ⊖	d			22p55			23p28						07 36										08 50
Slough 3	d			23p21	23p17		23p54		23p50				07 58				08 25				09 01		09 21
Maidenhead 3	d			23p32			00 05						08 08				08 33						09 31
Twyford 3	d			23p39		←	00 13				←		08 16						←				09 39
Reading 7	d	23p12		23p49	23p34	23p49	00 20	23p59	00 08	00 15	00 20	08 14	08 51	08 34	08 38	08 44	08 47		08 51	09 11	09 23		09 47
Reading West	d	23p14		→			→			00s18		08 17	→										→
Theale	d	23p20								00s24		08 23				08 51							
Aldermaston	d	23p25								00s29		08 28											
Midgham	d	23p29								00s32		08 31											
Thatcham	d	23p34								00s37		08 36				09 00							
Newbury Racecourse	d	23p38								00s42													
Newbury	a	23p41								00 45		08 43				09 05							
	d	23p41														09 06							
Kintbury	d	23p48														09 12							
Hungerford	d	23p52														09 17							
Bedwyn	a	00 01														09 24							
Tilehurst	d					23p53					00 24								08 55				
Pangbourne	d					23p58													09 00				
Goring & Streatley	d					00 03					00 31								09 05				
Cholsey	d					00 08					00 36								09 11				
Didcot Parkway	a				23p51	00 14		00 18	00 22		00 44			08 50	08 52		09 02		09 16		09 38		
	d				23p51	00 15			00 24		00 45						09 04		09 27		09 39		
Appleford	d										00s49												
Culham	d										00s51												
Radley	d					00s22					00s55								09 34				
Oxford	a				00 03	00 32			00 38		01 05						09 15		09 43	09 34	09 53		
	d		23p47															09 36		09 37		10 00	
Islip	d																	09 49					
Bicester Town	a																	10 01					
Tackley	d		00s06																			10 09	
Heyford	d		00s20																			10 13	
Kings Sutton	d																					10 22	
Banbury	a		00 45																	09 53		10 30	
Leamington Spa 8	a																			10 11			
Coventry	a																			10 22			
Birmingham International	a																			10 38			
Birmingham New Street 12	a																			10 50			

A 1 to Twyford

Table 116

London and Reading - Bedwyn, Oxford, Bicester, Banbury and Birmingham

Sundays 26 June to 31 July

Station		GW ◇1 🍴	GW ◇1 🍴	GW 1	GW 1	GW ◇1 🍴	XC ◇1 🛒	GW ◇1 🍴	CH 1	GW 1	GW ◇1 🍴	GW 1	GW 1	GW ◇1 🍴	XC ◇1 🛒	GW ◇1 🍴	GW 1	GW ◇1 🍴	GW 1	GW 1	GW ◇1 🍴	CH 1	XC ◇1 🛒
London Paddington 15 ⊖	d	08 57	09 00		09 04	09 30		09 35		09 43	10 00		10 04	10 30		10 42	10 43	11 00		11 04	11 30		
Ealing Broadway ⊖	d									09 50							10 50						
Slough 3	d				09 26			09 55		10 22			10 26			10 59	11 22			11 26			
Maidenhead 3	d				09 35					10 32			10 34				11 31			11 35			
Twyford 3	d			←						10 40		←					11 39		←				
Reading 7	d	09 34	09 38	09 47	09 49	10 05	10 11	10 15		10 47	10 38	10 47	10 51	11 05	11 11	11 22	11 47	11 38	11 47	11 50	12 06		12 11
Reading West	d				09 52					→			10 54				→						
Theale	d				09 58								11 00							11 57			
Aldermaston	d				10 03								11 05										
Midgham	d				10 06								11 08										
Thatcham	d				10 11								11 13							12 06			
Newbury Racecourse	d												11 18										
Newbury	a	09 50			10 17								11 22							12 11			
	d				10 17															12 12			
Kintbury	d				10 23															12 18			
Hungerford	d				10 28															12 23			
Bedwyn	a				10 37															12 32			
Tilehurst	d			09 51								10 51							11 51				
Pangbourne	d			09 56								10 57							11 56				
Goring & Streatley	d			10 01								11 02							12 01				
Cholsey	d			10 06								11 07							12 06				
Didcot Parkway	a		09 52	10 13		10 19		10 29			10 52	11 14		11 19		11 36		11 52	12 13		12 19		
	d			10 14				10 29				11 14				11 37			12 14				
Appleford	d			10 18																			
Culham	d																						
Radley	d			10 23								11 21							12 21				
Oxford	a			10 31			10 35	10 43				11 31			11 35	11 50			12 32				12 35
	d						10 37		10 56						11 37							12 33	12 37
Islip	d								11 09													12 46	
Bicester Town	a								11 21													12 58	
Tackley	d																						
Heyford	d																						
Kings Sutton	d																						
Banbury	a						10 53								11 53								12 53
Leamington Spa 8	a						11 11								12 11								13 11
Coventry	a						11 22								12 22								13 22
Birmingham International	a						11 38								12 38								13 37
Birmingham New Street 12	a						11 50								12 50								13 48

Station		GW ◇1	GW 1	GW ◇1 🍴	GW ◇1 🍴	GW 1	GW 1	XC ◇1 🛒	GW ◇1 🍴	XC ◇1 🛒	GW ◇1 🍴	CH 1	GW 1	GW ◇1 🍴	XC ◇1 🛒	GW 1	GW 1	GW 1	GW ◇1 🍴	XC ◇1 🛒	GW ◇1 🍴	GW 1
London Paddington 15 ⊖	d	11 42	11 43	11 57	12 00		12 04		12 30		12 42		12 43	13 00				13 04	13 30		13 42	13 43
Ealing Broadway ⊖	d		11 50										12 50									13 50
Slough 3	d	12 01	12 22				12 26				12 59		13 22					13 26			14 01	14 22
Maidenhead 3	d		12 31				12 36						13 31					13 34				14 32
Twyford 3	d		12 39			←							13 39				←					14 40
Reading 7	d	12 24	12 47	12 34	12 38	12 47	12 51	12 54	13 05	13 11	13 22		13 47	13 38	13 40		13 47	13 50	14 05	14 11	14 23	14 47
Reading West	d		→				12 54						→									→
Theale	d						13 00											13 57				
Aldermaston	d						13 05															
Midgham	d						13 09															
Thatcham	d						13 14											14 06				
Newbury Racecourse	d						13 18															
Newbury	a			12 49			13 22											14 11				
	d																	14 12				
Kintbury	d																	14 18				
Hungerford	d																	14 23				
Bedwyn	a																	14 32				
Tilehurst	d					12 50											13 50					
Pangbourne	d					12 56											13 55					
Goring & Streatley	d					13 01											14 00					
Cholsey	d					13 06											14 05					
Didcot Parkway	a	12 39			12 52	13 12			13 19		13 36			13 52			14 12		14 19		14 38	
	d	12 40				13 13					13 37						14 13				14 39	
Appleford	d					13 18																
Culham	d																					
Radley	d					13 22											14 20					
Oxford	a	12 52				13 31		13 15		13 35	13 51				14 03		14 30			14 35	14 53	
	d							13 17		13 37		13 56			14 06	14 20				14 37		
Islip	d											14 09										
Bicester Town	a											14 21										
Tackley	d															14 29						
Heyford	d															14 33						
Kings Sutton	d															14 42						
Banbury	a							13 33		13 53					14 23	14 50				14 53		
Leamington Spa 8	a							13 51		14 11					14 41					15 11		
Coventry	a									14 22										15 22		
Birmingham International	a									14 35										15 35		
Birmingham New Street 12	a							14 19		14 48					15 13					15 48		

London and Reading - Bedwyn, Oxford, Bicester, Banbury and Birmingham

		GW	GW	XC	GW	GW	GW	CH	XC	GW	GW	GW	XC	GW	GW	GW	XC	GW	CH	GW	GW	GW	XC
		◇1 ⊐	◇1 ⊐	◇1 ⌶	1	1	◇1 ⊐	1	◇1 ⌶	◇1 ⌶	1	◇1 ⊐	◇1 ⌶	1	1	◇1 ⊐	◇1 ⌶	◇1 ⊐	1	1	◇1 ⊐	◇1 ⊐	◇1 ⌶
London Paddington 15 ⊖	d	13 57	14 00			14 02	14 30			14 42	14 43	15 00			15 04	15 30		15 42		15 43	15 57	16 00	
Ealing Broadway ⊖	d										14 50									15 50			
Slough 3	d					14 26				15 02	15 21				15 25			16 01		16 21			
Maidenhead 3	d					14 35					15 31				15 35					16 31			
Twyford 3	d				←						15 39			←						16 39			
Reading 7	d	14 34	14 38	14 40	14 47	14 50	15 10		15 11	15 22	15 46 →	15 38	15 40	15 46	15 50	16 05	16 11	16 21		16 46 →	16 34	16 38	16 40
Reading West	d					14 53																	
Theale	d					14 59									15 57								
Aldermaston	d					15 04																	
Midgham	d					15 08																	
Thatcham	d					15 13									16 06								
Newbury Racecourse	d					15 17																	
Newbury	a	14 49				15 21									16 11						16 49		
	d														16 12								
Kintbury	d														16 18								
Hungerford	d														16 23								
Bedwyn	a														16 32								
Tilehurst	d				14 51									15 50									
Pangbourne	d				14 56									15 55									
Goring & Streatley	d				15 01									16 00									
Cholsey	d				15 06									16 05									
Didcot Parkway	a		14 52		15 13		15 23			15 36		15 52		16 12		16 19		16 37				16 52	
	d				15 14					15 37				16 13				16 37					
Appleford	d				15 18																		
Culham	d																						
Radley	d				15 23									16 20									
Oxford	a			15 03	15 31				15 35	15 51			16 03	16 28			16 35	16 51					17 03
	d			15 06				15 33	15 37				16 06				16 37		16 56				17 06
Islip	d							15 46											17 09				
Bicester Town	a							15 58											17 21				
Tackley	d																						
Heyford	d																						
Kings Sutton	d																						
Banbury	a			15 23					15 53				16 23				16 53						17 23
Leamington Spa 8	a			15 41					16 11				16 41				17 11						17 41
Coventry	a								16 22								17 22						
Birmingham International	a								16 35								17 35						
Birmingham New Street 12	a			16 12					16 48				17 12				17 48						18 09

		GW	GW	GW	GW	XC	GW	XC	GW	GW	GW	GW	GW	XC	CH	GW	GW	GW	GW	XC	GW	GW
		1	1	1	◇1 ⊐	◇1 ⌶	◇1 ⌶	◇1 ⌶	1	◇1 ⊐	1	1	◇1 ⊐	◇1 A ⌶	1	◇1 ⌶	1	◇1 ⊐	◇1 ⊐	◇1 ⌶	1	1
London Paddington 15 ⊖	d			16 02	16 30		16 42		16 43	17 00		17 04	17 30			17 42	17 43	17 57	18 00			18 12
Ealing Broadway ⊖	d								16 50								17 50					
Slough 3	d			16 25			17 01		17 21			17 25				18 01	18 22					18 30
Maidenhead 3	d			16 34					17 31			17 34					18 31					18 42
Twyford 3	d		←						17 39		←						18 39				←	
Reading 7	d		16 46	16 49	17 10	17 11	17 22	17 40	17 46 →	17 40	17 46	17 51	18 05	18 11		18 21	18 47 →	18 34	18 38	18 40	18 47	18 57
Reading West	d			16 52																		19 00
Theale	d			16 58								17 58										19 06
Aldermaston	d			17 03																		19 11
Midgham	d			17 07																		19 15
Thatcham	d			17 12								18 07										19 20
Newbury Racecourse	d			17 16																		19 24
Newbury	a			17 20								18 12						18 49				19 29
	d											18 13										
Kintbury	d											18 19										
Hungerford	d											18 24										
Bedwyn	a											18 33										
Tilehurst	d		16 50								17 50										18 51	
Pangbourne	d		16 55								17 55										18 56	
Goring & Streatley	d		17 00								18 00										19 01	
Cholsey	d		17 05								18 05										19 06	
Didcot Parkway	a		17 12		17 23		17 37			17 52	18 12		18 19			18 36			18 52		19 13	
	d		17 13				17 37				18 13					18 36					19 14	
Appleford	d										18 17											
Culham	d																					
Radley	d		17 20								18 22										19 21	
Oxford	a		17 28			17 35	17 51	18 03			18 30			18 35		18 51				19 03	19 29	
	d	17 19				17 37		18 06						18 37	18 35					19 06		
Islip	d														18 48							
Bicester Town	a														19 00							
Tackley	d	17 28																				
Heyford	d	17 32																				
Kings Sutton	d	17 41																				
Banbury	a	17 47				17 53		18 23						18 53						19 23		
Leamington Spa 8	a					18 11		18 41						19 11						19 41		
Coventry	a					18 22								19 22						19 53		
Birmingham International	a					18 35								19 35						20 03		
Birmingham New Street 12	a					18 48		19 11						19 48						20 15		

A ⌶ to Birmingham International

Table 116

Sundays
26 June to 31 July

London and Reading - Bedwyn, Oxford, Bicester, Banbury and Birmingham

		XC	GW	GW	CH	GW	GW	XC	GW	GW	GW	XC	GW	GW	GW	GW	XC	GW	GW	GW	CH	XC	GW
		◇1 A ⌶	◇1 ⊐	◇1 ⊐	1	1	◇1 ⊐	◇1 ⌶	1	1	◇1 ⊐	◇1	◇1 ⊐	1	◇1 ⊐	◇1 ⊐	◇1	1	1	◇1 ⊐	1	◇1	◇1
London Paddington 15 ⊖	d		18 30	18 42		18 43	19 00			19 04	19 30		19 42	19 43	19 57	20 00				20 30			20 42
Ealing Broadway ⊖	d					18 50								19 50									
Slough 3	d			19 01		19 22				19 25			19 59	20 22									21 03
Maidenhead 3	d					19 31				19 35				20 31									
Twyford 3	d					19 39			←					20 40					←				
Reading 7	d	19 11	19 15	19 24		19 47 →	19 38	19 40	19 47	19 51	20 05	20 11	20 22	20 47 →	20 34	20 38	20 40	20 44	20 47	21 05		21 11	21 23
Reading West	d																	20 47					
Theale	d									19 59								20 53					
Aldermaston	d																	20 58					
Midgham	d																	21 01					
Thatcham	d									20 07								21 06					
Newbury Racecourse	d																	21 11					
Newbury	a									20 13					20 49			21 15					
	d									20 13													
Kintbury	d									20 20													
Hungerford	d									20 24													
Bedwyn	a									20 34													
Tilehurst	d								19 51										20 51				
Pangbourne	d								19 56										20 56				
Goring & Streatley	d								20 01										21 01				
Cholsey	d								20 06										21 06				
Didcot Parkway	a		19 29	19 37			19 52		20 13		20 19		20 36			20 52			21 13	21 19			21 38
	d			19 38					20 14				20 37						21 14				21 39
Appleford	d																						
Culham	d																						
Radley	d								20 21										21 21				
Oxford	a	19 35		19 52				20 03	20 30			20 35	20 51				21 03		21 32			21 35	21 51
	d	19 37			19 56			20 06				20 37					21 06				21 33	21 37	
Islip	d				20 09																21 46		
Bicester Town	a				20 21																21 58		
Tackley	d																						
Heyford	d																						
Kings Sutton	d																						
Banbury	a	19 53						20 24				20 53					21 23					21 53	
Leamington Spa 8	a	20 11						20 41				21 11					21 41					22 11	
Coventry	a	20 22						20 53				21 22					21 53					22 22	
Birmingham International	a	20 35						21 03				21 35					22 03					22 32	
Birmingham New Street 12	a	20 48						21 15				21 48					22 15					22 42	

		GW	GW	XC	GW	GW	GW	GW	GW	GW	GW	GW	GW	GW	GW	GW	GW	GW	GW
		1	◇1 ⊐	◇1	1	1	◇1 ⊐	◇1	1	◇1 ⊐	1	1	1 B	🚌	◇1	🚌	1	◇1 ⊐	◇1 ⊐
London Paddington 15 ⊖	d	20 43	21 00				21 30	21 42	21 43	22 03			22 15		22 42		22 43	23 03	23 37
Ealing Broadway ⊖	d	20 50							21 50				22 24				22 50		
Slough 3	d	21 22						22 00	22 23				22 46		23 01		23 16		
Maidenhead 3	d	21 32							22 33				22 56				23 24		
Twyford 3	d	21 40				←			22 41			←	23 04				23 33		
Reading 7	d	21 49 →	21 38	21 40	21 44	21 49	22 08	22 24	22 49 →	22 42	22 44	22 49	23 12		23 21		23 53	23 47	00 15
Reading West	d										22 47		23 15						
Theale	d				21 51						22 53		23 21						
Aldermaston	d										22 58								
Midgham	d										23 01								
Thatcham	d				22 00						23 06		23 30						
Newbury Racecourse	d										23 11								
Newbury	a				22 05						23 15		23 37						
	d				22 06														
Kintbury	d				22 12														
Hungerford	d				22 17														
Bedwyn	a				22 25														
Tilehurst	d					21 53						22 53					23 57		
Pangbourne	d					21 57						22 59					00 01		
Goring & Streatley	d					22 02						23 03					00 07		
Cholsey	d					22 07						23 08					00 12		
Didcot Parkway	a		21 52			22 14	22 23	22 40		22 57		23 18			23 36		00 18	00s02	00s32
	d					22 15		22 40						23 27		23 45			
Appleford	d																		
Culham	d																		
Radley	d					22 22								23 42					
Oxford	a			22 03		22 30		22 52						23 57		00 10			
	d			22 06															
Islip	d																		
Bicester Town	a																		
Tackley	d																		
Heyford	d																		
Kings Sutton	d																		
Banbury	a			22 23															
Leamington Spa 8	a			22 41															
Coventry	a			22 53															
Birmingham International	a			23 03															
Birmingham New Street 12	a			23 14															

A ⌶ to Birmingham International

B 1 to Twyford

London and Reading - Bedwyn, Oxford, Bicester, Banbury and Birmingham

		GW	GW	GW	GW	GW	GW	GW	GW	GW	GW	GW	GW	GW	CH	GW	GW	XC	GW	GW	GW	GW	GW
		1	(bus)	1	◇1	1	1	◇1 ⌂	◇1	1	1	1	◇1 ⌂	◇1 ✕	1	1	◇1 ⌂	◇1 ✕	◇1	1	1	◇1 ⌂	1
London Paddington 15 ⊖	d			22p45	23p00		23p20	23p30	23p33			07 28	08 00	08 03			08 30		08 42		08 43	09 00	
Ealing Broadway ⊖	d			22p55			23p28					07 36									08 50		
Slough 3	d			23p21	23p17		23p54		23p50			07 58		08 22					09 00		09 20		
Maidenhead 3	d			23p32			00 05					08 08		08 31							09 30		
Twyford 3	d			23p39		←	00 13				←	08 16				←					09 38		←
Reading 7	d	23p12		23p49	23p34	23p49	00 20	23p59	00 08	00 15	00 20	08 51	08 38	08 44		08 51	09 06	09 11	09 22		09 47	09 35	09 47
Reading West	d	23p14		→			→			00s18		→									→		
Theale	d	23p20								00s24													
Aldermaston	d	23p25								00s29													
Midgham	d	23p29								00s32													
Thatcham	d	23p34								00s37													
Newbury Racecourse	d	23p38								00s42													
Newbury	a	23p41								00 45													
	d	23p41																					
Kintbury	d	23p48																					
Hungerford	d	23p52																					
Bedwyn	a	00 01																					
Tilehurst	d					23p53					00 24					08 55							09 51
Pangbourne	d					23p58										09 00							09 56
Goring & Streatley	d					00 03					00 31					09 05							10 01
Cholsey	d					00 08					00 36					09 11							10 06
Didcot Parkway	a				23p51	00 14		00 18	00 22		00 44		08 52	08 59		09 16	09 22		09 37			09 49	10 13
	d				23p51	00 15			00 24		00 45			09 02		09 27			09 38				10 14
Appleford	d										00s49												10 18
Culham	d										00s51												
Radley	d					00s22					00s55					09 34							10 23
Oxford	a				00 03	00 32			00 38		01 05			09 13		09 43		09 34	09 52				10 31
	d		23p47												09 36			09 37		10 00			
Islip	d														09 49								
Bicester Town	a														10 01								
Tackley	d		00s06																	10 09			
Heyford	d		00s20																	10 13			
Kings Sutton	d																			10 22			
Banbury	a		00 45															09 53		10 30			
Leamington Spa 8	a																						
Coventry	a																						
Birmingham International	a																						
Birmingham New Street 12	a																						

		XC	GW	GW	CH	GW	GW	GW	XC	GW	GW	GW	GW	GW	GW	CH	XC	GW	GW	GW	GW	GW	XC
		◇1 ✕	◇1 ⌂	◇1 ⌂	1	1	◇1 ⌂	1	◇1 ✕	◇1 ⌂	◇1 ⌂	1	◇1 ⌂	1	1	1	◇1 ✕	◇1 ⌂	◇1	1	◇1 ⌂	1	◇1 ✕
London Paddington 15 ⊖	d		09 35	09 42		09 43	10 00			10 37	10 42	10 43	11 00		11 13			11 37	11 42	11 43	12 00		
Ealing Broadway ⊖	d					09 50						10 50								11 50			
Slough 3	d		09 53			10 22					10 58	11 22			11 31				12 01	12 22			
Maidenhead 3	d					10 31						11 31			11 43					12 31			
Twyford 3	d					10 39		←				11 39		←						12 39		←	
Reading 7	d	10 11	10 17	10 21		10 47	10 38	10 47	11 11	11 15	11 21	11 47	11 38	11 47	12 01		12 11	12 15	12 23	12 47	12 38	12 47	13 11
Reading West	d					→						→			12 04					→			
Theale	d														12 22								
Aldermaston	d														12 27								
Midgham	d														12 32								
Thatcham	d														12 39								
Newbury Racecourse	d														12 52								
Newbury	a														12 55								
	d														12 55								
Kintbury	d														13 02								
Hungerford	d														13 06								
Bedwyn	a														13 15								
Tilehurst	d							10 51						11 51								12 51	
Pangbourne	d							10 56						11 56								12 56	
Goring & Streatley	d							11 01						12 01								13 01	
Cholsey	d							11 06						12 06								13 06	
Didcot Parkway	a		10 31	10 35			10 52	11 13		11 29	11 36		11 52	12 13				12 28	12 39		12 52	13 13	
	d		10 31					11 14			11 37			12 14					12 40			13 14	
Appleford	d																					13 18	
Culham	d																						
Radley	d							11 21						12 21								13 22	
Oxford	a	10 35	10 45					11 31	11 35		11 50			12 31			12 35		12 52			13 32	13 35
	d	10 37			10 56				11 37							12 33	12 37						13 37
Islip	d				11 09											12 46							
Bicester Town	a				11 21											12 58							
Tackley	d																						
Heyford	d																						
Kings Sutton	d																						
Banbury	a	10 53							11 53								12 53						13 53
Leamington Spa 8	a																						
Coventry	a																						
Birmingham International	a																						
Birmingham New Street 12	a																						

London and Reading - Bedwyn, Oxford, Bicester, Banbury and Birmingham

		GW	GW	CH	GW	GW	GW	XC	GW	GW	XC	GW	GW	GW	GW	XC	GW	GW	CH	XC	GW	GW
		◇1 ⌂	◇1 ⌂	1	1	1	◇1 ⌂	◇1 ✕	1	1	◇1 ✕	◇1 ⌂	◇1 ⌂	1	◇1 ⌂	◇1 ✕	1	1	1	◇1 ✕	◇1 ⌂	◇1 ✕
London Paddington 15 ⊖	d	12 37	12 42		12 43	12 51	13 00					13 37	13 42	13 43	14 00			14 04			14 37	14 42
Ealing Broadway ⊖	d				12 50									13 50								
Slough 3	d		12 58		13 22	13 09							14 00	14 22				14 26				15 02
Maidenhead 3	d				13 31	13 18								14 31				14 34				
Twyford 3	d				13 39					←				14 39			←					
Reading 7	d	13 16	13 22		13 47	13 33	13 38	13 40		13 47	14 11	14 17	14 23	14 47	14 38	14 40	14 47	14 54		15 11	15 15	15 22
Reading West	d				→	13 36								→				14 57				
Theale	d					13 51												15 16				
Aldermaston	d																	15 23				
Midgham	d																	15 26				
Thatcham	d					14 02												15 33				
Newbury Racecourse	d					14 16												15 49				
Newbury	a					14 19												15 51				
	d					14 19												15 52				
Kintbury	d					14 26												15 58				
Hungerford	d					14 30												16 03				
Bedwyn	a					14 38												16 09				
Tilehurst	d									13 51							14 50					
Pangbourne	d									13 56							14 56					
Goring & Streatley	d									14 01							15 01					
Cholsey	d									14 06							15 06					
Didcot Parkway	a	13 30	13 36				13 52			14 13		14 30	14 38		14 52		15 13				15 29	15 36
	d		13 37							14 14			14 39				15 13					15 37
Appleford	d																15 18					
Culham	d																					
Radley	d									14 21							15 23					
Oxford	a		13 51					14 03		14 31	14 35		14 53			15 03	15 31			15 35		15 51
	d			13 56				14 06	14 20		14 37					15 06			15 33	15 37		
Islip	d			14 09															15 46			
Bicester Town	a			14 21															15 58			
Tackley	d								14 29													
Heyford	d								14 33													
Kings Sutton	d								14 42													
Banbury	a							14 23	14 50		14 53					15 23				15 53		
Leamington Spa 8	a							14 41			15 11					15 41				16 11		
Coventry	a										15 22									16 22		
Birmingham International	a										15 35									16 35		
Birmingham New Street 12	a							15 13			15 48					16 12				16 48		

		GW	GW	XC	GW	XC	GW	GW	CH	GW	GW	GW	XC	GW	GW	GW	XC	GW	GW	GW	GW	XC	GW
		1	◇1 ⌂	◇1 ✕	1	◇1 ✕	◇1 ⌂	◇1 ⌂	1	1	◇1 ⌂	◇1 ⌂	◇1 ✕	1	1	1	◇1 ✕	◇1 ⌂	◇1 ✕	1	◇1 ⌂	◇1 ✕	1
London Paddington 15 ⊖	d	14 43	15 00				15 37	15 42		15 43	15 57	16 00		16 04				16 37	16 42	16 43	17 00		
Ealing Broadway ⊖	d	14 50								15 50										16 50			
Slough 3	d	15 22						16 01		16 20				16 24					17 01	17 22			
Maidenhead 3	d	15 31								16 29				16 33						17 31			
Twyford 3	d	15 39			←					16 37						←				17 39			←
Reading 7	d	15 47	15 38	15 40	15 47	16 11	16 17	16 21		16 47	16 33	16 38	16 40	16 47		16 47	17 11	17 19	17 22	17 47	17 38	17 40	17 47
Reading West	d	→								→				16 50						→			
Theale	d													16 56									
Aldermaston	d													17 01									
Midgham	d													17 05									
Thatcham	d													17 10									
Newbury Racecourse	d													17 14									
Newbury	a										16 49			17 18									
	d																						
Kintbury	d																						
Hungerford	d																						
Bedwyn	a																						
Tilehurst	d				15 50											16 50							17 51
Pangbourne	d				15 56											16 56							17 56
Goring & Streatley	d				16 01											17 01							18 01
Cholsey	d				16 06											17 06							18 06
Didcot Parkway	a		15 52		16 13		16 31	16 37				16 52				17 13		17 33	17 37		17 52		18 13
	d				16 13			16 37								17 13			17 37				18 14
Appleford	d																						18 18
Culham	d																						
Radley	d				16 21											17 21							18 23
Oxford	a			16 03	16 29	16 35		16 51					17 03			17 30	17 35		17 52			18 03	18 31
	d			16 06		16 37			16 56				17 06		17 19		17 37					18 06	
Islip	d								17 09														
Bicester Town	a								17 21														
Tackley	d														17 28								
Heyford	d														17 32								
Kings Sutton	d														17 41								
Banbury	a			16 23		16 53							17 23		17 47		17 53					18 23	
Leamington Spa 8	a			16 41		17 11							17 41				18 11					18 41	
Coventry	a					17 22											18 22						
Birmingham International	a					17 35											18 35						
Birmingham New Street 12	a			17 12		17 48							18 09				18 48					19 11	

Sundays
7 August to 11 September

London and Reading - Bedwyn, Oxford, Bicester, Banbury and Birmingham

		GW 1	XC ◇1 A ✠	GW ◇1 ☕	CH 1	GW ◇1 ✠	GW 1	GW ◇1 ☕	GW ◇1 ☕	XC ◇1 ✠	GW 1	GW 1	XC ◇1 A ✠	GW ◇1 ☕	GW ◇1 ☕	CH 1	GW 1	GW ◇1 ☕	XC ◇1 ✠	GW 1	GW 1	XC ◇1
London Paddington 15 ⊖	d	17 04		17 37		17 42	17 43	17 57	18 00			18 12		18 37	18 42		18 43	19 00			19 04	
Ealing Broadway ⊖	d						17 50										18 50					
Slough 3	d	17 26				18 01	18 21					18 30			18 59		19 22				19 25	
Maidenhead 3	d	17 36					18 31					18 44					19 31				19 35	
Twyford 3	d						18 39				←						19 39			←		
Reading 7	d	17 51	18 11	18 17		18 25	18 47	18 34	18 38	18 40	18 47	19 01	19 11	19 14	19 24		19 47	19 38	19 40	19 47	19 51	20 11
Reading West	d						→					19 04					→					
Theale	d	17 59										19 10									19 59	
Aldermaston	d											19 15										
Midgham	d											19 18										
Thatcham	d	18 07										19 23									20 07	
Newbury Racecourse	d											19 28										
Newbury	a	18 13						18 49				19 32									20 13	
	d	18 14																			20 13	
Kintbury	d	18 20																			20 20	
Hungerford	d	18 25																			20 24	
Bedwyn	a	18 34																			20 34	
Tilehurst	d										18 50									19 51		
Pangbourne	d										18 55									19 56		
Goring & Streatley	d										19 00									20 01		
Cholsey	d										19 05									20 06		
Didcot Parkway	a			18 31		18 40			18 52		19 12			19 28	19 39			19 52		20 13		
	d					18 40					19 13				19 40					20 14		
Appleford	d																					
Culham	d																					
Radley	d										19 20									20 21		
Oxford	a		18 35			18 53				19 03	19 28		19 35		19 54				20 03	20 30		20 35
	d		18 37		18 35					19 06			19 37			19 56			20 06			20 37
Islip	d				18 48											20 09						
Bicester Town	a				19 00											20 21						
Tackley	d																					
Heyford	d																					
Kings Sutton	d																					
Banbury	a		18 53							19 23			19 53						20 24			20 53
Leamington Spa 8	a		19 11							19 41			20 11						20 41			21 11
Coventry	a		19 22							19 53			20 22						20 53			21 22
Birmingham International	a		19 35							20 03			20 35						21 03			21 35
Birmingham New Street 12	a		19 48							20 15			20 48						21 15			21 48

		GW ◇1 ☕	GW ◇1 ☕	GW 1	GW ◇1 ☕	GW ◇1 ☕	XC ◇1	GW 1	GW 1	CH 1	XC ◇1	GW ◇1 ☕	GW ◇1	GW 1	GW ◇1 ☕	XC ◇1	GW 1	GW 1	GW ◇1 ☕	GW ◇1	GW 1	GW 1	GW ◇1 ☕
London Paddington 15 ⊖	d	19 37	19 42	19 43	19 57	20 00						20 37	20 42	20 43	21 00				21 37	21 42		21 43	22 03
Ealing Broadway ⊖	d			19 50										20 50								21 50	
Slough 3	d		19 59	20 22									21 02	21 19						21 59		22 16	
Maidenhead 3	d			20 31										21 28								22 25	
Twyford 3	d			20 39					←					21 36			←					22 33	
Reading 7	d	20 17	20 21	20 46	20 32	20 38	20 40	20 44	20 46		21 11	21 17	21 24	21 48	21 38	21 40	21 48	21 44	22 14	22 22	22 44	22 54	22 50
Reading West	d			→				20 47						→							22 47	→	
Theale	d							20 53										21 51			22 53		
Aldermaston	d							20 58													22 58		
Midgham	d							21 01													23 01		
Thatcham	d							21 06										22 00			23 06		
Newbury Racecourse	d							21 11													23 11		
Newbury	a				20 49			21 15										22 05			23 15		
	d																	22 06					
Kintbury	d																	22 12					
Hungerford	d																	22 17					
Bedwyn	a																	22 25					
Tilehurst	d								20 50								21 52						
Pangbourne	d								20 56								21 57						
Goring & Streatley	d								21 01								22 02						
Cholsey	d								21 05								22 07						
Didcot Parkway	a	20 30	20 36			20 52			21 12			21 31	21 40		21 52		22 14		22 30	22 38			23 05
	d		20 37						21 13				21 40				22 14			22 38			
Appleford	d																						
Culham	d																						
Radley	d								21 20								22 22						
Oxford	a		20 51				21 03		21 30		21 35		21 52			22 03	22 30			22 51			
	d						21 06			21 33	21 37					22 06							
Islip	d									21 46													
Bicester Town	a									21 58													
Tackley	d																						
Heyford	d																						
Kings Sutton	d																						
Banbury	a						21 23				21 53					22 23							
Leamington Spa 8	a						21 41				22 11					22 41							
Coventry	a						21 53				22 22					22 53							
Birmingham International	a						22 03				22 32					23 03							
Birmingham New Street 12	a						22 15				22 42					23 14							

A ✠ to Birmingham International

Table 116

Sundays
7 August to 11 September

London and Reading - Bedwyn, Oxford, Bicester, Banbury and Birmingham

		GW 1	GW 1	GW 🚌	GW ◇1	GW 🚌	GW 1	GW ◇1 ☕	GW 1	GW ◇1 ☕
London Paddington 15 ⊖	d		22 15		22 42		22 43	23 03		23 37
Ealing Broadway ⊖	d		22 24				22 50			
Slough 3	d		22 46		23 00		23 16			
Maidenhead 3	d		22 56				23 24			
Twyford 3	d	←	23 04				23 34		←	
Reading 7	d	22 54	23 11		23 21		23 53	23 47	23 53	00 15
Reading West	d		23 14				→			
Theale	d		23 20							
Aldermaston	d									
Midgham	d									
Thatcham	d		23 29							
Newbury Racecourse	d									
Newbury	a		23 36							
	d									
Kintbury	d									
Hungerford	d									
Bedwyn	a									
Tilehurst	d	22 58							23 57	
Pangbourne	d	23 03							00 01	
Goring & Streatley	d	23 07							00 07	
Cholsey	d	23 12							00 12	
Didcot Parkway	a	23 22			23 36			00s02	00 18	00s32
	d			23 27		23 45				
Appleford	d									
Culham	d									
Radley	d			23 42						
Oxford	a			23 57		00 10				
	d									
Islip	d									
Bicester Town	a									
Tackley	d									
Heyford	d									
Kings Sutton	d									
Banbury	a									
Leamington Spa 8	a									
Coventry	a									
Birmingham International	a									
Birmingham New Street 12	a									

Sundays
18 September to 23 October

		GW 1	GW 🚌	GW 🚌	GW 1	GW 1	GW ◇1 ☕	GW 1	GW 🚌	GW 1	GW 1	GW ◇1 ☕	GW ◇1 ✠	GW 1	GW ◇1 ☕	XC ◇1 ✠	CH 1	XC 🚌	GW ◇1	GW 1	GW ◇1 ☕	GW 1	XC ◇1 ✠
London Paddington 15 ⊖	d				22p45	23p20	23p30				07 28	08 00	08 03		08 30				08 42	08 43	09 00		
Ealing Broadway ⊖	d				22p55	23p28					07 36									08 50			
Slough 3	d				23p21	23p54					07 58		08 22						09 00	09 20			
Maidenhead 3	d				23p32	00 05					08 08		08 30							09 30			
Twyford 3	d				23p39	00 13				←	08 16			←						09 38		←	
Reading 7	d	23p12			23p49	00 20	23p59	00 15		00 20	08 50	08 38	08 44	08 50	09 06	09 11			09 22	09 47	09 35	09 47	10 11
Reading West	d	23p14				→		00s18			→									→			
Theale	d	23p20						00s24															
Aldermaston	d	23p25						00s29															
Midgham	d	23p29						00s32															
Thatcham	d	23p34						00s37															
Newbury Racecourse	d	23p38						00s42															
Newbury	a	23p41						00 45															
	d	23p41																					
Kintbury	d	23p48																					
Hungerford	d	23p52																					
Bedwyn	a	00 01																					
Tilehurst	d				23p53					00 24				08 54								09 51	
Pangbourne	d				23p58									08 59								09 56	
Goring & Streatley	d				00 03					00 31				09 04								10 01	
Cholsey	d				00 08					00 36				09 10								10 06	
Didcot Parkway	a				00 17		00 18			00 47		08 52	08 59	09 15	09 22				09 37		09 49	10 13	
	d			00 01					00 28				09 02	09 27					09 38			10 14	
Appleford	d																					10 18	
Culham	d																						
Radley	d								00s43					09 34								10 23	
Oxford	a			00 26					00 58				09 13	09 43		09 33			09 52			10 31	10 34
	d		23p47														09 36	09 40					
Islip	d																09 49						
Bicester Town	a																10 01						
Tackley	d		00s06																				
Heyford	d		00s20																				
Kings Sutton	d																						
Banbury	a		00 45															10 30					
Leamington Spa 8	a																	11 11					
Coventry	a																						
Birmingham International	a																						
Birmingham New Street 12	a																						

Table 116

Sundays

18 September to 23 October

London and Reading - Bedwyn, Oxford, Bicester, Banbury and Birmingham

		XC	GW	GW	CH	GW	GW	GW	XC	GW	XC	GW	GW	GW	GW	CH	XC	GW	XC	GW	GW	GW	GW
London Paddington ⊖	d		09 35	09 42		09 43	10 00			10 37		10 42	10 43	11 00				11 37		11 42	11 43	12 00	
Ealing Broadway ⊖	d					09 50							10 50								11 50		
Slough	d		09 53			10 22						10 58	11 22							12 01	12 22		
Maidenhead	d					10 31							11 31								12 31		
Twyford	d					10 39		←					11 39		←						12 39		←
Reading	d		10 17	10 21		10 47	10 38	10 47	11 11	11 15		11 22	11 47	11 38	11 47		12 11	12 15		12 23	12 47	12 38	12 47
Reading West	d					→							→								→		
Theale	d																						
Aldermaston	d																						
Midgham	d																						
Thatcham	d																						
Newbury Racecourse	d																						
Newbury	a																						
	d																						
Kintbury	d																						
Hungerford	d																						
Bedwyn	a																						
Tilehurst	d							10 51							11 51								12 51
Pangbourne	d							10 56							11 56								12 56
Goring & Streatley	d							11 01							12 01								13 01
Cholsey	d							11 06							12 06								13 06
Didcot Parkway	a		10 31	10 35			10 52	11 13		11 29		11 36		11 52	12 13			12 28		12 39		12 52	13 13
	d		10 31					11 14				11 37			12 14					12 40			13 14
Appleford	d																						13 18
Culham	d																						
Radley	d							11 21							12 21								13 22
Oxford	a		10 45					11 31	11 35			11 50			12 31		12 34			12 52			13 32
	d	10 40			10 56						11 40					12 33			12 40				
Islip	d				11 09											12 46							
Bicester Town	a				11 21											12 58							
Tackley	d																						
Heyford	d																						
Kings Sutton	d																						
Banbury	a	11 25									12 25								13 25				
Leamington Spa	a	12 00									13 00								14 00				
Coventry	a																						
Birmingham International	a																						
Birmingham New Street	a																						

		XC	GW	XC	GW	CH	GW	GW	GW	XC	GW	GW	GW	GW	XC	GW	CH	XC	GW	GW	GW	GW
London Paddington ⊖	d		12 37		12 42		12 43	13 00			13 37	13 42	13 43	14 00					14 37	14 42	14 43	15 00
Ealing Broadway ⊖	d						12 50						13 50								14 50	
Slough	d				12 58		13 22					13 59	14 22							15 02	15 22	
Maidenhead	d						13 31						14 31								15 31	
Twyford	d						13 39		←				14 39			←					15 39	
Reading	d	13 11	13 16		13 22		13 47	13 38	13 47	14 11	14 17	14 23	14 47	14 38	14 40	14 47		15 11	15 15	15 22	15 47	15 38
Reading West	d						→						→								→	
Theale	d																					
Aldermaston	d																					
Midgham	d																					
Thatcham	d																					
Newbury Racecourse	d																					
Newbury	a																					
	d																					
Kintbury	d																					
Hungerford	d																					
Bedwyn	a																					
Tilehurst	d								13 51							14 50						
Pangbourne	d								13 56							14 56						
Goring & Streatley	d								14 01							15 01						
Cholsey	d								14 06							15 06						
Didcot Parkway	a		13 30		13 36			13 52	14 13		14 30	14 38		14 52		15 13			15 29	15 36		15 52
	d				13 37				14 14			14 39				15 13				15 37		
Appleford	d															15 18						
Culham	d																					
Radley	d								14 21							15 23						
Oxford	a	13 35			13 51				14 31	14 35		14 53			15 03	15 31		15 35		15 51		
	d			13 40		13 56				14 37					15 06		15 33	15 37				
Islip	d					14 09											15 46					
Bicester Town	a					14 21											15 58					
Tackley	d																					
Heyford	d																					
Kings Sutton	d																					
Banbury	a			14 30						14 53					15 23			15 53				
Leamington Spa	a									15 11					15 41			16 11				
Coventry	a									15 22								16 22				
Birmingham International	a									15 35								16 35				
Birmingham New Street	a									15 48					16 12			16 48				

Table 116

Sundays

18 September to 23 October

London and Reading - Bedwyn, Oxford, Bicester, Banbury and Birmingham

		XC	GW	XC	GW	GW	CH	GW	GW	XC	GW	XC	GW	GW	GW	GW	XC	GW	XC A	GW	CH	GW	GW
London Paddington ⊖	d				15 37	15 42		15 43	16 00				16 37	16 42	16 43	17 00				17 37		17 42	17 43
Ealing Broadway ⊖	d							15 50							16 50								17 50
Slough	d					16 01		16 22						17 01	17 22							18 01	18 21
Maidenhead	d							16 31							17 31								18 31
Twyford	d		←					16 39			←				17 39			←					18 39
Reading	d	15 40	15 47	16 11	16 17	16 21		16 47	16 38	16 40	16 47	17 11	17 19	17 22	17 47	17 38	17 40	17 47	18 11	18 17		18 25	18 47
Reading West	d							→							→								→
Theale	d																						
Aldermaston	d																						
Midgham	d																						
Thatcham	d																						
Newbury Racecourse	d																						
Newbury	a																						
	d																						
Kintbury	d																						
Hungerford	d																						
Bedwyn	a																						
Tilehurst	d		15 50								16 50							17 51					
Pangbourne	d		15 56								16 56							17 56					
Goring & Streatley	d		16 01								17 01							18 01					
Cholsey	d		16 06								17 06							18 06					
Didcot Parkway	a		16 13		16 31	16 37			16 52		17 13		17 33	17 37		17 52		18 13		18 31		18 40	
	d		16 13			16 37					17 13			17 37				18 14				18 40	
Appleford	d																	18 18					
Culham	d																						
Radley	d		16 21								17 21							18 23					
Oxford	a	16 03	16 29	16 35		16 51				17 03	17 30	17 35		17 52			18 03	18 31	18 35			18 52	
	d	16 06		16 37			16 56			17 06		17 37					18 06		18 37		18 35		
Islip	d						17 09														18 48		
Bicester Town	a						17 21														19 00		
Tackley	d																						
Heyford	d																						
Kings Sutton	d																						
Banbury	a	16 23		16 53						17 23		17 53					18 23		18 53				
Leamington Spa	a	16 41		17 11						17 41		18 11					18 41		19 11				
Coventry	a			17 22								18 22							19 22				
Birmingham International	a			17 35								18 35							19 35				
Birmingham New Street	a	17 12		17 48						18 09		18 48					19 11		19 48				

		GW	XC	GW	XC A	GW	GW	CH	GW	GW	XC	GW	XC	GW	GW	GW	GW	XC	GW	CH	XC	GW
London Paddington ⊖	d	18 00				18 37	18 42		18 43	19 00				19 37	19 42	19 43	20 00					20 37
Ealing Broadway ⊖	d								18 50							19 50						
Slough	d						18 59		19 22						19 59	20 22						
Maidenhead	d								19 31							20 31						
Twyford	d			←					19 39			←				20 39			←			
Reading	d	18 38	18 40	18 47	19 11	19 14	19 24		19 47	19 38	19 40	19 47	20 11	20 17	20 21	20 46	20 38	20 40	20 46		21 11	21 17
Reading West	d								→							→						
Theale	d																					
Aldermaston	d																					
Midgham	d																					
Thatcham	d																					
Newbury Racecourse	d																					
Newbury	a																					
	d																					
Kintbury	d																					
Hungerford	d																					
Bedwyn	a																					
Tilehurst	d			18 50								19 51							20 50			
Pangbourne	d			18 55								19 56							20 56			
Goring & Streatley	d			19 00								20 01							21 01			
Cholsey	d			19 05								20 06							21 05			
Didcot Parkway	a	18 52		19 12		19 28	19 39			19 52		20 13		20 30	20 36		20 52		21 12			21 31
	d			19 13			19 40					20 14			20 37				21 13			
Appleford	d																					
Culham	d																					
Radley	d			19 20								20 21							21 20			
Oxford	a		19 03	19 28	19 35		19 54				20 03	20 30	20 35		20 51			21 03	21 30		21 35	
	d		19 06		19 37			19 56			20 06		20 37					21 06		21 33	21 37	
Islip	d							20 09												21 46		
Bicester Town	a							20 21												21 58		
Tackley	d																					
Heyford	d																					
Kings Sutton	d																					
Banbury	a		19 23		19 53						20 24		20 53					21 23			21 53	
Leamington Spa	a		19 41		20 11						20 41		21 11					21 41			22 11	
Coventry	a		19 53		20 22						20 53		21 22					21 53			22 22	
Birmingham International	a		20 03		20 35						21 03		21 35					22 03			22 32	
Birmingham New Street	a		20 15		20 48						21 15		21 48					22 15			22 42	

A to Birmingham International

Table 116

Sundays

18 September to 23 October

London and Reading - Bedwyn, Oxford, Bicester, Banbury and Birmingham

		GW	GW	GW	XC	GW	GW	GW	GW	GW	GW	GW	GW	GW	GW	GW
		◇1	1	◇1 🍴	◇1	1	◇1 🍴	◇1	1	◇1 🍴	1	◇1 🍴	◇1	◇1 🍴	◇1 🍴	◇1
London Paddington 15 ⊖	d	20 42	20 43	21 00			21 37	21 39	21 43	22 03		22 37	22 42	23 03	23 37	23 47
Ealing Broadway ⊖	d		20 50						21 50							23 55
Slough 3	d	21 02	21 19					21 59	22 16				23 01			00 09
Maidenhead 3	d		21 28						22 25							00 17
Twyford 3	d		21 36			←			22 33		←					
Reading 7	d	21 24	21 48	21 38	21 40	21 48	22 14	22 22	22 54	22 50	22 54	23 15	23 21	23 47	00 15	00 31
Reading West	d		→						→							
Theale	d															
Aldermaston	d															
Midgham	d															
Thatcham	d															
Newbury Racecourse	d															
Newbury	a															
	d															
Kintbury	d															
Hungerford	d															
Bedwyn	a															
Tilehurst	d					21 52					22 58					
Pangbourne	d					21 57					23 03					
Goring & Streatley	d					22 02					23 07					
Cholsey	d					22 07					23 12					
Didcot Parkway	a	21 40		21 52		22 14	22 30	22 38		23 05	23 19	23s30	23 35	00s02	00s32	00 49
	d	21 40				22 14		22 38			23 19		23 38			00 51
Appleford	d															
Culham	d															
Radley	d					22 22					23 29					
Oxford	a	21 52			22 03	22 30		22 51			23 37		23 49			01 02
	d				22 06											
Islip	d															
Bicester Town	a															
Tackley	d															
Heyford	d															
Kings Sutton	d															
Banbury	a				22 23											
Leamington Spa 5	a				22 41											
Coventry	a				22 53											
Birmingham International	a				23 03											
Birmingham New Street 12	a				23 14											

Sundays

from 30 October

		GW	GW	GW	GW	GW	GW	GW	GW	GW	GW	GW	GW	GW	XC	CH	XC	GW	GW	GW	GW	GW	XC
		1	🚌	🚌	1	1	◇1 🍴	1	🚌	1		1		◇1 🛒	◇1 🛒	1	🚌	◇1	1	◇1 🍴	1	1	◇1 🛒
London Paddington 15 ⊖	d				22p45	23p20	23p30					07 28		08 06				08 42	08 43	08 57			
Ealing Broadway ⊖	d				22p55	23p28						07 36							08 50				
Slough 3	d				23p21	23p54						07 58		08 28				09 04	09 16				
Maidenhead 3	d				23p32	00 05						08 08		08 36					09 27				
Twyford 3	d				23p39	00 13				←		08 16							09 35		←		
Reading 7	d	23p12			23p49	00 20	23p59	00 15		00 20	08 14	08 27	08 40	08 49	09 11			09 21	09 43	09 32	09 43	09 42	10 11
Reading West	d	23p14				→		00s18			08 17		08 43						→				
Theale	d	23p20						00s24			08 23		08 49									09 49	
Aldermaston	d	23p25						00s29			08 28		08 54										
Midgham	d	23p29						00s32			08 31		08 58										
Thatcham	d	23p34						00s37			08 36		09 03									09 58	
Newbury Racecourse	d	23p38						00s42															
Newbury	a	23p41						00 45			08 43		09 08							09 48		10 03	
	d	23p41											09 09									10 04	
Kintbury	d	23p48											09 15									10 10	
Hungerford	d	23p52											09 20									10 15	
Bedwyn	a	00 01											09 27									10 23	
Tilehurst	d				23p53					00 24		08 31									09 47		
Pangbourne	d				23p58							08 35									09 52		
Goring & Streatley	d				00 03					00 31		08 41									09 57		
Cholsey	d				00 08					00 36		08 46									10 02		
Didcot Parkway	a				00 17		00 18			00 47		08 51		09 04				09 36			10 09		
	d			00 01					00 28			08 54		09 07				09 37			10 10		
Appleford	d																				10 14		
Culham	d																						
Radley	d								00s43			09 01									10 19		
Oxford	a			00 26					00 58			09 10		09 18	09 34			09 51			10 27		10 34
	d		23p47													09 36	09 40						
Islip	d															09 49							
Bicester Town	a															10 01							
Tackley	d		00s06																				
Heyford	d		00s20																				
Kings Sutton	d																						
Banbury	a		00 45														10 30						
Leamington Spa 5	a																11 11						
Coventry	a																						
Birmingham International	a																						
Birmingham New Street 12	a																						

Table 116

Sundays

from 30 October

London and Reading - Bedwyn, Oxford, Bicester, Banbury and Birmingham

		XC	GW	GW	CH	GW	XC	XC	GW	GW	GW	CH	XC	XC	GW	GW	GW	GW	GW	XC	XC	GW	GW
		🚌	◇1 🍴	1	1	1	◇1 🛒	🚌	◇1 🍴	1	1	1	◇1 🛒	🚌	◇1	1	◇1 🍴	1	1	◇1 🛒	🚌	◇1 🍴	1
London Paddington 15 ⊖	d		09 35			09 43			10 42		10 43				11 42	11 43	11 57					12 42	
Ealing Broadway ⊖	d					09 50					10 50					11 50							
Slough 3	d		09 59			10 16			11 06		11 16				12 03	12 16						13 06	
Maidenhead 3	d					10 27					11 27					12 27							
Twyford 3	d					10 35					11 35					12 35			←				
Reading 7	d		10 12	10 43		10 43	11 11		11 21	11 42	11 43		12 11		12 19	12 43	12 32	12 42	12 43	13 11		13 21	13 42
Reading West	d			10 46												→		12 45					
Theale	d			10 52						11 50								12 51					13 50
Aldermaston	d			10 57														12 56					
Midgham	d			11 00														12 59					
Thatcham	d			11 05						11 58								13 04					13 58
Newbury Racecourse	d			11 10														13 09					
Newbury	a			11 14						12 04							12 47	13 13					14 04
	d									12 04													14 04
Kintbury	d									12 11													14 11
Hungerford	d									12 15													14 15
Bedwyn	a									12 24													14 24
Tilehurst	d					10 47					11 47								12 47				
Pangbourne	d					10 52					11 52								12 52				
Goring & Streatley	d					10 57					11 57								12 57				
Cholsey	d					11 02					12 02								13 02				
Didcot Parkway	a		10 28			11 09			11 36		12 09				12 34				13 09			13 36	
	d		10 28			11 10			11 37		12 10				12 35				13 10			13 37	
Appleford	d																		13 15				
Culham	d																						
Radley	d					11 17					12 17								13 19				
Oxford	a		10 42			11 27	11 35		11 50		12 27		12 34		12 47				13 29	13 34		13 51	
	d	10 40			10 56			11 40				12 33		12 40							13 40		
Islip	d				11 09							12 46											
Bicester Town	a				11 21							12 58											
Tackley	d																						
Heyford	d																						
Kings Sutton	d																						
Banbury	a	11 25						12 25						13 25							14 30		
Leamington Spa 5	a	12 00						13 00						14 00									
Coventry	a																						
Birmingham International	a																						
Birmingham New Street 12	a																						

		CH	GW	XC	GW	GW	GW	XC	GW	GW	CH	XC	GW	XC	GW	GW	XC	GW	CH	GW	GW	XC
		1	1	◇1 🛒	◇1 🍴	1	◇1 🍴	◇1 🛒	1	1	1	◇1 🛒	◇1 🛒	◇1 🛒	1	1	◇1 🛒	◇1 🍴	1	1	◇1 🍴	◇1 🛒
London Paddington 15 ⊖	d		12 43		13 42	13 43	13 57						14 42		14 43			15 42		15 43	15 57	
Ealing Broadway ⊖	d		12 50			13 50									14 50					15 50		
Slough 3	d		13 16		14 06	14 16							15 03		15 16			16 05		16 16		
Maidenhead 3	d		13 27			14 27									15 27					16 27		
Twyford 3	d		13 35			14 35				←					15 35					16 35		
Reading 7	d		13 43	14 11	14 21	14 43	14 35	14 40	14 42	14 43		15 11	15 18	15 40	15 43	15 44	16 11	16 21		16 43	16 32	16 40
Reading West	d					→			14 45											→		
Theale	d								14 51							15 52						
Aldermaston	d								14 56													
Midgham	d								14 59													
Thatcham	d								15 04							16 01						
Newbury Racecourse	d								15 09													
Newbury	a						14 50		15 13							16 06					16 48	
	d															16 07						
Kintbury	d															16 13						
Hungerford	d															16 18						
Bedwyn	a															16 26						
Tilehurst	d		13 47							14 47					15 47							
Pangbourne	d		13 52							14 52					15 52							
Goring & Streatley	d		13 57							14 57					15 57							
Cholsey	d		14 02							15 02					16 02							
Didcot Parkway	a		14 09		14 36					15 09			15 32		16 09			16 36				
	d		14 10		14 37					15 10			15 33		16 10			16 37				
Appleford	d									15 14												
Culham	d																					
Radley	d		14 17							15 19					16 17							
Oxford	a		14 27	14 35	14 51			15 03		15 28		15 35	15 47	16 03	16 26		16 35	16 50				17 03
	d	13 56		14 37				15 06			15 33	15 37		16 06			16 37		16 56			17 06
Islip	d	14 09									15 46								17 09			
Bicester Town	a	14 21									15 58								17 21			
Tackley	d																					
Heyford	d																					
Kings Sutton	d																					
Banbury	a			14 53				15 23				15 53		16 23			16 53					17 23
Leamington Spa 5	a			15 11				15 41				16 11		16 41			17 11					17 41
Coventry	a			15 22								16 22					17 22					
Birmingham International	a			15 35								16 35					17 35					
Birmingham New Street 12	a			15 48				16 12				16 48		17 12			17 48					18 09

Sundays from 30 October

London and Reading - Bedwyn, Oxford, Bicester, Banbury and Birmingham

		GW	GW	XC	GW	XC	GW	GW	XC	CH	GW	GW	GW	XC	GW	GW	XC	GW	CH	XC	GW	GW	XC
		1	1	◇1	◇1	◇1	1	1	◇1	1	◇1	1	◇1	◇1	1	1	◇1	◇1	1	◇1	1	1	◇1
									A								A						
				🛒	🛒	🛒			🛒		🛒		☕	🛒			🛒	☕		🛒			
London Paddington 15 ⊖	d				16 42		16 43				17 42	17 43	17 57					18 42			18 43		
Ealing Broadway ⊖	d						16 50					17 50									18 50		
Slough 3	d				17 02		17 16				18 02	18 16						19 05			19 16		
Maidenhead 3	d						17 27					18 27									19 27		
Twyford 3	d	←					17 35					18 35			←						19 35		
Reading 7	d	16 43	16 44	17 11	17 18	17 40	17 43	17 44	18 11		18 18	18 43	18 32	18 40	18 43	18 44	19 11	19 21		19 40	19 43	19 44	20 11
Reading West	d		16 47									→				18 47							
Theale	d		16 53					17 52								18 53						19 53	
Aldermaston	d		16 58													18 58							
Midgham	d		17 01													19 01							
Thatcham	d		17 06					18 01								19 06						20 01	
Newbury Racecourse	d		17 11													19 11							
Newbury	a		17 15					18 06					18 47			19 15						20 07	
	d							18 07														20 07	
Kintbury	d							18 13														20 14	
Hungerford	d							18 18														20 18	
Bedwyn	a							18 27														20 26	
Tilehurst	d	16 47					17 47								18 47						19 47		
Pangbourne	d	16 52					17 52								18 52						19 52		
Goring & Streatley	d	16 57					17 57								18 57						19 57		
Cholsey	d	17 02					18 02								19 02						20 02		
Didcot Parkway	a	17 09			17 33		18 09				18 33				19 09			19 36			20 09		
	d	17 10			17 33		18 10				18 33				19 10			19 37			20 10		
Appleford	d						18 14																
Culham	d																						
Radley	d	17 17					18 19								19 17						20 17		
Oxford	a	17 26		17 35	17 47	18 03	18 27		18 35		18 48			19 03	19 26		19 35	19 51		20 03	20 27		20 35
	d			17 37		18 06			18 37	18 35				19 06			19 37		19 56	20 06			20 37
Islip	d									18 48									20 09				
Bicester Town	a									19 00									20 21				
Tackley	d																						
Heyford	d																						
Kings Sutton	d																						
Banbury	a			17 53		18 23			18 53					19 23			19 53			20 24			20 53
Leamington Spa 8	a			18 11		18 41			19 11					19 41			20 11			20 41			21 11
Coventry	a			18 22					19 22					19 53			20 22			20 53			21 22
Birmingham International	a			18 35					19 35					20 03			20 35			21 03			21 35
Birmingham New Street 12	a			18 48		19 11			19 48					20 15			20 48			21 15			21 48

		GW	GW	GW	XC	GW	GW	CH	XC	GW	XC	GW	GW	GW	GW	GW	GW	GW	GW	GW	GW	GW
		◇1	1	◇1	◇1	1	1	1	◇1	◇1	◇1	1	1	◇1	1	1		1	◇1			1
																		B				
		☕		☕													🚌				🚌	
London Paddington 15 ⊖	d	19 42	19 43	19 57						20 42		20 43		21 42		21 43		22 15	22 42			22 43
Ealing Broadway ⊖	d		19 50									20 50				21 50		22 24				22 50
Slough 3	d	20 05	20 16							21 01		21 16		22 03		22 16		22 46	23 01			23 16
Maidenhead 3	d		20 27									21 27				22 31		22 56				23 24
Twyford 3	d		20 35			←						21 35				22 39		23 04		←		23 32
Reading 7	d	20 21	20 43	20 32	20 40	20 43	20 44		21 11	21 17	21 40	21 47	21 44	22 19	22 44	22 54		23 24	23 21	23 24		23 53
Reading West	d		→				20 47								22 47			→		23 27		
Theale	d						20 53						21 51		22 53					23 33		
Aldermaston	d						20 58								22 58							
Midgham	d						21 01								23 01							
Thatcham	d						21 06						22 00		23 06					23 42		
Newbury Racecourse	d						21 11								23 11							
Newbury	a			20 48			21 15						22 05		23 15					23 48		
	d												22 06									
Kintbury	d												22 12									
Hungerford	d												22 17									
Bedwyn	a												22 25									
Tilehurst	d					20 47						21 52				22 58						23 57
Pangbourne	d					20 52						21 56				23 03						00 01
Goring & Streatley	d					20 57						22 01				23 07						00 07
Cholsey	d					21 02						22 06				23 12						00 12
Didcot Parkway	a	20 36				21 09				21 33		22 13		22 35		23 22			23 36			00 18
	d	20 37				21 10				21 33		22 14		22 35			23 27				23 45	
Appleford	d																					
Culham	d																					
Radley	d					21 17						22 21					23 42					
Oxford	a	20 51			21 03	21 26			21 35	21 45	22 03	22 30		22 48			23 57				00 10	
	d				21 06			21 33	21 37		22 06											
Islip	d							21 46														
Bicester Town	a							21 58														
Tackley	d																					
Heyford	d																					
Kings Sutton	d																					
Banbury	a				21 23				21 53		22 23											
Leamington Spa 8	a				21 41				22 11		22 41											
Coventry	a				21 53				22 22		22 53											
Birmingham International	a				22 03				22 32		23 03											
Birmingham New Street 12	a				22 15				22 42		23 14											

A 🛒 to Birmingham International
B 1 to Twyford

Mondays to Fridays

Birmingham, Banbury, Bicester, Oxford and Bedwyn - Reading and London

Miles	Miles			GW	GW	GW	GW	GW	GW MX	GW	GW MX	GW	GW	GW	GW	GW	GW	GW	GW MX	GW	GW MX	CH	GW
				◇1	◇1	◇1	◇1	◇1	◇1	1	◇1	1	1	1	1	1	◇1		◇1	◇1	1		
				A	B	C	D	E		F		F	G	E	H	I	J	K	L	M		N	K
							☕	☕			☕							🚌					🚌
0	—	**Birmingham New Street** 12	d																				
8½	—	Birmingham International	d																				
19¼	—	Coventry	d																				
28¾	—	Leamington Spa 8	d																			23p38	
48¾	—	**Banbury**	d																		23p45	23p55	
52¼	—	Kings Sutton	d																		23p50		
59¾	—	Heyford	d																		23p58		
62½	—	Tackley	d																		00 03		
—	0	**Bicester Town**	d																				
—	6	Islip	d																				
71½	11¾	**Oxford**	a																		00 14	00 22	
—	—		d	22p47	22p47	22p47			23p05	23p15							00 01	00 05	00 07		00 27		03 38
76½	—	Radley	d							23p22											00 33		
78¾	—	Culham	d																		00 37		
79¾	—	Appleford	d																		00 39		
81½	—	**Didcot Parkway**	a	22p59	22p59	22p59			23p18	23p30							00 19	00 30	00 20		00 46		04 03
—	—		d	23p00	23p00	23p00	23p11	23p11	23p18	23p30	23p35		23p50	23p50			00 20		00 21	00 35	00 46		
86¾	—	Cholsey	d							23p36			23p56	23p56							00 52		
90¼	—	Goring & Streatley	d							23p42			00 01	00 01							00 57		
93½	—	Pangbourne	d							23p46			00 05	00 05							01 01		
96¼	—	Tilehurst	d							23p50			00 10	00 10							01 06		
—	0	**Bedwyn**	d																				
—	5	Hungerford	d																				
—	8	Kintbury	d																				
—	13½	**Newbury**	a																				
—	—		d												23p45	23p57							
—	14	Newbury Racecourse	d												23p47	23p59							
—	17	Thatcham	d												23p52	00 04							
—	19¾	Midgham	d												23p57	00 09							
—	21¾	Aldermaston	d												00 01	00 13							
—	25¾	Theale	d												00 06	00 18							
—	29½	Reading West	d									←			00s13	00s25							
99	30½	**Reading** 7	a	23p20	23p16	23p16	23p27	23p27	23p35	23p56	23p53	23p56	00 15	00 15	00 17	00 29	00 36		00 38	00 51	01 12		
—	—		d	23p23	23p23	23p23	23p28	23p28	23p40	23p56	23p55	23p56	00 15	00 15			00 38		00 39	00 53	01 12		
104	—	Twyford 3	a							→		00 02	00 21	00 22			00 44			00 59	01 18		
110¾	—	Maidenhead 3	a						23p53			00 10	00 29	00 30			00 51			01 06	01 26		
116½	—	Slough 3	a	23p45	23p43	23p45			00 01			00 20	00 36	00 37			00 59		00 56	01 14	01 34		
129¼	—	Ealing Broadway ⊖	a									00 43	00 59	01 01			01 15			01 30	01 50		
135	—	**London Paddington** 15 ⊖	a	00 04	00 10	00 11	00 11	00 16	00 26		00 33	00 52	01 11	01 13			01 24		01 17	01 39	02 01		

A MO from 8 August
B MO from 27 June until 1 August
C MO until 20 June
D MO from 8 August until 24 October
E MO until 1 August
F MO from 19 September until 24 October
G MO from 8 August until 12 September, MO from 31 October
H MO until 12 September
I MO from 31 October
J MO from 19 September until 17 October
K MO until 12 September, MO from 31 October
L not 24 May
M MO until 12 September, MO from 24 October
N MX until 2 September

Birmingham, Banbury, Bicester, Oxford and Bedwyn - Reading and London

Station		GW	GW	GW	GW	GW	GW	GW	GW	GW	GW	GW	GW	GW	GW	GW	GW	GW	GW	GW	GW	GW	GW
		■	■	■	◇■	■	■	■	■	◇■	■	■	◇■	■	■	◇■	◇■	◇■	■	◇■	■	◇■	◇■
		A	B																				
					⊐								⊐				⊐	⊐				⊐	⊐
Birmingham New Street	d																						
Birmingham International	d																						
Coventry	d																						
Leamington Spa	d																						
Banbury	d																						
Kings Sutton	d																						
Heyford	d																						
Tackley	d																						
Bicester Town	d																						
Islip	d																						
Oxford	a																						
	d	04 00		05 03		05 24		05 43		05 59					06 07		06 27						
Radley	d			05 09				05 49							06 13								
Culham	d														06 17								
Appleford	d														06 19								
Didcot Parkway	a	04 12		05 17		05 36		05 58		06 12					06 26		06 39						
	d	04 12	04 12	05 18	05 41	05 46		06 00		06 13		06 20	06 29		06 31	06 34	06 39	06 47				06 59	
Cholsey	d	04 18	04 18	05 23		05 52						06 25			06 37	06 40							
Goring & Streatley	d	04 23	04 23	05 28		05 57						06 30			06 42	06 46							
Pangbourne	d	04 28	04 28	05 33		06 02						06 35			06 47	06 52							
Tilehurst	d	04 32	04 32	05 37		06 06						06 40			06 51	06 59							
Bedwyn	d										05 55								06 13				
Hungerford	d										06 01								06 18				06 39
Kintbury	d										06 05								06 23				
Newbury	a										06 12								06 30				06 49
	d						05 40		05 58		06 12								06 30				06 50
Newbury Racecourse	d						05 42												06 32				
Thatcham	d						05 47		06 02		06 17								06 37				06 57
Midgham	d						05 51												06 42				
Aldermaston	d						05 55												06 45				
Theale	d						06 00		06 10		06 25								06 50				07 07
Reading West	d						06 07		06 17		06 32			←					06 57	←	←		
Reading	a	04 38	04 38	05 43	05 56	06 12	06 12	06 16	06 21	06 30	06 36	06 46	06 43	06 46	06 58	07 05	06 54	07 00	07 02	07 05	06 58	07 13	07 19
	d	04 39	04 39	05 44	05 57	06 15		06 16	06 22	06 31	06 36	06 46	06 44	06 46	07 10	07 07	06 56	07 01		07 07	07 10	07 15	07 21
Twyford	a	04 45	04 45	05 50		06 21		06 23				→		06 53	→	→					07 16		
Maidenhead	a	04 53	04 53	05 58		06 28		06 31		06 42				07 01			07 07			07 17	07 24		
Slough	a	05 00	05 00	06 10		06 40			06 40	06 50			06 58								07 36		
Ealing Broadway	a	05 25	05 25	06 35		07 05															08 03		
London Paddington	a	05 41	05 41	06 49	06 24	07 18		06 54	07 01	07 08	07 16		07 17	07 27			07 29	07 32		07 40	08 17	07 44	07 53

Station		GW	CH	GW	GW	GW	GW	GW	GW	GW	XC	GW	GW	GW	GW	GW	GW	GW	XC	GW	GW	GW
		■	■	◇■	■	◇■	■	◇■	◇■	■	◇■	◇■	■	■	■	◇■	◇■	◇■	◇■	◇■	◇■	■
																		C				
				⊐				⊐	⊐		⊤	⊐				⊤	⊐	⊐⊘	⊤	⊐	⊐	
Birmingham New Street	d										06 03								06 33			
Birmingham International	d										06 14											
Coventry	d										06 25											
Leamington Spa	d										06 38								07 00			
Banbury	d	06 07								06 30	06 57								07 22			
Kings Sutton	d	06 11								06 36												
Heyford	d	06 21								06 44												
Tackley	d	06 25								06 49												
Bicester Town	d		06 23																			
Islip	d		06 34																			
Oxford	a	06 36	06 49							06 59	07 14								07 41			
	d	06 37		06 56						07 00	07 16				07 21	07 31			07 43			
Radley	d	06 43								07 06					07 27							
Culham	d	06 47								07 10					07 31							
Appleford	d	06 49								07 13					07 33							
Didcot Parkway	a	06 56		07 07						07 19					07 40							
	d	07 01		07 09		07 15		07 20		07 28		07 29			07 49		07 47			07 55	08 01	
Cholsey	d	07 07				07 21				07 34					07 55							
Goring & Streatley	d	07 12				07 28				07 39					08 00							
Pangbourne	d	07 17				07 35				07 44					08 04							
Tilehurst	d	07 21				07 42				07 48					08 09							
Bedwyn	d								06 46					07 07				07 32				
Hungerford	d								06 53					07 12								
Kintbury	d								06 59					07 17								
Newbury	a								07 08					07 24				07 46				
	d				06 56				07 09					07 24				07 47				
Newbury Racecourse	d				06 58									07 26								
Thatcham	d				07 03				07 16					07 32								
Midgham	d				07 07									07 36								
Aldermaston	d				07 11									07 40								
Theale	d				07 16				07 25					07 45								
Reading West	d				07 23		←		07 34				←	07 52								←
Reading	a	07 28		07 25	07 28		07 28	07 34	07 37	07 53	07 39	07 43	07 53	07 56	08 17	07 55	08 00	08 06	08 10	08 12	08 16	08 17
	d	07 30		07 27			07 30	07 36	07 39	07 55		07 45	07 55		08 19	07 56	08 02	08 08		08 14	08 17	08 19
Twyford	a	→					07 37			→			08 02		→							08 25
Maidenhead	a					07 58	07 45						08 10									08 33
Slough	a						07 55						08 20									
Ealing Broadway	a						08 18															
London Paddington	a			07 59		08 26	08 32	08 07	08 09			08 14	08 52			08 31	08 33	08 38		08 40	08 44	08 59

A MX until 9 September, from 13 September until 28 October, MX from 1 November

B MO until 12 September, MO from 31 October

C ⊐ from Reading ⊘ to Newbury

Station		GW	GW	GW	GW	GW	XC	GW	GW	GW	GW	CH	GW	GW	GW	GW	GW	XC	GW	GW	GW	GW	GW
		◇■	■	■	■	■	◇■	◇■	■	◇■	■	■	◇■	■	■	◇■	■	◇■	◇■	◇■	■	■	◇■
		A						B					A							A			
		⊐					⊤	⊐		⊐			⊐			⊐		⊤	⊐	⊐			
Birmingham New Street	d						07 03											07 33					
Birmingham International	d						07 14																
Coventry	d						07 25																
Leamington Spa	d						07 38											08 05					
Banbury	d				07 27		07 55											08 22					
Kings Sutton	d				07 31																		
Heyford	d				07 40																		
Tackley	d				07 44																		
Bicester Town	d											07 57											
Islip	d											08 08											
Oxford	a				07 55		08 14					08 23						08 41					
	d	07 52			07 56	08 06	08 16				08 21						08 36	08 44		08 51			09 01
Radley	d				08 02						08 27												
Culham	d				08 06																		
Appleford	d				08 09												08 45						
Didcot Parkway	a				08 15	08 18					08 36						08 51						09 14
	d				08 15	08 20		08 29			08 37		08 47			08 53	09 01		08 59				09 15
Cholsey	d				08 22						08 43						09 07						
Goring & Streatley	d				08 27						08 48						09 12						
Pangbourne	d				08 32						08 53						09 17						
Tilehurst	d				08 37						08 57						09 21						
Bedwyn	d			07 56																	08 40		
Hungerford	d			08 01																	08 45		
Kintbury	d			08 06																	08 50		
Newbury	a			08 14																	08 57		
	d		07 55							08 29					08 36						08 57		
Newbury Racecourse	d		07 57												08 38								
Thatcham	d		08 02												08 43						09 02		
Midgham	d		08 07												08 47								
Aldermaston	d		08 10												08 51								
Theale	d		08 16												08 56						09 10		
Reading West	d		08 23						←					←	09 03							←	
Reading	a	08 21	08 27		08 46	08 36	08 39	08 44	08 46	08 50	09 03		09 01	09 03	09 08	09 07	09 27	09 09	09 13	09 14	09 20	09 27	09 32
	d	08 23			08 48	08 38		08 45	08 48	08 52	09 03		09 02	09 03		09 08	09 33		09 15	09 18	09 21	09 33	09 37
Twyford	a				→				08 54		→			09 09			→					09 39	
Maidenhead	a								09 02					09 17								09 47	
Slough	a													09 29								09 54	09 52
Ealing Broadway	a													09 54								10 19	
London Paddington	a	08 51				09 06		09 14	09 27	09 21			09 29	10 04		09 39			09 44	09 47	09 56	10 32	10 12

Station		GW	XC	GW	GW	GW	GW	CH	GW	GW	XC	GW	GW	GW	GW	GW	GW	GW	GW	XC	GW	GW
		■	◇■	◇■	■	◇■	■	■	◇■	■	◇■	■	◇■	◇■	◇■	◇■	■	■	■	◇■	■	◇■
													C	D	C	D						
			⊤	⊐					⊐		⊤			⊤	⊐	⊐				⊤		⊐
Birmingham New Street	d		08 03								08 33									09 03		
Birmingham International	d		08 14																	09 14		
Coventry	d		08 25																	09 25		
Leamington Spa	d		08 38								09 00									09 38		
Banbury	d		08 55								09 19								09 39	09 55		
Kings Sutton	d																		09 45			
Heyford	d																		09 53			
Tackley	d																		09 58			
Bicester Town	d							09 07														
Islip	d							09 18														
Oxford	a		09 14					09 32			09 41								10 10	10 14		
	d	09 07	09 16			09 31				09 37	09 43		10 01	10 01				10 07		10 16		
Radley	d	09 13																10 13				
Culham	d	09 17																				
Appleford	d																	10 17				
Didcot Parkway	a	09 24								09 50								10 24				
	d	09 31		09 29					09 53	10 01					10 16	10 16		10 31				10 29
Cholsey	d	09 37								10 07								10 37				
Goring & Streatley	d	09 42								10 12								10 42				
Pangbourne	d	09 47								10 17								10 47				
Tilehurst	d	09 51								10 21								10 51				
Bedwyn	d											09 36										
Hungerford	d											09 41										
Kintbury	d											09 46										
Newbury	a											09 53										
	d				09 22							09 53									10 13	
Newbury Racecourse	d				09 25																10 15	
Thatcham	d				09 30							09 58									10 20	
Midgham	d				09 34																10 24	
Aldermaston	d				09 38																10 28	
Theale	d				09 43							10 06									10 33	
Reading West	d				09 50		←										←				10 40	
Reading	a	09 57	09 39	09 44	09 54	09 54	09 57		10 06	10 28	10 10	10 16	10 24	10 25	10 31	10 31	10 28	10 58		10 39	10 45	10 44
	d	10 03		09 45		09 55	10 03		10 08	10 33		10 18	10 25	10 25	10 32	10 32	10 33	11 03				10 45
Twyford	a	→					10 09			→							10 39	→				
Maidenhead	a						10 17										10 47					
Slough	a					10 10	10 24						10 39	10 39			10 54					
Ealing Broadway	a						10 49										11 19					
London Paddington	a			10 15		10 29	11 02		10 37			10 54	10 58	11 00	11 01	11 07	11 32					11 14

A ⊐ from Reading

B The Bristolian

C until 9 September

D from 12 September

Birmingham, Banbury, Bicester, Oxford and Bedwyn - Reading and London

		GW	GW	GW	GW	XC	CH	GW	GW	GW	GW	GW	XC	GW	GW	GW	GW	GW	GW	XC	CH
		◇1	◇1	1	1	◇1	1	1	◇1	◇1	1	1	◇1	◇1	1	◇1	1	◇1	1	◇1	1
		H	A ☕			H			H	☕			H	☕		H		☕		H	
Birmingham New Street 12	d					09 33							10 03							10 33	
Birmingham International	d												10 14								
Coventry	d												10 25								
Leamington Spa 8	d					10 00							10 38							11 00	
Banbury	d					10 19							10 55							11 19	
Kings Sutton	d																				
Heyford	d																				
Tackley	d																				
Bicester Town	d						10 30														11 30
Islip	d						10 41														11 41
Oxford	a					10 41	10 56						11 14							11 40	11 56
	d	10 31			10 37	10 43			11 01			11 07	11 16			11 31			11 37	11 43	
Radley	d											11 13									
Culham	d																				
Appleford	d																				
Didcot Parkway	a				10 51							11 22							11 51		
	d		10 47		11 01					11 16		11 31		11 29				11 53	12 01		
Cholsey	d				11 07							11 37							12 07		
Goring & Streatley	d				11 12							11 42							12 12		
Pangbourne	d				11 17							11 47							12 17		
Tilehurst	d				11 21							11 51							12 21		
Bedwyn	d							10 36													
Hungerford	d							10 41													
Kintbury	d							10 46													
Newbury	a							10 53													
	d							10 53							11 13						
Newbury Racecourse	d														11 15						
Thatcham	d							10 58							11 20						
Midgham	d														11 24						
Aldermaston	d														11 28						
Theale	d							11 06							11 33						
Reading West	d			←							←				11 40		←				
Reading 7	a	10 54	11 00	10 58	11 27	11 08		11 16	11 24	11 30	11 27	11 58	11 39	11 43	11 45	11 54	11 58	12 06	12 27	12 10	
	d	10 55	11 02	11 03	11 33			11 18	11 25	11 32	11 33	12 03		11 44		11 55	12 03	12 08	12 33		
Twyford 3	a			11 09	→						11 39	→					12 09		→		
Maidenhead 3	a			11 17							11 47						12 17				
Slough 3	a	11 09		11 24					11 39		11 54					12 09	12 24				
Ealing Broadway ⊖	a			11 49							12 19						12 49				
London Paddington 15 ⊖	a	11 29	11 32	12 02				11 55	11 59	12 02	12 32			12 14		12 29	13 03	12 37			

		GW	GW	GW	GW	GW	XC	GW	GW	GW	GW	GW	GW	XC	GW	GW	GW	GW	GW	GW	XC
		1	◇1	◇1	1	1	◇1	◇1	1	◇1	◇1	1	1	◇1	◇1	1	◇1	1	1	1	◇1
			H	☕			H	☕		H	☕			H	H		☕				H
Birmingham New Street 12	d						11 03							11 33							12 03
Birmingham International	d						11 14														12 14
Coventry	d						11 25														12 25
Leamington Spa 8	d						11 38							12 00							12 38
Banbury	d						11 55							12 19						12 42	12 55
Kings Sutton	d																			12 48	
Heyford	d																			12 56	
Tackley	d																			13 01	
Bicester Town	d																				
Islip	d																				
Oxford	a						12 14							12 40						13 12	13 14
	d		12 01			12 07	12 16			12 31			12 37	12 43	13 01				13 07		13 16
Radley	d					12 13													13 13		
Culham	d																				
Appleford	d					12 17													13 17		
Didcot Parkway	a					12 24							12 49						13 24		
	d			12 16		12 31		12 29			12 47		13 01				13 16		13 31		
Cholsey	d					12 37							13 07						13 37		
Goring & Streatley	d					12 42							13 12						13 42		
Pangbourne	d					12 47							13 17						13 47		
Tilehurst	d					12 51							13 21						13 51		
Bedwyn	d	11 36														12 36					
Hungerford	d	11 41														12 41					
Kintbury	d	11 46														12 46					
Newbury	a	11 53														12 53					
	d	11 53							12 13							13 04					
Newbury Racecourse	d								12 15												
Thatcham	d	11 58							12 20							13 09					
Midgham	d								12 24												
Aldermaston	d								12 28												
Theale	d	12 06							12 33							13 17					
Reading West	d				←				12 40			←						←			
Reading 7	a	12 16	12 24	12 30	12 27	12 57	12 39	12 43	12 45	12 54	13 00	12 57	13 29	13 08	13 24	13 27	13 31	13 29	13 58		13 39
	d	12 18	12 25	12 32	12 33	13 03		12 44		12 55	13 02	13 03	13 33		13 25	13 29	13 32	13 33	14 03		
Twyford 3	a				12 39	→						13 09	→					13 39	→		
Maidenhead 3	a				12 47							13 17						13 47			
Slough 3	a		12 39		12 54					13 09		13 24			13 39			13 54			
Ealing Broadway ⊖	a				13 19							13 49						14 19			
London Paddington 15 ⊖	a	12 52	12 57	13 00	13 32			13 14		13 29	13 32	14 02			14 01	14 09	14 06	14 32			

A The Red Dragon

Birmingham, Banbury, Bicester, Oxford and Bedwyn - Reading and London

		GW	GW	GW	GW	GW	GW	XC	GW	GW	GW	GW	GW	XC	CH	GW	GW	GW	GW	GW	GW	XC
		◇1	1	◇1	1	◇1	1	◇1	◇1	◇1	◇1	1	1	◇1	1	◇1	1	◇1	◇1	1	1	◇1
		☕		H		☕		H	☕	H	☕			H		☕			☕			H
Birmingham New Street 12	d							12 33						13 03								13 33
Birmingham International	d													13 14								
Coventry	d													13 25								
Leamington Spa 8	d							13 00						13 38								14 00
Banbury	d							13 21						13 55								14 19
Kings Sutton	d																					
Heyford	d																					
Tackley	d																					
Bicester Town	d														14 00							
Islip	d														14 11							
Oxford	a							13 40						14 14	14 28							14 40
	d			13 31			13 37	13 43		14 01			14 07	14 16				14 31			14 37	14 43
Radley	d												14 13									
Culham	d																					
Appleford	d												14 17									
Didcot Parkway	a						13 49						14 24								14 51	
	d	13 29				13 53	14 01				14 16		14 31			14 29			14 47		15 01	
Cholsey	d						14 07						14 37								15 07	
Goring & Streatley	d						14 12						14 42								15 12	
Pangbourne	d						14 17						14 47								15 17	
Tilehurst	d						14 21						14 51								15 21	
Bedwyn	d								13 32													
Hungerford	d								13 39													
Kintbury	d																					
Newbury	a								13 49													
	d		13 13						13 49								14 13					
Newbury Racecourse	d		13 15														14 15					
Thatcham	d		13 20						13 56								14 20					
Midgham	d		13 24														14 24					
Aldermaston	d		13 28														14 28					
Theale	d		13 33						14 05								14 33					
Reading West	d		13 40		←							←					14 40			←		
Reading 7	a	13 43	13 45	13 54	13 58	14 06	14 27	14 10	14 15	14 24	14 31	14 27	14 58	14 39		14 43	14 45	14 54	15 00	14 58	15 27	15 08
	d	13 44		13 55	14 03	14 08	14 33		14 17	14 25	14 32	14 33	15 03			14 44		14 55	15 02	15 03	15 33	
Twyford 3	a				14 09		→					14 39	→							15 09	→	
Maidenhead 3	a				14 17							14 47								15 17		
Slough 3	a			14 09	14 24					14 39		14 54						15 09		15 24		
Ealing Broadway ⊖	a				14 49							15 19								15 49		
London Paddington 15 ⊖	a	14 14		14 29	15 02	14 37			14 44	15 00	15 08	15 33				15 14		15 29	15 32	16 03		

		GW	GW	GW	GW	GW	GW	XC	GW	GW	GW	GW	GW	GW	GW	XC	CH	GW	GW	GW	GW	GW
		1	1	◇1	◇1	1	1	◇1	◇1	1	◇1	1	◇1	1	1	◇1	1	1	1	1	◇1	1
		A	B	H	☕			H	☕		☕		C ☕			H			D H		☕	
Birmingham New Street 12	d							14 03								14 33						
Birmingham International	d							14 14														
Coventry	d							14 25														
Leamington Spa 8	d							14 38								15 00						
Banbury	d							14 55							15 08	15 19						
Kings Sutton	d														15 14							
Heyford	d														15 22							
Tackley	d														15 27							
Bicester Town	d																15 30					
Islip	d																15 41					
Oxford	a							15 14							15 39	15 42	15 56					
	d			15 01			15 07	15 16			15 31			15 37		15 44			16 01			16 07
Radley	d						15 13							15 43								16 13
Culham	d						15 17															
Appleford	d																					16 17
Didcot Parkway	a						15 24							15 51								16 24
	d				15 16		15 31		15 29				15 53	16 01							16 16	16 31
Cholsey	d						15 37							16 07								16 37
Goring & Streatley	d						15 42							16 12								16 42
Pangbourne	d						15 47							16 17								16 47
Tilehurst	d						15 51							16 21								16 51
Bedwyn	d	14 36	14 36															15 36				
Hungerford	d	14 41	14 41															15 41				
Kintbury	d	14 46	14 46															15 46				
Newbury	a	14 53	14 53															15 53				
	d	14 53	14 53							15 13								15 53				
Newbury Racecourse	d									15 15												
Thatcham	d	14 58	14 58							15 20								15 58				
Midgham	d									15 24												
Aldermaston	d									15 28												
Theale	d	15 06	15 06							15 33								16 06				
Reading West	d					←				15 40		←								←		
Reading 7	a	15 17	15 16	15 24	15 31	15 27	15 58	15 39	15 43	15 45	15 54	15 58	16 06	16 27		16 10		16 16	16 24	16 27	16 31	16 59
	d	15 18	15 18	15 25	15 32	15 33	16 03		15 44		15 55	16 03	16 08	16 33				16 19	16 25	16 33	16 34	17 03
Twyford 3	a					15 39	→					16 09		→						16 39		→
Maidenhead 3	a					15 47						16 17								16 47		
Slough 3	a			15 39		15 54					16 09	16 24							16 40	16 54		
Ealing Broadway ⊖	a					16 19						16 49								17 21		
London Paddington 15 ⊖	a	15 54	15 54	16 01	16 09	16 32			16 14		16 27	17 02	16 39					16 57	17 00	17 32	17 09	

A FO from 8 July until 2 September

B until 7 July, FX from 11 July until 1 September, from 5 September

C The Cheltenham Spa Express

Birmingham, Banbury, Bicester, Oxford and Bedwyn - Reading and London

		XC	GW	GW	GW	GW	GW	GW	GW	XC	GW	GW	GW	GW	GW	GW	GW	XC	CH	GW	GW	GW	GW
		◇1	◇1	1	◇1	◇1	◇1	1	1	◇1	◇1	1	1	1	◇1	1	1	◇1	1	1	◇1	1	◇1
					A	B														A			B
		T	□		T		□			T	□			T	□			T			□		□
Birmingham New Street 12	d	15 03								15 33								16 03					
Birmingham International	d	15 14																16 14					
Coventry	d	15 25																16 25					
Leamington Spa 5	d	15 38								16 00								16 38					
Banbury	d	15 55								16 19								16 55		17 00			
Kings Sutton	d																			17 05			
Heyford	d																			17 14			
Tackley	d																			17 17			
Bicester Town	d																		16 54				
Islip	d																		17 05				
Oxford	a	16 14								16 40								17 14	17 20	17 28			
	d	16 16			16 31	16 31			16 37	16 43			16 47	17 01			17 07	17 16					17 31
Radley	d								16 43								17 13						
Culham	d																17 17						
Appleford	d																						
Didcot Parkway	a								16 51				17 04				17 24						
	d		16 29				16 47		17 01						17 16		17 31				17 29		
Cholsey	d								17 07								17 37						
Goring & Streatley	d								17 12								17 42						
Pangbourne	d								17 17								17 47						
Tilehurst	d								17 21								17 51						
Bedwyn	d											16 44											
Hungerford	d										16 39	16 49											
Kintbury	d											16 54											
Newbury	a										16 49	17 03											
	d			16 13							16 49											17 13	
Newbury Racecourse	d			16 15																		17 15	
Thatcham	d			16 20							16 56											17 20	
Midgham	d			16 24																		17 24	
Aldermaston	d			16 28																		17 28	
Theale	d			16 33							17 05											17 33	
Reading West	d			16 40				←								←						17 40	
Reading 7	a	16 39	16 43	16 45	16 54	16 54	17 00	16 59	17 29	17 08	17 15			17 24	17 31	17 29	17 57	17 39			17 43	17 45	17 54
	d		16 44		16 55	16 55	17 02	17 03	17 33		17 17			17 25	17 32	17 33	18 00				17 44		17 56
Twyford 3	a							17 09	→							17 39	→						
Maidenhead 3	a							17 17			17 28					17 47							
Slough 3	a				17 09	17 09		17 24						17 39		17 54							18 10
Ealing Broadway ⊖	a							17 49								18 19							
London Paddington 15 ⊖	a		17 14		17 34	17 34	17 30	18 02			17 54			17 59	18 02	18 32					18 14		18 28

		GW	GW	GW	GW	GW	XC	GW	GW	GW	GW	GW	GW	XC	GW	GW	GW	GW	GW	GW	XC	CH
		1	1	◇1	◇1	1	◇1	1	1	◇1	1	1	1	◇1	1	◇1	1	◇1	1	1	◇1	1
			A	A		B					B	A										
				□	□		T		T	□				T		□		□			T	
Birmingham New Street 12	d						16 33							17 03							17 33	
Birmingham International	d													17 14								
Coventry	d													17 25								
Leamington Spa 5	d						17 00							17 38							18 00	
Banbury	d						17 19							17 55							18 19	
Kings Sutton	d																					
Heyford	d																					
Tackley	d																					
Bicester Town	d																					18 18
Islip	d																					18 29
Oxford	a						17 41							18 14							18 40	18 44
	d		17 31	17 36		17 37	17 43		18 01				18 07	18 16			18 31			18 37	18 43	
Radley	d		17 37			17 43							18 13							18 43		
Culham	d												18 17									
Appleford	d		17 41			17 47														18 47		
Didcot Parkway	a		17 48			17 54							18 24							18 56		
	d		18 01		17 53	18 01				18 16			18 31			18 29		18 47		19 01		
Cholsey	d		18 07			18 07							18 37							19 07		
Goring & Streatley	d		18 12			18 12							18 42							19 12		
Pangbourne	d		18 17			18 17							18 47							19 17		
Tilehurst	d		18 21			18 21							18 51							19 21		
Bedwyn	d							17 36							17 55							
Hungerford	d							17 41							18 00							
Kintbury	d							17 46							18 05							
Newbury	a							17 53							18 12							
	d							17 53							18 13							
Newbury Racecourse	d														18 15							
Thatcham	d							17 58							18 20							
Midgham	d														18 24							
Aldermaston	d							18 04							18 28							
Theale	d							18 09							18 33							
Reading West	d	←									←	←			18 40				←			
Reading 7	a	17 57	18 27	18 01	18 06	18 27	18 10	18 21	18 24	18 31	18 27	18 27	19 00	18 39	18 45	18 44	18 54	19 01	19 00	19 27	19 08	
	d	18 00	18 33	18 02	18 08	18 33		18 22	18 25	18 32	18 33	18 33	19 03			18 45	18 55	19 02	19 03	19 33		
Twyford 3	a	18 06	→			→					18 39	18 39	→						19 09	→		
Maidenhead 3	a	18 17									18 47	18 47							19 21			
Slough 3	a	18 24							18 39		18 54	18 54					19 09		19 29			
Ealing Broadway ⊖	a	18 49									19 19	19 19							19 53			
London Paddington 15 ⊖	a	19 01		18 30	18 39			18 54	18 59	19 02	19 31	19 32				19 14	19 31	19 32	20 03			

A until 9 September

B from 12 September

Birmingham, Banbury, Bicester, Oxford and Bedwyn - Reading and London

		GW	GW	GW	GW	GW	GW	XC	GW	GW	GW	GW	GW FX	GW FO	GW	GW	GW	XC	GW	GW	GW	GW	GW
		1	1	1	◇1	1	1	◇1	◇1	◇1	◇1	1	◇1	◇1	◇1	◇1	1	◇1	◇1	◇1	1	1	1
										A	B				C	D							
					T			T	□				□	□	□	□		T	□				
Birmingham New Street 12	d							18 03										18 33					
Birmingham International	d							18 14															
Coventry	d							18 25															
Leamington Spa 5	d							18 38										19 00					
Banbury	d						18 37	18 55										19 19					
Kings Sutton	d						18 43																
Heyford	d						18 51																
Tackley	d						18 56																
Bicester Town	d																						
Islip	d																						
Oxford	a						19 08	19 14										19 41					
	d			19 01	19 06			19 16		19 31	19 31						19 37	19 43		20 01			
Radley	d			19 07																			
Culham	d																						
Appleford	d																						
Didcot Parkway	a			19 16													19 49						
	d			19 32					19 29				19 47	19 47			20 01		19 59				
Cholsey	d			19 37													20 07						
Goring & Streatley	d			19 42													20 12						
Pangbourne	d			19 47													20 17						
Tilehurst	d			19 51													20 21						
Bedwyn	d		19 03																				19 55
Hungerford	d		19 08																				20 00
Kintbury	d		19 13																				20 05
Newbury	a		19 22																				20 12
	d	18 53													19 49	19 49						19 55	20 12
Newbury Racecourse	d																					19 57	
Thatcham	d	18 58																				20 02	20 17
Midgham	d																					20 06	
Aldermaston	d																					20 10	
Theale	d	19 06																				20 15	20 25
Reading West	d					←						←									←	20 21	
Reading 7	a	19 16		19 57	19 32	19 27		19 39	19 44	19 54	19 54	19 57	20 00	20 00	20 06	20 06	20 27	20 08	20 13	20 24	20 27	20 27	20 34
	d	19 18		19 58	19 32	19 33			19 45	19 54	19 54	19 58	20 02	20 02	20 08	20 08	20 33		20 15	20 25	20 33		20 34
Twyford 3	a			→		19 42						20 04					→				20 39		
Maidenhead 3	a					19 50						20 12									20 47		
Slough 3	a				19 47	19 57				20 09	20 09	20 19								20 39	20 54		
Ealing Broadway ⊖	a					20 22						20 49									21 19		
London Paddington 15 ⊖	a	19 54			20 06	20 32			20 14	20 27	20 29	21 00	20 30	20 32	20 39	20 39			20 46	21 01	21 31		21 08

		GW	XC	CH	GW	GW	GW	GW	GW	GW	XC	GW	GW	GW	GW	XC	GW	GW	GW	GW	GW FX	GW FO
		1	◇1	1	◇1	◇1	1	◇1	1	1	◇1	1	◇1	1	1	◇1	◇1	1	◇1	◇1	◇1	◇1
			E																			
			T		□	□		□			T						□		□		□	□
Birmingham New Street 12	d		19 03								19 33					20 03						
Birmingham International	d		19 14													20 14						
Coventry	d		19 25													20 25						
Leamington Spa 5	d		19 38								20 05					20 38						
Banbury	d		19 55				20 01				20 23					20 55						
Kings Sutton	d						20 07															
Heyford	d						20 15															
Tackley	d						20 20															
Bicester Town	d			20 00																		
Islip	d			20 11																		
Oxford	a		20 14	20 26			20 32				20 41					21 14						
	d	20 07	20 16			20 31				20 37	20 43		21 01		21 07	21 16				21 31		
Radley	d	20 13													21 13							
Culham	d	20 17													21 17							
Appleford	d									20 45												
Didcot Parkway	a	20 24								20 51					21 24							
	d	20 31			20 29			20 47		21 01					21 31		21 29				21 50	21 51
Cholsey	d	20 37								21 07					21 37							
Goring & Streatley	d	20 42								21 12					21 42							
Pangbourne	d	20 47								21 17					21 47							
Tilehurst	d	20 51								21 21					21 51							
Bedwyn	d											20 33						21 06				
Hungerford	d											20 38						21 11				
Kintbury	d											20 43						21 16				
Newbury	a											20 50						21 23				
	d											20 50						21 23	21 42			
Newbury Racecourse	d											20 52						21 25				
Thatcham	d											20 57						21 30				
Midgham	d											21 02						21 35				
Aldermaston	d											21 05						21 38				
Theale	d											21 10						21 43				
Reading West	d								←			21 17		←				21 50				
Reading 7	a	20 58	20 39		20 44	20 54		21 00	20 58	21 29	21 07	21 22	21 24	21 29	22 03	21 40	21 43	21 55	21 59	22 06	22 09	22 09
	d	21 14			20 45	20 55		21 02	21 14	21 33			21 25	21 33			21 44		22 01	22 06	22 11	22 11
Twyford 3	a	→							21 20	→				21 39								
Maidenhead 3	a								21 28					21 47								
Slough 3	a					21 09			21 40				21 39	21 58						22 22		
Ealing Broadway ⊖	a								22 04					22 21								
London Paddington 15 ⊖	a				21 14	21 29		21 32	22 18				22 00	22 33			22 14		22 30	22 43	22 45	22 45

A until 7 July, FX from 11 July until 1 September, from 5 September

B FO from 8 July until 2 September

C from 4 July until 2 September. The Atlantic Coast Express

D until 1 July, from 5 September

E T to Oxford

Table 116

Mondays to Fridays

Birmingham, Banbury, Bicester, Oxford and Bedwyn - Reading and London

		GW	XC	CH	GW FO	GW FX	XC	GW	GW FO	GW FX	GW FO	GW FX	GW	GW	GW FO	GW FX	GW	GW	XC	GW FO	GW FX	CH FO	GW
		■	◇■	■	◇	◇■	◇■	■	◇■	◇■	◇■	◇■	■	■	◇■	◇■	■	■	◇■	◇■	◇■	■	■
						A																	
											☕	☕								☕	☕		
Birmingham New Street	d		20 33				21 03												22 03				
Birmingham International	d						21 14												22 14				
Coventry	d						21 25												22 25				
Leamington Spa	d		21 00				21 38												22 38				
Banbury	d		21 19		21 38	21 38	21 55							22 25					22 55				23 45
Kings Sutton	d				21 42	21 42								22 31									23 50
Heyford	d				21 51	21 51								22 39									23 58
Tackley	d				21 55	21 55								22 44									00 03
Bicester Town	d			21 30																		23 40	
Islip	d			21 41																		23 51	
Oxford	a		21 40	21 56	22 06	22 06	22 14							22 56					23 14			00 06	00 14
	d	21 37	21 43		22 11	22 11	22 16		22 34	22 34			22 55		23 05	23 05			23 15				00 27
Radley	d	21 43											23 01										00 33
Culham	d												23 05										00 37
Appleford	d												23 07				←						00 39
Didcot Parkway	a	21 52			22 24	22 24							23 14		23 18	23 18	23 14						00 46
	d	22 01			22 27	22 27					22 52	22 52	23 21		23 18	23 18	23 21			23 35	23 35		00 46
Cholsey	d	22 07											→				23 27						00 52
Goring & Streatley	d	22 12															23 32						00 57
Pangbourne	d	22 17															23 37						01 01
Tilehurst	d	22 21															23 41						01 06
Bedwyn	d							21 55										23 00					
Hungerford	d							22 00										23 05					
Kintbury	d							22 05										23 10					
Newbury	a							22 12										23 17					
	d							22 13										23 17					
Newbury Racecourse	d							22 15										23 19					
Thatcham	d							22 20										23 24					
Midgham	d							22 24										23 29					
Aldermaston	d							22 28										23 32					
Theale	d							22 33										23 37					
Reading West	d							22 40										23 44					
Reading	a	22 27	22 16		22 44	22 44	22 41	22 45	22 58	22 58	23 06	23 06			23 34	23 35	23 48	23 49	23 52	23 53	23 53		01 12
	d				22 46	22 46			22 59	22 59	23 08	23 07			23 35	23 40				23 55	23 55		01 12
Twyford	a																						01 18
Maidenhead	a														23 46	23 53							01 26
Slough	a				23 02	23 02			23 12	23 18					23 54	00 01							01 34
Ealing Broadway ⊖	a																						01 50
London Paddington ⊖	a				23 21	23 25			23 30	23 37	23 42	23 50			00 22	00 26				00 27	00 33		02 01

		CH B
Birmingham New Street	d	
Birmingham International	d	
Coventry	d	
Leamington Spa	d	23 38
Banbury	d	23 55
Kings Sutton	d	
Heyford	d	
Tackley	d	
Bicester Town	d	
Islip	d	
Oxford	a	00 22
	d	
Radley	d	
Culham	d	
Appleford	d	
Didcot Parkway	a	
	d	
Cholsey	d	
Goring & Streatley	d	
Pangbourne	d	
Tilehurst	d	
Bedwyn	d	
Hungerford	d	
Kintbury	d	
Newbury	a	
	d	
Newbury Racecourse	d	
Thatcham	d	
Midgham	d	
Aldermaston	d	
Theale	d	
Reading West	d	
Reading	a	
	d	
Twyford	a	
Maidenhead	a	
Slough	a	
Ealing Broadway ⊖	a	
London Paddington ⊖	a	

A ■ from Reading ◇ from Reading

B until 2 September

Table 116

Saturdays until 10 September

Birmingham, Banbury, Bicester, Oxford and Bedwyn - Reading and London

		GW	GW	CH	GW	GW	CH	GW	GW	GW	GW	GW	GW	GW	GW	GW	GW	GW	GW	GW	GW	GW	XC
		◇■	◇■	■	◇■	■		■	■	■	◇■	■	■	◇■	■	◇■	■	■	◇■	◇■	■	■	◇■
							A																
			☕								☕					☕				☕			🍴
Birmingham New Street	d																						06 03
Birmingham International	d																						06 14
Coventry	d																						06 25
Leamington Spa	d						23p38																06 38
Banbury	d					23p45	23p55																06 55
Kings Sutton	d					23p50																	
Heyford	d					23p58																	
Tackley	d					00 03																	
Bicester Town	d			23p40																			
Islip	d			23p51																			
Oxford	a			00 06		00 14	00 22																07 14
	d	23p05			00 07	00 27		03 59	05 14	05 49			06 07	06 31				06 42	07 01			07 07	07 16
Radley	d					00 33			05 20				06 13									07 13	
Culham	d					00 37			05 24													07 17	
Appleford	d					00 39							06 18										
Didcot Parkway	a	23p18			00 20	00 46		04 10	05 31	06 01			06 24					06 54				07 24	
	d	23p18	23p35		00 21	00 46		04 10	05 31	06 01	06 29		06 31			06 59		07 01		07 17		07 31	
Cholsey	d					00 52			05 37	06 07			06 37					07 07				07 37	
Goring & Streatley	d					00 57			05 42	06 12			06 42					07 12				07 42	
Pangbourne	d					01 01			05 47	06 17			06 47					07 17				07 47	
Tilehurst	d					01 06			05 51	06 21			06 51					07 21				07 51	
Bedwyn	d											06 05					06 39						
Hungerford	d											06 11					06 43						
Kintbury	d											06 15					06 48						
Newbury	a											06 22					06 55						
	d											06 22					06 55						
Newbury Racecourse	d											06 24											
Thatcham	d											06 29					07 00						
Midgham	d											06 34											
Aldermaston	d											06 37											
Theale	d											06 42					07 08						
Reading West	d											06 49			←						←		
Reading	a	23p34	23p53		00 38	01 12		04 27	05 57	06 27	06 43	06 52	06 57	07 00	06 57	07 14	07 20	07 27	07 27	07 31	07 27	07 59	07 39
	d	23p35	23p55		00 39	01 12		04 40	06 03	06 33	06 45	06 52	07 03	07 00	07 03	07 15	07 21	07 33	07 27	07 32	07 33	08 03	
Twyford	a					01 18		04 46	06 09	06 39			→		07 09			→			07 39	→	
Maidenhead	a	23p46				01 26		04 54	06 17	06 47					07 17						07 47		
Slough	a	23p54			00 53	01 34		05 01	06 24	06 54				07 16	07 24				07 42		07 54		
Ealing Broadway ⊖	a					01 50		05 19	06 49	07 19					07 49						08 19		
London Paddington ⊖	a	00 22	00 27		01 11	02 01		05 31	07 01	07 32	07 14	07 22		07 37	08 02	07 44	07 54		08 01	08 07	08 32		

		GW	GW	GW	GW	GW	GW	GW	XC	GW	GW	GW	CH	GW	GW	GW	XC	GW	GW	GW	GW	GW	GW
		■	◇■	◇■	■	◇■	■	■	◇■	◇■	■	◇■	■	◇■	■	■	◇■	■	◇■	◇■	◇■	◇■	■
			☕	☕		☕			🍴	☕				☕			🍴		☕	☕	☕	☕	
Birmingham New Street	d								06 33								07 03						
Birmingham International	d																07 14						
Coventry	d																07 25						
Leamington Spa	d								07 00								07 38						
Banbury	d				07 02				07 19								07 55						
Kings Sutton	d				07 08																		
Heyford	d				07 17																		
Tackley	d				07 21																		
Bicester Town	d												07 36										
Islip	d												07 47										
Oxford	a				07 32				07 40				08 02				08 14						
	d			07 31				07 37	07 43			08 01				08 07	08 16				08 31		
Radley	d															08 13							
Culham	d																						
Appleford	d															08 17							
Didcot Parkway	a							07 49								08 24							
	d		07 29			07 47		08 01		08 00				08 17		08 31			08 29			08 47	
Cholsey	d							08 07								08 37							
Goring & Streatley	d							08 12								08 42							
Pangbourne	d							08 17								08 47							
Tilehurst	d							08 21								08 51							
Bedwyn	d										07 37												
Hungerford	d										07 41												
Kintbury	d										07 46												
Newbury	a										07 53												
	d	07 13									07 53							08 13		08 34			
Newbury Racecourse	d	07 15																08 15					
Thatcham	d	07 20									07 58							08 20					
Midgham	d	07 24																08 24					
Aldermaston	d	07 28																08 28					
Theale	d	07 33									08 06							08 33					
Reading West	d	07 42					←								←			08 40					←
Reading	a	07 45	07 44	07 54		08 00	07 59	08 27	08 06	08 14	08 19	08 25		08 31	08 27	08 57	08 39	08 44	08 44	08 52	08 54	09 00	08 57
	d		07 46	07 54		08 02	08 03	08 33		08 16	08 20	08 26		08 32	08 33	09 03			08 46	08 52	08 55	09 02	09 03
Twyford	a						08 09	→							08 39	→							09 09
Maidenhead	a						08 17								08 47								09 17
Slough	a			08 09			08 24					08 40			08 54						09 09		09 24
Ealing Broadway ⊖	a						08 49								09 19								09 49
London Paddington ⊖	a		08 14	08 29		08 32	09 02			08 44	08 52	08 59		09 02	09 32				09 14	09 21	09 29	09 32	10 02

A not 10 September

Table 116

Saturdays until 10 September

Birmingham, Banbury, Bicester, Oxford and Bedwyn - Reading and London

Station		GW ◇1 ⊡		GW 1	XC ◇1 ⚯	GW ◇1 ⊡	GW 1	GW ◇1 ⚯	GW ◇1 A ⊡	GW 1	GW 1	CH 1		XC ◇1 ⚯	GW ◇1 ⊡	GW 1	GW ◇1 A ⊡	GW 1	GW ◇1 A ⊡	GW 1	GW 1	XC ◇1 ⚯		GW 1	GW ◇1 ⚯
Birmingham New Street [12]	d				07 33									08 03								08 33			
Birmingham International	d													08 14											
Coventry	d													08 25											
Leamington Spa [3]	d				08 00									08 38								09 00			
Banbury	d				08 19									08 55				09 02				09 19			
Kings Sutton	d																	09 08							
Heyford	d																	09 17							
Tackley	d																	09 21							
Bicester Town	d											08 45													
Islip	d											08 56													
Oxford	a				08 40							09 11		09 14				09 32				09 40			
	d			08 37	08 43			09 01			09 07			09 16			09 31				09 37	09 43			10 01
Radley	d										09 13														
Culham	d										09 17														
Appleford	d																								
Didcot Parkway	a			08 49							09 24										09 49				
	d	08 52		09 01		09 00			09 18		09 31				09 29				09 47		10 01				
Cholsey	d			09 07							09 37										10 07				
Goring & Streatley	d			09 12							09 42										10 12				
Pangbourne	d			09 17							09 47										10 17				
Tilehurst	d			09 21							09 51										10 21				
Bedwyn	d						08 37																	09 37	
Hungerford	d						08 41																	09 41	
Kintbury	d						08 46																	09 46	
Newbury	a						08 53																	09 53	
	d						08 53									09 23								09 53	
Newbury Racecourse	d															09 26									
Thatcham	d						08 58									09 31								09 58	
Midgham	d															09 36									
Aldermaston	d															09 39									
Theale	d						09 06									09 44								10 06	
Reading West	d									←						09 51				←					
Reading [7]	a	09 07		09 27	09 08	09 14	09 20	09 24	09 32	09 27	09 57			09 39	09 44	09 55	09 54		10 00	09 57	10 27	10 09		10 17	10 25
	d	09 09		09 33		09 16	09 20	09 24	09 33	09 33	10 03				09 45		09 55		10 02	10 03	10 33			10 18	10 25
Twyford [3]	a			→						09 39	→									10 09	→				
Maidenhead [3]	a									09 47										10 17					
Slough [3]	a							09 40		09 54							10 09			10 24					10 40
Ealing Broadway ⊖	a									10 19										10 49					
London Paddington [15] ⊖	a	09 37				09 44	09 52	09 59	10 02	10 32					10 14		10 29		10 32	11 02				10 52	10 59

Station		GW 1	GW ◇1 ⊡	GW 1	XC ◇1 ⚯	CH 1	GW 1	GW ◇1 ⊡		GW ◇1 ⊡	GW ◇1 ⊡	GW 1	GW 1	XC ◇1 ⚯	GW 1	GW ◇1	GW 1	GW 1		XC ◇1 ⚯	GW 1	GW ◇1 ⊡	GW ◇1 ⚯	GW 1	GW ◇1 ⊡
Birmingham New Street [12]	d				09 03									09 33						10 03					
Birmingham International	d				09 14															10 14					
Coventry	d				09 25															10 25					
Leamington Spa [3]	d				09 38									10 00						10 38					
Banbury	d				09 55									10 19						10 55				11 02	
Kings Sutton	d																							11 08	
Heyford	d																							11 17	
Tackley	d																							11 21	
Bicester Town	d					09 57																			
Islip	d					10 08																			
Oxford	a				10 14	10 23								10 40						11 14				11 32	
	d			10 07	10 16					10 31			10 37	10 43		11 01		11 07		11 16			11 31		
Radley	d			10 13														11 13							
Culham	d																								
Appleford	d			10 17																					
Didcot Parkway	a			10 23									10 49					11 24							
	d		10 22	10 31				10 29			10 47		11 01					11 31				11 29			11 47
Cholsey	d			10 37									11 07					11 37							
Goring & Streatley	d			10 42									11 12					11 42							
Pangbourne	d			10 47									11 17					11 47							
Tilehurst	d			10 51									11 21					11 51							
Bedwyn	d														10 40										
Hungerford	d														10 46										
Kintbury	d														10 50										
Newbury	a														10 57										
	d						10 13								10 57						11 13				
Newbury Racecourse	d						10 15														11 15				
Thatcham	d						10 20								11 02						11 20				
Midgham	d						10 24														11 24				
Aldermaston	d						10 28														11 28				
Theale	d						10 33								11 10						11 33				
Reading West	d	←					10 40					←					←				11 40				
Reading [7]	a	10 27	10 36	10 58	10 39		10 44	10 45		10 54	11 01	10 58	11 27	11 09	11 21	11 24	11 27	11 58		11 39	11 44	11 44	11 54		12 00
	d	10 33	10 39	11 03				10 46		10 55	11 02	11 03	11 33		11 21	11 25	11 33	12 03				11 45	11 55		12 02
Twyford [3]	a	10 39		→								11 09	→				11 39	→							
Maidenhead [3]	a	10 47										11 17					11 47								
Slough [3]	a	10 54								11 09		11 24				11 39	11 54						12 09		
Ealing Broadway ⊖	a	11 19										11 49					12 19								
London Paddington [15] ⊖	a	11 32	11 08					11 14		11 29	11 33	12 02			11 52	11 59	12 32					12 14	12 29		12 32

A ⊡ from Reading

Table 116

Saturdays until 10 September

Birmingham, Banbury, Bicester, Oxford and Bedwyn - Reading and London

Station		GW 1	GW 1	XC ◇1 ⚯		CH 1	GW 1	GW ◇1 ⚯	GW 1	GW ◇1 ⊡	GW 1	XC ◇1 ⚯	GW ◇1 ⊡	GW 1		GW ◇1 ⚯	GW 1	GW ◇1 ⊡	GW 1	GW 1	XC ◇1 ⚯	GW ◇1 ⚯	GW 1	GW 1	
Birmingham New Street [12]	d			10 33								11 03									11 33				
Birmingham International	d											11 14													
Coventry	d											11 25													
Leamington Spa [3]	d			11 00								11 38									12 00				
Banbury	d			11 19								11 55									12 19				
Kings Sutton	d																								
Heyford	d																								
Tackley	d																								
Bicester Town	d					11 30																			
Islip	d					11 41																			
Oxford	a			11 40		11 56						12 14									12 40				
	d		11 37	11 43				12 01			12 07	12 16				12 31				12 37	12 43	13 01		13 07	
Radley	d										12 13													13 13	
Culham	d																							13 17	
Appleford	d										12 17														
Didcot Parkway	a		11 49								12 24									12 49				13 24	
	d		12 01							12 22	12 31		12 28					12 47		13 01				13 31	
Cholsey	d		12 07								12 37									13 07				13 37	
Goring & Streatley	d		12 12								12 42									13 12				13 42	
Pangbourne	d		12 17								12 47									13 17				13 47	
Tilehurst	d		12 21								12 51									13 21				13 51	
Bedwyn	d						11 37										12 32								
Hungerford	d						11 41										12 38								
Kintbury	d						11 46										12 42								
Newbury	a						11 53										12 50								
	d						11 53							12 24											
Newbury Racecourse	d													12 26											
Thatcham	d						11 58							12 31											
Midgham	d													12 36											
Aldermaston	d													12 39											
Theale	d						12 06							12 44											
Reading West	d	←							←					12 51					←				←		
Reading [7]	a	11 58	12 28	12 09			12 15	12 25	12 28	12 37	12 57	12 39	12 43	12 55		12 53		13 00	12 57	13 27	13 08	13 25	13 27	13 59	
	d	12 03	12 33				12 17	12 25	12 33	12 39	13 03		12 45			12 55		13 02	13 03	13 33		13 25	13 33	14 03	
Twyford [3]	a	12 09	→						12 39		→								13 09	→			13 39	→	
Maidenhead [3]	a	12 17							12 47										13 17				13 47		
Slough [3]	a	12 24						12 40	12 54							13 09			13 24			13 40	13 54		
Ealing Broadway ⊖	a	12 49							13 19										13 49				14 19		
London Paddington [15] ⊖	a	13 02					12 52	12 59	13 32	13 07			13 13			13 30		13 33	14 02			13 59	14 32		

Station		XC ◇1 ⚯	CH 1	GW 1	GW ◇1 ⊡	GW 1	GW ◇1	GW 1	GW ◇1 ⊡	GW 1		GW 1	XC ◇1 ⚯	GW 1	GW ◇1 ⚯	GW 1	GW ◇1 ⊡	GW 1	XC ◇1 ⚯	GW 1		GW ◇1 ⊡	GW ◇1 ⊡	GW ◇1 ⊡	GW 1
Birmingham New Street [12]	d	12 03											12 33						13 03						
Birmingham International	d	12 14																	13 14						
Coventry	d	12 25																	13 25						
Leamington Spa [3]	d	12 38											13 02						13 38						
Banbury	d	12 55						13 02					13 21						13 55						
Kings Sutton	d							13 08																	
Heyford	d							13 17																	
Tackley	d							13 21																	
Bicester Town	d		12 59																						
Islip	d		13 10																						
Oxford	a	13 14	13 25					13 32					13 40						14 14						
	d	13 16					13 31					13 37	13 43		14 01			14 07	14 16				14 31		
Radley	d																	14 13							
Culham	d																								
Appleford	d																	14 17							
Didcot Parkway	a											13 49						14 24							
	d				13 29				13 47			14 01					14 22	14 31				14 29		14 47	
Cholsey	d											14 07						14 37							
Goring & Streatley	d											14 12						14 42							
Pangbourne	d											14 17						14 47							
Tilehurst	d											14 21						14 51							
Bedwyn	d													13 40											
Hungerford	d													13 46											
Kintbury	d													13 50											
Newbury	a													13 57											
	d			13 12		13 28								13 57						14 13					
Newbury Racecourse	d			13 15																14 15					
Thatcham	d			13 20		13 33								14 02						14 20					
Midgham	d			13 24																14 24					
Aldermaston	d			13 28																14 28					
Theale	d			13 33		13 41								14 10						14 33					
Reading West	d			13 40						←						←				14 40					←
Reading [7]	a	13 39		13 44	13 44	13 51	13 54		14 00	13 59		14 27	14 09	14 18	14 25	14 27	14 38	14 58	14 39	14 44		14 44	14 53	15 00	14 58
	d				13 45	13 51	13 55		14 02	14 03		14 33		14 18	14 25	14 33	14 39	15 03				14 45	14 55	15 02	15 03
Twyford [3]	a									14 09		→				14 39		→							15 09
Maidenhead [3]	a									14 17						14 47									15 17
Slough [3]	a						14 09			14 24					14 40	14 54							15 10		15 24
Ealing Broadway ⊖	a									14 49						15 19									15 49
London Paddington [15] ⊖	a				14 14	14 23	14 29		14 32	15 02				14 54	14 59	15 32	15 09					15 14	15 29	15 32	16 02

Birmingham, Banbury, Bicester, Oxford and Bedwyn - Reading and London

		GW ■	XC ◇■ ⊼	CH ■	GW ■	GW ◇■	GW ■	GW ■	XC ◇■ ⊼	GW ■	GW ◇■ ☐	GW ◇■ ⊼	GW ■	GW ◇■ ☐	GW ■	GW ■	XC ◇■ ⊼	CH ■	GW ■	GW ◇■	GW ◇■ ☐	GW ■	GW ◇■ ☐
Birmingham New Street ■	d		13 33						14 03								14 33						
Birmingham International	d								14 14														
Coventry	d								14 25														
Leamington Spa ■	d		14 00						14 38								15 00						
Banbury	d		14 19						14 55				15 02				15 20						
Kings Sutton	d												15 08										
Heyford	d												15 17										
Tackley	d												15 21										
Bicester Town	d			14 18														15 28					
Islip	d			14 29														15 39					
Oxford	a		14 40	14 44					15 14				15 32				15 41	15 54					
	d	14 37	14 43			15 01		15 07	15 16			15 31				15 37	15 43			16 01			
Radley	d							15 13															
Culham	d							15 17															
Appleford	d																						
Didcot Parkway	a	14 49						15 24								15 49							
	d	15 01						15 31			15 29			15 47		16 01							16 22
Cholsey	d	15 07						15 37								16 07							
Goring & Streatley	d	15 12						15 42								16 12							
Pangbourne	d	15 17						15 47								16 17							
Tilehurst	d	15 21						15 51								16 21							
Bedwyn	d				14 37														15 37				
Hungerford	d				14 41														15 41				
Kintbury	d				14 46														15 46				
Newbury	a				14 53														15 53				
	d				14 53					15 13									15 53		16 06		
Newbury Racecourse	d									15 15													
Thatcham	d				14 58					15 20									15 58				
Midgham	d									15 24													
Aldermaston	d									15 28													
Theale	d				15 06					15 33									16 06				
Reading West	d						←			15 40					←							←	
Reading ■	a	15 27	15 08		15 17	15 25	15 27	15 59	15 39	15 44	15 44	15 54		16 01	15 59	16 29	16 09		16 16	16 25	16 25	16 29	16 38
	d	15 33			15 19	15 25	15 33	16 03			15 45	15 55		16 02	16 03	16 33			16 18	16 26	16 28	16 33	16 39
Twyford ■	a	→					15 39	→							16 09	→						16 39	
Maidenhead ■	a						15 47								16 17							16 47	
Slough ■	a					15 40	15 54					16 10			16 24					16 40		16 54	
Ealing Broadway ⊖	a						16 19								16 49							17 19	
London Paddington ■ ⊖	a				15 54	15 59	16 32				16 14	16 29		16 37	17 02				16 52	16 59	17 02	17 32	17 07

		GW ■	XC ◇■ ⊼	GW ■	GW ◇■ ☐	GW ◇■ ⊼	GW ◇■ ☐	GW ■	GW ■	XC ◇■ ⊼	CH ■	GW ■	GW ◇■	GW ■	GW ■	XC ◇■ ⊼	GW ◇■ ☐	GW ■	GW ◇■ ☐	GW ◇■ ☐	GW ■	GW ■
Birmingham New Street ■	d		15 03							15 33						16 03						
Birmingham International	d		15 14													16 14						
Coventry	d		15 25													16 25						
Leamington Spa ■	d		15 38							16 02						16 38						
Banbury	d		15 55							16 20						16 55						
Kings Sutton	d																					
Heyford	d																					
Tackley	d																					
Bicester Town	d										16 30											
Islip	d										16 41											
Oxford	a		16 14							16 40	16 56					17 14						
	d	16 07	16 16			16 31			16 37	16 43			17 01		17 07	17 16			17 31			17 37
Radley	d	16 13													17 13							
Culham	d														17 17							
Appleford	d	16 17																				
Didcot Parkway	a	16 24							16 49						17 24							17 49
	d	16 31			16 29		16 47		17 01						17 31		17 29			17 47		18 01
Cholsey	d	16 37							17 07						17 37							18 07
Goring & Streatley	d	16 42							17 12						17 42							18 12
Pangbourne	d	16 47							17 17						17 47							18 17
Tilehurst	d	16 51							17 21						17 51							18 21
Bedwyn	d											16 43										
Hungerford	d											16 49										
Kintbury	d											16 53										
Newbury	a											17 00										
	d			16 13								17 01						17 15				
Newbury Racecourse	d			16 15														17 17				
Thatcham	d			16 20								17 06						17 22				
Midgham	d			16 24														17 27				
Aldermaston	d			16 28														17 30				
Theale	d			16 33								17 14						17 35				
Reading West	d			16 40				←						←				17 42			←	
Reading ■	a	16 58	16 39	16 44	16 44	16 54	17 00	16 58	17 27	17 08		17 22	17 26	17 27	17 57	17 39	17 44	17 46	17 54	18 00	17 57	18 27
	d	17 03			16 45	16 55	17 02	17 03	17 33			17 22	17 27	17 33	18 03		17 45		17 56	18 02	18 03	18 33
Twyford ■	a	→						17 09	→					17 39	→						18 09	→
Maidenhead ■	a							17 17						17 47							18 17	
Slough ■	a					17 09		17 24					17 41	17 54					18 09		18 24	
Ealing Broadway ⊖	a							17 49						18 19							18 49	
London Paddington ■ ⊖	a				17 14	17 29	17 32	18 02				17 54	18 00	18 32			18 14		18 29	18 32	19 02	

Birmingham, Banbury, Bicester, Oxford and Bedwyn - Reading and London

		XC ◇■ ⊼	GW ■	GW ■	GW ◇■	GW ■	GW ◇■ ☐	GW ■	XC ◇■ ⊼	CH ■	GW ■	GW ◇■ ☐	GW ◇■ ⊼	GW ◇■ ☐	GW ■	GW ■	XC ◇■ ⊼	GW ■	GW ◇■	GW ■	GW ■	XC ◇■ ⊼	GW ■
Birmingham New Street ■	d	16 33							17 03								17 33					18 03	
Birmingham International	d								17 14													18 14	
Coventry	d								17 25													18 25	
Leamington Spa ■	d	17 00							17 38								18 02					18 38	
Banbury	d	17 19	17 23						17 55								18 19					18 55	
Kings Sutton	d		17 29																				
Heyford	d		17 38																				
Tackley	d		17 42																				
Bicester Town	d									18 04													
Islip	d									18 15													
Oxford	a	17 41	17 53						18 14	18 30							18 40					19 14	
	d	17 43			18 01			18 07	18 16				18 31			18 37	18 43		19 01		19 07	19 16	
Radley	d							18 13													19 13		
Culham	d																				19 17		
Appleford	d							18 17															
Didcot Parkway	a							18 24								18 49					19 24		
	d						18 22	18 31				18 29		18 47		19 01					19 31		
Cholsey	d							18 37								19 07					19 37		
Goring & Streatley	d							18 42								19 12					19 42		
Pangbourne	d							18 47								19 17					19 47		
Tilehurst	d							18 51								19 21					19 51		
Bedwyn	d			17 37														18 37					
Hungerford	d			17 41														18 41					
Kintbury	d			17 46														18 46					
Newbury	a			17 53														18 53					
	d			17 53							18 13							18 53					19 13
Newbury Racecourse	d										18 15												19 15
Thatcham	d			17 58							18 20							18 58					19 20
Midgham	d										18 24												19 24
Aldermaston	d										18 28												19 28
Theale	d			18 06							18 33							19 06					19 33
Reading West	d					←					18 40				←					←			19 40
Reading ■	a	18 09		18 17	18 25	18 27	18 38	18 58	18 39		18 44	18 44	18 54	19 00	18 58	19 29	19 08	19 17	19 25	19 29	19 57	19 39	19 44
	d			18 19	18 25	18 33	18 39	19 03				18 45	18 55	19 02	19 03	19 33		19 20	19 25	19 33	20 03		
Twyford ■	a					18 39		→							19 09	→				19 39	→		
Maidenhead ■	a					18 47									19 17					19 47			
Slough ■	a				18 40	18 54							19 09		19 24				19 40	19 54			
Ealing Broadway ⊖	a					19 19									19 49					20 19			
London Paddington ■ ⊖	a			18 52	18 59	19 32	19 08					19 14	19 29	19 32	20 02			19 52	19 59	20 32			

		GW ◇■ ☐	GW ◇■ ⊼	GW ■	GW ■	GW ◇■ ☐	GW ■	XC ◇■ ⊼	CH ■	GW ◇■	GW ■	GW ■	GW ◇■ ☐	GW ■	XC ◇■ A ⊼	GW ◇■ ☐	GW ◇■	GW ■	GW ◇■ ☐	GW ■	XC ◇■ ⊼	CH ■
Birmingham New Street ■	d							18 33							19 03						19 33	
Birmingham International	d														19 14							
Coventry	d														19 25							
Leamington Spa ■	d							19 00							19 38						20 03	
Banbury	d				19 02			19 19							19 55						20 21	
Kings Sutton	d				19 08																	
Heyford	d				19 17																	
Tackley	d				19 21																	
Bicester Town	d								19 18													20 30
Islip	d								19 29													20 41
Oxford	a				19 32			19 40	19 44						20 14						20 40	20 56
	d		19 31				19 37	19 43		20 01				20 07	20 16		20 31			20 37	20 43	
Radley	d													20 13								
Culham	d																					
Appleford	d													20 17								
Didcot Parkway	a						19 49							20 24						20 49		
	d	19 29					20 01						20 23	20 31		20 29			20 47	21 01		
Cholsey	d						20 07							20 37						21 07		
Goring & Streatley	d						20 12							20 42						21 12		
Pangbourne	d						20 17							20 47						21 17		
Tilehurst	d						20 21							20 51						21 21		
Bedwyn	d										19 41											
Hungerford	d										19 47											
Kintbury	d										19 51											
Newbury	a										19 58											
	d					19 46					19 58											
Newbury Racecourse	d										20 00											
Thatcham	d										20 05											
Midgham	d										20 10											
Aldermaston	d										20 13											
Theale	d										20 18											
Reading West	d			←							20 25	←						←				
Reading ■	a	19 44	19 54	19 57		20 07	20 29	20 08		20 25	20 28	20 29	20 38	20 57	20 39	20 44	20 54	20 57	21 06	21 27	21 08	
	d	19 45	19 55	20 03		20 09	20 33			20 25		20 33	20 39	21 03		20 45	20 54	21 03	21 08	21 33		
Twyford ■	a			20 09			→					20 39		→				21 09		→		
Maidenhead ■	a			20 17								20 47						21 17				
Slough ■	a		20 09	20 24						20 40		20 54					21 09	21 24				
Ealing Broadway ⊖	a			20 49								21 19						21 49				
London Paddington ■ ⊖	a	20 14	20 29	21 02		20 37				20 59		21 32	21 07			21 14	21 29	22 02	21 36			

A ⊼ to Oxford

Table 116

Saturdays
until 10 September

Birmingham, Banbury, Bicester, Oxford and Bedwyn - Reading and London

		GW ◇1	GW 1	GW 1	GW 1	XC ◇1 A ⌶	GW ◇1 ⊥P	GW ◇1 ⊥P	GW ◇1	GW 1	GW ◇1	GW 1	CH 1	XC ◇1	GW 1	GW ◇1	GW 1	GW ◇1 ⊥P	GW ◇1	GW 1	GW ◇1 B ⊥P	GW 1
Birmingham New Street 12	d					20 03								21 03								
Birmingham International	d					20 14								21 14								
Coventry	d					20 25								21 25								
Leamington Spa 8	d					20 38								21 38								
Banbury	d			20 38		20 55								21 55			22 02					
Kings Sutton	d			20 44													22 08					
Heyford	d			20 53													22 17					
Tackley	d			20 57													22 21					
Bicester Town	d												21 37									
Islip	d												21 48									
Oxford	a			21 08		21 14							22 03	22 16			22 32					
	d	21 01				21 16			21 36	21 50	22 01			22 18		22 31			23 01			23 07
Radley	d									21 56												23 13
Culham	d																					23 17
Appleford	d																					23 20
Didcot Parkway	a								21 49	22 04	22 12								23 13			23 25
	d						21 34	21 47	21 50	22 04	22 13							22 49	23 14		23 30	23 36
Cholsey	d									22 10												23 42
Goring & Streatley	d									22 15												23 47
Pangbourne	d									22 21												23 51
Tilehurst	d									22 24												23 56
Bedwyn	d				20 48										22 00					23 00		
Hungerford	d				20 54										22 06					23 06		
Kintbury	d				20 58										22 10					23 10		
Newbury	a				21 05										22 17					23 17		
	d				21 05										22 17					23 17		
Newbury Racecourse	d				21 07										22 19					23 19		
Thatcham	d				21 12										22 24					23 24		
Midgham	d				21 17										22 29					23 29		
Aldermaston	d				21 20										22 32					23 32		
Theale	d				21 25										22 37					23 37		
Reading West	d		←		21 32							←			22 44					23 44		
Reading 7	a	21 25	21 27		21 36	21 39	21 48	21 59	22 04	22 31	22 28	22 31		22 41	22 48	22 54		23 04	23 30	23 48	23 51	00 01
	d	21 25	21 33				21 50	22 02	22 05	22 33	22 29	22 33				22 55		23 05	23 31		23 52	00 03
Twyford 3	a		21 39							→		22 39										00 09
Maidenhead 3	a		21 47									22 47										00 17
Slough 3	a	21 40	21 54						22 22		22 43	22 54				23 09			23 48			00 28
Ealing Broadway ⊖	a		22 19									23 19										00 52
London Paddington 15 ⊖	a	21 59	22 32				22 16	22 37	22 41		23 02	23 29				23 29		23 36	00 13		00 33	01 03

		CH 1
Birmingham New Street 12	d	
Birmingham International	d	
Coventry	d	
Leamington Spa 8	d	
Banbury	d	
Kings Sutton	d	
Heyford	d	
Tackley	d	
Bicester Town	d	22 53
Islip	d	23 04
Oxford	a	23 19
	d	
Radley	d	
Culham	d	
Appleford	d	
Didcot Parkway	a	
	d	
Cholsey	d	
Goring & Streatley	d	
Pangbourne	d	
Tilehurst	d	
Bedwyn	d	
Hungerford	d	
Kintbury	d	
Newbury	a	
	d	
Newbury Racecourse	d	
Thatcham	d	
Midgham	d	
Aldermaston	d	
Theale	d	
Reading West	d	
Reading 7	a	
	d	
Twyford 3	a	
Maidenhead 3	a	
Slough 3	a	
Ealing Broadway ⊖	a	
London Paddington 15 ⊖	a	

A ⌶ to Oxford

Table 116

Saturdays
from 17 September

Birmingham, Banbury, Bicester, Oxford and Bedwyn - Reading and London

		GW ◇1	GW ◇1 ⊥P	CH 1	GW ◇1	GW 1	GW 1	GW 1	GW 1	GW ◇1 ⊥P	GW 1	GW 1	GW ◇1	GW 1	GW ◇1 ⊥P	GW 1	GW 1	GW ◇1	GW ◇1 ⊥P	GW 1	GW 1	XC ◇1 ⌶	GW 1
Birmingham New Street 12	d																					06 03	
Birmingham International	d																					06 14	
Coventry	d																					06 25	
Leamington Spa 8	d																					06 38	
Banbury	d					23p45																06 55	
Kings Sutton	d					23p50																	
Heyford	d					23p58																	
Tackley	d					00 03																	
Bicester Town	d			23p40																			
Islip	d			23p51																			
Oxford	a			00 06		00 14																07 14	
	d	23p05			00 07	00 27	03 59	05 14	05 49			06 07	06 31				06 42	07 01			07 07	07 16	
Radley	d					00 33		05 20				06 13									07 13		
Culham	d					00 37		05 24													07 17		
Appleford	d					00 39						06 18											
Didcot Parkway	a	23p18			00 20	00 46	04 10	05 31	06 01			06 24					06 54				07 24		
	d	23p18	23p35		00 21	00 46	04 10	05 31	06 01	06 29		06 31			06 59		07 01		07 17		07 31		
Cholsey	d					00 52		05 37	06 07			06 37					07 07				07 37		
Goring & Streatley	d					00 57		05 42	06 12			06 42					07 12				07 42		
Pangbourne	d					01 01		05 47	06 17			06 47					07 17				07 47		
Tilehurst	d					01 06		05 51	06 21			06 51					07 21				07 51		
Bedwyn	d										06 05					06 39							
Hungerford	d										06 11					06 43							
Kintbury	d										06 15					06 48							
Newbury	a										06 22					06 55							
	d										06 22					06 55							07 13
Newbury Racecourse	d										06 24												07 15
Thatcham	d										06 29					07 00							07 20
Midgham	d										06 34												07 24
Aldermaston	d										06 37												07 28
Theale	d										06 42					07 08							07 33
Reading West	d										06 49			←						←			07 42
Reading 7	a	23p34	23p53		00 38	01 12	04 27	05 57	06 27	06 43	06 52	06 57	07 00	06 57	07 14	07 20	07 27	07 27	07 31	07 27	07 59	07 39	07 45
	d	23p35	23p55		00 39	01 12	04 40	06 03	06 33	06 45	06 52	07 03	07 00	07 03	07 15	07 21	07 33	07 27	07 32	07 33	08 03		
Twyford 3	a					01 18	04 46	06 09	06 39			→		07 09			→			07 39	→		
Maidenhead 3	a	23p46				01 26	04 54	06 17	06 47					07 17						07 47			
Slough 3	a	23p54			00 53	01 34	05 01	06 24	06 54				07 16	07 24				07 42		07 54			
Ealing Broadway ⊖	a					01 50	05 19	06 49	07 19					07 49						08 19			
London Paddington 15 ⊖	a	00 22	00 27		01 11	02 01	05 31	07 01	07 32	07 14	07 22		07 37	08 02	07 44	07 54		08 01	08 07	08 32			

		GW ◇1 ⊥P	GW ◇1 ⊥P	GW 1	GW ◇1 ⊥P	GW 1	GW 1	XC ◇1 ⌶	GW ◇1 ⊥P	GW 1	GW ◇1	CH 1	GW ◇1 ⊥P	GW 1	GW 1	XC ◇1 ⌶	GW 1	GW ◇1 ⊥P	GW ◇1 ⊥P	GW ◇1 ⊥P	GW ◇1 ⊥P	GW 1	GW ◇1 ⊥P
Birmingham New Street 12	d							06 33								07 03							
Birmingham International	d															07 14							
Coventry	d															07 25							
Leamington Spa 8	d							07 00								07 38							
Banbury	d			07 02				07 19								07 55							
Kings Sutton	d			07 08																			
Heyford	d			07 17																			
Tackley	d			07 21																			
Bicester Town	d											07 36											
Islip	d											07 47											
Oxford	a			07 32				07 40				08 02				08 14							
	d		07 31				07 37	07 43			08 01				08 07	08 16				08 31			
Radley	d														08 13								
Culham	d																						
Appleford	d														08 17								
Didcot Parkway	a						07 49								08 24								
	d	07 29			07 47		08 01		08 00				08 17		08 31			08 29			08 47		08 52
Cholsey	d						08 07								08 37								
Goring & Streatley	d						08 12								08 42								
Pangbourne	d						08 17								08 47								
Tilehurst	d						08 21								08 51								
Bedwyn	d									07 37													
Hungerford	d									07 41													
Kintbury	d									07 46													
Newbury	a									07 53													
	d									07 53							08 13		08 34				
Newbury Racecourse	d																08 15						
Thatcham	d									07 58							08 20						
Midgham	d																08 24						
Aldermaston	d																08 28						
Theale	d									08 06							08 33						
Reading West	d					←								←			08 40					←	
Reading 7	a	07 44	07 54		08 00	07 59	08 27	08 06	08 14	08 19	08 25		08 31	08 27	08 57	08 39	08 44	08 44	08 52	08 54	09 00	08 57	09 07
	d	07 46	07 54		08 02	08 03	08 33		08 16	08 20	08 26		08 32	08 33	09 03			08 46	08 52	08 55	09 02	09 03	09 09
Twyford 3	a					08 09	→							08 39	→							09 09	
Maidenhead 3	a					08 17								08 47								09 17	
Slough 3	a		08 09			08 24					08 40			08 54						09 09		09 24	
Ealing Broadway ⊖	a					08 49								09 19								09 49	
London Paddington 15 ⊖	a	08 14	08 29		08 32	09 02			08 44	08 52	08 59		09 02	09 32				09 14	09 21	09 29	09 32	10 02	09 37

Table 116

Saturdays from 17 September

Birmingham, Banbury, Bicester, Oxford and Bedwyn - Reading and London

		GW		XC	GW	GW	GW	GW	GW	GW	CH	XC		GW	GW	GW	GW	GW	GW	GW	XC	GW		GW	GW
		1		◇1 ⊼	◇1 ⊐	1	◇1 ⊼	◇1 A ⊐	1	1	1	◇1 ⊼		◇1 ⊐	1	◇1 A ⊐	1	◇1 A ⊐	1	1	◇1 ⊼	1		◇1 ⊼	◇1 ⊐
Birmingham New Street 12	d			07 33								08 03									08 33				
Birmingham International	d											08 14													
Coventry	d											08 25													
Leamington Spa 8	d			08 00								08 38									09 00				
Banbury	d			08 19								08 55					09 02				09 19				
Kings Sutton	d																09 08								
Heyford	d																09 17								
Tackley	d																09 21								
Bicester Town	d										08 45														
Islip	d										08 56														
Oxford	a			08 40							09 11	09 14					09 32				09 40				
	d	08 37		08 43			09 01			09 07		09 16				09 31				09 37	09 43			10 01	
Radley	d									09 13															
Culham	d									09 17															
Appleford	d																								
Didcot Parkway	a	08 49								09 24										09 49					
	d	09 01			09 00			09 18		09 31				09 29				09 47		10 01					10 16
Cholsey	d	09 07								09 37										10 07					
Goring & Streatley	d	09 12								09 42										10 12					
Pangbourne	d	09 17								09 47										10 17					
Tilehurst	d	09 21								09 51										10 21					
Bedwyn	d					08 37																09 37			
Hungerford	d					08 41																09 41			
Kintbury	d					08 46																09 46			
Newbury	a					08 53																09 53			
	d					08 53									09 23							09 53			
Newbury Racecourse	d														09 26										
Thatcham	d					08 58									09 31							09 58			
Midgham	d														09 36										
Aldermaston	d														09 39										
Theale	d					09 06									09 44							10 06			
Reading West	d								←						09 51				←						
Reading 7	a	09 27		09 08	09 14	09 20	09 24	09 32	09 27	09 57		09 39		09 44	09 55	09 54		10 00	09 57	10 27	10 09	10 17		10 25	10 32
	d	09 33			09 16	09 20	09 24	09 33	09 33	10 03				09 45		09 55		10 02	10 03	10 33		10 18		10 25	10 33
Twyford 3	a	→							09 39	→									10 09	→					
Maidenhead 3	a								09 47										10 17						
Slough 3	a						09 40		09 54							10 09			10 24					10 40	
Ealing Broadway ⊖	a								10 19										10 49						
London Paddington 15 ⊖	a				09 44	09 52	09 59	10 02	10 32					10 14		10 29		10 32	11 02			10 52		10 59	11 02

		GW	GW	GW	XC	CH	GW	GW		GW	GW	GW	GW	XC	GW	GW	GW	GW		XC	GW	GW	GW	GW	GW
		1	◇1 ⊐	1	◇1 ⊼	1	1	◇1 ⊐		◇1 ⊐	◇1 ⊐	1	1	◇1 ⊼	1	◇1	1	1		◇1 ⊼	1	◇1 ⊐	◇1 ⊼	1	◇1 ⊐
Birmingham New Street 12	d				09 03									09 33						10 03					
Birmingham International	d				09 14															10 14					
Coventry	d				09 25															10 25					
Leamington Spa 8	d				09 38									10 00						10 38					
Banbury	d				09 55									10 19						10 55				11 02	
Kings Sutton	d																							11 08	
Heyford	d																							11 17	
Tackley	d																							11 21	
Bicester Town	d					09 57																			
Islip	d					10 08																			
Oxford	a				10 14	10 23								10 40						11 14				11 32	
	d			10 07	10 16					10 31			10 37	10 43		11 01		11 07		11 16			11 31		
Radley	d			10 13														11 13							
Culham	d																								
Appleford	d			10 17																					
Didcot Parkway	a			10 23									10 49					11 24							
	d		10 22	10 31				10 29			10 47		11 01					11 31				11 29			11 47
Cholsey	d			10 37									11 07					11 37							
Goring & Streatley	d			10 42									11 12					11 42							
Pangbourne	d			10 47									11 17					11 47							
Tilehurst	d			10 51									11 21					11 51							
Bedwyn	d														10 40										
Hungerford	d														10 46										
Kintbury	d														10 50										
Newbury	a														10 57										
	d						10 13								10 57						11 13				
Newbury Racecourse	d						10 15														11 15				
Thatcham	d						10 20								11 02						11 20				
Midgham	d						10 24														11 24				
Aldermaston	d						10 28														11 28				
Theale	d						10 33								11 10						11 33				
Reading West	d	←					10 40					←					←				11 40				
Reading 7	a	10 27	10 36	10 58	10 39		10 44	10 45		10 54	11 01	10 58	11 27	11 09	11 21	11 24	11 27	11 58		11 39	11 44	11 44	11 54		12 00
	d	10 33	10 39	11 03				10 46		10 55	11 02	11 03	11 33		11 21	11 25	11 33	12 03				11 45	11 55		12 02
Twyford 3	a	10 39		→								11 09	→				11 39	→							
Maidenhead 3	a	10 47										11 17					11 47								
Slough 3	a	10 54								11 09		11 24				11 39	11 54						12 09		
Ealing Broadway ⊖	a	11 19										11 49					12 19								
London Paddington 15 ⊖	a	11 32	11 08					11 14		11 29	11 33	12 02			11 52	11 59	12 32					12 14	12 29		12 32

A ⊐ from Reading

Table 116

Saturdays from 17 September

Birmingham, Banbury, Bicester, Oxford and Bedwyn - Reading and London

		GW	GW	XC		CH	GW	GW	GW	GW	GW	XC	GW	GW		GW	GW	GW	GW	XC	GW	GW	GW	XC
		1	1	◇1 ⊼		1	1	◇1 ⊼	1	◇1 ⊐	1	◇1 ⊼	1	◇1 ⊐		◇1 ⊼	◇1 ⊐	1	1	◇1 ⊼	◇1 ⊼	1	1	◇1 ⊼
Birmingham New Street 12	d			10 33								11 03								11 33				12 03
Birmingham International	d											11 14												12 14
Coventry	d											11 25												12 25
Leamington Spa 8	d			11 00								11 38								12 00				12 38
Banbury	d			11 19								11 55								12 19				12 55
Kings Sutton	d																							
Heyford	d																							
Tackley	d																							
Bicester Town	d					11 30																		
Islip	d					11 41																		
Oxford	a			11 40		11 56						12 14								12 40				13 14
	d		11 37	11 43				12 01			12 07	12 16				12 31			12 37	12 43	13 01		13 07	13 16
Radley	d										12 13												13 13	
Culham	d																						13 17	
Appleford	d										12 17													
Didcot Parkway	a		11 49								12 24								12 49				13 24	
	d		12 01							12 22	12 31			12 28			12 47		13 01				13 31	
Cholsey	d		12 07								12 37								13 07				13 37	
Goring & Streatley	d		12 12								12 42								13 12				13 42	
Pangbourne	d		12 17								12 47								13 17				13 47	
Tilehurst	d		12 21								12 51								13 21				13 51	
Bedwyn	d						11 37																	
Hungerford	d						11 41																	
Kintbury	d						11 46																	
Newbury	a						11 53																	
	d						11 53						12 13											
Newbury Racecourse	d												12 15											
Thatcham	d						11 58						12 20											
Midgham	d												12 24											
Aldermaston	d												12 28											
Theale	d						12 06						12 33											
Reading West	d	←							←				12 40					←				←		
Reading 7	a	11 58	12 28	12 09			12 15	12 25	12 28	12 37	12 57	12 39	12 44	12 43		12 53	13 00	12 57	13 27	13 08	13 25	13 27	13 59	13 39
	d	12 03	12 33				12 17	12 25	12 33	12 39	13 03			12 44		12 55	13 02	13 03	13 33		13 25	13 33	14 03	
Twyford 3	a	12 09	→						12 39		→							13 09	→			13 39	→	
Maidenhead 3	a	12 17							12 47									13 17				13 47		
Slough 3	a	12 24						12 40	12 54							13 09		13 24			13 40	13 54		
Ealing Broadway ⊖	a	12 49							13 19									13 49				14 19		
London Paddington 15 ⊖	a	13 02					12 52	12 59	13 32	13 07				13 14		13 30	13 33	14 02			13 59	14 32		

		CH	GW	GW	GW	GW	GW	GW	GW	GW		XC	GW	GW	GW	GW	GW	XC	GW	GW		GW	GW	GW	GW
		1	1	◇1 ⊐	1	◇1	1	◇1 ⊐	1	1		◇1 ⊼	◇1 ⊐	◇1 ⊼	1	◇1 ⊐	1	◇1 ⊼	1	◇1 ⊐		◇1 ⊐	◇1 ⊐	1	1
Birmingham New Street 12	d											12 33						13 03							
Birmingham International	d																	13 14							
Coventry	d																	13 25							
Leamington Spa 8	d											13 02						13 38							
Banbury	d						13 02					13 21						13 55							
Kings Sutton	d						13 08																		
Heyford	d						13 17																		
Tackley	d						13 21																		
Bicester Town	d	12 59																							
Islip	d	13 10																							
Oxford	a	13 25					13 32					13 40						14 14							
	d					13 31				13 37		13 43		14 01			14 07	14 16				14 31			14 37
Radley	d																14 13								
Culham	d																								
Appleford	d																14 17								
Didcot Parkway	a									13 49							14 24								14 49
	d			13 29				13 47		14 01						14 22	14 31			14 29			14 47		15 01
Cholsey	d									14 07							14 37								15 07
Goring & Streatley	d									14 12							14 42								15 12
Pangbourne	d									14 17							14 47								15 17
Tilehurst	d									14 21							14 51								15 21
Bedwyn	d				13 07								13 33												
Hungerford	d				13 13								13 40												
Kintbury	d				13 17																				
Newbury	a				13 24								13 49												
	d		13 13		13 28								13 50						14 13						
Newbury Racecourse	d		13 15																14 15						
Thatcham	d		13 20		13 33								13 57						14 20						
Midgham	d		13 24																14 24						
Aldermaston	d		13 28																14 28						
Theale	d		13 33		13 41								14 06						14 33						
Reading West	d		13 40						←						←				14 40					←	
Reading 7	a		13 44	13 44	13 51	13 54		14 00	13 59	14 27		14 09	14 19	14 25	14 27	14 38	14 58	14 39	14 44	14 44		14 53	15 00	14 58	15 27
	d			13 45	13 51	13 55		14 02	14 03	14 33			14 19	14 25	14 33	14 39	15 03			14 45		14 55	15 02	15 03	15 33
Twyford 3	a								14 09	→					14 39		→							15 09	→
Maidenhead 3	a								14 17						14 47									15 17	
Slough 3	a					14 09			14 24					14 40	14 54							15 10		15 24	
Ealing Broadway ⊖	a								14 49						15 19									15 49	
London Paddington 15 ⊖	a			14 14	14 23	14 29		14 32	15 02				14 45	14 59	15 32	15 09				15 14		15 29	15 32	16 02	

Birmingham, Banbury, Bicester, Oxford and Bedwyn - Reading and London

Station		XC ◇1 H	CH 1	GW 1	GW ◇1	GW 1	GW 1	XC ◇1 H	GW 1	GW ◇1 ⊐	GW ◇1 H	GW 1	GW ◇1 ⊐	GW 1	GW 1	XC ◇1 H	CH 1	GW 1	GW ◇1	GW 1	GW ◇1 ⊐	GW 1	XC ◇1 H
Birmingham New Street	d	13 33						14 03								14 33							15 03
Birmingham International	d							14 14															15 14
Coventry	d							14 25															15 25
Leamington Spa	d	14 00						14 38								15 00							15 38
Banbury	d	14 19						14 55				15 02				15 20							15 55
Kings Sutton	d											15 08											
Heyford	d											15 17											
Tackley	d											15 21											
Bicester Town	d		14 18														15 28						
Islip	d		14 29														15 39						
Oxford	a	14 40	14 44					15 14				15 32				15 41	15 54						16 14
	d	14 43			15 01		15 07	15 16			15 31				15 37	15 43			16 01			16 07	16 16
Radley	d						15 13															16 13	
Culham	d						15 17																
Appleford	d																					16 17	
Didcot Parkway	a						15 24								15 49							16 24	
	d						15 31			15 29			15 47		16 01						16 22	16 31	
Cholsey	d						15 37								16 07							16 37	
Goring & Streatley	d						15 42								16 12							16 42	
Pangbourne	d						15 47								16 17							16 47	
Tilehurst	d						15 51								16 21							16 51	
Bedwyn	d			14 37														15 37					
Hungerford	d			14 41														15 41					
Kintbury	d			14 46														15 46					
Newbury	a			14 53														15 53					
	d			14 53					15 13									15 53					
Newbury Racecourse	d								15 15														
Thatcham	d			14 58					15 20									15 58					
Midgham	d								15 24														
Aldermaston	d								15 28														
Theale	d			15 06					15 33									16 06					
Reading West	d					←			15 40					←						←			
Reading	a	15 08		15 17	15 25	15 27	15 59	15 39	15 44	15 44	15 54		16 00	15 59	16 29	16 09		16 16	16 25	16 29	16 38	16 58	16 39
	d			15 19	15 25	15 33	16 03			15 45	15 55		16 01	16 03	16 33			16 18	16 26	16 33	16 39	17 03	
Twyford	a					15 39	→							16 09	→					16 39		→	
Maidenhead	a					15 47								16 17						16 47			
Slough	a				15 40	15 54					16 10			16 24					16 40	16 54			
Ealing Broadway ⊖	a					16 19								16 49						17 19			
London Paddington ⊖	a			15 54	15 59	16 32				16 14	16 29		16 32	17 02				16 52	16 59	17 32	17 07		

Station		GW 1	GW ◇1 ⊐	GW ◇1 H	GW ◇1 ⊐	GW 1	GW 1	XC ◇1 H	CH 1	GW ◇1 ⊐	GW ◇1	GW 1	GW 1	XC ◇1 H	GW 1	GW ◇1 ⊐	GW ◇1 ⊐	GW ◇1 ⊐	GW 1	GW 1	XC ◇1 H	GW 1
Birmingham New Street	d							15 33						16 03							16 33	
Birmingham International	d													16 14								
Coventry	d													16 25								
Leamington Spa	d							16 02						16 38							17 00	
Banbury	d							16 20						16 55							17 19	17 23
Kings Sutton	d																					17 29
Heyford	d																					17 38
Tackley	d																					17 42
Bicester Town	d								16 30													
Islip	d								16 41													
Oxford	a							16 40	16 56					17 14							17 41	17 53
	d			16 31			16 37	16 43			17 01		17 07	17 16			17 31			17 37	17 43	
Radley	d												17 13									
Culham	d												17 17									
Appleford	d																					
Didcot Parkway	a						16 49						17 24							17 49		
	d		16 29		16 47		17 01						17 31			17 29		17 47		18 01		
Cholsey	d						17 07						17 37							18 07		
Goring & Streatley	d						17 12						17 42							18 12		
Pangbourne	d						17 17						17 47							18 17		
Tilehurst	d						17 21						17 51							18 21		
Bedwyn	d									16 35					16 56							
Hungerford	d									16 42					17 00							
Kintbury	d														17 05							
Newbury	a									16 52					17 13							
	d	16 13								16 53					17 13							
Newbury Racecourse	d	16 15													17 15							
Thatcham	d	16 20								16 59					17 20							
Midgham	d	16 24													17 25							
Aldermaston	d	16 28													17 28							
Theale	d	16 33								17 08					17 33							
Reading West	d	16 40				←						←			17 40				←			
Reading	a	16 44	16 44	16 55	17 00	16 58	17 27	17 08		17 17	17 26	17 27	17 57	17 39	17 44	17 44	17 55	18 00	17 57	18 27	18 09	
	d		16 45	16 55	17 02	17 03	17 33			17 18	17 27	17 33	18 03			17 45	17 57	18 02	18 03	18 33		
Twyford	a					17 09	→					17 39	→						18 09	→		
Maidenhead	a					17 17						17 47							18 17			
Slough	a			17 10		17 24					17 41	17 54					18 10		18 24			
Ealing Broadway ⊖	a					17 49						18 19							18 49			
London Paddington ⊖	a		17 14	17 29	17 32	18 02				17 51	18 00	18 32				18 14	18 29	18 32	19 02			

Table 116

Saturdays
from 17 September

Birmingham, Banbury, Bicester, Oxford and Bedwyn - Reading and London

Station		GW 1	GW ◇1	GW 1	GW ◇1 ⊐	GW 1	XC ◇1 H	CH 1	GW 1	GW ◇1 ⊐	GW ◇1 H	GW ◇1 ⊐	GW 1	GW 1	XC ◇1 H	GW 1	GW ◇1	GW 1	GW 1	XC ◇1 H	GW 1	GW ◇1 ⊐	GW ◇1 H
Birmingham New Street	d						17 03								17 33					18 03			
Birmingham International	d						17 14													18 14			
Coventry	d						17 25													18 25			
Leamington Spa	d						17 38								18 02					18 38			
Banbury	d						17 55								18 19					18 55			
Kings Sutton	d																						
Heyford	d																						
Tackley	d																						
Bicester Town	d							18 04															
Islip	d							18 15															
Oxford	a						18 14	18 30							18 40					19 14			
	d		18 01			18 07	18 16				18 31			18 37	18 43		19 01		19 07	19 16			19 31
Radley	d					18 13													19 13				
Culham	d																		19 17				
Appleford	d					18 17																	
Didcot Parkway	a					18 24								18 49					19 24				
	d				18 22	18 31				18 29		18 47		19 01					19 31			19 29	
Cholsey	d					18 37								19 07					19 37				
Goring & Streatley	d					18 42								19 12					19 42				
Pangbourne	d					18 47								19 17					19 47				
Tilehurst	d					18 51								19 21					19 51				
Bedwyn	d	17 37														18 37							
Hungerford	d	17 41														18 41							
Kintbury	d	17 46														18 46							
Newbury	a	17 53														18 53							
	d	17 53							18 13							18 53					19 13		
Newbury Racecourse	d								18 15												19 15		
Thatcham	d	17 58							18 20							18 58					19 20		
Midgham	d								18 24												19 24		
Aldermaston	d								18 28												19 28		
Theale	d	18 06							18 33							19 06					19 33		
Reading West	d			←					18 40				←					←			19 40		
Reading	a	18 17	18 25	18 27	18 38	18 58	18 39		18 44	18 44	18 55	19 00	18 58	19 29	19 08	19 17	19 25	19 29	19 57	19 39	19 44	19 44	19 55
	d	18 19	18 25	18 33	18 39	19 03				18 45	18 56	19 02	19 03	19 33		19 20	19 25	19 33	20 03			19 45	19 55
Twyford	a			18 39		→							19 09	→				19 39	→				
Maidenhead	a			18 47									19 17					19 47					
Slough	a		18 40	18 54							19 10		19 24				19 40	19 54					20 10
Ealing Broadway ⊖	a			19 19									19 49					20 19					
London Paddington ⊖	a	18 52	18 59	19 32	19 08					19 14	19 29	19 32	20 02			19 52	19 59	20 32				20 14	20 29

Station		GW 1	GW ◇1 ⊐	GW 1	GW ◇1 ⊐	GW 1	XC ◇1 H	CH 1	GW ◇1	GW 1	GW 1	GW ◇1 ⊐	GW 1	XC ◇1 A H	GW ◇1 ⊐	GW ◇1	GW 1	GW ◇1 ⊐	GW 1	XC ◇1 H	CH 1	GW ◇1
Birmingham New Street	d						18 33							19 03						19 33		
Birmingham International	d													19 14								
Coventry	d													19 25								
Leamington Spa	d						19 00							19 38						20 03		
Banbury	d	19 02					19 19							19 55						20 21		
Kings Sutton	d	19 08																				
Heyford	d	19 17																				
Tackley	d	19 21																				
Bicester Town	d							19 18													20 30	
Islip	d							19 29													20 41	
Oxford	a	19 32					19 40	19 44						20 14						20 40	20 56	
	d					19 37	19 43		20 01				20 07	20 16		20 31			20 37	20 43		21 01
Radley	d												20 13									
Culham	d																					
Appleford	d												20 17									
Didcot Parkway	a					19 49							20 24						20 49			
	d		19 47			20 01						20 23	20 31		20 29			20 47	21 01			
Cholsey	d					20 07							20 37						21 07			
Goring & Streatley	d					20 12							20 42						21 12			
Pangbourne	d					20 17							20 47						21 17			
Tilehurst	d					20 21							20 51						21 21			
Bedwyn	d									19 41												
Hungerford	d									19 47												
Kintbury	d									19 51												
Newbury	a									19 58												
	d				19 46					19 58												
Newbury Racecourse	d									20 00												
Thatcham	d									20 05												
Midgham	d									20 10												
Aldermaston	d									20 13												
Theale	d									20 18												
Reading West	d			←						20 25	←						←					
Reading	a		20 00	19 57	20 07	20 29	20 08		20 25	20 28	20 29	20 38	20 57	20 39	20 44	20 54	20 57	21 06	21 27	21 08		21 25
	d		20 03	20 03	20 09	20 33			20 25		20 33	20 39	21 03		20 45	20 54	21 03	21 08	21 33			21 25
Twyford	a			20 09		→					20 39		→				21 09		→			
Maidenhead	a			20 17							20 47						21 17					
Slough	a			20 24					20 40		20 54					21 09	21 24					21 40
Ealing Broadway ⊖	a			20 49							21 19						21 49					
London Paddington ⊖	a		20 32	21 02	20 37				20 59		21 32	21 07			21 14	21 29	22 02	21 36				21 59

A H to Oxford

Saturdays
from 17 September

Birmingham, Banbury, Bicester, Oxford and Bedwyn - Reading and London

	GW	GW	GW	XC	GW	GW	GW	XC	GW	GW	GW
	[1]	[1]	[1]	◇[1]	◇[1]	◇[1]	◇[1]	◇[1]	[1]	◇[1]	[1]
				A				A			
				🍴	☕		☕	🍴			
Birmingham New Street [12] d				20 03				20 33			
Birmingham International d				20 14							
Coventry d				20 25							
Leamington Spa [8] d				20 38				21 00			
Banbury d		20 38		20 55				21 20			
Kings Sutton d		20 44									
Heyford d		20 53									
Tackley d		20 57									
Bicester Town d											
Islip d											
Oxford a		21 08		21 14				21 41			
d				21 16		21 31		21 43	21 50	22 01	
Radley d									21 56		
Culham d											
Appleford d											
Didcot Parkway a						21 43			22 04	22 12	
d					21 34	21 45	21 47		22 04	22 13	
Cholsey d									22 10		
Goring & Streatley d									22 15		
Pangbourne d									22 21		
Tilehurst d									22 24		
Bedwyn d			20 48								
Hungerford d			20 54								
Kintbury d			20 58								
Newbury a			21 05								
d			21 05								
Newbury Racecourse d			21 07								
Thatcham d			21 12								
Midgham d			21 17								
Aldermaston d			21 20								
Theale d			21 25								
Reading West d	←		21 32								←
Reading [7] a	21 27		21 36	21 39	21 48	21 59	21 59	22 10	22 31	22 28	22 31
d	21 33				21 50	22 01	22 02		22 33	22 29	22 33
Twyford [8] a	21 39								→		22 39
Maidenhead [8] a	21 47										22 47
Slough [8] a	21 54					22 14				22 43	22 54
Ealing Broadway ⊖ a	22 19										23 19
London Paddington [15] ⊖ a	22 32				22 16	22 32	22 37			23 02	23 29

	CH	XC	GW	GW	GW	GW	GW	GW	GW	GW
	[1]	◇[1]	[1]	[1]	◇[1]	◇[1]	◇[1]	[1]	◇[1]	[1]
						☕			☕	
Birmingham New Street [12] d		21 03								
Birmingham International d		21 14								
Coventry d		21 25								
Leamington Spa [8] d		21 38								
Banbury d		21 55	22 00							
Kings Sutton d			22 06							
Heyford d			22 15							
Tackley d			22 19							
Bicester Town d	21 37									
Islip d	21 48									
Oxford a	22 03	22 16	22 30							
d		22 18			22 35		23 01			23 07
Radley d										23 13
Culham d										23 17
Appleford d										23 20
Didcot Parkway a					22 47		23 13			23 25
d					22 48	22 49	23 14		23 30	23 36
Cholsey d										23 42
Goring & Streatley d										23 47
Pangbourne d										23 51
Tilehurst d										23 56
Bedwyn d				22 00				23 00		
Hungerford d				22 06				23 06		
Kintbury d				22 10				23 10		
Newbury a				22 17				23 17		
d				22 17				23 17		
Newbury Racecourse d				22 19				23 19		
Thatcham d				22 24				23 24		
Midgham d				22 29				23 29		
Aldermaston d				22 32				23 32		
Theale d				22 37				23 37		
Reading West d				22 44				23 44		
Reading [7] a		22 41		22 48	23 04	23 04	23 30	23 48	23 51	00 01
d					23 05	23 05	23 31		23 52	00 03
Twyford [8] a										00 09
Maidenhead [8] a										00 17
Slough [8] a					23 23		23 48			00 28
Ealing Broadway ⊖ a										00 52
London Paddington [15] ⊖ a					23 43	23 36	00 10		00 33	01 03

	CH
	[1]
Birmingham New Street [12] d	
Birmingham International d	
Coventry d	
Leamington Spa [8] d	
Banbury d	
Kings Sutton d	
Heyford d	
Tackley d	
Bicester Town d	22 53
Islip d	23 04
Oxford a	23 19
d	
Radley d	
Culham d	
Appleford d	
Didcot Parkway a	
d	
Cholsey d	
Goring & Streatley d	
Pangbourne d	
Tilehurst d	
Bedwyn d	
Hungerford d	
Kintbury d	
Newbury a	
d	
Newbury Racecourse d	
Thatcham d	
Midgham d	
Aldermaston d	
Theale d	
Reading West d	
Reading [7] a	
d	
Twyford [8] a	
Maidenhead [8] a	
Slough [8] a	
Ealing Broadway ⊖ a	
London Paddington [15] ⊖ a	

A 🍴 to Oxford

Sundays
until 19 June

Birmingham, Banbury, Bicester, Oxford and Bedwyn - Reading and London

	GW	GW	GW	GW	GW	GW	GW	GW	GW	GW	GW
	◇[1]	◇[1]	[1]	[1]	[1]	◇[1]	◇[1]	◇[1]	[1]	[1]	◇[1]
	A	A	A								
		☕				☕		☕			☕
Birmingham New Street [12] d											
Birmingham International d											
Coventry d											
Leamington Spa [8] d											
Banbury d											
Kings Sutton d											
Heyford d											
Tackley d											
Bicester Town d											
Islip d											
Oxford a											
d	23p01		23p07		08 05		08 38			09 05	
Radley d			23p13		08 12					09 12	
Culham d			23p17								
Appleford d			23p20								
Didcot Parkway a	23p13		23p25		08 20		08 51			09 20	
d	23p14	23p30	23p36	07 45	08 21	08 43	08 53	09 14		09 21	09 45
Cholsey d			23p42		08 26					09 26	
Goring & Streatley d			23p47	07 53	08 32					09 32	
Pangbourne d			23p51		08 36					09 36	
Tilehurst d			23p56		08 42					09 42	
Bedwyn d											
Hungerford d											
Kintbury d											
Newbury a											
d									09 05		
Newbury Racecourse d									09 07		
Thatcham d									09 12		
Midgham d									09 17		
Aldermaston d									09 20		
Theale d									09 25		
Reading West d									09 32		
Reading [7] a	23p30	23p51	00 01	08 03	08 47	09 01	09 10	09 28	09 35	09 46	10 00
d	23p31	23p52	00 03	08 03	08 50	09 01	09 10	09 29	09 36	09 50	10 00
Twyford [8] a			00 09		08 56					09 56	
Maidenhead [8] a			00 17		09 04				09 52	10 04	
Slough [8] a	23p48		00 28	08 22	09 11		09 30		10 01	10 11	
Ealing Broadway ⊖ a			00 52		09 37					10 37	
London Paddington [15] ⊖ a	00 13	00 34	01 03	08 44	09 47	09 38	09 51	10 08	10 21	10 47	10 39

	GW	GW	GW	XC	CH	GW	GW	GW	GW	GW
	◇[1]	[1]	[1]	◇[1]	[1]	◇[1]	◇[1]	◇[1]	[1]	[1]
				🍴		☕	☕	🍴		
Birmingham New Street [12] d										
Birmingham International d										
Coventry d										
Leamington Spa [8] d										
Banbury d										
Kings Sutton d										
Heyford d										
Tackley d										
Bicester Town d					10 04					
Islip d					10 15					
Oxford a					10 31					
d	09 38		10 05	10 16				10 38		11 05
Radley d			10 11							11 11
Culham d										
Appleford d			10 16							
Didcot Parkway a	09 50		10 21					10 50		11 20
d	09 51		10 21				10 45	10 51		11 21
Cholsey d			10 27							11 27
Goring & Streatley d			10 33							11 33
Pangbourne d			10 37							11 37
Tilehurst d			10 42							11 42
Bedwyn d		09 35							10 54	
Hungerford d		09 41							11 00	
Kintbury d		09 46							11 04	
Newbury a		09 52							11 11	
d		09 53				10 27			11 11	
Newbury Racecourse d		09 55								
Thatcham d		10 00							11 16	
Midgham d		10 05								
Aldermaston d		10 08								
Theale d		10 13							11 24	
Reading West d		10 21								
Reading [7] a	10 06	10 26	10 51	10 42		10 47	11 00	11 08	11 34	11 49
d	10 07	10 27	10 53			10 49	11 00	11 08	11 34	11 53
Twyford [8] a			10 59							→
Maidenhead [8] a		10 45	11 07						11 52	
Slough [8] a	10 28	10 53	11 15					11 31	12 00	
Ealing Broadway ⊖ a			11 37							
London Paddington [15] ⊖ a	10 52	11 15	11 47			11 27	11 39	11 52	12 22	

	XC	GW	GW	GW	GW	GW	GW	CH	GW	GW	XC
	◇[1]	[1]	◇[1]	◇[1]	[1]	◇[1]	◇[1]	[1]	[1]	[1]	◇[1]
	🍴		☕	☕		☕					🍴
Birmingham New Street [12] d											
Birmingham International d											
Coventry d											
Leamington Spa [8] d											
Banbury d	10 55	11 00									11 55
Kings Sutton d		11 05									
Heyford d		11 14									
Tackley d		11 19									
Bicester Town d								11 33			
Islip d								11 44			
Oxford a	11 14	11 29						12 00			12 14
d	11 16						11 38			12 05	12 16
Radley d										12 11	
Culham d											
Appleford d										12 16	
Didcot Parkway a							11 50			12 21	
d			11 29			11 47	11 51			12 21	
Cholsey d										12 27	
Goring & Streatley d										12 33	
Pangbourne d										12 37	
Tilehurst d										12 42	
Bedwyn d											
Hungerford d											
Kintbury d											
Newbury a											
d				11 26					12 03		
Newbury Racecourse d									12 05		
Thatcham d									12 10		
Midgham d									12 15		
Aldermaston d									12 18		
Theale d									12 23		
Reading West d					←				12 31		
Reading [7] a	11 42		11 44	11 47	11 49	12 01	12 06		12 34	12 47	12 42
d			11 44	11 49	11 53	12 02	12 07		12 35	12 52	
Twyford [8] a					12 00					→	
Maidenhead [8] a					12 08				12 48		
Slough [8] a					12 15		12 29		12 56		
Ealing Broadway ⊖ a					12 38						
London Paddington [15] ⊖ a			12 24	12 27	12 48	12 38	12 51		13 16		

	GW	GW	GW	GW	GW	GW	XC	CH	GW	GW	GW
	◇[1]	[1]	◇[1]	◇[1]	[1]	[1]	◇[1]	[1]	◇[1]	◇[1]	[1]
	☕		☕	🍴			🍴		☕	☕	
Birmingham New Street [12] d											
Birmingham International d											
Coventry d											
Leamington Spa [8] d											
Banbury d							12 55				
Kings Sutton d											
Heyford d											
Tackley d											
Bicester Town d								13 03			
Islip d								13 14			
Oxford a							13 14	13 30			
d				12 45		13 05	13 16				
Radley d						13 11					
Culham d											
Appleford d											
Didcot Parkway a				12 56		13 20					
d	12 29		12 47	12 57		13 21			13 29		
Cholsey d						13 27					
Goring & Streatley d						13 33					
Pangbourne d						13 37					
Tilehurst d						13 42					
Bedwyn d					12 45						
Hungerford d					12 51						
Kintbury d					12 55						
Newbury a					13 02						
d					13 02					13 31	
Newbury Racecourse d											
Thatcham d					13 07						
Midgham d											
Aldermaston d											
Theale d					13 15						
Reading West d		←									←
Reading [7] a	12 44	12 47	13 00	13 13	13 24	13 46	13 42		13 44	13 48	13 46
d	12 44	12 52	13 02	13 13	13 25	13 52			13 44	13 49	13 52
Twyford [8] a		12 58				→					13 59
Maidenhead [8] a		13 06			13 42						14 07
Slough [8] a		13 14		13 35	13 50						14 15
Ealing Broadway ⊖ a		13 37									14 38
London Paddington [15] ⊖ a	13 24	13 47	13 39	13 54	14 11				14 22	14 29	14 47

A not 22 May

Birmingham, Banbury, Bicester, Oxford and Bedwyn - Reading and London

		GW ◇1 ☕	GW ◇1	GW 1	GW 1	XC ◇1 🛒	GW ◇1 ☕	GW 1	GW ◇1 ☕	XC ◇1 🛒	GW ◇1	CH 1	GW 1	GW 1	XC ◇1 🛒	GW ◇1 ☕	GW 1	GW ◇1 ☕	XC ◇1 🛒	GW ◇1 ☕	GW 1	GW 1
Birmingham New Street 12	d														14 03				14 33			
Birmingham International	d														14 14							
Coventry	d														14 25							
Leamington Spa 8	d														14 38				15 00			
Banbury	d					13 55				14 19					14 55				15 19			
Kings Sutton	d																					
Heyford	d																					
Tackley	d																					
Bicester Town	d											14 33										
Islip	d											14 44										
Oxford	a					14 14				14 38		15 00			15 14				15 41			
	d		13 38		14 05	14 16				14 43	14 41			15 05	15 16				15 43	15 50		16 05
Radley	d				14 11									15 11								16 11
Culham	d																					
Appleford	d				14 16																	16 16
Didcot Parkway	a		13 50		14 20						14 53			15 20						16 01		16 20
	d	13 47	13 51		14 21		14 29		14 47		14 54			15 21		15 30		15 47		16 03		16 21
Cholsey	d				14 27									15 27								16 27
Goring & Streatley	d				14 33									15 33								16 33
Pangbourne	d				14 37									15 37								16 37
Tilehurst	d				14 42									15 42								16 42
Bedwyn	d												14 45									
Hungerford	d												14 51									
Kintbury	d												14 55									
Newbury	a												15 02									
	d			14 03									15 02								16 03	
Newbury Racecourse	d			14 05																	16 05	
Thatcham	d			14 10									15 07								16 10	
Midgham	d			14 15																	16 15	
Aldermaston	d			14 18																	16 18	
Theale	d			14 23									15 15								16 23	
Reading West	d			14 31				←									←				16 31	
Reading 7	a	14 00	14 08	14 34	14 46	14 42	14 44	14 46	15 00	15 09	15 10		15 24	15 48	15 42	15 45	15 48	16 00	16 09	16 20	16 34	16 46
	d	14 02	14 08	14 36	14 52		14 44	14 52	15 02		15 11		15 25	15 52		15 45	15 52	16 02		16 20	16 36	16 52
Twyford 3	a				→			14 59						→			15 59					→
Maidenhead 3	a			14 50				15 07					15 40				16 07				16 52	
Slough 3	a		14 29	14 58				15 15			15 31		15 49				16 16			16 49	17 00	
Ealing Broadway ⊖	a							15 38									16 39					
London Paddington 15 ⊖	a	14 39	14 51	15 21			15 24	15 47	15 39		15 52		16 10			16 20	16 48	16 39		17 07	17 21	

		XC ◇1 🛒	CH 1	GW 1	GW ◇1 ☕	GW ◇1 ☕	GW 1	GW ◇1 ☕	XC ◇1 🛒	GW ◇1 ☕	GW ◇1 ☕	GW 1	GW 1	XC ◇1 🛒	GW ◇1 ☕	GW 1	GW ◇1 ☕	XC ◇1 🛒	GW ◇1 ☕	GW ◇1 ☕	CH 1	GW 1	GW 1
Birmingham New Street 12	d	15 03							15 33					16 03				16 33					
Birmingham International	d	15 14												16 14									
Coventry	d	15 25												16 25									
Leamington Spa 8	d	15 38							16 00					16 38				17 00					
Banbury	d	15 55		16 00					16 19					16 55				17 19					
Kings Sutton	d			16 05																			
Heyford	d			16 14																			
Tackley	d			16 18																			
Bicester Town	d		16 03																		17 33		
Islip	d		16 14																		17 44		
Oxford	a	16 14	16 30	16 33					16 41					17 14				17 38			18 00		
	d	16 16							16 43		16 50		17 05	17 16				17 43		17 50			18 05
Radley	d												17 11										18 11
Culham	d																						
Appleford	d																						18 16
Didcot Parkway	a										17 02		17 20							18 02			18 20
	d				16 29			16 47		16 59	17 03		17 21		17 29		17 47		17 59	18 03			18 21
Cholsey	d												17 27										18 27
Goring & Streatley	d												17 33										18 33
Pangbourne	d												17 37										18 37
Tilehurst	d												17 42										18 42
Bedwyn	d											16 54											
Hungerford	d											17 00											
Kintbury	d											17 04											
Newbury	a											17 11											
	d					16 31						17 11										18 03	
Newbury Racecourse	d																					18 05	
Thatcham	d											17 16										18 10	
Midgham	d																					18 15	
Aldermaston	d																					18 18	
Theale	d											17 24										18 23	
Reading West	d						←									←						18 31	
Reading 7	a	16 42			16 44	16 48	16 46	17 00	17 09	17 12	17 20	17 36	17 47	17 39	17 42	17 47	18 00	18 09	18 12	18 19		18 34	18 46
	d				16 44	16 49	16 52	17 02		17 13	17 20	17 36	17 52		17 44	17 52	18 02		18 14	18 23		18 37	18 52
Twyford 3	a						16 59						→			17 59							18 58
Maidenhead 3	a						17 07					17 52				18 07						18 51	19 06
Slough 3	a						17 15				17 44	18 00				18 16				18 50		18 59	19 15
Ealing Broadway ⊖	a						17 39									18 40							19 37
London Paddington 15 ⊖	a				17 24	17 27	17 49	17 39		17 50	18 07	18 22			18 24	18 48	18 39		18 53	19 09		19 21	19 47

		XC ◇1 🛒	GW 1	GW ◇1 ☕	GW ◇1 ☕	GW ◇1 ☕	XC ◇1 🛒	GW ◇1 ☕	GW ◇1 ☕	GW 1	GW 1	XC ◇1 🛒	CH 1	XC ◇1 🛒	GW ◇1 ☕	GW ◇1 ☕	GW 1	GW ◇1 ☕	GW ◇1 ☕	GW 1	XC ◇1 A 🛒	XC ◇1 🛒
Birmingham New Street 12	d	17 03					17 33					18 03		18 33							19 03	19 33
Birmingham International	d	17 14										18 14									19 14	
Coventry	d	17 25										18 25									19 25	
Leamington Spa 8	d	17 38					18 01					18 38		19 00							19 38	20 00
Banbury	d	17 55	18 00				18 20					18 55		19 19							19 55	20 19
Kings Sutton	d		18 07																			
Heyford	d		18 16																			
Tackley	d		18 20																			
Bicester Town	d												19 03									
Islip	d												19 14									
Oxford	a	18 14	18 31				18 40					19 14	19 30	19 38							20 14	20 40
	d	18 16				18 39	18 43				19 05	19 16		19 43		19 50				20 05	20 16	20 43
Radley	d										19 11									20 11		
Culham	d																					
Appleford	d																					
Didcot Parkway	a					18 52					19 20					20 02				20 20		
	d				18 47	18 56		18 59	19 17		19 21				19 59	20 03		20 17		20 21		
Cholsey	d										19 27									20 27		
Goring & Streatley	d										19 33									20 33		
Pangbourne	d										19 37									20 37		
Tilehurst	d										19 42									20 42		
Bedwyn	d									18 54												
Hungerford	d									19 00												
Kintbury	d									19 04												
Newbury	a									19 11												
	d			18 35						19 11							19 53		20 18			
Newbury Racecourse	d																19 55					
Thatcham	d									19 16							20 00					
Midgham	d																20 05					
Aldermaston	d																20 08					
Theale	d									19 24							20 13					
Reading West	d																20 21					
Reading 7	a	18 42		18 54	19 00	19 11	19 06	19 12	19 30	19 35	19 46	19 42		20 09	20 12	20 20	20 24	20 32	20 35	20 46	20 42	21 09
	d			18 56	19 03	19 13		19 13	19 32	19 37	19 52				20 14	20 20		20 32	20 37	20 52		
Twyford 3	a										19 58									20 57		
Maidenhead 3	a									19 53	20 06									21 05		
Slough 3	a					19 33				20 01	20 14					20 51				21 13		
Ealing Broadway ⊖	a										20 40									21 39		
London Paddington 15 ⊖	a			19 37	19 40	19 51		19 54	20 11	20 22	20 50				20 53	21 12		21 16	21 20	21 48		

		GW ◇1 ☕	GW ◇1 🛒	CH 1	GW ◇1 ☕	GW ◇1 ☕	GW 1	XC ◇1 A 🛒	GW 1	XC ◇1 🛒	GW ◇1 ☕	GW ◇1	GW 1	GW ◇1 ☕	XC ◇1	GW 1	CH 1	GW 1	GW ◇1	GW ◇1 ☕	GW 🚌	GW	GW 1
Birmingham New Street 12	d							20 03		20 33					21 03								
Birmingham International	d							20 14							21 14								
Coventry	d							20 25							21 24								
Leamington Spa 8	d							20 38		21 00					21 35								
Banbury	d							20 55		21 19													
Kings Sutton	d																						
Heyford	d																						
Tackley	d																						
Bicester Town	d			20 33													22 03						
Islip	d			20 44													22 14						
Oxford	a			21 00				21 14		21 38					22 08		22 30						
	d		20 50					21 16	21 21	21 40		21 50			22 10	22 21			22 47		23 00		
Radley	d								21 27							22 27					23 15		
Culham	d																						
Appleford	d																						
Didcot Parkway	a		21 02						21 35			22 02				22 35			22 59		23 35		
	d	20 58	21 03		21 10	21 17			21 35		22 01	22 03				22 35			23 00	23 11			23 50
Cholsey	d								21 41							22 41							23 56
Goring & Streatley	d								21 46							22 46							00 01
Pangbourne	d								21 51							22 51							00 05
Tilehurst	d								21 55							22 55							00 10
Bedwyn	d						20 54											22 35					
Hungerford	d						21 00											22 41					
Kintbury	d						21 04											22 45					
Newbury	a						21 11											22 52					
	d						21 12						21 53	22 13				22 53				23 23	
Newbury Racecourse	d												21 55										
Thatcham	d						21 17						22 00					22 58				23 28	
Midgham	d												22 05										
Aldermaston	d												22 08										
Theale	d						21 25						22 13					23 06				23 36	
Reading West	d												22 21										
Reading 7	a	21 17	21 23		21 24	21 32	21 33	21 43	22 02	22 07	22 17	22 20	22 24	22 30	22 35	23 00		23 15	23 16	23 27		23 44	00 15
	d	21 18	21 25		21 25	21 32			22 10		22 19	22 24		22 30		23 00			23 23	23 28			00 15
Twyford 3	a								22 16							23 06							00 22
Maidenhead 3	a		21 43						22 24							23 14							00 30
Slough 3	a		21 51						22 33			22 47				23 22			23 45				00 37
Ealing Broadway ⊖	a								22 56							23 45							01 01
London Paddington 15 ⊖	a	21 57	22 12		22 04	22 15			23 06		22 57	23 05		23 15		23 55			00 11	00 16			01 13

A 🛒 to Oxford

Table 116

Birmingham, Banbury, Bicester, Oxford and Bedwyn - Reading and London

Sundays
until 19 June

		GW 1
Birmingham New Street 12	d	
Birmingham International	d	
Coventry	d	
Leamington Spa 6	d	
Banbury	d	
Kings Sutton	d	
Heyford	d	
Tackley	d	
Bicester Town	d	
Islip	d	
Oxford	a	
	d	
Radley	d	
Culham	d	
Appleford	d	
Didcot Parkway	a	
	d	
Cholsey	d	
Goring & Streatley	d	
Pangbourne	d	
Tilehurst	d	
Bedwyn	d	
Hungerford	d	
Kintbury	d	
Newbury	a	
	d	23 45
Newbury Racecourse	d	23 47
Thatcham	d	23 52
Midgham	d	23 57
Aldermaston	d	00 01
Theale	d	00 06
Reading West	d	00s13
Reading 7	a	00 17
	d	
Twyford 3	a	
Maidenhead 3	a	
Slough 3	a	
Ealing Broadway ⊖	a	
London Paddington 15 ⊖	a	

Sundays
26 June to 31 July

		GW ◇1	GW ◇1 ☕	GW 1	GW 1	GW 1	GW ◇1 ☕	GW ◇1	GW ◇1 ☕	GW 1	GW 1	GW ◇1 ☕	GW ◇1	GW 1	GW 1	XC ◇1 🛒	CH 1	GW ◇1 ☕	GW ◇1 ☕	GW ◇1 🛒	GW 1	GW 1	XC ◇1 🛒
Birmingham New Street 12	d															09 03							10 03
Birmingham International	d															09 14							10 14
Coventry	d															09 25							10 25
Leamington Spa 6	d															09 38							10 38
Banbury	d															09 55							10 55
Kings Sutton	d																						
Heyford	d																						
Tackley	d																						
Bicester Town	d																10 04						
Islip	d																10 15						
Oxford	a															10 14	10 31						11 14
	d	23p01		23p07		08 05		08 38			09 05		09 38		10 05	10 16				10 38		11 05	11 16
Radley	d			23p13		08 12					09 12				10 11							11 11	
Culham	d			23p17																			
Appleford	d			23p20											10 16								
Didcot Parkway	a	23p13		23p25		08 20		08 51			09 20		09 50		10 21					10 50		11 20	
	d	23p14	23p30	23p36	07 45	08 21	08 43	08 53	09 14		09 21	09 45	09 51		10 21				10 45	10 51		11 21	
Cholsey	d			23p42		08 26					09 26				10 27							11 27	
Goring & Streatley	d			23p47	07 53	08 32					09 32				10 33							11 33	
Pangbourne	d			23p51		08 36					09 36				10 37							11 37	
Tilehurst	d			23p56		08 42					09 42				10 42							11 42	
Bedwyn	d													09 35							10 54		
Hungerford	d													09 41							11 00		
Kintbury	d													09 46							11 04		
Newbury	a													09 52							11 11		
	d									09 05				09 53				10 27			11 11		
Newbury Racecourse	d									09 07				09 55									
Thatcham	d									09 12				10 00							11 16		
Midgham	d									09 17				10 05									
Aldermaston	d									09 20				10 08									
Theale	d									09 25				10 13							11 24		
Reading West	d									09 32				10 21									
Reading 7	a	23p30	23p51	00 01	08 03	08 47	09 01	09 10	09 28	09 35	09 46	10 00	10 06	10 26	10 51	10 42		10 47	11 00	11 08	11 34	11 49	11 42
	d	23p31	23p52	00 03	08 03	08 50	09 02	09 10	09 29	09 36	09 50	10 00	10 07	10 27	10 53			10 49	11 00	11 08	11 34	11 53	
Twyford 3	a			00 09		08 56					09 56				10 59							→	
Maidenhead 3	a			00 17		09 04				09 52	10 04			10 45	11 07						11 52		
Slough 3	a	23p48		00 28	08 22	09 11		09 30		10 01	10 11		10 28	10 53	11 15					11 31	12 00		
Ealing Broadway ⊖	a			00 52		09 37					10 37				11 37								
London Paddington 15 ⊖	a	00 13	00 34	01 03	08 44	09 47	09 39	09 51	10 08	10 21	10 47	10 39	10 52	11 15	11 47			11 27	11 39	11 52	12 22		

Table 116

Birmingham, Banbury, Bicester, Oxford and Bedwyn - Reading and London

Sundays
26 June to 31 July

		GW 1	GW ◇1 ☕	GW ◇1 ☕	GW 1	GW ◇1 ☕	GW ◇1	CH 1	GW 1	GW 1	XC ◇1 🛒	GW ◇1 ☕	GW 1	GW ◇1 ☕	XC ◇1 🛒	GW ◇1 🛒	GW 1	GW 1	XC ◇1 🛒	CH 1	GW ◇1 ☕	GW ◇1 ☕	GW 1
Birmingham New Street 12	d										11 03				11 33				12 03				
Birmingham International	d										11 14								12 14				
Coventry	d										11 25								12 25				
Leamington Spa 6	d										11 38				12 00				12 38				
Banbury	d	11 00									11 55				12 19				12 55				
Kings Sutton	d	11 05																					
Heyford	d	11 14																					
Tackley	d	11 19																					
Bicester Town	d							11 33												13 03			
Islip	d							11 44												13 14			
Oxford	a	11 29						12 00			12 14				12 38				13 14	13 30			
	d						11 38			12 05	12 16				12 43	12 45		13 05	13 16				
Radley	d									12 11								13 11					
Culham	d																						
Appleford	d									12 16													
Didcot Parkway	a						11 50			12 21						12 56		13 20					
	d		11 31			11 47	11 51			12 21		12 29		12 48		12 57		13 21			13 29		
Cholsey	d									12 27								13 27					
Goring & Streatley	d									12 33								13 33					
Pangbourne	d									12 37								13 37					
Tilehurst	d									12 42								13 42					
Bedwyn	d																12 45						
Hungerford	d																12 51						
Kintbury	d																12 55						
Newbury	a																13 02						
	d			11 26					12 03								13 02					13 31	
Newbury Racecourse	d								12 05														
Thatcham	d								12 10								13 07						
Midgham	d								12 15														
Aldermaston	d								12 18														
Theale	d								12 23								13 15						
Reading West	d				←				12 31				←										←
Reading 7	a		11 44	11 47	11 49	12 00	12 06		12 34	12 47	12 42	12 44	12 47	13 01	13 09	13 13	13 24	13 46	13 42		13 44	13 48	13 46
	d		11 45	11 49	11 53	12 00	12 07		12 35	12 52		12 44	12 52	13 03		13 13	13 25	13 52			13 44	13 49	13 52
Twyford 3	a				12 00					→			12 58					→					13 59
Maidenhead 3	a				12 08				12 48				13 06				13 42						14 07
Slough 3	a				12 15		12 29		12 56				13 14			13 35	13 50						14 15
Ealing Broadway ⊖	a				12 38								13 37										14 38
London Paddington 15 ⊖	a		12 24	12 27	12 48	12 39	12 51		13 16			13 24	13 47	13 40		13 54	14 11				14 22	14 29	14 47

		GW ◇1 ☕	GW ◇1	XC ◇1 🛒	GW 1	GW 1	XC ◇1 🛒	GW ◇1 ☕	GW 1	GW ◇1 ☕	XC ◇1 🛒	GW ◇1	CH 1	GW 1	GW 1	XC ◇1 🛒	GW ◇1 ☕	GW 1	GW ◇1 ☕	XC ◇1 🛒	GW ◇1 ☕	GW 1
Birmingham New Street 12	d			12 33			13 03				13 33					14 03				14 33		
Birmingham International	d						13 14									14 14						
Coventry	d						13 25									14 25						
Leamington Spa 6	d			13 00			13 38				14 00					14 38				15 00		
Banbury	d			13 19			13 55				14 19					14 55				15 19		
Kings Sutton	d																					
Heyford	d																					
Tackley	d																					
Bicester Town	d												14 33									
Islip	d												14 44									
Oxford	a			13 41			14 14				14 38		15 00			15 14				15 41		
	d		13 38	13 43		14 05	14 16				14 43	14 41			15 05	15 16				15 43	15 50	
Radley	d					14 11									15 11							
Culham	d																					
Appleford	d					14 16																
Didcot Parkway	a		13 50			14 20						14 53			15 20						16 01	
	d	13 47	13 51			14 21		14 29		14 47		14 54			15 21		15 30		15 47		16 03	
Cholsey	d					14 27									15 27							
Goring & Streatley	d					14 33									15 33							
Pangbourne	d					14 37									15 37							
Tilehurst	d					14 42									15 42							
Bedwyn	d													14 45								
Hungerford	d													14 51								
Kintbury	d													14 55								
Newbury	a													15 02								
	d				14 03									15 02								16 03
Newbury Racecourse	d				14 05																	16 05
Thatcham	d				14 10									15 07								16 10
Midgham	d				14 15																	16 15
Aldermaston	d				14 18																	16 18
Theale	d				14 23									15 15								16 23
Reading West	d				14 31				←									←				16 31
Reading 7	a	14 00	14 08	14 10	14 34	14 46	14 42	14 44	14 46	15 00	15 09	15 10		15 24	15 48	15 42	15 45	15 48	16 00	16 09	16 20	16 34
	d	14 02	14 08		14 36	14 52		14 44	14 52	15 02		15 11		15 25	15 52		15 45	15 52	16 02		16 20	16 36
Twyford 3	a					→			14 59						→			15 59				
Maidenhead 3	a				14 50				15 07					15 40				16 07				16 52
Slough 3	a		14 29		14 58				15 15			15 31		15 49				16 16			16 49	17 00
Ealing Broadway ⊖	a								15 38									16 39				
London Paddington 15 ⊖	a	14 40	14 51		15 21			15 24	15 47	15 40		15 52		16 10			16 20	16 48	16 40		17 07	17 21

Birmingham, Banbury, Bicester, Oxford and Bedwyn - Reading and London

		GW	XC	CH	GW	GW	GW	GW	GW	XC	GW	GW	GW	GW	XC	GW	GW	GW	XC	GW	GW	CH	GW
		1	◇1	1	1	◇1	◇1	1	◇1	◇1	◇1	◇1	1	1	◇1	◇1	1	◇1	◇1	◇1	◇1	1	1
			⌶			☕	☕		☕	⌶	☕	☕			⌶	☕		☕	⌶	☕	☕		
Birmingham New Street 12	d		15 03							15 33					16 03				16 33				
Birmingham International	d		15 14												16 14								
Coventry	d		15 25												16 25								
Leamington Spa 8	d		15 38							16 00					16 38				17 00				
Banbury	d		15 55		16 00					16 19					16 55				17 19				
Kings Sutton	d				16 05																		
Heyford	d				16 14																		
Tackley	d				16 18																		
Bicester Town	d			16 03																		17 33	
Islip	d			16 14																		17 44	
Oxford	a		16 14	16 30	16 33					16 41					17 14				17 38			18 00	
	d	16 05	16 16							16 43		16 50		17 05	17 16				17 43		17 50		
Radley	d	16 11												17 11									
Culham	d																						
Appleford	d	16 16																					
Didcot Parkway	a	16 20										17 02		17 20							18 02		
	d	16 21				16 29			16 47		16 59	17 03		17 21		17 29		17 47		17 59	18 03		
Cholsey	d	16 27												17 27									
Goring & Streatley	d	16 33												17 33									
Pangbourne	d	16 37												17 37									
Tilehurst	d	16 42												17 42									
Bedwyn	d												16 54										
Hungerford	d												17 00										
Kintbury	d												17 04										
Newbury	a												17 11										
	d						16 31						17 11										18 03
Newbury Racecourse	d																						18 05
Thatcham	d												17 16										18 10
Midgham	d																						18 15
Aldermaston	d																						18 18
Theale	d												17 24										18 23
Reading West	d							←									←						18 31
Reading 7	a	16 46	16 42			16 44	16 48	16 46	17 00	17 09	17 12	17 20	17 36	17 47	17 39	17 42	17 47	18 00	18 09	18 12	18 19		18 34
	d	16 52				16 44	16 49	16 52	17 02		17 13	17 20	17 36	17 52		17 44	17 52	18 02		18 14	18 23		18 37
Twyford 3	a	→						16 59						→			17 59						
Maidenhead 3	a							17 07					17 52				18 07						18 51
Slough 3	a							17 15				17 44	18 00				18 16				18 50		18 59
Ealing Broadway ⊖	a							17 39									18 40						
London Paddington 15 ⊖	a					17 24	17 27	17 49	17 39		17 50	18 07	18 22			18 24	18 48	18 40		18 53	19 09		19 21

		GW	XC	GW	GW	GW	GW	XC	GW	GW	GW	GW	XC	CH	XC	GW	GW	GW	GW	GW	GW	XC
		1	◇1	1	◇1	◇1	◇1	◇1	◇1	◇1	1	1	◇1	1	◇1	◇1	◇1	1	◇1	◇1	1	◇1
																						A
			⌶		☕	☕	☕	⌶	☕	☕			⌶		⌶	☕	☕		☕	☕		⌶
Birmingham New Street 12	d		17 03					17 33					18 03		18 33							19 03
Birmingham International	d		17 14										18 14									19 14
Coventry	d		17 25										18 25									19 25
Leamington Spa 8	d		17 38					18 01					18 38		19 00							19 38
Banbury	d		17 55	18 00				18 20					18 55		19 19							19 55
Kings Sutton	d			18 07																		
Heyford	d			18 16																		
Tackley	d			18 20																		
Bicester Town	d													19 03								
Islip	d													19 14								
Oxford	a		18 14	18 31				18 40					19 14	19 30	19 38							20 14
	d	18 05	18 16				18 39	18 43				19 05	19 16		19 43		19 50				20 05	20 16
Radley	d	18 11										19 11									20 11	
Culham	d																					
Appleford	d	18 16																				
Didcot Parkway	a	18 20					18 52					19 20					20 02				20 20	
	d	18 21				18 47	18 56		18 59	19 17		19 21				19 59	20 03		20 17		20 21	
Cholsey	d	18 27										19 27									20 27	
Goring & Streatley	d	18 33										19 33									20 33	
Pangbourne	d	18 37										19 37									20 37	
Tilehurst	d	18 42										19 42									20 42	
Bedwyn	d										18 54											
Hungerford	d										19 00											
Kintbury	d										19 04											
Newbury	a										19 11											
	d				18 35						19 11							19 53		20 18		
Newbury Racecourse	d																	19 55				
Thatcham	d										19 16							20 00				
Midgham	d																	20 05				
Aldermaston	d																	20 08				
Theale	d										19 24							20 13				
Reading West	d																	20 21				
Reading 7	a	18 46	18 42		18 54	19 00	19 11	19 06	19 12	19 30	19 35	19 46	19 42		20 09	20 12	20 20	20 24	20 30	20 35	20 46	20 42
	d	18 52			18 56	19 02	19 13		19 13	19 32	19 37	19 52				20 14	20 20		20 32	20 37	20 52	
Twyford 3	a	18 58										19 58									20 57	
Maidenhead 3	a	19 06									19 53	20 06									21 05	
Slough 3	a	19 15					19 33				20 01	20 14					20 51				21 13	
Ealing Broadway ⊖	a	19 37										20 40									21 39	
London Paddington 15 ⊖	a	19 47			19 37	19 39	19 51		19 54	20 11	20 22	20 50				20 53	21 12		21 13	21 20	21 48	

A ⌶ to Oxford

Table 116

Sundays
26 June to 31 July

Birmingham, Banbury, Bicester, Oxford and Bedwyn - Reading and London

		XC	GW	GW	CH	GW	GW	GW	XC	GW	XC	GW	GW	GW	GW	XC	GW	CH	GW	GW	GW	GW	GW
		◇1	◇1	◇1	1	◇1	◇1	1	◇1	1	◇1	◇1	◇1	1	◇1	◇1	1	1	1	◇1	◇1		
									A														
		⌶	☕	⌶		☕	☕		⌶		⌶	☕			☕						☕	🚌	
Birmingham New Street 12	d	19 33							20 03		20 33					21 03							
Birmingham International	d								20 14							21 14							
Coventry	d								20 25							21 24							
Leamington Spa 8	d	20 00							20 38		21 00					21 35							
Banbury	d	20 19							20 55		21 19												
Kings Sutton	d																						
Heyford	d																						
Tackley	d																						
Bicester Town	d				20 33													22 03					
Islip	d				20 44													22 14					
Oxford	a	20 40			21 00				21 14		21 38					22 08		22 30					
	d	20 43		20 50					21 16	21 21	21 40		21 50			22 10	22 14			22 47		23 00	
Radley	d									21 27							22 20					23 15	
Culham	d																						
Appleford	d																						
Didcot Parkway	a			21 02						21 35			22 02				22 28			22 59		23 35	
	d		20 58	21 03		21 10	21 16			21 35		22 01	22 03				22 28			23 00	23 11		
Cholsey	d									21 41							22 34						
Goring & Streatley	d									21 46							22 39						
Pangbourne	d									21 51							22 44						
Tilehurst	d									21 55							22 48						
Bedwyn	d							20 54											22 35				
Hungerford	d							21 00											22 41				
Kintbury	d							21 04											22 45				
Newbury	a							21 11											22 52				
	d							21 12						21 53	22 13				22 53				23 23
Newbury Racecourse	d													21 55									
Thatcham	d							21 17						22 00					22 58				23 28
Midgham	d													22 05									
Aldermaston	d													22 08									
Theale	d							21 25						22 13					23 06				23 36
Reading West	d													22 21									
Reading 7	a	21 09	21 17	21 23		21 24	21 31	21 33	21 43	22 02	22 10	22 17	22 20	22 24	22 30	22 35	22 53		23 15	23 16	23 27		23 44
	d		21 18	21 25		21 25	21 31			22 10		22 19	22 24		22 30		23 00			23 23	23 28		
Twyford 3	a									22 16							23 07						
Maidenhead 3	a			21 43						22 24							23 15						
Slough 3	a			21 51						22 33			22 47				23 22			23 43			
Ealing Broadway ⊖	a									22 56							23 45						
London Paddington 15 ⊖	a		21 57	22 12		22 03	22 21			23 06		22 57	23 05		23 15		23 54			00 10	00 16		

		GW	GW
		1	1
Birmingham New Street 12	d		
Birmingham International	d		
Coventry	d		
Leamington Spa 8	d		
Banbury	d		
Kings Sutton	d		
Heyford	d		
Tackley	d		
Bicester Town	d		
Islip	d		
Oxford	a		
	d		
Radley	d		
Culham	d		
Appleford	d		
Didcot Parkway	a		
	d	23 50	
Cholsey	d	23 56	
Goring & Streatley	d	00 01	
Pangbourne	d	00 05	
Tilehurst	d	00 10	
Bedwyn	d		
Hungerford	d		
Kintbury	d		
Newbury	a		
	d		23 45
Newbury Racecourse	d		23 47
Thatcham	d		23 52
Midgham	d		23 57
Aldermaston	d		00 01
Theale	d		00 06
Reading West	d		00s13
Reading 7	a	00 15	00 17
	d	00 15	
Twyford 3	a	00 22	
Maidenhead 3	a	00 30	
Slough 3	a	00 37	
Ealing Broadway ⊖	a	01 01	
London Paddington 15 ⊖	a	01 13	

A ⌶ to Oxford

Birmingham, Banbury, Bicester, Oxford and Bedwyn - Reading and London

		GW	GW	GW	GW	GW	GW	GW	GW	GW	GW	GW	GW	XC	CH	GW	GW	GW	XC	GW	GW	GW	GW
		◇1	◇1	1	1	1	◇1	◇1	◇1	1	◇1	◇1	1	◇1	1	◇1	◇1	1	◇1	1	◇1	1	◇1
			⊐				⊐		⊐		⊐			⊼		⊐	⊼		⊼		⊐		⊐
Birmingham New Street 12	d																						
Birmingham International	d																						
Coventry	d																						
Leamington Spa 8	d																						
Banbury	d																		10 55	11 00			
Kings Sutton	d																			11 05			
Heyford	d																			11 14			
Tackley	d																			11 19			
Bicester Town	d														10 04								
Islip	d														10 15								
Oxford	a														10 31				11 14	11 29			
	d	23p01		23p07		08 05		08 38		09 05		09 38	10 05	10 16			10 38	11 05	11 16				
Radley	d			23p13		08 12				09 12			10 11					11 11					
Culham	d			23p17																			
Appleford	d			23p20									10 16										
Didcot Parkway	a	23p13		23p25		08 20		08 51		09 20		09 50	10 21				10 50	11 20					
	d	23p14	23p30	23p36	07 45	08 21	08 43	08 53	09 14	09 21	09 45	09 51	10 21			10 45	10 51	11 21			11 29		11 51
Cholsey	d			23p42		08 26				09 26			10 27					11 27					
Goring & Streatley	d			23p47	07 53	08 32				09 32			10 33					11 33					
Pangbourne	d			23p51		08 36				09 36			10 37					11 37					
Tilehurst	d			23p56		08 42				09 42			10 42					11 42					
Bedwyn	d																						
Hungerford	d																						
Kintbury	d																						
Newbury	a																						
	d																						
Newbury Racecourse	d																						
Thatcham	d																						
Midgham	d																						
Aldermaston	d																						
Theale	d																						
Reading West	d																					←	
Reading 7	a	23p30	23p51	00 01	08 03	08 47	09 01	09 10	09 28	09 46	10 00	10 06	10 49	10 42		11 00	11 08	11 46	11 42		11 44	11 46	12 05
	d	23p31	23p52	00 03	08 03	08 50	09 02	09 11	09 29	09 50	10 00	10 07	10 53			11 00	11 08	11 52			11 44	11 52	12 06
Twyford 3	a			00 09		08 56				09 58			10 59					→				11 58	
Maidenhead 3	a			00 17		09 04				10 06			11 07									12 06	
Slough 3	a	23p48		00 28	08 24	09 11		09 30		10 13		10 28	11 15				11 31					12 13	
Ealing Broadway ⊖	a			00 52		09 37				10 38			11 38									12 37	
London Paddington 15 ⊖	a	00 13	00 33	01 03	08 43	09 46	09 39	09 49	10 08	10 47	10 38	10 52	11 47			11 42	11 52				12 23	12 47	12 42

		GW	CH	GW	XC	GW	GW	GW	GW	GW	XC	CH	GW	GW	GW	GW	GW	XC	GW	GW	GW	XC	GW
		◇1	1	1	◇1	◇1	1	◇1	◇1	1	◇1	1	◇1	1	◇1	◇1	1	◇1	◇1	1	◇1	◇1	◇1
					⊼	⊐		⊐	⊼		⊼		⊐		⊐			⊼	⊐		⊐	⊼	
Birmingham New Street 12	d																						
Birmingham International	d																						
Coventry	d																						
Leamington Spa 8	d																						
Banbury	d				11 55						12 55							13 55				14 19	
Kings Sutton	d																						
Heyford	d																						
Tackley	d																						
Bicester Town	d		11 33									13 03											
Islip	d		11 44									13 14											
Oxford	a		12 00		12 14						13 14	13 30						14 14				14 38	
	d	11 38		12 05	12 16				12 45	13 05	13 16					13 38	14 05	14 16				14 43	14 41
Radley	d			12 11						13 11							14 11						
Culham	d																						
Appleford	d			12 16													14 16						
Didcot Parkway	a	11 53		12 21					12 56	13 20						13 54	14 20						14 53
	d	11 54		12 21		12 29		12 47	12 57	13 21			13 29		13 47	13 55	14 21		14 29		14 47		14 54
Cholsey	d			12 27						13 27							14 27						
Goring & Streatley	d			12 33						13 33							14 33						
Pangbourne	d			12 37						13 37							14 37						
Tilehurst	d			12 42						13 42							14 42						
Bedwyn	d													12 28									
Hungerford	d													12 34									
Kintbury	d													12 38									
Newbury	a													12 45									
	d													12 46									
Newbury Racecourse	d													12 58									
Thatcham	d													13 05									
Midgham	d													13 11									
Aldermaston	d													13 17									
Theale	d													13 41									
Reading West	d						←							13 47						←			
Reading 7	a	12 10		12 47	12 42	12 44	12 47	13 00	13 14	13 44	13 42		13 44	13 50	14 00	14 11	14 46	14 42	14 44	14 46	15 00	15 09	15 10
	d	12 11		12 52		12 44	12 52	13 02	13 14	13 49			13 44	13 53	14 02	14 11	14 53		14 44	14 53	15 02		15 11
Twyford 3	a			→			12 58			13 55							→			14 59			
Maidenhead 3	a						13 06			14 03				14 09						15 07			
Slough 3	a	12 33					13 14		13 33	14 10				14 17		14 31				15 15			15 31
Ealing Broadway ⊖	a						13 38			14 36										15 38			
London Paddington 15 ⊖	a	12 52				13 23	13 47	13 38	13 52	14 46			14 21	14 39	14 40	14 52			15 22	15 47	15 38		15 52

Table 116

Sundays

7 August to 11 September

Birmingham, Banbury, Bicester, Oxford and Bedwyn - Reading and London

		GW	CH	GW	XC	GW	GW	GW	XC	GW	GW	XC	CH	GW	GW	GW	GW	GW	GW	XC	GW	GW
		1	1	1	◇1	◇1	1	◇1	◇1	◇1	1	◇1	1	1	◇1	1	◇1	1	◇1	◇1	◇1	◇1
					⊼	⊐		⊐	⊼	⊐		⊼			⊐		⊐		⊐	⊼	⊐	⊐
Birmingham New Street 12	d				14 03				14 33			15 03								15 33		
Birmingham International	d				14 14							15 14										
Coventry	d				14 25							15 25										
Leamington Spa 8	d				14 38				15 00			15 38								16 00		
Banbury	d				14 55				15 19			15 55		16 00						16 19		
Kings Sutton	d													16 05								
Heyford	d													16 14								
Tackley	d													16 18								
Bicester Town	d		14 33										16 03									
Islip	d		14 44										16 14									
Oxford	a		15 00		15 14				15 41			16 14	16 30	16 33						16 41		
	d			15 05	15 16				15 43	15 50	16 05	16 16								16 43		16 50
Radley	d			15 11							16 11											
Culham	d																					
Appleford	d										16 16											
Didcot Parkway	a			15 20						16 01	16 20											17 02
	d			15 21		15 29		15 47		16 03	16 21				16 29				16 47		16 59	17 03
Cholsey	d			15 27							16 27											
Goring & Streatley	d			15 33							16 33											
Pangbourne	d			15 37							16 37											
Tilehurst	d			15 42							16 42											
Bedwyn	d	13 56														15 28						
Hungerford	d	14 02														15 34						
Kintbury	d	14 06														15 38						
Newbury	a	14 13														15 45						
	d	14 14														15 46	16 31					
Newbury Racecourse	d	14 26														15 58						
Thatcham	d	14 33														16 03						
Midgham	d	14 39														16 07						
Aldermaston	d	14 45														16 30						
Theale	d	15 09														16 35						
Reading West	d	15 15					←									16 41		←				
Reading 7	a	15 18		15 46	15 42	15 44	15 46	16 00	16 09	16 20	16 46	16 42			16 42	16 48	16 51	16 46	17 00	17 09	17 12	17 20
	d	15 18		15 52		15 44	15 52	16 02		16 20	16 53				16 44	16 48	16 53	16 53	17 02		17 14	17 20
Twyford 3	a			→			15 58				→							17 05				
Maidenhead 3	a	15 32					16 06									17 04		17 15				
Slough 3	a	15 40					16 16			16 51						17 12		17 23				17 44
Ealing Broadway ⊖	a						16 38											17 47				
London Paddington 15 ⊖	a	16 00				16 23	16 47	16 38		17 07					17 22	17 32	17 36	17 55	17 43		17 53	18 05

		GW	GW	XC	GW	GW	GW	XC	GW	GW	CH	GW	GW	XC	GW	GW	GW	GW	XC	GW	GW	GW	GW
		1	1	◇1	◇1	1	◇1	◇1	◇1	◇1	1	1	1	◇1	1	◇1	◇1	◇1	◇1	◇1	◇1	1	1
				⊼	⊐		⊐	⊼	⊐	⊐				⊼		⊐	⊐	⊐	⊼	⊐	⊐		
Birmingham New Street 12	d			16 03				16 33						17 03					17 33				
Birmingham International	d			16 14										17 14									
Coventry	d			16 25										17 25									
Leamington Spa 8	d			16 38				17 00						17 38					18 01				
Banbury	d			16 55				17 19						17 55	18 00				18 20				
Kings Sutton	d														18 07								
Heyford	d														18 16								
Tackley	d														18 20								
Bicester Town	d										17 33												
Islip	d										17 44												
Oxford	a			17 14				17 38			18 00			18 14	18 31				18 40				
	d		17 05	17 16				17 43		17 50			18 05	18 16				18 39	18 43				19 05
Radley	d		17 11										18 11										19 11
Culham	d																						
Appleford	d												18 16										
Didcot Parkway	a		17 20							18 02			18 20					18 52					19 20
	d		17 21		17 29		17 47		17 59	18 03			18 21				18 47	18 56		18 59	19 17		19 21
Cholsey	d		17 27										18 27										19 27
Goring & Streatley	d		17 33										18 33										19 33
Pangbourne	d		17 37										18 37										19 37
Tilehurst	d		17 42										18 42										19 42
Bedwyn	d	16 54																				18 54	
Hungerford	d	17 00																				19 00	
Kintbury	d	17 04																				19 04	
Newbury	a	17 11																				19 11	
	d	17 11										18 03				18 35						19 11	
Newbury Racecourse	d											18 05											
Thatcham	d	17 16										18 10										19 18	
Midgham	d											18 15											
Aldermaston	d											18 18											
Theale	d	17 24										18 23										19 27	
Reading West	d					←						18 31											
Reading 7	a	17 35	17 46	17 39	17 42	17 46	18 00	18 09	18 12	18 20		18 34	18 46	18 42		18 52	19 00	19 11	19 06	19 12	19 30	19 38	19 46
	d	17 36	17 53		17 44	17 53	18 02		18 14	18 23		18 37	18 52			18 53	19 02	19 13		19 13	19 32	19 39	19 52
Twyford 3	a		→			17 59							18 58										19 58
Maidenhead 3	a	17 52				18 07						18 51	19 06									19 51	20 06
Slough 3	a	18 00				18 16				18 49		18 59	19 15					19 33				19 59	20 14
Ealing Broadway ⊖	a					18 38							19 37										20 38
London Paddington 15 ⊖	a	18 20			18 22	18 47	18 38		18 53	19 06		19 21	19 47			19 35	19 38	19 51		19 53	20 12	20 23	20 48

Table 116

Sundays — 7 August to 11 September

Birmingham, Banbury, Bicester, Oxford and Bedwyn - Reading and London

		XC ◇1 ⊼	CH 1	XC ◇1 ⊼	GW ◇1 ⊡	GW ◇1 ⊡	GW 1	GW ◇1 ⊡	GW ◇1 ⊡	GW 1	XC ◇1 A ⊼	XC ◇1 ⊼	GW ◇1 ⊡	GW ◇1 ⊼	CH 1	GW ◇1 ⊡	GW ◇1 ⊡	GW 1	XC ◇1 A ⊼	GW 1	XC ◇1 ⊼	GW ◇1 ⊡
Birmingham New Street 12	d	18 03		18 33							19 03	19 33							20 03		20 33	
Birmingham International	d	18 14									19 14								20 14			
Coventry	d	18 25									19 25								20 25			
Leamington Spa 8	d	18 38		19 00							19 38	20 00							20 38		21 00	
Banbury	d	18 55		19 19							19 55	20 19							20 55		21 19	
Kings Sutton	d																					
Heyford	d																					
Tackley	d																					
Bicester Town	d		19 03												20 33							
Islip	d		19 14												20 44							
Oxford	a	19 14	19 30	19 38							20 14	20 40			21 00				21 14		21 38	
	d	19 16		19 43		19 50				20 05	20 16	20 43		20 50					21 16	21 21	21 40	
Radley	d									20 11										21 27		
Culham	d																					
Appleford	d																					
Didcot Parkway	a					20 02				20 20				21 02						21 36		
	d				19 59	20 03		20 17		20 21			20 59	21 03		21 10	21 17			21 37		22 01
Cholsey	d									20 27										21 43		
Goring & Streatley	d									20 33										21 48		
Pangbourne	d									20 37										21 52		
Tilehurst	d									20 42										21 57		
Bedwyn	d																	20 54				
Hungerford	d																	21 00				
Kintbury	d																	21 04				
Newbury	a																	21 11				
	d						19 53		20 18									21 12				
Newbury Racecourse	d						19 55															
Thatcham	d						20 00											21 17				
Midgham	d						20 05															
Aldermaston	d						20 08															
Theale	d						20 13											21 25				
Reading West	d						20 21															
Reading 7	a	19 42		20 09	20 12	20 20	20 24	20 32	20 35	20 46	20 42	21 09	21 18	21 24		21 24	21 32	21 33	21 43	22 03	22 06	22 17
	d				20 14	20 20		20 32	20 37	20 51			21 20	21 29		21 25	21 32			22 10		22 19
Twyford 3	a									20 57										22 16		
Maidenhead 3	a									21 05				21 45						22 25		
Slough 3	a					20 50				21 13				21 53						22 35		
Ealing Broadway ⊖	a									21 37										22 57		
London Paddington 15 ⊖	a				20 51	21 08		21 11	21 13	21 47			21 56	22 12		22 03	22 14			23 07		22 56

		GW ◇1	GW 1	GW ◇1 ⊡	XC ◇1	GW 1	CH 1	GW 1	GW ◇1	GW ◇1 ⊡	GW 🚌	GW	GW 1	GW 1
Birmingham New Street 12	d				21 03									
Birmingham International	d				21 14									
Coventry	d				21 24									
Leamington Spa 8	d				21 35									
Banbury	d													
Kings Sutton	d													
Heyford	d													
Tackley	d													
Bicester Town	d						22 03							
Islip	d						22 14							
Oxford	a				22 08		22 30							
	d	21 50			22 10	22 21			22 47		23 00			
Radley	d					22 27					23 15			
Culham	d													
Appleford	d													
Didcot Parkway	a	22 02				22 39			22 59		23 35			
	d	22 03				22 39			23 00	23 11			23 50	
Cholsey	d					22 45							23 56	
Goring & Streatley	d					22 50							00 01	
Pangbourne	d					22 55							00 05	
Tilehurst	d					22 59							00 10	
Bedwyn	d							22 35						
Hungerford	d							22 41						
Kintbury	d							22 45						
Newbury	a							22 52						
	d		21 53	22 13				22 53				23 23		23 45
Newbury Racecourse	d		21 55											23 47
Thatcham	d		22 00					22 58				23 28		23 52
Midgham	d		22 05											23 57
Aldermaston	d		22 08											00 01
Theale	d		22 13					23 06				23 36		00 06
Reading West	d		22 21											00s13
Reading 7	a	22 20	22 24	22 30	22 35	23 04		23 15	23 20	23 27		23 44	00 15	00 17
	d	22 24		22 30		23 04			23 23	23 28			00 15	
Twyford 3	a					23 10							00 21	
Maidenhead 3	a					23 18							00 29	
Slough 3	a	22 46				23 26			23 45				00 36	
Ealing Broadway ⊖	a					23 48							00 59	
London Paddington 15 ⊖	a	23 05		23 12		23 58			00 04	00 11			01 11	

A ⊼ to Oxford

Table 116

Sundays — 18 September to 23 October

Birmingham, Banbury, Bicester, Oxford and Bedwyn - Reading and London

		GW ◇1	GW ◇1 ⊡	GW 1	GW 1	GW 🚌	GW 1	GW ◇1 ⊡	GW 1	GW ◇1 ⊡	GW ◇1	GW 1	XC ◇1 ⊼	CH 1	GW ◇1 ⊡	GW ◇1 ⊼	GW 1	XC 🚌	XC ◇1 ⊼	GW ◇1 ⊡	GW 1	GW ◇1 ⊡	GW ◇1
Birmingham New Street 12	d																						
Birmingham International	d																						
Coventry	d																						
Leamington Spa 8	d																	09 45					
Banbury	d																	10 25					
Kings Sutton	d																						
Heyford	d																						
Tackley	d																						
Bicester Town	d													10 04									
Islip	d													10 15									
Oxford	a													10 31				11 10					
	d	23p01		23p07		07 45			09 01		09 38	10 05	10 16			10 38	11 05		11 16				11 38
Radley	d			23p13					09 07			10 11					11 11						
Culham	d			23p17																			
Appleford	d			23p20								10 16											
Didcot Parkway	a	23p13		23p25		08 10			09 16		09 50	10 21				10 50	11 20						11 53
	d	23p14	23p30	23p36	07 45		08 21	08 43	09 16	09 45	09 51	10 21			10 45	10 51	11 21			11 29		11 51	11 54
Cholsey	d			23p42			08 26		09 21			10 27					11 27						
Goring & Streatley	d			23p47	07 53		08 32		09 27			10 33					11 33						
Pangbourne	d			23p51			08 36		09 31			10 37					11 37						
Tilehurst	d			23p56			08 42		09 36			10 42					11 42						
Bedwyn	d																						
Hungerford	d																						
Kintbury	d																						
Newbury	a																						
	d																						
Newbury Racecourse	d																						
Thatcham	d																						
Midgham	d																						
Aldermaston	d																						
Theale	d																						
Reading West	d																				←		
Reading 7	a	23p30	23p51	00 01	08 03		08 47	09 01	09 41	10 00	10 06	10 49	10 42		11 00	11 08	11 46		11 42	11 44	11 46	12 05	12 10
	d	23p31	23p52	00 03	08 03		08 52	09 02	09 52	10 00	10 07	10 52			11 00	11 08	11 52			11 44	11 52	12 06	12 11
Twyford 3	a			00 09			08 58		09 58			10 58					→				11 58		
Maidenhead 3	a			00 17			09 06		10 06			11 06									12 06		
Slough 3	a	23p48		00 28	08 24		09 11		10 11		10 28	11 13				11 30					12 13		12 33
Ealing Broadway ⊖	a			00 52			09 37		10 37			11 38									12 37		
London Paddington 15 ⊖	a	00 10	00 33	01 03	08 43		09 46	09 39	10 46	10 38	10 52	11 47			11 42	11 52				12 23	12 47	12 42	12 52

		CH 1	GW 1	XC 🚌	XC ◇1 ⊼	GW ◇1 ⊡	GW 1	GW ◇1 ⊡	GW ◇1 ⊼	GW 1	XC 🚌	XC ◇1 ⊼	CH 1	GW ◇1 ⊡	GW 1	GW ◇1 ⊡	GW ◇1	GW 1	XC 🚌	XC ◇1 ⊼	GW ◇1 ⊡	GW 1	GW ◇1 ⊡
Birmingham New Street 12	d																						
Birmingham International	d																						
Coventry	d																						
Leamington Spa 8	d			10 45							11 45								12 45				
Banbury	d			11 25							12 25								13 24				
Kings Sutton	d																						
Heyford	d																						
Tackley	d																						
Bicester Town	d	11 33											13 03										
Islip	d	11 44											13 14										
Oxford	a	12 00		12 10							13 10		13 30						14 10				
	d		12 05		12 16				12 45	13 05		13 16					13 38	14 05		14 16			
Radley	d		12 11							13 11								14 11					
Culham	d																						
Appleford	d		12 16															14 16					
Didcot Parkway	a		12 21						12 56	13 20							13 54	14 20					
	d		12 21			12 29		12 47	12 57	13 21				13 29		13 47	13 55	14 21			14 29		14 47
Cholsey	d		12 27							13 27								14 27					
Goring & Streatley	d		12 33							13 33								14 33					
Pangbourne	d		12 37							13 37								14 37					
Tilehurst	d		12 42							13 42								14 45					
Bedwyn	d																						
Hungerford	d																						
Kintbury	d																						
Newbury	a																						
	d																						
Newbury Racecourse	d																						
Thatcham	d																						
Midgham	d																						
Aldermaston	d																						
Theale	d																						
Reading West	d						←								←							←	
Reading 7	a		12 47		12 42	12 44	12 47	13 00	13 14	13 45		13 42		13 44	13 45	14 00	14 11	14 48		14 42	14 44	14 48	15 00
	d		12 52			12 44	12 52	13 02	13 14	13 52				13 44	13 52	14 02	14 11	14 52			14 44	14 52	15 02
Twyford 3	a		→				12 58			→					13 58			→				14 58	
Maidenhead 3	a						13 06								14 06							15 06	
Slough 3	a						13 13		13 35						14 13		14 31					15 13	
Ealing Broadway ⊖	a						13 38								14 37							15 38	
London Paddington 15 ⊖	a					13 23	13 47	13 38	13 53					14 21	14 47	14 40	14 52				15 22	15 47	15 38

Table 116

Sundays
18 September to 23 October

Birmingham, Banbury, Bicester, Oxford and Bedwyn - Reading and London

		XC		GW	CH	GW	XC	GW	GW	GW	XC	GW		GW	XC	CH	GW	GW	GW	XC	GW	GW		GW	XC
		◇1		◇1	1	1	◇1	◇1	1	◇1	◇1	◇1		1	◇1	1	◇1	1	◇1	◇1	◇1	◇1		1	◇1
		⊼		⊡			⊼	⊡		⊡	⊼	⊡			⊼		⊡		⊡	⊼	⊡	⊡			⊼
Birmingham New Street 12	d	13 33					14 03				14 33				15 03					15 33					16 03
Birmingham International	d						14 14								15 14										16 14
Coventry	d						14 25								15 25										16 25
Leamington Spa 8	d	14 00					14 38				15 00				15 38					16 00					16 38
Banbury	d	14 19					14 55				15 19				15 55					16 19					16 55
Kings Sutton	d																								
Heyford	d																								
Tackley	d																								
Bicester Town	d				14 33											16 03									
Islip	d				14 44											16 14									
Oxford	a	14 38			15 00		15 14				15 41				16 14	16 30				16 41					17 14
	d	14 43		14 41		15 05	15 16				15 43	15 50		16 05	16 16					16 43		16 50		17 05	17 16
Radley	d					15 11								16 11										17 11	
Culham	d																								
Appleford	d													16 16											
Didcot Parkway	a			14 53		15 20						16 01		16 20								17 02		17 20	
	d			14 54		15 21		15 29		15 47		16 03		16 21			16 29		16 53		16 59	17 03		17 21	
Cholsey	d					15 27								16 27										17 27	
Goring & Streatley	d					15 33								16 34										17 33	
Pangbourne	d					15 37								16 37										17 37	
Tilehurst	d					15 42								16 42										17 42	
Bedwyn	d																								
Hungerford	d																								
Kintbury	d																								
Newbury	a																								
	d																								
Newbury Racecourse	d																								
Thatcham	d																								
Midgham	d																								
Aldermaston	d																								
Theale	d																								
Reading West	d								←									←							
Reading 7	a	15 09		15 10		15 46	15 42	15 44	15 46	16 00	16 09	16 19		16 46	16 42		16 42	16 46	17 06	17 09	17 12	17 21		17 46	17 39
	d			15 11		15 52		15 44	15 52	16 02		16 19		16 52			16 44	16 52	17 08		17 14	17 21		17 53	
Twyford 3	a					→			15 58					→				17 10						→	
Maidenhead 3	a								16 06									17 18							
Slough 3	a			15 31					16 16			16 50						17 27				17 44			
Ealing Broadway ⊖	a								16 38									17 51							
London Paddington 15 ⊖	a			15 52				16 23	16 47	16 38		17 07					17 22	17 59	17 49		17 53	18 05			

		GW	GW	GW	XC	GW	GW	CH		GW	XC	GW	GW	XC	GW	GW	GW	XC		CH	XC	GW	GW	GW	GW
		◇1	1	◇1	◇1	◇1	◇1	1		1	◇1	◇1	◇1	◇1	◇1	◇1	1	◇1		1	◇1	◇1	◇1	◇1	1
		⊡		⊡	⊼	⊡	⊡				⊼	⊡	⊡	⊼	⊡	⊡		⊼			⊼	⊡	⊡	⊡	
Birmingham New Street 12	d				16 33						17 03			17 33				18 03			18 33				
Birmingham International	d										17 14							18 14							
Coventry	d										17 25							18 25							
Leamington Spa 8	d				17 00						17 38			18 01				18 38			19 00				
Banbury	d				17 19						17 55			18 20				18 55			19 19				
Kings Sutton	d																								
Heyford	d																								
Tackley	d																								
Bicester Town	d							17 33												19 03					
Islip	d							17 44												19 14					
Oxford	a				17 38			18 00			18 14			18 40				19 14		19 30	19 38				
	d				17 43		17 50			18 05	18 16		18 39	18 43			19 05	19 16			19 43		19 50		20 05
Radley	d									18 11							19 11								20 11
Culham	d																								
Appleford	d									18 16															
Didcot Parkway	a						18 02			18 20			18 52				19 20						20 02		20 20
	d	17 29		17 47		17 59	18 03			18 21		18 47	18 56		18 59	19 17	19 21					19 59	20 03	20 17	20 21
Cholsey	d									18 27							19 27								20 27
Goring & Streatley	d									18 33							19 33								20 33
Pangbourne	d									18 37							19 37								20 37
Tilehurst	d									18 42							19 42								20 42
Bedwyn	d																								
Hungerford	d																								
Kintbury	d																								
Newbury	a																								
	d																								
Newbury Racecourse	d																								
Thatcham	d																								
Midgham	d																								
Aldermaston	d																								
Theale	d																								
Reading West	d		←																						
Reading 7	a	17 42	17 46	18 00	18 09	18 12	18 20			18 46	18 42	19 00	19 11	19 06	19 12	19 30	19 46	19 42			20 09	20 12	20 20	20 32	20 46
	d	17 44	17 53	18 02		18 14	18 23			18 52		19 02	19 13		19 13	19 32	19 52					20 14	20 23	20 32	20 52
Twyford 3	a		17 59							18 58							19 58								20 58
Maidenhead 3	a		18 07							19 06							20 06								21 06
Slough 3	a		18 16				18 50			19 15			19 33				20 14						20 53		21 14
Ealing Broadway ⊖	a		18 38							19 37							20 38								21 38
London Paddington 15 ⊖	a	18 22	18 47	18 38		18 53	19 06			19 47		19 38	19 51		19 53	20 12	20 48					20 51	21 11	21 14	21 47

Table 116

Sundays
18 September to 23 October

Birmingham, Banbury, Bicester, Oxford and Bedwyn - Reading and London

		XC	XC	GW		GW	CH	GW	GW	GW	XC	GW	XC	GW		GW	XC	GW	CH	GW	GW	GW			
		◇1	◇1	◇1		◇1	1	◇1	◇1	◇1	◇1	1	◇1	◇1		◇1	◇1	1	1	◇1	◇1	1			
		A									A		A												
		⊼	⊼	⊡		⊼		⊡	⊼	⊡	⊼		⊼	⊡							⊡				
Birmingham New Street 12	d	19 03	19 33								20 03		20 33				21 03								
Birmingham International	d	19 14									20 14						21 14								
Coventry	d	19 25									20 25						21 24								
Leamington Spa 8	d	19 38	20 00								20 38		21 00				21 35								
Banbury	d	19 55	20 19								20 55		21 19												
Kings Sutton	d																								
Heyford	d																								
Tackley	d																								
Bicester Town	d						20 33												22 03						
Islip	d						20 44												22 14						
Oxford	a	20 14	20 40				21 00				21 14		21 38				22 08		22 30						
	d	20 16	20 43			20 50					21 16	21 21	21 40			21 50	22 10	22 21		22 47		23 15			
Radley	d											21 27						22 27				23 22			
Culham	d																								
Appleford	d																								
Didcot Parkway	a					21 02						21 36				22 02		22 39		22 59		23 30			
	d			20 59		21 03		21 10		21 17		21 37		22 01		22 03		22 39		23 00	23 11	23 30			
Cholsey	d											21 43						22 45				23 36			
Goring & Streatley	d											21 48						22 50				23 42			
Pangbourne	d											21 52						22 55				23 46			
Tilehurst	d											21 57						22 59				23 50			
Bedwyn	d																								
Hungerford	d																								
Kintbury	d																								
Newbury	a																								
	d																								
Newbury Racecourse	d																								
Thatcham	d																								
Midgham	d																								
Aldermaston	d																								
Theale	d																								
Reading West	d								←																
Reading 7	a	20 42	21 09	21 15		21 25		21 24	21 25	21 32	21 43	22 03	22 07	22 17		22 20	22 35	23 04		23 20	23 27	23 56			
	d			21 17		21 30		21 25	21 30	21 32		22 10		22 19		22 24		23 04		23 23	23 28	23 56			
Twyford 3	a					→						22 16						23 10				00 02			
Maidenhead 3	a								21 44			22 25						23 18				00 10			
Slough 3	a								21 51			22 35				22 46		23 26		23 45		00 20			
Ealing Broadway ⊖	a											22 57						23 48				00 43			
London Paddington 15 ⊖	a			21 53				22 03	22 11	22 14		23 07		22 56		23 05		23 58		00 04	00 11	00 52			

Sundays
from 30 October

		GW	GW	GW	GW	GW	GW	GW	GW	GW		GW	GW	XC	CH	GW	GW	GW	GW	XC		XC	GW	GW	GW
		◇1	◇1	1	1		1	1	1	◇1		1	1	◇1	1	◇1	1	◇1	1			◇1	◇1	1	◇1
						bus														bus					
			⊡											⊼		⊡		⊼				⊼	⊡		
Birmingham New Street 12	d																								
Birmingham International	d																								
Coventry	d																								
Leamington Spa 8	d																			09 45					
Banbury	d																			10 25					
Kings Sutton	d																								
Heyford	d																								
Tackley	d																								
Bicester Town	d														10 04										
Islip	d														10 15										
Oxford	a														10 31					11 10					
	d	23p01		23p07		07 45			09 05	09 34			10 05	10 16				10 52	11 05			11 16			11 50
Radley	d			23p13					09 11				10 11						11 11						
Culham	d			23p17																					
Appleford	d			23p20					09 16				10 16						11 16						
Didcot Parkway	a	23p13		23p25		08 10			09 21	09 46			10 21					11 04	11 21						12 04
	d	23p14	23p30	23p36	07 45		08 21		09 21	09 47			10 21					11 05	11 21						12 05
Cholsey	d			23p42			08 26		09 27				10 27						11 27						
Goring & Streatley	d			23p47	07 53		08 32		09 33				10 33						11 33						
Pangbourne	d			23p51			08 36		09 37				10 37						11 37						
Tilehurst	d			23p56			08 42		09 42				10 42						11 42						
Bedwyn	d											09 42					10 35								
Hungerford	d											09 48					10 41								
Kintbury	d											09 53					10 45								
Newbury	a											09 59					10 52								
	d							08 53				10 07				10 27	10 53						11 26	11 45	
Newbury Racecourse	d							08 55				10 10												11 47	
Thatcham	d							09 00				10 15					10 58							11 52	
Midgham	d							09 05				10 19												11 57	
Aldermaston	d							09 08				10 23												12 00	
Theale	d							09 13				10 28					11 06							12 05	
Reading West	d							09 21				10 35												12 13	
Reading 7	a	23p30	23p51	00 01	08 03		08 47	09 24	09 49	10 01		10 39	10 49	10 42		10 43	11 14	11 22	11 49			11 42	11 43	12 16	12 19
	d	23p31	23p52	00 03	08 03		08 50		09 52	10 02			10 52			10 44		11 22	11 52				11 45		12 19
Twyford 3	a			00 09			08 56		09 58				10 58						11 58						
Maidenhead 3	a			00 17			09 04		10 06				11 06						12 06						
Slough 3	a	23p48		00 28	08 20		09 12		10 15	10 17			11 14					11 38	12 14						12 37
Ealing Broadway ⊖	a			00 52			09 41		10 43				11 43						12 43						
London Paddington 15 ⊖	a	00 10	00 34	01 03	08 44		09 50		10 52	10 44			11 52			11 28		12 01	12 52				12 29		13 03

A ⊼ to Oxford

Table 116

Sundays
from 30 October

Birmingham, Banbury, Bicester, Oxford and Bedwyn - Reading and London

	CH	GW	XC	XC	GW	GW	GW	XC	XC	CH	GW	GW	GW	GW	XC	XC	XC	GW	GW	CH	GW	XC
	■	■		◇■	■	◇■	■		◇■	■	◇■	■	◇■	■		◇■	◇■	■	◇■	■	■	◇■
			🚌	⊼		⊼		🚌	⊼		⊡				🚌	⊼	⊼					⊼
Birmingham New Street ■ d																	13 33					14 03
Birmingham International d																						14 14
Coventry d																						14 25
Leamington Spa ■ d			10 45					11 45							12 45		14 00					14 38
Banbury d			11 25					12 25							13 24		14 19					14 55
Kings Sutton d																						
Heyford d																						
Tackley d																						
Bicester Town d	11 33									13 03										14 33		
Islip d	11 44									13 14										14 44		
Oxford a	12 00		12 10					13 10		13 30					14 10		14 38			15 00		15 14
d		12 05		12 16		12 50	13 05		13 16				13 50	14 05		14 16	14 43		14 50		15 05	15 16
Radley d		12 11					13 11							14 11							15 11	
Culham d																						
Appleford d		12 16					13 16							14 16							15 16	
Didcot Parkway a		12 21				13 02	13 21						14 04	14 21					15 02		15 21	
d		12 21				13 03	13 21						14 05	14 21					15 03		15 21	
Cholsey d		12 27					13 27							14 27							15 27	
Goring & Streatley d		12 33					13 33							14 33							15 33	
Pangbourne d		12 37					13 37							14 37							15 37	
Tilehurst d		12 42					13 42							14 42							15 42	
Bedwyn d					12 35													14 35				
Hungerford d					12 41													14 41				
Kintbury d					12 45													14 45				
Newbury a					12 52													14 52				
d					12 53						13 31	13 45						14 53				
Newbury Racecourse d												13 47										
Thatcham d					12 58							13 52						14 58				
Midgham d												13 57										
Aldermaston d												14 00										
Theale d					13 06							14 05						15 06				
Reading West d												14 13										
Reading ■ a		12 49		12 42	13 14	13 24	13 49		13 42		13 48	14 16	14 25	14 49		14 42	15 09	15 14	15 25		15 49	15 42
d		12 52				13 26	13 52				13 49		14 25	14 52					15 26		15 52	
Twyford ■ a		12 58					13 58							14 58							15 58	
Maidenhead ■ a		13 06					14 06							15 06							16 06	
Slough ■ a		13 14				13 40	14 14						14 41	15 14					15 40		16 17	
Ealing Broadway ⊖ a		13 43					14 43							15 43							16 43	
London Paddington ■ ⊖ a		13 52				14 02	14 52				14 28		15 03	15 52					16 02		16 52	

	XC	GW	GW	GW	XC	CH	GW	XC	GW	GW	GW	XC	XC	GW	GW	CH	GW	XC	GW	GW	GW
	◇■	■	◇■	■	◇■	■	◇■	◇■	◇■	■	■	◇■	◇■	■	◇■	■	■	◇■	◇■	◇■	■
	⊼		⊡		⊼		⊡	⊼	⊡			⊼	⊼		⊡			⊼	⊡	⊡	
Birmingham New Street ■ d	14 33				15 03			15 33				16 03	16 33					17 03			
Birmingham International d					15 14							16 14						17 14			
Coventry d					15 25							16 25						17 25			
Leamington Spa ■ d	15 00				15 38			16 00				16 38	17 00					17 38			
Banbury d	15 19				15 55			16 19				16 55	17 19					17 55			
Kings Sutton d																					
Heyford d																					
Tackley d																					
Bicester Town d						16 03										17 33					
Islip d						16 14										17 44					
Oxford a	15 41				16 14	16 30		16 41				17 14	17 38			18 00		18 14			
d	15 43		15 50	16 05	16 16			16 43	16 50		17 05	17 16	17 43		17 50		18 05	18 16		18 50	
Radley d				16 11							17 11						18 11				
Culham d																					
Appleford d				16 16							17 16						18 16				
Didcot Parkway a			16 05	16 21					17 02		17 21				18 02		18 21			19 02	
d			16 07	16 21					17 03		17 21				18 03		18 21			19 03	
Cholsey d				16 27							17 27						18 27				
Goring & Streatley d				16 33							17 33						18 33				
Pangbourne d				16 37							17 37						18 37				
Tilehurst d				16 42							17 42						18 42				
Bedwyn d										16 42											18 42
Hungerford d										16 48											18 48
Kintbury d										16 52											18 52
Newbury a										16 59											18 59
d		15 45					16 31			17 09				17 45					18 34		19 09
Newbury Racecourse d		15 47												17 47							
Thatcham d		15 52								17 14				17 52							19 14
Midgham d		15 57												17 57							
Aldermaston d		16 00												18 00							
Theale d		16 05								17 22				18 05							19 22
Reading West d		16 13												18 13							
Reading ■ a	16 09	16 16	16 25	16 49	16 42		16 48	17 09	17 21	17 34	17 49	17 39	18 09	18 16	18 24		18 49	18 42	18 52	19 25	19 35
d			16 26	16 52			16 50		17 23		17 52				18 26		18 52		18 53	19 26	
Twyford ■ a				16 58							17 58						18 58				
Maidenhead ■ a				17 06							18 06						19 06				
Slough ■ a			16 41	17 17					17 39		18 16				18 40		19 17			19 40	
Ealing Broadway ⊖ a				17 43							18 43						19 43				
London Paddington ■ ⊖ a			17 06	17 52			17 29		18 04		18 52				19 05		19 52		19 29	20 06	

Table 116

Sundays
from 30 October

Birmingham, Banbury, Bicester, Oxford and Bedwyn - Reading and London

	GW	XC	CH	XC	GW	GW	GW	GW	XC	XC	GW	GW	CH	XC	GW	XC	GW	GW	XC	GW	GW	CH
	■	◇■	■	◇■	■	◇■	◇■	■	◇■	◇■	■	◇■	■	◇■	■	◇■	■	◇■	◇■	◇■	■	■
		⊼		⊼		⊡	⊡		A ⊼	⊼		⊼		A ⊼		A ⊼				⊡		
Birmingham New Street ■ d		18 03		18 33					19 03	19 33				20 03		20 33			21 03			
Birmingham International d		18 14							19 14					20 14					21 14			
Coventry d		18 25							19 25					20 25					21 24			
Leamington Spa ■ d		18 38		19 00					19 38	20 00				20 38		21 00			21 35			
Banbury d		18 55		19 19					19 55	20 19				20 55		21 19						
Kings Sutton d																						
Heyford d																						
Tackley d																						
Bicester Town d			19 03										20 33									22 03
Islip d			19 14										20 44									22 14
Oxford a		19 14	19 30	19 38					20 14	20 40			21 00	21 14		21 38			22 08			22 30
d	19 05	19 16		19 43		19 50		20 05	20 16	20 43		20 50		21 16	21 21	21 40		21 50	22 10		22 21	
Radley d	19 11							20 11							21 27						22 27	
Culham d																						
Appleford d	19 16							20 16														
Didcot Parkway a	19 21					20 02		20 21				21 02			21 35			22 02			22 35	
d	19 21					20 03		20 21				21 03			21 35			22 03			22 35	
Cholsey d	19 27							20 27							21 41						22 41	
Goring & Streatley d	19 33							20 33							21 46						22 46	
Pangbourne d	19 37							20 37							21 51						22 51	
Tilehurst d	19 42							20 42							21 55						22 55	
Bedwyn d											20 35											
Hungerford d											20 41											
Kintbury d											20 45											
Newbury a											20 52											
d					19 50		20 24				21 00						21 53			22 23		
Newbury Racecourse d					19 52												21 55					
Thatcham d					19 57						21 05						22 00					
Midgham d					20 02												22 05					
Aldermaston d					20 05												22 08					
Theale d					20 10						21 13						22 13					
Reading West d					20 18												22 21					
Reading ■ a	19 49	19 42		20 09	20 21	20 22	20 42	20 49	20 42	21 09	21 21	21 29		21 43	22 02	22 07	22 24	22 25	22 35	22 40	23 00	
d	19 52					20 23	20 47	20 52				21 30			22 10			22 33		22 41	23 00	
Twyford ■ a	19 58							20 58							22 16						23 06	
Maidenhead ■ a	20 06							21 06				21 42			22 24						23 14	
Slough ■ a	20 17					20 43		21 17				21 48			22 33			22 49			23 22	
Ealing Broadway ⊖ a	20 43							21 43							22 56						23 44	
London Paddington ■ ⊖ a	20 52					21 07	21 28	21 52				22 13			23 05			23 13		23 17	23 54	

	GW	GW	GW	GW	GW	GW
	■	◇■			■	■
			🚌			
Birmingham New Street ■ d						
Birmingham International d						
Coventry d						
Leamington Spa ■ d						
Banbury d						
Kings Sutton d						
Heyford d						
Tackley d						
Bicester Town d						
Islip d						
Oxford a						
d		22 47	23 00			
Radley d			23 15			
Culham d						
Appleford d						
Didcot Parkway a		22 59	23 35			
d		23 00			23 50	
Cholsey d					23 56	
Goring & Streatley d					00 01	
Pangbourne d					00 05	
Tilehurst d					00 10	
Bedwyn d	22 35					
Hungerford d	22 41					
Kintbury d	22 45					
Newbury a	22 52					
d	22 53			23 23		23 57
Newbury Racecourse d						23 59
Thatcham d	22 58			23 28		00 04
Midgham d						00 09
Aldermaston d						00 13
Theale d	23 06			23 36		00 18
Reading West d						00s25
Reading ■ a	23 15	23 20		23 44	00 15	00 29
d		23 23			00 15	
Twyford ■ a					00 21	
Maidenhead ■ a					00 29	
Slough ■ a		23 45			00 36	
Ealing Broadway ⊖ a					00 59	
London Paddington ■ ⊖ a		00 04			01 11	

A ⊼ to Oxford

Table 116A

Mondays to Fridays

Reading - Wallingford

Bus Service

		GW BHX Bus	GW BHX Bus	GW BHX Bus	GW BHX Bus	GW BHX Bus	GW BHX Bus	GW BHX Bus	GW BHX Bus	GW BHX Bus		GW BHX Bus	GW BHX Bus	GW BHX Bus	GW BHX Bus	GW BHX Bus	GW BHX Bus	GW BHX Bus	GW BHX Bus	GW BHX Bus		GW BHX Bus	GW BHX Bus	GW BHX Bus	GW BHX Bus
Reading	d	06 55	07 20	07 50	08 25	09 05	09 30	10 05	10 30	11 05		11 30	12 05	12 30	13 05	13 30	14 05	14 30	15 05	15 30		16 05	16 35	17 05	17 35
Wallingford Town Hall	a	07 23	07 55	08 20	09 00	09 35	10 05	10 35	11 05	11 35		12 05	12 35	13 05	13 35	14 05	14 35	15 05	15 35	16 05		16 35	17 14	17 39	18 14

		GW BHX Bus	GW BHX Bus	GW BHX Bus	GW BHX Bus	GW BHX Bus		GW BHX Bus	GW BHX Bus	GW BHX Bus
Reading	d	18 05	18 35	19 05	19 35	20 05		21 05	22 05	23 05
Wallingford Town Hall	a	18 37	19 10	19 35	20 08	20 38		21 38	22 38	23 38

Saturdays

		GW BHX Bus	GW BHX Bus	GW BHX Bus	GW Bus	GW Bus	GW Bus	GW Bus	GW Bus	GW Bus		GW Bus	GW Bus	GW Bus	GW Bus	GW Bus	GW Bus	GW Bus	GW Bus	GW Bus		GW Bus	GW Bus	GW Bus	GW Bus
Reading	d	00 05	01 05	02 05	07 00	08 30	09 30	10 05	10 30	11 05		11 30	12 05	12 30	13 05	13 30	14 05	14 30	15 05	15 30		16 05	16 30	17 05	17 30
Wallingford Town Hall	a	00 38	01 38	02 38	07 27	09 05	10 05	10 35	11 05	11 35		12 05	12 35	13 05	13 35	14 05	14 35	15 05	15 35	16 05		16 35	17 05	17 39	18 09

		GW Bus	GW Bus	GW Bus	GW Bus	GW Bus		GW Bus	GW Bus	GW Bus
Reading	d	18 05	18 35	19 05	19 35	20 05		21 05	22 05	23 05
Wallingford Town Hall	a	18 37	19 10	19 32	20 08	20 38		21 38	22 38	23 38

Sundays

		GW Bus	GW Bus	GW Bus	GW Bus	GW Bus	GW Bus	GW Bus	GW Bus	GW Bus		GW Bus	GW Bus	GW Bus	GW Bus	GW Bus	GW Bus	GW Bus
Reading	d	00 05	01 05	02 05	09 35	10 35	11 35	12 35	13 35	14 35		15 35	16 35	17 35	19 35	20 35	22 05	23 05
Wallingford Town Hall	a	00 38	01 38	02 38	10 08	11 08	12 08	13 08	14 08	15 08		16 08	17 08	18 08	20 08	21 08	22 38	23 38

Table 116A

Mondays to Fridays

Wallingford - Reading

Bus Service

		GW BHX	GW BHX	GW BHX	GW BHX	GW BHX	GW BHX	GW BHX	GW BHX	GW BHX		GW BHX	GW BHX	GW BHX	GW BHX	GW BHX	GW BHX	GW BHX	GW BHX	GW BHX		GW BHX	GW BHX	GW BHX	GW BHX
Wallingford Market Place	d	06 10	06 35	07 15	07 40	08 10	08 50	09 25	09 50	10 20		10 50	11 20	11 50	12 20	12 50	13 20	13 50	14 20	14 50		15 20	15 50	16 20	16 50
Reading	a	06 48	07 13	07 45	08 20	08 40	09 28	09 55	10 28	10 50		11 28	11 50	12 28	12 50	13 28	13 50	14 28	14 50	15 28		15 50	16 28	16 50	17 28

		GW BHX	GW BHX	GW BHX	GW BHX	GW BHX		GW BHX	GW BHX	GW BHX	GW FO BHX														
Wallingford Market Place	d	17 25	17 55	18 25	18 50	19 50		20 50	21 55	22 55	23 55														
Reading	a	17 55	18 33	18 55	19 28	20 28		21 28	22 33	23 33	00 33														

Saturdays

		GW BHX	GW BHX	GW BHX	GW	GW	GW	GW	GW	GW		GW	GW	GW	GW	GW	GW	GW	GW	GW		GW	GW	GW	GW
Wallingford Market Place	d	23p55	00 55	01 55	07 50	08 50	09 20	09 50	10 20	10 50		11 20	11 50	12 20	12 50	13 20	13 50	14 20	14 50	15 20		15 50	16 20	16 50	17 20
Reading	a	00 33	01 33	02 33	08 25	09 28	09 50	10 28	10 50	11 28		11 50	12 28	12 50	13 28	13 50	14 28	14 50	15 28	15 50		16 28	16 50	17 28	17 50

		GW	GW	GW	GW	GW		GW	GW	GW	GW														
Wallingford Market Place	d	17 50	18 20	18 50	19 20	19 50		20 50	21 55	22 55	23 55														
Reading	a	18 28	18 50	19 28	19 50	20 28		21 28	22 33	23 33	00 33														

Sundays

		GW A	GW	GW	GW	GW	GW	GW	GW	GW		GW	GW	GW	GW	GW	GW	GW							
Wallingford Market Place	d	23p55	00 55	01 55	09 20	10 20	11 20	12 20	13 20	14 20		15 20	16 20	17 20	18 20	19 25	21 25	22 25							
Reading	a	00 33	01 33	02 33	09 53	10 53	11 53	12 53	13 53	14 53		15 53	16 53	17 53	18 53	19 58	21 58	22 58							

mber 12

Oxford - Abingdon

Bus Service

	GW	GW	GW	GW	GW	GW	GW	GW	GW		GW	GW	GW	GW	GW	GW	GW	GW	GW		GW	GW	GW	GW
	MX																							
	BHX	BHX	BHX	BHX	BHX	BHX	BHX	BHX	BHX		BHX	BHX	BHX	BHX	BHX	BHX	BHX	BHX	BHX		BHX	BHX	BHX	BHX
	🚌	🚌	🚌	🚌	🚌	🚌	🚌	🚌	🚌		🚌	🚌	🚌	🚌	🚌	🚌	🚌	🚌	🚌		🚌	🚌	🚌	🚌
Oxford d	23p40	06 15	06 35	06 55	07 13	07 33	07 53	08 13	08 33		08 53	09 15	09 38	10 00	10 20	10 40	11 00	11 20	11 40		12 00	12 20	12 40	13 00
Abingdon Stratton Way a	00 10	06 50	07 10	07 30	07 50	08 10	08 30	08 52	09 12		09 32	09 54	10 13	10 35	10 55	11 15	11 35	11 55	12 15		12 35	12 55	13 15	13 35

	GW	GW	GW	GW	GW		GW	GW	GW	GW	GW	GW	GW	GW	GW		GW	GW	GW	GW	GW	GW	GW	GW
	BHX	BHX	BHX	BHX	BHX		BHX	BHX	BHX	BHX	BHX	BHX	BHX	BHX	BHX		BHX	BHX	BHX	BHX	BHX	BHX	BHX	BHX
	🚌	🚌	🚌	🚌	🚌		🚌	🚌	🚌	🚌	🚌	🚌	🚌	🚌	🚌		🚌	🚌	🚌	🚌	🚌	🚌	🚌	🚌
Oxford d	13 20	13 40	14 00	14 20	14 40		15 00	15 15	15 25	15 45	16 05	16 25	16 45	17 05	17 25		17 45	18 05	18 23	18 40	19 10	19 40	20 10	20 40
Abingdon Stratton Way a	13 55	14 15	14 35	14 55	15 15		15 35	15 55	16 03	16 25	16 47	17 03	17 25	17 47	18 03		18 25	18 47	19 03	19 10	19 40	20 10	20 40	21 10

	GW		GW	GW	GW	GW	GW																	
	BHX		BHX	BHX	BHX	BHX	BHX																	
	🚌		🚌	🚌	🚌	🚌	🚌																	
Oxford d	21 10		21 40	22 10	22 40	23 10	23 40																	
Abingdon Stratton Way a	21 40		22 10	22 40	23 10	23 40	00 10																	

Saturdays

	GW	GW	GW	GW	GW	GW	GW	GW	GW		GW	GW	GW	GW	GW	GW	GW	GW	GW		GW	GW	GW	GW
	BHX																							
	🚌	🚌	🚌	🚌	🚌	🚌	🚌	🚌	🚌		🚌	🚌	🚌	🚌	🚌	🚌	🚌	🚌	🚌		🚌	🚌	🚌	🚌
Oxford d	23p40	06 40	07 10	07 40	08 10	08 40	09 00	09 20	09 40		10 00	10 20	10 40	11 00	11 20	11 40	12 00	12 20	12 40		13 00	13 20	13 40	14 00
Abingdon Stratton Way a	00 10	07 10	07 40	08 10	08 40	09 15	09 35	09 55	10 15		10 35	10 55	11 15	11 35	11 55	12 15	12 35	12 55	13 15		13 35	13 55	14 15	14 35

	GW	GW	GW	GW	GW		GW	GW	GW	GW	GW	GW	GW	GW	GW		GW	GW	GW	GW	GW	GW	GW	GW
	🚌	🚌	🚌	🚌	🚌		🚌	🚌	🚌	🚌	🚌	🚌	🚌	🚌	🚌		🚌	🚌	🚌	🚌	🚌	🚌	🚌	🚌
Oxford d	14 20	14 40	15 00	15 20	15 40		16 00	16 20	16 40	17 00	17 20	17 40	18 00	18 20	18 40		19 10	19 40	20 10	20 40	21 10	21 40	22 10	22 40
Abingdon Stratton Way a	14 55	15 15	15 35	15 55	16 15		16 35	16 55	17 15	17 35	17 55	18 15	18 35	18 55	19 10		19 40	20 10	20 40	21 10	21 40	22 10	22 40	23 10

	GW		GW																					
	🚌		🚌																					
Oxford d	23 10		23 40																					
Abingdon Stratton Way a	23 40		00 10																					

Sundays

	GW	GW	GW	GW	GW	GW	GW	GW	GW		GW	GW	GW	GW	GW	GW	GW	GW	GW		GW	GW	GW	GW
	A																							
	🚌	🚌	🚌	🚌	🚌	🚌	🚌	🚌	🚌		🚌	🚌	🚌	🚌	🚌	🚌	🚌	🚌	🚌		🚌	🚌	🚌	🚌
Oxford d	23p40	08 10	08 40	09 10	09 40	10 10	10 40	11 10	11 40		12 10	12 40	13 10	13 40	14 10	14 40	15 10	15 40	16 10		16 40	17 10	17 40	18 10
Abingdon Stratton Way a	00 10	08 40	09 10	09 40	10 10	10 40	11 10	11 40	12 10		12 40	13 10	13 40	14 10	14 40	15 10	15 40	16 10	16 40		17 10	17 40	18 10	18 40

	GW	GW	GW	GW	GW		GW	GW	GW	GW	GW													
	🚌	🚌	🚌	🚌	🚌		🚌	🚌	🚌	🚌	🚌													
Oxford d	18 40	19 10	19 40	20 10	20 40		21 10	21 40	22 10	22 40	23 10													
Abingdon Stratton Way a	19 10	19 40	20 10	20 40	21 10		21 40	22 10	22 40	23 10	23 40													

A not 22 May

Table 116B

Mondays to Fridays

Abingdon - Oxford

Bus Service

		GW BHX 🚌	GW BHX 🚌	GW BHX 🚌	GW BHX 🚌	GW BHX 🚌	GW BHX 🚌	GW BHX 🚌	GW BHX 🚌	GW BHX 🚌		GW BHX 🚌	GW BHX 🚌	GW BHX 🚌	GW BHX 🚌	GW BHX 🚌	GW BHX 🚌	GW BHX 🚌	GW BHX 🚌	GW BHX 🚌		GW BHX 🚌	GW BHX 🚌	GW BHX 🚌	GW BHX 🚌
Abingdon Stratton Way	d	05 35	05 55	06 15	06 35	06 53	07 08	07 28	07 48	08 06		08 28	08 50	09 10	09 20	09 40	10 00	10 20	10 40	11 00		11 20	11 40	12 00	12 20
Oxford	a	06 05	06 25	06 45	07 05	07 23	07 48	08 08	08 28	08 46		09 08	09 30	09 50	10 00	10 10	10 30	10 50	11 10	11 30		11 50	12 10	12 30	12 50

		GW BHX 🚌	GW BHX 🚌	GW BHX 🚌	GW BHX 🚌	GW BHX 🚌		GW BHX 🚌	GW BHX 🚌	GW BHX 🚌	GW BHX 🚌	GW BHX 🚌	GW BHX 🚌	GW BHX 🚌	GW BHX 🚌	GW BHX 🚌		GW BHX 🚌	GW BHX 🚌	GW BHX 🚌	GW BHX 🚌	GW BHX 🚌	GW BHX 🚌	GW BHX 🚌	GW BHX 🚌
Abingdon Stratton Way	d	12 40	13 00	13 20	13 40	14 00		14 20	14 40	15 00	15 20	15 40	16 00	16 20	16 40	17 00		17 20	17 40	18 00	18 20	18 30	19 00	19 30	20 00
Oxford	a	13 10	13 30	13 50	14 10	14 30		14 50	15 10	15 30	15 50	16 10	16 30	16 52	17 12	17 32		17 52	18 12	18 32	18 52	19 02	19 28	19 58	20 28

		GW BHX 🚌		GW BHX 🚌	GW BHX 🚌	GW BHX 🚌	GW BHX 🚌	GW BHX 🚌																	
Abingdon Stratton Way	d	20 30		21 00	21 30	22 00	22 30	23 00																	
Oxford	a	20 58		21 28	21 58	22 28	22 58	23 28																	

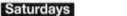

Saturdays

		GW 🚌	GW 🚌	GW 🚌	GW 🚌	GW 🚌	GW 🚌	GW 🚌	GW 🚌	GW 🚌		GW 🚌	GW 🚌	GW 🚌	GW 🚌	GW 🚌	GW 🚌	GW 🚌	GW 🚌	GW 🚌		GW 🚌	GW 🚌	GW 🚌	GW 🚌
Abingdon Stratton Way	d	06 00	06 30	07 00	07 30	08 00	08 20	08 40	09 00	09 20		09 40	10 00	10 20	10 40	11 00	11 20	11 40	12 00	12 20		12 40	13 00	13 20	13 40
Oxford	a	06 28	06 58	07 28	07 58	08 28	08 50	09 10	09 30	09 50		10 10	10 30	10 50	11 10	11 30	11 50	12 10	12 30	12 50		13 10	13 30	13 50	14 10

		GW 🚌	GW 🚌	GW 🚌	GW 🚌	GW 🚌		GW 🚌	GW 🚌	GW 🚌	GW 🚌	GW 🚌	GW 🚌	GW 🚌	GW 🚌	GW 🚌		GW 🚌	GW 🚌	GW 🚌	GW 🚌	GW 🚌	GW 🚌	GW 🚌	GW 🚌
Abingdon Stratton Way	d	14 00	14 20	14 40	15 00	15 20		15 40	16 00	16 20	16 40	17 00	17 20	17 40	18 00	18 20		18 40	19 00	19 30	20 00	20 30	21 00	21 30	22 00
Oxford	a	14 30	14 50	15 10	15 30	15 50		16 10	16 30	16 50	17 10	17 30	17 50	18 10	18 30	18 50		19 08	19 28	19 58	20 28	20 58	21 28	21 58	22 28

		GW 🚌		GW 🚌																					
Abingdon Stratton Way	d	22 30		23 00																					
Oxford	a	22 58		23 28																					

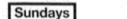

Sundays

		GW BHX 🚌	GW BHX 🚌	GW BHX 🚌	GW BHX 🚌	GW BHX 🚌	GW BHX 🚌	GW BHX 🚌	GW BHX 🚌	GW BHX 🚌		GW BHX 🚌	GW BHX 🚌	GW BHX 🚌	GW BHX 🚌	GW BHX 🚌	GW BHX 🚌	GW BHX 🚌	GW BHX 🚌	GW BHX 🚌		GW BHX 🚌	GW BHX 🚌	GW BHX 🚌	GW BHX 🚌
Abingdon Stratton Way	d	07 30	08 00	08 30	09 00	09 30	10 00	10 30	11 00	11 30		12 00	12 30	13 00	13 30	14 00	14 30	15 00	15 30	16 00		16 30	17 00	17 30	18 00
Oxford	a	07 58	08 28	08 58	09 28	09 58	10 28	10 58	11 28	11 58		12 28	12 58	13 28	13 58	14 28	14 58	15 28	15 58	16 28		16 58	17 28	17 58	18 28

		GW BHX 🚌	GW BHX 🚌	GW BHX 🚌	GW BHX 🚌	GW BHX 🚌		GW BHX 🚌	GW BHX 🚌	GW BHX 🚌	GW BHX 🚌	GW BHX 🚌													
Abingdon Stratton Way	d	18 30	19 00	19 30	20 00	20 30		21 00	21 30	22 00	22 30	23 00													
Oxford	a	18 58	19 28	19 58	20 28	20 58		21 28	21 58	22 28	22 58	23 28													

Table 116C

Mondays to Fridays

Oxford - Eynsham - Witney

Bus Service

		GW	GW	GW	GW	GW	GW	GW	GW	GW		GW	GW	GW	GW	GW	GW	GW	GW	GW		GW	GW	GW	GW
		MX BHX	MO	MO	MX	BHX	BHX	BHX	BHX	BHX		BHX	BHX	BHX	BHX	BHX	BHX	BHX	BHX	BHX		BHX	BHX	BHX	BHX
Oxford Frideswide Square	d	23p52	23p52	00 47	00 42	05 39	06 24	06 54	07 14	07 22	.....	07 40	08 00	08 15	08 30	08 45	09 00	09 15	09 30	09 45	.....	10 00	10 15	10 30	10 45
Eynsham Church	a	00 07	00 08	01 00	00 57	05 54	06 39	07 09	07 31	07 40	.	07 58	08 18	08 33	08 48	09 03	09 18	09 33	09 48	10 03	.	10 18	10 33	10 48	11 03
Witney Market Place	a	00 24	00 24	01 12	01 14	06 07	06 51	07 24	07 49	08 03	.....	08 23	08 43	08 55	09 05	09 20	09 35	09 50	10 05	10 20	.....	10 35	10 50	11 05	11 20

		GW	GW	GW	GW	GW		GW	GW	GW	GW	GW	GW	GW	GW	GW		GW	GW	GW	GW	GW	GW	GW	GW
		BHX	BHX	BHX	BHX	BHX		BHX	BHX	BHX	BHX	BHX	BHX	BHX	BHX	BHX		BHX	BHX	BHX	BHX	BHX	BHX	BHX	BHX
Oxford Frideswide Square	d	11 00	11 15	11 30	11 45	12 00	.....	12 15	12 30	12 45	13 00	13 15	13 30	13 45	14 00	14 15	.....	14 30	14 45	15 00	15 15	15 30	15 45	16 00	16 15
Eynsham Church	a	11 18	11 33	11 48	12 03	12 18	.	12 33	12 48	13 03	13 18	13 33	13 48	14 03	14 18	14 33	.	14 48	15 03	15 18	15 33	15 48	16 08	16 23	16 40
Witney Market Place	a	11 35	11 50	12 05	12 20	12 35	.....	12 50	13 05	13 20	13 35	13 50	14 05	14 20	14 35	14 50	.....	15 05	15 22	15 37	15 52	16 07	16 25	16 40	17 00

		GW		GW	GW	GW	GW	GW	GW	GW	GW	GW		GW	GW	GW	GW	GW	GW	GW	GW	GW		GW	GW
		BHX		BHX	BHX	BHX	BHX	BHX	BHX	BHX	BHX	BHX		BHX	BHX	BHX	BHX	BHX	BHX	BHX	BHX	BHX		BHX	BHX
Oxford Frideswide Square	d	16 27	.....	16 37	16 47	16 57	17 07	17 17	17 27	17 37	17 47	18 02	.....	18 22	18 42	19 02	19 22	19 52	20 22	20 52	21 22	21 52	.....	22 22	22 52
Eynsham Church	a	16 51	.	17 01	17 12	17 22	17 32	17 42	17 52	18 02	18 12	18 27	.	18 45	19 00	19 18	19 37	20 07	20 37	21 07	21 37	22 07	.	22 37	23 07
Witney Market Place	a	17 12	.....	17 22	17 32	17 41	17 51	18 01	18 11	18 21	18 31	18 46	.....	19 03	19 17	19 32	19 49	20 19	20 49	21 19	21 49	22 19	.....	22 49	23 19

		GW	GW																						
		BHX	BHX																						
Oxford Frideswide Square	d	23 22	23 52	.....	.....	.....	.....	.....	.....	.....	.....	.....	.....	.....	.....	.....	.....	.....	.....	.....	.....	.....	.....	.....	.....
Eynsham Church	a	23 37	00 07	.	.	.	.	.	.	.	.	.	.	.	.	.	.	.	.	.	.	.	.	.	.
Witney Market Place	a	23 54	00 24	.....	.....	.....	.....	.....	.....	.....	.....	.....	.....	.....	.....	.....	.....	.....	.....	.....	.....	.....	.....	.....	.....

Saturdays

		GW	GW	GW	GW	GW	GW	GW	GW	GW		GW	GW	GW	GW	GW	GW	GW	GW	GW		GW	GW	GW	GW
Oxford Frideswide Square	d	23p52	00 22	00 42	01 02	01 32	02 02	02 47	03 17	06 37	.....	07 22	07 52	08 19	08 45	09 00	09 15	09 30	09 45	10 00	.....	10 15	10 30	10 45	11 00
Eynsham Church	a	00 07	00 37	00 57	01 17	01 47	02 17	03 02	03 32	06 52	.	07 37	08 07	08 35	09 02	09 17	09 33	09 48	10 03	10 18	.	10 33	10 48	11 03	11 18
Witney Market Place	a	00 24	00 54	01 14	01 34	02 04	02 34	03 19	03 49	07 05	.....	07 50	08 20	08 50	09 20	09 35	09 50	10 05	10 20	10 35	.....	10 50	11 05	11 20	11 35

		GW	GW	GW	GW	GW		GW	GW	GW	GW	GW	GW	GW	GW	GW		GW	GW	GW	GW	GW	GW	GW	GW
Oxford Frideswide Square	d	11 15	11 30	11 45	12 00	12 15	.....	12 30	12 45	13 00	13 15	13 30	13 45	14 00	14 15	14 30	.....	14 45	15 00	15 15	15 30	15 45	16 00	16 15	16 30
Eynsham Church	a	11 33	11 48	12 03	12 18	12 33	.	12 48	13 03	13 18	13 33	13 48	14 03	14 18	14 33	14 48	.	15 03	15 18	15 33	15 48	16 03	16 18	16 33	16 48
Witney Market Place	a	11 50	12 05	12 20	12 35	12 50	.....	13 05	13 20	13 35	13 50	14 05	14 20	14 35	14 50	15 05	.....	15 20	15 35	15 50	16 05	16 20	16 35	16 50	17 05

		GW		GW	GW	GW	GW	GW	GW	GW	GW	GW		GW	GW	GW	GW	GW	GW	GW	GW	GW			
Oxford Frideswide Square	d	16 45	.....	17 00	17 15	17 30	17 45	18 00	18 15	18 30	18 52	19 22	.....	19 52	20 22	20 52	21 22	21 52	22 22	22 52	23 22	23 52	.....	.....	.....
Eynsham Church	a	17 03	.	17 18	17 33	17 48	18 03	18 18	18 33	18 48	19 10	19 37	.	20 07	20 37	21 07	21 37	22 07	22 37	23 07	23 37	00 07	.	.	.
Witney Market Place	a	17 20	.....	17 35	17 50	18 05	18 20	18 35	18 50	19 05	19 27	19 49	.....	20 19	20 49	21 19	21 49	22 19	22 49	23 19	23 54	00 24	.....	.....	.....

Sundays

		GW	GW	GW	GW	GW	GW	GW	GW	GW		GW	GW	GW	GW	GW	GW	GW	GW	GW		GW	GW	GW	GW
		A																							
Oxford Frideswide Square	d	23p52	00 22	00 42	01 02	01 32	02 02	02 22	02 47	03 17	.....	08 22	09 22	10 22	10 52	11 12	11 32	11 52	12 12	12 32	.....	12 52	13 12	13 32	13 52
Eynsham Church	a	00 07	00 37	00 57	01 17	01 47	02 17	02 37	03 02	03 32	.	08 40	09 40	10 40	11 10	11 30	11 50	12 10	12 30	12 50	.	13 10	13 30	13 50	14 10
Witney Market Place	a	00 24	00 54	01 14	01 34	02 04	02 34	02 54	03 19	03 49	.....	08 56	09 56	10 56	11 26	11 46	12 06	12 26	12 46	13 06	.....	13 26	13 46	14 06	14 26

		GW	GW	GW	GW	GW		GW	GW	GW	GW	GW	GW	GW	GW	GW		GW	GW	GW	GW	GW	GW	GW	
Oxford Frideswide Square	d	14 12	14 32	14 52	15 12	15 32	.....	15 52	16 12	16 32	16 52	17 12	17 32	17 52	18 22	18 52	.....	19 22	19 52	20 22	21 22	22 22	23 12	23 52	.....
Eynsham Church	a	14 30	14 50	15 10	15 30	15 50	.	16 10	16 30	16 50	17 10	17 30	17 50	18 10	18 40	19 10	.	19 38	20 08	20 38	21 38	22 38	23 28	00 08	.
Witney Market Place	a	14 46	15 06	15 26	15 46	16 06	.....	16 26	16 46	17 06	17 26	17 46	18 06	18 26	18 56	19 26	.....	19 54	20 24	20 54	21 54	22 54	23 44	00 24	.....

A not 22 May

Witney - Eynsham - Oxford

Bus Service

		GW	GW	GW	GW	GW	GW	GW	GW	GW		GW	GW	GW	GW	GW	GW	GW	GW	GW		GW	GW	GW	GW
		MX BHX	BHX	BHX	BHX	BHX	BHX	BHX	BHX	BHX		BHX	BHX	BHX	BHX	BHX	BHX	BHX	BHX	BHX		BHX	BHX	BHX	BHX
Witney Market Place	d	23p32	05 02	05 42	06 12	06 28	06 45	07 00	07 15	07 25		07 35	07 45	07 55	08 05	08 15	08 30	08 45	08 56	09 11		09 26	09 41	09 56	10 11
Eynsham Church	d	23p46	05 11	05 56	06 26	06 42	06 59	07 14	07 29	07 39		07 49	07 59	08 09	08 19	08 29	08 44	08 59	09 10	09 25		09 40	09 55	10 10	10 25
Oxford Frideswide Square	a	00 06	05 33	06 18	06 48	07 08	07 29	07 44	08 09	08 19		08 33	08 49	08 59	09 06	09 11	09 20	09 30	09 35	09 50		10 05	10 20	10 35	10 50

		GW	GW	GW	GW	GW		GW	GW	GW	GW	GW	GW	GW	GW	GW		GW	GW	GW	GW	GW	GW	GW	GW
		BHX	BHX	BHX	BHX	BHX		BHX	BHX	BHX	BHX	BHX	BHX	BHX	BHX	BHX		BHX	BHX	BHX	BHX	BHX	BHX	BHX	BHX
Witney Market Place	d	10 26	10 41	10 56	11 11	11 26		11 41	11 56	12 11	12 26	12 41	12 56	13 11	13 26	13 41		13 56	14 11	14 26	14 41	14 56	15 11	15 26	15 41
Eynsham Church	d	10 40	10 55	11 10	11 25	11 40		11 55	12 10	12 25	12 40	12 55	13 10	13 25	13 40	13 55		14 10	14 25	14 40	14 55	15 10	15 25	15 40	15 55
Oxford Frideswide Square	a	11 05	11 20	11 35	11 50	12 05		12 20	12 35	12 50	13 05	13 20	13 35	13 50	14 05	14 20		14 35	14 50	15 05	15 20	15 35	15 50	16 05	16 20

		GW		GW	GW	GW	GW	GW	GW	GW	GW	GW		GW	GW	GW	GW	GW	GW	GW	GW	GW		GW	GW
		BHX		BHX	BHX	BHX	BHX	BHX	BHX	BHX	BHX	BHX		BHX	BHX	BHX	BHX	BHX	BHX	BHX	BHX	BHX		BHX	BHX
Witney Market Place	d	15 56		16 11	16 26	16 41	17 01	17 16	17 34	17 46	17 51	18 06		18 25	18 45	19 07	19 37	20 07	20 37	21 02	21 32	22 02		22 32	23 02
Eynsham Church	d	16 13		16 27	16 42	17 00	17 20	17 35	17 50	18 00	18 05	18 20		18 40	19 00	19 22	19 51	20 21	20 51	21 16	21 46	22 16		22 46	23 16
Oxford Frideswide Square	a	16 38		16 53	17 08	17 25	17 45	18 00	18 16	18 26	18 31	18 45		18 59	19 19	19 41	20 11	20 41	21 11	21 36	22 06	22 36		23 06	23 36

		GW	GW
		BHX	FO BHX
Witney Market Place	d	23 32	23 59
Eynsham Church	d	23 46	00 10
Oxford Frideswide Square	a	00 06	00 26

Saturdays

		GW	GW	GW	GW	GW	GW	GW	GW	GW		GW	GW	GW	GW	GW	GW	GW	GW	GW		GW	GW	GW	GW
Witney Market Place	d	23p32	23p59	05 52	06 38	07 08	07 28	07 49	08 11	08 24		08 41	08 56	09 11	09 21	09 31	09 41	09 56	10 11	10 26		10 41	10 56	11 11	11 26
Eynsham Church	d	23p46	00 10	06 01	06 51	07 21	07 41	08 04	08 26	08 38		08 56	09 11	09 26	09 36	09 46	09 56	10 11	10 29	10 44		10 59	11 14	11 29	11 44
Oxford Frideswide Square	a	00 06	00 26	06 23	07 08	07 38	07 57	08 27	08 49	09 02		09 19	09 34	09 49	09 59	10 09	10 19	10 34	10 52	11 07		11 22	11 37	11 52	12 07

		GW	GW	GW	GW	GW		GW	GW	GW	GW	GW	GW	GW	GW	GW		GW	GW	GW	GW	GW	GW	GW	GW
Witney Market Place	d	11 41	11 56	12 11	12 28	12 42		12 57	13 12	13 27	13 42	13 57	14 12	14 27	14 42	14 57		15 12	15 27	15 42	15 57	16 12	16 27	16 42	16 57
Eynsham Church	d	11 59	12 14	12 29	12 46	12 56		13 11	13 26	13 41	13 56	14 11	14 26	14 41	14 56	15 11		15 26	15 41	15 56	16 11	16 26	16 41	16 56	17 11
Oxford Frideswide Square	a	12 22	12 37	12 52	13 09	13 17		13 32	13 47	14 02	14 17	14 32	14 47	15 02	15 17	15 32		15 47	16 02	16 17	16 32	16 47	17 02	17 17	17 32

		GW		GW	GW	GW	GW	GW	GW	GW	GW	GW		GW	GW	GW	GW	GW	GW	GW
Witney Market Place	d	17 14		17 29	17 44	18 04	18 25	18 45	19 07	19 37	20 07	20 37		21 02	21 32	22 02	22 32	23 02	23 32	23 59
Eynsham Church	d	17 28		17 43	17 58	18 18	18 40	19 00	19 22	19 52	20 22	20 52		21 16	21 46	22 16	22 46	23 16	23 46	00 10
Oxford Frideswide Square	a	17 46		18 01	18 16	18 36	19 04	19 24	19 46	20 16	20 46	21 16		21 36	22 06	22 36	23 06	23 36	00 06	00 26

Sundays

		GW	GW	GW	GW	GW	GW	GW	GW	GW		GW	GW	GW	GW	GW	GW	GW	GW	GW		GW	GW	GW	GW
		A	A																						
Witney Market Place	d	23p32	23p59	07 38	08 38	09 08	09 38	10 08	10 28	10 48		11 08	11 28	11 48	12 08	12 28	12 48	13 08	13 28	13 48		14 08	14 28	14 48	15 08
Eynsham Church	d	23p46	00 10	07 54	08 54	09 24	09 54	10 24	10 44	11 04		11 24	11 44	12 04	12 24	12 44	13 04	13 24	13 44	14 04		14 24	14 44	15 04	15 24
Oxford Frideswide Square	a	00 06	00 26	08 09	09 09	09 39	10 11	10 41	11 01	11 21		11 41	12 01	12 21	12 41	13 01	13 21	13 41	14 01	14 21		14 41	15 01	15 21	15 41

		GW	GW	GW	GW	GW		GW	GW	GW	GW	GW	GW	GW	GW
Witney Market Place	d	15 28	15 48	16 08	16 28	16 48		17 08	17 38	18 08	18 35	19 35	20 35	21 35	22 35
Eynsham Church	d	15 44	16 04	16 24	16 44	17 04		17 24	17 54	18 24	18 51	19 51	20 51	21 51	22 51
Oxford Frideswide Square	a	16 01	16 21	16 41	17 01	17 21		17 41	18 11	18 41	19 07	20 06	21 06	22 06	23 06

A not 22 May

Table 117

Mondays to Fridays

London - Greenford and Reading

Miles	Miles	Miles			GW	GW	GW	GW	GW	GW	GW	GW	GW		GW	GW	GW	GW	GW	GW	GW	GW	GW		GW
						MX	MX	MX		MX			MX				MX	MX	MX						
					1	1	◇1	1	1	1	1	1	◇1		1	1	1	1	◇1	◇1	◇1	◇1	◇1		◇1
					A				A		B	C			C	B				D	E	F	A		E
																			🛏	🛏	🛏				
0	0	0	**London Paddington** 15 ⊖	d	22p43	22p45	22p49			22p59	23p15	23p15	23p20					23p29	23p30	23p37	23p37	23p47	23p47		23p47
4¼	4¼	4¼	Acton Main Line	d		22p51																			
5¾	5¾	5¾	**Ealing Broadway** ⊖	d	22p50	22p54				23p07	23p24	23p24						23p37				23p55	23p55		23p55
6½	6½	6½	West Ealing	d																					
—	7¼	—	Drayton Green	d																					
—	7½	—	Castle Bar Park	d																					
—	8¼	—	South Greenford	d																					
—	9¼	—	**Greenford** ⊖	a																					
7¼	—	7¼	Hanwell	d																					
9	—	9	Southall	d	22p56					23p12	23p29	23p29													
10¾	—	10¾	Hayes & Harlington	d	23p02	23p02				23p18	23p33	23p33						23p44							
—	—	14¾	**Heathrow Term 1-2-3** 2 ✈	a																					
—	—	16½	**Heathrow Terminal 4** ✈	a																					
13¼	—	—	West Drayton	d	23p06					23p22	23p37	23p37													
14¾	—	—	Iver	d						23p25															
16¼	—	—	Langley	d	23p10			←	←	23p28	23p42	23p42			←	←									
18½	—	—	**Slough** 3	a	23p14	23p12	23p07	23p12	23p14	23p34	23p46	23p46	23p38		23p46	23p46		23p53				00 08	00 08		00 12
—	—	—		d	23p16	23p12	23p07	23p12	23p16	23p34	23p46	23p46	23p39		23p46	23p46		23p54				00 09	00 09		00 13
21	—	—	Burnham	d	→	→		23p16	23p20		→	→			23p51	23p51									
22½	—	—	Taplow	d				23p19																	
24¼	—	—	**Maidenhead** 3	d				23p23	23p24	23p41					23p56	23p56		00 01				00 17	00 17		00 20
31	—	—	**Twyford** 3	d				23p31	23p32	23p49					00 04	00 04	00 07	00 09							
36	—	—	**Reading** 7	a			23p34	23p40	23p43	00 01			00 04		00 13	00 14	00 16	00 19	00 06	00 15	00 16	00 31	00 31		00 31
—	—	—	Oxford	a			00 11	00 23	00 35				00 32					01 08					01 04		

		GW	GW	GW	GW	GW	GW	GW	GW		HC	HC	GW	GW	GW	HC	GW	GW	GW		GW	GW	GW	GW	HC
		MX	MO	MX	MX	MO	MX																		
		1	1	1	◇1	1	1	1	1				1	1	◇1		◇1	1	1		1	◇1	1	1	
															🛏		🛏								
London Paddington 15 ⊖	d	23p48	23p53		00 22	00 34	00 34	01 34	03 34		04 42	05 13	05 17	05 22	05 27	05 33	05 36		05 42		05 45	05 48		05 57	06 03
Acton Main Line	d	23p54																			05 51				
Ealing Broadway ⊖	d	23p57	00 02			00 42	00 42	01 42	03 42		04 50	05 21		05 30		05 41			05 50		05 54			06 05	06 11
West Ealing	d	23p59														05 43					05 57				06 13
Drayton Green	d																				05 59				
Castle Bar Park	d																				06 01				
South Greenford	d																				06 04				
Greenford ⊖	a																				06 09				
Hanwell	d	00 02														05 45									06 15
Southall	d	00 06	00 07			00 47	00 47	01 47	03 48		04 54	05 25		05 35		05 49			05 58					06 10	06 19
Hayes & Harlington	d	00 10	00 11			00 51	00 51	01 51	03 52		04 58	05 29		05 39		05 53			06 02					06 14	06 23
Heathrow Term 1-2-3 2 ✈	a										05 04	05 35				06 05									06 35
Heathrow Terminal 4 ✈	a										05 10	05 41													
West Drayton	d	00 14	00 15			00 55	00 55	01 55	03 56					05 43					06 06					06 18	
Iver	d	00 17												05 46										06 21	
Langley	d	00 21	00 20	←		01 00	01 00							05 50				←					←	06 25	
Slough 3	a	00 26	00 24	00 26	00 39	01 05	01 05	02 04	04 04				05 33	05 54			05 51	05 54	06 13			06 05	06 13	06 29	
	d	00 26	00 24	00 26	00 39	01 05	01 05	02 04	04 05				05 33	05 54			05 52	05 54	06 13			06 05	06 13	06 29	
Burnham	d	→	00 28	00 30		01 09	01 09							→					→				06 17		
Taplow	d			00 34			01 13																06 21		
Maidenhead 3	d		00 34	00 40		01 15	01 16	02 11	04 12									06 02					06 28	06 37	
Twyford 3	d		00 42	00 48		01 23	01 24	02 19	04 20									06 10					06 35	06 45	
Reading 7	a		00 49	00 57	01 00	01 32	01 35	02 29	04 30				05 51		05 55		06 05	06 20				06 19	06 45	06 53	
Oxford	a				01 33								06 22					07 03				06 56		07 47	

		GW	GW	GW	GW		GW	GW	HC	GW	GW	GW	GW	GW	GW		GW	HC	GW	GW	GW	GW	GW	GW	GW
		1	1	1	1		1	◇1		1	1	◇1	1	1	1		◇1		◇1		1	1	◇1	1	1
																			G						
								🛏				🛏					🛏		🛏				🛏		
London Paddington 15 ⊖	d	06 12	06 15	06 20			06 27	06 30	06 33	06 42	06 45	06 45	06 48		06 57		07 00	07 03	07 06	07 09	07 12	07 15	07 15	07 18	07 21
Acton Main Line	d		06 21								06 51											07 21			
Ealing Broadway ⊖	d	06 20	06 24				06 35		06 41	06 50	06 54				07 05			07 11			07 20	07 24			
West Ealing	d		06 27						06 43		06 57							07 13				07 27			
Drayton Green	d		06 29								06 59											07 29			
Castle Bar Park	d		06 31								07 01											07 31			
South Greenford	d		06 34								07 04											07 34			
Greenford ⊖	a		06 39								07 09											07 39			
Hanwell	d								06 45									07 15							
Southall	d	06 28							06 49	06 58					07 10			07 19			07 28				
Hayes & Harlington	d	06 32					06 45		06 53	07 02					07 14			07 23			07 32				
Heathrow Term 1-2-3 2 ✈	a								07 05									07 35							
Heathrow Terminal 4 ✈	a																								
West Drayton	d	06 40					06 49			07 06					07 18						07 36				
Iver	d						06 52								07 21										
Langley	d				←		06 56							←	07 25										
Slough 3	a	06 47		06 34	06 47		07 00			07 13			07 04	07 13	07 29						07 43				07 36
	d	06 47		06 35	06 47		07 00			07 13			07 04	07 13	07 29						07 43				07 36
Burnham	d	→			06 51					→				07 17							→				
Taplow	d				06 54									07 21											
Maidenhead 3	d				06 58		07 08							07 25	07 37					07 47					
Twyford 3	d				07 06		07 16							07 33	07 45					07 55					
Reading 7	a			06 49	07 15		07 27	06 54				07 09	07 19	07 45	07 52		07 24		07 30	08 04			07 39	07 47	07 51
Oxford	a			07 21									08 02		08 43										08 19

A MO from 19 September until 24 October
B MO from 8 August
C MO until 1 August
D MO until 24 October
E MO from 31 October
F MO until 12 September
G The Devon Express

London - Greenford and Reading

			GW 1	GW 1	GW ◇1 A Ø	HC	GW 1	GW 1	GW ◇1 B Ø	GW ◇1 ☕	GW 1		GW 1	GW ◇1 ☕	GW 1	HC	GW 1	GW 1	GW 1	GW ◇1 ☕	GW 1		GW 1	GW ◇1 ☕	GW 1
London Paddington 15 ⊖	d			07 27	07 30	07 33	07 42	07 45	07 45	07 48	07 50		07 57	08 00		08 03	08 06	08 12	08 15	08 15	08 18			08 22	
Acton Main Line	d							07 51											08 21						
Ealing Broadway ⊖	d			07 35		07 41	07 50	07 54					08 05			08 11		08 20	08 24						
West Ealing	d					07 43		07 57								08 13			08 27						
Drayton Green	d							07 59											08 29						
Castle Bar Park	d							08 01											08 31						
South Greenford	d							08 04											08 34						
Greenford ⊖	a							08 09											08 39						
Hanwell	d					07 45										08 15									
Southall	d			07 40		07 49	07 58						08 10			08 19		08 28							
Hayes & Harlington	d			07 44		07 53	08 02						08 14			08 23		08 32							
Heathrow Term 1-2-3 2 ✈	a					08 05										08 35									
Heathrow Terminal 4 ✈	a																								
West Drayton	d			07 48			08 06						08 18					08 36							
Iver	d			07 51									08 21												
Langley	d		←	07 55									08 25		←								←		←
Slough 3	a		07 43	07 59			08 13				08 06		08 29		08 13		08 25	08 43					08 29	08 36	08 43
	d		07 43	07 59			08 13				08 06		08 29		08 13		08 26	08 43					08 29	08 36	08 43
Burnham	d		07 47				→						→		08 17			→							08 47
Taplow	d		07 51												08 21										08 51
Maidenhead 3	d		07 55	08 07											08 25		08 34						08 38		08 55
Twyford 3	d		08 03	08 15											08 33		08 43						08 46		09 03
Reading 7	a		08 13	08 23	07 57				08 09	08 14	08 21			08 25	08 44		08 51			08 39	08 48		08 55	08 51	09 13
Oxford	a			09 15							08 49						09 26						09 44	09 20	

		GW 1	GW ◇1 ☕	HC	GW 1	GW 1	GW ◇1 ☕		GW 1	GW 1	GW 1	GW 1	GW ◇1 ☕	HC	GW ◇1 C Ø	GW ◇1 D Ø	GW ◇1 E Ø		GW ◇1 F Ø	GW 1	GW 1	GW ◇1 ☕	GW 1	GW ◇1 🍴	GW 1
London Paddington 15 ⊖	d	08 27	08 30	08 33	08 38	08 42	08 45		08 45	08 51		08 57	09 00	09 03	09 06	09 06	09 06		09 06	09 12	09 15	09 15	09 18	09 21	
Acton Main Line	d								08 51												09 21				
Ealing Broadway ⊖	d	08 35		08 41	08 47	08 50			08 54			09 05		09 11						09 20	09 24				
West Ealing	d			08 43		08 53			08 57					09 13							09 27				
Drayton Green	d								08 59												09 29				
Castle Bar Park	d								09 01												09 31				
South Greenford	d								09 04												09 34				
Greenford ⊖	a								09 10												09 39				
Hanwell	d			08 45		08 56								09 15											
Southall	d	08 40		08 49	08 53	09 00								09 19						09 28					
Hayes & Harlington	d	08 44		08 53	08 57	09 04						09 12		09 23						09 32					
Heathrow Term 1-2-3 2 ✈	a			09 05										09 35											
Heathrow Terminal 4 ✈	a																								
West Drayton	d	08 48				09 08						09 16								09 36					
Iver	d	08 51				09 11						09 19													
Langley	d	08 55				09 14					←	09 22													←
Slough 3	a	08 59			09 05	09 19				09 06	09 19	09 27								09 43				09 36	09 43
	d	08 59			09 05	09 19				09 06	09 19	09 27								09 43				09 36	09 43
Burnham	d				09 10	→														→					09 45
Taplow	d				09 13																				09 51
Maidenhead 3	d	09 06			09 17						09 26	09 34													09 55
Twyford 3	d	09 16			09 25						09a35	09 42													10 03
Reading 7	a	09 23	08 56		09 35		09 09			09 20		09 52	09 25		09 30		09 30					09 39	09 48	09 52	10 17
Oxford	a	10 14								09 52		10 41												10 18	

		GW 1	GW ◇1 ☕		HC	GW 1	GW 1	GW ◇1 Ø	GW ◇1 ☕	GW ◇1 G	GW ◇1 H	GW 1	GW 1		GW ◇1 I ☕	HC	GW FO ◇1 J Ø	GW FX ◇1 J Ø	GW 1	GW 1	GW ◇1 ☕	GW 1	GW ◇1 ☕		GW 1
London Paddington 15 ⊖	d	09 27	09 30		09 33	09 42	09 45	09 45	09 48	09 50	09 50		09 57		10 00	10 03	10 06	10 06	10 12	10 15	10 15	10 18	10 22		
Acton Main Line	d						09 51													10 21					
Ealing Broadway ⊖	d	09 35			09 41	09 50	09 54						10 05			10 11			10 20	10 24					
West Ealing	d				09 43		09 57									10 13				10 27					
Drayton Green	d						09 59													10 29					
Castle Bar Park	d						10 01													10 31					
South Greenford	d						10 04													10 34					
Greenford ⊖	a						10 09													10 39					
Hanwell	d				09 45											10 15									
Southall	d				09 49	09 58										10 19			10 28						
Hayes & Harlington	d	09 42			09 53	10 02							10 12			10 23			10 32						
Heathrow Term 1-2-3 2 ✈	a				10 05											10 35									
Heathrow Terminal 4 ✈	a																								
West Drayton	d	09 46				10 06							10 16						10 36						
Iver	d	09 49											10 19												
Langley	d	09 52										←	10 22												←
Slough 3	a	09 57				10 13				10 06	10 06	10 13	10 27						10 43				10 36		10 43
	d	09 57				10 13				10 06	10 06	10 13	10 27						10 43				10 36		10 43
Burnham	d					→						10 17							→						10 47
Taplow	d											10 21													10 51
Maidenhead 3	d	10 04										10 25	10 34												10 55
Twyford 3	d	10 12										10 33	10 42												11 03
Reading 7	a	10 22	09 56					10 09	10 14	10 21	10 22	10 45	10 52		10 25			10 30			10 39	10 48	10 51		11 13
Oxford	a	11 14								10 47	10 48		11 41										11 18		

A The Merchant Venturer
B The St. David
C FX until 30 June, FX from 5 September
D FO until 1 July, FO from 9 September
E FX from 4 July until 1 September. The Atlantic Coast Express
F FO from 8 July until 2 September. The Atlantic Coast Express
G from 12 September
H until 9 September
I The Torbay Express
J The Cornish Riveira

London - Greenford and Reading

		GW	GW	HC	GW	GW	GW	GW	GW		GW	GW	HC	GW	GW	GW	GW	GW	GW		GW	GW	GW	GW	HC
														FX	FO										
		1	◇1		1	1	◇1	◇1	1		1	◇1		◇1	◇1	1	1	◇1	1		◇1	1	1	◇1	
														A	A										
			⊡				Ø					⊡		Ø	Ø			⊡			⊼			⊡	
London Paddington 15 ⊖	d	10 27	10 30	10 33	10 42	10 45	10 45	10 50			10 57	11 00	11 03	11 06	11 06	11 12	11 15	11 15	11 18		11 20		11 27	11 30	11 33
Acton Main Line	d					10 51											11 21								
Ealing Broadway ⊖	d	10 35		10 41	10 50	10 54					11 05		11 11			11 20	11 24						11 35		11 41
West Ealing	d			10 43		10 57							11 13				11 27								11 43
Drayton Green	d					10 59											11 29								
Castle Bar Park	d					11 01											11 31								
South Greenford	d					11 04											11 34								
Greenford ⊖	a					11 09											11 39								
Hanwell	d			10 45									11 15												11 45
Southall	d			10 49	10 58								11 19			11 28									11 49
Hayes & Harlington	d	10 42		10 53	11 02						11 12		11 23			11 32							11 42		11 53
Heathrow Term 1-2-3 2 ✈	a			11 05									11 35												12 05
Heathrow Terminal 4 ✈	a																								
West Drayton	d	10 46			11 06						11 16					11 36							11 46		
Iver	d	10 49									11 19												11 49		
Langley	d	10 52							←		11 22											←	11 52		
Slough 3	a	10 57			11 13			11 06	11 13		11 27					11 43					11 36	11 43	11 57		
	d	10 57			11 13			11 06	11 13		11 27					11 43					11 36	11 43	11 57		
Burnham	d				→				11 17							→						11 47			
Taplow	d								11 21													11 51			
Maidenhead 3	d	11 04							11 25		11 34											11 55	12 04		
Twyford 3	d	11 12							11 33		11 42											12 03	12 12		
Reading 7	a	11 22	10 56				11 09	11 21	11 45		11 52	11 25		11 30				11 39	11 47		11 52	12 17	12 22	11 56	
Oxford	a	12 14						11 50			12 41										12 18		13 14		

		GW	GW	GW	GW		GW	GW	GW	GW	HC	GW	GW	GW	GW		GW	GW	GW	GW	GW	GW	GW	HC	GW
												FX	FO												
		1	1	◇1	◇1		◇1	1	1	◇1		◇1	◇1	1	1		◇1	◇1	◇1	◇1	1	1	◇1		1
					B							C	C						D	E					
				Ø	⊡		⊼			⊡		Ø	Ø				⊡	⊡	⊼	⊼			⊡		
London Paddington 15 ⊖	d	11 42	11 45	11 45	11 48		11 50		11 57	12 00	12 03	12 06	12 06	12 12	12 15		12 15	12 18	12 21	12 21		12 27	12 30	12 33	12 42
Acton Main Line	d		11 51												12 21										
Ealing Broadway ⊖	d	11 50	11 54						12 05		12 11			12 20	12 24							12 35		12 41	12 50
West Ealing	d		11 57								12 13				12 27									12 43	
Drayton Green	d		11 59												12 29										
Castle Bar Park	d		12 01												12 31										
South Greenford	d		12 04												12 34										
Greenford ⊖	a		12 09												12 39										
Hanwell	d										12 15													12 45	
Southall	d	11 58									12 19			12 28										12 49	12 58
Hayes & Harlington	d	12 02							12 12		12 23			12 32								12 42		12 53	13 02
Heathrow Term 1-2-3 2 ✈	a										12 35													13 05	
Heathrow Terminal 4 ✈	a																								
West Drayton	d	12 06							12 16					12 36								12 46			13 06
Iver	d								12 19													12 49			
Langley	d							←	12 22												←	12 52			
Slough 3	a	12 13					12 06	12 13	12 27					12 43					12 36	12 36	12 43	12 57			13 13
	d	12 13					12 06	12 13	12 27					12 43					12 36	12 36	12 43	12 57			13 13
Burnham	d	→						12 17						→							12 47				→
Taplow	d							12 21													12 51				
Maidenhead 3	d							12 25	12 34												12 55	13 04			
Twyford 3	d							12 33	12 42												13 03	13 12			
Reading 7	a			12 09	12 14		12 22	12 45	12 50	12 25		12 30					12 39	12 44	12 51	12 51	13 14	13 22	12 56		
Oxford	a						12 48		13 41										13 18	13 19		14 14			

			GW	GW	GW	GW	GW	GW	HC	GW			GW	GW	GW	GW	GW	GW	GW	GW	HC		GW	GW	GW
										FX															
			1	◇1	◇1	1	1	◇1		◇1			1	1	◇1	1	◇1	1	1	◇1			1	1	◇1
				Ø	⊼			⊡		Ø					⊡		⊼			⊡					⊡
London Paddington 15 ⊖	d		12 45	12 45	12 50		12 57	13 00	13 03	13 06			13 12	13 15	13 15	13 18	13 21		13 27	13 30	13 33		13 42	13 45	13 45
Acton Main Line	d		12 51											13 21										13 51	
Ealing Broadway ⊖	d		12 54				13 05		13 11				13 20	13 24					13 35		13 41		13 50	13 54	
West Ealing	d		12 57						13 13					13 27							13 43			13 57	
Drayton Green	d		12 59											13 29										13 59	
Castle Bar Park	d		13 01											13 31										14 01	
South Greenford	d		13 04											13 34										14 04	
Greenford ⊖	a		13 10											13 39										14 09	
Hanwell	d								13 15												13 45				
Southall	d								13 19				13 28								13 49		13 58		
Hayes & Harlington	d						13 12		13 23				13 32						13 42		13 53		14 02		
Heathrow Term 1-2-3 2 ✈	a								13 35												14 05				
Heathrow Terminal 4 ✈	a																								
West Drayton	d						13 16						13 36						13 46				14 06		
Iver	d						13 19												13 49						
Langley	d					←	13 22											←	13 52						
Slough 3	a				13 06	13 13	13 27						13 43				13 36	13 43	13 57				14 13		
	d				13 06	13 13	13 27						13 43				13 36	13 43	13 57				14 13		
Burnham	d					13 17							→					13 47					→		
Taplow	d					13 21												13 51							
Maidenhead 3	d					13 25	13 34											13 55	14 04						
Twyford 3	d					13 33	13 42											14 03	14 12						
Reading 7	a			13 09	13 22	13 45	13 51	13 25		13 30					13 39	13 47	13 52	14 17	14 21	13 56					14 09
Oxford	a				13 50		14 42										14 18		15 14						

A The Mayflower
B The Cheltenham Spa Express
C The Royal Duchy
D from 12 September
E until 9 September

Table 117

London - Greenford and Reading

		GW	GW	GW	GW	GW	HC		GW FX	GW FO	GW	GW	GW	GW	GW	GW	GW		GW	HC	GW	GW	GW	GW	GW
		◇1	◇1	1	1	◇1			◇1	◇1	1	1	◇1	1	◇1	1	1		◇1		◇1	1	1	◇1	◇1
															A						B				
		☕	🛒			☕			Ø	Ø			☕		🛒				☕		☕			☕	🛒
London Paddington 15 ⊖	d	13 48	13 50		13 57	14 00	14 03		14 06	14 06	14 12	14 15	14 15	14 18	14 21		14 27		14 30	14 33	14 36	14 42	14 45	14 45	14 50
Acton Main Line	d											14 21											14 51		
Ealing Broadway ⊖	d				14 05		14 11				14 20	14 24					14 35			14 41		14 50	14 54		
West Ealing	d						14 13					14 27								14 43			14 57		
Drayton Green	d											14 29											14 59		
Castle Bar Park	d											14 31											15 01		
South Greenford	d											14 34											15 04		
Greenford ⊖	a											14 39											15 09		
Hanwell	d						14 15													14 45					
Southall	d						14 19				14 28									14 49		14 58			
Hayes & Harlington	d				14 12		14 23				14 32						14 42			14 53		15 02			
Heathrow Term 1-2-3 2 ✈	a						14 37													15 05					
Heathrow Terminal 4 ✈	a																								
West Drayton	d				14 16						14 36						14 46					15 06			
Iver	d				14 19												14 49								
Langley	d			←	14 22											←	14 52								
Slough 3	a		14 06	14 13	14 27						14 43				14 36	14 43	14 57					15 13			15 06
	d		14 06	14 13	14 27						14 43				14 36	14 43	14 57					15 13			15 06
Burnham	d			14 17							↪					14 47						↪			
Taplow	d			14 21												14 51									
Maidenhead 3	d			14 25	14 34											14 55	15 04								
Twyford 3	d			14 33	14 42											15 03	15 12								
Reading 7	a	14 14	14 21	14 45	14 52	14 25			14 30				14 39	14 47	14 52	15 13	15 22		14 56					15 09	15 22
Oxford	a		14 48		15 41										15 18		16 14								15 50

		GW	GW		GW	HC	GW FX	GW FO	GW	GW	GW	GW	GW		GW	GW	GW	HC	GW	GW	GW	GW	GW		GW
		1	1		◇1		◇1	◇1	1	1	◇1	1	◇1		1	1	◇1		1	1	◇1	◇1	◇1		1
					☕		Ø	Ø			☕		🛒				☕				☕	☕	☕		
London Paddington 15 ⊖	d		14 57		15 00	15 03	15 06	15 06	15 12	15 15	15 15	15 18	15 22			15 27	15 30	15 33	15 42	15 45	15 45	15 48	15 51		
Acton Main Line	d									15 21										15 51					
Ealing Broadway ⊖	d		15 05			15 11			15 20	15 24						15 35		15 41	15 50	15 54					
West Ealing	d					15 13				15 27								15 43		15 57					
Drayton Green	d									15 29										15 59					
Castle Bar Park	d									15 31										16 01					
South Greenford	d									15 34										16 04					
Greenford ⊖	a									15 39										16 09					
Hanwell	d					15 15												15 45							
Southall	d					15 19			15 28							15 40		15 49	15 58						
Hayes & Harlington	d		15 12			15 23			15 32							15 44		15 53	16 02						
Heathrow Term 1-2-3 2 ✈	a					15 35												16 05							
Heathrow Terminal 4 ✈	a																								
West Drayton	d		15 16						15 36							15 48			16 06						
Iver	d		15 19													15 51									
Langley	d	←	15 22												←	15 55									←
Slough 3	a	15 13	15 27						15 43				15 36		15 43	15 59			16 13				16 06		16 13
	d	15 13	15 27						15 43				15 36		15 43	15 59			16 13				16 06		16 13
Burnham	d	15 17							↪						15 47				↪						16 17
Taplow	d	15 21													15 51										16 21
Maidenhead 3	d	15 25	15 34												15 55	16 07									16 25
Twyford 3	d	15 33	15 42												16 03	16 15									16 33
Reading 7	a	15 44	15 52		15 25		15 30				15 39	15 47	15 51		16 13	16 23	15 56				16 09	16 14	16 20		16 44
Oxford	a		16 43										16 18			17 15							16 47		

		GW	GW	HC	GW FX		GW	GW	GW		GW	GW	GW	GW	GW	HC	GW	GW	GW		GW	GW	GW	GW	GW
		1	◇1		◇1		1	1	◇1		1	◇1	1	1	◇1		◇1	1	1		◇1	◇1	1	1	◇1
																					C				
			☕		☕				☕			🛒			☕		☕				☕				☕
London Paddington 15 ⊖	d	15 57	16 00	16 03	16 06		16 12	16 15	16 15		16 18	16 22		16 27	16 30	16 33	16 36	16 42	16 45		16 45	16 49		16 55	17 00
Acton Main Line	d							16 21											16 51						
Ealing Broadway ⊖	d	16 05		16 11			16 20	16 24						16 35		16 41		16 50	16 54					17 03	
West Ealing	d			16 13				16 27								16 43			16 57						
Drayton Green	d							16 29											16 59						
Castle Bar Park	d							16 31											17 01						
South Greenford	d							16 34											17 04						
Greenford ⊖	a							16 39											17 09						
Hanwell	d			16 15												16 45									
Southall	d			16 19			16 28							16 40		16 49		16 58						17 08	
Hayes & Harlington	d	16 11		16 23			16 32							16 44		16 53		17 02						17 12	
Heathrow Term 1-2-3 2 ✈	a			16 35												17 05									
Heathrow Terminal 4 ✈	a																								
West Drayton	d	16 16					16 36											17 07						17 17	
Iver	d	16 19												16 49				17 10						17 20	
Langley	d	16 22											←	16 52				17 14					←	17 24	
Slough 3	a	16 27					16 43					16 36	16 43	16 57				17 18				17 04	17 18	17 27	
	d	16 27					16 43					16 36	16 43	16 57				17 18				17 04	17 18	17 28	
Burnham	d						↪						16 47					↪					17 22	17 33	
Taplow	d												16 51										17 26	17 36	
Maidenhead 3	d	16 34											16 55	17 04									17 30	17 43	
Twyford 3	d	16 42											17 03	17 12									17 38	17 51	
Reading 7	a	16 52	16 25		16 30				16 39		16 47	16 52	17 14	17 21	16 56		17 01				17 09	17 19	↪	↪	17 24
Oxford	a	17 44										17 23		18 13								17 50			

A 🛒 to Reading

B FO from 8 July until 2 September

C The Capitals United

London - Greenford and Reading

		HC	GW FX		GW		GW	GW	GW	GW	GW	GW	GW	GW	GW		GW	HC	GW	GW	GW	GW	GW	GW	GW
			◇1		◇1		1	1	1	◇1	1	1	◇1	1	◇1		1		◇1	◇1	1	◇1 A	1	1	◇1
			☕		☕					☕			☕		☕					☕		☕			☕
London Paddington 15 ⊖	d	17 03	17 03		17 06			17 12	17 15	17 15	17 18	17 18	17 22	17 25	17 30			17 33	17 33	17 36	17 42	17 45	17 45	17 48	17 48
Acton Main Line	d										17 24													17 54	
Ealing Broadway ⊖	d	17 11							17 23		17 27			17 33				17 41					17 53	17 57	
West Ealing	d	17 13									17 30							17 43						18 00	
Drayton Green	d										17 32													18 02	
Castle Bar Park	d										17 34													18 04	
South Greenford	d										17 37													18 07	
Greenford ⊖	a										17 42													18 12	
Hanwell	d	17 15																17 45							
Southall	d	17 19							17 29					17 38				17 49					17 59		
Hayes & Harlington	d	17 23							17 33					17 42				17 53					18 03		
Heathrow Term 1-2-3 2 ✈	a	17 35																18 05							
Heathrow Terminal 4 ✈	a																								
West Drayton	d								17 38					17 47									18 08		
Iver	d								17 41					17 50											
Langley	d								17 44					17 54									18 12		
Slough 3	a							17 34	17 49					17 58							18 04		18 16		
	d							17 35	17 49					17 58							18 05		18 16		
Burnham	d							17 40	17 53					18 02									18 21		
Taplow	d							17 43	17 57					18 06											
Maidenhead 3	d						←	17 47	18a05			17 40		18 10			←		17 53		18a13		18 26		
Twyford 3	d				17 28		17 38	17a57				17 48		18 17			17 51		18 07				18 34		
Reading 7	a		17 29		17 35		17 46			17 40		17 56	17 49	→	17 54		18 00		18 15	18 01		18 09	→		18 14
Oxford	a											18 45	18 15						19 06						

			GW	GW	GW	GW	HC	GW FX		GW	GW		GW	GW	GW	GW	GW	GW	GW FO	GW FX	GW		HC	GW	GW
			◇1	1	◇1 B	1		◇1 C		◇1	1		1	◇1	1	1	1	◇1 D	1	1	◇1			◇1	1
			☕		☕			🍽		☕				☕				☕			☕			☕	
London Paddington 15 ⊖	d		17 50	17 57	18 00		18 03	18 03		18 06			18 12	18 15	18 15	18 18	18 18	18 22	18 25	18 25	18 30		18 33	18 33	
Acton Main Line	d															18 24									
Ealing Broadway ⊖	d			18 05			18 11								18 23	18 27			18 33	18 33			18 41		
West Ealing	d						18 13									18 30							18 43		
Drayton Green	d															18 32									
Castle Bar Park	d															18 34									
South Greenford	d															18 37									
Greenford ⊖	a															18 42									
Hanwell	d						18 15																18 45		
Southall	d			18 10			18 19								18 29				18 38	18 38			18 49		
Hayes & Harlington	d			18 14			18 23								18 33				18 42	18 42			18 53		
Heathrow Term 1-2-3 2 ✈	a						18 35																19 05		
Heathrow Terminal 4 ✈	a																								
West Drayton	d			18 19											18 38				18 46	18 46					
Iver	d			18 22															18 49	18 49					
Langley	d			18 26											18 42				18 52	18 52					
Slough 3	a			18 30									18 35		18 47				18 59	18 59					
	d			18 30									18 36		18 47				18 59	18 59					
Burnham	d			18 35											18 51				→	→					
Taplow	d			18 39																					
Maidenhead 3	d		18 09	18 45		←					←		18 49		18 57		18 40								←
Twyford 3	d			18 52		18 17				18 28	18 34		18a58		19 05		18 48								18 52
Reading 7	a		18 20	→	18 25	18 26		18 30		18 35	18 44			18 40	→		18 56	18 49			18 54			18 59	19 01
Oxford	a		18 47			19 17											19 43	19 21							

		GW	20b26	GW	GW	GW	GW		GW FO	GW FX	GW	GW	GW	GW	GW	GW FO	HC		GW FX	GW	GW FO	GW	GW	GW FX	GW FO
			21 07													■			■						
		1		◇1	1	1	◇1		1	1	1	◇1	1	1	◇1	1			1	1	1	1	1	◇1	◇1
				☕			☕					🛒			☕	🍽			🍽					☕	☕
London Paddington 15 ⊖	d	18 36		18 45		18 45	18 47				18 48	18 51		18 57	19 00	19 03	19 03		19 03	19 06	19 12	19 12	19 15	19 15	19 15
Acton Main Line	d										18 54												19 21		
Ealing Broadway ⊖	d					18 53					18 57			19 05			19 11					19 20	19 24		
West Ealing	d										19 00						19 13						19 27		
Drayton Green	d										19 02												19 29		
Castle Bar Park	d										19 04												19 31		
South Greenford	d										19 07												19 34		
Greenford ⊖	a										19 12												19 39		
Hanwell	d																19 15								
Southall	d					18 59								19 10			19 19					19 28			
Hayes & Harlington	d					19 03								19 14			19 23					19 32			
Heathrow Term 1-2-3 2 ✈	a																19 35								
Heathrow Terminal 4 ✈	a																								
West Drayton	d													19 19											
Iver	d													19 22											
Langley	d								←	←			←	19 26											
Slough 3	a	18 54				19 11			18 59	18 59		19 06	19 11	19 30								19 41			
	d	18 55				19 11			18 59	18 59		19 06	19 11	19 30								19 41			
Burnham	d					→			19 03	19 03			19 15	19 34								→			
Taplow	d								19 06	19 06				19 38											
Maidenhead 3	d	19a03			←				19 10	19 10			19 21	19 43						19 27					
Twyford 3	d				19 05		19 09		19 18	19 18			19c37	19 51						19a38					
Reading 7	a			19 09	19 13		19 17		19 26	19 26		19 22	19 47	→	19 27				19 32		19 41			19 39	19 44
Oxford	a				20 13				20 18	20 27		19 48									20 28				

A The Red Dragon
B The Bristolian
C The Golden Hind
D The Cathedrals Express
b Arr. 1903
c Arr. 1929

Table 117

London - Greenford and Reading

		GW	GW		GW	GW	GW	GW	GW	HC	GW	GW	GW		GW	GW	GW	GW	GW	HC	GW	GW	GW		GW
			FX		FO																				
		1	◇1		◇1	1	1	1	◇1		1	1	◇1		◇1	◇1	1	1	◇1		1	1	◇1		◇1
			☕		☕				☕				☕		☕	⊼			☕				☕		☕
London Paddington 15 ⊖	d	19 18	19 22		19 22			19 27	19 30	19 33	19 42	19 45	19 45		19 48	19 50		19 57	20 00	20 03	20 12	20 15	20 15		20 20
Acton Main Line	d											19 51										20 21			
Ealing Broadway ⊖	d							19 35		19 41	19 50	19 54						20 05		20 11	20 20	20 24			
West Ealing	d									19 43		19 57								20 13		20 27			
Drayton Green	d											19 59										20 29			
Castle Bar Park	d											20 01										20 31			
South Greenford	d											20 04										20 34			
Greenford ⊖	a											20 09										20 39			
Hanwell	d									19 45										20 15					
Southall	d							19 40		19 49	19 58									20 19	20 28				
Hayes & Harlington	d							19 44		19 53	20 02							20 12		20 23	20 32				
Heathrow Term 1-2-3 2 ✈	a									20 05										20 35					
Heathrow Terminal 4 ✈	a																								
West Drayton	d							19 48			20 06							20 16			20 36				
Iver	d							19 51			20 09							20 19							
Langley	d						←	19 55			20 13						←	20 22							
Slough 3	a		19 36		19 36		19 41	19 59			20 17					20 06	20 17	20 27			20 43				20 35
	d		19 36		19 36		19 41	19 59			20 17					20 06	20 17	20 27			20 43				20 36
Burnham	d						19 45	20 03			→						20 20				→				
Taplow	d						19 48										20 25								
Maidenhead 3	d	19 40				←	19 52	20 09							20 06		20 29	20 34							
Twyford 3	d	19 48				19 51	20 00	20 17									20 37	20 42							
Reading 7	a	19 56	19 51		19 51	20 00	20 11	20 23	19 56				20 09		20 17	20 22	20 45	20 52	20 25				20 39		20 50
Oxford	a	20 46	20 18		20 21			21 13								20 47		21 43							21 16

		GW	GW	HC	GW	GW	GW	GW	GW		GW	GW	HC	GW	GW	GW	GW	GW	GW		HC	GW	GW	GW	GW
																									FO
		1	1		◇1	1	1	◇1	◇1		1	1		1	◇1	1	◇1	1	1			1	1	◇1	◇1
																						A	B	C	
					☕			☕	⊼						☕									☕	⊼
London Paddington 15 ⊖	d		20 27	20 33	20 35	20 42	20 45	20 45	20 51			20 57	21 03	21 12	21 15	21 15	21 21		21 27		21 33	21 42	21 42	21 45	21 48
Acton Main Line	d						20 51									21 21						21 48	21 48		
Ealing Broadway ⊖	d		20 35	20 41		20 50	20 54					21 05	21 11	21 20		21 24			21 35		21 41	21 51	21 51		
West Ealing	d			20 43			20 57						21 13			21 27					21 43				
Drayton Green	d						20 59									21 29									
Castle Bar Park	d						21 01									21 31									
South Greenford	d						21 04									21 34									
Greenford ⊖	a						21 09									21 39									
Hanwell	d			20 45									21 15								21 45				
Southall	d			20 49		20 58							21 19	21 28							21 49	21 58	21 58		
Hayes & Harlington	d		20 42	20 53		21 02						21 12	21 23	21 32					21 42		21 53	22 02	22 02		
Heathrow Term 1-2-3 2 ✈	a			21 05									21 35								22 05				
Heathrow Terminal 4 ✈	a																								
West Drayton	d		20 46			21 06						21 16		21 36					21 46			22 06	22 06		
Iver	d		20 49									21 19										22 09	22 09		
Langley	d	←	20 52								←	21 22						←				22 13	22 13		
Slough 3	a	20 43	20 57			21 13			21 06		21 13	21 27		21 43			21 36	21 43	21 54			22 18	22 18		22 03
	d	20 43	20 57			21 13			21 06		21 13	21 27		21 43			21 36	21 43	21 54			22 19	22 19		22 03
Burnham	d	20 47				→					21 17			→				21 47				→	→		
Taplow	d	20 51									21 21							21 51							
Maidenhead 3	d	20 55	21 04								21 25	21 34						21 55	22 01						
Twyford 3	d	21 03	21 12								21 33	21 42						22 03	22 09						
Reading 7	a	21 13	21 21		20 59			21 09	21 22		21 45	21 51			21 39		21 52	22 13	22 20					22 09	22 22
Oxford	a		22 16						21 53			22 40					22 24		23 17						22 47

		GW	GW	GW	GW		GW	HC	GW	GW	GW	GW	GW	GW	HC		GW	GW	GW	GW	GW	GW	GW	GW	GW
									FO	FX	FO	FX	FO	FX			FO	FO	FX	FX		FO	FX		
		◇1	◇1	1	1		1		1	1	◇1	◇1	◇1	◇1			◇1	1	1	◇1	1	◇1	◇1	1	1
		D	E	B	A																				
		☕									☕	☕					☕			☕					
London Paddington 15 ⊖	d	21 48	21 48				21 57	22 03	22 10	22 10	22 15	22 15	22 21	22 21	22 33		22 45			22 45	22 45	22 49	22 49		22 59
Acton Main Line	d																				22 51				
Ealing Broadway ⊖	d						22 05	22 11	22 18	22 18					22 41						22 54				23 07
West Ealing	d							22 13							22 43										
Drayton Green	d																								
Castle Bar Park	d																								
South Greenford	d																								
Greenford ⊖	a																								
Hanwell	d							22 15							22 45										
Southall	d							22 19	22 23	22 23					22 49										23 12
Hayes & Harlington	d						22 12	22 23	22 27	22 27					22 53						23 02				23 18
Heathrow Term 1-2-3 2 ✈	a							22 35							23 05										
Heathrow Terminal 4 ✈	a																								
West Drayton	d						22 16		22 31	22 31															23 22
Iver	d						22 19		22 34																23 25
Langley	d			←	←		22 22		22 38									←	←					←	23 28
Slough 3	a	22 03	22 03	22 18	22 18		22 28		22 43	22 39			22 36	22 42				22 43	22 39		23 12	23 06	23 07	23 12	23 34
	d	22 03	22 03	22 19	22 19		22 33		22 45	22 45			22 36	22 42				22 45	22 45		23 12	23 06	23 07	23 12	23 34
Burnham	d			22 22	22 22				→	→								22 49	22 49		→			23 16	
Taplow	d			22 26	22 26													22 52	22 52					23 19	
Maidenhead 3	d			22 30	22 30		22 41											22 56	22 56					23 23	23 41
Twyford 3	d			22 38	22 38		22 49											23 04	23 04					23 31	23 49
Reading 7	a	22 22	22 22	22 46	22 48		22 58				22 39	22 48	22 52	23 06			23 09	23 14	23 14	23 19		23 21	23 34	23 40	00 01
Oxford	a	22 47	22 47				23 44						23 25	23 37								23 48	00 11	00 23	

A FX until 30 June, from 4 July until 8 September, FX from 12 September

B FO until 1 July, FO from 9 September

C not 23 May

D FX from 12 September

E FX until 8 September

London - Greenford and Reading

		HC	GW FO	GW FX	GW FO	GW FX	GW FO	GW FX	GW FO	GW
			◇1	◇1	1	1	◇1	◇1	1	1
							☕	☕		
London Paddington [15] ⊖	d	23 03	23 20	23 20	23 29	23 29	23 30	23 30	23 42	23 48
Acton Main Line	d									23 54
Ealing Broadway ⊖	d	23 11			23 37	23 37				23 57
West Ealing	d	23 13								23 59
Drayton Green	d									
Castle Bar Park	d									
South Greenford	d									
Greenford ⊖	a									
Hanwell	d	23 15								00 02
Southall	d	23 19								00 06
Hayes & Harlington	d	23 23			23 44	23 44				00 10
Heathrow Term 1-2-3 [2] ✈	a	23 35								
Heathrow Terminal 4 ✈	a	23 41								
West Drayton	d									00 14
Iver	d									00 17
Langley	d									00 21
Slough [3]	a		23 36	23 38	23 53	23 53			23 58	00 26
	d		23 39	23 39	23 54	23 54			23 59	00 26
Burnham	d									00 30
Taplow	d									00 34
Maidenhead [3]	d				00 01	00 01			00 06	00 40
Twyford [3]	d				00 09	00 09				00 48
Reading [7]	a		23 54	00 04	00 18	00 19	00 03	00 06	00 17	00 57
Oxford	a		00 28	00 32	01 10	01 08			01 00	

Saturdays

		GW	GW	GW	GW	GW	GW	GW	GW	GW	GW	GW	GW	HC	HC	GW	GW	HC	GW	GW	GW	HC	GW
		1	1	◇1	1	1	◇1	1	1	◇1	1	1	1			◇1	1		1	◇1	1		1
							☕																
London Paddington [15] ⊖	d	22p45	22p59	23p20		23p29	23p30	23p42	23p48	00 22	00 34	01 44	03 34	04 42	05 13	05 21	05 25	05 33	05 45	05 50	05 57	06 03	06 12
Acton Main Line	d	22p51							23p54										05 51				
Ealing Broadway ⊖	d	22p54	23p07			23p37			23p57		00 42	01 52	03 42	04 50	05 21		05 33	05 41	05 54		06 05	06 11	06 20
West Ealing	d								23p59									05 43	05 57			06 13	
Drayton Green	d																		05 59				
Castle Bar Park	d																		06 01				
South Greenford	d																		06 04				
Greenford ⊖	a																		06 09				
Hanwell	d								00 02									05 45				06 15	
Southall	d		23p12						00 06		00 47	01 57	03 47	04 54	05 25		05 38	05 49			06 10	06 19	06 28
Hayes & Harlington	d	23p02	23p18			23p44			00 10		00 51	02 01	03 51	04 58	05 29		05 42	05 53			06 14	06 23	06 32
Heathrow Term 1-2-3 [2] ✈	a													05 04	05 35			06 05				06 35	
Heathrow Terminal 4 ✈	a													05 10	05 41								
West Drayton	d		23p22						00 14		00 55	02 05	03 55								06 18		06 36
Iver	d		23p25						00 17												06 21		
Langley	d		23p28						00 21		01 00										06 25		
Slough [3]	a	23p12	23p34	23p36		23p53		23p58	00 26	00 38	01 05	02 13	04 03			05 37	05 50			06 06	06 30		06 43
	d	23p12	23p34	23p39		23p54		23p59	00 26	00 39	01 05	02 13	04 03			05 38	05 51			06 06	06 31		06 43
Burnham	d	23p16							00 30		01 09						05 55				06 35		↪
Taplow	d	23p19							00 34		01 13						05 58				06 38		
Maidenhead [3]	d	23p23	23p41			00 01		00 06	00 40		01 16	02 21	04 11				06 02				06 42		
Twyford [3]	d	23p31	23p49		00 07	00 09			00 48		01 24	02 29	04 19				06 10				06 50		
Reading [7]	a	23p40	00 01	23p54	00 16	00 18	00 03	00 17	00 57	00 55	01 35	02 38	04 30			05 52	06 17			06 22	06 56		
Oxford	a	00 23		00 28		01 10		01 00		01 27						06 22	07 03			06 52	07 43		

		GW	GW	GW	GW	GW	GW	HC	GW	GW	GW	GW	GW	GW	HC	GW	GW	GW	GW	GW	GW	HC	GW
																					R		R
		1	◇1	◇1	1	1	◇1		1	1	◇1	1	1	◇1		1	1	◇1	1	1	1		1
			B	C																			C
							☕							☕							☕		☕
London Paddington [15] ⊖	d	06 15	06 21	06 21		06 27	06 30	06 33	06 42	06 45	06 50		06 57	07 00	07 03	07 12	07 15	07 21		07 27	07 30	07 33	07 36
Acton Main Line	d	06 21								06 51							07 21						
Ealing Broadway ⊖	d	06 24				06 35		06 41	06 50	06 54			07 05		07 11	07 20	07 24			07 35		07 41	
West Ealing	d	06 27						06 43		06 57					07 13		07 27					07 43	
Drayton Green	d	06 29								06 59							07 29						
Castle Bar Park	d	06 31								07 01							07 31						
South Greenford	d	06 34								07 04							07 34						
Greenford ⊖	a	06 39								07 09							07 39						
Hanwell	d							06 45							07 15							07 45	
Southall	d							06 49	06 58						07 19	07 28						07 49	
Hayes & Harlington	d					06 42		06 53	07 02				07 12		07 23	07 32				07 42		07 53	
Heathrow Term 1-2-3 [2] ✈	a							07 05							07 35							08 05	
Heathrow Terminal 4 ✈	a																						
West Drayton	d					06 46			07 06				07 16			07 36				07 46			
Iver	d					06 49							07 19							07 49			
Langley	d				←	06 52						←	07 22						←	07 52			
Slough [3]	a		06 37	06 37	06 43	06 57			07 13		07 06	07 13	07 27			07 43		07 37	07 43	07 57			
	d		06 38	06 38	06 43	06 57			07 13		07 06	07 13	07 27			07 43		07 38	07 43	07 57			
Burnham	d				06 47				↪			07 17				↪			07 47				
Taplow	d				06 51							07 21							07 51				
Maidenhead [3]	d				06 55	07 04						07 25	07 34						07 55	08 04			
Twyford [3]	d				07 03	07 12						07 33	07 42						08 03	08 12			
Reading [7]	a		06 53	06 53	07 13	07 20	06 57				07 22	07 43	07 52	07 26				07 53	08 13	08 22	07 57		
Oxford	a		07 18	07 19		08 09					07 48		08 40					08 19		09 14			

B from 17 September

C until 10 September

Table 117

Saturdays

London - Greenford and Reading

		GW		GW	GW	GW	GW	GW	GW	HC	GW	GW		GW	GW	GW	GW	GW	GW	GW	HC			GW	GW
		■1		■1	◇■1	◇■1	■1	■1	◇■1		■1	■1		◇■1	◇■1	■1	◇■1	■1	■1	◇■1				■1	■1
															A	B									
					☕				☕					☕	☕		☕			☕					
London Paddington 15 ⊖	d	07 42		07 45	07 45	07 50		07 57	08 00	08 03	08 12	08 15		08 15	08 18	08 18	08 21		08 27	08 30	08 33			08 42	08 45
Acton Main Line	d			07 51								08 21													08 51
Ealing Broadway ⊖	d	07 50		07 54				08 05		08 11	08 20	08 24							08 35		08 41			08 50	08 54
West Ealing	d			07 57						08 13		08 27									08 43				08 57
Drayton Green	d			07 59								08 29													08 59
Castle Bar Park	d			08 01								08 31													09 01
South Greenford	d			08 04								08 34													09 04
Greenford ⊖	a			08 09								08 39													09 09
Hanwell	d									08 15											08 45				
Southall	d	07 58								08 19	08 28										08 49			08 58	
Hayes & Harlington	d	08 02						08 12		08 23	08 32								08 42		08 53			09 02	
Heathrow Term 1-2-3 2 ✈	a									08 35											09 05				
Heathrow Terminal 4 ✈	a																								
West Drayton	d	08 06						08 16			08 36								08 46					09 06	
Iver	d							08 19											08 49						
Langley	d						←	08 22										←	08 52						
Slough 3	a	08 13				08 06	08 13	08 27			08 43						08 38	08 43	08 57					09 13	
	d	08 13				08 06	08 13	08 27			08 43						08 39	08 43	08 57					09 13	
Burnham	d	↦					08 17				↦							08 47						↦	
Taplow	d						08 21											08 51							
Maidenhead 3	d						08 25	08 34										08 55	09 04						
Twyford 3	d						08 33	08 42										09 03	09 12						
Reading 7	a				08 09	08 22	08 43	08 52	08 26					08 40	08 45	08 47	08 53	09 13	09 23	08 56					
Oxford	a					08 48		09 40									09 18		10 14						

		GW	GW	GW	GW	GW	GW	HC		GW	GW	GW	GW	GW	GW	GW	GW	GW		HC	GW	GW	GW	GW	GW
											■														
		◇■1	◇■1	◇■1	■1	■1	◇■1			◇■1	■1	■1	■1	■1	◇■1	■1	■1	◇■1			■1	■1	◇■1	◇■1	■1
		A	B							A	B														
		☕	☕				☕			⊘	⊘							☕					☕		
London Paddington 15 ⊖	d	08 45	08 45	08 50		08 57	09 00	09 03		09 06	09 06	09 12	09 15	09 18	09 21		09 27	09 30		09 33	09 42	09 45	09 45	09 50	
Acton Main Line	d												09 21									09 51			
Ealing Broadway ⊖	d					09 05		09 11				09 20	09 24				09 35			09 41	09 50	09 54			
West Ealing	d							09 13					09 27							09 43		09 57			
Drayton Green	d												09 29									09 59			
Castle Bar Park	d												09 31									10 01			
South Greenford	d												09 34									10 04			
Greenford ⊖	a												09 39									10 09			
Hanwell	d							09 15												09 45					
Southall	d							09 19				09 28								09 49	09 58				
Hayes & Harlington	d					09 12		09 23				09 32					09 42			09 53	10 02				
Heathrow Term 1-2-3 2 ✈	a							09 35												10 05					
Heathrow Terminal 4 ✈	a																								
West Drayton	d					09 16						09 36					09 46				10 06				
Iver	d					09 19											09 49								
Langley	d				←	09 22										←	09 52								←
Slough 3	a			09 06	09 13	09 27						09 43			09 38	09 43	09 57				10 13			10 06	10 13
	d			09 06	09 13	09 27						09 43			09 39	09 43	09 57				10 13			10 06	10 13
Burnham	d				09 17							↦				09 47					↦				10 17
Taplow	d				09 21											09 51									10 21
Maidenhead 3	d				09 25	09 34										09 55	10 04								10 25
Twyford 3	d				09 33	09 42										10 03	10 12								10 33
Reading 7	a	09 09	09 10	09 22	09 43	09 52	09 26			09 30				09 48	09 54	10 13	10 22	09 57					10 09	10 22	10 43
Oxford	a			09 48		10 40									10 19		11 14							10 48	

A from 17 September

B until 10 September

Table 117

Saturdays

London - Greenford and Reading

		GW	GW	HC		GW	GW	GW	GW	GW	GW	GW	GW	GW		GW	HC	GW	GW	GW	GW	GW	GW	GW
							R											R						
		1	◇1			◇1	1	1	1	◇1	1	◇1	1	1		◇1		1	1	1	◇1	◇1	1	1
						A	B											B						
			☕			⊘	⊘			☕		☕				☕		☕			⊘	🛒		
London Paddington 15 ⊖	d	09 57	10 00	10 03		10 06	10 06	10 12	10 15	10 15	10 18	10 21		10 27		10 30	10 33	10 35	10 42	10 45	10 45	10 50		10 57
Acton Main Line	d								10 21											10 51				
Ealing Broadway ⊖	d	10 05		10 11				10 20	10 24					10 35			10 41		10 50	10 54				11 05
West Ealing	d			10 13					10 27								10 43			10 57				
Drayton Green	d								10 29											10 59				
Castle Bar Park	d								10 31											11 01				
South Greenford	d								10 34											11 04				
Greenford ⊖	a								10 39											11 09				
Hanwell	d			10 15													10 45							
Southall	d			10 19				10 28									10 49		10 58					
Hayes & Harlington	d	10 12		10 23				10 32						10 42			10 53		11 02					11 12
Heathrow Term 1-2-3 2 ✈	a			10 35													11 05							
Heathrow Terminal 4 ✈	a																							
West Drayton	d	10 16						10 36						10 46					11 06					11 16
Iver	d	10 19												10 49										11 19
Langley	d	10 22											←	10 52									←	11 22
Slough 3	a	10 27						10 43				10 38	10 43	10 57					11 13			11 06	11 13	11 27
	d	10 27						10 43				10 39	10 43	10 57					11 13			11 06	11 13	11 27
Burnham	d							→					10 47						→				11 17	
Taplow	d												10 51										11 21	
Maidenhead 3	d	10 34											10 55	11 04									11 25	11 34
Twyford 3	d	10 42											11 03	11 12									11 33	11 42
Reading 7	a	10 52	10 26			10 30				10 40	10 48	10 53	11 13	11 22		10 57					11 09	11 22	11 43	11 52
Oxford	a	11 40										11 19		12 14								11 48		12 40

		GW	HC	GW	GW	GW	GW	GW	GW	GW		GW	GW	HC	GW	GW	GW	GW	GW	GW		GW	GW	HC	GW
					R										R										
		◇1		◇1	1	1	1	1	◇1	1		1	◇1		1	1	1	◇1	◇1	1		1	◇1		◇1
				A	B										B										A
		☕		⊘	⊘				🛒				⊘		☕			⊘					☕		⊘
London Paddington 15 ⊖	d	11 00	11 03	11 06	11 06	11 12	11 15	11 18	11 21			11 27	11 30	11 33	11 35	11 42	11 45	11 45	11 50			11 57	12 00	12 03	12 06
Acton Main Line	d						11 21										11 51								
Ealing Broadway ⊖	d		11 11			11 20	11 24					11 35		11 41		11 50	11 54					12 05		12 11	
West Ealing	d		11 13				11 27							11 43			11 57							12 13	
Drayton Green	d						11 29										11 59								
Castle Bar Park	d						11 31										12 01								
South Greenford	d						11 34										12 04								
Greenford ⊖	a						11 39										12 09								
Hanwell	d		11 15											11 45										12 15	
Southall	d		11 19			11 28								11 49		11 58								12 19	
Hayes & Harlington	d		11 23			11 32						11 42		11 53		12 02						12 12		12 23	
Heathrow Term 1-2-3 2 ✈	a		11 35											12 05										12 35	
Heathrow Terminal 4 ✈	a																								
West Drayton	d					11 36						11 46				12 06						12 16			
Iver	d											11 49										12 19			
Langley	d									←		11 52								←		12 22			
Slough 3	a					11 43			11 38	11 43		11 57				12 13			12 06	12 13		12 27			
	d					11 43			11 39	11 43		11 57				12 13			12 06	12 13		12 27			
Burnham	d					→				11 47						→				12 17					
Taplow	d									11 51										12 21					
Maidenhead 3	d									11 55		12 04								12 25		12 34			
Twyford 3	d									12 03		12 12								12 33		12 42			
Reading 7	a	11 26		11 30				11 48	11 54	12 13		12 22	11 58					12 09	12 22	12 43		12 52	12 26		12 30
Oxford	a								12 20			13 14							12 48			13 40			

A from 17 September

B until 10 September

Table 117

London - Greenford and Reading

		GW	GW	GW	GW	GW		GW	GW	GW	GW	GW	HC	GW	GW	GW		GW	GW	GW	GW	GW	HC	GW	GW
		R												R										R	R
		1	1	1	◇1	◇1		1	◇1	1	1	◇1		1	1	1		◇1	◇1	1	1	◇1		1	1
		A				B		A						A										B	A
		⊘			⊐P	⊐P						⊐P		⊐P				⊐P	⊤			⊐P		⊐P	⊐P
London Paddington 15 ⊖	d	12 06	12 12	12 15	12 15	12 18		12 18	12 21		12 27	12 30	12 33	12 35	12 42	12 45		12 45	12 50		12 57	13 00	13 03	13 06	13 06
Acton Main Line	d			12 21												12 51									
Ealing Broadway ⊖	d		12 20	12 24							12 35		12 41		12 50	12 54					13 05		13 11		
West Ealing	d			12 27									12 43			12 57							13 13		
Drayton Green	d			12 29												12 59									
Castle Bar Park	d			12 31												13 01									
South Greenford	d			12 34												13 04									
Greenford ⊖	a			12 39												13 09									
Hanwell	d												12 45										13 15		
Southall	d		12 28										12 49		12 58								13 19		
Hayes & Harlington	d		12 32								12 42		12 53		13 02						13 12		13 23		
Heathrow Term 1-2-3 2 ✈	a												13 05										13 35		
Heathrow Terminal 4 ✈	a																								
West Drayton	d		12 36								12 46				13 06						13 16				
Iver	d										12 49										13 19				
Langley	d									←	12 52									←	13 22				
Slough 3	a		12 43						12 38	12 43	12 57				13 13				13 06	13 13	13 27				
	d		12 43						12 39	12 43	12 57				13 13				13 06	13 13	13 27				
Burnham	d		↪							12 47					↪					13 17					
Taplow	d									12 51										13 21					
Maidenhead 3	d									12 55	13 04									13 25	13 34				
Twyford 3	d									13 03	13 12									13 33	13 42				
Reading 7	a				12 40	12 45		12 48	12 54	13 13	13 22	12 57						13 09	13 22	13 43	13 52	13 26		13 30	
Oxford	a								13 19		14 14								13 48		14 40				

		GW		GW	GW	GW	GW	GW	GW	HC	GW	GW		GW	GW	GW	GW	GW	HC	GW	GW	GW		GW	GW
		1		1	1	◇1	1	1	◇1		1	1		◇1	◇1	1	1	◇1		◇1	◇1	1		1	◇1
																				A	B				
						⊤			⊐P					⊐P	⊤			⊐P		⊐P	⊐P				⊐P
London Paddington 15 ⊖	d	13 12		13 15	13 18	13 21		13 27	13 30	13 33	13 42	13 45		13 45	13 50		13 57	14 00	14 03	14 06	14 06	14 12		14 15	14 15
Acton Main Line	d			13 21								13 51												14 21	
Ealing Broadway ⊖	d	13 20		13 24				13 35		13 41	13 50	13 54					14 05		14 11			14 20		14 24	
West Ealing	d			13 27						13 43		13 57							14 13					14 27	
Drayton Green	d			13 29								13 59												14 29	
Castle Bar Park	d			13 31								14 01												14 31	
South Greenford	d			13 34								14 04												14 34	
Greenford ⊖	a			13 39								14 09												14 39	
Hanwell	d									13 45									14 15						
Southall	d	13 28								13 49	13 58								14 19			14 28			
Hayes & Harlington	d	13 32						13 42		13 53	14 02						14 12		14 23			14 32			
Heathrow Term 1-2-3 2 ✈	a									14 05									14 35						
Heathrow Terminal 4 ✈	a																								
West Drayton	d	13 36						13 46			14 06						14 16					14 36			
Iver	d							13 49									14 19								
Langley	d						←	13 52								←	14 22								
Slough 3	a	13 43				13 38	13 43	13 57			14 13				14 06	14 13	14 27					14 43			
	d	13 43				13 39	13 43	13 57			14 13				14 06	14 13	14 27					14 43			
Burnham	d	↪					13 47				↪					14 17						↪			
Taplow	d						13 51									14 21									
Maidenhead 3	d						13 55	14 04								14 25	14 34								
Twyford 3	d						14 03	14 12								14 33	14 42								
Reading 7	a				13 48	13 54	14 13	14 22	13 58					14 09	14 22	14 43	14 52	14 26			14 30				14 40
Oxford	a					14 19		15 14							14 48		15 40								

		GW	GW	GW	GW	GW	HC	GW		GW	GW	GW	GW	GW	GW	HC	GW	GW		GW	GW	GW	GW	GW	GW
		1	◇1	1	1	◇1		1		1	◇1	◇1	1	1	◇1		◇1	◇1		1	1	1	◇1	1	1
																	A	B					C		
			⊤			⊐P					⊐P				⊐P		⊐P	⊐P					⊤		
London Paddington 15 ⊖	d	14 18	14 21		14 27	14 30	14 33	14 42		14 45	14 45	14 50		14 57	15 00	15 03	15 06	15 06		15 12	15 15	15 18	15 21		15 27
Acton Main Line	d									14 51											15 21				
Ealing Broadway ⊖	d				14 35		14 41	14 50		14 54				15 05		15 11				15 20	15 24				15 35
West Ealing	d						14 43			14 57						15 13					15 27				
Drayton Green	d									14 59											15 29				
Castle Bar Park	d									15 01											15 31				
South Greenford	d									15 04											15 34				
Greenford ⊖	a									15 09											15 39				
Hanwell	d						14 45									15 15									
Southall	d						14 49	14 58								15 19				15 28					
Hayes & Harlington	d				14 42		14 53	15 02						15 12		15 23				15 32					15 42
Heathrow Term 1-2-3 2 ✈	a						15 05									15 35									
Heathrow Terminal 4 ✈	a																								
West Drayton	d				14 46			15 06						15 16						15 36					15 46
Iver	d				14 49									15 19											15 49
Langley	d			←	14 52								←	15 22										←	15 52
Slough 3	a		14 38	14 43	14 57			15 13				15 06	15 13	15 27						15 43			15 38	15 43	15 57
	d		14 39	14 43	14 57			15 13				15 06	15 13	15 27						15 43			15 39	15 43	15 57
Burnham	d			14 47				↪					15 17							↪				15 47	
Taplow	d			14 51									15 21											15 51	
Maidenhead 3	d			14 55	15 04								15 25	15 34										15 55	16 04
Twyford 3	d			15 03	15 12								15 33	15 42										16 03	16 12
Reading 7	a	14 48	14 53	15 13	15 22	14 57					15 09	15 22	15 43	15 52	15 26			15 29				15 48	15 54	16 13	16 22
Oxford	a		15 18		16 14							15 48		16 40									16 19		17 14

A until 10 September

B from 17 September

C ⊤ to Reading

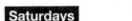

Table 117

Saturdays

London - Greenford and Reading

		GW	HC	GW	GW	GW	GW	GW	GW	GW	HC	GW	GW	GW	GW	GW	GW	GW	GW	GW	GW	HC
		◇1 ⊡		1	1	◇1 ⊡	◇1	1	1	◇1 ⊡		◇1 A ⊡	◇1 B ⊡	1	1	◇1 ⊡	1	◇1 ⊡	1	1	◇1 ⊡	
London Paddington 15 ⊖	d	15 30	15 33	15 42	15 45	15 45	15 50		15 57	16 00	16 03	16 06	16 06	16 12	16 15	16 15	16 18	16 21		16 27	16 30	16 33
Acton Main Line	d				15 51										16 21							
Ealing Broadway ⊖	d		15 41	15 50	15 54				16 05		16 11			16 20	16 24					16 35		16 41
West Ealing	d		15 43		15 57						16 13				16 27							16 43
Drayton Green	d				15 59										16 29							
Castle Bar Park	d				16 01										16 31							
South Greenford	d				16 04										16 34							
Greenford ⊖	a				16 09										16 39							
Hanwell	d		15 45								16 15											16 45
Southall	d		15 49	15 58							16 19			16 28								16 49
Hayes & Harlington	d		15 53	16 02					16 12		16 23			16 32						16 42		16 53
Heathrow Term 1-2-3 2 ✈	a		16 05								16 35											17 05
Heathrow Terminal 4 ✈	a																					
West Drayton	d			16 06					16 16					16 36						16 46		
Iver	d								16 19											16 49		
Langley	d							←	16 22										←	16 52		
Slough 3	a			16 13			16 06	16 13	16 27					16 43				16 38	16 43	16 57		
	d			16 13			16 06	16 13	16 27					16 43				16 39	16 43	16 57		
Burnham	d			→				16 17						→					16 47			
Taplow	d							16 21											16 51			
Maidenhead 3	d							16 25	16 34										16 55	17 04		
Twyford 3	d							16 33	16 42										17 03	17 12		
Reading 7	a	15 58				16 09	16 22	16 43	16 52	16 26		16 31				16 40	16 48	16 53	17 13	17 22	16 57	
Oxford	a						16 48		17 40									17 18		18 14		

		GW	GW	GW	GW	GW	GW	GW	HC	GW	GW	GW	GW	GW	GW	GW	GW	GW	HC	GW	GW	GW	GW
		1	1	◇1 ⊡	◇1 ⊥	1	1	◇1 ⊡		◇1 B ⊡	◇1 A ⊡	1	1	1	◇1 ⊡	1	1	◇1 ⊡		1	1	◇1 ⊡	◇1 ⊥
London Paddington 15 ⊖	d	16 42	16 45	16 45	16 50		16 57	17 00	17 03	17 06	17 06	17 12	17 15	17 18	17 21		17 27	17 30	17 33	17 42	17 45	17 45	17 50
Acton Main Line	d		16 51										17 21								17 51		
Ealing Broadway ⊖	d	16 50	16 54				17 05		17 11			17 20	17 24				17 35		17 41	17 50	17 54		
West Ealing	d		16 57						17 13				17 27						17 43		17 57		
Drayton Green	d		16 59										17 29								17 59		
Castle Bar Park	d		17 01										17 31								18 01		
South Greenford	d		17 04										17 34								18 04		
Greenford ⊖	a		17 09										17 39								18 09		
Hanwell	d								17 15										17 45				
Southall	d	16 58							17 19			17 28							17 49	17 58			
Hayes & Harlington	d	17 02					17 12		17 23			17 32					17 42		17 53	18 02			
Heathrow Term 1-2-3 2 ✈	a								17 35										18 05				
Heathrow Terminal 4 ✈	a																						
West Drayton	d	17 06					17 16					17 36					17 46			18 06			
Iver	d						17 19										17 49						
Langley	d					←	17 22									←	17 52						
Slough 3	a	17 13			17 06	17 13	17 27					17 43			17 38	17 43	17 57			18 13			18 06
	d	17 13			17 06	17 13	17 27					17 43			17 39	17 43	17 57			18 13			18 06
Burnham	d	→				17 17						→				17 47				→			
Taplow	d					17 21										17 51							
Maidenhead 3	d					17 25	17 34									17 55	18 04						
Twyford 3	d					17 33	17 42									18 03	18 12						
Reading 7	a			17 09	17 22	17 43	17 52	17 26			17 30			17 48	17 53	18 13	18 22	17 57				18 09	18 22
Oxford	a				17 47		18 40								18 18		19 14						18 48

		GW	GW	GW	HC	GW	GW	GW	GW	GW	GW	GW	GW	GW	GW	GW	HC	GW	GW	GW	GW	GW	GW
		1	1	◇1 ⊡		◇1 A ⊡	◇1 B ⊡	1	1	◇1 ⊡	1	◇1 ⊡	1	1 A	1 B	◇1 ⊡		1	1	◇1 ⊡	◇1	1	1
London Paddington 15 ⊖	d		17 57	18 00	18 03	18 06	18 06	18 12	18 15	18 15	18 18	18 21		18 27	18 27	18 30	18 33	18 42	18 45	18 45	18 50		18 57
Acton Main Line	d								18 21										18 51				
Ealing Broadway ⊖	d		18 05		18 11			18 20	18 24					18 35	18 35		18 41	18 50	18 54				19 05
West Ealing	d				18 13				18 27								18 43		18 57				
Drayton Green	d								18 29										18 59				
Castle Bar Park	d								18 31										19 01				
South Greenford	d								18 34										19 04				
Greenford ⊖	a								18 39										19 09				
Hanwell	d				18 15												18 45						
Southall	d				18 19			18 28									18 49	18 58					
Hayes & Harlington	d		18 12		18 23			18 32						18 42	18 42		18 53	19 02					19 12
Heathrow Term 1-2-3 2 ✈	a				18 35												19 05						
Heathrow Terminal 4 ✈	a																						
West Drayton	d		18 16					18 36						18 46	18 46			19 06					19 16
Iver	d		18 19											18 49	18 49								19 19
Langley	d	←	18 22										←	18 52	18 52							←	19 22
Slough 3	a	18 13	18 27					18 43				18 38	18 43	18 57	18 57			19 13			19 06	19 13	19 27
	d	18 13	18 27					18 43				18 39	18 43	18 57	18 57			19 13			19 06	19 13	19 27
Burnham	d	18 17						→					18 47					→				19 17	
Taplow	d	18 21											18 51									19 21	
Maidenhead 3	d	18 25	18 34										18 55	19 04	19 04							19 25	19 34
Twyford 3	d	18 33	18 42										19 03	19 12	19 12							19 33	19 42
Reading 7	a	18 43	18 52	18 27		18 30				18 40	18 48	18 53	19 13	19 22	19 23	18 57				19 09	19 22	19 43	19 52
Oxford	a		19 40									19 18		20 14	20 14						19 48		20 40

A from 17 September

B until 10 September

Table 117

Saturdays

London - Greenford and Reading

		GW		HC	GW	GW	GW	GW	GW	GW	GW	GW		GW	HC	GW	GW	GW	GW	GW	GW	GW		HC	GW
		◇1			◇1	1	1	◇1	◇1	1	1	1		◇1		1	1	◇1	◇1	1	1	◇1			◇1
								A			A	B							C						
		🍴			🍴			🍴						🍴				🍴	🛒			🍴			🍴
London Paddington 15 ⊖	d	19 00		19 03	19 06	19 12	19 15	19 15	19 21		19 27	19 27		19 30	19 33	19 42	19 45	19 45	19 50		19 57	20 00		20 03	20 06
Acton Main Line	d						19 21										19 51								
Ealing Broadway ⊖	d			19 11		19 20	19 24				19 35	19 35			19 41	19 50	19 54				20 05			20 11	
West Ealing	d			19 13			19 27								19 43		19 57							20 13	
Drayton Green	d						19 29										19 59								
Castle Bar Park	d						19 31										20 01								
South Greenford	d						19 34										20 04								
Greenford ⊖	a						19 39										20 09								
Hanwell	d			19 15											19 45									20 15	
Southall	d			19 19		19 28									19 49	19 58								20 19	
Hayes & Harlington	d			19 23		19 32					19 42	19 42			19 53	20 02					20 12			20 23	
Heathrow Term 1-2-3 2 ✈	a			19 35											20 05									20 35	
Heathrow Terminal 4 ✈	a																								
West Drayton	d					19 36					19 46	19 46				20 06					20 16				
Iver	d										19 49	19 49									20 19				
Langley	d									←	19 52	19 52								←	20 22				
Slough 3	a					19 43			19 37	19 43	19 57	19 57				20 13			20 06	20 13	20 27				
	d					19 43			19 38	19 43	19 57	19 57				20 13			20 06	20 13	20 27				
Burnham	d					→				19 47						→				20 17					
Taplow	d									19 51										20 21					
Maidenhead 3	d									19 55	20 04	20 04								20 25	20 34				
Twyford 3	d									20 03	20 12	20 12								20 33	20 42				
Reading 7	a	19 26			19 30			19 39	19 52	20 13	20 20	20 23		19 57				20 09	20 21	20 43	20 52	20 27			20 31
Oxford	a								20 20		21 14	21 14							20 47		21 40				

		GW	GW	GW	GW	GW	GW	GW		HC	GW	GW	GW	GW	GW	GW	HC	GW		GW	GW	GW	GW	HC	GW
		1	1	◇1	◇1	1	1	◇1			1	◇1	1	◇1	1	1		1		1	◇1	◇1	1		1
				🍴				🍴				🍴		🛒								🍴			
London Paddington 15 ⊖	d	20 12	20 15	20 15	20 20		20 27	20 30		20 33	20 42	20 45	20 45	20 50		20 57	21 03	21 12		21 15	21 17	21 30		21 33	21 42
Acton Main Line	d		20 21										20 51							21 21					21 48
Ealing Broadway ⊖	d	20 20	20 24				20 35			20 41	20 50		20 54			21 05	21 11	21 20		21 24				21 41	21 52
West Ealing	d		20 27							20 43			20 57				21 13			21 27				21 43	
Drayton Green	d		20 29										20 59							21 29					
Castle Bar Park	d		20 31										21 01							21 31					
South Greenford	d		20 34										21 04							21 34					
Greenford ⊖	a		20 39										21 09							21 39					
Hanwell	d									20 45							21 15							21 45	
Southall	d	20 28								20 49	20 58						21 19	21 28						21 49	21 58
Hayes & Harlington	d	20 32					20 42			20 53	21 02					21 12	21 23	21 32						21 53	22 02
Heathrow Term 1-2-3 2 ✈	a									21 05							21 35							22 05	
Heathrow Terminal 4 ✈	a																								
West Drayton	d	20 36					20 46				21 06					21 16		21 36							22 06
Iver	d						20 49									21 19									
Langley	d					←	20 52								←	21 22							←		
Slough 3	a	20 43			20 35	20 43	20 57				21 13			21 06	21 13	21 27		21 43			21 34		21 43		22 13
	d	20 43			20 35	20 43	20 57				21 13			21 06	21 13	21 27		21 43			21 35		21 43		22 13
Burnham	d	→				20 47					→				21 17			→					21 47		→
Taplow	d					20 51									21 21								21 51		
Maidenhead 3	d					20 55	21 04								21 25	21 34							21 55		
Twyford 3	d					21 03	21 12								21 33	21 42							22 03		
Reading 7	a			20 40	20 51	21 13	21 22	20 57				21 09		21 22	21 43	21 52					21 51	21 55	22 13		
Oxford	a				21 19		22 14							21 53		22 43					22 20				

		GW	GW	GW		GW	HC	GW	GW	HC	GW	GW	GW	GW		GW	GW	GW	GW	HC	GW	GW	GW	GW	
		◇1	1	1		◇1		1	◇1		◇1	1	1	1		◇1	◇1	1	1		1	1	◇1	◇1	
													A	B		B	A	A	B		A	B		A	
						🍴					🍴												🍴		
London Paddington 15 ⊖	d	21 50		21 57		22 00	22 03	22 12	22 15	22 33	22 35		22 45	22 45		23 00	23 00			23 03	23 20	23 20	23 30	23 33	
Acton Main Line	d												22 51	22 51											
Ealing Broadway ⊖	d			22 05			22 11	22 20		22 41			22 55	22 55						23 11	23 28	23 28			
West Ealing	d						22 13			22 43										23 13					
Drayton Green	d																								
Castle Bar Park	d																								
South Greenford	d																								
Greenford ⊖	a																								
Hanwell	d						22 15			22 45										23 15					
Southall	d						22 19	22 28		22 49			23 00	23 00						23 19	23 33	23 33			
Hayes & Harlington	d			22 12			22 25	22 32		22 53			23 04	23 04						23 23	23 37	23 37			
Heathrow Term 1-2-3 2 ✈	a						22 35			23 05										23 35					
Heathrow Terminal 4 ✈	a																			23 41					
West Drayton	d			22 16				22 36					23 08	23 08							23 41	23 41			
Iver	d			22 19									23 11	23 11							23 44	23 44			
Langley	d		←	22 22								←	23 14	23 14				←	←		23 48	23 48			
Slough 3	a	22 06	22 13	22 27				22 43	22 31			22 43	23 19	23 19		23 16	23 16	23 19	23 19		23 53	23 53		23 49	
	d	22 06	22 13	22 27				22 43	22 32			22 43	23 21	23 21		23 17	23 17	23 21	23 21		23 54	23 54		23 50	
Burnham	d		22 17					→				22 47	→	→				23 25	23 25		→	→			
Taplow	d		22 21									22 51													
Maidenhead 3	d		22 25	22 34								22 55						23 32	23 32						
Twyford 3	d		22 33	22 42								23 03						23 39	23 39						
Reading 7	a	22 22	22 41	22 52		22 27			22 48		23 00	23 13				23 33	23 33	23 46	23 46				23 59	00 06	
Oxford	a	22 49		23 36					23 20							00 03			00 31						

A from 17 September

B until 10 September

C 🛒 to Reading

Table 117

Saturdays

London - Greenford and Reading

		GW ◇1 A	GW 1 B	GW 1 A	GW 1
London Paddington 15 ⊖	d	23 33			23 42
Acton Main Line	d				
Ealing Broadway ⊖	d				23 50
West Ealing	d				
Drayton Green	d				
Castle Bar Park	d				
South Greenford	d				
Greenford ⊖	a				
Hanwell	d				
Southall	d				23 56
Hayes & Harlington	d				00 01
Heathrow Term 1-2-3 2 ✈	a				
Heathrow Terminal 4 ✈	a				
West Drayton	d				00 06
Iver	d				
Langley	d		←	←	
Slough 3	a	23 49	23 53	23 53	00 13
	d	23 50	23 54	23 54	00 14
Burnham	d		23 57	23 57	00 18
Taplow	d		00 01	00 01	00 21
Maidenhead 3	d		00 05	00 05	00 25
Twyford 3	d		00 13	00 13	00 33
Reading 7	a	00 06	00 20	00 20	00 43
Oxford	a	00 38		01 04	

Sundays

until 19 June

		GW 1 C	GW ◇1 C	GW 1 C	GW 1 C	GW ◇1 C	GW 1 C	GW 1 C	GW 1	GW 1	GW 1	HC	HC	GW 1	HC	GW 1	GW ◇1 ☕	GW ◇1 🛒	HC	GW 1	GW ◇1 ☕	GW ◇1 ☕	GW ◇1
London Paddington 15 ⊖	d	22p45	23p00		23p20	23p33		23p42	00 05	00 30	01 00	05 12	06 12	06 43	07 12	07 28	08 00	08 03	08 12	08 15	08 30	08 37	08 42
Acton Main Line	d	22p51																					
Ealing Broadway ⊖	d	22p55			23p28			23p50	00 13	00 38	01 08	05 20	06 20	06 52	07 20	07 36			08 20	08 24			
West Ealing	d																						
Drayton Green	d																						
Castle Bar Park	d																						
South Greenford	d																						
Greenford ⊖	a																						
Hanwell	d																						
Southall	d	23p00			23p33			23p56	00 19	00 44	01 13	05 24	06 24	06 58	07 24	07 42			08 24	08 29			
Hayes & Harlington	d	23p04			23p37			00 01	00 23	00 48	01 17	05 28	06 28	07 02	07 28	07 46			08 28	08 33			
Heathrow Term 1-2-3 2 ✈	a											05 34	06 34		07 34				08 34				
Heathrow Terminal 4 ✈	a											05 40	06 41		07 41				08 41				
West Drayton	d	23p08			23p41			00 06	00 27	00 52				07 06		07 50				08 37			
Iver	d	23p11			23p44				00 30														
Langley	d	23p14		←	23p48		←		00 33	00 56				07 11		07 55				08 42			
Slough 3	a	23p19	23p16	23p19	23p53	23p49	23p53	00 13	00 37	01 00	01 25			07 16		07 58		08 24		08 46			09 00
	d	23p21	23p17	23p21	23p54	23p50	23p54	00 14	00 38	01 01	01 26			07 16		07 58		08 25		08 46			09 01
Burnham	d	→		23p25	→		23p57	00 18	00 42					07 20		08 03							
Taplow	d						00 01	00 21	00 45														
Maidenhead 3	d			23p32			00 05	00 25	00 49	01 08	01 33			07 27		08 08		08 33		08 54			
Twyford 3	d			23p39			00 13	00 33	00 57	01 16	01 41			07 35		08 16				09 02			
Reading 7	a		23p33	23p46		00 06	00 20	00 43	01 05	01 24	01 50			07 42		08 25	08 38	08 47		09 10	09 11	09 14	09 22
Oxford	a		00 03	00 31		00 38	01 04									09 43		09 15					09 53

		GW 1	GW ◇1 ☕	GW ◇1 ☕	GW 1	HC	GW 1	GW ◇1 ☕	GW ◇1 ☕	HC	GW 1	GW ◇1 ☕	GW ◇1 ☕	GW 1	HC	GW 1	GW ◇1 ☕	HC	GW ◇1 ☕	GW ◇1 ☕	GW 1	GW ◇1 ☕	GW ◇1 ☕
London Paddington 15 ⊖	d	08 43	08 57	09 00	09 04	09 07	09 15	09 30	09 35	09 37	09 43	09 57	10 00	10 04	10 07	10 15	10 30	10 37	10 37	10 42	10 43	10 57	11 00
Acton Main Line	d																						
Ealing Broadway ⊖	d	08 50				09 15	09 23			09 45	09 50				10 15	10 24		10 45			10 50		
West Ealing	d																						
Drayton Green	d																						
Castle Bar Park	d																						
South Greenford	d																						
Greenford ⊖	a																						
Hanwell	d																						
Southall	d	08 56				09 19	09 29			09 49	09 56				10 19	10 29		10 49			10 56		
Hayes & Harlington	d	09 02				09 24	09 33			09 54	10 02				10 24	10 33		10 54			11 06		
Heathrow Term 1-2-3 2 ✈	a					09 29				09 59					10 29			10 59					
Heathrow Terminal 4 ✈	a					09 39				10 09					10 39			11 09					
West Drayton	d	09 11					09 37				10 10					10 40					11 12		
Iver	d																						
Langley	d	09 16					09 44				10 16					10 44					11 16		
Slough 3	a	09 20			09 26		09 48		09 54		10 20			10 25		10 48				10 58	11 20		
	d	09 21			09 26		09 49		09 55		10 22			10 26		10 49				10 59	11 22		
Burnham	d	09 25									10 26										11 26		
Taplow	d																						
Maidenhead 3	d	09 31			09 35		09 56				10 32			10 34		10 56					11 31		
Twyford 3	d	09 39					10 04				10 40					11 04					11 39		
Reading 7	a	09 46	09 32	09 38	09 48		10 11	10 05	10 14		10 47	10 32	10 38	10 50		11 12	11 04		11 13	11 20	11 47	11 32	11 38
Oxford	a	10 31							10 43		11 31									11 50	12 32		

A until 10 September

B from 17 September

C not 22 May

Table 117

Sundays
until 19 June

London - Greenford and Reading

		GW		HC	GW	GW	HC	GW	GW	GW	GW	GW		GW	HC	GW	GW	HC	GW	GW	GW	GW		GW	GW
		1			1	◇1 ⊡		◇1 ⊡	◇1	1	◇1 ⊡	◇1 ⊡		1		1	◇1 ⊡		◇1 ⊡	◇1 ⊡	1	◇1 ⊡		◇1 ⊡	1
London Paddington 15 ⊖	d	11 04		11 07	11 15	11 30	11 37	11 37	11 42	11 43	11 57	12 00		12 04	12 07	12 15	12 30	12 37	12 37	12 42	12 43	12 57		13 00	13 04
Acton Main Line	d																								
Ealing Broadway ⊖	d			11 15	11 24		11 45			11 50					12 15	12 24		12 45			12 50				
West Ealing	d																								
Drayton Green	d																								
Castle Bar Park	d																								
South Greenford	d																								
Greenford ⊖	a																								
Hanwell	d																								
Southall	d			11 19	11 29		11 49			11 56					12 19	12 29		12 49			12 56				
Hayes & Harlington	d			11 24	11 33		11 54			12 02					12 24	12 33		12 54			13 02				
Heathrow Term 1-2-3 2 ✈	a			11 29			11 59								12 29			12 59							
Heathrow Terminal 4 ✈	a			11 39			12 09								12 39			13 09							
West Drayton	d				11 38					12 06						12 37					13 06				
Iver	d																								
Langley	d				11 44					12 15						12 44					13 14				
Slough 3	a	11 26			11 48				12 00	12 20				12 26		12 48				12 58	13 20				13 25
	d	11 26			11 49				12 01	12 22				12 26		12 49				12 59	13 22				13 26
Burnham	d									12 26											13 26				
Taplow	d																								
Maidenhead 3	d	11 35			11 57					12 31				12 36		12 57					13 31				13 34
Twyford 3	d				12 05					12 39						13 05					13 39				
Reading 7	a	11 49			12 12	12 05		12 13	12 22	12 47	12 32	12 38		12 51		13 12	13 04		13 14	13 21	13 47	13 32		13 38	13 49
Oxford	a								12 52	13 31										13 51	14 30				

		HC	GW	HC	GW	GW	GW	GW		GW	GW	HC	GW	GW	HC	GW	GW	GW		GW	GW	GW	HC	GW	HC
			1		◇1 ⊡	◇1 ⊡	1	◇1 ⊡		◇1 ⊡	1		1	◇1 ⊡		◇1 ⊡	◇1 ⊥	1		◇1 ⊡	◇1 ⊡	1		1	
London Paddington 15 ⊖	d	13 07	13 15	13 37	13 37	13 42	13 43	13 57		14 00	14 02	14 07	14 15	14 27	14 37	14 37	14 42	14 43		14 57	15 00	15 04	15 07	15 15	15 37
Acton Main Line	d																								
Ealing Broadway ⊖	d	13 15	13 24	13 45			13 50					14 15	14 24		14 45			14 50					15 15	15 24	15 45
West Ealing	d																								
Drayton Green	d																								
Castle Bar Park	d																								
South Greenford	d																								
Greenford ⊖	a																								
Hanwell	d																								
Southall	d	13 19	13 29	13 49			13 56					14 19	14 29		14 49			14 56					15 19	15 29	15 49
Hayes & Harlington	d	13 24	13 33	13 54			14 02					14 24	14 35		14 54			15 02					15 24	15 33	15 54
Heathrow Term 1-2-3 2 ✈	a	13 29		13 59								14 29			14 59								15 29		15 59
Heathrow Terminal 4 ✈	a	13 39		14 09								14 39			15 09								15 39		16 09
West Drayton	d		13 37				14 09						14 40					15 09						15 40	
Iver	d																								
Langley	d		13 42				14 17						14 45					15 16						15 44	
Slough 3	a		13 46			14 00	14 21				14 26		14 49				15 01	15 20				15 25		15 48	
	d		13 46			14 01	14 22				14 26		14 49				15 02	15 21				15 25		15 49	
Burnham	d						14 26											15 25						15 53	
Taplow	d																								
Maidenhead 3	d		13 54				14 32				14 35		14 57					15 31				15 35		15 59	
Twyford 3	d		14 02				14 40						15 05					15 39						16 07	
Reading 7	a		14 10		14 11	14 23	14 47	14 32		14 38	14 50		15 12	15 03		15 15	15 20	15 46		15 32	15 38	15 49		16 14	
Oxford	a					14 53	15 31										15 51	16 28							

		GW	GW	GW		GW	GW	GW	HC	GW	GW	HC	GW	GW		GW	GW	GW	GW	HC	GW	GW	HC	GW	
		◇1 ⊡	◇1 ⊡	1		◇1 ⊡	◇1 ⊡	1		1	◇1 ⊡		◇1 ⊡	◇1 ⊥		1	◇1 ⊡	◇1 ⊡	1		1	◇1 ⊡		◇1 ⊡	
London Paddington 15 ⊖	d	15 37	15 42	15 43		15 57	16 00	16 02	16 07	16 15	16 27	16 37	16 37	16 42		16 43	16 57	17 00	17 04	17 07	17 15	17 30	17 37	17 37	
Acton Main Line	d																								
Ealing Broadway ⊖	d			15 50					16 15	16 24		16 45				16 50				17 15	17 24		17 45		
West Ealing	d																								
Drayton Green	d																								
Castle Bar Park	d																								
South Greenford	d																								
Greenford ⊖	a																								
Hanwell	d																								
Southall	d			15 56					16 19	16 29		16 49				16 56				17 19	17 29		17 49		
Hayes & Harlington	d			16 02					16 24	16 34		16 54				17 02				17 24	17 33		17 54		
Heathrow Term 1-2-3 2 ✈	a								16 29			16 59								17 29			17 59		
Heathrow Terminal 4 ✈	a								16 39			17 09								17 39			18 09		
West Drayton	d			16 11						16 38						17 11					17 37				
Iver	d																								
Langley	d			16 16						16 43						17 16					17 42				
Slough 3	a		16 01	16 20				16 25		16 47				17 01		17 20			17 25		17 46				
	d		16 01	16 21				16 25		16 47				17 01		17 21			17 25		17 46				
Burnham	d			16 25						16 52						17 25					17 51				
Taplow	d																								
Maidenhead 3	d			16 31				16 34		16 57						17 31			17 34		17 56				
Twyford 3	d			16 39						17 05						17 39					18 04				
Reading 7	a	16 16	16 19	16 46		16 32	16 38	16 49		17 13	17 03		17 13	17 20		17 46	17 32	17 38	17 49		18 12	18 12		18 15	
Oxford	a		16 51	17 28										17 51		18 30									

Table 117

Sundays
until 19 June

London - Greenford and Reading

		GW	GW	GW	GW	HC	GW	GW	GW	HC		GW	GW	GW	GW	GW	GW	HC	GW	GW		HC	GW	GW	GW
		◇[1] 🚲	[1]	◇[1] ⊡	◇[1] ⊡		[1]	[1]	◇[1] ⊡			◇[1] ⊡	◇[1] ⊡	[1]	◇[1] ⊡	◇[1] ⊡	[1]		[1]	◇[1] ⊡			◇[1] ⊡	◇[1] ⊡	[1]
London Paddington [15] ⊖	d	17 42	17 43	17 57	18 00	18 07	18 12	18 15	18 27	18 37		18 37	18 42	18 43	18 57	19 00	19 04	19 07	19 15	19 30		19 37	19 37	19 42	19 43
Acton Main Line	d																								
Ealing Broadway ⊖	d		17 50			18 15		18 24		18 45				18 50				19 15	19 24			19 45			19 50
West Ealing	d																								
Drayton Green	d																								
Castle Bar Park	d																								
South Greenford	d																								
Greenford ⊖	a																								
Hanwell	d																								
Southall	d		17 56			18 19		18 29		18 49				18 56				19 19	19 29			19 49			19 56
Hayes & Harlington	d		18 02			18 24		18 33		18 54				19 02				19 24	19 33			19 54			20 02
Heathrow Term 1-2-3 [2] ✈	a					18 29				18 59								19 29				19 59			
Heathrow Terminal 4 ✈	a					18 39				19 09								19 39				20 09			
West Drayton	d		18 10					18 37						19 10					19 38						20 10
Iver	d																								
Langley	d		18 16					18 42						19 16					19 45						20 16
Slough [3]	a	18 01	18 20				18 30	18 46					19 00	19 20			19 25		19 49					19 58	20 20
	d	18 01	18 22				18 30	18 46					19 01	19 22			19 25		19 49					19 59	20 22
Burnham	d		18 26					18 51						19 26					19 54						20 26
Taplow	d																								
Maidenhead [3]	d		18 31				18 42	18 56						19 31			19 35		19 59						20 31
Twyford [3]	d		18 39					19 04						19 39					20 07						20 40
Reading [7]	a	18 20	18 47	18 32	18 38		18 56	19 12	19 02			19 14	19 22	19 47	19 31	19 38	19 50		20 15	20 05			20 16	20 20	20 47
Oxford	a	18 51	19 29										19 52	20 30										20 51	21 32

		GW	GW	HC	GW	GW		HC	GW	GW	GW	GW	GW	HC	GW	GW		GW	GW	GW	HC	GW	GW	GW	GW
		◇[1] ⊡	◇[1] ⊡		[1]	◇[1] ⊡			◇[1] ⊡	◇[1]	[1]	◇[1] ⊡	◇[1] ⊡		[1]	◇[1] ⊡		◇[1]	[1]	◇[1] ⊡		[1] A	◇[1]	[1]	◇[1] ⊡
London Paddington [15] ⊖	d	19 57	20 00	20 07	20 15	20 30		20 37	20 37	20 42	20 43	20 57	21 00	21 07	21 15	21 37		21 42	21 43	22 03	22 12	22 15	22 42	22 43	23 03
Acton Main Line	d																								
Ealing Broadway ⊖	d			20 15	20 24			20 45			20 50			21 15	21 24				21 50		22 20	22 24		22 50	
West Ealing	d																								
Drayton Green	d																								
Castle Bar Park	d																								
South Greenford	d																								
Greenford ⊖	a																								
Hanwell	d																								
Southall	d			20 19	20 29			20 49			20 56			21 19	21 29				21 56		22 24	22 29		22 56	
Hayes & Harlington	d			20 24	20 33			20 54			21 02			21 24	21 33				22 02		22 28	22 33		23 02	
Heathrow Term 1-2-3 [2] ✈	a			20 29				20 59						21 29							22 34				
Heathrow Terminal 4 ✈	a			20 39				21 09						21 39							22 41				
West Drayton	d				20 37						21 06				21 37				22 09			22 37		23 06	
Iver	d																								
Langley	d				20 44						21 15				21 42				22 17			22 42		23 10	
Slough [3]	a				20 48					21 02	21 20				21 46			21 59	22 21			22 46	23 00	23 14	
	d				20 49					21 03	21 22				21 46			22 00	22 23			22 46	23 01	23 16	
Burnham	d				20 53						21 26				21 51				22 27			22 50		23 20	
Taplow	d																								
Maidenhead [3]	d				20 59						21 32				21 56				22 33			22 56		23 24	
Twyford [3]	d				21 07						21 40				22 04				22 41			23 04		23 33	
Reading [7]	a	20 32	20 38		21 14	21 07			21 14	21 21	21 45	21 31	21 38		22 11	22 13		22 22	22 48	22 39		23 11	23 20	23 43	23 43
Oxford	a									21 51	22 30							22 52							

		HC		GW	GW	GW	GW	GW
				[1]	◇[1] ⊡	◇[1]	■ 🛏 ⊡	[1]
London Paddington [15] ⊖	d	23 12		23 15	23 37	23 47	23 50	23 53
Acton Main Line	d							
Ealing Broadway ⊖	d	23 20		23 24		23 55		00 02
West Ealing	d							
Drayton Green	d							
Castle Bar Park	d							
South Greenford	d							
Greenford ⊖	a							
Hanwell	d							
Southall	d	23 24		23 29				00 07
Hayes & Harlington	d	23 28		23 33				00 11
Heathrow Term 1-2-3 [2] ✈	a	23 34						
Heathrow Terminal 4 ✈	a	23 41						
West Drayton	d			23 37				00 15
Iver	d							
Langley	d			23 42				00 20
Slough [3]	a			23 46		00 08		00 24
	d			23 46		00 09		00 24
Burnham	d			23 51				00 28
Taplow	d							
Maidenhead [3]	d			23 56		00 17		00 34
Twyford [3]	d			00 04				00 42
Reading [7]	a			00 13	00 15	00 31		00 49
Oxford	a							

A [1] to Twyford

Table 117

Sundays

26 June to 31 July

London - Greenford and Reading

		GW 1	GW ◇1	GW 1	GW 1	GW ◇1	GW 1	GW 1	GW 1	GW 1	GW 1	HC	HC	GW 1	HC	GW 1	GW ◇1 ☕	GW ◇1 ☕	GW ◇1 trolley	HC	GW 1	GW ◇1	GW 1
London Paddington 15 ⊖	d	22p45	23p00		23p20	23p33		23p42	00 05	00 30	01 00	05 12	06 12	06 43	07 12	07 28	07 57	08 00	08 03	08 12	08 15	08 42	08 43
Acton Main Line	d	22p51																					
Ealing Broadway ⊖	d	22p55			23p28			23p50	00 13	00 38	01 08	05 20	06 20	06 52	07 20	07 36				08 20	08 24		08 50
West Ealing	d																						
Drayton Green	d																						
Castle Bar Park	d																						
South Greenford	d																						
Greenford ⊖	a																						
Hanwell	d																						
Southall	d	23p00			23p33			23p56	00 19	00 44	01 13	05 24	06 24	06 58	07 24	07 42				08 24	08 29		08 56
Hayes & Harlington	d	23p04			23p37			00 01	00 23	00 48	01 17	05 28	06 28	07 02	07 28	07 46				08 28	08 33		09 02
Heathrow Term 1-2-3 2 ✈	a											05 34	06 34		07 34					08 34			
Heathrow Terminal 4 ✈	a											05 40	06 41		07 41					08 41			
West Drayton	d	23p08			23p41			00 06	00 27	00 52				07 06		07 50					08 37		09 11
Iver	d	23p11			23p44				00 30														
Langley	d	23p14		←	23p48		←		00 33	00 56				07 11		07 55					08 42		09 16
Slough 3	a	23p19	23p16	23p19	23p53	23p49	23p53	00 13	00 37	01 00	01 25			07 16		07 58			08 24		08 46	09 00	09 20
	d	23p21	23p17	23p21	23p54	23p50	23p54	00 14	00 38	01 01	01 26			07 16		07 58			08 25		08 46	09 01	09 21
Burnham	d	→		23p25	→		23p57	00 18	00 42					07 20		08 03							09 25
Taplow	d						00 01	00 21	00 45														
Maidenhead 3	d			23p32			00 05	00 25	00 49	01 08	01 33			07 27		08 08			08 33		08 54		09 31
Twyford 3	d			23p39			00 13	00 33	00 57	01 16	01 41			07 35		08 16					09 02		09 39
Reading 7	a		23p33	23p46		00 06	00 20	00 43	01 05	01 24	01 50			07 42		08 25	08 32	08 38	08 47		09 10	09 22	09 46
Oxford	a		00 03	00 31		00 38	01 04									09 43			09 15			09 53	10 31

		GW ◇1 ☕	GW ◇1 ☕	GW 1	HC	GW 1	GW ◇1 ☕	GW ◇1 ☕	HC	GW 1	GW ◇1 ☕	GW ◇1 ☕	GW 1	HC	GW 1	GW ◇1 ☕	HC	GW ◇1 ☕	GW 1	GW ◇1 ☕	GW ◇1 ☕	GW 1	HC
London Paddington 15 ⊖	d	08 57	09 00	09 04	09 07	09 15	09 30	09 35	09 37	09 43	09 57	10 00	10 04	10 07	10 15	10 30	10 37	10 42	10 43	10 57	11 00	11 04	11 07
Acton Main Line	d																						
Ealing Broadway ⊖	d				09 15	09 23			09 45	09 50				10 15	10 24		10 45		10 50				11 15
West Ealing	d																						
Drayton Green	d																						
Castle Bar Park	d																						
South Greenford	d																						
Greenford ⊖	a																						
Hanwell	d																						
Southall	d				09 19	09 29			09 49	09 56				10 19	10 29		10 49		10 56				11 19
Hayes & Harlington	d				09 24	09 33			09 54	10 02				10 24	10 33		10 54		11 06				11 24
Heathrow Term 1-2-3 2 ✈	a				09 29				09 59					10 29			10 59						11 29
Heathrow Terminal 4 ✈	a				09 39				10 09					10 39			11 09						11 39
West Drayton	d					09 37				10 10					10 40				11 12				
Iver	d																						
Langley	d					09 41				10 16					10 44				11 16				
Slough 3	a			09 26		09 48		09 54		10 20			10 25		10 48			10 58	11 20			11 26	
	d			09 26		09 48		09 55		10 22			10 26		10 49			10 59	11 22			11 26	
Burnham	d									10 26									11 26				
Taplow	d																						
Maidenhead 3	d			09 35		09 56				10 32			10 34		10 56				11 31			11 35	
Twyford 3	d					10 04				10 40					11 04				11 39				
Reading 7	a	09 32	09 38	09 48		10 11	10 05	10 14		10 47	10 32	10 38	10 50		11 12	11 04		11 20	11 47	11 32	11 38	11 49	
Oxford	a							10 43		11 31								11 50	12 32				

		GW 1	GW ◇1 ☕	HC	GW ◇1 ☕	GW ◇1	GW 1	GW ◇1 ☕	GW ◇1 ☕	GW 1	HC	GW 1	GW ◇1 ☕	HC	GW ◇1 ☕	GW ◇1 ☕	GW 1	GW ◇1 ☕	GW ◇1 ☕	GW 1	HC	GW 1
London Paddington 15 ⊖	d	11 15	11 30	11 37	11 37	11 42	11 43	11 57	12 00	12 04	12 07	12 15	12 30	12 37	12 37	12 42	12 43	12 57	13 00	13 04	13 07	13 15
Acton Main Line	d																					
Ealing Broadway ⊖	d	11 24		11 45			11 50				12 15	12 24		12 45			12 50				13 15	13 24
West Ealing	d																					
Drayton Green	d																					
Castle Bar Park	d																					
South Greenford	d																					
Greenford ⊖	a																					
Hanwell	d																					
Southall	d	11 29		11 49			11 56				12 19	12 29		12 49			12 56				13 19	13 29
Hayes & Harlington	d	11 33		11 54			12 02				12 24	12 33		12 54			13 02				13 24	13 33
Heathrow Term 1-2-3 2 ✈	a			11 59							12 29			12 59							13 29	
Heathrow Terminal 4 ✈	a			12 09							12 39			13 09							13 39	
West Drayton	d	11 38					12 06					12 37					13 06					13 37
Iver	d																					
Langley	d	11 44					12 15					12 44					13 14					13 44
Slough 3	a	11 48				12 00	12 20			12 26		12 48				12 58	13 20			13 25		13 48
	d	11 49				12 01	12 22			12 26		12 49				12 59	13 22			13 26		13 48
Burnham	d						12 26										13 26					
Taplow	d																					
Maidenhead 3	d	11 57					12 31			12 36		12 57					13 31			13 34		13 56
Twyford 3	d	12 05					12 39					13 05					13 39					14 04
Reading 7	a	12 12	12 05		12 13	12 22	12 47	12 32	12 38	12 51		13 12	13 04		13 14	13 21	13 47	13 32	13 38	13 49		14 12
Oxford	a					12 52	13 31									13 51	14 30					

Table 117

Sundays

26 June to 31 July

London - Greenford and Reading

		GW	HC	GW	GW	GW	GW	GW		HC	GW	GW	GW	HC	GW	GW	GW	GW		GW	HC	GW	GW	HC	GW
		◇1 ☕		◇1 ☕	1	◇1 ☕	◇1 ☕	1			1	◇1 ☕	◇1 ☕		◇1 🛒	1	◇1 ☕	◇1 ☕		1		1	◇1 ☕		◇1 ☕
London Paddington 15 ⊖	d	13 30	13 37	13 42	13 43	13 57	14 00	14 02		14 07	14 15	14 27	14 30	14 37	14 42	14 43	14 57	15 00		15 04	15 07	15 15	15 30	15 37	15 42
Acton Main Line	d																								
Ealing Broadway ⊖	d		13 45		13 50					14 15	14 24			14 45		14 50					15 15	15 24		15 45	
West Ealing	d																								
Drayton Green	d																								
Castle Bar Park	d																								
South Greenford	d																								
Greenford ⊖	a																								
Hanwell	d																								
Southall	d		13 49		13 56					14 19	14 29			14 49		14 56					15 19	15 29		15 49	
Hayes & Harlington	d		13 54		14 02					14 24	14 35			14 54		15 02					15 24	15 33		15 54	
Heathrow Term 1-2-3 2 ✈	a		13 59							14 29				14 59							15 29			15 59	
Heathrow Terminal 4 ✈	a		14 09							14 39				15 09							15 39			16 09	
West Drayton	d				14 09						14 40					15 09						15 40			
Iver	d																								
Langley	d				14 17						14 45					15 16						15 44			
Slough 3	a			14 00	14 21			14 26			14 49				15 01	15 20				15 25		15 48			16 01
	d			14 01	14 22			14 26			14 49				15 02	15 21				15 25		15 49			16 01
Burnham	d				14 26											15 25						15 53			
Taplow	d																								
Maidenhead 3	d				14 32			14 35			14 57					15 31				15 35		15 59			
Twyford 3	d				14 40						15 05					15 39						16 07			
Reading 7	a	14 04		14 23	14 47	14 32	14 38	14 50			15 12	15 01	15 08		15 20	15 46	15 32	15 38		15 49		16 14	16 04		16 19
Oxford	a			14 53	15 31										15 51	16 28									16 51

		GW	GW	GW		GW	HC	GW	GW	GW	HC	GW	GW	GW		GW	GW	HC	GW	GW	GW	HC	GW	GW	
		1	◇1 ☕	◇1 ☕		1		1	◇1 ☕	◇1 ☕		◇1 🛒	1	◇1 ☕		◇1 ☕	1		1	◇1 ☕	◇1 ☕		◇1 🛒	1	
London Paddington 15 ⊖	d	15 43	15 57	16 00		16 02	16 07	16 15	16 27	16 30	16 37	16 42	16 43	16 57		17 00	17 04	17 07	17 15	17 30	17 30	17 37	17 42	17 43	
Acton Main Line	d																								
Ealing Broadway ⊖	d	15 50					16 15	16 24			16 45		16 50					17 15	17 24			17 45		17 50	
West Ealing	d																								
Drayton Green	d																								
Castle Bar Park	d																								
South Greenford	d																								
Greenford ⊖	a																								
Hanwell	d																								
Southall	d	15 56					16 19	16 29			16 49		16 56					17 19	17 29			17 49		17 56	
Hayes & Harlington	d	16 02					16 24	16 34			16 54		17 02					17 24	17 33			17 54		18 02	
Heathrow Term 1-2-3 2 ✈	a						16 29				16 59							17 29				17 59			
Heathrow Terminal 4 ✈	a						16 39				17 09							17 39				18 09			
West Drayton	d	16 11						16 38					17 11						17 40					18 10	
Iver	d																								
Langley	d	16 16						16 46					17 16						17 44					18 16	
Slough 3	a	16 20				16 25		16 50				17 01	17 20				17 25		17 48				18 01	18 20	
	d	16 21				16 25		16 51				17 01	17 21				17 25		17 49				18 01	18 22	
Burnham	d	16 25						16 55					17 25						17 53					18 26	
Taplow	d																								
Maidenhead 3	d	16 31				16 34		17 01					17 31				17 34		17 59					18 31	
Twyford 3	d	16 39						17 09					17 39						18 07					18 39	
Reading 7	a	16 46	16 32	16 38		16 49		17 16	17 03	17 08		17 20	17 46	17 32		17 38	17 49		18 14	18 04	18 16		18 20	18 47	
Oxford	a	17 28										17 51	18 30										18 51	19 29	

		GW	GW	HC	GW	GW	GW	GW	HC	GW		GW	GW	GW	GW	HC	GW	GW	HC	GW		GW	GW	GW	GW
		◇1 ☕	◇1 ☕		1	1	◇1 ☕	◇1 ☕		◇1 ☕		1	◇1 ☕	◇1 ☕	1		1	◇1 ☕		◇1 ☕		◇1 ☕	1	◇1 ☕	◇1 ☕
London Paddington 15 ⊖	d	17 57	18 00	18 07	18 12	18 15	18 27	18 30	18 37	18 42		18 43	18 57	19 00	19 04	19 07	19 15	19 30	19 37	19 37		19 42	19 43	19 57	20 00
Acton Main Line	d																								
Ealing Broadway ⊖	d			18 15		18 24			18 45			18 50				19 15	19 24		19 45				19 50		
West Ealing	d																								
Drayton Green	d																								
Castle Bar Park	d																								
South Greenford	d																								
Greenford ⊖	a																								
Hanwell	d																								
Southall	d			18 19		18 29			18 49			18 56				19 19	19 29		19 49				19 56		
Hayes & Harlington	d			18 24		18 33			18 54			19 02				19 24	19 33		19 54				20 02		
Heathrow Term 1-2-3 2 ✈	a			18 29					18 59							19 29			19 59						
Heathrow Terminal 4 ✈	a			18 39					19 09							19 39			20 09						
West Drayton	d					18 37						19 10					19 38						20 10		
Iver	d																								
Langley	d					18 42						19 16					19 45						20 16		
Slough 3	a				18 30	18 46				19 00		19 20			19 25		19 49					19 58	20 20		
	d				18 30	18 46				19 01		19 22			19 25		19 49					19 59	20 22		
Burnham	d					18 51						19 26					19 54						20 26		
Taplow	d																								
Maidenhead 3	d				18 42	18 56						19 31			19 35		19 59						20 31		
Twyford 3	d					19 04						19 39					20 07						20 40		
Reading 7	a	18 32	18 38		18 56	19 12	19 02	19 14		19 22		19 47	19 31	19 38	19 50		20 15	20 04		20 16		20 20	20 47	20 32	20 38
Oxford	a									19 52		20 30										20 51	21 32		

Table 117

Sundays
26 June to 31 July

London - Greenford and Reading

		HC	GW	GW	HC	GW		GW	GW	GW	GW	HC	GW	GW	GW	GW		GW	HC	GW	GW	GW	GW	HC	GW
			■1	◇■1 ☕		◇■1 ☕		◇■1	■1	◇■1 ☕	◇■1 ☕		■1	◇■1 ☕	◇■1	■1		◇■1 ☕		■1 A	◇■1	■1	◇■1 ☕		■1
London Paddington 15 ⊖	d	20 07	20 15	20 30	20 37	20 37		20 42	20 43	20 57	21 00	21 07	21 15	21 30	21 42	21 43		22 03	22 12	22 15	22 42	22 43	23 03	23 12	23 15
Acton Main Line	d																								
Ealing Broadway ⊖	d	20 15	20 24		20 45				20 50			21 15	21 24			21 50			22 20	22 24		22 50		23 20	23 24
West Ealing	d																								
Drayton Green	d																								
Castle Bar Park	d																								
South Greenford	d																								
Greenford ⊖	a																								
Hanwell	d																								
Southall	d	20 19	20 29		20 49				20 56			21 19	21 29			21 56			22 24	22 29		22 56		23 24	23 29
Hayes & Harlington	d	20 24	20 36		20 54				21 02			21 24	21 33			22 02			22 28	22 33		23 02		23 28	23 33
Heathrow Term 1-2-3 2 ✈	a	20 29			20 59							21 29							22 34					23 34	
Heathrow Terminal 4 ✈	a	20 39			21 09							21 39							22 41					23 41	
West Drayton	d		20 40						21 06				21 40			22 09				22 37		23 06			23 37
Iver	d																								
Langley	d		20 44						21 15				21 44			22 17				22 42		23 10			23 42
Slough 3	a		20 48					21 02	21 20				21 48		21 59	22 21				22 46	23 00	23 14			23 46
	d		20 49					21 03	21 22				21 49		22 00	22 23				22 46	23 01	23 16			23 46
Burnham	d		20 53						21 26				21 53			22 27				22 50		23 20			23 51
Taplow	d																								
Maidenhead 3	d		20 59						21 32				21 59			22 33				22 56		23 24			23 56
Twyford 3	d		21 07						21 40				22 06			22 41				23 04		23 33			00 04
Reading 7	a		21 14	21 04		21 15		21 21	21 45	21 31	21 38		22 14	22 06	22 22	22 48		22 39		23 11	23 20	23 43	23 43		00 13
Oxford	a							21 51	22 30						22 52										

		GW		GW	GW	GW
		◇■1 ☕		◇■1	■ 🛏 ☕	■1
London Paddington 15 ⊖	d	23 37		23 47	23 50	23 53
Acton Main Line	d					
Ealing Broadway ⊖	d			23 55		00 02
West Ealing	d					
Drayton Green	d					
Castle Bar Park	d					
South Greenford	d					
Greenford ⊖	a					
Hanwell	d					
Southall	d					00 07
Hayes & Harlington	d					00 11
Heathrow Term 1-2-3 2 ✈	a					
Heathrow Terminal 4 ✈	a					
West Drayton	d					00 15
Iver	d					
Langley	d					00 20
Slough 3	a			00 08		00 24
	d			00 09		00 24
Burnham	d					00 28
Taplow	d					
Maidenhead 3	d			00 17		00 34
Twyford 3	d					00 42
Reading 7	a	00 15		00 31		00 49
Oxford	a					

Sundays
7 August to 11 September

		GW	GW	GW	GW	GW	GW	GW	GW	GW		GW	HC	HC	GW	HC	GW	GW	GW	HC		GW	GW	GW	GW
		■1	◇■1	■1	■1	◇■1	■1	■1	■1	■1		■1			■1		■1	◇■1 ☕	◇■1 ⇄			■1	◇■1 ☕	◇■1 ☕	◇■1
London Paddington 15 ⊖	d	22p45	23p00		23p20	23p33		23p42	00 05	00 30		01 00	05 12	06 12	06 43	07 12	07 28	08 00	08 03	08 12		08 15	08 30	08 37	08 42
Acton Main Line	d	22p51																							
Ealing Broadway ⊖	d	22p55			23p28			23p50	00 13	00 38		01 08	05 20	06 20	06 52	07 20	07 36			08 20		08 24			
West Ealing	d																								
Drayton Green	d																								
Castle Bar Park	d																								
South Greenford	d																								
Greenford ⊖	a																								
Hanwell	d																								
Southall	d	23p00			23p33			23p56	00 19	00 44		01 13	05 24	06 24	06 58	07 24	07 42			08 24		08 29			
Hayes & Harlington	d	23p04			23p37			00 01	00 23	00 48		01 17	05 28	06 28	07 02	07 28	07 46			08 28		08 33			
Heathrow Term 1-2-3 2 ✈	a												05 34	06 34		07 34				08 34					
Heathrow Terminal 4 ✈	a												05 40	06 41		07 41				08 41					
West Drayton	d	23p08			23p41			00 06	00 27	00 52					07 06		07 50					08 37			
Iver	d	23p11			23p44				00 30																
Langley	d	23p14		←	23p48		←		00 33	00 56					07 11		07 55					08 44			
Slough 3	a	23p19	23p16	23p19	23p53	23p49	23p53	00 13	00 37	01 00		01 25			07 16		07 58		08 22			08 48			08 59
	d	23p21	23p17	23p21	23p54	23p50	23p54	00 14	00 38	01 01		01 26			07 16		07 58		08 22			08 49			09 00
Burnham	d	↪		23p25	↪		23p57	00 18	00 42						07 20		08 03								
Taplow	d						00 01	00 21	00 45																
Maidenhead 3	d			23p32			00 05	00 25	00 49	01 08		01 33			07 27		08 08		08 31			08 57			
Twyford 3	d			23p39			00 13	00 33	00 57	01 16		01 41			07 35		08 16					09 05			
Reading 7	a		23p33	23p46		00 06	00 20	00 43	01 05	01 24		01 50			07 42		08 25	08 38	08 44			09 13	09 05	09 15	09 21
Oxford	a		00 03	00 31		00 38	01 04										09 43		09 13						09 52

A ■1 to Twyford

Table 117

Sundays

7 August to 11 September

London - Greenford and Reading

		GW	GW	GW	HC	GW		GW	GW	HC	GW	GW	GW	HC	GW	GW		GW	HC	GW	GW	GW	GW	HC	GW
		1	◇1 ☕	◇1 ☕		1		◇1 ☕	◇1 ☕		◇1 ☕	1	◇1 ☕		1	◇1 ☕		◇1 ☕		◇1 ☕	◇1 ☕	1	◇1 ☕		1
London Paddington 15 ⊖	d	08 43	08 51	09 00	09 07	09 15		09 30	09 35	09 37	09 42	09 43	10 00	10 07	10 15	10 27		10 30	10 37	10 37	10 42	10 43	11 00	11 07	11 13
Acton Main Line	d																								
Ealing Broadway ⊖	d	08 50			09 15	09 24				09 45		09 50		10 15	10 24				10 45			10 50		11 15	
West Ealing	d																								
Drayton Green	d																								
Castle Bar Park	d																								
South Greenford	d																								
Greenford ⊖	a																								
Hanwell	d																								
Southall	d	08 56			09 19	09 29				09 49		09 56		10 19	10 29				10 49			10 56		11 19	
Hayes & Harlington	d	09 02			09 24	09 33				09 54		10 02		10 24	10 33				10 54			11 02		11 24	
Heathrow Term 1-2-3 2 ✈	a				09 29					09 59				10 29					10 59					11 29	
Heathrow Terminal 4 ✈	a				09 39					10 09				10 39					11 09					11 39	
West Drayton	d	09 06				09 37						10 06			10 37							11 08			
Iver	d																								
Langley	d	09 15				09 44						10 16			10 45							11 16			
Slough 3	a	09 19				09 48			09 52			10 20			10 49						10 57	11 20			11 31
	d	09 20				09 49			09 53			10 22			10 49						10 58	11 22			11 31
Burnham	d	09 24										10 26										11 26			
Taplow	d																								
Maidenhead 3	d	09 30				09 58						10 31			10 57							11 31			11 43
Twyford 3	d	09 38				10 06						10 39			11 05							11 39			
Reading 7	a	09 45	09 26	09 35		10 13		10 05	10 16		10 21	10 47	10 38		11 13	11 02		11 07		11 14	11 20	11 47	11 38		12 00
Oxford	a	10 31							10 45			11 31									11 50	12 31			

		GW		GW	HC	GW	GW	GW	GW	HC	GW	GW		GW	HC	GW	GW	GW	GW	GW	GW	HC		GW	GW
		1		◇1 ☕		◇1 ☕	◇1	1	◇1 ☕		1	◇1 ☕		◇1 ☕		◇1 ☕	◇1 ☕	1	1	◇1 ☕	1			1	◇1 ☕
London Paddington 15 ⊖	d	11 15		11 30	11 37	11 37	11 42	11 43	12 00	12 07	12 15	12 27		12 30	12 37	12 37	12 42	12 43	12 51	13 00		13 07		13 15	13 30
Acton Main Line	d																								
Ealing Broadway ⊖	d	11 24			11 45			11 50		12 15	12 24				12 45			12 50				13 15		13 24	
West Ealing	d																								
Drayton Green	d																								
Castle Bar Park	d																								
South Greenford	d																								
Greenford ⊖	a																								
Hanwell	d																								
Southall	d	11 29			11 49			11 56		12 19	12 29				12 49			12 56				13 19		13 29	
Hayes & Harlington	d	11 33			11 54			12 02		12 24	12 33				12 54			13 02				13 24		13 33	
Heathrow Term 1-2-3 2 ✈	a				11 59					12 29					12 59							13 29			
Heathrow Terminal 4 ✈	a				12 09					12 39					13 09							13 39			
West Drayton	d	11 37						12 06			12 37							13 09						13 37	
Iver	d																								
Langley	d	11 44						12 16			12 44							13 16			←			13 44	
Slough 3	a	11 48					12 00	12 20			12 49						12 57	13 20	13 09		13 20			13 48	
	d	11 49					12 01	12 22			12 50						12 58	13 22	13 09		13 22			13 49	
Burnham	d							12 26										→			13 26				
Taplow	d																								
Maidenhead 3	d	11 56						12 31			12 57								13 18		13 31			13 57	
Twyford 3	d	12 04						12 39			13 05										13 39			14 05	
Reading 7	a	12 12		12 05		12 14	12 22	12 47	12 38		13 13	13 02		13 07		13 15	13 21		13 32	13 38	13 47			14 13	14 05
Oxford	a						12 52	13 32									13 51				14 31				

		HC	GW	GW	GW	GW	GW	HC		GW	GW	HC	GW	GW	GW	GW	GW	GW		HC	GW	HC	GW	GW	GW
			◇1 ☕	◇1 ☕	1	◇1 ☕	1			1	◇1 ☕		◇1 ☕	◇1 🛒	1	◇1 ☕	◇1 ☕	1			1		◇1 ☕	◇1 ☕	1
London Paddington 15 ⊖	d	13 37	13 37	13 42	13 43	14 00	14 04	14 07		14 15	14 27	14 37	14 37	14 42	14 43	14 48	15 00	15 04		15 07	15 15	15 37	15 37	15 42	15 43
Acton Main Line	d																								
Ealing Broadway ⊖	d	13 45			13 50			14 15		14 24		14 45			14 50					15 15	15 24	15 45			15 50
West Ealing	d																								
Drayton Green	d																								
Castle Bar Park	d																								
South Greenford	d																								
Greenford ⊖	a																								
Hanwell	d																								
Southall	d	13 49			13 56			14 19		14 29		14 49			14 56					15 19	15 29	15 49			15 56
Hayes & Harlington	d	13 54			14 02			14 24		14 33		14 54			15 02					15 24	15 33	15 54			16 02
Heathrow Term 1-2-3 2 ✈	a	13 59						14 29				14 59								15 29		15 59			
Heathrow Terminal 4 ✈	a	14 09						14 39				15 09								15 39		16 09			
West Drayton	d				14 06					14 37					15 06						15 37				16 06
Iver	d																								
Langley	d				14 16					14 45					15 16						15 44				16 14
Slough 3	a			13 59	14 20		14 25			14 49				15 01	15 21			15 25			15 48			16 01	16 18
	d			14 00	14 22		14 26			14 49				15 02	15 22			15 26			15 49			16 01	16 20
Burnham	d				14 26										15 26						15 53				16 24
Taplow	d																								
Maidenhead 3	d				14 31		14 34			14 57					15 31			15 36			15 59				16 29
Twyford 3	d				14 39					15 05					15 39						16 07				16 37
Reading 7	a		14 15	14 23	14 47	14 37	14 51			15 12	15 02		15 14	15 20	15 47	15 25	15 38	15 51			16 14		16 16	16 19	16 44
Oxford	a			14 53	15 31									15 51	16 29									16 51	17 30

Table 117

Sundays

7 August to 11 September

London - Greenford and Reading

	GW	GW	GW		HC	GW	GW	HC	GW	GW	GW	GW	GW		GW	HC	GW	GW	HC	GW	GW	GW	GW	
	◇1 ☕	◇1 ☕	1			1	◇1 ☕		◇1 ☕	◇1 🛒	1	◇1 ☕	◇1 ☕		1		1	◇1 ☕		◇1 ☕	◇1 🛒	1	◇1 ☕	
London Paddington 15 ⊖ d	15 57	16 00	16 04		16 07	16 15	16 27	16 37	16 37	16 42	16 43	16 57	17 00		17 04	17 07	17 15	17 30	17 37	17 37	17 42	17 43	17 57	
Acton Main Line d																								
Ealing Broadway ⊖ d					16 15	16 24		16 45			16 50					17 15	17 23		17 45			17 50		
West Ealing d																								
Drayton Green d																								
Castle Bar Park d																								
South Greenford d																								
Greenford ⊖ a																								
Hanwell d																								
Southall d					16 19	16 29		16 49			16 56					17 19	17 29		17 49			17 56		
Hayes & Harlington d					16 24	16 33		16 54			17 02					17 24	17 33		17 54			18 02		
Heathrow Term 1-2-3 2 ✈ a					16 29			16 59								17 29			17 59					
Heathrow Terminal 4 ✈ a					16 39			17 09								17 39			18 09					
West Drayton d						16 37					17 07						17 40					18 09		
Iver d																								
Langley d						16 46					17 16						17 44					18 16		
Slough 3 a			16 24			16 50				17 01	17 20				17 25		17 48				18 01	18 20		
d			16 24			16 50				17 01	17 22				17 26		17 49				18 01	18 21		
Burnham d						16 55					17 26						17 53					18 25		
Taplow d																								
Maidenhead 3 d			16 33			17 00					17 31				17 36		17 59					18 31		
Twyford 3 d						17 08					17 39						18 07					18 39		
Reading 7 a	16 32	16 38	16 47			17 16	17 04		17 18	17 20	17 47	17 32	17 38		17 51		18 14	18 04		18 16	18 24	18 46	18 32	
Oxford a										17 52	18 31										18 53	19 28		

	GW	HC	GW	GW	GW	HC	GW	GW	GW		GW	GW	GW	HC	GW	GW	HC	GW	GW		GW	GW	GW	HC
	◇1 ☕		1	1	◇1 ☕		◇1 ☕	◇1 ☕	1		◇1 ☕	◇1 ☕	1		1	◇1 ☕		◇1 ☕	◇1 ☕		1	◇1 ☕	◇1 ☕	
London Paddington 15 ⊖ d	18 00	18 07	18 12	18 15	18 27	18 37	18 37	18 42	18 43		18 57	19 00	19 04	19 07	19 15	19 30	19 37	19 37	19 42		19 43	19 57	20 00	20 07
Acton Main Line d																								
Ealing Broadway ⊖ d		18 15		18 23		18 45			18 50					19 15	19 24		19 45				19 50			20 15
West Ealing d																								
Drayton Green d																								
Castle Bar Park d																								
South Greenford d																								
Greenford ⊖ a																								
Hanwell d																								
Southall d		18 19		18 29		18 49			18 56					19 19	19 29		19 49				19 56			20 19
Hayes & Harlington d		18 24		18 33		18 54			19 02					19 24	19 33		19 54				20 02			20 24
Heathrow Term 1-2-3 2 ✈ a		18 29				18 59								19 29			19 59							20 29
Heathrow Terminal 4 ✈ a		18 39				19 09								19 39			20 09							20 39
West Drayton d				18 37					19 10						19 39						20 09			
Iver d																								
Langley d				18 41					19 16						19 44						20 16			
Slough 3 a			18 30	18 45				18 58	19 20				19 25		19 48				19 58		20 20			
d			18 30	18 46				18 59	19 22				19 25		19 48				19 59		20 22			
Burnham d				18 50					19 26						19 53						20 26			
Taplow d																								
Maidenhead 3 d			18 44	18 56					19 31				19 35		19 58						20 31			
Twyford 3 d				19 04					19 39						20 06						20 39			
Reading 7 a	18 38		18 59	19 12	19 02		19 13	19 22	19 47		19 32	19 38	19 50		20 14	20 06		20 15	20 20		20 46	20 32	20 38	
Oxford a								19 54	20 30										20 51		21 30			

	GW	GW	GW	HC	GW		GW	GW	GW	HC	GW	GW	GW	GW	GW		HC	GW	GW	GW	GW	HC	GW	GW
	1	◇1 ☕	◇1 ☕		◇1		1	◇1 ☕	◇1 ☕		1	◇1 ☕	◇1	1	◇1 ☕			1	◇1	1	◇1 ☕		1	◇1 ☕
London Paddington 15 ⊖ d	20 15	20 30	20 37	20 37	20 42		20 43	20 57	21 00	21 07	21 15	21 37	21 42	21 43	22 03		22 12	22 15	22 42	22 43	23 03	23 12	23 15	23 37
Acton Main Line d																								
Ealing Broadway ⊖ d	20 24			20 45			20 50			21 15	21 24			21 50			22 20	22 24		22 50		23 20	23 24	
West Ealing d																								
Drayton Green d																								
Castle Bar Park d																								
South Greenford d																								
Greenford ⊖ a																								
Hanwell d																								
Southall d	20 30			20 49			20 56			21 19	21 29			21 56			22 24	22 29		22 56		23 24	23 29	
Hayes & Harlington d	20 34			20 54			21 02			21 24	21 33			22 02			22 28	22 33		23 02		23 28	23 33	
Heathrow Term 1-2-3 2 ✈ a				20 59						21 29							22 34					23 34		
Heathrow Terminal 4 ✈ a				21 09						21 39							22 41					23 41		
West Drayton d	20 38						21 06				21 37			22 06				22 37		23 06			23 37	
Iver d																								
Langley d	20 44						21 13				21 42			22 10				22 42		23 10			23 42	
Slough 3 a	20 48				21 01		21 17				21 46		21 58	22 14				22 46	23 00	23 14			23 46	
d	20 49				21 02		21 19				21 46		21 59	22 16				22 46	23 00	23 16			23 46	
Burnham d	20 53						21 23				21 51			22 20				22 50		23 20			23 51	
Taplow d																								
Maidenhead 3 d	20 59						21 28				21 56			22 25				22 56		23 24			23 56	
Twyford 3 d	21 07						21 36				22 04			22 33				23 04		23 34			00 04	
Reading 7 a	21 14	21 04	21 16		21 22		21 42	21 32	21 38		22 11	22 13	22 20	22 40	22 49			23 10	23 19	23 43	23 45		00 14	00 15
Oxford a					21 52		22 30						22 51											

Table 117

London - Greenford and Reading

Sundays

7 August to 11 September

	GW	GW
	◇1	1
London Paddington 15 ⊖ d	23 47	23 53
Acton Main Line d		
Ealing Broadway ⊖ d	23 55	00 02
West Ealing d		
Drayton Green d		
Castle Bar Park d		
South Greenford d		
Greenford ⊖ a		
Hanwell d		
Southall d		00 07
Hayes & Harlington d		00 11
Heathrow Term 1-2-3 2 ✈ a		
Heathrow Terminal 4 ✈ a		
West Drayton d		00 15
Iver d		
Langley d		00 20
Slough 3 a	00 08	00 24
d	00 09	00 24
Burnham d		00 28
Taplow d		
Maidenhead 3 d	00 17	00 34
Twyford 3 d		00 42
Reading 7 a	00 31	00 49
Oxford a		

Sundays

18 September to 23 October

	GW	GW	GW	GW	GW	GW	GW	HC	HC		GW	HC	GW	GW	GW	HC	GW	GW	GW		GW	GW	GW	HC
	1	◇1	1	1	1	1	1				1		1	◇1	◇1		1	◇1	◇1		1	◇1	◇1	
														☕	🛒			☕				☕	☕	
London Paddington 15 ⊖ d	23p20	23p33		23p42	00 05	00 30	01 00	05 12	06 12		06 43	07 12	07 28	08 00	08 03	08 12	08 15	08 30	08 42		08 43	08 51	09 00	09 07
Acton Main Line d																								
Ealing Broadway ⊖ d	23p28			23p50	00 13	00 38	01 08	05 20	06 20		06 52	07 20	07 36			08 20	08 24				08 50			09 15
West Ealing d																								
Drayton Green d																								
Castle Bar Park d																								
South Greenford d																								
Greenford ⊖ a																								
Hanwell d																								
Southall d	23p33			23p56	00 19	00 44	01 13	05 24	06 24		06 58	07 24	07 42			08 24	08 29				08 56			09 19
Hayes & Harlington d	23p37			00 01	00 23	00 48	01 17	05 28	06 28		07 02	07 28	07 46			08 28	08 33				09 02			09 24
Heathrow Term 1-2-3 2 ✈ a								05 34	06 34			07 34				08 34								09 29
Heathrow Terminal 4 ✈ a								05 40	06 41			07 41				08 41								09 39
West Drayton d	23p41			00 06	00 27	00 52					07 06		07 50				08 37				09 06			
Iver d	23p44				00 30																			
Langley d	23p48		←		00 33	00 56					07 11		07 55				08 44				09 15			
Slough 3 a	23p53	23p49	23p53	00 13	00 37	01 00	01 25				07 16		07 58		08 22		08 48		08 59		09 19			
d	23p54	23p50	23p54	00 14	00 38	01 01	01 26				07 16		07 58		08 22		08 49		09 00		09 20			
Burnham d	→		23p57	00 18	00 42						07 20		08 03								09 24			
Taplow d			00 01	00 21	00 45																			
Maidenhead 3 d			00 05	00 25	00 49	01 08	01 33				07 27		08 08		08 30		08 57				09 30			
Twyford 3 d			00 13	00 33	00 57	01 16	01 41				07 35		08 16				09 05				09 38			
Reading 7 a		00 06	00 20	00 43	01 05	01 24	01 50				07 42		08 25	08 38	08 44		09 13	09 05	09 21		09 45	09 26	09 35	
Oxford a													09 43		09 13				09 52		10 31			

	GW	GW	GW	HC	GW		GW	GW	HC	GW	GW	HC	GW	GW	GW		GW	HC	GW	GW	HC	GW	GW	GW
	1	◇1	◇1		◇1		1	◇1		1	◇1		◇1	◇1	1		◇1		1	◇1		◇1	◇1	1
		☕	☕		☕			☕			☕		☕	☕			☕			☕		☕		
London Paddington 15 ⊖ d	09 15	09 30	09 35	09 37	09 42		09 43	10 00	10 07	10 15	10 30	10 37	10 37	10 42	10 43		11 00	11 07	11 15	11 30	11 37	11 37	11 42	11 43
Acton Main Line d																								
Ealing Broadway ⊖ d	09 24			09 45			09 50		10 15	10 24		10 45			10 50			11 15	11 24		11 45			11 50
West Ealing d																								
Drayton Green d																								
Castle Bar Park d																								
South Greenford d																								
Greenford ⊖ a																								
Hanwell d																								
Southall d	09 29			09 49			09 56		10 19	10 29		10 49			10 56			11 19	11 29		11 49			11 56
Hayes & Harlington d	09 33			09 54			10 02		10 24	10 33		10 54			11 02			11 24	11 33		11 54			12 02
Heathrow Term 1-2-3 2 ✈ a				09 59					10 29			10 59						11 29			11 59			
Heathrow Terminal 4 ✈ a				10 09					10 39			11 09						11 39			12 09			
West Drayton d	09 37						10 06			10 37					11 08				11 37					12 06
Iver d																								
Langley d	09 44						10 16			10 45					11 16				11 44					12 16
Slough 3 a	09 48		09 52				10 20			10 49				10 57	11 20				11 48				12 00	12 20
d	09 49		09 53				10 22			10 49				10 58	11 22				11 49				12 01	12 22
Burnham d							10 26								11 26									12 26
Taplow d																								
Maidenhead 3 d	09 58						10 31			10 57					11 31				11 56					12 31
Twyford 3 d	10 06						10 39			11 05					11 39				12 04					12 39
Reading 7 a	10 13	10 05	10 16		10 21		10 47	10 38		11 13	11 05		11 14	11 20	11 47		11 38		12 12	12 05		12 14	12 22	12 47
Oxford a			10 45				11 31							11 50	12 31								12 52	13 32

Table 117

Sundays

18 September to 23 October

London - Greenford and Reading

		GW ◇1 ☕		HC	GW 1	GW ◇1 ☕	HC	GW ◇1 ☕	GW ◇1 ☕	GW 1	GW ◇1 ☕	HC		GW 1	GW ◇1 ☕	HC	GW ◇1 ☕	GW ◇1 ☕	GW 1	GW ◇1 ☕	HC	GW 1		GW ◇1 ☕	HC
London Paddington 15 ⊖	d	12 00		12 07	12 15	12 30	12 37	12 37	12 42	12 43	13 00	13 07		13 15	13 30	13 37	13 37	13 42	13 43	14 00	14 07	14 15		14 30	14 37
Acton Main Line	d																								
Ealing Broadway ⊖	d			12 15	12 24		12 45			12 50		13 15		13 24		13 45			13 50		14 15	14 24			14 45
West Ealing	d																								
Drayton Green	d																								
Castle Bar Park	d																								
South Greenford	d																								
Greenford ⊖	a																								
Hanwell	d																								
Southall	d			12 19	12 29		12 49			12 56		13 19		13 29		13 49			13 56		14 19	14 29			14 49
Hayes & Harlington	d			12 24	12 33		12 54			13 02		13 24		13 33		13 54			14 02		14 24	14 33			14 54
Heathrow Term 1-2-3 2 ✈	a			12 29			12 59					13 29				13 59					14 29				14 59
Heathrow Terminal 4 ✈	a			12 39			13 09					13 39				14 09					14 39				15 09
West Drayton	d				12 37					13 09				13 37					14 06			14 37			
Iver	d																								
Langley	d				12 44					13 16				13 44					14 16			14 45			
Slough 3	a				12 49				12 57	13 20				13 48				13 58	14 20			14 49			
	d				12 50				12 58	13 22				13 49				13 59	14 22			14 49			
Burnham	d									13 26									14 26						
Taplow	d																								
Maidenhead 3	d				12 57					13 31				13 57					14 31			14 57			
Twyford 3	d				13 05					13 39				14 05					14 39			15 05			
Reading 7	a	12 38			13 13	13 07		13 15	13 21	13 47	13 38			14 13	14 05		14 15	14 23	14 47	14 37		15 12		15 05	
Oxford	a								13 51	14 31								14 53	15 31						

		GW ◇1 ☕	GW ◇1 🛒	GW 1	GW ◇1 ☕	HC	GW 1	GW ◇1 ☕		HC	GW ◇1 ☕	GW ◇1 ☕	GW 1	GW ◇1 ☕	HC	GW 1	GW ◇1 ☕	GW ◇1 ☕		HC	GW ◇1 ☕	GW ◇1 🛒	GW 1	GW ◇1 ☕	HC
London Paddington 15 ⊖	d	14 37	14 42	14 43	15 00	15 07	15 15	15 30		15 37	15 37	15 42	15 43	16 00	16 07	16 15	16 27	16 30		16 37	16 37	16 42	16 43	17 00	17 07
Acton Main Line	d																								
Ealing Broadway ⊖	d			14 50		15 15	15 24			15 45			15 50		16 15	16 24				16 45			16 50		17 15
West Ealing	d																								
Drayton Green	d																								
Castle Bar Park	d																								
South Greenford	d																								
Greenford ⊖	a																								
Hanwell	d																								
Southall	d			14 56		15 19	15 29			15 49			15 56		16 19	16 29				16 49			16 56		17 19
Hayes & Harlington	d			15 02		15 24	15 33			15 54			16 02		16 24	16 33				16 54			17 02		17 24
Heathrow Term 1-2-3 2 ✈	a					15 29				15 59					16 29					16 59					17 29
Heathrow Terminal 4 ✈	a					15 39				16 09					16 39					17 09					17 39
West Drayton	d			15 06			15 37						16 06			16 37							17 07		
Iver	d																								
Langley	d			15 16			15 44						16 16			16 46							17 16		
Slough 3	a		15 01	15 21			15 48					16 01	16 20			16 50						17 01	17 20		
	d		15 02	15 22			15 49					16 01	16 22			16 50						17 01	17 22		
Burnham	d			15 26			15 53						16 26			16 55							17 26		
Taplow	d																								
Maidenhead 3	d			15 31			15 59						16 31			17 00							17 31		
Twyford 3	d			15 39			16 07						16 39			17 08							17 39		
Reading 7	a	15 14	15 20	15 47	15 38		16 14	16 05			16 16	16 20	16 47	16 38		17 16	17 04	17 08			17 18	17 21	17 47	17 38	
Oxford	a		15 51	16 29								16 51	17 30									17 52	18 31		

		GW 1	GW ◇1 ☕	HC		GW ◇1 ☕	GW ◇1 🛒	GW 1	GW ◇1 ☕	GW ◇1 ☕	HC	GW 1	GW ◇1 ☕	HC		GW ◇1 ☕	GW ◇1 ☕	GW 1	GW ◇1 ☕	GW ◇1 ☕	HC	GW 1	GW ◇1 ☕	HC	
London Paddington 15 ⊖	d	17 15	17 30	17 37		17 37	17 42	17 43	17 57	18 00	18 07	18 15	18 27	18 37		18 37	18 42	18 43	18 57	19 00	19 07	19 15	19 30	19 37	
Acton Main Line	d																								
Ealing Broadway ⊖	d	17 23		17 45				17 50			18 15	18 23		18 45				18 50			19 15	19 24		19 45	
West Ealing	d																								
Drayton Green	d																								
Castle Bar Park	d																								
South Greenford	d																								
Greenford ⊖	a																								
Hanwell	d																								
Southall	d	17 29		17 49				17 56			18 19	18 29		18 49				18 56			19 19	19 29		19 49	
Hayes & Harlington	d	17 33		17 54				18 02			18 24	18 33		18 54				19 02			19 24	19 33		19 54	
Heathrow Term 1-2-3 2 ✈	a			17 59							18 29			18 59							19 29			19 59	
Heathrow Terminal 4 ✈	a			18 09							18 39			19 09							19 39			20 09	
West Drayton	d	17 40						18 09				18 37						19 10				19 39			
Iver	d																								
Langley	d	17 44						18 16				18 41						19 16				19 44			
Slough 3	a	17 48					18 01	18 20				18 45					18 58	19 20				19 48			
	d	17 49					18 01	18 21				18 46					18 59	19 22				19 48			
Burnham	d	17 53						18 25				18 50						19 26				19 53			
Taplow	d																								
Maidenhead 3	d	17 59						18 31				18 56						19 31				19 58			
Twyford 3	d	18 07						18 39				19 04						19 39				20 06			
Reading 7	a	18 14	18 04			18 16	18 24	18 46	18 32	18 38		19 12	19 02			19 13	19 22	19 47	19 32	19 38		20 14	20 06		
Oxford	a						18 52	19 28									19 54	20 30							

Table 117

Sundays

18 September to 23 October

London - Greenford and Reading

		GW	GW	GW	GW	GW	HC	GW	GW	GW	HC	GW
		◇1 ☕	◇1 ☕	1	◇1 ☕	◇1 ☕		1	◇1 ☕	◇1 ☕		◇1
London Paddington 15 ⊖	d	19 37	19 42	19 43	19 57	20 00	20 07	20 15	20 30	20 37	20 37	20 42
Acton Main Line	d											
Ealing Broadway ⊖	d			19 50			20 15	20 24			20 45	
West Ealing	d											
Drayton Green	d											
Castle Bar Park	d											
South Greenford	d											
Greenford ⊖	a											
Hanwell	d											
Southall	d			19 56			20 19	20 30			20 49	
Hayes & Harlington	d			20 02			20 24	20 34			20 54	
Heathrow Term 1-2-3 2 ✈	a						20 29				20 59	
Heathrow Terminal 4 ✈	a						20 39				21 09	
West Drayton	d			20 09				20 38				
Iver	d											
Langley	d			20 16				20 44				
Slough 3	a		19 58	20 20				20 48				21 01
	d		19 59	20 22				20 49				21 02
Burnham	d			20 26				20 53				
Taplow	d											
Maidenhead 3	d			20 31				20 59				
Twyford 3	d			20 39				21 07				
Reading 7	a	20 15	20 20	20 46	20 32	20 38		21 14	21 04	21 16		21 22
Oxford	a		20 51	21 30								21 52

		GW	GW	GW	HC	GW	GW	GW	GW	GW	HC	GW
		1	◇1 ☕	◇1 ☕		1	◇1 ☕	◇1	1	◇1 ☕		1
London Paddington 15 ⊖	d	20 43	20 57	21 00	21 07	21 15	21 37	21 39	21 43	22 03	22 12	22 15
Acton Main Line	d											
Ealing Broadway ⊖	d	20 50			21 15	21 24			21 50		22 20	22 24
West Ealing	d											
Drayton Green	d											
Castle Bar Park	d											
South Greenford	d											
Greenford ⊖	a											
Hanwell	d											
Southall	d	20 56			21 19	21 29			21 56		22 24	22 29
Hayes & Harlington	d	21 02			21 24	21 33			22 02		22 28	22 33
Heathrow Term 1-2-3 2 ✈	a				21 29						22 34	
Heathrow Terminal 4 ✈	a				21 39						22 41	
West Drayton	d	21 06				21 37			22 06			22 37
Iver	d											
Langley	d	21 13				21 42			22 10			22 42
Slough 3	a	21 17				21 46		21 58	22 14			22 46
	d	21 19				21 46		21 59	22 16			22 46
Burnham	d	21 23				21 51			22 20			22 50
Taplow	d											
Maidenhead 3	d	21 28				21 56			22 25			22 56
Twyford 3	d	21 36				22 04			22 33			23 04
Reading 7	a	21 42	21 32	21 38		22 11	22 13	22 20	22 40	22 49		23 12
Oxford	a	22 30						22 51	23 37			

		GW	GW	GW	GW	HC	GW	GW	GW	GW	GW
		◇1 ☕	◇1	1	◇1 ☕		1	◇1 ☕	◇1	R 🛏 ☕	1
London Paddington 15 ⊖	d	22 37	22 42	22 43	23 03	23 12	23 15	23 37	23 47	23 50	23 53
Acton Main Line	d										
Ealing Broadway ⊖	d			22 50		23 20	23 24		23 55		00 02
West Ealing	d										
Drayton Green	d										
Castle Bar Park	d										
South Greenford	d										
Greenford ⊖	a										
Hanwell	d										
Southall	d			22 56		23 24	23 29				00 07
Hayes & Harlington	d			23 02		23 28	23 33				00 11
Heathrow Term 1-2-3 2 ✈	a					23 34					
Heathrow Terminal 4 ✈	a					23 41					
West Drayton	d			23 06			23 37				00 15
Iver	d										
Langley	d			23 10			23 42				00 20
Slough 3	a		23 01	23 14			23 46		00 08		00 24
	d		23 01	23 16			23 46		00 09		00 24
Burnham	d			23 20			23 51				00 28
Taplow	d										
Maidenhead 3	d			23 24			23 56		00 17		00 34
Twyford 3	d			23 32			00 04				00 42
Reading 7	a	23 15	23 19	23 43	23 45		00 14	00 15	00 31		00 49
Oxford	a		23 49	00 35					01 04		

Sundays

from 30 October

		GW	GW	GW	GW	GW	GW	GW	HC	HC	GW	HC
		1	◇1	1	1	1	1	1			1	
London Paddington 15 ⊖	d	23p20	23p33		23p42	00 05	00 30	01 00	05 12	06 12	06 43	07 12
Acton Main Line	d											
Ealing Broadway ⊖	d	23p28			23p50	00 13	00 38	01 08	05 20	06 20	06 52	07 20
West Ealing	d											
Drayton Green	d											
Castle Bar Park	d											
South Greenford	d											
Greenford ⊖	a											
Hanwell	d											
Southall	d	23p33			23p56	00 19	00 44	01 13	05 24	06 24	06 58	07 24
Hayes & Harlington	d	23p37			00 01	00 23	00 48	01 17	05 28	06 28	07 02	07 28
Heathrow Term 1-2-3 2 ✈	a								05 34	06 34		07 34
Heathrow Terminal 4 ✈	a								05 40	06 41		07 41
West Drayton	d	23p41			00 06	00 27	00 52				07 06	
Iver	d	23p44				00 30						
Langley	d	23p48		←		00 33	00 56				07 11	
Slough 3	a	23p53	23p49	23p53	00 13	00 37	01 00	01 25			07 16	
	d	23p54	23p50	23p54	00 14	00 38	01 01	01 26			07 16	
Burnham	d	→		23p57	00 18	00 42					07 20	
Taplow	d			00 01	00 21	00 45						
Maidenhead 3	d			00 05	00 25	00 49	01 08	01 33			07 27	
Twyford 3	d			00 13	00 33	00 57	01 16	01 41			07 35	
Reading 7	a		00 06	00 20	00 43	01 05	01 24	01 50			07 42	
Oxford	a											

		GW	GW	GW	HC	GW	GW	GW	GW	GW	HC	GW
		1	◇1 ☕	◇1 🚲		1	◇1 ☕	◇1	1	◇1 ☕		1
London Paddington 15 ⊖	d	07 28	08 00	08 06	08 12	08 15	08 30	08 42	08 43	08 57	09 12	09 15
Acton Main Line	d											
Ealing Broadway ⊖	d	07 36			08 20	08 24			08 50		09 20	09 24
West Ealing	d											
Drayton Green	d											
Castle Bar Park	d											
South Greenford	d											
Greenford ⊖	a											
Hanwell	d											
Southall	d	07 42			08 24	08 29			08 56		09 24	09 29
Hayes & Harlington	d	07 46			08 28	08 33			09 02		09 28	09 33
Heathrow Term 1-2-3 2 ✈	a				08 34						09 34	
Heathrow Terminal 4 ✈	a				08 41						09 41	
West Drayton	d	07 50				08 37			09 06			09 37
Iver	d											
Langley	d	07 55				08 42			09 10			09 42
Slough 3	a	07 58		08 28		08 46		09 03	09 14			09 46
	d	07 58		08 28		08 46		09 04	09 16			09 46
Burnham	d	08 03							09 20			
Taplow	d											
Maidenhead 3	d	08 08		08 36		08 54			09 27			09 54
Twyford 3	d	08 16				09 02			09 35			10 02
Reading 7	a	08 25	08 32	08 49		09 10	09 02	09 20	09 42	09 31		10 10
Oxford	a	09 10		09 18				09 51	10 27			

Table 117

Sundays
from 30 October

London - Greenford and Reading

	GW	GW	GW	GW	HC		GW	GW	GW	GW	GW	HC	GW	GW	GW		GW	GW	GW	HC	GW	GW	GW	GW
	◇1	◇1	1	◇1			1	◇1	◇1	1	◇1		1	◇1	◇1		◇1	1	◇1		1	◇1	◇1	1
	🛒	🛒		🛒				🛒	🛒		🛒			🛒	🛒				🛒			🛒	🛒	
London Paddington 15 ⊖ d	09 30	09 35	09 43	09 57	10 12		10 15	10 30	10 42	10 43	10 57	11 12	11 15	11 30	11 37		11 42	11 43	11 57	12 12	12 15	12 30	12 42	12 43
Acton Main Line d																								
Ealing Broadway ⊖ d			09 50		10 20		10 24			10 50		11 20	11 24					11 50		12 20	12 24			12 50
West Ealing d																								
Drayton Green d																								
Castle Bar Park d																								
South Greenford d																								
Greenford ⊖ a																								
Hanwell d																								
Southall d			09 56		10 24		10 29			10 56		11 24	11 29					11 56		12 24	12 29			12 56
Hayes & Harlington d			10 02		10 28		10 33			11 02		11 28	11 33					12 02		12 28	12 33			13 02
Heathrow Term 1-2-3 2 ✈ a					10 34							11 34								12 34				
Heathrow Terminal 4 ✈ a					10 41							11 41								12 41				
West Drayton d			10 06				10 37			11 06			11 37					12 06			12 37			13 06
Iver d																								
Langley d			10 10				10 42			11 10			11 42					12 10			12 42			13 10
Slough 3 a		09 58	10 14				10 46		11 05	11 14			11 46				12 01	12 14			12 46		13 05	13 14
d		09 59	10 16				10 46		11 06	11 16			11 46				12 03	12 16			12 46		13 06	13 16
Burnham d			10 20							11 20								12 20						13 20
Taplow d																								
Maidenhead 3 d			10 27				10 54			11 27			11 54					12 27			12 54			13 27
Twyford 3 d			10 35				11 02			11 35			12 02					12 35			13 02			13 35
Reading 7 a	10 02	10 11	10 43	10 30			11 10	11 03	11 20	11 43	11 32		12 10	12 03	12 11		12 17	12 43	12 30		13 10	13 04	13 21	13 43
Oxford a		10 42	11 27						11 50	12 27							12 47	13 29					13 51	14 27

	GW		HC	GW	GW	GW	GW	GW	HC	GW	GW		GW	GW	GW	GW	HC	GW	GW	GW	GW		GW	GW
	◇1			1	◇1	◇1	1	◇1		1	◇1		◇1	1	◇1	◇1		1	◇1	◇1	1		◇1	◇1
	🛒				🛒	🛒		🛒			🛒		🍴		🛒	🛒			🛒	🛒			🛒	🛒
London Paddington 15 ⊖ d	12 57		13 12	13 15	13 30	13 42	13 43	13 57	14 12	14 15	14 30		14 42	14 43	14 57	15 03	15 12	15 15	15 30	15 42	15 43		15 57	16 03
Acton Main Line d																								
Ealing Broadway ⊖ d			13 20	13 24			13 50		14 20	14 24				14 50			15 20	15 24			15 50			
West Ealing d																								
Drayton Green d																								
Castle Bar Park d																								
South Greenford d																								
Greenford ⊖ a																								
Hanwell d																								
Southall d			13 24	13 29			13 56		14 24	14 29				14 56			15 24	15 29			15 56			
Hayes & Harlington d			13 28	13 33			14 02		14 28	14 33				15 02			15 28	15 33			16 02			
Heathrow Term 1-2-3 2 ✈ a			13 34						14 34								15 34							
Heathrow Terminal 4 ✈ a			13 41						14 41								15 41							
West Drayton d				13 37			14 06			14 37				15 06				15 37			16 06			
Iver d																								
Langley d				13 42			14 10			14 42				15 10				15 42			16 10			
Slough 3 a				13 46		14 05	14 14			14 46			15 02	15 14				15 46		16 05	16 14			
d				13 46		14 06	14 16			14 46			15 03	15 16				15 46		16 05	16 16			
Burnham d							14 20							15 20				15 51			16 20			
Taplow d																								
Maidenhead 3 d				13 54			14 27			14 54				15 27				15 56			16 27			
Twyford 3 d				14 02			14 35			15 02				15 35				16 04			16 35			
Reading 7 a	13 30			14 10	14 03	14 21	14 43	14 30		15 10	15 04		15 16	15 43	15 30	15 37		16 12	16 03	16 19	16 43		16 31	16 35
Oxford a						14 51	15 28						15 47	16 26						16 50	17 26			

	HC	GW	GW	GW	GW	GW	GW		HC	GW	GW	GW	GW	GW	GW	HC	GW		GW	GW	GW	GW	GW	HC
		1	◇1	◇1	1	◇1	◇1			1	◇1	◇1	1	◇1	◇1		1		◇1	◇1	1	◇1	◇1	
			🛒	🍴		🛒	🛒				🛒	🍴		🛒	🛒				🛒	🛒		🛒	🛒	
London Paddington 15 ⊖ d	16 12	16 15	16 30	16 42	16 43	16 57	17 03		17 12	17 15	17 30	17 42	17 43	17 57	18 03	18 12	18 15		18 30	18 42	18 43	18 55	19 03	19 12
Acton Main Line d																								
Ealing Broadway ⊖ d	16 20	16 24			16 50				17 20	17 24			17 50			18 20	18 24				18 50			19 20
West Ealing d																								
Drayton Green d																								
Castle Bar Park d																								
South Greenford d																								
Greenford ⊖ a																								
Hanwell d																								
Southall d	16 24	16 29			16 56				17 24	17 29			17 56			18 24	18 29				18 56			19 24
Hayes & Harlington d	16 28	16 33			17 02				17 28	17 33			18 02			18 28	18 33				19 02			19 28
Heathrow Term 1-2-3 2 ✈ a	16 34								17 34							18 34								19 34
Heathrow Terminal 4 ✈ a	16 41								17 41							18 41								19 41
West Drayton d		16 37			17 06					17 37			18 06				18 37				19 06			
Iver d																								
Langley d		16 42			17 10					17 42			18 10				18 42				19 10			
Slough 3 a		16 46		17 02	17 14					17 46		18 02	18 14				18 46			19 04	19 14			
d		16 46		17 02	17 16					17 46		18 02	18 16				18 46			19 05	19 16			
Burnham d		16 51			17 20					17 51			18 20				18 51				19 20			
Taplow d																								
Maidenhead 3 d		16 56			17 27					17 56			18 27				18 56				19 27			
Twyford 3 d		17 04			17 35					18 04			18 35				19 04				19 35			
Reading 7 a		17 12	17 03	17 16	17 43	17 30	17 35			18 12	18 03	18 17	18 43	18 30	18 36		19 12		19 03	19 19	19 43	19 28	19 35	
Oxford a				17 47	18 27							18 48	19 26							19 51	20 27			

Table 117

Sundays

from 30 October

London - Greenford and Reading

		GW	GW	GW	GW	GW	HC	GW	GW	GW	GW	GW	HC	GW	GW	GW	GW	HC	GW	GW	GW	GW
		[1]	◇[1]	◇[1]	[1]	◇[1]		[1]	◇[1]	◇[1]	[1]	◇[1]		[1]	◇[1]	◇[1]	[1]		[1]	◇[1]	◇[1]	[1]
																			A			
			⊡	⊡		⊡			⊡			⊡			⊡					⊡		
London Paddington [15] ⊖	d	19 15	19 30	19 42	19 43	19 57	20 12	20 15	20 30	20 42	20 43	20 57	21 12	21 15	21 37	21 42	21 43	22 12	22 15	22 37	22 42	22 43
Acton Main Line	d																					
Ealing Broadway ⊖	d	19 24			19 50		20 20	20 24			20 50		21 20	21 24			21 50	22 20	22 24			22 50
West Ealing	d																					
Drayton Green	d																					
Castle Bar Park	d																					
South Greenford	d																					
Greenford ⊖	a																					
Hanwell	d																					
Southall	d	19 29			19 56		20 24	20 29			20 56		21 24	21 29			21 56	22 24	22 29			22 56
Hayes & Harlington	d	19 33			20 02		20 28	20 33			21 02		21 28	21 33			22 02	22 28	22 33			23 02
Heathrow Term 1-2-3 [2] ✈	a						20 34						21 34					22 34				
Heathrow Terminal 4 ✈	a						20 41						21 41					22 41				
West Drayton	d	19 37			20 06			20 37			21 06			21 37			22 06		22 37			23 06
Iver	d																					
Langley	d	19 42			20 10			20 42			21 10			21 42			22 10		22 42			23 10
Slough [3]	a	19 46		20 04	20 14			20 46		21 01	21 14			21 46		22 02	22 14		22 46		23 01	23 14
	d	19 46		20 05	20 16			20 46		21 01	21 16			21 46		22 03	22 16		22 46		23 01	23 16
Burnham	d	19 51			20 20			20 51			21 20			21 51			22 20		22 50			23 20
Taplow	d																					
Maidenhead [3]	d	19 56			20 27			20 56			21 27			21 56			22 31		22 56			23 24
Twyford [3]	d	20 04			20 35			21 04			21 35			22 04			22 39		23 04			23 32
Reading [7]	a	20 12	20 03	20 20	20 43	20 30		21 12	21 03	21 15	21 43	21 30		22 11	22 12	22 17	22 46		23 11	23 15	23 19	23 43
Oxford	a			20 51	21 26					21 45	22 30					22 48						

		HC	GW	GW	GW	GW
			[1]	◇[1]	◇[1]	[1]
				⊡		
London Paddington [15] ⊖	d	23 12	23 15	23 37	23 47	23 53
Acton Main Line	d					
Ealing Broadway ⊖	d	23 20	23 24		23 55	00 02
West Ealing	d					
Drayton Green	d					
Castle Bar Park	d					
South Greenford	d					
Greenford ⊖	a					
Hanwell	d					
Southall	d	23 24	23 29			00 07
Hayes & Harlington	d	23 28	23 33			00 11
Heathrow Term 1-2-3 [2] ✈	a	23 34				
Heathrow Terminal 4 ✈	a	23 41				
West Drayton	d		23 37			00 15
Iver	d					
Langley	d		23 42			00 20
Slough [3]	a		23 46		00 12	00 24
	d		23 46		00 13	00 24
Burnham	d		23 51			00 28
Taplow	d					
Maidenhead [3]	d		23 56		00 20	00 34
Twyford [3]	d		00 04			00 42
Reading [7]	a		00 14	00 16	00 31	00 49
Oxford	a					

A [1] to Twyford

Reading and Greenford - London

Miles	Miles	Miles			GW MX 1	GW MX 1	GW ◇1 A	GW ◇1 B	GW ◇1 C	GW ◇1 D	GW ◇1 E	GW ◇1 F	HC MO		HC MX	GW 1 F	GW 1 E	GW 1 D	GW MX ◇1	GW MX ◇1	GW 1 D	GW 1 E	GW 1 G		GW 1 H
—	—	—	Oxford	d			22p47	22p47	22p47										23p05				23p15		
0	—	—	**Reading** 7	d	22p46	23p15	23b23	23p23	23b23	23p28	23p28	23p34				23p35	23p35	23p35	23p40	23p55			23p56		00 15
5	—	—	**Twyford** 3	d	22p54	23p22										23p41	23p45	23p45					00 03		00 21
11¾	—	—	**Maidenhead** 3	d	23p02	23p29										23p49	23p53	23p53	23p53				00 11		00 29
13½	—	—	Taplow	d	23p06	23p33																			
15	—	—	Burnham	d	23p09	23p36										23p54	23p58	23p58			←	←	00 15		
17½	—	—	**Slough** 3	a	23p15	23p41	23p43	23p45	23p45							23p58	00 02	00 02	00 01		00 02	00 02	00 20		00 36
—	—	—		d	23p27	23p41	23p44	23p46	23p45							23p59	00 03	00 03	00 01		00 03	00 03	00 20		00 36
19¾	—	—	Langley	d	23p31	23p45										00 03	→	→			00 07	00 07	00 24		00 40
21¼	—	—	Iver	d	23p34	23p48																			
22¾	—	—	West Drayton	d	23p38	23p51										00 12					00 12	00 12	00 29		00 45
—	—	0	**Heathrow Terminal 4** ✈	d									00 01		00 01										
—	—	1¾	**Heathrow Term 1-2-3** 2 ✈	d									00 07		00 07										
25¼	—	5¾	Hayes & Harlington	d	23p43	23p56							00 13		00 13	00 16					00 16	00 17	00 34		00 50
27	—	7½	Southall	d	23p47	23p59							00 16		00 16	00 20					00 20	00 20	00 38		00 53
28¾	—	9¼	Hanwell	d																					
—	0	—	**Greenford** ⊖	d																					
—	1	—	South Greenford	d																					
—	1¾	—	Castle Bar Park	d																					
—	2	—	Drayton Green	d																					
29½	2¾	10	West Ealing	d																					
30¼	3½	11	**Ealing Broadway** ⊖	d	23p52	00 06							00 21		00 22	00 25					00 25	00 26	00 43		00 59
31¾	5	12¼	Acton Main Line	d																					
36	9¼	16½	**London Paddington** 15 ⊖	a	00 03	00 17	00 10	00 04	00 11	00 11	00 16	00 13	00 30		00 30	00 34			00 26	00 33	00 34	00 35	00 52		01 11

		GW 1 G	GW MX 1	GW 1 E	GW 1 G	GW MX 1	GW ◇1 I	GW MX ◇1 J	GW ◇1 I		GW ◇1 K	GW MX 1	GW 1	GW 1	GW MO	GW MX L	GW 1 M	GW 1 N	HC		GW 1	HC	GW 1	GW 1	GW 1
Oxford	d						00 01	00 07				00 27					04 00								05 03
Reading 7	d	00 15	00 15	00 15			00 38	00 39			00 53	01 12	02 24	03 54			04 39	04 39			05 14		05 39		05 44
Twyford 3	d	00 21	00 21	00 22			00 44				00 59	01 18	02 30	04 00			04 45	04 45			05 20		05 45		05 50
Maidenhead 3	d	00 29	00 29	00 30			00 52				01 07	01 26	02 38	04 08			04 53	04 53			05 28		05 53		05 58
Taplow	d		00 32																		05 32				06 02
Burnham	d		00 35		←	←			←												05 35				06 05
Slough 3	a	00 36	00 40	00 37	00 36	00 40	00 59	00 56	00 59		01 14	01 34	02 45	04 15			05 00	05 00			05 40		06 01		06 10
	d	00 40	00 40	00 37	00 40	00 40	00 59	00 57	00 59		01 14	01 34	02 45	04 15			05 00	05 00			05 40		06 01		06 10
Langley	d	→	→	00 41	00 44	00 44	→										05 04	05 04			05 44				06 14
Iver	d																05 07	05 07			05 47				06 17
West Drayton	d			00 47	00 49	00 49							02 52	04 22			05 11	05 11			05 51				06 21
Heathrow Terminal 4 ✈	d																		05 23			05 51			
Heathrow Term 1-2-3 2 ✈	d																		05 29			05 57			
Hayes & Harlington	d			00 52	00 54	00 54			01 08		01 23	01 43	02 57	04 27			05 16	05 16	05 35		05 56	06 03	06 10		06 26
Southall	d			00 55	00 57	00 57							03 00	04 30			05 19	05 19	05 38		05 59	06 06	06 13		06 29
Hanwell	d																		05 41			06 09			
Greenford ⊖	d																							06 16	
South Greenford	d																							06 19	
Castle Bar Park	d																							06 22	
Drayton Green	d																							06 24	
West Ealing	d																		05 43			06 11		06 26	
Ealing Broadway ⊖	d			01 01	01 03	01 03			01 15		01 30	01 50	03 06	04 36			05 28	05 28	05 46		06 05	06 14	06 19	06 29	06 35
Acton Main Line	d																05 31	05 31			06 08			06 33	06 38
London Paddington 15 ⊖	a			01 13	01 14	01 14		01 17	01 24		01 39	02 01	03 18	04 47	05 05	05 25	05 41	05 41	05 56		06 16	06 24	06 32	06 42	06 49

A MO from 27 June until 1 August
B MO from 8 August
C MO until 20 June
D MO from 8 August until 24 October
E MO until 1 August
F MO from 31 October
G MO from 19 September until 24 October
H MO from 8 August until 12 September, MO from 31 October
I MO from 19 September until 17 October
J not 24 May
K MO until 12 September, MO from 24 October
L **The Night Riviera**
M MX until 9 September, from 13 September until 28 October, MX from 1 November
N MO until 12 September, MO from 31 October
b Previous night, arr. 2316

Reading and Greenford - London

		GW	GW	HC	GW		GW	GW	GW	GW	GW	GW	GW	GW	HC		GW	GW	GW	GW	GW	GW	GW	GW	HC
		◇1 ☕	1		1		1	1	1	1	1	◇1	1	1			1	◇1 ☕	1	◇1 ☕	1	1	1	◇1 ☕	
Oxford	d							05 24	05 43			05 59								06 27					
Reading 7	d	05 57	05 59		06 07			06 15	06 16	06 22	06 30	06 31	06 35	06 36				06 44	06 46	06 56			06 57	07 01	
Twyford 3	d				06 13			06 21	06 23		06 36		06 41						06 53				07 03		
Maidenhead 3	d		06 10		06 21			06 29	06 31		06 46	06 43	06 53						07 02	07 08			07 11		
Taplow	d				06 24			06 32					06 57												
Burnham	d				06 27			06 35			06 50		07 01				←					←			
Slough 3	a		06 17		06 32			06 40		06 40	06 55	06 50	07 06				06 55	06 58				07 06	07 19		
	d		06 17		06 32			06 40		06 40	06 56	06 50	07 06				06 56	06 59				07 06	07 20		
Langley	d				06 36			06 44			→		→				06 59					07 11			
Iver	d							06 47									07 03					07 14			
West Drayton	d				06 41			06 51									07 07					07 18			
Heathrow Terminal 4 ✈	d																								
Heathrow Term 1-2-3 2 ✈	d			06 27											06 57										07 27
Hayes & Harlington	d			06 33	06 46			06 56							07 03		07 11					07 23			07 33
Southall	d			06 36	06 50			07 00							07 06		07 15					07 27			07 36
Hanwell	d			06 39											07 09										07 39
Greenford ⊖	d						06 46														07 16				
South Greenford	d						06 49														07 19				
Castle Bar Park	d						06 52														07 22				
Drayton Green	d						06 54														07 24				
West Ealing	d			06 41			06 56								07 11						07 26				07 41
Ealing Broadway ⊖	d			06 44	06 55		06 59	07 05							07 14		07 21				07 29	07 33			07 44
Acton Main Line	d						07 03														07 33				
London Paddington 15 ⊖	a	06 24	06 36	06 54	07 07		07 12	07 18	06 54	07 01		07 08		07 16	07 24		07 32	07 17	07 27	07 29	07 42	07 45	07 49	07 32	07 54

			GW	GW	GW	GW	GW	GW	GW	GW	GW		GW	HC	GW	GW	GW	GW	GW	GW	GW		GW	GW	
			1	◇1	1	1	◇1 ☕	◇1 ☕	1	◇1 ☕	◇1 ☕		1		1	◇1 ☕	◇1 ☕	1	1	◇1 ☕	◇1		1	1	
Oxford	d					06 07				06 56					06 37									07 00	
Reading 7	d		07 02	07 07		07b10	07 15	07 21		07 27	07 30				07 30	07 36	07 39		07 40	07 45				07 55	
Twyford 3	d		07 08			07 16			07 22						07 37				07 46				07 56	08 02	
Maidenhead 3	d		07 16	07 19		07 24			07 31				07 41		07 45				07 54		08 00		08 04	08 11	
Taplow	d					07 28													07 58						
Burnham	d		07 21			07 31									07 51				08 01					08 15	
Slough 3	a		07 26			07 36							07 49		07 55				08 06					08 20	
	d		07 26			07 36							07 50		07 56				08 08					08 20	
Langley	d		07 31			07 41									08 00				08 12						
Iver	d					07 44													08 15						
West Drayton	d		07 35			07 48									08 04				08 19						
Heathrow Terminal 4 ✈	d																								
Heathrow Term 1-2-3 2 ✈	d													07 57											
Hayes & Harlington	d		07 41			07 53								08 03	08 10				08 24						
Southall	d		07 45			07 57								08 06	08 13				08 28						
Hanwell	d													08 09											
Greenford ⊖	d				07 46													08 16							
South Greenford	d				07 49													08 19							
Castle Bar Park	d				07 52													08 22							
Drayton Green	d				07 54													08 24							
West Ealing	d				07 56									08 11				08 26							
Ealing Broadway ⊖	d		07 52		07 59	08 03								08 14	08 18			08 29	08 33						
Acton Main Line	d				08 03													08 33							
London Paddington 15 ⊖	a		08 05	07 40	08 12	08 17	07 44	07 53	07 57	07 59	08 02		08 21	08 24	08 32	08 07	08 09	08 42	08 47	08 14	08 26		08 29	08 52	

		GW	GW	GW	GW	HC	GW		GW	GW	GW	GW	GW		GW	GW	HC		GW	GW	GW	GW	GW		GW
		◇1	◇1	1	◇1		1		1	1	◇1	◇1	1		◇1	1			1	◇1	1	◇1	1		◇1
					A										B							C			
		✕	☕		☕						☕	☕			☕					☕		☕			☕
Oxford	d	07 31											07 21		07 52						08 06		07 56		
Reading 7	d	07 56	08 02	08 06	08 08					08 12	08 14	08 17	08 19		08 23				08 31	08 34	08 38	08 45	08 48		08 52
Twyford 3	d			08a12						08 18			08 26						08 37				08 54		
Maidenhead 3	d									08 26			08 34			08 41			08 45				09 03		
Taplow	d									08 29									08 49						
Burnham	d									08 32									08 50						
Slough 3	a									08 38						08 49			08 57						
	d						08 26			08 38						08 50			08 57						
Langley	d						08 30			08 42									09 01						
Iver	d									08 45									09 04						
West Drayton	d						08 35			08 49									09 08						
Heathrow Terminal 4 ✈	d																								
Heathrow Term 1-2-3 2 ✈	d					08 27											08 57								
Hayes & Harlington	d					08 33	08 39			08 53							09 03		09 13						
Southall	d					08 36	08 43			08 57							09 06		09 17						
Hanwell	d					08 39											09 09								
Greenford ⊖	d								08 46																
South Greenford	d								08 49																
Castle Bar Park	d								08 52																
Drayton Green	d								08 54																
West Ealing	d					08 41			08 56								09 11								
Ealing Broadway ⊖	d					08 44	08 49		08 59	09 03							09 14		09 23						
Acton Main Line	d								09 03																
London Paddington 15 ⊖	a	08 31	08 33		08 38	08 54	09 03		09 12	09 17	08 40	08 44	08 59		08 51	09 22	09 24		09 35	09 00	09 06	09 14	09 27		09 21

A not 30 May
B ☕ from Reading
C The Bristolian
b Arr. 0658

Reading and Greenford - London

		GW	GW		GW	HC	GW	GW	GW	GW	GW	GW	GW		GW	GW	GW	GW	GW	HC	GW	GW	GW		GW
		◇1	1		1		1	◇1	◇1	1	1	◇1	1		◇1	1	◇1	◇1	◇1		1	1	◇1		◇1
												A													
		☕						☕	☕			☕			☕		☕		☕						☕
Oxford	d						08 21					08 51				08 36		09 01					09 31		
Reading [7]	d	09 02					09 03	09 08	09 15		09 17	09 18	09 21		09 27	09b33	09 34	09 37	09 45			09 48	09 55		10 02
Twyford [3]	d						09 09				09 24					09 39						09 54			
Maidenhead [3]	d						09 17				09 33					09 47						10 02			
Taplow	d						09 21				09 36											10 06			
Burnham	d						09 24				09 39										←	10 09			
Slough [3]	a						09 29				09 44					09 54		09 52			09 54	10 14	10 10		
	d				09 14		09 29				09 44					09 54		09 52			09 54	10 14	10 11		
Langley	d						09 33									→					09 58	→			
Iver	d						09 36														10 01				
West Drayton	d				09 21		09 40				09 51										10 05				
Heathrow Terminal 4 ✈	d																								
Heathrow Term 1-2-3 [2] ✈	d					09 27														09 57					
Hayes & Harlington	d				09 26	09 33	09 45				09 56									10 03	10 10				
Southall	d				09 30	09 36	09 48													10 06	10 13				
Hanwell	d					09 39														10 09					
Greenford ⊖	d		09 16							09 46															
South Greenford	d		09 19							09 49															
Castle Bar Park	d		09 22							09 52															
Drayton Green	d		09 24							09 54															
West Ealing	d		09 26			09 41				09 56										10 11					
Ealing Broadway ⊖	d		09 29		09 36	09 44	09 54			09 59	10 03									10 14	10 19				
Acton Main Line	d		09 33							10 03															
London Paddington [15] ⊖	a	09 29	09 42		09 48	09 54	10 04	09 39	09 44	10 12	10 16	09 47	09 56		09 59		10 02	10 12	10 15	10 24	10 32		10 29		10 32

		GW	GW	HC	GW		GW	GW	GW		GW	GW	GW	GW	GW	GW	GW	HC	GW		GW		GW	GW	GW
		1	1		1		◇1	◇1	1		1	◇1	◇1	◇1	◇1	1	1		1		1		◇1	1	◇1
												B	C	B	C				C		B				
							☕	☕					🛒	☕	☕								☕		☕
Oxford	d				09 07							10 01	10 01						09 36		09 37				
Reading [7]	d				10c03		10 08	10 12	10 18		10 18	10 25	10 25	10 32	10 32				10 33		10 33		10 45	10 48	10 52
Twyford [3]	d				10 09						10 24								10 39		10 39			10 54	
Maidenhead [3]	d				10 17						10 32								10 47		10 47			11 02	
Taplow	d										10 36													11 06	
Burnham	d		←								10 39						←							11 09	
Slough [3]	a		10 14		10 24						10 44	10 39	10 39				10 44		10 54		10 54			11 14	
	d		10 14		10 24						10 44	10 40	10 40				10 44		10 54		10 54			11 14	
Langley	d				10 28						→								10 58		10 58			→	
Iver	d				10 31														11 01		11 01				
West Drayton	d		10 21		10 35												10 51		11 05		11 05				
Heathrow Terminal 4 ✈	d																								
Heathrow Term 1-2-3 [2] ✈	d			10 27														10 57							
Hayes & Harlington	d		10 26	10 33	10 40												10 56	11 03	11 10		11 10				
Southall	d			10 36	10 43													11 06	11 13		11 13				
Hanwell	d			10 39														11 09							
Greenford ⊖	d	10 16														10 46									
South Greenford	d	10 19														10 49									
Castle Bar Park	d	10 22														10 52									
Drayton Green	d	10 24														10 54									
West Ealing	d	10 26		10 41												10 56		11 11							
Ealing Broadway ⊖	d	10 29	10 33	10 44	10 49											10 59	11 03	11 14	11 19		11 19				
Acton Main Line	d	10 33														11 03									
London Paddington [15] ⊖	a	10 42	10 46	10 54	11 02		10 37	10 39	10 54			10 58	11 00	11 01	11 07	11 12	11 16	11 24	11 31		11 31		11 14		11 24

		GW	GW	GW	GW		HC	GW	GW		GW	GW	GW	GW	GW		GW	GW	HC	GW	GW	GW	GW	GW	GW
		◇1	◇1	1	1			1	1		◇1	1	1	◇1	◇1		1	1		1	1	◇1	1	◇1	◇1
			D					C	B											C	B				
		🛒	☕								☕			🛒	☕							☕		☕	🛒
Oxford	d	10 31						10 08	10 07					11 01						10 36	10 37				11 31
Reading [7]	d	10 55	11 02					11 03	11 03		11 09	11 18	11 18	11 25	11 32					11e33	11e33	11 44	11 48	11 52	11 55
Twyford [3]	d							11 09	11 09				11 24							11 39	11 39		11 54		
Maidenhead [3]	d							11 17	11 17				11 32							11 47	11 47		12 02		
Taplow	d												11 36										12 06		
Burnham	d				←								11 39					←					12 09		
Slough [3]	a	11 09			11 14			11 24	11 24				11 44	11 39				11 44		11 54	11 54		12 14		12 09
	d	11 10			11 14			11 24	11 24				11 44	11 40				11 44		11 54	11 54		12 14		12 10
Langley	d							11 28	11 28				→							11 58	11 58		→		
Iver	d							11 31	11 31											12 01	12 01				
West Drayton	d				11 21			11 35	11 35									11 51		12 05	12 05				
Heathrow Terminal 4 ✈	d																								
Heathrow Term 1-2-3 [2] ✈	d						11 27												11 57						
Hayes & Harlington	d				11 26		11 33	11 40	11 40									11 56	12 03	12 10	12 10				
Southall	d						11 36	11 43	11 43										12 06	12 13	12 13				
Hanwell	d						11 39												12 09						
Greenford ⊖	d			11 16													11 46								
South Greenford	d			11 19													11 49								
Castle Bar Park	d			11 22													11 52								
Drayton Green	d			11 24													11 54								
West Ealing	d			11 26			11 41										11 56		12 11						
Ealing Broadway ⊖	d			11 29	11 33		11 44	11 49	11 49								11 59	12 03	12 14	12 19	12 19				
Acton Main Line	d			11 33													12 03								
London Paddington [15] ⊖	a	11 29	11 32	11 42	11 46		11 54	12 01	12 04		11 38	11 55		11 59	12 02		12 12	12 16	12 24	12 31	12 31	12 14		12 23	12 29

A ☕ from Reading
B until 9 September
C from 12 September

D The Red Dragon
b Arr. 0927
c Arr. 0957

e Arr. 1127

Table 117

Reading and Greenford - London

			GW	GW	GW	HC	GW		GW	GW	GW		GW	GW	GW	GW	GW	GW	GW	HC	GW			GW	GW
			◇1	1	1		1		◇1	◇1	1		1	◇1	◇1	◇1	◇1	1	1		1			◇1	1
														A	B	A	B								
			⊏P						⊏P	⊏P				Ɪo	Ɪo	⊏P	⊏P							⊏P	
Oxford	d						11 07							12 01	12 01						11 37				
Reading 7	d		12 02				12 03		12 08	12 12	12 18		12 18	12 25	12 25	12 32	12 32				12b33			12 44	12 48
Twyford 3	d						12 09						12 24								12 39				12 54
Maidenhead 3	d						12 17						12 32								12 47				13 02
Taplow	d												12 36												13 06
Burnham	d				←								12 39						←						13 09
Slough 3	a				12 14		12 24						12 44	12 39	12 39				12 44		12 54				13 14
	d				12 14		12 24						12 44	12 40	12 40				12 44		12 54				13 14
Langley	d						12 28						→								12 58				→
Iver	d						12 31														13 01				
West Drayton	d				12 21		12 35												12 51		13 05				
Heathrow Terminal 4 ✈	d																								
Heathrow Term 1-2-3 2 ✈	d					12 27														12 57					
Hayes & Harlington	d				12 26	12 33	12 40												12 56	13 03	13 10				
Southall	d					12 36	12 43													13 06	13 13				
Hanwell	d					12 39														13 09					
Greenford ⊖	d			12 16														12 46							
South Greenford	d			12 19														12 49							
Castle Bar Park	d			12 22														12 52							
Drayton Green	d			12 24														12 54							
West Ealing	d			12 26		12 41												12 56		13 11					
Ealing Broadway ⊖	d			12 29	12 33	12 44	12 49											12 59	13 03	13 14	13 19				
Acton Main Line	d			12 33														13 03							
London Paddington 15 ⊖	a		12 32	12 42	12 46	12 54	13 03		12 37	12 40	12 52			12 57	13 00	13 00	13 06	13 12	13 16	13 24	13 32			13 14	

		GW	GW	GW	GW	HC	GW			GW	GW	GW	GW	GW	GW	GW	GW		HC	GW	GW	GW	GW	GW	GW
											R														
		◇1	◇1	1	1		1			◇1	1	1	◇1	1	◇1	1	1			1	◇1	1	◇1	◇1	1
											C													D	
		Ɪo	⊏P							⊏P	⊏P		Ɪo		⊏P						⊏P		Ɪo	⊏P	
Oxford	d	12 31					12 07						13 01							12 37			13 31		
Reading 7	d	12 55	13 02				13c03			13 09	13 17	13 18	13 25	13 29	13 32					13 33	13 44	13 48	13 55	14 02	
Twyford 3	d						13 09					13 24								13 39		13 54			
Maidenhead 3	d						13 17					13 32								13 47		14 02			
Taplow	d											13 36										14 06			
Burnham	d				←							13 39					←					14 09			
Slough 3	a	13 09			13 14		13 24					13 44	13 39				13 44			13 54		14 14	14 09		
	d	13 10			13 14		13 24					13 44	13 40				13 44			13 54		14 14	14 10		
Langley	d						13 28					→								13 58		→			
Iver	d						13 31													14 01					
West Drayton	d				13 21		13 35										13 51			14 05					
Heathrow Terminal 4 ✈	d																								
Heathrow Term 1-2-3 2 ✈	d					13 27													13 57						
Hayes & Harlington	d				13 26	13 33	13 40										13 56		14 03	14 10					
Southall	d					13 36	13 43												14 06	14 13					
Hanwell	d					13 39													14 09						
Greenford ⊖	d			13 16												13 46									14 16
South Greenford	d			13 19												13 49									14 19
Castle Bar Park	d			13 22												13 52									14 22
Drayton Green	d			13 24												13 54									14 24
West Ealing	d			13 26		13 41										13 56			14 11						14 26
Ealing Broadway ⊖	d			13 29	13 33	13 44	13 49									13 59	14 03		14 14	14 19					14 29
Acton Main Line	d			13 33												14 03									14 33
London Paddington 15 ⊖	a	13 29	13 32	13 42	13 46	13 54	14 02			13 38	13 44		14 01	14 09	14 06	14 12	14 16		14 24	14 32	14 14		14 29	14 32	14 42

		GW	HC		GW		GW	GW	GW	GW	GW	GW	GW		GW	HC	GW		GW	GW	GW	GW	GW		GW
																					R				
		1			1		◇1	◇1	◇1	1	◇1	◇1	1		1		1		◇1	1	1	◇1	◇1		1
							⊏P	⊏P	⊏P		Ɪo	⊏P							⊏P		⊏P		⊏P		
Oxford	d				13 07						14 01						13 37					14 31			
Reading 7	d				14 03		14 08	14 12	14 17	14 18	14 25	14 32					14e33		14 44	14 48	14 52	14 55	15 02		
Twyford 3	d				14 09					14 24							14 39			14 54					
Maidenhead 3	d				14 17					14 32							14 47			15 02					
Taplow	d									14 36										15 06					
Burnham	d	←								14 39					←					15 09					
Slough 3	a	14 14			14 24					14 44	14 39				14 44		14 54			15 14		15 09			
	d	14 14			14 24					14 44	14 40				14 44		14 54			15 14		15 10			
Langley	d				14 28					→							14 58			→					
Iver	d				14 31												15 01								
West Drayton	d	14 21			14 35										14 51		15 05								
Heathrow Terminal 4 ✈	d																								
Heathrow Term 1-2-3 2 ✈	d		14 27													14 57									
Hayes & Harlington	d	14 26	14 33		14 40										14 56	15 03	15 10								
Southall	d		14 36		14 43											15 06	15 13								
Hanwell	d		14 39													15 09									
Greenford ⊖	d												14 46												15 16
South Greenford	d												14 49												15 19
Castle Bar Park	d												14 52												15 22
Drayton Green	d												14 54												15 24
West Ealing	d		14 41										14 56			15 11									15 26
Ealing Broadway ⊖	d	14 33	14 44		14 49								14 59		15 03	15 14	15 19								15 29
Acton Main Line	d												15 03												15 33
London Paddington 15 ⊖	a	14 46	14 54		15 02		14 37	14 40	14 44		15 00	15 08	15 12		15 16	15 24	15 33		15 14		15 24	15 29	15 32		15 42

A from 12 September
B until 9 September
C The Cornish Riviera
D The St. David
b Arr. 1227
c Arr. 1257
e Arr. 1427

Table 117

Reading and Greenford - London

		GW 1	HC	GW 1		GW ◇1 ☕	GW 1	GW 1	GW ◇1 🛒		GW ◇1 ☕	GW 1	GW 1	HC	GW 1	GW ◇1 ☕	GW 1	GW ◇1 A ☕	GW ◇1 ☕		GW ◇1 ☕	GW 1	GW 1	HC	GW 1
Oxford	d			14 07					15 01						14 37				15 31						15 07
Reading 7	d			15 03		15 09	15 18	15 18	15 25		15 32				15b33	15 44	15 48	15 52	15 55		16 02				16 03
Twyford 3	d			15 09				15 24							15 39		15 54								16 09
Maidenhead 3	d			15 17				15 32							15 47		16 02								16 17
Taplow	d							15 36									16 06								
Burnham	d	←						15 39					←				16 09						←		
Slough 3	a	15 14		15 24				15 44	15 39				15 44		15 54		16 14		16 09				16 14		16 24
	d	15 14		15 24				15 44	15 40				15 44		15 54		16 14		16 10				16 14		16 24
								→									→								
Langley	d			15 28											15 58										16 28
Iver	d			15 31											16 01										16 31
West Drayton	d	15 21		15 35									15 51		16 05								16 21		16 35
Heathrow Terminal 4 ✈	d																								
Heathrow Term 1-2-3 2 ✈	d		15 27											15 57										16 27	
Hayes & Harlington	d	15 26	15 33	15 40									15 56	16 03	16 10								16 26	16 33	16 40
Southall	d		15 36	15 43										16 06	16 13									16 36	16 43
Hanwell	d		15 39											16 09										16 39	
Greenford ⊖	d											15 46										16 16			
South Greenford	d											15 49										16 19			
Castle Bar Park	d											15 52										16 22			
Drayton Green	d											15 54										16 24			
West Ealing	d		15 41									15 56		16 11								16 26		16 41	
Ealing Broadway ⊖	d	15 33	15 44	15 49								15 59	16 03	16 14	16 19							16 29	16 33	16 44	16 49
Acton Main Line	d											16 03										16 33			
London Paddington 15 ⊖	a	15 46	15 54	16 03		15 38	15 54		16 01		16 09	16 12	16 17	16 24	16 31	16 14		16 22	16 27		16 30	16 42	16 46	16 54	17 02

			GW ◇1 B ☕	GW ◇1 ☕	GW 1		GW 1	GW 1 C 🛒	GW 1 D	GW 1	GW 1	HC	GW 1		GW ◇1 ☕		GW ◇1 ☕	GW 1	GW ◇1 E ☕	GW ◇1 D 🛒	GW ◇1 C	GW ◇1 ☕	GW 1	GW 1	HC
Oxford	d							16 01	16 01				15 37							16 31	16 31				
Reading 7	d		16 08	16 15	16 18		16 19	16 25	16 25				16c33		16 34		16 44	16 48	16 52	16 55	16 55	17 02			
Twyford 3	d				16 24								16 39					16 54							
Maidenhead 3	d				16 32								16 47					17 02							
Taplow	d				16 36													17 06							
Burnham	d				16 39						←							17 09						←	
Slough 3	a				16 44			16 40	16 40		16 44		16 54					17 14		17 09	17 09			17 14	
	d				16 44			16 40	16 40		16 44		16 54					17 14		17 10	17 10			17 14	
					→													→							
Langley	d												16 58												
Iver	d												17 01												
West Drayton	d										16 51		17 05											17 21	
Heathrow Terminal 4 ✈	d																								
Heathrow Term 1-2-3 2 ✈	d											16 57													17 27
Hayes & Harlington	d										16 56	17 03	17 10											17 26	17 33
Southall	d											17 06	17 13												17 36
Hanwell	d											17 09													17 39
Greenford ⊖	d									16 46													17 16		
South Greenford	d									16 49													17 19		
Castle Bar Park	d									16 52													17 22		
Drayton Green	d									16 54													17 24		
West Ealing	d									16 56		17 11											17 26		17 41
Ealing Broadway ⊖	d									16 59	17 03	17 14	17 21										17 29	17 33	17 44
Acton Main Line	d									17 03													17 33		
London Paddington 15 ⊖	a		16 39	16 44			16 57	17 00	17 00	17 12	17 19	17 24	17 32		17 09		17 14		17 24	17 34	17 34	17 30	17 42	17 48	17 54

			GW 1		GW ◇1 F ☕	GW ◇1 ☕	GW 1	GW 1 🛒	GW ◇1 ☕	GW 1	GW 1		HC	GW 1	GW 1	GW ◇1 ☕	GW ◇1 G ☕	GW ◇1 H ☕	GW 1	GW ◇1 C ☕	GW ◇1 D ☕		GW 1	GW 1	HC
Oxford	d		16 07					17 01						16 37						17 31					
Reading 7	d		17 03		17 09	17 17	17 17	17 25	17 32					17 33	17 42	17 44	17 51	17 52	17 54	17 56	17 58				
Twyford 3	d		17 09				17 24							17 39	17 48										
Maidenhead 3	d		17 17			17 29	17 32							17 47	17 56				18 08						
Taplow	d						17 36								18 00										
Burnham	d						17 39				←				18 02									←	
Slough 3	a		17 24				17 44	17 39			17 44			17 54	18 07				18 14	18 10				18 14	
	d		17 24				17 44	17 40			17 44			17 54	18 07				18 14	18 11				18 14	
							→												→						
Langley	d		17 28											17 58											
Iver	d		17 31											18 01											
West Drayton	d		17 35								17 51			18 05	18 14										
Heathrow Terminal 4 ✈	d																								
Heathrow Term 1-2-3 2 ✈	d												17 57												18 27
Hayes & Harlington	d		17 40								17 56		18 03	18 10	18 19									18 26	18 33
Southall	d		17 43										18 06	18 13											18 36
Hanwell	d												18 09												18 39
Greenford ⊖	d									17 46													18 16		
South Greenford	d									17 49													18 19		
Castle Bar Park	d									17 52													18 22		
Drayton Green	d									17 54													18 24		
West Ealing	d									17 56			18 11										18 26		18 41
Ealing Broadway ⊖	d		17 49							17 59	18 03		18 14	18 19	18 26								18 29	18 33	18 44
Acton Main Line	d									18 03													18 33		
London Paddington 15 ⊖	a		18 02		17 39	17 54		17 59	18 02	18 12	18 14		18 24	18 32	18 37	18 14	18 21	18 21		18 28	18 24		18 42	18 47	18 54

A Restaurant available for customers joining until Castle Cary
B The Cheltenham Spa Express
C from 12 September
D until 9 September
E The Torbay Express
F The Merchant Venturer
G from 12 September. The Mayflower
H until 9 September. The Mayflower
b Arr. 1527
c Arr. 1627

Reading and Greenford - London

		GW	GW	GW	GW	GW	GW	GW	GW	GW	GW	GW	GW	HC	GW	GW	GW	GW	GW	GW	GW
		1	◇1	◇1	◇1	◇1	1	1	1	1	◇1	1	1		1	1	◇1	1	◇1	1	◇1
			A	B											A	B			C		
			☕	☕	☕	☕				🛒	☕						☕		☕		☕
Oxford	d	17 07		17 36						18 01					17 37	17 31				18 31	
Reading 7	d	18 00	18 01	18 02	18 08	18 12		18 18	18 22	18 25	18 32				18b33	18b33	18 45	18 48	18 51	18 55	19 02
Twyford 3	d	18 10						18 24							18 39	18 39		18 54			
Maidenhead 3	d	18 17					18 26	18 32							18 48	18 48		19 05			
Taplow	d							18 35										19 09			
Burnham	d							18 39					←					19 12			
Slough 3	a	18 24					18 33	18 44		18 39			18 44		18 54	18 54		19 17		19 09	
	d	18 24					18 33	18 44		18 40			18 44		18 54	18 54		19 17		19 10	
Langley	d	18 28						→							18 58	18 58		→			
Iver	d	18 32													19 01	19 01					
West Drayton	d	18 35											18 51		19 05	19 05					
Heathrow Terminal 4 ✈	d																				
Heathrow Term 1-2-3 2 ✈	d													18 57							
Hayes & Harlington	d	18 40					18 45						18 56	19 03	19 10	19 10					
Southall	d	18 43												19 06	19 13	19 13					
Hanwell	d													19 09							
Greenford ⊖	d											18 46									
South Greenford	d											18 49									
Castle Bar Park	d											18 52									
Drayton Green	d											18 54									
West Ealing	d											18 56		19 11							
Ealing Broadway ⊖	d	18 49					18 54					18 59	19 05	19 14	19 19	19 19					
Acton Main Line	d											19 03									
London Paddington 15 ⊖	a	19 01	18 30	18 30	18 39	18 44	19 04		18 54	18 59	19 02	19 12	19 18	19 24	19 31	19 32	19 14		19 24	19 31	19 32

		GW	GW	HC	GW	GW	GW	GW	GW	GW	GW	HC	GW	GW	GW	GW	GW	GW	GW	GW	HC
		1	1		1	◇1	1	1	1	◇1	◇1		1	1	◇1	1	◇1	◇1	1	1	
													D				E	F			
						☕				☕	🛒				☕						
Oxford	d				18 07						19 06		18 37	18 37			19 31	19 31			
Reading 7	d				19 03	19 09	19 18		19 18	19 25	19 32		19c33	19c33	19 45	19 48	19 54	19 54			
Twyford 3	d				19 09				19 24				19 39	19 42		19 54					
Maidenhead 3	d				19 21				19 32				19 47	19 50		20 02					
Taplow	d								19 36							20 06					
Burnham	d		←						19 39							20 09				←	
Slough 3	a		19 17		19 29				19 44		19 47		19 54	19 57		20 14	20 09	20 09		20 14	
	d		19 17		19 29				19 44		19 47		19 54	19 57		20 14	20 10	20 10		20 14	
Langley	d				19 33								19 58	20 01		→					
Iver	d				19 36								20 01	20 04							
West Drayton	d		19 24		19 39				19 51				20 05	20 08						20 21	
Heathrow Terminal 4 ✈	d																				
Heathrow Term 1-2-3 2 ✈	d			19 27								19 57									20 27
Hayes & Harlington	d		19 29	19 33	19 44				19 56			20 03	20 10	20 13						20 26	20 33
Southall	d			19 36	19 47							20 06	20 13	20 16							20 36
Hanwell	d			19 39								20 09									20 39
Greenford ⊖	d	19 16						19 46											20 16		
South Greenford	d	19 19						19 49											20 19		
Castle Bar Park	d	19 22						19 52											20 22		
Drayton Green	d	19 24						19 54											20 24		
West Ealing	d	19 26		19 41				19 56				20 11							20 26		20 41
Ealing Broadway ⊖	d	19 29	19 36	19 44	19 53			19 59	20 03			20 14	20 19	20 22					20 29	20 33	20 44
Acton Main Line	d	19 33						20 03											20 33		
London Paddington 15 ⊖	a	19 42	19 45	19 54	20 03	19 38	19 54	20 12	20 16	19 54	20 06	20 24	20 32	20 32	20 14		20 27	20 29	20 42	20 49	20 54

A from 12 September
B until 9 September
C The Royal Duchy
D 30 May
E until 7 July, FX from 11 July until 1 September, from 5 September
F FO from 8 July until 2 September
b Arr. 1827
c Arr. 1927

Reading and Greenford - London

		GW	GW FX	GW FO	GW	GW	GW	GW	GW	GW	GW	GW	HC	GW	GW	GW	GW	GW	GW	GW	GW	GW
		[1]	◇[1]	◇[1]	◇[1]	◇[1]	◇[1]	[1]	◇	◇[1]	[1]	[1]		[1]	[1]	◇[1]	[1]	◇[1]	◇[1]	◇[1]	[1]	[1]
					A	B			C													
			☕	☕	☕	☕	☕		☕							☕		☕	☕	☕		
Oxford	d	19 01								20 01				19 37					20 31			
Reading [7]	d	19 58	20 02	20 02	20 08	20 08	20 15	20 18	20 22	20 25				20b33	20 34	20 45	20 48	20 52	20 55	21 02		
Twyford [3]	d	20 04						20 24						20 39			20 54					
Maidenhead [3]	d	20 12						20 32						20 47			21 02					
Taplow	d							20 36									21 06					
Burnham	d							20 39				←					21 09					←
Slough [3]	a	20 19						20 44		20 39		20 44		20 54			21 13		21 09			21 13
	d	20 24						20 44		20 40		20 44		20 54			21 14		21 10			21 14
Langley	d	20 28						→						20 58			→					21 17
Iver	d	20 31												21 01								21 20
West Drayton	d	20 35										20 51		21 05								21 24
Heathrow Terminal 4 ✈	d																					
Heathrow Term 1-2-3 [2] ✈	d												20 57									
Hayes & Harlington	d	20 40										20 56	21 03	21 10								21 28
Southall	d	20 43											21 06	21 13								
Hanwell	d												21 09									
Greenford ⊖	d										20 46										21 16	
South Greenford	d										20 49										21 19	
Castle Bar Park	d										20 52										21 22	
Drayton Green	d										20 54										21 24	
West Ealing	d										20 56		21 11								21 26	
Ealing Broadway ⊖	d	20 49									20 59	21 03	21 14	21 19							21 29	21 35
Acton Main Line	d										21 03										21 33	
London Paddington [15] ⊖	a	21 00	20 30	20 32	20 39	20 39	20 46		20 52	21 01	21 12	21 15	21 24	21 31	21 08	21 14		21 21	21 29	21 32	21 42	21 48

		HC	GW	GW	GW	HC	GW	GW	GW	GW	GW	HC	GW	GW FO	HC	GW FX	GW	GW FO	GW FX
			[1]	[1]	◇[1]		[1]	◇[1]	◇[1]	◇[1]	◇[1]		[1]	◇		◇[1]	[1]	◇[1]	◇[1]
																D			
								☕	☕		☕								
Oxford	d			20 07	21 01		20 37			21 31				22 11		22 11		22 34	22 34
Reading [7]	d			21c14	21 25		21 33	21 44	22 01	22 06	22 11		22 15	22 46		22 46	22 46	22 59	22 59
Twyford [3]	d			21 20			21 39						22 22				22 54		
Maidenhead [3]	d			21 28			21 47						22 30				23 02		
Taplow	d			21 32			21 50						22 33				23 06		
Burnham	d			21 35			21 53						22 36				23 09		
Slough [3]	a			21 40	21 39		21 58			22 22			22 41	23 02		23 02	23 15	23 12	23 18
	d			21 40	21 40		21 59			22 22			22 41	23 02		23 02	23 27	23 13	23 19
Langley	d			21 44			22 02						22 45				→		
Iver	d			21 47			22 05						22 48						
West Drayton	d			21 51			22 09						22 51						
Heathrow Terminal 4 ✈	d																		
Heathrow Term 1-2-3 [2] ✈	d	21 27				21 57						22 27			22 57				
Hayes & Harlington	d	21 33		21 56		22 03	22 14					22 33	22 56		23 03				
Southall	d	21 36		21 59		22 06						22 36	23 00		23 06				
Hanwell	d	21 39				22 09						22 39			23 09				
Greenford ⊖	d		21 46																
South Greenford	d		21 49																
Castle Bar Park	d		21 52																
Drayton Green	d		21 54																
West Ealing	d	21 41	21 56			22 11						22 41			23 11				
Ealing Broadway ⊖	d	21 44	21 59	22 05		22 14	22 21					22 44	23 05		23 14				
Acton Main Line	d		22 03																
London Paddington [15] ⊖	a	21 54	22 13	22 18	22 00	22 24	22 33	22 14	22 30	22 43	22 45	22 54	23 17	23 21	23 24	23 25		23 30	23 37

		GW FO	GW FX	GW FX	GW FO	HC	GW	GW	GW FO	GW FX	GW FO	GW FX
		◇[1]	◇[1]	◇[1]	◇[1]		[1]	[1]	◇[1]	◇[1]	◇[1]	◇[1]
		☕	☕	☕	☕						☕	☕
Oxford	d								23 05	23 05		
Reading [7]	d	23 05	23 05	23 07	23 08			23 15	23 35	23 40	23 55	23 55
Twyford [3]	d							23 22				
Maidenhead [3]	d							23 29	23 47	23 53		
Taplow	d							23 33				
Burnham	d						←	23 36				
Slough [3]	a						23 15	23 41	23 54	00 01		
	d						23 27	23 41	23 55	00 01		
Langley	d						23 31	23 45				
Iver	d						23 34	23 48				
West Drayton	d						23 38	23 51				
Heathrow Terminal 4 ✈	d											
Heathrow Term 1-2-3 [2] ✈	d					23 27						
Hayes & Harlington	d					23 33	23 43	23 56				
Southall	d					23 36	23 47	23 59				
Hanwell	d					23 39						
Greenford ⊖	d											
South Greenford	d											
Castle Bar Park	d											
Drayton Green	d											
West Ealing	d					23 41						
Ealing Broadway ⊖	d					23 44	23 52	00 06				
Acton Main Line	d											
London Paddington [15] ⊖	a	23 36	23 40	23 50	23 42	23 54	00 03	00 17	00 22	00 26	00 27	00 33

A from 4 July until 2 September. The Atlantic Coast Express
B until 1 July, from 5 September
C FO from 8 July until 2 September
D [1] from Reading ◇ from Reading
b Arr. 2027
c Arr. 2058

Table 117

Reading and Greenford - London

Station		GW	GW	GW	GW	HC	GW	GW	GW	GW				GW	HC	GW	HC	GW	GW	GW		HC	GW	GW	GW
		1	1	◇1	◇1 ☕		1	◇1	1	1				1		1		1	1	1			1	1	1
Oxford	d			23p05				00 07	00 27					03 59									05 14		
Reading 7	d	22p46	23p15	23p35	23p55		00 15	00 39	01 12	04 10				04b40		05 10		05 33		05 48			06c03		06 18
Twyford 3	d	22p54	23p22				00 21		01 18	04 16				04 46		05 16		05 39		05 54			06 09		06 24
Maidenhead 3	d	23p02	23p29	23p47			00 29		01 26	04 24				04 54		05 24		05 47		06 02			06 17		06 32
Taplow	d	23p06	23p33				00 32									05 28				06 06					06 36
Burnham	d	23p09	23p36				00 35									05 31				06 09					06 39
Slough 3	a	23p15	23p41	23p54			00 40	00 53	01 34	04 31				05 01		05 35		05 54		06 14			06 24		06 44
	d	23p27	23p41	23p55			00 40	00 53	01 34	04 32				05 02		05 36		05 54		06 14			06 24		06 44
Langley	d	23p31	23p45				00 44									05 40		05 58					06 28		
Iver	d	23p34	23p48													05 43		06 01					06 31		
West Drayton	d	23p38	23p51				00 49			04 38						05 45		06 05		06 21			06 35		06 51
Heathrow Terminal 4 ✈	d					00 01									05 23		05 51								
Heathrow Term 1-2-3 2 ✈	d					00 07									05 29		05 57					06 27			
Hayes & Harlington	d	23p43	23p56			00 13	00 54		01 43	04 43				05 11	05 35	05 51	06 03	06 10		06 26		06 33	06 40		06 56
Southall	d	23p47	23p59			00 16	00 57			04 46				05 14	05 38	05 54	06 06	06 13				06 36	06 43		
Hanwell	d														05 41		06 09					06 39			
Greenford ⊖	d																		06 16					06 46	
South Greenford	d																		06 19					06 49	
Castle Bar Park	d																		06 22					06 52	
Drayton Green	d																		06 24					06 54	
West Ealing	d														05 43		06 11		06 26			06 41		06 56	
Ealing Broadway ⊖	d	23p52	00 06			00 21	01 03		01 50	04 52				05 20	05 46	06 00	06 14	06 19	06 29	06 33		06 44	06 49	06 59	07 03
Acton Main Line	d													05 23		06 03			06 33					07 03	
London Paddington 15 ⊖	a	00 03	00 17	00 22	00 27	00 30	01 14	01 11	02 01	05 01				05 31	05 56	06 11	06 24	06 31	06 42	06 46		06 54	07 01	07 12	07 16

Station		HC	GW	GW	GW	GW		GW	GW	HC	GW	GW	GW	GW	GW	GW		GW	GW	HC	GW	GW	GW	GW	GW
			1	◇1 ☕	1	1		1	◇1		1	◇1 ☕	1	1	◇1	◇1 ☕		1	1		1	◇1 ☕	1	◇1 ☕	◇1 ☕
Oxford	d		05 49						06 31		06 07				07 01						06 42			07 31	
Reading 7	d		06e33	06 45		06 48		06 52	07 00		07f03	07 15	07 18	07 21	07 27	07 32					07g33	07 46	07 48	07 54	08 02
Twyford 3	d		06 39			06 54					07 09		07 24								07 39		07 54		
Maidenhead 3	d		06 47			07 02					07 17		07 32								07 47		08 02		
Taplow	d					07 06							07 36										08 06		
Burnham	d					07 09							07 39						←				08 09		
Slough 3	a		06 54			07 14			07 16		07 24		07 44		07 42				07 44		07 54		08 14	08 09	
	d		06 54			07 14			07 17		07 24		07 44		07 42				07 44		07 54		08 14	08 09	
Langley	d		06 58								07 28		→								07 58		→		
Iver	d		07 01								07 31										08 01				
West Drayton	d		07 05			07 21					07 35								07 51		08 05				
Heathrow Terminal 4 ✈	d																								
Heathrow Term 1-2-3 2 ✈	d	06 57								07 27										07 57					
Hayes & Harlington	d	07 03	07 10			07 26				07 33	07 40								07 56	08 03	08 10				
Southall	d	07 06	07 13							07 36	07 43									08 06	08 13				
Hanwell	d	07 09								07 39										08 09					
Greenford ⊖	d				07 16													07 46							
South Greenford	d				07 19													07 49							
Castle Bar Park	d				07 22													07 52							
Drayton Green	d				07 24													07 54							
West Ealing	d	07 11			07 26					07 41								07 56		08 11					
Ealing Broadway ⊖	d	07 14	07 19		07 29	07 33				07 44	07 49							07 59	08 03	08 14	08 19				
Acton Main Line	d				07 33													08 03							
London Paddington 15 ⊖	a	07 24	07 31	07 14	07 42	07 46		07 22	07 37	07 54	08 01	07 44		07 54	08 01	08 07		08 12	08 16	08 24	08 31	08 14		08 29	08 32

Station		GW		GW	HC	GW		GW	GW	GW	GW	GW		GW	GW	HC	GW		GW	GW	GW	GW		GW	GW
		1		1		1		◇1 ☕	1	1	◇1	◇1 ☕		1	1		1		◇1 ☕	1	◇1 ☕	◇1 ☕		◇1 ☕	1
Oxford	d					07 07					08 01						07 37					08 31			
Reading 7	d					08 03		08 16	08 18	08 20	08 26	08 32					08h33		08 46	08 48	08 52	08 55		09 02	
Twyford 3	d					08 09			08 24								08 39			08 54					
Maidenhead 3	d					08 17			08 32								08 47			09 02					
Taplow	d								08 36											09 06					
Burnham	d			←					08 39						←					09 09					
Slough 3	a			08 14		08 24			08 44		08 40				08 44		08 54			09 14		09 09			
	d			08 14		08 24			08 44		08 41				08 44		08 54			09 14		09 11			
Langley	d					08 28			→								08 58			→					
Iver	d					08 31											09 01								
West Drayton	d			08 21		08 35									08 51		09 05								
Heathrow Terminal 4 ✈	d																								
Heathrow Term 1-2-3 2 ✈	d				08 27											08 57									
Hayes & Harlington	d			08 26	08 33	08 40									08 56	09 03	09 10								
Southall	d				08 36	08 43										09 06	09 13								
Hanwell	d				08 39											09 09									
Greenford ⊖	d	08 16												08 46											09 16
South Greenford	d	08 19												08 49											09 19
Castle Bar Park	d	08 22												08 52											09 22
Drayton Green	d	08 24												08 54											09 24
West Ealing	d	08 26			08 41									08 56		09 11									09 26
Ealing Broadway ⊖	d	08 29		08 33	08 44	08 49								08 59	09 03	09 14	09 19								09 29
Acton Main Line	d	08 33												09 03											09 33
London Paddington 15 ⊖	a	08 42		08 46	08 54	09 01		08 44		08 52	08 59	09 02		09 12	09 16	09 24	09 31		09 14		09 21	09 29		09 32	09 42

b Arr. 0427
c Arr. 0557
e Arr. 0627
f Arr. 0657
g Arr. 0727
h Arr. 0827

Table 117

Saturdays

Reading and Greenford - London

		GW 1	HC	GW 1	GW ◇1 ⊏P	GW ◇1 ⊏P	GW 1	GW 1	GW ◇1 ⊥o	GW ◇1 ⊏P	GW 1	GW 1	HC	GW 1	GW ◇1 ⊏P	GW ◇1 ⊏P	GW 1	GW ◇1 A ⊏P	GW ◇1 ⊏P	GW 1	GW 1	HC
Oxford	d			08 07					09 01					08 37				09 31				
Reading 7	d			09b03	09 09	09 16	09 18	09 20	09 24	09 33				09c33	09 37	09 45	09 48	09 55	10 02			
Twyford 3	d			09 09			09 24							09 39			09 54					
Maidenhead 3	d			09 17			09 32							09 47			10 02					
Taplow	d						09 36										10 06					
Burnham	d	←					09 39					←					10 09				←	
Slough 3	a	09 14		09 24			09 44		09 40			09 44		09 54			10 14	10 09			10 14	
	d	09 14		09 24			09 44		09 40			09 44		09 54			10 14	10 10			10 14	
Langley	d			09 28			→							09 58			→					
Iver	d			09 31										10 01								
West Drayton	d	09 21		09 35								09 51		10 05							10 21	
Heathrow Terminal 4 ✈	d																					
Heathrow Term 1-2-3 2 ✈	d		09 27										09 57									10 27
Hayes & Harlington	d	09 26	09 33	09 40								09 56	10 03	10 10							10 26	10 33
Southall	d		09 36	09 43									10 06	10 13								10 36
Hanwell	d		09 39										10 09									10 39
Greenford ⊖	d										09 46									10 16		
South Greenford	d										09 49									10 19		
Castle Bar Park	d										09 52									10 22		
Drayton Green	d										09 54									10 24		
West Ealing	d		09 41								09 56		10 11							10 26		10 41
Ealing Broadway ⊖	d	09 33	09 44	09 49							09 59	10 03	10 14	10 19						10 29	10 33	10 44
Acton Main Line	d										10 03									10 33		
London Paddington 15 ⊖	a	09 46	09 54	10 01	09 37	09 44		09 52	09 59	10 02	10 12	10 16	10 24	10 31	10 08	10 14		10 29	10 32	10 42	10 46	10 54

		GW 1	GW ◇1 ⊏P	GW 1	GW 1	GW ◇1 ⊥o	GW ◇1 B ⊏P	GW 1	GW 1	HC	GW 1	GW ◇1 ⊏P	GW ◇1 ⊏P	GW 1	GW ◇1 ⊏P	GW ◇1 ⊏P	GW ◇1 ⊏P	GW 1	GW 1	HC
Oxford	d	09 07				10 01					09 37					10 31				
Reading 7	d	10e03	10 13	10 18	10 18	10 25	10 33				10f33	10 39	10 46	10 48	10 53	10 55	11 02			
Twyford 3	d	10 09			10 24						10 39			10 54						
Maidenhead 3	d	10 17			10 32						10 47			11 02						
Taplow	d				10 36									11 06						
Burnham	d				10 39				←					11 09					←	
Slough 3	a	10 24			10 44	10 40			10 44		10 54			11 14		11 09			11 14	
	d	10 24			10 44	10 40			10 44		10 54			11 14		11 10			11 14	
Langley	d	10 28			→						10 58			→						
Iver	d	10 31									11 01									
West Drayton	d	10 35							10 51		11 05								11 21	
Heathrow Terminal 4 ✈	d																			
Heathrow Term 1-2-3 2 ✈	d									10 57										11 27
Hayes & Harlington	d	10 40							10 56	11 03	11 10								11 26	11 33
Southall	d	10 43								11 06	11 13									11 36
Hanwell	d									11 09										11 39
Greenford ⊖	d							10 46										11 16		
South Greenford	d							10 49										11 19		
Castle Bar Park	d							10 52										11 22		
Drayton Green	d							10 54										11 24		
West Ealing	d							10 56		11 11								11 26		11 41
Ealing Broadway ⊖	d	10 49						10 59	11 03	11 14	11 19							11 29	11 33	11 44
Acton Main Line	d							11 03										11 33		
London Paddington 15 ⊖	a	11 01	10 39	10 52		10 59	11 02	11 12	11 16	11 24	11 31	11 08	11 14		11 24	11 29	11 33	11 42	11 46	11 54

		GW 1	GW ◇1 ⊏P	GW 1	GW 1	GW ◇1	GW 1	GW 1	HC	GW 1	GW ◇1 ⊏P	GW 1	GW R 1 ⊏P	GW ◇1 ⊥o	GW ◇1 ⊏P	GW 1	GW 1	HC	GW 1	GW ◇1 ⊏P	GW 1
Oxford	d	10 07				11 01				10 37				11 31					11 07		
Reading 7	d	11 03	11 13	11 18	11 21	11 25				11g33	11 45	11 48	11 53	11 55	12 02				12 03	12 13	12 17
Twyford 3	d	11 09		11 24						11 39		11 54							12 09		
Maidenhead 3	d	11 17		11 32						11 47		12 02							12 17		
Taplow	d			11 36								12 06									
Burnham	d			11 39				←				12 09					←				
Slough 3	a	11 24		11 44		11 39		11 44		11 54		12 14		12 09			12 14		12 24		
	d	11 24		11 44		11 40		11 44		11 54		12 14		12 11			12 14		12 24		
Langley	d	11 28		→						11 58		→							12 28		
Iver	d	11 31								12 01									12 31		
West Drayton	d	11 35						11 51		12 05							12 21		12 35		
Heathrow Terminal 4 ✈	d																				
Heathrow Term 1-2-3 2 ✈	d								11 57									12 27			
Hayes & Harlington	d	11 40						11 56	12 03	12 10							12 26	12 33	12 40		
Southall	d	11 43							12 06	12 13								12 36	12 43		
Hanwell	d								12 09									12 39			
Greenford ⊖	d						11 46									12 16					
South Greenford	d						11 49									12 19					
Castle Bar Park	d						11 52									12 22					
Drayton Green	d						11 54									12 24					
West Ealing	d						11 56		12 11							12 26		12 41			
Ealing Broadway ⊖	d	11 49					11 59	12 03	12 14	12 19						12 29	12 33	12 44	12 49		
Acton Main Line	d						12 03									12 33					
London Paddington 15 ⊖	a	12 01	11 40		11 52	11 59	12 12	12 16	12 24	12 31	12 14		12 23	12 29	12 32	12 42	12 46	12 54	13 01	12 39	12 52

A ⊏P from Reading
B from 17 September
b Arr. 0857
c Arr. 0927
e Arr. 0957
f Arr. 1027
g Arr. 1127

Table 117

Saturdays

Reading and Greenford - London

		GW	GW	GW	GW	HC		GW		GW	GW	GW	GW	GW	GW	GW		GW	GW	GW	HC	GW		GW	GW
		1	◇1	1	1			1		◇1	R 1	◇1	◇1	1	◇1	◇1		◇1	1	1		1		◇1	1
											A	B	A		B										
			🛒							☕	☕	☕	☕		☕	🛒		☕						☕	
Oxford	d		12 01					11 37								12 31						12 07			
Reading 7	d	12 18	12 25					12 33		12 39	12 42	12 44	12 45	12 48	12 54	12 55		13 02				13b03		13 12	13 18
Twyford 3	d	12 24						12 39						12 54								13 09			13 24
Maidenhead 3	d	12 32						12 47						13 02								13 17			13 32
Taplow	d	12 36												13 06											13 36
Burnham	d	12 39			←									13 09						←					13 39
Slough 3	a	12 44	12 40		12 44			12 54						13 14		13 09				13 14		13 24			13 44
	d	12 44	12 40		12 44			12 54						13 14		13 11				13 14		13 24			13 44
Langley	d	→						12 58						→								13 28			→
Iver	d							13 01														13 31			
West Drayton	d				12 51			13 05												13 21		13 35			
Heathrow Terminal 4 ✈	d																								
Heathrow Term 1-2-3 2 ✈	d					12 57															13 27				
Hayes & Harlington	d				12 56	13 03		13 10												13 26	13 33	13 40			
Southall	d					13 06		13 13													13 36	13 43			
Hanwell	d					13 09															13 39				
Greenford ⊖	d			12 46															13 16						
South Greenford	d			12 49															13 19						
Castle Bar Park	d			12 52															13 22						
Drayton Green	d			12 54															13 24						
West Ealing	d			12 56		13 11													13 26		13 41				
Ealing Broadway ⊖	d			12 59	13 03	13 14		13 19											13 29	13 33	13 44	13 49			
Acton Main Line	d			13 03															13 33						
London Paddington 15 ⊖	a		12 59	13 12	13 16	13 24		13 31		13 07	13 09	13 14	13 13		13 21	13 30		13 33	13 42	13 46	13 54	14 01		13 41	

		GW		GW	GW	GW	GW	HC	GW	GW	GW	GW		GW	GW	GW	GW	HC	GW		GW	GW		GW	GW
		R 1		◇1	◇1	1	1		1	◇1	1	1		◇1	◇1	1	1		1		◇1	1		1	◇1
		A		B																		A			B
		☕		☕	🛒					☕					☕						☕				☕
Oxford	d				13 01				12 37					13 31					13 07						
Reading 7	d	13 19		13 20	13 25				13c33	13 45	13 48	13 51		13 55	14 02				14 03		14 13	14 18		14 18	14 19
Twyford 3	d								13 39		13 54								14 09					14 24	
Maidenhead 3	d								13 47		14 02								14 17					14 32	
Taplow	d										14 06													14 36	
Burnham	d						←				14 09						←							14 39	
Slough 3	a				13 40		13 44		13 54		14 14			14 09			14 14		14 24					14 44	
	d				13 40		13 44		13 54		14 14			14 10			14 14		14 24					14 44	
Langley	d								13 58		→								14 28					→	
Iver	d								14 01										14 31						
West Drayton	d						13 51		14 05								14 21		14 35						
Heathrow Terminal 4 ✈	d																								
Heathrow Term 1-2-3 2 ✈	d							13 57										14 27							
Hayes & Harlington	d						13 56	14 03	14 10								14 26	14 33	14 40						
Southall	d							14 06	14 13									14 36	14 43						
Hanwell	d							14 09										14 39							
Greenford ⊖	d					13 46										14 16									
South Greenford	d					13 49										14 19									
Castle Bar Park	d					13 52										14 22									
Drayton Green	d					13 54										14 24									
West Ealing	d					13 56		14 11								14 26		14 41							
Ealing Broadway ⊖	d					13 59	14 03	14 14	14 19							14 29	14 33	14 44	14 49						
Acton Main Line	d					14 03										14 33									
London Paddington 15 ⊖	a	13 46		13 46	13 59	14 12	14 16	14 24	14 31	14 14		14 23		14 29	14 32	14 42	14 46	14 54	15 01		14 39	14 54			14 45

A until 10 September
B from 17 September
b Arr. 1257
c Arr. 1327

Table 117

Reading and Greenford - London

		GW	GW	GW	HC	GW		GW		GW	GW	GW	GW	GW	GW	GW	GW	HC		GW		GW	GW	GW	GW
													R												
		◇1	1	1		1		◇1		◇1	1	◇1	1	◇1	◇1	1	1			1		◇1	1	1	◇1
												A	B												
		🛒						☕		☕		☕	☕	☕	☕							☕			
Oxford	d	14 01				13 37								14 31						14 07					15 01
Reading 7	d	14 25				14b33		14 39		14 45	14 48	14 53	14 53	14 55	15 02					15 03		15 11	15 18	15 19	15 25
Twyford 3	d					14 39					14 54									15 09			15 24		
Maidenhead 3	d					14 47					15 02									15 17			15 32		
Taplow	d										15 06												15 36		
Burnham	d			←							15 09						←						15 39		
Slough 3	a	14 40		14 44		14 54					15 14			15 10			15 14			15 24			15 44		15 40
	d	14 40		14 44		14 54					15 14			15 11			15 14			15 24			15 44		15 40
Langley	d					14 58					→									15 28			→		
Iver	d					15 01														15 31					
West Drayton	d			14 51		15 05											15 21			15 35					
Heathrow Terminal 4 ✈	d																								
Heathrow Term 1-2-3 2 ✈	d				14 57													15 27							
Hayes & Harlington	d			14 56	15 03	15 10											15 26	15 33		15 40					
Southall	d				15 06	15 13												15 36		15 43					
Hanwell	d				15 09													15 39							
Greenford ⊖	d		14 46													15 16									
South Greenford	d		14 49													15 19									
Castle Bar Park	d		14 52													15 22									
Drayton Green	d		14 54													15 24									
West Ealing	d		14 56		15 11											15 26		15 41							
Ealing Broadway ⊖	d		14 59	15 03	15 14	15 19										15 29	15 33	15 44		15 49					
Acton Main Line	d		15 03													15 33									
London Paddington 15 ⊖	a	14 59	15 12	15 16	15 24	15 31		15 09		15 14		15 22	15 23	15 29	15 32	15 42	15 46	15 54		16 01		15 39		15 54	15 59

		GW	GW	HC		GW	GW	GW	GW	GW	GW	GW	GW	GW		GW	HC	GW		GW	GW	GW	GW	GW	
											R														
		1	1			1	◇1	1	◇1	◇1	1	◇1	◇1	1		1		1		◇1	1	1	◇1	◇1	
											B	A	B											B	
							☕		☕	🛒	☕	☕	☕							☕				☕	
Oxford	d					14 37				15 31								15 07					16 01		
Reading 7	d					15c33	15 45	15 48	15 53	15 55	16 01	16 01	16 02					16 03		16 13	16 18	16 18	16 26	16 28	
Twyford 3	d					15 39		15 54										16 09				16 24			
Maidenhead 3	d					15 47		16 02										16 17				16 32			
Taplow	d							16 06														16 36			
Burnham	d		←					16 09								←						16 39			
Slough 3	a		15 44			15 54		16 14		16 10						16 14		16 24				16 44	16 40		
	d		15 44			15 54		16 14		16 11						16 14		16 24				16 44	16 41		
Langley	d					15 58		→										16 28				→			
Iver	d					16 01												16 31							
West Drayton	d		15 51			16 05										16 21		16 35							
Heathrow Terminal 4 ✈	d																								
Heathrow Term 1-2-3 2 ✈	d			15 57													16 27								
Hayes & Harlington	d		15 56	16 03		16 10										16 26	16 33	16 40							
Southall	d			16 06		16 13											16 36	16 43							
Hanwell	d			16 09													16 39								
Greenford ⊖	d	15 46												16 16											
South Greenford	d	15 49												16 19											
Castle Bar Park	d	15 52												16 22											
Drayton Green	d	15 54												16 24											
West Ealing	d	15 56		16 11										16 26			16 41								
Ealing Broadway ⊖	d	15 59	16 03	16 14		16 19								16 29		16 33	16 44	16 49							
Acton Main Line	d	16 03												16 33											
London Paddington 15 ⊖	a	16 12	16 16	16 24		16 31	16 14		16 23	16 29	16 32	16 32	16 37	16 42		16 46	16 54	17 01		16 39	16 52		16 59	17 02	

		GW	GW	HC	GW		GW	GW	GW	GW		GW	GW	GW	GW	GW	GW	HC	GW			GW	GW	GW	GW
		1	1		1		◇1	◇1	1	◇1		◇1	◇1	◇1	◇1	1	1		1			◇1	◇1	1	1
										A		B	B	A									A		B
							☕	☕		☕		☕	🛒	🛒	☕							☕	☕		
Oxford	d				15 37								16 31	16 31					16 07						
Reading 7	d				16 33		16 39	16 45	16 48	16 50		16 51	16 55	16 55	17 02				17 03			17 11	17 18	17 18	17 22
Twyford 3	d				16 39				16 54										17 09					17 24	
Maidenhead 3	d				16 47				17 02										17 17					17 32	
Taplow	d								17 06															17 36	
Burnham	d		←						17 09								←							17 39	
Slough 3	a		16 44		16 54				17 14				17 09	17 10			17 14		17 24					17 44	
	d		16 44		16 54				17 14				17 11	17 11			17 14		17 24					17 44	
Langley	d				16 58				→										17 28					→	
Iver	d				17 01														17 31						
West Drayton	d		16 51		17 05												17 21		17 35						
Heathrow Terminal 4 ✈	d																								
Heathrow Term 1-2-3 2 ✈	d			16 57														17 27							
Hayes & Harlington	d		16 56	17 03	17 10												17 26	17 33	17 40						
Southall	d			17 06	17 13													17 36	17 43						
Hanwell	d			17 09														17 39							
Greenford ⊖	d	16 46														17 16									
South Greenford	d	16 49														17 19									
Castle Bar Park	d	16 52														17 22									
Drayton Green	d	16 54														17 24									
West Ealing	d	16 56		17 11												17 26		17 41							
Ealing Broadway ⊖	d	16 59	17 03	17 14	17 19											17 29	17 33	17 44	17 49						
Acton Main Line	d	17 03														17 33									
London Paddington 15 ⊖	a	17 12	17 16	17 24	17 31		17 07	17 14		17 21		17 21	17 29	17 29	17 32	17 42	17 46	17 54	18 01			17 38	17 51		17 54

A from 17 September
B until 10 September

b Arr. 1427
c Arr. 1527

Table 117

Reading and Greenford - London

		GW	GW	GW	HC	GW		GW	GW	GW	GW	GW	GW	GW	GW	GW		GW	HC	GW		GW	GW	GW	GW
		◇1	1	1		1		◇1	◇1	1	◇1	R 1	◇1	◇1	◇1	1		1		1		◇1	1	1	◇1
								A			B	A	A	B											
								☕	☕		☕	☕	☕	☕	☕							☕			
Oxford	d	17 01				16 37							17 31	17 31						17 07					18 01
Reading 7	d	17 27				17b33		17 36	17 45	17 48	17 54	17 54	17 56	17 57	18 02					18c03		18 13	18 18	18 19	18 25
Twyford 3	d					17 39				17 54										18 09			18 24		
Maidenhead 3	d					17 47				18 02										18 17			18 32		
Taplow	d									18 06													18 36		
Burnham	d			←						18 09								←					18 39		
Slough 3	a	17 41		17 44		17 54				18 14			18 09	18 10				18 14		18 24			18 44		18 40
	d	17 42		17 44		17 54				18 14			18 11	18 11				18 14		18 24			18 44		18 40
Langley	d					17 58				→										18 28			→		
Iver	d					18 01														18 31					
West Drayton	d			17 51		18 05												18 21		18 35					
Heathrow Terminal 4 ✈	d																								
Heathrow Term 1-2-3 2 ✈	d				17 57														18 27						
Hayes & Harlington	d			17 56	18 03	18 10												18 26	18 33	18 40					
Southall	d				18 06	18 13													18 36	18 43					
Hanwell	d				18 09														18 39						
Greenford ⊖	d		17 46													18 16									
South Greenford	d		17 49													18 19									
Castle Bar Park	d		17 52													18 22									
Drayton Green	d		17 54													18 24									
West Ealing	d		17 56		18 11											18 26			18 41						
Ealing Broadway ⊖	d		17 59	18 03	18 14	18 19										18 29		18 33	18 44	18 49					
Acton Main Line	d		18 03													18 33									
London Paddington 15 ⊖	a	18 00	18 12	18 16	18 24	18 31		18 08	18 14		18 21	18 23	18 29	18 29	18 32	18 42		18 46	18 54	19 01		18 39		18 52	18 59

		GW		GW	HC	GW		GW	GW	GW	GW	GW		GW	GW	GW	GW	HC			GW	GW		GW	GW
		1		1		1		◇1	◇1	1	◇1	◇1		◇1	◇1	1	1				◇1	1		1	◇1
												A		B											
								☕	☕		☕	🛒		🛒	☕						☕				
Oxford	d					17 37						18 31		18 31											19 01
Reading 7	d					18e33		18 39	18 45	18 48	18 50	18 55		18 56	19 02						19 11	19 18		19 20	19 25
Twyford 3	d					18 39				18 54												19 24			
Maidenhead 3	d					18 47				19 02												19 32			
Taplow	d									19 06												19 36			
Burnham	d			←						19 09							←					19 39			
Slough 3	a			18 44		18 54				19 14		19 09		19 10			19 14					19 44			19 40
	d			18 44		18 54				19 14		19 10		19 11			19 14					19 44			19 40
Langley	d					18 58				→												→			
Iver	d					19 01																			
West Drayton	d			18 51		19 05											19 21								
Heathrow Terminal 4 ✈	d																								
Heathrow Term 1-2-3 2 ✈	d				18 57													19 27							
Hayes & Harlington	d			18 56	19 03	19 10											19 26	19 33							
Southall	d				19 06	19 13												19 36							
Hanwell	d				19 09													19 39							
Greenford ⊖	d	18 46														19 16									
South Greenford	d	18 49														19 19									
Castle Bar Park	d	18 52														19 22									
Drayton Green	d	18 54														19 24									
West Ealing	d	18 56			19 11											19 26		19 41							
Ealing Broadway ⊖	d	18 59		19 03	19 14	19 19										19 29	19 33	19 44							
Acton Main Line	d	19 03														19 33									
London Paddington 15 ⊖	a	19 12		19 16	19 24	19 31		19 08	19 14		19 22	19 29		19 29	19 32	19 42	19 46	19 54			19 39			19 52	19 59

		GW	GW	HC	GW	GW	GW	GW		GW	GW	GW	GW	GW	HC	GW		GW		GW	GW	GW	GW	HC	GW
		1	1		1	◇1	1	◇1		◇1	◇1	◇1	1	1		1		◇1		1	◇1	1	1		1
								A		B	A	B													
						☕		🛒		🛒	☕	☕						☕							
Oxford	d				18 37			19 31		19 31						19 07					20 01				19 37
Reading 7	d				19 33	19 45	19 48	19 55		19 55	20 01	20 03				20f03		20 09		20 18	20 25				20 33
Twyford 3	d				19 39		19 54									20 09				20 24					20 39
Maidenhead 3	d				19 47		20 02									20 17				20 32					20 47
Taplow	d						20 06													20 36					
Burnham	d		←				20 09							←						20 39			←		
Slough 3	a		19 44		19 54		20 14	20 09		20 10				20 14		20 24				20 44	20 40		20 44		20 54
	d		19 44		19 54		20 14	20 10		20 10				20 14		20 24				20 44	20 40		20 44		20 54
Langley	d				19 58		→									20 28				→					20 58
Iver	d				20 01											20 31									21 01
West Drayton	d		19 51		20 05									20 21		20 35							20 51		21 05
Heathrow Terminal 4 ✈	d																								
Heathrow Term 1-2-3 2 ✈	d			19 57											20 27									20 57	
Hayes & Harlington	d		19 56	20 03	20 10									20 26	20 33	20 40							20 56	21 03	21 10
Southall	d			20 06	20 13										20 36	20 43								21 06	21 13
Hanwell	d			20 09											20 39									21 09	
Greenford ⊖	d	19 46											20 16									20 46			
South Greenford	d	19 49											20 19									20 49			
Castle Bar Park	d	19 52											20 22									20 52			
Drayton Green	d	19 54											20 24									20 54			
West Ealing	d	19 56		20 11									20 26		20 41							20 56		21 11	
Ealing Broadway ⊖	d	19 59	20 03	20 14	20 19								20 29	20 33	20 44	20 49						20 59	21 03	21 14	21 19
Acton Main Line	d	20 03											20 33									21 03			
London Paddington 15 ⊖	a	20 12	20 16	20 24	20 31	20 14		20 29		20 29	20 32	20 32	20 42	20 46	20 54	21 01		20 37			20 59	21 12	21 16	21 24	21 31

A until 10 September
B from 17 September

b Arr. 1727
c Arr. 1757

e Arr. 1827
f Arr. 1957

Table 117

Saturdays

Reading and Greenford - London

		GW	GW	GW	GW	GW	GW	GW	HC	GW	GW	GW	GW	GW	GW	HC	GW	GW	GW	GW
		◇1	◇1	1	◇1	◇1	1	1		1	◇1	1	◇1	1	1		1	1	◇1	R 1
																				A
		☕	☕			☕					☕								☕	☕
Oxford	d				20 31					20 07			21 01				20 37			
Reading 7	d	20 39	20 45	20 48	20 54	21 01				21b03	21 08	21 18	21 25				21c33	21 48	21 50	22 00
Twyford 3	d			20 54						21 09		21 24					21 39	21 54		
Maidenhead 3	d			21 02						21 17		21 32					21 47	22 02		
Taplow	d			21 06								21 36						22 06		
Burnham	d			21 09				←				21 39			←			22 09		
Slough 3	a			21 14	21 09			21 14		21 24		21 44	21 40		21 44		21 54	22 14		
	d			21 14	21 09			21 14		21 24		21 44	21 40		21 44		21 54	22 14		
Langley	d			→						21 28		→					21 58			
Iver	d									21 31							22 01			
West Drayton	d							21 21		21 35					21 51		22 05	22 21		
Heathrow Terminal 4 ✈	d																			
Heathrow Term 1-2-3 2 ✈	d								21 27							21 57				
Hayes & Harlington	d							21 26	21 33	21 40					21 56	22 03	22 10	22 26		
Southall	d								21 36	21 43						22 06	22 13			
Hanwell	d								21 39							22 09				
Greenford ⊖	d						21 16							21 46						
South Greenford	d						21 19							21 49						
Castle Bar Park	d						21 22							21 52						
Drayton Green	d						21 24							21 54						
West Ealing	d						21 26		21 41					21 56		22 11				
Ealing Broadway ⊖	d						21 29	21 33	21 44	21 49				21 59	22 03	22 14	22 19	22 33		
Acton Main Line	d						21 33							22 03						
London Paddington 15 ⊖	a	21 07	21 14		21 29	21 32	21 42	21 46	21 54	22 02	21 36		21 59	22 12	22 16	22 24	22 31	22 46	22 16	22 26

		GW	GW	GW	HC	GW	GW	HC	GW	GW	GW	GW	GW	GW	HC	GW	GW	GW	GW	GW	GW
		◇1	◇1	◇1		1	◇1		1	1	◇1	◇1	1	◇1		1	◇1	◇1	◇1	◇1	1
		B		A							A			B			B	A	C	D	
			☕									☕							☕	☕	
Oxford	d	21 31		21 36			22 01		21 50		22 31			22 35			23 01	23 01			23 07
Reading 7	d	22 01	22 02	22 05		22 18	22 29		22 33	22 48	22 55	23 05		23 05		23 18	23 31	23 31	23 52	23 52	00 03
Twyford 3	d					22 24			22 39	22 54						23 24					00 09
Maidenhead 3	d					22 32			22 47	23 02						23 32					00 17
Taplow	d					22 36				23 06						23 36					00 21
Burnham	d					22 39				23 09			←			23 39					00 24
Slough 3	a	22 14		22 22		22 44	22 43		22 54	23 14	23 09		23 14	23 23		23 44	23 48	23 48			00 28
	d	22 15		22 22		22 44	22 44		22 54	23 14	23 10		23 14	23 24		23 44	23 49	23 49			00 29
Langley	d								22 59	→											00 33
Iver	d								23 01												00 36
West Drayton	d					22 51			23 05				23 21			23 51					00 39
Heathrow Terminal 4 ✈	d																				
Heathrow Term 1-2-3 2 ✈	d				22 27			22 57							23 27						
Hayes & Harlington	d				22 33	22 56		23 03	23 10				23 26		23 33	23 56					00 44
Southall	d				22 36			23 06	23 13						23 36						00 47
Hanwell	d				22 39			23 09							23 39						
Greenford ⊖	d																				
South Greenford	d																				
Castle Bar Park	d																				
Drayton Green	d																				
West Ealing	d				22 41			23 11							23 41						
Ealing Broadway ⊖	d				22 44	23 03		23 14	23 19				23 33		23 44	00 03					00 53
Acton Main Line	d																				
London Paddington 15 ⊖	a	22 32	22 37	22 41	22 54	23 16	23 02	23 24	23 28		23 29	23 36	23 46	23 43	23 54	00 16	00 10	00 13	00 33	00 34	01 02

A until 10 September
B from 17 September
C from 6 August until 22 October
D until 30 July, from 29 October
b Arr. 2057
c Arr. 2127

Table 117

Sundays
until 19 June

Reading and Greenford - London

	GW	GW	HC	GW	GW	HC	GW	HC	GW		HC	GW	GW	GW	GW	HC	GW	GW	GW		HC	GW	GW	GW
	1	◇1		◇1	1		1		1			1	1	1	◇1		◇1	1	◇1			1	◇1	1
	A	A		A ☕	A										☕				☕				☕	
Oxford d		23p01			23p07									08 05			08 38							09 05
Reading 7 d	23p18	23p31		23p52	00 03		06 22		07 22			08 03	08 18	08 50	09 01		09 10	09 18	09 29			09 36	09 47	09 50
Twyford 3 d	23p24				00 09		06 28		07 28				08 24	08 56				09 25						09 56
Maidenhead 3 d	23p32				00 17		06 36		07 36				08 36	09 04				09 36				09 53		10 04
Taplow d	23p36				00 21																			
Burnham d	23p39				00 24		06 40		07 40				08 40					09 41						
Slough 3 a	23p44	23p48			00 28		06 45		07 45			08 22	08 45	09 11			09 30	09 46				10 01		10 11
d	23p44	23p49			00 29		06 46		07 46			08 22	08 46	09 15			09 31	09 46				10 01		10 15
Langley d					00 33		06 50		07 50				08 50	09 19				09 48						10 19
Iver d					00 36																			
West Drayton d	23p51				00 39		06 55		07 55				08 55	09 24				09 53						10 24
Heathrow Terminal 4 ✈ d			00 01			06 07		07 07			08 07					09 21					09 51			
Heathrow Term 1-2-3 2 ✈ d			00 07			06 13		07 13			08 13					09 27					09 57			
Hayes & Harlington d	23p56		00 13		00 44	06 19	07 02	07 19	08 01		08 19		09 02	09 29		09 33		10 00			10 03			10 29
Southall d			00 16		00 47	06 22	07 06	07 22	08 04		08 22		09 05	09 32		09 36		10 04			10 06			10 32
Hanwell d																								
Greenford ⊖ d																								
South Greenford d																								
Castle Bar Park d																								
Drayton Green d																								
West Ealing d																								
Ealing Broadway ⊖ d	00 03		00 21		00 53	06 27	07 11	07 27	08 10		08 27		09 11	09 38		09 41		10 08			10 12			10 38
Acton Main Line d																								
London Paddington 15 ⊖ a	00 16	00 13	00 30	00 34	01 02	06 36	07 21	07 36	08 19		08 36	08 44	09 21	09 47	09 38	09 50	09 51	10 18	10 08		10 20	10 21	10 27	10 47

	GW	HC	GW	GW	GW		HC	GW	GW	GW	GW		GW	HC	GW		GW	HC	GW	GW	GW	GW		GW
	◇1		◇1	1	1			◇1	◇1	◇1	1		◇1		◇1		1		1	◇1	◇1	1		◇1
	☕							☕	B ☕	C ☕			☕		🛒					☕	☕			☕
Oxford d			09 38								10 05				10 38							11 05		
Reading 7 d	10 00		10 07	10 18	10 27			10 44	10 49	10 49	10 53		11 00		11 08		11 18		11 34	11 44	11 49	11 53		12 02
Twyford 3 d				10 26							10 59						11 25					12 00		
Maidenhead 3 d				10 36	10 45						11 07						11 36		11 52			12 08		
Taplow d																								
Burnham d				10 41													11 41							
Slough 3 a			10 28	10 45	10 53						11 15				11 31		11 45		12 00			12 15		
d			10 29	10 46	10 53						11 15				11 32		11 46		12 00			12 16		
Langley d				10 48							11 19						11 48					12 20		
Iver d																								
West Drayton d				10 54							11 24						11 54					12 25		
Heathrow Terminal 4 ✈ d		10 21					10 51							11 21				11 51						
Heathrow Term 1-2-3 2 ✈ d		10 27					10 57							11 27				11 57						
Hayes & Harlington d		10 33		10 59			11 03				11 29			11 33			11 59	12 03				12 30		
Southall d		10 36		11 04			11 06				11 32			11 36			12 04	12 06				12 33		
Hanwell d																								
Greenford ⊖ d																								
South Greenford d																								
Castle Bar Park d																								
Drayton Green d																								
West Ealing d																								
Ealing Broadway ⊖ d		10 41		11 08			11 12				11 38			11 41			12 08	12 13				12 39		
Acton Main Line d																								
London Paddington 15 ⊖ a	10 39	10 50	10 52	11 18	11 15		11 20	11 21	11 27	11 31	11 47		11 39	11 50	11 52		12 18	12 20	12 22	12 24	12 27	12 48		12 38

	HC		GW	GW	GW	HC	GW	GW		GW	HC		GW	GW	GW	GW	HC	GW	GW	GW			GW	HC
			◇1	1	1		◇1	1		◇1			◇1	1	1	◇1		◇1	◇1	1			◇1	
							☕			☕			🛒			☕		☕	☕				☕	
Oxford d			11 38					12 05					12 45							13 05				
Reading 7 d			12 07	12 18	12 35		12 44	12 52		13 02			13 13	13 18	13 25	13 33		13 44	13 49	13b52			14 02	
Twyford 3 d				12 25				12 58						13 25						14 00				
Maidenhead 3 d				12 36	12 48			13 06						13 36	13 43					14 08				
Taplow d																								
Burnham d				12 41										13 41										
Slough 3 a			12 29	12 45	12 56			13 14					13 35	13 45	13 50					14 15				
d			12 30	12 46	12 56			13 15					13 35	13 46	13 50					14 15				
Langley d				12 48				13 19						13 50						14 20				
Iver d																								
West Drayton d				12 54				13 24						13 54						14 25				
Heathrow Terminal 4 ✈ d	12 21					12 51					13 21						13 51							14 21
Heathrow Term 1-2-3 2 ✈ d	12 27					12 57					13 27						13 57							14 27
Hayes & Harlington d	12 33			12 59		13 03		13 29			13 33			13 59			14 03			14 29				14 33
Southall d	12 36			13 04		13 06		13 32			13 36			14 04			14 06			14 33				14 36
Hanwell d																								
Greenford ⊖ d																								
South Greenford d																								
Castle Bar Park d																								
Drayton Green d																								
West Ealing d																								
Ealing Broadway ⊖ d	12 42			13 08		13 11		13 38			13 41			14 08			14 11			14 38				14 41
Acton Main Line d																								
London Paddington 15 ⊖ a	12 50		12 51	13 18	13 16	13 20	13 24	13 47		13 39	13 50		13 54	14 18	14 11	14 13	14 20	14 22	14 29	14 47			14 39	14 50

A not 22 May
B not 5 June
C 5 June
b Arr. 1346

Table 117

Sundays until 19 June

Reading and Greenford - London

	GW	GW	HC	GW	GW	GW	GW	GW	HC	GW	GW	GW	GW	GW	HC	GW	GW	GW	HC	GW
	◇1	1		1	◇1 ☕	◇1 ☕	1	◇1 ☕		◇1	1	1	◇1 ☕	◇1 ☕		◇1 ☕	1	◇1 ☕		◇1 ☕
Oxford d	13 38						14 05			14 41							15 05			15 50
Reading 7 d	14 08	14 18		14 36	14 44	14 50	14b52	15 02		15 11	15 19	15 25	15 37	15 45		15 50	15 52	16 02		16 20
Twyford 3 d		14 25					14 59				15 25						16 00			
Maidenhead 3 d		14 36		14 50			15 07				15 34	15 40					16 08			
Taplow d																				
Burnham d		14 41									15 39						16 12			
Slough 3 a	14 29	14 45		14 58			15 15			15 31	15 43	15 49					16 16			16 49
d	14 29	14 46		14 58			15 15			15 32	15 44	15 50					16 16			16 50
Langley d		14 50					15 20				15 48						16 21			→
Iver d																				
West Drayton d		14 54					15 25				15 52						16 25			
Heathrow Terminal 4 ✈ d			14 51						15 21						15 51				16 21	
Heathrow Term 1-2-3 2 ✈ d			14 57						15 27						15 57				16 27	
Hayes & Harlington d		14 59	15 03				15 29		15 33		15 58				16 03		16 31		16 33	
Southall d		15 04	15 06				15 33		15 36		16 02				16 06		16 33		16 37	
Hanwell d																				
Greenford ⊖ d																				
South Greenford d																				
Castle Bar Park d																				
Drayton Green d																				
West Ealing d																				
Ealing Broadway ⊖ d		15 08	15 11				15 38		15 42		16 06				16 11		16 39		16 41	
Acton Main Line d																				
London Paddington 15 ⊖ a	14 51	15 18	15 20	15 21	15 24	15 27	15 47	15 39	15 50	15 52	16 18	16 10	16 15	16 20	16 20	16 26	16 48	16 39	16 50	

	GW	GW	HC	GW	GW	GW	GW	GW	GW	HC	GW	HC	GW	GW	GW	GW	GW	GW	GW
	1	◇1 ☕		1	◇1 ☕	◇1 ☕	1	◇1 ☕	◇1 ☕		◇1 ☕		1	◇1 ☕	1	◇1 ☕	◇1 ☕	1	◇1 ☕
Oxford d							16 05				16 50							17 05	
Reading 7 d	16 21			16 36	16 44	16 49	16c52	17 02	17 13		17 20		17 25	17 32	17 36	17 44	17 49	17 52	18 02
Twyford 3 d	16 27						16 59						17 32					18 00	
Maidenhead 3 d	16 36			16 52			17 07						17 42		17 53			18 08	
Taplow d																			
Burnham d	16 41	←					17 12						17 47					18 12	
Slough 3 a	16 45	16 49		17 00			17 15				17 44		17 51		18 00			18 16	
d	16 46	16 50		17 00			17 16				17 45		17 52		18 01			18 16	
Langley d	16 50						17 20						17 56					18 21	
Iver d																			
West Drayton d	16 54						17 26						18 00					18 26	
Heathrow Terminal 4 ✈ d			16 51							17 21		17 51							
Heathrow Term 1-2-3 2 ✈ d			16 57							17 27		17 57							
Hayes & Harlington d	16 59		17 03				17 31			17 33		18 03	18 05					18 31	
Southall d	17 04		17 06				17 33			17 36		18 06	18 10					18 34	
Hanwell d																			
Greenford ⊖ d																			
South Greenford d																			
Castle Bar Park d																			
Drayton Green d																			
West Ealing d																			
Ealing Broadway ⊖ d	17 08		17 11				17 40			17 43		18 11	18 14					18 40	
Acton Main Line d																			
London Paddington 15 ⊖ a	17 18	17 07	17 20	17 21	17 24	17 27	17 49	17 39	17 50	17 50	18 07	18 20	18 25	18 13	18 22	18 24	18 27	18 48	18 39

	HC	GW	GW	GW	HC	GW	GW	GW	GW	GW	HC	GW	GW	GW	GW	GW	HC	GW	GW	GW
		◇1 ☕	1	◇1 ☕		1	◇1 ☕	1	◇1 ☕	◇1 ☕		◇1 ☕	◇1 ☕	1	◇1 ☕	◇1 ☕		1	◇1 ☕	1
Oxford d				17 50				18 05				18 39								19 05
Reading 7 d		18 14	18 21	18 23		18 37	18 46	18e52	18 56	19 03		19 13	19 13	19 18	19 23	19 32		19 37	19 44	19f52
Twyford 3 d			18 27					18 58						19 24						19 58
Maidenhead 3 d			18 36			18 51		19 06						19 34				19 54		20 06
Taplow d																				
Burnham d			18 41					19 11						19 39						20 11
Slough 3 a			18 45	18 50		18 59		19 15				19 33		19 43				20 01		20 14
d			18 46	18 51		18 59		19 15				19 34		19 44				20 02		20 15
Langley d			18 50					19 19						19 48						20 19
Iver d																				
West Drayton d			18 54					19 23						19 52						20 24
Heathrow Terminal 4 ✈ d	18 21				18 51						19 21						19 51			
Heathrow Term 1-2-3 2 ✈ d	18 27				18 57						19 27						19 57			
Hayes & Harlington d	18 33		18 59		19 03			19 29			19 33			19 58			20 03			20 30
Southall d	18 36		19 04		19 06			19 31			19 36			20 03			20 06			20 32
Hanwell d																				
Greenford ⊖ d																				
South Greenford d																				
Castle Bar Park d																				
Drayton Green d																				
West Ealing d																				
Ealing Broadway ⊖ d	18 41		19 08		19 11			19 38			19 41			20 07			20 11			20 40
Acton Main Line d																				
London Paddington 15 ⊖ a	18 50	18 53	19 18	19 09	19 20	19 21	19 26	19 47	19 37	19 40	19 50	19 51	19 54	20 18	20 09	20 11	20 20	20 22	20 22	20 50

b Arr. 1446
c Arr. 1646
e Arr. 1846
f Arr. 1946

Table 117

Sundays

until 19 June

Reading and Greenford - London

		GW	GW	HC	GW	GW	GW	GW	GW	HC	GW	HC	GW	GW	GW	GW	GW	HC	GW	GW	GW
		◇1	◇1		◇1	1	◇1	◇1	◇1		1		◇1	◇1	◇1	◇1	◇1		1	1	◇1
		☕	☕		☕		☕	☕	☕				☕	☕	☕	trolley	☕				☕
Oxford	d				19 50						20 05					20 50				21 21	
Reading 7	d	19 55	20 14		20 20	20 21		20 32	20 37		20b52		21 14	21 18	21 25	21 25	21 32		21 40	22c10	22 19
Twyford 3	d					20 27					20 57								21 46	22 16	
Maidenhead 3	d					20 36					21 05					21 43			21 54	22 24	
Taplow	d																				
Burnham	d					20 41	↤				21 10								21 59	22 29	
Slough 3	a				20 51	20 45	20 51				21 13					21 51			22 03	22 33	
	d				20 51	20 46	20 51				21 16					21 51			22 04	22 34	
Langley	d				↦	20 50					21 21								22 08	22 38	
Iver	d																				
West Drayton	d					20 53					21 26								22 15	22 43	
Heathrow Terminal 4 ✈	d			20 21						20 51		21 21						22 07			
Heathrow Term 1-2-3 2 ✈	d			20 27						20 57		21 27						22 13			
Hayes & Harlington	d			20 33		20 57				21 03	21 30	21 33						22 19	22 21	22 48	
Southall	d			20 36		21 02				21 07	21 33	21 36						22 23	22 26	22 51	
Hanwell	d																				
Greenford ⊖	d																				
South Greenford	d																				
Castle Bar Park	d																				
Drayton Green	d																				
West Ealing	d																				
Ealing Broadway ⊖	d			20 44		21 06				21 12	21 39	21 42						22 27	22 31	22 57	
Acton Main Line	d																				
London Paddington 15 ⊖	a	20 37	20 53	20 53		21 16	21 12	21 16	21 20	21 20	21 48	21 50	21 52	21 57	22 04	22 12	22 15	22 36	22 40	23 06	22 57

		GW	GW	GW	HC	GW	GW	GW	GW	GW
		◇1	◇1	◇1		1	1	◇1	◇1	1
			☕	☕					☕	
Oxford	d	21 50					22 21	22 47		
Reading 7	d	22 24	22 30	22 39		22 40	23 00	23e23	23 28	23 35
Twyford 3	d					22 52	23 07			23 45
Maidenhead 3	d					23 00	23 15			23 53
Taplow	d									
Burnham	d					23 05				23 58
Slough 3	a	22 47				23 09	23 22	23 45		00 02
	d	22 47				23 10	23 22	23 45		00 03
Langley	d					23 14	23 27			00 07
Iver	d									
West Drayton	d					23 19	23 32			00 12
Heathrow Terminal 4 ✈	d				23 07					
Heathrow Term 1-2-3 2 ✈	d				23 13					
Hayes & Harlington	d				23 19	23 25	23 37			00 17
Southall	d				23 23		23 40			00 20
Hanwell	d									
Greenford ⊖	d									
South Greenford	d									
Castle Bar Park	d									
Drayton Green	d									
West Ealing	d									
Ealing Broadway ⊖	d				23 27	23 32	23 46			00 26
Acton Main Line	d									
London Paddington 15 ⊖	a	23 05	23 15	23 20	23 36	23 41	23 55	00 11	00 16	00 35

Sundays

26 June to 31 July

		GW	GW	HC	GW	GW	HC	GW	HC	GW	HC	GW	GW	GW	GW	HC	GW	GW	GW	HC	GW	GW	GW
		1	◇1		◇1	1		1		1		1	1	1	◇1		◇1	1	◇1		1	◇1	1
					☕										☕				☕			☕	
Oxford	d		23p01			23p07								08 05			08 38						09 05
Reading 7	d	23p18	23p31		23p52	00 03		06 22		07 22		08 03	08 18	08 50	09 02		09 10	09 18	09 29		09 36	09 41	09 50
Twyford 3	d	23p24				00 09		06 28		07 28			08 24	08 56				09 25					09 56
Maidenhead 3	d	23p32				00 17		06 36		07 36			08 36	09 04				09 36			09 53		10 04
Taplow	d	23p36				00 21																	
Burnham	d	23p39				00 24		06 40		07 40			08 40					09 41					
Slough 3	a	23p44	23p48			00 28		06 45		07 45		08 22	08 45	09 11			09 30	09 46			10 01		10 11
	d	23p44	23p49			00 29		06 46		07 46		08 22	08 46	09 15			09 31	09 46			10 01		10 15
Langley	d					00 33		06 50		07 50			08 50	09 19				09 48					10 19
Iver	d					00 36																	
West Drayton	d	23p51				00 39		06 55		07 55			08 55	09 24				09 53					10 24
Heathrow Terminal 4 ✈	d			00 01			06 07		07 07		08 07					09 21				09 51			
Heathrow Term 1-2-3 2 ✈	d			00 07			06 13		07 13		08 13					09 27				09 57			
Hayes & Harlington	d	23p56		00 13		00 44	06 19	07 02	07 19	08 01	08 19		09 02	09 29		09 33		10 00		10 03			10 29
Southall	d			00 16		00 47	06 22	07 06	07 22	08 04	08 22		09 05	09 32		09 36		10 04		10 06			10 32
Hanwell	d																						
Greenford ⊖	d																						
South Greenford	d																						
Castle Bar Park	d																						
Drayton Green	d																						
West Ealing	d																						
Ealing Broadway ⊖	d	00 03		00 21		00 53	06 27	07 11	07 27	08 10	08 27		09 11	09 38		09 41		10 08		10 12			10 38
Acton Main Line	d																						
London Paddington 15 ⊖	a	00 16	00 13	00 30	00 34	01 02	06 36	07 21	07 36	08 19	08 36	08 44	09 21	09 47	09 39	09 50	09 51	10 18	10 08	10 20	10 21	10 23	10 47

b Arr. 2046

c Arr. 2202

e Arr. 2316

Table 117

Reading and Greenford - London

Sundays

26 June to 31 July

		GW	HC	GW	GW	GW		HC	GW	GW	GW		GW	HC	GW	GW		HC	GW	GW	GW	GW		GW	HC
		◇1 ☕		◇1	1	1			◇1 ☕	◇1 ☕	1		◇1 ☕		◇1 🍴	1			1	◇1 ☕	◇1 ☕	1		◇1 ☕	
Oxford	d			09 38							10 05				10 38							11 05			
Reading 7	d	10 00		10 07	10 18	10 27			10 44	10 49	10 53		11 00		11 08	11 18			11 34	11 45	11 49	11 53		12 00	
Twyford 3	d				10 26						10 59					11 25						12 00			
Maidenhead 3	d				10 36	10 45					11 07					11 36			11 52			12 08			
Taplow	d																								
Burnham	d				10 41											11 41									
Slough 3	a			10 28	10 45	10 53					11 15				11 31	11 45			12 00			12 15			
	d			10 29	10 46	10 53					11 15				11 32	11 46			12 00			12 16			
Langley	d				10 48						11 19					11 48						12 20			
Iver	d																								
West Drayton	d				10 54						11 24					11 54						12 25			
Heathrow Terminal 4 ✈	d		10 21					10 51						11 21				11 51							12 21
Heathrow Term 1-2-3 2 ✈	d		10 27					10 57						11 27				11 57							12 27
Hayes & Harlington	d		10 33		10 59			11 03			11 29			11 33		11 59		12 03				12 30			12 33
Southall	d		10 36		11 04			11 06			11 32			11 36		12 04		12 06				12 33			12 36
Hanwell	d																								
Greenford ⊖	d																								
South Greenford	d																								
Castle Bar Park	d																								
Drayton Green	d																								
West Ealing	d																								
Ealing Broadway ⊖	d		10 41		11 08			11 12			11 38			11 41		12 08		12 13				12 39			12 42
Acton Main Line	d																								
London Paddington 15 ⊖	a	10 39	10 50	10 52	11 18	11 15		11 20	11 21	11 27	11 47		11 39	11 50	11 52	12 18		12 20	12 22	12 24	12 27	12 48		12 39	12 50

		GW		GW	GW	HC	GW	GW		GW	HC	GW		GW	GW	HC	GW	GW	GW		GW	HC		GW	GW
		◇1		1	1		◇1 ☕	1		◇1 ☕		◇1 🍴		1	1		◇1 ☕	◇1 ☕	1		◇1 ☕			◇1	1
Oxford	d	11 38						12 05				12 45							13 05					13 38	
Reading 7	d	12 07		12 18	12 35		12 44	12 52		13 03		13 13		13 18	13 25		13 44	13 49	13b52		14 02			14 08	14 18
Twyford 3	d			12 25				12 58						13 25					14 00						14 25
Maidenhead 3	d			12 36	12 48			13 06						13 36	13 43				14 08						14 36
Taplow	d																								
Burnham	d			12 41										13 41											14 41
Slough 3	a	12 29		12 45	12 56			13 14				13 35		13 45	13 50				14 15					14 29	14 45
	d	12 30		12 46	12 56			13 15				13 35		13 46	13 50				14 15					14 29	14 46
Langley	d			12 48				13 19						13 50					14 20						14 50
Iver	d																								
West Drayton	d			12 54				13 24						13 54					14 25						14 54
Heathrow Terminal 4 ✈	d					12 51					13 21					13 51						14 21			
Heathrow Term 1-2-3 2 ✈	d					12 57					13 27					13 57						14 27			
Hayes & Harlington	d			12 59		13 03		13 29			13 33			13 59		14 03			14 29			14 33			14 59
Southall	d			13 04		13 06		13 32			13 36			14 04		14 06			14 33			14 36			15 04
Hanwell	d																								
Greenford ⊖	d																								
South Greenford	d																								
Castle Bar Park	d																								
Drayton Green	d																								
West Ealing	d																								
Ealing Broadway ⊖	d			13 08		13 11		13 38			13 41			14 08		14 11			14 38			14 41			15 08
Acton Main Line	d																								
London Paddington 15 ⊖	a	12 51		13 18	13 16	13 20	13 24	13 47		13 40	13 50	13 54		14 18	14 11	14 20	14 22	14 29	14 47		14 40	14 50		14 51	15 18

		HC	GW	GW	GW	GW		GW		HC	GW	GW	GW	GW	GW	HC	GW	GW			GW	HC	GW	GW	GW
			1	◇1 ☕	◇1 ☕	1		◇1 ☕			◇1	1	◇1 ☕	1	◇1 ☕		◇1 ☕	1			◇1 ☕		◇1 ☕	1	◇1 ☕
Oxford	d					14 05					14 41							15 05					15 50		
Reading 7	d		14 36	14 44	14 50	14c52		15 02			15 11	15 19	15 23	15 25	15 45		15 50	15 52			16 02		16 20	16 21	
Twyford 3	d					14 59						15 25						16 00						16 27	
Maidenhead 3	d		14 50			15 07						15 34		15 40				16 08						16 36	
Taplow	d																								
Burnham	d											15 39						16 12						16 41	←
Slough 3	a		14 58			15 15					15 31	15 43		15 49				16 16					16 49	16 45	16 49
	d		14 58			15 15					15 32	15 44		15 50				16 16					16 50	16 46	16 50
Langley	d					15 20						15 48						16 21					→	16 50	
Iver	d																								
West Drayton	d					15 25						15 52						16 25						16 54	
Heathrow Terminal 4 ✈	d	14 51								15 21						15 51						16 21			
Heathrow Term 1-2-3 2 ✈	d	14 57								15 27						15 57						16 27			
Hayes & Harlington	d	15 03				15 29				15 33		15 58				16 03		16 31				16 33		16 59	
Southall	d	15 06				15 33				15 36		16 02				16 06		16 33				16 37		17 04	
Hanwell	d																								
Greenford ⊖	d																								
South Greenford	d																								
Castle Bar Park	d																								
Drayton Green	d																								
West Ealing	d																								
Ealing Broadway ⊖	d	15 11				15 38				15 42		16 06				16 11		16 39				16 41		17 08	
Acton Main Line	d																								
London Paddington 15 ⊖	a	15 20	15 21	15 24	15 27	15 47		15 40		15 50	15 52	16 18	16 08	16 14	16 20	16 20	16 26	16 48			16 40	16 50		17 18	17 07

b Arr. 1346

c Arr. 1446

Table 117

Sundays

26 June to 31 July

Reading and Greenford - London

		HC	GW 1	GW ◇1 ☕		GW ◇1 ☕	GW 1		GW ◇1 ☕	GW ◇1 ☕	HC	GW ◇1 ☕	GW ◇1 ☕	HC		GW 1	GW 1	GW ◇1 ☕	GW ◇1 ☕	GW 1		GW ◇1 ☕	HC	GW ◇1 ☕
Oxford	d						16 05						16 50							17 05				
Reading 7	d		16 36	16 44		16 49	16b52		17 02	17 13		17 19	17 20			17 25	17 36	17 44	17 49	17 52		18 02		18 14
Twyford 3	d						16 59									17 31				18 00				
Maidenhead 3	d		16 52				17 07									17 42	17 53			18 08				
Taplow	d																							
Burnham	d						17 12									17 47				18 12				
Slough 3	a		17 00				17 15						17 44			17 51	18 00			18 16				
	d		17 00				17 16						17 45			17 53	18 01			18 16				
Langley	d						17 20									17 57				18 21				
Iver	d																							
West Drayton	d						17 26									18 01				18 26				
Heathrow Terminal 4 ✈	d	16 51									17 21			17 51									18 21	
Heathrow Term 1-2-3 2 ✈	d	16 57									17 27			17 57									18 27	
Hayes & Harlington	d	17 03					17 31				17 33			18 03		18 06				18 31			18 33	
Southall	d	17 06					17 33				17 36			18 06		18 11				18 34			18 36	
Hanwell	d																							
Greenford ⊖	d																							
South Greenford	d																							
Castle Bar Park	d																							
Drayton Green	d																							
West Ealing	d																							
Ealing Broadway ⊖	d	17 11					17 40				17 43			18 11		18 15				18 40			18 41	
Acton Main Line	d																							
London Paddington 15 ⊖	a	17 20	17 21	17 24		17 27	17 49		17 39	17 50	17 50	18 00	18 07	18 20		18 25	18 22	18 24	18 27	18 48		18 40	18 50	18 53

		GW 1	GW ◇1 ☕	HC	GW 1	GW ◇1 ☕	GW 1		GW ◇1 ☕	GW ◇1 ☕		HC	GW ◇1 ☕	GW ◇1 ☕	GW 1	GW ◇1 ☕	GW ◇1 ☕	HC	GW 1	GW ◇1 ☕		GW 1		GW ◇1 ☕	GW ◇1 ☕
Oxford	d		17 50				18 05						18 39									19 05			
Reading 7	d	18 21	18 23		18 37	18 46	18c52		18 56	19 02			19 13	19 13	19 18	19 23	19 32		19 37	19 44		19e52		19 55	20 14
Twyford 3	d	18 27					18 58								19 24							19 58			
Maidenhead 3	d	18 36			18 51		19 06								19 34				19 54			20 06			
Taplow	d																								
Burnham	d	18 41					19 11								19 39							20 11			
Slough 3	a	18 45	18 50		18 59		19 15						19 33		19 43				20 01			20 14			
	d	18 46	18 51		18 59		19 15						19 34		19 44				20 02			20 15			
Langley	d	18 50					19 19								19 48							20 19			
Iver	d																								
West Drayton	d	18 54					19 23								19 52							20 24			
Heathrow Terminal 4 ✈	d			18 51								19 21						19 51							
Heathrow Term 1-2-3 2 ✈	d			18 57								19 27						19 57							
Hayes & Harlington	d	18 59		19 03			19 29					19 33			19 59			20 03				20 30			
Southall	d	19 04		19 06			19 31					19 36			20 03			20 06				20 32			
Hanwell	d																								
Greenford ⊖	d																								
South Greenford	d																								
Castle Bar Park	d																								
Drayton Green	d																								
West Ealing	d																								
Ealing Broadway ⊖	d	19 08		19 11			19 38					19 41			20 07			20 11				20 40			
Acton Main Line	d																								
London Paddington 15 ⊖	a	19 18	19 09	19 20	19 21	19 26	19 47		19 37	19 39		19 50	19 51	19 54	20 18	20 09	20 11	20 20	20 22	20 22		20 50		20 37	20 53

		HC	GW ◇1 ☕	GW 1	GW ◇1 ☕	GW ◇1 ☕		GW ◇1 ☕	HC	GW 1		HC	GW ◇1 ☕	GW ◇1 ☕	GW ◇1 ☕	GW ◇1 🛒			GW ◇1 ☕	HC	GW 1	GW 1	GW ◇1 ☕	GW ◇1	GW ◇1 ☕
Oxford	d		19 50						20 05						20 50						21 21		21 50	
Reading 7	d		20 20	20 21		20 32		20 37		20f52			21 14	21 18	21 25	21 25			21 31		21 40	22g10	22 19	22 24	22 30
Twyford 3	d			20 27						20 57											21 46	22 16			
Maidenhead 3	d			20 36						21 05						21 43					21 54	22 24			
Taplow	d																								
Burnham	d			20 41	←					21 10											21 59	22 29			
Slough 3	a		20 51	20 45	20 51					21 13						21 51					22 03	22 33		22 47	
	d		20 51	20 46	20 51					21 16						21 51					22 04	22 34		22 47	
Langley	d		→	20 50						21 21											22 08	22 38			
Iver	d																								
West Drayton	d			20 53						21 26											22 15	22 43			
Heathrow Terminal 4 ✈	d	20 21							20 51			21 21								22 07					
Heathrow Term 1-2-3 2 ✈	d	20 27							20 57			21 27								22 13					
Hayes & Harlington	d	20 33		20 57					21 03	21 30		21 33								22 19	22 21	22 48			
Southall	d	20 36		21 02					21 07	21 33		21 36								22 23	22 26	22 51			
Hanwell	d																								
Greenford ⊖	d																								
South Greenford	d																								
Castle Bar Park	d																								
Drayton Green	d																								
West Ealing	d																								
Ealing Broadway ⊖	d	20 44		21 06					21 12	21 39		21 42								22 27	22 31	22 57			
Acton Main Line	d																								
London Paddington 15 ⊖	a	20 53		21 16	21 12	21 13		21 20	21 20	21 48		21 50	21 52	21 57	22 03	22 12			22 21	22 36	22 40	23 06	22 57	23 05	23 15

b Arr. 1646
c Arr. 1846
e Arr. 1946
f Arr. 2046
g Arr. 2202

Table 117

Sundays
26 June to 31 July

Reading and Greenford - London

	HC	GW 1	GW ◇1 🍴	GW 1	GW ◇1	GW ◇1 🍴	GW 1
Oxford d				22 14	22 47		
Reading 7 d		22 40	22 57	23b00	23c23	23 28	23 35
Twyford 3 d		22 52		23 07			23 45
Maidenhead 3 d		23 00		23 15			23 53
Taplow d							
Burnham d		23 05					23 58
Slough 3 a		23 09		23 22	23 43		00 02
d		23 10		23 23	23 44		00 03
Langley d		23 14		23 27			00 07
Iver d							
West Drayton d		23 19		23 32			00 12
Heathrow Terminal 4 ✈ d	23 07						
Heathrow Term 1-2-3 2 ✈ d	23 13						
Hayes & Harlington d	23 19	23 25		23 37			00 17
Southall d	23 23			23 40			00 20
Hanwell d							
Greenford ⊖ d							
South Greenford d							
Castle Bar Park d							
Drayton Green d							
West Ealing d							
Ealing Broadway ⊖ d	23 27	23 32		23 46			00 26
Acton Main Line d							
London Paddington 15 ⊖ a	23 36	23 41	23 34	23 54	00 10	00 16	00 35

Sundays
7 August to 11 September

	GW 1	GW ◇1	HC	GW ◇1 🍴	GW 1	HC	GW 1	HC	GW 1
Oxford d		23p01			23p07				
Reading 7 d	23p18	23p31		23p52	00 03		06 22		07 22
Twyford 3 d	23p24				00 09		06 28		07 28
Maidenhead 3 d	23p32				00 17		06 36		07 36
Taplow d	23p36				00 21				
Burnham d	23p39				00 24		06 40		07 40
Slough 3 a	23p44	23p48			00 28		06 45		07 45
d	23p44	23p49			00 29		06 46		07 46
Langley d					00 33		06 50		07 50
Iver d					00 36				
West Drayton d	23p51				00 39		06 55		07 55
Heathrow Terminal 4 ✈ d			00 01			06 07		07 07	
Heathrow Term 1-2-3 2 ✈ d			00 07			06 13		07 13	
Hayes & Harlington d	23p56		00 13		00 44	06 19	07 02	07 19	08 01
Southall d			00 16		00 47	06 22	07 05	07 22	08 04
Hanwell d									
Greenford ⊖ d									
South Greenford d									
Castle Bar Park d									
Drayton Green d									
West Ealing d									
Ealing Broadway ⊖ d	00 03		00 21		00 53	06 27	07 11	07 27	08 10
Acton Main Line d									
London Paddington 15 ⊖ a	00 16	00 13	00 30	00 33	01 02	06 36	07 20	07 36	08 19

	HC	GW 1	GW 1	GW 1	GW ◇1 🍴	GW ◇1	HC	GW 1	GW ◇1 🍴	HC	GW 1	GW ◇1 🍴	GW 1
Oxford d				08 05		08 38							09 05
Reading 7 d		08 03	08 18	08 50	09 02	09 11		09 18	09 29		09 36	09 49	09 50
Twyford 3 d			08 24	08 56				09 25					09 58
Maidenhead 3 d			08 36	09 04				09 36			09 52		10 06
Taplow d													
Burnham d			08 40					09 41					
Slough 3 a		08 24	08 45	09 11		09 30		09 45			09 59		10 13
d		08 25	08 46	09 15		09 31		09 46			10 00		10 16
Langley d			08 50	09 19				09 48					10 20
Iver d													
West Drayton d			08 55	09 24				09 53					10 25
Heathrow Terminal 4 ✈ d	08 07						09 21			09 51			
Heathrow Term 1-2-3 2 ✈ d	08 13						09 27			09 57			
Hayes & Harlington d	08 19		09 02	09 28			09 33	09 59		10 03			10 29
Southall d	08 22		09 05	09 32			09 36	10 03		10 06			10 33
Hanwell d													
Greenford ⊖ d													
South Greenford d													
Castle Bar Park d													
Drayton Green d													
West Ealing d													
Ealing Broadway ⊖ d	08 27		09 11	09 37			09 41	10 08		10 12			10 38
Acton Main Line d													
London Paddington 15 ⊖ a	08 36	08 43	09 20	09 46	09 39	09 49	09 50	10 18	10 08	10 20	10 21	10 25	10 47

	GW ◇1 🍴	HC	GW ◇1	GW 1	GW ◇1 🍴	HC	GW 1
Oxford d			09 38				10 05
Reading 7 d	10 00		10 07	10 18	10 44		10 53
Twyford 3 d				10 25			10 59
Maidenhead 3 d				10 36			11 07
Taplow d							
Burnham d				10 41			
Slough 3 a			10 28	10 45			11 15
d			10 29	10 46			11 15
Langley d				10 48			11 19
Iver d							
West Drayton d				10 54			11 24
Heathrow Terminal 4 ✈ d		10 21				10 51	
Heathrow Term 1-2-3 2 ✈ d		10 27				10 57	
Hayes & Harlington d		10 33		10 58		11 03	11 29
Southall d		10 36		11 03		11 06	11 33
Hanwell d							
Greenford ⊖ d							
South Greenford d							
Castle Bar Park d							
Drayton Green d							
West Ealing d							
Ealing Broadway ⊖ d		10 41		11 08		11 12	11 38
Acton Main Line d							
London Paddington 15 ⊖ a	10 38	10 50	10 52	11 18	11 20	11 20	11 47

	GW ◇1 🍴	GW ◇1 🍴	HC	GW ◇1 🛒	GW 1	HC	GW 1	GW ◇1 🍴	GW 1	GW ◇1 🍴	GW ◇1 🍴	HC	GW ◇1
Oxford d				10 38					11 05				11 38
Reading 7 d	10 55	11 00		11 08	11 18		11 35	11 44	11e52	11 53	12 06		12 11
Twyford 3 d					11 25				11 58				
Maidenhead 3 d					11 36		11 53		12 06				
Taplow d													
Burnham d					11 41								
Slough 3 a				11 31	11 45		12 00		12 13				12 33
d				11 32	11 46		12 01		12 14				12 34
Langley d					11 48				12 18				
Iver d													
West Drayton d					11 54				12 23				
Heathrow Terminal 4 ✈ d			11 21			11 51						12 21	
Heathrow Term 1-2-3 2 ✈ d			11 27			11 57						12 27	
Hayes & Harlington d			11 33		11 58	12 03			12 28			12 33	
Southall d			11 36		12 03	12 06			12 32			12 36	
Hanwell d													
Greenford ⊖ d													
South Greenford d													
Castle Bar Park d													
Drayton Green d													
West Ealing d													
Ealing Broadway ⊖ d			11 41		12 08	12 13			12 37			12 42	
Acton Main Line d													
London Paddington 15 ⊖ a	11 35	11 42	11 50	11 52	12 18	12 20	12 21	12 23	12 47	12 35	12 42	12 50	12 52

b Arr. 2253 c Arr. 2316 e Arr. 1146

Table 117

Sundays

7 August to 11 September

Reading and Greenford - London

		GW	GW	HC	GW	GW	GW	HC	GW	GW	GW	HC	GW	GW	GW	GW	GW	HC	GW	GW
		■1	■1		◇■1 ☕	■1	◇■1 ☕		◇■1 trolley	■1	◇■1 ☕		◇■1 ☕	■1	■1	◇■1 ☕	◇■1 ☕		◇■1	■1
Oxford	d					12 05			12 45					13 05					13 38	
Reading 7	d	12 18	12 36		12 44	12 52	13 02		13 14	13 18	13 26		13 44	13 49	13 53	14 02	14 05		14 11	14 18
Twyford 3	d	12 25				12 58				13 27				13 55						14 25
Maidenhead 3	d	12 36	12 53			13 06				13 36				14 03	14 10					14 33
Taplow	d																			
Burnham	d	12 41								13 41										14 38
Slough 3	a	12 45	13 01			13 14			13 33	13 45				14 10	14 17				14 31	14 42
	d	12 46	13 01			13 15			13 34	13 46				14 11	14 17				14 32	14 46
Langley	d	12 48				13 19				13 50				14 15						14 50
Iver	d																			
West Drayton	d	12 54				13 24				13 54				14 23						14 54
Heathrow Terminal 4 ✈	d			12 51				13 21				13 51						14 21		
Heathrow Term 1-2-3 2 ✈	d			12 57				13 27				13 57						14 27		
Hayes & Harlington	d	12 58		13 03		13 29		13 33		13 58		14 03		14 27				14 33		14 58
Southall	d	13 03		13 06		13 33		13 36		14 03		14 06		14 31				14 36		15 03
Hanwell	d																			
Greenford ⊖	d																			
South Greenford	d																			
Castle Bar Park	d																			
Drayton Green	d																			
West Ealing	d																			
Ealing Broadway ⊖	d	13 08		13 11		13 38		13 41		14 08		14 11		14 36				14 41		15 08
Acton Main Line	d																			
London Paddington 15 ⊖	a	13 18	13 20	13 20	13 23	13 47	13 38	13 50	13 52	14 18	14 08	14 20	14 21	14 46	14 39	14 40	14 44	14 50	14 52	15 18

		HC	GW	GW	GW	GW	GW	HC	GW	GW	GW	GW	HC	GW	GW	GW	GW	HC	GW	GW	GW
			■1	◇■1 ☕	■1	◇■1 ☕	◇■1 ☕		◇■1	■1	■1	◇■1 ☕		◇■1 ☕	■1	◇■1 ☕	◇■1 ☕		◇■1 ☕	■1	◇■1 ☕
Oxford	d				14 05				14 41						15 05				15 50		
Reading 7	d		14 36	14 44	14b53	15 02	15 06		15 11	15 18	15 19	15 23		15 44	15c52	16 02	16 08		16 20	16 21	
Twyford 3	d				14 59						15 29				15 58					16 28	
Maidenhead 3	d		14 50		15 07					15 33	15 37				16 06					16 37	
Taplow	d																				
Burnham	d										15 42				16 11					16 42	←
Slough 3	a		14 57		15 15				15 31	15 40	15 46				16 16				16 51	16 46	16 51
	d		14 59		15 15				15 32	15 40	15 47				16 16				16 51	16 47	16 51
Langley	d				15 20						15 51				16 19				↦	16 51	
Iver	d																				
West Drayton	d				15 25						15 55				16 25					16 54	
Heathrow Terminal 4 ✈	d	14 51						15 21					15 51					16 21			
Heathrow Term 1-2-3 2 ✈	d	14 57						15 27					15 57					16 27			
Hayes & Harlington	d	15 03			15 29			15 33			16 00		16 03		16 29			16 33		16 58	
Southall	d	15 06			15 33			15 36			16 04		16 06		16 33			16 37		17 03	
Hanwell	d																				
Greenford ⊖	d																				
South Greenford	d																				
Castle Bar Park	d																				
Drayton Green	d																				
West Ealing	d																				
Ealing Broadway ⊖	d	15 11			15 38			15 42			16 09		16 11		16 38			16 41		17 07	
Acton Main Line	d																				
London Paddington 15 ⊖	a	15 20	15 21	15 22	15 47	15 38	15 43	15 50	15 52	16 00	16 18	16 06	16 20	16 23	16 47	16 38	16 44	16 50		17 16	17 07

		HC	GW	GW	GW	HC	GW	GW	GW	GW	GW	HC	GW	GW	GW	GW	GW	GW	HC	GW
			◇■1 ☕	■1	◇■1 ☕		■1	◇■1 ☕	◇■1 ☕	◇■1 ☕	◇■1 ☕		■1	■1	◇■1 ☕	◇■1 ☕	■1	◇■1 ☕		◇■1 ☕
Oxford	d						16 05				16 50						17 05			
Reading 7	d		16 44	16 48	16 53		16e53	17 02	17 14	17 19	17 20		17 25	17 36	17 44	17 48	17f53	18 02		18 14
Twyford 3	d						17 05						17 33				18 00			
Maidenhead 3	d			17 05			17 15						17 42	17 52			18 08			
Taplow	d																			
Burnham	d						17 20						17 47				18 12			
Slough 3	a			17 12			17 23				17 44		17 51	18 00			18 16			
	d			17 12			17 24				17 45		17 52	18 00			18 16			
Langley	d						17 28						17 56				18 20			
Iver	d																			
West Drayton	d						17 33						18 00				18 25			
Heathrow Terminal 4 ✈	d	16 51				17 21						17 51							18 21	
Heathrow Term 1-2-3 2 ✈	d	16 57				17 27						17 57							18 27	
Hayes & Harlington	d	17 03				17 33	17 38					18 03	18 05				18 29		18 33	
Southall	d	17 06				17 36	17 41					18 06	18 10				18 33		18 36	
Hanwell	d																			
Greenford ⊖	d																			
South Greenford	d																			
Castle Bar Park	d																			
Drayton Green	d																			
West Ealing	d																			
Ealing Broadway ⊖	d	17 11				17 43	17 47					18 11	18 15				18 38		18 41	
Acton Main Line	d																			
London Paddington 15 ⊖	a	17 20	17 22	17 32	17 36	17 50	17 55	17 43	17 53	17 57	18 05	18 20	18 25	18 20	18 22	18 24	18 47	18 38	18 50	18 53

b Arr. 1446
c Arr. 1546
e Arr. 1646
f Arr. 1746

Table 117

Sundays

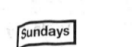

7 August to 11 September

Reading and Greenford - London

		GW ■1	GW ◇■1 ☕	HC	GW ■1	GW ◇■1 ☕	GW ■1	GW ◇■1 ☕	GW ◇■1 ☕	HC	GW ◇■1 ☕	GW ◇■1 ☕	GW ■1	GW ◇■1 ☕	GW ◇■1 ☕	HC	GW ■1	GW ◇■1 ☕	GW ■1	GW ◇■1 ☕	GW ◇■1 ☕
Oxford	d		17 50				18 05				18 39								19 05		
Reading 7	d	18 21	18 23		18 37	18 44	18b52	18 53	19 02		19 13	19 13	19 18	19 23	19 32		19 39	19 44	19c52	19 55	20 14
Twyford 3	d	18 27					18 58						19 25						19 58		
Maidenhead 3	d	18 36			18 52		19 06						19 36				19 52		20 06		
Taplow	d																				
Burnham	d	18 41					19 11						19 41						20 11		
Slough 3	a	18 45	18 49		18 59		19 15				19 33		19 45				19 59		20 14		
	d	18 46	18 50		18 59		19 15				19 34		19 46				20 00		20 15		
Langley	d	18 50					19 19						19 50						20 19		
Iver	d																				
West Drayton	d	18 54					19 23						19 54						20 24		
Heathrow Terminal 4 ✈	d			18 51						19 21						19 51					
Heathrow Term 1-2-3 2 ✈	d			18 57						19 27						19 57					
Hayes & Harlington	d	18 58		19 03			19 29			19 33			19 58			20 03			20 29		
Southall	d	19 03		19 06			19 31			19 36			20 03			20 06			20 32		
Hanwell	d																				
Greenford ⊖	d																				
South Greenford	d																				
Castle Bar Park	d																				
Drayton Green	d																				
West Ealing	d																				
Ealing Broadway ⊖	d	19 08		19 11			19 38			19 41			20 08			20 11			20 38		
Acton Main Line	d																				
London Paddington 15 ⊖	a	19 18	19 06	19 20	19 21	19 23	19 47	19 35	19 38	19 50	19 51	19 53	20 18	20 09	20 12	20 20	20 23	20 23	20 48	20 36	20 51

		HC	GW ◇■1 ☕	GW ■1	GW ◇■1 ☕	GW ◇■1 ☕	GW ◇■1 ☕	HC	GW ■1	HC	GW ◇■1 ☕	GW ◇■1 ☕	GW ◇■1 ☕	GW ◇■1 🛏	GW ◇■1 ☕	HC	GW ■1	GW ■1	GW ◇■1 ☕	GW ◇■1	GW ◇■1 ☕
Oxford	d		19 50						20 05					20 50				21 21		21 50	
Reading 7	d		20 20	20 21		20 32	20 37		20 51		21 17	21 20	21 25	21 29	21 32		21 40	22e10	22 19	22 24	22 30
Twyford 3	d			20 27					20 57								21 46	22 16			
Maidenhead 3	d			20 36					21 05					21 46			21 54	22 26			
Taplow	d																				
Burnham	d			20 41	←				21 10								21 59	22 30			
Slough 3	a		20 50	20 45	20 50				21 13					21 53			22 03	22 35		22 46	
	d		20 50	20 46	20 50				21 16					21 53			22 04	22 35		22 47	
Langley	d		→	20 50					21 20								22 08	22 39			
Iver	d																				
West Drayton	d			20 53					21 24								22 14	22 44			
Heathrow Terminal 4 ✈	d	20 21						20 51		21 21						22 07					
Heathrow Term 1-2-3 2 ✈	d	20 27						20 57		21 27						22 13					
Hayes & Harlington	d	20 33		20 57				21 03	21 29	21 33						22 19	22 21	22 49			
Southall	d	20 36		21 02				21 07	21 31	21 36						22 23	22 26	22 52			
Hanwell	d																				
Greenford ⊖	d																				
South Greenford	d																				
Castle Bar Park	d																				
Drayton Green	d																				
West Ealing	d																				
Ealing Broadway ⊖	d	20 44		21 06				21 12	21 38	21 42						22 27	22 31	22 58			
Acton Main Line	d																				
London Paddington 15 ⊖	a	20 53		21 16	21 08	21 11	21 13	21 20	21 47	21 50	21 54	21 56	22 03	22 12	22 14	22 36	22 40	23 07	22 56	23 05	23 12

		GW ◇■1 ☕	HC	GW ■1	GW ■1	GW ◇■1	GW ◇■1 ☕	GW ■1
Oxford	d				22 21	22 47		
Reading 7	d	22 39		22 40	23 04	23 23	23 28	23 35
Twyford 3	d			22 52	23 11			23 45
Maidenhead 3	d			23 00	23 19			23 53
Taplow	d							
Burnham	d			23 04				23 58
Slough 3	a			23 09	23 26	23 45		00 02
	d			23 09	23 26	23 46		00 03
Langley	d			23 13	23 30			00 07
Iver	d							
West Drayton	d			23 18	23 35			00 12
Heathrow Terminal 4 ✈	d		23 07					
Heathrow Term 1-2-3 2 ✈	d		23 13					
Hayes & Harlington	d		23 19	23 24	23 40			00 16
Southall	d		23 23		23 43			00 20
Hanwell	d							
Greenford ⊖	d							
South Greenford	d							
Castle Bar Park	d							
Drayton Green	d							
West Ealing	d							
Ealing Broadway ⊖	d		23 27	23 31	23 49			00 25
Acton Main Line	d							
London Paddington 15 ⊖	a	23 20	23 36	23 40	23 58	00 04	00 11	00 34

b Arr. 1846

c Arr. 1946

e Arr. 2203

Table 117

Sundays

18 September to 23 October

Reading and Greenford - London

		GW ■1	GW ◇■1	HC	GW ◇■1 ☕	GW ■1	HC	GW ■1	HC	GW ■1		HC	GW ■1	GW ■1	GW ■1	GW ◇■1 ☕	HC	GW ◇■1	GW ■1	HC		GW ◇■1 ☕	GW ■1	GW ◇■1 ☕	HC
Oxford	d		23p01			23p07																	09 01		
Reading 7	d	23p18	23p31		23p52	00 03		06 22		07 22			08 03	08 18	08 52	09 02		09 15	09 18			09 45	09b52	10 00	
Twyford 3	d	23p24				00 09		06 28		07 28				08 24	08 58				09 25				09 58		
Maidenhead 3	d	23p32				00 17		06 36		07 36				08 36	09 06				09 36				10 06		
Taplow	d	23p36				00 21																			
Burnham	d	23p39				00 24		06 40		07 40				08 40					09 41						
Slough 3	a	23p44	23p48			00 28		06 45		07 45			08 24	08 45	09 11			09 34	09 45				10 11		
	d	23p44	23p49			00 29		06 46		07 46			08 25	08 46	09 15			09 35	09 46				10 15		
Langley	d					00 33		06 50		07 50				08 50	09 19				09 48				10 19		
Iver	d					00 36																			
West Drayton	d	23p51				00 39		06 55		07 55				08 55	09 24				09 53				10 24		
Heathrow Terminal 4 ✈	d			00 01			06 07		07 07			08 07					09 21			09 51					10 21
Heathrow Term 1-2-3 2 ✈	d			00 07			06 13		07 13			08 13					09 27			09 57					10 27
Hayes & Harlington	d	23p56		00 13		00 44	06 19	07 02	07 19	08 01		08 19		09 02	09 28		09 33		09 59	10 03			10 28		10 33
Southall	d			00 16		00 47	06 22	07 05	07 22	08 04		08 22		09 05	09 32		09 36		10 03	10 06			10 32		10 36
Hanwell	d																								
Greenford ⊖	d																								
South Greenford	d																								
Castle Bar Park	d																								
Drayton Green	d																								
West Ealing	d																								
Ealing Broadway ⊖	d	00 03		00 21		00 53	06 27	07 11	07 27	08 10		08 27		09 11	09 37		09 41		10 08	10 12			10 37		10 41
Acton Main Line	d																								
London Paddington 15 ⊖	a	00 16	00 10	00 30	00 33	01 02	06 36	07 20	07 36	08 19		08 36	08 43	09 20	09 46	09 39	09 50	09 56	10 18	10 20		10 21	10 46	10 38	10 50

		GW ◇■1	GW ■1	GW ◇■1 ☕	HC	GW ■1			GW ◇■1 ☕	GW ◇■1 ☕	HC	GW ◇■1 🛒	GW ■1	HC	GW ◇■1 ☕	GW ■1			GW ◇■1 ☕	GW ◇■1 ☕	HC	GW ◇■1	GW ■1	HC	GW ◇■1 ☕
Oxford	d	09 38				10 05						10 38				11 05						11 38			
Reading 7	d	10 07	10 18	10 34		10 52			10 55	11 00		11 08	11 18		11 44	11c52			11 53	12 06		12 11	12 18		12 44
Twyford 3	d		10 25			10 58							11 25			11 58							12 25		
Maidenhead 3	d		10 36			11 06							11 36			12 06							12 36		
Taplow	d																								
Burnham	d		10 41										11 41										12 41		
Slough 3	a	10 28	10 45			11 13						11 30	11 45			12 13						12 33	12 45		
	d	10 29	10 46			11 15						11 31	11 46			12 14						12 34	12 46		
Langley	d		10 48			11 19							11 48			12 18							12 48		
Iver	d																								
West Drayton	d		10 54			11 24							11 54			12 23							12 54		
Heathrow Terminal 4 ✈	d				10 51						11 21			11 51							12 21			12 51	
Heathrow Term 1-2-3 2 ✈	d				10 57						11 27			11 57							12 27			12 57	
Hayes & Harlington	d		10 58		11 03	11 29					11 33		11 58	12 03		12 28					12 33		12 58	13 03	
Southall	d		11 03		11 06	11 33					11 36		12 03	12 06		12 32					12 36		13 03	13 06	
Hanwell	d																								
Greenford ⊖	d																								
South Greenford	d																								
Castle Bar Park	d																								
Drayton Green	d																								
West Ealing	d																								
Ealing Broadway ⊖	d		11 08		11 12	11 38					11 41		12 08	12 13		12 37					12 42		13 08	13 11	
Acton Main Line	d																								
London Paddington 15 ⊖	a	10 52	11 18	11 10	11 20	11 47			11 35	11 42	11 50	11 52	12 18	12 20	12 23	12 47			12 35	12 42	12 50	12 52	13 18	13 20	13 23

		GW ■1			GW ◇■1 ☕	HC	GW ◇■1 🛒	GW ■1	HC	GW ◇■1 ☕	GW ■1			GW ◇■1 ☕	GW ◇■1 ☕	HC	GW ◇■1	GW ■1	HC	GW ◇■1 ☕	GW ■1			GW ◇■1 ☕	GW ◇■1 ☕
Oxford	d	12 05					12 45				13 05						13 38				14 05				
Reading 7	d	12 52			13 02		13 14	13 18		13 44	13e52			14 02	14 06		14 11	14 18		14 44	14 52			15 02	15 06
Twyford 3	d	12 58						13 27			13 58							14 25			14 58				
Maidenhead 3	d	13 06						13 36			14 06							14 33			15 06				
Taplow	d																								
Burnham	d							13 41										14 38							
Slough 3	a	13 13					13 35	13 45			14 13						14 31	14 42			15 13				
	d	13 15					13 35	13 46			14 15						14 32	14 46			15 15				
Langley	d	13 19						13 50			14 19							14 50			15 20				
Iver	d																								
West Drayton	d	13 24						13 54			14 24							14 54			15 25				
Heathrow Terminal 4 ✈	d					13 21			13 51							14 21			14 51						
Heathrow Term 1-2-3 2 ✈	d					13 27			13 57							14 27			14 57						
Hayes & Harlington	d	13 29				13 33		13 58	14 03		14 28					14 33		14 58	15 03		15 29				
Southall	d	13 33				13 36		14 03	14 06		14 32					14 36		15 03	15 06		15 33				
Hanwell	d																								
Greenford ⊖	d																								
South Greenford	d																								
Castle Bar Park	d																								
Drayton Green	d																								
West Ealing	d																								
Ealing Broadway ⊖	d	13 38				13 41		14 08	14 11		14 37					14 41		15 08	15 11		15 38				
Acton Main Line	d																								
London Paddington 15 ⊖	a	13 47			13 38	13 50	13 53	14 18	14 20	14 21	14 47			14 40	14 43	14 50	14 52	15 18	15 20	15 22	15 47			15 38	15 43

b Arr. 0941 c Arr. 1146 e Arr. 1345

Table 117

Sundays

18 September to 23 October

Reading and Greenford - London

		HC	GW ◇1	GW 1	HC	GW ◇1 ☕	GW 1			GW ◇1 ☕	GW ◇1 ☕	HC	GW ◇1 ☕	GW 1	GW ◇1 ☕	HC	GW ◇1 ☕	HC		GW 1		GW ◇1 ☕	GW ◇1 ☕	GW ◇1 ☕	GW ◇1 ☕
Oxford	d		14 41				15 05						15 50							16 05					
Reading 7	d		15 11	15 19		15 44	15b52			16 02	16 08		16 19	16 21			16 44			16c52		16 54	17 08	17 14	17 19
Twyford 3	d			15 25			15 58							16 28						17 11					
Maidenhead 3	d			15 36			16 06							16 37						17 19					
Taplow	d																								
Burnham	d			15 41			16 11							16 42	←					17 23					
Slough 3	a		15 31	15 45			16 16						16 50	16 46	16 50					17 27					
	d		15 32	15 46			16 16						16 51	16 47	16 51					17 27					
Langley	d			15 50			16 19						→	16 51						17 31					
Iver	d																								
West Drayton	d			15 54			16 25							16 54						17 37					
Heathrow Terminal 4 ✈	d	15 21			15 51							16 21				16 51		17 21							
Heathrow Term 1-2-3 2 ✈	d	15 27			15 57							16 27				16 57		17 27							
Hayes & Harlington	d	15 33		15 59	16 03		16 29					16 33		16 58		17 03		17 33		17 42					
Southall	d	15 36		16 03	16 06		16 33					16 37		17 03		17 06		17 36		17 45					
Hanwell	d																								
Greenford ⊖	d																								
South Greenford	d																								
Castle Bar Park	d																								
Drayton Green	d																								
West Ealing	d																								
Ealing Broadway ⊖	d	15 42		16 08	16 11		16 38					16 41		17 07		17 11		17 43		17 51					
Acton Main Line	d																								
London Paddington 15 ⊖	a	15 50	15 52	16 18	16 20	16 23	16 47			16 38	16 44	16 50		17 16	17 07	17 20	17 22	17 50		17 59		17 34	17 49	17 53	17 57

		GW ◇1 ☕	HC	GW 1		GW ◇1 ☕	GW ◇1 ☕	GW 1		GW ◇1 ☕	HC	GW ◇1 ☕	GW 1	GW ◇1 ☕		HC	GW ◇1 ☕	GW 1		GW ◇1 ☕	GW ◇1 ☕	HC	GW ◇1 ☕	GW ◇1 ☕	
Oxford	d	16 50						17 05						17 50				18 05					18 39		
Reading 7	d	17 21		17 25		17 44	17 48	17e53		18 02		18 14	18 21	18 23			18 44	18f52		19 02	19 07		19 13	19 13	
Twyford 3	d			17 33				18 00					18 27					18 58							
Maidenhead 3	d			17 42				18 08					18 36					19 06							
Taplow	d																								
Burnham	d			17 47				18 12					18 41					19 11							
Slough 3	a	17 44		17 51				18 16					18 45	18 50				19 15					19 33		
	d	17 45		17 52				18 16					18 46	18 50				19 15					19 34		
Langley	d			17 56				18 20					18 50					19 19							
Iver	d																								
West Drayton	d			18 00				18 25					18 54					19 23							
Heathrow Terminal 4 ✈	d		17 51								18 21					18 51						19 21			
Heathrow Term 1-2-3 2 ✈	d		17 57								18 27					18 57						19 27			
Hayes & Harlington	d		18 03	18 05				18 29			18 33		18 58			19 03		19 29				19 33			
Southall	d		18 06	18 10				18 33			18 36		19 03			19 06		19 31				19 36			
Hanwell	d																								
Greenford ⊖	d																								
South Greenford	d																								
Castle Bar Park	d																								
Drayton Green	d																								
West Ealing	d																								
Ealing Broadway ⊖	d		18 11	18 15				18 38			18 41		19 08			19 11		19 38				19 41			
Acton Main Line	d																								
London Paddington 15 ⊖	a	18 05	18 20	18 25		18 22	18 24	18 47		18 38	18 50	18 53	19 18	19 06		19 20	19 23	19 47		19 38	19 43	19 50	19 51	19 53	

		GW 1	GW ◇1 ☕	GW ◇1 ☕	HC	GW ◇1 ☕	GW 1		GW ◇1 ☕	HC		GW ◇1 ☕	HC	GW 1	GW ◇1 ☕	GW ◇1 ☕	GW 1		GW ◇1 ☕	HC		GW ◇1 ☕	GW ◇1 ☕	GW ◇1 ☕	GW ◇1 trolley
Oxford	d						19 05								19 50		20 05								20 50
Reading 7	d	19 18	19 23	19 32		19 44	19g52		20 14			20 19		20 21	20 23	20 32	20h52		21 01			21 17	21 20	21 25	21 30
Twyford 3	d	19 25					19 58							20 29			20 58								
Maidenhead 3	d	19 36					20 06							20 39			21 06								21 44
Taplow	d																								
Burnham	d	19 41					20 11							20 44			21 11								
Slough 3	a	19 45					20 14							20 48	20 53		21 14								21 51
	d	19 46					20 15							20 49	20 53		21 15								21 52
Langley	d	19 50					20 19							20 53			21 19								
Iver	d																								
West Drayton	d	19 54					20 24							21 00			21 23								
Heathrow Terminal 4 ✈	d				19 51					20 21			20 51							21 21					
Heathrow Term 1-2-3 2 ✈	d				19 57					20 27			20 57							21 27					
Hayes & Harlington	d	19 58			20 03		20 29			20 33			21 03	21 05			21 29			21 33					
Southall	d	20 03			20 06		20 32			20 36			21 07	21 10			21 33			21 36					
Hanwell	d																								
Greenford ⊖	d																								
South Greenford	d																								
Castle Bar Park	d																								
Drayton Green	d																								
West Ealing	d																								
Ealing Broadway ⊖	d	20 08			20 11		20 38			20 44			21 12	21 14			21 38			21 42					
Acton Main Line	d																								
London Paddington 15 ⊖	a	20 18	20 09	20 12	20 20	20 23	20 48		20 51	20 53		20 55	21 20	21 24	21 11	21 14	21 47		21 38	21 50		21 53	21 57	22 03	22 11

b Arr. 1546
c Arr. 1646
e Arr. 1746
f Arr. 1846
g Arr. 1946
h Arr. 2046

Table 117

Reading and Greenford - London

Sundays

18 September to 23 October

		GW	HC	GW	GW	GW	GW	GW	HC	GW	GW	GW	GW	GW	GW	GW
		◇1 ☕		1	1	◇1 ☕	◇1	◇1 ☕		1	◇1 ☕	1	◇1	◇1 ☕	1	1
Oxford	d				21 21		21 50					22 21	22 47			23 15
Reading 7	d	21 32		21 40	22b10	22 19	22 24	22 39		22 40	22 55	23 04	23 23	23 28	23 35	23 56
Twyford 3	d			21 46	22 16					22 52		23 11			23 45	00 03
Maidenhead 3	d			21 54	22 26					23 00		23 19			23 53	00 11
Taplow	d															
Burnham	d			21 59	22 30					23 04					23 58	00 15
Slough 3	a			22 03	22 35		22 46			23 09		23 26	23 45		00 02	00 20
	d			22 04	22 35		22 47			23 09		23 26	23 46		00 03	00 20
Langley	d			22 08	22 39					23 13		23 30			00 07	00 24
Iver	d															
West Drayton	d			22 14	22 44					23 18		23 35			00 12	00 29
Heathrow Terminal 4 ✈	d		22 07						23 07							
Heathrow Term 1-2-3 2 ✈	d		22 13						23 13							
Hayes & Harlington	d		22 19	22 21	22 49				23 19	23 24		23 40			00 16	00 34
Southall	d		22 23	22 26	22 52				23 23			23 43			00 20	00 38
Hanwell	d															
Greenford ⊖	d															
South Greenford	d															
Castle Bar Park	d															
Drayton Green	d															
West Ealing	d															
Ealing Broadway ⊖	d		22 27	22 31	22 58				23 27	23 31		23 49			00 25	00 43
Acton Main Line	d															
London Paddington 15 ⊖	a	22 14	22 36	22 40	23 07	22 56	23 05	23 16	23 36	23 40	23 31	23 58	00 04	00 11	00 34	00 52

Sundays

from 30 October

		GW	GW	HC	GW	GW	HC	GW	HC	GW	HC	GW	GW	HC	GW	GW	GW	GW	GW	HC	GW	GW	GW
		1	◇1		◇1 ☕	1		1		1		1	1		1	◇1 ☕	1	◇1	1		1	◇1	1
Oxford	d		23p01			23p07															09 05	09 34	
Reading 7	d	23p18	23p31		23p52	00 03		06 22		07 22		08 03	08 18		08 50	09 01	09 18	09 20			09 52	10 02	
Twyford 3	d	23p24				00 09		06 28		07 28			08 24		08 56		09 24				09 58		
Maidenhead 3	d	23p32				00 17		06 36		07 36			08 36		09 05		09 36				10 07		
Taplow	d	23p36				00 21																	
Burnham	d	23p39				00 24		06 40		07 40			08 40				09 40		←				←
Slough 3	a	23p44	23p48			00 28		06 45		07 45		08 20	08 45		09 12		09 46	09 36	09 46		10 15	10 17	10 15
	d	23p44	23p49			00 29		06 46		07 46		08 20	08 46		09 19		09 46	09 36	09 46		10 21	10 18	10 21
Langley	d					00 33		06 50		07 50			08 50		09 23		→		09 50		→		10 25
Iver	d					00 36																	
West Drayton	d	23p51				00 39		06 55		07 55			08 55		09 28				09 55				10 30
Heathrow Terminal 4 ✈	d			00 01			06 07		07 07		08 07			09 07						10 07			
Heathrow Term 1-2-3 2 ✈	d			00 07			06 13		07 13		08 13			09 13						10 13			
Hayes & Harlington	d	23p56		00 13		00 44	06 19	07 02	07 19	08 02	08 19		09 02	09 19	09 32				10 02	10 19			10 34
Southall	d			00 16		00 47	06 22	07 05	07 22	08 05	08 22		09 05	09 22	09 36					10 22			10 38
Hanwell	d																						
Greenford ⊖	d																						
South Greenford	d																						
Castle Bar Park	d																						
Drayton Green	d																						
West Ealing	d																						
Ealing Broadway ⊖	d	00 03		00 21		00 53	06 27	07 11	07 27	08 11	08 27		09 11	09 27	09 41				10 08	10 27			10 43
Acton Main Line	d																						
London Paddington 15 ⊖	a	00 16	00 10	00 30	00 34	01 02	06 36	07 20	07 36	08 20	08 36	08 44	09 20	09 36	09 50	09 38		09 58	10 18	10 36		10 44	10 52

		GW	GW	GW	HC	GW	GW	GW	GW	GW	GW	HC	GW	GW	GW	GW	HC	GW	GW	GW
		1	◇1 ☕	◇1 ☕		1	1	◇1 ☕	◇1 🍴	1	◇1 ☕		1	◇1	◇1 ☕	1		1	1	◇1 ☕
Oxford	d					10 05			10 52				11 05	11 50				12 05		
Reading 7	d	10 18	10 21	10 44		10 52	11 18	11 21	11 22		11 45		11 52	12 19	12 21	12 23		12 52	13 18	13 21
Twyford 3	d	10 24				10 58	11 24						11 58			12 29		12 58	13 24	
Maidenhead 3	d	10 36				11 06	11 36						12 06			12 38		13 06	13 36	
Taplow	d																			
Burnham	d	10 40					11 40			←						12 42			13 40	
Slough 3	a	10 45				11 14	11 45		11 38	11 45			12 14	12 37		12 47		13 14	13 45	
	d	10 48				11 21	11 48		11 38	11 48			12 21	12 38		12 48		13 21	13 48	
Langley	d	10 50				11 25	→			11 50			12 25			12 50		13 25	→	
Iver	d																			
West Drayton	d	10 56				11 30				11 57			12 30			12 56		13 30		
Heathrow Terminal 4 ✈	d				11 07							12 07					13 07			
Heathrow Term 1-2-3 2 ✈	d				11 13							12 13					13 13			
Hayes & Harlington	d	11 01			11 19	11 34				12 01		12 19	12 34			13 01	13 19	13 34		
Southall	d				11 23	11 38						12 23	12 38				13 22	13 38		
Hanwell	d																			
Greenford ⊖	d																			
South Greenford	d																			
Castle Bar Park	d																			
Drayton Green	d																			
West Ealing	d																			
Ealing Broadway ⊖	d	11 08			11 28	11 43				12 08		12 28	12 43			13 08	13 27	13 43		
Acton Main Line	d																			
London Paddington 15 ⊖	a	11 18	10 58	11 28	11 36	11 52		11 58	12 01	12 18	12 29	12 36	12 52	13 03	12 58	13 18	13 36	13 52		13 58

b Arr. 2203

Table 117

Sundays

from 30 October

Reading and Greenford - London

		GW ◇1 ⊤o		GW 1	GW ◇1 ⊏P	HC	GW 1		GW 1	GW ◇1 ⊏P	GW ◇1	GW 1		GW ◇1 ⊏P	HC	GW 1		GW 1	GW ◇1 ⊏P	GW ◇1	GW 1	GW ◇1 ⊏P		HC	GW 1
Oxford	d	12 50					13 05				13 50					14 05				14 50					15 05
Reading 7	d	13 26			13 49		13 52		14 18	14 21	14 25			14 51		14 52		15 18	15 21	15 26		15 49			15 52
Twyford 3	d						13 58		14 24							14 58		15 24							15 58
Maidenhead 3	d						14 06		14 36							15 06		15 36							16 06
Taplow	d																								
Burnham	d			←					14 40			←						15 40			←				16 11
Slough 3	a	13 40		13 45			14 14		14 45		14 41	14 45				15 14		15 45		15 40	15 45				16 17
	d	13 41		13 48			14 21		14 48		14 41	14 48				15 21		15 48		15 41	15 48				16 21
Langley	d			13 52			14 25		→			14 52				15 25		→			15 52				16 25
Iver	d																								
West Drayton	d			13 56			14 30					14 56				15 30					15 56				16 30
Heathrow Terminal 4 ✈	d					14 07									15 07									16 07	
Heathrow Term 1-2-3 2 ✈	d					14 13									15 13									16 13	
Hayes & Harlington	d			14 02		14 19	14 34					15 01			15 19	15 34					16 01			16 19	16 34
Southall	d					14 23	14 38								15 23	15 38								16 23	16 38
Hanwell	d																								
Greenford ⊖	d																								
South Greenford	d																								
Castle Bar Park	d																								
Drayton Green	d																								
West Ealing	d																								
Ealing Broadway ⊖	d			14 09		14 28	14 43					15 08			15 28	15 43					16 08			16 28	16 43
Acton Main Line	d																								
London Paddington 15 ⊖	a	14 02		14 19	14 28	14 36	14 52			14 58	15 03	15 18		15 29	15 36	15 52			15 58	16 02	16 18	16 30		16 36	16 52

			GW 1	GW ◇1 ⊏P	GW ◇1 ⊏P	GW 1	GW ◇1 ⊏P	HC		GW 1		GW ◇1 ⊏P	GW 1	GW ◇1 ⊏P	GW ◇1 ⊏P	GW 1	GW ◇1 ⊏P	HC		GW 1		GW ◇1 ⊏P	GW 1	GW ◇1 ⊏P	GW ◇1 ⊏P
Oxford	d				15 50					16 05					16 50					17 05					17 50
Reading 7	d		16 18	16 21	16 26		16 50			16 52		17 01	17 18	17 21	17 23		17 44			17 52		17 57	18 18	18 21	18 26
Twyford 3	d		16 24							16 58			17 24							17 58			18 24		
Maidenhead 3	d		16 36							17 06			17 36							18 06			18 36		
Taplow	d																								
Burnham	d		16 40			←				17 11			17 40			←				18 11			18 40		
Slough 3	a		16 46		16 41	16 46				17 17			17 45		17 39	17 45				18 16			18 45		18 40
	d		16 48		16 42	16 48				17 21			17 48		17 39	17 48				18 21			18 48		18 40
Langley	d		→			16 52				17 25			→			17 52				18 25			→		
Iver	d																								
West Drayton	d					16 56				17 30						17 56				18 30					
Heathrow Terminal 4 ✈	d							17 07										18 07							
Heathrow Term 1-2-3 2 ✈	d							17 13										18 13							
Hayes & Harlington	d					17 01		17 19		17 34						18 01		18 19		18 34					
Southall	d							17 23		17 38								18 23		18 38					
Hanwell	d																								
Greenford ⊖	d																								
South Greenford	d																								
Castle Bar Park	d																								
Drayton Green	d																								
West Ealing	d																								
Ealing Broadway ⊖	d					17 08		17 28		17 43						18 08		18 28		18 43					
Acton Main Line	d																								
London Paddington 15 ⊖	a			16 58	17 06	17 19	17 29	17 36		17 52		17 43		17 58	18 04	18 18	18 28	18 36		18 52		18 42		18 58	19 05

		GW 1	HC	GW 1			GW ◇1 ⊏P	GW ◇1 ⊏P	GW 1	GW ◇1 ⊏P	GW ◇1 ⊏P	GW 1	GW ◇1 ⊏P	HC		GW 1		GW ◇1 ⊏P	GW 1	GW ◇1 ⊏P	GW ◇1 ⊏P	GW 1	GW ◇1 ⊏P	HC	
Oxford	d			18 05							18 50					19 05				19 50					
Reading 7	d			18 52			18 53	19 02	19 18	19 21	19 26		19 51			19 52		20 01	20 18	20 23	20 25		20 47		
Twyford 3	d			18 58					19 24							19 58			20 24						
Maidenhead 3	d			19 06					19 36							20 06			20 36						
Taplow	d																								
Burnham	d	←		19 11					19 40			←				20 11			20 40			←			
Slough 3	a	18 45		19 17					19 45		19 40	19 45				20 17			20 45	20 43		20 45			
	d	18 48		19 21					19 48		19 40	19 48				20 21			20 48	20 44		20 48			
Langley	d	18 52		19 25					→			19 52				20 25			→			20 52			
Iver	d																								
West Drayton	d	18 56		19 30								19 56				20 30						20 56			
Heathrow Terminal 4 ✈	d		19 07											20 07										21 07	
Heathrow Term 1-2-3 2 ✈	d		19 13											20 13										21 13	
Hayes & Harlington	d	19 01	19 19	19 34								20 01		20 19		20 34						21 01		21 19	
Southall	d		19 22	19 38										20 22		20 38								21 23	
Hanwell	d																								
Greenford ⊖	d																								
South Greenford	d																								
Castle Bar Park	d																								
Drayton Green	d																								
West Ealing	d																								
Ealing Broadway ⊖	d	19 08	19 27	19 43								20 08		20 27		20 43						21 08		21 28	
Acton Main Line	d																								
London Paddington 15 ⊖	a	19 18	19 36	19 52			19 29	19 43		19 58	20 06	20 18	20 27	20 36		20 52		20 43		21 07	21 00	21 18	21 28	21 36	

Table 117

Sundays
from 30 October

Reading and Greenford - London

		GW		GW	GW	GW	GW	GW		HC		GW		GW	GW	HC	GW	GW	GW	GW		GW	GW		
		1		◇1	1	◇1	◇1	1				1		◇1	◇1		1	◇1	1	◇1		◇1	1		
				☕		☕	🛒							☕				☕				☕			
Oxford	d	20 05					20 50					21 21			21 50				22 21	22 47					
Reading 7	d	20 52		21 12	21 24	21 25	21 30					22b10		22 27	22c33		22 40	22 41	23 00	23 23		23 34	23 35		
Twyford 3	d	20 58			21 30							22 16					22 49		23 07				23 41		
Maidenhead 3	d	21 06			21 38		21 42					22 24					22 57		23 15				23 49		
Taplow	d																								
Burnham	d	21 11			21 43			←				22 29					23 01						23 54		
Slough 3	a	21 17			21 51		21 48	21 51				22 33			22 49		23 06		23 22	23 45			23 58		
	d	21 21			21 52		21 48	21 52				22 34			22 50		23 06		23 22	23 46			23 59		
Langley	d	21 25			→			21 57				22 38					23 10		23 26				00 03		
Iver	d																								
West Drayton	d	21 30						22 00				22 43					23 15		23 31				00 12		
Heathrow Terminal 4 ✈	d									22 07						23 07									
Heathrow Term 1-2-3 2 ✈	d									22 13						23 13									
Hayes & Harlington	d	21 34						22 04		22 19		22 47				23 19	23 25		23 36				00 16		
Southall	d	21 38						22 09		22 23		22 51				23 23			23 39				00 20		
Hanwell	d																								
Greenford ⊖	d																								
South Greenford	d																								
Castle Bar Park	d																								
Drayton Green	d																								
West Ealing	d																								
Ealing Broadway ⊖	d	21 43						22 14		22 27		22 56				23 27	23 32		23 45				00 25		
Acton Main Line	d																								
London Paddington 15 ⊖	a	21 52		22 01		22 02	22 13	22 23		22 36		23 05		23 08	23 13	23 36	23 40	23 17	23 54	00 04		00 13	00 34		

b Arr. 2202

c Arr. 2225

London - Heathrow Airport

Miles		HX	HX	HX 1	HX	HX 1	HX	HX 1	HX	HX 1		HX	HX 1	HX	HX 1	HX	HX 1	HX	HX 1	HX		HX 1	HX	HX 1
0	London Paddington 15 ⊖ d	04 42		05 10	05 13	05 25		05 40		05 55			06 10		06 25		06 40		06 55			07 10		07 25
14¾	Heathrow Terminals 1-2-3 2 ✈ a	05 04		05 26	05 35	05 40		05 55		06 10			06 25		06 40		06 55		07 10			07 25		07 40
—	d	05 05	05 16	05 29	05 36	05 41	05 44	05 56	06 03	06 11		06 18	06 26	06 33	06 41	06 48	06 56	07 03	07 11	07 18		07 26	07 33	07 41
—	Heathrow Terminal 4 ✈ a	05 10	05 20		05 41		05 48		06 07			06 22		06 37		06 52		07 07		07 22			07 37	
16¼	Heathrow Terminal 5 ✈ a			05 33		05 46		06 01		06 16			06 31		06 46		07 01		07 16			07 31		07 46

	HX	HX 1	HX	HX 1	HX	HX 1		HX	HX 1	HX	HX 1	HX	HX 1	HX	HX 1	HX		HX 1	HX	HX 1	HX	HX 1	HX	HX 1
London Paddington 15 ⊖ d		07 40		07 55		08 10			08 25		08 40		08 55		09 10			09 25		09 40		09 55		10 10
Heathrow Terminals 1-2-3 2 ✈ a		07 55		08 10		08 25			08 40		08 55		09 10		09 25			09 40		09 55		10 10		10 25
d	07 48	07 56	08 03	08 11	08 18	08 26		08 33	08 41	08 48	08 56	09 03	09 11	09 18	09 26	09 33		09 41	09 48	09 56	10 03	10 11	10 18	10 26
Heathrow Terminal 4 ✈ a	07 52		08 07		08 22			08 37		08 52		09 07		09 22		09 37			09 52		10 07		10 22	
Heathrow Terminal 5 ✈ a		08 01		08 16		08 31			08 46		09 01		09 16		09 31			09 46		10 01		10 16		10 31

	HX	HX 1		HX	HX 1	HX	HX 1	HX	HX 1	HX	HX 1	HX		HX 1	HX	HX 1	HX	HX 1	HX	HX 1	HX	HX 1		HX
London Paddington 15 ⊖ d		10 25			10 40		10 55		11 10		11 25			11 40		11 55		12 10		12 25		12 40		
Heathrow Terminals 1-2-3 2 ✈ a		10 40			10 55		11 10		11 25		11 40			11 55		12 10		12 25		12 40		12 55		
d	10 33	10 41		10 48	10 56	11 03	11 11	11 18	11 26	11 33	11 41	11 48		11 56	12 03	12 11	12 18	12 26	12 33	12 41	12 48	12 56		13 03
Heathrow Terminal 4 ✈ a	10 37			10 52		11 07		11 22		11 37		11 52			12 07		12 22		12 37		12 52			13 07
Heathrow Terminal 5 ✈ a		10 46			11 01		11 16		11 31		11 46			12 01		12 16		12 31		12 46		13 01		

	HX 1	HX	HX 1	HX	HX 1	HX	HX 1	HX		HX 1	HX	HX 1	HX	HX 1	HX	HX 1	HX	HX 1		HX	HX 1	HX	HX 1	HX
London Paddington 15 ⊖ d	12 55		13 10		13 25		13 40			13 55		14 10		14 25		14 40		14 55			15 10		15 25	
Heathrow Terminals 1-2-3 2 ✈ a	13 10		13 25		13 40		13 55			14 10		14 25		14 40		14 55		15 10			15 25		15 40	
d	13 11	13 18	13 26	13 33	13 41	13 48	13 56	14 03		14 11	14 18	14 26	14 33	14 41	14 48	14 56	15 03	15 11		15 18	15 26	15 33	15 41	15 48
Heathrow Terminal 4 ✈ a		13 22		13 37		13 52		14 07			14 22		14 37		14 52		15 07			15 22		15 37		15 52
Heathrow Terminal 5 ✈ a	13 16		13 31		13 46		14 01			14 16		14 31		14 46		15 01		15 16			15 31		15 46	

	HX 1	HX	HX 1	HX		HX 1	HX	HX 1	HX	HX 1	HX	HX 1	HX	HX 1		HX	HX 1	HX	HX 1	HX	HX 1	HX	HX 1	HX
London Paddington 15 ⊖ d	15 40		15 55			16 10		16 25		16 40		16 55		17 10			17 25		17 40		17 55		18 10	
Heathrow Terminals 1-2-3 2 ✈ a	15 55		16 10			16 25		16 40		16 55		17 10		17 25			17 40		17 55		18 10		18 25	
d	15 56	16 03	16 11	16 18		16 26	16 33	16 41	16 48	16 56	17 03	17 11	17 18	17 26		17 33	17 41	17 48	17 56	18 03	18 11	18 18	18 26	18 33
Heathrow Terminal 4 ✈ a		16 07		16 22			16 37		16 52		17 07		17 22			17 37		17 52		18 07		18 22		18 37
Heathrow Terminal 5 ✈ a	16 01		16 16			16 31		16 46		17 01		17 16		17 31			17 46		18 01		18 16		18 31	

		HX 1	HX	HX 1	HX	HX 1	HX	HX 1	HX	HX 1		HX	HX 1	HX	HX 1	HX	HX 1	HX	HX 1	HX		HX 1	HX	HX 1
London Paddington 15 ⊖ d		18 25		18 40		18 55		19 10		19 25			19 40		19 55		20 10		20 25			20 40		20 55
Heathrow Terminals 1-2-3 2 ✈ a		18 40		18 55		19 10		19 25		19 40			19 55		20 10		20 25		20 40			20 55		21 10
d		18 41	18 48	18 56	19 03	19 11	19 18	19 26	19 33	19 41		19 48	19 56	20 03	20 11	20 18	20 26	20 33	20 41	20 48		20 56	21 03	21 11
Heathrow Terminal 4 ✈ a			18 52		19 07		19 22		19 37			19 52		20 07		20 22		20 37		20 52			21 07	
Heathrow Terminal 5 ✈ a		18 46		19 01		19 16		19 31		19 46			20 01		20 16		20 31		20 46			21 01		21 16

	HX	HX 1	HX	HX 1	HX	HX 1		HX	HX 1	HX	HX 1	HX	HX 1	HX	HX 1	HX		HX 1	HX	HX 1	HX	HX	HX 1	HX
London Paddington 15 ⊖ d		21 10		21 25		21 40			21 55		22 10		22 25		22 40			22 55		23 10		23 03	23 25	
Heathrow Terminals 1-2-3 2 ✈ a		21 25		21 40		21 55			22 10		22 25		22 40		22 55			23 10		23 25		23 35	23 40	
d	21 18	21 26	21 33	21 41	21 48	21 56		22 03	22 11	22 18	22 26	22 33	22 41	22 48	22 56	23 03		23 11	23 18	23 26	23 33	23 37	23 41	23 48
Heathrow Terminal 4 ✈ a	21 22		21 37		21 52			22 07		22 22		22 37		22 52		23 07			23 22		23 37	23 41		23 52
Heathrow Terminal 5 ✈ a		21 31		21 46		22 01			22 16		22 31		22 46		23 01			23 16		23 31			23 46	

Saturdays

	HX	HX	HX 1	HX	HX 1	HX	HX 1	HX	HX 1		HX	HX 1	HX	HX 1	HX	HX 1	HX	HX 1	HX		HX 1	HX	HX 1	HX
London Paddington 15 ⊖ d	04 42		05 10	05 13	05 25		05 40		05 55			06 10		06 25		06 40		06 55			07 10		07 25	
Heathrow Terminals 1-2-3 2 ✈ a	05 04		05 26	05 35	05 40		05 55		06 10			06 25		06 40		06 55		07 10			07 25		07 40	
d	05 05	05 16	05 29	05 36	05 41	05 44	05 56	06 03	06 11		06 18	06 26	06 33	06 41	06 48	06 56	07 03	07 11	07 18		07 26	07 33	07 41	07 48
Heathrow Terminal 4 ✈ a	05 10	05 20		05 41		05 48		06 07			06 22		06 37		06 52		07 07		07 22			07 37		07 52
Heathrow Terminal 5 ✈ a			05 33		05 46		06 01		06 16			06 31		06 46		07 01		07 16			07 31		07 46	

	HX 1	HX	HX 1	HX	HX 1		HX	HX 1	HX	HX 1	HX	HX 1	HX	HX 1	HX		HX 1	HX	HX 1	HX	HX 1	HX	HX 1	HX
London Paddington 15 ⊖ d	07 40		07 55		08 10			08 25		08 40		08 55		09 10			09 25		09 40		09 55		10 10	
Heathrow Terminals 1-2-3 2 ✈ a	07 55		08 10		08 25			08 40		08 55		09 10		09 25			09 40		09 55		10 10		10 25	
d	07 56	08 03	08 11	08 18	08 26		08 33	08 41	08 48	08 56	09 03	09 11	09 18	09 26	09 33		09 41	09 48	09 56	10 03	10 11	10 18	10 26	10 33
Heathrow Terminal 4 ✈ a		08 07		08 22			08 37		08 52		09 07		09 22		09 37			09 52		10 07		10 22		10 37
Heathrow Terminal 5 ✈ a	08 01		08 16		08 31			08 46		09 01		09 16		09 31			09 46		10 01		10 16		10 31	

Table 118

Saturdays

London - Heathrow Airport

	HX 1		HX	HX 1	HX	HX 1	HX	HX 1	HX	HX 1	HX		HX 1	HX	HX 1	HX	HX 1	HX	HX 1	HX	HX 1		HX	HX 1
London Paddington 15 ⊖ d	10 25			10 40		10 55		11 10		11 25			11 40		11 55		12 10		12 25		12 40			12 55
Heathrow Terminals 1-2-3 2 ✈ a	10 40			10 55		11 10		11 25		11 40			11 55		12 10		12 25		12 40		12 55			13 10
d	10 41		10 48	10 56	11 03	11 11	11 18	11 26	11 33	11 41	11 48		11 56	12 03	12 11	12 18	12 26	12 33	12 41	12 48	12 56		13 03	13 11
Heathrow Terminal 4 ✈ a			10 52		11 07		11 22		11 37		11 52			12 07		12 22		12 37		12 52			13 07	
Heathrow Terminal 5 ✈ a	10 46			11 01		11 16		11 31		11 46			12 01		12 16		12 31		12 46		13 01			13 16

	HX	HX 1	HX	HX 1	HX	HX 1	HX		HX 1	HX	HX 1	HX	HX 1	HX	HX 1	HX	HX 1		HX	HX 1	HX	HX 1	HX	HX 1
London Paddington 15 ⊖ d		13 10		13 25		13 40			13 55		14 10		14 25		14 40		14 55			15 10		15 25		15 40
Heathrow Terminals 1-2-3 2 ✈ a		13 25		13 40		13 55			14 10		14 25		14 40		14 55		15 10			15 25		15 40		15 55
d	13 18	13 26	13 33	13 41	13 48	13 56	14 03		14 11	14 18	14 26	14 33	14 41	14 48	14 56	15 03	15 11		15 18	15 26	15 33	15 41	15 48	15 56
Heathrow Terminal 4 ✈ a	13 22		13 37		13 52		14 07			14 22		14 37		14 52		15 07			15 22		15 37		15 52	
Heathrow Terminal 5 ✈ a		13 31		13 46		14 01			14 16		14 31		14 46		15 01		15 16			15 31		15 46		16 01

	HX	HX 1	HX		HX 1	HX	HX 1	HX	HX 1	HX	HX 1	HX	HX 1		HX	HX 1	HX	HX 1	HX	HX 1	HX	HX 1	HX	
London Paddington 15 ⊖ d		15 55			16 10		16 25		16 40		16 55		17 10			17 25		17 40		17 55		18 10		
Heathrow Terminals 1-2-3 2 ✈ a		16 10			16 25		16 40		16 55		17 10		17 25			17 40		17 55		18 10		18 25		
d	16 03	16 11	16 18		16 26	16 33	16 41	16 48	16 56	17 03	17 11	17 18	17 26		17 33	17 41	17 48	17 56	18 03	18 11	18 18	18 26	18 33	
Heathrow Terminal 4 ✈ a	16 07		16 22			16 37		16 52		17 07		17 22			17 37		17 52		18 07		18 22		18 37	
Heathrow Terminal 5 ✈ a		16 16			16 31		16 46		17 01		17 16		17 31			17 46		18 01		18 16		18 31		

	HX 1	HX	HX 1	HX	HX 1	HX	HX 1	HX	HX 1		HX	HX 1	HX	HX 1	HX	HX 1	HX	HX 1	HX		HX 1	HX	HX 1	HX
London Paddington 15 ⊖ d	18 25		18 40		18 55		19 10		19 25			19 40		19 55		20 10		20 25			20 40		20 55	
Heathrow Terminals 1-2-3 2 ✈ a	18 40		18 55		19 10		19 25		19 40			19 55		20 10		20 25		20 40			20 55		21 10	
d	18 41	18 48	18 56	19 03	19 11	19 18	19 26	19 33	19 41		19 48	19 56	20 03	20 11	20 18	20 26	20 33	20 41	20 48		20 56	21 03	21 11	21 18
Heathrow Terminal 4 ✈ a		18 52		19 07		19 22		19 37			19 52		20 07		20 22		20 37		20 52			21 07		21 22
Heathrow Terminal 5 ✈ a	18 46		19 01		19 16		19 31		19 46			20 01		20 16		20 31		20 46			21 01		21 16	

	HX 1	HX	HX 1	HX	HX 1		HX	HX 1	HX	HX 1	HX	HX 1	HX	HX 1	HX		HX 1	HX	HX 1	HX	HX	HX 1	HX	
London Paddington 15 ⊖ d	21 10		21 25		21 40			21 55		22 10		22 25		22 40			22 55		23 10		23 03	23 25		
Heathrow Terminals 1-2-3 2 ✈ a	21 25		21 40		21 55			22 10		22 25		22 40		22 55			23 10		23 25		23 35	23 40		
d	21 26	21 33	21 41	21 48	21 56		22 03	22 11	22 18	22 26	22 33	22 41	22 48	22 56	23 03		23 11	23 18	23 26	23 33	23 37	23 41	23 48	
Heathrow Terminal 4 ✈ a		21 37		21 52			22 07		22 22		22 37		22 52		23 07			23 22		23 37	23 41		23 52	
Heathrow Terminal 5 ✈ a	21 31		21 46		22 01			22 16		22 31		22 46		23 01			23 16		23 31			23 46		

Sundays

until 23 October

	HX	HX	HX	HX	HX	HX	HX	HX	HX		HX	HX	HX	HX	HX	HX	HX	HX	HX		HX	HX	HX	HX
London Paddington 15 ⊖ d	05 10	05 12	05 25	05 28	05 40		05 55		06 10			06 12	06 25		06 40		06 55		07 10			07 12	07 25	
Heathrow Terminals 1-2-3 2 ✈ a	05 26	05 34	05 41	05 45	05 56		06 11		06 26			06 34	06 41		06 56		07 11		07 26			07 34	07 41	
d	05 27	05 36	05 42	05 47	05 59	06 01	06 13	06 19	06 31		06 33	06 37	06 47	06 49	06 59	07 01	07 13	07 19	07 31		07 33	07 37	07 47	07 49
Heathrow Terminal 4 ✈ a		05 40		05 51		06 05		06 23			06 37	06 41		06 53		07 05		07 23			07 37	07 41		07 53
Heathrow Terminal 5 ✈ a	05 32		05 47		06 03		06 17		06 35				06 51		07 03		07 17		07 35				07 51	

	HX	HX	HX	HX	HX		HX	HX	HX	HX	HX	HX	HX	HX	HX		HX	HX	HX	HX	HX	HX	HX	HX
London Paddington 15 ⊖ d	07 40		07 55		08 10			08 12	08 25		08 40		08 55		09 10		09 07	09 25		09 40	09 37	09 55		10 10
Heathrow Terminals 1-2-3 2 ✈ a	07 56		08 11		08 26			08 34	08 41		08 56		09 11		09 25		09 29	09 40		09 55	09 59	10 10		10 25
d	07 59	08 01	08 13	08 19	08 31		08 33	08 37	08 47	08 49	08 59	09 01	09 13	09 15	09 26		09 35	09 41	09 44	09 56	10 05	10 11	10 14	10 26
Heathrow Terminal 4 ✈ a		08 05		08 23			08 37	08 41		08 53		09 05		09 19			09 39		09 48		10 09		10 18	
Heathrow Terminal 5 ✈ a	08 03		08 17		08 35				08 51		09 03		09 17		09 31			09 46		10 01		10 16		10 31

	HX		HX	HX	HX	HX	HX	HX	HX	HX	HX		HX	HX	HX	HX	HX	HX	HX	HX	HX		HX	HX
London Paddington 15 ⊖ d	10 07		10 25		10 40	10 37	10 55		11 10	11 07	11 25			11 40	11 37	11 55		12 10	12 07	12 25			12 40	12 37
Heathrow Terminals 1-2-3 2 ✈ a	10 29		10 40		10 55	10 59	11 10		11 25	11 29	11 40			11 55	11 59	12 10		12 25	12 29	12 40			12 55	12 59
d	10 35		10 41	10 44	10 56	11 05	11 11	11 14	11 26	11 35	11 41		11 44	11 56	12 05	12 11	12 14	12 26	12 35	12 41	12 44		12 56	13 05
Heathrow Terminal 4 ✈ a	10 39			10 48		11 09		11 18		11 39			11 48		12 09		12 18		12 39		12 48			13 09
Heathrow Terminal 5 ✈ a			10 46		11 01		11 16		11 31		11 46			12 01		12 16		12 31		12 46			13 01	

	HX	HX	HX	HX	HX	HX	HX		HX	HX	HX	HX	HX	HX	HX	HX	HX		HX	HX	HX	HX	HX	HX
London Paddington 15 ⊖ d	12 55		13 10	13 07	13 25		13 40		13 37	13 55		14 10	14 07	14 25		14 40	14 37		14 55		15 10	15 07	15 25	
Heathrow Terminals 1-2-3 2 ✈ a	13 10		13 25	13 29	13 40		13 55		13 59	14 10		14 25	14 29	14 40		14 55	14 59		15 10		15 25	15 29	15 40	
d	13 11	13 14	13 26	13 35	13 41	13 44	13 56		14 05	14 11	14 14	14 26	14 35	14 41	14 44	14 56	15 05		15 11	15 14	15 26	15 35	15 41	15 44
Heathrow Terminal 4 ✈ a		13 18		13 39		13 48			14 09		14 18		14 39		14 48		15 09			15 18		15 39		15 48
Heathrow Terminal 5 ✈ a	13 16		13 31		13 46		14 01			14 16		14 31		14 46		15 01			15 16		15 31		15 46	

Table 118

Sundays
until 23 October

London - Heathrow Airport

	HX	HX	HX		HX	HX	HX	HX	HX	HX	HX	HX	HX		HX	HX	HX	HX	HX	HX	HX	HX	HX	
London Paddington 15 ⊖ d	15 40	15 37	15 55			16 10	16 07	16 25		16 40	16 37	16 55			17 10	17 07	17 25		17 40	17 37	17 55		18 10	
Heathrow Terminals 1-2-3 2 ✈ a	15 55	15 59	16 10			16 25	16 29	16 40		16 55	16 59	17 10			17 25	17 29	17 40		17 55	17 59	18 10		18 25	
d	15 56	16 05	16 11		16 14	16 26	16 35	16 41	16 44	16 56	17 05	17 11	17 14		17 26	17 35	17 41	17 44	17 56	18 05	18 11	18 14	18 26	
Heathrow Terminal 4 ✈ a		16 09			16 18		16 39		16 48		17 09		17 18			17 39		17 48		18 09		18 18		
Heathrow Terminal 5 ✈ a	16 01		16 16			16 31		16 46		17 01		17 16			17 31		17 46		18 01		18 16		18 31	

	HX	HX	HX	HX	HX	HX	HX	HX	HX		HX	HX	HX	HX	HX	HX	HX	HX	HX		HX	HX	HX	HX
London Paddington 15 ⊖ d	18 07	18 25		18 40	18 37	18 55		19 10	19 07		19 25		19 40	19 37	19 55		20 10	20 07	20 25			20 40	20 37	20 55
Heathrow Terminals 1-2-3 2 ✈ a	18 29	18 40		18 55	18 59	19 10		19 25	19 29		19 40		19 55	19 59	20 10		20 25	20 29	20 40			20 55	20 59	21 10
d	18 35	18 41	18 44	18 56	19 05	19 11	19 14	19 26	19 35		19 41	19 44	19 56	20 05	20 11	20 14	20 26	20 35	20 41		20 44	20 56	21 05	21 11
Heathrow Terminal 4 ✈ a	18 39		18 48		19 09		19 18		19 39			19 48		20 09		20 18		20 39			20 48		21 09	
Heathrow Terminal 5 ✈ a		18 46		19 01		19 16		19 31			19 46		20 01		20 16		20 31		20 46			21 01		21 16

	HX	HX	HX	HX	HX		HX	HX	HX	HX	HX	HX	HX	HX	HX		HX	HX	HX	HX	HX	HX	HX	HX
London Paddington 15 ⊖ d		21 10	21 07	21 25			21 40		21 55		22 10		22 12	22 25			22 40		22 55		23 10		23 12	23 25
Heathrow Terminals 1-2-3 2 ✈ a		21 25	21 29	21 40			21 56		22 11		22 26		22 34	22 41			22 56		23 11		23 26		23 34	23 41
d	21 14	21 26	21 35	21 41	21 49		21 59	22 01	22 13	22 19	22 31	22 33	22 37	22 47	22 49		22 59	23 01	23 13	23 19	23 31	23 33	23 37	23 47
Heathrow Terminal 4 ✈ a	21 18		21 39		21 53			22 05		22 23		22 37	22 41		22 53			23 05		23 23		23 37	23 41	
Heathrow Terminal 5 ✈ a		21 31		21 46			22 03		22 17		22 35			22 51			23 03		23 17		23 35			23 51

	HX
London Paddington 15 ⊖ d	
Heathrow Terminals 1-2-3 2 ✈ a	
d	23 49
Heathrow Terminal 4 ✈ a	23 53
Heathrow Terminal 5 ✈ a	

Sundays
from 30 October

	HX	HX	HX	HX	HX	HX	HX	HX	HX		HX	HX	HX	HX	HX	HX	HX	HX	HX		HX	HX	HX	HX
London Paddington 15 ⊖ d	05 10	05 12	05 25	05 28	05 40		05 55		06 10			06 12	06 25		06 40		06 55		07 10			07 12	07 25	
Heathrow Terminals 1-2-3 2 ✈ a	05 26	05 34	05 41	05 45	05 56		06 11		06 26			06 34	06 41		06 56		07 11		07 26			07 34	07 41	
d	05 27	05 36	05 42	05 47	05 59	06 01	06 13	06 19	06 31		06 33	06 37	06 47	06 49	06 59	07 01	07 13	07 19	07 31		07 33	07 37	07 47	07 49
Heathrow Terminal 4 ✈ a		05 40		05 51		06 05		06 23			06 37	06 41		06 53		07 05		07 23			07 37	07 41		07 53
Heathrow Terminal 5 ✈ a	05 32		05 47		06 03		06 17		06 35				06 51		07 03		07 17		07 35				07 51	

	HX	HX	HX	HX	HX		HX	HX	HX	HX	HX	HX	HX	HX	HX		HX	HX	HX	HX	HX	HX	HX	HX
London Paddington 15 ⊖ d	07 40		07 55		08 10			08 12	08 25		08 40		08 55		09 10			09 12	09 25		09 40		09 55	
Heathrow Terminals 1-2-3 2 ✈ a	07 56		08 11		08 26			08 34	08 41		08 56		09 11		09 26			09 34	09 41		09 56		10 11	
d	07 59	08 01	08 13	08 19	08 31		08 33	08 37	08 47	08 49	08 59	09 01	09 13	09 19	09 31		09 33	09 37	09 47	09 49	09 59	10 01	10 13	10 19
Heathrow Terminal 4 ✈ a		08 05		08 23			08 37	08 41		08 53		09 05		09 23			09 37	09 41		09 53		10 05		10 23
Heathrow Terminal 5 ✈ a	08 03		08 17		08 35				08 51		09 03		09 17		09 35				09 51		10 03		10 17	

	HX		HX	HX	HX	HX	HX	HX	HX	HX	HX		HX	HX	HX	HX	HX	HX	HX	HX	HX		HX	HX
London Paddington 15 ⊖ d	10 10			10 12	10 25		10 40		10 55		11 10			11 12	11 25		11 40		11 55		12 10			12 12
Heathrow Terminals 1-2-3 2 ✈ a	10 26			10 34	10 41		10 56		11 11		11 26			11 34	11 41		11 56		12 11		12 26			12 34
d	10 31		10 33	10 37	10 47	10 49	10 59	11 01	11 13	11 19	11 31		11 33	11 37	11 47	11 49	11 59	12 01	12 13	12 19	12 31		12 33	12 37
Heathrow Terminal 4 ✈ a			10 37	10 41		10 53		11 05		11 23			11 37	11 41		11 53		12 05		12 23			12 37	12 41
Heathrow Terminal 5 ✈ a	10 35				10 51		11 03		11 17		11 35				11 51		12 03		12 17		12 35			

	HX	HX	HX	HX	HX	HX	HX		HX	HX	HX	HX	HX	HX	HX	HX	HX		HX	HX	HX	HX	HX	HX
London Paddington 15 ⊖ d	12 25		12 40		12 55		13 10			13 12	13 25		13 40		13 55		14 10			14 12	14 25		14 40	
Heathrow Terminals 1-2-3 2 ✈ a	12 41		12 56		13 11		13 26			13 34	13 41		13 56		14 11		14 26			14 34	14 41		14 56	
d	12 47	12 49	12 59	13 01	13 13	13 19	13 31		13 33	13 37	13 47	13 49	13 59	14 01	14 13	14 19	14 31		14 33	14 37	14 47	14 49	14 59	15 01
Heathrow Terminal 4 ✈ a		12 53		13 05		13 23			13 37	13 41		13 53		14 05		14 23			14 37	14 41		14 53		15 05
Heathrow Terminal 5 ✈ a	12 51		13 03		13 17		13 35				13 51		14 03		14 17		14 35				14 51		15 03	

	HX	HX	HX		HX	HX	HX	HX	HX	HX	HX	HX	HX		HX	HX	HX	HX	HX	HX	HX	HX	HX	
London Paddington 15 ⊖ d	14 55		15 10			15 12	15 25		15 40		15 55		16 10			16 12	16 25		16 40		16 55		17 10	
Heathrow Terminals 1-2-3 2 ✈ a	15 11		15 26			15 34	15 41		15 56		16 11		16 26			16 34	16 41		16 56		17 11		17 26	
d	15 13	15 19	15 31		15 33	15 37	15 47	15 49	15 59	16 01	16 13	16 19	16 31		16 33	16 37	16 47	16 49	16 59	17 01	17 13	17 19	17 31	
Heathrow Terminal 4 ✈ a		15 23			15 37	15 41		15 53		16 05		16 23			16 37	16 41		16 53		17 05		17 23		
Heathrow Terminal 5 ✈ a	15 17		15 35				15 51		16 03		16 17		16 35				16 51		17 03		17 17		17 35	

	HX	HX	HX	HX	HX	HX	HX	HX	HX		HX	HX	HX	HX	HX	HX	HX	HX	HX		HX	HX	HX	HX
London Paddington 15 ⊖ d		17 12	17 25		17 40		17 55		18 10			18 12	18 25		18 40		18 55		19 10			19 12	19 25	
Heathrow Terminals 1-2-3 2 ✈ a		17 34	17 41		17 56		18 11		18 26			18 34	18 41		18 56		19 11		19 26			19 34	19 41	
d	17 33	17 37	17 47	17 49	17 59	18 01	18 13	18 19	18 31		18 33	18 37	18 47	18 49	18 59	19 01	19 13	19 19	19 31		19 33	19 37	19 47	19 49
Heathrow Terminal 4 ✈ a	17 37	17 41		17 53		18 05		18 23			18 37	18 41		18 53		19 05		19 23			19 37	19 41		19 53
Heathrow Terminal 5 ✈ a			17 51		18 03		18 17		18 35				18 51		19 03		19 17		19 35				19 51	

Table 118

Sundays

from 30 October

London - Heathrow Airport

		HX	HX	HX	HX	HX		HX	HX	HX	HX	HX	HX	HX	HX	HX		HX	HX	HX	HX	HX	HX	HX	HX
London Paddington 15 ⊖	d	19 40		19 55		20 10			20 12	20 25		20 40		20 55		21 10			21 12	21 25		21 40		21 55	
Heathrow Terminals 1-2-3 2 ✈	a	19 56		20 11		20 26			20 34	20 41		20 56		21 11		21 26			21 34	21 41		21 56		22 11	
	d	19 59	20 01	20 13	20 19	20 31		20 33	20 37	20 47	20 49	20 59	21 01	21 13	21 19	21 31		21 33	21 37	21 47	21 49	21 59	22 01	22 13	22 19
Heathrow Terminal 4 ✈	a		20 05		20 23			20 37	20 41		20 53		21 05		21 23			21 37	21 41		21 53		22 05		22 23
Heathrow Terminal 5 ✈	a	20 03		20 17		20 35				20 51		21 03		21 17		21 35				21 51		22 03		22 17	

		HX		HX	HX	HX	HX	HX	HX	HX	HX	HX		HX	HX	HX	HX								
London Paddington 15 ⊖	d	22 10			22 12	22 25		22 40		22 55		23 10			23 12	23 25									
Heathrow Terminals 1-2-3 2 ✈	a	22 26			22 34	22 41		22 56		23 11		23 26			23 34	23 41									
	d	22 31		22 33	22 37	22 47	22 49	22 59	23 01	23 13	23 19	23 31		23 33	23 37	23 47	23 49								
Heathrow Terminal 4 ✈	a			22 37	22 41		22 53		23 05		23 23			23 37	23 41		23 53								
Heathrow Terminal 5 ✈	a	22 35				22 51		23 03		23 17		23 35				23 51									

Heathrow Airport - London

Miles		HX MX	HX MO	HX MX	HX MO	HX	HX 1	HX	HX 1	HX		HX 1	HX	HX	HX 1	HX	HX 1	HX	HX 1	HX		HX 1	HX	HX 1
0	Heathrow Terminal 5 d	23p42	23p48	23p53	23p58		05 07		05 27			05 42			05 57		06 12		06 27			06 42		06 57
—	Heathrow Terminal 4 d					00 01		05 23		05 32			05 51	05 57		06 12		06 27		06 42			06 57	
1½	Heathrow Terminals 1-2-3 2 a	23p46	23p52	23p57	00 02	00 05	05 11	05 27	05 31	05 36		05 46	05 55	06 01	06 01	06 16	06 16	06 31	06 31	06 46		06 46	07 01	07 01
—	d	23p48	23p53	23p57	00 02	00 07	05 12	05 29	05 33			05 48	05 57		06 03		06 18		06 33			06 48		07 03
16¼	London Paddington 15 ⊖ a	00 04	00 09	00 18	00 18	00 30	05 28	05 56	05 49			06 04	06 24		06 19		06 34		06 49			07 05		07 19

	HX	HX 1	HX	HX 1	HX	HX 1		HX	HX 1	HX	HX 1	HX	HX 1	HX	HX 1	HX		HX 1	HX	HX 1	HX	HX 1	HX	HX 1
Heathrow Terminal 5 d		07 12		07 27		07 42			07 57		08 12		08 27		08 42			08 57		09 12		09 27		09 42
Heathrow Terminal 4 d	07 12		07 27		07 42			07 57		08 12		08 27		08 42		08 57			09 12		09 27		09 42	
Heathrow Terminals 1-2-3 2 a	07 16	07 16	07 31	07 31	07 46	07 46		08 01	08 01	08 16	08 16	08 31	08 31	08 46	08 46	09 01		09 01	09 16	09 16	09 31	09 31	09 46	09 46
d		07 18		07 33		07 48			08 03		08 18		08 33		08 48			09 03		09 18		09 33		09 48
London Paddington 15 ⊖ a		07 35		07 49		08 04			08 19		08 35		08 49		09 04			09 19		09 35		09 49		10 05

	HX	HX 1		HX	HX 1	HX	HX 1	HX	HX 1	HX	HX 1	HX		HX 1	HX	HX 1	HX	HX 1	HX	HX 1	HX	HX 1		HX
Heathrow Terminal 5 d		09 57			10 12		10 27		10 42		10 57			11 12		11 27		11 42		11 57		12 12		
Heathrow Terminal 4 d	09 57			10 12		10 27		10 42		10 57		11 12			11 27		11 42		11 57		12 12			12 27
Heathrow Terminals 1-2-3 2 a	10 01	10 01		10 16	10 16	10 31	10 31	10 46	10 46	11 01	11 01	11 16		11 16	11 31	11 31	11 46	11 46	12 01	12 01	12 16	12 16		12 31
d		10 03			10 18		10 33		10 48		11 03			11 18		11 33		11 48		12 03		12 18		
London Paddington 15 ⊖ a		10 19			10 34		10 49		11 04		11 19			11 34		11 49		12 04		12 19		12 34		

	HX 1	HX	HX 1	HX	HX 1	HX	HX 1	HX		HX 1	HX	HX 1	HX	HX 1	HX	HX 1	HX	HX 1		HX	HX 1	HX	HX 1	HX
Heathrow Terminal 5 d	12 27		12 42		12 57		13 12			13 27		13 42		13 57		14 12		14 27			14 42		14 57	
Heathrow Terminal 4 d		12 42		12 57		13 12		13 27			13 42		13 57		14 12		14 27			14 42		14 57		15 12
Heathrow Terminals 1-2-3 2 a	12 31	12 46	12 46	13 01	13 01	13 16	13 16	13 31		13 31	13 46	13 46	14 01	14 01	14 16	14 16	14 31	14 31		14 46	14 46	15 01	15 01	15 16
d	12 33		12 48		13 03		13 18			13 33		13 48		14 03		14 18		14 33			14 48		15 03	
London Paddington 15 ⊖ a	12 49		13 04		13 19		13 35			13 49		14 04		14 19		14 34		14 49			15 04		15 19	

	HX 1	HX	HX 1	HX		HX 1	HX	HX 1	HX	HX 1	HX	HX 1	HX	HX 1		HX	HX 1	HX	HX 1	HX	HX 1	HX	HX 1	HX
Heathrow Terminal 5 d	15 12		15 27			15 42		15 57		16 12		16 27		16 42			16 57		17 12		17 27		17 42	
Heathrow Terminal 4 d		15 27		15 42			15 57		16 12		16 27		16 42			16 57		17 12		17 27		17 42		17 57
Heathrow Terminals 1-2-3 2 a	15 16	15 31	15 31	15 46		15 46	16 01	16 01	16 16	16 16	16 31	16 31	16 46	16 46		17 01	17 01	17 16	17 16	17 31	17 31	17 46	17 46	18 01
d	15 18		15 33			15 48		16 03		16 18		16 33		16 48			17 03		17 18		17 33		17 48	
London Paddington 15 ⊖ a	15 35		15 49			16 05		16 19		16 35		16 49		17 05			17 19		17 35		17 49		18 05	

		HX 1	HX	HX 1	HX	HX 1	HX	HX 1	HX	HX 1		HX	HX 1	HX	HX 1	HX	HX 1	HX	HX 1	HX		HX 1	HX	HX 1
Heathrow Terminal 5 d		17 57		18 12		18 27		18 42		18 57			19 12		19 27		19 42		19 57			20 12		20 27
Heathrow Terminal 4 d			18 12		18 27		18 42		18 57			19 12		19 27		19 42		19 57		20 12			20 27	
Heathrow Terminals 1-2-3 2 a		18 01	18 16	18 16	18 31	18 31	18 46	18 46	19 01	19 01		19 16	19 16	19 31	19 31	19 46	19 46	20 01	20 01	20 16		20 16	20 31	20 31
d		18 03		18 18		18 33		18 48		19 03			19 18		19 33		19 48		20 03			20 18		20 33
London Paddington 15 ⊖ a		18 19		18 35		18 49		19 05		19 19			19 35		19 49		20 04		20 19			20 34		20 49

	HX	HX 1	HX	HX 1	HX	HX 1		HX	HX 1	HX	HX 1	HX	HX 1	HX	HX 1	HX		HX 1	HX	HX 1	HX	HX 1	HX	HX 1
Heathrow Terminal 5 d		20 42		20 57		21 12			21 27		21 42		21 57		22 12			22 27		22 42		22 57		23 12
Heathrow Terminal 4 d	20 42		20 57		21 12			21 27		21 42		21 57		22 12		22 27			22 42		22 57		23 12	
Heathrow Terminals 1-2-3 2 a	20 46	20 46	21 01	21 01	21 16	21 16		21 31	21 31	21 46	21 46	22 01	22 01	22 16	22 16	22 31		22 31	22 46	22 46	23 01	23 01	23 16	23 16
d		20 48		21 03		21 18			21 33		21 48		22 03		22 18			22 33		22 48		23 03		23 18
London Paddington 15 ⊖ a		21 04		21 19		21 34			21 49		22 04		22 19		22 34			22 49		23 04		23 19		23 34

	HX	HX 1		HX	HX	HX
Heathrow Terminal 5 d		23 27		23 42		23 53
Heathrow Terminal 4 d	23 27				23 42	
Heathrow Terminals 1-2-3 2 a	23 31	23 31		23 46	23 46	23 57
d		23 33		23 48		23 57
London Paddington 15 ⊖ a		23 49		00 04		00 18

Saturdays

	HX	HX	HX	HX 1	HX	HX 1	HX	HX 1	HX		HX	HX 1	HX	HX 1	HX	HX 1	HX	HX 1	HX		HX 1	HX	HX 1	HX
Heathrow Terminal 5 d	23p42	23p53		05 07		05 27		05 42				05 57		06 12		06 27		06 42			06 57		07 12	
Heathrow Terminal 4 d			00 01		05 23		05 32		05 51		05 57		06 12		06 27		06 42		06 57			07 12		07 27
Heathrow Terminals 1-2-3 2 a	23p46	23p57	00 05	05 11	05 27	05 31	05 36	05 46	05 55		06 01	06 01	06 16	06 16	06 31	06 31	06 46	06 46	07 01		07 01	07 16	07 16	07 31
d	23p48	23p57	00 07	05 12	05 29	05 33		05 48	05 57			06 03		06 18		06 33		06 48			07 03		07 18	
London Paddington 15 ⊖ a	00 04	00 18	00 30	05 28	05 56	05 49		06 04	06 24			06 19		06 34		06 49		07 04			07 19		07 34	

Table 118

Saturdays

Heathrow Airport - London

	HX	HX	HX	HX	HX		HX	HX	HX	HX	HX	HX	HX	HX	HX		HX	HX	HX	HX	HX	HX	HX	HX
	1		1		1			1		1		1		1			1		1		1		1	
Heathrow Terminal 5 ✈ d	07 27		07 42		07 57			08 12		08 27		08 42		08 57			09 12		09 27		09 42		09 57	
Heathrow Terminal 4 ✈ d		07 42		07 57			08 12		08 27		08 42		08 57		09 12			09 27		09 42		09 57		10 12
Heathrow Terminals 1-2-3 2 ✈ a	07 31	07 46	07 46	08 01	08 01		08 16	08 16	08 31	08 31	08 46	08 46	09 01	09 01	09 16		09 16	09 31	09 31	09 46	09 46	10 01	10 01	10 16
d	07 33		07 48		08 03			08 18		08 33		08 48		09 03			09 18		09 33		09 48		10 03	
London Paddington 15 ⊖ a	07 49		08 04		08 19			08 34		08 49		09 04		09 19			09 34		09 49		10 04		10 19	

	HX		HX	HX	HX	HX	HX	HX	HX	HX	HX		HX	HX	HX	HX	HX	HX	HX	HX	HX		HX	HX
	1			1		1		1		1			1		1		1		1		1			1
Heathrow Terminal 5 ✈ d	10 12			10 27		10 42		10 57		11 12			11 27		11 42		11 57		12 12		12 27			12 42
Heathrow Terminal 4 ✈ d			10 27		10 42		10 57		11 12		11 27			11 42		11 57		12 12		12 27			12 42	
Heathrow Terminals 1-2-3 2 ✈ a	10 16		10 31	10 31	10 46	10 46	11 01	11 01	11 16	11 16	11 31		11 31	11 46	11 46	12 01	12 01	12 16	12 16	12 31	12 31		12 46	12 46
d	10 18			10 33		10 48		11 03		11 18			11 33		11 48		12 03		12 18		12 33			12 48
London Paddington 15 ⊖ a	10 34			10 49		11 04		11 19		11 34			11 49		12 04		12 19		12 34		12 49			13 04

	HX	HX	HX	HX	HX	HX	HX		HX	HX	HX	HX	HX	HX	HX	HX	HX		HX	HX	HX	HX	HX	HX
		1		1		1			1		1		1		1		1			1		1		1
Heathrow Terminal 5 ✈ d		12 57		13 12		13 27			13 42		13 57		14 12		14 27		14 42			14 57		15 12		15 27
Heathrow Terminal 4 ✈ d	12 57		13 12		13 27		13 42			13 57		14 12		14 27		14 42			14 57		15 12		15 27	
Heathrow Terminals 1-2-3 2 ✈ a	13 01	13 01	13 16	13 16	13 31	13 31	13 46		13 46	14 01	14 01	14 16	14 16	14 31	14 31	14 46	14 46		15 01	15 01	15 16	15 16	15 31	15 31
d		13 03		13 18		13 33			13 48		14 03		14 18		14 33		14 48			15 03		15 18		15 33
London Paddington 15 ⊖ a		13 19		13 35		13 49			14 04		14 19		14 34		14 49		15 04			15 19		15 34		15 49

	HX	HX	HX		HX	HX	HX	HX	HX	HX	HX	HX	HX		HX	HX	HX	HX	HX	HX	HX	HX	HX	
		1			1		1		1		1		1			1		1		1		1		
Heathrow Terminal 5 ✈ d		15 42			15 57		16 12		16 27		16 42		16 57			17 12		17 27		17 42		17 57		
Heathrow Terminal 4 ✈ d	15 42		15 57			16 12		16 27		16 42		16 57			17 12		17 27		17 42		17 57		18 12	
Heathrow Terminals 1-2-3 2 ✈ a	15 46	15 46	16 01		16 01	16 16	16 16	16 31	16 31	16 46	16 46	17 01	17 01		17 16	17 16	17 31	17 31	17 46	17 46	18 01	18 01	18 16	
d		15 48			16 03		16 18		16 33		16 48		17 03			17 18		17 33		17 48		18 03		
London Paddington 15 ⊖ a		16 04			16 19		16 34		16 49		17 04		17 19			17 34		17 49		18 04		18 19		

	HX	HX	HX	HX	HX	HX	HX	HX	HX		HX	HX	HX	HX	HX	HX	HX	HX	HX		HX	HX	HX	HX
	1		1		1		1		1			1		1		1		1			1		1	
Heathrow Terminal 5 ✈ d	18 12		18 27		18 42		18 57		19 12			19 27		19 42		19 57		20 12			20 27		20 42	
Heathrow Terminal 4 ✈ d		18 27		18 42		18 57		19 12			19 27		19 42		19 57		20 12		20 27			20 42		20 57
Heathrow Terminals 1-2-3 2 ✈ a	18 16	18 31	18 31	18 46	18 46	19 01	19 01	19 16	19 16		19 31	19 31	19 46	19 46	20 01	20 01	20 16	20 16	20 31		20 31	20 46	20 46	21 01
d	18 18		18 33		18 48		19 03		19 18			19 33		19 48		20 03		20 18			20 33		20 48	
London Paddington 15 ⊖ a	18 34		18 49		19 04		19 19		19 34			19 49		20 04		20 19		20 34			20 49		21 04	

	HX	HX	HX	HX	HX		HX	HX	HX	HX	HX	HX	HX	HX	HX		HX	HX	HX	HX	HX	HX	HX	HX
	1		1		1			1		1		1		1			1		1		1		1	1
Heathrow Terminal 5 ✈ d	20 57		21 12		21 27			21 42		21 57		22 12		22 27			22 42		22 57		23 12		23 27	23 42
Heathrow Terminal 4 ✈ d		21 12		21 27			21 42		21 57		22 12		22 27		22 42			22 57		23 12		23 27		
Heathrow Terminals 1-2-3 2 ✈ a	21 01	21 16	21 16	21 31	21 31		21 46	21 46	22 01	22 01	22 16	22 16	22 31	22 31	22 46		22 46	23 01	23 01	23 16	23 16	23 31	23 31	23 46
d	21 03		21 18		21 33			21 48		22 03		22 18		22 33			22 48		23 03		23 18		23 33	23 48
London Paddington 15 ⊖ a	21 19		21 34		21 49			22 04		22 19		22 35		22 49			23 05		23 19		23 34		23 49	00 04

	HX		HX
Heathrow Terminal 5 ✈ d			23 53
Heathrow Terminal 4 ✈ d	23 42		
Heathrow Terminals 1-2-3 2 ✈ a	23 46		23 57
d			23 57
London Paddington 15 ⊖ a			00 19

Sundays

until 23 October

	HX	HX	HX	HX	HX	HX	HX	HX	HX		HX	HX	HX	HX	HX	HX	HX	HX	HX		HX	HX	HX	HX
	1																							
	A	A																						
Heathrow Terminal 5 ✈ d	23p42	23p53		05 03	05 18	05 33	05 48		06 03				06 18		06 33		06 48		07 03				07 18	
Heathrow Terminal 4 ✈ d	⟆	⟆	00 01					05 53			06 07	06 13		06 25		06 41		06 53			07 07	07 13		07 25
Heathrow Terminals 1-2-3 2 ✈ a	23p46	23p57	00 05	05 07	05 22	05 37	05 52	05 57	06 07		06 11	06 17	06 22	06 29	06 37	06 45	06 52	06 57	07 07		07 11	07 17	07 22	07 29
d	23p48	23p57	00 07	05 08	05 23	05 38	05 53		06 08		06 13		06 23		06 38		06 53		07 08		07 13		07 23	
London Paddington 15 ⊖ a	00 04	00 19	00 30	05 24	05 39	05 54	06 09		06 24		06 36		06 39		06 54		07 09		07 24		07 36		07 39	

	HX	HX	HX	HX	HX		HX	HX	HX	HX	HX	HX	HX	HX	HX		HX	HX	HX	HX	HX	HX	HX	HX
Heathrow Terminal 5 ✈ d	07 33		07 48		08 03				08 18		08 33		08 48		09 00			09 13		09 27		09 42		09 57
Heathrow Terminal 4 ✈ d		07 41		07 53			08 07	08 13		08 25		08 41		08 53			09 06		09 21		09 31		09 51	
Heathrow Terminals 1-2-3 2 ✈ a	07 37	07 45	07 52	07 57	08 07		08 11	08 17	08 22	08 29	08 37	08 45	08 52	08 57	09 04		09 10	09 17	09 25	09 31	09 35	09 46	09 55	10 01
d	07 38		07 53		08 08		08 13		08 23		08 38		08 53		09 06			09 19	09 27	09 33		09 48	09 57	10 03
London Paddington 15 ⊖ a	07 54		08 09		08 24		08 36		08 39		08 54		09 09		09 22			09 35	09 50	09 49		10 04	10 20	10 19

A not 22 May

Table 118

Sundays
until 23 October

Heathrow Airport - London

	HX		HX	HX	HX	HX	HX	HX	HX	HX	HX		HX	HX	HX	HX	HX	HX	HX	HX	HX		HX	HX
Heathrow Terminal 5 ✈ d			10 12		10 27		10 42		10 57		11 12			11 27		11 42		11 57		12 12			12 27	
Heathrow Terminal 4 ✈ d	10 01			10 21		10 31		10 51		11 01			11 21		11 31		11 51		12 01		12 21			12 31
Heathrow Terminals 1-2-3 2 ✈ a	10 05		10 16	10 25	10 31	10 35	10 46	10 55	11 01	11 05	11 16		11 25	11 31	11 35	11 46	11 55	12 01	12 05	12 16	12 25		12 31	12 35
d			10 18	10 27	10 33		10 48	10 57	11 03		11 18		11 27	11 33		11 48	11 57	12 03		12 18	12 27		12 33	
London Paddington 15 ⊖ a			10 34	10 50	10 49		11 04	11 20	11 19		11 34		11 50	11 49		12 04	12 20	12 19		12 34	12 50		12 49	

	HX	HX	HX	HX	HX	HX	HX		HX	HX	HX	HX	HX	HX	HX	HX	HX		HX	HX	HX	HX	HX	HX
Heathrow Terminal 5 ✈ d	12 42		12 57		13 12		13 27			13 42		13 57		14 12		14 27			14 42		14 57		15 12	
Heathrow Terminal 4 ✈ d		12 51		13 01		13 21			13 31		13 51		14 01		14 21		14 31			14 51		15 01		15 21
Heathrow Terminals 1-2-3 2 ✈ a	12 46	12 55	13 01	13 05	13 16	13 25	13 31		13 35	13 46	13 55	14 01	14 05	14 16	14 25	14 31	14 35		14 46	14 55	15 01	15 05	15 16	15 25
d	12 48	12 57	13 03		13 18	13 27	13 33			13 48	13 57	14 03		14 18	14 27	14 33			14 48	14 57	15 03		15 18	15 27
London Paddington 15 ⊖ a	13 04	13 20	13 19		13 34	13 50	13 49			14 04	14 20	14 19		14 34	14 50	14 49			15 04	15 20	15 19		15 34	15 50

	HX	HX	HX		HX	HX	HX	HX	HX	HX	HX	HX	HX		HX	HX	HX	HX	HX	HX	HX	HX	HX	
Heathrow Terminal 5 ✈ d	15 27		15 42			15 57		16 12		16 27		16 42			16 57		17 12		17 27		17 42		17 57	
Heathrow Terminal 4 ✈ d		15 31			15 51		16 01		16 21		16 31		16 51			17 01		17 21		17 31		17 51		
Heathrow Terminals 1-2-3 2 ✈ a	15 31	15 35	15 46		15 55	16 01	16 05	16 16	16 25	16 31	16 35	16 46	16 55		17 01	17 05	17 16	17 25	17 31	17 35	17 46	17 55	18 01	
d	15 33		15 48		15 57	16 03		16 18	16 27	16 33		16 48	16 57		17 03		17 18	17 27	17 33		17 48	17 57	18 03	
London Paddington 15 ⊖ a	15 49		16 04		16 20	16 19		16 34	16 50	16 49		17 04	17 20		17 19		17 34	17 50	17 49		18 04	18 20	18 19	

	HX	HX	HX	HX	HX	HX	HX	HX	HX		HX	HX	HX	HX	HX	HX	HX	HX	HX		HX	HX	HX	HX
Heathrow Terminal 5 ✈ d		18 12		18 27		18 42		18 57			19 12		19 27		19 42		19 57		20 12			20 27		20 42
Heathrow Terminal 4 ✈ d	18 01		18 21		18 31		18 51		19 01			19 21		19 31		19 51		20 01			20 21		20 31	
Heathrow Terminals 1-2-3 2 ✈ a	18 05	18 16	18 25	18 31	18 35	18 46	18 55	19 01	19 05		19 16	19 25	19 31	19 35	19 46	19 55	20 01	20 05	20 16		20 25	20 31	20 35	20 46
d		18 18	18 27	18 33		18 48	18 57	19 03			19 18	19 27	19 33		19 48	19 57	20 03		20 18		20 27	20 33		20 48
London Paddington 15 ⊖ a		18 34	18 50	18 49		19 04	19 20	19 19			19 34	19 50	19 49		20 04	20 20	20 19		20 34		20 53	20 49		21 04

	HX	HX	HX	HX	HX		HX	HX	HX	HX	HX	HX	HX	HX	HX		HX	HX	HX	HX	HX	HX	HX	HX
Heathrow Terminal 5 ✈ d		20 57		21 12			21 27		21 48		22 03			22 18			22 33		22 48		23 03			23 18
Heathrow Terminal 4 ✈ d	20 51		21 01		21 21			21 41		21 53		22 07	22 13		22 25			22 41		22 53		23 07	23 13	
Heathrow Terminals 1-2-3 2 ✈ a	20 55	21 01	21 05	21 16	21 25		21 31	21 45	21 52	21 57	22 07	22 11	22 17	22 22	22 29		22 37	22 45	22 52	22 57	23 07	23 11	23 17	23 22
d	20 57	21 03		21 18	21 27		21 33		21 53		22 08	22 13		22 23			22 38		22 53		23 08	23 13		23 23
London Paddington 15 ⊖ a	21 20	21 19		21 34	21 50		21 49		22 09		22 24	22 36		22 39			22 54		23 09		23 24	23 36		23 43

	HX		HX	HX	HX	HX																		
Heathrow Terminal 5 ✈ d			23 33		23 48	23 58																		
Heathrow Terminal 4 ✈ d	23 25			23 41																				
Heathrow Terminals 1-2-3 2 ✈ a	23 29		23 37	23 45	23 52	00 02																		
d			23 38		23 53	00 02																		
London Paddington 15 ⊖ a			23 56		00 09	00 18																		

Sundays
from 30 October

	HX 1	HX	HX	HX	HX	HX	HX	HX	HX		HX	HX	HX	HX	HX	HX	HX	HX	HX		HX	HX	HX	HX
Heathrow Terminal 5 ✈ d	23p42	23p53		05 03	05 18	05 33	05 48		06 03				06 18		06 33		06 48		07 03				07 18	
Heathrow Terminal 4 ✈ d			00 01					05 53			06 07	06 13		06 25		06 41		06 53			07 07	07 13		07 25
Heathrow Terminals 1-2-3 2 ✈ a	23p46	23p57	00 05	05 07	05 22	05 37	05 52	05 57	06 07		06 11	06 17	06 22	06 29	06 37	06 45	06 52	06 57	07 07		07 11	07 17	07 22	07 29
d	23p48	23p57	00 07	05 08	05 23	05 38	05 53		06 08		06 13		06 23		06 38		06 53		07 08		07 13		07 23	
London Paddington 15 ⊖ a	00 04	00 19	00 30	05 24	05 39	05 54	06 09		06 24		06 36		06 39		06 54		07 09		07 24		07 36		07 39	

	HX	HX	HX	HX	HX		HX	HX	HX	HX	HX	HX	HX	HX	HX		HX	HX	HX	HX	HX	HX	HX	HX
Heathrow Terminal 5 ✈ d	07 33		07 48		08 03				08 18		08 33		08 48		09 03				09 18		09 33		09 48	
Heathrow Terminal 4 ✈ d		07 41		07 53			08 07	08 13		08 25		08 41		08 53			09 07	09 13		09 25		09 41		09 53
Heathrow Terminals 1-2-3 2 ✈ a	07 37	07 45	07 52	07 57	08 07		08 11	08 17	08 22	08 29	08 37	08 45	08 52	08 57	09 07		09 11	09 17	09 22	09 29	09 37	09 45	09 52	09 57
d	07 38		07 53		08 08		08 13		08 23		08 38		08 53		09 08		09 13		09 23		09 38		09 53	
London Paddington 15 ⊖ a	07 54		08 09		08 24		08 36		08 39		08 54		09 09		09 24		09 36		09 39		09 54		10 09	

	HX		HX	HX	HX	HX	HX	HX	HX	HX	HX		HX	HX	HX	HX	HX	HX	HX	HX	HX		HX	HX
Heathrow Terminal 5 ✈ d	10 03				10 18		10 33		10 48		11 03				11 18		11 33		11 48		12 03			
Heathrow Terminal 4 ✈ d			10 07	10 13		10 25		10 41		10 53			11 07	11 13		11 25		11 41		11 53			12 07	12 13
Heathrow Terminals 1-2-3 2 ✈ a	10 07		10 11	10 17	10 22	10 29	10 37	10 45	10 52	10 57	11 07		11 11	11 17	11 22	11 29	11 37	11 45	11 52	11 57	12 07		12 11	12 17
d	10 08		10 13		10 23		10 38		10 53		11 08		11 13		11 23		11 38		11 53		12 08		12 13	
London Paddington 15 ⊖ a	10 24		10 36		10 39		10 54		11 09		11 24		11 36		11 39		11 54		12 09		12 24		12 36	

	HX	HX	HX	HX	HX	HX	HX		HX	HX	HX	HX	HX	HX	HX	HX	HX		HX	HX	HX	HX	HX	HX
Heathrow Terminal 5 ✈ d	12 18		12 33		12 48		13 03				13 18		13 33		13 48		14 03				14 18		14 33	
Heathrow Terminal 4 ✈ d		12 25		12 41		12 53			13 07	13 13		13 25		13 41		13 53			14 07	14 13		14 25		14 41
Heathrow Terminals 1-2-3 2 ✈ a	12 22	12 29	12 37	12 45	12 52	12 57	13 07		13 11	13 17	13 22	13 29	13 37	13 45	13 52	13 57	14 07		14 11	14 17	14 22	14 29	14 37	14 45
d	12 23		12 38		12 53		13 08		13 13		13 23		13 38		13 53		14 08		14 13		14 23		14 38	
London Paddington 15 ⊖ a	12 39		12 54		13 09		13 24		13 36		13 39		13 54		14 09		14 24		14 36		14 39		14 54	

Table 118

Sundays

from 30 October

Heathrow Airport - London

		HX	HX	HX		HX	HX	HX	HX	HX	HX	HX	HX	HX		HX	HX	HX	HX	HX	HX	HX	HX	HX	
Heathrow Terminal 5	✈ d	14 48	...	15 03	...	...	...	15 18	...	15 33	...	15 48	...	16 03	...	...	...	16 18	...	16 33	...	16 48	...	17 03	...
Heathrow Terminal 4	✈ d	.	14 53	.		15 07	15 13		15 25	.	15 41	.	15 53	.		16 07	16 13	.	16 25	.	16 41	.	16 53	.	.
Heathrow Terminals 1-2-3 2	✈ a	14 52	14 57	15 07	...	15 11	15 17	15 22	15 29	15 37	15 45	15 52	15 57	16 07	...	16 11	16 17	16 22	16 29	16 37	16 45	16 52	16 57	17 07	...
	d	14 53	.	15 08	.	15 13	.	15 23	.	15 38	.	15 53	.	16 08	.	16 13	.	16 23	.	16 38	.	16 53	.	17 08	.
London Paddington 15	⊖ a	15 09	...	15 24	...	15 36	...	15 39	...	15 54	...	16 09	...	16 24	...	16 36	...	16 39	...	16 54	...	17 09	...	17 24	...

		HX	HX	HX	HX	HX	HX	HX	HX	HX		HX	HX	HX	HX	HX	HX	HX	HX	HX		HX	HX	HX	HX
Heathrow Terminal 5	✈ d	...	...	17 18	...	17 33	...	17 48	...	18 03	...	...	...	18 18	...	18 33	...	18 48	...	19 03	...	...	...	19 18	...
Heathrow Terminal 4	✈ d	17 07	17 13	.	17 25	.	17 41	.	17 53	.	.	18 07	18 13	.	18 25	.	18 41	.	18 53	.	.	19 07	19 13	.	19 25
Heathrow Terminals 1-2-3 2	✈ a	17 11	17 17	17 22	17 29	17 37	17 45	17 52	17 57	18 07	...	18 11	18 17	18 22	18 29	18 37	18 45	18 52	18 57	19 07	...	19 11	19 17	19 22	19 29
	d	17 13	.	17 23	.	17 38	.	17 53	.	18 08	.	18 13	.	18 23	.	18 38	.	18 53	.	19 08	.	19 13	.	19 23	.
London Paddington 15	⊖ a	17 36	...	17 39	...	17 54	...	18 09	...	18 24	...	18 36	...	18 39	...	18 54	...	19 09	...	19 24	...	19 36	...	19 39	...

		HX	HX	HX	HX	HX		HX	HX	HX	HX	HX	HX	HX	HX	HX		HX	HX	HX	HX	HX	HX	HX	HX
Heathrow Terminal 5	✈ d	19 33	...	19 48	...	20 03	...	...	...	20 18	...	20 33	...	20 48	...	21 03	...	...	...	21 18	...	21 33	...	21 48	...
Heathrow Terminal 4	✈ d	.	19 41	.	19 53	.	.	20 07	20 13	.	20 25	.	20 41	.	20 53	.	.	21 07	21 13	.	21 25	.	21 41	.	21 53
Heathrow Terminals 1-2-3 2	✈ a	19 37	19 45	19 52	19 57	20 07	...	20 11	20 17	20 22	20 29	20 37	20 45	20 52	20 57	21 07	...	21 11	21 17	21 22	21 29	21 37	21 45	21 52	21 57
	d	19 38	.	19 53	.	20 08	.	20 13	.	20 23	.	20 38	.	20 53	.	21 08	.	21 13	.	21 23	.	21 38	.	21 53	.
London Paddington 15	⊖ a	19 54	...	20 09	...	20 24	...	20 36	...	20 39	...	20 54	...	21 09	...	21 24	...	21 36	...	21 39	...	21 54	...	22 09	...

		HX		HX	HX	HX	HX	HX	HX	HX	HX	HX		HX	HX	HX	HX	HX	HX	HX	HX				
Heathrow Terminal 5	✈ d	22 03	...	...	...	22 18	...	22 33	...	22 48	...	23 03	...	...	...	23 18	...	23 33	...	23 48	23 58	...	...	...	...
Heathrow Terminal 4	✈ d	.	.	22 07	22 13	.	22 25	.	22 41	.	22 53	.	.	23 07	23 13	.	23 25	.	23 41	.	.	.	.	.	.
Heathrow Terminals 1-2-3 2	✈ a	22 07	...	22 11	22 17	22 22	22 29	22 37	22 45	22 52	22 57	23 07	...	23 11	23 17	23 22	23 29	23 37	23 45	23 52	00 02	...	...	...	...
	d	22 08	.	22 13	.	22 23	.	22 38	.	22 53	.	23 08	.	23 13	.	23 23	.	23 38	.	23 53	00 02	.	.	.	.
London Paddington 15	⊖ a	22 24	...	22 36	...	22 39	...	22 54	...	23 09	...	23 24	...	23 36	...	23 43	...	23 56	...	00 09	00 18	...	...	...	...

Table 119

Mondays to Fridays

Slough - Windsor & Eton

Miles			GW 1	GW 1	GW 1	GW 1	GW 1	GW 1	GW 1	GW 1	GW 1	GW 1	GW 1	GW 1	GW 1	GW 1	GW 1	GW 1	GW 1	GW 1	GW 1	GW 1	GW 1
0	Slough 3	d	05 38	05 58	06 18	06 37	06 55	07 13	07 31	07 54	08 13	08 31	08 54	09 14	09 33	09 53	10 11	10 30	10 50	11 10	11 30	11 50	12 10
2¼	Windsor & Eton Central	a	05 44	06 04	06 24	06 43	07 01	07 19	07 37	08 00	08 19	08 37	09 00	09 20	09 39	09 59	10 17	10 36	10 56	11 16	11 36	11 56	12 16

		GW 1	GW 1	GW 1	GW 1	GW 1	GW 1	GW 1	GW 1	GW 1	GW 1	GW 1	GW 1	GW 1	GW 1	GW 1	GW 1	GW 1	GW 1	GW 1	GW 1	GW 1	GW 1
Slough 3	d	12 30	12 50	13 10	13 30	13 50	14 10	14 30	14 50	15 10	15 30	15 50	16 21	16 43	17 01	17 21	17 40	17 58	18 16	18 40	18 58	19 16	19 40
Windsor & Eton Central	a	12 36	12 56	13 16	13 36	13 56	14 16	14 36	14 56	15 16	15 36	15 56	16 27	16 49	17 07	17 27	17 46	18 04	18 22	18 46	19 04	19 22	19 46

		GW 1	GW 1	GW 1	GW 1	GW 1	GW 1	GW 1	GW 1	GW 1	GW 1	GW 1
Slough 3	d	20 00	20 20	20 40	21 00	21 20	21 40	22 00	22 20	22 40	23 00	23 20
Windsor & Eton Central	a	20 06	20 26	20 46	21 06	21 26	21 46	22 06	22 26	22 46	23 06	23 26

Saturdays

		GW 1	GW 1	GW 1	GW 1	GW 1	GW 1	GW 1	GW 1	GW 1	GW 1	GW 1	GW 1	GW 1	GW 1	GW 1	GW 1	GW 1	GW 1	GW 1	GW 1	GW 1	GW 1
Slough 3	d	06 17	06 47	07 17	07 47	08 17	08 47	09 17	09 47	10 17	10 47	11 17	11 47	12 17	12 47	13 17	13 47	14 17	14 47	15 17	15 47	16 17	16 47
Windsor & Eton Central	a	06 23	06 53	07 23	07 53	08 23	08 53	09 23	09 53	10 23	10 53	11 23	11 53	12 23	12 53	13 23	13 53	14 23	14 53	15 23	15 53	16 23	16 53

		GW 1	GW 1	GW 1	GW 1	GW 1	GW 1	GW 1	GW 1	GW 1	GW 1	GW 1	GW 1	GW 1	GW 1
Slough 3	d	17 17	17 47	18 17	18 47	19 17	19 47	20 17	20 47	21 17	21 47	22 17	22 53	23 22	23 56
Windsor & Eton Central	a	17 23	17 53	18 23	18 53	19 23	19 53	20 23	20 53	21 23	21 53	22 23	22 59	23 28	00 02

Sundays

		GW 1 A	GW 1	GW 1	GW 1	GW 1	GW 1	GW 1	GW 1	GW 1	GW 1	GW 1	GW 1	GW 1	GW 1	GW 1	GW 1	GW 1	GW 1	GW 1	GW 1	GW 1	GW 1
Slough 3	d	23p56	08 22	08 52	09 22	09 52	10 22	10 52	11 22	11 52	12 22	12 52	13 22	13 52	14 22	14 52	15 22	15 52	16 22	16 52	17 22	17 52	18 22
Windsor & Eton Central	a	00 02	08 28	08 58	09 28	09 58	10 28	10 58	11 28	11 58	12 28	12 58	13 28	13 58	14 28	14 58	15 28	15 58	16 28	16 58	17 28	17 58	18 28

		GW 1	GW 1	GW 1	GW 1	GW 1	GW 1	GW 1	GW 1	GW 1	GW 1
Slough 3	d	18 52	19 22	19 52	20 22	20 52	21 22	21 52	22 22	22 52	23 22
Windsor & Eton Central	a	18 58	19 28	19 58	20 28	20 58	21 28	21 58	22 28	22 58	23 28

A not 22 May

Table 119

Windsor & Eton - Slough

Miles			GW	GW	GW	GW	GW	GW	GW	GW	GW		GW	GW	GW	GW	GW	GW	GW	GW	GW		GW	GW	GW
			1	1	1	1	1	1	1	1	1		1	1	1	1	1	1	1	1	1		1	1	1
0	Windsor & Eton Central	d	05 48	06 08	06 28	06 46	07 04	07 22	07 40	08 04	08 22		08 40	09 04	09 24	09 42	10 02	10 20	10 40	11 00	11 20		11 40	12 00	12 20
2¾	Slough 3	a	05 54	06 14	06 34	06 52	07 10	07 28	07 46	08 10	08 28		08 46	09 10	09 30	09 48	10 08	10 26	10 46	11 06	11 26		11 46	12 06	12 26

		GW	GW	GW	GW	GW	GW		GW	GW	GW	GW	GW	GW	GW	GW	GW		GW	GW	GW	GW	GW	GW	GW
		1	1	1	1	1	1		1	1	1	1	1	1	1	1	1		1	1	1	1	1	1	1
Windsor & Eton Central	d	12 40	13 00	13 20	13 40	14 00	14 20		14 40	15 00	15 20	15 40	16 00	16 30	16 52	17 10	17 30		17 49	18 07	18 28	18 49	19 07	19 27	19 50
Slough 3	a	12 46	13 06	13 26	13 46	14 06	14 26		14 46	15 06	15 26	15 46	16 06	16 36	16 58	17 16	17 36		17 55	18 13	18 34	18 55	19 13	19 33	19 56

		GW	GW		GW	GW	GW	GW	GW	GW	GW	GW	GW
		1	1		1	1	1	1	1	1	1	1	1
Windsor & Eton Central	d	20 10	20 30		20 50	21 10	21 30	21 50	22 10	22 30	22 50	23 10	23 30
Slough 3	a	20 16	20 36		20 56	21 16	21 36	21 56	22 16	22 36	22 56	23 16	23 36

Saturdays

		GW	GW	GW	GW	GW	GW	GW	GW	GW		GW	GW	GW	GW	GW	GW	GW	GW	GW		GW	GW	GW	GW
		1	1	1	1	1	1	1	1	1		1	1	1	1	1	1	1	1	1		1	1	1	1
Windsor & Eton Central	d	06 27	06 57	07 27	07 57	08 27	08 57	09 27	09 57	10 27		10 57	11 27	11 57	12 27	12 57	13 27	13 57	14 27	14 57		15 27	15 57	16 27	16 57
Slough 3	a	06 33	07 03	07 33	08 03	08 33	09 03	09 33	10 03	10 33		11 03	11 33	12 03	12 33	13 03	13 33	14 03	14 33	15 03		15 33	16 03	16 33	17 03

		GW	GW	GW	GW	GW		GW	GW	GW	GW	GW	GW	GW	GW
		1	1	1	1	1		1	1	1	1	1	1	1	1
Windsor & Eton Central	d	17 27	17 57	18 27	18 57	19 27		19 57	20 27	20 57	21 26	21 57	22 27	23 02	23 32
Slough 3	a	17 33	18 03	18 33	19 03	19 33		20 03	20 33	21 03	21 32	22 03	22 33	23 08	23 38

Sundays

		GW	GW	GW	GW	GW	GW	GW	GW	GW		GW	GW	GW	GW	GW	GW	GW	GW	GW		GW	GW	GW	GW
		1	1	1	1	1	1	1	1	1		1	1	1	1	1	1	1	1	1		1	1	1	1
Windsor & Eton Central	d	00 05	08 32	09 02	09 32	10 02	10 32	11 02	11 32	12 02		12 32	13 02	13 32	14 02	14 32	15 02	15 32	16 02	16 32		17 02	17 32	18 02	18 32
Slough 3	a	00 11	08 38	09 08	09 38	10 08	10 38	11 08	11 38	12 08		12 38	13 08	13 38	14 08	14 38	15 08	15 38	16 08	16 38		17 08	17 38	18 08	18 38

		GW	GW	GW	GW	GW		GW	GW	GW	GW	GW
		1	1	1	1	1		1	1	1	1	1
Windsor & Eton Central	d	19 02	19 32	20 02	20 32	21 02		21 32	22 02	22 32	23 02	23 32
Slough 3	a	19 08	19 38	20 08	20 38	21 08		21 38	22 08	22 38	23 08	23 38

Table 120

Mondays to Fridays

Maidenhead - Marlow

Miles			GW MX [1]	GW [1]	GW [1]	GW [1]	GW [1]	GW [1]	GW [1]	GW [1]	GW [1]	GW [1]	GW [1]	GW [1]	GW [1]	GW [1]	GW [1]	GW [1]	GW [1]	GW [1]	GW [1]	GW [1]	GW [1]
—	London Paddington [15] ⊖	d																					
0	**Maidenhead [3]**	d	23p45	05 25	05 49		06 31		07 09		07 42		08 13		09 04	09 38	10 38	11 38	12 38	13 38	14 38	15 38	16 40
1¼	Furze Platt	d	23p49	05 29	05 53		06 35		07 13		07 46		08 17		09 08	09 42	10 42	11 42	12 42	13 42	14 42	15 42	16 44
3	Cookham	d	23p52	05 32	05 57		06 39		07 17		07 49		08 20		09 11	09 45	10 45	11 45	12 45	13 45	14 45	15 45	16 47
4½	Bourne End [3]	a	23p56	05 36	06 01		06 43		07 21		07 53		08 24		09 15	09 49	10 49	11 49	12 49	13 49	14 49	15 49	16 51
—		d	00 01	05 40		06 18		06 49		07 28		07 58		08 27		09 53	10 53	11 53	12 53	13 53	14 53	15 53	16 55
7¼	**Marlow**	a	00 08	05 48		06 25		06 56		07 35		08 05		08 34		10 01	11 01	12 01	13 01	14 01	15 01	16 01	17 03

		GW [1]	GW [1]	GW [1]	GW [1]	GW [1]	GW [1]	GW [1]	GW [1]	GW [1]	GW [1]	GW [1]	GW [1]	GW [1]
London Paddington [15] ⊖	d		17 42				18 36							
Maidenhead [3]	d	17 46	18 14		18 46		19 14		19 47		20 42	21 38	22 46	23 45
Furze Platt	d	17 50	18 18		18 49		19 18		19 51		20 46	21 42	22 50	23 49
Cookham	d	17 53	18 22		18 53		19 22		19 54		20 49	21 45	22 53	23 52
Bourne End [3]	a	17 57	18 28		18 57		19 26		19 58		20 53	21 49	22 57	23 56
	d	18 01		18 31		19 02		19 31		20 01	20 57	21 53	23 01	00 01
Marlow	a	18 09		18 38		19 09		19 38		20 08	21 05	22 01	23 09	00 08

Saturdays

		GW [1]	GW [1]	GW [1]	GW [1]	GW [1]	GW [1]	GW [1]	GW [1]	GW [1]	GW [1]	GW [1]	GW [1]	GW [1]	GW [1]	GW [1]	GW [1]	GW [1]	GW [1]	GW [1]
London Paddington [15] ⊖	d																			
Maidenhead [3]	d	23p45	06 38	07 38	08 38	09 38	10 38	11 38	12 38	13 38	14 38	15 38	16 38	17 38	18 38	19 38	20 38	21 38	22 38	23 38
Furze Platt	d	23p49	06 42	07 42	08 42	09 42	10 42	11 42	12 42	13 42	14 42	15 42	16 42	17 42	18 42	19 42	20 42	21 42	22 42	23 42
Cookham	d	23p52	06 45	07 45	08 45	09 45	10 45	11 45	12 45	13 45	14 45	15 45	16 45	17 45	18 45	19 45	20 45	21 45	22 45	23 45
Bourne End [3]	a	23p56	06 49	07 49	08 49	09 49	10 49	11 49	12 49	13 49	14 49	15 49	16 49	17 49	18 49	19 49	20 49	21 49	22 49	23 49
	d	00 01	06 53	07 53	08 53	09 53	10 53	11 53	12 53	13 53	14 53	15 53	16 53	17 53	18 53	19 53	20 53	21 53	22 53	23 53
Marlow	a	00 08	07 01	08 01	09 01	10 01	11 01	12 01	13 01	14 01	15 01	16 01	17 01	18 01	19 01	20 01	21 01	22 01	23 01	00 01

Sundays

		GW [1] A	GW [1]	GW [1]	GW [1]	GW [1]	GW [1]	GW [1]	GW [1]	GW [1]	GW [1]	GW [1]	GW [1]	GW [1]	GW [1]	GW [1]
London Paddington [15] ⊖	d															
Maidenhead [3]	d	23p38	08 35	09 35	10 35	11 35	12 35	13 35	14 35	15 35	16 35	17 35	18 35	19 35	20 35	21 40
Furze Platt	d	23p42	08 39	09 39	10 39	11 39	12 39	13 39	14 39	15 39	16 39	17 39	18 39	19 39	20 39	21 44
Cookham	d	23p45	08 42	09 42	10 42	11 42	12 42	13 42	14 42	15 42	16 42	17 42	18 42	19 42	20 42	21 47
Bourne End [3]	a	23p49	08 47	09 47	10 47	11 47	12 47	13 47	14 47	15 47	16 47	17 47	18 47	19 47	20 47	21 52
	d	23p53	08 51	09 51	10 51	11 51	12 51	13 51	14 51	15 51	16 51	17 51	18 51	19 51	20 51	21 56
Marlow	a	00 01	08 58	09 58	10 58	11 58	12 58	13 58	14 58	15 58	16 58	17 58	18 58	19 58	20 58	22 03

A not 22 May

Table 120

Mondays to Fridays

Marlow - Maidenhead

Miles			GW MX 1	GW 1	GW 1	GW 1	GW 1	GW 1	GW 1	GW 1	GW 1		GW 1	GW 1	GW 1	GW 1	GW 1	GW 1	GW 1	GW 1	GW 1		GW 1	GW 1	GW 1
0	**Marlow**	d	00 11	06 04		06 39		07 18		07 47			08 17		08 37		10 06	11 06	12 06	13 06	14 06		15 06	16 06	17 06
2¾	Bourne End 3	a	00 18	06 11		06 46		07 25		07 54			08 24		08 44		10 13	11 13	12 13	13 13	14 13		15 13	16 13	17 13
—		d	00 22		06 14		06 49		07 28		07 57			08 28	08 48	09 19	10 17	11 17	12 17	13 17	14 17		15 17	16 17	17 17
4¼	Cookham	d	00 26		06 17		06 52		07 31		08 00			08 31	08 52	09 22	10 21	11 21	12 21	13 21	14 21		15 21	16 21	17 21
6	Furze Platt	d	00 29		06 21		06 56		07 35		08 04			08 35	08 55	09 26	10 24	11 24	12 24	13 24	14 24		15 24	16 24	17 24
7¼	**Maidenhead** 3	a	00 34		06 25		07 00		07 39		08 08			08 39	09 00	09 30	10 29	11 29	12 29	13 29	14 29		15 29	16 29	17 29
—	London Paddington 15 ⊖	a							08 19					09 20											

		GW 1	GW 1	GW 1	GW 1	GW 1	GW 1		GW 1	GW 1	GW 1	GW 1	GW 1	GW 1
Marlow	d	18 21		18 51		19 21			19 51		20 15	21 08	22 04	23 13
Bourne End 3	a	18 28		18 58		19 28			19 58		20 22	21 15	22 11	23 20
	d		18 31		19 01		19 32			20 05	20 26	21 19	22 15	23 24
Cookham	d		18 34		19 04		19 35			20 08	20 30	21 23	22 19	23 28
Furze Platt	d		18 37		19 07		19 38			20 12	20 33	21 26	22 22	23 31
Maidenhead 3	a		18 42		19 12		19 43			20 16	20 38	21 31	22 27	23 36
London Paddington 15 ⊖	a													

Saturdays

		GW 1	GW 1	GW 1	GW 1	GW 1	GW 1	GW 1	GW 1	GW 1		GW 1	GW 1	GW 1	GW 1	GW 1	GW 1	GW 1	GW 1	GW 1
Marlow	d	00 11	07 06	08 06	09 06	10 06	11 06	12 06	13 06	14 06		15 06	16 06	17 06	18 06	19 06	20 06	21 06	22 06	23 06
Bourne End 3	a	00 18	07 13	08 13	09 13	10 13	11 13	12 13	13 13	14 13		15 13	16 13	17 13	18 13	19 13	20 13	21 13	22 13	23 13
	d	00 22	07 17	08 17	09 17	10 17	11 17	12 17	13 17	14 17		15 17	16 17	17 17	18 17	19 17	20 17	21 17	22 17	23 17
Cookham	d	00 26	07 21	08 21	09 21	10 21	11 21	12 21	13 21	14 21		15 21	16 21	17 21	18 21	19 21	20 21	21 21	22 21	23 21
Furze Platt	d	00 29	07 24	08 24	09 24	10 24	11 24	12 24	13 24	14 24		15 24	16 24	17 24	18 24	19 24	20 24	21 24	22 24	23 24
Maidenhead 3	a	00 34	07 29	08 29	09 29	10 29	11 29	12 29	13 29	14 29		15 29	16 29	17 29	18 29	19 29	20 29	21 29	22 29	23 29
London Paddington 15 ⊖	a																			

Sundays

		GW 1	GW 1	GW 1	GW 1	GW 1	GW 1	GW 1	GW 1	GW 1		GW 1	GW 1	GW 1	GW 1	GW 1	GW 1
Marlow	d	00 06	09 01	10 01	11 01	12 01	13 01	14 01	15 01	16 01		17 01	18 01	19 01	20 01	21 01	22 06
Bourne End 3	a	00 13	09 08	10 08	11 08	12 08	13 08	14 08	15 08	16 08		17 08	18 08	19 08	20 08	21 08	22 13
	d	00 17	09 12	10 12	11 12	12 12	13 12	14 12	15 12	16 12		17 12	18 12	19 12	20 12	21 12	22 17
Cookham	d	00 21	09 16	10 16	11 16	12 16	13 16	14 16	15 16	16 16		17 16	18 16	19 16	20 16	21 16	22 20
Furze Platt	d	00 24	09 20	10 20	11 20	12 20	13 20	14 20	15 20	16 20		17 20	18 20	19 20	20 20	21 20	22 24
Maidenhead 3	a	00 29	09 24	10 24	11 24	12 24	13 24	14 24	15 24	16 24		17 24	18 24	19 24	20 24	21 24	22 28
London Paddington 15 ⊖	a																

Twyford - Henley-on-Thames

Miles			GW	GW	GW	GW	GW	GW	GW	GW	GW	GW	GW	GW	GW	GW	GW	GW	GW	GW	GW	GW	GW
			1	1	1	1	1	1	1	1	1	1	1	1	1	1	1	1	1	1	1	1	1
—	London Paddington 15 ⊖	d																			17 12		18 12
—	Reading 7	d					08 06																
0	**Twyford 3**	d	05 42	06 21	06 50	07 27	08 14	08 45	09 21	09 53	10 36	11 21	12 06	12 51	13 36	14 21	15 06	15 48	16 48	17 31	17 58	18 31	18 58
1¾	Wargrave	d	05 46	06 25	06 54	07 31	08 19	08 49	09 25	09 57	10 40	11 25	12 10	12 55	13 40	14 25	15 10	15 52	16 52	17 35	18 03	18 35	19 03
2¾	Shiplake	d	05 49	06 28	06 57	07 34	08 22	08 52	09 28	10 00	10 43	11 28	12 13	12 58	13 43	14 28	15 13	15 55	16 55	17 38	18 06	18 38	19 06
4½	**Henley-on-Thames**	a	05 54	06 33	07 02	07 39	08 26	08 57	09 33	10 05	10 48	11 33	12 18	13 03	13 48	14 33	15 18	16 00	17 00	17 43	18 13	18 43	19 13

		GW	GW	GW	GW	GW	GW
		1	1	1	1	1	1
London Paddington 15 ⊖	d	19 06					
Reading 7	d						
Twyford 3	d	19 38	20 09	20 48	21 48	22 52	23 37
Wargrave	d	19 42	20 13	20 52	21 52	22 56	23 41
Shiplake	d	19 45	20 16	20 55	21 55	22 59	23 44
Henley-on-Thames	a	19 52	20 21	21 00	22 00	23 04	23 49

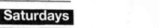

Saturdays

		GW	GW	GW	GW	GW	GW	GW	GW	GW	GW	GW	GW	GW	GW	GW	GW	GW	GW
		1	1	1	1	1	1	1	1	1	1	1	1	1	1	1	1	1	1
London Paddington 15 ⊖	d																		
Reading 7	d																		
Twyford 3	d	06 57	07 50	08 50	09 50	10 50	11 50	12 50	13 50	14 50	15 50	16 50	17 50	18 50	19 50	20 50	21 50	22 50	23 50
Wargrave	d	07 01	07 54	08 54	09 54	10 54	11 54	12 54	13 54	14 54	15 54	16 54	17 54	18 54	19 54	20 54	21 54	22 54	23 54
Shiplake	d	07 04	07 57	08 57	09 57	10 57	11 57	12 57	13 57	14 57	15 57	16 57	17 57	18 57	19 57	20 57	21 57	22 57	23 57
Henley-on-Thames	a	07 09	08 02	09 02	10 02	11 02	12 02	13 02	14 02	15 02	16 02	17 02	18 02	19 02	20 02	21 02	22 02	23 02	00 02

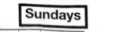

Sundays

		GW	GW	GW	GW	GW	GW	GW	GW	GW	GW	GW	GW	GW	GW
		1	1	1	1	1	1	1	1	1	1	1	1	1	1
		A													
London Paddington 15 ⊖	d														
Reading 7	d														
Twyford 3	d	23p50	09 38	10 38	11 38	12 38	13 38	14 38	15 38	16 38	17 38	18 38	19 38	20 38	21 38
Wargrave	d	23p54	09 42	10 42	11 42	12 42	13 42	14 42	15 42	16 42	17 42	18 42	19 42	20 42	21 42
Shiplake	d	23p57	09 45	10 45	11 45	12 45	13 45	14 45	15 45	16 45	17 45	18 45	19 45	20 45	21 45
Henley-on-Thames	a	00 02	09 50	10 50	11 50	12 50	13 50	14 50	15 50	16 50	17 50	18 50	19 50	20 50	21 50

A not 22 May

Table 121

Mondays to Fridays

Henley-on-Thames - Twyford

Miles			GW MX	GW	GW	GW	GW	GW	GW	GW	GW	GW	GW	GW	GW	GW	GW	GW	GW	GW	GW	GW	GW
			1	1	1	1	1	1	1	1	1	1	1	1	1	1	1	1	1	1	1	1	1
0	**Henley-on-Thames**	d	23p52	06 06	06 36	07 09	07 44	08 29	09 01	09 36	10 09	10 54	11 39	12 24	13 09	13 54	14 39	15 24	16 20	17 09	17 46	18 17	18 46
1¾	Shiplake	d	23p56	06 10	06 40	07 13	07 48	08 33	09 05	09 40	10 13	10 58	11 43	12 28	13 13	13 58	14 43	15 28	16 24	17 13	17 50	18 21	18 50
2¾	Wargrave	d	23p59	06 13	06 43	07 16	07 51	08 36	09 08	09 43	10 16	11 01	11 46	12 31	13 16	14 01	14 46	15 31	16 27	17 16	17 53	18 24	18 53
4½	**Twyford** 3	a	00 04	06 18	06 48	07 21	07 56	08 41	09 13	09 48	10 21	11 06	11 51	12 36	13 21	14 06	14 51	15 36	16 32	17 21	17 58	18 29	18 58
—	Reading 7	a	00 16																				
—	London Paddington 15 ⊖	a				07 57	08 29																

		GW	GW	GW	GW	GW	GW	GW
		1	1	1	1	1	1	1
Henley-on-Thames	d	19 16	19 55	20 24	21 05	22 07	23 07	23 52
Shiplake	d	19 20	19 59	20 28	21 09	22 11	23 11	23 56
Wargrave	d	19 23	20 02	20 31	21 12	22 14	23 14	23 59
Twyford 3	a	19 28	20 07	20 36	21 17	22 19	23 19	00 04
Reading 7	a							00 16
London Paddington 15 ⊖	a							

Saturdays

		GW	GW	GW	GW	GW	GW	GW	GW	GW	GW	GW	GW	GW	GW	GW	GW	GW	GW
		1	1	1	1	1	1	1	1	1	1	1	1	1	1	1	1	1	1
Henley-on-Thames	d	23p52	07 24	08 24	09 24	10 24	11 24	12 24	13 24	14 24	15 24	16 24	17 24	18 24	19 24	20 24	21 24	22 24	23 08
Shiplake	d	23p56	07 28	08 28	09 28	10 28	11 28	12 28	13 28	14 28	15 28	16 28	17 28	18 28	19 28	20 28	21 28	22 28	23 12
Wargrave	d	23p59	07 31	08 31	09 31	10 31	11 31	12 31	13 31	14 31	15 31	16 31	17 31	18 31	19 31	20 31	21 31	22 31	23 15
Twyford 3	a	00 04	07 36	08 36	09 36	10 36	11 36	12 36	13 36	14 36	15 36	16 36	17 36	18 36	19 36	20 36	21 36	22 36	23 20
Reading 7	a	00 16																	
London Paddington 15 ⊖	a																		

Sundays

		GW	GW	GW	GW	GW	GW	GW	GW	GW	GW	GW	GW	GW	GW
		1	1	1	1	1	1	1	1	1	1	1	1	1	1
Henley-on-Thames	d	00 08	10 03	11 03	12 03	13 03	14 03	15 03	16 03	17 03	18 03	19 03	20 03	21 03	22 01
Shiplake	d	00 12	10 07	11 07	12 07	13 07	14 07	15 07	16 07	17 07	18 07	19 07	20 07	21 07	22 05
Wargrave	d	00 15	10 10	11 10	12 10	13 10	14 10	15 10	16 10	17 10	18 10	19 10	20 10	21 10	22 08
Twyford 3	a	00 20	10 15	11 15	12 15	13 15	14 15	15 15	16 15	17 15	18 15	19 15	20 15	21 15	22 13
Reading 7	a														
London Paddington 15 ⊖	a														

Reading - Basingstoke

Miles			GW	GW	GW	GW	GW	GW	XC	GW	XC	GW	XC	GW	GW	XC	GW	XC	GW	XC	GW	GW	XC
			MO																				
			1	1	1	1	1	1	◇1	1	◇1	1	◇1	1	1	◇1	1	◇1	1	◇1	1	1	◇1
									T		T		T			T		T		T			T
0	Reading 7	d	23p37	05 39	06 07	06 39	07 07	07 39	07 46	08 07	08 15	08 39	08 46	09 08	09 39	09 46	10 07	10 15	10 39	10 46	11 07	11 39	11 46
1	Reading West	d	23p40	05 42	06 10	06 42	07 10	07 42	.	08 10	.	08 42	.	09 10	09 42	.	10 10	.	10 42	.	11 10	11 42	.
7¼	Mortimer	d	23p48	05 50	06 18	06 50	07 18	07 50	.	08 18	.	08 50	.	09 18	09 50	.	10 18	.	10 50	.	11 18	11 50	.
10½	Bramley (Hants)	d	23p53	05 55	06 23	06 55	07 23	07 55	.	08 23	.	08 55	.	09 23	09 55	.	10 23	.	10 55	.	11 23	11 55	.
15½	Basingstoke	a	00 01	06 03	06 31	07 03	07 31	08 03	08 08	08 31	08 40	09 03	09 08	09 34	10 03	10 08	10 31	10 39	11 03	11 08	11 31	12 03	12 08

		GW	XC	GW	XC	GW	GW	XC	GW	XC	GW	XC	GW	GW	XC	GW	XC	GW	XC	GW	GW	XC	GW
		1	◇1	1	◇1	1	1	◇1	1	◇1	1	◇1	1	1	◇1	1	◇1	1	◇1	1	1	◇1	1
																							A
			T		T			T		T		T			T		T		T			T	
Reading 7	d	12 07	12 15	12 39	12 46	13 07	13 39	13 46	14 07	14 15	14 39	14 46	15 07	15 39	15 46	16 07	16 15	16 39	16 46	17 07	17 41	17 46	18 07
Reading West	d	12 10	.	12 42	.	13 10	13 42	.	14 10	.	14 42	.	15 10	15 42	.	16 10	.	16 42	.	17 10	17 42	.	18 10
Mortimer	d	12 18	.	12 50	.	13 18	13 50	.	14 18	.	14 50	.	15 18	15 50	.	16 18	.	16 50	.	17 18	17 50	.	18 18
Bramley (Hants)	d	12 23	.	12 55	.	13 23	13 55	.	14 23	.	14 55	.	15 23	15 55	.	16 23	.	16 55	.	17 23	17 55	.	18 23
Basingstoke	a	12 32	12 39	13 03	13 08	13 31	14 03	14 08	14 31	14 39	15 03	15 08	15 31	16 03	16 08	16 31	16 39	17 03	17 08	17 31	18 05	18 08	18 31

		GW	XC	GW	XC	GW	GW	XC	GW	GW	XC	GW	GW	XC	GW	XC	GW	GW
		1	◇1	1	◇1	1	1	◇1	1	1	◇1	1	1	◇1	1	◇1	1	1
		B FO	T		T			T										
Reading 7	d	18 08	18 15	18 41	18 46	19 07	19 37	19 46	20 07	20 37	20 46	21 07	21 39	21 46	22 10	22 48	22 55	23 34
Reading West	d	18 10	.	18 42	.	19 10	19 40	.	20 10	20 40	.	21 10	21 42	.	22 13	.	22 58	23 37
Mortimer	d	18 18	.	18 50	.	19 18	19 48	.	20 18	20 48	.	21 18	21 50	.	22 21	.	23 06	23 45
Bramley (Hants)	d	18 23	.	18 55	.	19 23	19 53	.	20 23	20 53	.	21 23	21 55	.	22 26	.	23 11	23 50
Basingstoke	a	18 33	18 47	19 05	19 08	19 31	20 01	20 09	20 31	21 01	21 09	21 31	22 03	22 09	22 34	23 06	23 19	23 58

Saturdays

		GW	GW	GW	GW	XC	GW	XC	GW	XC	GW	GW	XC	GW	XC	GW	XC	GW	GW	XC	GW	XC	GW
		1	1	1	1	◇1	1	◇1	1	◇1	1	1	◇1	1	◇1	1	◇1	1	1	◇1	1	◇1	1
						T		T		T			T		T		T			T		T	
Reading 7	d	06 07	06 39	07 07	07 39	07 46	08 07	08 23	08 39	08 46	09 07	09 39	09 46	10 07	10 15	10 39	10 46	11 07	11 39	11 46	12 07	12 15	12 39
Reading West	d	06 10	06 42	07 10	07 42	.	08 10	.	08 42	.	09 10	09 42	.	10 10	.	10 42	.	11 10	11 42	.	12 10	.	12 42
Mortimer	d	06 18	06 50	07 18	07 50	.	08 18	.	08 50	.	09 18	09 50	.	10 18	.	10 50	.	11 18	11 50	.	12 18	.	12 50
Bramley (Hants)	d	06 23	06 55	07 23	07 55	.	08 23	.	08 55	.	09 23	09 55	.	10 23	.	10 55	.	11 23	11 55	.	12 23	.	12 55
Basingstoke	a	06 32	07 03	07 32	08 03	08 08	08 31	08 40	09 03	09 08	09 31	10 03	10 08	10 31	10 39	11 03	11 08	11 31	12 03	12 08	12 31	12 40	13 03

		XC	GW	GW	XC	GW	XC	GW	XC	GW	GW	XC	GW	XC	GW	XC	GW	GW	XC	GW	XC	GW	XC
		◇1	1	1	◇1	1	◇1	1	◇1	1	1	◇1	1	◇1	1	◇1	1	1	◇1	1	◇1	1	◇1
		T			T		T		T			T		T		T			T		T		T
Reading 7	d	12 46	13 07	13 39	13 46	14 07	14 15	14 39	14 46	15 07	15 39	15 46	16 07	16 15	16 39	16 46	17 07	17 39	17 46	18 07	18 15	18 39	18 46
Reading West	d	.	13 10	13 42	.	14 10	.	14 42	.	15 10	15 42	.	16 10	.	16 42	.	17 10	17 42	.	18 10	.	18 42	.
Mortimer	d	.	13 18	13 50	.	14 18	.	14 50	.	15 18	15 50	.	16 18	.	16 50	.	17 18	17 50	.	18 18	.	18 50	.
Bramley (Hants)	d	.	13 23	13 55	.	14 23	.	14 55	.	15 23	15 55	.	16 23	.	16 55	.	17 23	17 55	.	18 23	.	18 55	.
Basingstoke	a	13 08	13 31	14 03	14 08	14 31	14 40	15 03	15 08	15 31	16 03	16 08	16 31	16 40	17 03	17 08	17 31	18 03	18 08	18 31	18 40	19 03	19 08

		GW	GW	XC	GW	GW	XC	GW	GW	XC	GW	GW	XC	GW
		1	1	◇1	1	1	◇1	1	1	◇1	1	1	◇1	1
				T										
Reading 7	d	19 07	19 39	19 46	20 07	20 39	20 46	21 07	21 39	21 46	22 07	22 39	22 49	23 07
Reading West	d	19 10	19 42	.	20 10	20 42	.	21 10	21 42	.	22 10	22 42	.	23 10
Mortimer	d	19 18	19 50	.	20 18	20 50	.	21 18	21 50	.	22 18	22 50	.	23 18
Bramley (Hants)	d	19 23	19 55	.	20 23	20 55	.	21 23	21 55	.	22 23	22 55	.	23 23
Basingstoke	a	19 31	20 03	20 08	20 31	21 03	21 08	21 31	22 03	22 08	22 31	23 03	23 06	23 31

Sundays

		GW	GW	GW	XC	GW	XC	GW	GW	XC	GW	GW	XC	GW	GW	GW	XC	GW	XC	GW	XC	GW	XC
		1	1	1	◇1	1	◇1	1	1	◇1	1	1	◇1	1	1	1	◇1	1	◇1	1	◇1	1	◇1
								C	D		E	F		G	F	D							
					T		T			T			T				T		T		T		T
Reading 7	d	07 39	08 37	09 37	09 51	10 37	10 51	11 37	11 37	11 51	12 37	12 37	12 51	13 37	13 37	13 39	13 51	14 37	14 51	15 37	15 51	16 37	16 51
Reading West	d	07 40	08 40	09 40	.	10 40	.	11 40	11 42	.	12 40	12 42	.	13 40	13 42	13 42	.	14 40	.	15 40	.	16 40	.
Mortimer	d	07 48	08 48	09 48	.	10 48	.	11 48	11 50	.	12 48	12 50	.	13 48	13 50	13 50	.	14 48	.	15 48	.	16 48	.
Bramley (Hants)	d	07 53	08 53	09 53	.	10 53	.	11 53	11 55	.	12 53	12 55	.	13 53	13 55	13 55	.	14 53	.	15 53	.	16 53	.
Basingstoke	a	08 01	09 01	10 01	10 09	11 01	11 09	12 01	12 03	12 09	13 01	13 03	13 09	14 01	14 03	14 03	14 09	15 01	15 09	16 01	16 09	17 01	17 09

		GW	XC	GW	XC	GW	XC	GW	XC	GW	XC	GW	GW
		1	◇1	1	◇1	1	◇1	1	◇1	1	◇1	1	1
			T		T		T						
Reading 7	d	17 37	17 51	18 37	18 51	19 37	19 51	20 37	20 51	21 37	21 51	22 39	23 37
Reading West	d	17 40	.	18 40	.	19 40	.	20 40	.	21 40	.	22 41	23 40
Mortimer	d	17 48	.	18 48	.	19 48	.	20 48	.	21 48	.	22 49	23 48
Bramley (Hants)	d	17 53	.	18 53	.	19 53	.	20 53	.	21 53	.	22 54	23 53
Basingstoke	a	18 01	18 09	19 01	19 09	20 01	20 09	21 01	21 09	22 01	22 09	23 02	00 01

A Does not run on Fridays from 8 July until 2 September
B From 8 July until 2 September
C from 7 August
D until 31 July
E until 31 July, from 18 September
F from 7 August until 11 September
G from 18 September

Basingstoke - Reading

Miles			GW MX 1	GW MO 1	XC ◇1	GW 1	GW 1	XC ◇1 🛒	GW 1	GW 1	XC ◇1 🛒	GW 1	XC ◇1 🛒	GW 1	XC ◇1 🛒	GW 1	GW 1	XC ◇1 🛒	GW 1	XC ◇1 🛒	GW 1	XC ◇1 🛒	GW 1
0	**Basingstoke**	d	00 02	00 07	05 47	06 07	06 34	06 47	07 08	07 37	07 47	08 07	08 18	08 37	08 47	09 07	09 37	09 47	10 07	10 19	10 37	10 47	11 07
5	Bramley (Hants)	d	00 09	00 14	.	06 14	06 41	.	07 14	07 44	.	08 14	.	08 44	.	09 14	09 44	.	10 14	.	10 44	.	11 14
8¼	Mortimer	d	00 14	00 19	.	06 19	06 46	.	07 19	07 49	.	08 19	.	08 49	.	09 19	09 49	.	10 19	.	10 49	.	11 19
14½	Reading West	d	00 22	00 26	.	06 27	06 54	.	07 27	07 57	.	08 27	.	08 57	.	09 27	09 57	.	10 27	.	10 57	.	11 27
15½	**Reading 7**	a	00 26	00 30	06 04	06 32	06 57	07 04	07 31	08 00	08 04	08 30	08 36	09 00	09 04	09 30	10 00	10 04	10 30	10 35	11 00	11 04	11 30

		GW 1	XC ◇1 🛒	GW 1	XC ◇1 🛒	GW 1	XC ◇1 🛒	GW 1	GW 1	XC ◇1 🛒	GW 1	XC ◇1	GW 1	XC ◇1 🛒	GW 1	GW 1	XC ◇1 🛒	GW 1	XC ◇1 🛒	GW 1	XC ◇1 🛒	GW 1	GW 1
Basingstoke	d	11 37	11 47	12 07	12 18	12 37	12 47	13 07	13 37	13 47	14 07	14 18	14 37	14 47	15 07	15 37	15 47	16 07	16 18	16 37	16 47	17 07	17 37
Bramley (Hants)	d	11 44	.	12 14	.	12 44	.	13 14	13 44	.	14 14	.	14 44	.	15 14	15 44	.	16 14	.	16 44	.	17 14	17 44
Mortimer	d	11 49	.	12 19	.	12 49	.	13 19	13 49	.	14 19	.	14 49	.	15 19	15 49	.	16 19	.	16 49	.	17 19	17 49
Reading West	d	11 57	.	12 27	.	12 57	.	13 27	13 57	.	14 27	.	14 57	.	15 27	15 57	.	16 27	.	16 57	.	17 27	17 57
Reading 7	a	12 00	12 04	12 30	12 35	13 00	13 04	13 30	14 00	14 04	14 30	14 35	15 00	15 04	15 30	16 00	16 04	16 30	16 35	17 00	17 04	17 30	18 00

		XC ◇1 🛒	GW 1	XC ◇1 🛒	GW 1	XC ◇1 🛒	GW 1	GW 1	XC ◇1	GW 1	GW 1	XC ◇1	GW 1	GW 1	GW 1	GW 1	GW 1
Basingstoke	d	17 47	18 08	18 18	18 37	18 47	19 08	19 37	19 47	20 07	20 37	20 47	21 07	21 42	22 24	22 55	23 30
Bramley (Hants)	d	.	18 14	.	18 44	.	19 14	19 44	.	20 14	20 44	.	21 14	21 49	22 31	23 02	23 37
Mortimer	d	.	18 19	.	18 49	.	19 19	19 49	.	20 19	20 49	.	21 19	21 54	22 36	23 07	23 42
Reading West	d	.	18 27	.	18 57	.	19 27	19 57	.	20 27	20 57	.	21 27	22 02	22 44	23 15	23 50
Reading 7	a	18 04	18 31	18 35	19 00	19 04	19 31	20 01	20 04	20 30	21 01	21 04	21 30	22 05	22 47	23 18	23 53

Saturdays

		GW 1	XC ◇1	GW 1	XC ◇1 🛒	GW 1	XC ◇1 🛒	GW 1	XC ◇1 🛒	GW 1	XC ◇1 🛒	GW 1	XC ◇1 🛒	GW 1	GW 1	XC ◇1 🛒	GW 1	XC ◇1 🛒	GW 1	XC ◇1 🛒	GW 1	GW 1	XC ◇1 🛒
Basingstoke	d	00 02	05 41	06 37	06 47	07 07	07 25	07 37	07 47	08 07	08 19	08 37	08 47	09 07	09 37	09 47	10 07	10 19	10 37	10 47	11 07	11 37	11 47
Bramley (Hants)	d	00 09	.	06 44	.	07 14	.	07 44	.	08 14	.	08 44	.	09 14	09 44	.	10 14	.	10 44	.	11 14	11 44	.
Mortimer	d	00 14	.	06 49	.	07 19	.	07 49	.	08 19	.	08 49	.	09 19	09 49	.	10 19	.	10 49	.	11 19	11 49	.
Reading West	d	00 22	.	06 57	.	07 27	.	07 57	.	08 27	.	08 57	.	09 27	09 57	.	10 27	.	10 57	.	11 27	11 57	.
Reading 7	a	00 26	05 59	07 00	07 04	07 31	07 42	08 00	08 04	08 31	08 35	09 00	09 04	09 31	10 00	10 04	10 31	10 35	11 00	11 04	11 31	12 00	12 04

		GW 1	XC ◇1 🛒	GW 1	XC ◇1 🛒	GW 1	GW 1	XC ◇1 🛒	GW 1	XC ◇1 🛒	GW 1	XC ◇1 🛒	GW 1	GW 1	XC ◇1 🛒	GW 1	XC ◇1 🛒	GW 1	XC ◇1 🛒	GW 1	GW 1	XC ◇1 🛒	GW 1
Basingstoke	d	12 07	12 19	12 37	12 47	13 07	13 37	13 47	14 07	14 19	14 37	14 47	15 07	15 37	15 47	16 07	16 19	16 37	16 47	17 07	17 37	17 47	18 07
Bramley (Hants)	d	12 14	.	12 44	.	13 14	13 44	.	14 14	.	14 44	.	15 14	15 44	.	16 14	.	16 44	.	17 14	17 44	.	18 14
Mortimer	d	12 19	.	12 49	.	13 19	13 49	.	14 19	.	14 49	.	15 19	15 49	.	16 19	.	16 49	.	17 19	17 49	.	18 19
Reading West	d	12 27	.	12 57	.	13 27	13 57	.	14 28	.	14 57	.	15 27	15 57	.	16 27	.	16 57	.	17 27	17 57	.	18 27
Reading 7	a	12 31	12 35	13 00	13 04	13 31	14 00	14 04	14 32	14 35	15 00	15 04	15 31	16 00	16 05	16 31	16 35	17 00	17 04	17 31	18 00	18 04	18 31

		XC ◇1 🛒	GW 1	XC ◇1 🛒	GW 1	GW 1	XC ◇1	GW 1	GW 1	XC ◇1	GW 1	GW 1	GW 1	GW 1	GW 1	GW 1
Basingstoke	d	18 19	18 37	18 47	19 07	19 37	19 47	20 08	20 37	20 47	21 07	21 39	22 07	22 37	23 07	23 37
Bramley (Hants)	d	.	18 44	.	19 14	19 44	.	20 14	20 44	.	21 14	21 44	22 14	22 44	23 14	23 44
Mortimer	d	.	18 49	.	19 19	19 49	.	20 19	20 49	.	21 19	21 49	22 19	22 49	23 19	23 49
Reading West	d	.	18 57	.	19 27	19 57	.	20 27	20 57	.	21 27	21 57	22 27	22 57	23 27	23 57
Reading 7	a	18 35	19 00	19 04	19 31	20 01	20 04	20 32	21 01	21 04	21 31	22 02	22 31	23 00	23 31	00 01

Sundays

		GW 1 A	GW 1	GW 1	XC ◇1 🛒	GW 1	XC ◇1 🛒	GW 1	XC ◇1 🛒	GW 1	XC ◇1 🛒	GW 1	XC ◇1 🛒	GW 1	XC ◇1 🛒	GW 1	XC ◇1 🛒	GW 1	XC ◇1 🛒	GW 1	XC ◇1 🛒	GW 1	XC ◇1 🛒
Basingstoke	d	23p37	08 07	09 07	09 47	10 07	10 47	11 07	11 47	12 07	12 47	13 07	13 47	14 07	14 47	15 07	15 47	16 07	16 47	17 07	17 47	18 07	18 47
Bramley (Hants)	d	23p44	08 14	09 14	.	10 14	.	11 14	.	12 14	.	13 14	.	14 14	.	15 14	.	16 14	.	17 14	.	18 14	.
Mortimer	d	23p49	08 19	09 19	.	10 19	.	11 19	.	12 19	.	13 19	.	14 19	.	15 19	.	16 19	.	17 19	.	18 19	.
Reading West	d	23p57	08 27	09 27	.	10 27	.	11 27	.	12 27	.	13 27	.	14 34	.	15 27	.	16 27	.	17 27	.	18 27	.
Reading 7	a	00 01	08 30	09 30	10 04	10 30	11 04	11 30	12 04	12 30	13 04	13 30	14 04	14 37	15 04	15 30	16 04	16 30	17 04	17 30	18 04	18 30	19 04

		GW 1	XC ◇1	GW 1	XC ◇1	GW 1	GW 1	GW 1
Basingstoke	d	19 07	19 47	20 07	20 47	21 07	22 07	23 07
Bramley (Hants)	d	19 14	.	20 14	.	21 14	22 15	23 14
Mortimer	d	19 19	.	20 19	.	21 19	22 20	23 19
Reading West	d	19 28	.	20 27	.	21 27	22 30	23 27
Reading 7	a	19 31	20 04	20 30	21 04	21 30	22 33	23 30

A not 22 May

Network Diagram for Table 123

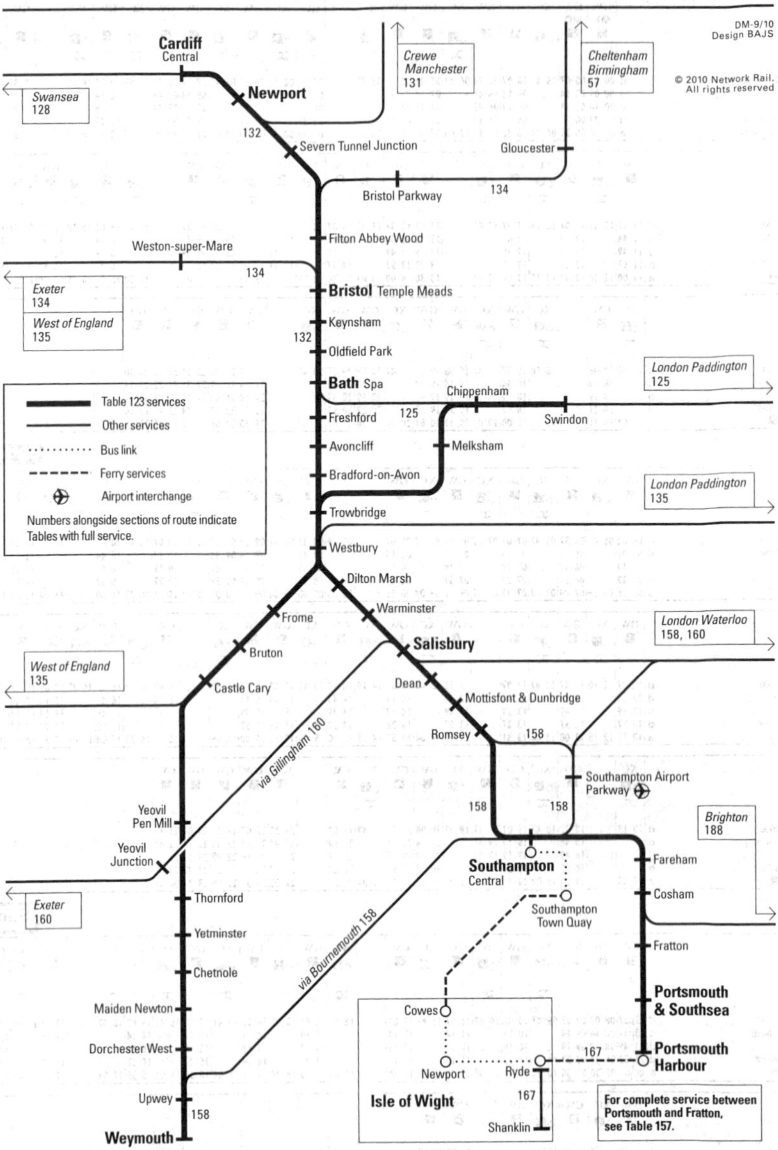

Table 123

Mondays to Fridays

until 1 July

South Wales and Bristol - Weymouth and Portsmouth

Miles	Miles	Miles			GW MX	GW MX	GW	GW	GW	GW	GW		GW		GW	GW	GW	GW	GW	GW	SW	GW	GW		GW
						R A 🛏 ☕			◇1 ☕		◇ B					◇ 🛒	◇1 C ☕		R 🛒		◇1		◇ 🛒		◇1 ⊘
0	0	—	**Cardiff Central 7**	d												06 28			07 30				08 30		
11¾	11¾	—	Newport (South Wales)	d												06 42			07 44				08 44		
21¾	21¾	—	Severn Tunnel Jn	d												06 53			07 55				08 55		
33¾	33¾	—	Filton Abbey Wood	d												07 09		07 28	08 09	08 23			09 09		
38¼	38¼	—	**Bristol Temple Meads 10**	d	23p20				05 20		05 44				06 48	07 23		07 49	08 23	08 41	08 51	09 05	09 23		
42¾	42¾	—	Keynsham	d	23p27						05 51				06 55			07 56		08 47	08 58				
48¾	48¾	—	Oldfield Park	d	23p34						05 58				07 02			08 03		08 54		09 17			
—	—	—	London Paddington 15 ⊖	d		23p45											07 06								09 06
—	—	0	Swindon	d									06 16												
—	—	16¾	Chippenham	d									06 32												
—	—	23	Melksham	d									06 41												
49¾	49¾	—	**Bath Spa 7**	d	23p38						06 02				07 06	07 36		08 07	08 36	08 58	09 07	09 21	09 36		
56¾	56¾	—	Freshford	d	23p47						06 12				07 16			08 16		09 07					
57¾	57¾	—	Avoncliff	d	23p50						06 14				07 18			08 18		09 09					
59	59	—	Bradford-on-Avon	d	23p53				05 44		06 18				07 22	07 47		08 22	08 47	09 13	09 20	09 33			
62¼	62¼	28½	Trowbridge	d	23p59				05 52		06 25		06 50		07 28	07 53		08 28	08 53	09 19	09 27	09 39	09 51		
66¼	66¼	32½	**Westbury**	a	00 06	01 35			05 59		06 32		06 57		07 35	08 00	08 26	08 36	09 01	09 27	09 33	09 49	09 58		
—	—	—																							
—	—	—		d	00 07		05 24	05 49		06 25	06 47	06 37	07 01			08 01			09 01	09 31	09 39		09 59		
—	72	—	Frome	d	00a18					06a35	06 56									09 40					
—	82½	—	Bruton	d							07 08									09 52					
—	86	—	Castle Cary	a							07 13									09 59					10 29
—	—	—		d							07 14									10 00					
—	97¾	—	Yeovil Pen Mill	d							07 35									10 14					
—	101	—	Thornford	d							07x39									10x18					
—	102	—	Yetminster	d							07x42									10x21					
—	104	—	Chetnole	d							07x46									10x25					
—	110½	—	Maiden Newton	d							07 58									10 37					
—	118¼	—	Dorchester West	d							08 09									10 48					
—	122¾	—	Upwey	a							08 16									10 55					
—	125¼	—	**Weymouth**	a							08 24									11 03					
67¾	—	—	Dilton Marsh	d									07x03												
71	—	—	Warminster	d			05 32	05 56				06 43	07 12			08 08			09 09		09 46		10 06		
90¾	—	—	**Salisbury**	a			05 53	06 19				07 10	07 36			08 32			09 32		10 09		10 29		
—	—	—		d				06 20				07 11	07 36			08 32			09 32				10 30		
107¼	—	—	Romsey	d				06 38				07 30	07 56			08 50			09 51				10 50		
115½	—	—	**Southampton Central**	a				06 49				07 41	08 09			09 04			10 04				11 04		
130	—	—	Fareham	a				07 14				08 05				09 27			10 27				11 27		
—	—	—		d				07 15				08 06				09 27			10 27				11 27		
135¾	—	—	Cosham	a				07 23				08 14				09 35			10 35				11 35		
139½	—	—	Fratton	a				07 34				08 21				09 42			10 42				11 42		
140½	—	—	Portsmouth & Southsea	a				07 38				08 24				09 46			10 46				11 46		
141¼	—	—	**Portsmouth Harbour**	a				07 45				08 30				09 55			10 54				11 54		
—	—	—	Havant	a																					
—	—	—	Chichester 4	a																					
—	—	—	Barnham	a																					
—	—	—	Worthing 4	a																					
—	—	—	Shoreham-by-Sea	a																					
—	—	—	Hove 2	a																					
—	—	—	Brighton 10	a																					

A The Night Riviera

B ◇ to Westbury

C The Devon Express

For connections from Swansea please refer to Table 128.
For connections from Plymouth and Exeter St Davids please refer to Table 135.
For connections to Bournemouth please refer to Table 158

Table 123

Mondays to Fridays

until 1 July

South Wales and Bristol - Weymouth and Portsmouth

		GW	GW	GW	GW	GW	GW	GW	GW	GW	GW	SW	GW	GW	GW	GW	GW	GW	GW	GW	GW	SW	GW
											■												
				◇			◇	◇■		◇		◇■	◇■	◇		◇			◇	◇■		◇■	◇
								A			B												
				T			T	Ø		T	T	T	⊓	T		T			T	Ø			T
Cardiff Central ■	d			09 30			10 30			11 30				12 30		13 30			14 30				15 30
Newport (South Wales)	d			09 44			10 44			11 44				12 44		13 44			14 44				15 44
Severn Tunnel Jn	d			09 55																			
Filton Abbey Wood	d		09 23	10 09		10 25	11 09		11 23	12 09	12 25			13 09	13 23	14 09		14 25	15 09		15 23		16 09
Bristol Temple Meads ■	d		09 49	10 23		10 49	11 23		11 49	12 23	12 39	13 15		13 23	13 49	14 23		14 48	15 23		15 44	15 51	16 23
Keynsham	d		09 56			10 56			11 56		12 46				13 56			14 55			15 51	15 58	
Oldfield Park	d		10 03			11 03			12 03		12 53				14 03			15 02			15 58		
London Paddington ■ ⊖	d							11 06					12 18							15 06			
Swindon	d																						
Chippenham	d																						
Melksham	d																						
Bath Spa ■	d		10 07	10 36		11 07	11 36		12 07	12 36	12 57	13 28		13 36	14 07	14 36		15 06	15 36		16 02	16 07	16 36
Freshford	d		10 16			11 16			12 16		13 06				14 16			15 15			16 10		
Avoncliff	d		10 18			11 18			12 18		13 07				14 18			15 17			16 13		
Bradford-on-Avon	d		10 22	10 47		11 22	11 47		12 22	12 47	13 12	13 40		13 47	14 22	14 47		15 22	15 47		16 16	16 22	16 47
Trowbridge	d		10 28	10 53		11 28	11 53		12 28	12 53	13 18	13 47		13 53	14 28	14 53		15 28	15 53		16 22	16 28	16 53
Westbury	a		10 36	11 00		11 36	12 01	12 21	12 36	13 01	13 25	13 53	13 57	14 01	14 36	15 01		15 36	16 01	16 22	16 29	16 36	17 01
	d	10 08	10 37	11 01	11 11		12 01	12 22	12 37	13 01	13 27	13 54	13 59	14 01	14 37	15 01	15 11	15 38	16 01	16 23		16 39	17 02
Frome	d		10 46						12 47						14a48			15 47					
Bruton	d		10 58						12 57									15 58					
Castle Cary	a		11 03					12 39	13 03				14 16					16 04		16 41			
	d		11 03						13 04									16 09					
Yeovil Pen Mill	d		11 17						13 17									16 24					
Thornford	d		11x22						13x22									16x28					
Yetminster	d		11x25						13x25									16x31					
Chetnole	d		11x29						13x29									16x35					
Maiden Newton	d		11 41						13 41									16 47					
Dorchester West	d		11 54						13 54									16 58					
Upwey	a		12 02						14 02									17 05					
Weymouth	a		12 09						14 09									17 10					
Dilton Marsh	d	10x10			11x13						13x29						15x13						
Warminster	d	10a19		11 09	11 20		12 09			13 09	13 36	14 02		14 09		15 09	15a22		16 09			16 47	17 09
Salisbury	a			11 32	11 42		12 32			13 32	13 58	14 28		14 32		15 32			16 32			17 09	17 32
	d			11 32	11 43		12 32			13 32	13 59			14 32		15 32			16 32				17 32
Romsey	d			11 51	12 11		12 51			13 51	14 20			14 51		15 51			16 51				17 51
Southampton Central	a			12 04	12 22		13 04			14 04	14 32			15 04		16 04			17 04				18 04
Fareham	a			12 27			13 27			14 27	14 55			15 27		16 27			17 27				18 27
	d			12 27			13 27			14 27	14 56			15 27		16 27			17 27				18 27
Cosham	a			12 35			13 35			14 35	15 04			15 35		16 35			17 35				18 35
Fratton	a			12 42			13 42			14 42				15 42		16 42			17 42				18 48
Portsmouth & Southsea	a			12 46			13 46			14 46				15 46		16 46			17 46				18 52
Portsmouth Harbour	a			12 54			13 54			14 54				15 54		16 54			17 54				19 00
Havant	a										15 10												
Chichester ■	a										15 21												
Barnham	a										15 29												
Worthing ■	a										15 45												
Shoreham-by-Sea	a										15 56												
Hove ■	a										16 07												
Brighton ■	a										16 14												

A The Mayflower

B T from Bristol Temple Meads

For connections from Swansea please refer to Table 128.
For connections from Plymouth and Exeter St Davids please refer to Table 135.
For connections to Bournemouth please refer to Table 158

Table 123

Mondays to Fridays

until 1 July

South Wales and Bristol - Weymouth and Portsmouth

		GW	GW	GW	GW	GW	GW	GW	GW	GW	GW	GW	GW	GW	GW	GW	GW	GW	GW	GW	GW	GW	GW
						◇1 ☕	R 🛒			◇1 ☕	R 🛒			◇1 ☕	◇ 🛒	◇1 ☕		◇	◇1 ☕		◇1 ☕	◇	
Cardiff Central 7	d						16 30				17 30				18 30			19 30				20 30	21 00
Newport (South Wales)	d						16 44				17 44				18 44			19 44				20 44	21 15
Severn Tunnel Jn.	d						16 55				17 55				18 55								21 25
Filton Abbey Wood	d		16 25	16 48	16 55		17 09	17 23	17 49		18 09		18 23		19 09		19 23	20 09		20 25		21 08	21 42
Bristol Temple Meads 10	d		16 49	17 06	17 14		17 23	17 49	18 07		18 23		18 49		19 23		19 49	20 23		20 49		21 23	22 00
Keynsham	d		16 56	17 13				17 56	18 14				18 56				19 56			20 56			22 07
Oldfield Park	d		17 03	17 21	17 26			18 03	18 21				19 03				20 03			21 03			22 14
London Paddington 15 ⊖	d					16 36				17 36				18 06		18 33			19 45		20 35		
Swindon	d											18 44											
Chippenham	d											19 01											
Melksham	d											19 11											
Bath Spa 7	d		17 07	17 25	17 31		17 36	18 07	18 25		18 36		19 07		19 36		20 07	20 36		21 07		21 36	22 18
Freshford	d		17 16		17 40			18 16	18 34				19 16				20 16			21 16			22 28
Avoncliff	d		17 18		17 42			18 18	18 36				19 18				20 18			21 18			22 29
Bradford-on-Avon	d		17 22	17 37			17 47	18 22	18 40		18 47		19 22		19 47		20 22	20 47		21 22		21 47	22 34
Trowbridge	d		17 28	17 43	17 50		17 56	18 28	18 46		18 53	19 20	19 28		19 53		20 28	20 53		21 28		21 53	22 40
Westbury	a		17 36	17 50	17 58	18 02	18 05	18 36	18 56	18 59	19 02	19 27	19 36	19 52	20 01	20 04	20 36	21 01	21 05	21 36	21 56	22 01	22 47
	d	17 11	17 38	17 54		18 04	18 05	18 39		19 01	19 04	19 41		19 53	20 01	20 05	20 36	21 01	21 05	21 38	21 57	22 01	
Frome	d		17 47					18 49						20a04			20a47			21 49			
Bruton	d		17 59					19 00												22 01			
Castle Cary	a		18 04			18 20		19 05		19 17						20 22			21 27	22 06	22 14		
	d		18 05					19 06												22 06			
Yeovil Pen Mill	d		18 21					19 19												22 20			
Thornford	d		18x26					19x24												22x25			
Yetminster	d		18x29					19x27												22x28			
Chetnole	d		18x33					19x31												22x32			
Maiden Newton	d		18 45					19 43												22 44			
Dorchester West	d		18 58					19 54												22 54			
Upwey	a		19 06					20 01												23 02			
Weymouth	a		19 14					20 09												23 10			
Dilton Marsh	d	17x13		17x56								19x43										22x04	
Warminster	d	17a21		18a05			18 12				19 09	19 50			20 09			21 09				22 09	
Salisbury	a						18 35				19 32	20 13			20 32			21 32				22 32	
	d						18 35				19 32	20 14			20 32			21 32				22 32	
Romsey	d						18 54				19 51	20 35			20 51			21 50				22 50	
Southampton Central	a						19 04				20 04	20 48			21 04			22 02				23 04	
Fareham	a						19 27				20 27				21 27			22 42				23 27	
	d						19 27				20 27				21 27			22 42				23 27	
Cosham	a						19 34																
Fratton	a						19 42				20 42				21 41			22 56				23 44	
Portsmouth & Southsea	a						19 46				20 46				21 45			22 59				23 48	
Portsmouth Harbour	a						19 54				20 54				21 52			23 04				23 54	
Havant	a																						
Chichester 4	a																						
Barnham	a																						
Worthing 4	a																						
Shoreham-by-Sea	a																						
Hove 2	a																						
Brighton 10	a																						

For connections from Swansea please refer to Table 128.
For connections from Plymouth and Exeter St Davids please refer to Table 135.
For connections to Bournemouth please refer to Table 158

Table 123

Mondays to Fridays

until 1 July

South Wales and Bristol - Weymouth and Portsmouth

		SW	GW	GW
		1		R A 🛏 🅿
Cardiff Central 7	d			
Newport (South Wales)	d			
Severn Tunnel Jn	d			
Filton Abbey Wood	d			
Bristol Temple Meads 10	d	22 25	23 20	
Keynsham	d		23 27	
Oldfield Park	d		23 34	
London Paddington 15 ⊖	d			23 45
Swindon	d			
Chippenham	d			
Melksham	d			
Bath Spa 7	d	22 38	23 38	
Freshford	d		23 47	
Avoncliff	d		23 50	
Bradford-on-Avon	d	22 51	23 53	
Trowbridge	d	22 57	23 59	
Westbury	a	23 04	00 06	01 35
	d	23 08	00 07	
Frome	d		00a18	
Bruton	d			
Castle Cary	a			
	d			
Yeovil Pen Mill	d			
Thornford	d			
Yetminster	d			
Chetnole	d			
Maiden Newton	d			
Dorchester West	d			
Upwey	a			
Weymouth	a			
Dilton Marsh	d			
Warminster	d	23 15		
Salisbury	a	23 35		
	d			
Romsey	d			
Southampton Central	a			
Fareham	a			
	d			
Cosham	a			
Fratton	a			
Portsmouth & Southsea	a			
Portsmouth Harbour	a			
Havant	a			
Chichester 4	a			
Barnham	a			
Worthing 4	a			
Shoreham-by-Sea	a			
Hove 2	a			
Brighton 10	a			

A The Night Riviera

For connections from Swansea please refer to Table 128.
For connections from Plymouth and Exeter St Davids please refer to Table 135.
For connections to Bournemouth please refer to Table 158

Table 123

Mondays to Fridays

4 July to 2 September

South Wales and Bristol - Weymouth and Portsmouth

		GW MX	GW MX	GW	GW	GW	GW	GW		GW		GW	GW	GW	GW	GW	GW	SW	GW	GW		GW	GW	GW	GW
			A			◇1		◇ B					◇	◇1 C				◇1		◇		◇1 D			◇
Cardiff Central 7	d												06 28			07 30				08 30					09 30
Newport (South Wales)	d												06 42			07 44				08 44					09 44
Severn Tunnel Jn.	d												06 53			07 55				08 55					09 55
Filton Abbey Wood	d												07 09		07 28	08 09	08 23			09 09				09 23	10 09
Bristol Temple Meads 10	d	23p20				05 20		05 44				06 48	07 23		07 49	08 23	08 41	08 51	09 05	09 23				09 49	10 23
Keynsham	d	23p27						05 51				06 55			07 56		08 47	08 58						09 56	
Oldfield Park	d	23p34						05 58				07 02			08 03		08 54		09 17					10 03	
London Paddington 15 ⊖	d		23p45											07 06								09 06			
Swindon	d									06 16															
Chippenham	d									06 32															
Melksham	d									06 41															
Bath Spa 7	d	23p38						06 02				07 06	07 36		08 07	08 36	08 58	09 07	09 21	09 36				10 07	10 36
Freshford	d	23p47						06 12				07 16			08 16		09 07							10 16	
Avoncliff	d	23p50						06 14				07 18			08 18		09 09							10 18	
Bradford-on-Avon	d	23p53				05 44		06 18				07 22	07 47		08 22	08 47	09 13	09 20	09 33					10 22	10 47
Trowbridge	d	23p59				05 52		06 25		06 50		07 28	07 53		08 28	08 53	09 19	09 27	09 39	09 51				10 28	10 53
Westbury	a	00 06	01 35			05 59		06 32		06 57		07 35	08 00	08 26	08 36	09 01	09 27	09 33	09 49	09 58				10 36	11 00
	d	00 07		05 24	05 49		06 25	06 47	06 37	07 01			08 01			09 01	09 31	09 39		09 59			10 08	10 37	11 01
Frome	d	00a18					06a35	06 56									09 40							10 46	
Bruton	d							07 08									09 52							10 58	
Castle Cary	a							07 13									09 59					10 29		11 03	
	d							07 14									10 00							11 03	
Yeovil Pen Mill	d							07 35									10 14							11 17	
Thornford	d							07x39									10x18							11x22	
Yetminster	d							07x42									10x21							11x25	
Chetnole	d							07x46									10x25							11x29	
Maiden Newton	d							07 58									10 37							11 41	
Dorchester West	d							08 09									10 48							11 54	
Upwey	a							08 16									10 55							12 02	
Weymouth	a							08 24									11 03							12 09	
Dilton Marsh	d									07x03													10x10		
Warminster	d			05 32	05 56				06 43	07 12			08 08			09 09		09 46		10 06			10a19		11 09
Salisbury	a			05 53	06 19				07 10	07 36			08 32			09 32		10 09		10 29					11 32
	d				06 20				07 11	07 36			08 32			09 32				10 30					11 32
Romsey	d				06 38				07 30	07 56			08 50			09 51				10 50					11 51
Southampton Central	a				06 49				07 41	08 09			09 04			10 04				11 04					12 04
Fareham	a				07 14				08 05				09 27			10 27				11 27					12 27
	d				07 15				08 06				09 27			10 27				11 27					12 27
Cosham	a				07 23				08 14				09 35			10 35				11 35					12 35
Fratton	a				07 34				08 21				09 42			10 42				11 42					12 42
Portsmouth & Southsea	a				07 38				08 24				09 46			10 46				11 46					12 46
Portsmouth Harbour	a				07 45				08 30				09 55			10 54				11 54					12 54
Havant	a																								
Chichester 4	a																								
Barnham	a																								
Worthing 4	a																								
Shoreham-by-Sea	a																								
Hove 2	a																								
Brighton 10	a																								

A The Night Riviera
B ◇ to Westbury
C The Devon Express
D The Atlantic Coast Express

For connections from Swansea please refer to Table 128.
For connections from Plymouth and Exeter St Davids please refer to Table 135.
For connections to Bournemouth please refer to Table 158

Table 123

Mondays to Fridays

4 July to 2 September

South Wales and Bristol - Weymouth and Portsmouth

		GW	GW	GW	GW	GW	GW	GW	SW	GW	GW	GW	GW	GW	GW	GW	GW	GW	GW	SW	GW	GW	GW
																	FO						
								■															
				◇	◇1		◇		◇1	◇1	◇		◇			◇	◇1	◇1		◇1	◇		
					A			B															
				trolley	Ø		trolley	trolley	trolley	restaurant	trolley		trolley			trolley	restaurant	Ø			trolley		
Cardiff Central 7	d			10 30			11 30				12 30		13 30			14 30					15 30		
Newport (South Wales)	d			10 44			11 44				12 44		13 44			14 44					15 44		
Severn Tunnel Jn.	d																						
Filton Abbey Wood	d		10 25	11 09		11 23	12 09	12 25			13 09	13 23	14 09		14 25	15 09			15 23		16 09		16 25
Bristol Temple Meads 10	d		10 49	11 23		11 49	12 23	12 39	13 15		13 23	13 49	14 23		14 48	15 23			15 44	15 51	16 23		16 49
Keynsham	d		10 56			11 56		12 46				13 56			14 55				15 51	15 58			16 56
Oldfield Park	d		11 03			12 03		12 53				14 03			15 02				15 58				17 03
London Paddington 15 ⊖	d				11 06					12 18							14 36	15 06					
Swindon	d																15 36						
Chippenham	d																						
Melksham	d																						
Bath Spa 7	d		11 07	11 36		12 07	12 36	12 57	13 28		13 36	14 07	14 36		15 06	15 36			16 02	16 07	16 36		17 07
Freshford	d		11 16			12 16		13 06				14 16			15 15				16 10				17 16
Avoncliff	d		11 18			12 18		13 07				14 18			15 17				16 13				17 18
Bradford-on-Avon	d		11 22	11 47		12 22	12 47	13 12	13 40		13 47	14 22	14 47		15 22	15 47			16 16	16 22	16 47		17 22
Trowbridge	d		11 28	11 53		12 28	12 53	13 18	13 47		13 53	14 28	14 53		15 28	15 53			16 22	16 28	16 53		17 28
Westbury	a		11 36	12 01	12 21	12 36	13 01	13 25	13 53	13 57	14 01	14 36	15 01		15 36	16 01	16 13	16 22	16 29	16 36	17 01		17 36
	d	11 11		12 01	12 22	12 37	13 01	13 27	13 54	13 59	14 01	14 37	15 01	15 11	15 38	16 01	16 15	16 23		16 39	17 02	17 11	17 38
Frome	d					12 47						14a48			15 47								17 47
Bruton	d					12 57									15 58								17 59
Castle Cary	a				12 39	13 03				14 16					16 04		16 31	16 41					18 04
	d					13 04									16 09								18 05
Yeovil Pen Mill	d					13 17									16 24								18 21
Thornford	d					13x22									16x28								18x26
Yetminster	d					13x25									16x31								18x29
Chetnole	d					13x29									16x35								18x33
Maiden Newton	d					13 41									16 47								18 45
Dorchester West	d					13 54									16 58								18 58
Upwey	a					14 02									17 05								19 06
Weymouth	a					14 09									17 10								19 14
Dilton Marsh	d	11x13						13x29						15x13								17x13	
Warminster	d	11 20		12 09			13 09	13 36	14 02		14 09		15 09	15a22		16 09				16 47	17 09	17a21	
Salisbury	a	11 42		12 32			13 32	13 58	14 28		14 32		15 32			16 32				17 09	17 32		
	d	11 43		12 32			13 32	13 59			14 32		15 32			16 32					17 32		
Romsey	d	12 11		12 51			13 51	14 20			14 51		15 51			16 51					17 51		
Southampton Central	a	12 22		13 04			14 04	14 32			15 04		16 04			17 04					18 04		
Fareham	a			13 27			14 27	14 55			15 27		16 27			17 27					18 27		
	d			13 27			14 27	14 56			15 27		16 27			17 27					18 27		
Cosham	a			13 35			14 35	15 04			15 35		16 35			17 35					18 35		
Fratton	a			13 42			14 42				15 42		16 42			17 42					18 48		
Portsmouth & Southsea	a			13 46			14 46				15 46		16 46			17 46					18 52		
Portsmouth Harbour	a			13 54			14 54				15 54		16 54			17 54					19 00		
Havant	a							15 10															
Chichester 4	a							15 21															
Barnham	a							15 29															
Worthing 4	a							15 45															
Shoreham-by-Sea	a							15 56															
Hove 2	a							16 07															
Brighton 10	a							16 14															

A The Mayflower

B trolley from Bristol Temple Meads

For connections from Swansea please refer to Table 128.
For connections from Plymouth and Exeter St Davids please refer to Table 135.
For connections to Bournemouth please refer to Table 158

Table 123

Mondays to Fridays

4 July to 2 September

South Wales and Bristol - Weymouth and Portsmouth

		GW		GW	GW	GW	GW	GW	GW	GW	GW	GW		GW	GW	GW	GW	GW	GW	GW	GW	GW		GW	SW
						R				R															
					◇1				◇1					◇1	◇	◇1		◇	◇1		◇1	◇			1
					☕	🛒			☕	🛒				☕	🛒	☕			☕		☕				
Cardiff Central 7	d					16 30				17 30					18 30			19 30				20 30		21 00	
Newport (South Wales)	d					16 44				17 44					18 44			19 44				20 44		21 15	
Severn Tunnel Jn.	d					16 55				17 55					18 55									21 25	
Filton Abbey Wood	d	16 48		16 55		17 09	17 23	17 49		18 09		18 23			19 09		19 23	20 09		20 25		21 08		21 42	
Bristol Temple Meads 10	d	17 06		17 14		17 23	17 49	18 07		18 23		18 49			19 23		19 49	20 23		20 49		21 23		22 00	22 25
Keynsham	d	17 13					17 56	18 14				18 56					19 56			20 56				22 07	
Oldfield Park	d	17 21		17 26			18 03	18 21				19 03					20 03			21 03				22 14	
London Paddington 15 ⊖	d				16 36				17 36					18 06		18 33			19 45		20 35				
Swindon	d										18 44														
Chippenham	d										19 01														
Melksham	d										19 11														
Bath Spa 7	d	17 25		17 31		17 36	18 07	18 25		18 36		19 07			19 36		20 07	20 36		21 07		21 36		22 18	22 38
Freshford	d			17 40			18 16	18 34				19 16					20 16			21 16				22 28	
Avoncliff	d			17 42			18 18	18 36				19 18					20 18			21 18				22 29	
Bradford-on-Avon	d	17 37				17 47	18 22	18 40		18 47		19 22			19 47		20 22	20 47		21 22		21 47		22 34	22 51
Trowbridge	d	17 43		17 50		17 56	18 28	18 46		18 53	19 20	19 28			19 53		20 28	20 53		21 28		21 53		22 40	22 57
Westbury	a	17 50		17 58	18 02	18 05	18 36	18 56	18 59	19 02	19 27	19 36		19 52	20 01	20 04	20 36	21 01	21 05	21 36	21 56	22 01		22 47	23 04
	d	17 54			18 04	18 05	18 39		19 01	19 04	19 41			19 53	20 01	20 05	20 36	21 01	21 05	21 38	21 57	22 01			23 08
Frome	d						18 49							20a04			20a47			21 49					
Bruton	d						19 00													22 01					
Castle Cary	a				18 20		19 05		19 17							20 22			21 27	22 06	22 14				
	d						19 06													22 06					
Yeovil Pen Mill	d						19 19													22 20					
Thornford	d						19x24													22x25					
Yetminster	d						19x27													22x28					
Chetnole	d						19x31													22x32					
Maiden Newton	d						19 43													22 44					
Dorchester West	d						19 54													22 54					
Upwey	a						20 01													23 02					
Weymouth	a						20 09													23 10					
Dilton Marsh	d	17x56									19x43											22x04			
Warminster	d	18a05				18 12				19 09	19 50				20 09			21 09				22 09			23 15
Salisbury	a					18 35				19 32	20 13				20 32			21 32				22 32			23 35
	d					18 35				19 32	20 14				20 32			21 32				22 32			
Romsey	d					18 54				19 51	20 35				20 51			21 50				22 50			
Southampton Central	a					19 04				20 04	20 48				21 04			22 02				23 04			
Fareham	a					19 27				20 27					21 27			22 42				23 27			
	d					19 27				20 27					21 27			22 42				23 27			
Cosham	a					19 34																			
Fratton	a					19 42				20 42					21 41			22 56				23 44			
Portsmouth & Southsea	a					19 46				20 46					21 45			22 59				23 48			
Portsmouth Harbour	a					19 54				20 54					21 52			23 04				23 54			
Havant	a																								
Chichester 4	a																								
Barnham	a																								
Worthing 4	a																								
Shoreham-by-Sea	a																								
Hove 2	a																								
Brighton 10	a																								

For connections from Swansea please refer to Table 128.
For connections from Plymouth and Exeter St Davids please refer to Table 135.
For connections to Bournemouth please refer to Table 158

Table 123

Mondays to Fridays

4 July to 2 September

South Wales and Bristol - Weymouth and Portsmouth

		GW	GW
			🛏 A 🛏 ☕
Cardiff Central 7	d		
Newport (South Wales)	d		
Severn Tunnel Jn	d		
Filton Abbey Wood	d		
Bristol Temple Meads 10	d	23 20	
Keynsham	d	23 27	
Oldfield Park	d	23 34	
London Paddington 15 ⊖	d		23 45
Swindon	d		
Chippenham	d		
Melksham	d		
Bath Spa 7	d	23 38	
Freshford	d	23 47	
Avoncliff	d	23 50	
Bradford-on-Avon	d	23 53	
Trowbridge	d	23 59	
Westbury	a	00 06	01 35
	d	00 07	
Frome	d	00a18	
Bruton	d		
Castle Cary	a		
	d		
Yeovil Pen Mill	d		
Thornford	d		
Yetminster	d		
Chetnole	d		
Maiden Newton	d		
Dorchester West	d		
Upwey	a		
Weymouth	a		
Dilton Marsh	d		
Warminster	d		
Salisbury	a		
	d		
Romsey	d		
Southampton Central	a		
Fareham	a		
	d		
Cosham	a		
Fratton	a		
Portsmouth & Southsea	a		
Portsmouth Harbour	a		
Havant	a		
Chichester 4	a		
Barnham	a		
Worthing 4	a		
Shoreham-by-Sea	a		
Hove 2	a		
Brighton 10	a		

A The Night Riviera

For connections from Swansea please refer to Table 128.
For connections from Plymouth and Exeter St Davids please refer to Table 135.
For connections to Bournemouth please refer to Table 158

Table 123

Mondays to Fridays

from 5 September

South Wales and Bristol - Weymouth and Portsmouth

Station		GW MX	GW	GW MX	GW	GW	GW	GW	GW			GW	GW	GW	GW	GW	GW	GW	SW	GW		GW	GW	GW	GW
			A 🛒	■R B 🛏 ☕			◇■1 ☕		◇ C					◇ 🛒	◇■1 D ☕		■R 🛒		◇■1			◇ 🛒	◇■1 ⊘		
Cardiff Central ■7	d													06 28			07 30					08 30			
Newport (South Wales)	d													06 42			07 44					08 44			
Severn Tunnel Jn.	d													06 53			07 55					08 55			
Filton Abbey Wood	d													07 09		07 28	08 09	08 23				09 09			09 23
Bristol Temple Meads ■10	d	23p20	23p38				05 20		05 44				06 48	07 23		07 49	08 23	08 41	08 51	09 05		09 23			09 49
Keynsham	d	23p27							05 51				06 55			07 56		08 47	08 58						09 56
Oldfield Park	d	23p34							05 58				07 02			08 03		08 54		09 17					10 03
London Paddington ■15 ⊖	d			23p45											07 06								09 06		
Swindon	d											06 16													
Chippenham	d											06 32													
Melksham	d											06 41													
Bath Spa ■7	d	23p38	23p50						06 02				07 06	07 36		08 07	08 36	08 58	09 07	09 21		09 36			10 07
Freshford	d	23p47							06 12				07 16			08 16		09 07							10 16
Avoncliff	d	23p50							06 14				07 18			08 18		09 09							10 18
Bradford-on-Avon	d	23p53	00 02				05 44		06 18				07 22	07 47		08 22	08 47	09 13	09 20	09 33					10 22
Trowbridge	d	23p59	00 08				05 52		06 25			06 50	07 28	07 53		08 28	08 53	09 19	09 27	09 39		09 51			10 28
Westbury	a	00 06	00 15	01 35			05 59		06 32			06 57	07 35	08 00	08 26	08 36	09 01	09 27	09 33	09 49		09 58			10 36
	d	00 07	00 18		05 24	05 49		06 25	06 47	06 37		07 01		08 01			09 01	09 31	09 39			09 59		10 08	10 37
Frome	d	00a18						06a35	06 56									09 40							10 46
Bruton	d								07 08									09 52							10 58
Castle Cary	a								07 13									09 59					10 29		11 03
	d								07 14									10 00							11 03
Yeovil Pen Mill	d								07 35									10 14							11 17
Thornford	d								07x39									10x18							11x22
Yetminster	d								07x42									10x21							11x25
Chetnole	d								07x46									10x25							11x29
Maiden Newton	d								07 58									10 37							11 41
Dorchester West	d								08 09									10 48							11 54
Upwey	a								08 16									10 55							12 02
Weymouth	a								08 24									11 03							12 09
Dilton Marsh	d		00x21									07x03												10x10	
Warminster	d		00a26		05 32	05 56				06 43		07 12		08 08			09 09		09 46			10 06		10a19	
Salisbury	a				05 53	06 19				07 10		07 36		08 32			09 32		10 09			10 29			
	d					06 20				07 11		07 36		08 32			09 32					10 30			
Romsey	d					06 38				07 30		07 56		08 50			09 51					10 50			
Southampton Central	a					06 49				07 41		08 09		09 04			10 04					11 04			
Fareham	a					07 14				08 05				09 27			10 27					11 27			
	d					07 15				08 06				09 27			10 27					11 27			
Cosham	a					07 23				08 14				09 35			10 35					11 35			
Fratton	a					07 34				08 21				09 42			10 42					11 42			
Portsmouth & Southsea	a					07 38				08 24				09 46			10 46					11 46			
Portsmouth Harbour	a					07 45				08 30				09 55			10 54					11 54			
Havant	a																								
Chichester ■4	a																								
Barnham	a																								
Worthing ■4	a																								
Shoreham-by-Sea	a																								
Hove ■2	a																								
Brighton ■10	a																								

A MO from 19 September until 24 October
B The Night Riviera
C ◇ to Westbury
D The Devon Express

For connections from Swansea please refer to Table 128.
For connections from Plymouth and Exeter St Davids please refer to Table 135.
For connections to Bournemouth please refer to Table 158

Table 123

Mondays to Fridays

from 5 September

South Wales and Bristol - Weymouth and Portsmouth

Station		GW	GW	GW	GW	GW	GW	GW	GW	SW	GW	GW	GW	GW	GW	GW	GW	GW	GW	SW	GW	GW	GW
									[R]														
		◇			◇	◇[1]		◇		◇[1]	◇[1]	◇		◇			◇	◇[1]		◇[1]	◇		
						A			B														
		⊼			⊼	Ø		⊼	⊼	⊼	⊡	⊼		⊼			⊼	Ø			⊼		
Cardiff Central [7]	d	09 30			10 30			11 30				12 30		13 30			14 30				15 30		
Newport (South Wales)	d	09 44			10 44			11 44				12 44		13 44			14 44				15 44		
Severn Tunnel Jn.	d	09 55																					
Filton Abbey Wood	d	10 09		10 25	11 09		11 23	12 09	12 25			13 09	13 23	14 09		14 25	15 09		15 23		16 09		16 25
Bristol Temple Meads [10]	d	10 23		10 49	11 23		11 49	12 23	12 39	13 15		13 23	13 49	14 23		14 48	15 23		15 44	15 51	16 23		16 49
Keynsham	d			10 56			11 56		12 46				13 56			14 55			15 51	15 58			16 56
Oldfield Park	d			11 03			12 03		12 53				14 03			15 02			15 58				17 03
London Paddington [15] ⊖	d					11 06					12 18							15 06					
Swindon	d																						
Chippenham	d																						
Melksham	d																						
Bath Spa [7]	d	10 36		11 07	11 36		12 07	12 36	12 57	13 28		13 36	14 07	14 36		15 06	15 36		16 02	16 07	16 36		17 07
Freshford	d			11 16			12 16		13 06				14 16			15 15			16 10				17 16
Avoncliff	d			11 18			12 18		13 07				14 18			15 17			16 13				17 18
Bradford-on-Avon	d	10 47		11 22	11 47		12 22	12 47	13 12	13 40		13 47	14 22	14 47		15 22	15 47		16 16	16 22	16 47		17 22
Trowbridge	d	10 53		11 28	11 53		12 28	12 53	13 18	13 47		13 53	14 28	14 53		15 28	15 53		16 22	16 28	16 53		17 28
Westbury	a	11 00		11 36	12 01	12 21	12 36	13 01	13 25	13 53	13 57	14 01	14 36	15 01		15 36	16 01	16 22	16 29	16 36	17 01		17 36
	d	11 01	11 11		12 01	12 22	12 37	13 01	13 27	13 54	13 59	14 01	14 37	15 01	15 11	15 38	16 01	16 23		16 39	17 02	17 11	17 38
Frome	d						12 47						14a48			15 47							17 47
Bruton	d						12 57									15 58							17 59
Castle Cary	a					12 39	13 03				14 16					16 04		16 41					18 04
	d						13 04									16 09							18 05
Yeovil Pen Mill	d						13 17									16 24							18 21
Thornford	d						13x22									16x28							18x26
Yetminster	d						13x25									16x31							18x29
Chetnole	d						13x29									16x35							18x33
Maiden Newton	d						13 41									16 47							18 45
Dorchester West	d						13 54									16 58							18 58
Upwey	a						14 02									17 05							19 06
Weymouth	a						14 09									17 10							19 14
Dilton Marsh	d		11x13						13x29						15x13							17x13	
Warminster	d	11 09	11 20		12 09			13 09	13 36	14 02		14 09		15 09	15a22		16 09			16 47	17 09	17a21	
Salisbury	a	11 32	11 42		12 32			13 32	13 58	14 28		14 32		15 32			16 32			17 09	17 32		
	d	11 32	11 43		12 32			13 32	13 59			14 32		15 32			16 32				17 32		
Romsey	d	11 51	12 11		12 51			13 51	14 20			14 51		15 51			16 51				17 51		
Southampton Central	a	12 04	12 22		13 04			14 04	14 32			15 04		16 04			17 04				18 04		
Fareham	a	12 27			13 27			14 27	14 55			15 27		16 27			17 27				18 27		
	d	12 27			13 27			14 27	14 56			15 27		16 27			17 27				18 27		
Cosham	a	12 35			13 35			14 35	15 04			15 35		16 35			17 35				18 35		
Fratton	a	12 42			13 42			14 42				15 42		16 42			17 42				18 48		
Portsmouth & Southsea	a	12 46			13 46			14 46				15 46		16 46			17 46				18 52		
Portsmouth Harbour	a	12 54			13 54			14 54				15 54		16 54			17 54				19 00		
Havant	a								15 10														
Chichester [4]	a								15 21														
Barnham	a								15 29														
Worthing [4]	a								15 45														
Shoreham-by-Sea	a								15 56														
Hove [2]	a								16 07														
Brighton [10]	a								16 14														

A The Mayflower

B ⊼ from Bristol Temple Meads

For connections from Swansea please refer to Table 128.
For connections from Plymouth and Exeter St Davids please refer to Table 135.
For connections to Bournemouth please refer to Table 158

Table 123

Mondays to Fridays

from 5 September

South Wales and Bristol - Weymouth and Portsmouth

		GW		GW	GW	GW	GW	GW	GW	GW	GW	GW		GW	GW	GW	GW	GW	GW	GW	GW	GW		GW	SW
					◇1	R			◇1	R				◇1	◇	◇1		◇	◇1		◇1	◇			1
					☕	🛒			☕	🛒				☕	🛒	☕			☕		☕				
Cardiff Central 7	d					16 30				17 30					18 30			19 30				20 30		21 00	
Newport (South Wales)	d					16 44				17 44					18 44			19 44				20 44		21 15	
Severn Tunnel Jn	d					16 55				17 55					18 55									21 25	
Filton Abbey Wood	d	16 48		16 55		17 09	17 23	17 49		18 09		18 23			19 09		19 23	20 09		20 25		21 08		21 42	
Bristol Temple Meads 10	d	17 06		17 14		17 23	17 49	18 07		18 23		18 49			19 23		19 49	20 23		20 49		21 23		22 00	22 25
Keynsham	d	17 13					17 56	18 14				18 56					19 56			20 56				22 07	
Oldfield Park	d	17 21		17 26			18 03	18 21				19 03					20 03			21 03				22 14	
London Paddington 15 ⊖	d				16 36				17 36					18 06		18 33			19 45		20 35				
Swindon	d										18 44														
Chippenham	d										19 01														
Melksham	d										19 11														
Bath Spa 7	d	17 25		17 31		17 36	18 07	18 25		18 36		19 07			19 36		20 07	20 36		21 07		21 36		22 18	22 38
Freshford	d			17 40			18 16	18 34				19 16					20 16			21 16				22 28	
Avoncliff	d			17 42			18 18	18 36				19 18					20 18			21 18				22 29	
Bradford-on-Avon	d	17 37				17 47	18 22	18 40		18 47		19 22			19 47		20 22	20 47		21 22		21 47		22 34	22 51
Trowbridge	d	17 43		17 50		17 56	18 28	18 46		18 53	19 20	19 28			19 53		20 28	20 53		21 28		21 53		22 40	22 57
Westbury	a	17 50		17 58	18 02	18 05	18 36	18 56	18 59	19 02	19 27	19 36		19 52	20 01	20 04	20 36	21 01	21 05	21 36	21 56	22 01		22 47	23 04
	d	17 54			18 04	18 05	18 39		19 01	19 04	19 41			19 53	20 01	20 05	20 36	21 01	21 05	21 38	21 57	22 01			23 08
Frome	d						18 49							20a04			20a47			21 49					
Bruton	d						19 00													22 01					
Castle Cary	a				18 20		19 05		19 17							20 22			21 27	22 06	22 14				
	d						19 06													22 06					
Yeovil Pen Mill	d						19 19													22 20					
Thornford	d						19x24													22x25					
Yetminster	d						19x27													22x28					
Chetnole	d						19x31													22x32					
Maiden Newton	d						19 43													22 44					
Dorchester West	d						19 54													22 54					
Upwey	a						20 01													23 02					
Weymouth	a						20 09													23 10					
Dilton Marsh	d	17x56									19x43											22x04			
Warminster	d	18a05				18 12				19 09	19 50				20 09			21 09				22 09			23 15
Salisbury	a					18 35				19 32	20 13				20 32			21 32				22 32			23 35
	d					18 35				19 32	20 14				20 32			21 32				22 32			
Romsey	d					18 54				19 51	20 35				20 51			21 50				22 50			
Southampton Central	a					19 04				20 04	20 48				21 04			22 02				23 04			
Fareham	a					19 27				20 27					21 27			22 42				23 27			
	d					19 27				20 27					21 27			22 42				23 27			
Cosham	a					19 34																			
Fratton	a					19 42				20 42					21 41			22 56				23 44			
Portsmouth & Southsea	a					19 46				20 46					21 45			22 59				23 48			
Portsmouth Harbour	a					19 54				20 54					21 52			23 04				23 54			
Havant	a																								
Chichester 4	a																								
Barnham	a																								
Worthing 4	a																								
Shoreham-by-Sea	a																								
Hove 2	a																								
Brighton 10	a																								

For connections from Swansea please refer to Table 128.
For connections from Plymouth and Exeter St Davids please refer to Table 135.
For connections to Bournemouth please refer to Table 158

Table 123

Mondays to Fridays

from 5 September

South Wales and Bristol - Weymouth and Portsmouth

		GW	GW
			A
Cardiff Central 7	d		
Newport (South Wales)	d		
Severn Tunnel Jn	d		
Filton Abbey Wood	d		
Bristol Temple Meads 10	d	23 20	
Keynsham	d	23 27	
Oldfield Park	d	23 34	
London Paddington 15 ⊖	d		23 45
Swindon	d		
Chippenham	d		
Melksham	d		
Bath Spa 7	d	23 38	
Freshford	d	23 47	
Avoncliff	d	23 50	
Bradford-on-Avon	d	23 53	
Trowbridge	d	23 59	
Westbury	a	00 06	01 35
	d	00 07	
Frome	d	00a18	
Bruton	d		
Castle Cary	a		
	d		
Yeovil Pen Mill	d		
Thornford	d		
Yetminster	d		
Chetnole	d		
Maiden Newton	d		
Dorchester West	d		
Upwey	a		
Weymouth	a		
Dilton Marsh	d		
Warminster	d		
Salisbury	a		
	d		
Romsey	d		
Southampton Central	a		
Fareham	a		
	d		
Cosham	a		
Fratton	a		
Portsmouth & Southsea	a		
Portsmouth Harbour	a		
Havant	a		
Chichester 4	a		
Barnham	a		
Worthing 4	a		
Shoreham-by-Sea	a		
Hove 2	a		
Brighton 10	a		

A The Night Riviera

For connections from Swansea please refer to Table 128.
For connections from Plymouth and Exeter St Davids please refer to Table 135.
For connections to Bournemouth please refer to Table 158

Table 123

Saturdays

until 10 September

South Wales and Bristol - Weymouth and Portsmouth

		GW	GW	GW	GW	GW	GW	GW	GW	GW		GW	GW	GW	SW	GW	GW	GW	GW	GW		GW	GW	GW	GW
			R A 🛏 ⊡			◇				◇			◇		◇1	R 1 B ⊡	◇			◇ C 🛒				R 1 ⊡	◇ C 🛒
Cardiff Central 7	d									06 30			07 30				08 30			09 30					10 30
Newport (South Wales)	d									06 44			07 44				08 44			09 44					10 44
Severn Tunnel Jn.	d									06 55			07 55				08 55			09 55					
Filton Abbey Wood	d									07 09			08 09	08 23			09 09		09 23	10 09			10 28		11 09
Bristol Temple Meads 10	d	23p20				05 49			06 49	07 23		07 49	08 23	08 40	08 51		09 23		09 49	10 23			10 49		11 23
Keynsham	d	23p27				05 56			06 56			07 56		08 47	08 58				09 56				10 56		
Oldfield Park	d	23p34				06 03			07 03			08 03		08 54					10 03				11 03		
London Paddington 15 ⊖	d		23p45													08 35								10 35	
Swindon	d																								
Chippenham	d																								
Melksham	d																								
Bath Spa 7	d	23p38				06 07			07 07	07 36		08 07	08 36	08 58	09 07		09 36		10 07	10 36			11 07		11 36
Freshford	d	23p47				06 16			07 16			08 16		09 07					10 16				11 16		
Avoncliff	d	23p50				06 18			07 18			08 18		09 09					10 18				11 18		
Bradford-on-Avon	d	23p53				06 22			07 22	07 47		08 22	08 47	09 13	09 20		09 47		10 22	10 47			11 22		11 47
Trowbridge	d	23p59				06 28			07 28	07 53		08 28	08 53	09 19	09 27		09 53		10 28	10 53			11 28		11 53
Westbury	a	00 06	01 35			06 35			07 35	08 01		08 35	09 01	09 27	09 34	09 56	10 03		10 36	11 00			11 35	11 53	12 01
	d	00 07		05 26	06 01	06 43	06 47	07 03		08 01			09 01	09 27	09 39	09 58	10 03	10 10	10 37	11 01		11 11		11 54	12 01
Frome	d	00a18					06 56							09 36					10 46						
Bruton	d						07 08							09 48					10 58						
Castle Cary	a						07 14							09 53		10 14			11 03					12 11	
	d						07 15							09 53					11 03						
Yeovil Pen Mill	d						07 29							10 07					11 17						
Thornford	d						07x33							10x12					11x22						
Yetminster	d						07x36							10x15					11x25						
Chetnole	d						07x40							10x19					11x29						
Maiden Newton	d						07 52							10 31					11 41						
Dorchester West	d						08 03							10 38					11 54						
Upwey	a						08 10							10 49					12 02						
Weymouth	a						08 17							10 57					12 09						
Dilton Marsh	d							07x06										10x13				11x13			
Warminster	d			05 34	06 08	06 50		07 12		08 09			09 08		09 46		10 09	10a19		11 09		11 20			12 09
Salisbury	a			05 58	06 32	07 15		07 35		08 32			09 32		10 09		10 31			11 32		11 42			12 32
	d				06 32	07 24		07 37		08 32			09 32				10 32			11 32		11 43			12 32
Romsey	d				06 50	07 44		07 56		08 51			09 50				10 51			11 51		12 04			12 51
Southampton Central	a				07 02	08 02		08 07		09 02			10 02				11 02			12 02		12 20			13 02
Fareham	a				07 27	08 27				09 27			10 27				11 27			12 27					13 27
	d				07 27	08 27				09 27			10 27				11 27			12 27					13 27
Cosham	a				07 35	08 35				09 35			10 35				11 35			12 35					13 35
Fratton	a				07 42	08 42				09 42			10 42				11 42			12 42					13 42
Portsmouth & Southsea	a				07 46	08 46				09 46			10 46				11 46			12 46					13 46
Portsmouth Harbour	a				07 52	08 52				09 52			10 52				11 52			12 51					13 51
Havant	a																								
Chichester 4	a																								
Barnham	a																								
Worthing 4	a																								
Shoreham-by-Sea	a																								
Hove 2	a																								
Brighton 10	a																								

A The Night Riviera

B The Torbay Express

C 🛒 from Bristol Temple Meads

For connections from Swansea please refer to Table 128.
For connections from Plymouth and Exeter St Davids please refer to Table 135.
For connections to Bournemouth please refer to Table 158

Table 123

Saturdays
until 10 September

South Wales and Bristol - Weymouth and Portsmouth

		GW	GW	GW	SW	GW	GW	GW	GW	GW	GW	GW	GW	GW	GW	SW	GW	GW	GW	GW	GW	GW	GW
			◇ A 🚲	◇ B	◇■1 🚲	R ■1 C ☕	◇		◇			◇		◇■1 ☕		◇■1	◇		R	◇■1 ☕		◇	
Cardiff Central 7	d		11 30				12 30		13 30			14 30					15 30		16 30			17 30	
Newport (South Wales)	d		11 44				12 44		13 44			14 44					15 44		16 44			17 44	
Severn Tunnel Jn	d																		16 55			17 55	
Filton Abbey Wood	d	11 23	12 09	12 28			13 09	13 23	14 09		14 25	15 09			15 22		16 09	16 28	17 09		17 23	18 09	
Bristol Temple Meads 10	d	11 49	12 23	12 43	13 15		13 23	13 49	14 23		14 49	15 25			15 38	15 51	16 23	16 49	17 23		17 49	18 23	
Keynsham	d	11 56		12 50				13 56			14 56				15 45	15 58		16 56			17 56		
Oldfield Park	d	12 03		12 57				14 03			15 03				15 52			17 03			18 03		
London Paddington 15 ⊖	d					12 35								15 06						17 06			
Swindon	d												15 22										
Chippenham	d												15 38										
Melksham	d												15 48										
Bath Spa 7	d	12 07	12 36	13 00	13 28		13 36	14 07	14 36		15 07	15 38			15 56	16 07	16 36	17 07	17 36		18 07	18 36	
Freshford	d	12 16						14 16			15 16				16 06			17 16			18 16		
Avoncliff	d	12 18						14 18			15 18				16 09			17 18			18 18		
Bradford-on-Avon	d	12 22	12 47	13 13	13 40		13 47	14 22	14 47		15 22	15 49			16 12	16 24	16 47	17 22	17 47		18 22	18 47	
Trowbridge	d	12 28	12 53	13 19	13 47		13 53	14 28	14 53		15 28	15 55	15 58		16 18	16 30	16 53	17 28	17 53		18 28	18 53	
Westbury	a	12 36	13 01	13 26	13 53	13 59	14 01	14 35	15 01		15 36	16 03	16 05	16 22	16 25	16 37	17 01	17 36	18 01	18 22	18 36	19 01	
	d	12 37	13 01	13 27	13 54	13 59	14 01	14 36	15 01	15 11	15 36	16 03	16 08	16 23		16 39	17 01	17 38	18 01	18 22	18 39	19 01	19 09
Frome	d	12 47						14a48			15 46							17 47			18 49		
Bruton	d	12 57									15 56							17 59			19 00		
Castle Cary	a	13 03				14 16					16 02			16 40				18 04		18 40	19 05		
	d	13 04									16 02							18 05			19 06		
Yeovil Pen Mill	d	13 17									16 17							18 21			19 19		
Thornford	d	13x22									16x21							18x26			19x24		
Yetminster	d	13x25									16x24							18x29			19x27		
Chetnole	d	13x29									16x28							18x33			19x31		
Maiden Newton	d	13 41									16f47							18 44			19 43		
Dorchester West	d	13 54									16 58							18 54			19 54		
Upwey	a	14 02									17 05							19 02			20 01		
Weymouth	a	14 08									17 11							19 10			20 09		
Dilton Marsh	d			13x30						15x13			16x11										19x12
Warminster	d		13 09	13 36	14 02		14 09		15 09	15a22		16 11	16a17			16 47	17 09		18 09			19 09	19 18
Salisbury	a		13 32	13 58	14 25		14 32		15 32			16 34				17 09	17 32		18 32			19 32	19 41
	d		13 32	13 59			14 32		15 32			16 34					17 32		18 32			19 32	19 41
Romsey	d		13 51	14 19			14 51		15 51			16 53					17 51		18 51			19 51	20 04
Southampton Central	a		14 02	14 32			15 02		16 02			17 04					18 02		19 02			20 02	20 18
Fareham	a		14 27	14 54			15 27		16 27			17 29					18 27		19 27			20 27	
	d		14 27	14 55			15 27		16 27			17 29					18 27		19 27			20 27	
Cosham	a		14 35	15 03			15 35		16 35			17 37					18 35		19 35				
Fratton	a		14 42				15 42		16 42			17 44					18 42		19 42			20 42	
Portsmouth & Southsea	a		14 46				15 46		16 46			17 48					18 46		19 46			20 46	
Portsmouth Harbour	a		14 51				15 51		16 51			17 53					18 52		19 52			20 52	
Havant	a			15 10																			
Chichester 4	a			15 21																			
Barnham	a			15 29																			
Worthing 4	a			15 44																			
Shoreham-by-Sea	a			15 55																			
Hove 2	a			16 07																			
Brighton 10	a			16 14																			

A 🚲 from Bristol Temple Meads

B ◇ from Bristol Temple Meads

C R to Westbury

For connections from Swansea please refer to Table 128.
For connections from Plymouth and Exeter St Davids please refer to Table 135.
For connections to Bournemouth please refer to Table 158

Table 123

Saturdays
until 10 September

South Wales and Bristol - Weymouth and Portsmouth

		GW	GW	GW	GW	GW	GW	GW	GW	GW	GW	SW	GW
			◇	◇[1] (catering)		◇	◇[1] (catering)			◇		[1]	
Cardiff Central [7]	d		18 30			19 30				20 30			
Newport (South Wales)	d		18 44			19 44				20 44			
Severn Tunnel Jn	d												
Filton Abbey Wood	d	18 28	19 09		19 24	20 09		20 28		21 08			
Bristol Temple Meads [10]	d	18 49	19 23		19 49	20 23		20 49		21 23	21 59	22 23	23 11
Keynsham	d	18 56			19 56			20 56			22 07		23 18
Oldfield Park	d	19 03			20 03			21 03			22 14		23 25
London Paddington [15] ⊖	d			19 06			20 06						
Swindon	d								21 08				
Chippenham	d								21 24				
Melksham	d								21 34				
Bath Spa [7]	d	19 07	19 36		20 07	20 36		21 07		21 36	22 18	22 36	23 29
Freshford	d	19 16			20 16			21 16			22 28		23 38
Avoncliff	d	19 18			20 18			21 18			22 29		23 41
Bradford-on-Avon	d	19 22	19 47		20 22	20 47		21 22		21 47	22 34	22 47	23 44
Trowbridge	d	19 28	19 53		20 28	20 53		21 28	21 43	21 53	22 40	22 53	23 50
Westbury	a	19 35	20 01	20 26	20 35	21 01	21 25	21 36	21 51	22 01	22 47	23 00	23 57
	d		20 01	20 27	20 37	21 01	21 26	21 38		22 01		23 04	23 57
Frome	d				20a46			21 49					00a07
Bruton	d							22 01					
Castle Cary	a			20 44			21 43	22 06					
	d							22 06					
Yeovil Pen Mill	d							22 20					
Thornford	d							22x25					
Yetminster	d							22x28					
Chetnole	d							22x32					
Maiden Newton	d							22 44					
Dorchester West	d							22 54					
Upwey	a							23 02					
Weymouth	a							23 10					
Dilton Marsh	d									22x04			
Warminster	d		20 09			21 09				22 09		23 11	
Salisbury	a		20 32			21 32				22 32		23 34	
	d		20 32			21 32				22 33			
Romsey	d		20 51			21 51				22 51			
Southampton Central	a		21 02			22 02				23 03			
Fareham	a		21 27			22 26				23 26			
	d		21 27			22 27				23 27			
Cosham	a												
Fratton	a		21 42			22 42				23 40			
Portsmouth & Southsea	a		21 46			22 46				23 44			
Portsmouth Harbour	a		21 52			22 52				23 52			
Havant	a												
Chichester [4]	a												
Barnham	a												
Worthing [4]	a												
Shoreham-by-Sea	a												
Hove [2]	a												
Brighton [10]	a												

For connections from Swansea please refer to Table 128.
For connections from Plymouth and Exeter St Davids please refer to Table 135.
For connections to Bournemouth please refer to Table 158

Table 123

Saturdays
from 17 September

South Wales and Bristol - Weymouth and Portsmouth

		GW	GW	GW	GW	GW	GW	GW	GW	GW		GW	GW	GW	SW	GW	GW	GW	GW	GW		GW	GW	GW	GW
			■ A 🛏 ☕			◇				◇			◇		◇1	◇1 ☕	◇			◇ B 🛒				◇ B 🛒	◇1 Ø
Cardiff Central 7	d									06 30			07 30				08 30			09 30				10 30	
Newport (South Wales)	d									06 44			07 44				08 44			09 44				10 44	
Severn Tunnel Jn	d									06 55			07 55				08 55			09 55					
Filton Abbey Wood	d									07 09			08 09	08 23			09 09		09 23	10 09			10 28	11 09	
Bristol Temple Meads 10	d	23p20				05 49			06 49	07 23		07 49	08 23	08 40	08 51		09 23		09 49	10 23			10 49	11 23	
Keynsham	d	23p27				05 56			06 56			07 56		08 47	08 58				09 56				10 56		
Oldfield Park	d	23p34				06 03			07 03			08 03		08 54					10 03				11 03		
London Paddington 15 ⊖	d		23p45													08 18									11 06
Swindon	d																								
Chippenham	d																								
Melksham	d																								
Bath Spa 7	d	23p38				06 07			07 07	07 36		08 07	08 36	08 58	09 07		09 36		10 07	10 36			11 07	11 36	
Freshford	d	23p47				06 16			07 16			08 16		09 07					10 16				11 16		
Avoncliff	d	23p50				06 18			07 18			08 18		09 09					10 18				11 18		
Bradford-on-Avon	d	23p53				06 22			07 22	07 47		08 22	08 47	09 13	09 20		09 47		10 22	10 47			11 22	11 47	
Trowbridge	d	23p59				06 28			07 28	07 53		08 28	08 53	09 19	09 27		09 53		10 28	10 53			11 28	11 53	
Westbury	a	00 06	01 35			06 35			07 35	08 01		08 35	09 01	09 27	09 34	09 59	10 03		10 36	11 00			11 35	12 01	12 22
	d	00 07		05 26	06 01	06 43	06 47	07 03		08 01			09 01	09 27	09 39	10 00	10 03	10 10	10 37	11 01		11 11		12 01	12 22
Frome	d	00a18					06 56							09 36					10 46						
Bruton	d						07 08							09 48					10 58						
Castle Cary	a						07 14							09 53		10 17			11 03						12 40
	d						07 15							09 53					11 03						
Yeovil Pen Mill	d						07 29							10 07					11 17						
Thornford	d						07x33							10x12					11x22						
Yetminster	d						07x36							10x15					11x25						
Chetnole	d						07x40							10x19					11x29						
Maiden Newton	d						07 52							10 31					11 41						
Dorchester West	d						08 03							10 38					11 54						
Upwey	a						08 10							10 49					12 02						
Weymouth	a						08 17							10 57					12 09						
Dilton Marsh	d							07x06										10x13				11x13			
Warminster	d			05 34	06 08	06 50		07 12		08 09			09 08		09 46		10 09	10a19		11 09		11 20		12 09	
Salisbury	a			05 58	06 32	07 15		07 35		08 32			09 32		10 09		10 31			11 32		11 42		12 32	
	d				06 32	07 24		07 37		08 32			09 32				10 32			11 32		11 43		12 32	
Romsey	d				06 50	07 44		07 56		08 51			09 50				10 51			11 51		12 04		12 51	
Southampton Central	a				07 02	08 02		08 07		09 02			10 02				11 02			12 02		12 20		13 02	
Fareham	a				07 27	08 27				09 27			10 27				11 27			12 27				13 27	
	d				07 27	08 27				09 27			10 27				11 27			12 27				13 27	
Cosham	a				07 35	08 35				09 35			10 35				11 35			12 35				13 35	
Fratton	a				07 42	08 42				09 42			10 42				11 42			12 42				13 42	
Portsmouth & Southsea	a				07 46	08 46				09 46			10 46				11 46			12 46				13 46	
Portsmouth Harbour	a				07 52	08 52				09 52			10 52				11 52			12 51				13 51	
Havant	a																								
Chichester 4	a																								
Barnham	a																								
Worthing 4	a																								
Shoreham-by-Sea	a																								
Hove 2	a																								
Brighton 10	a																								

A The Night Riviera

B 🛒 from Bristol Temple Meads

For connections from Swansea please refer to Table 128.
For connections from Plymouth and Exeter St Davids please refer to Table 135.
For connections to Bournemouth please refer to Table 158

Table 123

Saturdays

from 17 September

South Wales and Bristol - Weymouth and Portsmouth

		GW	GW	GW	SW	GW	GW	GW	GW	GW	GW	GW	GW	GW	GW	SW	GW	GW	GW	GW	GW	GW	GW
			◇ A [bus]	◇ B	◇[1] [bus]	◇[1] [catering]	◇		◇			◇		◇[1] [catering]		◇[1]	◇			[R]	◇[1] [catering]		◇
Cardiff Central [7]	d		11 30				12 30		13 30			14 30					15 30			16 30			17 30
Newport (South Wales)	d		11 44				12 44		13 44			14 44					15 44			16 44			17 44
Severn Tunnel Jn.	d																			16 55			17 55
Filton Abbey Wood	d	11 23	12 09	12 28			13 09	13 23	14 09		14 25	15 09			15 22		16 09		16 28	17 09		17 23	18 09
Bristol Temple Meads [10]	d	11 49	12 23	12 43	13 15		13 23	13 49	14 23		14 49	15 25			15 38	15 51	16 23		16 49	17 23		17 49	18 23
Keynsham	d	11 56		12 50				13 56			14 56				15 45	15 58			16 56			17 56	
Oldfield Park	d	12 03		12 57				14 03			15 03				15 52				17 03			18 03	
London Paddington [15] ⊖	d					12 18								15 06							17 06		
Swindon	d												15 22										
Chippenham	d												15 38										
Melksham	d												15 48										
Bath Spa [7]	d	12 07	12 36	13 00	13 28		13 36	14 07	14 36		15 07	15 38			15 56	16 07	16 36		17 07	17 36		18 07	18 36
Freshford	d	12 16						14 16			15 16				16 06				17 16			18 16	
Avoncliff	d	12 18						14 18			15 18				16 09				17 18			18 18	
Bradford-on-Avon	d	12 22	12 47	13 13	13 40		13 47	14 22	14 47		15 22	15 49			16 12	16 24	16 47		17 22	17 47		18 22	18 47
Trowbridge	d	12 28	12 53	13 19	13 47		13 53	14 28	14 53		15 28	15 55	15 58		16 18	16 30	16 53		17 28	17 53		18 28	18 53
Westbury	a	12 36	13 01	13 26	13 53	13 57	14 01	14 35	15 01		15 36	16 03	16 05	16 22	16 25	16 37	17 01		17 36	18 01	18 22	18 36	19 01
	d	12 37	13 01	13 27	13 54	13 58	14 01	14 36	15 01	15 11	15 36	16 03		16 23		16 39	17 01	17 08	17 38	18 01	18 22	18 39	19 01
Frome	d	12 47						14a48			15 46								17 47			18 49	
Bruton	d	12 57									15 57								17 59			19 00	
Castle Cary	a	13 03				14 14					16 03			16 40					18 04		18 40	19 05	
	d	13 04									16 09								18 05			19 06	
Yeovil Pen Mill	d	13 17									16 24								18 21			19 19	
Thornford	d	13x22									16x28								18x26			19x24	
Yetminster	d	13x25									16x31								18x29			19x27	
Chetnole	d	13x29									16x35								18x33			19x31	
Maiden Newton	d	13 41									16 47								18 44			19 43	
Dorchester West	d	13 54									16 58								18 54			19 54	
Upwey	a	14 02									17 05								19 02			20 01	
Weymouth	a	14 08									17 11								19 10			20 09	
Dilton Marsh	d			13x30						15x13								17x10					
Warminster	d		13 09	13 36	14 02		14 09		15 09	15a22		16 11				16 47	17 09	17a19		18 09			19 09
Salisbury	a		13 32	13 58	14 25		14 32		15 32			16 34				17 09	17 32			18 32			19 32
	d		13 32	13 59			14 32		15 32			16 34					17 32			18 32			19 32
Romsey	d		13 51	14 19			14 51		15 51			16 53					17 51			18 51			19 51
Southampton Central	a		14 02	14 32			15 02		16 02			17 04					18 02			19 02			20 02
Fareham	a		14 27	14 54			15 27		16 27			17 29					18 27			19 27			20 27
	d		14 27	14 55			15 27		16 27			17 29					18 27			19 27			20 27
Cosham	a		14 35	15 03			15 35		16 35			17 37					18 35			19 35			
Fratton	a		14 42				15 42		16 42			17 44					18 42			19 42			20 42
Portsmouth & Southsea	a		14 46				15 46		16 46			17 48					18 46			19 46			20 46
Portsmouth Harbour	a		14 51				15 51		16 51			17 53					18 52			19 52			20 52
Havant	a			15 10																			
Chichester [4]	a			15 21																			
Barnham	a			15 29																			
Worthing [4]	a			15 44																			
Shoreham-by-Sea	a			15 55																			
Hove [2]	a			16 07																			
Brighton [10]	a			16 14																			

A [bus] from Bristol Temple Meads

B ◇ from Bristol Temple Meads

For connections from Swansea please refer to Table 128.
For connections from Plymouth and Exeter St Davids please refer to Table 135.
For connections to Bournemouth please refer to Table 158

Table 123

Saturdays
from 17 September

South Wales and Bristol - Weymouth and Portsmouth

		GW		GW	GW	GW	GW	GW	GW	GW	GW	GW		GW	SW	GW
					◇	◇1		◇	◇1			◇			1	
Cardiff Central 7	d				18 30			19 30				20 30				
Newport (South Wales)	d				18 44			19 44				20 44				
Severn Tunnel Jn	d															
Filton Abbey Wood	d			18 28	19 09		19 24	20 09		20 28		21 08				
Bristol Temple Meads 10	d			18 49	19 23		19 49	20 23		20 49		21 23		21 59	22 23	23 11
Keynsham	d			18 56			19 56			20 56				22 07		23 18
Oldfield Park	d			19 03			20 03			21 03				22 14		23 25
London Paddington 15 ⊖	d					19 06			20 06							
Swindon	d										21 08					
Chippenham	d										21 24					
Melksham	d										21 34					
Bath Spa 7	d			19 07	19 36		20 07	20 36		21 07		21 36		22 18	22 36	23 29
Freshford	d			19 16			20 16			21 16				22 28		23 38
Avoncliff	d			19 18			20 18			21 18				22 29		23 41
Bradford-on-Avon	d			19 22	19 47		20 22	20 47		21 22		21 47		22 34	22 47	23 44
Trowbridge	d			19 28	19 53		20 28	20 53		21 28	21 43	21 53		22 40	22 53	23 50
Westbury	a			19 35	20 01	20 26	20 35	21 01	21 25	21 36	21 51	22 01		22 47	23 00	23 57
	d	19 09			20 01	20 27	20 37	21 01	21 26	21 38		22 01			23 04	23 57
Frome	d						20a46			21 49						00a07
Bruton	d									22 01						
Castle Cary	a					20 44			21 43	22 06						
	d									22 06						
Yeovil Pen Mill	d									22 20						
Thornford	d									22x25						
Yetminster	d									22x28						
Chetnole	d									22x32						
Maiden Newton	d									22 44						
Dorchester West	d									22 54						
Upwey	a									23 02						
Weymouth	a									23 10						
Dilton Marsh	d	19x12										22x04				
Warminster	d	19 18			20 09			21 09				22 09			23 11	
Salisbury	a	19 41			20 32			21 32				22 32			23 34	
	d	19 41			20 32			21 32				22 33				
Romsey	d	20 04			20 51			21 51				22 51				
Southampton Central	a	20 18			21 02			22 02				23 03				
Fareham	a				21 27			22 26				23 26				
	d				21 27			22 27				23 27				
Cosham	a															
Fratton	a				21 42			22 42				23 40				
Portsmouth & Southsea	a				21 46			22 46				23 44				
Portsmouth Harbour	a				21 52			22 52				23 52				
Havant	a															
Chichester 4	a															
Barnham	a															
Worthing 4	a															
Shoreham-by-Sea	a															
Hove 2	a															
Brighton 10	a															

For connections from Swansea please refer to Table 128.
For connections from Plymouth and Exeter St Davids please refer to Table 135.
For connections to Bournemouth please refer to Table 158

Table 123

Sundays
until 31 July

South Wales and Bristol - Weymouth and Portsmouth

		GW	GW	GW	GW	GW	GW	GW	GW	GW		GW	GW	GW	GW	GW	GW	GW	SW	GW		GW	GW	GW	GW
										■															
				◇		◇**1**	◇	◇**1**	◇	◇		◇**1**	◇	◇**1**		◇	◇**1**	◇	◇**1**	◇		◇**1**	◇	◇	
						☕		☕		🛒		☕		☕			☕					☕			
Cardiff Central 7	d			08 05			09 15		10 08	11 08			12 08			13 08		14 08		15 08			16 08	16 35	
Newport (South Wales)	d			08 23			09 29		10 22	11 22			12 22			13 22		14 23		15 22			16 22	16 49	
Severn Tunnel Jn.	d			08 40			09 46		10 39	11 39			12 39			13 39		14 40		15 39			16 39		
Filton Abbey Wood	d			08 55			10 03		10 54	11 54			12 57			13 54		14 56		15 55			16 55	17 20	
Bristol Temple Meads 10	d			09 10	09 20		10 15		11 10	12 15			13 10			14 15		15 10	16 04	16 15			17 15	17 40	17 44
Keynsham	d			09 18	09 27				11 17				13 17					15 18	16 11				17 22		17 51
Oldfield Park	d			09 25	09 35				11 24				13 24					15 25					17 29		17 58
London Paddington 15 ⊖	d					08 57		09 57				11 37		12 57			13 57					15 57			
Swindon	d																								
Chippenham	d																								
Melksham	d																								
Bath Spa 7	d			09 28	09 39		10 29		11 27	12 27			13 27			14 27		15 28	16 20	16 26			17 32	17 52	18 01
Freshford	d				09 49		10 39			12 37						14 38				16 37					18 11
Avoncliff	d				09 51		10 41			12 39						14 41				16 39					18 14
Bradford-on-Avon	d			09 40	09 55		10 45		11 39	12 43			13 39			14 44		15 40	16 31	16 43			17 44	18 04	18 17
Trowbridge	d			09 46	10 01		10 51		11 46	12 49			13 46			14 50		15 46	16 37	16 49			17 50	18 11	18 23
Westbury	a			09 53	10 08	10 25	10 58		11 53	12 59		13 04	13 53	14 16		14 57		15 53	16 44	16 56		17 25	17 57	18 18	18 30
	d	09 12		09 59	10 09		11 00		12 03	13 00		13 05	14 03		14 25	15 00		15 59	16 46	16 58		17 27	18 00	18 19	18 30
Frome	d	09 22			10 19										14 34										18 39
Bruton	d	09 34			10 31										14 46										18 51
Castle Cary	a	09 38			10 35			11 35				13 22			14 51		15 37					17 43			18 56
	d	09 40			10 37										14 51										18 58
Yeovil Pen Mill	d	09 54			10 51										15 06										19 12
Thornford	d	09x59			10x56										15 12										19x16
Yetminster	d	10x02			10x59										15 15										19x19
Chetnole	d	10x06			11x03										15 19										19x23
Maiden Newton	d	10 18			11 15										15 30										19 35
Dorchester West	d	10 26			11 30										15 41										19 47
Upwey	a	10 36			11 37										15 50										19 54
Weymouth	a	10 42			11 43										15 55										20 01
Dilton Marsh	d			10x02					12x06				14x06					16x02		17x01				18x22	
Warminster	d			10 08			11 07		12 12	13 07			14 12			15 07		16 08	16 53	17 07			18 07	18 28	
Salisbury	a			10 32			11 32		12 34	13 32			14 39			15 32		16 32	17 16	17 32			18 32	18 53	
	d			10 32			11 32		12 36	13 32			14 48			15 32		16 32		17 32			18 32	18 57	
Romsey	d			10 50			11 50		12 54	13 50			15 10			15 50		16 50		17 50			18 50	19 15	
Southampton Central	a			11 02			12 02		13 06	14 02			15 20			16 02		17 02		18 02			19 02	19 26	
Fareham	a			11 26			12 26		13 33	14 26			15 50			16 26		17 26		18 26			19 26	19 49	
	d			11 26			12 26		13 34	14 26			15 51			16 26		17 26		18 26			19 26	19 50	
Cosham	a			11 34			12 34		13 41	14 34			16 00			16 34		17 34		18 34			19 34	19 58	
Fratton	a			11 41			12 41			14 41						16 41		17 41		18 41			19 41		
Portsmouth & Southsea	a			11 45			12 45			14 45						16 45		17 45		18 45			19 45		
Portsmouth Harbour	a			11 52			12 52			14 55						16 52		17 52		18 52			19 52		
Havant	a								14 03				16 11											20 10	
Chichester 4	a								14 19				16 22											20 21	
Barnham	a								14 27				16 30											20 29	
Worthing 4	a								14 44				16 45											20 51	
Shoreham-by-Sea	a								14 51				16 51											20 57	
Hove 2	a								14 59				16 58											21 04	
Brighton 10	a								15 06				17 05											21 10	

For connections from Swansea please refer to Table 128.
For connections from Plymouth and Exeter St Davids please refer to Table 135.
For connections to Bournemouth please refer to Table 158

Table 123

Sundays
until 31 July

South Wales and Bristol - Weymouth and Portsmouth

		GW	GW	GW	GW	GW		GW	GW	GW	GW	GW	SW	GW	GW
				R											
			◇		◇1	◇		◇1	◇	◇1		◇	1		
					⊡			⊡		⊡					⊼
Cardiff Central 7	d		17 08	17 40		18 08			19 08			20 18			22 00
Newport (South Wales)	d		17 22	17 54		18 22			19 22			20 31			22 18
Severn Tunnel Jn	d		17 39			18 39			19 40			20 48			22 35
Filton Abbey Wood	d		17 54	18 23		18 55			19 55			21 05			22 52
Bristol Temple Meads 10	d		18 10	18 50		19 10			20 15		20 50	21 25	21 35	22 15	23 10
Keynsham	d		18 17			19 17					20 57			22 22	
Oldfield Park	d		18 24			19 24					21 04			22 29	
London Paddington 15 ⊖	d				17 57			18 57		19 57					
Swindon	d	18 06													
Chippenham	d	18 22													
Melksham	d	18 32													
Bath Spa 7	d		18 27	19 02		19 27			20 27		21 07	21 38	21 49	22 32	23 22
Freshford	d								20 37		21 18			22 43	
Avoncliff	d								20 39		21 21			22 45	
Bradford-on-Avon	d		18 39	19 14		19 39			20 43		21 24	21 49	22 00	22 49	23 34
Trowbridge	d	18 41	18 47	19 20		19 45			20 49		21 30	21 55	22 06	22 55	23 40
Westbury	a	18 49	18 56	19 27	19 28	19 52			20 56	21 28	21 37	22 02	22 13	23 02	23 47
	d		18 58	19 31		19 53			20 57	21 29	21 38	22 03	22 15		23 50
Frome	d										21 48				
Bruton	d										21 59				
Castle Cary	a							20 32		21 46	22 04				
	d										22 05				
Yeovil Pen Mill	d										22 19				
Thornford	d										22x23				
Yetminster	d										22x26				
Chetnole	d										22x30				
Maiden Newton	d										22 42				
Dorchester West	d										22 53				
Upwey	a										23 00				
Weymouth	a										23 06				
Dilton Marsh	d					19x56									23x53
Warminster	d		19 05	19 38		20 02			21 05			22 11	22 22		23a59
Salisbury	a		19 32	19 59		20 25			21 27			22 34	22 46		
	d		19 32	20 00		20 30			21 32			22 35			
Romsey	d		19 50	20 19		20 48			21 50			22 54			
Southampton Central	a		20 02	20 29		20 59			22 02			23 04			
Fareham	a		20 25	20 54		21 23			22 26			23 28			
	d		20 26	20 55		21 24			22 26			23 29			
Cosham	a														
Fratton	a		20 41	21 09		21 37			22 40			23 42			
Portsmouth & Southsea	a		20 45	21 15		21 41			22 43			23 46			
Portsmouth Harbour	a		20 52	21 26		21 48			22 49			23 52			
Havant	a														
Chichester 4	a														
Barnham	a														
Worthing 4	a														
Shoreham-by-Sea	a														
Hove 2	a														
Brighton 10	a														

For connections from Swansea please refer to Table 128.
For connections from Plymouth and Exeter St Davids please refer to Table 135.
For connections to Bournemouth please refer to Table 158

Table 123

Sundays

7 August to 11 September

South Wales and Bristol - Weymouth and Portsmouth

		GW	GW	GW	GW	GW	GW	GW	GW	GW	GW	GW	GW	GW	GW	GW	SW	GW	GW	GW	GW	GW	GW
			◇		◇1 ☕	◇	◇1 ☕	◇	R ◇ 🍴	◇1 ☕	◇	◇1 ☕		◇	◇1 ☕	◇	◇1	◇	◇1 ☕	◇	◇		
Cardiff Central [7]	d		08 05			09 15		10 08	11 08		12 08			13 08		14 08		15 08		16 08	16 35		
Newport (South Wales)	d		08 23			09 29		10 22	11 22		12 22			13 22		14 23		15 22		16 22	16 49		
Severn Tunnel Jn.	d		08 40			09 46		10 39	11 39		12 39			13 39		14 40		15 39		16 39			
Filton Abbey Wood	d		08 55			10 03		10 54	11 54		12 57			13 54		14 56		15 55		16 55	17 20		
Bristol Temple Meads [10]	d		09 10	09 20		10 15		11 10	12 15		13 10			14 15		15 10	16 04	16 15		17 15	17 40	17 44	
Keynsham	d		09 18	09 27				11 17			13 17					15 18	16 11			17 22		17 51	
Oldfield Park	d		09 25	09 35				11 24			13 24					15 25				17 29		17 58	
London Paddington [15] ⊖	d				08 51		09 30			11 30		12 30			13 30				15 57				
Swindon	d						10 36			12 36		13 38											18 06
Chippenham	d																						18 22
Melksham	d																						18 32
Bath Spa [7]	d		09 28	09 39		10 29		11 27	12 27		13 27			14 27		15 28	16 20	16 26		17 32	17 52	18 01	
Freshford	d			09 49		10 39			12 37					14 38				16 37				18 11	
Avoncliff	d			09 51		10 41			12 39					14 41				16 39				18 14	
Bradford-on-Avon	d		09 40	09 55		10 45		11 39	12 43		13 39			14 44		15 40	16 31	16 43		17 44	18 04	18 17	
Trowbridge	d		09 46	10 01		10 51		11 46	12 49		13 46			14 50		15 46	16 37	16 49		17 50	18 11	18 23	18 41
Westbury	a		09 53	10 08	10 25	10 58	11 09	11 53	12 59	13 10	13 53	14 10		14 57		15 53	16 44	16 56	17 24	17 57	18 18	18 30	18 49
	d	09 12	09 59	10 09		11 00	11 17	12 03	13 00		14 03		14 25	15 00		15 59	16 46	16 58	17 25	18 00	18 19	18 30	
Frome	d	09 22		10 19									14 34									18 39	
Bruton	d	09 34		10 31									14 46									18 51	
Castle Cary	a	09 38		10 35			11 34						14 51		15 18				17 42			18 56	
	d	09 40		10 37									14 51									18 58	
Yeovil Pen Mill	d	09 54		10 51									15 06									19 12	
Thornford	d	09x59		10x56									15 12									19x16	
Yetminster	d	10x02		10x59									15 15									19x19	
Chetnole	d	10x06		11x03									15 19									19x23	
Maiden Newton	d	10 18		11 15									15 30									19 35	
Dorchester West	d	10 26		11 30									15 41									19 47	
Upwey	a	10 36		11 37									15 50									19 54	
Weymouth	a	10 42		11 43									15 55									20 01	
Dilton Marsh	d		10x02					12x06			14x06					16x02		17x01			18x22		
Warminster	d		10 08			11 07		12 12	13 07		14 12			15 07		16 08	16 53	17 07		18 07	18 28		
Salisbury	a		10 32			11 32		12 34	13 32		14 39			15 32		16 32	17 16	17 32		18 32	18 53		
	d		10 32			11 32		12 36	13 32		14 48			15 32		16 32		17 32		18 32	18 57		
Romsey	d		10 50			11 50		12 54	13 50		15 10			15 50		16 50		17 50		18 50	19 15		
Southampton Central	a		11 02			12 02		13 06	14 02		15 20			16 02		17 02		18 02		19 02	19 26		
Fareham	a		11 26			12 26		13 33	14 26		15 50			16 26		17 26		18 26		19 26	19 49		
	d		11 26			12 26		13 34	14 26		15 51			16 26		17 26		18 26		19 26	19 50		
Cosham	a		11 34			12 34		13 41	14 34		16 00			16 34		17 34		18 34		19 34	19 58		
Fratton	a		11 41			12 41			14 41					16 41		17 41		18 41		19 41			
Portsmouth & Southsea	a		11 45			12 45			14 45					16 45		17 45		18 45		19 45			
Portsmouth Harbour	a		11 52			12 52			14 55					16 52		17 52		18 52		19 52			
Havant	a							14 03			16 11										20 10		
Chichester [4]	a							14 19			16 22										20 21		
Barnham	a							14 27			16 30										20 29		
Worthing [4]	a							14 44			16 45										20 51		
Shoreham-by-Sea	a							14 51			16 51										20 57		
Hove [2]	a							14 59			16 58										21 04		
Brighton [10]	a							15 06			17 05										21 10		

For connections from Swansea please refer to Table 128.
For connections from Plymouth and Exeter St Davids please refer to Table 135.
For connections to Bournemouth please refer to Table 158

Table 123

Sundays

7 August to 11 September

South Wales and Bristol - Weymouth and Portsmouth

		GW	GW	GW	GW	GW	GW	GW	GW	GW	SW	GW	GW
		◇	■	◇■ 🍴	◇	◇■ 🍴	◇	◇■ 🍴		◇	■		trolley
Cardiff Central ■	d	17 08	17 40		18 08		19 08			20 18			22 00
Newport (South Wales)	d	17 22	17 54		18 22		19 22			20 31			22 18
Severn Tunnel Jn.	d	17 39			18 39		19 40			20 48			22 35
Filton Abbey Wood	d	17 54	18 23		18 55		19 55			21 05			22 52
Bristol Temple Meads ■	d	18 10	18 50		19 10		20 15		20 50	21 25	21 35	22 15	23 10
Keynsham	d	18 17			19 17				20 57			22 22	
Oldfield Park	d	18 24			19 24				21 04			22 29	
London Paddington ■ ⊖	d			17 57		18 57		19 57					
Swindon	d												
Chippenham	d												
Melksham	d												
Bath Spa ■	d	18 27	19 02		19 27		20 27		21 07	21 38	21 49	22 32	23 22
Freshford	d						20 37		21 18			22 43	
Avoncliff	d						20 39		21 21			22 45	
Bradford-on-Avon	d	18 39	19 14		19 39		20 43		21 24	21 49	22 00	22 49	23 34
Trowbridge	d	18 47	19 20		19 45		20 49		21 30	21 55	22 06	22 55	23 40
Westbury	a	18 56	19 27	19 28	19 52		20 56	21 28	21 37	22 02	22 13	23 02	23 47
	d	18 58	19 31		19 53		20 57	21 29	21 38	22 03	22 15		23 50
Frome	d								21 48				
Bruton	d								21 59				
Castle Cary	a					20 32		21 46	22 04				
	d								22 05				
Yeovil Pen Mill	d								22 19				
Thornford	d								22x23				
Yetminster	d								22x26				
Chetnole	d								22x30				
Maiden Newton	d								22 42				
Dorchester West	d								22 53				
Upwey	a								23 00				
Weymouth	a								23 06				
Dilton Marsh	d				19x56								23x53
Warminster	d	19 05	19 38		20 02		21 05			22 11	22 22		23a59
Salisbury	a	19 32	19 59		20 25		21 27			22 34	22 46		
	d	19 32	20 00		20 30		21 32			22 35			
Romsey	d	19 50	20 19		20 48		21 50			22 54			
Southampton Central	a	20 02	20 29		20 59		22 02			23 04			
Fareham	a	20 25	20 54		21 23		22 26			23 28			
	d	20 26	20 55		21 24		22 26			23 29			
Cosham	a												
Fratton	a	20 41	21 09		21 37		22 40			23 42			
Portsmouth & Southsea	a	20 45	21 15		21 41		22 43			23 46			
Portsmouth Harbour	a	20 52	21 26		21 48		22 49			23 52			
Havant	a												
Chichester ■	a												
Barnham	a												
Worthing ■	a												
Shoreham-by-Sea	a												
Hove ■	a												
Brighton ■	a												

For connections from Swansea please refer to Table 128.
For connections from Plymouth and Exeter St Davids please refer to Table 135.
For connections to Bournemouth please refer to Table 158

Table 123

Sundays

18 September to 23 October

South Wales and Bristol - Weymouth and Portsmouth

		GW	GW	GW	GW	GW	GW	GW	GW	GW		GW	GW	GW	GW	SW	GW	GW	GW	GW		GW	GW	GW	GW
							■																		■
		◇	◇1	◇	◇1	◇	◇	◇1	◇	◇1			◇1	◇	◇	◇1	◇	◇1	◇	◇				◇	
			☕		☕		🛒	☕		☕			☕					☕							
Cardiff Central 7	d																								
Newport (South Wales)	d																								
Severn Tunnel Jn.	d																								
Filton Abbey Wood	d																								
Bristol Temple Meads 10	d	09 15		10 17		11 10	12 15		13 14			13 55		14 15	15 10	16 04	16 15		17 15	17 40		17 44		18 10	18 50
Keynsham	d	09 22				11 17			13 21			14 02			15 18	16 11			17 22			17 51		18 17	
Oldfield Park	d	09 29				11 24			13 28			14 09			15 25				17 29			17 58		18 24	
London Paddington 15 ⊖	d		08 51		09 30			11 30		12 30			13 30					15 30							
Swindon	d				10 36			12 36		13 38													18 06		
Chippenham	d																						18 22		
Melksham	d																						18 32		
Bath Spa 7	d	09 32		10 29		11 27	12 27		13 31			14 13		14 27	15 28	16 20	16 26		17 32	17 52		18 01		18 27	19 02
Freshford	d			10 39			12 37					14 23		14 37			16 37					18 11			
Avoncliff	d			10 41			12 39					14 26		14 39			16 39					18 14			
Bradford-on-Avon	d	09 44		10 45		11 39	12 43		13 43			14 29		14 43	15 40	16 31	16 43		17 46	18 04		18 17		18 39	19 14
Trowbridge	d	09 50		10 51		11 46	12 49		13 50			14 35		14 49	15 46	16 37	16 49		17 52	18 11		18 23	18 41	18 45	19 20
Westbury	a	09 58	10 30	10 58	11 07	11 53	12 59	13 10	13 59	14 10		14 42		14 56	15 53	16 44	16 56	17 03	17 59	18 18		18 30	18 49	18 54	19 27
	d	09 59		10 59	11 16	12 03	13 00		14 03			14 45		15 00	15 58	16 46	16 58	17 24	17 59	18 19		18 30		18 58	19 30
Frome	d											14 54										18 39			
Bruton	d											15 06										18 51			
Castle Cary	a				11 33							15 10	15 18					17 41				18 56			
	d											15 11										18 58			
Yeovil Pen Mill	d											15 26										19 12			
Thornford	d											15 32										19x16			
Yetminster	d											15 35										19x19			
Chetnole	d											15 39										19x23			
Maiden Newton	d											15 50										19 35			
Dorchester West	d											16 01										19 47			
Upwey	a											16 10										19 54			
Weymouth	a											16 15										20 01			
Dilton Marsh	d	10x02				12x06			14x06						16x01		17x01			18x22					
Warminster	d	10 08		11 06		12 12	13 07		14 12					15 07	16 07	16 53	17 07		18 07	18 28				19 05	19 38
Salisbury	a	10 32		11 29		12 34	13 32		14 39					15 32	16 31	17 16	17 32		18 32	18 53				19 32	19 59
	d	10 32		11 33		12 36	13 32		14 48					15 32	16 32		17 32		18 32	18 57				19 32	20 00
Romsey	d	10 50		11 52		12 54	13 50		15 10					15 50	16 50		17 50		18 50	19 15				19 50	20 19
Southampton Central	a	11 02		12 02		13 06	14 02		15 20					16 02	17 02		18 02		19 02	19 26				20 02	20 29
Fareham	a	11 26		12 26		13 33	14 26		15 50					16 26	17 26		18 26		19 26	19 49				20 25	20 54
	d	11 26		12 26		13 34	14 26		15 51					16 26	17 26		18 26		19 26	19 50				20 26	20 55
Cosham	a	11 34		12 34		13 41	14 34		16 00					16 34	17 34		18 34		19 34	19 58					
Fratton	a	11 41		12 41			14 41							16 41	17 41		18 41		19 41					20 41	21 09
Portsmouth & Southsea	a	11 45		12 45			14 45							16 45	17 45		18 45		19 45					20 45	21 15
Portsmouth Harbour	a	11 52		12 52			14 55							16 52	17 52		18 52		19 52					20 52	21 26
Havant	a					14 03			16 11											20 10					
Chichester 4	a					14 19			16 22											20 21					
Barnham	a					14 27			16 30											20 29					
Worthing 4	a					14 44			16 45											20 51					
Shoreham-by-Sea	a					14 51			16 51											20 57					
Hove 2	a					14 59			16 58											21 04					
Brighton 10	a					15 06			17 05											21 10					

For connections from Swansea please refer to Table 128.
For connections from Plymouth and Exeter St Davids please refer to Table 135.
For connections to Bournemouth please refer to Table 158

Table 123

Sundays

18 September to 23 October

South Wales and Bristol - Weymouth and Portsmouth

		GW	GW	GW	GW	GW	GW	GW	SW	GW	GW
		◇1	◇	◇1	◇	◇1		◇	1		
		⊡		⊡		⊡					⚲
Cardiff Central 7	d										
Newport (South Wales)	d										
Severn Tunnel Jn.	d										
Filton Abbey Wood	d										
Bristol Temple Meads 10	d		19 10		20 15		20 50	21 25	21 35	22 15	23 38
Keynsham	d		19 17				20 57			22 22	
Oldfield Park	d		19 24				21 04			22 29	
London Paddington 15 ⊖	d	17 57		18 57		19 57					
Swindon	d	19 03		20 03		21 03					
Chippenham	d										
Melksham	d										
Bath Spa 7	d		19 27		20 27		21 07	21 38	21 49	22 32	23 50
Freshford	d				20 37		21 18			22 43	
Avoncliff	d				20 39		21 21			22 45	
Bradford-on-Avon	d		19 39		20 43		21 24	21 49	22 00	22 49	00 02
Trowbridge	d		19 45		20 49		21 33	21 55	22 06	22 55	00 08
Westbury	a	19 35	19 52	20 36	20 56	21 37	21 40	22 02	22 13	23 02	00 15
	d	19 37	20 00	20 37	20 57	21 38	21 41	22 03	22 15		00 18
Frome	d						21 51				
Bruton	d						22 02				
Castle Cary	a	19 53		20 54		21 55	22 07				
	d						22 08				
Yeovil Pen Mill	d						22 22				
Thornford	d						22x26				
Yetminster	d						22x29				
Chetnole	d						22x33				
Maiden Newton	d						22 45				
Dorchester West	d						22 56				
Upwey	a						23 03				
Weymouth	a						23 09				
Dilton Marsh	d		20x03								00x21
Warminster	d		20 09		21 05			22 11	22 22		00a26
Salisbury	a		20 32		21 27			22 34	22 46		
	d		20 33		21 32			22 35			
Romsey	d		20 51		21 50			22 54			
Southampton Central	a		21 02		22 02			23 04			
Fareham	a		21 24		22 26			23 27			
	d		21 25		22 26			23 28			
Cosham	a										
Fratton	a		21 38		22 40			23 41			
Portsmouth & Southsea	a		21 42		22 43			23 44			
Portsmouth Harbour	a		21 48		22 49			23 53			
Havant	a										
Chichester 4	a										
Barnham	a										
Worthing 4	a										
Shoreham-by-Sea	a										
Hove 2	a										
Brighton 10	a										

For connections from Swansea please refer to Table 128.
For connections from Plymouth and Exeter St Davids please refer to Table 135.
For connections to Bournemouth please refer to Table 158

Table 123

Sundays

from 30 October

South Wales and Bristol - Weymouth and Portsmouth

		GW	GW	GW	GW	GW	GW	GW	GW	GW	GW	GW	GW	GW	GW	SW	GW	GW	GW	GW	GW	GW	GW
								R															
		◇	◇1	◇1	◇	◇1	◇	◇	◇1	◇	◇1		◇	◇1	◇	◇1	◇	◇1	◇	◇			◇
			☕	☕		☕		🍴	☕		☕			☕				☕					
Cardiff Central 7	d	08 05			09 15		10 08	11 08		12 08			13 08		14 08		15 08		16 08	16 35			17 08
Newport (South Wales)	d	08 23			09 29		10 22	11 22		12 22			13 22		14 23		15 22		16 22	16 49			17 22
Severn Tunnel Jn.	d	08 40			09 46		10 39	11 39		12 39			13 39		14 40		15 39		16 39				17 39
Filton Abbey Wood	d	08 55			10 03		10 54	11 54		12 57			13 54		14 56		15 55		16 55	17 20			17 54
Bristol Temple Meads 10	d	09 09			10 15		11 10	12 15		13 10		14 04	14 15		15 10	16 04	16 15		17 15	17 40	17 44		18 10
Keynsham	d	09 17					11 17			13 17		14 11			15 18	16 11			17 22		17 51		18 17
Oldfield Park	d	09 24					11 24			13 24		14 18			15 25				17 29		17 58		18 24
London Paddington 15 ⊖	d		08 30	08 57		09 57			11 37		12 57			13 57				15 57					
Swindon	d																					18 06	
Chippenham	d																					18 22	
Melksham	d																					18 32	
Bath Spa 7	d	09 27			10 29		11 27	12 27		13 27		14 22	14 27		15 28	16 20	16 26		17 32	17 52	18 01		18 27
Freshford	d				10 39			12 37				14 32	14 38				16 37				18 11		
Avoncliff	d				10 41			12 39				14 35	14 41				16 39				18 14		
Bradford-on-Avon	d	09 39			10 45		11 39	12 43		13 39		14 38	14 44		15 40	16 31	16 43		17 44	18 04	18 17		18 39
Trowbridge	d	09 45			10 51		11 46	12 49		13 46		14 44	14 50		15 46	16 37	16 49		17 50	18 11	18 23	18 41	18 47
Westbury	a	09 52	09 55	10 23	10 58		11 56	12 59	13 04	13 55	14 17	14 51	14 57		15 56	16 44	16 56	17 23	17 57	18 18	18 30	18 49	18 56
	d	09 59			11 00		12 03	13 00	13 05	14 03		14 52	15 00		15 59	16 46	16 58	17 25	18 00	18 19	18 30		18 58
Frome	d											15 03									18 39		
Bruton	d											15 15									18 51		
Castle Cary	a					11 35			13 22			15 19		15 37				17 41			18 56		
	d											15 20									18 58		
Yeovil Pen Mill	d											15 35									19 12		
Thornford	d											15 41									19x16		
Yetminster	d											15 44									19x19		
Chetnole	d											15 48									19x23		
Maiden Newton	d											15 59									19 35		
Dorchester West	d											16 10									19 47		
Upwey	a											16 19									19 54		
Weymouth	a											16 24									20 01		
Dilton Marsh	d	10x02					12x06			14x06					16x02		17x01			18x22			
Warminster	d	10 08			11 07		12 12	13 07		14 12			15 07		16 08	16 53	17 07		18 07	18 28			19 05
Salisbury	a	10 32			11 32		12 34	13 32		14 39			15 32		16 32	17 16	17 32		18 32	18 53			19 32
	d	10 32			11 32		12 36	13 32		14 48			15 32		16 32		17 32		18 32	18 57			19 32
Romsey	d	10 50			11 50		12 54	13 50		15 10			15 50		16 50		17 50		18 50	19 15			19 50
Southampton Central	a	11 02			12 02		13 06	14 02		15 20			16 02		17 02		18 02		19 02	19 26			20 02
Fareham	a	11 26			12 26		13 33	14 26		15 50			16 26		17 26		18 26		19 26	19 49			20 25
	d	11 26			12 26		13 34	14 26		15 51			16 26		17 26		18 26		19 26	19 50			20 26
Cosham	a	11 34			12 34		13 41	14 34		16 00			16 34		17 34		18 34		19 34	19 58			
Fratton	a	11 41			12 41			14 41					16 41		17 41		18 41		19 41				20 41
Portsmouth & Southsea	a	11 45			12 45			14 45					16 45		17 45		18 45		19 45				20 45
Portsmouth Harbour	a	11 52			12 52			14 55					16 52		17 52		18 52		19 52				20 52
Havant	a						14 03			16 11										20 10			
Chichester 4	a						14 19			16 22										20 21			
Barnham	a						14 27			16 30										20 29			
Worthing 4	a						14 44			16 45										20 51			
Shoreham-by-Sea	a						14 51			16 51										20 57			
Hove 2	a						14 59			16 58										21 04			
Brighton 10	a						15 06			17 05										21 10			

For connections from Swansea please refer to Table 128.
For connections from Plymouth and Exeter St Davids please refer to Table 135.
For connections to Bournemouth please refer to Table 158

Table 123

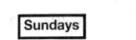

Sundays
from 30 October

South Wales and Bristol - Weymouth and Portsmouth

		GW	GW	GW	GW	GW		GW	GW	GW	SW	GW	GW
			R										
		◇1		◇	◇1	◇		◇1		◇	1		
		☕			☕			☕					🚃
Cardiff Central 7	d		17 40	18 08		19 08				20 18			22 00
Newport (South Wales)	d		17 54	18 22		19 22				20 31			22 18
Severn Tunnel Jn	d			18 39		19 40				20 48			22 35
Filton Abbey Wood	d		18 23	18 55		19 55				21 05			22 52
Bristol Temple Meads 10	d		18 50	19 10		20 15			20 50	21 25	21 35	22 20	23 10
Keynsham	d			19 17					20 57			22 27	
Oldfield Park	d			19 24					21 04			22 34	
London Paddington 15 ⊖	d	17 57			18 55			19 57					
Swindon	d												
Chippenham	d												
Melksham	d												
Bath Spa 7	d		19 02	19 27		20 27			21 07	21 38	21 49	22 37	23 22
Freshford	d					20 37			21 18			22 48	
Avoncliff	d					20 39			21 21			22 50	
Bradford-on-Avon	d		19 14	19 39		20 43			21 24	21 49	22 00	22 54	23 34
Trowbridge	d		19 20	19 45		20 49			21 30	21 55	22 06	23 00	23 40
Westbury	a	19 26	19 27	19 52		20 56		21 27	21 37	22 02	22 13	23 07	23 47
	d		19 31	19 53		20 57		21 28	21 38	22 03	22 15		23 50
Frome	d								21 48				
Bruton	d								21 59				
Castle Cary	a				20 30			21 45	22 04				
	d								22 05				
Yeovil Pen Mill	d								22 19				
Thornford	d								22x23				
Yetminster	d								22x26				
Chetnole	d								22x30				
Maiden Newton	d								22 42				
Dorchester West	d								22 53				
Upwey	a								23 00				
Weymouth	a								23 06				
Dilton Marsh	d			19x56									23x53
Warminster	d		19 38	20 02		21 05				22 11	22 22		23a59
Salisbury	a		19 59	20 25		21 27				22 33	22 46		
	d		20 00	20 30		21 32				22 35			
Romsey	d		20 19	20 48		21 50				22 53			
Southampton Central	a		20 29	20 59		22 02				23 04			
Fareham	a		20 54	21 23		22 26				23 26			
	d		20 55	21 24		22 26				23 27			
Cosham	a												
Fratton	a		21 09	21 37		22 40				23 40			
Portsmouth & Southsea	a		21 15	21 41		22 43				23 44			
Portsmouth Harbour	a		21 26	21 48		22 49				23 52			
Havant	a												
Chichester 4	a												
Barnham	a												
Worthing 4	a												
Shoreham-by-Sea	a												
Hove 2	a												
Brighton 10	a												

For connections from Swansea please refer to Table 128.
For connections from Plymouth and Exeter St Davids please refer to Table 135.
For connections to Bournemouth please refer to Table 158

Table 123

Mondays to Fridays

until 1 July

Portsmouth and Weymouth - Bristol and South Wales

Miles	Miles	Miles			GW	GW	GW	GW	GW	GW	GW	GW	GW		SW	GW	GW	GW	GW	GW	GW	GW	GW		GW
					MO		◇[1] ☕	◇[1] ☕				◇[1] A Ø			[1]			◇[1] ☕	[R] 🛒			◇ 🛒	◇		◇[1] A Ø
—	—	—	Brighton [10]	d																					
—	—	—	Hove [2]	d																					
—	—	—	Shoreham-by-Sea	d																					
—	—	—	Worthing [4]	d																					
—	—	—	Barnham	d																					
—	—	—	Chichester [4]	d																					
—	—	—	Havant	d																					
0	—	—	**Portsmouth Harbour** ⛴	d	22p03														06 00			07 05			
0¾	—	—	Portsmouth & Southsea	d	22p12														06 04			07 09			
1¾	—	—	Fratton	d	22p16														06 08			07 13			
5½	—	—	Cosham	d															06 15			07 21			
11¼	—	—	Fareham	a	22p31														06 23			07 28			
—	—	—		d	22p32														06 24			07 29			
25¾	—	—	**Southampton Central** ⛴	d	22p57														06 46			07 52	08 23		
34	—	—	Romsey	d	23p09														07 00			08 11	08 35		
50½	—	—	**Salisbury**	a	23p27														07 18			08 29	09 00		
—	—	—		d	23p28				06 04						06 40				07 19			08 30	09 03		
70¼	—	—	Warminster	d	23p53				06 25						07 00		07 23		07 39			08 52	09 23		
73½	—	—	Dilton Marsh	d	23b58				06x29								07x27		07x43				09x28		
—	0	—	**Weymouth**	d												05 33				06 40					
—	2½	—	Upwey	d												05 37				06 45					
—	7	—	Dorchester West	d												05 45				06 53					
—	14¾	—	Maiden Newton	d												05 57				07 05					
—	21¼	—	Chetnole	d												06x06				07x13					
—	23¼	—	Yetminster	d												06x08				07x16					
—	24¼	—	Thornford	d												06x10				07x18					
—	27½	—	Yeovil Pen Mill	d												06 20				07 30					
—	39¼	—	Castle Cary	a												06 33				07 43					
—	—	—		d								06 38				06 45		07 27		07 44					09 41
—	42¾	—	Bruton	d												06 51				07 49					
—	53¼	—	Frome	d				06 07			06 45					07 04				08 02					
75	59	—	**Westbury**	a	00 02			06 17	06 33		06 54	06 59			07 08	07 12	07 32	07 45	07 47	08 13		09 01	09 35		09 59
—	—	—		d		05 58	06 08	06 18		06 38	06 55	07 01	07 04		07 09	07 18	07 38	07 51	07 53	08 17	08 45	09 09	09 38		10 00
79	63	4	Trowbridge	d		06 04				06 44	07 01		07 10		07 15	07 24	07 44		08 00	08 23	08 51	09 15	09 44		
82¼	66¼	—	Bradford-on-Avon	d		06 10				06 49	07 07				07 21	07 30	07 50		08 06	08 29	08 57	09 21	09 50		
83½	67½	—	Avoncliff	d		06 12				06 52	07 09					07 32	07 52			08 31	08 59		09 52		
84½	68½	—	Freshford	d		06 15				06 55	07 13					07 36	07 55		08 10	08 34	09 02		09 55		
91½	75½	—	Bath Spa [7]	a		06 26				07 06	07 24				07 33	07 47	08 06		08 20	08 45	09 13	09 35	10 06		
—	—	9½	Melksham	d									07 19												
—	—	15¾	Chippenham	a									07 30												
—	—	32½	Swindon	a									07 48												
—	—	—	London Paddington [15] ⊖	a			07 53	08 09				08 38						09 21							11 24
92½	76½	—	Oldfield Park	a		06 30				07 10	07 28				07 37	07 51	08 10		08 23	08 49	09 17		10 10		
98½	82½	—	Keynsham	a		06 37				07 17	07 35				07 44	07 57	08 17		08 31	08 56	09 24	09 43	10 17		
103	87	—	**Bristol Temple Meads** [10]	a		06 45				07 27	07 45				07 52	08 06	08 29		08 39	09 05	09 35	09 50	10 29		
107½	91½	—	Filton Abbey Wood	a		07 01				07 42	08 00					08 21	08 48		09 01	09 21	09 48	10 00	10 48		
119½	119½	—	Severn Tunnel Jn	a		07 14																			
129½	113½	—	Newport (South Wales)	a		07 25					08 27								09 25			10 26			
141¼	125¼	—	**Cardiff Central** [7]	a		07 44					08 46								09 43			10 43			

A Ø to Westbury

b Previous night, stops on request

For connections to Swansea please refer to Table 128.
For connections to Exeter St Davids and Plymouth please refer to Table 135.
For connections from Bournemouth please refer to Table 158

Table 123

Mondays to Fridays

until 1 July

Portsmouth and Weymouth - Bristol and South Wales

		GW	GW	GW	GW	GW	SW	GW	GW	GW	GW	GW	GW	GW	SW	GW	GW	GW	GW	GW	GW	GW	GW
																						■	
		◇			◇1	◇	◇1	◇	◇		◇1	◇	◇	◇	◇1		◇1	◇		◇1	◇1		
								A									B			C			
		⊤				⊤		⊤	⊤		☕	⊤		⊤			☕	⊤		☕	☕	⊤	
Brighton 10	d							09 00															
Hove 2	d							09 04															
Shoreham-by-Sea	d							09 13															
Worthing 4	d							09 22															
Barnham	d							09 38															
Chichester 4	d							09 47															
Havant	d							09 59															
Portsmouth Harbour ⛴	d	08 23				09 23			10 23			11 23		12 23				13 23				14 23	
Portsmouth & Southsea	d	08 27				09 27			10 27			11 27		12 27				13 27				14 27	
Fratton	d	08 31				09 31			10 31			11 31		12 31				13 31				14 31	
Cosham	d	08 39				09 39		10 05	10 39			11 39		12 39				13 39				14 39	
Fareham	a	08 46				09 46		10 14	10 46			11 46		12 46				13 46				14 46	
	d	08 47				09 47		10 14	10 47			11 47		12 47				13 47				14 47	
Southampton Central ⛴	d	09 10				10 10		10 42	11 10			12 10	12 27	13 10				14 10				15 10	
Romsey	d	09 21				10 21		10 54	11 21			12 21	12 39	13 21				14 21				15 21	
Salisbury	a	09 40				10 40		11 13	11 40			12 40	13 02	13 40				14 40				15 40	
	d	09 41				10 41	10 52	11 14	11 41			12 41	13 06	13 41	13 52			14 41				15 41	
Warminster	d	10 01		10 25		11 01	11 12	11 33	12 01			13 01	13 33	14 01	14 12			15 01	15 28			16 01	
Dilton Marsh	d			10x29									13x38						15x32				
Weymouth	d		08 53							11 10													15 08
Upwey	d		08 58							11 15													15 13
Dorchester West	d		09 06							11 23													15 21
Maiden Newton	d		09 18							11 43													15 33
Chetnole	d		09x26							11x50													15x42
Yetminster	d		09x29							11x53													15x45
Thornford	d		09x31							11x55													15x47
Yeovil Pen Mill	d		09 41							12 05													15 56
Castle Cary	a		09 54							12 19													16 09
	d		09 55							12 22	12 45						14 44			15 51			16 10
Bruton	d		10 01							12 27													16 16
Frome	d		10 15							12 39											15 55		16 29
Westbury	a	10 09	10 24	10 33		11 09	11 20	11 38	12 09	12 48	13 04	13 09	13 42	14 09	14 20		15 02	15 09	15 36		16 06	16 09	16 38
	d	10 10	10 38		11 04	11 10	11 21	11 38	12 10	12 49	13 05	13 10	13 44	14 10	14 21	14 38	15 03	15 10	15 38		16 06	16 10	16 38
Trowbridge	d	10 16	10 44			11 16	11 27	11 44	12 16	12 55		13 16	13 50	14 16	14 27	14 44		15 16	15 44			16 16	16 44
Bradford-on-Avon	d	10 22	10 50			11 22	11 33	11 50	12 22	13 01		13 22	13 57	14 22	14 33	14 50		15 22	15 50			16 22	16 50
Avoncliff	d		10 52					11 52		13 03			13 59			14 52			15 52				16 52
Freshford	d		10 55					11 55		13 05			14 02			14 55			15 55				16 55
Bath Spa 7	a	10 34	11 06			11 34	11 46	12 06	12 34	13 17		13 34	14 13	14 34	14 46	15 06		15 34	16 06			16 34	17 06
Melksham	d																						
Chippenham	a																						
Swindon	a																						
London Paddington 15 ⊖	a				12 23						14 44						16 22			17 24	17 54		
Oldfield Park	a		11 09					12 10		13 20			14 17			15 10			16 09				17 10
Keynsham	a		11 16				11 54	12 17		13 27			14 25		14 54	15 17			16 17				17 17
Bristol Temple Meads 10	a	10 48	11 28			11 48	12 05	12 29	12 48	13 36		13 48	14 35	14 48	15 05	15 29		15 48	16 29			16 48	17 29
Filton Abbey Wood	a	11 00	11 48			12 00		12 48	13 00	13 48		14 00	14 47	15 00				16 00	16 48			17 00	17 48
Severn Tunnel Jn.	a																					17 13	
Newport (South Wales)	a	11 26				12 25			13 26			14 26		15 25				16 25				17 25	
Cardiff Central 7	a	11 43				12 43			13 43			14 43		15 43				16 43				17 43	

A ⊤ to Fareham

B Restaurant available for customers joining until Castle Cary. ☕ from Westbury

C The Torbay Express

For connections to Swansea please refer to Table 128.
For connections to Exeter St Davids and Plymouth please refer to Table 135.
For connections from Bournemouth please refer to Table 158

Portsmouth and Weymouth - Bristol and South Wales

		GW	GW	GW	GW		GW	GW FX	GW FO	GW	GW	GW	GW	GW	GW		GW	GW	GW	GW FO	GW FX	GW	SW	GW	GW
		R ⊥		R ⊥				◇ ⊥	◇ ⊥		◇[1] ⊓			◇ ⊥	◇ ⊥		[1]		◇[1] ⊓	◇	◇		◇[1]		◇
Brighton [10]	d													17 00											
Hove [2]	d													17 04											
Shoreham-by-Sea	d													17 13											
Worthing [4]	d													17 22											
Barnham	d													17 39											
Chichester [4]	d													17 47											
Havant	d													17 58											
Portsmouth Harbour ⛴	d	15 23		16 23				17 23	17 23						18 23					19 23	19 23				20 23
Portsmouth & Southsea	d	15 27		16 27				17 27	17 27						18 27					19 27	19 27				20 27
Fratton	d	15 31		16 31				17 31	17 31						18 31					19 31	19 31				20 31
Cosham	d	15 39		16 39				17 39	17 39					18 05	18 39					19 39	19 39				
Fareham	a	15 46		16 46				17 46	17 46					18 12	18 46					19 46	19 46				20 46
	d	15 47		16 47				17 47	17 47					18 13	18 47					19 47	19 47				20 47
Southampton Central ⛴	d	16 10		17 10				18 10	18 10					18 42	19 10					20 10	20 10				21 10
Romsey	d	16 21		17 21				18 21	18 21					18 54	19 21					20 21	20 21				21 21
Salisbury	a	16 40		17 40				18 40	18 40					19 12	19 40					20 40	20 40				21 40
	d	16 41		17 41				18 41	18 41					19 13	19 41					20 41	20 41		20 57		21 41
Warminster	d	17 01	17 28	18 01	18 18			19 01	19 01					19 32	20 01					21 01	21 01		21 17		22 01
Dilton Marsh	d		17x32		18x22									19x37											
Weymouth	d									17 30														20 21	
Upwey	d									17 35														20 26	
Dorchester West	d									17 43														20 34	
Maiden Newton	d									17 54														20 45	
Chetnole	d									18x03														20x54	
Yetminster	d									18x06														20x57	
Thornford	d									18x08														20x59	
Yeovil Pen Mill	d									18 23														21 09	
Castle Cary	a									18 36														21 22	
	d									18 37	18 53								20 45					21 23	
Bruton	d									18 43														21 29	
Frome	d									19 05		←					20 15					21 01		21 42	
Westbury	a	17 09	17 36	18 09	18 28			19 09	19 09	19 17	19 11	19 17		19 40	20 09		20 26		21 03	21 08	21 08	21 11	21 25	21 51	22 09
	d	17 10	17 38	18 10			18 38	19 10	19 10	19 17	19 11	19 17	19 32	19 41	20 10			20 38	21 04	21 10	21 10		21 25	21 55	22 10
Trowbridge	d	17 16	17 44	18 16			18 44	19 16	19 16	→		19 23	19 38	19 47	20 16			20 44		21 16	21 16		21 31	22 01	22 16
Bradford-on-Avon	d	17 22	17 50	18 22			18 50	19 22	19 22			19 29		19 53	20 22			20 50		21 22	21 22		21 37	22 07	22 22
Avoncliff	d		17 52				18 52					19 31		19 55				20 52						22 09	
Freshford	d		17 55				18 55					19 35		19 57				20 55						22 13	
Bath Spa [7]	a	17 34	18 06	18 34			19 06	19 34	19 34			19 46		20 11	20 35			21 06		21 34	21 34		21 50	22 24	22 35
Melksham	d												19 47												
Chippenham	a												20 01												
Swindon	a												20 21												
London Paddington [15] ⊖	a										20 39								22 30						
Oldfield Park	a		18 10				19 10					19 50		20 13				21 10						22 28	
Keynsham	a		18 16				19 17					19 57		20 20				21 17					21 58	22 35	
Bristol Temple Meads [10]	a	17 48	18 28	18 49			19 29	19 49	19 49			20 08		20 29	20 51			21 29		21 49	21 49		22 06	22 44	22 49
Filton Abbey Wood	a	18 00	18 48	19 00			19 48		20 00						21 00					21 59	22 00				23 00
Severn Tunnel Jn	a	18 13		19 13					20 16						21 13					22 17	22 17				23 16
Newport (South Wales)	a	18 25		19 26					20 27						21 26					22 29	22 36				23 34
Cardiff Central [7]	a	18 43		19 46					20 43						21 44					22 52	23 00				23 56

For connections to Swansea please refer to Table 128.
For connections to Exeter St Davids and Plymouth please refer to Table 135.
For connections from Bournemouth please refer to Table 158

Table 123

Mondays to Fridays

until 1 July

Portsmouth and Weymouth - Bristol and South Wales

Station		GW	GW	GW
Brighton 10	d			
Hove 2	d			
Shoreham-by-Sea	d			
Worthing 4	d			
Barnham	d			
Chichester 4	d			
Havant	d			
Portsmouth Harbour ⛴	d			21 23
Portsmouth & Southsea	d			21 27
Fratton	d			21 31
Cosham	d			
Fareham	a			21 47
	d			21 48
Southampton Central ⛴	d	21 20		22 22
Romsey	d	21 31		22 34
Salisbury	a	21 51		22 58
	d	21 53		23 00
Warminster	d	22 15		23 20
Dilton Marsh	d	22x20		23x24
Weymouth	d			
Upwey	d			
Dorchester West	d			
Maiden Newton	d			
Chetnole	d			
Yetminster	d			
Thornford	d			
Yeovil Pen Mill	d			
Castle Cary	a			
	d			
Bruton	d			
Frome	d			
Westbury	a	22 25		23 31
	d		22 32	
Trowbridge	d		22 38	
Bradford-on-Avon	d		22 44	
Avoncliff	d		22 46	
Freshford	d		22 49	
Bath Spa 7	a		23 00	
Melksham	d			
Chippenham	a			
Swindon	a			
London Paddington 15 ⊖	a			
Oldfield Park	a		23 04	
Keynsham	a		23 12	
Bristol Temple Meads 10	a		23 23	
Filton Abbey Wood	a			
Severn Tunnel Jn.	a			
Newport (South Wales)	a			
Cardiff Central 7	a			

For connections to Swansea please refer to Table 128.
For connections to Exeter St Davids and Plymouth please refer to Table 135.
For connections from Bournemouth please refer to Table 158

Table 123

Mondays to Fridays

4 July to 2 September

Portsmouth and Weymouth - Bristol and South Wales

		GW MO	GW	GW	GW	GW	GW	GW	GW	GW		SW	GW	GW	GW	GW	GW	GW	GW	GW		GW	GW	GW	GW
				◇1 ꟺ	◇1 ꟺ				◇1 A ⌀			1			◇1 ꟺ	R ⚲			◇ ⚲	◇		◇1 A ⌀	◇ ⚲		
Brighton 10	d																								
Hove 2	d																								
Shoreham-by-Sea	d																								
Worthing 4	d																								
Barnham	d																								
Chichester 4	d																								
Havant	d																								
Portsmouth Harbour ⛴	d	22p03														06 00			07 05				08 23		
Portsmouth & Southsea	d	22p12														06 04			07 09				08 27		
Fratton	d	22p16														06 08			07 13				08 31		
Cosham	d															06 15			07 21				08 39		
Fareham	a	22p31														06 23			07 28				08 46		
	d	22p32														06 24			07 29				08 47		
Southampton Central ⛴	d	22p57														06 46			07 52	08 23			09 10		
Romsey	d	23p09														07 00			08 11	08 35			09 21		
Salisbury	a	23p27														07 18			08 29	09 00			09 40		
	d	23p28				06 04						06 40				07 19			08 30	09 03			09 41		
Warminster	d	23p53				06 25						07 00		07 23		07 39			08 52	09 23			10 01		10 25
Dilton Marsh	d	23b58				06x29								07x27		07x43				09x28					10x29
Weymouth	d												05 33				06 40							08 53	
Upwey	d												05 37				06 45							08 58	
Dorchester West	d												05 45				06 53							09 06	
Maiden Newton	d												05 57				07 05							09 18	
Chetnole	d												06x06				07x13							09x26	
Yetminster	d												06x08				07x16							09x29	
Thornford	d												06x10				07x18							09x31	
Yeovil Pen Mill	d												06 20				07 30							09 41	
Castle Cary	a												06 33				07 43							09 54	
	d								06 38				06 45		07 27		07 44					09 41		09 55	
Bruton	d												06 51				07 49							10 01	
Frome	d				06 07			06 45					07 04				08 02							10 15	
Westbury	a	00 02			06 17	06 33		06 54	06 59			07 08	07 12	07 32	07 45	07 47	08 13		09 01	09 35		09 59	10 09	10 24	10 33
	d		05 58	06 08	06 18		06 38	06 55	07 01	07 04		07 09	07 18	07 38	07 51	07 53	08 17	08 45	09 09	09 38		10 00	10 10	10 38	
Trowbridge	d		06 04				06 44	07 01		07 10		07 15	07 24	07 44		08 00	08 23	08 51	09 15	09 44			10 16	10 44	
Bradford-on-Avon	d		06 10				06 49	07 07				07 21	07 30	07 50		08 06	08 29	08 57	09 21	09 50			10 22	10 50	
Avoncliff	d		06 12				06 52	07 09					07 32	07 52			08 31	08 59		09 52				10 52	
Freshford	d		06 15				06 55	07 13					07 36	07 55		08 10	08 34	09 02		09 55				10 55	
Bath Spa 7	a		06 26				07 06	07 24				07 33	07 47	08 06		08 20	08 45	09 13	09 35	10 06			10 34	11 06	
Melksham	d									07 19															
Chippenham	a									07 30															
Swindon	a									07 48															
London Paddington 15 ⊖	a			07 53	08 09				08 38						09 21							11 24			
Oldfield Park	a		06 30				07 10	07 28				07 37	07 51	08 10		08 23	08 49	09 17		10 10				11 09	
Keynsham	a		06 37				07 17	07 35				07 44	07 57	08 17		08 31	08 56	09 24	09 43	10 17				11 16	
Bristol Temple Meads 10	a		06 45				07 27	07 45				07 52	08 06	08 29		08 39	09 05	09 35	09 50	10 29			10 48	11 28	
Filton Abbey Wood	a		07 01				07 42	08 00					08 21	08 48		09 01	09 21	09 48	10 00	10 48			11 00	11 48	
Severn Tunnel Jn.	a		07 14																						
Newport (South Wales)	a		07 25					08 27								09 25			10 26				11 26		
Cardiff Central 7	a		07 44					08 46								09 43			10 43				11 43		

A ⌀ to Westbury

b Previous night, stops on request

For connections to Swansea please refer to Table 128.
For connections to Exeter St Davids and Plymouth please refer to Table 135.
For connections from Bournemouth please refer to Table 158

Table 123

Mondays to Fridays

4 July to 2 September

Portsmouth and Weymouth - Bristol and South Wales

		GW	GW	SW	GW	GW	GW	GW	GW	GW	GW	SW	GW	GW	GW	GW	GW	GW	GW	GW	GW	GW	GW
																			Ⓡ		Ⓡ		Ⓡ
		◇[1]	◇	◇[1]	◇	◇		◇[1]	◇	◇	◇	◇[1]		◇[1]	◇		◇[1]	◇[1]					
					A									B			C						
			T		T	T		R	T		T			R	T		R	R	T		T		T
Brighton [10]	d				09 00																		
Hove [2]	d				09 04																		
Shoreham-by-Sea	d				09 13																		
Worthing [4]	d				09 22																		
Barnham	d				09 38																		
Chichester [4]	d				09 47																		
Havant	d				09 59																		
Portsmouth Harbour	d		09 23			10 23			11 23		12 23				13 23				14 23		15 23		16 23
Portsmouth & Southsea	d		09 27			10 27			11 27		12 27				13 27				14 27		15 27		16 27
Fratton	d		09 31			10 31			11 31		12 31				13 31				14 31		15 31		16 31
Cosham	d		09 39		10 05	10 39			11 39		12 39				13 39				14 39		15 39		16 39
Fareham	a		09 46		10 14	10 46			11 46		12 46				13 46				14 46		15 46		16 46
	d		09 47		10 14	10 47			11 47		12 47				13 47				14 47		15 47		16 47
Southampton Central	d		10 10		10 42	11 10			12 10	12 27	13 10				14 10				15 10		16 10		17 10
Romsey	d		10 21		10 54	11 21			12 21	12 39	13 21				14 21				15 21		16 21		17 21
Salisbury	a		10 40		11 13	11 40			12 40	13 02	13 40				14 40				15 40		16 40		17 40
	d		10 41	10 52	11 14	11 41			12 41	13 06	13 41	13 52			14 41				15 41		16 41		17 41
Warminster	d		11 01	11 12	11 33	12 01			13 01	13 33	14 01	14 12			15 01	15 28			16 01		17 01	17 28	18 01
Dilton Marsh	d									13x38						15x32						17x32	
Weymouth	d						11 10													15 08			
Upwey	d						11 15													15 13			
Dorchester West	d						11 23													15 21			
Maiden Newton	d						11 43													15 33			
Chetnole	d						11x50													15x42			
Yetminster	d						11x53													15x45			
Thornford	d						11x55													15x47			
Yeovil Pen Mill	d						12 05													15 56			
Castle Cary	a						12 19													16 09			
	d						12 22	12 45						14 44			15 51			16 10			
Bruton	d						12 27													16 16			
Frome	d						12 39											15 55		16 29			
Westbury	a		11 09	11 20	11 38	12 09	12 48	13 04	13 09	13 42	14 09	14 20		15 02	15 09	15 36		16 06	16 09	16 38	17 09	17 36	18 09
	d	11 04	11 10	11 21	11 38	12 10	12 49	13 05	13 10	13 44	14 10	14 21	14 38	15 03	15 10	15 38		16 06	16 10	16 38	17 10	17 38	18 10
Trowbridge	d		11 16	11 27	11 44	12 16	12 55		13 16	13 50	14 16	14 27	14 44		15 16	15 44			16 16	16 44	17 16	17 44	18 16
Bradford-on-Avon	d		11 22	11 33	11 50	12 22	13 01		13 22	13 57	14 22	14 33	14 50		15 22	15 50			16 22	16 50	17 22	17 50	18 22
Avoncliff	d				11 52		13 03			13 59			14 52			15 52				16 52		17 52	
Freshford	d				11 55		13 05			14 02			14 55			15 55				16 55		17 55	
Bath Spa [7]	a		11 34	11 46	12 06	12 34	13 17		13 34	14 13	14 34	14 46	15 06		15 34	16 06			16 34	17 06	17 34	18 06	18 34
Melksham	d																						
Chippenham	a																						
Swindon	a																						
London Paddington [15]	a	12 23						14 44						16 22			17 24	17 54					
Oldfield Park	a				12 10		13 20			14 17			15 10			16 09				17 10		18 10	
Keynsham	a			11 54	12 17		13 27			14 25		14 54	15 17			16 17				17 17		18 16	
Bristol Temple Meads [10]	a		11 48	12 05	12 29	12 48	13 36		13 48	14 35	14 48	15 05	15 29		15 48	16 29			16 48	17 29	17 48	18 28	18 49
Filton Abbey Wood	a		12 00		12 48	13 00	13 48		14 00	14 47	15 00				16 00	16 48			17 00	17 48	18 00	18 48	19 00
Severn Tunnel Jn	a																		17 13		18 13		19 13
Newport (South Wales)	a		12 25			13 26			14 26		15 25				16 25				17 25		18 25		19 26
Cardiff Central [7]	a		12 43			13 43			14 43		15 43				16 43				17 43		18 43		19 46

A T to Fareham

B Restaurant available for customers joining until Castle Cary. R from Westbury

C The Torbay Express

For connections to Swansea please refer to Table 128.
For connections to Exeter St Davids and Plymouth please refer to Table 135.
For connections from Bournemouth please refer to Table 158

Table 123

Mondays to Fridays

4 July to 2 September

Portsmouth and Weymouth - Bristol and South Wales

		GW		GW	GW	GW	GW	GW	GW	GW	GW	GW		GW	GW	GW	GW	GW	GW	SW	GW	GW		GW	GW
					FX	FO											FO	FX							
					◇	◇		◇■1			◇	◇		■1		◇■1	◇	◇		◇■1		◇			
								A																	
					🛒	🛒		🍴			🛒	🛒				🍴									
Brighton ■10	d										17 00														
Hove ■2	d										17 04														
Shoreham-by-Sea	d										17 13														
Worthing ■4	d										17 22														
Barnham	d										17 39														
Chichester ■4	d										17 47														
Havant	d										17 58														
Portsmouth Harbour ⛴	d				17 23	17 23						18 23					19 23	19 23				20 23			
Portsmouth & Southsea	d				17 27	17 27						18 27					19 27	19 27				20 27			
Fratton	d				17 31	17 31						18 31					19 31	19 31				20 31			
Cosham	d				17 39	17 39					18 05	18 39					19 39	19 39							
Fareham	a				17 46	17 46					18 12	18 46					19 46	19 46				20 46			
	d				17 47	17 47					18 13	18 47					19 47	19 47				20 47			
Southampton Central ⛴	d				18 10	18 10					18 42	19 10					20 10	20 10				21 10		21 20	
Romsey	d				18 21	18 21					18 54	19 21					20 21	20 21				21 21		21 31	
Salisbury	a				18 40	18 40					19 12	19 40					20 40	20 40				21 40		21 51	
	d				18 41	18 41					19 13	19 41					20 41	20 41		20 57		21 41		21 53	
Warminster	d	18 18			19 01	19 01					19 32	20 01					21 01	21 01		21 17		22 01		22 15	
Dilton Marsh	d	18x22									19x37													22x20	
Weymouth	d						17 30														20 21				
Upwey	d						17 35														20 26				
Dorchester West	d						17 43														20 34				
Maiden Newton	d						17 54														20 45				
Chetnole	d						18x03														20x54				
Yetminster	d						18x06														20x57				
Thornford	d						18x08														20x59				
Yeovil Pen Mill	d						18 23														21 09				
Castle Cary	a						18 36														21 22				
	d						18 37	18 53								20 45					21 23				
Bruton	d						18 43														21 29				
Frome	d						19 05		←					20 15					21 01		21 42				
Westbury	a	18 28			19 09	19 09	19 17	19 11	19 17		19 40	20 09		20 26		21 03	21 08	21 08	21 11	21 25	21 51	22 09		22 25	
	d			18 38	19 10	19 10	19 17	19 11	19 17	19 32	19 41	20 10			20 38	21 04	21 10	21 10		21 25	21 55	22 10			22 32
Trowbridge	d			18 44	19 16	19 16	↪		19 23	19 38	19 47	20 16			20 44		21 16	21 16		21 31	22 01	22 16			22 38
Bradford-on-Avon	d			18 50	19 22	19 22			19 29		19 53	20 22			20 50		21 22	21 22		21 37	22 07	22 22			22 44
Avoncliff	d			18 52					19 31		19 55				20 52						22 09				22 46
Freshford	d			18 55					19 35		19 57				20 55						22 13				22 49
Bath Spa ■7	a			19 06	19 34	19 34			19 46		20 11	20 35			21 06		21 34	21 34		21 50	22 24	22 35			23 00
Melksham	d									19 47															
Chippenham	a									20 01															
Swindon	a									20 21															
London Paddington ■15 ⊖	a							20 39								22 30									
Oldfield Park	a			19 10					19 50		20 13				21 10						22 28				23 04
Keynsham	a			19 17					19 57		20 20				21 17					21 58	22 35				23 12
Bristol Temple Meads ■10	a			19 29	19 49	19 49			20 08		20 29	20 51			21 29		21 49	21 49		22 06	22 44	22 49			23 23
Filton Abbey Wood	a			19 48		20 00						21 00					21 59	22 00				23 00			
Severn Tunnel Jn.	a					20 16						21 13					22 17	22 17				23 16			
Newport (South Wales)	a					20 27						21 26					22 29	22 36				23 34			
Cardiff Central ■7	a					20 43						21 44					22 52	23 00				23 56			

A The Atlantic Coast Express

For connections to Swansea please refer to Table 128.
For connections to Exeter St Davids and Plymouth please refer to Table 135.
For connections from Bournemouth please refer to Table 158

Table 123

Mondays to Fridays

4 July to 2 September

Portsmouth and Weymouth - Bristol and South Wales

		GW
Brighton 10	d	
Hove 2	d	
Shoreham-by-Sea	d	
Worthing 4	d	
Barnham	d	
Chichester 4	d	
Havant	d	
Portsmouth Harbour ⛴	d	21 23
Portsmouth & Southsea	d	21 27
Fratton	d	21 31
Cosham	d	
Fareham	a	21 47
	d	21 48
Southampton Central ⛴	d	22 22
Romsey	d	22 34
Salisbury	a	22 58
	d	23 00
Warminster	d	23 20
Dilton Marsh	d	23x24
Weymouth	d	
Upwey	d	
Dorchester West	d	
Maiden Newton	d	
Chetnole	d	
Yetminster	d	
Thornford	d	
Yeovil Pen Mill	d	
Castle Cary	a	
	d	
Bruton	d	
Frome	d	
Westbury	a	23 31
	d	
Trowbridge	d	
Bradford-on-Avon	d	
Avoncliff	d	
Freshford	d	
Bath Spa 7	a	
Melksham	d	
Chippenham	a	
Swindon	a	
London Paddington 15 ⊖	a	
Oldfield Park	a	
Keynsham	a	
Bristol Temple Meads 10	a	
Filton Abbey Wood	a	
Severn Tunnel Jn	a	
Newport (South Wales)	a	
Cardiff Central 7	a	

For connections to Swansea please refer to Table 128.
For connections to Exeter St Davids and Plymouth please refer to Table 135.
For connections from Bournemouth please refer to Table 158

Table 123

Mondays to Fridays
from 5 September

Portsmouth and Weymouth - Bristol and South Wales

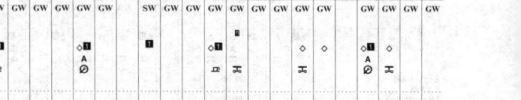

		GW MO	GW	GW	GW	GW	GW	GW	GW	GW		SW	GW	GW	GW	GW	GW	GW	GW	GW		GW	GW	GW	GW
				◇1	◇1				◇1 A ⌀			1			◇1	R			◇	◇		◇1 A ⌀	◇		
Brighton 10	d																								
Hove 2	d																								
Shoreham-by-Sea	d																								
Worthing 4	d																								
Barnham	d																								
Chichester 4	d																								
Havant	d																								
Portsmouth Harbour ⛴	d	22p03														06 00			07 05				08 23		
Portsmouth & Southsea	d	22p12														06 04			07 09				08 27		
Fratton	d	22p16														06 08			07 13				08 31		
Cosham	d															06 15			07 21				08 39		
Fareham	a	22p31														06 23			07 28				08 46		
	d	22p32														06 24			07 29				08 47		
Southampton Central ⛴	d	22p57														06 46			07 52	08 23			09 10		
Romsey	d	23p09														07 00			08 11	08 35			09 21		
Salisbury	a	23p27														07 18			08 29	09 00			09 40		
	d	23p28				06 04						06 40				07 19			08 30	09 03			09 41		
Warminster	d	23p53				06 25						07 00		07 23		07 39			08 52	09 23			10 01		10 25
Dilton Marsh	d	23b58				06x29								07x27		07x43				09x28					10x29
Weymouth	d												05 33				06 40							08 53	
Upwey	d												05 37				06 45							08 58	
Dorchester West	d												05 45				06 53							09 06	
Maiden Newton	d												05 57				07 05							09 18	
Chetnole	d												06x06				07x13							09x26	
Yetminster	d												06x08				07x16							09x29	
Thornford	d												06x10				07x18							09x31	
Yeovil Pen Mill	d												06 20				07 30							09 41	
Castle Cary	a												06 33				07 43							09 54	
	d								06 38				06 45		07 27		07 44					09 41		09 55	
Bruton	d												06 51				07 49							10 01	
Frome	d				06 07			06 45					07 04				08 02							10 15	
Westbury	a	00 02			06 17	06 33		06 54	06 59			07 08	07 12	07 32	07 45	07 47	08 13		09 01	09 35		09 59	10 09	10 24	10 33
	d		05 58	06 08	06 18		06 38	06 55	07 01	07 04		07 09	07 18	07 38	07 51	07 53	08 17	08 45	09 09	09 38		10 00	10 10	10 38	
Trowbridge	d		06 04				06 44	07 01		07 10		07 15	07 24	07 44		08 00	08 23	08 51	09 15	09 44			10 16	10 44	
Bradford-on-Avon	d		06 10				06 49	07 07				07 21	07 30	07 50		08 06	08 29	08 57	09 21	09 50			10 22	10 50	
Avoncliff	d		06 12				06 52	07 09					07 32	07 52			08 31	08 59		09 52				10 52	
Freshford	d		06 15				06 55	07 13					07 36	07 55		08 10	08 34	09 02		09 55				10 55	
Bath Spa 7	a		06 26				07 06	07 24				07 33	07 47	08 06		08 20	08 45	09 13	09 35	10 06			10 34	11 06	
Melksham	d									07 19															
Chippenham	a									07 30															
Swindon	a									07 48															
London Paddington 15 ⊖	a			07 53	08 09				08 38						09 21							11 24			
Oldfield Park	a		06 30				07 10	07 28				07 37	07 51	08 10		08 23	08 49	09 17		10 10				11 09	
Keynsham	a		06 37				07 17	07 35				07 44	07 57	08 17		08 31	08 56	09 24	09 43	10 17				11 16	
Bristol Temple Meads 10	a		06 45				07 27	07 45				07 52	08 06	08 29		08 39	09 05	09 35	09 50	10 29			10 48	11 28	
Filton Abbey Wood	a		07 01				07 42	08 00					08 21	08 48		09 01	09 21	09 48	10 00	10 48			11 00	11 48	
Severn Tunnel Jn.	a		07 14																						
Newport (South Wales)	a		07 25					08 27								09 25			10 26				11 26		
Cardiff Central 7	a		07 44					08 46								09 43			10 43				11 43		

A ⌀ to Westbury

b Previous night, stops on request

For connections to Swansea please refer to Table 128.
For connections to Exeter St Davids and Plymouth please refer to Table 135.
For connections from Bournemouth please refer to Table 158

Table 123

Mondays to Fridays

from 5 September

Portsmouth and Weymouth - Bristol and South Wales

		GW	GW	SW	GW	GW		GW	GW	GW	GW	GW	SW	GW	GW	GW		GW	GW	GW	GW	GW	GW	GW	GW
																					R		R		R
		◇1	◇	◇1	◇	◇			◇1	◇	◇	◇	◇1		◇1	◇			◇1	◇1					
					A										B				C						
			🛒		🛒	🛒			🍽	🛒		🛒			🍽	🛒			🍽	🍽	🛒		🛒		🛒
Brighton 10	d				09 00																				
Hove 2	d				09 04																				
Shoreham-by-Sea	d				09 13																				
Worthing 4	d				09 22																				
Barnham	d				09 38																				
Chichester 4	d				09 47																				
Havant	d				09 59																				
Portsmouth Harbour ⛴	d		09 23			10 23				11 23		12 23				13 23					14 23		15 23		16 23
Portsmouth & Southsea	d		09 27			10 27				11 27		12 27				13 27					14 27		15 27		16 27
Fratton	d		09 31			10 31				11 31		12 31				13 31					14 31		15 31		16 31
Cosham	d		09 39		10 05	10 39				11 39		12 39				13 39					14 39		15 39		16 39
Fareham	a		09 46		10 14	10 46				11 46		12 46				13 46					14 46		15 46		16 46
	d		09 47		10 14	10 47				11 47		12 47				13 47					14 47		15 47		16 47
Southampton Central ⛴	d		10 10		10 42	11 10				12 10	12 27	13 10				14 10					15 10		16 10		17 10
Romsey	d		10 21		10 54	11 21				12 21	12 39	13 21				14 21					15 21		16 21		17 21
Salisbury	a		10 40		11 13	11 40				12 40	13 02	13 40				14 40					15 40		16 40		17 40
	d		10 41	10 52	11 14	11 41				12 41	13 06	13 41	13 52			14 41					15 41		16 41		17 41
Warminster	d		11 01	11 12	11 33	12 01				13 01	13 33	14 01	14 12			15 01		15 28			16 01		17 01	17 28	18 01
Dilton Marsh	d										13x38							15x32						17x32	
Weymouth	d							11 10														15 08			
Upwey	d							11 15														15 13			
Dorchester West	d							11 23														15 21			
Maiden Newton	d							11 43														15 33			
Chetnole	d							11x50														15x42			
Yetminster	d							11x53														15x45			
Thornford	d							11x55														15x47			
Yeovil Pen Mill	d							12 05														15 56			
Castle Cary	a							12 19														16 09			
	d							12 22	12 45						14 44				15 51			16 10			
Bruton	d							12 27														16 16			
Frome	d							12 39												15 55		16 29			
Westbury	a		11 09	11 20	11 38	12 09		12 48	13 04	13 09	13 42	14 09	14 20		15 02	15 09		15 36		16 06	16 09	16 38	17 09	17 36	18 09
	d	11 04	11 10	11 21	11 38	12 10		12 49	13 05	13 10	13 44	14 10	14 21	14 38	15 03	15 10		15 38		16 06	16 10	16 38	17 10	17 38	18 10
Trowbridge	d		11 16	11 27	11 44	12 16		12 55		13 16	13 50	14 16	14 27	14 44		15 16		15 44			16 16	16 44	17 16	17 44	18 16
Bradford-on-Avon	d		11 22	11 33	11 50	12 22		13 01		13 22	13 57	14 22	14 33	14 50		15 22		15 50			16 22	16 50	17 22	17 50	18 22
Avoncliff	d				11 52			13 03			13 59			14 52				15 52				16 52		17 52	
Freshford	d				11 55			13 05			14 02			14 55				15 55				16 55		17 55	
Bath Spa 7	a		11 34	11 46	12 06	12 34		13 17		13 34	14 13	14 34	14 46	15 06		15 34		16 06			16 34	17 06	17 34	18 06	18 34
Melksham	d																								
Chippenham	a																								
Swindon	a																								
London Paddington 15 ⊖	a	12 23							14 44						16 22				17 24	17 54					
Oldfield Park	a				12 10			13 20			14 17			15 10				16 09				17 10		18 10	
Keynsham	a			11 54	12 17			13 27			14 25		14 54	15 17				16 17				17 17		18 16	
Bristol Temple Meads 10	a		11 48	12 05	12 29	12 48		13 36		13 48	14 35	14 48	15 05	15 29		15 48		16 29			16 48	17 29	17 48	18 28	18 49
Filton Abbey Wood	a		12 00		12 48	13 00		13 48		14 00	14 47	15 00				16 00		16 48			17 00	17 48	18 00	18 48	19 00
Severn Tunnel Jn	a																				17 13		18 13		19 13
Newport (South Wales)	a		12 25			13 26				14 26		15 25				16 25					17 25		18 25		19 26
Cardiff Central 7	a		12 43			13 43				14 43		15 43				16 43					17 43		18 43		19 46

A 🛒 to Fareham

B Restaurant available for customers joining until Castle Cary. 🍽 from Westbury

C The Torbay Express

For connections to Swansea please refer to Table 128.
For connections to Exeter St Davids and Plymouth please refer to Table 135.
For connections from Bournemouth please refer to Table 158

Table 123

Mondays to Fridays

from 5 September

Portsmouth and Weymouth - Bristol and South Wales

		GW		GW	GW FX	GW FO	GW	GW	GW	GW	GW	GW		GW	GW	GW	GW FO	GW FX	GW	SW	GW	GW		GW	GW
					◇ 🛒	◇ 🛒		◇[1] 🚌			◇ 🛒	◇ 🛒		[1]		◇[1] 🚌	◇	◇		◇[1]		◇			
Brighton [10]	d										17 00														
Hove [2]	d										17 04														
Shoreham-by-Sea	d										17 13														
Worthing [4]	d										17 22														
Barnham	d										17 39														
Chichester [4]	d										17 47														
Havant	d										17 58														
Portsmouth Harbour ⛴	d				17 23	17 23						18 23					19 23	19 23				20 23			
Portsmouth & Southsea	d				17 27	17 27						18 27					19 27	19 27				20 27			
Fratton	d				17 31	17 31						18 31					19 31	19 31				20 31			
Cosham	d				17 39	17 39					18 05	18 39					19 39	19 39							
Fareham	a				17 46	17 46					18 12	18 46					19 46	19 46				20 46			
	d				17 47	17 47					18 13	18 47					19 47	19 47				20 47			
Southampton Central ⛴	d				18 10	18 10					18 42	19 10					20 10	20 10				21 10		21 20	
Romsey	d				18 21	18 21					18 54	19 21					20 21	20 21				21 21		21 31	
Salisbury	a				18 40	18 40					19 12	19 40					20 40	20 40				21 40		21 51	
	d				18 41	18 41					19 13	19 41					20 41	20 41		20 57		21 41		21 53	
Warminster	d	18 18			19 01	19 01					19 32	20 01					21 01	21 01		21 17		22 01		22 15	
Dilton Marsh	d	18x22									19x37													22x20	
Weymouth	d						17 30														20 21				
Upwey	d						17 35														20 26				
Dorchester West	d						17 43														20 34				
Maiden Newton	d						17 54														20 45				
Chetnole	d						18x03														20x54				
Yetminster	d						18x06														20x57				
Thornford	d						18x08														20x59				
Yeovil Pen Mill	d						18 23														21 09				
Castle Cary	a						18 36														21 22				
	d						18 37	18 53								20 45					21 23				
Bruton	d						18 43														21 29				
Frome	d						19 05		←					20 15					21 01		21 42				
Westbury	a	18 28			19 09	19 09	19 17	19 11	19 17		19 40	20 09		20 26		21 03	21 08	21 08	21 11	21 25	21 51	22 09		22 25	
	d			18 38	19 10	19 10	19 17	19 11	19 17	19 32	19 41	20 10			20 38	21 04	21 10	21 10		21 25	21 55	22 10			22 32
Trowbridge	d			18 44	19 16	19 16	→		19 23	19 38	19 47	20 16			20 44		21 16	21 16		21 31	22 01	22 16			22 38
Bradford-on-Avon	d			18 50	19 22	19 22			19 29		19 53	20 22			20 50		21 22	21 22		21 37	22 07	22 22			22 44
Avoncliff	d			18 52					19 31		19 55				20 52						22 09				22 46
Freshford	d			18 55					19 35		19 57				20 55						22 13				22 49
Bath Spa [7]	a			19 06	19 34	19 34			19 46		20 11	20 35			21 06		21 34	21 34		21 50	22 24	22 35			23 00
Melksham	d									19 47															
Chippenham	a									20 01															
Swindon	a									20 21															
London Paddington [15] ⊖	a							20 39								22 30									
Oldfield Park	a			19 10					19 50		20 13				21 10						22 28				23 04
Keynsham	a			19 17					19 57		20 20				21 17					21 58	22 35				23 12
Bristol Temple Meads [10]	a			19 29	19 49	19 49			20 08		20 29	20 51			21 29		21 49	21 49		22 06	22 44	22 49			23 23
Filton Abbey Wood	a			19 48		20 00						21 00					21 59	22 00				23 00			
Severn Tunnel Jn	a					20 16						21 13					22 17	22 17				23 16			
Newport (South Wales)	a					20 27						21 26					22 29	22 36				23 34			
Cardiff Central [7]	a					20 43						21 44					22 52	23 00				23 56			

For connections to Swansea please refer to Table 128.
For connections to Exeter St Davids and Plymouth please refer to Table 135.
For connections from Bournemouth please refer to Table 158

Table 123

Mondays to Fridays

from 5 September

Portsmouth and Weymouth - Bristol and South Wales

		GW
Brighton 10	d	
Hove 2	d	
Shoreham-by-Sea	d	
Worthing 4	d	
Barnham	d	
Chichester 4	d	
Havant	d	
Portsmouth Harbour ⛴	d	21 23
Portsmouth & Southsea	d	21 27
Fratton	d	21 31
Cosham	d	
Fareham	a	21 47
	d	21 48
Southampton Central ⛴	d	22 22
Romsey	d	22 34
Salisbury	a	22 58
	d	23 00
Warminster	d	23 20
Dilton Marsh	d	23x24
Weymouth	d	
Upwey	d	
Dorchester West	d	
Maiden Newton	d	
Chetnole	d	
Yetminster	d	
Thornford	d	
Yeovil Pen Mill	d	
Castle Cary	a	
	d	
Bruton	d	
Frome	d	
Westbury	a	23 31
	d	
Trowbridge	d	
Bradford-on-Avon	d	
Avoncliff	d	
Freshford	d	
Bath Spa 7	a	
Melksham	d	
Chippenham	a	
Swindon	a	
London Paddington 15 ⊖	a	
Oldfield Park	a	
Keynsham	a	
Bristol Temple Meads 10	a	
Filton Abbey Wood	a	
Severn Tunnel Jn.	a	
Newport (South Wales)	a	
Cardiff Central 7	a	

For connections to Swansea please refer to Table 128.
For connections to Exeter St Davids and Plymouth please refer to Table 135.
For connections from Bournemouth please refer to Table 158

Table 123

Saturdays
until 10 September

Portsmouth and Weymouth - Bristol and South Wales

		GW	GW	GW	SW	GW	GW	GW	GW	GW	GW	GW	GW	GW	GW	GW	GW	GW	SW	GW	GW	GW	GW
					1		◇1 ☕	◇			◇ A ✕	◇	◇1 ☕	◇ A ✕			1 ☕	◇ A ✕	◇1	◇	1 ☕	◇	
Brighton 10	d																			09 00			
Hove 2	d																			09 04			
Shoreham-by-Sea	d																			09 13			
Worthing 4	d																			09 22			
Barnham	d																			09 41			
Chichester 4	d																			09 49			
Havant	d																			10 00			
Portsmouth Harbour ⛴	d							06 00			07 05			08 23				09 23				10 23	
Portsmouth & Southsea	d							06 04			07 09			08 27				09 27				10 27	
Fratton	d							06 08			07 14			08 31				09 31				10 31	
Cosham	d							06 19			07 21			08 39				09 39		10 06		10 39	
Fareham	a							06 27			07 29			08 46				09 46		10 15		10 46	
	d							06 28			07 30			08 47				09 47		10 16		10 47	
Southampton Central ⛴	d							06 53			07 54	08 27		09 10				10 10		10 42		11 10	
Romsey	d							07 11			08 12	08 38		09 21				10 21		10 53		11 21	
Salisbury	a							07 29			08 30	09 03		09 40				10 40		11 13		11 40	
	d	06 03	06 03		06 40			07 30			08 34	09 03		09 41				10 41	10 52	11 13		11 41	
Warminster	d	06 23			07 00	07 23		07 50			08 54	09 23		10 01		10 25		11 01	11 12	11 34		12 01	
Dilton Marsh	d	06x27				07x27		07x54				09x28				10x29							
Weymouth	d								06 40						08 46								11 10
Upwey	d								06 45						08 51								11 15
Dorchester West	d								06 53						08 59								11 26
Maiden Newton	d								07 05						09 11								11 43
Chetnole	d								07x13						09x19								11x50
Yetminster	d								07x16						09x22								11x53
Thornford	d								07x18						09x24								11x56
Yeovil Pen Mill	d								07 30						09 34								12 05
Castle Cary	a								07 43						09 47								12 19
	d						07 33		07 44				09 40		09 48						11 24		12 22
Bruton	d								07 49						09 54								12 27
Frome	d			06 37					08 02						10 07								12 39
Westbury	a	06 31	06 34	06 46	07 08	07 31	07 51	07 59	08 13		09 00	09 33	09 58	10 09	10 16	10 33		11 09	11 20	11 42	11 42	12 09	12 48
	d		06 38	06 51	07 09	07 38	07 56	08 10	08 17	09 05	09 10	09 38	09 59	10 10	10 38		11 02	11 10	11 21	11 42	11 45	12 10	12 49
Trowbridge	d		06 44	06 57	07 15	07 44		08 16	08 23	09 11	09 16	09 44		10 16	10 44			11 16	11 27	11 48		12 16	12 55
Bradford-on-Avon	d		06 50	07 03	07 21	07 50		08 22	08 29		09 22	09 50		10 22	10 50			11 22	11 33	11 54		12 22	13 01
Avoncliff	d		06 52	07 05		07 52			08 31			09 52			10 52					11 57			13 03
Freshford	d		06 55	07 09		07 55			08 34			09 55			10 55					12 00			13 05
Bath Spa 7	a		07 06	07 20	07 33	08 06		08 34	08 45		09 34	10 06		10 34	11 06			11 34	11 46	12 10		12 34	13 17
Melksham	d									09 20													
Chippenham	a									09 30													
Swindon	a									09 49													
London Paddington 15 ⊖	a						09 21						11 24				12 23				13 09		
Oldfield Park	a		07 10	07 24	07 37	08 10			08 49			10 10			11 10					12 14			13 20
Keynsham	a		07 17	07 31	07 44	08 17			08 56			10 17			11 17				11 54	12 21			13 27
Bristol Temple Meads 10	a		07 29	07 39	07 53	08 29		08 47	09 05		09 48	10 29		10 48	11 29			11 48	12 05	12 29		12 48	13 36
Filton Abbey Wood	a		07 48	08 00		08 48		09 00			10 00	10 48		11 00	11 48			12 00		12 48		13 00	13 48
Severn Tunnel Jn	a																						
Newport (South Wales)	a			08 26				09 25			10 24			11 24				12 24				13 25	
Cardiff Central 7	a			08 43				09 42			10 43			11 43				12 43				13 43	

A ✕ to Bath Spa

For connections to Swansea please refer to Table 128.
For connections to Exeter St Davids and Plymouth please refer to Table 135.
For connections from Bournemouth please refer to Table 158

Table 123

Saturdays
until 10 September

Portsmouth and Weymouth - Bristol and South Wales

		GW	GW	GW	SW	GW		GW	GW	GW	GW	GW	GW	GW	GW	GW		GW	GW	GW	GW	GW	GW	GW	GW
																			R					R	
		◇	◇	◇	◇1				◇	◇1		◇	1	◇1		◇				◇		◇1		◇	◇1
										🍴				🍴								🍴			🍴
Brighton 10	d																							17 00	
Hove 2	d																							17 04	
Shoreham-by-Sea	d																							17 13	
Worthing 4	d																							17 22	
Barnham	d																							17 38	
Chichester 4	d																							17 46	
Havant	d																							18 00	
Portsmouth Harbour ⛴	d	11 23		12 23					13 23			14 23				15 23			16 23	17 23					
Portsmouth & Southsea	d	11 27		12 27					13 27			14 27				15 27			16 27	17 27					
Fratton	d	11 31		12 31					13 31			14 31				15 31			16 31	17 31					
Cosham	d	11 39		12 39					13 39			14 39				15 39			16 39	17 39				18 06	
Fareham	a	11 46		12 46					13 46			14 46				15 46			16 46	17 46				18 14	
	d	11 47		12 47					13 47			14 47				15 47			16 47	17 47				18 15	
Southampton Central ⛴	d	12 10	12 27	13 10					14 10			15 10				16 10			17 10	18 10				18 45	
Romsey	d	12 21	12 38	13 21					14 21			15 21				16 21			17 21	18 21				18 56	
Salisbury	a	12 40	13 03	13 40					14 40			15 40				16 40			17 40	18 40				19 15	
	d	12 41	13 04	13 41	13 52				14 41			15 41				16 41			17 41	18 41				19 16	
Warminster	d	13 01	13 25	14 01	14 12				15 01		15 28	16 01			16 28	17 01			18 01	19 01				19 37	
Dilton Marsh	d		13x29								15x33				16x33									19x42	
Weymouth	d					13 10												16 08			17 28				
Upwey	d					13 15												16 13			17 33				
Dorchester West	d					13 23												16 23			17 41				
Maiden Newton	d					13 43												16 42			17 52				
Chetnole	d					13x51												16 51			18x01				
Yetminster	d					13x54												16 54			18x04				
Thornford	d					13x56												16 56			18x06				
Yeovil Pen Mill	d					14 06												17 05			18 18				
Castle Cary	a					14 19												17 18			18 31				
	d					14 20				15 08			15 50	16 19				17 19			18 32	18 53			19 47
Bruton	d					14 26												17 25			18 38				
Frome	d					14 39												17 38			19 05		←		
Westbury	a	13 09	13 33	14 09	14 20	14 48			15 09	15 26	15 36	16 09		16 36	16 36	17 09		17 47	18 09	19 09	19 14	19 11	19 14	19 46	20 05
	d	13 10	13 38	14 10	14 21	14 48		15 06	15 10	15 28	15 38	16 10		16 38	16 38	17 10		17 48	18 10	19 10	19 17	19 12	19 17	19 49	20 06
Trowbridge	d	13 16	13 44	14 16	14 27	14 54		15 12	15 16		15 44	16 16			16 44	17 16		17 54	18 16	19 16	→		19 23	19 55	
Bradford-on-Avon	d	13 22	13 50	14 22	14 33	15 00			15 22		15 50	16 22			16 50	17 22		18 00	18 22	19 22			19 29	20 01	
Avoncliff	d		13 52			15 02					15 52				16 52			18 02					19 31	20 03	
Freshford	d		13 55			15 06					15 55				16 55			18 05					19 35	20 06	
Bath Spa 7	a	13 34	14 06	14 34	14 46	15 17			15 35		16 06	16 34			17 06	17 34		18 16	18 34	19 34			19 46	20 16	
Melksham	d							15 21																	
Chippenham	a							15 29																	
Swindon	a							15 49																	
London Paddington 15 ⊖	a									17 02			17 21	18 08								20 37			21 32
Oldfield Park	a		14 10			15 21					16 10				17 10			18 20					19 50	20 20	
Keynsham	a		14 17		14 54	15 28					16 17				17 17			18 26					19 57	20 27	
Bristol Temple Meads 10	a	13 48	14 29	14 48	15 05	15 36			15 49		16 29	16 48			17 28	17 48		18 35	18 48	19 48			20 05	20 35	
Filton Abbey Wood	a	14 00	14 48	15 00		15 48			16 00		16 48	17 00			17 48	18 00		18 48	19 00	20 00					
Severn Tunnel Jn.	a											17 14				18 13									
Newport (South Wales)	a	14 24		15 25					16 24			17 26				18 25			19 26	20 25					
Cardiff Central 7	a	14 43		15 43					16 43			17 42				18 42			19 43	20 43					

For connections to Swansea please refer to Table 128.
For connections to Exeter St Davids and Plymouth please refer to Table 135.
For connections from Bournemouth please refer to Table 158

Table 123

Saturdays
until 10 September

Portsmouth and Weymouth - Bristol and South Wales

		GW ◇	GW	GW	GW ◇	SW ◇ 1	GW	GW ◇	GW
Brighton 10	d								
Hove 2	d								
Shoreham-by-Sea	d								
Worthing 4	d								
Barnham	d								
Chichester 4	d								
Havant	d								
Portsmouth Harbour ⛴	d	18 23			19 23			20 23	
Portsmouth & Southsea	d	18 27			19 27			20 27	
Fratton	d	18 31			19 31			20 31	
Cosham	d	18 39			19 39				
Fareham	a	18 46			19 46			20 45	
	d	18 47			19 47			20 47	
Southampton Central ⛴	d	19 10			20 10			21 10	21 27
Romsey	d	19 21			20 21			21 21	21 38
Salisbury	a	19 40			20 40			21 41	22 03
	d	19 41			20 41	20 57		21 41	22 04
Warminster	d	20 01			21 01	21 17		22 01	22 25
Dilton Marsh	d								22x29
Weymouth	d						20 21		
Upwey	d						20 26		
Dorchester West	d						20 34		
Maiden Newton	d						20 45		
Chetnole	d						20x54		
Yetminster	d						20x57		
Thornford	d						20x59		
Yeovil Pen Mill	d						21 09		
Castle Cary	a						21 22		
	d						21 23		
Bruton	d						21 29		
Frome	d			20 53			21 42		
Westbury	a	20 09		21 02	21 09	21 25	21 51	22 10	22 33
	d	20 10	20 38		21 10	21 25	21 55	22 10	22 38
Trowbridge	d	20 16	20 44		21 16	21 31	22 01	22 16	22 44
Bradford-on-Avon	d	20 22	20 50		21 22	21 37	22 07	22 22	22 50
Avoncliff	d		20 52				22 09		22 52
Freshford	d		20 55				22 13		22 55
Bath Spa 7	a	20 34	21 06		21 37	21 50	22 24	22 36	23 06
Melksham	d								
Chippenham	a								
Swindon	a								
London Paddington 15 ⊖	a								
Oldfield Park	a		21 10				22 28		23 10
Keynsham	a		21 17			21 58	22 35		23 17
Bristol Temple Meads 10	a	20 48	21 29		21 51	22 06	22 44	22 50	23 29
Filton Abbey Wood	a	21 00			22 00			23 00	
Severn Tunnel Jn.	a				22 17			23 17	
Newport (South Wales)	a	21 25			22 38			23 35	
Cardiff Central 7	a	21 43			22 58			23 55	

For connections to Swansea please refer to Table 128.
For connections to Exeter St Davids and Plymouth please refer to Table 135.
For connections from Bournemouth please refer to Table 158

Table 123

Saturdays
from 17 September

Portsmouth and Weymouth - Bristol and South Wales

		GW	GW	GW	SW	GW	GW	GW	GW	GW	GW	GW	GW	GW	GW	GW	GW	GW	SW	GW	GW	GW	GW
					1		◇1 ☕	◇			◇ A 🚲	◇	◇1 ☕	◇ A 🚲			R 1 ☕	◇ A 🚲	◇1	◇	◇		◇1 ☕
Brighton 10	d																			09 00			
Hove 2	d																			09 04			
Shoreham-by-Sea	d																			09 13			
Worthing 4	d																			09 22			
Barnham	d																			09 41			
Chichester 4	d																			09 49			
Havant	d																			10 00			
Portsmouth Harbour ⛴	d							06 00			07 05			08 23				09 23			10 23		
Portsmouth & Southsea	d							06 04			07 09			08 27				09 27			10 27		
Fratton	d							06 08			07 14			08 31				09 31			10 31		
Cosham	d							06 19			07 21			08 39				09 39		10 06	10 39		
Fareham	a							06 27			07 29			08 46				09 46		10 15	10 46		
	d							06 28			07 30			08 47				09 47		10 16	10 47		
Southampton Central ⛴	d							06 53			07 54	08 27		09 10				10 10		10 42	11 10		
Romsey	d							07 11			08 12	08 38		09 21				10 21		10 53	11 21		
Salisbury	a							07 29			08 30	09 03		09 40				10 40		11 13	11 40		
	d	06 03	06 03		06 40			07 30			08 34	09 03		09 41				10 41	10 52	11 13	11 41		
Warminster	d	06 23			07 00	07 23		07 50			08 54	09 23		10 01		10 25		11 01	11 12	11 34	12 01		
Dilton Marsh	d	06x27				07x27		07x54				09x28				10x29							
Weymouth	d								06 40						08 46							11 10	
Upwey	d								06 45						08 51							11 15	
Dorchester West	d								06 53						08 59							11 26	
Maiden Newton	d								07 05						09 11							11 43	
Chetnole	d								07x13						09x19							11x50	
Yetminster	d								07x16						09x22							11x53	
Thornford	d								07x18						09x24							11x56	
Yeovil Pen Mill	d								07 30						09 34							12 05	
Castle Cary	a								07 43						09 47							12 19	
	d						07 33		07 44				09 40		09 48							12 22	12 45
Bruton	d								07 49						09 54							12 27	
Frome	d			06 37					08 02						10 07							12 39	
Westbury	a	06 31	06 34	06 46	07 08	07 31	07 51	07 59	08 13		09 00	09 33	09 58	10 09	10 16	10 33		11 09	11 20	11 42	12 09	12 48	13 03
	d		06 38	06 51	07 09	07 38	07 56	08 10	08 17	09 05	09 10	09 38	09 59	10 10	10 38		11 02	11 10	11 21	11 42	12 10	12 49	13 05
Trowbridge	d		06 44	06 57	07 15	07 44		08 16	08 23	09 11	09 16	09 44		10 16	10 44			11 16	11 27	11 48	12 16	12 55	
Bradford-on-Avon	d		06 50	07 03	07 21	07 50		08 22	08 29		09 22	09 50		10 22	10 50			11 22	11 33	11 54	12 22	13 01	
Avoncliff	d		06 52	07 05		07 52			08 31			09 52			10 52					11 57		13 03	
Freshford	d		06 55	07 09		07 55			08 34			09 55			10 55					12 00		13 05	
Bath Spa 7	a		07 06	07 20	07 33	08 06		08 34	08 45		09 34	10 06		10 34	11 06			11 34	11 46	12 10	12 34	13 17	
Melksham	d									09 20													
Chippenham	a									09 30													
Swindon	a									09 49													
London Paddington 15 ⊖	a						09 21						11 24				12 23						14 45
Oldfield Park	a		07 10	07 24	07 37	08 10			08 49			10 10			11 10					12 14		13 20	
Keynsham	a		07 17	07 31	07 44	08 17			08 56			10 17			11 17				11 54	12 21		13 27	
Bristol Temple Meads 10	a		07 29	07 39	07 53	08 29		08 47	09 05		09 48	10 29		10 48	11 29			11 48	12 05	12 29	12 48	13 36	
Filton Abbey Wood	a		07 48	08 00		08 48		09 00			10 00	10 48		11 00	11 48			12 00		12 48	13 00	13 48	
Severn Tunnel Jn.	a																						
Newport (South Wales)	a			08 26				09 25			10 24			11 24				12 24			13 25		
Cardiff Central 7	a			08 43				09 42			10 43			11 43				12 43			13 43		

A 🚲 to Bath Spa

For connections to Swansea please refer to Table 128.
For connections to Exeter St Davids and Plymouth please refer to Table 135.
For connections from Bournemouth please refer to Table 158

Table 123

Saturdays

from 17 September

Portsmouth and Weymouth - Bristol and South Wales

		GW	GW	GW	SW	GW		GW	GW	GW	GW	GW	GW	GW	GW	GW		GW	GW	GW	GW	GW	GW	GW	GW
																			R						R
		◇	◇	◇	◇1			◇1		◇		◇1	◇1	◇		◇					◇		◇1		◇
								A ∅					🍴										🍴		
Brighton 10	d																								17 00
Hove 2	d																								17 04
Shoreham-by-Sea	d																								17 13
Worthing 4	d																								17 22
Barnham	d																								17 38
Chichester 4	d																								17 46
Havant	d																								18 00
Portsmouth Harbour ⛴	d	11 23		12 23						13 23				14 23		15 23			16 23		17 23				
Portsmouth & Southsea	d	11 27		12 27						13 27				14 27		15 27			16 27		17 27				
Fratton	d	11 31		12 31						13 31				14 31		15 31			16 31		17 31				
Cosham	d	11 39		12 39						13 39				14 39		15 39			16 39		17 39				18 06
Fareham	a	11 46		12 46						13 46				14 46		15 46			16 46		17 46				18 14
	d	11 47		12 47						13 47				14 47		15 47			16 47		17 47				18 15
Southampton Central ⛴	d	12 10	12 27	13 10						14 10				15 10		16 10			17 10		18 10				18 45
Romsey	d	12 21	12 38	13 21						14 21				15 21		16 21			17 21		18 21				18 56
Salisbury	a	12 40	13 03	13 40						14 40				15 40		16 40			17 40		18 40				19 15
	d	12 41	13 04	13 41	13 52					14 41				15 41		16 41			17 41		18 41				19 16
Warminster	d	13 01	13 25	14 01	14 12					15 01	15 28			16 01		17 01		17 28	18 01		19 01				19 37
Dilton Marsh	d		13x29								15x33							17 32							19x42
Weymouth	d					13 10									15 08							17 28			
Upwey	d					13 15									15 13							17 33			
Dorchester West	d					13 23									15 21							17 41			
Maiden Newton	d					13 43									15 33							17 52			
Chetnole	d					13x51									15x42							18x01			
Yetminster	d					13x54									15x45							18x04			
Thornford	d					13x56									15x47							18x06			
Yeovil Pen Mill	d					14 06									15 56							18 18			
Castle Cary	a					14 19									16 09							18 31			
	d					14 20		14 44				15 49			16 10							18 32	18 53		
Bruton	d					14 26									16 16							18 38			
Frome	d					14 39							15 55		16 29							19 05		←	
Westbury	a	13 09	13 33	14 09	14 20	14 48		15 02		15 09	15 36		16 05	16 09	16 38	17 09		17 36	18 09		19 09	19 14	19 11	19 14	19 46
	d	13 10	13 38	14 10	14 21	14 48		15 03	15 06	15 10	15 38		16 07	16 10	16 38	17 10		17 38	18 10	18 38	19 10	19 17	19 12	19 17	19 49
Trowbridge	d	13 16	13 44	14 16	14 27	14 54			15 12	15 16	15 44			16 16	16 44	17 16		17 44	18 16	18 44	19 16	↪		19 23	19 55
Bradford-on-Avon	d	13 22	13 50	14 22	14 33	15 00				15 22	15 50			16 22	16 50	17 22		17 50	18 22	18 50	19 22			19 29	20 01
Avoncliff	d		13 52			15 02					15 52				16 52			17 52		18 52				19 31	20 03
Freshford	d		13 55			15 06					15 55				16 55			17 55		18 55				19 35	20 06
Bath Spa 7	a	13 34	14 06	14 34	14 46	15 17				15 35	16 06			16 34	17 06	17 34		18 06	18 34	19 06	19 34			19 46	20 16
Melksham	d								15 21																
Chippenham	a								15 29																
Swindon	a								15 49																
London Paddington 15 ⊖	a							16 23				17 21	17 51										20 37		
Oldfield Park	a		14 10			15 21					16 10				17 10			18 10		19 10				19 50	20 20
Keynsham	a		14 17		14 54	15 28					16 17				17 17			18 16		19 17				19 57	20 27
Bristol Temple Meads 10	a	13 48	14 29	14 48	15 05	15 36				15 49	16 29			16 48	17 29	17 48		18 29	18 48	19 29	19 48			20 05	20 35
Filton Abbey Wood	a	14 00	14 48	15 00		15 48				16 00	16 48			17 00	17 48	18 00		18 48	19 00	19 48	20 00				
Severn Tunnel Jn.	a													17 14		18 13									
Newport (South Wales)	a	14 24		15 25						16 24				17 26		18 25			19 26		20 25				
Cardiff Central 7	a	14 43		15 43						16 43				17 42		18 42			19 43		20 43				

A ∅ to Westbury

For connections to Swansea please refer to Table 128.
For connections to Exeter St Davids and Plymouth please refer to Table 135.
For connections from Bournemouth please refer to Table 158

Table 123

Saturdays
from 17 September

Portsmouth and Weymouth - Bristol and South Wales

		GW	GW	GW	GW	GW	SW	GW	GW	GW
		◇[1]	◇			◇	◇[1]		◇	
		🍴								
Brighton [10]	d									
Hove [2]	d									
Shoreham-by-Sea	d									
Worthing [4]	d									
Barnham	d									
Chichester [4]	d									
Havant	d									
Portsmouth Harbour ⛴	d		18 23			19 23			20 23	
Portsmouth & Southsea	d		18 27			19 27			20 27	
Fratton	d		18 31			19 31			20 31	
Cosham	d		18 39			19 39				
Fareham	a		18 46			19 46			20 45	
	d		18 47			19 47			20 47	
Southampton Central ⛴	d		19 10			20 10			21 10	21 27
Romsey	d		19 21			20 21			21 21	21 38
Salisbury	a		19 40			20 40			21 41	22 03
	d		19 41			20 41	20 57		21 41	22 04
Warminster	d		20 01			21 01	21 17		22 01	22 25
Dilton Marsh	d									22x29
Weymouth	d							20 21		
Upwey	d							20 26		
Dorchester West	d							20 34		
Maiden Newton	d							20 45		
Chetnole	d							20x54		
Yetminster	d							20x57		
Thornford	d							20x59		
Yeovil Pen Mill	d							21 09		
Castle Cary	a							21 22		
	d	19 47						21 23		
Bruton	d							21 29		
Frome	d				20 53			21 42		
Westbury	a	20 05	20 09		21 02	21 09	21 25	21 51	22 10	22 33
	d	20 06	20 10	20 38		21 10	21 25	21 55	22 10	22 38
Trowbridge	d		20 16	20 44		21 16	21 31	22 01	22 16	22 44
Bradford-on-Avon	d		20 22	20 50		21 22	21 37	22 07	22 22	22 50
Avoncliff	d			20 52				22 09		22 52
Freshford	d			20 55				22 13		22 55
Bath Spa [7]	a		20 34	21 06		21 37	21 50	22 24	22 36	23 06
Melksham	d									
Chippenham	a									
Swindon	a									
London Paddington [15] ⊖	a	21 32								
Oldfield Park	a			21 10				22 28		23 10
Keynsham	a			21 17			21 58	22 35		23 17
Bristol Temple Meads [10]	a		20 48	21 29		21 51	22 06	22 44	22 50	23 29
Filton Abbey Wood	a		21 00			22 00			23 00	
Severn Tunnel Jn	a					22 17			23 17	
Newport (South Wales)	a		21 25			22 38			23 35	
Cardiff Central [7]	a		21 43			22 58			23 55	

For connections to Swansea please refer to Table 128.
For connections to Exeter St Davids and Plymouth please refer to Table 135.
For connections from Bournemouth please refer to Table 158

Table 123

Sundays
until 19 June

Portsmouth and Weymouth - Bristol and South Wales

		GW	GW	GW	GW	GW	GW	GW	GW	GW		GW	GW	SW	GW	GW	GW	GW	GW	GW		GW	GW	GW	GW
						Ⓡ													Ⓡ						
		◇1	◇1		◇1				◇1	◇		◇	◇1	◇1	◇		◇1	◇					◇1	◇	◇
		A	B																						
		☕	☕		☕				☕				☕				☕						☕		
Brighton 10	d											11 10													15 46
Hove 2	d											11 14													15 50
Shoreham-by-Sea	d											11 20													15 56
Worthing 4	d											11 29													16 08
Barnham	d											11 46													16 25
Chichester 4	d											11 54													16 34
Havant	d											12 10													16 48
Portsmouth Harbour ⛴	d					09 08				11 08					13 08			14 08	15 08					16 08	
Portsmouth & Southsea	d					09 12				11 12					13 12			14 12	15 12					16 12	
Fratton	d					09 16				11 16					13 16			14 16	15 16					16 16	
Cosham	d					09 23				11 23		12 23			13 23			14 23	15 23					16 23	16 55
Fareham	a					09 31				11 31		12 31			13 31			14 31	15 31					16 31	17 02
	d					09 32				11 32		12 32			13 32			14 32	15 32					16 32	17 03
Southampton Central ⛴	d					09 54				11 54		12 54			13 54			14 54	15 54					16 54	17 26
Romsey	d					10 06				12 06		13 06			14 06			15 06	16 06					17 06	17 39
Salisbury	a					10 24				12 24		13 24			14 24			15 24	16 24					17 24	18 01
	d					10 26				12 27		13 28		13 55	14 27			15 28	16 28					17 28	18 02
Warminster	d					10 46				12 48		13 47		14 15	14 48			15 48	16 48					17 48	18 22
Dilton Marsh	d					10x51									14x53			15x53	16x53						18x27
Weymouth	d							11 14								14 12						16 10			
Upwey	d							11 19								14 17						16 15			
Dorchester West	d							11 28								14 25						16 23			
Maiden Newton	d							11 40								14 37						16 35			
Chetnole	d							11x48								14x45						16x43			
Yetminster	d							11x51								14x48						16x46			
Thornford	d							11x53								14x50						16x48			
Yeovil Pen Mill	d							12 03								15 04						16 58			
Castle Cary	a							12 15								15 17						17 10			
	d	09 29	09 29					12 17	12 34							15 18	15 34					17 13	17 37		
Bruton	d							12 22								15 24						17 18			
Frome	d			09 35				12 35								15 37						17 31			
Westbury	a	09 46	09 46	09 44		10 54		12 44	12 52	12 54		13 55		14 23	14 58	15 46	15 51	15 56	16 56			17 40	17 54	17 58	18 31
	d	09 49	09 49	09 58	10 51	11 00	11 54		12 53	12 56		13 56	13 59	14 24	15 02	15 46	15 52	15 59	17 00	17 10		17 41	17 57	18 02	18 32
Trowbridge	d			10 04		11 06	12 00			13 02		14 02		14 30	15 08	15 52		16 05	17 06	17 16		17 47		18 08	18 38
Bradford-on-Avon	d			10 09		11 12	12 06			13 08		14 08		14 36	15 14	15 58		16 11	17 12			17 53			18 44
Avoncliff	d			10 12			12 09					14 11				16 01		16 14				17 56			18 47
Freshford	d			10 15			12 11					14 13				16 03		16 17				17 59			18 50
Bath Spa 7	a			10 26		11 25	12 21			13 22		14 24		14 49	15 27	16 14		16 28	17 25			18 10		18 27	19 01
Melksham	d																			17 25					
Chippenham	a																			17 39					
Swindon	a																			17 56					
London Paddington 15 ⊖	a	11 27	11 31		12 27				14 29				15 27				17 27						19 37		
Oldfield Park	a			10 30		11 28	12 25			13 25		14 27				16 17			17 28			18 13			19 05
Keynsham	a			10 37		11 35	12 32			13 32		14 35		14 57		16 25			17 35			18 21			19 12
Bristol Temple Meads 10	a			10 45		11 43	12 40			13 40		14 44		15 05	15 40	16 33		16 41	17 43			18 33		18 40	19 21
Filton Abbey Wood	a					11 55				13 55		14 55			15 55			16 55	17 55					18 55	
Severn Tunnel Jn.	a					12 10				14 09		15 07			16 09			17 10	18 08					19 07	
Newport (South Wales)	a					12 29				14 29		15 26			16 28			17 29	18 27					19 26	
Cardiff Central 7	a					12 44				14 53		15 41			16 46			17 46	18 45					19 42	

A not 5 June

B 5 June

For connections to Swansea please refer to Table 128.
For connections to Exeter St Davids and Plymouth please refer to Table 135.
For connections from Bournemouth please refer to Table 158

Table 123

Sundays
until 19 June

Portsmouth and Weymouth - Bristol and South Wales

		GW ◇	GW ◇1 ☕	GW	GW	GW ◇		SW ◇1	GW ◇1 ☕	GW ◇		GW ◇	GW ◇1 ☕	GW	GW ◇	GW
Brighton 10	d									17 46						
Hove 2	d									17 50						
Shoreham-by-Sea	d									17 56						
Worthing 4	d									18 08						
Barnham	d									18 25						
Chichester 4	d									18 34						
Havant	d									18 48						
Portsmouth Harbour ⛴	d	17 08				18 08						19 08			20 08	22 03
Portsmouth & Southsea	d	17 12				18 12						19 12			20 12	22 12
Fratton	d	17 16				18 16						19 16			20 16	22 16
Cosham	d	17 23				18 23				18 55		19 23				
Fareham	a	17 31				18 31				19 02		19 31			20 31	22 31
	d	17 32				18 32				19 03		19 32			20 32	22 32
Southampton Central ⛴	d	17 54				18 54				19 30		19 54			20 54	22 57
Romsey	d	18 06				19 06				19 42		20 06			21 06	23 09
Salisbury	a	18 24				19 24				20 00		20 24			21 24	23 27
	d	18 28				19 25		19 55		20 03		20 28			21 28	23 28
Warminster	d	18 48				19 48		20 15		20 23		20 48			21 48	23 53
Dilton Marsh	d									20x28					21x53	23x58
Weymouth	d			17 56										20 09		
Upwey	d			18 01										20 14		
Dorchester West	d			18 09										20 22		
Maiden Newton	d			18 21										20 34		
Chetnole	d			18x29										20x42		
Yetminster	d			18x32										20x45		
Thornford	d			18x34										20x47		
Yeovil Pen Mill	d			18 44										20 57		
Castle Cary	a			18 56										21 09		
	d			18 59					20 08				21 15	21 19		
Bruton	d			19 05										21 25		
Frome	d			19 18										21 38		
Westbury	a	18 55		19 27		19 55		20 23	20 27	20 32		20 56	21 33	21 47	21 56	00 02
	d	19 01	19 09	19 30	19 35	20 01		20 23	20 27	20 37		21 02	21 34	21 49	22 02	
Trowbridge	d	19 07		19 36	19 42	20 07		20 29		20 43		21 08		21 55	22 08	
Bradford-on-Avon	d	19 13		19 42		20 13		20 35		20 49		21 14		22 01	22 14	
Avoncliff	d			19 45						20 52				22 04		
Freshford	d			19 48						20 56				22 07		
Bath Spa 7	a	19 28		19 59		20 26		20 48		21 08		21 27		22 18	22 29	
Melksham	d				19 52											
Chippenham	a				20 02											
Swindon	a				20 20											
London Paddington 15 ⊖	a		20 37						21 52				23 15			
Oldfield Park	a			20 02						21 11				22 21		
Keynsham	a			20 10				20 56		21 19				22 29		
Bristol Temple Meads 10	a	19 41		20 18		20 39		21 04		21 27		21 40		22 37	22 42	
Filton Abbey Wood	a	19 55				20 55						21 55			22 55	
Severn Tunnel Jn.	a	20 10				21 07						22 12			23 07	
Newport (South Wales)	a	20 28				21 26						22 39			23 28	
Cardiff Central 7	a	20 46				21 42						23 02			23 49	

For connections to Swansea please refer to Table 128.
For connections to Exeter St Davids and Plymouth please refer to Table 135.
For connections from Bournemouth please refer to Table 158

Table 123

Sundays
26 June to 31 July

Portsmouth and Weymouth - Bristol and South Wales

		GW	GW	GW	GW	GW	GW	GW	GW	GW	GW	SW	GW	GW	GW	GW	GW	GW	GW	GW	GW	GW	GW
					■												■						
		◇1		◇1				◇1	◇	◇	◇1	◇1	◇		◇1	◇				◇1	◇	◇	◇
		🍴		🍴				🍴			🍴				🍴					🍴			
Brighton 10	d									11 10												15 46	
Hove 2	d									11 14												15 50	
Shoreham-by-Sea	d									11 20												15 56	
Worthing 4	d									11 29												16 08	
Barnham	d									11 46												16 25	
Chichester 4	d									11 54												16 34	
Havant	d									12 10												16 48	
Portsmouth Harbour ⛴	d				09 08				11 08				13 08			14 08	15 08				16 08		17 08
Portsmouth & Southsea	d				09 12				11 12				13 12			14 12	15 12				16 12		17 12
Fratton	d				09 16				11 16				13 16			14 16	15 16				16 16		17 16
Cosham	d				09 23				11 23	12 23			13 23			14 23	15 23				16 23	16 55	17 23
Fareham	a				09 31				11 31	12 31			13 31			14 31	15 31				16 31	17 02	17 31
	d				09 32				11 32	12 32			13 32			14 32	15 32				16 32	17 03	17 32
Southampton Central ⛴	d				09 54				11 54	12 54			13 54			14 54	15 54				16 54	17 26	17 54
Romsey	d				10 06				12 06	13 06			14 06			15 06	16 06				17 06	17 39	18 06
Salisbury	a				10 24				12 24	13 24			14 24			15 24	16 24				17 24	18 01	18 24
	d				10 26				12 27	13 28		13 55	14 27			15 28	16 28				17 28	18 02	18 28
Warminster	d				10 46				12 48	13 47		14 15	14 48			15 48	16 48				17 48	18 22	18 48
Dilton Marsh	d				10x51								14x53			15x53	16x53					18x27	
Weymouth	d						11 14							14 12					16 10				
Upwey	d						11 19							14 17					16 15				
Dorchester West	d						11 28							14 25					16 23				
Maiden Newton	d						11 40							14 37					16 35				
Chetnole	d						11x48							14x45					16x43				
Yetminster	d						11x51							14x48					16x46				
Thornford	d						11x53							14x50					16x48				
Yeovil Pen Mill	d						12 03							15 04					16 58				
Castle Cary	a						12 15							15 17					17 10				
	d	09 29					12 17	12 34						15 18	15 34				17 13	17 37			
Bruton	d						12 22							15 24					17 18				
Frome	d		09 35				12 35							15 37					17 31				
Westbury	a	09 46	09 44		10 54		12 44	12 52	12 54	13 55		14 23	14 58	15 46	15 51	15 56	16 56		17 40	17 54	17 58	18 31	18 55
	d	09 49	09 58	10 51	11 00	11 54		12 53	12 56	13 56	13 59	14 24	15 02	15 46	15 52	15 59	17 00	17 10	17 41	17 57	18 02	18 32	19 01
Trowbridge	d		10 04		11 06	12 00			13 02	14 02		14 30	15 08	15 52		16 05	17 06	17 16	17 47		18 08	18 38	19 07
Bradford-on-Avon	d		10 09		11 12	12 06			13 08	14 08		14 36	15 14	15 58		16 11	17 12		17 53			18 44	19 13
Avoncliff	d		10 12			12 09				14 11				16 01		16 14			17 56			18 47	
Freshford	d		10 15			12 11				14 13				16 03		16 17			17 59			18 50	
Bath Spa 7	a		10 26		11 25	12 21			13 22	14 24		14 49	15 27	16 14		16 28	17 25		18 10		18 27	19 01	19 28
Melksham	d																	17 25					
Chippenham	a																	17 39					
Swindon	a																	17 56					
London Paddington 15 ⊖	a	11 27		12 27				14 29			15 27				17 27					19 37			
Oldfield Park	a		10 30		11 28	12 25			13 25	14 27				16 17			17 28		18 13			19 05	
Keynsham	a		10 37		11 35	12 32			13 32	14 35		14 57		16 25			17 35		18 21			19 12	
Bristol Temple Meads 10	a		10 45		11 43	12 40			13 40	14 44		15 05	15 40	16 33		16 41	17 43		18 33		18 40	19 21	19 41
Filton Abbey Wood	a				11 55				13 55	14 55			15 55			16 55	17 55				18 55		19 55
Severn Tunnel Jn.	a				12 10				14 09	15 07			16 09			17 10	18 08				19 07		20 10
Newport (South Wales)	a				12 29				14 29	15 26			16 28			17 29	18 27				19 26		20 28
Cardiff Central 7	a				12 44				14 53	15 41			16 46			17 46	18 45				19 42		20 46

For connections to Swansea please refer to Table 128.
For connections to Exeter St Davids and Plymouth please refer to Table 135.
For connections from Bournemouth please refer to Table 158

Table 123

Sundays
26 June to 31 July

Portsmouth and Weymouth - Bristol and South Wales

		GW	GW	GW	GW	SW		GW	GW	GW	GW	GW	GW	GW
		◇■1			◇	◇■1		◇■1	◇	◇	◇■1		◇	
		⊡						⊡			⊡			
Brighton ■10	d								17 46					
Hove ■2	d								17 50					
Shoreham-by-Sea	d								17 56					
Worthing ■4	d								18 08					
Barnham	d								18 25					
Chichester ■4	d								18 34					
Havant	d								18 48					
Portsmouth Harbour ⛴	d				18 08					19 08			20 08	22 03
Portsmouth & Southsea	d				18 12					19 12			20 12	22 12
Fratton	d				18 16					19 16			20 16	22 16
Cosham	d				18 23				18 55	19 23				
Fareham	a				18 31				19 02	19 31			20 31	22 31
	d				18 32				19 03	19 32			20 32	22 32
Southampton Central ⛴	d				18 54				19 30	19 54			20 54	22 57
Romsey	d				19 06				19 42	20 06			21 06	23 09
Salisbury	a				19 24				20 00	20 24			21 24	23 27
	d				19 25	19 55			20 03	20 28			21 28	23 28
Warminster	d				19 48	20 15			20 23	20 48			21 48	23 53
Dilton Marsh	d								20x28				21x53	23x58
Weymouth	d		17 56									20 09		
Upwey	d		18 01									20 14		
Dorchester West	d		18 09									20 22		
Maiden Newton	d		18 21									20 34		
Chetnole	d		18x29									20x42		
Yetminster	d		18x32									20x45		
Thornford	d		18x34									20x47		
Yeovil Pen Mill	d		18 44									20 57		
Castle Cary	a		18 56									21 09		
	d		18 59					20 08			21 15	21 19		
Bruton	d		19 05									21 25		
Frome	d		19 18									21 38		
Westbury	a		19 27		19 55	20 23		20 27	20 32	20 56	21 33	21 47	21 56	00 02
	d	19 09	19 30	19 30	20 01	20 23		20 27	20 37	21 02	21 34	21 49	22 02	
Trowbridge	d		19 36	19 37	20 07	20 29			20 43	21 08		21 55	22 08	
Bradford-on-Avon	d		19 42		20 13	20 35			20 49	21 14		22 01	22 14	
Avoncliff	d		19 45						20 52			22 04		
Freshford	d		19 48						20 56			22 07		
Bath Spa ■7	a		19 59		20 26	20 48			21 08	21 27		22 18	22 29	
Melksham	d			19 47										
Chippenham	a			19 57										
Swindon	a			20 15										
London Paddington ■15 ⊖	a	20 37						21 52			23 15			
Oldfield Park	a		20 02						21 11			22 21		
Keynsham	a		20 10			20 56			21 19			22 29		
Bristol Temple Meads ■10	a		20 18		20 39	21 04			21 27	21 40		22 37	22 42	
Filton Abbey Wood	a				20 55					21 55			22 55	
Severn Tunnel Jn.	a				21 07					22 12			23 07	
Newport (South Wales)	a				21 26					22 36			23 28	
Cardiff Central ■7	a				21 42					22 59			23 49	

For connections to Swansea please refer to Table 128.
For connections to Exeter St Davids and Plymouth please refer to Table 135.
For connections from Bournemouth please refer to Table 158

Table 123

Sundays

7 August to 11 September

Portsmouth and Weymouth - Bristol and South Wales

		GW	GW	GW	GW	GW	GW	GW	GW	GW	GW	SW
		◇1 ☕		◇1 ☕	R			◇	◇1 ☕	◇	◇1 ☕	◇1
Brighton 10	d									11 10		
Hove 2	d									11 14		
Shoreham-by-Sea	d									11 20		
Worthing 4	d									11 29		
Barnham	d									11 46		
Chichester 4	d									11 54		
Havant	d									12 10		
Portsmouth Harbour ⛴	d				09 08			11 08				
Portsmouth & Southsea	d				09 12			11 12				
Fratton	d				09 16			11 16				
Cosham	d				09 23			11 23		12 23		
Fareham	a				09 31			11 31		12 31		
	d				09 32			11 32		12 32		
Southampton Central ⛴	d				09 54			11 54		12 54		
Romsey	d				10 06			12 06		13 06		
Salisbury	a				10 24			12 24		13 24		
	d				10 26			12 27		13 28		13 55
Warminster	d				10 46			12 48		13 47		14 15
Dilton Marsh	d				10x51							
Weymouth	d						11 14					
Upwey	d						11 19					
Dorchester West	d						11 28					
Maiden Newton	d						11 40					
Chetnole	d						11x48					
Yetminster	d						11x51					
Thornford	d						11x53					
Yeovil Pen Mill	d						12 03					
Castle Cary	a						12 15					
	d	09 21					12 17		12 34			
Bruton	d						12 22					
Frome	d		09 25				12 35					
Westbury	a	09 38	09 34		10 54		12 44	12 54	12 52	13 55		14 23
	d	09 41	09 46	10 51	11 00	11 54		12 56	12 59	13 56	13 59	14 24
Trowbridge	d		09 52		11 06	12 00		13 02		14 02		14 30
Bradford-on-Avon	d		09 57		11 12	12 06		13 08		14 08		14 36
Avoncliff	d		10 00			12 09				14 11		
Freshford	d		10 03			12 11				14 13		
Bath Spa 7	a		10 14		11 25	12 21		13 22		14 24		14 49
Melksham	d											
Chippenham	a											
Swindon	a	10 21							13 32			
London Paddington 15 ⊖	a	11 35		12 35					14 44		15 43	
Oldfield Park	a		10 18		11 28	12 25		13 25		14 27		
Keynsham	a		10 25		11 35	12 32		13 32		14 35		14 57
Bristol Temple Meads 10	a		10 33		11 43	12 40		13 40		14 44		15 05
Filton Abbey Wood	a				11 55			13 55		14 55		
Severn Tunnel Jn.	a				12 10			14 09		15 07		
Newport (South Wales)	a				12 29			14 29		15 26		
Cardiff Central 7	a				12 44			14 53		15 41		

		GW	GW	GW	GW	GW	GW	GW	GW	GW	GW	GW
		◇		◇1 ☕	◇	R			◇1 ☕	◇	◇	◇
Brighton 10	d										15 46	
Hove 2	d										15 50	
Shoreham-by-Sea	d										15 56	
Worthing 4	d										16 08	
Barnham	d										16 25	
Chichester 4	d										16 34	
Havant	d										16 48	
Portsmouth Harbour ⛴	d	13 08			14 08	15 08				16 08		17 08
Portsmouth & Southsea	d	13 12			14 12	15 12				16 12		17 12
Fratton	d	13 16			14 16	15 16				16 16		17 16
Cosham	d	13 23			14 23	15 23				16 23	16 55	17 23
Fareham	a	13 31			14 31	15 31				16 31	17 02	17 31
	d	13 32			14 32	15 32				16 32	17 03	17 32
Southampton Central ⛴	d	13 54			14 54	15 54				16 54	17 26	17 54
Romsey	d	14 06			15 06	16 06				17 06	17 39	18 06
Salisbury	a	14 24			15 24	16 24				17 24	18 01	18 24
	d	14 27			15 28	16 28				17 28	18 02	18 28
Warminster	d	14 48			15 48	16 48				17 48	18 22	18 48
Dilton Marsh	d	14x53			15x53	16x53					18x27	
Weymouth	d		14 12					16 10				
Upwey	d		14 17					16 15				
Dorchester West	d		14 25					16 23				
Maiden Newton	d		14 37					16 35				
Chetnole	d		14x45					16x43				
Yetminster	d		14x48					16x46				
Thornford	d		14x50					16x48				
Yeovil Pen Mill	d		15 04					16 58				
Castle Cary	a		15 17					17 10				
	d		15 18	15 34				17 13	17 37			
Bruton	d		15 24					17 18				
Frome	d		15 37					17 31				
Westbury	a	14 58	15 46	15 51	15 56	16 56		17 40	17 54	17 58	18 31	18 55
	d	15 02	15 46	15 52	15 59	17 00	17 10	17 41	17 57	18 02	18 32	19 01
Trowbridge	d	15 08	15 52		16 05	17 06	17 16	17 47		18 08	18 38	19 07
Bradford-on-Avon	d	15 14	15 58		16 11	17 12		17 53			18 44	19 13
Avoncliff	d		16 01		16 14			17 56			18 47	
Freshford	d		16 03		16 17			17 59			18 50	
Bath Spa 7	a	15 27	16 14		16 28	17 25		18 10		18 27	19 01	19 28
Melksham	d						17 25					
Chippenham	a						17 39					
Swindon	a						17 56					
London Paddington 15 ⊖	a			17 36					19 35			
Oldfield Park	a		16 17			17 28		18 13			19 05	
Keynsham	a		16 25			17 35		18 21			19 12	
Bristol Temple Meads 10	a	15 40	16 33		16 41	17 43		18 33		18 40	19 21	19 41
Filton Abbey Wood	a	15 55			16 55	17 55				18 55		19 55
Severn Tunnel Jn.	a	16 09			17 10	18 08				19 07		20 10
Newport (South Wales)	a	16 28			17 29	18 27				19 26		20 28
Cardiff Central 7	a	16 46			17 46	18 45				19 42		20 46

For connections to Swansea please refer to Table 128.
For connections to Exeter St Davids and Plymouth please refer to Table 135.
For connections from Bournemouth please refer to Table 158

Table 123

Sundays

7 August to 11 September

Portsmouth and Weymouth - Bristol and South Wales

		GW	GW	GW	GW	SW		GW	GW	GW	GW	GW	GW	GW
		◇■1 ⊡			◇	◇■1		◇■1 ⊡	◇	◇	◇■1 ⊡		◇	
Brighton ■10	d								17 46					
Hove ■2	d								17 50					
Shoreham-by-Sea	d								17 56					
Worthing ■4	d								18 08					
Barnham	d								18 25					
Chichester ■4	d								18 34					
Havant	d								18 48					
Portsmouth Harbour ⛴	d				18 08					19 08			20 08	22 03
Portsmouth & Southsea	d				18 12					19 12			20 12	22 12
Fratton	d				18 16					19 16			20 16	22 16
Cosham	d				18 23				18 55	19 23				
Fareham	a				18 31				19 02	19 31			20 31	22 31
	d				18 32				19 03	19 32			20 32	22 32
Southampton Central ⛴	d				18 54				19 30	19 54			20 54	22 57
Romsey	d				19 06				19 42	20 06			21 06	23 09
Salisbury	a				19 24				20 00	20 24			21 24	23 27
	d				19 25	19 55			20 03	20 28			21 28	23 28
Warminster	d				19 48	20 15			20 23	20 48			21 48	23 53
Dilton Marsh	d								20x28				21x53	23x58
Weymouth	d		17 56									20 09		
Upwey	d		18 01									20 14		
Dorchester West	d		18 09									20 22		
Maiden Newton	d		18 21									20 34		
Chetnole	d		18x29									20x42		
Yetminster	d		18x32									20x45		
Thornford	d		18x34									20x47		
Yeovil Pen Mill	d		18 44									20 57		
Castle Cary	a		18 56									21 09		
	d		18 59					20 08			21 15	21 19		
Bruton	d		19 05									21 25		
Frome	d		19 18									21 38		
Westbury	a		19 27		19 55	20 23		20 27	20 32	20 56	21 33	21 47	21 56	00 02
	d	19 09	19 30	19 35	20 01	20 23		20 28	20 37	21 02	21 34	21 49	22 02	
Trowbridge	d		19 36	19 42	20 07	20 29			20 43	21 08		21 55	22 08	
Bradford-on-Avon	d		19 42		20 13	20 35			20 49	21 14		22 01	22 14	
Avoncliff	d		19 45						20 52			22 04		
Freshford	d		19 48						20 56			22 07		
Bath Spa ■7	a		19 59		20 26	20 48			21 08	21 27		22 18	22 29	
Melksham	d			19 52										
Chippenham	a			20 02										
Swindon	a			20 20										
London Paddington ■15 ⊖	a	20 36						21 54			23 12			
Oldfield Park	a		20 02						21 11			22 21		
Keynsham	a		20 10			20 56			21 19			22 29		
Bristol Temple Meads ■10	a		20 18		20 39	21 04			21 27	21 40		22 37	22 42	
Filton Abbey Wood	a				20 55					21 55			22 55	
Severn Tunnel Jn.	a				21 07					22 12			23 07	
Newport (South Wales)	a				21 26					22 36			23 28	
Cardiff Central ■7	a				21 42					22 59			23 49	

For connections to Swansea please refer to Table 128.
For connections to Exeter St Davids and Plymouth please refer to Table 135.
For connections from Bournemouth please refer to Table 158

Table 123

Sundays

18 September to 23 October

Portsmouth and Weymouth - Bristol and South Wales

		GW	GW	GW	GW	GW	GW	GW	GW	GW		SW	GW	GW	GW	GW	GW	GW	GW	GW		GW	GW	GW	GW
					R												R								
		◇1		◇1			◇	◇1	◇	◇1		◇1	◇		◇1	◇			◇1	◇		◇	◇		
		☕		☕				☕		☕					☕				☕						
Brighton 10	d								11 10													15 46			
Hove 2	d								11 14													15 50			
Shoreham-by-Sea	d								11 20													15 56			
Worthing 4	d								11 29													16 08			
Barnham	d								11 46													16 25			
Chichester 4	d								11 54													16 34			
Havant	d								12 10													16 48			
Portsmouth Harbour ⛴	d				09 08		11 08						13 08			14 08	15 08			16 08			17 08		
Portsmouth & Southsea	d				09 12		11 12						13 12			14 12	15 12			16 12			17 12		
Fratton	d				09 16		11 16						13 16			14 16	15 16			16 16			17 16		
Cosham	d				09 23		11 23		12 23				13 23			14 23	15 23			16 23		16 55	17 23		
Fareham	a				09 31		11 31		12 31				13 31			14 31	15 31			16 31		17 02	17 31		
	d				09 32		11 32		12 32				13 32			14 32	15 32			16 32		17 03	17 32		
Southampton Central ⛴	d				09 54		11 54		12 54				13 54			14 54	15 54			16 54		17 26	17 54		
Romsey	d				10 06		12 06		13 06				14 06			15 06	16 06			17 06		17 39	18 06		
Salisbury	a				10 24		12 24		13 24				14 24			15 24	16 24			17 24		18 01	18 24		
	d				10 28		12 27		13 28			13 55	14 27			15 28	16 28			17 28		18 02	18 28		
Warminster	d				10 48		12 48		13 47			14 15	14 48			15 48	16 48			17 48		18 22	18 48		
Dilton Marsh	d				10x53								14x53			15x53	16x53					18x27			
Weymouth	d													14 00										17 56	
Upwey	d													14 05										18 01	
Dorchester West	d													14 13										18 09	
Maiden Newton	d													14 25										18 21	
Chetnole	d													14x33										18x29	
Yetminster	d													14x36										18x32	
Thornford	d													14x38										18x34	
Yeovil Pen Mill	d													14 48										18 44	
Castle Cary	a													15 01										18 56	
	d	09 21						12 34						15 03	15 34				17 37					18 59	
Bruton	d													15 08										19 05	
Frome	d		09 25											15 21										19 18	
Westbury	a	09 38	09 34		10 56		12 54	12 52	13 56			14 23	14 56	15 30	15 51	15 56	16 56		17 54	17 58		18 31	18 55	19 27	
	d	09 41	09 46	10 51	10 59	11 54	12 56	13 00	13 56	13 59		14 24	15 02	15 36	15 52	15 59	17 00	17 10	17 57	18 02		18 32	19 01	19 30	19 35
Trowbridge	d		09 52		11 05	12 00	13 02		14 02			14 30	15 08	15 42		16 05	17 06	17 16		18 08		18 38	19 07	19 36	19 42
Bradford-on-Avon	d		09 57		11 11	12 06	13 08		14 08			14 36	15 14	15 48		16 11	17 12					18 44	19 13	19 42	
Avoncliff	d		10 00			12 09			14 11					15 51		16 14						18 47		19 45	
Freshford	d		10 03			12 11			14 14					15 55		16 17						18 50		19 48	
Bath Spa 7	a		10 14		11 24	12 21	13 22		14 24			14 49	15 27	16 06		16 28	17 25			18 25		19 01	19 26	19 59	
Melksham	d																	17 25							19 52
Chippenham	a																	17 39							20 02
Swindon	a	10 21						13 35										17 56	18 32						20 20
London Paddington 15 ⊖	a	11 35		12 35				14 43		15 43					17 34				19 43						
Oldfield Park	a		10 18		11 27	12 25	13 25		14 27					16 09			17 28					19 05		20 02	
Keynsham	a		10 25		11 34	12 32	13 32		14 35			14 57		16 18			17 35					19 12		20 10	
Bristol Temple Meads 10	a		10 33		11 42	12 40	13 40		14 43			15 05	15 40	16 26		16 41	17 45			18 38		19 21	19 39	20 18	
Filton Abbey Wood	a																								
Severn Tunnel Jn.	a																								
Newport (South Wales)	a																								
Cardiff Central 7	a																								

For connections to Swansea please refer to Table 128.
For connections to Exeter St Davids and Plymouth please refer to Table 135.
For connections from Bournemouth please refer to Table 158

Table 123

Sundays

18 September to 23 October

Portsmouth and Weymouth - Bristol and South Wales

		GW	GW	SW	GW	GW	GW	GW	GW	GW
		◇1 ☕	◇	◇1	◇	◇	◇1 ☕		◇	
Brighton 10	d				17 46					
Hove 2	d				17 50					
Shoreham-by-Sea	d				17 56					
Worthing 4	d				18 08					
Barnham	d				18 25					
Chichester 4	d				18 34					
Havant	d				18 48					
Portsmouth Harbour	d		18 08			19 08			20 08	22 03
Portsmouth & Southsea	d		18 12			19 12			20 12	22 12
Fratton	d		18 16			19 16			20 16	22 16
Cosham	d		18 23		18 55	19 23				
Fareham	a		18 31		19 02	19 31			20 31	22 31
	d		18 32		19 03	19 32			20 32	22 32
Southampton Central	d		18 54		19 30	19 54			20 54	22 57
Romsey	d		19 06		19 42	20 06			21 06	23 09
Salisbury	a		19 24		20 00	20 24			21 24	23 27
	d		19 25	19 55	20 03	20 28			21 28	23 28
Warminster	d		19 48	20 15	20 23	20 48			21 48	23 53
Dilton Marsh	d				20x28				21x53	23x58
Weymouth	d							20 09		
Upwey	d							20 14		
Dorchester West	d							20 22		
Maiden Newton	d							20 34		
Chetnole	d							20x42		
Yetminster	d							20x45		
Thornford	d							20x47		
Yeovil Pen Mill	d							20 57		
Castle Cary	a							21 09		
	d	19 36					21 19	21 22		
Bruton	d							21 28		
Frome	d							21 41		
Westbury	a	19 53	19 55	20 23	20 32	20 56	21 37	21 50	21 56	00 02
	d	19 56	20 01	20 23	20 37	21 02	21 41	21 52	22 02	
Trowbridge	d		20 07	20 29	20 43	21 08		21 58	22 08	
Bradford-on-Avon	d		20 13	20 35	20 49	21 14		22 04	22 14	
Avoncliff	d				20 52			22 07		
Freshford	d				20 56			22 10		
Bath Spa 7	a		20 26	20 48	21 08	21 27		22 21	22 29	
Melksham	d									
Chippenham	a									
Swindon	a	20 31					22 16			
London Paddington 15 ⊖	a	21 38					23 31			
Oldfield Park	a				21 11			22 24		
Keynsham	a			20 56	21 19			22 32		
Bristol Temple Meads 10	a		20 39	21 04	21 27	21 40		22 40	22 45	
Filton Abbey Wood	a									
Severn Tunnel Jn.	a									
Newport (South Wales)	a									
Cardiff Central 7	a									

For connections to Swansea please refer to Table 128.
For connections to Exeter St Davids and Plymouth please refer to Table 135.
For connections from Bournemouth please refer to Table 158

Table 123

Sundays
from 30 October

Portsmouth and Weymouth - Bristol and South Wales

		GW	GW	GW	GW	GW	GW	GW	GW	GW	SW	GW	GW	GW	GW	GW	GW	GW	GW	GW	GW	GW	GW
					R											R							
		◇1		◇1			◇1	◇	◇	◇1	◇1	◇		◇1	◇			◇1	◇	◇	◇	◇1	
Brighton 10	d								11 10											15 46			
Hove 2	d								11 14											15 50			
Shoreham-by-Sea	d								11 20											15 56			
Worthing 4	d								11 29											16 08			
Barnham	d								11 46											16 25			
Chichester 4	d								11 54											16 34			
Havant	d								12 10											16 48			
Portsmouth Harbour	d				09 08			11 08				13 08			14 08	15 08			16 08		17 08		
Portsmouth & Southsea	d				09 12			11 12				13 12			14 12	15 12			16 12		17 12		
Fratton	d				09 16			11 16				13 16			14 16	15 16			16 16		17 16		
Cosham	d				09 23			11 23	12 23			13 23			14 23	15 23			16 23	16 55	17 23		
Fareham	a				09 31			11 31	12 31			13 31			14 31	15 31			16 31	17 02	17 31		
	d				09 32			11 32	12 32			13 32			14 32	15 32			16 32	17 03	17 32		
Southampton Central	d				09 54			11 54	12 54			13 54			14 54	15 54			16 54	17 26	17 54		
Romsey	d				10 06			12 06	13 06			14 06			15 06	16 06			17 06	17 39	18 06		
Salisbury	a				10 24			12 24	13 24			14 24			15 24	16 24			17 24	18 01	18 24		
	d				10 26			12 27	13 28		13 55	14 27			15 28	16 28			17 28	18 02	18 28		
Warminster	d				10 46			12 48	13 47		14 15	14 48			15 48	16 48			17 48	18 22	18 48		
Dilton Marsh	d				10x51							14x53			15x53	16x53				18x27			
Weymouth	d												14 00										17 56
Upwey	d												14 05										18 01
Dorchester West	d												14 13										18 09
Maiden Newton	d												14 25										18 21
Chetnole	d												14x33										18x29
Yetminster	d												14x36										18x32
Thornford	d												14x38										18x34
Yeovil Pen Mill	d												14 48										18 44
Castle Cary	a												15 01										18 56
	d	09 29					12 34						15 03	15 35				17 37					19 03
Bruton	d												15 08										19 08
Frome	d		09 35										15 21										19 21
Westbury	a	09 46	09 44		10 54		12 52	12 54	13 55		14 23	14 58	15 30	15 52	15 56	16 56		17 54	17 58	18 31	18 55		19 30
	d	09 49	09 58	10 53	11 00	11 54	12 53	12 56	13 56	13 59	14 24	15 02	15 36	15 52	15 59	17 00	17 10	17 56	18 02	18 32	19 01	19 14	19 37
Trowbridge	d		10 04		11 06	12 00		13 02	14 02		14 30	15 08	15 42		16 05	17 06	17 16		18 08	18 38	19 07		19 43
Bradford-on-Avon	d		10 09		11 12	12 06		13 08	14 08		14 36	15 14	15 48		16 11	17 12				18 44	19 13		19 49
Avoncliff	d		10 12			12 09			14 11				15 51		16 14					18 47			19 52
Freshford	d		10 15			12 11			14 13				15 55		16 17					18 50			19 55
Bath Spa 7	a		10 26		11 25	12 21		13 22	14 24		14 49	15 27	16 06		16 28	17 25			18 27	19 01	19 28		20 07
Melksham	d																17 25						
Chippenham	a																17 39						
Swindon	a																17 56						
London Paddington 15 ⊖	a	11 28		12 29			14 28			15 29				17 29				19 29				20 43	
Oldfield Park	a		10 30		11 28	12 25		13 25	14 27				16 09			17 28				19 05			20 10
Keynsham	a		10 37		11 35	12 32		13 32	14 35		14 57		16 18			17 35				19 12			20 18
Bristol Temple Meads 10	a		10 45		11 43	12 40		13 40	14 44		15 05	15 40	16 26		16 41	17 43			18 40	19 21	19 41		20 26
Filton Abbey Wood	a				11 55			13 55	14 55			15 55			16 55	17 55			18 55		19 55		
Severn Tunnel Jn.	a				12 10			14 09	15 09			16 09			17 10	18 08			19 11		20 10		
Newport (South Wales)	a				12 29			14 29	15 28			16 28			17 29	18 27			19 29		20 28		
Cardiff Central 7	a				12 44			14 53	15 45			16 46			17 46	18 45			19 45		20 48		

For connections to Swansea please refer to Table 128.
For connections to Exeter St Davids and Plymouth please refer to Table 135.
For connections from Bournemouth please refer to Table 158

Table 123

Sundays
from 30 October

Portsmouth and Weymouth - Bristol and South Wales

		GW	GW ◇	SW ◇1	GW ◇1 🍴	GW ◇	GW ◇	GW	GW ◇1 🍴	GW	GW ◇	GW
Brighton 10	d					17 46						
Hove 2	d					17 50						
Shoreham-by-Sea	d					17 56						
Worthing 4	d					18 08						
Barnham	d					18 25						
Chichester 4	d					18 34						
Havant	d					18 48						
Portsmouth Harbour ⛴	d		18 08				19 08				20 08	22 03
Portsmouth & Southsea	d		18 12				19 12				20 12	22 12
Fratton	d		18 16				19 16				20 16	22 16
Cosham	d		18 23			18 55	19 23					
Fareham	a		18 31			19 02	19 31				20 31	22 31
	d		18 32			19 03	19 32				20 32	22 32
Southampton Central ⛴	d		18 54			19 30	19 54				20 54	22 57
Romsey	d		19 06			19 42	20 06				21 06	23 09
Salisbury	a		19 24			20 00	20 24				21 24	23 27
	d		19 25	19 55		20 03	20 28				21 28	23 28
Warminster	d		19 48	20 15		20 23	20 48				21 48	23 53
Dilton Marsh	d					20x28					21x53	23x58
Weymouth	d							20 09				
Upwey	d							20 14				
Dorchester West	d							20 22				
Maiden Newton	d							20 34				
Chetnole	d							20x42				
Yetminster	d							20x45				
Thornford	d							20x47				
Yeovil Pen Mill	d							20 57				
Castle Cary	a							21 09				
	d				20 06			21 10	21 19			
Bruton	d							21 16				
Frome	d							21 31		←		
Westbury	a		19 55	20 23	20 25	20 32	20 56	21 41	21 37	21 41	21 56	00 02
	d	19 40	20 01	20 23	20 26	20 37	21 02	21 52	21 44	21 52	22 02	
Trowbridge	d	19 47	20 07	20 29		20 43	21 08	→		21 58	22 08	
Bradford-on-Avon	d		20 13	20 35		20 49	21 14			22 04	22 14	
Avoncliff	d					20 52				22 07		
Freshford	d					20 56				22 10		
Bath Spa 7	a		20 26	20 48		21 08	21 27			22 20	22 29	
Melksham	d	19 57										
Chippenham	a	20 07										
Swindon	a	20 25										
London Paddington 15 ⊖	a				22 01				23 17			
Oldfield Park	a					21 11				22 23		
Keynsham	a			20 56		21 19				22 32		
Bristol Temple Meads 10	a		20 39	21 04		21 27	21 40			22 40	22 45	
Filton Abbey Wood	a		20 55				21 58				22 57	
Severn Tunnel Jn.	a		21 09				22 15				23 09	
Newport (South Wales)	a		21 28				22 36				23 30	
Cardiff Central 7	a		21 46				22 59				23 51	

For connections to Swansea please refer to Table 128.
For connections to Exeter St Davids and Plymouth please refer to Table 135.
For connections from Bournemouth please refer to Table 158

Route Diagram for Table 125

DM-12/06
Design BAJS

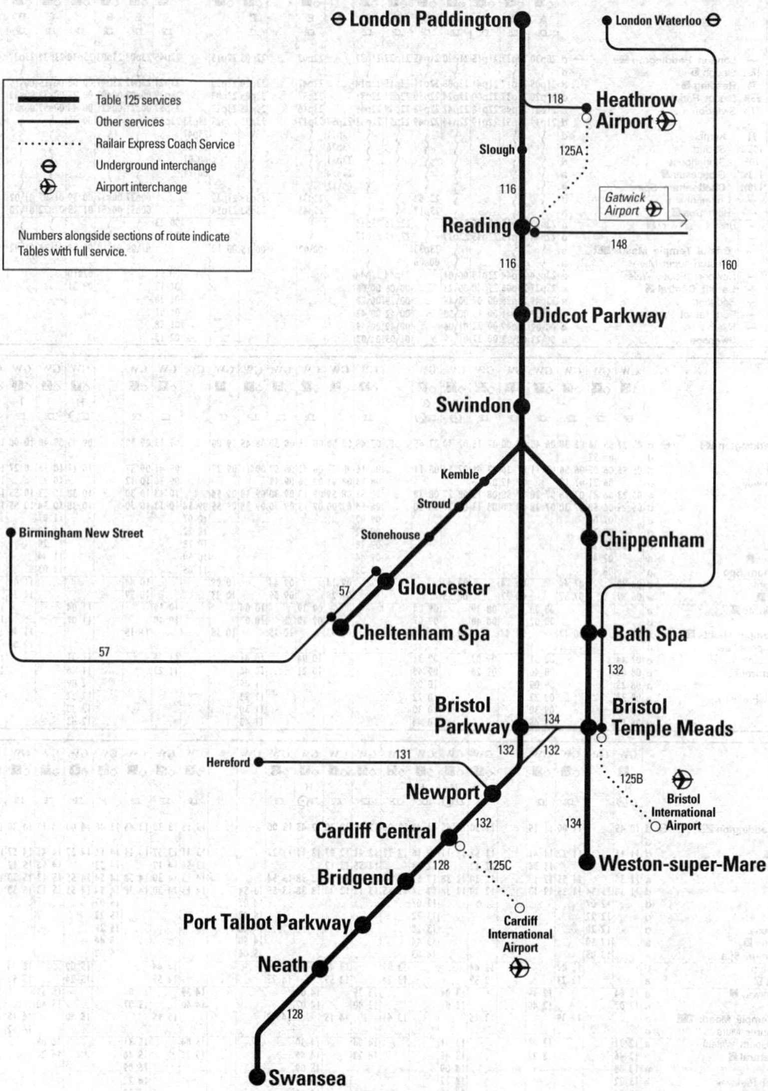

© Network Rail OPSU 2006. All rights reserved

London - Swindon, Cheltenham Spa, Bristol, Weston-super-Mare and South Wales

Miles	Miles	Miles			GW	GW	GW	GW	GW	GW	GW	GW	GW		GW	GW	GW	GW	GW	GW	GW	GW	GW		GW
					MO	MO	MX	MO	MX	MO	MO	MO	MO		MO	MX	MX	MX	MO	MO	MX	MO	MO		
					◇1	◇1	◇1	◇1	◇1	◇1	◇1		◇1		◇1	◇1		◇1	◇1	◇1	◇1	◇1	◇1		
					A	B		A	C	D	B	A	E		B				E	B		E	B		
					🛒	🛒	🛒	🛒	🛒	🛒	🛒		🛒		🛒	🛒		🛒	🛒	🛒	🛒	🛒	🛒		
—	—	—	**London Paddington** 15 ⊖	d	20p30	20p37	21p15	21p30	21p45	21p37	21p37		22p03		22p03	22p15		22p45	23p03	23p03	23p30	23p37	23p37		
18½	18½	18½	Slough 3	d																					
36	36	36	**Reading** 7	d	21p05	21p17	21p41	22p08	22p11	22p15	22p14		22p42		22p50	22p50		23p21	23p47	23p47	00 08	00⌇15	00⌇15		
53¼	53¼	53¼	Didcot Parkway	d	21p20	21p32	22p00	22p24	22p30	22p31	22p31		22p57		23p05	23p08		23p39	00s02	00s02	00 25	00s32	00s32		
77¼	77¼	77¼	**Swindon**	a	21p37	21p48	22p18	22p42	22p48	22p49	22p49		23p16		23p25	23p25		23p57	00s21	00s21	00 44	00s52	00s52		
—	—	—		d	21p39	21p51	22p19	22p44	22p49	22p51	22p51	22p57	23p17		23p25	23p25	23p33	23p58			00 45				06 16
—	—	91	Kemble	d								23p11					23p47								
—	—	102¼	Stroud	d								23p26					00 02								
—	—	105	Stonehouse	d								23p31					00 07								
—	—	113¾	Gloucester 7	a								23p54					00 24								
—	—	120¼	**Cheltenham Spa**	a								00⌇12													
—	94	—	Chippenham	d					23p03				23p31		23p39	23p39			00s37	00s37	00 59	01s07	01⌇07		06a32
—	107	—	Bath Spa 7	a					23p17				23p45		23p53	23p54			00s51	00s51	01 13	01s22	01⌇20		
111¾	—	—	Bristol Parkway 7	a	22p27	22p15	22p45	23p31		23p16	23p16							00 23							
—	—	—		d	22p34	22p16	22p45	23p37		23p17	23p17							00 24							
117¾	118½	—	**Bristol Temple Meads** 10	a					23p33				00⌇02		00⌇15	00 10			01⌇05	01⌇12	01 29	01⌇36	01⌇42		
—	137½	—	Weston-super-Mare	a					00s06																
133½	—	—	Newport (South Wales)	a	23p04	22p44	23p19	00⌇01		23p44	23p44							00 52			02s10				
145¼	—	—	**Cardiff Central** 7	a	23p27	23p06	23p40	00⌇23		00⌇06	00⌇06							01 12			02 31				
165½	—	—	Bridgend	a	23p49	23p28	00 02	00⌇45		00⌇29	00⌇29							01 38							
177¾	—	—	Port Talbot Parkway	a	00⌇02	23p41	00 15	00⌇58		00⌇42	00⌇42							01 51							
183¼	—	—	Neath	a	00⌇09	23p49	00 22	01⌇06		00⌇49	00⌇49							01 58							
192¾	—	—	**Swansea**	a	00⌇23	00⌇02	00 37	01⌇19		01⌇03	01⌇03							02 13							

		GW	GW	GW	GW	GW	GW	GW	GW		GW	GW	GW	GW	GW	GW	GW	GW	GW		GW	GW	GW	GW	GW
		◇1	◇1	◇1	◇1	◇1	◇1	◇1	◇1		◇1	◇1	◇1	◇1	◇1	◇1		◇1	◇1		◇1	◇1	◇1	◇1	◇1
								F	G												H		I		
		🛒	🛒	🛒	🛒	🛒	🛒	⊘	🛒⊘		🛒	🛒	🛒	🛒	🛒	🛒		🛒	🛒		🛒⊘	🛒	🛒	🛒	🛒
London Paddington 15 ⊖	d	05 27	05 36	06 30	06 45	07 00	07 15	07 30	07 45		07 48	08 00	08 15	08 30	08 45	09 00		09 15	09 30		09 45	09 48	10 00	10 15	10 30
Slough 3	d		05 52																						
Reading 7	d	05 56	06 07	06 56	07 11	07 26	07 41	07 57	08 11		08 16	08 27	08 41	08 57	09 11	09 27		09 41	09 57		10 11	10 16	10 27	10 41	10 57
Didcot Parkway	d		06 21	07 12		07 42	07 56				08 33	08 41	08 56	09 12				09 56	10 12			10 33		10 56	11 12
Swindon	a	06 23	06 41	07 28	07 38	07 58	08 13	08 27	08 38		08 53	08 59	09 13	09 30	09 38	09 54		10 13	10 30		10 38	10 53	10 55	11 13	11 30
	d	06 25	06 50	07 30	07 38	08 00	08 13	08 27	08 38		08 54	09 00	09 13	09 30	09 38	09 55	09 54	10 13	10 30		10 38	10 54	10 55	11 13	11 30
Kemble	d		07 07								09 07						10 07					11 07			
Stroud	d		07 22								09 22						10 22					11 22			
Stonehouse	d		07 28								09 28						10 28					11 28			
Gloucester 7	a		07 45								09 44						10 50					11 44			
Cheltenham Spa	a		08 01								10 03						11 05					12 03			
Chippenham	d	06 39		07 44		08 14		08 42				09 14		09 44		10 09			10 44				11 09		11 44
Bath Spa 7	a	06 52		07 57		08 27		08 55				09 28		09 59		10 23			10 59				11 24		11 59
Bristol Parkway 7	a				08 04		08 39		09 04				09 39		10 04			10 39			11 04			11 39	
	d				08 07		08 40		09 07				09 40		10 07			10 40			11 07			11 40	
Bristol Temple Meads 10	a	07 07		08 17		08 44		09 10				09 43		10 15		10 38			11 15				11 40		12 15
Weston-super-Mare	a																						12 06		
Newport (South Wales)	a	07 44			08 32		09 07		09 31				10 04		10 31			11 06			11 31			12 04	
Cardiff Central 7	a	08 00			08 46		09 24		09 48				10 21		10 46			11 23			11 46			12 21	
Bridgend	a	08 23			09 09				10 09						11 09						12 09				
Port Talbot Parkway	a	08 36			09 22				10 22						11 22						12 22				
Neath	a	08 44			09 30				10 30						11 30						12 30				
Swansea	a	08 57			09 45				10 44						11 43						12 43				

		GW	GW	GW	GW		GW	GW	GW	GW	GW	GW	GW	GW	GW		GW	GW	GW	GW	GW	GW	GW	GW	GW
		◇1		◇1	◇1		◇1	◇1	◇1	◇1	◇1	◇1	◇1	◇1			◇1	◇1	◇1	◇1	◇1	◇1	◇1	◇1	◇1
		H						H	J				H											K	
		🛒⊘		🛒	🛒		🛒	🛒⊘	🛒	🛒	🛒	🛒	🛒⊘	🛒			🛒	🛒	🛒	🛒	🛒	🛒	🛒	🛒 FO	🛒
London Paddington 15 ⊖	d	10 45		11 00	11 15		11 30	11 45	11 48	12 00	12 15	12 30	12 45	13 00			13 15	13 30	13 45	13 48	14 00	14 15	14 30	14⌇36	14 45
Slough 3	d																								
Reading 7	d	11 11		11 27	11 41		11 57	12 11	12 16	12 27	12 41	12 57	13 11	13 27			13 41	13 57	14 11	14 16	14 27	14 41	14 57	15u08	15 11
Didcot Parkway	d				11 56		12 12		12 33		12 56	13 12					13 56	14 12		14 33		14 56	15 12		
Swindon	a	11 38		11 55	12 13		12 30	12 38	12 53	12 55	13 13	13 30	13 38	13 54			14 13	14 30	14 38	14 54	14 55	15 13	15 30	15⌇35	15 38
	d	11 38	11 54	11 55	12 13		12 30	12 38	12 54	12 55	13 13	13 30	13 38	13 55	13 54		14 13	14 30	14 38	14 54	14 55	15 13	15 30		15 38
Kemble	d		12 07						13 07						14 07					15 07					
Stroud	d		12 22						13 22						14 22					15 22					
Stonehouse	d		12 28						13 28						14 28					15 28					
Gloucester 7	a		12 50						13 44						14 50					15 44					
Cheltenham Spa	a		13 05						14 03						15 05					16 03					
Chippenham	d			12 09			12 44			13 09		13 44		14 09				14 44			15 09		15 44		
Bath Spa 7	a			12 23			12 59			13 24		13 59		14 23				14 59			15 24		15 59		
Bristol Parkway 7	a	12 04			12 39			13 04			13 39		14 04				14 39		15 04			15 39			16 05
	d	12 07			12 40			13 07			13 40		14 07				14 40		15 07			15 40			16 07
Bristol Temple Meads 10	a			12 39			13 15			13 41		14 15		14 39				15 15			15 40		16 15		
Weston-super-Mare	a																						16 52		
Newport (South Wales)	a	12 31			13 06			13 31			14 04		14 30				15 04		15 31			16 05			16 30
Cardiff Central 7	a	12 46			13 22			13 46			14 22		14 46				15 22		15 46			16 24			16 46
Bridgend	a	13 09						14 09					15 09						16 09						17 09
Port Talbot Parkway	a	13 22						14 22					15 22						16 22						17 22
Neath	a	13 30						14 30					15 30						16 30						17 30
Swansea	a	13 43						14 43					15 43						16 43						17 43

A From 27 June until 1 August
B From 8 August until 5 September
C From 25 May until 9 September
D Until 20 June
E Until 1 August
F The Merchant Venturer
G The St. David. 🛒 from Bridgend ⊘ to Cardiff Central
H 🛒 from Bridgend ⊘ to Cardiff Central
I The Torbay Express
J The Cheltenham Spa Express
K From 8 July until 2 September

For connections from Heathrow Airport, Gatwick Airport and Oxford please refer to Tables 125A, 148 and 116.
For connections to Birmingham New Street and Hereford please refer to Tables 57 and 131

Table 125

Mondays to Fridays

until 9 September

London - Swindon, Cheltenham Spa, Bristol, Weston-super-Mare and South Wales

		GW	GW ◇1 🛒	GW ◇1 🛒	GW ◇1 🛒	GW ◇1 🛒	GW ◇1 🛒	GW ◇1 🛒	GW ◇1 🛒	GW ◇1 🛒	GW ◇1 A 🛒	GW	GW ◇1 🛒	GW ◇1 🛒	GW ◇1 🛒	GW ◇1 B 🛒	GW	GW ◇1 🛒	GW ◇1 C 🛒	GW ◇1 🛒	GW ◇1 🛒	GW FX ◇1 🛒
London Paddington 15 ⊖	d		15 00	15 15	15 30	15 45	15 48	16 00	16 15	16 30	16 45		17 00	17 15	17 30	17 45		17 48	18 00	18 15	18 30	18 45
Slough 3	d																					
Reading 7	d		15 27	15 41	15 57	16 11	16 16	16 27	16 41	16 57	17 11		17 26	17 41	17 56	18 11		18 16	18 27	18 41	18 56	19 11
Didcot Parkway	d			15 56	16 12		16 33		16 56	17 12			17 42	17 56	18 12			18 33	18 42	18 56	19 12	
Swindon	a		15 55	16 13	16 30	16 38	16 53	16 55	17 13	17 30	17 38		17 58	18 13	18 28	18 38		18 53	18 59	19 13	19 28	19 38
	d	15 54	15 55	16 13	16 30	16 38	16 54	16 55	17 13	17 30	17 38	17 54	18 00	18 13	18 30	18 38	18 44	18 54	19 00	19 13	19 30	19 38
Kemble	d	16 07					17 07					18 07						19 07				
Stroud	d	16 22					17 22					18 22						19 22				
Stonehouse	d	16 28					17 28					18 28						19 28				
Gloucester 7	a	16 50					17 46					18 49						19 45				
Cheltenham Spa	a	17 05					18 03					19 05						20 03				
Chippenham	d		16 10		16 44			17 13		17 44			18 14		18 44		19a01		19 14		19 44	
Bath Spa 7	a		16 24		16 59			17 26		17 59			18 27		18 57				19 28		19 57	
Bristol Parkway 7	a			16 39		17 04			17 40		18 04			18 40		19 04				19 40		20 04
	d			16 40		17 07			17 40		18 07			18 40		19 07				19 40		20 07
Bristol Temple Meads 10	a		16 39		17 15			17 41		18 14			18 44		19 12				19 43		20 13	
Weston-super-Mare	a				17 51					18 51					19 48						20 53	
Newport (South Wales)	a			17 06		17 31			18 04		18 30			19 11		19 31				20 07		20 31
Cardiff Central 7	a			17 22		17 46			18 19		18 48			19 26		19 47				20 22		20 45
Bridgend	a					18 09			18 44		19 09			19 49		20 10				20 45		21 09
Port Talbot Parkway	a					18 22			18 57		19 22			20 02		20 24				20 58		21 22
Neath	a					18 30			19 04		19 30			20 10		20 31				21 05		21 30
Swansea	a					18 48			19 18		19 45			20 23		20 45				21 19		21 43

		GW FO ◇1 🛒	GW ◇1 🛒	GW ◇1 🛒	GW FX ◇1 🛒	GW FO ◇1 🛒	GW ◇1 🛒	GW FO ◇1 🛒	GW FX ◇1 🛒	GW ◇1 🛒	GW ◇1 🛒	GW ◇1 🛒	GW	GW ◇1 🛒	GW ◇1 D 🛒	GW FO ◇1 🛒	GW FX ◇1 🛒	GW	GW FO ◇1 🛒	GW FX ◇1 🛒	GW FO ◇1 🛒	GW FX ◇1 🛒
London Paddington 15 ⊖	d	18 45	18 47	19 00	19 15	19 15	19 30	19 48	19 48	20 00	20 15	20 45		21 15	21 45	22 15	22 15		22 45	22 45	23 30	23 30
Slough 3	d																					
Reading 7	d	19 11	19 18	19 27	19 41	19 48	19 57	20 18	20 18	20 27	20 41	21 11		21 41	22 11	22 41	22 50		23 11	23 21	00 05	00 08
Didcot Parkway	d		19 33	19 42	19 56		20 12	20 33	20 33	20 42	20 56	21 26		22 00	22 30	23 01	23 08		23 30	23 39	00 25	00 25
Swindon	a	19 38	19 53	20 00	20 13	20 15	20 30	20 48	20 52	20 59	21 13	21 43		22 18	22 48	23 19	23 25		23 48	23 57	00 40	00 44
	d	19 38	19 54	20 00	20 13	20 16	20 30	20 54	20 54	21 00	21 13	21 43	21 54	22 19	22 49	23 20	23 25	23 33	23 49	23 58	00 42	00 45
Kemble	d		20 07					21 11	21 11				22 07					23 47				
Stroud	d		20 22					21 26	21 26				22 22					00 02				
Stonehouse	d		20 28					21 31	21 31				22 28					00 07				
Gloucester 7	a		20 45					21 46	21 46				22 45					00 24				
Cheltenham Spa	a		21 02					22 04	22 04				23 05									
Chippenham	d			20 14			20 44			21 15		21 58			23 03	23 33	23 39				00 56	00 59
Bath Spa 7	a			20 29			20 59			21 28		22 10			23 17	23 47	23 54				01 11	01 13
Bristol Parkway 7	a	20 04			20 39	20 42					21 39			22 45					00 14	00 23		
	d	20 07			20 40	20 43					21 40			22 45					00 16	00 24		
Bristol Temple Meads 10	a			20 44			21 15			21 44		22 30			23 33	00 03	00 10				01 27	01 29
Weston-super-Mare	a						21 50								00s06							
Newport (South Wales)	a	20 31			21 04	21 05					22 03			23 19					00 38	00 52	02s00	02s10
Cardiff Central 7	a	20 48			21 19	21 19					22 23			23 40					00 53	01 12	02 17	02 31
Bridgend	a	21 15			21 45	21 45					22 46			00 02					01 19	01 38		
Port Talbot Parkway	a	21 28			21 58	21 58					22 59			00 15					01 32	01 51		
Neath	a	21 36			22 06	22 06					23 07			00 22					01 39	01 58		
Swansea	a	21 49			22 19	22 19					23 20			00 37					01 53	02 13		

A The Capitals United
B The Red Dragon
C The Bristolian
D not 23 May

For connections from Heathrow Airport, Gatwick Airport and Oxford please refer to Tables 125A, 148 and 116.
For connections to Birmingham New Street and Hereford please refer to Tables 57 and 131

Table 125

Mondays to Fridays

from 12 September

London - Swindon, Cheltenham Spa, Bristol, Weston-super-Mare and South Wales

		GW	GW	GW	GW	GW	GW	GW	GW	GW		XC	GW	GW	GW	GW	GW	GW	GW	GW		GW	GW	GW	GW
		MO	MX	MX	MO	MO		MX	MO	MX		MO	MO	MX			MO	MX	MO			MO			
		◇1	◇1	◇1	◇1	◇1	◇1	◇1	◇1			◇1	◇1	◇1	◇1	◇1	🚌	◇1	◇1	◇1		🚌		◇1	◇1
		A			A	B	C		D			B	B		B	C	D		B	C		D			
		☕	☕	☕	☕	☕	☕	☕	☕				☕	☕	☕	☕		☕	☕	☕				☕	☕
London Paddington 15 ⊖	d	20p37	21p15	21p45	21p37	22p03	22p03	22p15					22p37	22p45	23p03	23p03		23p30	23p37	23p37				05 27	05 36
Slough 3	d	⌇			⌇	⌇	⌇						⌇		⌇	⌇			⌇	⌇					05 52
Reading 7	d	21p17	21p41	22p11	22p14	22p50	22p50	22p50					23p15	23p21	23p47	23p47	23p25	00 08	00 15	00 15		00 25		05 56	06 07
Didcot Parkway	d	21p32	22p00	22p30	22p31	23p05	23p05	23p08					23b30	23p39	00s02	00s02	⌇	00 25	00s32	00s32		⌇			06 21
Swindon	a	21p48	22p18	22p48	22p49	23p25	23p25	23p25					23b48	23p57	00s21	00s21	00 25	00 44	00s52	00s52		01 25		06 23	06 41
	d	21p51	22p19	22p49	22p51	23p25	23p25	23p25	23p29	23p33		23p38	⌇	23p58	⌇	⌇	00 25	00 45	⌇	⌇		01 25	06 16	06 25	06 50
Kemble	d	⌇			⌇	⌇	⌇		⌇	23p47		⌇	⌇		⌇	⌇	⌇		⌇	⌇		⌇			07 07
Stroud	d	⌇			⌇	⌇	⌇		⌇	00 02		⌇	⌇		⌇	⌇	⌇		⌇	⌇		⌇			07 22
Stonehouse	d	⌇			⌇	⌇	⌇		⌇	00 07		⌇	⌇		⌇	⌇	⌇		⌇	⌇		⌇			07 28
Gloucester 7	a	⌇			⌇	⌇	⌇		⌇	00 24		⌇	⌇		⌇	⌇	⌇		⌇	⌇		⌇			07 45
Cheltenham Spa	a	⌇			⌇	⌇	⌇		⌇			⌇	⌇		⌇	⌇	⌇		⌇	⌇		⌇			08 01
Chippenham	d	⌇		23p03	⌇	23p40	23p39	23p39	23p44			⌇	⌇		00s37	00s37	01a00	00 59	01s07	01 07		02a00	06a32	06 39	
Bath Spa 7	a	⌇		23p17	⌇	23p54	23p53	23p54	23p57			⌇	⌇		00s51	00s51		01 13	01s22	01 20				06 52	
Bristol Parkway 7	a	22p15	22p45		23p16	⌇	⌇		⌇			⌇	⌇	00 23	⌇	⌇			⌇	⌇					
	d	22p16	22p45		23p17	⌇	⌇		⌇			⌇	⌇	00 24	⌇	⌇			⌇	⌇					
Bristol Temple Meads 10	a	⌇		23p33	⌇	00 09	00 15	00 10	00 12			00 13	00 25		01 05	01 12		01 29	01 36	01 42				07 07	
Weston-super-Mare	a	⌇		00s06	⌇																				
Newport (South Wales)	a	22p44	23p19		23p44									00 52				02s10						07 44	
Cardiff Central 7	a	23p06	23p40		00 06									01 12				02 31						08 00	
Bridgend	a	23p28	00 02		00 29									01 38										08 23	
Port Talbot Parkway	a	23p41	00 15		00 42									01 51										08 36	
Neath	a	23p49	00 22		00 49									01 58										08 44	
Swansea	a	00 02	00 37		01 03									02 13										08 57	

		GW	GW	GW	GW	GW		GW	GW	GW	GW	GW	GW	GW	GW	GW		GW	GW	GW	GW	GW	GW	GW	GW
		◇1	◇1	◇1	◇1	◇1		◇1	◇1	◇1	◇1	◇1	◇1	◇1		◇1		◇1	◇1	◇1	◇1	◇1	◇1	◇1	
						E		F											G		H			G	
		☕	☕	☕	☕	⊘		☕⊘	☕	☕	☕	☕	☕	☕		☕		☕	☕⊘	☕	☕	☕	☕	☕⊘	
London Paddington 15 ⊖	d	06 30	06 45	07 00	07 15	07 30		07 45	07 48	08 00	08 15	08 30	08 45	09 00		09 15		09 30	09 45	09 48	10 00	10 15	10 30	10 45	
Slough 3	d																								
Reading 7	d	06 56	07 11	07 26	07 41	07 57		08 11	08 16	08 27	08 41	08 57	09 11	09 27		09 41		09 57	10 11	10 16	10 27	10 41	10 57	11 11	
Didcot Parkway	d	07 12		07 42	07 56				08 33	08 41	08 56	09 12				09 56		10 12		10 33		10 56	11 12		
Swindon	a	07 28	07 38	07 58	08 13	08 27		08 38	08 53	08 59	09 13	09 30	09 38	09 54		10 13		10 30	10 38	10 53	10 55	11 13	11 30	11 38	
	d	07 30	07 38	08 00	08 13	08 27		08 38	08 54	09 00	09 13	09 30	09 38	09 55	09 54	10 13		10 30	10 38	10 54	10 55	11 13	11 30	11 38	11 54
Kemble	d								09 07						10 07					11 07					12 07
Stroud	d								09 22						10 22					11 22					12 22
Stonehouse	d								09 28						10 28					11 28					12 28
Gloucester 7	a								09 44						10 50					11 44					12 50
Cheltenham Spa	a								10 03						11 05					12 03					13 05
Chippenham	d	07 44		08 14		08 42				09 14		09 44		10 09				10 44			11 09		11 44		
Bath Spa 7	a	07 57		08 27		08 55				09 28		09 59		10 23				10 59			11 24		11 59		
Bristol Parkway 7	a		08 04		08 39			09 04			09 39		10 04			10 39			11 04			11 39		12 04	
	d		08 07		08 40			09 07			09 40		10 07			10 40			11 07			11 40		12 07	
Bristol Temple Meads 10	a	08 17		08 44		09 10				09 43		10 15		10 38				11 15			11 40		12 15		
Weston-super-Mare	a																				12 06				
Newport (South Wales)	a		08 32		09 07			09 31			10 04		10 31			11 06			11 31			12 04		12 31	
Cardiff Central 7	a		08 46		09 24			09 48			10 21		10 46			11 23			11 46			12 21		12 46	
Bridgend	a		09 09					10 09					11 09						12 09					13 09	
Port Talbot Parkway	a		09 22					10 22					11 22						12 22					13 22	
Neath	a		09 30					10 30					11 30						12 30					13 30	
Swansea	a		09 45					10 44					11 43						12 43					13 43	

		GW		GW	GW	GW	GW	GW	GW	GW	GW	GW		GW	GW	GW	GW	GW	GW	GW	GW	GW		GW	GW
		◇1		◇1	◇1	◇1	◇1	◇1	◇1	◇1	◇1	◇1			◇1	◇1	◇1	◇1	◇1	◇1	◇1	◇1			◇1
						G	I				G														
		☕		☕	☕	☕⊘	☕	☕	☕	☕	☕⊘	☕			☕	☕	☕	☕	☕	☕	☕	☕			☕
London Paddington 15 ⊖	d	11 00		11 15	11 30	11 45	11 48	12 00	12 15	12 30	12 45	13 00			13 15	13 30	13 45	13 48	14 00	14 15	14 30	14 45			15 00
Slough 3	d																								
Reading 7	d	11 27		11 41	11 57	12 11	12 16	12 27	12 41	12 57	13 11	13 27			13 41	13 57	14 11	14 16	14 27	14 41	14 57	15 11			15 27
Didcot Parkway	d			11 56	12 12		12 33		12 56	13 12					13 56	14 12		14 33		14 56	15 12				
Swindon	a	11 55		12 13	12 30	12 38	12 53	12 55	13 13	13 30	13 38	13 54			14 13	14 30	14 38	14 54	14 55	15 13	15 30	15 38			15 55
	d	11 55		12 13	12 30	12 38	12 54	12 55	13 13	13 30	13 38	13 55		13 54	14 13	14 30	14 38	14 54	14 55	15 13	15 30	15 38		15 54	15 55
Kemble	d						13 07							14 07				15 07						16 07	
Stroud	d						13 22							14 22				15 22						16 22	
Stonehouse	d						13 28							14 28				15 28						16 28	
Gloucester 7	a						13 44							14 50				15 44						16 50	
Cheltenham Spa	a						14 03							15 05				16 03						17 05	
Chippenham	d	12 09			12 44			13 09		13 44		14 09				14 44			15 09		15 44				16 10
Bath Spa 7	a	12 23			12 59			13 24		13 59		14 23				14 59			15 24		15 59				16 24
Bristol Parkway 7	a			12 39		13 04			13 39		14 04				14 39		15 04			15 39		16 05			
	d			12 40		13 07			13 40		14 07				14 40		15 07			15 40		16 07			
Bristol Temple Meads 10	a	12 39			13 15			13 41		14 15		14 39				15 15			15 40		16 15				16 39
Weston-super-Mare	a																				16 52				
Newport (South Wales)	a			13 06		13 31			14 04		14 30				15 04		15 31			16 05		16 30			
Cardiff Central 7	a			13 22		13 46			14 22		14 46				15 22		15 46			16 24		16 46			
Bridgend	a					14 09					15 09						16 09					17 09			
Port Talbot Parkway	a					14 22					15 22						16 22					17 22			
Neath	a					14 30					15 30						16 30					17 30			
Swansea	a					14 43					15 43						16 43					17 43			

A Fom 12 September until 24 October
B From 19 September until 24 October
C 12 September
D From 31 October
E The Merchant Venturer
F The St. David. ☕ from Bridgend ⊘ to Cardiff Central
G ☕ from Bridgend ⊘ to Cardiff Central
H The Torbay Express
I The Cheltenham Spa Express
b Previous night, stops to set down only

For connections from Heathrow Airport, Gatwick Airport and Oxford please refer to Tables 125A, 148 and 116.
For connections to Birmingham New Street and Hereford please refer to Tables 57 and 131

Table 125

Mondays to Fridays

from 12 September

London - Swindon, Cheltenham Spa, Bristol, Weston-super-Mare and South Wales

		GW	GW	GW	GW	GW	GW	GW		GW	GW	GW	GW	GW	GW	GW	GW	GW		GW	GW	GW	GW	GW	GW
																						FX	FO		
		◇1	◇1	◇1	◇1	◇1	◇1	◇1		◇1		◇1	◇1	◇1	◇1		◇1	◇1		◇1	◇1	◇1	◇1	◇1	◇1
										A					B			C							
		🍴	🍴	🍴	🍴	🍴	🍴	🍴		🍴		🍴	🍴	🍴	🍴		🍴	🍴		🍴	🍴	🍴	🍴	🍴	🍴
London Paddington 15 ⊖	d	15 15	15 30	15 45	15 48	16 00	16 15	16 30		16 45		17 00	17 15	17 30	17 45		17 48	18 00		18 15	18 30	18 45	18 45	18 47	19 00
Slough 3	d																								
Reading 7	d	15 41	15 57	16 11	16 16	16 27	16 41	16 57		17 11		17 26	17 41	17 56	18 11		18 16	18 27		18 41	18 56	19 11	19 11	19 18	19 27
Didcot Parkway	d	15 56	16 12		16 33		16 56	17 12				17 42	17 56	18 12			18 33	18 42		18 56	19 12			19 33	19 42
Swindon	a	16 13	16 30	16 38	16 53	16 55	17 13	17 30		17 38		17 58	18 13	18 28	18 38		18 53	18 59		19 13	19 28	19 38	19 38	19 53	20 00
	d	16 13	16 30	16 38	16 54	16 55	17 13	17 30		17 38	17 54	18 00	18 13	18 30	18 38	18 44	18 54	19 00		19 13	19 30	19 38	19 38	19 54	20 00
Kemble	d				17 07						18 07						19 07							20 07	
Stroud	d				17 22						18 22						19 22							20 22	
Stonehouse	d				17 28						18 28						19 28							20 28	
Gloucester 7	a				17 46						18 49						19 45							20 45	
Cheltenham Spa	a				18 03						19 05						20 03							21 02	
Chippenham	d		16 44			17 13		17 44				18 14		18 44		19a01		19 14			19 44				20 14
Bath Spa 7	a		16 59			17 26		17 59				18 27		18 57				19 28			19 57				20 29
Bristol Parkway 7	a	16 39		17 04			17 40			18 04			18 40		19 04					19 40		20 04	20 04		
	d	16 40		17 07			17 40			18 07			18 40		19 07					19 40		20 07	20 07		
Bristol Temple Meads 10	a		17 15			17 41		18 14				18 44		19 12				19 43			20 13				20 44
Weston-super-Mare	a		17 51					18 51						19 48							20 53				
Newport (South Wales)	a	17 06		17 31			18 04			18 30			19 11		19 31					20 07		20 31	20 31		
Cardiff Central 7	a	17 22		17 46			18 19			18 48			19 26		19 47					20 22		20 45	20 48		
Bridgend	a			18 09			18 44			19 09			19 49		20 10					20 45		21 09	21 15		
Port Talbot Parkway	a			18 22			18 57			19 22			20 02		20 24					20 58		21 22	21 28		
Neath	a			18 30			19 04			19 30			20 10		20 31					21 05		21 30	21 36		
Swansea	a			18 48			19 18			19 45			20 23		20 45					21 19		21 43	21 49		

		GW	GW	GW		GW	GW	GW	GW	GW	GW	GW	GW	GW		GW	GW	GW	GW	GW	GW				
		FX	FO			FO	FX							FO		FX		FO	FX	FO	FX				
		◇1	◇1	◇1		◇1	◇1	◇1	◇1	◇1		◇1	◇1	◇1		◇1		◇1	◇1	◇1	◇1				
		🍴	🍴	🍴		🍴	🍴	🍴	🍴	🍴		🍴	🍴	🍴		🍴		🍴	🍴	🍴	🍴				
London Paddington 15 ⊖	d	19 15	19 15	19 30		19 48	19 48	20 00	20 15	20 45		21 15	21 45	22 15		22 15		22 45	22 45	23 30	23 30				
Slough 3	d																								
Reading 7	d	19 41	19 48	19 57		20 18	20 18	20 27	20 41	21 11		21 41	22 11	22 41		22 50		23 11	23 21	00 05	00 08				
Didcot Parkway	d	19 56		20 12		20 33	20 33	20 42	20 56	21 26		22 00	22 30	23 01		23 08		23 30	23 39	00 25	00 25				
Swindon	a	20 13	20 15	20 30		20 48	20 52	20 59	21 13	21 43		22 18	22 48	23 19		23 25		23 48	23 57	00 40	00 44				
	d	20 13	20 16	20 30		20 54	20 54	21 00	21 13	21 43	21 54	22 19	22 49	23 20		23 25	23 33	23 49	23 58	00 42	00 45				
Kemble	d					21 11	21 11				22 07						23 47								
Stroud	d					21 26	21 26				22 22						00 02								
Stonehouse	d					21 31	21 31				22 28						00 07								
Gloucester 7	a					21 46	21 46				22 45						00 24								
Cheltenham Spa	a					22 04	22 04				23 05														
Chippenham	d			20 44				21 15		21 58			23 03	23 33		23 39				00 56	00 59				
Bath Spa 7	a			20 59				21 28		22 10			23 17	23 47		23 54				01 11	01 13				
Bristol Parkway 7	a	20 39	20 42						21 39			22 45						00 14	00 23						
	d	20 40	20 43						21 40			22 45						00 16	00 24						
Bristol Temple Meads 10	a			21 15				21 44		22 30			23 33	00 03		00 10				01 27	01 29				
Weston-super-Mare	a			21 50									00s06												
Newport (South Wales)	a	21 04	21 05						22 03			23 19						00 38	00 52	02s00	02s10				
Cardiff Central 7	a	21 19	21 19						22 23			23 40						00 53	01 12	02 17	02 31				
Bridgend	a	21 45	21 45						22 46			00 02						01 19	01 38						
Port Talbot Parkway	a	21 58	21 58						22 59			00 15						01 32	01 51						
Neath	a	22 06	22 06						23 07			00 22						01 39	01 58						
Swansea	a	22 19	22 19						23 20			00 37						01 53	02 13						

Saturdays

		GW	GW	GW	GW	GW	GW	GW	GW	GW		GW	GW	GW	GW	GW	GW	GW	GW	GW		GW	GW	GW	GW
		◇1	◇1	◇1		◇1	◇1		◇1	◇1		■ 1	◇1	◇1	◇1	◇1	◇1	◇1	◇1	◇1			◇1	◇1	◇1
																	D	E	D	E					
		🍴	🍴	🍴		🍴	🍴		🍴	🍴		🍴	🍴	🍴	🍴	🍴	🍴	🍴	🍴	🍴			🍴	🍴	🍴
London Paddington 15 ⊖	d	21p15	21p45	22p15		22p45	23p30		06 30	07 00		07 30	07 45	08 00	08 15	08 30	08 45	08 45	09 00	09 00			09 30	09 45	10 00
Slough 3	d																								
Reading 7	d	21p41	22p11	22p41		23p11	00 05		06 59	07 27		07 57	08 11	08 27	08 41	08 57	09 11	09 11	09 27	09 27			09 57	10 11	10 27
Didcot Parkway	d	22p00	22p30	23p01		23p30	00 25		07 12			08 12			08 55	09 12							10 12		
Swindon	a	22p18	22p48	23p19		23p48	00 40		07 30	07 54		08 30	08 38	08 55	09 15	09 30	09 38	09 38	09 54	09 54			10 30	10 38	10 54
	d	22p19	22p49	23p20	23p33	23p49	00 42	07 16	07 30	07 55		08 30	08 38	08 55	09 15	09 30	09 38	09 38	09 55	09 55		10 14	10 30	10 38	10 55
Kemble	d				23p47			07 30							09 30							10 28			
Stroud	d				00 02			07 45							09 45							10 43			
Stonehouse	d				00 07			07 50							09 50							10 48			
Gloucester 7	a				00 24			08 06							10 06							11 07			
Cheltenham Spa	a							08 24							10 22							11 23			
Chippenham	d		23p03	23p33			00 56		07 44	08 09		08 44		09 09		09 44			10 09	10 09			10 44		11 09
Bath Spa 7	a		23p17	23p47			01 11		08 00	08 24		09 00		09 24		10 00			10 24	10 24			11 00		11 24
Bristol Parkway 7	a	22p45				00 14							09 04				10 04	10 05						11 04	
	d	22p45				00 16							09 07				10 07	10 07						11 07	
Bristol Temple Meads 10	a		23p33	00 03			01 27		08 15	08 39		09 15		09 39		10 15			10 39	10 39			11 15		11 39
Weston-super-Mare	a		00s06																	11 06					
Newport (South Wales)	a	23p19				00 38	02s00						09 30				10 31	10 31						11 31	
Cardiff Central 7	a	23p40				00 53	02 17						09 47				10 46	10 47						11 46	
Bridgend	a	00 02				01 19							10 09				11 09	11 09						12 09	
Port Talbot Parkway	a	00 15				01 32							10 22				11 22	11 22						12 22	
Neath	a	00 22				01 39							10 30				11 30	11 30						12 30	
Swansea	a	00 37				01 53							10 43				11 43	11 43						12 43	

A The Capitals United
B The Red Dragon
C The Bristolian
D from 17 September
E until 10 September

For connections from Heathrow Airport, Gatwick Airport and Oxford please refer to Tables 125A, 148 and 116.
For connections to Birmingham New Street and Hereford please refer to Tables 57 and 131

London - Swindon, Cheltenham Spa, Bristol, Weston-super-Mare and South Wales

		GW	GW	GW	GW	GW	GW	GW	GW	GW	GW	GW	GW	GW	GW	GW	GW	GW	GW	GW	GW	GW	GW
		◇1	◇1	◇1	◇1	◇1		◇1	◇1	◇1	◇1	◇1	◇1	◇1	◇1		◇1	◇1	◇1	◇1		◇1	◇1
			A	B	C			D	C			A	B									A	B
		☕	☕	☕	☕⊘	☕		☕⊘	☕⊘	☕	☕	☕	☕	☕	☕		☕	☕	☕	☕		☕	☕
London Paddington 15 ⊖	d	10 15	10 30	10 30	10 45	11 00		11 30	11 45	12 00	12 15	12 30	12 30	12 45	13 00		13 30	13 45	14 00	14 15		14 30	14 30
Slough 3	d																						
Reading 7	d	10 41	10 57	10 57	11 11	11 27		11 58	12 11	12 27	12 41	12 57	12 57	13 11	13 27		13 59	14 11	14 27	14 41		14 57	14 57
Didcot Parkway	d	10 55	11 12	11 12				12 12			12 55	13 12	13 12				14 12			14 55		15 12	15 12
Swindon	a	11 15	11 30	11 30	11 38	11 54		12 30	12 38	12 54	13 15	13 30	13 30	13 38	13 55		14 30	14 38	14 54	15 15		15 30	15 30
	d	11 15	11 30	11 30	11 38	11 55	12 14	12 30	12 38	12 55	13 15	13 30	13 30	13 38	13 55	14 14	14 30	14 38	14 55	15 15	15 22	15 30	15 30
Kemble	d	11 30					12 28				13 30					14 28				15 30			
Stroud	d	11 45					12 43				13 45					14 43				15 45			
Stonehouse	d	11 50					12 48				13 50					14 48				15 50			
Gloucester 7	a	12 07					13 03				14 06					15 03				16 06			
Cheltenham Spa	a	12 22					13 24				14 22					15 25				16 22			
Chippenham	d		11 44	11 44		12 09		12 43		13 09		13 44	13 44		14 09		14 44		15 09		15a38	15 44	15 44
Bath Spa 7	a		12 00	12 00		12 24		12 59		13 24		14 00	14 00		14 24		15 00		15 24			16 00	16 00
Bristol Parkway 7	a				12 04				13 04					14 04				15 04					
	d				12 07				13 07					14 07				15 07					
Bristol Temple Meads 10	a		12 15	12 15		12 39		13 14		13 42		14 15	14 15		14 39		15 15		15 41			16 15	16 15
Weston-super-Mare	a			12 35									14 35										16 35
Newport (South Wales)	a				12 31				13 31					14 31				15 31					
Cardiff Central 7	a				12 46				13 47					14 46				15 46					
Bridgend	a				13 09				14 09					15 09				16 09					
Port Talbot Parkway	a				13 22				14 22					15 22				16 22					
Neath	a				13 30				14 30					15 30				16 30					
Swansea	a				13 43				14 43					15 43				16 43					

		GW	GW	GW	GW	GW	GW	GW	GW	GW	GW	GW	GW	GW	GW	GW	GW	GW	GW	GW	GW
		◇1	◇1		◇1	◇1	◇1	◇1	◇1	◇1	◇1	◇1		◇1	◇1	◇1	◇1	◇1	◇1	◇1		◇1
					A	B																A
		☕	☕		☕	☕	☕	☕	☕	☕	☕	☕		☕	☕	☕	☕	☕	☕	☕		☕
London Paddington 15 ⊖	d	14 45	15 00		15 30	15 30	15 45	16 00	16 15	16 30	16 45	17 00		17 30	17 45	18 00	18 15	18 30	18 45	19 00		19 15
Slough 3	d																					
Reading 7	d	15 11	15 27		15 59	15 59	16 11	16 27	16 41	16 57	17 11	17 27		17 57	18 11	18 27	18 41	18 57	19 11	19 27		19 41
Didcot Parkway	d				16 12	16 12			16 55	17 12				18 12			18 55	19 12				19 55
Swindon	a	15 38	15 54		16 30	16 30	16 38	16 54	17 15	17 30	17 38	17 54		18 30	18 38	18 54	19 15	19 29	19 38	19 54		20 13
	d	15 38	15 55	16 14	16 30	16 30	16 38	16 55	17 15	17 30	17 38	17 55	18 14	18 30	18 38	18 55	19 15	19 30	19 38	19 55	20 00	20 13
Kemble	d			16 28					17 30				18 28				19 30				20 15	
Stroud	d			16 43					17 45				18 43				19 45				20 30	
Stonehouse	d			16 48					17 50				18 48				19 50				20 35	
Gloucester 7	a			17 03					18 06				19 03				20 06				20 50	
Cheltenham Spa	a			17 25					18 22				19 25				20 22				21 03	
Chippenham	d		16 09		16 44	16 44		17 09		17 44		18 09		18 44		19 09		19 44		20 09		
Bath Spa 7	a		16 24		17 00	17 00		17 24		18 00		18 24		19 00		19 24		19 59		20 24		
Bristol Parkway 7	a	16 04					17 04				18 04				19 05				20 05			20 40
	d	16 07					17 07				18 07				19 07				20 07			20 40
Bristol Temple Meads 10	a		16 39		17 15	17 15		17 39		18 15		18 39		19 15		19 38		20 15		20 40		
Weston-super-Mare	a					17 35				18 36				19 50				20 36		21 26		
Newport (South Wales)	a	16 31					17 29				18 30				19 30				20 30			21 05
Cardiff Central 7	a	16 47					17 46				18 46				19 46				20 44			21 23
Bridgend	a	17 09					18 09				19 09				20 09				21 09			21 46
Port Talbot Parkway	a	17 22					18 22				19 22				20 22				21 22			21 59
Neath	a	17 30					18 30				19 30				20 30				21 30			22 07
Swansea	a	17 43					18 46				19 43				20 43				21 43			22 19

		GW	GW	GW	GW	GW	GW	GW	GW	GW	GW	GW	GW	GW	GW	GW
		◇1	◇1	◇1		◇1	◇1	◇1	◇1		◇1	◇1	◇1		◇1	◇1
												E	F	E	E	F
														🚌		
		☕	☕	☕		☕	☕	☕	☕		☕	☕	☕		☕	☕
London Paddington 15 ⊖	d	19 30	19 45	20 00		20 15	20 30	20 45	21 30		22 00	22 35	22 35		23 30	23 30
Slough 3	d															
Reading 7	d	19 57	20 11	20 27		20 41	20 57	21 11	21 57		22 27	23 02	23 02		23 59	23 59
Didcot Parkway	d	20 12		20 42		20 55	21 12		22 12		22 41	23 22	23 22		00 18	00 18
Swindon	a	20 30	20 38	21 00		21 15	21 30	21 40	22 30		22 59	23 39	23 40		00 36	00 36
	d	20 30	20 38	21 00	21 08	21 15	21 30	21 41	22 30	22 35	22 59	23 40	23 41	23 49	00 36	00 36
Kemble	d					21 30				22 49						
Stroud	d					21 45				23 04						
Stonehouse	d					21 50				23 09						
Gloucester 7	a					22 05				23 25						
Cheltenham Spa	a					22 20										
Chippenham	d	20 45		21 14	21a24		21 45		22 44				23 55	00 24		00 51
Bath Spa 7	a	21 00		21 29			21 58		23 00				00 10	00 59		01 07
Bristol Parkway 7	a		21 04					22 06			23 27					
	d		21 07					22 11			23 28					
Bristol Temple Meads 10	a	21 16		21 45			22 14		23 15			00 15	00 25	01 29	01 09	01 21
Weston-super-Mare	a						22s47									
Newport (South Wales)	a		21 30					22 46			23 57					
Cardiff Central 7	a		21 47					23 06			00 18					
Bridgend	a		22 09					23 28								
Port Talbot Parkway	a		22 22					23 41								
Neath	a		22 30					23 49								
Swansea	a		22 43					00 02								

A from 17 September
B until 10 September
C ☕ from Bridgend ⊘ to Cardiff Central
D ☕ from Chippenham ⊘ to Swindon
E from 6 August until 10 September
F until 30 July, from 17 September

For connections from Heathrow Airport, Gatwick Airport and Oxford please refer to Tables 125A, 148 and 116.
For connections to Birmingham New Street and Hereford please refer to Tables 57 and 131

Table 125

Sundays
until 19 June

London - Swindon, Cheltenham Spa, Bristol, Weston-super-Mare and South Wales

		GW	GW	GW	GW	GW	GW	GW	GW	GW		GW	GW	GW	GW	GW	GW	GW	GW	GW		GW	GW	GW	GW
		◇1	◇1	◇1	◇1	◇1	◇1	◇1	◇1	◇1			◇1	◇1	◇1	◇1	◇1	◇1	◇1	◇1		◇1	◇1		◇1
		A	A	A	A																				
		🍴	🍴	🍴	🍴	🍴	🍴	🍴	🍴	🍴			🍴	🍴	🍴	🍴	🍴	🍴	🍴	🍴		🍴	🍴		🍴
London Paddington 15 ⊖	d	20p45	22p00	22p35	23p30	08 00	08 30	08 37	09 00	09 30			10 00	10 30	10 37	11 00	11 30	12 00	12 30	12 37		13 00	13 37		14 00
Slough 3	d	⌇	⌇	⌇	⌇																				
Reading 7	d	21p11	22p27	23p02	23p59	08 38	09 11	09 15	09 38	10 06			10 38	11 05	11 14	11 38	12 06	12 38	13 05	13 15		13 38	14 12		14 38
Didcot Parkway	d	⌇	22p41	23p22	00⌇18	08 53	09 27		09 53	10 22			10 53	11 20		11 53	12 20	12 53	13 20			13 53	14 27		14 53
Swindon	a	21p40	22p59	23p40	00⌇36	09 11	09 44	09 49	10 11	10 38			11 11	11 36	11 41	12 11	12 36	13 11	13 37	13 41		14 11	14 43		15 11
	d	21p41	22p59	23p41	00⌇36	09 11	09 45	09 50	10 11	10 40		10 47	11 11	11 38	11 42	12 11	12 38	13 11	13 38	13 43		14 11	14 46	15 04	15 11
Kemble	d	⌇	⌇	⌇	⌇			10 04				11 01			11 56					13 57				15 19	
Stroud	d	⌇	⌇	⌇	⌇			10 19				11 16			12 11					14 12				15 34	
Stonehouse	d	⌇	⌇	⌇	⌇			10 24				11 21			12 16					14 17				15 39	
Gloucester 7	a	⌇	⌇	⌇	⌇			11 01				12 00			13 19					15 10				15 57	
Cheltenham Spa	a	⌇	⌇	⌇	⌇			11 15				12 16			13 36					15 27				16 17	
Chippenham	d	⌇	⌇	23p55	00⌇51	09 26			10 26				11 26			12 26		13 26				14 26			15 26
Bath Spa 7	a	⌇	⌇	00⌇10	01⌇07	09 45			10 40				11 40			12 40		13 40				14 40			15 40
Bristol Parkway 7	a	22p06	23p27	⌇	⌇		10 09			11 04				12 03			13 05		14 03				15 10		
	d	22p11	23p28	⌇	⌇		10 11			11 06				12 04			13 06		14 04				15 11		
Bristol Temple Meads 10	a	⌇	⌇	00⌇25	01⌇21	09 55			10 55				11 55			12 55		13 55				14 55			15 55
Weston-super-Mare	a	⌇	⌇										12 33					14 27							
Newport (South Wales)	a	22p46	23p57				10 36			11 31				12 32			13 35		14 32				15 37		
Cardiff Central 7	a	23p06	00⌇18				10 53			11 48				12 51			13 55		14 51				15 56		
Bridgend	a	23p28					11 16			12 11				13 13			14 17		15 13				16 18		
Port Talbot Parkway	a	23p41					11 29			12 24				13 26			14 30		15 26				16 31		
Neath	a	23p49					11 38			12 33				13 33			14 37		15 33				16 38		
Swansea	a	00⌇02					11 51			12 46				13 47			14 51		15 47				16 52		

		GW	GW	GW	GW	GW		GW	GW	GW	GW	GW	GW	GW	GW	GW		GW	GW	GW	GW	GW	GW	GW	GW
		◇1	◇1	◇1	◇1	◇1		◇1	◇1	◇1			◇1	◇1	◇1	◇1		◇1	◇1	◇1	◇1	◇1	◇1	◇1	◇1
		🍴	🍴	🍴	🍴	🍴		🍴	🍴	🍴			🍴	🍴	🍴	🍴		🍴	🍴	🍴	🍴	🍴	🍴	🍴	🍴
London Paddington 15 ⊖	d	14 27	14 37	15 00	15 37	16 00		16 27	16 37	17 00			17 30	17 37	18 00	18 27		18 37	19 00	19 30	19 37	20 00	20 30	20 37	21 00
Slough 3	d																								
Reading 7	d	15 04	15 17	15 38	16 18	16 38		17 05	17 14	17 40			18 13	18 17	18 38	19 04		19 15	19 38	20 07	20 17	20 38	21 08	21 16	21 38
Didcot Parkway	d		15 31	15 53	16 32	16 53			17 29	17 53				18 31	18 53			19 30	19 53		20 32	20 53		21 30	21 53
Swindon	a	15 31	15 48	16 11	16 49	17 11		17 35	17 45	18 11			18 42	18 47	19 11	19 33		19 46	20 11	20 36	20 49	21 11	21 35	21 47	22 14
	d	15 35	15 49	16 11	16 51	17 11		17 36	17 48	18 11	18 19	18 22	18 42	18 49	19 11	19 43		19 49	20 11	20 36	20 50	21 11	21 38	21 49	22 15
Kemble	d	15 48						17 50				18 36				19 56							21 51		
Stroud	d	16 03						18 05				18 50				20 11							22 06		
Stonehouse	d	16 08						18 09				18 55				20 16							22 11		
Gloucester 7	a	16 25						18 25				19 16				20 31							22 26		
Cheltenham Spa	a	16 51						18 46								20 46							22 41		
Chippenham	d			16 26		17 26				18 26	18a35		18 56		19 26				20 26	20 50		21 26			22 27
Bath Spa 7	a			16 40		17 40				18 40			19 12		19 40				20 40	21 04		21 40			22 42
Bristol Parkway 7	a		16 14		17 16				18 12					19 15				20 13			21 15			22 13	
	d		16 14		17 16				18 13					19 16				20 14			21 16			22 15	
Bristol Temple Meads 10	a			16 54		17 57				18 55			19 26		19 55				20 55	21 19		21 55			22 57
Weston-super-Mare	a			17 27									19 59						21 27			22 27			
Newport (South Wales)	a		16 40		17 44				18 41					19 42				20 40			21 44			22 40	
Cardiff Central 7	a		16 59		18 01				18 58					20 00				20 59			22 06			23 02	
Bridgend	a		17 21		18 23				19 20					20 23				21 21			22 29			23 23	
Port Talbot Parkway	a		17 34		18 36				19 33					20 36				21 34			22 42			23 36	
Neath	a		17 41		18 44				19 40					20 44				21 41			22 50			23 43	
Swansea	a		17 56		18 57				19 54					20 58				21 55			23 03			23 57	

		GW		GW	GW	GW	GW
		◇1			◇1	◇1	◇1
		🍴			🍴	🍴	🍴
London Paddington 15 ⊖	d	21 37			22 03	23 03	23 37
Slough 3	d						
Reading 7	d	22 15			22 42	23 47	00 15
Didcot Parkway	d	22 31			22 57	00s02	00s32
Swindon	a	22 49			23 16	00s21	00s52
	d	22 51		22 57	23 17		
Kemble	d			23 11			
Stroud	d			23 26			
Stonehouse	d			23 31			
Gloucester 7	a			23 46			
Cheltenham Spa	a			23 58			
Chippenham	d				23 31	00s37	01s07
Bath Spa 7	a				23 45	00s51	01s22
Bristol Parkway 7	a	23 16					
	d	23 17					
Bristol Temple Meads 10	a				00 02	01 05	01 36
Weston-super-Mare	a						
Newport (South Wales)	a	23 44					
Cardiff Central 7	a	00 06					
Bridgend	a	00 29					
Port Talbot Parkway	a	00 42					
Neath	a	00 49					
Swansea	a	01 03					

A not 22 May

For connections from Heathrow Airport, Gatwick Airport and Oxford please refer to Tables 125A, 148 and 116.
For connections to Birmingham New Street and Hereford please refer to Tables 57 and 131

Table 125

Sundays

26 June to 31 July

London - Swindon, Cheltenham Spa, Bristol, Weston-super-Mare and South Wales

		GW ◇1 ⊏	GW ◇1 ⊏	GW ◇1 ⊏	GW ◇1 ⊏	GW ◇1 ⊏	GW ◇1 ⊏	GW	GW ◇1 ⊏	GW ◇1 ⊏	GW	GW ◇1 ⊏	GW ◇1 ⊏	GW ◇1 ⊏	GW ◇1 ⊏	GW	GW ◇1 ⊏	GW ◇1 ⊏	GW ◇1 ⊏	GW ◇1 ⊏	GW	GW ◇1 ⊏	GW ◇1 ⊏
London Paddington 15 ⊖	d	20p45	22p00	22p35	23p30	07 57	08 00		09 00	09 30		10 00	10 30	11 00	11 30		12 00	12 30	12 37	13 00		13 30	14 00
Slough 3	d																						
Reading 7	d	21p11	22p27	23p02	23p59	08 34	08 38		09 38	10 05		10 38	11 05	11 38	12 06		12 38	13 05	13 15	13 38		14 05	14 38
Didcot Parkway	d		22p41	23p22	00 18	08 51	08 53		09 53	10 20		10 53	11 20	11 53	12 20		12 53	13 20		13 53		14 20	14 53
Swindon	a	21p40	22p59	23p40	00 36	09 08	09 11		10 11	10 37		11 11	11 37	12 11	12 38		13 11	13 38	13 41	14 11		14 37	15 11
	d	21p41	22p59	23p41	00 36	09 10	09 11	09 45	10 11	10 38	10 47	11 11	11 39	12 11	12 39	12 45	13 11	13 40	13 43	14 11	14 21	14 39	15 11
Kemble	d							10a03			11a05					13a03			13 57		14 36		
Stroud	d																		14 12		14 51		
Stonehouse	d																		14 17		14 56		
Gloucester 7	a																		14 35		15 19		
Cheltenham Spa	a																		14 49		15 33		
Chippenham	d			23p55	00 51		09 26		10 26			11 26		12 26			13 26			14 26			15 26
Bath Spa 7	a			00 10	01 07		09 45		10 40			11 40		12 40			13 40			14 40			15 40
Bristol Parkway 7	a	22p06	23p27			10 00				11 19			12 20		13 20			14 26				15 25	
	d	22p11	23p28			10 08				11 26			12 27		13 29			14 33				15 32	
Bristol Temple Meads 10	a			00 25	01 21		09 55		10 55			11 55		12 55			13 55			14 55			15 55
Weston-super-Mare	a											12 33					14 27						
Newport (South Wales)	a	22p46	23p57			10 33				11 51			12 54		13 54			14 59				15 58	
Cardiff Central 7	a	23p06	00 18			10 51				12 08			13 12		14 12			15 17				16 17	
Bridgend	a	23p28				11 14				12 31			13 34		14 35			15 39				16 39	
Port Talbot Parkway	a	23p41				11 27				12 46			13 47		14 48			15 52				16 52	
Neath	a	23p49				11 35				12 55			13 55		14 56			16 00				16 58	
Swansea	a	00 02				11 49				13 08			14 08		15 09			16 13				17 13	

		GW ◇1 ⊏	GW ◇1 ⊏	GW ◇1 ⊏	GW ◇1 ⊏	GW ◇1 ⊏	GW ◇1 ⊏	GW ◇1 ⊏	GW ◇1 ⊏	GW	GW	GW ◇1 ⊏	GW ◇1 ⊏	GW ◇1 ⊏	GW ◇1 ⊏	GW ◇1 ⊏	GW ◇1 ⊏	GW ◇1 ⊏	GW ◇1 ⊏	GW ◇1 ⊏	GW ◇1 ⊏	GW ◇1 ⊏	GW ◇1 ⊏
London Paddington 15 ⊖	d	14 27	14 30	15 00	15 30	16 00	16 27	16 30	17 00			17 30	17 30	18 00	18 27	18 30	19 00	19 30	19 37	20 00	20 30	20 37	21 00
Slough 3	d																						
Reading 7	d	15 05	15 10	15 38	16 05	16 38	17 05	17 10	17 40			18 05	18 16	18 38	19 04	19 15	19 38	20 05	20 17	20 38	21 05	21 15	21 38
Didcot Parkway	d		15 24	15 53	16 20	16 53		17 24	17 53			18 20		18 53		19 30	19 53	20 20		20 53	21 20		21 53
Swindon	a	15 31	15 42	16 11	16 37	17 11	17 35	17 42	18 11			18 37	18 45	19 11	19 33	19 47	20 11	20 37	20 45	21 11	21 37	21 45	22 14
	d	15 35	15 43	16 11	16 39	17 11	17 36	17 43	18 11	18 19	18 22	18 39	18 45	19 11	19 43	19 49	20 11	20 39	20 45	21 11	21 39	21 45	22 15
Kemble	d	15 48					17 50				18 36				19 56							21 57	
Stroud	d	16 03					18 05				18 50				20 11							22 12	
Stonehouse	d	16 08					18 09				18 55				20 16							22 17	
Gloucester 7	a	16 25					18 25				19 16				20 31							22 35	
Cheltenham Spa	a	16 46					18 46								20 46							22 52	
Chippenham	d			16 26		17 26			18 26	18a35			18 59	19 26			20 26		20 59	21 26			22 27
Bath Spa 7	a			16 40		17 40			18 40				19 15	19 40			20 40		21 13	21 40			22 42
Bristol Parkway 7	a		16 24		17 23			18 24				19 19				20 29		21 27			22 27		
	d		16 32		17 32			18 32				19 26				20 36		21 34			22 34		
Bristol Temple Meads 10	a			16 54		17 57			18 55				19 29	19 55			20 55		21 31	21 55			22 57
Weston-super-Mare	a			17 27									20 02				21 27			22 27			
Newport (South Wales)	a		16 56		18 01			18 58				19 52				21 02		22 00			23 04		
Cardiff Central 7	a		17 15		18 18			19 16				20 09				21 20		22 22			23 27		
Bridgend	a		17 37		18 41			19 39				20 32				21 42		22 45			23 49		
Port Talbot Parkway	a		17 50		18 54			19 51				20 46				21 59		22 58			00 02		
Neath	a		17 57		19 02			19 59				20 54				22 07		23 05			00 09		
Swansea	a		18 12		19 16			20 13				21 07				22 21		23 19			00 23		

		GW ◇1 ⊏	GW	GW ◇1 ⊏	GW ◇1 ⊏	GW ◇1 ⊏
London Paddington 15 ⊖	d	21 30		22 03	23 03	23 37
Slough 3	d					
Reading 7	d	22 08		22 42	23 47	00 15
Didcot Parkway	d	22 24		22 57	00s02	00s32
Swindon	a	22 42		23 16	00s21	00s52
	d	22 44	22 57	23 17		
Kemble	d		23 11			
Stroud	d		23 26			
Stonehouse	d		23 31			
Gloucester 7	a		23 54			
Cheltenham Spa	a		00 12			
Chippenham	d			23 31	00s37	01s07
Bath Spa 7	a			23 45	00s51	01s22
Bristol Parkway 7	a	23 31				
	d	23 37				
Bristol Temple Meads 10	a			00 02	01 05	01 36
Weston-super-Mare	a					
Newport (South Wales)	a	00 01				
Cardiff Central 7	a	00 23				
Bridgend	a	00 45				
Port Talbot Parkway	a	00 58				
Neath	a	01 06				
Swansea	a	01 19				

For connections from Heathrow Airport, Gatwick Airport and Oxford please refer to Tables 125A, 148 and 116.
For connections to Birmingham New Street and Hereford please refer to Tables 57 and 131

Table 125

Sundays

7 August to 11 September

London - Swindon, Cheltenham Spa, Bristol, Weston-super-Mare and South Wales

		GW	GW	GW	GW	GW	GW	GW	GW	GW		GW	GW	GW	GW	GW	GW	GW	GW	GW		GW	GW	GW	GW
		◇1	◇1	◇1		◇1		◇1	◇1	◇1		◇1	◇1	◇1	◇1	◇1	◇1	◇1	◇1	◇1		◇1	◇1	◇1	◇1
		☕	☕	☕	🚌	☕	🚌	☕	☕	☕		☕	☕	☕	☕	☕	☕	☕	☕	☕		☕	☕	☕	☕
London Paddington 15 ⊖	d	20p45	22p00	22p35		23p30		08 00	08 30	08 37		09 00	09 30		09 42	10 00	10 27	10 37	11 00	11 30		11 37	12 00	12 27	12 30
Slough 3	d																								
Reading 7	d	21p11	22p27	23p02		23p59		08 38	09 06	09 17		09 35	10 06		10 21	10 38	11 04	11 15	11 38	12 06		12 15	12 38	13 04	13 09
Didcot Parkway	d		22p41	23p22		00 18		08 53	09 23			09 50			10 36	10 53		11 30	11 53			12 29	12 53		
Swindon	a	21p40	22p59	23p39		00 36		09 06	09 41	09 44		10 08	10 34		10 52	11 11	11 31	11 47	12 11	12 34		12 45	13 11	13 30	13 37
	d	21p41	22p59	23p40	23p49	00 36	00 46	09 06	09 42	09 49		10 08		10 47	10 54	11 11	11 31	11 48	12 11			12 47	13 11	13 33	
Kemble	d									10 03				11 01			11 46							13 48	
Stroud	d									10 18				11 16			12 01							14 03	
Stonehouse	d									10 23				11 21			12 06							14 08	
Gloucester 7	a									10 38				11 36			12 17							14 22	
Cheltenham Spa	a									10 52				11 49			12 34							14 46	
Chippenham	d				00 24		01 21	09 21				10 23				11 26			12 26				13 26		
Bath Spa 7	a				00 59		01 56	09 37				10 37				11 40			12 40				13 40		
Bristol Parkway 7	a	22p06	23p27						10 07						11 18			12 13				13 14			
	d	22p11	23p28						10 08						11 20			12 15				13 15			
Bristol Temple Meads 10	a			00 15	01 29	01 09	02 26	09 52				10 52				11 55			12 55				13 55		
Weston-super-Mare	a															12 31			13 18				14 28		
Newport (South Wales)	a	22p46	23p57						10 33						11 45			12 41				13 38			
Cardiff Central 7	a	23p06	00 18						10 51						12 02			12 59				13 57			
Bridgend	a	23p28							11 14						12 29			13 21				14 19			
Port Talbot Parkway	a	23p41							11 27						12 45			13 34				14 32			
Neath	a	23p49							11 35						12 54			13 42				14 38			
Swansea	a	00 02							11 49						13 07			13 55				14 53			

		GW	GW	GW	GW	GW		GW	GW	GW	GW	GW	GW	GW	GW	GW		GW	GW	GW	GW	GW	GW	GW	GW
		◇1	◇1		◇1	◇1		◇1	◇1	◇1	◇1	◇1	◇1	◇1	◇1				◇1	◇1	◇1	◇1	◇1	◇1	◇1
		☕	☕		☕	☕		☕	☕	☕	☕	☕	☕	☕	☕				☕	☕	☕	☕	☕	☕	☕
London Paddington 15 ⊖	d	12 37	13 00		13 37	14 00		14 27	14 37	15 00	15 37	16 00	16 27	16 37	17 00				17 30	17 37	18 00	18 27	18 37	19 00	19 30
Slough 3	d																								
Reading 7	d	13 16	13 38		14 17	14 38		15 05	15 15	15 38	16 17	16 38	17 06	17 19	17 38				18 04	18 17	18 38	19 04	19 14	19 38	20 06
Didcot Parkway	d	13 31	13 53		14 31	14 53			15 30	15 53	16 32	16 53		17 34	17 53					18 32	18 53		19 29	19 53	
Swindon	a	13 48	14 11		14 48	15 11		15 31	15 47	16 11	16 48	17 11	17 36	17 50	18 11				18 32	18 46	19 11	19 33	19 45	20 11	20 34
	d	13 49	14 11	14 21	14 50	15 11		15 35	15 48	16 11	16 51	17 11	17 36	17 53	18 11	18 19		18 22	18 32	18 49	19 11	19 43	19 47	20 11	20 34
Kemble	d			14 36				15 48					17 50					18 36				19 56			
Stroud	d			14 51				16 03					18 08					18 50				20 11			
Stonehouse	d			14 56				16 08					18 12					18 55				20 16			
Gloucester 7	a			15 19				16 25					18 29					19 16				20 31			
Cheltenham Spa	a			15 33				16 46					18 46									20 46			
Chippenham	d		14 26			15 26				16 26		17 26			18 26	18a35			18 47		19 26			20 26	20 49
Bath Spa 7	a		14 40			15 40				16 40		17 40			18 40				19 06		19 40			20 40	21 02
Bristol Parkway 7	a	14 14			15 14				16 13		17 15			18 17						19 14			20 11		
	d	14 15			15 16				16 14		17 15			18 19						19 15			20 13		
Bristol Temple Meads 10	a		14 55			15 55				16 55		17 55			18 55				19 23		19 56			20 55	21 17
Weston-super-Mare	a									17 28									19 57					21 27	
Newport (South Wales)	a	14 41			15 42				16 40		17 43			18 45						19 41			20 39		
Cardiff Central 7	a	15 00			16 00				17 00		18 00			19 03						19 59			20 57		
Bridgend	a	15 22			16 22				17 22		18 23			19 26						20 22			21 19		
Port Talbot Parkway	a	15 35			16 35				17 35		18 36			19 38						20 35			21 32		
Neath	a	15 42			16 42				17 41		18 44			19 46						20 43			21 40		
Swansea	a	15 56			16 56				17 57		19 00			19 59						20 56			21 53		

		GW		GW	GW	GW	GW	GW	GW	GW	GW	GW
		◇1		◇1	◇1	◇1	◇1	◇1		◇1	◇1	◇1
		☕		☕	☕	☕	☕	☕		☕	☕	☕
London Paddington 15 ⊖	d	19 37		20 00	20 30	20 37	21 00	21 37		22 03	23 03	23 37
Slough 3	d											
Reading 7	d	20 17		20 38	21 06	21 17	21 38	22 14		22 50	23 47	00 15
Didcot Parkway	d	20 31		20 53		21 32	21 53	22 31		23 05	00s02	00s32
Swindon	a	20 48		21 11	21 35	21 48	22 13	22 49		23 25	00s21	00s52
	d	20 50		21 11	21 36	21 51	22 13	22 51	22 57	23 25		
Kemble	d				21 50				23 11			
Stroud	d				22 05				23 26			
Stonehouse	d				22 10				23 31			
Gloucester 7	a				22 24				23 46			
Cheltenham Spa	a				22 40				23 58			
Chippenham	d			21 26			22 28			23 39	00s37	01 07
Bath Spa 7	a			21 40			22 43			23 53	00s51	01 20
Bristol Parkway 7	a	21 15				22 15		23 16				
	d	21 16				22 16		23 17				
Bristol Temple Meads 10	a			21 55			22 58			00 15	01 12	01 42
Weston-super-Mare	a			22 29								
Newport (South Wales)	a	21 44				22 44		23 44				
Cardiff Central 7	a	22 06				23 06		00 06				
Bridgend	a	22 29				23 28		00 29				
Port Talbot Parkway	a	22 42				23 41		00 42				
Neath	a	22 50				23 49		00 49				
Swansea	a	23 03				00 02		01 03				

For connections from Heathrow Airport, Gatwick Airport and Oxford please refer to Tables 125A, 148 and 116.
For connections to Birmingham New Street and Hereford please refer to Tables 57 and 131

Sundays

18 September to 23 October

London - Swindon, Cheltenham Spa, Bristol, Weston-super-Mare and South Wales

		GW	GW	GW	GW	GW	GW	GW	GW	GW	GW	GW	GW	GW	GW	GW	GW	GW	GW	GW	GW	GW	GW
		◇1	◇1	◇1	◇1	◇1	◇1	◇1	◇1	◇1		◇1	◇1	◇1		◇1	◇1	◇1	◇1		◇1	◇1	◇1
		🛒	🛒	🛒	🛒	🛒	🛒	🛒	🛒	🛒		🛒	🛒	🛒		🛒	🛒	🛒	🛒		🛒	🛒	🛒
London Paddington 15 ⊖	d	20p45	22p00	22p35	23p30	08 00	08 30		09 00	09 30		09 42	10 00	10 37		11 00	11 30	11 37	12 00		12 30	12 37	13 00
Slough 3	d																						
Reading 7	d	21p11	22p27	23p02	23p59	08 38	09 06		09 35	10 06		10 21	10 38	11 15		11 38	12 06	12 15	12 38		13 09	13 16	13 38
Didcot Parkway	d		22p41	23p22	00 18	08 53	09 23		09 50			10 36	10 53	11 30		11 53		12 29	12 53			13 31	13 53
Swindon	a	21p40	22p59	23p40	00 36	09 11	09 41		10 08	10 34		10 52	11 11	11 47		12 11	12 34	12 45	13 11		13 37	13 48	14 11
	d	21p41	22p59	23p41	00 36	09 11	09 42	09 50	10 08		10 47	10 54	11 11	11 48	11 47	12 11		12 47	13 11	13 21		13 49	14 11
Kemble	d							10 03			11 01				12 02					13 36			
Stroud	d							10 18			11 16				12 17					13 51			
Stonehouse	d							10 23			11 21				12 22					13 56			
Gloucester 7	a							10 40			11 36				12 39					14 19			
Cheltenham Spa	a							10 55			11 49				12 51					14 33			
Chippenham	d			23p55	00 51	09 26			10 23				11 26			12 26			13 26				14 26
Bath Spa 7	a			00 10	01 07	09 40			10 37				11 40			12 40			13 40				14 40
Bristol Parkway 7	a	22p06	23p27				10 07					11 18		12 13				13 14				14 14	
	d	22p11	23p28				10 08					11 20		12 15				13 15				14 15	
Bristol Temple Meads 10	a			00 25	01 21	09 55			10 52				11 55			12 53			13 55				14 55
Weston-super-Mare	a												12 31			13 18			14 28				
Newport (South Wales)	a	22p46	23p57				10 36					11 45		12 41				13 38				14 41	
Cardiff Central 7	a	23p06	00 18				10 54					12 02		12 59				13 57				15 00	
Bridgend	a	23p28					11 17					12 25		13 21				14 19				15 22	
Port Talbot Parkway	a	23p41					11 30					12 38		13 34				14 32				15 35	
Neath	a	23p49					11 38					12 47		13 42				14 38				15 42	
Swansea	a	00 02					11 52					13 01		13 55				14 53				15 56	

		GW	GW	GW	GW	GW	GW	GW	GW	GW	GW	GW	GW	GW	GW	GW	GW	GW	GW	GW	GW	GW	GW
			◇1	◇1	◇1		◇1	◇1	◇1	◇1	◇1	◇1			◇1	◇1	◇1	◇1	◇1	◇1	◇1	◇1	◇1
			🛒	🛒	🛒		🛒	🛒	🛒	🛒	🛒	🛒			🛒	🛒	🛒	🛒	🛒	🛒	🛒	🛒	🛒
London Paddington 15 ⊖	d		13 37	14 00	14 37		15 00	15 37	16 00	16 27	16 37	17 00			17 30	17 37	17 57	18 00	18 27	18 37	18 57	19 00	19 30
Slough 3	d																						
Reading 7	d		14 17	14 38	15 15		15 38	16 17	16 38	17 06	17 19	17 38			18 04	18 17	18 33	18 38	19 04	19 14	19 34	19 38	20 06
Didcot Parkway	d		14 31	14 53	15 30		15 53	16 32	16 53		17 34	17 53				18 32		18 53		19 29		19 53	
Swindon	a		14 48	15 11	15 47		16 11	16 48	17 11	17 36	17 50	18 11			18 32	18 46	19 01	19 11	19 33	19 45	20 02	20 11	20 34
	d	14 21	14 50	15 11	15 48	16 00	16 11	16 51	17 11	17 36	17 53	18 11	18 19	18 22	18 32	18 49		19 11	19 43	19 47		20 11	20 34
Kemble	d	14 36				16 15				17 50				18 36					19 56				
Stroud	d	14 51				16 30				18 08				18 50					20 11				
Stonehouse	d	14 56				16 35				18 12				18 55					20 16				
Gloucester 7	a	15 19				16 52				18 29				19 16					20 31				
Cheltenham Spa	a	15 33				17 04				18 46									20 46				
Chippenham	d			15 26			16 26		17 26			18 26	18a35		18 47			19 26				20 26	20 49
Bath Spa 7	a			15 40			16 40		17 40			18 40			19 06			19 40				20 40	21 02
Bristol Parkway 7	a		15 14		16 13			17 15			18 17					19 14				20 11			
	d		15 16		16 14			17 15			18 19					19 15				20 13			
Bristol Temple Meads 10	a			15 55			16 55		17 55			18 55			19 23			19 56				20 55	21 17
Weston-super-Mare	a						17 28								19 57							21 27	
Newport (South Wales)	a		15 42		16 40			17 43			18 45					19 41				20 39			
Cardiff Central 7	a		16 00		17 00			18 00			19 03					19 59				20 57			
Bridgend	a		16 22		17 22			18 23			19 26					20 22				21 19			
Port Talbot Parkway	a		16 35		17 35			18 36			19 38					20 35				21 32			
Neath	a		16 42		17 41			18 44			19 46					20 43				21 40			
Swansea	a		16 56		17 57			19 00			19 59					20 56				21 53			

		GW	GW	GW	GW	GW	GW	XC	GW	GW	GW	XC	GW	GW	GW
		◇1	◇1	◇1	◇1	◇1	◇1	◇1	◇1		◇1	◇1	◇1	◇1	◇1
		🛒	🛒	🛒	🛒	🛒	🛒		🛒		🛒		🛒	🛒	🛒
London Paddington 15 ⊖	d	19 37	19 57	20 00	20 30	20 37	21 00		21 37		22 03		22 37	23 03	23 37
Slough 3	d														
Reading 7	d	20 17	20 33	20 38	21 06	21 17	21 38		22 14		22 50		23 15	23 47	00 15
Didcot Parkway	d	20 31		20 53		21 32	21 53		22 31		23 05		23s30	00s02	00s32
Swindon	a	20 48	21 01	21 11	21 35	21 48	22 13		22 49		23 25		23s48	00s21	00s52
	d	20 50		21 11	21 36	21 51	22 13	22 47	22 51	22 57	23 25	23 38			
Kemble	d				21 50					23 11					
Stroud	d				22 05					23 26					
Stonehouse	d				22 10					23 31					
Gloucester 7	a				22 24					23 46					
Cheltenham Spa	a				22 40					23 58					
Chippenham	d			21 26			22 28				23 40			00s37	01s07
Bath Spa 7	a			21 40			22 43				23 54			00s51	01s22
Bristol Parkway 7	a	21 15				22 15			23 16						
	d	21 16				22 16			23 17						
Bristol Temple Meads 10	a			21 55			23 00	23 20			00 09	00 13	00 25	01 05	01 36
Weston-super-Mare	a			22 29											
Newport (South Wales)	a	21 44				22 44			23 44						
Cardiff Central 7	a	22 06				23 06			00 06						
Bridgend	a	22 29				23 28			00 29						
Port Talbot Parkway	a	22 42				23 41			00 42						
Neath	a	22 50				23 49			00 49						
Swansea	a	23 03				00 02			01 03						

For connections from Heathrow Airport, Gatwick Airport and Oxford please refer to Tables 125A, 148 and 116.
For connections to Birmingham New Street and Hereford please refer to Tables 57 and 131

London - Swindon, Cheltenham Spa, Bristol, Weston-super-Mare and South Wales

	GW	GW	GW	GW	GW	GW	GW	GW	GW		GW	GW	GW	GW	GW	GW	GW	GW	GW		GW	GW	GW	GW
	◇1	◇1	◇1	◇1		◇1					◇1					◇1						◇1		
					[bus]		[bus]		[bus]			[bus]		[bus]	[bus]		[bus]		[bus]		[bus]		[bus]	[bus]
	[cup]	[cup]	[cup]	[cup]		[cup]					[cup]					[cup]						[cup]		
London Paddington 15 ⊖ d	20p45	22p00	22p35	23p30																				
Slough 3 d																								
Reading 7 d	21p11	22p27	23p02	23p59			08 40					09 40			10 11		10 40		11 11				11 41	
Didcot Parkway d		22p41	23p22	00 18	08 05				09 15					10 15							11 30			12 20
Swindon a	21p40	22p59	23p40	00 36	08 55		09 40		10 05			10 40		11 05	11 11		11 40		12 16		12 20		12 46	13 10
d	21p41	22p59	23p41	00 36		09 08		09 50			10 14		10 50			11 15		11 47				12 29		
Kemble d								10 04					11 04					12 02						
Stroud d								10 19					11 19					12 17						
Stonehouse d								10 24					11 24					12 22						
Gloucester 7 a								10 43					11 42					12 39						
Cheltenham Spa a								10 55					11 54					12 51						
Chippenham d			23p55	00 51		09 23					10 29					11 29						12 43		
Bath Spa 7 a			00 10	01 07		09 38					10 44					11 43						12 57		
Bristol Parkway 7 a	22p06	23p27																						
d	22p11	23p28																						
Bristol Temple Meads 10 a			00 25	01 21		09 53					10 59					11 57						13 12		
Weston-super-Mare a																12 31								
Newport (South Wales) a	22p46	23p57																						
Cardiff Central 7 a	23p06	00 18																						
Bridgend a	23p28																							
Port Talbot Parkway a	23p41																							
Neath a	23p49																							
Swansea a	00 02																							

	GW	GW	GW	GW	GW		GW	GW	GW	GW	GW	GW	GW	GW	GW		GW	GW	GW	GW	GW	GW	GW	GW
			◇1						◇1				◇1						◇1					◇1
	[bus]			[bus]	[bus]		[bus]			[bus]	[bus]	[bus]		[bus]			[bus]	[bus]		[bus]	[bus]	[bus]		
			[cup]						[cup]				[cup]						[cup]					[cup]
London Paddington 15 ⊖ d																								
Slough 3 d																								
Reading 7 d	12 11			12 41			13 11			13 41	14 11			14 41			15 11			15 41	16 11			
Didcot Parkway d					13 20							14 30						15 30				16 30		
Swindon a	13 16			13 46	14 10		14 16			14 46	15 16	15 20		15 46			16 16	16 20		16 46	17 16	17 20		
d		13 21	13 25					14 21	14 30				15 29		16 00				16 29				17 27	17 29
Kemble d		13 35						14 36							16 15								17 46	
Stroud d		13 50						14 51							16 30								18 01	
Stonehouse d		13 55						14 56							16 35								18 06	
Gloucester 7 a		14 16						15 16							16 52								18 26	
Cheltenham Spa a		14 30						15 31							17 04								18 46	
Chippenham d			13 39						14 44				15 43						16 43					17 43
Bath Spa 7 a			13 52						14 58				15 57						16 57					17 57
Bristol Parkway 7 a																								
d																								
Bristol Temple Meads 10 a			14 07						15 12				16 12						17 11					18 12
Weston-super-Mare a			14 40																					
Newport (South Wales) a																								
Cardiff Central 7 a																								
Bridgend a																								
Port Talbot Parkway a																								
Neath a																								
Swansea a																								

	GW		GW	GW	GW	GW	GW	GW	GW	GW	GW		GW	GW	GW	GW	GW	GW	GW	GW	GW		GW	GW
							◇1				◇1						◇1				1			
	[bus]			[bus]	[bus]			[bus]	[bus]	[bus]				[bus]	[bus]	[bus]		[bus]	[bus]	[bus]				[bus]
							[cup]				[cup]						[cup]				[cup]			
London Paddington 15 ⊖ d																								
Slough 3 d																								
Reading 7 d	16 41			17 11				17 41	18 11					18 41	19 11			19 41		20 11				20 41
Didcot Parkway d					17 30					18 30						19 30			20 20					
Swindon a	17 46			18 16	18 20			18 46	19 16	19 20				19 46	20 16	20 20		20 41	21 10	21 11				21 41
d			18 07			18 22	18 27				19 30		19 35				20 29				21 19		21 22	
Kemble d						18 36							19 49										21 36	
Stroud d						18 50							20 04										21 51	
Stonehouse d						18 55							20 09										21 56	
Gloucester 7 a						19 16							20 25										22 12	
Cheltenham Spa a													20 36										22 23	
Chippenham d			18a23				18 41				19 44						20 44				21 37			
Bath Spa 7 a							18 55				20 01						20 57				21 51			
Bristol Parkway 7 a																								
d																								
Bristol Temple Meads 10 a							19 09				20 15						21 12				22 04			
Weston-super-Mare a																					22 34			
Newport (South Wales) a																								
Cardiff Central 7 a																								
Bridgend a																								
Port Talbot Parkway a																								
Neath a																								
Swansea a																								

For connections from Heathrow Airport, Gatwick Airport and Oxford please refer to Tables 125A, 148 and 116.
For connections to Birmingham New Street and Hereford please refer to Tables 57 and 131

Table 125

Sundays
from 30 October

London - Swindon, Cheltenham Spa, Bristol, Weston-super-Mare and South Wales

		GW	GW	GW	GW	GW	GW	GW		GW	GW
			◇1							◇1	
		🚌	☕	🚌	🚌		🚌	🚌		☕	🚌
London Paddington 15 ⊖	d										
Slough 3	d										
Reading 7	d			21 13	21 41		22 20				23 25
Didcot Parkway	d	21 15						22 30			
Swindon	a	22 05		22 18	22 41		23 20	23 20			00 25
	d		22 15			22 57				23 29	00 25
Kemble	d					23 11					
Stroud	d					23 26					
Stonehouse	d					23 31					
Gloucester 7	a					23 46					
Cheltenham Spa	a					23 58					
Chippenham	d		22 27							23 44	01a00
Bath Spa 7	a		22 42							23 57	
Bristol Parkway 7	a										
	d										
Bristol Temple Meads 10	a		22 57							00 12	
Weston-super-Mare	a										
Newport (South Wales)	a										
Cardiff Central 7	a										
Bridgend	a										
Port Talbot Parkway	a										
Neath	a										
Swansea	a										

For connections from Heathrow Airport, Gatwick Airport and Oxford please refer to Tables 125A, 148 and 116.
For connections to Birmingham New Street and Hereford please refer to Tables 57 and 131

Table 125

Mondays to Fridays

until 9 September

South Wales, Weston-super-Mare, Bristol, Cheltenham Spa and Swindon - London

Miles	Miles	Miles			GW MO ◇1 A ☕	GW MO ◇1 B ☕	GW MX ◇1 ☕	GW MX R C 🛏 ☕	GW MO R 🛏 ☕	GW MX R D 🛏 ☕	GW ◇1 ☕	GW ◇1 ☕	GW ◇1 ☕		GW ◇1 ☕	GW ◇1 ☕	GW ◇1 ☕	GW ◇1 ☕	GW ◇1 E ☕	GW ◇1 ☕	GW ◇1 ☕	GW ◇1 ☕	GW		GW ◇1 F Ø
0	—	—	**Swansea**	d									03 57			04 58				05 27					05 58
9½	—	—	Neath	d									04 09			05 10				05 39					06 10
15	—	—	Port Talbot Parkway	d									04 17			05 18				05 47					06 18
27¼	—	—	Bridgend	d									04 30			05 30				05 59					06 30
47½	—	—	**Cardiff Central 7**	d									05 14			05 55				06 24					06 55
59¼	—	—	Newport (South Wales)	d									05 32			06 09				06 38					07 09
—	0	—	Weston-super-Mare	d			22p01															06 20			
—	19	—	**Bristol Temple Meads 10**	d	22p10	22p10	22p35	02 35	02 39	03 00	04 47	05 30			06 00			06 30	06 40			07 00			
81	—	—	Bristol Parkway 7	a									05 59			06 29				06 58					07 29
—	—	—		d							04u57		06 01			06 31				07 01					07 31
—	30½	—	Bath Spa 7	d	22p23	22p23	22p47					05 43			06 13			06 43	06 52			07 13			
—	43½	—	Chippenham	d	22p35	22p35	23p00					05 55			06 25			06 55	07 05			07 25	07 30		
—	—	0	**Cheltenham Spa**	d													05 53				06 30				
—	—	6½	Gloucester 7	d													06 10				06 47				
—	—	15½	Stonehouse	d													06 23				06 59				
—	—	18	Stroud	d													06 29				07 05				
—	—	29¼	Kemble	d													06 43				07 19				
115½	60¼	43	**Swindon**	a	22p50	22p50	23p14	03 15	03 21	03 42	05 22	06 10	06 27		06 40	06 57	06 58	07 10	07 19	07 27	07 35	07 40	07 48		07 57
—	—	—		d	22p53	22p53	23p16	03 17	03 22	03 43	05 23	06 11	06 28		06 41	06 58	07 01	07 11	07 20	07 28	07 35	07 41			07 58
139½	84¼	67	Didcot Parkway	a	23p10	23p10	23p33				05 41	06 28	06 46		06 58		07 19	07 28		07 45	07 53	08 00			
156¾	101½	84½	**Reading 7**	a	23p27	23p27	23p53	04s05	04s02	04s27	05 56	06 43	07 00		07 13	07 28	07 34	07 43		08 00	08 12	08 16			
174¼	119	101¾	Slough 3	a								06 58													
192¾	137½	120¼	**London Paddington 15** ⊖	a	00 11	00 16	00 33	05 25	05 05	05 25	06 24	07 17	07 32		07 44	08 02	08 07	08 14	08 16	08 33	08 40	08 44			08 54

		GW ◇1 G ☕	GW ◇1 H ☕Ø	GW ◇1 ☕	GW ◇1 ☕	GW ◇1 I ☕Ø	GW	GW ◇1 ☕	GW ◇1 I ☕Ø		GW ◇1 ☕	GW ◇1 ☕	GW ◇1 ☕	GW ◇1 ☕	GW ◇1 J ☕	GW ◇1 ☕	GW	GW ◇1 ☕	GW ◇1 ☕		GW ◇1 ☕	GW ◇1 ☕	GW ◇1 ☕	GW ◇1 ☕	GW ◇1 ☕
Swansea	d		06 28			06 58			07 28				07 58		08 28						09 28				
Neath	d		06 40			07 10			07 40				08 10		08 40						09 40				
Port Talbot Parkway	d		06 48			07 18			07 48				08 18		08 48						09 48				
Bridgend	d		07 00			07 30			08 00				08 30		09 00						10 00				
Cardiff Central 7	d		07 25			07 55			08 25				08 55		09 25			09 55			10 25			10 55	
Newport (South Wales)	d		07 39			08 09			08 39				09 09		09 39			10 09			10 39			11 09	
Weston-super-Mare	d	06 49			07 24			07 49								09 29									
Bristol Temple Meads 10	d	07 30			08 00		08 13	08 30				09 00		09 30		10 00			10 30				11 00		11 30
Bristol Parkway 7	a		07 59			08 30			08 59				09 30		09 59			10 30			10 59			11 30	
	d		08 01			08 31			09 01				09 31		10 01			10 31			11 01			11 31	
Bath Spa 7	d	07 43			08 13		08 31	08 43				09 13		09 43		10 13			10 43				11 13		11 43
Chippenham	d	07 55			08 25		08 45	08 55				09 25		09 55		10 25			10 55				11 25		11 55
Cheltenham Spa	d			07 29							08 31						09 40					10 31			
Gloucester 7	d			07 45							08 46						09 54					10 46			
Stonehouse	d			07 59							08 59						10 06					10 59			
Stroud	d			08 05							09 05						10 11					11 05			
Kemble	d			08 19							09 19						10 27					11 19			
Swindon	a	08 10	08 27	08 33	08 40	08 57	09 04	09 10	09 27		09 33	09 40	09 57	10 10	10 27	10 40	10 44	10 57	11 10		11 27	11 33	11 40	11 57	12 10
	d	08 11	08 28	08 35	08 41	08 59		09 11	09 29		09 35	09 41	09 59	10 11	10 29	10 41		10 59	11 11		11 29	11 35	11 41	11 59	12 11
Didcot Parkway	a	08 28	08 46	08 52	08 58			09 28			09 52		10 16	10 28	10 46			11 16	11 28			11 52		12 16	12 28
Reading 7	a	08 44	09 01	09 07	09 13	09 25		09 44	09 59		10 06	10 10	10 31	10 44	11 00	11 08		11 30	11 43		11 59	12 06	12 10	12 30	12 43
Slough 3	a																								
London Paddington 15 ⊖	a	09 14	09 29	09 39	09 44	09 59		10 15	10 32		10 37	10 39	11 01	11 14	11 32	11 38		12 02	12 14		12 32	12 37	12 40	13 06	13 14

- **A** From 8 August until 5 September
- **B** Until 1 August
- **C** Until 29 July. The Night Riviera
- **D** From 2 August until 9 September. The Night Riviera
- **E** until 1 July, from 5 September until 9 September
- **F** The Capitals United
- **G** The Bristolian
- **H** ☕ from Reading Ø to Didcot Parkway
- **I** ☕ from Reading Ø to Swindon
- **J** The Red Dragon

For connections from Heathrow Airport, Gatwick Airport and Oxford please refer to Tables 125A, 148 and 116.
For connections to Birmingham New Street and Hereford please refer to Tables 57 and 131

Table 125

Mondays to Fridays

until 9 September

South Wales, Weston-super-Mare, Bristol, Cheltenham Spa and Swindon - London

		GW	GW	GW	GW		GW	GW	GW	GW	GW	GW	GW	GW	GW		GW	GW	GW	GW	GW	GW	GW	GW	GW
		◇1	◇1		◇1		◇1	◇1	◇1	◇1	◇1	◇1	◇1	◇1			◇1	◇1	◇1	◇1	◇1	◇1	◇1	◇1	◇1
								A												B					C
		☕	☕		☕		☕	☕⊘	☕	☕	☕	☕	☕	☕			☕	☕	☕	☕	☕	☕	☕	☕	☕
Swansea	d	10 28						11 28					12 28						13 28					14 28	
Neath	d	10 40						11 40					12 40						13 40					14 40	
Port Talbot Parkway	d	10 48						11 48					12 48						13 48					14 48	
Bridgend	d	11 00						12 00					13 00						14 00					15 00	
Cardiff Central 7	d	11 25			11 55			12 25			12 55		13 25				13 55		14 25			14 55		15 25	
Newport (South Wales)	d	11 39			12 09			12 39			13 09		13 39				14 09		14 39			15 09		15 39	
Weston-super-Mare	d																								
Bristol Temple Meads 10	d		12 00				12 30			13 00		13 30		14 00				14 30			15 00		15 30		16 00
Bristol Parkway 7	a	11 59			12 30			12 59			13 30		13 59				14 30		15 00			15 30		15 59	
	d	12 01			12 31			13 01			13 31		14 01				14 31		15 01			15 31		16 01	
Bath Spa 7	d		12 13				12 43			13 13		13 43		14 13				14 43			15 13		15 43		16 13
Chippenham	d		12 25				12 55			13 25		13 55		14 25				14 55			15 25		15 55		16 25
Cheltenham Spa	d			11 40					12 31						13 40					14 31					
Gloucester 7	d			11 54					12 46						13 54					14 46					
Stonehouse	d			12 06					12 59						14 06					14 59					
Stroud	d			12 11					13 05						14 11					15 05					
Kemble	d			12 27					13 19						14 27					15 19					
Swindon	a	12 27	12 41	12 44	12 57		13 10	13 27	13 33	13 40	13 57	14 10	14 27	14 40	14 44		14 57	15 10	15 27	15 33	15 40	15 57	16 10	16 27	16 40
	d	12 29	12 41		12 59		13 11	13 29	13 35	13 41	13 59	14 11	14 29	14 41			14 59	15 11	15 29	15 35	15 41	15 59	16 11	16 29	16 41
Didcot Parkway	a	12 46			13 16		13 28		13 52		14 15	14 28	14 46				15 15	15 28		15 52		16 16	16 28	16 46	
Reading 7	a	13 00	13 09		13 31		13 43	13 59	14 06	14 10	14 31	14 43	15 00	15 08			15 31	15 43	16 00	16 06	16 13	16 31	16 43	17 00	17 08
Slough 3	a																								
London Paddington 15 ⊖	a	13 32	13 38		14 06		14 14	14 32	14 37	14 40	15 08	15 14	15 32	15 38			16 09	16 14	16 30	16 39	16 44	17 09	17 14	17 30	17 39

			GW	GW	GW	GW	GW	GW	GW	GW	GW		GW	GW	GW	GW	GW	GW	GW	GW	GW		GW	GW	GW
																FX	FO								FX
				◇1	◇1	◇1	◇1	◇1	◇1	◇1	◇1		◇1	◇1	◇1	◇1	◇1	◇1	◇1		◇1			◇1	◇1
				☕	☕	☕	☕	☕	☕	☕	☕		☕	☕	☕	☕	☕	☕	☕		☕			☕	☕
Swansea	d					15 28					16 28					17 28	17 28				18 28				19 29
Neath	d					15 40					16 40					17 40	17 40				18 40				19 40
Port Talbot Parkway	d					15 48					16 48					17 48	17 48				18 48				19 48
Bridgend	d					16 00					17 00					18 00	18 00				19 00				20 00
Cardiff Central 7	d			15 55		16 25			16 55		17 25			17 55		18 25	18 25				19 25				20 25
Newport (South Wales)	d			16 09		16 39			17 09		17 39			18 09		18 39	18 39				19 39				20 39
Weston-super-Mare	d									17 10					18 08										
Bristol Temple Meads 10	d				16 30			17 00		17 30			18 00		18 30				19 30					20 30	
Bristol Parkway 7	a			16 30		16 59			17 30		17 59			18 30		18 59	18 59				19 59				21 01
	d			16 31		17 01			17 31		18 01			18 31		19 01	19 01				20 01				21 01
Bath Spa 7	d				16 43			17 13		17 43			18 13		18 43				19 43					20 43	
Chippenham	d				16 55			17 25		17 55			18 25		18 55				19 55	20 02				20 55	
Cheltenham Spa	d		15 40				16 31											18 34					20 00		
Gloucester 7	d		15 54				16 46											18 52					20 13		
Stonehouse	d		16 06				16 59											19 05					20 25		
Stroud	d		16 11				17 05											19 10					20 30		
Kemble	d		16 27				17 19											19 24					20 44		
Swindon	a		16 44	16 57	17 10	17 27	17 33	17 40	17 57	18 10	18 27		18 40	18 57	19 10	19 27	19 27	19 39	20 10	20 21	20 27		21 03	21 10	21 29
	d			16 59	17 11	17 29	17 35	17 41	17 59	18 11	18 29		18 41	18 59	19 11	19 29	19 29	19 41	20 11		20 29			21 11	21 29
Didcot Parkway	a			17 16	17 28		17 52		18 16	18 28	18 46				19 28	19 46	19 46	19 58	20 28		20 46			21 28	21 49
Reading 7	a			17 31	17 43	17 56	18 06	18 12	18 31	18 44	19 01		19 08	19 25	19 44	20 00	20 00	20 13	20 44		21 00			21 43	22 09
Slough 3	a																								
London Paddington 15 ⊖	a			18 02	18 14	18 24	18 39	18 44	19 02	19 14	19 32		19 38	19 54	20 14	20 30	20 32	20 46	21 14		21 32			22 14	22 45

		GW	GW	GW	GW	GW	GW		GW	GW	GW
		FO		FO	FX	FO	FX			FO	FX
		◇1	1	◇1	◇1	◇1	◇1			◇1	◇1
		☕		☕	☕	☕	☕			☕	☕
Swansea	d	19 29		20 28	20 28						
Neath	d	19 40		20 40	20 40						
Port Talbot Parkway	d	19 48		20 48	20 48						
Bridgend	d	20 00		21 00	21 00						
Cardiff Central 7	d	20 25		21 25	21 25						
Newport (South Wales)	d	20 39		21 39	21 39						
Weston-super-Mare	d									22 01	22 01
Bristol Temple Meads 10	d					21 50	21 50			22 35	22 35
Bristol Parkway 7	a	21 01		21 59	21 59						
	d	21 01		22 01	22 01						
Bath Spa 7	d					22 02	22 02			22 47	22 47
Chippenham	d					22 15	22 15			23 00	23 00
Cheltenham Spa	d		20 48						22 00		
Gloucester 7	d		21g05						22 13		
Stonehouse	d		21 17						22 26		
Stroud	d		21 23						22 31		
Kemble	d		21 37						22 46		
Swindon	a	21 29	21 51	22 27	22 27	22 33	22 33		23 05	23 14	23 14
	d	21 29		22 28	22 28	22 34	22 34			23 16	23 16
Didcot Parkway	a	21 50				22 50	22 50			23 33	23 33
Reading 7	a	22 09		23 03	23 03	23 06	23 06			23 53	23 53
Slough 3	a										
London Paddington 15 ⊖	a	22 45		23 36	23 40	23 42	23 50			00 27	00 33

A The St. David. ☕ from Reading ⊘ to Swindon

B The Cheltenham Spa Express

C The Merchant Venturer

For connections from Heathrow Airport, Gatwick Airport and Oxford please refer to Tables 125A, 148 and 116.
For connections to Birmingham New Street and Hereford please refer to Tables 57 and 131

Table 125

Mondays to Fridays

from 12 September

South Wales, Weston-super-Mare, Bristol, Cheltenham Spa and Swindon - London

Station		GW MO ◇1 A 🍴	GW MO B 🚌	GW MX ◇1 🍴	GW MX R C 🛏 🍴	GW MO R A 🛏 🍴	GW ◇1 🍴	GW ◇1 🍴	GW ◇1 🍴	GW ◇1 🍴		GW ◇1 🍴	GW ◇1 🍴	GW ◇1 🍴	GW ◇1 🍴	GW ◇1 🍴	GW ◇1 🍴	GW ◇1 🍴	GW	GW ◇1 D ⊘		GW ◇1 E 🍴	GW ◇1 F 🍴⊘	GW ◇1 🍴	GW ◇1 🍴
Swansea	d								03 57			04 58				05 27				05 58			06 28		
Neath	d								04 09			05 10				05 39				06 10			06 40		
Port Talbot Parkway	d								04 17			05 18				05 47				06 18			06 48		
Bridgend	d								04 30			05 30				05 59				06 30			07 00		
Cardiff Central 7	d								05 14			05 55				06 24				06 55			07 25		
Newport (South Wales)	d								05 32			06 09				06 38				07 09			07 39		
Weston-super-Mare	d			22p01														06 20				06 49			07 24
Bristol Temple Meads 10	d	22p10		22p35	02 35	02 39	04 47	05 30		06 00				06 30	06 40			07 00				07 30			08 00
Bristol Parkway 7	a								05 59			06 29				06 58				07 29			07 59		
	d						04u57		06 01			06 31				07 01				07 31			08 01		
Bath Spa 7	d	22p23		22p47				05 43		06 13				06 43	06 52			07 13				07 43			08 13
Chippenham	d	22p35		23p00				05 55		06 25				06 55	07 05			07 25	07 30			07 55			08 25
Cheltenham Spa	d												05 53				06 30							07 29	
Gloucester 7	d												06 10				06 47							07 45	
Stonehouse	d												06 23				06 59							07 59	
Stroud	d												06 29				07 05							08 05	
Kemble	d												06 43				07 19							08 19	
Swindon	a	22p50		23p14	03 15	03 21	05 22	06 10	06 27	06 40		06 57	06 58	07 10	07 19	07 27	07 35	07 40	07 48	07 57		08 10	08 27	08 33	08 40
	d	22p53	23p05	23p16	03 17	03 22	05 23	06 11	06 28	06 41		06 58	07 01	07 11	07 20	07 28	07 35	07 41		07 58		08 11	08 28	08 35	08 41
Didcot Parkway	a	23p10		23p33			05 41	06 28	06 46	06 58			07 19	07 28		07 45	07 53	08 00				08 28	08 46	08 52	08 58
Reading 7	a	23p27	00 05	23p53	04s05	04s02	05 56	06 43	07 00	07 13		07 28	07 34	07 43		08 00	08 12	08 16				08 44	09 01	09 07	09 13
Slough 3	a							06 58																	
London Paddington 15 ⊖	a	00 11		00 33	05 25	05 05	06 24	07 17	07 32	07 44		08 02	08 07	08 14	08 16	08 33	08 40	08 44		08 54		09 14	09 29	09 39	09 44

Station		GW ◇1 G 🍴⊘	GW	GW ◇1 🍴	GW ◇1 G 🍴⊘	GW ◇1 🍴		GW ◇1 🍴	GW ◇1 🍴	GW ◇1 🍴	GW ◇1 H 🍴	GW ◇1 🍴	GW	GW ◇1 🍴	GW ◇1 🍴	GW ◇1 🍴		GW ◇1 🍴	GW ◇1 🍴	GW ◇1 🍴	GW ◇1 🍴	GW ◇1 🍴	GW ◇1 🍴	GW	GW ◇1 🍴
Swansea	d	06 58			07 28				07 58		08 28					09 28						10 28			
Neath	d	07 10			07 40				08 10		08 40					09 40						10 40			
Port Talbot Parkway	d	07 18			07 48				08 18		08 48					09 48						10 48			
Bridgend	d	07 30			08 00				08 30		09 00					10 00						11 00			
Cardiff Central 7	d	07 55			08 25				08 55		09 25			09 55		10 25				10 55		11 25			11 55
Newport (South Wales)	d	08 09			08 39				09 09		09 39			10 09		10 39				11 09		11 39			12 09
Weston-super-Mare	d			07 49								09 29													
Bristol Temple Meads 10	d		08 13	08 30				09 00		09 30		10 00			10 30				11 00		11 30		12 00		
Bristol Parkway 7	a	08 30			08 59				09 30		09 59			10 30		10 59				11 30		11 59			12 30
	d	08 31			09 01				09 31		10 01			10 31		11 01				11 31		12 01			12 31
Bath Spa 7	d		08 31	08 43				09 13		09 43		10 13			10 43				11 13		11 43		12 13		
Chippenham	d		08 45	08 55				09 25		09 55		10 25			10 55				11 25		11 55		12 25		
Cheltenham Spa	d					08 31							09 40					10 31						11 40	
Gloucester 7	d					08 46							09 54					10 46						11 54	
Stonehouse	d					08 59							10 06					10 59						12 06	
Stroud	d					09 05							10 11					11 05						12 11	
Kemble	d					09 19							10 27					11 19						12 27	
Swindon	a	08 57	09 04	09 10	09 27	09 33		09 40	09 57	10 10	10 27	10 40	10 44	10 57	11 10	11 27		11 33	11 40	11 57	12 10	12 27	12 41	12 44	12 57
	d	08 59		09 11	09 29	09 35		09 41	09 59	10 11	10 29	10 41		10 59	11 11	11 29		11 35	11 41	11 59	12 11	12 29	12 41		12 59
Didcot Parkway	a			09 28		09 52			10 16	10 28	10 46			11 16	11 28			11 52		12 16	12 28	12 46			13 16
Reading 7	a	09 25		09 44	09 59	10 06		10 10	10 31	10 44	11 00	11 08		11 30	11 43	11 59		12 06	12 10	12 30	12 43	13 00	13 09		13 31
Slough 3	a																								
London Paddington 15 ⊖	a	09 59		10 15	10 32	10 37		10 39	11 07	11 14	11 32	11 38		12 02	12 14	12 32		12 37	12 40	13 00	13 14	13 32	13 38		14 06

A From 12 September until 24 October
B From 31 October
C The Night Riviera
D The Capitals United
E The Bristolian
F 🍴 from Reading ⊘ to Didcot Parkway
G 🍴 from Reading ⊘ to Swindon
H The Red Dragon

For connections from Heathrow Airport, Gatwick Airport and Oxford please refer to Tables 125A, 148 and 116.
For connections to Birmingham New Street and Hereford please refer to Tables 57 and 131

Table 125

Mondays to Fridays

from 12 September

South Wales, Weston-super-Mare, Bristol, Cheltenham Spa and Swindon - London

		GW		GW	GW	GW	GW	GW	GW	GW	GW	GW		GW	GW	GW	GW	GW	GW	GW	GW	GW		GW	GW
		◇1		◇1	◇1	◇1	◇1	◇1	◇1	◇1		◇1		◇1	◇1	◇1	◇1	◇1	◇1	◇1	◇1			◇1	◇1
				A												B					C				
		☕		☕⊘	☕	☕	☕	☕	☕	☕		☕		☕	☕	☕	☕	☕	☕	☕	☕			☕	☕
Swansea	d			11 28					12 28						13 28					14 28					
Neath	d			11 40					12 40						13 40					14 40					
Port Talbot Parkway	d			11 48					12 48						13 48					14 48					
Bridgend	d			12 00					13 00						14 00					15 00					
Cardiff Central 7	d			12 25			12 55		13 25			13 55			14 25			14 55		15 25				15 55	
Newport (South Wales)	d			12 39			13 09		13 39			14 09			14 39			15 09		15 39				16 09	
Weston-super-Mare	d																								
Bristol Temple Meads 10	d	12 30				13 00		13 30		14 00				14 30			15 00		15 30		16 00				16 30
Bristol Parkway 7	a			12 59			13 30		13 59			14 30			15 00			15 30		15 59				16 30	
	d			13 01			13 31		14 01			14 31			15 01			15 31		16 01				16 31	
Bath Spa 7	d	12 43				13 13		13 43		14 13				14 43			15 13		15 43		16 13				16 43
Chippenham	d	12 55				13 25		13 55		14 25				14 55			15 25		15 55		16 25				16 55
Cheltenham Spa	d				12 31						13 40					14 31						15 40			
Gloucester 7	d				12 46						13 54					14 46						15 54			
Stonehouse	d				12 59						14 06					14 59						16 06			
Stroud	d				13 05						14 11					15 05						16 11			
Kemble	d				13 19						14 27					15 19						16 27			
Swindon	a	13 10		13 27	13 33	13 40	13 57	14 10	14 27	14 40	14 44	14 57		15 10	15 27	15 33	15 40	15 57	16 10	16 27	16 40	16 44		16 57	17 10
	d	13 11		13 29	13 35	13 41	13 59	14 11	14 29	14 41		14 59		15 11	15 29	15 35	15 41	15 59	16 11	16 29	16 41			16 59	17 11
Didcot Parkway	a	13 28			13 52		14 15	14 28	14 46			15 15		15 28		15 52		16 16	16 28	16 46				17 16	17 28
Reading 7	a	13 43		13 59	14 06	14 10	14 31	14 43	15 00	15 08		15 31		15 43	16 00	16 06	16 13	16 31	16 43	17 00	17 08			17 31	17 43
Slough 3	a																								
London Paddington 15 ⊖	a	14 14		14 32	14 37	14 40	15 08	15 14	15 32	15 38		16 09		16 14	16 30	16 39	16 44	17 09	17 14	17 30	17 39			18 02	18 14

		GW	GW	GW	GW	GW	GW	GW		GW	GW	GW	GW	GW	GW	GW	GW	GW		GW	GW	GW	GW	GW	GW
												FX	FO								FX	FO		FO	FX
		◇1	◇1	◇1	◇1	◇1	◇1	◇1		◇1	◇1	◇1	◇1	◇1	◇1		◇1			◇1	◇1	◇1	1	◇1	◇1
		☕	☕	☕	☕	☕	☕	☕		☕	☕	☕	☕	☕	☕		☕			☕	☕	☕		☕	☕
Swansea	d	15 28					16 28					17 28	17 28				18 28				19 29	19 29		20 28	20 28
Neath	d	15 40					16 40					17 40	17 40				18 40				19 40	19 40		20 40	20 40
Port Talbot Parkway	d	15 48					16 48					17 48	17 48				18 48				19 48	19 48		20 48	20 48
Bridgend	d	16 00					17 00					18 00	18 00				19 00				20 00	20 00		21 00	21 00
Cardiff Central 7	d	16 25			16 55		17 25			17 55		18 25	18 25				19 25				20 25	20 25		21 25	21 25
Newport (South Wales)	d	16 39			17 09		17 39			18 09		18 39	18 39				19 39				20 39	20 39		21 39	21 39
Weston-super-Mare	d					17 10					18 08														
Bristol Temple Meads 10	d			17 00		17 30		18 00			18 30				19 30					20 30					
Bristol Parkway 7	a	16 59			17 30		17 59			18 30		18 59	18 59				19 59				21 01	21 01		21 59	21 59
	d	17 01			17 31		18 01			18 31		19 01	19 01				20 01				21 01	21 01		22 01	22 01
Bath Spa 7	d			17 13		17 43		18 13			18 43				19 43					20 43					
Chippenham	d			17 25		17 55		18 25			18 55				19 55	20 02				20 55					
Cheltenham Spa	d		16 31											18 34				20 00					20 48		
Gloucester 7	d		16 46											18 52				20 13					21 05		
Stonehouse	d		16 59											19 05				20 25					21 17		
Stroud	d		17 05											19 10				20 30					21 23		
Kemble	d		17 19											19 24				20 44					21 37		
Swindon	a	17 27	17 33	17 40	17 57	18 10	18 27	18 40		18 57	19 10	19 27	19 27	19 39	20 10	20 21	20 27	21 03		21 10	21 29	21 29	21 51	22 27	22 27
	d	17 29	17 35	17 41	17 59	18 11	18 29	18 41		18 59	19 11	19 29	19 29	19 41	20 11		20 29			21 11	21 29	21 29		22 28	22 28
Didcot Parkway	a		17 52		18 16	18 28	18 46				19 28	19 46	19 46	19 58	20 28		20 46			21 28	21 49	21 50			
Reading 7	a	18 00	18 06	18 12	18 31	18 44	19 01	19 08		19 25	19 44	20 00	20 00	20 13	20 44		21 00			21 43	22 09	22 09		23 03	23 03
Slough 3	a																								
London Paddington 15 ⊖	a	18 30	18 39	18 44	19 02	19 14	19 32	19 38		19 54	20 14	20 30	20 32	20 46	21 14		21 32			22 14	22 45	22 45		23 36	23 40

		GW	GW	GW		GW	GW
		FO	FX			FO	FX
		◇1	◇1			◇1	◇1
		☕	☕			☕	☕
Swansea	d						
Neath	d						
Port Talbot Parkway	d						
Bridgend	d						
Cardiff Central 7	d						
Newport (South Wales)	d						
Weston-super-Mare	d					22 01	22 01
Bristol Temple Meads 10	d	21 50	21 50			22 35	22 35
Bristol Parkway 7	a						
	d						
Bath Spa 7	d	22 02	22 02			22 47	22 47
Chippenham	d	22 15	22 15			23 00	23 00
Cheltenham Spa	d			22 00			
Gloucester 7	d			22 13			
Stonehouse	d			22 26			
Stroud	d			22 31			
Kemble	d			22 46			
Swindon	a	22 33	22 33	23 05		23 14	23 14
	d	22 34	22 34			23 16	23 16
Didcot Parkway	a	22 50	22 50			23 33	23 33
Reading 7	a	23 06	23 06			23 53	23 53
Slough 3	a						
London Paddington 15 ⊖	a	23 42	23 50			00 27	00 33

A The St. David. ☕ from Reading ⊘ to Swindon **B** The Cheltenham Spa Express **C** The Merchant Venturer

For connections from Heathrow Airport, Gatwick Airport and Oxford please refer to Tables 125A, 148 and 116.
For connections to Birmingham New Street and Hereford please refer to Tables 57 and 131

Table 125

Saturdays

South Wales, Weston-super-Mare, Bristol, Cheltenham Spa and Swindon - London

		GW	GW	GW	GW	GW	GW	GW	GW	GW	GW	GW	GW	GW	GW	GW	GW	GW	GW	GW	GW	GW	GW
		◇1	R	R	◇1		◇1	◇1	◇1	◇1	◇1	◇1	◇1	◇1	◇1	◇1	◇1	◇1	◇1	◇1		◇1	◇1
			A	B													C		C			D	
		☕	🛏 ☕	🛏 ☕	☕		☕	☕	☕	☕	☕	☕	☕	☕	☕	☕	☕⊘	☕	☕⊘	☕		☕	☕
Swansea	d						03 58	04 58		05 28		05 58		06 28			06 58		07 28			07 58	
Neath	d						04 10	05 10		05 40		06 10		06 40			07 10		07 40			08 10	
Port Talbot Parkway	d						04 18	05 18		05 48		06 18		06 48			07 18		07 48			08 18	
Bridgend	d						04 30	05 30		06 00		06 30		07 00			07 30		08 00			08 30	
Cardiff Central 7	d						04 55	05 55		06 25		06 55		07 25			07 55		08 25			08 55	
Newport (South Wales)	d						05 09	06 09		06 39		07 09		07 39			08 09		08 39			09 09	
Weston-super-Mare	d	22p01									06 24					07 24				08 29			
Bristol Temple Meads 10	d	22p35	02 35	03 00	05 30		06 00		06 30		07 00		07 30			08 00		08 30		09 00			
Bristol Parkway 7	a							06 29		06 59		07 29		07 59			08 30		08 59			09 30	
	d							06 31		07 01		07 31		08 01			08 31		09 01			09 31	
Bath Spa 7	d	22p47			05 43		06 13		06 43		07 13		07 43			08 13		08 43		09 13			
Chippenham	d	23p00			05 55		06 25		06 55		07 25		07 55			08 25		08 55		09 25	09 30		
Cheltenham Spa	d					05 30									07 30								08 59
Gloucester 7	d					05 44									07 46								09 16
Stonehouse	d					05 56									07 58								09 29
Stroud	d					06 01									08 03								09 34
Kemble	d					06 16									08 17								09 48
Swindon	a	23p14	03 15	03 39	06 09	06 32	06 39	06 57	07 09	07 27	07 40	07 57	08 09	08 27	08 33	08 39	08 58	09 09	09 27	09 40	09 49	09 57	10 02
	d	23p16	03 17	03 41	06 11		06 41	06 59	07 11	07 29	07 41	07 58	08 11	08 29	08 35	08 41	08 59	09 11	09 29	09 41		09 59	10 04
Didcot Parkway	a	23p33			06 28		06 58	07 16	07 28	07 46	07 59	08 16	08 28	08 46	08 51	08 58	09 16	09 28	09 46			10 15	10 21
Reading 7	a	23p53	04s05	04s24	06 43		07 14	07 31	07 44	08 00	08 14	08 31	08 44	09 00	09 07	09 14	09 32	09 44	10 00	10 11		10 32	10 36
Slough 3	a																						
London Paddington 15 ⊖	a	00 27	05 09	05 10	07 14		07 44	08 07	08 14	08 32	08 44	09 02	09 14	09 32	09 37	09 44	10 02	10 14	10 32	10 39		11 02	11 08

		GW	GW	GW	GW	GW	GW	GW	GW	GW	GW	GW	GW	GW	GW	GW	GW	GW	GW	GW	GW	GW	GW
		◇1	◇1	◇1	◇1		◇1	◇1	◇1	◇1	◇1	◇1	◇1	◇1	◇1		◇1	◇1	◇1	◇1	◇1	◇1	◇1
		D	E								E	D		E	D						E	D	
		☕	☕	☕	☕		☕	☕	☕	☕	☕	☕	☕	☕	☕		☕	☕	☕	☕	☕	☕	☕
Swansea	d			08 28				09 28					10 28					11 28					12 28
Neath	d			08 40				09 40					10 40					11 40					12 40
Port Talbot Parkway	d			08 48				09 48					10 48					11 48					12 48
Bridgend	d			09 00				10 00					11 00					12 00					13 00
Cardiff Central 7	d			09 25				10 25					11 25					12 25					13 25
Newport (South Wales)	d			09 39				10 39					11 39					12 39					13 39
Weston-super-Mare	d	09 02												11 30							13 01		
Bristol Temple Meads 10	d	09 30	09 30		10 00		10 30		11 00		11 30	11 30		12 00	12 00		12 30		13 00		13j30	13 30	
Bristol Parkway 7	a			09 59				10 59					11 59					12 59					13 59
	d			10 01				11 01					12 01					13 01					14 01
Bath Spa 7	d	09 43	09 43		10 13		10 43		11 13		11 43	11 43		12 13	12 13		12 43		13 13		13 43	13 43	
Chippenham	d	09 55	09 55		10 25		10 55		11 25		11 55	11 55		12 25	12 25		12 55		13 25		13 55	13 55	
Cheltenham Spa	d					10 01				11 00						12 01				13 00			
Gloucester 7	d					10 15				11 16						12 15				13 16			
Stonehouse	d					10 27				11 29						12 27				13 29			
Stroud	d					10 32				11 34						12 32				13 34			
Kemble	d					10 47				11 48						12 47				13 48			
Swindon	a	10 10	10 10	10 28	10 39	11 04	11 09	11 27	11 39	12 02	12 09	12 09	12 27	12 40	12 40	13 04	13 09	13 27	13 39	14 02	14 09	14 09	14 27
	d	10 11	10 11	10 29	10 41		11 11	11 29	11 41	12 04	12 11	12 11	12 29	12 41	12 41		13 11	13 29	13 41	14 04	14 11	14 11	14 29
Didcot Parkway	a	10 28	10 28	10 47			11 28	11 46		12 21	12 27	12 27	12 46				13 28	13 46		14 21	14 28	14 28	14 46
Reading 7	a	10 45	10 45	11 01	11 11		11 44	12 00	12 11	12 37	12 43	12 43	13 00	13 10	13 10		13 44	14 00	14 11	14 38	14 44	14 44	15 00
Slough 3	a																						
London Paddington 15 ⊖	a	11 14	11 14	11 33	11 40		12 14	12 32	12 39	13 07	13 13	13 14	13 33	13 41	13 41		14 14	14 32	14 39	15 09	15 14	15 14	15 32

A until 30 July, from 17 September. **The Night Riviera**
B from 6 August until 10 September. **The Night Riviera**
C ☕ from Reading ⊘ to Didcot Parkway
D from 17 September
E until 10 September

For connections from Heathrow Airport, Gatwick Airport and Oxford please refer to Tables 125A, 148 and 116.
For connections to Birmingham New Street and Hereford please refer to Tables 57 and 131

Table 125

Saturdays

South Wales, Weston-super-Mare, Bristol, Cheltenham Spa and Swindon - London

		GW		GW	GW	GW	GW	GW	GW	GW	GW	GW		GW	GW	GW	GW	GW	GW	GW	GW	GW		GW	GW
		◇1			◇1	◇1	◇1	◇1		◇1	◇1	◇1		◇1	◇1		◇1	◇1	◇1	◇1	◇1	◇1		◇1	◇1
						A	B				B	A									B	A			
		⊡			⊡	⊡	⊡	⊡		⊡	⊡	⊡		⊡	⊡		⊡	⊡	⊡	⊡	⊡	⊡		⊡	⊡
Swansea	d					13 28	13 28							14 28				15 28						16 28	
Neath	d					13 40	13 40							14 40				15 40						16 40	
Port Talbot Parkway	d					13 48	13 48							14 48				15 48						16 48	
Bridgend	d					14 00	14 00							15 00				16 00						17 00	
Cardiff Central 7	d					14 25	14 25							15 25				16 25						17 25	
Newport (South Wales)	d					14 39	14 39							15 39				16 39						17 39	
Weston-super-Mare	d										15 01										17 01				
Bristol Temple Meads 10	d	14 00			14 30			15 00			15 30	15 30			16 00		16 30		17 00		17 30	17 30			18 00
Bristol Parkway 7	a					14 59	14 59							15 59				16 59						17 59	
	d					15 01	15 01							16 01				17 01						18 01	
Bath Spa 7	d	14 13			14 43			15 13			15 43	15 43			16 13		16 43		17 13		17 43	17 43			18 13
Chippenham	d	14 25			14 55			15 25	15 29		15 55	15 55			16 25		16 55		17 25		17 55	17 55			18 25
Cheltenham Spa	d			14 01						15 00						16 01				17 00					
Gloucester 7	d			14 15						15b16						16 15				17e16					
Stonehouse	d			14 27						15 29						16 27				17 29					
Stroud	d			14 32						15 34						16 32				17 34					
Kemble	d			14 47						15 48						16 47				17 48					
Swindon	a	14 39		15 04	15 09	15 27	15 27	15 39	15 49	16 02	16 09	16 09		16 27	16 39	17 04	17 09	17 27	17 39	18 02	18 09	18 09		18 27	18 39
	d	14 41			15 11	15 29	15 29	15 41		16 04	16 11	16 11		16 29	16 41		17 11	17 29	17 41	18 04	18 11	18 11		18 29	18 41
Didcot Parkway	a				15 28	15 46	15 46			16 21	16 28	16 28		16 46			17 28	17 46		18 21	18 28	18 28		18 46	
Reading 7	a	15 09			15 44	16 00	16 01	16 11		16 38	16 44	16 44		17 00	17 09		17 44	18 00	18 11	18 38	18 44	18 44		19 00	19 09
Slough 3	a																								
London Paddington 15 ⊖	a	15 39			16 14	16 32	16 37	16 39		17 07	17 14	17 14		17 32	17 38		18 14	18 32	18 39	19 08	19 14	19 14		19 32	19 39

		GW	GW	GW	GW	GW	GW	GW		GW	GW	GW	GW	GW	GW	GW
			◇1	◇1	◇1	◇1	◇1	◇1		◇1	◇1	◇1		◇1	◇1	◇1
			B	A	B	A									C	D
			⊡	⊡	⊡	⊡	⊡	⊡		⊡	⊡	⊡		⊡	⊡	⊡
Swansea	d				17 28	17 28				18 28		19 28				
Neath	d				17 40	17 40				18 40		19 40				
Port Talbot Parkway	d				17 48	17 48				18 48		19 48				
Bridgend	d				18 00	18 00				19 00		20 00				
Cardiff Central 7	d				18 25	18 25				19 25		20 25				
Newport (South Wales)	d				18 39	18 39				19 39		20 39				
Weston-super-Mare	d		18 01								20 10				21 53	21 53
Bristol Temple Meads 10	d		18 30	18 30				19 30			20 33			21 47	22 30	22 30
Bristol Parkway 7	a				18 59	18 59				19 59		21 01				
	d				19 01	19 01				20 01		21 01				
Bath Spa 7	d		18 43	18 43				19 43			20 46			22 02	22 43	22 43
Chippenham	d		18 55	18 55				19 55			20 58			22 15	22 55	22 55
Cheltenham Spa	d	18 01					19 00						21 19			
Gloucester 7	d	18 15					19 16						21 35			
Stonehouse	d	18 27					19 29						21 47			
Stroud	d	18 32					19 34						21 52			
Kemble	d	18 47					19 48						22 07			
Swindon	a	19 04	19 09	19 09	19 27	19 27	20 03	20 09		20 27	21 13	21 29	22 24	22 29	23 10	23 10
	d		19 11	19 11	19 29	19 29	20 05	20 11		20 29	21 14	21 29		22 31	23 11	23 11
Didcot Parkway	a		19 28	19 28		19 46	20 22	20 28		20 46	21 31	21 47		22 48	23 28	23 28
Reading 7	a		19 44	19 44	19 58	20 00	20 38	20 44		21 06	21 48	21 59		23 04	23 51	23 51
Slough 3	a															
London Paddington 15 ⊖	a		20 14	20 14	20 32	20 32	21 07	21 14		21 36	22 16	22 37		23 36	00 33	00 34

A from 17 September
B until 10 September
C from 6 August until 22 October
D until 30 July, from 29 October

For connections from Heathrow Airport, Gatwick Airport and Oxford please refer to Tables 125A, 148 and 116.
For connections to Birmingham New Street and Hereford please refer to Tables 57 and 131

Table 125

Sundays
until 19 June

South Wales, Weston-super-Mare, Bristol, Cheltenham Spa and Swindon - London

	GW	GW	GW	GW	GW	GW	GW	GW	GW		GW	GW	GW	GW	GW	GW	GW	GW	GW		GW	GW	GW	GW
	◇1	◇1	◇1	◇1	◇1	◇1		◇1	◇1		◇1	◇1	◇1	◇1	◇1	◇1	◇1		◇1		◇1	◇1	◇1	◇1
	A																							
	☕	☕	☕	☕	☕	☕		☕	☕		☕	☕	☕	☕	☕	☕	☕		☕		☕	☕	☕	☕
Swansea d						08 07					09 21		10 21			11 22			12 21				13 21	
Neath d						08 19					09 33		10 33			11 34			12 33				13 33	
Port Talbot Parkway d						08 26					09 40		10 40			11 41			12 40				13 40	
Bridgend d						08 38					09 52		10 52			11 53			12 52				13 52	
Cardiff Central [7] d				07 56		09 05					10 15		11 15			12 15			13 15				14 15	
Newport (South Wales) d				08 15		09 19					10 32		11 32			12 32			13 32				14 32	
Weston-super-Mare d	21p53				08 11				09 56								12 51							14 52
Bristol Temple Meads [10] d	22 30	07 45	08 15		08 45			09 48	10 30			11 30			12 30		13 30					14 30		15 30
Bristol Parkway [7] a				08 44		09 46					10 59		11 59			12 59			13 59				14 59	
d				08 45		09 48					11 01		12 01			13 02			14 01				15 01	
Bath Spa [7] d	22p43	07 58	08 28		08 58			10 00	10 43			11 43			12 43		13 43					14 43		15 43
Chippenham d	22p55	08 10	08 40		09 10			10 12	10 55			11 55			12 55		13 55					14 55		15 55
Cheltenham Spa d							09 24							11 46				13 04			13 58			
Gloucester [7] d							09 38							12 10				13 25			14 12			
Stonehouse d							09 49							12 30				13 49			14 33			
Stroud d							09 54							12 36				13 54			14 38			
Kemble d							10 08							12 51				14 09			14 53			
Swindon a	23p10	08 25	08 55	09 10	09 24	10 14	10 23	10 27	11 10		11 25	12 10	12 26	13 04	13 10	13 27	14 10	14 24	14 27		15 08	15 11	15 27	16 10
d	23p11	08 26	08 55	09 11	09 29	10 14		10 29	11 11		11 29	12 11	12 29	13 05	13 11	13 29	14 11		14 29		15 09	15 12	15 29	16 11
Didcot Parkway a	23p28	08 43	09 13		09 45			10 45	11 29		11 46	12 28	12 46		13 28	13 46	14 29		14 46			15 30	15 46	16 29
Reading [7] a	23p51	09 01	09 28	09 46	10 00	10 42		11 00	11 44		12 01	12 44	13 00	13 32	13 44	14 00	14 44		15 00		15 35	15 45	16 00	16 44
Slough [3] a																								
London Paddington [15] ⊖ a	00 34	09 38	10 08	10 27	10 39	11 21		11 39	12 24		12 38	13 24	13 39	14 13	14 22	14 39	15 24		15 39		16 15	16 20	16 39	17 24

	GW	GW	GW	GW	GW		GW	GW	GW	GW	GW	GW	GW	GW	GW		GW	GW	GW	GW	GW	GW	GW	GW
	◇1	◇1	◇1	◇1	◇1			◇1		◇1	◇1	◇1	◇1	◇1	◇1		◇1	◇1			◇1	◇1	◇1	◇1
	☕	☕	☕	☕	☕			☕		☕	☕	☕	☕	☕	☕		☕	☕			☕	☕	☕	☕
Swansea d	14 21				15 21						16 21			16 51				17 51					18 51	
Neath d	14 33				15 33						16 33			17 03				18 03					19 03	
Port Talbot Parkway d	14 40				15 40						16 40			17 10				18 10					19 10	
Bridgend d	14 52				15 52						16 52			17 22				18 22					19 22	
Cardiff Central [7] d	15 15				16 15						17 15			17 50				18 50					19 50	
Newport (South Wales) d	15 32				16 32						17 32			18 04				19 04					20 04	
Weston-super-Mare d										17 02		17 29									19 27			20 26
Bristol Temple Meads [10] d		16 00		16 30				17 00		17 30		18 00			18 30		19 00				20 00			21 00
Bristol Parkway [7] a	15 59				16 59						17 59			18 31				19 31					20 31	
d	16 01				17 01						18 02			18 33				19 33					20 33	
Bath Spa [7] d		16 13		16 43				17 13		17 43		18 13			18 43		19 13				20 13			21 13
Chippenham d		16 25		16 55				17 25	17 39	17 55		18 25			18 55		19 25		20 04		20 25			21 25
Cheltenham Spa d			15 59				16 33						17 46									19 46		
Gloucester [7] d			16 13				16 49						18 02							19 34		20 02		
Stonehouse d			16 27				17 01						18 15							19 47		20 15		
Stroud d			16 31				17 06						18 20							19 52		20 23		
Kemble d			16 46				17 21						18 35							20 07		20 38		
Swindon a	16 27	16 40	17 01	17 10	17 27		17 36	17 40	17 56	18 10	18 27	18 39	18 48	18 59	19 10		19 39	19 58	20 20	20 29	20 39	20 51	20 59	21 39
d	16 29	16 41	17 03	17 11	17 29			17 41		18 11	18 29	18 41	18 50	18 59	19 11		19 41	19 59			20 40	20 52	20 59	21 41
Didcot Parkway a	16 46	16 58		17 28	17 46			17 58			18 46	18 58		19 16			19 58	20 16			20 57	21 09	21 16	22 00
Reading [7] a	17 00	17 12	17 30	17 42	18 00			18 12		18 42	19 00	19 12	19 21	19 30	19 42		20 12	20 32			21 17	21 24	21 32	22 17
Slough [3] a																								
London Paddington [15] ⊖ a	17 39	17 50	18 13	18 24	18 39			18 53		19 26	19 40	19 54	20 09	20 11	20 22		20 53	21 16			21 57	22 04	22 15	22 57

	GW		GW	GW
	◇1			◇1
	☕			☕
Swansea d	19 59			
Neath d	20 11			
Port Talbot Parkway d	20 18			
Bridgend d	20 30			
Cardiff Central [7] d	20 55			
Newport (South Wales) d	21 09			
Weston-super-Mare d				
Bristol Temple Meads [10] d				22 10
Bristol Parkway [7] a	21 36			
d	21 38			
Bath Spa [7] d				22 23
Chippenham d				22 35
Cheltenham Spa d			21 46	
Gloucester [7] d			21 59	
Stonehouse d			22 12	
Stroud d			22 17	
Kemble d			22 32	
Swindon a	22 04		22 47	22 50
d	22 05			22 53
Didcot Parkway a				23 10
Reading [7] a	22 37			23 27
Slough [3] a				
London Paddington [15] ⊖ a	23 20			00 16

A not 22 May

b Previous night, arr. 2212

For connections from Heathrow Airport, Gatwick Airport and Oxford please refer to Tables 125A, 148 and 116.
For connections to Birmingham New Street and Hereford please refer to Tables 57 and 131

Table 125

Sundays

26 June to 31 July

South Wales, Weston-super-Mare, Bristol, Cheltenham Spa and Swindon - London

		GW	GW	GW	GW	GW	GW	GW	GW	GW	GW	GW	GW	GW	GW	GW	GW	GW	GW	GW	GW	GW	GW
		◇1	◇1	◇1	◇1	◇1	◇1		◇1	◇1		◇1	◇1	◇1	◇1		◇1	◇1	◇1	◇1	◇1	◇1	◇1
		℗	℗	℗	℗	℗	℗		℗	℗		℗	℗	℗	℗		℗	℗	℗	℗	℗	℗	℗
Swansea	d						07 40			08 45				09 55			10 55		11 55			12 55	
Neath	d						07 52			08 57				10 07			11 07		12 07			13 07	
Port Talbot Parkway	d						07 59			09 04				10 14			11 14		12 14			13 14	
Bridgend	d						08 11			09 16				10 26			11 26		12 26			13 26	
Cardiff Central 7	d				07 35		08 35			09 40				10 50			11 49		12 49			13 49	
Newport (South Wales)	d				07 53		08 55			09 55				11 06			12 06		13 06			14 06	
Weston-super-Mare	d	21p53				08 11						10 14						12 51					14 52
Bristol Temple Meads 10	d	22b30	07 45	08 15		08 45			09 48			10 45	11 30		12 30			13 30			14 30		15 30
Bristol Parkway 7	a				08 22		09 22			10 23				11 34			12 34		13 37			14 36	
	d				08 30		09 30			10 30				11 45			12 45		13 45			14 45	
Bath Spa 7	d	22p43	07 58	08 28		08 58			10 00			11 01	11 43		12 43			13 43			14 43		15 43
Chippenham	d	22p55	08 10	08 40		09 10			10 12			11 13	11 55		12 55			13 55			14 55		15 55
Cheltenham Spa	d																			13 46			
Gloucester 7	d																			14 02			
Stonehouse	d																			14 15			
Stroud	d																			14 20			
Kemble	d							10 09			11 09					13 09				14 35			
Swindon	a	23p10	08 25	08 55	09 11	09 24	10 14	10 24	10 27	11 12	11 24	11 29	12 10	12 26	13 10	13 24	13 26	14 10	14 25	14 50	15 11	15 27	16 10
	d	23p11	08 26	08 55	09 11	09 29	10 14		10 29	11 14		11 29	12 11	12 30	13 11		13 29	14 11	14 29	14 51	15 12	15 29	16 11
Didcot Parkway	a	23p28	08 43	09 13		09 45			10 45	11 30		11 47	12 28	12 47	13 28		13 46	14 29	14 46		15 30	15 46	16 29
Reading 7	a	23p51	09 01	09 28	09 39	10 00	10 42		11 00	11 44		12 00	12 44	13 01	13 44		14 00	14 44	15 00	15 17	15 45	16 00	16 44
Slough 3	a																						
London Paddington 15 ⊖	a	00 34	09 39	10 08	10 23	10 39	11 21		11 39	12 24		12 39	13 24	13 40	14 22		14 40	15 24	15 40	16 08	16 20	16 40	17 24

		GW	GW	GW	GW	GW	GW	GW	GW	GW	GW	GW	GW	GW	GW	GW	GW	GW	GW	GW	GW	GW	GW
		◇1	◇1	◇1	◇1	◇1		◇1		◇1	◇1	◇1	◇1	◇1	◇1	◇1	◇1			◇1	◇1	◇1	◇1
		℗	℗	℗	℗	℗		℗		℗	℗	℗	℗	℗	℗	℗	℗			℗	℗	℗	℗
Swansea	d	13 55				14 55					15 55			16 29			17 21					18 25	
Neath	d	14 07				15 07					16 07			16 41			17 33					18 37	
Port Talbot Parkway	d	14 14				15 14					16 14			16 48			17 40					18 44	
Bridgend	d	14 26				15 26					16 26			17 00			17 52					18 56	
Cardiff Central 7	d	14 49				15 49					16 49			17 25			18 19					19 20	
Newport (South Wales)	d	15 06				16 06					17 06			17 39			18 33					19 38	
Weston-super-Mare	d									17 02		17 29								19 27			20 26
Bristol Temple Meads 10	d		16 00		16 30			17 00		17 30		18 00			18 30	19 00				20 00			21 00
Bristol Parkway 7	a	15 35				16 34					17 33			18 06			19 00					20 05	
	d	15 45				16 45					17 45			18 15			19 15					20 15	
Bath Spa 7	d		16 13		16 43			17 13		17 43		18 13			18 43	19 13				20 13			21 13
Chippenham	d		16 25		16 55			17 25	17 39	17 55		18 25			18 55	19 25		20 04		20 25			21 25
Cheltenham Spa	d			15 46			16 33						17 46								19 46		
Gloucester 7	d			16 00			16 47						18 02						19 34		20 04		
Stonehouse	d			16 14			16 59						18 15						19 47		20 17		
Stroud	d			16 18			17 04						18 20						19 52		20 23		
Kemble	d			16 33			17 19						18 35						20 07		20 38		
Swindon	a	16 26	16 40	16 48	17 10	17 27	17 34	17 40	17 56	18 10	18 25	18 39	18 48	18 56	19 10	19 39	19 58	20 20	20 29	20 39	20 52	20 55	21 39
	d	16 29	16 41	16 50	17 11	17 29		17 41		18 11	18 29	18 41	18 50	18 59	19 11	19 41	19 59			20 40	20 52	21 00	21 41
Didcot Parkway	a	16 46	16 58		17 28	17 46		17 58			18 46	18 58		19 16		19 58	20 16			20 57	21 09	21 15	22 00
Reading 7	a	17 00	17 12	17 17	17 42	18 00		18 12		18 42	19 00	19 12	19 21	19 30	19 42	20 12	20 30			21 17	21 24	21 31	22 17
Slough 3	a																						
London Paddington 15 ⊖	a	17 39	17 50	18 00	18 24	18 40		18 53		19 26	19 39	19 54	20 09	20 11	20 22	20 53	21 13			21 57	22 03	22 21	22 57

		GW	GW	GW
		◇1		◇1
		℗		℗
Swansea	d	19 53		
Neath	d	20 05		
Port Talbot Parkway	d	20 12		
Bridgend	d	20 24		
Cardiff Central 7	d	20 50		
Newport (South Wales)	d	21 05		
Weston-super-Mare	d			
Bristol Temple Meads 10	d			22 10
Bristol Parkway 7	a	21 33		
	d	21 40		
Bath Spa 7	d			22 23
Chippenham	d			22 35
Cheltenham Spa	d		21 46	
Gloucester 7	d		21 59	
Stonehouse	d		22 12	
Stroud	d		22 17	
Kemble	d		22 32	
Swindon	a	22 22	22 47	22 50
	d	22 24		22 53
Didcot Parkway	a			23 10
Reading 7	a	22 55		23 27
Slough 3	a			
London Paddington 15 ⊖	a	23 34		00 16

b Previous night, arr. 2212

For connections from Heathrow Airport, Gatwick Airport and Oxford please refer to Tables 125A, 148 and 116.
For connections to Birmingham New Street and Hereford please refer to Tables 57 and 131

Table 125

Sundays

7 August to 11 September

South Wales, Weston-super-Mare, Bristol, Cheltenham Spa and Swindon - London

		GW	GW	GW	GW	GW	GW	GW	GW	GW		GW	GW	GW	GW	GW	GW	GW	GW	GW		GW	GW	GW	GW
		◇1	◇1			◇1	◇1	◇1	◇1	◇1			◇1	◇1	◇1	◇1	◇1	◇1	◇1			◇1	◇1	◇1	◇1
				🚌	🚌																				
		☕	☕			☕	☕	☕	☕	☕			☕	☕	☕	☕	☕	☕	☕			☕	☕	☕	☕
Swansea	d								08 07						09 21		10 21					11 21			12 21
Neath	d								08 19						09 33		10 33					11 33			12 33
Port Talbot Parkway	d								08 26						09 40		10 40					11 40			12 40
Bridgend	d								08 38						09 52		10 52					11 52			12 52
Cardiff Central 7	d						07 56		09 05						10 15		11 15					12 15			13 15
Newport (South Wales)	d						08 15		09 19						10 32		11 32					12 32			13 32
Weston-super-Mare	d	21p53						08 11						09 56										12 51	
Bristol Temple Meads 10	d	22b30	07 50			08 20		08 45					09 48	10 30		11 30			12 30					13 30	
Bristol Parkway 7	a						08 44		09 46						10 59		11 59					12 59			13 59
	d						08 45		09 48						11 01		12 01					13 02			14 01
Bath Spa 7	d	22p43		07 35	07 55			08 58					10 00	10 43		11 43			12 43					13 43	
Chippenham	d	22p55		08 10				09 10					10 12	10 55		11 55			12 55					13 55	
Cheltenham Spa	d											09 24						11 46		12 24					
Gloucester 7	d											09 38						12 02		12 38					
Stonehouse	d											09 50						12 15		12 50					
Stroud	d											09 55						12 20		12 55					
Kemble	d											10 09						12 35		13 09					
Swindon	a	23p10	08 22	08 35	08 45	08 52	09 10	09 24	10 14			10 24	10 27	11 10	11 30	12 10	12 27	12 48	13 10	13 24		13 27		14 10	14 27
	d	23p11	08 26			08 55	09 11	09 29	10 14	10 23			10 29	11 11	11 33	12 11	12 29	12 53	13 11			13 29	13 35	14 11	14 29
Didcot Parkway	a	23p28	08 43			09 13		09 45					10 45	11 29	11 50	12 28	12 46		13 28			13 46		14 29	14 46
Reading 7	a	23p51	09 01			09 28	09 48	10 00	10 42	10 50			11 00	11 44	12 05	12 44	13 00	13 21	13 44			14 00	14 04	14 44	15 00
Slough 3	a																								
London Paddington 15 ⊖	a	00 33	09 39			10 08	10 25	10 38	11 20	11 35			11 42	12 23	12 42	13 23	13 38	14 08	14 21			14 40	14 44	15 22	15 38

		GW	GW	GW	GW	GW		GW	GW	GW	GW	GW	GW	GW	GW	GW		GW	GW	GW	GW	GW	GW	GW	GW
		◇1	◇1	◇1	◇1	◇1		◇1	◇1	◇1	◇1		◇1		◇1	◇1		◇1	◇1	◇1	◇1	◇1	◇1		
		☕	☕	☕	☕	☕		☕	☕	☕	☕		☕		☕	☕		☕	☕	☕	☕	☕	☕		
Swansea	d			13 21		14 21					15 21					16 21				16 51			17 51		
Neath	d			13 33		14 33					15 33					16 33				17 03			18 03		
Port Talbot Parkway	d			13 40		14 40					15 40					16 40				17 10			18 10		
Bridgend	d			13 52		14 52					15 52					16 52				17 22			18 22		
Cardiff Central 7	d			14 15		15 15					16 15					17 15				17 50			18 50		
Newport (South Wales)	d			14 32		15 32					16 32					17 32				18 04			19 04		
Weston-super-Mare	d				14 52										17 02			17 29							
Bristol Temple Meads 10	d		14 30		15 30			16 00		16 30			17 00		17 30			18 00			18 30	19 00			
Bristol Parkway 7	a			14 59		15 59					16 59					17 59				18 31			19 31		
	d			15 01		16 01					17 01					18 01				18 33			19 33		
Bath Spa 7	d		14 43		15 43			16 13		16 43			17 13		17 43			18 13			18 43	19 13			
Chippenham	d		14 55		15 55			16 25		16 55			17 25	17 39	17 55			18 25			18 55	19 25		20 04	
Cheltenham Spa	d	13 46							15 46			16 33							17 46						
Gloucester 7	d	14 02							16 00			16 47							18h02						19 34
Stonehouse	d	14 15							16 15			16 59							18 15						19 47
Stroud	d	14 20							16 19			17 04							18 20						19 52
Kemble	d	14 35							16 34			17 19							18 35						20 07
Swindon	a	14 50	15 10	15 27	16 10	16 27		16 40	16 49	17 10	17 27	17 34	17 40	17 56	18 10	18 27		18 39	18 48	18 59	19 10	19 39	19 58	20 20	20 29
	d	14 51	15 11	15 29	16 11	16 29		16 41	16 51	17 11	17 29		17 41		18 11	18 29		18 41	18 50	18 59	19 11	19 41	19 59		
Didcot Parkway	a		15 29	15 46	16 28	16 46		16 58		17 28	17 46		17 58			18 46		18 58		19 16		19 58	20 16		
Reading 7	a	15 21	15 44	16 00	16 42	17 00		17 12	17 18	17 42	18 00		18 12		18 42	19 00		19 12	19 21	19 30	19 42	20 12	20 32		
Slough 3	a																								
London Paddington 15 ⊖	a	16 06	16 23	16 38	17 22	17 43		17 53	17 57	18 22	18 38		18 53		19 23	19 38		19 53	20 09	20 12	20 23	20 51	21 11		

		GW		GW	GW	GW	GW	GW	GW
		◇1		◇1	◇1	◇1	◇1		◇1
		☕		☕	☕	☕	☕		☕
Swansea	d				18 51		19 59		
Neath	d				19 03		20 11		
Port Talbot Parkway	d				19 10		20 18		
Bridgend	d				19 22		20 30		
Cardiff Central 7	d				19 50		20 55		
Newport (South Wales)	d				20 04		21 09		
Weston-super-Mare	d	19 27				20 26			
Bristol Temple Meads 10	d	20 00				21 00			22 10
Bristol Parkway 7	a				20 31		21 36		
	d				20 33		21 38		
Bath Spa 7	d	20 13				21 13			22 23
Chippenham	d	20 25				21 25			22 35
Cheltenham Spa	d			19 46				21 46	
Gloucester 7	d			20 04				21 59	
Stonehouse	d			20 17				22 12	
Stroud	d			20 23				22 17	
Kemble	d			20 38				22 32	
Swindon	a	20 39		20 52	20 59	21 39	22 04	22 47	22 50
	d	20 41		20 52	20 59	21 41	22 05		22 53
Didcot Parkway	a	20 58		21 09	21 16	22 00			23 10
Reading 7	a	21 18		21 24	21 32	22 17	22 37		23 27
Slough 3	a								
London Paddington 15 ⊖	a	21 56		22 03	22 14	22 56	23 20		00 11

b Previous night, arr. 2212

For connections from Heathrow Airport, Gatwick Airport and Oxford please refer to Tables 125A, 148 and 116.
For connections to Birmingham New Street and Hereford please refer to Tables 57 and 131

Table 125

Sundays

18 September to 23 October

South Wales, Weston-super-Mare, Bristol, Cheltenham Spa and Swindon - London

		GW	GW	GW	GW	GW	GW	GW	GW	GW		GW	GW	GW	GW	GW	GW	GW	GW	GW		GW	GW	GW	GW
		◇1	◇1	1	◇1	◇1	◇1	◇1		◇1		◇1		◇1	◇1		◇1	◇1	◇1	◇1			◇1	◇1	◇1
		☕	☕	☕	☕	☕	☕	☕		☕		☕		☕	☕		☕	☕	☕	☕			☕	☕	☕
Swansea	d						07 55							09 21			10 21		11 21					12 21	
Neath	d						08 07							09 33			10 33		11 33					12 33	
Port Talbot Parkway	d						08 14							09 40			10 40		11 40					12 40	
Bridgend	d						08 26							09 52			10 52		11 52					12 52	
Cardiff Central 7	d				07 55		08 52							10 15			11 15		12 15					13 15	
Newport (South Wales)	d				08 13		09 06							10 32			11 32		12 32					13 32	
Weston-super-Mare	d	21p53				08 11						09 56											12 51		
Bristol Temple Meads 10	d	22b30	07 45	08 20		08 45				09 48		10 30			11 30			12 30					13 30		14 30
Bristol Parkway 7	a				08 44		09 36							10 59			11 59		12 59					13 59	
	d				08 45		09 38							11 01			12 01		13 02					14 01	
Bath Spa 7	d	22p43	07 57	08 33		08 58				10 00		10 43			11 43			12 43					13 43		14 43
Chippenham	d	22p55	08 10	08 45		09 10				10 12		10 55			11 55			12 55					13 55		14 55
Cheltenham Spa	d								09 24				10 24			11 24						13 01			
Gloucester 7	d								09 38				10 38			11 38						13 15			
Stonehouse	d								09 50				10 50			11 50						13 27			
Stroud	d								09 55				10 55			11 55						13 32			
Kemble	d								10 09				11 09			12 09						13 46			
Swindon	a	23p10	08 24	09 00	09 10	09 24	10 01		10 24	10 27		11 10	11 24	11 30	12 10	12 24	12 27	13 10	13 27			14 01	14 10	14 27	15 10
	d	23p11	08 26		09 11	09 29	10 01	10 23		10 29		11 11		11 33	12 11		12 29	13 11	13 29	13 36			14 11	14 29	15 11
Didcot Parkway	a	23p28	08 43			09 45				10 45		11 29		11 50	12 28		12 46	13 28	13 46				14 29	14 46	15 29
Reading 7	a	23p51	09 01		09 43	10 00	10 32	10 50		11 00		11 44		12 05	12 44		13 00	13 44	14 00	14 05			14 44	15 00	15 44
Slough 3	a																								
London Paddington 15 ⊖	a	00 33	09 39		10 21	10 38	11 10	11 35		11 42		12 23		12 42	13 23		13 38	14 21	14 40	14 43			15 22	15 38	16 23

		GW	GW	GW	GW	GW		GW	GW	GW	GW	GW	GW	GW	GW	GW		GW	GW	GW	GW	GW	GW	GW	GW
		◇1		◇1	◇1	◇1		◇1	◇1	◇1		◇1		◇1	◇1	◇1		◇1	◇1	◇1	◇1	◇1	◇1		
		☕		☕	☕	☕		☕	☕	☕		☕		☕	☕	☕		☕	☕	☕	☕	☕	☕		
Swansea	d	13 21			14 21					15 21					16 21					16 51			17 51		
Neath	d	13 33			14 33					15 33					16 33					17 03			18 03		
Port Talbot Parkway	d	13 40			14 40					15 40					16 40					17 10			18 10		
Bridgend	d	13 52			14 52					15 52					16 52					17 22			18 22		
Cardiff Central 7	d	14 15			15 15					16 15					17 15					17 50			18 50		
Newport (South Wales)	d	14 32			15 32					16 32					17 32					18 04			19 04		
Weston-super-Mare	d			14 52										17 02				17 29							
Bristol Temple Meads 10	d			15 30		16 00			16 30			17 00		17f 0				18 00			18 30	19 00			
Bristol Parkway 7	a	14 59			15 59					16 59					17 59					18 31			19 31		
	d	15 01			16 01					17 01					18 01					18 33			19 33		
Bath Spa 7	d			15 43		16 13			16 43			17 13		17 43				18 13			18 43	19 13			
Chippenham	d			15 55		16 25			16 55			17 25	17 39	17 55				18 25			18 55	19 25		20 04	
Cheltenham Spa	d		14 46					15 46			16 33								17 46						
Gloucester 7	d		15 00					16 00			16 47								18 02						19 34
Stonehouse	d		15 13					16 15			16 59								18 15						19 47
Stroud	d		15 18					16 19			17 04								18 20						19 52
Kemble	d		15 32					16 34			17 19								18 35						20 07
Swindon	a	15 27	15 47	16 10	16 33	16 40		16 49	17 10	17 27	17 34	17 40	17 56	18 10	18 27			18 39	18 48	18 59	19 10	19 39	19 58	20 20	20 29
	d	15 29		16 11	16 35	16 41		16 51	17 11	17 29		17 41		18 11	18 29	18 33		18 41	18 50	18 59	19 11	19 41	19 59		
Didcot Parkway	a	15 46		16 28	16 52	16 58			17 28	17 46		17 58			18 46			18 58		19 16		19 58	20 16		
Reading 7	a	16 00		16 42	17 06	17 12		17 18	17 42	18 00		18 12		18 42	19 00	19 06		19 12	19 21	19 30	19 42	20 12	20 32		
Slough 3	a																								
London Paddington 15 ⊖	a	16 38		17 22	17 49	17 53		17 57	18 22	18 38		18 53		19 23	19 38	19 43		19 53	20 09	20 12	20 23	20 51	21 14		

		GW		GW	GW	GW	GW	GW	GW	GW	GW
		◇1		◇1	◇1	◇1	◇1	◇1	◇1		◇1
		☕		☕	☕	☕	☕	☕	☕		☕
Swansea	d					18 51		19 59			
Neath	d					19 03		20 11			
Port Talbot Parkway	d					19 10		20 18			
Bridgend	d					19 22		20 30			
Cardiff Central 7	d					19 50		20 55			
Newport (South Wales)	d					20 04		21 09			
Weston-super-Mare	d			19 27			20 26				
Bristol Temple Meads 10	d			20 00			21 00				22 10
Bristol Parkway 7	a					20 31		21 36			
	d					20 33		21 38			
Bath Spa 7	d			20 13			21 13				22 23
Chippenham	d			20 26			21 25				22 35
Cheltenham Spa	d				19 46					21 46	
Gloucester 7	d				20 04					21 59	
Stonehouse	d				20 17					22 12	
Stroud	d				20 23					22 17	
Kemble	d				20 38					22 32	
Swindon	a			20 39	20 52	20 59	21 39	22 04		22 47	22 50
	d	20 32		20 41	20 52	20 59	21 41	22 05	22 20		22 53
Didcot Parkway	a			20 58	21 09	21 16	22 00				23 10
Reading 7	a	21 00		21 15	21 24	21 32	22 17	22 37	22 54		23 27
Slough 3	a										
London Paddington 15 ⊖	a	21 38		21 53	22 03	22 14	22 56	23 16	23 31		00 11

b Previous night, arr. 2212

For connections from Heathrow Airport, Gatwick Airport and Oxford please refer to Tables 125A, 148 and 116.
For connections to Birmingham New Street and Hereford please refer to Tables 57 and 131

Table 125

Sundays
from 30 October

South Wales, Weston-super-Mare, Bristol, Cheltenham Spa and Swindon - London

		GW ◇1 ☕	GW 🚌	GW 1 ☕	GW 🚌	GW 🚌	GW 1	GW 🚌	GW 1 ☕	GW 🚌		GW 🚌	GW	GW 🚌	GW 1 ☕	GW 🚌	GW 🚌	GW	GW 🚌	GW 🚌		GW 1 ☕	GW 🚌	GW	GW 🚌
Swansea	d																								
Neath	d																								
Port Talbot Parkway	d																								
Bridgend	d																								
Cardiff Central 7	d																								
Newport (South Wales)	d																								
Weston-super-Mare	d	21p53																							
Bristol Temple Meads 10	d	22b30		07 55			08 45		09 23						10 23							11 30			
Bristol Parkway 7	a																								
	d																								
Bath Spa 7	d	22p43		08 08			09 00		09 35						10 35							11 43			
Chippenham	d	22p55		08 20			09 15		09 48						10 48							11 55			
Cheltenham Spa	d												09 24					10 24						11 24	
Gloucester 7	d												09 38					10 38						11 38	
Stonehouse	d												09 50					10 50						11 50	
Stroud	d												09 55					10 55						11 55	
Kemble	d												10 09					11 09						12 09	
Swindon	a	23p10		08 35			09 32		10 03				10 24		11 03			11 24				12 10		12 24	
	d	23p11	07 55		09 10	09 10		09 40		10 10		10 13		10 40		11 05	11 13		11 35	12 05			12 20		12 35
Didcot Parkway	a	23p28			10 00							11 03					12 03						13 10		
Reading 7	a	23p51	08 55			10 10		10 40		11 10				11 40		12 10			12 40	13 10					13 40
Slough 3	a																								
London Paddington 15 ⊖	a	00 34																							

		GW 1 ☕	GW 🚌	GW 🚌	GW 🚌	GW		GW 🚌	GW 1 ☕	GW 🚌	GW 🚌	GW 🚌	GW 1 ☕	GW 🚌	GW 🚌	GW		GW 🚌	GW 1 ☕	GW 🚌	GW 🚌	GW	GW 🚌	GW 1 ☕	GW 🚌
Swansea	d																								
Neath	d																								
Port Talbot Parkway	d																								
Bridgend	d																								
Cardiff Central 7	d																								
Newport (South Wales)	d																								
Weston-super-Mare	d								12 51																
Bristol Temple Meads 10	d	12 25							13 30				14 30						15 40					16 30	
Bristol Parkway 7	a																								
	d																								
Bath Spa 7	d	12 38							13 43				14 43						15 53					16 43	
Chippenham	d	12 51							13 55				14 55						16 06					16 55	
Cheltenham Spa	d					13 01										14 46						15 46			
Gloucester 7	d					13 15										15 00						16 02			
Stonehouse	d					13 27										15 13						16 14			
Stroud	d					13 32										15 18						16 19			
Kemble	d					13 46										15 32						16 35			
Swindon	a	13 05				14 01			14 10				15 10			15 47			16 20			16 51		17 10	
	d		13 05	13 15	13 35			14 05		14 20	14 35	15 05		15 20	15 35			16 05		16 30	16 35		17 05		17 20
Didcot Parkway	a			14 05						15 10				16 10						17 20					18 10
Reading 7	a		14 10		14 40			15 10			15 40	16 10			16 40			17 10			17 40		18 10		
Slough 3	a																								
London Paddington 15 ⊖	a																								

		GW		GW 🚌	GW	GW 🚌	GW 1 ☕	GW 🚌	GW 🚌	GW	GW 🚌	GW 1 ☕		GW 🚌	GW 🚌	GW 🚌	GW 1 ☕	GW	GW 🚌	GW	GW 🚌	GW		GW 🚌	GW 1 ☕
Swansea	d																								
Neath	d																								
Port Talbot Parkway	d																								
Bridgend	d																								
Cardiff Central 7	d																								
Newport (South Wales)	d																								
Weston-super-Mare	d																								
Bristol Temple Meads 10	d						17 35					18 35					19 35								20 45
Bristol Parkway 7	a																								
	d																								
Bath Spa 7	d						17 49					18 49					19 49								20 58
Chippenham	d				17 39		18 01					19 01					20 01	20 08							21 10
Cheltenham Spa	d	16 33								17 46												20 05			
Gloucester 7	d	16 47								18 02										19 46		20 16			
Stonehouse	d	16 59								18 15										19 59		20 29			
Stroud	d	17 04								18 21										20 04		20 35			
Kemble	d	17 19								18 36										20 19		20 50			
Swindon	a	17 34			17 56		18 16			18 51		19 16					20 16	20 25		20 38		21 05			21 25
	d			17 35		18 05		18 20	18 35		19 10			19 30	19 40	20 05			20 30		20 45			21 15	
Didcot Parkway	a							19 10						20 20					21 20						
Reading 7	a			18 40		19 10			19 40		20 10				20 45	21 05					21 45			22 15	
Slough 3	a																								
London Paddington 15 ⊖	a																								

b Previous night, arr. 2212

For connections from Heathrow Airport, Gatwick Airport and Oxford please refer to Tables 125A, 148 and 116.
For connections to Birmingham New Street and Hereford please refer to Tables 57 and 131

Table 125

Sundays
from 30 October

South Wales, Weston-super-Mare, Bristol, Cheltenham Spa and Swindon - London

		GW	GW	GW	GW	GW	GW	GW
						1		
		🚌	🚌	🚌			🚌	🚌
						☕		
Swansea	d							
Neath	d							
Port Talbot Parkway	d							
Bridgend	d							
Cardiff Central 7	d							
Newport (South Wales)	d							
Weston-super-Mare	d							
Bristol Temple Meads 10	d					22 15		
Bristol Parkway 7	a							
	d							
Bath Spa 7	d					22 28		
Chippenham	d					22 40		
Cheltenham Spa	d				21 46			
Gloucester 7	d				21 59			
Stonehouse	d				22 12			
Stroud	d				22 17			
Kemble	d				22 32			
Swindon	a				22 47	22 55		
	d	21 35	21 35	22 15			23 05	23 10
Didcot Parkway	a	22 25						23 59
Reading 7	a		22 35	23 15			00 05	
Slough 3	a							
London Paddington 15 ⊖	a							

For connections from Heathrow Airport, Gatwick Airport and Oxford please refer to Tables 125A, 148 and 116.
For connections to Birmingham New Street and Hereford please refer to Tables 57 and 131

Table 125A

Mondays to Fridays

Reading - Heathrow Railair Link

Express Coach Service

Mondays to Fridays

		GW	GW	GW	GW	GW	GW	GW	GW	GW		GW	GW	GW	GW	GW	GW	GW	GW	GW		GW	GW	GW	GW
Reading 7	d	04 00	05 00	05 30	05 55	06 08	06 20	06 40	07 00	07 20		07 40	08 00	08 20	08 40	09 05	09 25	09 45	10 05	10 25		10 45	11 05	11 25	11 45
Heathrow Terminal 5 Bus	a	04 38	05 38	06 08	06 33	06 48	07 15	07 35	07 55	08 15		08 35	08 55	09 15	09 35	09 45	10 05	10 25	10 45	11 05		11 25	11 45	12 05	12 25
Heathrow Terminal 1 Bus	a																								
Heathrow Terminal 2 Bus	a																								
Heathrow Terminal 3 Bus	a																								

		GW	GW	GW	GW	GW		GW	GW	GW	GW	GW	GW	GW	GW	GW		GW	GW	GW	GW	GW	GW	GW	GW
Reading 7	d	12 05	12 25	12 45	13 05	13 25		13 45	14 05	14 25	14 45	15 05	15 25	15 45	16 05	16 25		16 45	17 05	17 25	17 45	18 05	18 35	19 05	19 35
Heathrow Terminal 5 Bus	a	12 45	13 05	13 25	13 45	14 05		14 25	14 45	15 05	15 25	15 45	16 05	16 25	16 45	17 05		17 25	17 45	18 05	18 25	18 45	19 15	19 45	20 15
Heathrow Terminal 1 Bus	a																								
Heathrow Terminal 2 Bus	a																								
Heathrow Terminal 3 Bus	a																								

		GW		GW	GW	GW	GW
Reading 7	d	20 05		20 35	21 05	22 05	23 05
Heathrow Terminal 5 Bus	a	20 43		21 13	21 43	22 43	23 43
Heathrow Terminal 1 Bus	a						
Heathrow Terminal 2 Bus	a						
Heathrow Terminal 3 Bus	a						

Saturdays

		GW	GW	GW	GW	GW	GW	GW	GW	GW		GW	GW	GW	GW	GW	GW	GW	GW	GW		GW	GW	GW	GW
Reading 7	d	04 00	05 00	05 45	06 15	06 45	07 15	07 45	08 15	08 45		09 15	09 45	10 15	10 45	11 15	11 45	12 15	12 45	13 15		13 45	14 15	14 45	15 15
Heathrow Terminal 5 Bus	a	04 38	05 38	06 25	06 55	07 25	07 55	08 25	08 55	09 25		09 55	10 25	10 55	11 25	11 55	12 25	12 55	13 25	13 55		14 25	14 55	15 25	15 55
Heathrow Terminal 1 Bus	a																								
Heathrow Terminal 2 Bus	a																								
Heathrow Terminal 3 Bus	a																								

		GW	GW	GW	GW	GW		GW	GW	GW	GW	GW	GW	GW	GW
Reading 7	d	15 45	16 15	16 45	17 15	17 45		18 15	18 45	19 15	19 45	20 25	20 55	22 05	23 05
Heathrow Terminal 5 Bus	a	16 25	16 55	17 25	17 55	18 25		18 55	19 25	19 55	20 25	21 05	21 35	22 43	23 43
Heathrow Terminal 1 Bus	a														
Heathrow Terminal 2 Bus	a														
Heathrow Terminal 3 Bus	a														

Sundays

		GW	GW	GW	GW	GW	GW	GW	GW	GW		GW	GW	GW	GW	GW	GW	GW	GW	GW		GW	GW	GW	GW
Reading 7	d	04 00	05 00	05 45	06 15	06 45	07 15	07 45	08 15	08 45		09 15	09 45	10 15	10 45	11 15	11 45	12 15	12 45	13 15		13 45	14 15	14 45	15 15
Heathrow Terminal 5 Bus	a	04 38	05 38	06 25	06 55	07 25	07 55	08 25	08 55	09 25		09 55	10 25	10 55	11 25	11 55	12 25	12 55	13 25	13 55		14 25	14 55	15 25	15 55
Heathrow Terminal 1 Bus	a																								
Heathrow Terminal 2 Bus	a																								
Heathrow Terminal 3 Bus	a																								

		GW	GW	GW	GW	GW		GW	GW	GW	GW	GW	GW	GW	GW
Reading 7	d	15 45	16 15	16 45	17 15	17 45		18 15	18 45	19 15	19 45	20 25	20 55	22 05	23 05
Heathrow Terminal 5 Bus	a	16 25	16 55	17 25	17 55	18 25		18 55	19 25	19 55	20 25	21 05	21 35	22 43	23 43
Heathrow Terminal 1 Bus	a														
Heathrow Terminal 2 Bus	a														
Heathrow Terminal 3 Bus	a														

Table 125A

Mondays to Fridays

Heathrow - Reading Railair Link

Express Coach Service

	GW	GW	GW	GW	GW	GW	GW	GW	GW		GW	GW	GW	GW	GW	GW	GW	GW	GW		GW	GW	GW	GW
Heathrow Central Bus Stn d	00 05	05 00	06 00	06 30	06 57	07 20	07 40	08 00	08 20	.....	08 40	09 00	09 20	09 40	10 00	10 15	10 35	10 55	11 15	.....	11 35	11 55	12 15	12 35
Heathrow Terminal 5 Bus d	00 13	05 08	06 08	06 38	07 05	07 28	07 50	08 10	08 30	.	08 50	09 10	09 30	09 50	10 10	10 25	10 45	11 05	11 25	.	11 45	12 05	12 25	12 45
Reading a	00 51	05 46	06 46	07 21	07 48	08 21	08 46	09 06	09 26	.....	09 39	09 59	10 13	10 33	10 53	11 08	11 28	11 48	12 08	.....	12 28	12 48	13 08	13 28

	GW	GW	GW	GW	GW		GW	GW	GW	GW	GW	GW	GW	GW	GW		GW	GW	GW	GW	GW	GW	GW	GW
Heathrow Central Bus Stn d	12 55	13 15	13 35	13 55	14 15	.....	14 35	14 55	15 15	15 35	15 55	16 15	16 35	16 55	17 15	.....	17 35	17 55	18 15	18 35	18 55	19 15	19 40	20 10
Heathrow Terminal 5 Bus d	13 05	13 25	13 45	14 05	14 25	.	14 45	15 05	15 25	15 45	16 05	16 25	16 45	17 05	17 25	.	17 45	18 05	18 25	18 45	19 05	19 25	19 50	20 20
Reading a	13 48	14 08	14 28	14 48	15 08	.....	15 28	15 48	16 08	16 28	16 48	17 14	17 34	17 54	18 14	.....	18 34	18 54	19 14	19 34	19 54	20 14	20 31	21 01

	GW		GW	GW	GW	GW																		
Heathrow Central Bus Stn d	20 40	.....	21 10	21 40	22 15	23 05																		
Heathrow Terminal 5 Bus d	20 50	.	21 20	21 50	22 23	23 13																		
Reading a	21 31	.....	22 01	22 31	23 01	23 51																		

Saturdays

	GW	GW	GW	GW	GW	GW	GW	GW	GW		GW	GW	GW	GW	GW	GW	GW	GW	GW		GW	GW	GW	GW
Heathrow Central Bus Stn d	00 05	05 00	06 00	07 00	07 30	08 00	08 30	09 00	09 30	.....	10 00	10 30	11 00	11 30	12 00	12 30	13 00	13 30	14 00	.....	14 30	15 00	15 30	16 00
Heathrow Terminal 5 Bus d	00 13	05 08	06 08	07 10	07 40	08 10	08 40	09 10	09 40	.	10 10	10 40	11 10	11 40	12 10	12 40	13 10	13 40	14 10	.	14 40	15 10	15 40	16 10
Reading a	00 51	05 46	06 46	07 53	08 23	08 53	09 23	09 53	10 23	.....	10 53	11 23	11 53	12 23	12 53	13 23	13 53	14 23	14 53	.....	15 23	15 53	16 23	16 53

	GW	GW	GW	GW	GW		GW	GW	GW	GW	GW	GW	GW	GW										
Heathrow Central Bus Stn d	16 30	17 00	17 30	18 00	18 30	.....	19 00	19 20	19 50	20 20	20 50	21 30	22 00	23 05										
Heathrow Terminal 5 Bus d	16 40	17 10	17 40	18 10	18 40	.	19 10	19 30	20 00	20 30	21 00	21 38	22 08	23 13										
Reading a	17 23	17 53	18 23	18 53	19 23	.....	19 53	20 13	20 43	21 13	21 43	22 19	22 49	23 51										

Sundays

	GW	GW	GW	GW	GW	GW	GW	GW	GW		GW	GW	GW	GW	GW	GW	GW	GW	GW		GW	GW	GW	GW
Heathrow Central Bus Stn d	00 05	05 00	06 00	07 00	07 30	08 00	08 30	09 00	09 30	.....	10 00	10 30	11 00	11 30	12 00	12 30	13 00	13 30	14 00	.....	14 30	15 00	15 30	16 00
Heathrow Terminal 5 Bus d	00 13	05 08	06 08	07 10	07 40	08 10	08 40	09 10	09 40	.	10 10	10 40	11 10	11 40	12 10	12 40	13 10	13 40	14 10	.	14 40	15 10	15 40	16 10
Reading a	00 51	05 46	06 46	07 53	08 23	08 53	09 23	09 53	10 23	.....	10 53	11 23	11 53	12 23	12 53	13 23	13 53	14 23	14 53	.....	15 23	15 53	16 23	16 53

	GW	GW	GW	GW	GW		GW	GW	GW	GW	GW	GW	GW	GW										
Heathrow Central Bus Stn d	16 30	17 00	17 30	18 00	18 30	.....	19 00	19 20	19 50	20 20	20 50	21 30	22 00	23 05										
Heathrow Terminal 5 Bus d	16 40	17 10	17 40	18 10	18 40	.	19 10	19 30	20 00	20 30	21 00	21 38	22 08	23 13										
Reading a	17 23	17 53	18 23	18 53	19 23	.....	19 53	20 13	20 43	21 13	21 43	22 19	22 49	23 51										

Bristol - Bristol International Airport

Bus Service

		GW	GW	GW	GW	GW	GW	GW	GW	GW		GW	GW	GW	GW	GW	GW	GW	GW	GW		GW	GW	GW	GW
Bristol Temple Meads 10	d	23p53	00 13	02 42	03 57	04 52	05 12	05 32	05 52	06 12		06 22	06 32	06 42	06 52	07 02	07 12	07 22	07 32	07 46		07 56	08 06	08 16	08 26
Bristol Internatl Airport ✈	a	00 13	00 33	03 01	04 16	05 11	05 31	05 51	06 11	06 31		06 41	06 51	07 01	07 11	07 21	07 31	07 44	07 57	08 11		08 21	08 31	08 41	08 51

		GW	GW	GW	GW	GW		GW	GW	GW	GW	GW	GW	GW	GW	GW		GW	GW	GW	GW	GW	GW	GW	GW
Bristol Temple Meads 10	d	08 36	08 46	08 56	09 06	09 16		09 26	09 36	09 45	09 55	10 05	10 15	10 25	10 35	10 45		10 55	11 05	11 15	11 25	11 35	11 45	11 55	12 05
Bristol Internatl Airport ✈	a	09 01	09 11	09 21	09 31	09 41		09 49	09 58	10 07	10 17	10 27	10 37	10 47	10 57	11 07		11 17	11 27	11 37	11 47	11 57	12 07	12 17	12 27

		GW		GW	GW	GW	GW	GW	GW	GW	GW	GW		GW	GW	GW	GW	GW	GW	GW	GW	GW		GW	GW
Bristol Temple Meads 10	d	12 15		12 25	12 35	12 45	12 55	13 05	13 15	13 25	13 35	13 45		13 55	14 05	14 15	14 25	14 35	14 45	14 55	15 05	15 15		15 25	15 35
Bristol Internatl Airport ✈	a	12 37		12 47	12 57	13 07	13 17	13 27	13 37	13 47	13 57	14 07		14 17	14 27	14 37	14 47	14 57	15 07	15 17	15 27	15 37		15 50	16 02

		GW	GW	GW	GW	GW	GW	GW		GW	GW	GW	GW	GW	GW	GW	GW	GW		GW	GW	GW	GW	GW	GW
Bristol Temple Meads 10	d	15 48	15 58	16 08	16 18	16 28	16 38	16 48		16 58	17 08	17 18	17 28	17 38	17 48	17 58	18 08	18 15		18 25	18 35	18 45	18 55	19 05	19 15
Bristol Internatl Airport ✈	a	16 15	16 25	16 35	16 45	16 55	17 05	17 15		17 25	17 35	17 45	17 55	18 05	18 12	18 22	18 30	18 37		18 47	18 57	19 07	19 17	19 27	19 37

		GW	GW	GW		GW	GW	GW	GW	GW	GW	GW	GW	GW		GW	GW								
Bristol Temple Meads 10	d	19 35	19 55	20 13		20 33	20 53	21 13	21 33	21 53	22 13	22 33	22 53	23 13		23 33	23 53								
Bristol Internatl Airport ✈	a	19 57	20 17	20 33		20 53	21 13	21 33	21 53	22 13	22 33	22 53	23 13	23 33		23 53	00 13								

Saturdays

		GW	GW	GW	GW	GW	GW	GW	GW	GW		GW	GW	GW	GW	GW	GW	GW	GW	GW		GW	GW	GW	GW
Bristol Temple Meads 10	d	23p53	00 13	02 42	03 57	04 52	05 12	05 32	05 52	06 12		06 22	06 32	06 42	06 52	07 02	07 12	07 22	07 32	07 44		07 54	08 04	08 14	08 24
Bristol Internatl Airport ✈	a	00 13	00 33	03 01	04 16	05 11	05 31	05 51	06 11	06 31		06 41	06 51	07 01	07 11	07 21	07 31	07 42	07 52	08 04		08 14	08 24	08 34	08 44

		GW	GW	GW	GW	GW		GW	GW	GW	GW	GW	GW	GW	GW	GW		GW	GW	GW	GW	GW	GW	GW	GW
Bristol Temple Meads 10	d	08 34	08 44	09 04	09 14	09 24		09 34	09 45	09 55	10 05	10 15	10 25	10 35	10 45	10 55		11 05	11 15	11 25	11 35	11 45	11 55	12 05	12 15
Bristol Internatl Airport ✈	a	08 54	09 04	09 24	09 34	09 44		09 57	10 08	10 18	10 28	10 38	10 48	10 58	11 08	11 18		11 28	11 38	11 48	11 58	12 08	12 18	12 28	12 38

		GW		GW	GW	GW	GW	GW	GW	GW	GW	GW		GW	GW	GW	GW	GW	GW	GW	GW	GW		GW	GW
Bristol Temple Meads 10	d	12 25		12 35	12 45	12 55	13 05	13 15	13 25	13 35	13 45	13 55		14 05	14 15	14 25	14 35	14 45	14 55	15 05	15 15	15 25		15 35	15 46
Bristol Internatl Airport ✈	a	12 48		12 58	13 08	13 18	13 28	13 38	13 48	13 58	14 08	14 18		14 28	14 38	14 48	14 58	15 08	15 18	15 28	15 38	15 48		15 57	16 08

		GW	GW	GW	GW	GW	GW	GW		GW	GW	GW	GW	GW	GW	GW	GW	GW		GW	GW	GW	GW	GW	GW
Bristol Temple Meads 10	d	15 56	16 16	16 36	16 56	17 16	17 36	17 56		18 15	18 35	18 55	19 15	19 35	19 55	20 13	20 33	20 53		21 13	21 33	21 53	22 13	22 33	22 53
Bristol Internatl Airport ✈	a	16 18	16 38	16 58	17 18	17 38	17 58	18 18		18 38	18 58	19 18	19 38	19 58	20 18	20 33	20 53	21 13		21 33	21 53	22 13	22 33	22 53	23 13

		GW	GW	GW																					
Bristol Temple Meads 10	d	23 13	23 33	23 53																					
Bristol Internatl Airport ✈	a	23 33	23 53	00 13																					

Sundays

		GW A	GW	GW	GW	GW	GW	GW	GW	GW		GW	GW	GW	GW	GW	GW	GW	GW	GW		GW	GW	GW	GW
Bristol Temple Meads 10	d	23p53	00 13	02 42	03 57	04 52	05 12	05 32	05 52	06 12		06 32	06 52	07 12	07 32	07 54	08 14	08 34	08 54	09 14		09 34	09 55	10 15	10 35
Bristol Internatl Airport ✈	a	00 13	00 33	03 01	04 16	05 11	05 31	05 51	06 11	06 31		06 51	07 11	07 31	07 51	08 13	08 33	08 53	09 13	09 33		09 56	10 17	10 37	10 57

		GW	GW	GW	GW	GW		GW	GW	GW	GW	GW	GW	GW	GW	GW		GW	GW	GW	GW	GW	GW	GW	GW
Bristol Temple Meads 10	d	10 55	11 15	11 25	11 35	11 45		11 55	12 05	12 15	12 25	12 35	12 45	12 55	13 05	13 15		13 25	13 35	13 45	13 55	14 05	14 15	14 25	14 35
Bristol Internatl Airport ✈	a	11 17	11 37	11 47	11 57	12 07		12 17	12 27	12 37	12 47	12 57	13 07	13 17	13 27	13 37		13 47	13 57	14 07	14 17	14 27	14 37	14 47	14 57

		GW		GW	GW	GW	GW	GW	GW	GW	GW	GW		GW	GW	GW	GW	GW	GW	GW	GW	GW		GW	GW
Bristol Temple Meads 10	d	14 45		14 55	15 05	15 15	15 25	15 35	15 45	15 55	16 15	16 35		16 55	17 15	17 35	17 55	18 15	18 35	18 55	19 15	19 35		19 55	20 13
Bristol Internatl Airport ✈	a	15 07		15 17	15 27	15 37	15 47	15 58	16 08	16 18	16 38	16 58		17 18	17 38	17 58	18 18	18 37	18 57	19 17	19 37	19 57		20 17	20 33

		GW	GW	GW	GW	GW	GW	GW		GW	GW	GW	GW												
Bristol Temple Meads 10	d	20 33	20 53	21 13	21 33	21 53	22 13	22 33		22 53	23 13	23 33	23 53												
Bristol Internatl Airport ✈	a	20 53	21 13	21 33	21 53	22 13	22 33	22 53		23 13	23 33	23 53	00 13												

A not 22 May

Table 125B

Bristol International Airport - Bristol

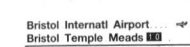

Bus Service

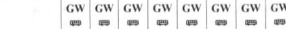

		GW	GW	GW	GW	GW	GW	GW	GW	GW		GW	GW	GW	GW	GW	GW	GW	GW	GW		GW	GW	GW	GW
Bristol Internatl Airport ✈	d	23p50	00 50	03 05	04 20	05 20	06 00	06 20	06 40	06 50	.....	07 00	07 10	07 20	07 30	07 40	07 50	08 00	08 10	08 20	.....	08 30	08 40	08 50	09 00
Bristol Temple Meads **10**	a	00 16	01 16	03 29	04 44	05 44	06 24	06 44	07 04	07 14	.	07 24	07 34	07 48	08 02	08 12	08 22	08 32	08 42	08 52	.	09 02	09 12	09 22	09 32

		GW	GW	GW	GW	GW		GW	GW	GW	GW	GW	GW	GW	GW	GW		GW	GW	GW	GW	GW	GW	GW	GW
Bristol Internatl Airport ✈	d	09 10	09 20	09 30	09 40	09 50	.....	10 00	10 10	10 20	10 30	10 40	10 50	11 00	11 10	11 20	.....	11 30	11 40	11 50	12 00	12 10	12 20	12 30	12 40
Bristol Temple Meads **10**	a	09 42	09 52	10 00	10 10	10 20	.	10 30	10 40	10 50	11 00	11 10	11 20	11 30	11 40	11 50	.	12 00	12 10	12 20	12 30	12 40	12 50	13 00	13 10

		GW		GW	GW	GW	GW	GW	GW	GW	GW	GW		GW	GW	GW	GW	GW	GW	GW	GW	GW		GW	GW
Bristol Internatl Airport ✈	d	12 50	.....	13 00	13 10	13 20	13 30	13 40	13 50	14 00	14 10	14 20	.....	14 30	14 40	14 50	15 00	15 10	15 20	15 30	15 40	15 50	.....	16 00	16 10
Bristol Temple Meads **10**	a	13 20	.	13 30	13 40	13 50	14 00	14 10	14 20	14 30	14 40	14 50	.	15 00	15 10	15 20	15 30	15 40	15 52	16 03	16 13	16 23	.	16 33	16 43

		GW	GW	GW	GW	GW	GW	GW		GW	GW	GW	GW	GW	GW	GW	GW	GW		GW	GW	GW	GW	GW	GW
Bristol Internatl Airport ✈	d	16 20	16 30	16 40	16 50	17 00	17 10	17 20	.....	17 30	17 40	17 50	18 00	18 10	18 20	18 30	18 40	18 50	.....	19 00	19 10	19 20	19 30	19 50	20 10
Bristol Temple Meads **10**	a	16 53	17 03	17 13	17 23	17 33	17 43	17 53	.	18 03	18 13	18 21	18 30	18 40	18 50	19 00	19 10	19 20	.	19 30	19 40	19 50	20 00	20 17	20 36

		GW	GW	GW		GW	GW	GW	GW	GW	GW	GW	GW												
Bristol Internatl Airport ✈	d	20 30	20 50	21 10	.....	21 30	21 50	22 10	22 30	22 50	23 10	23 30	23 50	.....	.....	.....	.....	.....	.....	.....	.....	.....	.....	.....	.....
Bristol Temple Meads **10**	a	20 56	21 16	21 36	.	21 56	22 16	22 36	22 56	23 16	23 36	23 56	00 16	.	.	.	.	.	.	.	.	.	.	.	.

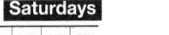

Saturdays

		GW	GW	GW	GW	GW	GW	GW	GW	GW		GW	GW	GW	GW	GW	GW	GW	GW	GW		GW	GW	GW	GW
Bristol Internatl Airport ✈	d	23p50	00 50	03 05	04 20	05 20	05 40	06 00	06 20	06 40	.....	06 50	07 00	07 10	07 20	07 30	07 40	07 50	08 00	08 10	.....	08 20	08 30	08 40	08 50
Bristol Temple Meads **10**	a	00 16	01 16	03 29	04 44	05 44	06 04	06 24	06 44	07 04	.	07 14	07 24	07 34	07 45	07 56	08 06	08 16	08 26	08 36	.	08 46	08 56	09 06	09 16

		GW	GW	GW	GW	GW		GW	GW	GW	GW	GW	GW	GW	GW	GW		GW	GW	GW	GW	GW	GW	GW	GW
Bristol Internatl Airport ✈	d	09 00	09 10	09 20	09 30	09 40	.....	09 50	10 00	10 10	10 20	10 30	10 40	10 50	11 00	11 10	.....	11 20	11 30	11 40	11 50	12 00	12 10	12 20	12 30
Bristol Temple Meads **10**	a	09 26	09 36	09 48	09 59	10 09	.	10 19	10 29	10 39	10 49	10 59	11 09	11 19	11 29	11 39	.	11 49	11 59	12 09	12 19	12 29	12 39	12 49	12 59

		GW		GW	GW	GW	GW	GW	GW	GW	GW	GW		GW	GW	GW	GW	GW	GW	GW	GW	GW		GW	GW
Bristol Internatl Airport ✈	d	12 40	.....	12 50	13 00	13 10	13 20	13 30	13 40	13 50	14 00	14 10	.....	14 20	14 30	14 40	14 50	15 00	15 10	15 20	15 30	15 40	.....	15 50	16 00
Bristol Temple Meads **10**	a	13 09	.	13 19	13 29	13 39	13 49	13 59	14 09	14 19	14 29	14 39	.	14 49	14 59	15 09	15 19	15 29	15 39	15 50	16 00	16 10	.	16 20	16 30

		GW	GW	GW	GW	GW	GW	GW		GW	GW	GW	GW	GW	GW	GW	GW	GW		GW	GW	GW	GW	GW	GW
Bristol Internatl Airport ✈	d	16 10	16 20	16 30	16 50	17 10	17 30	17 50	.....	18 10	18 30	18 50	19 10	19 30	19 50	20 10	20 30	20 50	.....	21 10	21 30	21 50	22 10	22 30	22 50
Bristol Temple Meads **10**	a	16 40	16 50	17 00	17 20	17 40	18 00	18 19	.	18 39	18 59	19 19	19 39	19 59	20 17	20 36	20 56	21 16	.	21 36	21 56	22 16	22 36	22 56	23 16

		GW	GW	GW																					
Bristol Internatl Airport ✈	d	23 10	23 30	23 50	.....	.....	.....	.....	.....	.....	.....	.....	.....	.....	.....	.....	.....	.....	.....	.....	.....	.....	.....	.....	.....
Bristol Temple Meads **10**	a	23 36	23 56	00 16	.	.	.	.	.	.	.	.	.	.	.	.	.	.	.	.	.	.	.	.	.

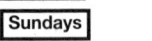

Sundays

		GW A	GW	GW	GW	GW	GW	GW	GW	GW		GW	GW	GW	GW	GW	GW	GW	GW	GW		GW	GW	GW	GW
Bristol Internatl Airport ✈	d	23p50	00 50	03 05	04 20	05 20	05 50	06 10	06 30	06 50	.....	07 10	07 30	07 50	08 10	08 30	08 50	09 10	09 30	09 50	.....	10 10	10 30	10 50	11 10
Bristol Temple Meads **10**	a	00 16	01 16	03 29	04 44	05 44	06 14	06 34	06 54	07 14	.	07 34	07 55	08 15	08 35	08 55	09 15	09 35	09 57	10 17	.	10 37	10 57	11 17	11 37

		GW	GW	GW	GW	GW		GW	GW	GW	GW	GW	GW	GW	GW	GW		GW	GW	GW	GW	GW	GW	GW	GW
Bristol Internatl Airport ✈	d	11 20	11 30	11 40	11 50	12 00	.....	12 10	12 20	12 30	12 40	12 50	13 00	13 10	13 20	13 30	.....	13 40	13 50	14 00	14 10	14 20	14 30	14 40	14 50
Bristol Temple Meads **10**	a	11 47	11 57	12 07	12 17	12 27	.	12 37	12 47	12 57	13 07	13 17	13 27	13 37	13 47	13 57	.	14 07	14 17	14 27	14 37	14 47	14 57	15 07	15 17

		GW		GW	GW	GW	GW	GW	GW	GW	GW	GW		GW	GW	GW	GW	GW	GW	GW	GW	GW		GW	GW
Bristol Internatl Airport ✈	d	15 00	.....	15 10	15 20	15 30	15 40	15 50	16 00	16 10	16 20	16 30	.....	16 50	17 10	17 30	17 50	18 10	18 30	18 50	19 10	19 30	.....	19 50	20 10
Bristol Temple Meads **10**	a	15 27	.	15 37	15 49	16 00	16 10	16 20	16 30	16 40	16 50	17 00	.	17 20	17 40	18 00	18 18	18 37	18 57	19 17	19 37	19 57	.	20 16	20 36

		GW	GW	GW	GW	GW	GW	GW		GW	GW	GW	GW												
Bristol Internatl Airport ✈	d	20 30	20 50	21 10	21 30	21 50	22 10	22 30	.....	22 50	23 10	23 30	23 50	.....	.....	.....	.....	.....	.....	.....	.....	.....	.....	.....	.....
Bristol Temple Meads **10**	a	20 56	21 16	21 36	21 56	22 16	22 36	22 56	.	23 16	23 36	23 56	00 16	.	.	.	.	.	.	.	.	.	.	.	.

A not 22 May

Table 125C

Mondays to Fridays

Cardiff - Cardiff International Airport

Bus Service

		GW BHX	GW BHX	GW BHX	GW BHX	GW BHX	GW BHX	GW BHX	GW BHX	GW BHX
Cardiff Central Bus Stn	d	08 05	08 57	10 52	12 02	14 02	14 37	16 02	17 12	18 10
Cardiff International Apt ✈	a	08 44	09 28	11 23	12 33	14 33	15 07	16 35	17 51	18 41

Saturdays

		GW	GW	GW	GW	GW	GW	GW	GW	GW
Cardiff Central Bus Stn	d	06 00	08 15	08 57	10 52	12 02	14 02	16 02	17 12	18 10
Cardiff International Apt ✈	a	06 26	08 44	09 28	11 23	12 33	14 33	16 35	17 42	18 41

Sundays

		GW	GW	GW	GW	GW	GW
Cardiff Central Bus Stn	d	10 02	12 02	14 02	16 02	18 02	19 32
Cardiff International Apt ✈	a	10 32	12 32	14 32	16 32	18 32	20 02

Table 125C

Mondays to Fridays

Cardiff International Airport - Cardiff

Bus Service

		GW BHX	GW BHX	GW BHX	GW BHX	GW BHX	GW BHX	GW BHX	GW BHX	GW BHX	GW BHX
Cardiff International Apt ✈	d	07 16	07 51	09 26	10 26	11 35	13 35	15 35	17 30	18 51	19 41
Cardiff Central Bus Stn	a	07 50	08 32	09 59	10 59	12 08	14 08	16 08	18 03	19 21	20 11

Saturdays

		GW	GW	GW	GW	GW	GW	GW	GW	GW
Cardiff International Apt ✈	d	08 00	09 26	10 26	11 35	13 35	15 35	17 30	18 51	19 41
Cardiff Central Bus Stn	a	08 31	09 59	10 59	12 08	14 08	16 08	18 03	19 21	20 11

Sundays

		GW	GW	GW	GW	GW	GW
Cardiff International Apt ✈	d	10 40	12 40	14 40	16 40	18 40	20 40
Cardiff Central Bus Stn	a	11 10	13 10	15 10	17 10	19 10	21 10

Table 126

Mondays to Fridays

until 9 September

London and Oxford - Worcester and Hereford

Miles			GW MX	GW	GW	GW	GW	GW	GW	GW	GW	GW	GW	GW	GW	GW	GW	GW	GW FX	GW FO	GW	GW	GW FX
			◇1	◇1	◇1	1	◇1	1	◇1	◇1	◇1	◇1	◇1	◇1	◇1	◇1	◇1	◇1	◇1	◇1	◇1	◇1	◇1
				A	B		C	C						D				E				F	
							trolley	trolley	buffet	trolley	buffet	trolley	trolley	trolley	buffet	buffet	buffet	buffet	buffet	buffet	buffet	trolley	
0	**London Paddington** 15 ⊖	d	21p48	21p42	21p42		05 48	06 48	08 22	09 21	10 22	11 20	13 21	14 21	15 51	17 22	17 50	18 22	19 22	19 22	20 20	21 48	21 48
18½	Slough 3	d	22p03	21p59	22p00		06 05	07 04	08 36	09 36	10 36	11 36	13 36	14 36	16 06				19 36	19 36	20 36	22 03	22 03
36	Reading 7	d	22p22	22p22	22p24		06 21	07 22	08 52	09 52	10 52	11 52	13 52	14 52	16 22	17 50	18 22	18 50	19 52	19 52	20 52	22 22	22 22
53¼	Didcot Parkway	d		22p38	22p40		06 39	07 50															
63½	**Oxford**	d	22p52	22p53	22p54		06 56	08 04	09 21	10b25	11 19	12 19	14 19	15 19	16 47	18 17	18c54	19 21	20 20	20 24	21 18	22 52	22 52
70½	Hanborough	d	23p02	23p04	23p05		07 06		09 31	10 35	11 29	12 28	14 29	15 30	16 58	18 26		19 31	20 30	20 34	21 27	23 03	23 02
71½	Combe	d																					
75	Finstock	d																					
76¾	Charlbury	d	23p10	23p12	23p13		07 13		09 39	10 42	11 37	12 36	14 37	15 37	17 06	18 35	19 09	19 40	20 38	20 42	21 35	23 11	23 10
80½	Ascott-under-Wychwood	d																					
81¾	Shipton	d	23p18														19 16					23 18	23 18
84¾	Kingham	d	23p24	23p21	23p22		07 22	08 25	09 49	10 51	11 47	12 45	14 46	15 46	17 15	18 45	19 23	19 50	20 48	20 52	21 45	23 24	23 24
91¾	Moreton-in-Marsh	a	23p33	23p29	23p30		07 31	08 33	09 58	11 00	11 56	12 54	14 54	15 56	17 24	18 54	19 32	19 59	20 57	21 01	21 54	23 33	23 33
—		d	23p34	23p32	23p33	05 37	07 32	08 34	09 59	11 01	11 57	12 55	14 58		17 25	18 55	19 35	20 00	20 58	21 02	21 54	23 35	23 34
101¾	Honeybourne	d	23p46	23p43	23p44		07 43	08 46	10 11		12 09	13 06	15 09		17 37	19 07		20 11	21 10	21 14	22 06	23 46	23 46
106¾	Evesham	a	23p54	23p50	23p51	05 51	07 50	08 52	10 19	11 16	12 17	13 15	15 16		17 45	19 15	19 52	20 19	21 18	21 22	22 14	23 55	23 54
—		d	23p56	23p52	23p53	06 06	07 57	08 53	10 29	11 18	12 29	13 16	15 19		17 47	19 21	19 57	20 20	21 25	21 25	22 15	23 56	23 56
112¾	Pershore	d	00 04	00 01	00 03	06 14	08 05	09 02	10 37		12 37	13 24	15 27		17 55	19 29	20 05	20 28	21 33	21 33	22 23	00 05	00 04
120½	**Worcester Shrub Hill** 7	a	00 18	00 12	00 14	06 32	08 17	09 15	10 51	11 35	12 50	13 36	15 39		18 09	19 44	20 25	20 41	21 46	21 46	22 39	00 17	00 18
121¼	**Worcester Foregate Street** 7	a				06 38	08 21	09 18	10 55	11 41	12 54	13 40	15 47			19 48		20 45	21 52	21 52	22 44		
128	Malvern Link	a					08 33	09 27	11 05		13 03	13 51	15 57			19 58		20 54	22 04	22 04	22 53		
128¾	Great Malvern	a					08 38	09 33	11 09		13 07	13 56	16 00			20 02		20 58	22 08	22 08	22 59		
131¾	Colwall	a							11 15		13 15					20 08		21 04	22 25	22 25			
136	Ledbury	a							11 23		13 23					20 16		21 12	22 33	22 33			
149¾	**Hereford** 7	a							11 43		13 50					20 36		21 33	22 54	22 54			

		GW
		◇1
		G
		trolley
London Paddington 15 ⊖	d	21 48
Slough 3	d	22 03
Reading 7	d	22 22
Didcot Parkway	d	
Oxford	d	22 52
Hanborough	d	23 03
Combe	d	
Finstock	d	
Charlbury	d	23 11
Ascott-under-Wychwood	d	
Shipton	d	23 18
Kingham	d	23 24
Moreton-in-Marsh	a	23 33
	d	23 35
Honeybourne	d	23 46
Evesham	a	23 55
	d	23 56
Pershore	d	00 05
Worcester Shrub Hill 7	a	00 18
Worcester Foregate Street 7	a	
Malvern Link	a	
Great Malvern	a	
Colwall	a	
Ledbury	a	
Hereford 7	a	

A MO from 8 August until 5 September
B MO until 1 August
C trolley from Oxford
D trolley to Reading
E The Cathedrals Express
F FO until 1 July, 9 September
G FO from 8 July until 2 September
b Arr. 1018
c Arr. 1847

Table 126

Mondays to Fridays

from 12 September

London and Oxford - Worcester and Hereford

		GW	GW	GW	GW	GW	GW	GW	GW	GW
			MX							
		◇**1**	◇**1**	◇**1**	◇**1**	**1**	◇**1**	**1**	**1**	◇**1**
		A		B	C		D	D		
			☕				🛒	🛒		☕
London Paddington 15 ⊖	d	21p42	21p48	21p39	21p42		05 48	06 48		08 22
Slough 3	d	22p03	22p03	21p59	21p59		06 05	07 04		08 36
Reading 7	d	22p19	22p22	22p22	22p22		06 21	07 22		08 52
Didcot Parkway	d	22p35		22p38	22p38		06 39	07 50		
Oxford	d	22p50	22p52	22p53	22p53		06 56	08 04	08 58	09 21
Hanborough	d	23p01	23p03	23p04	23p04		07 06	08 14	09 07	09 32
Combe	d	⌇		⌇	⌇					
Finstock	d	⌇		⌇	⌇					
Charlbury	d	23p09	23p11	23p12	23p12		07 13	08 21	09 14	09 40
Ascott-under-Wychwood	d	⌇		⌇	⌇					
Shipton	d	⌇	23p18	⌇	⌇					
Kingham	d	23p18	23p24	23p21	23p21		07 22	08 30	09 23	09 49
Moreton-in-Marsh	a	23p26	23p31	23p29	23p29		07 30	08 38	09 35	09 57
	d	23p27	23p32	23p30	23p32	05 46	07 30	08 38		09 58
Honeybourne	d	23p39	23p44	23p42	23p43		07 41	08 49		10 09
Evesham	a	23p45	23p50	23p48	23p50	06 00	07 48	08 56		10 17
	d	23p46	23p52	23p49	23p52	06 00	07 51	08 56		10 24
Pershore	d	23p54	23p59	23p57	00⌇01	06 08	07 58	09 03		10 32
Worcester Shrub Hill 7	a	00⌇06	00 14	00⌇09	00⌇12	06 19	08 10	09 15		10 44
Worcester Foregate Street 7	a					06 39	08 20	09 18		10 48
Malvern Link	a							09 27		11 02
Great Malvern	a							09 32		11 06
Colwall	a									11 14
Ledbury	a									11 22
Hereford 7	a									11 42

		GW	GW	GW	GW	GW	GW	GW	GW	GW	GW	GW	GW	GW
														FX
		◇**1**	◇**1**	◇**1**	◇**1**	◇**1**	◇**1**	◇**1**	◇**1**	**1**	◇**1**	◇**1**	◇**1**	◇**1**
								E					F	
		🛒		☕	🛒	🛒	🛒	🛒	☕		☕	☕	☕	☕
London Paddington 15 ⊖	d	09 21	09 50	10 22	11 20	12 21	13 21	14 21	15 51		17 22	17 50	18 22	19 22
Slough 3	d	09 36	10 06	10 36	11 36	12 36	13 36	14 36	16 06					19 36
Reading 7	d	09 52	10 22	10 52	11 52	12 52	13 52	14 52	16 22		17 50	18 22	18 50	19 52
Didcot Parkway	d													
Oxford	d	10b25	10 48	11 19	12 19	13 19	14 19	15 19	16 48	17 31	18 17	18 49	19 21	20 19
Hanborough	d	10 35	10 57	11 30	12 29	13 29	14 29	15 29	16 58	17 40	18 27		19 32	20 30
Combe	d									17 43				
Finstock	d									17 48				
Charlbury	d	10 42	11 04	11 38	12 36	13 36	14 36	15 36	17 07	17 52	18 35	19 03	19 40	20 38
Ascott-under-Wychwood	d									17 57				
Shipton	d									18 00		19 11		
Kingham	d	10 51	11 13	11 47	12 45	13 45	14 45	15 45	17 17	18 05	18 45	19 18	19 50	20 47
Moreton-in-Marsh	a	10 59	11 22	11 55	12 53	13 53	14 54	15 53	17 25	18 13	18 53	19 26	19 58	20 55
	d	10 59		11 56	12 53	13 53		15 53	17 26	18 13	18 54	19 27	19 59	20 56
Honeybourne	d			12 07	13 04	14 04		16 04	17 38	18 24	19 06		20 11	21 07
Evesham	a	11 14		12 15	13 11	14 11		16 11	17 45	18 30	19 13	19 43	20 18	21 15
	d	11 14		12 24	13 11	14 25		16 20	17 47	18 40	19 14	19 44	20 19	21 19
Pershore	d			12 32	13 18	14 33		16 27	17 55	18 47	19 22	19 52	20 27	21 27
Worcester Shrub Hill 7	a	11 31		12 44	13 31	14 47		16 39	18 09	18 59	19 34	20 05	20 41	21 46
Worcester Foregate Street 7	a	11 37		12 48	13 35	14 52		16 43		19 11	19 38		20 45	21 50
Malvern Link	a			12 58	13 50	15 06				19 20	19 48		20 54	22 02
Great Malvern	a			13 02	13 56	15 11				19 24	19 52		20 58	22 06
Colwall	a			13 16							19 58		21 04	22 25
Ledbury	a			13 24							20 06		21 12	22 33
Hereford 7	a			13 50							20 27		21 33	22 54

		GW	GW	GW	GW
		FO		FO	FX
		◇**1**	◇**1**	◇**1**	◇**1**
		☕	☕	🛒	☕
London Paddington 15 ⊖	d	19 22	20 20	21 48	21 48
Slough 3	d	19 36	20 36	22 03	22 03
Reading 7	d	19 52	20 52	22 22	22 22
Didcot Parkway	d				
Oxford	d	20 24	21 18	22 52	22 52
Hanborough	d	20 35	21 28	23 03	23 03
Combe	d				
Finstock	d				
Charlbury	d	20 43	21 36	23 11	23 11
Ascott-under-Wychwood	d				
Shipton	d			23 18	23 18
Kingham	d	20 52	21 45	23 24	23 24
Moreton-in-Marsh	a	21 00	21 53	23 31	23 31
	d	21 01	21 54	23 32	23 32
Honeybourne	d	21 12	22 05	23 44	23 44
Evesham	a	21 19	22 13	23 50	23 50
	d	21 19	22 13	23 52	23 52
Pershore	d	21 27	22 21	23 59	23 59
Worcester Shrub Hill 7	a	21 46	22 34	00 14	00 14
Worcester Foregate Street 7	a	21 50	22 43		
Malvern Link	a	22 02	22 52		
Great Malvern	a	22 06	22 58		
Colwall	a	22 25			
Ledbury	a	22 33			
Hereford 7	a	22 54			

A MO from 31 October
B MO from 19 September until 24 October
C 12 September
D 🛒 from Oxford
E 🛒 to Reading
F The Cathedrals Express
b Arr. 1018

Table 126

Saturdays
until 10 September

London and Oxford - Worcester and Hereford

		GW	GW	GW	GW	GW	GW	GW	GW	GW	GW	GW	GW	GW	GW	GW	GW
		◇1	◇1	◇1	◇1	◇1	◇1	◇1	◇1	◇1	◇1	◇1	◇1	◇1	◇1	◇1	◇1
		A	B		C	C						D				D	
		⊤	⊤		⊤	⊤	🍴	🍴	⊤	⊤	⊤	⊤	🍴	🍴	🍴	⊤	
London Paddington 15 ⊖	d	21p48	21p48	05 21	06 21	07 21	08 21	10 21	11 21	13 21	14 21	15 21	16 21	17 21	18 21	19 50	21 50
Slough 3	d	22p03	22p03	05 38	06 38	07 38	08 39	10 39	11 39	13 39	14 39	15 39	16 39	17 39	18 39	20 06	22 06
Reading 7	d	22p22	22p22	05 54	06 54	07 54	08 54	10 54	11 55	13 55	14 54	15 55	16 54	17 55	18 54	20 22	22 22
Didcot Parkway	d	⟆	⟆	06 08													22 37
Oxford	d	22p52	22p52	06 23	07 21	08 21	09 21	11 21	12 23	14 21	15 21	16 21	17 21	18 21	19 21	20 49	22 50
Hanborough	d	23p03	23p03	06 34	07 31	08 31	09 31	11 31	12 33	14 31	15 31	16 31	17 31	18 31	19 31	20 58	23 00
Combe	d	⟆	⟆														
Finstock	d	⟆	⟆														
Charlbury	d	23p11	23p11	06 42	07 39	08 39	09 39	11 39	12 41	14 39	15 39	16 39	17 39	18 39	19 39	21 06	23 07
Ascott-under-Wychwood	d	⟆	⟆														
Shipton	d	23p18	23p18							14 46			17 46			21 12	23 14
Kingham	d	23p24	23p24	06 52	07 49	08 49	09 49	11 49	12 51	14 49	15 49	16 49	17 50	18 49	19 49	21 17	23 19
Moreton-in-Marsh	a	23p33	23p33	07 00	07 58	08 58	09 59	11 58	13 00	14 59	15 57	16 57	18 00	18 57	19 58	21 25	23 27
	d	23p35	23p35	07 02	08 00	09 00	10 00	12 00	13 02	15 00	16 00	17 00	18 00	19 00	20 00	21 28	23 29
Honeybourne	d	23p46	23p46	07 13	08 11	09 11	10 11	12 11	13 13	15 11	16 11	17 11	18 11	19 11	20 11	21 39	23 40
Evesham	a	23p55	23p55	07 21	08 22	09 22	10 21	12 19	13 21	15 21	16 18	17 22	18 22	19 19	20 19	21 46	23 47
	d	23p56	23p56	07 23	08 24	09 24	10 24	12 24	13 24	15 24	16 24	17 24	18 24	19 22	20 27	21 49	23 49
Pershore	d	00⟆05	00⟆05	07 31	08 32	09 32	10 32	12 32	13 32	15 32	16 32	17 32	18 32	19 30	20 35	21 56	23 57
Worcester Shrub Hill 7	a	00⟆17	00⟆18	07 42	08 43	09 43	10 44	12 43	13 44	15 43	16 44	17 43	18 44	19 41	20 46	22 08	00 11
Worcester Foregate Street 7	a			07 46	08 47	09 46	10 48	12 48	13 47	15 47	16 48	17 47	18 54	19 45	20 50	22 11	
Malvern Link	a			07 56	08 57	09 57	10 57	12 57	13 57	15 57	16 57	17 57	19 03		21 00	22 20	
Great Malvern	a			08 01	09 04	10 04	11 04	13 04	14 04	16 04	17 04	18 04	19 07		21 04	22 27	
Colwall	a						11 13	13 13					19 13		21 10		
Ledbury	a						11 21	13 21					19 21		21 18		
Hereford 7	a						11 41	13 40					19 45		21 36		

Saturdays
from 17 September

		GW	GW	GW	GW	GW	GW	GW	GW	GW	GW	GW	GW	GW	GW	GW
		◇1	◇1	◇1	◇1	◇1	◇1	◇1	◇1	◇1	◇1	◇1	◇1	◇1	◇1	◇1
				C	C						D				D	
		⊤		⊤	⊤	🍴	🍴	⊤	⊤	⊤	⊤	🍴	🍴	🍴	⊤	
London Paddington 15 ⊖	d	21p48	05 21	06 21	07 21	08 21	10 21	11 21	13 21	14 21	15 21	16 21	17 21	18 21	19 50	21 50
Slough 3	d	22p03	05 38	06 38	07 38	08 39	10 39	11 39	13 39	14 39	15 39	16 39	17 39	18 39	20 06	22 06
Reading 7	d	22p22	05 54	06 54	07 53	08 54	10 54	11 55	13 55	14 54	15 55	16 54	17 55	18 54	20 22	22 22
Didcot Parkway	d		06 08													22 37
Oxford	d	22p52	06 23	07 23	08 23	09 23	11 23	12 23	14 23	15 23	16 23	17 23	18 23	19 23	20 49	22 50
Hanborough	d	23p03	06 34	07 32	08 32	09 34	11 33	12 33	14 32	15 32	16 32	17 33	18 33	19 33	20 58	23 00
Combe	d															
Finstock	d															
Charlbury	d	23p11	06 42	07 39	08 39	09 42	11 41	12 40	14 39	15 39	16 39	17 41	18 41	19 41	21 05	23 07
Ascott-under-Wychwood	d															
Shipton	d	23p18							14 46			17 48			21 12	23 14
Kingham	d	23p24	06 51	07 48	08 48	09 51	11 50	12 49	14 51	15 48	16 48	17 54	18 50	19 50	21 17	23 19
Moreton-in-Marsh	a	23p31	07 00	07 56	08 56	10 00	11 59	12 58	14 59	15 57	16 57	18 03	18 59	19 59	21 25	23 27
	d	23p32	07 00	07 56	08 56	10 00	11 59	12 58	14 59	15 57	16 57	18 03	18 59	19 59	21 25	23 27
Honeybourne	d	23p44	07 12	08 07	09 07	10 12	12 11	13 09	15 10	16 08	17 08	18 15	19 11	20 11	21 36	23 38
Evesham	a	23p50	07 20	08 15	09 15	10 20	12 19	13 17	15 18	16 16	17 16	18 23	19 19	20 19	21 43	23 45
	d	23p52	07 25	08 21	09 21	10 25	12 20	13 21	15 21	16 21	17 21	18 24	19 21	20 23	21 43	23 45
Pershore	d	23p59	07 32	08 28	09 28	10 32	12 27	13 28	15 28	16 28	17 28	18 31	19 28	20 30	21 50	23 53
Worcester Shrub Hill 7	a	00 14	07 44	08 40	09 40	10 44	12 39	13 40	15 40	16 40	17 40	18 43	19 40	20 42	22 02	00 07
Worcester Foregate Street 7	a		07 48	08 44	09 44	10 48	12 43	13 44	15 44	16 44	17 44	18 54	19 44	20 48	22 06	
Malvern Link	a		07 58	08 54	09 54	10 58	12 53	13 54	15 54	16 54	17 54	19 04		20 58	22 16	
Great Malvern	a		08 03	09 00	10 00	11 05	12 58	14 00	16 00	17 00	18 00	19 08		21 02	22 22	
Colwall	a					11 12	13 13					19 14		21 08		
Ledbury	a					11 20	13 21					19 22		21 16		
Hereford 7	a					11 41	13 40					19 45		21 34		

A until 2 July, 10 September
B from 9 July until 3 September
C ⊤ from Oxford
D ⊤ to Reading

Table 126

London and Oxford - Worcester and Hereford

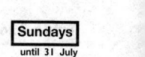

Sundays
until 31 July

		GW	GW	GW	GW	GW	GW	GW	GW	GW	GW	GW	GW	GW
		◇1	◇1	◇1	◇1	◇1	◇1	◇1	◇1	◇1	◇1	◇1	◇1	◇1
		A												
			🛒	☕	☕	☕	☕	🛒	☕	🛒	🛒	☕	☕	
London Paddington 15 ⊖	d	21p50	08 03	09 35	10 42	12 42	13 42	14 42	15 42	16 42	17 42	18 42	19 42	21 42
Slough 3	d	22p06	08 25	09 55	10 59	12 59	14 01	15 02	16 01	17 01	18 01	19 01	19 59	22 00
Reading 7	d	22p22	08 47	10 15	11 22	13 22	14 23	15 22	16 21	17 22	18 21	19 24	20 22	22 24
Didcot Parkway	d	22p37	09 04	10 29	11 37	13 37	14 39	15 37	16 37	17 37	18 36	19 38	20 37	22 40
Oxford	d	22p50	09 16	10 44	11 52	13 52	14 53	15 52	16 51	17 52	18 51	19 53	20 52	22 54
Hanborough	d	23p00	09 26	10 55	12 02	14 02		16 01		18 02	19 02	20 04	21 02	23 05
Combe	d													
Finstock	d													
Charlbury	d	23p07	09 33	11 03	12 10	14 10	15 07	16 10	17 05	18 10	19 09	20 12	21 10	23 13
Ascott-under-Wychwood	d													
Shipton	d	23p14												
Kingham	d	23p19	09 42	11 13	12 20	14 20	15 15	16 19	17 14	18 19	19 18	20 21	21 19	23 22
Moreton-in-Marsh	a	23p27	09 50	11 21	12 27	14 27	15 24	16 26	17 23	18 27	19 26	20 28	21 27	23 30
	d	23p29	09 59	11 22	12 29	14 29	15 25	16 28	17 24	18 29	19 27	20 29	21 29	23 33
Honeybourne	d	23p40	10 10	11 34	12 40		15 38	16 40		18 40	19 38	20 40	21 40	23 44
Evesham	a	23p47	10 16	11 41	12 48	14 48	15 47	16 48	17 40	18 47	19 46	20 48	21 48	23 51
	d	23p49	10 19	11 44	12 48	14 48	15 47	16 48	17 48	18 48	19 46	20 55	21 48	23 53
Pershore	d	23p57	10 26	11 52	12 57	14 58	15 56	16 57	17 56	18 57	19 56	21 03	21 57	00 03
Worcester Shrub Hill 7	a	00 11	10 38	12 03	13 11	15 08	16 08	17 08	18 08	19 11	20 07	21 15	22 11	00 14
Worcester Foregate Street 7	a		10 41	12 07	13 15	15 13		17 13	18 11	19 15	20 13	21 19	22 14	
Malvern Link	a		10 50	12 17	13 24	15 23		17 22		19 25	20 22	21 28	22 24	
Great Malvern	a		10 55	12 20	13 28	15 27		17 26		19 30	20 26	21 33	22 28	
Colwall	a			12 27	13 35	15 33		17 33				21 38		
Ledbury	a			12 35	13 43	15 41		17 41				21 46		
Hereford 7	a			12 54	14 06	16 07		18 01				22 06		

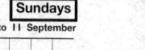

Sundays
7 August to 11 September

		GW	GW	GW	GW	GW	GW	GW	GW	GW	GW	GW	GW	GW
		◇1	◇1	◇1	◇1	◇1	◇1	◇1	◇1	◇1	◇1	◇1	◇1	◇1
			🛒	☕	☕	☕	☕	🛒	☕	🛒	🛒	☕	☕	
London Paddington 15 ⊖	d	21p50	08 03	09 35	10 42	12 42	13 42	14 42	15 42	16 42	17 42	18 42	19 42	21 42
Slough 3	d	22p06	08 22	09 53	10 58	12 58	14 00	15 02	16 01	17 01	18 01	18 59	19 59	21 59
Reading 7	d	22p22	08 44	10 17	11 21	13 22	14 23	15 22	16 21	17 22	18 25	19 24	20 21	22 22
Didcot Parkway	d	22p37	09 02	10 31	11 37	13 37	14 39	15 37	16 37	17 37	18 40	19 40	20 37	22 38
Oxford	d	22p50	09 16	10 47	11 51	13 52	14 53	15 52	16 51	17 52	18 55	19 54	20 51	22 53
Hanborough	d	23p00	09 26	10 58	12 02	14 02		16 01		18 02	19 06	20 06	21 02	23 04
Combe	d													
Finstock	d													
Charlbury	d	23p07	09 33	11 06	12 10	14 10	15 07	16 10	17 05	18 10	19 13	20 14	21 10	23 12
Ascott-under-Wychwood	d													
Shipton	d	23p14												
Kingham	d	23p19	09 42	11 16	12 19	14 20	15 17	16 19	17 14	18 19	19 22	20 22	21 18	23 21
Moreton-in-Marsh	a	23p27	09 50	11 24	12 26	14 27	15 26	16 27	17 23	18 28	19 30	20 29	21 26	23 29
	d	23p29	09 59	11 25	12 29	14 29	15 28	16 29	17 24	18 30	19 31	20 31	21 29	23 32
Honeybourne	d	23p40	10 10	11 37	12 40		15 39	16 41		18 41	19 42	20 43	21 40	23 43
Evesham	a	23p47	10 16	11 44	12 48	14 48	15 48	16 49	17 40	18 49	19 48	20 50	21 50	23 50
	d	23p49	10 19	11 47	12 48	14 48	15 48	16 49	17 48	18 53	19 48	20 55	21 52	23 52
Pershore	d	23p57	10 26	11 55	12 57	14 58	15 57	16 58	17 56	18 57	19 57	21 03	22 00	00 01
Worcester Shrub Hill 7	a	00 11	10 38	12 06	13 11	15 08	16 08	17 09	18 08	19 11	20 08	21 15	22 11	00 12
Worcester Foregate Street 7	a		10 41	12 10	13 15	15 13		17 14	18 11	19 15	20 15	21 19	22 14	
Malvern Link	a		10 51	12 20	13 24	15 23		17 23		19 25	20 24	21 28	22 24	
Great Malvern	a		10 56	12 23	13 28	15 27		17 27		19 30	20 27	21 33	22 28	
Colwall	a			12 29	13 35	15 33		17 34				21 38		
Ledbury	a			12 37	13 43	15 41		17 42				21 46		
Hereford 7	a			12 56	14 06	16 07		18 02				22 06		

A not 22 May

Table 126

Sundays

18 September to 23 October

London and Oxford - Worcester and Hereford

		GW	GW	GW	GW	GW	GW	GW	GW	GW	GW	GW	GW	GW
		◇1	◇1	◇1	◇1	◇1	◇1	◇1	◇1	◇1	◇1	◇1	◇1	◇1
			[trolley]	[buffet]	[buffet]	[buffet]	[buffet]	[trolley]	[buffet]	[trolley]	[trolley]	[buffet]	[buffet]	
London Paddington 15 ⊖	d	21p50	08 03	09 35	10 42	12 42	13 42	14 42	15 42	16 42	17 42	18 42	19 42	21 39
Slough 3	d	22p06	08 22	09 53	10 58	12 58	13 59	15 02	16 01	17 01	18 01	18 59	19 59	21 59
Reading 7	d	22p22	08 44	10 17	11 21	13 22	14 23	15 22	16 21	17 22	18 25	19 24	20 21	22 22
Didcot Parkway	d	22p37	09 02	10 31	11 37	13 37	14 39	15 37	16 37	17 37	18 40	19 40	20 37	22 38
Oxford	d	22p50	09b20	10 47	11 51	13 52	14 53	15 52	16 51	17 52	18 55	19 54	20 51	22 53
Hanborough	d	23p00	09 30	10 58	12 02	14 02		16 01		18 02	19 05	20 06	21 02	23 04
Combe	d													
Finstock	d													
Charlbury	d	23p07	09 37	11 06	12 10	14 10	15 07	16 10	17 05	18 10	19 13	20 14	21 10	23 12
Ascott-under-Wychwood	d													
Shipton	d	23p14												
Kingham	d	23p19	09 46	11 16	12 19	14 20	15 17	16 19	17 14	18 19	19 22	20 22	21 18	23 21
Moreton-in-Marsh	a	23p27	09 54	11 24	12 26	14 27	15 26	16 27	17 23	18 28	19 30	20 29	21 26	23 29
	d	23p27	09 55	11 25	12 29	14 29	15 28	16 29	17 24	18 30	19 30	20 31	21 27	23 30
Honeybourne	d	23p38	10 06	11 37	12 40		15 39	16 41		18 41	19 41	20 43	21 39	23 42
Evesham	a	23p45	10 12	11 44	12 48	14 48	15 48	16 49	17 40	18 48	19 49	20 50	21 48	23 48
	d	23p45	10 13	11 47	12 48	14 48	15 48	16 49	17 48	18 53	19 49	20 55	21 49	23 49
Pershore	d	23p53	10 20	11 55	12 57	14 58	15 57	16 58	17 56	18 57	19 57	21 03	21 57	23 57
Worcester Shrub Hill 7	a	00 07	10 32	12 06	13 11	15 08	16 08	17 09	18 08	19 11	20 08	21 15	22 08	00 09
Worcester Foregate Street 7	a		10 36	12 10	13 15	15 13		17 14	18 11	19 15	20 15	21 19	22 12	
Malvern Link	a		10 46	12 20	13 24	15 23		17 23		19 25	20 24	21 28	22 22	
Great Malvern	a		10 51	12 23	13 28	15 27		17 27		19 30	20 27	21 33	22 26	
Colwall	a			12 29	13 35	15 33		17 34				21 38		
Ledbury	a			12 37	13 43	15 41		17 42				21 46		
Hereford 7	a			12 56	14 06	16 07		18 02				22 06		

Sundays

from 30 October

		GW	GW	GW	GW	GW	GW	GW	GW	GW	GW	GW	GW	GW
		◇1	◇1	◇1	◇1	◇1	◇1	◇1	◇1	◇1	◇1	◇1	◇1	◇1
			[trolley]	[buffet]	[buffet]	[buffet]	[buffet]	[trolley]	[buffet]	[trolley]	[trolley]	[buffet]	[buffet]	
London Paddington 15 ⊖	d	21p50	08 06	09 35	10 42	12 42	13 42	14 42	15 42	16 42	17 42	18 42	19 42	21 42
Slough 3	d	22p06	08 28	09 59	11 06	13 06	14 06	15 03	16 02	17 02	18 02	19 05	20 05	22 03
Reading 7	d	22p22	08 49	10 12	11 21	13 21	14 21	15 18	16 17	17 18	18 18	19 21	20 21	22 19
Didcot Parkway	d	22p37	09 07	10 28	11 37	13 37	14 37	15 33	16 33	17 33	18 33	19 37	20 37	22 35
Oxford	d	22p50	09 20	10c49	11 51	13 51	14 51	15 48	16 47	17 47	18 48	19 51	20 51	22 50
Hanborough	d	23p00	09 30	11 00	12 02	14 02		15 57		17 57	18 58	20 03	21 02	23 01
Combe	d													
Finstock	d													
Charlbury	d	23p07	09 37	11 08	12 10	14 10	15 05	16 06	17 01	18 05	19 06	20 11	21 10	23 09
Ascott-under-Wychwood	d													
Shipton	d	23p14												
Kingham	d	23p19	09 46	11 18	12 19	14 19	15 14	16 15	17 10	18 14	19 15	20 19	21 18	23 18
Moreton-in-Marsh	a	23p27	09 54	11 26	12 26	14 26	15 22	16 23	17 19	18 23	19 23	20 26	21 26	23 26
	d	23p27	09 55	11 27	12 26	14 29	15 23	16 25	17 21	18 25	19 25	20 29	21 27	23 27
Honeybourne	d	23p38	10 06	11 38	12 38		15 35	16 37		18 36	19 37	20 40	21 39	23 39
Evesham	a	23p45	10 12	11 46	12 45	14 48	15 44	16 45	17 36	18 43	19 44	20 48	21 48	23 45
	d	23p45	10 13	11 47	12 46	14 48	15 44	16 47	17 45	18 44	19 47	20 53	21 52	23 46
Pershore	d	23p53	10 20	11 55	12 53	14 58	15 51	16 56	17 52	18 53	19 56	21 01	22 00	23 54
Worcester Shrub Hill 7	a	00 07	10 32	12 06	13 07	15 08	16 03	17 07	18 05	19 07	20 07	21 13	22 11	00 06
Worcester Foregate Street 7	a		10 36	12 10	13 11	15 13		17 12	18 08	19 11	20 14	21 16	22 15	
Malvern Link	a		10 46	12 20	13 20	15 23		17 21		19 21	20 23	21 25	22 24	
Great Malvern	a		10 51	12 23	13 24	15 27		17 25		19 26	20 26	21 30	22 28	
Colwall	a			12 29	13 31	15 33		17 32				21 35		
Ledbury	a			12 37	13 39	15 41		17 40				21 43		
Hereford 7	a			12 56	14 08	16 07		18 00				22 02		

b Arr. 0913

c Arr. 1042

Table 126

Mondays to Fridays

until 9 September

Hereford and Worcester - Oxford and London

Miles			GW	GW	GW	GW	GW	GW	GW	GW	GW	GW	GW	GW	GW	GW	GW	GW	GW	GW	GW	GW	GW
																							FO
			◇1	◇1	◇1	◇1	◇1	◇1	◇1	1	◇1	1	◇1	◇1	◇1	◇1	◇1	1	◇1	◇1	◇1	1	◇1
			A	B	C	D			E		E												
							☕	☕	☕Ø		☕Ø		🛒	🛒	🛒	☕	🛒		☕	🛒	☕		
0	**Hereford** 7	d				21p51			05 34		06 43					13 14			15 14				
13¾	Ledbury	d				22p09			05 50		07 00					13 31			15 30				
18	Colwall	d				22p16			05 58		07 09					13 38			15 38				
20¾	Great Malvern	d	20p55	20p55	20p55	22p22		05 17	06 03		07 14		08 58	09 54		13 47	14 35		15 43	17 00			
21¾	Malvern Link	d	20p59	20p59	20p59	⌇		05 20	06 07		07 18		09 00	09 56		13 51	14 37		15 47	17 02			
28½	**Worcester Foregate Street** 7	d	21p10	21p10	21p10	22p34		05 31	06 18	06 51	07 30		09 09	10 05	12 06	14 02	14 52		16 02	17 20	18 49	19 27	20 59
29¼	**Worcester Shrub Hill** 7	d	21b18	21b18	21b18	22p40	05 02	05 35	06 26	06 53	07 35		09 12	10 08	12 08	14 06	14 56		16 06	17 24	18 53	19 29	21 04
37	Pershore	d	21p28	21p28	21p28	22p49		05 44	06 35	07 02	07 44		09 21	10 17	12 17	14 15	15 05		16 16	17 34	19 08	19 45	21 13
43	Evesham	a	21p36	21p36	21p36	22p58	05 16	05 53	06 44	07 11	07 53		09 29	10 26	12 26	14 24	15 14		16 25	17 42	19 17	19 54	21 22
—		d	21p51	21p51	21p51	23p00	05 18	05 55	06 45	07 11	07 54		09 30	10 27	12 27	14 26	15 22		16 30	17 51	19 19	20 22	21 27
48	Honeybourne	d	21p59	21p59	21p59	23p07		06 02	06 52		08 01		09 37	10 34	12 34	14 33	15 28		16 37	17 57		20 29	21 34
58	Moreton-in-Marsh	a	22p12	22p12	22p12	23p19	05 34	06 14	07 05	07 27	08 14		09 49	10 47	12 47	14 45	15 41		16 49	18 09	19 35	20 42	21 46
—		d	22p12	22p12	22p12	23p21	05 48	06 16	07 06	07 28	08 15	09 29	09 50	10 47	12 47	14 47	15 43	16 14	16 51	18 12	19 36	20 43	21 48
65	Kingham	d	22p20	22p20	22p20	23p29	05 56	06 24	07 15	07 37	08 24	09 37	09 58	10 56	12 56	14 55	15 51	16 21	16 59	18 20	19 45	20 52	21 56
68	Shipton	d	⌇	⌇	⌇	⌇				07 40									17 05				
69¼	Ascott-under-Wychwood	d	⌇	⌇	⌇	⌇				07 44													
73	Charlbury	d	22p30	22p30	22p30	23p39	06 06	06 34	07 26	07 49	08 35	09 52	10 08	11 05	13 05	15 05	16 00	16 31	17 18	18 47	19 55	21 01	22 06
74¾	Finstock	d	⌇	⌇	⌇	⌇				07 53													
78¼	Combe	d	⌇	⌇	⌇	⌇				07 58													
79¼	Hanborough	d	22p38	22p38	22p38	⌇	06 14	06 42	07 34	08 01			10 15	11 13	13 13	15 13	16 08		17 26		20 03	21 09	22 14
86¼	**Oxford**	a	22p47	22p47	22p47	23p56	06 25	06 54	07 47	08 12	08 49	10 06	10 26	11 28	13 25	15 25	16 27	16 46	17 36	19 04	20 19	21 20	22 27
96½	Didcot Parkway	a	22p59	22p59	22p59	00⌇20	06 39	07 07				10 24						17 04					
113¾	Reading 7	a	23p16	23p20	23p16	00⌇38	06 54	07 25	08 21		09 14	10 58	10 54	11 54	13 54	15 54	16 54		18 01	19 32	20 54		22 58
131¼	Slough 3	a	23p43	23p45	23p45	00⌇56						11 24	11 09	12 09	14 09	16 09	17 09			19 47	21 09		23 12
149¾	**London Paddington** 15 ⊖	a	00⌇10	00⌇04	00⌇11	01⌇17	07 29	07 59	08 51		09 47	12 04	11 29	12 29	14 29	16 27	17 34		18 30	20 06	21 29		23 30

		GW	GW	GW
		FX	FO	
		◇1	◇1	◇1
				F
Hereford 7	d		21 51	21⌇51
Ledbury	d		22 09	22⌇09
Colwall	d		22 16	22⌇16
Great Malvern	d		22 22	22⌇22
Malvern Link	d			⌇
Worcester Foregate Street 7	d	20 59	22 34	22⌇34
Worcester Shrub Hill 7	d	21 04	22 40	22⌇40
Pershore	d	21 13	22 49	22⌇49
Evesham	a	21 22	22 58	22⌇58
	d	21 27	23 00	23⌇00
Honeybourne	d	21 34	23 07	23⌇07
Moreton-in-Marsh	a	21 46	23 19	23⌇19
	d	21 48	23 21	23⌇21
Kingham	d	21 56	23 29	23⌇29
Shipton	d			⌇
Ascott-under-Wychwood	d			⌇
Charlbury	d	22 06	23 39	23⌇39
Finstock	d			⌇
Combe	d			⌇
Hanborough	d	22 14		⌇
Oxford	a	22 27	23 56	23⌇56
Didcot Parkway	a		00 20	00⌇20
Reading 7	a	22 58	00 38	00⌇38
Slough 3	a	23 18	00 53	00⌇56
London Paddington 15 ⊖	a	23 37	01 11	01⌇17

A MO from 27 June until 1 August
B MO from 8 August until 5 September
C MO until 20 June
D MX from 25 May until 9 September
E ☕ from Reading Ø to Oxford
F FX from 24 May until 8 September
b Previous night, arr. 2112

Table 126

Mondays to Fridays

from 12 September

Hereford and Worcester - Oxford and London

		GW	GW	GW MX	GW	GW	GW	GW	GW	GW	GW	GW	GW	GW	GW	GW	GW	GW	GW	GW	GW	GW FO
		◇1	◇1	◇1	◇1	◇1	◇1	1	◇1	◇1	◇1	◇1	◇1	◇1	◇1	1	◇1	1	◇1	◇1	◇1	◇1
		A	B				C		C		D											
					[restaurant]	[restaurant]	[restaurant]⌀		[restaurant]⌀	[trolley]	[trolley]	[trolley]	[trolley]	[trolley]	[restaurant]	[trolley]			[restaurant]	[trolley]	[restaurant]	
Hereford 7	d			21p51			05 35		06 43						13 14				15 14			
Ledbury	d			22p09			05 52		07 02						13 31				15 31			
Colwall	d			22p17			05 59		07 09						13 39				15 38			
Great Malvern	d	21p15	20p55	22p22		05 18	06c10		07 15			09 54			13 44	14 26		15 22	15 44			19 44	
Malvern Link	d	21p18	20p59			05 21	06 14		07 19			09 56			13 48	14 28			15 48			19 46	
Worcester Foregate Street 7	d	21p31	21p10	22p34		05 32	06 25	06 53	07 30	08 26		10 05		12 06	13 59	14 38		15 34	15 59	17 28	18 49	19 54	20 59
Worcester Shrub Hill 7	d	21p34	21b18	22p43	05 11	05 38	06 31	06 56	07 34	08e39		10 08		12 08	14f09	14 41		15 42	16 03	17 31	18 55	20i03	21 03
Pershore	d	21p44	21p28	22p52		05 47	06 40	07 05	07 43	08 48		10 17		12 17	14 18	14 50		15 51	16 13	17 40	19 04	20 12	21 12
Evesham	a	21p51	21p36	23p00	05 24	05 55	06 48	07 13	07 51	08 56		10 25		12 25	14 26	14 58		15 59	16 21	17 48	19 12	20 20	21 20
	d	21p51	21p51	23p01	05 31	05 57	06 51	07 13	07 52	09 04		10 31		12 31	14 30	15 06		15 59	16 21	17 48	19 12	20 20	21 21
Honeybourne	d	21p58	21p59	23p08		06 04	06 58		07 59	09 11		10 37		12 38	14 37	15 12			16 28	17 54	19 20	20 27	21 28
Moreton-in-Marsh	a	22p11	22p12	23p19	05 46	06 16	07 09	07 28	08 11	09 23		10 49		12 50	14 48	15 24		16 14	16 40	18 06	19 31	20 39	21 39
	d	22p11	22p12	23p27	05 46	06 16	07 10	07 28	08 12	09 23	09 51	10 49	11 51	12 50	14 49	15 24	15 53	16 14	16 40	18 06	19 48	20 48	21 40
Kingham	d	22p19	22p20	23p36	05 55	06 25	07 19	07 36	08 21	09 31	09 58	10 57	11 58	12 58	14 57	15 32	16 00	16 22	16 49	18 14	19 56	20 56	21 48
Shipton	d	⌇	⌇					07 41											16 55				
Ascott-under-Wychwood	d	⌇	⌇					07 44															
Charlbury	d	22p29	22p30	23p45	06 04	06 34	07 30	07 49	08 31	09 40	10 07	11 06	12 07	13 06	15 07	15 41	16 09	16 31	17g06	18h37	20 06	21 05	22j07
Finstock	d	⌇	⌇					07 53															
Combe	d	⌇	⌇					07 58															
Hanborough	d	22p37	22p38		06 12	06 42	07 39	08 01	08 39	09 47	10 15	11 14	12 15	13 14	15 15	15 49	16 17		17 14	18 44	20 14	21 12	22 15
Oxford	a	22p46	22p47	23p58	06 23	06 54	07 49	08 12	08 49	09 58	10 25	11 28	12 29	13 25	15 25	15 59	16 27	16 46	17 24	19 04	20 24	21 22	22 27
Didcot Parkway	a	22p59	22p59	00 20	06 39	07 07												17 04					
Reading 7	a	23p20	23p20	00 38	06 54	07 25	08 21		09 14	10 25	10 54	11 54	12 54	13 54	15 54	16 24	16 54		17 54	19 32	20 54	22 06	22 58
Slough 3	a	23p45	23p45	00 56						10 39	11 09	12 09	13 09	14 09	16 09	16 40	17 09		18 09	19 47	21 09	22 22	23 12
London Paddington 15 ⊖	a	00⌇04	00⌇04	01 17	07 29	07 59	08 51		09 47	11 00	11 29	12 29	13 29	14 29	16 27	17 00	17 34		18 27	20 06	21 29	22 43	23 30

		GW FX	GW FO	GW FX
		◇1	◇1	◇1
Hereford 7	d		21 51	21 51
Ledbury	d		22 09	22 09
Colwall	d		22 17	22 17
Great Malvern	d		22 22	22 22
Malvern Link	d			
Worcester Foregate Street 7	d	20 59	22 34	22 34
Worcester Shrub Hill 7	d	21 03	22 43	22 43
Pershore	d	21 12	22 52	22 52
Evesham	a	21 20	23 00	23 00
	d	21 21	23 01	23 01
Honeybourne	d	21 28	23 08	23 08
Moreton-in-Marsh	a	21 39	23 19	23 19
	d	21 40	23 27	23 27
Kingham	d	21 48	23 36	23 36
Shipton	d			
Ascott-under-Wychwood	d			
Charlbury	d	22j07	23 45	23 45
Finstock	d			
Combe	d			
Hanborough	d	22 15		
Oxford	a	22 27	23 58	23 58
Didcot Parkway	a		00 20	00 20
Reading 7	a	22 58	00 38	00 38
Slough 3	a	23 18	00 53	00 56
London Paddington 15 ⊖	a	23 37	01 11	01 17

A MO from 19 September
B 12 September
C [restaurant] from Reading ⌀ to Oxford
D [trolley] from Oxford

b Previous night, arr. 2112
c Arr. 0604
e Arr. 0828
f Arr. 1403

g Arr. 1701
h Arr. 1823
i Arr. 1957
j Arr. 2157

Table 126

Saturdays
until 10 September

Hereford and Worcester - Oxford and London

		GW	GW	GW	GW	GW	GW	GW	GW	GW	GW	GW	GW	GW	GW	GW
		◇1	◇1	◇1	◇1	◇1	◇1	◇1	◇1	◇1	◇1	◇1	◇1	◇1	◇1	1
					A											
			⊐P	⊐P	⊐P⊘	⊐P	⊼	⊼	⊐P	⊐P	⊼	⊼				
Hereford 7	d	21p51			07 10				12 13	15 10					20 20	
Ledbury	d	22p09			07 30				12 31	15 29					20 40	
Colwall	d	22p16			07 38				12 39	15 36					20 48	
Great Malvern	d	22p22	05 39	06 35	07 43	08 43	09 43	10 32	12 43	15 42	16 32	17 44	18 29		20 53	22 41
Malvern Link	d		05 42	06 39	07 46	08 46	09 46	10 35	12 46	15 45	16 35	17 47	18 32		20 57	22 44
Worcester Foregate Street 7	d	22p34	05 52	06 50	07 57	08 57	09 57	10 57	12 57	15 57	16 57	17 57	18 46	20 02	21 12	22 53
Worcester Shrub Hill 7	d	22p40	05 56	06 54	08 02	09 02	10 02	11 02	13 02	16 02	17 02	18 03	19b00	20 06	21c25	22 57
Pershore	d	22p49	06 06	07 03	08 11	09 11	10 11	11 11	13 11	16 11	17 11	18 11	19 09	20 15	21 34	23 06
Evesham	a	22p58	06 14	07 11	08 20	09 20	10 19	11 19	13 21	16 20	17 19	18 20	19 17	20 23	21 42	23 15
	d	23p00	06 23	07 25	08 27	09 27	10 27	11 27	13 27	16 26	17 27	18 27	19 27	20 37	21 54	
Honeybourne	d	23p07	06 30	07 32	08 33	09 33	10 34	11 33	13 33	16 32	17 34	18 34	19 33	20 44	22 01	
Moreton-in-Marsh	a	23p19	06 42	07 43	08 45	09 46	10 46	11 46	13 45	16 46	17 46	18 46	19 45	20 57	22 13	
	d	23p21	06 45	07 45	08 48	09 48	10 49	11 48	13 48	16 47	17 48	18 48	19 48	20 58	22 15	
Kingham	d	23p29	06 54	07 54	08 56	09 56	10 58	11 56	13 56	16 56	17 57	18 57	19 57	21 07	22 24	
Shipton	d			08 00	09 02					17 01					22 30	
Ascott-under-Wychwood	d															
Charlbury	d	23p39	07 04	08 08	09 08	10 08	11 08	12 08	14 08	17 08	18 08	19 08	20 08	21 18	22 38	
Finstock	d															
Combe	d															
Hanborough	d		07 12	08 16	09 16	10 16	11 16	12 16	14 16	17 16	18 16	19 16	20 16	21 26	22 46	
Oxford	a	23p56	07 22	08 26	09 28	10 28	11 28	12 28	14 28	17 28	18 28	19 28	20 26	21 35	22 56	
Didcot Parkway	a	00 20												21 49	23 13	
Reading 7	a	00 38	07 54	08 54	09 54	10 54	11 54	12 53	14 53	17 54	18 54	19 54	20 54	22 04	23 30	
Slough 3	a	00 53	08 09	09 09	10 09	11 09	12 09	13 09	15 10	18 09	19 09	20 09	21 09	22 22	23 48	
London Paddington 15 ⊖	a	01 11	08 29	09 29	10 29	11 29	12 29	13 30	15 29	18 29	19 29	20 29	21 29	22 41	00 13	

Saturdays
from 17 September

		GW	GW	GW	GW	GW	GW	GW	GW	GW	GW	GW	GW	GW	GW	GW
		◇1	◇1	◇1	◇1	◇1	◇1	◇1	◇1	◇1	◇1	◇1	◇1	◇1	◇1	1
					A											
			⊐P	⊐P	⊐P⊘	⊐P	⊼	⊼	⊐P	⊐P	⊼	⊼				
Hereford 7	d	21p51			07 10				12 13	15 13					20 20	
Ledbury	d	22p09			07 30				12 31	15 31					20 40	
Colwall	d	22p17			07 37				12 38	15 38					20 47	
Great Malvern	d	22p22	05 56	06 49	07 43	08 43	09 51	10 58	12 44	15 44	16 34	17 49	18 35		20 53	22 41
Malvern Link	d		05 59	06 53	07 46	08 47	09 54	11 01	12 48	15 48	16 37	17 52	18 38		20 57	22 44
Worcester Foregate Street 7	d	22p34	06 09	07 04	07 59	08 58	10 04	11 11	12 59	15 59	16 54	18 02	18 48	20 02	21 11	22 53
Worcester Shrub Hill 7	d	22p43	06 12	07 08	08 04	09 02	10 08	11 15	13 04	16 04	17e02	18 06	19f02	20 06	21 15	22 57
Pershore	d	22p52	06 21	07 17	08 13	09 11	10 16	11 23	13 13	16 12	17 10	18 15	19 10	20 15	21 24	23 06
Evesham	a	23p00	06 29	07 25	08 21	09 19	10 25	11 32	13 21	16 21	17 19	18 23	19 19	20 23	21 32	23 15
	d	23p01	06 30	07 26	08 26	09 32	10 32	11 32	13 30	16 22	17 26	18 27	19 27	20 24	21 33	
Honeybourne	d	23p08	06 36	07 33	08 33	09 39	10 38	11 38	13 37	16 28	17 32	18 33	19 33	20 31	21 39	
Moreton-in-Marsh	a	23p19	06 48	07 45	08 45	09 51	10 50	11 51	13 49	16 40	17 45	18 46	19 46	20 43	21 51	
	d	23p27	06 48	07 45	08 45	09 51	10 50	11 51	13 49	16 41	17 45	18 46	19 46	20 43	21 51	
Kingham	d	23p36	06 56	07 54	08 54	10 00	10 58	11 59	13 58	16 49	17 53	18 54	19 54	20 52	22 00	
Shipton	d			07 59	08 59					16 55					22 05	
Ascott-under-Wychwood	d															
Charlbury	d	23p45	07 06	08 07	09 07	10 10	11 08	12 08	14 08	17 02	18 02	19 03	20 03	21 06	22 12	
Finstock	d															
Combe	d															
Hanborough	d		07 13	08 15	09 15	10 18	11 15	12 16	14 16	17 10	18 10	19 11	20 11	21 14	22 20	
Oxford	a	23p58	07 24	08 26	09 25	10 28	11 26	12 28	14 26	17 21	18 21	19 21	20 21	21 25	22 34	
Didcot Parkway	a	00 20												21 43	22 47	
Reading 7	a	00 38	07 54	08 54	09 54	10 54	11 54	12 53	14 53	17 55	18 55	19 55	20 54	21 59	23 04	
Slough 3	a	00 53	08 09	09 09	10 09	11 09	12 09	13 09	15 10	18 10	19 10	20 10	21 09	22 14	23 23	
London Paddington 15 ⊖	a	01 11	08 29	09 29	10 29	11 29	12 29	13 30	15 29	18 29	19 29	20 29	21 29	22 32	23 43	

A ⊐P from Reading ⊘ to Oxford
b Arr. 1845
c Arr. 2118
e Arr. 1656
f Arr. 1850

Table 126

Sundays
until 31 July

Hereford and Worcester - Oxford and London

		GW	GW	GW	GW	GW	GW	GW	GW	GW	GW	GW	GW	GW
		◇1	◇1	◇1	◇1	◇1	◇1	◇1	◇1	◇1	◇1	◇1	◇1	◇1
		A											B	C
			🛒	🛒		☕	☕	☕	☕	☕	🛒			
Hereford [7]	d	20p20				13 28	14 30		16 33		18 30			
Ledbury	d	20p40				13 46	14c55		16 50		18 48			
Colwall	d	20p48				13 53	15 02		16 58		18 55			
Great Malvern	d	20p53	09 00	11 07	13 10	13 59	15 08		17 03		19e11	20 10	20 55	20 55
Malvern Link	d	20p57	09 03	11 10	13 13	14 03	15 12		17 07		19 14	20 11	20 59	20 59
Worcester Foregate Street [7]	d	21p12	09 12	11 19	13 23	14 14	15 23		17 22	18 25	19 25	20 24	21 10	21 10
Worcester Shrub Hill [7]	d	21b25	09 17	11 22	13 27	14 19	15 27	16 27	17 27	18 27	19 27	20 27	21f18	21f18
Pershore	d	21p34	09 26	11 31	13 36	14 28	15 36	16 36	17 36	18 36	19 36	20 36	21 28	21 28
Evesham	a	21p42	09 34	11 40	13 44	14 36	15 45	16 45	17 45	18 45	19 45	20 46	21 36	21 36
	d	21p54	09 36	11 46	13 47	14 50	15 50	16 50	17 48	18 50	19 50	20 50	21 51	21 51
Honeybourne	d	22p01	09 42	11 52	13 52		15 57	16 57	17 55	18 57	19 57	20 57	21 59	21 59
Moreton-in-Marsh	a	22p13	09 55	12 03	14 04	15 05	16 11	17 11	18 10	19 11	20 11	21 11	22 12	22 12
	d	22p15	09 56	12 05	14 04	15 07	16 12	17 12	18 10	19 12	20 12	21 11	22 12	22 12
Kingham	d	22p24	10 04	12 13	14 12	15 15	16 20	17 20	18 16	19 20	20 20	21 20	22 20	22 20
Shipton	d	22p30												
Ascott-under-Wychwood	d													
Charlbury	d	22p38	10 15	12 22	14 22	15 25	16 29	17 29	18 25	19 29	20 29	21 29	22 30	22 30
Finstock	d													
Combe	d													
Hanborough	d	22p46	10 22	12 30	14 29	15 33	16 38	17 38		19 38	20 38	21 38	22 38	22 38
Oxford	a	22p56	10 34	12 45	14 41	15 49	16 49	17 49	18 44	19 49	20 49	21 49	22 47	22 47
Didcot Parkway	a	23p13	10 50	12 56	14 53	16 01	17 02	18 02	18 57	20 02	21 02	22 02	22 59	22 59
Reading [7]	a	23p30	11 08	13 13	15 10	16 20	17 20	18 19	19 13	20 20	21 23	22 20	23 16	23 16
Slough [3]	a	23p48	11 31	13 35	15 31	16 49	17 44	18 50	19 32	20 51	21 51	22 47	23 43	23 45
London Paddington [15] ⊖	a	00 13	11 52	13 54	15 52	17 07	18 07	19 09	19 51	21 12	22 12	23 05	00 10	00 11

Sundays
7 August to 11 September

		GW	GW	GW	GW	GW	GW	GW	GW	GW	GW	GW	GW
		◇1	◇1	◇1	◇1	◇1	◇1	◇1	◇1	◇1	◇1	◇1	◇1
			🛒	🛒		☕	☕	☕	☕	☕	🛒		
Hereford [7]	d	20p20				13 28	14 30		16 33		18 30		
Ledbury	d	20p40				13 46	14c55		16 50		18 48		
Colwall	d	20p48				13 53	15 02		16 58		18 55		
Great Malvern	d	20p53	09 00	11 07	13 10	13 59	15 08		17 03		19e11	20 10	20 55
Malvern Link	d	20p57	09 03	11 10	13 13	14 03	15 12		17 07		19 14	20 11	20 59
Worcester Foregate Street [7]	d	21p12	09 12	11 19	13 23	14 14	15 23		17 22	18 25	19 25	20 24	21 10
Worcester Shrub Hill [7]	d	21b25	09 17	11 22	13 27	14 19	15 27	16 27	17 27	18 27	19 27	20 27	21f18
Pershore	d	21p34	09 26	11 31	13 36	14 28	15 36	16 36	17 36	18 36	19 36	20 36	21 28
Evesham	a	21p42	09 34	11 40	13 44	14 36	15 45	16 45	17 45	18 45	19 45	20 46	21 36
	d	21p54	09 36	11 46	13 47	14 50	15 50	16 50	17 48	18 50	19 50	20 50	21 51
Honeybourne	d	22p01	09 42	11 52	13 52		15 57	16 57	17 55	18 57	19 57	20 57	21 59
Moreton-in-Marsh	a	22p13	09 55	12 03	14 04	15 05	16 11	17 11	18 10	19 11	20 11	21 11	22 12
	d	22p15	09 56	12 05	14 04	15 07	16 12	17 12	18 10	19 12	20 12	21 11	22 12
Kingham	d	22p24	10 04	12 13	14 12	15 15	16 20	17 20	18 16	19 20	20 20	21 20	22 20
Shipton	d	22p30											
Ascott-under-Wychwood	d												
Charlbury	d	22p38	10 15	12 22	14 21	15 25	16 29	17 29	18 25	19 29	20 29	21 29	22 30
Finstock	d												
Combe	d												
Hanborough	d	22p46	10 22	12 30	14 29	15 33	16 38	17 38		19 38	20 38	21 38	22 38
Oxford	a	22p56	10 34	12 41	14 41	15 49	16 49	17 49	18 44	19 49	20 49	21 49	22 47
Didcot Parkway	a	23p13	10 50	12 53	14 53	16 01	17 02	18 02	18 57	20 02	21 02	22 02	22 59
Reading [7]	a	23p30	11 08	13 11	15 10	16 20	17 20	18 20	19 13	20 20	21 24	22 20	23 20
Slough [3]	a	23p48	11 31	13 37	15 31	16 51	17 44	18 49	19 33	20 50	21 51	22 46	23 45
London Paddington [15] ⊖	a	00 13	11 52	13 57	15 52	17 07	18 05	19 06	19 50	21 08	22 12	23 05	00 04

A not 22 May
B from 26 June until 31 July
C until 19 June

b Previous night, arr. 2118
c Arr. 1447
e Arr. 1900

f Arr. 2112

Table 126

Hereford and Worcester - Oxford and London

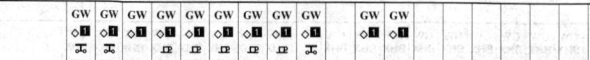

Sundays

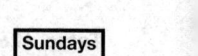

18 September to 23 October

		GW	GW	GW	GW	GW	GW	GW	GW	GW		GW	GW
		◇1	◇1	◇1	◇1	◇1	◇1	◇1	◇1	◇1		◇1	◇1
Hereford 7	d				13 28	14 30		16 33		18 30			
Ledbury	d				13 46	14b55		16 50		18 48			
Colwall	d				13 53	15 02		16 58		18 55			
Great Malvern	d	09 00	11 07	13 10	13 59	15 08		17 03		19c11		20 10	21 15
Malvern Link	d	09 03	11 10	13 13	14 03	15 12		17 07		19 14		20 11	21 18
Worcester Foregate Street 7	d	09 13	11 19	13 23	14 14	15 23		17 22	18 25	19 25		20 24	21 31
Worcester Shrub Hill 7	d	09 17	11 22	13 27	14 19	15 27	16 27	17 27	18 27	19 27		20 27	21 34
Pershore	d	09 26	11 31	13 36	14 28	15 36	16 36	17 36	18 36	19 36		20 36	21 44
Evesham	a	09 34	11 40	13 44	14 36	15 45	16 45	17 45	18 45	19 45		20 46	21 51
	d	09 34	11 46	13 47	14 50	15 50	16 50	17 48	18 50	19 50		20 50	21 51
Honeybourne	d	09 40	11 51	13 51		15 57	16 57	17 55	18 57	19 57		20 57	21 58
Moreton-in-Marsh	a	09 52	12 03	14 04	15 05	16 11	17 11	18 10	19 11	20 11		21 11	22 11
	d	09 52	12 05	14 04	15 07	16 12	17 12	18 10	19 12	20 12		21 11	22 11
Kingham	d	10 00	12 13	14 12	15 15	16 20	17 20	18 16	19 20	20 20		21 20	22 19
Shipton	d												
Ascott-under-Wychwood	d												
Charlbury	d	10 11	12 22	14 21	15 25	16 29	17 29	18 25	19 29	20 29		21 29	22 29
Finstock	d												
Combe	d												
Hanborough	d	10 18	12 30	14 29	15 33	16 38	17 38		19 38	20 38		21 38	22 37
Oxford	a	10 34	12 41	14 46	15 49	16 49	17 49	18 44	19 49	20 49		21 49	22 46
Didcot Parkway	a	10 50	12 53	14 57	16 01	17 02	18 02	18 57	20 02	21 02		22 02	22 59
Reading 7	a	11 08	13 11	15 15	16 19	17 21	18 20	19 13	20 20	21 25		22 20	23 20
Slough 3	a	11 30	13 32	15 34	16 50	17 44	18 50	19 33	20 53	21 51		22 46	23 45
London Paddington 15 ⊖	a	11 52	13 52	15 54	17 07	18 05	19 06	19 50	21 11	22 11		23 05	00 04

Sundays

from 30 October

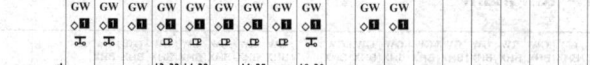

		GW	GW	GW	GW	GW	GW	GW	GW	GW		GW	GW
		◇1	◇1	◇1	◇1	◇1	◇1	◇1	◇1	◇1		◇1	◇1
Hereford 7	d				13 32	14 32		16 35		18 30			
Ledbury	d				13 50	14e55		16 52		18 48			
Colwall	d				13 58	15 02		17 00		18 55			
Great Malvern	d	09 15	11 15	13 15	14 04	15 08		17 05		19c15		20 15	21 15
Malvern Link	d	09 18	11 18	13 18	14 08	15 12		17 09		19 18		20 16	21 18
Worcester Foregate Street 7	d	09 28	11 27	13 26	14 19	15 23		17 22	18 25	19 29		20 29	21 31
Worcester Shrub Hill 7	d	09 32	11 30	13 32	14 23	15 27	16 27	17 27	18 27	19 31		20 32	21 34
Pershore	d	09 41	11 39	13 41	14 32	15 36	16 36	17 36	18 36	19 40		20 41	21 44
Evesham	a	09 49	11 48	13 49	14 39	15 45	16 45	17 45	18 45	19 49		20 51	21 51
	d	09 49	11 52	13 52	14 52	15 50	16 50	17 50	18 50	19 52		20 53	21 51
Honeybourne	d	09 55	11 57	13 57		15 57	16 57	17 57	18 57	19 57		20 57	21 58
Moreton-in-Marsh	a	10 07	12 09	14 10	15 07	16 11	17 11	18 11	19 11	20 11		21 11	22 11
	d	10 07	12 12	14 12	15 09	16 12	17 12	18 12	19 12	20 12		21 11	22 11
Kingham	d	10 15	12 20	14 20	15 17	16 20	17 20	18 20	19 20	20 20		21 20	22 19
Shipton	d												
Ascott-under-Wychwood	d												
Charlbury	d	10 26	12 30	14 30	15 27	16 29	17 29	18 29	19 29	20 29		21 29	22 29
Finstock	d												
Combe	d												
Hanborough	d	10 33	12 38	14 38	15 35	16 38	17 38		19 38	20 38		21 38	22 37
Oxford	a	10 46	12 48	14 49	15 50	16 49	17 49	18 49	19 49	20 49		21 49	22 46
Didcot Parkway	a	11 04	13 02	15 02	16 05	17 02	18 02	19 02	20 02	21 02		22 02	22 59
Reading 7	a	11 22	13 24	15 25	16 25	17 21	18 24	19 25	20 22	21 29		22 25	23 20
Slough 3	a	11 38	13 40	15 40	16 41	17 39	18 40	19 40	20 43	21 48		22 49	23 45
London Paddington 15 ⊖	a	12 01	14 02	16 02	17 06	18 04	19 05	20 06	21 07	22 13		23 13	00 04

b Arr. 1447

c Arr. 1900

e Arr. 1449

Table 126A

Mondays to Fridays

Kingham - Chipping Norton

Bus Service

		GW BHX	GW BHX	GW BHX	GW BHX	GW BHX	GW BHX	GW BHX	GW BHX	GW BHX		GW BHX	GW BHX	GW BHX	GW BHX	GW BHX	GW BHX	GW BHX	GW BHX
Kingham	d	06 30	07 00	07 30	08 30	09 55	10 55	11 55	12 55	13 55		14 55	15 50	16 40	17 20	18 10	18 50	19 25	19 50
Chipping Norton West St	a	06 43	07 13	07 43	08 43	10 08	11 08	12 08	13 08	14 08		15 08	16 03	16 53	17 33	18 23	19 03	19 38	20 03

Saturdays

		GW	GW	GW	GW	GW	GW	GW	GW	GW		GW	GW	GW	GW
Kingham	d	08 15	08 55	09 55	10 55	11 55	12 55	13 55	14 55	15 50		16 50	17 55	18 50	19 50
Chipping Norton West St	a	08 28	09 08	10 08	11 08	12 08	13 08	14 08	15 08	16 03		17 03	18 08	19 03	20 03

Sundays

			GW			GW			GW
Kingham	d		13 17			17 17			18 22
Chipping Norton West St	a		13 29			17 29			18 34

Table 126A

Mondays to Fridays

Chipping Norton - Kingham

Bus Service

		GW BHX	GW BHX	GW BHX	GW BHX	GW BHX	GW BHX	GW BHX	GW BHX	GW BHX		GW BHX	GW BHX	GW BHX	GW BHX	GW BHX	GW BHX	GW BHX
Chipping Norton West St	d	06 07	06 45	07 15	08 00	09 30	10 35	11 35	12 35	13 35		14 35	15 30	16 20	16 55	17 45	18 25	19 10
Kingham	a	06 19	06 58	07 28	08 14	09 44	10 50	11 50	12 50	13 50		14 50	15 45	16 35	17 10	18 00	18 40	19 25

Saturdays

		GW	GW	GW	GW	GW	GW	GW	GW	GW		GW	GW	GW	GW
Chipping Norton West St	d	08 00	08 30	09 30	10 35	11 35	12 35	13 35	14 35	15 30		16 35	17 30	18 25	19 10
Kingham	a	08 14	08 44	09 44	10 50	11 50	12 50	13 50	14 50	15 45		16 50	17 45	18 40	19 25

Sundays

			GW			GW			GW
Chipping Norton West St	d		09 25			13 33			17 59
Kingham	a		09 39			13 47			18 13

Route Diagram for Tables 127, 128

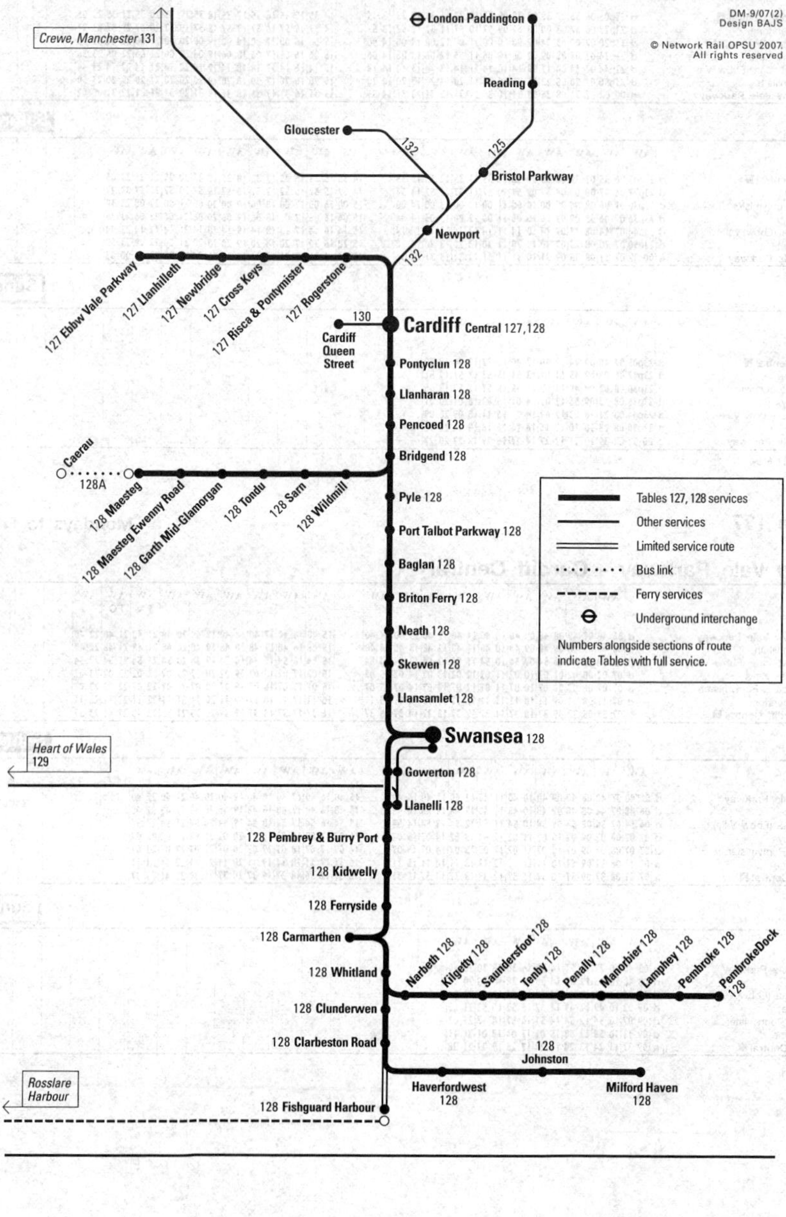

Table 127

Mondays to Fridays

Cardiff Central - Ebbw Vale Parkway

Miles			AW MX	AW	AW	AW	AW	AW	AW	AW	AW	AW	AW	AW	AW	AW	AW	AW	AW	AW
0	**Cardiff Central** 7	d	23p05	06 35	07 39	08 35	09 35	10 35	11 35	12 35	13 35	14 35	15 35	16 35	17 35	18 35	19 35	20 35	21 35	23 05
14	Rogerstone	d	23p27	06 57	08 00	08 57	09 57	10 57	11 57	12 57	13 57	14 57	15 57	16 57	17 57	18 57	19 57	20 57	21 57	23 27
15¼	Risca & Pontymister	d	23p30	07 00	08 04	09 00	10 00	11 00	12 00	13 00	14 00	15 00	16 00	17 00	18 00	19 00	20 00	21 00	22 00	23 30
17¼	Cross Keys	d	23p36	07 06	08 09	09 06	10 06	11 06	12 06	13 06	14 06	15 06	16 06	17 06	18 06	19 06	20 06	21 06	22 06	23 36
20¾	Newbridge (Ebbw Vale)	d	23p44	07 14	08 17	09 14	10 14	11 14	12 14	13 14	14 14	15 14	16 14	17 14	18 14	19 14	20 14	21 14	22 14	23 44
23½	Llanhilleth	d	23p50	07 20	08 23	09 20	10 20	11 20	12 20	13 20	14 20	15 20	16 20	17 20	18 20	19 20	20 20	21 20	22 20	23 50
28¾	**Ebbw Vale Parkway**	a	00 02	07 31	08 35	09 31	10 31	11 31	12 31	13 31	14 31	15 31	16 31	17 31	18 31	19 31	20 34	21 31	22 31	00 02

Saturdays

		AW	AW	AW	AW	AW	AW	AW	AW	AW	AW	AW	AW	AW	AW	AW	AW	AW	AW
Cardiff Central 7	d	23p05	06 35	07 39	08 35	09 35	10 35	11 35	12 35	13 35	14 35	15 35	16 35	17 35	18 35	19 35	20 35	21 35	23 05
Rogerstone	d	23p27	06 57	08 00	08 57	09 57	10 57	11 57	12 57	13 57	14 57	15 57	16 57	17 57	18 57	19 57	20 57	21 57	23 27
Risca & Pontymister	d	23p30	07 00	08 04	09 00	10 00	11 00	12 00	13 00	14 00	15 00	16 00	17 00	18 00	19 00	20 00	21 00	22 00	23 30
Cross Keys	d	23p36	07 06	08 09	09 06	10 06	11 06	12 06	13 06	14 06	15 06	16 06	17 06	18 06	19 06	20 06	21 06	22 06	23 36
Newbridge (Ebbw Vale)	d	23p44	07 14	08 17	09 14	10 14	11 14	12 14	13 14	14 14	15 14	16 14	17 14	18 14	19 14	20 14	21 14	22 14	23 44
Llanhilleth	d	23p50	07 20	08 23	09 20	10 20	11 20	12 20	13 20	14 20	15 20	16 20	17 20	18 20	19 20	20 20	21 20	22 20	23 50
Ebbw Vale Parkway	a	00 02	07 31	08 35	09 31	10 31	11 31	12 31	13 31	14 31	15 31	16 31	17 31	18 31	19 31	20 34	21 31	22 31	00 02

Sundays

		AW A	AW	AW	AW	AW	AW	AW	AW
Cardiff Central 7	d	23p05	07 40	09 24	11 30	13 30	15 32	17 30	19 30
Rogerstone	d	23p27	08 03	09 45	11 51	13 51	15 53	17 51	19 51
Risca & Pontymister	d	23p30	08 07	09 49	11 55	13 55	15 57	17 55	19 55
Cross Keys	d	23p36	08 13	09 55	12 01	14 01	16 03	18 01	20 01
Newbridge (Ebbw Vale)	d	23p44	08 21	10 03	12 09	14 09	16 11	18 09	20 09
Llanhilleth	d	23p50	08 28	10 10	12 16	14 16	16 18	18 16	20 16
Ebbw Vale Parkway	a	00 02	08 39	10 21	12 27	14 27	16 29	18 27	20 27

A not 22 May

Table 127

Mondays to Fridays

Ebbw Vale Parkway - Cardiff Central

Miles			AW	AW	AW	AW	AW	AW	AW	AW	AW	AW	AW	AW	AW	AW	AW	AW FX	AW FO	AW
0	**Ebbw Vale Parkway**	d	06 40	07 40	08 40	09 40	10 40	11 40	12 40	13 40	14 40	15 40	16 40	17 40	18 40	19 40	20 40	21 40	21 40	22 40
5¼	Llanhilleth	d	06 48	07 48	08 48	09 48	10 48	11 48	12 48	13 48	14 48	15 48	16 48	17 48	18 48	19 48	20 48	21 48	21 48	22 48
8	Newbridge (Ebbw Vale)	d	06 54	07 54	08 54	09 54	10 54	11 54	12 54	13 54	14 54	15 54	16 54	17 54	18 54	19 54	20 54	21 54	21 54	22 54
11½	Cross Keys	d	07 02	08 02	09 02	10 02	11 02	12 02	13 02	14 02	15 02	16 02	17 02	18 02	19 02	20 02	21 02	22 02	22 02	23 02
13½	Risca & Pontymister	d	07 07	08 07	09 07	10 07	11 07	12 07	13 07	14 07	15 07	16 07	17 07	18 07	19 07	20 07	21 07	22 07	22 07	23 07
14¾	Rogerstone	d	07 11	08 11	09 11	10 11	11 11	12 11	13 11	14 11	15 11	16 11	17 11	18 11	19 11	20 11	21 11	22 11	22 11	23 11
28¾	**Cardiff Central** 7	a	07 37	08 37	09 37	10 37	11 37	12 37	13 37	14 37	15 37	16 37	17 37	18 37	19 39	20 39	21 38	22 40	22 41	23 37

Saturdays

		AW	AW	AW	AW	AW	AW	AW	AW	AW	AW	AW	AW	AW	AW	AW	AW	AW
Ebbw Vale Parkway	d	06 40	07 40	08 40	09 40	10 40	11 40	12 40	13 40	14 40	15 40	16 40	17 40	18 40	19 40	20 40	21 40	22 40
Llanhilleth	d	06 48	07 48	08 48	09 48	10 48	11 48	12 48	13 48	14 48	15 48	16 48	17 48	18 48	19 48	20 48	21 48	22 48
Newbridge (Ebbw Vale)	d	06 54	07 54	08 54	09 54	10 54	11 54	12 54	13 54	14 54	15 54	16 54	17 54	18 54	19 54	20 54	21 54	22 54
Cross Keys	d	07 02	08 02	09 02	10 02	11 02	12 02	13 02	14 02	15 02	16 02	17 02	18 02	19 02	20 02	21 02	22 02	23 02
Risca & Pontymister	d	07 07	08 07	09 07	10 07	11 07	12 07	13 07	14 07	15 07	16 07	17 07	18 07	19 07	20 07	21 07	22 07	23 07
Rogerstone	d	07 11	08 11	09 11	10 11	11 11	12 11	13 11	14 11	15 11	16 11	17 11	18 11	19 11	20 11	21 11	22 11	23 11
Cardiff Central 7	a	07 37	08 37	09 37	10 37	11 37	12 37	13 37	14 37	15 37	16 37	17 36	18 37	19 37	20 37	21 37	22 41	23 37

Sundays

		AW	AW	AW	AW	AW	AW	AW
Ebbw Vale Parkway	d	08 40	10 27	12 27	14 30	16 30	18 30	20 40
Llanhilleth	d	08 48	10 35	12 35	14 38	16 38	18 38	20 48
Newbridge (Ebbw Vale)	d	08 54	10 41	12 41	14 44	16 44	18 44	20 54
Cross Keys	d	09 02	10 49	12 49	14 52	16 52	18 52	21 02
Risca & Pontymister	d	09 07	10 54	12 54	14 57	16 57	18 57	21 07
Rogerstone	d	09 11	10 58	12 58	15 01	17 01	19 01	21 11
Cardiff Central 7	a	09 37	11 24	13 24	15 23	17 25	19 23	21 38

Cardiff - Maesteg, Swansea and West Wales

Miles	Miles			AW	AW	AW	AW	GW	AW	GW	GW	GW		GW	GW	GW	AW	AW	AW	AW	AW	AW		AW	AW
				MX	MO	MX	MO	MO	MX	MO	MX	MO		MO		MX									
					◇	◇	◇	◇1		◇1	◇1	◇1		◇1	◇1	◇1	B	◇						◇	
								A		B		C		A	B										
								⊡		⊡	⊡	⊡		⊡	⊡	⊡					trolley	trolley		trolley	
—	—	London Paddington 15 ⊖	d					20p37		20p30	21p15	21p37		21p37	21p30	22p45									
—	—	Reading 7	d					21p17		21p05	21p41	22p15		22p14	22p08	23p21									
—	—	Manchester Piccadilly 10	d																						
—	—	Gloucester 7	d																						
—	—	Bristol Parkway 7	d					22p16		22c34	22p45	23p17		23p17	23e37	00 24									
—	—	Newport (South Wales)	d					22p44		23p05	23p19	23p45		23p45	00 02	00 54									
0	—	**Cardiff Central 7**	d	21p04	22p30			23p08	23p15	23p28	23p43	00 08		00 08	00 25	01 15								05 39	05 51
11	—	Pontyclun	d						23p29															05 51	06 03
14	—	Llanharan	d						23p34															05 56	06 08
16¼	—	Pencoed	d						23p39															06 01	06 12
20¼	0	Bridgend	d	21p27	22p51			23p28	23p45	23p49	00 02	00 30		00 30	00 46	01 38								06 07	06 20
—	1	Wildmill	d																						06 22
—	2¼	Sarn	d																						06 25
—	3	Tondu	d																						06 29
—	7	Garth (Mid Glamorgan)	d																						06 38
—	7¾	Maesteg (Ewenny Road)	d																						06 41
—	8¼	Maesteg	a																						06 45
26¼	—	Pyle	d	21p34					23p53															06 15	
32½	—	Port Talbot Parkway	d	21p45	23p05			23p42	00 01	00 03	00 15	00 43		00 43	00 59	01 51								06 23	
34½	—	Baglan	d						00 05															06 27	
36¼	—	Briton Ferry	d						00 09															06 30	
38	—	Neath	d	21p52	23p13			23p50	00 13	00 10	00 22	00 50		00 50	01 07	01 58								06 34	
41¾	—	Skewen	d						00 16															06 38	
43½	—	Llansamlet	d						00 20															06 42	
47½	—	**Swansea**	a	22p04	23p25			00 02	00 28	00 23	00 37	01 03		01 03	01 19	02 13								06 51	
—	—		d	22p27	23p38	23p45			00 45									04 36				05 50		06 53	
53	—	Gowerton	d	22b41	23b49	23b55			00x56													06x00			
58¾	—	Llanelli	a	22p47	23p56	00 03			01s02									04 52				06 07		07 10	
—	—		d	22p49	23p58	00 04																06 09		07 10	
62¾	—	Pembrey & Burry Port	d	22p54	00 04	00 09			01s09													06 15		07 16	
68	—	Kidwelly	d	23b00	00x11				01x16													06x22		07x22	
72¼	—	Ferryside	d	23b06	00x17		←		01x22													06x28		07x28	
79¼	—	**Carmarthen**	a	23p18	00 30	00 31	00 30		01 40													06 42		07 42	
—	—		d	23p21	00 34	00 33	00 34												04 53	05 43	05 58	06 43		07 44	
93¼	—	Whitland	a	23p35	→	00 48	00 50												05 06	05 59	06 13	07 00		07 58	
—	—		d	23p36		00 49	00 50												05 06	05 59	06 13	07 00		07 58	
—	5¼	Narberth	d																	06x08		07x09			
—	10¾	Kilgetty	d																	06x18		07x19			
—	11½	Saundersfoot	d																	06x20		07x21			
—	15¾	**Tenby**	a																	06 27		07 28			
—	—		d																	06 30		07 42			
—	17	Penally	d																	06x33		07x45			
—	20¼	Manorbier	d																	06 40		07 52			
—	23¾	Lamphey	d																	06x47		07x59			
—	25¼	Pembroke	d																	06 50		08 02			
—	27¼	**Pembroke Dock**	a																	07 05		08 17			
98¾	—	Clunderwen	d	23b42															05x13		06x19			08 05	
105¼	0	Clarbeston Road	d	23b51		01x02	01x03												05x21		06x27			08x12	
—	5¼	Haverfordwest	d	23p59															05 32		06 35			08 21	
—	10	Johnston	d	00x07															05x40		06x43			08x29	
—	14	**Milford Haven**	a	00 22															05 55		06 58			08 46	
121	—	**Fishguard Harbour** ⛴	a			01 29	01 30																		
—	—		d														02 45								
—	—	Rosslare Harbour ⛴	a														06 15								

A From 8 August until 5 September
B From 27 June until 1 August
C Until 20 June
b Previous night, stops on request
c Previous night, arr. 2227
e Previous night, arr. 2331

When events are being held at the Millenium Stadium, services are subject to alteration. Please check times before travelling.

Cardiff - Maesteg, Swansea and West Wales

		AW	AW	AW	AW	GW	AW	AW	GW	AW	AW	AW	AW	AW	GW	AW	AW	GW	AW	AW	AW	AW	AW
		◇ A	◇ B		◇ 🛒	◇1 🍽	◇	◇	◇1 🍽	◇ 🛒	🛒			◇ 🛒	◇1 C 🍽⊘		◇ 🛒	◇1 🍽	◇ 🛒	🛒			◇ 🛒
London Paddington 15 ⊖	d					05 27			06 45						07 45			08 45					
Reading 7	d					05 56			07 11						08 11			09 11					
Manchester Piccadilly 10	d																07 30						08 30
Gloucester 7	d			05 50									07 58			08 58							
Bristol Parkway 7	d								08 07						09 07			10 07					
Newport (South Wales)	d	06 17		06 44	07 35	07 44		08 01	08 32	08 38			08 52	09 03	09 32	09 52	10 22	10 31					11 22
Cardiff Central 7	d	06 42	06 42	07 04	07 58	08 02	08 09	08 20	08 48	09 04		09 14	09 18	09 39	09 48	10 18	10 39	10 48	10 54		11 14	11 18	11 39
Pontyclun	d			07 16				08 32					09 30			10 30						11 30	
Llanharan	d			07 21				08 37					09 35			10 35						11 35	
Pencoed	d			07 25				08 41					09 39			10 39						11 39	
Bridgend	d	07 02	07 02	07 32	08 17	08 23	08 29	08 49	09 09	09 23		09 34	09 46	09 58	10 09	10 46	10 59	11 09			11 34	11 46	12 00
Wildmill	d			07 35				08 51					09 49			10 49						11 49	
Sarn	d			07 38				08 54					09 52			10 52						11 52	
Tondu	d			07 41				08 58					09 55			10 55						11 55	
Garth (Mid Glamorgan)	d			07 51				09 07					10 05			11 05						12 05	
Maesteg (Ewenny Road)	d			07 53				09 10					10 07			11 07						12 07	
Maesteg	a			07 58				09 15					10 12			11 12						12 14	
Pyle	d	07 10	07 10				08 37					09 43									11 42		
Port Talbot Parkway	d	07 18	07 18		08 30	08 36	08 45		09 22	09 36		09 52		10 12	10 22		11 12	11 22			11 50		12 12
Baglan	d	07 22	07 22				08 49					09 55									11 54		
Briton Ferry	d	07 25	07 25				08 52					09 59									11 57		
Neath	d	07 29	07 29		08 37	08 44	08 56		09 30	09 43		10 03		10 19	10 30		11 19	11 30			12 01		12 19
Skewen	d	07 33	07 33				09 00					10 06									12 05		
Llansamlet	d	07 37	07 37				09 04					10 10									12 09		
Swansea	a	07 45	07 45		08 50	08 57	09 12		09 45	09 55		10 21		10 34	10 44		11 34	11 43			12 20		12 34
	d	07 50	07 50		09 02		09 15			10 00	10 05			10 38			11 37			12 00			12 37
Gowerton	d	08x00	08x00		09x14						10x16									12x11			
Llanelli	a	08 07	08 07		09 20		09 31			10 15	10 23			10 53			11 52		11 58	12 18			13 00
	d	08 08	08 08		09 22					10 17	10 25			10 55			11 54		12 02	12 20			13 02
Pembrey & Burry Port	d	08 14	08 14		09 28					10 23	10 31			11 01			12 00			12 26			13 08
Kidwelly	d	08x20	08x20		09x34					10x29							12x06						
Ferryside	d	08x26	08x26		09x39					10x34							12x11						
Carmarthen	a	08 40	08 40		09 51					10 51	10 54			11 20			12 26			12 49			13 25
	d	08 45	08 45		09 57						10 56			11 23						12 51			13 30
Whitland	a	08 59	08 59		10 13						11 10			11 37					12 44	13 05			13 45
	d	08 59	08 59		10 14						11 11			11 39					12 44	13 06			13 45
Narberth	d	09x08	09x08								11x20									13x15			
Kilgetty	d	09x18	09x18								11x30									13x25			
Saundersfoot	d	09x20	09x20								11x32									13x27			
Tenby	a	09 27	09 27								11 39									13 34			
	d	09 43	09 43								11 45									13 45			
Penally	d	09x46	09x46								11x48									13x48			
Manorbier	d	09 53	09 53								11 54									13 54			
Lamphey	d	10x00	10x00								12x02									14x02			
Pembroke	d	10 03	10 03								12 05									14 05			
Pembroke Dock	a	10 18	10 18								12 19									14 19			
Clunderwen	d				10x20									11x46									13x52
Clarbeston Road	d				10x28									11x54					12 58				13x59
Haverfordwest	d				10 36									12 03									14 08
Johnston	d				10x44									12x13									14x16
Milford Haven	a				10 57									12 27									14 31
Fishguard Harbour ⛴	a																		13 25				
	d																						
Rosslare Harbour ⛴	a																						

A until 22 July
B from 25 July until 9 September
C The St. David. 🍽 from Bridgend
⊘ to Cardiff Central

When events are being held at the Millenium Stadium, services are subject to alteration. Please check times before travelling.

Table 128

Mondays to Fridays

until 9 September

Cardiff - Maesteg, Swansea and West Wales

		GW	AW	AW		AW	GW	AW	AW	AW	AW	GW	AW	AW		GW	AW	AW	AW	AW	GW	AW	AW	AW
																	R					R		
		◇1		◇		◇	◇1				◇	◇1		◇		◇1					◇1			
		A					A					A				A								
		⊡⊘				🚲	⊡⊘	🚲			🚲	⊡⊘		🚲		⊡⊘		🚲			⊡	🚲		🚲
London Paddington 15 ⊖	d	09 45					10 45					11 45				12 45					13 45			
Reading 7	d	10 11					11 11					12 11				13 11					14 11			
Manchester Piccadilly 10	d					09 30					10 30			11 30								12 30		
Gloucester 7	d		10 58							11 58										13 58			14 58	
Bristol Parkway 7	d	11 07					12 07					13 07				14 07					15 07			
Newport (South Wales)	d	11 31	11 51			12 23	12 32			12 52	13 23	13 31		14 22		14 31				14 52	15 32	15 37	15 52	
Cardiff Central 7	d	11 48	12 18			12 39	12 48		13 14	13 18	13 39	13 48	14 21	14 39		14 48			15 14	15 18	15 48	16 04	16 18	
Pontyclun	d		12 30							13 30			14 33							15 30			16 30	
Llanharan	d		12 35							13 35			14 38							15 35			16 35	
Pencoed	d		12 39							13 39			14 42							15 39			16 39	
Bridgend	d	12 09	12 46			12 58	13 09		13 34	13 46	14 04	14 09	14 49	14 58		15 09			15 34	15 46	16 09	16 23	16 46	
Wildmill	d		12 49							13 49			14 52							15 49			16 49	
Sarn	d		12 52							13 52			14 55							15 52			16 52	
Tondu	d		12 55							13 55			14 58							15 55			16 55	
Garth (Mid Glamorgan)	d		13 05							14 05			15 08							16 05			17 05	
Maesteg (Ewenny Road)	d		13 07							14 07			15 10							16 07			17 07	
Maesteg	a		13 12							14 12			15 15							16 12			17 12	
Pyle	d								13 42										15 42			16 33		
Port Talbot Parkway	d	12 22				13 11	13 22		13 50		14 18	14 22		15 11		15 22			15 50		16 22	16 41		
Baglan	d								13 54										15 54					
Briton Ferry	d								13 57										15 57					
Neath	d	12 30				13 18	13 30		14 01		14 25	14 30		15 18		15 30			16 01		16 30	16 48		
Skewen	d								14 05										16 05					
Llansamlet	d								14 09										16 09					
Swansea	a	12 43				13 34	13 43		14 20		14 34	14 43		15 34		15 43			16 20		16 43	17 01		
	d			13 14		13 37		14 00			14 37			15 37				16 00				17 05		17 35
Gowerton	d							14x11										16x11				17x16		17x45
Llanelli	a			13 31		13 52		14 18			14 53			15 52				16 18				17 22		17 52
	d					13 54		14 20			14 54			15 54				16 20				17 24		17 54
Pembrey & Burry Port	d					14 00		14 26			15 00			16 00				16 26				17 30		18 00
Kidwelly	d					14x06								16x06										18x08
Ferryside	d					14x11								16x11										18x14
Carmarthen	a					14 28		14 49			15 20			16 28				16 49				17 49		18 30
	d							14 51			15 28							16 51				17 54		
Whitland	a							15 05			15 43							17 05				18 11		
	d							15 06			15 43							17 06				18 12		
Narberth	d							15x15										17x15						
Kilgetty	d							15x25										17x25						
Saundersfoot	d							15x27										17x27						
Tenby	a							15 34										17 34						
	d							15 45										17 45						
Penally	d							15x48										17x48						
Manorbier	d							15 54										17 54						
Lamphey	d							16x02										18x02						
Pembroke	d							16 05										18 05						
Pembroke Dock	a							16 19										18 19						
Clunderwen	d										15x50											18x18		
Clarbeston Road	d										15x57											18x26		
Haverfordwest	d										16 06											18 34		
Johnston	d										16x14											18x42		
Milford Haven	a										16 29											18 57		
Fishguard Harbour ⛴	a																							
	d																14 30							
Rosslare Harbour ⛴	a																18 00							

A ⊡ from Bridgend ⊘ to Cardiff Central

When events are being held at the Millenium Stadium, services are subject to alteration. Please check times before travelling.

Table 128

Mondays to Fridays

until 9 September

Cardiff - Maesteg, Swansea and West Wales

		GW	AW	AW	AW	AW	GW	AW	GW	AW		AW	GW	AW	AW	GW	AW	GW	AW	GW		GW FX	GW FO	AW	AW
		◇[1] ☕	[R] 🛒	◇ 🛒	◇	[R] 🛒	◇[1] ☕		◇[1] ☕				◇[1] A ☕	[R] 🛒		◇[1] ☕	[R] 🛒	◇[1] B ☕		◇[1] ☕		◇[1] ☕	◇[1] ☕		
London Paddington [15] ⊖	d	14 45					15 45		16 15				16 45			17 15		17 45		18 15		18 45	18 45		
Reading [7]	d	15 11					16 11		16 41				17 11			17 41		18 11		18 41		19 11	19 11		
Manchester Piccadilly [10]	d		13 30			14 30								15 30			16 30								
Gloucester [7]	d									16 58					17 59				18 58						19 58
Bristol Parkway [7]	d	16 07					17 07		17 40				18 07			18 40		19 07		19 40		20 07	20 07		
Newport (South Wales)	d	16 31	16 40	17 01		17 22	17 31		18 04	17 52			18 31	18 41	18 53	19 11	19 22	19 31	19 52	20 08		20 31	20 31		20 52
Cardiff Central [7]	d	16 48	17 04	17 18		17 39	17 48	18 04	18 22	18 12			18 50	19 04	19 12	19 28	19 45	19 50	20 13	20 24		20 49	20 55	21 04	21 10
Pontyclun	d			17 32						18 24					19 28				20 25						21 22
Llanharan	d			17 36						18 29					19 33				20 30						21 27
Pencoed	d			17 40						18 33					19 37				20 34						21 32
Bridgend	d	17 09	17 25	17 46		17 59	18 09	18 24	18 44	18 49			19 09	19 23	19 45	19 49	20 05	20 10	20 41	20 45		21 09	21 16	21 27	21 41
Wildmill	d			17 48						18 52					19 48				20 44						21 43
Sarn	d			17 51						18 55					19 51				20 47						21 46
Tondu	d			17 55						18 58					19 54				20 50						21 50
Garth (Mid Glamorgan)	d			18 04						19 08					20 04				21 00						21 59
Maesteg (Ewenny Road)	d			18 07						19 10					20 06				21 02						22 02
Maesteg	a			18 15						19 15					20 11				21 07						22 06
Pyle	d		17 32			18 07		18 32						19 30										21 34	
Port Talbot Parkway	d	17 22	17 40			18 17	18 22	18 40	18 57				19 22	19 38		20 02	20 20	20 24		20 58		21 22	21 29	21 45	
Baglan	d		17 42					18 42						19 41											
Briton Ferry	d		17 46					18 46						19 44											
Neath	d	17 30	17 50			18 25	18 30	18 50	19 04				19 30	19 48		20 10	20 27	20 31		21 05		21 30	21 37	21 52	
Skewen	d		17 54					18 53						19 53											
Llansamlet	d		17 58					18 57						19 57											
Swansea	a	17 43	18 05			18 37	18 48	19 08	19 18				19 45	20 04		20 23	20 40	20 45		21 19		21 43	21 49	22 04	
	d		18 09		18 21	18 41						19 35		20 08			20 52	21 02						22 27	
Gowerton	d		18 20			18x52								20x19										22x41	
Llanelli	a		18 26		18 35	18 59						19 51		20 25			21 07	21 18						22 47	
	d		18 28			19 00						19 53		20 27			21 09	21 18						22 49	
Pembrey & Burry Port	d		18 33			19 06						19 59		20 32			21 14	21 25						22 54	
Kidwelly	d		18 39									20x06												23x00	
Ferryside	d		18 45									20x12												23x06	
Carmarthen	a		18 57			19 27						20 28		20 55			21 34	21 50						23 18	
	d		19 02			19 30								20 58			21 38							23 21	
Whitland	a		19 18			19 45								21 13			21 52							23 35	
	d		19 18			19 46								21 14			21 53							23 36	
Narberth	d		19 28											21x22											
Kilgetty	d		19 38											21x31											
Saundersfoot	d		19 40											21x33											
Tenby	a		19 52											21 40											
	d													21 43											
Penally	d													21x46											
Manorbier	d													21 52											
Lamphey	d													22x00											
Pembroke	d													22 03											
Pembroke Dock	a													22 18											
Clunderwen	d					19x53											21x59							23x42	
Clarbeston Road	d					20x00											22x07							23x51	
Haverfordwest	d					20 09											22 20							23 59	
Johnston	d					20x17											22x28							00x07	
Milford Haven	a					20 32											22 43							00 22	
Fishguard Harbour ⛴	a																								
	d																								
Rosslare Harbour ⛴	a																								

A The Capitals United

B The Red Dragon

When events are being held at the Millenium Stadium, services are subject to alteration. Please check times before travelling.

Table 128

Mondays to Fridays

until 9 September

Cardiff - Maesteg, Swansea and West Wales

		GW	GW	AW	AW	GW	AW	AW	AW	GW	GW	GW
		FX	FO	FX	FO						FO	FX
		◇1	◇1	◇	◇	◇1		◇		◇1	◇1	◇1
		🍴	🍴	🛒	🛒	🍴				🍴	🍴	🍴
London Paddington 15 ⊖	d	19 15	19 15			20 15				21 15	22 45	22 45
Reading 7	d	19 41	19 48			20 41				21 41	23 11	23 21
Manchester Piccadilly 10	d			18 30	18 30							
Gloucester 7	d											
Bristol Parkway 7	d	20 40	20 43			21 40				22 45	00 16	00 24
Newport (South Wales)	d	21 04	21 07	21 52	21 52	22 05				23 19	00 38	00 54
Cardiff Central 7	d	21 22	21 22	22 09	22 09	22 26	22 35		23 15	23 43	00 55	01 15
Pontyclun	d			22 21	22 21				23 29			
Llanharan	d			22 25	22 25				23 34			
Pencoed	d			22 29	22 29				23 39			
Bridgend	d	21 45	21 45	22 35	22 35	22 46	22 59		23 45	00 02	01 19	01 38
Wildmill	d						23 01					
Sarn	d						23 04					
Tondu	d						23 08					
Garth (Mid Glamorgan)	d						23 17					
Maesteg (Ewenny Road)	d						23 20					
Maesteg	a						23 24					
Pyle	d								23 53			
Port Talbot Parkway	d	21 58	21 58	22 47	22 47	22 59			00 01	00 15	01 32	01 51
Baglan	d								00 05			
Briton Ferry	d								00 09			
Neath	d	22 06	22 06		22 54	23 07			00 13	00 22	01 39	01 58
Skewen	d								00 16			
Llansamlet	d								00 20			
Swansea	a	22 19	22 19		23 07	23 20			00 28	00 37	01 53	02 13
	d				23 11			23 45	00 45			
Gowerton	d				23x22			23x55	00x56			
Llanelli	a			23 16	23 29			00 03	01s02			
	d			23 18	23 30			00 04				
Pembrey & Burry Port	d			23 23	23 36			00 09	01s09			
Kidwelly	d			23x29	23x42				01x16			
Ferryside	d			23x35	23x47				01x22			
Carmarthen	a			23 55	00 04			00 31	01 40			
	d							00 33				
Whitland	a							00 48				
	d							00 49				
Narberth	d											
Kilgetty	d											
Saundersfoot	d											
Tenby	a											
	d											
Penally	d											
Manorbier	d											
Lamphey	d											
Pembroke	d											
Pembroke Dock	a											
Clunderwen	d											
Clarbeston Road	d							01x02				
Haverfordwest	d											
Johnston	d											
Milford Haven	a											
Fishguard Harbour ⛴	a							01 29				
	d											
Rosslare Harbour ⛴	a											

When events are being held at the Millenium Stadium, services are subject to alteration. Please check times before travelling.

Cardiff - Maesteg, Swansea and West Wales

		AW	AW	AW	AW	AW	GW	AW	GW	GW	GW	GW	GW	AW	AW	AW	AW	AW	AW	AW	AW	AW	AW
		MX	MO	MX	MO	MO		MX	MO	MX	MO	MO	MX										
			◇ A	◇	◇ A	◇ B	◇1 A 🍴		◇1 B 🍴	◇1 🍴	◇1 A 🍴	◇1 B 🍴	◇1 🍴	🚌	◇					◇		◇	
London Paddington 15 ⊖	d						20p37		20p30	21p15	21p37	21p37	22p45										
Reading 7	d						21p17		21p05	21p41	22p14	22p15	23p21										
Manchester Piccadilly 10	d																						
Gloucester 7	d																						05 50
Bristol Parkway 7	d						22p16		22c51	22p45	23p17	23e59	00 24										
Newport (South Wales)	d						22p44		23p16	23p19	23p45	00 27	00 54									06 17	06 44
Cardiff Central 7	d	21p04	22p30			22p30	23p08	23p15	23p42	23p43	00 08	00 53	01 15							05 39	05 51	06 42	07 04
Pontyclun	d							23p29												05 51	06 03		07 16
Llanharan	d							23p34												05 56	06 08		07 21
Pencoed	d							23p39												06 01	06 12		07 25
Bridgend	d	21p27	22p51			22p51	23p28	23p45	00 02	00 02	00 30	01 13	01 38							06 07	06 20	07 02	07 32
Wildmill	d																				06 22		07 35
Sarn	d																				06 25		07 38
Tondu	d																				06 29		07 41
Garth (Mid Glamorgan)	d																				06 38		07 51
Maesteg (Ewenny Road)	d																				06 41		07 53
Maesteg	a																				06 45		07 58
Pyle	d	21p34						23p53												06 15		07 10	
Port Talbot Parkway	d	21p45	23p05			23p05	23p42	00 01	00 15	00 15	00 43	01 26	01 51							06 23		07 18	
Baglan	d							00 05												06 27		07 22	
Briton Ferry	d							00 09												06 30		07 25	
Neath	d	21p52	23p13			23p13	23p50	00 13	00 24	00 22	00 50	01 35	01 58							06 34		07 29	
Skewen	d							00 16												06 38		07 33	
Llansamlet	d							00 20												06 42		07 37	
Swansea	a	22p04	23p25			23p25	00 02	00 28	00 36	00 37	01 03	01 47	02 13							06 51		07 45	
	d	22p27	23p38	23p45		23p48		00 45							04 36				05 50	06 53		07 50	
Gowerton	d	22b41	23b49	23b55		23b59		00x56											06x00			08x00	
Llanelli	a	22p47	23p56	00 03		00 06		01s02							04 52				06 07	07 10		08 07	
	d	22p49	23p58	00 04		00 08													06 09	07 10		08 08	
Pembrey & Burry Port	d	22p54	00 04	00 09		00 14		01s09											06 15	07 16		08 14	
Kidwelly	d	23b00	00x11			00x21		01x16											06x22	07x22		08x20	
Ferryside	d	23b06	00x17		←	00x27		01x22											06x28	07x28		08x26	
Carmarthen	a	23p18	00 30	00 31	00 30	00 40		01 40											06 42	07 42		08 40	
	d	23p21	00 34	00 33	00 34	00 44										04 53	05 43	05 58	06 43	07 44		08 45	
Whitland	a	23p35	→	00 48	00 50	01 00										05 06	05 59	06 13	07 00	07 58		08 59	
	d	23p36		00 49	00 50	01 00										05 06	05 59	06 13	07 00	07 58		08 59	
Narberth	d																06x08		07x09			09x08	
Kilgetty	d																06x18		07x19			09x18	
Saundersfoot	d																06x20		07x21			09x20	
Tenby	a																06 27		07 28			09 27	
	d																06 30		07 42			09 43	
Penally	d																06x33		07x45			09x46	
Manorbier	d																06 40		07 52			09 53	
Lamphey	d																06x47		07x59			10x00	
Pembroke	d																06 50		08 02			10 03	
Pembroke Dock	a																07 05		08 17			10 18	
Clunderwen	d	23b42														05x13		06x19		08 05			
Clarbeston Road	d	23b51		01x02	01x03	01x13										05x21		06x27		08x12			
Haverfordwest	d	23p59														05 32		06 35		08 21			
Johnston	d	00x07														05x40		06x43		08x29			
Milford Haven	a	00 22														05 55		06 58		08 46			
Fishguard Harbour ⛴	a			01 29	01 30	01 40																	
	d													02 45									
Rosslare Harbour ⛴	a													06 15									

A From 12 September until 24 October
B From 31 October

b Previous night, stops on request
c Previous night, arr. 2243

e Previous night, arr. 2352

When events are being held at the Millenium Stadium, services are subject to alteration. Please check times before travelling.

Table 128

Mondays to Fridays

from 12 September

Cardiff - Maesteg, Swansea and West Wales

		AW	GW	AW	AW	GW		AW	AW	AW	AW	AW	GW	AW	AW	GW		AW	AW	AW	AW	AW	GW	AW	AW
		◇	◇1	◇	◇	◇1		◇				◇	◇1		◇	◇1		◇				◇	◇1		◇
													A										B		
		⊥	⊡			⊡		⊥				⊥	⊡⊘		⊥	⊡		⊥				⊥	⊡⊘		
London Paddington 15 ⊖	d		05 27			06 45							07 45			08 45							09 45		
Reading 7	d		05 56			07 11							08 11			09 11							10 11		
Manchester Piccadilly 10	d														07 30							08 30			
Gloucester 7	d										07 58			08 58										10 58	
Bristol Parkway 7	d					08 07							09 07			10 07							11 07		
Newport (South Wales)	d	07 35	07 44		08 01	08 32		08 38			08 52	09 03	09 32	09 52	10 22	10 31						11 22	11 31	11 51	
Cardiff Central 7	d	07 58	08 02	08 09	08 20	08 48		09 04		09 14	09 18	09 39	09 48	10 18	10 39	10 48		10 54		11 14	11 18	11 39	11 48	12 18	
Pontyclun	d				08 32						09 30			10 30							11 30			12 30	
Llanharan	d				08 37						09 35			10 35							11 35			12 35	
Pencoed	d				08 41						09 39			10 39							11 39			12 39	
Bridgend	d	08 17	08 23	08 29	08 49	09 09		09 23		09 34	09 46	09 58	10 09	10 46	10 59	11 09				11 34	11 46	12 00	12 09	12 46	
Wildmill	d				08 51						09 49			10 49							11 49			12 49	
Sarn	d				08 54						09 52			10 52							11 52			12 52	
Tondu	d				08 58						09 55			10 55							11 55			12 55	
Garth (Mid Glamorgan)	d				09 07						10 05			11 05							12 05			13 05	
Maesteg (Ewenny Road)	d				09 10						10 07			11 07							12 07			13 07	
Maesteg	a				09 15						10 12			11 12							12 14			13 12	
Pyle	d			08 37						09 43										11 42					
Port Talbot Parkway	d	08 30	08 36	08 45		09 22		09 36		09 52		10 12	10 22		11 12	11 22				11 50		12 12	12 22		
Baglan	d			08 49						09 55										11 54					
Briton Ferry	d			08 52						09 59										11 57					
Neath	d	08 37	08 44	08 56		09 30		09 43		10 03		10 19	10 30		11 19	11 30				12 01		12 19	12 30		
Skewen	d			09 00						10 06										12 05					
Llansamlet	d			09 04						10 10										12 09					
Swansea	a	08 50	08 57	09 12		09 45		09 55		10 21		10 34	10 44		11 34	11 43				12 20		12 34	12 43		
	d	09 02		09 15				10 00	10 05			10 38			11 37				12 00			12 37			13 14
Gowerton	d	09x14							10x16										12x11						
Llanelli	a	09 20		09 31				10 15	10 23			10 53			11 52			11 58	12 18			13 00			13 31
	d	09 22						10 17	10 25			10 55			11 54			12 02	12 20			13 02			
Pembrey & Burry Port	d	09 28						10 23	10 31			11 01			12 00				12 26			13 08			
Kidwelly	d	09x34						10x29							12x06										
Ferryside	d	09x39						10x34							12x11										
Carmarthen	a	09 51						10 51	10 54			11 20			12 26				12 49			13 25			
	d	09 57							10 56			11 23							12 51			13 30			
Whitland	a	10 13							11 10			11 37						12 44	13 05			13 45			
	d	10 14							11 11			11 39						12 44	13 06			13 45			
Narberth	d								11x20										13x15						
Kilgetty	d								11x30										13x25						
Saundersfoot	d								11x32										13x27						
Tenby	a								11 39										13 34						
	d								11 45										13 45						
Penally	d								11x48										13x48						
Manorbier	d								11 54										13 54						
Lamphey	d								12x02										14x02						
Pembroke	d								12 05										14 05						
Pembroke Dock	a								12 19										14 19						
Clunderwen	d	10x20										11x46										13x52			
Clarbeston Road	d	10x28										11x54						12 58				13x59			
Haverfordwest	d	10 36										12 03										14 08			
Johnston	d	10x44										12x13										14x16			
Milford Haven	a	10 57										12 27										14 31			
Fishguard Harbour ⛴	a																	13 25							
	d																								
Rosslare Harbour ⛴	a																								

A The St. David. ⊡ from Bridgend ⊘ to Cardiff Central

B ⊡ from Bridgend ⊘ to Cardiff Central

When events are being held at the Millenium Stadium, services are subject to alteration. Please check times before travelling.

Table 128

Mondays to Fridays
from 12 September

Cardiff - Maesteg, Swansea and West Wales

		AW		GW	AW	AW	AW	AW	GW	AW	AW	GW		AW	AW	AW	AW	GW	AW	AW	AW	GW		AW	AW
														R					R					R	
		◇		◇1				◇	◇1		◇	◇1						◇1				◇1			◇
				A					A			A													
		🛒		☕⊘				🛒	☕⊘		🛒	☕⊘						☕	🛒			☕		🛒	🛒
London Paddington 15 ⊖	d			10 45					11 45			12 45						13 45				14 45			
Reading 7	d			11 11					12 11			13 11						14 11				15 11			
Manchester Piccadilly 10	d	09 30						10 30			11 30								12 30					13 30	
Gloucester 7	d						11 58										13 58			14 58					
Bristol Parkway 7	d			12 07					13 07			14 07						15 07				16 07			
Newport (South Wales)	d	12 23		12 32			12 52	13 23	13 31		14 22	14 31					14 52	15 32	15 37	15 52		16 31		16 40	17 01
Cardiff Central 7	d	12 39		12 48		13 14	13 18	13 39	13 48	14 21	14 39	14 48				15 14	15 18	15 48	16 04	16 18		16 48		17 04	17 18
Pontyclun	d						13 30			14 33							15 30			16 30					17 32
Llanharan	d						13 35			14 38							15 35			16 35					17 36
Pencoed	d						13 39			14 42							15 39			16 39					17 40
Bridgend	d	12 58		13 09		13 34	13 46	14 04	14 09	14 49	14 58	15 09				15 34	15 46	16 09	16 23	16 46		17 09		17 25	17 46
Wildmill	d						13 49			14 52							15 49			16 49					17 48
Sarn	d						13 52			14 55							15 52			16 52					17 51
Tondu	d						13 55			14 58							15 55			16 55					17 55
Garth (Mid Glamorgan)	d						14 05			15 08							16 05			17 05					18 04
Maesteg (Ewenny Road)	d						14 07			15 10							16 07			17 07					18 07
Maesteg	a						14 12			15 15							16 12			17 12					18 15
Pyle	d					13 42										15 42			16 33					17 32	
Port Talbot Parkway	d	13 11		13 22		13 50		14 18	14 22		15 11	15 22				15 50		16 22	16 41			17 22		17 40	
Baglan	d					13 54										15 54								17 42	
Briton Ferry	d					13 57										15 57								17 46	
Neath	d	13 18		13 30		14 01		14 25	14 30		15 18	15 30				16 01		16 30	16 48			17 30		17 50	
Skewen	d					14 05										16 05								17 54	
Llansamlet	d					14 09										16 09								17 58	
Swansea	a	13 34		13 43		14 20		14 34	14 43		15 34	15 43				16 20		16 43	17 01			17 43		18 05	
	d	13 37			14 00			14 37			15 37				16 00				17 05		17 35			18 09	
Gowerton	d				14x11										16x11				17x16		17x45			18 20	
Llanelli	a	13 52			14 18			14 53			15 52				16 18				17 22		17 52			18 26	
	d	13 54			14 20			14 54			15 54				16 20				17 24		17 54			18 28	
Pembrey & Burry Port	d	14 00			14 26			15 00			16 00				16 26				17 30		18 00			18 33	
Kidwelly	d	14x06									16x06										18x08			18 39	
Ferryside	d	14x11									16x11										18x14			18 45	
Carmarthen	a	14 28			14 49			15 20			16 28				16 49				17 49		18 30			18 57	
	d				14 51			15 28							16 51				17 54					19 02	
Whitland	a				15 05			15 43							17 05				18 11					19 18	
	d				15 06			15 43							17 06				18 12					19 18	
Narberth	d				15x15										17x15									19 28	
Kilgetty	d				15x25										17x25									19 38	
Saundersfoot	d				15x27										17x27									19 40	
Tenby	a				15 34										17 34									19 52	
	d				15 45										17 45										
Penally	d				15x48										17x48										
Manorbier	d				15 54										17 54										
Lamphey	d				16x02										18x02										
Pembroke	d				16 05										18 05										
Pembroke Dock	a				16 19										18 19										
Clunderwen	d							15x50											18x18						
Clarbeston Road	d							15x57											18x26						
Haverfordwest	d							16 06											18 34						
Johnston	d							16x14											18x42						
Milford Haven	a							16 29											18 57						
Fishguard Harbour ⛴	a																								
	d													14 30											
Rosslare Harbour ⛴	a													18 00											

A ☕ from Bridgend ⊘ to Cardiff Central

When events are being held at the Millenium Stadium, services are subject to alteration. Please check times before travelling.

Table 128

Mondays to Fridays

from 12 September

Cardiff - Maesteg, Swansea and West Wales

		AW ◇	AW R	GW ◇1	AW	GW ◇1	AW	AW	GW ◇1 A	AW R	AW	GW ◇1	AW R	GW ◇1 B	AW	GW ◇1	GW FX ◇1	GW FO ◇1	AW	AW	GW FX ◇1	GW FO ◇1	AW FX ◇
London Paddington 15 ⊖	d			15 45		16 15			16 45			17 15		17 45		18 15	18 45	18 45			19 15	19 15	
Reading 7	d			16 11		16 41			17 11			17 41		18 11		18 41	19 11	19 11			19 41	19 48	
Manchester Piccadilly 10	d		14 30							15 30			16 30										18 30
Gloucester 7	d						16 58				17 59				18 58					19 58			
Bristol Parkway 7	d			17 07		17 40			18 07			18 40		19 07		19 40	20 07	20 07			20 40	20 43	
Newport (South Wales)	d		17 22	17 31		18 04	17 52		18 31	18 41	18 53	19 11	19 22	19 31	19 52	20 08	20 31	20 31		20 52	21 04	21 07	21 52
Cardiff Central 7	d		17 39	17 48	18 04	18 22	18 12		18 50	19 04	19 12	19 28	19 45	19 50	20 13	20 24	20 49	20 55	21 04	21 10	21 22	21 22	22 09
Pontyclun	d						18 24				19 28				20 25					21 22			22 21
Llanharan	d						18 29				19 33				20 30					21 27			22 25
Pencoed	d						18 33				19 37				20 34					21 32			22 29
Bridgend	d		17 59	18 09	18 24	18 44	18 49		19 09	19 23	19 45	19 49	20 05	20 10	20 41	20 45	21 09	21 16	21 27	21 41	21 45	21 45	22 35
Wildmill	d						18 52				19 48				20 44					21 43			
Sarn	d						18 55				19 51				20 47					21 46			
Tondu	d						18 58				19 54				20 50					21 50			
Garth (Mid Glamorgan)	d						19 08				20 04				21 00					21 59			
Maesteg (Ewenny Road)	d						19 10				20 06				21 02					22 02			
Maesteg	a						19 15				20 11				21 07					22 06			
Pyle	d		18 07		18 32					19 30									21 34				
Port Talbot Parkway	d		18 17	18 22	18 40	18 57			19 22	19 38		20 02	20 20	20 24		20 58	21 22	21 29	21 45		21 58	21 58	22 47
Baglan	d				18 42					19 41													
Briton Ferry	d				18 46					19 44													
Neath	d		18 25	18 30	18 50	19 04			19 30	19 48		20 10	20 27	20 31		21 05	21 30	21 37	21 52		22 06	22 06	
Skewen	d				18 53					19 53													
Llansamlet	d				18 57					19 57													
Swansea	a		18 37	18 48	19 08	19 18			19 45	20 04		20 23	20 40	20 45		21 19	21 43	21 49	22 04		22 19	22 19	
	d	18 21	18 41					19 35		20 08			20 52	21 02					22 27				
Gowerton	d		18x52							20x19									22x41				
Llanelli	a	18 35	18 59					19 51		20 25			21 07	21 18					22 47				23 16
	d		19 00					19 53		20 27			21 09	21 18					22 49				23 18
Pembrey & Burry Port	d		19 06					19 59		20 32			21 14	21 25					22 54				23 23
Kidwelly	d							20x06											23x00				23x29
Ferryside	d							20x12											23x06				23x35
Carmarthen	a		19 27					20 28		20 55			21 34	21 50					23 18				23 55
	d		19 30							20 58			21 38						23 21				
Whitland	a		19 45							21 13			21 52						23 35				
	d		19 46							21 14			21 53						23 36				
Narberth	d									21x22													
Kilgetty	d									21x31													
Saundersfoot	d									21x33													
Tenby	a									21 40													
	d									21 43													
Penally	d									21x46													
Manorbier	d									21 52													
Lamphey	d									22x00													
Pembroke	d									22 03													
Pembroke Dock	a									22 18													
Clunderwen	d		19x53										21x59						23x42				
Clarbeston Road	d		20x00										22x07						23x51				
Haverfordwest	d		20 09										22 20						23 59				
Johnston	d		20x17										22x28						00x07				
Milford Haven	a		20 32										22 43						00 22				
Fishguard Harbour ⛴	a																						
	d																						
Rosslare Harbour ⛴	a																						

A The Capitals United

B The Red Dragon

When events are being held at the Millenium Stadium, services are subject to alteration. Please check times before travelling.

Table 128

Mondays to Fridays

from 12 September

Cardiff - Maesteg, Swansea and West Wales

		AW FO	GW	AW		AW	AW	GW	GW FO	GW FX
		◇	◇ 1			◇		◇ 1	◇ 1	◇ 1
		[trolley]	[catering]					[catering]	[catering]	[catering]
London Paddington 15	d		20 15					21 15	22 45	22 45
Reading 7	d		20 41					21 41	23 11	23 21
Manchester Piccadilly 10	d	18 30								
Gloucester 7	d									
Bristol Parkway 7	d		21 40					22 45	00 16	00 24
Newport (South Wales)	d	21 52	22 05					23 19	00 38	00 54
Cardiff Central 7	d	22 09	22 26	22 35			23 15	23 43	00 55	01 15
Pontyclun	d	22 21					23 29			
Llanharan	d	22 25					23 34			
Pencoed	d	22 29					23 39			
Bridgend	d	22 35	22 46	22 59			23 45	00 02	01 19	01 38
Wildmill	d			23 01						
Sarn	d			23 04						
Tondu	d			23 08						
Garth (Mid Glamorgan)	d			23 17						
Maesteg (Ewenny Road)	d			23 20						
Maesteg	a			23 24						
Pyle	d						23 53			
Port Talbot Parkway	d	22 47	22 59				00 01	00 15	01 32	01 51
Baglan	d						00 05			
Briton Ferry	d						00 09			
Neath	d	22 54	23 07				00 13	00 22	01 39	01 58
Skewen	d						00 16			
Llansamlet	d						00 20			
Swansea	a	23 07	23 20				00 28	00 37	01 53	02 13
	d	23 11				23 45	00 45			
Gowerton	d	23x22				23x55	00x56			
Llanelli	a	23 29				00 03	01s02			
	d	23 30				00 04				
Pembrey & Burry Port	d	23 36				00 09	01s09			
Kidwelly	d	23x42					01x16			
Ferryside	d	23x47					01x22			
Carmarthen	a	00 04				00 31	01 40			
	d					00 33				
Whitland	a					00 48				
	d					00 49				
Narberth	d									
Kilgetty	d									
Saundersfoot	d									
Tenby	a									
	d									
Penally	d									
Manorbier	d									
Lamphey	d									
Pembroke	d									
Pembroke Dock	a									
Clunderwen	d									
Clarbeston Road	d					01x02				
Haverfordwest	d									
Johnston	d									
Milford Haven	a									
Fishguard Harbour	a					01 29				
	d									
Rosslare Harbour	a									

When events are being held at the Millenium Stadium, services are subject to alteration. Please check times before travelling.

Table 128

Saturdays

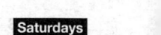

until 10 September

Cardiff - Maesteg, Swansea and West Wales

		AW	AW	AW	AW	AW	GW	GW	AW	AW		AW	AW	AW	AW	AW	AW	GW	AW	AW		GW	GW	AW	AW
			◇	◇			◇1	◇1	R	◇						◇		◇1	◇			1	◇1		◇
London Paddington 15 ⊖	d						21p15	22p45																	
Reading 7	d						21p41	23p11																	
Manchester Piccadilly 10	d		18p30																						
Gloucester 7	d																			05 50					
Bristol Parkway 7	d						22p45	00 16															07 11		
Newport (South Wales)	d		21p52				23p19	00 38												06 44			07 32		07 38
Cardiff Central 7	d	21p04	22p09			23p15	23p43	00 55								05 39	05 51		06 42	07 04			07 48		07 58
Pontyclun	d		22p21			23p29										05 51	06 03			07 16					
Llanharan	d		22p25			23p34										05 56	06 08			07 21					
Pencoed	d		22p29			23p39										06 01	06 12			07 25					
Bridgend	d	21p27	22p35			23p45	00 02	01 19								06 07	06 20		07 02	07 32			08 08		08 17
Wildmill	d																06 22			07 35					
Sarn	d																06 25			07 38					
Tondu	d																06 29			07 41					
Garth (Mid Glamorgan)	d																06 38			07 51					
Maesteg (Ewenny Road)	d																06 41			07 53					
Maesteg	a																06 45			07 58					
Pyle	d	21p34				23p53										06 15			07 10						
Port Talbot Parkway	d	21p45	22p47			00 01	00 15	01 32								06 23			07 18				08 21		08 30
Baglan	d					00 05										06 27			07 22						
Briton Ferry	d					00 09										06 30			07 25						
Neath	d	21p52	22p54			00 13	00 22	01 39								06 34			07 29				08 30		08 37
Skewen	d					00 16										06 38			07 33						
Llansamlet	d					00 20										06 42			07 37						
Swansea	a	22p04	23p07			00 28	00 37	01 53								06 51			07 45				08 44		08 51
	d	22p27	23p11	23p45	00 05	00 45				04 36					05 50	06 53		07 24	07 50			08 15			09 02
Gowerton	d	22b41	23b22	23b55	00x16	00x56									06x00				08x00						09x16
Llanelli	a	22p47	23p29	00 03	00 23	01s02				04 52					06 07	07 10		07 42	08 07			08 31			09 22
	d	22p49	23p30	00 04	00 25										06 09	07 10		07 43	08 08			08 36			09 24
Pembrey & Burry Port	d	22p54	23p36	00 09	00 31	01s09									06 15	07 16		07 50	08 14			08 43			09 30
Kidwelly	d	23b00	23b42		00x38	01x16									06x22	07x22			08x20						09x36
Ferryside	d	23b06	23b47		00x44	01x22									06x28	07x28			08x26						09x41
Carmarthen	a	23p18	00 04	00 31	01 00	01 40									06 42	07 42		08 11	08 42			09 08			09 53
	d	23p21		00 33								04 53	05 43	05 58	06 43	07 44		08 18						09 40	09 57
Whitland	a	23p35		00 48								05 06	05 59	06 13	07 00	07 58		08 35						09 54	10 11
	d	23p36		00 49								05 06	05 59	06 13	07 00	07 58		08 37						09 54	10 12
Narberth	d												06x08		07x09			08x46						10x03	
Kilgetty	d												06x18		07x19			08x55						10 12	
Saundersfoot	d												06x20		07x21			08x58						10x13	
Tenby	a												06 27		07 28			09 06						10 25	
	d												06 30		07 42			09 10							
Penally	d												06x33		07x45			09x14							
Manorbier	d												06 40		07 52			09 22							
Lamphey	d												06x47		07x59			09x31							
Pembroke	d												06 50		08 02			09 36							
Pembroke Dock	a												07 05		08 17			09 43							
Clunderwen	d	23b42										05x13		06x19		08 05									10x18
Clarbeston Road	d	23b51		01x02								05x21		06x27		08x12									10x26
Haverfordwest	d	23p59										05 32		06 35		08 21									10 34
Johnston	d	00x07										05x40		06x43		08x29									10x42
Milford Haven	a	00 22										05 55		06 58		08 46									10 55
Fishguard Harbour ⛴	a			01 29																					
	d								02 45																
Rosslare Harbour ⛴	a								06 15																

b Previous night, stops on request

When events are being held at the Millenium Stadium, services are subject to alteration. Please check times before travelling.

Table 128

Saturdays
until 10 September

Cardiff - Maesteg, Swansea and West Wales

		AW	AW	AW	AW	AW		AW	GW	AW	AW	AW	GW	AW	AW	AW		AW	GW	AW	AW	AW	AW	GW	AW
		◇			◇				◇ 1	◇		◇	◇ 1	◇					◇ 1	◇		◇		◇ 1	◇
																								A	
					[trolley]				[restaurant]	[trolley]		[trolley]	[restaurant]	[trolley]					[restaurant]	[trolley]				[restaurant] Ø	[trolley]
London Paddington 15 ⊖	d								07 45				08 45						09 45					10 45	
Reading 7	d								08 11				09 11						10 11					11 11	
Manchester Piccadilly 10	d									06 30				07 30						08 30					09 30
Gloucester 7	d							07 58			08 58										10 58				
Bristol Parkway 7	d								09 07				10 07						11 07					12 07	
Newport (South Wales)	d		08 01		08 33			08 52	09 31	09 38	09 52		10 31	10 36					11 31	11 37	11 52			12 31	12 37
Cardiff Central 7	d	08 09	08 22		09 04	09 14		09 18	09 48	10 04	10 18	10 54	10 48	11 04	11 14	11 21			11 48	12 04	12 18			12 48	13 04
Pontyclun	d		08 34					09 30			10 30					11 33					12 30				
Llanharan	d		08 39					09 35			10 35					11 38					12 35				
Pencoed	d		08 43					09 39			10 39					11 42					12 39				
Bridgend	d	08 29	08 51		09 23	09 34		09 46	10 09	10 23	10 46		11 09	11 23	11 34	11 49			12 09	12 23	12 46			13 09	13 23
Wildmill	d		08 53					09 49			10 49					11 52					12 49				
Sarn	d		08 56					09 52			10 52					11 55					12 52				
Tondu	d		09 00					09 55			10 55					11 58					12 55				
Garth (Mid Glamorgan)	d		09 09					10 05			11 05					12 08					13 05				
Maesteg (Ewenny Road)	d		09 12					10 07			11 07					12 10					13 07				
Maesteg	a		09 16					10 12			11 12					12 15					13 12				
Pyle	d	08 37				09 43									11 42										
Port Talbot Parkway	d	08 45			09 38	09 52			10 22	10 35			11 22	11 36	11 50				12 22	12 36				13 22	13 36
Baglan	d	08 49				09 55									11 54										
Briton Ferry	d	08 52				09 59									11 57										
Neath	d	08 56			09 45	10 03			10 30	10 42			11 30	11 43	12 01				12 30	12 43				13 30	13 43
Skewen	d	09 00				10 06									12 05										
Llansamlet	d	09 04				10 10									12 09										
Swansea	a	09 13			09 57	10 21			10 43	10 55			11 43	11 56	12 20				12 43	12 55				13 43	13 55
	d	09 16		09 41	10 01					11 00			11 50	12 05				12 35		13 03		13 16	13 35		14 05
Gowerton	d			09x51														12x52					13x45		
Llanelli	a	09 32		09 58	10 16					11 15		12 00	12 06	12 21				12 59		13 19		13 32	13 52		14 20
	d			10 00	10 18					11 17		12 00	12 08	12 22				13 01		13 20			13 53		14 22
Pembrey & Burry Port	d			10 06	10 24					11 23			12 14	12 28				13 07		13 26			13 59		14 28
Kidwelly	d			10x13	10x30									12x34											14x34
Ferryside	d			10x19	10x36									12x40											14x39
Carmarthen	a			10 36	10 53					11 42			12 39	12 55				13 33		13 46			14 27		14 56
	d			10 56						11 47			12 46							13 49			14 38		
Whitland	a			11 10						12 01		12 36	13 03							14 03			14 54		
	d			11 11						12 02		12 36	13 05							14 04			14 54		
Narberth	d			11x20																			15x03		
Kilgetty	d			11x30																			15x12		
Saundersfoot	d			11x32									13 25										15x13		
Tenby	a			11 39									13 35										15 20		
	d			11 45									13 41										15 34		
Penally	d			11x48																			15x37		
Manorbier	d			11 54									13 51										15 43		
Lamphey	d			12x02																			15x51		
Pembroke	d			12 05									14 03										15 54		
Pembroke Dock	a			12 20									14 14										16 09		
Clunderwen	d									12x08										14x10					
Clarbeston Road	d									12x16		12 49								14x18					
Haverfordwest	d									12 24										14 26					
Johnston	d									12x32										14x34					
Milford Haven	a									12 47										14 49					
Fishguard Harbour [ferry]	a											13 17													
	d																								
Rosslare Harbour [ferry]	a																								

A [restaurant] from Bridgend Ø to Cardiff Central

When events are being held at the Millenium Stadium, services are subject to alteration. Please check times before travelling.

Table 128

Saturdays
until 10 September

Cardiff - Maesteg, Swansea and West Wales

		AW		AW	GW	AW	AW	GW	AW	AW	AW	AW		AW	GW	AW	AW	GW	AW	AW	AW	AW		AW	GW
										B						B				B					
					◇1	◇		◇1	◇						◇1			◇1			◇	◇			◇1
					A																				
					🍴Ø	🛒		🍴	🛒						🍴	🛒		🍴		🛒	🛒				🍴
London Paddington 15 ⊖	d				11 45			12 45							13 45			14 45							15 45
Reading 7	d				12 11			13 11							14 11			15 11							16 11
Manchester Piccadilly 10	d					10 30			11 30							12 30				13 30					
Gloucester 7	d			11 58										13 58			14 58								
Bristol Parkway 7	d				13 07			14 07							15 07			16 07							17 07
Newport (South Wales)	d			12 52	13 31	13 37		14 31	14 37					14 52	15 31	15 37	15 52	16 31		16 37	16 56				17 31
Cardiff Central 7	d	13 14		13 18	13 48	14 04	14 21	14 48	15 04			15 14		15 18	15 48	16 04	16 18	16 48		17 04	17 16			17 38	17 48
Pontyclun	d			13 30			14 33							15 30			16 30				17 28				
Llanharan	d			13 35			14 38							15 35			16 35				17 33				
Pencoed	d			13 39			14 42							15 39			16 39				17 37				
Bridgend	d	13 34		13 46	14 09	14 23	14 49	15 09	15 23			15 34		15 46	16 09	16 23	16 46	17 09		17 25	17 44			17 58	18 09
Wildmill	d			13 49			14 52							15 49			16 49				17 47				
Sarn	d			13 52			14 55							15 52			16 52				17 50				
Tondu	d			13 55			14 58							15 55			16 55				17 53				
Garth (Mid Glamorgan)	d			14 05			15 08							16 05			17 05				18 03				
Maesteg (Ewenny Road)	d			14 07			15 10							16 07			17 07				18 05				
Maesteg	a			14 12			15 15							16 12			17 12				18 13				
Pyle	d	13 42										15 42				16 31				17 32				18 06	
Port Talbot Parkway	d	13 50			14 22	14 36		15 22	15 36			15 50			16 22	16 39		17 22		17 40				18 14	18 22
Baglan	d	13 54										15 54								17 42				18 18	
Briton Ferry	d	13 57										15 57								17 46				18 21	
Neath	d	14 01			14 30	14 43		15 30	15 43			16 01			16 30	16 46		17 30		17 50				18 25	18 30
Skewen	d	14 05										16 05								17 54				18 29	
Llansamlet	d	14 09										16 09								17 58				18 33	
Swansea	a	14 20			14 43	14 55		15 43	15 55			16 20			16 43	16 58		17 43		18 05				18 44	18 46
	d					15 00			16 00		16 05					17 05			17 51	18 09		18 21			
Gowerton	d										16x16					17x16			18x01	18x20					
Llanelli	a					15 20			16 15		16 23					17 22			18 08	18 26		18 37			
	d					15 22			16 17		16 24					17 24			18 10	18 28					
Pembrey & Burry Port	d					15 28			16 23		16 30					17 30			18 16	18 33					
Kidwelly	d								16x29		16x37								18x24	18x39					
Ferryside	d								16x34		16x43								18x30	18x45					
Carmarthen	a					15 46			16 51		16 57					17 49			18 46	18 57					
	d					15 49					17 06					17 54				19 02					
Whitland	a					16 03					17 22					18 09				19 18					
	d					16 04					17 32					18 10				19 18					
Narberth	d										17x41									19x28					
Kilgetty	d										17x50									19x38					
Saundersfoot	d										17x51									19x40					
Tenby	a										17 58									19 50					
	d										18 05									19 50					
Penally	d										18x08									19x53					
Manorbier	d										18 14									20 00					
Lamphey	d										18x22									20x07					
Pembroke	d										18 25									20 10					
Pembroke Dock	a										18 40									20 20					
Clunderwen	d					16x10										18x16									
Clarbeston Road	d					16x18										18x24									
Haverfordwest	d					16 26										18 32									
Johnston	d					16x34										18x40									
Milford Haven	a					16 49										18 54									
Fishguard Harbour ⛴	a																								
	d									14 30															
Rosslare Harbour ⛴	a									18 00															

A 🍴 from Bridgend Ø to Cardiff Central

When events are being held at the Millenium Stadium, services are subject to alteration. Please check times before travelling.

Table 128

Saturdays
until 10 September

Cardiff - Maesteg, Swansea and West Wales

		AW	AW	AW	GW	AW	AW	GW		AW	GW	AW	GW	AW	AW	GW	AW	AW		AW	GW
		■ ⊥			◇1 ☕	■ ⊥		◇1 ☕		■ ⊥	◇1 ☕		◇1 ☕			◇1 ☕	◇ ⊥				◇1 ☕
London Paddington 15 ⊖	d				16 45			17 45					18 45			19 45					20 45
Reading 7	d				17 11			18 11					19 11			20 11					21 11
Manchester Piccadilly 10	d	14 30				15 30				16 30							18 30				
Gloucester 7	d		16 58				17 58					18 58			19 58						
Bristol Parkway 7	d				18 07			19 07					20 07			21 07					22 11
Newport (South Wales)	d	17 37	17 52		18 31	18 37	18 52	19 31		19 37		19 52	20 31		20 52	21 31	21 44				22 46
Cardiff Central 7	d	18 04	18 18		18 48	19 04	19 16	19 48		20 04		20 13	20 48	21 04	21 10	21 48	22 06			22 43	23 07
Pontyclun	d		18 30				19 28					20 25			21 22		22 18			22 57	
Llanharan	d		18 35				19 33					20 30			21 27		22 22			23 02	
Pencoed	d		18 39				19 37					20 34			21 30		22 26			23 07	
Bridgend	d	18 25	18 46		19 09	19 23	19 45	20 09		20 23		20 41	21 09	21 23	21 41	22 09	22 32			23 13	23 28
Wildmill	d		18 49				19 48					20 44			21 43						
Sarn	d		18 52				19 51					20 47			21 46						
Tondu	d		18 55				19 54					20 50			21 50						
Garth (Mid Glamorgan)	d		19 05				20 04					21 00			21 59						
Maesteg (Ewenny Road)	d		19 07				20 06					21 02			22 02						
Maesteg	a		19 13				20 11					21 07			22 06						
Pyle	d	18 33				19 30								21 31						23 21	
Port Talbot Parkway	d	18 41			19 22	19 38		20 22		20 36			21 22	21 39		22 22	22 44			23 29	23 41
Baglan	d					19 41														23 33	
Briton Ferry	d					19 44														23 36	
Neath	d	18 49			19 30	19 48		20 30					21 30	21 46		22 30	22 51			23 40	23 49
Skewen	d					19 53														23 44	
Llansamlet	d					19 57														23 48	
Swansea	a	19 02			19 43	20 04		20 43					21 43	21 57		22 43	23 04			23 56	00 02
	d	19 05		19 35		20 08		21 00						22 25			23 10	23 45		00 08	
Gowerton	d	19x16				20x19					←			22x36			23x22			00x19	
Llanelli	a	19 23		19 51		20 25		21 16		21 05	21 16			22 42			23 29	00 01		00s25	
	d	19 24		19 53		20 27		21 16		21 06	21 16			22 44			23 30	00 02			
Pembrey & Burry Port	d	19 30		19 59		20 32		↦		21 12	21 23			22 50			23 36	00 07		00s32	
Kidwelly	d			20x06										22x56			23x42			00x39	
Ferryside	d			20x12										23x01			23x47			00x45	
Carmarthen	a	19 51		20 28		20 55				21 31	21 48			23 18			00 04	00 28		01 03	
	d	19 55				21 00				22 05								00 31			
Whitland	a	20 10				21 15				22 19								00 46			
	d	20 10				21 15				22 20								00 46			
Narberth	d					21x24															
Kilgetty	d					21x33															
Saundersfoot	d					21x35															
Tenby	a					21 42															
	d					21 43															
Penally	d					21x46															
Manorbier	d					21 52															
Lamphey	d					22x00															
Pembroke	d					22 03															
Pembroke Dock	a					22 18															
Clunderwen	d	20x17								22x26											
Clarbeston Road	d	20x25								22x34								01x00			
Haverfordwest	d	20 33								22 42											
Johnston	d	20x41								22x50											
Milford Haven	a	20 56								23 05											
Fishguard Harbour ⛴	a																	01 27			
	d																				
Rosslare Harbour ⛴	a																				

When events are being held at the Millenium Stadium, services are subject to alteration. Please check times before travelling.

Table 128

Saturdays
from 17 September

Cardiff - Maesteg, Swansea and West Wales

		AW	AW	AW	AW	AW	GW	GW	AW	AW		AW	AW	AW	AW	AW	AW	AW	AW	GW		GW	AW	AW	AW
			◇ 🚲	◇			◇[1] ☕	◇[1] ☕	[R]	◇						◇ 🚲		◇		[1]		◇[1]	◇ 🚲	◇	
London Paddington [15] ⊖	d						21p15	22p45																	
Reading [7]	d						21p41	23p11																	
Manchester Piccadilly [10]	d		18p30																						
Gloucester [7]	d																		05 50						
Bristol Parkway [7]	d						22p45	00 16														07 11			
Newport (South Wales)	d		21p52				23p19	00 38											06 44			07 32	07 38		08 01
Cardiff Central [7]	d	21p04	22p09			23p15	23p43	00 55								05 39	05 51	06 42	07 04			07 48	07 58	08 09	08 22
Pontyclun	d		22p21			23p29										05 51	06 03		07 16						08 34
Llanharan	d		22p25			23p34										05 56	06 08		07 21						08 39
Pencoed	d		22p29			23p39										06 01	06 12		07 25						08 43
Bridgend	d	21p27	22p35			23p45	00 02	01 19								06 07	06 20	07 02	07 32			08 08	08 17	08 29	08 51
Wildmill	d																06 22		07 35						08 53
Sarn	d																06 25		07 38						08 56
Tondu	d																06 29		07 41						09 00
Garth (Mid Glamorgan)	d																06 38		07 51						09 09
Maesteg (Ewenny Road)	d																06 41		07 53						09 12
Maesteg	a																06 45		07 58						09 16
Pyle	d	21p34				23p53										06 15		07 10						08 37	
Port Talbot Parkway	d	21p45	22p47			00 01	00 15	01 32								06 23		07 18				08 21	08 30	08 45	
Baglan	d					00 05										06 27		07 22						08 49	
Briton Ferry	d					00 09										06 30		07 25						08 52	
Neath	d	21p52	22p54			00 13	00 22	01 39								06 34		07 29				08 30	08 37	08 56	
Skewen	d					00 16										06 38		07 33						09 00	
Llansamlet	d					00 20										06 42		07 37						09 04	
Swansea	a	22p04	23p07			00 28	00 37	01 53								06 51		07 45				08 44	08 51	09 13	
	d	22p27	23p11	23p45	00 05	00 45				04 36					05 50	06 53		07 50		08 15			09 02	09 16	
Gowerton	d	22b41	23b22	23b55	00x16	00x56									06x00			08x00					09x16		
Llanelli	a	22p47	23p29	00 03	00 23	01s02				04 52					06 07	07 10		08 07		08 31			09 22	09 32	
	d	22p49	23p30	00 04	00 25										06 09	07 10		08 08		08 36			09 24		
Pembrey & Burry Port	d	22p54	23p36	00 09	00 31	01s09									06 15	07 16		08 14		08 43			09 30		
Kidwelly	d	23b00	23b42		00x38	01x16									06x22	07x22		08x20					09x36		
Ferryside	d	23b06	23b47		00x44	01x22									06x28	07x28		08x26					09x41		
Carmarthen	a	23p18	00 04	00 31	01 00	01 40									06 42	07 42		08 40		09 08			09 53		
	d	23p21		00 33								04 53	05 43	05 58	06 43	07 44		08 53					09 57		
Whitland	a	23p35		00 48								05 06	05 59	06 13	07 00	07 58		09 09					10 11		
	d	23p36		00 49								05 06	05 59	06 13	07 00	07 58		09 09					10 12		
Narberth	d												06x08		07x09			09x18							
Kilgetty	d												06x18		07x19			09x28							
Saundersfoot	d												06x20		07x21			09x30							
Tenby	a												06 27		07 28			09 37							
	d												06 30		07 42			09 43							
Penally	d												06x33		07x45			09x46							
Manorbier	d												06 40		07 52			09 53							
Lamphey	d												06x47		07x59			10x00							
Pembroke	d												06 50		08 02			10 03							
Pembroke Dock	a												07 05		08 17			10 17							
Clunderwen	d	23b42										05x13		06x19		08 05							10x18		
Clarbeston Road	d	23b51		01x02								05x21		06x27		08x12							10x26		
Haverfordwest	d	23p59										05 32		06 35		08 21							10 34		
Johnston	d	00x07										05x40		06x43		08x29							10x42		
Milford Haven	a	00 22										05 55		06 58		08 46							10 55		
Fishguard Harbour ⛴	a			01 29																					
	d								02 45																
Rosslare Harbour ⛴	a								06 15																

b Previous night, stops on request

When events are being held at the Millenium Stadium, services are subject to alteration. Please check times before travelling.

Table 128

Saturdays

from 17 September

Cardiff - Maesteg, Swansea and West Wales

		AW	AW	AW	AW	GW		AW	AW	GW	AW	AW	AW	AW	AW	GW		AW	AW	AW	GW	AW	AW	AW	AW
			◇			◇ 1		◇		◇ 1	◇		◇			◇ 1		◇		◇	◇ 1 A		◇		
London Paddington 15 ⊖	d					07 45				08 45						09 45					10 45				
Reading 7	d					08 11				09 11						10 11					11 11				
Manchester Piccadilly 10	d							06 30					07 30					08 30					09 30		
Gloucester 7	d				07 58				08 58										10 58						11 58
Bristol Parkway 7	d					09 07				10 07						11 07					12 07				
Newport (South Wales)	d		08 33		08 52	09 31		09 38	09 52	10 31			10 36			11 31		11 37	11 52		12 31		12 37		12 52
Cardiff Central 7	d		09 04	09 14	09 18	09 48		10 04	10 18	10 48	10 54		11 04	11 14	11 21	11 48		12 04	12 18		12 48		13 04	13 14	13 18
Pontyclun	d				09 30				10 30						11 33				12 30						13 30
Llanharan	d				09 35				10 35						11 38				12 35						13 35
Pencoed	d				09 39				10 39						11 42				12 39						13 39
Bridgend	d		09 23	09 34	09 46	10 09		10 23	10 46	11 09			11 23	11 34	11 49	12 09		12 23	12 46		13 09		13 23	13 34	13 46
Wildmill	d				09 49				10 49						11 52				12 49						13 49
Sarn	d				09 52				10 52						11 55				12 52						13 52
Tondu	d				09 55				10 55						11 58				12 55						13 55
Garth (Mid Glamorgan)	d				10 05				11 05						12 08				13 05						14 05
Maesteg (Ewenny Road)	d				10 07				11 07						12 10				13 07						14 07
Maesteg	a				10 12				11 12						12 15				13 12						14 12
Pyle	d			09 43										11 42										13 42	
Port Talbot Parkway	d		09 38	09 52		10 22		10 35		11 22			11 36	11 50		12 22		12 36			13 22		13 36	13 50	
Baglan	d			09 55										11 54										13 54	
Briton Ferry	d			09 59										11 57										13 57	
Neath	d		09 45	10 03		10 30		10 42		11 30			11 43	12 01		12 30		12 43			13 30		13 43	14 01	
Skewen	d			10 06										12 05										14 05	
Llansamlet	d			10 10										12 09										14 09	
Swansea	a		09 57	10 21		10 43		10 55		11 43			11 56	12 20		12 43		12 55			13 43		13 55	14 20	
	d	09 41	10 01					11 00				11 50	12 05					13 03		13 16		13 50	14 05		
Gowerton	d	09x51										12x00										14x00			
Llanelli	a	09 58	10 16					11 15			12 00	12 07	12 21					13 19		13 32		14 07	14 20		
	d	10 00	10 18					11 17			12 00	12 09	12 22					13 20				14 09	14 22		
Pembrey & Burry Port	d	10 06	10 24					11 23				12 15	12 28					13 26				14 15	14 28		
Kidwelly	d	10x13	10x30										12x34										14x34		
Ferryside	d	10x19	10x36										12x40										14x39		
Carmarthen	a	10 36	10 53					11 42				12 39	12 55					13 46				14 39	14 56		
	d	10 56						11 47				12 56						13 49				14 56			
Whitland	a	11 10						12 01			12 36	13 10						14 03				15 10			
	d	11 11						12 02			12 36	13 11						14 04				15 11			
Narberth	d	11x20										13x20										15x20			
Kilgetty	d	11x30										13x30										15x30			
Saundersfoot	d	11x32										13x32										15x32			
Tenby	a	11 39										13 39										15 39			
	d	11 45										13 45										15 45			
Penally	d	11x48										13x48										15x48			
Manorbier	d	11 54										13 54										15 54			
Lamphey	d	12x02										14x02										16x02			
Pembroke	d	12 05										14 05										16 05			
Pembroke Dock	a	12 20										14 19										16 20			
Clunderwen	d							12x08										14x10							
Clarbeston Road	d							12x16			12 49							14x18							
Haverfordwest	d							12 24										14 26							
Johnston	d							12x32										14x34							
Milford Haven	a							12 47										14 49							
Fishguard Harbour	a										13 17														
	d																								
Rosslare Harbour	a																								

A from Bridgend to Cardiff Central

When events are being held at the Millenium Stadium, services are subject to alteration. Please check times before travelling.

Table 128

Saturdays

from 17 September

Cardiff - Maesteg, Swansea and West Wales

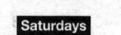

		GW		AW	AW	GW	AW	AW	AW	AW	AW	GW		AW	AW	GW	AW	AW	AW	AW	AW	GW		AW	AW
								R						R				R						R	
		◇1		◇		◇1	◇					◇1				◇1			◇	◇		◇1			
		A																							
		🍴⊘		🛒		🍴	🛒					🍴		🛒		🍴		🛒	🛒			🍴		🛒	
London Paddington 15 ⊖	d	11 45				12 45						13 45				14 45						15 45			
Reading 7	d	12 11				13 11						14 11				15 11						16 11			
Manchester Piccadilly 10	d			10 30			11 30							12 30				13 30						14 30	
Gloucester 7	d										13 58				14 58										16 58
Bristol Parkway 7	d	13 07				14 07						15 07				16 07						17 07			
Newport (South Wales)	d	13 31		13 37		14 31	14 37				14 52	15 31		15 37	15 52	16 31		16 37	16 56			17 31		17 37	17 52
Cardiff Central 7	d	13 48		14 04	14 21	14 48	15 04			15 14	15 18	15 48		16 04	16 18	16 48		17 04	17 16		17 38	17 48		18 04	18 18
Pontyclun	d				14 33						15 30				16 30				17 28						18 30
Llanharan	d				14 38						15 35				16 35				17 33						18 35
Pencoed	d				14 42						15 39				16 39				17 37						18 39
Bridgend	d	14 09		14 23	14 49	15 09	15 23			15 34	15 46	16 09		16 23	16 46	17 09		17 25	17 44		17 58	18 09		18 25	18 46
Wildmill	d				14 52						15 49				16 49				17 47						18 49
Sarn	d				14 55						15 52				16 52				17 50						18 52
Tondu	d				14 58						15 55				16 55				17 53						18 55
Garth (Mid Glamorgan)	d				15 08						16 05				17 05				18 03						19 05
Maesteg (Ewenny Road)	d				15 10						16 07				17 07				18 05						19 07
Maesteg	a				15 15						16 12				17 12				18 13						19 13
Pyle	d									15 42				16 31				17 32			18 06			18 33	
Port Talbot Parkway	d	14 22		14 36		15 22	15 36			15 50		16 22		16 39		17 22		17 40			18 14	18 22		18 41	
Baglan	d									15 54								17 42			18 18				
Briton Ferry	d									15 57								17 46			18 21				
Neath	d	14 30		14 43		15 30	15 43			16 01		16 30		16 46		17 30		17 50			18 25	18 30		18 49	
Skewen	d									16 05								17 54			18 29				
Llansamlet	d									16 09								17 58			18 33				
Swansea	a	14 43		14 55		15 43	15 55			16 20		16 43		16 58		17 43		18 05			18 44	18 46		19 02	
	d			15 00			16 00		16 05					17 05			17 51	18 09		18 21				19 05	
Gowerton	d								16x16					17x16			18x01	18x20						19x16	
Llanelli	a			15 20			16 15		16 23					17 22			18 08	18 26		18 37				19 23	
	d			15 22			16 17		16 24					17 24			18 10	18 28						19 24	
Pembrey & Burry Port	d			15 28			16 23		16 30					17 30			18 16	18 33						19 30	
Kidwelly	d						16x29										18x24	18x39							
Ferryside	d						16x34										18x30	18x45							
Carmarthen	a			15 46			16 51		16 54					17 49			18 46	18 57						19 51	
	d			15 49					16 56					17 54				19 02						19 55	
Whitland	a			16 03					17 10					18 09				19 18						20 10	
	d			16 04					17 11					18 10				19 18						20 10	
Narberth	d								17x20									19x28							
Kilgetty	d								17x30									19x38							
Saundersfoot	d								17x32									19x40							
Tenby	a								17 38									19 50							
	d								17 45									19 50							
Penally	d								17x48									19x53							
Manorbier	d								17 54									20 00							
Lamphey	d								18x02									20x07							
Pembroke	d								18 05									20 10							
Pembroke Dock	a								18 19									20 20							
Clunderwen	d			16x10										18x16										20x17	
Clarbeston Road	d			16x18										18x24										20x25	
Haverfordwest	d			16 26										18 32										20 33	
Johnston	d			16x34										18x40										20x41	
Milford Haven	a			16 49										18 54										20 56	
Fishguard Harbour ⛴	a																								
	d							14 30																	
Rosslare Harbour ⛴	a							18 00																	

A 🍴 from Bridgend ⊘ to Cardiff Central

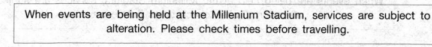

When events are being held at the Millenium Stadium, services are subject to alteration. Please check times before travelling.

Table 128

Saturdays
from 17 September

Cardiff - Maesteg, Swansea and West Wales

		AW	GW	AW	AW	GW	AW	GW	AW	GW	AW	AW	GW	GW	AW	AW	AW	GW
			◇1 🍴	R 🛒		◇1 🍴	R 🛒	◇1 🍴		◇1 🍴			◇1 🍴	◇1 🍴	◇ 🛒			◇1 🍴
London Paddington 15 ⊖	d		16 45			17 45				18 45			19 15	19 45				20 45
Reading 7	d		17 11			18 11				19 11			19 41	20 11				21 11
Manchester Piccadilly 10	d			15 30			16 30								18 30			
Gloucester 7	d				17 58				18 58			19 58						
Bristol Parkway 7	d		18 07			19 07				20 07			20 40	21 07				22 11
Newport (South Wales)	d		18 31	18 37	18 52	19 31	19 37		19 52	20 31		20 52	21 07	21 31	21 44			22 46
Cardiff Central 7	d		18 48	19 04	19 16	19 48	20 04		20 13	20 48	21 04	21 10	21 23	21 48	22 06		22 43	23 07
Pontyclun	d				19 28				20 25			21 22			22 18		22 57	
Llanharan	d				19 33				20 30			21 27			22 22		23 02	
Pencoed	d				19 37				20 34			21 30			22 26		23 07	
Bridgend	d		19 09	19 23	19 45	20 09	20 23		20 41	21 09	21 23	21 41	21 46	22 09	22 32		23 13	23 28
Wildmill	d				19 48				20 44			21 43						
Sarn	d				19 51				20 47			21 46						
Tondu	d				19 54				20 50			21 50						
Garth (Mid Glamorgan)	d				20 04				21 00			21 59						
Maesteg (Ewenny Road)	d				20 06				21 02			22 02						
Maesteg	a				20 11				21 07			22 06						
Pyle	d			19 30							21 31						23 21	
Port Talbot Parkway	d		19 22	19 38		20 22	20 36			21 22	21 39		21 59	22 22	22 44		23 29	23 41
Baglan	d			19 41													23 33	
Briton Ferry	d			19 44													23 36	
Neath	d		19 30	19 48		20 30				21 30	21 46		22 07	22 30	22 51		23 40	23 49
Skewen	d			19 53													23 44	
Llansamlet	d			19 57													23 48	
Swansea	a		19 43	20 04		20 43				21 43	21 57		22 19	22 43	23 04		23 56	00 02
	d	19 35		20 08		21 00					22 25				23 10	23 45	00 08	
Gowerton	d			20x19				←			22x36				23x22		00x19	
Llanelli	a	19 51		20 25		21 16	21 05	21 16			22 42				23 29	00 01	00s25	
	d	19 53		20 27		21 16	21 06	21 16			22 44				23 30	00 02		
Pembrey & Burry Port	d	19 59		20 32		→	21 12	21 23			22 50				23 36	00 07	00s32	
Kidwelly	d	20x06									22x56				23x42		00x39	
Ferryside	d	20x12									23x01				23x47		00x45	
Carmarthen	a	20 28		20 55			21 31	21 48			23 18				00 04	00 28	01 03	
	d			21 00			22 05									00 31		
Whitland	a			21 15			22 19									00 46		
	d			21 15			22 20									00 46		
Narberth	d			21x24														
Kilgetty	d			21x33														
Saundersfoot	d			21x35														
Tenby	a			21 42														
	d			21 43														
Penally	d			21x46														
Manorbier	d			21 52														
Lamphey	d			22x00														
Pembroke	d			22 03														
Pembroke Dock	a			22 18														
Clunderwen	d						22x26											
Clarbeston Road	d						22x34									01x00		
Haverfordwest	d						22 42											
Johnston	d						22x50											
Milford Haven	a						23 05											
Fishguard Harbour ⛴	a															01 27		
	d																	
Rosslare Harbour ⛴	a																	

When events are being held at the Millenium Stadium, services are subject to alteration. Please check times before travelling.

Table 128

Cardiff - Maesteg, Swansea and West Wales

Sundays
until 19 June

		AW	AW	AW	GW	AW	AW	AW	AW	AW	AW	AW	GW	AW	GW	AW	GW	AW	GW	AW	AW	AW	GW
						R														R	R		
		◇			◇1			◇			◇	◇	◇1	◇	◇1		◇1		◇1			◇	◇1
		A	A	A	A																		
		bike			catering						bike		catering	bike	catering		catering		catering	bike			catering
London Paddington 15 ⊖	d				20p45								08 30		09 30		10 30		11 30				12 30
Reading 7	d				21p11								09 11		10 06		11 05		12 06				13 05
Manchester Piccadilly 10	d	18p30																		10 30			
Gloucester 7	d																						
Bristol Parkway 7	d				22p11								10 11		11 06		12 04		13 06				14 04
Newport (South Wales)	d	21p44			22p46						09 27		10 36		11 32		12 32		13 35	13 29			14 32
Cardiff Central 7	d	22p06		22p43	23p07			07 10			09 50		10 57	11 25	11 52	12 05	12 52		13 56	14 02			14 52
Pontyclun	d	22p18		22p57							10 03									14 15			
Llanharan	d	22p22		23p02							10 08									14 20			
Pencoed	d	22p26		23p07							10 13									14 25			
Bridgend	d	22p32		23p13	23p28			07 31			10 20		11 17	11 45	12 12	12 26	13 14		14 18	14 32			15 14
Wildmill	d																						
Sarn	d																						
Tondu	d																						
Garth (Mid Glamorgan)	d																						
Maesteg (Ewenny Road)	d																						
Maesteg	a																						
Pyle	d			23p21							10 28					12 34				14 40			
Port Talbot Parkway	d	22p44		23p29	23p41			07 45			10 37		11 30	11 59	12 25	12 43	13 27		14 31	14 48			15 27
Baglan	d			23p33																			
Briton Ferry	d			23p36																			
Neath	d	22p51		23p40	23p49			07 53			10 45		11 39	12 07	12 34		13 34		14 38	14 56			15 34
Skewen	d			23p44																			
Llansamlet	d			23p48																			
Swansea	a	23p04		23p56	00ʃ02			08 06			10 58		11 51	12 19	12 46		13 47		14 51	15 09			15 47
	d	23p10	23p45	00ʃ08				08 15			11 01	11 06		12 26	12 59			14 11	14 58	15 12		15 26	
Gowerton	d	23b22		00x19				08x26				11x16		12x36				14x22				15x36	
Llanelli	a	23p29	00ʃ01	00s25				08 33			11 17	11 23		12 43	13 15	13 23		14 29	15 14	15 28		15 43	
	d	23p30	00ʃ02					08 35			11 19			12 43	13 16	13 23		14 31	15 15	15 29			
Pembrey & Burry Port	d	23p36	00ʃ07	00s32				08 41			11 25			12 49	13 23	13 29		14 37	15 22	15 35			
Kidwelly	d	23b42		00x39				08x48			11x32			12x55				14x43					
Ferryside	d	23b47		00x45				08x54			11x38			13x01				14x49					
Carmarthen	a	00ʃ04	00ʃ28	01ʃ03				09 07			11 51			13 15	13 44	13 56		15 04	15 43	15 58			
	d		00ʃ31				08 20	09 10	09 55	10 19	11 55			13 18		14 04		15 07		16 03			
Whitland	a		00ʃ46				08 36	09 26	10 11	10 34	12 11			13 33		14 20		15 21		16 19			
	d		00ʃ46				08 36	09 26	10 11	10 34	12 11			13 34		14 20		15 22		16 20			
Narberth	d							09x35		10x43								15x31					
Kilgetty	d							09x45		10x52								15x41					
Saundersfoot	d							09x47		10x54								15x43					
Tenby	a							09 54		11 01								15 50					
	d							09 56		11 17								15 54					
Penally	d							09x59		11x20								15x57					
Manorbier	d							10 06		11 26								16 03					
Lamphey	d							10x14		11x34								16x11					
Pembroke	d							10 17		11 37								16 14					
Pembroke Dock	a							10 32		11 52								16 29					
Clunderwen	d						08x44		10x19		12x19					14x28				16x28			
Clarbeston Road	d		01x00				08x52		10x27		12x27			13 49		14x36				16x36			
Haverfordwest	d						09 00		10 35		12 35					14 44				16 44			
Johnston	d						09x09		10x44		12x44					14x53				16x53			
Milford Haven	a						09 20		10 55		12 59					15 08				17 08			
Fishguard Harbour ⛴	a		01ʃ27											14 14									
	d					02 45															14 30		
Rosslare Harbour ⛴	a					06 15															18 00		

A not 22 May

b Previous night, stops on request

When events are being held at the Millenium Stadium, services are subject to alteration. Please check times before travelling.

Table 128

Sundays
until 19 June

Cardiff - Maesteg, Swansea and West Wales

		AW	GW	AW	GW	AW	GW	AW	GW	AW	AW	GW	AW	GW	GW	AW	GW	GW
				■				■										
			◇1		◇1		◇1		◇1			◇1	◇	◇1	◇1	◇	◇1	◇1
			☕	🛒	☕		☕	🛒	☕			☕		☕	☕		☕	☕
London Paddington 15 ⊖	d		13 37		14 37		15 37		16 37			17 37		18 37	19 37		20 37	21 37
Reading 7	d		14 12		15 17		16 18		17 14			18 17		19 15	20 17		21 16	22 15
Manchester Piccadilly 10	d			12 30				14 30										
Gloucester 7	d																	
Bristol Parkway 7	d		15 11		16 14		17 16		18 13			19 16		20 14	21 16		22 15	23 17
Newport (South Wales)	d		15 37	15 46	16 40		17 44	17 34	18 42			19 42		20 40	21 44		22 40	23 45
Cardiff Central 7	d		15 57	16 16	17 00		18 02	18 06	18 59			20 01	20 15	21 00	22 08	22 30	23 02	00 08
Pontyclun	d							18 21										
Llanharan	d							18 26										
Pencoed	d							18 30										
Bridgend	d		16 19	16 37	17 22		18 24	18 38	19 21			20 23	20 37	21 21	22 30	22 51	23 23	00 30
Wildmill	d																	
Sarn	d																	
Tondu	d																	
Garth (Mid Glamorgan)	d																	
Maesteg (Ewenny Road)	d																	
Maesteg	a																	
Pyle	d			16 45				18 46					20 45					
Port Talbot Parkway	d		16 32	16 54	17 35		18 37	18 54	19 34			20 36	20 54	21 35	22 42	23 05	23 37	00 43
Baglan	d																	
Briton Ferry	d																	
Neath	d		16 39	17 02	17 42		18 45	19 02	19 41			20 44	21 02	21 42	22 51	23 13	23 44	00 50
Skewen	d																	
Llansamlet	d																	
Swansea	a		16 52	17 14	17 56		18 57	19 15	19 54			20 58	21 14	21 55	23 03	23 25	23 57	01 03
	d	16 26	17 05	17 25		18 11		19 19			20 35		21 18			23 38		
Gowerton	d	16x37				18x22					20x46					23x49		
Llanelli	a	16 44	17 21	17 41		18 29		19 35			20 54		21 34			23 56		
	d	16 46	17 22	17 41		18 31		19 36			20 55		21 34			23 58		
Pembrey & Burry Port	d	16 52	17 29	17 48		18 37		19 43			21 01		21 41			00 04		
Kidwelly	d	16x59				18x44					21x08					00x11		
Ferryside	d	17x05				18x50					21x14					00x17		
Carmarthen	a	17 19	17 50	18 14		19 03		20 05			21 30		22 04			00 30		
	d	17 32		18 20		19 06		20 07					22 05			00 34		
Whitland	a	17 48		18 36		19 22		20 23					22 21			00 50		
	d	17 48		18 37		19 22		20 30		20 33			22 22			00 50		
Narberth	d	17x57								20x42								
Kilgetty	d	18x07								20x51								
Saundersfoot	d	18x09								20x53								
Tenby	a	18 16								21 00								
	d	18 19								21 04								
Penally	d	18x22								21x07								
Manorbier	d	18 29								21 13								
Lamphey	d	18x36								21x21								
Pembroke	d	18 40								21 24								
Pembroke Dock	a	18 55								21 39								
Clunderwen	d			18x45		19x30		20x37					22x29					
Clarbeston Road	d			18x53		19x38		20x45					22x37			01x03		
Haverfordwest	d			19 01		19a51		20 54					22 46					
Johnston	d			19x10				21x02					22x54					
Milford Haven	a			19 25				21 19					23 10					
Fishguard Harbour ⛴	a															01 30		
	d																	
Rosslare Harbour ⛴	a																	

When events are being held at the Millenium Stadium, services are subject to alteration. Please check times before travelling.

Table 128

Sundays
26 June to 31 July

Cardiff - Maesteg, Swansea and West Wales

		AW	AW	AW	GW	AW	AW	AW	AW	AW		AW	AW	GW	AW	AW	GW	GW	AW	AW		GW	AW	AW	GW
		◇			◇1	R		◇				◇	◇	◇1	◇		◇1	◇1		B		◇1	R	◇	◇1
London Paddington 15 ⊖	d				20p45									07 57			09 30	10 30				11 30			12 30
Reading 7	d				21p11									08 34			10 05	11 05				12 06			13 05
Manchester Piccadilly 10	d	18p30																		10 30					
Gloucester 7	d																								
Bristol Parkway 7	d				22p11									10 08			11 26	12 27				13 29			14 33
Newport (South Wales)	d	21p44			22p46							09 27		10 33			11 55	12 55		13 29		13 54			15 00
Cardiff Central 7	d	22p06		22p43	23p07			07 10				09 50		10 55	11 25	12 05	12 12	13 14		13 46		14 14			15 19
Pontyclun	d	22p18		22p57								10 03								14 00					
Llanharan	d	22p22		23p02								10 08								14 05					
Pencoed	d	22p26		23p07								10 13								14 09					
Bridgend	d	22p32		23p13	23p28			07 31				10 20		11 15	11 45	12 26	12 32	13 35		14 16		14 36			15 40
Wildmill	d																								
Sarn	d																								
Tondu	d																								
Garth (Mid Glamorgan)	d																								
Maesteg (Ewenny Road)	d																								
Maesteg	a																								
Pyle	d			23p21								10 28				12 34				14 24					
Port Talbot Parkway	d	22p44		23p29	23p41			07 45				10 37		11 28	11 59	12 43	12 47	13 48		14 33		14 49			15 53
Baglan	d			23p33																					
Briton Ferry	d			23p36																					
Neath	d	22p51		23p40	23p49			07 53				10 45		11 36	12 07		12 56	13 56		14 41		14 57			16 01
Skewen	d			23p44																					
Llansamlet	d			23p48																					
Swansea	a	23p04		23p56	00 02			08 06				10 58		11 49	12 19		13 08	14 08		14 53		15 09			16 13
	d	23p10	23p45	00 08				08 15				11 01	11 06		12 26		13 15		14 15	15 00		15 16		15 26	16 21
Gowerton	d	23b22		00x19				08x26					11x16		12x36				14x26					15x36	
Llanelli	a	23p29	00 01	00s25				08 33				11 17	11 23		12 43	13 12	13 31		14 33	15 16		15 32		15 43	16 37
	d	23p30	00 02					08 35				11 19			12 43	13 12	13 32		14 35	15 16		15 33			16 38
Pembrey & Burry Port	d	23p36	00 07	00s32				08 41				11 25			12 49	13 18	13 39		14 41	15 23		15 40			16 45
Kidwelly	d	23b42		00x39				08x48				11x32			12x55				14x47						
Ferryside	d	23b47		00x45				08x54				11x38			13x01				14x53						
Carmarthen	a	00 04	00 28	01 03				09 07				11 51			13 15	13 44	14 00		15 08	15 46		16 01			17 06
	d		00 31				08 20	09 10	09 55	10 19		11 55			13 18	14 04			15 18	16 03					
Whitland	a		00 46				08 36	09 26	10 11	10 34		12 11			13 33	14 20			15 32	16 19					
	d		00 46				08 36	09 26	10 11	10 34		12 11			13 34	14 20			15 33	16 20					
Narberth	d							09x35		10x43									15x42						
Kilgetty	d							09x45		10x52									15x52						
Saundersfoot	d							09x47		10x54									15x54						
Tenby	a							09 54		11 01									16 01						
	d							09 56		11 17									16 05						
Penally	d							09x59		11x20									16x08						
Manorbier	d							10 06		11 26									16 14						
Lamphey	d							10x14		11x34									16x22						
Pembroke	d							10 17		11 37									16 25						
Pembroke Dock	a							10 32		11 52									16 40						
Clunderwen	d						08x44		10x19			12x19				14x28				16x28					
Clarbeston Road	d		01x00				08x52		10x27			12x27			13 49	14x36				16x36					
Haverfordwest	d						09 00		10 35			12 35				14 44				16 44					
Johnston	d						09x09		10x44			12x44				14x53				16x53					
Milford Haven	a						09 20		10 55			12 59				15 08				17 08					
Fishguard Harbour ⛴	a		01 27												14 14										
	d					02 45																	14 30		
Rosslare Harbour ⛴	a					06 15																	18 00		

b Previous night, stops on request

When events are being held at the Millenium Stadium, services are subject to alteration. Please check times before travelling.

Table 128

Sundays

26 June to 31 July

Cardiff - Maesteg, Swansea and West Wales

		AW	AW	GW	GW	AW	AW	GW	GW	AW	AW	GW	AW	GW	GW	AW	GW	GW
			■				■											
				◇1	◇1			◇1	◇1			◇1	◇	◇1	◇1	◇	◇1	◇1
			trolley	restaurant	restaurant		trolley	restaurant	restaurant			restaurant		restaurant	restaurant		restaurant	restaurant
London Paddington 15 ⊖	d			13 30	14 30			15 30	16 30			17 30		18 30	19 30		20 30	21 30
Reading 7	d			14 05	15 10			16 05	17 10			18 05		19 15	20 05		21 05	22 08
Manchester Piccadilly 10	d		12 30				14 30											
Gloucester 7	d																	
Bristol Parkway 7	d			15 32	16 32			17 32	18 32			19 26		20 36	21 34		22 34	23 37
Newport (South Wales)	d		15 46	15 59	16 56		17 34	18 01	18 59			19 53		21 03	22 01		23 05	00 02
Cardiff Central 7	d		16 03	16 17	17 16		18e01	18 21	19 17			20 09	20 15	21 22	22 23	22 30	23 28	00 25
Pontyclun	d						18 15											
Llanharan	d						18 20											
Pencoed	d						18 25											
Bridgend	d		16 24	16 40	17 38		18 32	18 42	19 39			20 32	20 37	21 42	22 46	22 51	23 49	00 46
Wildmill	d																	
Sarn	d																	
Tondu	d																	
Garth (Mid Glamorgan)	d																	
Maesteg (Ewenny Road)	d																	
Maesteg	a																	
Pyle	d		16 32				18 40						20 45					
Port Talbot Parkway	d		16 41	16 53	17 51		18 49	18 55	19 52			20 46	20 54	22 00	22 58	23 05	00 03	00 59
Baglan	d																	
Briton Ferry	d																	
Neath	d		16 49	16 59	17 58		18 57	19 03	20 00			20 54	21 02	22 08	23 06	23 13	00 10	01 07
Skewen	d																	
Llansamlet	d																	
Swansea	a		17 01	17 13	18 12		19 09	19 16	20 13			21 07	21 14	22 21	23 19	23 25	00 23	01 19
	d	16 25	17 09	17 25		18 17	19 22				20 35		21 18			23 38		
Gowerton	d	16x36				18x28					20x46					23x49		
Llanelli	a	16 43	17 25	17 41		18 35	19 38				20 54		21 34			23 56		
	d	16 45	17 25	17 43		18 37	19 39				20 55		21 34			23 58		
Pembrey & Burry Port	d	16 51	17 32	17 49		18 43	19 46				21 01		21 41			00 04		
Kidwelly	d	16x58				18x50					21x08					00x11		
Ferryside	d	17x04				18x56					21x14					00x17		
Carmarthen	a	17 18	17 55	18 15		19 09	20 08				21 30		22 04			00 30		
	d	17 32	17 57			19 12	20 09						22 05			00 34		
Whitland	a	17 48	18 13			19 28	20 25						22 21			00 50		
	d	17 48	18 15			19 28	20 30			20 33			22 22			00 50		
Narberth	d	17x57								20x42								
Kilgetty	d	18x07								20x51								
Saundersfoot	d	18x09								20x53								
Tenby	a	18 16								21 00								
	d	18 19								21 04								
Penally	d	18x22								21x07								
Manorbier	d	18 29								21 13								
Lamphey	d	18x36								21x21								
Pembroke	d	18 40								21 24								
Pembroke Dock	a	18 55								21 39								
Clunderwen	d		18x22			19x36	20x37						22x29					
Clarbeston Road	d		18x30			19x44	20x45						22x37			01x03		
Haverfordwest	d		18 39			19a57	20 54						22 46					
Johnston	d		18x47				21x02						22x54					
Milford Haven	a		19 02				21 19						23 10					
Fishguard Harbour ⛴	a															01 30		
	d																	
Rosslare Harbour ⛴	a																	

When events are being held at the Millenium Stadium, services are subject to alteration. Please check times before travelling.

Table 128

Sundays

7 August to 11 September

Cardiff - Maesteg, Swansea and West Wales

		AW	AW	AW	GW	AW	AW	AW	AW	AW	AW	AW	GW	AW	AW	GW	GW	AW	GW	AW	AW	AW	GW
						B														■	B		
		◇			◇1			◇			◇	◇	◇1	◇		◇1	◇1		◇1			◇	◇1
		⊼			⊏						⊼		⊏	⊼		⊏	⊏		⊏	⊼			⊏
London Paddington 15 ⊖	d				20p45								08 30			09 42	10 37		11 37				12 37
Reading 7	d				21p11								09 06			10 21	11 15		12 15				13 16
Manchester Piccadilly 10	d	18p30																		10 30			
Gloucester 7	d																						
Bristol Parkway 7	d				22p11								10 08			11 20	12 15		13 15				14 15
Newport (South Wales)	d	21p44			22p46						09 27		10 33			11 49	12 41		13 39	13 29			14 42
Cardiff Central 7	d	22p06		22p43	23p07			07 10			09 50		10 54	11 25	12 05	12 08	13 01		13 57	14 03			15 01
Pontyclun	d	22p18		22p57							10 03									14 17			
Llanharan	d	22p22		23p02							10 08									14 22			
Pencoed	d	22p26		23p07							10 13									14 26			
Bridgend	d	22p32		23p13	23p28			07 31			10 20		11 15	11 45	12 26	12 30	13 22		14 20	14 33			15 23
Wildmill	d																						
Sarn	d																						
Tondu	d																						
Garth (Mid Glamorgan)	d																						
Maesteg (Ewenny Road)	d																						
Maesteg	a																						
Pyle	d			23p21							10 28				12 34					14 41			
Port Talbot Parkway	d	22p44		23p29	23p41			07 45			10 37		11 28	11 59	12 43	12 46	13 35		14 33	14 50			15 36
Baglan	d			23p33																			
Briton Ferry	d			23p36																			
Neath	d	22p51		23p40	23p49			07 53			10 45		11 36	12 07		12 55	13 43		14 39	14 58			15 43
Skewen	d			23p44																			
Llansamlet	d			23p48																			
Swansea	a	23p04		23p56	00 02			08 06			10 58		11 49	12 19		13 07	13 55		14 53	15 10			15 56
	d	23p10	23p45	00 08				08 15			11 01	11 06		12 26		13 17		14 11	14 59	15 13		15 26	
Gowerton	d	23b22		00x19				08x26				11x16		12x36				14x22				15x36	
Llanelli	a	23p29	00 01	00s25				08 33			11 17	11 23		12 43	13 12	13 33		14 29	15 15	15 29		15 43	
	d	23p30	00 02					08 35			11 19			12 43	13 12	13 34		14 31	15 17	15 29			
Pembrey & Burry Port	d	23p36	00 07	00s32				08 41			11 25			12 49	13 18	13 41		14 37	15 23	15 36			
Kidwelly	d	23b42		00x39				08x48			11x32			12x55				14x43					
Ferryside	d	23b47		00x45				08x54			11x38			13x01				14x49					
Carmarthen	a	00 04	00 28	01 03				09 07			11 51			13 15	13 44	14 03		15 04	15 45	15 59			
	d		00 31				08 20	09 10	09 55	10 19	11 55			13 18	14 04			15 07		16 03			
Whitland	a		00 46				08 36	09 26	10 11	10 34	12 11			13 33	14 20			15 21		16 19			
	d		00 46				08 36	09 26	10 11	10 34	12 11			13 34	14 20			15 22		16 20			
Narberth	d							09x35		10x43								15x31					
Kilgetty	d							09x45		10x52								15x41					
Saundersfoot	d							09x47		10x54								15x43					
Tenby	a							09 54		11 01								15 50					
	d							09 56		11 17								15 54					
Penally	d							09x59		11x20								15x57					
Manorbier	d							10 06		11 26								16 03					
Lamphey	d							10x14		11x34								16x11					
Pembroke	d							10 17		11 37								16 14					
Pembroke Dock	a							10 32		11 52								16 29					
Clunderwen	d						08x44		10x19		12x19				14x28					16x28			
Clarbeston Road	d		01x00				08x52		10x27		12x27			13 49	14x36					16x36			
Haverfordwest	d						09 00		10 35		12 35				14 44					16 44			
Johnston	d						09x09		10x44		12x44				14x53					16x53			
Milford Haven	a						09 20		10 55		12 59				15 08					17 08			
Fishguard Harbour ⛴	a		01 27											14 14									
	d					02 45															14 30		
Rosslare Harbour ⛴	a					06 15															18 00		

b Previous night, stops on request

When events are being held at the Millenium Stadium, services are subject to alteration. Please check times before travelling.

Table 128

Sundays

7 August to 11 September

Cardiff - Maesteg, Swansea and West Wales

		AW	GW	AW	GW	AW		GW	AW	GW	AW	AW	GW	AW	GW	GW		AW	GW	GW
				B					B											
			◇1		◇1			◇1		◇1			◇1	◇	◇1	◇1		◇	◇1	◇1
			⊡	🛒	⊡			⊡	🛒	⊡			⊡		⊡	⊡			⊡	⊡
London Paddington 15 ⊖	d		13 37		14 37			15 37		16 37			17 37		18 37	19 37			20 37	21 37
Reading 7	d		14 17		15 15			16 17		17 19			18 17		19 14	20 17			21 17	22 14
Manchester Piccadilly 10	d			12 30					14 30											
Gloucester 7	d																			
Bristol Parkway 7	d		15 16		16 14			17 15		18 19			19 15		20 13	21 16			22 16	23 17
Newport (South Wales)	d		15 42	15 50	16 41			17 43	17 34	18 45			19 41		20 39	21 45			22 44	23 45
Cardiff Central 7	d		16 01	16 16	17 00			18 03	18 07	19 04			20 00	20 15	20 59	22 08		22 30	23 08	00 08
Pontyclun	d								18 21											
Llanharan	d								18 26											
Pencoed	d								18 31											
Bridgend	d		16 23	16 37	17 23			18 24	18 38	19 26			20 22	20 37	21 19	22 30		22 51	23 28	00 30
Wildmill	d																			
Sarn	d																			
Tondu	d																			
Garth (Mid Glamorgan)	d																			
Maesteg (Ewenny Road)	d																			
Maesteg	a																			
Pyle	d			16 45					18 46					20 45						
Port Talbot Parkway	d		16 36	16 54	17 36			18 37	18 55	19 39			20 35	20 54	21 33	22 42		23 05	23 42	00 43
Baglan	d																			
Briton Ferry	d																			
Neath	d		16 43	17 02	17 42			18 45	19 03	19 47			20 43	21 02	21 41	22 51		23 13	23 50	00 50
Skewen	d																			
Llansamlet	d																			
Swansea	a		16 56	17 14	17 57			19 00	19 16	19 59			20 56	21 14	21 53	23 03		23 25	00 02	01 03
	d	16 25	17 06	17 25		18 11			19 19			20 35		21 18				23 38		
Gowerton	d	16x36				18x22						20x46						23x49		
Llanelli	a	16 43	17 22	17 41		18 29			19 35			20 54		21 34				23 56		
	d	16 45	17 23	17 41		18 31			19 37			20 55		21 34				23 58		
Pembrey & Burry Port	d	16 51	17 30	17 48		18 37			19 43			21 01		21 41				00 04		
Kidwelly	d	16x58				18x44						21x08						00x11		
Ferryside	d	17x04				18x50						21x14						00x17		
Carmarthen	a	17 18	17 51	18 17		19 03			20 05			21 30		22 04				00 30		
	d	17 32		18 20		19 06			20 07					22 05				00 34		
Whitland	a	17 48		18 36		19 22			20 23					22 21				00 50		
	d	17 48		18 37		19 22			20 30		20 33			22 22				00 50		
Narberth	d	17x57									20x42									
Kilgetty	d	18x07									20x51									
Saundersfoot	d	18x09									20x53									
Tenby	a	18 16									21 00									
	d	18 19									21 04									
Penally	d	18x22									21x07									
Manorbier	d	18 29									21 13									
Lamphey	d	18x36									21x21									
Pembroke	d	18 40									21 24									
Pembroke Dock	a	18 55									21 39									
Clunderwen	d			18x45		19x30			20x37					22x29						
Clarbeston Road	d			18x53		19x38			20x45					22x37				01x03		
Haverfordwest	d			19 01		19a51			20 54					22 46						
Johnston	d			19x10					21x02					22x54						
Milford Haven	a			19 25					21 19					23 10						
Fishguard Harbour ⛴	a																	01 30		
	d																			
Rosslare Harbour ⛴	a																			

When events are being held at the Millenium Stadium, services are subject to alteration. Please check times before travelling.

Table 128

Sundays

10 September to 23 October

Cardiff - Maesteg, Swansea and West Wales

		AW	AW	AW	GW	AW	AW	AW	AW	GW		AW	GW	AW	GW	AW	GW	AW	AW	AW		GW	AW	GW	AW
						R												R	R						R
		◇			◇1			◇	◇	◇1		◇	◇1		◇1		◇1			◇		◇1		◇1	
		🛒			☕			🛒		☕			☕		☕		☕	🛒				☕		☕	🛒
London Paddington 15 ⊖	d				20p45					08 30			09 42		10 37		11 37					12 37		13 37	
Reading 7	d				21p11					09 06			10 21		11 15		12 15					13 16		14 17	
Manchester Piccadilly 10	d	18p30																10 30							12 30
Gloucester 7	d																								
Bristol Parkway 7	d				22p11					10 08			11 20		12 15		13 15					14 15		15 16	
Newport (South Wales)	d	21p44			22p46			09 27		10 36		11 00	11 49		12 41		13 39	13 29				14 42		15 42	15 50
Cardiff Central 7	d	22p06		22p43	23p07			09 50		10 57		11 18	12 06	12 12	13 01		13 57	14 04				15 01		16 01	16 16
Pontyclun	d	22p18		22p57				10 03										14 17							
Llanharan	d	22p22		23p02				10 08										14 22							
Pencoed	d	22p26		23p07				10 13										14 27							
Bridgend	d	22p32		23p13	23p28			10 20		11 18		11 38	12 26	12 34	13 22		14 20	14 34				15 23		16 23	16 37
Wildmill	d																								
Sarn	d																								
Tondu	d																								
Garth (Mid Glamorgan)	d																								
Maesteg (Ewenny Road)	d																								
Maesteg	a																								
Pyle	d			23p21				10 28						12 42				14 42							16 45
Port Talbot Parkway	d	22p44		23p29	23p41			10 37		11 31		11 52	12 39	12 50	13 35		14 33	14 50				15 36		16 36	16 54
Baglan	d			23p33																					
Briton Ferry	d			23p36																					
Neath	d	22p51		23p40	23p49			10 45		11 39		12 00	12 48		13 43		14 39	14 58				15 43		16 43	17 02
Skewen	d			23p44																					
Llansamlet	d			23p48																					
Swansea	a	23p04		23p56	00 02			10 58		11 52		12 13	13 01		13 55		14 53	15 12				15 56		16 56	17 14
	d	23p10	23p45	00 08				11 01	11 06			12 15	13 07			14 11	14 59	15 15		15 26			16 25	17 06	17 25
Gowerton	d	23b22		00x19					11x16			12x26				14x22				15x36			16x36		
Llanelli	a	23p29	00 01	00s25				11 17	11 23			12 32	13 23	13 29		14 29	15 15	15 31		15 43			16 43	17 22	17 41
	d	23p30	00 02					11 19				12 34	13 25	13 31		14 31	15 17	15 31					16 45	17 23	17 41
Pembrey & Burry Port	d	23p36	00 07	00s32				11 25				12 39	13 31	13 37		14 37	15 23	15 38					16 51	17 30	17 48
Kidwelly	d	23b42		00x39				11x32				12x46				14x43							16x58		
Ferryside	d	23b47		00x45				11x38				12x52				14x49							17x04		
Carmarthen	a	00 04	00 28	01 03				11 51				13 05	13 53	14 03		15 04	15 45	16 01					17 18	17 51	18 17
	d		00 31				09 55	11 55				13 08		14 06		15 07		16 09					17 32		18 20
Whitland	a		00 46				10 11	12 11				13 23		14 22		15 21		16 25					17 48		18 36
	d		00 46				10 11	12 11				13 23		14 22		15 22		16 26					17 48		18 37
Narberth	d															15x31							17x57		
Kilgetty	d															15x41							18x07		
Saundersfoot	d															15x43							18x09		
Tenby	a															15 50							18 16		
	d															15 54							18 19		
Penally	d															15x57							18x22		
Manorbier	d															16 03							18 29		
Lamphey	d															16x11							18x36		
Pembroke	d															16 14							18 40		
Pembroke Dock	a															16 29							18 55		
Clunderwen	d						10x19	12x19						14x30				16x34							18x45
Clarbeston Road	d		01x00				10x27	12x27				13 36		14x38				16x42							18x53
Haverfordwest	d						10 35	12 35						14 46				16 50							19 01
Johnston	d						10x44	12x44						14x55				16x59							19x10
Milford Haven	a						10 55	12 59						15 10				17 14							19 25
Fishguard Harbour ⛴	a		01 27									14 03													
	d					02 45													14 30						
Rosslare Harbour ⛴	a					06 15													18 00						

b Previous night, stops on request

When events are being held at the Millenium Stadium, services are subject to alteration. Please check times before travelling.

Table 128

Sundays

18 September to 23 October

Cardiff - Maesteg, Swansea and West Wales

		GW	AW	GW	AW	GW		AW	AW	GW	AW	GW	GW	AW	GW	GW
		◇1		◇1		◇1				◇1	◇	◇1	◇1	◇	◇1	◇1
London Paddington 15 ⊖	d	14 37		15 37		16 37				17 37		18 37	19 37		20 37	21 37
Reading 7	d	15 15		16 17		17 19				18 17		19 14	20 17		21 17	22 14
Manchester Piccadilly 10	d				14 30											
Gloucester 7	d															
Bristol Parkway 7	d	16 14		17 15		18 19				19 15		20 13	21 16		22 16	23 17
Newport (South Wales)	d	16 41		17 43	17 34	18 45				19 41		20 39	21 45		22 44	23 45
Cardiff Central 7	d	17 00		18 03	18 07	19 04				20 00	20 15	20 59	22 08	22 30	23 08	00 08
Pontyclun	d				18 21											
Llanharan	d				18 26											
Pencoed	d				18 31											
Bridgend	d	17 23		18 24	18 38	19 26				20 22	20 37	21 19	22 30	22 51	23 28	00 30
Wildmill	d															
Sarn	d															
Tondu	d															
Garth (Mid Glamorgan)	d															
Maesteg (Ewenny Road)	d															
Maesteg	a															
Pyle	d				18 46						20 45					
Port Talbot Parkway	d	17 36		18 37	18 55	19 39				20 35	20 54	21 33	22 42	23 05	23 42	00 43
Baglan	d															
Briton Ferry	d															
Neath	d	17 42		18 45	19 03	19 47				20 43	21 02	21 41	22 51	23 13	23 50	00 50
Skewen	d															
Llansamlet	d															
Swansea	a	17 57		19 00	19 16	19 59				20 56	21 14	21 53	23 03	23 25	00 02	01 03
	d		18 11		19 19				20 35		21 18			23 38		
Gowerton	d		18x22						20x46					23x49		
Llanelli	a		18 29		19 35				20 54		21 34			23 56		
	d		18 31		19 37				20 55		21 34			23 58		
Pembrey & Burry Port	d		18 37		19 43				21 01		21 41			00 04		
Kidwelly	d		18x44						21x08					00x11		
Ferryside	d		18x50						21x14					00x17		
Carmarthen	a		19 03		20 05				21 30		22 04			00 30		
	d		19 06		20 07						22 05			00 34		
Whitland	a		19 22		20 23						22 21			00 50		
	d		19 22		20 30			20 33			22 22			00 50		
Narberth	d							20x42								
Kilgetty	d							20x51								
Saundersfoot	d							20x53								
Tenby	a							21 00								
	d							21 04								
Penally	d							21x07								
Manorbier	d							21 13								
Lamphey	d							21x21								
Pembroke	d							21 24								
Pembroke Dock	a							21 39								
Clunderwen	d		19x30		20x37						22x29					
Clarbeston Road	d		19x38		20x45						22x37			01x03		
Haverfordwest	d		19a51		20 54						22 46					
Johnston	d				21x02						22x54					
Milford Haven	a				21 19						23 10					
Fishguard Harbour ⛴	a													01 30		
	d															
Rosslare Harbour ⛴	a															

When events are being held at the Millenium Stadium, services are subject to alteration. Please check times before travelling.

Table 128

Sundays

from 30 October

Cardiff - Maesteg, Swansea and West Wales

		AW	AW	AW	GW	AW	AW	AW	AW	GW		AW	AW	GW	AW	GW	AW	AW	AW	GW		AW	GW	AW	GW
						R											R	R						R	
		◇			◇■1			◇	◇	◇■1		◇		◇■1		◇■1			◇	◇■1			◇■1		◇■1
		⊥o			⊥P			⊥o		⊥P				⊥P		⊥P	⊥o			⊥P			⊥P	⊥o	⊥P
London Paddington ■15 ⊖	d				20p45					08 00				09 30		10 30				11 30			12 30		13 30
Reading ■7	d				21p11					08 34				10 05		11 04				12 05			13 05		14 06
Manchester Piccadilly ■10	d	18p30															10 30							12 30	
Gloucester ■7	d																								
Bristol Parkway ■7	d				22p11					10 20				11 51		12 53				13 51			14 51		15 51
Newport (South Wales)	d	21p44			22p46			09 27		10 44		11 00		12 15		13 16	13 29			14 15			15 16	15 46	16 16
Cardiff Central ■7	d	22p06		22p43	23p07			09 50		11 05		11 18	12 05	12 36		13 38	14 01			14 36			15 41	16 16	16 38
Pontyclun	d	22p18		22p57				10 03									14 14								
Llanharan	d	22p22		23p02				10 08									14 19								
Pencoed	d	22p26		23p07				10 13									14 24								
Bridgend	d	22p32		23p13	23p28			10 20		11 25		11 38	12 26	12 57		13 58	14 31			14 56			16 01	16 37	16 58
Wildmill	d																								
Sarn	d																								
Tondu	d																								
Garth (Mid Glamorgan)	d																								
Maesteg (Ewenny Road)	d																								
Maesteg	a																								
Pyle	d			23p21				10 28					12 34				14 39							16 45	
Port Talbot Parkway	d	22p44		23p29	23p41			10 37		11 38		11 52	12 43	13 10		14 11	14 47			15 11			16 18	16 54	17 11
Baglan	d			23p33																					
Briton Ferry	d			23p36																					
Neath	d	22p51		23p40	23p49			10 45		11 47		12 00		13 18		14 20	14 55			15 20			16 27	17 02	17 20
Skewen	d			23p44																					
Llansamlet	d			23p48																					
Swansea	a	23p04		23p56	00 02			10 58		12 01		12 13		13 31		14 32	15 08			15 34			16 39	17 14	17 32
	d	23p10	23p45	00 08				11 01	11 06			12 15		13 50	14 11		15 10		15 26	15 52		16 25		17 25	17 39
Gowerton	d	23b22		00x19					11x16			12x26			14x22				15x36			16x36			
Llanelli	a	23p29	00 01	00s25				11 17	11 23			12 32	13 12	14 11	14 29		15 26		15 43	16 12		16 43		17 47	17 55
	d	23p30	00 02					11 19				12 34	13 12	14 13	14 31		15 27			16 13		16 45		17 48	17 56
Pembrey & Burry Port	d	23p36	00 07	00s32				11 25				12 39	13 18	14 19	14 37		15 33			16 20		16 51		17 54	18 04
Kidwelly	d	23b42		00x39				11x32				12x46			14x43							16x58			
Ferryside	d	23b47		00x45				11x38				12x52			14x49							17x04			
Carmarthen	a	00 04	00 28	01 03				11 51				13 05	13 44	14 41	15 04		15 56			16 41		17 18		18 17	18 31
	d		00 31				09 55	11 55				13 08	14 04		15 07		16 03					17 32		18 20	
Whitland	a		00 46				10 11	12 11				13 23	14 20		15 21		16 19					17 48		18 36	
	d		00 46				10 11	12 11				13 23	14 20		15 22		16 20					17 48		18 37	
Narberth	d														15x31							17x57			
Kilgetty	d														15x41							18x07			
Saundersfoot	d														15x43							18x09			
Tenby	a														15 50							18 16			
	d														15 54							18 19			
Penally	d														15x57							18x22			
Manorbier	d														16 03							18 29			
Lamphey	d														16x11							18x36			
Pembroke	d														16 14							18 40			
Pembroke Dock	a														16 29							18 55			
Clunderwen	d						10x19	12x19					14x28				16x28							18x45	
Clarbeston Road	d		01x00				10x27	12x27				13 36	14x36				16x36							18x53	
Haverfordwest	d						10 35	12 35					14 44				16 44							19 01	
Johnston	d						10x44	12x44					14x53				16x53							19x10	
Milford Haven	a						10 55	12 59					15 08				17 08							19 25	
Fishguard Harbour ⛴	a		01 27									14 03													
	d					02 45												14 30							
Rosslare Harbour ⛴	a					06 15												18 00							

b Previous night, stops on request

When events are being held at the Millenium Stadium, services are subject to alteration. Please check times before travelling.

Table 128

Sundays
from 30 October

Cardiff - Maesteg, Swansea and West Wales

		AW	GW	AW	GW	GW		AW	AW	AW	GW	GW	AW	GW	GW	GW
				R												
			◇1		◇1	◇1				◇	◇1	◇1	◇	◇1	◇1	◇1
			⊡	trolley	⊡	⊡					⊡	⊡		⊡	⊡	⊡
London Paddington 15 ⊖	d		14 30		15 30	16 30					17 30	18 30		19 30	20 30	21 37
Reading 7	d		15 05		16 05	17 05					18 05	19 05		20 05	21 05	22 15
Manchester Piccadilly 10	d			14 30												
Gloucester 7	d															
Bristol Parkway 7	d		16 51		17 51	18f51					19 51	20 51		21 55	22 51	23 59
Newport (South Wales)	d		17 16	17 34	18 16	19 20					20 17	21 17		22 20	23 16	00 27
Cardiff Central 7	d		17 38	18 01	18 38	19 41				20 15	20 39	21 43	22 30	22 47	23 42	00 53
Pontyclun	d			18 15												
Llanharan	d			18 20												
Pencoed	d			18 25												
Bridgend	d		17 58	18 32	18 58	20 01				20 37	20 59	22 03	22 51	23 07	00 02	01 13
Wildmill	d															
Sarn	d															
Tondu	d															
Garth (Mid Glamorgan)	d															
Maesteg (Ewenny Road)	d															
Maesteg	a															
Pyle	d			18 40						20 45						
Port Talbot Parkway	d		18 11	18 49	19 11	20 14				20 54	21 12	22 16	23 05	23 20	00 15	01 26
Baglan	d															
Briton Ferry	d															
Neath	d		18 20	18 57	19 20	20 22				21 02	21 21	22 25	23 13	23 29	00 24	01 35
Skewen	d															
Llansamlet	d															
Swansea	a		18 32	19 10	19 32	20 34				21 14	21 33	22 37	23 25	23 42	00 36	01 47
	d	18 11		19 13					20 35	21 18			23 48			
Gowerton	d	18x22							20x46				23x59			
Llanelli	a	18 29		19 34					20 54	21 34			00 06			
	d	18 31		19 36					20 55	21 34			00 08			
Pembrey & Burry Port	d	18 37		19 42					21 01	21 41			00 14			
Kidwelly	d	18x44							21x08				00x21			
Ferryside	d	18x50							21x14				00x27			
Carmarthen	a	19 03		20 04					21 30	22 04			00 40			
	d	19 06		20 05						22 05			00 44			
Whitland	a	19 22		20 21						22 21			01 00			
	d	19 22		20 26				20 33		22 22			01 00			
Narberth	d							20x42								
Kilgetty	d							20x51								
Saundersfoot	d							20x53								
Tenby	a							21 00								
	d							21 04								
Penally	d							21x07								
Manorbier	d							21 13								
Lamphey	d							21x21								
Pembroke	d							21 24								
Pembroke Dock	a							21 39								
Clunderwen	d	19x30		20x33						22x29						
Clarbeston Road	d	19x38		20x41						22x37			01x13			
Haverfordwest	d	19a51		20 50						22 46						
Johnston	d			20x58						22x54						
Milford Haven	a			21 15						23 10						
Fishguard Harbour (ferry)	a												01 40			
	d															
Rosslare Harbour (ferry)	a															

When events are being held at the Millenium Stadium, services are subject to alteration. Please check times before travelling.

Table 128

Mondays to Fridays

until 9 September

West Wales, Swansea and Maesteg - Cardiff

Miles	Miles			AW MO	AW MX	AW MX	AW MO	AW MO	AW MX	AW MX	AW	GW		GW	GW	AW	GW	GW	AW	GW	AW	AW		GW	AW
				🚌	◇		◇				◇	◇1		◇1	◇1	◇	◇1	◇1		◇1	◇			◇1	◇
																	A	B		B				B	
												🍽		🍽	🍽	🛒	⊘	🍽⊘		🍽⊘	🛒			🍽⊘	🛒
—	—	Rosslare Harbour ⛴	d	21p15	21p15																				
0	—	**Fishguard Harbour** ⛴	a	00 45	00 45																				
—	—		d								01 50														
—	0	**Milford Haven**	d				21p33	23p15	23p18	00 18															06 00
—	4	Johnston	d				21b41	23b23	23b26	00x26															06x08
—	8¾	Haverfordwest	d				21p49	23p30	23p33	00 33															06 15
15¾	14	Clarbeston Road	d				21b57	23b39	23b41	00x41	02x10														06x23
22¼	—	Clunderwen	d				22b05	23b46	23b48	00x48															06x30
—	0	**Pembroke Dock**	d																						
—	2	Pembroke	d																						
—	3½	Lamphey	d																						
—	7	Manorbier	d																						
—	10¼	Penally	d																						
—	11½	**Tenby**	a																						
—	—		d																						
—	15¾	Saundersfoot	d																						
—	16½	Kilgetty	d																						
—	22	Narberth	d																						
27¾	27¼	Whitland	a				22p11	23p53	23p54	00 54	02 22														06 36
—	—		d				22p14	23p53	23p54	00 54	02 22														06 36
41¾	—	**Carmarthen**	a				22p31	00 14	00 16	01 16	02 39														06 52
—	—		d				22p34				02 44					05 04					05 53	06 20			06 57
48¾	—	Ferryside	d				22b44														06x03	06x30			
53	—	Kidwelly	d				22b50														06x08	06x35			
58¼	—	Pembrey & Burry Port	d				22p58									05 22					06 15	06 42			07 15
62¼	—	Llanelli	a				23p04				03 06					05 27					06 20	06 47			07 20
—	—		d				23p04				03 06					05 29					06 22	06 48			07 22
68	—	Gowerton	d				23b12														06x28	06x55			07x28
73½	—	**Swansea**	a				23p27				03 29										06 41	07 09			07 41
—	—		d				23p30					03 57		04 58	05 27		05 58	06 28		06 58	07 03	07 12		07 28	07 45
77½	—	Llansamlet	d																			07 19			
79¼	—	Skewen	d																			07 23			
83	—	Neath	d				23p42					04 09		05 10	05 39		06 10	06 40		07 10	07 15	07 27		07 40	07 56
84¾	—	Briton Ferry	d																			07 30			
86½	—	Baglan	d																			07 34			
88½	—	Port Talbot Parkway	d				23p49					04 17		05 18	05 47	06 02	06 18	06 48		07 18	07 22	07 38		07 48	08 03
94¾	—	Pyle	d				23p56									06 08					07 28	07 45			08 09
—	0	Maesteg	d			22p15													06 46						
—	0½	Maesteg (Ewenny Road)	d			22p17													06 48						
—	1¼	Garth (Mid Glamorgan)	d			22p20													06 51						
—	5¼	Tondu	d			22p29													07 00						
—	6	Sarn	d			22p32													07 03						
—	7¼	Wildmill	d			22p34													07 05						
100¾	8¼	Bridgend	d			22p38	00 04					04 30		05 30	05 59	06 17	06 30	07 00	07 09	07 30	07 38	07 53		08 00	08 17
104¾	—	Pencoed	d			22p44										06 23			07 15			08 06			08 23
107	—	Llanharan	d			22p48										06 26					07 45	08 10			
110	—	Pontyclun	d			22p52										06 31			07 22			08 14			08 30
121	—	**Cardiff Central** 7	a			23p07	00 29					05 02		05 52	06 21	06 44	06 52	07 22	07 36	07 52	08 01	08 34		08 22	08 44
—	—	Newport (South Wales)	a			23p39						05 30		06 09	06 37	07 02	07 09	07 39		08 09	08 17			08 39	09 02
—	—	Bristol Parkway 7	a									05 59		06 29	06 58		07 29	07 59		08 30				08 59	
—	—	Gloucester 7	a			00 39																			
—	—	Manchester Piccadilly 10	a													10 15					11 15				12 15
—	—	Reading 7	a									07 00		07 28	08 00			09 01		09 25				09 59	
—	—	London Paddington 15 ⊖	a									07 32		08 02	08 33		08 54	09 29		09 59				10 32	

A The Capitals United

B 🍽 from Reading ⊘ to Bristol Parkway

b Previous night, stops on request

When events are being held at the Millenium Stadium, services are subject to alteration. Please check times before travelling.

Table 128

Mondays to Fridays

until 9 September

West Wales, Swansea and Maesteg - Cardiff

		AW	GW	GW	AW	AW	AW	AW	GW	AW	AW	AW	GW	AW	AW	AW	AW	GW	AW	AW	GW	AW	AW
						🚌																	
			◇1	◇1	◇			◇	◇1	◇			◇1	◇				◇1	◇		◇1	◇	
				A														B					
			🍴	🍴	🛒				🍴	🛒	🛒		🍴	🛒			🛒	🍴⊘	🛒		🍴	🛒	
Rosslare Harbour ⛴	d					09 00																	
Fishguard Harbour ⛴	a					12 30																	
	d																						
Milford Haven	d				07 05									09 08								11 08	
Johnston	d				07x13									09x16								11x16	
Haverfordwest	d				07 20									09 23								11 23	
Clarbeston Road	d				07x28									09x31								11x31	
Clunderwen	d				07x35									09x38								11x38	
Pembroke Dock	d									07 09							09 09						
Pembroke	d									07 17							09 17						
Lamphey	d									07x20							09x20						
Manorbier	d									07 28							09 29						
Penally	d									07x34							09x34						
Tenby	a									07 35							09 37						
	d									07 38							09 42						
Saundersfoot	d									07x44							09x50						
Kilgetty	d									07x46							09x51						
Narberth	d									07x56							10x01						
Whitland	a				07 41					08 04				09 44			10 09					11 44	
	d				07 41					08 05				09 44			10 09					11 44	
Carmarthen	a				07 55					08 23				10 02			10 27					12 00	
	d			07 30	08 01					08 30	09 00			10 04			10 31		11 04			12 05	
Ferryside	d			07 42	08x11					08x40	09x10								11x14				
Kidwelly	d			07 49	08x16					08x45	09x16								11x19				
Pembrey & Burry Port	d			07 56	08 23					08 51	09 23			10 24			10 50		11 25			12 23	
Llanelli	a			08 02	08 28					08 57	09 29			10 29			10 56		11 31			12 28	
	d			08 04	08 30			08 45		08 58	09 30			10 31			10 57		11 32			12 30	
Gowerton	d				08x36			08x53		09x05							11x04		11x39				
Swansea	a			08 21	08 49			09 08		09 23	09 51			10 48			11 22		11 51			12 47	
	d		07 58	08 28	08 55			09 11	09 28	09 55			10 28	10 55		11 10		11 28	11 55		12 28	12 55	
Llansamlet	d							09 18								11 17							
Skewen	d							09 22								11 21							
Neath	d		08 10	08 40	09 06			09 26	09 40	10 06			10 40	11 06		11 25		11 40	12 06		12 40	13 06	
Briton Ferry	d							09 30								11 28							
Baglan	d							09 33								11 32							
Port Talbot Parkway	d		08 18	08 48	09 13			09 37	09 48	10 13			10 48	11 13		11 36		11 48	12 13		12 48	13 13	
Pyle	d							09 44								11 43							
Maesteg	d	08 00					09 15					10 15			11 15					12 15			13 15
Maesteg (Ewenny Road)	d	08 02					09 17					10 17			11 17					12 17			13 17
Garth (Mid Glamorgan)	d	08 05					09 20					10 20			11 20					12 20			13 20
Tondu	d	08 14					09 29					10 29			11 29					12 29			13 29
Sarn	d	08 17					09 32					10 32			11 32					12 32			13 32
Wildmill	d	08 19					09 34					10 34			11 34					12 34			13 34
Bridgend	d	08 23	08 30	09 00	09 25		09 38	09 53	10 00	10 25		10 38	11 00	11 25	11 38	11 55		12 00	12 25	12 38	13 00	13 25	13 38
Pencoed	d						09 44					10 44			11 44					12 44			13 44
Llanharan	d	08 31					09 48					10 48			11 48					12 48			13 48
Pontyclun	d						09 52					10 52			11 52					12 52			13 52
Cardiff Central (7)	a	08 48	08 52	09 22	09 46		10 07	10 17	10 22	10 48		11 09	11 22	11 48	12 08	12 18		12 22	12 47	13 07	13 22	13 47	14 07
Newport (South Wales)	a	09 25	09 09	09 39	10 17		10 25		10 39	11 02			11 39	12 17	12 25			12 39	13 02	13 25	13 39	14 17	
Bristol Parkway (7)	a		09 30	09 59					10 59				11 59					12 59			13 59		
Gloucester (7)	a	10 20					11 20								13 20					14 20			
Manchester Piccadilly (10)	a				13 15					14 15				15 15					16 15			17 14	
Reading (7)	a		10 31	11 00					11 59				13 00					13 59			15 00		
London Paddington (15) ⊖	a		11 01	11 32					12 32				13 32					14 32			15 32		

A The Red Dragon

B The St. David. 🍴 from Reading
⊘ to Bristol Parkway

When events are being held at the Millenium Stadium, services are subject to alteration. Please check times before travelling.

Table 128

Mondays to Fridays

until 9 September

West Wales, Swansea and Maesteg - Cardiff

		AW	AW	GW	AW	AW	GW	AW	AW	AW	AW	AW	GW	AW	AW	GW	AW	AW	AW	AW	GW FX	GW FO
								R	R					R			R					
		◇		◇1	◇		◇1						◇1			◇1					◇1	◇1
			trolley	buffet	trolley		buffet	trolley	trolley			trolley	buffet	trolley		buffet	trolley			trolley	buffet	buffet
Rosslare Harbour ⛴	d																					
Fishguard Harbour ⛴	a																					
	d								13 30													
Milford Haven	d							13 08									15 08					
Johnston	d							13x16									15x16					
Haverfordwest	d							13 23									15 23					
Clarbeston Road	d							13x31	13 50								15x31					
Clunderwen	d							13x38									15x38					
Pembroke Dock	d		11 09									13 09								15 09		
Pembroke	d		11 17									13 17								15 17		
Lamphey	d		11x20									13x20								15x20		
Manorbier	d		11 29									13 29								15 29		
Penally	d		11x34									13x34								15x34		
Tenby	a		11 37									13 37								15 37		
	d		11 42									13 42								15 42		
Saundersfoot	d		11x50									13x50								15x50		
Kilgetty	d		11x51									13x51								15x51		
Narberth	d		12x01									14x01								16x01		
Whitland	a		12 09					13 44	14 02			14 09					15 44			16 09		
	d		12 09					13 44	14 02			14 09					15 44			16 09		
Carmarthen	a		12 27					14 00	14 19			14 27					16 00			16 27		
	d		12 31		13 02			14 05	14 25			14 31		15 05			16 05			16 31		
Ferryside	d				13x12									15x15								
Kidwelly	d				13x17									15x20								
Pembrey & Burry Port	d		12 50		13 23			14 23				14 50		15 27			16 23			16 50		
Llanelli	a		12 56		13 29			14 28	14 47			14 56		15 32			16 28			16 56		
	d	12 41	12 57		13 30			14 30	14 47			14 57		15 34			16 30			16 57		
Gowerton	d		13x04					14x36									16x36			17x04		
Swansea	a	13 01	13 22		13 51			14 49				15 22		15 51			16 49			17 22		
	d	13 10		13 28	13 55		14 28	14 55			15 10		15 28	15 55		16 28	16 55		17 10		17 28	17 28
Llansamlet	d	13 17									15 17								17 17			
Skewen	d	13 21									15 21								17 21			
Neath	d	13 25		13 40	14 06		14 40	15 06			15 25		15 40	16 06		16 40	17 06		17 25		17 40	17 40
Briton Ferry	d	13 28									15 28								17 28			
Baglan	d	13 32									15 32								17 32			
Port Talbot Parkway	d	13 36		13 48	14 13		14 48	15 13			15 36		15 48	16 13		16 48	17 13		17 36		17 48	17 48
Pyle	d	13 43									15 43								17 43			
Maesteg	d					14 15				15 17					16 15			17 15				
Maesteg (Ewenny Road)	d					14 17				15 19					16 17			17 17				
Garth (Mid Glamorgan)	d					14 20				15 22					16 20			17 20				
Tondu	d					14 29				15 31					16 29			17 29				
Sarn	d					14 32				15 34					16 32			17 32				
Wildmill	d					14 34				15 36					16 34			17 34				
Bridgend	d	13 52		14 00	14 25	14 38	15 00	15 25		15 40	15 52		16 00	16 25	16 38	17 00	17 25	17 38	17 54		18 00	18 00
Pencoed	d					14 44				15 46					16 44			17 44				
Llanharan	d					14 48				15 50					16 48			17 48				
Pontyclun	d					14 52				15 54					16 52			17 52				
Cardiff Central 7	a	14 15		14 22	14 47	15 07	15 22	15 47	16 04	16 09	16 15		16 22	16 46	17 07	17 22	17 47	18 07	18 20		18 22	18 22
Newport (South Wales)	a			14 39	15 02	15 26	15 39	16 02	16 18				16 39	17 02	17 25	17 39	18 02	18 25			18 39	18 39
Bristol Parkway 7	a			15 00			15 59						16 59			17 59					18 59	18 59
Gloucester 7	a					16 21			17 14						18 21			19 20				
Manchester Piccadilly 10	a				18 13			19 15						20 15			21 05					
Reading 7	a			16 00			17 00						17 56			19 01					20 00	20 00
London Paddington 15 ⊖	a			16 30			17 30						18 24			19 32					20 30	20 32

When events are being held at the Millenium Stadium, services are subject to alteration. Please check times before travelling.

Table 128

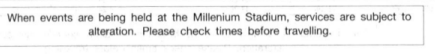

Mondays to Fridays

until 9 September

West Wales, Swansea and Maesteg - Cardiff

		AW	AW	AW	GW	AW	AW	AW	AW	GW		AW	AW	GW	GW	AW		AW	AW	AW		AW	AW	AW	AW
														FO	FX								FO	FX	
		◇	◇		◇1					◇1				◇1	◇1							◇			
Rosslare Harbour ⛴	d																								
Fishguard Harbour ⛴	a																								
	d																								
Milford Haven	d					17 08										19 08				20 36					
Johnston	d					17x16										19x16				20x44					
Haverfordwest	d					17 23										19 23				20 51					
Clarbeston Road	d					17x31										19x31				20x59					
Clunderwen	d					17x38										19x38				21x06					
Pembroke Dock	d								17 09																
Pembroke	d								17 17																
Lamphey	d								17x20																
Manorbier	d								17 29																
Penally	d								17x34																
Tenby	a								17 37																
	d								17 42										19 57						
Saundersfoot	d								17x50										20x05						
Kilgetty	d								17x51										20x07						
Narberth	d								18x01										20x17						
Whitland	a					17 44			18 09							19 44			20 25	21 12					
	d					17 45			18 09							19 44			20 27	21 12					
Carmarthen	a					18 02			18 27							20 00			20 45	21 34					
	d	17 04				18 07			18 31			19 06				20 05			20 47						
Ferryside	d	17x14				18x17													20x58						
Kidwelly	d	17x19				18x22													21x04						
Pembrey & Burry Port	d	17 25				18 29			18 50			19 25				20 23			21 11						
Llanelli	a	17 31				18 35			18 56			19 31				20 28			21 17						
	d	17 32	17 48			18 35			18 57			19 33				20 29			21 17			21 43			
Gowerton	d		17x57						19x04													21x50			
Swansea	a	17 49	18 18			18 53			19 22			19 51				20 47			21 39			22 10			
	d	17 55			18 28	19 00		19 10		19 29		19 55		20 28	20 28	20 57			21 45						22 32
Llansamlet	d							19 17											21 52						22 39
Skewen	d							19 21											21 56						22 43
Neath	d	18 06			18 40	19 11		19 25		19 40		20 06		20 40	20 40	21 08			22 00						22 47
Briton Ferry	d							19 28											22 03						22 50
Baglan	d							19 32											22 07						22 54
Port Talbot Parkway	d	18 13			18 48	19 19		19 36		19 48		20 13		20 48	20 48	21 15			22 11						22 58
Pyle	d							19 43											22 18						23 05
Maesteg	d			18 20			19 17						20 15					21 15					22 15	22 15	
Maesteg (Ewenny Road)	d			18 22			19 19						20 17					21 17					22 17	22 17	
Garth (Mid Glamorgan)	d			18 25			19 22						20 20					21 20					22 20	22 20	
Tondu	d			18 34			19 31						20 29					21 29					22 29	22 29	
Sarn	d			18 37			19 34						20 32					21 32					22 32	22 32	
Wildmill	d			18 39			19 36						20 34					21 34					22 34	22 34	
Bridgend	d	18 25		18 43	19 00	19 32	19 40	19 51		20 00		20 26	20 38	21 00	21 00	21 27		21 38	22 26				22 38	22 38	23 13
Pencoed	d			18 49			19 46						20 44					21 44					22 44	22 44	
Llanharan	d			18 53			19 49						20 48					21 48					22 48	22 48	
Pontyclun	d			18 57			19 54						20 52					21 52					22 52	22 52	
Cardiff Central 7	a	18 46		19 13	19 22	19 57	20 10	20 17		20 22		20 51	21 07	21 22	21 22	21 50		22 10	22 49				23 07	23 07	23 38
Newport (South Wales)	a	19 03			19 39					20 38			21 25	21 38	21 38								23 38	23 39	
Bristol Parkway 7	a				19 59					21 01				21 59	21 59										
Gloucester 7	a												22 21										00 39	00 39	
Manchester Piccadilly 10	a	22 13																							
Reading 7	a				21 00					22 09				23 03	23 03										
London Paddington 15 ⊖	a				21 32					22 45				23 36	23 40										

When events are being held at the Millenium Stadium, services are subject to alteration. Please check times before travelling.

Table 128

Mondays to Fridays

until 9 September

West Wales, Swansea and Maesteg - Cardiff

		AW	AW	AW	AW ◇
Rosslare Harbour ⛴	d				21 15
Fishguard Harbour ⛴	a				00 45
	d				
Milford Haven	d			23 18	
Johnston	d			23x26	
Haverfordwest	d			23 33	
Clarbeston Road	d			23x41	
Clunderwen	d			23x48	
Pembroke Dock	d	21 09	22 23		
Pembroke	d	21 17	22 31		
Lamphey	d	21x20	22x34		
Manorbier	d	21 29	22 42		
Penally	d	21x34	22x48		
Tenby	a	21 37	22 50		
	d	21 42	22 50		
Saundersfoot	d	21x50	22x58		
Kilgetty	d	21x52	23x00		
Narberth	d	22x02	23x09		
Whitland	a	22 10	23 17	23 54	
	d	22 10	23 20	23 54	
Carmarthen	a	22 28	23 39	00 16	
	d	22 35			
Ferryside	d	22x45			
Kidwelly	d	22x51			
Pembrey & Burry Port	d	22 58			
Llanelli	a	23 04			
	d	23 05			
Gowerton	d	23x12			
Swansea	a	23 32			
	d				
Llansamlet	d				
Skewen	d				
Neath	d				
Briton Ferry	d				
Baglan	d				
Port Talbot Parkway	d				
Pyle	d				
Maesteg	d				
Maesteg (Ewenny Road)	d				
Garth (Mid Glamorgan)	d				
Tondu	d				
Sarn	d				
Wildmill	d				
Bridgend	d				
Pencoed	d				
Llanharan	d				
Pontyclun	d				
Cardiff Central 7	a				
Newport (South Wales)	a				
Bristol Parkway 7	a				
Gloucester 7	a				
Manchester Piccadilly 10	a				
Reading 7	a				
London Paddington 15 ⊖	a				

When events are being held at the Millenium Stadium, services are subject to alteration. Please check times before travelling.

Table 128

Mondays to Fridays

from 12 September

West Wales, Swansea and Maesteg - Cardiff

		GW MO ◇1 A 🍽	AW MO ▣	AW MX ◇	AW MX	AW MO ◇	AW MO	AW MX	AW MX	AW ◇	GW ◇1 🍽	GW ◇1 🍽	GW ◇1 🍽	AW ◇ 🛒	GW ◇1 B Ø	GW ◇1 C 🍽Ø	AW	GW ◇1 C 🍽Ø	AW ◇ 🛒	AW	GW ◇1 C 🍽Ø	AW ◇ 🛒	AW
Rosslare Harbour ⛴	d		21p15	21p15																			
Fishguard Harbour ⛴	a		00 45	00 45																			
	d									01 50													
Milford Haven	d					21p33	23p15	23p18	00 18													06 00	
Johnston	d					21b41	23b23	23b26	00x26													06x08	
Haverfordwest	d					21p49	23p30	23p33	00 33													06 15	
Clarbeston Road	d					21b57	23b39	23b41	00x41	02x10												06x23	
Clunderwen	d					22b05	23b46	23b48	00x48													06x30	
Pembroke Dock	d																						
Pembroke	d																						
Lamphey	d																						
Manorbier	d																						
Penally	d																						
Tenby	a																						
	d																						
Saundersfoot	d																						
Kilgetty	d																						
Narberth	d																						
Whitland	a					22p11	23p53	23p54	00 54	02 22												06 36	
	d					22p14	23p53	23p54	00 54	02 22												06 36	
Carmarthen	a					22p31	00 14	00 16	01 16	02 39												06 52	
	d	19p09				22p34				02 44				05 04					05 53	06 20		06 57	
Ferryside	d					22b44													06x03	06x30			
Kidwelly	d					22b50													06x08	06x35			
Pembrey & Burry Port	d	19p29				22p58								05 22					06 15	06 42		07 15	
Llanelli	a	19p35				23p04				03 06				05 27					06 20	06 47		07 20	
	d	19p36				23p04				03 06				05 29					06 22	06 48		07 22	
Gowerton	d					23b12													06x28	06x55		07x28	
Swansea	a	19p53				23p27				03 29									06 41	07 09		07 41	
	d	19p59				23p30					03 57	04 58	05 27		05 58	06 28		06 58	07 03	07 12	07 28	07 45	
Llansamlet	d																			07 19			
Skewen	d																			07 23			
Neath	d	20p11				23p42					04 09	05 10	05 39		06 10	06 40		07 10	07 15	07 27	07 40	07 56	
Briton Ferry	d																			07 30			
Baglan	d																			07 34			
Port Talbot Parkway	d	20p18				23p49					04 17	05 18	05 47	06 02	06 18	06 48		07 18	07 22	07 38	07 48	08 03	
Pyle	d					23p56								06 08					07 28	07 45		08 09	
Maesteg	d				22p15												06 46						08 00
Maesteg (Ewenny Road)	d				22p17												06 48						08 02
Garth (Mid Glamorgan)	d				22p20												06 51						08 05
Tondu	d				22p29												07 00						08 14
Sarn	d				22p32												07 03						08 17
Wildmill	d				22p34												07 05						08 19
Bridgend	d	20p30			22p38	00 04					04 30	05 30	05 59	06 17	06 30	07 00	07 09	07 30	07 38	07 53	08 00	08 17	08 23
Pencoed	d				22p44									06 23			07 15			08 06		08 23	
Llanharan	d				22p48									06 26					07 45	08 10			08 31
Pontyclun	d				22p52									06 31			07 22			08 14		08 30	
Cardiff Central 7	a	20p53			23p07	00 29					05 02	05 52	06 21	06 44	06 52	07 22	07 36	07 52	08 01	08 34	08 22	08 44	08 48
Newport (South Wales)	a	21p08			23p39						05 30	06 09	06 37	07 02	07 09	07 39		08 09	08 17		08 39	09 02	09 25
Bristol Parkway 7	a	21p37									05 59	06 29	06 58		07 29	07 59		08 30			08 59		
Gloucester 7	a				00 39																		10 20
Manchester Piccadilly 10	a													10 15					11 15			12 15	
Reading 7	a	23p32									07 00	07 28	08 00			09 01		09 25			09 59		
London Paddington 15 ⊖	a	00 13									07 32	08 02	08 33		08 54	09 29		09 59			10 32		

A From 31 October
B The Capitals United
C 🍽 from Reading Ø to Bristol Parkway
b Previous night, stops on request

When events are being held at the Millenium Stadium, services are subject to alteration. Please check times before travelling.

Table 128

Mondays to Fridays

from 12 September

West Wales, Swansea and Maesteg - Cardiff

		GW	GW	AW	AW	AW		AW	GW	AW	AW	AW	GW	AW	AW	AW		AW	GW	AW	AW	GW	AW	AW	AW
					R																				
		◇1	◇1	◇				◇	◇1	◇			◇1	◇					◇1	◇		◇1	◇		◇
			A		B														C						
		🍴	🍴	🛒					🍴	🛒			🍴	🛒					🍴Ø	🛒		🍴	🛒		
Rosslare Harbour ⛴	d				09 00																				
Fishguard Harbour ⛴	a				12 30																				
	d																								
Milford Haven	d			07 05										09 08									11 08		
Johnston	d			07x13										09x16									11x16		
Haverfordwest	d			07 20										09 23									11 23		
Clarbeston Road	d			07x28										09x31									11x31		
Clunderwen	d			07x35										09x38									11x38		
Pembroke Dock	d									07 09								09 09							
Pembroke	d									07 17								09 17							
Lamphey	d									07x20								09x20							
Manorbier	d									07 28								09 29							
Penally	d									07x34								09x34							
Tenby	a									07 35								09 37							
	d									07 38								09 38							
Saundersfoot	d									07x44								09x46							
Kilgetty	d									07x46								09x48							
Narberth	d									07x56								09x58							
Whitland	a			07 41						08 04				09 44				10 06					11 44		
	d			07 41						08 05				09 44				10 07					11 44		
Carmarthen	a			07 55						08 23				10 02				10 24					12 00		
	d		07 30	08 01						08 30	09 00			10 04				10 29		11 04			12 05		
Ferryside	d		07 42	08x11						08x40	09x10									11x14					
Kidwelly	d		07 49	08x16						08x45	09x16									11x19					
Pembrey & Burry Port	d		07 56	08 23						08 51	09 23			10 24				10 48		11 25			12 23		
Llanelli	a		08 02	08 28						08 57	09 29			10 29				10 54		11 31			12 28		
	d		08 04	08 30				08 45		08 58	09 30			10 31				10 55		11 32			12 30		12 41
Gowerton	d			08x36				08x53		09x05								11x02		11x39					
Swansea	a		08 21	08 49				09 08		09 23	09 51			10 48				11 22		11 51			12 47		13 01
	d	07 58	08 28	08 55				09 11	09 28	09 55			10 28	10 55		11 10			11 28	11 55		12 28	12 55		13 10
Llansamlet	d							09 18								11 17									13 17
Skewen	d							09 22								11 21									13 21
Neath	d	08 10	08 40	09 06				09 26	09 40	10 06			10 40	11 06		11 25			11 40	12 06		12 40	13 06		13 25
Briton Ferry	d							09 30								11 28									13 28
Baglan	d							09 33								11 32									13 32
Port Talbot Parkway	d	08 18	08 48	09 13				09 37	09 48	10 13			10 48	11 13		11 36			11 48	12 13		12 48	13 13		13 36
Pyle	d							09 44								11 43									13 43
Maesteg	d					09 15						10 15			11 15						12 15			13 15	
Maesteg (Ewenny Road)	d					09 17						10 17			11 17						12 17			13 17	
Garth (Mid Glamorgan)	d					09 20						10 20			11 20						12 20			13 20	
Tondu	d					09 29						10 29			11 29						12 29			13 29	
Sarn	d					09 32						10 32			11 32						12 32			13 32	
Wildmill	d					09 34						10 34			11 34						12 34			13 34	
Bridgend	d	08 30	09 00	09 25		09 38		09 53	10 00	10 25		10 38	11 00	11 25	11 38	11 55			12 00	12 25	12 38	13 00	13 25	13 38	13 52
Pencoed	d					09 44						10 44			11 44						12 44			13 44	
Llanharan	d					09 48						10 48			11 48						12 48			13 48	
Pontyclun	d					09 52						10 52			11 52						12 52			13 52	
Cardiff Central 7	a	08 52	09 22	09 46		10 07		10 17	10 22	10 48		11 09	11 22	11 48	12 08	12 18			12 22	12 47	13 07	13 22	13 47	14 07	14 15
Newport (South Wales)	a	09 09	09 39	10 17		10 25			10 39	11 02			11 39	12 17	12 25				12 39	13 02	13 25	13 39	14 17		
Bristol Parkway 7	a	09 30	09 59						10 59				11 59						12 59			13 59			
Gloucester 7	a					11 20									13 20						14 20				
Manchester Piccadilly 10	a			13 15						14 15				15 15						16 15			17 14		
Reading 7	a	10 31	11 00						11 59				13 00						13 59			15 00			
London Paddington 15 ⊖	a	11 07	11 32						12 32				13 32						14 32			15 32			

A The Red Dragon
B from 12 September until 2 December
C The St. David. 🍴 from Reading
Ø to Bristol Parkway

When events are being held at the Millenium Stadium, services are subject to alteration. Please check times before travelling.

Table 128

Mondays to Fridays

from 12 September

West Wales, Swansea and Maesteg - Cardiff

		AW		GW	AW	AW	GW	AW	AW	AW	AW	AW		GW	AW	AW	GW	AW	AW	AW	AW	GW FX		GW FO	AW
								■	■						■			■							
				◇1	◇		◇1							◇1			◇1					◇1		◇1	◇
				🍴	🛒		🍴	🛒	🛒					🍴	🛒		🍴	🛒				🍴		🍴	🛒
Rosslare Harbour ⛴	d																								
Fishguard Harbour ⛴	a																								
	d								13 30																
Milford Haven	d							13 08										15 08							
Johnston	d							13x16										15x16							
Haverfordwest	d							13 23										15 23							
Clarbeston Road	d							13x31	13 50									15x31							
Clunderwen	d							13x38										15x38							
Pembroke Dock	d	11 09										13 09									15 09				
Pembroke	d	11 17										13 17									15 17				
Lamphey	d	11x20										13x20									15x20				
Manorbier	d	11 29										13 29									15 29				
Penally	d	11x34										13x34									15x34				
Tenby	a	11 37										13 37									15 37				
	d	11 42										13 42									15 42				
Saundersfoot	d	11x50										13x50									15x50				
Kilgetty	d	11x51										13x51									15x51				
Narberth	d	12x01										14x01									16x01				
Whitland	a	12 09						13 44	14 02			14 09						15 44			16 09				
	d	12 09						13 44	14 02			14 09						15 44			16 09				
Carmarthen	a	12 27						14 00	14 19			14 27						16 00			16 27				
	d	12 31			13 02			14 05	14 25			14 31			15 05			16 05			16 31				17 04
Ferryside	d				13x12										15x15										17x14
Kidwelly	d				13x17										15x20										17x19
Pembrey & Burry Port	d	12 50			13 23			14 23				14 50			15 27			16 23			16 50				17 25
Llanelli	a	12 56			13 29			14 28	14 47			14 56			15 32			16 28			16 56				17 31
	d	12 57			13 30			14 30	14 47			14 57			15 34			16 30			16 57				17 32
Gowerton	d	13x04						14x36										16x36			17x04				
Swansea	a	13 22			13 51			14 49				15 22			15 51			16 49			17 22				17 49
	d			13 28	13 55		14 28	14 55			15 10			15 28	15 55		16 28	16 55		17 10		17 28		17 28	17 55
Llansamlet	d										15 17									17 17					
Skewen	d										15 21									17 21					
Neath	d			13 40	14 06		14 40	15 06			15 25			15 40	16 06		16 40	17 06		17 25		17 40		17 40	18 06
Briton Ferry	d										15 28									17 28					
Baglan	d										15 32									17 32					
Port Talbot Parkway	d			13 48	14 13		14 48	15 13			15 36			15 48	16 13		16 48	17 13		17 36		17 48		17 48	18 13
Pyle	d										15 43									17 43					
Maesteg	d					14 15				15 17						16 15			17 15						
Maesteg (Ewenny Road)	d					14 17				15 19						16 17			17 17						
Garth (Mid Glamorgan)	d					14 20				15 22						16 20			17 20						
Tondu	d					14 29				15 31						16 29			17 29						
Sarn	d					14 32				15 34						16 32			17 32						
Wildmill	d					14 34				15 36						16 34			17 34						
Bridgend	d			14 00	14 25	14 38	15 00	15 25		15 40	15 52			16 00	16 25	16 38	17 00	17 25	17 38	17 54		18 00		18 00	18 25
Pencoed	d					14 44				15 46						16 44			17 44						
Llanharan	d					14 48				15 50						16 48			17 48						
Pontyclun	d					14 52				15 54						16 52			17 52						
Cardiff Central 7	a			14 22	14 47	15 07	15 22	15 47	16 04	16 09	16 15			16 22	16 46	17 07	17 22	17 47	18 07	18 20		18 22		18 22	18 46
Newport (South Wales)	a			14 39	15 02	15 26	15 39	16 02	16 18					16 39	17 02	17 25	17 39	18 02	18 25			18 39		18 39	19 03
Bristol Parkway 7	a			15 00			15 59							16 59			17 59					18 59		18 59	
Gloucester 7	a					16 21			17 14							18 21			19 20						
Manchester Piccadilly 10	a				18 13			19 15							20 15			21 05							22 13
Reading 7	a			16 00			17 00							18 00			19 01					20 00		20 00	
London Paddington 15 ⊖	a			16 30			17 30							18 30			19 32					20 30		20 32	

When events are being held at the Millenium Stadium, services are subject to alteration. Please check times before travelling.

Table 128

Mondays to Fridays

from 12 September

West Wales, Swansea and Maesteg - Cardiff

		AW	AW	GW	AW	AW	AW	AW	GW	AW	AW	GW	GW	AW	AW	AW	AW	AW	AW	AW	AW	AW	AW
												FO	FX							FO	FX		
		◇		◇1 🍴					◇1 🍴			◇1 🍴	◇1 🍴		◇				◇				
Rosslare Harbour ⛴	d														21 15								
Fishguard Harbour ⛴	a														00 45								
	d																						
Milford Haven	d				17 08									19 08				20 36					
Johnston	d				17x16									19x16				20x44					
Haverfordwest	d				17 23									19 23				20 51					
Clarbeston Road	d				17x31									19x31				20x59					
Clunderwen	d				17x38									19x38				21x06					
Pembroke Dock	d							17 09															21 09
Pembroke	d							17 17															21 17
Lamphey	d							17x20															21x20
Manorbier	d							17 29															21 29
Penally	d							17x34															21x34
Tenby	a							17 37															21 37
	d							17 42									19 57						21 42
Saundersfoot	d							17x50									20x05						21x50
Kilgetty	d							17x51									20x07						21x52
Narberth	d							18x01									20x17						22x02
Whitland	a				17 44			18 09						19 44			20 25	21 12					22 10
	d				17 45			18 09						19 44			20 27	21 12					22 10
Carmarthen	a				18 02			18 27						20 00			20 45	21 34					22 28
	d				18 07			18 31		19 06				20 05			20 47						22 35
Ferryside	d				18x17												20x58						22x45
Kidwelly	d				18x22												21x04						22x51
Pembrey & Burry Port	d				18 29			18 50		19 25				20 23			21 11						22 58
Llanelli	a				18 35			18 56		19 31				20 28			21 17						23 04
	d	17 48			18 35			18 57		19 33				20 29			21 17		21 43				23 05
Gowerton	d	17x57						19x04											21x50				23x12
Swansea	a	18 18			18 53			19 22		19 51				20 47			21 39		22 10				23 32
	d			18 28	19 00		19 10		19 29	19 55		20 28	20 28	20 57			21 45					22 32	
Llansamlet	d						19 17										21 52					22 39	
Skewen	d						19 21										21 56					22 43	
Neath	d			18 40	19 11		19 25		19 40	20 06		20 40	20 40	21 08			22 00					22 47	
Briton Ferry	d						19 28										22 03					22 50	
Baglan	d						19 32										22 07					22 54	
Port Talbot Parkway	d			18 48	19 19		19 36		19 48	20 13		20 48	20 48	21 15			22 11					22 58	
Pyle	d						19 43										22 18					23 05	
Maesteg	d		18 20			19 17					20 15					21 15				22 15	22 15		
Maesteg (Ewenny Road)	d		18 22			19 19					20 17					21 17				22 17	22 17		
Garth (Mid Glamorgan)	d		18 25			19 22					20 20					21 20				22 20	22 20		
Tondu	d		18 34			19 31					20 29					21 29				22 29	22 29		
Sarn	d		18 37			19 34					20 32					21 32				22 32	22 32		
Wildmill	d		18 39			19 36					20 34					21 34				22 34	22 34		
Bridgend	d		18 43	19 00	19 32	19 40	19 51		20 00	20 26	20 38	21 00	21 00	21 27		21 38	22 26			22 38	22 38	23 13	
Pencoed	d		18 49			19 46					20 44					21 44				22 44	22 44		
Llanharan	d		18 53			19 49					20 48					21 48				22 48	22 48		
Pontyclun	d		18 57			19 54					20 52					21 52				22 52	22 52		
Cardiff Central 7	a		19 13	19 22	19 57	20 10	20 17		20 22	20 51	21 07	21 22	21 22	21 50		22 10	22 49			23 07	23 07	23 38	
Newport (South Wales)	a			19 39					20 38		21 25	21 38	21 38							23 38	23 39		
Bristol Parkway 7	a			19 59					21 01			21 59	21 59										
Gloucester 7	a										22 21									00 39	00 39		
Manchester Piccadilly 10	a																						
Reading 7	a			21 00					22 09			23 03	23 03										
London Paddington 15 ⊖	a			21 32					22 45			23 36	23 40										

When events are being held at the Millenium Stadium, services are subject to alteration. Please check times before travelling.

Table 128

Mondays to Fridays

from 12 September

West Wales, Swansea and Maesteg - Cardiff

		AW	AW
Rosslare Harbour ⛴	d		
Fishguard Harbour ⛴	a		
	d		
Milford Haven	d		23 18
Johnston	d		23x26
Haverfordwest	d		23 33
Clarbeston Road	d		23x41
Clunderwen	d		23x48
Pembroke Dock	d	22 23	
Pembroke	d	22 31	
Lamphey	d	22x34	
Manorbier	d	22 42	
Penally	d	22x48	
Tenby	a	22 50	
	d	22 50	
Saundersfoot	d	22x58	
Kilgetty	d	23x00	
Narberth	d	23x09	
Whitland	a	23 17	23 54
	d	23 20	23 54
Carmarthen	a	23 39	00 16
	d		
Ferryside	d		
Kidwelly	d		
Pembrey & Burry Port	d		
Llanelli	a		
	d		
Gowerton	d		
Swansea	a		
	d		
Llansamlet	d		
Skewen	d		
Neath	d		
Briton Ferry	d		
Baglan	d		
Port Talbot Parkway	d		
Pyle	d		
Maesteg	d		
Maesteg (Ewenny Road)	d		
Garth (Mid Glamorgan)	d		
Tondu	d		
Sarn	d		
Wildmill	d		
Bridgend	d		
Pencoed	d		
Llanharan	d		
Pontyclun	d		
Cardiff Central 7	a		
Newport (South Wales)	a		
Bristol Parkway 7	a		
Gloucester 7	a		
Manchester Piccadilly 10	a		
Reading 7	a		
London Paddington 15 ⊖	a		

When events are being held at the Millenium Stadium, services are subject to alteration. Please check times before travelling.

Table 128

Saturdays
until 10 September

West Wales, Swansea and Maesteg - Cardiff

		AW	AW	AW	AW	AW	GW	GW	GW	AW		GW	GW	AW	AW	GW	AW	GW	AW	AW		GW	AW	AW	AW
																								[B]	
		◇				◇	◇**1**	◇**1**	◇**1**	◇		◇**1**	◇**1**		◇	◇**1**		◇**1**	◇			◇**1**	◇		
																A		A							
							catering	catering	catering	trolley		catering	catering		trolley	catering Ø		catering Ø	trolley			catering	trolley		
Rosslare Harbour ⛴	d	21p15																						09 00	
Fishguard Harbour ⛴	a	00 45																						12 30	
	d					01 50																			
Milford Haven	d			23p18	00 18														06 00				07 05		
Johnston	d			23b26	00x26														06x08				07x13		
Haverfordwest	d			23p33	00 33														06 15				07 20		
Clarbeston Road	d			23b41	00x41	02x10													06x23				07x28		
Clunderwen	d			23b48	00x48														06x30				07x35		
Pembroke Dock	d																								
Pembroke	d																								
Lamphey	d																								
Manorbier	d																								
Penally	d																								
Tenby	a																								
	d																								
Saundersfoot	d																								
Kilgetty	d																								
Narberth	d																								
Whitland	a			23p54	00 54	02 22													06 36				07 41		
	d			23p54	00 54	02 22													06 36				07 41		
Carmarthen	a			00 16	01 16	02 39													06 52				07 55		
	d					02 44				05 04					05 55		06 20		06 57				08 01		
Ferryside	d														06x05		06x30						08x11		
Kidwelly	d														06x10		06x35						08x16		
Pembrey & Burry Port	d									05 22					06 17		06 42		07 15				08 23		
Llanelli	a					03 06				05 27					06 22		06 47		07 20				08 28		
	d					03 06				05 29					06 24		06 48		07 22				08 30		
Gowerton	d														06x30		06x55		07x28				08x36		
Swansea	a					03 29									06 43		07 09		07 41				08 49		
	d						03 58	04 58	05 28			05 58	06 28		06 47	06 58	07 12	07 28	07 45			08 28	08 55		
Llansamlet	d																07 19								
Skewen	d																07 23								
Neath	d						04 10	05 10	05 40			06 10	06 40		06 58	07 10	07 27	07 40	07 56			08 40	09 06		
Briton Ferry	d																07 30								
Baglan	d																07 34								
Port Talbot Parkway	d						04 18	05 18	05 48	06 02		06 18	06 48		07 05	07 18	07 38	07 48	08 03			08 48	09 13		
Pyle	d									06 08					07 11		07 45		08 09						
Maesteg	d		22p15											06 46						08 00					09 17
Maesteg (Ewenny Road)	d		22p17											06 48						08 02					09 19
Garth (Mid Glamorgan)	d		22p20											06 51						08 05					09 22
Tondu	d		22p29											07 00						08 14					09 31
Sarn	d		22p32											07 03						08 17					09 34
Wildmill	d		22p34											07 05						08 19					09 36
Bridgend	d		22p38				04 30	05 30	06 00	06 16		06 30	07 00	07 09	07 19	07 30	07 53	08 00	08 17	08 23		09 00	09 25		09 40
Pencoed	d		22p44							06 22				07 15			08 06		08 23						09 46
Llanharan	d		22p48							06 25					07 26		08 10			08 30					09 50
Pontyclun	d		22p52							06 30				07 22			08 14		08 30						09 54
Cardiff Central 7	a		23p07				04 52	05 52	06 22	06 43		06 52	07 22	07 36	07 42	07 52	08 34	08 22	08 44	08 47		09 22	09 44		10 09
Newport (South Wales)	a		23p38				05 09	06 09	06 38	07 02		07 08	07 39		08 02	08 08		08 38	09 02	09 24		09 39	10 07		10 25
Bristol Parkway 7	a						05 36	06 29	06 59			07 29	07 59			08 30		08 59				09 59			
Gloucester 7	a		00 39																	10 19					11 21
Manchester Piccadilly 10	a									10 14					11 15				12 15				13 15		
Reading 7	a						07 14	07 31	08 00			08 31	09 00			09 32		10 00				11 01			
London Paddington 15 ⊖	a						07 44	08 07	08 32			09 02	09 32			10 02		10 32				11 33			

A catering from Reading Ø to Bristol Parkway

b Previous night, stops on request

When events are being held at the Millenium Stadium, services are subject to alteration. Please check times before travelling.

Table 128

Saturdays
until 10 September

West Wales, Swansea and Maesteg - Cardiff

		AW	AW	GW	AW	AW		AW	GW	AW	AW	AW	AW	GW	AW	AW		GW	AW	AW	AW	AW	GW	AW	AW
		◇		◇1	◇				◇1	◇				◇1	◇			◇1	◇		◇		◇1	◇	
				☕	🛒				☕	🛒				☕	🛒			☕	🛒				☕	🛒	
Rosslare Harbour ⛴	d																								
Fishguard Harbour ⛴	a																								
	d																								
Milford Haven	d									09 08									11 08						
Johnston	d									09x16									11x16						
Haverfordwest	d									09 23									11 23						
Clarbeston Road	d									09x31									11x31						
Clunderwen	d									09x38									11x38						
Pembroke Dock	d				07 09	08 35												10 00							
Pembroke	d				07 17	08 43												10 10							
Lamphey	d				07x20	08x46																			
Manorbier	d				07 28	08 55												10 23							
Penally	d				07x34	09x00																			
Tenby	a				07 35	09 03												10 32							
	d				07 38	09 08												10 36				11 39			
Saundersfoot	d				07x44	09x16												10 46				11x46			
Kilgetty	d				07x46	09x18																11x48			
Narberth	d				07x56	09x28																11x57			
Whitland	a				08 04	09 38				09 44								11 06	11 44			12 05			
	d				08 05					09 44			10 07					11 07	11 44			12 06			
Carmarthen	a				08 23					10 02			10 24					11 25	12 00			12 23			
	d		08 30		09 00				09 35	10 04			10 29		11 09			11 35	12 05			12 31		13 02	
Ferryside	d				09x10										11x19									13x12	
Kidwelly	d				09x15										11x24									13x17	
Pembrey & Burry Port	d		08 49		09 21				09 56	10 24			10 48		11 30			11 56	12 23			12 50		13 23	
Llanelli	a		08 55		09 27				10 01	10 29			10 54		11 36			12 01	12 28			12 56		13 29	
	d	08 45	08 55		09 28				10 03	10 31			10 55		11 37			12 03	12 30		12 37	12 57		13 30	
Gowerton	d	08x53			09x36								11x02		11x44							13x04			
Swansea	a	09 08	09 23		09 48				10 21	10 48			11 22		11 56			12 21	12 47		13 01	13 24		13 48	
	d	09 11		09 28	09 55				10 28	10 55		11 10		11 28	12 00			12 28	12 55		13 10		13 28	14 00	
Llansamlet	d	09 19										11 17									13 17				
Skewen	d	09 23										11 21									13 21				
Neath	d	09 27		09 40	10 06				10 40	11 06		11 25		11 40	12 11			12 40	13 06		13 25		13 40	14 11	
Briton Ferry	d	09 31										11 28									13 28				
Baglan	d	09 34										11 32									13 32				
Port Talbot Parkway	d	09 38		09 48	10 13				10 48	11 13		11 36		11 48	12 18			12 48	13 13		13 36		13 48	14 18	
Pyle	d	09 46										11 43									13 43				
Maesteg	d							10 15			11 15					12 17				13 15					14 15
Maesteg (Ewenny Road)	d							10 17			11 17					12 19				13 17					14 17
Garth (Mid Glamorgan)	d							10 20			11 20					12 22				13 20					14 20
Tondu	d							10 29			11 29					12 31				13 29					14 29
Sarn	d							10 32			11 32					12 34				13 32					14 32
Wildmill	d							10 34			11 34					12 36				13 34					14 34
Bridgend	d	09 54		10 00	10 25			10 38	11 00	11 25	11 38	11 55		12 00	12 30	12 40		13 00	13 25	13 38	13 52		14 00	14 30	14 38
Pencoed	d							10 44			11 44					12 46				13 44					14 44
Llanharan	d							10 48			11 48					12 50				13 48					14 48
Pontyclun	d							10 52			11 52					12 54				13 52					14 52
Cardiff Central 7	a	10 20		10 22	10 48			11 13	11 22	11 48	12 07	12 18		12 22	12 52	13 09		13 22	13 46	14 09	14 15		14 22	14 52	15 07
Newport (South Wales)	a			10 39	11 07				11 39	12 07	12 25			12 39	13 07	13 25		13 38	14 07				14 39	15 07	15 25
Bristol Parkway 7	a			10 59					11 59					12 59				13 59					14 59		
Gloucester 7	a										13 21					14 21									16 19
Manchester Piccadilly 10	a				14 15					15 15					16 15				17 14					18 15	
Reading 7	a			12 00					13 00					14 00				15 00					16 01		
London Paddington 15 ⊖	a			12 32					13 33					14 32				15 32					16 37		

When events are being held at the Millenium Stadium, services are subject to alteration. Please check times before travelling.

Table 128

Saturdays
until 10 September

West Wales, Swansea and Maesteg - Cardiff

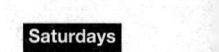

		GW		AW	AW	AW	AW	AW	GW	AW	AW	GW		AW	AW	AW	GW	AW	AW	GW	AW	AW		AW	AW
				R	R					R				R											
		◇1							◇1			◇1					◇1	◇		◇1	◇				◇
																									A
		🍽		🛒	🛒				🍽	🛒		🍽		🛒			🍽			🍽					
Rosslare Harbour ⛴	d																				21 15				
Fishguard Harbour ⛴	a																				00 45				
	d				13 30																				
Milford Haven	d			13 08										15 08										17 08	
Johnston	d			13x16										15x16										17x16	
Haverfordwest	d			13 23										15 23										17 23	
Clarbeston Road	d			13x31	13 50									15x31										17x31	
Clunderwen	d			13x38										15x38										17x38	
Pembroke Dock	d							13 09									14 55					16 25			
Pembroke	d							13 17									15 05					16 33			
Lamphey	d							13x20									15x08					16x36			
Manorbier	d							13 29									15 20					16 45			
Penally	d							13x34									15x26					16x50			
Tenby	a							13 37									15 29					16 53			
	d							13 42									15 36					16 55			
Saundersfoot	d							13x50									15 46					17x03			
Kilgetty	d							13x51									15x49					17x05			
Narberth	d							14x01									15x58					17x15			
Whitland	a			13 44	14 02			14 09						15 44			16 08					17 23		17 44	
	d			13 44	14 02			14 09						15 44			16 09					17 25		17 45	
Carmarthen	a			14 00	14 17			14 27						16 00			16 27					17 43		18 02	
	d			14 05	14 19			14 31		15 05				16 05			16 33					18 30		18 07	
Ferryside	d							14x42		15x15							16x45					→		18x17	
Kidwelly	d							14x48		15x20							16x50							18x22	
Pembrey & Burry Port	d			14 23				14 55		15 27				16 23			16 58							18 29	
Llanelli	a			14 28	14 41			15 01		15 32				16 28			17 03							18 35	
	d			14 30	14 42			15 01		15 34				16 30			17 05	17 41						18 35	
Gowerton	d			14x36										16x36				17x51							
Swansea	a			14 49				15 23		15 51				16 49			17 21	18 10						18 53	
	d	14 28		14 55			15 10		15 28	15 55		16 28		16 55		17 10	17 28			18 28				19 00	
Llansamlet	d						15 17									17 17									
Skewen	d						15 21									17 21									
Neath	d	14 40		15 06			15 25		15 40	16 06		16 40		17 06		17 25	17 40			18 40				19 11	
Briton Ferry	d						15 28									17 28									
Baglan	d						15 32									17 32									
Port Talbot Parkway	d	14 48		15 13			15 36		15 48	16 13		16 48		17 13		17 36	17 48			18 48				19 19	
Pyle	d						15 43									17 43									
Maesteg	d					15 17					16 15				17 15				18 20						19 15
Maesteg (Ewenny Road)	d					15 19					16 17				17 17				18 22						19 17
Garth (Mid Glamorgan)	d					15 22					16 20				17 20				18 25						19 20
Tondu	d					15 31					16 29				17 29				18 34						19 29
Sarn	d					15 34					16 32				17 32				18 37						19 32
Wildmill	d					15 36					16 34				17 34				18 39						19 34
Bridgend	d	15 00		15 25		15 40	15 52		16 00	16 25	16 38	17 00		17 25	17 38	17 54	18 00		18 43	19 00				19 32	19 38
Pencoed	d					15 46					16 44				17 44				18 49						19 44
Llanharan	d					15 50					16 48				17 48				18 53						19 47
Pontyclun	d					15 54					16 52				17 52				18 57						19 52
Cardiff Central 7	a	15 22		15 47	16 06	16 09	16 15		16 22	16 46	17 07	17 22		17 47	18 07	18 20	18 22		19 13	19 22				19 57	20 05
Newport (South Wales)	a	15 39		16 07		16 23	16 32		16 39	17 07	17 27	17 39		18 07	18 25		18 39			19 39					
Bristol Parkway 7	a	15 59							16 59			17 59					18 59			19 59					
Gloucester 7	a					17 19					18 20				19 20										
Manchester Piccadilly 10	a			19 15						20 15				21 10											
Reading 7	a	17 00							18 00			19 00					19 58			21 06					
London Paddington 15 ⊖	a	17 32							18 32			19 32					20 32			21 36					

A from 6 August until 10 September

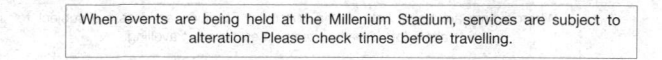

When events are being held at the Millenium Stadium, services are subject to alteration. Please check times before travelling.

Table 128

Saturdays
until 10 September

West Wales, Swansea and Maesteg - Cardiff

		AW	AW	AW	GW	AW	AW	AW	AW	AW	AW	AW	AW	AW	AW	AW	AW	AW
		◇			◇1	◇	◇						◇					
		A				A	B											
Rosslare Harbour	d																	
Fishguard Harbour	a																	
	d																	
Milford Haven	d								19 08			21 16						23 16
Johnston	d								19x16			21x24						23x24
Haverfordwest	d								19 23			21 31						23 31
Clarbeston Road	d								19x31			21x39						23x39
Clunderwen	d								19x38			21x46						23x46
Pembroke Dock	d										19 09					21 09	22 23	
Pembroke	d										19 17					21 17	22 31	
Lamphey	d										19 21					21x20	22x34	
Manorbier	d										19 29					21 29	22 42	
Penally	d										19 34					21x34	22x48	
Tenby	a										19 37					21 37	22 50	
	d										19 49					21 42	22 50	
Saundersfoot	d										19x57					21x50	22x58	
Kilgetty	d										19x59					21x52	23x00	
Narberth	d										20x09					22x02	23x09	
Whitland	a			←					19 44		20 17	21 52				22 10	23 17	23 52
	d								19 44		20 19	21 52				22 10	23 20	23 52
Carmarthen	a			17 43					20 00		20 37	22 14				22 28	23 39	00 14
	d			18 30		19 08	19 08		20 05		20 47					22 35		
Ferryside	d										20x58					22x45		
Kidwelly	d										21x04					22x51		
Pembrey & Burry Port	d			18 49		19 26	19 26		20 23		21 11					22 58		
Llanelli	a			18 55		19 31	19 31		20 28		21 17					23 04		
	d			18 55		19 32	19 32		20 29		21 17		21 40			23 05		
Gowerton	d			19x03									21x47			23x12		
Swansea	a			19 18		19 50	19 50		20 47		21 39		22 10			23 32		
	d		19 10		19 28	20 00	20 00		20 55		21 43				22 20			
Llansamlet	d		19 17								21 50				22 27			
Skewen	d		19 21								21 54				22 31			
Neath	d		19 25		19 40	20 11	20 11		21 06		21 58				22 35			
Briton Ferry	d		19 28								22 02				22 38			
Baglan	d		19 32								22 05				22 42			
Port Talbot Parkway	d		19 36		19 48	20 18	20 18		21 13		22 09				22 46			
Pyle	d		19 43								22 16				22 53			
Maesteg	d	19 15						20 15		21 15				22 15				
Maesteg (Ewenny Road)	d	19 17						20 17		21 17				22 17				
Garth (Mid Glamorgan)	d	19 20						20 20		21 20				22 20				
Tondu	d	19 29						20 29		21 29				22 29				
Sarn	d	19 32						20 32		21 32				22 32				
Wildmill	d	19 34						20 34		21 34				22 34				
Bridgend	d	19 38	19 51		20 00	20 30	20 30	20 38	21 25	21 38	22 25			22 38	23 01			
Pencoed	d	19 44						20 44		21 44				22 44				
Llanharan	d	19 47						20 48		21 48				22 48				
Pontyclun	d	19 52						20 52		21 52				22 52				
Cardiff Central 7	a	20 05	20 17		20 23	20 51	20 51	21 07	21 48	22 09	22 47			23 08	23 26			
Newport (South Wales)	a	20 24			20 39	21 08	21 09	21 25						23 36				
Bristol Parkway 7	a				21 01													
Gloucester 7	a							22 22						00 40				
Manchester Piccadilly 10	a	23 50																
Reading 7	a				21 59													
London Paddington 15 ⊖	a				22 37													

A until 30 July

B from 6 August until 10 September

When events are being held at the Millenium Stadium, services are subject to alteration. Please check times before travelling.

Table 128

Saturdays

from 17 September

West Wales, Swansea and Maesteg - Cardiff

		AW	AW	AW	AW	AW	GW	GW	GW	AW		GW	GW	AW	AW	GW	AW	GW	AW	AW		GW	GW	AW	AW
																									[illegible]
		◇				◇	◇1	◇1	◇1	◇		◇1	◇1		◇	◇1		◇1	◇			◇1	◇1	◇	
																A		A							B
							🍴	🍴	🍴	☕		🍴	🍴		☕	🍴⊘		🍴⊘	☕			🍴	🍴	☕	
Rosslare Harbour ⛴	d	21p15																							09(00
Fishguard Harbour ⛴	a	00 45																							12)30
	d					01 50																			
Milford Haven	d			23p18	00 18														06 00					07 05	
Johnston	d			23b26	00x26														06x08					07x13	
Haverfordwest	d			23p33	00 33														06 15					07 20	
Clarbeston Road	d			23b41	00x41	02x10													06x23					07x28	
Clunderwen	d			23b48	00x48														06x30					07x35	
Pembroke Dock	d																								
Pembroke	d																								
Lamphey	d																								
Manorbier	d																								
Penally	d																								
Tenby	a																								
	d																								
Saundersfoot	d																								
Kilgetty	d																								
Narberth	d																								
Whitland	a			23p54	00 54	02 22													06 36					07 41	
	d			23p54	00 54	02 22													06 36					07 41	
Carmarthen	a			00 16	01 16	02 39													06 52					07 55	
	d					02 44				05 04					05 55		06 20		06 57					08 01	
Ferryside	d														06x05		06x30							08x11	
Kidwelly	d														06x10		06x35							08x16	
Pembrey & Burry Port	d									05 22					06 17		06 42		07 15					08 23	
Llanelli	a					03 06				05 27					06 22		06 47		07 20					08 28	
	d					03 06				05 29					06 24		06 48		07 22					08 30	
Gowerton	d														06x30		06x55		07x28					08x36	
Swansea	a					03 29									06 43		07 09		07 41					08 49	
	d						03 58	04 58	05 28			05 58	06 28		06 47	06 58	07 12	07 28	07 45			07 58	08 28	08 55	
Llansamlet	d																07 19								
Skewen	d																07 23								
Neath	d						04 10	05 10	05 40			06 10	06 40		06 58	07 10	07 27	07 40	07 56			08 10	08 40	09 06	
Briton Ferry	d																07 30								
Baglan	d																07 34								
Port Talbot Parkway	d						04 18	05 18	05 48	06 02		06 18	06 48		07 05	07 18	07 38	07 48	08 03			08 18	08 48	09 13	
Pyle	d									06 08					07 11		07 45		08 09						
Maesteg	d		22p15											06 46						08 00					
Maesteg (Ewenny Road)	d		22p17											06 48						08 02					
Garth (Mid Glamorgan)	d		22p20											06 51						08 05					
Tondu	d		22p29											07 00						08 14					
Sarn	d		22p32											07 03						08 17					
Wildmill	d		22p34											07 05						08 19					
Bridgend	d		22p38				04 30	05 30	06 00	06 16		06 30	07 00	07 09	07 19	07 30	07 53	08 00	08 17	08 23		08 30	09 00	09 25	
Pencoed	d		22p44							06 22				07 15			08 06		08 23						
Llanharan	d		22p48							06 25					07 26		08 10			08 30					
Pontyclun	d		22p52							06 30				07 22			08 14		08 30						
Cardiff Central 7	a		23p07				04 52	05 52	06 22	06 43		06 52	07 22	07 36	07 42	07 52	08 34	08 22	08 44	08 47		08 52	09 22	09 44	
Newport (South Wales)	a		23p38				05 09	06 09	06 38	07 02		07 08	07 39		08 02	08 08		08 38	09 02	09 24		09 08	09 39	10 07	
Bristol Parkway 7	a						05 36	06 29	06 59			07 29	07 59			08 30		08 59				09 30	09 59		
Gloucester 7	a		00 39																	10 19					
Manchester Piccadilly 10	a									10 14					11 15				12 15					13 15	
Reading 7	a						07 14	07 31	08 00			08 31	09 00			09 32		10 00				10 32	11 01		
London Paddington 15 ⊖	a						07 44	08 07	08 32			09 02	09 32			10 02		10 32				11 02	11 33		

A 🍴 from Reading ⊘ to Bristol Parkway **B** not 10 December **b** Previous night, stops on request

When events are being held at the Millenium Stadium, services are subject to alteration. Please check times before travelling.

Table 128

Saturdays

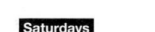

from 17 September

West Wales, Swansea and Maesteg - Cardiff

		AW	AW ◇	AW	GW ◇1	AW ◇	AW	GW ◇1	AW ◇	AW	AW	AW	GW ◇1	AW ◇	AW	GW ◇1	AW ◇	AW	AW ◇	AW	GW ◇1	AW ◇	AW
Rosslare Harbour	d																						
Fishguard Harbour	a																						
	d																						
Milford Haven	d								09 08								11 08						
Johnston	d								09x16								11x16						
Haverfordwest	d								09 23								11 23						
Clarbeston Road	d								09x31								11x31						
Clunderwen	d								09x38								11x38						
Pembroke Dock	d					07 09						09 07								11 09			
Pembroke	d					07 17						09 15								11 17			
Lamphey	d					07x20						09x18								11x20			
Manorbier	d					07 28						09 27								11 29			
Penally	d					07x34						09x32								11x34			
Tenby	a					07 35						09 35								11 37			
	d					07 38						09 36								11 41			
Saundersfoot	d					07x44						09x44								11x49			
Kilgetty	d					07x46						09x46								11x51			
Narberth	d					07x56						09x56								12x01			
Whitland	a					08 04			09 44			10 04					11 44			12 09			
	d					08 05			09 44			10 07					11 44			12 09			
Carmarthen	a					08 23			10 02			10 24					12 00			12 27			
	d			08 30		09 00		09 35	10 04			10 29		11 09			12 05			12 31		13 02	
Ferryside	d					09x10								11x19								13x12	
Kidwelly	d					09x15								11x24								13x17	
Pembrey & Burry Port	d			08 49		09 21		09 56	10 24			10 48		11 30			12 23			12 50		13 23	
Llanelli	a			08 55		09 27		10 01	10 29			10 54		11 36			12 28			12 56		13 29	
	d		08 45	08 55		09 28		10 03	10 31			10 55		11 37			12 30		12 37	12 57		13 30	
Gowerton	d		08x53			09x36						11x02		11x44						13x04			
Swansea	a		09 08	09 23		09 48		10 21	10 48			11 22		11 56			12 47		13 01	13 23		13 48	
	d		09 11		09 28	09 55		10 28	10 55		11 10		11 28	12 00		12 28	12 55		13 10		13 28	14 00	
Llansamlet	d		09 19								11 17								13 17				
Skewen	d		09 23								11 21								13 21				
Neath	d		09 27		09 40	10 06		10 40	11 06		11 25		11 40	12 11		12 40	13 06		13 25		13 40	14 11	
Briton Ferry	d		09 31								11 28								13 28				
Baglan	d		09 34								11 32								13 32				
Port Talbot Parkway	d		09 38		09 48	10 13		10 48	11 13		11 36		11 48	12 18		12 48	13 13		13 36		13 48	14 18	
Pyle	d		09 46								11 43								13 43				
Maesteg	d	09 17					10 15			11 15					12 17			13 15					14 15
Maesteg (Ewenny Road)	d	09 19					10 17			11 17					12 19			13 17					14 17
Garth (Mid Glamorgan)	d	09 22					10 20			11 20					12 22			13 20					14 20
Tondu	d	09 31					10 29			11 29					12 31			13 29					14 29
Sarn	d	09 34					10 32			11 32					12 34			13 32					14 32
Wildmill	d	09 36					10 34			11 34					12 36			13 34					14 34
Bridgend	d	09 40	09 54		10 00	10 25	10 38	11 00	11 25	11 38	11 55		12 00	12 30	12 40	13 00	13 25	13 38	13 52		14 00	14 30	14 38
Pencoed	d	09 46					10 44			11 44					12 46			13 44					14 44
Llanharan	d	09 50					10 48			11 48					12 50			13 48					14 48
Pontyclun	d	09 54					10 52			11 52					12 54			13 52					14 52
Cardiff Central 7	a	10 09	10 20		10 22	10 48	11 13	11 22	11 48	12 07	12 18		12 22	12 52	13 09	13 22	13 46	14 09	14 15		14 22	14 52	15 07
Newport (South Wales)	a	10 25			10 39	11 07		11 39	12 07	12 25			12 39	13 07	13 25	13 38	14 07				14 39	15 07	15 25
Bristol Parkway 7	a				10 59			11 59					12 59			13 59					14 59		
Gloucester 7	a	11 21								13 21					14 21								16 19
Manchester Piccadilly 10	a					14 15			15 15					16 15			17 14					18 15	
Reading 7	a				12 00			13 00					14 00			15 00					16 00		
London Paddington 15 ⊖	a				12 32			13 33					14 32			15 32					16 32		

When events are being held at the Millenium Stadium, services are subject to alteration. Please check times before travelling.

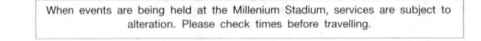

Table 128

Saturdays

from 17 September

West Wales, Swansea and Maesteg - Cardiff

		GW		AW	AW	AW	AW	AW	GW	AW	AW	GW		AW	AW	AW	AW	GW	AW	AW	GW	AW		AW	AW
				R	R					R				R											
		◇1							◇1			◇1						◇1	◇		◇1			◇	
		☕		🛒	🛒				☕	🛒		☕		🛒				☕			☕				
Rosslare Harbour ⛴	d																								
Fishguard Harbour ⛴	a																								
	d				13 30																				
Milford Haven	d			13 08										15 08								17 08			
Johnston	d			13x16										15x16								17x16			
Haverfordwest	d			13 23										15 23								17 23			
Clarbeston Road	d			13x31	13 50									15x31								17x31			
Clunderwen	d			13x38										15x38								17x38			
Pembroke Dock	d							13 09									15 09								
Pembroke	d							13 17									15 17								
Lamphey	d							13x20									15x20								
Manorbier	d							13 29									15 29								
Penally	d							13x34									15x34								
Tenby	a							13 37									15 37								
	d							13 42									15 42								
Saundersfoot	d							13x50									15x49								
Kilgetty	d							13x51									15x51								
Narberth	d							14x01									16x00								
Whitland	a			13 44	14 02			14 09						15 44			16 08					17 44			
	d			13 44	14 02			14 09						15 44			16 09					17 45			
Carmarthen	a			14 00	14 17			14 27						16 00			16 26					18 02			
	d			14 05	14 19			14 31		15 05				16 05			16 31					18 07			
Ferryside	d							14x42		15x15												18x17			
Kidwelly	d							14x48		15x20												18x22			
Pembrey & Burry Port	d			14 23				14 55		15 27				16 23			16 50					18 29			
Llanelli	a			14 28	14 41			15 01		15 32				16 28			16 56					18 35			
	d			14 30	14 42			15 01		15 34				16 30			16 57		17 41			18 35			
Gowerton	d			14x36										16x36			17x04		17x51						
Swansea	a			14 49				15 23		15 51				16 49			17 19		18 10			18 53			
	d	14 28		14 55			15 10		15 28	15 55		16 28		16 55		17 10		17 28			18 28	19 00			19 10
Llansamlet	d						15 17									17 17									19 17
Skewen	d						15 21									17 21									19 21
Neath	d	14 40		15 06			15 25		15 40	16 06		16 40		17 06		17 25		17 40			18 40	19 11			19 25
Briton Ferry	d						15 28									17 28									19 28
Baglan	d						15 32									17 32									19 32
Port Talbot Parkway	d	14 48		15 13			15 36		15 48	16 13		16 48		17 13		17 36		17 48			18 48	19 19			19 36
Pyle	d						15 43									17 43									19 43
Maesteg	d					15 17					16 15				17 15					18 20				19 15	
Maesteg (Ewenny Road)	d					15 19					16 17				17 17					18 22				19 17	
Garth (Mid Glamorgan)	d					15 22					16 20				17 20					18 25				19 20	
Tondu	d					15 31					16 29				17 29					18 34				19 29	
Sarn	d					15 34					16 32				17 32					18 37				19 32	
Wildmill	d					15 36					16 34				17 34					18 39				19 34	
Bridgend	d	15 00		15 25		15 40	15 52		16 00	16 25	16 38	17 00		17 25	17 38	17 54		18 00		18 43	19 00	19 32		19 38	19 51
Pencoed	d					15 46					16 44				17 44					18 49				19 44	
Llanharan	d					15 50					16 48				17 48					18 53				19 47	
Pontyclun	d					15 54					16 52				17 52					18 57				19 52	
Cardiff Central 7	a	15 22		15 47	16 06	16 09	16 15		16 22	16 46	17 07	17 22		17 47	18 07	18 20		18 22		19 13	19 22	19 57		20 05	20 17
Newport (South Wales)	a	15 39		16 07		16 23	16 32		16 39	17 07	17 27	17 39		18 07	18 25			18 39			19 39			20 24	
Bristol Parkway 7	a	15 59							16 59			17 59						18 59			19 59				
Gloucester 7	a					17 19					18 20				19 20										
Manchester Piccadilly 10	a			19 15						20 15				21 10										23 50	
Reading 7	a	17 00							18 00			19 00						20 00			21 06				
London Paddington 15 ⊖	a	17 32							18 32			19 32						20 32			21 36				

When events are being held at the Millenium Stadium, services are subject to alteration. Please check times before travelling.

Table 128

Saturdays
from 17 September

West Wales, Swansea and Maesteg - Cardiff

		AW	GW	AW	AW	AW	AW	AW		AW	AW	AW	AW	AW	AW	AW	AW
			◇1	◇			◇					◇					
			🍴														
Rosslare Harbour ⛴	d						21 15										
Fishguard Harbour ⛴	a						00 45										
	d																
Milford Haven	d					19 08					21 16						23 16
Johnston	d					19x16					21x24						23x24
Haverfordwest	d					19 23					21 31						23 31
Clarbeston Road	d					19x31					21x39						23x39
Clunderwen	d					19x38					21x46						23x46
Pembroke Dock	d	17 07								19 09					21 09	22 23	
Pembroke	d	17 15								19 17					21 17	22 31	
Lamphey	d	17x18								19 21					21x20	22x34	
Manorbier	d	17 27								19 29					21 29	22 42	
Penally	d	17x32								19 34					21x34	22x48	
Tenby	a	17 35								19 37					21 37	22 50	
	d	17 40								19 49					21 42	22 50	
Saundersfoot	d	17x47								19x57					21x50	22x58	
Kilgetty	d	17x49								19x59					21x52	23x00	
Narberth	d	17x58								20x09					22x02	23x09	
Whitland	a	18 06				19 44				20 17	21 52				22 10	23 17	23 52
	d	18 07				19 44				20 19	21 52				22 10	23 20	23 52
Carmarthen	a	18 24				20 00				20 37	22 14				22 28	23 39	00 14
	d	18 30		19 08		20 05				20 47					22 35		
Ferryside	d	18x40								20x58					22x45		
Kidwelly	d	18x46								21x04					22x51		
Pembrey & Burry Port	d	18 53		19 26		20 23				21 11					22 58		
Llanelli	a	19 00		19 31		20 28				21 17					23 04		
	d	19 00		19 32		20 29				21 17		21 40			23 05		
Gowerton	d	19x07										21x47			23x12		
Swansea	a	19 22		19 50		20 47				21 39		22 10			23 32		
	d		19 28	20 00		20 55				21 43				22 20			
Llansamlet	d									21 50				22 27			
Skewen	d									21 54				22 31			
Neath	d		19 40	20 11		21 06				21 58				22 35			
Briton Ferry	d									22 02				22 38			
Baglan	d									22 05				22 42			
Port Talbot Parkway	d		19 48	20 18		21 13				22 09				22 46			
Pyle	d									22 16				22 53			
Maesteg	d				20 15			21 15					22 15				
Maesteg (Ewenny Road)	d				20 17			21 17					22 17				
Garth (Mid Glamorgan)	d				20 20			21 20					22 20				
Tondu	d				20 29			21 29					22 29				
Sarn	d				20 32			21 32					22 32				
Wildmill	d				20 34			21 34					22 34				
Bridgend	d		20 00	20 30	20 38	21 25		21 38		22 25			22 38	23 01			
Pencoed	d				20 44			21 44					22 44				
Llanharan	d				20 48			21 48					22 48				
Pontyclun	d				20 52			21 52					22 52				
Cardiff Central 7	a		20 23	20 51	21 07	21 48		22 09		22 47			23 07	23 26			
Newport (South Wales)	a		20 39	21 08	21 25								23 41				
Bristol Parkway 7	a		21 01														
Gloucester 7	a				22 22												
Manchester Piccadilly 10	a																
Reading 7	a		21 59														
London Paddington 15 ⊖	a		22 37														

When events are being held at the Millenium Stadium, services are subject to alteration. Please check times before travelling.

Table 128

Sundays
until 19 June

West Wales, Swansea and Maesteg - Cardiff

		AW	AW	AW	AW	GW	AW	GW	AW	GW	AW	GW	AW	AW	AW	GW	GW	AW	AW	GW	GW	AW	AW
		◇ A	A	A	◇	◇1 (bistro)	R	◇1 (bistro)	◇ (trolley)	◇1 (bistro)		◇1 (bistro)	◇ (trolley)			◇1 (bistro)	◇1 (bistro)	R (trolley)		◇1 (bistro)	◇1 (bistro)	R (trolley)	◇
Rosslare Harbour ⛴	d	21p15					09 00																
Fishguard Harbour ⛴	a	00 45					12 30																
	d				01 50																		
Milford Haven	d			23p16									09 28					11 28				13 23	
Johnston	d			23b24									09x38					11x36				13x29	
Haverfordwest	d			23p31									09 45					11 43				13 36	
Clarbeston Road	d			23b39	02 10								09x54					11x52				13x45	
Clunderwen	d			23b46									10x01					11x59				13x52	
Pembroke Dock	d														10 45				11 53				
Pembroke	d														10 53				12 01				
Lamphey	d														10x56				12x04				
Manorbier	d														11 05				12 13				
Penally	d														11x10				12x18				
Tenby	a														11 13				12 21				
	d														11 14				12 21				
Saundersfoot	d														11x22				12x29				
Kilgetty	d														11x24				12x31				
Narberth	d														11x34				12x41				
Whitland	a			23p52	02s22								10 08		11 42			12 06	12 49			13 59	
	d			23p52									10 08		11 45			12 08	12 52			14 02	
Carmarthen	a			00 14	02s40								10 26		12 06			12 26	13 10			14 20	
	d								08 40		09 40		10 30	11 18				12 29	13 17			14 23	
Ferryside	d										09x50			11x28					13x27				
Kidwelly	d										09x56			11x34					13x33				
Pembrey & Burry Port	d								08 59		10 03		10 49	11 42				12 49	13 40			14 42	
Llanelli	a				03s06				09 05		10 09		10 54	11 48				12 55	13 46			14 48	
	d								09 07		10 10		10 56	11 48				12 55	13 47			14 49	15 41
Gowerton	d										10x17			11x56					13x54				
Swansea	a				03s26				09 28		10 35		11 15	12 14				13 15	14 14			15 08	16 04
	d					08 07		09 21	09 32	10 21		11 22	11 32			12 21	13 21	13 43		14 21	15 21	15 33	
Llansamlet	d																						
Skewen	d																						
Neath	d				03s45	08 19		09 33	09 43	10 33		11 34	11 43			12 33	13 33	13 54		14 33	15 33	15 44	
Briton Ferry	d																						
Baglan	d																						
Port Talbot Parkway	d				03s52	08 26		09 40	09 50	10 40		11 41	11 50			12 40	13 40	14 01		14 40	15 40	15 51	
Pyle	d								09 57				11 57					14 09				15 58	
Maesteg	d		22p15																				
Maesteg (Ewenny Road)	d		22p17																				
Garth (Mid Glamorgan)	d		22p20																				
Tondu	d		22p29																				
Sarn	d		22p32																				
Wildmill	d		22p34																				
Bridgend	d		22p38		04s06	08 38		09 52	10 05	10 52		11 53	12 05			12 52	13 52	14 17		14 52	15 52	16 06	
Pencoed	d		22p44										12 11									16 12	
Llanharan	d		22p48										12 15									16 16	
Pontyclun	d		22p52										12 20									16 21	
Cardiff Central 7	a		23p08		04 35	09 01		10 14	10 29	11 14		12 15	12 35			13 14	14 14	14 40		15 14	16 14	16 36	
Newport (South Wales)	a		23p36			09 18		10 31	10 48	11 31		12 31	12 52			13 31	14 31	15 12		15 31	16 31	16 52	
Bristol Parkway 7	a					09 46		10 59		11 59		12 59				13 59	14 59			15 59	16 59		
Gloucester 7	a		00 40																				
Manchester Piccadilly 10	a								14 19				16 17					18 17				20 17	
Reading 7	a					10 42		12 01		13 00		14 00				15 00	16 00			17 00	18 00		
London Paddington 15 ⊖	a					11 21		12 38		13 39		14 39				15 39	16 39			17 39	18 39		

A not 22 May

b Previous night, stops on request

When events are being held at the Millenium Stadium, services are subject to alteration. Please check times before travelling.

Table 128

Sundays
until 19 June

West Wales, Swansea and Maesteg - Cardiff

		AW	GW	GW	AW	GW		GW	AW	AW	GW	AW	AW	AW	AW	AW		AW	AW	AW
					[illegible]											🅱				
			◇1	◇1		◇1		◇1			◇1	◇			◇			◇		
			🍴	🍴	🛒	🍴		🍴			🍴									
Rosslare Harbour ⛴	d															21 15				
Fishguard Harbour ⛴	a															00 45				
	d	14 23																		
Milford Haven	d				15 28					17 30				19 38				21 33		23 15
Johnston	d				15x36					17x38				19x46				21x41		23x23
Haverfordwest	d				15 43					17 45				19 53				21 49		23 30
Clarbeston Road	d	14 43			15x52					17x53				20x01				21x57		23x39
Clunderwen	d				15x59					18x00				20x08				22x05		23x46
Pembroke Dock	d								16 45				19 00						21 45	
Pembroke	d								16 53				19 08						21 53	
Lamphey	d								16x56				19x11						21x56	
Manorbier	d								17 05				19 20						22 05	
Penally	d								17x10				19x25						22x10	
Tenby	a								17 13				19 28						22 13	
	d								17 13				19 28						22 13	
Saundersfoot	d								17x21				19x36						22x21	
Kilgetty	d								17x23				19x38						22x23	
Narberth	d								17x33				19x48						22x33	
Whitland	a	14 55			16 06				17 41	18 06			19 56	20 14				22 11	22 41	23 53
	d	14 55			16 09				17 44	18 08			19 59	20 17				22 14	22 44	23 53
Carmarthen	a	15 13			16 26				18 04	18 29			20 16	20 36				22 31	23 05	00 14
	d	15 16	15 30		16 30	16 55			18 07		19 09		20 19		21 05			22 34		
Ferryside	d	15x26			16x40				18x17				20x30					22x44		
Kidwelly	d	15x32			16x46				18x23				20x36					22x50		
Pembrey & Burry Port	d	15 39	15 50		16 54	17 15			18 31		19 29		20 43		21 24			22 58		
Llanelli	a	15 45	15 56		17 00	17 21			18 37		19 35		20 49		21 30			23 04		
	d	15 46	15 58		17 00	17 22			18 38		19 36	19 55	20 51		21 31			23 04		
Gowerton	d	15x55							18x46			20x02	20x58					23x12		
Swansea	a	16 14	16 14		17 19	17 39			19 06		19 53	20 16	21 17		21 48			23 27		
	d		16 21	16 51	17 30	17 51		18 51			19 59	20 40			21 52			23 30		
Llansamlet	d																			
Skewen	d																			
Neath	d		16 33	17 03	17 41	18 03		19 03			20 11	20 51			22 03			23 42		
Briton Ferry	d																			
Baglan	d																			
Port Talbot Parkway	d		16 40	17 10	17 48	18 10		19 10			20 18	20 58			22 10			23 49		
Pyle	d				17 55										22 17			23 56		
Maesteg	d																			
Maesteg (Ewenny Road)	d																			
Garth (Mid Glamorgan)	d																			
Tondu	d																			
Sarn	d																			
Wildmill	d																			
Bridgend	d		16 52	17 22	18 03	18 22		19 22			20 30	21 11			22 25			00 04		
Pencoed	d				18 09															
Llanharan	d				18 13															
Pontyclun	d				18 18															
Cardiff Central 7	a		17 14	17 45	18 34	18 45		19 45			20 53	21 36			22 49			00 29		
Newport (South Wales)	a		17 31	18 03	18 52	19 03		20 03			21 08				23 18					
Bristol Parkway 7	a		17 59	18 31		19 31		20 31			21 36									
Gloucester 7	a																			
Manchester Piccadilly 10	a				22 19															
Reading 7	a		19 00	19 30		20 32		21 32			22 37									
London Paddington 15 ⊖	a		19 40	20 11		21 16		22 15			23 20									

When events are being held at the Millenium Stadium, services are subject to alteration. Please check times before travelling.

Table 128

Sundays

26 June to 31 July

West Wales, Swansea and Maesteg - Cardiff

		AW	AW	AW	AW	GW	GW	AW	AW	GW	AW	GW	AW	GW	AW	AW	GW	AW	GW	AW	GW	AW	GW
		◇			◇	◇1	◇1	◇	R	◇1		◇1	◇	◇1			◇1	R	◇1		◇1	R	◇1
Rosslare Harbour ⛴	d	21p15							09 00														
Fishguard Harbour ⛴	a	00 45							12 30														
	d				01 50																		
Milford Haven	d			23p16									09 28					11 28				13 23	
Johnston	d			23b24									09x38					11x36				13x29	
Haverfordwest	d			23p31									09 45					11 43				13 36	
Clarbeston Road	d			23b39	02 10								09x54					11x52				13x45	
Clunderwen	d			23b46									10x01					11x59				13x52	
Pembroke Dock	d															10 45				11 53			
Pembroke	d															10 53				12 01			
Lamphey	d															10x56				12x04			
Manorbier	d															11 05				12 13			
Penally	d															11x10				12x18			
Tenby	a															11 13				12 21			
	d															11 14				12 21			
Saundersfoot	d															11x22				12x29			
Kilgetty	d															11x24				12x31			
Narberth	d															11x34				12x41			
Whitland	a			23p52	02s22								10 08			11 42		12 06		12 49		13 59	
	d			23p52									10 08			11 45		12 08		12 52		14 02	
Carmarthen	a			00 14	02s40								10 26			12 06		12 26		13 10		14 20	
	d							08 40			09 40		10 30		11 18			12 29		13 17		14 23	
Ferryside	d										09x50				11x28					13x27			
Kidwelly	d										09x56				11x34					13x33			
Pembrey & Burry Port	d							08 59			10 03		10 49		11 42			12 49		13 40		14 42	
Llanelli	a				03s06			09 05			10 09		10 54		11 48			12 55		13 46		14 48	
	d							09 07			10 10		10 56		11 48			12 55		13 47		14 49	
Gowerton	d										10x17				11x56					13x54			
Swansea	a				03s26			09 28			10 35		11 15		12 14			13 21		14 14		15 08	
	d					07 40	08 45	09 32		09 55		10 55	11 32	11 55			12 55	13 43	13 55		14 55	15 33	15 55
Llansamlet	d																						
Skewen	d																						
Neath	d				03s45	07 52	08 57	09 43		10 07		11 07	11 43	12 07			13 07	13 54	14 07		15 07	15 44	16 07
Briton Ferry	d																						
Baglan	d																						
Port Talbot Parkway	d				03s52	07 59	09 04	09 50		10 14		11 14	11 50	12 14			13 14	14 01	14 14		15 14	15 51	16 14
Pyle	d							09 57					11 57					14 09				15 58	
Maesteg	d		22p15																				
Maesteg (Ewenny Road)	d		22p17																				
Garth (Mid Glamorgan)	d		22p20																				
Tondu	d		22p29																				
Sarn	d		22p32																				
Wildmill	d		22p34																				
Bridgend	d		22p38		04s06	08 11	09 16	10 05		10 26		11 26	12 05	12 26			13 26	14 17	14 26		15 26	16 06	16 26
Pencoed	d		22p44										12 11									16 12	
Llanharan	d		22p48										12 15									16 16	
Pontyclun	d		22p52										12 20									16 21	
Cardiff Central 7	a		23p08		04 35	08 34	09 38	10 29		10 48		11 48	12 35	12 48			13 48	14 40	14 48		15 48	16 36	16 48
Newport (South Wales)	a		23p36			08 53	09 55	10 48		11 04		12 05	12 52	13 05			14 05	15 12	15 05		16 05	16 52	17 05
Bristol Parkway 7	a					09 22	10 23			11 34		12 34		13 37			14 36		15 35		16 34		17 33
Gloucester 7	a		00 40																				
Manchester Piccadilly 10	a							14 19					16 17					18 17				20 17	
Reading 7	a					10 42	11 44			13 01		14 00		15 00			16 00		17 00		18 00		19 00
London Paddington 15 ⊖	a					11 21	12 24			13 40		14 40		15 40			16 40		17 39		18 40		19 39

b Previous night, stops on request

When events are being held at the Millenium Stadium, services are subject to alteration. Please check times before travelling.

Table 128

Sundays

26 June to 31 July

West Wales, Swansea and Maesteg - Cardiff

		AW	AW	GW	GW	AW		GW	AW	AW	GW	AW	AW	AW	AW	AW		AW	AW	AW
						R										R				
		◇		◇1	◇1			◇1			◇1	◇			◇			◇		
				☕	☕	🛒		☕			☕									
Rosslare Harbour ⛴	d															21 15				
Fishguard Harbour ⛴	a															00 45				
	d		14 23																	
Milford Haven	d					15 28				17 30				19 38				21 33		23 15
Johnston	d					15x36				17x38				19x46				21x41		23x23
Haverfordwest	d					15 43				17 45				19 53				21 49		23 30
Clarbeston Road	d		14 43			15x52				17x53				20x01				21x57		23x39
Clunderwen	d					15x59				18x00				20x08				22x05		23x46
Pembroke Dock	d								16 45				19 00						21 45	
Pembroke	d								16 53				19 08						21 53	
Lamphey	d								16x56				19x11						21x56	
Manorbier	d								17 05				19 20						22 05	
Penally	d								17x10				19x25						22x10	
Tenby	a								17 13				19 28						22 13	
	d								17 13				19 28						22 13	
Saundersfoot	d								17x21				19x36						22x21	
Kilgetty	d								17x23				19x38						22x23	
Narberth	d								17x33				19x48						22x33	
Whitland	a		14 55			16 06			17 41	18 06			19 56	20 14				22 11	22 41	23 53
	d		14 55			16 09			17 44	18 08			19 59	20 17				22 14	22 44	23 53
Carmarthen	a		15 13			16 26			18 04	18 29			20 16	20 36				22 31	23 05	00 14
	d		15 16	15 35		16 30		17 25	18 07		18 50		20 19		21 05			22 34		
Ferryside	d		15x26			16x40			18x17				20x30					22x44		
Kidwelly	d		15x32			16x46			18x23				20x36					22x50		
Pembrey & Burry Port	d		15 39	15 55		16 54		17 45	18 31		19 10		20 43		21 24			22 58		
Llanelli	a		15 45	16 01		17 00		17 51	18 37		19 16		20 49		21 30			23 04		
	d	15 41	15 46	16 03		17 00		17 52	18 38		19 17	19 55	20 51		21 31			23 04		
Gowerton	d		15x55						18x46			20x02	20x58					23x12		
Swansea	a	16 04	16 14	16 19		17 19		18 09	19 06		19 34	20 16	21 17		21 48			23 27		
	d			16 29	17 21	17 30		18 25			19 53	20 40			21 52			23 30		
Llansamlet	d																			
Skewen	d																			
Neath	d			16 41	17 33	17 41		18 37			20 05	20 51			22 03			23 42		
Briton Ferry	d																			
Baglan	d																			
Port Talbot Parkway	d			16 48	17 40	17 48		18 44			20 12	20 58			22 10			23 49		
Pyle	d					17 55									22 17			23 56		
Maesteg	d																			
Maesteg (Ewenny Road)	d																			
Garth (Mid Glamorgan)	d																			
Tondu	d																			
Sarn	d																			
Wildmill	d																			
Bridgend	d			17 00	17 52	18 03		18 56			20 24	21 11			22 25			00 04		
Pencoed	d					18 09														
Llanharan	d					18 13														
Pontyclun	d					18 18														
Cardiff Central 7	a			17 22	18 15	18 34		19 20			20 47	21 36			22 49			00 29		
Newport (South Wales)	a			17 38	18 32	18 52		19 37			21 03				23 18					
Bristol Parkway 7	a			18 06	19 00			20 05			21 33									
Gloucester 7	a																			
Manchester Piccadilly 10	a					22 19														
Reading 7	a			19 30	20 30			21 31			22 55									
London Paddington 15 ⊖	a			20 11	21 13			22 21			23 34									

When events are being held at the Millenium Stadium, services are subject to alteration. Please check times before travelling.

Table 128

Sundays

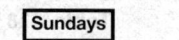

7 August to 11 September

West Wales, Swansea and Maesteg - Cardiff

		AW	AW	AW	AW	GW	AW	GW	AW	GW		AW	GW	AW	AW	AW	GW	GW	AW	AW		GW	GW	AW	AW
							R												R					R	
		◇			◇	◇1		◇1	◇	◇1			◇1	◇			◇1	◇1				◇1	◇1		◇
						🍽		🍽	🛒	🍽			🍽	🛒			🍽	🍽	🛒			🍽	🍽	🛒	
Rosslare Harbour ⛴	d	21p15					09 00																		
Fishguard Harbour ⛴	a	00 45					12 30																		
	d				01 50																				
Milford Haven	d			23p16										09 28					11 28					13 23	
Johnston	d			23b24										09x38					11x36					13x29	
Haverfordwest	d			23p31										09 45					11 43					13 36	
Clarbeston Road	d			23b39	02 10									09x54					11x52					13x45	
Clunderwen	d			23b46										10x01					11x59					13x52	
Pembroke Dock	d															10 45				11 53					
Pembroke	d															10 53				12 01					
Lamphey	d															10x56				12x04					
Manorbier	d															11 05				12 13					
Penally	d															11x10				12x18					
Tenby	a															11 13				12 21					
	d															11 14				12 21					
Saundersfoot	d															11x22				12x29					
Kilgetty	d															11x24				12x31					
Narberth	d															11x34				12x41					
Whitland	a			23p52	02s22									10 08		11 42			12 06	12 49				13 59	
	d			23p52										10 08		11 45			12 08	12 52				14 02	
Carmarthen	a			00 14	02s40									10 26		12 06			12 26	13 10				14 20	
	d								08 40			09 40		10 30	11 18				12 29	13 17				14 23	
Ferryside	d											09x50			11x28					13x27					
Kidwelly	d											09x56			11x34					13x33					
Pembrey & Burry Port	d								08 59			10 03		10 49	11 42				12 49	13 40				14 42	
Llanelli	a				03s06				09 05			10 09		10 54	11 48				12 55	13 46				14 48	
	d								09 07			10 10		10 56	11 48				12 55	13 47				14 49	15 41
Gowerton	d											10x17			11x56					13x54					
Swansea	a				03s26				09 28			10 35		11 15	12 14				13 15	14 14				15 08	16 04
	d					08 07		09 21	09 32	10 21			11 21	11 32			12 21	13 21	13 43			14 21	15 21	15 33	
Llansamlet	d																								
Skewen	d																								
Neath	d				03s45	08 19		09 33	09 43	10 33			11 33	11 43			12 33	13 33	13 54			14 33	15 33	15 44	
Briton Ferry	d																								
Baglan	d																								
Port Talbot Parkway	d				03s52	08 26		09 40	09 50	10 40			11 40	11 50			12 40	13 40	14 01			14 40	15 40	15 51	
Pyle	d								09 57					11 57					14 09					15 58	
Maesteg	d		22p15																						
Maesteg (Ewenny Road)	d		22p17																						
Garth (Mid Glamorgan)	d		22p20																						
Tondu	d		22p29																						
Sarn	d		22p32																						
Wildmill	d		22p34																						
Bridgend	d		22p38		04s06	08 38		09 52	10 05	10 52			11 52	12 05			12 52	13 52	14 17			14 52	15 52	16 06	
Pencoed	d		22p44											12 11										16 12	
Llanharan	d		22p48											12 15										16 16	
Pontyclun	d		22p52											12 20										16 21	
Cardiff Central 7	a		23p08		04 35	09 01		10 14	10 29	11 14			12 14	12 35			13 14	14 14	14 40			15 14	16 14	16 36	
Newport (South Wales)	a		23p36			09 18		10 31	10 48	11 31			12 31	12 52			13 31	14 31	15 12			15 31	16 31	16 52	
Bristol Parkway 7	a					09 46		10 59		11 59			12 59				13 59	14 59				15 59	16 59		
Gloucester 7	a		00 40																						
Manchester Piccadilly 10	a								14 19					16 17					18 17					20 17	
Reading 7	a					10 42		12 05		13 00			14 00				15 00	16 00				17 00	18 00		
London Paddington 15 ⊖	a					11 20		12 42		13 38			14 40				15 38	16 38				17 43	18 38		

b Previous night, stops on request

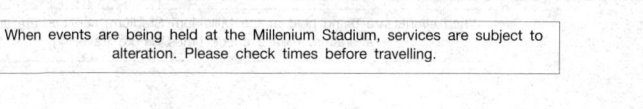

When events are being held at the Millenium Stadium, services are subject to alteration. Please check times before travelling.

Table 128

Sundays

7 August to 11 September

West Wales, Swansea and Maesteg - Cardiff

		AW	GW	GW	AW	GW		GW	AW	AW	GW	AW	AW	AW	AW	AW		AW	AW	AW
					■											B				
			◇1	◇1		◇1		◇1			◇1	◇		◇				◇		
			☕	☕	🛒	☕		☕			☕									
Rosslare Harbour ⛴	d															21 15				
Fishguard Harbour ⛴	a															00 45				
	d	14 23																		
Milford Haven	d				15 28					17 30				19 38				21 33		23 15
Johnston	d				15x36					17x38				19x46				21x41		23x23
Haverfordwest	d				15 43					17 45				19 53				21 49		23 30
Clarbeston Road	d	14 43			15x52					17x53				20x01				21x57		23x39
Clunderwen	d				15x59					18x00				20x08				22x05		23x46
Pembroke Dock	d								16 45				19 00						21 45	
Pembroke	d								16 53				19 08						21 53	
Lamphey	d								16x56				19x11						21x56	
Manorbier	d								17 05				19 20						22 05	
Penally	d								17x10				19x25						22x10	
Tenby	a								17 13				19 28						22 13	
	d								17 13				19 28						22 13	
Saundersfoot	d								17x21				19x36						22x21	
Kilgetty	d								17x23				19x38						22x23	
Narberth	d								17x33				19x48						22x33	
Whitland	a	14 55			16 06				17 41	18 06			19 56	20 14				22 11	22 41	23 53
	d	14 55			16 09				17 44	18 08			19 59	20 17				22 14	22 44	23 53
Carmarthen	a	15 13			16 26				18 04	18 29			20 16	20 36				22 31	23 05	00 14
	d	15 16	15 30		16 30	16 55			18 07		19 09		20 19		21 05			22 34		
Ferryside	d	15x26			16x40				18x17				20x30					22x44		
Kidwelly	d	15x32			16x46				18x23				20x36					22x50		
Pembrey & Burry Port	d	15 39	15 50		16 54	17 15			18 31		19 29		20 43		21 24			22 58		
Llanelli	a	15 45	15 56		17 00	17 21			18 37		19 35		20 49		21 30			23 04		
	d	15 46	15 58		17 00	17 22			18 38		19 36	19 55	20 51		21 31			23 04		
Gowerton	d	15x55							18x46			20x02	20x58					23x12		
Swansea	a	16 14	16 14		17 19	17 39			19 06		19 53	20 16	21 17		21 48			23 27		
	d		16 21	16 51	17 30	17 51		18 51			19 59	20 40			21 52			23 30		
Llansamlet	d																			
Skewen	d																			
Neath	d		16 33	17 03	17 41	18 03		19 03			20 11	20 51			22 03			23 42		
Briton Ferry	d																			
Baglan	d																			
Port Talbot Parkway	d		16 40	17 10	17 48	18 10		19 10			20 18	20 58			22 10			23 49		
Pyle	d				17 55										22 17			23 56		
Maesteg	d																			
Maesteg (Ewenny Road)	d																			
Garth (Mid Glamorgan)	d																			
Tondu	d																			
Sarn	d																			
Wildmill	d																			
Bridgend	d		16 52	17 22	18 03	18 22		19 22			20 30	21 11			22 25			00 04		
Pencoed	d				18 09															
Llanharan	d				18 13															
Pontyclun	d				18 18															
Cardiff Central 7	a		17 14	17 45	18 34	18 45		19 45			20 53	21 36			22 49			00 29		
Newport (South Wales)	a		17 31	18 03	18 52	19 03		20 03			21 08				23 18					
Bristol Parkway 7	a		17 59	18 31		19 31		20 31			21 36									
Gloucester 7	a																			
Manchester Piccadilly 10	a				22 19															
Reading 7	a		19 00	19 30		20 32		21 32			22 37									
London Paddington 15 ⊖	a		19 38	20 12		21 11		22 14			23 20									

When events are being held at the Millenium Stadium, services are subject to alteration. Please check times before travelling.

Table 128

Sundays

18 September to 23 October

West Wales, Swansea and Maesteg - Cardiff

Station		AW	AW	AW	GW	AW	GW	GW	AW	GW		AW	AW	GW	GW	AW	AW	GW	GW	AW		AW	AW	GW	GW
		◇		◇	◇1 🍽	R	◇1 🍽	◇1 🍽		◇1 🍽		◇ 🛒		◇1 🍽	◇1 🍽	R 🛒		◇1 🍽	◇1 🍽	R 🛒		◇		◇1 🍽	◇1 🍽
Rosslare Harbour ⛴	d	21p15				09 00																			
Fishguard Harbour ⛴	a	00 45				12 30																			
	d			01 50																			14 23		
Milford Haven	d		23p16													11 28				13 23					
Johnston	d		23b24													11x36				13x29					
Haverfordwest	d		23p31													11 43				13 36					
Clarbeston Road	d		23b39	02 10												11x52				13x45			14 43		
Clunderwen	d		23b46													11x59				13x52					
Pembroke Dock	d																								
Pembroke	d																								
Lamphey	d																								
Manorbier	d																								
Penally	d																								
Tenby	a																								
	d																								
Saundersfoot	d																								
Kilgetty	d																								
Narberth	d																								
Whitland	a		23p52	02s22												12 06				13 59			14 55		
	d		23p52													12 08				14 02			14 55		
Carmarthen	a		00 14	02s40												12 26				14 20			15 13		
	d								09 40			10 30	11 18			12 29	13 17			14 23			15 16	15 30	
Ferryside	d								09x50				11x28				13x27						15x26		
Kidwelly	d								09x56				11x34				13x33						15x32		
Pembrey & Burry Port	d								10 03			10 49	11 42			12 49	13 40			14 42			15 39	15 50	
Llanelli	a			03s06					10 09			10 54	11 48			12 55	13 46			14 48			15 45	15 56	
	d								10 10			10 56	11 48			12 55	13 47			14 49		15 41	15 46	15 58	
Gowerton	d								10x17				11x56				13x54						15x55		
Swansea	a			03s26					10 35			11 15	12 14			13 15	14 14			15 08		16 04	16 14	16 14	
	d				07 55		09 21	10 21		11 21		11 32		12 21	13 21	13 43		14 21	15 21	15 33				16 21	16 51
Llansamlet	d																								
Skewen	d																								
Neath	d			03s45	08 07		09 33	10 33		11 33		11 43		12 33	13 33	13 54		14 33	15 33	15 44				16 33	17 03
Briton Ferry	d																								
Baglan	d																								
Port Talbot Parkway	d			03s52	08 14		09 40	10 40		11 40		11 50		12 40	13 40	14 01		14 40	15 40	15 51				16 40	17 10
Pyle	d											11 57				14 09				15 58					
Maesteg	d																								
Maesteg (Ewenny Road)	d																								
Garth (Mid Glamorgan)	d																								
Tondu	d																								
Sarn	d																								
Wildmill	d																								
Bridgend	d			04s06	08 26		09 52	10 52		11 52		12 05		12 52	13 52	14 17		14 52	15 52	16 06				16 52	17 22
Pencoed	d											12 11								16 12					
Llanharan	d											12 15								16 16					
Pontyclun	d											12 20								16 21					
Cardiff Central 7	a			04 35	08 49		10 14	11 14		12 14		12 35		13 14	14 14	14 40		15 14	16 14	16 36				17 14	17 45
Newport (South Wales)	a				09 05		10 31	11 31		12 31		12 52		13 31	14 31	15 12		15 31	16 31	16 52				17 31	18 03
Bristol Parkway 7	a				09 36		10 59	11 59		12 59				13 59	14 59			15 59	16 59					17 59	18 31
Gloucester 7	a																								
Manchester Piccadilly 10	a											16 17				18 17				20 17					
Reading 7	a				10 32		12 05	13 00		14 00				15 00	16 00			17 06	18 00					19 00	19 30
London Paddington 15 ⊖	a				11 10		12 42	13 38		14 40				15 38	16 38			17 49	18 38					19 38	20 12

b Previous night, stops on request

When events are being held at the Millenium Stadium, services are subject to alteration. Please check times before travelling.

Table 128

Sundays

18 September to 23 October

West Wales, Swansea and Maesteg - Cardiff

		AW	GW	GW	AW	AW		GW	AW	AW	AW	AW	AW	AW	AW	AW
		■											R			
			◇1	◇1				◇1	◇			◇		◇		
		🛒	☕	☕				☕								
Rosslare Harbour ⛴	d												21 15			
Fishguard Harbour ⛴	a												00 45			
	d															
Milford Haven	d	15 28				17 30					19 38			21 33		23 15
Johnston	d	15x36				17x38					19x46			21x41		23x23
Haverfordwest	d	15 43				17 45					19 53			21 49		23 30
Clarbeston Road	d	15x52				17x53					20x01			21x57		23x39
Clunderwen	d	15x59				18x00					20x08			22x05		23x46
Pembroke Dock	d				16 45					19 00					21 45	
Pembroke	d				16 53					19 08					21 53	
Lamphey	d				16x56					19x11					21x56	
Manorbier	d				17 05					19 20					22 05	
Penally	d				17x10					19x25					22x10	
Tenby	a				17 13					19 28					22 13	
	d				17 13					19 28					22 13	
Saundersfoot	d				17x21					19x36					22x21	
Kilgetty	d				17x23					19x38					22x23	
Narberth	d				17x33					19x48					22x33	
Whitland	a	16 06			17 41	18 06				19 56	20 14			22 11	22 41	23 53
	d	16 09			17 44	18 08				19 59	20 17			22 14	22 44	23 53
Carmarthen	a	16 26			18 04	18 29				20 16	20 36			22 31	23 05	00 14
	d	16 30	16 55		18 07			19 09		20 19		21 05		22 34		
Ferryside	d	16x40			18x17					20x30				22x44		
Kidwelly	d	16x46			18x23					20x36				22x50		
Pembrey & Burry Port	d	16 54	17 15		18 31			19 29		20 43		21 24		22 58		
Llanelli	a	17 00	17 21		18 37			19 35		20 49		21 30		23 04		
	d	17 00	17 22		18 38			19 36	19 55	20 51		21 31		23 04		
Gowerton	d				18x46				20x02	20x58				23x12		
Swansea	a	17 19	17 39		19 06			19 53	20 16	21 17		21 48		23 27		
	d	17 30	17 51	18 51				19 59	20 40			21 52		23 30		
Llansamlet	d															
Skewen	d															
Neath	d	17 41	18 03	19 03				20 11	20 51			22 03		23 42		
Briton Ferry	d															
Baglan	d															
Port Talbot Parkway	d	17 48	18 10	19 10				20 18	20 58			22 10		23 49		
Pyle	d	17 55										22 17		23 56		
Maesteg	d															
Maesteg (Ewenny Road)	d															
Garth (Mid Glamorgan)	d															
Tondu	d															
Sarn	d															
Wildmill	d															
Bridgend	d	18 03	18 22	19 22				20 30	21 11			22 25		00 04		
Pencoed	d	18 09														
Llanharan	d	18 13														
Pontyclun	d	18 18														
Cardiff Central 7	a	18 34	18 45	19 45				20 53	21 36			22 49		00 29		
Newport (South Wales)	a	18 52	19 03	20 03				21 08				23 18				
Bristol Parkway 7	a		19 31	20 31				21 36								
Gloucester 7	a															
Manchester Piccadilly 10	a	22 19														
Reading 7	a		20 32	21 32				22 37								
London Paddington 15 ⊖	a		21 14	22 14				23 16								

When events are being held at the Millenium Stadium, services are subject to alteration. Please check times before travelling.

Table 128

Sundays

from 30 October

West Wales, Swansea and Maestog - Cardiff

		AW	AW	AW	GW	GW	AW	GW	AW	GW		AW	GW	AW	GW	AW	GW	AW	GW	AW		GW	AW	AW	GW
							R									R				R					
		◇		◇	◇1	◇1		◇1		◇1		◇	◇1		◇1		◇1		◇1			◇1	◇		◇1
					🍽	🍽		🍽		🍽		🛒	🍽		🍽	🛒	🍽		🍽	🛒		🍽			🍽
Rosslare Harbour ⛴	d	21p15					09 00																		
Fishguard Harbour ⛴	a	00 45					12 30																		
	d			01 50																				14 23	
Milford Haven	d		23p16													11 28				13 23					
Johnston	d		23b24													11x36				13x29					
Haverfordwest	d		23p31													11 43				13 36					
Clarbeston Road	d		23b39	02 10												11x52				13x45				14 43	
Clunderwen	d		23b46													11x59				13x52					
Pembroke Dock	d																								
Pembroke	d																								
Lamphey	d																								
Manorbier	d																								
Penally	d																								
Tenby	a																								
	d																								
Saundersfoot	d																								
Kilgetty	d																								
Narberth	d																								
Whitland	a		23p52	02s22												12 06				13 59				14 55	
	d		23p52													12 08				14 02				14 55	
Carmarthen	a		00 14	02s40												12 26				14 20				15 13	
	d								09 40			10 30		11 18		12 29		13 17		14 23		14 55		15 16	
Ferryside	d								09x50					11x28				13x27						15x26	
Kidwelly	d								09x56					11x34				13x33						15x32	
Pembrey & Burry Port	d								10 03			10 49		11 42		12 49		13 40		14 42		15 16		15 39	
Llanelli	a			03s06					10 09			10 54		11 48		12 55		13 46		14 48		15 22		15 45	
	d								10 10			10 56		11 48		12 55		13 47		14 49		15 25	15 41	15 46	
Gowerton	d								10x17					11x56				13x54						15x55	
Swansea	a			03s26					10 35			11 15		12 14		13 15		14 14		15 08		15 40	16 04	16 14	
	d				07 59	08 55		09 55		10 55		11 32	11 55		12 55	13 43	13 55		14 55	15 33		16 00			16 55
Llansamlet	d																								
Skewen	d																								
Neath	d			03s45	08 11	09 07		10 07		11 07		11 43	12 07		13 07	13 54	14 07		15 07	15 44		16 13			17 07
Briton Ferry	d																								
Baglan	d																								
Port Talbot Parkway	d			03s52	08 18	09 14		10 14		11 14		11 50	12 14		13 14	14 01	14 14		15 14	15 51		16 20			17 14
Pyle	d											11 57				14 09				15 58					
Maesteg	d																								
Maesteg (Ewenny Road)	d																								
Garth (Mid Glamorgan)	d																								
Tondu	d																								
Sarn	d																								
Wildmill	d																								
Bridgend	d			04s06	08 30	09 26		10 26		11 26		12 05	12 26		13 26	14 17	14 26		15 26	16 06		16 32			17 26
Pencoed	d											12 11								16 12					
Llanharan	d											12 15								16 16					
Pontyclun	d											12 20								16 21					
Cardiff Central 7	a			04 35	08 53	09 48		10 48		11 48		12 35	12 48		13 48	14 40	14 48		15 48	16 36		16 54			17 49
Newport (South Wales)	a				09 09	10 05		11 05		12 05		12 52	13 05		14 05	15 12	15 05		16 05	16 52		17 10			18 05
Bristol Parkway 7	a				09 34	10 34		11 34		12 34			13 34		14 34		15 34		16 34			17 40			18 34
Gloucester 7	a																								
Manchester Piccadilly 10	a											16 17				18 17				20 17					
Reading 7	a				11 19	12 19		13 19		14 19			15 19		16 19		17 19		18 20			19 17			20 24
London Paddington 15 ⊖	a				11 58	12 58		13 58		14 58			15 58		16 58		17 58		18 58			19 58			21 00

b Previous night, stops on request

When events are being held at the Millenium Stadium, services are subject to alteration. Please check times before travelling.

Table 128

Sundays
from 30 October

West Wales, Swansea and Maesteg - Cardiff

		AW	GW	GW	AW	AW	GW	AW	AW	AW	AW	AW	AW	AW	AW
		R										R			
			◇1	◇1			◇1	◇			◇		◇		
		⊼	☕	☕			☕								
Rosslare Harbour ⛴	d											21 15			
Fishguard Harbour ⛴	a											00 45			
	d														
Milford Haven	d	15 28				17 30				19 38			21 33		23 15
Johnston	d	15x36				17x38				19x46			21x41		23x23
Haverfordwest	d	15 43				17 45				19 53			21 49		23 30
Clarbeston Road	d	15x52				17x53				20x01			21x57		23x39
Clunderwen	d	15x59				18x00				20x08			22x05		23x46
Pembroke Dock	d				16 45				19 00					21 45	
Pembroke	d				16 53				19 08					21 53	
Lamphey	d				16x56				19x11					21x56	
Manorbier	d				17 05				19 20					22 05	
Penally	d				17x10				19x25					22x10	
Tenby	a				17 13				19 28					22 13	
	d				17 13				19 28					22 13	
Saundersfoot	d				17x21				19x36					22x21	
Kilgetty	d				17x23				19x38					22x23	
Narberth	d				17x33				19x48					22x33	
Whitland	a	16 06			17 41	18 06			19 56	20 14			22 11	22 41	23 53
	d	16 09			17 44	18 08			19 59	20 17			22 14	22 44	23 53
Carmarthen	a	16 26			18 04	18 29			20 16	20 36			22 31	23 05	00 14
	d	16 30	17 03		18 07		19 09		20 19		21 05		22 34		
Ferryside	d	16x40			18x17				20x30				22x44		
Kidwelly	d	16x46			18x23				20x36				22x50		
Pembrey & Burry Port	d	16 54	17 23		18 31		19 29		20 43		21 24		22 58		
Llanelli	a	17 00	17 29		18 37		19 35		20 49		21 30		23 04		
	d	17 00	17 30		18 38		19 36	19 55	20 51		21 31		23 04		
Gowerton	d				18x46			20x02	20x58				23x12		
Swansea	a	17 19	17 48		19 06		19 53	20 16	21 17		21 48		23 27		
	d	17 30	17 55	18 55			19 59	20 40			21 52		23 30		
Llansamlet	d														
Skewen	d														
Neath	d	17 41	18 07	19 07			20 11	20 51			22 03		23 42		
Briton Ferry	d														
Baglan	d														
Port Talbot Parkway	d	17 48	18 14	19 14			20 18	20 58			22 10		23 49		
Pyle	d	17 55									22 17		23 56		
Maesteg	d														
Maesteg (Ewenny Road)	d														
Garth (Mid Glamorgan)	d														
Tondu	d														
Sarn	d														
Wildmill	d														
Bridgend	d	18 03	18 26	19 26			20 30	21 11			22 25		00 04		
Pencoed	d	18 09													
Llanharan	d	18 13													
Pontyclun	d	18 18													
Cardiff Central [7]	a	18 34	18 49	19 49			20 53	21 36			22 49		00 29		
Newport (South Wales)	a	18 52	19 05	20 05			21 08				23 18				
Bristol Parkway [7]	a		19 34	20 34			21 37								
Gloucester [7]	a														
Manchester Piccadilly [10]	a	22 19													
Reading [7]	a		21 25	22 26			23 32								
London Paddington [15] ⊖	a		22 02	23 08			00 13								

When events are being held at the Millenium Stadium, services are subject to alteration. Please check times before travelling.

Table 128A

Mondays to Fridays

Maesteg - Caerau

Bus Service

		AW	AW	AW	AW	AW	AW	AW	AW	AW		AW	AW	AW	AW	AW	AW	AW	AW
Maesteg	d	06 51	08 05	09 20	10 20	11 20	12 20	13 20	14 20	15 20	....	16 20	17 20	18 20	19 20	20 20	21 20	22 11	23 34
Caerau (Square)	a	07 01	08 15	09 30	10 30	11 30	12 30	13 30	14 30	15 30		16 30	17 30	18 30	19 30	20 30	21 30	22 21	23 43
Caerau Park	a	07 10	08 24	09 39	10 39	11 39	12 39	13 39	14 39	15 39	....	16 39	17 39	18 39	19 39	20 39	21 39	22 30	23 53

Saturdays

		AW	AW	AW	AW	AW	AW	AW	AW	AW		AW	AW	AW	AW	AW	AW	AW
Maesteg	d	06 51	08 05	09 20	10 20	11 20	12 20	13 20	14 20	15 20	....	16 20	17 20	18 20	19 20	20 20	21 20	22 11
Caerau (Square)	a	07 01	08 15	09 30	10 30	11 30	12 30	13 30	14 30	15 30		16 30	17 30	18 30	19 30	20 30	21 30	22 21
Caerau Park	a	07 10	08 24	09 39	10 39	11 39	12 39	13 39	14 39	15 39	....	16 39	17 39	18 39	19 39	20 39	21 39	22 30

No Sunday Service

For connections from Cardiff and Bridgend please refer to Table 128

Table 128A

Mondays to Fridays

Caerau - Maesteg

Bus Service

		AW	AW	AW	AW	AW	AW	AW	AW	AW		AW	AW	AW	AW	AW	AW	AW
Caerau Park	d	06 21	07 35	08 50	09 50	10 50	11 50	12 50	13 50	14 50	....	15 50	16 50	17 50	18 40	19 40	20 40	21 40
Caerau (Square)	d	06 31	07 45	09 00	10 00	11 00	12 00	13 00	14 00	15 00		16 00	17 00	18 00	18 50	19 50	20 50	21 50
Maesteg	a	06 41	07 55	09 10	10 10	11 10	12 10	13 10	14 10	15 10	....	16 10	17 10	18 10	19 00	20 00	21 00	22 00

Saturdays

		AW	AW	AW	AW	AW	AW	AW	AW	AW		AW	AW	AW	AW	AW	AW	AW
Caerau Park	d	06 21	07 35	08 50	09 50	10 50	11 50	12 50	13 50	14 50	....	15 50	16 50	17 50	18 40	19 40	20 40	21 40
Caerau (Square)	d	06 31	07 45	09 00	10 00	11 00	12 00	13 00	14 00	15 00		16 00	17 00	18 00	18 50	19 50	20 50	21 50
Maesteg	a	06 41	07 55	09 10	10 10	11 10	12 10	13 10	14 10	15 10	....	16 10	17 10	18 10	19 00	20 00	21 00	22 00

No Sunday Service

For connections to Bridgend and Cardiff please refer to Table 128

Network Diagram for Tables 129, 131

DM-10/10
Design BAJS

© 2010 Network Rail.
All rights reserved

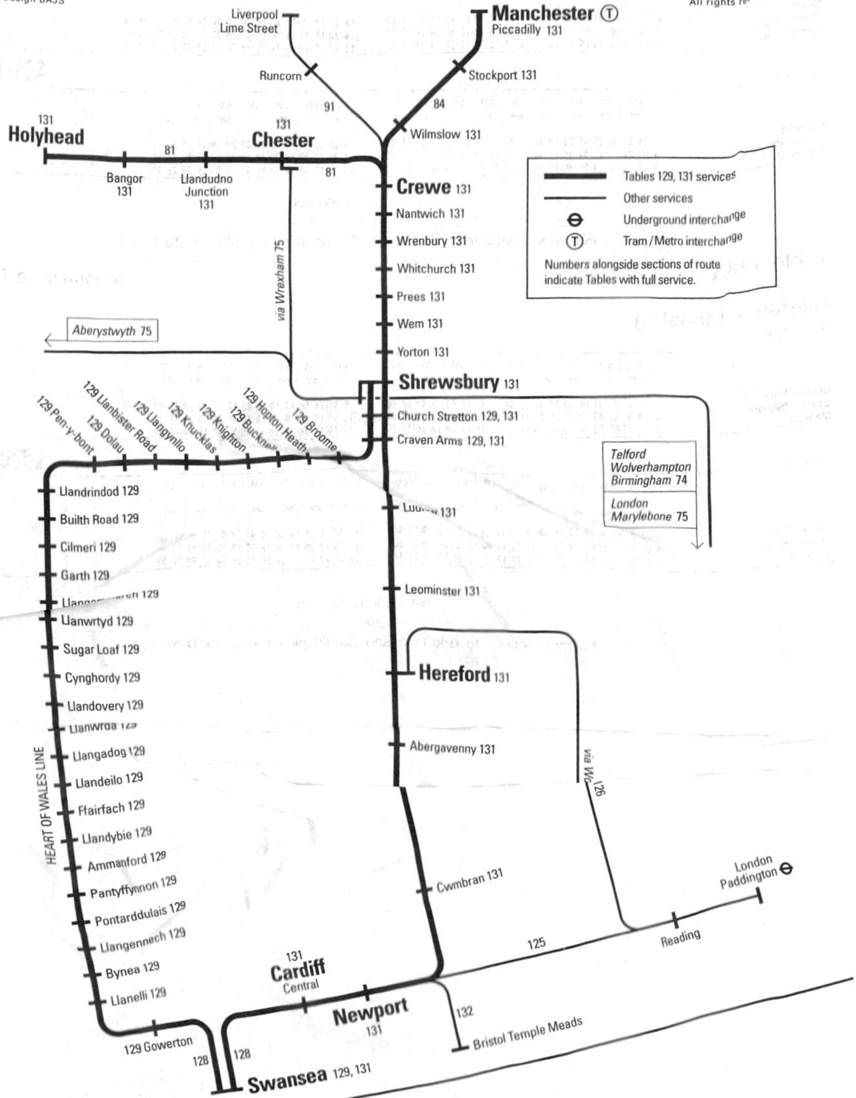

Table 128A

Mondays to Fridays

Maesteg - Caerau

Bus Service

		AW	AW	AW	AW	AW	AW	AW	AW	AW	AW	AW	AW	AW	AW	AW	AW	AW
Maesteg	d	06 51	08 05	09 20	10 20	11 20	12 20	13 20	14 20	15 20	16 20	17 20	18 20	19 20	20 20	21 20	22 11	23 34
Caerau (Square)	a	07 01	08 15	09 30	10 30	11 30	12 30	13 30	14 30	15 30	16 30	17 30	18 30	19 30	20 30	21 30	22 21	23 43
Caerau Park	a	07 10	08 24	09 39	10 39	11 39	12 39	13 39	14 39	15 39	16 39	17 39	18 39	19 39	20 39	21 39	22 30	23 53

Saturdays

		AW	AW	AW	AW	AW	AW	AW	AW	AW	AW	AW	AW	AW	AW	AW	AW
Maesteg	d	06 51	08 05	09 20	10 20	11 20	12 20	13 20	14 20	15 20	16 20	17 20	18 20	19 20	20 20	21 20	22 11
Caerau (Square)	a	07 01	08 15	09 30	10 30	11 30	12 30	13 30	14 30	15 30	16 30	17 30	18 30	19 30	20 30	21 30	22 21
Caerau Park	a	07 10	08 24	09 39	10 39	11 39	12 39	13 39	14 39	15 39	16 39	17 39	18 39	19 39	20 39	21 39	22 30

No Sunday Service

For connections from Cardiff and Bridgend please refer to Table 128

Table 128A

Mondays to Fridays

Caerau - Maesteg

Bus Service

		AW	AW	AW	AW	AW	AW	AW	AW	AW	AW	AW	AW	AW	AW	AW	AW
Caerau Park	d	06 21	07 35	08 50	09 50	10 50	11 50	12 50	13 50	14 50	15 50	16 50	17 50	18 40	19 40	20 40	21 40
Caerau (Square)	d	06 31	07 45	09 00	10 00	11 00	12 00	13 00	14 00	15 00	16 00	17 00	18 00	18 50	19 50	20 50	21 50
Maesteg	a	06 41	07 55	09 10	10 10	11 10	12 10	13 10	14 10	15 10	16 10	17 10	18 10	19 00	20 00	21 00	22 00

Saturdays

		AW	AW	AW	AW	AW	AW	AW	AW	AW	AW	AW	AW	AW	AW	AW	AW
Caerau Park	d	06 21	07 35	08 50	09 50	10 50	11 50	12 50	13 50	14 50	15 50	16 50	17 50	18 40	19 40	20 40	21 40
Caerau (Square)	d	06 31	07 45	09 00	10 00	11 00	12 00	13 00	14 00	15 00	16 00	17 00	18 00	18 50	19 50	20 50	21 50
Maesteg	a	06 41	07 55	09 10	10 10	11 10	12 10	13 10	14 10	15 10	16 10	17 10	18 10	19 00	20 00	21 00	22 00

No Sunday Service

For connections to Bridgend and Cardiff please refer to Table 128

Network Diagram for Tables 129, 131

DM-10/10
Design BAJS

© 2010 Network Rail.
All rights reserved

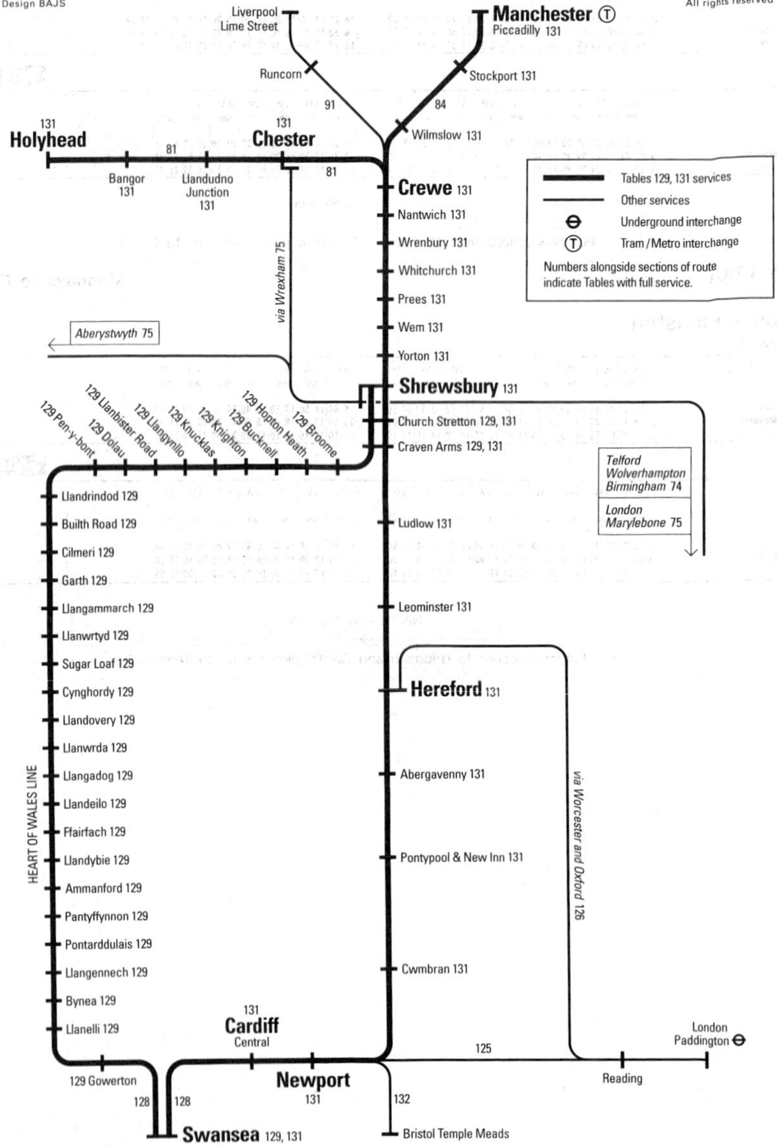

Table 129

Mondays to Fridays

Swansea - Shrewsbury

HEART OF WALES LINE

Miles			AW ◇	AW ◇	AW ◇	AW ◇
0	**Swansea**	d	04 36	09 15	13 14	18 21
5½	Gowerton	d				
11¼	Llanelli	d	04 53	09 34	13 35	18 39
14	Bynea	d	04x58	09x39	13x40	18x44
16	Llangennech	d	05x01	09x43	13x44	18x47
18¼	Pontarddulais	d	05x05	09x47	13x48	18x51
23	Pantyffynnon	d	05 13	09 55	13 56	18 59
24¼	Ammanford	d	05 16	09 58	13 59	19 02
26	Llandybie	d	05 20	10 02	14 03	19 06
30	Ffairfach	d	05x27	10x10	14x11	19x13
30¾	Llandeilo	a	05 30	10 12	14 13	19 16
—		d	05 32	10 15	14 16	19 18
36½	Llangadog	d	05 42	10 24	14 25	19 28
38¼	Llanwrda	d	05 45	10 28	14 29	19 31
42	Llandovery	a	05 52	10 34	14 35	19 38
—		d	05 54	10 37	14 38	19 40
46¾	Cynghordy	d	06x02	10x45	14x46	19x48
49½	Sugar Loaf	d	06x10	10x54	14x55	19x56
53½	Llanwrtyd	a	06 16	11 00	15 01	20 02
—		d	06 19	11 05	15 03	20 07
56¾	Llangammarch	d	06x24	11x11	15x09	20x12
58½	Garth (Powys)	d	06x28	11x17	15x13	20x16
62	Cilmeri	d	06x33	11x21	15x19	20x21
64	Builth Road	d	06x36	11x24	15x22	20x24
69¾	Llandrindod	a	06 47	11 36	15 34	20 36
—		d	06 55	11 40	15 40	20 40
73¼	Pen-y-bont	d	07x02	11x48	15x48	20x47
76¼	Dolau	d	07 07	11 53	15 53	20 52
79¾	Llanbister Road	d	07x13	11x59	15x59	20x58
82¾	Llangynllo	d	07x18	12x05	16x04	21x03
86¾	Knucklas	d	07x24	12x11	16x11	21x09
89¼	Knighton	a	07 30	12 16	16 16	21 14
—		d	07 32	12 18	16 19	21 17
93½	Bucknell	d	07 38	12 24	16 25	21 23
96½	Hopton Heath	d	07x42	12x28	16x29	21x27
99	Broome	d	07x46	12x32	16x34	21x31
101½	Craven Arms	a	07 53	12 39	16 40	21 38
108¾	Church Stretton	a	08 06	12 52	16 53	21 51
121½	**Shrewsbury**	a	08 22	13 08	17 09	22 08

Saturdays

		AW ◇	AW ◇	AW ◇	AW ◇
Swansea	d	04 36	09 16	13 16	18 21
Gowerton	d				
Llanelli	d	04 53	09 34	13 35	18 39
Bynea	d	04x58	09x39	13x39	18x44
Llangennech	d	05x01	09x43	13x43	18x47
Pontarddulais	d	05x05	09x47	13x48	18x51
Pantyffynnon	d	05 13	09 55	13 55	18 59
Ammanford	d	05 16	09 58	13 58	19 02
Llandybie	d	05 20	10 02	14 03	19 06
Ffairfach	d	05x27	10x10	14x10	19x13
Llandeilo	a	05 30	10 12	14 12	19 16
	d	05 32	10 15	14 15	19 18
Llangadog	d	05 42	10 24	14 24	19 28
Llanwrda	d	05 45	10 28	14 28	19 31
Llandovery	a	05 52	10 34	14 34	19 38
	d	05 54	10 37	14 37	19 40
Cynghordy	d	06x02	10x45	14x45	19x48
Sugar Loaf	d	06x10	10x54	14x53	19x56
Llanwrtyd	a	06 16	11 00	14 59	20 02
	d	06 19	11 05	15 01	20 07
Llangammarch	d	06x24	11x11	15x07	20x13
Garth (Powys)	d	06x28	11x15	15x11	20x16
Cilmeri	d	06x33	11x20	15x16	20x21
Builth Road	d	06x36	11x23	15x19	20x24
Llandrindod	a	06 47	11 35	15 31	20 36
	d	06 55	11 39	15 40	20 40
Pen-y-bont	d	07x02	11x46	15x47	20x47
Dolau	d	07x07	11 51	15 52	20 52
Llanbister Road	d	07x12	11x57	15x57	20x58
Llangynllo	d	07x17	12x02	16x02	21x03
Knucklas	d	07x23	12x08	16x08	21x09
Knighton	a	07 29	12 13	16 14	21 14
	d	07 32	12 16	16 16	21 17
Bucknell	d	07 38	12 22	16 22	21 23
Hopton Heath	d	07x42	12x26	16x26	21x27
Broome	d	07x46	12x30	16x30	21x31
Craven Arms	a	07 53	12 37	16 37	21 38
Church Stretton	a	08 06	12 51	16 51	21 51
Shrewsbury	a	08 22	13 09	17 11	22 08

When events are being held at the Millenium Stadium, services are subject to alteration. Please check times before travelling.

Table 129

Swansea - Shrewsbury

HEART OF WALES LINE

		AW ◇	AW ◇
Swansea	d	11 06	15 26
Gowerton	d	11x16	15x36
Llanelli	d	11 29	15 51
Bynea	d	11x34	15x56
Llangennech	d	11x38	16x00
Pontarddulais	d	11x42	16x04
Pantyffynnon	d	11 50	16 11
Ammanford	d	11 53	16 14
Llandybie	d	11 57	16 19
Ffairfach	d	12x05	16x26
Llandeilo	a	12 07	16 29
	d	12 10	16 31
Llangadog	d	12 19	16 41
Llanwrda	d	12 23	16 44
Llandovery	a	12 29	16 51
	d	12 32	16 53
Cynghordy	d	12x40	17x02
Sugar Loaf	d	12x49	17x10
Llanwrtyd	a	12 55	17 16
	d	12 57	17 19
Llangammarch	d	13x03	17x25
Garth (Powys)	d	13x07	17x29
Cilmeri	d	13x13	17x34
Builth Road	d	13x16	17x38
Llandrindod	a	13 28	17 49
	d	13 52	17 56
Pen-y-bont	d	14x00	18x04
Dolau	d	14 05	18 09
Llanbister Road	d	14x11	18x15
Llangynllo	d	14x16	18x20
Knucklas	d	14x23	18x27
Knighton	a	14 28	18 32
	d	14 31	18 35
Bucknell	d	14 37	18 41
Hopton Heath	d	14x41	18x45
Broome	d	14x46	18x50
Craven Arms	a	14 53	18 59
Church Stretton	a	15 04	19 12
Shrewsbury	a	15 22	19 31

When events are being held at the Millenium Stadium, services are subject to alteration. Please check times before travelling.

Table 129

Mondays to Fridays

Shrewsbury - Swansea

HEART OF WALES LINE

Miles			AW ◇	AW ◇	AW ◇	AW ◇
0	**Shrewsbury**	d	05 19	09 00	14 04	18 05
12¾	Church Stretton	d	05 36	09 18	14 22	18 23
20	Craven Arms	d	05 50	09 28	14 33	18 35
22½	Broome	d	05x55	09x34	14x39	18x40
25	Hopton Heath	d	05x59	09x38	14x43	18x44
28	Bucknell	d	06x03	09x43	14x48	18x48
32¼	Knighton	a	06 10	09 50	14 55	18 55
—		d	06 12	09 52	14 57	18 57
34¾	Knucklas	d	06x17	09x58	15x03	19x02
38¾	Llangynllo	d	06x25	10x06	15x11	19x10
41¾	Llanbister Road	d	06x30	10x11	15x16	19x15
45¼	Dolau	d	06x35	10x17	15x22	19x20
48½	Pen-y-bont	d	06x39	10x21	15x26	19x24
51¾	Llandrindod	a	06 46	10 28	15 35	19 31
—		d	06 52	10 31	15 40	19 34
57½	Builth Road	d	07x01	10x40	15x50	19x43
59½	Cilmeri	d	07x04	10x44	15x53	19x46
63	Garth (Powys)	d	07x09	10x49	15x59	19x52
64¾	Llangammarch	d	07x12	10x53	16x03	19x55
68	Llanwrtyd	a	07 18	10 59	16 09	20 01
—		d	07 21	11 07	16 11	20 10
70¾	Sugar Loaf	d	07x27	11x13	16x18	20x16
74¾	Cynghordy	d	07x33	11x20	16x25	20x23
79½	Llandovery	a	07 43	11 30	16 34	20 33
—		d	07 45	11 32	16 37	20 35
83¼	Llanwrda	d	07x51	11x38	16x43	20x41
85	Llangadog	d	07x54	11x42	16x47	20x45
90¾	Llandeilo	a	08 03	11 51	16 56	20 54
—		d	08 06	11 54	16 58	20 57
91½	Ffairfach	d	08 08	11 56	17 01	20 59
95½	Llandybie	d	08x15	12x04	17x08	21x07
97¼	Ammanford	d	08x20	12x08	17x13	21x11
98½	Pantyffynnon	d	08 23	12 11	17 16	21 14
103¼	Pontarddulais	d	08x30	12x18	17x23	21x21
105½	Llangennech	d	08x34	12x23	17x27	21x26
107½	Bynea	d	08x37	12x26	17x31	21x29
110¼	Llanelli	a	08 42	12 35	17 38	21 34
116	Gowerton	a	08x53		17x57	21x50
121½	**Swansea**	a	09 08	13 01	18 18	22 10

Saturdays

		AW ◇	AW ◇	AW ◇	AW ◇
Shrewsbury	d	05 19	09 00	14 05	18 05
Church Stretton	d	05 36	09 17	14 23	18 23
Craven Arms	d	05 47	09 30	14 36	18 36
Broome	d	05x52	09x35	14x42	18x42
Hopton Heath	d	05x56	09x39	14x45	18x45
Bucknell	d	06x00	09x43	14x50	18x50
Knighton	a	06 09	09 50	14 56	18 56
	d	06 11	09 52	14 59	18 59
Knucklas	d	06x15	09x57	15x04	19x04
Llangynllo	d	06x22	10x05	15x11	19x11
Llanbister Road	d	06x27	10x10	15x16	19x16
Dolau	d	06x33	10x15	15x21	19x22
Pen-y-bont	d	06x37	10x20	15x25	19x26
Llandrindod	a	06 48	10 29	15 34	19 35
	d	06 52	10 29	15 37	19 35
Builth Road	d	07x01	10x39	15x46	19x45
Cilmeri	d	07x04	10x42	15x50	19x48
Garth (Powys)	d	07x09	10x47	15x55	19x53
Llangammarch	d	07x12	10x51	15x59	19x57
Llanwrtyd	a	07 18	10 57	16 05	20 03
	d	07 21	11 06	16 08	20 10
Sugar Loaf	d	07x27	11x13	16x14	20x16
Cynghordy	d	07x33	11x20	16x21	20x23
Llandovery	a	07 43	11 29	16 31	20 33
	d	07 45	11 32	16 33	20 35
Llanwrda	d	07x51	11x37	16x39	20x41
Llangadog	d	07x54	11x41	16x43	20x45
Llandeilo	a	08 03	11 50	16 52	20 54
	d	08 06	11 53	16 55	20 57
Ffairfach	d	08 08	11 55	16 57	20 59
Llandybie	d	08x15	12x02	17x05	21x07
Ammanford	d	08x20	12x07	17x09	21x11
Pantyffynnon	d	08 23	12 10	17 12	21 14
Pontarddulais	d	08x30	12x17	17x19	21x21
Llangennech	d	08x34	12x21	17x24	21x26
Bynea	d	08x37	12x24	17x27	21x29
Llanelli	a	08 42	12 29	17 32	21 34
Gowerton	a	08x53		17x51	21x47
Swansea	a	09 08	13 01	18 10	22 10

When events are being held at the Millenium Stadium, services are subject to alteration. Please check times before travelling.

Table 129

Sundays

Shrewsbury - Swansea

HEART OF WALES LINE

		AW ◇	AW ◇
Shrewsbury	d	12 07	16 18
Church Stretton	d	12 25	16 36
Craven Arms	d	12 36	16 47
Broome	d	12x42	16x53
Hopton Heath	d	12x46	16x57
Bucknell	d	12x51	17x02
Knighton	a	12 58	17 08
	d	13 00	17 11
Knucklas	d	13x06	17x16
Llangynllo	d	13x14	17x24
Llanbister Road	d	13x19	17x29
Dolau	d	13x25	17x35
Pen-y-bont	d	13x29	17x40
Llandrindod	a	13 38	17 49
	d	13 41	17 54
Builth Road	d	13x50	18x04
Cilmeri	d	13x54	18x07
Garth (Powys)	d	13x59	18x13
Llangammarch	d	14x03	18x17
Llanwrtyd	a	14 09	18 23
	d	14 12	18 25
Sugar Loaf	d	14x18	18x32
Cynghordy	d	14x25	18x39
Llandovery	a	14 35	18 48
	d	14 37	18 51
Llanwrda	d	14x43	18x57
Llangadog	d	14x47	19x01
Llandeilo	a	14 56	19 10
	d	14 59	19 12
Ffairfach	d	15 01	19 15
Llandybie	d	15x09	19x22
Ammanford	d	15x13	19x27
Pantyffynnon	d	15 16	19 30
Pontarddulais	d	15x23	19x37
Llangennech	d	15x28	19x41
Bynea	d	15x31	19x45
Llanelli	a	15 36	19 50
Gowerton	a		20x02
Swansea	a	16 04	20 16

When events are being held at the Millenium Stadium, services are subject to alteration. Please check times before travelling.

Network Diagram for Table 130

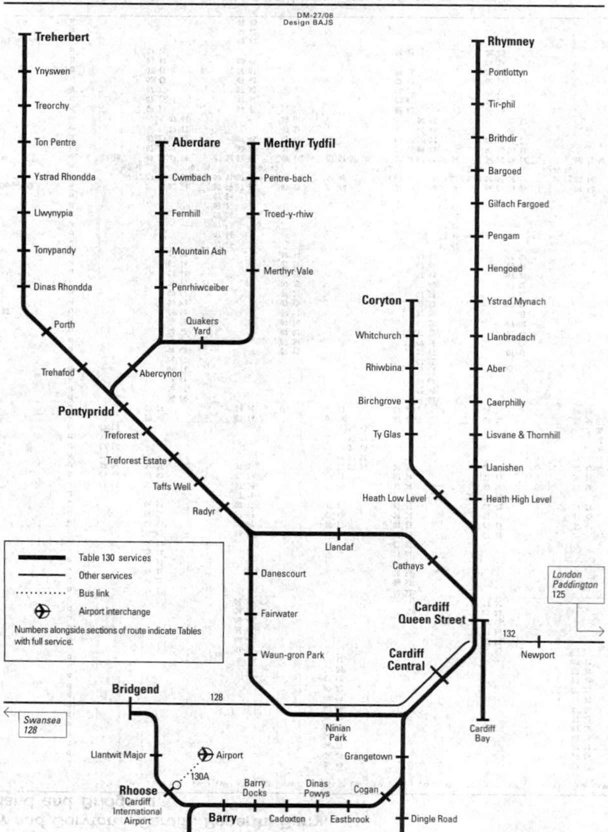

© Network Rail OPSU 2008.
All rights reserved

Treherbert, Aberdare, Merthyr, Pontypridd, Rhymney and Coryton - Cardiff, Penarth, Barry, Barry Island and Bridgend

Miles	Miles	Miles	Miles	Miles			AW MX	AW	AW	AW	AW	AW	AW	AW	AW		AW	AW	AW	AW	AW	AW	AW	AW	AW
0	—	—	—	—	**Treherbert**	d												05 47							06 17
0½	—	—	—	—	Ynyswen	d												05 49							06 19
1¼	—	—	—	—	Treorchy	d												05 51							06 21
2¾	—	—	—	—	Ton Pentre	d												05 53							06 23
3¼	—	—	—	—	Ystrad Rhondda	a												05 56							06 26
—	—	—	—	—		d												05 58							06 28
4½	—	—	—	—	Llwynypia	d												06 00							06 30
5½	—	—	—	—	Tonypandy	d												06 03							06 33
6	—	—	—	—	Dinas Rhondda	d												06 05							06 35
7½	—	—	—	—	Porth	a												06 08							06 38
—	—	—	—	—		d												06 09							06 39
8¾	—	—	—	—	Trehafod	d												06 12							06 42
—	—	0	—	—	**Merthyr Tydfil**	d																			
—	—	1½	—	—	Pentre-bach	d																			
—	—	2¾	—	—	Troed Y Rhiw	d																			
—	—	4½	—	—	Merthyr Vale	a																			
—	—	—	—	—		d																			
—	—	6¾	—	—	Quakers Yard	d																			
—	—	—	—	0	**Aberdare** 3	d																			
—	—	—	—	1½	Cwmbach	d																			
—	—	—	—	2¾	Fernhill	d																			
—	—	—	—	3¾	Mountain Ash	a																			
—	—	—	—	—		d																			
—	—	—	—	5	Penrhiwceiber	d																			
—	—	8¼	—	7¾	Abercynon	d																			
10¾	—	11½	—	11	**Pontypridd** 3	a												06 17							06 47
—	—	—	—	—		d					05 24							06 18							06 48
11½	—	—	—	—	Trefforest	d					05 27							06 21							06 51
14	—	—	—	—	Trefforest Estate	d					05 31														
16¼	—	—	—	—	Taffs Well 3	d					05 35							06 28							06 58
18¼	—	—	0	—	Radyr 3	a					05 39							06 31							07 01
—	—	—	—	—		d	23p10				05 39							06 31							07 01
—	—	—	1½	—	Danescourt	d																			
—	—	—	2	—	Fairwater	d																			
—	—	—	2¼	—	Waun-gron Park	d																			
—	—	—	3¾	—	Ninian Park	d																			
19¼	—	—	—	—	Llandaf	d	23p12				05 42							06 34							07 04
21¾	—	—	—	—	Cathays	d	23p16				05 46							06 39							07 09
—	0	—	—	—	**Rhymney** 3	d																		06 10	
—	1	—	—	—	Pontlottyn	d																		06 13	
—	3½	—	—	—	Tir-phil	d																		06 17	
—	4½	—	—	—	Brithdir	d																		06 20	
—	6	—	—	—	Bargoed	a																		06 23	
—	—	—	—	—		d																		06 27	
—	6½	—	—	—	Gilfach Fargoed	d																		06 29	
—	7½	—	—	—	Pengam	d																		06 32	
—	9¼	—	—	—	Hengoed	d																		06 35	
—	10½	—	—	—	Ystrad Mynach 3	d																		06 38	
—	13	—	—	—	Llanbradach	d																		06 43	
—	15	—	—	—	Aber	d																		06 47	
—	15¾	—	—	—	Caerphilly 3	d									06 10									06 50	
—	18¼	—	—	—	Lisvane & Thornhill	d									06 14									06 54	
—	19¾	—	—	—	Llanishen	d									06 16									06 56	
—	20¼	—	—	—	Heath High Level	d									06 19									06 59	
—	—	0	—	—	**Coryton**	d																	06 45		
—	—	0½	—	—	Whitchurch (Cardiff)	d																	06 46		
—	—	0¾	—	—	Rhiwbina	d																	06 48		
—	—	1¼	—	—	Birchgrove	d																	06 50		
—	—	1½	—	—	Ty Glas	d																	06 51		
—	—	2¼	—	—	Heath Low Level	d																	06 54		
22½	22¾	4¾	—	—	**Cardiff Queen Street** 3	a	23p20				05 51				06 25			06 42					06 59	07 04	07 12
—	—	—	—	—		d	23p20				05 51				06 26		06 36	06 43	06 48		07 00		07 01	07 06	07 14
—	—	5¾	—	—	**Cardiff Bay**	a											06 40		06 52		07 04				
23	23¼	—	4¾	—	**Cardiff Central** 7	a	23p25				05 54				06 29			06 48					07 04	07 09	07 16
—	—	—	—	—		d	23p30	05 20	05 41	05 46	05 55	06 16	06 25	06 36	06 41					06 35		07 01		07 10	07 16
24	24¼	—	—	—	Grangetown	d	23p34	05 24	05 45	05 50	05 59	06 20	06 29	06 40	06 45					06 39		07 05		07 14	07 20
—	26¾	—	—	—	Dingle Road	d				05 54		06 24		06 44								07 11			07 26
—	27	—	—	—	**Penarth**	a				05 59		06 29		06 49								07 16			07 32
25¾	—	—	—	—	Cogan	d	23p37	05 28	05 48		06 03		06 33		06 48					07 [illegible]				07 18	
26½	—	—	—	—	Eastbrook	d	23p40	05 30	05 51		06 05		06 35		06 51					07 [illegible]				07 20	
27½	—	—	—	—	Dinas Powys	d	23p42	05 32	05 53		06 07		06 37		06 53					07 [illegible]				07 22	
29½	—	—	—	—	Cadoxton	d	23p46	05 37	05 57		06 12		06 42		06 57					07 12				07 27	
30¼	—	—	—	—	Barry Docks	d	23p49	05 40	06 00		06 15		06 45		07 00					07 15				07 30	
31½	—	0	—	—	**Barry** 3	d	23p54	05 44	06 05		06 19		06 49		07 05					07 19				07 34	
32¼	—	—	—	—	**Barry Island**	a	00 01	05 50			06 25		06 55							07 25				07 40	
—	—	3¼	—	—	Rhoose Cardiff Int Airport ✈	d			06 12						07 12										
—	—	9¾	—	—	Llantwit Major	d			06 22						07 22										
—	—	19	—	—	**Bridgend**	a			06 40						07 40										

When events are being held at the Millenium Stadium, services are subject to alteration. Please check times before travelling.

Table 130

Mondays to Fridays
until 9 September

Treherbert, Aberdare, Merthyr, Pontypridd, Rhymney and Coryton - Cardiff, Penarth, Barry, Barry Island and Bridgend

Station		AW	AW	AW	AW	AW	AW	AW	AW	AW	AW	AW	AW	AW	AW	AW	AW	AW	AW	AW	AW	AW
Treherbert	d										06 47										07 17	
Ynyswen	d										06 49										07 19	
Treorchy	d										06 51										07 21	
Ton Pentre	d										06 53										07 23	
Ystrad Rhondda	a										06 56										07 26	
	d										06 58										07 28	
Llwynypia	d										07 00										07 30	
Tonypandy	d										07 03										07 33	
Dinas Rhondda	d										07 05										07 35	
Porth	a										07 08										07 38	
	d										07 09										07 39	
Trehafod	d										07 12										07 42	
Merthyr Tydfil	d							06 38										07 08				
Pentre-bach	d							06 42										07 12				
Troed Y Rhiw	d							06 45										07 15				
Merthyr Vale	a							06 48										07 18				
	d							06 50										07 20				
Quakers Yard	d							06 55										07 25				
Aberdare 3	d			06 22										06 52								
Cwmbach	d			06 25										06 55								
Fernhill	d			06 28										06 58								
Mountain Ash	a			06 31										07 01								
	d			06 34										07 04								
Penrhiwceiber	d			06 37										07 07								
Abercynon	d			06 43				06 59						07 13				07 29				
Pontypridd 3	a			06 53				07 07			07 17			07 23				07 37			07 47	
	d			06 54				07 09			07 18			07 24				07 39			07 48	
Trefforest	d			06 57				07 12			07 21			07 27				07 42			07 51	
Trefforest Estate	d							07 16										07 46				
Taffs Well 3	d	06 53		07 04				07 20			07 28			07 34				07 50			07 58	
Radyr 3	a	06 56		07 07				07 23			07 31			07 37				07 53			08 01	
	d	07 04		07 07				07 23			07 31	07 34		07 37				07 53			08 01	08 04
Danescourt	d	07 08										07 38										08 08
Fairwater	d	07 10										07 40										08 10
Waun-gron Park	d	07 12										07 42										08 12
Ninian Park	d	07 15										07 45										08 15
Llandaf	d			07 10				07 26			07 34			07 40				07 56			08 04	
Cathays	d			07 15				07 31			07 39			07 45				08 01			08 09	
Rhymney 3	d				06 34										07 02							
Pontlottyn	d				06 37										07 05							
Tir-phil	d				06 41										07 09							
Brithdir	d				06 44										07 12							
Bargoed	a				06 47										07 15							
	d				06 48					07 02					07 17				07 32			
Gilfach Fargoed	d									07 04					07 19							
Pengam	d				06 52					07 07					07 22				07 37			
Hengoed	d				06 56					07 10					07 25				07 40			
Ystrad Mynach 3	d				06 58					07 13					07 28				07 43			
Llanbradach	d				07 03					07 18					07 33				07 48			
Aber	d				07 07					07 22					07 37				07 52			
Caerphilly 3	d				07 10					07 25					07 40				07 55			
Lisvane & Thornhill	d				07 14					07 29					07 44				07 59			
Llanishen	d				07 16					07 31					07 46				08 01			
Heath High Level	d				07 19					07 34					07 49				08 04			
Coryton	d						07 15									07 45						
Whitchurch (Cardiff)	d						07 16									07 46						
Rhiwbina	d						07 18									07 48						
Birchgrove	d						07 20									07 50						
Ty Glas	d						07 21									07 51						
Heath Low Level	d						07 24									07 54						
Cardiff Queen Street 3	a			07 19	07 24		07 29	07 35		07 39	07 44			07 49	07 54	07 59		08 04	08 09		08 14	
	d		07 12	07 21	07 26	07 24	07 31	07 36	07 36	07 41	07 46		07 48	07 51	07 56	08 01	08 00	08 06	08 11	08 12	08 16	
Cardiff Bay	a		07 16			07 28			07 40				07 52				08 04			08 16		
Cardiff Central 7	a	07 20		07 24	07 29		07 34	07 40		07 44	07 51	07 50		07 54	07 59	08 04		08 09	08 14		08 22	08 20
	d			07 25	07 31			07 41		07 46				07 55	08 01			08 10	08 16			
Grangetown	d			07 29	07 33			07 45		07 50				07 59	08 04			08 14	08 20			
Dingle Road	d				07 42					07 56					08 11				08 26			
Penarth	a				07 46					08 01					08 15				08 32			
Cogan	d			07 33				07 49						08 03				08 18				
Eastbrook	d			07 35				07 51						08 05				08 20				
Dinas Powys	d			07 37				07 53						08 07				08 22				
Cadoxton	d			07 42				07 58						08 12				08 27				
Barry Docks	d			07 45				08 01						08 15				08 30				
Barry 3	d			07 49				08 05						08 19				08 34				
Barry Island	a			07 55										08 25				08 40				
Rhoose Cardiff Int Airport ✈	d							08 12														
Llantwit Major	d							08 22														
Bridgend	a							08 40														

When events are being held at the Millenium Stadium, services are subject to alteration. Please check times before travelling.

Table 130

Mondays to Fridays
until 9 September

Treherbert, Aberdare, Merthyr, Pontypridd, Rhymney and Coryton - Cardiff, Penarth, Barry, Barry Island and Bridgend

Station		AW	AW	AW	AW	AW	AW	AW	AW	AW	AW	AW	AW	AW	AW	AW	AW	AW	AW	AW	AW	AW	AW
Treherbert	d								07 45										08 17				
Ynyswen	d								07 47										08 19				
Treorchy	d								07 49										08 21				
Ton Pentre	d								07 51										08 23				
Ystrad Rhondda	a								07 54										08 26				
	d								07 58										08 28				
Llwynypia	d								08 00										08 30				
Tonypandy	d								08 03										08 33				
Dinas Rhondda	d								08 05										08 35				
Porth	a								08 08										08 38				
	d								08 09										08 39				
Trehafod	d								08 12										08 42				
Merthyr Tydfil	d					07 38										08 08							
Pentre-bach	d					07 42										08 12							
Troed Y Rhiw	d					07 45										08 15							
Merthyr Vale	a					07 48										08 18							
	d					07 50										08 20							
Quakers Yard	d					07 55										08 25							
Aberdare 3	d	07 22										07 52									08 22		
Cwmbach	d	07 25										07 55									08 25		
Fernhill	d	07 28										07 58									08 28		
Mountain Ash	a	07 31										08 01									08 31		
	d	07 34										08 04									08 34		
Penrhiwceiber	d	07 37										08 07									08 37		
Abercynon	d	07 43				07 59						08 13				08 29					08 43		
Pontypridd 3	a	07 53				08 07			08 17			08 23				08 37			08 47		08 53		
	d	07 54				08 09			08 18			08 24				08 39			08 48		08 54		
Trefforest	d	07 57				08 12			08 21			08 27				08 42			08 51		08 57		
Trefforest Estate	d					08 16										08 46							
Taffs Well 3	d	08 04				08 20			08 28			08 34				08 50			08 58		09 04		
Radyr 3	a	08 07				08 23			08 31			08 37				08 53			09 01		09 07		
	d	08 07				08 23			08 31	08 34		08 37				08 53			09 01	09 04	09 07		
Danescourt	d									08 38										09 08			
Fairwater	d									08 40										09 10			
Waun-gron Park	d									08 42										09 12			
Ninian Park	d									08 45										09 15			
Llandaf	d	08 10				08 26			08 34			08 40				08 56			09 04		09 10		
Cathays	d	08 15				08 31			08 39			08 45				09 01			09 09		09 15		
Rhymney 3	d		07 24					07 44														08 30	
Pontlottyn	d		07 27					07 47														08 33	
Tir-phil	d		07 31					07 51														08 37	
Brithdir	d		07 34					07 54														08 40	
Bargoed	a		07 37					08 00														08 44	
	d		07 45					08 02					08 17				08 32					08 47	
Gilfach Fargoed	d		07 47										08 19										
Pengam	d		07 50					08 07					08 22				08 37					08 52	
Hengoed	d		07 54					08 10					08 25				08 40					08 55	
Ystrad Mynach 3	d		07 57					08 13					08 28				08 43					08 58	
Llanbradach	d		08 02					08 18					08 33				08 48					09 03	
Aber	d		08 07					08 22					08 37				08 52					09 07	
Caerphilly 3	d		08 10					08 25					08 40				08 55					09 10	
Lisvane & Thornhill	d		08 14					08 29					08 44				08 59					09 14	
Llanishen	d		08 16					08 31					08 46				09 01					09 16	
Heath High Level	d		08 19					08 34					08 49				09 04					09 19	
Coryton	d				08 15									08 45									
Whitchurch (Cardiff)	d				08 16									08 46									
Rhiwbina	d				08 18									08 48									
Birchgrove	d				08 20									08 50									
Ty Glas	d				08 21									08 51									
Heath Low Level	d				08 24									08 54									
Cardiff Queen Street 3	a	08 19	08 24		08 29	08 34		08 39	08 44			08 49	08 54	08 59		09 04	09 09		09 14		09 19	09 24	
	d	08 21	08 26	08 24	08 31	08 36	08 36	08 41	08 46		08 48	08 51	08 56	09 01	09 00	09 06	09 11	09 12	09 16		09 21	09 26	09 24
Cardiff Bay	a			08 28			08 40				08 52				09 04			09 16					09 28
Cardiff Central 7	a	08 24	08 29		08 34	08 39		08 47	08 52	08 50		08 54	08 59	09 04		09 09	09 14		09 22	09 20	09 24	09 29	
	d	08 25	08 31			08 41						08 55	09 01			09 10	09 16				09 25	09 31	
Grangetown	d	08 29	08 35			08 45						08 59	09 05			09 14	09 20				09 29	09 35	
Dingle Road	d		08 41										09 11				09 26					09 41	
Penarth	a		08 46										09 17				09 31					09 46	
Cogan	d	08 33				08 48						09 03				09 18					09 33		
Eastbrook	d	08 35				08 51						09 05				09 20					09 35		
Dinas Powys	d	08 37				08 53						09 07				09 22					09 37		
Cadoxton	d	08 42				08 57						09 12				09 27					09 42		
Barry Docks	d	08 45				09 00						09 15				09 30					09 45		
Barry 3	d	08 49				09 05						09 19				09 34					09 49		
Barry Island	a	08 55										09 25				09 40					09 55		
Rhoose Cardiff Int Airport ✈	d					09 12																	
Llantwit Major	d					09 22																	
Bridgend	a					09 40																	

When events are being held at the Millenium Stadium, services are subject to alteration. Please check times before travelling.

Treherbert, Aberdare, Merthyr, Pontypridd, Rhymney and Coryton - Cardiff, Penarth, Barry, Barry Island and Bridgend

		AW	AW		AW	AW	AW	AW	AW	AW	AW	AW	AW		AW	AW	AW	AW	AW	AW	AW	AW	AW		AW
Treherbert	d						08 47											09 17							
Ynyswen	d						08 49											09 19							
Treorchy	d						08 51											09 21							
Ton Pentre	d						08 53											09 23							
Ystrad Rhondda	a						08 56											09 26							
	d						08 58											09 28							
Llwynypia	d						09 00											09 30							
Tonypandy	d						09 03											09 33							
Dinas Rhondda	d						09 05											09 35							
Porth	a						09 08											09 38							
	d						09 09											09 39							
Trehafod	d						09 12											09 42							
Merthyr Tydfil	d		08 38												09 08										09 38
Pentre-bach	d		08 42												09 12										09 42
Troed Y Rhiw	d		08 45												09 15										09 45
Merthyr Vale	a		08 48												09 18										09 48
	d		08 50												09 20										09 50
Quakers Yard	d		08 55												09 25										09 55
Aberdare	d									08 52										09 22					
Cwmbach	d									08 55										09 25					
Fernhill	d									08 58										09 28					
Mountain Ash	a									09 01										09 31					
	d									09 04										09 34					
Penrhiwceiber	d									09 07										09 37					
Abercynon	d		08 59							09 13					09 29					09 43					09 59
Pontypridd	a		09 07				09 17			09 23					09 37			09 47		09 53					10 07
	d		09 09				09 18			09 24					09 39			09 48		09 54					10 09
Trefforest	d		09 12				09 21			09 27					09 42			09 51		09 57					10 12
Trefforest Estate	d		09 16												09 46										10 16
Taffs Well	d		09 20				09 28			09 34					09 50			09 58		10 04					10 20
Radyr	a		09 23				09 31			09 37					09 53			10 01		10 07					10 23
	d		09 23				09 31	09 34		09 37					09 53			10 01	10 04	10 07					10 23
Danescourt	d							09 38											10 08						
Fairwater	d							09 40											10 10						
Waun-gron Park	d							09 42											10 12						
Ninian Park	d							09 45											10 15						
Llandaf	d		09 26				09 34			09 40					09 56			10 04		10 10					10 26
Cathays	d		09 31				09 39			09 45					10 01			10 09		10 15					10 31
Rhymney	d																				09 29				
Pontlottyn	d																				09 32				
Tir-phil	d																				09 36				
Brithdir	d																				09 39				
Bargoed	a																				09 42				
	d					09 02					09 17					09 32					09 47				
Gilfach Fargoed	d										09 19														
Pengam	d					09 07					09 22					09 37					09 52				
Hengoed	d					09 10					09 25					09 40					09 55				
Ystrad Mynach	d					09 13					09 28					09 43					09 58				
Llanbradach	d					09 18					09 33					09 48					10 03				
Aber	d					09 22					09 37					09 52					10 07				
Caerphilly	d					09 25					09 40					09 55					10 10				
Lisvane & Thornhill	d					09 29					09 44					09 59					10 14				
Llanishen	d					09 31					09 46					10 01					10 16				
Heath High Level	d					09 34					09 49					10 04					10 19				
Coryton	d	09 15										09 45											10 15		
Whitchurch (Cardiff)	d	09 16										09 46											10 16		
Rhiwbina	d	09 18										09 48											10 18		
Birchgrove	d	09 20										09 50											10 20		
Ty Glas	d	09 21										09 51											10 21		
Heath Low Level	d	09 24										09 54											10 24		
Cardiff Queen Street	a	09 29	09 34			09 39	09 44			09 49	09 54	09 59			10 04	10 09		10 14		10 19	10 24		10 29		10 34
	d	09 31	09 36		09 36	09 41	09 46		09 48	09 51	09 56	10 01	10 00		10 06	10 11	10 12	10 16		10 21	10 26	10 24	10 31		10 36
Cardiff Bay	a				09 40				09 52				10 04				10 16					10 28			
Cardiff Central	a	09 34	09 39			09 44	09 52	09 50		09 54	09 59	10 04			10 09	10 14		10 22	10 20	10 24	10 29		10 34		10 39
	d		09 41			09 46				09 55	10 01				10 10	10 16				10 25	10 31				10 41
Grangetown	d		09 45			09 50				09 59	10 05				10 14	10 20				10 29	10 35				10 45
Dingle Road	d					09 56					10 11					10 26					10 41				
Penarth	a					10 02					10 16					10 31					10 46				
Cogan	d		09 48							10 03					10 18					10 33					10 48
Eastbrook	d		09 51							10 05					10 20					10 35					10 51
Dinas Powys	d		09 53							10 07					10 22					10 37					10 53
Cadoxton	d		09 57							10 12					10 27					10 42					10 57
Barry Docks	d		10 00							10 15					10 30					10 45					11 00
Barry	d		10 05							10 19					10 34					10 49					11 05
Barry Island	a									10 25					10 40					10 55					
Rhoose Cardiff Int Airport	d		10 12																						11 12
Llantwit Major	d		10 22																						11 22
Bridgend	a		10 40																						11 40

When events are being held at the Millenium Stadium, services are subject to alteration. Please check times before travelling.

Treherbert, Aberdare, Merthyr, Pontypridd, Rhymney and Coryton - Cardiff, Penarth, Barry, Barry Island and Bridgend

		AW	AW	AW	AW	AW	AW	AW	AW		AW	AW	AW	AW	AW	AW	AW	AW	AW		AW	AW	AW	AW	AW
Treherbert	d			09 47															10 17						
Ynyswen	d			09 49															10 19						
Treorchy	d			09 51															10 21						
Ton Pentre	d			09 53															10 23						
Ystrad Rhondda	a			09 56															10 26						
	d			09 58															10 28						
Llwynypia	d			10 00															10 30						
Tonypandy	d			10 03															10 33						
Dinas Rhondda	d			10 05															10 35						
Porth	a			10 08															10 38						
	d			10 09															10 52						
Trehafod	d			10 12															10 55						
Merthyr Tydfil	d							10 04															10 38		
Pentre-bach	d							10 08															10 42		
Troed Y Rhiw	d							10 11															10 45		
Merthyr Vale	a							10 14															10 48		
	d							10 16															10 50		
Quakers Yard	d							10 22															10 55		
Aberdare	d						09 52										10 22								
Cwmbach	d						09 55										10 25								
Fernhill	d						09 58										10 28								
Mountain Ash	a						10 01										10 31								
	d						10 04										10 34								
Penrhiwceiber	d						10 07										10 37								
Abercynon	d						10 13	10 26									10 43						10 59		
Pontypridd	a			10 17			10 23	10 32									10 53		11 00				11 08		
	d			10 18			10 24						10 39				10 54		11 04				11 09		
Trefforest	d			10 21			10 27						10 42				10 57		11 07				11 12		
Trefforest Estate	d																						11 16		
Taffs Well	d			10 28			10 34						10 50				11 04		11 13				11 20		
Radyr	a			10 31			10 37						10 53				11 07		11 17				11 23		
	d			10 31	10 34		10 37						10 53		11 04		11 07		11 17				11 23		
Danescourt	d				10 38										11 08										
Fairwater	d				10 40										11 10										
Waun-gron Park	d				10 42										11 12										
Ninian Park	d				10 45										11 15										
Llandaf	d			10 34			10 40						10 56				11 10						11 26		
Cathays	d			10 39			10 45						11 01				11 15						11 31		
Rhymney	d																	10 29							
Pontlottyn	d																	10 32							
Tir-phil	d																	10 36							
Brithdir	d																	10 39							
Bargoed	a																	10 42							
	d		10 02						10 17					10 32				10 47							11 02
Gilfach Fargoed	d								10 19																
Pengam	d		10 07						10 22					10 37				10 52							11 07
Hengoed	d		10 10						10 25					10 40				10 55							11 10
Ystrad Mynach	d		10 13						10 28					10 43				10 58							11 13
Llanbradach	d		10 18						10 33					10 48				11 03							11 18
Aber	d		10 22						10 37					10 52				11 07							11 22
Caerphilly	d		10 25						10 40					10 55				11 10							11 25
Lisvane & Thornhill	d		10 29						10 44					10 59				11 14							11 29
Llanishen	d		10 31						10 46					11 01				11 16							11 31
Heath High Level	d		10 34						10 49					11 04				11 19							11 34
Coryton	d										10 45											11 15			
Whitchurch (Cardiff)	d										10 46											11 16			
Rhiwbina	d										10 48											11 18			
Birchgrove	d										10 50											11 20			
Ty Glas	d										10 51											11 21			
Heath Low Level	d										10 54											11 24			
Cardiff Queen Street	a		10 39	10 44			10 49		10 54		10 59		11 04	11 09			11 19	11 24				11 29	11 34		11 39
	d	10 36	10 41	10 46		10 48	10 51		10 56		11 01	11 00	11 06	11 11		11 12	11 21	11 26			11 24	11 31	11 36	11 36	11 41
Cardiff Bay	a	10 40				10 52						11 04				11 16					11 28			11 40	
Cardiff Central	a		10 44	10 52	10 50		10 54		10 59		11 04		11 09	11 14	11 20		11 24	11 29	11 34			11 34	11 39		11 44
	d		10 46				10 55		11 01				11 10	11 16			11 25	11 31					11 41		11 46
Grangetown	d		10 50				10 59		11 05				11 14	11 20			11 29	11 35					11 45		11 50
Dingle Road	d		10 56						11 11					11 26				11 41							11 56
Penarth	a		11 01						11 17					11 31				11 46							12 01
Cogan	d						11 03						11 18				11 33						11 48		
Eastbrook	d						11 05						11 20				11 35						11 51		
Dinas Powys	d						11 07						11 22				11 37						11 53		
Cadoxton	d						11 12						11 27				11 42						11 57		
Barry Docks	d						11 15						11 30				11 45						12 00		
Barry	d						11 19						11 34				11 49						12 05		
Barry Island	a						11 25						11 40				11 55								
Rhoose Cardiff Int Airport	d																						12 12		
Llantwit Major	d																						12 22		
Bridgend	a																						12 40		

When events are being held at the Millenium Stadium, services are subject to alteration. Please check times before travelling.

Table 130

Mondays to Fridays

until 9 September

Treherbert, Aberdare, Merthyr, Pontypridd, Rhymney and Coryton - Cardiff, Penarth, Barry, Barry Island and Bridgend

		AW	AW	AW	AW		AW	AW	AW	AW	AW	AW	AW	AW	AW		AW	AW	AW	AW	AW	AW	AW	AW	AW
Treherbert	d	10 47											11 17										11 47		
Ynyswen	d	10 49											11 19										11 49		
Treorchy	d	10 51											11 21										11 51		
Ton Pentre	d	10 53											11 23										11 53		
Ystrad Rhondda	a	10 56											11 26										11 56		
	d	10 58											11 28										11 58		
Llwynypia	d	11 00											11 30										12 00		
Tonypandy	d	11 03											11 33										12 03		
Dinas Rhondda	d	11 05											11 35										12 05		
Porth	a	11 08											11 38										12 08		
	d	11 09											11 39										12 09		
Trehafod	d	11 12											11 42										12 12		
Merthyr Tydfil	d									11 08										11 38					
Pentre-bach	d									11 12										11 42					
Troed Y Rhiw	d									11 15										11 45					
Merthyr Vale	a									11 18										11 48					
	d									11 20										11 50					
Quakers Yard	d									11 25										11 55					
Aberdare [3]	d				10 52										11 22										
Cwmbach	d				10 55										11 25										
Fernhill	d				10 58										11 28										
Mountain Ash	a				11 01										11 31										
	d				11 04										11 34										
Penrhiwceiber	d				11 07										11 37										
Abercynon	d				11 13					11 29					11 43					11 59					
Pontypridd [3]	a	11 17			11 23					11 37			11 47		11 53					12 07			12 17		
	d	11 18			11 24					11 39			11 48		11 54					12 09			12 18		
Trefforest	d	11 21			11 27					11 42			11 51		11 57					12 12			12 21		
Trefforest Estate	d									11 46										12 16					
Taffs Well [3]	d	11 28			11 34					11 50			11 58		12 04					12 20			12 28		
Radyr [3]	a	11 31			11 37					11 53			12 01		12 07					12 23			12 31		
	d	11 31	11 34		11 37					11 53			12 01	12 04	12 07					12 23			12 31	12 34	
Danescourt	d		11 38											12 08										12 38	
Fairwater	d		11 40											12 10										12 40	
Waun-gron Park	d		11 42											12 12										12 42	
Ninian Park	d		11 45											12 15										12 45	
Llandaf	d	11 34			11 40					11 56			12 04		12 10					12 26			12 34		
Cathays	d	11 39			11 45					12 01			12 09		12 15					12 31			12 39		
Rhymney [3]	d																11 29								
Pontlottyn	d																11 32								
Tir-phil	d																11 36								
Brithdir	d																11 39								
Bargoed	a																11 42								
	d						11 17				11 32						11 47					12 02			
Gilfach Fargoed	d						11 19																		
Pengam	d						11 22				11 37						11 52					12 07			
Hengoed	d						11 25				11 40						11 55					12 10			
Ystrad Mynach [3]	d						11 28				11 43						11 58					12 13			
Llanbradach	d						11 33				11 48						12 03					12 18			
Aber	d						11 37				11 52						12 07					12 22			
Caerphilly [3]	d						11 40				11 55						12 10					12 25			
Lisvane & Thornhill	d						11 44				11 59						12 14					12 29			
Llanishen	d						11 46				12 01						12 16					12 31			
Heath High Level	d						11 49				12 04						12 19					12 34			
Coryton	d							11 45											12 15						
Whitchurch (Cardiff)	d							11 46											12 16						
Rhiwbina	d							11 48											12 18						
Birchgrove	d							11 50											12 20						
Ty Glas	d							11 51											12 21						
Heath Low Level	d							11 54											12 24						
Cardiff Queen Street [3]	a	11 44			11 49		11 54	11 59		12 04	12 09		12 14		12 19		12 24		12 29	12 34		12 39	12 44		
	d	11 46		11 48	11 51		11 56	12 01	12 00	12 06	12 11	12 12	12 16		12 21		12 26	12 24	12 31	12 36	12 36	12 41	12 46		12 48
Cardiff Bay	a			11 52					12 04			12 16						12 28			12 40				12 52
Cardiff Central [7]	a	11 52	11 50		11 54		11 59	12 04		12 09	12 14		12 22	12 20	12 24		12 29		12 34	12 39		12 44	12 52	12 50	
	d				11 55		12 01			12 10	12 16				12 25		12 31			12 41		12 46			
Grangetown	d				11 59		12 05			12 14	12 20				12 29		12 35			12 45		12 50			
Dingle Road	d						12 11				12 26						12 41					12 56			
Penarth	a						12 16				12 31						12 46					13 01			
Cogan	d				12 03					12 18					12 33					12 48					
Eastbrook	d				12 05					12 20					12 35					12 51					
Dinas Powys	d				12 07					12 22					12 37					12 53					
Cadoxton	d				12 12					12 27					12 42					12 57					
Barry Docks	d				12 15					12 30					12 45					13 00					
Barry [3]	d				12 19					12 34					12 49					13 05					
Barry Island	a				12 25					12 40					12 55										
Rhoose Cardiff Int Airport ✈	d																			13 12					
Llantwit Major	d																			13 22					
Bridgend	a																			13 40					

When events are being held at the Millenium Stadium, services are subject to alteration. Please check times before travelling.

Table 130

Mondays to Fridays

until 9 September

Treherbert, Aberdare, Merthyr, Pontypridd, Rhymney and Coryton - Cardiff, Penarth, Barry, Barry Island and Bridgend

			AW	AW	AW	AW	AW	AW	AW	AW	AW		AW	AW	AW	AW	AW	AW	AW	AW	AW		AW	AW	AW
Treherbert	d									12 17										12 47					
Ynyswen	d									12 19										12 49					
Treorchy	d									12 21										12 51					
Ton Pentre	d									12 23										12 53					
Ystrad Rhondda	a									12 26										12 56					
	d									12 28										12 58					
Llwynypia	d									12 30										13 00					
Tonypandy	d									12 33										13 03					
Dinas Rhondda	d									12 35										13 05					
Porth	a									12 38										13 08					
	d									12 39										13 09					
Trehafod	d									12 42										13 12					
Merthyr Tydfil	d						12 08										12 38								
Pentre-bach	d						12 12										12 42								
Troed Y Rhiw	d						12 15										12 45								
Merthyr Vale	a						12 18										12 48								
	d						12 20										12 50								
Quakers Yard	d						12 25										12 55								
Aberdare [3]	d												12 22											12 52	
Cwmbach	d												12 25											12 55	
Fernhill	d												12 28											12 58	
Mountain Ash	a												12 31											13 01	
	d												12 34											13 04	
Penrhiwceiber	d												12 37											13 07	
Abercynon	d						12 29						12 43				12 59							13 13	
Pontypridd [3]	a						12 37			12 48			12 53				13 07			13 17				13 23	
	d						12 39			12 48			12 54				13 09			13 18				13 24	
Trefforest	d						12 42			12 51			12 57				13 12			13 21				13 27	
Trefforest Estate	d						12 46										13 16								
Taffs Well [3]	d						12 50			12 58			13 04				13 20			13 28				13 34	
Radyr [3]	a						12 53			13 01			13 07				13 23			13 31				13 37	
	d						12 53			13 01	13 04		13 07				13 23			13 31	13 34			13 37	
Danescourt	d										13 08										13 38				
Fairwater	d										13 10										13 40				
Waun-gron Park	d										13 12										13 42				
Ninian Park	d										13 15										13 45				
Llandaf	d						12 56			13 04			13 10				13 26			13 34				13 40	
Cathays	d						13 01			13 09			13 15				13 31			13 39				13 45	
Rhymney [3]	d													12 29											
Pontlottyn	d													12 32											
Tir-phil	d													12 36											
Brithdir	d													12 39											
Bargoed	a													12 42											
	d			12 17				12 32						12 47					13 02						13 17
Gilfach Fargoed	d			12 19																					13 19
Pengam	d			12 22				12 37						12 52					13 07						13 22
Hengoed	d			12 25				12 40						12 55					13 10						13 25
Ystrad Mynach [3]	d			12 28				12 43						12 58					13 13						13 28
Llanbradach	d			12 33				12 48						13 03					13 18						13 33
Aber	d			12 37				12 52						13 07					13 22						13 37
Caerphilly [3]	d			12 40				12 55						13 10					13 25						13 40
Lisvane & Thornhill	d			12 44				12 59						13 14					13 29						13 44
Llanishen	d			12 46				13 01						13 16					13 31						13 46
Heath High Level	d			12 49				13 04						13 19					13 34						13 49
Coryton	d				12 45											13 15									
Whitchurch (Cardiff)	d				12 46											13 16									
Rhiwbina	d				12 48											13 18									
Birchgrove	d				12 50											13 20									
Ty Glas	d				12 51											13 21									
Heath Low Level	d				12 54											13 24									
Cardiff Queen Street [3]	a			12 54	12 59		13 04	13 09		13 14			13 19	13 24		13 29	13 34		13 39	13 44				13 49	13 54
	d			12 56	13 01	13 00	13 06	13 11	13 12	13 16			13 21	13 26	13 24	13 31	13 36	13 36	13 41	13 46			13 48	13 51	13 56
Cardiff Bay	a					13 04			13 16						13 28			13 40					13 52		
Cardiff Central [7]	a			12 59	13 04		13 09	13 14		13 22	13 20		13 24	13 29		13 34	13 39		13 44	13 52	13 50			13 54	13 59
	d		12 55	13 01			13 10	13 16					13 25	13 31			13 41		13 46					13 55	14 01
Grangetown	d		12 59	13 05			13 14	13 20					13 29	13 35			13 45		13 50					13 59	14 05
Dingle Road	d			13 11				13 26						13 41					13 56						14 11
Penarth	a			13 16				13 31						13 46					14 01						14 16
Cogan	d		13 03				13 18						13 33				13 48							14 03	
Eastbrook	d		13 05				13 20						13 35				13 51							14 05	
Dinas Powys	d		13 07				13 22						13 37				13 53							14 07	
Cadoxton	d		13 12				13 27						13 42				13 57							14 12	
Barry Docks	d		13 15				13 30						13 45				14 00							14 15	
Barry [3]	d		13 19				13 34						13 49				14 05							14 19	
Barry Island	a		13 25				13 40						13 55											14 25	
Rhoose Cardiff Int Airport ✈	d																14 12								
Llantwit Major	d																14 22								
Bridgend	a																14 40								

When events are being held at the Millenium Stadium, services are subject to alteration. Please check times before travelling.

Table 130

Mondays to Fridays
until 9 September

Treherbert, Aberdare, Merthyr, Pontypridd, Rhymney and Coryton - Cardiff, Penarth, Barry, Barry Island and Bridgend

		AW	AW	AW	AW	AW	AW		AW	AW	AW	AW	AW	AW	AW	AW	AW		AW	AW	AW	AW	AW	AW	AW
Treherbert	d						13 17										13 47								
Ynyswen	d						13 19										13 49								
Treorchy	d						13 21										13 51								
Ton Pentre	d						13 23										13 53								
Ystrad Rhondda	a						13 26										13 56								
	d						13 28										13 58								
Llwynypia	d						13 30										14 00								
Tonypandy	d						13 33										14 03								
Dinas Rhondda	d						13 35										14 05								
Porth	a						13 38										14 08								
	d						13 39										14 09								
Trehafod	d						13 42										14 12								
Merthyr Tydfil	d			13 08										13 38											14 08
Pentre-bach	d			13 12										13 42											14 12
Troed Y Rhiw	d			13 15										13 45											14 15
Merthyr Vale	a			13 18										13 48											14 18
	d			13 20										13 50											14 20
Quakers Yard	d			13 25										13 55											14 25
Aberdare 3	d																				13 52				
Cwmbach	d																				13 55				
Fernhill	d																				13 58				
Mountain Ash	a																				14 01				
	d																				14 04				
Penrhiwceiber	d																				14 07				
Abercynon	d			13 29						13 45				13 59							14 13				14 29
Pontypridd 3	a			13 37			13 47			13 53				14 07			14 17				14 23				14 37
	d			13 39			13 48			13 54				14 09			14 18				14 24				14 39
Trefforest	d			13 42			13 51			13 57				14 12			14 21				14 27				14 42
Trefforest Estate	d			13 46										14 16											14 46
Taffs Well 3	d			13 50			13 58			14 04				14 20			14 28				14 34				14 50
Radyr 3	a			13 53			14 01			14 07				14 23			14 31				14 37				14 53
	d			13 53			14 01		14 04	14 07				14 23			14 31		14 34		14 37				14 53
Danescourt	d								14 08										14 38						
Fairwater	d								14 10										14 40						
Waun-gron Park	d								14 12										14 42						
Ninian Park	d								14 15										14 45						
Llandaf	d			13 56			14 04			14 10				14 26			14 34				14 40				14 56
Cathays	d			14 01			14 09			14 15				14 31			14 39				14 45				15 01
Rhymney 3	d										13 29														
Pontlottyn	d										13 32														
Tir-phil	d										13 36														
Brithdir	d										13 39														
Bargoed	a										13 42														
	d				13 32						13 47					14 02						14 17			
Gilfach Fargoed	d																					14 19			
Pengam	d				13 37						13 52					14 07						14 22			
Hengoed	d				13 40						13 55					14 10						14 25			
Ystrad Mynach 3	d				13 43						13 58					14 13						14 28			
Llanbradach	d				13 48						14 03					14 18						14 33			
Aber	d				13 52						14 07					14 22						14 37			
Caerphilly 3	d				13 55						14 10					14 25						14 40			
Lisvane & Thornhill	d				13 59						14 14					14 29						14 44			
Llanishen	d				14 01						14 16					14 31						14 46			
Heath High Level	d				14 04						14 19					14 34						14 49			
Coryton	d	13 45											14 15											14 45	
Whitchurch (Cardiff)	d	13 46											14 16											14 46	
Rhiwbina	d	13 48											14 18											14 48	
Birchgrove	d	13 50											14 20											14 50	
Ty Glas	d	13 51											14 21											14 51	
Heath Low Level	d	13 54											14 24											14 54	
Cardiff Queen Street 3	a	13 59		14 04	14 09		14 14			14 19	14 24		14 29	14 34		14 39	14 44				14 49	14 54		15 01	15 04
	d	14 01	14 00	14 06	14 11	14 12	14 16			14 21	14 26	14 24	14 31	14 36	14 36	14 41	14 46			14 48	14 51	14 56	15 00	15 02	15 06
Cardiff Bay	a		14 04			14 16						14 28			14 40					14 52			15 04		
Cardiff Central 7	a	14 04		14 09	14 14		14 22		14 20	14 24	14 29		14 34	14 39		14 44	14 52		14 50		14 54	14 59		15 05	15 09
	d			14 10	14 16					14 25	14 31			14 41		14 46					14 55	15 01			15 10
Grangetown	d			14 14	14 20					14 29	14 35			14 45		14 50					14 59	15 05			15 14
Dingle Road	d				14 26						14 41					14 56						15 11			
Penarth	a				14 31						14 46					15 01						15 16			
Cogan	d			14 18						14 33				14 48							15 03				15 18
Eastbrook	d			14 20						14 35				14 51							15 05				15 20
Dinas Powys	d			14 22						14 37				14 53							15 07				15 22
Cadoxton	d			14 27						14 42				14 57							15 12				15 27
Barry Docks	d			14 30						14 45				15 00							15 15				15 30
Barry 3	d			14 34						14 49				15 05							15 19				15 34
Barry Island	a			14 40						14 55											15 25				15 40
Rhoose Cardiff Int Airport ✈	d													15 12											
Llantwit Major	d													15 22											
Bridgend	a													15 40											

When events are being held at the Millenium Stadium, services are subject to alteration. Please check times before travelling.

Table 130

Mondays to Fridays
until 9 September

Treherbert, Aberdare, Merthyr, Pontypridd, Rhymney and Coryton - Cardiff, Penarth, Barry, Barry Island and Bridgend

		AW	AW		AW	AW	AW	AW	AW	AW	AW	AW	AW		AW	AW	AW	AW	AW	AW	AW	AW	AW		AW
Treherbert	d							14 17							14 47										
Ynyswen	d							14 19							14 49										
Treorchy	d							14 21							14 51										
Ton Pentre	d							14 23							14 53										
Ystrad Rhondda	a							14 26							14 56										
	d							14 28							14 58										
Llwynypia	d							14 30							15 00										
Tonypandy	d							14 33							15 03										
Dinas Rhondda	d							14 35							15 05										
Porth	a							14 38							15 08										
	d							14 52							15 09										
Trehafod	d							14 55							15 12										
Merthyr Tydfil	d										14 38											15 08			
Pentre-bach	d										14 42											15 12			
Troed Y Rhiw	d										14 45											15 15			
Merthyr Vale	a										14 48											15 18			
	d										14 50											15 20			
Quakers Yard	d										14 55											15 25			
Aberdare 3	d					14 22												14 52							
Cwmbach	d					14 25												14 55							
Fernhill	d					14 28												14 58							
Mountain Ash	a					14 31												15 01							
	d					14 34												15 04							
Penrhiwceiber	d					14 37												15 07							
Abercynon	d					14 43					14 59							15 13				15 29			
Pontypridd 3	a					14 53		15 00			15 07				15 17			15 23				15 37			
	d					14 54		15 04			15 09				15 18			15 24				15 39			
Trefforest	d					14 57		15 07			15 12				15 21			15 27				15 42			
Trefforest Estate	d										15 16											15 46			
Taffs Well 3	d					15 04		15 13			15 20				15 28			15 34				15 50			
Radyr 3	a					15 07		15 17			15 23				15 31			15 37				15 53			
	d		15 04			15 07		15 17			15 23				15 31	15 34		15 37				15 53			
Danescourt	d		15 08													15 38									
Fairwater	d		15 10													15 40									
Waun-gron Park	d		15 12													15 42									
Ninian Park	d		15 15													15 45									
Llandaf	d					15 10					15 26				15 34			15 40				15 56			
Cathays	d					15 15					15 31				15 39			15 45				16 01			
Rhymney 3	d						14 29																		
Pontlottyn	d						14 32																		
Tir-phil	d						14 36																		
Brithdir	d						14 39																		
Bargoed	a						14 42																		
	d	14 32					14 47						15 02						15 17				15 32		
Gilfach Fargoed	d																		15 19						
Pengam	d	14 37					14 52						15 07						15 22				15 37		
Hengoed	d	14 40					14 55						15 10						15 25				15 40		
Ystrad Mynach 3	d	14 43					14 58						15 13						15 28				15 43		
Llanbradach	d	14 48					15 03						15 18						15 33				15 48		
Aber	d	14 52					15 07						15 22						15 37				15 52		
Caerphilly 3	d	14 55					15 10						15 25						15 40				15 55		
Lisvane & Thornhill	d	14 59					15 14						15 29						15 44				15 59		
Llanishen	d	15 01					15 16						15 31						15 46				16 01		
Heath High Level	d	15 04					15 19						15 34						15 49				16 04		
Coryton	d									15 15										15 45					
Whitchurch (Cardiff)	d									15 16										15 46					
Rhiwbina	d									15 18										15 48					
Birchgrove	d									15 20										15 50					
Ty Glas	d									15 21										15 51					
Heath Low Level	d									15 24										15 54					
Cardiff Queen Street 3	a	15 09				15 19	15 24			15 29	15 34		15 39		15 44			15 49	15 54	15 59		16 04	16 09		
	d	15 11			15 12	15 21	15 26		15 24	15 31	15 36	15 36	15 41		15 46		15 48	15 51	15 56	16 01	16 00	16 06	16 11		16 12
Cardiff Bay	a				15 16				15 28			15 40					15 52				16 04				16 16
Cardiff Central 7	a	15 14	15 20			15 24	15 29	15 34		15 34	15 39		15 44		15 52	15 50		15 54	15 59	16 05		16 09	16 14		
	d	15 16				15 25	15 31				15 41		15 46					15 55	16 01			16 10	16 16		
Grangetown	d	15 20				15 29	15 35				15 45		15 50					15 59	16 05			16 14	16 20		
Dingle Road	d	15 26					15 41						15 56						16 11				16 26		
Penarth	a	15 31					15 46						16 01						16 17				16 31		
Cogan	d					15 33					15 48							16 03				16 18			
Eastbrook	d					15 35					15 51							16 05				16 20			
Dinas Powys	d					15 37					15 53							16 07				16 22			
Cadoxton	d					15 42					15 57							16 12				16 27			
Barry Docks	d					15 45					16 00							16 15				16 30			
Barry 3	d					15 49					16 05							16 19				16 34			
Barry Island	a					15 55												16 25				16 40			
Rhoose Cardiff Int Airport ✈	d										16 12														
Llantwit Major	d										16 22														
Bridgend	a										16 40														

When events are being held at the Millenium Stadium, services are subject to alteration. Please check times before travelling.

Table 130

Mondays to Fridays
until 9 September

Treherbert, Aberdare, Merthyr, Pontypridd, Rhymney and Coryton - Cardiff, Penarth, Barry, Barry Island and Bridgend

		AW	AW	AW	AW	AW	AW	AW	AW	AW	AW	AW	AW	AW	AW	AW	AW	AW	AW	AW	AW	AW	AW
Treherbert	d	15 13									15 47										16 17		
Ynyswen	d	15 15									15 49										16 19		
Treorchy	d	15 21									15 51										16 21		
Ton Pentre	d	15 23									15 53										16 23		
Ystrad Rhondda	a	15 26									15 56										16 26		
	d	15 28									15 58										16 28		
Llwynypia	d	15 30									16 00										16 30		
Tonypandy	d	15 33									16 03										16 33		
Dinas Rhondda	d	15 35									16 05										16 35		
Porth	a	15 38									16 08										16 38		
	d	15 39									16 09										16 39		
Trehafod	d	15 42									16 12										16 42		
Merthyr Tydfil	d							15 38										16 08					
Pentre-bach	d							15 42										16 12					
Troed Y Rhiw	d							15 45										16 15					
Merthyr Vale	a							15 48										16 18					
	d							15 50										16 20					
Quakers Yard	d							15 55										16 25					
Aberdare 3	d			15 22										15 52									16 22
Cwmbach	d			15 25										15 55									16 25
Fernhill	d			15 28										15 58									16 28
Mountain Ash	a			15 31										16 01									16 31
	d			15 34										16 04									16 34
Penrhiwceiber	d			15 37										16 07									16 37
Abercynon	d			15 44				15 59						16 13				16 29					16 43
Pontypridd 3	a	15 47		15 53				16 08			16 17			16 23				16 37			16 47		16 53
	d	15 48		15 54				16 09			16 18			16 24				16 39			16 48		16 54
Trefforest	d	15 51		15 57				16 12			16 21			16 27				16 42			16 51		16 57
Trefforest Estate	d							16 16										16 46					
Taffs Well 3	d	15 58		16 04				16 20			16 28			16 34				16 50			16 58		17 04
Radyr 3	a	16 01		16 07				16 23			16 31			16 37				16 53			17 01		17 07
	d	16 01	16 04	16 07				16 23			16 31	16 34		16 37				16 53			17 01	17 04	17 07
Danescourt	d		16 08									16 38										17 08	
Fairwater	d		16 10									16 40										17 10	
Waun-gron Park	d		16 12									16 42										17 12	
Ninian Park	d		16 15									16 45										17 15	
Llandaf	d	16 04		16 10				16 26			16 34			16 40				16 56			17 04		17 10
Cathays	d	16 09		16 15				16 31			16 39			16 45				17 01			17 09		17 15
Rhymney 3	d				15 29																		
Pontlottyn	d				15 32																		
Tir-phil	d				15 36																		
Brithdir	d				15 39																		
Bargoed	a				15 42																		
	d				15 47					16 02					16 17				16 32				
Gilfach Fargoed	d														16 19								
Pengam	d				15 52					16 07					16 22				16 37				
Hengoed	d				15 55					16 10					16 25				16 40				
Ystrad Mynach 3	d				15 58					16 13					16 28				16 43				
Llanbradach	d				16 03					16 18					16 33				16 48				
Aber	d				16 07					16 22					16 37				16 52				
Caerphilly 3	d				16 10					16 25					16 40				16 55				
Lisvane & Thornhill	d				16 14					16 29					16 44				16 59				
Llanishen	d				16 16					16 31					16 46				17 01				
Heath High Level	d				16 19					16 34					16 49				17 04				
Coryton	d						16 15									16 45							
Whitchurch (Cardiff)	d						16 16									16 46							
Rhiwbina	d						16 18									16 48							
Birchgrove	d						16 20									16 50							
Ty Glas	d						16 21									16 51							
Heath Low Level	d						16 24									16 54							
Cardiff Queen Street 3	a	16 14		16 19	16 24		16 29	16 34		16 39	16 44			16 49	16 54	16 59		17 04	17 09		17 14		17 19
	d	16 16		16 21	16 26	16 24	16 31	16 36	16 36	16 41	16 46		16 48	16 51	16 56	17 01	17 00	17 06	17 11	17 12	17 16		17 21
Cardiff Bay	a					16 28			16 40				16 52				17 04			17 16			
Cardiff Central 7	a	16 22	16 20	16 24	16 32		16 34	16 39		16 44	16 52	16 50		16 54	16 59	17 04		17 09	17 14		17 22	17 20	17 24
	d			16 25				16 41		16 46				16 55	17 01			17 10	17 16				17 25
Grangetown	d			16 29				16 45		16 50				16 59	17 07			17 14	17 20				17 29
Dingle Road	d									16 56					17 11				17 26				
Penarth	a									17 01					17 16				17 31				
Cogan	d			16 33				16 48						17 03				17 18					17 33
Eastbrook	d			16 35				16 51						17 05				17 20					17 35
Dinas Powys	d			16 37				16 53						17 07				17 22					17 37
Cadoxton	d			16 42				16 57						17 12				17 27					17 42
Barry Docks	d			16 45				17 00						17 15				17 30					17 45
Barry 3	d			16 49				17 05						17 19				17 34					17 49
Barry Island	a			16 55										17 25				17 40					17 55
Rhoose Cardiff Int Airport ✈	d							17 12															
Llantwit Major	d							17 22															
Bridgend	a							17 40															

When events are being held at the Millenium Stadium, services are subject to alteration. Please check times before travelling.

Table 130

Mondays to Fridays
until 9 September

Treherbert, Aberdare, Merthyr, Pontypridd, Rhymney and Coryton - Cardiff, Penarth, Barry, Barry Island and Bridgend

		AW	AW	AW	AW	AW	AW	AW	AW	AW	AW	AW	AW	AW	AW	AW	AW	AW	AW	AW	AW	AW	AW
Treherbert	d							16 47										17 17					
Ynyswen	d							16 49										17 19					
Treorchy	d							16 51										17 21					
Ton Pentre	d							16 53										17 23					
Ystrad Rhondda	a							16 56										17 26					
	d							16 58										17 28					
Llwynypia	d							17 00										17 30					
Tonypandy	d							17 03										17 33					
Dinas Rhondda	d							17 05										17 35					
Porth	a							17 08										17 38					
	d							17 09										17 39					
Trehafod	d							17 12										17 42					
Merthyr Tydfil	d				16 38										17 08								
Pentre-bach	d				16 42										17 12								
Troed Y Rhiw	d				16 45										17 15								
Merthyr Vale	a				16 48										17 18								
	d				16 50										17 20								
Quakers Yard	d				16 55										17 25								
Aberdare 3	d										16 52									17 22			
Cwmbach	d										16 55									17 25			
Fernhill	d										16 58									17 28			
Mountain Ash	a										17 01									17 31			
	d										17 04									17 34			
Penrhiwceiber	d										17 07									17 37			
Abercynon	d				16 59						17 13				17 29					17 43			
Pontypridd 3	a				17 07			17 17			17 23				17 37			17 47		17 53			
	d				17 09			17 18			17 24				17 39			17 48		17 54			
Trefforest	d				17 12			17 21			17 27				17 42			17 51		17 57			
Trefforest Estate	d				17 16										17 46								
Taffs Well 3	d				17 20			17 28			17 34				17 50			17 58		18 04			
Radyr 3	a				17 23			17 31			17 37				17 53			18 01		18 07			
	d				17 23			17 31	17 34		17 37				17 53			18 01	18 04	18 07			
Danescourt	d								17 38										18 08				
Fairwater	d								17 40										18 10				
Waun-gron Park	d								17 42										18 12				
Ninian Park	d								17 45										18 15				
Llandaf	d				17 26			17 34			17 40				17 56			18 04		18 10			
Cathays	d				17 31			17 39			17 45				18 01			18 09		18 15			
Rhymney 3	d	16 29																			17 29		
Pontlottyn	d	16 32																			17 32		
Tir-phil	d	16 36																			17 36		
Brithdir	d	16 39																			17 39		
Bargoed	a	16 42																			17 42		
	d	16 47					17 02					17 17				17 32					17 47		
Gilfach Fargoed	d											17 19											
Pengam	d	16 52					17 07					17 22				17 37					17 52		
Hengoed	d	16 55					17 10					17 25				17 40					17 55		
Ystrad Mynach 3	d	16 58					17 13					17 28				17 43					17 58		
Llanbradach	d	17 03					17 18					17 33				17 48					18 03		
Aber	d	17 07					17 22					17 37				17 52					18 07		
Caerphilly 3	d	17 10					17 25					17 40				17 55					18 10		
Lisvane & Thornhill	d	17 14					17 29					17 44				17 59					18 14		
Llanishen	d	17 16					17 31					17 46				18 01					18 16		
Heath High Level	d	17 19					17 34					17 49				18 04					18 19		
Coryton	d			17 15									17 45										18 15
Whitchurch (Cardiff)	d			17 16									17 46										18 16
Rhiwbina	d			17 18									17 48										18 18
Birchgrove	d			17 20									17 50										18 20
Ty Glas	d			17 21									17 51										18 21
Heath Low Level	d			17 24									17 54										18 24
Cardiff Queen Street 3	a	17 24		17 29	17 34		17 39	17 44			17 49	17 54	17 59		18 04	18 09		18 14		18 19	18 24		18 29
	d	17 26	17 24	17 31	17 36	17 36	17 41	17 46		17 48	17 51	17 56	18 01	18 00	18 06	18 11	18 12	18 16		18 21	18 26	18 24	18 31
Cardiff Bay	a		17 28			17 40				17 52				18 04			18 16					18 28	
Cardiff Central 7	a	17 29		17 34	17 39		17 44	17 52	17 50		17 54	17 59	18 04		18 09	18 14		18 22	18 20	18 24	18 29		18 34
	d	17 31			17 41		17 46				17 55	18 01			18 10	18 16				18 25	18 31		
Grangetown	d	17 35			17 45		17 50				17 59	18 05			18 14	18 20				18 29	18 35		
Dingle Road	d	17 41					17 56					18 11				18 26					18 41		
Penarth	a	17 46					18 02					18 16				18 31					18 46		
Cogan	d				17 48						18 03				18 18					18 33			
Eastbrook	d				17 51						18 05				18 20					18 35			
Dinas Powys	d				17 53						18 07				18 22					18 37			
Cadoxton	d				17 57						18 12				18 27					18 42			
Barry Docks	d				18 00						18 15				18 30					18 45			
Barry 3	d				18 05						18 19				18 34					18 49			
Barry Island	a										18 25				18 40					18 55			
Rhoose Cardiff Int Airport ✈	d				18 12																		
Llantwit Major	d				18 22																		
Bridgend	a				18 40																		

When events are being held at the Millenium Stadium, services are subject to alteration. Please check times before travelling.

Treherbert, Aberdare, Merthyr, Pontypridd, Rhymney and Coryton - Cardiff, Penarth, Barry, Barry Island and Bridgend

		AW	AW	AW	AW	AW	AW	AW	AW	AW	AW	AW	AW	AW	AW	AW	AW	AW	AW	AW	AW	AW
Treherbert	d			17 47									18 17								18 47	
Ynyswen	d			17 49									18 19								18 49	
Treorchy	d			17 51									18 21								18 51	
Ton Pentre	d			17 53									18 23								18 53	
Ystrad Rhondda	a			17 56									18 26								18 56	
	d			17 58									18 28								18 58	
Llwynypia	d			18 00									18 30								19 00	
Tonypandy	d			18 03									18 33								19 03	
Dinas Rhondda	d			18 05									18 35								19 05	
Porth	a			18 08									18 38								19 08	
	d			18 09									18 39								19 09	
Trehafod	d			18 12									18 42								19 12	
Merthyr Tydfil	d	17 38									18 08								18 38			
Pentre-bach	d	17 42									18 12								18 42			
Troed Y Rhiw	d	17 45									18 15								18 45			
Merthyr Vale	a	17 48									18 18								18 48			
	d	17 50									18 20								18 50			
Quakers Yard	d	17 55									18 25								18 55			
Aberdare 3	d						17 52								18 22							
Cwmbach	d						17 55								18 25							
Fernhill	d						17 58								18 28							
Mountain Ash	a						18 01								18 31							
	d						18 04								18 34							
Penrhiwceiber	d						18 07								18 37							
Abercynon	d	17 59					18 13				18 29				18 43				18 59			
Pontypridd 3	a	18 07		18 17			18 23				18 37		18 47		18 53				19 07		19 17	
	d	18 09		18 18			18 24				18 39		18 48		18 54				19 09		19 18	
Trefforest	d	18 12		18 21			18 27				18 42		18 51		18 57				19 12		19 21	
Trefforest Estate	d	18 16									18 46								19 16			
Taffs Well 3	d	18 20		18 28			18 34				18 50		18 58		19 04				19 20		19 28	
Radyr 3	a	18 23		18 31			18 37				18 53		19 01		19 07				19 23		19 31	
	d	18 23		18 31	18 34		18 37				18 53		19 01	19 04	19 07				19 23		19 31	
Danescourt	d				18 38									19 08								
Fairwater	d				18 40									19 10								
Waun-gron Park	d				18 42									19 12								
Ninian Park	d				18 45									19 15								
Llandaf	d	18 26		18 34			18 40				18 56		19 04		19 10				19 26		19 34	
Cathays	d	18 31		18 39			18 45				19 01		19 09		19 15				19 31		19 39	
Rhymney 3	d																					
Pontlottyn	d																					
Tir-phil	d																					
Brithdir	d																					
Bargoed	a																					
	d							18 17								18 48						
Gilfach Fargoed	d							18 19								18 50						
Pengam	d							18 22								18 53						
Hengoed	d							18 25								18 56						
Ystrad Mynach 3	d							18 28								18 59						
Llanbradach	d							18 33								19 04						
Aber	d							18 37								19 08						
Caerphilly 3	d							18 40								19 11						
Lisvane & Thornhill	d							18 44								19 15						
Llanishen	d							18 46								19 17						
Heath High Level	d							18 49								19 20						
Coryton	d								18 45									19 15				
Whitchurch (Cardiff)	d								18 46									19 16				
Rhiwbina	d								18 48									19 18				
Birchgrove	d								18 50									19 20				
Ty Glas	d								18 51									19 21				
Heath Low Level	d								18 54									19 24				
Cardiff Queen Street 3	a	18 34		18 44			18 49	18 54	18 59		19 04		19 14		19 19	19 24		19 29	19 35		19 44	
	d	18 36	18 36	18 46		18 48	18 51	18 56	19 01	19 00	19 06	19 12	19 16		19 21	19 26	19 24	19 31	19 36	19 36	19 46	19 48
Cardiff Bay	a		18 40			18 52				19 04		19 16					19 28			19 40		19 52
Cardiff Central 7	a	18 39		18 53	18 50		18 54	18 59	19 06		19 10		19 22	19 22	19 24	19 29		19 34	19 40		19 52	
	d	18 41					18 55	19 01							19 25	19 31			19 41			
Grangetown	d	18 45					18 59	19 05							19 29	19 35			19 45			
Dingle Road	d							19 11								19 41						
Penarth	a							19 16								19 46						
Cogan	d	18 48					19 03								19 33				19 48			
Eastbrook	d	18 51					19 05								19 35				19 51			
Dinas Powys	d	18 53					19 07								19 37				19 53			
Cadoxton	d	18 57					19 12								19 42				19 57			
Barry Docks	d	19 00					19 15								19 45				20 00			
Barry 3	d	19 05					19 19								19 49				20 05			
Barry Island	a						19 25								19 55							
Rhoose Cardiff Int Airport ✈	d	19 12																	20 12			
Llantwit Major	d	19 22																	20 22			
Bridgend	a	19 40																	20 40			

When events are being held at the Millenium Stadium, services are subject to alteration. Please check times before travelling.

Treherbert, Aberdare, Merthyr, Pontypridd, Rhymney and Coryton - Cardiff, Penarth, Barry, Barry Island and Bridgend

		AW	AW	AW	AW	AW	AW	AW	AW	AW	AW	AW	AW	AW	AW	AW	AW	AW	AW	AW	AW	AW	AW
Treherbert	d						19 17								19 47						20 17		
Ynyswen	d						19 19								19 49						20 19		
Treorchy	d						19 21								19 51						20 21		
Ton Pentre	d						19 23								19 53						20 23		
Ystrad Rhondda	a						19 26								19 56						20 26		
	d						19 28								19 58						20 28		
Llwynypia	d						19 30								20 00						20 30		
Tonypandy	d						19 33								20 03						20 33		
Dinas Rhondda	d						19 35								20 05						20 35		
Porth	a						19 38								20 08						20 38		
	d						19 39								20 09						20 39		
Trehafod	d						19 42								20 12						20 42		
Merthyr Tydfil	d				19 08							19 38											
Pentre-bach	d				19 12							19 42											
Troed Y Rhiw	d				19 15							19 45											
Merthyr Vale	a				19 18							19 48											
	d				19 20							19 50											
Quakers Yard	d				19 25							19 55											
Aberdare 3	d	18 52															19 52						20 22
Cwmbach	d	18 55															19 55						20 25
Fernhill	d	18 58															19 58						20 28
Mountain Ash	a	19 01															20 01						20 31
	d	19 04															20 04						20 34
Penrhiwceiber	d	19 07															20 07						20 37
Abercynon	d	19 13			19 29				19 43			19 59					20 13						20 43
Pontypridd 3	a	19 23			19 37		19 47		19 53			20 07			20 18		20 23				20 47		20 53
	d	19 24			19 39		19 48		19 54			20 09			20 18		20 24				20 48		20 54
Trefforest	d	19 27			19 42		19 51		19 57			20 12			20 21		20 27				20 51		20 57
Trefforest Estate	d				19 46							20 16											
Taffs Well 3	d	19 34			19 50		19 58		20 04			20 20			20 28		20 34				20 58		21 04
Radyr 3	a	19 37			19 53		20 01		20 07			20 23			20 31		20 37				21 01		21 07
	d	19 37			19 53		20 01	20 04	20 07			20 23			20 31		20 37				21 01	21 04	21 07
Danescourt	d							20 08														21 08	
Fairwater	d							20 10														21 10	
Waun-gron Park	d							20 12														21 12	
Ninian Park	d							20 15														21 15	
Llandaf	d	19 40			19 56		20 04		20 10			20 26			20 34		20 40				21 04		21 10
Cathays	d	19 45			20 01		20 09		20 15			20 31			20 39		20 45				21 09		21 15
Rhymney 3	d													19 45									
Pontlottyn	d													19 48									
Tir-phil	d													19 52									
Brithdir	d													19 55									
Bargoed	a													19 58									
	d													19 59									
Gilfach Fargoed	d													20 01									
Pengam	d													20 04									
Hengoed	d													20 07									
Ystrad Mynach 3	d													20 10									
Llanbradach	d													20 15									
Aber	d													20 19									
Caerphilly 3	d		19 40											20 22				20 40					
Lisvane & Thornhill	d		19 44											20 26				20 44					
Llanishen	d		19 46											20 28				20 46					
Heath High Level	d		19 49											20 31				20 49					
Coryton	d										20 15												
Whitchurch (Cardiff)	d										20 16												
Rhiwbina	d										20 18												
Birchgrove	d										20 20												
Ty Glas	d										20 21												
Heath Low Level	d										20 24												
Cardiff Queen Street 3	a	19 49	19 54		20 04		20 14		20 19		20 29	20 34		20 39	20 44		20 49	20 54			21 14		21 19
	d	19 51	19 56	20 00	20 06	20 12	20 16		20 21	20 24	20 31	20 36	20 36	20 41	20 46	20 48	20 51	20 56	21 00	21 12	21 16		21 21
Cardiff Bay	a			20 04		20 16				20 28			20 40			20 52			21 04	21 16			
Cardiff Central 7	a	19 57	19 59		20 09		20 22	20 22	20 24		20 34	20 39		20 47	20 52		20 57	20 59			21 21	21 25	21 24
	d		20 06		20 10				20 31			20 41					21 06	21 10					
Grangetown	d		20 10		20 14				20 37			20 45					21 10	21 14					
Dingle Road	d		20 14						20 41								21 14						
Penarth	a		20 19						20 46								21 19						
Cogan	d				20 18							20 48						21 17					
Eastbrook	d				20 20							20 51						21 20					
Dinas Powys	d				20 22							20 53						21 22					
Cadoxton	d				20 27							20 57						21 26					
Barry Docks	d				20 30							21 00						21 29					
Barry 3	d				20 34							21 05						21 34					
Barry Island	a				20 40													21 40					
Rhoose Cardiff Int Airport ✈	d											21 12											
Llantwit Major	d											21 22											
Bridgend	a											21 42											

When events are being held at the Millenium Stadium, services are subject to alteration. Please check times before travelling.

Table 130

Mondays to Fridays
until 9 September

Treherbert, Aberdare, Merthyr, Pontypridd, Rhymney and Coryton - Cardiff, Penarth, Barry, Barry Island and Bridgend

		AW	AW	AW	AW	AW	AW	AW	AW	AW	AW	AW	AW	AW	AW	AW	AW	AW	AW	AW	AW	AW
Treherbert	d											21 17										
Ynyswen	d											21 19										
Treorchy	d											21 21										
Ton Pentre	d											21 23										
Ystrad Rhondda	a											21 26										
	d											21 28										
Llwynypia	d											21 30										
Tonypandy	d											21 33										
Dinas Rhondda	d											21 35										
Porth	a											21 38										
	d											21 39										
Trehafod	d											21 42										
Merthyr Tydfil	d				20 38											21 38						
Pentre-bach	d				20 42											21 42						
Troed Y Rhiw	d				20 45											21 45						
Merthyr Vale	a				20 48											21 48						
	d				20 50											21 50						
Quakers Yard	d				20 55											21 55						
Aberdare [3]	d								20 54										21 54			
Cwmbach	d								20 57										21 57			
Fernhill	d								21 00										22 00			
Mountain Ash	a								21 03										22 03			
	d								21 04										22 04			
Penrhiwceiber	d								21 07										22 07			
Abercynon	d				20 59				21 13							21 59			22 13			
Pontypridd [3]	a				21 07				21 22				21 47			22 07			22 22			
	d				21 09				21 24				21 48			22 09			22 24			
Trefforest	d				21 12				21 27				21 51			22 12			22 27			
Trefforest Estate	d				21 16											22 16						
Taffs Well [3]	d				21 20				21 34				21 58			22 20			22 34			
Radyr [3]	a				21 23				21 37				22 01			22 23			22 37			
	d				21 23				21 37				22 01	22 04		22 23			22 37			
Danescourt	d													22 08								
Fairwater	d													22 10								
Waun-gron Park	d													22 12								
Ninian Park	d													22 15								
Llandaf	d				21 26				21 40				22 04			22 26			22 40			
Cathays	d				21 31				21 45				22 09			22 31			22 45			
Rhymney [3]	d						20 48								21 33							
Pontlottyn	d						20 51								21 36							
Tir-phil	d						20 55								21 40							
Brithdir	d						20 58								21 43							
Bargoed	a						21 01								21 46							
	d						21 02								21 47							
Gilfach Fargoed	d						21 04								21 49							
Pengam	d						21 07								21 52							
Hengoed	d						21 10								21 55							
Ystrad Mynach [3]	d						21 13								21 58							
Llanbradach	d						21 18								22 03							
Aber	d						21 22								22 07							
Caerphilly [3]	d						21 25			21 45					22 10							
Lisvane & Thornhill	d						21 29			21 50					22 14							
Llanishen	d						21 31			21 52					22 16							
Heath High Level	d						21 34			21 54					22 19							
Coryton	d			21 15																	22 45	
Whitchurch (Cardiff)	d			21 16																	22 46	
Rhiwbina	d			21 18																	22 48	
Birchgrove	d			21 20																	22 50	
Ty Glas	d			21 21																	22 51	
Heath Low Level	d			21 24																	22 54	
Cardiff Queen Street [3]	a			21 29	21 34		21 39		21 49	22 00			22 14		22 24		22 34		22 48		22 59	
	d	21 24		21 31	21 36	21 36	21 44	21 48	21 51	22 01	22 00	22 12	22 16		22 26	22 24	22 36	22 36	22 54	22 48	23 01	23 00
Cardiff Bay	a	21 28				21 40		21 52			22 04	22 16				22 28		22 40		22 52		23 04
Cardiff Central [7]	a			21 34	21 39		21 47		21 54	22 04			22 22	22 20	22 30		22 39		23 00		23 06	
	d		21 31		21 41				21 56	22 10					22 31		22 41		23 12			
Grangetown	d		21 35		21 45				22 00	22 14					22 35		22 45		23 16			
Dingle Road	d		21 41						22 04						22 41				23 20			
Penarth	a		21 46						22 09						22 48				23 25			
Cogan	d				21 48					22 18							22 48					
Eastbrook	d				21 51					22 20							22 51					
Dinas Powys	d				21 53					22 22							22 53					
Cadoxton	d				21 57					22 27							22 57					
Barry Docks	d				22 00					22 30							23 00					
Barry [3]	d				22 05					22 34							23 05					
Barry Island	a									22 40												
Rhoose Cardiff Int Airport ✈	d				22 12												23 12					
Llantwit Major	d				22 22												23 22					
Bridgend	a				22 40												23 40					

When events are being held at the Millenium Stadium, services are subject to alteration. Please check times before travelling.

Table 130

Mondays to Fridays
until 9 September

Treherbert, Aberdare, Merthyr, Pontypridd, Rhymney and Coryton - Cardiff, Penarth, Barry, Barry Island and Bridgend

		AW	AW	AW	AW	AW	AW	AW
Treherbert	d							
Ynyswen	d							
Treorchy	d							
Ton Pentre	d							
Ystrad Rhondda	a							
	d							
Llwynypia	d							
Tonypandy	d							
Dinas Rhondda	d							
Porth	a							
	d							
Trehafod	d							
Merthyr Tydfil	d				22 38			
Pentre-bach	d				22 42			
Troed Y Rhiw	d				22 45			
Merthyr Vale	a				22 48			
	d				22 50			
Quakers Yard	d				22 55			
Aberdare [3]	d					22 51		
Cwmbach	d					22 54		
Fernhill	d					22 58		
Mountain Ash	a					23 01		
	d					23 04		
Penrhiwceiber	d					23 08		
Abercynon	d				22 59	23 14		
Pontypridd [3]	a				23 07	23 22		
	d				23 09			
Trefforest	d				23 12			
Trefforest Estate	d				23 16			
Taffs Well [3]	d				23 20			
Radyr [3]	a				23 23			
	d		23 10		23 23			
Danescourt	d							
Fairwater	d							
Waun-gron Park	d							
Ninian Park	d							
Llandaf	d		23 12		23 26			
Cathays	d		23 16		23 31			
Rhymney [3]	d							
Pontlottyn	d							
Tir-phil	d							
Brithdir	d							
Bargoed	a							
	d							
Gilfach Fargoed	d							
Pengam	d							
Hengoed	d							
Ystrad Mynach [3]	d							
Llanbradach	d							
Aber	d							
Caerphilly [3]	d							
Lisvane & Thornhill	d							
Llanishen	d							
Heath High Level	d							
Coryton	d							
Whitchurch (Cardiff)	d							
Rhiwbina	d							
Birchgrove	d							
Ty Glas	d							
Heath Low Level	d							
Cardiff Queen Street [3]	a		23 20		23 34			
	d	23 12	23 20	23 24	23 36		23 36	23 48
Cardiff Bay	a	23 16		23 28			23 40	23 52
Cardiff Central [7]	a		23 25		23 42			
	d		23 30					
Grangetown	d		23 34					
Dingle Road	d							
Penarth	a							
Cogan	d		23 37					
Eastbrook	d		23 40					
Dinas Powys	d		23 42					
Cadoxton	d		23 46					
Barry Docks	d		23 49					
Barry [3]	d		23 54					
Barry Island	a		00 01					
Rhoose Cardiff Int Airport ✈	d							
Llantwit Major	d							
Bridgend	a							

When events are being held at the Millenium Stadium, services are subject to alteration. Please check times before travelling.

Table 130

Mondays to Fridays
from 12 September

Treherbert, Aberdare, Merthyr, Pontypridd, Rhymney and Coryton - Cardiff, Penarth, Barry, Barry Island and Bridgend

		AW MX	AW	AW	AW	AW	AW	AW	AW	AW		AW	AW	AW	AW	AW	AW	AW	AW	AW		AW	AW	AW	AW
Treherbert	d												05 47							06 17					
Ynyswen	d												05 49							06 19					
Treorchy	d												05 51							06 21					
Ton Pentre	d												05 53							06 23					
Ystrad Rhondda	a												05 56							06 26					
	d												05 58							06 28					
Llwynypia	d												06 00							06 30					
Tonypandy	d												06 03							06 33					
Dinas Rhondda	d												06 05							06 35					
Porth	a												06 08							06 38					
	d												06 09							06 39					
Trehafod	d												06 12							06 42					
Merthyr Tydfil	d																								
Pentre-bach	d																								
Troed Y Rhiw	d																								
Merthyr Vale	a																								
	d																								
Quakers Yard	d																								
Aberdare 3	d																							06 21	
Cwmbach	d																							06 24	
Fernhill	d																							06 28	
Mountain Ash	a																							06 31	
	d																							06 34	
Penrhiwceiber	d																							06 38	
Abercynon	d																							06 44	
Pontypridd 3	a												06 17							06 47				06 53	
	d					05 24							06 18							06 48				06 54	
Trefforest	d					05 27							06 21							06 51				06 57	
Trefforest Estate	d					05 31																			
Taffs Well 3	d					05 35							06 28							06 58		06 53		07 04	
Radyr 3	a					05 39							06 31							07 01		06 56		07 07	
	d	23p10				05 39							06 31							07 01		07 04		07 07	
Danescourt	d																					07 08			
Fairwater	d																					07 10			
Waun-gron Park	d																					07 12			
Ninian Park	d																					07 15			
Llandaf	d	23p12				05 42							06 34							07 04				07 10	
Cathays	d	23p16				05 46							06 39							07 09				07 15	
Rhymney 3	d																		06 10						06 34
Pontlottyn	d																		06 13						06 37
Tir-phil	d																		06 17						06 41
Brithdir	d																		06 20						06 44
Bargoed	a																		06 23						06 47
	d																		06 27						06 48
Gilfach Fargoed	d																		06 29						
Pengam	d																		06 32						06 52
Hengoed	d																		06 35						06 56
Ystrad Mynach 3	d																		06 38						06 58
Llanbradach	d																		06 43						07 03
Aber	d																		06 47						07 07
Caerphilly 3	d									06 10									06 50						07 10
Lisvane & Thornhill	d									06 14									06 54						07 14
Llanishen	d									06 16									06 56						07 16
Heath High Level	d									06 19									06 59						07 19
Coryton	d																	06 45							
Whitchurch (Cardiff)	d																	06 46							
Rhiwbina	d																	06 48							
Birchgrove	d																	06 50							
Ty Glas	d																	06 51							
Heath Low Level	d																	06 54							
Cardiff Queen Street 3	a	23p19				05 51				06 25			06 42					06 59	07 04	07 12				07 19	07 24
	d	23p20				05 51				06 26		06 36	06 43	06 48		07 00		07 00	07 06	07 14			07 12	07 21	07 26
Cardiff Bay	a											06 40		06 52		07 04							07 16		
Cardiff Central 7	a	23p25				05 54				06 29			06 48					07 04	07 09	07 16		07 20		07 24	07 29
	d	23p30	05 20	05 41	05 46	05 55	06 16	06 25	06 36	06 41					06 55		07 01		07 10	07 16				07 25	07 31
Grangetown	d	23p34	05 24	05 45	05 50	05 59	06 20	06 29	06 40	06 45					06 59		07 05		07 14	07 20				07 29	07 35
Dingle Road	d				05 54		06 24		06 44								07 11			07 26					07 42
Penarth	a				06 00		06 30		06 50								07 17			07 33					07 47
Cogan	d	23p37	05 28	05 48		06 03		06 33		06 48					07 03				07 18					07 33	
Eastbrook	d	23p40	05 30	05 51		06 05		06 35		06 51					07 05				07 20					07 35	
Dinas Powys	d	23p42	05 32	05 53		06 07		06 37		06 53					07 07				07 22					07 37	
Cadoxton	d	23p46	05 37	05 57		06 12		06 42		06 57					07 12				07 27					07 42	
Barry Docks	d	23p49	05 40	06 00		06 15		06 45		07 00					07 15				07 30					07 45	
Barry 3	d	23p54	05 44	06 05		06 19		06 49		07 05					07 19				07 34					07 49	
Barry Island	a	00 01	05 51			06 26		06 56							07 26				07 41					07 56	
Rhoose Cardiff Int Airport ✈	d			06 12						07 12															
Llantwit Major	d			06 22						07 22															
Bridgend	a			06 41						07 41															

When events are being held at the Millenium Stadium, services are subject to alteration. Please check times before travelling.

Table 130

Mondays to Fridays
from 12 September

Treherbert, Aberdare, Merthyr, Pontypridd, Rhymney and Coryton - Cardiff, Penarth, Barry, Barry Island and Bridgend

		AW	AW	AW	AW	AW		AW	AW	AW	AW	AW	AW	AW	AW	AW		AW	AW	AW	AW	AW	AW	AW	AW
Treherbert	d							06 47											07 17						
Ynyswen	d							06 49											07 19						
Treorchy	d							06 51											07 21						
Ton Pentre	d							06 53											07 23						
Ystrad Rhondda	a							06 56											07 26						
	d							06 58											07 28						
Llwynypia	d							07 00											07 30						
Tonypandy	d							07 03											07 33						
Dinas Rhondda	d							07 05											07 35						
Porth	a							07 08											07 38						
	d							07 09											07 39						
Trehafod	d							07 12											07 42						
Merthyr Tydfil	d			06 38											07 08										07 38
Pentre-bach	d			06 42											07 12										07 42
Troed Y Rhiw	d			06 45											07 15										07 45
Merthyr Vale	a			06 48											07 18										07 48
	d			06 50											07 20										07 50
Quakers Yard	d			06 55											07 25										07 55
Aberdare 3	d										06 51										07 21				
Cwmbach	d										06 54										07 24				
Fernhill	d										06 58										07 28				
Mountain Ash	a										07 01										07 31				
	d										07 04										07 34				
Penrhiwceiber	d										07 08										07 38				
Abercynon	d			06 59							07 14				07 29						07 44				07 59
Pontypridd 3	a			07 07				07 17			07 23				07 37				07 47		07 53				08 07
	d			07 09				07 18			07 24				07 39				07 48		07 54				08 09
Trefforest	d			07 12				07 21			07 27				07 42				07 51		07 57				08 12
Trefforest Estate	d			07 16											07 46										08 16
Taffs Well 3	d			07 20				07 28			07 34				07 50				07 58		08 04				08 20
Radyr 3	a			07 23				07 31			07 37				07 53				08 01		08 07				08 23
	d			07 23				07 31	07 34		07 37				07 53				08 01	08 04	08 07				08 23
Danescourt	d								07 38											08 08					
Fairwater	d								07 40											08 10					
Waun-gron Park	d								07 42											08 12					
Ninian Park	d								07 45											08 15					
Llandaf	d			07 26				07 34			07 40				07 56				08 04		08 10				08 26
Cathays	d			07 31				07 39			07 45				08 01				08 09		08 15				08 31
Rhymney 3	d											07 02										07 24			
Pontlottyn	d											07 05										07 27			
Tir-phil	d											07 09										07 31			
Brithdir	d											07 12										07 34			
Bargoed	a											07 15										07 37			
	d					07 02						07 17				07 32						07 45			
Gilfach Fargoed	d					07 04						07 19										07 47			
Pengam	d					07 07						07 22				07 37						07 50			
Hengoed	d					07 10						07 25				07 40						07 54			
Ystrad Mynach 3	d					07 13						07 28				07 43						07 57			
Llanbradach	d					07 18						07 33				07 48						08 02			
Aber	d					07 22						07 37				07 52						08 07			
Caerphilly 3	d					07 25						07 40				07 55						08 10			
Lisvane & Thornhill	d					07 29						07 44				07 59						08 14			
Llanishen	d					07 31						07 46				08 01						08 16			
Heath High Level	d					07 34						07 49				08 04						08 19			
Coryton	d		07 15										07 45											08 15	
Whitchurch (Cardiff)	d		07 16										07 46											08 16	
Rhiwbina	d		07 18										07 48											08 18	
Birchgrove	d		07 20										07 50											08 20	
Ty Glas	d		07 21										07 51											08 21	
Heath Low Level	d		07 24										07 54											08 24	
Cardiff Queen Street 3	a		07 29	07 35		07 39		07 44			07 49	07 54	07 59		08 04	08 09			08 14		08 19	08 24		08 29	08 34
	d	07 24	07 31	07 36	07 36	07 41		07 46		07 48	07 51	07 56	08 01	08 00	08 06	08 11		08 12	08 16		08 21	08 26	08 24	08 31	08 36
Cardiff Bay	a	07 28			07 40					07 52				08 04				08 16					08 28		
Cardiff Central 7	a		07 34	07 40		07 44		07 52	07 50		07 54	07 59	08 04		08 09	08 14			08 23	08 2[illegible]	08 24	08 29		08 34	08 39
	d			07 41		07 46					07 55	08 01			08 10	08 16					08 25	08 31			08 41
Grangetown	d			07 45		07 50					07 59	08 05			08 14	08 20					08 29	08 35			08 45
Dingle Road	d					07 56						08 11				08 26						08 41			
Penarth	a					08 02						08 16				08 33						08 47			
Cogan	d			07 48							08 03				08 18						08 33				08 48
Eastbrook	d			07 51							08 05				08 20						08 35				08 51
Dinas Powys	d			07 53							08 07				08 22						08 37				08 53
Cadoxton	d			07 57							08 12				08 27						08 42				08 57
Barry Docks	d			08 00							08 15				08 30						08 45				09 00
Barry 3	d			08 05							08 19				08 34						08 49				09 05
Barry Island	a										08 26				08 41						08 56				
Rhoose Cardiff Int Airport ✈	d			08 12																					09 12
Llantwit Major	d			08 22																					09 22
Bridgend	a			08 41																					09 41

When events are being held at the Millenium Stadium, services are subject to alteration. Please check times before travelling.

Table 130

Mondays to Fridays

from 12 September

Treherbert, Aberdare, Merthyr, Pontypridd, Rhymney and Coryton - Cardiff, Penarth, Barry, Barry Island and Bridgend

		AW		AW	AW	AW	AW	AW	AW	AW	AW	AW		AW	AW	AW	AW	AW	AW	AW	AW	AW		AW	AW
Treherbert	d				07 45											08 17									
Ynyswen	d				07 47											08 19									
Treorchy	d				07 49											08 21									
Ton Pentre	d				07 51											08 23									
Ystrad Rhondda	a				07 54											08 26									
	d				07 58											08 28									
Llwynypia	d				08 00											08 30									
Tonypandy	d				08 03											08 33									
Dinas Rhondda	d				08 05											08 35									
Porth	a				08 08											08 38									
	d				08 09											08 39									
Trehafod	d				08 12											08 42									
Merthyr Tydfil	d											08 08										08 38			
Pentre-bach	d											08 12										08 42			
Troed Y Rhiw	d											08 15										08 45			
Merthyr Vale	a											08 18										08 48			
	d											08 20										08 50			
Quakers Yard	d											08 25										08 55			
Aberdare ■	d							07 51										08 21							
Cwmbach	d							07 54										08 24							
Fernhill	d							07 58										08 28							
Mountain Ash	a							08 01										08 31							
	d							08 04										08 34							
Penrhiwceiber	d							08 08										08 38							
Abercynon	d							08 14				08 29						08 44				08 59			
Pontypridd ■	a				08 17			08 23				08 37				08 47		08 53				09 07			
	d				08 18			08 24				08 39				08 48		08 54				09 09			
Trefforest	d				08 21			08 27				08 42				08 51		08 57				09 12			
Trefforest Estate	d											08 46										09 16			
Taffs Well ■	d				08 28			08 34				08 50				08 58		09 04				09 20			
Radyr ■	a				08 31			08 37				08 53				09 01		09 07				09 23			
	d				08 31	08 34		08 37				08 53				09 01	09 04	09 07				09 23			
Danescourt	d					08 38											09 08								
Fairwater	d					08 40											09 10								
Waun-gron Park	d					08 42											09 12								
Ninian Park	d					08 45											09 15								
Llandaf	d				08 34			08 40				08 56				09 04		09 10				09 26			
Cathays	d				08 39			08 45				09 01				09 09		09 15				09 31			
Rhymney ■	d			07 44															08 30						
Pontlottyn	d			07 47															08 33						
Tir-phil	d			07 51															08 37						
Brithdir	d			07 54															08 40						
Bargoed	a			08 00															08 44						
	d			08 02					08 17					08 32					08 47						09 02
Gilfach Fargoed	d								08 19																
Pengam	d			08 07					08 22					08 37					08 52						09 07
Hengoed	d			08 10					08 25					08 40					08 55						09 10
Ystrad Mynach ■	d			08 13					08 28					08 43					08 58						09 13
Llanbradach	d			08 18					08 33					08 48					09 03						09 18
Aber	d			08 22					08 37					08 52					09 07						09 22
Caerphilly ■	d			08 25					08 40					08 55					09 10						09 25
Lisvane & Thornhill	d			08 29					08 44					08 59					09 14						09 29
Llanishen	d			08 31					08 46					09 01					09 16						09 31
Heath High Level	d			08 34					08 49					09 04					09 19						09 34
Coryton	d									08 45											09 15				
Whitchurch (Cardiff)	d									08 46											09 16				
Rhiwbina	d									08 48											09 18				
Birchgrove	d									08 50											09 20				
Ty Glas	d									08 51											09 21				
Heath Low Level	d									08 54											09 24				
Cardiff Queen Street ■	a			08 39	08 44			08 49	08 54	08 59		09 04		09 09		09 14		09 19	09 24		09 29	09 34			09 39
	d	08 36		08 41	08 46		08 48	08 51	08 56	09 01	09 00	09 06		09 11	09 12	09 16		09 21	09 26	09 24	09 31	09 36		09 36	09 41
Cardiff Bay	a	08 40					08 52				09 04				09 16					09 28				09 40	
Cardiff Central ■	a			08 48	08 53	08 50		08 54	08 59	09 04		09 09		09 14		09 23	09 20	09 24	09 29		09 34	09 39			09 44
	d							08 55	09 01			09 10		09 16				09 25	09 31			09 41			09 46
Grangetown	d							08 59	09 05			09 14		09 20				09 29	09 35			09 45			09 50
Dingle Road	d								09 11					09 26					09 41						09 56
Penarth	a								09 18					09 32					09 47						10 03
Cogan	d							09 03				09 18						09 33				09 48			
Eastbrook	d							09 05				09 20						09 35				09 51			
Dinas Powys	d							09 07				09 22						09 37				09 53			
Cadoxton	d							09 12				09 27						09 42				09 57			
Barry Docks	d							09 15				09 30						09 45				10 00			
Barry ■	d							09 19				09 34						09 49				10 05			
Barry Island	a							09 26				09 41						09 56							
Rhoose Cardiff Int Airport ✈	d																					10 12			
Llantwit Major	d																					10 22			
Bridgend	a																					10 41			

When events are being held at the Millenium Stadium, services are subject to alteration. Please check times before travelling.

Table 130

Mondays to Fridays

from 12 September

Treherbert, Aberdare, Merthyr, Pontypridd, Rhymney and Coryton - Cardiff, Penarth, Barry, Barry Island and Bridgend

		AW	AW	AW	AW	AW	AW	AW		AW	AW	AW	AW	AW	AW	AW	AW	AW		AW	AW	AW	AW	AW	AW
Treherbert	d	08 47											09 17										09 47		
Ynyswen	d	08 49											09 19										09 49		
Treorchy	d	08 51											09 21										09 51		
Ton Pentre	d	08 53											09 23										09 53		
Ystrad Rhondda	a	08 56											09 26										09 56		
	d	08 58											09 28										09 58		
Llwynypia	d	09 00											09 30										10 00		
Tonypandy	d	09 03											09 33										10 03		
Dinas Rhondda	d	09 05											09 35										10 05		
Porth	a	09 08											09 38										10 08		
	d	09 09											09 39										10 09		
Trehafod	d	09 12											09 42										10 12		
Merthyr Tydfil	d									09 08										09 38					
Pentre-bach	d									09 12										09 42					
Troed Y Rhiw	d									09 15										09 45					
Merthyr Vale	a									09 18										09 48					
	d									09 20										09 50					
Quakers Yard	d									09 25										09 55					
Aberdare ■	d				08 51										09 21										
Cwmbach	d				08 54										09 24										
Fernhill	d				08 58										09 28										
Mountain Ash	a				09 01										09 31										
	d				09 04										09 34										
Penrhiwceiber	d				09 08										09 38										
Abercynon	d				09 14					09 29					09 44					09 59					
Pontypridd ■	a	09 17			09 23					09 37			09 47		09 53					10 07			10 17		
	d	09 18			09 24					09 39			09 48		09 54					10 09			10 18		
Trefforest	d	09 21			09 27					09 42			09 51		09 57					10 12			10 21		
Trefforest Estate	d									09 46										10 16					
Taffs Well ■	d	09 28			09 34					09 50			09 58		10 04					10 20			10 28		
Radyr ■	a	09 31			09 37					09 53			10 01		10 07					10 23			10 31		
	d	09 31	09 34		09 37					09 53			10 01	10 04	10 07					10 23			10 31	10 34	
Danescourt	d		09 38											10 08										10 38	
Fairwater	d		09 40											10 10										10 40	
Waun-gron Park	d		09 42											10 12										10 42	
Ninian Park	d		09 45											10 15										10 45	
Llandaf	d	09 34			09 40					09 56			10 04		10 10					10 26			10 34		
Cathays	d	09 39			09 45					10 01			10 09		10 15					10 31			10 39		
Rhymney ■	d															09 29									
Pontlottyn	d															09 32									
Tir-phil	d															09 36									
Brithdir	d															09 39									
Bargoed	a															09 42									
	d										09 25					09 47						10 02			
Gilfach Fargoed	d										09 27														
Pengam	d										09 30					09 52						10 07			
Hengoed	d										09 33					09 55						10 10			
Ystrad Mynach ■	d					09 28					09b43					09 58						10 13			
Llanbradach	d					09 33					09 48					10 03						10 18			
Aber	d					09 37					09 52					10 07						10 22			
Caerphilly ■	d					09 40					09 55					10 10						10 25			
Lisvane & Thornhill	d					09 44					09 59					10 14						10 29			
Llanishen	d					09 46					10 01					10 16						10 31			
Heath High Level	d					09 49					10 04					10 19						10 34			
Coryton	d						09 45											10 15							
Whitchurch (Cardiff)	d						09 46											10 16							
Rhiwbina	d						09 48											10 18							
Birchgrove	d						09 50											10 20							
Ty Glas	d						09 51											10 21							
Heath Low Level	d						09 54											10 24							
Cardiff Queen Street ■	a	09 44			09 49	09 54	09 59			10 04	10 09		10 14		10 19	10 24		10 29		10 34		10 39	10 44		
	d	09 46		09 48	09 51	09 56	10 01	10 00		10 06	10 11	10 12	10 16		10 21	10 26	10 24	10 31		10 36	10 36	10 41	10 46		10 48
Cardiff Bay	a			09 52				10 04				10 16					10 28				10 40				10 52
Cardiff Central ■	a	09 53	09 50		09 54	09 59	10 04			10 09	10 14		10 23	10 20	10 24	10 29		10 34		10 39		10 44	10 53	10 50	
	d				09 55	10 01				10 10	10 16				10 25	10 31				10 41		10 46			
Grangetown	d				09 59	10 05				10 14	10 20				10 29	10 35				10 45		10 50			
Dingle Road	d					10 11					10 26					10 41						10 56			
Penarth	a					10 17					10 32					10 47						11 02			
Cogan	d				10 03					10 18					10 33					10 48					
Eastbrook	d				10 05					10 20					10 35					10 51					
Dinas Powys	d				10 07					10 22					10 37					10 53					
Cadoxton	d				10 12					10 27					10 42					10 57					
Barry Docks	d				10 15					10 30					10 45					11 00					
Barry ■	d				10 19					10 34					10 49					11 05					
Barry Island	a				10 26					10 41					10 56										
Rhoose Cardiff Int Airport ✈	d																			11 12					
Llantwit Major	d																			11 22					
Bridgend	a																			11 41					

b Arr. 0936

When events are being held at the Millenium Stadium, services are subject to alteration. Please check times before travelling.

Table 130

Mondays to Fridays
from 12 September

Treherbert, Aberdare, Merthyr, Pontypridd, Rhymney and Coryton - Cardiff, Penarth, Barry, Barry Island and Bridgend

		AW	AW	AW	AW	AW	AW	AW	AW	AW	AW	AW	AW	AW	AW	AW	AW	AW	AW	AW	AW	AW
Treherbert	d												10 17						10 47			
Ynyswen	d												10 19						10 49			
Treorchy	d												10 21						10 51			
Ton Pentre	d												10 23						10 53			
Ystrad Rhondda	a												10 26						10 56			
	d												10 28						10 58			
Llwynypia	d												10 30						11 00			
Tonypandy	d												10 33						11 03			
Dinas Rhondda	d												10 35						11 05			
Porth	a												10 38						11 08			
	d												10 52						11 09			
Trehafod	d												10 55						11 12			
Merthyr Tydfil	d		10 04													10 38						
Pentre-bach	d		10 08													10 42						
Troed Y Rhiw	d		10 11													10 45						
Merthyr Vale	a		10 14													10 48						
	d		10 16													10 50						
Quakers Yard	d		10 22													10 55						
Aberdare 3	d	09 51									10 21											10 51
Cwmbach	d	09 54									10 24											10 54
Fernhill	d	09 58									10 28											10 58
Mountain Ash	a	10 01									10 31											11 01
	d	10 04									10 34											11 04
Penrhiwceiber	d	10 08									10 38											11 08
Abercynon	d	10 14	10 26								10 44					10 59						11 14
Pontypridd 3	a	10 23	10 32								10 53		11 00			11 08			11 17			11 23
	d	10 24					10 39				10 54		11 04			11 09			11 18			11 24
Trefforest	d	10 27					10 42				10 57		11 07			11 12			11 21			11 27
Trefforest Estate	d															11 16						
Taffs Well 3	d	10 34					10 50				11 04		11 13			11 20			11 28			11 34
Radyr 3	a	10 37					10 53				11 07		11 17			11 23			11 31			11 37
	d	10 37					10 53		11 04		11 07		11 17			11 23			11 31	11 34		11 37
Danescourt	d								11 08											11 38		
Fairwater	d								11 10											11 40		
Waun-gron Park	d								11 12											11 42		
Ninian Park	d								11 15											11 45		
Llandaf	d	10 40					10 56				11 10					11 26			11 34			11 40
Cathays	d	10 45					11 01				11 15					11 31			11 39			11 45
Rhymney 3	d											10 29										
Pontlottyn	d											10 32										
Tir-phil	d											10 36										
Brithdir	d											10 39										
Bargoed	a											10 42										
	d							10 25				10 47						11 02				
Gilfach Fargoed	d							10 27														
Pengam	d							10 30				10 52						11 07				
Hengoed	d							10 33				10 55						11 10				
Ystrad Mynach 3	d			10 28				10b43				10 58						11 13				
Llanbradach	d			10 33				10 48				11 03						11 18				
Aber	d			10 37				10 52				11 07						11 22				
Caerphilly 3	d			10 40				10 55				11 10						11 25				
Lisvane & Thornhill	d			10 44				10 59				11 14						11 29				
Llanishen	d			10 46				11 01				11 16						11 31				
Heath High Level	d			10 49				11 04				11 19						11 34				
Coryton	d				10 45										11 15							
Whitchurch (Cardiff)	d				10 46										11 16							
Rhiwbina	d				10 48										11 18							
Birchgrove	d				10 50										11 20							
Ty Glas	d				10 51										11 21							
Heath Low Level	d				10 54										11 24							
Cardiff Queen Street 3	a	10 49		10 54	10 59		11 04	11 09			11 19	11 24			11 29	11 34		11 39	11 44			11 49
	d	10 51		10 56	11 01	11 00	11 06	11 11		11 12	11 21	11 26		11 24	11 31	11 36	11 36	11 41	11 46		11 48	11 51
Cardiff Bay	a					11 04				11 16				11 28			11 40				11 52	
Cardiff Central 7	a	10 54		10 59	11 04		11 09	11 14	11 20		11 24	11 29	11 34		11 34	11 39		11 44	11 53	11 50		11 54
	d	10 55		11 01			11 10	11 16			11 25	11 31				11 41		11 46				11 55
Grangetown	d	10 59		11 05			11 14	11 20			11 29	11 35				11 45		11 50				11 59
Dingle Road	d			11 11				11 26				11 41						11 56				
Penarth	a			11 18				11 32				11 47						12 02				
Cogan	d	11 03					11 18				11 33					11 48						12 03
Eastbrook	d	11 05					11 20				11 35					11 51						12 05
Dinas Powys	d	11 07					11 22				11 37					11 53						12 07
Cadoxton	d	11 12					11 27				11 42					11 57						12 12
Barry Docks	d	11 15					11 30				11 45					12 00						12 15
Barry 3	d	11 19					11 34				11 49					12 05						12 19
Barry Island	a	11 26					11 41				11 56											12 26
Rhoose Cardiff Int Airport ✈	d															12 12						
Llantwit Major	d															12 22						
Bridgend	a															12 41						

b Arr. 1036

When events are being held at the Millenium Stadium, services are subject to alteration. Please check times before travelling.

Table 130

Mondays to Fridays
from 12 September

Treherbert, Aberdare, Merthyr, Pontypridd, Rhymney and Coryton - Cardiff, Penarth, Barry, Barry Island and Bridgend

		AW	AW	AW	AW	AW	AW	AW	AW	AW	AW	AW	AW	AW	AW	AW	AW	AW	AW	AW	AW	AW	AW
Treherbert	d							11 17									11 47						
Ynyswen	d							11 19									11 49						
Treorchy	d							11 21									11 51						
Ton Pentre	d							11 23									11 53						
Ystrad Rhondda	a							11 26									11 56						
	d							11 28									11 58						
Llwynypia	d							11 30									12 00						
Tonypandy	d							11 33									12 03						
Dinas Rhondda	d							11 35									12 05						
Porth	a							11 38									12 08						
	d							11 39									12 09						
Trehafod	d							11 42									12 12						
Merthyr Tydfil	d				11 08									11 38									
Pentre-bach	d				11 12									11 42									
Troed Y Rhiw	d				11 15									11 45									
Merthyr Vale	a				11 18									11 48									
	d				11 20									11 50									
Quakers Yard	d				11 25									11 55									
Aberdare 3	d									11 21													
Cwmbach	d									11 24													
Fernhill	d									11 28													
Mountain Ash	a									11 31													
	d									11 34													
Penrhiwceiber	d									11 38													
Abercynon	d				11 29					11 44				11 59									
Pontypridd 3	a				11 37			11 47		11 53				12 07			12 17						
	d				11 39			11 48		11 54				12 09			12 18						
Trefforest	d				11 42			11 51		11 57				12 12			12 21						
Trefforest Estate	d				11 46									12 16									
Taffs Well 3	d				11 50			11 58		12 04				12 20			12 28						
Radyr 3	a				11 53			12 01		12 07				12 23			12 31						
	d				11 53			12 01	12 04	12 07				12 23			12 31	12 34					
Danescourt	d								12 08									12 38					
Fairwater	d								12 10									12 40					
Waun-gron Park	d								12 12									12 42					
Ninian Park	d								12 15									12 45					
Llandaf	d				11 56			12 04		12 10				12 26			12 34						
Cathays	d				12 01			12 09		12 15				12 31			12 39						
Rhymney 3	d										11 29												
Pontlottyn	d										11 32												
Tir-phil	d										11 36												
Brithdir	d										11 39												
Bargoed	a										11 42												
	d					11 20					11 47					12 02							
Gilfach Fargoed	d					11 22																	
Pengam	d					11 25					11 52					12 07							
Hengoed	d					11 28					11 55					12 10							
Ystrad Mynach 3	d	11 28				11b39					11 58					12 13					12 28		
Llanbradach	d	11 33				11 43					12 03					12 18					12 33		
Aber	d	11 37				11 48					12 07					12 22					12 37		
Caerphilly 3	d	11 40				11 55					12 10					12 25					12 40		
Lisvane & Thornhill	d	11 44				11 59					12 14					12 29					12 44		
Llanishen	d	11 46				12 01					12 16					12 31					12 46		
Heath High Level	d	11 49				12 04					12 19					12 34					12 49		
Coryton	d		11 45										12 15									12 45	
Whitchurch (Cardiff)	d		11 46										12 16									12 46	
Rhiwbina	d		11 48										12 18									12 48	
Birchgrove	d		11 50										12 20									12 50	
Ty Glas	d		11 51										12 21									12 51	
Heath Low Level	d		11 54										12 24									12 54	
Cardiff Queen Street 3	a	11 54	11 59		12 04	12 09		12 14		12 19	12 24		12 29	12 34		12 39	12 44				12 54	12 59	
	d	11 56	12 01	12 00	12 06	12 11	12 12	12 16		12 21	12 26	12 24	12 31	12 36	12 36	12 41	12 46		12 43		12 56	13 01	13 00
Cardiff Bay	a			12 04			12 16					12 28			12 40				12 52				13 04
Cardiff Central 7	a	11 59	12 04		12 09	12 14		12 23	12 20	12 24	12 29		12 34	12 39		12 44	12 53	12 50			12 59	13 04	
	d	12 01			12 10	12 16				12 25	12 31			12 41		12 46				12 55	13 01		
Grangetown	d	12 05			12 14	12 20				12 29	12 35			12 45		12 50				12 59	13 05		
Dingle Road	d	12 11				12 26					12 41					12 56					13 11		
Penarth	a	12 17				12 32					12 47					13 02					13 17		
Cogan	d				12 18					12 33				12 48						13 03			
Eastbrook	d				12 20					12 35				12 51						13 05			
Dinas Powys	d				12 22					12 37				12 53						13 07			
Cadoxton	d				12 27					12 42				12 57						13 12			
Barry Docks	d				12 30					12 45				13 00						13 15			
Barry 3	d				12 34					12 49				13 05						13 19			
Barry Island	a				12 41					12 56										13 25			
Rhoose Cardiff Int Airport ✈	d													13 12									
Llantwit Major	d													13 22									
Bridgend	a													13 41									

b Arr. 1131

When events are being held at the Millenium Stadium, services are subject to alteration. Please check times before travelling.

Table 130

Mondays to Fridays

from 12 September

Treherbert, Aberdare, Merthyr, Pontypridd, Rhymney and Coryton - Cardiff, Penarth, Barry, Barry Island and Bridgend

		AW	AW	AW	AW	AW	AW	AW	AW	AW	AW	AW	AW	AW	AW	AW	AW	AW	AW	AW	AW	AW	AW
Treherbert	d				12 17									12 47									
Ynyswen	d				12 19									12 49									
Treorchy	d				12 21									12 51									
Ton Pentre	d				12 23									12 53									
Ystrad Rhondda	a				12 26									12 56									
	d				12 28									12 58									
Llwynypia	d				12 30									13 00									
Tonypandy	d				12 33									13 03									
Dinas Rhondda	d				12 35									13 05									
Porth	a				12 38									13 08									
	d				12 39									13 09									
Trehafod	d				12 42									13 12									
Merthyr Tydfil	d	12 08									12 38										13 08		
Pentre-bach	d	12 12									12 42										13 12		
Troed Y Rhiw	d	12 15									12 45										13 15		
Merthyr Vale	a	12 18									12 48										13 18		
	d	12 20									12 50										13 20		
Quakers Yard	d	12 25									12 55										13 25		
Aberdare [3]	d						12 21										12 51						
Cwmbach	d						12 24										12 54						
Fernhill	d						12 28										12 58						
Mountain Ash	a						12 31										13 01						
	d						12 34										13 04						
Penrhiwceiber	d						12 38										13 08						
Abercynon	d	12 29					12 44				12 59						13 14				13 29		
Pontypridd [3]	a	12 37			12 48		12 53				13 07			13 17			13 23				13 37		
	d	12 39			12 48		12 54				13 09			13 18			13 24				13 39		
Trefforest	d	12 42			12 51		12 57				13 12			13 21			13 27				13 42		
Trefforest Estate	d	12 46									13 16										13 46		
Taffs Well [3]	d	12 50			12 58		13 04				13 20			13 28			13 34				13 50		
Radyr [3]	a	12 53			13 01		13 07				13 23			13 31			13 37				13 53		
	d	12 53			13 01	13 04	13 07				13 23			13 31	13 34		13 37				13 53		
Danescourt	d					13 08									13 38								
Fairwater	d					13 10									13 40								
Waun-gron Park	d					13 12									13 42								
Ninian Park	d					13 15									13 45								
Llandaf	d	12 56			13 04		13 10				13 26			13 34			13 40				13 56		
Cathays	d	13 01			13 09		13 15				13 31			13 39			13 45				14 01		
Rhymney [3]	d							12 29															
Pontlottyn	d							12 32															
Tir-phil	d							12 36															
Brithdir	d							12 39															
Bargoed	a							12 42															
	d		12 25					12 47					13 02									13 25	
Gilfach Fargoed	d		12 27																			13 27	
Pengam	d		12 30					12 52					13 07									13 30	
Hengoed	d		12 33					12 55					13 10									13 33	
Ystrad Mynach [3]	d		12b43					12 58					13 13					13 28				13c43	
Llanbradach	d		12 48					13 03					13 18					13 33				13 48	
Aber	d		12 52					13 07					13 22					13 37				13 52	
Caerphilly [3]	d		12 55					13 10					13 25					13 40				13 55	
Lisvane & Thornhill	d		12 59					13 14					13 29					13 44				13 59	
Llanishen	d		13 01					13 16					13 31					13 46				14 01	
Heath High Level	d		13 04					13 19					13 34					13 49				14 04	
Coryton	d									13 15									13 45				
Whitchurch (Cardiff)	d									13 16									13 46				
Rhiwbina	d									13 18									13 48				
Birchgrove	d									13 20									13 50				
Ty Glas	d									13 21									13 51				
Heath Low Level	d									13 24									13 54				
Cardiff Queen Street [3]	a	13 04	13 09		13 14		13 19	13 24		13 29	13 34		13 39	13 44			13 49	13 54	13 59		14 04	14 09	
	d	13 06	13 11	13 12	13 16		13 21	13 26	13 24	13 31	13 36	13 36	13 41	13 46		13 48	13 51	13 56	14 01	14 00	14 06	14 11	14 12
Cardiff Bay	a			13 16					13 28			13 40				13 52				14 04			14 16
Cardiff Central [7]	a	13 09	13 14		13 23	13 20	13 24	13 29		13 34	13 39		13 44	13 53	13 50		13 54	13 59	14 04		14 09	14 14	
	d	13 10	13 16				13 25	13 31			13 41		13 46				13 55	14 01			14 10	14 16	
Grangetown	d	13 14	13 20				13 29	13 35			13 45		13 50				13 59	14 05			14 14	14 20	
Dingle Road	d		13 26					13 41					13 56					14 11				14 26	
Penarth	a		13 32					13 47					14 02					14 17				14 32	
Cogan	d	13 18					13 33				13 48						14 03				14 18		
Eastbrook	d	13 20					13 35				13 51						14 05				14 20		
Dinas Powys	d	13 22					13 37				13 53						14 07				14 22		
Cadoxton	d	13 27					13 42				13 57						14 12				14 27		
Barry Docks	d	13 30					13 45				14 00						14 15				14 30		
Barry [3]	d	13 34					13 49				14 05						14 19				14 34		
Barry Island	a	13 41					13 56										14 26				14 41		
Rhoose Cardiff Int Airport ✈	d										14 12												
Llantwit Major	d										14 22												
Bridgend	a										14 41												

b Arr. 1236 c Arr. 1336

When events are being held at the Millenium Stadium, services are subject to alteration. Please check times before travelling.

Table 130

Mondays to Fridays

from 12 September

Treherbert, Aberdare, Merthyr, Pontypridd, Rhymney and Coryton - Cardiff, Penarth, Barry, Barry Island and Bridgend

		AW		AW	AW	AW	AW	AW	AW	AW	AW		AW	AW	AW	AW	AW	AW	AW	AW		AW	AW
Treherbert	d	13 17									13 47												
Ynyswen	d	13 19									13 49												
Treorchy	d	13 21									13 51												
Ton Pentre	d	13 23									13 53												
Ystrad Rhondda	a	13 26									13 56												
	d	13 28									13 58												
Llwynypia	d	13 30									14 00												
Tonypandy	d	13 33									14 03												
Dinas Rhondda	d	13 35									14 05												
Porth	a	13 38									14 08												
	d	13 39									14 09												
Trehafod	d	13 42									14 12												
Merthyr Tydfil	d								13 38											14 08				
Pentre-bach	d								13 42											14 12				
Troed Y Rhiw	d								13 45											14 15				
Merthyr Vale	a								13 48											14 18				
	d								13 50											14 20				
Quakers Yard	d								13 55											14 25				
Aberdare [3]	d														13 51									14 21
Cwmbach	d														13 54									14 24
Fernhill	d														13 58									14 28
Mountain Ash	a														14 01									14 31
	d														14 04									14 34
Penrhiwceiber	d														14 08									14 38
Abercynon	d				13 45				13 59						14 14				14 29				14 44
Pontypridd [3]	a	13 47		13 53				14 07			14 17			14 23				14 37				14 53
	d	13 48		13 54				14 09			14 18			14 24				14 39				14 54
Trefforest	d	13 51		13 57				14 12			14 21			14 27				14 42				14 57
Trefforest Estate	d							14 16										14 46				
Taffs Well [3]	d	13 58		14 04				14 20			14 28			14 34				14 50				15 04
Radyr [3]	a	14 01		14 07				14 23			14 31			14 37				14 53				15 07
	d	14 01	14 04	14 07				14 23			14 31	14 34		14 37				14 53		15 04		15 07
Danescourt	d		14 08									14 38								15 08		
Fairwater	d		14 10									14 40								15 10		
Waun-gron Park	d		14 12									14 42								15 12		
Ninian Park	d		14 15									14 45								15 15		
Llandaf	d	14 04		14 10				14 26			14 34			14 40				14 56				15 10
Cathays	d	14 09		14 15				14 31			14 39			14 45				15 01				15 15
Rhymney [3]	d				13 29																	
Pontlottyn	d				13 32																	
Tir-phil	d				13 36																	
Brithdir	d				13 39																	
Bargoed	a				13 42																	
	d				13 47					14 02									14 25			
Gilfach Fargoed	d																		14 27			
Pengam	d				13 52					14 07									14 30			
Hengoed	d				13 55					14 10									14 33			
Ystrad Mynach [3]	d				13 58					14 13					14 28				14b43			
Llanbradach	d				14 03					14 18					14 33				14 48			
Aber	d				14 07					14 22					14 37				14 52			
Caerphilly [3]	d				14 10					14 25					14 40				14 55			
Lisvane & Thornhill	d				14 14					14 29					14 44				14 59			
Llanishen	d				14 16					14 31					14 46				15 01			
Heath High Level	d				14 19					14 34					14 49				15 04			
Coryton	d						14 15									14 45						
Whitchurch (Cardiff)	d						14 16									14 46						
Rhiwbina	d						14 18									14 48						
Birchgrove	d						14 20									14 50						
Ty Glas	d						14 21									14 51						
Heath Low Level	d						14 24									14 54						
Cardiff Queen Street [3]	a	14 14		14 19	14 24		14 29	14 34		14 39	14 44			14 49	14 54	14 59		15 04	15 09			15 19
	d	14 16		14 21	14 26	14 24	14 31	14 36	14 36	14 41	14 46		14 48	14 51	14 56	15 01	15 00	15 06	15 11		15 12	15 21
Cardiff Bay	a					14 28			14 40				14 52				15 04				15 16	
Cardiff Central [7]	a	14 23	14 20	14 24	14 29		14 34	14 39		14 44	14 53	14 50		14 54	14 59	15 05		15 09	15 14	15 20		15 24
	d			14 25	14 31			14 41		14 46				14 55	15 01			15 10	15 16			15 25
Grangetown	d			14 29	14 35			14 45		14 50				14 59	15 09			15 14	15 20			15 29
Dingle Road	d				14 41					14 56					15 13				15 26			
Penarth	a				14 47					15 02					15 17				15 32			
Cogan	d			14 33				14 48						15 03				15 18				15 33
Eastbrook	d			14 35				14 51						15 05				15 20				15 35
Dinas Powys	d			14 37				14 53						15 07				15 22				15 37
Cadoxton	d			14 42				14 57						15 12				15 27				15 42
Barry Docks	d			14 45				15 00						15 15				15 30				15 45
Barry [3]	d			14 49				15 05						15 19				15 34				15 49
Barry Island	a			14 56										15 26				15 41				15 56
Rhoose Cardiff Int Airport ✈	d							15 12														
Llantwit Major	d							15 22														
Bridgend	a							15 41														

b Arr. 1436

When events are being held at the Millenium Stadium, services are subject to alteration. Please check times before travelling.

Table 130

Mondays to Fridays

from 12 September

Treherbert, Aberdare, Merthyr, Pontypridd, Rhymney and Coryton - Cardiff, Penarth, Barry, Barry Island and Bridgend

		AW	AW	AW	AW	AW	AW	AW		AW	AW	AW	AW	AW	AW	AW	AW	AW		AW	AW	AW	AW	AW	AW
Treherbert	d		14 17							14 47											15 13				
Ynyswen	d		14 19							14 49											15 15				
Treorchy	d		14 21							14 51											15 21				
Ton Pentre	d		14 23							14 53											15 23				
Ystrad Rhondda	a		14 26							14 56											15 26				
	d		14 28							14 58											15 28				
Llwynypia	d		14 30							15 00											15 30				
Tonypandy	d		14 33							15 03											15 33				
Dinas Rhondda	d		14 35							15 05											15 35				
Porth	a		14 38							15 08											15 38				
	d		14 52							15 09											15 39				
Trehafod	d		14 55							15 12											15 42				
Merthyr Tydfil	d					14 38											15 08								
Pentre-bach	d					14 42											15 12								
Troed Y Rhiw	d					14 45											15 15								
Merthyr Vale	a					14 48											15 18								
	d					14 50											15 20								
Quakers Yard	d					14 55											15 25								
Aberdare 🅱	d												14 51										15 21		
Cwmbach	d												14 54										15 24		
Fernhill	d												14 58										15 28		
Mountain Ash	a												15 01										15 31		
	d												15 04										15 34		
Penrhiwceiber	d												15 08										15 38		
Abercynon	d					14 59							15 14				15 29						15 44		
Pontypridd 🅱	a		15 00			15 07				15 17			15 23				15 37				15 47		15 53		
	d		15 04			15 09				15 18			15 24				15 39				15 48		15 54		
Trefforest	d		15 07			15 12				15 21			15 27				15 42				15 51		15 57		
Trefforest Estate	d					15 16											15 46								
Taffs Well 🅱	d		15 13			15 20				15 28			15 34				15 50				15 58		16 04		
Radyr 🅱	a		15 17			15 23				15 31			15 37				15 53				16 01		16 07		
	d		15 17			15 23				15 31	15 34		15 37				15 53				16 01	16 04	16 07		
Danescourt	d										15 38											16 08			
Fairwater	d										15 40											16 10			
Waun-gron Park	d										15 42											16 12			
Ninian Park	d										15 45											16 15			
Llandaf	d					15 26				15 34			15 40				15 56				16 04		16 10		
Cathays	d					15 31				15 39			15 45				16 01				16 09		16 15		
Rhymney 🅱	d	14 29																						15 29	
Pontlottyn	d	14 32																						15 32	
Tir-phil	d	14 36																						15 36	
Brithdir	d	14 39																						15 39	
Bargoed	a	14 42																						15 42	
	d	14 47						15 02										15 25						15 47	
Gilfach Fargoed	d																	15 27							
Pengam	d	14 52						15 07										15 30						15 52	
Hengoed	d	14 55						15 10										15 33						15 55	
Ystrad Mynach 🅱	d	14 58						15 13						15 28				15b43						15 58	
Llanbradach	d	15 03						15 18						15 33				15 48						16 03	
Aber	d	15 07						15 22						15 37				15 52						16 07	
Caerphilly 🅱	d	15 10						15 25						15 40				15 55						16 10	
Lisvane & Thornhill	d	15 14						15 29						15 44				15 59						16 14	
Llanishen	d	15 16						15 31						15 46				16 01						16 16	
Heath High Level	d	15 19						15 34						15 49				16 04						16 19	
Coryton	d				15 15										15 45										
Whitchurch (Cardiff)	d				15 16										15 46										
Rhiwbina	d				15 18										15 48										
Birchgrove	d				15 20										15 50										
Ty Glas	d				15 21										15 51										
Heath Low Level	d				15 24										15 54										
Cardiff Queen Street 🅱	a	15 24			15 29	15 34		15 39		15 44			15 49	15 54	15 59		16 04	16 09			16 14		16 19	16 24	
	d	15 26		15 24	15 31	15 36	15 36	15 41		15 46		15 48	15 51	15 56	16 01	16 00	16 06	16 11		16 12	16 16		16 21	16 26	16 24
Cardiff Bay	a			15 28			15 40					15 52				16 04				16 16					16 28
Cardiff Central 🅱	a	15 29	15 34		15 34	15 39		15 44		15 52	15 50		15 54	15 59	16 05		16 09	16 14			16 23	16 20	16 24	16 33	
	d	15 31				15 41		15 46					15 55	16 01			16 10	16 16					16 25		
Grangetown	d	15 35				15 45		15 50					15 59	16 05			16 14	16 20					16 29		
Dingle Road	d	15 41						15 56						16 11				16 26							
Penarth	a	15 47						16 02						16 18				16 32							
Cogan	d					15 48							16 03				16 18						16 33		
Eastbrook	d					15 51							16 05				16 20						16 35		
Dinas Powys	d					15 53							16 07				16 22						16 37		
Cadoxton	d					15 57							16 12				16 27						16 42		
Barry Docks	d					16 00							16 15				16 30						16 45		
Barry 🅱	d					16 05							16 19				16 34						16 49		
Barry Island	a												16 26				16 41						16 56		
Rhoose Cardiff Int Airport ✈	d					16 12																			
Llantwit Major	d					16 22																			
Bridgend	a					16 41																			

b Arr. 1536

When events are being held at the Millenium Stadium, services are subject to alteration. Please check times before travelling.

Table 130

Mondays to Fridays

from 12 September

Treherbert, Aberdare, Merthyr, Pontypridd, Rhymney and Coryton - Cardiff, Penarth, Barry, Barry Island and Bridgend

		AW	AW	AW		AW	AW	AW	AW	AW	AW	AW	AW	AW		AW	AW	AW	AW	AW	AW	AW	AW	AW	
Treherbert	d						15 47											16 17							
Ynyswen	d						15 49											16 19							
Treorchy	d						15 51											16 21							
Ton Pentre	d						15 53											16 23							
Ystrad Rhondda	a						15 56											16 26							
	d						15 58											16 28							
Llwynypia	d						16 00											16 30							
Tonypandy	d						16 03											16 33							
Dinas Rhondda	d						16 05											16 35							
Porth	a						16 08											16 38							
	d						16 09											16 39							
Trehafod	d						16 12											16 42							
Merthyr Tydfil	d		15 38											16 08										16 38	
Pentre-bach	d		15 42											16 12										16 42	
Troed Y Rhiw	d		15 45											16 15										16 45	
Merthyr Vale	a		15 48											16 18										16 48	
	d		15 50											16 20										16 50	
Quakers Yard	d		15 55											16 25										16 55	
Aberdare 🅱	d									15 51										16 21					
Cwmbach	d									15 54										16 24					
Fernhill	d									15 58										16 28					
Mountain Ash	a									16 01										16 31					
	d									16 04										16 34					
Penrhiwceiber	d									16 08										15 38					
Abercynon	d		15 59							16 14				16 29						15 44				16 59	
Pontypridd 🅱	a		16 08				16 17			16 23				16 37				16 47		15 53				17 07	
	d		16 09				16 18			16 24				16 39				16 48		15 54				17 09	
Trefforest	d		16 12				16 21			16 27				16 42				16 51		15 57				17 12	
Trefforest Estate	d		16 16											16 46										17 16	
Taffs Well 🅱	d		16 20				16 28			16 34				16 50				16 58		17 04				17 20	
Radyr 🅱	a		16 23				16 31			16 37				16 53				17 01		17 07				17 23	
	d		16 23				16 31	16 34		16 37				16 53				17 01	17 04	17 07				17 23	
Danescourt	d							16 38											17 08						
Fairwater	d							16 40											17 10						
Waun-gron Park	d							16 42											17 12						
Ninian Park	d							16 45											17 15						
Llandaf	d		16 26				16 34			16 40				16 56				17 04		17 10				17 26	
Cathays	d		16 31				16 39			16 45				17 01				17 09		17 15				17 31	
Rhymney 🅱	d																				16 29				
Pontlottyn	d																				16 32				
Tir-phil	d																				16 36				
Brithdir	d																				16 39				
Bargoed	a																				16 42				
	d					16 02					16 17					16 32					16 47				
Gilfach Fargoed	d										16 19														
Pengam	d					16 07					16 22					16 37					16 52				
Hengoed	d					16 10					16 25					16 40					16 55				
Ystrad Mynach 🅱	d					16 13					16 28					16 43					16 58				
Llanbradach	d					16 18					16 33					16 48					17 03				
Aber	d					16 22					16 37					16 52					17 07				
Caerphilly 🅱	d					16 25					16 40					16 55					17 10				
Lisvane & Thornhill	d					16 29					16 44					16 59					17 14				
Llanishen	d					16 31					16 46					17 01					17 16				
Heath High Level	d					16 34					16 49					17 04					17 19				
Coryton	d	16 15										16 45											17 15		
Whitchurch (Cardiff)	d	16 16										16 46											17 16		
Rhiwbina	d	16 18										16 48											17 18		
Birchgrove	d	16 20										16 50											17 20		
Ty Glas	d	16 21										16 51											17 21		
Heath Low Level	d	16 24										16 54											17 24		
Cardiff Queen Street 🅱	a	16 29	16 34			16 39	16 44			16 49	16 54	16 59		17 04		17 09		17 14		17 19	17 24		17 29	17 34	
	d	16 31	16 36	16 36		16 41	16 46		16 48	16 51	16 56	17 01	17 00	17 06		17 11	17 12	17 16		17 21	17 26	17 24	17 31	17 36	
Cardiff Bay	a			16 40					16 52				17 04				17 16					17 28			
Cardiff Central 🅱	a	16 34	16 39			16 44	16 53	16 50		16 54	16 59	17 04		17 09		17 14		17 23	17 20	17 24	17 29		17 34	17 39	
	d		16 41			16 46				16 55	17 01			17 10		17 16				17 25	17 31			17 41	
Grangetown	d		16 45			16 50				16 59	17 05			17 14		17 20				17 29	17 35			17 45	
Dingle Road	d					16 56					17 11					17 26					17 41				
Penarth	a					17 02					17 17					17 32					17 47				
Cogan	d		16 48							17 03				17 18						17 33				17 48	
Eastbrook	d		16 51							17 05				17 20						17 35				17 51	
Dinas Powys	d		16 53							17 07				17 22						17 37				17 53	
Cadoxton	d		16 57							17 12				17 27						17 42				17 57	
Barry Docks	d		17 00							17 15				17 30						17 45				18 00	
Barry 🅱	d		17 05							17 19				17 34						17 49				18 05	
Barry Island	a									17 26				17 41						17 56					
Rhoose Cardiff Int Airport ✈	d		17 12																					18 12	
Llantwit Major	d		17 22																					18 22	
Bridgend	a		17 41																					18 41	

When events are being held at the Millenium Stadium, services are subject to alteration. Please check times before travelling.

Table 130

Mondays to Fridays from 12 September

Treherbert, Aberdare, Merthyr, Pontypridd, Rhymney and Coryton - Cardiff, Penarth, Barry, Barry Island and Bridgend

Station		AW	AW	AW	AW	AW	AW	AW	AW	AW	AW	AW	AW	AW	AW	AW	AW	AW	AW	AW	AW	AW	AW
Treherbert	d			16 47										17 17								17 47	
Ynyswen	d			16 49										17 19								17 49	
Treorchy	d			16 51										17 21								17 51	
Ton Pentre	d			16 53										17 23								17 53	
Ystrad Rhondda	a			16 56										17 26								17 56	
	d			16 58										17 28								17 58	
Llwynypia	d			17 00										17 30								18 00	
Tonypandy	d			17 03										17 33								18 03	
Dinas Rhondda	d			17 05										17 35								18 05	
Porth	a			17 08										17 38								18 08	
	d			17 09										17 39								18 09	
Trehafod	d			17 12										17 42								18 12	
Merthyr Tydfil	d										17 08									17 38			
Pentre-bach	d										17 12									17 42			
Troed Y Rhiw	d										17 15									17 45			
Merthyr Vale	a										17 18									17 48			
	d										17 20									17 50			
Quakers Yard	d										17 25									17 55			
Aberdare 3	d						16 51									17 21							
Cwmbach	d						16 54									17 24							
Fernhill	d						16 58									17 28							
Mountain Ash	a						17 01									17 31							
	d						17 04									17 34							
Penrhiwceiber	d						17 08									17 38							
Abercynon	d						17 14				17 29					17 44				17 59			
Pontypridd 3	a			17 17			17 23				17 37			17 47		17 53				18 07		18 17	
	d			17 18			17 24				17 39			17 48		17 54				18 09		18 18	
Trefforest	d			17 21			17 27				17 42			17 51		17 57				18 12		18 21	
Trefforest Estate	d										17 46									18 16			
Taffs Well 3	d			17 28			17 34				17 50			17 58		18 04				18 20		18 28	
Radyr 3	a			17 31			17 37				17 53			18 01		18 07				18 23		18 31	
	d			17 31	17 34		17 37				17 53			18 01	18 04	18 07				18 23		18 31	18 34
Danescourt	d				17 38										18 08								18 38
Fairwater	d				17 40										18 10								18 40
Waun-gron Park	d				17 42										18 12								18 42
Ninian Park	d				17 45										18 15								18 45
Llandaf	d			17 34			17 40				17 56			18 04		18 10				18 26		18 34	
Cathays	d			17 39			17 45				18 01			18 09		18 15				18 31		18 39	
Rhymney 3	d																17 29						
Pontlottyn	d																17 32						
Tir-phil	d																17 36						
Brithdir	d																17 39						
Bargoed	a																17 42						
	d		17 02					17 17				17 32					17 47						
Gilfach Fargoed	d							17 19															
Pengam	d		17 07					17 22				17 37					17 52						
Hengoed	d		17 10					17 25				17 40					17 55						
Ystrad Mynach 3	d		17 13					17 28				17 43					17 58						
Llanbradach	d		17 18					17 33				17 48					18 03						
Aber	d		17 22					17 37				17 52					18 07						
Caerphilly 3	d		17 25					17 40				17 55					18 10						
Lisvane & Thornhill	d		17 29					17 44				17 59					18 14						
Llanishen	d		17 31					17 46				18 01					18 16						
Heath High Level	d		17 34					17 49				18 04					18 19						
Coryton	d								17 45										18 15				
Whitchurch (Cardiff)	d								17 46										18 16				
Rhiwbina	d								17 48										18 18				
Birchgrove	d								17 50										18 20				
Ty Glas	d								17 51										18 21				
Heath Low Level	d								17 54										18 24				
Cardiff Queen Street 3	a		17 39	17 44			17 49	17 54	17 59		18 04	18 09		18 14		18 19	18 24		18 29	18 34		18 44	
	d	17 36	17 41	17 46		17 48	17 51	17 56	18 01	18 00	18 06	18 11	18 12	18 16		18 21	18 26	18 24	18 31	18 36	18 36	18 46	
Cardiff Bay	a	17 40				17 52				18 04			18 16					18 28			18 40		
Cardiff Central 7	a		17 44	17 53	17 50		17 54	17 59	18 04		18 09	18 14		18 23	18 20	18 24	18 29		18 34	18 39		18 53	18 50
	d		17 46				17 55	18 01			18 10	18 16				18 25	18 31			18 41			
Grangetown	d		17 50				17 59	18 05			18 14	18 20				18 29	18 35			18 45			
Dingle Road	d		17 56					18 11				18 26					18 41						
Penarth	a		18 03					18 17				18 32					18 47						
Cogan	d						18 03				18 18					18 33				18 48			
Eastbrook	d						18 05				18 20					18 35				18 51			
Dinas Powys	d						18 07				18 22					18 37				18 53			
Cadoxton	d						18 12				18 27					18 42				18 57			
Barry Docks	d						18 15				18 30					18 45				19 00			
Barry 3	d						18 19				18 34					18 49				19 05			
Barry Island	a						18 26				18 41					18 56							
Rhoose Cardiff Int Airport ✈	d																			19 12			
Llantwit Major	d																			19 22			
Bridgend	a																			19 41			

When events are being held at the Millenium Stadium, services are subject to alteration. Please check times before travelling.

Table 130

Mondays to Fridays from 12 September

Treherbert, Aberdare, Merthyr, Pontypridd, Rhymney and Coryton - Cardiff, Penarth, Barry, Barry Island and Bridgend

Station		AW	AW	AW	AW	AW	AW	AW	AW	AW	AW	AW	AW	AW	AW	AW	AW	AW	AW	AW	AW	AW	AW
Treherbert	d								18 17								18 47						
Ynyswen	d								18 19								18 49						
Treorchy	d								18 21								18 51						
Ton Pentre	d								18 23								18 53						
Ystrad Rhondda	a								18 26								18 56						
	d								18 28								18 58						
Llwynypia	d								18 30								19 00						
Tonypandy	d								18 33								19 03						
Dinas Rhondda	d								18 35								19 05						
Porth	a								18 38								19 08						
	d								18 39								19 09						
Trehafod	d								18 42								19 12						
Merthyr Tydfil	d						18 08								18 38							19 08	
Pentre-bach	d						18 12								18 42							19 12	
Troed Y Rhiw	d						18 15								18 45							19 15	
Merthyr Vale	a						18 18								18 48							19 18	
	d						18 20								18 50							19 20	
Quakers Yard	d						18 25								18 55							19 25	
Aberdare 3	d		17 51								18 21								18 51				
Cwmbach	d		17 54								18 24								18 54				
Fernhill	d		17 58								18 28								18 58				
Mountain Ash	a		18 01								18 31								19 01				
	d		18 04								18 34								19 04				
Penrhiwceiber	d		18 08								18 38								19 08				
Abercynon	d		18 14				18 29				18 44				18 59				19 14			19 29	
Pontypridd 3	a		18 23				18 37		18 47		18 53				19 07		19 17		19 23			19 37	
	d		18 24				18 39		18 48		18 54				19 09		19 18		19 24			19 39	
Trefforest	d		18 27				18 42		18 51		18 57				19 12		19 21		19 27			19 42	
Trefforest Estate	d						18 46								19 16							19 46	
Taffs Well 3	d		18 34				18 50		18 58		19 04				19 20		19 28		19 34			19 50	
Radyr 3	a		18 37				18 53		19 01		19 07				19 23		19 31		19 37			19 53	
	d		18 37				18 53		19 01	19 04	19 07				19 23		19 31		19 37			19 53	
Danescourt	d									19 08													
Fairwater	d									19 10													
Waun-gron Park	d									19 12													
Ninian Park	d									19 15													
Llandaf	d		18 40				18 56		19 04		19 10				19 26		19 34		19 40			19 56	
Cathays	d		18 45				19 01		19 09		19 15				19 31		19 39		19 45			20 01	
Rhymney 3	d																						
Pontlottyn	d																						
Tir-phil	d																						
Brithdir	d																						
Bargoed	a																						
	d			18 17								18 48											
Gilfach Fargoed	d			18 19								18 50											
Pengam	d			18 22								18 53											
Hengoed	d			18 25								18 56											
Ystrad Mynach 3	d			18 28								18 59											
Llanbradach	d			18 33								19 04											
Aber	d			18 37								19 08											
Caerphilly 3	d			18 40								19 11								19 40			
Lisvane & Thornhill	d			18 44								19 15								19 44			
Llanishen	d			18 46								19 17								19 46			
Heath High Level	d			18 49								19 20								19 49			
Coryton	d				18 45									19 15									
Whitchurch (Cardiff)	d				18 46									19 16									
Rhiwbina	d				18 48									19 18									
Birchgrove	d				18 50									19 20									
Ty Glas	d				18 51									19 21									
Heath Low Level	d				18 54									19 24									
Cardiff Queen Street 3	a		18 49	18 54	18 59		19 04		19 14		19 19	19 24		19 29	19 35		19 42		19 49	19 54		20 04	
	d	18 48	18 51	18 56	19 01	19 00	19 06	19 12	19 16		19 21	19 26	19 24	19 31	19 36	19 36	19 46	19 48	19 51	19 56	20 00	20 06	20 12
Cardiff Bay	a	18 52				19 04		19 16					19 28			19 40		19 52			20 04		20 16
Cardiff Central 7	a		18 54	18 59	19 07		19 10		19 23	19 22	19 24	19 29		19 34	19 40		19 53		19 57	19 59		20 10	
	d		18 55	19 01							19 25	19 31			19 41					20 06		20 10	
Grangetown	d		18 59	19 05							19 29	19 35			19 45					20 10		20 14	
Dingle Road	d			19 11								19 41								20 14			
Penarth	a			19 17								19 47								20 20			
Cogan	d		19 03								19 33				19 48							20 18	
Eastbrook	d		19 05								19 35				19 51							20 20	
Dinas Powys	d		19 07								19 37				19 53							20 22	
Cadoxton	d		19 12								19 42				19 57							20 27	
Barry Docks	d		19 15								19 45				20 00							20 30	
Barry 3	d		19 19								19 49				20 05							20 34	
Barry Island	a		19 26								19 56											20 41	
Rhoose Cardiff Int Airport ✈	d														20 12								
Llantwit Major	d														20 22								
Bridgend	a														20 41								

When events are being held at the Millenium Stadium, services are subject to alteration. Please check times before travelling.

Table 130

Mondays to Fridays
from 12 September

Treherbert, Aberdare, Merthyr, Pontypridd, Rhymney and Coryton - Cardiff, Penarth, Barry, Barry Island and Bridgend

Station		AW		AW	AW	AW	AW	AW	AW	AW	AW		AW	AW	AW	AW	AW	AW	AW	AW	AW		AW	AW
Treherbert	d	19 17									19 47							20 17							
Ynyswen	d	19 19									19 49							20 19							
Treorchy	d	19 21									19 51							20 21							
Ton Pentre	d	19 23									19 53							20 23							
Ystrad Rhondda	a	19 26									19 56							20 26							
	d	19 28									19 58							20 28							
Llwynypia	d	19 30									20 00							20 30							
Tonypandy	d	19 33									20 03							20 33							
Dinas Rhondda	d	19 35									20 05							20 35							
Porth	a	19 38									20 08							20 38							
	d	19 39									20 09							20 39							
Trehafod	d	19 42									20 12							20 42							
Merthyr Tydfil	d							19 38																	20 38
Pentre-bach	d							19 42																	20 42
Troed Y Rhiw	d							19 45																	20 45
Merthyr Vale	a							19 48																	20 48
	d							19 50																	20 50
Quakers Yard	d							19 55																	20 55
Aberdare [3]	d													19 51						20 21					
Cwmbach	d													19 54						20 24					
Fernhill	d													19 58						20 28					
Mountain Ash	a													20 01						20 31					
	d													20 04						20 34					
Penrhiwceiber	d													20 08						20 38					
Abercynon	d				19 43			19 59						20 14						20 44					20 59
Pontypridd [3]	a	19 47			19 53			20 07			20 17			20 23				20 47		20 53					21 07
	d	19 48			19 54			20 09			20 18			20 24				20 48		20 54					21 09
Trefforest	d	19 51			19 57			20 12			20 21			20 27				20 51		20 57					21 12
Trefforest Estate	d							20 16																	21 16
Taffs Well [3]	d	19 58			20 04			20 20			20 28			20 34				20 58		21 04					21 20
Radyr [3]	a	20 01			20 07			20 23			20 31			20 37				21 01		21 07					21 23
	d	20 01		20 04	20 07			20 23			20 31			20 37				21 01	21 04	21 07					21 23
Danescourt	d			20 08															21 08						
Fairwater	d			20 10															21 10						
Waun-gron Park	d			20 12															21 12						
Ninian Park	d			20 15															21 15						
Llandaf	d	20 04			20 10			20 26			20 34			20 40				21 04		21 10					21 26
Cathays	d	20 09			20 15			20 31			20 39			20 45				21 09		21 15					21 31
Rhymney [3]	d									19 45															
Pontlottyn	d									19 48															
Tir-phil	d									19 52															
Brithdir	d									19 55															
Bargoed	a									19 58															
	d									19 59															
Gilfach Fargoed	d									20 01															
Pengam	d									20 04															
Hengoed	d									20 07															
Ystrad Mynach [3]	d									20 10															
Llanbradach	d									20 15															
Aber	d									20 19															
Caerphilly [3]	d									20 22					20 40										
Lisvane & Thornhill	d									20 26					20 44										
Llanishen	d									20 28					20 46										
Heath High Level	d									20 31					20 49										
Coryton	d						20 15																	21 15	
Whitchurch (Cardiff)	d						20 16																	21 16	
Rhiwbina	d						20 18																	21 18	
Birchgrove	d						20 20																	21 20	
Ty Glas	d						20 21																	21 21	
Heath Low Level	d						20 24																	21 24	
Cardiff Queen Street [3]	a	20 14			20 19		20 29	20 34		20 39	20 44			20 49	20 54			21 14		21 19				21 29	21 34
	d	20 16			20 21	20 24	20 31	20 36	20 36	20 41	20 46	20 48		20 51	20 56	21 00	21 12	21 16		21 21	21 24			21 31	21 36
Cardiff Bay	a					20 28			20 40			20 52				21 04	21 16				21 28				
Cardiff Central [7]	a	20 21		20 22	20 24		20 34	20 39		20 48	20 53			20 53	20 59			21 22	21 25	21 24				21 34	21 39
	d				20 31			20 41						21 02	21 10							21 31			21 41
Grangetown	d				20 37			20 45						21 06	21 14							21 35			21 45
Dingle Road	d				20 41									21 10								21 41			
Penarth	a				20 47									21 20								21 47			
Cogan	d							20 48							21 17										21 48
Eastbrook	d							20 51							21 20										21 51
Dinas Powys	d							20 53							21 22										21 53
Cadoxton	d							20 57							21 26										21 57
Barry Docks	d							21 00							21 29										22 00
Barry [3]	d							21 05							21 34										22 05
Barry Island	a														21 41										
Rhoose Cardiff Int Airport ✈	d							21 12																	22 12
Llantwit Major	d							21 22																	22 22
Bridgend	a							21 43																	22 41

When events are being held at the Millenium Stadium, services are subject to alteration. Please check times before travelling.

Table 130

Mondays to Fridays
from 12 September

Treherbert, Aberdare, Merthyr, Pontypridd, Rhymney and Coryton - Cardiff, Penarth, Barry, Barry Island and Bridgend

Station		AW	AW	AW	AW	AW	AW	AW	AW	AW	AW	AW	AW	AW	AW	AW	AW	AW	AW	AW	AW	AW	AW	AW	AW
Treherbert	d								21 17																
Ynyswen	d								21 19																
Treorchy	d								21 21																
Ton Pentre	d								21 23																
Ystrad Rhondda	a								21 26																
	d								21 28																
Llwynypia	d								21 30																
Tonypandy	d								21 33																
Dinas Rhondda	d								21 35																
Porth	a								21 38																
	d								21 39																
Trehafod	d								21 42																
Merthyr Tydfil	d												21 38									22 38			
Pentre-bach	d												21 42									22 42			
Troed Y Rhiw	d												21 45									22 45			
Merthyr Vale	a												21 48									22 48			
	d												21 50									22 50			
Quakers Yard	d												21 55									22 55			
Aberdare [3]	d				20 51											21 51							22 51		
Cwmbach	d				20 54											21 54							22 54		
Fernhill	d				20 58											21 58							22 58		
Mountain Ash	a				21 01											22 01							23 01		
	d				21 04											22 04							23 04		
Penrhiwceiber	d				21 08											22 08							23 08		
Abercynon	d				21 14								21 59			22 14						22 59	23 14		
Pontypridd [3]	a				21 23				21 47				22 07			22 22						23 07	23 22		
	d				21 24				21 48				22 09			22 29						23 09			
Trefforest	d				21 27				21 51				22 12			22 32						23 12			
Trefforest Estate	d												22 16									23 16			
Taffs Well [3]	d				21 34				21 58				22 20			22 39						23 20			
Radyr [3]	a				21 37				22 01				22 23			22 42						23 23			
	d				21 37				22 01	22 04			22 23			22 42				23 10		23 23			
Danescourt	d									22 08															
Fairwater	d									22 10															
Waun-gron Park	d									22 12															
Ninian Park	d									22 15															
Llandaf	d				21 40				22 04				22 26			22 45				23 12		23 26			
Cathays	d				21 45				22 09				22 31			22 50				23 16		23 31			
Rhymney [3]	d		20 48								21 33														
Pontlottyn	d		20 51								21 36														
Tir-phil	d		20 55								21 40														
Brithdir	d		20 58								21 43														
Bargoed	a		21 01								21 46														
	d		21 02								21 47														
Gilfach Fargoed	d		21 04								21 49														
Pengam	d		21 07								21 52														
Hengoed	d		21 10								21 55														
Ystrad Mynach [3]	d		21 13								21 58														
Llanbradach	d		21 18								22 03														
Aber	d		21 22								22 07														
Caerphilly [3]	d		21 25			21 45					22 10														
Lisvane & Thornhill	d		21 29			21 50					22 14														
Llanishen	d		21 31			21 52					22 16														
Heath High Level	d		21 34			21 54					22 19														
Coryton	d																22 45								
Whitchurch (Cardiff)	d																22 46								
Rhiwbina	d																22 48								
Birchgrove	d																22 50								
Ty Glas	d																22 51								
Heath Low Level	d																22 54								
Cardiff Queen Street [3]	a		21 42		21 49	22 00			22 14		22 24		22 34			22 54	22 59			23 19		23 34			
	d	21 36	21 44	21 48	21 51	22 01	22 00	22 12	22 16		22 26	22 24	22 36	22 36	22 48	22 55	23 01	23 00	23 12	23 20	23 24	23 36		23 36	23 48
Cardiff Bay	a	21 40		21 52			22 04	22 16				22 28		22 40	22 52			23 04	23 16		23 28			23 40	23 52
Cardiff Central [7]	a		21 51		21 54	22 04			22 22	22 20	22 29		22 39			23 01	23 07			23 25		23 43			
	d				21 56	22 10					22 31		22 41			23 12				23 30					
Grangetown	d				22 00	22 14					22 35		22 45			23 16				23 34					
Dingle Road	d				22 04						22 41					23 20									
Penarth	a				22 10						22 49					23 26									
Cogan	d					22 18							22 48							23 37					
Eastbrook	d					22 20							22 51							23 40					
Dinas Powys	d					22 22							22 53							23 42					
Cadoxton	d					22 27							22 57							23 46					
Barry Docks	d					22 30							23 00							23 49					
Barry [3]	d					22 34							23 05							23 54					
Barry Island	a					22 41														00 01					
Rhoose Cardiff Int Airport ✈	d												23 12												
Llantwit Major	d												23 22												
Bridgend	a												23 41												

When events are being held at the Millenium Stadium, services are subject to alteration. Please check times before travelling.

Table 130

Saturdays
until 10 September

Treherbert, Aberdare, Merthyr, Pontypridd, Rhymney and Coryton - Cardiff, Penarth, Barry, Barry Island and Bridgend

		AW	AW	AW	AW	AW	AW	AW	AW	AW	AW	AW	AW	AW	AW	AW	AW	AW	AW	AW	AW	AW	AW
Treherbert	d											05 47							06 17				
Ynyswen	d											05 49							06 19				
Treorchy	d											05 51							06 21				
Ton Pentre	d											05 53							06 23				
Ystrad Rhondda	a											05 56							06 26				
	d											05 58							06 28				
Llwynypia	d											06 00							06 30				
Tonypandy	d											06 03							06 33				
Dinas Rhondda	d											06 05							06 35				
Porth	a											06 08							06 38				
	d											06 09							06 39				
Trehafod	d											06 12							06 42				
Merthyr Tydfil	d																						
Pentre-bach	d																						
Troed Y Rhiw	d																						
Merthyr Vale	a																						
	d																						
Quakers Yard	d																						
Aberdare 3	d																					06 22	
Cwmbach	d																					06 25	
Fernhill	d																					06 28	
Mountain Ash	a																					06 31	
	d																					06 34	
Penrhiwceiber	d																					06 37	
Abercynon	d																					06 43	
Pontypridd 3	a											06 17							06 47			06 53	
	d					05 24						06 18							06 48			06 54	
Trefforest	d					05 27						06 21							06 51			06 57	
Trefforest Estate	d					05 31																	
Taffs Well 3	d					05 35						06 28							06 58	06 53		07 04	
Radyr 3	a					05 39						06 31							07 01	06 56		07 07	
	d	23p10				05 39						06 31							07 01	07 04		07 07	
Danescourt	d																			07 08			
Fairwater	d																			07 10			
Waun-gron Park	d																			07 12			
Ninian Park	d																			07 15			
Llandaf	d	23p12				05 42						06 34							07 04			07 10	
Cathays	d	23p16				05 46						06 39							07 09			07 15	
Rhymney 3	d																	06 10					06 34
Pontlottyn	d																	06 13					06 37
Tir-phil	d																	06 17					06 41
Brithdir	d																	06 20					06 44
Bargoed	a																	06 23					06 47
	d																	06 27					06 48
Gilfach Fargoed	d																	06 29					
Pengam	d																	06 32					06 52
Hengoed	d																	06 35					06 56
Ystrad Mynach 3	d																	06 38					06 58
Llanbradach	d																	06 43					07 03
Aber	d																	06 47					07 07
Caerphilly 3	d									06 10								06 50					07 10
Lisvane & Thornhill	d									06 14								06 54					07 14
Llanishen	d									06 16								06 56					07 16
Heath High Level	d									06 19								06 59					07 19
Coryton	d																06 45						
Whitchurch (Cardiff)	d																06 46						
Rhiwbina	d																06 48						
Birchgrove	d																06 50						
Ty Glas	d																06 51						
Heath Low Level	d																06 54						
Cardiff Queen Street 3	a	23p20				05 51				06 25		06 42					06 59	07 04	07 12			07 19	07 24
	d	23p20				05 51				06 26	06 36	06 43	06 48		07 00		07 01	07 06	07 13		07 12	07 21	07 26
Cardiff Bay	a										06 40		06 52		07 04						07 16		
Cardiff Central 7	a	23p25				05 54				06 29		06 48					07 04	07 09	07 16	07 20		07 24	07 29
	d	23p30	05 20	05 41	05 46	05 55	06 16	06 25	06 36	06 41				06 55		07 01		07 10	07 16			07 25	07 31
Grangetown	d	23p34	05 24	05 45	05 50	05 59	06 20	06 29	06 40	06 45				06 59		07 05		07 14	07 20			07 29	07 35
Dingle Road	d				05 54		06 24		06 44							07 11			07 26				07 41
Penarth	a				05 59		06 29		06 49							07 16			07 32				07 46
Cogan	d	23p37	05 28	05 48		06 03		06 33		06 48				07 03				07 18				07 33	
Eastbrook	d	23p40	05 30	05 51		06 05		06 35		06 51				07 05				07 20				07 35	
Dinas Powys	d	23p42	05 32	05 53		06 07		06 37		06 53				07 07				07 22				07 37	
Cadoxton	d	23p46	05 37	05 57		06 12		06 42		06 57				07 12				07 27				07 42	
Barry Docks	d	23p49	05 40	06 00		06 15		06 45		07 00				07 15				07 30				07 45	
Barry 3	d	23p54	05 44	06 05		06 19		06 49		07 05				07 19				07 34				07 49	
Barry Island	a	00 01	05 50			06 25		06 55						07 25				07 40				07 55	
Rhoose Cardiff Int Airport ✈	d			06 12						07 12													
Llantwit Major	d			06 22						07 22													
Bridgend	a			06 40						07 40													

When events are being held at the Millenium Stadium, services are subject to alteration. Please check times before travelling.

Table 130

Saturdays
until 10 September

Treherbert, Aberdare, Merthyr, Pontypridd, Rhymney and Coryton - Cardiff, Penarth, Barry, Barry Island and Bridgend

		AW	AW	AW	AW	AW	AW	AW	AW	AW	AW	AW	AW	AW	AW	AW	AW	AW	AW	AW	AW	AW	AW
Treherbert	d						06 47										07 17						
Ynyswen	d						06 49										07 19						
Treorchy	d						06 51										07 21						
Ton Pentre	d						06 53										07 23						
Ystrad Rhondda	a						06 56										07 26						
	d						06 58										07 28						
Llwynypia	d						07 00										07 30						
Tonypandy	d						07 03										07 33						
Dinas Rhondda	d						07 05										07 35						
Porth	a						07 08										07 38						
	d						07 09										07 39						
Trehafod	d						07 12										07 42						
Merthyr Tydfil	d			06 38										07 08									07 38
Pentre-bach	d			06 42										07 12									07 42
Troed Y Rhiw	d			06 45										07 15									07 45
Merthyr Vale	a			06 48										07 18									07 48
	d			06 50										07 20									07 50
Quakers Yard	d			06 55										07 25									07 55
Aberdare 3	d									06 52									07 22				
Cwmbach	d									06 55									07 25				
Fernhill	d									06 58									07 28				
Mountain Ash	a									07 01									07 31				
	d									07 04									07 34				
Penrhiwceiber	d									07 07									07 37				
Abercynon	d			06 59						07 13				07 29					07 43				07 59
Pontypridd 3	a			07 07			07 17			07 23				07 37			07 47		07 53				08 07
	d			07 09			07 18			07 24				07 39			07 48		07 54				08 09
Trefforest	d			07 12			07 21			07 27				07 42			07 51		07 57				08 12
Trefforest Estate	d			07 16										07 46									08 16
Taffs Well 3	d			07 20			07 28			07 34				07 50			07 58		08 04				08 20
Radyr 3	a			07 23			07 31			07 37				07 53			08 01		08 07				08 23
	d			07 23			07 31	07 34		07 37				07 53			08 01	08 04	08 07				08 23
Danescourt	d							07 38										08 08					
Fairwater	d							07 40										08 10					
Waun-gron Park	d							07 42										08 12					
Ninian Park	d							07 45										08 15					
Llandaf	d			07 26			07 34			07 40				07 56			08 04		08 10				08 26
Cathays	d			07 31			07 39			07 45				08 01			08 09		08 15				08 31
Rhymney 3	d										07 02									07 24			
Pontlottyn	d										07 05									07 27			
Tir-phil	d										07 09									07 31			
Brithdir	d										07 12									07 34			
Bargoed	a										07 15									07 37			
	d					07 02					07 17				07 32					07 45			
Gilfach Fargoed	d					07 04					07 19									07 47			
Pengam	d					07 07					07 22				07 37					07 50			
Hengoed	d					07 10					07 25				07 40					07 54			
Ystrad Mynach 3	d					07 13					07 28				07 43					07 57			
Llanbradach	d					07 18					07 33				07 48					08 02			
Aber	d					07 22					07 37				07 52					08 07			
Caerphilly 3	d					07 25					07 40				07 55					08 10			
Lisvane & Thornhill	d					07 29					07 44				07 59					08 14			
Llanishen	d					07 31					07 46				08 01					08 16			
Heath High Level	d					07 34					07 49				08 04					08 19			
Coryton	d		07 15									07 45										08 15	
Whitchurch (Cardiff)	d		07 16									07 46										08 16	
Rhiwbina	d		07 18									07 48										08 18	
Birchgrove	d		07 20									07 50										08 20	
Ty Glas	d		07 21									07 51										08 21	
Heath Low Level	d		07 24									07 54										08 24	
Cardiff Queen Street 3	a		07 29	07 34		07 39	07 44			07 49	07 54	07 59		08 04	08 09		08 14		08 19	08 24		08 29	08 34
	d	07 24	07 31	07 36	07 36	07 41	07 46		07 48	07 51	07 56	08 01	08 00	08 06	08 11	08 12	08 16		08 21	08 26	08 24	08 31	08 36
Cardiff Bay	a	07 28			07 40				07 52				08 04			08 16					08 28		
Cardiff Central 7	a		07 34	07 39		07 44	07 52	07 50		07 54	07 59	08 04		08 09	08 14		08 22	08 20	08 24	08 29		08 34	08 39
	d			07 41		07 46				07 55	08 01			08 10	08 16				08 25	08 31			08 41
Grangetown	d			07 45		07 50				07 59	08 05			08 14	08 20				08 29	08 35			08 45
Dingle Road	d					07 56					08 11				08 26					08 41			
Penarth	a					08 01					08 16				08 31					08 46			
Cogan	d			07 48						08 03				08 18					08 33				08 48
Eastbrook	d			07 51						08 05				08 20					08 35				08 51
Dinas Powys	d			07 53						08 07				08 22					08 37				08 53
Cadoxton	d			07 57						08 12				08 27					08 42				08 57
Barry Docks	d			08 00						08 15				08 30					08 45				09 00
Barry 3	d			08 05						08 19				08 34					08 49				09 05
Barry Island	a									08 25				08 40					08 55				
Rhoose Cardiff Int Airport ✈	d			08 12																			09 12
Llantwit Major	d			08 22																			09 22
Bridgend	a			08 40																			09 40

When events are being held at the Millenium Stadium, services are subject to alteration. Please check times before travelling.

Table 130

Saturdays
until 10 September

Treherbert, Aberdare, Merthyr, Pontypridd, Rhymney and Coryton - Cardiff, Penarth, Barry, Barry Island and Bridgend

		AW		AW	AW	AW	AW	AW	AW	AW	AW	AW		AW	AW	AW	AW	AW	AW	AW	AW	AW		AW	AW
Treherbert	d				07 45											08 17									
Ynyswen	d				07 47											08 19									
Treorchy	d				07 49											08 21									
Ton Pentre	d				07 51											08 23									
Ystrad Rhondda	a				07 54											08 26									
	d				07 58											08 28									
Llwynypia	d				08 00											08 30									
Tonypandy	d				08 03											08 33									
Dinas Rhondda	d				08 05											08 35									
Porth	a				08 08											08 38									
	d				08 09											08 39									
Trehafod	d				08 12											08 42									
Merthyr Tydfil	d											08 08										08 38			
Pentre-bach	d											08 12										08 42			
Troed Y Rhiw	d											08 15										08 45			
Merthyr Vale	a											08 18										08 48			
	d											08 20										08 50			
Quakers Yard	d											08 25										08 55			
Aberdare [3]	d							07 52										08 22							
Cwmbach	d							07 55										08 25							
Fernhill	d							07 58										08 28							
Mountain Ash	a							08 01										08 31							
	d							08 04										08 34							
Penrhiwceiber	d							08 07										08 37							
Abercynon	d							08 13				08 29						08 43				08 59			
Pontypridd [3]	a				08 17			08 23				08 37				08 47		08 53				09 07			
	d				08 18			08 24				08 39				08 48		08 54				09 09			
Trefforest	d				08 21			08 27				08 42				08 51		08 57				09 12			
Trefforest Estate	d											08 46										09 16			
Taffs Well [3]	d				08 28			08 34				08 50				08 58		09 04				09 20			
Radyr [3]	a				08 31			08 37				08 53				09 01		09 07				09 23			
	d				08 31	08 34		08 37				08 53				09 01	09 04	09 07				09 23			
Danescourt	d					08 38											09 08								
Fairwater	d					08 40											09 10								
Waun-gron Park	d					08 42											09 12								
Ninian Park	d					08 45											09 15								
Llandaf	d				08 34			08 40				08 56				09 04		09 10				09 26			
Cathays	d				08 39			08 45				09 01				09 09		09 15				09 31			
Rhymney [3]	d			07 44															08 30						
Pontlottyn	d			07 47															08 33						
Tir-phil	d			07 51															08 37						
Brithdir	d			07 54															08 40						
Bargoed	a			08 00															08 44						
	d			08 02					08 17					08 32					08 47						09 02
Gilfach Fargoed	d								08 19																
Pengam	d			08 07					08 22					08 37					08 52						09 07
Hengoed	d			08 10					08 25					08 40					08 55						09 10
Ystrad Mynach [3]	d			08 13					08 28					08 43					08 58						09 13
Llanbradach	d			08 18					08 33					08 48					09 03						09 18
Aber	d			08 22					08 37					08 52					09 07						09 22
Caerphilly [3]	d			08 25					08 40					08 55					09 10						09 25
Lisvane & Thornhill	d			08 29					08 44					08 59					09 14						09 29
Llanishen	d			08 31					08 46					09 01					09 16						09 31
Heath High Level	d			08 34					08 49					09 04					09 19						09 34
Coryton	d									08 45											09 15				
Whitchurch (Cardiff)	d									08 46											09 16				
Rhiwbina	d									08 48											09 18				
Birchgrove	d									08 50											09 20				
Ty Glas	d									08 51											09 21				
Heath Low Level	d									08 54											09 24				
Cardiff Queen Street [3]	a			08 39	08 44			08 49	08 54	08 59		09 04		09 09		09 14		09 19	09 24		09 29	09 34			09 39
	d	08 36		08 41	08 46		08 48	08 51	08 56	09 01	09 00	09 06		09 11	09 12	09 16		09 21	09 26	09 24	09 31	09 36		09 36	09 41
Cardiff Bay	a	08 40					08 52				09 04				09 16					09 28				09 40	
Cardiff Central [7]	a			08 47	08 52	08 50		08 54	08 59	09 04		09 09		09 14		09 22	09 20	09 24	09 29		09 34	09 39			09 44
	d							08 55	09 01			09 10		09 16				09 25	09 31			09 41			09 46
Grangetown	d							08 59	09 05			09 14		09 20				09 29	09 35			09 45			09 50
Dingle Road	d								09 11					09 26					09 41						09 56
Penarth	a								09 16					09 31					09 46						10 02
Cogan	d							09 03				09 18						09 33				09 48			
Eastbrook	d							09 05				09 20						09 35				09 51			
Dinas Powys	d							09 07				09 22						09 37				09 53			
Cadoxton	d							09 12				09 27						09 42				09 57			
Barry Docks	d							09 15				09 30						09 45				10 00			
Barry [3]	d							09 19				09 34						09 49				10 05			
Barry Island	a							09 25				09 40						09 55							
Rhoose Cardiff Int Airport ✈	d																					10 12			
Llantwit Major	d																					10 22			
Bridgend	a																					10 40			

When events are being held at the Millenium Stadium, services are subject to alteration. Please check times before travelling.

Table 130

Saturdays
until 10 September

Treherbert, Aberdare, Merthyr, Pontypridd, Rhymney and Coryton - Cardiff, Penarth, Barry, Barry Island and Bridgend

		AW	AW	AW	AW	AW	AW	AW		AW	AW	AW	AW	AW	AW	AW	AW	AW		AW	AW	AW	AW	AW	AW
Treherbert	d	08 47											09 17										09 47		
Ynyswen	d	08 49											09 19										09 49		
Treorchy	d	08 51											09 21										09 51		
Ton Pentre	d	08 53											09 23										09 53		
Ystrad Rhondda	a	08 56											09 26										09 56		
	d	08 58											09 28										09 58		
Llwynypia	d	09 00											09 30										10 00		
Tonypandy	d	09 03											09 33										10 03		
Dinas Rhondda	d	09 05											09 35										10 05		
Porth	a	09 08											09 38										10 08		
	d	09 09											09 39										10 09		
Trehafod	d	09 12											09 42										10 12		
Merthyr Tydfil	d									09 08										09 38					
Pentre-bach	d									09 12										09 42					
Troed Y Rhiw	d									09 15										09 45					
Merthyr Vale	a									09 18										09 48					
	d									09 20										09 50					
Quakers Yard	d									09 25										09 55					
Aberdare [3]	d				08 52										09 22										
Cwmbach	d				08 55										09 25										
Fernhill	d				08 58										09 28										
Mountain Ash	a				09 01										09 31										
	d				09 04										09 34										
Penrhiwceiber	d				09 07										09 37										
Abercynon	d				09 13					09 29					09 43					09 59					
Pontypridd [3]	a	09 17			09 23					09 37			09 47		09 53					10 07			10 17		
	d	09 18			09 24					09 39			09 48		09 54					10 09			10 18		
Trefforest	d	09 21			09 27					09 42			09 51		09 57					10 12			10 21		
Trefforest Estate	d									09 46										10 16					
Taffs Well [3]	d	09 28			09 34					09 50			09 58		10 04					10 20			10 28		
Radyr [3]	a	09 31			09 37					09 53			10 01		10 07					10 23			10 31		
	d	09 31	09 34		09 37					09 53			10 01	10 04	10 07					10 23			10 31	10 34	
Danescourt	d		09 38											10 08										10 38	
Fairwater	d		09 40											10 10										10 40	
Waun-gron Park	d		09 42											10 12										10 42	
Ninian Park	d		09 45											10 15										10 45	
Llandaf	d	09 34			09 40					09 56			10 04		10 10					10 26			10 34		
Cathays	d	09 39			09 45					10 01			10 09		10 15					10 31			10 39		
Rhymney [3]	d															09 29									
Pontlottyn	d															09 32									
Tir-phil	d															09 36									
Brithdir	d															09 39									
Bargoed	a															09 42									
	d					09 17					09 32					09 47						10 02			
Gilfach Fargoed	d					09 19																			
Pengam	d					09 22					09 37					09 52						10 07			
Hengoed	d					09 25					09 40					09 55						10 10			
Ystrad Mynach [3]	d					09 28					09 43					09 58						10 13			
Llanbradach	d					09 33					09 48					10 03						10 18			
Aber	d					09 37					09 52					10 07						10 22			
Caerphilly [3]	d					09 40					09 55					10 10						10 25			
Lisvane & Thornhill	d					09 44					09 59					10 14						10 29			
Llanishen	d					09 46					10 01					10 16						10 31			
Heath High Level	d					09 49					10 04					10 19						10 34			
Coryton	d						09 45											10 15							
Whitchurch (Cardiff)	d						09 46											10 16							
Rhiwbina	d						09 48											10 18							
Birchgrove	d						09 50											10 20							
Ty Glas	d						09 51											10 21							
Heath Low Level	d						09 54											10 24							
Cardiff Queen Street [3]	a	09 44			09 49	09 54	09 59			10 04	10 09		10 14		10 19	10 24		10 29		10 34		10 39	10 44		
	d	09 46		09 48	09 51	09 56	10 01	10 00		10 06	10 11	10 12	10 16		10 21	10 26	10 24	10 31		10 36	10 36	10 41	10 46		10 48
Cardiff Bay	a			09 52				10 04				10 16					10 28				10 40				10 52
Cardiff Central [7]	a	09 52	09 50		09 54	09 59	10 04			10 09	10 14		10 22	10 20	10 24	10 29		10 34		10 39		10 44	10 52	10 50	
	d				09 55	10 01				10 10	10 16				10 25	10 31				10 41		10 46			
Grangetown	d				09 59	10 05				10 14	10 20				10 29	10 35				10 45		10 50			
Dingle Road	d					10 11					10 26					10 41						10 56			
Penarth	a					10 16					10 31					10 46						11 01			
Cogan	d				10 03					10 18					10 33					10 48					
Eastbrook	d				10 05					10 20					10 35					10 51					
Dinas Powys	d				10 07					10 22					10 37					10 53					
Cadoxton	d				10 12					10 27					10 42					10 57					
Barry Docks	d				10 15					10 30					10 45					11 00					
Barry [3]	d				10 19					10 34					10 49					11 05					
Barry Island	a				10 25					10 40					10 55										
Rhoose Cardiff Int Airport ✈	d																			11 12					
Llantwit Major	d																			11 22					
Bridgend	a																			11 40					

When events are being held at the Millenium Stadium, services are subject to alteration. Please check times before travelling.

Table 130

Saturdays
until 10 September

Treherbert, Aberdare, Merthyr, Pontypridd, Rhymney and Coryton - Cardiff, Penarth, Barry, Barry Island and Bridgend

		AW	AW	AW		AW	AW	AW	AW	AW	AW	AW	AW	AW		AW	AW	AW	AW	AW	AW	AW	AW	AW
Treherbert	d													10 17							10 47			
Ynyswen	d													10 19							10 49			
Treorchy	d													10 21							10 51			
Ton Pentre	d													10 23							10 53			
Ystrad Rhondda	a													10 26							10 56			
	d													10 28							10 58			
Llwynypia	d													10 30							11 00			
Tonypandy	d													10 33							11 03			
Dinas Rhondda	d													10 35							11 05			
Porth	a													10 38							11 08			
	d													10 52							11 09			
Trehafod	d													10 55							11 12			
Merthyr Tydfil	d		10 04															10 38						
Pentre-bach	d		10 08															10 42						
Troed Y Rhiw	d		10 11															10 45						
Merthyr Vale	a		10 14															10 48						
	d		10 16															10 50						
Quakers Yard	d		10 22															10 55						
Aberdare 3	d	09 52										10 22												10 52
Cwmbach	d	09 55										10 25												10 55
Fernhill	d	09 58										10 28												10 58
Mountain Ash	a	10 01										10 31												11 01
	d	10 04										10 34												11 04
Penrhiwceiber	d	10 07										10 37												11 07
Abercynon	d	10 13	10 26									10 43						10 59						11 13
Pontypridd 3	a	10 23	10 32									10 53		11 00				11 08			11 17			11 23
	d	10 24						10 39				10 54		11 04				11 09			11 18			11 24
Trefforest	d	10 27						10 42				10 57		11 07				11 12			11 21			11 27
Trefforest Estate	d																	11 16						
Taffs Well 3	d	10 34						10 50				11 04		11 13				11 20			11 28			11 34
Radyr 3	a	10 37						10 53				11 07		11 17				11 23			11 31			11 37
	d	10 37						10 53		11 04		11 07		11 17				11 23			11 31	11 34		11 37
Danescourt	d									11 08												11 38		
Fairwater	d									11 10												11 40		
Waun-gron Park	d									11 12												11 42		
Ninian Park	d									11 15												11 45		
Llandaf	d	10 40						10 56				11 10						11 26			11 34			11 40
Cathays	d	10 45						11 01				11 15						11 31			11 39			11 45
Rhymney 3	d												10 29											
Pontlottyn	d												10 32											
Tir-phil	d												10 36											
Brithdir	d												10 39											
Bargoed	a												10 42											
	d			10 17					10 32				10 47							11 02				
Gilfach Fargoed	d			10 19																				
Pengam	d			10 22					10 37				10 52							11 07				
Hengoed	d			10 25					10 40				10 55							11 10				
Ystrad Mynach 3	d			10 28					10 43				10 58							11 13				
Llanbradach	d			10 33					10 48				11 03							11 18				
Aber	d			10 37					10 52				11 07							11 22				
Caerphilly 3	d			10 40					10 55				11 10							11 25				
Lisvane & Thornhill	d			10 44					10 59				11 14							11 29				
Llanishen	d			10 46					11 01				11 16							11 31				
Heath High Level	d			10 49					11 04				11 19							11 34				
Coryton	d					10 45											11 15							
Whitchurch (Cardiff)	d					10 46											11 16							
Rhiwbina	d					10 48											11 18							
Birchgrove	d					10 50											11 20							
Ty Glas	d					10 51											11 21							
Heath Low Level	d					10 54											11 24							
Cardiff Queen Street 3	a	10 49		10 54		10 59		11 04	11 09			11 19	11 24				11 29	11 34		11 39	11 44			11 49
	d	10 51		10 56		11 01	11 00	11 06	11 11		11 12	11 21	11 26			11 24	11 31	11 36	11 36	11 41	11 46		11 48	11 51
Cardiff Bay	a						11 04				11 16					11 28			11 40				11 52	
Cardiff Central 7	a	10 54		10 59		11 04		11 09	11 14	11 20		11 24	11 29	11 34			11 34	11 39		11 44	11 52	11 50		11 54
	d	10 55		11 01				11 10	11 16			11 25	11 31					11 41		11 46				11 55
Grangetown	d	10 59		11 05				11 14	11 20			11 29	11 35					11 45		11 50				11 59
Dingle Road	d			11 11					11 26				11 41							11 56				
Penarth	a			11 17					11 31				11 46							12 01				
Cogan	d	11 03						11 18				11 33						11 48						12 03
Eastbrook	d	11 05						11 20				11 35						11 51						12 05
Dinas Powys	d	11 07						11 22				11 37						11 53						12 07
Cadoxton	d	11 12						11 27				11 42						11 57						12 12
Barry Docks	d	11 15						11 30				11 45						12 00						12 15
Barry 3	d	11 19						11 34				11 49						12 05						12 19
Barry Island	a	11 25						11 40				11 55												12 25
Rhoose Cardiff Int Airport ✈	d																	12 12						
Llantwit Major	d																	12 22						
Bridgend	a																	12 40						

When events are being held at the Millenium Stadium, services are subject to alteration. Please check times before travelling.

Table 130

Saturdays
until 10 September

Treherbert, Aberdare, Merthyr, Pontypridd, Rhymney and Coryton - Cardiff, Penarth, Barry, Barry Island and Bridgend

		AW	AW	AW	AW	AW	AW	AW	AW	AW		AW	AW	AW	AW	AW	AW	AW	AW	AW		AW	AW	AW	AW
Treherbert	d							11 17										11 47							
Ynyswen	d							11 19										11 49							
Treorchy	d							11 21										11 51							
Ton Pentre	d							11 23										11 53							
Ystrad Rhondda	a							11 26										11 56							
	d							11 28										11 58							
Llwynypia	d							11 30										12 00							
Tonypandy	d							11 33										12 03							
Dinas Rhondda	d							11 35										12 05							
Porth	a							11 38										12 08							
	d							11 39										12 09							
Trehafod	d							11 42										12 12							
Merthyr Tydfil	d				11 08										11 38										12 08
Pentre-bach	d				11 12										11 42										12 12
Troed Y Rhiw	d				11 15										11 45										12 15
Merthyr Vale	a				11 18										11 48										12 18
	d				11 20										11 50										12 20
Quakers Yard	d				11 25										11 55										12 25
Aberdare 3	d									11 22															
Cwmbach	d									11 25															
Fernhill	d									11 28															
Mountain Ash	a									11 31															
	d									11 34															
Penrhiwceiber	d									11 37															
Abercynon	d				11 29					11 43					11 59										12 29
Pontypridd 3	a				11 37			11 47		11 53					12 07			12 17							12 37
	d				11 39			11 48		11 54					12 09			12 18							12 39
Trefforest	d				11 42			11 51		11 57					12 12			12 21							12 42
Trefforest Estate	d				11 46										12 16										12 46
Taffs Well 3	d				11 50			11 58		12 04					12 20			12 28							12 50
Radyr 3	a				11 53			12 01		12 07					12 23			12 31							12 53
	d				11 53			12 01	12 04	12 07					12 23			12 31	12 34						12 53
Danescourt	d								12 08										12 38						
Fairwater	d								12 10										12 40						
Waun-gron Park	d								12 12										12 42						
Ninian Park	d								12 15										12 45						
Llandaf	d				11 56			12 04		12 10					12 26			12 34							12 56
Cathays	d				12 01			12 09		12 15					12 31			12 39							13 01
Rhymney 3	d											11 29													
Pontlottyn	d											11 32													
Tir-phil	d											11 36													
Brithdir	d											11 39													
Bargoed	a											11 42													
	d	11 17				11 32						11 47					12 02					12 17			
Gilfach Fargoed	d	11 19																				12 19			
Pengam	d	11 22				11 37						11 52					12 07					12 22			
Hengoed	d	11 25				11 40						11 55					12 10					12 25			
Ystrad Mynach 3	d	11 28				11 43						11 58					12 13					12 28			
Llanbradach	d	11 33				11 48						12 03					12 18					12 33			
Aber	d	11 37				11 52						12 07					12 22					12 37			
Caerphilly 3	d	11 40				11 55						12 10					12 25					12 40			
Lisvane & Thornhill	d	11 44				11 59						12 14					12 29					12 44			
Llanishen	d	11 46				12 01						12 16					12 31					12 46			
Heath High Level	d	11 49				12 04						12 19					12 34					12 49			
Coryton	d		11 45											12 15									12 45		
Whitchurch (Cardiff)	d		11 46											12 16									12 46		
Rhiwbina	d		11 48											12 18									12 48		
Birchgrove	d		11 50											12 20									12 50		
Ty Glas	d		11 51											12 21									12 51		
Heath Low Level	d		11 54											12 24									12 54		
Cardiff Queen Street 3	a	11 54	11 59		12 04	12 09		12 14		12 19		12 24		12 29	12 34		12 39	12 44				12 54	12 59		13 04
	d	11 56	12 01	12 00	12 06	12 11	12 12	12 16		12 21		12 26	12 24	12 31	12 36	12 36	12 41	12 46		12 48		12 56	13 01	13 00	13 06
Cardiff Bay	a			12 04			12 16						12 28			12 40				2 52				13 04	
Cardiff Central 7	a	11 59	12 04		12 09	12 14		12 22	12 20	12 24		12 29		12 34	12 39		12 44	12 52	12 50			12 59	13 04		13 09
	d	12 01			12 10	12 16				12 25		12 31			12 41		12 46	12 55				13 01			13 10
Grangetown	d	12 05			12 14	12 20				12 29		12 35			12 45		12 50	12 59				13 05			13 14
Dingle Road	d	12 11				12 26						12 41					12 56					13 11			
Penarth	a	12 16				12 31						12 46					13 01					13 16			
Cogan	d				12 18					12 33					12 48			13 03							13 18
Eastbrook	d				12 20					12 35					12 51			13 05							13 20
Dinas Powys	d				12 22					12 37					12 53			13 07							13 22
Cadoxton	d				12 27					12 42					12 57			13 12							13 27
Barry Docks	d				12 30					12 45					13 00			13 15							13 30
Barry 3	d				12 34					12 49					13 05			13 19							13 34
Barry Island	a				12 40					12 55								13 25							13 40
Rhoose Cardiff Int Airport ✈	d														13 12										
Llantwit Major	d														13 22										
Bridgend	a														13 40										

When events are being held at the Millenium Stadium, services are subject to alteration. Please check times before travelling.

Treherbert, Aberdare, Merthyr, Pontypridd, Rhymney and Coryton - Cardiff, Penarth, Barry, Barry Island and Bridgend

		AW	AW	AW	AW	AW		AW	AW	AW	AW	AW	AW	AW	AW	AW		AW	AW	AW	AW	AW	AW	AW	AW
Treherbert	d			12 17										12 47											13 17
Ynyswen	d			12 19										12 49											13 19
Treorchy	d			12 21										12 51											13 21
Ton Pentre	d			12 23										12 53											13 23
Ystrad Rhondda	a			12 26										12 56											13 26
	d			12 28										12 58											13 28
Llwynypia	d			12 30										13 00											13 30
Tonypandy	d			12 33										13 03											13 33
Dinas Rhondda	d			12 35										13 05											13 35
Porth	a			12 38										13 08											13 38
	d			12 39										13 09											13 39
Trehafod	d			12 42										13 12											13 42
Merthyr Tydfil	d										12 38											13 08			
Pentre-bach	d										12 42											13 12			
Troed Y Rhiw	d										12 45											13 15			
Merthyr Vale	a										12 48											13 18			
	d										12 50											13 20			
Quakers Yard	d										12 55											13 25			
Aberdare ■	d					12 22												12 52							
Cwmbach	d					12 25												12 55							
Fernhill	d					12 28												12 58							
Mountain Ash	a					12 31												13 01							
	d					12 34												13 04							
Penrhiwceiber	d					12 37												13 07							
Abercynon	d					12 43					12 59							13 13				13 29			
Pontypridd ■	a			12 48		12 53					13 07			13 17				13 23				13 37			13 47
	d			12 48		12 54					13 09			13 18				13 24				13 39			13 48
Trefforest	d			12 51		12 57					13 12			13 21				13 27				13 42			13 51
Trefforest Estate	d										13 16											13 46			
Taffs Well ■	d			12 58		13 04					13 20			13 28				13 34				13 50			13 58
Radyr ■	a			13 01		13 07					13 23			13 31				13 37				13 53			14 01
	d			13 01	13 04	13 07					13 23			13 31	13 34			13 37				13 53			14 01
Danescourt	d				13 08										13 38										
Fairwater	d				13 10										13 40										
Waun-gron Park	d				13 12										13 42										
Ninian Park	d				13 15										13 45										
Llandaf	d			13 04		13 10					13 26			13 34				13 40				13 56			14 04
Cathays	d			13 09		13 15					13 31			13 39				13 45				14 01			14 09
Rhymney ■	d							12 29																	
Pontlottyn	d							12 32																	
Tir-phil	d							12 36																	
Brithdir	d							12 39																	
Bargoed	a							12 42																	
	d	12 32						12 47					13 02						13 17				13 32		
Gilfach Fargoed	d																		13 19						
Pengam	d	12 37						12 52					13 07						13 22				13 37		
Hengoed	d	12 40						12 55					13 10						13 25				13 40		
Ystrad Mynach ■	d	12 43						12 58					13 13						13 28				13 43		
Llanbradach	d	12 48						13 03					13 18						13 33				13 48		
Aber	d	12 52						13 07					13 22						13 37				13 52		
Caerphilly ■	d	12 55						13 10					13 25						13 40				13 55		
Lisvane & Thornhill	d	12 59						13 14					13 29						13 44				13 59		
Llanishen	d	13 01						13 16					13 31						13 46				14 01		
Heath High Level	d	13 04						13 19					13 34						13 49				14 04		
Coryton	d									13 15										13 45					
Whitchurch (Cardiff)	d									13 16										13 46					
Rhiwbina	d									13 18										13 48					
Birchgrove	d									13 20										13 50					
Ty Glas	d									13 21										13 51					
Heath Low Level	d									13 24										13 54					
Cardiff Queen Street ■	a	13 09		13 14		13 19		13 24		13 29	13 34		13 39	13 44				13 49	13 54	13 59		14 04	14 09		14 14
	d	13 11	13 12	13 16		13 21		13 26	13 24	13 31	13 36	13 36	13 41	13 46		13 48		13 51	13 56	14 01	14 00	14 06	14 11	14 12	14 16
Cardiff Bay	a		13 16						13 28			13 40				13 52					14 04			14 16	
Cardiff Central ■	a	13 14		13 22	13 20	13 24		13 29		13 34	13 39		13 44	13 52	13 50			13 54	13 59	14 04		14 09	14 14		14 22
	d	13 16				13 25		13 31			13 41		13 46					13 55	14 01			14 10	14 16		
Grangetown	d	13 20				13 29		13 35			13 45		13 50					13 59	14 05			14 14	14 20		
Dingle Road	d	13 26						13 41					13 56						14 11				14 26		
Penarth	a	13 31						13 46					14 01						14 16				14 31		
Cogan	d					13 33					13 48							14 03				14 18			
Eastbrook	d					13 35					13 51							14 05				14 20			
Dinas Powys	d					13 37					13 53							14 07				14 22			
Cadoxton	d					13 42					13 57							14 12				14 27			
Barry Docks	d					13 45					14 00							14 15				14 30			
Barry ■	d					13 49					14 05							14 19				14 34			
Barry Island	a					13 55												14 25				14 40			
Rhoose Cardiff Int Airport ✈	d										14 12														
Llantwit Major	d										14 22														
Bridgend	a										14 40														

When events are being held at the Millenium Stadium, services are subject to alteration. Please check times before travelling.

Treherbert, Aberdare, Merthyr, Pontypridd, Rhymney and Coryton - Cardiff, Penarth, Barry, Barry Island and Bridgend

		AW		AW	AW	AW	AW	AW	AW	AW	AW	AW		AW	AW	AW	AW	AW	AW	AW	AW	AW		AW	AW
Treherbert	d										13 47														
Ynyswen	d										13 49														
Treorchy	d										13 51														
Ton Pentre	d										13 53														
Ystrad Rhondda	a										13 56														
	d										13 58														
Llwynypia	d										14 00														
Tonypandy	d										14 03														
Dinas Rhondda	d										14 05														
Porth	a										14 08														
	d										14 09														
Trehafod	d										14 12														
Merthyr Tydfil	d							13 38											14 08						
Pentre-bach	d							13 42											14 12						
Troed Y Rhiw	d							13 45											14 15						
Merthyr Vale	a							13 48											14 18						
	d							13 50											14 20						
Quakers Yard	d							13 55											14 25						
Aberdare ■	d														13 52									14 22	
Cwmbach	d														13 55									14 25	
Fernhill	d														13 58									14 28	
Mountain Ash	a														14 01									14 31	
	d														14 04									14 34	
Penrhiwceiber	d														14 07									14 37	
Abercynon	d			13 45				13 59							14 13				14 25					14 43	
Pontypridd ■	a			13 53				14 07			14 17				14 23				14 37					14 53	
	d			13 54				14 09			14 18				14 24				14 39					14 54	
Trefforest	d			13 57				14 12			14 21				14 27				14 42					14 57	
Trefforest Estate	d							14 16											14 46						
Taffs Well ■	d			14 04				14 20			14 28				14 34				14 50					15 04	
Radyr ■	a			14 07				14 23			14 31				14 37				14 53					15 07	
	d	14 04		14 07				14 23			14 31	14 34			14 37				14 53		15 04			15 07	
Danescourt	d	14 08										14 38									15 08				
Fairwater	d	14 10										14 40									15 10				
Waun-gron Park	d	14 12										14 42									15 12				
Ninian Park	d	14 15										14 45									15 15				
Llandaf	d			14 10				14 26			14 34				14 40				14 56					15 10	
Cathays	d			14 15				14 31			14 39				14 45				15 01					15 15	
Rhymney ■	d				13 29																				14 29
Pontlottyn	d				13 32																				14 32
Tir-phil	d				13 36																				14 36
Brithdir	d				13 39																				14 39
Bargoed	a				13 42																				14 42
	d				13 47					14 02						14 17				14 32					14 47
Gilfach Fargoed	d															14 19									
Pengam	d				13 52					14 07						14 22				14 37					14 52
Hengoed	d				13 55					14 10						14 25				14 40					14 55
Ystrad Mynach ■	d				13 58					14 13						14 28				14 43					14 58
Llanbradach	d				14 03					14 18						14 33				14 48					15 03
Aber	d				14 07					14 22						14 38				14 52					15 07
Caerphilly ■	d				14 10					14 25						14 40				14 55					15 10
Lisvane & Thornhill	d				14 14					14 29						14 45				14 59					15 14
Llanishen	d				14 16					14 31						14 47				15 01					15 16
Heath High Level	d				14 19					14 34						14 50				15 04					15 19
Coryton	d						14 15										14 45								
Whitchurch (Cardiff)	d						14 16										14 46								
Rhiwbina	d						14 18										14 48								
Birchgrove	d						14 20										14 50								
Ty Glas	d						14 21										14 51								
Heath Low Level	d						14 24										14 54								
Cardiff Queen Street ■	a			14 19	14 24		14 29	14 34		14 39	14 44				14 49	14 55	14 59		15 04	15 09				15 19	15 24
	d			14 21	14 26	14 24	14 31	14 36	14 36	14 41	14 46			14 48	14 51	14 56	15 01	15 00	15 06	15 11		15 12		15 21	15 26
Cardiff Bay	a					14 28			14 40					14 52				15 04				15 16			
Cardiff Central ■	a	14 20		14 24	14 29		14 34	14 39		14 44	14 52	14 50			14 54	14 59	15 04		15 09	15 14	15 20			15 24	15 29
	d			14 25	14 31			14 41		14 46					14 55	15 01			15 10	15 16				15 25	15 31
Grangetown	d			14 29	14 35			14 45		14 50					14 59	15 05			15 14	15 20				15 29	15 35
Dingle Road	d				14 41					14 56						15 12				15 26					15 41
Penarth	a				14 46					15 01						15 17				15 31					15 46
Cogan	d			14 33				14 48							15 03				15 18					15 33	
Eastbrook	d			14 35				14 51							15 05				15 20					15 35	
Dinas Powys	d			14 37				14 53							15 07				15 22					15 37	
Cadoxton	d			14 42				14 57							15 12				15 27					15 42	
Barry Docks	d			14 45				15 00							15 15				15 30					15 45	
Barry ■	d			14 49				15 05							15 19				15 34					15 49	
Barry Island	a			14 55											15 25				15 40					15 55	
Rhoose Cardiff Int Airport ✈	d							15 12																	
Llantwit Major	d							15 22																	
Bridgend	a							15 40																	

When events are being held at the Millenium Stadium, services are subject to alteration. Please check times before travelling.

Table 130

Saturdays
until 10 September

Treherbert, Aberdare, Merthyr, Pontypridd, Rhymney and Coryton - Cardiff, Penarth, Barry, Barry Island and Bridgend

		AW	AW	AW	AW	AW	AW	AW	AW	AW	AW	AW	AW	AW	AW	AW	AW	AW	AW	AW	AW	AW	AW
Treherbert	d	14 17						14 47										15 13					
Ynyswen	d	14 19						14 49										15 15					
Treorchy	d	14 21						14 51										15 21					
Ton Pentre	d	14 23						14 53										15 23					
Ystrad Rhondda	a	14 26						14 56										15 26					
	d	14 28						14 58										15 28					
Llwynypia	d	14 30						15 00										15 30					
Tonypandy	d	14 33						15 03										15 33					
Dinas Rhondda	d	14 35						15 05										15 35					
Porth	a	14 38						15 08										15 38					
	d	14 52						15 09										15 39					
Trehafod	d	14 55						15 12										15 42					
Merthyr Tydfil	d				14 38										15 08								
Pentre-bach	d				14 42										15 12								
Troed Y Rhiw	d				14 45										15 15								
Merthyr Vale	a				14 48										15 18								
	d				14 50										15 20								
Quakers Yard	d				14 55										15 25								
Aberdare	d										14 52									15 22			
Cwmbach	d										14 55									15 25			
Fernhill	d										14 58									15 28			
Mountain Ash	a										15 01									15 31			
	d										15 04									15 34			
Penrhiwceiber	d										15 07									15 37			
Abercynon	d				14 59						15 13				15 29					15 43			
Pontypridd	a	15 00			15 07			15 17			15 23				15 37			15 47		15 53			
	d	15 04			15 09			15 18			15 24				15 39			15 48		15 54			
Trefforest	d	15 07			15 12			15 21			15 27				15 42			15 51		15 57			
Trefforest Estate	d				15 16										15 46								
Taffs Well	d	15 13			15 20			15 28			15 34				15 50			15 58		16 04			
Radyr	a	15 17			15 23			15 31			15 37				15 53			16 01		16 07			
	d	15 17			15 23			15 31	15 34		15 37				15 53			16 01	16 04	16 07			
Danescourt	d								15 38										16 08				
Fairwater	d								15 40										16 10				
Waun-gron Park	d								15 42										16 12				
Ninian Park	d								15 45										16 15				
Llandaf	d				15 26			15 34			15 40				15 56			16 04		16 10			
Cathays	d				15 31			15 39			15 45				16 01			16 09		16 15			
Rhymney	d																				15 29		
Pontlottyn	d																				15 32		
Tir-phil	d																				15 36		
Brithdir	d																				15 39		
Bargoed	a																				15 42		
	d						15 02					15 17				15 32					15 47		
Gilfach Fargoed	d											15 19											
Pengam	d						15 07					15 22				15 37					15 52		
Hengoed	d						15 10					15 25				15 40					15 55		
Ystrad Mynach	d						15 13					15 28				15 43					15 58		
Llanbradach	d						15 18					15 33				15 48					16 03		
Aber	d						15 22					15 37				15 52					16 07		
Caerphilly	d						15 25					15 40				15 55					16 10		
Lisvane & Thornhill	d						15 29					15 44				15 59					16 14		
Llanishen	d						15 31					15 46				16 01					16 16		
Heath High Level	d						15 34					15 49				16 04					16 19		
Coryton	d			15 15									15 45										16 15
Whitchurch (Cardiff)	d			15 16									15 46										16 16
Rhiwbina	d			15 18									15 48										16 18
Birchgrove	d			15 20									15 50										16 20
Ty Glas	d			15 21									15 51										16 21
Heath Low Level	d			15 24									15 54										16 24
Cardiff Queen Street	a			15 29	15 34		15 39	15 44			15 49	15 54	15 59		16 04	16 09		16 14		16 19	16 24		16 29
	d		15 24	15 31	15 36	15 36	15 41	15 46		15 48	15 51	15 56	16 01	16 00	16 06	16 11	16 12	16 16		16 21	16 26	16 24	16 31
Cardiff Bay	a		15 28			15 40				15 52				16 04			16 16					16 28	
Cardiff Central	a	15 34		15 34	15 39		15 44	15 52	15 50		15 54	15 59	16 05		16 09	16 14		16 22	16 20	16 24	16 32		16 34
	d				15 41		15 46				15 55	16 01			16 10	16 16				16 25			
Grangetown	d				15 45		15 50				15 59	16 05			16 14	16 20				16 29			
Dingle Road	d						15 56					16 11				16 26							
Penarth	a						16 01					16 17				16 31							
Cogan	d				15 48						16 03				16 18					16 33			
Eastbrook	d				15 51						16 05				16 20					16 35			
Dinas Powys	d				15 53						16 07				16 22					16 37			
Cadoxton	d				15 57						16 12				16 27					16 42			
Barry Docks	d				16 00						16 15				16 30					16 45			
Barry	d				16 05						16 19				16 34					16 49			
Barry Island	a										16 25				16 40					16 55			
Rhoose Cardiff Int Airport	d				16 12																		
Llantwit Major	d				16 22																		
Bridgend	a				16 40																		

When events are being held at the Millenium Stadium, services are subject to alteration. Please check times before travelling.

Table 130

Saturdays
until 10 September

Treherbert, Aberdare, Merthyr, Pontypridd, Rhymney and Coryton - Cardiff, Penarth, Barry, Barry Island and Bridgend

		AW	AW	AW	AW	AW	AW	AW	AW	AW	AW	AW	AW	AW	AW	AW	AW	AW	AW	AW	AW	AW
Treherbert	d					15 47									16 17							
Ynyswen	d					15 49									16 19							
Treorchy	d					15 51									16 21							
Ton Pentre	d					15 53									16 23							
Ystrad Rhondda	a					15 56									16 26							
	d					15 58									16 28							
Llwynypia	d					16 00									16 30							
Tonypandy	d					16 03									16 33							
Dinas Rhondda	d					16 05									16 35							
Porth	a					16 08									16 38							
	d					16 09									16 39							
Trehafod	d					16 12									16 42							
Merthyr Tydfil	d	15 38										16 08									16 38	
Pentre-bach	d	15 42										16 12									16 42	
Troed Y Rhiw	d	15 45										16 15									16 45	
Merthyr Vale	a	15 48										16 18									16 48	
	d	15 50										16 20									16 50	
Quakers Yard	d	15 55										16 25									16 55	
Aberdare	d							15 52									16 22					
Cwmbach	d							15 55									16 25					
Fernhill	d							15 58									16 28					
Mountain Ash	a							16 01									16 31					
	d							16 04									16 34					
Penrhiwceiber	d							16 07									16 37					
Abercynon	d	15 59						16 13				16 29					16 43				16 59	
Pontypridd	a	16 08				16 17		16 23				16 37			16 47		16 53				17 07	
	d	16 09				16 18		16 24				16 39			16 48		16 54				17 09	
Trefforest	d	16 12				16 21		16 27				16 42			16 51		16 57				17 12	
Trefforest Estate	d	16 16										16 46									17 16	
Taffs Well	d	16 20				16 28		16 34				16 50			16 58		17 04				17 20	
Radyr	a	16 23				16 31		16 37				16 53			17 01		17 07				17 23	
	d	16 23			16 30	16 37		16 37				16 53			17 01	17 04	17 07				17 23	
Danescourt	d				16 34											17 08						
Fairwater	d				16 36											17 10						
Waun-gron Park	d				16 38											17 12						
Ninian Park	d				16 45	16b59										17 15						
Llandaf	d	16 26						16 40				16 56			17 04		17 10				17 26	
Cathays	d	16 31						16 45				17 01			17 09		17 15				17 31	
Rhymney	d																	16 29				
Pontlottyn	d																	16 32				
Tir-phil	d																	16 36				
Brithdir	d																	16 39				
Bargoed	a																	16 42				
	d			16 02					16 17				16 32					16 47				
Gilfach Fargoed	d								16 19													
Pengam	d			16 07					16 22				16 37					16 52				
Hengoed	d			16 10					16 25				16 40					16 55				
Ystrad Mynach	d			16 13					16 28				16 43					16 58				
Llanbradach	d			16 18					16 33				16 48					17 03				
Aber	d			16 22					16 37				16 52					17 07				
Caerphilly	d			16 25					16 40				16 55					17 10				
Lisvane & Thornhill	d			16 29					16 44				16 59					17 14				
Llanishen	d			16 31					16 46				17 01					17 16				
Heath High Level	d			16 34					16 49				17 04					17 19				
Coryton	d									16 45										17 15		
Whitchurch (Cardiff)	d									16 46										17 16		
Rhiwbina	d									16 48										17 18		
Birchgrove	d									16 50										17 20		
Ty Glas	d									16 51										17 21		
Heath Low Level	d									16 54										17 24		
Cardiff Queen Street	a	16 34		16 39				16 49	16 54	16 59		17 04	17 09		17 14		17 19	17 24		17 29	17 34	
	d	16 36	16 36	16 41			16 48	16 51	16 56	17 01	17 00	17 06	17 11	17 12	17 16		17 21	17 26	17 24	17 31	17 36	17 36
Cardiff Bay	a		16 40				16 52				17 04			17 16					17 28			17 40
Cardiff Central	a	16 39		16 44	16 50	17 04		16 54	16 59	17 04		17 09	17 14		17 22	17 20	17 24	17 29		17 34	17 39	
	d	16 41		16 46				16 55	17 01			17 10	17 16				17 25	17 31			17 41	
Grangetown	d	16 45		16 50				16 59	17 05			17 14	17 20				17 29	17 35			17 45	
Dingle Road	d			16 56					17 11				17 26					17 41				
Penarth	a			17 01					17 16				17 31					17 46				
Cogan	d	16 48						17 03				17 18					17 33				17 48	
Eastbrook	d	16 51						17 05				17 20					17 35				17 51	
Dinas Powys	d	16 53						17 07				17 22					17 37				17 53	
Cadoxton	d	16 57						17 12				17 27					17 42				17 57	
Barry Docks	d	17 00						17 15				17 30					17 45				18 00	
Barry	d	17 05						17 19				17 34					17 49				18 05	
Barry Island	a							17 25				17 40					17 55					
Rhoose Cardiff Int Airport	d	17 12																			18 12	
Llantwit Major	d	17 22																			18 22	
Bridgend	a	17 40																			18 40	

b Arr. 1648

When events are being held at the Millenium Stadium, services are subject to alteration. Please check times before travelling.

Table 130

Saturdays until 10 September

Treherbert, Aberdare, Merthyr, Pontypridd, Rhymney and Coryton - Cardiff, Penarth, Barry, Barry Island and Bridgend

		AW	AW	AW	AW	AW	AW	AW	AW	AW		AW	AW	AW	AW	AW	AW	AW	AW	AW		AW	AW	AW	AW
Treherbert	d		16 47											17 17									17 47		
Ynyswen	d		16 49											17 19									17 49		
Treorchy	d		16 51											17 21									17 51		
Ton Pentre	d		16 53											17 23									17 53		
Ystrad Rhondda	a		16 56											17 26									17 56		
	d		16 58											17 28									17 58		
Llwynypia	d		17 00											17 30									18 00		
Tonypandy	d		17 03											17 33									18 03		
Dinas Rhondda	d		17 05											17 35									18 05		
Porth	a		17 08											17 38									18 08		
	d		17 09											17 39									18 09		
Trehafod	d		17 12											17 42									18 12		
Merthyr Tydfil	d									17 08										17 38					
Pentre-bach	d									17 12										17 42					
Troed Y Rhiw	d									17 15										17 45					
Merthyr Vale	a									17 18										17 48					
	d									17 20										17 50					
Quakers Yard	d									17 25										17 55					
Aberdare [3]	d					16 52										17 22									
Cwmbach	d					16 55										17 25									
Fernhill	d					16 58										17 28									
Mountain Ash	a					17 01										17 31									
	d					17 04										17 34									
Penrhiwceiber	d					17 07										17 37									
Abercynon	d					17 13				17 29						17 43				17 59					
Pontypridd [3]	a		17 17			17 23				17 37				17 47		17 53				18 07			18 17		
	d		17 18			17 24				17 39				17 48		17 54				18 09			18 18		
Trefforest	d		17 21			17 27				17 42				17 51		17 57				18 12			18 21		
Trefforest Estate	d									17 46										18 16					
Taffs Well [3]	d		17 28			17 34				17 50				17 58		18 04				18 20			18 28		
Radyr [3]	a		17 31			17 37				17 53				18 01		18 07				18 23			18 31		
	d		17 31	17 34		17 37				17 53				18 01	18 04	18 07				18 23			18 31	18 34	
Danescourt	d			17 38											18 08									18 38	
Fairwater	d			17 40											18 10									18 40	
Waun-gron Park	d			17 42											18 12									18 42	
Ninian Park	d			17 45											18 15									18 45	
Llandaf	d		17 34			17 40				17 56				18 04		18 10				18 26			18 34		
Cathays	d		17 39			17 45				18 01				18 09		18 15				18 31			18 39		
Rhymney [3]	d																17 29								
Pontlottyn	d																17 32								
Tir-phil	d																17 36								
Brithdir	d																17 39								
Bargoed	a																17 42								
	d	17 02					17 17					17 32					17 47								
Gilfach Fargoed	d						17 19																		
Pengam	d	17 07					17 22					17 37					17 52								
Hengoed	d	17 10					17 25					17 40					17 55								
Ystrad Mynach [3]	d	17 13					17 28					17 43					17 58								
Llanbradach	d	17 18					17 33					17 48					18 03								
Aber	d	17 22					17 37					17 52					18 07								
Caerphilly [3]	d	17 25					17 40					17 55					18 10								
Lisvane & Thornhill	d	17 29					17 44					17 59					18 14								
Llanishen	d	17 31					17 46					18 01					18 16								
Heath High Level	d	17 34					17 49					18 04					18 19								
Coryton	d							17 45											18 15						
Whitchurch (Cardiff)	d							17 46											18 16						
Rhiwbina	d							17 48											18 18						
Birchgrove	d							17 50											18 20						
Ty Glas	d							17 51											18 21						
Heath Low Level	d							17 54											18 24						
Cardiff Queen Street [3]	a	17 39	17 44			17 49	17 54	17 59		18 04		18 09		18 14		18 19	18 24		18 29	18 34			18 44		
	d	17 41	17 46		17 48	17 51	17 56	18 01	18 00	18 06		18 11	18 12	18 16		18 21	18 26	18 24	18 31	18 36		18 36	18 46		18 48
Cardiff Bay	a				17 52				18 04				18 16					18 28				18 40			18 52
Cardiff Central [7]	a	17 44	17 52	17 50		17 54	17 59	18 04		18 09		18 15		18 22	18 20	18 24	18 29		18 34	18 39			18 52	18 50	
	d	17 46				17 55	18 01			18 10		18 16				18 25	18 31			18 41					
Grangetown	d	17 50				17 59	18 05			18 14		18 20				18 29	18 35			18 45					
Dingle Road	d	17 56					18 11					18 26					18 41								
Penarth	a	18 01					18 17					18 33					18 46								
Cogan	d					18 03				18 18						18 33				18 48					
Eastbrook	d					18 05				18 20						18 35				18 51					
Dinas Powys	d					18 07				18 22						18 37				18 53					
Cadoxton	d					18 12				18 27						18 42				18 57					
Barry Docks	d					18 15				18 30						18 45				19 00					
Barry [3]	d					18 19				18 34						18 49				19 05					
Barry Island	a					18 25				18 40						18 55									
Rhoose Cardiff Int Airport ✈	d																			19 12					
Llantwit Major	d																			19 22					
Bridgend	a																			19 40					

When events are being held at the Millenium Stadium, services are subject to alteration. Please check times before travelling.

Table 130

Saturdays until 10 September

Treherbert, Aberdare, Merthyr, Pontypridd, Rhymney and Coryton - Cardiff, Penarth, Barry, Barry Island and Bridgend

		AW	AW	AW	AW	AW		AW	AW	AW	AW	AW	AW	AW	AW	AW		AW	AW	AW	AW	AW	AW	AW	AW
Treherbert	d								18 17									18 47							19 17
Ynyswen	d								18 19									18 49							19 19
Treorchy	d								18 21									18 51							19 21
Ton Pentre	d								18 23									18 53							19 23
Ystrad Rhondda	a								18 26									18 56							19 26
	d								18 28									18 58							19 28
Llwynypia	d								18 30									19 00							19 30
Tonypandy	d								18 33									19 03							19 33
Dinas Rhondda	d								18 35									19 05							19 35
Porth	a								18 38									19 08							19 38
	d								18 39									19 09							19 39
Trehafod	d								18 42									19 12							19 42
Merthyr Tydfil	d					18 08									18 38								19 08		
Pentre-bach	d					18 12									18 42								19 12		
Troed Y Rhiw	d					18 15									18 45								19 15		
Merthyr Vale	a					18 18									18 48								19 18		
	d					18 20									18 50								19 20		
Quakers Yard	d					18 25									18 55								19 25		
Aberdare [3]	d	17 52									18 22									18 52					
Cwmbach	d	17 55									18 25									18 55					
Fernhill	d	17 58									18 28									18 58					
Mountain Ash	a	18 01									18 31									19 01					
	d	18 04									18 34									19 04					
Penrhiwceiber	d	18 07									18 37									19 07					
Abercynon	d	18 13				18 29					18 43				18 59					19 13			19 29		
Pontypridd [3]	a	18 23				18 37			18 47		18 53				19 07			19 17		19 23			19 37		19 47
	d	18 24				18 39			18 48		18 54				19 09			19 18		19 24			19 39		19 48
Trefforest	d	18 27				18 42			18 51		18 57				19 12			19 21		19 27			19 42		19 51
Trefforest Estate	d					18 46									19 16								19 46		
Taffs Well [3]	d	18 34				18 50			18 58		19 04				19 20			19 28		19 34			19 50		19 58
Radyr [3]	a	18 37				18 53			19 01		19 07				19 23			19 31		19 37			19 53		20 01
	d	18 37				18 53			19 01	19 04	19 07				19 23			19 31		19 37			19 53		20 01
Danescourt	d									19 08															
Fairwater	d									19 10															
Waun-gron Park	d									19 12															
Ninian Park	d									19 15															
Llandaf	d	18 40				18 56			19 04		19 10				19 26			19 34		19 40			19 56		20 04
Cathays	d	18 45				19 01			19 09		19 15				19 31			19 39		19 45			20 01		20 09
Rhymney [3]	d																								
Pontlottyn	d																								
Tir-phil	d																								
Brithdir	d																								
Bargoed	a																								
	d		18 17									18 48													
Gilfach Fargoed	d		18 19									18 50													
Pengam	d		18 22									18 53													
Hengoed	d		18 25									18 56													
Ystrad Mynach [3]	d		18 28									18 59													
Llanbradach	d		18 33									19 04													
Aber	d		18 37									19 08													
Caerphilly [3]	d		18 40									19 11									19 40				
Lisvane & Thornhill	d		18 44									19 15									19 44				
Llanishen	d		18 46									19 17									19 46				
Heath High Level	d		18 49									19 20									19 49				
Coryton	d			18 45										19 15											
Whitchurch (Cardiff)	d			18 46										19 16											
Rhiwbina	d			18 48										19 18											
Birchgrove	d			18 50										19 20											
Ty Glas	d			18 51										19 21											
Heath Low Level	d			18 54										19 24											
Cardiff Queen Street [3]	a	18 49	18 54	18 59		19 04			19 14		19 19	19 24		19 29	19 35			19 44		19 49	19 54		20 04		20 14
	d	18 51	18 56	19 01	19 00	19 06		19 12	19 16		19 21	19 26	19 24	19 31	19 36	19 36		19 46	19 48	19 51	19 56	20 00	20 06	20 12	20 16
Cardiff Bay	a				19 04			19 16					19 28			19 40			19 52			20 04		20 16	
Cardiff Central [7]	a	18 54	18 59	19 06		19 10			19 22	19 22	19 24	19 29		19 34	19 40			19 52		19 57	19 59		20 09		20 22
	d	18 55	19 01								19 25	19 31			19 41						20 06		20 10		
Grangetown	d	18 59	19 05								19 29	19 35			19 45						20 10		20 14		
Dingle Road	d		19 11									19 41									20 14				
Penarth	a		19 16									19 46									20 19				
Cogan	d	19 03									19 33				19 48								20 18		
Eastbrook	d	19 05									19 35				19 51								20 20		
Dinas Powys	d	19 07									19 37				19 53								20 22		
Cadoxton	d	19 12									19 42				19 57								20 27		
Barry Docks	d	19 15									19 45				20 00								20 30		
Barry [3]	d	19 19									19 49				20 05								20 34		
Barry Island	a	19 25									19 55												20 40		
Rhoose Cardiff Int Airport ✈	d														20 12										
Llantwit Major	d														20 22										
Bridgend	a														20 40										

When events are being held at the Millenium Stadium, services are subject to alteration. Please check times before travelling.

Table 130

Saturdays
until 10 September

Treherbert, Aberdare, Merthyr, Pontypridd, Rhymney and Coryton - Cardiff, Penarth, Barry, Barry Island and Bridgend

		AW		AW	AW	AW	AW	AW	AW	AW	AW	AW		AW	AW	AW	AW	AW	AW	AW	AW	AW		AW	AW
Treherbert	d									19 47							20 17								
Ynyswen	d									19 49							20 19								
Treorchy	d									19 51							20 21								
Ton Pentre	d									19 53							20 23								
Ystrad Rhondda	a									19 56							20 26								
	d									19 58							20 28								
Llwynypia	d									20 00							20 30								
Tonypandy	d									20 03							20 33								
Dinas Rhondda	d									20 05							20 35								
Porth	a									20 08							20 38								
	d									20 09							20 39								
Trehafod	d									20 12							20 42								
Merthyr Tydfil	d						19 38																	20 38	
Pentre-bach	d						19 42																	20 42	
Troed Y Rhiw	d						19 45																	20 45	
Merthyr Vale	a						19 48																	20 48	
	d						19 50																	20 50	
Quakers Yard	d						19 55																	20 55	
Aberdare 3	d											19 52							20 22						
Cwmbach	d											19 55							20 25						
Fernhill	d											19 58							20 28						
Mountain Ash	a											20 01							20 31						
	d											20 04							20 34						
Penrhiwceiber	d											20 07							20 37						
Abercynon	d			19 43			19 59					20 13							20 43					20 59	
Pontypridd 3	a			19 53			20 07			20 18		20 23					20 47		20 53					21 07	
	d			19 54			20 09			20 18		20 24					20 48		20 54					21 09	
Trefforest	d			19 57			20 12			20 21		20 27					20 51		20 57					21 12	
Trefforest Estate	d						20 16																	21 16	
Taffs Well 3	d			20 04			20 20			20 28		20 34					20 58		21 04					21 20	
Radyr 3	a			20 07			20 23			20 31		20 37					21 01		21 07					21 23	
	d	20 04		20 07			20 23			20 31		20 37					21 01	21 04	21 07					21 23	
Danescourt	d	20 08																21 08							
Fairwater	d	20 10																21 10							
Waun-gron Park	d	20 12																21 12							
Ninian Park	d	20 15																21 15							
Llandaf	d			20 10			20 26			20 34		20 40					21 04		21 10					21 26	
Cathays	d			20 15			20 31			20 39		20 45					21 09		21 15					21 31	
Rhymney 3	d								19 45																
Pontlottyn	d								19 48																
Tir-phil	d								19 52																
Brithdir	d								19 55																
Bargoed	a								19 58																
	d								19 59																
Gilfach Fargoed	d								20 01																
Pengam	d								20 04																
Hengoed	d								20 07																
Ystrad Mynach 3	d								20 10																
Llanbradach	d								20 15																
Aber	d								20 19																
Caerphilly 3	d								20 22					20 40											
Lisvane & Thornhill	d								20 26					20 44											
Llanishen	d								20 28					20 46											
Heath High Level	d								20 31					20 49											
Coryton	d					20 15																21 15			
Whitchurch (Cardiff)	d					20 16																21 16			
Rhiwbina	d					20 18																21 18			
Birchgrove	d					20 20																21 20			
Ty Glas	d					20 21																21 21			
Heath Low Level	d					20 24																21 24			
Cardiff Queen Street 3	a			20 19		20 29	20 34		20 39	20 44		20 49		20 54			21 14		21 19			21 29		21 34	
	d			20 21	20 24	20 31	20 36	20 36	20 41	20 46	20 48	20 51		20 56	21 00	21 12	21 16		21 21	21 24		21 31		21 36	21 36
Cardiff Bay	a				20 28			20 40			20 52				21 04	21 16				21 28					21 40
Cardiff Central 7	a	20 25		20 24		20 34	20 39		20 47	20 52		20 54		20 59			21 21	21 25	21 27			21 34		21 39	
	d			20 31			20 41					21 06		21 10							21 31			21 41	
Grangetown	d			20 35			20 45					21 10		21 14							21 35			21 45	
Dingle Road	d			20 41								21 14									21 41				
Penarth	a			20 46								21 19									21 46				
Cogan	d						20 48							21 18										21 48	
Eastbrook	d						20 51							21 20										21 51	
Dinas Powys	d						20 53							21 22										21 53	
Cadoxton	d						20 57							21 27										21 57	
Barry Docks	d						21 00							21 30										22 00	
Barry 3	d						21 05							21 34										22 05	
Barry Island	a													21 40											
Rhoose Cardiff Int Airport ✈	d						21 12																	22 12	
Llantwit Major	d						21 22																	22 22	
Bridgend	a						21 42																	22 40	

When events are being held at the Millenium Stadium, services are subject to alteration. Please check times before travelling.

Table 130

Saturdays
until 10 September

Treherbert, Aberdare, Merthyr, Pontypridd, Rhymney and Coryton - Cardiff, Penarth, Barry, Barry Island and Bridgend

		AW	AW	AW	AW	AW	AW	AW		AW	AW	AW	AW	AW	AW	AW	AW	AW	AW	AW	AW	AW	AW	AW	AW
Treherbert	d							21 17																	
Ynyswen	d							21 19																	
Treorchy	d							21 21																	
Ton Pentre	d							21 23																	
Ystrad Rhondda	a							21 26																	
	d							21 28																	
Llwynypia	d							21 30																	
Tonypandy	d							21 33																	
Dinas Rhondda	d							21 35																	
Porth	a							21 38																	
	d							21 39																	
Trehafod	d							21 42																	
Merthyr Tydfil	d												21 38									22 38			
Pentre-bach	d												21 42									22 42			
Troed Y Rhiw	d												21 45									22 45			
Merthyr Vale	a												21 48									22 48			
	d												21 50									22 50			
Quakers Yard	d												21 55									22 55			
Aberdare 3	d			20 54												21 54							22 51		
Cwmbach	d			20 57												21 57							22 54		
Fernhill	d			21 00												22 00							22 58		
Mountain Ash	a			21 03												22 03							23 01		
	d			21 04												22 04							23 04		
Penrhiwceiber	d			21 07												22 07							23 08		
Abercynon	d			21 13									21 59			22 13						22 59	23 14		
Pontypridd 3	a			21 22				21 47					22 07			22 22						23 07	23 22		
	d			21 24				21 48					22 09			22 24						23 09			
Trefforest	d			21 27				21 51					22 12			22 27						23 12			
Trefforest Estate	d												22 16									23 16			
Taffs Well 3	d			21 34				21 58					22 20			22 34						23 20			
Radyr 3	a			21 37				22 01					22 23			22 37						23 23			
	d			21 37				22 01		22 04			22 23			22 37				23 10		23 23			
Danescourt	d									22 08															
Fairwater	d									22 10															
Waun-gron Park	d									22 12															
Ninian Park	d									22 15															
Llandaf	d			21 40				22 04					22 26			22 40				23 12		23 26			
Cathays	d			21 45				22 09					22 31			22 45				23 16		23 31			
Rhymney 3	d	20 48									21 33														
Pontlottyn	d	20 51									21 36														
Tir-phil	d	20 55									21 40														
Brithdir	d	20 58									21 43														
Bargoed	a	21 01									21 46														
	d	21 02									21 47														
Gilfach Fargoed	d	21 04									21 49														
Pengam	d	21 07									21 52														
Hengoed	d	21 10									21 55														
Ystrad Mynach 3	d	21 13									21 58														
Llanbradach	d	21 18									22 03														
Aber	d	21 22									22 07														
Caerphilly 3	d	21 25			21 45						22 10														
Lisvane & Thornhill	d	21 29			21 50						22 14														
Llanishen	d	21 31			21 52						22 16														
Heath High Level	d	21 34			21 54						22 19														
Coryton	d																22 45								
Whitchurch (Cardiff)	d																22 46								
Rhiwbina	d																22 48								
Birchgrove	d																22 50								
Ty Glas	d																22 51								
Heath Low Level	d																22 54								
Cardiff Queen Street 3	a	21 42		21 49	22 00			22 14			22 24		22 34			22 49	22 59			23 19		23 34			
	d	21 44	21 48	21 51	22 01	22 00	22 12	22 16			22 26	22 24	22 36	22 36	22 48	22 54	23 01	23 00	23 12	23 20	23 24	23 36		23 36	23 48
Cardiff Bay	a		21 52			22 04	22 16					22 28		22 40	22 52			23 04	23 16		23 28			23 40	23 52
Cardiff Central 7	a	21 51		21 54	22 04			22 22		22 20	22 30		22 41			22 59	23 06			23 25		23 42			
	d			22 06	22 10						22 31					23 12				23 30					
Grangetown	d			22 10	22 14						22 35					23 16				23 34					
Dingle Road	d			22 14							22 41					23 20									
Penarth	a			22 19							22 49					23 25									
Cogan	d				22 18															23 37					
Eastbrook	d				22 20															23 40					
Dinas Powys	d				22 22															23 42					
Cadoxton	d				22 27															23 46					
Barry Docks	d				22 30															23 49					
Barry 3	d				22 34															23 54					
Barry Island	a				22 40															23 59					
Rhoose Cardiff Int Airport ✈	d																								
Llantwit Major	d																								
Bridgend	a																								

When events are being held at the Millenium Stadium, services are subject to alteration. Please check times before travelling.

Table 130

Saturdays
from 17 September

Treherbert, Aberdare, Merthyr, Pontypridd, Rhymney and Coryton - Cardiff, Penarth, Barry, Barry Island and Bridgend

Station		AW	AW	AW	AW	AW	AW	AW	AW	AW	AW	AW	AW	AW	AW	AW	AW	AW	AW	AW	AW	AW	AW
Treherbert	d											05 47							06 17				
Ynyswen	d											05 49							06 19				
Treorchy	d											05 51							06 21				
Ton Pentre	d											05 53							06 23				
Ystrad Rhondda	a											05 56							06 26				
	d											05 58							06 28				
Llwynypia	d											06 00							06 30				
Tonypandy	d											06 03							06 33				
Dinas Rhondda	d											06 05							06 35				
Porth	a											06 08							06 38				
	d											06 09							06 39				
Trehafod	d											06 12							06 42				
Merthyr Tydfil	d																						
Pentre-bach	d																						
Troed Y Rhiw	d																						
Merthyr Vale	a																						
	d																						
Quakers Yard	d																						
Aberdare 3	d																					06 21	
Cwmbach	d																					06 24	
Fernhill	d																					06 28	
Mountain Ash	a																					06 31	
	d																					06 34	
Penrhiwceiber	d																					06 38	
Abercynon	d																					06 44	
Pontypridd 3	a											06 17							06 47			06 53	
	d					05 24						06 18							06 48			06 54	
Trefforest	d					05 27						06 21							06 51			06 57	
Trefforest Estate	d					05 31																	
Taffs Well 3	d					05 35						06 28							06 58	06 53		07 04	
Radyr 3	a					05 39						06 31							07 01	06 56		07 07	
	d	23p10				05 39						06 31							07 01	07 04		07 07	
Danescourt	d																			07 08			
Fairwater	d																			07 10			
Waun-gron Park	d																			07 12			
Ninian Park	d																			07 15			
Llandaf	d	23p12				05 42						06 34							07 04			07 10	
Cathays	d	23p16				05 46						06 39							07 09			07 15	
Rhymney 3	d																	06 10					06 34
Pontlottyn	d																	06 13					06 37
Tir-phil	d																	06 17					06 41
Brithdir	d																	06 20					06 44
Bargoed	a																	06 23					06 47
	d																	06 27					06 48
Gilfach Fargoed	d																	06 29					
Pengam	d																	06 32					06 52
Hengoed	d																	06 35					06 56
Ystrad Mynach 3	d																	06 38					06 58
Llanbradach	d																	06 43					07 03
Aber	d																	06 47					07 07
Caerphilly 3	d									06 10								06 50					07 10
Lisvane & Thornhill	d									06 14								06 54					07 14
Llanishen	d									06 16								06 56					07 16
Heath High Level	d									06 19								06 59					07 19
Coryton	d																06 45						
Whitchurch (Cardiff)	d																06 46						
Rhiwbina	d																06 48						
Birchgrove	d																06 50						
Ty Glas	d																06 51						
Heath Low Level	d																06 54						
Cardiff Queen Street 3	a	23p19				05 51				06 25		06 42					06 59	07 04	07 12			07 19	07 24
	d	23p20				05 51				06 26	06 36	06 43	06 48		07 00		07 00	07 06	07 14		07 12	07 21	07 26
Cardiff Bay	a										06 40		06 52		07 04						07 16		
Cardiff Central 7	a	23p25				05 54				06 29		06 48					07 04	07 09	07 16	07 20		07 24	07 29
	d	23p30	05 20	05 41	05 46	05 55	06 16	06 25	06 36	06 41				06 55		07 01		07 10	07 16			07 25	07 31
Grangetown	d	23p34	05 24	05 45	05 50	05 59	06 22	06 29	06 40	06 45				06 59		07 05		07 14	07 20			07 29	07 35
Dingle Road	d				05 54		06 27		06 44							07 11			07 26				07 41
Penarth	a				06 00		06 33		06 50							07 17			07 33				07 47
Cogan	d	23p37	05 28	05 48		06 03		06 33		06 48				07 03				07 18				07 33	
Eastbrook	d	23p40	05 30	05 51		06 05		06 35		06 51				07 05				07 20				07 35	
Dinas Powys	d	23p42	05 32	05 53		06 07		06 37		06 53				07 07				07 22				07 37	
Cadoxton	d	23p46	05 37	05 57		06 12		06 42		06 57				07 12				07 27				07 42	
Barry Docks	d	23p49	05 40	06 00		06 15		06 45		07 00				07 15				07 30				07 45	
Barry 3	d	23p54	05 44	06 05		06 19		06 49		07 05				07 19				07 34				07 49	
Barry Island	a	00 01	05 51			06 26		06 56						07 26				07 41				07 56	
Rhoose Cardiff Int Airport ✈	d			06 12						07 12													
Llantwit Major	d			06 22						07 22													
Bridgend	a			06 41						07 41													

When events are being held at the Millenium Stadium, services are subject to alteration. Please check times before travelling.

Table 130

Saturdays
from 17 September

Treherbert, Aberdare, Merthyr, Pontypridd, Rhymney and Coryton - Cardiff, Penarth, Barry, Barry Island and Bridgend

Station		AW	AW	AW	AW	AW	AW	AW	AW	AW	AW	AW	AW	AW	AW	AW	AW	AW	AW	AW	AW	AW	AW
Treherbert	d						06 47										07 17						
Ynyswen	d						06 49										07 19						
Treorchy	d						06 51										07 21						
Ton Pentre	d						06 53										07 23						
Ystrad Rhondda	a						06 56										07 25						
	d						06 58										07 23						
Llwynypia	d						07 00										07 30						
Tonypandy	d						07 03										07 33						
Dinas Rhondda	d						07 05										07 35						
Porth	a						07 08										07 38						
	d						07 09										07 39						
Trehafod	d						07 12										07 42						
Merthyr Tydfil	d			06 38										07 08									07 38
Pentre-bach	d			06 42										07 12									07 42
Troed Y Rhiw	d			06 45										07 15									07 45
Merthyr Vale	a			06 48										07 18									07 48
	d			06 50										07 20									07 50
Quakers Yard	d			06 55										07 25									07 55
Aberdare 3	d									06 51									07 21				
Cwmbach	d									06 54									07 24				
Fernhill	d									06 58									07 28				
Mountain Ash	a									07 01									07 31				
	d									07 04									07 34				
Penrhiwceiber	d									07 08									07 38				
Abercynon	d			06 59						07 14				07 29					07 44				07 59
Pontypridd 3	a			07 07			07 17			07 23				07 37			07 47		07 53				08 07
	d			07 09			07 18			07 24				07 39			07 48		07 54				08 09
Trefforest	d			07 12			07 21			07 27				07 42			07 51		07 57				08 12
Trefforest Estate	d			07 16										07 46									08 16
Taffs Well 3	d			07 20			07 28			07 34				07 50			07 58		08 04				08 20
Radyr 3	a			07 23			07 31			07 37				07 53			08 01		08 07				08 23
	d			07 23			07 31	07 34		07 37				07 53			08 01	08 04	08 07				08 23
Danescourt	d							07 38										08 08					
Fairwater	d							07 40										08 10					
Waun-gron Park	d							07 42										08 12					
Ninian Park	d							07 45										08 15					
Llandaf	d			07 26			07 34			07 40				07 56			08 04		08 10				08 26
Cathays	d			07 31			07 39			07 45				08 01			08 09		08 15				08 31
Rhymney 3	d										07 02									07 24			
Pontlottyn	d										07 05									07 27			
Tir-phil	d										07 09									07 31			
Brithdir	d										07 12									07 34			
Bargoed	a										07 15									07 37			
	d					07 02					07 17				07 32					07 45			
Gilfach Fargoed	d					07 04					07 19									07 47			
Pengam	d					07 07					07 22				07 37					07 50			
Hengoed	d					07 10					07 25				07 40					07 54			
Ystrad Mynach 3	d					07 13					07 28				07 43					07 57			
Llanbradach	d					07 18					07 33				07 48					08 02			
Aber	d					07 22					07 37				07 52					08 07			
Caerphilly 3	d					07 25					07 40				07 55					08 10			
Lisvane & Thornhill	d					07 29					07 44				07 59					08 14			
Llanishen	d					07 31					07 46				08 01					08 16			
Heath High Level	d					07 34					07 49				08 04					08 19			
Coryton	d		07 15									07 45										08 15	
Whitchurch (Cardiff)	d		07 16									07 46										08 16	
Rhiwbina	d		07 18									07 48										08 18	
Birchgrove	d		07 20									07 50										08 20	
Ty Glas	d		07 21									07 51										08 21	
Heath Low Level	d		07 24									07 54										08 24	
Cardiff Queen Street 3	a		07 29	07 35		07 39	07 44			07 49	07 54	07 59		08 04	08 09		08 14		08 19	08 24		08 29	08 34
	d	07 24	07 31	07 36	07 36	07 41	07 46		07 48	07 51	07 56	08 01	08 00	08 06	08 11	08 12	08 16		08 21	08 26	08 24	08 31	08 36
Cardiff Bay	a	07 28			07 40				07 52				08 04			08 16					08 28		
Cardiff Central 7	a		07 34	07 39		07 44	07 53	07 50		07 54	07 59	08 04		08 09	08 14		08 23	08 20	08 24	08 29		08 34	08 39
	d			07 41		07 46				07 55	08 01			08 10	08 16				08 25	08 31			08 41
Grangetown	d			07 45		07 50				07 59	08 05			08 14	08 20				08 29	08 35			08 45
Dingle Road	d					07 56					08 11				08 26					08 41			
Penarth	a					08 02					08 17				08 32					08 47			
Cogan	d			07 48						08 03				08 18					08 33				08 48
Eastbrook	d			07 51						08 05				08 20					08 35				08 51
Dinas Powys	d			07 53						08 07				08 22					08 37				08 53
Cadoxton	d			07 57						08 12				08 27					08 42				08 57
Barry Docks	d			08 00						08 15				08 30					08 45				09 00
Barry 3	d			08 05						08 19				08 34					08 49				09 05
Barry Island	a									08 26				08 41					08 56				
Rhoose Cardiff Int Airport ✈	d			08 12																			09 12
Llantwit Major	d			08 22																			09 22
Bridgend	a			08 41																			09 41

When events are being held at the Millenium Stadium, services are subject to alteration. Please check times before travelling.

Table 130

Saturdays
from 17 September

Treherbert, Aberdare, Merthyr, Pontypridd, Rhymney and Coryton - Cardiff, Penarth, Barry, Barry Island and Bridgend

		AW		AW	AW	AW	AW	AW	AW	AW	AW	AW		AW	AW	AW	AW	AW	AW	AW	AW	AW		AW	AW
Treherbert	d				07 45											08 17									
Ynyswen	d				07 47											08 19									
Treorchy	d				07 49											08 21									
Ton Pentre	d				07 51											08 23									
Ystrad Rhondda	a				07 54											08 26									
	d				07 58											08 28									
Llwynypia	d				08 00											08 30									
Tonypandy	d				08 03											08 33									
Dinas Rhondda	d				08 05											08 35									
Porth	a				08 08											08 38									
	d				08 09											08 39									
Trehafod	d				08 12											08 42									
Merthyr Tydfil	d											08 08										08 38			
Pentre-bach	d											08 12										08 42			
Troed Y Rhiw	d											08 15										08 45			
Merthyr Vale	a											08 18										08 48			
	d											08 20										08 50			
Quakers Yard	d											08 25										08 55			
Aberdare 3	d							07 51										08 21							
Cwmbach	d							07 54										08 24							
Fernhill	d							07 58										08 28							
Mountain Ash	a							08 01										08 31							
	d							08 04										08 34							
Penrhiwceiber	d							08 08										08 38							
Abercynon	d							08 14				08 29						08 44				08 59			
Pontypridd 3	a				08 17			08 23				08 37				08 47		08 53				09 07			
	d				08 18			08 24				08 39				08 48		08 54				09 09			
Trefforest	d				08 21			08 27				08 42				08 51		08 57				09 12			
Trefforest Estate	d											08 46										09 16			
Taffs Well 3	d				08 28			08 34				08 50				08 58		09 04				09 20			
Radyr 3	a				08 31			08 37				08 53				09 01		09 07				09 23			
	d				08 31	08 34		08 37				08 53				09 01	09 04	09 07				09 23			
Danescourt	d					08 38											09 08								
Fairwater	d					08 40											09 10								
Waun-gron Park	d					08 42											09 12								
Ninian Park	d					08 45											09 15								
Llandaf	d				08 34			08 40				08 56				09 04		09 10				09 26			
Cathays	d				08 39			08 45				09 01				09 09		09 15				09 31			
Rhymney 3	d			07 44															08 30						
Pontlottyn	d			07 47															08 33						
Tir-phil	d			07 51															08 37						
Brithdir	d			07 54															08 40						
Bargoed	a			08 00															08 44						
	d			08 02					08 17					08 32					08 47						09 02
Gilfach Fargoed	d								08 19																
Pengam	d			08 07					08 22					08 37					08 52						09 07
Hengoed	d			08 10					08 25					08 40					08 55						09 10
Ystrad Mynach 3	d			08 13					08 28					08 43					08 58						09 13
Llanbradach	d			08 18					08 33					08 48					09 03						09 18
Aber	d			08 22					08 37					08 52					09 07						09 22
Caerphilly 3	d			08 25					08 40					08 55					09 10						09 25
Lisvane & Thornhill	d			08 29					08 44					08 59					09 14						09 29
Llanishen	d			08 31					08 46					09 01					09 16						09 31
Heath High Level	d			08 34					08 49					09 04					09 19						09 34
Coryton	d									08 45											09 15				
Whitchurch (Cardiff)	d									08 46											09 16				
Rhiwbina	d									08 48											09 18				
Birchgrove	d									08 50											09 20				
Ty Glas	d									08 51											09 21				
Heath Low Level	d									08 54											09 24				
Cardiff Queen Street 3	a			08 39	08 44			08 49	08 54	08 59		09 04		09 09		09 14		09 19	09 24		09 29	09 34			09 39
	d	08 36		08 41	08 46		08 48	08 51	08 56	09 01	09 00	09 06		09 11	09 12	09 16		09 21	09 26	09 24	09 31	09 36		09 36	09 41
Cardiff Bay	a	08 40					08 52				09 04				09 16					09 28				09 40	
Cardiff Central 7	a			08 48	08 53	08 50		08 54	08 59	09 04		09 09		09 14		09 23	09 20	09 24	09 29		09 34	09 39			09 44
	d							08 55	09 01			09 10		09 16				09 25	09 31			09 41			09 46
Grangetown	d							08 59	09 05			09 14		09 20				09 29	09 35			09 45			09 50
Dingle Road	d								09 11					09 26					09 41						09 56
Penarth	a								09 17					09 32					09 47						10 03
Cogan	d							09 03				09 18						09 33				09 48			
Eastbrook	d							09 05				09 20						09 35				09 51			
Dinas Powys	d							09 07				09 22						09 37				09 53			
Cadoxton	d							09 12				09 27						09 42				09 57			
Barry Docks	d							09 15				09 30						09 45				10 00			
Barry 3	d							09 19				09 34						09 49				10 05			
Barry Island	a							09 26				09 41						09 56							
Rhoose Cardiff Int Airport ✈	d																					10 12			
Llantwit Major	d																					10 22			
Bridgend	a																					10 41			

When events are being held at the Millenium Stadium, services are subject to alteration. Please check times before travelling.

Table 130

Saturdays
from 17 September

Treherbert, Aberdare, Merthyr, Pontypridd, Rhymney and Coryton - Cardiff, Penarth, Barry, Barry Island and Bridgend

		AW	AW	AW	AW	AW	AW	AW		AW	AW	AW	AW	AW	AW	AW	AW	AW		AW	AW	AW	AW	AW	AW
Treherbert	d	08 47											09 17										09 47		
Ynyswen	d	08 49											09 19										09 49		
Treorchy	d	08 51											09 21										09 51		
Ton Pentre	d	08 53											09 23										09 53		
Ystrad Rhondda	a	08 56											09 26										09 56		
	d	08 58											09 28										09 58		
Llwynypia	d	09 00											09 30										10 00		
Tonypandy	d	09 03											09 33										10 03		
Dinas Rhondda	d	09 05											09 35										10 05		
Porth	a	09 08											09 38										10 08		
	d	09 09											09 39										10 09		
Trehafod	d	09 12											09 42										10 12		
Merthyr Tydfil	d									09 08										09 38					
Pentre-bach	d									09 12										09 42					
Troed Y Rhiw	d									09 15										09 45					
Merthyr Vale	a									09 18										09 48					
	d									09 20										09 50					
Quakers Yard	d									09 25										09 55					
Aberdare 3	d				08 51										09 21										
Cwmbach	d				08 54										09 24										
Fernhill	d				08 58										09 28										
Mountain Ash	a				09 01										09 31										
	d				09 04										09 34										
Penrhiwceiber	d				09 08										09 38										
Abercynon	d				09 14					09 29					09 44					09 59					
Pontypridd 3	a	09 17			09 23					09 37			09 47		09 53					10 07			10 17		
	d	09 18			09 24					09 39			09 48		09 54					10 09			10 18		
Trefforest	d	09 21			09 27					09 42			09 51		09 57					10 12			10 21		
Trefforest Estate	d									09 46										10 16					
Taffs Well 3	d	09 28			09 34					09 50			09 58		10 04					10 20			10 28		
Radyr 3	a	09 31			09 37					09 53			10 01		10 07					10 23			10 31		
	d	09 31	09 34		09 37					09 53			10 01	10 04	10 07					10 23			10 31	10 34	
Danescourt	d		09 38											10 08										10 38	
Fairwater	d		09 40											10 10										10 40	
Waun-gron Park	d		09 42											10 12										10 42	
Ninian Park	d		09 45											10 15										10 45	
Llandaf	d	09 34			09 40					09 56			10 04		10 10					10 26			10 34		
Cathays	d	09 39			09 45					10 01			10 09		10 15					10 31			10 39		
Rhymney 3	d															09 29									
Pontlottyn	d															09 32									
Tir-phil	d															09 36									
Brithdir	d															09 39									
Bargoed	a															09 42									
	d										09 25					09 47						10 02			
Gilfach Fargoed	d										09 27														
Pengam	d										09 30					09 52						10 07			
Hengoed	d										09 33					09 55						10 10			
Ystrad Mynach 3	d					09 28					09b43					09 58						10 13			
Llanbradach	d					09 33					09 48					10 03						10 18			
Aber	d					09 37					09 52					10 07						10 22			
Caerphilly 3	d					09 40					09 55					10 10						10 25			
Lisvane & Thornhill	d					09 44					09 59					10 14						10 29			
Llanishen	d					09 46					10 01					10 16						10 31			
Heath High Level	d					09 49					10 04					10 19						10 34			
Coryton	d						09 45											10 15							
Whitchurch (Cardiff)	d						09 46											10 16							
Rhiwbina	d						09 48											10 18							
Birchgrove	d						09 50											10 20							
Ty Glas	d						09 51											10 21							
Heath Low Level	d						09 54											10 24							
Cardiff Queen Street 3	a	09 44			09 49	09 54	09 59			10 04	10 09		10 14		10 19	10 24		10 29		10 34		10 39	10 44		
	d	09 46		09 48	09 51	09 56	10 01	10 00		10 06	10 11	10 12	10 16		10 21	10 26	10 24	10 31		10 36	10 36	10 41	10 46		10 48
Cardiff Bay	a			09 52				10 04				10 16					10 28				10 40				10 52
Cardiff Central 7	a	09 53	09 50		09 54	09 59	10 04			10 09	10 14		10 23	10 20	10 24	10 29		10 34		10 39		10 44	10 53	10 50	
	d				09 55	10 01				10 10	10 16				10 25	10 31				10 41		10 46			
Grangetown	d				09 59	10 05				10 14	10 20				10 29	10 35				10 45		10 50			
Dingle Road	d					10 11					10 26					10 41						10 56			
Penarth	a					10 17					10 32					10 47						11 02			
Cogan	d				10 03					10 18					10 33					10 48					
Eastbrook	d				10 05					10 20					10 35					10 51					
Dinas Powys	d				10 07					10 22					10 37					10 53					
Cadoxton	d				10 12					10 27					10 42					10 57					
Barry Docks	d				10 15					10 30					10 45					11 00					
Barry 3	d				10 19					10 34					10 49					11 05					
Barry Island	a				10 26					10 41					10 56										
Rhoose Cardiff Int Airport ✈	d																			11 12					
Llantwit Major	d																			11 22					
Bridgend	a																			11 41					

b Arr. 0936

When events are being held at the Millenium Stadium, services are subject to alteration. Please check times before travelling.

Table 130

Saturdays from 17 September

Treherbert, Aberdare, Merthyr, Pontypridd, Rhymney and Coryton - Cardiff, Penarth, Barry, Barry Island and Bridgend

		AW	AW	AW	AW	AW	AW	AW	AW	AW	AW	AW	AW	AW	AW	AW	AW	AW	AW	AW	AW	AW
Treherbert	d												10 17						10 47			
Ynyswen	d												10 19						10 49			
Treorchy	d												10 21						10 51			
Ton Pentre	d												10 23						10 53			
Ystrad Rhondda	a												10 26						10 56			
	d												10 28						10 58			
Llwynypia	d												10 30						11 00			
Tonypandy	d												10 33						11 03			
Dinas Rhondda	d												10 35						11 05			
Porth	a												10 38						11 08			
	d												10 52						11 09			
Trehafod	d												10 55						11 12			
Merthyr Tydfil	d		10 04													10 38						
Pentre-bach	d		10 08													10 42						
Troed Y Rhiw	d		10 11													10 45						
Merthyr Vale	a		10 14													10 48						
	d		10 16													10 50						
Quakers Yard	d		10 22													10 55						
Aberdare ■	d	09 51									10 21											10 51
Cwmbach	d	09 54									10 24											10 54
Fernhill	d	09 58									10 28											10 58
Mountain Ash	a	10 01									10 31											11 01
	d	10 04									10 34											11 04
Penrhiwceiber	d	10 08									10 38											11 08
Abercynon	d	10 14	10 26								10 44					10 59						11 14
Pontypridd ■	a	10 23	10 32								10 53		11 00			11 08			11 17			11 23
	d	10 24					10 39				10 54		11 04			11 09			11 18			11 24
Trefforest	d	10 27					10 42				10 57		11 07			11 12			11 21			11 27
Trefforest Estate	d															11 16						
Taffs Well ■	d	10 34					10 50				11 04		11 13			11 20			11 28			11 34
Radyr ■	a	10 37					10 53				11 07		11 17			11 23			11 31			11 37
	d	10 37					10 53		11 04		11 07		11 17			11 23			11 31	11 34		11 37
Danescourt	d								11 08											11 38		
Fairwater	d								11 10											11 40		
Waun-gron Park	d								11 12											11 42		
Ninian Park	d								11 15											11 45		
Llandaf	d	10 40					10 56				11 10					11 26			11 34			11 40
Cathays	d	10 45					11 01				11 15					11 31			11 39			11 45
Rhymney ■	d											10 29										
Pontlottyn	d											10 32										
Tir-phil	d											10 36										
Brithdir	d											10 39										
Bargoed	a											10 42										
	d							10 25				10 47						11 02				
Gilfach Fargoed	d							10 27														
Pengam	d							10 30				10 52						11 07				
Hengoed	d							10 33				10 55						11 10				
Ystrad Mynach ■	d			10 28				10b43				10 58						11 13				
Llanbradach	d			10 33				10 48				11 03						11 18				
Aber	d			10 37				10 52				11 07						11 22				
Caerphilly ■	d			10 40				10 55				11 10						11 25				
Lisvane & Thornhill	d			10 44				10 59				11 14						11 29				
Llanishen	d			10 46				11 01				11 16						11 31				
Heath High Level	d			10 49				11 04				11 19						11 34				
Coryton	d				10 45										11 15							
Whitchurch (Cardiff)	d				10 46										11 16							
Rhiwbina	d				10 48										11 18							
Birchgrove	d				10 50										11 20							
Ty Glas	d				10 51										11 21							
Heath Low Level	d				10 54										11 24							
Cardiff Queen Street ■	a	10 49		10 54	10 59		11 04	11 09			11 19	11 24			11 29	11 34		11 39	11 44			11 49
	d	10 51		10 56	11 01	11 00	11 06	11 11		11 12	11 21	11 26		11 24	11 31	11 36	11 36	11 41	11 46		11 48	11 51
Cardiff Bay	a					11 04				11 16				11 28			11 40				11 52	
Cardiff Central ■	a	10 54		10 59	11 04		11 09	11 14	11 20		11 24	11 29	11 34		11 34	11 39		11 44	11 53	11 50		11 54
	d	10 55		11 01			11 10	11 16			11 25	11 31				11 41		11 46				11 55
Grangetown	d	10 59		11 05			11 14	11 20			11 29	11 35				11 45		11 50				11 59
Dingle Road	d			11 11				11 26				11 41						11 56				
Penarth	a			11 18				11 32				11 47						12 02				
Cogan	d	11 03					11 18				11 33					11 48						12 03
Eastbrook	d	11 05					11 20				11 35					11 51						12 05
Dinas Powys	d	11 07					11 22				11 37					11 53						12 07
Cadoxton	d	11 12					11 27				11 42					11 57						12 12
Barry Docks	d	11 15					11 30				11 45					12 00						12 15
Barry ■	d	11 19					11 34				11 49					12 05						12 19
Barry Island	a	11 26					11 41				11 56											12 26
Rhoose Cardiff Int Airport ✈	d															12 12						
Llantwit Major	d															12 22						
Bridgend	a															12 41						

b Arr. 1036

When events are being held at the Millenium Stadium, services are subject to alteration. Please check times before travelling.

Table 130

Saturdays from 17 September

Treherbert, Aberdare, Merthyr, Pontypridd, Rhymney and Coryton - Cardiff, Penarth, Barry, Barry Island and Bridgend

		AW	AW	AW	AW	AW	AW	AW	AW	AW	AW	AW	AW	AW	AW	AW	AW	AW	AW	AW	AW	AW	AW
Treherbert	d							11 17									11 47						
Ynyswen	d							11 19									11 49						
Treorchy	d							11 21									11 51						
Ton Pentre	d							11 23									11 53						
Ystrad Rhondda	a							11 26									11 56						
	d							11 28									11 58						
Llwynypia	d							11 30									12 00						
Tonypandy	d							11 33									12 03						
Dinas Rhondda	d							11 35									12 05						
Porth	a							11 38									12 08						
	d							11 39									12 09						
Trehafod	d							11 42									12 12						
Merthyr Tydfil	d				11 08									11 38									12 08
Pentre-bach	d				11 12									11 42									12 12
Troed Y Rhiw	d				11 15									11 45									12 15
Merthyr Vale	a				11 18									11 48									12 18
	d				11 20									11 50									12 20
Quakers Yard	d				11 25									11 55									12 25
Aberdare ■	d									11 21													
Cwmbach	d									11 24													
Fernhill	d									11 28													
Mountain Ash	a									11 31													
	d									11 34													
Penrhiwceiber	d									11 38													
Abercynon	d				11 29					11 44				11 59									12 29
Pontypridd ■	a				11 37			11 47		11 53				12 07			12 17						12 37
	d				11 39			11 48		11 54				12 09			12 18						12 39
Trefforest	d				11 42			11 51		11 57				12 12			12 21						12 42
Trefforest Estate	d				11 46									12 16									12 46
Taffs Well ■	d				11 50			11 58		12 04				12 20			12 28						12 50
Radyr ■	a				11 53			12 01		12 07				12 23			12 31						12 53
	d				11 53			12 01	12 04	12 07				12 23			12 31	12 34					12 53
Danescourt	d								12 08									12 38					
Fairwater	d								12 10									12 40					
Waun-gron Park	d								12 12									12 42					
Ninian Park	d								12 15									12 45					
Llandaf	d				11 56			12 04		12 10				12 26			12 34						12 56
Cathays	d				12 01			12 09		12 15				12 31			12 39						13 01
Rhymney ■	d										11 29												
Pontlottyn	d										11 32												
Tir-phil	d										11 36												
Brithdir	d										11 39												
Bargoed	a										11 42												
	d					11 25					11 47					12 02							
Gilfach Fargoed	d					11 27																	
Pengam	d					11 30					11 52					12 07							
Hengoed	d					11 33					11 55					12 10							
Ystrad Mynach ■	d	11 28				11b43					11 58					12 13				12 28			
Llanbradach	d	11 33				11 48					12 03					12 18				12 33			
Aber	d	11 37				11 52					12 07					12 22				12 37			
Caerphilly ■	d	11 40				11 55					12 10					12 25				12 40			
Lisvane & Thornhill	d	11 44				11 59					12 14					12 29				12 44			
Llanishen	d	11 46				12 01					12 16					12 31				12 46			
Heath High Level	d	11 49				12 04					12 19					12 34				12 49			
Coryton	d		11 45										12 15								12 45		
Whitchurch (Cardiff)	d		11 46										12 16								12 46		
Rhiwbina	d		11 48										12 18								12 48		
Birchgrove	d		11 50										12 20								12 50		
Ty Glas	d		11 51										12 21								12 51		
Heath Low Level	d		11 54										12 24								12 54		
Cardiff Queen Street ■	a	11 54	11 59		12 04	12 09		12 14		12 19	12 24		12 29	12 34		12 39	12 44			12 54	12 59		13 04
	d	11 56	12 01	12 00	12 06	12 11	12 12	12 16		12 21	12 26	12 24	12 31	12 36	12 36	12 41	12 46		12 48	12 56	13 01	13 00	13 06
Cardiff Bay	a			12 04			12 16					12 28			12 40				12 52			13 04	
Cardiff Central ■	a	11 59	12 04		12 09	12 14		12 23	12 20	12 24	12 29		12 34	12 39		12 44	12 52	12 50		12 59	13 04		13 09
	d	12 01			12 10	12 16				12 25	12 31			12 41		12 46	12 55			13 01			13 10
Grangetown	d	12 05			12 14	12 20				12 29	12 35			12 45		12 50	12 59			13 05			13 14
Dingle Road	d	12 11				12 26					12 41					12 56				13 11			
Penarth	a	12 17				12 32					12 47					13 02				13 17			
Cogan	d				12 18					12 33				12 48			13 03						13 18
Eastbrook	d				12 20					12 35				12 51			13 05						13 20
Dinas Powys	d				12 22					12 37				12 53			13 07						13 22
Cadoxton	d				12 27					12 42				12 57			13 12						13 27
Barry Docks	d				12 30					12 45				13 00			13 15						13 30
Barry ■	d				12 34					12 49				13 05			13 19						13 34
Barry Island	a				12 41					12 56							13 26						13 41
Rhoose Cardiff Int Airport ✈	d													13 12									
Llantwit Major	d													13 22									
Bridgend	a													13 41									

b Arr. 1136

When events are being held at the Millenium Stadium, services are subject to alteration. Please check times before travelling.

Table 130

Saturdays
from 17 September

Treherbert, Aberdare, Merthyr, Pontypridd, Rhymney and Coryton - Cardiff, Penarth, Barry, Barry Island and Bridgend

		AW	AW	AW	AW	AW		AW	AW	AW	AW	AW	AW	AW	AW	AW		AW	AW	AW	AW	AW	AW	AW	AW
Treherbert	d			12 17										12 47											13 17
Ynyswen	d			12 19										12 49											13 19
Treorchy	d			12 21										12 51											13 21
Ton Pentre	d			12 23										12 53											13 23
Ystrad Rhondda	a			12 26										12 56											13 26
	d			12 28										12 58											13 28
Llwynypia	d			12 30										13 00											13 30
Tonypandy	d			12 33										13 03											13 33
Dinas Rhondda	d			12 35										13 05											13 35
Porth	a			12 38										13 08											13 38
	d			12 39										13 09											13 39
Trehafod	d			12 42										13 12											13 42
Merthyr Tydfil	d										12 38											13 08			
Pentre-bach	d										12 42											13 12			
Troed Y Rhiw	d										12 45											13 15			
Merthyr Vale	a										12 48											13 18			
	d										12 50											13 20			
Quakers Yard	d										12 55											13 25			
Aberdare 3	d					12 21												12 51							
Cwmbach	d					12 24												12 54							
Fernhill	d					12 28												12 58							
Mountain Ash	a					12 31												13 01							
	d					12 34												13 04							
Penrhiwceiber	d					12 38												13 08							
Abercynon	d					12 44					12 59							13 14				13 29			
Pontypridd 3	a			12 48		12 53					13 07			13 17				13 23				13 37			13 47
	d			12 48		12 54					13 09			13 18				13 24				13 39			13 48
Trefforest	d			12 51		12 57					13 12			13 21				13 27				13 42			13 51
Trefforest Estate	d										13 16											13 46			
Taffs Well 3	d			12 58		13 04					13 20			13 28				13 34				13 50			13 58
Radyr 3	a			13 01		13 07					13 23			13 31				13 37				13 53			14 01
	d			13 01	13 04	13 07					13 23			13 31	13 34			13 37				13 53			14 01
Danescourt	d				13 08										13 38										
Fairwater	d				13 10										13 40										
Waun-gron Park	d				13 12										13 42										
Ninian Park	d				13 15										13 45										
Llandaf	d			13 04		13 10					13 26			13 34				13 40				13 56			14 04
Cathays	d			13 09		13 15					13 31			13 39				13 45				14 01			14 09
Rhymney 3	d							12 29																	
Pontlottyn	d							12 32																	
Tir-phil	d							12 36																	
Brithdir	d							12 39																	
Bargoed	a							12 42																	
	d	12 25						12 47					13 02										13 25		
Gilfach Fargoed	d	12 27																					13 27		
Pengam	d	12 30						12 52					13 07										13 30		
Hengoed	d	12 33						12 55					13 10										13 33		
Ystrad Mynach 3	d	12b43						12 58					13 13						13 28				13c43		
Llanbradach	d	12 48						13 03					13 18						13 33				13 48		
Aber	d	12 52						13 07					13 22						13 37				13 52		
Caerphilly 3	d	12 55						13 10					13 25						13 40				13 55		
Lisvane & Thornhill	d	12 59						13 14					13 29						13 44				13 59		
Llanishen	d	13 01						13 16					13 31						13 46				14 01		
Heath High Level	d	13 04						13 19					13 34						13 49				14 04		
Coryton	d									13 15										13 45					
Whitchurch (Cardiff)	d									13 16										13 46					
Rhiwbina	d									13 18										13 48					
Birchgrove	d									13 20										13 50					
Ty Glas	d									13 21										13 51					
Heath Low Level	d									13 24										13 54					
Cardiff Queen Street 3	a	13 09		13 14		13 19		13 24		13 29	13 34		13 39	13 44				13 49	13 54	13 59		14 04	14 09		14 14
	d	13 11	13 12	13 16		13 21		13 26	13 24	13 31	13 36	13 36	13 41	13 46		13 48		13 51	13 56	14 01	14 00	14 06	14 11	14 12	14 16
Cardiff Bay	a		13 16						13 28			13 40				13 52					14 04			14 16	
Cardiff Central 7	a	13 14		13 23	13 20	13 24		13 29		13 34	13 39		13 44	13 53	13 50			13 54	13 59	14 04		14 09	14 14		14 23
	d	13 16				13 25		13 31			13 41		13 46					13 55	14 01			14 10	14 16		
Grangetown	d	13 20				13 29		13 35			13 45		13 50					13 59	14 05			14 14	14 20		
Dingle Road	d	13 26						13 41					13 56						14 11				14 26		
Penarth	a	13 32						13 47					14 02						14 17				14 32		
Cogan	d					13 33					13 48							14 03				14 18			
Eastbrook	d					13 35					13 51							14 05				14 20			
Dinas Powys	d					13 37					13 53							14 07				14 22			
Cadoxton	d					13 42					13 57							14 12				14 27			
Barry Docks	d					13 45					14 00							14 15				14 30			
Barry 3	d					13 49					14 05							14 19				14 34			
Barry Island	a					13 56												14 26				14 41			
Rhoose Cardiff Int Airport ✈	d										14 12														
Llantwit Major	d										14 22														
Bridgend	a										14 41														

b Arr. 1236 c Arr. 1336

When events are being held at the Millenium Stadium, services are subject to alteration. Please check times before travelling.

Table 130

Saturdays
from 17 September

Treherbert, Aberdare, Merthyr, Pontypridd, Rhymney and Coryton - Cardiff, Penarth, Barry, Barry Island and Bridgend

		AW		AW	AW	AW	AW	AW	AW	AW	AW	AW		AW	AW	AW	AW	AW	AW	AW	AW	AW		AW	AW
Treherbert	d										13 47														
Ynyswen	d										13 49														
Treorchy	d										13 51														
Ton Pentre	d										13 53														
Ystrad Rhondda	a										13 56														
	d										13 58														
Llwynypia	d										14 00														
Tonypandy	d										14 03														
Dinas Rhondda	d										14 05														
Porth	a										14 08														
	d										14 09														
Trehafod	d										14 12														
Merthyr Tydfil	d							13 38											14 08						
Pentre-bach	d							13 42											14 12						
Troed Y Rhiw	d							13 45											14 15						
Merthyr Vale	a							13 48											14 18						
	d							13 50											14 20						
Quakers Yard	d							13 55											14 25						
Aberdare 3	d														13 51									14 21	
Cwmbach	d														13 54									14 24	
Fernhill	d														13 58									14 28	
Mountain Ash	a														14 01									14 31	
	d														14 04									14 34	
Penrhiwceiber	d														14 08									14 38	
Abercynon	d			13 45				13 59							14 14				14 29					14 44	
Pontypridd 3	a			13 53				14 07			14 17				14 23				14 37					14 53	
	d			13 54				14 09			14 18				14 24				14 39					14 54	
Trefforest	d			13 57				14 12			14 21				14 27				14 42					14 57	
Trefforest Estate	d							14 16											14 46						
Taffs Well 3	d			14 04				14 20			14 28				14 34				14 50					15 04	
Radyr 3	a			14 07				14 23			14 31				14 37				14 53					15 07	
	d	14 04		14 07				14 23			14 31	14 34			14 37				14 53		15 04			15 07	
Danescourt	d	14 08										14 38									15 08				
Fairwater	d	14 10										14 40									15 10				
Waun-gron Park	d	14 12										14 42									15 12				
Ninian Park	d	14 15										14 45									15 15				
Llandaf	d			14 10				14 26			14 34				14 40				14 56					15 10	
Cathays	d			14 15				14 31			14 39				14 45				15 01					15 15	
Rhymney 3	d				13 29																				14 29
Pontlottyn	d				13 32																				14 32
Tir-phil	d				13 36																				14 36
Brithdir	d				13 39																				14 39
Bargoed	a				13 42																				14 42
	d				13 47					14 02										14 25					14 47
Gilfach Fargoed	d																			14 27					
Pengam	d				13 52					14 07										14 30					14 52
Hengoed	d				13 55					14 10										14 33					14 55
Ystrad Mynach 3	d				13 58					14 13						14 28				14b43					14 58
Llanbradach	d				14 03					14 18						14 33				14 48					15 03
Aber	d				14 07					14 22						14 37				14 52					15 07
Caerphilly 3	d				14 10					14 25						14 40				14 55					15 10
Lisvane & Thornhill	d				14 14					14 29						14 44				14 59					15 14
Llanishen	d				14 16					14 31						14 46				15 01					15 16
Heath High Level	d				14 19					14 34						14 49				15 04					15 19
Coryton	d						14 15										14 45								
Whitchurch (Cardiff)	d						14 16										14 46								
Rhiwbina	d						14 18										14 48								
Birchgrove	d						14 20										14 50								
Ty Glas	d						14 21										14 51								
Heath Low Level	d						14 24										14 54								
Cardiff Queen Street 3	a			14 19	14 24		14 29	14 34		14 39	14 44				14 49	14 54	14 59		15 04	15 09				15 19	15 24
	d			14 21	14 26	14 24	14 31	14 36	14 36	14 41	14 46			14 48	14 51	14 56	15 01	15 00	15 06	15 11		15 12		15 21	15 26
Cardiff Bay	a					14 28			14 40					14 52				15 04				15 16			
Cardiff Central 7	a	14 20		14 24	14 29		14 34	14 39		14 44	14 53	14 50			14 54	14 59	15 04		15 09	15 14	15 20			15 24	15 29
	d			14 25	14 31			14 41		14 46					14 55	15 01			15 10	15 16				15 25	15 31
Grangetown	d			14 29	14 35			14 45		14 50					14 59	15 05			15 14	15 20				15 29	15 35
Dingle Road	d				14 41					14 56						15 11				15 26					15 41
Penarth	a				14 47					15 02						15 17				15 32					15 47
Cogan	d			14 33				14 48							15 03				15 18					15 33	
Eastbrook	d			14 35				14 51							15 05				15 20					15 35	
Dinas Powys	d			14 37				14 53							15 07				15 22					15 37	
Cadoxton	d			14 42				14 57							15 12				15 27					15 42	
Barry Docks	d			14 45				15 00							15 15				15 30					15 45	
Barry 3	d			14 49				15 05							15 19				15 34					15 49	
Barry Island	a			14 56											15 26				15 41					15 56	
Rhoose Cardiff Int Airport ✈	d							15 12																	
Llantwit Major	d							15 22																	
Bridgend	a							15 41																	

b Arr. 1436

When events are being held at the Millenium Stadium, services are subject to alteration. Please check times before travelling.

Table 130

Saturdays from 17 September

Treherbert, Aberdare, Merthyr, Pontypridd, Rhymney and Coryton - Cardiff, Penarth, Barry, Barry Island and Bridgend

		AW	AW	AW	AW	AW	AW	AW	AW	AW	AW	AW	AW	AW	AW	AW	AW	AW	AW	AW	AW	AW	AW
Treherbert	d	14 17						14 47										15 13					
Ynyswen	d	14 19						14 49										15 15					
Treorchy	d	14 21						14 51										15 21					
Ton Pentre	d	14 23						14 53										15 23					
Ystrad Rhondda	a	14 26						14 56										15 26					
	d	14 28						14 58										15 28					
Llwynypia	d	14 30						15 00										15 30					
Tonypandy	d	14 33						15 03										15 33					
Dinas Rhondda	d	14 35						15 05										15 35					
Porth	a	14 38						15 08										15 38					
	d	14 52						15 09										15 39					
Trehafod	d	14 55						15 12										15 42					
Merthyr Tydfil	d				14 38										15 08								
Pentre-bach	d				14 42										15 12								
Troed Y Rhiw	d				14 45										15 15								
Merthyr Vale	a				14 48										15 18								
	d				14 50										15 20								
Quakers Yard	d				14 55										15 25								
Aberdare [3]	d										14 51									15 21			
Cwmbach	d										14 54									15 24			
Fernhill	d										14 58									15 28			
Mountain Ash	a										15 01									15 31			
	d										15 04									15 34			
Penrhiwceiber	d										15 08									15 38			
Abercynon	d				14 59						15 14				15 29					15 44			
Pontypridd [3]	a	15 00			15 07			15 17			15 23				15 37			15 47		15 53			
	d	15 04			15 09			15 18			15 24				15 39			15 48		15 54			
Trefforest	d	15 07			15 12			15 21			15 27				15 42			15 51		15 57			
Trefforest Estate	d				15 16										15 46								
Taffs Well [3]	d	15 13			15 20			15 28			15 34				15 50			15 58		16 04			
Radyr [3]	a	15 17			15 23			15 31			15 37				15 53			16 01		16 07			
	d	15 17			15 23			15 31	15 34		15 37				15 53			16 01	16 04	16 07			
Danescourt	d								15 38										16 08				
Fairwater	d								15 40										16 10				
Waun-gron Park	d								15 42										16 12				
Ninian Park	d								15 45										16 15				
Llandaf	d				15 26			15 34			15 40				15 56			16 04		16 10			
Cathays	d				15 31			15 39			15 45				16 01			16 09		16 15			
Rhymney [3]	d																				15 29		
Pontlottyn	d																				15 32		
Tir-phil	d																				15 36		
Brithdir	d																				15 39		
Bargoed	a																				15 42		
	d						15 02									15 25					15 47		
Gilfach Fargoed	d															15 27							
Pengam	d						15 07									15 30					15 52		
Hengoed	d						15 10									15 33					15 55		
Ystrad Mynach [3]	d						15 13					15 28				15b43					15 58		
Llanbradach	d						15 18					15 33				15 48					16 03		
Aber	d						15 22					15 37				15 52					16 07		
Caerphilly [3]	d						15 25					15 40				15 55					16 10		
Lisvane & Thornhill	d						15 29					15 44				15 59					16 14		
Llanishen	d						15 31					15 46				16 01					16 16		
Heath High Level	d						15 34					15 49				16 04					16 19		
Coryton	d			15 15									15 45										16 15
Whitchurch (Cardiff)	d			15 16									15 46										16 16
Rhiwbina	d			15 18									15 48										16 18
Birchgrove	d			15 20									15 50										16 20
Ty Glas	d			15 21									15 51										16 21
Heath Low Level	d			15 24									15 54										16 24
Cardiff Queen Street [3]	a			15 29	15 34		15 39	15 44			15 49	15 54	15 59		16 04	16 09		16 14		16 19	16 24		16 29
	d		15 24	15 31	15 36	15 36	15 41	15 46		15 48	15 51	15 56	16 01	16 00	16 06	16 11	16 12	16 16		16 21	16 26	16 24	16 31
Cardiff Bay	a		15 28			15 40				15 52				16 04			16 16					16 28	
Cardiff Central [7]	a	15 34		15 34	15 39		15 44	15 53	15 50		15 54	15 59	16 05		16 09	16 14		16 23	16 20	16 24	16 33		16 34
	d				15 41		15 46				15 55	16 01			16 10	16 16				16 25			
Grangetown	d				15 45		15 50				15 59	16 05			16 14	16 20				16 29			
Dingle Road	d						15 56					16 11				16 26							
Penarth	a						16 02					16 18				16 32							
Cogan	d				15 48						16 03				16 18					16 33			
Eastbrook	d				15 51						16 05				16 20					16 35			
Dinas Powys	d				15 53						16 07				16 22					16 37			
Cadoxton	d				15 57						16 12				16 27					16 42			
Barry Docks	d				16 00						16 15				16 30					16 45			
Barry [3]	d				16 05						16 19				16 34					16 49			
Barry Island	a										16 26				16 41					16 56			
Rhoose Cardiff Int Airport ✈	d				16 12																		
Llantwit Major	d				16 22																		
Bridgend	a				16 41																		

b Arr. 1536

When events are being held at the Millenium Stadium, services are subject to alteration. Please check times before travelling.

Table 130

Saturdays from 17 September

Treherbert, Aberdare, Merthyr, Pontypridd, Rhymney and Coryton - Cardiff, Penarth, Barry, Barry Island and Bridgend

		AW	AW	AW	AW	AW	AW	AW	AW	AW	AW	AW	AW	AW	AW	AW	AW	AW	AW	AW	AW	AW
Treherbert	d					15 47									16 17							
Ynyswen	d					15 49									16 19							
Treorchy	d					15 51									16 21							
Ton Pentre	d					15 53									16 23							
Ystrad Rhondda	a					15 56									16 26							
	d					15 58									16 28							
Llwynypia	d					16 00									16 30							
Tonypandy	d					16 03									16 33							
Dinas Rhondda	d					16 05									16 35							
Porth	a					16 08									16 38							
	d					16 09									16 39							
Trehafod	d					16 12									16 42							
Merthyr Tydfil	d	15 38										16 08									16 38	
Pentre-bach	d	15 42										16 12									16 42	
Troed Y Rhiw	d	15 45										16 15									16 45	
Merthyr Vale	a	15 48										16 18									16 48	
	d	15 50										16 20									16 50	
Quakers Yard	d	15 55										16 25									16 55	
Aberdare [3]	d							15 51									16 21					
Cwmbach	d							15 54									16 24					
Fernhill	d							15 58									16 28					
Mountain Ash	a							16 01									16 31					
	d							16 04									16 34					
Penrhiwceiber	d							16 08									16 38					
Abercynon	d	15 59						16 14				16 29					16 44				16 59	
Pontypridd [3]	a	16 08				16 17		16 23				16 37			16 47		16 53				17 07	
	d	16 09				16 18		16 24				16 39			16 48		16 54				17 09	
Trefforest	d	16 12				16 21		16 27				16 42			16 51		16 57				17 12	
Trefforest Estate	d	16 16										16 46									17 16	
Taffs Well [3]	d	16 20				16 28		16 34				16 50			16 58		17 04				17 20	
Radyr [3]	a	16 23				16 31		16 37				16 53			17 01		17 07				17 23	
	d	16 23			16 30	16 37		16 37				16 53			17 01	17 04	17 07				17 23	
Danescourt	d				16 34											17 08						
Fairwater	d				16 36											17 10						
Waun-gron Park	d				16 38											17 12						
Ninian Park	d				16 45	16b59										17 15						
Llandaf	d	16 26						16 40				16 56			17 04		17 10				17 26	
Cathays	d	16 31						16 45				17 01			17 09		17 15				17 31	
Rhymney [3]	d																	16 29				
Pontlottyn	d																	16 32				
Tir-phil	d																	16 36				
Brithdir	d																	16 39				
Bargoed	a																	16 42				
	d			16 02					16 17				16 32					16 47				
Gilfach Fargoed	d								16 19													
Pengam	d			16 07					16 22				16 37					16 52				
Hengoed	d			16 10					16 25				16 40					16 55				
Ystrad Mynach [3]	d			16 13					16 28				16 43					16 58				
Llanbradach	d			16 18					16 33				16 48					17 03				
Aber	d			16 22					16 37				16 52					17 07				
Caerphilly [3]	d			16 25					16 40				16 55					17 10				
Lisvane & Thornhill	d			16 29					16 44				16 59					17 14				
Llanishen	d			16 31					16 46				17 01					17 16				
Heath High Level	d			16 34					16 49				17 04					17 19				
Coryton	d									16 45										17 15		
Whitchurch (Cardiff)	d									16 46										17 16		
Rhiwbina	d									16 48										17 18		
Birchgrove	d									16 50										17 20		
Ty Glas	d									16 51										17 21		
Heath Low Level	d									16 54										17 24		
Cardiff Queen Street [3]	a	16 34		16 39				16 49	16 54	16 59		17 04	17 09		17 14		17 19	17 24		17 29	17 34	
	d	16 36	16 36	16 41			16 48	16 51	16 56	17 01	17 00	17 06	17 11	17 12	17 16		17 21	17 26	17 24	17 31	17 36	17 36
Cardiff Bay	a		16 40				16 52				17 04			17 16					17 28			17 40
Cardiff Central [7]	a	16 39		16 44	16 50	17 04		16 54	16 59	17 05		17 09	17 14		17 23	17 20	17 24	17 29		17 34	17 39	
	d	16 41		16 46				16 55	17 01			17 10	17 16				17 25	17 31			17 41	
Grangetown	d	16 45		16 50				16 59	17 05			17 14	17 20				17 29	17 35			17 45	
Dingle Road	d			16 56					17 11				17 26					17 41				
Penarth	a			17 02					17 17				17 32					17 47				
Cogan	d	16 48						17 03				17 18					17 33				17 48	
Eastbrook	d	16 51						17 05				17 20					17 35				17 51	
Dinas Powys	d	16 53						17 07				17 22					17 37				17 53	
Cadoxton	d	16 57						17 12				17 27					17 42				17 57	
Barry Docks	d	17 00						17 15				17 30					17 45				18 00	
Barry [3]	d	17 05						17 19				17 34					17 49				18 05	
Barry Island	a							17 26				17 41					17 56					
Rhoose Cardiff Int Airport ✈	d	17 12																			18 12	
Llantwit Major	d	17 22																			18 22	
Bridgend	a	17 41																			18 41	

b Arr. 1648

When events are being held at the Millenium Stadium, services are subject to alteration. Please check times before travelling.

Table 130

Saturdays
from 17 September

Treherbert, Aberdare, Merthyr, Pontypridd, Rhymney and Coryton - Cardiff, Penarth, Barry, Barry Island and Bridgend

		AW	AW	AW	AW	AW	AW	AW	AW	AW	AW	AW	AW	AW	AW	AW	AW	AW	AW	AW	AW	AW	AW
Treherbert	d		16 47										17 17								17 47		
Ynyswen	d		16 49										17 19								17 49		
Treorchy	d		16 51										17 21								17 51		
Ton Pentre	d		16 53										17 23								17 53		
Ystrad Rhondda	a		16 56										17 26								17 56		
	d		16 58										17 28								17 58		
Llwynypia	d		17 00										17 30								18 00		
Tonypandy	d		17 03										17 33								18 03		
Dinas Rhondda	d		17 05										17 35								18 05		
Porth	a		17 08										17 38								18 08		
	d		17 09										17 39								18 09		
Trehafod	d		17 12										17 42								18 12		
Merthyr Tydfil	d									17 08									17 38				
Pentre-bach	d									17 12									17 42				
Troed Y Rhiw	d									17 15									17 45				
Merthyr Vale	a									17 18									17 48				
	d									17 20									17 50				
Quakers Yard	d									17 25									17 55				
Aberdare 3	d					16 51									17 21								
Cwmbach	d					16 54									17 24								
Fernhill	d					16 58									17 28								
Mountain Ash	a					17 01									17 31								
	d					17 04									17 34								
Penrhiwceiber	d					17 08									17 38								
Abercynon	d					17 14				17 29					17 44				17 59				
Pontypridd 3	a		17 17			17 23				17 37			17 47		17 53				18 07		18 17		
	d		17 18			17 24				17 39			17 48		17 54				18 09		18 18		
Trefforest	d		17 21			17 27				17 42			17 51		17 57				18 12		18 21		
Trefforest Estate	d									17 46									18 16				
Taffs Well 3	d		17 28			17 34				17 50			17 58		18 04				18 20		18 28		
Radyr 3	a		17 31			17 37				17 53			18 01		18 07				18 23		18 31		
	d		17 31	17 34		17 37				17 53			18 01	18 04	18 07				18 23		18 31	18 34	
Danescourt	d			17 38										18 08								18 38	
Fairwater	d			17 40										18 10								18 40	
Waun-gron Park	d			17 42										18 12								18 42	
Ninian Park	d			17 45										18 15								18 45	
Llandaf	d		17 34			17 40				17 56			18 04		18 10				18 26		18 34		
Cathays	d		17 39			17 45				18 01			18 09		18 15				18 31		18 39		
Rhymney 3	d															17 29							
Pontlottyn	d															17 32							
Tir-phil	d															17 36							
Brithdir	d															17 39							
Bargoed	a															17 42							
	d	17 02					17 17				17 32					17 47							
Gilfach Fargoed	d						17 19																
Pengam	d	17 07					17 22				17 37					17 52							
Hengoed	d	17 10					17 25				17 40					17 55							
Ystrad Mynach 3	d	17 13					17 28				17 43					17 58							
Llanbradach	d	17 18					17 33				17 48					18 03							
Aber	d	17 22					17 37				17 52					18 07							
Caerphilly 3	d	17 25					17 40				17 55					18 10							
Lisvane & Thornhill	d	17 29					17 44				17 59					18 14							
Llanishen	d	17 31					17 46				18 01					18 16							
Heath High Level	d	17 34					17 49				18 04					18 19							
Coryton	d							17 45										18 15					
Whitchurch (Cardiff)	d							17 46										18 16					
Rhiwbina	d							17 48										18 18					
Birchgrove	d							17 50										18 20					
Ty Glas	d							17 51										18 21					
Heath Low Level	d							17 54										18 24					
Cardiff Queen Street 3	a	17 39	17 44			17 49	17 54	17 59		18 04	18 09		18 14		18 19	18 24		18 29	18 34		18 44		
	d	17 41	17 46		17 48	17 51	17 56	18 01	18 00	18 06	18 11	18 12	18 16		18 21	18 26	18 24	18 31	18 36	18 36	18 46		18 48
Cardiff Bay	a				17 52				18 04			18 16					18 28			18 40			18 52
Cardiff Central 7	a	17 44	17 53	17 50		17 54	17 59	18 05		18 09	18 14		18 23	18 20	18 24	18 29		18 34	18 39		18 53	18 50	
	d	17 46				17 55	18 01			18 10	18 16				18 25	18 31			18 41				
Grangetown	d	17 50				17 59	18 05			18 14	18 20				18 29	18 35			18 45				
Dingle Road	d	17 56					18 11				18 26					18 41							
Penarth	a	18 02					18 18				18 34					18 47							
Cogan	d					18 03				18 18					18 33				18 48				
Eastbrook	d					18 05				18 20					18 35				18 51				
Dinas Powys	d					18 07				18 22					18 37				18 53				
Cadoxton	d					18 12				18 27					18 42				18 57				
Barry Docks	d					18 15				18 30					18 45				19 00				
Barry 3	d					18 19				18 34					18 49				19 05				
Barry Island	a					18 26				18 41					18 56								
Rhoose Cardiff Int Airport ✈	d																		19 12				
Llantwit Major	d																		19 22				
Bridgend	a																		19 41				

When events are being held at the Millenium Stadium, services are subject to alteration. Please check times before travelling.

Table 130

Saturdays
from 17 September

Treherbert, Aberdare, Merthyr, Pontypridd, Rhymney and Coryton - Cardiff, Penarth, Barry, Barry Island and Bridgend

		AW	AW	AW	AW	AW	AW	AW	AW	AW	AW	AW	AW	AW	AW	AW	AW	AW	AW	AW	AW	AW	AW
Treherbert	d							18 17								18 47							19 17
Ynyswen	d							18 19								18 49							19 19
Treorchy	d							18 21								18 51							19 21
Ton Pentre	d							18 23								18 53							19 23
Ystrad Rhondda	a							18 26								18 56							19 26
	d							18 28								18 58							19 28
Llwynypia	d							18 30								19 00							19 30
Tonypandy	d							18 33								19 03							19 33
Dinas Rhondda	d							18 35								19 05							19 35
Porth	a							18 38								19 08							19 38
	d							18 39								19 09							19 39
Trehafod	d							18 42								19 12							19 42
Merthyr Tydfil	d					18 08								18 38							19 08		
Pentre-bach	d					18 12								18 42							19 12		
Troed Y Rhiw	d					18 15								18 45							19 15		
Merthyr Vale	a					18 18								18 48							19 18		
	d					18 20								18 50							19 20		
Quakers Yard	d					18 25								18 55							19 25		
Aberdare 3	d	17 51								18 21								18 51					
Cwmbach	d	17 54								18 24								18 54					
Fernhill	d	17 58								18 28								18 58					
Mountain Ash	a	18 01								18 31								19 01					
	d	18 04								18 34								19 04					
Penrhiwceiber	d	18 08								18 38								19 08					
Abercynon	d	18 14				18 29				18 44				18 59				19 14			19 29		
Pontypridd 3	a	18 23				18 37		18 47		18 53				19 07		19 17		19 23			19 37		19 47
	d	18 24				18 39		18 48		18 54				19 09		19 18		19 24			19 39		19 48
Trefforest	d	18 27				18 42		18 51		18 57				19 12		19 21		19 27			19 42		19 51
Trefforest Estate	d					18 46								19 16							19 46		
Taffs Well 3	d	18 34				18 50		18 58		19 04				19 20		19 28		19 34			19 50		19 58
Radyr 3	a	18 37				18 53		19 01		19 07				19 23		19 31		19 37			19 53		20 01
	d	18 37				18 53		19 01	19 04	19 07				19 23		19 31		19 37			19 53		20 01
Danescourt	d								19 08														
Fairwater	d								19 10														
Waun-gron Park	d								19 12														
Ninian Park	d								19 15														
Llandaf	d	18 40				18 56		19 04		19 10				19 26		19 34		19 40			19 56		20 04
Cathays	d	18 45				19 01		19 09		19 15				19 31		19 39		19 45			20 01		20 09
Rhymney 3	d																						
Pontlottyn	d																						
Tir-phil	d																						
Brithdir	d																						
Bargoed	a																						
	d		18 17								18 48												
Gilfach Fargoed	d		18 19								18 50												
Pengam	d		18 22								18 53												
Hengoed	d		18 25								18 56												
Ystrad Mynach 3	d		18 28								18 59												
Llanbradach	d		18 33								19 04												
Aber	d		18 37								19 08												
Caerphilly 3	d		18 40								19 11								19 40				
Lisvane & Thornhill	d		18 44								19 15								19 44				
Llanishen	d		18 46								19 17								19 46				
Heath High Level	d		18 49								19 20								19 49				
Coryton	d			18 45									19 15										
Whitchurch (Cardiff)	d			18 46									19 16										
Rhiwbina	d			18 48									19 18										
Birchgrove	d			18 50									19 20										
Ty Glas	d			18 51									19 21										
Heath Low Level	d			18 54									19 24										
Cardiff Queen Street 3	a	18 49	18 54	18 59		19 04		19 14		19 19	19 24		19 29	19 35		19 44		19 49	19 54		20 04		20 14
	d	18 51	18 56	19 01	19 00	19 06	19 12	19 16		19 21	19 26	19 24	19 31	19 36	19 36	19 46	19 48	19 51	19 56	20 00	20 06	20 12	20 16
Cardiff Bay	a				19 04		19 16					19 28			19 40		19 52			20 04		20 16	
Cardiff Central 7	a	18 54	18 59	19 07		19 10		19 23	19 22	19 24	19 29		19 34	19 40		19 53		19 57	19 59		20 10		20 20
	d	18 55	19 01							19 25	19 31			19 41					20 06		20 10		
Grangetown	d	18 59	19 05							19 29	19 35			19 45					20 10		20 14		
Dingle Road	d		19 11								19 41								20 14				
Penarth	a		19 17								19 47								20 20				
Cogan	d	19 03								19 33				19 48							20 18		
Eastbrook	d	19 05								19 35				19 51							20 20		
Dinas Powys	d	19 07								19 37				19 53							20 22		
Cadoxton	d	19 12								19 42				19 57							20 27		
Barry Docks	d	19 15								19 45				20 00							20 30		
Barry 3	d	19 19								19 49				20 05							20 34		
Barry Island	a	19 26								19 56											20 41		
Rhoose Cardiff Int Airport ✈	d													20 12									
Llantwit Major	d													20 22									
Bridgend	a													20 41									

When events are being held at the Millenium Stadium, services are subject to alteration. Please check times before travelling.

Table 130

Saturdays from 17 September

Treherbert, Aberdare, Merthyr, Pontypridd, Rhymney and Coryton - Cardiff, Penarth, Barry, Barry Island and Bridgend

		AW	AW	AW	AW	AW	AW	AW	AW	AW	AW	AW	AW	AW	AW	AW	AW	AW	AW	AW	AW	AW
Treherbert	d								19 47						20 17							
Ynyswen	d								19 49						20 19							
Treorchy	d								19 51						20 21							
Ton Pentre	d								19 53						20 23							
Ystrad Rhondda	a								19 56						20 26							
	d								19 58						20 28							
Llwynypia	d								20 00						20 30							
Tonypandy	d								20 03						20 33							
Dinas Rhondda	d								20 05						20 35							
Porth	a								20 08						20 38							
	d								20 09						20 39							
Trehafod	d								20 12						20 42							
Merthyr Tydfil	d					19 38															20 38	
Pentre-bach	d					19 42															20 42	
Troed Y Rhiw	d					19 45															20 45	
Merthyr Vale	a					19 48															20 48	
	d					19 50															20 50	
Quakers Yard	d					19 55															20 55	
Aberdare [3]	d										19 51						20 21					
Cwmbach	d										19 54						20 24					
Fernhill	d										19 58						20 28					
Mountain Ash	a										20 01						20 31					
	d										20 04						20 34					
Penrhiwceiber	d										20 08						20 38					
Abercynon	d		19 43			19 59					20 14						20 44				20 59	
Pontypridd [3]	a		19 53			20 07			20 17		20 23				20 47		20 53				21 07	
	d		19 54			20 09			20 18		20 24				20 48		20 54				21 09	
Trefforest	d		19 57			20 12			20 21		20 27				20 51		20 57				21 12	
Trefforest Estate	d					20 16															21 16	
Taffs Well [3]	d		20 04			20 20			20 28		20 34				20 58		21 04				21 20	
Radyr [3]	a		20 07			20 23			20 31		20 37				21 01		21 07				21 23	
	d	20 04	20 07			20 23			20 31		20 37				21 01	21 04	21 07				21 23	
Danescourt	d	20 08														21 08						
Fairwater	d	20 10														21 10						
Waun-gron Park	d	20 12														21 12						
Ninian Park	d	20 15														21 15						
Llandaf	d		20 10			20 26			20 34		20 40				21 04		21 10				21 26	
Cathays	d		20 15			20 31			20 39		20 45				21 09		21 15				21 31	
Rhymney [3]	d							19 45														
Pontlottyn	d							19 48														
Tir-phil	d							19 52														
Brithdir	d							19 55														
Bargoed	a							19 58														
	d							19 59														
Gilfach Fargoed	d							20 01														
Pengam	d							20 04														
Hengoed	d							20 07														
Ystrad Mynach [3]	d							20 10														
Llanbradach	d							20 15														
Aber	d							20 19														
Caerphilly [3]	d							20 22				20 40										
Lisvane & Thornhill	d							20 26				20 44										
Llanishen	d							20 28				20 46										
Heath High Level	d							20 31				20 49										
Coryton	d				20 15															21 15		
Whitchurch (Cardiff)	d				20 16															21 16		
Rhiwbina	d				20 18															21 18		
Birchgrove	d				20 20															21 20		
Ty Glas	d				20 21															21 21		
Heath Low Level	d				20 24															21 24		
Cardiff Queen Street [3]	a		20 19		20 29	20 34		20 39	20 44		20 49	20 54			21 14		21 19			21 29	21 34	
	d		20 21	20 24	20 31	20 36	20 36	20 41	20 46	20 48	20 51	20 56	21 00	21 12	21 16		21 21	21 24		21 31	21 36	21 36
Cardiff Bay	a			20 28			20 40			20 52			21 04	21 16				21 28				21 40
Cardiff Central [7]	a	20 25	20 24		20 34	20 39		20 48	20 53		20 57	20 59			21 22	21 25	21 24			21 34	21 39	
	d		20 31			20 41					21 06	21 10							21 32		21 41	
Grangetown	d		20 35			20 45					21 10	21 14							21 36		21 45	
Dingle Road	d		20 41								21 14								21 41			
Penarth	a		20 47								21 20								21 47			
Cogan	d					20 48						21 18									21 48	
Eastbrook	d					20 51						21 20									21 51	
Dinas Powys	d					20 53						21 22									21 53	
Cadoxton	d					20 57						21 27									21 57	
Barry Docks	d					21 00						21 30									22 00	
Barry [3]	d					21 05						21 34									22 05	
Barry Island	a											21 41										
Rhoose Cardiff Int Airport ✈	d					21 12															22 12	
Llantwit Major	d					21 22															22 22	
Bridgend	a					21 43															22 41	

When events are being held at the Millenium Stadium, services are subject to alteration. Please check times before travelling.

Table 130

Saturdays from 17 September

Treherbert, Aberdare, Merthyr, Pontypridd, Rhymney and Coryton - Cardiff, Penarth, Barry, Barry Island and Bridgend

		AW	AW	AW	AW	AW	AW	AW	AW	AW	AW	AW	AW	AW	AW	AW	AW	AW	AW	AW	AW	AW	AW	AW
Treherbert	d							21 17																
Ynyswen	d							21 19																
Treorchy	d							21 21																
Ton Pentre	d							21 23																
Ystrad Rhondda	a							21 26																
	d							21 28																
Llwynypia	d							21 30																
Tonypandy	d							21 33																
Dinas Rhondda	d							21 35																
Porth	a							21 38																
	d							21 39																
Trehafod	d							21 42																
Merthyr Tydfil	d											21 38									22 38			
Pentre-bach	d											21 42									22 42			
Troed Y Rhiw	d											21 45									22 45			
Merthyr Vale	a											21 48									22 48			
	d											21 50									22 50			
Quakers Yard	d											21 55									22 55			
Aberdare [3]	d			20 51											21 51							22 51		
Cwmbach	d			20 54											21 54							22 54		
Fernhill	d			20 58											21 57							22 58		
Mountain Ash	a			21 01											22 00							23 01		
	d			21 04											22 04							23 04		
Penrhiwceiber	d			21 08											22 07							23 08		
Abercynon	d			21 14								21 59			22 13						22 59	23 14		
Pontypridd [3]	a			21 24				21 47				22 07			22 22						23 07	23 22		
	d			21 24				21 48				22 09			22 24						23 09			
Trefforest	d			21 27				21 51				22 12			22 27						23 12			
Trefforest Estate	d											22 16									23 16			
Taffs Well [3]	d			21 34				21 58				22 20			22 34						23 20			
Radyr [3]	a			21 37				22 01				22 23			22 37						23 23			
	d			21 37				22 01	22 04			22 23			22 37				23 10		23 23			
Danescourt	d								22 08															
Fairwater	d								22 10															
Waun-gron Park	d								22 12															
Ninian Park	d								22 15															
Llandaf	d			21 40				22 04				22 26			22 40				23 12		23 26			
Cathays	d			21 45				22 09				22 31			22 45				23 16		23 31			
Rhymney [3]	d	20 48									21 34													
Pontlottyn	d	20 51									21 37													
Tir-phil	d	20 55									21 41													
Brithdir	d	20 58									21 44													
Bargoed	a	21 01									21 47													
	d	21 02									21 48													
Gilfach Fargoed	d	21 04									21 50													
Pengam	d	21 07									21 53													
Hengoed	d	21 10									21 56													
Ystrad Mynach [3]	d	21 13									21 59													
Llanbradach	d	21 18									22 04													
Aber	d	21 22									22 08													
Caerphilly [3]	d	21 25			21 45						22 11													
Lisvane & Thornhill	d	21 29			21 50						22 15													
Llanishen	d	21 31			21 52						22 17													
Heath High Level	d	21 34			21 54						22 20													
Coryton	d															22 45								
Whitchurch (Cardiff)	d															22 46								
Rhiwbina	d															22 48								
Birchgrove	d															22 50								
Ty Glas	d															22 51								
Heath Low Level	d															22 54								
Cardiff Queen Street [3]	a	21 42		21 49	22 00			22 14			22 25	22 34			22 49	22 59			23 19		23 34			
	d	21 44	21 48	21 51	22 01	22 00	22 12	22 16		22 24	22 27	22 36	22 36	22 48	22 54	23 01	23 00	23 12	23 20	23 24	23 36		23 36	23 48
Cardiff Bay	a		21 52			22 04	22 16			22 28			22 40	22 52			23 04	23 16		23 28			23 40	23 52
Cardiff Central [7]	a	21 51		21 54	22 04			22 22	22 20		22 30	22 41			22 59	23 07			23 25		23 43			
	d			22 06	22 10						22 31				23 12				23 30					
Grangetown	d			22 10	22 14						22 35				23 16				23 34					
Dingle Road	d			22 14							22 41				23 20									
Penarth	a			22 20							22 49				23 26									
Cogan	d				22 18														23 37					
Eastbrook	d				22 20														23 40					
Dinas Powys	d				22 22														23 42					
Cadoxton	d				22 27														23 46					
Barry Docks	d				22 30														23 49					
Barry [3]	d				22 34														23 54					
Barry Island	a				22 41														00 01					
Rhoose Cardiff Int Airport ✈	d																							
Llantwit Major	d																							
Bridgend	a																							

When events are being held at the Millenium Stadium, services are subject to alteration. Please check times before travelling.

Table 130

Sundays
until 31 July

Treherbert, Aberdare, Merthyr, Pontypridd, Rhymney and Coryton - Cardiff, Penarth, Barry, Barry Island and Bridgend

		AW	AW	AW	AW	AW	AW	AW	AW	AW	AW	AW	AW	AW	AW	AW	AW	AW	AW	AW	AW	AW
Treherbert	d					08 17																10 07
Ynyswen	d					08 19																10 09
Treorchy	d					08 21																10 11
Ton Pentre	d					08 23																10 13
Ystrad Rhondda	a					08 26																10 16
	d					08 28																10 18
Llwynypia	d					08 30																10 20
Tonypandy	d					08 33																10 23
Dinas Rhondda	d					08 35																10 25
Porth	a					08 38																10 28
	d					08 39																10 29
Trehafod	d					08 42																10 32
Merthyr Tydfil	d															09 38						
Pentre-bach	d															09 42						
Troed Y Rhiw	d															09 45						
Merthyr Vale	a															09 48						
	d															09 50						
Quakers Yard	d															09 55						
Aberdare ■	d																		09 52			
Cwmbach	d																		09 55			
Fernhill	d																		09 58			
Mountain Ash	a																		10 01			
	d																		10 04			
Penrhiwceiber	d																		10 07			
Abercynon	d															09 59			10 13			
Pontypridd ■	a					08 47										10 07			10 23			10 37
	d					08 48										10 09			10 24			10 38
Trefforest	d					08 51										10 12			10 27			10 41
Trefforest Estate	d																					
Taffs Well ■	d					08 58										10 20			10 34			10 48
Radyr ■	a					09 01										10 23			10 37			10 51
	d					09 01										10 23			10 37			10 51
Danescourt	d																					
Fairwater	d																					
Waun-gron Park	d																					
Ninian Park	d																					
Llandaf	d					09 04										10 26			10 40			10 54
Cathays	d					09 09										10 31			10 45			10 59
Rhymney ■	d												09 22									
Pontlottyn	d												09 25									
Tir-phil	d												09 29									
Brithdir	d												09 32									
Bargoed	a												09 35									
	d												09 37									
Gilfach Fargoed	d												09 39									
Pengam	d												09 42									
Hengoed	d												09 45									
Ystrad Mynach ■	d												09 48									
Llanbradach	d												09 53									
Aber	d												09 57									
Caerphilly ■	d												10 00									
Lisvane & Thornhill	d												10 04									
Llanishen	d												10 06									
Heath High Level	d												10 09									
Coryton	d																					
Whitchurch (Cardiff)	d																					
Rhiwbina	d																					
Birchgrove	d																					
Ty Glas	d																					
Heath Low Level	d																					
Cardiff Queen Street ■	a					09 14							10 14			10 34			10 49			11 02
	d			09 00	09 12	09 16	09 24	09 36	09 48		10 00	10 12	10 16	10 24		10 36	10 36	10 48	10 51	11 00		11 04
Cardiff Bay	a			09 04	09 16		09 28	09 40	09 52		10 04	10 16		10 28			10 40	10 52		11 04		
Cardiff Central ■	a					09 18							10 18			10 39			10 54			11 07
	d	08 25	08 41			09 25				09 55			10 25		10 31	10 41			10 55		11 15	11 25
Grangetown	d	08 29	08 45			09 29				09 59			10 29		10 35	10 45			10 59			11 29
Dingle Road	d														10 41							
Penarth	a														10 46							
Cogan	d	08 33	08 48			09 33				10 03			10 33			10 48			11 03			11 33
Eastbrook	d	08 35	08 51			09 35				10 05			10 35			10 51			11 05			11 35
Dinas Powys	d	08 37	08 53			09 37				10 07			10 37			10 53			11 07			11 37
Cadoxton	d	08 42	08 57			09 42				10 12			10 42			10 57			11 12			11 42
Barry Docks	d	08 45	09 00			09 45				10 15			10 45			11 00			11 15			11 45
Barry ■	d	08 49	09 05			09 49				10 19			10 49			11 05			11 19		11 34	11 49
Barry Island	a	08 55				09 55				10 25			10 55						11 25		11 41	11 55
Rhoose Cardiff Int Airport ✈	d		09 12													11 12						
Llantwit Major	d		09 22													11 22						
Bridgend	a		09 40													11 40						

When events are being held at the Millenium Stadium, services are subject to alteration. Please check times before travelling.

Table 130

Sundays
until 31 July

Treherbert, Aberdare, Merthyr, Pontypridd, Rhymney and Coryton - Cardiff, Penarth, Barry, Barry Island and Bridgend

		AW	AW	AW	AW	AW	AW	AW	AW	AW	AW	AW	AW	AW	AW	AW	AW	AW	AW	AW	AW	AW	AW
Treherbert	d																12 07						
Ynyswen	d																12 09						
Treorchy	d																12 11						
Ton Pentre	d																12 13						
Ystrad Rhondda	a																12 16						
	d																12 18						
Llwynypia	d																12 20						
Tonypandy	d																12 23						
Dinas Rhondda	d																12 25						
Porth	a																12 28						
	d																12 29						
Trehafod	d																12 32						
Merthyr Tydfil	d											11 38											
Pentre-bach	d											11 42											
Troed Y Rhiw	d											11 45											
Merthyr Vale	a											11 48											
	d											11 50											
Quakers Yard	d											11 55											
Aberdare ■	d					10 52																12 52	
Cwmbach	d					10 55																12 55	
Fernhill	d					10 58																12 58	
Mountain Ash	a					11 01																13 01	
	d					11 04																13 04	
Penrhiwceiber	d					11 07																13 07	
Abercynon	d					11 13						11 59										13 13	
Pontypridd ■	a					11 23						12 07					12 37					13 23	
	d					11 24						12 09					12 38					13 24	
Trefforest	d					11 27						12 12					12 41					13 27	
Trefforest Estate	d																						
Taffs Well ■	d					11 34						12 20					12 48					13 34	
Radyr ■	a					11 37						12 23					12 51					13 37	
	d					11 37						12 23					12 51					13 37	
Danescourt	d																						
Fairwater	d																						
Waun-gron Park	d																						
Ninian Park	d																						
Llandaf	d					11 40						12 26					12 54					13 40	
Cathays	d					11 45						12 31					12 59					13 45	
Rhymney ■	d							11 10															
Pontlottyn	d							11 13															
Tir-phil	d							11 17															
Brithdir	d							11 20															
Bargoed	a							11 23															
	d							11 25															
Gilfach Fargoed	d							11 27															
Pengam	d							11 30															
Hengoed	d							11 33															
Ystrad Mynach ■	d							11 36															
Llanbradach	d							11 41															
Aber	d							11 45															
Caerphilly ■	d							11 48															
Lisvane & Thornhill	d							11 52															
Llanishen	d							11 54															
Heath High Level	d							11 57															
Coryton	d																						
Whitchurch (Cardiff)	d																						
Rhiwbina	d																						
Birchgrove	d																						
Ty Glas	d																						
Heath Low Level	d																						
Cardiff Queen Street ■	a					11 49		12 02				12 34					13 04					13 49	
	d	11 12	11 24	11 36	11 48	11 51	12 00	12 04	12 12	12 24		12 36	12 36	12 48		13 00	13 04	13 12	13 24	13 36	13 48	13 51	14 00
Cardiff Bay	a	11 16	11 28	11 40	11 52		12 04		12 16	12 28			12 40	12 52		13 04		13 16	13 28	13 40	13 52		14 04
Cardiff Central ■	a					11 54		12 07				12 39					13 06					13 54	
	d					11 55		12 25			12 31	12 41			12 55		13 25					13 55	
Grangetown	d					11 59		12 29			12 35	12 45			12 59		13 29					13 59	
Dingle Road	d										12 41												
Penarth	a										12 46												
Cogan	d					12 03		12 33				12 48			13 03		13 33					14 03	
Eastbrook	d					12 05		12 35				12 51			13 05		13 35					14 05	
Dinas Powys	d					12 07		12 37				12 53			13 07		13 37					14 07	
Cadoxton	d					12 12		12 42				12 57			13 12		13 42					14 12	
Barry Docks	d					12 15		12 45				13 00			13 15		13 45					14 15	
Barry ■	d					12 19		12 49				13 05			13 19		13 49					14 19	
Barry Island	a					12 25		12 55							13 25		13 55					14 25	
Rhoose Cardiff Int Airport ✈	d											13 12											
Llantwit Major	d											13 22											
Bridgend	a											13 40											

When events are being held at the Millenium Stadium, services are subject to alteration. Please check times before travelling.

Table 130

Sundays until 31 July

Treherbert, Aberdare, Merthyr, Pontypridd, Rhymney and Coryton - Cardiff, Penarth, Barry, Barry Island and Bridgend

		AW		AW	AW	AW	AW	AW	AW	AW	AW	AW		AW	AW	AW	AW	AW	AW	AW	AW	AW		AW	AW
Treherbert	d													14 17											
Ynyswen	d													14 19											
Treorchy	d													14 21											
Ton Pentre	d													14 23											
Ystrad Rhondda	a													14 26											
	d													14 28											
Llwynypia	d													14 30											
Tonypandy	d													14 33											
Dinas Rhondda	d													14 35											
Porth	a													14 38											
	d													14 39											
Trehafod	d													14 42											
Merthyr Tydfil	d						13 38																		15 38
Pentre-bach	d						13 42																		15 42
Troed Y Rhiw	d						13 45																		15 45
Merthyr Vale	a						13 48																		15 48
	d						13 50																		15 50
Quakers Yard	d						13 55																		15 55
Aberdare 3	d																	14 52							
Cwmbach	d																	14 55							
Fernhill	d																	14 58							
Mountain Ash	a																	15 01							
	d																	15 04							
Penrhiwceiber	d																	15 07							
Abercynon	d						13 59											15 13							15 59
Pontypridd 3	a						14 07							14 47				15 23							16 07
	d						14 09							14 48				15 24							16 09
Trefforest	d						14 12							14 51				15 27							16 12
Trefforest Estate	d																								
Taffs Well 3	d						14 20							14 58				15 34							16 20
Radyr 3	a						14 23							15 01				15 37							16 23
	d						14 23							15 01				15 37							16 23
Danescourt	d																								
Fairwater	d																								
Waun-gron Park	d																								
Ninian Park	d																								
Llandaf	d						14 26							15 04				15 40							16 26
Cathays	d						14 31							15 09				15 45							16 31
Rhymney 3	d	13 10																			15 22				
Pontlottyn	d	13 13																			15 25				
Tir-phil	d	13 17																			15 29				
Brithdir	d	13 20																			15 32				
Bargoed	a	13 23																			15 35				
	d	13 25																			15 37				
Gilfach Fargoed	d	13 27																			15 39				
Pengam	d	13 30																			15 42				
Hengoed	d	13 33																			15 45				
Ystrad Mynach 3	d	13 36																			15 48				
Llanbradach	d	13 41																			15 53				
Aber	d	13 45																			15 57				
Caerphilly 3	d	13 48																			16 00				
Lisvane & Thornhill	d	13 52																			16 04				
Llanishen	d	13 54																			16 06				
Heath High Level	d	13 57																			16 09				
Coryton	d																								
Whitchurch (Cardiff)	d																								
Rhiwbina	d																								
Birchgrove	d																								
Ty Glas	d																								
Heath Low Level	d																								
Cardiff Queen Street 3	a	14 02					14 34							15 14				15 49			16 14				16 34
	d	14 04		14 12	14 24		14 36	14 36	14 48		15 00	15 12		15 16	15 24	15 36	15 48	15 51	16 00	16 12	16 16	16 24			16 36
Cardiff Bay	a			14 16	14 28			14 40	14 52		15 04	15 16			15 28	15 40	15 52		16 04	16 16		16 28			
Cardiff Central 7	a	14 07					14 39							15 18				15 54			16 18				16 39
	d	14 25				14 31	14 41			14 55				15 25				15 55			16 25			16 31	16 41
Grangetown	d	14 29				14 35	14 45			14 59				15 29				15 59			16 29			16 35	16 45
Dingle Road	d					14 41																		16 41	
Penarth	a					14 46																		16 46	
Cogan	d	14 33					14 48			15 03				15 33				16 03			16 33				16 48
Eastbrook	d	14 35					14 51			15 05				15 35				16 05			16 35				16 51
Dinas Powys	d	14 37					14 53			15 07				15 37				16 07			16 37				16 53
Cadoxton	d	14 42					14 57			15 12				15 42				16 12			16 42				16 57
Barry Docks	d	14 45					15 00			15 15				15 45				16 15			16 45				17 00
Barry 3	d	14 49					15 05			15 19				15 49				16 19			16 49				17 05
Barry Island	a	14 55								15 25				15 55				16 25			16 55				
Rhoose Cardiff Int Airport ✈	d						15 12																		17 12
Llantwit Major	d						15 22																		17 22
Bridgend	a						15 40																		17 40

When events are being held at the Millenium Stadium, services are subject to alteration. Please check times before travelling.

Table 130

Sundays until 31 July

Treherbert, Aberdare, Merthyr, Pontypridd, Rhymney and Coryton - Cardiff, Penarth, Barry, Barry Island and Bridgend

		AW	AW	AW	AW	AW	AW	AW		AW	AW	AW	AW	AW	AW	AW	AW	AW		AW	AW	AW	AW	AW	AW
Treherbert	d						16 17																	18 17	
Ynyswen	d						16 19																	18 19	
Treorchy	d						16 21																	18 21	
Ton Pentre	d						16 23																	18 23	
Ystrad Rhondda	a						16 26																	18 26	
	d						16 28																	18 28	
Llwynypia	d						16 30																	18 30	
Tonypandy	d						16 33																	18 33	
Dinas Rhondda	d						16 35																	18 35	
Porth	a						16 38																	18 38	
	d						16 39																	18 39	
Trehafod	d						16 42																	18 42	
Merthyr Tydfil	d																	17 38							
Pentre-bach	d																	17 42							
Troed Y Rhiw	d																	17 45							
Merthyr Vale	a																	17 48							
	d																	17 50							
Quakers Yard	d																	17 55							
Aberdare 3	d											16 52													18 52
Cwmbach	d											16 55													18 55
Fernhill	d											16 58													18 58
Mountain Ash	a											17 01													19 01
	d											17 04													19 04
Penrhiwceiber	d											17 07													19 07
Abercynon	d											17 13						17 59							19 13
Pontypridd 3	a						16 47					17 23						18 07						18 47	19 23
	d						16 48					17 24						18 09						18 48	19 24
Trefforest	d						16 51					17 27						18 12						18 51	19 27
Trefforest Estate	d																								
Taffs Well 3	d						16 58					17 34						18 20						18 58	19 34
Radyr 3	a						17 01					17 37						18 23						19 01	19 37
	d						17 01					17 37						18 23						19 01	19 37
Danescourt	d																								
Fairwater	d																								
Waun-gron Park	d																								
Ninian Park	d																								
Llandaf	d						17 04					17 40						18 26						19 04	19 40
Cathays	d						17 09					17 45						18 31						19 09	19 45
Rhymney 3	d														17 22										
Pontlottyn	d														17 25										
Tir-phil	d														17 29										
Brithdir	d														17 32										
Bargoed	a														17 35										
	d														17 37										
Gilfach Fargoed	d														17 39										
Pengam	d														17 42										
Hengoed	d														17 45										
Ystrad Mynach 3	d														17 48										
Llanbradach	d														17 53										
Aber	d														17 57										
Caerphilly 3	d														18 00										
Lisvane & Thornhill	d														18 04										
Llanishen	d														18 06										
Heath High Level	d														18 09										
Coryton	d																								
Whitchurch (Cardiff)	d																								
Rhiwbina	d																								
Birchgrove	d																								
Ty Glas	d																								
Heath Low Level	d																								
Cardiff Queen Street 3	a						17 14					17 49			18 14			18 34						19 14	19 49
	d	16 36	16 48		17 00	17 12	17 16	17 24		17 36	17 48	17 51	18 00	18 12	18 16	18 24		18 36		18 36	18 48		19 00	19 16	19 51
Cardiff Bay	a	16 40	16 52		17 04	17 16		17 28		17 40	17 52		18 04	18 16		18 28				18 40	18 52				
Cardiff Central 7	a						17 18					17 54			18 18			18 39					19 03	19 18	19 54
	d			16 55			17 25					17 55			18 25		18 31	18 41				18 55		19 25	19 55
Grangetown	d			16 59			17 29					17 59			18 29		18 35	18 45				18 59		19 29	19 59
Dingle Road	d																18 41								
Penarth	a																18 46								
Cogan	d			17 03			17 33					18 03			18 33			18 48				19 03		19 33	20 03
Eastbrook	d			17 05			17 35					18 05			18 35			18 51				19 05		19 35	20 05
Dinas Powys	d			17 07			17 37					18 07			18 37			18 53				19 07		19 37	20 07
Cadoxton	d			17 12			17 42					18 12			18 42			18 57				19 12		19 42	20 12
Barry Docks	d			17 15			17 45					18 15			18 45			19 00				19 15		19 45	20 15
Barry 3	d			17 19			17 49					18 19			18 49			19 05				19 19		19 49	20 19
Barry Island	a			17 25			17 55					18 25			18 55							19 25		19 55	20 25
Rhoose Cardiff Int Airport ✈	d																	19 12							
Llantwit Major	d																	19 22							
Bridgend	a																	19 40							

When events are being held at the Millenium Stadium, services are subject to alteration. Please check times before travelling.

Table 130

Sundays
until 31 July

Treherbert, Aberdare, Merthyr, Pontypridd, Rhymney and Coryton - Cardiff, Penarth, Barry, Barry Island and Bridgend

		AW	AW	AW	AW	AW	AW	AW	AW
Treherbert	d					20 17			
Ynyswen	d					20 19			
Treorchy	d					20 21			
Ton Pentre	d					20 23			
Ystrad Rhondda	a					20 26			
	d					20 28			
Llwynypia	d					20 30			
Tonypandy	d					20 33			
Dinas Rhondda	d					20 35			
Porth	a					20 38			
	d					20 39			
Trehafod	d					20 42			
Merthyr Tydfil	d			19 38					21 38
Pentre-bach	d			19 42					21 42
Troed Y Rhiw	d			19 45					21 45
Merthyr Vale	a			19 48					21 48
	d			19 50					21 50
Quakers Yard	d			19 55					21 55
Aberdare 3	d						20 54		
Cwmbach	d						20 57		
Fernhill	d						21 00		
Mountain Ash	a						21 03		
	d						21 04		
Penrhiwceiber	d						21 07		
Abercynon	d			19 59			21 13		21 59
Pontypridd 3	a			20 07		20 47	21 23		22 07
	d			20 09		20 48	21 24		22 09
Trefforest	d			20 12		20 51	21 27		22 12
Trefforest Estate	d								
Taffs Well 3	d			20 20		20 58	21 34		22 20
Radyr 3	a			20 23		21 01	21 37		22 23
	d			20 23		21 01	21 37		22 23
Danescourt	d								
Fairwater	d								
Waun-gron Park	d								
Ninian Park	d					21 12			
Llandaf	d			20 26					22 26
Cathays	d			20 31					22 31
Rhymney 3	d	19 22							
Pontlottyn	d	19 25							
Tir-phil	d	19 29							
Brithdir	d	19 32							
Bargoed	a	19 35							
	d	19 37							
Gilfach Fargoed	d	19 39							
Pengam	d	19 42							
Hengoed	d	19 45							
Ystrad Mynach 3	d	19 48							
Llanbradach	d	19 53							
Aber	d	19 57							
Caerphilly 3	d	20 00							
Lisvane & Thornhill	d	20 04							
Llanishen	d	20 06							
Heath High Level	d	20 09							
Coryton	d								
Whitchurch (Cardiff)	d								
Rhiwbina	d								
Birchgrove	d								
Ty Glas	d								
Heath Low Level	d								
Cardiff Queen Street 3	a	20 14		20 34					22 34
	d	20 16		20 36					22 36
Cardiff Bay	a								
Cardiff Central 7	a	20 18		20 39		21 15	21 51		22 41
	d	20 25	20 31	20 41	20 55	21 26		22 25	
Grangetown	d	20 29	20 35	20 45	20 59	21 30		22 29	
Dingle Road	d		20 41						
Penarth	a		20 46						
Cogan	d	20 33		20 48	21 03	21 33		22 33	
Eastbrook	d	20 35		20 51	21 05	21 36		22 35	
Dinas Powys	d	20 37		20 53	21 07	21 38		22 37	
Cadoxton	d	20 42		20 57	21 12	21 42		22 42	
Barry Docks	d	20 45		21 00	21 15	21 45		22 45	
Barry 3	d	20 49		21 05	21 19	21 49		22 49	
Barry Island	a	20 55			21 25	21 55		22 55	
Rhoose Cardiff Int Airport ✈	d			21 12					
Llantwit Major	d			21 22					
Bridgend	a			21 40					

When events are being held at the Millenium Stadium, services are subject to alteration. Please check times before travelling.

Table 130

Sundays
7 August to 11 September

Treherbert, Aberdare, Merthyr, Pontypridd, Rhymney and Coryton - Cardiff, Penarth, Barry, Barry Island and Bridgend

		AW	AW	AW	AW	AW	AW	AW	AW	AW	AW	AW	AW	AW	AW	AW	AW	AW	AW	AW	AW	AW	AW
Treherbert	d						08 17																
Ynyswen	d						08 19																
Treorchy	d						08 21																
Ton Pentre	d						08 23																
Ystrad Rhondda	a						08 26																
	d						08 28																
Llwynypia	d						08 30																
Tonypandy	d						08 33																
Dinas Rhondda	d						08 35																
Porth	a						08 38																
	d						08 39																
Trehafod	d						08 42																
Merthyr Tydfil	d																09 38						
Pentre-bach	d																09 42						
Troed Y Rhiw	d																09 45						
Merthyr Vale	a																09 48						
	d																09 50						
Quakers Yard	d																09 55						
Aberdare 3	d																			09 52			
Cwmbach	d																			09 55			
Fernhill	d																			09 58			
Mountain Ash	a																			10 01			
	d																			10 04			
Penrhiwceiber	d																			10 07			
Abercynon	d																09 59			10 13			
Pontypridd 3	a						08 47										10 07			10 23			
	d						08 48										10 09			10 24			
Trefforest	d						08 51										10 12			10 27			
Trefforest Estate	d																						
Taffs Well 3	d						08 58										10 20			10 34			
Radyr 3	a						09 01										10 23			10 37			
	d						09 01										10 23			10 37			
Danescourt	d																						
Fairwater	d																						
Waun-gron Park	d																						
Ninian Park	d																						
Llandaf	d						09 04										10 26			10 40			
Cathays	d						09 09										10 31			10 45			
Rhymney 3	d													09 22									
Pontlottyn	d													09 25									
Tir-phil	d													09 29									
Brithdir	d													09 32									
Bargoed	a													09 35									
	d													09 37									
Gilfach Fargoed	d													09 39									
Pengam	d													09 42									
Hengoed	d													09 45									
Ystrad Mynach 3	d													09 48									
Llanbradach	d													09 53									
Aber	d													09 57									
Caerphilly 3	d													10 00									
Lisvane & Thornhill	d													10 04									
Llanishen	d													10 06									
Heath High Level	d													10 09									
Coryton	d																						
Whitchurch (Cardiff)	d																						
Rhiwbina	d																						
Birchgrove	d																						
Ty Glas	d																						
Heath Low Level	d																						
Cardiff Queen Street 3	a						09 14							10 14			10 34			10 49			
	d		09 00			09 12	09 16	09 24	09 36	09 48		10 00	10 12	10 16	10 24		10 36	10 36	10 48	10 51	11 00		
Cardiff Bay	a		09 04			09 16		09 28	09 40	09 52		10 04	10 16		10 28			10 40	10 52		11 04		
Cardiff Central 7	a						09 18							10 18			10 39			10 54			
	d	08 25			08 41		09 25				09 55			10 25		10 31				10 55			11 15
Grangetown	d	08 29			08 45		09 29				09 59			10 29		10 35				10 59			
Dingle Road	d															10 41							
Penarth	a															10 46							
Cogan	d	08 33			08 48		09 33				10 03			10 33						11 03			
Eastbrook	d	08 35			08 51		09 35				10 05			10 35						11 05			
Dinas Powys	d	08 37			08 53		09 37				10 07			10 37						11 07			
Cadoxton	d	08 42			08 57		09 42				10 12			10 42						11 12			
Barry Docks	d	08 45			09 00		09 45				10 15			10 45						11 15			
Barry 3	d	08 49		09 00	09 05		09 49				10 19			10 49						11 19		11 30	11 34
Barry Island	a	08 55					09 55				10 25			10 55						11 25			11 41
Rhoose Cardiff Int Airport ✈	d			09 15	09 12																	11 45	
Llantwit Major	d			09 30	09 22																	12 00	
Bridgend	a			09 55	09 40																	12 25	

When events are being held at the Millenium Stadium, services are subject to alteration. Please check times before travelling.

Table 130

Sundays
7 August to 11 September

Treherbert, Aberdare, Merthyr, Pontypridd, Rhymney and Coryton - Cardiff, Penarth, Barry, Barry Island and Bridgend

		AW	AW	AW	AW	AW		AW	AW	AW	AW	AW	AW	AW	AW	AW		AW	AW	AW (bus)	AW	AW	AW	AW	AW
Treherbert	d	10 07																			12 07				
Ynyswen	d	10 09																			12 09				
Treorchy	d	10 11																			12 11				
Ton Pentre	d	10 13																			12 13				
Ystrad Rhondda	a	10 16																			12 16				
	d	10 18																			12 18				
Llwynypia	d	10 20																			12 20				
Tonypandy	d	10 23																			12 23				
Dinas Rhondda	d	10 25																			12 25				
Porth	a	10 28																			12 28				
	d	10 29																			12 29				
Trehafod	d	10 32																			12 32				
Merthyr Tydfil	d													11 38											
Pentre-bach	d													11 42											
Troed Y Rhiw	d													11 45											
Merthyr Vale	a													11 48											
	d													11 50											
Quakers Yard	d													11 55											
Aberdare 3	d							10 52																	
Cwmbach	d							10 55																	
Fernhill	d							10 58																	
Mountain Ash	a							11 01																	
	d							11 04																	
Penrhiwceiber	d							11 07																	
Abercynon	d							11 13						11 59											
Pontypridd 3	a	10 37						11 23						12 07							12 37				
	d	10 38						11 24						12 09							12 38				
Trefforest	d	10 41						11 27						12 12							12 41				
Trefforest Estate	d																								
Taffs Well 3	d	10 48						11 34						12 20							12 48				
Radyr 3	a	10 51						11 37						12 23							12 51				
	d	10 51						11 37						12 23							12 51				
Danescourt	d																								
Fairwater	d																								
Waun-gron Park	d																								
Ninian Park	d																								
Llandaf	d	10 54						11 40						12 26							12 54				
Cathays	d	10 59						11 45						12 31							12 59				
Rhymney 3	d									11 10															
Pontlottyn	d									11 13															
Tir-phil	d									11 17															
Brithdir	d									11 20															
Bargoed	a									11 23															
	d									11 25															
Gilfach Fargoed	d									11 27															
Pengam	d									11 30															
Hengoed	d									11 33															
Ystrad Mynach 3	d									11 36															
Llanbradach	d									11 41															
Aber	d									11 45															
Caerphilly 3	d									11 48															
Lisvane & Thornhill	d									11 52															
Llanishen	d									11 54															
Heath High Level	d									11 57															
Coryton	d																								
Whitchurch (Cardiff)	d																								
Rhiwbina	d																								
Birchgrove	d																								
Ty Glas	d																								
Heath Low Level	d																								
Cardiff Queen Street 3	a	11 02						11 49		12 02				12 34							13 04				
	d	11 04	11 12	11 24	11 36	11 48		11 51	12 00	12 04	12 12	12 24		12 36	12 36	12 48			13 00		13 04	13 12	13 24	13 36	13 48
Cardiff Bay	a		11 16	11 28	11 40	11 52			12 04		12 16	12 28			12 40	12 52			13 04			13 16	13 28	13 40	13 52
Cardiff Central 7	a	11 07						11 54		12 07				12 39							13 06				
	d	11 25						11 55		12 25			12 31					12 55			13 25				
Grangetown	d	11 29						11 59		12 29			12 35					12 59			13 29				
Dingle Road	d												12 41												
Penarth	a												12 46												
Cogan	d	11 33						12 03		12 33								13 03			13 33				
Eastbrook	d	11 35						12 05		12 35								13 05			13 35				
Dinas Powys	d	11 37						12 07		12 37								13 07			13 37				
Cadoxton	d	11 42						12 12		12 42								13 12			13 42				
Barry Docks	d	11 45						12 15		12 45								13 15			13 45				
Barry 3	d	11 49						12 19		12 49								13 19		13 30	13 49				
Barry Island	a	11 55						12 25		12 55								13 25			13 55				
Rhoose Cardiff Int Airport ✈	d																			13 45					
Llantwit Major	d																			14 00					
Bridgend	a																			14 25					

When events are being held at the Millenium Stadium, services are subject to alteration. Please check times before travelling.

Table 130

Sundays
7 August to 11 September

Treherbert, Aberdare, Merthyr, Pontypridd, Rhymney and Coryton - Cardiff, Penarth, Barry, Barry Island and Bridgend

		AW		AW	AW	AW	AW	AW	AW	AW	AW	AW		AW	AW	AW (bus)	AW	AW	AW	AW	AW	AW		AW	AW
Treherbert	d																14 17								
Ynyswen	d																14 19								
Treorchy	d																14 21								
Ton Pentre	d																14 23								
Ystrad Rhondda	a																14 26								
	d																14 28								
Llwynypia	d																14 30								
Tonypandy	d																14 33								
Dinas Rhondda	d																14 35								
Porth	a																14 38								
	d																14 39								
Trehafod	d																14 42								
Merthyr Tydfil	d								13 38																
Pentre-bach	d								13 42																
Troed Y Rhiw	d								13 45																
Merthyr Vale	a								13 48																
	d								13 50																
Quakers Yard	d								13 55																
Aberdare 3	d	12 52																			14 52				
Cwmbach	d	12 55																			14 55				
Fernhill	d	12 58																			14 58				
Mountain Ash	a	13 01																			15 01				
	d	13 04																			15 04				
Penrhiwceiber	d	13 07																			15 07				
Abercynon	d	13 13							13 59												15 13				
Pontypridd 3	a	13 23							14 07								14 47				15 23				
	d	13 24							14 09								14 48				15 24				
Trefforest	d	13 27							14 12								14 51				15 27				
Trefforest Estate	d																								
Taffs Well 3	d	13 34							14 20								14 58				15 34				
Radyr 3	a	13 37							14 23								15 01				15 37				
	d	13 37							14 23								15 01				15 37				
Danescourt	d																								
Fairwater	d																								
Waun-gron Park	d																								
Ninian Park	d																								
Llandaf	d	13 40							14 26								15 04				15 40				
Cathays	d	13 45							14 31								15 09				15 45				
Rhymney 3	d				13 10																				15 22
Pontlottyn	d				13 13																				15 25
Tir-phil	d				13 17																				15 29
Brithdir	d				13 20																				15 32
Bargoed	a				13 23																				15 35
	d				13 25																				15 37
Gilfach Fargoed	d				13 27																				15 39
Pengam	d				13 30																				15 42
Hengoed	d				13 33																				15 45
Ystrad Mynach 3	d				13 36																				15 48
Llanbradach	d				13 41																				15 53
Aber	d				13 45																				15 57
Caerphilly 3	d				13 48																				16 00
Lisvane & Thornhill	d				13 52																				16 04
Llanishen	d				13 54																				16 06
Heath High Level	d				13 57																				16 09
Coryton	d																								
Whitchurch (Cardiff)	d																								
Rhiwbina	d																								
Birchgrove	d																								
Ty Glas	d																								
Heath Low Level	d																								
Cardiff Queen Street 3	a	13 49			14 02				14 34								15 14				15 49				16 14
	d	13 51		14 00	14 04	14 12	14 24		14 36	14 36	14 48			15 00	15 12		15 16	15 24	15 36	15 48	15 51	16 00		16 12	16 16
Cardiff Bay	a			14 04		14 16	14 28			14 40	14 52			15 04	15 16			15 28	15 40	15 52		16 04		16 16	
Cardiff Central 7	a	13 54			14 07				14 39								15 18				15 54				16 18
	d	13 55			14 25			14 31				14 55					15 25				15 55				16 25
Grangetown	d	13 59			14 29			14 35				14 59					15 29				15 59				16 29
Dingle Road	d							14 41																	
Penarth	a							14 46																	
Cogan	d	14 03			14 33							15 03					15 33				16 03				16 33
Eastbrook	d	14 05			14 35							15 05					15 35				16 05				16 35
Dinas Powys	d	14 07			14 37							15 07					15 37				16 07				16 37
Cadoxton	d	14 12			14 42							15 12					15 42				16 12				16 42
Barry Docks	d	14 15			14 45							15 15					15 45				16 15				16 45
Barry 3	d	14 19			14 49							15 19				15 30	15 49				16 19				16 49
Barry Island	a	14 25			14 55							15 25					15 55				16 25				16 55
Rhoose Cardiff Int Airport ✈	d															15 45									
Llantwit Major	d															16 00									
Bridgend	a															16 25									

When events are being held at the Millenium Stadium, services are subject to alteration. Please check times before travelling.

Table 130

Treherbert, Aberdare, Merthyr, Pontypridd, Rhymney and Coryton - Cardiff, Penarth, Barry, Barry Island and Bridgend

		AW	AW	AW	AW	AW	AW	AW		AW	AW (bus)	AW	AW	AW	AW	AW	AW	AW		AW	AW	AW	AW	AW	AW
Treherbert	d											16 17													
Ynyswen	d											16 19													
Treorchy	d											16 21													
Ton Pentre	d											16 23													
Ystrad Rhondda	a											16 26													
	d											16 28													
Llwynypia	d											16 30													
Tonypandy	d											16 33													
Dinas Rhondda	d											16 35													
Porth	a											16 38													
	d											16 39													
Trehafod	d											16 42													
Merthyr Tydfil	d			15 38																			17 38		
Pentre-bach	d			15 42																			17 42		
Troed Y Rhiw	d			15 45																			17 45		
Merthyr Vale	a			15 48																			17 48		
	d			15 50																			17 50		
Quakers Yard	d			15 55																			17 55		
Aberdare ■	d															16 52									
Cwmbach	d															16 55									
Fernhill	d															16 58									
Mountain Ash	a															17 01									
	d															17 04									
Penrhiwceiber	d															17 07									
Abercynon	d			15 59												17 13							17 59		
Pontypridd ■	a			16 07								16 47				17 23							18 07		
	d			16 09								16 48				17 24							18 09		
Trefforest	d			16 12								16 51				17 27							18 12		
Trefforest Estate	d																								
Taffs Well ■	d			16 20								16 58				17 34							18 20		
Radyr ■	a			16 23								17 01				17 37							18 23		
	d			16 23								17 01				17 37							18 23		
Danescourt	d																								
Fairwater	d																								
Waun-gron Park	d																								
Ninian Park	d																								
Llandaf	d			16 26								17 04				17 40							18 26		
Cathays	d			16 31								17 09				17 45							18 31		
Rhymney ■	d																			17 22					
Pontlottyn	d																			17 25					
Tir-phil	d																			17 29					
Brithdir	d																			17 32					
Bargoed	a																			17 35					
	d																			17 37					
Gilfach Fargoed	d																			17 39					
Pengam	d																			17 42					
Hengoed	d																			17 45					
Ystrad Mynach ■	d																			17 48					
Llanbradach	d																			17 53					
Aber	d																			17 57					
Caerphilly ■	d																			18 00					
Lisvane & Thornhill	d																			18 04					
Llanishen	d																			18 06					
Heath High Level	d																			18 09					
Coryton	d																								
Whitchurch (Cardiff)	d																								
Rhiwbina	d																								
Birchgrove	d																								
Ty Glas	d																								
Heath Low Level	d																								
Cardiff Queen Street ■	a			16 34								17 14				17 49				18 14			18 34		
	d	16 24		16 36	16 36	16 48		17 00		17 12		17 16	17 24	17 36	17 48	17 51	18 00	18 12		18 16	18 24		18 36	18 36	18 48
Cardiff Bay	a	16 28			16 40	16 52		17 04		17 16			17 28	17 40	17 52		18 04	18 16			18 28			18 40	18 52
Cardiff Central ■	a			16 39								17 18				17 54				18 18			18 39		
	d		16 31				16 55					17 25				17 55				18 25		18 31			
Grangetown	d		16 35				16 59					17 29				17 59				18 29		18 35			
Dingle Road	d		16 41																			18 41			
Penarth	a		16 46																			18 46			
Cogan	d						17 03					17 33				18 03				18 33					
Eastbrook	d						17 05					17 35				18 05				18 35					
Dinas Powys	d						17 07					17 37				18 07				18 37					
Cadoxton	d						17 12					17 42				18 12				18 42					
Barry Docks	d						17 15					17 45				18 15				18 45					
Barry ■	d						17 19				17 30	17 49				18 19				18 49					
Barry Island	a						17 25					17 55				18 25				18 55					
Rhoose Cardiff Int Airport ✈	d										17 45														
Llantwit Major	d										18 00														
Bridgend	a										18 25														

When events are being held at the Millenium Stadium, services are subject to alteration. Please check times before travelling.

Table 130

Treherbert, Aberdare, Merthyr, Pontypridd, Rhymney and Coryton - Cardiff, Penarth, Barry, Barry Island and Bridgend

		AW	AW	AW (bus)		AW	AW	AW	AW	AW	AW	AW (bus)	AW	AW		AW	AW
Treherbert	d					18 17							20 17				
Ynyswen	d					18 19							20 19				
Treorchy	d					18 21							20 21				
Ton Pentre	d					18 23							20 23				
Ystrad Rhondda	a					18 26							20 26				
	d					18 28							20 28				
Llwynypia	d					18 30							20 30				
Tonypandy	d					18 33							20 33				
Dinas Rhondda	d					18 35							20 35				
Porth	a					18 38							20 38				
	d					18 39							20 39				
Trehafod	d					18 42							20 42				
Merthyr Tydfil	d									19 38							21 38
Pentre-bach	d									19 42							21 42
Troed Y Rhiw	d									19 45							21 45
Merthyr Vale	a									19 48							21 48
	d									19 50							21 50
Quakers Yard	d									19 55							21 55
Aberdare ■	d						18 52							20 54			
Cwmbach	d						18 55							20 57			
Fernhill	d						18 58							21 00			
Mountain Ash	a						19 01							21 03			
	d						19 04							21 04			
Penrhiwceiber	d						19 07							21 07			
Abercynon	d						19 13			19 59				21 13			21 59
Pontypridd ■	a					18 47	19 23			20 07			20 47	21 23			22 07
	d					18 48	19 24			20 09			20 48	21 24			22 09
Trefforest	d					18 51	19 27			20 12			20 51	21 27			22 12
Trefforest Estate	d																
Taffs Well ■	d					18 58	19 34			20 20			20 58	21 34			22 20
Radyr ■	a					19 01	19 37			20 23			21 01	21 37			22 23
	d					19 01	19 37			20 23			21 01	21 37			22 23
Danescourt	d																
Fairwater	d																
Waun-gron Park	d																
Ninian Park	d												21 12				
Llandaf	d					19 04	19 40			20 26				21 40			22 26
Cathays	d					19 09	19 45			20 31				21 45			22 31
Rhymney ■	d							19 22									
Pontlottyn	d							19 25									
Tir-phil	d							19 29									
Brithdir	d							19 32									
Bargoed	a							19 35									
	d							19 37									
Gilfach Fargoed	d							19 39									
Pengam	d							19 42									
Hengoed	d							19 45									
Ystrad Mynach ■	d							19 48									
Llanbradach	d							19 53									
Aber	d							19 57									
Caerphilly ■	d							20 00									
Lisvane & Thornhill	d							20 04									
Llanishen	d							20 06									
Heath High Level	d							20 09									
Coryton	d																
Whitchurch (Cardiff)	d																
Rhiwbina	d																
Birchgrove	d																
Ty Glas	d																
Heath Low Level	d																
Cardiff Queen Street ■	a					19 14	19 49	20 14		20 34				21 49			22 34
	d		19 00			19 16	19 51	20 16		20 36				21 51			22 36
Cardiff Bay	a																
Cardiff Central ■	a		19 03			19 18	19 54	20 18		20 39			21 15	21 57			22 41
	d	18 55				19 25	19 55	20 25	20 31		20 55		21 26			22 25	
Grangetown	d	18 59				19 29	19 59	20 29	20 35		20 59		21 30			22 29	
Dingle Road	d								20 41								
Penarth	a								20 46								
Cogan	d	19 03				19 33	20 03	20 33			21 03		21 33			22 33	
Eastbrook	d	19 05				19 35	20 05	20 35			21 05		21 36			22 35	
Dinas Powys	d	19 07				19 37	20 07	20 37			21 07		21 38			22 37	
Cadoxton	d	19 12				19 42	20 12	20 42			21 12		21 42			22 42	
Barry Docks	d	19 15				19 45	20 15	20 45			21 15		21 45			22 45	
Barry ■	d	19 19		19 30		19 49	20 19	20 49			21 19	21 30	21 49			22 49	
Barry Island	a	19 25				19 55	20 25	20 55			21 25		21 55			22 55	
Rhoose Cardiff Int Airport ✈	d			19 45								21 45					
Llantwit Major	d			20 00								22 00					
Bridgend	a			20 25								22 25					

When events are being held at the Millenium Stadium, services are subject to alteration. Please check times before travelling.

Table 130

Sundays
from 18 September

Treherbert, Aberdare, Merthyr, Pontypridd, Rhymney and Coryton - Cardiff, Penarth, Barry, Barry Island and Bridgend

		AW	AW	AW	AW	AW	AW	AW	AW	AW	AW	AW	AW	AW	AW	AW	AW	AW	AW	AW	AW	AW	AW
					A 🚌	B												A	B				
Treherbert	d							08 17															
Ynyswen	d							08 19															
Treorchy	d							08 21															
Ton Pentre	d							08 23															
Ystrad Rhondda	a							08 26															
	d							08 28															
Llwynypia	d							08 30															
Tonypandy	d							08 33															
Dinas Rhondda	d							08 35															
Porth	a							08 38															
	d							08 39															
Trehafod	d							08 42															
Merthyr Tydfil	d																	09 38	09 38				
Pentre-bach	d																	09 42	09 42				
Troed Y Rhiw	d																	09 45	09 45				
Merthyr Vale	a																	09 48	09 48				
	d																	09 50	09 50				
Quakers Yard	d																	09 55	09 55				
Aberdare 3	d																					09 54	
Cwmbach	d																					09 57	
Fernhill	d																					10 00	
Mountain Ash	a																					10 03	
	d																					10 04	
Penrhiwceiber	d																					10 07	
Abercynon	d																	09 59	09 59			10 13	
Pontypridd 3	a							08 47										10 07	10 07			10 23	
	d							08 48										10 09	10 09			10 24	
Trefforest	d							08 51										10 12	10 12			10 27	
Trefforest Estate	d																						
Taffs Well 3	d							08 58										10 20	10 20			10 34	
Radyr 3	a							09 01										10 23	10 23			10 37	
	d	23p10						09 01										10 23	10 23			10 37	
Danescourt	d																						
Fairwater	d																						
Waun-gron Park	d																						
Ninian Park	d																						
Llandaf	d	23p12						09 04										10 26	10 26			10 40	
Cathays	d	23p16						09 09										10 31	10 31			10 45	
Rhymney 3	d														09 22								
Pontlottyn	d														09 25								
Tir-phil	d														09 29								
Brithdir	d														09 32								
Bargoed	a														09 35								
	d														09 37								
Gilfach Fargoed	d														09 39								
Pengam	d														09 42								
Hengoed	d														09 45								
Ystrad Mynach 3	d														09 48								
Llanbradach	d														09 53								
Aber	d														09 57								
Caerphilly 3	d														10 00								
Lisvane & Thornhill	d														10 04								
Llanishen	d														10 06								
Heath High Level	d														10 09								
Coryton	d																						
Whitchurch (Cardiff)	d																						
Rhiwbina	d																						
Birchgrove	d																						
Ty Glas	d																						
Heath Low Level	d																						
Cardiff Queen Street 3	a	23p19						09 14							10 14			10 34	10 34			10 49	
	d	23p20		09 00			09 12	09 16	09 24	09 36	09 48		10 00	10 12	10 16	10 24		10 36	10 36	10 36	10 48	10 51	11 00
Cardiff Bay	a			09 04			09 16		09 28	09 40	09 52		10 04	10 16		10 28				10 40	10 52		11 04
Cardiff Central 7	a	23p25						09 18							10 18			10 39	10 39			10 54	
	d	23p30	08 25			08 41		09 25				09 55			10 25		10 31		10 41			10 55	
Grangetown	d	23p34	08 29			08 45		09 29				09 59			10 29		10 35		10 45			10 59	
Dingle Road	d																10 41						
Penarth	a																10 47						
Cogan	d	23p37	08 33			08 48		09 33				10 03			10 33				10 48			11 03	
Eastbrook	d	23p40	08 35			08 51		09 35				10 05			10 35				10 51			11 05	
Dinas Powys	d	23p42	08 37			08 53		09 37				10 07			10 37				10 53			11 07	
Cadoxton	d	23p46	08 42			08 57		09 42				10 12			10 42				10 57			11 12	
Barry Docks	d	23p49	08 45			09 00		09 45				10 15			10 45				11 00			11 15	
Barry 3	d	23p54	08 49		09 00	09 05		09 49				10 19			10 49				11 05			11 19	
Barry Island	a	00 01	08 56					09 56				10 26			10 56							11 26	
Rhoose Cardiff Int Airport ✈	d				09 15	09 12													11 12				
Llantwit Major	d				09 30	09 22													11 22				
Bridgend	a				09 55	09 41													11 41				

A from 30 October
B from 18 September until 23 October

When events are being held at the Millenium Stadium, services are subject to alteration. Please check times before travelling.

Table 130

Sundays
from 18 September

Treherbert, Aberdare, Merthyr, Pontypridd, Rhymney and Coryton - Cardiff, Penarth, Barry, Barry Island and Bridgend

		AW	AW	AW	AW	AW	AW	AW	AW	AW	AW	AW	AW	AW	AW	AW	AW	AW	AW	AW	AW	AW	AW
		A 🚌																					
Treherbert	d		10 07																12 07				
Ynyswen	d		10 09																12 09				
Treorchy	d		10 11																12 11				
Ton Pentre	d		10 13																12 13				
Ystrad Rhondda	a		10 16																12 16				
	d		10 18																12 18				
Llwynypia	d		10 20																12 20				
Tonypandy	d		10 23																12 23				
Dinas Rhondda	d		10 25																12 25				
Porth	a		10 28																12 28				
	d		10 29																12 29				
Trehafod	d		10 32																12 32				
Merthyr Tydfil	d													11 38									
Pentre-bach	d													11 42									
Troed Y Rhiw	d													11 45									
Merthyr Vale	a													11 48									
	d													11 50									
Quakers Yard	d													11 55									
Aberdare 3	d							10 54															
Cwmbach	d							10 57															
Fernhill	d							11 00															
Mountain Ash	a							11 03															
	d							11 04															
Penrhiwceiber	d							11 07															
Abercynon	d							11 13						11 59									
Pontypridd 3	a		10 37					11 23						12 07					12 37				
	d		10 38					11 24						12 09					12 38				
Trefforest	d		10 41					11 27						12 12					12 41				
Trefforest Estate	d																						
Taffs Well 3	d		10 48					11 34						12 20					12 48				
Radyr 3	a		10 51					11 37						12 23					12 51				
	d		10 51					11 37						12 23					12 51				
Danescourt	d																						
Fairwater	d																						
Waun-gron Park	d																						
Ninian Park	d																						
Llandaf	d		10 54					11 40						12 26					12 54				
Cathays	d		10 59					11 45						12 31					12 59				
Rhymney 3	d									11 10													
Pontlottyn	d									11 13													
Tir-phil	d									11 17													
Brithdir	d									11 20													
Bargoed	a									11 23													
	d									11 25													
Gilfach Fargoed	d									11 27													
Pengam	d									11 30													
Hengoed	d									11 33													
Ystrad Mynach 3	d									11 36													
Llanbradach	d									11 41													
Aber	d									11 45													
Caerphilly 3	d									11 48													
Lisvane & Thornhill	d									11 52													
Llanishen	d									11 54													
Heath High Level	d									11 57													
Coryton	d																						
Whitchurch (Cardiff)	d																						
Rhiwbina	d																						
Birchgrove	d																						
Ty Glas	d																						
Heath Low Level	d																						
Cardiff Queen Street 3	a		11 02					11 49		12 02				12 34					13 04				
	d		11 04	11 12	11 24	11 36	11 48	11 51	12 00	12 04	12 12	12 24		12 36	12 36	12 48		13 00	13 04	13 12	13 24	13 36	13 48
Cardiff Bay	a			11 16	11 28	11 40	11 52		12 04		12 16	12 28			12 40	12 52		13 04		13 16	13 28	13 40	13 52
Cardiff Central 7	a		11 07					11 54		12 07				12 39					13 06				
	d		11 25					11 55		12 25			12 31	12 41			12 55		13 25				
Grangetown	d		11 29					11 59		12 29			12 35	12 45			12 59		13 29				
Dingle Road	d												12 41										
Penarth	a												12 47										
Cogan	d		11 33					12 03		12 33				12 48			13 03		13 33				
Eastbrook	d		11 35					12 05		12 35				12 51			13 05		13 35				
Dinas Powys	d		11 37					12 07		12 37				12 53			13 07		13 37				
Cadoxton	d		11 42					12 12		12 42				12 57			13 12		13 42				
Barry Docks	d		11 45					12 15		12 45				13 00			13 15		13 45				
Barry 3	d	11 30	11 49					12 19		12 49				13 05			13 19		13 49				
Barry Island	a		11 56					12 26		12 55							13 26		13 56				
Rhoose Cardiff Int Airport ✈	d	11 45												13 12									
Llantwit Major	d	12 00												13 22									
Bridgend	a	12 25												13 41									

A from 30 October

When events are being held at the Millenium Stadium, services are subject to alteration. Please check times before travelling.

Table 130

Sundays
from 18 September

Treherbert, Aberdare, Merthyr, Pontypridd, Rhymney and Coryton - Cardiff, Penarth, Barry, Barry Island and Bridgend

		AW		AW	AW	AW	AW	AW	AW	AW	AW	AW		AW	AW	AW	AW	AW	AW	AW	AW	AW		AW	AW
Treherbert	d															14 17									
Ynyswen	d															14 19									
Treorchy	d															14 21									
Ton Pentre	d															14 23									
Ystrad Rhondda	a															14 26									
	d															14 28									
Llwynypia	d															14 30									
Tonypandy	d															14 33									
Dinas Rhondda	d															14 35									
Porth	a															14 38									
	d															14 39									
Trehafod	d															14 42									
Merthyr Tydfil	d								13 38																
Pentre-bach	d								13 42																
Troed Y Rhiw	d								13 45																
Merthyr Vale	a								13 48																
	d								13 50																
Quakers Yard	d								13 55																
Aberdare 3	d	12 54																		14 54					
Cwmbach	d	12 57																		14 57					
Fernhill	d	13 00																		15 00					
Mountain Ash	a	13 03																		15 03					
	d	13 04																		15 04					
Penrhiwceiber	d	13 07																		15 07					
Abercynon	d	13 13							13 59											15 13					
Pontypridd 3	a	13 23							14 07							14 47				15 23					
	d	13 24							14 09							14 48				15 24					
Trefforest	d	13 27							14 12							14 51				15 27					
Trefforest Estate	d																								
Taffs Well 3	d	13 34							14 20							14 58				15 34					
Radyr 3	a	13 37							14 23							15 01				15 37					
	d	13 37							14 23							15 01				15 37					
Danescourt	d																								
Fairwater	d																								
Waun-gron Park	d																								
Ninian Park	d																								
Llandaf	d	13 40							14 26							15 04				15 40					
Cathays	d	13 45							14 31							15 09				15 45					
Rhymney 3	d				13 10																			15 22	
Pontlottyn	d				13 13																			15 25	
Tir-phil	d				13 17																			15 29	
Brithdir	d				13 20																			15 32	
Bargoed	a				13 23																			15 35	
	d				13 25																			15 37	
Gilfach Fargoed	d				13 27																			15 39	
Pengam	d				13 30																			15 42	
Hengoed	d				13 33																			15 45	
Ystrad Mynach 3	d				13 36																			15 48	
Llanbradach	d				13 41																			15 53	
Aber	d				13 45																			15 57	
Caerphilly 3	d				13 48																			16 00	
Lisvane & Thornhill	d				13 52																			16 04	
Llanishen	d				13 54																			16 06	
Heath High Level	d				13 57																			16 09	
Coryton	d																								
Whitchurch (Cardiff)	d																								
Rhiwbina	d																								
Birchgrove	d																								
Ty Glas	d																								
Heath Low Level	d																								
Cardiff Queen Street 3	a	13 49			14 02				14 34							15 14				15 49				16 14	
	d	13 51		14 00	14 04	14 12	14 24		14 36	14 36	14 48			15 00	15 12	15 16	15 24	15 36	15 48	15 51	16 00	16 12		16 16	16 24
Cardiff Bay	a			14 04		14 16	14 28			14 40	14 52			15 04	15 16		15 28	15 40	15 52		16 04	16 16			16 28
Cardiff Central 7	a	13 54			14 07				14 39							15 18				15 54				16 18	
	d	13 55			14 25			14 31	14 41			14 55				15 25				15 55				16 25	
Grangetown	d	13 59			14 29			14 35	14 45			14 59				15 29				15 59				16 29	
Dingle Road	d							14 41																	
Penarth	a							14 47																	
Cogan	d	14 03			14 33				14 48			15 03				15 33				16 03				16 33	
Eastbrook	d	14 05			14 35				14 51			15 05				15 35				16 05				16 35	
Dinas Powys	d	14 07			14 37				14 53			15 07				15 37				16 07				16 37	
Cadoxton	d	14 12			14 42				14 57			15 12				15 42				16 12				16 42	
Barry Docks	d	14 15			14 45				15 00			15 15				15 45				16 15				16 45	
Barry 3	d	14 19			14 49				15 05			15 19				15 49				16 19				16 49	
Barry Island	a	14 26			14 56							15 26				15 56				16 26				16 56	
Rhoose Cardiff Int Airport ✈	d								15 12																
Llantwit Major	d								15 22																
Bridgend	a								15 41																

When events are being held at the Millenium Stadium, services are subject to alteration. Please check times before travelling.

Table 130

Sundays
from 18 September

Treherbert, Aberdare, Merthyr, Pontypridd, Rhymney and Coryton - Cardiff, Penarth, Barry, Barry Island and Bridgend

		AW	AW	AW	AW	AW	AW	AW		AW	AW	AW	AW	AW	AW	AW	AW	AW		AW	AW	AW	AW	AW	AW
Treherbert	d									16 17															
Ynyswen	d									16 19															
Treorchy	d									16 21															
Ton Pentre	d									16 23															
Ystrad Rhondda	a									16 26															
	d									16 28															
Llwynypia	d									16 30															
Tonypandy	d									16 33															
Dinas Rhondda	d									16 35															
Porth	a									16 38															
	d									16 39															
Trehafod	d									16 42															
Merthyr Tydfil	d		15 38																		17 38				
Pentre-bach	d		15 42																		17 42				
Troed Y Rhiw	d		15 45																		17 45				
Merthyr Vale	a		15 48																		17 48				
	d		15 50																		17 50				
Quakers Yard	d		15 55																		17 55				
Aberdare 3	d													16 54											
Cwmbach	d													16 57											
Fernhill	d													17 00											
Mountain Ash	a													17 03											
	d													17 04											
Penrhiwceiber	d													17 07											
Abercynon	d		15 59											17 13							17 59				
Pontypridd 3	a		16 07							16 47				17 23							18 07				
	d		16 09							16 48				17 24							18 09				
Trefforest	d		16 12							16 51				17 27							18 12				
Trefforest Estate	d																								
Taffs Well 3	d		16 20							16 58				17 34							18 20				
Radyr 3	a		16 23							17 01				17 37							18 23				
	d		16 23							17 01				17 37							18 23				
Danescourt	d																								
Fairwater	d																								
Waun-gron Park	d																								
Ninian Park	d																								
Llandaf	d		16 26							17 04				17 40							18 26				
Cathays	d		16 31							17 09				17 45							18 31				
Rhymney 3	d																17 22								
Pontlottyn	d																17 25								
Tir-phil	d																17 29								
Brithdir	d																17 32								
Bargoed	a																17 35								
	d																17 37								
Gilfach Fargoed	d																17 39								
Pengam	d																17 42								
Hengoed	d																17 45								
Ystrad Mynach 3	d																17 48								
Llanbradach	d																17 53								
Aber	d																17 57								
Caerphilly 3	d																18 00								
Lisvane & Thornhill	d																18 04								
Llanishen	d																18 06								
Heath High Level	d																18 09								
Coryton	d																								
Whitchurch (Cardiff)	d																								
Rhiwbina	d																								
Birchgrove	d																								
Ty Glas	d																								
Heath Low Level	d																								
Cardiff Queen Street 3	a		16 34							17 14				17 49			18 14				18 34				
	d		16 36	16 36	16 48		17 00	17 12		17 16	17 24	17 36	17 48	17 51	18 00	18 12	18 16	18 24			18 36	18 36	18 48		19 00
Cardiff Bay	a			16 40	16 52		17 04	17 16			17 28	17 40	17 52		18 04	18 16		18 28				18 40	18 52		
Cardiff Central 7	a		16 39							17 18				17 54			18 18				18 39				19 03
	d	16 31	16 41			16 55				17 25				17 55			18 25			18 31	18 41			18 55	
Grangetown	d	16 35	16 45			16 59				17 29				17 59			18 29			18 35	18 45			18 59	
Dingle Road	d	16 41																		18 41					
Penarth	a	16 47																		18 47					
Cogan	d		16 48			17 03				17 33				18 03			18 33				18 48			19 03	
Eastbrook	d		16 51			17 05				17 35				18 05			18 35				18 51			19 05	
Dinas Powys	d		16 53			17 07				17 37				18 07			18 37				18 53			19 07	
Cadoxton	d		16 57			17 12				17 42				18 12			18 42				18 57			19 12	
Barry Docks	d		17 00			17 15				17 45				18 15			18 45				19 00			19 15	
Barry 3	d		17 05			17 19				17 49				18 19			18 49				19 05			19 19	
Barry Island	a					17 26				17 56				18 26			18 56							19 26	
Rhoose Cardiff Int Airport ✈	d		17 12																		19 12				
Llantwit Major	d		17 22																		19 22				
Bridgend	a		17 41																		19 41				

When events are being held at the Millenium Stadium, services are subject to alteration. Please check times before travelling.

Table 130

Sundays
from 18 September

Treherbert, Aberdare, Merthyr, Pontypridd, Rhymney and Coryton - Cardiff, Penarth, Barry, Barry Island and Bridgend

		AW	AW	AW		AW	AW	AW	AW	AW	AW	AW
Treherbert	d	18 17							20 17			
Ynyswen	d	18 19							20 19			
Treorchy	d	18 21							20 21			
Ton Pentre	d	18 23							20 23			
Ystrad Rhondda	a	18 26							20 26			
	d	18 28							20 28			
Llwynypia	d	18 30							20 30			
Tonypandy	d	18 33							20 33			
Dinas Rhondda	d	18 35							20 35			
Porth	a	18 38							20 38			
	d	18 39							20 39			
Trehafod	d	18 42							20 42			
Merthyr Tydfil	d						19 38					21 38
Pentre-bach	d						19 42					21 42
Troed Y Rhiw	d						19 45					21 45
Merthyr Vale	a						19 48					21 48
	d						19 50					21 50
Quakers Yard	d						19 55					21 55
Aberdare ■	d		18 54							20 54		
Cwmbach	d		18 57							20 57		
Fernhill	d		19 00							21 00		
Mountain Ash	a		19 03							21 03		
	d		19 04							21 04		
Penrhiwceiber	d		19 07							21 07		
Abercynon	d		19 13				19 59			21 13		21 59
Pontypridd ■	a	18 47	19 23				20 07		20 47	21 23		22 07
	d	18 48	19 24				20 09		20 48	21 24		22 09
Trefforest	d	18 51	19 27				20 12		20 51	21 27		22 12
Trefforest Estate	d											
Taffs Well ■	d	18 58	19 34				20 20		20 58	21 34		22 20
Radyr ■	a	19 01	19 37				20 23		21 01	21 37		22 23
	d	19 01	19 37				20 23		21 01	21 37		22 23
Danescourt	d											
Fairwater	d											
Waun-gron Park	d											
Ninian Park	d											
Llandaf	d	19 04	19 40				20 26		21 04	21 40		22 26
Cathays	d	19 09	19 45				20 31		21 09	21 45		22 31
Rhymney ■	d			19 22								
Pontlottyn	d			19 25								
Tir-phil	d			19 29								
Brithdir	d			19 32								
Bargoed	a			19 35								
	d			19 37								
Gilfach Fargoed	d			19 39								
Pengam	d			19 42								
Hengoed	d			19 45								
Ystrad Mynach ■	d			19 48								
Llanbradach	d			19 53								
Aber	d			19 57								
Caerphilly ■	d			20 00								
Lisvane & Thornhill	d			20 04								
Llanishen	d			20 06								
Heath High Level	d			20 09								
Coryton	d											
Whitchurch (Cardiff)	d											
Rhiwbina	d											
Birchgrove	d											
Ty Glas	d											
Heath Low Level	d											
Cardiff Queen Street ■	a	19 14	19 49	20 14			20 34		21 14	21 49		22 34
	d	19 16	19 51	20 16			20 36		21 16	21 51		22 36
Cardiff Bay	a											
Cardiff Central ■	a	19 18	19 54	20 18			20 39		21 18	21 57		22 41
	d	19 25	19 55	20 25		20 31	20 41	20 55	21 25		22 25	
Grangetown	d	19 29	19 59	20 29		20 35	20 45	20 59	21 29		22 29	
Dingle Road	d					20 41						
Penarth	a					20 47						
Cogan	d	19 33	20 03	20 33			20 48	21 03	21 33		22 33	
Eastbrook	d	19 35	20 05	20 35			20 51	21 05	21 35		22 35	
Dinas Powys	d	19 37	20 07	20 37			20 53	21 07	21 37		22 37	
Cadoxton	d	19 42	20 12	20 42			20 57	21 12	21 42		22 42	
Barry Docks	d	19 45	20 15	20 45			21 00	21 15	21 45		22 45	
Barry ■	d	19 49	20 19	20 49			21 05	21 19	21 49		22 49	
Barry Island	a	19 56	20 26	20 55				21 26	21 56		22 56	
Rhoose Cardiff Int Airport ✈	d						21 12					
Llantwit Major	d						21 22					
Bridgend	a						21 41					

When events are being held at the Millenium Stadium, services are subject to alteration. Please check times before travelling.

Table 130

Mondays to Fridays
until 9 September

Bridgend, Barry Island, Barry, Penarth and Cardiff - Coryton, Rhymney, Pontypridd, Merthyr, Aberdare and Treherbert

Miles	Miles	Miles	Miles	Miles			AW		AW	AW	AW	AW	AW	AW	AW		AW	AW	AW	AW	AW	AW	AW	AW	AW
—	—	0	—	—	**Bridgend**	d											05 42								
—	—	9¼	—	—	Llantwit Major	d											05 56								
—	—	15¾	—	—	Rhoose Cardiff Int Airport ✈	d											06 06								
0	—	—	—	—	**Barry Island**	d								05 52								06 25			
0¾	—	19	—	—	**Barry** ■	d								05 57			06 15					06 30			
2	—	—	—	—	Barry Docks	d								06 01			06 19					06 34			
2¾	—	—	—	—	Cadoxton	d								06 04			06 22					06 37			
4¾	—	—	—	—	Dinas Powys	d								06 08			06 26					06 41			
5¾	—	—	—	—	Eastbrook	d								06 10			06 28					06 43			
6½	—	—	—	—	Cogan	d								06 12			06 30					06 45			
—	0	—	—	—	**Penarth**	d						06 02							06 32						
—	0¼	—	—	—	Dingle Road	d						06 04							06 34						
8¼	2¾	—	—	—	Grangetown	d						06 08		06 16			06 34		06 38			06 49			
9¼	3¾	—	0	—	**Cardiff Central** ■	a						06 13		06 21			06 39		06 44			06 54			
—	—	—	—	—		d	05 26		05 46	05 56	06 11	06 15	06 19	06 26	06 36		06 41		06 46	06 51		06 56		07 06	07 06
—	—	0	—	—	**Cardiff Bay**	d												06 42			06 54		07 06		
9¾	4¼	1	—	—	**Cardiff Queen Street** ■	a	05 29		05 49	05 59	06 14	06 19	06 24	06 29	06 39		06 44	06 46	06 45	06 54	06 58	07 00	07 10	07 09	
—	—	—	—	—		d	05 30		05 50	06 00	06 15	06 20	06 25	06 30	06 40		06 45		06 50	06 55		07 00		07 10	
—	—	3½	—	—	Heath Low Level	d							06 30							07 00					
—	4½	—	—	—	Ty Glas	d							06 33							07 03					
—	—	4¾	—	—	Birchgrove	d							06 34							07 04					
—	—	5¼	—	—	Rhiwbina	d							06 36							07 06					
—	—	5½	—	—	Whitchurch (Cardiff)	d							06 38							07 08					
—	—	6	—	—	**Coryton**	a							06 43							07 13					
—	6¾	—	—	—	Heath High Level	d			05 54			06 25							06 55						
—	7¾	—	—	—	Llanishen	d			05 57			06 28							06 58						
—	8¾	—	—	—	Lisvane & Thornhill	d			06 00			06 30							07 00						
—	11¼	—	—	—	Caerphilly ■	d			06a08			06 36							07 06						
—	12	—	—	—	Aber	d						06 38							07 08						
—	14	—	—	—	Llanbradach	d						06 42							07 12						
—	16¾	—	—	—	Ystrad Mynach ■	d						06 47							07 17						
—	17¾	—	—	—	Hengoed	d						06 50							07 20						
—	19½	—	—	—	Pengam	d						06 53							07 23						
—	20½	—	—	—	Gilfach Fargoed	d																			
—	21	—	—	—	Bargoed	a						07 01							07 31						
—	—	—	—	—		d																			
—	22½	—	—	—	Brithdir	d																			
—	23½	—	—	—	Tir-phil	d																			
—	26	—	—	—	Pontlottyn	d																			
—	27	—	—	—	**Rhymney** ■	a																			
10½	—	—	—	—	Cathays	d	05 33			06 03	06 18			06 33	06 43		06 48					07 03		07 13	
13	—	—	—	—	Llandaf	d	05 37			06 07	06 22			06 37	06 47		06 52					07 07		07 17	
—	—	—	1	—	Ninian Park	d																			07 10
—	—	—	2½	—	Waun-gron Park	d																			07 13
—	—	—	3	—	Fairwater	d																			07 15
—	—	—	3½	—	Danescourt	d																			07 17
14	—	—	4¾	—	Radyr ■	a	05 39			06 10	06 24			06 40	06 50		06 54					07 10		07 20	07 24
—	—	—	—	—		d	05 40			06 10	06 24			06 40	06 50		06 55					07 10		07 20	
16	—	—	—	—	Taffs Well ■	d	05 43			06 14	06 28			06 44	06 54		06 59					07 14		07 24	
18¼	—	—	—	—	Trefforest Estate	d	05 47			06 18				06 48								07 18			
20¾	—	—	—	—	Trefforest	d	05 52			06 22	06 35			06 52	07 01		07 06					07 22		07 31	
21¾	—	0	—	0	**Pontypridd** ■	a	05 55			06 25	06 38			06 55	07 04		07 09					07 27		07 34	
—	—	—	—	—		d	05 57	06 11		06 27	06 41			06 57	07 06		07 11					07 27		07 36	
—	—	3¼	—	3¼	Abercynon	d	06 04	06 19		06 34	06 49			07 04			07 19					07 34			
—	—	—	—	6	Penrhiwceiber	d		06 24			06 54						07 24								
—	—	—	—	7¼	Mountain Ash	a		06 28			06 58						07 28								
—	—	—	—	—		d		06 33			07 03						07 33								
—	—	—	—	8¼	Fernhill	d		06 35			07 05						07 35								
—	—	—	—	9½	Cwmbach	d		06 39			07 09						07 39								
—	—	—	—	11	**Aberdare** ■	a		06 46			07 16						07 46								
—	—	4¾	—	—	Quakers Yard	d	06 09			06 39				07 09								07 39			
—	—	7	—	—	Merthyr Vale	a	06 14			06 44				07 14								07 44			
—	—	—	—	—		d	06 17			06 47				07 17								07 47			
—	—	8¾	—	—	Troed Y Rhiw	d	06 20			06 50				07 20								07 50			
—	—	10	—	—	Pentre-bach	d	06 23			06 53				07 23								07 53			
—	—	11½	—	—	**Merthyr Tydfil**	a	06 31			07 01				07 31								08 01			
23½	—	—	—	—	Trehafod	d									07 11									07 41	
24¾	—	—	—	—	Porth	a									07 14									07 44	
—	—	—	—	—		d									07 15									07 45	
26¼	—	—	—	—	Dinas Rhondda	d									07 19									07 49	
26¾	—	—	—	—	Tonypandy	d									07 21									07 51	
27¾	—	—	—	—	Llwynypia	d									07 23									07 53	
29	—	—	—	—	Ystrad Rhondda	a									07 26									07 56	
—	—	—	—	—		d									07 29									07 59	
29½	—	—	—	—	Ton Pentre	d									07 31									08 01	
30¾	—	—	—	—	Treorchy	d									07 34									08 04	
31¾	—	—	—	—	Ynyswen	d									07 37									08 07	
32¼	—	—	—	—	**Treherbert**	a									07 43									08 13	

When events are being held at the Millenium Stadium, services are subject to alteration. Please check times before travelling.

Bridgend, Barry Island, Barry, Penarth and Cardiff - Coryton, Rhymney, Pontypridd, Merthyr, Aberdare and Treherbert

		AW	AW	AW	AW	AW	AW	AW	AW	AW	AW	AW	AW	AW	AW	AW	AW	AW	AW	AW	AW	AW
Bridgend	d										06 42											
Llantwit Major	d										06 56											
Rhoose Cardiff Int Airport ✈	d										07 06											
Barry Island	d					06 55										07 25					07 40	
Barry 3	d					07 00					07 15					07 30					07 45	
Barry Docks	d					07 04					07 19					07 34					07 49	
Cadoxton	d					07 07					07 22					07 37					07 52	
Dinas Powys	d					07 11					07 26					07 41					07 56	
Eastbrook	d					07 13					07 28					07 43					07 58	
Cogan	d					07 15					07 30					07 45					08 00	
Penarth	d		07 02				07 17						07 32				07 47					08 02
Dingle Road	d		07 04				07 19						07 34				07 49					08 04
Grangetown	d		07 08			07 19	07 23				07 34		07 38			07 49	07 53				08 04	08 08
Cardiff Central 7	a		07 14			07 24	07 29				07 39		07 44			07 54	08 00				08 09	08 14
	d	07 11	07 16		07 21	07 26	07 31		07 36	07 36	07 41		07 46	07 51		07 56	08 01		08 06	08 06	08 11	08 16
Cardiff Bay	d			07 18				07 30				07 42			07 54			08 06				
Cardiff Queen Street 3	a	07 14	07 19	07 22	07 24	07 29	07 34	07 34	07 39		07 44	07 46	07 49	07 54	07 58	07 59	08 04	08 10	08 09		08 14	08 19
	d	07 15	07 20		07 25	07 30	07 35		07 40		07 45		07 50	07 55		08 00	08 05		08 10		08 15	08 20
Heath Low Level	d				07 30									08 00								
Ty Glas	d				07 33									08 03								
Birchgrove	d				07 34									08 04								
Rhiwbina	d				07 36									08 06								
Whitchurch (Cardiff)	d				07 38									08 08								
Coryton	a				07 43									08 13								
Heath High Level	d		07 25				07 40						07 55				08 10					08 25
Llanishen	d		07 28				07 43						07 58				08 13					08 28
Lisvane & Thornhill	d		07 30				07 45						08 00				08 15					08 30
Caerphilly 3	d		07 36				07 51						08 06				08 21					08 36
Aber	d		07 38				07 53						08 08				08 23					08 38
Llanbradach	d		07 42				07 57						08 12				08 27					08 42
Ystrad Mynach 3	d		07 47				08 02						08 17				08 32					08 47
Hengoed	d		07 50				08 05						08 20				08 35					08 50
Pengam	d		07 53				08 08						08 23				08 38					08 53
Gilfach Fargoed	d																08 41					
Bargoed	a		08 02				08 13						08 31				08 48					08 58
	d						08 14															08 59
Brithdir	d						08 18															09 03
Tir-phil	d						08 21															09 06
Pontlottyn	d						08 25															09 10
Rhymney 3	a						08 31															09 16
Cathays	d	07 18				07 33			07 43		07 48					08 03			08 13		08 18	
Llandaf	d	07 22				07 37			07 47		07 52					08 07			08 17		08 22	
Ninian Park	d									07 40										08 10		
Waun-gron Park	d									07 43										08 13		
Fairwater	d									07 45										08 15		
Danescourt	d									07 47										08 17		
Radyr 3	a	07 25				07 40			07 50	07 54	07 55					08 10			08 20	08 24	08 25	
	d	07 25				07 40			07 50		07 55					08 10			08 20		08 25	
Taffs Well 3	d	07 29				07 44			07 54		07 59					08 14			08 24		08 29	
Trefforest Estate	d					07 48										08 18						
Trefforest	d	07 36				07 52			08 01		08 06					08 23			08 31		08 36	
Pontypridd 3	a	07 39				07 55			08 04		08 09					08 26			08 34		08 39	
	d	07 41				07 57			08 06		08 11					08 27			08 36		08 41	
Abercynon	d	07 49				08 04					08 19					08 34					08 49	
Penrhiwceiber	d	07 54									08 24										08 54	
Mountain Ash	a	07 58									08 28										08 58	
	d	08 03									08 33										09 03	
Fernhill	d	08 05									08 35										09 05	
Cwmbach	d	08 09									08 39										09 09	
Aberdare 3	a	08 16									08 46										09 16	
Quakers Yard	d					08 09										08 39						
Merthyr Vale	a					08 14										08 44						
	d					08 17										08 47						
Troed Y Rhiw	d					08 20										08 50						
Pentre-bach	d					08 23										08 53						
Merthyr Tydfil	a					08 31										09 01						
Trehafod	d								08 11										08 41			
Porth	a								08 14										08 44			
	d								08 15										08 45			
Dinas Rhondda	d								08 19										08 49			
Tonypandy	d								08 21										08 51			
Llwynypia	d								08 23										08 53			
Ystrad Rhondda	a								08 26										08 56			
	d								08 29										08 59			
Ton Pentre	d								08 31										09 01			
Treorchy	d								08 34										09 04			
Ynyswen	d								08 37										09 07			
Treherbert	a								08 43										09 13			

When events are being held at the Millenium Stadium, services are subject to alteration. Please check times before travelling.

Bridgend, Barry Island, Barry, Penarth and Cardiff - Coryton, Rhymney, Pontypridd, Merthyr, Aberdare and Treherbert

		AW	AW	AW	AW	AW	AW	AW	AW	AW	AW	AW	AW	AW	AW	AW	AW	AW	AW	AW	AW	AW	AW
Bridgend	d								07 42														
Llantwit Major	d								07 56														
Rhoose Cardiff Int Airport ✈	d								08 06														
Barry Island	d			07 55										08 25					08 40				08 55
Barry 3	d			08 00					08 15					08 30					08 45				09 00
Barry Docks	d			08 04					08 19					08 34					08 49				09 04
Cadoxton	d			08 07					08 22					08 37					08 52				09 07
Dinas Powys	d			08 11					08 26					08 41					08 56				09 11
Eastbrook	d			08 13					08 28					08 43					08 58				09 13
Cogan	d			08 15					08 30					08 45					09 00				09 15
Penarth	d				08 17						08 32				08 47								
Dingle Road	d				08 19						08 34				08 49								
Grangetown	d			08 19	08 23				08 34		08 38			08 49	08 53				09 04				09 19
Cardiff Central 7	a			08 25	08 29				08 39		08 44			08 54	08 59				09 09				09 24
	d		08 21	08 26	08 31		08 36	08 36	08 41		08 46	08 51		08 56	09 01		09 06	09 06	09 11	09 16		09 21	09 26
Cardiff Bay	d	08 18				08 30				08 42			08 54			09 06					09 18		
Cardiff Queen Street 3	a	08 22	08 24	08 29	08 34	08 34	08 39		08 44	08 46	08 49	08 54	08 58	08 59	09 04	09 10	09 09		09 14	09 19	09 22	09 24	09 29
	d		08 25	08 30	08 35		08 40		08 45		08 50	08 55		09 00	09 05		09 10		09 15	09 20		09 25	09 30
Heath Low Level	d		08 30									09 00										09 30	
Ty Glas	d		08 33									09 03										09 33	
Birchgrove	d		08 34									09 04										09 34	
Rhiwbina	d		08 36									09 06										09 36	
Whitchurch (Cardiff)	d		08 38									09 08										09 38	
Coryton	a		08 43									09 13										09 43	
Heath High Level	d				08 40						08 55				09 10					09 25			
Llanishen	d				08 43						08 58				09 13					09 28			
Lisvane & Thornhill	d				08 45						09 00				09 15					09 30			
Caerphilly 3	d				08 51						09 06				09 21					09 36			
Aber	d				08 53						09 08				09 23					09 38			
Llanbradach	d				08 57						09 12				09 27					09 42			
Ystrad Mynach 3	d				09 02						09 17				09 32					09 47			
Hengoed	d				09 05						09 20				09 35					09 50			
Pengam	d				09 08						09 23				09 38					09 53			
Gilfach Fargoed	d														09 41								
Bargoed	a				09 16						09 31				09 48					09 58			
	d																			09 59			
Brithdir	d																			10 03			
Tir-phil	d																			10 06			
Pontlottyn	d																			10 10			
Rhymney 3	a																			10 16			
Cathays	d			08 33			08 43		08 48					09 03			09 13		09 18				09 33
Llandaf	d			08 37			08 47		08 52					09 07			09 17		09 22				09 37
Ninian Park	d							08 40										09 10					
Waun-gron Park	d							08 43										09 13					
Fairwater	d							08 45										09 15					
Danescourt	d							08 47										09 17					
Radyr 3	a			08 40			08 50	08 54	08 55					09 10			09 20	09 24	09 25				09 40
	d			08 40			08 50		08 55					09 10			09 20		09 25				09 40
Taffs Well 3	d			08 44			08 54		08 59					09 14			09 24		09 29				09 44
Trefforest Estate	d			08 48										09 18									09 48
Trefforest	d			08 52			09 01		09 06					09 22			09 31		09 36				09 52
Pontypridd 3	a			08 55			09 04		09 09					09 25			09 34		09 39				09 55
	d			08 57			09 06		09 11					09 27			09 36		09 41				09 57
Abercynon	d			09 04					09 19					09 34					09 49				10 04
Penrhiwceiber	d								09 24										09 54				
Mountain Ash	a								09 28										09 58				
	d								09 33										10 03				
Fernhill	d								09 35										10 05				
Cwmbach	d								09 39										10 09				
Aberdare 3	a								09 46										10 16				
Quakers Yard	d			09 09										09 39									10 09
Merthyr Vale	a			09 14										09 44									10 14
	d			09 17										09 47									10 17
Troed Y Rhiw	d			09 20										09 50									10 20
Pentre-bach	d			09 23										09 53									10 23
Merthyr Tydfil	a			09 31										10 01									10 31
Trehafod	d						09 11										09 41						
Porth	a						09 14										09 44						
	d						09 15										09 45						
Dinas Rhondda	d						09 19										09 49						
Tonypandy	d						09 21										09 51						
Llwynypia	d						09 23										09 53						
Ystrad Rhondda	a						09 26										09 56						
	d						09 29										09 59						
Ton Pentre	d						09 31										10 01						
Treorchy	d						09 34										10 04						
Ynyswen	d						09 37										10 07						
Treherbert	a						09 43										10 13						

When events are being held at the Millenium Stadium, services are subject to alteration. Please check times before travelling.

Table 130

Mondays to Fridays

until 9 September

Bridgend, Barry Island, Barry, Penarth and Cardiff - Coryton, Rhymney, Pontypridd, Merthyr, Aberdare and Treherbert

		AW	AW	AW	AW	AW	AW	AW	AW	AW	AW	AW	AW	AW	AW	AW	AW	AW	AW	AW	AW	AW
Bridgend	d					08 42																
Llantwit Major	d					08 56																
Rhoose Cardiff Int Airport ✈	d					09 06																
Barry Island	d										09 25						09 40				09 55	
Barry 3	d					09 15					09 30						09 45				10 00	
Barry Docks	d					09 19					09 34						09 49				10 04	
Cadoxton	d					09 22					09 37						09 52				10 07	
Dinas Powys	d					09 26					09 41						09 56				10 11	
Eastbrook	d					09 28					09 43						09 58				10 13	
Cogan	d					09 30					09 45						10 00				10 15	
Penarth	d	09 17						09 32				09 47						10 02				10 17
Dingle Road	d	09 19						09 34				09 49						10 04				10 19
Grangetown	d	09 23				09 34		09 38			09 49	09 53					10 04	10 08			10 19	10 23
Cardiff Central 7	a	09 29				09 39		09 44			09 54	09 59					10 09	10 14			10 24	10 29
	d	09 31		09 36	09 36	09 41		09 46	09 51		09 56	10 01		10 06	10 06		10 11	10 16		10 21	10 26	10 31
Cardiff Bay	d		09 30				09 42			09 54			10 06						10 18			
Cardiff Queen Street 3	a	09 34	09 34	09 39		09 44	09 46	09 49	09 54	09 58	09 59	10 04	10 10	10 09			10 14	10 19	10 22	10 24	10 29	10 34
	d	09 35		09 40		09 45		09 50	09 55		10 00	10 05		10 10			10 15	10 20		10 25	10 30	10 35
Heath Low Level	d								10 00											10 30		
Ty Glas	d								10 03											10 33		
Birchgrove	d								10 04											10 34		
Rhiwbina	d								10 06											10 36		
Whitchurch (Cardiff)	d								10 08											10 38		
Coryton	a								10 13											10 43		
Heath High Level	d	09 40						09 55				10 10						10 25				10 40
Llanishen	d	09 43						09 58				10 13						10 28				10 43
Lisvane & Thornhill	d	09 45						10 00				10 15						10 30				10 45
Caerphilly 3	d	09 51						10 06				10 21						10 36				10 51
Aber	d	09 53						10 08				10 23						10 38				10 53
Llanbradach	d	09 57						10 12				10 27						10 42				10 57
Ystrad Mynach 3	d	10 02						10 17				10 32						10 47				11 02
Hengoed	d	10 05						10 19				10 35						10 50				11 05
Pengam	d	10 08						10 23				10 38						10 53				11 08
Gilfach Fargoed	d											10 41										
Bargoed	a	10 16						10 31				10 48						10 58				11 16
	d																	10 59				
Brithdir	d																	11 03				
Tir-phil	d																	11 06				
Pontlottyn	d																	11 10				
Rhymney 3	a																	11 16				
Cathays	d			09 43		09 48					10 03			10 13			10 18				10 33	
Llandaf	d			09 47		09 52					10 07			10 17			10 22				10 37	
Ninian Park	d				09 40										10 10							
Waun-gron Park	d				09 43										10 13							
Fairwater	d				09 45										10 15							
Danescourt	d				09 47										10 17							
Radyr 3	a			09 50	09 54	09 55					10 10			10 20	10 25		10 25				10 40	
	d			09 50		09 55					10 10			10 20			10 25				10 40	
Taffs Well 3	d			09 54		09 59					10 14			10 24			10 29				10 44	
Trefforest Estate	d																				10 48	
Trefforest	d			10 01		10 06					10 22			10 31			10 36				10 52	
Pontypridd 3	a			10 04		10 09					10 30			10 34			10 39				10 55	
	d			10 06		10 11								10 36		10 35	10 41				10 57	
Abercynon	d					10 19										10 41	10 49				11 04	
Penrhiwceiber	d					10 24											10 54					
Mountain Ash	a					10 28											10 58					
	d					10 33											11 03					
Fernhill	d					10 35											11 05					
Cwmbach	d					10 39											11 09					
Aberdare 3	a					10 46											11 16					
Quakers Yard	d															10 45					11 09	
Merthyr Vale	a															10 50					11 14	
	d															10 52					11 17	
Troed Y Rhiw	d															10 55					11 20	
Pentre-bach	d															10 58					11 23	
Merthyr Tydfil	a															11 06					11 31	
Trehafod	d			10 11										10 41								
Porth	a			10 14										10 44								
	d			10 15										10 45								
Dinas Rhondda	d			10 19										10 49								
Tonypandy	d			10 21										10 51								
Llwynypia	d			10 23										10 53								
Ystrad Rhondda	a			10 26										10 56								
	d			10 29										10 59								
Ton Pentre	d			10 31										11 01								
Treorchy	d			10 34										11 04								
Ynyswen	d			10 37										11 07								
Treherbert	a			10 43										11 13								

When events are being held at the Millenium Stadium, services are subject to alteration. Please check times before travelling.

Table 130

Mondays to Fridays

until 9 September

Bridgend, Barry Island, Barry, Penarth and Cardiff - Coryton, Rhymney, Pontypridd, Merthyr, Aberdare and Treherbert

		AW	AW	AW	AW	AW	AW	AW	AW	AW	AW	AW	AW	AW	AW	AW	AW	AW	AW	AW	AW	AW	AW
Bridgend	d				09 42																		
Llantwit Major	d				09 56																		
Rhoose Cardiff Int Airport ✈	d				10 06																		
Barry Island	d									10 25					10 40				10 55				
Barry 3	d				10 15					10 30					10 45				11 00				
Barry Docks	d				10 19					10 34					10 49				11 04				
Cadoxton	d				10 22					10 37					10 52				11 07				
Dinas Powys	d				10 26					10 41					10 56				11 11				
Eastbrook	d				10 28					10 43					10 58				11 13				
Cogan	d				10 30					10 45					11 00				11 15				
Penarth	d						10 32					10 47				11 02				11 17			
Dingle Road	d						10 34					10 49				11 04				11 19			
Grangetown	d				10 34		10 38			10 49		10 53			11 04	11 08			11 19	11 23			
Cardiff Central 7	a				10 42		10 44			10 54		10 59			11 09	11 14			11 24	11 29			
	d		10 36	10 36			10 46	10 51		10 56	10 54	11 01	11 06		11 11	11 16		11 21	11 26	11 31		11 36	11 36
Cardiff Bay	d	10 30				10 42			10 54					11 06			11 18				11 30		
Cardiff Queen Street 3	a	10 34	10 39			10 46	10 49	10 54	10 58	10 59		11 04		11 10	11 14	11 19	11 22	11 24	11 29	11 34	11 34	11 39	
	d		10 40				10 50	10 55		11 00		11 05			11 15	11 20		11 25	11 30	11 35		11 40	
Heath Low Level	d							11 00										11 30					
Ty Glas	d							11 03										11 33					
Birchgrove	d							11 04										11 34					
Rhiwbina	d							11 06										11 36					
Whitchurch (Cardiff)	d							11 08										11 38					
Coryton	a							11 13										11 43					
Heath High Level	d						10 55					11 10				11 25				11 40			
Llanishen	d						10 58					11 13				11 28				11 43			
Lisvane & Thornhill	d						11 00					11 15				11 30				11 45			
Caerphilly 3	d						11 06					11 21				11 36				11 51			
Aber	d						11 08					11 23				11 38				11 53			
Llanbradach	d						11 12					11 27				11 42				11 57			
Ystrad Mynach 3	d						11 17					11 32				11 47				12 02			
Hengoed	d						11 19					11 35				11 50				12 05			
Pengam	d						11 23					11 38				11 53				12 08			
Gilfach Fargoed	d											11 41											
Bargoed	a						11 31					11 48				11 58				12 16			
	d															11 59							
Brithdir	d															12 03							
Tir-phil	d															12 06							
Pontlottyn	d															12 10							
Rhymney 3	a															12 16							
Cathays	d		10 43							11 03					11 18				11 33			11 43	
Llandaf	d		10 47							11 07					11 22				11 37			11 47	
Ninian Park	d			10 40									11 10										11 40
Waun-gron Park	d			10 43									11 13										11 43
Fairwater	d			10 45									11 15										11 45
Danescourt	d			10 47									11 17										11 47
Radyr 3	a		10 50	10 54						11 10	11 02		11 24		11 25				11 40			11 50	11 54
	d		10 50							11 10	11 20				11 25				11 40			11 50	
Taffs Well 3	d		10 54							11 14	11 24				11 29				11 44			11 54	
Trefforest Estate	d									11 18									11 48				
Trefforest	d		11 01							11 22	11 31				11 36				11 52			12 01	
Pontypridd 3	a		11 04							11 25	11 34				11 39				11 55			12 04	
	d		11 06							11 27	11 36				11 41				11 57			12 06	
Abercynon	d									11 34					11 49				12 04				
Penrhiwceiber	d														11 54								
Mountain Ash	a														11 58								
	d														12 03								
Fernhill	d														12 05								
Cwmbach	d														12 09								
Aberdare 3	a														12 16								
Quakers Yard	d									11 39									12 09				
Merthyr Vale	a									11 44									12 14				
	d									11 47									12 17				
Troed Y Rhiw	d									11 50									12 20				
Pentre-bach	d									11 53									12 23				
Merthyr Tydfil	a									12 01									12 31				
Trehafod	d		11 11								11 41											12 11	
Porth	a		11 14								11 44											12 14	
	d		11 15								11 45											12 15	
Dinas Rhondda	d		11 19								11 49											12 19	
Tonypandy	d		11 21								11 51											12 21	
Llwynypia	d		11 23								11 53											12 23	
Ystrad Rhondda	a		11 26								11 56											12 26	
	d		11 29								11 59											12 29	
Ton Pentre	d		11 31								12 01											12 31	
Treorchy	d		11 34								12 04											12 34	
Ynyswen	d		11 37								12 07											12 37	
Treherbert	a		11 43								12 13											12 43	

When events are being held at the Millenium Stadium, services are subject to alteration. Please check times before travelling.

Table 130

Mondays to Fridays
until 9 September

Bridgend, Barry Island, Barry, Penarth and Cardiff - Coryton, Rhymney, Pontypridd, Merthyr, Aberdare and Treherbert

Station		AW	AW	AW	AW	AW	AW	AW	AW	AW	AW	AW	AW	AW	AW	AW	AW	AW	AW	AW	AW	AW	AW
Bridgend	d	10 42																				11 42	
Llantwit Major	d	10 56																				11 56	
Rhoose Cardiff Int Airport ✈	d	11 06																				12 06	
Barry Island	d						11 25					11 40				11 55							
Barry [3]	d	11 15					11 30					11 45				12 00						12 15	
Barry Docks	d	11 19					11 34					11 49				12 04						12 19	
Cadoxton	d	11 22					11 37					11 52				12 07						12 22	
Dinas Powys	d	11 26					11 41					11 56				12 11						12 26	
Eastbrook	d	11 28					11 43					11 58				12 13						12 28	
Cogan	d	11 30					11 45					12 00				12 15						12 30	
Penarth	d			11 32				11 47					12 02				12 17						
Dingle Road	d			11 34				11 49					12 04				12 19						
Grangetown	d	11 34		11 38			11 49	11 53				12 04	12 08			12 19	12 23					12 34	
Cardiff Central [7]	a	11 39		11 44			11 54	11 59				12 09	12 14			12 25	12 29					12 46	
	d	11 41		11 46	11 51		11 56	12 01		12 06	12 06	12 11	12 16		12 21	12 26	12 31		12 36	12 36	12 41		
Cardiff Bay	d		11 42			11 54			12 06					12 18				12 30					12 42
Cardiff Queen Street [3]	a	11 44	11 46	11 49	11 54	11 58	11 59	12 04	12 10	12 09		12 14	12 19	12 22	12 24	12 29	12 34	12 34	12 39		12 44		12 46
	d	11 45		11 50	11 55		12 00	12 05		12 10		12 15	12 20		12 25	12 30	12 35		12 40		12 45		
Heath Low Level	d				12 00										12 30								
Ty Glas	d				12 03										12 33								
Birchgrove	d				12 04										12 34								
Rhiwbina	d				12 06										12 36								
Whitchurch (Cardiff)	d				12 08										12 38								
Coryton	a				12 13										12 43								
Heath High Level	d			11 55				12 10					12 25				12 40						
Llanishen	d			11 58				12 13					12 28				12 43						
Lisvane & Thornhill	d			12 00				12 15					12 30				12 45						
Caerphilly [3]	d			12 06				12 21					12 36				12 51						
Aber	d			12 08				12 23					12 38				12 53						
Llanbradach	d			12 12				12 27					12 42				12 57						
Ystrad Mynach [3]	d			12 17				12 32					12 47				13 02						
Hengoed	d			12 20				12 35					12 50				13 05						
Pengam	d			12 23				12 38					12 53				13 08						
Gilfach Fargoed	d							12 41															
Bargoed	a			12 31				12 48					12 58				13 16						
	d												12 59										
Brithdir	d												13 03										
Tir-phil	d												13 06										
Pontlottyn	d												13 10										
Rhymney [3]	a												13 16										
Cathays	d	11 48					12 03			12 13		12 18				12 33			12 43		12 48		
Llandaf	d	11 52					12 07			12 17		12 22				12 37			12 47		12 52		
Ninian Park	d										12 10									12 40			
Waun-gron Park	d										12 13									12 43			
Fairwater	d										12 15									12 45			
Danescourt	d										12 17									12 47			
Radyr [3]	a	11 55					12 10			12 20	12 24	12 25				12 40			12 50	12 54	12 55		
	d	11 55					12 10			12 20		12 25				12 40			12 50		12 55		
Taffs Well [3]	d	11 59					12 14			12 24		12 29				12 44			12 54		12 59		
Trefforest Estate	d						12 18									12 48							
Trefforest	d	12 06					12 22			12 31		12 36				12 52			13 01		13 06		
Pontypridd [3]	a	12 09					12 25			12 34		12 42				12 55			13 04		13 09		
	d	12 11					12 27			12 36						12 57			13 06		13 11		
Abercynon	d	12 19					12 34									13 04					13 19		
Penrhiwceiber	d	12 24																			13 24		
Mountain Ash	a	12 28																			13 28		
	d	12 33																			13 33		
Fernhill	d	12 35																			13 35		
Cwmbach	d	12 39																			13 39		
Aberdare [3]	a	12 46																			13 46		
Quakers Yard	d						12 39									13 09							
Merthyr Vale	a						12 44									13 14							
	d						12 47									13 17							
Troed Y Rhiw	d						12 50									13 20							
Pentre-bach	d						12 53									13 23							
Merthyr Tydfil	a						13 01									13 31							
Trehafod	d									12 41									13 11				
Porth	a									12 44									13 14				
	d									12 45									13 15				
Dinas Rhondda	d									12 49									13 19				
Tonypandy	d									12 51									13 21				
Llwynypia	d									12 53									13 23				
Ystrad Rhondda	a									12 56									13 26				
	d									12 59									13 29				
Ton Pentre	d									13 01									13 31				
Treorchy	d									13 04									13 34				
Ynyswen	d									13 07									13 37				
Treherbert	a									13 13									13 43				

When events are being held at the Millenium Stadium, services are subject to alteration. Please check times before travelling.

Table 130

Mondays to Fridays
until 9 September

Bridgend, Barry Island, Barry, Penarth and Cardiff - Coryton, Rhymney, Pontypridd, Merthyr, Aberdare and Treherbert

Station		AW	AW	AW	AW	AW	AW	AW	AW	AW	AW	AW	AW	AW	AW	AW	AW	AW	AW	AW	AW	AW
Bridgend	d																		12 42			
Llantwit Major	d																		12 56			
Rhoose Cardiff Int Airport ✈	d																		13 06			
Barry Island	d				12 25					12 40				12 55								
Barry [3]	d				12 30					12 45				13 00					13 15			
Barry Docks	d				12 34					12 49				13 04					13 19			
Cadoxton	d				12 37					12 52				13 07					13 22			
Dinas Powys	d				12 41					12 56				13 11					13 26			
Eastbrook	d				12 43					12 58				13 13					13 28			
Cogan	d				12 45					13 00				13 15					13 30			
Penarth	d	12 32				12 47					13 02				13 17						13 32	
Dingle Road	d	12 34				12 49					13 04				13 19						13 34	
Grangetown	d	12 38			12 49	12 53				13 04	13 08			13 19	13 23				13 34		13 38	
Cardiff Central [7]	a	12 44			12 54	12 59				13 09	13 14			13 24	13 29				13 39		13 44	
	d	12 46	12 51		12 56	13 01		13 06	13 06	13 11	13 16		13 21	13 26	13 31		13 36	13 36	13 41		13 46	13 51
Cardiff Bay	d			12 54			13 06					13 18				13 30				13 42		
Cardiff Queen Street [3]	a	12 49	12 54	12 58	12 59	13 04	13 10	13 09		13 14	13 19	13 22	13 24	13 29	13 34	13 34	13 39		13 44	13 46	13 49	13 54
	d	12 50	12 55		13 00	13 05		13 10		13 15	13 20		13 25	13 30	13 35		13 40		13 45		13 50	13 55
Heath Low Level	d		13 00										13 30									14 00
Ty Glas	d		13 03										13 33									14 03
Birchgrove	d		13 04										13 34									14 04
Rhiwbina	d		13 06										13 36									14 06
Whitchurch (Cardiff)	d		13 08										13 38									14 08
Coryton	a		13 13										13 43									14 13
Heath High Level	d	12 55				13 10					13 25				13 40						13 55	
Llanishen	d	12 58				13 13					13 28				13 43						13 58	
Lisvane & Thornhill	d	13 00				13 15					13 30				13 45						14 00	
Caerphilly [3]	d	13 06				13 21					13 36				13 51						14 06	
Aber	d	13 08				13 23					13 38				13 53						14 08	
Llanbradach	d	13 12				13 27					13 42				13 57						14 12	
Ystrad Mynach [3]	d	13 17				13 32					13 47				14 02						14 17	
Hengoed	d	13 20				13 35					13 50				14 05						14 20	
Pengam	d	13 23				13 38					13 53				14 08						14 23	
Gilfach Fargoed	d					13 41																
Bargoed	a	13 31				13 48					13 58				14 16						14 31	
	d										13 59											
Brithdir	d										14 03											
Tir-phil	d										14 06											
Pontlottyn	d										14 10											
Rhymney [3]	a										14 16											
Cathays	d				13 03			13 13		13 18				13 33			13 43		13 48			
Llandaf	d				13 07			13 17		13 22				13 37			13 47		13 52			
Ninian Park	d								13 10									13 40				
Waun-gron Park	d								13 13									13 43				
Fairwater	d								13 15									13 45				
Danescourt	d								13 17									13 47				
Radyr [3]	a				13 10			13 20	13 24	13 25				13 40			13 50	13 54	13 55			
	d				13 10			13 20		13 25				13 40			13 50		13 55			
Taffs Well [3]	d				13 14			13 24		13 29				13 44			13 54		13 59			
Trefforest Estate	d				13 18									13 48								
Trefforest	d				13 22			13 31		13 36				13 52			14 01		14 06			
Pontypridd [3]	a				13 25			13 34		13 39				13 55			14 04		14 09			
	d				13 27			13 36		13 41				13 57			14 06		14 11			
Abercynon	d				13 34					13 49				14 04					14 19			
Penrhiwceiber	d									13 54									14 24			
Mountain Ash	a									13 58									14 28			
	d									14 03									14 33			
Fernhill	d									14 05									14 35			
Cwmbach	d									14 09									14 39			
Aberdare [3]	a									14 16									14 46			
Quakers Yard	d				13 39									14 09								
Merthyr Vale	a				13 44									14 14								
	d				13 47									14 17								
Troed Y Rhiw	d				13 50									14 20								
Pentre-bach	d				13 53									14 23								
Merthyr Tydfil	a				14 01									14 31								
Trehafod	d							13 41									14 11					
Porth	a							13 44									14 14					
	d							13 45									14 15					
Dinas Rhondda	d							13 49									14 19					
Tonypandy	d							13 51									14 21					
Llwynypia	d							13 53									14 23					
Ystrad Rhondda	a							13 56									14 26					
	d							13 59									14 29					
Ton Pentre	d							14 01									14 31					
Treorchy	d							14 04									14 34					
Ynyswen	d							14 07									14 37					
Treherbert	a							14 13									14 43					

When events are being held at the Millenium Stadium, services are subject to alteration. Please check times before travelling.

Bridgend, Barry Island, Barry, Penarth and Cardiff - Coryton, Rhymney, Pontypridd, Merthyr, Aberdare and Treherbert

		AW	AW	AW	AW	AW	AW		AW	AW	AW	AW	AW	AW	AW	AW	AW		AW	AW	AW	AW	AW	AW	AW
Bridgend	d																		13 42						
Llantwit Major	d																		13 56						
Rhoose Cardiff Int Airport ✈	d																		14 06						
Barry Island	d		13 25						13 40				13 55												14 25
Barry ■	d		13 30						13 45				14 00						14 15						14 30
Barry Docks	d		13 34						13 49				14 04						14 19						14 34
Cadoxton	d		13 37						13 52				14 07						14 22						14 37
Dinas Powys	d		13 41						13 56				14 11						14 26						14 41
Eastbrook	d		13 43						13 58				14 13						14 28						14 43
Cogan	d		13 45						14 00				14 15						14 30						14 45
Penarth	d			13 47						14 02				14 17							14 32				
Dingle Road	d			13 49						14 04				14 19							14 34				
Grangetown	d		13 49	13 53					14 04	14 08			14 19	14 23					14 34		14 38				14 49
Cardiff Central ■	a		13 54	13 59					14 09	14 14			14 24	14 29					14 39		14 44				14 54
	d		13 56	14 01		14 06	14 06		14 11	14 16		14 21	14 26	14 31		14 36	14 36		14 41		14 46	14 51		14 51	14 56
Cardiff Bay	d	13 54			14 06						14 18				14 30					14 42			14 54		
Cardiff Queen Street ■	a	13 58	13 59	14 04	14 10	14 09			14 14	14 19	14 22	14 24	14 29	14 34	14 34	14 39			14 44	14 46	14 49	14 54	14 58		14 59
	d		14 00	14 05		14 10			14 15	14 20		14 25	14 30	14 35		14 40			14 45		14 50	14 55			15 00
Heath Low Level	d											14 30										15 00			
Ty Glas	d											14 33										15 03			
Birchgrove	d											14 34										15 04			
Rhiwbina	d											14 36										15 06			
Whitchurch (Cardiff)	d											14 38										15 08			
Coryton	a											14 43										15 13			
Heath High Level	d			14 10						14 25				14 40							14 55				
Llanishen	d			14 13						14 28				14 43							14 58				
Lisvane & Thornhill	d			14 15						14 30				14 45							15 00				
Caerphilly ■	d			14 21						14 36				14 51							15 06				
Aber	d			14 23						14 38				14 53							15 08				
Llanbradach	d			14 27						14 42				14 57							15 12				
Ystrad Mynach ■	d			14 32						14 47				15 02							15 17				
Hengoed	d			14 35						14 50				15 05							15 20				
Pengam	d			14 38						14 53				15 08							15 23				
Gilfach Fargoed	d			14 41																					
Bargoed	a			14 48						14 58				15 16							15 31				
	d									14 59															
Brithdir	d									15 03															
Tir-phil	d									15 06															
Pontlottyn	d									15 10															
Rhymney ■	a									15 16															
Cathays	d		14 03			14 13			14 18				14 33			14 43			14 48						15 03
Llandaf	d		14 07			14 17			14 22				14 37			14 47			14 52						15 07
Ninian Park	d						14 10										14 40								
Waun-gron Park	d						14 13										14 43								
Fairwater	d						14 15										14 45								
Danescourt	d						14 17										14 47								
Radyr ■	a		14 10			14 20	14 24		14 25				14 40			14 50	14 54		14 55					15 08	15 10
	d		14 10			14 20			14 25				14 40			14 50			14 55					15 20	15 10
Taffs Well ■	d		14 14			14 24			14 29				14 44			14 54			14 59					→	15 14
Trefforest Estate	d		14 18										14 48												15 18
Trefforest	d		14 22			14 31			14 36				14 52			15 01			15 06						15 22
Pontypridd ■	a		14 25			14 34			14 39				14 55			15 04			15 09						15 25
	d		14 27			14 36			14 41				14 57			15 06			15 11						15 27
Abercynon	d		14 34						14 49				15 04						15 19						15 34
Penrhiwceiber	d								14 54										15 24						
Mountain Ash	a								14 58										15 28						
	d								15 03										15 33						
Fernhill	d								15 05										15 35						
Cwmbach	d								15 09										15 39						
Aberdare ■	a								15 16										15 46						
Quakers Yard	d		14 39										15 09												15 39
Merthyr Vale	a		14 44										15 14												15 44
	d		14 47										15 17												15 47
Troed Y Rhiw	d		14 50										15 20												15 50
Pentre-bach	d		14 53										15 23												15 53
Merthyr Tydfil	a		15 01										15 31												16 01
Trehafod	d					14 41										15 11									
Porth	a					14 44										15 14									
	d					14 45										15 15									
Dinas Rhondda	d					14 49										15 19									
Tonypandy	d					14 51										15 21									
Llwynypia	d					14 53										15 23									
Ystrad Rhondda	a					14 56										15 26									
	d					14 59										15 29									
Ton Pentre	d					15 01										15 31									
Treorchy	d					15 04										15 34									
Ynyswen	d					15 07										15 37									
Treherbert	a					15 13										15 43									

When events are being held at the Millenium Stadium, services are subject to alteration. Please check times before travelling.

Bridgend, Barry Island, Barry, Penarth and Cardiff - Coryton, Rhymney, Pontypridd, Merthyr, Aberdare and Treherbert

		AW	AW		AW	AW	AW	AW	AW	AW	AW	AW	AW		AW	AW	AW	AW	AW	AW	AW	AW	AW		AW
Bridgend	d																14 42								
Llantwit Major	d																14 56								
Rhoose Cardiff Int Airport ✈	d																15 06								
Barry Island	d						14 40				14 55											15 25			
Barry ■	d						14 45				15 00						15 15					15 30			
Barry Docks	d						14 49				15 04						15 19					15 34			
Cadoxton	d						14 52				15 07						15 22					15 37			
Dinas Powys	d						14 56				15 11						15 26					15 41			
Eastbrook	d						14 58				15 13						15 28					15 43			
Cogan	d						15 00				15 15						15 30					15 45			
Penarth	d		14 47					15 02				15 17							15 32				15 47		
Dingle Road	d		14 49					15 04				15 19							15 34				15 49		
Grangetown	d		14 53				15 04	15 08			15 19	15 23					15 34		15 38			15 49	15 53		
Cardiff Central ■	a		14 59				15 09	15 14			15 24	15 29					15 39		15 44			15 54	15 59		
	d		15 01		15 06		15 11	15 16		15 21	15 26	15 31			15 36	15 36	15 41		15 46	15 51		15 56	16 01		
Cardiff Bay	d					15 06			15 18				15 30					15 42			15 54				16 06
Cardiff Queen Street ■	a		15 04			15 10	15 14	15 19	15 22	15 24	15 29	15 34	15 34		15 39		15 44	15 46	15 49	15 54	15 58	15 59	16 04		16 10
	d		15 05				15 15	15 20		15 25	15 30	15 35			15 40		15 45		15 50	15 55		16 00	16 05		
Heath Low Level	d									15 30										16 00					
Ty Glas	d									15 33										16 03					
Birchgrove	d									15 34										16 04					
Rhiwbina	d									15 36										16 06					
Whitchurch (Cardiff)	d									15 38										16 08					
Coryton	a									15 43										16 13					
Heath High Level	d		15 10					15 25				15 40							15 55				16 10		
Llanishen	d		15 13					15 28				15 43							15 58				16 13		
Lisvane & Thornhill	d		15 15					15 30				15 45							16 00				16 15		
Caerphilly ■	d		15 21					15 36				15 51							16 06				16 21		
Aber	d		15 23					15 38				15 53							16 08				16 23		
Llanbradach	d		15 27					15 42				15 57							16 12				16 27		
Ystrad Mynach ■	d		15 32					15 47				16 02							16 17				16 32		
Hengoed	d		15 35					15 50				16 05							16 20				16 35		
Pengam	d		15 38					15 53				16 08							16 23				16 38		
Gilfach Fargoed	d		15 41																				16 41		
Bargoed	a		15 48					15 58				16 16							16 31				16 48		
	d							15 59																	
Brithdir	d							16 03																	
Tir-phil	d							16 06																	
Pontlottyn	d							16 10																	
Rhymney ■	a							16 16																	
Cathays	d						15 18				15 33				15 43		15 48					16 03			
Llandaf	d						15 22				15 37				15 47		15 52					16 07			
Ninian Park	d				15 10											15 40									
Waun-gron Park	d				15 13											15 43									
Fairwater	d				15 15											15 45									
Danescourt	d	←			15 17											15 47									
Radyr ■	a	15 08			15 24		15 25				15 40				15 50	15 54	15 55					16 10			
	d	15 20					15 25				15 40				15 50		15 55					16 10			
Taffs Well ■	d	15 24					15 29				15 44				15 54		15 59					16 14			
Trefforest Estate	d										15 48											16 18			
Trefforest	d	15 31					15 36				15 52				16 01		16 06					16 22			
Pontypridd ■	a	15 34					15 39				15 55				16 04		16 09					16 25			
	d	15 36					15 41				15 57				16 06		16 11					16 27			
Abercynon	d						15 49				16 04						16 19					16 34			
Penrhiwceiber	d						15 54										16 24								
Mountain Ash	a						15 58										16 28								
	d						16 03										16 33								
Fernhill	d						16 05										16 35								
Cwmbach	d						16 09										16 39								
Aberdare ■	a						16 16										16 46								
Quakers Yard	d										16 09											16 39			
Merthyr Vale	a										16 14											16 44			
	d										16 17											16 47			
Troed Y Rhiw	d										16 20											16 50			
Pentre-bach	d										16 23											16 53			
Merthyr Tydfil	a										16 31											17 01			
Trehafod	d	15 41													16 11										
Porth	a	15 44													16 14										
	d	15 45													16 15										
Dinas Rhondda	d	15 49													16 19										
Tonypandy	d	15 51													16 21										
Llwynypia	d	15 53													16 23										
Ystrad Rhondda	a	15 56													16 26										
	d	15 59													16 29										
Ton Pentre	d	16 01													16 31										
Treorchy	d	16 04													16 34										
Ynyswen	d	16 07													16 37										
Treherbert	a	16 13													16 43										

When events are being held at the Millenium Stadium, services are subject to alteration. Please check times before travelling.

Table 130

Bridgend, Barry Island, Barry, Penarth and Cardiff - Coryton, Rhymney, Pontypridd, Merthyr, Aberdare and Treherbert

		AW	AW	AW	AW	AW	AW	AW	AW		AW	AW	AW	AW	AW	AW	AW	AW	AW		AW	AW	AW	AW	AW
Bridgend	d													15 42											
Llantwit Major	d													15 56											
Rhoose Cardiff Int Airport ✈	d													16 06											
Barry Island	d			15 40				15 55											16 25						16 40
Barry 3	d			15 45				16 00						16 15					16 30						16 45
Barry Docks	d			15 49				16 04						16 19					16 34						16 49
Cadoxton	d			15 52				16 07						16 22					16 37						16 52
Dinas Powys	d			15 56				16 11						16 26					16 41						16 56
Eastbrook	d			15 58				16 13						16 28					16 43						16 58
Cogan	d			16 00				16 15						16 30					16 45						17 00
Penarth	d				16 02				16 17							16 32									
Dingle Road	d				16 04				16 19							16 34									
Grangetown	d			16 04	16 08			16 19	16 23					16 34		16 38			16 49						17 04
Cardiff Central 7	a			16 09	16 14			16 24	16 29					16 39		16 44			16 54						17 09
	d	16 06	16 06	16 11	16 16		16 21	16 26	16 31			16 36	16 36	16 41		16 46	16 51		16 56		17 01		17 06	17 06	17 11
Cardiff Bay	d					16 18					16 30				16 42			16 54				17 06			
Cardiff Queen Street 3	a	16 09		16 14	16 19	16 22	16 24	16 29	16 34		16 34	16 39		16 44	16 46	16 49	16 54	16 58	16 59		17 04	17 10	17 09		17 14
	d	16 10		16 15	16 20		16 25	16 30	16 35			16 40		16 45		16 50	16 55		17 00		17 05		17 10		17 15
Heath Low Level	d						16 30										17 00								
Ty Glas	d						16 33										17 03								
Birchgrove	d						16 34										17 04								
Rhiwbina	d						16 36										17 06								
Whitchurch (Cardiff)	d						16 38										17 08								
Coryton	a						16 43										17 13								
Heath High Level	d				16 25				16 40							16 55					17 10				
Llanishen	d				16 28				16 43							16 58					17 13				
Lisvane & Thornhill	d				16 30				16 45							17 00					17 15				
Caerphilly 3	d				16 36				16 51							17 06					17 21				
Aber	d				16 38				16 53							17 08					17 23				
Llanbradach	d				16 42				16 57							17 12					17 27				
Ystrad Mynach 3	d				16 47				17 02							17 17					17 33				
Hengoed	d				16 50				17 05							17 20					17 35				
Pengam	d				16 53				17 08							17 23					17 39				
Gilfach Fargoed	d																				17 42				
Bargoed	a				16 58				17 16							17 31					17 45				
	d				16 59																17 47				
Brithdir	d				17 03																17 50				
Tir-phil	d				17 06																17 53				
Pontlottyn	d				17 10																17 58				
Rhymney 3	a				17 16																18 04				
Cathays	d	16 13		16 18				16 33				16 43		16 48					17 03				17 13		17 18
Llandaf	d	16 17		16 22				16 37				16 47		16 52					17 07				17 17		17 22
Ninian Park	d		16 10										16 40											17 10	
Waun-gron Park	d		16 13										16 43											17 13	
Fairwater	d		16 15										16 45											17 15	
Danescourt	d		16 17										16 47											17 17	
Radyr 3	a	16 20	16 24	16 25				16 40				16 50	16 54	16 55					17 10				17 20	17 24	17 25
	d	16 20		16 25				16 40				16 50		16 55					17 10				17 20		17 25
Taffs Well 3	d	16 24		16 29				16 44				16 54		16 59					17 14				17 24		17 29
Trefforest Estate	d							16 48											17 18						
Trefforest	d	16 31		16 36				16 52				17 01		17 06					17 22				17 31		17 36
Pontypridd 3	a	16 34		16 39				16 55				17 04		17 09					17 25				17 34		17 39
	d	16 36		16 41				16 57				17 06		17 11					17 27				17 36		17 41
Abercynon	d			16 49				17 04						17 19					17 34						17 49
Penrhiwceiber	d			16 54										17 24											17 54
Mountain Ash	a			16 58										17 28											17 58
	d			17 03										17 33											18 03
Fernhill	d			17 05										17 35											18 05
Cwmbach	d			17 09										17 39											18 09
Aberdare 3	a			17 16										17 46											18 16
Quakers Yard	d							17 09											17 39						
Merthyr Vale	a							17 14											17 44						
	d							17 17											17 47						
Troed Y Rhiw	d							17 20											17 50						
Pentre-bach	d							17 23											17 53						
Merthyr Tydfil	a							17 31											18 01						
Trehafod	d	16 41										17 11											17 41		
Porth	a	16 44										17 14											17 44		
	d	16 45										17 15											17 45		
Dinas Rhondda	d	16 49										17 19											17 49		
Tonypandy	d	16 51										17 21											17 51		
Llwynypia	d	16 53										17 23											17 53		
Ystrad Rhondda	a	16 56										17 26											17 56		
	d	16 59										17 29											17 59		
Ton Pentre	d	17 01										17 31											18 01		
Treorchy	d	17 04										17 34											18 04		
Ynyswen	d	17 07										17 37											18 07		
Treherbert	a	17 13										17 43											18 13		

When events are being held at the Millenium Stadium, services are subject to alteration. Please check times before travelling.

Table 130

Bridgend, Barry Island, Barry, Penarth and Cardiff - Coryton, Rhymney, Pontypridd, Merthyr, Aberdare and Treherbert

		AW	AW	AW	AW		AW	AW	AW	AW	AW	AW	AW	AW	AW		AW	AW	AW	AW	AW	AW	AW	AW	AW
Bridgend	d										16 42														
Llantwit Major	d										16 56														
Rhoose Cardiff Int Airport ✈	d										17 06														
Barry Island	d				16 55												17 25					17 40			
Barry 3	d				17 00						17 15						17 30					17 45			
Barry Docks	d				17 04						17 19						17 34					17 49			
Cadoxton	d				17 07						17 22						17 37					17 52			
Dinas Powys	d				17 11						17 26						17 41					17 56			
Eastbrook	d				17 13						17 28						17 43					17 58			
Cogan	d				17 15						17 30						17 45					18 00			
Penarth	d	17 02					17 17						17 32					17 47					18 02		
Dingle Road	d	17 04					17 19						17 34					17 49					18 04		
Grangetown	d	17 08			17 19		17 23				17 34		17 38				17 49	17 53				18 04	18 08		
Cardiff Central 7	a	17 14			17 24		17 29				17 39		17 44				17 54	17 59				18 09	18 14		
	d	17 16		17 21	17 26		17 31		17 36	17 36	17 41		17 46	17 51			17 56	18 01		18 06	18 06	18 11	18 16		18 21
Cardiff Bay	d		17 18					17 30				17 42			17 54				18 06					18 18	
Cardiff Queen Street 3	a	17 19	17 22	17 24	17 29		17 34	17 34	17 39		17 44	17 46	17 49	17 54	17 58		17 59	18 04	18 10	18 09		18 14	18 19	18 22	18 24
	d	17 20		17 25	17 30		17 35		17 40		17 45		17 50	17 55			18 00	18 05		18 10		18 15	18 20		18 25
Heath Low Level	d			17 30										18 00											18 30
Ty Glas	d			17 33										18 03											18 33
Birchgrove	d			17 34										18 04											18 34
Rhiwbina	d			17 36										18 06											18 36
Whitchurch (Cardiff)	d			17 38										18 08											18 38
Coryton	a			17 43										18 13											18 43
Heath High Level	d	17 25					17 40						17 55					18 10					18 25		
Llanishen	d	17 28					17 43						17 59					18 13					18 28		
Lisvane & Thornhill	d	17 30					17 45						18 02					18 15					18 30		
Caerphilly 3	d	17 36					17 51						18 07					18 21					18 36		
Aber	d	17 38					17 53						18 10					18 23					18 38		
Llanbradach	d	17 42					17 57						18 14					18 27					18 42		
Ystrad Mynach 3	d	17 47					18 02						18 20					18 32					18a51		
Hengoed	d	17 50					18 05						18 23					18 35							
Pengam	d	17 53					18 08						18 27					18 38							
Gilfach Fargoed	d						18 11						18 30					18 41							
Bargoed	a	18 01					18 14						18 34					18 48							
	d						18 16						18 44												
Brithdir	d						18 20						18 48												
Tir-phil	d						18 23						18 51												
Pontlottyn	d						18 27						18 55												
Rhymney 3	a						18 33						19 01												
Cathays	d				17 33				17 43		17 48						18 03			18 13		18 18			
Llandaf	d				17 37				17 47		17 52						18 07			18 17		18 22			
Ninian Park	d									17 40											18 10				
Waun-gron Park	d									17 43											18 13				
Fairwater	d									17 45											18 15				
Danescourt	d									17 47											18 17				
Radyr 3	a				17 40				17 50	17 54	17 55						18 10			18 20	18 24	18 25			
	d				17 40				17 50		17 55						18 10			18 20		18 25			
Taffs Well 3	d				17 44				17 54		17 59						18 14			18 24		18 29			
Trefforest Estate	d				17 48												18 18								
Trefforest	d				17 52				18 01		18 06						18 22			18 31		18 36			
Pontypridd 3	a				17 55				18 04		18 09						18 25			18 34		18 42			
	d				17 57				18 06		18 11						18 27			18 36					
Abercynon	d				18 04						18 19						18 34								
Penrhiwceiber	d										18 24														
Mountain Ash	a										18 28														
	d										18 33														
Fernhill	d										18 35														
Cwmbach	d										18 39														
Aberdare 3	a										18 46														
Quakers Yard	d				18 09												18 39								
Merthyr Vale	a				18 14												18 44								
	d				18 17												18 47								
Troed Y Rhiw	d				18 20												18 50								
Pentre-bach	d				18 23												18 53								
Merthyr Tydfil	a				18 31												19 01								
Trehafod	d								18 11											18 41					
Porth	a								18 14											18 44					
	d								18 15											18 45					
Dinas Rhondda	d								18 19											18 49					
Tonypandy	d								18 21											18 51					
Llwynypia	d								18 23											18 53					
Ystrad Rhondda	a								18 26											18 56					
	d								18 29											18 59					
Ton Pentre	d								18 31											19 01					
Treorchy	d								18 34											19 04					
Ynyswen	d								18 37											19 07					
Treherbert	a								18 43											19 13					

When events are being held at the Millenium Stadium, services are subject to alteration. Please check times before travelling.

Table 130

Mondays to Fridays

until 9 September

Bridgend, Barry Island, Barry, Penarth and Cardiff - Coryton, Rhymney, Pontypridd, Merthyr, Aberdare and Treherbert

		AW	AW	AW	AW	AW	AW	AW	AW	AW	AW	AW	AW	AW	AW	AW	AW	AW	AW	AW	AW	AW
Bridgend	d						17 42															18 42
Llantwit Major	d						17 56															18 56
Rhoose Cardiff Int Airport ✈	d						18 06															19 06
Barry Island	d	17 55									18 25					18 40		18 55				
Barry [3]	d	18 00					18 15				18 30					18 45		19 00				19 15
Barry Docks	d	18 04					18 19				18 34					18 49		19 04				19 19
Cadoxton	d	18 07					18 22				18 37					18 52		19 07				19 22
Dinas Powys	d	18 11					18 26				18 41					18 56		19 11				19 26
Eastbrook	d	18 13					18 28				18 43					18 58		19 13				19 28
Cogan	d	18 15					18 30				18 45					19 00		19 15				19 30
Penarth	d		18 17					18 32					18 47						19 17			
Dingle Road	d		18 19					18 34					18 49						19 19			
Grangetown	d	18 19	18 23				18 34	18 38			18 49		18 53			19 04		19 19	19 23			19 34
Cardiff Central [7]	a	18 24	18 29				18 39	18 47			18 55		18 59			19 09		19 24	19 29			19 39
	d	18 26	18 31		18 36	18 36	18 41			18 51			19 01		19 06	19 11		19 26	19 31		19 36	19 41
Cardiff Bay	d			18 30					18 42			18 54		19 06			19 18			19 30		
Cardiff Queen Street [3]	a	18 29	18 34	18 34	18 38		18 44		18 46	18 54		18 58	19 04	19 10	19 09	19 14	19 22	19 29	19 34	19 34		19 44
	d	18 30	18 35		18 40		18 50			18 55			19 05		19 10	19 15		19 30	19 35			19 45
Heath Low Level	d									19 00												
Ty Glas	d									19 03												
Birchgrove	d									19 04												
Rhiwbina	d									19 06												
Whitchurch (Cardiff)	d									19 08												
Coryton	a									19 13												
Heath High Level	d		18 40										19 10						19 40			
Llanishen	d		18 43										19 13						19 43			
Lisvane & Thornhill	d		18 45										19 15						19 45			
Caerphilly [3]	d		18 51										19a23						19 51			
Aber	d		18 53																19 53			
Llanbradach	d		18 57																19 57			
Ystrad Mynach [3]	d		19 02																20 02			
Hengoed	d		19 05																20 05			
Pengam	d		19 08																20 08			
Gilfach Fargoed	d		19 11																20 11			
Bargoed	a		19 14																20 15			
	d		19 16																20 16			
Brithdir	d		19 20																20 20			
Tir-phil	d		19 23																20 23			
Pontlottyn	d		19 27																20 27			
Rhymney [3]	a		19 34																20 33			
Cathays	d	18 33			18 43		18 52								19 13	19 18		19 33				19 48
Llandaf	d	18 37			18 47		18 56								19 17	19 22		19 37				19 52
Ninian Park	d					18 40															19 40	
Waun-gron Park	d					18 43															19 43	
Fairwater	d					18 45															19 45	
Danescourt	d					18 47															19 47	
Radyr [3]	a	18 40			18 50	18 54	18 58								19 20	19 25		19 40			19 54	19 55
	d	18 40			18 50		18 58								19 20	19 25		19 40				19 55
Taffs Well [3]	d	18 44			18 54		19 03								19 24	19 29		19 44				19 59
Trefforest Estate	d	18 48																19 48				
Trefforest	d	18 52			19 01		19 10								19 31	19 36		19 52				20 06
Pontypridd [3]	a	18 55			19 04		19 13								19 34	19 39		19 55				20 09
	d	18 57			19 06		19 14								19 36	19 41		19 57				20 11
Abercynon	d	19 04					19 21									19 49		20 04				20 21
Penrhiwceiber	d						19 26									19 54						20 26
Mountain Ash	a						19 30									19 56						20 30
	d						19 33									20 03						20 33
Fernhill	d						19 35									20 05						20 35
Cwmbach	d						19 39									20 09						20 39
Aberdare [3]	a						19 46									20 16						20 46
Quakers Yard	d	19 09																20 08				
Merthyr Vale	a	19 14																20 13				
	d	19 17																20 15				
Troed Y Rhiw	d	19 20																20 19				
Pentre-bach	d	19 23																20 22				
Merthyr Tydfil	a	19 31																20 30				
Trehafod	d				19 11										19 41							
Porth	a				19 14										19 44							
	d				19 15										19 45							
Dinas Rhondda	d				19 19										19 49							
Tonypandy	d				19 21										19 51							
Llwynypia	d				19 23										19 53							
Ystrad Rhondda	a				19 26										19 56							
	d				19 29										19 59							
Ton Pentre	d				19 31										20 01							
Treorchy	d				19 34										20 04							
Ynyswen	d				19 37										20 07							
Treherbert	a				19 43										20 13							

When events are being held at the Millenium Stadium, services are subject to alteration. Please check times before travelling.

Table 130

Mondays to Fridays

until 9 September

Bridgend, Barry Island, Barry, Penarth and Cardiff - Coryton, Rhymney, Pontypridd, Merthyr, Aberdare and Treherbert

		AW	AW	AW	AW	AW	AW	AW	AW	AW	AW	AW	AW	AW	AW	AW	AW	AW	AW	AW	AW	AW	AW
Bridgend	d												19 42										
Llantwit Major	d												19 56										
Rhoose Cardiff Int Airport ✈	d												20 06										
Barry Island	d				19 25				19 55												20 55		
Barry [3]	d				19 30				20 00				20 15								21 00		
Barry Docks	d				19 34				20 04				20 19								21 04		
Cadoxton	d				19 37				20 07				20 22								21 07		
Dinas Powys	d				19 41				20 11				20 26								21 11		
Eastbrook	d				19 43				20 13				20 28								21 13		
Cogan	d				19 45				20 15				20 30								21 15		
Penarth	d					19 47				20 20							20 47						
Dingle Road	d					19 49				20 22							20 49						
Grangetown	d				19 49	19 54			20 19	20 26			20 34				20 53				21 19		
Cardiff Central [7]	a				19 56	19 59			20 24	20 31			20 39				20 59				21 24		
	d		19 51		20 00	20 06			20 26	20 31		20 36	20 41		20 51		21 01		21 06		21 26		21 31
Cardiff Bay	d	19 42		19 54			20 06	20 18			20 30			20 42		20 54		21 06		21 18		21 30	
Cardiff Queen Street [3]	a	19 46	19 54	19 58	20 04	20 09	20 10	20 22	20 29	20 34	20 34		20 44	20 46	20 54	20 58	21 04	21 10	21 09	21 22	21 29	21 34	21 34
	d		19 55		20 05	20 10			20 30	20 35			20 45		20 55		21 05		21 10		21 30		21 35
Heath Low Level	d		20 00												21 00								
Ty Glas	d		20 03												21 03								
Birchgrove	d		20 04												21 04								
Rhiwbina	d		20 06												21 06								
Whitchurch (Cardiff)	d		20 08												21 08								
Coryton	a		20 13												21 13								
Heath High Level	d				20 10					20 40							21 10						21 40
Llanishen	d				20 13					20 43							21 13						21 43
Lisvane & Thornhill	d				20 15					20 45							21 16						21 45
Caerphilly [3]	d				20a27					20 51							21a36						21 51
Aber	d									20 53													21 53
Llanbradach	d									20 57													21 57
Ystrad Mynach [3]	d									21 02													22 02
Hengoed	d									21 05													22 05
Pengam	d									21 08													22 08
Gilfach Fargoed	d									21 11													22 11
Bargoed	a									21 15													22 15
	d									21 16													22 16
Brithdir	d									21 20													22 20
Tir-phil	d									21 23													22 23
Pontlottyn	d									21 27													22 27
Rhymney [3]	a									21 34													22 34
Cathays	d					20 13			20 33				20 48						21 13		21 33		
Llandaf	d					20 17			20 37				20 52						21 17		21 37		
Ninian Park	d											20 40											
Waun-gron Park	d											20 43											
Fairwater	d											20 45											
Danescourt	d											20 47											
Radyr [3]	a					20 20			20 40			20 54	20 55						21 20		21 40		
	d					20 20			20 40				20 55						21 20		21 40		
Taffs Well [3]	d					20 24			20 44				20 59						21 24		21 44		
Trefforest Estate	d								20 48												21 48		
Trefforest	d					20 31			20 52				21 06						21 31		21 52		
Pontypridd [3]	a					20 34			20 55				21 09						21 34		21 55		
	d					20 36			20 57				21 11						21 36		21 57		
Abercynon	d								21 04				21 19								22 04		
Penrhiwceiber	d												21 24										
Mountain Ash	a												21 28										
	d												21 29										
Fernhill	d												21 31										
Cwmbach	d												21 35										
Aberdare [3]	a												21 42										
Quakers Yard	d								21 08												22 08		
Merthyr Vale	a								21 13												22 13		
	d								21 15												22 15		
Troed Y Rhiw	d								21 19												22 19		
Pentre-bach	d								21 22												22 22		
Merthyr Tydfil	a								21 30												22 30		
Trehafod	d					20 41													21 41				
Porth	a					20 44													21 44				
	d					20 45													21 45				
Dinas Rhondda	d					20 49													21 49				
Tonypandy	d					20 51													21 51				
Llwynypia	d					20 53													21 53				
Ystrad Rhondda	a					20 56													21 56				
	d					20 59													21 59				
Ton Pentre	d					21 01													22 01				
Treorchy	d					21 04													22 04				
Ynyswen	d					21 07													22 07				
Treherbert	a					21 13													22 13				

When events are being held at the Millenium Stadium, services are subject to alteration. Please check times before travelling.

Bridgend, Barry Island, Barry, Penarth and Cardiff - Coryton, Rhymney, Pontypridd, Merthyr, Aberdare and Treherbert

		AW	AW	AW	AW	AW	AW	AW	AW	AW	AW	AW	AW	AW	AW	AW	AW	AW	AW	AW	AW	AW
Bridgend	d			20 42											21 42							
Llantwit Major	d			20 56											21 56							
Rhoose Cardiff Int Airport ✈	d			21 06											22 06							
Barry Island	d											21 55										22 44
Barry 3	d			21 15								22 00			22 15							22 48
Barry Docks	d			21 19								22 04			22 19							22 52
Cadoxton	d			21 22								22 07			22 22							22 55
Dinas Powys	d			21 26								22 11			22 26							22 59
Eastbrook	d			21 28								22 13			22 28							23 01
Cogan	d			21 30								22 15			22 30							23 03
Penarth	d		21 20				21 47							22 20						22 47		
Dingle Road	d		21 22				21 49							22 22						22 49		
Grangetown	d		21 26	21 34			21 53					22 19		22 26	22 34					22 53		23 07
Cardiff Central 7	a		21 37	21 39			21 59					22 24		22 33	22 39					23 00		23 12
	d	21 36		21 41			22 01		22 06		22 21	22 26		22 35	22 41		22 46			23 15		23 26
Cardiff Bay	d				21 42	21 54		22 06		22 18			22 30			22 42		22 54	23 06		23 18	
Cardiff Queen Street 3	a			21 44	21 46	21 58	22 04	22 10	22 09	22 22	22 24	22 29	22 34	22 38	22 44	22 46	22 49	22 58	23 10	23 18	23 22	23 29
	d			21 45			22 05		22 10		22 25	22 30		22 39	22 45		22 50			23 19		23 30
Heath Low Level	d										22 30											
Ty Glas	d										22 33											
Birchgrove	d										22 34											
Rhiwbina	d										22 36											
Whitchurch (Cardiff)	d										22 38											
Coryton	a										22 43											
Heath High Level	d						22 10							22 44						23 24		
Llanishen	d						22 13							22 47						23 27		
Lisvane & Thornhill	d						22 15							22 49						23 29		
Caerphilly 3	d						22a23							22 55						23 35		
Aber	d													22 57						23 37		
Llanbradach	d													23 01						23 41		
Ystrad Mynach 3	d													23 06						23a50		
Hengoed	d													23 09								
Pengam	d													23 12								
Gilfach Fargoed	d													23 15								
Bargoed	a													23 19								
	d													23 20								
Brithdir	d													23 24								
Tir-phil	d													23 27								
Pontlottyn	d													23 31								
Rhymney 3	a													23 37								
Cathays	d			21 48					22 13			22 33			22 48		22 53					23 33
Llandaf	d			21 52					22 17			22 37			22 52		22 57					23 37
Ninian Park	d	21 40																				
Waun-gron Park	d	21 43																				
Fairwater	d	21 45																				
Danescourt	d	21 47																				
Radyr 3	a	21 54		21 55					22 20			22 40			22 55		22 59					23 40
	d			21 55					22 20			22 40			22 55		22 59					23 40
Taffs Well 3	d			21 59					22 24			22 44			22 59		23 03					23 44
Trefforest Estate	d											22 48										
Trefforest	d			22 06					22 31			22 52			23 06		23 10					23 52
Pontypridd 3	a			22 09					22 34			22 55			23 09		23 14					23 58
	d			22 11					22 36			22 57			23 11		23 15					
Abercynon	d			22 19								23 04			23 19							
Penrhiwceiber	d			22 24											23 24							
Mountain Ash	a			22 28											23 28							
	d			22 29											23 29							
Fernhill	d			22 31											23 31							
Cwmbach	d			22 35											23 35							
Aberdare 3	a			22 42											23 42							
Quakers Yard	d											23 08										
Merthyr Vale	a											23 13										
	d											23 15										
Troed Y Rhiw	d											23 19										
Pentre-bach	d											23 22										
Merthyr Tydfil	a											23 30										
Trehafod	d								22 41								23 20					
Porth	a								22 44								23 23					
	d								22 45								23 24					
Dinas Rhondda	d								22 49								23 28					
Tonypandy	d								22 51								23 30					
Llwynypia	d								22 53								23 32					
Ystrad Rhondda	a								22 56								23 35					
	d								22 59								23 38					
Ton Pentre	d								23 01								23 40					
Treorchy	d								23 04								23 43					
Ynyswen	d								23 07								23 46					
Treherbert	a								23 13								23 52					

When events are being held at the Millenium Stadium, services are subject to alteration. Please check times before travelling.

Bridgend, Barry Island, Barry, Penarth and Cardiff - Coryton, Rhymney, Pontypridd, Merthyr, Aberdare and Treherbert

		AW	AW	AW	AW	AW
Bridgend	d		22 42			
Llantwit Major	d		22 56			
Rhoose Cardiff Int Airport ✈	d		23 06			
Barry Island	d					
Barry 3	d		23 15			
Barry Docks	d		23 19			
Cadoxton	d		23 22			
Dinas Powys	d		23 26			
Eastbrook	d		23 28			
Cogan	d		23 30			
Penarth	d	23 26				
Dingle Road	d	23 28				
Grangetown	d	23 32	23 34			
Cardiff Central 7	a	23 40	23 42			
	d					
Cardiff Bay	d			23 30	23 42	23 54
Cardiff Queen Street 3	a			23 34	23 46	23 58
	d					
Heath Low Level	d					
Ty Glas	d					
Birchgrove	d					
Rhiwbina	d					
Whitchurch (Cardiff)	d					
Coryton	a					
Heath High Level	d					
Llanishen	d					
Lisvane & Thornhill	d					
Caerphilly 3	d					
Aber	d					
Llanbradach	d					
Ystrad Mynach 3	d					
Hengoed	d					
Pengam	d					
Gilfach Fargoed	d					
Bargoed	a					
	d					
Brithdir	d					
Tir-phil	d					
Pontlottyn	d					
Rhymney 3	a					
Cathays	d					
Llandaf	d					
Ninian Park	d					
Waun-gron Park	d					
Fairwater	d					
Danescourt	d					
Radyr 3	a					
	d					
Taffs Well 3	d					
Trefforest Estate	d					
Trefforest	d					
Pontypridd 3	a					
	d					
Abercynon	d					
Penrhiwceiber	d					
Mountain Ash	a					
	d					
Fernhill	d					
Cwmbach	d					
Aberdare 3	a					
Quakers Yard	d					
Merthyr Vale	a					
	d					
Troed Y Rhiw	d					
Pentre-bach	d					
Merthyr Tydfil	a					
Trehafod	d					
Porth	a					
	d					
Dinas Rhondda	d					
Tonypandy	d					
Llwynypia	d					
Ystrad Rhondda	a					
	d					
Ton Pentre	d					
Treorchy	d					
Ynyswen	d					
Treherbert	a					

When events are being held at the Millenium Stadium, services are subject to alteration. Please check times before travelling.

Table 130

Mondays to Fridays
from 12 September

Bridgend, Barry Island, Barry, Penarth and Cardiff - Coryton, Rhymney, Pontypridd, Merthyr, Aberdare and Treherbert

Station		AW		AW	AW	AW	AW	AW	AW	AW	AW	AW	AW	AW	AW	AW	AW	AW	AW	AW	AW	AW	AW
Bridgend	d										05 42												
Llantwit Major	d										05 56												
Rhoose Cardiff Int Airport	d										06 06												
Barry Island	d								05 52							06 25							
Barry	d								05 57		06 15					06 30							
Barry Docks	d								06 01		06 19					06 34							
Cadoxton	d								06 04		06 22					06 37							
Dinas Powys	d								06 08		06 26					06 41							
Eastbrook	d								06 10		06 28					06 43							
Cogan	d								06 12		06 30					06 45							
Penarth	d						06 02						06 32								07 02		
Dingle Road	d						06 04						06 34								07 04		
Grangetown	d						06 08		06 16		06 34		06 38			06 49					07 08		
Cardiff Central	a						06 13		06 21		06 39		06 44			06 54					07 14		
	d	05 26		05 46	05 56	06 11	06 15	06 19	06 26	06 36	06 41		06 46	06 51		06 56		07 06	07 06	07 11	07 16		07 21
Cardiff Bay	d											06 42			06 54		07 06					07 18	
Cardiff Queen Street	a	05 29		05 49	05 59	06 14	06 19	06 24	06 29	06 39	06 44	06 46	06 49	06 54	06 58	06 59	07 10	07 09		07 14	07 19	07 22	07 24
	d	05 30		05 50	06 00	06 15	06 20	06 25	06 30	06 40	06 45		06 50	06 55		07 00		07 10		07 15	07 20		07 25
Heath Low Level	d							06 30						07 00									07 30
Ty Glas	d							06 33						07 03									07 33
Birchgrove	d							06 34						07 04									07 34
Rhiwbina	d							06 36						07 06									07 36
Whitchurch (Cardiff)	d							06 38						07 08									07 38
Coryton	a							06 44						07 14									07 44
Heath High Level	d			05 54			06 25						06 55								07 25		
Llanishen	d			05 57			06 28						06 58								07 28		
Lisvane & Thornhill	d			06 00			06 30						07 00								07 30		
Caerphilly	d			06a09			06 36						07 06								07 36		
Aber	d						06 38						07 08								07 38		
Llanbradach	d						06 42						07 12								07 42		
Ystrad Mynach	d						06 47						07 17								07 47		
Hengoed	d						06 50						07 20								07 50		
Pengam	d						06 53						07 23								07 53		
Gilfach Fargoed	d																						
Bargoed	a						07 02						07 32								08 03		
	d																						
Brithdir	d																						
Tir-phil	d																						
Pontlottyn	d																						
Rhymney	a																						
Cathays	d	05 33			06 03	06 18			06 33	06 43	06 48					07 03		07 13		07 18			
Llandaf	d	05 37			06 07	06 22			06 37	06 47	06 52					07 07		07 17		07 22			
Ninian Park	d																		07 10				
Waun-gron Park	d																		07 14				
Fairwater	d																		07 16				
Danescourt	d																		07 19				
Radyr	a	05 39			06 10	06 24			06 40	06 50	06 54					07 10		07 20	07 27	07 25			
	d	05 40			06 10	06 24			06 40	06 50	06 55					07 10		07 20		07 25			
Taffs Well	d	05 43			06 14	06 28			06 44	06 54	06 59					07 14		07 24		07 29			
Trefforest Estate	d	05 47			06 18				06 48							07 18							
Trefforest	d	05 52			06 22	06 35			06 52	07 01	07 06					07 22		07 31		07 36			
Pontypridd	a	05 55			06 25	06 38			06 55	07 04	07 09					07 25		07 34		07 39			
	d	05 57	06 11		06 27	06 41			06 57	07 06	07 11					07 27		07 36		07 41			
Abercynon	d	06 04	06 19		06 34	06 49			07 04		07 19					07 34				07 49			
Penrhiwceiber	d		06 25			06 55					07 25									07 55			
Mountain Ash	a		06 28			06 58					07 28									07 58			
	d		06 34			07 04					07 34									08 04			
Fernhill	d		06 37			07 07					07 37									08 07			
Cwmbach	d		06 41			07 11					07 41									08 11			
Aberdare	a		06 49			07 19					07 49									08 19			
Quakers Yard	d	06 09			06 39				07 09							07 39							
Merthyr Vale	a	06 14			06 44				07 14							07 44							
	d	06 17			06 47				07 17							07 47							
Troed Y Rhiw	d	06 21			06 51				07 21							07 51							
Pentre-bach	d	06 24			06 54				07 24							07 54							
Merthyr Tydfil	a	06 33			07 03				07 33							08 03							
Trehafod	d									07 11								07 41					
Porth	a									07 14								07 44					
	d									07 15								07 45					
Dinas Rhondda	d									07 19								07 49					
Tonypandy	d									07 21								07 51					
Llwynypia	d									07 23								07 53					
Ystrad Rhondda	a									07 26								07 56					
	d									07 29								07 59					
Ton Pentre	d									07 31								08 01					
Treorchy	d									07 34								08 04					
Ynyswen	d									07 37								08 07					
Treherbert	a									07 44								08 14					

When events are being held at the Millenium Stadium, services are subject to alteration. Please check times before travelling.

Table 130

Mondays to Fridays
from 12 September

Bridgend, Barry Island, Barry, Penarth and Cardiff - Coryton, Rhymney, Pontypridd, Merthyr, Aberdare and Treherbert

Station		AW	AW	AW	AW	AW	AW	AW	AW	AW	AW	AW	AW	AW	AW	AW	AW	AW	AW	AW	AW	AW	AW
Bridgend	d						06 42																
Llantwit Major	d						06 56																
Rhoose Cardiff Int Airport	d						07 06																
Barry Island	d	06 55										07 25					07 40				07 55		
Barry	d	07 00					07 15					07 30					07 45				08 00		
Barry Docks	d	07 04					07 19					07 34					07 49				08 04		
Cadoxton	d	07 07					07 22					07 37					07 52				08 07		
Dinas Powys	d	07 11					07 26					07 41					07 56				08 11		
Eastbrook	d	07 13					07 28					07 43					07 58				08 13		
Cogan	d	07 15					07 30					07 45					08 00				08 15		
Penarth	d		07 17						07 32				07 47					08 02				08 17	
Dingle Road	d		07 19						07 34				07 49					08 04				08 19	
Grangetown	d	07 19	07 23				07 34		07 38			07 49	07 54				08 04	08 08			08 19	08 23	
Cardiff Central	a	07 24	07 29				07 39		07 44			07 54	08 00				08 09	08 14			08 24	08 29	
	d	07 26	07 31		07 36	07 36	07 41		07 46	07 51		07 56	08 01		08 06	08 06	08 11	08 16		08 21	08 26	08 31	
Cardiff Bay	d			07 30				07 42			07 54			08 06					08 18				08 30
Cardiff Queen Street	a	07 29	07 34	07 34	07 39		07 44	07 46	07 49	07 54	07 58	07 59	08 04	08 10	08 09		08 14	08 19	08 22	08 24	08 29	08 34	08 34
	d	07 30	07 35		07 40		07 45		07 50	07 55		08 00	08 05		08 10		08 15	08 20		08 25	08 30	08 35	
Heath Low Level	d									08 00										08 30			
Ty Glas	d									08 03										08 33			
Birchgrove	d									08 04										08 34			
Rhiwbina	d									08 06										08 36			
Whitchurch (Cardiff)	d									08 08										08 38			
Coryton	a									08 14										08 44			
Heath High Level	d		07 40						07 55				08 10					08 25				08 40	
Llanishen	d		07 43						07 58				08 13					08 28				08 43	
Lisvane & Thornhill	d		07 45						08 00				08 15					08 30				08 45	
Caerphilly	d		07 51						08 06				08 21					08 36				08 51	
Aber	d		07 53						08 08				08 23					08 38				08 53	
Llanbradach	d		07 57						08 12				08 27					08 42				08 57	
Ystrad Mynach	d		08 02						08 17				08 32					08 47				09 07	
Hengoed	d		08 05						08 20				08 35					08 50				09 10	
Pengam	d		08 08						08 23				08 38					08 53				09 13	
Gilfach Fargoed	d												08 41										
Bargoed	a		08 13						08 32				08 49					08 58				09 22	
	d		08 14															08 59					
Brithdir	d		08 18															09 03					
Tir-phil	d		08 21															09 06					
Pontlottyn	d		08 25															09 10					
Rhymney	a		08 32															09 17					
Cathays	d	07 33			07 43		07 48					08 03			08 13		08 18				08 33		
Llandaf	d	07 37			07 47		07 52					08 07			08 17		08 22				08 37		
Ninian Park	d					07 40										08 10							
Waun-gron Park	d					07 44										08 14							
Fairwater	d					07 46										08 16							
Danescourt	d					07 49										08 19							
Radyr	a	07 40			07 50	07 57	07 55					08 10			08 20	08 27	08 25				08 40		
	d	07 40			07 50		07 55					08 10			08 20		08 25				08 40		
Taffs Well	d	07 44			07 54		07 59					08 14			08 24		08 29				08 44		
Trefforest Estate	d	07 48										08 18									08 48		
Trefforest	d	07 52			08 01		08 06					08 23			08 31		08 36				08 52		
Pontypridd	a	07 55			08 04		08 09					08 26			08 34		08 39				08 55		
	d	07 57			08 06		08 11					08 27			08 36		08 41				08 57		
Abercynon	d	08 04					08 19					08 34					08 49				09 04		
Penrhiwceiber	d						08 25										08 55						
Mountain Ash	a						08 28										08 58						
	d						08 34										09 04						
Fernhill	d						08 37										09 07						
Cwmbach	d						08 41										09 11						
Aberdare	a						08 49										09 19						
Quakers Yard	d	08 09										08 39									09 09		
Merthyr Vale	a	08 14										08 44									09 14		
	d	08 17										08 47									09 17		
Troed Y Rhiw	d	08 21										08 51									09 21		
Pentre-bach	d	08 24										08 54									09 24		
Merthyr Tydfil	a	08 33										09 03									09 33		
Trehafod	d				08 11										08 41								
Porth	a				08 14										08 44								
	d				08 15										08 45								
Dinas Rhondda	d				08 19										08 49								
Tonypandy	d				08 21										08 51								
Llwynypia	d				08 23										08 53								
Ystrad Rhondda	a				08 26										08 56								
	d				08 29										08 59								
Ton Pentre	d				08 31										09 01								
Treorchy	d				08 34										09 04								
Ynyswen	d				08 37										09 07								
Treherbert	a				08 44										09 14								

When events are being held at the Millenium Stadium, services are subject to alteration. Please check times before travelling.

Bridgend, Barry Island, Barry, Penarth and Cardiff - Coryton, Rhymney, Pontypridd, Merthyr, Aberdare and Treherbert

		AW		AW	AW	AW	AW	AW	AW	AW	AW	AW		AW	AW	AW	AW	AW	AW	AW	AW	AW		AW	AW
Bridgend	d				07 42																				
Llantwit Major	d				07 56																				
Rhoose Cardiff Int Airport ✈	d				08 06																				
Barry Island	d									08 25						08 40				08 55					
Barry ■	d				08 15					08 30						08 45				09 00					
Barry Docks	d				08 19					08 34						08 49				09 04					
Cadoxton	d				08 22					08 37						08 52				09 07					
Dinas Powys	d				08 26					08 41						08 56				09 11					
Eastbrook	d				08 28					08 43						08 58				09 13					
Cogan	d				08 30					08 45						09 00				09 15					
Penarth	d						08 32				08 47										09 17				
Dingle Road	d						08 34				08 49										09 19				
Grangetown	d				08 34		08 38			08 49	08 53					09 04				09 19	09 23				
Cardiff Central ■	a				08 39		08 44			08 54	08 59					09 09				09 24	09 29				
	d	08 36		08 36	08 41		08 46	08 51		08 56	09 01			09 06	09 06	09 11	09 16		09 21	09 26	09 31			09 36	09 36
Cardiff Bay	d					08 42			08 54			09 06						09 18				09 30			
Cardiff Queen Street ■	a	08 39			08 44	08 46	08 49	08 54	08 58	08 59	09 04	09 10		09 09		09 14	09 19	09 22	09 24	09 29	09 34	09 34		09 39	
	d	08 40			08 45		08 50	08 55		09 00	09 05			09 10		09 15	09 20		09 25	09 30	09 35			09 40	
Heath Low Level	d							09 00											09 30						
Ty Glas	d							09 03											09 33						
Birchgrove	d							09 04											09 34						
Rhiwbina	d							09 06											09 36						
Whitchurch (Cardiff)	d							09 08											09 38						
Coryton	a							09 14											09 44						
Heath High Level	d						08 55				09 10						09 25				09 40				
Llanishen	d						08 58				09 13						09 28				09 43				
Lisvane & Thornhill	d						09 00				09 15						09 30				09 45				
Caerphilly ■	d						09 06				09 21						09 36				09 51				
Aber	d						09 08				09 23						09 38				09 53				
Llanbradach	d						09 12				09 27						09 42				09 57				
Ystrad Mynach ■	d						09a22				09 32						09 47				10 07				
Hengoed	d										09 35						09 50				10 10				
Pengam	d										09 38						09 53				10 13				
Gilfach Fargoed	d										09 41														
Bargoed	a										09 49						09 58				10 22				
	d																09 59								
Brithdir	d																10 03								
Tir-phil	d																10 06								
Pontlottyn	d																10 10								
Rhymney ■	a																10 17								
Cathays	d	08 43			08 48					09 03				09 13		09 18				09 33				09 43	
Llandaf	d	08 47			08 52					09 07				09 17		09 22				09 37				09 47	
Ninian Park	d			08 40											09 10										09 40
Waun-gron Park	d			08 44											09 14										09 44
Fairwater	d			08 46											09 16										09 46
Danescourt	d			08 49											09 19										09 49
Radyr ■	a	08 50		08 57	08 55					09 10				09 20	09 27	09 25				09 40				09 50	09 57
	d	08 50			08 55					09 10				09 20		09 25				09 40				09 50	
Taffs Well ■	d	08 54			08 59					09 14				09 24		09 29				09 44				09 54	
Trefforest Estate	d									09 18										09 48					
Trefforest	d	09 01			09 06					09 22				09 31		09 36				09 52				10 01	
Pontypridd ■	a	09 04			09 09					09 25				09 34		09 39				09 55				10 04	
	d	09 06			09 11					09 27				09 36		09 41				09 57				10 06	
Abercynon	d				09 19					09 34						09 49				10 04					
Penrhiwceiber	d				09 25											09 55									
Mountain Ash	a				09 28											09 58									
	d				09 34											10 04									
Fernhill	d				09 37											10 07									
Cwmbach	d				09 41											10 11									
Aberdare ■	a				09 49											10 19									
Quakers Yard	d									09 39										10 09					
Merthyr Vale	a									09 44										10 14					
	d									09 47										10 17					
Troed Y Rhiw	d									09 51										10 21					
Pentre-bach	d									09 54										10 24					
Merthyr Tydfil	a									10 03										10 33					
Trehafod	d	09 11												09 41										10 11	
Porth	a	09 14												09 44										10 14	
	d	09 15												09 45										10 15	
Dinas Rhondda	d	09 19												09 49										10 19	
Tonypandy	d	09 21												09 51										10 21	
Llwynypia	d	09 23												09 53										10 23	
Ystrad Rhondda	a	09 26												09 56										10 26	
	d	09 29												09 59										10 29	
Ton Pentre	d	09 31												10 01										10 31	
Treorchy	d	09 34												10 04										10 34	
Ynyswen	d	09 37												10 07										10 37	
Treherbert	a	09 44												10 14										10 44	

When events are being held at the Millenium Stadium, services are subject to alteration. Please check times before travelling.

Bridgend, Barry Island, Barry, Penarth and Cardiff - Coryton, Rhymney, Pontypridd, Merthyr, Aberdare and Treherbert

		AW	AW	AW	AW	AW	AW	AW		AW	AW	AW	AW	AW	AW	AW	AW	AW		AW	AW	AW	AW	AW	AW
Bridgend	d	08 42																						09 42	
Llantwit Major	d	08 56																						09 56	
Rhoose Cardiff Int Airport ✈	d	09 06																						10 06	
Barry Island	d						09 25							09 40				09 55							
Barry ■	d	09 15					09 30							09 45				10 00						10 15	
Barry Docks	d	09 19					09 34							09 49				10 04						10 19	
Cadoxton	d	09 22					09 37							09 52				10 07						10 22	
Dinas Powys	d	09 26					09 41							09 56				10 11						10 26	
Eastbrook	d	09 28					09 43							09 58				10 13						10 28	
Cogan	d	09 30					09 45							10 00				10 15						10 30	
Penarth	d			09 32				09 47							10 02					10 17					
Dingle Road	d			09 34				09 49							10 04					10 19					
Grangetown	d	09 34		09 38			09 49	09 53						10 04	10 08			10 19		10 23				10 34	
Cardiff Central ■	a	09 39		09 44			09 54	09 59						10 09	10 14			10 24		10 29				10 42	
	d	09 41		09 46	09 51		09 56	10 01			10 06	10 06		10 11	10 16		10 21	10 26		10 31		10 36	10 36		
Cardiff Bay	d		09 42			09 54				10 06						10 18					10 30				10 42
Cardiff Queen Street ■	a	09 44	09 46	09 49	09 54	09 58	09 59	10 04		10 10	10 09			10 14	10 19	10 22	10 24	10 29		10 34	10 34	10 39			10 46
	d	09 45		09 50	09 55		10 00	10 05			10 10			10 15	10 20		10 25	10 30		10 35		10 40			
Heath Low Level	d				10 00												10 30								
Ty Glas	d				10 03												10 33								
Birchgrove	d				10 04												10 34								
Rhiwbina	d				10 06												10 36								
Whitchurch (Cardiff)	d				10 08												10 38								
Coryton	a				10 14												10 44								
Heath High Level	d			09 55				10 10							10 25					10 40					
Llanishen	d			09 58				10 13							10 28					10 43					
Lisvane & Thornhill	d			10 00				10 15							10 30					10 45					
Caerphilly ■	d			10 06				10 21							10 36					10 51					
Aber	d			10 08				10 23							10 38					10 53					
Llanbradach	d			10 12				10 27							10 42					10 57					
Ystrad Mynach ■	d			10a22				10 32							10 47					11 07					
Hengoed	d							10 35							10 50					11 10					
Pengam	d							10 38							10 53					11 13					
Gilfach Fargoed	d							10 41																	
Bargoed	a							10 49							10 58					11 22					
	d														10 59										
Brithdir	d														11 03										
Tir-phil	d														11 06										
Pontlottyn	d														11 10										
Rhymney ■	a														11 17										
Cathays	d	09 48					10 03				10 13			10 18				10 33				10 43			
Llandaf	d	09 52					10 07				10 17			10 22				10 37				10 47			
Ninian Park	d											10 10											10 40		
Waun-gron Park	d											10 14											10 44		
Fairwater	d											10 16											10 46		
Danescourt	d											10 19											10 49		
Radyr ■	a	09 55					10 10				10 20	10 27		10 25				10 40				10 50	10 57		
	d	09 55					10 10				10 20			10 25				10 40				10 50			
Taffs Well ■	d	09 59					10 14				10 24			10 29				10 44				10 54			
Trefforest Estate	d																	10 48							
Trefforest	d	10 06					10 22				10 31			10 36				10 52				11 01			
Pontypridd ■	a	10 09					10 30				10 34			10 39				10 55				11 04			
	d	10 11									10 36		10 35	10 41				10 57				11 06			
Abercynon	d	10 19											10 41	10 49				11 04							
Penrhiwceiber	d	10 25												10 55											
Mountain Ash	a	10 28												10 58											
	d	10 34												11 04											
Fernhill	d	10 37												11 07											
Cwmbach	d	10 41												11 11											
Aberdare ■	a	10 49												11 19											
Quakers Yard	d												10 45					11 09							
Merthyr Vale	a												10 50					11 14							
	d												10 52					11 17							
Troed Y Rhiw	d												10 56					11 21							
Pentre-bach	d												10 59					11 24							
Merthyr Tydfil	a												11 08					11 33							
Trehafod	d										10 41											11 11			
Porth	a										10 44											11 14			
	d										10 45											11 15			
Dinas Rhondda	d										10 49											11 19			
Tonypandy	d										10 51											11 21			
Llwynypia	d										10 53											11 23			
Ystrad Rhondda	a										10 56											11 26			
	d										10 59											11 29			
Ton Pentre	d										11 01											11 31			
Treorchy	d										11 04											11 34			
Ynyswen	d										11 07											11 37			
Treherbert	a										11 14											11 44			

When events are being held at the Millenium Stadium, services are subject to alteration. Please check times before travelling.

Bridgend, Barry Island, Barry, Penarth and Cardiff - Coryton, Rhymney, Pontypridd, Merthyr, Aberdare and Treherbert

		AW	AW	AW	AW	AW	AW	AW	AW	AW	AW	AW	AW	AW	AW	AW	AW	AW	AW	AW	AW	AW
Bridgend	d																		10 42			
Llantwit Major	d																		10 56			
Rhoose Cardiff Int Airport	d																		11 06			
Barry Island	d				10 25					10 40				10 55								
Barry [3]	d				10 30					10 45				11 00					11 15			
Barry Docks	d				10 34					10 49				11 04					11 19			
Cadoxton	d				10 37					10 52				11 07					11 22			
Dinas Powys	d				10 41					10 56				11 11					11 26			
Eastbrook	d				10 43					10 58				11 13					11 28			
Cogan	d				10 45					11 00				11 15					11 30			
Penarth	d	10 32					10 47				11 02				11 17						11 32	
Dingle Road	d	10 34					10 49				11 04				11 19						11 34	
Grangetown	d	10 38			10 49		10 53			11 04	11 08			11 19	11 23				11 34		11 38	
Cardiff Central [7]	a	10 44			10 54		10 59			11 09	11 14			11 24	11 29				11 39		11 44	
	d	10 46	10 51		10 56	10 54	11 01	11 06		11 11	11 16		11 21	11 26	11 31		11 36	11 36	11 41		11 46	11 51
Cardiff Bay	d			10 54					11 06			11 18				11 30				11 42		
Cardiff Queen Street [3]	a	10 49	10 54	10 58	10 59		11 04		11 10	11 14	11 19	11 22	11 24	11 29	11 34	11 34	11 39		11 44	11 46	11 49	11 54
	d	10 50	10 55		11 00		11 05			11 15	11 20		11 25	11 30	11 35		11 40		11 45		11 50	11 55
Heath Low Level	d		11 00										11 30									12 00
Ty Glas	d		11 03										11 33									12 03
Birchgrove	d		11 04										11 34									12 04
Rhiwbina	d		11 06										11 36									12 06
Whitchurch (Cardiff)	d		11 08										11 38									12 08
Coryton	a		11 14										11 44									12 14
Heath High Level	d	10 55					11 10				11 25				11 40						11 55	
Llanishen	d	10 58					11 13				11 28				11 43						11 58	
Lisvane & Thornhill	d	11 00					11 15				11 30				11 45						12 00	
Caerphilly [3]	d	11 06					11 21				11 36				11 51						12 06	
Aber	d	11 08					11 23				11 38				11 53						12 08	
Llanbradach	d	11 12					11 27				11 42				11 57						12 12	
Ystrad Mynach [3]	d	11a22					11 32				11 47				12 07						12a22	
Hengoed	d						11 35				11 50				12 10							
Pengam	d						11 38				11 53				12 13							
Gilfach Fargoed	d						11 41															
Bargoed	a						11 49				11 58				12 25							
	d										11 59											
Brithdir	d										12 03											
Tir-phil	d										12 06											
Pontlottyn	d										12 10											
Rhymney [3]	a										12 17											
Cathays	d				11 03					11 18				11 33			11 43		11 48			
Llandaf	d				11 07					11 22				11 37			11 47		11 52			
Ninian Park	d							11 10										11 40				
Waun-gron Park	d							11 14										11 44				
Fairwater	d							11 16										11 46				
Danescourt	d							11 19										11 49				
Radyr [3]	a				11 10	11 02		11 27		11 25				11 40			11 50	11 57	11 55			
	d				11 10	11 20				11 25				11 40			11 50		11 55			
Taffs Well [3]	d				11 14	11 24				11 29				11 44			11 54		11 59			
Trefforest Estate	d				11 18									11 48								
Trefforest	d				11 22	11 31				11 36				11 52			12 01		12 06			
Pontypridd [3]	a				11 25	11 34				11 39				11 55			12 04		12 09			
	d				11 27	11 36				11 41				11 57			12 06		12 11			
Abercynon	d				11 34					11 49				12 04					12 20			
Penrhiwceiber	d									11 55									12 25			
Mountain Ash	a									11 58									12 29			
	d									12 04									12 34			
Fernhill	d									12 07									12 37			
Cwmbach	d									12 11									12 41			
Aberdare [3]	a									12 19									12 49			
Quakers Yard	d				11 39									12 09								
Merthyr Vale	a				11 44									12 14								
	d				11 47									12 17								
Troed Y Rhiw	d				11 51									12 21								
Pentre-bach	d				11 54									12 24								
Merthyr Tydfil	a				12 03									12 33								
Trehafod	d					11 41										12 11						
Porth	a					11 44										12 14						
	d					11 45										12 15						
Dinas Rhondda	d					11 49										12 19						
Tonypandy	d					11 51										12 21						
Llwynypia	d					11 53										12 23						
Ystrad Rhondda	a					11 56										12 26						
	d					11 59										12 29						
Ton Pentre	d					12 01										12 31						
Treorchy	d					12 04										12 34						
Ynyswen	d					12 07										12 37						
Treherbert	a					12 14										12 44						

When events are being held at the Millenium Stadium, services are subject to alteration. Please check times before travelling.

Bridgend, Barry Island, Barry, Penarth and Cardiff - Coryton, Rhymney, Pontypridd, Merthyr, Aberdare and Treherbert

		AW	AW	AW	AW	AW	AW	AW	AW	AW	AW	AW	AW	AW	AW	AW	AW	AW	AW	AW	AW	AW	AW
Bridgend	d																	11 42					
Llantwit Major	d																	11 56					
Rhoose Cardiff Int Airport	d																	12 06					
Barry Island	d		11 25					11 40				11 55											12 25
Barry [3]	d		11 30					11 45				12 00						12 15					12 30
Barry Docks	d		11 34					11 49				12 04						12 19					12 34
Cadoxton	d		11 37					11 52				12 07						12 22					12 37
Dinas Powys	d		11 41					11 56				12 11						12 26					12 41
Eastbrook	d		11 43					11 58				12 13						12 28					12 43
Cogan	d		11 45					12 00				12 15						12 30					12 45
Penarth	d			11 47					12 02				12 17							12 32			
Dingle Road	d			11 49					12 04				12 19							12 34			
Grangetown	d		11 49	11 53				12 04	12 08			12 19	12 23					12 34		12 38			12 49
Cardiff Central [7]	a		11 54	12 00				12 09	12 14			12 24	12 29					12 44		12 44			12 54
	d		11 56	12 01		12 06	12 06	12 11	12 16		12 21	12 26	12 31		12 36	12 36	12 41			12 46	12 51		12 56
Cardiff Bay	d	11 54			12 06					12 18				12 30					12 42			12 54	
Cardiff Queen Street [3]	a	11 58	11 59	12 04	12 10	12 09		12 14	12 19	12 22	12 24	12 29	12 34	12 34	12 39		12 44		12 46	12 49	12 54	12 58	12 59
	d		12 00	12 05		12 10		12 15	12 20		12 25	12 30	12 35		12 40		12 45			12 50	12 55		13 00
Heath Low Level	d										12 30										13 00		
Ty Glas	d										12 33										13 03		
Birchgrove	d										12 34										13 04		
Rhiwbina	d										12 36										13 06		
Whitchurch (Cardiff)	d										12 38										13 08		
Coryton	a										12 44										13 14		
Heath High Level	d			12 10					12 25				12 40							12 55			
Llanishen	d			12 13					12 28				12 43							12 58			
Lisvane & Thornhill	d			12 15					12 30				12 45							13 00			
Caerphilly [3]	d			12 21					12 36				12 51							13 06			
Aber	d			12 23					12 38				12 53							13 08			
Llanbradach	d			12 27					12 42				12 57							13 12			
Ystrad Mynach [3]	d			12 32					12 47				13 07							13a22			
Hengoed	d			12 35					12 50				13 10										
Pengam	d			12 38					12 53				13 13										
Gilfach Fargoed	d			12 41																			
Bargoed	a			12 49					12 58				13 22										
	d								12 59														
Brithdir	d								13 03														
Tir-phil	d								13 06														
Pontlottyn	d								13 10														
Rhymney [3]	a								13 17														
Cathays	d		12 03			12 13		12 18				12 33			12 43		12 48						13 03
Llandaf	d		12 07			12 17		12 22				12 37			12 47		12 52						13 07
Ninian Park	d						12 10									12 39							
Waun-gron Park	d						12 14									12 43							
Fairwater	d						12 16									12 45							
Danescourt	d						12 19									12 48							
Radyr [3]	a		12 10			12 20	12 27	12 25				12 40			12 50	12 56	12 55						13 10
	d		12 10			12 20		12 25				12 40			12 50		12 55						13 10
Taffs Well [3]	d		12 14			12 24		12 29				12 44			12 54		12 59						13 14
Trefforest Estate	d		12 18									12 48											13 18
Trefforest	d		12 22			12 31		12 36				12 52			13 01		13 06						13 22
Pontypridd [3]	a		12 25			12 34		12 42				12 55			13 04		13 09						13 25
	d		12 27			12 36						12 57			13 06		13 11						13 27
Abercynon	d		12 34									13 04					13 19						13 34
Penrhiwceiber	d																13 25						
Mountain Ash	a																13 28						
	d																13 34						
Fernhill	d																13 37						
Cwmbach	d																13 41						
Aberdare [3]	a																13 49						
Quakers Yard	d		12 39									13 09											13 39
Merthyr Vale	a		12 44									13 14											13 44
	d		12 47									13 17											13 47
Troed Y Rhiw	d		12 51									13 21											13 51
Pentre-bach	d		12 54									13 24											13 54
Merthyr Tydfil	a		13 03									13 33											14 03
Trehafod	d					12 41									13 11								
Porth	a					12 44									13 14								
	d					12 45									13 15								
Dinas Rhondda	d					12 49									13 19								
Tonypandy	d					12 51									13 21								
Llwynypia	d					12 53									13 23								
Ystrad Rhondda	a					12 56									13 26								
	d					12 59									13 29								
Ton Pentre	d					13 01									13 31								
Treorchy	d					13 04									13 34								
Ynyswen	d					13 07									13 37								
Treherbert	a					13 14									13 44								

When events are being held at the Millenium Stadium, services are subject to alteration. Please check times before travelling.

Table 130

Mondays to Fridays
from 12 September

Bridgend, Barry Island, Barry, Penarth and Cardiff - Coryton, Rhymney, Pontypridd, Merthyr, Aberdare and Treherbert

		AW	AW	AW	AW	AW	AW	AW	AW	AW	AW	AW	AW	AW	AW	AW	AW	AW	AW	AW	AW	AW	AW
Bridgend	d														12 42								
Llantwit Major	d														12 56								
Rhoose Cardiff Int Airport ✈	d														13 06								
Barry Island	d					12 40				12 55										13 25			
Barry 3	d					12 45				13 00					13 15					13 30			
Barry Docks	d					12 49				13 04					13 19					13 34			
Cadoxton	d					12 52				13 07					13 22					13 37			
Dinas Powys	d					12 56				13 11					13 26					13 41			
Eastbrook	d					12 58				13 13					13 28					13 43			
Cogan	d					13 00				13 15					13 30					13 45			
Penarth	d	12 47					13 02				13 17						13 32				13 47		
Dingle Road	d	12 49					13 04				13 19						13 34				13 49		
Grangetown	d	12 53				13 04	13 08			13 19	13 23				13 34		13 38			13 49	13 53		
Cardiff Central 7	a	12 59				13 09	13 14			13 24	13 29				13 39		13 44			13 54	13 59		
	d	13 01		13 06	13 06	13 11	13 16		13 21	13 26	13 31		13 36	13 36	13 41		13 46	13 51		13 56	14 01		14 06
Cardiff Bay	d		13 06					13 18				13 30				13 42			13 54			14 06	
Cardiff Queen Street 3	a	13 04	13 10	13 09		13 14	13 19	13 22	13 24	13 29	13 34	13 34	13 39		13 44	13 46	13 49	13 54	13 58	13 59	14 04	14 10	14 09
	d	13 05		13 10		13 15	13 20		13 25	13 30	13 35		13 40		13 45		13 50	13 55		14 00	14 05		14 10
Heath Low Level	d								13 30									14 00					
Ty Glas	d								13 33									14 03					
Birchgrove	d								13 34									14 04					
Rhiwbina	d								13 36									14 06					
Whitchurch (Cardiff)	d								13 38									14 08					
Coryton	a								13 44									14 14					
Heath High Level	d	13 10					13 25				13 40						13 55				14 10		
Llanishen	d	13 13					13 28				13 43						13 58				14 13		
Lisvane & Thornhill	d	13 15					13 30				13 45						14 00				14 15		
Caerphilly 3	d	13 21					13 36				13 51						14 06				14 21		
Aber	d	13 23					13 38				13 53						14 08				14 23		
Llanbradach	d	13 27					13 42				13 57						14 12				14 27		
Ystrad Mynach 3	d	13 32					13 47				14 07						14a22				14 32		
Hengoed	d	13 35					13 50				14 10										14 35		
Pengam	d	13 38					13 53				14 13										14 38		
Gilfach Fargoed	d	13 41																			14 41		
Bargoed	a	13 49					13 58				14 22										14 49		
	d						13 59																
Brithdir	d						14 03																
Tir-phil	d						14 06																
Pontlottyn	d						14 10																
Rhymney 3	a						14 17																
Cathays	d			13 13		13 18				13 33			13 43		13 48					14 03			14 13
Llandaf	d			13 17		13 22				13 37			13 47		13 52					14 07			14 17
Ninian Park	d				13 10									13 40									
Waun-gron Park	d				13 14									13 44									
Fairwater	d				13 16									13 46									
Danescourt	d				13 19									13 49									
Radyr 3	a			13 20	13 27	13 25				13 40			13 50	13 57	13 55					14 10			14 20
	d			13 20		13 25				13 40			13 50		13 55					14 10			14 20
Taffs Well 3	d			13 24		13 29				13 44			13 54		13 59					14 14			14 24
Trefforest Estate	d									13 48										14 18			
Trefforest	d			13 31		13 36				13 52			14 01		14 06					14 22			14 31
Pontypridd 3	a			13 34		13 39				13 55			14 04		14 09					14 25			14 34
	d			13 36		13 41				13 57			14 06		14 11					14 27			14 36
Abercynon	d					13 49				14 04					14 19					14 34			
Penrhiwceiber	d					13 55									14 25								
Mountain Ash	a					13 58									14 28								
	d					14 04									14 34								
Fernhill	d					14 07									14 37								
Cwmbach	d					14 11									14 41								
Aberdare 3	a					14 19									14 49								
Quakers Yard	d									14 09										14 39			
Merthyr Vale	a									14 14										14 44			
	d									14 17										14 47			
Troed Y Rhiw	d									14 21										14 51			
Pentre-bach	d									14 24										14 54			
Merthyr Tydfil	a									14 33										15 03			
Trehafod	d			13 41									14 11										14 41
Porth	a			13 44									14 14										14 44
	d			13 45									14 15										14 45
Dinas Rhondda	d			13 49									14 19										14 49
Tonypandy	d			13 51									14 21										14 51
Llwynypia	d			13 53									14 23										14 53
Ystrad Rhondda	a			13 56									14 26										14 56
	d			13 59									14 29										14 59
Ton Pentre	d			14 01									14 31										15 01
Treorchy	d			14 04									14 34										15 04
Ynyswen	d			14 07									14 37										15 07
Treherbert	a			14 14									14 44										15 14

When events are being held at the Millenium Stadium, services are subject to alteration. Please check times before travelling.

Table 130

Mondays to Fridays
from 12 September

Bridgend, Barry Island, Barry, Penarth and Cardiff - Coryton, Rhymney, Pontypridd, Merthyr, Aberdare and Treherbert

		AW	AW	AW	AW	AW	AW	AW	AW	AW	AW	AW	AW	AW	AW	AW	AW	AW	AW	AW	AW	AW
Bridgend	d											13 42										
Llantwit Major	d											13 56										
Rhoose Cardiff Int Airport ✈	d											14 06										
Barry Island	d		13 40				13 55											14 25				
Barry 3	d		13 45				14 00					14 15						14 30				
Barry Docks	d		13 49				14 04					14 19						14 34				
Cadoxton	d		13 52				14 07					14 22						14 37				
Dinas Powys	d		13 56				14 11					14 26						14 41				
Eastbrook	d		13 58				14 13					14 28						14 43				
Cogan	d		14 00				14 15					14 30						14 45				
Penarth	d			14 02				14 17						14 32						14 47		
Dingle Road	d			14 04				14 19						14 34						14 49		
Grangetown	d		14 04	14 08			14 19	14 23				14 34		14 38				14 49		14 53		
Cardiff Central 7	a		14 09	14 14			14 24	14 29				14 39		14 44				14 54		14 58		
	d	14 06	14 11	14 16		14 21	14 26	14 31		14 36	14 36	14 41		14 46	14 51		14 51	14 56		15 01	15 06	
Cardiff Bay	d				14 18				14 30				14 42			14 54						15 06
Cardiff Queen Street 3	a		14 14	14 19	14 22	14 24	14 29	14 34	14 34	14 39		14 44	14 46	14 49	14 54	14 58		14 59		15 05		15 10
	d		14 15	14 20		14 25	14 30	14 35		14 40		14 45		14 50	14 55			15 00		15 05		
Heath Low Level	d					14 30									15 00							
Ty Glas	d					14 33									15 03							
Birchgrove	d					14 34									15 04							
Rhiwbina	d					14 36									15 06							
Whitchurch (Cardiff)	d					14 38									15 08							
Coryton	a					14 44									15 14							
Heath High Level	d			14 25				14 40						14 55						15 10		
Llanishen	d			14 28				14 43						14 58						15 13		
Lisvane & Thornhill	d			14 30				14 45						15 00						15 15		
Caerphilly 3	d			14 36				14 51						15 06						15 21		
Aber	d			14 38				14 53						15 08						15 23		
Llanbradach	d			14 42				14 57						15 12						15 27		
Ystrad Mynach 3	d			14 47				15 07						15a22						15 32		
Hengoed	d			14 50				15 10												15 35		
Pengam	d			14 53				15 13												15 38		
Gilfach Fargoed	d																			15 41		
Bargoed	a			14 58				15 22												15 49		
	d			14 59																		
Brithdir	d			15 03																		
Tir-phil	d			15 06																		
Pontlottyn	d			15 10																		
Rhymney 3	a			15 17																		
Cathays	d		14 18				14 33			14 43		14 48						15 03				
Llandaf	d		14 22				14 37			14 47		14 52						15 07				
Ninian Park	d	14 10									14 40										15 12	
Waun-gron Park	d	14 14									14 44										15 14	
Fairwater	d	14 16									14 46										15 16	
Danescourt	d	14 19									14 49								←		15 19	
Radyr 3	a	14 27	14 25				14 40			14 50	14 57	14 55					15 08	15 10	15 08		15 27	
	d		14 25				14 40			14 50		14 55					15 20	15 10	15 20			
Taffs Well 3	d		14 29				14 44			14 54		14 59					→	15 14	15 24			
Trefforest Estate	d						14 48											15 18				
Trefforest	d		14 36				14 52			15 01		15 06						15 22	15 31			
Pontypridd 3	a		14 39				14 55			15 04		15 09						15 25	15 34			
	d		14 41				14 57			15 06		15 11						15 27	15 36			
Abercynon	d		14 49				15 04					15 19						15 34				
Penrhiwceiber	d		14 55									15 25										
Mountain Ash	a		14 58									15 28										
	d		15 04									15 34										
Fernhill	d		15 07									15 37										
Cwmbach	d		15 11									15 41										
Aberdare 3	a		15 19									15 49										
Quakers Yard	d						15 09											15 39				
Merthyr Vale	a						15 14											15 44				
	d						15 17											15 47				
Troed Y Rhiw	d						15 21											15 51				
Pentre-bach	d						15 24											15 54				
Merthyr Tydfil	a						15 33											16 03				
Trehafod	d									15 11									15 41			
Porth	a									15 14									15 44			
	d									15 15									15 45			
Dinas Rhondda	d									15 19									15 49			
Tonypandy	d									15 21									15 51			
Llwynypia	d									15 23									15 53			
Ystrad Rhondda	a									15 26									15 56			
	d									15 29									15 59			
Ton Pentre	d									15 31									16 01			
Treorchy	d									15 34									16 04			
Ynyswen	d									15 37									16 07			
Treherbert	a									15 44									16 14			

When events are being held at the Millenium Stadium, services are subject to alteration. Please check times before travelling.

Bridgend, Barry Island, Barry, Penarth and Cardiff - Coryton, Rhymney, Pontypridd, Merthyr, Aberdare and Treherbert

		AW	AW	AW	AW	AW	AW	AW		AW	AW	AW	AW	AW	AW	AW	AW	AW		AW	AW	AW	AW	AW	AW
Bridgend	d											14 42													
Llantwit Major	d											14 56													
Rhoose Cardiff Int Airport ✈	d											15 06													
Barry Island	d	14 40				14 55											15 25						15 40		
Barry 3	d	14 45				15 00						15 15					15 30						15 45		
Barry Docks	d	14 49				15 04						15 19					15 34						15 49		
Cadoxton	d	14 52				15 07						15 22					15 37						15 52		
Dinas Powys	d	14 56				15 11						15 26					15 41						15 56		
Eastbrook	d	14 58				15 13						15 28					15 43						15 58		
Cogan	d	15 00				15 15						15 30					15 45						16 00		
Penarth	d		15 02				15 17							15 32				15 47						16 02	
Dingle Road	d		15 04				15 19							15 34				15 49						16 04	
Grangetown	d	15 04	15 08			15 19	15 23					15 34		15 38			15 49	15 53					16 04	16 08	
Cardiff Central 7	a	15 09	15 14			15 24	15 29					15 39		15 44			15 54	15 59					16 09	16 14	
	d	15 11	15 16		15 21	15 26	15 31			15 36	15 36	15 41		15 46	15 51		15 56	16 01			16 06	16 06	16 11	16 16	
Cardiff Bay	d			15 18				15 30					15 42			15 54				16 06					16 18
Cardiff Queen Street 3	a	15 14	15 19	15 22	15 24	15 29	15 34	15 34		15 39		15 44	15 46	15 49	15 54	15 58	15 59	16 04		16 10	16 09		16 14	16 19	16 22
	d	15 15	15 20		15 25	15 30	15 35			15 40		15 45		15 50	15 55		16 00	16 05			16 10		16 15	16 20	
Heath Low Level	d				15 30										16 00										
Ty Glas	d				15 33										16 03										
Birchgrove	d				15 34										16 04										
Rhiwbina	d				15 36										16 06										
Whitchurch (Cardiff)	d				15 38										16 08										
Coryton	a				15 44										16 14										
Heath High Level	d		15 25				15 40							15 55				16 10						16 25	
Llanishen	d		15 28				15 43							15 58				16 13						16 28	
Lisvane & Thornhill	d		15 30				15 45							16 00				16 15						16 30	
Caerphilly 3	d		15 36				15 51							16 06				16 21						16 36	
Aber	d		15 38				15 53							16 08				16 23						16 38	
Llanbradach	d		15 42				15 57							16 12				16 27						16 42	
Ystrad Mynach 3	d		15 47				16 02							16 17				16 32						16 47	
Hengoed	d		15 50				16 05							16 20				16 35						16 50	
Pengam	d		15 53				16 08							16 23				16 38						16 53	
Gilfach Fargoed	d																	16 41							
Bargoed	a		15 58				16 17							16 32				16 49						16 58	
	d		15 59																					16 59	
Brithdir	d		16 03																					17 03	
Tir-phil	d		16 06																					17 06	
Pontlottyn	d		16 10																					17 10	
Rhymney 3	a		16 17																					17 17	
Cathays	d	15 18				15 33				15 43		15 48					16 03				16 13		16 18		
Llandaf	d	15 22				15 37				15 47		15 52					16 07				16 17		16 22		
Ninian Park	d										15 40											16 10			
Waun-gron Park	d										15 44											16 14			
Fairwater	d										15 46											16 16			
Danescourt	d										15 49											16 19			
Radyr 3	a	15 25				15 40				15 50	15 57	15 55					16 10				16 20	16 27	16 25		
	d	15 25				15 40				15 50		15 55					16 10				16 20		16 25		
Taffs Well 3	d	15 29				15 44				15 54		15 59					16 14				16 24		16 29		
Trefforest Estate	d					15 48											16 18								
Trefforest	d	15 36				15 52				16 01		16 06					16 22				16 31		16 36		
Pontypridd 3	a	15 39				15 55				16 04		16 09					16 25				16 34		16 39		
	d	15 41				15 57				16 06		16 11					16 27				16 36		16 41		
Abercynon	d	15 49				16 04						16 19					16 34						16 49		
Penrhiwceiber	d	15 55										16 25											16 55		
Mountain Ash	a	15 58										16 28											16 58		
	d	16 04										16 34											17 04		
Fernhill	d	16 07										16 37											17 07		
Cwmbach	d	16 11										16 41											17 11		
Aberdare 3	a	16 19										16 49											17 19		
Quakers Yard	d					16 09											16 39								
Merthyr Vale	a					16 14											16 44								
	d					16 17											16 47								
Troed Y Rhiw	d					16 21											16 51								
Pentre-bach	d					16 24											16 54								
Merthyr Tydfil	a					16 33											17 03								
Trehafod	d									16 11											16 41				
Porth	a									16 14											16 44				
	d									16 15											16 45				
Dinas Rhondda	d									16 19											16 49				
Tonypandy	d									16 21											16 51				
Llwynypia	d									16 23											16 53				
Ystrad Rhondda	a									16 26											16 56				
	d									16 29											16 59				
Ton Pentre	d									16 31											17 01				
Treorchy	d									16 34											17 04				
Ynyswen	d									16 37											17 07				
Treherbert	a									16 44											17 14				

When events are being held at the Millenium Stadium, services are subject to alteration. Please check times before travelling.

Bridgend, Barry Island, Barry, Penarth and Cardiff - Coryton, Rhymney, Pontypridd, Merthyr, Aberdare and Treherbert

		AW	AW	AW		AW	AW	AW	AW	AW	AW	AW	AW	AW		AW	AW	AW	AW	AW	AW	AW	AW	AW
Bridgend	d								15 42															
Llantwit Major	d								15 56															
Rhoose Cardiff Int Airport ✈	d								16 06															
Barry Island	d		15 55											16 25						16 40				16 55
Barry 3	d		16 00						16 15					16 30						16 45				17 00
Barry Docks	d		16 04						16 19					16 34						16 49				17 04
Cadoxton	d		16 07						16 22					16 37						16 52				17 07
Dinas Powys	d		16 11						16 26					16 41						16 56				17 11
Eastbrook	d		16 13						16 28					16 43						16 58				17 13
Cogan	d		16 15						16 30					16 45						17 00				17 15
Penarth	d			16 17							16 32										17 02			
Dingle Road	d			16 19							16 34										17 04			
Grangetown	d		16 19	16 23					16 34		16 38			16 49						17 04	17 08			17 19
Cardiff Central 7	a		16 24	16 29					16 39		16 44			16 54						17 09	17 14			17 24
	d	16 21	16 26	16 31			16 36	16 36	16 41		16 46	16 51		16 56		17 01		17 06	17 06	17 11	17 16		17 21	17 26
Cardiff Bay	d					16 30				16 42			16 54				17 06					17 18		
Cardiff Queen Street 3	a	16 24	16 29	16 34		16 34	16 39		16 44	16 46	16 49	16 54	16 58	16 59		17 04	17 10	17 09		17 14	17 19	17 22	17 24	17 29
	d	16 25	16 30	16 35			16 40		16 45		16 50	16 55		17 00		17 05		17 10		17 15	17 20		17 25	17 30
Heath Low Level	d	16 30										17 00											17 30	
Ty Glas	d	16 33										17 03											17 33	
Birchgrove	d	16 34										17 04											17 34	
Rhiwbina	d	16 36										17 06											17 36	
Whitchurch (Cardiff)	d	16 38										17 08											17 38	
Coryton	a	16 44										17 14											17 44	
Heath High Level	d			16 40							16 55					17 10					17 25			
Llanishen	d			16 43							16 58					17 13					17 28			
Lisvane & Thornhill	d			16 45							17 00					17 15					17 30			
Caerphilly 3	d			16 51							17 06					17 21					17 36			
Aber	d			16 53							17 08					17 23					17 38			
Llanbradach	d			16 57							17 12					17 27					17 42			
Ystrad Mynach 3	d			17 02							17 17					17 33					17 47			
Hengoed	d			17 05							17 20					17 35					17 50			
Pengam	d			17 08							17 23					17 39					17 53			
Gilfach Fargoed	d															17 42								
Bargoed	a			17 17							17 32					17 45					18 02			
	d															17 47								
Brithdir	d															17 50								
Tir-phil	d															17 53								
Pontlottyn	d															17 58								
Rhymney 3	a															18 05								
Cathays	d		16 33				16 43		16 48					17 03				17 13		17 18				17 33
Llandaf	d		16 37				16 47		16 52					17 07				17 17		17 22				17 37
Ninian Park	d							16 40											17 10					
Waun-gron Park	d							16 44											17 14					
Fairwater	d							16 46											17 16					
Danescourt	d							16 49											17 19					
Radyr 3	a		16 40				16 50	16 57	16 55					17 10				17 20	17 27	17 25				17 40
	d		16 40				16 50		16 55					17 10				17 20		17 25				17 40
Taffs Well 3	d		16 44				16 54		16 59					17 14				17 24		17 29				17 44
Trefforest Estate	d		16 48											17 18										17 48
Trefforest	d		16 52				17 01		17 06					17 22				17 31		17 36				17 52
Pontypridd 3	a		16 55				17 04		17 09					17 25				17 34		17 39				17 55
	d		16 57				17 06		17 11					17 27				17 36		17 41				17 57
Abercynon	d		17 04						17 19					17 34						17 49				18 04
Penrhiwceiber	d								17 25											17 55				
Mountain Ash	a								17 28											17 58				
	d								17 34											18 04				
Fernhill	d								17 37											18 07				
Cwmbach	d								17 41											18 11				
Aberdare 3	a								17 49											18 19				
Quakers Yard	d		17 09											17 39										18 09
Merthyr Vale	a		17 14											17 44										18 14
	d		17 17											17 47										18 17
Troed Y Rhiw	d		17 21											17 51										18 21
Pentre-bach	d		17 24											17 54										18 24
Merthyr Tydfil	a		17 33											18 03										18 33
Trehafod	d						17 11											17 41						
Porth	a						17 14											17 44						
	d						17 15											17 45						
Dinas Rhondda	d						17 19											17 49						
Tonypandy	d						17 21											17 51						
Llwynypia	d						17 23											17 53						
Ystrad Rhondda	a						17 26											17 56						
	d						17 29											17 59						
Ton Pentre	d						17 31											18 01						
Treorchy	d						17 34											18 04						
Ynyswen	d						17 37											18 07						
Treherbert	a						17 44											18 14						

When events are being held at the Millenium Stadium, services are subject to alteration. Please check times before travelling.

Bridgend, Barry Island, Barry, Penarth and Cardiff - Coryton, Rhymney, Pontypridd, Merthyr, Aberdare and Treherbert

		AW	AW	AW	AW	AW	AW	AW	AW	AW	AW	AW	AW	AW	AW	AW	AW	AW	AW	AW	AW	AW	AW
Bridgend	d					16 42																	
Llantwit Major	d					16 56																	
Rhoose Cardiff Int Airport ✈	d					17 06																	
Barry Island	d										17 25					17 40				17 55			
Barry ■	d					17 15					17 30					17 45				18 00			
Barry Docks	d					17 19					17 34					17 49				18 04			
Cadoxton	d					17 22					17 37					17 52				18 07			
Dinas Powys	d					17 26					17 41					17 56				18 11			
Eastbrook	d					17 28					17 43					17 58				18 13			
Cogan	d					17 30					17 45					18 00				18 15			
Penarth	d	17 17						17 32				17 47					18 02				18 17		
Dingle Road	d	17 19						17 34				17 49					18 04				18 19		
Grangetown	d	17 23				17 34		17 38			17 49	17 53				18 04	18 08			18 19	18 23		
Cardiff Central ■	a	17 29				17 39		17 44			17 54	17 59				18 09	18 14			18 24	18 29		
	d	17 31		17 36	17 36	17 41		17 46	17 51		17 56	18 01		18 06	18 06	18 11	18 16		18 21	18 26	18 31		18 36
Cardiff Bay	d		17 30				17 42			17 54			18 06					18 18				18 30	
Cardiff Queen Street ■	a	17 34	17 34	17 39		17 44	17 46	17 49	17 54	17 58	17 59	18 04	18 10	18 09		18 14	18 19	18 22	18 24	18 29	18 34	18 34	18 38
	d	17 35		17 40		17 45		17 50	17 55		18 00	18 05		18 10		18 15	18 20		18 25	18 30	18 35		18 40
Heath Low Level	d								18 00										18 30				
Ty Glas	d								18 03										18 33				
Birchgrove	d								18 04										18 34				
Rhiwbina	d								18 06										18 36				
Whitchurch (Cardiff)	d								18 08										18 38				
Coryton	a								18 14										18 44				
Heath High Level	d	17 40						17 55				18 10					18 25				18 40		
Llanishen	d	17 43						17 59				18 13					18 28				18 43		
Lisvane & Thornhill	d	17 45						18 02				18 15					18 30				18 45		
Caerphilly ■	d	17 51						18 07				18 21					18 36				18 51		
Aber	d	17 53						18 10				18 23					18 38				18 53		
Llanbradach	d	17 57						18 14				18 27					18 42				18 57		
Ystrad Mynach ■	d	18 02						18 20				18 32					18a52				19 02		
Hengoed	d	18 05						18 23				18 35									19 05		
Pengam	d	18 08						18 27				18 38									19 08		
Gilfach Fargoed	d	18 11						18 30				18 41									19 11		
Bargoed	a	18 14						18 34				18 49									19 14		
	d	18 16						18 44													19 16		
Brithdir	d	18 20						18 48													19 20		
Tir-phil	d	18 23						18 51													19 23		
Pontlottyn	d	18 27						18 55													19 27		
Rhymney ■	a	18 34						19 02													19 35		
Cathays	d			17 43		17 48					18 03			18 13		18 18				18 33			18 43
Llandaf	d			17 47		17 52					18 07			18 17		18 22				18 37			18 47
Ninian Park	d				17 40										18 10								
Waun-gron Park	d				17 44										18 14								
Fairwater	d				17 46										18 16								
Danescourt	d				17 49										18 19								
Radyr ■	a			17 50	17 57	17 55					18 10			18 20	18 27	18 25				18 40			18 50
	d			17 50		17 55					18 10			18 20		18 25				18 40			18 50
Taffs Well ■	d			17 54		17 59					18 14			18 24		18 29				18 44			18 54
Trefforest Estate	d										18 18									18 48			
Trefforest	d			18 01		18 06					18 22			18 31		18 36				18 52			19 01
Pontypridd ■	a			18 04		18 09					18 25			18 34		18 42				18 55			19 04
	d			18 06		18 11					18 27			18 36						18 57			19 06
Abercynon	d					18 19					18 34									19 04			
Penrhiwceiber	d					18 25																	
Mountain Ash	a					18 28																	
	d					18 34																	
Fernhill	d					18 37																	
Cwmbach	d					18 41																	
Aberdare ■	a					18 49																	
Quakers Yard	d										18 39									19 09			
Merthyr Vale	a										18 44									19 14			
	d										18 47									19 17			
Troed Y Rhiw	d										18 51									19 21			
Pentre-bach	d										18 54									19 24			
Merthyr Tydfil	a										19 03									19 33			
Trehafod	d			18 11										18 41									19 11
Porth	a			18 14										18 44									19 14
	d			18 15										18 45									19 15
Dinas Rhondda	d			18 19										18 49									19 19
Tonypandy	d			18 21										18 51									19 21
Llwynypia	d			18 23										18 53									19 23
Ystrad Rhondda	a			18 26										18 56									19 26
	d			18 29										18 59									19 29
Ton Pentre	d			18 31										19 01									19 31
Treorchy	d			18 34										19 04									19 34
Ynyswen	d			18 37										19 07									19 37
Treherbert	a			18 44										19 14									19 44

When events are being held at the Millenium Stadium, services are subject to alteration. Please check times before travelling.

Bridgend, Barry Island, Barry, Penarth and Cardiff - Coryton, Rhymney, Pontypridd, Merthyr, Aberdare and Treherbert

		AW	AW	AW	AW	AW	AW	AW	AW	AW	AW	AW	AW	AW	AW	AW	AW	AW	AW	AW	AW	AW	AW
Bridgend	d		17 42															18 42					
Llantwit Major	d		17 56															18 56					
Rhoose Cardiff Int Airport ✈	d		18 06															19 06					
Barry Island	d						18 25					18 40		18 55								19 25	
Barry ■	d		18 15				18 30					18 45		19 00				19 15				19 30	
Barry Docks	d		18 19				18 34					18 49		19 04				19 19				19 34	
Cadoxton	d		18 22				18 37					18 52		19 07				19 22				19 37	
Dinas Powys	d		18 26				18 41					18 56		19 11				19 26				19 41	
Eastbrook	d		18 28				18 43					18 58		19 13				19 28				19 43	
Cogan	d		18 30				18 45					19 00		19 15				19 30				19 45	
Penarth	d			18 32					18 47						19 17								19 47
Dingle Road	d			18 34					18 49						19 19								19 49
Grangetown	d		18 34	18 38			18 49		18 53			19 04		19 19	19 23			19 34				19 49	19 54
Cardiff Central ■	a		18 39	18 47			18 55		18 59			19 09		19 24	19 29			19 39				19 56	19 59
	d	18 36	18 41			18 51			19 01		19 06	19 11		19 26	19 31		19 36	19 41		19 51		20 01	20 06
Cardiff Bay	d				18 42			18 54		19 06			19 18			19 30			19 42		19 54		
Cardiff Queen Street ■	a		18 44		18 46	18 54		18 58	19 04	19 10	19 09	19 14	19 22	19 29	19 34	19 34		19 44	19 46	19 54	19 58	20 04	20 09
	d		18 50			18 55			19 05		19 10	19 15		19 30	19 35			19 45		19 55		20 05	20 10
Heath Low Level	d					19 00														20 00			
Ty Glas	d					19 03														20 03			
Birchgrove	d					19 04														20 04			
Rhiwbina	d					19 06														20 06			
Whitchurch (Cardiff)	d					19 08														20 08			
Coryton	a					19 14														20 14			
Heath High Level	d								19 10						19 40							20 10	
Llanishen	d								19 13						19 43							20 13	
Lisvane & Thornhill	d								19 15						19 45							20 15	
Caerphilly ■	d								19a24						19 51							20a28	
Aber	d														19 53								
Llanbradach	d														19 57								
Ystrad Mynach ■	d														20 02								
Hengoed	d														20 05								
Pengam	d														20 08								
Gilfach Fargoed	d														20 11								
Bargoed	a														20 15								
	d														20 16								
Brithdir	d														20 20								
Tir-phil	d														20 23								
Pontlottyn	d														20 27								
Rhymney ■	a														20 34								
Cathays	d		18 52								19 13	19 18		19 33				19 48					20 13
Llandaf	d		18 56								19 17	19 22		19 37				19 52					20 17
Ninian Park	d	18 40															19 40						
Waun-gron Park	d	18 44															19 44						
Fairwater	d	18 46															19 46						
Danescourt	d	18 49															19 49						
Radyr ■	a	18 57	18 58								19 20	19 25		19 40			19 57	19 55					20 20
	d		18 58								19 20	19 25		19 40				19 55					20 20
Taffs Well ■	d		19 03								19 24	19 29		19 44				19 59					20 24
Trefforest Estate	d													19 48									
Trefforest	d		19 10								19 31	19 36		19 52				20 06					20 31
Pontypridd ■	a		19 13								19 34	19 39		19 55				20 09					20 35
	d		19 14								19 36	19 41		19 57				20 11					20 36
Abercynon	d		19 21									19 49		20 04				20 21					
Penrhiwceiber	d		19 27									19 55						20 27					
Mountain Ash	a		19 30									19 59						20 31					
	d		19 34									20 03						20 34					
Fernhill	d		19 37									20 07						20 37					
Cwmbach	d		19 41									20 11						20 41					
Aberdare ■	a		19 49									20 19						20 49					
Quakers Yard	d													20 09									
Merthyr Vale	a													20 14									
	d													20 14									
Troed Y Rhiw	d													20 18									
Pentre-bach	d													20 22									
Merthyr Tydfil	a													20 31									
Trehafod	d										19 41												20 41
Porth	a										19 44												20 44
	d										19 45												20 45
Dinas Rhondda	d										19 49												20 49
Tonypandy	d										19 51												20 51
Llwynypia	d										19 53												20 53
Ystrad Rhondda	a										19 56												20 56
	d										19 59												20 59
Ton Pentre	d										20 01												21 01
Treorchy	d										20 04												21 04
Ynyswen	d										20 07												21 07
Treherbert	a										20 14												21 14

When events are being held at the Millenium Stadium, services are subject to alteration. Please check times before travelling.

Table 130

Mondays to Fridays
from 12 September

Bridgend, Barry Island, Barry, Penarth and Cardiff - Coryton, Rhymney, Pontypridd, Merthyr, Aberdare and Treherbert

		AW	AW	AW	AW	AW	AW	AW	AW	AW	AW	AW	AW	AW	AW	AW	AW	AW	AW	AW	AW	AW
Bridgend	d							19 42													20 42	
Llantwit Major	d							19 56													20 56	
Rhoose Cardiff Int Airport ✈	d							20 06													21 06	
Barry Island	d			19 55												20 55						
Barry 3	d			20 00				20 15								21 00					21 15	
Barry Docks	d			20 04				20 19								21 04					21 19	
Cadoxton	d			20 07				20 22								21 07					21 22	
Dinas Powys	d			20 11				20 26								21 11					21 26	
Eastbrook	d			20 13				20 28								21 13					21 28	
Cogan	d			20 15				20 30								21 15					21 30	
Penarth	d					20 19						20 47								21 20		
Dingle Road	d					20 21						20 49								21 22		
Grangetown	d			20 19		20 24		20 34				20 53				21 19				21 26	21 34	
Cardiff Central 7	a			20 26		20 31		20 39				20 59				21 23				21 37	21 39	
	d			20 27		20 32	20 36	20 41		20 51		21 01		21 06		21 26		21 31	21 36		21 41	
Cardiff Bay	d	20 06	20 18		20 30				20 42		20 54		21 06		21 18		21 30					21 42
Cardiff Queen Street 3	a	20 10	20 22	20 30	20 34	20 35		20 44	20 46	20 54	20 58	21 04	21 10	21 09	21 21	21 29	21 33	21 34			21 44	21 45
	d			20 31		20 36		20 45		20 55		21 05		21 10		21 30		21 35			21 45	
Heath Low Level	d									21 00												
Ty Glas	d									21 03												
Birchgrove	d									21 04												
Rhiwbina	d									21 06												
Whitchurch (Cardiff)	d									21 08												
Coryton	a									21 14												
Heath High Level	d					20 41						21 10						21 40				
Llanishen	d					20 44						21 13						21 43				
Lisvane & Thornhill	d					20 46						21 15						21 45				
Caerphilly 3	d					20 52						21a37						21 51				
Aber	d					20 54												21 53				
Llanbradach	d					20 58												21 57				
Ystrad Mynach 3	d					21 03												22 02				
Hengoed	d					21 06												22 05				
Pengam	d					21 09												22 08				
Gilfach Fargoed	d					21 12												22 11				
Bargoed	a					21 16												22 15				
	d					21 17												22 16				
Brithdir	d					21 21												22 20				
Tir-phil	d					21 24												22 23				
Pontlottyn	d					21 28												22 27				
Rhymney 3	a					21 35												22 35				
Cathays	d			20 34				20 48						21 13		21 33					21 48	
Llandaf	d			20 38				20 52						21 17		21 37					21 52	
Ninian Park	d						20 40												21 40			
Waun-gron Park	d						20 44												21 44			
Fairwater	d						20 46												21 46			
Danescourt	d						20 49												21 49			
Radyr 3	a			20 41			20 57	20 55						21 20		21 40			21 57		21 55	
	d			20 41				20 55						21 20		21 40					21 55	
Taffs Well 3	d			20 45				20 59						21 24		21 44					21 59	
Trefforest Estate	d			20 49												21 48						
Trefforest	d			20 53				21 06						21 31		21 52					22 06	
Pontypridd 3	a			20 56				21 09						21 34		21 55					22 09	
	d			20 57				21 11						21 36		21 57					22 11	
Abercynon	d			21 04				21 19								22 04					22 19	
Penrhiwceiber	d							21 25													22 25	
Mountain Ash	a							21 28													22 28	
	d							21 29													22 29	
Fernhill	d							21 32													22 32	
Cwmbach	d							21 36													22 36	
Aberdare 3	a							21 44													22 44	
Quakers Yard	d			21 09												22 09						
Merthyr Vale	a			21 14												22 14						
	d			21 14												22 14						
Troed Y Rhiw	d			21 18												22 18						
Pentre-bach	d			21 22												22 22						
Merthyr Tydfil	a			21 31												22 31						
Trehafod	d													21 41								
Porth	a													21 44								
	d													21 45								
Dinas Rhondda	d													21 49								
Tonypandy	d													21 51								
Llwynypia	d													21 53								
Ystrad Rhondda	a													21 56								
	d													21 59								
Ton Pentre	d													22 01								
Treorchy	d													22 04								
Ynyswen	d													22 07								
Treherbert	a													22 14								

When events are being held at the Millenium Stadium, services are subject to alteration. Please check times before travelling.

Table 130

Mondays to Fridays
from 12 September

Bridgend, Barry Island, Barry, Penarth and Cardiff - Coryton, Rhymney, Pontypridd, Merthyr, Aberdare and Treherbert

		AW	AW	AW	AW	AW	AW	AW	AW	AW	AW	AW	AW	AW	AW	AW	AW	AW	AW	AW	AW	AW	AW
Bridgend	d										21 42									22 42			
Llantwit Major	d										21 56									22 56			
Rhoose Cardiff Int Airport ✈	d										22 06									23 06			
Barry Island	d							21 55										22 45					
Barry 3	d							22 00			22 15							22 49		23 15			
Barry Docks	d							22 04			22 19							22 53		23 19			
Cadoxton	d							22 07			22 22							22 56		23 22			
Dinas Powys	d							22 11			22 26							23 00		23 26			
Eastbrook	d							22 13			22 28							23 02		23 28			
Cogan	d							22 15			22 30							23 04		23 30			
Penarth	d		21 47							22 19						22 47			23 26				
Dingle Road	d		21 49							22 21						22 49			23 28				
Grangetown	d		21 53					22 19		22 25	22 34					22 53		23 08	23 32	23 34			
Cardiff Central 7	a		21 59					22 24		22 33	22 39					23 00		23 13	23 40	23 42			
	d		22 01		22 06		22 21	22 26		22 35	22 41		22 46			23 15		23 26					
Cardiff Bay	d	21 54		22 06		22 18			22 30			22 42		22 54	23 06		23 18				23 30	23 42	23 54
Cardiff Queen Street 3	a	21 57	22 04	22 10	22 09	22 22	22 24	22 29	22 34	22 38	22 44	22 46	22 49	22 58	23 10	23 18	23 22	23 29			23 34	23 46	23 58
	d		22 05		22 10		22 25	22 30		22 39	22 45		22 50			23 19		23 30					
Heath Low Level	d						22 30																
Ty Glas	d						22 33																
Birchgrove	d						22 34																
Rhiwbina	d						22 36																
Whitchurch (Cardiff)	d						22 38																
Coryton	a						22 44																
Heath High Level	d		22 10							22 44						23 24							
Llanishen	d		22 13							22 47						23 27							
Lisvane & Thornhill	d		22 15							22 49						23 29							
Caerphilly 3	d		22a24							22 55						23 35							
Aber	d									22 57						23 37							
Llanbradach	d									23 01						23 41							
Ystrad Mynach 3	d									23 06						23a51							
Hengoed	d									23 09													
Pengam	d									23 12													
Gilfach Fargoed	d									23 15													
Bargoed	a									23 19													
	d									23 20													
Brithdir	d									23 24													
Tir-phil	d									23 27													
Pontlottyn	d									23 31													
Rhymney 3	a									23 38													
Cathays	d				22 13			22 33			22 48		22 53					23 33					
Llandaf	d				22 17			22 37			22 52		22 57					23 37					
Ninian Park	d																						
Waun-gron Park	d																						
Fairwater	d																						
Danescourt	d																						
Radyr 3	a				22 20			22 40			22 55		22 59					23 40					
	d				22 20			22 40			22 55		22 59					23 40					
Taffs Well 3	d				22 24			22 44			22 59		23 03					23 44					
Trefforest Estate	d							22 48															
Trefforest	d				22 31			22 52			23 06		23 10					23 52					
Pontypridd 3	a				22 34			22 55			23 09		23 14					23 58					
	d				22 36			22 57			23 11		23 15										
Abercynon	d							23 04			23 19												
Penrhiwceiber	d										23 25												
Mountain Ash	a										23 28												
	d										23 34												
Fernhill	d										23 37												
Cwmbach	d										23 41												
Aberdare 3	a										23 49												
Quakers Yard	d							23 09															
Merthyr Vale	a							23 14															
	d							23 14															
Troed Y Rhiw	d							23 18															
Pentre-bach	d							23 22															
Merthyr Tydfil	a							23 31															
Trehafod	d				22 41								23 20										
Porth	a				22 44								23 23										
	d				22 45								23 24										
Dinas Rhondda	d				22 49								23 28										
Tonypandy	d				22 51								23 30										
Llwynypia	d				22 53								23 32										
Ystrad Rhondda	a				22 56								23 35										
	d				22 59								23 38										
Ton Pentre	d				23 01								23 40										
Treorchy	d				23 04								23 43										
Ynyswen	d				23 07								23 46										
Treherbert	a				23 14								23 53										

When events are being held at the Millenium Stadium, services are subject to alteration. Please check times before travelling.

Table 130

Saturdays until 10 September

Bridgend, Barry Island, Barry, Penarth and Cardiff - Coryton, Rhymney, Pontypridd, Merthyr, Aberdare and Treherbert

Station		AW		AW	AW	AW	AW	AW	AW	AW	AW	AW	AW	AW	AW	AW	AW	AW	AW	AW	AW	AW	AW
Bridgend	d										05 42												
Llantwit Major	d										05 56												
Rhoose Cardiff Int Airport ✈	d										06 06												
Barry Island	d								05 52							06 25							
Barry 3	d								05 57		06 15					06 30							
Barry Docks	d								06 01		06 19					06 34							
Cadoxton	d								06 04		06 22					06 37							
Dinas Powys	d								06 08		06 26					06 41							
Eastbrook	d								06 10		06 28					06 43							
Cogan	d								06 12		06 30					06 45							
Penarth	d						06 02						06 32								07 02		
Dingle Road	d						06 04						06 34								07 04		
Grangetown	d						06 08		06 16		06 34		06 38			06 49					07 08		
Cardiff Central 7	a						06 13		06 21		06 39		06 44			06 54					07 14		
	d	05 26		05 46	05 56	06 11	06 15	06 19	06 26	06 36	06 41		06 46	06 51		06 56		07 06	07 06	07 11	07 16		07 21
Cardiff Bay	d											06 42			06 54		07 06					07 18	
Cardiff Queen Street 3	a	05 29		05 49	05 59	06 14	06 19	06 24	06 29	06 39	06 44	06 46	06 49	06 54	06 58	06 59	07 10	07 09		07 14	07 19	07 22	07 24
	d	05 30		05 50	06 00	06 15	06 20	06 25	06 30	06 40	06 45		06 50	06 55		07 00		07 10		07 15	07 20		07 25
Heath Low Level	d							06 30						07 00									07 30
Ty Glas	d							06 33						07 03									07 33
Birchgrove	d							06 34						07 04									07 34
Rhiwbina	d							06 36						07 06									07 36
Whitchurch (Cardiff)	d							06 38						07 08									07 38
Coryton	a							06 43						07 13									07 43
Heath High Level	d			05 54			06 25						06 55								07 25		
Llanishen	d			05 57			06 28						06 58								07 28		
Lisvane & Thornhill	d			06 00			06 30						07 00								07 30		
Caerphilly 3	d			06a08			06 36						07 06								07 36		
Aber	d						06 38						07 08								07 38		
Llanbradach	d						06 42						07 12								07 42		
Ystrad Mynach 3	d						06 47						07 17								07 47		
Hengoed	d						06 50						07 20								07 50		
Pengam	d						06 53						07 23								07 53		
Gilfach Fargoed	d																						
Bargoed	a						07 01						07 31								08 02		
	d																						
Brithdir	d																						
Tir-phil	d																						
Pontlottyn	d																						
Rhymney 3	a																						
Cathays	d	05 33			06 03	06 18			06 33	06 43	06 48					07 03		07 13		07 18			
Llandaf	d	05 37			06 07	06 22			06 37	06 47	06 52					07 07		07 17		07 22			
Ninian Park	d																		07 10				
Waun-gron Park	d																		07 13				
Fairwater	d																		07 15				
Danescourt	d																		07 17				
Radyr 3	a	05 39			06 10	06 24			06 40	06 50	06 54					07 10		07 20	07 24	07 25			
	d	05 40			06 10	06 24			06 40	06 50	06 55					07 10		07 20		07 25			
Taffs Well 3	d	05 43			06 14	06 28			06 44	06 54	06 59					07 14		07 24		07 29			
Trefforest Estate	d	05 47			06 18				06 48							07 18							
Trefforest	d	05 52			06 22	06 35			06 52	07 01	07 06					07 22		07 31		07 36			
Pontypridd 3	a	05 55			06 25	06 38			06 55	07 04	07 09					07 25		07 34		07 39			
	d	05 57	06 11		06 27	06 41			06 57	07 06	07 11					07 27		07 36		07 41			
Abercynon	d	06 04	06 19		06 34	06 49			07 04		07 19					07 34				07 49			
Penrhiwceiber	d		06 24			06 54					07 24									07 54			
Mountain Ash	a		06 28			06 58					07 28									07 58			
	d		06 33			07 03					07 33									08 03			
Fernhill	d		06 35			07 05					07 35									08 05			
Cwmbach	d		06 39			07 09					07 39									08 09			
Aberdare 3	a		06 46			07 16					07 46									08 16			
Quakers Yard	d	06 09			06 39				07 09							07 39							
Merthyr Vale	a	06 14			06 44				07 14							07 44							
	d	06 17			06 47				07 17							07 47							
Troed Y Rhiw	d	06 20			06 50				07 20							07 50							
Pentre-bach	d	06 23			06 53				07 23							07 53							
Merthyr Tydfil	a	06 31			07 01				07 31							08 01							
Trehafod	d									07 11								07 41					
Porth	a									07 14								07 44					
	d									07 15								07 45					
Dinas Rhondda	d									07 19								07 49					
Tonypandy	d									07 21								07 51					
Llwynypia	d									07 23								07 53					
Ystrad Rhondda	a									07 26								07 56					
	d									07 29								07 59					
Ton Pentre	d									07 31								08 01					
Treorchy	d									07 34								08 04					
Ynyswen	d									07 37								08 07					
Treherbert	a									07 43								08 13					

When events are being held at the Millenium Stadium, services are subject to alteration. Please check times before travelling.

Table 130

Saturdays until 10 September

Bridgend, Barry Island, Barry, Penarth and Cardiff - Coryton, Rhymney, Pontypridd, Merthyr, Aberdare and Treherbert

Station		AW	AW	AW	AW	AW	AW	AW	AW	AW	AW	AW	AW	AW	AW	AW	AW	AW	AW	AW	AW	AW	AW
Bridgend	d						06 42																
Llantwit Major	d						06 56																
Rhoose Cardiff Int Airport ✈	d						07 06																
Barry Island	d	06 55										07 25					07 40				07 55		
Barry 3	d	07 00					07 15					07 30					07 45				08 00		
Barry Docks	d	07 04					07 19					07 34					07 49				08 04		
Cadoxton	d	07 07					07 22					07 37					07 52				08 07		
Dinas Powys	d	07 11					07 26					07 41					07 56				08 11		
Eastbrook	d	07 13					07 28					07 43					07 58				08 13		
Cogan	d	07 15					07 30					07 45					08 00				08 15		
Penarth	d		07 17						07 32				07 47					08 02				08 17	
Dingle Road	d		07 19						07 34				07 49					08 04				08 19	
Grangetown	d	07 19	07 23				07 34		07 38			07 49	07 53				08 04	08 08			08 20	08 23	
Cardiff Central 7	a	07 24	07 30				07 39		07 44			07 55	07 59				08 09	08 14			08 24	08 29	
	d	07 26	07 31		07 36	07 36	07 41		07 46	07 51		07 56	08 01		08 06	08 06	08 11	08 16		08 21	08 26	08 31	
Cardiff Bay	d			07 30				07 42			07 54			08 06					08 18				08 30
Cardiff Queen Street 3	a	07 29	07 34	07 34	07 39		07 44	07 46	07 49	07 54	07 58	07 59	08 04	08 10	08 09		08 14	08 19	08 22	08 24	08 29	08 34	08 34
	d	07 30	07 35		07 40		07 45		07 50	07 55		08 00	08 05		08 10		08 15	08 20		08 25	08 30	08 35	
Heath Low Level	d									08 00										08 30			
Ty Glas	d									08 03										08 33			
Birchgrove	d									08 04										08 34			
Rhiwbina	d									08 06										08 36			
Whitchurch (Cardiff)	d									08 08										08 38			
Coryton	a									08 13										08 43			
Heath High Level	d		07 40						07 55				08 10					08 25				08 40	
Llanishen	d		07 43						07 58				08 13					08 28				08 43	
Lisvane & Thornhill	d		07 45						08 00				08 15					08 30				08 45	
Caerphilly 3	d		07 51						08 06				08 21					08 36				08 51	
Aber	d		07 53						08 08				08 23					08 38				08 53	
Llanbradach	d		07 57						08 12				08 27					08 42				08 57	
Ystrad Mynach 3	d		08 02						08 17				08 32					08 47				09 02	
Hengoed	d		08 05						08 20				08 35					08 50				09 05	
Pengam	d		08 08						08 23				08 38					08 53				09 08	
Gilfach Fargoed	d												08 41										
Bargoed	a		08 13						08 31				08 48					08 58				09 16	
	d		08 14															08 59					
Brithdir	d		08 18															09 03					
Tir-phil	d		08 21															09 06					
Pontlottyn	d		08 25															09 10					
Rhymney 3	a		08 31															09 16					
Cathays	d	07 33			07 43		07 48					08 03			08 13		08 18				08 33		
Llandaf	d	07 37			07 47		07 52					08 07			08 17		08 22				08 37		
Ninian Park	d					07 40										08 10							
Waun-gron Park	d					07 44										08 13							
Fairwater	d					07 46										08 15							
Danescourt	d					07 49										08 17							
Radyr 3	a	07 40			07 50	07 56	07 55					08 10			08 20	08 24	08 25				08 40		
	d	07 40			07 50		07 55					08 10			08 20		08 25				08 40		
Taffs Well 3	d	07 44			07 54		07 59					08 14			08 24		08 29				08 44		
Trefforest Estate	d	07 48										08 18									08 48		
Trefforest	d	07 52			08 01		08 06					08 22			08 31		08 36				08 52		
Pontypridd 3	a	07 55			08 04		08 09					08 25			08 34		08 39				08 55		
	d	07 57			08 06		08 11					08 27			08 36		08 41				08 57		
Abercynon	d	08 04					08 19					08 34					08 49				09 04		
Penrhiwceiber	d						08 24										08 54						
Mountain Ash	a						08 28										08 58						
	d						08 33										09 03						
Fernhill	d						08 35										09 05						
Cwmbach	d						08 39										09 09						
Aberdare 3	a						08 46										09 16						
Quakers Yard	d	08 09										08 39									09 09		
Merthyr Vale	a	08 14										08 44									09 14		
	d	08 17										08 47									09 17		
Troed Y Rhiw	d	08 20										08 50									09 20		
Pentre-bach	d	08 23										08 53									09 23		
Merthyr Tydfil	a	08 31										09 01									09 31		
Trehafod	d				08 11										08 41								
Porth	a				08 14										08 44								
	d				08 15										08 45								
Dinas Rhondda	d				08 19										08 49								
Tonypandy	d				08 21										08 51								
Llwynypia	d				08 23										08 53								
Ystrad Rhondda	a				08 26										08 56								
	d				08 29										08 59								
Ton Pentre	d				08 31										09 01								
Treorchy	d				08 34										09 04								
Ynyswen	d				08 37										09 07								
Treherbert	a				08 43										09 13								

When events are being held at the Millenium Stadium, services are subject to alteration. Please check times before travelling.

Table 130

Saturdays
until 10 September

Bridgend, Barry Island, Barry, Penarth and Cardiff - Coryton, Rhymney, Pontypridd, Merthyr, Aberdare and Treherbert

		AW		AW	AW	AW	AW	AW	AW	AW	AW	AW		AW	AW	AW	AW	AW	AW	AW	AW	AW		AW	AW
Bridgend	d				07 42																				
Llantwit Major	d				07 56																				
Rhoose Cardiff Int Airport ✈	d				08 06																				
Barry Island	d									08 25						08 40				08 55					
Barry ■	d				08 15					08 30						08 45				09 00					
Barry Docks	d				08 19					08 34						08 49				09 04					
Cadoxton	d				08 22					08 37						08 52				09 07					
Dinas Powys	d				08 26					08 41						08 56				09 11					
Eastbrook	d				08 28					08 43						08 58				09 13					
Cogan	d				08 30					08 45						09 00				09 15					
Penarth	d						08 32				08 47										09 17				
Dingle Road	d						08 34				08 49										09 19				
Grangetown	d				08 34		08 38			08 49	08 53					09 04				09 19	09 23				
Cardiff Central ■	a				08 39		08 44			08 54	08 59					09 09				09 24	09 29				
	d	08 36		08 36	08 41		08 46	08 51		08 56	09 01			09 06	09 06	09 11	09 16		09 21	09 26	09 31			09 36	09 36
Cardiff Bay	d					08 42			08 54			09 06						09 18				09 30			
Cardiff Queen Street ■	a	08 39			08 44	08 46	08 49	08 54	08 58	08 59	09 04	09 10		09 09		09 14	09 19	09 22	09 24	09 29	09 34	09 34		09 39	
	d	08 40			08 45		08 50	08 55		09 00	09 05			09 '0		09 15	09 20		09 25	09 30	09 35			09 40	
Heath Low Level	d							09 00											09 30						
Ty Glas	d							09 03											09 33						
Birchgrove	d							09 04											09 34						
Rhiwbina	d							09 06											09 36						
Whitchurch (Cardiff)	d							09 08											09 38						
Coryton	a							09 13											09 43						
Heath High Level	d						08 55				09 10						09 25				09 40				
Llanishen	d						08 58				09 13						09 28				09 43				
Lisvane & Thornhill	d						09 00				09 15						09 30				09 45				
Caerphilly ■	d						09 06				09 21						09 36				09 51				
Aber	d						09 08				09 23						09 38				09 53				
Llanbradach	d						09 12				09 27						09 42				09 57				
Ystrad Mynach ■	d						09 17				09 32						09 47				10 02				
Hengoed	d						09 20				09 35						09 50				10 05				
Pengam	d						09 23				09 38						09 53				10 08				
Gilfach Fargoed	d										09 41														
Bargoed	a						09 31				09 48						09 58				10 16				
	d																09 59								
Brithdir	d																10 03								
Tir-phil	d																10 06								
Pontlottyn	d																10 10								
Rhymney ■	a																10 16								
Cathays	d	08 43			08 48					09 03				09 13		09 18				09 33				09 43	
Llandaf	d	08 47			08 52					09 07				09 17		09 22				09 37				09 47	
Ninian Park	d			08 40											09 10										09 40
Waun-gron Park	d			08 43											09 13										09 43
Fairwater	d			08 45											09 15										09 45
Danescourt	d			08 47											09 17										09 47
Radyr ■	a	08 50		08 54	08 55					09 10				09 20	09 24	09 25				09 40				09 50	09 54
	d	08 50			08 55					09 10				09 20		09 25				09 40				09 50	
Taffs Well ■	d	08 54			08 59					09 14				09 24		09 29				09 44				09 54	
Trefforest Estate	d									09 18										09 48					
Trefforest	d	09 01			09 06					09 22				09 31		09 36				09 52				10 01	
Pontypridd ■	a	09 04			09 09					09 25				09 34		09 39				09 55				10 04	
	d	09 06			09 11					09 27				09 36		09 41				09 57				10 06	
Abercynon	d				09 19					09 34						09 49				10 04					
Penrhiwceiber	d				09 24											09 54									
Mountain Ash	a				09 28											09 58									
	d				09 33											10 03									
Fernhill	d				09 35											10 05									
Cwmbach	d				09 39											10 09									
Aberdare ■	a				09 46											10 16									
Quakers Yard	d									09 39										10 09					
Merthyr Vale	a									09 44										10 14					
	d									09 47										10 17					
Troed Y Rhiw	d									09 50										10 20					
Pentre-bach	d									09 53										10 23					
Merthyr Tydfil	a									10 01										10 31					
Trehafod	d	09 11												09 41										10 11	
Porth	a	09 14												09 44										10 14	
	d	09 15												09 45										10 15	
Dinas Rhondda	d	09 19												09 49										10 19	
Tonypandy	d	09 21												09 51										10 21	
Llwynypia	d	09 23												09 53										10 23	
Ystrad Rhondda	a	09 26												09 56										10 26	
	d	09 29												09 59										10 29	
Ton Pentre	d	09 31												10 01										10 31	
Treorchy	d	09 34												10 04										10 34	
Ynyswen	d	09 37												10 07										10 37	
Treherbert	a	09 43												10 13										10 43	

When events are being held at the Millenium Stadium, services are subject to alteration. Please check times before travelling.

Table 130

Saturdays
until 10 September

Bridgend, Barry Island, Barry, Penarth and Cardiff - Coryton, Rhymney, Pontypridd, Merthyr, Aberdare and Treherbert

		AW	AW	AW	AW	AW	AW	AW		AW	AW	AW	AW	AW	AW	AW	AW	AW		AW	AW	AW	AW	AW	AW
Bridgend	d	08 42																						09 42	
Llantwit Major	d	08 56																						09 56	
Rhoose Cardiff Int Airport ✈	d	09 06																						10 06	
Barry Island	d						09 25							09 40				09 55							
Barry ■	d	09 15					09 30							09 45				10 00						10 15	
Barry Docks	d	09 19					09 34							09 49				10 04						10 19	
Cadoxton	d	09 22					09 37							09 52				10 07						10 22	
Dinas Powys	d	09 26					09 41							09 56				10 11						10 26	
Eastbrook	d	09 28					09 43							09 58				10 13						10 28	
Cogan	d	09 30					09 45							10 00				10 15						10 30	
Penarth	d			09 32				09 47							10 02					10 17					
Dingle Road	d			09 34				09 49							10 04					10 19					
Grangetown	d	09 34		09 38			09 49	09 53						10 04	10 08			10 19		10 23				10 34	
Cardiff Central ■	a	09 39		09 44			09 54	09 59						10 09	10 14			10 24		10 29				10 42	
	d	09 41		09 46	09 51		09 56	10 01			10 06	10 06		10 11	10 16		10 21	10 26		10 31		10 36	10 36		10 42
Cardiff Bay	d		09 42			09 54				10 06						10 18					10 30				
Cardiff Queen Street ■	a	09 44	09 46	09 49	09 54	09 58	09 59	10 04		10 10	10 09			10 14	10 19	10 22	10 24	10 29		10 34	10 34	10 39			10 46
	d	09 45		09 50	09 55		10 00	10 05			10 10			10 15	10 20		10 25	10 30		10 35		10 40			
Heath Low Level	d				10 00												10 30								
Ty Glas	d				10 03												10 33								
Birchgrove	d				10 04												10 34								
Rhiwbina	d				10 06												10 36								
Whitchurch (Cardiff)	d				10 08												10 38								
Coryton	a				10 13												10 43								
Heath High Level	d			09 55				10 10							10 25					10 40					
Llanishen	d			09 58				10 13							10 28					10 43					
Lisvane & Thornhill	d			10 00				10 15							10 30					10 45					
Caerphilly ■	d			10 06				10 21							10 36					10 51					
Aber	d			10 08				10 23							10 38					10 53					
Llanbradach	d			10 12				10 27							10 42					10 57					
Ystrad Mynach ■	d			10 17				10 32							10 47					11 02					
Hengoed	d			10 20				10 35							10 50					11 05					
Pengam	d			10 23				10 38							10 53					11 08					
Gilfach Fargoed	d							10 41																	
Bargoed	a			10 31				10 48							10 58					11 16					
	d														10 59										
Brithdir	d														11 03										
Tir-phil	d														11 06										
Pontlottyn	d														11 10										
Rhymney ■	a														11 16										
Cathays	d	09 48					10 03				10 13			10 18				10 33				10 43			
Llandaf	d	09 52					10 07				10 17			10 22				10 37				10 47			
Ninian Park	d											10 10											10 40		
Waun-gron Park	d											10 13											10 43		
Fairwater	d											10 15											10 45		
Danescourt	d											10 17											10 47		
Radyr ■	a	09 55					10 10				10 20	10 24		10 25				10 40				10 50	10 54		
	d	09 55					10 10				10 20			10 25				10 40				10 50			
Taffs Well ■	d	09 59					10 14				10 24			10 29				10 44				10 54			
Trefforest Estate	d																	10 48							
Trefforest	d	10 06					10 22				10 31			10 36				10 52				11 01			
Pontypridd ■	a	10 09					10 30				10 34			10 39				10 55				11 04			
	d	10 11									10 36		10 35	10 41				10 57				11 06			
Abercynon	d	10 19											10 41	10 49				11 04							
Penrhiwceiber	d	10 24												10 54											
Mountain Ash	a	10 28												10 58											
	d	10 33												11 03											
Fernhill	d	10 35												11 05											
Cwmbach	d	10 39												11 09											
Aberdare ■	a	10 46												11 16											
Quakers Yard	d												10 45					11 09							
Merthyr Vale	a												10 50					11 14							
	d												10 52					11 17							
Troed Y Rhiw	d												10 55					11 20							
Pentre-bach	d												10 58					11 23							
Merthyr Tydfil	a												11 06					11 31							
Trehafod	d										10 41											11 11			
Porth	a										10 44											11 14			
	d										10 45											11 15			
Dinas Rhondda	d										10 49											11 19			
Tonypandy	d										10 51											11 21			
Llwynypia	d										10 53											11 23			
Ystrad Rhondda	a										10 56											11 26			
	d										10 59											11 29			
Ton Pentre	d										11 01											11 31			
Treorchy	d										11 04											11 34			
Ynyswen	d										11 07											11 37			
Treherbert	a										11 13											11 43			

When events are being held at the Millenium Stadium, services are subject to alteration. Please check times before travelling.

Table 130

Saturdays
until 10 September

Bridgend, Barry Island, Barry, Penarth and Cardiff - Coryton, Rhymney, Pontypridd, Merthyr, Aberdare and Treherbert

		AW	AW	AW	AW	AW	AW	AW	AW	AW	AW	AW	AW	AW	AW	AW	AW	AW	AW	AW	AW	AW
Bridgend	d																			10 42		
Llantwit Major	d																			10 56		
Rhoose Cardiff Int Airport ✈	d																			11 06		
Barry Island	d					10 25					10 40				10 55							
Barry ■	d					10 30					10 45				11 00					11 15		
Barry Docks	d					10 34					10 49				11 04					11 19		
Cadoxton	d					10 37					10 52				11 07					11 22		
Dinas Powys	d					10 41					10 56				11 11					11 26		
Eastbrook	d					10 43					10 58				11 13					11 28		
Cogan	d					10 45					11 00				11 15					11 30		
Penarth	d	10 32						10 47				11 02				11 17						11 32
Dingle Road	d	10 34						10 49				11 04				11 19						11 34
Grangetown	d	10 38				10 49		10 53			11 04	11 08			11 19	11 23				11 34		11 38
Cardiff Central ■	a	10 44				10 54		10 59			11 09	11 14			11 24	11 29				11 39		11 44
	d	10 46	10 51		10 51	10 56		11 01	11 06		11 11	11 16		11 21	11 26	11 31		11 36	11 36	11 41		11 46
Cardiff Bay	d			10 54						11 06			11 18				11 30				11 42	
Cardiff Queen Street ■	a	10 49	10 54	10 58		10 59		11 04		11 10	11 14	11 19	11 22	11 24	11 29	11 34	11 34	11 39		11 44	11 46	11 49
	d	10 50	10 55			11 00		11 05			11 15	11 20		11 25	11 30	11 35		11 40		11 45		11 50
Heath Low Level	d		11 00											11 30								
Ty Glas	d		11 03											11 33								
Birchgrove	d		11 04											11 34								
Rhiwbina	d		11 06											11 36								
Whitchurch (Cardiff)	d		11 08											11 38								
Coryton	a		11 13											11 43								
Heath High Level	d	10 55						11 10				11 25				11 40						11 55
Llanishen	d	10 58						11 13				11 28				11 4						11 58
Lisvane & Thornhill	d	11 00						11 15				11 30				11 6						12 00
Caerphilly ■	d	11 06						11 21				11 36				11 ,1						12 06
Aber	d	11 08						11 23				11 38				1153						12 08
Llanbradach	d	11 12						11 27				11 42				1 57						12 12
Ystrad Mynach ■	d	11 17						11 32				11 47				1 02						12 17
Hengoed	d	11 20						11 35				11 50				2 05						12 20
Pengam	d	11 23						11 38				11 53				12 08						12 23
Gilfach Fargoed	d							11 41														
Bargoed	a	11 31						11 48				11 58				12 16						12 31
	d											11 59										
Brithdir	d											12 03										
Tir-phil	d											12 06										
Pontlottyn	d											12 10										
Rhymney ■	a											12 16										
Cathays	d					11 03					11 18				11 33			11 43		11 48		
Llandaf	d					11 07					11 22				11 37			11 47		11 52		
Ninian Park	d								11 10										11 40			
Waun-gron Park	d								11 13										11 43			
Fairwater	d								11 15										11 45			
Danescourt	d						←		11 17										11 47			
Radyr ■	a				11 02	11 10	11 02		11 24		11 25				11 40			11 50	11 54	11 55		
	d				11 20	11 10	11 20				11 25				11 40			11 50		11 55		
Taffs Well ■	d				→	11 14	11 24				11 29				11 44			11 54		11 59		
Trefforest Estate	d					11 18									11 48							
Trefforest	d					11 22	11 31				11 36				11 52			12 01		12 06		
Pontypridd ■	a					11 25	11 34				11 39				11 55			12 04		12 09		
	d					11 27	11 36				11 41				11 57			12 06		12 11		
Abercynon	d					11 34					11 49				12 04					12 19		
Penrhiwceiber	d										11 54									12 24		
Mountain Ash	a										11 58									12 28		
	d										12 03									12 33		
Fernhill	d										12 05									12 35		
Cwmbach	d										12 09									12 39		
Aberdare ■	a										12 16									12 46		
Quakers Yard	d					11 39									12 09							
Merthyr Vale	a					11 44									12 14							
	d					11 47									12 17							
Troed Y Rhiw	d					11 50									12 20							
Pentre-bach	d					11 53									12 23							
Merthyr Tydfil	a					12 01									12 31							
Trehafod	d						11 41											12 11				
Porth	a						11 44											12 14				
	d						11 45											12 15				
Dinas Rhondda	d						11 49											12 19				
Tonypandy	d						11 51											12 21				
Llwynypia	d						11 53											12 23				
Ystrad Rhondda	a						11 56											12 26				
	d						11 59											12 29				
Ton Pentre	d						12 01											12 31				
Treorchy	d						12 04											12 34				
Ynyswen	d						12 07											12 37				
Treherbert	a						12 13											12 43				

When events are being held at the Millenium Stadium, services are subject to alteration. Please check times before travelling.

Table 130

Saturdays
until 10 September

Bridgend, Barry Island, Barry, Penarth and Cardiff - Coryton, Rhymney, Pontypridd, Merthyr, Aberdare and Treherbert

		AW	AW	AW	AW	AW	AW	AW	AW	AW	AW	AW	AW	AW	AW	AW	AW	AW	AW	AW	AW	AW	AW
Bridgend	d																	11 42					
Llantwit Major	d																	11 56					
Rhoose Cardiff Int Airport ✈	d																	12 06					
Barry Island	d			11 25					11 40				11 55										12 25
Barry ■	d			11 30					11 45				12 00					12 15					12 30
Barry Docks	d			11 34					11 49				12 04					12 19					12 34
Cadoxton	d			11 37					11 52				12 07					12 22					12 37
Dinas Powys	d			11 41					11 56				12 11					12 26					12 41
Eastbrook	d			11 43					11 58				12 13					12 28					12 43
Cogan	d			11 45					12 00				12 15					12 30					12 45
Penarth	d				11 47					12 02				12 17						12 32			
Dingle Road	d				11 49					12 04				12 19						12 34			
Grangetown	d			11 49	11 53				12 04	12 08			12 19	12 23				12 34		12 38			12 49
Cardiff Central ■	a			11 54	11 59				12 09	12 14			12 24	12 29				12 39		12 44			12 54
	d	11 51		11 56	12 01		12 06	12 06	12 11	12 16		12 21	12 26	12 31		12 36	12 36	12 41		12 46	12 51		12 56
Cardiff Bay	d		11 54			12 06					12 18				12 30				12 42			12 54	
Cardiff Queen Street ■	a	11 54	11 58	11 59	12 04	12 10	12 09		12 14	12 19	12 22	12 24	12 29	12 34	12 34	12 39		12 44	12 46	12 49	12 54	12 58	12 59
	d	11 55		12 00	12 05		12 10		12 15	12 20		12 25	12 30	12 35		12 40		12 45		12 50	12 55		13 00
Heath Low Level	d	12 00										12 30									13 00		
Ty Glas	d	12 03										12 33									13 03		
Birchgrove	d	12 04										12 34									13 04		
Rhiwbina	d	12 06										12 36									13 06		
Whitchurch (Cardiff)	d	12 08										12 38									13 08		
Coryton	a	12 13										12 43									13 13		
Heath High Level	d				12 10					12 25				12 40						12 55			
Llanishen	d				12 13					12 28				12 43						12 58			
Lisvane & Thornhill	d				12 15					12 30				12 45						13 00			
Caerphilly ■	d				12 21					12 36				12 51						13 06			
Aber	d				12 23					12 38				12 53						13 08			
Llanbradach	d				12 27					12 42				12 57						13 12			
Ystrad Mynach ■	d				12 32					12 47				13 02						13 17			
Hengoed	d				12 35					12 50				13 05						13 20			
Pengam	d				12 38					12 53				13 08						13 23			
Gilfach Fargoed	d				12 41																		
Bargoed	a				12 48					12 58				13 16						13 31			
	d									12 59													
Brithdir	d									13 03													
Tir-phil	d									13 06													
Pontlottyn	d									13 10													
Rhymney ■	a									13 16													
Cathays	d			12 03			12 13		12 18				12 33			12 43		12 48					13 03
Llandaf	d			12 07			12 17		12 22				12 37			12 47		12 52					13 07
Ninian Park	d							12 10									12 40						
Waun-gron Park	d							12 13									12 43						
Fairwater	d							12 15									12 45						
Danescourt	d							12 17									12 47						
Radyr ■	a			12 10			12 20	12 24	12 25				12 40			12 50	12 54	12 55					13 10
	d			12 10			12 20		12 25				12 40			12 50		12 55					13 10
Taffs Well ■	d			12 14			12 24		12 29				12 44			12 54		12 59					13 14
Trefforest Estate	d			12 18									12 48										13 18
Trefforest	d			12 22			12 31		12 36				12 52			13 01		13 06					13 22
Pontypridd ■	a			12 25			12 34		12 42				12 55			13 04		13 09					13 25
	d			12 27			12 36						12 57			13 06		13 11					13 27
Abercynon	d			12 34									13 04					13 19					13 34
Penrhiwceiber	d																	13 24					
Mountain Ash	a																	13 28					
	d																	13 33					
Fernhill	d																	13 35					
Cwmbach	d																	13 39					
Aberdare ■	a																	13 46					
Quakers Yard	d			12 39									13 09										13 39
Merthyr Vale	a			12 44									13 14										13 44
	d			12 47									13 17										13 47
Troed Y Rhiw	d			12 50									13 20										13 50
Pentre-bach	d			12 53									13 23										13 53
Merthyr Tydfil	a			13 01									13 31										14 01
Trehafod	d						12 41									13 11							
Porth	a						12 44									13 14							
	d						12 45									13 15							
Dinas Rhondda	d						12 49									13 19							
Tonypandy	d						12 51									13 21							
Llwynypia	d						12 53									13 23							
Ystrad Rhondda	a						12 56									13 26							
	d						12 59									13 29							
Ton Pentre	d						13 01									13 31							
Treorchy	d						13 04									13 34							
Ynyswen	d						13 07									13 37							
Treherbert	a						13 13									13 43							

When events are being held at the Millenium Stadium, services are subject to alteration. Please check times before travelling.

Table 130

Saturdays
until 10 September

Bridgend, Barry Island, Barry, Penarth and Cardiff - Coryton, Rhymney, Pontypridd, Merthyr, Aberdare and Treherbert

		AW	AW	AW	AW	AW	AW	AW	AW	AW	AW	AW	AW	AW	AW	AW	AW	AW	AW	AW	AW	AW	AW
Bridgend	d														12 42								
Llantwit Major	d														12 56								
Rhoose Cardiff Int Airport ✈	d														13 06								
Barry Island	d					12 40				12 55										13 25			
Barry [3]	d					12 45				13 00					13 15					13 31			
Barry Docks	d					12 49				13 04					13 19					13 34			
Cadoxton	d					12 52				13 07					13 22					13 37			
Dinas Powys	d					12 56				13 11					13 26					13 41			
Eastbrook	d					12 58				13 13					13 28					13 43			
Cogan	d					13 00				13 15					13 30					13 46			
Penarth	d	12 47					13 02				13 17						13 32				13 47		
Dingle Road	d	12 49					13 04				13 19						13 34				13 49		
Grangetown	d	12 53				13 04	13 08			13 20	13 23				13 34		13 38			13 50	13 53		
Cardiff Central [7]	a	12 59				13 09	13 14			13 24	13 29				13 39		13 44			13 55	13 59		
	d	13 01		13 06	13 06	13 11	13 16		13 21	13 26	13 31		13 36	13 36	13 41		13 46	13 51		13 56	14 01		14 06
Cardiff Bay	d		13 06					13 18				13 30				13 42			13 54			14 06	
Cardiff Queen Street [3]	a	13 04	13 10	13 09		13 14	13 19	13 22	13 24	13 29	13 34	13 34	13 39		13 44	13 46	13 49	13 54	13 58	13 59	14 04	14 10	14 09
	d	13 05		13 10		13 15	13 20		13 25	13 30	13 35		13 40		13 45		13 50	13 55		14 00	14 05		14 10
Heath Low Level	d								13 30									14 00					
Ty Glas	d								13 33									14 03					
Birchgrove	d								13 34									14 04					
Rhiwbina	d								13 36									14 06					
Whitchurch (Cardiff)	d								13 38									14 08					
Coryton	a								13 43									14 13					
Heath High Level	d	13 10					13 25				13 40						13 55				14 10		
Llanishen	d	13 13					13 28				13 43						13 58				14 13		
Lisvane & Thornhill	d	13 15					13 30				13 45						14 00				14 15		
Caerphilly [3]	d	13 21					13 36				13 51						14 06				14 21		
Aber	d	13 23					13 38				13 53						14 08				14 23		
Llanbradach	d	13 27					13 42				13 57						14 12				14 27		
Ystrad Mynach [3]	d	13 32					13 47				14 02						14 17				14 32		
Hengoed	d	13 35					13 50				14 05						14 20				14 35		
Pengam	d	13 38					13 53				14 08						14 23				14 38		
Gilfach Fargoed	d	13 41																			14 41		
Bargoed	a	13 48					13 58				14 16						14 31				14 48		
	d						13 59																
Brithdir	d						14 03																
Tir-phil	d						14 06																
Pontlottyn	d						14 10																
Rhymney [3]	a						14 16																
Cathays	d			13 13		13 18				13 33			13 43		13 48					14 03			14 13
Llandaf	d			13 17		13 22				13 37			13 47		13 52					14 07			14 17
Ninian Park	d				13 10									13 40									
Waun-gron Park	d				13 13									13 43									
Fairwater	d				13 15									13 45									
Danescourt	d				13 17									13 47									
Radyr [3]	a			13 20	13 24	13 25				13 40			13 50	13 54	13 55					14 10			14 20
	d			13 20		13 25				13 40			13 50		13 55					14 10			14 20
Taffs Well [3]	d			13 24		13 29				13 44			13 54		13 59					14 14			14 24
Trefforest Estate	d									13 48										14 18			
Trefforest	d			13 31		13 36				13 52			14 01		14 06					14 22			14 31
Pontypridd [3]	a			13 34		13 39				13 55			14 04		14 09					14 25			14 34
	d			13 36		13 41				13 57			14 06		14 11					14 27			14 36
Abercynon	d					13 49				14 04					14 19					14 34			
Penrhiwceiber	d					13 54									14 24								
Mountain Ash	a					13 58									14 28								
	d					14 03									14 33								
Fernhill	d					14 05									14 35								
Cwmbach	d					14 09									14 39								
Aberdare [3]	a					14 16									14 46								
Quakers Yard	d									14 09										14 39			
Merthyr Vale	a									14 14										14 44			
	d									14 17										14 47			
Troed Y Rhiw	d									14 20										14 50			
Pentre-bach	d									14 23										14 53			
Merthyr Tydfil	a									14 31										15 01			
Trehafod	d			13 41									14 11										14 41
Porth	a			13 44									14 14										14 44
	d			13 45									14 15										14 45
Dinas Rhondda	d			13 49									14 19										14 49
Tonypandy	d			13 51									14 21										14 51
Llwynypia	d			13 53									14 23										14 53
Ystrad Rhondda	a			13 56									14 26										14 56
	d			13 59									14 29										14 59
Ton Pentre	d			14 01									14 31										15 01
Treorchy	d			14 04									14 34										15 04
Ynyswen	d			14 07									14 37										15 07
Treherbert	a			14 13									14 43										15 13

When events are being held at the Millenium Stadium, services are subject to alteration. Please check times before travelling.

Table 130

Saturdays
until 10 September

Bridgend, Barry Island, Barry, Penarth and Cardiff - Coryton, Rhymney, Pontypridd, Merthyr, Aberdare and Treherbert

		AW	AW	AW	AW	AW	AW	AW	AW	AW	AW	AW	AW	AW	AW	AW	AW	AW	AW	AW	AW	AW
Bridgend	d											13 42										
Llantwit Major	d											13 56										
Rhoose Cardiff Int Airport ✈	d											14 06										
Barry Island	d		13 40				13 55											14 25				
Barry [3]	d		13 45				14 00					14 15						14 30				
Barry Docks	d		13 49				14 04					14 19						14 34				
Cadoxton	d		13 52				14 07					14 22						14 37				
Dinas Powys	d		13 56				14 11					14 26						14 41				
Eastbrook	d		13 58				14 13					14 28						14 43				
Cogan	d		14 00				14 15					14 30						14 45				
Penarth	d			14 02				14 17						14 32						14 47		
Dingle Road	d			14 04				14 19						14 34						14 49		
Grangetown	d		14 04	14 08			14 20	14 23				14 34		14 38				14 49		14 53		
Cardiff Central [7]	a		14 09	14 14			14 24	14 29				14 39		14 44				14 54		14 59		
	d	14 06	14 11	14 16		14 21	14 26	14 31		14 36	14 36	14 41		14 46	14 51		14 51	14 56		15 01	15 06	
Cardiff Bay	d				14 18				14 30				14 42			14 54						15 06
Cardiff Queen Street [3]	a		14 14	14 19	14 22	14 24	14 29	14 34	14 34	14 39		14 44	14 46	14 49	14 54	14 58		14 59		15 04		15 10
	d		14 15	14 20		14 25	14 30	14 35		14 40		14 45		14 50	14 55			15 00		15 05		
Heath Low Level	d					14 30									15 00							
Ty Glas	d					14 33									15 03							
Birchgrove	d					14 34									15 04							
Rhiwbina	d					14 36									15 06							
Whitchurch (Cardiff)	d					14 38									15 08							
Coryton	a					14 43									15 13							
Heath High Level	d			14 25				14 40						14 55						15 10		
Llanishen	d			14 28				14 43						14 58						15 13		
Lisvane & Thornhill	d			14 30				14 45						15 00						15 15		
Caerphilly [3]	d			14 36				14 51						15 06						15 21		
Aber	d			14 38				14 53						15 08						15 23		
Llanbradach	d			14 42				14 57						15 12						15 27		
Ystrad Mynach [3]	d			14 47				15 02						15 17						15 32		
Hengoed	d			14 50				15 05						15 20						15 35		
Pengam	d			14 53				15 08						15 23						15 38		
Gilfach Fargoed	d																			15 41		
Bargoed	a			14 58				15 16						15 31						15 48		
	d			14 59																		
Brithdir	d			15 03																		
Tir-phil	d			15 06																		
Pontlottyn	d			15 10																		
Rhymney [3]	a			15 16																		
Cathays	d		14 18				14 33			14 43		14 48						15 03				
Llandaf	d		14 22				14 37			14 47		14 52						15 07				
Ninian Park	d	14 10									14 40										15 10	
Waun-gron Park	d	14 13									14 43										15 13	
Fairwater	d	14 15									14 45										15 15	
Danescourt	d	14 17									14 47								←		15 17	
Radyr [3]	a	14 24		14 25				14 40		14 50	14 54	14 55					15 08	15 09	15 08		15 24	
	d			14 25				14 40		14 50		14 55					15 20	15 10	15 20			
Taffs Well [3]	d			14 29				14 44		14 54		14 59					→	15 14	15 24			
Trefforest Estate	d							14 48										15 18				
Trefforest	d			14 36				14 52		15 01		15 06						15 22	15 31			
Pontypridd [3]	a			14 39				14 55		15 04		15 09						15 25	15 34			
	d			14 41				14 57		15 06		15 11						15 27	15 36			
Abercynon	d			14 49				15 04				15 19						15 34				
Penrhiwceiber	d			14 54								15 24										
Mountain Ash	a			14 58								15 28										
	d			15 03								15 33										
Fernhill	d			15 05								15 35										
Cwmbach	d			15 09								15 39										
Aberdare [3]	a			15 16								15 46										
Quakers Yard	d							15 09										15 39				
Merthyr Vale	a							15 14										15 44				
	d							15 17										15 47				
Troed Y Rhiw	d							15 20										15 50				
Pentre-bach	d							15 23										15 53				
Merthyr Tydfil	a							15 31										16 01				
Trehafod	d									15 11									15 41			
Porth	a									15 14									15 44			
	d									15 15									15 45			
Dinas Rhondda	d									15 19									15 49			
Tonypandy	d									15 21									15 51			
Llwynypia	d									15 23									15 53			
Ystrad Rhondda	a									15 26									15 56			
	d									15 29									15 59			
Ton Pentre	d									15 31									16 01			
Treorchy	d									15 34									16 04			
Ynyswen	d									15 37									16 07			
Treherbert	a									15 43									16 13			

When events are being held at the Millenium Stadium, services are subject to alteration. Please check times before travelling.

Table 130

Saturdays
until 10 September

Bridgend, Barry Island, Barry, Penarth and Cardiff - Coryton, Rhymney, Pontypridd, Merthyr, Aberdare and Treherbert

		AW	AW	AW	AW	AW	AW	AW	AW	AW	AW	AW	AW	AW	AW	AW	AW	AW	AW	AW	AW	AW	AW
Bridgend	d										14 42												
Llantwit Major	d										14 56												
Rhoose Cardiff Int Airport ✈	d										15 06												
Barry Island	d	14 40				14 55										15 25					15 40		
Barry	d	14 45				15 00					15 15					15 30					15 45		
Barry Docks	d	14 49				15 04					15 19					15 34					15 49		
Cadoxton	d	14 52				15 07					15 22					15 37					15 52		
Dinas Powys	d	14 56				15 11					15 26					15 41					15 56		
Eastbrook	d	14 58				15 13					15 28					15 43					15 58		
Cogan	d	15 00				15 15					15 30					15 45					16 00		
Penarth	d		15 02				15 17						15 32				15 47					16 02	
Dingle Road	d		15 04				15 19						15 34				15 49					16 04	
Grangetown	d	15 04	15 08			15 19	15 23				15 34		15 38			15 49	15 53				16 04	16 08	
Cardiff Central	a	15 09	15 14			15 24	15 29				15 39		15 44			15 54	15 59				16 09	16 14	
	d	15 11	15 16		15 21	15 26	15 31		15 36	15 36	15 41		15 46	15 51		15 56	16 01		16 06	16 06	16 11	16 16	
Cardiff Bay	d			15 18				15 30				15 42			15 54			16 06					16 18
Cardiff Queen Street	a	15 14	15 19	15 22	15 24	15 29	15 34	15 34	15 39		15 44	15 46	15 49	15 54	15 58	15 59	16 04	16 10	16 09		16 14	16 19	16 22
	d	15 15	15 20		15 25	15 30	15 35		15 40		15 45		15 50	15 55		16 00	16 05		16 10		16 15	16 20	
Heath Low Level	d				15 30									16 00									
Ty Glas	d				15 33									16 03									
Birchgrove	d				15 34									16 04									
Rhiwbina	d				15 36									16 06									
Whitchurch (Cardiff)	d				15 38									16 08									
Coryton	a				15 43									16 13									
Heath High Level	d		15 25				15 40						15 55				16 10					16 25	
Llanishen	d		15 28				15 43						15 58				16 13					16 28	
Lisvane & Thornhill	d		15 30				15 45						16 00				16 15					16 30	
Caerphilly	d		15 36				15 51						16 06				16 21					16 36	
Aber	d		15 38				15 53						16 08				16 23					16 38	
Llanbradach	d		15 42				15 57						16 12				16 27					16 42	
Ystrad Mynach	d		15 47				16 02						16 17				16 32					16 47	
Hengoed	d		15 50				16 05						16 20				16 35					16 50	
Pengam	d		15 53				16 08						16 23				16 38					16 53	
Gilfach Fargoed	d																16 41						
Bargoed	a		15 58				16 16						16 31				16 48					16 58	
	d		15 59																			16 59	
Brithdir	d		16 03																			17 03	
Tir-phil	d		16 06																			17 06	
Pontlottyn	d		16 10																			17 10	
Rhymney	a		16 16																			17 16	
Cathays	d	15 18				15 33			15 43		15 48					16 03			16 13		16 18		
Llandaf	d	15 22				15 37			15 47		15 52					16 07			16 17		16 22		
Ninian Park	d									15 40										16 10			
Waun-gron Park	d									15 43										16 13			
Fairwater	d									15 45										16 15			
Danescourt	d									15 47										16 17			
Radyr	a	15 25				15 40			15 50	15 54	15 55					16 10			16 20	16 24	16 25		
	d	15 25				15 40			15 50		15 55					16 10			16 20		16 25		
Taffs Well	d	15 29				15 44			15 54		15 59					16 14			16 24		16 29		
Trefforest Estate	d					15 48										16 18							
Trefforest	d	15 36				15 52			16 01		16 06					16 22			16 31		16 36		
Pontypridd	a	15 39				15 55			16 04		16 09					16 25			16 34		16 39		
	d	15 41				15 57			16 06		16 11					16 27			16 36		16 41		
Abercynon	d	15 49				16 04					16 19					16 34					16 49		
Penrhiwceiber	d	15 54									16 24										16 54		
Mountain Ash	a	15 58									16 28										16 58		
	d	16 03									16 33										17 03		
Fernhill	d	16 05									16 35										17 05		
Cwmbach	d	16 09									16 39										17 09		
Aberdare	a	16 16									16 46										17 16		
Quakers Yard	d					16 09										16 39							
Merthyr Vale	a					16 14										16 44							
	d					16 17										16 47							
Troed Y Rhiw	d					16 20										16 50							
Pentre-bach	d					16 23										16 53							
Merthyr Tydfil	a					16 31										17 01							
Trehafod	d								16 11										16 41				
Porth	a								16 14										16 44				
	d								16 15										16 45				
Dinas Rhondda	d								16 19										16 49				
Tonypandy	d								16 21										16 51				
Llwynypia	d								16 23										16 53				
Ystrad Rhondda	a								16 26										16 56				
	d								16 29										16 59				
Ton Pentre	d								16 31										17 01				
Treorchy	d								16 34										17 04				
Ynyswen	d								16 37										17 07				
Treherbert	a								16 43										17 13				

When events are being held at the Millenium Stadium, services are subject to alteration. Please check times before travelling.

Table 130

Saturdays
until 10 September

Bridgend, Barry Island, Barry, Penarth and Cardiff - Coryton, Rhymney, Pontypridd, Merthyr, Aberdare and Treherbert

		AW	AW	AW	AW	AW	AW	AW	AW	AW	AW	AW	AW	AW	AW	AW	AW	AW	AW	AW	AW	AW
Bridgend	d							15 42														
Llantwit Major	d							15 56														
Rhoose Cardiff Int Airport ✈	d							16 06														
Barry Island	d		15 55										16 25					16 40				16 55
Barry	d		16 00					16 15					16 30					16 45				17 00
Barry Docks	d		16 04					16 19					16 34					16 49				17 04
Cadoxton	d		16 07					16 22					16 37					16 52				17 07
Dinas Powys	d		16 11					16 26					16 41					16 56				17 11
Eastbrook	d		16 13					16 28					16 43					16 58				17 13
Cogan	d		16 15					16 30					16 45					17 00				17 15
Penarth	d			16 17						16 32									17 02			
Dingle Road	d			16 19						16 34									17 04			
Grangetown	d		16 19	16 23				16 34		16 38			16 49					17 04	17 08			17 19
Cardiff Central	a		16 24	16 29				16 39		16 44			16 54					17 09	17 14			17 24
	d	16 21	16 26	16 31		16 36	16 36	16 41		16 46	16 51		16 56	17 01		17 06	17 06	17 11	17 16		17 21	17 26
Cardiff Bay	d				16 30				16 42			16 54			17 06					17 18		
Cardiff Queen Street	a	16 24	16 29	16 34	16 34	16 39		16 44	16 46	16 49	16 54	16 58	16 59	17 04	17 10	17 09		17 14	17 19	17 22	17 24	17 29
	d	16 25	16 30	16 35		16 40		16 45		16 50	16 55		17 00	17 05		17 10		17 15	17 20		17 25	17 30
Heath Low Level	d	16 30									17 00										17 30	
Ty Glas	d	16 33									17 03										17 33	
Birchgrove	d	16 34									17 04										17 34	
Rhiwbina	d	16 36									17 06										17 36	
Whitchurch (Cardiff)	d	16 38									17 08										17 38	
Coryton	a	16 43									17 13										17 43	
Heath High Level	d			16 40						16 55				17 10					17 25			
Llanishen	d			16 43						16 58				17 13					17 28			
Lisvane & Thornhill	d			16 45						17 00				17 15					17 30			
Caerphilly	d			16 51						17 06				17 21					17 36			
Aber	d			16 53						17 08				17 23					17 38			
Llanbradach	d			16 57						17 12				17 27					17 42			
Ystrad Mynach	d			17 02						17 17				17 33					17 47			
Hengoed	d			17 05						17 20				17 35					17 50			
Pengam	d			17 08						17 23				17 39					17 53			
Gilfach Fargoed	d													17 42								
Bargoed	a			17 16						17 31				17 45					18 01			
	d													17 47								
Brithdir	d													17 50								
Tir-phil	d													17 53								
Pontlottyn	d													17 58								
Rhymney	a													18 04								
Cathays	d		16 33			16 43		16 48					17 03			17 13		17 18				17 33
Llandaf	d		16 37			16 47		16 52					17 07			17 17		17 22				17 37
Ninian Park	d						16 40										17 10					
Waun-gron Park	d						16 43										17 13					
Fairwater	d						16 45										17 15					
Danescourt	d						16 47										17 17					
Radyr	a		16 40			16 50	16 54	16 55					17 10			17 20	17 24	17 25				17 40
	d		16 40			16 50		16 55					17 10			17 20		17 25				17 40
Taffs Well	d		16 44			16 54		16 59					17 14			17 24		17 29				17 44
Trefforest Estate	d		16 48										17 18									17 48
Trefforest	d		16 52			17 01		17 06					17 22			17 31		17 36				17 52
Pontypridd	a		16 55			17 04		17 09					17 25			17 34		17 39				17 55
	d		16 57			17 06		17 11					17 27			17 36		17 41				17 57
Abercynon	d		17 04					17 19					17 34					17 49				18 04
Penrhiwceiber	d							17 24										17 54				
Mountain Ash	a							17 28										17 58				
	d							17 33										18 03				
Fernhill	d							17 35										18 05				
Cwmbach	d							17 39										18 09				
Aberdare	a							17 46										18 16				
Quakers Yard	d		17 09										17 39									18 09
Merthyr Vale	a		17 14										17 44									18 14
	d		17 17										17 47									18 17
Troed Y Rhiw	d		17 20										17 50									18 20
Pentre-bach	d		17 23										17 53									18 23
Merthyr Tydfil	a		17 31										18 01									18 31
Trehafod	d					17 11										17 41						
Porth	a					17 14										17 44						
	d					17 15										17 45						
Dinas Rhondda	d					17 19										17 49						
Tonypandy	d					17 21										17 51						
Llwynypia	d					17 23										17 53						
Ystrad Rhondda	a					17 26										17 56						
	d					17 29										17 59						
Ton Pentre	d					17 31										18 01						
Treorchy	d					17 34										18 04						
Ynyswen	d					17 37										18 07						
Treherbert	a					17 43										18 13						

When events are being held at the Millenium Stadium, services are subject to alteration. Please check times before travelling.

Table 130

Saturdays
until 10 September

Bridgend, Barry Island, Barry, Penarth and Cardiff - Coryton, Rhymney, Pontypridd, Merthyr, Aberdare and Treherbert

		AW	AW	AW	AW	AW	AW	AW	AW	AW	AW	AW	AW	AW	AW	AW	AW	AW	AW	AW	AW	AW	AW
Bridgend	d					16 42																	
Llantwit Major	d					16 56																	
Rhoose Cardiff Int Airport	d					17 06																	
Barry Island	d										17 25					17 40				17 55			
Barry	d					17 15					17 30					17 45				18 00			
Barry Docks	d					17 19					17 34					17 49				18 04			
Cadoxton	d					17 22					17 37					17 52				18 07			
Dinas Powys	d					17 26					17 41					17 56				18 11			
Eastbrook	d					17 28					17 43					17 58				18 13			
Cogan	d					17 30					17 45					18 00				18 15			
Penarth	d	17 17						17 32				17 47					18 02				18 17		
Dingle Road	d	17 19						17 34				17 49					18 04				18 19		
Grangetown	d	17 23				17 34		17 38			17 49	17 53				18 04	18 08			18 19	18 23		
Cardiff Central	a	17 29				17 39		17 44			17 54	17 59				18 09	18 14			18 23	18 29		
	d	17 31		17 36	17 36	17 41		17 46	17 51		17 56	18 01		18 06	18 06	18 11	18 16		18 21	18 26	18 31		18 36
Cardiff Bay	d		17 30				17 42			17 54			18 06					18 18				18 30	
Cardiff Queen Street	a	17 34	17 34	17 39		17 44	17 46	17 49	17 54	17 58	17 59	18 04	18 10	18 09		18 14	18 19	18 22	18 24	18 29	18 34	18 34	18 38
	d	17 35		17 40		17 45		17 50	17 55		18 00	18 05		18 10		18 15	18 20		18 25	18 30	18 35		18 40
Heath Low Level	d								18 00										18 30				
Ty Glas	d								18 03										18 33				
Birchgrove	d								18 04										18 34				
Rhiwbina	d								18 06										18 36				
Whitchurch (Cardiff)	d								18 08										18 38				
Coryton	a								18 13										18 43				
Heath High Level	d	17 40						17 55				18 10					18 25				18 40		
Llanishen	d	17 43						17 59				18 13					18 28				18 43		
Lisvane & Thornhill	d	17 45						18 02				18 15					18 30				18 45		
Caerphilly	d	17 51						18 07				18 21					18 36				18 51		
Aber	d	17 53						18 10				18 23					18 38				18 53		
Llanbradach	d	17 57						18 14				18 27					18 42				18 57		
Ystrad Mynach	d	18 02						18 20				18 32					18a51				19 02		
Hengoed	d	18 05						18 23				18 35									19 05		
Pengam	d	18 08						18 27				18 38									19 08		
Gilfach Fargoed	d	18 11						18 30				18 41									19 11		
Bargoed	a	18 14						18 34				18 48									19 14		
	d	18 16						18 44													19 16		
Brithdir	d	18 20						18 48													19 20		
Tir-phil	d	18 23						18 51													19 23		
Pontlottyn	d	18 27						18 55													19 27		
Rhymney	a	18 33						19 01													19 34		
Cathays	d			17 43		17 48					18 03			18 13		18 18				18 33			18 43
Llandaf	d			17 47		17 52					18 07			18 17		18 22				18 37			18 47
Ninian Park	d				17 40										18 10								
Waun-gron Park	d				17 43										18 13								
Fairwater	d				17 45										18 15								
Danescourt	d				17 47										18 17								
Radyr	a			17 50	17 54	17 55					18 10			18 20	18 24	18 25				18 40			18 50
	d			17 50		17 55					18 10			18 20		18 25				18 40			18 50
Taffs Well	d			17 54		17 59					18 14			18 24		18 29				18 44			18 54
Trefforest Estate	d										18 18									18 48			
Trefforest	d			18 01		18 06					18 22			18 31		18 36				18 52			19 01
Pontypridd	a			18 04		18 09					18 25			18 34		18 42				18 55			19 04
	d			18 06		18 11					18 27			18 36						18 57			19 06
Abercynon	d					18 19					18 34									19 04			
Penrhiwceiber	d					18 24																	
Mountain Ash	a					18 28																	
	d					18 33																	
Fernhill	d					18 35																	
Cwmbach	d					18 39																	
Aberdare	a					18 46																	
Quakers Yard	d										18 39									19 09			
Merthyr Vale	a										18 44									19 14			
	d										18 47									19 17			
Troed Y Rhiw	d										18 50									19 20			
Pentre-bach	d										18 53									19 23			
Merthyr Tydfil	a										19 01									19 31			
Trehafod	d			18 11										18 41									19 11
Porth	a			18 14										18 44									19 14
	d			18 15										18 45									19 15
Dinas Rhondda	d			18 19										18 49									19 19
Tonypandy	d			18 21										18 51									19 21
Llwynypia	d			18 23										18 53									19 23
Ystrad Rhondda	a			18 26										18 56									19 26
	d			18 29										18 59									19 29
Ton Pentre	d			18 31										19 01									19 31
Treorchy	d			18 34										19 04									19 34
Ynyswen	d			18 37										19 07									19 37
Treherbert	a			18 43										19 13									19 43

When events are being held at the Millenium Stadium, services are subject to alteration. Please check times before travelling.

Table 130

Saturdays
until 10 September

Bridgend, Barry Island, Barry, Penarth and Cardiff - Coryton, Rhymney, Pontypridd, Merthyr, Aberdare and Treherbert

		AW	AW	AW	AW	AW	AW	AW	AW	AW	AW	AW	AW	AW	AW	AW	AW	AW	AW	AW	AW	AW	AW
Bridgend	d		17 42															18 42					
Llantwit Major	d		17 56															18 56					
Rhoose Cardiff Int Airport	d		18 06															19 06					
Barry Island	d						18 25					18 40		18 55								19 25	
Barry	d		18 15				18 30					18 45		19 00				19 15				19 30	
Barry Docks	d		18 19				18 34					18 49		19 04				19 19				19 34	
Cadoxton	d		18 22				18 37					18 52		19 07				19 22				19 37	
Dinas Powys	d		18 26				18 41					18 56		19 11				19 26				19 41	
Eastbrook	d		18 28				18 43					18 58		19 13				19 28				19 43	
Cogan	d		18 30				18 45					19 00		19 15				19 30				19 45	
Penarth	d			18 32					18 47						19 17								19 47
Dingle Road	d			18 34					18 49						19 19								19 49
Grangetown	d		18 34	18 38			18 49		18 53			19 04		19 19	19 23			19 34				19 49	19 54
Cardiff Central	a		18 39	18 45			18 55		18 59			19 09		19 24	19 29			19 39				19 55	19 59
	d	18 36	18 41			18 51			19 01		19 06	19 11		19 26	19 31		19 36	19 41		19 51		20 01	20 06
Cardiff Bay	d				18 42			18 54		19 06			19 18			19 30			19 42		19 54		
Cardiff Queen Street	a		18 44		18 46	18 54		18 58	19 04	19 10	19 09	19 14	19 22	19 29	19 33	19 34		19 44	19 46	19 54	19 58	20 04	20 09
	d		18 50			18 55			19 05		19 10	19 15		19 30	19 35			19 45		19 55		20 06	20 10
Heath Low Level	d					19 00														20 00			
Ty Glas	d					19 03														20 03			
Birchgrove	d					19 04														20 04			
Rhiwbina	d					19 06														20 06			
Whitchurch (Cardiff)	d					19 08														20 08			
Coryton	a					19 13														20 13			
Heath High Level	d								19 10						19 40							20 10	
Llanishen	d								19 13						19 43							20 13	
Lisvane & Thornhill	d								19 15						19 45							20 16	
Caerphilly	d								19a23						19 51							20a27	
Aber	d														19 53								
Llanbradach	d														19 57								
Ystrad Mynach	d														20 02								
Hengoed	d														20 05								
Pengam	d														20 08								
Gilfach Fargoed	d														20 11								
Bargoed	a														20 15								
	d														20 16								
Brithdir	d														20 20								
Tir-phil	d														20 23								
Pontlottyn	d														20 27								
Rhymney	a														20 33								
Cathays	d		18 52								19 13	19 18		19 33				19 48					20 13
Llandaf	d		18 56								19 17	19 22		19 37				19 52					20 17
Ninian Park	d	18 40															19 40						
Waun-gron Park	d	18 43															19 43						
Fairwater	d	18 45															19 45						
Danescourt	d	18 47															19 47						
Radyr	a	18 54	18 58								19 20	19 25		19 40			19 54	19 55					20 20
	d		18 58								19 20	19 25		19 40				19 55					20 20
Taffs Well	d		19 03								19 24	19 29		19 44				19 59					20 24
Trefforest Estate	d													19 48									
Trefforest	d		19 10								19 31	19 36		19 52				20 06					20 31
Pontypridd	a		19 13								19 34	19 39		19 55				20 09					20 34
	d		19 14								19 36	19 41		19 57				20 11					20 36
Abercynon	d		19 21									19 49		20 04				20 21					
Penrhiwceiber	d		19 26									19 54						20 26					
Mountain Ash	a		19 30									19 56						20 30					
	d		19 33									20 03						20 33					
Fernhill	d		19 35									20 05						20 35					
Cwmbach	d		19 39									20 09						20 39					
Aberdare	a		19 46									20 16						20 46					
Quakers Yard	d													20 08									
Merthyr Vale	a													20 13									
	d													20 15									
Troed Y Rhiw	d													20 19									
Pentre-bach	d													20 22									
Merthyr Tydfil	a													20 30									
Trehafod	d										19 41												20 41
Porth	a										19 44												20 44
	d										19 45												20 45
Dinas Rhondda	d										19 49												20 49
Tonypandy	d										19 51												20 51
Llwynypia	d										19 53												20 53
Ystrad Rhondda	a										19 56												20 56
	d										19 59												20 59
Ton Pentre	d										20 01												21 01
Treorchy	d										20 04												21 04
Ynyswen	d										20 07												21 07
Treherbert	a										20 13												21 13

When events are being held at the Millenium Stadium, services are subject to alteration. Please check times before travelling.

Table 130

Bridgend, Barry Island, Barry, Penarth and Cardiff - Coryton, Rhymney, Pontypridd, Merthyr, Aberdare and Treherbert

		AW		AW	AW	AW	AW	AW	AW	AW	AW	AW		AW	AW	AW	AW	AW	AW	AW	AW	AW		AW	AW
Bridgend	d								19 42															20 42	
Llantwit Major	d								19 56															20 56	
Rhoose Cardiff Int Airport ✈	d								20 06															21 06	
Barry Island	d				19 55													20 55							
Barry 3	d				20 00				20 15									21 00						21 15	
Barry Docks	d				20 04				20 19									21 04						21 19	
Cadoxton	d				20 07				20 22									21 07						21 22	
Dinas Powys	d				20 11				20 26									21 11						21 26	
Eastbrook	d				20 13				20 28									21 13						21 28	
Cogan	d				20 15				20 30									21 15						21 30	
Penarth	d					20 19								20 47								21 20			
Dingle Road	d					20 21								20 49								21 22			
Grangetown	d				20 19	20 25			20 34					20 53				21 19				21 26		21 34	
Cardiff Central 7	a				20 24	20 31			20 39					20 59				21 24				21 37		21 39	
	d				20 26	20 31		20 36	20 41		20 51			21 01		21 06		21 26		21 31	21 36			21 41	
Cardiff Bay	d	20 06		20 18			20 30			20 42		20 54			21 06		21 18		21 30						21 42
Cardiff Queen Street 3	a	20 10		20 22	20 29	20 34	20 34		20 44	20 46	20 54	20 58		21 04	21 10	21 09	21 22	21 29	21 34	21 34				21 44	21 46
	d				20 30	20 35			20 45		20 55			21 05		21 10		21 30		21 35				21 45	
Heath Low Level	d										21 00														
Ty Glas	d										21 03														
Birchgrove	d										21 04														
Rhiwbina	d										21 06														
Whitchurch (Cardiff)	d										21 08														
Coryton	a										21 13														
Heath High Level	d					20 40								21 10						21 40					
Llanishen	d					20 43								21 13						21 43					
Lisvane & Thornhill	d					20 45								21 15						21 45					
Caerphilly 3	d					20 51								21a30						21 51					
Aber	d					20 53														21 53					
Llanbradach	d					20 57														21 57					
Ystrad Mynach 3	d					21 02														22 02					
Hengoed	d					21 05														22 05					
Pengam	d					21 08														22 08					
Gilfach Fargoed	d					21 11														22 11					
Bargoed	a					21 15														22 15					
	d					21 16														22 16					
Brithdir	d					21 20														22 20					
Tir-phil	d					21 23														22 23					
Pontlottyn	d					21 27														22 27					
Rhymney 3	a					21 34														22 34					
Cathays	d				20 33				20 48							21 13		21 33						21 48	
Llandaf	d				20 37				20 52							21 17		21 37						21 52	
Ninian Park	d							20 40													21 40				
Waun-gron Park	d							20 43													21 43				
Fairwater	d							20 45													21 45				
Danescourt	d							20 47													21 47				
Radyr 3	a				20 40			20 54	20 55							21 20		21 40			21 54			21 55	
	d				20 40				20 55							21 20		21 40						21 55	
Taffs Well 3	d				20 44				20 59							21 24		21 44						21 59	
Trefforest Estate	d				20 48													21 48							
Trefforest	d				20 52				21 06							21 31		21 52						22 06	
Pontypridd 3	a				20 55				21 09							21 34		21 55						22 09	
	d				20 57				21 11							21 36		21 57						22 11	
Abercynon	d				21 04				21 19									22 04						22 19	
Penrhiwceiber	d								21 24															22 24	
Mountain Ash	a								21 28															22 28	
	d								21 29															22 29	
Fernhill	d								21 31															22 31	
Cwmbach	d								21 35															22 35	
Aberdare 3	a								21 42															22 42	
Quakers Yard	d				21 08													22 08							
Merthyr Vale	a				21 13													22 13							
	d				21 15													22 15							
Troed Y Rhiw	d				21 19													22 19							
Pentre-bach	d				21 22													22 22							
Merthyr Tydfil	a				21 30													22 30							
Trehafod	d															21 41									
Porth	a															21 44									
	d															21 45									
Dinas Rhondda	d															21 49									
Tonypandy	d															21 51									
Llwynypia	d															21 53									
Ystrad Rhondda	a															21 56									
	d															21 59									
Ton Pentre	d															22 01									
Treorchy	d															22 04									
Ynyswen	d															22 07									
Treherbert	a															22 13									

When events are being held at the Millenium Stadium, services are subject to alteration. Please check times before travelling.

Table 130

Saturdays
until 10 September

Bridgend, Barry Island, Barry, Penarth and Cardiff - Coryton, Rhymney, Pontypridd, Merthyr, Aberdare and Treherbert

		AW	AW	AW	AW	AW	AW	AW		AW	AW	AW	AW	AW	AW	AW	AW	AW		AW	AW	AW	AW	AW	AW
Bridgend	d											21 42										22 42			
Llantwit Major	d											21 56										22 56			
Rhoose Cardiff Int Airport ✈	d											22 06										23 06			
Barry Island	d							21 55												22 44					
Barry 3	d							22 00				22 15								22 48		23 15			
Barry Docks	d							22 04				22 19								22 52		23 19			
Cadoxton	d							22 07				22 22								22 55		23 22			
Dinas Powys	d							22 11				22 26								22 59		23 26			
Eastbrook	d							22 13				22 28								23 01		23 28			
Cogan	d							22 15				22 30								23 03		23 30			
Penarth	d		21 47								22 20						22 47				23 26				
Dingle Road	d		21 49								22 22						22 49				23 28				
Grangetown	d		21 53					22 19			22 26	22 34					22 53			23 07	23 32	23 34			
Cardiff Central 7	a		21 59					22 24			22 31	22 39					23 00			23 12	23 40	23 42			
	d		22 01		22 06		22 21	22 26			22 35	22 41		22 46			23 15			23 26					
Cardiff Bay	d	21 54		22 06		22 18				22 30			22 42		22 54	23 06		23 18					23 30	23 42	23 54
Cardiff Queen Street 3	a	21 58	22 04	22 10	22 09	22 22	22 24	22 29		22 34	22 38	22 44	22 46	22 49	22 58	23 10	23 18	23 22		23 29			23 34	23 46	23 58
	d		22 05		22 10		22 25	22 30			22 39	22 45		22 50			23 19			23 30					
Heath Low Level	d						22 30																		
Ty Glas	d						22 33																		
Birchgrove	d						22 34																		
Rhiwbina	d						22 36																		
Whitchurch (Cardiff)	d						22 38																		
Coryton	a						22 43																		
Heath High Level	d		22 10								22 44						23 24								
Llanishen	d		22 13								22 47						23 27								
Lisvane & Thornhill	d		22 15								22 49						23 29								
Caerphilly 3	d		22a23								22 55						23 35								
Aber	d										22 57						23 37								
Llanbradach	d										23 01						23 41								
Ystrad Mynach 3	d										23 06						23a50								
Hengoed	d										23 09														
Pengam	d										23 12														
Gilfach Fargoed	d										23 15														
Bargoed	a										23 19														
	d										23 20														
Brithdir	d										23 24														
Tir-phil	d										23 27														
Pontlottyn	d										23 31														
Rhymney 3	a										23 37														
Cathays	d				22 13			22 33				22 48		22 53						23 33					
Llandaf	d				22 17			22 37				22 52		22 57						23 37					
Ninian Park	d																								
Waun-gron Park	d																								
Fairwater	d																								
Danescourt	d																								
Radyr 3	a				22 20			22 40				22 55		22 59						23 40					
	d				22 20			22 40				22 55		22 59						23 40					
Taffs Well 3	d				22 24			22 44				22 59		23 03						23 44					
Trefforest Estate	d							22 48																	
Trefforest	d				22 31			22 52				23 06		23 10						23 52					
Pontypridd 3	a				22 34			22 55				23 09		23 14						23 58					
	d				22 36			22 57				23 11		23 15											
Abercynon	d							23 04				23 19													
Penrhiwceiber	d											23 24													
Mountain Ash	a											23 28													
	d											23 29													
Fernhill	d											23 31													
Cwmbach	d											23 35													
Aberdare 3	a											23 42													
Quakers Yard	d							23 08																	
Merthyr Vale	a							23 13																	
	d							23 15																	
Troed Y Rhiw	d							23 19																	
Pentre-bach	d							23 22																	
Merthyr Tydfil	a							23 30																	
Trehafod	d				22 41									23 20											
Porth	a				22 44									23 23											
	d				22 45									23 24											
Dinas Rhondda	d				22 49									23 28											
Tonypandy	d				22 51									23 30											
Llwynypia	d				22 53									23 32											
Ystrad Rhondda	a				22 56									23 35											
	d				22 59									23 38											
Ton Pentre	d				23 01									23 40											
Treorchy	d				23 04									23 43											
Ynyswen	d				23 07									23 46											
Treherbert	a				23 13									23 52											

When events are being held at the Millenium Stadium, services are subject to alteration. Please check times before travelling.

Table 130

Saturdays
from 17 September

Bridgend, Barry Island, Barry, Penarth and Cardiff - Coryton, Rhymney, Pontypridd, Merthyr, Aberdare and Treherbert

		AW		AW	AW	AW	AW	AW	AW	AW	AW	AW	AW	AW	AW	AW	AW	AW	AW	AW	AW	AW	AW
Bridgend	d										05 42												
Llantwit Major	d										05 56												
Rhoose Cardiff Int Airport ✈	d										06 06												
Barry Island	d								05 52							06 25							
Barry ■	d								05 57		06 15					06 30							
Barry Docks	d								06 01		06 19					06 34							
Cadoxton	d								06 04		06 22					06 37							
Dinas Powys	d								06 08		06 26					06 41							
Eastbrook	d								06 10		06 28					06 43							
Cogan	d								06 12		06 30					06 45							
Penarth	d						06 02						06 32								07 02		
Dingle Road	d						06 04						06 34								07 04		
Grangetown	d						06 08		06 16		06 34		06 38			06 49					07 08		
Cardiff Central ■	a						06 13		06 21		06 39		06 44			06 54					07 14		
	d	05 26		05 46	05 56	06 11	06 15	06 19	06 26	06 36	06 41		06 46	06 51		06 56		07 06	07 06	07 11	07 16		07 21
Cardiff Bay	d											06 42			06 54		07 06					07 18	
Cardiff Queen Street ■	a	05 29		05 49	05 59	06 14	06 19	06 24	06 29	06 39	06 44	06 46	06 49	06 54	06 58	06 59	07 10	07 09		07 14	07 19	07 22	07 24
	d	05 30		05 50	06 00	06 15	06 20	06 25	06 30	06 40	06 45		06 50	06 55		07 00		07 10		07 15	07 20		07 25
Heath Low Level	d							06 30						07 00									07 30
Ty Glas	d							06 33						07 03									07 33
Birchgrove	d							06 34						07 04									07 34
Rhiwbina	d							06 36						07 06									07 36
Whitchurch (Cardiff)	d							06 38						07 08									07 38
Coryton	a							06 44						07 14									07 44
Heath High Level	d			05 54			06 25						06 55								07 25		
Llanishen	d			05 57			06 28						06 58								07 28		
Lisvane & Thornhill	d			06 00			06 30						07 00								07 30		
Caerphilly ■	d			06a09			06 36						07 06								07 36		
Aber	d						06 38						07 08								07 38		
Llanbradach	d						06 42						07 12								07 42		
Ystrad Mynach ■	d						06 47						07 17								07 47		
Hengoed	d						06 50						07 20								07 50		
Pengam	d						06 53						07 23								07 53		
Gilfach Fargoed	d																						
Bargoed	a						07 02						07 32								08 02		
	d																						
Brithdir	d																						
Tir-phil	d																						
Pontlottyn	d																						
Rhymney ■	a																						
Cathays	d	05 33			06 03	06 18			06 33	06 43	06 48					07 03		07 13		07 18			
Llandaf	d	05 37			06 07	06 22			06 37	06 47	06 52					07 07		07 17		07 22			
Ninian Park	d																		07 10				
Waun-gron Park	d																		07 14				
Fairwater	d																		07 16				
Danescourt	d																		07 19				
Radyr ■	a	05 39			06 10	06 24			06 40	06 50	06 54					07 10		07 20	07 27	07 25			
	d	05 40			06 10	06 24			06 40	06 50	06 55					07 10		07 20		07 25			
Taffs Well ■	d	05 43			06 14	06 28			06 44	06 54	06 59					07 14		07 24		07 29			
Trefforest Estate	d	05 47			06 18				06 48							07 18							
Trefforest	d	05 52			06 22	06 35			06 52	07 01	07 06					07 22		07 31		07 36			
Pontypridd ■	a	05 55			06 25	06 38			06 55	07 04	07 09					07 25		07 34		07 39			
	d	05 57	06 11		06 27	06 41			06 57	07 06	07 11					07 27		07 36		07 41			
Abercynon	d	06 04	06 19		06 34	06 49			07 04		07 19					07 34				07 49			
Penrhiwceiber	d		06 24			06 55					07 25									07 55			
Mountain Ash	a		06 28			06 58					07 28									07 58			
	d		06 34			07 04					07 34									08 04			
Fernhill	d		06 37			07 07					07 37									08 07			
Cwmbach	d		06 41			07 11					07 41									08 11			
Aberdare ■	a		06 49			07 19					07 49									08 19			
Quakers Yard	d	06 09			06 39				07 09							07 39							
Merthyr Vale	a	06 14			06 44				07 14							07 44							
	d	06 17			06 47				07 17							07 47							
Troed Y Rhiw	d	06 21			06 51				07 21							07 51							
Pentre-bach	d	06 24			06 54				07 24							07 54							
Merthyr Tydfil	a	06 33			07 03				07 33							08 03							
Trehafod	d									07 11								07 41					
Porth	a									07 14								07 44					
	d									07 15								07 45					
Dinas Rhondda	d									07 19								07 49					
Tonypandy	d									07 21								07 51					
Llwynypia	d									07 23								07 53					
Ystrad Rhondda	a									07 26								07 56					
	d									07 29								07 59					
Ton Pentre	d									07 31								08 01					
Treorchy	d									07 34								08 04					
Ynyswen	d									07 37								08 07					
Treherbert	a									07 44								08 14					

When events are being held at the Millenium Stadium, services are subject to alteration. Please check times before travelling.

Table 130

Saturdays
from 17 September

Bridgend, Barry Island, Barry, Penarth and Cardiff - Coryton, Rhymney, Pontypridd, Merthyr, Aberdare and Treherbert

		AW	AW	AW	AW	AW	AW	AW	AW	AW	AW	AW	AW	AW	AW	AW	AW	AW	AW	AW	AW	AW	AW
Bridgend	d						06 42																
Llantwit Major	d						06 56																
Rhoose Cardiff Int Airport ✈	d						07 06																
Barry Island	d	06 55										07 25					07 40				07 55		
Barry ■	d	07 00					07 15					07 30					07 45				08 00		
Barry Docks	d	07 04					07 19					07 34					07 49				08 04		
Cadoxton	d	07 07					07 22					07 37					07 52				08 07		
Dinas Powys	d	07 11					07 26					07 41					07 56				08 11		
Eastbrook	d	07 13					07 28					07 43					07 58				08 13		
Cogan	d	07 15					07 30					07 45					08 00				08 15		
Penarth	d		07 17						07 32				07 47					08 02				08 17	
Dingle Road	d		07 19						07 34				07 49					08 04				08 19	
Grangetown	d	07 19	07 23				07 34		07 38			07 49	07 53				08 04	08 08			08 19	08 23	
Cardiff Central ■	a	07 24	07 29				07 39		07 44			07 55	07 59				08 09	08 14			08 24	08 29	
	d	07 26	07 31		07 36	07 36	07 41		07 46	07 51		07 56	08 01		08 06	08 06	08 11	08 16		08 21	08 26	08 31	
Cardiff Bay	d			07 30				07 42			07 54			08 06					08 18				08 30
Cardiff Queen Street ■	a	07 29	07 34	07 34	07 39		07 44	07 46	07 49	07 54	07 58	07 59	08 04	08 10	08 09		08 14	08 19	08 22	08 24	08 29	08 34	08 34
	d	07 30	07 35		07 40		07 45		07 50	07 55		08 00	08 05		08 10		08 15	08 20		08 25	08 30	08 35	
Heath Low Level	d									08 00										08 30			
Ty Glas	d									08 03										08 33			
Birchgrove	d									08 04										08 34			
Rhiwbina	d									08 06										08 36			
Whitchurch (Cardiff)	d									08 08										08 38			
Coryton	a									08 14										08 44			
Heath High Level	d		07 40						07 55				08 10					08 25				08 40	
Llanishen	d		07 43						07 58				08 13					08 28				08 43	
Lisvane & Thornhill	d		07 45						08 00				08 15					08 30				08 45	
Caerphilly ■	d		07 51						08 06				08 21					08 36				08 51	
Aber	d		07 53						08 08				08 23					08 38				08 53	
Llanbradach	d		07 57						08 12				08 27					08 42				08 57	
Ystrad Mynach ■	d		08 02						08 17				08 32					08 47				09 07	
Hengoed	d		08 05						08 20				08 35					08 50				09 10	
Pengam	d		08 08						08 23				08 38					08 53				09 13	
Gilfach Fargoed	d												08 41										
Bargoed	a		08 13						08 32				08 49					08 58				09 22	
	d		08 14															08 59					
Brithdir	d		08 18															09 03					
Tir-phil	d		08 21															09 06					
Pontlottyn	d		08 25															09 10					
Rhymney ■	a		08 32															09 17					
Cathays	d	07 33			07 43		07 48					08 03			08 13		08 18				08 33		
Llandaf	d	07 37			07 47		07 52					08 07			08 17		08 22				08 37		
Ninian Park	d					07 40										08 10							
Waun-gron Park	d					07 44										08 14							
Fairwater	d					07 46										08 16							
Danescourt	d					07 49										08 19							
Radyr ■	a	07 40			07 50	07 57	07 55					08 10			08 20	08 27	08 25				08 40		
	d	07 40			07 50		07 55					08 10			08 20		08 25				08 40		
Taffs Well ■	d	07 44			07 54		07 59					08 14			08 24		08 29				08 44		
Trefforest Estate	d	07 48										08 18									08 48		
Trefforest	d	07 52			08 01		08 06					08 22			08 31		08 36				08 52		
Pontypridd ■	a	07 55			08 04		08 09					08 25			08 34		08 39				08 55		
	d	07 57			08 06		08 11					08 27			08 36		08 41				08 57		
Abercynon	d	08 04					08 19					08 34					08 49				09 04		
Penrhiwceiber	d						08 25										08 55						
Mountain Ash	a						08 28										08 58						
	d						08 34										09 04						
Fernhill	d						08 37										09 07						
Cwmbach	d						08 41										09 11						
Aberdare ■	a						08 49										09 19						
Quakers Yard	d	08 09										08 39									09 09		
Merthyr Vale	a	08 14										08 44									09 14		
	d	08 17										08 47									09 17		
Troed Y Rhiw	d	08 21										08 51									09 21		
Pentre-bach	d	08 24										08 54									09 24		
Merthyr Tydfil	a	08 33										09 03									09 33		
Trehafod	d				08 11										08 41								
Porth	a				08 14										08 44								
	d				08 15										08 45								
Dinas Rhondda	d				08 19										08 49								
Tonypandy	d				08 21										08 51								
Llwynypia	d				08 23										08 53								
Ystrad Rhondda	a				08 26										08 56								
	d				08 29										08 59								
Ton Pentre	d				08 31										09 01								
Treorchy	d				08 34										09 04								
Ynyswen	d				08 37										09 07								
Treherbert	a				08 44										09 14								

When events are being held at the Millenium Stadium, services are subject to alteration. Please check times before travelling.

Table 130

Saturdays from 17 September

Bridgend, Barry Island, Barry, Penarth and Cardiff - Coryton, Rhymney, Pontypridd, Merthyr, Aberdare and Treherbert

Station		AW		AW	AW	AW	AW	AW	AW	AW	AW	AW		AW	AW	AW	AW	AW	AW	AW	AW	AW		AW	AW
Bridgend	d				07 42																				
Llantwit Major	d				07 56																				
Rhoose Cardiff Int Airport ✈	d				08 06																				
Barry Island	d									08 25						08 40				08 55					
Barry 3	d				08 15					08 30						08 45				09 00					
Barry Docks	d				08 19					08 34						08 49				09 04					
Cadoxton	d				08 22					08 37						08 52				09 07					
Dinas Powys	d				08 26					08 41						08 56				09 11					
Eastbrook	d				08 28					08 43						08 58				09 13					
Cogan	d				08 30					08 45						09 00				09 15					
Penarth	d						08 32				08 47										09 17				
Dingle Road	d						08 34				08 49										09 19				
Grangetown	d				08 34		08 38			08 49	08 53					09 04				09 19	09 23				
Cardiff Central 7	a				08 39		08 44			08 54	08 59					09 09				09 24	09 29				
	d	08 36		08 36	08 41		08 46	08 51		08 56	09 01			09 06	09 06	09 11	09 16		09 21	09 26	09 31			09 36	09 36
Cardiff Bay	d					08 42			08 54			09 06						09 18				09 30			
Cardiff Queen Street 3	a	08 39			08 44	08 46	08 49	08 54	08 58	08 59	09 04	09 10		09 09		09 14	09 19	09 22	09 24	09 29	09 34	09 34		09 39	
	d	08 40			08 45		08 50	08 55		09 00	09 05			09 10		09 15	09 20		09 25	09 30	09 35			09 40	
Heath Low Level	d							09 00											09 30						
Ty Glas	d							09 03											09 33						
Birchgrove	d							09 04											09 34						
Rhiwbina	d							09 06											09 36						
Whitchurch (Cardiff)	d							09 08											09 38						
Coryton	a							09 14											09 44						
Heath High Level	d						08 55				09 10						09 25				09 40				
Llanishen	d						08 58				09 13						09 28				09 43				
Lisvane & Thornhill	d						09 00				09 15						09 30				09 45				
Caerphilly 3	d						09 06				09 21						09 36				09 51				
Aber	d						09 08				09 23						09 38				09 53				
Llanbradach	d						09 12				09 27						09 42				09 57				
Ystrad Mynach 3	d						09a22				09 32						09 47				10 07				
Hengoed	d										09 35						09 50				10 10				
Pengam	d										09 38						09 53				10 13				
Gilfach Fargoed	d										09 41														
Bargoed	a										09 49						09 58				10 22				
	d																09 59								
Brithdir	d																10 03								
Tir-phil	d																10 06								
Pontlottyn	d																10 10								
Rhymney 3	a																10 17								
Cathays	d	08 43			08 48					09 03				09 13		09 18				09 33				09 43	
Llandaf	d	08 47			08 52					09 07				09 17		09 22				09 37				09 47	
Ninian Park	d			08 40											09 10										09 40
Waun-gron Park	d			08 44											09 14										09 44
Fairwater	d			08 46											09 16										09 46
Danescourt	d			08 49											09 19										09 49
Radyr 3	a	08 50		08 57	08 55					09 10				09 20	09 27	09 25				09 40				09 50	09 57
	d	08 50			08 55					09 10				09 20		09 25				09 40				09 50	
Taffs Well 3	d	08 54			08 59					09 14				09 24		09 29				09 44				09 54	
Trefforest Estate	d									09 18										09 48					
Trefforest	d	09 01			09 06					09 22				09 31		09 36				09 52				10 01	
Pontypridd 3	a	09 04			09 09					09 25				09 34		09 39				09 55				10 04	
	d	09 06			09 11					09 27				09 36		09 41				09 57				10 06	
Abercynon	d				09 19					09 34						09 49				10 04					
Penrhiwceiber	d				09 25											09 55									
Mountain Ash	a				09 28											09 58									
	d				09 34											10 04									
Fernhill	d				09 37											10 07									
Cwmbach	d				09 41											10 11									
Aberdare 3	a				09 49											10 19									
Quakers Yard	d									09 39										10 09					
Merthyr Vale	a									09 44										10 14					
	d									09 47										10 17					
Troed Y Rhiw	d									09 51										10 21					
Pentre-bach	d									09 54										10 24					
Merthyr Tydfil	a									10 03										10 33					
Trehafod	d	09 11												09 41										10 11	
Porth	a	09 14												09 44										10 14	
	d	09 15												09 45										10 15	
Dinas Rhondda	d	09 19												09 49										10 19	
Tonypandy	d	09 21												09 51										10 21	
Llwynypia	d	09 23												09 53										10 23	
Ystrad Rhondda	a	09 26												09 56										10 26	
	d	09 29												09 59										10 29	
Ton Pentre	d	09 31												10 01										10 31	
Treorchy	d	09 34												10 04										10 34	
Ynyswen	d	09 37												10 07										10 37	
Treherbert	a	09 44												10 14										10 44	

When events are being held at the Millenium Stadium, services are subject to alteration. Please check times before travelling.

Table 130

Saturdays from 17 September

Bridgend, Barry Island, Barry, Penarth and Cardiff - Coryton, Rhymney, Pontypridd, Merthyr, Aberdare and Treherbert

Station		AW	AW	AW	AW	AW	AW	AW		AW	AW	AW	AW	AW	AW	AW	AW	AW		AW	AW	AW	AW	AW	AW
Bridgend	d	08 42																						09 42	
Llantwit Major	d	08 56																						09 56	
Rhoose Cardiff Int Airport ✈	d	09 06																						10 06	
Barry Island	d						09 25							09 40				09 55							
Barry 3	d	09 15					09 30							09 45				10 00						10 15	
Barry Docks	d	09 19					09 34							09 49				10 04						10 19	
Cadoxton	d	09 22					09 37							09 52				10 07						10 22	
Dinas Powys	d	09 26					09 41							09 56				10 11						10 26	
Eastbrook	d	09 28					09 43							09 58				10 13						10 28	
Cogan	d	09 30					09 45							10 00				10 15						10 30	
Penarth	d			09 32				09 47							10 02					10 17					
Dingle Road	d			09 34				09 49							10 04					10 19					
Grangetown	d	09 34		09 38			09 49	09 53						10 04	10 08			10 19		10 23				10 34	
Cardiff Central 7	a	09 39		09 44			09 54	09 59						10 09	10 14			10 24		10 29				10 42	
	d	09 41		09 46	09 51		09 56	10 01			10 06	10 06		10 11	10 16		10 21	10 26		10 31		10 36	10 36		
Cardiff Bay	d		09 42			09 54				10 06						10 18					10 30				10 42
Cardiff Queen Street 3	a	09 44	09 46	09 49	09 54	09 58	09 59	10 04		10 10	10 09			10 14	10 19	10 22	10 24	10 29		10 34	10 34	10 39			10 46
	d	09 45		09 50	09 55		10 00	10 05			10 10			10 15	10 20		10 25	10 30		10 35		10 40			
Heath Low Level	d				10 00												10 30								
Ty Glas	d				10 03												10 33								
Birchgrove	d				10 04												10 34								
Rhiwbina	d				10 06												10 36								
Whitchurch (Cardiff)	d				10 08												10 38								
Coryton	a				10 14												10 44								
Heath High Level	d			09 55				10 10							10 25					10 40					
Llanishen	d			09 58				10 13							10 28					10 43					
Lisvane & Thornhill	d			10 00				10 15							10 30					10 45					
Caerphilly 3	d			10 06				10 21							10 36					10 51					
Aber	d			10 08				10 23							10 38					10 53					
Llanbradach	d			10 12				10 27							10 42					10 57					
Ystrad Mynach 3	d			10a22				10 32							10 47					11 07					
Hengoed	d							10 35							10 50					11 10					
Pengam	d							10 38							10 53					11 13					
Gilfach Fargoed	d							10 41																	
Bargoed	a							10 49							10 58					11 22					
	d														10 59										
Brithdir	d														11 03										
Tir-phil	d														11 06										
Pontlottyn	d														11 10										
Rhymney 3	a														11 17										
Cathays	d	09 48					10 03				10 13			10 18				10 33				10 43			
Llandaf	d	09 52					10 07				10 17			10 22				10 37				10 47			
Ninian Park	d											10 10											10 40		
Waun-gron Park	d											10 14											10 44		
Fairwater	d											10 16											10 46		
Danescourt	d											10 19											10 49		
Radyr 3	a	09 55					10 10				10 20	10 27		10 25				10 40				10 50	10 57		
	d	09 55					10 10				10 20			10 25				10 40				10 50			
Taffs Well 3	d	09 59					10 14				10 24			10 29				10 44				10 54			
Trefforest Estate	d																	10 48							
Trefforest	d	10 06					10 22				10 31			10 36				10 52				11 01			
Pontypridd 3	a	10 09					10 30				10 34			10 39				10 55				11 04			
	d	10 11									10 36		10 35	10 41				10 57				11 06			
Abercynon	d	10 19											10 41	10 49				11 04							
Penrhiwceiber	d	10 25												10 55											
Mountain Ash	a	10 28												10 58											
	d	10 34												11 04											
Fernhill	d	10 37												11 07											
Cwmbach	d	10 41												11 11											
Aberdare 3	a	10 49												11 19											
Quakers Yard	d												10 45					11 09							
Merthyr Vale	a												10 50					11 14							
	d												10 52					11 17							
Troed Y Rhiw	d												10 56					11 21							
Pentre-bach	d												10 59					11 24							
Merthyr Tydfil	a												11 08					11 33							
Trehafod	d										10 41											11 11			
Porth	a										10 44											11 14			
	d										10 45											11 15			
Dinas Rhondda	d										10 49											11 19			
Tonypandy	d										10 51											11 21			
Llwynypia	d										10 53											11 23			
Ystrad Rhondda	a										10 56											11 26			
	d										10 59											11 29			
Ton Pentre	d										11 01											11 31			
Treorchy	d										11 04											11 34			
Ynyswen	d										11 07											11 37			
Treherbert	a										11 14											11 44			

When events are being held at the Millenium Stadium, services are subject to alteration. Please check times before travelling.

Bridgend, Barry Island, Barry, Penarth and Cardiff - Coryton, Rhymney, Pontypridd, Merthyr, Aberdare and Treherbert

		AW	AW	AW	AW	AW	AW	AW	AW	AW	AW	AW	AW	AW	AW	AW	AW	AW	AW	AW	AW	AW
Bridgend	d																			10 42		
Llantwit Major	d																			10 56		
Rhoose Cardiff Int Airport ✈	d																			11 06		
Barry Island	d					10 25					10 40				10 55							
Barry 3	d					10 30					10 45				11 00					11 15		
Barry Docks	d					10 34					10 49				11 04					11 19		
Cadoxton	d					10 37					10 52				11 07					11 22		
Dinas Powys	d					10 41					10 56				11 11					11 26		
Eastbrook	d					10 43					10 58				11 13					11 28		
Cogan	d					10 45					11 00				11 15					11 30		
Penarth	d	10 32						10 47				11 02				11 17						11 32
Dingle Road	d	10 34						10 49				11 04				11 19						11 34
Grangetown	d	10 38				10 49		10 53			11 04	11 08			11 19	11 23				11 34		11 38
Cardiff Central 7	a	10 44				10 54		10 59			11 09	11 14			11 24	11 29				11 38		11 44
	d	10 46	10 51		10 51	10 56		11 01	11 06		11 11	11 16		11 21	11 26	11 31		11 36	11 36	11 40		11 46
Cardiff Bay	d			10 54						11 06			11 18				11 30				11 42	
Cardiff Queen Street 3	a	10 49	10 54	10 58		10 59		11 04		11 10	11 14	11 19	11 22	11 24	11 29	11 34	11 34	11 39		11 43	11 46	11 49
	d	10 50	10 55			11 00		11 05			11 15	11 20		11 25	11 30	11 35		11 40		11 44		11 50
Heath Low Level	d		11 00											11 30								
Ty Glas	d		11 03											11 33								
Birchgrove	d		11 04											11 34								
Rhiwbina	d		11 06											11 36								
Whitchurch (Cardiff)	d		11 08											11 38								
Coryton	a		11 14											11 44								
Heath High Level	d	10 55						11 10				11 25				11 40						11 55
Llanishen	d	10 58						11 13				11 28				11 43						11 58
Lisvane & Thornhill	d	11 00						11 15				11 30				11 45						12 00
Caerphilly 3	d	11 06						11 21				11 36				11 51						12 06
Aber	d	11 08						11 23				11 38				11 53						12 08
Llanbradach	d	11 12						11 27				11 42				11 57						12 12
Ystrad Mynach 3	d	11a22						11 32				11 47				12 07						12a22
Hengoed	d							11 35				11 50				12 10						
Pengam	d							11 38				11 53				12 13						
Gilfach Fargoed	d							11 41														
Bargoed	a							11 49				11 58				12 22						
	d											11 59										
Brithdir	d											12 03										
Tir-phil	d											12 06										
Pontlottyn	d											12 10										
Rhymney 3	a											12 17										
Cathays	d					11 03					11 18				11 33			11 43		11 48		
Llandaf	d					11 07					11 22				11 37			11 47		11 52		
Ninian Park	d								11 10										11 40			
Waun-gron Park	d								11 14										11 44			
Fairwater	d								11 16										11 46			
Danescourt	d						⟵		11 19										11 49			
Radyr 3	a				11 02	11 10	11 02		11 27		11 25				11 40			11 50	11 57	11 54		
	d				11 20	11 10	11 20				11 25				11 40			11 50		11 55		
Taffs Well 3	d				→	11 14	11 24				11 29				11 44			11 54		11 59		
Trefforest Estate	d					11 18									11 48							
Trefforest	d					11 22	11 31				11 36				11 52			12 01		12 06		
Pontypridd 3	a					11 25	11 34				11 39				11 55			12 04		12 09		
	d					11 27	11 36				11 41				11 57			12 06		12 11		
Abercynon	d					11 34					11 49				12 04					12 19		
Penrhiwceiber	d										11 55									12 25		
Mountain Ash	a										11 58									12 28		
	d										12 04									12 34		
Fernhill	d										12 07									12 37		
Cwmbach	d										12 11									12 41		
Aberdare 3	a										12 19									12 49		
Quakers Yard	d					11 39									12 09							
Merthyr Vale	a					11 44									12 14							
	d					11 47									12 17							
Troed Y Rhiw	d					11 51									12 21							
Pentre-bach	d					11 54									12 24							
Merthyr Tydfil	a					12 03									12 33							
Trehafod	d						11 41											12 11				
Porth	a						11 44											12 14				
	d						11 45											12 15				
Dinas Rhondda	d						11 49											12 19				
Tonypandy	d						11 51											12 21				
Llwynypia	d						11 53											12 23				
Ystrad Rhondda	a						11 56											12 26				
	d						11 59											12 29				
Ton Pentre	d						12 01											12 31				
Treorchy	d						12 04											12 34				
Ynyswen	d						12 07											12 37				
Treherbert	a						12 14											12 44				

When events are being held at the Millenium Stadium, services are subject to alteration. Please check times before travelling.

Bridgend, Barry Island, Barry, Penarth and Cardiff - Coryton, Rhymney, Pontypridd, Merthyr, Aberdare and Treherbert

		AW	AW	AW	AW	AW	AW	AW	AW	AW	AW	AW	AW	AW	AW	AW	AW	AW	AW	AW	AW	AW	AW
Bridgend	d																	11 42					
Llantwit Major	d																	11 56					
Rhoose Cardiff Int Airport ✈	d																	12 06					
Barry Island	d			11 25					11 40				11 55										12 25
Barry 3	d			11 30					11 45				12 00					12 15					12 30
Barry Docks	d			11 34					11 49				12 04					12 19					12 34
Cadoxton	d			11 37					11 52				12 07					12 22					12 37
Dinas Powys	d			11 41					11 56				12 11					12 26					12 41
Eastbrook	d			11 43					11 58				12 13					12 28					12 43
Cogan	d			11 45					12 00				12 15					12 30					12 45
Penarth	d				11 47					12 02				12 17						12 32			
Dingle Road	d				11 49					12 04				12 19						12 34			
Grangetown	d			11 49	11 53				12 04	12 08			12 19	12 23				12 34		12 38			12 49
Cardiff Central 7	a			11 54	12 00				12 09	12 14			12 24	12 29				12 39		12 44			12 54
	d	11 51		11 56	12 01		12 06	12 06	12 11	12 16		12 21	12 26	12 31		12 36	12 36	12 41		12 46	12 51		12 56
Cardiff Bay	d		11 54			12 06					12 18				12 30				12 42			12 54	
Cardiff Queen Street 3	a	11 54	11 58	11 59	12 04	12 10	12 09		12 14	12 19	12 22	12 24	12 29	12 34	12 34	12 39		12 44	12 46	12 49	12 54	12 58	12 59
	d	11 55		12 00	12 05		12 10		12 15	12 20		12 25	12 30	12 35		12 40		12 45		12 50	12 55		13 00
Heath Low Level	d	12 00										12 30									13 00		
Ty Glas	d	12 03										12 33									13 03		
Birchgrove	d	12 04										12 34									13 04		
Rhiwbina	d	12 06										12 36									13 06		
Whitchurch (Cardiff)	d	12 08										12 38									13 08		
Coryton	a	12 14										12 44									13 14		
Heath High Level	d				12 10					12 25				12 40						12 55			
Llanishen	d				12 13					12 28				12 43						12 58			
Lisvane & Thornhill	d				12 15					12 30				12 45						13 00			
Caerphilly 3	d				12 21					12 36				12 51						13 06			
Aber	d				12 23					12 38				12 53						13 08			
Llanbradach	d				12 27					12 42				12 57						13 12			
Ystrad Mynach 3	d				12 32					12 47				13 07						13a22			
Hengoed	d				12 35					12 50				13 10									
Pengam	d				12 38					12 53				13 13									
Gilfach Fargoed	d				12 41																		
Bargoed	a				12 49					12 58				13 22									
	d									12 59													
Brithdir	d									13 03													
Tir-phil	d									13 06													
Pontlottyn	d									13 10													
Rhymney 3	a									13 17													
Cathays	d			12 03			12 13		12 18				12 33			12 43		12 48					13 03
Llandaf	d			12 07			12 17		12 22				12 37			12 47		12 52					13 07
Ninian Park	d							12 10									12 40						
Waun-gron Park	d							12 14									12 44						
Fairwater	d							12 16									12 46						
Danescourt	d							12 19									12 49						
Radyr 3	a			12 10			12 20	12 27	12 25				12 40			12 50	12 57	12 55					13 10
	d			12 10			12 20		12 25				12 40			12 50		12 55					13 10
Taffs Well 3	d			12 14			12 24		12 29				12 44			12 54		12 59					13 14
Trefforest Estate	d			12 18									12 48										13 18
Trefforest	d			12 22			12 31		12 36				12 52			13 01		13 06					13 22
Pontypridd 3	a			12 25			12 34		12 42				12 55			13 04		13 09					13 25
	d			12 27			12 36						12 57			13 06		13 11					13 27
Abercynon	d			12 34									13 04					13 19					13 34
Penrhiwceiber	d																	13 25					
Mountain Ash	a																	13 28					
	d																	13 34					
Fernhill	d																	13 37					
Cwmbach	d																	13 41					
Aberdare 3	a																	13 49					
Quakers Yard	d			12 39									13 09										13 39
Merthyr Vale	a			12 44									13 14										13 44
	d			12 47									13 17										13 47
Troed Y Rhiw	d			12 51									13 21										13 51
Pentre-bach	d			12 54									13 24										13 54
Merthyr Tydfil	a			13 03									13 33										14 03
Trehafod	d						12 41									13 11							
Porth	a						12 44									13 14							
	d						12 45									13 15							
Dinas Rhondda	d						12 49									13 19							
Tonypandy	d						12 51									13 21							
Llwynypia	d						12 53									13 23							
Ystrad Rhondda	a						12 56									13 26							
	d						12 59									13 29							
Ton Pentre	d						13 01									13 31							
Treorchy	d						13 04									13 34							
Ynyswen	d						13 07									13 37							
Treherbert	a						13 14									13 44							

When events are being held at the Millenium Stadium, services are subject to alteration. Please check times before travelling.

Table 130

Saturdays from 17 September

Bridgend, Barry Island, Barry, Penarth and Cardiff - Coryton, Rhymney, Pontypridd, Merthyr, Aberdare and Treherbert

		AW	AW	AW	AW	AW		AW	AW	AW	AW	AW	AW	AW	AW	AW		AW	AW	AW	AW	AW	AW	AW	AW
Bridgend	d															12 42									
Llantwit Major	d															12 56									
Rhoose Cardiff Int Airport ✈	d															13 06									
Barry Island	d					12 40					12 55											13 25			
Barry	d					12 45					13 00					13 15						13 30			
Barry Docks	d					12 49					13 04					13 19						13 34			
Cadoxton	d					12 52					13 07					13 22						13 37			
Dinas Powys	d					12 56					13 11					13 26						13 41			
Eastbrook	d					12 58					13 13					13 28						13 43			
Cogan	d					13 00					13 15					13 30						13 45			
Penarth	d	12 47						13 02				13 17							13 32				13 47		
Dingle Road	d	12 49						13 04				13 19							13 34				13 49		
Grangetown	d	12 53				13 04		13 08			13 19	13 23				13 34			13 38			13 49	13 53		
Cardiff Central	a	12 59				13 09		13 14			13 24	13 29				13 39			13 44			13 54	13 59		
	d	13 01		13 06	13 06	13 11		13 16		13 21	13 26	13 31		13 36	13 36	13 41			13 46	13 51		13 56	14 01		14 06
Cardiff Bay	d		13 06						13 18				13 30					13 42			13 54			14 06	
Cardiff Queen Street	a	13 04	13 10	13 09		13 14		13 19	13 22	13 24	13 29	13 34	13 34	13 39		13 44		13 46	13 49	13 54	13 58	13 59	14 04	14 10	14 09
	d	13 05		13 10		13 15		13 20		13 25	13 30	13 35		13 40		13 45			13 50	13 55		14 00	14 05		14 10
Heath Low Level	d									13 30										14 00					
Ty Glas	d									13 33										14 03					
Birchgrove	d									13 34										14 04					
Rhiwbina	d									13 36										14 06					
Whitchurch (Cardiff)	d									13 38										14 08					
Coryton	a									13 44										14 14					
Heath High Level	d	13 10						13 25				13 40							13 55				14 10		
Llanishen	d	13 13						13 28				13 43							13 58				14 13		
Lisvane & Thornhill	d	13 15						13 30				13 45							14 00				14 15		
Caerphilly	d	13 21						13 36				13 51							14 06				14 21		
Aber	d	13 23						13 38				13 53							14 08				14 23		
Llanbradach	d	13 27						13 42				13 57							14 12				14 27		
Ystrad Mynach	d	13 32						13 47				14 07							14a22				14 32		
Hengoed	d	13 35						13 50				14 10											14 35		
Pengam	d	13 38						13 53				14 13											14 38		
Gilfach Fargoed	d	13 41																					14 41		
Bargoed	a	13 49						13 58				14 22											14 49		
	d							13 59																	
Brithdir	d							14 03																	
Tir-phil	d							14 06																	
Pontlottyn	d							14 10																	
Rhymney	a							14 17																	
Cathays	d			13 13		13 18					13 33			13 43		13 48						14 03			14 13
Llandaf	d			13 17		13 22					13 37			13 47		13 52						14 07			14 17
Ninian Park	d				13 10										13 40										
Waun-gron Park	d				13 14										13 44										
Fairwater	d				13 16										13 46										
Danescourt	d				13 19										13 49										
Radyr	a			13 20	13 27	13 25					13 40			13 50	13 57	13 55						14 10			14 20
	d			13 20		13 25					13 40			13 50		13 55						14 10			14 20
Taffs Well	d			13 24		13 29					13 44			13 54		13 59						14 14			14 24
Trefforest Estate	d										13 48											14 18			
Trefforest	d			13 31		13 36					13 52			14 01		14 06						14 22			14 31
Pontypridd	a			13 34		13 39					13 55			14 04		14 09						14 25			14 34
	d			13 36		13 41					13 57			14 06		14 11						14 27			14 36
Abercynon	d					13 49					14 04					14 19						14 34			
Penrhiwceiber	d					13 55										14 25									
Mountain Ash	a					13 58										14 28									
	d					14 04										14 34									
Fernhill	d					14 07										14 37									
Cwmbach	d					14 11										14 41									
Aberdare	a					14 19										14 49									
Quakers Yard	d										14 09											14 39			
Merthyr Vale	a										14 14											14 44			
	d										14 17											14 47			
Troed Y Rhiw	d										14 21											14 51			
Pentre-bach	d										14 24											14 54			
Merthyr Tydfil	a										14 33											15 03			
Trehafod	d			13 41										14 11											14 41
Porth	a			13 44										14 14											14 44
	d			13 45										14 15											14 45
Dinas Rhondda	d			13 49										14 19											14 49
Tonypandy	d			13 51										14 21											14 51
Llwynypia	d			13 53										14 23											14 53
Ystrad Rhondda	a			13 56										14 26											14 56
	d			13 59										14 29											14 59
Ton Pentre	d			14 01										14 31											15 01
Treorchy	d			14 04										14 34											15 04
Ynyswen	d			14 07										14 37											15 07
Treherbert	a			14 14										14 44											15 14

When events are being held at the Millenium Stadium, services are subject to alteration. Please check times before travelling.

Table 130

Saturdays from 17 September

Bridgend, Barry Island, Barry, Penarth and Cardiff - Coryton, Rhymney, Pontypridd, Merthyr, Aberdare and Treherbert

		AW		AW	AW	AW	AW	AW	AW	AW	AW	AW		AW	AW	AW	AW	AW	AW	AW	AW	AW		AW	AW
Bridgend	d													13 42											
Llantwit Major	d													13 56											
Rhoose Cardiff Int Airport ✈	d													14 06											
Barry Island	d			13 40				13 55												14 25					
Barry	d			13 45				14 00						14 15						14 30					
Barry Docks	d			13 49				14 04						14 19						14 34					
Cadoxton	d			13 52				14 07						14 22						14 37					
Dinas Powys	d			13 56				14 11						14 26						14 41					
Eastbrook	d			13 58				14 13						14 28						14 43					
Cogan	d			14 00				14 15						14 30						14 45					
Penarth	d				14 02				14 17							14 32						14 47			
Dingle Road	d				14 04				14 19							14 34						14 49			
Grangetown	d			14 04	14 08			14 19	14 23					14 34		14 38				14 49		14 53			
Cardiff Central	a			14 09	14 14			14 24	14 29					14 39		14 44				14 54		14 59			
	d	14 06		14 11	14 16		14 21	14 26	14 31		14 36	14 36		14 41		14 46	14 51		14 51	14 56		15 01		15 06	
Cardiff Bay	d					14 18				14 30					14 42			14 54							15 06
Cardiff Queen Street	a			14 14	14 19	14 22	14 24	14 29	14 34	14 34	14 39			14 44	14 46	14 49	14 54	14 58		14 59		15 04			15 10
	d			14 15	14 20		14 25	14 30	14 35		14 40			14 45		14 50	14 55			15 00		15 05			
Heath Low Level	d						14 30										15 00								
Ty Glas	d						14 33										15 03								
Birchgrove	d						14 34										15 04								
Rhiwbina	d						14 36										15 06								
Whitchurch (Cardiff)	d						14 38										15 08								
Coryton	a						14 44										15 14								
Heath High Level	d				14 25				14 40							14 55						15 10			
Llanishen	d				14 28				14 43							14 58						15 13			
Lisvane & Thornhill	d				14 30				14 45							15 00						15 15			
Caerphilly	d				14 36				14 51							15 06						15 21			
Aber	d				14 38				14 53							15 08						15 23			
Llanbradach	d				14 42				14 57							15 12						15 27			
Ystrad Mynach	d				14 47				15 07							15a22						15 32			
Hengoed	d				14 50				15 10													15 35			
Pengam	d				14 53				15 13													15 38			
Gilfach Fargoed	d																					15 41			
Bargoed	a				14 58				15 22													15 49			
	d				14 59																				
Brithdir	d				15 03																				
Tir-phil	d				15 06																				
Pontlottyn	d				15 10																				
Rhymney	a				15 17																				
Cathays	d			14 18				14 33			14 43			14 48						15 03					
Llandaf	d			14 22				14 37			14 47			14 52						15 07					
Ninian Park	d	14 10										14 40												15 10	
Waun-gron Park	d	14 14										14 44												15 14	
Fairwater	d	14 16										14 46												15 16	
Danescourt	d	14 19										14 49									←			15 19	
Radyr	a	14 27		14 25				14 40			14 50	14 57		14 55					15 08	15 10	15 08			15 27	
	d			14 25				14 40			14 50			14 55					15 20	15 10	15 20				
Taffs Well	d			14 29				14 44			14 54			14 59					→	15 14	15 24				
Trefforest Estate	d							14 48												15 18					
Trefforest	d			14 36				14 52			15 01			15 06						15 22	15 31				
Pontypridd	a			14 39				14 55			15 04			15 09						15 25	15 34				
	d			14 41				14 57			15 06			15 11						15 27	15 36				
Abercynon	d			14 49				15 04						15 19						15 34					
Penrhiwceiber	d			14 55										15 25											
Mountain Ash	a			14 58										15 28											
	d			15 04										15 34											
Fernhill	d			15 07										15 37											
Cwmbach	d			15 11										15 41											
Aberdare	a			15 19										15 49											
Quakers Yard	d							15 09												15 39					
Merthyr Vale	a							15 14												15 44					
	d							15 17												15 47					
Troed Y Rhiw	d							15 21												15 51					
Pentre-bach	d							15 24												15 54					
Merthyr Tydfil	a							15 33												16 03					
Trehafod	d										15 11										15 41				
Porth	a										15 14										15 44				
	d										15 15										15 45				
Dinas Rhondda	d										15 19										15 49				
Tonypandy	d										15 21										15 51				
Llwynypia	d										15 23										15 53				
Ystrad Rhondda	a										15 26										15 56				
	d										15 29										15 59				
Ton Pentre	d										15 31										16 01				
Treorchy	d										15 34										16 04				
Ynyswen	d										15 37										16 07				
Treherbert	a										15 44										16 14				

When events are being held at the Millenium Stadium, services are subject to alteration. Please check times before travelling.

Table 130

Bridgend, Barry Island, Barry, Penarth and Cardiff - Coryton, Rhymney, Pontypridd, Merthyr, Aberdare and Treherbert

Saturdays
from 17 September

Station		AW	AW	AW	AW	AW	AW	AW	AW	AW	AW		AW	AW	AW	AW	AW	AW	AW	AW	AW
Bridgend	d										14 4[illegible]										
Llantwit Major	d										14 5[illegible]										
Rhoose Cardiff Int Airport ✈	d										15 0[illegible]										
Barry Island	d	14 40				14 55							15 25					15 40		
Barry ■	d	14 45				15 00					15 1[illegible]		15 30					15 45		
Barry Docks	d	14 49				15 04					15 1[illegible]		15 34					15 49		
Cadoxton	d	14 52				15 07					15 2[illegible]		15 37					15 52		
Dinas Powys	d	14 56				15 11					15 2[illegible]		15 41					15 56		
Eastbrook	d	14 58				15 13					15 28		15 43					15 58		
Cogan	d	15 00				15 15					15 30		15 45					16 00		
Penarth	d		15 02				15 17							15 47					16 02	
Dingle Road	d		15 04				15 19							15 49					16 04	
Grangetown	d	15 04	15 08			15 19	15 23				15 34		15 49	15 53				16 04	16 08	
Cardiff Central ■	a	15 09	15 14			15 24	15 29				15 39		15 54	15 59				16 09	16 14	
	d	15 11	15 16		15 21	15 26	15 31		15 36	15 36	15 41		15 56	16 01		16 06	16 06	16 11	16 16	
Cardiff Bay	d			15 18				15 30				5 54			16 06					16 18
Cardiff Queen Street ■	a	15 14	15 19	15 22	15 24	15 29	15 34	15 34	15 39		15 44	5 58	15 59	16 04	16 10	16 09		16 14	16 19	16 22
	d	15 15	15 20		15 25	15 30	15 35		15 40		15 45		16 00	16 05		16 10		16 15	16 20	
Heath Low Level	d				15 30															
Ty Glas	d				15 33															
Birchgrove	d				15 34															
Rhiwbina	d				15 36															
Whitchurch (Cardiff)	d				15 38															
Coryton	a				15 44															
Heath High Level	d		15 25				15 40							16 10					16 25	
Llanishen	d		15 28				15 43							16 13					16 28	
Lisvane & Thornhill	d		15 30				15 45							16 15					16 30	
Caerphilly ■	d		15 36				15 51							16 21					16 36	
Aber	d		15 38				15 53							16 23					16 38	
Llanbradach	d		15 42				15 57							16 27					16 42	
Ystrad Mynach ■	d		15 47				16 02							16 32					16 47	
Hengoed	d		15 50				16 05							16 35					16 50	
Pengam	d		15 53				16 08							16 38					16 53	
Gilfach Fargoed	d													16 41						
Bargoed	a		15 58				16 17							16 49					16 58	
	d		15 59																16 59	
Brithdir	d		16 03																17 03	
Tir-phil	d		16 06																17 06	
Pontlottyn	d		16 10																17 10	
Rhymney ■	a		16 17																17 17	
Cathays	d	15 18				15 33			15 43		15 48		[illegible]			16 13		16 18		
Llandaf	d	15 22				15 37			15 47		15 52		[illegible]			16 17		16 22		
Ninian Park	d									15 40							16 10			
Waun-gron Park	d									15 44							16 13			
Fairwater	d									15 46							16 15			
Danescourt	d									15 49							16 17			
Radyr ■	a	15 25				15 40			15 50	15 57	15 55		16 [illegible]			16 20	16 27	16 25		
	d	15 25				15 40			15 50		15 55		16 1[illegible]			16 20		16 25		
Taffs Well ■	d	15 29				15 44			15 54		15 59		16 14			16 24		16 29		
Trefforest Estate	d					15 48							16 18							
Trefforest	d	15 36				15 52			16 01		16 06		16 22			16 31		16 36		
Pontypridd ■	a	15 39				15 55			16 04		16 09		16 25			16 34		16 39		
	d	15 41				15 57			16 06		16 11		16 27			16 36		16 41		
Abercynon	d	15 49				16 04					16 19		16 34					16 49		
Penrhiwceiber	d	15 55									16 25							16 55		
Mountain Ash	a	15 58									16 28							16 58		
	d	16 04									16 34							17 04		
Fernhill	d	16 07									16 37							17 07		
Cwmbach	d	16 11									16 41							17 11		
Aberdare ■	a	16 19									16 49							17 19		
Quakers Yard	d					16 09							16 39							
Merthyr Vale	a					16 14							16 44							
	d					16 17							16 47							
Troed Y Rhiw	d					16 21							16 51							
Pentre-bach	d					16 24							16 54							
Merthyr Tydfil	a					16 33							17 03							
Trehafod	d								16 11							16 41				
Porth	a								16 14							16 44				
	d								16 15							16 45				
Dinas Rhondda	d								16 19							16 49				
Tonypandy	d								16 21							16 51				
Llwynypia	d								16 23							16 53				
Ystrad Rhondda	a								16 26							16 56				
	d								16 29							16 59				
Ton Pentre	d								16 31							17 01				
Treorchy	d								16 34							17 04				
Ynyswen	d								16 37							17 07				
Treherbert	a								16 44							17 14				

When events are being held at the Millenium Stadium, services are subject to alteration. Please check times before travelling.

Table 130

Bridgend, Barry Island, Barry, Penarth and Cardiff - Coryton, Rhymney, Pontypridd, Merthyr, Aberdare and Treherbert

Saturdays
from 17 September

Station		AW	AW	AW	AW	AW	AW	AW	AW	AW	AW	AW	AW	AW	AW	AW	AW	AW	AW	AW	AW	AW
Bridgend	d							15 42														
Llantwit Major	d							15 56														
Rhoose Cardiff Int Airport ✈	d							16 06														
Barry Island	d		15 55										16 25					16 40				16 55
Barry ■	d		16 00					16 15					16 30					16 45				17 00
Barry Docks	d		16 04					16 19					16 34					16 49				17 04
Cadoxton	d		16 07					16 22					16 37					16 52				17 07
Dinas Powys	d		16 11					16 26					16 41					16 56				17 11
Eastbrook	d		16 13					16 28					16 43					16 58				17 13
Cogan	d		16 15					16 30					16 45					17 00				17 15
Penarth	d			16 17						16 32									17 02			
Dingle Road	d			16 19						16 34									17 04			
Grangetown	d		16 19	16 23				16 34		16 38			16 49					17 04	17 08			17 19
Cardiff Central ■	a		16 24	16 29				16 39		16 44			16 54					17 09	17 14			17 24
	d	16 21	16 26	16 31		16 36	16 36	16 41		16 46	16 51		16 56	17 01		17 06	17 06	17 11	17 16		17 21	17 26
Cardiff Bay	d				16 30				16 42			16 54			17 06					17 18		
Cardiff Queen Street ■	a	16 24	16 29	16 34	16 34	16 39		16 44	16 46	16 49	16 54	16 58	16 59	17 04	17 10	17 09		17 14	17 19	17 22	17 24	17 29
	d	16 25	16 30	16 35		16 40		16 45		16 50	16 55		17 00	17 05		17 10		17 15	17 20		17 25	17 30
Heath Low Level	d	16 30									17 00										17 30	
Ty Glas	d	16 33									17 03										17 33	
Birchgrove	d	16 34									17 04										17 34	
Rhiwbina	d	16 36									17 06										17 36	
Whitchurch (Cardiff)	d	16 38									17 08										17 38	
Coryton	a	16 44									17 14										17 44	
Heath High Level	d			16 40						16 55				17 10					17 25			
Llanishen	d			16 43						16 58				17 13					17 28			
Lisvane & Thornhill	d			16 45						17 00				17 15					17 30			
Caerphilly ■	d			16 51						17 06				17 21					17 36			
Aber	d			16 53						17 08				17 23					17 38			
Llanbradach	d			16 57						17 12				17 27					17 42			
Ystrad Mynach ■	d			17 02						17 17				17 33					17 47			
Hengoed	d			17 05						17 20				17 35					17 50			
Pengam	d			17 08						17 23				17 39					17 53			
Gilfach Fargoed	d													17 42								
Bargoed	a			17 17						17 32				17 45					18 02			
	d													17 47								
Brithdir	d													17 50								
Tir-phil	d													17 53								
Pontlottyn	d													17 58								
Rhymney ■	a													18 05								
Cathays	d		16 33			16 43		16 48					17 03			17 13		17 18				17 33
Llandaf	d		16 37			16 47		16 52					17 07			17 17		17 22				17 37
Ninian Park	d						16 40										17 10					
Waun-gron Park	d						16 44										17 14					
Fairwater	d						16 46										17 16					
Danescourt	d						16 49										17 19					
Radyr ■	a		16 40			16 50	16 57	16 55					17 10			17 20	17 27	17 25				17 40
	d		16 40			16 50		16 55					17 10			17 20		17 25				17 40
Taffs Well ■	d		16 44			16 54		16 59					17 14			17 24		17 29				17 44
Trefforest Estate	d		16 48										17 18									17 48
Trefforest	d		16 52			17 01		17 06					17 22			17 31		17 36				17 52
Pontypridd ■	a		16 56			17 04		17 09					17 25			17 34		17 39				17 55
	d		16 57			17 06		17 11					17 27			17 36		17 41				17 57
Abercynon	d		17 04					17 19					17 34					17 49				18 04
Penrhiwceiber	d							17 25										17 55				
Mountain Ash	a							17 28										17 58				
	d							17 34										18 04				
Fernhill	d							17 37										18 07				
Cwmbach	d							17 41										18 11				
Aberdare ■	a							17 49										18 19				
Quakers Yard	d		17 09										17 39									18 09
Merthyr Vale	a		17 14										17 44									18 14
	d		17 17										17 47									18 17
Troed Y Rhiw	d		17 21										17 51									18 21
Pentre-bach	d		17 24										17 54									18 24
Merthyr Tydfil	a		17 33										18 03									18 33
Trehafod	d					17 11										17 41						
Porth	a					17 14										17 44						
	d					17 15										17 45						
Dinas Rhondda	d					17 19										17 49						
Tonypandy	d					17 21										17 51						
Llwynypia	d					17 23										17 53						
Ystrad Rhondda	a					17 26										17 56						
	d					17 29										17 59						
Ton Pentre	d					17 31										18 01						
Treorchy	d					17 34										18 04						
Ynyswen	d					17 37										18 07						
Treherbert	a					17 44										18 14						

When events are being held at the Millenium Stadium, services are subject to alteration. Please check times before travelling.

Table 130

Saturdays
from 17 September

Bridgend, Barry Island, Barry, Penarth and Cardiff - Coryton, Rhymney, Pontypridd, Merthyr, Aberdare and Treherbert

		AW	AW	AW	AW	AW	AW	AW	AW	AW		AW	AW	AW	AW	AW	AW	AW	AW	AW		AW	AW	AW	AW
Bridgend	d					16 42																			
Llantwit Major	d					16 56																			
Rhoose Cardiff Int Airport ✈	d					17 06																			
Barry Island	d											17 25					17 40					17 55			
Barry	d					17 15						17 30					17 45					18 00			
Barry Docks	d					17 19						17 34					17 49					18 04			
Cadoxton	d					17 22						17 37					17 52					18 07			
Dinas Powys	d					17 26						17 41					17 56					18 11			
Eastbrook	d					17 28						17 43					17 58					18 13			
Cogan	d					17 30						17 45					18 00					18 15			
Penarth	d	17 17						17 32					17 47					18 02					18 16		
Dingle Road	d	17 19						17 34					17 49					18 04					18 18		
Grangetown	d	17 23				17 34		17 38				17 49	17 53				18 04	18 08				18 19	18 22		
Cardiff Central	a	17 29				17 39		17 44				17 54	17 59				18 10	18 14				18 24	18 29		
	d	17 31		17 36	17 36	17 41		17 46	17 51			17 56	18 01		18 06	18 06	18 11	18 16		8 21		18 26	18 31		18 36
Cardiff Bay	d		17 30				17 42			17 54				18 06					18					18 30	
Cardiff Queen Street	a	17 34	17 34	17 39		17 44	17 46	17 49	17 54	17 58		17 59	18 04	18 10	18 09		18 14	18 19	18	18 24		18 29	18 34	18 34	18 38
	d	17 35		17 40		17 45		17 50	17 55			18 00	18 05		18 10		18 15	18 20		18 25		18 30	18 35		18 40
Heath Low Level	d								18 00											18 30					
Ty Glas	d								18 03											18 33					
Birchgrove	d								18 04											18 34					
Rhiwbina	d								18 06											18 36					
Whitchurch (Cardiff)	d								18 08											18 38					
Coryton	a								18 14											18 44					
Heath High Level	d	17 40						17 55					18 10					18					18 40		
Llanishen	d	17 43						17 59					18 13					18					18 43		
Lisvane & Thornhill	d	17 45						18 02					18 15					[illegible]					18 45		
Caerphilly	d	17 51						18 07					18 21					[illegible]					18 51		
Aber	d	17 53						18 10					18 23										18 53		
Llanbradach	d	17 57						18 14					18 27										18 57		
Ystrad Mynach	d	18 02						18 20					18 32										19 02		
Hengoed	d	18 05						18 23					18 35										19 05		
Pengam	d	18 08						18 27					[illegible]										19 08		
Gilfach Fargoed	d	18 11						18 30															19 11		
Bargoed	a	18 14						18 34															19 14		
	d	18 16						18 44															19 16		
Brithdir	d	18 20						18 48															19 20		
Tir-phil	d	18 23						18 51															19 23		
Pontlottyn	d	18 27						18 55															19 27		
Rhymney	a	18 34						19 02															19 35		
Cathays	d			17 43		17 48						18 03			18 13		18 18					18 33			18 43
Llandaf	d			17 47		17 52						18 07			18 17		18 22					18 37			18 47
Ninian Park	d				17 40											18									
Waun-gron Park	d				17 44											18									
Fairwater	d				17 46											[illegible]									
Danescourt	d				17 49											[illegible]									
Radyr	a			17 50	17 57	17 55						18			18 20	[illegible]	18 25					18 40			18 50
	d			17 50		17 55						18			18 20		18 25					18 40			18 50
Taffs Well	d			17 54		17 59						18			18 24		18 29					18 44			18 54
Trefforest Estate	d																					18 48			
Trefforest	d			18 01		18 06									18 31		18 36					18 52			19 01
Pontypridd	a			18 04		18 09									18 34		18 42					18 55			19 04
	d			18 06		18 11									18 36							18 57			19 06
Abercynon	d					18 19																19 04			
Penrhiwceiber	d					18 25																19 09			
Mountain Ash	a					18 28																19 14			
	d					18 34																19 17			
Fernhill	d					18 37																19 21			
Cwmbach	d					18 41																19 24			
Aberdare	a					18 49																19 33			
Quakers Yard	d																								
Merthyr Vale	a																								
	d																								
Troed Y Rhiw	d																								
Pentre-bach	d																								
Merthyr Tydfil	a																								
Trehafod	d			18 11											18 41										19 11
Porth	a			18 14											18 44										19 14
	d			18 15											18 45										19 15
Dinas Rhondda	d			18 19											18 49										19 19
Tonypandy	d			18 21											18 51										19 21
Llwynypia	d			18 23											18 53										19 23
Ystrad Rhondda	a			18 26											18 56										19 26
	d			18 29											18 59										19 29
Ton Pentre	d			18 31											19 01										19 31
Treorchy	d			18 34											19 04										19 34
Ynyswen	d			18 37											19 07										19 37
Treherbert	a			18 44											19 14										19 44

When events are being held at the Millenium Stadium, services are subject to alteration. Please check times before travelling.

Table 130

Saturdays
from 17 September

Bridgend, Barry Island, Barry, Penarth and Cardiff - Coryton, Rhymney, Pontypridd, Merthyr, Aberdare and Treherbert

		AW	AW	AW	AW	AW		AW	AW	AW	AW	AW	AW	AW	AW	AW		AW	AW	AW	AW	AW	AW	AW	AW
Bridgend	d		17 42																	18 42					
Llantwit Major	d		17 56																	18 56					
Rhoose Cardiff Int Airport ✈	d		18 06																	19 06					
Barry Island	d							18 25					18 40		18 55									19 25	
Barry	d		18 15					18 30					18 45		19 00					19 15				19 30	
Barry Docks	d		18 19					18 34					18 49		19 04					19 19				19 34	
Cadoxton	d		18 22					18 37					18 52		19 07					19 22				19 37	
Dinas Powys	d		18 26					18 41					18 56		19 11					19 26				19 41	
Eastbrook	d		18 28					18 43					18 58		19 13					19 28				19 43	
Cogan	d		18 30					18 45					19 00		19 15					19 30				19 45	
Penarth	d			18 32						18 47						19 17									19 47
Dingle Road	d			18 34						18 49						19 19									19 49
Grangetown	d		18 34	18 38				18 49		18 53			19 04		19 19	19 23				19 34				19 49	19 54
Cardiff Central	a		18 39	18 47				18 55		18 59			19 09		19 24	19 29				19 39				19 55	19 59
	d	18 36	18 41			18 51				19 01		19 06	19 11		19 26	19 31			19 36	19 41		19 51		20 01	20 06
Cardiff Bay	d				18 42				18 54		19 06			19 18				19 30			19 42		19 54		
Cardiff Queen Street	a		18 44		18 46	18 54			18 58	19 04	19 10	19 09	19 14	19 22	19 29	19 34		19 34		19 44	19 46	19 54	19 58	20 04	20 09
	d		18 50			18 55				19 05		19 10	19 15		19 30	19 35				19 45		19 55		20 06	20 10
Heath Low Level	d					19 00																20 00			
Ty Glas	d					19 03																20 03			
Birchgrove	d					19 04																20 04			
Rhiwbina	d					19 06																20 06			
Whitchurch (Cardiff)	d					19 08																20 08			
Coryton	a					19 14																20 14			
Heath High Level	d									19 10						19 40								20 10	
Llanishen	d									19 13						19 43								20 13	
Lisvane & Thornhill	d									19 15						19 45								20 16	
Caerphilly	d									19a24						19 51								20a28	
Aber	d															19 53									
Llanbradach	d															19 57									
Ystrad Mynach	d															20 02									
Hengoed	d															20 05									
Pengam	d															20 08									
Gilfach Fargoed	d															20 11									
Bargoed	a															20 15									
	d															20 16									
Brithdir	d															20 20									
Tir-phil	d															20 23									
Pontlottyn	d															20 27									
Rhymney	a															20 34									
Cathays	d		18 52									19 13	19 18		19 33					19 48					20 13
Llandaf	d		18 56									19 17	19 22		19 37					19 52					20 17
Ninian Park	d	18 40																	19 40						
Waun-gron Park	d	18 44																	19 44						
Fairwater	d	18 46																	19 46						
Danescourt	d	18 49																	19 49						
Radyr	a	18 57	18 58									19 20	19 25		19 40				19 57	19 55					20 20
	d		18 58									19 20	19 25		19 40					19 55					20 20
Taffs Well	d		19 03									19 24	19 29		19 44					19 59					20 24
Trefforest Estate	d														19 48										
Trefforest	d		19 10									19 31	19 36		19 52					20 06					20 31
Pontypridd	a		19 13									19 34	19 39		19 55					20 09					20 35
	d		19 14									19 36	19 41		19 57					20 11					20 36
Abercynon	d		19 21										19 49		20 04					20 21					
Penrhiwceiber	d		19 27										19 55							20 27					
Mountain Ash	a		19 30										19 58							20 31					
	d		19 34										20 04							20 34					
Fernhill	d		19 37										20 07							20 37					
Cwmbach	d		19 41										20 11							20 41					
Aberdare	a		19 49										20 19							20 49					
Quakers Yard	d														20 08										
Merthyr Vale	a														20 13										
	d														20 15										
Troed Y Rhiw	d														20 19										
Pentre-bach	d														20 22										
Merthyr Tydfil	a														20 31										
Trehafod	d											19 41													20 41
Porth	a											19 44													20 44
	d											19 45													20 45
Dinas Rhondda	d											19 49													20 49
Tonypandy	d											19 51													20 51
Llwynypia	d											19 53													20 53
Ystrad Rhondda	a											19 56													20 56
	d											19 59													20 59
Ton Pentre	d											20 01													21 01
Treorchy	d											20 04													21 04
Ynyswen	d											20 07													21 07
Treherbert	a											20 14													21 14

When events are being held at the Millenium Stadium, services are subject to alteration. Please check times before travelling.

Table 130

Bridgend, Barry Island, Barry, Penarth and Cardiff - Coryton, Rhymney, Pontypridd, Merthyr, Aberdare and Treherbert

		AW	AW	AW	AW	AW	AW	AW	AW	AW	AW	AW	AW	AW	AW	AW	AW	AW	AW
Bridgend	d							19 42									20 42		
Llantwit Major	d							19 56									20 56		
Rhoose Cardiff Int Airport ✈	d							20 06									21 06		
Barry Island	d			19 55									20 [illegible]						
Barry [3]	d			20 00				20 15					21 [illegible]				21 15		
Barry Docks	d			20 04				20 19					[illegible]				21 19		
Cadoxton	d			20 07				20 22					[illegible]				21 22		
Dinas Powys	d			20 11				20 26					[illegible]				21 26		
Eastbrook	d			20 13				20 28					[illegible]				21 28		
Cogan	d			20 15				20 30					[illegible]				21 30		
Penarth	d					20 19										21 20			
Dingle Road	d					20 21										21 22			
Grangetown	d			20 19		20 25		20 34					21 [illegible]			21 26	21 34		
Cardiff Central [7]	a			20 24		20 31		20 39					2[illegible]			21 37	21 39		
	d			20 26		20 31	20 36	20 41	20 42	20 51			21 [illegible]		21 3[illegible]	21 36	21 41		
Cardiff Bay	d	20 06	20 18		20 30						20 54		[illegible]	[illegible]30				21 42	
Cardiff Queen Street [3]	a	20 10	20 22	20 29	20 34	20 35		20 44	20 46	20 54	20 58		[illegible]	[illegible]34	21 3[illegible]		21 44	21 46	
	d			20 30		20 36		20 45		20 55			[illegible]		21 3[illegible]		21 45		
Heath Low Level	d									21 00									
Ty Glas	d									21 03									
Birchgrove	d									21 04									
Rhiwbina	d									21 06									
Whitchurch (Cardiff)	d									21 08									
Coryton	a									21 14									
Heath High Level	d					20 41					21 [illegible]				21 4[illegible]				
Llanishen	d					20 44					21 [illegible]				21 4[illegible]				
Lisvane & Thornhill	d					20 46					21 15				21 45				
Caerphilly [3]	d					20 52					21a31				21 51				
Aber	d					20 54									21 53				
Llanbradach	d					20 58									21 57				
Ystrad Mynach [3]	d					21 03									22 02				
Hengoed	d					21 06									22 05				
Pengam	d					21 09									22 08				
Gilfach Fargoed	d					21 12									22 11				
Bargoed	a					21 16									22 15				
	d					21 17									22 16				
Brithdir	d					21 21									22 20				
Tir-phil	d					21 24									22 23				
Pontlottyn	d					21 28									22 27				
Rhymney [3]	a					21 35									22 35				
Cathays	d			20 33				20 48					21 33				21 48		
Llandaf	d			20 37				20 52					21 37				21 52		
Ninian Park	d						20 40									21 40			
Waun-gron Park	d						20 44									21 44			
Fairwater	d						20 46									21 46			
Danescourt	d						20 49									21 49			
Radyr [3]	a			20 40			20 57	20 55				21 [illegible]	21 40			21 57	21 55		
	d			20 40				20 55				21 [illegible]	21 40				21 55		
Taffs Well [3]	d			20 44				20 59				21 2[illegible]	21 44				21 59		
Trefforest Estate	d			20 48									21 48						
Trefforest	d			20 52				21 06				21 3[illegible]	21 52				22 06		
Pontypridd [3]	a			20 55				21 09				21 34	21 55				22 09		
	d			20 57				21 11				21 36	21 57				22 11		
Abercynon	d			21 04				21 19					22 04				22 19		
Penrhiwceiber	d							21 25									22 25		
Mountain Ash	a							21 28									22 28		
	d							21 29									22 29		
Fernhill	d							21 32									22 32		
Cwmbach	d							21 36									22 36		
Aberdare [3]	a							21 44									22 44		
Quakers Yard	d			21 08									22 08						
Merthyr Vale	a			21 13									22 13						
	d			21 15									22 15						
Troed Y Rhiw	d			21 19									22 19						
Pentre-bach	d			21 22									22 22						
Merthyr Tydfil	a			21 31									22 31						
Trehafod	d											21 41							
Porth	a											21 44							
	d											21 45							
Dinas Rhondda	d											21 49							
Tonypandy	d											21 51							
Llwynypia	d											21 53							
Ystrad Rhondda	a											21 56							
	d											21 59							
Ton Pentre	d											22 01							
Treorchy	d											22 04							
Ynyswen	d											22 07							
Treherbert	a											22 14							

When events are being held at the Millenium Stadium, services are subject to alteration. Please check times before travelling.

Table 130

Bridgend, Barry Island, Barry, Penarth and Cardiff - Coryton, Rhymney, Pontypridd, Merthyr, Aberdare and Treherbert

		AW	AW	AW	AW	AW	AW	AW	AW	AW	AW	AW	AW	AW	AW	AW	AW	AW	AW	AW	AW	AW	AW
Bridgend	d										21 42									22 42			
Llantwit Major	d										21 56									22 56			
Rhoose Cardiff Int Airport ✈	d										22 06									23 06			
Barry Island	d							21 55										22 45					
Barry [3]	d							22 00			22 15							22 49		23 15			
Barry Docks	d							22 04			22 19							22 53		23 19			
Cadoxton	d							22 07			22 22							22 56		23 22			
Dinas Powys	d							22 11			22 26							23 00		23 26			
Eastbrook	d							22 13			22 28							23 02		23 28			
Cogan	d							22 15			22 30							23 04		23 30			
Penarth	d		21 47							22 20						22 47			23 26				
Dingle Road	d		21 49							22 22						22 49			23 29				
Grangetown	d		21 53					22 19		22 26	22 34					22 53		23 08	23 32	23 34			
Cardiff Central [7]	a		21 59					22 24		22 33	22 39					23 00		23 13	23 40	23 42			
	d		22 01		22 06		22 21	22 26		22 35	22 41		22 46			23 15		23 26					
Cardiff Bay	d	21 54		22 06		22 18			22 30			22 42		22 54	23 06		23 18				23 30	23 42	23 54
Cardiff Queen Street [3]	a	21 58	22 04	22 10	22 09	22 22	22 24	22 29	22 34	22 38	22 44	22 46	22 49	22 58	23 10	23 18	23 22	23 29			23 34	23 46	23 58
	d		22 05		22 10		22 25	22 30		22 39	22 45		22 50			23 19		23 30					
Heath Low Level	d						22 30																
Ty Glas	d						22 33																
Birchgrove	d						22 34																
Rhiwbina	d						22 36																
Whitchurch (Cardiff)	d						22 38																
Coryton	a						22 44																
Heath High Level	d		22 10							22 44						23 24							
Llanishen	d		22 13							22 47						23 27							
Lisvane & Thornhill	d		22 15							22 49						23 29							
Caerphilly [3]	d		22a24							22 55						23 35							
Aber	d									22 57						23 37							
Llanbradach	d									23 01						23 41							
Ystrad Mynach [3]	d									23 06						23a51							
Hengoed	d									23 09													
Pengam	d									23 12													
Gilfach Fargoed	d									23 15													
Bargoed	a									23 19													
	d									23 20													
Brithdir	d									23 24													
Tir-phil	d									23 27													
Pontlottyn	d									23 31													
Rhymney [3]	a									23 38													
Cathays	d				22 13			22 33			22 48		22 53					23 33					
Llandaf	d				22 17			22 37			22 52		22 57					23 37					
Ninian Park	d																						
Waun-gron Park	d																						
Fairwater	d																						
Danescourt	d																						
Radyr [3]	a				22 20			22 40			22 55		22 59					23 40					
	d				22 20			22 40			22 55		22 59					23 40					
Taffs Well [3]	d				22 24			22 44			22 59		23 03					23 44					
Trefforest Estate	d							22 48															
Trefforest	d				22 31			22 52			23 06		23 10					23 52					
Pontypridd [3]	a				22 34			22 55			23 09		23 14					23 58					
	d				22 36			22 57			23 11		23 15										
Abercynon	d							23 04			23 19												
Penrhiwceiber	d										23 25												
Mountain Ash	a										23 28												
	d										23 34												
Fernhill	d										23 37												
Cwmbach	d										23 41												
Aberdare [3]	a										23 49												
Quakers Yard	d							23 08															
Merthyr Vale	a							23 13															
	d							23 15															
Troed Y Rhiw	d							23 19															
Pentre-bach	d							23 22															
Merthyr Tydfil	a							23 31															
Trehafod	d				22 41								23 20										
Porth	a				22 44								23 23										
	d				22 45								23 24										
Dinas Rhondda	d				22 49								23 28										
Tonypandy	d				22 51								23 30										
Llwynypia	d				22 53								23 32										
Ystrad Rhondda	a				22 56								23 35										
	d				22 59								23 38										
Ton Pentre	d				23 01								23 40										
Treorchy	d				23 04								23 43										
Ynyswen	d				23 07								23 46										
Treherbert	a				23 14								23 53										

When events are being held at the Millenium Stadium, services are subject to alteration. Please check times before travelling.

Table 130

Bridgend, Barry Island, Barry, Penarth and Cardiff - Coryton, Rhymney, Pontypridd, Merthyr, Aberdare and Treherbert

		AW	AW	AW	AW	AW	AW	AW	AW	AW	AW	AW	AW	AW	AW	AW	AW	AW	AW	AW	AW	AW	AW
Bridgend	d															09 42							
Llantwit Major	d															09 56							
Rhoose Cardiff Int Airport ✈	d															10 06							
Barry Island	d								08 55						09 55		10 25						
Barry ■	d								09 00						10 00	10 15	10 30						
Barry Docks	d								09 04						10 04	10 19	10 34						
Cadoxton	d								09 07						10 07	10 22	10 37						
Dinas Powys	d								09 11						10 11	10 26	10 41						
Eastbrook	d								09 13						10 13	10 28	10 43						
Cogan	d								09 15						10 15	10 30	10 45						
Penarth	d																			10 47			
Dingle Road	d																			10 49			
Grangetown	d								09 19						10 19	10 34	10 49			10 53			
Cardiff Central ■	a								09 24						10 24	10 42	10 56			10 59			
	d	08 26	08 41	08 54	09 00				09 41				10 06		10 26							11 00	
Cardiff Bay	d					09 06	09 18	09 30		09 42	09 54	10 06		10 18				10 30	10 42		10 54		11 06
Cardiff Queen Street ■	a	08 29	08 44	08 57	09 03	09 10	09 22	09 34	09 44	09 46	09 58	10 10	10 09	10 22	10 29			10 34	10 46		10 58	11 03	11 10
	d	08 30	08 45		09 04				09 45				10 10		10 30							11 04	
Heath Low Level	d																						
Ty Glas	d																						
Birchgrove	d																						
Rhiwbina	d																						
Whitchurch (Cardiff)	d																						
Coryton	a																						
Heath High Level	d												10 15										
Llanishen	d												10 18										
Lisvane & Thornhill	d												10 20										
Caerphilly ■	d												10 26										
Aber	d												10 28										
Llanbradach	d												10 32										
Ystrad Mynach ■	d												10 37										
Hengoed	d												10 40										
Pengam	d												10 43										
Gilfach Fargoed	d												10 46										
Bargoed	a												10 49										
	d												10 49										
Brithdir	d												10 53										
Tir-phil	d												10 5[illegible]										
Pontlottyn	d												11 0[illegible]										
Rhymney ■	a												11 [illegible]										
Cathays	d	08 33	08 48		09 07				09 48													11 07	
Llandaf	d	08 37	08 52		09 11				09 52													11 11	
Ninian Park	d																						
Waun-gron Park	d																						
Fairwater	d																						
Danescourt	d																						
Radyr ■	a	08 40	08 55		09 14				09 55						40							11 14	
	d	08 40	08 55		09 14				09 55						40							11 14	
Taffs Well ■	d	08 44	08 59		09 18				09 59						44							11 18	
Trefforest Estate	d																						
Trefforest	d	08 52	09 06		09 25				10 06						52							11 25	
Pontypridd ■	a	08 55	09 09		09 28				10 09						55							11 28	
	d	08 57	09 11		09 30				10 11						57							11 30	
Abercynon	d	09 05	09 19						10 19						04								
Penrhiwceiber	d		09 24						10 24														
Mountain Ash	a		09 28						10 28														
	d		09 31						10 31														
Fernhill	d		09 33						10 33														
Cwmbach	d		09 37						10 37														
Aberdare ■	a		09 44						10 44														
Quakers Yard	d	09 09													11 09								
Merthyr Vale	a	09 14													11 14								
	d	09 17													11 17								
Troed Y Rhiw	d	09 20													11 20								
Pentre-bach	d	09 23													11 23								
Merthyr Tydfil	a	09 31													11 31								
Trehafod	d				09 35																	11 35	
Porth	a				09 38																	11 38	
	d				09 39																	11 39	
Dinas Rhondda	d				09 43																	11 43	
Tonypandy	d				09 45																	11 45	
Llwynypia	d				09 47																	11 47	
Ystrad Rhondda	a				09 50																	11 50	
	d				09 53																	11 53	
Ton Pentre	d				09 55																	11 55	
Treorchy	d				09 58																	11 58	
Ynyswen	d				10 01																	12 01	
Treherbert	a				10 07																	12 07	

When events are being held [illegible]um, services are su[illegible] alteration. Ple[illegible]re travelling.

Table 130

Bridgend, Barry Island, Barry, Penarth and Cardiff - Coryton, Rhymney, Pontypridd, Merthyr, Aberdare and Treherbert

		AW	AW	AW	AW	AW	AW	AW	AW	AW	AW	AW	AW	AW	AW	AW	AW	AW	AW	AW	AW	AW	AW
Bridgend	d										11 42												
Llantwit Major	d										11 56												
Rhoose Cardiff Int Airport ✈	d										12 06												
Barry Island	d			10 55			11 25			11 55		12 25									12 55		
Barry ■	d			11 00			11 30			12 00	12 15	12 30									13 00		
Barry Docks	d			11 04			11 34			12 04	12 19	12 34									13 04		
Cadoxton	d			11 07			11 37			12 07	12 22	12 37									13 07		
Dinas Powys	d			11 11			11 41			12 11	12 26	12 41									13 11		
Eastbrook	d			11 13			11 43			12 13	12 28	12 43									13 13		
Cogan	d			11 15			11 45			12 15	12 30	12 45									13 15		
Penarth	d														12 47								
Dingle Road	d														12 49								
Grangetown	d			11 19			11 49			12 19	12 34	12 49			12 53						13 19		
Cardiff Central ■	a			11 24			11 57			12 24	12 42	12 56			12 59						13 24		
	d			11 41			12 06			12 26								13 06			13 41		
Cardiff Bay	d	11 18	11 30		11 42	11 54		12 06	12 18				12 30	12 42		12 54	13 06		13 18	13 30		13 42	13 54
Cardiff Queen Street ■	a	11 22	11 34	11 44	11 46	11 58	12 09	12 10	12 22	12 29			12 34	12 46		12 58	13 10	13 09	13 22	13 34	13 44	13 46	13 58
	d			11 45			12 10			12 30								13 10			13 45		
Heath Low Level	d																						
Ty Glas	d																						
Birchgrove	d																						
Rhiwbina	d																						
Whitchurch (Cardiff)	d																						
Coryton	a																						
Heath High Level	d						12 15																
Llanishen	d						12 18																
Lisvane & Thornhill	d						12 20																
Caerphilly ■	d						12 26																
Aber	d						12 28																
Llanbradach	d						12 32																
Ystrad Mynach ■	d						12 37																
Hengoed	d						12 40																
Pengam	d						12 43																
Gilfach Fargoed	d						12 46																
Bargoed	a						12 49																
	d						12 49																
Brithdir	d						12 53																
Tir-phil	d						12 56																
Pontlottyn	d						13 00																
Rhymney ■	a						13 07																
Cathays	d			11 48						12 33								13 13			13 48		
Llandaf	d			11 52						12 37								13 17			13 52		
Ninian Park	d																						
Waun-gron Park	d																						
Fairwater	d																						
Danescourt	d																						
Radyr ■	a			11 55						12 40								13 20			13 55		
	d			11 55						12 40								13 20			13 55		
Taffs Well ■	d			11 59						12 44								13 24			13 59		
Trefforest Estate	d																						
Trefforest	d			12 06						12 52								13 31			14 06		
Pontypridd ■	a			12 09						12 55								13 34			14 09		
	d			12 11						12 57								13 36			14 11		
Abercynon	d			12 19						13 04											14 19		
Penrhiwceiber	d			12 24																	14 24		
Mountain Ash	a			12 28																	14 28		
	d			12 31																	14 31		
Fernhill	d			12 33																	14 33		
Cwmbach	d			12 37																	14 37		
Aberdare ■	a			12 44																	14 44		
Quakers Yard	d									13 09													
Merthyr Vale	a									13 14													
	d									13 17													
Troed Y Rhiw	d									13 20													
Pentre-bach	d									13 23													
Merthyr Tydfil	a									13 31													
Trehafod	d																	13 41					
Porth	a																	13 44					
	d																	13 45					
Dinas Rhondda	d																	13 49					
Tonypandy	d																	13 51					
Llwynypia	d																	13 53					
Ystrad Rhondda	a																	13 56					
	d																	13 59					
Ton Pentre	d																	14 01					
Treorchy	d																	14 04					
Ynyswen	d																	14 07					
Treherbert	a																	14 13					

When events are being held at the Millenium Stadium, services are subject to alteration. Please check times before travelling.

Saturdays
from 17 September

Bridgend, Barry Island, Barry, Penarth and Cardiff - Coryton, Rhymney, Pontypridd, Merthyr, Aberdare and Treherbert

Station		AW		AW	AW	AW	AW	AW	AW	AW	AW	AW		AW	AW	AW	AW	AW	AW	AW	AW	AW		AW	AW
Bridgend	d								19 42															20 42	
Llantwit Major	d								19 56															20 56	
Rhoose Cardiff Int Airport ✈	d								20 06															21 06	
Barry Island	d				19 55													20 55							
Barry [3]	d				20 00				20 15									21 00						21 15	
Barry Docks	d				20 04				20 19									21 04						21 19	
Cadoxton	d				20 07				20 22									21 07						21 22	
Dinas Powys	d				20 11				20 26									21 11						21 26	
Eastbrook	d				20 13				20 28									21 13						21 28	
Cogan	d				20 15				20 30									21 15						21 30	
Penarth	d						20 19							20 47								21 20			
Dingle Road	d						20 21							20 49								21 22			
Grangetown	d				20 19		20 25		20 34					20 53				21 19				21 26		21 34	
Cardiff Central [7]	a				20 24		20 31		20 39					20 59				21 24				21 37		21 39	
	d				20 26		20 31	20 36	20 41		20 51			21 01		21 06		21 26		21 31	21 36			21 41	
Cardiff Bay	d	20 06		20 18		20 30				20 42		20 54			21 06		21 18		21 30						21 42
Cardiff Queen Street [3]	a	20 10		20 22	20 29	20 34	20 35		20 44	20 46	20 54	20 58		21 04	21 10	21 09	21 22	21 29	21 34	21 34				21 44	21 46
	d				20 30		20 36		20 45		20 55			21 05		21 10		21 30		21 35				21 45	
Heath Low Level	d										21 00														
Ty Glas	d										21 03														
Birchgrove	d										21 04														
Rhiwbina	d										21 06														
Whitchurch (Cardiff)	d										21 08														
Coryton	a										21 14														
Heath High Level	d						20 41							21 10						21 40					
Llanishen	d						20 44							21 13						21 43					
Lisvane & Thornhill	d						20 46							21 15						21 45					
Caerphilly [3]	d						20 52							21a31						21 51					
Aber	d						20 54													21 53					
Llanbradach	d						20 58													21 57					
Ystrad Mynach [3]	d						21 03													22 02					
Hengoed	d						21 06													22 05					
Pengam	d						21 09													22 08					
Gilfach Fargoed	d						21 12													22 11					
Bargoed	a						21 16													22 15					
	d						21 17													22 16					
Brithdir	d						21 21													22 20					
Tir-phil	d						21 24													22 23					
Pontlottyn	d						21 28													22 27					
Rhymney [3]	a						21 35													22 35					
Cathays	d				20 33				20 48							21 13		21 33						21 48	
Llandaf	d				20 37				20 52							21 17		21 37						21 52	
Ninian Park	d							20 40													21 40				
Waun-gron Park	d							20 44													21 44				
Fairwater	d							20 46													21 46				
Danescourt	d							20 49													21 49				
Radyr [3]	a				20 40			20 57	20 55							21 20		21 40			21 57			21 55	
	d				20 40				20 55							21 20		21 40						21 55	
Taffs Well [3]	d				20 44				20 59							21 24		21 44						21 59	
Trefforest Estate	d				20 48													21 48							
Trefforest	d				20 52				21 06							21 31		21 52						22 06	
Pontypridd [3]	a				20 55				21 09							21 34		21 55						22 09	
	d				20 57				21 11							21 36		21 57						22 11	
Abercynon	d				21 04				21 19									22 04						22 19	
Penrhiwceiber	d								21 25															22 25	
Mountain Ash	a								21 28															22 28	
	d								21 29															22 29	
Fernhill	d								21 32															22 32	
Cwmbach	d								21 36															22 36	
Aberdare [3]	a								21 44															22 44	
Quakers Yard	d				21 08													22 08							
Merthyr Vale	a				21 13													22 13							
	d				21 15													22 15							
Troed Y Rhiw	d				21 19													22 19							
Pentre-bach	d				21 22													22 22							
Merthyr Tydfil	a				21 31													22 31							
Trehafod	d															21 41									
Porth	a															21 44									
	d															21 45									
Dinas Rhondda	d															21 49									
Tonypandy	d															21 51									
Llwynypia	d															21 53									
Ystrad Rhondda	a															21 56									
	d															21 59									
Ton Pentre	d															22 01									
Treorchy	d															22 04									
Ynyswen	d															22 07									
Treherbert	a															22 14									

When events are being held at the Millenium Stadium, services are subject to alteration. Please check times before travelling.

Saturdays
from 17 September

Bridgend, Barry Island, Barry, Penarth and Cardiff - Coryton, Rhymney, Pontypridd, Merthyr, Aberdare and Treherbert

Station		AW	AW	AW	AW	AW	AW	AW		AW	AW	AW	AW	AW	AW	AW	AW	AW		AW	AW	AW	AW	AW	AW
Bridgend	d											21 42										22 42			
Llantwit Major	d											21 56										22 56			
Rhoose Cardiff Int Airport ✈	d											22 06										23 06			
Barry Island	d							21 55												22 45					
Barry [3]	d							22 00				22 15								22 49		23 15			
Barry Docks	d							22 04				22 19								22 53		23 19			
Cadoxton	d							22 07				22 22								22 56		23 22			
Dinas Powys	d							22 11				22 26								23 00		23 26			
Eastbrook	d							22 13				22 28								23 02		23 28			
Cogan	d							22 15				22 30								23 04		23 30			
Penarth	d		21 47								22 20						22 47				23 26				
Dingle Road	d		21 49								22 22						22 49				23 28				
Grangetown	d		21 53					22 19			22 26	22 34					22 53			23 08	23 32	23 34			
Cardiff Central [7]	a		21 59					22 24			22 33	22 39					23 00			23 13	23 40	23 42			
	d		22 01		22 06		22 21	22 26			22 35	22 41		22 46			23 15			23 26					
Cardiff Bay	d	21 54		22 06		22 18				22 30			22 42		22 54	23 06		23 18					23 30	23 42	23 54
Cardiff Queen Street [3]	a	21 58	22 04	22 10	22 09	22 22	22 24	22 29		22 34	22 38	22 44	22 46	22 49	22 58	23 10	23 18	23 22		23 29			23 34	23 46	23 58
	d		22 05		22 10		22 25	22 30			22 39	22 45		22 50			23 19			23 30					
Heath Low Level	d						22 30																		
Ty Glas	d						22 33																		
Birchgrove	d						22 34																		
Rhiwbina	d						22 36																		
Whitchurch (Cardiff)	d						22 38																		
Coryton	a						22 44																		
Heath High Level	d		22 10								22 44						23 24								
Llanishen	d		22 13								22 47						23 27								
Lisvane & Thornhill	d		22 15								22 49						23 29								
Caerphilly [3]	d		22a24								22 55						23 35								
Aber	d										22 57						23 37								
Llanbradach	d										23 01						23 41								
Ystrad Mynach [3]	d										23 06						23a51								
Hengoed	d										23 09														
Pengam	d										23 12														
Gilfach Fargoed	d										23 15														
Bargoed	a										23 19														
	d										23 20														
Brithdir	d										23 24														
Tir-phil	d										23 27														
Pontlottyn	d										23 31														
Rhymney [3]	a										23 38														
Cathays	d				22 13			22 33				22 48		22 53						23 33					
Llandaf	d				22 17			22 37				22 52		22 57						23 37					
Ninian Park	d																								
Waun-gron Park	d																								
Fairwater	d																								
Danescourt	d																								
Radyr [3]	a				22 20			22 40				22 55		22 59						23 40					
	d				22 20			22 40				22 55		22 59						23 40					
Taffs Well [3]	d				22 24			22 44				22 59		23 03						23 44					
Trefforest Estate	d							22 48																	
Trefforest	d				22 31			22 52				23 06		23 10						23 52					
Pontypridd [3]	a				22 34			22 55				23 09		23 14						23 58					
	d				22 36			22 57				23 11		23 15											
Abercynon	d							23 04				23 19													
Penrhiwceiber	d											23 25													
Mountain Ash	a											23 28													
	d											23 34													
Fernhill	d											23 37													
Cwmbach	d											23 41													
Aberdare [3]	a											23 49													
Quakers Yard	d							23 08																	
Merthyr Vale	a							23 13																	
	d							23 15																	
Troed Y Rhiw	d							23 19																	
Pentre-bach	d							23 22																	
Merthyr Tydfil	a							23 31																	
Trehafod	d				22 41									23 20											
Porth	a				22 44									23 23											
	d				22 45									23 24											
Dinas Rhondda	d				22 49									23 28											
Tonypandy	d				22 51									23 30											
Llwynypia	d				22 53									23 32											
Ystrad Rhondda	a				22 56									23 35											
	d				22 59									23 38											
Ton Pentre	d				23 01									23 40											
Treorchy	d				23 04									23 43											
Ynyswen	d				23 07									23 46											
Treherbert	a				23 14									23 53											

When events are being held at the Millenium Stadium, services are subject to alteration. Please check times before travelling.

Table 130

Sundays
until 31 July

Bridgend, Barry Island, Barry, Penarth and Cardiff - Coryton, Rhymney, Pontypridd, Merthyr, Aberdare and Treherbert

		AW	AW	AW	AW	AW	AW	AW	AW	AW		AW	AW	AW	AW	AW	AW	AW	AW	AW		AW	AW	AW	AW
Bridgend	d																09 42								
Llantwit Major	d																09 56								
Rhoose Cardiff Int Airport ✈	d																10 06								
Barry Island	d								08 55							09 55		10 25							
Barry 3	d								09 00							10 00	10 15	10 30							
Barry Docks	d								09 04							10 04	10 19	10 34							
Cadoxton	d								09 07							10 07	10 22	10 37							
Dinas Powys	d								09 11							10 11	10 26	10 41							
Eastbrook	d								09 13							10 13	10 28	10 43							
Cogan	d								09 15							10 15	10 30	10 45							
Penarth	d																					10 47			
Dingle Road	d																					10 49			
Grangetown	d								09 19							10 19	10 34	10 49				10 53			
Cardiff Central 7	a								09 24							10 24	10 42	10 56				10 59			
	d	08 26	08 41	08 54	09 00				09 41					10 06		10 26								11 00	
Cardiff Bay	d					09 06	09 18	09 30		09 42		09 54	10 06		10 18				10 30	10 42			10 54		11 06
Cardiff Queen Street 3	a	08 29	08 44	08 57	09 03	09 10	09 22	09 34	09 44	09 46		09 58	10 10	10 09	10 22	10 29			10 34	10 46			10 58	11 03	11 10
	d	08 30	08 45		09 04				09 45					10 10		10 30								11 04	
Heath Low Level	d																								
Ty Glas	d																								
Birchgrove	d																								
Rhiwbina	d																								
Whitchurch (Cardiff)	d																								
Coryton	a																								
Heath High Level	d													10 15											
Llanishen	d													10 18											
Lisvane & Thornhill	d													10 20											
Caerphilly 3	d													10 26											
Aber	d													10 28											
Llanbradach	d													10 32											
Ystrad Mynach 3	d													10 37											
Hengoed	d													10 40											
Pengam	d													10 43											
Gilfach Fargoed	d													10 46											
Bargoed	a													10 49											
	d													10 49											
Brithdir	d													10 53											
Tir-phil	d													10 56											
Pontlottyn	d													11 00											
Rhymney 3	a													11 07											
Cathays	d	08 33	08 48		09 07				09 48							10 33								11 07	
Llandaf	d	08 37	08 52		09 11				09 52							10 37								11 11	
Ninian Park	d																								
Waun-gron Park	d																								
Fairwater	d																								
Danescourt	d																								
Radyr 3	a	08 40	08 55		09 14				09 55							10 40								11 14	
	d	08 40	08 55		09 14				09 55							10 40								11 14	
Taffs Well 3	d	08 44	08 59		09 18				09 59							10 44								11 18	
Trefforest Estate	d																								
Trefforest	d	08 52	09 06		09 25				10 06							10 52								11 25	
Pontypridd 3	a	08 55	09 09		09 28				10 09							10 55								11 28	
	d	08 57	09 11		09 30				10 11							10 57								11 30	
Abercynon	d	09 05	09 19						10 19							11 04									
Penrhiwceiber	d		09 24						10 24																
Mountain Ash	a		09 28						10 28																
	d		09 31						10 31																
Fernhill	d		09 33						10 33																
Cwmbach	d		09 37						10 37																
Aberdare 3	a		09 44						10 44																
Quakers Yard	d	09 09														11 09									
Merthyr Vale	a	09 14														11 14									
	d	09 17														11 17									
Troed Y Rhiw	d	09 20														11 20									
Pentre-bach	d	09 23														11 23									
Merthyr Tydfil	a	09 31														11 31									
Trehafod	d				09 35																			11 35	
Porth	a				09 38																			11 38	
	d				09 39																			11 39	
Dinas Rhondda	d				09 43																			11 43	
Tonypandy	d				09 45																			11 45	
Llwynypia	d				09 47																			11 47	
Ystrad Rhondda	a				09 50																			11 50	
	d				09 53																			11 53	
Ton Pentre	d				09 55																			11 55	
Treorchy	d				09 58																			11 58	
Ynyswen	d				10 01																			12 01	
Treherbert	a				10 07																			12 07	

When events are being held at the Millenium Stadium, services are subject to alteration. Please check times before travelling.

Table 130

Sundays
until 31 July

Bridgend, Barry Island, Barry, Penarth and Cardiff - Coryton, Rhymney, Pontypridd, Merthyr, Aberdare and Treherbert

		AW	AW	AW	AW	AW		AW	AW	AW	AW	AW	AW	AW	AW	AW		AW	AW	AW	AW	AW	AW	AW	AW
Bridgend	d											11 42													
Llantwit Major	d											11 56													
Rhoose Cardiff Int Airport ✈	d											12 06													
Barry Island	d			10 55				11 25			11 55		12 25										12 55		
Barry 3	d			11 00				11 30			12 00	12 15	12 30										13 00		
Barry Docks	d			11 04				11 34			12 04	12 19	12 34										13 04		
Cadoxton	d			11 07				11 37			12 07	12 22	12 37										13 07		
Dinas Powys	d			11 11				11 41			12 11	12 26	12 41										13 11		
Eastbrook	d			11 13				11 43			12 13	12 28	12 43										13 13		
Cogan	d			11 15				11 45			12 15	12 30	12 45										13 15		
Penarth	d															12 47									
Dingle Road	d															12 49									
Grangetown	d			11 19				11 49			12 19	12 34	12 49			12 53							13 19		
Cardiff Central 7	a			11 24				11 57			12 24	12 42	12 56			12 59							13 24		
	d			11 41				12 06			12 26									13 06			13 41		
Cardiff Bay	d	11 18	11 30		11 42	11 54			12 06	12 18				12 30	12 42			12 54	13 06		13 18	13 30		13 42	13 54
Cardiff Queen Street 3	a	11 22	11 34	11 44	11 46	11 58		12 09	12 10	12 22	12 29			12 34	12 46			12 58	13 10	13 09	13 22	13 34	13 44	13 46	13 58
	d			11 45				12 10			12 30									13 10			13 45		
Heath Low Level	d																								
Ty Glas	d																								
Birchgrove	d																								
Rhiwbina	d																								
Whitchurch (Cardiff)	d																								
Coryton	a																								
Heath High Level	d							12 15																	
Llanishen	d							12 18																	
Lisvane & Thornhill	d							12 20																	
Caerphilly 3	d							12 26																	
Aber	d							12 28																	
Llanbradach	d							12 32																	
Ystrad Mynach 3	d							12 37																	
Hengoed	d							12 40																	
Pengam	d							12 43																	
Gilfach Fargoed	d							12 46																	
Bargoed	a							12 49																	
	d							12 49																	
Brithdir	d							12 53																	
Tir-phil	d							12 56																	
Pontlottyn	d							13 00																	
Rhymney 3	a							13 07																	
Cathays	d			11 48							12 33									13 13			13 48		
Llandaf	d			11 52							12 37									13 17			13 52		
Ninian Park	d																								
Waun-gron Park	d																								
Fairwater	d																								
Danescourt	d																								
Radyr 3	a			11 55							12 40									13 20			13 55		
	d			11 55							12 40									13 20			13 55		
Taffs Well 3	d			11 59							12 44									13 24			13 59		
Trefforest Estate	d																								
Trefforest	d			12 06							12 52									13 31			14 06		
Pontypridd 3	a			12 09							12 55									13 34			14 09		
	d			12 11							12 57									13 36			14 11		
Abercynon	d			12 19							13 04												14 19		
Penrhiwceiber	d			12 24																			14 24		
Mountain Ash	a			12 28																			14 28		
	d			12 31																			14 31		
Fernhill	d			12 33																			14 33		
Cwmbach	d			12 37																			14 37		
Aberdare 3	a			12 44																			14 44		
Quakers Yard	d										13 09														
Merthyr Vale	a										13 14														
	d										13 17														
Troed Y Rhiw	d										13 20														
Pentre-bach	d										13 23														
Merthyr Tydfil	a										13 31														
Trehafod	d																			13 41					
Porth	a																			13 44					
	d																			13 45					
Dinas Rhondda	d																			13 49					
Tonypandy	d																			13 51					
Llwynypia	d																			13 53					
Ystrad Rhondda	a																			13 56					
	d																			13 59					
Ton Pentre	d																			14 01					
Treorchy	d																			14 04					
Ynyswen	d																			14 07					
Treherbert	a																			14 13					

When events are being held at the Millenium Stadium, services are subject to alteration. Please check times before travelling.

Table 130

Sundays until 31 July

Bridgend, Barry Island, Barry, Penarth and Cardiff - Coryton, Rhymney, Pontypridd, Merthyr, Aberdare and Treherbert

		AW		AW	AW	AW	AW	AW	AW	AW	AW	AW		AW	AW	AW	AW	AW	AW	AW	AW	AW		AW	AW
Bridgend	d						13 42																		
Llantwit Major	d						13 56																		
Rhoose Cardiff Int Airport ✈	d						14 10																		
Barry Island	d	13 25				13 55		14 25										14 55			15 25				15 55
Barry 3	d	13 30				14 00	14 19	14 30										15 00			15 30				16 00
Barry Docks	d	13 34				14 04	14 23	14 34										15 04			15 34				16 04
Cadoxton	d	13 37				14 07	14 26	14 37										15 07			15 37				16 07
Dinas Powys	d	13 41				14 11	14 30	14 41										15 11			15 41				16 11
Eastbrook	d	13 43				14 13	14 32	14 43										15 13			15 43				16 13
Cogan	d	13 45				14 15	14 34	14 45										15 15			15 45				16 15
Penarth	d										14 47														
Dingle Road	d										14 49														
Grangetown	d	13 49				14 19	14 38	14 49			14 53							15 19			15 49				16 19
Cardiff Central 7	a	13 57				14 24	14 46	14 56			14 59							15 24			15 57				16 24
	d	14 06				14 26									15 06			15 41			16 06				16 26
Cardiff Bay	d			14 06	14 18				14 30	14 42		14 54		15 06		15 18	15 30		15 42	15 54		16 06		16 18	
Cardiff Queen Street 3	a	14 09		14 10	14 22	14 29			14 34	14 46		14 58		15 10	15 09	15 22	15 34	15 44	15 46	15 58	16 09	16 10		16 22	16 29
	d	14 10				14 30									15 10			15 45			16 10				16 30
Heath Low Level	d																								
Ty Glas	d																								
Birchgrove	d																								
Rhiwbina	d																								
Whitchurch (Cardiff)	d																								
Coryton	a																								
Heath High Level	d	14 15																			16 15				
Llanishen	d	14 18																			16 18				
Lisvane & Thornhill	d	14 20																			16 20				
Caerphilly 3	d	14 26																			16 26				
Aber	d	14 28																			16 28				
Llanbradach	d	14 32																			16 32				
Ystrad Mynach 3	d	14 37																			16 37				
Hengoed	d	14 40																			16 40				
Pengam	d	14 43																			16 43				
Gilfach Fargoed	d	14 46																			16 46				
Bargoed	a	14 49																			16 49				
	d	14 49																			16 49				
Brithdir	d	14 53																			16 53				
Tir-phil	d	14 56																			16 56				
Pontlottyn	d	15 00																			17 00				
Rhymney 3	a	15 07																			17 07				
Cathays	d					14 33									15 13			15 48							16 33
Llandaf	d					14 37									15 17			15 52							16 37
Ninian Park	d																								
Waun-gron Park	d																								
Fairwater	d																								
Danescourt	d																								
Radyr 3	a					14 40									15 20			15 55							16 40
	d					14 40									15 20			15 55							16 40
Taffs Well 3	d					14 44									15 24			15 59							16 44
Trefforest Estate	d																								
Trefforest	d					14 52									15 31			16 06							16 52
Pontypridd 3	a					14 55									15 34			16 09							16 55
	d					14 57									15 36			16 11							16 57
Abercynon	d					15 04												16 19							17 04
Penrhiwceiber	d																	16 24							
Mountain Ash	a																	16 28							
	d																	16 31							
Fernhill	d																	16 33							
Cwmbach	d																	16 37							
Aberdare 3	a																	16 44							
Quakers Yard	d					15 09																			17 09
Merthyr Vale	a					15 14																			17 14
	d					15 17																			17 17
Troed Y Rhiw	d					15 20																			17 20
Pentre-bach	d					15 23																			17 23
Merthyr Tydfil	a					15 31																			17 31
Trehafod	d														15 41										
Porth	a														15 44										
	d														15 45										
Dinas Rhondda	d														15 49										
Tonypandy	d														15 51										
Llwynypia	d														15 53										
Ystrad Rhondda	a														15 56										
	d														15 59										
Ton Pentre	d														16 01										
Treorchy	d														16 04										
Ynyswen	d														16 07										
Treherbert	a														16 13										

When events are being held at the Millenium Stadium, services are subject to alteration. Please check times before travelling.

Table 130

Sundays until 31 July

Bridgend, Barry Island, Barry, Penarth and Cardiff - Coryton, Rhymney, Pontypridd, Merthyr, Aberdare and Treherbert

		AW	AW	AW	AW	AW	AW	AW		AW	AW	AW	AW	AW	AW	AW	AW	AW		AW	AW	AW	AW	AW	AW
Bridgend	d	15 42																				17 42			
Llantwit Major	d	15 56																				17 56			
Rhoose Cardiff Int Airport ✈	d	16 06																				18 06			
Barry Island	d		16 25				16 40							16 55			17 25				17 55		18 25		
Barry 3	d	16 15	16 30				16 45							17 00			17 30				18 00	18 15	18 30		
Barry Docks	d	16 19	16 34											17 04			17 34				18 04	18 19	18 34		
Cadoxton	d	16 22	16 37											17 07			17 37				18 07	18 22	18 37		
Dinas Powys	d	16 26	16 41											17 11			17 41				18 11	18 26	18 41		
Eastbrook	d	16 28	16 43											17 13			17 43				18 13	18 28	18 43		
Cogan	d	16 30	16 45											17 15			17 45				18 15	18 30	18 45		
Penarth	d					16 47																			
Dingle Road	d					16 49																			
Grangetown	d	16 34	16 49			16 53								17 19			17 49				18 19	18 34	18 49		
Cardiff Central 7	a	16 42	16 56			16 59	17 02							17 24			17 57				18 24	18 42	18 56		
	d										17 06			17 41			18 06				18 26				
Cardiff Bay	d			16 30	16 42			16 54		17 06		17 18	17 30		17 42	17 54		18 06		18 18				18 30	18 42
Cardiff Queen Street 3	a			16 34	16 46			16 58		17 10	17 09	17 22	17 34	17 44	17 46	17 58	18 09	18 10		18 22	18 29			18 34	18 46
	d										17 10			17 45			18 10				18 30				
Heath Low Level	d																								
Ty Glas	d																								
Birchgrove	d																								
Rhiwbina	d																								
Whitchurch (Cardiff)	d																								
Coryton	a																								
Heath High Level	d																18 15								
Llanishen	d																18 18								
Lisvane & Thornhill	d																18 20								
Caerphilly 3	d																18 26								
Aber	d																18 28								
Llanbradach	d																18 32								
Ystrad Mynach 3	d																18 37								
Hengoed	d																18 40								
Pengam	d																18 43								
Gilfach Fargoed	d																18 46								
Bargoed	a																18 49								
	d																18 49								
Brithdir	d																18 53								
Tir-phil	d																18 56								
Pontlottyn	d																19 00								
Rhymney 3	a																19 07								
Cathays	d										17 13			17 48							18 33				
Llandaf	d										17 17			17 52							18 37				
Ninian Park	d																								
Waun-gron Park	d																								
Fairwater	d																								
Danescourt	d																								
Radyr 3	a										17 20			17 55							18 40				
	d										17 20			17 55							18 40				
Taffs Well 3	d										17 24			17 59							18 44				
Trefforest Estate	d																								
Trefforest	d										17 31			18 06							18 52				
Pontypridd 3	a										17 34			18 09							18 55				
	d										17 36			18 11							18 57				
Abercynon	d													18 19							19 04				
Penrhiwceiber	d													18 24											
Mountain Ash	a													18 28											
	d													18 31											
Fernhill	d													18 33											
Cwmbach	d													18 37											
Aberdare 3	a													18 44											
Quakers Yard	d																				19 09				
Merthyr Vale	a																				19 14				
	d																				19 17				
Troed Y Rhiw	d																				19 20				
Pentre-bach	d																				19 23				
Merthyr Tydfil	a																				19 31				
Trehafod	d										17 41														
Porth	a										17 44														
	d										17 45														
Dinas Rhondda	d										17 49														
Tonypandy	d										17 51														
Llwynypia	d										17 53														
Ystrad Rhondda	a										17 56														
	d										17 59														
Ton Pentre	d										18 01														
Treorchy	d										18 04														
Ynyswen	d										18 07														
Treherbert	a										18 13														

When events are being held at the Millenium Stadium, services are subject to alteration. Please check times before travelling.

Table 130

Sundays until 31 July

Bridgend, Barry Island, Barry, Penarth and Cardiff - Coryton, Rhymney, Pontypridd, Merthyr, Aberdare and Treherbert

		AW	AW	AW	AW	AW	AW	AW	AW	AW	AW A	AW	AW	AW	AW	AW B	AW
Bridgend	d							19 42							21 42		
Llantwit Major	d							19 56							21 56		
Rhoose Cardiff Int Airport ✈	d							20 06							22 06		
Barry Island	d				18 55	19 25	19 55		20 25			20 55	21 25	21 55			22 55
Barry	d				19 00	19 30	20 00	20 15	20 30			21 00	21 30	22 00	22 15		23 00
Barry Docks	d				19 04	19 34	20 04	20 19	20 34			21 04	21 34	22 04	22 19		23 04
Cadoxton	d				19 07	19 37	20 07	20 22	20 37			21 07	21 37	22 07	22 22		23 07
Dinas Powys	d				19 11	19 41	20 11	20 26	20 41			21 11	21 41	22 11	22 26		23 11
Eastbrook	d				19 13	19 43	20 13	20 28	20 43			21 13	21 43	22 13	22 28		23 13
Cogan	d				19 15	19 45	20 15	20 30	20 45			21 15	21 45	22 15	22 30		23 15
Penarth	d	18 47								20 47							
Dingle Road	d	18 49								20 49							
Grangetown	d	18 53			19 19	19 49	20 19	20 34	20 49	20 53		21 19	21 49	22 19	22 34		23 19
Cardiff Central	a	18 59			19 24	19 57	20 24	20 42	20 54	21 01		21 27	21 54	22 27	22 42		23 27
	d			19 06	19 41	20 06	20 26		21 06		21 16		22 06				
Cardiff Bay	d		18 54														
Cardiff Queen Street	a		18 57	19 09	19 44	20 09	20 29		21 09		21 19		22 09				
	d			19 10	19 45	20 10	20 30		21 10		21 20		22 10				
Heath Low Level	d																
Ty Glas	d																
Birchgrove	d																
Rhiwbina	d																
Whitchurch (Cardiff)	d																
Coryton	a																
Heath High Level	d					20 15					21 25					22 12	
Llanishen	d					20 18					21 28					22 15	
Lisvane & Thornhill	d					20 20					21 30					22 17	
Caerphilly	d					20 26					21 36					22 23	
Aber	d					20 28					21 38					22 25	
Llanbradach	d					20 32					21 42					22 29	
Ystrad Mynach	d					20 37					21 47					22 34	
Hengoed	d					20 40					21 50					22 37	
Pengam	d					20 43					21 53					22 40	
Gilfach Fargoed	d					20 46					21 56					22 43	
Bargoed	a					20 49					21 59					22 46	
	d					20 49					21 59					22 46	
Brithdir	d					20 53					22 03					22 50	
Tir-phil	d					20 56					22 06					22 53	
Pontlottyn	d					21 00					22 10					22 57	
Rhymney	a					21 07					22 17					23 04	
Cathays	d			19 13	19 48		20 33		21 13				22 13				
Llandaf	d			19 17	19 52		20 37		21 17				22 17				
Ninian Park	d																
Waun-gron Park	d																
Fairwater	d																
Danescourt	d																
Radyr	a			19 20	19 55		20 40		21 20				22 20				
	d			19 20	19 55		20 40		21 20				22 20				
Taffs Well	d			19 24	19 59		20 44		21 24				22 24				
Trefforest Estate	d																
Trefforest	d			19 31	20 06		20 52		21 31				22 31				
Pontypridd	a			19 34	20 09		20 55		21 34				22 34				
	d			19 36	20 11		20 57		21 36				22 36				
Abercynon	d				20 19		21 04										
Penrhiwceiber	d				20 24												
Mountain Ash	a				20 28												
	d				20 31												
Fernhill	d				20 33												
Cwmbach	d				20 37												
Aberdare	a				20 44												
Quakers Yard	d						21 09										
Merthyr Vale	a						21 14										
	d						21 17										
Troed Y Rhiw	d						21 20										
Pentre-bach	d						21 23										
Merthyr Tydfil	a						21 31										
Trehafod	d			19 41					21 41				22 41				
Porth	a			19 44					21 44				22 44				
	d			19 45					21 45				22 45				
Dinas Rhondda	d			19 49					21 49				22 49				
Tonypandy	d			19 51					21 51				22 51				
Llwynypia	d			19 53					21 53				22 53				
Ystrad Rhondda	a			19 56					21 56				22 56				
	d			19 59					21 59				22 59				
Ton Pentre	d			20 01					22 01				23 01				
Treorchy	d			20 04					22 04				23 04				
Ynyswen	d			20 07					22 07				23 07				
Treherbert	a			20 13					22 13				23 13				

A not from 29 May until 5 June

B 29 May, 5 June

When events are being held at the Millenium Stadium, services are subject to alteration. Please check times before travelling.

Table 130

Sundays 7 August to 11 September

Bridgend, Barry Island, Barry, Penarth and Cardiff - Coryton, Rhymney, Pontypridd, Merthyr, Aberdare and Treherbert

		AW	AW	AW	AW	AW	AW	AW	AW	AW	AW	AW	AW	AW	AW	AW	AW	AW	AW	AW	AW	AW	AW
Bridgend	d															09 25							
Llantwit Major	d															09 50							
Rhoose Cardiff Int Airport ✈	d															10 05							
Barry Island	d								08 55						09 55		10 25						
Barry	d								09 00						10 00	10a20	10 30						
Barry Docks	d								09 04						10 04		10 34						
Cadoxton	d								09 07						10 07		10 37						
Dinas Powys	d								09 11						10 11		10 41						
Eastbrook	d								09 13						10 13		10 43						
Cogan	d								09 15						10 15		10 45						
Penarth	d																			10 47			
Dingle Road	d																			10 49			
Grangetown	d								09 19						10 19		10 49			10 53			
Cardiff Central	a								09 24						10 24		10 56			10 59			
	d	08 26	08 41	08 54	09 00				09 41				10 06		10 26							11 00	
Cardiff Bay	d					09 06	09 18	09 30		09 42	09 54	10 06		10 18				10 30	10 42		10 54		11 06
Cardiff Queen Street	a	08 29	08 44	08 57	09 03	09 10	09 22	09 34	09 44	09 46	09 58	10 10	10 09	10 22	10 29			10 34	10 46		10 58	11 03	11 10
	d	08 30	08 45		09 04				09 45				10 10		10 30							11 04	
Heath Low Level	d																						
Ty Glas	d																						
Birchgrove	d																						
Rhiwbina	d																						
Whitchurch (Cardiff)	d																						
Coryton	a																						
Heath High Level	d												10 15										
Llanishen	d												10 18										
Lisvane & Thornhill	d												10 20										
Caerphilly	d												10 26										
Aber	d												10 28										
Llanbradach	d												10 32										
Ystrad Mynach	d												10 37										
Hengoed	d												10 40										
Pengam	d												10 43										
Gilfach Fargoed	d												10 46										
Bargoed	a												10 49										
	d												10 49										
Brithdir	d												10 53										
Tir-phil	d												10 56										
Pontlottyn	d												11 00										
Rhymney	a												11 07										
Cathays	d	08 33	08 48		09 07				09 48						10 33							11 07	
Llandaf	d	08 37	08 52		09 11				09 52						10 37							11 11	
Ninian Park	d																						
Waun-gron Park	d																						
Fairwater	d																						
Danescourt	d																						
Radyr	a	08 40	08 55		09 14				09 55						10 40							11 14	
	d	08 40	08 55		09 14				09 55						10 40							11 14	
Taffs Well	d	08 44	08 59		09 18				09 59						10 44							11 18	
Trefforest Estate	d																						
Trefforest	d	08 52	09 06		09 25				10 06						10 52							11 25	
Pontypridd	a	08 55	09 09		09 28				10 09						10 55							11 28	
	d	08 57	09 11		09 30				10 11						10 57							11 30	
Abercynon	d	09 05	09 19						10 19						11 04								
Penrhiwceiber	d		09 24						10 24														
Mountain Ash	a		09 28						10 28														
	d		09 31						10 31														
Fernhill	d		09 33						10 33														
Cwmbach	d		09 37						10 37														
Aberdare	a		09 44						10 44														
Quakers Yard	d	09 09													11 09								
Merthyr Vale	a	09 14													11 14								
	d	09 17													11 17								
Troed Y Rhiw	d	09 20													11 20								
Pentre-bach	d	09 23													11 23								
Merthyr Tydfil	a	09 31													11 31								
Trehafod	d				09 35																	11 35	
Porth	a				09 38																	11 38	
	d				09 39																	11 39	
Dinas Rhondda	d				09 43																	11 43	
Tonypandy	d				09 45																	11 45	
Llwynypia	d				09 47																	11 47	
Ystrad Rhondda	a				09 50																	11 50	
	d				09 53																	11 53	
Ton Pentre	d				09 55																	11 55	
Treorchy	d				09 58																	11 58	
Ynyswen	d				10 01																	12 01	
Treherbert	a				10 07																	12 07	

When events are being held at the Millenium Stadium, services are subject to alteration. Please check times before travelling.

Table 130

Sundays
7 August to 11 September

Bridgend, Barry Island, Barry, Penarth and Cardiff - Coryton, Rhymney, Pontypridd, Merthyr, Aberdare and Treherbert

		AW	AW	AW	AW	AW	AW	AW	AW	AW	AW 🚌	AW	AW	AW	AW	AW	AW	AW	AW	AW	AW	AW	AW
Bridgend	d										11 25												
Llantwit Major	d										11 50												
Rhoose Cardiff Int Airport ✈	d										12 05												
Barry Island	d			10 55			11 25			11 55		12 25									12 55		
Barry 3	d			11 00			11 30			12 00	12a20	12 30									13 00		
Barry Docks	d			11 04			11 34			12 04		12 34									13 04		
Cadoxton	d			11 07			11 37			12 07		12 37									13 07		
Dinas Powys	d			11 11			11 41			12 11		12 41									13 11		
Eastbrook	d			11 13			11 43			12 13		12 43									13 13		
Cogan	d			11 15			11 45			12 15		12 45									13 15		
Penarth	d														12 47								
Dingle Road	d														12 49								
Grangetown	d			11 19			11 49			12 19		12 49			12 53						13 19		
Cardiff Central 7	a			11 24			11 57			12 24		12 56			12 59						13 24		
	d			11 41			12 06			12 26								13 06			13 41		
Cardiff Bay	d	11 18	11 30		11 42	11 54		12 06	12 18				12 30	12 42		12 54	13 06		13 18	13 30		13 42	13 54
Cardiff Queen Street 3	a	11 22	11 34	11 44	11 46	11 58	12 09	12 10	12 22	12 29			12 34	12 46		12 58	13 10	13 09	13 22	13 34	13 44	13 46	13 58
	d			11 45			12 10			12 30								13 10			13 45		
Heath Low Level	d																						
Ty Glas	d																						
Birchgrove	d																						
Rhiwbina	d																						
Whitchurch (Cardiff)	d																						
Coryton	a																						
Heath High Level	d						12 15																
Llanishen	d						12 18																
Lisvane & Thornhill	d						12 20																
Caerphilly 3	d						12 26																
Aber	d						12 28																
Llanbradach	d						12 32																
Ystrad Mynach 3	d						12 37																
Hengoed	d						12 40																
Pengam	d						12 43																
Gilfach Fargoed	d						12 46																
Bargoed	a						12 49																
	d						12 49																
Brithdir	d						12 53																
Tir-phil	d						12 56																
Pontlottyn	d						13 00																
Rhymney 3	a						13 07																
Cathays	d			11 48						12 33								13 13			13 48		
Llandaf	d			11 52						12 37								13 17			13 52		
Ninian Park	d																						
Waun-gron Park	d																						
Fairwater	d																						
Danescourt	d																						
Radyr 3	a			11 55						12 40								13 20			13 55		
	d			11 55						12 40								13 20			13 55		
Taffs Well 3	d			11 59						12 44								13 24			13 59		
Trefforest Estate	d																						
Trefforest	d			12 06						12 52								13 31			14 06		
Pontypridd 3	a			12 09						12 55								13 34			14 09		
	d			12 11						12 57								13 36			14 11		
Abercynon	d			12 19						13 04											14 19		
Penrhiwceiber	d			12 24																	14 24		
Mountain Ash	a			12 28																	14 28		
	d			12 31																	14 31		
Fernhill	d			12 33																	14 33		
Cwmbach	d			12 37																	14 37		
Aberdare 3	a			12 44																	14 44		
Quakers Yard	d									13 09													
Merthyr Vale	a									13 14													
	d									13 17													
Troed Y Rhiw	d									13 20													
Pentre-bach	d									13 23													
Merthyr Tydfil	a									13 31													
Trehafod	d																	13 41					
Porth	a																	13 44					
	d																	13 45					
Dinas Rhondda	d																	13 49					
Tonypandy	d																	13 51					
Llwynypia	d																	13 53					
Ystrad Rhondda	a																	13 56					
	d																	13 59					
Ton Pentre	d																	14 01					
Treorchy	d																	14 04					
Ynyswen	d																	14 07					
Treherbert	a																	14 13					

When events are being held at the Millenium Stadium, services are subject to alteration. Please check times before travelling.

Table 130

Sundays
7 August to 11 September

Bridgend, Barry Island, Barry, Penarth and Cardiff - Coryton, Rhymney, Pontypridd, Merthyr, Aberdare and Treherbert

		AW	AW	AW	AW	AW 🚌	AW	AW	AW	AW	AW	AW	AW	AW	AW	AW	AW	AW	AW	AW	AW	AW
Bridgend	d					13 25																
Llantwit Major	d					13 50																
Rhoose Cardiff Int Airport ✈	d					14 05																
Barry Island	d	13 25			13 55		14 25									14 55			15 25			15 55
Barry 3	d	13 30			14 00	14a20	14 30									15 00			15 30			16 00
Barry Docks	d	13 34			14 04		14 34									15 04			15 34			16 04
Cadoxton	d	13 37			14 07		14 37									15 07			15 37			16 07
Dinas Powys	d	13 41			14 11		14 41									15 11			15 41			16 11
Eastbrook	d	13 43			14 13		14 43									15 13			15 43			16 13
Cogan	d	13 45			14 15		14 45									15 15			15 45			16 15
Penarth	d									14 47												
Dingle Road	d									14 49												
Grangetown	d	13 49			14 19		14 49			14 53						15 19			15 49			16 19
Cardiff Central 7	a	13 57			14 24		14 56			14 59						15 24			15 57			16 24
	d	14 06			14 26								15 06			15 41			16 06			16 26
Cardiff Bay	d		14 06	14 18				14 30	14 42		14 54	15 06		15 18	15 30		15 42	15 54		16 06	16 18	
Cardiff Queen Street 3	a	14 09	14 10	14 22	14 29			14 34	14 46		14 58	15 10	15 09	15 22	15 34	15 44	15 46	15 58	16 09	16 10	16 22	16 29
	d	14 10			14 30								15 10			15 45			16 10			16 30
Heath Low Level	d																					
Ty Glas	d																					
Birchgrove	d																					
Rhiwbina	d																					
Whitchurch (Cardiff)	d																					
Coryton	a																					
Heath High Level	d	14 15																	16 15			
Llanishen	d	14 18																	16 18			
Lisvane & Thornhill	d	14 20																	16 20			
Caerphilly 3	d	14 26																	16 26			
Aber	d	14 28																	16 28			
Llanbradach	d	14 32																	16 32			
Ystrad Mynach 3	d	14 37																	16 37			
Hengoed	d	14 40																	16 40			
Pengam	d	14 43																	16 43			
Gilfach Fargoed	d	14 46																	16 46			
Bargoed	a	14 49																	16 49			
	d	14 49																	16 49			
Brithdir	d	14 53																	16 53			
Tir-phil	d	14 56																	16 56			
Pontlottyn	d	15 00																	17 00			
Rhymney 3	a	15 07																	17 07			
Cathays	d				14 33								15 13			15 48						16 33
Llandaf	d				14 37								15 17			15 52						16 37
Ninian Park	d																					
Waun-gron Park	d																					
Fairwater	d																					
Danescourt	d																					
Radyr 3	a				14 40								15 20			15 55						16 40
	d				14 40								15 20			15 55						16 40
Taffs Well 3	d				14 44								15 24			15 59						16 44
Trefforest Estate	d																					
Trefforest	d				14 52								15 31			16 06						16 52
Pontypridd 3	a				14 55								15 34			16 09						16 55
	d				14 57								15 36			16 11						16 57
Abercynon	d				15 04											16 19						17 04
Penrhiwceiber	d															16 24						
Mountain Ash	a															16 28						
	d															16 31						
Fernhill	d															16 33						
Cwmbach	d															16 37						
Aberdare 3	a															16 44						
Quakers Yard	d				15 09																	17 09
Merthyr Vale	a				15 14																	17 14
	d				15 17																	17 17
Troed Y Rhiw	d				15 20																	17 20
Pentre-bach	d				15 23																	17 23
Merthyr Tydfil	a				15 31																	17 31
Trehafod	d												15 41									
Porth	a												15 44									
	d												15 45									
Dinas Rhondda	d												15 49									
Tonypandy	d												15 51									
Llwynypia	d												15 53									
Ystrad Rhondda	a												15 56									
	d												15 59									
Ton Pentre	d												16 01									
Treorchy	d												16 04									
Ynyswen	d												16 07									
Treherbert	a												16 13									

When events are being held at the Millenium Stadium, services are subject to alteration. Please check times before travelling.

Table 130

Sundays

7 August to 11 September

Bridgend, Barry Island, Barry, Penarth and Cardiff - Coryton, Rhymney, Pontypridd, Merthyr, Aberdare and Treherbert

Station		AW [bus]	AW	AW	AW	AW	AW	AW		AW	AW	AW	AW	AW	AW	AW	AW	AW		AW	AW	AW [bus]	AW	AW	AW
Bridgend	d	15 25																				17 25			
Llantwit Major	d	15 50																				17 50			
Rhoose Cardiff Int Airport ✈	d	16 05																				18 05			
Barry Island	d		16 25				16 40							16 55			17 25				17 55		18 25		
Barry 3	d	16a20	16 30				16 45							17 00			17 30				18 00	18a20	18 30		
Barry Docks	d		16 34											17 04			17 34				18 04		18 34		
Cadoxton	d		16 37											17 07			17 37				18 07		18 37		
Dinas Powys	d		16 41											17 11			17 41				18 11		18 41		
Eastbrook	d		16 43											17 13			17 43				18 13		18 43		
Cogan	d		16 45											17 15			17 45				18 15		18 45		
Penarth	d					16 47																			
Dingle Road	d					16 49																			
Grangetown	d		16 49			16 53								17 19			17 49				18 19		18 49		
Cardiff Central 7	a		16 56			16 59	17 02							17 24			17 57				18 24		18 56		
	d										17 06			17 41			18 06				18 26				
Cardiff Bay	d			16 30	16 42			16 54		17 06		17 18	17 30		17 42	17 54		18 06		18 18				18 30	18 42
Cardiff Queen Street 3	a			16 34	16 46			16 58		17 10	17 09	17 22	17 34	17 44	17 46	17 58	18 09	18 10		18 22	18 29			18 34	18 46
	d										17 10			17 45			18 10				18 30				
Heath Low Level	d																								
Ty Glas	d																								
Birchgrove	d																								
Rhiwbina	d																								
Whitchurch (Cardiff)	d																								
Coryton	a																								
Heath High Level	d																18 15								
Llanishen	d																18 18								
Lisvane & Thornhill	d																18 20								
Caerphilly 3	d																18 26								
Aber	d																18 28								
Llanbradach	d																18 32								
Ystrad Mynach 3	d																18 37								
Hengoed	d																18 40								
Pengam	d																18 43								
Gilfach Fargoed	d																18 46								
Bargoed	a																18 49								
	d																18 49								
Brithdir	d																18 53								
Tir-phil	d																18 56								
Pontlottyn	d																19 00								
Rhymney 3	a																19 07								
Cathays	d										17 13			17 48							18 33				
Llandaf	d										17 17			17 52							18 37				
Ninian Park	d																								
Waun-gron Park	d																								
Fairwater	d																								
Danescourt	d																								
Radyr 3	a										17 20			17 55							18 40				
	d										17 20			17 55							18 40				
Taffs Well 3	d										17 24			17 59							18 44				
Trefforest Estate	d																								
Trefforest	d										17 31			18 06							18 52				
Pontypridd 3	a										17 34			18 09							18 55				
	d										17 36			18 11							18 57				
Abercynon	d													18 19							19 04				
Penrhiwceiber	d													18 24											
Mountain Ash	a													18 28											
	d													18 31											
Fernhill	d													18 33											
Cwmbach	d													18 37											
Aberdare 3	a													18 44											
Quakers Yard	d																				19 09				
Merthyr Vale	a																				19 14				
	d																				19 17				
Troed Y Rhiw	d																				19 20				
Pentre-bach	d																				19 23				
Merthyr Tydfil	a																				19 31				
Trehafod	d										17 41														
Porth	a										17 44														
	d										17 45														
Dinas Rhondda	d										17 49														
Tonypandy	d										17 51														
Llwynypia	d										17 53														
Ystrad Rhondda	a										17 56														
	d										17 59														
Ton Pentre	d										18 01														
Treorchy	d										18 04														
Ynyswen	d										18 07														
Treherbert	a										18 13														

When events are being held at the Millenium Stadium, services are subject to alteration. Please check times before travelling.

Table 130

Sundays

7 August to 11 September

Bridgend, Barry Island, Barry, Penarth and Cardiff - Coryton, Rhymney, Pontypridd, Merthyr, Aberdare and Treherbert

Station		AW	AW	AW		AW	AW	AW	AW [bus]	AW	AW	AW	AW	AW		AW	AW [bus]	AW
Bridgend	d								19 25								21 55	
Llantwit Major	d								19 50								22 20	
Rhoose Cardiff Int Airport ✈	d								20 05								22 35	
Barry Island	d					18 55	19 25	19 55		20 25			20 55	21 25		21 55		22 55
Barry 3	d					19 00	19 30	20 00	20a20	20 30			21 00	21 30		22 00	22a50	23 00
Barry Docks	d					19 04	19 34	20 04		20 34			21 04	21 34		22 04		23 04
Cadoxton	d					19 07	19 37	20 07		20 37			21 07	21 37		22 07		23 07
Dinas Powys	d					19 11	19 41	20 11		20 41			21 11	21 41		22 11		23 11
Eastbrook	d					19 13	19 43	20 13		20 43			21 13	21 43		22 13		23 13
Cogan	d					19 15	19 45	20 15		20 45			21 15	21 45		22 15		23 15
Penarth	d	18 47									20 47							
Dingle Road	d	18 49									20 49							
Grangetown	d	18 53				19 19	19 49	20 19		20 49	20 53		21 19	21 49		22 19		23 19
Cardiff Central 7	a	18 59				19 24	19 57	20 24		20 54	21 01		21 27	21 54		22 27		23 27
	d			19 06		19 41	20 06	20 26		21 06		21 16		22 06				
Cardiff Bay	d		18 54															
Cardiff Queen Street 3	a		18 57	19 09		19 44	20 09	20 29		21 09		21 19		22 09				
	d			19 10		19 45	20 10	20 30		21 10		21 20		22 10				
Heath Low Level	d																	
Ty Glas	d																	
Birchgrove	d																	
Rhiwbina	d																	
Whitchurch (Cardiff)	d																	
Coryton	a																	
Heath High Level	d						20 15					21 25						
Llanishen	d						20 18					21 28						
Lisvane & Thornhill	d						20 20					21 30						
Caerphilly 3	d						20 26					21 36						
Aber	d						20 28					21 38						
Llanbradach	d						20 32					21 42						
Ystrad Mynach 3	d						20 37					21 47						
Hengoed	d						20 40					21 50						
Pengam	d						20 43					21 53						
Gilfach Fargoed	d						20 46					21 56						
Bargoed	a						20 49					21 59						
	d						20 49					21 59						
Brithdir	d						20 53					22 03						
Tir-phil	d						20 56					22 06						
Pontlottyn	d						21 00					22 10						
Rhymney 3	a						21 07					22 17						
Cathays	d			19 13		19 48		20 33		21 13				22 13				
Llandaf	d			19 17		19 52		20 37		21 17				22 17				
Ninian Park	d																	
Waun-gron Park	d																	
Fairwater	d																	
Danescourt	d																	
Radyr 3	a			19 20		19 55		20 40		21 20				22 20				
	d			19 20		19 55		20 40		21 20				22 20				
Taffs Well 3	d			19 24		19 59		20 44		21 24				22 24				
Trefforest Estate	d																	
Trefforest	d			19 31		20 06		20 52		21 31				22 31				
Pontypridd 3	a			19 34		20 09		20 55		21 34				22 34				
	d			19 36		20 11		20 57		21 36				22 36				
Abercynon	d					20 19		21 04										
Penrhiwceiber	d					20 24												
Mountain Ash	a					20 28												
	d					20 31												
Fernhill	d					20 33												
Cwmbach	d					20 37												
Aberdare 3	a					20 44												
Quakers Yard	d							21 09										
Merthyr Vale	a							21 14										
	d							21 17										
Troed Y Rhiw	d							21 20										
Pentre-bach	d							21 23										
Merthyr Tydfil	a							21 31										
Trehafod	d			19 41						21 41				22 41				
Porth	a			19 44						21 44				22 44				
	d			19 45						21 45				22 45				
Dinas Rhondda	d			19 49						21 49				22 49				
Tonypandy	d			19 51						21 51				22 51				
Llwynypia	d			19 53						21 53				22 53				
Ystrad Rhondda	a			19 56						21 56				22 56				
	d			19 59						21 59				22 59				
Ton Pentre	d			20 01						22 01				23 01				
Treorchy	d			20 04						22 04				23 04				
Ynyswen	d			20 07						22 07				23 07				
Treherbert	a			20 13						22 13				23 13				

When events are being held at the Millenium Stadium, services are subject to alteration. Please check times before travelling.

Table 130

Sundays from 18 September

Bridgend, Barry Island, Barry, Penarth and Cardiff - Coryton, Rhymney, Pontypridd, Merthyr, Aberdare and Treherbert

Station		AW	AW	AW	AW	AW	AW	AW	AW	AW	AW	AW	AW	AW	AW	AW A	AW B 🚌	AW	AW	AW	AW	AW	AW
Bridgend	d															09 42	09 25						
Llantwit Major	d															09 56	09 50						
Rhoose Cardiff Int Airport ✈	d															10 06	10 05						
Barry Island	d								08 55						09 55			10 25					
Barry [3]	d								09 00						10 00	10 15	10a20	10 30					
Barry Docks	d								09 04						10 04	10 19		10 34					
Cadoxton	d								09 07						10 07	10 22		10 37					
Dinas Powys	d								09 11						10 11	10 26		10 41					
Eastbrook	d								09 13						10 13	10 28		10 43					
Cogan	d								09 15						10 15	10 30		10 45					
Penarth	d																				10 47		
Dingle Road	d																				10 49		
Grangetown	d								09 19						10 19	10 34		10 49			10 53		
Cardiff Central [7]	a								09 24						10 24	10 42		10 56			10 59		
	d	08 26	08 41	08 54	09 00				09 41				10 06		10 26								11 00
Cardiff Bay	d					09 06	09 18	09 30		09 42	09 54	10 06		10 18					10 30	10 42		10 54	
Cardiff Queen Street [3]	a	08 29	08 44	08 57	09 03	09 10	09 22	09 34	09 44	09 46	09 58	10 10	10 09	10 22	10 29				10 34	10 46		10 58	11 03
	d	08 30	08 45		09 04				09 45				10 10		10 30								11 04
Heath Low Level	d																						
Ty Glas	d																						
Birchgrove	d																						
Rhiwbina	d																						
Whitchurch (Cardiff)	d																						
Coryton	a																						
Heath High Level	d												10 15										
Llanishen	d												10 18										
Lisvane & Thornhill	d												10 20										
Caerphilly [3]	d												10 26										
Aber	d												10 28										
Llanbradach	d												10 32										
Ystrad Mynach [3]	d												10 37										
Hengoed	d												10 40										
Pengam	d												10 43										
Gilfach Fargoed	d												10 46										
Bargoed	a												10 49										
	d												10 49										
Brithdir	d												10 53										
Tir-phil	d												10 56										
Pontlottyn	d												11 00										
Rhymney [3]	a												11 07										
Cathays	d	08 33	08 48		09 07				09 48						10 33								11 07
Llandaf	d	08 37	08 52		09 11				09 52						10 37								11 11
Ninian Park	d																						
Waun-gron Park	d																						
Fairwater	d																						
Danescourt	d																						
Radyr [3]	a	08 40	08 55		09 14				09 55						10 40								11 14
	d	08 40	08 55		09 14				09 55						10 40								11 14
Taffs Well [3]	d	08 44	08 59		09 18				09 59						10 44								11 18
Trefforest Estate	d																						
Trefforest	d	08 52	09 06		09 25				10 06						10 52								11 25
Pontypridd [3]	a	08 55	09 09		09 28				10 09						10 55								11 28
	d	08 57	09 11		09 30				10 11						10 57								11 30
Abercynon	d	09 05	09 19						10 19						11 04								
Penrhiwceiber	d		09 25						10 25														
Mountain Ash	a		09 28						10 28														
	d		09 31						10 31														
Fernhill	d		09 34						10 34														
Cwmbach	d		09 38						10 38														
Aberdare [3]	a		09 46						10 46														
Quakers Yard	d	09 09													11 09								
Merthyr Vale	a	09 14													11 14								
	d	09 17													11 17								
Troed Y Rhiw	d	09 20													11 20								
Pentre-bach	d	09 23													11 23								
Merthyr Tydfil	a	09 32													11 32								
Trehafod	d				09 35																		11 35
Porth	a				09 38																		11 38
	d				09 39																		11 39
Dinas Rhondda	d				09 43																		11 43
Tonypandy	d				09 45																		11 45
Llwynypia	d				09 47																		11 47
Ystrad Rhondda	a				09 50																		11 50
	d				09 53																		11 53
Ton Pentre	d				09 55																		11 55
Treorchy	d				09 58																		11 58
Ynyswen	d				10 01																		12 01
Treherbert	a				10 08																		12 08

A from 18 September until 23 October **B** from 30 October

When events are being held at the Millenium Stadium, services are subject to alteration. Please check times before travelling.

Table 130

Sundays from 18 September

Bridgend, Barry Island, Barry, Penarth and Cardiff - Coryton, Rhymney, Pontypridd, Merthyr, Aberdare and Treherbert

Station		AW	AW	AW	AW	AW	AW	AW	AW	AW	AW	AW A	AW B 🚌	AW	AW	AW	AW	AW	AW	AW	AW	AW	AW
Bridgend	d											11 42	11 25										
Llantwit Major	d											11 56	11 50										
Rhoose Cardiff Int Airport ✈	d											12 06	12 05										
Barry Island	d				10 55			11 25			11 55			12 25									12 55
Barry [3]	d				11 00			11 30			12 00	12 15	12a20	12 30									13 00
Barry Docks	d				11 04			11 34			12 04	12 19		12 34									13 04
Cadoxton	d				11 07			11 37			12 07	12 22		12 37									13 07
Dinas Powys	d				11 11			11 41			12 11	12 26		12 41									13 11
Eastbrook	d				11 13			11 43			12 13	12 28		12 43									13 13
Cogan	d				11 15			11 45			12 15	12 30		12 45									13 15
Penarth	d																12 47						
Dingle Road	d																12 49						
Grangetown	d				11 19			11 49			12 19	12 34		12 49			12 53						13 19
Cardiff Central [7]	a				11 24			11 57			12 24	12 42		12 56			12 59						13 24
	d				11 41			12 06			12 26									13 06			13 41
Cardiff Bay	d	11 06	11 18	11 30		11 42	11 54		12 06	12 18					12 30	12 42		12 54	13 06		13 18	13 30	
Cardiff Queen Street [3]	a	11 10	11 22	11 34	11 44	11 46	11 58	12 09	12 10	12 22	12 29				12 34	12 46		12 58	13 10	13 09	13 22	13 34	13 44
	d				11 45			12 10			12 30									13 10			13 45
Heath Low Level	d																						
Ty Glas	d																						
Birchgrove	d																						
Rhiwbina	d																						
Whitchurch (Cardiff)	d																						
Coryton	a																						
Heath High Level	d							12 15															
Llanishen	d							12 18															
Lisvane & Thornhill	d							12 20															
Caerphilly [3]	d							12 26															
Aber	d							12 28															
Llanbradach	d							12 32															
Ystrad Mynach [3]	d							12 37															
Hengoed	d							12 40															
Pengam	d							12 43															
Gilfach Fargoed	d							12 46															
Bargoed	a							12 49															
	d							12 49															
Brithdir	d							12 53															
Tir-phil	d							12 56															
Pontlottyn	d							13 00															
Rhymney [3]	a							13 08															
Cathays	d				11 48						12 33									13 13			13 48
Llandaf	d				11 52						12 37									13 17			13 52
Ninian Park	d																						
Waun-gron Park	d																						
Fairwater	d																						
Danescourt	d																						
Radyr [3]	a				11 55						12 40									13 20			13 55
	d				11 55						12 40									13 20			13 55
Taffs Well [3]	d				11 59						12 44									13 24			13 59
Trefforest Estate	d																						
Trefforest	d				12 06						12 52									13 31			14 06
Pontypridd [3]	a				12 09						12 55									13 34			14 09
	d				12 11						12 57									13 36			14 11
Abercynon	d				12 19						13 04												14 19
Penrhiwceiber	d				12 25																		14 25
Mountain Ash	a				12 28																		14 28
	d				12 31																		14 31
Fernhill	d				12 34																		14 34
Cwmbach	d				12 38																		14 38
Aberdare [3]	a				12 46																		14 46
Quakers Yard	d										13 09												
Merthyr Vale	a										13 14												
	d										13 17												
Troed Y Rhiw	d										13 20												
Pentre-bach	d										13 23												
Merthyr Tydfil	a										13 32												
Trehafod	d																			13 41			
Porth	a																			13 44			
	d																			13 45			
Dinas Rhondda	d																			13 49			
Tonypandy	d																			13 51			
Llwynypia	d																			13 53			
Ystrad Rhondda	a																			13 56			
	d																			13 59			
Ton Pentre	d																			14 01			
Treorchy	d																			14 04			
Ynyswen	d																			14 07			
Treherbert	a																			14 14			

A from 18 September until 23 October **B** from 30 October

When events are being held at the Millenium Stadium, services are subject to alteration. Please check times before travelling.

Table 130

Sundays
from 18 September

Bridgend, Barry Island, Barry, Penarth and Cardiff - Coryton, Rhymney, Pontypridd, Merthyr, Aberdare and Treherbert

		AW		AW	AW	AW	AW	AW	AW	AW	AW	AW		AW	AW	AW	AW	AW	AW	AW	AW	AW		AW	AW
Bridgend	d								13 42																
Llantwit Major	d								13 56																
Rhoose Cardiff Int Airport ✈	d								14 10																
Barry Island	d				13 25			13 55		14 25										14 55				15 25	
Barry 🅱	d				13 30			14 00	14 19	14 30										15 00				15 30	
Barry Docks	d				13 34			14 04	14 23	14 34										15 04				15 34	
Cadoxton	d				13 37			14 07	14 26	14 37										15 07				15 37	
Dinas Powys	d				13 41			14 11	14 30	14 41										15 11				15 41	
Eastbrook	d				13 43			14 13	14 32	14 43										15 13				15 43	
Cogan	d				13 45			14 15	14 34	14 45										15 15				15 45	
Penarth	d													14 47											
Dingle Road	d													14 49											
Grangetown	d				13 49			14 19	14 38	14 49				14 53						15 19				15 49	
Cardiff Central 🅱	a				13 57			14 24	14 46	14 56				14 59						15 24				15 57	
	d				14 06			14 26									15 06			15 41				16 06	
Cardiff Bay	d	13 42		13 54		14 06	14 18				14 30	14 42			14 54	15 06		15 18	15 30		15 42	15 54			16 06
Cardiff Queen Street 🅱	a	13 46		13 58	14 09	14 10	14 22	14 29			14 34	14 46			14 58	15 10	15 09	15 22	15 34	15 44	15 46	15 58		16 09	16 10
	d				14 10			14 30									15 10			15 45				16 10	
Heath Low Level	d																								
Ty Glas	d																								
Birchgrove	d																								
Rhiwbina	d																								
Whitchurch (Cardiff)	d																								
Coryton	a																								
Heath High Level	d				14 15																			16 15	
Llanishen	d				14 18																			16 18	
Lisvane & Thornhill	d				14 20																			16 20	
Caerphilly 🅱	d				14 26																			16 26	
Aber	d				14 28																			16 28	
Llanbradach	d				14 32																			16 32	
Ystrad Mynach 🅱	d				14 37																			16 37	
Hengoed	d				14 40																			16 40	
Pengam	d				14 43																			16 43	
Gilfach Fargoed	d				14 46																			16 46	
Bargoed	a				14 49																			16 49	
	d				14 49																			16 49	
Brithdir	d				14 53																			16 53	
Tir-phil	d				14 56																			16 56	
Pontlottyn	d				15 00																			17 00	
Rhymney 🅱	a				15 08																			17 08	
Cathays	d							14 33									15 13			15 48					
Llandaf	d							14 37									15 17			15 52					
Ninian Park	d																								
Waun-gron Park	d																								
Fairwater	d																								
Danescourt	d																								
Radyr 🅱	a							14 40									15 20			15 55					
	d							14 40									15 20			15 55					
Taffs Well 🅱	d							14 44									15 24			15 59					
Trefforest Estate	d																								
Trefforest	d							14 52									15 31			16 06					
Pontypridd 🅱	a							14 55									15 34			16 09					
	d							14 57									15 36			16 11					
Abercynon	d							15 04												16 19					
Penrhiwceiber	d																			16 25					
Mountain Ash	a																			16 28					
	d																			16 31					
Fernhill	d																			16 34					
Cwmbach	d																			16 38					
Aberdare 🅱	a																			16 46					
Quakers Yard	d							15 09																	
Merthyr Vale	a							15 14																	
	d							15 17																	
Troed Y Rhiw	d							15 20																	
Pentre-bach	d							15 23																	
Merthyr Tydfil	a							15 32																	
Trehafod	d																15 41								
Porth	a																15 44								
	d																15 45								
Dinas Rhondda	d																15 49								
Tonypandy	d																15 51								
Llwynypia	d																15 53								
Ystrad Rhondda	a																15 56								
	d																15 59								
Ton Pentre	d																16 01								
Treorchy	d																16 04								
Ynyswen	d																16 07								
Treherbert	a																16 14								

When events are being held at the Millenium Stadium, services are subject to alteration. Please check times before travelling.

Table 130

Sundays
from 18 September

Bridgend, Barry Island, Barry, Penarth and Cardiff - Coryton, Rhymney, Pontypridd, Merthyr, Aberdare and Treherbert

		AW	AW	AW	AW	AW	AW	AW		AW	AW	AW	AW	AW	AW	AW	AW	AW		AW	AW	AW	AW	AW	AW
Bridgend	d			15 42																			17 42		
Llantwit Major	d			15 56																			17 56		
Rhoose Cardiff Int Airport ✈	d			16 06																			18 06		
Barry Island	d		15 55		16 25										16 55			17 25				17 55		18 25	
Barry 🅱	d		16 00	16 15	16 30										17 00			17 30				18 00	18 15	18 30	
Barry Docks	d		16 04	16 19	16 34										17 04			17 34				18 04	18 19	18 34	
Cadoxton	d		16 07	16 22	16 37										17 07			17 37				18 07	18 22	18 37	
Dinas Powys	d		16 11	16 26	16 41										17 11			17 41				18 11	18 26	18 41	
Eastbrook	d		16 13	16 28	16 43										17 13			17 43				18 13	18 28	18 43	
Cogan	d		16 15	16 30	16 45										17 15			17 45				18 15	18 30	18 45	
Penarth	d							16 47																	
Dingle Road	d							16 49																	
Grangetown	d		16 19	16 34	16 49			16 53							17 19			17 49				18 19	18 34	18 49	
Cardiff Central 🅱	a		16 24	16 42	16 56			16 59							17 24			17 57				18 24	18 42	18 56	
	d		16 26									17 06			17 41			18 06				18 26			
Cardiff Bay	d	16 18				16 30	16 42			16 54	17 06		17 18	17 30		17 42	17 54			18 06	18 18				18 30
Cardiff Queen Street 🅱	a	16 22	16 29			16 34	16 46			16 58	17 10	17 09	17 22	17 34	17 44	17 46	17 58	18 09		18 10	18 22	18 29			18 34
	d		16 30									17 10			17 45			18 10				18 30			
Heath Low Level	d																								
Ty Glas	d																								
Birchgrove	d																								
Rhiwbina	d																								
Whitchurch (Cardiff)	d																								
Coryton	a																								
Heath High Level	d																	18 15							
Llanishen	d																	18 18							
Lisvane & Thornhill	d																	18 20							
Caerphilly 🅱	d																	18 26							
Aber	d																	18 28							
Llanbradach	d																	18 32							
Ystrad Mynach 🅱	d																	18 37							
Hengoed	d																	18 40							
Pengam	d																	18 43							
Gilfach Fargoed	d																	18 46							
Bargoed	a																	18 49							
	d																	18 49							
Brithdir	d																	18 53							
Tir-phil	d																	18 56							
Pontlottyn	d																	19 00							
Rhymney 🅱	a																	19 08							
Cathays	d		16 33									17 13			17 48							18 33			
Llandaf	d		16 37									17 17			17 52							18 37			
Ninian Park	d																								
Waun-gron Park	d																								
Fairwater	d																								
Danescourt	d																								
Radyr 🅱	a		16 40									17 20			17 55							18 40			
	d		16 40									17 20			17 55							18 40			
Taffs Well 🅱	d		16 44									17 24			17 59							18 44			
Trefforest Estate	d																								
Trefforest	d		16 52									17 31			18 06							18 52			
Pontypridd 🅱	a		16 55									17 34			18 09							18 55			
	d		16 57									17 36			18 11							18 57			
Abercynon	d		17 04												18 19							19 04			
Penrhiwceiber	d														18 25										
Mountain Ash	a														18 28										
	d														18 31										
Fernhill	d														18 34										
Cwmbach	d														18 38										
Aberdare 🅱	a														18 46										
Quakers Yard	d		17 09																			19 09			
Merthyr Vale	a		17 14																			19 14			
	d		17 17																			19 17			
Troed Y Rhiw	d		17 20																			19 20			
Pentre-bach	d		17 23																			19 23			
Merthyr Tydfil	a		17 32																			19 32			
Trehafod	d											17 41													
Porth	a											17 44													
	d											17 45													
Dinas Rhondda	d											17 49													
Tonypandy	d											17 51													
Llwynypia	d											17 53													
Ystrad Rhondda	a											17 56													
	d											17 59													
Ton Pentre	d											18 01													
Treorchy	d											18 04													
Ynyswen	d											18 07													
Treherbert	a											18 14													

When events are being held at the Millenium Stadium, services are subject to alteration. Please check times before travelling.

Table 130

Sundays
from 18 September

Bridgend, Barry Island, Barry, Penarth and Cardiff - Coryton, Rhymney, Pontypridd, Merthyr, Aberdare and Treherbert

		AW	AW	AW	AW	AW	AW	AW	AW	AW	AW	AW	AW	AW	AW	AW	AW
Bridgend	d								19 42							21 42	
Llantwit Major	d								19 56							21 56	
Rhoose Cardiff Int Airport ✈	d								20 06							22 06	
Barry Island	d					18 55	19 25	19 55		20 25			20 55	21 25	21 55		22 55
Barry 3	d					19 00	19 30	20 00	20 15	20 30			21 00	21 30	22 00	22 15	23 00
Barry Docks	d					19 04	19 34	20 04	20 19	20 34			21 04	21 34	22 04	22 19	23 04
Cadoxton	d					19 07	19 37	20 07	20 22	20 37			21 07	21 37	22 07	22 22	23 07
Dinas Powys	d					19 11	19 41	20 11	20 26	20 41			21 11	21 41	22 11	22 26	23 11
Eastbrook	d					19 13	19 43	20 13	20 28	20 43			21 13	21 43	22 13	22 28	23 13
Cogan	d					19 15	19 45	20 15	20 30	20 45			21 15	21 45	22 15	22 30	23 15
Penarth	d		18 47								20 47						
Dingle Road	d		18 49								20 49						
Grangetown	d		18 53			19 19	19 49	20 19	20 34	20 49	20 53		21 19	21 49	22 19	22 34	23 19
Cardiff Central 7	a		18 59			19 24	19 57	20 24	20 42	20 54	21 01		21 27	21 54	22 27	22 42	23 27
	d				19 06	19 41	20 06	20 26		21 06		21 16		22 06			
Cardiff Bay	d	18 42		18 54													
Cardiff Queen Street 3	a	18 46		18 57	19 09	19 44	20 09	20 29		21 09		21 19		22 09			
	d				19 10	19 45	20 10	20 30		21 10		21 20		22 10			
Heath Low Level	d																
Ty Glas	d																
Birchgrove	d																
Rhiwbina	d																
Whitchurch (Cardiff)	d																
Coryton	a																
Heath High Level	d						20 15					21 25					
Llanishen	d						20 18					21 28					
Lisvane & Thornhill	d						20 20					21 30					
Caerphilly 3	d						20 26					21 36					
Aber	d						20 28					21 38					
Llanbradach	d						20 32					21 42					
Ystrad Mynach 3	d						20 37					21 47					
Hengoed	d						20 40					21 50					
Pengam	d						20 43					21 53					
Gilfach Fargoed	d						20 46					21 56					
Bargoed	a						20 49					21 59					
	d						20 49					21 59					
Brithdir	d						20 53					22 03					
Tir-phil	d						20 56					22 06					
Pontlottyn	d						21 00					22 10					
Rhymney 3	a						21 08					22 18					
Cathays	d				19 13	19 48		20 33		21 13				22 13			
Llandaf	d				19 17	19 52		20 37		21 17				22 17			
Ninian Park	d																
Waun-gron Park	d																
Fairwater	d																
Danescourt	d																
Radyr 3	a				19 20	19 55		20 40		21 20				22 20			
	d				19 20	19 55		20 40		21 20				22 20			
Taffs Well 3	d				19 24	19 59		20 44		21 24				22 24			
Trefforest Estate	d																
Trefforest	d				19 31	20 06		20 52		21 31				22 31			
Pontypridd 3	a				19 34	20 09		20 55		21 34				22 34			
	d				19 36	20 11		20 57		21 36				22 36			
Abercynon	d					20 19		21 04									
Penrhiwceiber	d					20 25											
Mountain Ash	a					20 28											
	d					20 31											
Fernhill	d					20 34											
Cwmbach	d					20 38											
Aberdare 3	a					20 46											
Quakers Yard	d							21 09									
Merthyr Vale	a							21 14									
	d							21 17									
Troed Y Rhiw	d							21 20									
Pentre-bach	d							21 23									
Merthyr Tydfil	a							21 32									
Trehafod	d				19 41					21 41				22 41			
Porth	a				19 44					21 44				22 44			
	d				19 45					21 45				22 45			
Dinas Rhondda	d				19 49					21 49				22 49			
Tonypandy	d				19 51					21 51				22 51			
Llwynypia	d				19 53					21 53				22 53			
Ystrad Rhondda	a				19 56					21 56				22 56			
	d				19 59					21 59				22 59			
Ton Pentre	d				20 01					22 01				23 01			
Treorchy	d				20 04					22 04				23 04			
Ynyswen	d				20 07					22 07				23 07			
Treherbert	a				20 14					22 14				23 14			

When events are being held at the Millenium Stadium, services are subject to alteration. Please check times before travelling.

Cardiff - Crewe, Liverpool and Manchester

Miles	Miles			AW MX	AW MX	AW MO	AW MX	AW MO	AW MX	AW	AW	AW		AW	AW	AW	AW	AW	AW	AW	AW	AW		AW	GW
				◇	◇	◇	◇	◇			◇	◇ 🛒		◇ 🛒		◇	◇ 🛒	◇ 🛒	◇ 🛒		◇ 🛒	◇ 🛒		◇ 🛒	◇■1 🍴
—	—	Swansea	d					21p52								04 36			07 03		07 45			08 55	
0	0	**Cardiff Central ■7**	d	19p34	20p55	21p04	21p55	23c00	00 30		04 35	05 10		05 40			06 50	07 21	08 05		08f50	09 21		10g05	
—	—	London Paddington ■15 ⊖	d																						08 22
—	—	Reading ■7	d																						08 52
11¾	11¾	**Newport (South Wales)**	d	19p48	21p10	21p19	22p11	23p20	00e59		04 52	05 28		05 57			07 04	07 36	08 19		09 04	09 36		10 19	
18¾	18¾	Cwmbran	d	19p58	21p20	21p30	22p23	23p29	01 10		05 03	05 38		06 08			07 14	07 46	08 29		09 14	09 46		10 29	
21¾	21¾	Pontypool and New Inn	d	20p03		21p36	22p29	23p35	01 16		05 09	05 44		06 13				07 52				09 52			
31¼	31¼	Abergavenny	d	20p12	21p33	21p46	22p39	23p45	01 27		05 18	05 53		06 23			07 27	08 01	08 42		09 27	10 01		10 42	
55¼	55¼	**Hereford ■7**	a	20p38	21p57	22p12	23p05	00 17	01 57		05 46	06 17		06 47			07 51	08 25	09 06		09 51	10 25		11 06	11 43
—	—		d	20p39	21p59	22p14	23p07				05 47	06 25		06 49			07 53	08 27	09 08		09 53	10 27		11 08	
67¾	67¾	Leominster	d	20p52	22p12	22p27	23p20				06 00	06 38		07 02			08 06		09 21		10 06			11 21	
78¾	78¾	Ludlow	d	21p03	22p23	22p38	23p31				06 11	06 49		07 13			08 17	08 48	09 32		10 17	10 48		11 32	
86	86	Craven Arms	d	21p12	22p31	22p48	23p41				06 20	06 57		07 21		07 54	08 25	08 56			10 25	10 56			
93¼	93¼	Church Stretton	d	21p21	22p40	22p57	23p50				06 29	07 06		07 30		08 07	08 34	09 05			10 39	11 05			
106	106	**Shrewsbury**	a	21p37	22p54	23p14	00 05				06 43	07 20		07 44		08 22	08 48	09 19	09 58		10 52	11 19		11 58	
—	—		d	21p39	23p06	23p14	00 10			05 44	06 44	07 24		07 46	07 57		08 50	09 24	09 59	10 18	10 53	11 24		11 59	
113¼	113¼	Yorton	d		23b15	23b23	00x19			05x52					08x06					10x28					
116¾	116¾	Wem	d		23p20	23p29	00 24			05 58	06 56			07 57	08 12					10 34					
120	120	Prees	d		23b25	23b34	00x29			06x03					08x17					10x39					
125	125	Whitchurch (Shrops)	d		23p32	23p41	00 36			06 10	07 04			08 06	08 25		09 06			10 46	11 11				
129¾	129¾	Wrenbury	d		23b38	23b47	00x42			06x17					08x31					10x53					
134¼	134¼	Nantwich	d		23p44	23p54	00 49			06 23	07 13			08 15	08 38		09 16			10 59	11 19				
138¾	138¾	**Crewe ■10**	a		23p53	00 02	01 04			06 35	07 22			08 24	08 47		09 25		10 30	11 09	11 29			12 29	
—	—	Chester	a	22p34	00 27	00 25						08 19						10 19				12 19			
—	—	Llandudno Junction	a	23p49								09 11						11 14				13 11			
—	—	Bangor (Gwynedd)	a	00 13								09 33						11 38				13 28			
—	—	Holyhead	a	00 58								10 14						12 14				14 13			
157¾	—	Wilmslow	a								07 44			08 45			09 48		10 48		11 48			12 48	
163¾	—	Stockport	a								07 54			08 55			09 58		10 58		11 58			12 58	
169¾	—	**Manchester Piccadilly ■10** 🚊	a								08 10			09 11			10 15		11 15		12 15			13 15	

		AW	AW	AW	AW	AW	GW	AW		AW	AW	AW	AW	AW	AW	AW	AW	AW BHX		AW	AW	AW	AW	AW	AW
			◇ 🛒	◇	◇ 🛒	◇ 🛒	◇■1 🍴			◇ 🛒	◇ 🛒	◇ 🛒		◇ 🛒	◇	■ 🛒	■ 🛒	■ ⊠			■ 🛒	■ 🛒	■ 🛒	■ 🛒	
Swansea	d		09 55	09 15		10 55				11 55		12 55		13 55	13 14		14 55				15 55		16 55		
Cardiff Central ■7	d		10 50		11 21	12h05				12 50	13 21	14i05		14 50		15 21	15 50	16 15			16 50	17 21	17 50	18 18	
London Paddington ■15 ⊖	d						10 22																		
Reading ■7	d						10 52																		
Newport (South Wales)	d		11 04		11 36	12 19				13 04	13 36	14 19		15 04		15 36	16 04	16 29			17 04	17 36	18 04	18 32	
Cwmbran	d		11 14		11 46	12 29				13 14	13 46	14 29		15 14		15 46	16 14	16 40			17 14	17 46	18 14		
Pontypool and New Inn	d				11 52						13 52					15 52	16 19					17 52	18 19		
Abergavenny	d		11 27		12 01	12 42				13 26	14 01	14 43		15 27		16 01	16 29	16 54			17 27	18 01	18 29	18 53	
Hereford ■7	a		11 51		12 25	13 06	13 50			13 53	14 25	15 06		15 51		16 25	16 53				17 51	18 25	18 53	19 17	
	d		11 53		12 27	13 08				13 55	14 27	15 08		15 53		16 27	16 54				17 53	18 27	18 54	19 18	
Leominster	d		12 06			13 21				14 08		15 21		16 06		16 40	17 07				18 06		19 07		
Ludlow	d		12 17		12 48	13 32				14 19	14 48	15 32		16 17		16 51	17 18				18 17	18 48	19 18		
Craven Arms	d		12 25	12 39	12 56					14 27	14 56			16 25	16 40		17 27				18 25		19 27		
Church Stretton	d		12 38	12 52	13 05					14 36	15 05				16 53	17 06	17 36				18 34		19 36		
Shrewsbury	a		12 52	13 08	13 19	13 58				14 50	15 19	15 58		16 48	17 09	17 20	17 50	18 05			18 48	19 14	19 50	20 03	
	d	12 18	12 54		13 24	13 59		14 18		14 52	15 24	15 59	16 23	16 50		17 24	17 51	18 06		18 25	18 50	19 24	19 51	20 05	20 32
Yorton	d	12x28						14x28					16x33							18 35					20x39
Wem	d	12 34						14 34					16 39	17 01						18 41					20 44
Prees	d	12x39						14x39					16x44							18 46					20x49
Whitchurch (Shrops)	d	12 46	13 10					14 46		15 08			16 51	17 10			18 09			18 53	19 06				20 56
Wrenbury	d	12x53						14x53					16x58							19x00					21x02
Nantwich	d	12 59	13 20					14 59		15 18			17 04	17 19			18 19			19 06	19 16				21 08
Crewe ■10	a	13 09	13 29			14 29		15 09		15 27		16 29	17 14	17 28			18 28	18 42		19 16	19 25		20 22		21 19
Chester	a				14 19						16 20					18 20		19 06				20 20		20 57	
Llandudno Junction	a				15 11						17 12					19 12		19 52				21 24		21 44	
Bangor (Gwynedd)	a				15 28						17 33					19 33		20 09				21 40		22 02	
Holyhead	a				16 15						18 18					20 18		20 49				22 25		22 34	
Wilmslow	a		13 48			14 48				15 47		16 48		17 47			18 48				19 48		20 40		
Stockport	a		13 58			14 58				15 58		16 58		17 57			18 58				19 58		20 50		
Manchester Piccadilly ■10 🚊	a		14 15			15 15				16 15		17 14		18 13			19 15				20 15		21 05		

b Previous night, stops on request
c Previous night, arr. 2249
e Arr. 0048
f Arr. 0844
g Arr. 0946
h Arr. 1148
i Arr. 1347

For connections from Bristol Temple Meads please refer to Table 132. For connections to Runcorn and Liverpool Lime Street please refer to Table 91

When events are being held at the Millenium Stadium, services are subject to alteration. Please check times before travelling.

Table 131

Cardiff - Crewe, Liverpool and Manchester

Mondays to Fridays

until 9 September

		AW	GW	AW		AW	AW	GW	AW	GW	AW
		◇	◇1	◇		◇	◇	◇1	◇	◇1	◇
								A			
		⚲	⊡					⊡		⊡	
Swansea	d	17 55				18 21					
Cardiff Central 7	d	18 50		19 34			20 17		20 55		21 55
London Paddington 15 ⊖	d		17 22					18 22		19 22	
Reading 7	d		17 50					18 50		19 52	
Newport (South Wales)	d	19 05		19 48			20 31		21 10		22 11
Cwmbran	d	19 15		19 58			20 41		21 20		22 23
Pontypool and New Inn	d	19 20		20 03			20 47				22 29
Abergavenny	d	19 30		20 12			20 58		21 33		22 39
Hereford 7	a	19 54	20 36	20 38			21 22	21 33	21 57	22 54	23 05
	d	19 55		20 39			21 24		21 59		23 07
Leominster	d	20 08		20 52			21 37		22 12		23 20
Ludlow	d	20 19		21 03			21 48		22 23		23 31
Craven Arms	d	20 28		21 12		21 38	21 56		22 31		23 41
Church Stretton	d	20 37		21 21		21 51	22 05		22 40		23 50
Shrewsbury	a	20 51		21 37		22 08	22 19		22 54		00 05
	d	20 52		21 39			22 21		23 06		00 10
Yorton	d						22x29		23x15		00x19
Wem	d						22 34		23 20		00 24
Prees	d						22x38		23x25		00x29
Whitchurch (Shrops)	d	21 10					22 45		23 32		00 36
Wrenbury	d						22x51		23x38		00x42
Nantwich	d	21 20					22 56		23 44		00 49
Crewe 10	a	21 29					23 06		23 53		01 04
Chester	a			22 34					00 27		
Llandudno Junction	a			23 49							
Bangor (Gwynedd)	a			00 13							
Holyhead	a			00 58							
Wilmslow	a	21 48					23 24				
Stockport	a	21 58					23 35				
Manchester Piccadilly 10 ⛴	a	22 13					23 53				

Mondays to Fridays

from 12 September

		AW MX	AW MX	AW MO	AW MX	AW MO	AW MX	AW	AW	AW		AW	AW
		◇	◇	◇	◇	◇			◇	◇		◇	
										⚲		⚲	
Swansea	d					21p52							
Cardiff Central 7	d	19p34	20p55	21p04	21p55	23c00	00 30		04 35	05 10		05 40	
London Paddington 15 ⊖	d												
Reading 7	d												
Newport (South Wales)	d	19p48	21p10	21p19	22p11	23p20	00e59		04 52	05 28		05 57	
Cwmbran	d	19p58	21p20	21p30	22p23	23p29	01 10		05 03	05 38		06 08	
Pontypool and New Inn	d	20p03		21p36	22p29	23p35	01 16		05 09	05 44		06 13	
Abergavenny	d	20p12	21p33	21p46	22p39	23p45	01 27		05 18	05 53		06 23	
Hereford 7	a	20p38	21p57	22p12	23p05	00 17	01 57		05 46	06 17		06 47	
	d	20p39	21p59	22p14	23p07				05 47	06 25		06 49	
Leominster	d	20p52	22p12	22p27	23p20				06 00	06 38		07 02	
Ludlow	d	21p03	22p23	22p38	23p31				06 11	06 49		07 13	
Craven Arms	d	21p12	22p31	22p48	23p41				06 20	06 57		07 21	
Church Stretton	d	21p21	22p40	22p57	23p50				06 29	07 06		07 30	
Shrewsbury	a	21p37	22p54	23p14	00 05				06 43	07 20		07 44	
	d	21p39	23p06	23p14	00 10			05 44	06 44	07 24		07 46	07 57
Yorton	d		23b15	23b23	00x19			05x52					08x06
Wem	d		23p20	23p29	00 24			05 58	06 56			07 57	08 12
Prees	d		23b25	23b34	00x29			06x03					08x17
Whitchurch (Shrops)	d		23p32	23p41	00 36			06 10	07 04			08 06	08 25
Wrenbury	d		23b38	23b47	00x42			06x17					08x31
Nantwich	d		23p44	23p54	00 49			06 23	07 13			08 15	08 38
Crewe 10	a		23p53	00 02	01 04			06 35	07 22			08 24	08 47
Chester	a	22p34	00 27	00 25						08 19			
Llandudno Junction	a	23p49								09 11			
Bangor (Gwynedd)	a	00 13								09 33			
Holyhead	a	00 58								10 14			
Wilmslow	a								07 44			08 45	
Stockport	a								07 54			08 55	
Manchester Piccadilly 10 ⛴	a								08 10			09 11	

		AW	AW	AW	AW	AW	AW	AW		AW	GW	AW	AW
		◇	◇	◇	◇		◇	◇		◇	◇1		◇
			⚲	⚲	⚲		⚲	⚲		⚲	⊡		⚲
Swansea	d	04 36			07 03		07 45			08 55			09 55
Cardiff Central 7	d		06 50	07 21	08 05		08f50	09 21		10g05			10 50
London Paddington 15 ⊖	d										08 22		
Reading 7	d										08 52		
Newport (South Wales)	d		07 04	07 36	08 19		09 04	09 36		10 19			11 04
Cwmbran	d		07 14	07 46	08 29		09 14	09 46		10 29			11 14
Pontypool and New Inn	d			07 52				09 52					
Abergavenny	d		07 27	08 01	08 42		09 27	10 01		10 42			11 27
Hereford 7	a		07 51	08 25	09 06		09 51	10 25		11 06	11 42		11 51
	d		07 53	08 27	09 08		09 53	10 27		11 08			11 53
Leominster	d		08 06		09 21		10 06			11 21			12 06
Ludlow	d		08 17	08 48	09 32		10 17	10 48		11 32			12 17
Craven Arms	d	07 54	08 25	08 56			10 25	10 56					12 25
Church Stretton	d	08 07	08 34	09 05			10 39	11 05					12 38
Shrewsbury	a	08 22	08 48	09 19	09 58		10 52	11 19		11 58			12 52
	d		08 50	09 24	09 59	10 18	10 53	11 24		11 59		12 18	12 54
Yorton	d					10x28						12x28	
Wem	d					10 34						12 34	
Prees	d					10x39						12x39	
Whitchurch (Shrops)	d		09 06			10 46	11 11					12 46	13 10
Wrenbury	d					10x53						12x53	
Nantwich	d		09 16			10 59	11 19					12 59	13 20
Crewe 10	a		09 25		10 30	11 09	11 29			12 29		13 09	13 29
Chester	a			10 19				12 19					
Llandudno Junction	a			11 14				13 11					
Bangor (Gwynedd)	a			11 38				13 28					
Holyhead	a			12 14				14 13					
Wilmslow	a		09 48		10 48		11 48			12 48			13 48
Stockport	a		09 58		10 58		11 58			12 58			13 58
Manchester Piccadilly 10 ⛴	a		10 15		11 15		12 15			13 15			14 15

A The Cathedrals Express
b Previous night, stops on request
c Previous night, arr. 2249
e Arr. 0048
f Arr. 0844
g Arr. 0946

For connections from Bristol Temple Meads please refer to Table 132. For connections to Runcorn and Liverpool Lime Street please refer to Table 91

When events are being held at the Millenium Stadium, services are subject to alteration. Please check times before travelling.

Cardiff - Crewe, Liverpool and Manchester

		AW	AW	AW	GW	AW		AW	AW	AW	AW	AW	AW	AW	AW	AW		AW	AW	AW	AW	AW	AW	AW	GW
																BHX									
														■	■	■			■	■	■	■			
		◇	◇ ⊥	◇ ⊥	◇■1 ⊐			◇ ⊥	◇ ⊥	◇ ⊥		◇ ⊥	◇	⊥	⊥	⊠			⊥	⊥	⊥	⊥		◇ ⊥	◇■1 ⊐
Swansea	d	09 15		10 55				11 55		12 55		13 55	13 14		14 55				15 55		16 55			17 55	
Cardiff Central [7]	d		11 21	12b05				12 50	13 21	14c05		14 50		15 21	15 50	16 15			16 50	17 21	17 50	18 18		18 50	
London Paddington [15] ⊖	d				10 22																				17 22
Reading [7]	d				10 52																				17 50
Newport (South Wales)	d		11 36	12 19				13 04	13 36	14 19		15 04		15 36	16 04	16 29			17 04	17 36	18 04	18 32		19 05	
Cwmbran	d		11 46	12 29				13 14	13 46	14 29		15 14		15 46	16 14	16 40			17 14	17 46	18 14			19 15	
Pontypool and New Inn	d		11 52						13 52					15 52	16 19					17 52	18 19			19 20	
Abergavenny	d		12 01	12 42				13 26	14 01	14 43		15 27		16 01	16 29	16 54			17 27	18 01	18 29	18 53		19 30	
Hereford [7]	a		12 25	13 06	13 50			13 53	14 25	15 06		15 51		16 25	16 53				17 51	18 25	18 53	19 17		19 54	20 27
	d		12 27	13 08				13 55	14 27	15 08		15 53		16 27	16 54				17 53	18 27	18 54	19 18		19 55	
Leominster	d			13 21				14 08		15 21		16 06		16 40	17 07				18 06		19 07			20 08	
Ludlow	d		12 48	13 32				14 19	14 48	15 32		16 17		16 51	17 18				18 17	18 48	19 18			20 19	
Craven Arms	d	12 39	12 56					14 27	14 56			16 25	16 40		17 27				18 25		19 27			20 28	
Church Stretton	d	12 52	13 05					14 36	15 05				16 53	17 06	17 36				18 34		19 36			20 37	
Shrewsbury	a	13 08	13 19	13 58				14 50	15 19	15 58		16 48	17 09	17 20	17 50	18 05			18 48	19 14	19 50	20 03		20 51	
	d		13 24	13 59		14 18		14 52	15 24	15 59	16 23	16 50		17 24	17 51	18 06		18 25	18 50	19 24	19 51	20 05	20 32	20 52	
Yorton	d					14x28					16x33							18 35					20x39		
Wem	d					14 34					16 39	17 01						18 41					20 44		
Prees	d					14x39					16x44							18 46					20x49		
Whitchurch (Shrops)	d					14 46		15 08			16 51	17 10			18 09			18 53	19 06				20 56	21 10	
Wrenbury	d					14x53					16x58							19x00					21x02		
Nantwich	d					14 59		15 18			17 04	17 19			18 19			19 06	19 16				21 08	21 20	
Crewe [10]	a			14 29		15 09		15 27		16 29	17 14	17 28			18 28	18 42		19 16	19 25		20 22		21 19	21 29	
Chester	a		14 19						16 20					18 20		19 06				20 20		20 57			
Llandudno Junction	a		15 11						17 12					19 12		19 52				21 24		21 44			
Bangor (Gwynedd)	a		15 28						17 33					19 33		20 09				21 40		22 02			
Holyhead	a		16 15						18 18					20 18		20 49				22 25		22 34			
Wilmslow	a			14 48				15 47		16 48		17 47			18 48				19 48		20 40			21 48	
Stockport	a			14 58				15 58		16 58		17 57			18 58				19 58		20 50			21 58	
Manchester Piccadilly [10] ⛴	a			15 15				16 15		17 14		18 13			19 15				20 15		21 05			22 13	

		AW		AW	AW	GW	AW	GW	AW
		◇		◇	◇	◇■1	◇	◇■1	◇
						A			
						⊐		⊐	
Swansea	d			18 21					
Cardiff Central [7]	d	19 34			20 17		20 55		21 55
London Paddington [15] ⊖	d					18 22		19 22	
Reading [7]	d					18 50		19 52	
Newport (South Wales)	d	19 48			20 31		21 10		22 11
Cwmbran	d	19 58			20 41		21 20		22 23
Pontypool and New Inn	d	20 03			20 47				22 29
Abergavenny	d	20 12			20 58		21 33		22 39
Hereford [7]	a	20 38			21 22	21 33	21 57	22 54	23 05
	d	20 39			21 24		21 59		23 07
Leominster	d	20 52			21 37		22 12		23 20
Ludlow	d	21 03			21 48		22 23		23 31
Craven Arms	d	21 12		21 38	21 56		22 31		23 41
Church Stretton	d	21 21		21 51	22 05		22 40		23 50
Shrewsbury	a	21 37		22 08	22 19		22 54		00 05
	d	21 39			22 21		23 06		00 10
Yorton	d				22x29		23x15		00x19
Wem	d				22 34		23 20		00 24
Prees	d				22x38		23x25		00x29
Whitchurch (Shrops)	d				22 45		23 32		00 36
Wrenbury	d				22x51		23x38		00x42
Nantwich	d				22 56		23 44		00 49
Crewe [10]	a				23 06		23 53		01 04
Chester	a	22 34					00 27		
Llandudno Junction	a	23 49							
Bangor (Gwynedd)	a	00 13							
Holyhead	a	00 58							
Wilmslow	a				23 24				
Stockport	a				23 35				
Manchester Piccadilly [10] ⛴	a				23 53				

A The Cathedrals Express

b Arr. 1148

c Arr. 1347

For connections from Bristol Temple Meads please refer to Table 132. For connections to Runcorn and Liverpool Lime Street please refer to Table 91

When events are being held at the Millenium Stadium, services are subject to alteration. Please check times before travelling.

Table 131

Saturdays

until 30 July

Cardiff - Crewe, Liverpool and Manchester

		AW	AW	AW	AW	AW	AW	AW	AW	AW		AW	AW	AW	AW	AW	AW	AW	AW	GW		AW	AW	AW	AW
		◇	◇	◇			◇	◇ ⚲	◇ ⚲			◇	◇ ⚲	◇ ⚲	◇ ⚲		◇ ⚲	◇ ⚲	◇ ⚲	◇ 1 ⊒			◇ ⚲	◇	◇ ⚲
Swansea	d											04 36			06 47		07 45		08 55				09 55	09 16	
Cardiff Central 7	d	19p34	20p55	21p55	00 30		04 35	05 20	05 40				06 50	07 21	07c50		08e50	09 21	09f55				10g55		11 21
London Paddington 15 ⊖	d																			08 21					
Reading 7	d																			08 54					
Newport (South Wales)	d	19p48	21p10	22p11	00 52		04 52	05 35	05 57				07 04	07 36	08 04		09 04	09 36	10 09				11 09		11 36
Cwmbran	d	19p58	21p20	22p23	01 02		05 03	05 45	06 08				07 14	07 46	08 14		09 14	09 46	10 19				11 19		11 46
Pontypool and New Inn	d	20p03		22p29	01 08		05 09	05 51	06 13					07 51				09 51							11 50
Abergavenny	d	20p12	21p33	22p39	01 19		05 18	06 00	06 23				07 27	08 01	08 27		09 27	10 01	10 32				11 32		12 01
Hereford 7	a	20p38	21p57	23p05	01 49		05 46	06 24	06 47				07 51	08 26	08 51		09 51	10 26	10 56	11 41			11 56		12 26
	d	20p39	21p59	23p07			05 47	06 26	06 49				07 53	08 27	08 53		09 53	10 27	10 58				11 58		12 27
Leominster	d	20p52	22p12	23p20			06 00	06 40	07 02				08 06		09 06		10 06		11 11				12 11		
Ludlow	d	21p03	22p23	23p31			06 11	06 51	07 13				08 17	08 48	09 17		10 17	10 48	11 22				12 22		12 48
Craven Arms	d	21p12	22p31	23p41			06 20	06 59	07 21			07 54	08 25	08 56			10 25	10 56					12 30	12 37	12 56
Church Stretton	d	21p21	22p40	23p50			06 29	07 08	07 30			08 07	08 34	09 05			10 34	11 05					12 39	12 51	13 05
Shrewsbury	a	21p37	22p54	00 05			06 43	07 22	07 44			08 22	08 51	09 19	09 43		10 48	11 19	11 48				12 53	13 09	13 19
	d	21p39	23p06	00 10		05 44	06 44	07 24	07 46	07 57			08 52	09 24	09 44	10 18	10 50	11 24	11 49			12 23	12 55		13 24
Yorton	d		23b15	00x19		05x52				08x06						10x28						12x33			
Wem	d		23p20	00 24		05 58	06 56		07 57	08 12						10 34						12 39			
Prees	d		23b25	00x29		06x03				08x17						10x39						12x44			
Whitchurch (Shrops)	d		23p32	00 36		06 10	07 04		08 06	08 25			09 09		10 01	10 46	11 06		12 06			12 51			
Wrenbury	d		23b38	00x42		06x17				08x31						10x53						12x58			
Nantwich	d		23p44	00 49		06 23	07 13		08 15	08 38			09 18		10 10	10 59	11 16		12 15			13 04			
Crewe 10	a		23p53	01 04		06 35	07 22		08 24	08 47			09 27		10 20	11 09	11 25		12 24			13 14	13 25		
Chester	a	22p34	00 27					08 18						10 19				12 19							14 19
Llandudno Junction	a	23p49						09 11						11 11				13 11							15 11
Bangor (Gwynedd)	a	00 13						09 33						11 33				13 28							15 28
Holyhead	a	00 58						10 14						12 09				14 13							16 13
Wilmslow	a						07 44		08 45				09 47		10 48		11 48		12 48				13 48		
Stockport	a						08 01		08 58				09 57		10 58		11 58		12 58				13 58		
Manchester Piccadilly 10 ✈	a						08 20		09 15				10 14		11 15		12 15		13 15				14 15		

		AW	GW	AW	AW	AW		AW	AW	AW	AW	AW	AW	AW	AW	AW		AW	AW	GW	AW	AW	AW	AW	GW
		◇ ⚲	◇ 1 ⊒		◇ ⚲	◇ ⚲		◇ ⚲		◇ ⚲	◇	R ⚲	R ⚲			R ⚲		R ⚲	R ⚲	◇ 1 ⊒		◇	◇	◇	◇ 1 ⊒
Swansea	d	10 55			12 00			12 55		14 00	13 16		14 55	15 10		15 55			16 55				18 21		
Cardiff Central 7	d	11h55			12 55	13 21		13i55		14 55		15 21	15j55	16 19		16k55		17 21	17l55			19 34		20 10	
London Paddington 15 ⊖	d		10 21																	16 21					18 21
Reading 7	d		10 54																	16 54					18 54
Newport (South Wales)	d	12 09			13 09	13 36		14 09		15 09		15 36	16 09	16 34		17 09		17 36	18 09			19 48		20 26	
Cwmbran	d	12 19			13 19	13 46		14 19		15 19		15 46	16 19	16 44		17 19		17 46	18 19			19 58		20 37	
Pontypool and New Inn	d					13 50						15 52	16 24	16 50				17 52	18 24			20 03		20 42	
Abergavenny	d	12 32			13 32	14 01		14 32		15 32		16 01	16 34	17a02		17 32		18 01	18 34			20 12		20 52	
Hereford 7	a	12 56	13 40		13 56	14 26		14 56		15 56		16 25	16 58			17 56		18 25	18 58	19 45		20 38		21 17	21 36
	d	12 58			13 58	14 27		14 58		15 58		16 27	16 59			17 58		18 27	18 59			20 39		21 20	
Leominster	d	13 11			14 11			15 11		16 11		16 40	17 12			18 11			19 12			20 52		21 33	
Ludlow	d	13 22			14 22	14 48		15 22		16 22		16 51	17 23			18 22		18 48	19 23			21 03		21 44	
Craven Arms	d				14 30	14 56				16 30	16 38					18 30		18 56				21 12	21 38	21 53	
Church Stretton	d				14 39	15 05				16 39	16 51	17 06				18 39		19 05				21 21	21 51	22 03	
Shrewsbury	a	13 48			14 53	15 19		15 48		16 53	17 11	17 20	17 49			18 53		19 19	19 49			21 35	22 08	22 17	
	d	13 49		14 18	14 55	15 24		15 49	16 23	16 55		17 24	17 51		18 25	18 55		19 24	19 51		20 32	21 37		22 19	
Yorton	d			14x28					16x33						18 35						20x39			22x27	
Wem	d			14 34					16 39						18 41						20 44			22 32	
Prees	d			14x39					16x44						18 46						20x49			22x36	
Whitchurch (Shrops)	d	14 06		14 46				16 06	16 51				18 07		18 53				20 07		20 56			22 44	
Wrenbury	d			14x53					16x58						19x00						21x02			22x49	
Nantwich	d	14 15		14 59				16 15	17 04				18 17		19 06				20 17		21 08			22 55	
Crewe 10	a	14 29		15 09	15 25			16 24	17 14	17 25			18 28		19 16	19 25			20 26		21 19			23 04	
Chester	a					16 22						18 19						20 19				22 31			
Llandudno Junction	a					17 14						19 14						21 22				23 38			
Bangor (Gwynedd)	a					17 35						19 32						21 38							
Holyhead	a					18 20						20 18						22 23							
Wilmslow	a	14 48			15 45			16 48		17 45			18 48			19 48			20 45					23 24	
Stockport	a	14 58			15 58			16 58		17 58			18 58			19 58			20 55					23 32	
Manchester Piccadilly 10 ✈	a	15 15			16 15			17 14		18 15			19 15			20 15			21 10					23 50	

b Previous night, stops on request
c Arr. 0742
e Arr. 0844
f Arr. 0944
g Arr. 1048
h Arr. 1148
i Arr. 1346
j Arr. 1547
k Arr. 1646
l Arr. 1747

For connections from Bristol Temple Meads please refer to Table 132. For connections to Runcorn and Liverpool Lime Street please refer to Table 91

When events are being held at the Millenium Stadium, services are subject to alteration. Please check times before travelling.

Table 131

Saturdays
until 30 July

Cardiff - Crewe, Liverpool and Manchester

		AW ◇		AW
Swansea	d	20 00		
Cardiff Central 7	d	20 55		
London Paddington 15 ⊖	d			
Reading 7	d			
Newport (South Wales)	d	21 10		
Cwmbran	d	21 21		
Pontypool and New Inn	d			
Abergavenny	d	21 34		
Hereford 7	a	21 58		
	d	22 00		
Leominster	d	22 14		
Ludlow	d	22 25		
Craven Arms	d	22 33		
Church Stretton	d	22 42		
Shrewsbury	a	22 57		
	d	23 06		23 50
Yorton	d	23x14		23x58
Wem	d	23 20		00 04
Prees	d	23x24		00x07
Whitchurch (Shrops)	d	23 31		00 15
Wrenbury	d	23x36		00x20
Nantwich	d	23 42		00 26
Crewe 10	a	23 53		00 38
Chester	a	00 24		
Llandudno Junction	a			
Bangor (Gwynedd)	a			
Holyhead	a			
Wilmslow	a			
Stockport	a			
Manchester Piccadilly 10 ⇌	a			

Saturdays
6 August to 10 September

		AW ◇	AW ◇	AW ◇	AW	AW	AW ◇	AW ◇ 🍴	AW ◇ 🍴	AW		AW ◇	AW ◇ 🍴	AW ◇ 🍴	AW ◇ 🍴	AW	AW ◇ 🍴	AW ◇ 🍴	AW ◇ 🍴	GW ◇1 buffet		AW	AW ◇ 🍴	AW ◇	AW ◇ 🍴
Swansea	d											04 36			06 47		07 45		08 55				09 55	09 16	
Cardiff Central 7	d	19p34	20p55	21p55	00 30		04 35	05 20	05 40				06 50	07 21	07c50		08e50	09 21	09f55				10g55		11 21
London Paddington 15 ⊖	d																			08 21					
Reading 7	d																			08 54					
Newport (South Wales)	d	19p48	21p10	22p11	00 52		04 52	05 35	05 57				07 04	07 36	08 04		09 04	09 36	10 09				11 09		11 36
Cwmbran	d	19p58	21p20	22p23	01 02		05 03	05 45	06 08				07 14	07 46	08 14		09 14	09 46	10 19				11 19		11 46
Pontypool and New Inn	d	20p03		22p29	01 08		05 09	05 51	06 13					07 51				09 51							11 50
Abergavenny	d	20p12	21p33	22p39	01 19		05 18	06 00	06 23				07 27	08 01	08 27		09 27	10 01	10 32				11 32		12 01
Hereford 7	a	20p38	21p57	23p05	01 49		05 46	06 24	06 47				07 51	08 26	08 51		09 51	10 26	10 56	11 41			11 56		12 26
	d	20p39	21p59	23p07			05 47	06 26	06 49				07 53	08 27	08 53		09 53	10 27	10 58				11 58		12 27
Leominster	d	20p52	22p12	23p20			06 00	06 40	07 02				08 06		09 06		10 06		11 11				12 11		
Ludlow	d	21p03	22p23	23p31			06 11	06 51	07 13				08 17	08 48	09 17		10 17	10 48	11 22				12 22		12 48
Craven Arms	d	21p12	22p31	23p41			06 20	06 59	07 21			07 54	08 25	08 56			10 25	10 56					12 30	12 37	12 56
Church Stretton	d	21p21	22p40	23p50			06 29	07 08	07 30			08 07	08 34	09 05			10 34	11 05					12 39	12 51	13 05
Shrewsbury	a	21p37	22p54	00 05			06 43	07 22	07 44			08 22	08 51	09 19	09 43		10 48	11 19	11 48				12 53	13 09	13 19
	d	21p39	23p06	00 10		05 44	06 44	07 24	07 46	07 57			08 52	09 24	09 44	10 18	10 50	11 24	11 49			12 23	12 55		13 24
Yorton	d		23b15	00x19		05x52				08x06						10x28						12x33			
Wem	d		23p20	00 24		05 58	06 56		07 57	08 12						10 34						12 39			
Prees	d		23b25	00x29		06x03				08x17						10x39						12x44			
Whitchurch (Shrops)	d		23p32	00 36		06 10	07 04		08 06	08 25			09 09		10 01	10 46	11 06		12 06			12 51			
Wrenbury	d		23b38	00x42		06x17				08x31						10x53						12x58			
Nantwich	d		23p44	00 49		06 23	07 13		08 15	08 38			09 18		10 10	10 59	11 16		12 15			13 04			
Crewe 10	a		23p53	01 04		06 35	07 22		08 24	08 47			09 27		10 20	11 09	11 25		12 24			13 14	13 25		
Chester	a	22p34	00 27					08 18						10 19				12 19							14 19
Llandudno Junction	a	23p49						09 11						11 11				13 11							15 11
Bangor (Gwynedd)	a	00 13						09 33						11 33				13 28							15 28
Holyhead	a	00 58						10 14						12 09				14 13							16 13
Wilmslow	a						07 44		08 45				09 47		10 48		11 48		12 48				13 48		
Stockport	a						08 01		08 58				09 57		10 58		11 58		12 58				13 58		
Manchester Piccadilly 10 ⇌	a						08 20		09 15				10 14		11 15		12 15		13 15				14 15		

b Previous night, stops on request
c Arr. 0742
e Arr. 0844
f Arr. 0944
g Arr. 1048

For connections from Bristol Temple Meads please refer to Table 132. For connections to Runcorn and Liverpool Lime Street please refer to Table 91

When events are being held at the Millenium Stadium, services are subject to alteration. Please check times before travelling.

Table 131

Saturdays

6 August to 10 September

Cardiff - Crewe, Liverpool and Manchester

		AW	GW	AW	AW	AW		AW	AW	AW	AW	AW	AW	AW	AW	AW		AW	AW	GW	AW	AW	AW	AW	GW
												R	R			R		R	R						
		◇	◇1		◇	◇		◇		◇	◇									◇1		◇	◇	◇	◇1
Swansea	d	10 55			12 00			12 55		14 00	13 16		14 55	15 10		15 55			16 55				18 21		
Cardiff Central 7	d	11b55			12 55	13 21		13c55		14 55		15 21	15e55	16 19		16f55		17 21	17g55			19 34			
London Paddington 15 ⊖	d		10 21																	16 21					18 21
Reading 7	d		10 54																	16 54					18 54
Newport (South Wales)	d	12 09			13 09	13 36		14 09		15 09		15 36	16 09	16 34		17 09		17 36	18 09			19 48			
Cwmbran	d	12 19			13 19	13 46		14 19		15 19		15 46	16 19	16 44		17 19		17 46	18 19			19 58			
Pontypool and New Inn	d					13 50						15 52	16 24	16 50				17 52	18 24			20 03			
Abergavenny	d	12 32			13 32	14 01		14 32		15 32		16 01	16 34	17a02		17 32		18 01	18 34			20 12			
Hereford 7	a	12 56	13 40		13 56	14 26		14 56		15 56		16 25	16 58			17 56		18 25	18 58	19 45		20 38			21 36
	d	12 58			13 58	14 27		14 58		15 58		16 27	16 59			17 58		18 27	18 59			20 39		21 20	
Leominster	d	13 11			14 11			15 11		16 11		16 40	17 12			18 11			19 12			20 52		21 33	
Ludlow	d	13 22			14 22	14 48		15 22		16 22		16 51	17 23			18 22		18 48	19 23			21 03		21 44	
Craven Arms	d				14 30	14 56				16 30	16 38					18 30		18 56				21 12	21 38	21 53	
Church Stretton	d				14 39	15 05				16 39	16 51	17 06				18 39		19 05				21 21	21 51	22 03	
Shrewsbury	a	13 48			14 53	15 19		15 48		16 53	17 11	17 20	17 49			18 53		19 19	19 49			21 35	22 08	22 17	
	d	13 49		14 18	14 55	15 24		15 49	16 23	16 55		17 24	17 51		18 25	18 55		19 24	19 51		20 32	21 37		22 19	
Yorton	d			14x28					16x33						18 35						20x39			22x27	
Wem	d			14 34					16 39						18 41						20 44			22 32	
Prees	d			14x39					16x44						18 46						20x49			22x36	
Whitchurch (Shrops)	d	14 06		14 46				16 06	16 51				18 07		18 53				20 07		20 56			22 44	
Wrenbury	d			14x53					16x58						19x00						21x02			22x49	
Nantwich	d	14 15		14 59				16 15	17 04				18 17		19 06				20 17		21 08			22 55	
Crewe 10	a	14 29		15 09	15 25			16 24	17 14	17 25			18 28		19 16	19 25			20 26		21 19			23 04	
Chester	a					16 22						18 19						20 19				22 31			
Llandudno Junction	a					17 14						19 14						21 22				23 38			
Bangor (Gwynedd)	a					17 35						19 32						21 38							
Holyhead	a					18 20						20 18						22 23							
Wilmslow	a	14 48			15 45			16 48		17 45			18 48			19 48			20 45					23 24	
Stockport	a	14 58			15 58			16 58		17 58			18 58			19 58			20 55					23 32	
Manchester Piccadilly 10	a	15 15			16 15			17 14		18 15			19 15			20 15			21 10					23 50	

		AW		AW	AW
		Bus		Bus	
Swansea	d				
Cardiff Central 7	d			21 55	
London Paddington 15 ⊖	d				
Reading 7	d				
Newport (South Wales)	d	21 20		22 25	
Cwmbran	d	21 35		22 43	
Pontypool and New Inn	d			22 55	
Abergavenny	d	22 00		23 10	
Hereford 7	a	22 40		23 50	
	d				
Leominster	d				
Ludlow	d				
Craven Arms	d				
Church Stretton	d				
Shrewsbury	a				
	d				23 50
Yorton	d				23x58
Wem	d				00 04
Prees	d				00x07
Whitchurch (Shrops)	d				00 15
Wrenbury	d				00x20
Nantwich	d				00 26
Crewe 10	a				00 38
Chester	a				
Llandudno Junction	a				
Bangor (Gwynedd)	a				
Holyhead	a				
Wilmslow	a				
Stockport	a				
Manchester Piccadilly 10	a				

b Arr. 1148
c Arr. 1346
e Arr. 1547
f Arr. 1646
g Arr. 1747

For connections from Bristol Temple Meads please refer to Table 132. For connections to Runcorn and Liverpool Lime Street please refer to Table 91

When events are being held at the Millenium Stadium, services are subject to alteration. Please check times before travelling.

Table 131

Saturdays

from 17 September

Cardiff - Crewe, Liverpool and Manchester

		AW ◇	AW ◇	AW ◇	AW	AW	AW ◇	AW ◇ 🍴	AW ◇ 🍴	AW		AW ◇	AW ◇ 🍴	AW ◇ 🍴	AW ◇ 🍴	AW	AW ◇ 🍴	AW ◇ 🍴	AW ◇ 🍴	GW ◇1 🍴		AW	AW ◇ 🍴	AW ◇	AW ◇ 🍴
Swansea	d											04 36			06 47		07 45		08 55				09 55	09 16	
Cardiff Central 7	d	19p34	20p55	21p55	00 30		04 35	05 20	05 40				06 50	07 21	07c50		08e50	09 21	09f55				10g55		11 21
London Paddington 15 ⊖	d																			08 21					
Reading 7	d																			08 54					
Newport (South Wales)	d	19p48	21p10	22p11	00 52		04 52	05 35	05 57				07 04	07 36	08 04		09 04	09 36	10 09				11 09		11 36
Cwmbran	d	19p58	21p20	22p23	01 02		05 03	05 45	06 08				07 14	07 46	08 14		09 14	09 46	10 19				11 19		11 46
Pontypool and New Inn	d	20p03		22p29	01 08		05 09	05 51	06 13					07 51				09 51							11 50
Abergavenny	d	20p12	21p33	22p39	01 19		05 18	06 00	06 23				07 27	08 01	08 27		09 27	10 01	10 32				11 32		12 01
Hereford 7	a	20p38	21p57	23p05	01 49		05 46	06 24	06 47				07 51	08 26	08 51		09 51	10 26	10 56	11 41			11 56		12 26
	d	20p39	21p59	23p07			05 47	06 26	06 49				07 53	08 27	08 53		09 53	10 27	10 58				11 58		12 27
Leominster	d	20p52	22p12	23p20			06 00	06 40	07 02				08 06		09 06		10 06		11 11				12 11		
Ludlow	d	21p03	22p23	23p31			06 11	06 51	07 13				08 17	08 48	09 17		10 17	10 48	11 22				12 22		12 48
Craven Arms	d	21p12	22p31	23p41			06 20	06 59	07 21			07 54	08 25	08 56			10 25	10 56					12 30	12 37	12 56
Church Stretton	d	21p21	22p40	23p50			06 29	07 08	07 30			08 07	08 34	09 05			10 34	11 05					12 39	12 51	13 05
Shrewsbury	a	21p37	22p54	00 05			06 43	07 22	07 44			08 22	08 51	09 19	09 43		10 48	11 19	11 48				12 53	13 09	13 19
	d	21p39	23p06	00 10		05 44	06 44	07 24	07 46	07 57			08 52	09 24	09 44	10 18	10 50	11 24	11 49			12 23	12 55		13 24
Yorton	d		23b15	00x19		05x52				08x06						10x28						12x33			
Wem	d		23p20	00 24		05 58	06 56		07 57	08 12						10 34						12 39			
Prees	d		23b25	00x29		06x03				08x17						10x39						12x44			
Whitchurch (Shrops)	d		23p32	00 36		06 10	07 04		08 06	08 25			09 09		10 01	10 46	11 06		12 06			12 51			
Wrenbury	d		23b38	00x42		06x17				08x31						10x53						12x58			
Nantwich	d		23p44	00 49		06 23	07 13		08 15	08 38			09 18		10 10	10 59	11 16		12 15			13 04			
Crewe 10	a		23p53	01 04		06 35	07 22		08 24	08 47			09 27		10 20	11 09	11 25		12 24			13 14	13 25		
Chester	a	22p34	00 27					08 18						10 19				12 19							14 19
Llandudno Junction	a	23p49						09 11						11 11				13 11							15 11
Bangor (Gwynedd)	a	00 13						09 33						11 33				13 28							15 28
Holyhead	a	00 58						10 14						12 09				14 13							16 13
Wilmslow	a						07 44		08 45				09 47		10 48		11 48		12 48				13 48		
Stockport	a						08 01		08 58				09 57		10 58		11 58		12 58				13 58		
Manchester Piccadilly 10 ⇌	a						08 20		09 15				10 14		11 15		12 15		13 15				14 15		

		AW ◇ 🍴	GW ◇1 🍴	AW	AW ◇ 🍴	AW ◇ 🍴		AW ◇ 🍴	AW	AW ◇ 🍴	AW ◇	AW R 🍴	AW R 🍴	AW	AW	AW R 🍴		AW R 🍴	AW R 🍴	GW ◇1 🍴	AW	AW ◇	AW ◇	AW ◇	GW ◇1 🍴
Swansea	d	10 55			12 00			12 55		14 00	13 16		14 55	15 10		15 55			16 55				18 21		
Cardiff Central 7	d	11h55			12 55	13 21		13i55		14 55		15 21	15j55	16 19		16k55		17 21	17l55			19 34		20 10	
London Paddington 15 ⊖	d		10 21																	16 21					18 21
Reading 7	d		10 54																	16 54					18 54
Newport (South Wales)	d	12 09			13 09	13 36		14 09		15 09		15 36	16 09	16 34		17 09		17 36	18 09			19 48		20 26	
Cwmbran	d	12 19			13 19	13 46		14 19		15 19		15 46	16 19	16 44		17 19		17 46	18 19			19 58		20 37	
Pontypool and New Inn	d					13 50						15 52	16 24	16 50				17 52	18 24			20 03		20 42	
Abergavenny	d	12 32			13 32	14 01		14 32		15 32		16 01	16 34	17a02		17 32		18 01	18 34			20 12		20 52	
Hereford 7	a	12 56	13 40		13 56	14 26		14 56		15 56		16 25	16 58			17 56		18 25	18 58	19 45		20 38		21 17	21 34
	d	12 58			13 58	14 27		14 58		15 58		16 27	16 59			17 58		18 27	18 59			20 39		21 20	
Leominster	d	13 11			14 11			15 11		16 11		16 40	17 12			18 11			19 12			20 52		21 33	
Ludlow	d	13 22			14 22	14 48		15 22		16 22		16 51	17 23			18 22		18 48	19 23			21 03		21 44	
Craven Arms	d				14 30	14 56				16 30	16 38					18 30		18 56				21 12	21 38	21 53	
Church Stretton	d				14 39	15 05				16 39	16 51	17 06				18 39		19 05				21 21	21 51	22 03	
Shrewsbury	a	13 48			14 53	15 19		15 48		16 53	17 11	17 20	17 49			18 53		19 19	19 49			21 35	22 08	22 17	
	d	13 49		14 18	14 55	15 24		15 49	16 23	16 55		17 24	17 51		18 25	18 55		19 24	19 51		20 32	21 37		22 19	
Yorton	d			14x28					16x33						18 35						20x39			22x27	
Wem	d			14 34					16 39						18 41						20 44			22 32	
Prees	d			14x39					16x44						18 46						20x49			22x36	
Whitchurch (Shrops)	d	14 06		14 46				16 06	16 51				18 07		18 53				20 07		20 56			22 44	
Wrenbury	d			14x53					16x58						19x00						21x02			22x49	
Nantwich	d	14 15		14 59				16 15	17 04				18 17		19 06				20 17		21 08			22 55	
Crewe 10	a	14 29		15 09	15 25			16 24	17 14	17 25			18 28		19 16	19 25			20 26		21 19			23 04	
Chester	a					16 22						18 19						20 19				22 31			
Llandudno Junction	a					17 14						19 14						21 22				23 38			
Bangor (Gwynedd)	a					17 35						19 32						21 38							
Holyhead	a					18 20						20 18						22 23							
Wilmslow	a	14 48			15 45			16 48		17 45			18 48			19 48			20 45					23 24	
Stockport	a	14 58			15 58			16 58		17 58			18 58			19 58			20 55					23 32	
Manchester Piccadilly 10 ⇌	a	15 15			16 15			17 14		18 15			19 15			20 15			21 10					23 50	

b Previous night, stops on request
c Arr. 0742
e Arr. 0844
f Arr. 0944
g Arr. 1048
h Arr. 1148
i Arr. 1346
j Arr. 1547
k Arr. 1646
l Arr. 1747

For connections from Bristol Temple Meads please refer to Table 132. For connections to Runcorn and Liverpool Lime Street please refer to Table 91

When events are being held at the Millenium Stadium, services are subject to alteration. Please check times before travelling.

Table 131

Cardiff - Crewe, Liverpool and Manchester

Saturdays
from 17 September

		AW	AW
		◇	
Swansea	d	20 00	
Cardiff Central 7	d	20 55	
London Paddington 15 ⊖	d		
Reading 7	d		
Newport (South Wales)	d	21 10	
Cwmbran	d	21 21	
Pontypool and New Inn	d		
Abergavenny	d	21 34	
Hereford 7	a	21 58	
	d	22 00	
Leominster	d	22 14	
Ludlow	d	22 25	
Craven Arms	d	22 33	
Church Stretton	d	22 42	
Shrewsbury	a	22 57	
	d	23 06	23 50
Yorton	d	23x14	23x58
Wem	d	23 20	00 04
Prees	d	23x24	00x07
Whitchurch (Shrops)	d	23 31	00 15
Wrenbury	d	23x36	00x20
Nantwich	d	23 42	00 26
Crewe 10	a	23 53	00 38
Chester	a	00 24	
Llandudno Junction	a		
Bangor (Gwynedd)	a		
Holyhead	a		
Wilmslow	a		
Stockport	a		
Manchester Piccadilly 10 ⛴	a		

Sundays
until 19 June

		AW	AW	AW	AW	AW	AW	GW	AW	AW
		◇		◇	◇	◇	◇	◇1	◇	◇
		A	A							
					trolley	trolley	trolley	restaurant	trolley	trolley
Swansea	d	20p00					09 32			11 32
Cardiff Central 7	d	20p55			08 30	09 30	10c35		11 35	12 40
London Paddington 15 ⊖	d	⟆						09 35		
Reading 7	d	⟆						10 15		
Newport (South Wales)	d	21p10			08 49	09 50	10 51		11 50	12 54
Cwmbran	d	21p21			09 00	10 00	11 02		12 04	13 09
Pontypool and New Inn	d	⟆			09 06	10 06	11 08		12 10	13 15
Abergavenny	d	21p34			09 15	10 16	11 18		12 20	13 25
Hereford 7	a	21p58			09 40	10 40	11 44	12 54	12 44	13 49
	d	22p00			09 41	10 43	11 50		12 57	13 55
Leominster	d	22p14			09 55	10 56	12 03		13 10	14 08
Ludlow	d	22p25			10 06	11 07	12 14		13 21	14 19
Craven Arms	d	22p33			10 14		12 24			14 28
Church Stretton	d	22p42			10 23		12 33			14 37
Shrewsbury	a	22p57			10 37	11 36	12 48		13 47	14 51
	d	23p06	23p50	09 55	10 39	11 37	12 51		13 50	14 53
Yorton	d	23b14	23b58			11x45				
Wem	d	23p20	00⟆04		10 51	11 51				
Prees	d	23b24	00x07			11x55				
Whitchurch (Shrops)	d	23p31	00⟆15		11 00	12 03				
Wrenbury	d	23b36	00x20			12x08				
Nantwich	d	23p42	00⟆26		11 09	12 15				
Crewe 10	a	23p53	00⟆38	10 25	11 22	12 25	13 26		14 22	15 25
Chester	a	00⟆24								
Llandudno Junction	a									
Bangor (Gwynedd)	a									
Holyhead	a									
Wilmslow	a			10 46	11 41	12 46	13 49		14 46	15 46
Stockport	a			10 58		12 58	14 00		14 58	15 58
Manchester Piccadilly 10 ⛴	a			11 15	12 02	13 15	14 19		15 15	16 17

		GW	AW	AW	AW	AW	AW	GW	AW	AW	AW	GW	AW	AW
			R	R		R	R		R	R	R			R
		◇1			◇			◇1				◇1	◇	
			B	C										D
		restaurant				trolley	trolley	restaurant	trolley	trolley	trolley	trolley		
Swansea	d				11 06		13 43				15 33		15 26	
Cardiff Central 7	d		13⟆13	13⟆18		13 40	14e56		15 22	15 56	16 40			17⟆22
London Paddington 15 ⊖	d	10 42	⟆	⟆				12 42				14 42		⟆
Reading 7	d	11 22	⟆	⟆				13 22				15 22		⟆
Newport (South Wales)	d		13⟆27	13⟆32		13 54	15 14		15 36	16 14	16 54			17⟆36
Cwmbran	d		13⟆37	13⟆42		14 09	15 24		15 46	16 24	17 09			17⟆46
Pontypool and New Inn	d		⟆	⟆					15 51		17 15			⟆
Abergavenny	d		13⟆51	13⟆56		14 22	15 38		16 01	16 37	17 25			18⟆00
Hereford 7	a	14 06	14⟆16	14⟆21		14 47	16 02	16 07	16 27	17 02	17 49	18 01		18⟆25
	d		14⟆17	14⟆22		14 48	16 04		16 27	17 04	17 53			18⟆26
Leominster	d		⟆	⟆		15 01			16 40		18 07			⟆
Ludlow	d		14⟆38	14⟆43		15 12	16 25		16 51	17 26	18 18			18⟆47
Craven Arms	d		⟆	⟆	14 53				17 00		18 26		18 59	⟆
Church Stretton	d		⟆	⟆	15 04				17 09		18 35		19 12	⟆
Shrewsbury	a		15⟆04	15⟆09	15 22	15 38	16 51		17 23	17 52	18 49		19 31	19⟆13
	d		15⟆20	15⟆20		15 40	16 53		17 30	17 54	18 54			19⟆32
Yorton	d		⟆	⟆		15x48								⟆
Wem	d		⟆	⟆		15 54								⟆
Prees	d		⟆	⟆		15x58								⟆
Whitchurch (Shrops)	d		⟆	⟆		16 06								⟆
Wrenbury	d		⟆	⟆		16x11								⟆
Nantwich	d		⟆	⟆		16 18								⟆
Crewe 10	a		⟆	⟆		16 27	17 25			18 25	19 24			⟆
Chester	a		16⟆25	16⟆24					18 25					20⟆29
Llandudno Junction	a		17⟆28	17⟆29					19 22					21⟆29
Bangor (Gwynedd)	a		17⟆51	17⟆52					19 45					21⟆52
Holyhead	a		18⟆40	18⟆37					20 20					22⟆37
Wilmslow	a					16 46	17 45			18 46	19 46			
Stockport	a					16 58	17 58			18 58	19 58			
Manchester Piccadilly 10 ⛴	a					17 15	18 17			19 15	20 17			

A not 22 May
B not until 29 May
C 29 May
D 22 May
b Previous night, stops on request
c Arr. 1029
e Arr. 1440

For connections from Bristol Temple Meads please refer to Table 132. For connections to Runcorn and Liverpool Lime Street please refer to Table 91

When events are being held at the Millenium Stadium, services are subject to alteration. Please check times before travelling.

Table 131

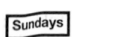

Sundays until 19 June

Cardiff - Crewe, Liverpool and Manchester

		AW	AW	AW	GW	AW		AW	AW
		R	R						
				◇	◇1	◇		◇	◇
			🚲		☕				
Swansea	d		17 30						21 52
Cardiff Central 7	d	17 35	18b40	19 40				21 04	23c00
London Paddington 15 ⊖	d				18 42				
Reading 7	d				19 24				
Newport (South Wales)	d	17 49	18 54	19 55				21 19	23 20
Cwmbran	d	18 04	19 09	20 10				21 30	23 29
Pontypool and New Inn	d	18 10		20 16				21 36	23 35
Abergavenny	d	18 20	19 22	20 26				21 46	23 45
Hereford 7	a	18 44	19 47	20 52	22 06			22 12	00 17
	d	18 49	19 49	20 54				22 14	
Leominster	d	19 03	20 03	21 08				22 27	
Ludlow	d	19 14	20 14	21 19				22 38	
Craven Arms	d		20 22	21 29				22 48	
Church Stretton	d		20 31	21 38				22 57	
Shrewsbury	a	19 40	20 45	21 55				23 14	
	d	19 41	20 48			22 32		23 14	
Yorton	d	19x49						23x23	
Wem	d	19 55						23 29	
Prees	d	19x59						23x34	
Whitchurch (Shrops)	d	20 06						23 41	
Wrenbury	d	20x11						23x47	
Nantwich	d	20 18						23 54	
Crewe 10	a	20 27	21 21			23 03		00 02	
Chester	a					23 31		00 25	
Llandudno Junction	a								
Bangor (Gwynedd)	a								
Holyhead	a								
Wilmslow	a	20 45	21 45						
Stockport	a	20 58	21 58						
Manchester Piccadilly 10 ⛴	a	21 14	22 19						

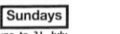

Sundays 26 June to 31 July

		AW	AW	AW	AW	AW	AW	GW	AW	AW		GW	AW	AW	AW	GW	AW	AW	AW	GW		AW	AW	AW	AW
														R	R		R	R	R				R	R	
		◇		◇	◇	◇	◇	◇1	◇	◇		◇1	◇			◇1				◇1		◇			◇
					🚲	🚲	🚲	☕	🚲	🚲		☕		🚲	🚲	☕	🚲	🚲	🚲	🚲				🚲	
Swansea	d	20p00					09 32			11 32			11 06		13 43				15 33			15 26		17 30	
Cardiff Central 7	d	20p55			08 30	09 30	10f35		11 35	12 40				13 40	14g56		15 22	15 56	16 40				17 35	18b40	19 40
London Paddington 15 ⊖	d							09 35				10 42				12 42				14 42					
Reading 7	d							10 15				11 22				13 22				15 22					
Newport (South Wales)	d	21p10			08 49	09 50	10 51		11 50	12 54				13 54	15 14		15 36	16 14	16 54				17 49	18 54	19 55
Cwmbran	d	21p21			09 00	10 00	11 02		12 04	13 09				14 09	15 24		15 46	16 24	17 09				18 04	19 09	20 10
Pontypool and New Inn	d				09 06	10 06	11 08		12 10	13 15							15 51		17 15				18 10		20 16
Abergavenny	d	21p34			09 15	10 16	11 18		12 20	13 25				14 22	15 38		16 01	16 37	17 25				18 20	19 22	20 26
Hereford 7	a	21p58			09 40	10 40	11 44	12 54	12 44	13 49		14 06		14 47	16 02	16 07	16 27	17 02	17 49	18 01			18 44	19 47	20 52
	d	22p00			09 41	10 43	11 50		12 57	13 55				14 48	16 04		16 27	17 04	17 53				18 49	19 49	20 54
Leominster	d	22p14			09 55	10 56	12 03		13 10	14 08				15 01			16 40		18 07				19 03	20 03	21 08
Ludlow	d	22p25			10 06	11 07	12 14		13 21	14 19				15 12	16 25		16 51	17 26	18 18				19 14	20 14	21 19
Craven Arms	d	22p33			10 14		12 24			14 28			14 53				17 00		18 26			18 59		20 22	21 29
Church Stretton	d	22p42			10 23		12 33			14 37			15 04				17 09		18 35			19 12		20 31	21 38
Shrewsbury	a	22p57			10 37	11 36	12 48		13 47	14 51			15 22	15 38	16 51		17 23	17 52	18 49			19 31	19 40	20 45	21 55
	d	23p06	23p50	09 55	10 39	11 37	12 51		13 50	14 53				15 40	16 53		17 30	17 54	18 54				19 41	20 48	
Yorton	d	23e14	23e58			11x45								15x48									19x49		
Wem	d	23p20	00 04		10 51	11 51								15 54									19 55		
Prees	d	23e24	00x07			11x55								15x58									19x59		
Whitchurch (Shrops)	d	23p31	00 15		11 00	12 03								16 06									20 06		
Wrenbury	d	23e36	00x20			12x08								16x11									20x11		
Nantwich	d	23p42	00 26		11 09	12 15								16 18									20 18		
Crewe 10	a	23p53	00 38	10 25	11 22	12 25	13 26		14 22	15 25				16 27	17 25		18 00	18 25	19 24				20 27	21 21	
Chester	a	00 24															18 22								
Llandudno Junction	a																19 22								
Bangor (Gwynedd)	a																19 45								
Holyhead	a																20 20								
Wilmslow	a			10 46	11 41	12 46	13 49		14 46	15 46				16 46	17 45			18 46	19 46				20 45	21 45	
Stockport	a			10 58		12 58	14 00		14 58	15 58				16 58	17 58			18 58	19 58				20 58	21 58	
Manchester Piccadilly 10 ⛴	a			11 15	12 02	13 15	14 19		15 15	16 17				17 15	18 17			19 15	20 17				21 14	22 19	

b Arr. 1834
c Arr. 2249
e Previous night, stops on request
f Arr. 1029
g Arr. 1440

For connections from Bristol Temple Meads please refer to Table 132. For connections to Runcorn and Liverpool Lime Street please refer to Table 91

When events are being held at the Millenium Stadium, services are subject to alteration. Please check times before travelling.

Table 131

Sundays

26 June to 31 July

Cardiff - Crewe, Liverpool and Manchester

		GW	AW	AW	AW
		◇1 ☕	◇	◇	◇
Swansea	d				21 52
Cardiff Central 7	d			21 04	23b00
London Paddington 15 ⊖	d	18 42			
Reading 7	d	19 24			
Newport (South Wales)	d			21 19	23 20
Cwmbran	d			21 30	23 29
Pontypool and New Inn	d			21 36	23 35
Abergavenny	d			21 46	23 45
Hereford 7	a	22 06		22 12	00 17
	d			22 14	
Leominster	d			22 27	
Ludlow	d			22 38	
Craven Arms	d			22 48	
Church Stretton	d			22 57	
Shrewsbury	a			23 14	
	d		22 32	23 14	
Yorton	d			23x23	
Wem	d			23 29	
Prees	d			23x34	
Whitchurch (Shrops)	d			23 41	
Wrenbury	d			23x47	
Nantwich	d			23 54	
Crewe 10	a		23 03	00 02	
Chester	a		23 31	00 25	
Llandudno Junction	a				
Bangor (Gwynedd)	a				
Holyhead	a				
Wilmslow	a				
Stockport	a				
Manchester Piccadilly 10	a				

Sundays

7 August to 11 September

		AW	AW	AW	AW	AW	GW	AW	AW	GW		AW	AW
												R	
			◇	◇	◇	◇	◇1	◇	◇	◇1			◇
				🚲	🚲	🚲	☕	🚲	🚲	☕			
Swansea	d					09 32			11 32				11 06
Cardiff Central 7	d			08 30	09 30	10e35		11 35	12 40			13 13	
London Paddington 15 ⊖	d						09 35			10 42			
Reading 7	d						10 17			11 21			
Newport (South Wales)	d			08 49	09 50	10 51		11 50	12 54			13 27	
Cwmbran	d			09 00	10 00	11 02		12 04	13 09			13 37	
Pontypool and New Inn	d			09 06	10 06	11 08		12 10	13 15				
Abergavenny	d			09 15	10 16	11 18		12 20	13 25			13 51	
Hereford 7	a			09 40	10 40	11 44	12 56	12 44	13 49	14 06		14 16	
	d			09 41	10 43	11 50		12 57	13 55			14 17	
Leominster	d			09 55	10 56	12 03		13 10	14 08				
Ludlow	d			10 06	11 07	12 14		13 21	14 19			14 38	
Craven Arms	d			10 14		12 24			14 28				14 53
Church Stretton	d			10 23		12 33			14 37				15 04
Shrewsbury	a			10 37	11 36	12 48		13 47	14 51			15 04	15 22
	d	23p50	09 55	10 39	11 37	12 51		13 50	14 53			15 20	
Yorton	d	23c58			11x45								
Wem	d	00 04		10 51	11 51								
Prees	d	00x07			11x55								
Whitchurch (Shrops)	d	00 15		11 00	12 03								
Wrenbury	d	00x20			12x08								
Nantwich	d	00 26		11 09	12 15								
Crewe 10	a	00 38	10 25	11 22	12 25	13 26		14 22	15 25				
Chester	a											16 25	
Llandudno Junction	a											17 28	
Bangor (Gwynedd)	a											17 51	
Holyhead	a											18 40	
Wilmslow	a		10 46	11 41	12 46	13 49		14 46	15 46				
Stockport	a		10 58		12 58	14 00		14 58	15 58				
Manchester Piccadilly 10	a		11 15	12 02	13 15	14 19		15 15	16 17				

		AW	AW	GW	AW	AW	AW	GW		AW	AW	AW	AW
		R	R		R	R	R				R	R	
				◇1				◇1		◇			◇
		🚲	🚲	☕	🚲	🚲	🚲	🚲				🚲	
Swansea	d		13 43				15 33			15 26		17 30	
Cardiff Central 7	d	13 40	14f56		15 22	15 56	16 40				17 35	18g40	19 40
London Paddington 15 ⊖	d			12 42				14 42					
Reading 7	d			13 22				15 22					
Newport (South Wales)	d	13 54	15 14		15 36	16 14	16 54				17 49	18 54	19 55
Cwmbran	d	14 09	15 24		15 46	16 24	17 09				18 04	19 09	20 10
Pontypool and New Inn	d				15 51		17 15				18 10		20 16
Abergavenny	d	14 22	15 38		16 01	16 37	17 25				18 20	19 22	20 26
Hereford 7	a	14 47	16 02	16 07	16 27	17 02	17 49	18 02			18 44	19 47	20 52
	d	14 48	16 04		16 27	17 04	17 53				18 49	19 49	20 54
Leominster	d	15 01			16 40		18 07				19 03	20 03	21 08
Ludlow	d	15 12	16 25		16 51	17 26	18 18				19 14	20 14	21 19
Craven Arms	d				17 00		18 26			18 59		20 22	21 29
Church Stretton	d				17 09		18 35			19 12		20 31	21 38
Shrewsbury	a	15 38	16 51		17 23	17 52	18 49			19 31	19 40	20 45	21 55
	d	15 40	16 53		17 30	17 54	18 54				19 41	20 48	
Yorton	d	15x48									19x49		
Wem	d	15 54									19 55		
Prees	d	15x58									19x59		
Whitchurch (Shrops)	d	16 06									20 06		
Wrenbury	d	16x11									20x11		
Nantwich	d	16 18									20 18		
Crewe 10	a	16 27	17 25			18 25	19 24				20 27	21 21	
Chester	a				18 25								
Llandudno Junction	a				19 22								
Bangor (Gwynedd)	a				19 45								
Holyhead	a				20 20								
Wilmslow	a	16 46	17 45			18 46	19 46				20 45	21 45	
Stockport	a	16 58	17 58			18 58	19 58				20 58	21 58	
Manchester Piccadilly 10	a	17 15	18 17			19 15	20 17				21 14	22 19	

b Arr. 2249
c Previous night, stops on request
e Arr. 1029
f Arr. 1440
g Arr. 1834

For connections from Bristol Temple Meads please refer to Table 132. For connections to Runcorn and Liverpool Lime Street please refer to Table 91

When events are being held at the Millenium Stadium, services are subject to alteration. Please check times before travelling.

Table 131

Sundays

7 August to 11 September

Cardiff - Crewe, Liverpool and Manchester

		GW	AW	AW	AW
		◇[1]	◇	◇	◇
		☕			
Swansea	d				21 52
Cardiff Central [7]	d			21 04	23b00
London Paddington [15] ⊖	d	18 42			
Reading [7]	d	19 24			
Newport (South Wales)	d			21 19	23 20
Cwmbran	d			21 30	23 29
Pontypool and New Inn	d			21 36	23 35
Abergavenny	d			21 46	23 45
Hereford [7]	a	22 06		22 12	00 17
	d			22 14	
Leominster	d			22 27	
Ludlow	d			22 38	
Craven Arms	d			22 48	
Church Stretton	d			22 57	
Shrewsbury	a			23 14	
	d		22 32	23 14	
Yorton	d			23x23	
Wem	d			23 29	
Prees	d			23x34	
Whitchurch (Shrops)	d			23 41	
Wrenbury	d			23x47	
Nantwich	d			23 54	
Crewe [10]	a		23 03	00 02	
Chester	a		23 31	00 25	
Llandudno Junction	a				
Bangor (Gwynedd)	a				
Holyhead	a				
Wilmslow	a				
Stockport	a				
Manchester Piccadilly [10] 🚢	a				

Sundays

18 September to 23 October

		AW	AW	AW	AW	AW	AW	GW	AW	AW		GW	AW	AW	AW	AW	GW	AW	AW	AW		GW	AW	AW	AW
													[R]		[R]	[R]		[R]	[R]	[R]				[R]	[R]
		◇		◇	◇	◇	◇	◇[1]	◇	◇		◇[1]		◇			◇[1]					◇[1]	◇		
					🛒	🛒	🛒	☕	🛒	🛒		☕			🛒	🛒	☕	🛒	🛒	🛒		🛒			🛒
Swansea	d	20p00								11 32				11 06		13 43				15 33			15 26		17 30
Cardiff Central [7]	d	20p55			08 30	09 30	10 35		11 35	12 40			13 13		13 40	14e56		15 22	15 56	16 40				17 35	18f40
London Paddington [15] ⊖	d							09 35				10 42					12 42					14 42			
Reading [7]	d							10 17				11 22					13 22					15 22			
Newport (South Wales)	d	21p10			08 49	09 50	10 51		11 50	12 54			13 27		13 54	15 14		15 36	16 14	16 54				17 49	18 54
Cwmbran	d	21p21			09 00	10 00	11 02		12 04	13 09			13 37		14 09	15 24		15 46	16 24	17 09				18 04	19 09
Pontypool and New Inn	d				09 06	10 06	11 08		12 10	13 15								15 51		17 15				18 10	
Abergavenny	d	21p34			09 15	10 16	11 18		12 20	13 25			13 51		14 22	15 38		16 01	16 37	17 25				18 20	19 22
Hereford [7]	a	21p58			09 40	10 40	11 44	12 56	12 44	13 49		14 06	14 16		14 47	16 02	16 07	16 27	17 02	17 49		18 02		18 44	19 47
	d	22p00			09 41	10 43	11 50		12 57	13 55			14 17		14 48	16 04		16 27	17 04	17 53				18 49	19 49
Leominster	d	22p14			09 55	10 56	12 03		13 10	14 08					15 01			16 40		18 07				19 03	20 03
Ludlow	d	22p25			10 06	11 07	12 14		13 21	14 19			14 38		15 12	16 25		16 51	17 26	18 18				19 14	20 14
Craven Arms	d	22p33			10 14		12 24			14 28				14 53				17 00		18 26			18 59		20 22
Church Stretton	d	22p42			10 23		12 33			14 37				15 04				17 09		18 35			19 12		20 31
Shrewsbury	a	22p57			10 37	11 36	12 48		13 47	14 51			15 04	15 22	15 38	16 51		17 23	17 52	18 49			19 31	19 40	20 45
	d	23p06	23p50	09 55	10 39	11 37	12 51		13 50	14 53			15 20		15 40	16 53		17 30	17 54	18 54				19 41	20 48
Yorton	d	23c14	23c58			11x45									15x48									19x49	
Wem	d	23p20	00 04		10 51	11 51									15 54									19 55	
Prees	d	23c24	00x07			11x55									15x58									19x59	
Whitchurch (Shrops)	d	23p31	00 15		11 00	12 03									16 06									20 06	
Wrenbury	d	23c36	00x20			12x08									16x11									20x11	
Nantwich	d	23p42	00 26		11 09	12 15									16 18									20 18	
Crewe [10]	a	23p53	00 38	10 25	11 22	12 25	13 26		14 22	15 25					16 27	17 25			18 25	19 24				20 27	21 21
Chester	a	00 24											16 25					18 25							
Llandudno Junction	a												17 28					19 22							
Bangor (Gwynedd)	a												17 51					19 45							
Holyhead	a												18 40					20 20							
Wilmslow	a			10 46	11 41	12 46	13 49		14 46	15 46					16 46	17 45			18 46	19 46				20 45	21 45
Stockport	a			10 58		12 58	14 00		14 58	15 58					16 58	17 58			18 58	19 58				20 58	21 58
Manchester Piccadilly [10] 🚢	a			11 15	12 02	13 15	14 19		15 15	16 17					17 15	18 17			19 15	20 17				21 14	22 19

b Arr. 2249
c Previous night, stops on request
e Arr. 1440
f Arr. 1834

For connections from Bristol Temple Meads please refer to Table 132. For connections to Runcorn and Liverpool Lime Street please refer to Table 91

When events are being held at the Millenium Stadium, services are subject to alteration. Please check times before travelling.

Table 131

Cardiff - Crewe, Liverpool and Manchester

Sundays
18 September to 23 October

		AW	GW	AW	AW	AW
		◇	◇1	◇	◇	◇
Swansea	d					21 52
Cardiff Central 7	d	19 40			21 04	23b00
London Paddington 15 ⊖	d		18 42			
Reading 7	d		19 24			
Newport (South Wales)	d	19 55			21 19	23 20
Cwmbran	d	20 10			21 30	23 29
Pontypool and New Inn	d	20 16			21 36	23 35
Abergavenny	d	20 26			21 46	23 45
Hereford 7	a	20 52	22 06		22 12	00 17
	d	20 54			22 14	
Leominster	d	21 08			22 27	
Ludlow	d	21 19			22 38	
Craven Arms	d	21 29			22 48	
Church Stretton	d	21 38			22 57	
Shrewsbury	a	21 55			23 14	
	d			22 32	23 14	
Yorton	d				23x23	
Wem	d				23 29	
Prees	d				23x34	
Whitchurch (Shrops)	d				23 41	
Wrenbury	d				23x47	
Nantwich	d				23 54	
Crewe 10	a			23 03	00 02	
Chester	a			23 31	00 25	
Llandudno Junction	a					
Bangor (Gwynedd)	a					
Holyhead	a					
Wilmslow	a					
Stockport	a					
Manchester Piccadilly 10	a					

Sundays
from 30 October

		AW	AW	AW	AW	AW	AW	GW	AW	AW		GW	AW	AW	AW	AW	GW	AW	AW	AW		GW	AW	AW	AW
													R		R	R		R	R	R				R	R
		◇		◇	◇	◇	◇	◇1	◇	◇		◇1		◇			◇1					◇1	◇		
Swansea	d	20p00								11 32				11 06		13 43				15 33			15 26		17 30
Cardiff Central 7	d	20p55			08 30	09 30	10 35		11 35	12 40			13 13		13 40	14e56		15 22	15 56	16 40				17 35	18f40
London Paddington 15 ⊖	d							09 35				10 42					12 42					14 42			
Reading 7	d							10 12				11 21					13 21					15 18			
Newport (South Wales)	d	21p10			08 49	09 50	10 51		11 50	12 54			13 27		13 54	15 14		15 36	16 14	16 54				17 49	18 54
Cwmbran	d	21p21			09 00	10 00	11 02		12 04	13 09			13 37		14 09	15 24		15 46	16 24	17 09				18 04	19 09
Pontypool and New Inn	d				09 06	10 06	11 08		12 10	13 15								15 51		17 15				18 10	
Abergavenny	d	21p34			09 15	10 16	11 18		12 20	13 25			13 51		14 22	15 38		16 01	16 37	17 25				18 20	19 22
Hereford 7	a	21p58			09 40	10 40	11 44	12 56	12 44	13 49		14 08	14 16		14 47	16 02	16 07	16 27	17 02	17 49		18 00		18 44	19 47
	d	22p00			09 41	10 43	11 50		12 57	13 55			14 17		14 48	16 04		16 27	17 04	17 53				18 49	19 49
Leominster	d	22p14			09 55	10 56	12 03		13 10	14 08					15 01			16 40		18 07				19 03	20 03
Ludlow	d	22p25			10 06	11 07	12 14		13 21	14 19			14 38		15 12	16 25		16 51	17 26	18 18				19 14	20 14
Craven Arms	d	22p33			10 14		12 24			14 28				14 53				17 00		18 26			18 59		20 22
Church Stretton	d	22p42			10 23		12 33			14 37				15 04				17 09		18 35			19 12		20 31
Shrewsbury	a	22p57			10 37	11 36	12 48		13 47	14 51			15 04	15 22	15 38	16 51		17 23	17 52	18 49			19 31	19 40	20 45
	d	23p06	23p50	09 55	10 39	11 37	12 51		13 50	14 53			15 20		15 40	16 53		17 30	17 54	18 54				19 41	20 48
Yorton	d	23c14	23c58			11x45									15x48									19x49	
Wem	d	23p20	00 04		10 51	11 51									15 54									19 55	
Prees	d	23c24	00x07			11x55									15x58									19x59	
Whitchurch (Shrops)	d	23p31	00 15		11 00	12 03									16 06									20 06	
Wrenbury	d	23c36	00x20			12x08									16x11									20x11	
Nantwich	d	23p42	00 26		11 09	12 15									16 18									20 18	
Crewe 10	a	23p53	00 38	10 25	11 22	12 25	13 26		14 22	15 25					16 27	17 25			18 25	19 24				20 27	21 21
Chester	a	00 24											16 25					18 25							
Llandudno Junction	a												17 28					19 22							
Bangor (Gwynedd)	a												17 51					19 45							
Holyhead	a												18 40					20 20							
Wilmslow	a			10 46	11 41	12 46	13 49		14 46	15 46					16 46	17 45			18 46	19 46				20 45	21 45
Stockport	a			10 58		12 58	14 00		14 58	15 58					16 58	17 58			18 58	19 58				20 58	21 58
Manchester Piccadilly 10	a			11 15	12 02	13 15	14 19		15 15	16 17					17 15	18 17			19 15	20 17				21 14	22 19

b Arr. 2249
c Previous night, stops on request
e Arr. 1440
f Arr. 1834

For connections from Bristol Temple Meads please refer to Table 132. For connections to Runcorn and Liverpool Lime Street please refer to Table 91

When events are being held at the Millenium Stadium, services are subject to alteration. Please check times before travelling.

Table 131

Sundays
from 30 October

Cardiff - Crewe, Liverpool and Manchester

		AW	GW	AW	AW	AW
		◇	◇1 🍵	◇	◇	◇
Swansea	d					21 52
Cardiff Central 7	d	19 40			21 04	23b00
London Paddington 15 ⊖	d		18 42			
Reading 7	d		19 21			
Newport (South Wales)	d	19 55			21 19	23 20
Cwmbran	d	20 10			21 30	23 29
Pontypool and New Inn	d	20 16			21 36	23 35
Abergavenny	d	20 26			21 46	23 45
Hereford 7	a	20 52	22 02		22 12	00 17
	d	20 54			22 14	
Leominster	d	21 08			22 27	
Ludlow	d	21 19			22 38	
Craven Arms	d	21 29			22 48	
Church Stretton	d	21 38			22 57	
Shrewsbury	a	21 55			23 14	
	d			22 32	23 14	
Yorton	d				23x23	
Wem	d				23 29	
Prees	d				23x34	
Whitchurch (Shrops)	d				23 41	
Wrenbury	d				23x47	
Nantwich	d				23 54	
Crewe 10	a			23 03	00 02	
Chester	a			23 31	00 25	
Llandudno Junction	a					
Bangor (Gwynedd)	a					
Holyhead	a					
Wilmslow	a					
Stockport	a					
Manchester Piccadilly 10 ⛴	a					

b Arr. 2249

For connections from Bristol Temple Meads please refer to Table 132. For connections to Runcorn and Liverpool Lime Street please refer to Table 91

When events are being held at the Millenium Stadium, services are subject to alteration. Please check times before travelling.

Table 131

Mondays to Fridays

until 9 September

Manchester, Liverpool and Crewe - Cardiff

Miles	Miles			GW ◇1 A	AW MX ◇	AW MO ◇	AW MX ◇	AW MX ◇	AW MO	AW	AW ◇ B	AW ◇		AW C	GW ◇1 D ꟾP	AW ◇ ⚲	XC ◇1 ⚲	XC ◇1 ⚲	GW ◇1 D ꟾP	AW ◇	AW ◇ ⚲	AW ◇ ⚲		AW ◇ ⚲	AW BHX ◇ ⊠
0	—	**Manchester Piccadilly** 10 ⛴	d		20p30	20p30		22p35									05 00	06 00						06 30	
6	—	Stockport	d		20p39	20p39		22p44										06 08						06 39	
12	—	Wilmslow	d		20p46	20p47		22p52																06 46	
—	—	Holyhead	d																			04 25			05 32
—	—	Bangor (Gwynedd)	d																			04 57			06 02
—	—	Llandudno Junction	d																			05 15			06 21
—	—	Chester	d						23p00	04 22										05 15		06e18			07 08
31	35½	**Crewe** 10	d		21p08	21c13		23p14	23p23	04a44						04 54	05 47	06a32			05 55			07 08	07 33
35½	40	Nantwich	d		21p17	21p21		23p22	23p31							05 02					06 03			07 17	
40	44½	Wrenbury	d		21b23	21b26		23b27	23b37												06x09				
44¾	49¼	Whitchurch (Shrops)	d		21p30	21p35		23p34	23p45							05 13					06 16				
49¾	54¼	Prees	d		21b36	21b40		23b40	23b51												06x22				
53	57½	Wem	d		21p41	21p47		23p45	23p57							05 22					06 27				
56½	61	Yorton	d		21b46	21b51		23b50	00x02												06x32				
63¾	68¼	**Shrewsbury**	a		21p55	22p03		00 04	00 14							05 33				06 10	06 42	07 17		07 42	08 09
—	—		d		21p57	22p04	23p08					05 19				05 40				06 13	06 44	07 19		07 44	08 10
76½	81	Church Stretton	d		22p12	22p20	23p24					05 36				05 55				06 29	06 59			07 59	
83¾	88¼	Craven Arms	d		22p20	22p29	23p32					05 50				06 03				06 37	07 07			08 07	
91	95½	Ludlow	d		22p27	22p37	23p41									06 10				06 45	07 14	07 46		08 14	
102	106½	Leominster	d		22p38	22p49	23p52									06 21				06 56	07 25	07 56		08 25	
114½	119	**Hereford** 7	a		22p56	23p03	00 07									06 36				07 10	07 43	08 12		08 40	
—	—		d	21p51	22p58	23p05	00 09				05 25			05 26	05 34	06 42			06 43	07 13	07 45	08 13		08 42	
138½	143	Abergavenny	d		23p21	23p29	00 33				05 49			05 51		07 05				07 36	08 08	08 36		09 05	
148	152½	Pontypool and New Inn	d		23p30	23p39					05 59			06 02		07 15				07 46	08 17	08 46			
151	155½	Cwmbran	d		23p35	23p44	00 46				06 04			06 07		07 20				07 51	08 22	08 51		09 17	
158	162½	**Newport (South Wales)**	a		23p46	23p54	00 57				06 16			06 19		07 33				08 01	08 37	09 02		09 35	09 40
—	—	Reading 7	a	00 38											08 21		08 39		09 14						
—	—	London Paddington 15 ⊖	a	01 17											08 51				09 47						
169¾	174½	**Cardiff Central** 7	a		00 02	00 20	01 18				06 33			06 40		07 49				08 17	08 53	09 18		09 57	09 58
—	—	Swansea	a								07 45	09 08				08 50					09 55	10 34			

		AW	AW ◇ ⚲	AW ◇	AW ◇ ⚲	AW ◇ ⚲	AW	AW ◇ ⚲		AW ◇ ⚲	AW ◇ ⚲	AW ◇ ⚲	AW	GW ◇1 ꟾP	AW ◇ ⚲	AW R ⚲	AW R ⚲	AW ◇		AW	GW ◇1 ꟾP	AW R ⚲	AW ◇ ⚲	AW R ⚲	AW
Manchester Piccadilly 10 ⛴	d		07 30			08 30				09 30		10 30			11 30		12 30					13 30		14 30	
Stockport	d		07 39			08 39				09 39		10 39			11 39		12 39					13 39		14 39	
Wilmslow	d		07 46			08 46				09 46		10 46			11 46		12 46					13 46		14 46	
Holyhead	d				06 29			07 15			08 05					10 33							12 39		
Bangor (Gwynedd)	d				07 07			08f02			09h02					11 05							13 07		
Llandudno Junction	d				07 25			08 25			09 25					11 25							13 25		
Chester	d				08 19			09 19			10 20					12 19							14 19		
Crewe 10	d	07 40	08 08			09 08	09 20	09g51		10 08		11 08	11 20		12 08		13 08			13 20		14 08		15 08	15 20
Nantwich	d	07 47					09 28	09 58					11 28							13 28		14 17			15 28
Wrenbury	d	07x53					09x34						11x35							13x35					15x35
Whitchurch (Shrops)	d	08 00					09 42	10 09					11 43							13 43		14 28			15 43
Prees	d	08x07					09x48						11x49							13x49					15x49
Wem	d	08 12					09 54	10 18					11 55							13 55					15 55
Yorton	d	08x17					10x00						12x01							14x01					16x01
Shrewsbury	a	08 28	08 37		09 13	09 37	10 12	10 27		10 37	11 14	11 37	12 11		12 37	13 14	13 37			14 11		14 45	15 13	15 37	16 11
	d		08 40	09 00	09 15	09 40				10 39	11 16	11 39			12 40	13 15	13 40	14 04				14 53	15 15	15 40	
Church Stretton	d			09 18	09 30					10 54		11 54				13 30		14 22				15 08	15 30		
Craven Arms	d			09 28	09 38						11 36					13 38		14 33				15 16	15 38		
Ludlow	d		09 06		09 45	10 06				11 08	11 42	12 08			13 06	13 45	14 06					15 23	15 46	16 06	
Leominster	d		09 16			10 16				11 18		12 18			13 16		14 16					15 34		16 16	
Hereford 7	a		09 32		10 09	10 32				11 34	12 06	12 34			13 32	14 09	14 32					15 49	16 09	16 32	
	d		09 33		10 10	10 33				11 35	12 07	12 35		13 14	13 33	14 11	14 33				15 14	15 51	16 11	16 33	
Abergavenny	d		09 56		10 33	10 56				11 58	12 30	12 58			13 56	14 33	14 56					16 14	16 34	16 56	
Pontypool and New Inn	d				10 43						12 41					14 44						16 23	16 44		
Cwmbran	d		10 09		10 48	11 09				12 11	12 46	13 11			14 09	14 49	15 09					16 28	16 49	17 09	
Newport (South Wales)	a		10 20		11 01	11 20				12 22	13 00	13 22			14 20	14 58	15 22					16 39	16 59	17 21	
Reading 7	a													15 54							18 01				
London Paddington 15 ⊖	a													16 27							18 30				
Cardiff Central 7	a		10 37		11 15	11 37				12 38	13 22	13 39			14 37	15 21	15 53					16 55	17 15	17 36	
Swansea	a		11 34	13 01		12 34				13 34		14 34			15 34		17 01	18 18				18 05		18 37	

A MX from 25 May until 9 September
B until 22 July
C from 25 July until 9 September
D ꟾP from Reading
b Previous night, stops on request
c Previous night, arr. 2107
e Arr. 0605
f Arr. 0752
g Arr. 0940
h Arr. 0842

For connections from Liverpool Lime Street and Runcorn please refer to Table 91. For connections to Bristol Temple Meads please refer to Table 132

When events are being held at the Millenium Stadium, services are subject to alteration. Please check times before travelling.

Table 131

Manchester, Liverpool and Crewe - Cardiff

Mondays to Fridays

until 9 September

		AW	AW	AW		AW	AW	XC	AW	AW	AW	AW	AW	AW		AW	VT	GW	GW	AW	AW	AW	AW		
									FX	FO		FO	FX	FO		FX		FO							
		R		R					R	R															
			◇			◇		◇1			◇	◇	◇	◇		◇	◇1	◇1	◇1	◇		◇	◇		
								A											B						
		trolley	trolley	trolley				trolley	trolley	trolley	trolley	trolley	trolley				catering								
Manchester Piccadilly 10	d	15 30		16 30				17 27	17 30	17 30		18 30	18 30	19 30		19 30				20 30	21 35		22 35		
Stockport	d	15 39		16 39				17 35	17 39	17 39		18 39	18 39	19 39		19 39				20 39	21 44		22 44		
Wilmslow	d	15 46		16 46				17 44	17 46	17 46		18 46	18 46	19 46		19 46				20 46	21 51		22 52		
Holyhead	d		14 34								16 38														
Bangor (Gwynedd)	d		15 04								17 06						20 20								
Llandudno Junction	d		15 27								17 25						20 38								
Chester	d		16 19								18 18						21b35								
Crewe 10	d	16 08		17 08			17 20	18 07	18 08	18 08		19 08	19 08	20 08		20 08	21a54			21 08	22 12		23 14		
Nantwich	d	16 17					17 28		18 17	18 17		19 17	19 17	20 17		20 17				21 17	22 20		23 22		
Wrenbury	d						17x35					19x23	19x23							21x23	22x26		23x27		
Whitchurch (Shrops)	d	16 28					17 43		18 28	18 28		19 29	19 29	20 28		20 28				21 30	22 33		23 34		
Prees	d						17x49					19x35	19x35							21x36	22x39		23x40		
Wem	d	16 36					17 55		18 36	18 36		19 40	19 40	20 36		20 36				21 41	22 44		23 45		
Yorton	d						18x01					19x45	19x45							21x46	22x49		23x50		
Shrewsbury	a	16 47	17 14	17 37			18 11		18 47	18 47	19 15	19 55	19 55	20 47		20 47				21 55	23 01		00 04		
	d	16 50	17 16	17 40		18 05			18 50	18 50	19 17	19 56	19 56	20 50		20 50				21 57		23 08			
Church Stretton	d	17 06	17 31			18 23			19 05	19 05		20 11	20 11	21 05		21 05				22 12		23 24			
Craven Arms	d	17 14	17 39			18 35			19 13	19 13		20 19	20 19	21 13		21 13				22 20		23 32			
Ludlow	d	17 21	17 46	18 06					19 20	19 20	19 43	20 27	20 27	21 20		21 20				22 27		23 41			
Leominster	d	17 32		18 16					19 31	19 31		20 37	20 37	21 31		21 31				22 38		23 52			
Hereford 7	a	17 49	18 10	18 32					19 46	19 46	20 06	20 53	20 53	21 46		21 46				22 56		00 07			
	d	17 51	18 11	18 33					19 48	19 48	20 09	20 54	20 54	21 50		21 50		21 51	21 51	22 58		00 09			
Abergavenny	d	18 14	18 34	18 56					20 11	20 11	20 32	21 22	21 22	22 16		22 16				23 21		00 33			
Pontypool and New Inn	d	18 24	18 44						20 21	20 21		21 32	21 32							23 30					
Cwmbran	d	18 29	18 49	19 09					20 26	20 26	20 44	21 37	21 37	22 28		22 28				23 35		00 46			
Newport (South Wales)	a	18 39	19 00	19 22					20 36	20 37	20 58	21 50	21 50	22 39		22 41				23 46		00 57			
Reading 7	a							20 39										00 38	00 38						
London Paddington 15 ⊖	a																	01 11	01 17						
Cardiff Central 7	a	18 55	19 21	19 42					20 59	20 58	21 20	22 06	22 06	22 55		23 02				00 02		01 18			
Swansea	a	20 04		20 40		22 10						23 07													

Mondays to Fridays

from 12 September

		GW	AW	AW	AW	AW	AW	AW	AW	AW		GW	AW	XC	XC	GW	AW	AW	AW	AW		AW	AW	AW	AW
		MX	MX	MO	MX	MX	MO															BHX			
		◇1	◇	◇	◇	◇			◇	◇		◇1	◇	◇1	◇1	◇1	◇	◇	◇	◇		◇		◇	◇
												C				C									
												catering	trolley	trolley	trolley	catering		trolley	trolley	trolley		⊠		trolley	
Manchester Piccadilly 10	d		20p30	20p30		22p35								05 00	06 00					06 30				07 30	
Stockport	d		20p39	20p39		22p44									06 08					06 39				07 39	
Wilmslow	d		20p46	20p47		22p52														06 46				07 46	
Holyhead	d																		04 25			05 32			
Bangor (Gwynedd)	d																		04 57			06 02			
Llandudno Junction	d																		05 15			06 21			
Chester	d						23p00	04 22									05 15		06f18			07 08			
Crewe 10	d		21p08	21e13		23p14	23p23	04a44					04 54	05 47	06a32			05 55		07 08		07 33	07 40	08 08	
Nantwich	d		21p17	21p21		23p22	23p31						05 02					06 03		07 17			07 47		
Wrenbury	d		21c23	21c26		23c27	23c37											06x09					07x53		
Whitchurch (Shrops)	d		21p30	21p35		23p34	23p45						05 13					06 16					08 00		
Prees	d		21c36	21c40		23c40	23c51											06x22					08x07		
Wem	d		21p41	21p47		23p45	23p57						05 22					06 27					08 12		
Yorton	d		21c46	21c51		23c50	00x02											06x32					08x17		
Shrewsbury	a		21p55	22p03		00 04	00 14						05 33				06 10	06 42	07 17	07 42		08 09	08 28	08 37	
	d		21p57	22p04	23p08					05 19			05 40				06 13	06 44	07 19	07 44		08 10		08 40	09 00
Church Stretton	d		22p12	22p20	23p24					05 36			05 55				06 29	06 59		07 59					09 18
Craven Arms	d		22p20	22p29	23p32					05 50			06 03				06 37	07 07		08 07					09 28
Ludlow	d		22p27	22p37	23p41								06 10				06 45	07 14	07 46	08 14				09 06	
Leominster	d		22p38	22p49	23p52								06 21				06 56	07 25	07 56	08 25				09 16	
Hereford 7	a		22p56	23p03	00 07								06 36				07 10	07 43	08 12	08 40				09 32	
	d	21p51	22p58	23p05	00 09				05 25			05 35	06 42			06 43	07 13	07 45	08 13	08 42				09 33	
Abergavenny	d		23p21	23p29	00 33				05 49				07 05				07 36	08 08	08 36	09 05				09 56	
Pontypool and New Inn	d		23p30	23p39					05 59				07 15				07 46	08 17	08 46						
Cwmbran	d		23p35	23p44	00 46				06 04				07 20				07 51	08 22	08 51	09 17				10 09	
Newport (South Wales)	a		23p46	23p54	00 57				06 16				07 33				08 01	08 37	09 02	09 35		09 40		10 20	
Reading 7	a	00 38										08 21		08 39		09 14									
London Paddington 15 ⊖	a	01 17										08 51				09 47									
Cardiff Central 7	a		00 02	00 20	01 18				06 33				07 49				08 17	08 53	09 18	09 57		09 58		10 37	
Swansea	a								07 45	09 08			08 50					09 55	10 34					11 34	13 01

A trolley to Crewe
B FX from 24 May until 8 September
C catering from Reading
b Arr. 2128
c Previous night, stops on request
e Previous night, arr. 2107
f Arr. 0605

For connections from Liverpool Lime Street and Runcorn please refer to Table 91. For connections to Bristol Temple Meads please refer to Table 132

When events are being held at the Millenium Stadium, services are subject to alteration. Please check times before travelling.

Table 131

Mondays to Fridays

from 12 September

Manchester, Liverpool and Crewe - Cardiff

		AW	AW	AW	AW	AW		AW	AW	AW	GW	AW	AW	AW	AW	AW		GW	AW	AW	AW	AW	AW	AW	AW
													[R]	[R]					[R]		[R]		[R]		[R]
		◇	◇		◇	◇		◇	◇		◇[1]	◇			◇			◇[1]		◇				◇	
		🛒	🛒		🛒	🛒		🛒	🛒		🍽	🛒	🛒	🛒				🍽	🛒	🛒	🛒		🛒	🛒	🛒
Manchester Piccadilly [10] ⛴	d		08 30			09 30			10 30			11 30		12 30					13 30		14 30		15 30		16 30
Stockport	d		08 39			09 39			10 39			11 39		12 39					13 39		14 39		15 39		16 39
Wilmslow	d		08 46			09 46			10 46			11 46		12 46					13 46		14 46		15 46		16 46
Holyhead	d	06 29			07 15			08 05					10 33							12 39				14 34	
Bangor (Gwynedd)	d	07 07			08b02			09e02					11 05							13 07				15 04	
Llandudno Junction	d	07 25			08 25			09 25					11 25							13 25				15 27	
Chester	d	08 19			09 19			10 20					12 19							14 19				16 19	
Crewe [10]	d		09 08	09 20	09c51	10 08			11 08	11 20		12 08		13 08		13 20			14 08		15 08	15 20	16 08		17 08
Nantwich	d			09 28	09 58					11 28						13 28			14 17			15 28	16 17		
Wrenbury	d			09x34						11x35						13x35						15x35			
Whitchurch (Shrops)	d			09 42	10 09					11 43						13 43			14 28			15 43	16 28		
Prees	d			09x48						11x49						13x49						15x49			
Wem	d			09 54	10 18					11 55						13 55						15 55	16 36		
Yorton	d			10x00						12x01						14x01						16x01			
Shrewsbury	a	09 13	09 37	10 12	10 27	10 37		11 14	11 37	12 11		12 37	13 14	13 37		14 11			14 45	15 13	15 37	16 11	16 47	17 14	17 37
	d	09 15	09 40			10 39		11 16	11 39			12 40	13 15	13 40	14 04				14 53	15 15	15 40		16 50	17 16	17 40
Church Stretton	d	09 30				10 54			11 54				13 30		14 22				15 08	15 30			17 06	17 31	
Craven Arms	d	09 38						11 36					13 38		14 33				15 16	15 38			17 14	17 39	
Ludlow	d	09 45	10 06			11 08		11 42	12 08			13 06	13 45	14 06					15 23	15 46	16 06		17 21	17 46	18 06
Leominster	d		10 16			11 18			12 18			13 16		14 16					15 34		16 16		17 32		18 16
Hereford [7]	a	10 09	10 32			11 34		12 06	12 34			13 32	14 09	14 32					15 49	16 09	16 32		17 49	18 10	18 32
	d	10 10	10 33			11 35		12 07	12 35		13 14	13 33	14 11	14 33				15 14	15 51	16 11	16 33		17 51	18 11	18 33
Abergavenny	d	10 33	10 56			11 58		12 30	12 58			13 56	14 33	14 56					16 14	16 34	16 56		18 14	18 34	18 56
Pontypool and New Inn	d	10 43						12 41					14 44						16 23	16 44			18 24	18 44	
Cwmbran	d	10 48	11 09			12 11		12 46	13 11			14 09	14 49	15 09					16 28	16 49	17 09		18 29	18 49	19 09
Newport (South Wales)	a	11 01	11 20			12 22		13 00	13 22			14 20	14 58	15 22					16 39	16 59	17 21		18 39	19 00	19 22
Reading [7]	a										15 54							17 54							
London Paddington [15] ⊖	a										16 27							18 28							
Cardiff Central [7]	a	11 15	11 37			12 38		13 22	13 39			14 37	15 21	15 53					16 55	17 15	17 36		18 55	19 21	19 42
Swansea	a		12 34			13 34			14 34			15 34		17 01	18 18				18 05		18 37		20 04		20 40

		AW		AW	XC	AW	AW	AW	AW	AW	AW	AW		VT	GW	GW	AW	AW	AW	AW					
						FX	FO		FO	FX	FO	FX			FO	FX									
						[R]	[R]																		
		◇			◇[1]			◇	◇	◇	◇	◇		◇[1]	◇[1]	◇[1]	◇		◇	◇					
					A																				
					🛒	🛒	🛒	🛒	🛒	🛒				🍽											
Manchester Piccadilly [10] ⛴	d				17 27	17 30	17 30		18 30	18 30	19 30	19 30					20 30	21 35		22 35					
Stockport	d				17 35	17 39	17 39		18 39	18 39	19 39	19 39					20 39	21 44		22 44					
Wilmslow	d				17 44	17 46	17 46		18 46	18 46	19 46	19 46					20 46	21 51		22 52					
Holyhead	d							16 38																	
Bangor (Gwynedd)	d							17 06						20 20											
Llandudno Junction	d							17 25						20 38											
Chester	d							18 18						21f35											
Crewe [10]	d			17 20	18 07	18 08	18 08		19 08	19 08	20 08	20 08		21a54			21 08	22 12		23 14					
Nantwich	d			17 28		18 17	18 17		19 17	19 17	20 17	20 17					21 17	22 20		23 22					
Wrenbury	d			17x35					19x23	19x23							21x23	22x26		23x27					
Whitchurch (Shrops)	d			17 43		18 28	18 28		19 29	19 29	20 28	20 28					21 30	22 33		23 34					
Prees	d			17x49					19x35	19x35							21x36	22x39		23x40					
Wem	d			17 55		18 36	18 36		19 40	19 40	20 36	20 36					21 41	22 44		23 45					
Yorton	d			18x01					19x45	19x45							21x46	22x49		23x50					
Shrewsbury	a			18 11		18 47	18 47	19 15	19 55	19 55	20 47	20 47					21 55	23 01		00 04					
	d	18 05				18 50	18 50	19 17	19 56	19 56	20 50	20 50					21 57		23 08						
Church Stretton	d	18 23				19 05	19 05		20 11	20 11	21 05	21 05					22 12		23 24						
Craven Arms	d	18 35				19 13	19 13		20 19	20 19	21 13	21 13					22 20		23 32						
Ludlow	d					19 20	19 20	19 43	20 27	20 27	21 20	21 20					22 27		23 41						
Leominster	d					19 31	19 31		20 37	20 37	21 31	21 31					22 38		23 52						
Hereford [7]	a					19 46	19 46	20 06	20 53	20 53	21 46	21 46					22 56		00 07						
	d					19 48	19 48	20 09	20 54	20 54	21 50	21 50			21 51	21 51	22 58		00 09						
Abergavenny	d					20 11	20 11	20 32	21 22	21 22	22 16	22 16					23 21		00 33						
Pontypool and New Inn	d					20 21	20 21		21 32	21 32							23 30								
Cwmbran	d					20 26	20 26	20 44	21 37	21 37	22 28	22 28					23 35		00 46						
Newport (South Wales)	a					20 36	20 37	20 58	21 50	21 50	22 39	22 41					23 46		00 57						
Reading [7]	a				20 39										00 38	00 38									
London Paddington [15] ⊖	a														01 11	01 17									
Cardiff Central [7]	a					20 59	20 58	21 20	22 06	22 06	22 55	23 02					00 02		01 18						
Swansea	a	22 10							23 07																

A 🛒 to Crewe
b Arr. 0752
c Arr. 0940
e Arr. 0842
f Arr. 2128

For connections from Liverpool Lime Street and Runcorn please refer to Table 91. For connections to Bristol Temple Meads please refer to Table 132

When events are being held at the Millenium Stadium, services are subject to alteration. Please check times before travelling.

Table 131

Saturdays
until 30 July

Manchester, Liverpool and Crewe - Cardiff

		GW ◇1	AW ◇	AW ◇	AW ◇	AW	AW ◇	AW	AW ◇ 🛒	XC ◇1 🛒	AW	GW ◇1 A ⊒
Manchester Piccadilly 10 ⇌	d		20p30		22p35					05 11		
Stockport	d		20p39		22p44							
Wilmslow	d		20p46		22p52							
Holyhead	d											
Bangor (Gwynedd)	d											
Llandudno Junction	d											
Chester	d					04 22						
Crewe 10	d		21p08		23p14	04a44			04 54	05c47		
Nantwich	d		21p17		23p22				05 02			
Wrenbury	d		21b23		23b27							
Whitchurch (Shrops)	d		21p30		23p34				05 13			
Prees	d		21b36		23b40							
Wem	d		21p41		23p45				05 22			
Yorton	d		21b46		23b50							
Shrewsbury	a		21p55		00 04				05 33			
	d		21p57	23p08			05 19		05 40		06 13	
Church Stretton	d		22p12	23p24			05 36		05 55		06 28	
Craven Arms	d		22p20	23p32			05 47		06 03		06 36	
Ludlow	d		22p27	23p41					06 10		06 44	
Leominster	d		22p38	23p52					06 21		06 55	
Hereford 7	a		22p56	00 07					06 36		07 09	
	d	21p51	22p58	00 09				05 42	06 42		07 11	07 10
Abergavenny	d		23p21	00 33				06 07	07 05		07 34	
Pontypool and New Inn	d		23p30					06 18	07 15		07 44	
Cwmbran	d		23p35	00 46				06 23	07 20		07 49	
Newport (South Wales)	a		23p46	00 57				06 34	07 37		08 00	
Reading 7	a	00 38								08 39		09 54
London Paddington 15 ⊖	a	01 11										10 29
Cardiff Central 7	a		00 02	01 18				06 54	07 54		08 19	
Swansea	a						09 08		08 51			

		AW ◇ 🛒	AW ◇ 🛒	AW ◇ 🛒	AW	AW ◇ 🛒	AW ◇	AW ◇ 🛒	AW ◇ 🛒	AW	AW ◇ 🛒	AW ◇ 🛒
Manchester Piccadilly 10 ⇌	d			06 30		07 30			08 30		09 30	
Stockport	d			06 39		07 39			08 39		09 39	
Wilmslow	d			06 46		07 46			08 46		09 46	
Holyhead	d		04 25					06 35				08 20
Bangor (Gwynedd)	d		04 57					07 07				09 02
Llandudno Junction	d		05 15					07 25				09 25
Chester	d		06e12					08 19				10 19
Crewe 10	d	05 55		07 08	07 20	08 08			09 08	09 20	10 08	
Nantwich	d	06 03		07 17	07 27	08 17				09 28		
Wrenbury	d	06x09			07x34					09x34		
Whitchurch (Shrops)	d	06 16		07 28	07 41	08 27				09 42	10 23	
Prees	d	06x22			07x47					09x48		
Wem	d	06 27		07 36	07 53					09 54		
Yorton	d	06x32			07x58					10x00		
Shrewsbury	a	06 42	07 17	07 47	08 08	08 45		09 13	09 37	10 12	10 40	11 13
	d	06 44	07 19	07 50		08 46	09 00	09 15	09 40		10 41	11 16
Church Stretton	d	06 59		08 05		09 01	09 17		09 55		10 57	
Craven Arms	d	07 07		08 13		09 09	09 30		10 03		11 05	
Ludlow	d	07 14	07 45	08 20		09 17		09 41	10 10		11 13	11 41
Leominster	d	07 25	07 55	08 31		09 27			10 21		11 23	
Hereford 7	a	07 40	08 11	08 49		09 43		10 05	10 36		11 43	12 05
	d	07 44	08 12	08 51		09 44		10 06	10 38		11 46	12 06
Abergavenny	d	08 07	08 35	09 14		10 07		10 29	11 01		12 09	12 29
Pontypool and New Inn	d	08 16	08 45					10 39				12 39
Cwmbran	d	08 21	08 50	09 26		10 20		10 44	11 13		12 21	12 44
Newport (South Wales)	a	08 31	09 01	09 37		10 35		10 55	11 27		12 34	12 55
Reading 7	a											
London Paddington 15 ⊖	a											
Cardiff Central 7	a	08 50	09 22	09 58		10 53		11 15	11 53		12 53	13 15
Swansea	a	09 57		10 55		11 56	13 01		12 55		13 55	

		GW ◇1 ⊒	AW ◇ 🛒	AW	AW ◇ 🛒	AW R 🛒	AW R 🛒	AW ◇	AW	GW ◇1 ⊒	AW R 🛒	AW ◇ 🛒
Manchester Piccadilly 10 ⇌	d		10 30		11 30		12 30				13 30	
Stockport	d		10 39		11 39		12 39				13 39	
Wilmslow	d		10 46		11 46		12 46				13 46	
Holyhead	d					10 33						12 38
Bangor (Gwynedd)	d					11 05						13 07
Llandudno Junction	d					11 25						13 25
Chester	d					12 19						14 19
Crewe 10	d		11 08	11 20	12 08		13 08		13 20		14 08	
Nantwich	d			11 31	12 17				13 28		14 17	
Wrenbury	d			11x42					13x35			
Whitchurch (Shrops)	d			11 49	12 27				13 43		14 28	
Prees	d			11x56					13x49			
Wem	d			12 02					13 55			
Yorton	d			12x08					14x01			
Shrewsbury	a		11 37	12 18	12 43	13 13	13 37		14 11		14 45	15 13
	d		11 40		12 45	13 15	13 40	14 05			14 45	15 15
Church Stretton	d		11 55		13 01		13 55	14 23			15 02	
Craven Arms	d		12 03		13 09		14 03	14 36			15 10	
Ludlow	d		12 10		13 17	13 40	14 10				15 17	15 41
Leominster	d		12 21		13 27		14 21				15 28	
Hereford 7	a		12 36		13 44	14 04	14 36				15 43	16 05
	d	12 13	12 38		13 45	14 06	14 38			15 10	15 45	16 06
Abergavenny	d		13 01		14 08	14 28	15 01				16 08	16 29
Pontypool and New Inn	d					14 39						16 39
Cwmbran	d		13 13		14 21	14 44	15 13				16 20	16 44
Newport (South Wales)	a		13 28		14 35	15 05	15 34				16 35	16 55
Reading 7	a	14 53								17 54		
London Paddington 15 ⊖	a	15 29								18 29		
Cardiff Central 7	a		13 53		14 53	15 26	15 53				16 53	17 15
Swansea	a		14 55		15 55		16 58	18 10			18 05	

		AW R 🛒	AW	AW R 🛒	AW ◇ 🛒	AW R 🛒	AW ◇	AW	AW R 🛒	AW ◇ 🛒	GW ◇1	AW ◇ 🛒
Manchester Piccadilly 10 ⇌	d	14 30		15 30		16 30			17 30			18 30
Stockport	d	14 39		15 39		16 39			17 39			18 39
Wilmslow	d	14 46		15 46		16 46			17 46			18 46
Holyhead	d				14 32					16 37		
Bangor (Gwynedd)	d				15 00					17 06		
Llandudno Junction	d				15 23					17 24		
Chester	d				16f19					18 20		
Crewe 10	d	15 08	15 20	16 08		17 08		17 20	18 08			19 08
Nantwich	d		15 27	16 17		17 17		17 28	18 17			19 17
Wrenbury	d		15x34					17x35				19x23
Whitchurch (Shrops)	d		15 42	16 28		17 27		17 43	18 28			19 29
Prees	d		15x48					17x49				19x35
Wem	d		15 54					17 55				19 40
Yorton	d		16x00					18x01				19x45
Shrewsbury	a	15 37	16 08	16 45	17 14	17 43		18 11	18 45	19 16		19 55
	d	15 40		16 45	17 16	17 45	18 05		18 48	19 17		19 56
Church Stretton	d	15 55		17 02		18 00	18 23		19 03			20 11
Craven Arms	d	16 03		17 10		18 08	18 36		19 11			20 19
Ludlow	d	16 10		17 17	17 42	18 15			19 19	19 41		20 27
Leominster	d	16 21		17 28		18 26			19 29			20 37
Hereford 7	a	16 36		17 43	18 05	18 41			19 49	20 10		20 53
	d	16 38		17 46	18 07	18 43			19 51	20 11	20 20	20 54
Abergavenny	d	17 01		18 09	18 30	19 06			20 14	20 34		21 17
Pontypool and New Inn	d				18 40				20 23			21 27
Cwmbran	d	17 13		18 21	18 45	19 18			20 28	20 47		21 32
Newport (South Wales)	a	17 33		18 36	18 55	19 37			20 39	21 00		21 42
Reading 7	a										23 30	
London Paddington 15 ⊖	a										00 13	
Cardiff Central 7	a	17 53		18 53	19 15	19 53			20 58	21 15		22 03
Swansea	a	19 02		20 04			22 10					23 04

A ⊒ from Reading
b Previous night, stops on request
c Arr. 0541
e Arr. 0604
f Arr. 1612

For connections from Liverpool Lime Street and Runcorn please refer to Table 91. For connections to Bristol Temple Meads please refer to Table 132

When events are being held at the Millenium Stadium, services are subject to alteration. Please check times before travelling.

Table 131

Manchester, Liverpool and Crewe - Cardiff

Saturdays
from 17 September

		AW		AW	AW	AW
Manchester Piccadilly 10 ⇌	d	19 30		20 30	21 35	22 35
Stockport	d	19 39		20 39	21 44	22 44
Wilmslow	d	19 46		20 46	21 51	22 52
Holyhead	d					
Bangor (Gwynedd)	d					
Llandudno Junction	d					
Chester	d					
Crewe 10	d	20 08		21 08	22 12	23 14
Nantwich	d	20 17		21 17	22 20	23 22
Wrenbury	d			21x23	22x26	23x27
Whitchurch (Shrops)	d	20 27		21 29	22 33	23 34
Prees	d			21x35	22x39	23x40
Wem	d	20 36		21 40	22 44	23 45
Yorton	d			21x45	22x49	23x50
Shrewsbury	a	20 47		21 55	23 01	00 04
	d	20 48		21 56		
Church Stretton	d	21 03		22 11		
Craven Arms	d	21 11		22 19		
Ludlow	d	21 19		22 27		
Leominster	d	21 29		22 37		
Hereford 7	a	21 45		22 53		
	d	21 46		22 54		
Abergavenny	d	22 09		23 17		
Pontypool and New Inn	d			23 27		
Cwmbran	d	22 22		23 32		
Newport (South Wales)	a	22 33		23 45		
Reading 7	a					
London Paddington 15 ⊖	a					
Cardiff Central 7	a	22 53		00 05		
Swansea	a					

Sundays
until 19 June

		GW	AW	AW	XC	AW	AW	AW	AW	GW		AW	AW	GW	AW	AW	GW	AW	AW	AW		GW	AW	AW	AW
								R				R			R	R		R		R			R	R	R
		◇1			◇1		◇		◇	◇1			◇	◇1			◇1		◇			◇1			
		A	A	A																					
					⌶		⌶	⌶		⊡		⌶		⊡	⌶	⌶	⊡	⌶		⌶		⌶	⌶	⌶	⌶
Manchester Piccadilly 10 ⇌	d		20p30	22p35	08 27		09 30	10 30				11 24			12 30	13 30		14 30		15 30			16 30	17 30	
Stockport	d		20p39	22p44	08 36		09 39	10 40				11e40			12 40	13 40		14 39		15 39			16 39	17 39	
Wilmslow	d		20p46	22p52	08 43		09 47	10 48				11 47			12 48	13 47		14 47		15 47			16 47	17 47	
Holyhead	d												10 20												16 25
Bangor (Gwynedd)	d												10 59												17 04
Llandudno Junction	d												11 22												17 25
Chester	d												12 21												18 24
Crewe 10	d		21p08	23p14	09a01		10c13	11 11				12f13			13g13	14h13		15 10		16i13			17j13	18k13	
Nantwich	d		21p17	23p22			10 22								13 21								17 21		
Wrenbury	d		21b23	23b27			10x27								13x26								17x26		
Whitchurch (Shrops)	d		21p29	23p34			10 35								13 34								17 34		
Prees	d		21b35	23b40			10x40								13x39								17x39		
Wem	d		21p40	23p45			10 46								13 45								17 45		
Yorton	d		21b45	23b50			10x50								13x49								17x49		
Shrewsbury	a		21p55	00 04			11 01	11 41				12 43	13 18		13 59	14 43		15 44		16 43			18 00	18 43	19 20
	d		21p56				11 03	11 45	12 07			12 44	13 19		14 01	14 44		15 47	16 18	16 44			18 01	18 44	19 21
Church Stretton	d		22p11				11 19		12 25				13 35			15 00			16 36	17 00					19 37
Craven Arms	d		22p19				11 27		12 36				13 43			15 08			16 47	17 08					19 45
Ludlow	d		22p27				11 36	12 13				13 12	13 51		14 28	15 16		16 17		17 16			18 29	19 12	19 53
Leominster	d		22p37				11 47	12 23				13 22	14 02		14 39	15 26		16 28		17 26			18 39		20 04
Hereford 7	a		22p53				12 02	12 38				13 37	14 17		14 53	15 41		16 43		17 41			18 54	19 34	20 18
	d	20p20	22p54			10 09	12 03	12 39		13 28		13 39	14 19	14 30	14 56	15 43	16 33	16 44		17 43		18 30	18 57	19 36	20 21
Abergavenny	d		23p17			10 33	12 27	13 02				14 02	14 42		15 19	16 06		17 08		18 06			19 20	19 59	20 46
Pontypool and New Inn	d		23p27			10 43		13 12					14 52			16 16				18 16					20 56
Cwmbran	d		23p32			10 48	12 40	13 17				14 14	14 57		15 31	16 21		17 21		18 21			19 33	20 11	21 01
Newport (South Wales)	a		23p45			10 59	12 51	13 28				14 28	15 07		15 45	16 32		17 33		18 31			19 49	20 22	21 14
Reading 7	a	23p30								16 20				17 20			19 11					21 23			
London Paddington 15 ⊖	a	00 13								17 07				18 07			19 51					22 12			
Cardiff Central 7	a		00 05			11 16	13 13	13 44				14 49	15 31		16 02	16 53		17 50		18 50			20 10	20 43	21 36
Swansea	a							15 09	16 04						17 14			19 15	20 16						

nt 22 May
evious night, stops on request
. 1006
1134

f Arr. 1207
g Arr. 1307
h Arr. 1407
i Arr. 1606
j Arr. 1706
k Arr. 1807

For connections from Liverpool Lime Street and Runcorn please refer to Table 91. For connections to Bristol Temple Meads please refer to Table 132

When events are being held at the Millenium Stadium, services are subject to alteration. Please check times before travelling.

Table 131

Manchester, Liverpool and Crewe - Cardiff

Saturdays
until 30 July

		AW		AW	AW	AW
Manchester Piccadilly 10 ⇌	d	19 30		20 30	21 35	22 35
Stockport	d	19 39		20 39	21 44	22 44
Wilmslow	d	19 46		20 46	21 51	22 52
Holyhead	d					
Bangor (Gwynedd)	d					
Llandudno Junction	d					
Chester	d					
Crewe 10	d	20 08		21 08	22 12	23 14
Nantwich	d	20 17		21 17	22 20	23 22
Wrenbury	d			21x23	22x26	23x27
Whitchurch (Shrops)	d	20 27		21 29	22 33	23 34
Prees	d			21x35	22x39	23x40
Wem	d	20 36		21 40	22 44	23 45
Yorton	d			21x45	22x49	23x50
Shrewsbury	a	20 47		21 55	23 01	00 04
	d	20 48		21 56		
Church Stretton	d	21 03		22 11		
Craven Arms	d	21 11		22 19		
Ludlow	d	21 19		22 27		
Leominster	d	21 29		22 37		
Hereford 7	a	21 45		22 53		
	d	21 46		22 54		
Abergavenny	d	22 09		23 17		
Pontypool and New Inn	d			23 27		
Cwmbran	d	22 22		23 32		
Newport (South Wales)	a	22 33		23 45		
Reading 7	a					
London Paddington 15 ⊖	a					
Cardiff Central 7	a	22 53		00 05		
Swansea	a					

Saturdays
6 August to 10 September

		GW	AW	AW	AW	AW	AW	AW	AW	XC		AW	GW	AW	AW	AW	AW	AW	AW	AW		AW	AW	AW	AW
		◇1	◇	◇	◇		◇		◇	◇1			◇1	◇	◇	◇		◇	◇	◇		◇		◇	◇
													A												
									⌶	⌶			⊡	⌶	⌶	⌶		⌶		⌶		⌶		⌶	⌶
Manchester Piccadilly 10 ⇌	d		20p30		22p35					05 11						06 30		07 30				08 30		09 30	
Stockport	d		20p39		22p44											06 39		07 39				08 39		09 39	
Wilmslow	d		20p46		22p52											06 46		07 46				08 46		09 46	
Holyhead	d														04 25					06 35					08 20
Bangor (Gwynedd)	d														04 57					07 07					09 02
Llandudno Junction	d														05 15					07 25					09 25
Chester	d					04 22									06e12					08 19					10 19
Crewe 10	d		21p08		23p14	04a44			04 54	05c47				05 55		07 08	07 20	08 08				09 08	09 20	10 08	
Nantwich	d		21p17		23p22				05 02					06 03		07 17	07 27	08 17					09 28		
Wrenbury	d		21b23		23b27									06x09			07x34						09x34		
Whitchurch (Shrops)	d		21p30		23p34				05 13					06 16		07 28	07 41	08 27					09 42	10 23	
Prees	d		21b36		23b40									06x22			07x47						09x48		
Wem	d		21p41		23p45				05 22					06 27		07 36	07 53						09 54		
Yorton	d		21b46		23b50									06x32			07x58						10x00		
Shrewsbury	a		21p55		00 04				05 33					06 42	07 17	07 47	08 08	08 45		09 13		09 37	10 12	10 40	11 13
	d		21p57	23p08			05 19		05 40			06 13		06 44	07 19	07 50		08 46	09 00	09 15		09 40		10 41	11 16
Church Stretton	d		22p12	23p24			05 36		05 55			06 28		06 59		08 05		09 01	09 17			09 55		10 57	
Craven Arms	d		22p20	23p32			05 47		06 03			06 36		07 07		08 13		09 09	09 30			10 03		11 05	
Ludlow	d		22p27	23p41					06 10			06 44		07 14	07 45	08 20		09 17		09 41		10 10		11 13	11 41
Leominster	d		22p38	23p52					06 21			06 55		07 25	07 55	08 31		09 27				10 21		11 23	
Hereford 7	a		22p56	00 07					06 36			07 09		07 40	08 11	08 49		09 43		10 05		10 36		11 43	12 05
	d	21p51	22p58	00 09				05 42	06 42			07 11	07 10	07 44	08 12	08 51		09 44		10 06		10 38		11 46	12 06
Abergavenny	d		23p21	00 33				06 07	07 05			07 34		08 07	08 35	09 14		10 07		10 29		11 01		12 09	12 29
Pontypool and New Inn	d		23p30					06 18	07 15			07 44		08 16	08 45					10 39					12 39
Cwmbran	d		23p35	00 46				06 23	07 20			07 49		08 21	08 50	09 26		10 20		10 44		11 13		12 21	12 44
Newport (South Wales)	a		23p46	00 57				06 34	07 37			08 00		08 31	09 01	09 37		10 35		10 55		11 27		12 34	12 55
Reading 7	a	00 38								08 39			09 54												
London Paddington 15 ⊖	a	01 11											10 29												
Cardiff Central 7	a		00 02	01 18				06 54	07 54			08 19		08 50	09 22	09 58		10 53		11 15		11 53		12 53	13 15
Swansea	a						09 08		08 51					09 57		10 55		11 56	13 01			12 55		13 55	

A ⊡ from Reading
b Previous night, stops on request
c Arr. 0541
e Arr. 0604

For connections from Liverpool Lime Street and Runcorn please refer to Table 91. For connections to Bristol Temple Meads please refer to Table 132

When events are being held at the Millenium Stadium, services are subject to alteration. Please check times before travelling.

Table 131

Saturdays

6 August to 10 September

Manchester, Liverpool and Crewe - Cardiff

		GW	AW	AW	AW	AW	AW	AW	AW	GW	AW	AW	AW	AW	AW	AW	AW	AW	AW	AW	AW	GW	AW
		◇1 ⊡	◇ ⊥		◇ ⊥	R ⊥	R ⊥	◇		◇1 ⊡	R ⊥	◇ ⊥	R ⊥		R ⊥	◇ ⊥	R ⊥	◇		R ⊥	◇ ⊥	◇1	◇ ⊥
Manchester Piccadilly 10 ⇌	d		10 30		11 30		12 30				13 30		14 30		15 30		16 30			17 30			18 30
Stockport	d		10 39		11 39		12 39				13 39		14 39		15 39		16 39			17 39			18 39
Wilmslow	d		10 46		11 46		12 46				13 46		14 46		15 46		16 46			17 46			18 46
Holyhead	d					10 33						12 38				14 32					16 37		
Bangor (Gwynedd)	d					11 05						13 07				15 00					17 06		
Llandudno Junction	d					11 25						13 25				15 23					17 24		
Chester	d					12 19						14 19				16b19					18 20		
Crewe 10	d		11 08	11 20	12 08		13 08		13 20		14 08		15 08	15 20	16 08		17 08		17 20	18 08			19 08
Nantwich	d			11 31	12 17				13 28		14 17			15 27	16 17		17 17		17 28	18 17			19 17
Wrenbury	d			11x42					13x35					15x34					17x35				19x23
Whitchurch (Shrops)	d			11 49	12 27				13 43		14 28			15 42	16 28		17 27		17 43	18 28			19 29
Prees	d			11x56					13x49					15x48					17x49				19x35
Wem	d			12 02					13 55					15 54					17 55				19 40
Yorton	d			12x08					14x01					16x00					18x01				19x45
Shrewsbury	a		11 37	12 18	12 43	13 13	13 37		14 11		14 45	15 13	15 37	16 08	16 45	17 14	17 43		18 11	18 45	19 16		19 55
	d		11 40		12 45	13 15	13 40	14 05			14 45	15 15	15 40		16 45	17 16	17 45	18 05		18 48	19 17		19 56
Church Stretton	d		11 55		13 01		13 55	14 23			15 02		15 55		17 02		18 00	18 23		19 03			20 11
Craven Arms	d		12 03		13 09		14 03	14 36			15 10		16 03		17 10		18 08	18 36		19 11			20 19
Ludlow	d		12 10		13 17	13 40	14 10				15 17	15 41	16 10		17 17	17 42	18 15			19 19	19 41		20 27
Leominster	d		12 21		13 27		14 21				15 28		16 21		17 28		18 26			19 29			20 37
Hereford 7	a		12 36		13 44	14 04	14 36				15 43	16 05	16 36		17 43	18 05	18 41			19 49	20 10		20 53
	d	12 13	12 38		13 45	14 06	14 38			15 10	15 45	16 06	16 38		17 46	18 07	18 43			19 51	20 11	20 20	20 54
Abergavenny	d		13 01		14 08	14 28	15 01				16 08	16 29	17 01		18 09	18 30	19 06			20 14	20 34		21 17
Pontypool and New Inn	d					14 39						16 39				18 40				20 23			21 27
Cwmbran	d		13 13		14 21	14 44	15 13				16 20	16 44	17 13		18 21	18 45	19 18			20 28	20 47		21 32
Newport (South Wales)	a		13 28		14 35	15 05	15 34				16 35	16 55	17 33		18 36	18 55	19 37			20 39	21 00		21 42
Reading 7	a	14 53								17 54												23 30	
London Paddington 15 ⊖	a	15 29								18 29												00 13	
Cardiff Central 7	a		13 53		14 53	15 26	15 53				16 53	17 15	17 53		18 53	19 15	19 53			20 58	21 15		22 03
Swansea	a		14 55		15 55		16 58	18 10			18 05		19 02		20 04			22 10					23 04

		AW	AW	AW	AW
Manchester Piccadilly 10 ⇌	d	19 30	20 30	21 35	22 35
Stockport	d	19 39	20 39	21 44	22 44
Wilmslow	d	19 46	20 46	21 51	22 52
Holyhead	d				
Bangor (Gwynedd)	d				
Llandudno Junction	d				
Chester	d				
Crewe 10	d	20 08	21 08	22 12	23 14
Nantwich	d	20 17	21 17	22 20	23 22
Wrenbury	d		21x23	22x26	23x27
Whitchurch (Shrops)	d	20 27	21 29	22 33	23 34
Prees	d		21x35	22x39	23x40
Wem	d	20 36	21 40	22 44	23 45
Yorton	d		21x45	22x49	23x50
Shrewsbury	a	20 47	21 55	23 01	00 04
	d	20 48	21 56		
Church Stretton	d	21 03	22 11		
Craven Arms	d	21 11	22 19		
Ludlow	d	21 19	22 27		
Leominster	d	21 29	22 37		
Hereford 7	a	21 45	22 53		
	d	21 46			
Abergavenny	d	22 09			
Pontypool and New Inn	d				
Cwmbran	d	22 22			
Newport (South Wales)	a	22 33			
Reading 7	a				
London Paddington 15 ⊖	a				
Cardiff Central 7	a	22 53			
Swansea	a				

b Arr. 1612

For connections from Liverpool Lime Street and Runcorn please refer to Table 91. For connections to Bristol Temple Meads please refer to Table 132

When events are being held at the Millenium Stadium, services are subject to alteration. Please check times before travelling.

Table 131

Saturdays

from 17 September

Manchester, Liverpool and Crewe - Cardiff

		GW	AW	AW	AW	AW	AW	AW	AW	XC	AW	GW	AW	AW	AW	AW	AW	AW	AW	AW	AW	AW	AW
		◇1	◇	◇	◇		◇		◇ ⊥	◇1 ⊥		◇1 A ⊡	◇ ⊥	◇ ⊥	◇ ⊥		◇ ⊥	◇	◇ ⊥	◇ ⊥		◇ ⊥	◇ ⊥
Manchester Piccadilly 10 ⇌	d		20p30		22p35					05 11					06 30		07 30			08 30		09 30	
Stockport	d		20p39		22p44										06 39		07 39			08 39		09 39	
Wilmslow	d		20p46		22p52										06 46		07 46			08 46		09 46	
Holyhead	d													04 25					06 35				08 20
Bangor (Gwynedd)	d													04 57					07 07				09 02
Llandudno Junction	d													05 15					07 25				09 25
Chester	d					04 22								06e12					08 19				10 19
Crewe 10	d		21p08		23p14	04a44			04 54	05c47			05 55		07 08	07 20	08 08			09 08	09 20	10 08	
Nantwich	d		21p17		23p22				05 02				06 03		07 17	07 27	08 17				09 28		
Wrenbury	d		21b23		23b27								06x09			07x34					09x34		
Whitchurch (Shrops)	d		21p30		23p34				05 13				06 16		07 28	07 41	08 27				09 42	10 23	
Prees	d		21b36		23b40								06x22			07x47					09x48		
Wem	d		21p41		23p45				05 22				06 27		07 36	07 53					09 54		
Yorton	d		21b46		23b50								06x32			07x58					10x00		
Shrewsbury	a		21p55		00 04				05 33				06 42	07 17	07 47	08 08	08 45		09 13	09 37	10 12	10 40	11 13
	d		21p57	23p08			05 19		05 40		06 13		06 44	07 19	07 50		08 46	09 00	09 15	09 40		10 41	11 16
Church Stretton	d		22p12	23p24			05 36		05 55		06 28		06 59		08 05		09 01	09 17		09 55		10 57	
Craven Arms	d		22p20	23p32			05 47		06 03		06 36		07 07		08 13		09 09	09 30		10 03		11 05	
Ludlow	d		22p27	23p41					06 10		06 44		07 14	07 45	08 20		09 17		09 41	10 10		11 13	11 41
Leominster	d		22p38	23p52					06 21		06 55		07 25	07 55	08 31		09 27			10 21		11 23	
Hereford 7	a		22p56	00 07					06 36		07 09		07 40	08 11	08 49		09 43		10 05	10 36		11 43	12 05
	d	21p51	22p58	00 09				05 42	06 42		07 11	07 10	07 44	08 12	08 51		09 44		10 06	10 38		11 46	12 06
Abergavenny	d		23p21	00 33				06 07	07 05		07 34		08 07	08 35	09 14		10 07		10 29	11 01		12 09	12 29
Pontypool and New Inn	d		23p30					06 18	07 15		07 44		08 16	08 45					10 39				12 39
Cwmbran	d		23p35	00 46				06 23	07 20		07 49		08 21	08 50	09 26		10 20		10 44	11 13		12 21	12 44
Newport (South Wales)	a		23p46	00 57				06 34	07 37		08 00		08 31	09 01	09 37		10 35		10 55	11 27		12 34	12 55
Reading 7	a	00 38								08 39		09 54											
London Paddington 15 ⊖	a	01 11										10 29											
Cardiff Central 7	a		00 02	01 18				06 54	07 54		08 19		08 50	09 22	09 58		10 53		11 15	11 53		12 53	13 15
Swansea	a						09 08		08 51				09 57		10 55		11 56	13 01		12 55		13 55	

		GW	AW	AW	AW	AW	AW	AW	AW	GW	AW	AW	AW	AW	AW	AW	AW	AW	AW	AW	AW	GW	AW
		◇1 ⊡	◇ ⊥		◇ ⊥	R ⊥	R ⊥	◇		◇1 ⊡	R ⊥	◇ ⊥	R ⊥		R ⊥	◇ ⊥	R ⊥	◇		R ⊥	◇ ⊥	◇1	◇ ⊥
Manchester Piccadilly 10 ⇌	d		10 30		11 30		12 30				13 30		14 30		15 30		16 30			17 30			18 30
Stockport	d		10 39		11 39		12 39				13 39		14 39		15 39		16 39			17 39			18 39
Wilmslow	d		10 46		11 46		12 46				13 46		14 46		15 46		16 46			17 46			18 46
Holyhead	d					10 33						12 38				14 32					16 37		
Bangor (Gwynedd)	d					11 05						13 07				15 00					17 06		
Llandudno Junction	d					11 25						13 25				15 23					17 24		
Chester	d					12 19						14 19				16f19					18 20		
Crewe 10	d		11 08	11 20	12 08		13 08		13 20		14 08		15 08	15 20	16 08		17 08		17 20	18 08			19 08
Nantwich	d			11 31	12 17				13 28		14 17			15 27	16 17		17 17		17 28	18 17			19 17
Wrenbury	d			11x42					13x35					15x34					17x35				19x23
Whitchurch (Shrops)	d			11 49	12 27				13 43		14 28			15 42	16 28		17 27		17 43	18 28			19 29
Prees	d			11x56					13x49					15x48					17x49				19x35
Wem	d			12 02					13 55					15 54					17 55				19 40
Yorton	d			12x08					14x01					16x00					18x01				19x45
Shrewsbury	a		11 37	12 18	12 43	13 13	13 37		14 11		14 45	15 13	15 37	16 08	16 45	17 14	17 43		18 11	18 45	19 16		19 55
	d		11 40		12 45	13 15	13 40	14 05			14 45	15 15	15 40		16 45	17 16	17 45	18 05		18 48	19 17		19 56
Church Stretton	d		11 55		13 01		13 55	14 23			15 02		15 55		17 02		18 00	18 23		19 03			20 1
Craven Arms	d		12 03		13 09		14 03	14 36			15 10		16 03		17 10		18 08	18 36		19 11			20
Ludlow	d		12 10		13 17	13 40	14 10				15 17	15 41	16 10		17 17	17 42	18 15			19 19	19 41		20
Leominster	d		12 21		13 27		14 21				15 28		16 21		17 28		18 26			19 29			2
Hereford 7	a		12 36		13 44	14 04	14 36				15 43	16 05	16 36		17 43	18 05	18 41			19 49	20 10		
	d	12 13	12 38		13 45	14 06	14 38			15 13	15 45	16 06	16 38		17 46	18 07	18 43			19 51	20 11	20 2	
Abergavenny	d		13 01		14 08	14 28	15 01				16 08	16 29	17 01		18 09	18 30	19 06			20 14	20 34		
Pontypool and New Inn	d					14 39						16 39				18 40				20 23			
Cwmbran	d		13 13		14 21	14 44	15 13				16 20	16 44	17 13		18 21	18 45	19 18			20 28	20 47		
Newport (South Wales)	a		13 28		14 35	15 05	15 34				16 35	16 55	17 33		18 36	18 55	19 37			20 39	2		
Reading 7	a	14 53								17 55													
London Paddington 15 ⊖	a	15 29								18 29													
Cardiff Central 7	a		13 53		14 53	15 26	15 53				16 53	17 15	17 53		18 53	19 15	19 53						
Swansea	a		14 55		15 55		16 58	18 10			18 05		19 02		20 04			22 10					

A ⊡ from Reading
b Previous night, stops on request
c Arr. 0541
e Arr. 0604
f Arr. 1612

For connections from Liverpool Lime Street and Runcorn please refer to Table 91. For connections to Bristol Temple Meads please refer to Table

When events are being held at the Millenium Stadium, servic alteration. Please check times before travelling.

Table 131

Manchester, Liverpool and Crewe - Cardiff

Saturdays
until 30 July

		AW		AW	AW	AW
Manchester Piccadilly 10	d	19 30		20 30	21 35	22 35
Stockport	d	19 39		20 39	21 44	22 44
Wilmslow	d	19 46		20 46	21 51	22 52
Holyhead	d					
Bangor (Gwynedd)	d					
Llandudno Junction	d					
Chester	d					
Crewe 10	d	20 08		21 08	22 12	23 14
Nantwich	d	20 17		21 17	22 20	23 22
Wrenbury	d			21x23	22x26	23x27
Whitchurch (Shrops)	d	20 27		21 29	22 33	23 34
Prees	d			21x35	22x39	23x40
Wem	d	20 36		21 40	22 44	23 45
Yorton	d			21x45	22x49	23x50
Shrewsbury	a	20 47		21 55	23 01	00 04
	d	20 48		21 56		
Church Stretton	d	21 03		22 11		
Craven Arms	d	21 11		22 19		
Ludlow	d	21 19		22 27		
Leominster	d	21 29		22 37		
Hereford 7	a	21 45		22 53		
	d	21 46		22 54		
Abergavenny	d	22 09		23 17		
Pontypool and New Inn	d			23 27		
Cwmbran	d	22 22		23 32		
Newport (South Wales)	a	22 33		23 45		
Reading 7	a					
London Paddington 15 ⊖	a					
Cardiff Central 7	a	22 53		00 05		
Swansea	a					

Saturdays
6 August to 10 September

		GW	AW	AW	AW	AW	AW	AW	AW	XC		AW	GW	AW	AW	AW	AW	AW	AW	AW		AW	AW	AW	AW
		◇1	◇	◇	◇		◇		◇	◇1			◇1	◇	◇	◇		◇	◇	◇		◇		◇	◇
													A												
									🛒	🛒				🛒	🛒	🛒		🛒		🛒		🛒		🛒	🛒
Manchester Piccadilly 10	d		20p30		22p35					05 11						06 30		07 30				08 30		09 30	
Stockport	d		20p39		22p44											06 39		07 39				08 39		09 39	
Wilmslow	d		20p46		22p52											06 46		07 46				08 46		09 46	
Holyhead	d														04 25					06 35					08 20
Bangor (Gwynedd)	d														04 57					07 07					09 02
Llandudno Junction	d														05 15					07 25					09 25
Chester	d					04 22									06e12					08 19					10 19
Crewe 10	d		21p08		23p14	04a44			04 54	05c47				05 55		07 08	07 20	08 08				09 08	09 20	10 08	
Nantwich	d		21p17		23p22				05 02					06 03		07 17	07 27	08 17					09 28		
Wrenbury	d		21b23		23b27									06x09			07x34						09x34		
Whitchurch (Shrops)	d		21p30		23p34				05 13					06 16		07 28	07 41	08 27					09 42	10 23	
Prees	d		21b36		23b40									06x22			07x47						09x48		
Wem	d		21p41		23p45				05 22					06 27		07 36	07 53						09 54		
Yorton	d		21b46		23b50									06x32			07x58						10x00		
Shrewsbury	a		21p55		00 04				05 33					06 42	07 17	07 47	08 08	08 45		09 13		09 37	10 12	10 40	11 13
	d		21p57	23p08			05 19		05 40			06 13		06 44	07 19	07 50		08 46	09 00	09 15		09 40		10 41	11 16
Church Stretton	d		22p12	23p24			05 36		05 55			06 28		06 59		08 05		09 01	09 17			09 55		10 57	
Craven Arms	d		22p20	23p32			05 47		06 03			06 36		07 07		08 13		09 09	09 30			10 03		11 05	
Ludlow	d		22p27	23p41					06 10			06 44		07 14	07 45	08 20		09 17		09 41		10 10		11 13	11 41
Leominster	d		22p38	23p52					06 21			06 55		07 25	07 55	08 31		09 27				10 21		11 23	
Hereford 7	a		22p56	00 07					06 36			07 09		07 40	08 11	08 49		09 43		10 05		10 36		11 43	12 05
	d	21p51	22p58	00 09				05 42	06 42			07 11	07 10	07 44	08 12	08 51		09 44		10 06		10 38		11 46	12 06
Abergavenny	d		23p21	00 33				06 07	07 05			07 34		08 07	08 35	09 14		10 07		10 29		11 01		12 09	12 29
Pontypool and New Inn	d		23p30					06 18	07 15			07 44		08 16	08 45					10 39					12 39
Cwmbran	d		23p35	00 46				06 23	07 20			07 49		08 21	08 50	09 26		10 20		10 44		11 13		12 21	12 44
Newport (South Wales)	a		23p46	00 57				06 34	07 37			08 00		08 31	09 01	09 37		10 35		10 55		11 27		12 34	12 55
Reading 7	a	00 38								08 39			09 54												
London Paddington 15 ⊖	a	01 11											10 29												
Cardiff Central 7	a		00 02	01 18				06 54	07 54			08 19		08 50	09 22	09 58		10 53		11 15		11 53		12 53	13 15
Swansea	a						09 08		08 51					09 57		10 55		11 56	13 01			12 55		13 55	

A ⊡ from Reading
b Previous night, stops on request
c Arr. 0541
e Arr. 0604

For connections from Liverpool Lime Street and Runcorn please refer to Table 91. For connections to Bristol Temple Meads please refer to Table 132

When events are being held at the Millenium Stadium, services are subject to alteration. Please check times before travelling.

Table 131

Saturdays

6 August to 10 September

Manchester, Liverpool and Crewe - Cardiff

		GW	AW	AW	AW	AW		AW	AW	AW	GW	AW	AW
						■		■				■	
		◇1	◇		◇				◇		◇1		◇
		🍴	🛒		🛒	🛒		🛒			🍴	🛒	🛒
Manchester Piccadilly 10	d		10 30		11 30			12 30				13 30	
Stockport	d		10 39		11 39			12 39				13 39	
Wilmslow	d		10 46		11 46			12 46				13 46	
Holyhead	d					10 33							12 38
Bangor (Gwynedd)	d					11 05							13 07
Llandudno Junction	d					11 25							13 25
Chester	d					12 19							14 19
Crewe 10	d		11 08	11 20	12 08			13 08		13 20		14 08	
Nantwich	d			11 31	12 17					13 28		14 17	
Wrenbury	d			11x42						13x35			
Whitchurch (Shrops)	d			11 49	12 27					13 43		14 28	
Prees	d			11x56						13x49			
Wem	d			12 02						13 55			
Yorton	d			12x08						14x01			
Shrewsbury	a		11 37	12 18	12 43	13 13		13 37		14 11		14 45	15 13
	d		11 40		12 45	13 15		13 40	14 05			14 45	15 15
Church Stretton	d		11 55		13 01			13 55	14 23			15 02	
Craven Arms	d		12 03		13 09			14 03	14 36			15 10	
Ludlow	d		12 10		13 17	13 40		14 10				15 17	15 41
Leominster	d		12 21		13 27			14 21				15 28	
Hereford 7	a		12 36		13 44	14 04		14 36				15 43	16 05
	d	12 13	12 38		13 45	14 06		14 38			15 10	15 45	16 06
Abergavenny	d		13 01		14 08	14 28		15 01				16 08	16 29
Pontypool and New Inn	d					14 39							16 39
Cwmbran	d		13 13		14 21	14 44		15 13				16 20	16 44
Newport (South Wales)	a		13 28		14 35	15 05		15 34				16 35	16 55
Reading 7	a	14 53									17 54		
London Paddington 15 ⊖	a	15 29									18 29		
Cardiff Central 7	a		13 53		14 53	15 26		15 53				16 53	17 15
Swansea	a		14 55		15 55			16 58	18 10			18 05	

		AW	AW	AW		AW	AW	AW	AW	AW	AW	GW	AW
		■		■			■			■			
						◇		◇			◇	◇1	◇
		🛒		🛒		🛒	🛒			🛒	🛒		🛒
Manchester Piccadilly 10	d	14 30		15 30			16 30			17 30			18 30
Stockport	d	14 39		15 39			16 39			17 39			18 39
Wilmslow	d	14 46		15 46			16 46			17 46			18 46
Holyhead	d					14 32					16 37		
Bangor (Gwynedd)	d					15 00					17 06		
Llandudno Junction	d					15 23					17 24		
Chester	d					16b19					18 20		
Crewe 10	d	15 08	15 20	16 08			17 08		17 20	18 08			19 08
Nantwich	d		15 27	16 17			17 17		17 28	18 17			19 17
Wrenbury	d		15x34						17x35				19x23
Whitchurch (Shrops)	d		15 42	16 28			17 27		17 43	18 28			19 29
Prees	d		15x48						17x49				19x35
Wem	d		15 54						17 55				19 40
Yorton	d		16x00						18x01				19x45
Shrewsbury	a	15 37	16 08	16 45		17 14	17 43		18 11	18 45	19 16		19 55
	d	15 40		16 45		17 16	17 45	18 05		18 48	19 17		19 56
Church Stretton	d	15 55		17 02			18 00	18 23		19 03			20 11
Craven Arms	d	16 03		17 10			18 08	18 36		19 11			20 19
Ludlow	d	16 10		17 17		17 42	18 15			19 19	19 41		20 27
Leominster	d	16 21		17 28			18 26			19 29			20 37
Hereford 7	a	16 36		17 43		18 05	18 41			19 49	20 10		20 53
	d	16 38		17 46		18 07	18 43			19 51	20 11	20 20	20 54
Abergavenny	d	17 01		18 09		18 30	19 06			20 14	20 34		21 17
Pontypool and New Inn	d					18 40				20 23			21 27
Cwmbran	d	17 13		18 21		18 45	19 18			20 28	20 47		21 32
Newport (South Wales)	a	17 33		18 36		18 55	19 37			20 39	21 00		21 42
Reading 7	a											23 30	
London Paddington 15 ⊖	a											00 13	
Cardiff Central 7	a	17 53		18 53		19 15	19 53			20 58	21 15		22 03
Swansea	a	19 02		20 04				22 10					23 04

		AW		AW	AW	AW
Manchester Piccadilly 10	d	19 30		20 30	21 35	22 35
Stockport	d	19 39		20 39	21 44	22 44
Wilmslow	d	19 46		20 46	21 51	22 52
Holyhead	d					
Bangor (Gwynedd)	d					
Llandudno Junction	d					
Chester	d					
Crewe 10	d	20 08		21 08	22 12	23 14
Nantwich	d	20 17		21 17	22 20	23 22
Wrenbury	d			21x23	22x26	23x27
Whitchurch (Shrops)	d	20 27		21 29	22 33	23 34
Prees	d			21x35	22x39	23x40
Wem	d	20 36		21 40	22 44	23 45
Yorton	d			21x45	22x49	23x50
Shrewsbury	a	20 47		21 55	23 01	00 04
	d	20 48		21 56		
Church Stretton	d	21 03		22 11		
Craven Arms	d	21 11		22 19		
Ludlow	d	21 19		22 27		
Leominster	d	21 29		22 37		
Hereford 7	a	21 45		22 53		
	d	21 46				
Abergavenny	d	22 09				
Pontypool and New Inn	d					
Cwmbran	d	22 22				
Newport (South Wales)	a	22 33				
Reading 7	a					
London Paddington 15 ⊖	a					
Cardiff Central 7	a	22 53				
Swansea	a					

b Arr. 1612

For connections from Liverpool Lime Street and Runcorn please refer to Table 91. For connections to Bristol Temple Meads please refer to Table 132

When events are being held at the Millenium Stadium, services are subject to alteration. Please check times before travelling.

Table 131

Saturdays

from 17 September

Manchester, Liverpool and Crewe - Cardiff

		GW	AW	AW	AW	AW	AW	AW	AW	XC		AW	GW	AW	AW	AW	AW	AW	AW	AW		AW	AW	AW	AW
		◇1	◇	◇	◇		◇		◇	◇1			◇1	◇	◇	◇		◇	◇	◇		◇		◇	◇
													A												
									🛒	🛒			⊡	🛒	🛒	🛒		🛒		🛒		🛒		🛒	🛒
Manchester Piccadilly 10 ⛴	d		20p30		22p35					05 11						06 30		07 30				08 30		09 30	
Stockport	d		20p39		22p44											06 39		07 39				08 39		09 39	
Wilmslow	d		20p46		22p52											06 46		07 46				08 46		09 46	
Holyhead	d														04 25					06 35					08 20
Bangor (Gwynedd)	d														04 57					07 07					09 02
Llandudno Junction	d														05 15					07 25					09 25
Chester	d					04 22									06e12					08 19					10 19
Crewe 10	d		21p08		23p14	04a44			04 54	05c47				05 55		07 08	07 20	08 08				09 08	09 20	10 08	
Nantwich	d		21p17		23p22				05 02					06 03		07 17	07 27	08 17					09 28		
Wrenbury	d		21b23		23b27									06x09			07x34						09x34		
Whitchurch (Shrops)	d		21p30		23p34				05 13					06 16		07 28	07 41	08 27					09 42	10 23	
Prees	d		21b36		23b40									06x22			07x47						09x48		
Wem	d		21p41		23p45				05 22					06 27		07 36	07 53						09 54		
Yorton	d		21b46		23b50									06x32			07x58						10x00		
Shrewsbury	a		21p55		00 04				05 33					06 42	07 17	07 47	08 08	08 45		09 13		09 37	10 12	10 40	11 13
	d		21p57	23p08			05 19		05 40			06 13		06 44	07 19	07 50		08 46	09 00	09 15		09 40		10 41	11 16
Church Stretton	d		22p12	23p24			05 36		05 55			06 28		06 59		08 05		09 01	09 17			09 55		10 57	
Craven Arms	d		22p20	23p32			05 47		06 03			06 36		07 07		08 13		09 09	09 30			10 03		11 05	
Ludlow	d		22p27	23p41					06 10			06 44		07 14	07 45	08 20		09 17		09 41		10 10		11 13	11 41
Leominster	d		22p38	23p52					06 21			06 55		07 25	07 55	08 31		09 27				10 21		11 23	
Hereford 7	a		22p56	00 07					06 36			07 09		07 40	08 11	08 49		09 43		10 05		10 36		11 43	12 05
	d	21p51	22p58	00 09				05 42	06 42			07 11	07 10	07 44	08 12	08 51		09 44		10 06		10 38		11 46	12 06
Abergavenny	d		23p21	00 33				06 07	07 05			07 34		08 07	08 35	09 14		10 07		10 29		11 01		12 09	12 29
Pontypool and New Inn	d		23p30					06 18	07 15			07 44		08 16	08 45					10 39					12 39
Cwmbran	d		23p35	00 46				06 23	07 20			07 49		08 21	08 50	09 26		10 20		10 44		11 13		12 21	12 44
Newport (South Wales)	a		23p46	00 57				06 34	07 37			08 00		08 31	09 01	09 37		10 35		10 55		11 27		12 34	12 55
Reading 7	a	00 38								08 39			09 54												
London Paddington 15 ⊖	a	01 11											10 29												
Cardiff Central 7	a		00 02	01 18				06 54	07 54			08 19		08 50	09 22	09 58		10 53		11 15		11 53		12 53	13 15
Swansea	a						09 08		08 51					09 57		10 55		11 56	13 01			12 55		13 55	

		GW	AW	AW	AW	AW		AW	AW	AW	GW	AW	AW	AW	AW	AW		AW	AW	AW	AW	AW	AW	GW	AW
						R		R				R		R		R			R			R			
		◇1	◇		◇				◇		◇1		◇					◇		◇			◇	◇1	◇
		⊡	🛒		🛒	🛒		🛒			⊡	🛒	🛒	🛒		🛒		🛒	🛒			🛒	🛒		🛒
Manchester Piccadilly 10 ⛴	d		10 30		11 30			12 30				13 30		14 30		15 30			16 30			17 30			18 30
Stockport	d		10 39		11 39			12 39				13 39		14 39		15 39			16 39			17 39			18 39
Wilmslow	d		10 46		11 46			12 46				13 46		14 46		15 46			16 46			17 46			18 46
Holyhead	d					10 33							12 38					14 32					16 37		
Bangor (Gwynedd)	d					11 05							13 07					15 00					17 06		
Llandudno Junction	d					11 25							13 25					15 23					17 24		
Chester	d					12 19							14 19					16f19					18 20		
Crewe 10	d		11 08	11 20	12 08			13 08		13 20		14 08		15 08	15 20	16 08			17 08		17 20	18 08			19 08
Nantwich	d			11 31	12 17					13 28		14 17			15 27	16 17			17 17		17 28	18 17			19 17
Wrenbury	d			11x42						13x35					15x34						17x35				19x23
Whitchurch (Shrops)	d			11 49	12 27					13 43		14 28			15 42	16 28			17 27		17 43	18 28			19 29
Prees	d			11x56						13x49					15x48						17x49				19x35
Wem	d			12 02						13 55					15 54						17 55				19 40
Yorton	d			12x08						14x01					16x00						18x01				19x45
Shrewsbury	a		11 37	12 18	12 43	13 13		13 37		14 11		14 45	15 13	15 37	16 08	16 45		17 14	17 43		18 11	18 45	19 16		19 55
	d		11 40		12 45	13 15		13 40	14 05			14 45	15 15	15 40		16 45		17 16	17 45	18 05		18 48	19 17		19 56
Church Stretton	d		11 55		13 01			13 55	14 23			15 02		15 55		17 02			18 00	18 23		19 03			20 11
Craven Arms	d		12 03		13 09			14 03	14 36			15 10		16 03		17 10			18 08	18 36		19 11			20 19
Ludlow	d		12 10		13 17	13 40		14 10				15 17	15 41	16 10		17 17		17 42	18 15			19 19	19 41		20 27
Leominster	d		12 21		13 27			14 21				15 28		16 21		17 28			18 26			19 29			20 37
Hereford 7	a		12 36		13 44	14 04		14 36				15 43	16 05	16 36		17 43		18 05	18 41			19 49	20 10		20 53
	d	12 13	12 38		13 45	14 06		14 38			15 13	15 45	16 06	16 38		17 46		18 07	18 43			19 51	20 11	20 20	20 54
Abergavenny	d		13 01		14 08	14 28		15 01				16 08	16 29	17 01		18 09		18 30	19 06			20 14	20 34		21 17
Pontypool and New Inn	d					14 39							16 39					18 40				20 23			21 27
Cwmbran	d		13 13		14 21	14 44		15 13				16 20	16 44	17 13		18 21		18 45	19 18			20 28	20 47		21 32
Newport (South Wales)	a		13 28		14 35	15 05		15 34				16 35	16 55	17 33		18 36		18 55	19 37			20 39	21 00		21 42
Reading 7	a	14 53									17 55													23 04	
London Paddington 15 ⊖	a	15 29									18 29													23 43	
Cardiff Central 7	a		13 53		14 53	15 26		15 53				16 53	17 15	17 53		18 53		19 15	19 53			20 58	21 15		22 03
Swansea	a		14 55		15 55			16 58	18 10			18 05		19 02		20 04				22 10					23 04

A ⊡ from Reading

b Previous night, stops on request

c Arr. 0541

e Arr. 0604

f Arr. 1612

For connections from Liverpool Lime Street and Runcorn please refer to Table 91. For connections to Bristol Temple Meads please refer to Table 132

When events are being held at the Millenium Stadium, services are subject to alteration. Please check times before travelling.

Table 131

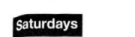

Saturdays
from 17 September

Manchester, Liverpool and Crewe - Cardiff

		AW	AW	AW	AW
Manchester Piccadilly 10 ⛴	d	19 30	20 30	21 35	22 35
Stockport	d	19 39	20 39	21 44	22 44
Wilmslow	d	19 46	20 46	21 51	22 52
Holyhead	d				
Bangor (Gwynedd)	d				
Llandudno Junction	d				
Chester	d				
Crewe 10	d	20 08	21 08	22 12	23 14
Nantwich	d	20 17	21 17	22 20	23 22
Wrenbury	d		21x23	22x26	23x27
Whitchurch (Shrops)	d	20 27	21 29	22 33	23 34
Prees	d		21x35	22x39	23x40
Wem	d	20 36	21 40	22 44	23 45
Yorton	d		21x45	22x49	23x50
Shrewsbury	a	20 47	21 55	23 01	00 04
	d	20 48	21 56		
Church Stretton	d	21 03	22 11		
Craven Arms	d	21 11	22 19		
Ludlow	d	21 19	22 27		
Leominster	d	21 29	22 37		
Hereford 7	a	21 45	22 53		
	d	21 46	22 54		
Abergavenny	d	22 09	23 17		
Pontypool and New Inn	d		23 27		
Cwmbran	d	22 22	23 32		
Newport (South Wales)	a	22 33	23 45		
Reading 7	a				
London Paddington 15 ⊖	a				
Cardiff Central 7	a	22 53	00 05		
Swansea	a				

Sundays
until 19 June

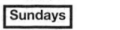

		GW	AW	AW	XC	AW	AW	AW	AW	GW	AW	AW	GW	AW	AW	GW	AW	AW	AW	GW	AW	AW	AW
		◇1 A	A	A	◇1 trolley		◇ trolley	R trolley	◇	◇1 buffet	R trolley	◇	◇1 buffet	R trolley	R trolley	◇1 buffet	R trolley	◇	R trolley	◇1 trolley	R trolley	R trolley	R trolley
Manchester Piccadilly 10 ⛴	d		20p30	22p35	08 27		09 30	10 30			11 24			12 30	13 30		14 30		15 30		16 30	17 30	
Stockport	d		20p39	22p44	08 36		09 39	10 40			11e40			12 40	13 40		14 39		15 39		16 39	17 39	
Wilmslow	d		20p46	22p52	08 43		09 47	10 48			11 47			12 48	13 47		14 47		15 47		16 47	17 47	
Holyhead	d											10 20											16 25
Bangor (Gwynedd)	d											10 59											17 04
Llandudno Junction	d											11 22											17 25
Chester	d											12 21											18 24
Crewe 10	d		21p08	23p14	09a01		10c13	11 11			12f13			13g13	14h13		15 10		16i13		17j13	18k13	
Nantwich	d		21p17	23p22			10 22							13 21							17 21		
Wrenbury	d		21b23	23b27			10x27							13x26							17x26		
Whitchurch (Shrops)	d		21p29	23p34			10 35							13 34							17 34		
Prees	d		21b35	23b40			10x40							13x39							17x39		
Wem	d		21p40	23p45			10 46							13 45							17 45		
Yorton	d		21b45	23b50			10x50							13x49							17x49		
Shrewsbury	a		21p55	00§04			11 01	11 41			12 43	13 18		13 59	14 43		15 44		16 43		18 00	18 43	19 20
	d		21p56				11 03	11 45	12 07		12 44	13 19		14 01	14 44		15 47	16 18	16 44		18 01	18 44	19 21
Church Stretton	d		22p11				11 19		12 25			13 35			15 00			16 36	17 00				19 37
Craven Arms	d		22p19				11 27		12 36			13 43			15 08			16 47	17 08				19 45
Ludlow	d		22p27				11 36	12 13			13 12	13 51		14 28	15 16		16 17		17 16		18 29	19 12	19 53
Leominster	d		22p37				11 47	12 23			13 22	14 02		14 39	15 26		16 28		17 26		18 39		20 04
Hereford 7	a		22p53				12 02	12 38			13 37	14 17		14 53	15 41		16 43		17 41		18 54	19 34	20 18
	d	20p20	22p54			10 09	12 03	12 39		13 28	13 39	14 19	14 30	14 56	15 43	16 33	16 44		17 43	18 30	18 57	19 36	20 21
Abergavenny	d		23p17			10 33	12 27	13 02			14 02	14 42		15 19	16 06		17 08		18 06		19 20	19 59	20 46
Pontypool and New Inn	d		23p27			10 43		13 12				14 52			16 16				18 16				20 56
Cwmbran	d		23p32			10 48	12 40	13 17			14 14	14 57		15 31	16 21		17 21		18 21		19 33	20 11	21 01
Newport (South Wales)	a		23p45			10 59	12 51	13 28			14 28	15 07		15 45	16 32		17 33		18 31		19 49	20 22	21 14
Reading 7	a	23p30								16 20			17 20			19 11				21 23			
London Paddington 15 ⊖	a	00§13								17 07			18 07			19 51				22 12			
Cardiff Central 7	a		00§05			11 16	13 13	13 44			14 49	15 31		16 02	16 53		17 50		18 50		20 10	20 43	21 36
Swansea	a							15 09	16 04					17 14			19 15	20 16					

A not 22 May
b Previous night, stops on request
c Arr. 1006
e Arr. 1134
f Arr. 1207
g Arr. 1307
h Arr. 1407
i Arr. 1606
j Arr. 1706
k Arr. 1807

For connections from Liverpool Lime Street and Runcorn please refer to Table 91. For connections to Bristol Temple Meads please refer to Table 132

When events are being held at the Millenium Stadium, services are subject to alteration. Please check times before travelling.

Table 131

Sundays until 19 June

Manchester, Liverpool and Crewe - Cardiff

		AW	AW	AW	AW	AW
			R			
		◇		◇	◇	
		T	T			
Manchester Piccadilly 10 ⇌	d		18 30	19 30	20 30	
Stockport	d		18 39	19 39	20 39	
Wilmslow	d		18 47	19 47	20 47	
Holyhead	d	18 25				
Bangor (Gwynedd)	d	19 04				
Llandudno Junction	d	19 24				
Chester	d	20b27				23 00
Crewe 10	d	20a48	19c13	20e13	21f13	23 23
Nantwich	d		19 21		21 21	23 31
Wrenbury	d		19x26		21x26	23x37
Whitchurch (Shrops)	d		19 34		21 35	23 45
Prees	d		19x39		21x40	23x51
Wem	d		19 45		21 47	23 57
Yorton	d		19x49		21x51	00x02
Shrewsbury	a		20 00	20 43	22 03	00 14
	d		20 01	20 44	22 04	
Church Stretton	d			21 00	22 20	
Craven Arms	d			21 08	22 29	
Ludlow	d		20 29	21 16	22 37	
Leominster	d		20 39	21 26	22 49	
Hereford 7	a		20 54	21 41	23 03	
	d		20 55	21 43	23 05	
Abergavenny	d		21 18	22 06	23 29	
Pontypool and New Inn	d			22 16	23 39	
Cwmbran	d		21 31	22 21	23 44	
Newport (South Wales)	a		21 41	22 30	23 54	
Reading 7	a					
London Paddington 15 ⊖	a					
Cardiff Central 7	a		22 06	22 57	00 20	
Swansea	a					

Sundays 26 June to 31 July

		GW	AW	AW	XC	AW	AW	AW	AW	GW
								R		
		◇1			◇1		◇		◇	◇1
					T		T	T		P
Manchester Piccadilly 10 ⇌	d		20p30	22p35	08 27		09 30	10 30		
Stockport	d		20p39	22p44	08 36		09 39	10 40		
Wilmslow	d		20p46	22p52	08 43		09 47	10 48		
Holyhead	d									
Bangor (Gwynedd)	d									
Llandudno Junction	d									
Chester	d									
Crewe 10	d		21p08	23p14	09 05		10h13	11 11		
Nantwich	d		21p17	23p22			10 22			
Wrenbury	d		21g23	23g27			10x27			
Whitchurch (Shrops)	d		21p29	23p34			10 35			
Prees	d		21g35	23g40			10x40			
Wem	d		21p40	23p45			10 46			
Yorton	d		21g45	23g50			10x50			
Shrewsbury	a		21p55	00 04			11 01	11 41		
	d		21p56				11 03	11 45	12 07	
Church Stretton	d		22p11				11 19		12 25	
Craven Arms	d		22p19				11 27		12 36	
Ludlow	d		22p27				11 36	12 13		
Leominster	d		22p37				11 47	12 23		
Hereford 7	a		22p53				12 02	12 38		
	d	20p20	22p54			10 09	12 03	12 39		13 28
Abergavenny	d		23p17			10 33	12 27	13 02		
Pontypool and New Inn	d		23p27			10 43		13 12		
Cwmbran	d		23p32			10 48	12 40	13 17		
Newport (South Wales)	a		23p45			10 59	12 51	13 28		
Reading 7	a	23p30			11 42					16 20
London Paddington 15 ⊖	a	00 13								17 07
Cardiff Central 7	a		00 05			11 16	13 13	13 44		
Swansea	a							14 53	16 04	

		AW	AW	GW	AW	AW	GW	AW	AW	AW	GW	AW	AW	AW
		R			R	R		R		R		R	R	R
			◇	◇1			◇1		◇		◇1			
		T		P	T	T	P	T		T	T	T	T	T
Manchester Piccadilly 10 ⇌	d	11 24			12 30	13 30		14 30		15 30		16 30	17 30	
Stockport	d	11i40			12 40	13 40		14 39		15 39		16 39	17 39	
Wilmslow	d	11 47			12 48	13 47		14 47		15 47		16 47	17 47	
Holyhead	d		10 20											16 25
Bangor (Gwynedd)	d		10 59											17 04
Llandudno Junction	d		11 22											17 25
Chester	d		12 18											18 24
Crewe 10	d	12j13	12 43		13k13	14l13		15 10		16m13		17n13	18o13	18 48
Nantwich	d				13 21							17 21		
Wrenbury	d				13x26							17x26		
Whitchurch (Shrops)	d				13 34							17 34		
Prees	d				13x39							17x39		
Wem	d				13 45							17 45		
Yorton	d				13x49							17x49		
Shrewsbury	a	12 43	13 17		13 59	14 43		15 44		16 43		18 00	18 43	19 19
	d	12 44	13 19		14 01	14 44		15 47	16 18	16 44		18 01	18 44	19 21
Church Stretton	d		13 35			15 00			16 36	17 00				19 37
Craven Arms	d		13 43			15 08			16 47	17 08				19 45
Ludlow	d	13 12	13 51		14 28	15 16		16 17		17 16		18 29	19 12	19 53
Leominster	d	13 22	14 02		14 39	15 26		16 28		17 26		18 39		20 04
Hereford 7	a	13 37	14 17		14 53	15 41		16 43		17 41		18 54	19 34	20 18
	d	13 39	14 19	14 30	14 56	15 43	16 33	16 44		17 43	18 30	18 57	19 36	20 21
Abergavenny	d	14 02	14 42		15 19	16 06		17 08		18 06		19 20	19 59	20 46
Pontypool and New Inn	d		14 52			16 16				18 16				20 56
Cwmbran	d	14 14	14 57		15 31	16 21		17 21		18 21		19 33	20 11	21 01
Newport (South Wales)	a	14 28	15 07		15 45	16 32		17 33		18 31		19 49	20 22	21 14
Reading 7	a			17 20			19 11				21 23			
London Paddington 15 ⊖	a			18 07			19 51				22 12			
Cardiff Central 7	a	14 49	15 31		16 00	16 53		17 50		18 50		20 10	20 43	21 36
Swansea	a				17 01			19 09	20 16					

b Arr. 2019
c Arr. 1906
e Arr. 2007
f Arr. 2107
g Previous night, stops on request
h Arr. 1006
i Arr. 1134
j Arr. 1207
k Arr. 1307
l Arr. 1407
m Arr. 1606
n Arr. 1706
o Arr. 1807

For connections from Liverpool Lime Street and Runcorn please refer to Table 91. For connections to Bristol Temple Meads please refer to Table 132

When events are being held at the Millenium Stadium, services are subject to alteration. Please check times before travelling.

Table 131

Sundays

26 June to 31 July

Manchester, Liverpool and Crewe - Cardiff

		AW	AW	AW	AW	AW
			R			
		◇		◇	◇	
		T	T			
Manchester Piccadilly 10	d		18 30	19 30	20 30	
Stockport	d		18 39	19 39	20 39	
Wilmslow	d		18 47	19 47	20 47	
Holyhead	d	18 25				
Bangor (Gwynedd)	d	19 04				
Llandudno Junction	d	19 24				
Chester	d	20b27				23 00
Crewe 10	d	20a48	19c13	20e13	21f13	23 23
Nantwich	d		19 21		21 21	23 31
Wrenbury	d		19x26		21x26	23x37
Whitchurch (Shrops)	d		19 34		21 35	23 45
Prees	d		19x39		21x40	23x51
Wem	d		19 45		21 47	23 57
Yorton	d		19x49		21x51	00x02
Shrewsbury	a		20 00	20 43	22 03	00 14
	d		20 01	20 44	22 04	
Church Stretton	d			21 00	22 20	
Craven Arms	d			21 08	22 29	
Ludlow	d		20 29	21 16	22 37	
Leominster	d		20 39	21 26	22 49	
Hereford 7	a		20 54	21 41	23 03	
	d		20 55	21 43	23 05	
Abergavenny	d		21 18	22 06	23 29	
Pontypool and New Inn	d			22 16	23 39	
Cwmbran	d		21 31	22 21	23 44	
Newport (South Wales)	a		21 41	22 30	23 54	
Reading 7	a					
London Paddington 15 ⊖	a					
Cardiff Central 7	a		22 06	22 57	00 20	
Swansea	a					

Sundays

7 August to 11 September

		GW	AW	XC	AW	AW	AW	AW	GW	AW	AW	GW	AW	AW	GW	AW	AW	AW	GW	AW	AW	AW	AW
							R			R			R	R		R		R		R	R	R	
		◇1		◇1		◇		◇	◇1		◇	◇1			◇1		◇		◇1				◇
				T		T	T		RB	T		RB	T	T	RB	T		T	T	T	T	T	T
Manchester Piccadilly 10	d		22p35	08 27		09 30	10 30			11 24			12 30	13 30		14 30		15 30		16 30	17 30		
Stockport	d		22p44	08 36		09 39	10 40			11i40			12 40	13 40		14 39		15 39		16 39	17 39		
Wilmslow	d		22p52	08 43		09 47	10 48			11 47			12 48	13 47		14 47		15 47		16 47	17 47		
Holyhead	d										10 20											16 25	18 25
Bangor (Gwynedd)	d										10 59											17 04	19 04
Llandudno Junction	d										11 22											17 25	19 24
Chester	d										12 21											18 24	20b27
Crewe 10	d		23p14	09a01		10h13	11 11			12j13			13k13	14l13		15 10		16m13		17n13	18o13		20a48
Nantwich	d		23p22			10 22							13 21							17 21			
Wrenbury	d		23g27			10x27							13x26							17x26			
Whitchurch (Shrops)	d		23p34			10 35							13 34							17 34			
Prees	d		23g40			10x40							13x39							17x39			
Wem	d		23p45			10 46							13 45							17 45			
Yorton	d		23g50			10x50							13x49							17x49			
Shrewsbury	a		00 04			11 01	11 41			12 43	13 18		13 59	14 43		15 44		16 43		18 00	18 43	19 20	
	d					11 03	11 45	12 07		12 44	13 19		14 01	14 44		15 47	16 18	16 44		18 01	18 44	19 21	
Church Stretton	d					11 19		12 25			13 35			15 00			16 36	17 00				19 37	
Craven Arms	d					11 27		12 36			13 43			15 08			16 47	17 08				19 45	
Ludlow	d					11 36	12 13			13 12	13 51		14 28	15 16		16 17		17 16		18 29	19 12	19 53	
Leominster	d					11 47	12 23			13 22	14 02		14 39	15 26		16 28		17 26		18 39		20 04	
Hereford 7	a					12 02	12 38			13 37	14 17		14 53	15 41		16 43		17 41		18 54	19 34	20 18	
	d	20p20			10 09	12 03	12 39		13 28	13 39	14 19	14 30	14 56	15 43	16 33	16 44		17 43	18 30	18 57	19 36	20 21	
Abergavenny	d				10 33	12 27	13 02			14 02	14 42		15 19	16 06		17 08		18 06		19 20	19 59	20 46	
Pontypool and New Inn	d				10 43		13 12				14 52			16 16				18 16				20 56	
Cwmbran	d				10 48	12 40	13 17			14 14	14 57		15 31	16 21		17 21		18 21		19 33	20 11	21 01	
Newport (South Wales)	a				10 59	12 51	13 28			14 28	15 07		15 50	16 32		17 33		18 31		19 49	20 22	21 14	
Reading 7	a	23p30							16 20			17 20			19 11				21 24				
London Paddington 15 ⊖	a	00 13							17 07			18 05			19 51				22 12				
Cardiff Central 7	a				11 16	13 13	13 44			14 49	15 31		16 07	16 53		17 50		18 50		20 10	20 43	21 36	
Swansea	a						15 10	16 04					17 14			19 16	20 16						

b Arr. 2019
c Arr. 1906
e Arr. 2007
f Arr. 2107
g Previous night, stops on request
h Arr. 1006
i Arr. 1134
j Arr. 1207
k Arr. 1307
l Arr. 1407
m Arr. 1606
n Arr. 1706
o Arr. 1807

For connections from Liverpool Lime Street and Runcorn please refer to Table 91. For connections to Bristol Temple Meads please refer to Table 132

When events are being held at the Millenium Stadium, services are subject to alteration. Please check times before travelling.

Table 131

Sundays

7 August to 11 September

Manchester, Liverpool and Crewe - Cardiff

		AW R	AW ◇	AW ◇	AW
Manchester Piccadilly 10	d	18 30	19 30	20 30	
Stockport	d	18 39	19 39	20 39	
Wilmslow	d	18 47	19 47	20 47	
Holyhead	d				
Bangor (Gwynedd)	d				
Llandudno Junction	d				
Chester	d				23 00
Crewe 10	d	19b13	20c13	21e13	23 23
Nantwich	d	19 21		21 21	23 31
Wrenbury	d	19x26		21x26	23x37
Whitchurch (Shrops)	d	19 34		21 35	23 45
Prees	d	19x39		21x40	23x51
Wem	d	19 45		21 47	23 57
Yorton	d	19x49		21x51	00x02
Shrewsbury	a	20 00	20 43	22 03	00 14
	d	20 01	20 44	22 04	
Church Stretton	d		21 00	22 20	
Craven Arms	d		21 08	22 29	
Ludlow	d	20 29	21 16	22 37	
Leominster	d	20 39	21 26	22 49	
Hereford 7	a	20 54	21 41	23 03	
	d	20 55	21 43	23 05	
Abergavenny	d	21 18	22 06	23 29	
Pontypool and New Inn	d		22 16	23 39	
Cwmbran	d	21 31	22 21	23 44	
Newport (South Wales)	a	21 41	22 30	23 54	
Reading 7	a				
London Paddington 15 ⊖	a				
Cardiff Central 7	a	22 06	22 57	00 20	
Swansea	a				

Sundays

18 September to 23 October

		AW	AW	XC ◇1	AW ◇	AW ◇	AW R	AW ◇	GW ◇1	AW R	AW ◇	GW ◇1	AW R	AW R	GW ◇1	AW R	AW ◇	AW R	GW ◇1	AW R	AW R	AW R	AW ◇
Manchester Piccadilly 10	d	20p30	22p35	08 27		09 30	10 30			11 24			12 30	13 30		14 30		15 30		16 30	17 30		
Stockport	d	20p39	22p44	08 36		09 39	10 39			11h40			12 40	13 40		14 39		15 39		16 39	17 39		
Wilmslow	d	20p46	22p52	08 43		09 47	10 48			11 47			12 48	13 47		14 47		15 47		16 47	17 47		
Holyhead	d										10 20											16 25	18 25
Bangor (Gwynedd)	d										10 59											17 04	19 04
Llandudno Junction	d										11 22											17 25	19 24
Chester	d										12 21											18 24	20o27
Crewe 10	d	21p08	23p14	09a01		10g13	11 11			12i13			13j13	14k13		15 10		16l13		17m13	18n13		20a48
Nantwich	d	21p17	23p22			10 22							13 21							17 21			
Wrenbury	d	21f23	23f27			10x27							13x26							17x26			
Whitchurch (Shrops)	d	21p29	23p34			10 35							13 34							17 34			
Prees	d	21f35	23f40			10x40							13x39							17x39			
Wem	d	21p40	23p45			10 46							13 45							17 45			
Yorton	d	21f45	23f50			10x50							13x49							17x49			
Shrewsbury	a	21p55	00 04			11 01	11 41			12 43	13 18		13 59	14 43		15 44		16 43		18 00	18 43	19 20	
	d	21p56				11 03	11 45	12 07		12 44	13 19		14 01	14 44		15 47	16 18	16 44		18 01	18 44	19 21	
Church Stretton	d	22p11				11 19		12 25			13 35			15 00			16 36	17 00				19 37	
Craven Arms	d	22p19				11 27		12 36			13 43			15 08			16 47	17 08				19 45	
Ludlow	d	22p27				11 36	12 13			13 12	13 51		14 28	15 16		16 17		17 16		18 29	19 12	19 53	
Leominster	d	22p37				11 47	12 23			13 22	14 02		14 39	15 26		16 28		17 26		18 39		20 04	
Hereford 7	a	22p53				12 02	12 38			13 37	14 17		14 53	15 41		16 43		17 41		18 54	19 34	20 18	
	d	22p54			10 09	12 03	12 39		13 28	13 39	14 19	14 30	14 56	15 43	16 33	16 44		17 43	18 30	18 57	19 36	20 21	
Abergavenny	d	23p17			10 33	12 27	13 02			14 02	14 42		15 19	16 06		17 08		18 06		19 20	19 59	20 46	
Pontypool and New Inn	d	23p27			10 43		13 12				14 52			16 16				18 16				20 56	
Cwmbran	d	23p32			10 48	12 40	13 17			14 14	14 57		15 31	16 21		17 21		18 21		19 33	20 11	21 01	
Newport (South Wales)	a	23p45			10 59	12 51	13 28			14 28	15 07		15 50	16 32		17 33		18 31		19 49	20 22	21 14	
Reading 7	a								16 19			17 21			19 11				21 25				
London Paddington 15 ⊖	a								17 07			18 05			19 51				22 11				
Cardiff Central 7	a	00 05			11 16	13 13	13 44			14 49	15 31		16 07	16 53		17 50		18 50		20 10	20 43	21 36	
Swansea	a				12 13		15 12	16 04					17 14			19 16	20 16						

b Arr. 1906
c Arr. 2007
e Arr. 2107
f Previous night, stops on request
g Arr. 1006
h Arr. 1134
i Arr. 1207
j Arr. 1307
k Arr. 1407
l Arr. 1606
m Arr. 1706
n Arr. 1807
o Arr. 2019

For connections from Liverpool Lime Street and Runcorn please refer to Table 91. For connections to Bristol Temple Meads please refer to Table 132

When events are being held at the Millenium Stadium, services are subject to alteration. Please check times before travelling.

Table 131

Sundays

18 September to 23 October

Manchester, Liverpool and Crewe - Cardiff

		AW	AW	AW	AW
		R			
			◇	◇	
		trolley			
Manchester Piccadilly 10	d	18 30	19 30	20 30	
Stockport	d	18 39	19 39	20 39	
Wilmslow	d	18 47	19 47	20 47	
Holyhead	d				
Bangor (Gwynedd)	d				
Llandudno Junction	d				
Chester	d				23 00
Crewe 10	d	19b13	20c13	21e13	23 23
Nantwich	d	19 21		21 21	23 31
Wrenbury	d	19x26		21x26	23x37
Whitchurch (Shrops)	d	19 34		21 35	23 45
Prees	d	19x39		21x40	23x51
Wem	d	19 45		21 47	23 57
Yorton	d	19x49		21x51	00x02
Shrewsbury	a	20 00	20 43	22 03	00 14
	d	20 01	20 44	22 04	
Church Stretton	d		21 00	22 20	
Craven Arms	d		21 08	22 29	
Ludlow	d	20 29	21 16	22 37	
Leominster	d	20 39	21 26	22 49	
Hereford 7	a	20 54	21 41	23 03	
	d	20 55	21 43	23 05	
Abergavenny	d	21 18	22 06	23 29	
Pontypool and New Inn	d		22 16	23 39	
Cwmbran	d	21 31	22 21	23 44	
Newport (South Wales)	a	21 41	22 30	23 54	
Reading 7	a				
London Paddington 15 ⊖	a				
Cardiff Central 7	a	22 06	22 57	00 20	
Swansea	a				

Sundays

from 30 October

		AW	AW	XC	AW	AW	AW	AW	GW	AW	AW	GW	AW	AW	GW	AW	AW	AW	GW	AW	AW	AW	AW
							R			R			R	R		R		R		R	R	R	
				◇1	◇	◇		◇	◇1		◇	◇1			◇1		◇		◇1				◇
				trolley		trolley	trolley		buffet	trolley		buffet	trolley	trolley	buffet	trolley		trolley	trolley	trolley	trolley	trolley	trolley
Manchester Piccadilly 10	d	20p30	22p35	08 27		09 30	10 30			11 24			12 30	13 30		14 30		15 30		16 30	17 30		
Stockport	d	20p39	22p44	08 36		09 39	10 39			11h40			12 40	13 40		14 39		15 39		16 39	17 39		
Wilmslow	d	20p46	22p52	08 43		09 47	10 48			11 47			12 48	13 47		14 47		15 47		16 47	17 47		
Holyhead	d										10 20											16 25	18 25
Bangor (Gwynedd)	d										10 59											17 04	19 04
Llandudno Junction	d										11 22											17 25	19 24
Chester	d										12 21											18 24	20o27
Crewe 10	d	21p08	23p14	09a01		10g13	11 11			12i13			13j13	14k13		15 10		16l13		17m13	18n13		20a48
Nantwich	d	21p17	23p22			10 22							13 21							17 21			
Wrenbury	d	21f23	23f27			10x27							13x26							17x26			
Whitchurch (Shrops)	d	21p29	23p34			10 35							13 34							17 34			
Prees	d	21f35	23f40			10x40							13x39							17x39			
Wem	d	21p40	23p45			10 46							13 45							17 45			
Yorton	d	21f45	23f50			10x50							13x49							17x49			
Shrewsbury	a	21p55	00 04			11 01	11 41			12 43	13 18		13 59	14 43		15 44		16 43		18 00	18 43	19 20	
	d	21p56				11 03	11 45	12 07		12 44	13 19		14 01	14 44		15 47	16 18	16 44		18 01	18 44	19 21	
Church Stretton	d	22p11				11 19		12 25			13 35			15 00			16 36	17 00				19 37	
Craven Arms	d	22p19				11 27		12 36			13 43			15 08			16 47	17 08				19 45	
Ludlow	d	22p27				11 36	12 13			13 12	13 51		14 28	15 16		16 17		17 16		18 29	19 12	19 53	
Leominster	d	22p37				11 47	12 23			13 22	14 02		14 39	15 26		16 28		17 26		18 39		20 04	
Hereford 7	a	22p53				12 02	12 38			13 37	14 17		14 53	15 41		16 43		17 41		18 54	19 34	20 18	
	d	22p54			10 09	12 03	12 39		13 32	13 39	14 19	14 32	14 56	15 43	16 35	16 44		17 43	18 30	18 57	19 36	20 21	
Abergavenny	d	23p17			10 33	12 27	13 02			14 02	14 42		15 19	16 06		17 08		18 06		19 20	19 59	20 46	
Pontypool and New Inn	d	23p27			10 43		13 12				14 52			16 16				18 16				20 56	
Cwmbran	d	23p32			10 48	12 40	13 17			14 14	14 57		15 31	16 21		17 21		18 21		19 33	20 11	21 01	
Newport (South Wales)	a	23p45			10 59	12 51	13 28			14 28	15 07		15 45	16 32		17 33		18 31		19 49	20 22	21 14	
Reading 7	a								16 25			17 21			19 25				21 29				
London Paddington 15 ⊖	a								17 06			18 04			20 06				22 13				
Cardiff Central 7	a	00 05			11 16	13 13	13 44			14 49	15 31		16 02	16 53		17 50		18 50		20 10	20 43	21 36	
Swansea	a				12 13		15 08	16 04					17 14			19 10	20 16						

b Arr. 1906
c Arr. 2007
e Arr. 2107
f Previous night, stops on request
g Arr. 1006
h Arr. 1134
i Arr. 1207
j Arr. 1307
k Arr. 1407
l Arr. 1606
m Arr. 1706
n Arr. 1807
o Arr. 2019

For connections from Liverpool Lime Street and Runcorn please refer to Table 91. For connections to Bristol Temple Meads please refer to Table 132

When events are being held at the Millenium Stadium, services are subject to alteration. Please check times before travelling.

Table 131

Sundays
from 30 October

Manchester, Liverpool and Crewe - Cardiff

		AW	AW	AW	AW
		R	◇	◇	
		⚲			
Manchester Piccadilly 10	d	18 30	19 30	20 30	
Stockport	d	18 39	19 39	20 39	
Wilmslow	d	18 47	19 47	20 47	
Holyhead	d				
Bangor (Gwynedd)	d				
Llandudno Junction	d				
Chester	d				23 00
Crewe 10	d	19b13	20c13	21e13	23 23
Nantwich	d	19 21		21 21	23 31
Wrenbury	d	19x26		21x26	23x37
Whitchurch (Shrops)	d	19 34		21 35	23 45
Prees	d	19x39		21x40	23x51
Wem	d	19 45		21 47	23 57
Yorton	d	19x49		21x51	00x02
Shrewsbury	a	20 00	20 43	22 03	00 14
	d	20 01	20 44	22 04	
Church Stretton	d		21 00	22 20	
Craven Arms	d		21 08	22 29	
Ludlow	d	20 29	21 16	22 37	
Leominster	d	20 39	21 26	22 49	
Hereford 7	a	20 54	21 41	23 03	
	d	20 55	21 43	23 05	
Abergavenny	d	21 18	22 06	23 29	
Pontypool and New Inn	d		22 16	23 39	
Cwmbran	d	21 31	22 21	23 44	
Newport (South Wales)	a	21 41	22 30	23 54	
Reading 7	a				
London Paddington 15 ⊖	a				
Cardiff Central 7	a	22 06	22 57	00 20	
Swansea	a				

b Arr. 1906 c Arr. 2007 e Arr. 2107

For connections from Liverpool Lime Street and Runcorn please refer to Table 91. For connections to Bristol Temple Meads please refer to Table 132

When events are being held at the Millenium Stadium, services are subject to alteration. Please check times before travelling.

Network Diagram for Tables 132, 133 ,134

DM-26/05
Design BAJS

© Network Rail
OPSU 2005.
All rights reserved

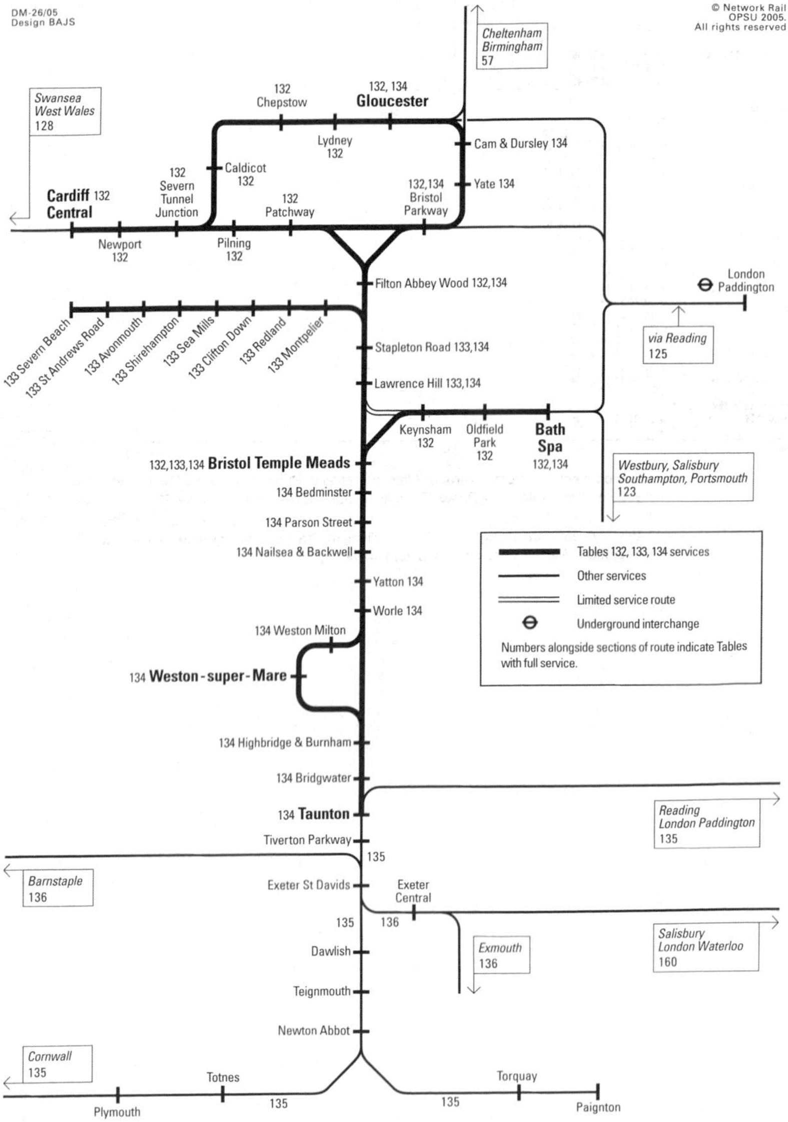

Table 132

Mondays to Fridays

until 1 July

Cardiff - Gloucester, Bristol and Bath Spa

Miles	Miles	Miles			AW	GW	AW	AW	AW	GW	GW	AW	GW	GW	GW	AW	GW	GW	GW	GW	GW	GW	XC
					MX	MX	MX																
								◇	◇	◇1	◇1	◇	◇	◇1	◇1		◇1	◇1	◇1		◇1	◇	◇1
									trolley	buffet	buffet	trolley		buffet	buffet		buffet	buffet	buffet		buffet	trolley	
0	0	0	**Cardiff Central 7**	d	23p19	23p27	00 30	04 35	05 10	05 14		05 40		05 55		06 12	06 24					06 28	06 40
11¾	11¾	11¾	Newport (South Wales)	a	23p39	23p44	00 48	04 50	05 25	05 30		05 55		06 09		06 26	06 37					06 41	06 53
—	—	—		d	23p40	23p45				05 32				06 09		06 28	06 38					06 42	06 55
21¾	21¾	21¾	Severn Tunnel Jn	d	23p58	00 03										06 38						06 53	07 05
—	—	22½	Caldicot	d	00 01											06 40							07 08
—	—	29¼	Chepstow	d	00 10											06 49							07 16
—	—	37	Lydney	d	00 19											06 58							07 25
—	—	56½	**Gloucester 7**	a	00 39											07 20							07 44
28¾	28¾	—	Pilning	d																			
32¼	32¼	—	Patchway	d		00 16																07 06	
—	33½	—	**Bristol Parkway 7**	a						05 59				06 29			06 58						
—	—	—		d																			
33¾	—	—	Filton Abbey Wood	d		00 20																07 09	
38¼	—	—	**Bristol Temple Meads 10**	a		00 33																07 18	
—	—	—		d							05 30		05 44		06 00			06 30	06 40	06 48	07 00	07 23	
42¾	—	—	Keynsham	d									05 51							06 55			
48¾	—	—	Oldfield Park	d									05 58							07 02			
49¾	—	—	**Bath Spa 7**	a							05 41		06 01		06 11			06 41	06 51	07 05	07 11	07 34	

		AW	GW	GW	GW	XC	AW	AW	GW	GW	GW	GW	XC	GW	GW	GW	GW	AW	GW	SW	GW	GW	GW
												R											
		◇	◇1		◇1	◇1		◇	◇1		◇1		◇1	◇1		◇1		◇	◇1	◇1	◇1		◇
			A		B								C										
		trolley	buffet		Ø			trolley	buffet		Ø	trolley	trolley	buffet		Ø		trolley	Ø		buffet		trolley
Cardiff Central 7	d	06 50			06 55	07 00	07 12	07 21			07 25	07 30	07 45			07 55	08 00	08 05	08 25				08 30
Newport (South Wales)	a	07 02			07 09	07 13	07 26	07 34			07 39	07 44	07 59			08 09	08 13	08 17	08 39				08 42
	d				07 09	07 15	07 27				07 39	07 44	08 02			08 09	08 15		08 39				08 44
Severn Tunnel Jn	d					07 25	07 38					07 55					08 25						08 55
Caldicot	d						07 40																
Chepstow	d						07 49																
Lydney	d						07 58						08 25										
Gloucester 7	a						08 20						08 44										
Pilning	d																						
Patchway	d					07 37											08 39						
Bristol Parkway 7	a				07 29						07 59					08 30			08 59				
	d			07 25						07 49					08 19								
Filton Abbey Wood	d			07 28		07 41				07 53		08 09			08 23		08 42						09 09
Bristol Temple Meads 10	a			07 40		07 51				08 01		08 18			08 36		08 51						09 18
	d		07 30	07 49					08 00	08 13		08 23		08 30	08 41					08 51	09 00	09 05	09 23
Keynsham	d			07 56						08 20					08 47					08 58			
Oldfield Park	d			08 03						08 27					08 54							09 17	
Bath Spa 7	a		07 41	08 05					08 11	08 29		08 35		08 41	08 56					09 05	09 11	09 19	09 34

		XC	AW	GW	GW	GW	GW	AW	AW	GW	GW	GW	XC	GW	GW	GW	GW	AW	AW	GW	GW	GW	XC
		◇1	◇	◇1		◇1	◇		◇	◇1	◇1	◇	◇1	◇1		◇1		◇		◇1	◇1	◇	◇1
		C								D			C										C
		trolley	trolley	buffet		buffet			trolley	buffet	buffet	trolley	trolley	buffet		buffet		trolley		buffet	buffet	trolley	trolley
Cardiff Central 7	d	08 45	08 50			08 55	09 00	09 12	09 21	09 25		09 30	09 45			09 55	10 00	10 05	10 12	10 25		10 30	10 45
Newport (South Wales)	a	08 59	09 02			09 09	09 13	09 25	09 34	09 39		09 42	09 58			10 08	10 13	10 17	10 25	10 39		10 42	10 58
	d	09 02				09 09	09 15	09 27		09 39		09 44	10 00			10 09	10 15		10 27	10 39		10 44	11 00
Severn Tunnel Jn	d						09 25	09 37				09 55					10 25		10 38				
Caldicot	d							09 39											10 40				
Chepstow	d							09 48					10 18						10 49				
Lydney	d							09 57											10 58				11 25
Gloucester 7	a	09 44						10 20					10 44						11 20				11 44
Pilning	d																						
Patchway	d						09 39										10 39						
Bristol Parkway 7	a					09 30				09 59						10 30				10 59			
	d				09 20										10 22								
Filton Abbey Wood	d				09 23		09 42					10 09			10 25		10 42					11 09	
Bristol Temple Meads 10	a				09 35		09 53					10 18			10 38		10 51					11 18	
	d			09 30	09 49						10 00	10 23		10 30	10 49						11 00	11 23	
Keynsham	d				09 56										10 56								
Oldfield Park	d				10 03										11 03								
Bath Spa 7	a			09 41	10 05						10 11	10 34		10 41	11 06						11 11	11 34	

A The Bristolian

B The Capitals United

C trolley from Newport (South Wales)

D The Red Dragon

When events are being held at the Millenium Stadium, services are subject to alteration. Please check times before travelling.

Table 132

Mondays to Fridays

until 1 July

Cardiff - Gloucester, Bristol and Bath Spa

		AW	GW	GW	GW	GW	AW	GW	GW	GW	XC	GW	GW	GW	GW	AW	AW	GW	GW	SW	GW	XC
													R									
		◇	◇1		◇1		◇	◇1	◇1	◇	◇1	◇1		◇1		◇		◇1	◇1	◇1	◇	◇1
											A		B					C				A
		🛒	☕		☕		🛒	☕	☕	🛒	🛒	☕	🛒	☕		🛒		Ø	☕	🛒	🛒	🛒
Cardiff Central 7	d	10 50			10 55	11 00	11 21	11 25		11 30	11 45			11 55	12 00	12 05	12 12	12 25			12 30	12 45
Newport (South Wales)	a	11 02			11 08	11 13	11 34	11 39		11 42	11 59			12 08	12 13	12 17	12 25	12 39			12 42	12 59
	d				11 09	11 15		11 39		11 44	12 02			12 09	12 15		12 28	12 39			12 44	13 01
Severn Tunnel Jn	d					11 25									12 25		12 39					
Caldicot	d																12 42					
Chepstow	d										12 18						12 51					13 18
Lydney	d																13 00					
Gloucester 7	a										12 44						13 20					13 44
Pilning	d																					
Patchway	d					11 39									12 39							
Bristol Parkway 7	a				11 30			11 59						12 30				12 59				
	d			11 20									12 22									
Filton Abbey Wood	d			11 23		11 42				12 09			12 25		12 42						13 09	
Bristol Temple Meads 10	a			11 35		11 51				12 18			12 35		12 51						13 18	
	d		11 30	11 49					12 00	12 23		12 30	12 39						13 00	13 15	13 23	
Keynsham	d			11 56									12 46									
Oldfield Park	d			12 03									12 53									
Bath Spa 7	a		11 41	12 05					12 13	12 34		12 41	12 56						13 11	13 26	13 34	

		AW	GW	GW	GW	GW	AW	AW	GW	GW	GW	XC	GW	GW	GW	GW	AW	GW	GW	GW	XC	AW	GW
		◇	◇1		◇1	◇		◇	◇1	◇1	◇	◇1	◇1		◇1		◇	◇1	◇1	◇	◇1	◇	◇1
												A									A		
		🛒	☕		☕			🛒	☕	☕	🛒	🛒	☕		☕		🛒	☕	☕	🛒	🛒	🛒	☕
Cardiff Central 7	d	12 50			12 55	13 00	13 12	13 21	13 25		13 30	13 45			13 55	14 00	14 05	14 25		14 30	14 45	14 50	
Newport (South Wales)	a	13 02			13 08	13 13	13 25	13 34	13 39		13 42	13 58			14 08	14 13	14 17	14 39		14 42	14 59	15 02	
	d				13 09	13 15	13 28		13 39		13 44	14 00			14 09	14 15		14 39		14 44	15 01		
Severn Tunnel Jn	d					13 25	13 39									14 25							
Caldicot	d						13 41																
Chepstow	d						13 50														15 18		
Lydney	d						13 59					14 25											
Gloucester 7	a						14 20					14 44									15 44		
Pilning	d																						
Patchway	d					13 39										14 39							
Bristol Parkway 7	a				13 30				13 59						14 30			15 00					
	d			13 20										14 22									
Filton Abbey Wood	d			13 23		13 42					14 09			14 25		14 42				15 09			
Bristol Temple Meads 10	a			13 36		13 51					14 18			14 38		14 51				15 18			
	d		13 30	13 49						14 00	14 23		14 30	14 48					15 00	15 23			15 30
Keynsham	d			13 56										14 55									
Oldfield Park	d			14 03										15 02									
Bath Spa 7	a		13 41	14 06						14 11	14 34		14 41	15 04					15 11	15 34			15 41

		GW	GW	GW	AW	AW	SW	GW	GW	GW	GW	XC	AW	GW	GW	GW	GW	AW	AW BHX	GW	GW	GW
						R							R					R	R			
			◇1				◇1	◇1		◇1	◇	◇1		◇1		◇1				◇1		◇1
								D														
			☕			🛒		☕		☕	🛒		🛒	☕		☕		🛒	⊠	☕		☕
Cardiff Central 7	d		14 55	15 00	15 12	15 21				15 25	15 30	15 45	15 50			15 55	16 00	16 05	16 15			16 25
Newport (South Wales)	a		15 08	15 13	15 26	15 34				15 39	15 43	15 58	16 02			16 08	16 13	16 18	16 28			16 39
	d		15 09	15 15	15 28					15 39	15 44	16 00				16 09	16 15	16 21				16 39
Severn Tunnel Jn	d			15 25	15 37												16 25	16 32				
Caldicot	d				15 40													16 34				
Chepstow	d				15 49							16 18						16 43				
Lydney	d				15 58													16 52				
Gloucester 7	a				16 21							16 44						17 14				
Pilning	d																					
Patchway	d			15 39													16 39					
Bristol Parkway 7	a		15 30							15 59						16 30						16 59
	d	15 20							15 53						16 22						16 45	
Filton Abbey Wood	d	15 23		15 42					15 56		16 09				16 25		16 42				16 48	
Bristol Temple Meads 10	a	15 37		15 51							16 19				16 38		16 51				17 02	
	d	15 44					15 51	16 00			16 23			16 30	16 49					17 00	17 06	
Keynsham	d	15 51					15 58		16 11						16 56						17 13	
Oldfield Park	d	15 58							16 18						17 03						17 21	
Bath Spa 7	a	16 00					16 05	16 11	16 21		16 34			16 41	17 06					17 11	17 24	

A 🛒 from Newport (South Wales)

B 🛒 from Bristol Temple Meads

C The St. David

D The Merchant Venturer

When events are being held at the Millenium Stadium, services are subject to alteration. Please check times before travelling.

Cardiff - Gloucester, Bristol and Bath Spa

		GW	GW	XC	AW	GW	GW	GW	GW		AW	AW	GW	GW	GW	GW	XC	AW	GW		GW	GW	GW	AW	AW
			R	◇1	R	◇1		◇1				R	◇1		◇1	R	◇1	R	◇1			◇1			R
																	A								
			🚲		🚲	☕		☕				🚲	☕		☕	🚲	🚲	🚲	☕			☕			🚲
Cardiff Central 7	d		16 30	16 45	16 50			16 55	17 00		17 12	17 21			17 25	17 30	17 45	17 50				17 55	18 00	18 12	18 18
Newport (South Wales)	a		16 42	16 58	17 02			17 08	17 13		17 25	17 34			17 39	17 42	17 58	18 02				18 08	18 13	18 25	18 30
	d		16 44	17 00				17 09	17 15		17 28				17 39	17 44	18 00					18 09	18 15	18 27	
Severn Tunnel Jn	d		16 55						17 25		17 39					17 55							18 25	18 38	
Caldicot	d										17 41													18 40	
Chepstow	d										17 50						18 18							18 49	
Lydney	d			17 24							17 59													18 58	
Gloucester 7	a			17 43							18 21						18 44							19 20	
Pilning	d																								
Patchway	d								17 39														18 39		
Bristol Parkway 7	a							17 30							17 59							18 30			
	d						17 20							17 46							18 20				
Filton Abbey Wood	d	16 55	17 09				17 23		17 42					17 49		18 09					18 23		18 42		
Bristol Temple Meads 10	a	17 05	17 18				17 37		17 53					18 02		18 18					18 37		18 53		
	d	17 14	17 23			17 30	17 49						18 00	18 07		18 23			18 30		18 49				
Keynsham	d						17 56							18 14							18 56				
Oldfield Park	d	17 26					18 03							18 21							19 03				
Bath Spa 7	a	17 30	17 35			17 41	18 06						18 11	18 24		18 34			18 41		19 06				

		GW	GW	XC	AW		GW	GW	GW	GW	GW	AW	XC	GW	GW		GW	AW	GW	GW	AW	GW	GW	XC	AW
		◇1	◇	◇1	◇		◇1			◇1	◇	◇	◇1	◇1				◇	◇1	◇	◇	◇1		◇1	
		☕	🚲		🚲		☕			☕				☕					☕			☕			
Cardiff Central 7	d	18 25	18 30	18 45	18 50				19 00	19 25	19 30	19 34	19 50				20 00	20 17	20 25	20 30	20 55		21 00	21 05	21 12
Newport (South Wales)	a	18 39	18 42	18 59	19 03				19 13	19 39	19 42	19 46	20 03				20 13	20 29	20 38	20 44	21 08		21 13	21 18	21 25
	d	18 39	18 44	19 01					19 15	19 39	19 44		20 05				20 15		20 39	20 44			21 15	21 21	21 27
Severn Tunnel Jn	d		18 55						19 25				20 15				20 25						21 25		21 38
Caldicot	d												20 18												21 40
Chepstow	d			19 19									20 26												21 49
Lydney	d												20 35												21 58
Gloucester 7	a			19 45									20 53											22 02	22 21
Pilning	d																								
Patchway	d								19 39								20 39						21 39		
Bristol Parkway 7	a	18 59								19 59									21 01						
	d							19 20							20 22										
Filton Abbey Wood	d		19 09					19 23	19 42		20 09				20 25		20 42			21 08			21 42		
Bristol Temple Meads 10	a		19 18					19 36	19 51		20 18				20 38		20 53			21 19			21 51		
	d		19 23				19 30	19 49			20 23			20 30	20 49					21 23		21 50	22 00		
Keynsham	d							19 56							20 56								22 07		
Oldfield Park	d							20 03							21 03								22 14		
Bath Spa 7	a		19 35				19 41	20 05			20 34			20 41	21 06					21 35		22 01	22 17		

			GW	GW	SW	XC	XC	AW	GW	GW	GW		GW	AW	AW	GW
														FX	FO	
			◇1		1		◇1	◇	◇1							
			☕						☕							
Cardiff Central 7	d		21 25	21 30		21 40	21 50	21 55		22 04			22 49	23 19	23 20	23 27
Newport (South Wales)	a		21 38	21 43		21 55	22 03	22 08		22 16			23 06	23 39	23 38	23 44
	d		21 39	21 44		21 56	22 05			22 18			23 06	23 40	23 40	23 45
Severn Tunnel Jn	d			21 55						22 35			23 25	23 58	23 58	00 03
Caldicot	d													00 01	00 01	
Chepstow	d													00 10	00 09	
Lydney	d													00 19	00 18	
Gloucester 7	a						22 46							00 39	00 39	
Pilning	d															
Patchway	d									22 48						00 16
Bristol Parkway 7	a		21 59													
	d															
Filton Abbey Wood	d			22 09						22 52			23 40			00 20
Bristol Temple Meads 10	a			22 22		22 29				23 05			23 49			00 33
	d				22 25				22 35		23 20					
Keynsham	d										23 27					
Oldfield Park	d										23 34					
Bath Spa 7	a				22 37				22 46		23 36					

A 🚲 from Newport (South Wales)

When events are being held at the Millenium Stadium, services are subject to alteration. Please check times before travelling.

Cardiff - Gloucester, Bristol and Bath Spa

		AW	AW	GW	AW	AW	AW	GW	GW	AW		GW	GW	GW	AW	GW	GW	GW	GW	GW		XC	AW	GW	GW
		MO	MX	MX	MX																				
						◇	◇	◇1	◇1	◇		◇	◇1	◇1		◇1	◇1		◇1	◇		◇1	◇	◇1	
		A																						B	
		🚌					🛒	☕	☕	🛒			☕	☕		☕	☕		☕	🛒			🛒	☕	
Cardiff Central 7	d		23p19	23p27	00 30	04 35	05 10	05 14		05 40			05 55		06 12	06 24				06 28		06 40	06 50		
Newport (South Wales)	a		23p39	23p44	00 48	04 50	05 25	05 30		05 55			06 09		06 26	06 37				06 41		06 53	07 02		
	d	22p57	23p40	23p45				05 32					06 09		06 28	06 38				06 42		06 55			
Severn Tunnel Jn	d	23p22	23p58	00 03											06 38					06 53		07 05			
Caldicot	d	23p32	00 01												06 40							07 08			
Chepstow	d	23p47	00 10												06 49							07 16			
Lydney	d	00 07	00 19												06 58							07 25			
Gloucester 7	a	00 47	00 39												07 20							07 44			
Pilning	d																								
Patchway	d			00 16																07 06					
Bristol Parkway 7	a							05 59					06 29			06 58									
	d																								07 25
Filton Abbey Wood	d			00 20																07 09					07 28
Bristol Temple Meads 10	a			00 33																07 18					07 40
	d								05 30			05 44		06 00			06 30	06 48	07 00	07 23				07 30	07 49
Keynsham	d											05 51						06 55							07 56
Oldfield Park	d											05 58						07 02							08 03
Bath Spa 7	a								05 41			06 01		06 11			06 41	07 05	07 11	07 34				07 41	08 05

		GW	XC	AW	AW	GW		GW	GW	GW	XC	GW	GW	GW	GW	AW		GW	SW	GW	GW	GW	XC	AW	GW
										R															
		◇1	◇1		◇	◇1			◇1		◇1	◇1		◇1		◇		◇1	◇1	◇1		◇	◇1	◇	◇1
		C									D												D		
		Ø			🛒	☕			Ø	🛒	🛒	☕		Ø		🛒		Ø		☕		🛒	🛒	🛒	☕
Cardiff Central 7	d	06 55	07 00	07 12	07 21				07 25	07 30	07 45			07 55	08 00	08 05		08 25				08 30	08 45	08 50	
Newport (South Wales)	a	07 09	07 13	07 26	07 34				07 39	07 44	07 59			08 09	08 13	08 17		08 39				08 42	08 59	09 02	
	d	07 09	07 15	07 27					07 39	07 44	08 02			08 09	08 15			08 39				08 44	09 02		
Severn Tunnel Jn	d		07 25	07 38						07 55					08 25							08 55			
Caldicot	d			07 40																					
Chepstow	d			07 49																					
Lydney	d			07 58							08 25														
Gloucester 7	a			08 20							08 44												09 44		
Pilning	d																								
Patchway	d		07 37												08 39										
Bristol Parkway 7	a	07 29							07 59					08 30				08 59							
	d							07 49					08 19												
Filton Abbey Wood	d		07 41					07 53		08 09			08 23		08 42							09 09			
Bristol Temple Meads 10	a		07 51					08 01		08 18			08 36		08 51							09 18			
	d					08 00		08 13		08 23		08 30	08 41						08 51	09 00	09 05	09 23			09 30
Keynsham	d							08 20					08 47						08 58						
Oldfield Park	d							08 27					08 54								09 17				
Bath Spa 7	a					08 11		08 29		08 35		08 41	08 56						09 05	09 11	09 19	09 34			09 41

		GW		GW	GW	AW	AW	GW	GW	GW	XC	GW		GW	GW	GW	AW	AW	GW	GW	GW	XC		AW	GW
				◇1	◇		◇	◇1	◇1	◇	◇1	◇1			◇1		◇		◇1	◇1	◇	◇1		◇	◇1
								E			D											D			
				☕			🛒	☕	☕	🛒	🛒	☕			☕		🛒		☕	☕	🛒	🛒		🛒	☕
Cardiff Central 7	d			08 55	09 00	09 12	09 21	09 25		09 30	09 45				09 55	10 00	10 05	10 12	10 25		10 30	10 45		10 50	
Newport (South Wales)	a			09 09	09 13	09 25	09 34	09 39		09 42	09 58				10 08	10 13	10 17	10 25	10 39		10 42	10 58		11 02	
	d			09 09	09 15	09 27		09 39		09 44	10 00				10 09	10 15		10 27	10 39		10 44	11 00			
Severn Tunnel Jn	d				09 25	09 37				09 55						10 25		10 38							
Caldicot	d					09 39												10 40							
Chepstow	d					09 48					10 18							10 49							
Lydney	d					09 57												10 58				11 25			
Gloucester 7	a					10 20					10 44							11 20				11 44			
Pilning	d																								
Patchway	d				09 39											10 39									
Bristol Parkway 7	a			09 30				09 59							10 30				10 59						
	d	09 20												10 22											
Filton Abbey Wood	d	09 23			09 42					10 09				10 25		10 42					11 09				
Bristol Temple Meads 10	a	09 35			09 53					10 18				10 38		10 51					11 18				
	d	09 49							10 00	10 23		10 30		10 49						11 00	11 23				11 30
Keynsham	d	09 56												10 56											
Oldfield Park	d	10 03												11 03											
Bath Spa 7	a	10 05							10 11	10 34		10 41		11 06						11 11	11 34				11 41

A From 8 August until 29 August

B The Bristolian

C The Capitals United

D 🛒 from Newport (South Wales)

E The Red Dragon

When events are being held at the Millenium Stadium, services are subject to alteration. Please check times before travelling.

Cardiff - Gloucester, Bristol and Bath Spa

		GW	GW	GW	AW	GW	GW	GW		XC	GW	GW	GW	GW	AW	AW	GW	GW		SW	GW	XC	AW	GW	GW
			◇1 ☕		◇ 🛒	◇1 ☕	◇1 ☕	◇ 🛒		◇1 A 🛒	◇1 ☕	Ⓡ B 🛒	◇1 ☕		◇ 🛒		◇1 C ⌀	◇1 ☕		◇1 🛒	◇ 🛒	◇1 A 🛒	◇ 🛒	◇1 ☕	
Cardiff Central 7	d		10 55	11 00	11 21	11 25		11 30		11 45			11 55	12 00	12 05	12 12	12 25				12 30	12 45	12 50		
Newport (South Wales)	a		11 08	11 13	11 34	11 39		11 42		11 59			12 08	12 13	12 17	12 25	12 39				12 42	12 59	13 02		
	d		11 09	11 15		11 39		11 44		12 02			12 09	12 15		12 28	12 39				12 44	13 01			
Severn Tunnel Jn	d			11 25										12 25		12 39									
Caldicot	d															12 42									
Chepstow	d									12 18						12 51						13 18			
Lydney	d															13 00									
Gloucester 7	a									12 44						13 20						13 44			
Pilning	d																								
Patchway	d			11 39										12 39											
Bristol Parkway 7	a		11 30			11 59							12 30				12 59								
	d	11 20										12 22													13 20
Filton Abbey Wood	d	11 23		11 42				12 09				12 25		12 42							13 09				13 23
Bristol Temple Meads 10	a	11 35		11 51				12 18				12 35		12 51							13 18				13 36
	d	11 49					12 00	12 23			12 30	12 39						13 00		13 15	13 23			13 30	13 49
Keynsham	d	11 56										12 46													13 56
Oldfield Park	d	12 03										12 53													14 03
Bath Spa 7	a	12 05					12 13	12 34			12 41	12 56						13 11		13 26	13 34			13 41	14 06

		GW	GW	AW		AW	GW	GW	GW	XC	GW	GW	GW	GW		AW	GW	GW	GW	XC	AW	GW	GW	GW	
		◇1 ☕	◇			◇ 🛒	◇1 ☕	◇1 ☕	◇ 🛒	◇1 A 🛒	◇1 ☕		◇1 ☕			◇ 🛒	◇1 ☕	◇1 ☕	◇ 🛒	◇1 A 🛒	◇ 🛒	◇1 ☕		◇1 ☕	
Cardiff Central 7	d	12 55	13 00	13 12		13 21	13 25		13 30	13 45			13 55	14 00		14 05	14 25		14 30	14 45	14 50			14 55	
Newport (South Wales)	a	13 08	13 13	13 25		13 34	13 39		13 42	13 58			14 08	14 13		14 17	14 39		14 42	14 59	15 02			15 08	
	d	13 09	13 15	13 28			13 39		13 44	14 00			14 09	14 15			14 39		14 44	15 01				15 09	
Severn Tunnel Jn	d		13 25	13 39										14 25											
Caldicot	d			13 41																					
Chepstow	d			13 50																15 18					
Lydney	d			13 59						14 25															
Gloucester 7	a			14 20						14 44										15 44					
Pilning	d																								
Patchway	d		13 39											14 39											
Bristol Parkway 7	a	13 30					13 59						14 30				15 00							15 30	
	d											14 22											15 20		
Filton Abbey Wood	d		13 42						14 09			14 25		14 42					15 09				15 23		
Bristol Temple Meads 10	a		13 51						14 18			14 38		14 51					15 18				15 37		
	d							14 00	14 23		14 30	14 48						15 00	15 23			15 30	15 44		
Keynsham	d											14 55											15 51		
Oldfield Park	d											15 02											15 58		
Bath Spa 7	a							14 11	14 34		14 41	15 04						15 11	15 34			15 41	16 00		

		GW	AW	AW	SW	GW	GW	GW	GW	XC		AW	GW	GW	GW	GW	AW	AW BHX	GW	GW		GW	GW	GW	XC
				Ⓡ 🛒	◇1	◇1 D ☕		◇1 ☕	◇ 🛒	◇1		Ⓡ 🛒	◇1 ☕		◇1 ☕		Ⓡ 🛒	Ⓡ ⊠	◇1 ☕			◇1 ☕		Ⓡ 🛒	◇1
Cardiff Central 7	d	15 00	15 12	15 21				15 25	15 30	15 45		15 50			15 55	16 00	16 05	16 15				16 25		16 30	16 45
Newport (South Wales)	a	15 13	15 26	15 34				15 39	15 43	15 58		16 02			16 08	16 13	16 18	16 28				16 39		16 42	16 58
	d	15 15	15 28					15 39	15 44	16 00					16 09	16 15	16 21					16 39		16 44	17 00
Severn Tunnel Jn	d	15 25	15 37													16 25	16 32							16 55	
Caldicot	d		15 40														16 34								
Chepstow	d		15 49							16 18							16 43								
Lydney	d		15 58														16 52								17 24
Gloucester 7	a		16 21							16 44							17 14								17 43
Pilning	d																								
Patchway	d	15 39														16 39									
Bristol Parkway 7	a							15 59							16 30							16 59			
	d						15 53							16 22						16 45					
Filton Abbey Wood	d	15 42					15 56		16 09					16 25		16 42				16 48			16 55	17 09	
Bristol Temple Meads 10	a	15 51							16 19					16 38		16 51				17 02			17 05	17 18	
	d				15 51	16 00			16 23				16 30	16 49					17 00	17 06			17 14	17 23	
Keynsham	d				15 58		16 11							16 56						17 13					
Oldfield Park	d						16 18							17 03						17 21			17 26		
Bath Spa 7	a				16 05	16 11	16 21		16 34				16 41	17 06					17 11	17 24			17 30	17 35	

A 🛒 from Newport (South Wales)

B 🛒 from Bristol Temple Meads

C The St. David

D The Merchant Venturer

When events are being held at the Millenium Stadium, services are subject to alteration. Please check times before travelling.

Cardiff - Gloucester, Bristol and Bath Spa

		AW	GW	GW	GW	GW		AW	AW	GW	GW	GW	GW	XC	AW	GW		GW	GW	GW	AW	AW	GW	GW	XC
		■							■				■		■							■			
			◇1		◇1					◇1		◇1		◇1		◇1			◇1				◇1	◇	◇1
														A											
		🛒	☕		☕				🛒	☕		☕	🛒	🛒	🛒	☕			☕			🛒	☕	🛒	
Cardiff Central 7	d	16 50			16 55	17 00		17 12	17 21			17 25	17 30	17 45	17 50				17 55	18 00	18 12	18 18	18 25	18 30	18 45
Newport (South Wales)	a	17 02			17 08	17 13		17 25	17 34			17 39	17 42	17 58	18 02				18 08	18 13	18 25	18 30	18 39	18 42	18 59
	d				17 09	17 15		17 28				17 39	17 44	18 00					18 09	18 15	18 27		18 39	18 44	19 01
Severn Tunnel Jn	d					17 25		17 39					17 55							18 25	18 38			18 55	
Caldicot	d							17 41													18 40				
Chepstow	d							17 50						18 18							18 49				19 19
Lydney	d							17 59													18 58				
Gloucester 7	a							18 21						18 44							19 20				19 45
Pilning	d																								
Patchway	d					17 40														18 39					
Bristol Parkway 7	a				17 30							17 59							18 30				18 59		
	d			17 20							17 46							18 20							
Filton Abbey Wood	d			17 23		17 42					17 49		18 09					18 23		18 42				19 09	
Bristol Temple Meads 10	a			17 37		17 53					18 02		18 18					18 37		18 53				19 18	
	d		17 30	17 49						18 00	18 07		18 23			18 30		18 49						19 23	
Keynsham	d			17 56							18 14							18 56							
Oldfield Park	d			18 03							18 21							19 03							
Bath Spa 7	a		17 41	18 06						18 11	18 24		18 34			18 41		19 06						19 35	

		AW		GW	GW	GW	GW	GW	AW	XC	GW	GW		GW	AW	GW	GW	AW	GW	GW	XC	AW		GW	GW
		◇		◇1			◇1	◇	◇	◇1	◇1				◇	◇1	◇	◇	◇1		◇1			◇1	
		🛒		☕			☕				☕					☕			☕					☕	
Cardiff Central 7	d	18 50				19 00	19 25	19 30	19 34	19 50				20 00	20 17	20 25	20 30	20 55		21 00	21 05	21 12		21 25	21 30
Newport (South Wales)	a	19 03				19 13	19 39	19 42	19 46	20 03				20 13	20 29	20 38	20 44	21 08		21 13	21 18	21 25		21 38	21 43
	d					19 15	19 39	19 44		20 05				20 15		20 39	20 44			21 15	21 21	21 27		21 39	21 44
Severn Tunnel Jn	d					19 25				20 15				20 25						21 25		21 38			21 55
Caldicot	d									20 18												21 40			
Chepstow	d									20 26												21 49			
Lydney	d									20 35												21 58			
Gloucester 7	a									20 53											22 02	22 21			
Pilning	d																								
Patchway	d					19 39								20 39						21 39					
Bristol Parkway 7	a						19 59									21 01								21 59	
	d				19 20							20 22													
Filton Abbey Wood	d				19 23	19 42		20 09				20 25		20 42			21 08			21 42					22 09
Bristol Temple Meads 10	a				19 36	19 51		20 18				20 38		20 53			21 19			21 51					22 22
	d			19 30	19 49			20 23			20 30	20 49					21 23		21 50	22 00					
Keynsham	d				19 56							20 56								22 07					
Oldfield Park	d				20 03							21 03								22 14					
Bath Spa 7	a			19 41	20 05			20 34			20 41	21 06					21 35		22 01	22 17					

		SW	XC	XC	AW	GW	GW	GW		GW	AW	AW	GW
											FX	FO	
		1		◇1	◇	◇1							
						☕							
Cardiff Central 7	d		21 40	21 50	21 55		22 04			22 49	23 19	23 20	23 27
Newport (South Wales)	a		21 55	22 03	22 08		22 16			23 06	23 39	23 38	23 44
	d		21 56	22 05			22 18			23 06	23 40	23 40	23 45
Severn Tunnel Jn	d						22 35			23 25	23 58	23 58	00 03
Caldicot	d										00 01	00 01	
Chepstow	d										00 10	00 09	
Lydney	d										00 19	00 18	
Gloucester 7	a			22 46							00 39	00 39	
Pilning	d												
Patchway	d						22 48						00 16
Bristol Parkway 7	a												
	d												
Filton Abbey Wood	d						22 52			23 40			00 20
Bristol Temple Meads 10	a		22 29				23 05			23 49			00 33
	d	22 25				22 35		23 20					
Keynsham	d							23 27					
Oldfield Park	d							23 34					
Bath Spa 7	a	22 37				22 46		23 36					

A 🛒 from Newport (South Wales)

When events are being held at the Millenium Stadium, services are subject to alteration. Please check times before travelling.

Table 132

Mondays to Fridays

from 5 September

Cardiff - Gloucester, Bristol and Bath Spa

Station		AW	AW	GW	AW	AW	AW	GW	GW	AW		GW	GW	GW	AW	GW	GW	GW	GW	GW		GW	XC	AW	GW
		A 🚌	MX	MX	MX	◇	◇ 🛒	◇1 ☕	◇1 ☕	◇ 🛒		◇	◇1 ☕	◇1 ☕		◇1 ☕	◇1 ☕	◇1 ☕		◇1 ☕		◇ 🛒	◇1	◇ 🛒	◇1 B ☕
Cardiff Central 7	d		23p19	23p27	00 30	04 35	05 10	05 14		05 40			05 55		06 12	06 24						06 28	06 40	06 50	
Newport (South Wales)	a		23p39	23p44	00 48	04 50	05 25	05 30		05 55			06 09		06 26	06 37						06 41	06 53	07 02	
	d	22p57	23p40	23p45				05 32					06 09		06 28	06 38						06 42	06 55		
Severn Tunnel Jn	d	23p22	23p58	00 03											06 38							06 53	07 05		
Caldicot	d	23p32	00 01												06 40								07 08		
Chepstow	d	23p47	00 10												06 49								07 16		
Lydney	d	00 07	00 19												06 58								07 25		
Gloucester 7	a	00 47	00 39												07 20								07 44		
Pilning	d																								
Patchway	d			00 16																		07 06			
Bristol Parkway 7	a							05 59					06 29			06 58									
	d																								
Filton Abbey Wood	d			00 20																		07 09			
Bristol Temple Meads 10	a			00 33																		07 18			
	d								05 30			05 44		06 00			06 30	06 40	06 48	07 00		07 23			07 30
Keynsham	d											05 51							06 55						
Oldfield Park	d											05 58							07 02						
Bath Spa 7	a								05 41			06 01		06 11			06 41	06 51	07 05	07 11		07 34			07 41

Station		GW	GW	XC	AW	AW		GW	GW	GW	GW	XC	GW	GW	GW	GW		AW	GW	SW	GW	GW	GW	XC	AW
			◇1 C Ø	◇1		◇ 🛒		◇1 ☕		◇1 Ø	■ 🛒	◇1 D 🛒	◇1 ☕		◇1 Ø			◇ 🛒	◇1 Ø	◇1	◇1 ☕		◇ 🛒	◇1 D 🛒	◇ 🛒
Cardiff Central 7	d		06 55	07 00	07 12	07 21				07 25	07 30	07 45			07 55	08 00		08 05	08 25				08 30	08 45	08 50
Newport (South Wales)	a		07 09	07 13	07 26	07 34				07 39	07 44	07 59			08 09	08 13		08 17	08 39				08 42	08 59	09 02
	d		07 09	07 15	07 27					07 39	07 44	08 02			08 09	08 15			08 39				08 44	09 02	
Severn Tunnel Jn	d			07 25	07 38						07 55					08 25							08 55		
Caldicot	d				07 40																				
Chepstow	d				07 49																				
Lydney	d				07 58							08 25													
Gloucester 7	a				08 20							08 44												09 44	
Pilning	d																								
Patchway	d			07 37												08 39									
Bristol Parkway 7	a		07 29							07 59					08 30				08 59						
	d	07 25							07 49					08 19											
Filton Abbey Wood	d	07 28		07 41					07 53		08 09			08 23		08 42							09 09		
Bristol Temple Meads 10	a	07 40		07 51					08 01		08 18			08 36		08 51							09 18		
	d	07 49						08 00	08 13		08 23		08 30	08 41						08 51	09 00	09 05	09 23		
Keynsham	d	07 56							08 20					08 47						08 58					
Oldfield Park	d	08 03							08 27					08 54								09 17			
Bath Spa 7	a	08 05						08 11	08 29		08 35		08 41	08 56						09 05	09 11	09 19	09 34		

Station		GW		GW	GW	GW	AW	AW	GW	GW	GW	XC		GW	GW	GW	GW	AW	AW	GW	GW	GW		XC	AW
		◇1 ☕			◇1 ☕	◇		◇ 🛒	◇1 E ☕	◇1 ☕	◇ 🛒	◇1 D 🛒		◇1 ☕		◇1 ☕		◇ 🛒		◇1 ☕	◇1 ☕	◇ 🛒		◇1 D 🛒	◇ 🛒
Cardiff Central 7	d				08 55	09 00	09 12	09 21	09 25		09 30	09 45				09 55	10 00	10 05	10 12	10 25		10 30		10 45	10 50
Newport (South Wales)	a				09 09	09 13	09 25	09 34	09 39		09 42	09 58				10 08	10 13	10 17	10 25	10 39		10 42		10 58	11 02
	d				09 09	09 15	09 27		09 39		09 44	10 00				10 09	10 15		10 27	10 39		10 44		11 00	
Severn Tunnel Jn	d					09 25	09 37				09 55						10 25		10 38						
Caldicot	d						09 39												10 40						
Chepstow	d						09 48					10 18							10 49						
Lydney	d						09 57												10 58					11 25	
Gloucester 7	a						10 20					10 44							11 20					11 44	
Pilning	d																								
Patchway	d					09 39											10 39								
Bristol Parkway 7	a				09 30				09 59							10 30				10 59					
	d			09 20											10 22										
Filton Abbey Wood	d			09 23		09 42					10 09				10 25		10 42					11 09			
Bristol Temple Meads 10	a			09 35		09 53					10 18				10 38		10 51					11 18			
	d	09 30		09 49						10 00	10 23			10 30	10 49						11 00	11 23			
Keynsham	d			09 56											10 56										
Oldfield Park	d			10 03											11 03										
Bath Spa 7	a	09 41		10 05						10 11	10 34			10 41	11 06						11 11	11 34			

A 5 September, 12 September
B The Bristolian
C The Capitals United
D 🛒 from Newport (South Wales)
E The Red Dragon

When events are being held at the Millenium Stadium, services are subject to alteration. Please check times before travelling.

Table 132 — Mondays to Fridays from 5 September

Cardiff - Gloucester, Bristol and Bath Spa

		GW	GW	GW	GW	AW	GW	GW		GW	XC	GW	GW	GW	GW	AW	AW	GW		GW	SW	GW	XC	AW	GW
													R												
		◇1		◇1		◇	◇1	◇1		◇	◇1	◇1		◇1		◇		◇1		◇1	◇1	◇	◇1	◇	◇1
											A		B					C					A		
		[restaurant]		[restaurant]		[trolley]	[restaurant]	[restaurant]		[trolley]	[trolley]	[restaurant]	[trolley]	[restaurant]		[trolley]		Ø		[restaurant]	[trolley]	[trolley]	[trolley]	[trolley]	[restaurant]
Cardiff Central 7	d			10 55	11 00	11 21	11 25			11 30	11 45			11 55	12 00	12 05	12 12	12 25				12 30	12 45	12 50	
Newport (South Wales)	a			11 08	11 13	11 34	11 39			11 42	11 59			12 08	12 13	12 17	12 25	12 39				12 42	12 59	13 02	
	d			11 09	11 15		11 39			11 44	12 02			12 09	12 15		12 28	12 39				12 44	13 01		
Severn Tunnel Jn	d				11 25										12 25		12 39								
Caldicot	d																12 42								
Chepstow	d										12 18						12 51						13 18		
Lydney	d																13 00								
Gloucester 7	a										12 44						13 20						13 44		
Pilning	d																								
Patchway	d				11 39										12 39										
Bristol Parkway 7	a			11 30			11 59							12 30				12 59							
	d		11 20										12 22												
Filton Abbey Wood	d		11 23		11 42					12 09			12 25		12 42							13 09			
Bristol Temple Meads 10	a		11 35		11 51					12 18			12 35		12 51							13 18			
	d	11 30	11 49					12 00		12 23		12 30	12 39							13 00	13 15	13 23			13 30
Keynsham	d		11 56										12 46												
Oldfield Park	d		12 03										12 53												
Bath Spa 7	a	11 41	12 05					12 13		12 34		12 41	12 56							13 11	13 26	13 34			13 41

		GW	GW	GW		AW	AW	GW	GW	GW	XC	GW	GW	GW		GW	AW	GW	GW	GW	XC	AW	GW	GW	
			◇1	◇			◇	◇1	◇1	◇	◇1	◇1		◇1			◇	◇1	◇1	◇	◇1	◇	◇1		
											A										A				
			[restaurant]				[trolley]	[restaurant]	[restaurant]	[trolley]	[trolley]	[restaurant]		[restaurant]			[trolley]	[restaurant]	[restaurant]	[trolley]	[trolley]	[trolley]	[restaurant]		
Cardiff Central 7	d		12 55	13 00		13 12	13 21	13 25		13 30	13 45			13 55		14 00	14 05	14 25		14 30	14 45	14 50			
Newport (South Wales)	a		13 08	13 13		13 25	13 34	13 39		13 42	13 58			14 08		14 13	14 17	14 39		14 42	14 59	15 02			
	d		13 09	13 15		13 28		13 39		13 44	14 00			14 09		14 15		14 39		14 44	15 01				
Severn Tunnel Jn	d			13 25		13 39										14 25									
Caldicot	d					13 41																			
Chepstow	d					13 50															15 18				
Lydney	d					13 59					14 25														
Gloucester 7	a					14 20					14 44										15 44				
Pilning	d																								
Patchway	d			13 39												14 39									
Bristol Parkway 7	a		13 30					13 59						14 30				15 00							
	d	13 20											14 22											15 20	
Filton Abbey Wood	d	13 23		13 42						14 09			14 25			14 42				15 09				15 23	
Bristol Temple Meads 10	a	13 36		13 51						14 18			14 38			14 51				15 18				15 37	
	d	13 49							14 00	14 23		14 30	14 48						15 00	15 23			15 30	15 44	
Keynsham	d	13 56											14 55											15 51	
Oldfield Park	d	14 03											15 02											15 58	
Bath Spa 7	a	14 06							14 11	14 34		14 41	15 04						15 11	15 34			15 41	16 00	

		GW	GW	AW	AW	SW	GW	GW	GW	GW		XC	AW	GW	GW	GW	GW	AW	AW	GW		GW	GW	GW	GW
					R								R					R	BHX R						R
		◇1				◇1	◇1		◇1	◇		◇1		◇1		◇1				◇1			◇1		
							D																		
		[restaurant]			[trolley]		[restaurant]		[restaurant]	[trolley]			[trolley]	[restaurant]		[restaurant]		[trolley]	⊠	[restaurant]			[restaurant]		[trolley]
Cardiff Central 7	d	14 55	15 00	15 12	15 21				15 25	15 30		15 45	15 50			15 55	16 00	16 05	16 15				16 25		16 30
Newport (South Wales)	a	15 08	15 13	15 26	15 34				15 39	15 43		15 58	16 02			16 08	16 13	16 18	16 28				16 39		16 42
	d	15 09	15 15	15 28					15 39	15 44		16 00				16 09	16 15	16 21					16 39		16 44
Severn Tunnel Jn	d		15 25	15 37													16 25	16 32							16 55
Caldicot	d			15 40														16 34							
Chepstow	d			15 49								16 18						16 43							
Lydney	d			15 58														16 52							
Gloucester 7	a			16 21								16 44						17 14							
Pilning	d																								
Patchway	d		15 39														16 39								
Bristol Parkway 7	a	15 30							15 59							16 30							16 59		
	d							15 53							16 22							16 45			
Filton Abbey Wood	d		15 42					15 56		16 09					16 25		16 42					16 48		16 55	17 09
Bristol Temple Meads 10	a		15 51							16 19					16 38		16 51					17 02		17 05	17 18
	d					15 51	16 00			16 23				16 30	16 49					17 00		17 06		17 14	17 23
Keynsham	d					15 58		16 11							16 56							17 13			
Oldfield Park	d							16 18							17 03							17 21		17 26	
Bath Spa 7	a					16 05	16 11	16 21		16 34				16 41	17 06					17 11		17 24		17 30	17 35

A [trolley] from Newport (South Wales)
B [trolley] from Bristol Temple Meads
C The St. David
D The Merchant Venturer

When events are being held at the Millenium Stadium, services are subject to alteration. Please check times before travelling.

Table 132

Mondays to Fridays

from 5 September

Cardiff - Gloucester, Bristol and Bath Spa

		XC	AW	GW	GW	GW		GW	AW	AW	GW	GW	GW	GW	XC	AW		GW	GW	GW	GW	AW	AW	GW	GW
			R							R				R		R							R		
		◇1		◇1		◇1					◇1		◇1		◇1			◇1		◇1				◇1	◇
															A										
			🛒	☕		☕				🛒	☕		☕	🛒	🛒	🛒		☕		☕			🛒	☕	🛒
Cardiff Central [7]	d	16 45	16 50			16 55		17 00	17 12	17 21			17 25	17 30	17 45	17 50				17 55	18 00	18 12	18 18	18 25	18 30
Newport (South Wales)	a	16 58	17 02			17 08		17 13	17 25	17 34			17 39	17 42	17 58	18 02				18 08	18 13	18 25	18 30	18 39	18 42
	d	17 00				17 09		17 15	17 28				17 39	17 44	18 00					18 09	18 15	18 27		18 39	18 44
Severn Tunnel Jn	d							17 25	17 39					17 55							18 25	18 38			18 55
Caldicot	d								17 41													18 40			
Chepstow	d								17 50						18 18							18 49			
Lydney	d	17 24							17 59													18 58			
Gloucester [7]	a	17 43							18 21						18 44							19 20			
Pilning	d																								
Patchway	d							17 39													18 39				
Bristol Parkway [7]	a					17 30							17 59							18 30				18 59	
	d				17 20							17 46							18 20						
Filton Abbey Wood	d				17 23			17 42				17 49		18 09					18 23		18 42				19 09
Bristol Temple Meads [10]	a				17 37			17 53				18 02		18 18					18 37		18 53				19 18
	d			17 30	17 49						18 00	18 07		18 23				18 30	18 49						19 23
Keynsham	d				17 56							18 14							18 56						
Oldfield Park	d				18 03							18 21							19 03						
Bath Spa [7]	a			17 41	18 06						18 11	18 24		18 34				18 41	19 06						19 35

		XC		AW	GW	GW	GW	GW	GW	AW	XC	GW		GW	GW	AW	GW	GW	AW	GW	GW	XC		AW	GW
		◇1		◇	◇1			◇1	◇	◇	◇1	◇1				◇	◇1	◇	◇	◇1		◇1			◇1
				🛒	☕			☕				☕					☕			☕					☕
Cardiff Central [7]	d	18 45		18 50			19 00	19 25	19 30	19 34	19 50				20 00	20 17	20 25	20 30	20 55		21 00	21 05		21 12	21 25
Newport (South Wales)	a	18 59		19 03			19 13	19 39	19 42	19 46	20 03				20 13	20 29	20 38	20 44	21 08		21 13	21 18		21 25	21 38
	d	19 01					19 15	19 39	19 44		20 05				20 15		20 39	20 44			21 15	21 21		21 27	21 39
Severn Tunnel Jn	d						19 25				20 15				20 25						21 25			21 38	
Caldicot	d										20 18													21 40	
Chepstow	d	19 19									20 26													21 49	
Lydney	d										20 35													21 58	
Gloucester [7]	a	19 45									20 53											22 02		22 21	
Pilning	d																								
Patchway	d						19 39								20 39						21 39				
Bristol Parkway [7]	a							19 59									21 01								21 59
	d					19 20								20 22											
Filton Abbey Wood	d					19 23	19 42		20 09					20 25	20 42			21 08			21 42				
Bristol Temple Meads [10]	a					19 36	19 51		20 18					20 38	20 53			21 19			21 51				
	d				19 30	19 49			20 23			20 30		20 49				21 23		21 50	22 00				
Keynsham	d					19 56								20 56							22 07				
Oldfield Park	d					20 03								21 03							22 14				
Bath Spa [7]	a				19 41	20 05			20 34			20 41		21 06				21 35		22 01	22 17				

		GW	SW	XC	XC	AW	GW	GW		GW	GW	AW FX	AW FO	GW
			1		◇1	◇	◇1							
							☕							
Cardiff Central [7]	d	21 30		21 40	21 50	21 55		22 04			22 49	23 19	23 20	23 27
Newport (South Wales)	a	21 43		21 55	22 03	22 08		22 16			23 06	23 39	23 38	23 44
	d	21 44		21 56	22 05			22 18			23 06	23 40	23 40	23 45
Severn Tunnel Jn	d	21 55						22 35			23 25	23 58	23 58	00 03
Caldicot	d											00 01	00 01	
Chepstow	d											00 10	00 09	
Lydney	d											00 19	00 18	
Gloucester [7]	a				22 46							00 39	00 39	
Pilning	d													
Patchway	d							22 48						00 16
Bristol Parkway [7]	a													
	d													
Filton Abbey Wood	d	22 09						22 52			23 40			00 20
Bristol Temple Meads [10]	a	22 22		22 29				23 05			23 49			00 33
	d		22 25				22 35			23 20				
Keynsham	d									23 27				
Oldfield Park	d									23 34				
Bath Spa [7]	a		22 37				22 46			23 36				

A 🛒 from Newport (South Wales)

When events are being held at the Millenium Stadium, services are subject to alteration. Please check times before travelling.

Table 132

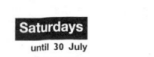

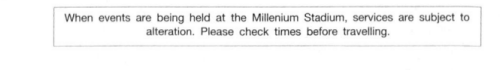

Cardiff - Gloucester, Bristol and Bath Spa

		AW	GW	AW	AW	GW	GW	GW	AW	AW		GW	AW	GW	GW	GW	GW	GW	XC	AW		GW	GW	GW	XC
					◇	◇1 🍴	◇	◇1 🍴	◇ 🛒	◇ 🛒		◇1 🍴		◇1 🍴	◇1 🍴		◇1 🍴	◇	◇1	◇ 🛒		◇1 🍴	◇1 🍴		◇1 🛒
Cardiff Central 7	d	23p20	23p27	00 30	04 35			04 55	05 20	05 40		05 55	06 12	06 25				06 30	06 40	06 50		06 55			07 00
Newport (South Wales)	a	23p38	23p44	00 48	04 50			05 09	05 33	05 55		06 09	06 25	06 38				06 43	06 53	07 02		07 08			07 13
	d	23p40	23p45					05 09				06 09	06 28	06 39				06 44	06 55			07 09			07 15
Severn Tunnel Jn	d	23p58	00 03										06 39					06 55	07 05						07 25
Caldicot	d	00 01											06 41						07 08						
Chepstow	d	00 09											06 50						07 16						
Lydney	d	00 18											06 59						07 25						
Gloucester 7	a	00 39											07 20						07 44						
Pilning	d																								
Patchway	d		00 16																						07 37
Bristol Parkway 7	a							05 36				06 29		06 59								07 29			
	d							05 42																	
Filton Abbey Wood	d		00 20															07 09							07 41
Bristol Temple Meads 10	a		00 33					05 53										07 18							07 51
	d					05 30	05 49	06 00							06 30	06 49	07 00	07 23					07 30	07 49	
Keynsham	d						05 56									06 56								07 56	
Oldfield Park	d						06 03									07 03								08 03	
Bath Spa 7	a					05 41	06 05	06 11							06 41	07 05	07 11	07 34					07 41	08 05	

		AW	AW	GW	GW	GW		XC	AW	GW	GW	GW	SW	GW	GW	GW		GW	XC	AW	GW	GW	GW	AW	AW
			◇ 🛒	◇1 🍴	◇1 🍴	◇		◇1 A 🛒	◇ 🛒	◇1 🍴		◇1 ⊘	◇1		◇1 ⊘	◇1 🍴		◇	◇1 A 🛒	◇ 🛒	◇1 🍴				◇ 🛒
Cardiff Central 7	d	07 12	07 21	07 25		07 30		07 45	07 50			07 55		08 00	08 25			08 30	08 45	08 50			09 00	09 12	09 21
Newport (South Wales)	a	07 25	07 34	07 39		07 42		07 59	08 02			08 08		08 13	08 38			08 42	08 58	09 02			09 13	09 24	09 34
	d	07 27		07 39		07 44		08 00				08 09		08 15	08 39			08 44	09 00				09 15	09 26	
Severn Tunnel Jn	d	07 38				07 55								08 25				08 55					09 25	09 36	
Caldicot	d	07 40																						09 38	
Chepstow	d	07 49																						09 48	
Lydney	d	07 58						08 26																09 56	
Gloucester 7	a	08 21						08 45											09 44					10 19	
Pilning	d													08 32											
Patchway	d													08 39									09 39		
Bristol Parkway 7	a			07 59								08 30			08 59										
	d										08 19											09 20			
Filton Abbey Wood	d					08 09					08 23			08 42				09 09				09 23	09 42		
Bristol Temple Meads 10	a					08 18					08 34			08 52				09 18				09 34	09 51		
	d				08 00	08 23				08 30	08 40		08 51			09 00		09 23			09 30	09 49			
Keynsham	d										08 47		08 58									09 56			
Oldfield Park	d										08 54											10 03			
Bath Spa 7	a				08 11	08 34				08 41	08 56		09 05			09 11		09 34			09 41	10 05			

		GW		GW	GW	XC	AW	GW	GW	GW	AW	GW		GW	GW	XC	AW	GW	GW	GW	AW	GW		GW	GW
		◇1 🍴		◇1 🍴	◇ B 🛒	◇1 A 🛒	◇ 🛒	◇1 🍴				◇1 🍴		◇1 🍴	◇ B 🛒	◇1 A 🛒	◇ 🛒	◇1 🍴			◇ 🛒	◇1 🍴		◇1 🍴	◇ B 🛒
Cardiff Central 7	d	09 25			09 30	09 45	09 55			10 00	10 12	10 25			10 30	10 45	10 55			11 00	11 21	11 25			11 30
Newport (South Wales)	a	09 39			09 42	09 58	10 07			10 13	10 25	10 39			10 42	10 58	11 07			11 13	11 34	11 39			11 42
	d	09 39			09 44	10 00				10 15	10 27	10 39			10 44	11 00				11 15		11 39			11 44
Severn Tunnel Jn	d				09 55					10 25	10 38									11 25					
Caldicot	d										10 40														
Chepstow	d					10 18					10 49														
Lydney	d										10 58					11 25									
Gloucester 7	a					10 44					11 21					11 44									
Pilning	d																								
Patchway	d									10 39										11 39					
Bristol Parkway 7	a	09 59										10 59										11 59			
	d								10 25										11 20						
Filton Abbey Wood	d				10 09				10 28	10 42					11 09				11 23	11 42					12 09
Bristol Temple Meads 10	a				10 18				10 39	10 51					11 18				11 34	11 51					12 19
	d			10 00	10 23			10 30	10 49					11 00	11 23			11 30	11 49					12 00	12 23
Keynsham	d								10 56										11 56						
Oldfield Park	d								11 03										12 03						
Bath Spa 7	a			10 11	10 34			10 41	11 05					11 11	11 34			11 41	12 05					12 11	12 34

		XC	AW	GW	GW	GW	AW	GW		GW	SW	GW	XC	AW	GW	GW	GW	AW		AW	GW	GW	GW	XC	AW
		◇1 A 🛒	◇ 🛒	◇1 🍴	R ◇			◇1 🍴		◇1 🍴	◇1 🛒	◇	◇1 A 🛒	◇ 🛒	◇1 🍴					◇ 🛒	◇1 🍴	◇1 🍴	◇	◇1 A 🛒	◇ 🛒
Cardiff Central 7	d	11 45	11 55			12 00	12 12	12 25				12 30	12 45	12 55			13 00	13 12		13 21	13 25		13 30	13 45	13 55
Newport (South Wales)	a	11 58	12 07			12 13	12 25	12 39				12 42	12 59	13 07			13 13	13 25		13 34	13 38		13 42	13 58	14 07
	d	12 00				12 15	12 27	12 39				12 44	13 00				13 15	13 27			13 39		13 44	14 00	
Severn Tunnel Jn	d					12 25	12 38										13 25	13 39							
Caldicot	d						12 40											13 40							
Chepstow	d	12 18					12 49						13 18					13 49							
Lydney	d						12 58											13 58						14 25	
Gloucester 7	a	12 44					13 21						13 44					14 21						14 44	
Pilning	d																								
Patchway	d					12 39											13 39								
Bristol Parkway 7	a							12 59													13 59				
	d				12 25											13 20									
Filton Abbey Wood	d				12 28	12 42						13 09				13 23	13 42						14 09		
Bristol Temple Meads 10	a				12 39	12 51						13 18				13 34	13 53						14 18		
	d			12 30	12 43					13 00	13 15	13 23			13 30	13 49						14 00	14 23		
Keynsham	d				12 50											13 56									
Oldfield Park	d				12 57											14 03									
Bath Spa 7	a			12 41	13 00					13 11	13 26	13 34			13 41	14 05						14 11	14 34		

A 🛒 from Newport (South Wales)
B 🛒 from Bristol Temple Meads

When events are being held at the Millenium Stadium, services are subject to alteration. Please check times before travelling.

Table 132

Saturdays
until 30 July

Cardiff - Gloucester, Bristol and Bath Spa

Station		GW	GW	GW		GW	GW	GW	XC	AW	GW	GW	GW	AW		AW	GW	SW	GW	GW	XC	AW	GW	GW	
		◇1				◇1	◇1	◇	◇1	◇	◇1					R	◇1	◇1	◇1	◇	◇1	R	◇1		
									A																
		☕				☕	☕		🛒	🛒	☕					🛒	☕		☕			🛒	☕		
Cardiff Central 7	d			14 00		14 25		14 30	14 45	14 55			15 00	15 12		15 21	15 25			15 30	15 45	15 55			
Newport (South Wales)	a			14 13		14 39		14 42	14 59	15 07			15 13	15 25		15 34	15 39			15 42	15 58	16 07			
	d			14 15		14 39		14 44	15 00				15 15	15 27			15 39			15 44	16 00				
Severn Tunnel Jn	d			14 25									15 25	15 37											
Caldicot	d													15 38											
Chepstow	d								15 18					15 47							16 18				
Lydney	d													15 56											
Gloucester 7	a								15 44					16 19							16 44				
Pilning	d																								
Patchway	d			14 39									15 39												
Bristol Parkway 7	a					14 59											15 59								
	d		14 20									15 19												16 25	
Filton Abbey Wood	d		14 25	14 42				15 09				15 22	15 42							16 09				16 28	
Bristol Temple Meads 10	a		14 36	14 51				15 18				15 33	15 51							16 18				16 39	
	d	14 30	14 49				15 00	15 25			15 30	15 38						15 51	16 00	16 23			16 30	16 49	
Keynsham	d		14 56									15 45						15 58						16 56	
Oldfield Park	d		15 03									15 52												17 03	
Bath Spa 7	a	14 41	15 05				15 11	15 36			15 41	15 54						16 05	16 11	16 34			16 41	17 06	

Station		GW	AW	AW	GW	GW	GW	XC	AW	GW		GW	GW	AW	AW	GW	GW	GW	XC	AW		GW	GW	GW	AW
					◇1	◇1	R	◇1	R	◇1					R	◇1	◇1	◇	◇1	R		◇1			
					☕	☕			🛒	☕					🛒	☕	☕		🛒	🛒		☕			
Cardiff Central 7	d	16 00	16 12	16 19	16 25		16 30	16 45	16 55				17 00	17 12	17 21	17 25		17 30	17 45	17 55				18 00	18 12
Newport (South Wales)	a	16 13	16 23	16 32	16 39		16 42	16 58	17 07				17 13	17 27	17 34	17 39		17 42	17 58	18 07				18 13	18 25
	d	16 15	16 26		16 39		16 44	17 00					17 15	17 27		17 39		17 44	18 00					18 15	18 27
Severn Tunnel Jn	d	16 25	16 38				16 55						17 25	17 38				17 55						18 25	18 38
Caldicot	d		16 40											17 40											18 40
Chepstow	d		16 49											17 49					18 18						18 49
Lydney	d		16 58					17 24						17 58											18 58
Gloucester 7	a		17 19					17 43						18 20					18 44						19 20
Pilning	d																								
Patchway	d	16 39											17 39											18 39	
Bristol Parkway 7	a				16 59											17 59									
	d											17 20											18 25		
Filton Abbey Wood	d	16 42					17 09					17 23	17 42					18 09					18 28	18 42	
Bristol Temple Meads 10	a	16 51					17 18					17 34	17 51					18 18					18 39	18 51	
	d					17 00	17 23			17 30		17 49					18 00	18 23				18 30	18 49		
Keynsham	d											17 56											18 56		
Oldfield Park	d											18 03											19 03		
Bath Spa 7	a					17 11	17 34			17 41		18 06					18 11	18 34				18 41	19 05		

Station		GW	GW	XC	AW	GW		GW	GW	GW	GW	AW	GW	GW	GW	XC		AW	GW	GW	XC	AW	GW	GW	AW
		◇1	◇	◇1	◇	◇1				◇1	◇	◇	◇1			◇1		◇	◇1	◇	◇1	◇	◇1	◇	
		☕			🛒	☕				☕			☕						☕				☕		
Cardiff Central 7	d	18 25	18 30	18 45	18 50				19 00	19 25	19 30	19 34			19 55	20 00		20 10	20 25	20 30	20 50	20 55		21 00	21 12
Newport (South Wales)	a	18 39	18 42	18 59	19 02				19 13	19 39	19 42	19 46			20 08	20 13		20 24	20 39	20 42	21 03	21 08		21 13	21 25
	d	18 39	18 44	19 00					19 15	19 39	19 44				20 10	20 15			20 39	20 44	21 05			21 15	21 27
Severn Tunnel Jn	d								19 25						20 20	20 25								21 25	21 38
Caldicot	d															20 28									21 40
Chepstow	d			19 17												20 36									21 49
Lydney	d															20 45									21 58
Gloucester 7	a			19 43												21 04					21 48				22 22
Pilning	d																								
Patchway	d								19 39						20 34									21 38	
Bristol Parkway 7	a	18 59								19 59									21 01						
	d							19 21						20 25											
Filton Abbey Wood	d		19 09					19 24	19 42		20 09			20 28	20 40					21 08				21 42	
Bristol Temple Meads 10	a		19 18					19 36	19 51		20 18			20 39	20 48					21 18				21 49	
	d		19 23			19 30		19 49			20 23		20 33	20 49						21 23			21 47		
Keynsham	d							19 56						20 56											
Oldfield Park	d							20 03						21 03											
Bath Spa 7	a		19 34			19 41		20 05			20 34		20 44	21 06						21 34			22 01		

Station		GW		XC	AW	SW	GW	GW	GW	AW
						1	◇1			
							☕			
Cardiff Central 7	d			21 30	21 49			22 00		23 20
Newport (South Wales)	a			21 42	22 05			22 14		23 36
	d			21 44				22 17		23 38
Severn Tunnel Jn	d							22 31		23 55
Caldicot	d									23 58
Chepstow	d									00 07
Lydney	d									00 16
Gloucester 7	a									00 40
Pilning	d									
Patchway	d							22 45		
Bristol Parkway 7	a									
	d									
Filton Abbey Wood	d							22 49		
Bristol Temple Meads 10	a			22 17				22 57		
	d	21 59				22 23	22 30		23 11	
Keynsham	d	22 07							23 18	
Oldfield Park	d	22 14							23 25	
Bath Spa 7	a	22 17				22 34	22 41		23 27	

A 🛒 from Newport (South Wales)

When events are being held at the Millenium Stadium, services are subject to alteration. Please check times before travelling.

Table 132

Saturdays

6 August to 10 September

Cardiff - Gloucester, Bristol and Bath Spa

		AW	GW	AW	AW	GW	GW	GW	AW	AW		GW	AW	GW	GW	GW	GW	GW	XC	AW		GW	GW	GW	XC
					◇	◇ [1] ☕	◇	◇ [1] ☕	◇ 🛒	◇ 🛒		◇ [1] ☕		◇ [1] ☕	◇ [1] ☕		◇ [1] ☕	◇	◇ [1]	◇ 🛒		◇ [1] ☕	◇ [1] ☕		◇ [1] 🛒
Cardiff Central [7]	d	23p20	23p27	00 30	04 35			04 55	05 20	05 40		05 55	06 12	06 25				06 30	06 40	06 50		06 55			07 00
Newport (South Wales)	a	23p38	23p44	00 48	04 50			05 09	05 33	05 55		06 09	06 25	06 38				06 43	06 53	07 02		07 08			07 13
	d	23p40	23p45					05 09				06 09	06 28	06 39				06 44	06 55			07 09			07 15
Severn Tunnel Jn	d	23p58	00 03										06 39					06 55	07 05						07 25
Caldicot	d	00 01											06 41						07 08						
Chepstow	d	00 09											06 50						07 16						
Lydney	d	00 18											06 59						07 25						
Gloucester [7]	a	00 39											07 20						07 44						
Pilning	d																								
Patchway	d		00 16																						07 37
Bristol Parkway [7]	a							05 36				06 29		06 59								07 29			
	d							05 42																	
Filton Abbey Wood	d		00 20															07 09							07 41
Bristol Temple Meads [10]	a		00 33					05 53										07 18							07 51
	d					05 30	05 49	06 00							06 30	06 49	07 00	07 23					07 30	07 49	
Keynsham	d						05 56									06 56								07 56	
Oldfield Park	d						06 03									07 03								08 03	
Bath Spa [7]	a					05 41	06 05	06 11							06 41	07 05	07 11	07 34					07 41	08 05	

		AW	AW	GW	GW	GW		XC	AW	GW	GW	GW	SW	GW	GW	GW		GW	XC	AW	GW	GW	GW	AW	AW
			◇ 🛒	◇ [1] ☕	◇ [1] ☕	◇		◇ [1] A 🛒	◇ 🛒	◇ [1] ☕		◇ [1] ⊘	◇ [1]		◇ [1] ⊘	◇ [1] ☕		◇	◇ [1] A 🛒	◇ 🛒	◇ [1] ☕				◇ 🛒
Cardiff Central [7]	d	07 12	07 21	07 25		07 30		07 45	07 50			07 55		08 00	08 25			08 30	08 45	08 50			09 00	09 12	09 21
Newport (South Wales)	a	07 25	07 34	07 39		07 42		07 59	08 02			08 08		08 13	08 38			08 42	08 58	09 02			09 13	09 24	09 34
	d	07 27		07 39		07 44		08 00				08 09		08 15	08 39			08 44	09 00				09 15	09 26	
Severn Tunnel Jn	d	07 38				07 55								08 25				08 55					09 25	09 36	
Caldicot	d	07 40																						09 38	
Chepstow	d	07 49																						09 48	
Lydney	d	07 58						08 26																09 56	
Gloucester [7]	a	08 21						08 45											09 44					10 19	
Pilning	d													08 32											
Patchway	d													08 39									09 39		
Bristol Parkway [7]	a			07 59								08 30			08 59										
	d										08 19											09 20			
Filton Abbey Wood	d					08 09					08 23			08 42				09 09				09 23	09 42		
Bristol Temple Meads [10]	a					08 18					08 34			08 52				09 18				09 34	09 51		
	d				08 00	08 23				08 30	08 40		08 51			09 00		09 23			09 30	09 49			
Keynsham	d										08 47		08 58									09 56			
Oldfield Park	d										08 54											10 03			
Bath Spa [7]	a				08 11	08 34				08 41	08 56		09 05			09 11		09 34			09 41	10 05			

		GW		GW	GW	XC	AW	GW	GW	GW	AW	GW		GW	GW	XC	AW	GW	GW	GW	AW	GW		GW	GW
		◇ [1] ☕		◇ [1] ☕	◇ B 🛒	◇ [1] A 🛒	◇ 🛒	◇ [1] ☕				◇ [1] ☕		◇ [1] ☕	◇ B 🛒	◇ [1] A 🛒	◇ 🛒	◇ [1] ☕			◇ 🛒	◇ [1] ☕		◇ [1] ☕	◇ B 🛒
Cardiff Central [7]	d	09 25			09 30	09 45	09 55			10 00	10 12	10 25			10 30	10 45	10 55			11 00	11 21	11 25			11 30
Newport (South Wales)	a	09 39			09 42	09 58	10 07			10 13	10 25	10 39			10 42	10 58	11 07			11 13	11 34	11 39			11 42
	d	09 39			09 44	10 00				10 15	10 27	10 39			10 44	11 00				11 15		11 39			11 44
Severn Tunnel Jn	d				09 55					10 25	10 38									11 25					
Caldicot	d										10 40														
Chepstow	d					10 18					10 49														
Lydney	d										10 58					11 25									
Gloucester [7]	a					10 44					11 21					11 44									
Pilning	d																								
Patchway	d									10 39										11 39					
Bristol Parkway [7]	a	09 59										10 59										11 59			
	d								10 25										11 20						
Filton Abbey Wood	d				10 09				10 28	10 42					11 09				11 23	11 42					12 09
Bristol Temple Meads [10]	a				10 18				10 39	10 51					11 18				11 34	11 51					12 19
	d			10 00	10 23			10 30	10 49					11 00	11 23			11 30	11 49					12 00	12 23
Keynsham	d								10 56										11 56						
Oldfield Park	d								11 03										12 03						
Bath Spa [7]	a			10 11	10 34			10 41	11 05					11 11	11 34			11 41	12 05					12 11	12 34

		XC	AW	GW	GW	GW	AW	GW		GW	SW	GW	XC	AW	GW	GW	GW	AW		AW	GW	GW	GW	XC	AW
		◇ [1] A 🛒	◇ 🛒	◇ [1] ☕	R ◇			◇ [1] ☕		◇ [1] ☕	◇ [1] 🛒	◇	◇ [1] A 🛒	◇ 🛒	◇ [1] ☕					◇ 🛒	◇ [1] ☕	◇ [1] ☕	◇	◇ [1] A 🛒	◇ 🛒
Cardiff Central [7]	d	11 45	11 55			12 00	12 12	12 25				12 30	12 45	12 55			13 00	13 12		13 21	13 25		13 30	13 45	13 55
Newport (South Wales)	a	11 58	12 07			12 13	12 25	12 39				12 42	12 59	13 07			13 13	13 25		13 34	13 38		13 42	13 58	14 07
	d	12 00				12 15	12 27	12 39				12 44	13 00				13 15	13 27			13 39		13 44	14 00	
Severn Tunnel Jn	d					12 25	12 38										13 25	13 39							
Caldicot	d						12 40											13 40							
Chepstow	d	12 18					12 49						13 18					13 49							
Lydney	d						12 58											13 58						14 25	
Gloucester [7]	a	12 44					13 21						13 44					14 21						14 44	
Pilning	d																								
Patchway	d					12 39											13 39								
Bristol Parkway [7]	a							12 59													13 59				
	d				12 25											13 20									
Filton Abbey Wood	d				12 28	12 42						13 09				13 23	13 42						14 09		
Bristol Temple Meads [10]	a				12 39	12 51						13 18				13 34	13 53						14 18		
	d			12 30	12 43					13 00	13 15	13 23			13 30	13 49						14 00	14 23		
Keynsham	d				12 50											13 56									
Oldfield Park	d				12 57											14 03									
Bath Spa [7]	a			12 41	13 00					13 11	13 26	13 34			13 41	14 05						14 11	14 34		

A 🛒 from Newport (South Wales)

B 🛒 from Bristol Temple Meads

When events are being held at the Millenium Stadium, services are subject to alteration. Please check times before travelling.

Table 132

Saturdays

6 August to 10 September

Cardiff - Gloucester, Bristol and Bath Spa

		GW	GW	GW		GW	GW	GW	XC	AW	GW	GW	GW	AW		AW	GW	SW	GW	GW	XC	AW	GW	GW	
																R						R			
		◇1				◇1	◇1	◇	◇1	◇	◇1						◇1	◇1	◇1	◇	◇1		◇1		
									A																
		☕				☕	☕		🛒	🛒	☕					🛒	☕		☕			🛒	☕		
Cardiff Central 7	d			14 00		14 25		14 30	14 45	14 55			15 00	15 12		15 21	15 25			15 30	15 45	15 55			
Newport (South Wales)	a			14 13		14 39		14 42	14 59	15 07			15 13	15 25		15 34	15 39			15 42	15 58	16 07			
	d			14 15		14 39		14 44	15 00				15 15	15 27			15 39			15 44	16 00				
Severn Tunnel Jn	d			14 25									15 25	15 37											
Caldicot	d													15 38											
Chepstow	d								15 18					15 47							16 18				
Lydney	d													15 56											
Gloucester 7	a								15 44					16 19							16 44				
Pilning	d																								
Patchway	d			14 39									15 39												
Bristol Parkway 7	a					14 59											15 59								
	d		14 20									15 19												16 25	
Filton Abbey Wood	d		14 25	14 42				15 09				15 22	15 42							16 09				16 28	
Bristol Temple Meads 10	a		14 36	14 51				15 18				15 33	15 51							16 18				16 39	
	d	14 30	14 49				15 00	15 25			15 30	15 38						15 51	16 00	16 23			16 30	16 49	
Keynsham	d		14 56									15 45						15 58						16 56	
Oldfield Park	d		15 03									15 52												17 03	
Bath Spa 7	a	14 41	15 05				15 11	15 36			15 41	15 54						16 05	16 11	16 34			16 41	17 06	

		GW	AW	AW	GW	GW	GW	XC	AW	GW		GW	GW	AW	AW	GW	GW	GW	XC	AW		GW	GW	GW	AW
							R		R						R					R					
					◇1	◇1		◇1		◇1						◇1	◇1	◇	◇1			◇1			
																			A						
					☕	☕			🛒	☕					🛒	☕	☕		🛒	🛒		☕			
Cardiff Central 7	d	16 00	16 12	16 19	16 25		16 30	16 45	16 55				17 00	17 12	17 21	17 25		17 30	17 45	17 55				18 00	18 12
Newport (South Wales)	a	16 13	16 23	16 32	16 39		16 42	16 58	17 07				17 13	17 27	17 34	17 39		17 42	17 58	18 07				18 13	18 25
	d	16 15	16 26		16 39		16 44	17 00					17 15	17 27		17 39		17 44	18 00					18 15	18 27
Severn Tunnel Jn	d	16 25	16 38				16 55						17 25	17 38				17 55						18 25	18 38
Caldicot	d		16 40											17 40											18 40
Chepstow	d		16 49											17 49					18 18						18 49
Lydney	d		16 58					17 24						17 58											18 58
Gloucester 7	a		17 19					17 43						18 20					18 44						19 20
Pilning	d																								
Patchway	d	16 39											17 39											18 39	
Bristol Parkway 7	a				16 59											17 59									
	d											17 20											18 25		
Filton Abbey Wood	d	16 42					17 09					17 23	17 42					18 09					18 28	18 42	
Bristol Temple Meads 10	a	16 51					17 18					17 34	17 51					18 18					18 39	18 51	
	d					17 00	17 23			17 30		17 49					18 00	18 23				18 30	18 49		
Keynsham	d											17 56											18 56		
Oldfield Park	d											18 03											19 03		
Bath Spa 7	a					17 11	17 34			17 41		18 06					18 11	18 34				18 41	19 05		

		GW	GW	XC	AW	GW		GW	GW	GW	GW	AW	GW	GW	GW	XC		GW	GW	XC	GW	GW	AW	GW	XC
		◇1	◇	◇1	◇	◇1				◇1	◇	◇	◇1			◇1		◇1	◇	◇1	◇1	◇			
		☕			🛒	☕				☕			☕					☕			☕				
Cardiff Central 7	d	18 25	18 30	18 45	18 50				19 00	19 25	19 30	19 34			19 55	20 00		20 25	20 30	20 50		21 00	21 12		21 30
Newport (South Wales)	a	18 39	18 42	18 59	19 02				19 13	19 39	19 42	19 46			20 08	20 13		20 39	20 42	21 03		21 13	21 25		21 42
	d	18 39	18 44	19 00					19 15	19 39	19 44				20 10	20 15		20 39	20 44	21 05		21 15	21 27		21 44
Severn Tunnel Jn	d								19 25						20 20	20 25						21 25	21 38		
Caldicot	d															20 28							21 40		
Chepstow	d			19 17												20 36							21 49		
Lydney	d															20 45							21 58		
Gloucester 7	a			19 43												21 04				21 48			22 22		
Pilning	d																								
Patchway	d								19 39						20 34							21 38			
Bristol Parkway 7	a	18 59								19 59								21 01							
	d							19 21						20 25											
Filton Abbey Wood	d		19 09					19 24	19 42		20 09			20 28	20 40				21 08			21 42			
Bristol Temple Meads 10	a		19 18					19 36	19 51		20 18			20 39	20 48				21 18			21 49			22 17
	d		19 23			19 30		19 49			20 23		20 33	20 49					21 23		21 47			21 59	
Keynsham	d							19 56						20 56										22 07	
Oldfield Park	d							20 03						21 03										22 14	
Bath Spa 7	a		19 34			19 41		20 05			20 34		20 44	21 06					21 34		22 01			22 17	

		SW		GW	GW	AW	GW	AW
		1		◇1				
				☕		🚌		
Cardiff Central 7	d				22 00	21 55		23 20
Newport (South Wales)	a				22 14	22 25		23 36
	d				22 17			23 38
Severn Tunnel Jn	d				22 31			23 55
Caldicot	d							23 58
Chepstow	d							00 07
Lydney	d							00 16
Gloucester 7	a							00 40
Pilning	d							
Patchway	d				22 45			
Bristol Parkway 7	a							
	d							
Filton Abbey Wood	d				22 49			
Bristol Temple Meads 10	a				22 57			
	d	22 23		22 30			23 11	
Keynsham	d						23 18	
Oldfield Park	d						23 25	
Bath Spa 7	a	22 34		22 41			23 27	

A 🛒 from Newport (South Wales)

When events are being held at the Millenium Stadium, services are subject to alteration. Please check times before travelling.

Table 132

Saturdays

from 17 September

Cardiff - Gloucester, Bristol and Bath Spa

		AW	GW	AW	AW	GW	GW	GW	AW	AW		GW	AW	GW	GW	GW	GW	GW	XC	AW		GW	GW	GW	XC
					◇	◇1	◇	◇1	◇	◇		◇1		◇1	◇1		◇1	◇	◇1	◇		◇1	◇1		◇1
						☕		☕	🛒	🛒		☕		☕	☕		☕			🛒		☕	☕		🛒
Cardiff Central [7]	d	23p20	23p27	00 30	04 35			04 55	05 20	05 40		05 55	06 12	06 25				06 30	06 40	06 50		06 55			07 00
Newport (South Wales)	a	23p38	23p44	00 48	04 50			05 09	05 33	05 55		06 09	06 25	06 38				06 43	06 53	07 02		07 08			07 13
	d	23p40	23p45					05 09				06 09	06 28	06 39				06 44	06 55			07 09			07 15
Severn Tunnel Jn	d	23p58	00 03										06 39					06 55	07 05						07 25
Caldicot	d	00 01											06 41						07 08						
Chepstow	d	00 09											06 50						07 16						
Lydney	d	00 18											06 59						07 25						
Gloucester [7]	a	00 39											07 20						07 44						
Pilning	d																								
Patchway	d		00 16																						07 37
Bristol Parkway [7]	a							05 36				06 29		06 59								07 29			
	d							05 42																	
Filton Abbey Wood	d		00 20															07 09							07 41
Bristol Temple Meads [10]	a		00 33					05 53										07 18							07 51
	d					05 30	05 49	06 00							06 30	06 49	07 00	07 23					07 30	07 49	
Keynsham	d						05 56									06 56								07 56	
Oldfield Park	d						06 03									07 03								08 03	
Bath Spa [7]	a					05 41	06 05	06 11							06 41	07 05	07 11	07 34					07 41	08 05	

		AW	AW	GW	GW	GW		XC	AW	GW	GW	GW	SW	GW	GW	GW		GW	XC	AW	GW	GW	GW	GW	AW
			◇	◇1	◇1	◇		◇1	◇	◇1		◇1	◇1		◇1	◇1		◇	◇1	◇	◇1		◇1		
								A											A						
Cardiff Central [7]	d	07 12	07 21	07 25		07 30		07 45	07 50			07 55		08 00	08 25			08 30	08 45	08 50			08 55	09 00	09 12
Newport (South Wales)	a	07 25	07 34	07 39		07 42		07 59	08 02			08 08		08 13	08 38			08 42	08 58	09 02			09 08	09 13	09 24
	d	07 27		07 39		07 44		08 00				08 09		08 15	08 39			08 44	09 00				09 09	09 15	09 26
Severn Tunnel Jn	d	07 38				07 55								08 25				08 55						09 25	09 36
Caldicot	d	07 40																							09 38
Chepstow	d	07 49																							09 48
Lydney	d	07 58						08 26																	09 56
Gloucester [7]	a	08 21						08 45											09 44						10 19
Pilning	d													08 32											
Patchway	d													08 39										09 39	
Bristol Parkway [7]	a			07 59								08 30			08 59								09 30		
	d										08 19											09 20			
Filton Abbey Wood	d					08 09					08 23			08 42				09 09				09 23		09 42	
Bristol Temple Meads [10]	a					08 18					08 34			08 52				09 18				09 34		09 51	
	d				08 00	08 23				08 30	08 40		08 51			09 00		09 23			09 30	09 49			
Keynsham	d										08 47		08 58									09 56			
Oldfield Park	d										08 54											10 03			
Bath Spa [7]	a				08 11	08 34				08 41	08 56		09 05			09 11		09 34			09 41	10 05			

		AW		GW	GW	GW	XC	AW	GW	GW	GW	AW		GW	GW	GW	XC	AW	GW	GW	GW	AW		GW	GW
		◇		◇1	◇1	◇	◇1	◇	◇1					◇1	◇1	◇	◇1	◇	◇1			◇		◇1	◇1
						B	A									B	A								
		🛒		☕	☕	🛒	🛒	🛒	☕					☕	☕	🛒	🛒	🛒	☕			🛒		☕	☕
Cardiff Central [7]	d	09 21		09 25		09 30	09 45	09 55			10 00	10 12		10 25		10 30	10 45	10 55			11 00	11 21		11 25	
Newport (South Wales)	a	09 34		09 39		09 42	09 58	10 07			10 13	10 25		10 39		10 42	10 58	11 07			11 13	11 34		11 39	
	d			09 39		09 44	10 00				10 15	10 27		10 39		10 44	11 00				11 15			11 39	
Severn Tunnel Jn	d					09 55					10 25	10 38									11 25				
Caldicot	d											10 40													
Chepstow	d						10 18					10 49													
Lydney	d											10 58					11 25								
Gloucester [7]	a						10 44					11 21					11 44								
Pilning	d																								
Patchway	d										10 39										11 39				
Bristol Parkway [7]	a			09 59										10 59										11 59	
	d									10 25										11 20					
Filton Abbey Wood	d					10 09				10 28	10 42					11 09				11 23	11 42				
Bristol Temple Meads [10]	a					10 18				10 39	10 51					11 18				11 34	11 51				
	d				10 00	10 23			10 30	10 49					11 00	11 23			11 30	11 49					12 00
Keynsham	d									10 56										11 56					
Oldfield Park	d									11 03										12 03					
Bath Spa [7]	a				10 11	10 34			10 41	11 05					11 11	11 34			11 41	12 05					12 11

		GW	XC	AW	GW	GW	GW	AW		GW	GW	SW	GW	XC	AW	GW	GW	GW		AW	AW	GW	GW	GW	XC
						■																			
		◇	◇1	◇	◇1	◇				◇1	◇1	◇1	◇	◇1	◇	◇1					◇	◇1	◇1	◇	◇1
		B	A											A											A
		🛒	🛒	🛒	☕					☕	☕	🛒		🛒	🛒	☕					🛒	☕	☕		🛒
Cardiff Central [7]	d	11 30	11 45	11 55			12 00	12 12		12 25			12 30	12 45	12 55			13 00		13 12	13 21	13 25		13 30	13 45
Newport (South Wales)	a	11 42	11 58	12 07			12 13	12 25		12 39			12 42	12 59	13 07			13 13		13 25	13 34	13 38		13 42	13 58
	d	11 44	12 00				12 15	12 27		12 39			12 44	13 00				13 15		13 27		13 39		13 44	14 00
Severn Tunnel Jn	d						12 25	12 38										13 25		13 39					
Caldicot	d							12 40												13 40					
Chepstow	d		12 18					12 49						13 18						13 49					
Lydney	d							12 58												13 58					14 25
Gloucester [7]	a		12 44					13 21						13 44						14 21					14 44
Pilning	d																								
Patchway	d						12 39											13 39							
Bristol Parkway [7]	a									12 59												13 59			
	d					12 25											13 20								
Filton Abbey Wood	d	12 09				12 28	12 42						13 09				13 23	13 42						14 09	
Bristol Temple Meads [10]	a	12 19				12 39	12 51						13 18				13 34	13 53						14 18	
	d	12 23			12 30	12 43					13 00	13 15	13 23			13 30	13 49						14 00	14 23	
Keynsham	d					12 50											13 56								
Oldfield Park	d					12 57											14 03								
Bath Spa [7]	a	12 34			12 41	13 00					13 11	13 26	13 34			13 41	14 05						14 11	14 34	

A 🛒 from Newport (South Wales)

B 🛒 from Bristol Temple Meads

When events are being held at the Millenium Stadium, services are subject to alteration. Please check times before travelling.

Table 132

Saturdays
from 17 September

Cardiff - Gloucester, Bristol and Bath Spa

		AW	GW	GW		GW	GW	GW	GW	XC	AW	GW	GW	GW		AW	AW	GW	SW	GW	GW	XC	AW	GW	
																	R						R		
		◇	◇1				◇1	◇1	◇	◇1	◇	◇1						◇1	◇1	◇1	◇	◇1		◇1	
										A															
		🛒	☕				☕	☕		🛒	🛒	☕					🛒	☕		☕			🛒	☕	
Cardiff Central 7	d	13 55				14 00	14 25		14 30	14 45	14 55			15 00		15 12	15 21	15 25			15 30	15 45	15 55		
Newport (South Wales)	a	14 07				14 13	14 39		14 42	14 59	15 07			15 13		15 25	15 34	15 39			15 42	15 58	16 07		
	d					14 15	14 39		14 44	15 00				15 15		15 27		15 39			15 44	16 00			
Severn Tunnel Jn	d					14 25								15 25		15 37									
Caldicot	d															15 38									
Chepstow	d									15 18						15 47						16 18			
Lydney	d															15 56									
Gloucester 7	a									15 44						16 19						16 44			
Pilning	d																								
Patchway	d					14 39								15 39											
Bristol Parkway 7	a						14 59											15 59							
	d			14 20									15 19												
Filton Abbey Wood	d			14 25		14 42			15 09				15 22	15 42							16 09				
Bristol Temple Meads 10	a			14 36		14 51			15 18				15 33	15 51							16 18				
	d		14 30	14 49				15 00	15 25			15 30	15 38						15 51	16 00	16 23			16 30	
Keynsham	d			14 56									15 45						15 58						
Oldfield Park	d			15 03									15 52												
Bath Spa 7	a		14 41	15 05				15 11	15 36			15 41	15 54						16 05	16 11	16 34			16 41	

		GW	GW	AW	AW	GW	GW	GW	XC	AW		GW	GW	GW	AW	AW	GW	GW	GW	XC		AW	GW	GW	GW
								R		R						R						R			
						◇1	◇1		◇1			◇1					◇1	◇1	◇	◇1			◇1		
																				A					
Cardiff Central 7	d		16 00	16 12	16 19	16 25		16 30	16 45	16 55				17 00	17 12	17 21	17 25		17 30	17 45		17 55			18 00
Newport (South Wales)	a		16 13	16 23	16 32	16 39		16 42	16 58	17 07				17 13	17 27	17 34	17 39		17 42	17 58		18 07			18 13
	d		16 15	16 26		16 39		16 44	17 00					17 15	17 27		17 39		17 44	18 00					18 15
Severn Tunnel Jn	d		16 25	16 38				16 55						17 25	17 38				17 55						18 25
Caldicot	d			16 40											17 40										
Chepstow	d			16 49											17 49					18 18					
Lydney	d			16 58					17 24						17 58										
Gloucester 7	a			17 19					17 43						18 20					18 44					
Pilning	d																								
Patchway	d		16 39											17 39											18 39
Bristol Parkway 7	a					16 59											17 59								
	d	16 25											17 20											18 25	
Filton Abbey Wood	d	16 28	16 42					17 09					17 23	17 42					18 09					18 28	18 42
Bristol Temple Meads 10	a	16 39	16 51					17 18					17 34	17 51					18 18					18 39	18 51
	d	16 49					17 00	17 23				17 30	17 49					18 00	18 23				18 30	18 49	
Keynsham	d	16 56											17 56											18 56	
Oldfield Park	d	17 03											18 03											19 03	
Bath Spa 7	a	17 06					17 11	17 34				17 41	18 06					18 11	18 34				18 41	19 05	

		AW	GW	GW	XC	AW		GW	GW	GW	GW	GW	AW	GW	GW	GW		XC	AW	GW	GW	XC	AW	GW	GW
			◇1	◇	◇1	◇		◇1			◇1	◇	◇	◇1				◇1	◇	◇1	◇	◇1	◇	◇1	◇
			☕			🛒		☕			☕			☕						☕				☕	
Cardiff Central 7	d	18 12	18 25	18 30	18 45	18 50				19 00	19 25	19 30	19 34			19 55		20 00	20 10	20 25	20 30	20 50	20 55		21 00
Newport (South Wales)	a	18 25	18 39	18 42	18 59	19 02				19 13	19 39	19 42	19 46			20 08		20 13	20 24	20 39	20 42	21 03	21 08		21 13
	d	18 27	18 39	18 44	19 00					19 15	19 39	19 44				20 10		20 15		20 39	20 44	21 05			21 15
Severn Tunnel Jn	d	18 38								19 25						20 20		20 25							21 25
Caldicot	d	18 40																20 28							
Chepstow	d	18 49			19 17													20 36							
Lydney	d	18 58																20 45							
Gloucester 7	a	19 20			19 43													21 04				21 48			
Pilning	d																								
Patchway	d									19 39						20 34									21 38
Bristol Parkway 7	a		18 59								19 59									21 01					
	d								19 21						20 25										
Filton Abbey Wood	d			19 09					19 24	19 42		20 09			20 28	20 40					21 08				21 42
Bristol Temple Meads 10	a			19 18					19 36	19 51		20 18			20 39	20 48					21 18				21 49
	d			19 23				19 30	19 49			20 23		20 33	20 49						21 23			21 47	
Keynsham	d								19 56						20 56										
Oldfield Park	d								20 03						21 03										
Bath Spa 7	a			19 34				19 41	20 05			20 34		20 44	21 06						21 34			22 01	

		AW		GW	XC	AW	SW	GW	GW	GW	AW	AW
							1	◇1				
								☕				🚌
Cardiff Central 7	d	21 12			21 30	21 49			22 00		23 20	
Newport (South Wales)	a	21 25			21 42	22 05			22 14		23 41	
	d	21 27			21 44				22 17			23 50
Severn Tunnel Jn	d	21 38							22 31			00 15
Caldicot	d	21 40										00 25
Chepstow	d	21 49										00 40
Lydney	d	21 58										01 00
Gloucester 7	a	22 22										01 40
Pilning	d											
Patchway	d								22 45			
Bristol Parkway 7	a											
	d											
Filton Abbey Wood	d								22 49			
Bristol Temple Meads 10	a				22 17				22 57			
	d			21 59			22 23	22 30		23 11		
Keynsham	d			22 07						23 18		
Oldfield Park	d			22 14						23 25		
Bath Spa 7	a			22 17			22 34	22 41		23 27		

A 🛒 from Newport (South Wales)

When events are being held at the Millenium Stadium, services are subject to alteration. Please check times before travelling.

Table 132

Sundays
until 19 June

Cardiff - Gloucester, Bristol and Bath Spa

		AW	GW	GW	GW	GW		GW	AW	GW		GW	GW	GW	AW	GW	GW	GW	AW	AW		GW	XC	XC	GW
		A	◇1 ☕	◇1 ☕	◇1 ☕	◇1 ☕		◇	◇ 🛒	◇1 ☕			◇1 ☕	◇	◇ 🛒	◇1 ☕	◇	◇1 ☕		◇ 🛒		◇1 ☕	◇1 🛒	◇1	R ◇ D 🛒
Cardiff Central 7	d	23p20		07 56				08 05	08 30	09 05				09 15	09 30		10 08	10 15	10 23	10 35				10 45	11 08
Newport (South Wales)	a	23p36		08 13				08 21	08 47	09 18				09 27	09 48		10 20	10 31	10 36	10 48				10 57	11 20
	d	23p38		08 15				08 23		09 19				09 29			10 22	10 32	10 38				10 49	10 59	11 22
Severn Tunnel Jn	d	23p55						08 40						09 46			10 39		10 56						11 39
Caldicot	d	23p58																	10 58						
Chepstow	d	00 07																	11 07						
Lydney	d	00 16																	11 16						
Gloucester 7	a	00 40																	11 42					11 49	
Pilning	d																								
Patchway	d													09 59											
Bristol Parkway 7	a			08 44						09 46								10 59					11 11		
	d																						11 29		
Filton Abbey Wood	d							08 55						10 03			10 54								11 54
Bristol Temple Meads 10	a							09 05						10 13			11 03						11 40		12 04
	d		07 45		08 15	08 45		09 10				09 20	09 48	10 15		10 30	11 10					11 30			12 15
Keynsham	d							09 18				09 27					11 17								
Oldfield Park	d							09 25				09 35					11 24								
Bath Spa 7	a		07 57		08 26	08 57		09 27				09 38	09 58	10 28		10 41	11 26					11 42			12 26

		GW	AW	GW	XC	XC		GW	GW	AW	AW	GW	XC	XC	GW				GW	AW	GW	XC	XC	GW	GW
		◇1 ☕	◇ 🛒	◇1 ☕	◇1 🛒	◇1 E 🛒		◇	◇1 ☕		◇ 🛒	◇1 ☕	◇1 🛒	◇1	◇				◇1 ☕	R 🛒	◇1 ☕	◇1 🛒	◇1 E 🛒	◇	◇1 ☕
Cardiff Central 7	d	11 15	11 35			11 45		12 08	12 15	12 23	12 40			12 45	13 08				13 15	13 40			13 45	14 08	14 15
Newport (South Wales)	a	11 31	11 49			11 57		12 20	12 31	12 36	12 52			12 57	13 20				13 31	13 52			13 57	14 20	14 31
	d	11 32			11 52	11 59		12 22	12 32	12 38			12 53	12 59	13 22				13 32			13 52	13 59	14 23	14 32
Severn Tunnel Jn	d							12 39		12 56					13 39									14 40	
Caldicot	d									12 58															
Chepstow	d									13 07															
Lydney	d									13 16															
Gloucester 7	a					12 46				13 34				13 47									14 46		
Pilning	d																								
Patchway	d							12 52																	
Bristol Parkway 7	a	11 59			12 13				12 59				13 17						13 59			14 18			14 59
	d				12 25								13 25									14 25			
Filton Abbey Wood	d							12 57							13 54									14 56	
Bristol Temple Meads 10	a				12 35			13 05					13 37		14 04							14 36		15 05	
	d			12 30				13 10				13 30			14 15						14 30			15 10	
Keynsham	d							13 17																15 18	
Oldfield Park	d							13 24																15 25	
Bath Spa 7	a			12 41				13 26				13 41			14 26						14 41			15 27	

		AW		XC	XC	AW	GW	GW	SW	GW	GW	AW		XC	AW	GW	GW	GW	GW	AW	GW	GW		AW	XC
				◇1 🛒	◇1 E 🛒	R 🛒	◇1 ☕	◇1 ☕	◇1	◇	◇1 ☕	R 🛒		◇1 E 🛒	R 🛒	◇1 ☕	◇1 ☕	◇	◇1 ☕		◇1 ☕	◇		R 🛒	◇1
Cardiff Central 7	d	14 23			14 45	14 56				15 08	15 15	15 22		15 45	15 56			16 08	16 15	16 23		16 35		16 40	16 45
Newport (South Wales)	a	14 36			14 57	15 12				15 20	15 31	15 34		15 57	16 12			16 20	16 31	16 36		16 47		16 52	16 57
	d	14 38		14 48	14 59					15 22	15 32			15 59				16 22	16 32	16 38		16 49			16 59
Severn Tunnel Jn	d	14 56								15 39								16 39		16 56					
Caldicot	d	14 58																		16 58					
Chepstow	d	15 07																		17 07					
Lydney	d	15 16																		17 16					
Gloucester 7	a	15 37			15 46									16 46						17 37					17 46
Pilning	d																								
Patchway	d									15 52															
Bristol Parkway 7	a			15 08							15 59								16 59						
	d			15 12																					
Filton Abbey Wood	d									15 55								16 55				17 20			
Bristol Temple Meads 10	a			15 23						16 04								17 06				17 29			
	d						15 30	16 00	16 04	16 15						16 30	17 00	17 15			17 30	17 40			
Keynsham	d								16 11									17 22							
Oldfield Park	d																	17 29							
Bath Spa 7	a						15 41	16 11	16 18	16 26						16 41	17 11	17 30			17 41	17 51			

A not 22 May

D 🛒 from Bristol Temple Meads

E 🛒 from Newport (South Wales)

When events are being held at the Millenium Stadium, services are subject to alteration. Please check times before travelling.

Table 132

Sundays
until 19 June

Cardiff - Gloucester, Bristol and Bath Spa

		GW	GW	GW	AW	GW		AW		GW	GW	XC	GW	GW	GW	AW	AW	XC		GW	GW	GW	AW	XC	GW
								R			R						R								
			◇1	◇		◇1				◇1		◇1	◇1	◇1	◇			◇1		◇1	◇1	◇	◇	◇1	◇1
			☕			☕				☕			☕	☕			🛒			☕	☕				☕
Cardiff Central 7	d			17 08	17 05	17 15		17 35			17 40	17 45	17 50		18 08	18 23	18 40	18 45		18 50		19 08	19 40	19 45	19 50
Newport (South Wales)	a			17 20	17 24	17 31		17 48			17 52	17 57	18 03		18 20	18 36	18 52	18 57		19 03		19 20	19 53	19 58	20 03
	d			17 22		17 32					17 54	17 59	18 04		18 22	18 38		18 59		19 04		19 22		20 00	20 04
Severn Tunnel Jn	d			17 39											18 39	18 56						19 40			
Caldicot	d															18 58									
Chepstow	d															19 07									
Lydney	d															19 16									
Gloucester 7	a											18 46				19 38		19 47						20 49	
Pilning	d																								
Patchway	d														18 52										
Bristol Parkway 7	a					17 59							18 31							19 31					20 31
	d																								
Filton Abbey Wood	d			17 54							18 23				18 55							19 55			
Bristol Temple Meads 10	a			18 04							18 33				19 06							20 05			
	d	17 44	18 00	18 10						18 30	18 50			19 00	19 10						20 00	20 15			
Keynsham	d	17 51		18 17											19 17										
Oldfield Park	d	17 58		18 24											19 24										
Bath Spa 7	a	18 00	18 12	18 26						18 41	19 01			19 11	19 26						20 11	20 26			

		GW	GW	GW		AW	XC	GW	AW	SW	GW	GW	GW	AW		AW
			◇1	◇			◇1	◇1	◇	1	◇1					◇
			☕					☕			☕		🛒			
Cardiff Central 7	d			20 18		20 23	20 45	20 55	21 04				22 00	22 30		23 00
Newport (South Wales)	a			20 30		20 36	20 57	21 08	21 17				22 16	22 47		23 18
	d			20 31		20 38	20 59	21 09					22 18	22 49		
Severn Tunnel Jn	d			20 48		20 56							22 35	23 06		
Caldicot	d					20 58								23 09		
Chepstow	d					21 07								23 18		
Lydney	d					21 16								23 27		
Gloucester 7	a					21 41	21 47							23 51		
Pilning	d															
Patchway	d												22 48			
Bristol Parkway 7	a							21 36								
	d															
Filton Abbey Wood	d			21 05									22 52			
Bristol Temple Meads 10	a			21 13									23 00			
	d	20 50	21 00	21 25						21 35	22 10	22 15	23 10			
Keynsham	d	20 57										22 22				
Oldfield Park	d	21 04										22 29				
Bath Spa 7	a	21 07	21 13	21 36						21 47	22 22	22 31	23 21			

Sundays
26 June to 31 July

		AW	GW	GW	GW	GW	GW	AW	GW	GW		GW	GW	AW	GW	GW	GW	AW	AW	GW		XC	XC	GW	GW
																									R
			◇1	◇1	◇1	◇1	◇	◇	◇1			◇1	◇	◇	◇1	◇1	◇		◇	◇1		◇1	◇1	◇1	◇
																							B		C
			☕	☕	☕	☕		🛒	☕			☕		🛒	☕	☕			🛒	☕		🛒	🛒	☕	🛒
Cardiff Central 7	d	23p20	07 35				08 05	08 30	08 35				09 15	09 30	09 40		10 08	10 23	10 35				10 45	10 50	11 08
Newport (South Wales)	a	23p36	07 51				08 21	08 47	08 53				09 27	09 48	09 55		10 20	10 36	10 48				10 57	11 04	11 20
	d	23p38	07 53				08 23		08 55				09 29		09 55		10 22	10 38				10 49	10 59	11 06	11 22
Severn Tunnel Jn	d	23p55					08 40						09 46				10 39	10 56							11 39
Caldicot	d	23p58																10 58							
Chepstow	d	00 07																11 07							
Lydney	d	00 16																11 16							
Gloucester 7	a	00 40																11 42					11 49		
Pilning	d																								
Patchway	d												09 59												
Bristol Parkway 7	a		08 22						09 22						10 23							11 11		11 34	
	d																					11 29			
Filton Abbey Wood	d						08 55						10 03				10 54								11 54
Bristol Temple Meads 10	a						09 05						10 13				11 03					11 40			12 04
	d			07 45	08 15	08 45	09 10			09 20		09 48	10 15			10 45	11 10			11 30					12 15
Keynsham	d						09 18			09 27							11 17								
Oldfield Park	d						09 25			09 35							11 24								
Bath Spa 7	a			07 57	08 26	08 57	09 27			09 38		09 58	10 28			10 59	11 26			11 42					12 26

B 🛒 from Newport (South Wales)

C 🛒 from Bristol Temple Meads

When events are being held at the Millenium Stadium, services are subject to alteration. Please check times before travelling.

Table 132

Sundays

26 June to 31 July

Cardiff - Gloucester, Bristol and Bath Spa

		AW	XC	GW	GW	GW		AW	AW	GW	XC	XC	GW	GW	AW	GW		XC	XC	GW	GW	AW	GW	XC	XC
															R										
		◇	◇1	◇1	◇1	◇			◇	◇1	◇1	◇1	◇1	◇		◇1		◇1	◇1	◇1	◇		◇1	◇1	◇1
			A									A							A						A
		🛒	🛒	☕	☕				🛒	☕	🛒	🛒	☕		🛒	☕		🛒	🛒	☕			☕	🛒	🛒
Cardiff Central 7	d	11 35	11 45	11 49		12 08		12 23	12 40			12 45	12 49	13 08	13 40				13 45	13 49	14 08	14 23			14 45
Newport (South Wales)	a	11 49	11 57	12 05		12 20		12 36	12 52			12 57	13 05	13 20	13 52				13 57	14 05	14 20	14 36			14 57
	d		11 59	12 06		12 22		12 38			12 53	12 59	13 06	13 22				13 53	13 59	14 06	14 23	14 38		14 48	14 59
Severn Tunnel Jn	d					12 39		12 56						13 39							14 40	14 56			
Caldicot	d							12 58														14 58			
Chepstow	d							13 07														15 07			
Lydney	d							13 16														15 16			
Gloucester 7	a		12 46					13 34				13 47							14 46			15 37			15 46
Pilning	d																								
Patchway	d					12 52																			
Bristol Parkway 7	a			12 34							13 17		13 37					14 17		14 36				15 12	
	d										13 25							14 29						15 25	
Filton Abbey Wood	d					12 57								13 54							14 56				
Bristol Temple Meads 10	a					13 05					13 36			14 04				14 40			15 05			15 35	
	d				12 30	13 10				13 30				14 15		14 30					15 10		15 30		
Keynsham	d					13 17															15 18				
Oldfield Park	d					13 24															15 25				
Bath Spa 7	a				12 41	13 26				13 41				14 26		14 41					15 27		15 41		

		GW		AW	GW	SW	GW	AW	GW	XC	XC	GW		AW	GW	GW	AW	GW	GW	AW	XC	XC		GW	GW
				R				R						R						R					
		◇1			◇1	◇1	◇		◇1	◇1	◇1	◇1			◇1	◇		◇1	◇		◇1	◇1		◇1	
		☕		🛒	☕			🛒	☕	🛒		☕		🛒	☕			☕		🛒	🛒			☕	
Cardiff Central 7	d	14 49		14 56			15 08	15 22			15 45	15 49		15 56		16 08	16 23		16 35	16 40		16 45		16 49	
Newport (South Wales)	a	15 05		15 12			15 20	15 34			15 57	16 05		16 12		16 20	16 36		16 47	16 52		16 57		17 05	
	d	15 06					15 22			15 54	15 59	16 06				16 22	16 38		16 49		16 52	16 59		17 06	
Severn Tunnel Jn	d						15 39									16 39	16 56								
Caldicot	d																16 58								
Chepstow	d																17 07								
Lydney	d																17 16								
Gloucester 7	a										16 46						17 37					17 46			
Pilning	d																								
Patchway	d						15 52																		
Bristol Parkway 7	a	15 35								16 16		16 34									17 21			17 33	
	d									16 25											17 26				
Filton Abbey Wood	d						15 55									16 55			17 20						
Bristol Temple Meads 10	a						16 04			16 36						17 06			17 29		17 36				
	d				16 00	16 04	16 15		16 30						17 00	17 15		17 30	17 40						17 44
Keynsham	d					16 11										17 22									17 51
Oldfield Park	d															17 29									17 58
Bath Spa 7	a				16 11	16 18	16 26		16 41						17 11	17 30		17 41	17 51						18 00

		GW	GW	AW	GW	AW	GW	XC		GW	XC	GW	GW	GW	AW	XC	AW	XC		GW	GW	GW	AW	XC	XC
						R				R							R								
		◇1	◇		◇1		◇1	◇1			◇1	◇1	◇	◇1		◇1		◇1		◇1	◇	◇1	◇	◇1	◇1
																								B	
		☕			☕		☕	🛒				☕		☕		🛒	🛒			☕		☕		🛒	
Cardiff Central 7	d		17 08	17 05	17 25	17 35				17 40	17 45		18 08	18 19	18 23		18 40	18 45			19 08	19 20	19 40		19 45
Newport (South Wales)	a		17 20	17 24	17 38	17 48				17 52	17 57		18 20	18 32	18 36		18 52	18 57			19 20	19 37	19 53		19 58
	d		17 22		17 39			17 49		17 54	17 59		18 22	18 33	18 38	18 49		18 59			19 22	19 38		19 53	20 00
Severn Tunnel Jn	d		17 39										18 39		18 56						19 40				
Caldicot	d														18 58										
Chepstow	d														19 07										
Lydney	d														19 16										
Gloucester 7	a										18 46				19 38			19 47							20 49
Pilning	d																								
Patchway	d												18 52												
Bristol Parkway 7	a				18 06			18 12						19 00		19 12						20 05		20 15	
	d							18 26								19 25								20 25	
Filton Abbey Wood	d		17 54							18 23			18 55								19 55				
Bristol Temple Meads 10	a		18 04					18 39		18 33			19 06			19 35					20 05			20 35	
	d	18 00	18 10				18 30			18 50		19 00	19 10							20 00	20 15				
Keynsham	d		18 17										19 17												
Oldfield Park	d		18 24										19 24												
Bath Spa 7	a	18 12	18 26				18 41			19 01		19 11	19 26							20 11	20 26				

A 🛒 from Newport (South Wales)

B 🛒 to Bristol Parkway

When events are being held at the Millenium Stadium, services are subject to alteration. Please check times before travelling.

Table 132

Cardiff - Gloucester, Bristol and Bath Spa

Sundays

26 June to 31 July

		GW	GW	GW		AW	XC	XC	GW	AW	SW	GW	GW	XC		GW	AW	XC	AW						
			◇1 ☕	◇			◇1 A 🛒	◇1	◇1 ☕	◇	1	◇1 ☕		◇1 🛒		🛒		◇1	◇						
Cardiff Central 7	d			20 18		20 23		20 45	20 50	21 04						22 00	22 30		23 00						
Newport (South Wales)	a			20 30		20 36		20 57	21 03	21 17						22 16	22 47		23 18						
	d			20 31		20 38	20 52	20 59	21 05					21 50		22 18	22 49	22 55							
Severn Tunnel Jn	d			20 48		20 56										22 35	23 06								
Caldicot	d					20 58											23 09								
Chepstow	d					21 07											23 18								
Lydney	d					21 16											23 27								
Gloucester 7	a					21 41		21 47									23 51								
Pilning	d																								
Patchway	d															22 48									
Bristol Parkway 7	a						21 12		21 33					22 12				23 22							
	d						21 25							22 16				23 29							
Filton Abbey Wood	d			21 05												22 52									
Bristol Temple Meads 10	a			21 13			21 35							22 25		23 00		23 41							
	d	20 50	21 00	21 25							21 35	22 10	22 15			23 10									
Keynsham	d	20 57											22 22												
Oldfield Park	d	21 04											22 29												
Bath Spa 7	a	21 07	21 13	21 36							21 47	22 22	22 31			23 21									

Sundays

7 August to 11 September

		AW	GW	GW	GW	AW	GW	GW	GW	GW		AW	GW	GW	XC	GW	AW	AW	AW	GW		GW	GW	XC	AW
			◇1 ☕	◇1 ☕	◇	◇ 🛒	◇1 ☕		◇1 ☕	◇		◇ 🛒	◇1 ☕	◇	🚌	◇1 ☕		🚌	◇ 🛒	◇1 ☕		R ◇ B 🛒	◇1 ☕	◇1 C 🛒	◇ 🛒
Cardiff Central 7	d	23p20	07 56		08 05	08 30	09 05			09 15		09 30		10 08		10 15	10 23		10 35			11 08	11 15	11 25	11 35
Newport (South Wales)	a	23p36	08 13		08 21	08 47	09 18			09 27		09 48		10 20		10 31	10 36		10 48			11 20	11 31	11 37	11 49
	d	23p38	08 15		08 23		09 19			09 29				10 22	10 30	10 32		10 46				11 22	11 32	11 39	
Severn Tunnel Jn	d	23p55			08 40					09 46				10 39				11 11				11 39			
Caldicot	d	23p58																11 21							
Chepstow	d	00 07																11 36							
Lydney	d	00 16																11 56							
Gloucester 7	a	00 40													11 40			12 36						12 35	
Pilning	d																								
Patchway	d									09 59															
Bristol Parkway 7	a		08 44				09 46									10 59							11 59		
	d																								
Filton Abbey Wood	d				08 55					10 03				10 54								11 54			
Bristol Temple Meads 10	a				09 05					10 13				11 03								12 04			
	d			08 45	09 10			09 20	09 48	10 15			10 30	11 10						11 30		12 15			
Keynsham	d				09 18			09 27						11 17											
Oldfield Park	d				09 25			09 35						11 24											
Bath Spa 7	a			08 57	09 27			09 38	09 58	10 28			10 41	11 26						11 42		12 26			

		GW	GW	XC	GW	AW		AW	AW	GW	GW	AW	XC	GW	AW	GW		GW	XC	GW	AW	AW	AW	GW	GW
		◇1 ☕	◇	🚌	◇1 ☕			🚌	◇ 🛒	◇1 ☕	◇	R	🚌	◇1 ☕	R 🛒	◇1 ☕		◇	🚌	◇1 ☕		🚌	R 🛒	◇1 ☕	◇1 ☕
Cardiff Central 7	d		12 08		12 15	12 23			12 40		13 08	13 13		13 15	13 40			14 08		14 15	14 23		14 56		
Newport (South Wales)	a		12 20		12 31	12 36			12 52		13 20	13 25		13 31	13 52			14 20		14 31	14 36		15 12		
	d		12 22	12 30	12 32			12 46			13 22		13 30	13 32				14 23	14 30	14 32		14 46			
Severn Tunnel Jn	d		12 39					13 11			13 39							14 40				15 11			
Caldicot	d							13 21														15 21			
Chepstow	d							13 36														15 36			
Lydney	d							13 56														15 56			
Gloucester 7	a			13 40				14 36					14 40						15 40			16 36			
Pilning	d																								
Patchway	d		12 52																						
Bristol Parkway 7	a				12 59									13 59						14 59					
	d																								
Filton Abbey Wood	d		12 57								13 54							14 56							
Bristol Temple Meads 10	a		13 05								14 04							15 05							
	d	12 30	13 10							13 30	14 15					14 30		15 10						15 30	16 00
Keynsham	d		13 17															15 18							
Oldfield Park	d		13 24															15 25							
Bath Spa 7	a	12 41	13 26							13 41	14 26					14 41		15 27						15 41	16 11

A 🛒 to Bristol Parkway

B 🛒 from Bristol Temple Meads

C 🛒 from Newport (South Wales)

When events are being held at the Millenium Stadium, services are subject to alteration. Please check times before travelling.

Table 132

Sundays

7 August to 11 September

Cardiff - Gloucester, Bristol and Bath Spa

Station		SW		GW	XC	GW	AW	AW	GW	GW	GW	XC		GW	AW	AW	GW	GW	AW	GW	GW	GW		AW	XC
		◇1		◇	bus	◇1 cup	R trolley	R trolley	◇1 cup	◇1 cup	◇	bus		◇1 cup		bus	◇1 cup	◇	R trolley		◇1 cup	◇			bus
Cardiff Central 7	d			15 08		15 15	15 22	15 56			16 08			16 15	16 23			16 35	16 40			17 08		17 05	
Newport (South Wales)	a			15 20		15 31	15 34	16 12			16 20			16 31	16 36			16 47	16 52			17 20		17 24	
	d			15 22	15 30	15 32					16 22	16 30		16 32		16 46		16 49				17 22			17 30
Severn Tunnel Jn	d			15 39							16 39					17 11						17 39			
Caldicot	d															17 21									
Chepstow	d															17 36									
Lydney	d															17 56									
Gloucester 7	a				16 40							17 40				18 36									18 40
Pilning	d																								
Patchway	d			15 52																					
Bristol Parkway 7	a					15 59								16 59											
	d																								
Filton Abbey Wood	d			15 55							16 55							17 20				17 54			
Bristol Temple Meads 10	a			16 04							17 06							17 29				18 04			
	d	16 04		16 15					16 30	17 00	17 15						17 30	17 40		17 44	18 00	18 10			
Keynsham	d	16 11									17 22									17 51		18 17			
Oldfield Park	d										17 29									17 58		18 24			
Bath Spa 7	a	16 18		16 26					16 41	17 11	17 30						17 41	17 51		18 00	18 12	18 26			

Station		GW	AW	GW	GW	GW	GW	GW		XC	AW	AW	AW	GW	GW	GW	XC	AW		GW	XC	GW	GW	GW	AW
		◇1 cup	R	◇1 cup	R	◇1 cup	◇1 cup	◇		bus		bus	R trolley	◇1 cup	◇1 cup	◇	bus	◇		◇1 cup	bus		◇1 cup	◇	
Cardiff Central 7	d	17 15	17 35		17 40	17 50		18 08			18 23		18 40	18 50		19 08		19 40		19 50				20 18	20 23
Newport (South Wales)	a	17 31	17 48		17 52	18 03		18 20			18 36		18 52	19 03		19 20		19 53		20 03				20 30	20 36
	d	17 32			17 54	18 04		18 22		18 30		18 46		19 04		19 22	19 30			20 04	20 30			20 31	
Severn Tunnel Jn	d							18 39				19 11				19 40								20 48	
Caldicot	d											19 21													
Chepstow	d											19 36													
Lydney	d											19 56													
Gloucester 7	a									19 40		20 36					20 40				21 40				
Pilning	d																								
Patchway	d							18 52																	
Bristol Parkway 7	a	17 59				18 31								19 31						20 31					
	d																								
Filton Abbey Wood	d				18 23			18 55								19 55								21 05	
Bristol Temple Meads 10	a				18 33			19 06								20 05								21 13	
	d			18 30	18 50		19 00	19 10							20 00	20 15						20 50	21 00	21 25	
Keynsham	d							19 17														20 57			
Oldfield Park	d							19 24														21 04			
Bath Spa 7	a			18 41	19 01		19 11	19 26							20 11	20 26						21 07	21 13	21 36	

Station		AW	GW	AW		SW	GW	GW	GW	AW	AW	AW
		bus	◇1 cup	◇		1	◇1 cup		trolley		bus	◇
Cardiff Central 7	d		20 55	21 04					22 00	22 30		23 00
Newport (South Wales)	a		21 08	21 17					22 16	22 47		23 18
	d	20 46	21 09						22 18		22 57	
Severn Tunnel Jn	d	21 11							22 35		23 22	
Caldicot	d	21 21									23 32	
Chepstow	d	21 36									23 47	
Lydney	d	21 56									00 07	
Gloucester 7	a	22 36									00 47	
Pilning	d											
Patchway	d								22 48			
Bristol Parkway 7	a		21 36									
	d											
Filton Abbey Wood	d								22 52			
Bristol Temple Meads 10	a								23 00			
	d					21 35	22 10	22 15	23 10			
Keynsham	d							22 22				
Oldfield Park	d							22 29				
Bath Spa 7	a					21 47	22 22	22 31	23 21			

When events are being held at the Millenium Stadium, services are subject to alteration. Please check times before travelling.

Table 132

Sundays

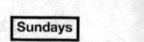

18 September to 23 October

Cardiff - Gloucester, Bristol and Bath Spa

		AW	GW	GW	GW	AW	GW	GW	GW	GW		AW	GW	AW	GW	GW	GW	GW	AW	GW		GW	GW	AW	GW
		🚌	◇1 ☕	◇1 ☕	1 ☕	◇ 🛒	◇1 ☕	◇1 ☕	◇			◇ 🛒	◇1 ☕		◇1 ☕	◇	◇1 ☕		◇ 🛒	◇		◇1 ☕	◇1 ☕	◇ 🛒	
Cardiff Central 7	d			07 55		08 30		08 52		09 20		09 30		10 12	10 15			10 30	10 35			11 15		11 35	11 40
Newport (South Wales)	a			08 13		08 47		09 05		09 33		09 48		10 25	10 31			10 43	10 49			11 31		11 49	11 53
	d	23p50		08 13				09 06		09 35				10 27	10 32			10 45				11 32			11 55
Severn Tunnel Jn	d	00 15						09 25		09 52				10 45				11 03							12 13
Caldicot	d	00 25												10 47											
Chepstow	d	00 40												10 56											
Lydney	d	01 00												11 19											
Gloucester 7	a	01 40												12 20											
Pilning	d																								
Patchway	d									10 05								11 16							
Bristol Parkway 7	a			08 44				09 36		10 08					10 59			11 19				11 59			12 29
	d																								
Filton Abbey Wood	d																								
Bristol Temple Meads 10	a																								
	d		07 45		08 20		08 45		09 15				09 48			10 17	10 30			11 10			11 30		
Keynsham	d								09 22											11 17					
Oldfield Park	d								09 29											11 24					
Bath Spa 7	a		07 57		08 31		08 57		09 31				09 58			10 29	10 41			11 26			11 42		

		GW	GW	AW	GW	GW		AW	AW	GW	GW	GW	GW	AW	XC	GW		GW	GW	AW	GW	GW	XC	AW	GW
		◇1 ☕	R		◇1 ☕			◇ 🛒	R	◇	◇1 ☕	◇1 ☕		R 🛒	◇1 A 🛒			◇1 ☕	◇		◇1 ☕		◇1 A 🛒	R 🛒	◇
Cardiff Central 7	d	12 15		12 23		12 30		12 40	13 13		13 15		13 35	13 40	13 45			14 15		14 23		14 31	14 45	14 56	
Newport (South Wales)	a	12 31		12 36		12 43		12 52	13 25		13 31		13 48	13 52	13 57			14 31		14 36		14 44	14 57	15 12	
	d	12 32		12 38		12 45					13 32		13 50		13 59			14 32		14 38		14 46	14 59		
Severn Tunnel Jn	d			12 56		13 03							14 08							14 56		15 04			
Caldicot	d			12 58																14 58					
Chepstow	d			13 07																15 07					
Lydney	d			13 25																15 16					
Gloucester 7	a			14 28											14 47					15 37			15 46		
Pilning	d																								
Patchway	d					13 16																			
Bristol Parkway 7	a	12 59				13 19					13 59		14 22					14 59				15 18			
	d																								
Filton Abbey Wood	d																								
Bristol Temple Meads 10	a																								
	d		12 15		12 30					13 14		13 30				13 55			14 15		14 30				15 10
Keynsham	d									13 21						14 02									15 18
Oldfield Park	d									13 28						14 09									15 25
Bath Spa 7	a		12 26		12 41					13 30		13 41				14 12			14 26		14 41				15 27

		GW		AW	GW	GW	XC	AW	GW	SW	GW	GW		AW	GW	GW	AW	XC	GW	GW	GW	GW		GW	AW
		◇1 ☕		R 🛒		◇1 ☕	◇1 🛒	R 🛒	◇1 ☕	◇1	◇1 ☕	◇				◇1 ☕	R 🛒	◇1	◇1 ☕	◇1 ☕	◇			◇1 ☕	R
Cardiff Central 7	d	15 15		15 22	15 29			15 56			16 15			16 23	16 30		16 40	16 45		17 15		17 26			17 35
Newport (South Wales)	a	15 31		15 34	15 43			16 12			16 31			16 36	16 43		16 52	16 57		17 31		17 39			17 48
	d	15 32			15 44		15 59				16 32			16 38	16 45			16 59		17 32		17 41			
Severn Tunnel Jn	d				16 02									16 56	17 03							17 59			
Caldicot	d													16 58											
Chepstow	d													17 07											
Lydney	d													17 16											
Gloucester 7	a						16 46							17 37				17 46							
Pilning	d																								
Patchway	d				16 15																				
Bristol Parkway 7	a	15 59			16 18						16 59				17 17					17 59		18 13			
	d																								
Filton Abbey Wood	d																								
Bristol Temple Meads 10	a																								
	d					15 30			16 00	16 04		16 15				16 30			17 00		17 15			17 30	
Keynsham	d									16 11											17 22				
Oldfield Park	d																				17 29				
Bath Spa 7	a					15 41			16 11	16 18		16 26				16 41			17 11		17 30			17 41	

A 🛒 from Newport (South Wales)

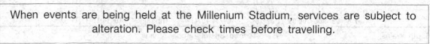

When events are being held at the Millenium Stadium, services are subject to alteration. Please check times before travelling.

Table 132

Sundays

18 September to 23 October

Cardiff - Gloucester, Bristol and Bath Spa

		GW	GW	XC	GW	GW	GW	AW		GW	GW	AW	XC	GW	GW	GW	GW	GW		AW	XC	GW	GW	GW	AW
		◇		◇1	◇1 ☕	◇1 ☕	◇			◇1 ☕		R 🛒	◇1	◇1 ☕	R	◇1 ☕	◇			◇	◇1	◇1 ☕	◇1 ☕	◇	
Cardiff Central 7	d			17 45	17 50			18 23			18 30	18 40	18 45	18 50				19 35		19 40	19 45	19 50			20 23
Newport (South Wales)	a			17 57	18 03			18 36			18 43	18 52	18 57	19 03				19 48		19 53	19 58	20 03			20 36
	d			17 59	18 04			18 38			18 45		18 59	19 04				19 50			20 00	20 04			20 38
Severn Tunnel Jn	d							18 56			19 03							20 08							20 56
Caldicot	d							18 58																	20 58
Chepstow	d							19 07																	21 07
Lydney	d							19 16																	21 16
Gloucester 7	a			18 46				19 38					19 47								20 49				21 41
Pilning	d																								
Patchway	d										19 16														
Bristol Parkway 7	a				18 31						19 19			19 31				20 22				20 31			
	d																								
Filton Abbey Wood	d																								
Bristol Temple Meads 10	a																								
	d	17 40	17 44			18 00	18 10			18 30					18 50	19 00	19 10						20 00	20 15	
Keynsham	d		17 51				18 17										19 17								
Oldfield Park	d		17 58				18 24										19 24								
Bath Spa 7	a	17 51	18 00			18 12	18 26			18 41					19 01	19 11	19 26						20 11	20 26	

		GW	XC	GW		GW	GW	AW	GW	SW	GW	GW	GW	AW		AW	GW
			◇1			◇1 ☕	◇1 ☕	◇	◇	1		◇1 ☕				◇	🛒
Cardiff Central 7	d	20 35	20 45			20 55		21 04			22 00			22 30		23 00	
Newport (South Wales)	a	20 48	20 57			21 08		21 17			22 17			22 47		23 18	
	d	20 50	20 59			21 09					22 19			22 49			
Severn Tunnel Jn	d	21 08									22 42			23 06			
Caldicot	d													23 09			
Chepstow	d													23 18			
Lydney	d													23 27			
Gloucester 7	a		21 47											23 51			
Pilning	d																
Patchway	d										22 55						
Bristol Parkway 7	a	21 22				21 36					22 58						
	d																
Filton Abbey Wood	d																
Bristol Temple Meads 10	a																
	d			20 50			21 00		21 25	21 35		22 10	22 15				23 38
Keynsham	d			20 57									22 22				
Oldfield Park	d			21 04									22 29				
Bath Spa 7	a			21 07			21 13		21 36	21 47		22 22	22 31				23 49

Sundays

from 30 October

		AW	GW	GW	GW	GW	GW	AW	GW	GW		GW	AW	GW	GW	GW	AW	AW	XC	GW		GW	GW	AW	XC
		🚌	◇1 ☕	1 ☕	1	◇1 ☕	◇	◇ 🛒	1 ☕	◇1 ☕		◇	◇ 🛒	1 ☕	◇1 ☕	◇		◇ 🛒	◇1 A 🛒	1 ☕		◇1 ☕	R ◇ B 🛒	◇ 🛒	◇1 A 🛒
Cardiff Central 7	d					07 45	08 05	08 30		08 55		09 15	09 30		09 50	10 08	10 23	10 35	10 45			10 50	11 08	11 35	11 45
Newport (South Wales)	a					08 01	08 21	08 47		09 09		09 27	09 48		10 05	10 20	10 36	10 49	10 57			11 05	11 20	11 49	11 57
	d	23p50				08 03	08 23			09 10		09 29			10 05	10 22	10 38		10 59			11 05	11 22		11 59
Severn Tunnel Jn	d	00 15					08 40					09 46				10 39	10 56						11 39		
Caldicot	d	00 25															10 58								
Chepstow	d	00 40															11 07								
Lydney	d	01 00															11 16								
Gloucester 7	a	01 40															11 42		11 49						12 46
Pilning	d																								
Patchway	d											09 59													
Bristol Parkway 7	a					08 34				09 34					10 34							11 34			
	d					08 40				09 40					10 40							11 40			
Filton Abbey Wood	d						08 55					10 03				10 54							11 54		
Bristol Temple Meads 10	a					08 52	09 05			09 52		10 13			10 52	11 03						11 52	12 04		
	d		07 40	07 55	08 45	09 00	09 09		09 23	10 00		10 15		10 23	11 00	11 10				11 30		12 00	12 15		
Keynsham	d						09 17									11 17									
Oldfield Park	d						09 24									11 24									
Bath Spa 7	a		07 51	08 06	09 00	09 11	09 26		09 34	10 11		10 28		10 34	11 11	11 26				11 41		12 11	12 26		

A 🛒 from Newport (South Wales)

B 🛒 from Bristol Temple Meads

When events are being held at the Millenium Stadium, services are subject to alteration. Please check times before travelling.

Table 132

Sundays

from 30 October

Cardiff - Gloucester, Bristol and Bath Spa

		GW	GW	GW	AW	AW		XC	GW	GW	GW	GW	AW	AW	XC	GW		GW	GW	AW	XC	GW	GW	GW	AW
													[R]	[R]											[R]
		[1]	◇[1]	◇		◇		◇[1]	[1]	◇[1]		◇			◇[1]	[1]		◇[1]	◇		◇[1]	◇[1]	[1]	◇[1]	
								A							A						A				
		⊡	⊡			🛒		🛒	⊡	⊡				🛒	🛒	⊡		⊡			🛒	⊡	⊡	⊡	🛒
Cardiff Central [7]	d		11 50	12 08	12 23	12 40		12 45		12 50		13 08	13 13	13 40	13 45			13 50	14 08	14 23	14 45			14 50	14 56
Newport (South Wales)	a		12 05	12 20	12 36	12 52		12 57		13 05		13 20	13 25	13 52	13 57			14 05	14 20	14 36	14 57			15 05	15 12
	d		12 05	12 22	12 38			12 59		13 05		13 22			13 59			14 05	14 23	14 38	14 59			15 05	
Severn Tunnel Jn	d			12 39	12 56							13 39							14 40	14 56					
Caldicot	d				12 58															14 58					
Chepstow	d				13 07															15 07					
Lydney	d				13 16															15 16					
Gloucester [7]	a				13 34			13 47							14 46					15 37	15 46				
Pilning	d																								
Patchway	d			12 52																					
Bristol Parkway [7]	a		12 34							13 34								14 34						15 34	
	d		12 40							13 40								14 40						15 40	
Filton Abbey Wood	d			12 57								13 54							14 56						
Bristol Temple Meads [10]	a		12 52	13 05						13 52		14 04						14 52	15 05					15 52	
	d	12 25	13 00	13 10					13 30	14 00	14 04	14 15				14 30		15 00	15 10			15 35	15 40	16 00	
Keynsham	d			13 17							14 11								15 18						
Oldfield Park	d			13 24							14 18								15 25						
Bath Spa [7]	a	12 37	13 11	13 26					13 41	14 11	14 21	14 26				14 41		15 11	15 27			15 46	15 52	16 11	

		SW		GW	AW	XC	GW	GW	GW	AW	GW	AW		GW	GW	GW	AW	XC	GW	GW	GW	AW		GW	GW
					[R]					[R]							[R]					[R]			
		◇[1]		◇		◇[1]	[1]	◇[1]	◇[1]		◇			◇[1]	[1]	◇		◇[1]		◇[1]	◇			◇[1]	[1]
					🛒		⊡	⊡	⊡	🛒				⊡	⊡		🛒			⊡				⊡	⊡
Cardiff Central [7]	d			15 08	15 22	15 45			15 50	15 56	16 08	16 23				16 35	16 40	16 45		16 55	17 08	17 35			
Newport (South Wales)	a			15 20	15 34	15 57			16 05	16 12	16 20	16 36				16 47	16 52	16 57		17 10	17 20	17 48			
	d			15 22		15 59			16 05		16 22	16 38				16 49		16 59		17 10	17 22				
Severn Tunnel Jn	d			15 39							16 39	16 56									17 39				
Caldicot	d											16 58													
Chepstow	d											17 07													
Lydney	d											17 16													
Gloucester [7]	a					16 46						17 37						17 46							
Pilning	d																								
Patchway	d			15 52																					
Bristol Parkway [7]	a								16 34											17 40					
	d								16 40											17 40					
Filton Abbey Wood	d			15 55							16 55					17 20					17 54				
Bristol Temple Meads [10]	a			16 04							17 06					17 29					18 04				
	d	16 04		16 15			16 30	16 35			17 15			17 30	17 35	17 40			17 44		18 10			18 30	18 35
Keynsham	d	16 11									17 22								17 51		18 17				
Oldfield Park	d										17 29								17 58		18 24				
Bath Spa [7]	a	16 18		16 26			16 41	16 47	17 03		17 30			17 41	17 47	17 51			18 00	18 11	18 26			18 41	18 47

		GW	XC	GW	GW	AW	AW	XC		GW	GW	GW	AW	XC	GW	GW	GW	GW		AW	XC	SW	GW	AW	GW
		[R]					[R]																		
			◇[1]	◇[1]	◇			◇[1]		[1]	◇[1]	◇	◇	◇[1]	[1]		◇[1]	◇			◇[1]	[1]	◇[1]	◇	[1]
				⊡			🛒			⊡	⊡				⊡		⊡						⊡		⊡
Cardiff Central [7]	d	17 40	17 45	17 50	18 08	18 23	18 40	18 45			18 52	19 08	19 40	19 45			19 52	20 18		20 23	20 45		20 55	21 04	
Newport (South Wales)	a	17 52	17 57	18 05	18 20	18 36	18 52	18 57			19 05	19 20	19 53	19 58			20 05	20 30		20 36	20 57		21 08	21 17	
	d	17 54	17 59	18 05	18 22	18 38		18 59			19 06	19 22		20 00			20 06	20 31		20 38	20 59		21 09		
Severn Tunnel Jn	d				18 39	18 56						19 40						20 48		20 56					
Caldicot	d					18 58														20 58					
Chepstow	d					19 07														21 07					
Lydney	d					19 16														21 16					
Gloucester [7]	a		18 46			19 38		19 47						20 49						21 41	21 47				
Pilning	d																								
Patchway	d				18 52																				
Bristol Parkway [7]	a			18 34							19 34						20 34						21 37		
	d			18 40							19 41						20 40						21 44		
Filton Abbey Wood	d	18 23			18 55							19 55						21 05							
Bristol Temple Meads [10]	a	18 33		18 52	19 06						19 52	20 05					20 52	21 13					21 55		
	d	18 50		19 00	19 10					19 35	20 05	20 15			20 45	20 50	21 05	21 25				21 35	22 10		22 15
Keynsham	d				19 17											20 57									
Oldfield Park	d				19 24											21 04									
Bath Spa [7]	a	19 01		19 11	19 26					19 47	20 16	20 26			20 56	21 07	21 16	21 36				21 47	22 21		22 26

		GW	GW	AW		AW
						◇
			🛒			
Cardiff Central [7]	d		22 00	22 30		23 00
Newport (South Wales)	a		22 16	22 47		23 18
	d		22 18	22 49		
Severn Tunnel Jn	d		22 35	23 06		
Caldicot	d			23 09		
Chepstow	d			23 18		
Lydney	d			23 27		
Gloucester [7]	a			23 51		
Pilning	d					
Patchway	d		22 48			
Bristol Parkway [7]	a					
	d					
Filton Abbey Wood	d		22 52			
Bristol Temple Meads [10]	a		23 00			
	d	22 20	23 10			
Keynsham	d	22 27				
Oldfield Park	d	22 34				
Bath Spa [7]	a	22 36	23 21			

A 🛒 from Newport (South Wales)

When events are being held at the Millenium Stadium, services are subject to alteration. Please check times before travelling.

Table 132

Mondays to Fridays

until 1 July

Bath Spa, Bristol and Gloucester - Cardiff

Miles	Miles	Miles			GW	AW		AW		AW		GW	AW			GW		XC	XC	AW	GW	AW	GW		XC
					MO	MX		MO		MX		MX	MX			MX		MX	MO						
					◇1	◇		◇				◇1	◇			◇1		1	1	◇					◇1
					A																				C
					☕							☕				☕									🛒
0	—	—	**Bath Spa 7**	d												01 15									06 09
1	—	—	Oldfield Park	d																					
7	—	—	Keynsham	d																					
11½	—	—	**Bristol Temple Meads 10**	a												01 29									06 20
—	—	—		d												01 36		05 19	05 19		05 54		06 19		06 27
16	—	—	Filton Abbey Wood	d																	06 01		06 31		
—	0	—	**Bristol Parkway 7**	a														05 28	05 28						06 37
—	—	—		d	23p17							00 24						05 38	05 38						
17½	—	—	Patchway	d																	06 06		06 35		
21	4¾	—	Pilning	d																					
—	—	0	**Gloucester 7**	d						23p13												05 50			
—	—	19½	Lydney	d						23p33												06 09			
—	—	27¼	Chepstow	d						23p42												06 19			
—	—	34	Caldicot	d						23p51												06 26			
28	11¾	34¾	Severn Tunnel Jn	d						23p54											06 17	06 29	06 47		
38	21¾	44¾	Newport (South Wales)	a	23p44					00 05		00 52				02s10		05 58	06 08		06 28	06 41	06 58		
—	—	—		d	23p45	23p47		23p55		00 07		00 54	00 59					06 00	06 10	06 17	06 29	06 44	07 00		
49¾	33½	56½	**Cardiff Central 7**	a	00 06	00 02		00 20		00 29		01 12	01 18			02 31		06 18	06 24	06 33	06 48	07 00	07 20		

		XC	GW	AW	GW	XC	AW	GW	GW		GW	SW	GW	GW	GW	AW	AW	AW	GW		GW	XC	GW	GW	GW
																								R	
		◇1		◇	◇1	◇1	◇					1	◇1		◇1	◇		◇			◇1	◇1			◇1
																						D			
				🛒	☕								☕		☕	🛒		🛒			☕	🛒		🛒	☕
Bath Spa 7	d		06 28		06 54				07 07		07 25	07 35		07 48	07 59								08 07	08 21	08 29
Oldfield Park	d		06 31						07 10		07 28	07 38		07 51									08 10	08 23	
Keynsham	d		06 38						07 17		07 35	07 45		07 58	08 08								08 17	08 33	
Bristol Temple Meads 10	a		06 45		07 07				07 27		07 45	07 52		08 06	08 17								08 29	08 39	08 44
	d		06 50		07 14			07 19	07 34		07 54			08 10					08 21				08 41	08 54	
Filton Abbey Wood	d		07 02		07 22			07 30	07 43		08 00			08 22					08 30				08 48	09 01	
Bristol Parkway 7	a							07 33	07 47					08 29									08 52		
	d							07 40	07 48				08 07								08 40		08 52		
Patchway	d							07 44			08 05								08 35						
Pilning	d																								
Gloucester 7	d	06 18				07 01			08a29								07 58					08 28	09a33		
Lydney	d	06 37				07 20											08 17								
Chepstow	d	06 46				07 29											08 27					08 54			
Caldicot	d	06 55				07 38											08 35								
Severn Tunnel Jn	d	06 58	07 14			07 41		07 56									08 38		08 46						
Newport (South Wales)	a	07 09	07 25		07 44	07 52		08 07			08 27		08 32				08 50		09 02		09 07	09 12		09 25	
	d	07 10	07 27	07 35	07 44	07 53	08 01	08 09			08 27		08 32			08 38	08 52	09 03	09 03		09 08	09 14		09 25	
Cardiff Central 7	a	07 26	07 44	07 49	08 00	08 08	08 17	08 24			08 46		08 46			08 53	09 07	09 18	09 24		09 24	09 30		09 43	

		GW	GW	GW	AW		AW	AW	GW	GW	XC	GW	GW	AW	GW		GW	GW	AW	GW	GW	XC	GW	GW	AW
							BHX																		
		◇1		◇1	◇		◇			◇1	◇1		◇1	◇	◇		◇1	◇1	◇		◇1	◇1	◇	◇1	◇
		E		F							D											G			
		Ø		Ø	🛒		⊠			☕	🛒		☕	🛒	🛒		☕	☕	🛒		☕	🛒		☕	🛒
Bath Spa 7	d		08 47	08 57								09 15	09 29		09 36		10 00						10 07	10 24	
Oldfield Park	d		08 49									09 17											10 10		
Keynsham	d		08 57									09 25			09 44								10 17		
Bristol Temple Meads 10	a		09 05	09 10								09 35	09 43		09 50		10 15						10 29	10 38	
	d		09 10						09 21			09 41			09 55					10 21			10 41		
Filton Abbey Wood	d		09 22						09 30			09 48			10 00					10 30			10 48		
Bristol Parkway 7	a		09 28									09 52											10 52		
	d	09 07								09 40		09 52						10 07			10 40		10 52		
Patchway	d								09 35											10 35					
Pilning	d																								
Gloucester 7	d							08 58			09 24	10a33										10 24	11a34		
Lydney	d							09 17														10 43			
Chepstow	d							09 27			09 50														
Caldicot	d							09 36																	
Severn Tunnel Jn	d							09 38	09 46											10 46					
Newport (South Wales)	a	09 31						09 51	09 58	10 04	10 09				10 26			10 31		11 02	11 06	11 11			
	d	09 32			09 37		09 41	09 52	10 00	10 04	10 10			10 22	10 26			10 31	11 01	11 02	11 06	11 12			11 22
Cardiff Central 7	a	09 48			09 57		09 58	10 07	10 18	10 21	10 25			10 37	10 43			10 46	11 15	11 23	11 23	11 27			11 37

A Until 20 June
C 🛒 from Bristol Temple Meads
D 🛒 to Chepstow
E The St. David
F The Merchant Venturer
G 🛒 to Lydney

When events are being held at the Millenium Stadium, services are subject to alteration. Please check times before travelling.

Table 132

Mondays to Fridays

until 1 July

Bath Spa, Bristol and Gloucester - Cardiff

		GW	GW	GW	AW	AW	GW	GW	XC	GW	GW	AW	GW	SW	GW	GW	AW	GW	AW	GW	XC	GW
		◇	◇1	◇1		R	◇	◇1	◇1		◇1	◇	◇	◇1	◇1	◇1			◇	◇1	◇1	◇
									A		B										A	
		🛒	☕	Ø		🛒		☕	🛒		☕	🛒	🛒		☕	Ø			🛒	☕	🛒	
Bath Spa 7	d	10 36	11 00							11 08	11 24		11 36	11 47	12 00							12 08
Oldfield Park	d									11 09												12 10
Keynsham	d									11 16				11 55								12 17
Bristol Temple Meads 10	a	10 48	11 15							11 28	11 40		11 48	12 05	12 15							12 29
	d	10 54					11 21			11 41			11 54					12 21				12 41
Filton Abbey Wood	d	11 00					11 30			11 48			12 00					12 30				12 48
Bristol Parkway 7	a									11 52												12 52
	d			11 07				11 40		11 52						12 07				12 40		12 52
Patchway	d						11 35											12 35				
Pilning	d																					
Gloucester 7	d				10 58				11 24	12a33							11 58				12 24	13a31
Lydney	d				11 17												12 17					
Chepstow	d				11 27				11 50								12 27				12 50	
Caldicot	d				11 35												12 35					
Severn Tunnel Jn.	d				11 38		11 46										12 38	12 46				
Newport (South Wales)	a	11 26		11 31	11 50		11 58	12 04	12 10				12 25			12 31	12 50	13 00		13 06	13 11	
	d	11 27		11 31	11 51	11 53	12 00	12 04	12 11			12 23	12 26			12 32	12 52	13 01	13 00	13 06	13 12	
Cardiff Central 7	a	11 43		11 46	12 10	12 08	12 18	12 21	12 28			12 38	12 43			12 46	13 07	13 22	13 22	13 22	13 29	

		GW	AW	GW	GW	GW	GW	GW	XC	GW	GW	AW	GW	GW	GW	AW	AW	GW	GW	XC	GW	GW	GW
		◇1	◇	◇	◇1	◇1		◇1	◇1		◇1	◇	◇	◇1	◇1		R		◇1	◇1	◇	◇1	◇
									C											A			
		☕	🛒	🛒	☕	Ø		☕	🛒		☕	🛒	🛒	☕	Ø		🛒		☕	🛒		☕	🛒
Bath Spa 7	d	12 24		12 36	13 00					13 19	13 24		13 36	14 00							14 15	14 24	14 36
Oldfield Park	d									13 21											14 18		
Keynsham	d									13 28											14 25		
Bristol Temple Meads 10	a	12 39		12 48	13 15					13 36	13 41		13 48	14 15							14 35	14 39	14 48
	d			12 54			13 21			13 41			13 54					14 21			14 41		14 54
Filton Abbey Wood	d			13 00			13 30			13 48			14 00					14 30			14 48		15 00
Bristol Parkway 7	a									13 52											14 51		
	d					13 07		13 40		13 52					14 07				14 40		14 52		
Patchway	d						13 35											14 35					
Pilning	d																						
Gloucester 7	d								13 24	14a33						13 58				14 24	15a32		
Lydney	d								13 43							14 17							
Chepstow	d															14 27				14 50			
Caldicot	d															14 35							
Severn Tunnel Jn.	d						13 46									14 38		14 46					
Newport (South Wales)	a			13 26		13 31	13 58	14 04	14 09				14 26		14 30	14 50		15 02	15 04	15 11			15 25
	d		13 23	13 26		13 31	14 00	14 04	14 10			14 22	14 27		14 31	14 52	15 00	15 03	15 04	15 12			15 26
Cardiff Central 7	a		13 39	13 43		13 46	14 18	14 22	14 27			14 37	14 43		14 46	15 07	15 21	15 24	15 22	15 29			15 43

		SW	GW	GW	AW	AW	GW	GW	GW	XC	GW	GW	GW	GW	AW	AW	GW	GW	XC	GW	GW	AW
					R										R							R
		◇1	◇1	◇1			◇	◇1		◇1	◇1	◇	◇1	◇1		◇		◇1	◇1		◇1	
										A									A			
			☕	☕	🛒			☕		🛒	☕	🛒	☕	☕	🛒	🛒		☕	🛒		☕	🛒
Bath Spa 7	d	14 47	15 00						15 07		15 24	15 36	16 00							16 07	16 24	
Oldfield Park	d								15 10											16 10		
Keynsham	d	14 55							15 17											16 17		
Bristol Temple Meads 10	a	15 05	15 15						15 29		15 40	15 48	16 15							16 29	16 39	
	d						15 21		15 34			15 54					16 24			16 41		
Filton Abbey Wood	d						15 30					16 00					16 30			16 48		
Bristol Parkway 7	a								15 48											16 52		
	d			15 07				15 40						16 07				16 40		16 52		
Patchway	d						15 35										16 35					
Pilning	d																					
Gloucester 7	d					14 58				15 24									16 24	17a33		
Lydney	d					15 17													16 43			
Chepstow	d					15 27				15 50									16 52			
Caldicot	d					15 35																
Severn Tunnel Jn.	d					15 38	15 46										16 46					
Newport (South Wales)	a			15 31		15 50	15 58	16 05		16 10		16 25		16 30			17 00	17 06	17 11			
	d			15 32	15 37	15 52	16 00	16 06		16 12		16 25		16 31	16 40	17 01	17 01	17 06	17 12			17 22
Cardiff Central 7	a			15 46	15 53	16 10	16 18	16 24		16 29		16 43		16 46	16 55	17 15	17 25	17 22	17 28			17 36

A 🛒 to Chepstow

B The Torbay Express

C 🛒 to Lydney

When events are being held at the Millenium Stadium, services are subject to alteration. Please check times before travelling.

Bath Spa, Bristol and Gloucester - Cardiff

		GW	GW	GW	AW	GW	GW	XC	GW		GW	GW	GW	GW	AW	AW	AW	GW	GW		XC	GW	GW	AW	GW
		[R] [trolley]	◇[1] [buffet]	◇[1] [buffet]			◇[1] [buffet]	◇[1]			◇[1] [buffet]	[R] [trolley]	◇[1] [buffet]	◇[1] A [buffet]	[R] [trolley]		◇ [trolley]		◇[1] [buffet]		◇[1]		◇[1] [buffet]	[R] [trolley]	[R] [trolley]
Bath Spa [7]	d	16 36	17 00						17 07		17 27	17 36	18 00									18 07	18 29		18 36
Oldfield Park	d								17 10													18 10			
Keynsham	d								17 17													18 17			
Bristol Temple Meads [10]	a	16 48	17 15						17 29		17 41	17 48	18 14									18 28	18 44		18 49
	d	16 54				17 21			17 41			17 54						18 21				18 41			18 54
Filton Abbey Wood	d	17 00				17 30			17 48			18 00						18 30				18 48			19 00
Bristol Parkway [7]	a								17 52													18 52			
	d			17 07			17 40		17 52					18 07					18 40			18 52			
Patchway	d					17 35												18 35							
Pilning	d																								
Gloucester [7]	d				16 58			17 27	18a33							17 59					18 31	19a30			
Lydney	d				17 17											18 18									
Chepstow	d				17 27											18 28									
Caldicot	d				17 35											18 36									
Severn Tunnel Jn.	d	17 14			17 38	17 46						18 14				18 39		18 50							19 14
Newport (South Wales)	a	17 25		17 31	17 50	17 58	18 04	18 10				18 25		18 30		18 51		19 06	19 11		19 16				19 26
	d	17 27		17 31	17 52	18 00	18 04	18 11				18 26		18 31	18 41	18 53	19 01	19 06	19 11		19 17			19 22	19 26
Cardiff Central [7]	a	17 43		17 46	18 10	18 17	18 19	18 27				18 43		18 48	18 55	19 09	19 21	19 24	19 26		19 33			19 42	19 46

		GW	GW	AW	GW		GW	XC	GW	GW	GW	GW	GW	GW	GW		AW	AW	GW	GW	GW	XC	AW	GW	GW
												FX	FO	FX	FO		FX	FO	FX						
		◇[1] [buffet]	◇[1] B [buffet]				◇[1] [buffet]	◇[1]		◇[1] [buffet]	◇[1] C [buffet]	◇ [trolley]	◇ [trolley]	◇[1] [buffet]	◇[1] [buffet]		[R] [trolley]	[R] [trolley]			◇[1] [buffet]	◇[1]		◇ [trolley]	◇[1] [buffet]
Bath Spa [7]	d	18 59							19 07	19 24	19 30	19 36	19 36							19 47	19 59			20 11	20 30
Oldfield Park	d								19 10											19 50				20 13	
Keynsham	d								19 17											19 58				20 20	
Bristol Temple Meads [10]	a	19 12							19 29	19 41	19 43	19 49	19 49							20 08	20 13			20 29	20 44
	d				19 21				19 41				19 54						20 04			20 15			
Filton Abbey Wood	d				19 30				19 48				20 00						20 11			20 22			
Bristol Parkway [7]	a								19 52																
	d		19 07				19 40		19 52					20 07	20 07										
Patchway	d				19 35																	20 25			
Pilning	d																								
Gloucester [7]	d			18 58				19 28	20a32														19 58		
Lydney	d			19 17																			20 17		
Chepstow	d			19 27																			20 27		
Caldicot	d			19 34																			20 36		
Severn Tunnel Jn.	d			19 37	19 46								20 16						20 26			20 37	20 39		
Newport (South Wales)	a		19 31	19 50	20 01		20 07	20 11					20 27	20 31	20 31				20 41			20 47	20 51		
	d		19 31	19 52	20 02		20 08	20 13					20 28	20 31	20 31		20 38	20 39	20 42			20 49	20 52		
Cardiff Central [7]	a		19 47	20 09	20 20		20 22	20 27					20 43	20 45	20 48		20 59	20 58	21 00			21 02	21 10		

			AW	GW	GW	XC	XC	GW	GW	AW	GW		GW	GW	GW	XC	XC	GW	GW	SW	GW		GW	AW	AW
				FX	FO	FX	FO									FO	FX	FO	FX					FO	FX
			◇ [trolley]	◇[1] [buffet]	◇[1] [buffet]	◇[1]	◇[1]	◇ [trolley]	◇[1] [buffet]	◇ [trolley]				◇[1] [buffet]	◇[1] [buffet]	◇[1]	◇[1]	◇	◇	◇[1]	◇[1] [buffet]			◇	◇
Bath Spa [7]	d							20 36	21 00				21 07	21 29				21 36	21 36	21 51	22 13		22 26		
Oldfield Park	d												21 10										22 28		
Keynsham	d												21 17							21 59			22 35		
Bristol Temple Meads [10]	a							20 51	21 15				21 29	21 44				21 49	21 49	22 06	22 30		22 44		
	d							20 55			21 19							21 54	21 54						
Filton Abbey Wood	d							21 00			21 30							22 00	22 00						
Bristol Parkway [7]	a																								
	d			20 40	20 43										21 40										
Patchway	d										21 34							22 06	22 06						
Pilning	d																								
Gloucester [7]	d					20 24	20 24									21 24	21 24								
Lydney	d															21 43	21 43								
Chepstow	d															21 52	21 52								
Caldicot	d															22 01	22 01								
Severn Tunnel Jn.	d							21 14			21 46					22 04	22 04	22 18	22 18						
Newport (South Wales)	a			21 04	21 05	21 11	21 11	21 26			21 58				22 03	22 15	22 15	22 29	22 36						
	d		20 59	21 04	21 07	21 13	21 13	21 26		21 52	21 59				22 05	22 16	22 16	22 30	22 37					22 40	22 42
Cardiff Central [7]	a		21 20	21 19	21 19	21 27	21 29	21 44		22 06	22 18				22 23	22 31	22 35	22 52	23 00					22 55	23 02

A The Capitals United

B The Red Dragon

C The Bristolian

When events are being held at the Millenium Stadium, services are subject to alteration. Please check times before travelling.

Table 132

Mondays to Fridays

until 1 July

Bath Spa, Bristol and Gloucester - Cardiff

		GW ◇1 ☕	GW ◇	GW	GW ◇1 A ☕	AW ◇	AW FX	AW FO	GW FO ◇1 ☕	GW FX ◇1 ☕
Bath Spa 7	d		22 36	23 02	23 19				23 49	23 55
Oldfield Park	d			23 05						
Keynsham	d			23 12						
Bristol Temple Meads 10	a		22 49	23 23	23 33				00 03	00 10
	d		22 54							
Filton Abbey Wood	d		23 00							
Bristol Parkway 7	a									
	d	22 45								
Patchway	d		23 06							
Pilning	d									
Gloucester 7	d						23 13	23 13		
Lydney	d						23 33	23 33		
Chepstow	d						23 42	23 42		
Caldicot	d						23 51	23 51		
Severn Tunnel Jn.	d		23 17				23 54	23 54		
Newport (South Wales)	a	23 19	23 34				00 05	00 07		
	d	23 19	23 35			23 47	00 07	00 08		
Cardiff Central 7	a	23 40	23 56			00 02	00 29	00 35		

Mondays to Fridays

4 July to 2 September

		GW MO ◇1 B ☕	AW MX ◇	GW ◇1 C ☕	AW MO ◇	GW MO ◇1 C ☕	AW MX	AW MO B 🚌	GW MX ◇1 ☕	GW MO ◇1 B ☕	GW MX ◇1 ☕	AW MX ◇	GW MX ◇1 ☕	GW MO ◇1 B ☕	XC MX 1	XC MO 1	AW ◇ D	AW E	GW	AW
Bath Spa 7	d			23p47					23p55	23p55			01 15	01 22						
Oldfield Park	d																			
Keynsham	d																			
Bristol Temple Meads 10	a			00 02					00 10	00 15			01 29	01 42						
	d												01 36		05 19	05 19			05 54	
Filton Abbey Wood	d																		06 01	
Bristol Parkway 7	a														05 28	05 28				
	d	23p17				23p37					00 24				05 38	05 38				
Patchway	d																		06 06	
Pilning	d																			
Gloucester 7	d						23p13	22p35												05 50
Lydney	d						23p33	23p15												06 09
Chepstow	d						23p42	23p35												06 19
Caldicot	d						23p51	23p50												06 26
Severn Tunnel Jn.	d						23p54	23p59											06 17	06 29
Newport (South Wales)	a	23p44				00 01	00 05	00 25			00 52		02s10		05 58	06 08			06 28	06 41
	d	23p45	23p47		23p55	00 02	00 07	00 25			00 54	00 59			06 00	06 10	06 17	06 23	06 29	06 44
Cardiff Central 7	a	00 06	00 02		00 20	00 23	00 29	00 55			01 12	01 18	02 31		06 18	06 24	06 33	06 40	06 48	07 00

		GW	XC ◇1 F 🛒	XC ◇1	GW	AW ◇ 🛒	GW ◇1 ☕	XC ◇1	AW ◇	GW	GW	GW	SW 1	GW ◇1 ☕	GW	GW ◇1 ☕	AW ◇ 🛒	AW	AW ◇ 🛒	GW	GW ◇1 ☕	XC ◇1 G 🛒	GW
Bath Spa 7	d		06 09		06 28		06 54				07 07	07 25	07 35		07 48	07 59							08 07
Oldfield Park	d				06 31						07 10	07 28	07 38		07 51								08 10
Keynsham	d				06 38						07 17	07 35	07 45		07 58	08 08							08 17
Bristol Temple Meads 10	a		06 20		06 45		07 07				07 27	07 45	07 52		08 06	08 17							08 29
	d	06 19	06 27		06 50		07 14			07 19	07 34	07 54			08 10					08 21			08 41
Filton Abbey Wood	d	06 31			07 02		07 22			07 30	07 43	08 00			08 22					08 30			08 48
Bristol Parkway 7	a		06 37							07 33	07 47				08 29								08 52
	d									07 40	07 48			08 07							08 40		08 52
Patchway	d	06 35								07 44		08 05								08 35			
Pilning	d																						
Gloucester 7	d			06 18				07 01			08a29							07 58				08 28	09a33
Lydney	d			06 37				07 20										08 17					
Chepstow	d			06 46				07 29										08 27				08 54	
Caldicot	d			06 55				07 38										08 35					
Severn Tunnel Jn.	d	06 47		06 58	07 14			07 41		07 56								08 38		08 46			
Newport (South Wales)	a	06 58		07 09	07 25		07 44	07 52		08 07		08 27		08 32				08 50		09 02	09 07	09 12	
	d	07 00		07 10	07 27	07 35	07 44	07 53	08 01	08 09		08 27		08 32			08 38	08 52	09 03	09 03	09 08	09 14	
Cardiff Central 7	a	07 20		07 26	07 44	07 49	08 00	08 08	08 17	08 24		08 46		08 46			08 53	09 07	09 18	09 24	09 24	09 30	

A not 23 May
B From 8 August until 29 August
C From 4 July until 1 August
D from 4 July until 22 July
E from 25 July until 2 September
F 🛒 from Bristol Temple Meads
G 🛒 to Chepstow

When events are being held at the Millenium Stadium, services are subject to alteration. Please check times before travelling.

Table 132

Mondays to Fridays

4 July to 2 September

Bath Spa, Bristol and Gloucester - Cardiff

		GW		GW	GW	GW	GW	AW	AW BHX	AW	GW	GW		XC	GW	GW	AW	GW	GW	GW	AW	GW		GW	XC
		R																							
				◇1	◇1		◇1	◇	◇			◇1		◇1		◇1	◇	◇	◇1	◇1	◇			◇1	◇1
					A		B							C											D
		🚲		☕	Ø		Ø	🚲	⊠			☕		🚲		☕	🚲	🚲	☕	☕	🚲			☕	🚲
Bath Spa 7	d	08 21		08 29		08 47	08 57								09 15	09 29		09 36	10 00						
Oldfield Park	d	08 23				08 49									09 17										
Keynsham	d	08 33				08 57									09 25			09 44							
Bristol Temple Meads 10	a	08 39		08 44		09 05	09 10								09 35	09 43		09 50	10 15						
	d	08 54				09 10					09 21				09 41			09 55				10 21			
Filton Abbey Wood	d	09 01				09 22					09 30				09 48			10 00				10 30			
Bristol Parkway 7	a					09 28									09 52										
	d				09 07							09 40			09 52					10 07				10 40	
Patchway	d										09 35											10 35			
Pilning	d																								
Gloucester 7	d									08 58				09 24	10a33										10 24
Lydney	d									09 17															10 43
Chepstow	d									09 27				09 50											
Caldicot	d									09 36															
Severn Tunnel Jn	d									09 38	09 46											10 46			
Newport (South Wales)	a	09 25			09 31					09 51	09 58	10 04		10 09				10 26		10 31		11 02		11 06	11 11
	d	09 25			09 32			09 37	09 41	09 52	10 00	10 04		10 10			10 22	10 26		10 31	11 01	11 02		11 06	11 12
Cardiff Central 7	a	09 43			09 48			09 57	09 58	10 07	10 18	10 21		10 25			10 37	10 43		10 46	11 15	11 23		11 23	11 27

		GW	GW	AW	GW	GW	GW	AW		AW	GW	GW	XC	GW	GW	AW	GW	SW		GW	GW	AW	GW	AW	GW
										R															
		◇	◇1	◇	◇	◇1	◇1				◇	◇1	◇1		◇1	◇	◇	◇1		◇1	◇1			◇	◇1
													C		E										
			☕	🚲	🚲	☕	Ø			🚲		☕	🚲		☕	🚲	🚲			☕	Ø			🚲	☕
Bath Spa 7	d	10 07	10 24		10 36	11 00								11 08	11 24		11 36	11 47		12 00					
Oldfield Park	d	10 10												11 09											
Keynsham	d	10 17												11 16				11 55							
Bristol Temple Meads 10	a	10 29	10 38		10 48	11 15								11 28	11 40		11 48	12 05		12 15					
	d	10 41			10 54						11 21			11 41			11 54						12 21		
Filton Abbey Wood	d	10 48			11 00						11 30			11 48			12 00						12 30		
Bristol Parkway 7	a	10 52												11 52											
	d	10 52					11 07					11 40		11 52							12 07				12 40
Patchway	d										11 35												12 35		
Pilning	d																								
Gloucester 7	d	11a34						10 58					11 24	12a33								11 58			
Lydney	d							11 17														12 17			
Chepstow	d							11 27					11 50									12 27			
Caldicot	d							11 35														12 35			
Severn Tunnel Jn	d							11 38			11 46											12 38	12 46		
Newport (South Wales)	a				11 26		11 31	11 50			11 58	12 04	12 10				12 25				12 31	12 50	13 00		13 06
	d			11 22	11 27		11 31	11 51		11 53	12 00	12 04	12 11			12 23	12 26				12 32	12 52	13 01	13 00	13 06
Cardiff Central 7	a			11 37	11 43		11 46	12 10		12 08	12 18	12 21	12 28			12 38	12 43				12 46	13 07	13 22	13 22	13 22

		XC	GW	GW		AW	GW	GW	GW	GW	GW	XC	GW	GW		AW	GW	GW	GW	AW	AW	GW	GW	XC	
																					R				
		◇1	◇	◇1		◇	◇	◇1	◇1		◇1	◇1		◇1		◇	◇	◇1	◇1				◇1	◇1	
		C										D												C	
		🚲		☕		🚲	🚲	☕	Ø		☕	🚲		☕		🚲	🚲	☕	Ø		🚲		☕	🚲	
Bath Spa 7	d		12 08	12 24			12 36	13 00					13 19	13 24			13 36	14 00							
Oldfield Park	d		12 10										13 21												
Keynsham	d		12 17										13 28												
Bristol Temple Meads 10	a		12 29	12 39			12 48	13 15					13 36	13 41			13 48	14 15							
	d		12 41				12 54			13 21			13 41				13 54					14 21			
Filton Abbey Wood	d		12 48				13 00			13 30			13 48				14 00					14 30			
Bristol Parkway 7	a		12 52										13 52												
	d		12 52						13 07		13 40		13 52						14 07				14 40		
Patchway	d									13 35												14 35			
Pilning	d																								
Gloucester 7	d	12 24	13a31									13 24	14a33							13 58				14 24	
Lydney	d											13 43								14 17					
Chepstow	d	12 50																		14 27				14 50	
Caldicot	d																			14 35					
Severn Tunnel Jn	d									13 46										14 38		14 46			
Newport (South Wales)	a	13 11					13 26		13 31	13 58	14 04	14 09					14 26		14 30	14 50		15 02	15 04	15 11	
	d	13 12				13 23	13 26		13 31	14 00	14 04	14 10				14 22	14 27		14 31	14 52	15 00	15 03	15 04	15 12	
Cardiff Central 7	a	13 29				13 39	13 43		13 46	14 18	14 22	14 27				14 37	14 43		14 46	15 07	15 21	15 24	15 22	15 29	

A The St. David
B The Merchant Venturer
C 🚲 to Chepstow
D 🚲 to Lydney
E The Torbay Express

When events are being held at the Millenium Stadium, services are subject to alteration. Please check times before travelling.

Bath Spa, Bristol and Gloucester - Cardiff

		GW	GW	GW	SW	GW	GW	AW	AW	GW		GW	GW	XC	GW	GW	GW	GW	AW	AW		GW	GW	XC	GW
		◇	◇1 ☕	◇ 🛒	◇1	◇1 ☕	◇1 ☕	R 🛒		◇		◇1 ☕		◇1 A 🛒	◇1 ☕	◇ 🛒	◇1 ☕	◇1 ☕	R 🛒	◇ 🛒			◇1 ☕	◇1 A 🛒	
Bath Spa 7	d	14 15	14 24	14 36	14 47	15 00							15 07		15 24	15 36	16 00								16 07
Oldfield Park	d	14 18											15 10												16 10
Keynsham	d	14 25			14 55								15 17												16 17
Bristol Temple Meads 10	a	14 35	14 39	14 48	15 05	15 15							15 29		15 40	15 48	16 15								16 29
	d	14 41		14 54						15 21			15 34			15 54						16 24			16 41
Filton Abbey Wood	d	14 48		15 00						15 30						16 00						16 30			16 48
Bristol Parkway 7	a	14 51											15 48												16 52
	d	14 52					15 07					15 40						16 07					16 40		16 52
Patchway	d									15 35												16 35			
Pilning	d																								
Gloucester 7	d	15a32							14 58					15 24										16 24	17a33
Lydney	d								15 17															16 43	
Chepstow	d								15 27					15 50										16 52	
Caldicot	d								15 35																
Severn Tunnel Jn.	d								15 38	15 46												16 46			
Newport (South Wales)	a			15 25			15 31		15 50	15 58		16 05		16 10		16 25		16 30				17 00	17 06	17 11	
	d			15 26			15 32	15 37	15 52	16 00		16 06		16 12		16 25		16 31	16 40	17 01		17 01	17 06	17 12	
Cardiff Central 7	a			15 43			15 46	15 53	16 10	16 18		16 24		16 29		16 43		16 46	16 55	17 15		17 25	17 22	17 28	

		GW	AW	GW	GW	GW		AW	GW	GW	XC	GW	GW	GW	GW	GW		AW	AW	AW	GW	GW	XC	GW	GW
		◇1 ☕	R 🛒	R 🛒	◇1 ☕	◇1 ☕				◇1 ☕	◇1		◇1 ☕	R 🛒	◇1 ☕	◇1 B ☕		R 🛒		◇ 🛒		◇1 ☕	◇1		◇1 ☕
Bath Spa 7	d	16 24		16 36	17 00							17 07	17 27	17 36	18 00									18 07	18 29
Oldfield Park	d											17 10												18 10	
Keynsham	d											17 17												18 17	
Bristol Temple Meads 10	a	16 39		16 48	17 15							17 29	17 41	17 48	18 14									18 28	18 44
	d			16 54					17 21			17 41		17 54							18 21			18 41	
Filton Abbey Wood	d			17 00					17 30			17 48		18 00							18 30			18 48	
Bristol Parkway 7	a											17 52												18 52	
	d					17 07				17 40		17 52				18 07						18 40		18 52	
Patchway	d								17 35												18 35				
Pilning	d																								
Gloucester 7	d							16 58			17 27	18a33							17 59				18 31	19a30	
Lydney	d							17 17											18 18						
Chepstow	d							17 27											18 28						
Caldicot	d							17 35											18 36						
Severn Tunnel Jn.	d			17 14				17 38	17 46					18 14					18 39		18 50				
Newport (South Wales)	a			17 25		17 31		17 50	17 58	18 04	18 10			18 25		18 30			18 51		19 06	19 11	19 16		
	d		17 22	17 27		17 31		17 52	18 00	18 04	18 11			18 26		18 31		18 41	18 53	19 01	19 06	19 11	19 17		
Cardiff Central 7	a		17 36	17 43		17 46		18 10	18 17	18 19	18 27			18 43		18 48		18 55	19 09	19 21	19 24	19 26	19 33		

		AW		GW	GW	GW	AW	GW	GW	XC	GW	GW		GW	GW FX	GW FO	GW FX	GW FO	AW FX	AW FO	GW FX	GW		GW	XC
		R 🛒		R 🛒	◇1 ☕	◇1 C ☕			◇1 ☕	◇1		◇1 ☕		◇1 D ☕	◇ 🛒	◇ 🛒	◇1 ☕	◇1 ☕	R 🛒	R 🛒				◇1 ☕	◇1
Bath Spa 7	d			18 36	18 59						19 07	19 24		19 30	19 36	19 36						19 47		19 59	
Oldfield Park	d										19 10											19 50			
Keynsham	d										19 17											19 58			
Bristol Temple Meads 10	a			18 49	19 12						19 29	19 41		19 43	19 49	19 49						20 08		20 13	
	d			18 54				19 21			19 41					19 54					20 04				20 15
Filton Abbey Wood	d			19 00				19 30			19 48					20 00					20 11				20 22
Bristol Parkway 7	a										19 52														
	d					19 07			19 40		19 52						20 07	20 07							
Patchway	d							19 35																	20 25
Pilning	d																								
Gloucester 7	d						18 58			19 28	20a32														
Lydney	d						19 17																		
Chepstow	d						19 27																		
Caldicot	d						19 34																		
Severn Tunnel Jn.	d			19 14			19 37	19 46								20 16					20 26				20 37
Newport (South Wales)	a			19 26		19 31	19 50	20 01	20 07	20 11						20 27	20 31	20 31			20 41				20 47
	d	19 22		19 26		19 31	19 52	20 02	20 08	20 13						20 28	20 31	20 31	20 38	20 39	20 42				20 49
Cardiff Central 7	a	19 42		19 46		19 47	20 09	20 20	20 22	20 27						20 43	20 45	20 48	20 59	20 58	21 00				21 02

A 🛒 to Chepstow
B The Capitals United
C The Red Dragon
D The Bristolian

When events are being held at the Millenium Stadium, services are subject to alteration. Please check times before travelling.

Table 132 — Mondays to Fridays

4 July to 2 September

Bath Spa, Bristol and Gloucester - Cardiff

		AW	GW	GW	AW	GW	GW	XC		XC	GW	GW	AW	GW	GW	GW	GW	XC		XC	GW	GW	SW	GW	GW
						FX	FO	FX		FO								FO		FX	FO	FX			
			◇	◇1	◇	◇1	◇1	◇1		◇1	◇	◇1	◇			◇1	◇1	◇1		◇1	◇	◇	◇1	◇1	
			🛒	☕	🛒	☕	☕				🛒	☕	🛒			☕	☕							☕	
Bath Spa 7	d		20 11	20 30							20 36	21 00			21 07	21 29					21 36	21 36	21 51	22 13	22 26
Oldfield Park	d		20 13												21 10										22 28
Keynsham	d		20 20												21 17								21 59		22 35
Bristol Temple Meads 10	a		20 29	20 44							20 51	21 15			21 29	21 44					21 49	21 49	22 06	22 30	22 44
	d										20 55			21 19							21 54	21 54			
Filton Abbey Wood	d										21 00			21 30							22 00	22 00			
Bristol Parkway 7	a																								
	d					20 40	20 43										21 40								
Patchway	d													21 34							22 06	22 06			
Pilning	d																								
Gloucester 7	d	19 58						20 24		20 24								21 24		21 24					
Lydney	d	20 17																21 43		21 43					
Chepstow	d	20 27																21 52		21 52					
Caldicot	d	20 36																22 01		22 01					
Severn Tunnel Jn.	d	20 39									21 14			21 46				22 04		22 04	22 18	22 18			
Newport (South Wales)	a	20 51				21 04	21 05	21 11		21 11	21 26			21 58			22 03	22 15		22 15	22 29	22 36			
	d	20 52			20 59	21 04	21 07	21 13		21 13	21 26		21 52	21 59			22 05	22 16		22 16	22 30	22 37			
Cardiff Central 7	a	21 10			21 20	21 19	21 19	21 27		21 29	21 44		22 06	22 18			22 23	22 31		22 35	22 52	23 00			

		AW	AW	GW		GW	GW	GW	AW	AW	AW	GW	GW
		FO	FX							FX	FO	FO	FX
		◇	◇	◇1		◇		◇1	◇			◇1	◇1
				☕				☕				☕	☕
Bath Spa 7	d					22 36	23 02	23 19				23 49	23 55
Oldfield Park	d						23 05						
Keynsham	d						23 12						
Bristol Temple Meads 10	a					22 49	23 23	23 33				00 03	00 10
	d					22 54							
Filton Abbey Wood	d					23 00							
Bristol Parkway 7	a												
	d			22 45									
Patchway	d					23 06							
Pilning	d												
Gloucester 7	d									23 13	23 13		
Lydney	d									23 33	23 33		
Chepstow	d									23 42	23 42		
Caldicot	d									23 51	23 51		
Severn Tunnel Jn.	d					23 17				23 54	23 54		
Newport (South Wales)	a			23 19		23 34				00 05	00 07		
	d	22 40	22 42	23 19		23 35			23 47	00 07	00 08		
Cardiff Central 7	a	22 55	23 02	23 40		23 56			00 02	00 29	00 35		

Mondays to Fridays

from 5 September

		GW	AW	AW	GW	AW	AW	GW	GW	GW		GW	GW	GW	GW	AW			GW			GW	GW	XC	XC
		MO	MX	MO	MO	MX		MO	MO	MX			MO	MO	MX	MX			MX				MO	MX	MO
		◇1	◇	◇				◇1	◇1	◇1		◇1	◇1	◇1	◇1	◇			◇1			◇1	◇1	1	1
		A			B		C	D	B			C	D	D								C	D		
							🚌																		
		☕						☕	☕	☕		☕	☕	☕	☕				☕			☕	☕		
Bath Spa 7	d							23p26	23p55	23p55		23p55	23p59	00 24					01 15			01 22	01 27		
Oldfield Park	d							⌇	⌇			⌇	⌇	⌇								⌇	⌇		
Keynsham	d							⌇	⌇			⌇	⌇	⌇								⌇	⌇		
Bristol Temple Meads 10	a							23p38	00 09	00 10		00 15	00 12	00 38					01 29			01 42	01 41		
	d							23p45											01 36					05 19	05 19
Filton Abbey Wood	d							⌇																	
Bristol Parkway 7	a							23p52																05 28	05 28
	d	23p17			23p30			23p59							00 24									05 38	05 38
Patchway	d	⌇			⌇			⌇																	
Pilning	d	⌇			⌇			⌇																	
Gloucester 7	d	⌇			⌇	23p13	22p35	⌇																	
Lydney	d	⌇			⌇	23p33	23p15	⌇																	
Chepstow	d	⌇			⌇	23p42	23p35	⌇																	
Caldicot	d	⌇			⌇	23p51	23p50	⌇																	
Severn Tunnel Jn.	d	⌇			23p42	23p54	23p59	⌇																	
Newport (South Wales)	a	23p44			00 05	00 05	00 25	00 27							00 52				02s10					05 58	06 08
	d	23p45	23p47	23p55	00 07	00 07	00 25	00 27							00 54	00 59								06 00	06 10
Cardiff Central 7	a	00 06	00 02	00 20	00 26	00 29	00 55	00 49							01 12	01 18			02 31					06 18	06 24

A From 5 September until 24 October
B From 19 September until 24 October
C 5 September, 12 September
D From 31 October

When events are being held at the Millenium Stadium, services are subject to alteration. Please check times before travelling.

Table 132

Mondays to Fridays

from 5 September

Bath Spa, Bristol and Gloucester - Cardiff

		AW	AW	GW	AW	GW		XC	XC	GW	AW	GW	XC	AW	GW	GW		GW	SW	GW	GW	GW	AW	AW	AW
		◇						◇[1]	◇[1]		◇	◇[1]	◇[1]	◇					[1]	◇[1]		◇[1]	◇		◇
		A	B					C																	
								[trolley]			[trolley]	[buffet]								[buffet]		[buffet]	[trolley]		[trolley]
Bath Spa [7]	d							06 09		06 28		06 54				07 07		07 25	07 35		07 48	07 59			
Oldfield Park	d									06 31						07 10		07 28	07 38		07 51				
Keynsham	d									06 38						07 17		07 35	07 45		07 58	08 08			
Bristol Temple Meads [10]	a							06 20		06 45		07 07				07 27		07 45	07 52		08 06	08 17			
	d			05 54		06 19		06 27		06 50		07 14			07 19	07 34		07 54			08 10				
Filton Abbey Wood	d			06 01		06 31				07 02		07 22			07 30	07 43		08 00			08 22				
Bristol Parkway [7]	a							06 37							07 33	07 47					08 29				
	d														07 40	07 48				08 07					
Patchway	d			06 06		06 35									07 44			08 05							
Pilning	d																								
Gloucester [7]	d				05 50				06 18				07 01			08a29								07 58	
Lydney	d				06 09				06 37				07 20											08 17	
Chepstow	d				06 19				06 46				07 29											08 27	
Caldicot	d				06 26				06 55				07 38											08 35	
Severn Tunnel Jn.	d			06 17	06 29	06 47			06 58	07 14			07 41		07 56									08 38	
Newport (South Wales)	a			06 28	06 41	06 58			07 09	07 25		07 44	07 52		08 07			08 27		08 32				08 50	
	d	06{17	06{23	06 29	06 44	07 00			07 10	07 27	07 35	07 44	07 53	08 01	08 09			08 27		08 32			08 38	08 52	09 03
Cardiff Central [7]	a	06{33	06{40	06 48	07 00	07 20			07 26	07 44	07 49	08 00	08 08	08 17	08 24			08 46		08 46			08 53	09 07	09 18

		GW		GW	XC	GW	GW	GW	GW	GW	GW	AW		AW BHX	AW	GW	GW	XC	GW	GW	AW	GW		GW	GW
							[R]																		
				◇[1]	◇[1]			◇[1]	◇[1]		◇[1]	◇		◇			◇[1]	◇[1]		◇[1]	◇	◇		◇[1]	◇[1]
					D				E		F							D							
				[buffet]	[trolley]		[trolley]	[buffet]	⊘		⊘	[trolley]		☒			[buffet]	[trolley]		[buffet]	[trolley]	[trolley]		[buffet]	[buffet]
Bath Spa [7]	d					08 07	08 21	08 29		08 47	08 57								09 15	09 29		09 36		10 00	
Oldfield Park	d					08 10	08 23			08 49									09 17						
Keynsham	d					08 17	08 33			08 57									09 25			09 44			
Bristol Temple Meads [10]	a					08 29	08 39	08 44		09 05	09 10								09 35	09 43		09 50		10 15	
	d	08 21				08 41	08 54			09 10						09 21			09 41			09 55			
Filton Abbey Wood	d	08 30				08 48	09 01			09 22						09 30			09 48			10 00			
Bristol Parkway [7]	a					08 52				09 28									09 52						
	d			08 40		08 52			09 07								09 40		09 52						10 07
Patchway	d	08 35														09 35									
Pilning	d																								
Gloucester [7]	d				08 28	09a33									08 58			09 24	10a33						
Lydney	d														09 17										
Chepstow	d				08 54										09 27			09 50							
Caldicot	d														09 36										
Severn Tunnel Jn.	d	08 46													09 38	09 46									
Newport (South Wales)	a	09 02		09 07	09 12		09 25		09 31						09 51	09 58	10 04	10 09				10 26			10 31
	d	09 03		09 08	09 14		09 25		09 32			09 37		09 41	09 52	10 00	10 04	10 10			10 22	10 26			10 31
Cardiff Central [7]	a	09 24		09 24	09 30		09 43		09 48			09 57		09 58	10 07	10 18	10 21	10 25			10 37	10 43			10 46

		AW	GW	GW	XC	GW	GW	AW		GW	GW	GW	AW	AW	GW	GW	XC	GW		GW	AW	GW	SW	GW	GW
														[R]											
		◇		◇[1]	◇[1]	◇	◇[1]	◇		◇	◇[1]	◇[1]			◇	◇[1]	◇[1]			◇[1]	◇	◇	◇[1]	◇[1]	◇[1]
					G												D			H					
		[trolley]		[buffet]	[trolley]		[buffet]	[trolley]		[trolley]	[buffet]	⊘		[trolley]		[buffet]	[trolley]			[buffet]	[trolley]	[trolley]		[buffet]	⊘
Bath Spa [7]	d					10 07	10 24			10 36	11 00							11 08		11 24		11 36	11 47	12 00	
Oldfield Park	d					10 10												11 09							
Keynsham	d					10 17												11 16					11 55		
Bristol Temple Meads [10]	a					10 29	10 38			10 48	11 15							11 28		11 40		11 48	12 05	12 15	
	d		10 21			10 41				10 54					11 21			11 41				11 54			
Filton Abbey Wood	d		10 30			10 48				11 00					11 30			11 48				12 00			
Bristol Parkway [7]	a					10 52												11 52							
	d			10 40		10 52						11 07				11 40		11 52							12 07
Patchway	d		10 35												11 35										
Pilning	d																								
Gloucester [7]	d				10 24	11a34							10 58				11 24	12a33							
Lydney	d				10 43								11 17												
Chepstow	d												11 27				11 50								
Caldicot	d												11 35												
Severn Tunnel Jn.	d		10 46										11 38		11 46										
Newport (South Wales)	a		11 02	11 06	11 11					11 26		11 31	11 50		11 58	12 04	12 10					12 25			12 31
	d	11 01	11 02	11 06	11 12			11 22		11 27		11 31	11 51	11 53	12 00	12 04	12 11				12 23	12 26			12 32
Cardiff Central [7]	a	11 15	11 23	11 23	11 27			11 37		11 43		11 46	12 10	12 08	12 18	12 21	12 28				12 38	12 43			12 46

A from 12 September
B from 5 September until 9 September
C [trolley] from Bristol Temple Meads
D [trolley] to Chepstow
E The St. David
F The Merchant Venturer
G [trolley] to Lydney
H The Torbay Express

When events are being held at the Millenium Stadium, services are subject to alteration. Please check times before travelling.

Table 132

Mondays to Fridays

from 5 September

Bath Spa, Bristol and Gloucester - Cardiff

		AW	GW	AW		GW	XC	GW	GW	AW	GW	GW	GW	GW		GW	XC	GW	GW	AW	GW	GW	GW	AW	
				◇		◇1	◇1	◇	◇1	◇	◇	◇1	◇1			◇1	◇1		◇1	◇	◇	◇1	◇1		
							A										B								
				🛒		☕	🛒		☕	🛒	🛒	☕	Ø			☕	🛒		☕	🛒	🛒	☕	Ø		
Bath Spa 7	d							12 08	12 24		12 36	13 00						13 19	13 24		13 36	14 00			
Oldfield Park	d							12 10										13 21							
Keynsham	d							12 17										13 28							
Bristol Temple Meads 10	a							12 29	12 39		12 48	13 15						13 36	13 41		13 48	14 15			
	d		12 21					12 41			12 54			13 21				13 41			13 54				
Filton Abbey Wood	d		12 30					12 48			13 00			13 30				13 48			14 00				
Bristol Parkway 7	a							12 52										13 52							
	d					12 40		12 52					13 07			13 40		13 52					14 07		
Patchway	d		12 35											13 35											
Pilning	d																								
Gloucester 7	d	11 58					12 24	13a31									13 24	14a33						13 58	
Lydney	d	12 17															13 43							14 17	
Chepstow	d	12 27					12 50																	14 27	
Caldicot	d	12 35																						14 35	
Severn Tunnel Jn.	d	12 38	12 46											13 46										14 38	
Newport (South Wales)	a	12 50	13 00			13 06	13 11				13 26		13 31	13 58		14 04	14 09				14 26		14 30	14 50	
	d	12 52	13 01	13 00		13 06	13 12			13 23	13 26		13 31	14 00		14 04	14 10			14 22	14 27		14 31	14 52	
Cardiff Central 7	a	13 07	13 22	13 22		13 22	13 29			13 39	13 43		13 46	14 18		14 22	14 27			14 37	14 43		14 46	15 07	

		AW	GW	GW	XC	GW	GW	GW	SW	GW		GW	AW	AW	GW	GW	GW	XC	GW	GW		GW	GW	AW	AW
		■											■											■	
				◇1	◇1	◇	◇1	◇	◇1	◇1		◇1			◇	◇1		◇1	◇1	◇		◇1	◇1		◇
					A													A							
		🛒		☕	🛒		☕	🛒		☕		☕	🛒			☕		🛒	☕	🛒		☕	☕	🛒	🛒
Bath Spa 7	d					14 15	14 24	14 36	14 47	15 00							15 07		15 24	15 36		16 00			
Oldfield Park	d					14 18											15 10								
Keynsham	d					14 25			14 55								15 17								
Bristol Temple Meads 10	a					14 35	14 39	14 48	15 05	15 15							15 29		15 40	15 48		16 15			
	d		14 21			14 41		14 54							15 21		15 34			15 54					
Filton Abbey Wood	d		14 30			14 48		15 00							15 30					16 00					
Bristol Parkway 7	a					14 51											15 48								
	d			14 40		14 52						15 07				15 40							16 07		
Patchway	d		14 35												15 35										
Pilning	d																								
Gloucester 7	d				14 24	15a32								14 58				15 24							
Lydney	d													15 17											
Chepstow	d				14 50									15 27				15 50							
Caldicot	d													15 35											
Severn Tunnel Jn.	d		14 46											15 38	15 46										
Newport (South Wales)	a		15 02	15 04	15 11			15 25				15 31		15 50	15 58	16 05		16 10		16 25			16 30		
	d	15 00	15 03	15 04	15 12			15 26				15 32	15 37	15 52	16 00	16 06		16 12		16 25			16 31	16 40	17 01
Cardiff Central 7	a	15 21	15 24	15 22	15 29			15 43				15 46	15 53	16 10	16 18	16 24		16 29		16 43			16 46	16 55	17 15

		GW	GW	XC	GW	GW		AW	GW	GW	GW	AW	GW	GW	XC	GW		GW	GW	GW	GW	AW	AW	AW	GW
								■	■										■			■			
			◇1	◇1		◇1				◇1	◇1			◇1	◇1			◇1		◇1	◇1			◇	
				A																	C				
			☕	🛒		☕		🛒	🛒	☕	☕			☕				☕	🛒	☕	☕	🛒		🛒	
Bath Spa 7	d				16 07	16 24			16 36	17 00						17 07		17 27	17 36	18 00					
Oldfield Park	d				16 10											17 10									
Keynsham	d				16 17											17 17									
Bristol Temple Meads 10	a				16 29	16 39			16 48	17 15						17 29		17 41	17 48	18 14					
	d	16 24			16 41				16 54				17 21			17 41			17 54						18 21
Filton Abbey Wood	d	16 30			16 48				17 00				17 30			17 48			18 00						18 30
Bristol Parkway 7	a				16 52											17 52									
	d		16 40		16 52						17 07			17 40		17 52					18 07				
Patchway	d	16 35											17 35												18 35
Pilning	d																								
Gloucester 7	d			16 24	17a33							16 58			17 27	18a33							17 59		
Lydney	d			16 43								17 17											18 18		
Chepstow	d			16 52								17 27											18 28		
Caldicot	d											17 35											18 36		
Severn Tunnel Jn.	d	16 46							17 14			17 38	17 46						18 14				18 39		18 50
Newport (South Wales)	a	17 00	17 06	17 11					17 25		17 31	17 50	17 58	18 04	18 10				18 25		18 30		18 51		19 06
	d	17 01	17 06	17 12				17 22	17 27		17 31	17 52	18 00	18 04	18 11				18 26		18 31	18 41	18 53	19 01	19 06
Cardiff Central 7	a	17 25	17 22	17 28				17 36	17 43		17 46	18 10	18 17	18 19	18 27				18 43		18 48	18 55	19 09	19 21	19 24

A 🛒 to Chepstow

B 🛒 to Lydney

C The Capitals United

When events are being held at the Millenium Stadium, services are subject to alteration. Please check times before travelling.

Table 132

Mondays to Fridays

from 5 September

Bath Spa, Bristol and Gloucester - Cardiff

		GW ◇1 ☕		XC ◇1	GW	GW ◇1 ☕	AW R 🛒	GW R 🛒	GW ◇1 ☕	GW ◇1 A ☕	AW	GW		GW ◇1 ☕	XC ◇1	GW	GW ◇1 ☕	GW ◇1 B ☕	GW FX ◇ 🛒	GW FO ◇ 🛒	GW FX ◇1 ☕	GW FO ◇1 ☕		AW FX R 🛒	AW FO R 🛒
Bath Spa 7	d				18 07	18 29		18 36	18 59							19 07	19 24	19 30	19 36	19 36					
Oldfield Park	d				18 10											19 10									
Keynsham	d				18 17											19 17									
Bristol Temple Meads 10	a				18 28	18 44		18 49	19 12							19 29	19 41	19 43	19 49	19 49					
	d				18 41			18 54				19 21				19 41				19 54					
Filton Abbey Wood	d				18 48			19 00				19 30				19 48				20 00					
Bristol Parkway 7	a				18 52											19 52									
	d	18 40			18 52					19 07				19 40		19 52					20 07	20 07			
Patchway	d											19 35													
Pilning	d																								
Gloucester 7	d			18 31	19a30						18 58				19 28	20a32									
Lydney	d										19 17														
Chepstow	d										19 27														
Caldicot	d										19 34														
Severn Tunnel Jn.	d							19 14			19 37	19 46								20 16					
Newport (South Wales)	a	19 11		19 16				19 26		19 31	19 50	20 01		20 07	20 11					20 27	20 31	20 31			
	d	19 11		19 17			19 22	19 26		19 31	19 52	20 02		20 08	20 13					20 28	20 31	20 31		20 38	20 39
Cardiff Central 7	a	19 26		19 33			19 42	19 46		19 47	20 09	20 20		20 22	20 27					20 43	20 45	20 48		20 59	20 58

		GW FX	GW	GW ◇1 ☕	XC ◇1	AW	GW ◇ 🛒	GW ◇1 ☕		AW ◇ 🛒	GW FX ◇1 ☕	GW FO ◇1 ☕	XC FX ◇1	XC FO ◇1	GW ◇ 🛒	GW ◇1 ☕	AW ◇ 🛒	GW		GW	GW ◇1 ☕	GW ◇1 ☕	XC FO ◇1	XC FX ◇1	GW FO ◇
Bath Spa 7	d		19 47	19 59			20 11	20 30							20 36	21 00				21 07	21 29				21 36
Oldfield Park	d		19 50				20 13													21 10					
Keynsham	d		19 58				20 20													21 17					
Bristol Temple Meads 10	a		20 08	20 13			20 29	20 44							20 51	21 15				21 29	21 44				21 49
	d	20 04			20 15										20 55			21 19							21 54
Filton Abbey Wood	d	20 11			20 22										21 00			21 30							22 00
Bristol Parkway 7	a																								
	d										20 40	20 43										21 40			
Patchway	d				20 25													21 34							22 06
Pilning	d																								
Gloucester 7	d					19 58							20 24	20 24									21 24	21 24	
Lydney	d					20 17																	21 43	21 43	
Chepstow	d					20 27																	21 52	21 52	
Caldicot	d					20 36																	22 01	22 01	
Severn Tunnel Jn.	d	20 26			20 37	20 39									21 14			21 46					22 04	22 04	22 18
Newport (South Wales)	a	20 41			20 47	20 51					21 04	21 05	21 11	21 11	21 26			21 58				22 03	22 15	22 15	22 29
	d	20 42			20 49	20 52				20 59	21 04	21 07	21 13	21 13	21 26		21 52	21 59				22 05	22 16	22 16	22 30
Cardiff Central 7	a	21 00			21 02	21 10				21 20	21 19	21 19	21 27	21 29	21 44		22 06	22 18				22 23	22 31	22 35	22 52

		GW FX ◇	SW ◇1	GW ◇1 ☕		GW	AW FO ◇	AW FX ◇	GW ◇1 ☕	GW ◇	GW	GW ◇1 ☕	AW ◇	AW FX		AW FO	GW FO ◇1 ☕	GW FX ◇1 ☕
Bath Spa 7	d	21 36	21 51	22 13		22 26				22 36	23 02	23 19					23 49	23 55
Oldfield Park	d					22 28					23 05							
Keynsham	d		21 59			22 35					23 12							
Bristol Temple Meads 10	a	21 49	22 06	22 30		22 44				22 49	23 23	23 33					00 03	00 10
	d	21 54								22 54								
Filton Abbey Wood	d	22 00								23 00								
Bristol Parkway 7	a																	
	d								22 45									
Patchway	d	22 06								23 06								
Pilning	d																	
Gloucester 7	d													23 13		23 13		
Lydney	d													23 33		23 33		
Chepstow	d													23 42		23 42		
Caldicot	d													23 51		23 51		
Severn Tunnel Jn.	d	22 18								23 17				23 54		23 54		
Newport (South Wales)	a	22 36							23 19	23 34				00 05		00 07		
	d	22 37					22 40	22 42	23 19	23 35			23 47	00 07		00 08		
Cardiff Central 7	a	23 00					22 55	23 02	23 40	23 56			00 02	00 29		00 35		

A The Red Dragon

B The Bristolian

When events are being held at the Millenium Stadium, services are subject to alteration. Please check times before travelling.

Table 132

Saturdays
until 30 July

Bath Spa, Bristol and Gloucester - Cardiff

		AW	AW	GW	GW	AW	GW	AW	AW	XC		GW	GW	AW	XC	GW	GW	AW	GW	SW		GW	AW	AW	GW
		◇		◇1 ☕	◇1 ☕	◇	◇1 ☕			◇1		◇1		◇ 🛒	◇1					1		◇1 ☕	◇ 🛒		
Bath Spa 7	d			23p49			01 13										07 07		07 22	07 35		08 00			
Oldfield Park	d																07 10		07 25	07 38					
Keynsham	d																07 17		07 32	07 45					
Bristol Temple Meads 10	a			00 03			01 27										07 29		07 39	07 53		08 15			
	d						01 34					06 46	06 50			07 21	07 41		07 54						08 20
Filton Abbey Wood	d											06 54	07 02			07 30	07 48		08 01						08 30
Bristol Parkway 7	a											06 58					07 52								
	d				00 16							07 11					07 52								
Patchway	d															07 34									08 35
Pilning	d																								
Gloucester 7	d		23p13						05 50	06 15					07 00		08a32							07 58	
Lydney	d		23p33						06 09	06 34					07 20									08 17	
Chepstow	d		23p42						06 19	06 43					07 29									08 27	
Caldicot	d		23p51						06 27	06 52					07 38									08 35	
Severn Tunnel Jn.	d		23p54						06 30	06 55			07 14		07 41	07 46								08 38	08 46
Newport (South Wales)	a		00 07		00 38		02s00		06 42	07 06		07 31	07 25		07 52	07 58			08 26					08 50	09 01
	d	23p47	00 08		00 38	00 59		06 38	06 44	07 07		07 32	07 26	07 38	07 53	07 58		08 01	08 27				08 33	08 52	09 01
Cardiff Central 7	a	00 02	00 35		00 53	01 18	02 17	06 54	07 00	07 22		07 47	07 44	07 54	08 08	08 18		08 19	08 43				08 50	09 10	09 21

		AW	XC	GW	GW	GW		GW	GW	GW	AW	AW	GW	XC	GW	GW		GW	GW	AW	AW	GW	XC	GW	GW
		◇ 🛒	◇1 A 🛒		◇1 ☕	◇			R 1 ☕	◇1 ☕	◇ 🛒			◇1 A 🛒	◇1 ☕	◇		◇1 ☕	◇1 ☕	◇ 🛒	◇ 🛒		◇1 B 🛒	◇	◇1 ☕
Bath Spa 7	d			08 07	08 24	08 36		08 47	09 00						09 24	09 36		10 00						10 07	10 24
Oldfield Park	d			08 10				08 49																10 10	
Keynsham	d			08 17				08 57																10 17	
Bristol Temple Meads 10	a			08 29	08 39	08 47		09 05	09 15						09 39	09 48		10 15						10 29	10 39
	d			08 41		08 54							09 21			09 54						10 21		10 41	
Filton Abbey Wood	d			08 48		09 00							09 30			10 00						10 30		10 48	
Bristol Parkway 7	a			08 52																				10 52	
	d			08 52						09 07									10 07					10 52	
Patchway	d												09 35									10 35			
Pilning	d																								
Gloucester 7	d		08 24	09a33								08 58		09 24									10 24	11a32	
Lydney	d											09 17											10 43		
Chepstow	d		08 50									09 27		09 50											
Caldicot	d											09 35													
Severn Tunnel Jn.	d											09 38	09 46									10 46			
Newport (South Wales)	a		09 07			09 25				09 30		09 50	09 58	10 07		10 24			10 31			11 00	11 08		
	d	09 02	09 09			09 25				09 31	09 38	09 52	09 59	10 09		10 24			10 31	10 36	10 56	11 01	11 09		
Cardiff Central 7	a	09 22	09 23			09 42				09 47	09 58	10 07	10 18	10 23		10 43			10 47	10 53	11 15	11 22	11 24		

		GW		GW	GW	AW	AW	GW	XC	GW	GW	GW		SW	GW	GW	AW	AW	AW	GW	XC	GW		GW	GW
		◇		◇1 ☕	◇1 ☕	◇ 🛒			◇1 A 🛒		◇1 ☕	◇		◇1	◇1 ☕	◇1 ⊘	◇ 🛒		◇ 🛒		◇1 A 🛒	◇		◇1 ☕	◇
Bath Spa 7	d	10 36		11 00						11 07	11 24	11 36		11 47	12 00							12 11		12 24	12 36
Oldfield Park	d									11 10												12 14			
Keynsham	d									11 17				11 55								12 21			
Bristol Temple Meads 10	a	10 48		11 15						11 29	11 39	11 48		12 05	12 15							12 29		12 39	12 48
	d	10 54						11 21		11 41		11 54								12 21		12 41			12 54
Filton Abbey Wood	d	11 00						11 30		11 48		12 00								12 30		12 48			13 00
Bristol Parkway 7	a									11 52												12 52			
	d				11 07					11 52						12 07						12 52			
Patchway	d							11 35												12 35					
Pilning	d																								
Gloucester 7	d						10 58		11 24	12a33								11 58			12 24	13a34			
Lydney	d						11 17											12 17							
Chepstow	d						11 27		11 50									12 27			12 50				
Caldicot	d						11 35											12 35							
Severn Tunnel Jn.	d						11 38	11 46										12 38		12 46					
Newport (South Wales)	a	11 24			11 31		11 50	11 58	12 07			12 24				12 31		12 50		13 00	13 11				13 25
	d	11 24			11 31	11 37	11 52	11 59	12 09			12 24				12 31	12 37	12 52	12 56	13 01	13 12				13 25
Cardiff Central 7	a	11 43			11 46	11 53	12 07	12 18	12 23			12 43				12 46	12 53	13 07	13 15	13 18	13 27				13 43

		GW	GW	AW	GW	XC	GW	GW		GW	GW	GW	AW	AW	GW	AW	XC	GW		GW	GW	SW	GW	GW	AW
		◇1 ☕	◇1 ⊘	◇ 🛒		◇1 B 🛒		◇1 ☕		◇	◇1 ☕	◇1 ☕	◇ 🛒			R 🛒	◇1 A 🛒	◇		◇1 ☕	◇	◇1	◇1 ☕	◇1 ☕	R 🛒
Bath Spa 7	d	12 59					13 19	13 24		13 36	14 00							14 07		14 24	14 36	14 47	15 00		
Oldfield Park	d						13 21											14 10							
Keynsham	d						13 28											14 17				14 55			
Bristol Temple Meads 10	a	13 14					13 36	13 42		13 48	14 15							14 29		14 39	14 48	15 05	15 15		
	d				13 21		13 41			13 54					14 21			14 41			14 54				
Filton Abbey Wood	d				13 30		13 48			14 00					14 30			14 48			15 00				
Bristol Parkway 7	a						13 52											14 52							
	d		13 07				13 52					14 07						14 52						15 07	
Patchway	d				13 35										14 35										
Pilning	d																								
Gloucester 7	d					13 24	14a33							13 58			14 24	15a32							
Lydney	d					13 43								14 17											
Chepstow	d													14 27			14 50								
Caldicot	d													14 35											
Severn Tunnel Jn.	d				13 46									14 38	14 46										
Newport (South Wales)	a		13 31		13 58	14 08				14 24		14 31		14 50	14 59		15 11				15 25			15 31	
	d		13 31	13 37	13 59	14 09				14 24		14 31	14 37	14 52	15 00	15 06	15 12				15 25			15 31	15 37
Cardiff Central 7	a		13 47	13 53	14 18	14 24				14 43		14 46	14 53	15 09	15 18	15 26	15 27				15 43			15 46	15 53

A 🛒 to Chepstow

B 🛒 to Lydney

When events are being held at the Millenium Stadium, services are subject to alteration. Please check times before travelling.

Table 132

Saturdays until 30 July

Bath Spa, Bristol and Gloucester - Cardiff

		AW	GW	XC		GW	GW	GW	GW	GW	AW	AW	GW
				◇1 A 🚌			◇1 ☕	◇	◇1 ☕	◇1 ☕	R 🚌	◇ 🚌	
Bath Spa 7	d					15 18	15 24	15 36	16 00				
Oldfield Park	d					15 21							
Keynsham	d					15 28							
Bristol Temple Meads 10	a					15 36	15 41	15 49	16 15				
	d		15 21			15 41		15 54					16 21
Filton Abbey Wood	d		15 30			15 48		16 00					16 30
Bristol Parkway 7	a					15 52							
	d					15 52				16 07			
Patchway	d		15 35										16 35
Pilning	d		15 41										
Gloucester 7	d	14 58		15 24		16a33							
Lydney	d	15 17											
Chepstow	d	15 27		15 50									
Caldicot	d	15 35											
Severn Tunnel Jn	d	15 38	15 46										16 46
Newport (South Wales)	a	15 50	16 01	16 08				16 24		16 31			17 01
	d	15 52	16 01	16 10				16 24		16 31	16 37	16 56	17 01
Cardiff Central 7	a	16 07	16 18	16 25				16 43		16 47	16 53	17 15	17 22

		XC		GW	GW	GW	GW	GW	AW	AW	GW	XC	
		◇1 A 🚌			◇1 ☕	◇	◇1 ☕	◇1 ☕	R 🚌			◇1 🚌	
Bath Spa 7	d			16 07	16 24	16 36	17 00						
Oldfield Park	d			16 10									
Keynsham	d			16 17									
Bristol Temple Meads 10	a			16 29	16 39	16 48	17 15						
	d			16 41		16 54					17 21		
Filton Abbey Wood	d			16 48		17 00					17 30		
Bristol Parkway 7	a			16 52									
	d			16 52				17 07					
Patchway	d										17 35		
Pilning	d												
Gloucester 7	d	16 24		17a33						16 58		17 24	
Lydney	d	16 43								17 17			
Chepstow	d	16 52								17 27			
Caldicot	d									17 35			
Severn Tunnel Jn	d					17 14				17 38	17 46		
Newport (South Wales)	a	17 10				17 26		17 29		17 50	17 58	18 05	
	d	17 11				17 26		17 31	17 37	17 52	18 00	18 07	
Cardiff Central 7	a	17 26				17 42		17 46	17 53	18 10	18 18	18 21	

		GW	GW	GW	GW	GW	AW	AW	AW	GW		XC	GW
			◇1 ☕	◇	◇1 ☕	◇1 ☕	R 🚌		◇ 🚌			◇1	
Bath Spa 7	d	17 07	17 24	17 36	18 00								18 18
Oldfield Park	d	17 10											18 20
Keynsham	d	17 17											18 27
Bristol Temple Meads 10	a	17 28	17 39	17 48	18 15								18 35
	d	17 41		17 54						18 21			18 41
Filton Abbey Wood	d	17 48		18 00						18 30			18 48
Bristol Parkway 7	a	17 52											18 52
	d	17 52				18 07							18 52
Patchway	d									18 35			
Pilning	d												
Gloucester 7	d	18a33						17 58				18 31	19a33
Lydney	d							18 17					
Chepstow	d							18 27					
Caldicot	d							18 35					
Severn Tunnel Jn	d			18 14				18 38		18 47			
Newport (South Wales)	a			18 25		18 30		18 50		19 05		19 12	
	d			18 25		18 31	18 37	18 52	18 57	19 05		19 14	
Cardiff Central 7	a			18 42		18 46	18 53	19 10	19 15	19 23		19 29	

		GW	GW	GW	GW	AW	AW	GW		XC	GW	GW	GW
		◇1 ☕	R	◇1 ☕	◇1 ☕	R 🚌				◇1	◇1 ☕	◇	
Bath Spa 7	d	18 24	18 36	19 00							19 24	19 36	19 47
Oldfield Park	d												19 50
Keynsham	d												19 58
Bristol Temple Meads 10	a	18 39	18 48	19 15							19 38	19 48	20 05
	d		18 54					19 21				19 54	
Filton Abbey Wood	d		19 00					19 28				20 00	
Bristol Parkway 7	a												
	d				19 07								
Patchway	d							19 33					
Pilning	d												
Gloucester 7	d						18 58			19 24			
Lydney	d						19 17						
Chepstow	d						19 27						
Caldicot	d						19 34						
Severn Tunnel Jn	d						19 37	19 46					
Newport (South Wales)	a		19 26		19 30		19 50	19 58		20 05		20 25	
	d		19 26		19 31	19 37	19 52	19 58		20 07		20 25	
Cardiff Central 7	a		19 43		19 46	19 53	20 11	20 18		20 21		20 43	

		GW	GW	AW	AW	XC		GW	GW	AW	XC	GW	GW
		◇1 ☕	◇1 ☕	R 🚌		◇1 🚌		R	◇1 ☕	◇ 🚌	◇1	◇	◇1 ☕
Bath Spa 7	d	20 00						20 18	20 25			20 36	21 00
Oldfield Park	d							20 20					
Keynsham	d							20 27					
Bristol Temple Meads 10	a	20 15						20 35	20 40			20 48	21 16
	d					20 21						20 54	
Filton Abbey Wood	d					20 28						21 00	
Bristol Parkway 7	a												
	d		20 07										
Patchway	d					20 32							
Pilning	d												
Gloucester 7	d				19 58						20 24		
Lydney	d				20 17								
Chepstow	d				20 27								
Caldicot	d				20 35								
Severn Tunnel Jn	d				20 38	20 42							
Newport (South Wales)	a		20 30		20 50	20 55					21 11	21 25	
	d		20 31	20 40	20 52	20 57				21 02	21 13	21 25	
Cardiff Central 7	a		20 44	20 58	21 09	21 11				21 15	21 29	21 43	

		GW	GW	AW		GW	XC	GW	AW	GW	SW	GW	GW
		◇1 ☕		◇ 🚌			◇1	◇1 ☕		◇	◇1	◇1 ☕	◇1 ☕
Bath Spa 7	d		21 07					21 30		21 39	21 51	22 00	
Oldfield Park	d		21 10										
Keynsham	d		21 17								21 59		
Bristol Temple Meads 10	a		21 29					21 45		21 51	22 06	22 14	
	d					21 29				21 54			
Filton Abbey Wood	d					21 36				22 00			
Bristol Parkway 7	a												
	d	21 07											22 11
Patchway	d					21 41				22 06			
Pilning	d												
Gloucester 7	d						21 24						
Lydney	d						21 43						
Chepstow	d						21 52						
Caldicot	d						22 01						
Severn Tunnel Jn	d					21 52	22 04			22 18			
Newport (South Wales)	a	21 30				22 09	22 16			22 38			22 46
	d	21 31		21 44		22 11	22 19		22 34	22 38			22 46
Cardiff Central 7	a	21 47		22 03		22 30	22 41		22 53	22 58			23 06

		GW		GW	GW	GW	AW	GW	AW
				◇	◇1 ☕			◇1 ☕	
Bath Spa 7	d	22 26		22 36	23 00	23 07			
Oldfield Park	d	22 28				23 10			
Keynsham	d	22 35				23 17			
Bristol Temple Meads 10	a	22 44		22 50	23 15	23 29			
	d			22 54					
Filton Abbey Wood	d			23 00					
Bristol Parkway 7	a								
	d							23 28	
Patchway	d			23 07					
Pilning	d								
Gloucester 7	d								23 09
Lydney	d								23 28
Chepstow	d								23 38
Caldicot	d								23 46
Severn Tunnel Jn	d			23 18					23 49
Newport (South Wales)	a			23 35				23 57	00 07
	d			23 36			23 46	23 58	00 09
Cardiff Central 7	a			23 55			00 05	00 18	00 35

A 🚌 to Chepstow

When events are being held at the Millenium Stadium, services are subject to alteration. Please check times before travelling.

Table 132

Saturdays

6 August to 10 September

Bath Spa, Bristol and Gloucester - Cardiff

		AW	AW	GW	GW	AW	GW	AW	AW	XC		GW	GW	AW	XC	GW	GW	AW	GW	SW		GW	AW	AW	GW
		◇		◇■1	◇■1	◇	◇■1			◇■1		◇■1		◇	◇■1					■1		◇■1	◇		
				☕	☕		☕							🛒								☕	🛒		
Bath Spa ■7	d			23p49			01 13										07 07		07 22	07 35		08 00			
Oldfield Park	d																07 10		07 25	07 38					
Keynsham	d																07 17		07 32	07 45					
Bristol Temple Meads ■10	a			00 03			01 27										07 29		07 39	07 53		08 15			
	d						01 34					06 46	06 50			07 21	07 41		07 54						08 20
Filton Abbey Wood	d											06 54	07 02			07 30	07 48		08 01						08 30
Bristol Parkway ■7	a											06 58					07 52								
	d				00 16							07 11					07 52								
Patchway	d															07 34									08 35
Pilning	d																								
Gloucester ■7	d		23p13						05 50	06 15					07 00		08a32							07 58	
Lydney	d		23p33						06 09	06 34					07 20									08 17	
Chepstow	d		23p42						06 19	06 43					07 29									08 27	
Caldicot	d		23p51						06 27	06 52					07 38									08 35	
Severn Tunnel Jn.	d		23p54						06 30	06 55			07 14		07 41	07 46								08 38	08 46
Newport (South Wales)	a		00 07		00 38		02s00		06 42	07 06		07 31	07 25		07 52	07 58			08 26					08 50	09 01
	d	23p47	00 08		00 38	00 59		06 38	06 44	07 07		07 32	07 26	07 38	07 53	07 58		08 01	08 27				08 33	08 52	09 01
Cardiff Central ■7	a	00 02	00 35		00 53	01 18	02 17	06 54	07 00	07 22		07 47	07 44	07 54	08 08	08 18		08 19	08 43				08 50	09 10	09 21

		AW	XC	GW	GW	GW		GW	GW	GW	AW	AW	GW	XC	GW	GW		GW	GW	AW	AW	GW	XC	GW	GW
									R																
		◇	◇■1		◇■1	◇			■1	◇■1	◇			◇■1	◇■1	◇		◇■1	◇■1	◇	◇		◇■1	◇	◇■1
			A											A									B		
		🛒	🛒		☕				☕	☕	🛒			🛒	☕			☕	☕	🛒	🛒		🛒		☕
Bath Spa ■7	d			08 07	08 24	08 36		08 47	09 00						09 24	09 36		10 00						10 07	10 24
Oldfield Park	d			08 10				08 49																10 10	
Keynsham	d			08 17				08 57																10 17	
Bristol Temple Meads ■10	a			08 29	08 39	08 47		09 05	09 15						09 39	09 48		10 15						10 29	10 39
	d			08 41		08 54							09 21			09 54						10 21		10 41	
Filton Abbey Wood	d			08 48		09 00							09 30			10 00						10 30		10 48	
Bristol Parkway ■7	a			08 52																				10 52	
	d			08 52						09 07									10 07					10 52	
Patchway	d												09 35									10 35			
Pilning	d																								
Gloucester ■7	d		08 24	09a33								08 58		09 24									10 24	11a32	
Lydney	d											09 17											10 43		
Chepstow	d		08 50									09 27		09 50											
Caldicot	d											09 35													
Severn Tunnel Jn.	d											09 38	09 46									10 46			
Newport (South Wales)	a		09 07			09 25				09 30		09 50	09 58	10 07		10 24			10 31			11 00	11 08		
	d	09 02	09 09			09 25				09 31	09 38	09 52	09 59	10 09		10 24			10 31	10 36	10 56	11 01	11 09		
Cardiff Central ■7	a	09 22	09 23			09 42				09 47	09 58	10 07	10 18	10 23		10 43			10 47	10 53	11 15	11 22	11 24		

		GW		GW	GW	AW	AW	GW	XC	GW	GW	GW		SW	GW	GW	AW	AW	AW	GW	XC	GW		GW	GW
		◇		◇■1	◇■1	◇			◇■1		◇■1	◇		◇■1	◇■1	◇■1	◇		◇		◇■1	◇		◇■1	◇
									A												A				
				☕	☕	🛒			🛒		☕				☕	Ø	🛒		🛒		🛒			☕	
Bath Spa ■7	d	10 36		11 00						11 07	11 24	11 36		11 47	12 00							12 11		12 24	12 36
Oldfield Park	d									11 10												12 14			
Keynsham	d									11 17				11 55								12 21			
Bristol Temple Meads ■10	a	10 48		11 15						11 29	11 39	11 48		12 05	12 15							12 29		12 39	12 48
	d	10 54						11 21		11 41		11 54								12 21		12 41			12 54
Filton Abbey Wood	d	11 00						11 30		11 48		12 00								12 30		12 48			13 00
Bristol Parkway ■7	a									11 52												12 52			
	d				11 07					11 52						12 07						12 52			
Patchway	d							11 35												12 35					
Pilning	d																								
Gloucester ■7	d						10 58		11 24	12a33									11 58		12 24	13a34			
Lydney	d						11 17												12 17						
Chepstow	d						11 27		11 50										12 27		12 50				
Caldicot	d						11 35												12 35						
Severn Tunnel Jn.	d						11 38	11 46											12 38	12 46					
Newport (South Wales)	a	11 24			11 31		11 50	11 58	12 07			12 24				12 31			12 50	13 00	13 11				13 25
	d	11 24			11 31	11 37	11 52	11 59	12 09			12 24				12 31	12 37	12 56	12 52	13 01	13 12				13 25
Cardiff Central ■7	a	11 43			11 46	11 53	12 07	12 18	12 23			12 43				12 46	12 53	13 15	13 07	13 18	13 27				13 43

		GW	GW	AW	GW	XC	GW	GW		GW	GW	GW	AW	AW	GW	AW	XC	GW		GW	GW	SW	GW	GW	AW
																R									R
		◇■1	◇■1	◇		◇■1		◇■1		◇	◇■1	◇■1	◇				◇■1	◇		◇■1	◇	◇■1	◇■1	◇■1	
						B											A								
		☕	Ø	🛒		🛒		☕			☕	☕	🛒			🛒	🛒			☕			☕	☕	🛒
Bath Spa ■7	d	12 59					13 19	13 24		13 36	14 00							14 07		14 24	14 36	14 47	15 00		
Oldfield Park	d						13 21											14 10							
Keynsham	d						13 28											14 17				14 55			
Bristol Temple Meads ■10	a	13 14					13 36	13 42		13 48	14 15							14 29		14 39	14 48	15 05	15 15		
	d				13 21		13 41			13 54					14 21			14 41			14 54				
Filton Abbey Wood	d				13 30		13 48			14 00					14 30			14 48			15 00				
Bristol Parkway ■7	a						13 52											14 52							
	d		13 07				13 52					14 07						14 52						15 07	
Patchway	d				13 35										14 35										
Pilning	d																								
Gloucester ■7	d					13 24	14a33							13 58			14 24	15a32							
Lydney	d					13 43								14 17											
Chepstow	d													14 27			14 50								
Caldicot	d													14 35											
Severn Tunnel Jn.	d				13 46									14 38	14 46										
Newport (South Wales)	a		13 31		13 58	14 08				14 24		14 31		14 50	14 59		15 11				15 25			15 31	
	d		13 31	13 37	13 59	14 09				14 24		14 31	14 37	14 52	15 00	15 06	15 12				15 25			15 31	15 37
Cardiff Central ■7	a		13 47	13 53	14 18	14 24				14 43		14 46	14 53	15 09	15 18	15 26	15 27				15 43			15 46	15 53

A 🛒 to Chepstow

B 🛒 to Lydney

When events are being held at the Millenium Stadium, services are subject to alteration. Please check times before travelling.

Table 132

Saturdays

6 August to 10 September

Bath Spa, Bristol and Gloucester - Cardiff

		AW	GW	XC		GW	GW	GW	GW	GW	AW	AW	GW	XC		GW	GW	GW	GW	GW	AW	AW	GW	XC	
				◇1 A ⍑			◇1 ⊡	◇	◇1 ⊡	◇1 ⊡	R ⍑	◇ ⍑		◇1 A ⍑			◇1 ⊡	◇	◇1 ⊡	◇1 ⊡	R ⍑			◇1 ⍑	
Bath Spa 7	d					15 18	15 24	15 36	16 00							16 07	16 24	16 36	17 00						
Oldfield Park	d					15 21										16 10									
Keynsham	d					15 28										16 17									
Bristol Temple Meads 10	a					15 36	15 41	15 49	16 15							16 29	16 39	16 48	17 15						
	d		15 21			15 41		15 54					16 21			16 41		16 54					17 21		
Filton Abbey Wood	d		15 30			15 48		16 00					16 30			16 48		17 00					17 30		
Bristol Parkway 7	a					15 52										16 52									
	d					15 52				16 07						16 52				17 07					
Patchway	d		15 35										16 35										17 35		
Pilning	d		15 41																						
Gloucester 7	d	14 58		15 24		16a33								16 24		17a33						16 58		17 24	
Lydney	d	15 17												16 43								17 17			
Chepstow	d	15 27		15 50										16 52								17 27			
Caldicot	d	15 35																				17 35			
Severn Tunnel Jn.	d	15 38	15 46										16 46					17 14				17 38	17 46		
Newport (South Wales)	a	15 50	16 01	16 08				16 24		16 31			17 01	17 10				17 26		17 29		17 50	17 58	18 05	
	d	15 52	16 01	16 10				16 24		16 31	16 37	16 56	17 01	17 11				17 26		17 31	17 37	17 52	18 00	18 07	
Cardiff Central 7	a	16 07	16 18	16 25				16 43		16 47	16 53	17 15	17 22	17 26				17 42		17 46	17 53	18 10	18 18	18 21	

		GW	GW	GW	GW	GW	AW	AW	AW	GW		XC	GW	GW	GW	GW	GW	AW	AW	GW		XC	GW	GW	GW
			◇1 ⊡	◇	◇1 ⊡	◇1 ⊡	R ⍑		◇ ⍑			◇1		◇1 ⊡	R	◇1 ⊡	◇1 ⊡	R ⍑				◇1	◇1 ⊡	◇	
Bath Spa 7	d	17 07	17 24	17 36	18 00								18 18	18 24	18 36	19 00							19 24	19 36	19 47
Oldfield Park	d	17 10											18 20												19 50
Keynsham	d	17 17											18 27												19 58
Bristol Temple Meads 10	a	17 28	17 39	17 48	18 15								18 35	18 39	18 48	19 15							19 38	19 48	20 05
	d	17 41		17 54						18 21			18 41		18 54					19 21				19 54	
Filton Abbey Wood	d	17 48		18 00						18 30			18 48		19 00					19 28				20 00	
Bristol Parkway 7	a	17 52											18 52												
	d	17 52				18 07							18 52				19 07								
Patchway	d									18 35										19 33					
Pilning	d																								
Gloucester 7	d	18a33						17 58				18 31	19a33						18 58			19 24			
Lydney	d							18 17											19 17						
Chepstow	d							18 27											19 27						
Caldicot	d							18 35											19 34						
Severn Tunnel Jn.	d			18 14				18 38		18 47									19 37	19 46					
Newport (South Wales)	a			18 25		18 30		18 50		19 05		19 12			19 26		19 30		19 50	19 58		20 05		20 25	
	d			18 25		18 31	18 37	18 52	18 57	19 05		19 14			19 26		19 31	19 37	19 52	19 58		20 07		20 25	
Cardiff Central 7	a			18 42		18 46	18 53	19 10	19 15	19 23		19 29			19 43		19 46	19 53	20 11	20 18		20 21		20 43	

		GW	GW	AW	AW	XC		GW	GW	AW	XC	GW	GW	GW	GW	AW		GW	XC	GW	AW	GW	SW	GW	GW
		◇1 ⊡	◇1 ⊡	R ⍑		◇1 ⍑		R	◇1 ⊡	◇ ⍑	◇1	◇	◇1 ⊡	◇1 ⊡		◇ ⍑			◇1	◇1 ⊡		◇	◇1	◇1 ⊡	◇1 ⊡
Bath Spa 7	d	20 00						20 18	20 25			20 36	21 00		21 07					21 30		21 39	21 51	22 00	
Oldfield Park	d							20 20							21 10										
Keynsham	d							20 27							21 17								21 59		
Bristol Temple Meads 10	a	20 15						20 35	20 40			20 48	21 16		21 29					21 45		21 51	22 06	22 14	
	d					20 21						20 54						21 29				21 54			
Filton Abbey Wood	d					20 28						21 00						21 36				22 00			
Bristol Parkway 7	a																								
	d		20 07											21 07											22 11
Patchway	d					20 32												21 41				22 06			
Pilning	d																								
Gloucester 7	d				19 58						20 24								21 24						
Lydney	d				20 17														21 43						
Chepstow	d				20 27														21 52						
Caldicot	d				20 35														22 01						
Severn Tunnel Jn.	d				20 38	20 42												21 52	22 04			22 18			
Newport (South Wales)	a		20 30		20 50	20 55					21 11	21 25		21 30				22 09	22 16			22 38			22 46
	d		20 31	20 40	20 52	20 57				21 02	21 13	21 25		21 31		21 44		22 11	22 19		22 34	22 38			22 46
Cardiff Central 7	a		20 44	20 58	21 09	21 11				21 15	21 29	21 43		21 47		22 03		22 30	22 41		22 53	22 58			23 06

		GW		GW	GW	GW	GW	AW
				◇	◇1 ⊡		◇1 ⊡	
Bath Spa 7	d	22 26		22 36	23 00	23 07		
Oldfield Park	d	22 28				23 10		
Keynsham	d	22 35				23 17		
Bristol Temple Meads 10	a	22 44		22 50	23 15	23 29		
	d			22 54				
Filton Abbey Wood	d			23 00				
Bristol Parkway 7	a							
	d						23 28	
Patchway	d			23 07				
Pilning	d							
Gloucester 7	d							23 09
Lydney	d							23 28
Chepstow	d							23 38
Caldicot	d							23 46
Severn Tunnel Jn.	d			23 18				23 49
Newport (South Wales)	a			23 35			23 57	00 07
	d			23 36			23 58	00 09
Cardiff Central 7	a			23 55			00 18	00 35

A ⍑ to Chepstow

When events are being held at the Millenium Stadium, services are subject to alteration. Please check times before travelling.

Table 132

Saturdays
from 17 September

Bath Spa, Bristol and Gloucester - Cardiff

		AW	AW	GW	GW	AW	GW	AW	AW	XC		GW	GW	AW	XC	GW	GW	AW	GW	SW		GW	AW	AW	GW
		◇		◇ [1]	◇ [1]	◇	◇ [1]			◇ [1]		◇ [1]		◇	◇ [1]					[1]		◇ [1]	◇		
Bath Spa [7]	d			23p49			01 13										07 07		07 22	07 35		08 00			
Oldfield Park	d																07 10		07 25	07 38					
Keynsham	d																07 17		07 32	07 45					
Bristol Temple Meads [10]	a			00 03			01 27										07 29		07 39	07 53		08 15			
	d						01 34					06 46	06 50			07 21	07 41		07 54						08 20
Filton Abbey Wood	d											06 54	07 02			07 30	07 48		08 01						08 30
Bristol Parkway [7]	a											06 58					07 52								
	d				00 16							07 11					07 52								
Patchway	d															07 34									08 35
Pilning	d																								
Gloucester [7]	d		23p13						05 50	06 15					07 00		08a32							07 58	
Lydney	d		23p33						06 09	06 34					07 20									08 17	
Chepstow	d		23p42						06 19	06 43					07 29									08 27	
Caldicot	d		23p51						06 27	06 52					07 38									08 35	
Severn Tunnel Jn.	d		23p54						06 30	06 55			07 14		07 41	07 46								08 38	08 46
Newport (South Wales)	a		00 07		00 38		02s00		06 42	07 06		07 31	07 25		07 52	07 58			08 26					08 50	09 01
	d	23p47	00 08		00 38	00 59		06 38	06 44	07 07		07 32	07 26	07 38	07 53	07 58		08 01	08 27				08 33	08 52	09 01
Cardiff Central [7]	a	00 02	00 35		00 53	01 18	02 17	06 54	07 00	07 22		07 47	07 44	07 54	08 08	08 18		08 19	08 43				08 50	09 10	09 21

		AW	XC	GW	GW	GW		GW	GW	GW	AW	AW	GW	XC	GW	GW		GW	GW	AW	AW	GW	XC	GW	GW
		◇ 🛒	◇ [1] A 🛒		◇ [1] 🍴	◇			Ⓡ [1] 🍴	◇ [1] 🍴	◇ 🛒			◇ [1] A 🛒	◇ [1] 🍴	◇		◇ [1] 🍴	◇ [1] 🍴	◇ 🛒	◇ 🛒		◇ [1] B 🛒	◇	◇ [1] 🍴
Bath Spa [7]	d			08 07	08 24	08 36		08 47	09 00						09 24	09 36		10 00						10 07	10 24
Oldfield Park	d			08 10				08 49																10 10	
Keynsham	d			08 17				08 57																10 17	
Bristol Temple Meads [10]	a			08 29	08 39	08 47		09 05	09 15						09 39	09 48		10 15						10 29	10 39
	d			08 41		08 54							09 21			09 54						10 21		10 41	
Filton Abbey Wood	d			08 48		09 00							09 30			10 00						10 30		10 48	
Bristol Parkway [7]	a			08 52																				10 52	
	d			08 52						09 07									10 07					10 52	
Patchway	d												09 35									10 35			
Pilning	d																								
Gloucester [7]	d		08 24	09a33								08 58		09 24									10 24	11a32	
Lydney	d											09 17											10 43		
Chepstow	d		08 50									09 27		09 50											
Caldicot	d											09 35													
Severn Tunnel Jn.	d											09 38	09 46									10 46			
Newport (South Wales)	a		09 07			09 25				09 30		09 50	09 58	10 07		10 24			10 31			11 00	11 08		
	d	09 02	09 09			09 25				09 31	09 38	09 52	09 59	10 09		10 24			10 31	10 36	10 56	11 01	11 09		
Cardiff Central [7]	a	09 22	09 23			09 42				09 47	09 58	10 07	10 18	10 23		10 43			10 46	10 53	11 15	11 22	11 24		

		GW		GW	GW	AW	AW	GW	XC	GW	GW	GW		SW	GW	GW	AW	AW	AW	GW	XC	GW		GW	GW
		◇		◇ [1] 🍴	◇ [1] 🍴	◇ 🛒			◇ [1] A 🛒		◇ [1] 🍴	◇		◇ [1]	◇ [1] 🍴	◇ [1] Ø	◇ 🛒		◇ 🛒		◇ [1] A 🛒	◇		◇ [1] 🍴	◇
Bath Spa [7]	d	10 36		11 00						11 07	11 24	11 36		11 47	12 00							12 11		12 24	12 36
Oldfield Park	d									11 10												12 14			
Keynsham	d									11 17				11 55								12 21			
Bristol Temple Meads [10]	a	10 48		11 15						11 29	11 39	11 48		12 05	12 15							12 29		12 39	12 48
	d	10 54						11 21		11 41		11 54								12 21		12 41			12 54
Filton Abbey Wood	d	11 00						11 30		11 48		12 00								12 30		12 48			13 00
Bristol Parkway [7]	a									11 52												12 52			
	d				11 07					11 52						12 07						12 52			
Patchway	d							11 35												12 35					
Pilning	d																								
Gloucester [7]	d						10 58		11 24	12a33								11 58			12 24	13a34			
Lydney	d						11 17											12 17							
Chepstow	d						11 27		11 50									12 27			12 50				
Caldicot	d						11 35											12 35							
Severn Tunnel Jn.	d						11 38	11 46										12 38		12 46					
Newport (South Wales)	a	11 24			11 31		11 50	11 58	12 07			12 24				12 31		12 50		13 00	13 11				13 25
	d	11 24			11 31	11 37	11 52	11 59	12 09			12 24				12 31	12 37	12 52	12 56	13 01	13 12				13 25
Cardiff Central [7]	a	11 43			11 46	11 53	12 07	12 18	12 23			12 43				12 46	12 53	13 07	13 15	13 18	13 27				13 43

		GW	GW	AW	GW	XC	GW	GW		GW	GW	GW	AW	AW	GW	AW	XC	GW		GW	GW	SW	GW	GW	AW
		◇ [1] 🍴	◇ [1] Ø	◇ 🛒		◇ [1] B 🛒		◇ [1] 🍴		◇	◇ [1] 🍴	◇ [1] 🍴	◇ 🛒			Ⓡ 🛒	◇ [1] A 🛒	◇		◇ [1] 🍴	◇	◇ [1]	◇ [1] 🍴	◇ [1] 🍴	Ⓡ 🛒
Bath Spa [7]	d	12 59					13 19	13 24		13 36	14 00							14 07		14 24	14 36	14 47	15 00		
Oldfield Park	d						13 21											14 10							
Keynsham	d						13 28											14 17				14 55			
Bristol Temple Meads [10]	a	13 14					13 36	13 42		13 48	14 15							14 29		14 39	14 48	15 05	15 15		
	d				13 21		13 41			13 54					14 21			14 41			14 54				
Filton Abbey Wood	d				13 30		13 48			14 00					14 30			14 48			15 00				
Bristol Parkway [7]	a						13 52											14 52							
	d		13 07				13 52					14 07						14 52						15 07	
Patchway	d				13 35										14 35										
Pilning	d																								
Gloucester [7]	d					13 24	14a33							13 58			14 24	15a32							
Lydney	d					13 43								14 17											
Chepstow	d													14 27			14 50								
Caldicot	d													14 35											
Severn Tunnel Jn.	d				13 46									14 38	14 46										
Newport (South Wales)	a		13 31		13 58	14 08				14 24		14 31		14 50	14 59		15 11				15 25			15 31	
	d		13 31	13 37	13 59	14 09				14 24		14 31	14 37	14 52	15 00	15 06	15 12				15 25			15 31	15 37
Cardiff Central [7]	a		13 47	13 53	14 18	14 24				14 43		14 46	14 53	15 09	15 18	15 26	15 27				15 43			15 46	15 53

A 🛒 to Chepstow

B 🛒 to Lydney

When events are being held at the Millenium Stadium, services are subject to alteration. Please check times before travelling.

Table 132

Saturdays
from 17 September

Bath Spa, Bristol and Gloucester - Cardiff

		AW	GW	XC		GW	GW	GW	GW	GW	AW	AW	GW	XC		GW	GW	GW	GW	GW	AW	AW	GW	XC	
											R										R				
				◇1			◇1	◇	◇1	◇1		◇		◇1			◇1	◇	◇1	◇1				◇1	
				A										A											
				🛒			☕		☕	☕	🛒	🛒		🛒			☕		☕	☕	🛒			🛒	
Bath Spa 7	d					15 18	15 24	15 36	16 00							16 07	16 24	16 36	17 00						
Oldfield Park	d					15 21										16 10									
Keynsham	d					15 28										16 17									
Bristol Temple Meads 10	a					15 36	15 41	15 49	16 15							16 29	16 39	16 48	17 15						
	d		15 21			15 41		15 54					16 21			16 41		16 54					17 21		
Filton Abbey Wood	d		15 30			15 48		16 00					16 30			16 48		17 00					17 30		
Bristol Parkway 7	a					15 52										16 52									
	d					15 52				16 07						16 52				17 07					
Patchway	d		15 35										16 35										17 35		
Pilning	d		15 41																						
Gloucester 7	d	14 58		15 24		16a33								16 24		17a33						16 58		17 24	
Lydney	d	15 17												16 43								17 17			
Chepstow	d	15 27		15 50										16 52								17 27			
Caldicot	d	15 35																				17 35			
Severn Tunnel Jn.	d	15 38	15 46										16 46					17 14				17 38	17 46		
Newport (South Wales)	a	15 50	16 01	16 08				16 24		16 31			17 01	17 10				17 26		17 29		17 50	17 58	18 05	
	d	15 52	16 01	16 10				16 24		16 31	16 37	16 56	17 01	17 11				17 26		17 31	17 37	17 52	18 00	18 07	
Cardiff Central 7	a	16 07	16 18	16 25				16 43		16 47	16 53	17 15	17 22	17 26				17 42		17 46	17 53	18 10	18 18	18 21	

		GW	GW	GW	GW	GW	AW	AW	AW	GW		XC	GW	GW	GW	GW	GW	AW	AW	GW		XC	GW	GW	GW
							R								R			R							
			◇1	◇	◇1	◇1			◇			◇1		◇1		◇1	◇1					◇1		◇1	◇
			☕		☕	☕	🛒		🛒					☕		☕	☕	🛒						☕	
Bath Spa 7	d	17 07	17 24	17 36	18 00								18 07	18 24	18 36	19 00							19 07	19 24	19 36
Oldfield Park	d	17 10											18 10										19 10		
Keynsham	d	17 17											18 17										19 17		
Bristol Temple Meads 10	a	17 29	17 39	17 48	18 15								18 29	18 39	18 48	19 15							19 29	19 38	19 48
	d	17 41		17 54						18 21			18 41		18 54					19 21			19 41		19 54
Filton Abbey Wood	d	17 48		18 00						18 30			18 48		19 00					19 28			19 48		20 00
Bristol Parkway 7	a	17 52											18 52										19 52		
	d	17 52				18 07							18 52				19 07						19 52		
Patchway	d									18 35										19 33					
Pilning	d																								
Gloucester 7	d	18a33						17 58				18 31	19a33						18 58			19 24	20a33		
Lydney	d							18 17											19 17						
Chepstow	d							18 27											19 27						
Caldicot	d							18 35											19 34						
Severn Tunnel Jn.	d			18 14				18 38		18 47									19 37	19 46					
Newport (South Wales)	a			18 25		18 30		18 50		19 05		19 12			19 26		19 30		19 50	19 58		20 05			20 25
	d			18 25		18 31	18 37	18 52	18 57	19 05		19 14			19 26		19 31	19 37	19 52	19 58		20 07			20 25
Cardiff Central 7	a			18 42		18 46	18 53	19 10	19 15	19 23		19 29			19 43		19 46	19 53	20 11	20 18		20 21			20 43

		GW	GW	GW	AW	AW		XC	GW	GW	AW	GW	XC	GW	GW	GW		GW	AW	GW	XC	GW	AW	GW	SW
					R				R																
			◇1	◇1				◇1		◇1	◇	◇1	◇1	◇	◇1	◇1			◇		◇1	◇1		◇	◇1
			☕	☕	🛒			🛒		☕	🛒	☕			☕	☕			🛒			☕			
Bath Spa 7	d	19 47	20 00						20 18	20 25				20 36	21 00			21 07				21 30		21 39	21 51
Oldfield Park	d	19 50							20 20									21 10							
Keynsham	d	19 58							20 27									21 17							21 59
Bristol Temple Meads 10	a	20 05	20 15						20 35	20 40				20 48	21 16			21 29				21 45		21 51	22 06
	d							20 21						20 54						21 29				21 54	
Filton Abbey Wood	d							20 28						21 00						21 36				22 00	
Bristol Parkway 7	a																								
	d			20 07								20 40				21 07									
Patchway	d							20 32												21 41				22 06	
Pilning	d																								
Gloucester 7	d					19 58							20 24								21 24				
Lydney	d					20 17															21 43				
Chepstow	d					20 27															21 52				
Caldicot	d					20 35															22 01				
Severn Tunnel Jn.	d					20 38		20 42												21 52	22 04			22 18	
Newport (South Wales)	a			20 30		20 50		20 55				21 05	21 11	21 25		21 30				22 09	22 16			22 38	
	d			20 31	20 40	20 52		20 57			21 02	21 07	21 13	21 25		21 31			21 44	22 11	22 19		22 34	22 38	
Cardiff Central 7	a			20 44	20 58	21 09		21 11			21 15	21 23	21 29	21 43		21 47			22 03	22 30	22 41		22 53	22 58	

A 🛒 to Chepstow

When events are being held at the Millenium Stadium, services are subject to alteration. Please check times before travelling.

Table 132

Saturdays
from 17 September

Bath Spa, Bristol and Gloucester - Cardiff

		GW		GW	GW	GW	GW	GW	AW	GW	AW
		◇1 ☕		◇1 ☕		◇	◇1 ☕			◇1 ☕	🚌
Bath Spa 7	d	22 00			22 26	22 36	23 00	23 07			
Oldfield Park	d				22 28			23 10			
Keynsham	d				22 35			23 17			
Bristol Temple Meads 10	a	22 14			22 44	22 50	23 15	23 29			
	d					22 54					
Filton Abbey Wood	d					23 00					
Bristol Parkway 7	a										
	d			22 11						23 28	
Patchway	d					23 07					
Pilning	d										
Gloucester 7	d										23 09
Lydney	d										23 49
Chepstow	d										00 09
Caldicot	d										00 24
Severn Tunnel Jn	d					23 18					00 34
Newport (South Wales)	a			22 46		23 35				23 57	00 59
	d			22 46		23 36			23 46	23 58	00 59
Cardiff Central 7	a			23 06		23 55			00 05	00 18	01 29

Sundays
until 19 June

		AW	GW	AW	AW	GW	GW	AW	XC	GW		GW	GW	AW	AW	XC	GW	GW	GW	AW		XC	XC	GW	GW
		A	◇1 A ☕	A	A	◇1 A ☕	◇1 A ☕	◇ 🛒	◇1 🛒	◇		◇1 ☕	◇1 ☕			◇1 🛒		◇1 ☕	◇1 ☕			◇1	◇1 🛒	R	◇1 ☕
Bath Spa 7	d					00 10	01 07					09 45					10 27	10 40						11 26	11 40
Oldfield Park	d																10 30							11 29	
Keynsham	d																10 37							11 36	
Bristol Temple Meads 10	a					00 25	01 21					09 55					10 45	10 55						11 43	11 55
	d								09 30	09 48						10 30							11 30	11 48	
Filton Abbey Wood	d									09 56														11 55	
Bristol Parkway 7	a								09 40							10 38							11 38		
	d		23p28						09 48				10 11			10 43			11 06				11 43		
Patchway	d																							12 00	
Pilning	d																								
Gloucester 7	d				23p09															10 48		11 23			
Lydney	d				23p28															11 07					
Chepstow	d				23p38															11 17					
Caldicot	d				23p46															11 25					
Severn Tunnel Jn	d				23p49					10 09										11 29				12 11	
Newport (South Wales)	a		23p57		00 07				10 12	10 26			10 36			11 07			11 31	11 47		12 06	12 09	12 29	
	d	23p46	23p58	00 04	00 09			09 27		10 27			10 36	10 55	11 00				11 32	11 49		12 08		12 29	
Cardiff Central 7	a	00 05	00 18	00 23	00 35			09 42		10 42			10 53	11 11	11 16				11 48	12 07		12 26		12 44	

		GW	AW	XC	XC	GW		GW	AW	AW	GW	XC	XC	XC	AW	GW		GW	GW	AW	XC	GW	AW	GW	SW
		◇1 ☕	◇ 🛒	◇1 🛒	◇1 🛒			◇1 ☕	R 🛒		◇1 ☕	◇1 🛒	◇1	◇1 🛒	R 🛒	◇		◇1 ☕	◇1 ☕	◇	◇1	◇		◇1 ☕	◇1
Bath Spa 7	d					12 23		12 40								13 23		13 40				14 26		14 40	14 50
Oldfield Park	d					12 25										13 26						14 28			
Keynsham	d					12 33										13 33						14 36			14 58
Bristol Temple Meads 10	a					12 40		12 55								13 40		13 55				14 44		14 55	15 05
	d				12 30							13 00		13 30		13 48						14 48			
Filton Abbey Wood	d															13 55						14 55			
Bristol Parkway 7	a				12 38							13 08		13 38											
	d	12 04			12 43						13 06	13 13		13 43					14 04						
Patchway	d																								
Pilning	d																								
Gloucester 7	d			12 23						12 30			13 23								14 24		14 33		
Lydney	d									12 49													14 52		
Chepstow	d									12 59													15 02		
Caldicot	d									13 07													15 10		
Severn Tunnel Jn	d									13 10						14 09						15 08	15 13		
Newport (South Wales)	a	12 32		13 06	13 10					13 33	13 35	13 40	14 06	14 08		14 29			14 32		15 08	15 26	15 31		
	d	12 32	12 52	13 08					13 29	13 34	13 35		14 08		14 30	14 30			14 32	15 07	15 09	15 26	15 33		
Cardiff Central 7	a	12 51	13 13	13 26					13 44	13 52	13 55		14 26		14 49	14 53			14 51	15 31	15 31	15 41	15 51		

A not 22 May

When events are being held at the Millenium Stadium, services are subject to alteration. Please check times before travelling.

Table 132

Sundays until 19 June

Bath Spa, Bristol and Gloucester - Cardiff

		GW		AW	XC	GW	GW	GW	AW	GW	XC	GW		GW	AW	AW	GW	XC	GW	GW	GW	AW		GW	XC
		◇1 ☕		R 🛒	◇1	◇	◇1 ☕		R 🛒	◇1 ☕	◇1	◇		◇1 ☕	R 🛒		◇1 ☕	◇1	R	◇1 ☕		R 🛒		◇1 ☕	◇1
Bath Spa 7	d					15 28	15 40	16 16				16 28		16 40					17 26	17 40	18 11				
Oldfield Park	d							16 17											17 29		18 13				
Keynsham	d							16 26											17 36		18 22				
Bristol Temple Meads 10	a					15 40	15 55	16 33				16 41		16 54					17 43	17 57	18 33				
	d					15 48						16 48							17 48						
Filton Abbey Wood	d					15 55						16 55							17 55						
Bristol Parkway 7	a																								
	d	15 11								16 14							17 16							18 13	
Patchway	d											17 00													
Pilning	d																								
Gloucester 7	d				15 23						16 23					16 37		17 23							18 23
Lydney	d															16 56									
Chepstow	d															17 07									
Caldicot	d															17 13									
Severn Tunnel Jn	d					16 10						17 11				17 16			18 09						
Newport (South Wales)	a	15 37			16 06	16 28				16 40	17 06	17 29				17 37	17 44	18 06	18 27					18 41	19 07
	d	15 37		15 46	16 08	16 28			16 32	16 40	17 08	17 29			17 34	17 38	17 44	18 08	18 27			18 33		18 42	19 08
Cardiff Central 7	a	15 56		16 02	16 26	16 46			16 53	16 59	17 27	17 46			17 50	17 55	18 01	18 28	18 45			18 50		18 58	19 27

		GW	GW	GW	GW	GW	AW	AW		XC	AW	GW	GW	GW	GW	XC	AW	GW		AW	GW	SW	GW	GW	AW
		◇	◇1 ☕	◇	◇1 ☕	◇1 ☕	R 🛒			◇1	R 🛒	◇	◇1 ☕		◇1 ☕	◇1	R 🛒	◇			◇1 ☕	◇1	◇1 ☕	◇	R 🛒
Bath Spa 7	d	18 27	18 40	19 03	19 13							19 29	19 40	20 00				20 27			20 40	20 49	21 05	21 10	
Oldfield Park	d			19 06										20 02										21 12	
Keynsham	d			19 13										20 11								20 57		21 20	
Bristol Temple Meads 10	a	18 40	18 55	19 21	19 26							19 41	19 55	20 18				20 39			20 55	21 04	21 19	21 27	
	d	18 48										19 48						20 48							
Filton Abbey Wood	d	18 55										19 55						20 55							
Bristol Parkway 7	a																								
	d					19 16									20 14										
Patchway	d											20 00													
Pilning	d																								
Gloucester 7	d							18 48		19 28						20 23				20 31					
Lydney	d							19 07												20 50					
Chepstow	d							19 17												21 00					
Caldicot	d							19 25												21 10					
Severn Tunnel Jn	d	19 08						19 32				20 11						21 08		21 13					
Newport (South Wales)	a	19 26				19 42		19 54		20 11		20 28			20 40	21 06		21 26		21 31					
	d	19 26				19 42	19 51	19 56		20 13	20 23	20 29			20 40	21 08	21 14	21 26		21 33					21 43
Cardiff Central 7	a	19 42				20 00	20 10	20 12		20 31	20 43	20 46			20 59	21 26	21 36	21 42		21 49					22 06

		GW	AW	GW			GW	GW	GW	GW	AW	GW	GW	GW		AW
		◇1 ☕	◇	◇ A			◇1 ☕	◇1 ☕		◇		◇1 ☕	◇1 ☕	◇1 ☕		◇
Bath Spa 7	d			21 28			21 40		22 19	22 29		22 44		23 47		
Oldfield Park	d								22 21							
Keynsham	d								22 30							
Bristol Temple Meads 10	a			21 40			21 55		22 37	22 42		22 57		00 02		
	d			21 48						22 48						
Filton Abbey Wood	d			21 55						22 55						
Bristol Parkway 7	a															
	d	21 16						22 15					23 17			
Patchway	d			22 02												
Pilning	d															
Gloucester 7	d										22 33					
Lydney	d										22 52					
Chepstow	d										23 02					
Caldicot	d										23 10					
Severn Tunnel Jn	d			22 13						23 08	23 14					
Newport (South Wales)	a	21 44		22 36				22 40		23 28	23 33		23 44			
	d	21 44	22 31	22 37				22 40		23 28	23 34		23 45			23 55
Cardiff Central 7	a	22 06	22 57	22 59				23 02		23 49	23 54		00 06			00 20

When events are being held at the Millenium Stadium, services are subject to alteration. Please check times before travelling.

Table 132

Sundays
26 June to 31 July

Bath Spa, Bristol and Gloucester - Cardiff

		AW	GW	AW	AW	GW	GW	AW	XC	GW		GW	GW	AW	AW	XC	GW	GW	AW	GW		XC	XC	GW	GW
																								R	
			◇1			◇1	◇1	◇	◇1	◇		◇1	◇1			◇1		◇1		◇1		◇1	◇1		◇1
			☕			☕	☕	🛒	🛒			☕	☕			🛒		☕		☕			🛒		☕
Bath Spa 7	d					00 10	01 07					09 45					10 27	10 40						11 26	11 40
Oldfield Park	d																10 30							11 29	
Keynsham	d																10 37							11 36	
Bristol Temple Meads 10	a					00 25	01 21					09 55					10 45	10 55						11 43	11 55
	d								09 30	09 48						10 30							11 30	11 48	
Filton Abbey Wood	d									09 56														11 55	
Bristol Parkway 7	a								09 38							10 38							11 38		
	d		23p28						09 43				10 08			10 43				11 26			11 43		
Patchway	d																							12 00	
Pilning	d																								
Gloucester 7	d				23p09														10 48			11 23			
Lydney	d				23p28														11 07						
Chepstow	d				23p38														11 17						
Caldicot	d				23p46														11 25						
Severn Tunnel Jn.	d				23p49					10 09									11 29					12 11	
Newport (South Wales)	a		23p57		00 07				10 02	10 26			10 33			11 07			11 47	11 51		12 06	12 09	12 29	
	d	23p46	23p58	00 04	00 09			09 27		10 27			10 33	10 55	11 00				11 49	11 55		12 08		12 29	
Cardiff Central 7	a	00 05	00 18	00 23	00 35			09 42		10 42			10 51	11 11	11 16				12 07	12 08		12 26		12 44	

		AW	GW	XC	XC	GW		GW	AW	AW	GW	XC	XC	AW	GW	GW		GW	XC	AW	XC	GW	AW	GW	SW
									R					R											
		◇	◇1	◇1	◇1			◇1			◇1	◇1	◇1		◇	◇1		◇1	◇1	◇	◇1	◇		◇1	◇1
		🛒	☕	🛒	🛒			☕	🛒		☕		🛒	🛒		☕		☕			🛒			☕	
Bath Spa 7	d					12 23		12 40							13 23	13 40						14 26		14 40	14 50
Oldfield Park	d					12 25									13 26							14 28			
Keynsham	d					12 33									13 33							14 36			14 58
Bristol Temple Meads 10	a					12 40		12 55							13 40	13 55						14 44		14 55	15 05
	d				12 30								13 30		13 48						14 30	14 48			
Filton Abbey Wood	d														13 55							14 55			
Bristol Parkway 7	a				12 38								13 41								14 40				
	d		12 27		12 43						13 29		13 48					14 33			14 47				
Patchway	d																								
Pilning	d																								
Gloucester 7	d			12 23						12 30		13 23							14 24				14 33		
Lydney	d									12 49													14 52		
Chepstow	d									12 59													15 02		
Caldicot	d									13 07													15 10		
Severn Tunnel Jn.	d									13 10					14 09							15 08	15 13		
Newport (South Wales)	a		12 54	13 06	13 11					13 33	13 54	14 06	14 10		14 29			14 59	15 07		15 11	15 26	15 31		
	d	12 52	12 55	13 08					13 29	13 34	13 54	14 08		14 30	14 30			15 00	15 09	15 07		15 26	15 33		
Cardiff Central 7	a	13 13	13 12	13 26					13 44	13 52	14 12	14 26		14 49	14 53			15 17	15 31	15 31		15 41	15 51		

		AW		GW	XC	XC	GW	GW	AW	GW	XC	XC		GW	GW	GW	AW	AW	GW	XC	XC	GW		GW	AW
		R							R								R					R			R
				◇1	◇1	◇1	◇	◇1		◇1	◇1	◇1			◇	◇1			◇1	◇1	◇1			◇1	
		🛒		☕		🛒		☕	🛒	☕		🛒				☕	🛒		☕	🛒				☕	🛒
Bath Spa 7	d						15 28	15 40						16 16	16 28	16 40						17 26		17 40	
Oldfield Park	d													16 17								17 29			
Keynsham	d													16 26								17 36			
Bristol Temple Meads 10	a						15 40	15 55						16 33	16 41	16 54						17 43		17 57	
	d					15 30	15 48					16 30			16 48					17 30		17 48			
Filton Abbey Wood	d						15 55								16 55							17 55			
Bristol Parkway 7	a					15 38						16 38								17 38					
	d			15 32		15 45				16 32		16 45							17 32	17 43					
Patchway	d														17 00										
Pilning	d																								
Gloucester 7	d				15 23						16 23							16 37			17 23				
Lydney	d																	16 56							
Chepstow	d																	17 07							
Caldicot	d																	17 13							
Severn Tunnel Jn.	d						16 10								17 11			17 16				18 09			
Newport (South Wales)	a			15 58	16 06	16 10	16 28			16 56	17 06	17 09			17 29			17 37	18 01	18 03	18 07	18 27			
	d	15 46		15 59	16 08		16 28		16 32	16 56	17 08				17 29		17 34	17 38	18 01		18 09	18 27			18 33
Cardiff Central 7	a	16 00		16 17	16 26		16 46		16 53	17 15	17 27				17 46		17 50	17 55	18 18		18 29	18 45			18 50

		GW	XC	XC	GW	GW	GW	GW		GW	AW	GW	AW	XC	XC	AW	GW	GW		GW	GW	XC	XC	AW	GW
											R					R								R	
		◇1	◇1	◇1		◇	◇1	◇		◇1		◇1		◇1	◇1		◇	◇1			◇1	◇1	◇1		◇
		☕		🛒			☕			☕	🛒	☕			🛒	🛒		☕			☕		🛒	🛒	
Bath Spa 7	d				18 11	18 27	18 40	19 03		19 16							19 29	19 40		20 00					20 27
Oldfield Park	d				18 13			19 06												20 02					
Keynsham	d				18 22			19 13												20 11					
Bristol Temple Meads 10	a				18 33	18 40	18 55	19 21		19 29							19 41	19 55		20 18					20 39
	d			18 30		18 48									19 30		19 48						20 30		20 48
Filton Abbey Wood	d					18 55											19 55								20 55
Bristol Parkway 7	a			18 41											19 38								20 38		
	d	18 32		18 48								19 26			19 45						20 36		20 43		
Patchway	d																20 00								
Pilning	d																								
Gloucester 7	d		18 23										18 48	19 28								20 23			
Lydney	d												19 07												
Chepstow	d												19 17												
Caldicot	d												19 25												
Severn Tunnel Jn.	d					19 08							19 32				20 11								21 08
Newport (South Wales)	a	18 58	19 07	19 11		19 26						19 52	19 54	20 11	20 12		20 28				21 02	21 06	21 09		21 26
	d	18 59	19 08			19 26					19 51	19 53	19 56	20 13		20 23	20 29				21 03	21 08		21 14	21 26
Cardiff Central 7	a	19 16	19 27			19 42					20 10	20 09	20 12	20 31		20 43	20 46				21 20	21 26		21 36	21 42

When events are being held at the Millenium Stadium, services are subject to alteration. Please check times before travelling.

Table 132

Sundays

26 June to 31 July

Bath Spa, Bristol and Gloucester - Cardiff

		AW	GW	SW		GW	GW	AW	GW	AW	GW	GW	GW	GW		GW	AW	GW	GW	AW	GW				
			◇1 ⊏	◇1		◇	◇1 ⊏	R ⚲	◇1 ⊏	◇	◇	◇1 ⊏		◇1 ⊏		◇		◇1 ⊏	◇1 ⊏	◇	◇1 ⊏				
Bath Spa 7	d		20 40	20 49		21 10	21 14				21 28	21 40	22 19			22 29		22 44	23 47						
Oldfield Park	d					21 12							22 21												
Keynsham	d			20 57		21 20							22 30												
Bristol Temple Meads 10	a		20 55	21 04		21 27	21 31				21 40	21 55	22 37			22 42		22 57	00 02						
	d										21 48					22 48									
Filton Abbey Wood	d										21 55					22 55									
Bristol Parkway 7	a																								
	d								21 34					22 34							23 37				
Patchway	d										22 02														
Pilning	d																								
Gloucester 7	d	20 31															22 33								
Lydney	d	20 50															22 52								
Chepstow	d	21 00															23 02								
Caldicot	d	21 10															23 10								
Severn Tunnel Jn.	d	21 13									22 13					23 08	23 14								
Newport (South Wales)	a	21 31							22 00		22 36			23 04		23 28	23 33				00 01				
	d	21 33						21 43	22 01	22 31	22 37			23 05		23 28	23 34			23 55	00 02				
Cardiff Central 7	a	21 49						22 06	22 22	22 57	22 59			23 27		23 49	23 54			00 20	00 23				

Sundays

7 August to 11 September

		GW	AW	GW	GW	AW	GW	GW	GW	GW		GW	AW	AW	GW	AW	GW	AW	XC	GW		GW	GW	GW	AW
		◇1 ⊏		🚌	🚌	◇ ⚲	◇	◇1 ⊏	◇1 ⊏			◇1 ⊏			◇1 ⊏		R	🚌	🚌	◇1 ⊏		◇1 ⊏		◇1 ⊏	◇ ⚲
Bath Spa 7	d			00 59	01 56			09 38		10 15		10 37					11 26			11 40			12 23	12 40	
Oldfield Park	d									10 18							11 29						12 25		
Keynsham	d									10 25							11 36						12 33		
Bristol Temple Meads 10	a			01 29	02 26			09 52		10 33		10 52					11 43			11 55			12 40	12 55	
	d						09 48										11 48								
Filton Abbey Wood	d						09 56										11 55								
Bristol Parkway 7	a																								
	d	23p28							10 08						11 20							12 15			
Patchway	d																12 00								
Pilning	d																								
Gloucester 7	d		23p09															10 48	11 30						
Lydney	d		23p28															11 28							
Chepstow	d		23p38															11 48							
Caldicot	d		23p46															12 03							
Severn Tunnel Jn.	d		23p49				10 09										12 11	12 13							
Newport (South Wales)	a	23p57	00 07				10 26		10 33						11 45		12 29	12 38	12 40			12 41			
	d	23p58	00 09			09 27	10 27		10 33				10 55	11 00	11 49	11 55	12 29					12 41			12 52
Cardiff Central 7	a	00 18	00 35			09 42	10 42		10 51				11 11	11 16	12 02	12 11	12 44					12 59			13 13

		AW	AW	GW	XC	AW		AW	GW	XC	GW	GW	AW	GW	GW	SW		AW	XC	GW	AW	AW	GW	GW	GW
		R ⚲		◇1 ⊏	🚌	🚌		R ⚲	◇	🚌	◇1 ⊏	◇1 ⊏	◇	◇	◇1 ⊏	◇1			🚌	◇1 ⊏	R ⚲	🚌	◇	◇1 ⊏	
Bath Spa 7	d								13 23		13 40			14 26	14 40	14 50							15 28	15 40	16 16
Oldfield Park	d								13 26					14 28											16 17
Keynsham	d								13 33					14 36		14 58									16 26
Bristol Temple Meads 10	a								13 40		13 55			14 44	14 55	15 05							15 40	15 55	16 33
	d								13 48					14 48									15 48		
Filton Abbey Wood	d								13 55					14 55									15 55		
Bristol Parkway 7	a																								
	d			13 15								14 15								15 16					
Patchway	d																								
Pilning	d																								
Gloucester 7	d				12 30	12 35				13 30									14 30			14 35			
Lydney	d					13 15																15 15			
Chepstow	d					13 35																15 35			
Caldicot	d					13 50																15 50			
Severn Tunnel Jn.	d					14 00			14 09					15 08								16 00	16 10		
Newport (South Wales)	a			13 38	13 40	14 25			14 29	14 40		14 41		15 26					15 40	15 42		16 25	16 28		
	d	13 29	13 34	13 39				14 30	14 30			14 42	15 07	15 26				15 33		15 42	15 50		16 28		
Cardiff Central 7	a	13 44	13 52	13 57				14 49	14 53			15 00	15 31	15 41				15 52		16 00	16 07		16 46		

When events are being held at the Millenium Stadium, services are subject to alteration. Please check times before travelling.

Table 132

Sundays

7 August to 11 September

Bath Spa, Bristol and Gloucester - Cardiff

		AW		XC	GW	GW	GW	AW	AW	XC	GW	AW		GW	GW	GW	AW	XC	GW	GW	XC	GW		GW	GW
		R 🛒		🚌	◇1 ☕	◇	◇1 ☕	R 🛒		🚌	◇1 ☕	🚌		R	◇1 ☕		R 🛒	🚌	◇1 ☕	◇	🚌	◇1 ☕		◇	◇1 ☕
Bath Spa 7	d					16 28	16 40							17 26	17 40	18 11				18 27		18 40		19 03	19 10
Oldfield Park	d													17 29		18 13								19 06	
Keynsham	d													17 36		18 22								19 13	
Bristol Temple Meads 10	a					16 41	16 55							17 43	17 55	18 33				18 40		18 55		19 21	19 23
	d					16 48								17 48						18 48					
Filton Abbey Wood	d					16 55								17 55						18 55					
Bristol Parkway 7	a																								
	d				16 14						17 15								18 19						
Patchway	d					17 00																			
Pilning	d																								
Gloucester 7	d			15 30						16 30		16 35						17 30			18 30				
Lydney	d											17 15													
Chepstow	d											17 35													
Caldicot	d											17 50													
Severn Tunnel Jn	d					17 11						18 00		18 09						19 08					
Newport (South Wales)	a			16 40	16 40	17 29				17 40	17 43	18 25		18 27				18 40	18 45	19 26	19 40				
	d	16 32			16 41	17 29		17 34	17 38		17 43			18 27			18 33		18 45	19 26					
Cardiff Central 7	a	16 53			17 00	17 46		17 50	17 56		18 00			18 45			18 50		19 03	19 42					

		GW	AW	AW	AW	AW	GW	GW		GW	GW	XC	AW	GW	GW	SW	GW	GW		AW	XC	AW	GW	AW	AW
		◇1 ☕	R 🛒		R 🛒	🚌	◇	◇1 ☕			◇1 ☕	🚌	R 🛒	◇	◇1 ☕	◇1	◇1 ☕	◇			🚌	R 🛒	◇1 ☕	🚌	◇
Bath Spa 7	d						19 29	19 40		20 00				20 27	20 40	20 49	21 04	21 10							
Oldfield Park	d									20 02								21 12							
Keynsham	d									20 11						20 57		21 20							
Bristol Temple Meads 10	a						19 41	19 56		20 18				20 39	20 55	21 04	21 17	21 27							
	d						19 48							20 48											
Filton Abbey Wood	d						19 55							20 55											
Bristol Parkway 7	a																								
	d	19 15									20 13												21 16		
Patchway	d						20 00																		
Pilning	d																								
Gloucester 7	d					18 35						19 31									20 30			20 35	
Lydney	d					19 15																		21 15	
Chepstow	d					19 35																		21 35	
Caldicot	d					19 50																		21 50	
Severn Tunnel Jn	d					20 00	20 11							21 08										22 00	
Newport (South Wales)	a	19 41				20 25	20 28				20 39	20 41		21 26							21 40		21 44	22 25	
	d	19 41	19 51	19 56	20 23		20 29				20 39		21 14	21 26						21 33		21 43	21 45		22 31
Cardiff Central 7	a	19 59	20 10	20 13	20 43		20 46				20 57		21 36	21 42						21 50		22 06	22 06		22 57

		GW	GW	GW		GW	GW	GW	AW	GW	AW	AW	GW
		◇	◇1 ☕	◇1 ☕			◇	◇1 ☕		◇1 ☕	◇	🚌	◇1 ☕
Bath Spa 7	d	21 28	21 40			22 19	22 29	22 44					23 55
Oldfield Park	d					22 21							
Keynsham	d					22 30							
Bristol Temple Meads 10	a	21 40	21 55			22 37	22 42	22 58					00 15
	d	21 48					22 48						
Filton Abbey Wood	d	21 55					22 55						
Bristol Parkway 7	a												
	d			22 16						23 17			
Patchway	d	22 02											
Pilning	d												
Gloucester 7	d											22 35	
Lydney	d											23 15	
Chepstow	d											23 35	
Caldicot	d											23 50	
Severn Tunnel Jn	d	22 13					23 08					23 59	
Newport (South Wales)	a	22 36		22 44			23 28			23 44		00 25	
	d	22 37		22 44			23 28		23 34	23 45	23 55	00 25	
Cardiff Central 7	a	22 59		23 06			23 49		23 54	00 06	00 20	00 55	

When events are being held at the Millenium Stadium, services are subject to alteration. Please check times before travelling.

Table 132

Sundays

18 September to 23 October

Bath Spa, Bristol and Gloucester - Cardiff

		AW	GW	AW	AW	GW	GW	AW	GW	GW		GW	GW	AW	GW	AW	GW	GW	GW	GW		GW	GW	AW	GW
																	R								
			◇1			◇1	◇1	◇	◇1	◇1			◇1	◇	◇1				◇1	◇1			◇1	◇	
			🍴		🚌	🍴	🍴	🛒	🍴	🍴			🍴		🍴				🍴	🍴			🍴	🛒	
Bath Spa 7	d					00 10	01 07		09 40			10 15	10 37				11 25		11 40			12 23	12 40		
Oldfield Park	d											10 18					11 28					12 25			
Keynsham	d											10 25					11 35					12 33			
Bristol Temple Meads 10	a					00 25	01 21		09 55			10 33	10 52				11 42		11 55			12 40	12 53		
	d																								
Filton Abbey Wood	d																								
Bristol Parkway 7	a																								
	d		23p28							10 08					11 20			11 30		12 15					12 25
Patchway	d																								12 28
Pilning	d																								
Gloucester 7	d				23p09											10 32									
Lydney	d				23p49											11 13									
Chepstow	d				00 09											11 23									
Caldicot	d				00 24											11 31									
Severn Tunnel Jn.	d				00 34					10 22						11 34		11 42							12 40
Newport (South Wales)	a		23p57		00 59					10 36					11 45	11 53		12 00		12 41					12 57
	d	23p46	23p58	00 07	00 59			09 27		10 36				11 00	11 49	11 55		12 01		12 41				12 52	12 59
Cardiff Central 7	a	00 05	00 18	00 26	01 29			09 42		10 54				11 16	12 02	12 13		12 17		12 59				13 13	13 14

		GW	AW	GW	AW	GW		GW	GW	AW	GW	GW	GW	SW	AW	XC		AW	GW	GW	GW	AW	GW	XC	GW
			R							R												R			
		◇		◇1				◇1	◇		◇1		◇1	◇1	◇	◇1			◇1	◇	◇1			◇1	
			🛒	🍴				🍴		🛒	🍴		🍴			🛒			🍴		🍴	🛒			
Bath Spa 7	d	13 23						13 40	14 25				14 40	14 50						15 28	15 40				16 08
Oldfield Park	d	13 26							14 27																16 10
Keynsham	d	13 33							14 35					14 58											16 18
Bristol Temple Meads 10	a	13 40						13 55	14 43				14 55	15 05						15 40	15 55				16 26
	d																								
Filton Abbey Wood	d																								
Bristol Parkway 7	a																								
	d			13 15		13 30					14 15	14 30							15 16				15 30		
Patchway	d																								
Pilning	d																								
Gloucester 7	d				12 27											14 30		14 34						15 23	
Lydney	d				13 09													14 53							
Chepstow	d				13 19													15 03							
Caldicot	d				13 27													15 11							
Severn Tunnel Jn.	d				13 30	13 42						14 42						15 14					15 42		
Newport (South Wales)	a			13 38	13 53	14 02					14 41	15 00				15 14		15 32	15 42				16 00	16 06	
	d		13 29	13 39	13 54	14 03				14 30	14 42	15 01			15 07			15 34	15 42			15 50	16 01	16 08	
Cardiff Central 7	a		13 44	13 57	14 12	14 19				14 49	15 00	15 17			15 31			15 52	16 00			16 07	16 17	16 26	

		GW		AW	GW	GW	XC	GW	GW	AW	AW	GW		GW	XC	GW	GW	AW	GW	GW	XC	GW		GW	GW
				R					R	R								R							
		◇			◇1		◇1	◇1				◇1			◇1	◇1	◇		◇1		◇1	◇1		◇	◇1
				🛒	🍴			🍴		🛒		🍴				🍴		🛒	🍴			🍴			🍴
Bath Spa 7	d	16 28						16 40	17 26							17 40	18 25					18 40		19 03	19 10
Oldfield Park	d								17 29															19 06	
Keynsham	d								17 36															19 13	
Bristol Temple Meads 10	a	16 41						16 55	17 45							17 55	18 38					18 55		19 21	19 23
	d																								
Filton Abbey Wood	d																								
Bristol Parkway 7	a																								
	d				16 14	16 28						17 15		17 30					18 19	18 28					
Patchway	d													17 33											
Pilning	d																								
Gloucester 7	d						16 23				16 37				17 23						18 23				
Lydney	d										16 56														
Chepstow	d										17 07														
Caldicot	d										17 13														
Severn Tunnel Jn.	d					16 40					17 16			17 45						18 40					
Newport (South Wales)	a				16 40	16 58	17 06				17 37	17 43		18 02	18 07				18 45	18 58	19 07				
	d			16 32	16 41	16 59	17 08			17 34	17 38	17 43		18 04	18 09			18 33	18 45	18 59	19 08				
Cardiff Central 7	a			16 53	17 00	17 15	17 27			17 50	17 55	18 00		18 19	18 29			18 50	19 03	19 15	19 27				

		GW	GW	GW	AW	AW	GW	XC		GW	AW	GW	GW	GW	XC	GW	SW	GW		GW	AW	AW	GW	GW	AW
					R						R										R				R
		◇1	◇	◇1				◇1				◇1	◇		◇1	◇1	◇1	◇1		◇			◇	◇1	
		🍴		🍴	🛒						🛒	🍴				🍴		🍴			🛒			🍴	🛒
Bath Spa 7	d		19 27	19 40						20 00			20 27			20 40	20 49	21 04		21 10			21 28	21 40	
Oldfield Park	d									20 02										21 12					
Keynsham	d									20 11							20 57			21 20					
Bristol Temple Meads 10	a		19 39	19 56						20 18			20 39			20 55	21 04	21 17		21 27			21 40	21 55	
	d																								
Filton Abbey Wood	d																								
Bristol Parkway 7	a																								
	d	19 15					19 28					20 13		20 28											
Patchway	d													20 31											
Pilning	d																								
Gloucester 7	d					18 48		19 28							20 23							20 31			
Lydney	d					19 07																20 50			
Chepstow	d					19 17																21 00			
Caldicot	d					19 25																21 10			
Severn Tunnel Jn.	d					19 32	19 40							20 43								21 13			
Newport (South Wales)	a	19 41				19 54	19 59	20 11				20 39		21 00	21 06							21 31			
	d	19 41			19 51	19 56	20 01	20 13			20 23	20 39		21 02	21 08						21 14	21 33			21 43
Cardiff Central 7	a	19 59			20 10	20 12	20 16	20 31			20 43	20 57		21 17	21 26						21 36	21 49			22 06

When events are being held at the Millenium Stadium, services are subject to alteration. Please check times before travelling.

Table 132

Sundays
18 September to 23 October

Bath Spa, Bristol and Gloucester - Cardiff

		GW	GW	GW		GW	AW	GW	GW	AW	GW	GW	AW	GW		GW
		◇1				◇	◇	◇1			◇1	◇1	◇			◇1
		☕						☕			☕	☕				☕
Bath Spa 7	d			22 22		22 29					22 44					23 55
Oldfield Park	d			22 24												
Keynsham	d			22 33												
Bristol Temple Meads 10	a			22 40		22 45					23 00					00 09
	d															
Filton Abbey Wood	d															
Bristol Parkway 7	a															
	d	21 16	21 33					22 16	22 30			23 17		23 30		
Patchway	d								22 33							
Pilning	d															
Gloucester 7	d									22 33						
Lydney	d									22 52						
Chepstow	d									23 02						
Caldicot	d									23 10						
Severn Tunnel Jn.	d		21 45						22 45	23 14				23 42		
Newport (South Wales)	a	21 44	22 03					22 44	23 02	23 33		23 44		00 05		
	d	21 45	22 04				22 31	22 44	23 04	23 34		23 45	23 55	00 07		
Cardiff Central 7	a	22 06	22 23				22 57	23 06	23 23	23 54		00 06	00 20	00 26		

Sundays
from 30 October

		AW	GW	AW	AW	GW	GW	AW	GW	GW		GW	GW	GW	AW	AW	XC	GW	GW	GW		AW	XC	GW	GW
																			R						
			◇1			◇1	◇1	◇	◇	◇1		◇1		◇1	◇		◇1	◇1		◇1		◇	◇1	◇1	
			☕		🚌	☕	☕	🛒		☕		☕		☕				☕		☕		🛒	🛒	☕	
Bath Spa 7	d					00 10	01 07			09 40		09 47	10 27	10 45				11 16	11 26	11 45				12 14	12 23
Oldfield Park	d												10 30						11 29						12 25
Keynsham	d												10 37						11 36						12 33
Bristol Temple Meads 10	a					00 25	01 21			09 53		09 58	10 45	10 59				11 28	11 43	11 57				12 27	12 40
	d								09 48			10 05						11 35	11 48					12 35	
Filton Abbey Wood	d								09 56										11 55						
Bristol Parkway 7	a											10 13						11 44						12 44	
	d		23p28									10 20						11 51						12 53	
Patchway	d																		12 00						
Pilning	d																								
Gloucester 7	d				23p09											10 48	11 23						12 23		
Lydney	d				23p49											11 07									
Chepstow	d				00 09											11 17									
Caldicot	d				00 24											11 25									
Severn Tunnel Jn.	d				00 34				10 09							11 29			12 11						
Newport (South Wales)	a		23p57		00 59				10 26			10 44				11 47	12 06	12 15	12 29				13 06	13 16	
	d	23p46	23p58	00 07	00 59			09 27	10 27			10 44			11 00	11 49	12 08	12 15	12 29			12 52	13 08	13 16	
Cardiff Central 7	a	00 05	00 18	00 26	01 29			09 42	10 42			11 01			11 16	12 07	12 26	12 33	12 44			13 13	13 26	13 34	

		GW	AW	AW	XC	GW		AW	GW	GW	AW	XC	GW	GW	AW	SW		GW	AW	XC	GW	GW	GW	GW	AW
			R					R											R						R
		◇1			◇1	◇1			◇	◇1	◇	◇1	◇1	◇		◇1		◇1		◇1	◇1	◇	◇1		
		☕	🛒			☕		🛒		☕			☕					☕	🛒		☕		☕		🛒
Bath Spa 7	d	12 59				13 16			13 23	13 54			14 17	14 26		14 50		15 00			15 17	15 28	15 59	16 08	
Oldfield Park	d								13 26					14 28										16 10	
Keynsham	d								13 33					14 36		14 58								16 18	
Bristol Temple Meads 10	a	13 12				13 29			13 40	14 07			14 29	14 44		15 05		15 12			15 29	15 40	16 12	16 26	
	d					13 35			13 48				14 35	14 48							15 35	15 48			
Filton Abbey Wood	d								13 55					14 55								15 55			
Bristol Parkway 7	a					13 44							14 44								15 44				
	d					13 51							14 51								15 51				
Patchway	d																								
Pilning	d																								
Gloucester 7	d			12 30	13 23							14 24			14 33					15 23					
Lydney	d			12 49											14 52										
Chepstow	d			12 59											15 02										
Caldicot	d			13 07											15 10										
Severn Tunnel Jn.	d			13 10					14 09					15 10	15 13							16 10			
Newport (South Wales)	a			13 33	14 06	14 15			14 29			15 08	15 16	15 28	15 31					16 06	16 16	16 28			
	d		13 29	13 34	14 08	14 15		14 30	14 30		15 07	15 09	15 16	15 28	15 33				15 46	16 08	16 16	16 28			16 32
Cardiff Central 7	a		13 44	13 52	14 26	14 33		14 49	14 53		15 31	15 31	15 37	15 45	15 51				16 02	16 26	16 34	16 46			16 53

When events are being held at the Millenium Stadium, services are subject to alteration. Please check times before travelling.

Table 132

Sundays

from 30 October

Bath Spa, Bristol and Gloucester - Cardiff

		XC		GW	GW	GW	GW	AW	AW	XC	GW	GW		GW	GW	AW	XC	GW	GW	GW	GW	GW		AW	AW
		◇[1]		◇[1] ☕	◇	◇[1] ☕	◇[1] ☕	[R] 🛒		◇[1] 🛒	◇[1] ☕	[R]		◇[1] ☕	◇[1] ☕	[R] 🛒	◇[1]	◇[1] ☕	◇	◇[1] ☕	◇[1] ☕	◇		[R] 🛒	
Bath Spa [7]	d			16 17	16 28	16 48	16 58				17 20	17 26		17 52	17 59			18 17	18 27	18 50	18 56	19 03			
Oldfield Park	d											17 29										19 06			
Keynsham	d											17 36										19 13			
Bristol Temple Meads [10]	a			16 31	16 41	17 01	17 11					17 43		18 06	18 12				18 40	19 04	19 09	19 21			
	d			16 38	16 48							17 48							18 48						
Filton Abbey Wood	d				16 55							17 55							18 55						
Bristol Parkway [7]	a			16 45							17 44							18 45							
	d			16 51							17 51							18 51							
Patchway	d				17 00																				
Pilning	d																								
Gloucester [7]	d	16 23							16 37	17 23							18 23								18 48
Lydney	d								16 56																19 07
Chepstow	d								17 07																19 17
Caldicot	d								17 13																19 25
Severn Tunnel Jn.	d				17 11				17 16			18 09							19 11						19 32
Newport (South Wales)	a	17 06		17 16	17 29				17 37	18 07	18 16	18 27					19 07	19 19	19 29						19 54
	d	17 08		17 16	17 29			17 34	17 38	18 09	18 16	18 27				18 33	19 08	19 20	19 30					19 51	19 56
Cardiff Central [7]	a	17 27		17 34	17 46			17 50	17 55	18 29	18 34	18 45				18 50	19 27	19 38	19 45					20 10	20 12

		XC	GW	AW	GW	GW	GW	GW		XC	AW	GW	GW	AW	SW	GW	GW	GW		AW	GW	AW	GW	GW	GW
		◇[1]	◇[1] ☕	[R] 🛒	◇	◇[1] ☕	◇[1] ☕			◇[1]	[R] 🛒	◇[1] ☕	◇		◇[1]	◇[1] ☕	◇[1] ☕	◇		[R] 🛒	◇[1] ☕	◇	◇	[1] ☕	◇[1] ☕
Bath Spa [7]	d		19 21		19 29	19 56	20 02	20 08				20 18	20 27		20 49	20 54	20 59	21 10			21 20		21 28	21 52	22 16
Oldfield Park	d							20 10										21 12							
Keynsham	d							20 19							20 57			21 20							
Bristol Temple Meads [10]	a				19 41	20 10	20 15	20 26					20 39		21 04	21 07	21 12	21 27			21 33		21 40	22 04	22 29
	d				19 48								20 48								21 40		21 50		22 35
Filton Abbey Wood	d				19 55								20 55										21 58		
Bristol Parkway [7]	a		19 44									20 44									21 48				22 43
	d		19 51									20 51									21 55				22 51
Patchway	d				20 00																		22 05		
Pilning	d																								
Gloucester [7]	d	19 28								20 23				20 31											
Lydney	d													20 50											
Chepstow	d													21 00											
Caldicot	d													21 10											
Severn Tunnel Jn.	d				20 11								21 10	21 13									22 16		
Newport (South Wales)	a	20 11	20 16		20 28					21 06		21 16	21 28	21 31							22 20		22 36		23 16
	d	20 13	20 17	20 23	20 30					21 08	21 14	21 17	21 28	21 33						21 43	22 20	22 31	22 37		23 16
Cardiff Central [7]	a	20 31	20 36	20 43	20 48					21 26	21 36	21 39	21 46	21 49						22 06	22 43	22 57	22 59		23 38

		GW	GW	AW		GW	AW	GW	GW
			◇			◇[1] ☕	◇	◇[1] ☕	◇[1] ☕
Bath Spa [7]	d	22 22	22 29			22 44		23 26	23 59
Oldfield Park	d	22 24							
Keynsham	d	22 32							
Bristol Temple Meads [10]	a	22 40	22 45			22 57		23 38	00 12
	d		22 50					23 45	
Filton Abbey Wood	d		22 57						
Bristol Parkway [7]	a							23 52	
	d							23 59	
Patchway	d								
Pilning	d								
Gloucester [7]	d			22 33					
Lydney	d			22 52					
Chepstow	d			23 02					
Caldicot	d			23 10					
Severn Tunnel Jn.	d		23 10	23 14					
Newport (South Wales)	a		23 30	23 33				00 27	
	d		23 30	23 34			23 55	00 27	
Cardiff Central [7]	a		23 51	23 54			00 20	00 49	

When events are being held at the Millenium Stadium, services are subject to alteration. Please check times before travelling.

Gloucester - Taunton

Miles			GW	GW	XC	XC	GW	GW	GW	XC	GW	GW	GW	GW	GW	GW	GW	XC	GW	GW	GW	XC	GW
			MX	MX	MO	MX	MX																
				◇1	◇1	◇1		◇	1	◇1	◇			◇				◇1	R			◇1	
				A 🍴	B	C								🛒				🛒	🛒			🛒	D
0	**Gloucester [7]**	d			23p04								06 17		06 42		07 11				07 40		
13	Cam & Dursley	d			⌇								06 32		06 58		07 25				07 54		
28	Yate	d			⌇								06 45		07 12		07 40				08 09		
34	**Bristol Parkway [7]**	a			23p55								06 54		07 23		07 48				08 19		
—		d			23p58	00⌇03					06 26		06 58		07 25		07 49	07 58		08 12	08 19	08 26	
35¼	Filton Abbey Wood	d			⌇	⌇	00 20						07 01	07 09	07 28		07 53		08 09	08 15	08 23		08⌇42
38¼	Stapleton Road	d			⌇	⌇	00 26						07 07		07 33								⌇
38¾	Lawrence Hill	d			⌇	⌇	00 28						07 09		07 35								⌇
39¾	**Bristol Temple Meads [10]**	a			00⌇10	00⌇14	00 33				06 37		07 13	07 18	07 40		08 01	08 08	08 18	08 23	08 36	08 40	08⌇51
—		d	23p06	23p36				05 24	06 03	06 34	06 42	06 48	07 18			07 51		08 11		08 25		08 44	08⌇53
40¾	Bedminster	d	23p10	⌇								06 50				07 53				08 27			⌇
41½	Parson Street	d	23p12	⌇								06 53				07 55				08 29			⌇
47¾	Nailsea & Backwell	d	23p20	23b46					06 14			07 02	07 28			08 04				08 38			09⌇03
51¾	Yatton	d	23p26	23b53					06 21			07 07	07 33			08 09				08 44			09⌇08
55¾	Worle	d	23p32	23b59					06 27			07 12	07 39			08 15				08 50			09⌇14
58½	Weston Milton	d	23p37	⌇								07 18				08 20				08 55			⌇
59¾	**Weston-super-Mare**	a	23p40	00s06				05 43	06 36		07 02	07 23	07 47			08 26				08 58			09⌇22
—		d	23p42	⌇				05 45			07 06		07 49							09 00			09⌇29
67¼	Highbridge & Burnham	d	23p54	00s17				05 55			07 17		08 00							09 10			09⌇40
73½	Bridgwater	d	00 02	00s25				06 03			07 25		08 08							09 18			09⌇48
85¼	**Taunton**	a	00s14	00s37				06 16		07 06	07 38		08 24					08 42		09 32		09 15	10⌇01

		GW	GW	GW	XC	GW	GW	GW	XC	GW	GW	XC	GW	GW	GW	XC	GW	XC	GW	GW	GW	XC	GW
				◇1	◇1	◇			◇1		◇	◇1	◇			◇1		◇1	◇			◇1	◇1
		E		F	🛒	🛒			🛒			🛒	🛒			🛒		🛒	🛒			🛒	G 🍴
Gloucester [7]	d							08 42							09 45						10 42		
Cam & Dursley	d							08 56							09 59						10 56		
Yate	d							09 10							10 13						11 10		
Bristol Parkway [7]	a							09 19							10 22						11 19		
	d		08 45		08 56		09 12	09 20	09 26	09 34		09 56		10 12	10 22	10 27		10 56		11 12	11 20	11 28	
Filton Abbey Wood	d	08⌇42	08 48			09 09	09 15	09 23		09 37	09 42		10 09	10 15	10 25		10 42		11 09	11 15	11 23		
Stapleton Road	d	⌇	08 53					09 29		09 42					10 31						11 29		
Lawrence Hill	d	⌇	08 55					09 31							10 33						11 31		
Bristol Temple Meads [10]	a	08⌇51	09 01		09 14	09 18	09 23	09 35	09 39	09 50	09 53	10 08	10 18	10 23	10 38	10 41	10 51	11 12	11 18	11 23	11 35	11 38	
	d	08⌇53		09 13			09 25		09 44		09 55			10 25		10 44	10 53	11 15		11 25		11 44	11 47
Bedminster	d	⌇					09 27							10 27						11 27			
Parson Street	d	⌇					09 29							10 29						11 29			
Nailsea & Backwell	d	09⌇03					09 38				10 03			10 38			11 03			11 38			
Yatton	d	09⌇08					09 44				10 08			10 44			11 08			11 44			
Worle	d	09⌇14					09 50				10 14			10 50			11 14			11 50			
Weston Milton	d	⌇					09 55							10 55						11 55			
Weston-super-Mare	a	09⌇22					10 00				10 22			11 00			11 21	11 32		12 00			12 06
	d	09⌇28									10 23						11 23	11 37					12 07
Highbridge & Burnham	d	09⌇40									10 34						11 34						
Bridgwater	d	09⌇48									10 42						11 42						
Taunton	a	10⌇01		09 45					10 16		10 58					11 16	11 57	12 00				12 15	12 29

		GW	XC	GW	GW	GW	XC	GW	XC	GW	GW	GW	XC	GW	XC	GW	GW	GW	XC	GW	XC	GW
			◇1	◇			◇1		◇1	◇			◇1	◇	◇1	◇			◇1		◇1	◇
			🛒	🛒			🛒		🛒	🛒			🛒		🛒	🛒			🛒		🛒	🛒
Gloucester [7]	d					11 45						12 42						13 45				
Cam & Dursley	d					11 59						12 56						13 59				
Yate	d					12 13						13 10						14 13				
Bristol Parkway [7]	a					12 22						13 19						14 22				
	d		11 56		12 12	12 22	12 30		12 56		13 12	13 20	13 27		13 59		14 12	14 22	14 29		14 58	
Filton Abbey Wood	d	11 42		12 09	12 15	12 25		12 42		13 09	13 15	13 23		13 42		14 09	14 15	14 25		14 42		15 09
Stapleton Road	d											13 29						14 31				
Lawrence Hill	d											13 31						14 33				
Bristol Temple Meads [10]	a	11 51	12 08	12 18	12 23	12 35	12 41	12 51	13 10	13 18	13 23	13 36	13 39	13 51	14 09	14 18	14 23	14 38	14 41	14 51	15 10	15 18
	d	11 53			12 25		12 44	12 53			13 25		13 44	13 54			14 25		14 44	14 53	15 13	
Bedminster	d				12 27						13 27						14 27					
Parson Street	d				12 29						13 29						14 29					
Nailsea & Backwell	d	12 03			12 38			13 03			13 38			14 03			14 38			15 03		
Yatton	d	12 08			12 44			13 08			13 44			14 08			14 44			15 08		
Worle	d	12 14			12 50			13 14			13 50			14 14			14 50			15 14		
Weston Milton	d				12 55						13 55						14 55					
Weston-super-Mare	a	12 20			13 00			13 21			14 00			14 21			15 00			15 22		
	d	12 22						13 23						14 23						15 28		
Highbridge & Burnham	d	12 33						13 34						14 34						15 38		
Bridgwater	d	12 41						13 42						14 42						15 46		
Taunton	a	12 57					13 16	13 59					14 15	14 55					15 16	16 01	15 44	

A not 24 May
B From 27 June until 1 August
C Until 17 June
D until 1 July, from 5 September
E from 4 July until 2 September
F The Merchant Venturer
G The Torbay Express
b Previous night, stops to set down only

For connections from London Paddington please refer to Table 125

Table 134

Gloucester - Taunton

		GW	GW	XC	GW	GW	XC	GW	GW	GW	GW	XC	GW	GW	GW	XC	GW	GW	GW	GW	XC	GW	GW
																	R						
				◇1			◇1	◇1	◇			◇1				◇1		◇1			◇1	A	B
				🛒			🛒	☕	🛒			🛒				🛒	🛒	☕			🛒		
Gloucester 7	d		14 42								15 45									16 42			
Cam & Dursley	d		14 56								15 59									16 56			
Yate	d		15 10								16 13									17 10			
Bristol Parkway 7	a		15 20								16 22									17 20			
	d	15 12	15 20	15 26		15 53	15 57			16 12	16 22	16 29		16 45		16 58			17 12	17 20	17 27		
Filton Abbey Wood	d	15 15	15 23		15 42	15a56			16 09	16 15	16 25		16 42	16 48	16 55		17 09		17 15	17 23		17 42	17 42
Stapleton Road	d		15 29								16 31			16 53						17 29			
Lawrence Hill	d		15 31								16 33			16 55						17 31			
Bristol Temple Meads 10	a	15 23	15 37	15 40	15 51		16 08		16 19	16 23	16 38	16 42	16 51	17 02	17 05	17 11	17 18		17 23	17 37	17 40	17 53	17 53
	d	15 25		15 44	15 53			16 18		16 25		16 45	16 53			17 14		17 18	17 25		17 44	17 55	17 55
Bedminster	d	15 27			15 55					16 27			16 55						17 27			17 58	17 58
Parson Street	d	15 29			15 57					16 29			16 57						17 29			18 01	18 01
Nailsea & Backwell	d	15 38			16 03			16 29		16 38			17 03					17 28	17 38			18 09	18 09
Yatton	d	15 44			16 08			16 36		16 44			17 08					17 34	17 44			18 15	18 15
Worle	d	15 50			16 14			16 43		16 50			17 14					17 41	17 50			18 21	18 21
Weston Milton	d	15 55			16 21					16 55			17 22						17 55			18 25	18 25
Weston-super-Mare	a	16 00			16 24			16 52		17 00			17 27					17 51	18 00			18 29	18 29
	d				16 24								17 28									18 30	18 30
Highbridge & Burnham	d				16 37								17 38									18 41	18 41
Bridgwater	d				16 45								17 46									18 49	18 49
Taunton	a			16 15	17 00							17 16	18 01			17 45					18 16	19 03	19 08

		GW	XC	GW	GW	GW	GW	GW	XC	GW	XC	GW	GW	GW	XC	GW	XC	GW	GW	GW	GW	XC	GW
				R																			
			◇1		◇1	A	B		◇1		◇1	◇1	◇		◇1		◇1	◇	◇1			◇1	
			🛒	🛒	☕				🛒		🛒	☕	🛒		🛒				☕				
Gloucester 7	d							17 42						18 42							19 45		
Cam & Dursley	d							17 56						18 56							19 59		
Yate	d							18 10						19 10							20 13		
Bristol Parkway 7	a							18 20						19 20							20 22		
	d	17 46	18 00			18 12	18 12	18 20	18 28		18 57			19 20	19 29		19 58			20 11	20 22	20 29	
Filton Abbey Wood	d	17 49		18 09		18 15	18 15	18 23		18 42			19 09	19 23		19 42		20 09		20 14	20 25		20 42
Stapleton Road	d	17 54				18 19	18 19	18 29						19 29							20 31		
Lawrence Hill	d	17 56						18 31						19 31							20 33		
Bristol Temple Meads 10	a	18 02	18 10	18 18		18 24	18 24	18 37	18 40	18 53	19 07		19 18	19 36	19 39	19 51	20 10	20 18		20 24	20 38	20 41	20 53
	d				18 20	18 26	18 26		18 44	18 56		19 15			19 45	19 55			20 18			20 45	20 55
Bedminster	d					18 27	18 27			18 57						19 57							20 57
Parson Street	d					18 29	18 29			18 59						19 59							20 59
Nailsea & Backwell	d				18 31	18 38	18 38			19 08		19 25				20 08			20 29				21 08
Yatton	d				18 38	18 44	18 44			19 13		19 32				20 13			20 36				21 13
Worle	d				18 45	18 50	18 50			19 19		19 38				20 19			20 44				21 19
Weston Milton	d					18 54	18 54			19 23		19 43				20 23			20 49				21 23
Weston-super-Mare	a				18 51	19 00	19 09			19 28		19 48				20 27			20 53				21 27
	d				18 55					19 29		19 57				20 29							21 33
Highbridge & Burnham	d				19 07					19 40						20 39							21 44
Bridgwater	d				19 14					19 48						20 47							21 52
Taunton	a				19 28				19 15	20 03		20 23			20 16	21 02						21 16	22 07

		XC	GW	GW	XC	GW	GW	GW	XC	GW	XC	GW	GW	GW	GW	XC	GW
		◇1	◇1	◇	◇1		◇		◇1		◇1				◇1	◇1	
															C	D	
			☕												☕		
Gloucester 7	d							21 15			22 6			22 29			
Cam & Dursley	d							21 29									
Yate	d							21 43									
Bristol Parkway 7	a							21 52			22 32			23 04			
	d	20 57			21 26			21 52	22 02		22 34			23 05		23 24	
Filton Abbey Wood	d			21 08		21 42		21 5[illegible]		22 09		22 52					23 40
Stapleton Road	d											22 59					
Lawrence Hill	d											23 01					
Bristol Temple Meads 10	a	21 08		21 19	21 38	21 51		22 10	22 14	22 22	22 45	23 05		23 19		23 40	23 49
	d	21 13	21 18		21 44		21 56						23 06		23 36		
Bedminster	d						21 58						23 10				
Parson Street	d						22 00						23 12				
Nailsea & Backwell	d		21 27				22 09						23 20		23s46		
Yatton	d		21 34				22 13						23 26		23s53		
Worle	d		21 40				22 19						23 32		23s59		
Weston Milton	d						22 24						23 37				
Weston-super-Mare	a		21 50				22 29						23 40		00s06		
	d						22 30						23 42				
Highbridge & Burnham	d						22 41						23 54		00s17		
Bridgwater	d						22 49						00 02		00s25		
Taunton	a	21 44			22 15		23 02						00s14		00s37		

A until 1 July, from 5 September
B from 4 July until 2 September
C not 23 May
D from 20 June

For connections from London Paddington please refer to Table 125

Table 134

Gloucester - Taunton

		GW	GW	XC	GW	GW	GW	XC	GW	GW	GW	GW	GW	GW	XC	GW	GW	GW	XC	GW	XC	GW	GW
			◇1 ☕	◇1 A		◇	◇1 ☕	◇1 🛒		◇			◇		◇1 🛒	◇			◇1 🛒		◇1 🛒	R 1 ☕	◇
Gloucester 7	d											06 19		07 02				07 40					
Cam & Dursley	d											06 35		07 15				07 54					
Yate	d											06 48		07 30				08 09					
Bristol Parkway 7	a											06 58		07 39				08 19					
	d			00 03			05 42					06 58		07 40	07 57		08 12	08 19	08 26		08 57		
Filton Abbey Wood	d				00 20							07 02	07 09	07 46		08 09	08 15	08 23		08 42			09 09
Stapleton Road	d				00 26																		
Lawrence Hill	d				00 28																		
Bristol Temple Meads 10	a			00 14	00 33		05 53					07 11	07 18	07 54	08 07	08 18	08 23	08 34	08 38	08 52	09 08		09 18
	d	23p06	23p36			05 24		06 08	06 18	06 36	06 48	07 18		07 56	08 11		08 25		08 44	08 56		09 17	
Bedminster	d	23p10									06 50	07 21					08 27						
Parson Street	d	23p12									06 53	07 23					08 29						
Nailsea & Backwell	d	23p20	23b46						06 28		07 01	07 28		08 03			08 38			09 03			
Yatton	d	23p26	23b53						06 34		07 06	07 34		08 08			08 44			09 07			
Worle	d	23p32	23b59						06 40		07 12	07 40		08 14			08 50			09 13			
Weston Milton	d	23p37									07 17	07 46					08 55						
Weston-super-Mare	a	23p40	00s06			05 43			06 45	06 55	07 22	07 47		08 23			09 00			09 23			
	d	23p42				05 45			06 47	06 56		07 50								09 32			
Highbridge & Burnham	d	23p54	00s17			05 55			06 58			08 01								09 44			
Bridgwater	d	00 02	00s25			06 03			07 06			08 09								09 52			
Taunton	a	00s14	00s37			06 16		07 14	07 20	07 24		08 24			08 42				09 15	10 06		09 50	

		GW	GW	XC	GW	XC	GW	GW	GW	XC	GW	GW	XC	GW	GW	GW	XC	GW	XC	GW	GW	GW	GW
				◇1 🛒		◇1 🛒	◇			◇1 🛒	◇1 ☕		◇1 🛒	◇			◇1 🛒		◇1 🛒	◇1 ☕	◇		
Gloucester 7	d		08 42						09 46							10 42							11 46
Cam & Dursley	d		08 56						10 02							10 56							12 01
Yate	d		09 11						10 16							11 10							12 16
Bristol Parkway 7	a		09 19						10 24							11 19							12 24
	d	09 12	09 20	09 26		09 57		10 12	10 25	10 31			10 59		11 12	11 20	11 26		11 57			12 12	12 25
Filton Abbey Wood	d	09 15	09 23		09 42		10 09	10 15	10 28			10 42		11 09	11 15	11 23		11 42			12 09	12 15	12 28
Stapleton Road	d		09 29						10 32							11 29							12 32
Lawrence Hill	d		09 31						10 34							11 31							12 34
Bristol Temple Meads 10	a	09 23	09 34	09 38	09 51	10 11	10 18	10 23	10 39	10 42		10 51	11 10	11 18	11 23	11 34	11 39	11 51	12 08		12 19	12 23	12 39
	d	09 25		09 44	09 55	10 20		10 25		10 44	10 48	10 53	11 14		11 25		11 44	11 53		12 18		12 25	
Bedminster	d	09 27						10 27							11 27							12 27	
Parson Street	d	09 29						10 29							11 29							12 29	
Nailsea & Backwell	d	09 38			10 03			10 38				11 03			11 38			12 03				12 38	
Yatton	d	09 44			10 08			10 44				11 08			11 44			12 08				12 44	
Worle	d	09 50			10 14			10 50				11 14			11 50			12 14				12 50	
Weston Milton	d	09 55						10 55							11 55							12 55	
Weston-super-Mare	a	10 00			10 22			11 00			11 06	11 21	11 31		12 00			12 22		12 35		13 00	
	d				10 23							11 23	11 39					12 23					
Highbridge & Burnham	d				10 34							11 34						12 34					
Bridgwater	d				10 42							11 42						12 42					
Taunton	a			10 17	10 59	10 59				11 15		11 56	11 59				12 15	12 57					

		XC	GW	XC	GW	GW	GW	XC	GW	XC	GW	GW	GW	GW	XC	GW	XC	GW	GW	GW	XC	GW
		◇1 🛒		◇1 🛒	◇			◇1 🛒		◇1 🛒	◇	◇1 ☕			◇1 🛒		◇1 🛒	◇			◇1 🛒	
Gloucester 7	d						12 42							13 42						14 42		
Cam & Dursley	d						12 56							13 57						14 56		
Yate	d						13 11							14 11						15 10		
Bristol Parkway 7	a						13 19							14 20						15 18		
	d	12 31		12 57		13 12	13 20	13 27		13 58			14 12	14 20	14 28		14 59		15 12	15 19	15 26	
Filton Abbey Wood	d		12 42		13 09	13 15	13 23		13 42		14 09		14 15	14 25		14 42		15 09	15 15	15 22		15 42
Stapleton Road	d						[illegible]							14 31						15 27		
Lawrence Hill	d						[illegible]							14 33						15 29		
Bristol Temple Meads 10	a	12 42	12 51	13 07	13 18	13 23	[illegible]	13 40	13 53	14 09			14 23	14 36	14 41	14 51	15 10	15 18	15 23	15 33	15 38	15 51
	d	12 44	12 53			13 25		13 44	13 55			14 16	[illegible]			[illegible]	15 13		15 25		15 44	15 53
Bedminster	d					13 27							14 27						15 27			
Parson Street	d					13 29							14 29						15 29			
Nailsea & Backwell	d		13 03			13 38			14 03				14 38			15 03			15 38			16 03
Yatton	d		13 08			13 44			14 08				14 44			15 08			15 44			16 08
Worle	d		13 14			13 50			14 14				14 50			15 14			15 50			16 14
Weston Milton	d					13 55							14 55						15 55			
Weston-super-Mare	a		13 22			14 00			14 21			14 35	15 00			15 22			16 00			16 22
	d		13 23						14 23							15 23						16 23
Highbridge & Burnham	d		13 34						14 34							15 34						16 34
Bridgwater	d		13 42						14 42							15 42						16 42
Taunton	a	13 15	13 59					14 15	14 59						15 16	15 59		15 52			16 15	16 57

A until 18 June

b Previous night, stops to set down only

For connections from London Paddington please refer to Table 125

Table 134

Gloucester - Taunton

Saturdays
until 10 September

		XC	GW	GW	GW	GW	XC	GW		XC	GW	GW	GW	GW	XC	GW	XC	GW		GW	GW	GW	XC	GW	XC
		◇1	◇	◇1			◇1			◇1	R	◇1			◇1		◇1	◇		◇1			◇1		◇1
		🛒		🍴			🛒			🛒		🍴			🛒		🛒			🍴			🛒		🛒
Gloucester 7	d					15 45								16 42								17 46			
Cam & Dursley	d					15 59								16 56								18 01			
Yate	d					16 13								17 10								18 16			
Bristol Parkway 7	a					16 24								17 18								18 24			
	d	15 57			16 12	16 25	16 31			16 57			17 12	17 20	17 26		17 57				18 12	18 25	18 31		18 57
Filton Abbey Wood	d		16 09		16 15	16 28		16 42			17 09		17 15	17 23		17 42		18 09			18 15	18 28		18 42	
Stapleton Road	d					16 34								17 29								18 34			
Lawrence Hill	d					16 36								17 31								18 36			
Bristol Temple Meads 10	a	16 08	16 18		16 23	16 39	16 42	16 51		17 07	17 18		17 23	17 34	17 38	17 51	18 07	18 18			18 23	18 39	18 42	18 51	19 07
	d			16 18	16 25		16 44	16 53				17 18	17 25		17 44	17 53				18 18	18 25		18 44	18 53	
Bedminster	d				16 27								17 27								18 27				
Parson Street	d				16 29								17 29								18 29				
Nailsea & Backwell	d				16 38			17 03					17 38			18 03					18 38			19 03	
Yatton	d				16 44			17 08					17 44			18 08					18 44			19 08	
Worle	d				16 50			17 14					17 50			18 14					18 50			19 14	
Weston Milton	d				16 55								17 55								18 55			19 20	
Weston-super-Mare	a			16 35	17 00			17 22				17 35	18 00			18 22				18 36	19 00			19 23	
	d							17 23								18 23				18 40				19 23	
Highbridge & Burnham	d							17 34								18 34								19 34	
Bridgwater	d							17 42								18 42								19 42	
Taunton	a						17 17	17 59							18 15	18 56				19 06			19 15	19 59	

		GW	GW	GW		GW	XC	GW	XC	GW	GW	GW	GW	XC		XC	GW	GW	XC	GW	XC	GW	GW	XC	
		◇	◇1				◇1		◇1	◇1	◇			◇1		◇1		◇1	◇1	◇	◇1	◇		◇1	
														A		B									
			🍴				🛒		🛒	🍴								🍴	🛒					🛒	
Gloucester 7	d					18 42							19 45										21 16		
Cam & Dursley	d					18 56							19 59										21 30		
Yate	d					19 11							20 13										21 44		
Bristol Parkway 7	a					19 20							20 24										21 53		
	d			19 12		19 21	19 29		19 57			20 17	20 25	20 31		20 31			20 57		21 26		21 53	21 59	
Filton Abbey Wood	d	19 09		19 15		19 24		19 42			20 09	20 20	20 28				20 40			21 08		21 42	21 57		
Stapleton Road	d					19 29							20 34												
Lawrence Hill	d					19 31							20 36												
Bristol Temple Meads 10	a	19 18		19 24		19 36	19 41	19 51	20 07		20 18	20 29	20 39	20 42		20 42	20 48		21 09	21 18	21 38	21 49	22 05	22 12	
	d		19 18				19 44	19 53		20 15				20 44		20 44		20 55			21 44	21 55			
Bedminster	d																					21 57			
Parson Street	d																					21 59			
Nailsea & Backwell	d		19 30					20 03										21 04				22 08			
Yatton	d		19 37					20 08										21 11				22 14			
Worle	d		19 43					20 14										21 17				22 20			
Weston Milton	d							20 20										21 22							
Weston-super-Mare	a		19 50					20 23		20 36								21 26				22 25			
	d							20 24		20 38								21 26				22 27			
Highbridge & Burnham	d							20 34										21 39				22 38			
Bridgwater	d							20 42										21 46				22 46			
Taunton	a						20 15	20 59		21 03				21 15		21 17		21 58			22 15	22 59			

		GW	XC	GW
		◇1	◇1	
		🍴		
Gloucester 7	d		22 06	
Cam & Dursley	d			
Yate	d			
Bristol Parkway 7	a		22 32	
	d		22 34	
Filton Abbey Wood	d			22 49
Stapleton Road	d			
Lawrence Hill	d			
Bristol Temple Meads 10	a		22 45	22 57
	d	22 17		
Bedminster	d			
Parson Street	d			
Nailsea & Backwell	d	22s27		
Yatton	d	22s34		
Worle	d	22s40		
Weston Milton	d			
Weston-super-Mare	a	22s47		
	d			
Highbridge & Burnham	d	22s58		
Bridgwater	d	23s05		
Taunton	a	23 17		

A from 6 August until 10 September

B until 30 July

For connections from London Paddington please refer to Table 125

Table 134

Saturdays from 17 September

Gloucester - Taunton

		GW	GW	GW	GW	GW	XC	GW	GW	GW	GW	GW	GW	XC	GW	GW	GW	XC	GW	XC	GW	GW	GW
			◇1 ⊏		◇	◇1 ⊏	◇1 ⊼		◇			◇		◇1 ⊼	◇			◇1 ⊼		◇1 ⊼	1 ⊏	◇	
Gloucester 7	d										06 19		07 02				07 40						
Cam & Dursley	d										06 35		07 15				07 54						
Yate	d										06 48		07 30				08 09						
Bristol Parkway 7	a										06 58		07 39				08 19						
	d					05 42					06 58		07 40	07 57		08 12	08 19	08 26		08 57			09 12
Filton Abbey Wood	d			00 20							07 02	07 09	07 46		08 09	08 15	08 23		08 42			09 09	09 15
Stapleton Road	d			00 26																			
Lawrence Hill	d			00 28																			
Bristol Temple Meads 10	a			00 33		05 53					07 11	07 18	07 54	08 07	08 18	08 23	08 34	08 38	08 52	09 08		09 18	09 23
	d	23p06	23p36		05 24		06 08	06 18	06 36	06 48	07 18		07 56	08 11		08 25		08 44	08 56		09 17		09 25
Bedminster	d	23p10								06 50	07 21					08 27							09 27
Parson Street	d	23p12								06 53	07 23					08 29							09 29
Nailsea & Backwell	d	23p20	23b46					06 28		07 01	07 28		08 03			08 38			09 03				09 38
Yatton	d	23p26	23b53					06 34		07 06	07 34		08 08			08 44			09 07				09 44
Worle	d	23p32	23b59					06 40		07 12	07 40		08 14			08 50			09 13				09 50
Weston Milton	d	23p37								07 17	07 46					08 55							09 55
Weston-super-Mare	a	23p40	00s06		05 43			06 45	06 55	07 22	07 47		08 23			09 00			09 23				10 00
	d	23p42			05 45			06 47	06 56		07 50								09 32				
Highbridge & Burnham	d	23p54	00s17		05 55			06 58			08 01								09 44				
Bridgwater	d	00 02	00s25		06 03			07 06			08 09								09 52				
Taunton	a	00s14	00s37		06 16		07 14	07 20	07 24		08 24			08 42				09 15	10 06		09 50		

		GW	XC	GW	XC	GW	GW	GW	XC	GW	XC	GW	GW	GW	XC	GW	XC	GW	GW	GW	XC	GW	XC
			◇1 ⊼		◇1 ⊼	◇			◇1 ⊼		◇1 ⊼	◇			◇1 ⊼		◇1 ⊼	◇			◇1 ⊼		◇1 ⊼
Gloucester 7	d	08 42						09 46						10 42						11 46			
Cam & Dursley	d	08 56						10 02						10 56						12 01			
Yate	d	09 11						10 16						11 10						12 16			
Bristol Parkway 7	a	09 19						10 24						11 19						12 24			
	d	09 20	09 26		09 57		10 12	10 25	10 31		10 59		11 12	11 20	11 26		11 57		12 12	12 25	12 31		12 57
Filton Abbey Wood	d	09 23		09 42		10 09	10 15	10 28		10 42		11 09	11 15	11 23		11 42		12 09	12 15	12 28		12 42	
Stapleton Road	d	09 29						10 32						11 29						12 32			
Lawrence Hill	d	09 31						10 34						11 31						12 34			
Bristol Temple Meads 10	a	09 34	09 38	09 51	10 07	10 18	10 23	10 39	10 42	10 51	11 10	11 18	11 23	11 34	11 38	11 51	12 08	12 19	12 23	12 39	12 42	12 51	13 07
	d		09 44	09 55			10 25		10 44	10 53	11 14		11 25		11 44	11 53			12 25		12 44	12 53	
Bedminster	d						10 27						11 27						12 27				
Parson Street	d						10 29						11 29						12 29				
Nailsea & Backwell	d			10 03			10 38			11 03			11 38			12 03			12 38			13 03	
Yatton	d			10 08			10 44			11 08			11 44			12 08			12 44			13 08	
Worle	d			10 14			10 50			11 14			11 50			12 14			12 50			13 14	
Weston Milton	d						10 55						11 55						12 55				
Weston-super-Mare	a			10 22			11 00			11 21	11 31		12 00			12 22			13 00			13 22	
	d			10 23						11 23	11 39					12 23						13 23	
Highbridge & Burnham	d			10 34						11 34						12 34						13 34	
Bridgwater	d			10 42						11 42						12 42						13 42	
Taunton	a		10 17	10 59					11 15	11 56	11 59				12 15	12 57					13 15	13 59	

		GW	GW	GW	XC	GW	XC	GW	GW	GW	XC	GW	XC	GW	GW	GW	XC	GW	XC	GW	GW	GW
		◇			◇1 ⊼		◇1 ⊼	◇			◇1 ⊼		◇1 ⊼	◇			◇1 ⊼		◇1 ⊼	◇		
Gloucester 7	d			12 42						13 42						14 42						15 45
Cam & Dursley	d			12 56						13 57						14 56						15 59
Yate	d			13 11						14 11						15 10						16 13
Bristol Parkway 7	a			13 19						14 20						15 18						16 24
	d		13 12	13 20	13 26		13 58		14 12	14 20	14 28		14 59		15 12	15 19	15 25		15 57		16 12	16 25
Filton Abbey Wood	d	13 09	13 15	13 23		13 42		14 09	14 15	14 25		14 42		15 09	15 15	15 22		15 42		16 09	16 15	16 28
Stapleton Road	d			13 27						14 31						15 27						16 34
Lawrence Hill	d			13 29						14 33						15 29						16 36
Bristol Temple Meads 10	a	13 18	13 23	13 34	13 38	13 53	14 09	14 18	14 23	14 36	14 41	14 51	15 10	15 18	15 23	15 33	15 37	15 51	16 08	16 18	16 23	16 39
	d		13 25		13 44	13 55			14 25		14 44	14 53	15 13		15 25		15 44	15 53			16 25	
Bedminster	d		13 27						14 27						15 27						16 27	
Parson Street	d		13 29						14 29						15 29						16 29	
Nailsea & Backwell	d		13 38			14 03			14 38			15 03			15 38			16 03			16 38	
Yatton	d		13 44			14 08			14 44			15 08			15 44			16 08			16 44	
Worle	d		13 50			14 14			14 50			15 14			15 50			16 14			16 50	
Weston Milton	d		13 55						14 55						15 55						16 55	
Weston-super-Mare	a		14 00			14 21			15 00			15 22			16 00			16 22			17 00	
	d					14 23						15 23						16 23				
Highbridge & Burnham	d					14 34						15 34						16 34				
Bridgwater	d					14 42						15 42						16 42				
Taunton	a				14 15	14 59					15 16	15 59	15 52				16 15	16 57				

b Previous night, stops to set down only

For connections from London Paddington please refer to Table 125

Table 134

Gloucester - Taunton

Saturdays
from 17 September

		XC	GW	XC	GW	GW	GW	XC	GW	XC	GW	GW	GW	GW	XC	GW	XC	GW	GW	GW	GW	XC	GW
		◇1 bike		◇1 bike	R			◇1 bike		◇1 bike	◇	◇1 catering			◇1 bike		◇1 bike	◇	◇1 catering			◇1 bike	
Gloucester 7	d						16 42							17 46							18 42		
Cam & Dursley	d						16 56							18 01							18 56		
Yate	d						17 10							18 16							19 11		
Bristol Parkway 7	a						17 18							18 24							19 20		
	d	16 31		16 57		17 12	17 20	17 26		17 57			18 12	18 25	18 31		18 57			19 12	19 21	19 29	
Filton Abbey Wood	d		16 42		17 09	17 15	17 23		17 42		18 09		18 15	18 28		18 42		19 09		19 15	19 24		19 42
Stapleton Road	d						17 29							18 34							19 29		
Lawrence Hill	d						17 31							18 36							19 31		
Bristol Temple Meads 10	a	16 42	16 51	17 07	17 18	17 23	17 34	17 38	17 51	18 07	18 18		18 23	18 39	18 42	18 51	19 07	19 18		19 24	19 36	19 41	19 51
	d	16 44	16 53	17 10		17 25		17 44	17 53			18 18	18 25		18 44	18 53			19 18			19 44	19 53
Bedminster	d					17 27							18 27										
Parson Street	d					17 29							18 29										
Nailsea & Backwell	d		17 03			17 38			18 03				18 38			19 03			19 30				20 03
Yatton	d		17 08			17 44			18 08				18 44			19 08			19 37				20 08
Worle	d		17 14			17 50			18 14				18 50			19 14			19 43				20 14
Weston Milton	d					17 55							18 55			19 20							20 20
Weston-super-Mare	a		17 22			18 00			18 22			18 36	19 00			19 23			19 50				20 23
	d		17 23						18 23			18 40				19 23							20 24
Highbridge & Burnham	d		17 34						18 34							19 34							20 34
Bridgwater	d		17 42						18 42							19 42							20 42
Taunton	a	17 17	17 59	17 41				18 15	18 56			19 06			19 15	19 59						20 15	20 59

		XC	GW	GW	GW	GW	XC	GW	GW	XC	GW	XC	GW	GW	GW	XC	GW	XC	GW
		◇1 bike	◇1 catering	◇			◇1		◇1 catering	◇1	◇	◇1	◇ B	A		◇1 bike	◇1 catering	◇1	
Gloucester 7	d					19 45									21 16			22 06	
Cam & Dursley	d					19 59									21 30				
Yate	d					20 13									21 44				
Bristol Parkway 7	a					20 24									21 53			22 32	
	d	19 57			20 17	20 25	20 31			20 57		21 26			21 53	21 59		22 34	
Filton Abbey Wood	d			20 09	20 20	20 28		20 40			21 08		21 42		21 57				22 49
Stapleton Road	d					20 34													
Lawrence Hill	d					20 36													
Bristol Temple Meads 10	a	20 07		20 18	20 29	20 39	20 42	20 48		21 07	21 18	21 38	21 49		22 05	22 12		22 45	22 57
	d		20 15				20 44		20 55	21 11		21 44	21 55	21 59			22 17		
Bedminster	d												21 57	22 01					
Parson Street	d												21 59	22 03					
Nailsea & Backwell	d								21 04				22 08	22 12			22s27		
Yatton	d								21 11				22 14	22 18			22s34		
Worle	d								21 17				22 20	22 24			22s40		
Weston Milton	d								21 22										
Weston-super-Mare	a		20 36						21 26				22 25	22 29			22s47		
	d		20 38						21 26				22 27	22 31					
Highbridge & Burnham	d								21 39				22 38	22 42			22s58		
Bridgwater	d								21 46				22 46	22 50			23s05		
Taunton	a		21 03				21 15		21 58	21 42		22 15	22 59	23 03			23 17		

Sundays
until 19 June

		GW	GW	XC	GW	GW	GW	XC	GW	GW	GW	XC	GW	GW	XC	GW	GW	GW	GW	XC	GW	GW	XC
		◇	◇	◇1 bike	◇		bus	◇1 bike	◇1 catering	◇			◇		◇1 bike	bus	◇1 catering			◇1 bike	◇		◇1 bike
Gloucester 7	d						09 15								10 02	10 23				11 02			12 05
Cam & Dursley	d						09 45									10 53							
Yate	d						10 25									11 33							
Bristol Parkway 7	a						10 45								11 11	11 53				12 13			13 17
	d													10 56	11 29				12 02	12 25			13 25
Filton Abbey Wood	d				08 55					10 03			10 54	11 00				11 54	12 07		12 57		
Stapleton Road	d										10 16												
Lawrence Hill	d										10 18												
Bristol Temple Meads 10	a				09 05					10 13	10 21		11 03	11 08	11 40			12 04	12 14	12 35	13 05		13 37
	d	07 45	08 28	08 44		09 05		09 48	10 01		10 23	10 44		11 09	11 44		11 55			12 44		13 05	13 44
Bedminster	d										10 26												
Parson Street	d										10 29												
Nailsea & Backwell	d		08 38			09 13					10 37			11 19			12 07					13 15	
Yatton	d	07 58	08 43			09 20					10 42			11 24			12 14					13 20	
Worle	d		08 49			09 26					10 48			11 30			12 19					13 26	
Weston Milton	d																						
Weston-super-Mare	a	08 07	08 55			09 37					10 53			11 36			12 33					13 31	
	d	08 08	08 59								10 58			11 37								13 33	
Highbridge & Burnham	d		09 10								11 09			11 47								13 44	
Bridgwater	d	08 24	09 18								11 17			11 55								13 52	
Taunton	a	08 37	09 31	09 15				10 19	10 35		11 31	11 15		12 09	12 15					13 15		14 06	14 16

A from 29 October

B from 17 September until 22 October

For connections from London Paddington please refer to Table 125

Table 134

Sundays

until 19 June

Gloucester - Taunton

		GW	GW	GW	GW	XC		GW	GW	GW	XC	XC	GW	GW	XC	GW		XC	GW	GW	XC	GW	GW	XC	GW
			◇1	◇		◇1		◇1	◇		◇1	◇1		◇	◇1			◇1	◇1	◇	◇1		◇	◇1	◇
		(bus)	(buffet)			(trolley)		(buffet)			(trolley)	(trolley)			(trolley)			(trolley)	(buffet)		(trolley)			(trolley)	
Gloucester 7	d	12 30				13 04					14 04	15 08				15 28									
Cam & Dursley	d	13 00														15 47									
Yate	d	13 40														16 01									
Bristol Parkway 7	a	13 59				14 18					15 08	15 33				16 09									
	d				14 15	14 25					15 12	15 34			15 56	16 10		16 25			16 58			17 25	
Filton Abbey Wood	d			13 54	14 19				14 56					15 55		16 13				16 55			17 20		17 54
Stapleton Road	d																								
Lawrence Hill	d																								
Bristol Temple Meads 10	a			14 04	14 25	14 36			15 05		15 23	15 45		16 04	16 09	16 24		16 37		17 06	17 09		17 29	17 35	18 04
	d		13 55			14 44		14 55		15 10		15 47	15 55		16 14	16 25		16 44	16 55			17 25		17 44	
Bedminster	d									15 13			15 58									17 28			
Parson Street	d												16 00												
Nailsea & Backwell	d		14 07							15 22			16 08			16 35			17 07			17 37			
Yatton	d		14 14							15 28			16 14			16 40			17 14			17 43			
Worle	d		14 19							15 34			16 20			16 46			17 19			17 49			
Weston Milton	d									15 39						16 52						17 58			
Weston-super-Mare	a		14 27							15 42			16 25			16 56			17 27			18 01			
	d												16 28						17 31						
Highbridge & Burnham	d												16 40												
Bridgwater	d												16 48												
Taunton	a					15 16		15 30				16 18	17 03		16 45			17 16	17 53					18 19	

		GW		XC	GW	XC	GW	GW	GW	XC	GW	XC		GW	GW	XC	GW	XC	GW	XC	GW	XC		GW	GW
					R																				
		◇		◇1		◇1		◇		◇1	◇1	◇1		◇		◇1		◇1	◇1	◇1	◇	◇1		◇1	
				(trolley)		(trolley)				(trolley)	(buffet)	(trolley)				(trolley)		(trolley)	(buffet)	(trolley)				(buffet)	
Gloucester 7	d								18 19						19 20										21 15
Cam & Dursley	d								18 34						19 34										21 31
Yate	d								18 49						19 48										21 45
Bristol Parkway 7	a								18 57						19 56										21 53
	d			18 02		18 25			18 58	19 04		19 25			19 57	20 02		20 25		20 58		21 25			21 55
Filton Abbey Wood	d				18 23			18 55	19 01					19 55	20 00						21 05				21 58
Stapleton Road	d																20 16								
Lawrence Hill	d																20 18								
Bristol Temple Meads 10	a			18 14	18 33	18 37		19 06	19 10	19 14		19 37		20 05	20 10	20 14	20 21	20 35		21 09	21 13	21 35			22 07
	d	18 07				18 44	19 05				19 29	19 44				20 19	20 25	20 44	20 55			21 44		21 57	
Bedminster	d						19 08										20 28								
Parson Street	d						19 10																		
Nailsea & Backwell	d	18 17					19 18				19 39						20 36		21 07					22 07	
Yatton	d	18 23					19 24				19 45						20 42		21 14					22 14	
Worle	d	18 29					19 30				19 52						20 48		21 19					22 19	
Weston Milton	d						19 34																		
Weston-super-Mare	a	18 35					19 38				19 59					20 36	20 53		21 27					22 27	
	d	18 36					19 39									20 37	20 58		21 27						
Highbridge & Burnham	d	18 47					19 50										21 09								
Bridgwater	d	18 55					19 58										21 17								
Taunton	a	19 09				19 15	20 13					20 19				20 59	21 33	21 15	21 50			22 15			

		XC	XC	GW	XC	GW	XC
		◇1	◇1		◇1		◇1
			(trolley)	(trolley)			
Gloucester 7	d		22 07				
Cam & Dursley	d						
Yate	d						
Bristol Parkway 7	a		22 35				
	d	22 00	22 37		22 58		23 24
Filton Abbey Wood	d			22 52			
Stapleton Road	d						
Lawrence Hill	d						
Bristol Temple Meads 10	a	22 11	22 45	23 00	23 10		23 36
	d					23 10	
Bedminster	d					23 13	
Parson Street	d					23 15	
Nailsea & Backwell	d					23 23	
Yatton	d					23 29	
Worle	d					23 35	
Weston Milton	d					23 40	
Weston-super-Mare	a					23 43	
	d						
Highbridge & Burnham	d						
Bridgwater	d						
Taunton	a						

For connections from London Paddington please refer to Table 125

Table 134

Sundays

26 June to 31 July

Gloucester - Taunton

		GW	GW	XC	GW	GW	XC	GW	GW	GW		XC	GW	GW	XC	GW	GW	GW	XC	GW		GW	GW	XC	GW
		◇	◇	◇1	◇		◇1	◇1	◇				◇		◇1		◇1		◇1	◇				◇1	◇1
				[trolley]			[trolley]	[restaurant]							[trolley]	[bus]	[restaurant]		[trolley]					[trolley]	[restaurant]
Gloucester 7	d														10 02	10 23								12 05	
Cam & Dursley	d															10 53									
Yate	d															11 33									
Bristol Parkway 7	a														11 11	11 53								13 17	
	d													10 56	11 29								13 11	13 25	
Filton Abbey Wood	d				08 55				10 03				10 54	10 59				11 54		12 57			13 14		
Stapleton Road	d									10 16															
Lawrence Hill	d									10 18															
Bristol Temple Meads 10	a				09 05				10 13	10 21			11 03	11 08	11 40			12 04		13 05			13 23	13 36	
	d	07 45	08 28	08 44		09 24	09 48	10 01		10 23		10 44		11 10	11 44		11 55		12 57			13 05		13 44	13 55
Bedminster	d									10 26															
Parson Street	d									10 29															
Nailsea & Backwell	d		08 38			09 32				10 37				11 19			12 07					13 15			14 07
Yatton	d	07 58	08 43			09 39				10 42				11 24			12 14					13 20			14 14
Worle	d		08 49			09 45				10 48				11 30			12 19					13 26			14 19
Weston Milton	d																								
Weston-super-Mare	a	08 07	08 55			09 56				10 53				11 36			12 33		13 14			13 31			14 27
	d	08 08	08 59							10 58				11 37					13 15			13 33			
Highbridge & Burnham	d		09 10							11 09				11 47								13 44			
Bridgwater	d	08 24	09 18							11 17				11 55								13 52			
Taunton	a	08 37	09 31	09 15			10 19	10 35		11 31		11 15		12 09	12 15				13 36			14 06		14 16	

		GW	XC	GW	GW	GW		XC	GW	GW	GW	XC	GW	GW	GW	GW		XC	GW	GW	GW	XC	GW	GW	GW
																					R				
		◇	◇1	◇1	◇			◇1		◇		◇1	◇1	◇		◇		◇1	◇	◇		◇1		◇	
			[trolley]	[restaurant]				[trolley]				[trolley]	[restaurant]					[trolley]				[trolley]			
Gloucester 7	d		13 04					14 04				15 05						16 03				17 03			
Cam & Dursley	d																								
Yate	d																								
Bristol Parkway 7	a		14 17					15 12				16 16						17 21				18 12			
	d		14 29			14 58		15 25				16 25			17 05			17 26				18 26			19 06
Filton Abbey Wood	d	13 54			14 56					15 55				16 55		17 20			17 54		18 23			18 55	19 10
Stapleton Road	d																								
Lawrence Hill	d																								
Bristol Temple Meads 10	a	14 04	14 40		15 05	15 08		15 35		16 04		16 36		17 06	17 15	17 29		17 36	18 04		18 33	18 39		19 06	19 24
	d		14 44	14 55		15 10		15 44	15 55		16 25	16 44	16 55		17 25			17 44		18 07		18 44	19 05		
Bedminster	d					15 13			15 58						17 28								19 08		
Parson Street	d								16 00														19 10		
Nailsea & Backwell	d					15 22			16 08		16 36		17 07		17 37					18 17			19 18		
Yatton	d					15 28			16 14		16 41		17 14		17 43					18 23			19 24		
Worle	d					15 34			16 20		16 47		17 19		17 49					18 29			19 30		
Weston Milton	d					15 39					16 53				17 58								19 34		
Weston-super-Mare	a					15 42			16 25		16 57		17 27		18 01					18 35			19 38		
	d								16 28				17 31							18 36			19 39		
Highbridge & Burnham	d								16 40											18 47			19 50		
Bridgwater	d								16 48											18 55			19 58		
Taunton	a		15 16	15 30				16 15	17 03			17 16	17 53					18 19		19 09		19 15	20 13		

		GW		XC	GW	GW	XC	GW	GW	GW	XC	GW		XC	GW	GW	XC	XC
		◇1		◇1	◇		◇1	◇1	◇		◇1	◇1		◇1			◇1	◇1
							A				A							
		[restaurant]		[trolley]			[trolley]	[restaurant]			[trolley]	[restaurant]		[trolley]	[trolley]			
Gloucester 7	d			18 03			19 03				20 03			21 03			22 03	23 04
Cam & Dursley	d																	
Yate	d																	
Bristol Parkway 7	a			19 12			20 15				21 12			22 12			23 22	23 55
	d			19 25			20 25			21 08	21 25			22 16			23 29	23 58
Filton Abbey Wood	d				19 55				21 05	21 12					22 52			
Stapleton Road	d					20 16												
Lawrence Hill	d					20 18												
Bristol Temple Meads 10	a			19 35	20 05	20 21	20 35		21 13	21 19	21 35			22 25	23 00		23 41	00 10
	d	19 32		19 44		20 25	20 44	20 55			21 44	21 57				23 10		
Bedminster	d					20 28										23 13		
Parson Street	d															23 15		
Nailsea & Backwell	d	19 41				20 36		21 07				22 07				23 23		
Yatton	d	19 48				20 42		21 14				22 14				23 29		
Worle	d	19 54				20 48		21 19				22 19				23 35		
Weston Milton	d															23 40		
Weston-super-Mare	a	20 02				20 53		21 27				22 27				23 43		
	d					20 58		21 27										
Highbridge & Burnham	d					21 09												
Bridgwater	d					21 17												
Taunton	a			20 19		21 33	21 15	21 50			22 15							

A [trolley] to Bristol Parkway

For connections from London Paddington please refer to Table 125

Table 134

Sundays

7 August to 11 September

Gloucester - Taunton

		GW	GW	XC	GW	GW	XC	GW	GW	GW		XC	GW	GW	XC	GW	GW	GW	XC	GW		GW	GW	GW	XC
		◇	◇	◇[1]	◇		◇[1]	◇[1]	◇			◇[1]	◇		◇[1]	(bus)	◇[1]		◇[1]	◇[1]		◇			◇[1]
				(bike)			(bike)	(cup)				(bike)			(bike)		(cup)		(bike)	(cup)					(bike)
Gloucester [7]	d													10 19		10 23								12 14	
Cam & Dursley	d													10 32		10 53								12 28	
Yate	d													10 47		11 33								12 42	
Bristol Parkway [7]	a													10 55		11 53								12 51	
	d											10 24		10 56	11 29				12 25					12 57	13 25
Filton Abbey Wood	d				08 55				10 03				10 54	11 00				11 54				12 57		13 01	
Stapleton Road	d									10 16															
Lawrence Hill	d									10 18															
Bristol Temple Meads [10]	a				09 05				10 13	10 21		10 34	11 03	11 08	11 41			12 04	12 36			13 05		13 10	13 35
	d	07 45	08 28	08 44		09 05	09 48	10 01		10 23		10 44		11 12	11 44		11 57		12 44	12 58			13 05		13 44
Bedminster	d									10 26															
Parson Street	d									10 29															
Nailsea & Backwell	d		08 38			09 13				10 37				11 22			12 07						13 15		
Yatton	d	07 58	08 43			09 20				10 42				11 27			12 14						13 20		
Worle	d		08 49			09 26				10 48				11 33			12 19						13 26		
Weston Milton	d																								
Weston-super-Mare	a	08 07	08 55			09 37				10 53				11 38			12 31			13 18			13 31		
	d	08 08	08 59							10 58				11 39						13 19			13 33		
Highbridge & Burnham	d		09 10							11 09				11 49									13 44		
Bridgwater	d	08 24	09 18							11 17				11 57									13 52		
Taunton	a	08 37	09 31	09 15			10 19	10 35		11 31		11 15		12 11	12 16				13 16	13 41			14 06		14 15

		GW	GW	XC	GW	GW		XC	GW	XC	GW	GW	GW	XC	XC	GW		GW	XC	GW	GW	XC	GW	GW	GW
		◇[1]	◇	◇[1]	◇[1]	◇		◇[1]		◇[1]		◇		◇[1]	◇[1]	◇[1]		◇	◇[1]		◇	◇[1]	◇	◇	
		(cup)		(bike)	(cup)			(bike)		(bike)				(bike)	(bike)	(cup)			(bike)			(bike)			
Gloucester [7]	d												15 13												17 20
Cam & Dursley	d												15 28												17 34
Yate	d												15 41												17 49
Bristol Parkway [7]	a												15 49												17 57
	d			14 25				14 57		15 26			15 55	15 56	16 25				16 58			17 25			17 58
Filton Abbey Wood	d		13 54			14 56						15 55	15 58					16 55			17 20		17 54		18 01
Stapleton Road	d																								
Lawrence Hill	d																								
Bristol Temple Meads [10]	a		14 04	14 39		15 05		15 08		15 38		16 04	16 09	16 09	16 35			17 06	17 09		17 29	17 35	18 04		18 10
	d	13 58		14 44	14 57				15 10	15 44	15 55		16 25	16 14	16 44	16 58				17 25		17 44		18 07	
Bedminster	d								15 13		15 58									17 28					
Parson Street	d										16 00														
Nailsea & Backwell	d	14 07							15 22		16 08		16 36			17 07				17 37				18 17	
Yatton	d	14 15							15 28		16 14		16 41			17 14				17 43				18 23	
Worle	d	14 19							15 34		16 20		16 47			17 19				17 49				18 29	
Weston Milton	d								15 39				16 53							17 58					
Weston-super-Mare	a	14 28							15 42		16 25		16 57			17 28				18 01				18 35	
	d										16 28					17 32								18 36	
Highbridge & Burnham	d										16 40													18 47	
Bridgwater	d										16 48													18 55	
Taunton	a			15 15	15 29					16 16	17 05			16 45	17 15	17 55						18 18		19 09	

		XC		GW	XC	GW	GW	XC	GW	XC	GW	GW		XC	GW	XC	GW	XC	GW	XC	GW	GW		XC	XC
				[R]																					
		◇[1]			◇[1]		◇	◇[1]	◇[1]	◇[1]	◇			◇[1]		◇[1]	◇[1]	◇[1]	◇	◇[1]	◇[1]			◇[1]	◇[1]
		(bike)			(bike)			(bike)	(cup)	(bike)				(bike)			(cup)	(bike)			(cup)				
Gloucester [7]	d											19 20										21 15			22 07
Cam & Dursley	d											19 34										21 31			
Yate	d											19 48										21 45			
Bristol Parkway [7]	a											19 56										21 53			22 34
	d	18 02			18 25			18 58		19 25		19 57		20 02		20 25		20 58		21 25		21 55		22 00	22 34
Filton Abbey Wood	d			18 23			18 55				19 55	20 00							21 05			21 58			
Stapleton Road	d														20 16										
Lawrence Hill	d														20 18										
Bristol Temple Meads [10]	a	18 14		18 33	18 37		19 06	19 09		19 35	20 05	20 10		20 14	20 21	20 35		21 09	21 13	21 35		22 07		22 11	22 46
	d				18 44	19 05			19 25	19 44				20 19	20 25	20 44	20 55			21 44	21 55				
Bedminster	d					19 08									20 28										
Parson Street	d					19 10																			
Nailsea & Backwell	d					19 18			19 36						20 36		21 07				22 07				
Yatton	d					19 24			19 43						20 42		21 14				22 14				
Worle	d					19 30			19 49						20 48		21 19				22 19				
Weston Milton	d					19 34																			
Weston-super-Mare	a					19 38			19 57					20 36	20 53		21 27				22 29				
	d					19 39								20 37	20 58		21 27								
Highbridge & Burnham	d					19 50									21 09										
Bridgwater	d					19 58									21 17										
Taunton	a				19 15	20 13				20 18				20 59	21 33	21 15	21 50			22 15					

For connections from London Paddington please refer to Table 125

Table 134

Gloucester - Taunton

Sundays

7 August to 11 September

		GW	XC	GW	XC
			◇1		◇1
		🛒			
Gloucester 7	d				
Cam & Dursley	d				
Yate	d				
Bristol Parkway 7	a				
	d		22 58		23 25
Filton Abbey Wood	d	22 52			
Stapleton Road	d				
Lawrence Hill	d				
Bristol Temple Meads 10	a	23 00	23 10		23 36
	d			23 10	
Bedminster	d			23 13	
Parson Street	d			23 15	
Nailsea & Backwell	d			23 23	
Yatton	d			23 29	
Worle	d			23 35	
Weston Milton	d			23 40	
Weston-super-Mare	a			23 43	
	d				
Highbridge & Burnham	d				
Bridgwater	d				
Taunton	a				

Sundays

18 September to 23 October

		GW	GW	XC	GW	GW	XC	GW	GW	GW		GW	XC	GW	GW	XC	GW	GW	GW	XC		GW	XC	GW	XC
		◇	◇	◇1			◇1	◇1								◇1		◇1					◇1	◇1	
					🚌				🚌			🚌	🚌		🚌				🚌	🚌		🚌			🚌
				🛒			🛒	🍴								🛒		🍴					🛒	🍴	
Gloucester 7	d													09 59								10 23			
Cam & Dursley	d													10 12								10 53			
Yate	d													10 27								11 33			
Bristol Parkway 7	a													10 37								11 53			
	d				08 42				09 47			10 20	10 30		10 44				11 30	11 35					12 30
Filton Abbey Wood	d				08 47				09 52			10 25			10 49				11 35						
Stapleton Road	d																								
Lawrence Hill	d																								
Bristol Temple Meads 10	a				09 04				10 09			10 50	11 00		11 09				12 00	12 00					13 00
	d	07 45	08 28	08 44		09 05	09 48	10 03		10 23						11 15	11 19	11 57					12 15	12 58	
Bedminster	d																								
Parson Street	d																								
Nailsea & Backwell	d		08 38			09 13				10 34							11 29	12 07							
Yatton	d	07 58	08 43			09 20				10 39							11 34	12 14							
Worle	d		08 49			09 26				10 45							11 40	12 19							
Weston Milton	d																								
Weston-super-Mare	a	08 07	08 55			09 37				10 50							11 45	12 31						13 18	
	d	08 08	08 59							10 58							11 46							13 19	
Highbridge & Burnham	d		09 10							11 09							11 57								
Bridgwater	d	08 24	09 18							11 17							12 05								
Taunton	a	08 37	09 31	09 15			10 19	10 38		11 31						11 46	12 19						12 48	13 41	

		GW	GW	GW	XC	GW		GW	XC	GW	XC	GW	XC	GW	GW	XC		GW	GW	XC	GW	XC	GW	GW	GW
					◇1			◇1			◇1	◇1				◇1						◇1			◇1
			🚌			🚌			🚌	🚌			🚌	🚌					🚌	🚌				🚌	
					🛒			🍴			🛒	🍴				🛒						🛒			🍴
Gloucester 7	d			12 14																	15 13				
Cam & Dursley	d			12 28																	15 27				
[illegible]	d			12 42																	15 41				
[illegible] Parkway 7	a			12 52																	15 51				
[illegible]	d		12 38			13 01			13 30	13 30			14 30	14 32					15 30	15 30				16 01	
[illegible]	d		12 43			13 06				13 35				14 37					15 35					16 06	
[illegible]	d																								
[illegible]	[illegible]	[illegible]	[illegible]	[illegible]	[illegible]	[illegible]	[illegible]																		
[illegible]	[illegible]	[illegible]	13 04			13 31			14 00	14 00			15 00	15 00					16 00	16 00				16 31	
[illegible]	[illegible]	[illegible]	[illegible]	[illegible]	13 15			13 58			14 15	14 57			15 03	15 15		15 55				16 15	16 26		16 58
[illegible]	[illegible]	[illegible]	[illegible]	[illegible]	[illegible]	[illegible]	[illegible]								15 06			15 58							
[illegible]	[illegible]	[illegible]	[illegible]	[illegible]	[illegible]	[illegible]	[illegible]											16 00							
[illegible]	[illegible]	[illegible]	[illegible]	[illegible]	[illegible]	[illegible]	[illegible]	14 07							15 15			16 08					16 36		17 07
[illegible]	[illegible]	[illegible]	[illegible]	[illegible]	[illegible]	[illegible]	[illegible]	[illegible]							15 21			16 14					16 41		17 14
[illegible]	[illegible]	[illegible]	[illegible]	[illegible]	[illegible]	[illegible]	[illegible]	[illegible]							15 27			16 20					16 47		17 19
[illegible]	[illegible]	[illegible]	[illegible]	[illegible]	[illegible]	[illegible]	[illegible]	[illegible]							15 32								16 53		
[illegible]	[illegible]	[illegible]	[illegible]	[illegible]	[illegible]	[illegible]	[illegible]	[illegible]							15 35			16 25					16 57		17 28
[illegible]	[illegible]	[illegible]	[illegible]	[illegible]	[illegible]	[illegible]	[illegible]	[illegible]										16 28							17 32
[illegible]	[illegible]	[illegible]	[illegible]	[illegible]	[illegible]	[illegible]	[illegible]	[illegible]										16 40							
[illegible]	[illegible]	[illegible]	[illegible]	[illegible]	[illegible]	[illegible]	[illegible]	[illegible]										16 48							
[illegible]	[illegible]	[illegible]	[illegible]	[illegible]	[illegible]	[illegible]	[illegible]	[illegible]			14 46	15 29				15 51		17 03				16 46			17 55

ondon Paddington please refer to Table 125

Sundays

18 September to 23 October

Gloucester - Taunton

		XC		GW	XC	GW	GW	XC	GW	GW	XC	GW		GW	XC	GW	XC	GW	GW	XC	GW	XC		GW	GW
										◇	◇1							◇1				◇1			
		bus		bus	trolley		bus	bus			trolley	bus			bus	bus	trolley	cafe	bus	bus					bus
Gloucester 7	d								17 20												19 20				
Cam & Dursley	d								17 34												19 34				
Yate	d								17 49												19 48				
Bristol Parkway 7	a								17 57												19 57				
	d	16 30		16 40			17 27	17 30				18 07			18 30	18 38			19 29	19 30					20 07
Filton Abbey Wood	d			16 45			17 32					18 12				18 43			19 34						20 12
Stapleton Road	d																								
Lawrence Hill	d																								
Bristol Temple Meads 10	a	17 00		17 05			17 57	18 00				18 37			19 00	19 00			19 51	20 00					20 29
	d				17 15	17 25				18 07	18 15			18 59			19 15	19 25				20 15		20 25	
Bedminster	d					17 28								19 02										20 28	
Parson Street	d													19 04											
Nailsea & Backwell	d					17 37				18 17				19 12				19 36						20 36	
Yatton	d					17 43				18 23				19 18				19 43						20 42	
Worle	d					17 49				18 39				19 38				19 49						20 48	
Weston Milton	d					17 58								19 42											
Weston-super-Mare	a					18 01				18 45				19 46				19 57						20 53	
	d									18 46				19 49										20 58	
Highbridge & Burnham	d									18 57				19 59										21 09	
Bridgwater	d									19 05				20 07										21 17	
Taunton	a				17 46					19 19	18 52			20 21			19 46					20 46		21 33	

		GW	XC	GW	XC	GW	XC	GW		GW	GW	XC	GW	GW
		◇1			◇1	◇1								
		cafe	bus	bus		cafe	bus	bus			bus	bus		bus
Gloucester 7	d									21 15				
Cam & Dursley	d									21 31				
Yate	d									21 45				
Bristol Parkway 7	a									21 53				
	d		20 30	20 45			21 30	21 35			22 03	22 05		23 08
Filton Abbey Wood	d			20 50				21 40			22 08			23 13
Stapleton Road	d													
Lawrence Hill	d													
Bristol Temple Meads 10	a		21 00	21 07			22 00	21 57			22 25	22 25		23 30
	d	20 55			21 15	21 55							23 10	
Bedminster	d												23 13	
Parson Street	d												23 15	
Nailsea & Backwell	d	21 07				22 07							23 23	
Yatton	d	21 14				22 14							23 29	
Worle	d	21 19				22 19							23 35	
Weston Milton	d												23 40	
Weston-super-Mare	a	21 27				22 29							23 43	
	d	21 27												
Highbridge & Burnham	d													
Bridgwater	d													
Taunton	a	21 50			21 46									

Sundays

from 30 October

		GW	GW	GW	GW	XC	GW	GW	GW	GW		GW	GW	XC	GW	GW	GW	XC	GW	GW		GW	GW	XC	GW
			◇		◇	◇1	◇1	◇		◇1		◇		◇1	◇1	◇		◇1	◇1			◇1		◇1	◇1
		bus		bus		trolley	cafe		bus	cafe				trolley	cafe			trolley	cafe	bus		cafe		trolley	cafe
Gloucester 7	d																10 19			10 23					
Cam & Dursley	d																10 32			10 53					
Yate	d																10 47			11 33					
Bristol Parkway 7	a																10 55			11 53					
	d						08 40			09 40				10 25	10 40		10 56	11 29	11 40					12 25	12 40
Filton Abbey Wood	d							08 55				10 03				10 54	11 00						11 54		
Stapleton Road	d												10 16												
Lawrence Hill	d												10 18												
Bristol Temple Meads 10	a						08 52	09 05		09 52		10 13	10 21	10 35	10 52	11 03	11 08	11 41	11 52				12 04	12 36	12 52
	d	07 20		07 45		08 44			09 05				10 30	10 44			11 10	11 44				11 59		12 44	
Bedminster	d																								[illegible]
Parson Street	d																								[illegible]
Nailsea & Backwell	d			08 05					09 25				10 40				11 22					12 10		[illegible]	[illegible]
Yatton	d			08 20					09 40				10 45				11 27					12 16		[illegible]	[illegible]
Worle	d			08 35					09 55				10 51				11 33					12 22		[illegible]	[illegible]
Weston Milton	d																							[illegible]	[illegible]
Weston-super-Mare	a	08 00		08 50					10 10				10 56				11 38					12 31	[illegible]	[illegible]	[illegible]
	d		08 08		08 58								10 58				11 39						[illegible]	[illegible]	[illegible]
Highbridge & Burnham	d				09 09								11 09				11 49						[illegible]	[illegible]	[illegible]
Bridgwater	d		08 24		09 17								11 17				11 57						[illegible]	[illegible]	[illegible]
Taunton	a		08 37		09 30	09 48							11 31	11 15			12 11	12 16				[illegible]	[illegible]	[illegible]	[illegible]

For connections from London Paddington please refer to Table 125

Table 134

Sundays
from 30 October

Gloucester - Taunton

		GW	GW	GW	XC	GW		GW	GW	XC	GW	GW	XC	GW	XC	GW		GW	GW	GW	XC	GW	XC	GW	GW
		◇			◇1	◇1		◇	◇1	◇1	◇1	◇	◇1		◇1	◇1			◇		◇1		◇1		◇
					🛒	🍴			🍴	🛒	🍴		🛒		🛒	🍴					🛒		🛒		
Gloucester 7	d			12 14																15 13					
Cam & Dursley	d			12 28																15 28					
Yate	d			12 42																15 41					
Bristol Parkway 7	a			12 51																15 49					
	d			12 57	13 25	13 40				14 25	14 40		14 57		15 26	15 40				15 55	16 00		16 25		
Filton Abbey Wood	d	12 57		13 01				13 54				14 56							15 55	15 58					16 55
Stapleton Road	d																								
Lawrence Hill	d																					←			
Bristol Temple Meads 10	a	13 05		13 10	13 35	13 52		14 04		14 39	14 52	15 05	15 08		15 38	15 52			16 04	16 09	16 11	16 09	16 35		17 06
	d		13 05		13 44				14 10	14 44				15 25	15 44			15 55		16 25	16 14	16 25	16 44	16 55	
Bedminster	d													15 28				15 58		→				16 58	
Parson Street	d																	16 00						17 00	
Nailsea & Backwell	d		13 15						14 20					15 37				16 08				16 36		17 08	
Yatton	d		13 20						14 27					15 43				16 14				16 41		17 14	
Worle	d		13 26						14 32					15 49				16 20				16 47		17 20	
Weston Milton	d													15 57								16 53			
Weston-super-Mare	a		13 31						14 40					16 00				16 25				16 57		17 25	
	d		13 33															16 28							
Highbridge & Burnham	d		13 44															16 40							
Bridgwater	d		13 52															16 48							
Taunton	a		14 06		14 15					15 15					16 16			17 03			16 45		17 15		

		XC		GW	GW	XC	GW	GW	XC	GW	GW	XC		GW	GW	GW	XC	GW	XC	GW	GW	GW		GW	XC
											R														
		◇1			◇	◇1	◇		◇1	◇		◇1		◇1	◇1	◇	◇1		◇1	◇1	◇				◇1
		🛒				🛒			🛒			🛒		🍴	🍴		🛒		🛒	🍴					
Gloucester 7	d							17 20														19 20			
Cam & Dursley	d							17 34														19 34			
Yate	d							17 49														19 48			
Bristol Parkway 7	a							17 57														19 56			
	d	16 58				17 25		17 58	18 02			18 25		18 40			18 58		19 25	19 41		19 57			20 25
Filton Abbey Wood	d				17 20		17 54	18 01			18 23					18 55					19 55	20 00			
Stapleton Road	d																								
Lawrence Hill	d																								
Bristol Temple Meads 10	a	17 09			17 29	17 35	18 04	18 10	18 14		18 33	18 40		18 52		19 06	19 09		19 35	19 52	20 05	20 10			20 35
	d			17 25		17 44				18 25		18 44			19 05			19 25	19 44					20 25	20 44
Bedminster	d			17 28														19 28						20 28	
Parson Street	d																	19 30							
Nailsea & Backwell	d			17 36						18 35					19 17			19 38						20 36	
Yatton	d			17 42						18 41					19 23			19 44						20 42	
Worle	d			17 48						18 47					19 30			19 50						20 48	
Weston Milton	d			17 53														19 54							
Weston-super-Mare	a			17 56						18 53					19 37			19 58						20 53	
	d			18 01						18 58								19 59						20 58	
Highbridge & Burnham	d			18 12						19 09								20 10						21 09	
Bridgwater	d			18 20						19 17								20 18						21 17	
Taunton	a			18 34		18 18				19 32		19 15						20 33	20 18					21 33	21 15

		GW	XC	GW	GW	XC	GW	GW		GW	XC	XC	GW	XC	GW	XC
		◇1	◇1	◇1	◇	◇1	◇1	1			◇1	◇1		◇1		◇1
		🍴	🛒	🍴			🍴	🍴					🛒			
Gloucester 7	d									21 15		22 07				
Cam & Dursley	d									21 31						
Yate	d									21 45						
Bristol Parkway 7	a									21 53		22 34				
	d	20 40	20 58			21 25	21 44			21 55	22 00	22 34		22 58		23 25
Filton Abbey Wood	d				21 05					21 58			22 52			
Stapleton Road	d															
Lawrence Hill	d															
Bristol Temple Meads 10	a	20 52	21 09		21 13	21 35	21 55			22 07	22 11	22 46	23 00	23 10		23 36
	d			21 10		21 44		22 06							23 10	
Bedminster	d														23 13	
Parson Street	d														23 15	
Nailsea & Backwell	d			21 20				22 16							23 23	
Yatton	d			21 27				22 21							23 29	
Worle	d			21 33				22 27							23 35	
Weston Milton	d														23 40	
Weston-super-Mare	a			21 40				22 34							23 43	
	d			21 40												
Highbridge & Burnham	d															
Bridgwater	d															
Taunton	a			22 02		22 15										

For connections from London Paddington please refer to Table 125

Taunton - Gloucester

Miles			GW MO	GW MX	GW MX	GW	XC	GW	GW	GW	XC	GW	GW	GW	XC	GW	GW	GW	GW	XC	GW	GW	GW
				R	R																		
						◇1	1				◇1			◇1	◇1	◇1		◇1		◇1			
				A	B				C	D								E					
				🛏	🛏																		
				☕	☕	☕					🛒			☕	🛒	☕		☕		🛒			
0	**Taunton**	d		01 30	02 18							05 30					06 02		06 34	06 51			
11¾	Bridgwater	d										05 42					06 14		06 46				
18	Highbridge & Burnham	d										05 49					06 21		06 54				
25¾	**Weston-super-Mare**	a										06 00					06 32		07 04				
—		d	23p47									06 01		06 20			06 36	06 49	07 08				
27	Weston Milton	d	23p50											06 25			06 39	06 53	07 11				
29½	Worle	d	23p54									06 07		06 30			06 43	06 59	07 15				
33½	Yatton	d	23p59									06 12		06 37			06 49	07 06	07 21				
37½	Nailsea & Backwell	d	00 06									06 18		06 44			06 55	07 13	07 27				
43¾	Parson Street	d															07 02		07 36				
44½	Bedminster	d	00 15														07 05		07 38			←	
45½	**Bristol Temple Meads 10**	a	00 19	02 34	02 59							06 30		06 55			07 10	07 24	07 41	07 26		07 41	
—		d				04 47	05 19	05 54	06 19	06 19	06 27		06 50		07 00	07 14	07 19		07 47	07 30	07 34	07 47	07 54
46½	Lawrence Hill	d							06 22	06 22			06 53				07 22		→			07 50	
47	Stapleton Road	d							06 25	06 24			06 56				07 24					07 52	
50	Filton Abbey Wood	d						06a01	06a30	06a30			07a01			07a21	07 30				07 43	07 59	08a00
51¼	**Bristol Parkway 7**	a					05 28				06 37				07 08		07 33			07 38	07 47	08 05	
—		d																			07 48		
57½	Yate	d																			07 57		
72¼	Cam & Dursley	d																			08 10		
85¼	**Gloucester 7**	a																			08 29		

		GW	XC	GW	GW	GW	GW	XC	GW	GW	GW	XC	GW	GW	GW	XC	GW	GW	GW	GW	XC	GW	GW
											R												
		◇1	◇1			◇1		◇1				◇1				◇1			◇	◇1	◇1		
		☕	🛒			☕		🛒			🛒	🛒				🛒			🛒	☕	🛒		
Taunton	d	06 54				07 12	07 36	07 51				08 12			08 36	08 51				09 05			09 37
Bridgwater	d	07 05				07 23	07 48								08 48								09 49
Highbridge & Burnham	d	07 12				07 31	07 56								08 56								09 56
Weston-super-Mare	a	07 24				07 41	08 06					08 31			09 08					09 27			10 07
	d	07 24			07 37	07 49	08 08					08 33		08 40	09 10					09 29		09 45	10 10
Weston Milton	d				07 40	07 53	08 11							08 43	09 13								10 13
Worle	d	07 32			07 44	07 59	08 15							08 45	09 17							09 50	10 17
Yatton	d	07 39			07 49	08 06	08 21							08 51	09 23					09 40		09 56	10 23
Nailsea & Backwell	d	07 46			07 55	08 13	08 27							08 57	09 29					09 46		10 02	10 29
Parson Street	d				08 02		08 35							09 05	09 37								10 36
Bedminster	d				08 04		08 37			←				09 07	09 39			←					10 39
Bristol Temple Meads 10	a	07 58			08 10	08 25	08 42	08 27		08 42		08 55		09 16	09 43	09 27		09 43		09 57		10 14	10 43
	d		08 00	08 10	08 21		08 44	08 30	08 41	08 44	08 54	09 00	09 10	09 21	09 47	09 30	09 41	09 47	09 55		10 00	10 21	10 44
Lawrence Hill	d			08 13			→			08 47			09 13		→			09 49					→
Stapleton Road	d			08 16						08 49			09 15					09 50					
Filton Abbey Wood	d			08 22	08a30				08 48	08 55	09a01		09 22	09a30			09 48	09 55	10a00			10a30	
Bristol Parkway 7	a		08 08	08 29				08 38	08 52	09 02		09 08	09 28			09 38	09 52	10 03			10 08		
	d								08 52								09 52						
Yate	d								09 01								10 01						
Cam & Dursley	d								09 14								10 14						
Gloucester 7	a								09 33								10 33						

		XC	GW	GW	GW	XC	GW	XC	GW	GW	GW	GW	XC	GW	GW	XC	GW	GW	GW	XC	GW	XC
		◇1	◇		◇	◇1	◇	◇1			◇		◇1	◇1		◇1	◇		◇	◇1		◇1
		🛒			🛒	🛒		🛒			🛒		🛒	☕		🛒			🛒	🛒		🛒
Taunton	d	09 51					10 07	10 51				11 04	11 17	11 26		11 51					12 07	12 51
Bridgwater	d						10 19					11 16									12 19	
Highbridge & Burnham	d						10 27					11 24									12 27	
Weston-super-Mare	a						10 38					11 34									12 38	
	d						10 39			11 10		11 45						12 10			12 39	
Weston Milton	d									11 13								12 13				
Worle	d						10 45			11 17		11 50						12 17			12 45	
Yatton	d						10 51			11 23		11 56						12 23			12 51	
Nailsea & Backwell	d						10 57			11 29		12 02						12 29			12 57	
Parson Street	d									11 36								12 36				
Bedminster	d			←						11 39					←			12 39				
Bristol Temple Meads 10	a	10 26		10 43			11 09	11 24		11 43		12 12	11 53	11 59	12 12	12 24		12 43			13 10	13 24
	d	10 30	10 41	10 44	10 54	11 00	11 21	11 30	11 41	11 44	11 54	12 21	12 00		12 21	12 30	12 41	12 44	12 54	13 00	13 21	13 30
Lawrence Hill	d			10 47						11 47		→						12 47				
Stapleton Road	d			10 50						11 50								12 50				
Filton Abbey Wood	d		10 48	10 55	11a00		11a30		11 48	11 55	12a00				12a30		12 48	12 55	13a00		13a30	
Bristol Parkway 7	a	10 38	10 52	11 03		11 08		11 38	11 52	12 03			12 08			12 38	12 52	13 03		13 08		13 38
	d		10 52						11 52								12 52					
Yate	d		11 01						12 01								13 01					
Cam & Dursley	d		11 14						12 14								13 14					
Gloucester 7	a		11 34						12 33								13 31					

A Until 29 July, and from 13 September. **The Night Riviera**
B From 2 August until 9 September. **The Night Riviera**
C until 1 July, from 5 September
D from 4 July until 2 September
E The Bristolian

For connections to London Paddington please refer to Table 125

Table 134

Taunton - Gloucester

		GW	GW	GW	GW	XC	GW	XC	GW		GW	GW	XC	GW	GW	XC	GW	GW	GW		XC	GW	GW	XC	GW
				◇ 🍴		◇1 🍴		◇1 🍴	◇			◇ 🍴	◇1 🍴	◇ A	◇ B	◇1 🍴			◇ 🍴		◇1 🍴			◇1 🍴	
Taunton	d				13 07	13 16		13 54						14 07	14 07	14 54					15 12		15 15	15 51	
Bridgwater	d				13 19									14 19	14 19								15 27		
Highbridge & Burnham	d				13 27									14 27	14 27								15 34		
Weston-super-Mare	a				13 38									14 37	14 37						15 37		15 45		
	d		13 10		13 39						14 10			14 39	14 39			15 10			15 38		15 45		
Weston Milton	d		13 13								14 13							15 13							
Worle	d		13 17		13 45						14 17			14 45	14 45			15 17					15 50		
Yatton	d		13 23		13 51						14 23			14 51	14 51			15 23					15 56		
Nailsea & Backwell	d		13 29		13 57						14 29			14 57	14 57			15 29					16 02		
Parson Street	d		13 36								14 36							15 36							
Bedminster	d		13 39				←				14 39							15 39							
Bristol Temple Meads 10	a		13 42		14 12	13 56	14 12	14 27			14 43			15 09	15 15	15 27		15 43			15 57		16 17	16 27	
	d	13 41	13 46	13 54	14 21	14 00	14 21	14 30	14 41		14 45	14 54	15 00	15 21	15 21	15 30	15 34	15 45	15 54		16 00	16 15	16 24	16 30	16 41
Lawrence Hill	d		13 47		→						14 47							15 47				16 18			
Stapleton Road	d		13 50								14 50							15 50				16 20			
Filton Abbey Wood	d	13 48	13 55	14a00			14a30		14 48		14 55	15a00		15a30	15a30			15 55	16a00			16 26	16a30		16 48
Bristol Parkway 7	a	13 52	14 03			14 08		14 38	14 51		15 03		15 08			15 38	15 48	16 03			16 08	16 34		16 38	16 52
	d	13 52							14 52																16 52
Yate	d	14 01							15 01																17 01
Cam & Dursley	d	14 14							15 14																17 14
Gloucester 7	a	14 33							15 32																17 33

		GW	GW	XC	GW		GW	XC	GW	GW	GW	GW	GW	XC	GW		XC	GW	GW	GW	GW	XC	GW	GW	XC
			R 🍴	◇1 🍴				◇1 🍴	◇1 ☕			R 🍴		◇1 🍴			◇1 🍴	◇1 ☕			R 🍴	◇1 🍴	A	B	◇1 🍴
Taunton	d						16 07	16 54					17 06	17 21			17 51						18 08	18 08	18 54
Bridgwater	d						16 19						17 17										18 19	18 19	
Highbridge & Burnham	d						16 27						17 25										18 27	18 27	
Weston-super-Mare	a						16 37						17 37										18 38	18 38	
	d	16 10					16 39		17 10		17 15		17 38					18 08		18 15			18 39	18 39	
Weston Milton	d	16 13					16 42						17 41										18 43	18 43	
Worle	d	16 17					16 45				17 21		17 45							18 21			18 45	18 45	
Yatton	d	16 23					16 51				17 26		17 51							18 27			18 51	18 51	
Nailsea & Backwell	d	16 29					16 57				17 32		17 57							18 33			18 57	18 57	
Parson Street	d	16 36											18 04										19 07	19 07	
Bedminster	d	16 39					17 07						18 06		←								19 09	19 09	
Bristol Temple Meads 10	a	16 43					17 12	17 27	17 30		17 44		18 14	17 54	18 14		18 24	18 28		18 44			19 14	19 18	19 27
	d	16 44	16 54	17 00	17 10		17 21	17 30		17 41	17 46	17 54	18 21	18 00	18 21		18 30		18 41	18 48	18 54	19 00	19 21	19 21	19 30
Lawrence Hill	d	16 47			17 13						17 47		→		18 24					18 51			19 24	19 24	
Stapleton Road	d	16 50			17 16						17 49				18 26					18a53			19 26	19 26	
Filton Abbey Wood	d	16 55	17a00		17 22		17a30			17 48	17 55	18a00			18a30				18 48		19a00		19a30	19a30	
Bristol Parkway 7	a	17 03		17 08	17 27			17 38		17 52	18 03			18 08			18 38		18 52			19 08			19 38
	d									17 52									18 52						
Yate	d									18 01									19 01						
Cam & Dursley	d									18 14									19 14						
Gloucester 7	a									18 33									19 30						

			GW	GW	GW	GW	XC	GW	GW	GW	XC		GW	GW	GW	GW	GW	XC	GW	GW	GW		GW	GW	GW
				A	B	FO ◇ 🍴	◇1	FX	A	B	◇1			◇ 🍴			◇1 ☕	◇1	◇	1			◇1 ☕	◇	◇ C
Taunton	d								19 10	19 17	19 51					20 30	21 14	21 18					21 29		22 00
Bridgwater	d								19 22	19 30						20 42							21 39		
Highbridge & Burnham	d								19 31	19 38						20 50							21 47		
Weston-super-Mare	a								19 42	19 50						21 00							21 57		22 24
	d			19 10	19 10				19 49	20 08						21 02				21 33			22 01		22 30
Weston Milton	d			19 13	19 13											21 05				21 37					
Worle	d			19 17	19 17				19 55	20 14						21 09				21 42			22 08		
Yatton	d			19 23	19 23				20 01	20 21						21 14				21 49			22 15		
Nailsea & Backwell	d			19 29	19 29				20 07	20 27						21 20				21 55			22 21		
Parson Street	d			19 36						20 38						21 28									
Bedminster	d			19 39						20 41						21 30									
Bristol Temple Meads 10	a			19 43	19 43				20 19	20 45	20 25					21 35	21 47	21 51		22 06			22 32		22 56
	d		19 41	19 45	19 45	19 54	20 00	20 04			20 30		20 41	20 55	21 19			22 00	21 54		22 11			22 54	
Lawrence Hill	d			19 47	19 47										21 22										
Stapleton Road	d			19 50	19 50										21 24										
Filton Abbey Wood	d		19 48	19 55	19 55	20a00		20a11					20 48	21a00	21a30				21a59		22 18			23a00	
Bristol Parkway 7	a		19 52	20 03	20 03		20 08				20 38		20 52					22 08			22 22				
	d		19 52				20 10						20 52								22 22				
Yate	d		20 01										21 01								22 31				
Cam & Dursley	d		20 14										21 14								22 44				
Gloucester 7	a		20 32				20 38						21 32								23 03				

A until 1 July, from 5 September **B** from 4 July until 2 September **C** until 29 July

For connections to London Paddington please refer to Table 125

Table 134

Taunton - Gloucester

		GW	GW	GW
			◇	
		A	B	
Taunton	d	22§00	22§23	22 45
Bridgwater	d	§	§	22 57
Highbridge & Burnham	d	§	§	23 05
Weston-super-Mare	a	22§24	22§47	23 15
	d	22§30	22§49	23 17
Weston Milton	d	§	§	23 20
Worle	d	§	§	23 24
Yatton	d	§	§	23 30
Nailsea & Backwell	d	§	§	23 36
Parson Street	d	§	§	23 43
Bedminster	d	§	§	23 46
Bristol Temple Meads 10	a	22§56	23§16	23 51
	d			
Lawrence Hill	d			
Stapleton Road	d			
Filton Abbey Wood	d			
Bristol Parkway 7	a			
	d			
Yate	d			
Cam & Dursley	d			
Gloucester 7	a			

Saturdays

until 10 September

		GW	GW	XC	GW	GW	GW	GW	XC	GW		GW	XC	GW	GW	GW	GW	XC	GW	GW		XC	GW	GW	GW
		R	R																						
				◇1		◇1		◇1	◇1				◇1				◇1	◇1				◇1			◇
		C	D																						
		🛏	🛏																						
		⊡	⊡	🛒				⊡	🛒				🛒				⊡	🛒				🛒			
Taunton	d	01§30	02§18		05 28							06 35	06 51				06 54			07 35		07 51			
Bridgwater	d	§	§		05 40							06 48					07 05			07 47					
Highbridge & Burnham	d	§	§		05 48							06 55					07 12			07 55					
Weston-super-Mare	a	§	§		05 59							07 06					07 24			08 06					
	d	§	§		06 01			06 24				07 08					07 24		07 37	08 06					
Weston Milton	d	§	§		06 04							07 11							07 40	08 09					
Worle	d	§	§		06 07			06 32				07 16					07 32		07 44	08 15					
Yatton	d	§	§		06 12			06 39				07 22					07 39		07 49	08 21					
Nailsea & Backwell	d	§	§		06 18			06 45				07 28					07 46		07 55	08 27					
Parson Street	d	§	§		06 29							07 35							08 02	08 36					
Bedminster	d	§	§		06 31							07 38			←				08 04	08 38				←	
Bristol Temple Meads 10	a	02§34	02§59		06 34			06 56				07 42	07 25		07 42		07 58		08 10	08 41		08 24		08 41	
	d			06 15		06 46	06 50		07 00	07 21		07 47	07 30	07 41	07 47	07 54		08 00	08 20	08 45		08 30	08 41	08 45	08 54
Lawrence Hill	d						06 53					→			07 50				08 23	→				08 48	
Stapleton Road	d						06 56								07 52				08 25					08 50	
Filton Abbey Wood	d					06 54	07a01			07a29				07 48	07 59	08a00			08a30				08 48	08 56	09a00
Bristol Parkway 7	a			06 23		06 58			07 08				07 38	07 52	08 05			08 08				08 38	08 52	09 03	
	d			06 25										07 52									08 52		
Yate	d													08 01									09 01		
Cam & Dursley	d													08 14									09 14		
Gloucester 7	a			06 54										08 32									09 33		

		GW	XC	GW	XC	GW		GW	GW	XC	GW	XC	GW	GW	XC	GW		GW	GW	XC	GW	GW	GW	GW	GW
		◇1	◇1		◇1				◇	◇1		◇1	◇		◇1	◇			◇1	◇1			◇1	◇	
		⊡	🛒		🛒					🛒		🛒			🛒				⊡	🛒			⊡		
Taunton	d	07 58	08 12		08 51						09 10	09 51			10 09			10 12	10 45	10 53					11 07
Bridgwater	d	08 09									09 22							10 24							11 19
Highbridge & Burnham	d	08 16									09 30							10 32							11 27
Weston-super-Mare	a	08 26									09 42				10 32			10 40							11 37
	d	08 29		08 39				09 10			09 44			10 10	10 33			10 40				11 10	11 30		11 39
Weston Milton	d							09 13						10 13								11 13			
Worle	d			08 45				09 18			09 49			10 18				10 46				11 18			11 45
Yatton	d	08 40		08 51				09 23			09 55			10 23				10 52				11 23			11 51
Nailsea & Backwell	d	08 46		08 57				09 29			10 01			10 29				10 58				11 29			11 57
Parson Street	d							09 36						10 36								11 36			
Bedminster	d							09 38						10 38								11 38			
Bristol Temple Meads 10	a	08 57	08 49	09 08	09 26			09 43			10 13	10 26		10 43	10 52			11 13	11 24	11 26		11 43	11 47		12 10
	d		09 00	09 21	09 30	09 41		09 45	09 54	10 00	10 21	10 30	10 41	10 45	11 00	10 54		11 21		11 30	11 41	11 45		11 54	12 21
Lawrence Hill	d							09 48						10 48								11 48			→
Stapleton Road	d			09 25				09 50			10 25			10 50				11 25				11 50			
Filton Abbey Wood	d			09a30		09 48		09 56	10a00		10a30		10 48	10 56		11a00		11a30			11 48	11 56		12a00	
Bristol Parkway 7	a		09 08		09 38	09 52		10 03		10 08		10 38	10 52	11 03	11 08					11 38	11 52	12 03			
	d					09 52							10 52								11 52				
Yate	d					10 01							11 01								12 01				
Cam & Dursley	d					10 14							11 14								12 14				
Gloucester 7	a					10 33							11 32								12 33				

A from 1 August until 9 September
B from 12 September
C until 30 July. **The Night Riviera**
D from 6 August until 10 September. **The Night Riviera**

For connections to London Paddington please refer to Table 125

Table 134

Saturdays

until 10 September

Taunton - Gloucester

		XC		GW	XC	GW	GW	GW	XC	GW	GW	XC		GW	GW	GW	XC	GW	XC	GW	GW	GW		XC	GW
		◇1			◇1	◇		◇	◇1		◇1	◇1				◇	◇1		◇1	◇		◇		◇1	
		🛒			🛒				🛒		☕	🛒					🛒		🛒					🛒	
Taunton	d	11 17			11 51					12 07		12 51						13 07	13 54						14 07
Bridgwater	d									12 19								13 19							14 19
Highbridge & Burnham	d									12 27								13 27							14 27
Weston-super-Mare	a									12 37								13 37							14 37
	d						12 10			12 39	13 01				13 10			13 39			14 10				14 39
Weston Milton	d						12 13								13 13						14 13				
Worle	d						12 18			12 45					13 18			13 45			14 18				14 45
Yatton	d						12 23			12 51					13 23			13 51			14 23				14 51
Nailsea & Backwell	d						12 29			12 57					13 29			13 57			14 29				14 57
Parson Street	d						12 36								13 36						14 36				
Bedminster	d			←			12 38								13 38						14 38				
Bristol Temple Meads [10]	a	11 55		12 10	12 25		12 43			13 09	13 19	13 24			13 43			14 11	14 27		14 43				15 10
	d	12 00		12 21	12 30	12 41	12 45	12 54	13 00	13 21		13 30		13 41	13 45	13 54	14 00	14 21	14 30	14 41	14 45	14 54		15 00	15 21
Lawrence Hill	d						12 48								13 48						14 48				
Stapleton Road	d			12 25			12 50			13 25					13 50			14 25			14 50				15 25
Filton Abbey Wood	d			12a29		12 48	12 56	13a00		13a30				13 48	13 56	14a00		14a30		14 48	14 56	15a00			15a30
Bristol Parkway [7]	a	12 08			12 38	12 52	13 03		13 08			13 38		13 52	14 03		14 08		14 38	14 52	15 03			15 08	
	d					12 52								13 52						14 52					
Yate	d					13 01								14 01						15 01					
Cam & Dursley	d					13 14								14 14						15 14					
Gloucester [7]	a					13 34								14 33						15 32					

		GW	XC	GW	GW	XC	GW	GW		XC	GW	GW	GW	XC	GW	GW	XC	GW		GW	GW	XC	GW	GW	XC
		◇1	◇1			◇1	◇			◇1			◇	◇1		◇1	◇1				◇	◇1		◇1	◇1
		☕	🛒			🛒				🛒				🛒		☕	🛒					🛒		☕	🛒
Taunton	d		14 52			15 04		15 07		15 51					16 07		16 51						17 07		17 54
Bridgwater	d							15 19							16 19								17 17		
Highbridge & Burnham	d							15 27							16 27								17 25		
Weston-super-Mare	a					15 23		15 37							16 37								17 37		
	d	15 01			15 10	15 30		15 39				16 10			16 39	17 01				17 10			17 40	18 01	
Weston Milton	d				15 13							16 13								17 13					
Worle	d				15 18			15 45				16 18			16 45					17 18			17 45		
Yatton	d				15 23			15 51				16 23			16 51					17 23			17 51		
Nailsea & Backwell	d				15 29			15 57				16 29			16 57					17 29			17 57		
Parson Street	d				15 36							16 36								17 36					
Bedminster	d				15 38							16 38								17 38					
Bristol Temple Meads [10]	a	15 19	15 25		15 43	15 49		16 09		16 25		16 43			17 09	17 19	17 25			17 43			18 11	18 18	18 27
	d		15 30	15 41	15 45	16 00	15 54	16 21		16 30	16 41	16 45	16 54	17 00	17 21		17 30	17 41		17 45	17 54	18 00	18 21		18 30
Lawrence Hill	d				15 48							16 48								17 48					
Stapleton Road	d				15 50			16 25				16 50			17 25					17 50			18 25		
Filton Abbey Wood	d			15 48	15 56		16a00	16a30			16 48	16 56	17a00		17a30			17 48		17 56	18a00		18a30		
Bristol Parkway [7]	a		15 38	15 52	16 03	16 08				16 38	16 52	17 03		17 08			17 38	17 52		18 03		18 08			18 38
	d			15 52							16 52							17 52							
Yate	d			16 01							17 01							18 01							
Cam & Dursley	d			16 14							17 14							18 14							
Gloucester [7]	a			16 33							17 33							18 33							

		GW	GW	GW		XC	GW	XC	GW	GW	GW	GW	XC	XC		GW	GW	GW	GW	GW	GW	GW	GW	GW	
				R																					
						◇1		◇1			◇		◇1	◇1		◇1		◇		◇1	◇		◇1		
						🛒		🛒								☕				☕			☕		
Taunton	d						18 07	18 51				19 07	19 18	19 54					20 17	21 14			21 30	21 35	
Bridgwater	d						18 19					19 19							20 29					21 47	
Highbridge & Burnham	d						18 27					19 27							20 37					21 55	
Weston-super-Mare	a						18 37					19 37							20 48				21 51	22 05	
	d		18 10				18 39			19 10		19 39				20 10			20 50				21 53	22 07	
Weston Milton	d		18 13							19 13									20 53					22 10	
Worle	d		18 18				18 45			19 18		19 45							20 57					22 14	
Yatton	d		18 23				18 51			19 23		19 51							21 03					22 20	
Nailsea & Backwell	d		18 29				18 57			19 29		19 57							21 09					22 26	
Parson Street	d		18 36							19 36									21 17					22 33	
Bedminster	d		18 38							19 38									21 19					22 36	
Bristol Temple Meads [10]	a		18 43				19 09	19 23		19 43		20 09	19 54	20 27		20 30			21 24	21 47			22 12	22 42	
	d	18 41	18 45	18 54		19 00	19 21	19 30	19 41	19 45	19 54		20 00	20 30			20 41	20 54	21 29		21 54	22 06			
Lawrence Hill	d		18 48							19 48															
Stapleton Road	d		18 50							19 50															
Filton Abbey Wood	d	18 48	18 56	19a00			19a28		19 48	19 56	20a00						20 48	21a00	21a36		22a00	22 14			
Bristol Parkway [7]	a	18 52	19 03			19 08		19 38	19 52	20 03			20 08	20 38			20 52					22 17			
	d	18 52							19 52								20 52					22 18			
Yate	d	19 01							20 01								21 01					22 28			
Cam & Dursley	d	19 14							20 14								21 14					22 43			
Gloucester [7]	a	19 33							20 33								21 33					23 01			

For connections to London Paddington please refer to Table 125

Table 134

Saturdays
until 10 September

Taunton - Gloucester

Station		GW ◇
Taunton	d	
Bridgwater	d	
Highbridge & Burnham	d	
Weston-super-Mare	a	
	d	
Weston Milton	d	
Worle	d	
Yatton	d	
Nailsea & Backwell	d	
Parson Street	d	
Bedminster	d	
Bristol Temple Meads 10	a	
	d	22 54
Lawrence Hill	d	
Stapleton Road	d	
Filton Abbey Wood	d	23a00
Bristol Parkway 7	a	
	d	
Yate	d	
Cam & Dursley	d	
Gloucester 7	a	

Saturdays
from 17 September

Station		GW	XC	GW	GW	GW	GW	XC	GW	GW		XC	GW	GW	GW	GW	XC	GW	GW	XC		GW	GW	GW	GW
		R A 🛏 🍴	◇1 ☕		◇1		◇1 🍴	◇1 ☕				◇1 ☕				◇1 🍴	◇1 ☕			◇1 ☕				◇	◇1 🍴
Taunton	d	01 30		05 28						06 35		06 51				06 54			07 35	07 51					07 58
Bridgwater	d			05 40						06 48						07 05			07 47						08 09
Highbridge & Burnham	d			05 48						06 55						07 12			07 55						08 16
Weston-super-Mare	a			05 59						07 06						07 24			08 06						08 26
	d			06 01			06 24			07 08						07 24		07 37	08 06						08 29
Weston Milton	d			06 04						07 11								07 40	08 09						
Worle	d			06 07			06 32			07 16						07 32		07 44	08 15						
Yatton	d			06 12			06 39			07 22						07 39		07 49	08 21						08 40
Nailsea & Backwell	d			06 18			06 45			07 28						07 46		07 55	08 27						08 46
Parson Street	d			06 29						07 35								08 02	08 36						
Bedminster	d			06 31						07 38				←				08 04	08 38				←		
Bristol Temple Meads 10	a	02 34		06 34			06 56			07 42		07 25		07 42		07 58		08 10	08 41	08 24			08 41		08 57
	d		06 15		06 46	06 50		07 00	07 21	07 47		07 30	07 41	07 47	07 54		08 00	08 20	08 45	08 30		08 41	08 45	08 54	
Lawrence Hill	d					06 53				→				07 50				08 23	→				08 48		
Stapleton Road	d					06 56								07 52				08 25					08 50		
Filton Abbey Wood	d				06 54	07a01			07a29				07 48	07 59	08a00			08a30				08 48	08 56	09a00	
Bristol Parkway 7	a		06 23		06 58			07 08				07 38	07 52	08 05			08 08			08 38		08 52	09 03		
	d		06 25										07 52									08 52			
Yate	d												08 01									09 01			
Cam & Dursley	d												08 14									09 14			
Gloucester 7	a		06 54										08 32									09 33			

Station		XC	GW	GW	XC	GW		GW	GW	XC	GW	XC	GW	GW	GW	XC		GW	XC	GW	GW	GW	GW	XC	GW
		◇1 ☕		◇1 🍴	◇1 ☕				◇	◇1 ☕		◇1 ☕	◇		◇	◇1 ☕			◇1 ☕			◇		◇1 ☕	
Taunton	d	08 12		08 38	08 51						09 10	09 51						10 12	10 51				11 07	11 17	
Bridgwater	d										09 22							10 24					11 19		
Highbridge & Burnham	d										09 30							10 32					11 27		
Weston-super-Mare	a			08 58							09 42							10 40					11 37		
	d		08 39	09 02				09 10			09 44			10 10				10 40			11 10		11 39		
Weston Milton	d							09 13						10 13							11 13				
Worle	d		08 45					09 18			09 49			10 18				10 46			11 18		11 45		
Yatton	d		08 51					09 23			09 55			10 23				10 52			11 23		11 51		
Nailsea & Backwell	d		08 57					09 29			10 01			10 29				10 58			11 29		11 57		
Parson Street	d							09 36						10 36							11 36				
Bedminster	d							09 38						10 38							11 38				←
Bristol Temple Meads 10	a	08 49	09 08	09 23	09 26			09 43			10 13	10 26		10 43				11 13	11 26		11 43		12 10	11 55	12 10
	d	09 00	09 21		09 30	09 41		09 45	09 54	10 00	10 21	10 30	10 41	10 45	10 54	11 00		11 21	11 30	11 41	11 45	11 54	12 21	12 00	12 21
Lawrence Hill	d							09 48						10 48							11 48		→		
Stapleton Road	d		09 25					09 50			10 25			10 50				11 25			11 50				12 25
Filton Abbey Wood	d		09a30			09 48		09 56	10a00		10a30		10 48	10 56	11a00			11a30		11 48	11 56	12a00			12a29
Bristol Parkway 7	a	09 08			09 38	09 52		10 03		10 08		10 38	10 52	11 03		11 08			11 38	11 52	12 03			12 08	
	d					09 52							10 52							11 52					
Yate	d					10 01							11 01							12 01					
Cam & Dursley	d					10 14							11 14							12 14					
Gloucester 7	a					10 33							11 32							12 33					

A The Night Riviera

For connections to London Paddington please refer to Table 125

Table 134

Saturdays

from 17 September

Taunton - Gloucester

		XC		GW	GW	GW	XC	GW	XC	GW	GW	GW		GW	XC	GW	XC	GW	GW	GW	XC	GW		XC	GW
		◇[1]		◇		◇	◇[1]		◇[1]			◇			◇[1]		◇[1]	◇		◇	◇[1]			◇[1]	
		🛒					🛒		🛒						🛒		🛒				🛒			🛒	
Taunton	d	11 51						12 07	12 51					13 07	13 16		13 54					14 07		14 52	
Bridgwater	d							12 19						13 19								14 19			
Highbridge & Burnham	d							12 27						13 27								14 27			
Weston-super-Mare	a							12 37						13 37								14 37			
	d				12 10			12 39			13 10			13 39					14 10			14 39			
Weston Milton	d				12 13						13 13								14 13						
Worle	d				12 18			12 45			13 18			13 45					14 18			14 45			
Yatton	d				12 23			12 51			13 23			13 51					14 23			14 51			
Nailsea & Backwell	d				12 29			12 57			13 29			13 57					14 29			14 57			
Parson Street	d				12 36						13 36								14 36						
Bedminster	d				12 38						13 38					←			14 38						
Bristol Temple Meads [10]	a	12 25			12 43			13 09	13 24		13 43			14 11	13 56	14 11	14 27		14 43			15 10		15 25	
	d	12 30		12 41	12 45	12 54	13 00	13 21	13 30	13 41	13 45	13 54		14 21	14 00	14 21	14 30	14 41	14 45	14 54	15 00	15 21		15 30	15 41
Lawrence Hill	d				12 48						13 48			→					14 48						
Stapleton Road	d				12 50			13 25			13 50					14 25			14 50			15 25			
Filton Abbey Wood	d			12 48	12 56	13a00		13a30		13 48	13 56	14a00				14a30		14 48	14 56	15a00		15a30			15 48
Bristol Parkway [7]	a	12 38		12 52	13 03		13 08		13 38	13 52	14 03				14 08		14 38	14 52	15 03		15 08			15 38	15 52
	d			12 52						13 52								14 52							15 52
Yate	d			13 01						14 01								15 01							16 01
Cam & Dursley	d			13 14						14 14								15 14							16 14
Gloucester [7]	a			13 34						14 33								15 32							16 33

		GW	XC	GW	GW	XC	GW	GW		GW	XC	GW	XC	GW	GW	GW	GW	XC		GW	XC	GW	GW	GW	XC
																								R	
			◇[1]	◇		◇[1]				◇	◇[1]		◇[1]			◇		◇[1]			◇[1]				◇[1]
			🛒			🛒					🛒		🛒					🛒			🛒				🛒
Taunton	d		15 04		15 07	15 51						16 07	16 51				17 07	17 21			17 51				
Bridgwater	d				15 19							16 19					17 17								
Highbridge & Burnham	d				15 27							16 27					17 25								
Weston-super-Mare	a		15 23		15 37							16 37					17 37								
	d	15 10	15 30		15 39			16 10				16 39			17 10		17 40						18 10		
Weston Milton	d	15 13						16 13							17 13								18 13		
Worle	d	15 18			15 45			16 18				16 45			17 18		17 45						18 18		
Yatton	d	15 23			15 51			16 23				16 51			17 23		17 51						18 23		
Nailsea & Backwell	d	15 29			15 57			16 29				16 57			17 29		17 57						18 29		
Parson Street	d	15 36						16 36							17 36								18 36		
Bedminster	d	15 38						16 38							17 38					←			18 38		
Bristol Temple Meads [10]	a	15 43	15 49		16 09	16 25		16 43				17 09	17 25		17 43		18 11	17 54		18 11	18 25		18 43		
	d	15 45	16 00	15 54	16 21	16 30	16 41	16 45		16 54	17 00	17 21	17 30	17 41	17 45	17 54	18 21	18 00		18 21	18 30	18 41	18 45	18 54	19 00
Lawrence Hill	d	15 48						16 48							17 48		→						18 48		
Stapleton Road	d	15 50			16 25			16 50				17 25			17 50					18 25			18 50		
Filton Abbey Wood	d	15 56		16a00	16a30		16 48	16 56		17a00		17a30		17 48	17 56	18a00				18a30		18 48	18 56	19a00	
Bristol Parkway [7]	a	16 03	16 08			16 38	16 52	17 03			17 08		17 38	17 52	18 03			18 08			18 38	18 52	19 03		19 08
	d						16 52							17 52								18 52			
Yate	d						17 01							18 01								19 01			
Cam & Dursley	d						17 14							18 14								19 14			
Gloucester [7]	a						17 33							18 33								19 33			

		GW	XC	GW		GW	GW	XC	GW	XC	GW	GW	GW	GW		GW	GW	GW	GW	GW	GW				
			◇[1]				◇	◇[1]		◇[1]	◇[1]		◇			◇[1]	◇		◇[1]		◇				
			🛒							🛒	☕					☕			☕						
Taunton	d	18 07	18 54						19 07	19 51				20 17		21 14			21 30	21 35					
Bridgwater	d	18 19							19 19					20 29						21 47					
Highbridge & Burnham	d	18 27							19 27					20 37						21 55					
Weston-super-Mare	a	18 37							19 37					20 48					21 51	22 05					
	d	18 39				19 10			19 39		20 10			20 50					21 53	22 07					
Weston Milton	d					19 13								20 53						22 10					
Worle	d	18 45				19 18			19 45					20 57						22 14					
Yatton	d	18 51				19 23			19 51					21 03						22 20					
Nailsea & Backwell	d	18 57				19 29			19 57					21 09						22 26					
Parson Street	d					19 36								21 17						22 33					
Bedminster	d					19 38								21 19						22 36					
Bristol Temple Meads [10]	a	19 09	19 27			19 43			20 09	20 25	20 30			21 24		21 47			22 12	22 42					
	d	19 21	19 30	19 41		19 45	19 54	20 00		20 30		20 41	20 54	21 29			21 54	22 06			22 54				
Lawrence Hill	d					19 48																			
Stapleton Road	d					19 50																			
Filton Abbey Wood	d	19a28		19 48		19 56	20a00					20 48	21a00	21a36			22a00	22 14			23a00				
Bristol Parkway [7]	a		19 38	19 52		20 03		20 08		20 38		20 52						22 17							
	d			19 52								20 52						22 18							
Yate	d			20 01								21 01						22 28							
Cam & Dursley	d			20 14								21 14						22 43							
Gloucester [7]	a			20 33								21 33						23 01							

For connections to London Paddington please refer to Table 125

Table 134

Sundays

until 19 June

Taunton - Gloucester

		GW	XC	GW	GW	GW	GW	XC	GW	XC		GW	GW	GW	GW	GW	XC	GW	GW	XC		GW	XC	GW	GW
													R												
		◇1 ☕	◇1 🛒		◇	◇1 ☕	🚌	◇1 🛒		◇1 🛒				🚌		◇1 ☕	◇1 🛒		🚌	◇1 🛒		◇1 ☕	◇1 🛒	◇	
Taunton	d				08 35				10 11	10 51					11 36	11 48	11 53			12 01			12 51		13 11
Bridgwater	d				08 47				10 23						11 48										13 23
Highbridge & Burnham	d				08 55				10 31						11 55										13 30
Weston-super-Mare	a				09 06				10 41						12 05					12 22					13 41
	d	08 11			09 08	09 56			10 45						12 07					12 23		12 51			13 43
Weston Milton	d				09 11										12 10										13 46
Worle	d	08 18			09 15	10 03			10 51						12 18										13 50
Yatton	d	08 25			09 21	10 10			10 56						12 23							13 02			13 56
Nailsea & Backwell	d	08 31			09 27	10 16			11 02						12 29							13 08			14 02
Parson Street	d																								
Bedminster	d														12 40			←							
Bristol Temple Meads 10	a	08 42			09 38	10 27			11 14	11 24					12 43	12 23	12 27	12 43		12 47		13 20	13 26		14 14
	d		09 30	09 41	09 48			10 30	11 23	11 30		11 35	11 48		12 45		12 30	12 45		13 00			13 30	13 48	
Lawrence Hill	d								11 26						→										
Stapleton Road	d								11a28																
Filton Abbey Wood	d			09 48	09a55							11 42	11a55					12 53						13a55	
Bristol Parkway 7	a		09 40	09 53				10 38		11 38		11 46					12 38	12 57		13 08			13 38		
	d		09 48				10 02	10 43		11 43				11 56			12 43		13 02	13 13			13 43		
Yate	d						10 20							12 16					13 22						
Cam & Dursley	d						11 00							12 56					14 02						
Gloucester 7	a		10 58				11 32	11 56		12 58				13 26			13 56		14 32	14 29			14 56		

		XC	GW	GW	XC	GW		GW	XC	GW	XC	GW	GW	GW	XC	GW		XC	GW	GW	GW	XC	GW	GW	XC
																				R					
		◇1 🛒	◇	◇1 ☕	◇1 🛒			◇	◇1 🛒		◇1 🛒		◇		◇1 🛒	◇1 ☕		◇1 🛒			◇1 ☕	◇1 🛒		◇1 ☕	◇1
Taunton	d	13 51			14 54					15 18	15 54				16 01	16 40		16 51			16 59		17 20	17 48	17 54
Bridgwater	d									15 30											17 10		17 31		
Highbridge & Burnham	d									15 37											17 18		17 38		
Weston-super-Mare	a									15 47					16 20	17 01					17 28		17 49		
	d			14 52						15 49				16 14	16 30	17 02			17 07		17 29		17 51		
Weston Milton	d									15 52				16 17					17 10						
Worle	d			14 59						15 56				16 22					17 17				17 57		
Yatton	d			15 06						16 02				16 28					17 22		17 41		18 03		
Nailsea & Backwell	d			15 12						16 08				16 34					17 28		17 47		18 09		
Parson Street	d													16 41											
Bedminster	d													16 44					17 39						
Bristol Temple Meads 10	a	14 24		15 23	15 27					16 20	16 28			16 49	16 53	17 22		17 26	17 42		17 57		18 21	18 23	18 28
	d	15 00	14 48		15 30	15 34		15 48	16 00		16 30	16 41	16 48	16 53	17 00			17 30		17 48		18 00			18 30
Lawrence Hill	d													16 56											
Stapleton Road	d													16a58											
Filton Abbey Wood	d		14a55			15 41		15a55				16 48	16a55							17a55					
Bristol Parkway 7	a	15 08			15 38	15 45			16 08		16 38	16 52			17 08			17 38				18 08			18 39
	d					15 46						16 52													
Yate	d					15 56						17 02													
Cam & Dursley	d					16 10						17 16													
Gloucester 7	a					16 28						17 32													

		GW		GW	GW	XC	GW	XC	GW	GW	XC	XC		GW	GW	GW	GW	GW	GW	XC	GW	GW		GW	
				◇		◇1 🛒	◇	◇1 🛒	◇	◇1 ☕	◇1 🛒	◇1 🛒			◇	◇1 ☕		◇	◇1 ☕	◇1		◇			
Taunton	d						18 22	18 52		18 57	19 23	19 54					20 20		21 23		21 35				
Bridgwater	d						18 34			19 07							20 32				21 48				
Highbridge & Burnham	d						18 41			19 14							20 40				21 55				
Weston-super-Mare	a						18 52			19 25							20 51				22 05				
	d				18 16		18 53			19 27						20 26	20 55				22 07			23 47	
Weston Milton	d				18 19												20 58				22 10			23 50	
Worle	d				18 24		18 59									20 33	21 03							23 54	
Yatton	d				18 30		19 04			19 36						20 39	21 09				22 18			23 59	
Nailsea & Backwell	d				18 36		19 10			19 42						20 46	21 15				22 24			00 06	
Parson Street	d				18 43																				
Bedminster	d				18 46												21 26				22 34			00 15	
Bristol Temple Meads 10	a				18 50		19 22	19 27		19 54	19 57	20 27				20 58	21 29		22 00		22 38			00 19	
	d	18 41		18 48	18 53	19 00		19 30	19 48		20 00	20 30		20 41	20 48			21 48		22 10		22 48			
Lawrence Hill	d				18 56																				
Stapleton Road	d				18a58																				
Filton Abbey Wood	d	18 48		18a55					19a55					20 48	20a55			21a55				22a55			
Bristol Parkway 7	a	18 52				19 08		19 38			20 08	20 38		20 52						22 18					
	d	18 52												20 52											
Yate	d	19 02												21 02											
Cam & Dursley	d	19 16												21 16											
Gloucester 7	a	19 33												21 31											

For connections to London Paddington please refer to Table 125

Table 134

Taunton - Gloucester

Sundays

26 June to 31 July

		GW	XC	GW	GW	XC	GW	GW	XC	GW		GW	GW	GW	XC	GW	XC	GW	XC	GW		GW	XC	GW	GW
										R		🚌													
		◇1	◇1		◇	◇1	◇1		◇1					◇1	◇1		◇1	◇1	◇1	◇			◇1		◇
		☕	🛒			🛒	☕		🛒					☕	🛒		🛒	☕	🛒				🛒		
Taunton	d				08 35			10 11	10 51				11 36	11 48	11 51		12 00		12 51			13 11	13 53		
Bridgwater	d				08 47			10 23					11 48									13 23			
Highbridge & Burnham	d				08 55			10 31					11 55									13 30			
Weston-super-Mare	a				09 06			10 41					12 05				12 20					13 41			
	d	08 11			09 08		10 14	10 45					12 07				12 21	12 51				13 43			
Weston Milton	d				09 11								12 10									13 46			
Worle	d	08 18			09 15		10 21	10 51					12 18									13 50			
Yatton	d	08 25			09 21		10 28	10 56					12 23					13 02				13 56			
Nailsea & Backwell	d	08 31			09 27		10 34	11 02					12 29					13 08				14 02			
Parson Street	d																								
Bedminster	d												12 40			←								←	
Bristol Temple Meads [10]	a	08 42			09 38		10 45	11 14	11 24				12 43	12 23	12 27	12 43	12 46	13 20	13 26			14 14	14 26	14 14	
	d		09 30	09 41	09 48	10 30		11 23	11 30	11 48			12 45		12 30	12 45			13 30	13 48		14 41	14 30	14 41	14 48
Lawrence Hill	d							11 26					→									→			
Stapleton Road	d							11a28																	
Filton Abbey Wood	d			09 48	09a55					11a55						12 53				13a55				14 48	14a55
Bristol Parkway [7]	a		09 38	09 52		10 38			11 38						12 38	12 57			13 41				14 40	14 52	
	d		09 43			10 43			11 43			11 56			12 43				13 48				14 47		
Yate	d											12 16													
Cam & Dursley	d											12 56													
Gloucester [7]	a		10 51			11 59			12 58			13 26			13 59				15 00				15 59		

		GW	XC	GW	GW	XC		GW	GW	GW	XC	GW	XC	GW	GW	GW		GW	GW	XC	GW	GW	GW	XC	GW
															R										
		◇1	◇1	◇		◇1			◇		◇1	◇1	◇1			◇1			◇1	◇1	◇		◇	◇1	◇
		☕	🛒			🛒					🛒	☕	🛒			☕			☕	🛒				🛒	
Taunton	d		14 54		15 18	15 54					16 01	16 40	16 51			16 59		17 19	17 48	17 54			18 22	18 54	
Bridgwater	d				15 30											17 10		17 30					18 34		
Highbridge & Burnham	d				15 37											17 18		17 37					18 41		
Weston-super-Mare	a				15 47						16 20	17 01				17 28		17 48					18 52		
	d	14 52			15 49					16 14	16 30	17 02		17 07		17 29		17 50				18 16	18 53		
Weston Milton	d				15 52					16 17				17 10								18 19			
Worle	d	14 59			15 56					16 22				17 17				17 56				18 24	18 59		
Yatton	d	15 06			16 02					16 28				17 22		17 41		18 02				18 30	19 04		
Nailsea & Backwell	d	15 12			16 08					16 34				17 28		17 47		18 08				18 36	19 10		
Parson Street	d									16 41												18 43			
Bedminster	d							←		16 44				17 39								18 46			
Bristol Temple Meads [10]	a	15 23	15 27		16 20	16 28		16 20		16 49	16 53	17 22	17 26	17 42		17 57		18 20	18 23	18 27		18 50	19 22	19 27	
	d		15 30	15 48	16 41	16 30		16 41	16 48	16 53			17 30		17 48			18 25		18 30	18 48	18 53		19 30	19 48
Lawrence Hill	d				→					16 56												18 56			
Stapleton Road	d									16a58												18a58			
Filton Abbey Wood	d			15a55				16 48	16a55						17a55			18 32			18a55				19a55
Bristol Parkway [7]	a		15 38			16 38		16 52					17 38					18 36		18 41				19 38	
	d		15 45			16 45							17 43							18 48				19 45	
Yate	d																								
Cam & Dursley	d																								
Gloucester [7]	a		17 00			17 58							18 58							20 01				21 02	

		GW		XC	GW	GW	GW	GW	GW	GW	XC	GW		GW	GW
		◇1		◇1		◇	◇1		◇	◇1	◇1			◇	
		☕		🛒			☕			☕					
Taunton	d	18 57		19 54				20 20		21 23		21 35			
Bridgwater	d	19 07						20 32				21 48			
Highbridge & Burnham	d	19 14						20 40				21 55			
Weston-super-Mare	a	19 25						20 51				22 05			
	d	19 27					20 26	20 55				22 07			23 47
Weston Milton	d							20 58				22 10			23 50
Worle	d						20 33	21 03							23 54
Yatton	d	19 36					20 39	21 09				22 18			23 59
Nailsea & Backwell	d	19 42					20 46	21 15				22 24			00 06
Parson Street	d														
Bedminster	d							21 26				22 34			00 15
Bristol Temple Meads [10]	a	19 54		20 27			20 58	21 29		22 00		22 38			00 19
	d			20 30	20 41	20 48			21 48		22 10			22 48	
Lawrence Hill	d														
Stapleton Road	d														
Filton Abbey Wood	d				20 48	20a55			21a55					22a55	
Bristol Parkway [7]	a			20 38	20 52						22 19				
	d			20 43							22 24				
Yate	d														
Cam & Dursley	d														
Gloucester [7]	a			22 01							23 19				

For connections to London Paddington please refer to Table 125

Table 134

Sundays

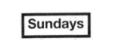

7 August to 11 September

Taunton - Gloucester

		GW	XC	GW	GW	GW	XC	GW	XC	GW	GW	GW	GW
		◇1 ☕	◇1 🛒		◇	◇1 ☕	◇1 🛒		◇1 🛒	R		◇1 ☕	🚌
Taunton	d				08 35			10 11	10 51		11 36	11 48	
Bridgwater	d				08 47			10 23			11 48		
Highbridge & Burnham	d				08 55			10 31			11 55		
Weston-super-Mare	a				09 06			10 41			12 05		
	d	08 11			09 08	09 56		10 45			12 07		
Weston Milton	d				09 11						12 10		
Worle	d	08 18			09 15	10 03		10 51			12 18		
Yatton	d	08 25			09 21	10 10		10 56			12 23		
Nailsea & Backwell	d	08 31			09 27	10 16		11 02			12 29		
Parson Street	d												
Bedminster	d										12 40		
Bristol Temple Meads 10	a	08 42			09 38	10 27		11 14	11 27		12 43	12 23	
	d		09 15	09 41	09 48		10 30	11 23	11 30	11 48			
Lawrence Hill	d							11 26					
Stapleton Road	d							11a28					
Filton Abbey Wood	d			09 48	09a55					11a55			
Bristol Parkway 7	a		09 23	09 53			10 38		11 38				
	d		09 25	09 53									11 56
Yate	d			10 03									12 16
Cam & Dursley	d			10 17									12 56
Gloucester 7	a		09 54	10 33									13 26

		XC	GW	XC	GW	XC	GW	GW	XC	XC	GW
		◇1 🛒		◇1 🛒	◇1 ☕	◇1 🛒	◇		◇1 🛒	◇1 🛒	
Taunton	d	11 51		12 00		12 51		13 11	13 25	13 51	
Bridgwater	d							13 23			
Highbridge & Burnham	d							13 30			
Weston-super-Mare	a			12 20				13 41			
	d			12 21	12 51			13 43			
Weston Milton	d							13 46			
Worle	d							13 50			
Yatton	d				13 02			13 56			
Nailsea & Backwell	d				13 08			14 02			
Parson Street	d										
Bedminster	d										
Bristol Temple Meads 10	a	12 27		12 46	13 20	13 24		14 14	13 57	14 26	
	d	12 30	12 41	13 00		13 30	13 48		14 00	14 30	14 41
Lawrence Hill	d										
Stapleton Road	d										
Filton Abbey Wood	d		12 48				13a55				14 48
Bristol Parkway 7	a	12 38	12 52	13 08		13 38			14 08	14 38	14 52
	d		12 52								14 53
Yate	d		13 02								15 03
Cam & Dursley	d		13 16								15 17
Gloucester 7	a		13 31								15 35

		GW	XC	GW	XC	GW	XC	GW	XC	GW	GW	GW
		◇	◇1 🛒	◇1 ☕	◇1 🛒	◇	◇1 🛒		◇1 🛒		◇	
Taunton	d				14 54			15 18	15 54			
Bridgwater	d							15 30				
Highbridge & Burnham	d							15 37				
Weston-super-Mare	a							15 47				
	d			14 52				15 49				16 14
Weston Milton	d							15 52				16 17
Worle	d			14 59				15 56				16 22
Yatton	d			15 06				16 02				16 28
Nailsea & Backwell	d			15 12				16 08				16 34
Parson Street	d											16 41
Bedminster	d											16 44
Bristol Temple Meads 10	a			15 23	15 27			16 20	16 27			16 49
	d	14 48	15 00		15 30	15 48	16 00		16 30	16 41	16 48	16 53
Lawrence Hill	d											16 56
Stapleton Road	d											16a58
Filton Abbey Wood	d	14a55				15a55				16 48	16a55	
Bristol Parkway 7	a		15 08		15 38		16 08		16 38	16 53		
	d									16 54		
Yate	d									17 04		
Cam & Dursley	d									17 18		
Gloucester 7	a									17 34		

		XC	GW	XC	GW	GW	GW	XC	GW	GW	XC	GW
		◇1 🛒	◇1 ☕	◇1 🛒		R	◇1 ☕	◇1 🛒		◇1 ☕	◇1 🛒	
Taunton	d	16 01	16 40	16 54			16 59		17 20	17 49	17 51	
Bridgwater	d						17 10		17 31			
Highbridge & Burnham	d						17 18		17 38			
Weston-super-Mare	a	16 20	17 01				17 28		17 49			
	d	16 30	17 02		17 07		17 29		17 51			
Weston Milton	d				17 10							
Worle	d				17 17				17 57			
Yatton	d				17 22		17 41		18 03			
Nailsea & Backwell	d				17 28		17 47		18 09			
Parson Street	d											
Bedminster	d				17 39							
Bristol Temple Meads 10	a	16 53	17 22	17 27	17 42		17 57		18 21	18 25	18 27	
	d	17 00		17 30		17 48		18 00			18 30	18 41
Lawrence Hill	d											
Stapleton Road	d											
Filton Abbey Wood	d					17a55						18 48
Bristol Parkway 7	a	17 08		17 38				18 08			18 38	18 52
	d											18 52
Yate	d											19 02
Cam & Dursley	d											19 16
Gloucester 7	a											19 33

		GW	GW	XC	GW	XC	GW	GW	XC	XC	GW
		◇		◇1 🛒	◇	◇1 🛒	◇	◇1 ☕	◇1 🛒	◇1 🛒	
Taunton	d				18 22	18 52		18 57	19 23	19 54	
Bridgwater	d				18 34			19 07			
Highbridge & Burnham	d				18 41			19 14			
Weston-super-Mare	a				18 52			19 25			
	d		18 16		18 53			19 27			
Weston Milton	d		18 19								
Worle	d		18 24		18 59						
Yatton	d		18 30		19 04			19 36			
Nailsea & Backwell	d		18 36		19 10			19 42			
Parson Street	d		18 43								
Bedminster	d		18 46								
Bristol Temple Meads 10	a		18 50		19 22	19 27		19 54	19 57	20 27	
	d	18 48	18 53	19 00		19 30	19 48		20 00	20 30	20 41
Lawrence Hill	d		18 56								
Stapleton Road	d		18a58								
Filton Abbey Wood	d	18a55					19a55				20 48
Bristol Parkway 7	a			19 08		19 38			20 08	20 38	20 52
	d										20 52
Yate	d										21 02
Cam & Dursley	d										21 16
Gloucester 7	a										21 31

		GW	GW	GW	GW	GW	XC	GW	GW	GW
		◇	◇1 ☕		◇	◇1 ☕	◇1		◇	
Taunton	d			20 20		21 23		21 35		
Bridgwater	d			20 32				21 48		
Highbridge & Burnham	d			20 40				21 55		
Weston-super-Mare	a			20 51				22 05		
	d		20 26	20 55				22 07		23 47
Weston Milton	d			20 58				22 10		23 50
Worle	d		20 33	21 03						23 54
Yatton	d		20 39	21 09				22 18		23 59
Nailsea & Backwell	d		20 46	21 15				22 24		00 06
Parson Street	d									
Bedminster	d			21 26				22 34		00 15
Bristol Temple Meads 10	a		20 58	21 29		22 00		22 38		00 19
	d	20 48			21 48		22 10		22 48	
Lawrence Hill	d									
Stapleton Road	d									
Filton Abbey Wood	d	20a55			21a55				22a55	
Bristol Parkway 7	a						22 18			
	d									
Yate	d									
Cam & Dursley	d									
Gloucester 7	a									

For connections to London Paddington please refer to Table 125

Table 134

Taunton - Gloucester

Sundays

18 September to 23 October

		GW ◇1 ☕	GW ◇	GW 🚌	GW	GW 🚌	XC 🚌	GW ◇1 ☕	XC ◇1 🛒	GW 🚌		XC 🚌	GW	XC ◇1 🛒	GW 🚌	GW 🚌	XC 🚌	GW 🚌	GW	GW ◇1 ☕		XC ◇1 🛒	GW	GW 🚌	XC 🚌
Taunton	d		08 24						09 58				10 19	11 03					11 36	11 48		11 59			
Bridgwater	d		08 36										10 31						11 48						
Highbridge & Burnham	d		08 44										10 39						11 55						
Weston-super-Mare	a		08 53										10 49						12 05						
	d	08 11	08 56					09 56					10 51						12 07						
Weston Milton	d		08 59																12 10						
Worle	d	08 18	09 03					10 03					10 57						12 14						
Yatton	d	08 25	09 09					10 10					11 03						12 20						
Nailsea & Backwell	d	08 31	09 15					10 16					11 09						12 26						
Parson Street	d																								
Bedminster	d																		12 36						
Bristol Temple Meads 10	a	08 42	09 27					10 27	10 32				11 20	11 36					12 39	12 23		12 43			
	d			09 37		09 53	10 00			10 50		11 00				11 52	12 00	12 12						12 50	13 00
Lawrence Hill	d																								
Stapleton Road	d																								
Filton Abbey Wood	d			09 57		10 13				11 10						12 12		12 32						13 10	
Bristol Parkway 7	a			10 02		10 18	10 30			11 20		11 30				12 17	12 30	12 42						13 20	13 30
	d				10 08										11 56								12 52		
Yate	d				10 18										12 16								13 02		
Cam & Dursley	d				10 32										12 56								13 16		
Gloucester 7	a				10 51										13 26								13 31		

		GW ◇1 ☕	XC ◇1 🛒	GW 🚌	XC 🚌	GW		GW 🚌	XC ◇1 🛒	GW	GW 🚌	XC 🚌	GW ◇1 ☕	XC ◇1 🛒	GW 🚌	XC 🚌		GW 🚌	GW	XC ◇1 🛒	GW	GW	GW 🚌	XC 🚌	GW ◇1 ☕
Taunton	d		13 03			13 11			14 02					14 59					15 18	15 57					16 40
Bridgwater	d					13 23													15 30						
Highbridge & Burnham	d					13 30													15 37						
Weston-super-Mare	a					13 41													15 47						17 01
	d	12 51				13 43							14 52						15 49		16 14				17 02
Weston Milton	d					13 46													15 52		16 17				
Worle	d					13 50							14 59						15 56		16 22				
Yatton	d	13 02				13 56							15 06						16 02		16 28				
Nailsea & Backwell	d	13 08				14 02							15 12						16 08		16 34				
Parson Street	d																				16 41				
Bedminster	d																				16 44				
Bristol Temple Meads 10	a	13 20	13 37			14 14			14 39				15 23	15 33					16 20	16 31	16 49				17 22
	d			13 50	14 00			14 25			14 53	15 00			15 53	16 00		16 12					16 51	17 00	
Lawrence Hill	d																								
Stapleton Road	d																								
Filton Abbey Wood	d			14 10				14 45			15 13				16 13			16 32					17 11		
Bristol Parkway 7	a			14 20	14 30			14 55			15 23	15 30			16 18	16 30		16 42					17 21	17 30	
	d									15 05												16 52			
Yate	d									15 14												17 02			
Cam & Dursley	d									15 28												17 16			
Gloucester 7	a									15 44												17 32			

		XC ◇1 🛒		GW	GW 🚌	GW ◇1 ☕	XC 🚌	GW 🚌	GW	GW ◇1 ☕	XC ◇1 🛒	GW		GW	GW 🚌	XC 🚌	GW ◇	GW ◇1 ☕	XC ◇1 🛒	GW 🚌	XC 🚌	GW 🚌		XC ◇1 🛒	GW
Taunton	d	16 50				16 59			17 20	17 49	17 57						18 22	18 57	19 00					19 57	
Bridgwater	d					17 10			17 31								18 34	19 07							
Highbridge & Burnham	d					17 18			17 38								18 41	19 14							
Weston-super-Mare	a					17 28			17 49								18 54	19 25							
	d			17 07		17 29			17 51			18 13					19 02	19 27							
Weston Milton	d			17 10								18 16													
Worle	d			17 17					17 57			18 21					19 08								
Yatton	d			17 22		17 41			18 03			18 27					19 14	19 36							
Nailsea & Backwell	d			17 28		17 47			18 09			18 33					19 20	19 42							
Parson Street	d											18 40													
Bedminster	d			17 39								18 43													
Bristol Temple Meads 10	a	17 26		17 42		17 57			18 21	18 25	18 30	18 47					19 32	19 54	19 42					20 35	
	d				17 55		18 00	18 12							18 48	19 00				19 53	20 00	20 17			
Lawrence Hill	d																								
Stapleton Road	d																								
Filton Abbey Wood	d				18 15			18 32							19 08					20 13		20 37			
Bristol Parkway 7	a				18 20		18 30	18 42							19 18	19 30				20 18	20 30	20 42			
	d													18 52											20 52
Yate	d													19 02											21 02
Cam & Dursley	d													19 16											21 16
Gloucester 7	a													19 33											21 31

For connections to London Paddington please refer to Table 125

Table 134

Taunton - Gloucester

Sundays

18 September to 23 October

		GW	GW	XC	XC	GW	XC	GW		GW	GW	GW	GW
			◇1	◇1						◇1			
		🚌			🚌		🚌	🚌				🚌	
			☕	trolley						☕			
Taunton	d			20 20		20 26				21 23	21 35		
Bridgwater	d					20 38					21 48		
Highbridge & Burnham	d					20 46					21 55		
Weston-super-Mare	a					20 57					22 05		
	d		20 26			21 01					22 07		23 47
Weston Milton	d					21 04					22 10		23 50
Worle	d		20 33			21 09							23 54
Yatton	d		20 39			21 15					22 18		23 59
Nailsea & Backwell	d		20 46			21 21					22 24		00 06
Parson Street	d												
Bedminster	d					21 32					22 34		00 15
Bristol Temple Meads 10	a		20 58	21 02		21 35				22 00	22 38		00 19
	d	20 53			21 15		21 50	21 53				22 53	
Lawrence Hill	d												
Stapleton Road	d												
Filton Abbey Wood	d	21 13						22 13				23 13	
Bristol Parkway 7	a	21 18			21 35		22 10	22 18				23 18	
	d												
Yate	d												
Cam & Dursley	d												
Gloucester 7	a												

Sundays

from 30 October

		GW	GW	XC	GW	GW	GW	GW	XC	GW		XC	GW	GW	GW	GW	GW	XC	GW	GW		XC	GW	XC	GW
														■											
			◇	◇1		◇	◇1		◇1	◇		◇1	◇1			1		◇1	◇1			◇1	1	◇1	◇1
		🚌						🚌									🚌								
				trolley			☕		trolley			trolley	☕			☕		trolley	☕			trolley	☕	trolley	☕
Taunton	d		08 16							10 19		10 51			11 36	11 48		11 53				12 00		12 51	
Bridgwater	d		08 28							10 31					11 48										
Highbridge & Burnham	d		08 36							10 39					11 55										
Weston-super-Mare	a		08 46							10 49					12 05							12 20			
	d	07 40						08 56		10 51					12 07							12 21	12 51		
Weston Milton	d							09 06							12 10										
Worle	d	07 55						09 16		10 57					12 18								12 58		
Yatton	d	08 10						09 31		11 03					12 23								13 05		
Nailsea & Backwell	d	08 25						09 46		11 09					12 29								13 11		
Parson Street	d																								
Bedminster	d														12 40										
Bristol Temple Meads 10	a	08 50						10 11		11 20		11 27			12 43	12 22		12 27				12 46	13 22	13 24	
	d			09 15	09 41	09 48	10 05		10 30	11 23		11 30	11 35	11 48				12 30	12 35	12 41		13 00		13 30	13 35
Lawrence Hill	d									11 26															
Stapleton Road	d									11a28															
Filton Abbey Wood	d				09 48	09a55								11a55						12 48					
Bristol Parkway 7	a			09 23	09 53		10 13		10 38			11 38	11 44					12 38	12 44	12 52		13 08		13 38	13 44
	d			09 25	09 53												11 56			12 52					
Yate	d				10 03												12 16			13 02					
Cam & Dursley	d				10 17												12 56			13 16					
Gloucester 7	a			09 54	10 33												13 26			13 31					

		GW	GW	XC	XC	GW		GW	GW	XC	GW	XC	GW	GW	XC	GW		XC	GW	GW	GW	GW	XC	GW	XC
		◇		◇1	◇1	◇1			◇	◇1	◇1	◇1	◇1	◇	◇1			◇1	◇1		◇		◇1	◇1	◇1
				trolley	trolley	☕				trolley	☕	trolley	☕		trolley			trolley	☕				trolley	☕	trolley
Taunton	d		13 11	13 25	13 51							14 54				15 17		15 54					16 01	16 34	16 54
Bridgwater	d		13 23													15 29									
Highbridge & Burnham	d		13 30													15 36									
Weston-super-Mare	a		13 41													15 46							16 20	16 55	
	d		13 43								14 56					15 48						16 14	16 30	16 56	
Weston Milton	d		13 46													15 51						16 17			
Worle	d		13 50													15 55						16 22			
Yatton	d		13 56								15 06					16 01						16 28		17 08	
Nailsea & Backwell	d		14 02								15 13					16 07						16 34		17 14	
Parson Street	d																					16 41			
Bedminster	d																					16 44			
Bristol Temple Meads 10	a		14 14	13 57	14 26						15 24	15 27				16 19		16 27				16 49	16 53	17 24	17 27
	d	13 48		14 00	14 30	14 35		14 41	14 48	15 00		15 30	15 35	15 48	16 00			16 30	16 38	16 41	16 48	16 53	17 00		17 30
Lawrence Hill	d																					16 56			
Stapleton Road	d																					16a58			
Filton Abbey Wood	d	13a55						14 48	14a55					15a55						16 48	16a55				
Bristol Parkway 7	a			14 08	14 38	14 44		14 52		15 08		15 38	15 44		16 08			16 38	16 45	16 53			17 08		17 38
	d							14 53												16 54					
Yate	d							15 03												17 04					
Cam & Dursley	d							15 17												17 18					
Gloucester 7	a							15 35												17 34					

For connections to London Paddington please refer to Table 125

Table 134

Sundays

from 30 October

Taunton - Gloucester

		GW		GW	XC	GW	GW	XC	GW	GW	GW	XC		GW	GW	XC	GW	XC	XC	GW	GW	GW		GW	GW
				R	◇1		◇1	◇1		◇		◇1		◇		◇1	◇	◇1	◇1		◇	◇1		◇1	
Taunton	d					17 19	17 41	17 51						18 22	18 42	18 52		19 23	19 54						20 40
Bridgwater	d					17 30	17 53							18 34	18 54										20 52
Highbridge & Burnham	d					17 37	18 00							18 41											21 00
Weston-super-Mare	a					17 48								18 52	19 10										21 11
	d	17 07				17 51					18 16			18 53	19 26							20 25			21 12
Weston Milton	d	17 10									18 19														21 15
Worle	d	17 17				17 56					18 24			18 59								20 32			21 20
Yatton	d	17 22				18 02					18 30			19 04	19 35							20 38			21 26
Nailsea & Backwell	d	17 28				18 08					18 36			19 10	19 41							20 45			21 32
Parson Street	d										18 43														
Bedminster	d	17 39									18 46														21 43
Bristol Temple Meads 10	a	17 42				18 20	18 24	18 27			18 50			19 22	19 53	19 27		19 57	20 27			20 55			21 46
	d			17 48	18 00			18 30	18 41	18 48		19 00				19 30	19 48	20 00	20 30	20 41	20 48			21 40	
Lawrence Hill	d																								
Stapleton Road	d																								
Filton Abbey Wood	d			17a55					18 48	18a55							19a55			20 48	20a55				
Bristol Parkway 7	a				18 08			18 38	18 52			19 08				19 38		20 08	20 38	20 52				21 48	
	d								18 52											20 52					
Yate	d								19 02											21 02					
Cam & Dursley	d								19 16											21 16					
Gloucester 7	a								19 33											21 31					

		GW	GW	XC	GW	GW	GW	GW		GW
		◇	1	◇1	◇1		◇	◇1		
Taunton	d		21 25			21 35				
Bridgwater	d					21 48				
Highbridge & Burnham	d					21 55				
Weston-super-Mare	a					22 05				
	d					22 07				23 47
Weston Milton	d					22 10				23 50
Worle	d									23 54
Yatton	d					22 18				23 59
Nailsea & Backwell	d					22 24				00 06
Parson Street	d									
Bedminster	d					22 34				00 15
Bristol Temple Meads 10	a		21 58			22 38				00 19
	d	21 50		22 10	22 35		22 50	23 45		
Lawrence Hill	d									
Stapleton Road	d									
Filton Abbey Wood	d	21a58					22a57			
Bristol Parkway 7	a			22 18	22 43			23 52		
	d									
Yate	d									
Cam & Dursley	d									
Gloucester 7	a									

For connections to London Paddington please refer to Table 125

Route Diagram for Tables 135, 136, 139, 140, 142, 143, 144

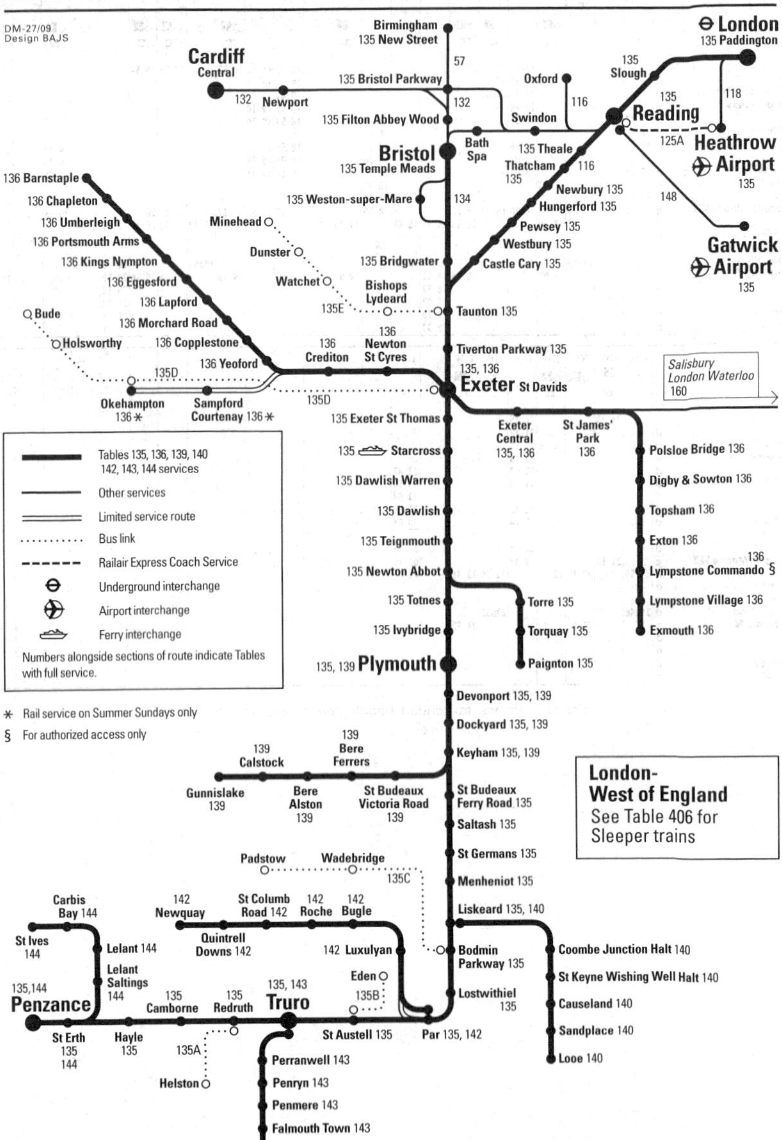

© Network Rail OPSU 2009. All rights reserved

London and Birmingham - Devon and Cornwall

Miles	Miles			GW	XC	GW	GW	GW	GW	GW	GW	GW		GW	XC	XC	GW	GW	GW	GW	GW	GW		GW	GW
				MX	MX	MX	MX	MX	MX	MX	MX	MX		MX	MO	MX		MO	MO	MO	MO				
												R		R				R	R	R	R				
					◇1	◇1	◇1			◇1	◇1				◇1	◇1									
					A	B	C	B	C	D	C	E		F				G	H	I	J				
0	—	**London Paddington** 15 ⊖	d			20p35	20p35			21p45	21p45	23p45		23p45				23p50	23p50	23p50	23p50				
18½	—	Slough 3	d																						
36	—	**Reading** 7	d			21p02	21p02			22p11	22p11	00u37		00u37				00u40	00u37	00u38	00u41				
41¼	—	Theale	d																						
49½	—	Thatcham	d																						
53	—	Newbury	d			21p18	21p18																		
61½	—	Hungerford	d																						
75¼	—	Pewsey	d			21p38	21p38																		
95½	—	Westbury	d			21p57	21p57					01e45		01e45											
115¼	—	Castle Cary	d			22p15	22p15																		
—	0	**Birmingham New Street** 12	d		20p12																				
—	—	Cardiff Central 7	d																						
—	—	Newport (South Wales)	d																						
—	—	Swindon	d							22p49	22p49														
—	87	Bristol Parkway 7	d		21p26																				
—	88¼	Filton Abbey Wood	d																						
—	—	Bath Spa 7	d							23p19	23p19														
—	92¾	**Bristol Temple Meads** 10	d		21b44			23p06	23p06	23p36	23p36							02g55	02i55	02j55	02k55				
—	112¾	Weston-super-Mare	d					23p42	23p42	00s06	00s06														
—	126½	Bridgwater	d					00 02	00 02	00s25	00s25														
143	138¼	Taunton	d		22c27	22p37	22p37	00s14	00 15	00s37	00 38	02 35		03f06											
157¼	—	Tiverton Parkway	d		22p51	22p50	23p03	00s30	00 39	00s50	01 03														
173¾	—	**Exeter St Davids** 6	a		23p04	23p06	23p20	00 51	00 59	01 09	01 21	03 06		03 59				04 05	04 05	04 05	04 05				
—	—	Exmouth	d																						
—	—	Exeter Central	d																						
—	—	**Exeter St Davids** 6	d		23p06	23p08	23p21					04 11		04 11				04 35	04 35	04 35	04 35			05 34	06 11
174¾	—	Exeter St Thomas	d																					05 38	06 14
182¼	—	Starcross	d																					05 46	06 22
184¼	—	Dawlish Warren	d																					05 51	06 27
185¾	—	Dawlish	d																					05 55	06 31
188¾	—	Teignmouth	d																					06 00	06 36
193¾	—	Newton Abbot	a		23p24	23p28	23p42					04 32		04 32				04 55	04 55	04 55	04 55			06 07	06 44
—	—		d		23p25	23p29	23p42					04 34		04 34				04 56	04 56	04 56	04 56	05 42		06 09	06 45
—	5¼	Torre	d																			05 50		06 17	06 53
—	6	Torquay	d																			05 53		06 20	06 56
—	8¼	Paignton	a																			06 00		06 28	07 06
202½	—	Totnes	d		23p38	23p43	23p56																		
214	—	Ivybridge	d																						
225¾	—	**Plymouth**	a		00 03	00 11	00 25					05 13		05 13				05 35	05 35	05 35	05 35				
—	—		d	22p33								05 43		05 43	05 43	06 28		06 28	06 28	06 28	06 28				
227	—	Devonport	d																						
227½	—	Dockyard	d																						
228	—	Keyham	d																						
228¾	—	St Budeaux Ferry Road	d																						
230	—	Saltash	d	22p39																					
235	—	St Germans	d	22p47																					
240¼	—	Menheniot	d																						
243½	—	Liskeard 6	d	22p59								06 08		06 08	06 08	06 51		07h09	07h09	07h09	07h09				
252½	—	Bodmin Parkway	d	23p13								06 22		06 22	06 23	07 03		07 23	07 23	07 23	07 23				
256	—	Lostwithiel	d	23p18								06 28		06 28	06 28	07 08		07 29	07 29	07 29	07 29				
260½	—	Par	d	23p26								06 37		06 37	06 37	07 15		07 38	07 38	07 38	07 38				
—	—	Newquay	a																						
265	—	St Austell	d	23p33								06 46		06 46	06 46	07 21		07 46	07 46	07 46	07 46				
279½	—	Truro	d	23p52								07 06		07 06	07 06	07 38		08 06	08 06	08 06	08 06				
288½	—	Redruth	d	00 05								07 18		07 18	07 18	07 50		08 20	08 20	08 20	08 20				
292	—	Camborne	d	00 11								07 26		07 26	07 26	07 56		08 27	08 27	08 27	08 27				
298	—	Hayle	d	00 18								07 35		07 35	07 35	08 04		08 38	08 38	08 38	08 38				
299½	—	St Erth	d	00 22								07 41		07 41	07 41	08 10	08 28	08 45	08 45	08 45	08 45				
305¼	—	**Penzance**	a	00 40								07 53		07 53	07 53	08 19	08 40	08 58	08 59	08 59	08 59				

A from 2 August until 9 September. to Bristol Parkway
B until 29 July, and then from 13 September
C from 2 August until 9 September
D from 25 May until 29 July, from 13 September
E until 29 July, MX from 13 September. **The Night Riviera**
F from 2 August until 9 September. **The Night Riviera**
G from 8 August until 12 September
H from 31 October
I from 19 September until 24 October
J until 1 August
b Previous night, arr. 2138
c Previous night, arr. 2215
e Arr. 0135
f Arr. 0232
g Arr. 0157
h Arr. 0652
i Arr. 0207
j Arr. 0156
k Arr. 0158

For connections to Oxford, Gatwick Airport and Heathrow Airport please refer to Tables 116, 148 and 125A

London and Birmingham - Devon and Cornwall

		GW	GW	GW	GW	GW	GW	XC	GW	GW	GW	XC	GW	GW	GW	XC	GW	GW	GW	GW	XC	GW	GW
		■1	■1	◇	◇		■1	◇■1		◇		◇■1		◇■1		◇■1		◇■1			◇■1		◇■1
				A	B		A				B		A	C				D	B	A			E
		🍴					🍴					🛒		🍴		🛒		🍴⊘			🛒		🍴⊘
London Paddington 15 ⊖	d													07 06				07 30					09 06
Slough 3	d																						
Reading 7	d													07 33				07 57					09 33
Theale	d																						
Thatcham	d																						
Newbury	d													07 48									
Hungerford	d																						
Pewsey	d													08 08									
Westbury	d													08 26									
Castle Cary	d																						10 29
Birmingham New Street 12	d											06 42				07 12					08 12		
Cardiff Central 7	d																		08 00	08 00			
Newport (South Wales)	d																		08 15	08 15			
Swindon	d																	08 27					
Bristol Parkway 7	d									06 26		07 58				08 26					09 26		
Filton Abbey Wood	d																		08 42	08 42			
Bath Spa 7	d																	08 57					
Bristol Temple Meads 10	d			05 24	05 24			06 34		06 42		08 11				08 44		09 13	08 53	08 53	09 44		
Weston-super-Mare	d			05 45	05 45					07 06									09f29	09f28			
Bridgwater	d			06 03	06 03					07 25									09 48	09 48			
Taunton	d			06 18	06 18			07 08		07 39		08 43		09 03		09 17		09 46	10 02	10 02	10 18		10 51
Tiverton Parkway	d			06 33	06 33			07 20		07 54		08 55				09 29					10 30		11 04
Exeter St Davids 6	a			06 51	06 51			07 34		08 12		09 10		09 30		09 43		10 12	10 33	10 33	10 46		11 20
Exmouth	d					06 45			07 14		08 23		08 23				09 23					10 23	
Exeter Central	d					07 12			07 43		08 50		08 50				09 50					10 50	
Exeter St Davids 6	d			06 55	06 55	07 18		07 36	07 50	08 13	08 59	09 11	09e16	09 32	09 36	09 45	09 56	10 15	10 34	10 34	10 48	10 56	11 22
Exeter St Thomas	d			06 58	06 58	07 21			07 53		09 02		09 17				09 59					10 59	
Starcross	d			07 07	07 07	07 29			08 01		09 10		09 25				10 07					11 07	
Dawlish Warren	d			07 12	07 12	07 34			08 06		09c23		09 32				10 12		10 46	10 46		11 12	
Dawlish	d			07 16	07 16	07 38			08 10		09 27		09 36				10 16		10 50	10 50		11 16	
Teignmouth	d			07 21	07 21	07 43			08 15		09 32		09 39				10 21		10 55	10 55		11 21	
Newton Abbot	a			07 29	07 29	07 50		07 54	08 22	08 35	09 39		09 46	09 52	09 56	10 03	10 30	10 34	11 03	11 03	11 08	11 29	11 42
	d		07 06	07 29	07 29	07 52		07 55	08 24	08 35	09 40		09 48	09 55	09 57	10 04	10 39	10 36	11 04	11 04	11 09	11 30	11 43
Torre	d		07 15			08 00			08 32		09 49		09 56	10 04			10 47		11 13	11 13		11 38	
Torquay	d		07 20			08 03			08 35		09 52	09 41	09 59	10 08			10 50		11 16	11 16		11 41	
Paignton	a		07 29			08 12			08 44		09 59	09 46	10 10	10 18			10 59		11 24	11 25		11 51	
Totnes	d			07 43	07 43			08 07		08 49					10 10	10 17		10 49			11 23		11 56
Ivybridge	d			07 59	07 59					09 05					10 27								
Plymouth	a			08 12	08 12			08 35		09 19					10 41	10 46		11 17			11 51		12 25
	d	07 02		08 15	08 15		08 20			09 21					10 42			11 20					
Devonport	d	07 07			08 18		08 24			09 24													
Dockyard	d																						
Keyham	d																						
St Budeaux Ferry Road	d														10 48								
Saltash	d	07 15			08 25		08 33			09 31					10 53								
St Germans	d	07 23			08 32		08 41			09 38					11 00								
Menheniot	d																						
Liskeard 6	d	07 36		08 39	08 44		08 53			09 50					11 12			11 44					
Bodmin Parkway	d	07 49		08 51	08 56					10 02					11 24			11 57					
Lostwithiel	d	07 55		08 56	09 01					10 07					11 29								
Par	d	08 04		09b17	09 09		09 14			10 15					11 37			12 09					
Newquay	a			10 09																			
St Austell	d	08 11			09 17		09 23			10 22					11 44			12 16					
Truro	d	08 30			09 35		09 41			10 40					12 02			12 34					
Redruth	d	08 42			09 48		09 55			10 53					12 15			12 46					
Camborne	d	08 48			09 54		10 02			10 59					12 21			12 53					
Hayle	d	08 57			10 01		10 10			11 06					12 28								
St Erth	d	09 02			10 08		10 16			11 10					12 32			13 05					
Penzance	a	09 12			10 17		10 27			11 23					12 42			13 17					

A from 4 July until 2 September
B until 1 July, from 5 September
C The Devon Express
D The Merchant Venturer. 🍴 from Taunton ⊘ to Bristol Temple Meads
E until 1 July, from 5 September. 🍴 from Taunton ⊘ to Castle Cary
b Arr. 0906
c Arr. 0915
e Arr. 0854
f Arr. 0922

For connections to Oxford, Gatwick Airport and Heathrow Airport please refer to Tables 116, 148 and 125A

Table 135

Mondays to Fridays

London and Birmingham - Devon and Cornwall

		GW	GW	GW	XC	GW	GW	GW	XC	XC	GW	GW	GW	GW	XC	GW	GW	GW	XC	GW	GW	GW
		◇1		◇	◇1			◇1	◇1	◇1	◇1			◇1	◇1		◇1		◇1	◇1		
		A	B				C	D			E			F			G					C
		[restaurant] ⊘			[trolley]			[restaurant] ⊘	[trolley]	[trolley]	[restaurant]			[restaurant] ⊘	[trolley]		[restaurant] ⊘		[trolley]	[restaurant]		
London Paddington 15 ⊖	d	09 06						10 06			10 00			11 06			12 06			12 18		
Slough 3	d																					
Reading 7	d	09 33						10u33			10 27			11 33			12 33			12 48		
Theale	d																			12 56		
Thatcham	d																			13 04		
Newbury	d																			13 12		
Hungerford	d																			13 21		
Pewsey	d													12 03						13 40		
Westbury	d													12 22						13 59		
Castle Cary	d	10 29												12 39						14 16		
Birmingham New Street 12	d				09 12				09 42	10 12					11 12				12 12			
Cardiff Central 7	d			09 00																		
Newport (South Wales)	d			09 15																		
Swindon	d										10 55											
Bristol Parkway 7	d				10 27				10 56	11 28					12 30				13 27			
Filton Abbey Wood	d			09 42																		
Bath Spa 7	d										11 24											
Bristol Temple Meads 10	d			09 55	10 44				11 15	11c44	11e47				12 44				13 44			
Weston-super-Mare	d			10 23					11 37		12 07											
Bridgwater	d			10 42																		
Taunton	d	10 51		10 58	11 18				12 02	12 17	12 29			13 02	13 18				14 17	14a41		
Tiverton Parkway	d	11 04		11 14	11 30				12 14	12 29				13 15	13 30				14 29			
Exeter St Davids 6	a	11 20		11 33	11 46			12 08	12 30	12 43	12 55			13 31	13 46		14 08		14 43			
Exmouth	d					11 23						12 23				13 23					14 23	
Exeter Central	d					11 50						12 50				13 50					14 50	
Exeter St Davids 6	d	11 22		11 35	11 48	11 56		12 08	12 32	12 45	12 56	13f03		13 33	13 48	13 56	14 08		14 45		14 56	
Exeter St Thomas	d					11 59						13 06				13 59					14 59	
Starcross	d					12 07						13 15				14 07					15 07	
Dawlish Warren	d					12b23						13 20				14g23					15 12	
Dawlish	d					12 28			12 44		13 08	13 24				14 27					15 16	
Teignmouth	d					12 33			12 49		13 14	13 29				14 32					15 21	
Newton Abbot	a	11 42		11 55	12 07	12 40		12 28	12 55	13 03	13 23	13 36		13 53	14 07	14 40	14 28		15 03		15 29	
	d	11 43		11 56	12 08	12 41		12 30	12 56	13 04	13 23	13 38		13 54	14 08	14 41	14 30	14 50	15 04		15 30	
Torre	d					12 50						13 46				14 49					15 38	
Torquay	d					12 53			13 08		13 35	13 49				14 52					15 41	
Paignton	a					13 00			13 14		13 43	13 58				15 00					15 51	
Totnes	d	11 56		12 09	12 22					13 17				14 07	14 22			15 02	15 17			
Ivybridge	d			12 26														15 19				
Plymouth	a	12 25		12 42	12 50			13 06		13 43				14 36	14 50		15 06	15 37	15 43			
	d	12 29	12 39					13 12					13 53				15 12					15 53
Devonport	d																					15 56
Dockyard	d																					15x57
Keyham	d																					15 59
St Budeaux Ferry Road	d																					16 02
Saltash	d	12 39	12 48										14 02									16 07
St Germans	d	12 47	12 55										14 09									16 14
Menheniot	d																					16x21
Liskeard 6	d	12 59	13 07					13 36					14 21				15 36					16a27
Bodmin Parkway	d	13 12	13 19					13 49					14 33				15 49					
Lostwithiel	d	13 18	13 24										14 38									
Par	d	13 29	13 32				13 37	14 01					14 46				16 01					
Newquay	a	14 29																				
St Austell	d		13 39				13 44	14 08					14 53				16 08					
Truro	d		13 57				14 02	14 26					15 11				16 26					
Redruth	d		14 10				14 15	14 38					15 24				16 38					
Camborne	d		14 16				14 21	14 46					15 30				16 46					
Hayle	d		14 23				14 28	14 55					15 37				16 55					
St Erth	d		14 28				14 33	15 00					15 42				17 00					
Penzance	a		14 39				14 44	15 12					15 53				17 12					

A from 4 July until 2 September.
The Atlantic Coast Express. [restaurant] from Taunton
⊘ to Castle Cary
B until 1 July, from 5 September
C from 4 July until 2 September

D The Cornish Riveira. [restaurant] from Newton Abbot
⊘ to Exeter St Davids
E The Torbay Express
F The Mayflower. [restaurant] from Taunton ⊘ to Castle Cary

G The Royal Duchy.
[restaurant] from Newton Abbot
⊘ to Exeter St Davids
b Arr. 1212
c Arr. 1138
e Arr. 1140
f Arr. 1254
g Arr. 1412

For connections to Oxford, Gatwick Airport and Heathrow Airport please refer to Tables 116, 148 and 125A

London and Birmingham - Devon and Cornwall

		GW	GW	GW	GW	GW	GW	XC	XC	GW		GW	GW	GW	XC	GW FO	GW	GW	GW	GW		GW	GW	XC	GW
			◇1	◇1	◇1	◇		◇1	◇1				◇1		◇1	◇	◇1						◇1	◇1	
		A	B	C	D								E				F						E	G	
			🍴⊘	🍴⊘	🍴⊘			🛒	🛒				🍴⊘		🛒		🍴						🍴⊘	🛒	
London Paddington 15 ⊖	d		13 06	13 06	13 06								14 06				14 36						15 06		
Slough 3	d																								
Reading 7	d		13 33	13 33	13u33								14 33				15u08						15 33		
Theale	d																								
Thatcham	d																								
Newbury	d																								
Hungerford	d																								
Pewsey	d																						16 03		
Westbury	d															15 20	16 15						16 23		
Castle Cary	d																16 32						16 41		
Birmingham New Street 12	d							13 12	13 42						14 12									15 12	
Cardiff Central 7	d					13 00																			
Newport (South Wales)	d					13 15																			
Swindon	d																								
Bristol Parkway 7	d							14 29	14 58						15 26									16 29	
Filton Abbey Wood	d					13 42																			
Bath Spa 7	d																								
Bristol Temple Meads 10	d					13 54		14 44	15 13						15 44									16 45	
Weston-super-Mare	d					14 23																			
Bridgwater	d					14 42																			
Taunton	d		14 48	14 48	14 48	14 56		15 18	15 46				15 50		16 17	16 24	16 55						17 05	17 18	
Tiverton Parkway	d		15 01	15 01	15 01	15 11		15 30	15 58				16 03		16 29		17 08						17 18	17 30	
Exeter St Davids 6	a		15 17	15 17	15 17	15 30		15 46	16 13				16 19		16 43	17 01	17 28						17 34	17 44	
Exmouth	d									15 23				15 53					16 55						
Exeter Central	d									15 50				16 20				16 46	17 21						17 45
Exeter St Davids 6	d		15 18	15 18	15 18			15 48		15 56		16 07	16 21	16 26	16 45			16b56	17 26				17 35	17 46	17 50
Exeter St Thomas	d									15 59				16 29				16 59	17 29						17 54
Starcross	d									16 07				16 37				17 07	17 37						18 02
Dawlish Warren	d									16 12		16 20		16 42				17 12	17c49						18 07
Dawlish	d									16 16		16 24		16 46				17 16	17 53						18 11
Teignmouth	d									16 21		16 29		16 51				17 21	17 58						18 16
Newton Abbot	a		15 39	15 39	15 39			16 07		16 30		16 37	16 41	16 58	17 03			17 29	18 05				17 56	18 11	18 23
	d		15 40	15 40	15 40		15 58	16 08		16 30		16 50	16 42	17 00	17 04			17 30	18 09				17 57	18 13	18 25
Torre	d									16 38				17 08				17 38	18 17						18 33
Torquay	d									16 41				17 11				17 41	18 20						18 36
Paignton	a									16 51				17 20				17 51	18 30						18 45
Totnes	d		15 53	15 53	15 53		16 11	16 22				17 04	16 55		17 17								18 10	18 25	
Ivybridge	d						16 28					17 21													
Plymouth	a		16 22	16 22	16 22		16 42	16 50				17 36	17 23		17 43								18 38	18 52	
	d	15 57		16 28	16 28		17 04						17 25							17 55		18 17	18 41	19 01	
Devonport	d	16 00					17 07															18 20			
Dockyard	d	16x01					17x08															18x21			
Keyham	d	16 03					17 10															18x23			
St Budeaux Ferry Road	d	16 06					17 13															18 25			
Saltash	d	16 11					17 17						17 36							18 03		18 31			
St Germans	d	16 18					17 24						17 43									18 38			
Menheniot	d	16x25					17x32															18x45			
Liskeard 6	d	16 32		16 53	16 53		17a40						17 56							18 20		18a53	19 07	19 24	
Bodmin Parkway	d	16 44		17 06	17 06								18 09							18 32			19 19	19 36	
Lostwithiel	d	16 49		17 12	17 12								18 15							18 37					
Par	d	16 57		17 21	17 21								18 24							18 45			19 31	19 47	
Newquay	a																								
St Austell	d	17 06		17 28	17 28								18 31							18 52			19 39	19 54	
Truro	d	17 23		17 46	17 46								18 49							19 10			20 00	20 11	
Redruth	d	17 36		17 59	17 59								19 01							19 23			20 10	20 26	
Camborne	d	17 42		18 07	18 07								19 09							19 29			20 18	20 33	
Hayle	d	17 50		18 15	18 15								19 18							19 36					
St Erth	d	17 54		18 21	18 22								19 23							19 42			20 28	20 43	
Penzance	a	18 07		18 33	18 33								19 35							19 54			20 40	20 52	

A until 1 July, from 5 September
B until 1 July, from 5 September. 🍴 from Newton Abbot ⊘ to Exeter St Davids
C from 4 July until 1 September. 🍴 from Newton Abbot ⊘ to Exeter St Davids
D from 8 July until 2 September. 🍴 from Newton Abbot ⊘ to Exeter St Davids
E 🍴 from Newton Abbot ⊘ to Exeter St Davids
F from 8 July until 2 September
G 🛒 to Totnes
b Arr. 1649
c Arr. 1743

For connections to Oxford, Gatwick Airport and Heathrow Airport please refer to Tables 116, 148 and 125A

Table 135

London and Birmingham - Devon and Cornwall

		XC	GW	GW	XC	GW FO	GW FX	GW	GW	XC	GW	GW	GW	GW	GW	XC	GW FX	GW FO	GW FO	GW FX	GW	GW FX	XC
																			R	R			
		◇1	◇1		◇1	◇1	◇1	◇1		◇1	◇1	◇1		◇1	◇1	◇1	◇1	◇1	1	1			◇1
					A					A				B					C	D			E
		(trolley)	(buffet)		(trolley)	(buffet)	(buffet)	(buffet)		(trolley)	(buffet)	(buffet)		✕ (buffet)	(buffet)	(trolley)	(buffet)	(buffet)	✕ (buffet)	✕ (buffet)			(trolley)
London Paddington 15 ⊖	d		16 06			16 36	16 36	17 03			17 06	17 36		18 03	18 06		18 33	18 33	19 03	19 03			
Slough 3	d																						
Reading 7	d		16 33			17 04	17 04	17 32			17 36	18 04		18 33	18 37		19 02	19 02	19u33	19 33			
Theale	d										17 45				18 45								
Thatcham	d										17 55				18 55								
Newbury	d					17 19	17 19	17 48			18 02	18 19			19 02		19 17	19 17	19 49	19 49			
Hungerford	d					17 29	17 29				18 16				19 16		19 27	19 27					
Pewsey	d					17 44	17 44				18 34	18 41			19 34		19 46	19 46					
Westbury	d					18 04	18 04					19 01			19a52		20 05	20 05					
Castle Cary	d					18 21	18 21					19 19					20 22	20 22					
Birmingham New Street 12	d	15 42			16 12					17 12						18 12							19 12
Cardiff Central 7	d																						
Newport (South Wales)	d																						
Swindon	d																						
Bristol Parkway 7	d	16 58			17 27					18 28						19 29							20 29
Filton Abbey Wood	d																						
Bath Spa 7	d										19 24												
Bristol Temple Meads 10	d	17 14			17 44					18 44	19a41					19b45							20 45
Weston-super-Mare	d																						
Bridgwater	d																						
Taunton	d	17 46	17 50		18 18	18 43	18 43	18 52		19 17		19 41		19 48		20 18	20 45	20 45	20 53	20 53			21 17
Tiverton Parkway	d	17 58	18 03		18 30	18 56	18 56	19 05		19 29		19 54				20 30	20 58	20 58	21 06	21 06			21 30
Exeter St Davids 6	a	18 13	18 19		18 44	19 12	19 14	19 21		19 43		20 09		20 13		20 44	21 15	21 15	21 22	21 22			21 44
Exmouth	d			17 55					18 55														
Exeter Central	d			18 21					19 21												21 21		
Exeter St Davids 6	d	18 15	18 21	18 28	18 47	19 13		19 22	19 28	19 45		20 19		20 15		20 46		21 17	21 24	21 24	21 28		21 46
Exeter St Thomas	d			18 31					19 31			20 23									21 31		
Starcross	d			18 39					19 39			20 32									21 39		
Dawlish Warren	d			18 44					19 44			20 36									21 44		
Dawlish	d	18 27		18 48					19 48			20 41									21 48		
Teignmouth	d	18 32		18 53					19 53			20 47									21 53		
Newton Abbot	a	18 38	18 42	19 01	19 06	19 34		19 43	20 00	20 04		20 56		20 35		21 03		21 36	21 44	21 44	22 00		22 04
	d	18 39	18 43	19 10	19 07	19 35		19 43	20 09	20 06		20 56		20 36		21 05		21 37	21 45	21 45	22 01		22 06
Torre	d			19 18					20 17			21 06									22 09		
Torquay	d	18 51		19 21					20 20			21 10									22 12		
Paignton	a	18 57		19 30					20 29			21 18									22 21		
Totnes	d		18 56		19 20			19 57		20 18				20 49		21 18			21 58	21 58			22 18
Ivybridge	d		19 12																				
Plymouth	a		19 26		19 45	20 14		20 25		20 45				21 17		21 44		22 15	22 26	22 27			22 45
	d		19 31		19 49			20 27		20 51				21 20					22 30			22 33	
Devonport	d																						
Dockyard	d																						
Keyham	d																						
St Budeaux Ferry Road	d																						
Saltash	d		19 40					20 38											22 39			22 39	
St Germans	d							20 45											22 47			22 47	
Menheniot	d																						
Liskeard 6	d		19 57		20 12			20 57		21 14				21 45					22 59			22 59	
Bodmin Parkway	d		20 10		20 25			21 10		21 27				21 59					23 13			23 13	
Lostwithiel	d									21 32									23 18			23 18	
Par	d		20 22		20 36			21 22		21 40				22 11					23 26			23 26	
Newquay	a																						
St Austell	d		20 29		20 44			21 29		21 47				22 19					23 33			23 33	
Truro	d		20 47		21 02			21 47		22 04				22 37					23 52			23 52	
Redruth	d		20 59		21 16			21 59		22 15				22 49					00 05			00 05	
Camborne	d		21 07		21 23					22 22									00 11			00 11	
Hayle	d							22 12		22 30									00 18			00 18	
St Erth	d		21 20		21 34			22 17		22 35			22 45						00 22			00 22	
Penzance	a		21 31		21 42			22 29		22 43			22 57	23 13					00 40			00 40	

A (trolley) to Totnes
B The Golden Hind. (buffet) from Taunton ✕ to Reading
C (buffet) from Taunton ✕ to Newbury
D (buffet) from Taunton ✕ to Newbury
E (trolley) to Bristol Parkway
b Arr. 1939

For connections to Oxford, Gatwick Airport and Heathrow Airport please refer to Tables 116, 148 and 125A

London and Birmingham - Devon and Cornwall

		XC	GW	GW	XC	XC	GW	GW	GW	GW	GW	GW	GW	GW FO	GW FX	GW FX	GW FO
		◇1 A	◇1		◇1 B	◇1 C	◇1 D	◇1 E	◇ D	D	E	◇1 F	◇1 E	R G	R H	R I	R J
														🛏	🛏	🛏	🛏
		🛒	☕		🛒	🛒	☕	☕				☕	☕	☕	☕	☕	☕
London Paddington 15 ⊖	d		19 45				20§35	20§35				21§45	21§45	23§45	23§45	23§45	23§45
Slough 3	d																
Reading 7	d		20 12				21§02	21§02				22§11	22§11	00u37	00u37	00u37	00u37
Theale	d																
Thatcham	d																
Newbury	d		20 27				21§18	21§18									
Hungerford	d																
Pewsey	d		20 47				21§38	21§38									
Westbury	d		21 05				21§57	21§57						01§37	01g45	01g45	01§37
Castle Cary	d		21 27				22§15	22§15									
Birmingham New Street 12	d	19 42			20§12	20§12											
Cardiff Central 7	d																
Newport (South Wales)	d																
Swindon	d											22§49	22§49				
Bristol Parkway 7	d	20 57			21§26	21§26											
Filton Abbey Wood	d																
Bath Spa 7	d											23§19	23§19				
Bristol Temple Meads 10	d	21 13			21c44	21c44			21§56	23§06	23§06	23§36	23§36				
Weston-super-Mare	d								22§30	23§42	23§42	00s06	00s06				
Bridgwater	d								22§49	00§02	00§02	00s25	00s25				
Taunton	d	21 46	21 49		22§17	22e27	22§37	22§37	23§04	00s14	00§15	00s37	00§38	02f35	02§35	03h06	03i06
Tiverton Parkway	d	21 58	22 02		22§29	22§51	22§50	23§03	23§19	00s30	00§39	00s50	01§03				
Exeter St Davids 6	a	22 11	22 19		22§44	23§04	23§06	23§20	23§37	00§51	00§59	01§09	01§21	03§06	03§06	03§59	03§59
Exmouth	d			22 05													
Exeter Central	d			22 31													
Exeter St Davids 6	d	22 12	22 21	22 37	22§46	23§06	23§08	23§21						04§11	04§11	04§11	04§11
Exeter St Thomas	d			22 40													
Starcross	d			22 48													
Dawlish Warren	d			22b59													
Dawlish	d			23 03													
Teignmouth	d			23 08													
Newton Abbot	a	22 30	22 40	23 15	23§04	23§24	23§28	23§42						04§32	04§32	04§32	04§32
	d	22 32	22 41	23 16	23§06	23§25	23§29	23§42						04§34	04§34	04§34	04§34
Torre	d			23 24													
Torquay	d			23 27													
Paignton	a			23 37													
Totnes	d	22 44	22 54		23§18	23§38	23§43	23§56									
Ivybridge	d		23 11														
Plymouth	a	23 15	23 26		23§44	00§03	00§11	00§25						05§13	05§13	05§13	05§13
	d													05§43	05§43	05§43	05§43
Devonport	d																
Dockyard	d																
Keyham	d																
St Budeaux Ferry Road	d																
Saltash	d																
St Germans	d																
Menheniot	d																
Liskeard 6	d													06§08	06§08	06§08	06§08
Bodmin Parkway	d													06§22	06§22	06§22	06§22
Lostwithiel	d													06§28	06§28	06§28	06§28
Par	d													06§37	06§37	06§37	06§37
Newquay	a																
St Austell	d													06§46	06§46	06§46	06§46
Truro	d													07§06	07§06	07§06	07§06
Redruth	d													07§18	07§18	07§18	07§18
Camborne	d													07§26	07§26	07§26	07§26
Hayle	d													07§35	07§35	07§35	07§35
St Erth	d													07§41	07§41	07§41	07§41
Penzance	a													07§53	07§53	07§53	07§53

A 🛒 to Bristol Parkway
B until 29 July, from 12 September. 🛒 to Bristol Parkway
C from 1 August until 9 September. 🛒 to Bristol Parkway
D until 29 July, from 12 September
E from 1 August until 9 September
F from 24 May until 29 July, from 12 September
G until 29 July, FO from 16 September. **The Night Riviera**
H until 28 July, FX from 12 September. **The Night Riviera**
I from 1 August until 8 September. **The Night Riviera**
J from 5 August until 9 September. **The Night Riviera**
b Arr. 2253
c Arr. 2138
e Arr. 2215
f Arr. 0222
g Arr. 0135
h Arr. 0232
i Arr. 0230

For connections to Oxford, Gatwick Airport and Heathrow Airport please refer to Tables 116, 148 and 125A

Table 135

Saturdays

until 10 September

London and Birmingham - Devon and Cornwall

		GW	XC	GW	GW	GW	GW	GW	GW	GW		GW	GW	GW	GW	XC	GW	GW	GW	XC		GW	GW	GW	GW
		R								R		R													
		1	◇1	◇1	◇1			◇1	◇1							◇1		◇		◇1			◇1	◇	
		A	B	C	D	C	D	C	D	E		F													
										🛏		🛏													
		✕ ☕	🛒	☕	☕			☕	☕	☕		☕								🛒			☕		
London Paddington 15 ⊖	d	19p03		20p35	20p35			21p45	21p45	23p45		23p45													
Slough 3	d																								
Reading 7	d	19b33		21p02	21p02			22p11	22p11	00u37		00u37													
Theale	d																								
Thatcham	d																								
Newbury	d	19p49		21p18	21p18																				
Hungerford	d																								
Pewsey	d			21p38	21p38																				
Westbury	d			21p57	21p57					01 37		01 37													
Castle Cary	d			22p15	22p15																				
Birmingham New Street 12	d		20p12																						
Cardiff Central 7	d																								
Newport (South Wales)	d																								
Swindon	d							22p49	22p49																
Bristol Parkway 7	d		21p26																						
Filton Abbey Wood	d																								
Bath Spa 7	d							23p19	23p19																
Bristol Temple Meads 10	d		21c44			23p06	23p06	23p36	23p36									05 24		06 08				06 36	
Weston-super-Mare	d					23p42	23p42	00s06	00s06									05 45						06 56	
Bridgwater	d					00 02	00 02	00s25	00s25									06 03							
Taunton	d	20p53	22e27	22p37	22p37	00s14	00 15	00s37	00 38	02f35		03g06						06 18		07 17				07 25	
Tiverton Parkway	d	21p06	22p51	22p50	23p03	00s30	00 39	00s50	01 03									06 33		07 29				07 41	
Exeter St Davids 6	a	21p22	23p04	23p06	23p20	00 51	00 59	01 09	01 21	03 06		03 59						06 52		07 43				08 00	
Exmouth	d																					07 15			
Exeter Central	d																					07 43			
Exeter St Davids 6	d	21p24	23p06	23p08	23p21					04 11		04 11	05 18	05 36	06 11			06 56		07 45		07 50		08 01	08 37
Exeter St Thomas	d												05 22	05 40	06 14			06 59				07 53		08 05	
Starcross	d												05 30	05 48	06 22			07 05				08 01			
Dawlish Warren	d												05 35	05 53	06 27			07 10				08 06			
Dawlish	d												05 39	05 57	06 31			07 14				08 10		08 18	08 51
Teignmouth	d												05 44	06 02	06 36			07 19				08 15		08 23	08 56
Newton Abbot	a	21p44	23p24	23p28	23p42					04 32		04 32	05 51	06 09	06 45			07 26		08 03		08 22		08 30	09 03
	d	21p45	23p25	23p29	23p42					04 34		04 34	05 52	06 11	06 45			07 26	07 40	08 04		08 24		08 32	09 06
Torre	d												06 00	06 19	06 53				07 48			08 32			
Torquay	d												06 03	06 22	06 56				07 51			08 35			09 16
Paignton	a												06 11	06 30	07 06				07 59			08 44			09 25
Totnes	d	21p58	23p38	23p43	23p56													07 40		08 17				08 46	
Ivybridge	d																	07 56						09 03	
Plymouth	a	22p26	00 03	00 11	00 25					05 13		05 13						08 13		08 43				09 17	
	d	22p30								05 43		05 43				06 35		08 15					08 57		
Devonport	d																	08 18							
Dockyard	d																								
Keyham	d																								
St Budeaux Ferry Road	d																								
Saltash	d	22p39																08 25							
St Germans	d	22p47																08 32							
Menheniot	d																								
Liskeard 6	d	22p59								06 08		06 08				06 59		08 44					09 23		
Bodmin Parkway	d	23p13								06 22		06 22				07 12		08 56					09 36		
Lostwithiel	d	23p18								06 28		06 28				07 18		09 01							
Par	d	23p26								06 37		06 37				07 28		09 09					09 46		
Newquay	a															08 27							10 55		
St Austell	d	23p33								06 46		06 46						09 17							
Truro	d	23p52								07 06		07 06						09 34							
Redruth	d	00 05								07 18		07 18						09 47							
Camborne	d	00 11								07 26		07 26						09 53							
Hayle	d	00 18								07 35		07 35						10 00							
St Erth	d	00 22								07 41		07 41					08 28	10 05							
Penzance	a	00 40								07 53		07 53					08 40	10 15							

A ☕ from Taunton ✕ to Newbury
B from 6 August until 10 September.
🛒 to Bristol Parkway
C until 30 July
D from 6 August until 10 September
E until 30 July. **The Night Riviera**
F from 6 August until 10 September. **The Night Riviera**
b Previous night, stops to pick up only
c Previous night, arr. 2138
e Previous night, arr. 2215
f Arr. 0222
g Arr. 0230

For connections to Oxford, Gatwick Airport and Heathrow Airport please refer to Tables 116, 148 and 125A

Table 135

Saturdays
until 10 September

London and Birmingham - Devon and Cornwall

		GW	XC	GW	GW	GW	XC	GW	GW	GW	GW	GW	XC	GW	GW	GW	XC	XC	GW	GW	XC	XC	GW
				R				R		R					R	R				R			
			◇1	1			◇1	◇1		◇1			◇1		◇1	◇1	◇1	◇1		◇1	◇1	◇1	
								A		B					C	D				D		E	
			🛒	⊘			🛒	🍴		🍴			🛒		🍴	🍴⊘	🛒	🛒		🍴⊘	🛒	🛒	
London Paddington 15 ⊖	d							07 36		07 30					08 35	09 06				10 06			
Slough 3	d																						
Reading 7	d							08u06		07 57					09u04	09u34				10u32			
Theale	d																						
Thatcham	d																						
Newbury	d														09 21								
Hungerford	d																						
Pewsey	d														09 40								
Westbury	d														09 58								
Castle Cary	d														10 15								
Birmingham New Street 12	d		06 42				07 12						08 12				08 42	09 12			09 42	10 12	
Cardiff Central 7	d																						
Newport (South Wales)	d																						
Swindon	d									08 30													
Bristol Parkway 7	d		07 57				08 26						09 26				09 57	10 31			10 59	11 26	
Filton Abbey Wood	d																						
Bath Spa 7	d									09 00													
Bristol Temple Meads 10	d		08 11				08c44			09 17			09e44				10f20	10 44			11 14	11 44	
Weston-super-Mare	d																				11g39		
Bridgwater	d																						
Taunton	d		08 43				09 17			09 51			10 18		10 37	10 50	11 01	11 17			12 01	12 17	
Tiverton Parkway	d		08 55				09 29						10 30		10 50	11 03	11 13	11 29			12 13	12 30	
Exeter St Davids 6	a		09 10				09 43	09 51		10 16			10 46		11 06	11 19	11 26	11 43		12 09	12 27	12 44	
Exmouth	d	08 23							09 23					10 23					11 23				
Exeter Central	d	08 50							09 52			10 30		10 50					11 50				
Exeter St Davids 6	d	08 57	09 12			09 28	09 45	09 54	09 58	10 19	10 25	10 35	10 48	10 56	11 08	11 22	11 29	11 45	11 56	12 11	12 29	12 47	12 52
Exeter St Thomas	d	08 59							09 59					10 59					11 59				
Starcross	d	09 07							10 08					11 07					12 07				
Dawlish Warren	d	09b24							10 13			10 47		11 13	11 19				12 13				13 04
Dawlish	d	09 28							10 18			10 51	11 01	11 17	11 24				12 17		12 41		13 08
Teignmouth	d	09 33							10 23			10 56	11 07	11 23	11 31				12 23		12 46		13 13
Newton Abbot	a	09 40				09 48	10 03		10 32	10 39	10 46	11 03	11 15	11 31	11 39	11 44	11 49	12 03	12 31	12 33	12 52	13 10	13 20
	d	09 41				09 49	10 05		10 33	10 40	10 48	11 03	11 16	11 32	11 40	11 44	11 51	12 05	12 38	12 34	12 53	13 12	13 21
Torre	d	09 50							10 41		10 56			11 40					12 45				
Torquay	d	09 53	09 40						10 44		10 59	11 14	11 29	11 43	11 52				12 48		13 05		
Paignton	a	10 01	09 46						10 52		11 07	11 23	11 36	11 51	12 02				12 56		13 11		
Totnes	d					10 02	10 17			10 53						11 57	12 07	12 17				13 24	13 34
Ivybridge	d					10 19																	13 50
Plymouth	a					10 32	10 44	10 51		11 21						12 25	12 34	12 44		13 14		13 50	14 05
	d			09 24	09 58	10 33		10 53		11 24						12 28	12 41			13 15		13 53	
Devonport	d				10 01																		
Dockyard	d																						
Keyham	d																						
St Budeaux Ferry Road	d					10 39																	
Saltash	d			09 34	10 08	10 44																	
St Germans	d				10 15	10 51																	
Menheniot	d				10x22																		
Liskeard 6	d			09 51	10 29	11 03				11 48						12 53	13 04			13 40		14 16	
Bodmin Parkway	d			10 04	10 41	11 15				12 01						13 06	13 20			13 54		14 28	
Lostwithiel	d			10 10	10 46	11 20										13 12						14 34	
Par	d			10 17	10a53	11 28		11 41		12 12							13 34			14 06		14 43	
Newquay	a							12 44									14 36						
St Austell	d			10 25		11 37				12 20						13 24				14 14		14 51	
Truro	d			10 43		11 55				12 38						13 42				14 30		15 09	
Redruth	d			10 55		12 08				12 50						13 56				14 44		15 21	
Camborne	d			11 02		12 14				12 57						14 03				14 50		15 28	
Hayle	d			11 11		12 21										14 12				15 00		15 37	
St Erth	d			11 18		12 25				13 10						14 19				15 06		15 42	
Penzance	a			11 28		12 36				13 22						14 29				15 18		15 52	

A ◇ from Exeter St Davids R to Reading

B ◇ from Exeter St Davids R to Taunton

C **The Torbay Express**. ◇ from Exeter St Davids R to Tiverton Parkway

D 🍴 from Newton Abbot ⊘ to Exeter St Davids ◇ from Newton Abbot R to Exeter St Davids

E 🛒 to Totnes

b Arr. 0914

c Arr. 0838

e Arr. 0938

f Arr. 1011

g Arr. 1131

For connections to Oxford, Gatwick Airport and Heathrow Airport please refer to Tables 116, 148 and 125A

Table 135

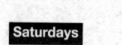

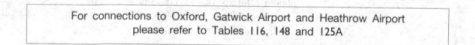

Saturdays
until 10 September

London and Birmingham - Devon and Cornwall

		GW		GW	GW	XC	GW	GW	GW	GW	GW	XC		GW	GW	GW	GW	XC	GW	GW	GW	GW		XC	XC
				■	■		■	■	■						■		■								
				◇1	◇1	◇1	1	1	◇1			◇1			◇1		1	◇1				◇1		◇1	◇1
				A	B		C	D	B						E										F
				RB	RB∅	T	RB	RB	RB∅			T			RB		RB	T				RB		T	T
London Paddington [15] ⊖	d			10 35	11 06		11 35	11 35	12 06						12 35		13 06					14 06			
Slough [3]	d																								
Reading [7]	d			11u04	11u34		12u06	12u06	12u32						13u06		13u32					14u32			
Theale	d																								
Thatcham	d																								
Newbury	d																								
Hungerford	d														13 22										
Pewsey	d			11 36											13 40										
Westbury	d			11 54											13 59										
Castle Cary	d			12 12											14 16										
Birmingham New Street [12]	d					11 12						12 12						13 12						13 42	14 12
Cardiff Central [7]	d																								
Newport (South Wales)	d																								
Swindon	d																								
Bristol Parkway [7]	d					12 31						13 27						14 28						14 59	15 26
Filton Abbey Wood	d																								
Bath Spa [7]	d																								
Bristol Temple Meads [10]	d					12 44						13 44						14 44						15 13	15c44
Weston-super-Mare	d																								
Bridgwater	d																								
Taunton	d			12 35	12 50	13 17						14 17			14 39		14 48	15 18				15 48		15 54	16 17
Tiverton Parkway	d			12 49		13 29						14 30					15 01	15 30				16 01		16 08	
Exeter St Davids [6]	a			13 04	13 15	13 43		13 52	14 09			14 45			15 03		15 17	15 46				16 17		16 23	16 40
Exmouth	d	12 23								13 23				14 23						15 23					
Exeter Central	d	12 50								13 50				14 50						15 50					
Exeter St Davids [6]	d	12 56		13 08	13 18	13 45	13u55	13 55	14 11	14b16	14 30	14 47		14 56	15 06		15 19	15 48		15 57		16 19		16 26	16 42
Exeter St Thomas	d	12 59								14 18				14 59						15 59					
Starcross	d	13 07								14 26				15 07						16 07					
Dawlish Warren	d	13 12								14 32	14 42	15 00		15 12	15 18					16 12				16 37	
Dawlish	d	13 16		13 22						14 36	14 46	15 05		15 16	15 24					16 16				16 42	
Teignmouth	d	13 21		13 28						14 41	14 51	15 12		15 21	15 30					16 21				16 47	
Newton Abbot	a	13 29		13 36	13 39	14 03			14 31	14 49	14 58	15 18		15 29	15 38		15 43	16 07		16 29		16 39		16 54	
	d	13 30		13 38	13 40	14 05			14 33	14 50	15 00	15 20		15 30	15 39		15 43	16 08	16 18	16 30		16 41		16 56	
Torre	d	13 38								14 58	15 08			15 38						16 38					
Torquay	d	13 41		13 51						15 01	15 11	15 32		15 41	15 52					16 41				17 08	
Paignton	a	13 51		14 01						15 09	15 19	15 40		15 51	15 58					16 51				17 15	
Totnes	d				13 53	14 17											15 57	16 22	16 31			16 53			17 11
Ivybridge	d																		16 47			17 10			
Plymouth	a				14 21	14 44		14 52	15 10								16 24	16 48	17 05			17 24			17 37
	d				14 24		14u55	14 55	15 12							16 03	16 29	16 52				17 27			17 42
Devonport	d																								
Dockyard	d																								
Keyham	d																								
St Budeaux Ferry Road	d																								
Saltash	d															16 12									
St Germans	d															16 19									
Menheniot	d															16x27									
Liskeard [6]	d				14 49				15 37							16 33	16 53	17 16				17 52			18 05
Bodmin Parkway	d				15 02				15 50							16 45	17 06	17 28				18 04			18 18
Lostwithiel	d						15 33	15 33								16 50									
Par	d						15 43	15 43	16 02							16a56		17 41				18 17			18 28
Newquay	a						16 52	16 52										18 45							
St Austell	d				15 17				16 09								17 23					18 23			18 34
Truro	d				15 35				16 27								17 40					18 42			18 52
Redruth	d				15 48				16 39								17 53					18 53			19 09
Camborne	d				15 55				16 47								18 00					19 02			19 16
Hayle	d				16 04												18 09								
St Erth	d				16 10				16 59								18 16				18 32	19 12			19 26
Penzance	a				16 21				17 11								18 28				18 44	19 24			19 36

A ◇ from Exeter St Davids ■ to Tiverton Parkway
B RB from Newton Abbot ∅ to Exeter St Davids
◇ from Newton Abbot ■ to Exeter St Davids
C until 9 July
D from 16 July until 10 September
E ◇ from Castle Cary ■ to Westbury
F T to Totnes
b Arr. 1354
c Arr. 1538

For connections to Oxford, Gatwick Airport and Heathrow Airport please refer to Tables 116, 148 and 125A

Table 135

Saturdays

until 10 September

London and Birmingham - Devon and Cornwall

		GW	GW	GW	GW	XC	GW	GW	GW	XC	GW	GW	GW	GW	GW	GW	XC	GW	GW	XC	GW	GW	XC
					◇1	◇1	1	◇1		◇1			◇1	◇1			◇1		◇1	◇1		◇1	◇1
						A	B			A													C
					☕	🛒		☕		🛒			☕	☕			🛒		☕	🛒		☕	🛒
London Paddington 15 ⊖	d				15 06			16 06					17 06	16 30					18 06			19 06	
Slough 3	d																						
Reading 7	d				15u32			16u32					17u32	16 57					18u32			19 32	
Theale	d																						
Thatcham	d																						
Newbury	d																					19 49	
Hungerford	d																						
Pewsey	d				16 04								18 03									20 09	
Westbury	d				16 23								18 22									20 27	
Castle Cary	d				16 40								18 41									20 44	
Birmingham New Street 12	d					15 12				16 12							17 12			18 12			19 12
Cardiff Central 7	d																						
Newport (South Wales)	d																						
Swindon	d													17 30									
Bristol Parkway 7	d					16 31				17 26							18 31			19 29			20 31
Filton Abbey Wood	d																						
Bath Spa 7	d													18 00									
Bristol Temple Meads 10	d					16 44				17c44				18 18			18 44			19 44			20 44
Weston-super-Mare	d													18 40									
Bridgwater	d																						
Taunton	d				17 03	17 18		17 49		18 17			19 02	19 06			19 17		19 47	20 17		21 07	21 17
Tiverton Parkway	d				17 16	17 31		18 02		18 29			19 15	19 21			19 29			20 29		21 20	21 29
Exeter St Davids 6	a				17 31	17 47		18 18		18 43			19 31	19 36			19 43		20 13	20 43		21 36	21 43
Exmouth	d		16 55						17 55									19 38			20 08		
Exeter Central	d	16 48	17 21						18 21									20 01			20 35		
Exeter St Davids 6	d	16 56	17 27		17 34	17 48	17 53	18 19	18 27	18 47	18 56	19 16	19 33	19 38			19 45	20 07	20 15	20 45	20f56	21 37	21 46
Exeter St Thomas	d	16 59	17 30						18 29			19 19						20 10			20 59		
Starcross	d	17 07	17 35						18 37			19 27						20 18			21 07		
Dawlish Warren	d	17 12	17b49				18 05		18 42			19 32						20e32			21 12		
Dawlish	d	17 16	17 53				18 09		18 46		19 09	19 36						20 36			21 16		
Teignmouth	d	17 21	17 58				18 14		18 51		19 14	19 41						20 41			21 21		
Newton Abbot	a	17 29	18 05		17 53	18 10	18 21	18 40	18 59	19 05	19 21	19 48	19 53	19 58			20 03	20 48	20 37	21 03	21 28	21 58	22 05
	d	17 30	18 09		17 55	18 12	18 22	18 41	19 01	19 06	19 22	19 50	19 54	19 59			20 05	20 49	20 37	21 05	21 30	21 58	22 10
Torre	d	17 38	18 17						19 09			19 58		20 09				20 57			21 38		
Torquay	d	17 41	18 20						19 12		19 32	20 01		20 13				21 00			21 41		
Paignton	a	17 51	18 27						19 21		19 40	20 09		20 22				21 07			21 48		
Totnes	d				18 08	18 25	18 35	18 54		19 19			20 07				20 17		20 51	21 17		22 12	22 23
Ivybridge	d						18 51	19 11															
Plymouth	a				18 37	18 52	19 05	19 24		19 44			20 36				20 43		21 19	21 44		22 41	22 49
	d			17 52		18 59	19 08	19 28		19 48						20 42			21 20				
Devonport	d			17 55																			
Dockyard	d			17x57																			
Keyham	d			17 59																			
St Budeaux Ferry Road	d			18 01																			
Saltash	d			18 06			19 17									20 51							
St Germans	d			18 12			19 24									20 58							
Menheniot	d			18x19																			
Liskeard 6	d			18 26		19 22	19 36	19 53		20 11						21 10			21 45				
Bodmin Parkway	d			18 38		19 35	19 48	20 06		20 23						21 22			21 59				
Lostwithiel	d			18 44			19 53			20 29						21 27							
Par	d			18 52		19 46	20 01	20 17		20 36						21 35			22 11				
Newquay	a																						
St Austell	d			18 59		19 54	20 08	20 25		20 43						21 44			22 18				
Truro	d			19 17		20 13	20 26	20 43		21 02						22 03			22 36				
Redruth	d			19 30		20 25	20 41	20 56		21 13						22 16			22 48				
Camborne	d			19 36		20 33	20 47	21 03		21 19						22 22			22 56				
Hayle	d			19 43						21 27						22 29			23 03				
St Erth	d			19 48		20 44	20 57	21 15		21 32					22 20	22 33			23 09				
Penzance	a			19 57		20 54	21 06	21 25		21 43					22 32	22 42			23 22				

A 🛒 to Totnes
B 1 from Plymouth
C from 6 August until 10 September. 🛒 to Bristol Parkway
b Arr. 1741
c Arr. 1738
e Arr. 2023
f Arr. 2038

For connections to Oxford, Gatwick Airport and Heathrow Airport please refer to Tables 116, 148 and 125A

Table 135

Saturdays

until 10 September

London and Birmingham - Devon and Cornwall

		GW	XC	GW		GW
		◇1	◇1	◇		◇1
			A			
		🍴	🚲			🍴
London Paddington 15 ⊖	d	20 06				20 30
Slough 3	d					
Reading 7	d	20 33				20 57
Theale	d					
Thatcham	d					
Newbury	d	20 47				
Hungerford	d					
Pewsey	d	21 07				
Westbury	d	21 26				
Castle Cary	d	21 43				
Birmingham New Street 12	d		20 12			
Cardiff Central 7	d			21 00		
Newport (South Wales)	d			21 15		
Swindon	d					21 30
Bristol Parkway 7	d		21 26			
Filton Abbey Wood	d			21 42		
Bath Spa 7	d					22 00
Bristol Temple Meads 10	d		21b44	21c55		22 17
Weston-super-Mare	d			22 27		22s47
Bridgwater	d			22 46		23s05
Taunton	d	22 06	22 17	22 59		23 18
Tiverton Parkway	d	22 19	22 29	23 14		23 31
Exeter St Davids 6	a	22 35	22 44	23 33		23 48
Exmouth	d					
Exeter Central	d					
Exeter St Davids 6	d	22 38	22 46			
Exeter St Thomas	d					
Starcross	d					
Dawlish Warren	d					
Dawlish	d	22 48				
Teignmouth	d	22 54				
Newton Abbot	a	23 03	23 11			
	d	23 03	23 12			
Torre	d					
Torquay	d					
Paignton	a					
Totnes	d	23 17	23 28			
Ivybridge	d					
Plymouth	a	23 48	23 54			
	d					
Devonport	d					
Dockyard	d					
Keyham	d					
St Budeaux Ferry Road	d					
Saltash	d					
St Germans	d					
Menheniot	d					
Liskeard 6	d					
Bodmin Parkway	d					
Lostwithiel	d					
Par	d					
Newquay	a					
St Austell	d					
Truro	d					
Redruth	d					
Camborne	d					
Hayle	d					
St Erth	d					
Penzance	a					

A 🚲 to Bristol Parkway

b Arr. 2138

c Arr. 2149

For connections to Oxford, Gatwick Airport and Heathrow Airport please refer to Tables 116, 148 and 125A

Table 135

Saturdays

from 17 September

London and Birmingham - Devon and Cornwall

		GW	GW	GW	GW	GW	GW	GW	GW	GW		XC	GW	GW	GW	XC	GW	GW	GW	GW		XC	GW	GW	XC
		R 1 A ✕ ⊐⊏	◇1 ⊐⊏		◇1 ⊐⊏		R B 🛏 ⊐⊏					◇1		◇		◇1 ⚲		◇				◇1 ⚲			◇1 ⚲
London Paddington 15 ⊖	d	19p03	20p35		21p45		23p45																		
Slough 3	d																								
Reading 7	d	19b33	21p02		22p11		00u37																		
Theale	d																								
Thatcham	d																								
Newbury	d	19p49	21p18																						
Hungerford	d																								
Pewsey	d		21p38																						
Westbury	d		21p57				01 37																		
Castle Cary	d		22p15																						
Birmingham New Street 12	d																					06 42			07 12
Cardiff Central 7	d																								
Newport (South Wales)	d																								
Swindon	d				22p49																				
Bristol Parkway 7	d																					07 57			08 26
Filton Abbey Wood	d																								
Bath Spa 7	d				23p19																				
Bristol Temple Meads 10	d			23p06	23p36									05 24		06 08		06 36				08 11			08g44
Weston-super-Mare	d			23p42	00s06									05 45				06 56							
Bridgwater	d			00 02	00s25									06 03											
Taunton	d	20p53	22p37	00s14	00s37		02e35							06 18		07 17		07 25				08 43			09 17
Tiverton Parkway	d	21p06	22p50	00s30	00s50									06 33		07 29		07 41				08 55			09 29
Exeter St Davids 6	a	21p22	23p06	00 51	01 09		03 06							06 52		07 43		08 00				09 10			09 43
Exmouth	d																07 15			08 23					
Exeter Central	d																07 43			08 50					
Exeter St Davids 6	d	21p24	23p08				04 11	05 18	05 36	06 11				06 56		07 45	07 50	08 01	08 37	08 56		09 12		09 28	09 45
Exeter St Thomas	d							05 22	05 40	06 14				06 59			07 53	08 05		08 59					
Starcross	d							05 30	05 48	06 22				07 05			08 01			09 07					
Dawlish Warren	d							05 35	05 53	06 27				07 10			08 06			09f24					
Dawlish	d							05 39	05 57	06 31				07 14			08 10	08 18	08 51	09 28					
Teignmouth	d							05 44	06 02	06 36				07 19			08 15	08 23	08 56	09 33					
Newton Abbot	a	21p44	23p28				04 32	05 51	06 09	06 45				07 26		08 03	08 22	08 30	09 03	09 40				09 48	10 03
	d	21p45	23p29				04 34	05 52	06 11	06 45				07 26	07 40	08 04	08 24	08 32	09 06	09 41				09 49	10 05
Torre	d							06 00	06 19	06 53					07 48		08 32			09 50					
Torquay	d							06 03	06 22	06 56					07 51		08 35		09 16	09 53		09 40			
Paignton	a							06 11	06 30	07 06					07 59		08 44		09 25	10 01		09 46			
Totnes	d	21p58	23p43											07 40		08 17		08 46						10 02	10 17
Ivybridge	d													07 56				09 03						10 19	
Plymouth	a	22p26	00 11				05 13							08 13		08 43		09 17						10 32	10 44
	d	22p30					05 43					06 28		08 15				09 20					09 51	10 33	
Devonport	d													08 18									09 54		
Dockyard	d																								
Keyham	d																								
St Budeaux Ferry Road	d																							10 39	
Saltash	d	22p39												08 25				09 29					10 01	10 44	
St Germans	d	22p47												08 32				09 37					10 08	10 51	
Menheniot	d																						10x15		
Liskeard 6	d	22p59					06 08					06 51		08 44				09 50					10 22	11 03	
Bodmin Parkway	d	23p13					06 22					07 03		08 56				10 03					10 34	11 15	
Lostwithiel	d	23p18					06 28					07 08		09 01									10 39	11 20	
Par	d	23p26				06 09	06 37					07 15		09 09				10 15					10 46	11 28	
Newquay	a																								
St Austell	d	23p33				06 16	06 46					07 21		09 17				10 23					10 54	11 37	
Truro	d	23p52				06c41	07 06					07 38		09 34				10 41					11 10	11 55	
Redruth	d	00 05				06 54	07 18					07 50		09 47				10 56					11 24	12 08	
Camborne	d	00 11				07 00	07 26					07 56		09 53				11 03					11 30	12 14	
Hayle	d	00 18				07 07	07 35					08 04		10 00				11 11					11 38	12 21	
St Erth	d	00 22				07 10	07 41					08 11	08 28	10 05				11 18					11 42	12 25	
Penzance	a	00 40				07 22	07 53					08 19	08 40	10 15				11 26					11 55	12 36	

A ⊐⊏ from Taunton ✕ to Newbury
B **The Night Riviera**
b Previous night, stops to pick up only
c Arr. 0634
e Arr. 0222
f Arr. 0914
g Arr. 0838

For connections to Oxford, Gatwick Airport and Heathrow Airport please refer to Tables 116, 148 and 125A

Table 135

Saturdays
from 17 September

London and Birmingham - Devon and Cornwall

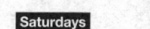

		GW	GW	GW	GW	XC		GW	GW	GW	XC	GW	GW	GW	XC	XC		GW	GW	GW	GW	XC	GW	GW	GW
			■																						
			◇1			◇1		◇1		◇1	◇1			◇1	◇1	◇1					◇1	◇1		◇1	
			A							B				B							B			B	
			🍴			🛒		🍴		🍴⊘	🛒			🍴⊘	🛒	🛒					🍴⊘	🛒		🍴⊘	
London Paddington 15 ⊖	d		07 30					08 18		09 06				10 06							11 06			12 06	
Slough 3	d																								
Reading 7	d		07 57					08 49		09 32				10 32							11 32			12 32	
Theale	d							08 58																	
Thatcham	d							09 07																	
Newbury	d							09 14																	
Hungerford	d							09 23																	
Pewsey	d							09 41													12 03				
Westbury	d							10 00													12 22				
Castle Cary	d							10 18													12 40				
Birmingham New Street 12	d					08 12					09 12				09 42	10 12						11 12			
Cardiff Central 7	d																								
Newport (South Wales)	d																								
Swindon	d		08 30																						
Bristol Parkway 7	d					09 26					10 31				10 59	11 26						12 31			
Filton Abbey Wood	d																								
Bath Spa 7	d		09 00																						
Bristol Temple Meads 10	d		09 17			09b44					10 44				11 14	11e44						12 44			
Weston-super-Mare	d														11c39										
Bridgwater	d																								
Taunton	d		09 51			10 18		10 40		10 48	11 17				12 01	12 17					13 02	13 17			
Tiverton Parkway	d					10 30		10 53		11 01	11 29				12 13	12 29					13 15	13 29			
Exeter St Davids 6	a		10 16			10 46		11 09		11 17	11 43			12 09	12 27	12 43					13 31	13 43		14 09	
Exmouth	d	09 23							10 23			11 23							12 23				13 23		
Exeter Central	d	09 52			10 30				10 50			11 50							12 50				13 50		
Exeter St Davids 6	d	09 58	10 19	10 25	10 35	10 48			10 56	11 19	11 45	11 56		12 10	12 29	12 45		12 52	12 56		13 33	13 45	13 57	14 10	14 30
Exeter St Thomas	d	09 59							10 59			11 59							12 59				13 59		
Starcross	d	10 07							11 07			12 07							13 07				14 07		
Dawlish Warren	d	10 12			10 47				11 12			12 12						13 04	13 12				14f24		14 42
Dawlish	d	10 16			10 51				11 16			12 16			12 41			13 08	13 16				14 28		14 46
Teignmouth	d	10 21			10 56				11 21			12 21			12 46			13 13	13 21				14 33		14 51
Newton Abbot	a	10 30	10 39	10 46	11 03	11 08			11 29	11 39	12 03	12 29		12 31	12 52	13 03		13 20	13 29		13 52	14 03	14 41	14 30	14 58
	d	10 31	10 40	10 48	11 04	11 09			11 30	11 39	12 05	12 36		12 31	12 53	13 05		13 21	13 30		13 54	14 05	14 42	14 32	15 00
Torre	d	10 39		10 56					11 38			12 43							13 38				14 50		15 08
Torquay	d	10 42		10 59	11 14				11 41			12 46			13 05				13 41				14 53		15 11
Paignton	a	10 50		11 07	11 23				11 51			12 54			13 11				13 51				15 01		15 19
Totnes	d		10 53			11 23				11 53	12 17					13 17		13 34			14 06	14 17			
Ivybridge	d									12 08								13 50							
Plymouth	a		11 21			11 51				12 25	12 44			13 11		13 44		14 05			14 36	14 44		15 09	
	d		11 24										12 44	13 13						14 15				15 11	
Devonport	d																								
Dockyard	d																								
Keyham	d																								
St Budeaux Ferry Road	d																								
Saltash	d												12 53							14 24					
St Germans	d												13 00							14 32					
Menheniot	d																								
Liskeard 6	d		11 48										13 12	13 38						14 45				15 36	
Bodmin Parkway	d		12 01										13 24	13 52						14 58				15 49	
Lostwithiel	d												13 29							15 04					
Par	d		12 12										13 37	14 04						15 12				16 01	
Newquay	a																								
St Austell	d		12 20										13 45	14 11						15 21				16 08	
Truro	d		12 38										14 02	14 28						15 39				16 26	
Redruth	d		12 50										14 15	14 41						15 53				16 38	
Camborne	d		12 57										14 21	14 48						16 00				16 46	
Hayle	d												14 28	14 58											
St Erth	d		13 09										14 33	15 03						16 12				16 57	
Penzance	a		13 21										14 42	15 15						16 21				17 09	

A ◇ from Exeter St Davids ■ to Taunton
B 🍴 from Newton Abbot ⊘ to Exeter St Davids

b Arr. 0938
c Arr. 1131
e Arr. 1138
f Arr. 1412

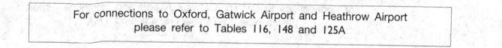

For connections to Oxford, Gatwick Airport and Heathrow Airport please refer to Tables 116, 148 and 125A

Table 135

Saturdays

from 17 September

London and Birmingham - Devon and Cornwall

		XC		GW	GW	GW	GW	XC	GW	GW	GW	GW		XC	XC	GW	GW	GW	GW	XC	GW	XC		GW	GW
		◇1 [trolley]		◇1 [buffet]			R 1 [buffet]	◇1 [trolley]				◇1 [buffet]		◇1 [trolley]	◇1 [trolley]				◇1 [buffet]	◇1 A [trolley]	1 B	◇1 [trolley]		◇1 [buffet]	
London Paddington 15 ⊖	d			12 18			13 06					14 06							15 06					16 06	
Slough 3	d																								
Reading 7	d			12 49			13 32					14 32							15 32					16 32	
Theale	d			12 57																					
Thatcham	d			13 05																					
Newbury	d			13 13																					
Hungerford	d			13 21																					
Pewsey	d			13 39															16 04						
Westbury	d			13 58															16 23						
Castle Cary	d			14 14															16 40						
Birmingham New Street 12	d	12 12						13 12						13 42	14 12					15 12		15 42			
Cardiff Central 7	d																								
Newport (South Wales)	d																								
Swindon	d																								
Bristol Parkway 7	d	13 26						14 28						14 59	15 25					16 31		16 57			
Filton Abbey Wood	d																								
Bath Spa 7	d																								
Bristol Temple Meads 10	d	13b44						14 44						15 13	15c44					16 44		17 10			
Weston-super-Mare	d																								
Bridgwater	d																								
Taunton	d	14 17		14a37			14 48	15 18				15 48		15 54	16 17				17 03	17 18		17 42		17 49	
Tiverton Parkway	d	14 29					15 01	15 30				16 01		16 08	16 29				17 16	17 31		17 54		18 02	
Exeter St Davids 6	a	14 43					15 17	15 46				16 17		16 26	16 43				17 31	17 47		18 09		18 18	
Exmouth	d				14 23					15 23							16 55								17 55
Exeter Central	d				14 50					15 50						16 48	17 21								18 21
Exeter St Davids 6	d	14 45			14 56		15 18	15 48		15 57		16 19			16 45	16 56	17 27		17 34	17 48	17 53	18 10		18 19	18 27
Exeter St Thomas	d				14 59					15 59						16 59	17 30								18 29
Starcross	d				15 07					16 07						17 07	17 35								18 37
Dawlish Warren	d				15 12					16 12						17 12	17e49				18 05				18 42
Dawlish	d				15 16					16 16						17 16	17 53				18 09	18 22			18 46
Teignmouth	d				15 21					16 21						17 21	17 58				18 14	18 27			18 51
Newton Abbot	a	15 03			15 29		15 40	16 07		16 29		16 39			17 03	17 29	18 05		17 53	18 10	18 21	18 33		18 40	18 59
	d	15 05			15 30		15 40	16 08	16 18	16 30		16 41			17 05	17 30	18 09		17 55	18 12	18 22	18 35		18 41	19 01
Torre	d				15 38					16 38						17 38	18 17								19 09
Torquay	d				15 41					16 41						17 41	18 20					18 46			19 12
Paignton	a				15 51					16 51						17 51	18 27					18 53			19 21
Totnes	d	15 17					15 54	16 22	16 31			16 53			17 17				18 08	18 25	18 35			18 54	
Ivybridge	d								16 47			17 10									18 51			19 11	
Plymouth	a	15 44					16 21	16 50	17 05			17 24			17 44				18 36	18 52	19 05			19 26	
	d					16 03	16 26					17 27						17 52	18 40	18 59	19 08				
Devonport	d																	17 55							
Dockyard	d																	17x57							
Keyham	d																	17 59							
St Budeaux Ferry Road	d																	18 01							
Saltash	d					16 12												18 06			19 17				
St Germans	d					16 19												18 12			19 24				
Menheniot	d					16x27												18x19							
Liskeard 6	d					16 33	16 50					17 52						18 26	19 05	19 22	19 36				
Bodmin Parkway	d					16 45	17 03					18 04						18 38	19 18	19 35	19 48				
Lostwithiel	d					16 50												18 44			19 53				
Par	d					16 57						18 17						18 52	19 30	19 46	20 01				
Newquay	a																								
St Austell	d					17 05	17 20					18 23						18 59	19 38	19 54	20 08				
Truro	d					17 23	17 37					18 42						19 17	20 00	20 13	20 26				
Redruth	d					17 36	17 50					18 53						19 30	20 10	20 25	20 41				
Camborne	d					17 42	17 57					19 02						19 36	20 18	20 33	20 47				
Hayle	d					17 49	18 06											19 43							
St Erth	d					17 54	18 12				18 32	19 12						19 48	20 29	20 44	20 57				
Penzance	a					18 03	18 24				18 44	19 24						19 57	20 40	20 54	21 06				

A [trolley] to Totnes

B 1 from Plymouth

b Arr. 1338

c Arr. 1537

e Arr. 1741

For connections to Oxford, Gatwick Airport and Heathrow Airport please refer to Tables 116, 148 and 125A

Table 135

Saturdays
from 17 September

London and Birmingham - Devon and Cornwall

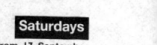

		XC	GW	GW	GW	GW	GW	XC		GW	GW	XC	GW	GW	XC	XC	GW	XC		GW	GW	GW
		◇1				◇1	◇1	◇1			◇1	◇1		◇1	◇1	◇1	◇1	◇1		◇		◇1
		A						A							B	B		B		C	D	
		🛒				☕	☕	🛒			☕	🛒		☕	🛒	🛒	☕	🛒				☕
London Paddington [15] ⊖	d					17 06	16 30				18 06			19 06			20 06					20 30
Slough [3]	d																					
Reading [7]	d					17 32	16 57				18 32			19 32			20 33					20 57
Theale	d																					
Thatcham	d																					
Newbury	d													19 49			20 47					
Hungerford	d																					
Pewsey	d					18 03								20 09			21 07					
Westbury	d					18 22								20 27			21 26					
Castle Cary	d					18 41								20 44			21 43					
Birmingham New Street [12]	d	16 12						17 12				18 12			19 12	19 42		20 12				
Cardiff Central [7]	d																			21 00		
Newport (South Wales)	d																			21 15		
Swindon	d						17 30															21 30
Bristol Parkway [7]	d	17 26						18 31				19 29			20 31	20 57		21 26				
Filton Abbey Wood	d																			21 42		
Bath Spa [7]	d						18 00															22 00
Bristol Temple Meads [10]	d	17b44					18 18	18 44				19 44			20 44	21 11		21f44		21g55	21 59	22 17
Weston-super-Mare	d						18 40													22 27	22 31	22s47
Bridgwater	d																			22 46	22 50	23s05
Taunton	d	18 17				19 02	19 06	19 17			19 47	20 17		21 07	21 17	21 44	22 06	22 17		22 59	23 03	23 18
Tiverton Parkway	d	18 29				19 15	19 21	19 29				20 29		21 20	21 29	21 56	22 19	22 29		23 14	23 18	23 31
Exeter St Davids [6]	a	18 43				19 31	19 36	19 43			20 13	20 43		21 36	21 43	22 10	22 35	22 44		23 33	23 37	23 48
Exmouth	d									19 38			20 08									
Exeter Central	d									20 01			20 35									
Exeter St Davids [6]	d	18 47	18 56	19 16		19 33	19 38	19 45		20 07	20 15	20 45	20e56	21 37	21 46	22 12	22 38	22 46				
Exeter St Thomas	d			19 19						20 10			20 59									
Starcross	d			19 27						20 18			21 07									
Dawlish Warren	d			19 32						20c32			21 12									
Dawlish	d		19 09	19 36						20 36			21 16				22 48					
Teignmouth	d		19 14	19 41						20 41			21 21				22 54					
Newton Abbot	a	19 05	19 21	19 48		19 53	19 58	20 03		20 48	20 37	21 03	21 28	21 58	22 05	22 30	23 03	23 11				
	d	19 06	19 22	19 50		19 54	19 59	20 05		20 49	20 37	21 05	21 30	21 58	22 10	22 31	23 03	23 12				
Torre	d			19 58			20 09			20 57			21 38									
Torquay	d		19 32	20 01			20 12			21 00			21 41									
Paignton	a		19 40	20 09			20 21			21 07			21 48									
Totnes	d	19 19				20 07		20 17			20 51	21 17		22 12	22 23	22 44	23 17	23 28				
Ivybridge	d																					
Plymouth	a	19 44				20 35		20 43			21 19	21 44		22 41	22 49	23 10	23 48	23 54				
	d	19 48				20 38		20 58			21 20											
Devonport	d																					
Dockyard	d																					
Keyham	d																					
St Budeaux Ferry Road	d																					
Saltash	d					20 49																
St Germans	d					20 56																
Menheniot	d																					
Liskeard [6]	d	20 11				21 08		21 25			21 45											
Bodmin Parkway	d	20 23				21 21		21 38			21 59											
Lostwithiel	d	20 29																				
Par	d	20 36				21 33		21 49			22 11											
Newquay	a																					
St Austell	d	20 43				21 43		21 56			22 18											
Truro	d	21 02				22 03		22 13			22 36											
Redruth	d	21 13				22 13		22 28			22 48											
Camborne	d	21 19						22 34			22 56											
Hayle	d	21 27									23 03											
St Erth	d	21 32			22 20	22 30		22 45			23 09											
Penzance	a	21 43			22 32	22 42		22 54			23 22											

A 🛒 to Totnes
B 🛒 to Bristol Parkway
C from 17 September until 22 October
D from 29 October
b Arr. 1738
c Arr. 2023
e Arr. 2038
f Arr. 2138
g Arr. 2149

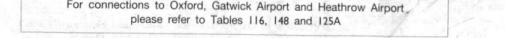

For connections to Oxford, Gatwick Airport and Heathrow Airport please refer to Tables 116, 148 and 125A

Table 135

Sundays
until 19 June

London and Birmingham - Devon and Cornwall

		GW	XC	GW	GW	XC	GW	GW	XC	GW	GW	GW	XC	GW	GW	GW	XC	GW	GW	GW	XC	GW	GW
			[R] ◇ A		◇	◇[1]		◇	◇[1]		◇[1]	◇[1]	◇[1] B			◇[1]	◇[1]		◇[1]		◇[1]		◇[1]
				🚲		🚲			🚲		☕	☕				☕	🚲		☕		🚲		☕
London Paddington [15] ⊖	d										08 00	08 57				09 57			10 57				11 37
Slough [3]	d																						
Reading [7]	d										08 38	09 34				10 34			11 34				12 14
Theale	d																						
Thatcham	d																						
Newbury	d											09 51											
Hungerford	d																						12 46
Pewsey	d															11 06							13 05
Westbury	d											10 25											13 22
Castle Cary	d															11 36							
Birmingham New Street [12]	d																09 12				10 12		
Cardiff Central [7]	d																						
Newport (South Wales)	d																10e49				11 52		
Swindon	d										09 11												
Bristol Parkway [7]	d																11f29				12h25		
Filton Abbey Wood	d																						
Bath Spa [7]	d										09 45												
Bristol Temple Meads [10]	d				07 45	08 44		08 28	09 48		10c01		10 44				11 44				12i44		
Weston-super-Mare	d				08 08			08 59															
Bridgwater	d				08 24			09 18															
Taunton	d				08 39	09 16		09 32	10 21		10 36	11 02	11 16			11 58	12 15		12 49		13 16		13 44
Tiverton Parkway	d				08 54	09 28		09 48	10 33		10 49	11 15	11 29				12 27				13 29		
Exeter St Davids [6]	a				09 11	09 42		10 05	10 46		11 06	11 30	11 42			12 23	12 42		13 15		13 42		14 10
Exmouth	d						09 10			10 21				11 24				12 29				13 24	
Exeter Central	d						09 36			10 48				11 53				12 55		13 20		13 50	
Exeter St Davids [6]	d	08 54			09 13	09 44	09b56	10 09	10 48	10 53	11 08	11 30	11 44	11 58	12 15	12 24	12 44	13 01	13 15	13 25	13 44	13 56	14 10
Exeter St Thomas	d	08 57					09 59			10 56				12 01								13 59	
Starcross	d	09 05					10 07			11 05				12 09								14 07	
Dawlish Warren	d	09 10					10 12			11 09				12 14				13 12				14 12	14 24
Dawlish	d	09 14			09 26		10 16	10 23		11 13	11 22			12 18				13 16		13 38		14 16	14 27
Teignmouth	d	09 19			09 31		10 21	10 28		11 18	11 28			12 23				13 21		13 43		14 21	14 34
Newton Abbot	a	09 26			09 39	10 03	10 28	10 34	11 07	11 25	11 36	11 52	12 03	12 30	12 35	12 46	13 03	13 28	13 38	13 50	14 03	14 28	14 42
	d	09 28			09 39	10 04	10 39	10 36	11 09	11 27	11 36	11 53	12 04	12 32	12 36	12 46	13 05	13 29	13 39	13 52	14 04	14 30	14 42
Torre	d	09 36					10 47			11 35				12 40				13 37		14 00		14 38	
Torquay	d	09 39					10 50			11 38				12 43				13 40		14 03		14 41	14 54
Paignton	a	09 46					10 55			11 45				12 50				13 47		14 10		14 48	15 03
Totnes	d				09 52	10 17		10 49	11 21		11 50	12 07	12 17		12 48	12 59	13 17				14 17		
Ivybridge	d				10 09										13 04								
Plymouth	a				10 22	10 43		11 18	11 48		12 18	12 35	12 44		13 17	13 28	13 44		14 17		14 45		
	d		09 05	09 15	10 22			11 22			12 20	12 35	12 55			13 31			14 20				
Devonport	d				10 28																		
Dockyard	d																						
Keyham	d																						
St Budeaux Ferry Road	d			09 21																			
Saltash	d			09 25	10 38			11 31															
St Germans	d			09 31	10 45			11 38															
Menheniot	d				10x53			11x46															
Liskeard [6]	d		09 30	09 47	10 59			11 52			12 45	13 01	13 18			13 56			14 44				
Bodmin Parkway	d		09 43	09 59	11 11			12 04			12 57	13 15	13 30			14 08			14 58				
Lostwithiel	d			10 05	11 16			12 09															
Par	d		09 56	10 13	11 24			12 16			13 09	13 25	13 41			14 21							
Newquay	a		11 10													15 26							
St Austell	d			10 20	11 31			12 24			13 17	13 32	13 48						15 13				
Truro	d			10 39	11 49			12 41			13 35	13 51	14 05						15 32				
Redruth	d			10 52	12 02			12 54			13 48	14 03	14 17						15 42				
Camborne	d			10 58	12 08			13 00				14 12	14 25						15 50				
Hayle	d			11 05	12 15			13 07															
St Erth	d			11 10	12 19			13 11			14 04	14 23	14 37						16g06				
Penzance	a			11 22	12 30			13 25			14 13	14 35	14 49						16 20				

A ◇ to Bodmin Parkway [R] from Par
B [1] from Plymouth ◇ from Plymouth
b Arr. 0940
c Arr. 0955
e Arr. 1042
f Arr. 1111
g Arr. 1600
h Arr. 1213
i Arr. 1235

For connections to Oxford, Gatwick Airport and Heathrow Airport please refer to Tables 116, 148 and 125A

Table 135

Sundays

until 19 June

London and Birmingham - Devon and Cornwall

		GW	GW	XC	GW	GW	GW	XC	GW	GW	GW	GW	XC	GW	XC	GW	GW	XC	GW	GW	GW	XC	GW
			◇1	◇1		◇1		◇1	◇1			◇1	◇1		◇1		◇1	◇1		◇1		◇1	
																		A					
		[trolley]	[restaurant]	[trolley]		[restaurant]		[trolley]	[restaurant]			[restaurant]	[trolley]		[trolley]		[restaurant]	[trolley]		[restaurant]		[trolley]	
London Paddington 15 ⊖	d		11 57			12 57			13 00			13 57					14 57			15 57			
Slough 3	d																						
Reading 7	d		12 34			13 34			13 38			14 34					15 34			16 34			
Theale	d																						
Thatcham	d																						
Newbury	d		12 50									14 51								16 51			
Hungerford	d																						
Pewsey	d																						
Westbury	d					14 19														17 27			
Castle Cary	d											15 38								17 44			
Birmingham New Street 12	d			11 12				12 12					14 12		14 42			15 12				16 12	
Cardiff Central 7	d																						
Newport (South Wales)	d			12b53				13g52															
Swindon	d								14 11														
Bristol Parkway 7	d			13c25				14h25					15 34		15 56			16 25				17 25	
Filton Abbey Wood	d																						
Bath Spa 7	d								14 40														
Bristol Temple Meads 10	d			13e44				14i44	14 55				15 47		16 14			16k44				17l44	
Weston-super-Mare	d																						
Bridgwater	d																						
Taunton	d		13 55	14 17		14 55		15 16	15 30			15 58	16 20		16 46		16 51	17 17		18 07		18 21	
Tiverton Parkway	d			14 29		15 08		15 29					16 33		16 58		17 04	17 28		18 20		18 33	
Exeter St Davids 6	a		14 19	14 46		15 23		15 45	15 56			16 24	16 46		17 12		17 19	17 46		18 36		18 48	
Exmouth	d				14 31					15 24				16 24					17 24				18 24
Exeter Central	d				14 57		15 20			15 50				16 50					17 50				18 49
Exeter St Davids 6	d		14 21	14 48	15 03	15 24	15f31	15 47	15 56	16j00	16 10	16 24	16 48	16 56	17 14		17 21	17 47	17 56	18 37		18 49	18 56
Exeter St Thomas	d									16 03	16 12								17 59				18 59
Starcross	d									16 11									18 07				19 07
Dawlish Warren	d									16 16									18 12				19 12
Dawlish	d				15 15		15 43			16 20	16 25			17 09	17 26				18 16				19 16
Teignmouth	d				15 20		15 48			16 25	16 30			17 14	17 31				18 21				19 21
Newton Abbot	a		14 46	15 08	15 27	15 46	15 55	16 07	16 18	16 32	16 36	16 44	17 07	17 21	17 38		17 42	18 07	18 28	18 57		19 07	19 28
	d		14 48	15 09	15 28	15 46	15 56	16 09	16 18	16 33	16 36	16 44	17 07	17 22	17 39		17 42	18 09	18 29	18 59		19 08	19 30
Torre	d				15 37		16 04			16 41				17 31					18 37				19 38
Torquay	d				15 40		16 07			16 44				17 34	17 51				18 40				19 41
Paignton	a				15 50		16 15			16 51				17 41	17 57				18 47				19 48
Totnes	d		15 00	15 23		16 00		16 22			16 52	17 02	17 21				17 57	18 22				19 21	
Ivybridge	d										17 08												
Plymouth	a		15 35	15 53		16 31		16 50	16 57		17 22	17 30	17 47				18 24	18 51		19 37		19 48	
	d	14 58	15 35			16 35					17 35						18 25	18 55			19 43		
Devonport	d																						
Dockyard	d																						
Keyham	d																						
St Budeaux Ferry Road	d																						
Saltash	d	15 07									17 45										19 52		
St Germans	d	15 14									17 52										19 59		
Menheniot	d										18x00												
Liskeard 6	d	15 26	16 00			16 58					18 06						18 50	19 18			20 11		
Bodmin Parkway	d	15 39	16 13			17 11					18 18						19 04	19 30			20 23		
Lostwithiel	d	15 45									18 23										20 28		
Par	d	15 53	16 25			17 23					18 31						19 14	19 41			20 36		
Newquay	a																						
St Austell	d	16 00	16 32			17 29					18 39						19 21	19 52			20 43		
Truro	d	16 19	16 51			17 48					18 56						19 39	20 09			21 00		
Redruth	d	16 32	17 03			18 00					19 09						19 51	20 20			21 14		
Camborne	d	16 38	17 10			18 08					19 15						20 01	20 28			21 20		
Hayle	d	16 45									19 22										21 27		
St Erth	d	16 50	17 22			18 20					19 27					20 05	20 14	20 39			21 32		
Penzance	a	17 00	17 32			18 32					19 38					20 14	20 25	20 47			21 42		

A [trolley] to Totnes
b Arr. 1247
c Arr. 1317
e Arr. 1337
f Arr. 1523
g Arr. 1346
h Arr. 1418
i Arr. 1436
j Arr. 1553
k Arr. 1637
l Arr. 1735

For connections to Oxford, Gatwick Airport and Heathrow Airport please refer to Tables 116, 148 and 125A

Table 135

Sundays
until 19 June

London and Birmingham - Devon and Cornwall

		GW	GW	XC	GW	GW	XC	GW	GW	XC	XC	GW	GW	GW	XC	GW	GW
																	[R]
		◇■1	◇	◇■1		◇■1	◇■1		◇■1	◇■1	◇■1	◇■1		◇■1	◇■1	◇■1	
				A											B		
																	🛏
		☕		🛒		☕	🛒		☕	🛒	🛒	☕		☕	🛒	☕	☕
London Paddington ■15 ⊖	d	16 57				17 57			18 57			19 00		19 57		20 57	23 50
Slough ■3	d																
Reading ■7	d	17 34				18 34			19 32			19 38		20 34		21 34	00u41
Theale	d																
Thatcham	d																
Newbury	d					18 50								20 50			
Hungerford	d																
Pewsey	d					19 11								21 10			
Westbury	d					19 29								21 29			
Castle Cary	d								20 32					21 47			
Birmingham New Street ■12	d			17 12			18 12			18 42	19 12				20 12		
Cardiff Central ■7	d																
Newport (South Wales)	d																
Swindon	d											20 11					
Bristol Parkway ■7	d			18 25			19 25			20 02	20 25				21 25		
Filton Abbey Wood	d																
Bath Spa ■7	d											20 40					
Bristol Temple Meads ■10	d		18 07	18b44			19c44			20 19	20e44	20 55			21f44		02g55
Weston-super-Mare	d		18 36							20 37		21 27					
Bridgwater	d		18 55														
Taunton	d	18 50	19 10	19 17		20 04	20 21		20 55	21 01	21 17	21 51		22 08	22 17	22s49	
Tiverton Parkway	d	19 02	19 25	19 29		20 18	20 31		21 07	21 13	21 29	22 04		22 21	22 29	23s03	
Exeter St Davids ■6	a	19 18	19 44	19 48		20 34	20 48		21 24	21 28	21 43	22 20		22 38	22 45	23 20	04 05
Exmouth	d				19 24			20 24					21 25				
Exeter Central	d				19 50			20 50					21 50				
Exeter St Davids ■6	d	19 20		19 49	19 56	20 35	20 49	20 56	21 24	21 30	21 44		21 56	22 38	22 48		04 35
Exeter St Thomas	d				19 59								21 59				
Starcross	d				20 07								22 07				
Dawlish Warren	d				20 12								22 12				
Dawlish	d				20 16			21 09	21 37	21 43			22 16				
Teignmouth	d				20 21			21 14	21 43	21 48			22 21				
Newton Abbot	a	19 40		20 07	20 28	20 56	21 07	21 21	21 52	21 55	22 03		22 28	23 00	23 07		04 55
	d	19 41		20 09	20 30	20 56	21 09	21 22	21 52	21 57	22 05		22 30	23 00	23 08		04 56
Torre	d				20 38			21 31					22 38				
Torquay	d				20 41			21 34		22 08			22 41				
Paignton	a				20 48			21 41		22 13			22 49				
Totnes	d	19 54		20 21		21 12	21 22		22 05		22 20			23 13	23 21		
Ivybridge	d																
Plymouth	a	20 22		20 48		21 39	21 49		22 33		22 46			23 43	23 50		05 35
	d	20 25		20 50		21 40											06 28
Devonport	d																
Dockyard	d																
Keyham	d																
St Budeaux Ferry Road	d																
Saltash	d																
St Germans	d																
Menheniot	d																
Liskeard ■6	d	20 49		21 13		22 04											07h09
Bodmin Parkway	d	21 02		21 25		22 19											07 23
Lostwithiel	d																07 29
Par	d	21 13		21 36		22 31											07 38
Newquay	a																
St Austell	d	21 20		21 43		22 39											07 46
Truro	d	21 37		22 01		22 56											08 06
Redruth	d	21 50		22 12		23 09											08 20
Camborne	d	21 58		22 19		23 16											08 27
Hayle	d																08 38
St Erth	d	22 10		22 30		23 27											08 45
Penzance	a	22 22		22 38		23 40											08 59

A 🛒 to Totnes
B 🛒 to Bristol Parkway
b Arr. 1837
c Arr. 1937
e Arr. 2035
f Arr. 2135
g Arr. 0158
h Arr. 0652

For connections to Oxford, Gatwick Airport and Heathrow Airport please refer to Tables 116, 148 and 125A

Table 135

Sundays

26 June to 31 July

London and Birmingham - Devon and Cornwall

Station		GW	XC	GW	GW	XC	GW	GW	XC	GW	GW	GW	XC	GW	GW	GW	XC	GW	GW	GW	GW	GW	XC
			R ◇ A	🚲	◇	◇1 🚲		◇	◇1 🚲		◇1 ☕	◇1 ☕	◇1 B			◇1 ☕	◇1 🚲		◇1 ☕			🚲	◇1 🚲
London Paddington 15 ⊖	d										08 00	08 57				09 57			10 57				
Slough 3	d																						
Reading 7	d										08 38	09 34				10 34			11 34				
Theale	d																						
Thatcham	d																						
Newbury	d											09 51											
Hungerford	d																						
Pewsey	d															11 06							
Westbury	d											10 25											
Castle Cary	d															11 36							
Birmingham New Street 12	d																09 12						
Cardiff Central 7	d																						
Newport (South Wales)	d																10e49						
Swindon	d										09 11												
Bristol Parkway 7	d																11f29						
Filton Abbey Wood	d																						
Bath Spa 7	d										09 45												
Bristol Temple Meads 10	d				07 45	08 44		08 28	09 48		10c01		10 44				11 44						12 57
Weston-super-Mare	d				08 08			08 59															13 15
Bridgwater	d				08 24			09 18															
Taunton	d				08 39	09 16		09 32	10 21		10 36	11 02	11 16			11 58	12 15		12 49				13 37
Tiverton Parkway	d				08 54	09 28		09 48	10 33		10 49	11 15	11 29				12 27						13 49
Exeter St Davids 6	a				09 11	09 42		10 05	10 46		11 06	11 30	11 42			12 23	12 42		13 15				14 03
Exmouth	d						09 10			10 21				11 24				12 29			13 24		
Exeter Central	d						09 36			10 48				11 53				12 55		13 20	13 50		
Exeter St Davids 6	d	08 54			09 13	09 44	09b56	10 09	10 48	10 53	11 08	11 30	11 44	11 58	12 15	12 24	12 44	13 01	13 15	13 25	13 56		14 05
Exeter St Thomas	d	08 57					09 59			10 56				12 01							13 59		
Starcross	d	09 05					10 07			11 05				12 09							14 07		
Dawlish Warren	d	09 10					10 12			11 09				12 14				13 12			14 12		
Dawlish	d	09 14			09 26		10 16	10 23		11 13	11 22			12 18				13 16		13 38	14 16		
Teignmouth	d	09 19			09 31		10 21	10 28		11 18	11 28			12 23				13 21		13 43	14 21		
Newton Abbot	a	09 26			09 39	10 03	10 28	10 34	11 07	11 25	11 36	11 52	12 03	12 30	12 35	12 46	13 03	13 28	13 38	13 50	14 28		14 31
	d	09 28			09 39	10 04	10 39	10 36	11 09	11 27	11 36	11 53	12 04	12 32	12 36	12 46	13 05	13 29	13 39	13 52	14 30		14 32
Torre	d	09 36					10 47			11 35				12 40				13 37		14 00	14 38		
Torquay	d	09 39					10 50			11 38				12 43				13 40		14 03	14 41		
Paignton	a	09 46					10 55			11 45				12 50				13 47		14 10	14 48		
Totnes	d				09 52	10 17		10 49	11 21		11 50	12 07	12 17		12 48	12 59	13 17						14 44
Ivybridge	d				10 09										13 04								
Plymouth	a				10 22	10 43		11 18	11 48		12 18	12 35	12 44		13 17	13 28	13 44		14 17				15 12
	d		09 05	09 15	10 22			11 22			12 20	12 35	12 55			13 31			14 20			14 58	
Devonport	d				10 28																		
Dockyard	d																						
Keyham	d																						
St Budeaux Ferry Road	d			09 21																			
Saltash	d			09 25	10 38			11 31														15 07	
St Germans	d			09 31	10 45			11 38														15 14	
Menheniot	d				10x53			11x46															
Liskeard 6	d		09 30	09 47	10 59			11 52			12 45	13 01	13 18			13 56			14 44			15 26	
Bodmin Parkway	d		09 43	09 59	11 11			12 04			12 57	13 15	13 30			14 08			14 58			15 39	
Lostwithiel	d			10 05	11 16			12 09														15 45	
Par	d		09 56	10 13	11 24			12 16			13 09	13 25	13 41			14 21						15 53	
Newquay	a		11 10													15 26							
St Austell	d			10 20	11 31			12 24			13 17	13 32	13 48						15 13			16 00	
Truro	d			10 39	11 49			12 41			13 35	13 51	14 05						15 32			16 19	
Redruth	d			10 52	12 02			12 54			13 48	14 03	14 17						15 42			16 32	
Camborne	d			10 58	12 08			13 00				14 12	14 25						15 50			16 38	
Hayle	d			11 05	12 15			13 07														16 45	
St Erth	d			11 10	12 19			13 11			14 04	14 23	14 37						16g06			16 50	
Penzance	a			11 22	12 30			13 25			14 13	14 35	14 49						16 20			17 00	

A ◇ to Bodmin Parkway R from Par

B 1 from Plymouth ◇ from Plymouth

b Arr. 0940

c Arr. 0955

e Arr. 1042

f Arr. 1111

g Arr. 1600

For connections to Oxford, Gatwick Airport and Heathrow Airport please refer to Tables 116, 148 and 125A

Table 135

Sundays

26 June to 31 July

London and Birmingham - Devon and Cornwall

		GW	GW	XC	GW	GW		GW	XC	GW	GW	GW	GW	XC	GW	GW		GW	XC	GW	GW	GW	XC	GW	GW
		◇1	◇1	◇1		◇1			◇1	◇1			◇1	◇1				◇1	◇1		◇1		◇1		◇1
																			A						
		☕	☕	🛒		☕			🛒	☕			☕	🛒				☕	🛒		☕		🛒		☕
London Paddington 15 ⊖	d	11 37	11 57			12 57				13 00			13 57					14 57			15 57				16 57
Slough 3	d																								
Reading 7	d	12 14	12 34			13 34				13 38			14 34					15 34			16 34				17 34
Theale	d																								
Thatcham	d																								
Newbury	d		12 50										14 51								16 51				
Hungerford	d																								
Pewsey	d	12 46																							
Westbury	d	13 05				14 19															17 27				
Castle Cary	d	13 22											15 38								17 44				
Birmingham New Street 12	d			11 12					12 12					13 12					14 12				15 12		
Cardiff Central 7	d																								
Newport (South Wales)	d			12b53					13g53					14 48					15l54				16o52		
Swindon	d									14 11															
Bristol Parkway 7	d			13c25					14h29					15j25					16m25				17 26		
Filton Abbey Wood	d																								
Bath Spa 7	d									14 40															
Bristol Temple Meads 10	d			13e44					14 44	14 55				15k44					16n44				17q44		
Weston-super-Mare	d																								
Bridgwater	d																								
Taunton	d	13 44	13 55	14 17		14 55			15 18	15 30			15 58	16 16				16 51	17 18		18 07		18 21		18 50
Tiverton Parkway	d			14 29		15 08			15 31					16 27				17 04	17 31		18 20		18 33		19 02
Exeter St Davids 6	a	14 10	14 19	14 46		15 23			15 46	15 56			16 24	16 43				17 19	17 46		18 36		18 48		19 18
Exmouth	d				14 31						15 24				16 24					17 24				18 24	
Exeter Central	d				14 57			15 20			15 50				16 50					17 50				18 49	
Exeter St Davids 6	d	14 10	14 21	14 48	15 03	15 24		15f31	15 47	15 56	16i00	16 10	16 24	16 44	16 56			17 21	17 47	17 56	18 37		18 49	18 56	19 20
Exeter St Thomas	d										16 03	16 12								17 59				18 59	
Starcross	d										16 11									18 07				19 07	
Dawlish Warren	d	14 24									16 16									18 12				19 12	
Dawlish	d	14 27			15 15			15 43			16 20	16 25			17 09					18 16				19 16	
Teignmouth	d	14 34			15 20			15 48			16 25	16 30			17 14					18 21				19 21	
Newton Abbot	a	14 42	14 46	15 08	15 27	15 46		15 55	16 07	16 18	16 32	16 36	16 44	17 03	17 21			17 42	18 07	18 28	18 57		19 07	19 28	19 40
	d	14 42	14 48	15 09	15 28	15 46		15 56	16 08	16 18	16 33	16 36	16 44	17 05	17 22			17 42	18 08	18 29	18 59		19 08	19 30	19 41
Torre	d				15 37			16 04			16 41				17 31					18 37				19 38	
Torquay	d	14 54			15 40			16 07			16 44				17 34					18 40				19 41	
Paignton	a	15 03			15 50			16 15			16 51				17 41					18 47				19 48	
Totnes	d		15 00	15 23		16 00			16 22			16 52	17 02	17 17				17 57	18 22				19 21		19 54
Ivybridge	d											17 08													
Plymouth	a		15 35	15 53		16 31			16 50	16 57		17 22	17 30	17 44				18 24	18 51		19 37		19 48		20 22
	d		15 35			16 35						17 35						18 25	18 55			19 43			20 25
Devonport	d																								
Dockyard	d																								
Keyham	d																								
St Budeaux Ferry Road	d																								
Saltash	d											17 45										19 52			
St Germans	d											17 52										19 59			
Menheniot	d											18x00													
Liskeard 6	d		16 00			16 58						18 06						18 50	19 18			20 11			20 49
Bodmin Parkway	d		16 13			17 11						18 18						19 04	19 30			20 23			21 02
Lostwithiel	d											18 23										20 28			
Par	d		16 25			17 23						18 31						19 14	19 41			20 36			21 13
Newquay	a																								
St Austell	d		16 32			17 29						18 39						19 21	19 52			20 43			21 20
Truro	d		16 51			17 48						18 56						19 39	20 09			21 00			21 37
Redruth	d		17 03			18 00						19 09						19 51	20 20			21 14			21 50
Camborne	d		17 10			18 08						19 15						20 01	20 28			21 20			21 58
Hayle	d											19 22										21 27			
St Erth	d		17 22			18 20						19 27				20 05		20 14	20 39			21 32			22 10
Penzance	a		17 32			18 32						19 38				20 14		20 25	20 47			21 42			22 22

A 🛒 to Totnes
b Arr. 1247
c Arr. 1317
e Arr. 1336
f Arr. 1523
g Arr. 1347
h Arr. 1417
i Arr. 1553
j Arr. 1512
k Arr. 1535
l Arr. 1548
m Arr. 1616
n Arr. 1636
o Arr. 1645
q Arr. 1736

For connections to Oxford, Gatwick Airport and Heathrow Airport please refer to Tables 116, 148 and 125A

Table 135

Sundays

26 June to 31 July

London and Birmingham - Devon and Cornwall

		GW		XC	GW	GW	XC	GW	GW	XC	GW	GW		GW	XC	GW	GW
																	R
		◇		◇1		◇1	◇1		◇1	◇1	◇1			◇1	◇1	◇1	
				A						B					B		
				🛒		☕	🛒		☕	🛒	☕			☕	🛒	☕	🛏 ☕
London Paddington 15 ⊖	d					17 57			18 57		19 00			19 57		20 57	23 50
Slough 3	d																
Reading 7	d					18 34			19 32		19 38			20 34		21 34	00u41
Theale	d																
Thatcham	d																
Newbury	d					18 50								20 50			
Hungerford	d																
Pewsey	d					19 11								21 10			
Westbury	d					19 29								21 29			
Castle Cary	d								20 32					21 47			
Birmingham New Street 12	d			16 12			17 12			18 12					19 12		
Cardiff Central 7	d																
Newport (South Wales)	d			17 49			18 49			19 53					20h52		
Swindon	d										20 11						
Bristol Parkway 7	d			18b26			19c25			20f25					21i25		
Filton Abbey Wood	d																
Bath Spa 7	d										20 40						
Bristol Temple Meads 10	d	18 07		18 44			19e44			20g44	20 55				21j44		02k55
Weston-super-Mare	d	18 36									21 27						
Bridgwater	d	18 55															
Taunton	d	19 10		19 17		20 04	20 21		20 55	21 17	21 51			22 08	22 17	22s49	
Tiverton Parkway	d	19 25		19 29		20 18	20 33		21 07	21 29	22 04			22 21	22 29	23s03	
Exeter St Davids 6	a	19 44		19 48		20 34	20 48		21 24	21 43	22 20			22 38	22 45	23 20	04 05
Exmouth	d				19 24			20 24				21 25					
Exeter Central	d				19 50			20 50				21 50					
Exeter St Davids 6	d			19 49	19 56	20 35	20 49	20 56	21 24	21 44		21 56		22 38	22 48		04 35
Exeter St Thomas	d				19 59							21 59					
Starcross	d				20 07							22 07					
Dawlish Warren	d				20 12							22 12					
Dawlish	d				20 16			21 09	21 37			22 16					
Teignmouth	d				20 21			21 14	21 43			22 21					
Newton Abbot	a			20 07	20 28	20 56	21 07	21 21	21 52	22 03		22 28		23 00	23 06		04 55
	d			20 09	20 30	20 56	21 09	21 22	21 52	22 05		22 30		23 00	23 07		04 56
Torre	d				20 38			21 31				22 38					
Torquay	d				20 41			21 34				22 41					
Paignton	a				20 48			21 41				22 49					
Totnes	d			20 21		21 12	21 22		22 05	22 20				23 13	23 21		
Ivybridge	d																
Plymouth	a			20 48		21 39	21 49		22 33	22 46				23 43	23 51		05 35
	d			20 50		21 40											06 28
Devonport	d																
Dockyard	d																
Keyham	d																
St Budeaux Ferry Road	d																
Saltash	d																
St Germans	d																
Menheniot	d																
Liskeard 6	d			21 13		22 04											07l09
Bodmin Parkway	d			21 25		22 19											07 23
Lostwithiel	d																07 29
Par	d			21 36		22 31											07 38
Newquay	a																
St Austell	d			21 43		22 39											07 46
Truro	d			22 01		22 56											08 06
Redruth	d			22 12		23 09											08 20
Camborne	d			22 19		23 16											08 27
Hayle	d																08 38
St Erth	d			22 30		23 27											08 45
Penzance	a			22 38		23 40											08 59

A 🛒 to Totnes
B 🛒 to Bristol Parkway
b Arr. 1812
c Arr. 1912
e Arr. 1935
f Arr. 2015
g Arr. 2035
h Arr. 2044
i Arr. 2112
j Arr. 2135
k Arr. 0158
l Arr. 0652

For connections to Oxford, Gatwick Airport and Heathrow Airport please refer to Tables 116, 148 and 125A

Table 135

Sundays

7 August to 11 September

London and Birmingham - Devon and Cornwall

		GW	XC	GW	GW	XC	GW	GW	XC	GW	GW	GW	XC	GW	GW	GW	GW	XC	GW	GW	GW	XC	GW
			■ ◇ A	(trolley)	◇	◇1 (trolley)		◇	◇1 (trolley)		◇1 (restaurant)	◇1 (restaurant)	◇1 B (trolley)	(bus)			◇1 (restaurant)	◇1 (trolley)		◇1 (restaurant)		◇1 (trolley)	
London Paddington 15 ⊖	d										08 00	08 51					09 30			10 30			
Slough 3	d																						
Reading 7	d										08 38	09 27					10 06			11 09			
Theale	d																						
Thatcham	d																						
Newbury	d																						
Hungerford	d																						
Pewsey	d													09 30									
Westbury	d											10 25					11f17						
Castle Cary	d																11 35						
Birmingham New Street 12	d												09 12					10 12				11 12	
Cardiff Central 7	d																						
Newport (South Wales)	d																						
Swindon	d										09 06			10a15									
Bristol Parkway 7	d												10 24					11 29				12 25	
Filton Abbey Wood	d																						
Bath Spa 7	d										09 38												
Bristol Temple Meads 10	d				07 45	08 44		08 28	09 48		10c01		10e44					11 44				12i44	
Weston-super-Mare	d				08 08			08 59															
Bridgwater	d				08 24			09 18															
Taunton	d				08 39	09 16		09 32	10 21		10 36	11 01	11 16				11 57	12 16		12g49		13 16	
Tiverton Parkway	d				08 54	09 28		09 48	10 33		10 49	11 14	11 29					12 28				13 29	
Exeter St Davids 6	a				09 11	09 42		10 05	10 46		11 06	11 29	11 42				12 22	12 45		13 15		13 45	
Exmouth	d						09 10			10 21					11 24				12 29				13 24
Exeter Central	d						09 36			10 48					11 53				12 55		13 20		13 50
Exeter St Davids 6	d	08 54			09 13	09 44	09b56	10 09	10 48	10 53	11 08	11 29	11 44		11 58	12 15	12 23	12 47	13 01	13 15	13 25	13 47	13 56
Exeter St Thomas	d	08 57					09 59			10 56					12 01								13 59
Starcross	d	09 05					10 07			11 05					12 09								14 07
Dawlish Warren	d	09 10					10 12			11 09					12 14				13 12				14 12
Dawlish	d	09 14			09 26		10 16	10 23		11 13	11 22				12 18				13 16		13 38		14 16
Teignmouth	d	09 19			09 31		10 21	10 28		11 18	11 28				12 23				13 21		13 43		14 21
Newton Abbot	a	09 26			09 39	10 03	10 28	10 34	11 07	11 25	11 36	11 52	12 03		12 30	12 35	12 45	13 07	13 28	13 38	13 50	14 07	14 28
	d	09 28			09 39	10 04	10 39	10 36	11 09	11 27	11 36	11 54	12 04		12 32	12 36	12 45	13 09	13 29	13 40	13 52	14 09	14 30
Torre	d	09 36					10 47			11 35					12 40				13 37		14 00		14 38
Torquay	d	09 39					10 50			11 38					12 43				13 40		14 03		14 41
Paignton	a	09 46					10 55			11 45					12 50				13 47		14 10		14 48
Totnes	d				09 52	10 17		10 49	11 21		11 50	12 06	12 17			12 48	12 59	13 22				14 22	
Ivybridge	d				10 09											13 04							
Plymouth	a				10 22	10 43		11 18	11 48		12 18	12 34	12 44			13 17	13 28	13 50		14 17		14 50	
	d		09 05	09 15	10 22			11 22			12 20	12 34	12 55				13 31			14 20			
Devonport	d				10 28																		
Dockyard	d																						
Keyham	d																						
St Budeaux Ferry Road	d			09 21																			
Saltash	d			09 25	10 38			11 31															
St Germans	d			09 31	10 45			11 38															
Menheniot	d				10x53			11x46															
Liskeard 6	d		09 30	09 47	10 59			11 52			12 45	13 00	13 18				13 55			14 44			
Bodmin Parkway	d		09 43	09 59	11 11			12 04			12 57	13 15	13 30				14 08			14 58			
Lostwithiel	d			10 05	11 16			12 09															
Par	d		09 56	10 13	11 24			12 16			13 09	13 26	13 41				14 21						
Newquay	a		11 10														15 26						
St Austell	d			10 20	11 31			12 24			13 17	13 33	13 48							15 13			
Truro	d			10 39	11 49			12 41			13 35	13 52	14 05							15 32			
Redruth	d			10 52	12 02			12 54			13 48	14 04	14 20							15 42			
Camborne	d			10 58	12 08			13 00				14 11	14 27							15 50			
Hayle	d			11 05	12 15			13 07															
St Erth	d			11 10	12 19			13 11			14 04	14 23	14 38							16h06			
Penzance	a			11 22	12 30			13 25			14 13	14 35	14 49							16 20			

A ◇ to Bodmin Parkway ■ from Par
B (trolley) to Totnes
b Arr. 0940
c Arr. 0952
e Arr. 1034
f Arr. 1109
g Arr. 1240
h Arr. 1600
i Arr. 1236

For connections to Oxford, Gatwick Airport and Heathrow Airport please refer to Tables 116, 148 and 125A

Table 135

London and Birmingham - Devon and Cornwall

Sundays

18 September to 23 October

		GW	XC	GW	GW	XC	GW	GW	XC	GW	GW	GW	GW	GW	XC	GW	GW	GW	GW	XC	GW	GW	GW
			◇		◇	◇1		◇	◇1		◇1	◇1			◇1	◇1			◇1	◇1			◇1
				trolley		trolley			trolley		restaurant	restaurant	bus		trolley	restaurant			restaurant	trolley			restaurant
London Paddington 15 ⊖	d										08 00	08 51				09 30			10 30				11 00
Slough 3	d																						
Reading 7	d										08 38	09 27				10 06			11 06				11 38
Theale	d																						
Thatcham	d																						
Newbury	d																						
Hungerford	d																						
Pewsey	d												09 30										
Westbury	d											10 34				11e16							
Castle Cary	d															11 34							
Birmingham New Street 12	d																						
Cardiff Central 7	d																						
Newport (South Wales)	d																						
Swindon	d										09 11		10a15										12 11
Bristol Parkway 7	d																						
Filton Abbey Wood	d																						
Bath Spa 7	d										09 40												12 40
Bristol Temple Meads 10	d				07 45	08 44		08 28	09 48		10c03				11 15					12 15			12 58
Weston-super-Mare	d				08 08			08 59															13 19
Bridgwater	d				08 24			09 18															
Taunton	d				08 39	09 16		09 32	10 21		10 38	11 11			11 47	11 55			12 38	12 49			13 41
Tiverton Parkway	d				08 54	09 28		09 48	10 33		10 51	11 24			11 59					13 01			
Exeter St Davids 6	a				09 11	09 42		10 05	10 46		11 08	11 40			12 13	12 20			13 04	13 15			14 07
Exmouth	d						09 10			10 21				11 24				12 29				13 24	
Exeter Central	d						09 36			10 48				11 53				12 55			13 20	13 50	
Exeter St Davids 6	d	08 54			09 13	09 44	09b56	10 06	10 48	10 53	11 11	11 40		11 58	12 15	12 22	12 27	13 01	13 08	13 17	13 25	13 56	14 07
Exeter St Thomas	d	08 57					09 59			10 56				12 01								13 59	
Starcross	d	09 05					10 07			11 05				12 09								14 07	
Dawlish Warren	d	09 10					10 12			11 09				12 14				13 12				14 12	
Dawlish	d	09 14			09 26		10 16	10 20		11 13	11 27			12 18				13 16			13 38	14 16	14 19
Teignmouth	d	09 19			09 31		10 21	10 25		11 18	11 33			12 23				13 21			13 43	14 21	14 26
Newton Abbot	a	09 26			09 39	10 03	10 28	10 31	11 07	11 25	11 40	12 02		12 30	12 34	12 43	12 49	13 28	13 32	13 37	13 50	14 28	14 35
	d	09 28			09 39	10 04	10 39	10 33	11 09	11 27	11 41	12 03		12 32	12 35	12 44	12 52	13 29	13 34	13 39	13 52	14 30	14 36
Torre	d	09 36					10 47			11 35				12 40				13 37			14 00	14 38	
Torquay	d	09 39					10 50			11 38				12 43				13 40			14 03	14 41	14 47
Paignton	a	09 46					10 55			11 45				12 50				13 47			14 10	14 48	14 55
Totnes	d				09 52	10 17		10 46	11 21		11 54	12 16			12 48	12 57	13 05			13 53			
Ivybridge	d				10 09												13 21						
Plymouth	a				10 22	10 43		11 15	11 48		12 22	12 44			13 14	13 26	13 34		14 10	14 19			
	d		09 01	09 14	10 22			11 16				12 50							14 20				
Devonport	d				10 28																		
Dockyard	d																						
Keyham	d																						
St Budeaux Ferry Road	d																						
Saltash	d			09 23	10 38			11 25															
St Germans	d			09 30	10 45			11 32															
Menheniot	d				10x53			11x40															
Liskeard 6	d		09 26	09 42	10 59			11 46				13 17							14 44				
Bodmin Parkway	d		09 39	09 54	11 11			11 58				13 30							14 58				
Lostwithiel	d			10 00	11 16			12 03															
Par	d		09 50	10 08	11 24			12 11				13 40											
Newquay	a																						
St Austell	d		09 58	10 15	11 31			12 19				13 48							15 13				
Truro	d		10 17	10 34	11 49			12 36				14 06							15 32				
Redruth	d		10 29	10 47	12 02			12 49				14 19							15 42				
Camborne	d		10 36	10 53	12 08			12 55				14 26							15 50				
Hayle	d			11 01	12 15			13 02															
St Erth	d		10 47	11 05	12 19			13 06				14 37							16f06				
Penzance	a		10 56	11 18	12 30			13 18				14 52							16 20				

b Arr. 0940
c Arr. 0955
e Arr. 1107
f Arr. 1600

For connections to Oxford, Gatwick Airport and Heathrow Airport please refer to Tables 116, 148 and 125A

Table 135

Sundays

18 September to 23 October

London and Birmingham - Devon and Cornwall

		GW	GW	GW	XC	GW		XC	GW	GW	GW	GW	GW	XC	GW	GW		GW	GW	GW	GW	GW	XC	GW	XC
				◇1	◇1			◇1	◇1		◇1		◇1	◇1								◇1	◇1		◇1
																A		B							C
		[bus]	[trolley]	[restaurant]	[trolley]			[trolley]	[restaurant]		[restaurant]		[restaurant]	[trolley]	[bus]					[bus]		[restaurant]	[trolley]		[trolley]
London Paddington 15 ⊖	d			11 30					12 30		13 00		13 30									14 30			
Slough 3	d																								
Reading 7	d			12 06					13 09		13 38		14 06									15 06			
Theale	d																								
Thatcham	d																								
Newbury	d																								
Hungerford	d																								
Pewsey	d	11 34													15 30					17 55					
Westbury	d																								
Castle Cary	d												15e25												
Birmingham New Street 12	d																								
Cardiff Central 7	d																								
Newport (South Wales)	d																								
Swindon	d	12a19		12 36					13 38		14 11				16a15					18a40					
Bristol Parkway 7	d																								
Filton Abbey Wood	d																								
Bath Spa 7	d										14 40														
Bristol Temple Meads 10	d				13 15			14 15			14 57			15 15									16 15		17 15
Weston-super-Mare	d																								
Bridgwater	d																								
Taunton	d			13 49	13 55			14 47	14 55		15 30		15 45	15 53								16 39	16 47		17 47
Tiverton Parkway	d				14 07			14 59	15 08					16 05								16 52	16 59		18 00
Exeter St Davids 6	a			14 13	14 20			15 13	15 23		15 55		16 12	16 18								17 07	17 13		18 13
Exmouth	d					14 31						15 24							16 24					17 24	
Exeter Central	d					14 57				15 20		15 50							16 50					17 50	
Exeter St Davids 6	d			14 14	14 22	15 03		15 17	15 24	15b31	15 56	16c00	16 13	16 20		16 23		16 23	16 56			17 09	17 15	17 56	18 15
Exeter St Thomas	d											16 03				16 25		16 25						17 59	
Starcross	d											16 11												18 07	
Dawlish Warren	d											16 16												18 12	
Dawlish	d					15 15				15 43		16 20				16 38		16 38	17 09					18 16	
Teignmouth	d					15 20				15 48		16 25				16 43		16 43	17 14					18 21	
Newton Abbot	a			14 39	14 51	15 27		15 36	15 46	15 55	16 17	16 32	16 34	16 42		16 49		16 49	17 21			17 29	17 35	18 28	18 34
	d			14 40	14 53	15 28		15 37	15 47	15 56	16 18	16 33	16 34	16 43		16 49		16 49	17 22			17 29	17 37	18 29	18 35
Torre	d					15 37				16 04		16 41							17 31					18 37	
Torquay	d					15 40				16 07		16 44							17 34					18 40	
Paignton	a					15 50				16 15		16 51							17 41					18 47	
Totnes	d			14 53	15 09			15 50	16 00				16 51	16 59		17 07		17 07				17 44	17 52		18 48
Ivybridge	d															17 23		17 23							
Plymouth	a			15 21	15 35			16 16	16 31		16 55		17 19	17 28		17 37		17 37				18 11	18 20		19 15
	d		14 58	15 33					16 35							17 39		17 49				18 25			19 20
Devonport	d																								
Dockyard	d																								
Keyham	d																								
St Budeaux Ferry Road	d																								
Saltash	d		15 07													17 48		17 58							
St Germans	d		15 14													17 55		18 05							
Menheniot	d															18x03		18x13							
Liskeard 6	d		15 26	16 00					16 58							18 09		18 19				18 50			19 43
Bodmin Parkway	d		15 39	16 13					17 11							18 21		18 31				19 04			19 55
Lostwithiel	d		15 45													18 26		18 36							
Par	d		15 53	16 25					17 23							18 34		18 44				19 14			20 06
Newquay	a																								
St Austell	d		16 00	16 32					17 29							18 41		18 51				19 21			20 13
Truro	d		16 19	16 51					17 48							18 59		19 09				19 39			20 30
Redruth	d		16 32	17 03					18 00							19 12		19 22				19 51			20 41
Camborne	d		16 38	17 11					18 08							19 18		19 28				20 01			20 48
Hayle	d		16 45													19 25		19 35							
St Erth	d		16 50	17 22					18 20							19 29		19 39			20 05	20 16			20 59
Penzance	a		17 00	17 32					18 32							19 41		19 51			20 14	20 27			21 07

A not from 18 September until 25 September
B 18 September, 25 September
C 1 from Plymouth [trolley] to Totnes ◇ from Plymouth
b Arr. 1523
c Arr. 1553
e Arr. 1518

For connections to Oxford, Gatwick Airport and Heathrow Airport please refer to Tables 116, 148 and 125A

Table 135

Sundays

London and Birmingham - Devon and Cornwall

18 September to 23 October

		GW		GW	GW	GW	XC	GW	GW	XC	GW	GW		XC	GW	GW	XC	GW	GW	GW	GW	GW		GW
																								R
		◇1				◇1	◇1	◇		◇1	◇1			◇1	◇1		◇1	◇1	◇1		◇1			
										A														
		🍴				🍴	🛒			🛒	🍴				🍴			🍴	🍴	🚌	🍴	🚌		🛏 🍴
London Paddington 15 ⊖	d	15 30				16 30					17 57				18 57			19 00	19 57		20 57			23 50
Slough 3	d																							
Reading 7	d	16 06				17 09					18 33				19 34			19 38	20 33		21 34			00u38
Theale	d																							
Thatcham	d																							
Newbury	d																							
Hungerford	d																							
Pewsey	d																			20 05		22 00		
Westbury	d	17b24									19 37				20 37				21 38					
Castle Cary	d	17 42									19 54				20 55				21 56					
Birmingham New Street 12	d																							
Cardiff Central 7	d																							
Newport (South Wales)	d																							
Swindon	d																	20 11		20a50		22a45		
Bristol Parkway 7	d																							
Filton Abbey Wood	d																							
Bath Spa 7	d																	20 40						
Bristol Temple Meads 10	d						18 15	18 07		19 15				20 15			21 15	20 55						02c55
Weston-super-Mare	d							18 46										21 27						
Bridgwater	d							19 05																
Taunton	d	18 04				18 46	18 54	19 20		19 47	20 15			20 47	21 17		21 47	21 51	22 16		23s09			
Tiverton Parkway	d	18 17				18 58	19 06	19 35		20 00	20 29			20 59	21 30		21 59	22 04	22 29		23s23			
Exeter St Davids 6	a	18 36				19 14	19 19	19 54		20 13	20 45			21 13	21 46		22 13	22 20	22 46		23 40			04 05
Exmouth	d			18 24					19 24			20 24				21 25								
Exeter Central	d			18 49					19 50			20 50				21 50								
Exeter St Davids 6	d	18 36		18 56		19 15	19 21		19 56	20 15	20 45	20 56		21 15	21 46	21 56	22 15		22 47					04 35
Exeter St Thomas	d			18 59					19 59							21 59								
Starcross	d			19 07					20 07							22 07								
Dawlish Warren	d			19 12					20 12							22 12								
Dawlish	d			19 16					20 16			21 09			21 59	22 16								
Teignmouth	d			19 21					20 21			21 14			22 06	22 21								
Newton Abbot	a	18 57		19 28		19 36	19 41		20 28	20 34	21 07	21 21		21 34	22 14	22 28	22 35		23 08					04 55
	d	18 58		19 30		19 36	19 43		20 30	20 35	21 07	21 22		21 35	22 14	22 30	22 37		23 09					04 56
Torre	d			19 38					20 38			21 31				22 38								
Torquay	d			19 41					20 41			21 34				22 41								
Paignton	a			19 48					20 48			21 41				22 49								
Totnes	d					19 50	19 57			20 48	21 22			21 48	22 28		22 49		23 21					
Ivybridge	d																							
Plymouth	a	19 36				20 18	20 26			21 15	21 49			22 14	22 59		23 16		23 51					05 35
	d				19 43	20 19				21 20	21 50													06 28
Devonport	d																							
Dockyard	d																							
Keyham	d																							
St Budeaux Ferry Road	d																							
Saltash	d				19 52																			
St Germans	d				19 59																			
Menheniot	d																							
Liskeard 6	d				20 11	20 44				21 43	22 16													07e09
Bodmin Parkway	d				20 23	20 57				21 55	22 29													07 23
Lostwithiel	d				20 28																			07 29
Par	d				20 36	21 09				22 06	22 42													07 38
Newquay	a																							
St Austell	d				20 43	21 15				22 13	22 49													07 46
Truro	d				21 00	21 33				22 30	23 07													08 06
Redruth	d				21 14	21 46				22 41	23 19													08 20
Camborne	d				21 20	21 53				22 48	23 26													08 27
Hayle	d				21 27																			08 38
St Erth	d				21 32	22 05				22 59	23 38													08 45
Penzance	a				21 42	22 17				23 07	23 51													08 59

A 1 from Plymouth 🛒 to Totnes ◇ from Plymouth

b Arr. 1703

c Arr. 0156

e Arr. 0652

For connections to Oxford, Gatwick Airport and Heathrow Airport please refer to Tables 116, 148 and 125A

Table 135

Sundays
from 30 October

London and Birmingham - Devon and Cornwall

		GW	XC	GW	GW	GW	GW	XC	GW	GW		GW	XC	GW	GW	GW	XC	GW	GW	GW		XC	GW	GW	GW
			◇		◇		◇	◇1		◇1		◇1	◇1			◇1	◇1		◇1			◇1		◇1	
													A												
				trolley				trolley		restaurant		restaurant	trolley			restaurant	trolley		restaurant			trolley		restaurant	trolley
London Paddington 15 ⊖	d									08 30		08 57				09 57			10 57					11 37	
Slough 3	d																								
Reading 7	d									09 04		09 32				10 32			11 32					12 12	
Theale	d																								
Thatcham	d																								
Newbury	d											09 49													
Hungerford	d																								
Pewsey	d															11 04								12 44	
Westbury	d									09 57		10 23												13 05	
Castle Cary	d															11 36								13 22	
Birmingham New Street 12	d												09 12				10 12					11 12			
Cardiff Central 7	d																								
Newport (South Wales)	d																								
Swindon	d																								
Bristol Parkway 7	d												10 25				11 29					12 25			
Filton Abbey Wood	d																								
Bath Spa 7	d																								
Bristol Temple Meads 10	d							08 44					10b44				11 44					12e44			
Weston-super-Mare	d				08 08		08 58																		
Bridgwater	d				08 24		09 17																		
Taunton	d				08 38		09 31	09 50		10 32		11 00	11 16			11 58	12 16		12 49			13 16		13 44	
Tiverton Parkway	d				08 53		09 47	10 02		10 45		11 13	11 29				12 28					13 29			
Exeter St Davids 6	a				09 12		10 04	10 15		11 02		11 29	11 42			12 23	12 45		13 16			13 45		14 10	
Exmouth	d																								
Exeter Central	d																								
Exeter St Davids 6	d	08 54			09 13	09 53	10 05	10 17	10 53	11 04		11 29	11 44	11 58	12 15	12 24	12 47	13 00	13 16	13 25		13 47	13 56	14 10	
Exeter St Thomas	d	08 57				09 56			10 56					12 01									13 59		
Starcross	d	09 05				10 04			11 05					12 09									14 07		
Dawlish Warren	d	09 10				10 09			11 09					12 14				13 11					14 12		
Dawlish	d	09 14			09 26	10 13	10 19		11 13	11 19				12 18				13 15		13 38			14 16	14 22	
Teignmouth	d	09 19			09 31	10 18	10 24		11 18	11 25				12 23				13 20		13 43			14 21	14 29	
Newton Abbot	a	09 26			09 38	10 25	10 30	10 41	11 25	11 31		11 51	12 03	12 30	12 35	12 46	13 07	13 27	13 37	13 50		14 07	14 28	14 37	
	d	09 28			09 39	10 36	10 32	10 42	11 27	11 32		11 52	12 04	12 32	12 36	12 46	13 09	13 28	13 38	13 52		14 09	14 30	14 37	
Torre	d	09 36				10 44			11 35					12 40				13 36		14 00			14 38		
Torquay	d	09 39				10 47			11 38					12 43				13 39		14 03			14 41	14 50	
Paignton	a	09 46				10 52			11 45					12 50				13 46		14 10			14 48	14 58	
Totnes	d				09 52		10 45	10 58		11 45		12 05	12 17		12 48	12 59	13 22					14 22			
Ivybridge	d				10 08										13 04										
Plymouth	a				10 22		11 14	11 25		12 13		12 33	12 44		13 17	13 28	13 50		14 15			14 50			
	d		09 01	09 14	10 24		11 15					12 35	12 55						14 20						14 58
Devonport	d				10 30																				
Dockyard	d																								
Keyham	d																								
St Budeaux Ferry Road	d																								
Saltash	d			09 23	10 40		11 24																		15 07
St Germans	d			09 30	10 47		11 31																		15 14
Menheniot	d				10x56		11x39																		
Liskeard 6	d		09 26	09 42	11 02		11 45					12 58	13 18						14 44						15 26
Bodmin Parkway	d		09 39	09 54	11 14		11 57					13 12	13 30						14 58						15 39
Lostwithiel	d			10 00	11 19		12 02																		15 45
Par	d		09 50	10 08	11 26		12 09					13 23	13 41												15 53
Newquay	a																								
St Austell	d		09 58	10 15	11 33		12 17					13 29	13 48						15 13						16 00
Truro	d		10 17	10 34	11 51		12 34					13 49	14 05						15 32						16 19
Redruth	d		10 29	10 47	12 05		12 47					14 00	14 19						15 42						16 32
Camborne	d		10 36	10 53	12 11		12 53					14 09	14 25						15 50						16 38
Hayle	d			11 01	12 18		13 00																		16 45
St Erth	d		10 47	11 05	12 24		13 04					14 21	14 37						16c06						16 50
Penzance	a		10 56	11 18	12 42		13 18					14 33	14 49						16 20						17 00

A trolley to Totnes
b Arr. 1035
c Arr. 1600
e Arr. 1236

For connections to Oxford, Gatwick Airport and Heathrow Airport please refer to Tables 116, 148 and 125A

Table 135

Sundays
from 30 October

London and Birmingham - Devon and Cornwall

		GW	XC	GW	GW	GW		XC	GW	GW	GW	XC	GW	XC	GW	GW		XC	GW	GW	GW	XC	GW	GW	XC
		◇1	◇1		◇1			◇1			◇1	◇1		◇1		◇1		◇1		◇1		◇1		◇1	◇1
																		A							A
		☕	🛒		☕			🛒			☕	🛒		🛒		☕		🛒		☕		🛒		☕	🛒
London Paddington 15 ⊖	d	11 57			12 57						13 57					14 57				15 57				16 57	
Slough 3	d																								
Reading 7	d	12 32			13 32						14 35					15 32				16 32				17 32	
Theale	d																								
Thatcham	d																								
Newbury	d	12 48									14 51									16 49					
Hungerford	d																								
Pewsey	d																								
Westbury	d				14 19															17 25					
Castle Cary	d										15 38									17 42					
Birmingham New Street 12	d		12 12					13 12				14 12		14 42				15 12				16 12			17 12
Cardiff Central 7	d																								
Newport (South Wales)	d																								
Swindon	d																								
Bristol Parkway 7	d		13 25					14 25				15 26		16 00				16 25				17 25			18 25
Filton Abbey Wood	d																								
Bath Spa 7	d																								
Bristol Temple Meads 10	d		13b44					14 44				15c44		16 14				16e44				17f44			18 44
Weston-super-Mare	d																								
Bridgwater	d																								
Taunton	d	13 54	14 17		14 55			15 17			15 58	16 17		16 46		16 49		17 17		18 05		18 20		18 50	19 17
Tiverton Parkway	d	14 07	14 29		15 08			15 29				16 28		16 58		17 02		17 29		18 18		18 32		19 02	19 29
Exeter St Davids 6	a	14 23	14 44		15 24			15 43			16 25	16 46		17 12		17 17		17 43		18 36		18 46		19 18	19 48
Exmouth	d																								
Exeter Central	d																								
Exeter St Davids 6	d	14 24	14 46	15 03	15 25	15 31		15 44	16 00	16 10	16 26	16 47	16 56	17 14		17 19		17 44	17 56	18 37		18 47	18 56	19 20	19 49
Exeter St Thomas	d								16 03	16 12									17 59				18 59		
Starcross	d								16 11										18 07				19 07		
Dawlish Warren	d								16 16										18 12				19 12		
Dawlish	d			15 15		15 43			16 20	16 25			17 09	17 26					18 16				19 16		
Teignmouth	d			15 20		15 48			16 25	16 30			17 14	17 31					18 21				19 21		
Newton Abbot	a	14 46	15 04	15 27	15 47	15 55		16 03	16 32	16 36	16 45	17 07	17 21	17 38		17 39		18 03	18 28	18 57		19 06	19 28	19 40	20 07
	d	14 48	15 04	15 28	15 47	15 56		16 04	16 33	16 36	16 45	17 09	17 22	17 39		17 39		18 04	18 29	18 59		19 08	19 30	19 41	20 09
Torre	d			15 37		16 04			16 41				17 31						18 37				19 38		
Torquay	d			15 40		16 07			16 44				17 34	17 51					18 40				19 41		
Paignton	a			15 50		16 15			16 51				17 41	17 57					18 47				19 48		
Totnes	d	15 00	15 18		16 01			16 17		16 52	17 01	17 22				17 54		18 17				19 20		19 54	20 21
Ivybridge	d									17 08															
Plymouth	a	15 28	15 44		16 29			16 44		17 22	17 30	17 50				18 21		18 44		19 37		19 47		20 22	20 48
	d	15 31			16 35					17 35						18 25		18 55			19 43			20 24	20 50
Devonport	d																								
Dockyard	d																								
Keyham	d																								
St Budeaux Ferry Road	d																								
Saltash	d									17 45											19 52				
St Germans	d									17 52											19 59				
Menheniot	d									18x00															
Liskeard 6	d	16 00			16 58					18 06						18 48		19 18			20 11			20 49	21 13
Bodmin Parkway	d	16 13			17 11					18 18						19 02		19 30			20 23			21 02	21 25
Lostwithiel	d									18 23											20 28				
Par	d	16 25			17 23					18 31						19 12		19 41			20 36			21 13	21 36
Newquay	a																								
St Austell	d	16 32			17 29					18 38						19 19		19 52			20 43			21 20	21 43
Truro	d	16 49			17 48					18 56						19 37		20 09			21 00			21 37	22 01
Redruth	d	17 03			18 00					19 09						19 49		20 20			21 14			21 50	22 12
Camborne	d	17 11			18 08					19 15						19 58		20 28			21 20			21 58	22 19
Hayle	d									19 22											21 27				
St Erth	d	17 22			18 20					19 26					20 05	20 14		20 39			21 32			22 10	22 30
Penzance	a	17 36			18 32					19 38					20 14	20 25		20 47			21 42			22 22	22 38

A 🛒 to Totnes
b Arr. 1335
c Arr. 1538
e Arr. 1635
f Arr. 1735

For connections to Oxford, Gatwick Airport and Heathrow Airport please refer to Tables 116, 148 and 125A

Table 135

Sundays
from 30 October

London and Birmingham - Devon and Cornwall

		GW		GW	GW	XC	GW	GW	XC	GW	GW	GW		XC	GW	GW
		◇			◇1 ⊏	◇1 ⚲		◇1 ⊏	◇1 A ⚲	◇1 ⊏		◇1 ⊏		◇1 A ⚲	◇1 ⊏	▪ ⊏
London Paddington 15 ⊖	d				17 57			18 55		19 03		19 57			20 57	23 50
Slough 3	d															
Reading 7	d				18 32			19 32		19 39		20 32			21 32	00u37
Theale	d															
Thatcham	d															
Newbury	d				18 48							20 49				
Hungerford	d															
Pewsey	d				19 09							21 09				
Westbury	d				19 29							21 28				
Castle Cary	d							20 30				21 46				
Birmingham New Street 12	d					18 12			19 12					20 12		
Cardiff Central 7	d															
Newport (South Wales)	d															
Swindon	d															
Bristol Parkway 7	d					19 25			20 25					21 25		
Filton Abbey Wood	d															
Bath Spa 7	d									20 54						
Bristol Temple Meads 10	d	18 25				19b44			20c44	21 10				21e44		02f55
Weston-super-Mare	d	18 58								21 40						
Bridgwater	d	19 17														
Taunton	d	19 32			20 03	20 20		20 52	21 17	22 03		22 06		22 17	22s48	
Tiverton Parkway	d	19 48			20 17	20 32		21 05	21 29	22 16		22 19		22 29	23s02	
Exeter St Davids 6	a	20 07			20 33	20 46		21 22	21 43	22 32		22 37		22 45	23 19	04 05
Exmouth	d															
Exeter Central	d															
Exeter St Davids 6	d			19 56	20 35	20 47	20 56	21 23	21 44		21 56	22 37		22 48		04 35
Exeter St Thomas	d			19 59							21 59					
Starcross	d			20 07							22 07					
Dawlish Warren	d			20 12							22 12					
Dawlish	d			20 16			21 09	21 37			22 16					
Teignmouth	d			20 21			21 14	21 43			22 21					
Newton Abbot	a			20 28	20 55	21 06	21 21	21 49	22 03		22 28	22 58		23 06		04 55
	d			20 30	20 56	21 08	21 22	21 50	22 05		22 30	22 58		23 07		04 56
Torre	d			20 38			21 31				22 38					
Torquay	d			20 41			21 34				22 41					
Paignton	a			20 48			21 41				22 49					
Totnes	d				21 11	21 20		22 04	22 20			23 11		23 21		
Ivybridge	d															
Plymouth	a				21 38	21 47		22 32	22 46			23 41		23 49		05 35
	d				21 40											06 28
Devonport	d															
Dockyard	d															
Keyham	d															
St Budeaux Ferry Road	d															
Saltash	d															
St Germans	d															
Menheniot	d															
Liskeard 6	d				22 05											07g09
Bodmin Parkway	d				22 20											07 23
Lostwithiel	d															07 29
Par	d				22 32											07 38
Newquay	a															
St Austell	d				22 40											07 46
Truro	d				22 57											08 06
Redruth	d				23 10											08 20
Camborne	d				23 17											08 27
Hayle	d															08 38
St Erth	d				23 28											08 45
Penzance	a				23 41											08 59

A ⚲ to Bristol Parkway
b Arr. 1935
c Arr. 2035
e Arr. 2135
f Arr. 0207
g Arr. 0652

For connections to Oxford, Gatwick Airport and Heathrow Airport please refer to Tables 116, 148 and 125A

Cornwall and Devon - Birmingham and London

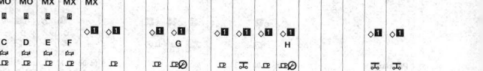

Miles	Miles			GW MO	GW MO	GW MX	GW MO	GW MO	GW MX	GW MX	XC MX	GW	GW	GW	GW	GW	XC	GW	GW	GW	GW	XC	XC
							R	R	R	R													
				◇1	◇1						◇1	◇1	◇1	◇1		◇1	◇1	◇1	◇1			◇1	◇1
				A	B		C	D	E	F				G					H				
							sleeper	sleeper	sleeper	sleeper													
				⊐	⊐		⊐	⊐	⊐	⊐		⊐	⊐	⊐⊘		⊐	trolley	⊐	⊐⊘			trolley	trolley
0	—	**Penzance**	d				21p15	21p15	21p45	21p45	22p08												
5¾	—	St Erth	d				21p25	21p25	21p55	21p55	22p16												
7¼	—	Hayle	d								22p20												
13¼	—	Camborne	d				21p38	21p38	22p07	22p07	22p30												
16¾	—	Redruth	d				21p45	21p45	22p14	22p14	22p36												
25¾	—	Truro	d				22p00	22p00	22p27	22p27	22p48												
40¼	—	St Austell	d				22p18	22p18	22p45	22p45	23p04												
—	—	Newquay	d																				
44¾	—	Par	d						22p54	22p54	23p12												
49¼	—	Lostwithiel	d								23p19												
52¾	—	Bodmin Parkway	d				22p35	22p35	23p06	23p06	23p26												
61¾	—	Liskeard 6	d				22p50	22p50	23p21	23p21	23p39												
65	—	Menheniot	d																				
70¼	—	St Germans	d																				
75¼	—	Saltash	d																				
76½	—	St Budeaux Ferry Road	d																				
77¼	—	Keyham	d																				
77¾	—	Dockyard	d																				
78¼	—	Devonport	d																				
79½	—	**Plymouth**	a				23p15	23p15	23p45	23p45	00 04												
—	—		d	19p55	19p55		23p20	23p20	23p51	23p51						05 10	05 20	05 30	05 53			06 25	
90¼	—	Ivybridge	d																				
102¾	—	Totnes	d				23p48	23p48	00 19	00 19							05 45	05 57				06 50	
—	0	Paignton	d			23p41														06 09	06 34		07 01
—	2¼	Torquay	d			23p46														06 14	06 39		07 07
—	3	Torre	d			23p49														06 17	06 42		
111½	8¼	Newton Abbot	a	20p31	20p31	23p57	23p59	23p59	00 31	00 31						05 45	05 56	06 08	06 28	06 25	06 50	07 01	07 17
—	—		d	20p32	20p32	23p59	00 01	00 01	00 32	00 32						05 47	06 03	06 10	06 30	06 33	06 52	07 03	07 18
116½	—	Teignmouth	d			00 06										05 54				06 40	06 59		07 25
119¼	—	Dawlish	d			00 11												06 20		06 45	07 04		07 30
121	—	Dawlish Warren	d			00 16														06 50	07f15		
123	—	Starcross	d			00 20														06 54	07 19		
130½	—	Exeter St Thomas	d			00 29														07 02	07 28		
131½	—	**Exeter St Davids 6**	a	20p53	20p53	00 34	00 40	00 40	00 54	00 54						06 10	06 21	06 33	06 50	07 08	07 33	07 21	07 42
—	—	Exeter Central	a																	07 14	07 39		
—	—	Exmouth	a																	07 43	08 18		
—	—	**Exeter St Davids 6**	d	20p55	20p55		00 57	00 57	01 00	01 00				05 46	06 00	06 12	06 23	06 35	06 51			07 23	07 44
148	—	Tiverton Parkway	d	21p10	21p10									06 02	06 17	06 27	06 37	06 50				07 37	07 57
162¼	—	Taunton	d	21p23	21p23				01 30	02b18				06 17	06 34	06c54	06 51	07 05	07 17			07 51	08 12
—	11¾	Bridgwater	a												06 46	07 05							
—	25¾	Weston-super-Mare	a												07 04	07 24							08 31
—	45½	**Bristol Temple Meads 10**	a	22p00	22p00		02 08	02 08	02 34	02 59					07 41	07 58	07 26					08 27	08 55
—	—	Bath Spa 7	a	22p22	22p22											08 11							
—	—	Filton Abbey Wood	a												07 58								
—	51¼	Bristol Parkway 7	a												08 05		07 38					08 38	09 08
—	—	Swindon	a	22p50	22p50		03 21		03 15	03 42						08 40							
—	—	Newport (South Wales)	a																				
—	—	Cardiff Central 7	a																				
—	138¾	**Birmingham New Street 12**	a														08 56					09 56	10 26
190	—	Castle Cary	d											06 38				07 27					
209¾	—	Westbury	d									06 08	06 18	07 01				07e51					
230	—	Pewsey	d									06 25	06 35	07 18				08 08					
243¾	—	Hungerford	a									06 38	06 53	07 31									
252¼	—	Newbury	a									06 49	07 08	07 46				08 29					
255¾	—	Thatcham	a									06 56	07 15										
264½	—	Theale	a									07 06	07 25										
269¼	—	**Reading 7**	a	23p27	23p27		04s02	04s18	04s05	04s27		07 19	07 37	08 06		09 13		08 50	08 32				
286¾	—	Slough 3	a																				
305¼	—	**London Paddington 15** ⊖	a	00 11	00 16		05 05	05 05	05 25	05 25		07 53	08 09	08 38		09 44		09 21	09 00				

A from 8 August until 24 October
B until 1 August
C until 24 October
D from 31 October
E until 29 July, and then from 13 September. **The Night Riviera**
F from 2 August until 9 September. **The Night Riviera**
G not 30 May. ⊐ from Reading ⊘ to Newbury
H ⊐ from Reading ⊘ to Taunton
b Arr. 0208
c Arr. 0641
e Arr. 0745
f Arr. 0708

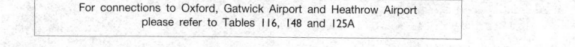

For connections to Oxford, Gatwick Airport and Heathrow Airport please refer to Tables 116, 148 and 125A

Cornwall and Devon - Birmingham and London

		GW	GW	GW	XC	GW	GW	GW	GW	XC	GW	GW	GW	GW	XC	XC	GW	GW	XC	GW	GW	GW	GW
		◇1 A 🍴⌀			◇1 🛒	◇1 🍴	◇1 B 🍴⌀			◇1 C 🛒	◇	◇1 D 🍴⌀			◇1 🛒	◇1 🛒	◇1 🍴		◇1 C 🛒	R 1 E 🍴⌀		◇1 🍴	
Penzance	d	05 05	05 21				05 41		06 00	06 28		06 45	06 55				07 41		08 28	08 44	08 57		
St Erth	d								06 09	06 36		06 55	07a03				07 51		08 36	08 54	09a05		
Hayle	d		05 31						06 12								07 55						
Camborne	d		05 40				05 58		06 21	06 46		07 06					08 05		08 46	09 06			
Redruth	d	05 25					06 05		06 27	06 52		07 13					08 12		08 52	09 13			
Truro	d	05 38	05a55				06 18		06 39	07 04		07 26					08 25		09 04	09 26			
St Austell	d	05 55					06 35		06 56	07 20		07 44					08 43		09 20	09 43			
Newquay	d																						
Par	d						06 43		07 03	07 28		07 52					08 51		09 28	09 51			
Lostwithiel	d						06 51		07 10			08 00											
Bodmin Parkway	d	06 11					06 57		07 16	07 39		08 06					09 03		09 39	10 03			
Liskeard 6	d	06 26					07 11		07 29	07 53		08 20					09 16		09 51	10 16			
Menheniot	d								07x33														
St Germans	d						07 22		07 41			08 31					09 27						
Saltash	d						07 30		07 48			08 39					09 35						
St Budeaux Ferry Road	d								07 52														
Keyham	d								07 54														
Dockyard	d								07x56														
Devonport	d								07 58														
Plymouth	a	06 51					07 41		08 04	08 20		08 49					09 46		10 15	10 41			
	d	06 55			07 25		07 48		08 06	08 25		08 53			09 25		09 48		10 25	10 44			
Ivybridge	d								08 21			09 08					10 03						
Totnes	d				07 50		08 15		08 35	08 50		09 22			09 50		10 18		10 50				
Paignton	d			07 09		07 40		08 23						09 13		10 06		10 14				11 06	11 23
Torquay	d			07 14		07 46		08 28						09 18		10 12		10 23				11 12	11 28
Torre	d			07 17		07 50		08 31						09 21				10 26				11 16	11 31
Newton Abbot	a	07 29		07 24	08 01	07 58	08 26	08 39	08 47	09 01		09 33		09 29	10 01	10 22	10 30	10 33	11 01			11 24	11 39
	d	07 31		07 34	08 03	08 06	08 28	08 41	08 49	09 03		09 35		09 38	10 03	10 23	10 31	10 35	11 03			11 26	11 41
Teignmouth	d			07 41		08 13		08 48	08 56					09 45		10 30		10 42				11 33	11 48
Dawlish	d			07 46		08 19		08 53	09 01					09 50		10 35		10 47				11 39	11 53
Dawlish Warren	d			07 51				08 58						09 54				10 52					11 58
Starcross	d			07 55		08 25		09 02						09 58				10 56					12 02
Exeter St Thomas	d			08 05		08 34		09 11						10 08				11 05					12 11
Exeter St Davids 6	a	07 51		08 11	08 21	08 39	08 48	09 15	09 19	09 22		09 55		10 14	10 21	10 47	10 54	11 09	11 21	11 37		11 52	12 16
Exeter Central	a			08 16				09 21						10 21				11 21					12 21
Exmouth	a							09 50						10 50				11 50					12 50
Exeter St Davids 6	d	07 52			08 23	08 41	08 50			09 23	09 33	09 57			10 23	10 49	10 56		11 23	11 39		11 55	
Tiverton Parkway	d				08 37		09 05			09 37	09 50	10 12			10 37	11 02	11 11		11 37			12 09	
Taunton	d	08 18			08 51	09 05	09 20			09 51	10 07	10 27			10 51	11 17	11 26		11 51			12 24	
Bridgwater	a										10 19												
Weston-super-Mare	a					09 27					10 38												
Bristol Temple Meads 10	a				09 27	09 57				10 26	11 09				11 24	11 53	11 59		12 24				
Bath Spa 7	a					10 11											12 13						
Filton Abbey Wood	a										11 30												
Bristol Parkway 7	a				09 38					10 38					11 38	12 08			12 38				
Swindon	a					10 40											12 41						
Newport (South Wales)	a										11 58												
Cardiff Central 7	a										12 18												
Birmingham New Street 12	a				10 56					11 58					12 56	13 26			13 56				
Castle Cary	d						09 41															12 45	
Westbury	d						10 00					11 04										13 05	
Pewsey	d						10 17															13 21	
Hungerford	a																					13 39	
Newbury	a																					13 49	
Thatcham	a																					13 56	
Theale	a																					14 05	
Reading 7	a	09 32				11 08	10 50					11 50					13 09			13 15		14 15	
Slough 3	a																						
London Paddington 15 ⊖	a	10 02				11 38	11 24					12 23					13 38			13 44		14 44	

A 🍴 to Liskeard 🍴 from Reading
⌀ from Plymouth to Taunton

B 🍴 to Saltash 🍴 from Reading
⌀ from Plymouth to Pewsey

C 🛒 from Plymouth

D 🍴 to Saltash 🍴 from Reading
⌀ from Plymouth to Westbury

E **The Cornish Riviera.** 🍴 to Liskeard

🍴 from Reading
⌀ from Plymouth to Exeter St Davids

For connections to Oxford, Gatwick Airport and Heathrow Airport please refer to Tables 116, 148 and 125A

Table 135

Mondays to Fridays

Cornwall and Devon - Birmingham and London

		XC	XC	GW		GW	XC	GW	GW	GW	GW	GW	GW	XC		XC	GW	GW	GW	GW	XC	GW	GW	GW
		◇1	◇1			R 1	◇1		◇	◇	◇1	◇1		◇1		◇1	◇	◇1	◇1		◇1		◇1	◇1
			A			B		C	D	C	E	F							G				H	I
		🛒	🛒			✕☕	🛒				✕☕	✕☕		🛒		🛒		☕	☕		🛒		☕	☕
Penzance	d		09 40			10 00		10 46			10 47						11 41							
St Erth	d		09 48			10 10		10 55			10 57						11 50							
Hayle	d		09 52					10 58			11 01						11 53							
Camborne	d		10 01			10 21		11 07			11 11						12 02							
Redruth	d		10 08			10 28		11 13			11 18						12 08							
Truro	d		10 19			10 41		11 25			11 31						12 19							
St Austell	d		10 35			10 58		11 42			11 49						12 36							
Newquay	d																							
Par	d		10 43			11 07		11 50			11 57						12 44							
Lostwithiel	d		10 50					11 56									12 50							
Bodmin Parkway	d		10 57			11 19		12 02			12 08						12 56							
Liskeard 6	d		11 09			11 33		12 16			12 21						13 09							
Menheniot	d																13x13							
St Germans	d							12 27			12 33						13 22							
Saltash	d							12 34			12 41						13 29							
St Budeaux Ferry Road	d																							
Keyham	d																							
Dockyard	d																							
Devonport	d																							
Plymouth	a		11 39			11 59		12 45			12 51						13 39							
	d	11 25	11 50			12 02	12 23				12 55	12 55		13 23			13 41				14 25		15 00	15 00
Ivybridge	d																13 56							
Totnes	d	11 50	12 15			12 29	12 49				13 22	13 22		13 49			14 10				14 50		15 27	15 27
Paignton	d			12 13					12 48	12 48			13 13			14 01			14 15	14 23		15 13		
Torquay	d			12 18					12 53	12 53			13 18			14 07			14 21	14 28		15 18		
Torre	d			12 21					12 56	12 56			13 21							14 31		15 21		
Newton Abbot	a	12 01	12 26	12 30		12 40	13 01		13 04	13 04	13 33	13 33	13 30	14 01		14 17	14 24		14 31	14 39	15 01	15 29	15 38	15 38
	d	12 03	12 28	12 31		12 42	13 03		13 06	13 06	13 35	13 35	13 41	14 03		14 18			14 33	14 41	15 03	15 31	15 40	15 40
Teignmouth	d			12 38					13 13	13 13			13 48			14 25			14 40	14 48		15 38		
Dawlish	d			12 43					13 18	13 18			13 53			14 30			14 46	14 53		15 43		
Dawlish Warren	d			12b54									13 58							14 58		15c54		
Starcross	d			12 58									14 02							15 02		15 58		
Exeter St Thomas	d			13 07									14 11							15 11		16 07		
Exeter St Davids 6	a	12 21	12 46	13 13		13 02	13 23		13 31	13 31	13 55	13 55	14 16	14 23		14 42			14 59	15 16	15 21	16 13	16 00	16 00
Exeter Central	a			13 21									14 21							15 21		16 21		
Exmouth	a			13 50									14 50							15 50		16 50		
Exeter St Davids 6	d	12 23	12 48			13 04	13 25		13 33	13 33	13 57	13 57		14 25		14 44			15 01		15 23		16 02	16 02
Tiverton Parkway	d	12 37	13 02			13 19	13 39		13 50	13 50				14 39		14 57			15 15		15 37		16 16	16 16
Taunton	d	12 51	13 16			13 34	13 54		14 07	14 07	14 23	14 23		14 54		15 12		15 23	15 30		15 51		16 30	16 30
Bridgwater	a								14 18	14 18														
Weston-super-Mare	a								14 37	14 37						15 37								
Bristol Temple Meads 10	a	13 24	13 56				14 27		15 15	15 09				15 27		15 57					16 27			
Bath Spa 7	a																							
Filton Abbey Wood	a								15 30	15 30														
Bristol Parkway 7	a	13 38	14 08				14 38							15 38		16 08					16 38			
Swindon	a																							
Newport (South Wales)	a								15 58	15 58														
Cardiff Central 7	a								16 18	16 18														
Birmingham New Street 12	a	14 56	15 26				15 56							16 58		17 26					17 56			
Castle Cary	d										14 44	14 44							15 51					
Westbury	d										15 03	15 03						16 06						
Pewsey	d																	16 25						
Hungerford	a																	16 39						
Newbury	a																	16 49						
Thatcham	a																	16 56						
Theale	a																	17 05						
Reading 7	a					14 50					15 50	15 50						17 15	16 50				17 49	17 50
Slough 3	a																							
London Paddington 15 ⊖	a					15 24					16 22	16 22						17 54	17 24				18 21	18 21

A 🛒 from Plymouth
B Restaurant available after PLY for customers joining until TAU. ☕ to Liskeard ☕ from Reading ✕ from Plymouth to Taunton
C until 1 July, from 5 September
D from 4 July until 2 September
E from 4 July until 2 September. Restaurant available for customers joining until Castle Cary. ☕ to Saltash ☕ from Westbury ✕ from Plymouth to Castle Cary
F until 1 July, from 5 September. Restaurant available for customers joining until Castle Cary. ☕ from Westbury ✕ to Castle Cary
G **The Torbay Express**
H from 12 September. **The Mayflower**
I until 9 September. **The Mayflower**
b Arr. 1248
c Arr. 1547

For connections to Oxford, Gatwick Airport and Heathrow Airport please refer to Tables 116, 148 and 125A

Cornwall and Devon - Birmingham and London

		GW	XC	GW	XC	GW	XC	GW	GW	GW	GW	GW	GW	GW	GW	XC	GW	GW	GW	GW	GW	XC	GW
			◇1		◇1	◇1	◇1				◇1	◇1			◇	◇1			◇1			◇1	
						A	B	C	D		E	C	D		F	B			G			H	
			🍴		🍴	☕	🍴				☕	☕			☕	🍴			☕⊘			🍴	
Penzance	d	12 54				14 00		14 49	14 52										16 00				
St Erth	d	13 03				14 10		14 58	15 01										16 10				
Hayle	d	13 06						15 01	15 04														
Camborne	d	13 15				14 21		15 10	15 13										16 20				
Redruth	d	13 21				14 28		15 16	15 19										16 28				
Truro	d	13 32				14 41		15 27	15 30										16 41				
St Austell	d	13 49				14 58		15 44	15 47										16 58				
Newquay	d										15 00												
Par	d	13 57				15 06		15 52	15a54		16 00								17 07				
Lostwithiel	d	14 04						15 58			16 09								17 14				
Bodmin Parkway	d	14 10				15 18		16 04			16 16								17 21				
Liskeard 6	d	14 23				15 31		16 17			16 29		16 43						17 34	17 49			
Menheniot	d							16x21					16x48										
St Germans	d	14 34						16 30					16 55							18 00			
Saltash	d	14 42						16 37					17 02							18 07			
St Budeaux Ferry Road	d							16 41					17 06							18 12			
Keyham	d							16 43					17 08										
Dockyard	d							16x45					17x10										
Devonport	d							16 47					17 12										
Plymouth	a	14 51				15 56		16 52			16 54		17 18						17 58	18 19			
	d	15 08	15 23			16 00	16 25				16 57	16 57				17 23		17 45	18 00			18 25	
Ivybridge	d	15 23									17 12	17 12						18 02					
Totnes	d	15 37	15 49			16 27	16 50				17 27	17 27				17 49		18 16	18 30			18 50	
Paignton	d			16 13						16 55				17 25			17 52				18 35		18 52
Torquay	d			16 18						17 00				17 30			17 57				18 40		18 57
Torre	d			16 21						17 03				17 33			18 00				18 43		
Newton Abbot	a	15 52	16 01	16 29		16 39	17 01			17 11	17 38	17 38		17 41		18 01	18 08	18 28	18 42		18 50	19 01	19 07
	d		16 03	16 31		16 40	17 03			17 13	17 40	17 40		17 43		18 03	18 10	18 29	18 43		18 53	19 03	19 09
Teignmouth	d			16 38						17 20				17 50			18 17	18 36			19 00		19 16
Dawlish	d			16 43						17 25				17 55			18 22	18 42			19 05		19 21
Dawlish Warren	d			16b54						17 30				18 00			18 27	18 46			19c16		19 26
Starcross	d			16 58						17 34				18 04			18 31				19 20		
Exeter St Thomas	d			17 07						17 43				18 13			18 40				19 29		
Exeter St Davids 6	a		16 23	17 13		17 00	17 21			17 50	18 00	18 00		18 17		18 23	18 46	18 59	19 03		19 33	19 21	19 40
Exeter Central	a			17 21						17 55				18 23			18 53						
Exmouth	a			17 51						18 25				18 52			19 23						
Exeter St Davids 6	d		16 25		16 53	17 02	17 23				18 02	18 02			18 20	18 25			19 05			19 23	
Tiverton Parkway	d		16 39		17 07	17 17	17 37				18 16	18 16				18 39			19 20			19 37	
Taunton	d		16 54		17 21	17 31	17 51				18 30	18 30			18 48	18 54			19 35			19 51	
Bridgwater	a																						
Weston-super-Mare	a																						
Bristol Temple Meads 10	a		17 27		17 54		18 24									19 27						20 25	
Bath Spa 7	a																						
Filton Abbey Wood	a																						
Bristol Parkway 7	a		17 38		18 08		18 38									19 38						20 38	
Swindon	a																						
Newport (South Wales)	a																						
Cardiff Central 7	a																						
Birmingham New Street 12	a		18 55		19 26		19 56									20 52						22 09	
Castle Cary	d										18 53	18 53											
Westbury	d										19 11	19 11											
Pewsey	d										19 28	19 28											
Hungerford	a																						
Newbury	a										19 49	19 49											
Thatcham	a																						
Theale	a																						
Reading 7	a					18 49					20 06	20 06			20 21				20 50				
Slough 3	a																						
London Paddington 15 ⊖	a					19 24					20 39	20 39			20 52				21 21				

A The Royal Duchy
B 🍴 to Bristol Parkway
C until 1 July, from 5 September
D from 4 July until 2 September
E from 4 July until 2 September. The Atlantic Coast Express
F FO from 8 July until 2 September
G ☕ to Liskeard ☕ from Reading ⊘ from Plymouth to Taunton
H 🍴 to Taunton
b Arr. 1647
c Arr. 1909

For connections to Oxford, Gatwick Airport and Heathrow Airport please refer to Tables 116, 148 and 125A

Table 135

Mondays to Fridays

Cornwall and Devon - Birmingham and London

		GW	GW	GW	GW	GW		GW	GW	GW	GW	XC	GW	GW	GW	GW		GW	GW	GW	GW	GW	GW	GW	GW
		FO	FX		FX	FO		FO	FX											FX	FO				FO
		◇	◇		◇1	◇1		◇1	◇1			◇1		◇		1					1	◇			1
										A	B			C	D				A			E			F
					☕	☕		☕	☕																🛏 ☕
Penzance	d	16 44	16 44					17 39	17 39	19 13	19 16									20 18	20 18				21 45
St Erth	d	16 53	16 53					17 49	17 49	19 23	19 24									20 27	20 27				21 55
Hayle	d	16 56	16 56					17 53	17 53	19 27	19 27									20 32	20 32				
Camborne	d	17 05	17 05					18 03	18 03	19 38	19 37									20 41	20 41				22 07
Redruth	d	17 11	17 11					18 11	18 11	19 45	19 43									20 49	20 49				22 14
Truro	d	17 24	17 24					18 23	18 23	19 58	19 54									21 02	21 02				22 27
St Austell	d	17 41	17 41					18 40	18 40	20 15	20 11									21 19	21 19				22 45
Newquay	d																								
Par	d	17 48	17 48					18 49	18 49	20 24	20 19									21 27	21 27				22 54
Lostwithiel	d	17 55	17 55							20 31	20 25									21 34	21 34				
Bodmin Parkway	d	18 01	18 01					19 01	19 01	20 38	20 31									21 40	21 40				23 06
Liskeard 8	d	18 14	18 14					19 14	19 14	20 51	20 44								21 03	21 53	21 53				23 21
Menheniot	d										20x49								21x08						
St Germans	d	18 25	18 25								20 57								21 15	22 04	22 04				
Saltash	d	18 32	18 32								21 04								21b30	22 12	22 12				
St Budeaux Ferry Road	d										21 08								21 34						
Keyham	d										21 10								21 36						
Dockyard	d										21x12								21x38						
Devonport	d										21 14								21 40						
Plymouth	a	18 42	18 42					19 39	19 39	21 16	21 20								21 46	22 25	22 25				23 45
	d	18 44	18 44					19 42	19 42									21 25							23 51
Ivybridge	d	18 59	18 59															21 40							
Totnes	d	19 13	19 13					20 09	20 09									21 54							00 19
Paignton	d			19 32								20 12	20 34			21 31							22 30	23 41	
Torquay	d			19 37								20 18	20 39			21 37							22 35	23 46	
Torre	d			19 40									20 42			21 41							22 38	23 49	
Newton Abbot	a	19 25	19 25	19 48				20 20	20 20			20 28	20 50			21 52		22 02					22 46	23 57	00 31
	d	19 26	19 26	19 50				20 22	20 22			20 29	20 52					22 02					22 48	23 59	00 32
Teignmouth	d			19 57									20 59					22 13					22 55	00 06	
Dawlish	d			20 02									21 04					22 18					23 00	00 11	
Dawlish Warren	d			20 07									21 09					22 23					23 05	00 16	
Starcross	d			20 11									21 13					22 27					23 09	00 20	
Exeter St Thomas	d			20 20									21 22					22 36					23 18	00 29	
Exeter St Davids 6	a	19 47	19 48	20 26				20 42	20 42			20 48	21 27					22 40					23 22	00 34	00 54
Exeter Central	a			20 33									21 35												
Exmouth	a			21 01									22 02												
Exeter St Davids 6	d	19 48			19 54			20 44	20 44			20 50		21 26	21 26							21 49			01 00
Tiverton Parkway	d	20 05			20 09			20 59	20 59			21 03		21 43	21 43							22 06			
Taunton	d	20a21			20 24	20 26		21 14	21 14			21 18		22 00	22 00							22 23			01 30
Bridgwater	a																								
Weston-super-Mare	a													22 24	22 24							22 47			
Bristol Temple Meads 10	a							21 47	21 47			21 51		22 56	22 56							23 16			02 34
Bath Spa 7	a							22 01	22 01																
Filton Abbey Wood	a																								
Bristol Parkway 7	a											22 08													
Swindon	a							22 33	22 33																03 15
Newport (South Wales)	a																								
Cardiff Central 7	a																								
Birmingham New Street 12	a											23 44													
Castle Cary	d				20 45	20 45																			
Westbury	d				21 04	21 04																			
Pewsey	d				21 21	21 21																			
Hungerford	a																								
Newbury	a				21 42	21 42																			
Thatcham	a																								
Theale	a																								
Reading 7	a				21 59	21 59		23 06	23 06																04s05
Slough 3	a																								
London Paddington 15 ⊖	a				22 30	22 30		23 42	23 50																05 09

A from 4 July until 2 September
B until 1 July, from 5 September until 8 December
C until 29 July
D from 1 August until 9 September
E from 12 September
F until 29 July, FO from 16 September. **The Night Riviera**
b Arr. 2122

For connections to Oxford, Gatwick Airport and Heathrow Airport please refer to Tables 116, 148 and 125A

Table 135

Cornwall and Devon - Birmingham and London

		GW	GW	GW	XC
		R	R	R	
		FX	FO	FX	◇1
		A	B	C	
		🛏	🛏	🛏	
		☕	☕	☕	
Penzance	d	21 45	21 45	21 45	22 08
St Erth	d	21 55	21 55	21 55	22 16
Hayle	d				22 20
Camborne	d	22 07	22 07	22 07	22 30
Redruth	d	22 14	22 14	22 14	22 36
Truro	d	22 27	22 27	22 27	22 48
St Austell	d	22 45	22 45	22 45	23 04
Newquay	d				
Par	d	22 54	22 54	22 54	23 12
Lostwithiel	d				23 19
Bodmin Parkway	d	23 06	23 06	23 06	23 26
Liskeard 6	d	23 21	23 21	23 21	23 39
Menheniot	d				
St Germans	d				
Saltash	d				
St Budeaux Ferry Road	d				
Keyham	d				
Dockyard	d				
Devonport	d				
Plymouth	a	23 45	23 45	23 45	00 04
	d	23 51	23 51	23 51	
Ivybridge	d				
Totnes	d	00 19	00 19	00 19	
Paignton	d				
Torquay	d				
Torre	d				
Newton Abbot	a	00 31	00 31	00 31	
	d	00 32	00 32	00 32	
Teignmouth	d				
Dawlish	d				
Dawlish Warren	d				
Starcross	d				
Exeter St Thomas	d				
Exeter St Davids 6	a	00 54	00 54	00 54	
Exeter Central	a				
Exmouth	a				
Exeter St Davids 6	d	01 00	01 00	01 00	
Tiverton Parkway	d				
Taunton	d	01 30	02b18	02b18	
Bridgwater	a				
Weston-super-Mare	a				
Bristol Temple Meads 10	a	02 34	02 59	02 59	
Bath Spa 7	a				
Filton Abbey Wood	a				
Bristol Parkway 7	a				
Swindon	a	03 15	03 39	03 42	
Newport (South Wales)	a				
Cardiff Central 7	a				
Birmingham New Street 12	a				
Castle Cary	d				
Westbury	d				
Pewsey	d				
Hungerford	a				
Newbury	a				
Thatcham	a				
Theale	a				
Reading 7	a	04s05	04s24	04s27	
Slough 3	a				
London Paddington 15 ⊖	a	05 25	05 10	05 25	

A until 28 July, FX from 12 September. The Night Riviera

B from 5 August until 9 September. The Night Riviera

C from 1 August until 8 September. The Night Riviera

b Arr. 0208

For connections to Oxford, Gatwick Airport and Heathrow Airport please refer to Tables 116, 148 and 125A

Table 135

Cornwall and Devon - Birmingham and London

Saturdays
until 10 September

		GW	GW	GW	XC	GW	GW	XC	GW	GW	GW	XC	GW	XC	GW	GW	XC	GW	GW	GW	GW	XC	GW
			R	R																			
					◇1			◇1	◇1			◇1	◇1	◇1		◇1	◇1		◇1			◇1	
			A	B												C			D			E	
			🛏	🛏																			
			🍴	🍴				🛒	🍴			🛒	🍴	🛒		🍴⊘	🛒		🍴⊘			🛒	
Penzance	d		21p45	21p45	22p08	05 20												05 37				06 30	06 41
St Erth	d		21p55	21p55	22p16													05 44				06 38	06a49
Hayle	d				22p20													05 48				06 41	
Camborne	d		22p07	22p07	22p30	05 37												05 57				06 51	
Redruth	d		22p14	22p14	22p36	05 43												06 03				06 57	
Truro	d		22p27	22p27	22p48	05a55												06 14				07 09	
St Austell	d		22p45	22p45	23p04													06 31				07 25	
Newquay	d																						
Par	d		22p54	22p54	23p12													06 39				07 32	
Lostwithiel	d				23p19													06 46				07 39	
Bodmin Parkway	d		23p06	23p06	23p26													06 52				07 46	
Liskeard 6	d		23p21	23p21	23p39													07 06				07 58	
Menheniot	d																	07x10					
St Germans	d																	07 17					
Saltash	d																	07 24					
St Budeaux Ferry Road	d																	07 28					
Keyham	d																	07 30					
Dockyard	d																	07x32					
Devonport	d																	07 34					
Plymouth	a		23p45	23p45	00 04													07 41				08 22	
	d		23p51	23p51				05 25	05 40			06 25				06 55	07 25		07 47		08 06	08 25	
Ivybridge	d																				08 21		
Totnes	d		00 19	00 19				05 50	06 07			06 50					07 50		08 14		08 35	08 50	
Paignton	d	23p41								06 13	06 34			07 00	07 08					08 06			
Torquay	d	23p46								06 18	06 39			07 06	07 13					08 11			
Torre	d	23p49								06 21	06 42				07 16					08 14			
Newton Abbot	a	23p57	00 31	00 31				06 01	06 18	06 29	06 50	07 01		07 16	07 24	07 30	08 01		08 26	08 22	08 47	09 01	
	d	23p59	00 32	00 32				06 03	06 20	06 31	06 52	07 03		07 18		07 31	08 03		08 27	08 34	08 48	09 03	
Teignmouth	d	00 06								06 38	06 59			07 25						08 41	08 55		
Dawlish	d	00 11								06 43	07 04			07 30						08 46	09 00		
Dawlish Warren	d	00 16								06 48	07c15									08 51			
Starcross	d	00 20								06 52	07 19									08 55			
Exeter St Thomas	d	00 29								07 01	07 28									09 04			
Exeter St Davids 6	a	00 34	00 54	00 54				06 21	06 40	07 06	07 33	07 21		07 41		07 52	08 21		08 47	09 09	09 16	09 21	
Exeter Central	a									07 14	07 39									09 21			
Exmouth	a									07 43	08 18									09 50			
Exeter St Davids 6	d		01 00	01 00			06 00	06 23	06 41			07 23	07 28	07 47		07 54	08 23		08 49			09 23	
Tiverton Parkway	d						06 18	06 37	06 56			07 37	07 43				08 37		09 04			09 37	
Taunton	d		01 30	02b18			06 35	06 51	07 11			07 51	07 58	08 12		08 19	08 51		09 19			09 51	
Bridgwater	a						06 47						08 08										
Weston-super-Mare	a						07 06						08 26										
Bristol Temple Meads 10	a		02 34	02 59			07 42	07 25				08 24	08 57	08 49			09 26					10 26	
Bath Spa 7	a												09 11										
Filton Abbey Wood	a						07 58																
Bristol Parkway 7	a						08 05	07 38				08 38		09 08			09 38					10 38	
Swindon	a		03 15	03 39									09 40										
Newport (South Wales)	a																						
Cardiff Central 7	a																						
Birmingham New Street 12	a							08 56				09 56		10 26			10 56					11 56	
Castle Cary	d								07 33										09 40				
Westbury	d								07 56										09 59				
Pewsey	d								08 13										10 16				
Hungerford	a																						
Newbury	a								08 33														
Thatcham	a																						
Theale	a																						
Reading 7	a		04s05	04s24					08 52				10 11			09 35			10 51				
Slough 3	a																						
London Paddington 15 ⊖	a		05 09	05 10					09 21				10 39			10 08			11 24				

A until 30 July. **The Night Riviera**
B from 6 August until 10 September. **The Night Riviera**
C 🍴 from Reading ⊘ to Taunton
D 🍴 from Castle Cary ⊘ to Taunton
E 🛒 from Plymouth
b Arr. 0208
c Arr. 0708

For connections to Oxford, Gatwick Airport and Heathrow Airport please refer to Tables 116, 148 and 125A

Table 135

Saturdays

until 10 September

Cornwall and Devon - Birmingham and London

		XC	GW	GW	GW	GW	XC	GW	XC	GW	XC	GW	GW	GW	GW	XC	GW	GW	XC	GW	GW	GW	GW
		◇1 A [trolley]	R 1 [restaurant]		◇1 [restaurant]		◇1 [trolley]	R 1 [restaurant]	◇1 [trolley]		◇1 B [trolley]	R 1 [restaurant]				◇1 B [trolley]		R 1 [restaurant]	◇1 [trolley]				◇1 [restaurant]
Penzance	d		06 50					07 18			08 28	08 39	08 54					09 54					
St Erth	d		07 00					07 29			08 36	08 50	09a02					10 05					
Hayle	d							07 34				08 55						10 10					
Camborne	d		07 11					07 44			08 46	09 05						10 20					
Redruth	d		07 18					07 51			08 52	09 12						10 27					
Truro	d		07 31					08 05			09 04	09 25						10 40					
St Austell	d		07 48					08 22			09 20	09 43						10 58					
Newquay	d															09 27							
Par	d		07 56					08 30			09 28	09 51				10 26		11 06			11 31		
Lostwithiel	d		08 04					08 38													11 38		
Bodmin Parkway	d		08 10					08 44			09 39	10 02				10b43		11 18			11 44		
Liskeard 6	d		08 23					08 57			09 51	10 15				10 55		11 31			11 58		
Menheniot	d																				12x02		
St Germans	d							09 09													12 09		
Saltash	d							09 17													12 15		
St Budeaux Ferry Road	d																						
Keyham	d																						
Dockyard	d																						
Devonport	d																						
Plymouth	a		08 49					09 26			10 15	10 40				11 19		11 56			12 27		
	d	08 39	08 52				09 18	09 33			10 25	10 43				11 25		12 00			12 35		
Ivybridge	d							09 48										12 15			12 50		
Totnes	d	09 04	09 19				09 43	10 02			10 50					11 50		12 29			13 04		
Paignton	d			09 04	09 18	09 30			10 06	10 23				10 56	11 13		12 13		12 34	12 49		12 58	13 07
Torquay	d			09 09	09 25	09 35			10 12	10 28				11 01	11 18		12 18		12 41	12 54		13 03	13 15
Torre	d			09 12	09 29	09 38				10 31				11 04	11 21		12 21					13 06	
Newton Abbot	a	09 15	09 30	09 20	09 38	09 47	09 54	10 14	10 22	10 38	11 01			11 12	11 29	12 01	12 30	12 41	12 51	13 04	13 16	13 14	13 25
	d	09 17	09 32	09 35	09 39	09 48	09 56	10 15	10 23	10 41	11 03			11 23	11 41	12 03	12 32	12 42	12 53	13 06	13 16	13 21	13 26
Teignmouth	d			09 42	09 49	09 56	10 03		10 30	10 48				11 30	11 48		12 39		13 02	13 13		13 28	13 35
Dawlish	d			09 47	09 57	10 02	10 09		10 35	10 53				11 35	11 53		12 44		13 09	13 18		13 33	13 43
Dawlish Warren	d	09 28		09 52	10 02	10 07	10 13			10 58				11 40	11 58		12c55			13 23		13 38	13e55
Starcross	d			09 56						11 02				11 44	12 02		12 59					13 42	
Exeter St Thomas	d			10 05						11 11				11 53	12 11		13 08					13 51	
Exeter St Davids 6	a	09 38	09 52	10 10	10 13	10 18	10 23	10 35	10 47	11 15	11 21	11 37		11 58	12 16	12 21	13 13	13 02	13 22	13 35	13 38	13 59	14 08
Exeter Central	a			10 21						11 21					12 21		13 21					14 21	
Exmouth	a			10 50						11 50					12 50		13 50					14 50	
Exeter St Davids 6	d	09 41	09 54		10 15		10 25	10 38	10 49		11 23	11 40				12 23		13 05	13 25				14 11
Tiverton Parkway	d	09 54	10 09		10 30		10 39		11 02		11 37					12 37		13 20	13 39				
Taunton	d	10 09	10 24		10 45		10 53	11 03	11 17		11 51					12 51		13 35	13 54				14f44
Bridgwater	a																						
Weston-super-Mare	a	10 32																					
Bristol Temple Meads 10	a	10 52			11 24		11 26		11 55		12 25					13 24			14 27				
Bath Spa 7	a				11 41																		
Filton Abbey Wood	a																						
Bristol Parkway 7	a	11 08					11 38		12 08		12 38					13 38			14 38				
Swindon	a				12 09																		
Newport (South Wales)	a																						
Cardiff Central 7	a																						
Birmingham New Street 12	a	12 26					12 56		13 26		13 56					14 56			15 55				
Castle Cary	d							11 24															15 08
Westbury	d		11 02					11 45															15 28
Pewsey	d							12 01															15 45
Hungerford	a																						
Newbury	a																						16 05
Thatcham	a																						
Theale	a																						
Reading 7	a		11 51		12 43			12 40				13 17						14 52					16 25
Slough 3	a																						
London Paddington 15 ⊖	a		12 23		13 13			13 09				13 46						15 23					17 02

A [trolley] to Bristol Parkway
B [trolley] from Plymouth

b Arr. 1037
c Arr. 1248

e Arr. 1347
f Arr. 1435

For connections to Oxford, Gatwick Airport and Heathrow Airport please refer to Tables 116, 148 and 125A

Table 135

Cornwall and Devon - Birmingham and London

Saturdays
until 10 September

		GW	GW	GW	XC	XC	GW	GW	GW	XC	GW	GW	GW	XC	GW	GW	GW	GW	GW	XC	GW	GW
		R	R	R			R		R			R										
		◇1	1	1	◇1	◇1	◇1		◇1	◇1		1		◇1				◇1		◇1	◇1	
		A	B	C			D		E											F		
		☕⊘	☕	☕	🛒	🛒	☕⊘		☕	🛒		☕		🛒				☕		🛒	☕	
Penzance	d	11 00					11 58						13 00					14 01	14 52			
St Erth	d	11 11					12 09						13 09					14 11	15 01			
Hayle	d	11 16					12 14						13 12						15 04			
Camborne	d	11 26					12 24						13 21					14 22	15 14			
Redruth	d	11 33					12 31						13 27					14 29	15 20			
Truro	d	11 46					12 44						13 38					14 42	15 31			
St Austell	d	12 04					13 02						13 55					14 59	15 48			
Newquay	d		11 22	11 22								13 14										
Par	d		12 26	12 26								14 16	14e25					15 07	15 55			
Lostwithiel	d												14 31						16 02			
Bodmin Parkway	d	12 21					13 19						14 37					15 19	16 08			
Liskeard 6	d	12 34					13 32						14 50					15 32	16 21			
Menheniot	d																		16x25			
St Germans	d												15 01						16 33			
Saltash	d												15 09						16 39			
St Budeaux Ferry Road	d																					
Keyham	d																					
Dockyard	d																					
Devonport	d												15 15									
Plymouth	a	12 58	13 10	13s10			13 56					15 00	15 20					15 57	16 51			
	d	13 00	13 14		13 25		14 00			14 25		15 07		15 25		15 32		16 01				
Ivybridge	d															15 47						
Totnes	d	13 28			13 50					14 50				15 50		16 01		16 28				
Paignton	d					13 53		14 13	14 31		15 13				15 43		16 13			16 34	17 03	17 13
Torquay	d					13 59		14 18	14 38		15 18				15 48		16 18			16 41	17 10	17 19
Torre	d							14 21			15 21						16 21					17 22
Newton Abbot	a	13 40			14 01	14 09	14 35	14 29	14 48	15 01	15 29	15 42		16 01	15 58	16 13	16 29	16 40		16 51	17 21	17 30
	d	13 42			14 03	14 10	14 36	14 40	14 50	15 03	15 34	15 44		16 03	16 09		16 31	16 41		16 53	17 22	17 41
Teignmouth	d					14 17		14 48	14 58		15 42				16 16		16 39			17 02	17 30	17 49
Dawlish	d					14 22		14 53	15 04		15 48				16 21		16 44			17 09	17 37	17 54
Dawlish Warren	d							14 57	15b17		15c58						16f55				17 42	17 59
Starcross	d							15 01			16 02						16 59					18 04
Exeter St Thomas	d							15 11			16 12						17 09					18 13
Exeter St Davids 6	a	14 02	14 15	14s15	14 21	14 34	14 56	15 15	15 28	15 21	16 15	16 04		16 21	16 34		17 15	17 01		17 22	17 54	18 18
Exeter Central	a							15 21			16 21				16 44		17 21					18 23
Exmouth	a							15 50			16 50						17 50					18 52
Exeter St Davids 6	d	14 05	14 18		14 23	14 36	14 59		15 32	15 23		16 06		16 23				17 03		17 25	18 02	
Tiverton Parkway	d				14 37	14 49	15 14			15 37		16 21		16 37				17 17		17 39	18 17	
Taunton	d	14 30			14 52	15 04	15 29		15 57	15 51		16 36		16 51				17 32		17 54	18 32	
Bridgwater	a																					
Weston-super-Mare	a					15 23																
Bristol Temple Meads 10	a				15 25	15 49				16 25				17 25						18 27		
Bath Spa 7	a																					
Filton Abbey Wood	a																					
Bristol Parkway 7	a				15 38	16 08				16 38				17 38						18 38		
Swindon	a																					
Newport (South Wales)	a																					
Cardiff Central 7	a																					
Birmingham New Street 12	a				16 56	17 26				17 56				18 56						19 58		
Castle Cary	d						15 50		16 19												18 53	
Westbury	d								16 38												19 12	
Pewsey	d								16 54													
Hungerford	a																					
Newbury	a																				19 45	
Thatcham	a																					
Theale	a																					
Reading 7	a	15 51	15 59	15 59			16 50		17 34			17 53						18 49			20 07	
Slough 3	a																					
London Paddington 15 ⊖	a	16 23	16 32	16 32			17 21		18 08			18 23						19 22			20 37	

A ☕ to Liskeard ☕ from Reading ⊘ from Plymouth to Taunton ◇ from Plymouth R to Liskeard
B from 16 July until 10 September
C until 9 July
D ☕ from Reading ⊘ to Castle Cary ◇ from Reading R to Castle Cary
E ◇ from Exeter St Davids R to Dawlish Warren
F 🛒 to Bristol Parkway
b Arr. 1509
c Arr. 1552
e Arr. 1402
f Arr. 1648

For connections to Oxford, Gatwick Airport and Heathrow Airport please refer to Tables 116, 148 and 125A

Table 135

Saturdays
until 10 September

Cornwall and Devon - Birmingham and London

		XC	GW	GW	XC	GW	XC	GW	GW	GW	GW	GW	GW	GW	GW	GW	GW	GW	GW	XC	GW	GW	XC	GW
		◇1			◇1	◇1	◇1					■ 1		◇1						◇1			◇1	
							A																	
		🛒				☕	🛒					☕		☕										
Penzance	d					15 52	16 25	16 44						17 40	18 50				19 06				21 32	
St Erth	d					16 02	16 35	16 54						17 50	18a58				19 15				21 42	
Hayle	d							16 58						17 54					19 18					
Camborne	d					16 13	16 46	17 09						18 04					19 27				21 53	
Redruth	d					16 20	16 53	17 16						18 11					19 33				22 00	
Truro	d					16 33	17 06	17 29						18 24					19 44				22 13	
St Austell	d					16 51	17 23	17 46						18 41					20 01				22 30	
Newquay	d	15 25										17 18								19 55		21 21		
Par	d	16 27				16 59		17 54				18 22		18 49		19 00			20 09	20 55		22 09	22 38	
Lostwithiel	d					17 06		18 02								19 07			20 15			22 18		
Bodmin Parkway	d	16 37				17 13	17 40	18 08				18 34		19 01		19 13			20 21	21 07		22 24	22 49	
Liskeard 6	d	16 51				17 26	17 53	18 21				18 47		19 14		19 27			20 34	21 20	21 53	22 37	23 02	
Menheniot	d																		20x39			22x41		
St Germans	d							18 33								19 36			20 47			22 49		
Saltash	d							18 40								19 42			20 54			22 55		
St Budeaux Ferry Road	d																		20 58			22 59		
Keyham	d																		21 00			23 01		
Dockyard	d																		21x02			23x03		
Devonport	d																		21 04			23 05		
Plymouth	a	17 15				17 51	18 19	18 50				19 14		19 39		19 55			21 10	21 46	22 18	23 12	23 27	
	d	17 25		17 38		17 54	18 23			18 56		19 18		19 42					21 15					
Ivybridge	d			17 53						19 13									21 30					
Totnes	d	17 50		18 07		18 21	18 49			19 27				20 09					21 44					
Paignton	d		17 52		18 05				18 53		19 21		19 50				20 13	21 13						21 53
Torquay	d		17 57		18 12				18 58		19 26		19 55				20 18	21 18						21 58
Torre	d		18 00						19 01		19 29						20 21	21 21						22 01
Newton Abbot	a	18 01	18 08	18 19	18 22	18 32	19 01		19 10	19 39	19 38	19 53	20 05	20 20			20 29	21 29	21 56					22 09
	d	18 03	18 10	18 19	18 23	18 34	19 03		19 12	19 40	19 44	19 55	20 07	20 22			20 31	21 31	21 56					22 11
Teignmouth	d		18 18	18 26					19 19	19 47	19 51		20 14				20 38	21 38	22 03					22 18
Dawlish	d		18 23	18 31					19 24	19 53	19 56		20 19				20 43	21 43	22 08					22 23
Dawlish Warren	d		18 28	18b47					19 29		20c06		20 24				20 48	21 48						22 28
Starcross	d		18 33						19 33		20 10						20 52	21 52						22 32
Exeter St Thomas	d		18 42						19 42		20 20						21 01	22 01						22 41
Exeter St Davids 6	a	18 21	18 47	18 59	18 48	18 54	19 23		19 45	20 06	20 25	20 14	20 36	20 42			21 05	22 05	22 22					22 45
Exeter Central	a		18 53								20 33													
Exmouth	a		19 22								21 01													
Exeter St Davids 6	d	18 23			18 50	18 56	19 25					20 16		20 44										
Tiverton Parkway	d	18 37			19 04	19 11	19 39							20 59										
Taunton	d	18 51			19 18	19 26	19 54					20 42		21 14										
Bridgwater	a																							
Weston-super-Mare	a																							
Bristol Temple Meads 10	a	19 23			19 54		20 27							21 47										
Bath Spa 7	a													22 01										
Filton Abbey Wood	a																							
Bristol Parkway 7	a	19 38			20 08		20 38																	
Swindon	a													22 29										
Newport (South Wales)	a																							
Cardiff Central 7	a																							
Birmingham New Street 12	a	20 54			21 38		21 53																	
Castle Cary	d					19 47																		
Westbury	d					20 06																		
Pewsey	d					20 23																		
Hungerford	a																							
Newbury	a																							
Thatcham	a																							
Theale	a																							
Reading 7	a					20 58						21 59		23 04										
Slough 3	a																							
London Paddington 15 ⊖	a					21 32						22 26		23 36										

A 🛒 from Plymouth to Taunton

b Arr. 1835

c Arr. 2000

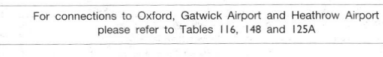

For connections to Oxford, Gatwick Airport and Heathrow Airport please refer to Tables 116, 148 and 125A

Table 135

Saturdays
from 17 September

Cornwall and Devon - Birmingham and London

		GW	GW	XC	GW	GW	XC	GW	GW	GW	XC	GW	XC	GW	GW	GW	XC	GW	GW	GW	GW	XC	GW
			R	◇1			◇1	◇1			◇1	◇1	◇1		◇1	◇1	◇1		◇1			◇1	
			A												B				C			D	
			🛏 🍴				🛒	🍴			🛒	🍴	🛒		🍴Ø	🍴	🛒		🍴Ø			🛒	
Penzance	d		21p45	22p08	05 20													05 37				06 30	06 41
St Erth	d		21p55	22p16														05 44				06 38	06a49
Hayle	d			22p20														05 48				06 41	
Camborne	d		22p07	22p30	05 37													05 57				06 51	
Redruth	d		22p14	22p36	05 43													06 03				06 57	
Truro	d		22p27	22p48	05a55													06 14				07 09	
St Austell	d		22p45	23p04														06 31				07 25	
Newquay	d																						
Par	d		22p54	23p12														06 39				07 32	
Lostwithiel	d			23p19														06 46				07 39	
Bodmin Parkway	d		23p06	23p26														06 52				07 46	
Liskeard 6	d		23p21	23p39														07 06				07 58	
Menheniot	d																	07x10					
St Germans	d																	07 17					
Saltash	d																	07 24					
St Budeaux Ferry Road	d																	07 28					
Keyham	d																	07 30					
Dockyard	d																	07x32					
Devonport	d																	07 34					
Plymouth	a		23p45	00 04														07 41				08 22	
	d		23p51				05 25	05 40			06 25				06 55		07 25		07 47		08 06	08 25	
Ivybridge	d																				08 21		
Totnes	d		00 19				05 50	06 07			06 50						07 50		08 14		08 35	08 50	
Paignton	d	23p41							06 13	06 34			07 00	07 08		07 20				08 06			
Torquay	d	23p46							06 18	06 39			07 06	07 13		07 26				08 11			
Torre	d	23p49							06 21	06 42				07 16		07 30				08 14			
Newton Abbot	a	23p57	00 31				06 01	06 18	06 29	06 50	07 01		07 16	07 24	07 30	07 39	08 01		08 26	08 22	08 47	09 01	
	d	23p59	00 32				06 03	06 20	06 31	06 52	07 03		07 18		07 31	07 40	08 03		08 27	08 34	08 48	09 03	
Teignmouth	d	00 06							06 38	06 59			07 25			07 48				08 41	08 55		
Dawlish	d	00 11							06 43	07 04			07 30			07 54				08 46	09 00		
Dawlish Warren	d	00 16							06 48	07b15										08 51			
Starcross	d	00 20							06 52	07 19										08 55			
Exeter St Thomas	d	00 29							07 01	07 28										09 04			
Exeter St Davids 6	a	00 34	00 54				06 21	06 40	07 06	07 33	07 21		07 41		07 52	08 06	08 21		08 47	09 09	09 16	09 21	
Exeter Central	a								07 14	07 39										09 21			
Exmouth	a								07 43	08 18										09 50			
Exeter St Davids 6	d		01 00			06 00	06 23	06 41			07 23	07 28	07 47		07 54	08 08	08 23		08 49			09 23	
Tiverton Parkway	d					06 18	06 37	06 56			07 37	07 43				08 23	08 37		09 04			09 37	
Taunton	d		01 30			06 35	06 51	07 11			07 51	07 58	08 12		08 19	08 38	08 51		09 19			09 51	
Bridgwater	a					06 47						08 08											
Weston-super-Mare	a					07 06						08 26				08 58							
Bristol Temple Meads 10	a		02 34			07 42	07 25				08 24	08 57	08 49			09 23	09 26					10 26	
Bath Spa 7	a											09 11				09 41							
Filton Abbey Wood	a					07 58																	
Bristol Parkway 7	a					08 05	07 38				08 38		09 08				09 38					10 38	
Swindon	a		03 15									09 40				10 10							
Newport (South Wales)	a																						
Cardiff Central 7	a																						
Birmingham New Street 12	a						08 56				09 56		10 26				10 56					11 56	
Castle Cary	d							07 33											09 40				
Westbury	d							07 56											09 59				
Pewsey	d							08 13											10 16				
Hungerford	a																						
Newbury	a							08 33															
Thatcham	a																						
Theale	a																						
Reading 7	a		04s05					08 52				10 11			09 35	10 45			10 51				
Slough 3	a																						
London Paddington 15 ⊖	a		05 09					09 21				10 39			10 08	11 14			11 24				

A The Night Riviera
B 🍴 from Reading Ø to Taunton
C 🍴 from Castle Cary Ø to Taunton
D 🛒 from Plymouth
b Arr. 0708

For connections to Oxford, Gatwick Airport and Heathrow Airport please refer to Tables 116, 148 and 125A

Table 135

Saturdays

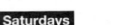

from 17 September

Cornwall and Devon - Birmingham and London

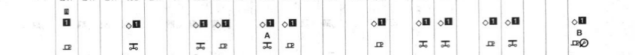

		GW	GW	GW	XC	GW		XC	GW	GW	XC	GW	GW	GW	GW	GW		XC	XC	GW	GW	XC	GW	GW	GW
		1			◇1			◇1	◇1		◇1	◇1				◇1		◇1	◇1		◇1	◇1			◇1
											A														B
		☕			🛒			🛒	☕		🛒	☕				☕		🛒	🛒		☕	🛒			☕⊘
Penzance	d	06 50				07 35			07 59		08 28	08 45	08 54						09 43		10 00		10 36		10 58
St Erth	d	07 00				07 48			08 09		08 36	08 55	09a02						09 51		10 10		10 45		11 08
Hayle	d					07 52			08 13														10 48		
Camborne	d	07 11				08 02			08 23		08 46	09 06							10 01		10 21		10 58		11 19
Redruth	d	07 18				08 09			08 30		08 52	09 13							10 07		10 28		11 04		11 26
Truro	d	07 31				08 20			08 43		09 04	09 26							10 19		10 41		11 15		11 39
St Austell	d	07 48				08 36			09 01		09 20	09 43							10 35		10 58		11 32		11 56
Newquay	d																								
Par	d	07 56				08 44			09 09		09 28	09 51							10 42		11 07		11 39		
Lostwithiel	d	08 04				08 51													10 49				11 46		
Bodmin Parkway	d	08 10				08 57			09 20		09 39	10 03							10 56		11 18		11 52		12 13
Liskeard 6	d	08 23				09 10			09 33		09 51	10 16							11 09		11 31		12 06		12 26
Menheniot	d																						12x10		
St Germans	d					09 22																	12 17		
Saltash	d					09 29																	12 23		
St Budeaux Ferry Road	d																								
Keyham	d																								
Dockyard	d																								
Devonport	d																								
Plymouth	a	08 49				09 40			09 59		10 15	10 40							11 33		11 59		12 36		12 52
	d	08 52			09 25				10 02		10 25	10 44						11 25	11 48		12 00	12 23			12 54
Ivybridge	d								10 17												12 15				
Totnes	d	09 19			09 50				10 31		10 50							11 50	12 13		12 29	12 49			13 21
Paignton	d		09 11	09 30				10 06		10 23				10 56	11 13					12 13				12 43	
Torquay	d		09 16	09 35				10 12		10 28				11 01	11 18					12 18				12 48	
Torre	d		09 19	09 38						10 31				11 04	11 21					12 21					
Newton Abbot	a	09 30	09 27	09 47	10 01			10 22	10 43	10 38	11 01			11 12	11 29			12 01	12 24	12 30	12 41	13 01		12 58	13 34
	d	09 32	09 35	09 48	10 03			10 23	10 44	10 47	11 03			11 23	11 41			12 03	12 25	12 32	12 42	13 03		13 06	13 35
Teignmouth	d		09 42	09 56				10 30		10 55				11 30	11 48					12 39				13 13	
Dawlish	d		09 47	10 02				10 35		11 00				11 35	11 53					12 44				13 18	
Dawlish Warren	d		09 52	10 07						11 04				11 40	11 58					12 55				13 23	
Starcross	d		09 56											11 44	12 02					12 59					
Exeter St Thomas	d		10 05											11 53	12 11					13 08					
Exeter St Davids 6	a	09 52	10 10	10 18	10 21			10 47	11 04	11 16	11 21	11 38		11 58	12 16			12 21	12 44	13 13	13 02	13 23		13 35	13 55
Exeter Central	a		10 21							11 21					12 21					13 21					
Exmouth	a		10 50							11 50					12 50					13 50					
Exeter St Davids 6	d	09 54			10 23			10 49	11 06		11 23	11 40				11 54		12 23	12 48		13 04	13 25			13 57
Tiverton Parkway	d	10 09			10 37			11 02	11 21		11 37					12 09		12 37	13 02		13 19	13 39			
Taunton	d	10 24			10 51			11 17	11 36		11 51					12 24		12 51	13 16		13 34	13 54			14 23
Bridgwater	a																								
Weston-super-Mare	a																								
Bristol Temple Meads 10	a				11 26			11 55			12 25							13 24	13 56			14 27			
Bath Spa 7	a																								
Filton Abbey Wood	a																								
Bristol Parkway 7	a				11 38			12 08			12 38							13 38	14 08			14 38			
Swindon	a																								
Newport (South Wales)	a																								
Cardiff Central 7	a																								
Birmingham New Street 12	a				12 56			13 26			13 56							14 56	15 26			15 55			
Castle Cary	d															12 45									14 44
Westbury	d	11 02														13 05									15 03
Pewsey	d															13 22									
Hungerford	a															13 39									
Newbury	a															13 49									
Thatcham	a															13 56									
Theale	a															14 05									
Reading 7	a	11 51							12 52			13 17				14 19					14 51				15 51
Slough 3	a																								
London Paddington 15 ⊖	a	12 23							13 21			13 46				14 45					15 22				16 23

A 🛒 from Plymouth

B ☕ to Liskeard ☕ from Reading
⊘ from Plymouth to Westbury

For connections to Oxford, Gatwick Airport and Heathrow Airport please refer to Tables 116, 148 and 125A

Table 135

Saturdays
from 17 September

Cornwall and Devon - Birmingham and London

		GW	XC	GW	XC	GW	GW	GW	XC	GW	GW	GW	XC	GW	GW	GW	XC	GW	XC	GW	GW	GW
			◇1 [trolley]		◇1 [trolley]	◇1 [buffet]	◇1 A [buffet]⊘		◇1 [trolley]			◇1 [buffet]	◇1 [trolley]				◇1 B [trolley]	◇1 [buffet]	◇1 B [trolley]		◇1 [buffet]	
Penzance	d			11 46						13 00								14 01		14 52		
St Erth	d			11 56						13 09								14 11		15 01		
Hayle	d			12 00						13 12										15 04		
Camborne	d			12 10						13 21								14 22		15 14		
Redruth	d			12 16						13 27								14 29		15 20		
Truro	d			12 29						13 38								14 42		15 31		
St Austell	d			12 47						13 55								14 59		15 48		
Newquay	d																					
Par	d			12 55						14 03								15 07		15 55		
Lostwithiel	d			13 02						14 09										16 02		
Bodmin Parkway	d			13 09						14 15								15 19		16 08		
Liskeard 6	d			13 23						14 28								15 32		16 21		
Menheniot	d			13x28																16x25		
St Germans	d			13 36						14 39										16 33		
Saltash	d			13 45						14 47										16 39		
St Budeaux Ferry Road	d																					
Keyham	d																					
Dockyard	d																					
Devonport	d									14 52												
Plymouth	a			13 55						14 58								15 57		16 51		
	d		13 25				14 00		14 25			15 04	15 25		15 32			16 01	16 25		16 57	
Ivybridge	d														15 47						17 12	
Totnes	d		13 50						14 50			15 31	15 50		16 01			16 28	16 50		17 27	
Paignton	d	13 13			13 53			14 13			15 13			15 43		16 13						17 13
Torquay	d	13 18			13 59			14 18			15 18			15 48		16 18						17 18
Torre	d	13 21						14 21			15 21					16 21						17 21
Newton Abbot	a	13 29	14 01		14 09		14 35	14 29	15 01		15 29	15 42	16 01	15 58	16 13	16 29		16 40	17 01		17 38	17 29
	d	13 41	14 03		14 10		14 36	14 40	15 03		15 34	15 44	16 03	16 09		16 31		16 41	17 03		17 40	17 43
Teignmouth	d	13 48			14 17			14 48			15 42			16 16		16 38						17 50
Dawlish	d	13 53			14 22			14 53			15 47			16 21		16 43						17 55
Dawlish Warren	d	13 58						14 57			15b58					16c55						18 00
Starcross	d	14 02						15 01			16 02					16 59						18 04
Exeter St Thomas	d	14 11						15 11			16 12					17 08						18 13
Exeter St Davids 6	a	14 16	14 21		14 34		14 56	15 15	15 21		16 15	16 04	16 21	16 34		17 15		17 01	17 21		18 00	18 18
Exeter Central	a	14 21						15 21			16 21			16 44		17 21						18 23
Exmouth	a	14 50						15 50			16 50					17 50						18 52
Exeter St Davids 6	d		14 23		14 36		14 58		15 23			16 06	16 23				16 53	17 03	17 23		18 02	
Tiverton Parkway	d		14 37		14 49		15 13		15 37			16 21	16 37				17 07	17 17	17 37		18 17	
Taunton	d		14 52		15 04	15 19	15 28		15 51			16 36	16 51				17 21	17 32	17 51		18 32	
Bridgwater	a																					
Weston-super-Mare	a				15 23																	
Bristol Temple Meads 10	a		15 25		15 49				16 25				17 25				17 54		18 25			
Bath Spa 7	a																					
Filton Abbey Wood	a																					
Bristol Parkway 7	a		15 38		16 08				16 38				17 38				18 08		18 38			
Swindon	a																					
Newport (South Wales)	a																					
Cardiff Central 7	a																					
Birmingham New Street 12	a		16 56		17 26				17 56				18 56				19 26		19 56			
Castle Cary	d						15 49															
Westbury	d					16 07															18 53	
Pewsey	d					16 25															19 12	
Hungerford	a					16 41																
Newbury	a					16 52																
Thatcham	a					16 58															19 45	
Theale	a					17 07																
Reading 7	a					17 17	16 50					17 53						18 49			20 07	
Slough 3	a																					
London Paddington 15 ⊖	a					17 51	17 21					18 21						19 22			20 37	

A [buffet] from Reading ⊘ to Castle Cary

B [trolley] to Bristol Parkway

b Arr. 1551

c Arr. 1647

For connections to Oxford, Gatwick Airport and Heathrow Airport please refer to Tables 116, 148 and 125A

Table 135

Saturdays
from 17 September

Cornwall and Devon - Birmingham and London

		XC	GW	GW	GW	XC	GW	GW	GW	GW	GW	GW	GW	GW	GW	GW	GW	XC	GW
		◇1			◇1	◇1					◇1			1				◇1	
		A																	
		[trolley]			[restaurant]	[trolley]					[restaurant]								
Penzance	d				15 52			16 41			17 40	18 50				19 06		21 32	
St Erth	d				16 02			16 51			17 50	18a58				19 15		21 42	
Hayle	d							16 55			17 54					19 18			
Camborne	d				16 13			17 05			18 04					19 27		21 53	
Redruth	d				16 20			17 12			18 11					19 33		22 00	
Truro	d				16 33			17 25			18 24					19 44		22 13	
St Austell	d				16 51			17 43			18 41					20 01		22 30	
Newquay	d																21 18		
Par	d				16 59			17 51			18 49					20 09	22 09	22 38	
Lostwithiel	d				17 06			17 58								20 15	22 18		
Bodmin Parkway	d				17 13			18 05			19 01					20 21	22 24	22 49	
Liskeard 6	d				17 26			18 19			19 14					20 34	22 37	23 02	
Menheniot	d															20x39	22x41		
St Germans	d							18 31								20 47	22 49		
Saltash	d							18 38								20 54	22 55		
St Budeaux Ferry Road	d															20 58	22 59		
Keyham	d															21 00	23 01		
Dockyard	d															21x02	23x03		
Devonport	d															21 04	23 05		
Plymouth	a				17 51			18 49			19 39					21 10	23 12	23 27	
	d	17 23		17 38	17 54	18 25		18 51			19 42					21 15			
Ivybridge	d			17 53				19 07								21 30			
Totnes	d	17 49		18 07	18 21	18 50		19 22			20 09					21 44			
Paignton	d		17 52				18 53		19 21	19 50			20 13	20 46	21 13				21 53
Torquay	d		17 57				18 58		19 26	19 55			20 18	20 52	21 18				21 58
Torre	d		18 00				19 01		19 29				20 21		21 21				22 01
Newton Abbot	a	18 01	18 08	18 19	18 32	19 01	19 10	19 34	19 38	20 05	20 20		20 29	21 02	21 29	21 56			22 09
	d	18 03	18 10	18 19	18 34	19 03	19 12	19 35	19 40	20 07	20 22		20 31	21 04	21 31	21 56			22 11
Teignmouth	d		18 17	18 26			19 19	19 43	19 47	20 14			20 38		21 38	22 03			22 18
Dawlish	d		18 22	18 31			19 24	19 48	19 52	20 19			20 43		21 43	22 08			22 23
Dawlish Warren	d		18 27	18b47			19 29		20c06	20 24			20 48		21 48				22 28
Starcross	d		18 31				19 33		20 10				20 52		21 52				22 32
Exeter St Thomas	d		18 40				19 42		20 20				21 01		22 01				22 41
Exeter St Davids 6	a	18 23	18 46	18 59	18 54	19 21	19 45	20 01	20 25	20 36	20 42		21 05	21 24	22 05	22 22			22 45
Exeter Central	a		18 53						20 33										
Exmouth	a		19 22						21 01										
Exeter St Davids 6	d	18 25			18 56	19 23					20 44								
Tiverton Parkway	d	18 39			19 11	19 37					20 59								
Taunton	d	18 54			19 26	19 51					21 14								
Bridgwater	a																		
Weston-super-Mare	a																		
Bristol Temple Meads 10	a	19 27				20 25					21 47								
Bath Spa 7	a										22 01								
Filton Abbey Wood	a																		
Bristol Parkway 7	a	19 38				20 38													
Swindon	a										22 29								
Newport (South Wales)	a																		
Cardiff Central 7	a																		
Birmingham New Street 12	a	20 53				21 53													
Castle Cary	d				19 47														
Westbury	d				20 06														
Pewsey	d				20 23														
Hungerford	a																		
Newbury	a																		
Thatcham	a																		
Theale	a																		
Reading 7	a				20 58						23 04								
Slough 3	a																		
London Paddington 15 ⊖	a				21 32						23 36								

A [trolley] to Bristol Parkway

b Arr. 1835

c Arr. 1956

For connections to Oxford, Gatwick Airport and Heathrow Airport please refer to Tables 116, 148 and 125A

Table 135

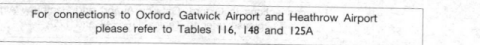

Sundays
until 19 June

Cornwall and Devon - Birmingham and London

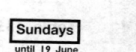

		GW	GW		GW	GW	XC	GW	GW	XC		XC	GW	GW	GW	XC	GW	GW	XC	GW		GW	XC	GW	GW
		◇	◇1			◇1	◇1		◇1	◇1		◇1	◇1			◇1		◇1	◇1			◇1	◇1		◇1
																C									
			⊡			⊡	⊥		⊡	⊥		⊥	⊡			⊥		⊡	⊥			⊡	⊥		⊡
Penzance	d												08 35	08 45		09 30		09 47				11 00			11 40
St Erth	d												08 44	08a53		09 38		09 57				11 09			11 50
Hayle	d												08 49												
Camborne	d												09 00			09 48		10 09				11 22			12 02
Redruth	d												09 06			09 54		10 15				11 28			12 09
Truro	d												09 20			10 06		10 28				11 41			12 22
St Austell	d												09 36			10 22		10 45				11 58			12 39
Newquay	d																						11 35		
Par	d												09 45			10 30		10 53				12 06			12 47
Lostwithiel	d																								
Bodmin Parkway	d												09 57			10 41		11 06				12 18	12 41		12 59
Liskeard 6	d												10 10			10 53		11 19				12 32	12 54		13 12
Menheniot	d																								
St Germans	d																	11 30							
Saltash	d												10 28												
St Budeaux Ferry Road	d																								
Keyham	d																								
Dockyard	d																								
Devonport	d																								
Plymouth	a												10 35			11 17		11 45				12 57	13 19		13 37
	d					08 40	09 25		10 10	10 25			10 40			11 25		11 45	12 25			13 00	13 23		13 44
Ivybridge	d																								
Totnes	d					09 07	09 50		10 40	10 50			11 07			11 50		12 16	12 50			13 28	13 49		14 10
Paignton	d							09 49				10 50			11 00		11 49			12 57				13 51	
Torquay	d							09 54				10 56			11 05		11 54			13 02				13 56	
Torre	d							09 57							11 08		11 57			13 05				13 59	
Newton Abbot	a					09 19	10 01	10 05	10 52	11 01		11 05	11 19		11 16	12 01	12 05	12 28	13 01	13 13		13 39	14 01	14 07	14 23
	d					09 20	10 03	10 07	10 54	11 03		11 08	11 21		11 26	12 03	12 07	12 30	13 03	13 15		13 41	14 03	14 08	14 24
Teignmouth	d					09 27		10 14				11 15			11 33		12 14			13 22				14 15	
Dawlish	d					09 33		10 19				11 20			11 38		12 19			13 27				14 20	
Dawlish Warren	d							10 24									12 24							14 25	
Starcross	d							10 28									12 28							14 29	
Exeter St Thomas	d							10 37									12 37							14 38	
Exeter St Davids 6	a					09 47	10 21	10 42	11 14	11 21		11 31	11 41		11 52	12 21	12 43	12 50	13 21	13 41		14 01	14 23	14 43	14 46
Exeter Central	a							10 50							11 58		12 51			13 51				14 51	
Exmouth	a							11 17							12 25		13 20			14 18				15 18	
Exeter St Davids 6	d	08 01	08 38		09 35	09 48	10 23		11 18	11 23		11 33	11 43			12 23		12 51	13 23			14 03	14 25		14 47
Tiverton Parkway	d	08 18	08 53		09 53		10 37		11 33	11 38		11 47	11 58			12 37			13 37			14 17	14 39		
Taunton	d	08 35	09 07		10 11	10 14	10 51		11 48	11 53		12 01	12 13			12 51		13 16	13 51			14 32	14 54		15 12
Bridgwater	a	08 46			10 23																				
Weston-super-Mare	a	09 06			10 41							12 22													
Bristol Temple Meads 10	a	09 38			11 14		11 24		12 23	12 27		12 47				13 26			14 24				15 27		
Bath Spa 7	a								12 41																
Filton Abbey Wood	a	09 55																							
Bristol Parkway 7	a						11 38			12 38		13 08				13 38			15 08				15 38		
Swindon	a								13 10																
Newport (South Wales)	a	10 26					12 09			13 10		13 40				14 08									
Cardiff Central 7	a	10 42																							
Birmingham New Street 12	a						13 50			14 48		15 26				15 50			16 26				16 50		
Castle Cary	d		09 29										12 34												
Westbury	d		09 49			10 51							12 53					13b59							15 34
Pewsey	d		10 06										13 10												15 52
Hungerford	a																								16 10
Newbury	a		10 26			11 26							13 30												
Thatcham	a																								16 31
Theale	a																								
Reading 7	a		10 47			11 47			13 44				13 48					14 49				15 47			16 48
Slough 3	a																								
London Paddington 15 ⊖	a		1127			12 27			14 22				14 29					15 27				16 26			17 27

C ⊥ from Plymouth

b Arr. 1352

For connections to Oxford, Gatwick Airport and Heathrow Airport please refer to Tables 116, 148 and 125A

Table 135

Sundays
until 19 June

Cornwall and Devon - Birmingham and London

		GW	GW	XC	XC	GW	GW	GW	XC	GW	GW	GW	GW	GW	GW	XC	GW	GW	GW	XC	GW	GW	XC
				◇1	◇1		◇1	◇1	◇1	◇1		◇1			◇1	◇1		◇	◇1	◇1		◇1	◇1
					A				B											A			
				🚲	🚲		🍴	🍴	🚲	🍴		🍴			🍴				🍴	🚲		🍴	🚲
Penzance	d		12 05		12 30		12 56						13 40					14 40	15 00	15 30		15 50	
St Erth	d		12 14		12 40		13 05						13 50					14 49	15 10	15 38		16 00	
Hayle	d				12 44								13 53					14 52					
Camborne	d		12 25		12 56		13 19						14 02					15 01	15 22	15 51		16 12	
Redruth	d		12 31		13 02		13 25						14 08					15 07	15 29	15 57		16 19	
Truro	d		12 42		13 14		13 38						14 19					15 18	15 41	16 09		16 32	
St Austell	d		12 59		13 30		13 56						14 36					15 35	15 59	16 25		16 49	
Newquay	d																						
Par	d		13 06		13 38		14 03						14 44					15 43	16 07	16 33		16 56	
Lostwithiel	d		13 13		13 45								14 50					15 49					
Bodmin Parkway	d		13 19		13 52		14 16						14 56					15 55	16 18	16 44		17 08	
Liskeard 6	d		13 33		14 04		14 29						15 09					16 08	16 31	16 56		17 21	
Menheniot	d												15x14										
St Germans	d		13 44										15 21					16 19					
Saltash	d		13 52										15 29					16 27					
St Budeaux Ferry Road	d																						
Keyham	d																						
Dockyard	d																						
Devonport	d																						
Plymouth	a		14 01		14 28		14 55						15 38					16 37	16 57	17 20		17 43	
	d		14 06	14 23	14 35		14 55	15 05	15 25			15 43	15 49		16 10	16 25		16 38	17 00	17 25		17 45	
Ivybridge	d		14 21										16 07					16 53					
Totnes	d		14 35	14 49	15 00		15 25	15 35	15 50			16 11	16 21		16 42	16 51		17 07	17 27	17 51		18 13	
Paignton	d	14 19				14 57				15 45	15 54			16 22			16 55				17 49		18 18
Torquay	d	14 24				15 02				15 51	15 59			16 27			17 00				17 54		18 24
Torre	d	14 27				15 05				15 56	16 02			16 30			17 03				17 57		
Newton Abbot	a	14 35	14 47	15 01	15 11	15 13	15 37	15 47	16 01	16 04	16 10	16 22	16 33	16 38	16 53	17 03	17 11	17 19	17 39	18 02	18 05	18 25	18 34
	d	14 37	14 48	15 03	15 12	15 15	15 38	15 48	16 03	16 05	16 11	16 24	16 34	16 39	16 55	17 04	17 12	17 20	17 40	18 03	18 07	18 26	18 35
Teignmouth	d	14 44	14 55			15 22				16 13	16 18			16 47			17 19	17 27			18 14		
Dawlish	d	14 49	15 00			15 27				16 18	16 23			16 52			17 24	17 32			18 19		
Dawlish Warren	d	14 54									16 28			16 56			17 29				18 24		
Starcross	d	14 58												17 00							18 28		
Exeter St Thomas	d	15 07												17 10							18 37		
Exeter St Davids 6	a	15 12	15 16	15 23	15 31	15 41	15 58	16 08	16 21	16 32	16 41	16 44	16 55	17 14	17 17	17 23	17 42	17 46	18 00	18 22	18 40	18 47	18 54
Exeter Central	a	15 17				15 51					16 51			17 21			17 51				18 51		
Exmouth	a					16 18					17 18						18 18				19 18		
Exeter St Davids 6	d			15 25	15 33		16 01	16 10	16 23	16 34		16 45			17 19	17 25		17 51	18 02	18 24		18 49	18 56
Tiverton Parkway	d			15 38	15 46		16 16	16 25	16 37			17 01			17 34	17 41			18 17	18 36			19 09
Taunton	d			15 54	16 01		16 31	16 40	16 51	16 59		17 15			17 48	17 54		18 22	18 32	18 52		19 10	19 23
Bridgwater	a									17 09								18 33					
Weston-super-Mare	a				16 20			17 01		17 28								18 52					
Bristol Temple Meads 10	a			16 28	16 53			17 22	17 26	17 57					18 23	18 28		19 22		19 27			19 57
Bath Spa 7	a							17 41		18 12					18 41								
Filton Abbey Wood	a																						
Bristol Parkway 7	a			16 38	17 08				17 38							18 39				19 38			20 08
Swindon	a							18 10		18 39					19 10								
Newport (South Wales)	a																						
Cardiff Central 7	a																						
Birmingham New Street 12	a			17 51	18 27				18 50							19 53				20 50			21 20
Castle Cary	d											17 37											
Westbury	d											17 57							19 09				
Pewsey	d											18 14											
Hungerford	a																						
Newbury	a											18 34										20 17	
Thatcham	a																						
Theale	a																						
Reading 7	a						17 47	18 42		19 12		18 54			19 42				19 54			20 35	
Slough 3	a																						
London Paddington 15 ⊖	a						18 27	19 26		19 54		19 37			20 22				20 37			21 20	

A 🚲 from Plymouth to Bristol Parkway

B 🚲 to Bristol Parkway

For connections to Oxford, Gatwick Airport and Heathrow Airport please refer to Tables 116, 148 and 125A

Table 135

Sundays

until 19 June

Cornwall and Devon - Birmingham and London

		GW		XC	GW	GW	GW	GW	GW	GW	GW	GW		GW	GW	GW
																■
		◇1		◇1		◇1			◇1							
		🍽		🛒		🍽	🛒		🍽			🛒				🛏 🍽
Penzance	d					17 20	17 50				19 00	20 05				21 15
St Erth	d					17 29	17 59				19 09	20 14				21 25
Hayle	d						18 02					20 17				
Camborne	d					17 42	18 12				19 20	20 26				21 38
Redruth	d					17 49	18 18				19 26	20 32				21 45
Truro	d					18 01	18 30				19 38	20 44				22 00
St Austell	d					18 19	18 47				19 55	21 01				22 18
Newquay	d	16 15														
Par	d	17 15				18 27	18 54				20 02	21 08				
Lostwithiel	d	17 25					19 01				20 09					
Bodmin Parkway	d	17 30				18 39	19 08				20 15	21 20				22 35
Liskeard 6	d	17 43				18 52	19 22				20 28	21 34				22 50
Menheniot	d										20x33					
St Germans	d										20 40					
Saltash	d										20 47					
St Budeaux Ferry Road	d						19 43									
Keyham	d															
Dockyard	d															
Devonport	d						19 47				20 55					
Plymouth	a	18 10				19 16	19 50				20 59	22 00				23 15
	d	18 10		18 23		19 21			19 55		21 15					23 20
Ivybridge	d															
Totnes	d	18 41		18 49		19 48					21 42					23 48
Paignton	d				18 55			19 55		20 55				21 52	23 00	
Torquay	d				19 00			20 00		21 00				21 57	23 05	
Torre	d				19 03			20 03		21 03				22 00	23 08	
Newton Abbot	a	18 53		19 01	19 11	20 00		20 11	20 31	21 11	21 54			22 08	23 16	23 59
	d	18 53		19 03	19 13	20 01		20 13	20 32	21 13	21 55			22 10	23 18	00 01
Teignmouth	d				19 20			20 20		21 20	22 02			22 17	23 25	
Dawlish	d				19 25			20 25		21 25	22 07			22 22	23 30	
Dawlish Warren	d				19 30			20 30						22 27	23 35	
Starcross	d				19 34			20 34						22 31	23 39	
Exeter St Thomas	d				19 43			20 43						22 40	23 48	
Exeter St Davids 6	a	19 15		19 23	19 48	20 21		20 48	20 53	21 40	22 21			22 43	23 52	00 40
Exeter Central	a				19 54			20 54		21 51				22 51		
Exmouth	a				20 21			21 21		22 18				23 18		
Exeter St Davids 6	d	19 17		19 25		20 22			20 55							00 57
Tiverton Parkway	d	19 32		19 38		20 38			21 10							
Taunton	d	19 46		19 54		20 53			21 23							
Bridgwater	a															
Weston-super-Mare	a															
Bristol Temple Meads 10	a			20 27					22 00							02 08
Bath Spa 7	a								22 22							
Filton Abbey Wood	a															
Bristol Parkway 7	a			20 38												
Swindon	a								22 50							03 21
Newport (South Wales)	a															
Cardiff Central 7	a															
Birmingham New Street 12	a			21 51												
Castle Cary	d	20 08				21 15										
Westbury	d	20 27				21 34										
Pewsey	d					21 52										
Hungerford	a															
Newbury	a					22 12										
Thatcham	a															
Theale	a															
Reading 7	a	21 13				22 30			23 27							04s02
Slough 3	a															
London Paddington 15 ⊖	a	21 52				23 15			00 16							05 05

For connections to Oxford, Gatwick Airport and Heathrow Airport please refer to Tables 116, 148 and 125A

Table 135

Sundays

26 June to 31 July

Cornwall and Devon - Birmingham and London

		GW	GW	GW	GW	XC	GW	GW	XC	XC	GW	GW	GW	XC	GW	GW	XC	GW	GW	XC	GW	GW	GW
		◇	◇[1]		◇[1]	◇[1]		◇[1]	◇[1]	◇[1]	◇[1]			◇[1]		◇[1]	◇[1]		◇[1]	◇[1]		◇[1]	
														A									
			🍽		🍽	🛒		🍽	🛒	🛒	🍽			🛒		🍽	🛒		🍽	🛒		🍽	
Penzance	d										08 35	08 45		09 30		09 47			11 00			11 40	
St Erth	d										08 44	08a53		09 38		09 57			11 09			11 50	
Hayle	d										08 49												
Camborne	d										09 00			09 48		10 09			11 22			12 02	
Redruth	d										09 06			09 54		10 15			11 28			12 09	
Truro	d										09 20			10 06		10 28			11 41			12 22	
St Austell	d										09 36			10 22		10 45			11 58			12 39	
Newquay	d																			11 35			
Par	d										09 45			10 30		10 53			12 06			12 47	
Lostwithiel	d																						
Bodmin Parkway	d										09 57			10 41		11 06			12 18	12 41		12 59	
Liskeard [6]	d										10 10			10 53		11 19			12 32	12 54		13 12	
Menheniot	d																						
St Germans	d															11 30							
Saltash	d										10 28												
St Budeaux Ferry Road	d																						
Keyham	d																						
Dockyard	d																						
Devonport	d																						
Plymouth	a										10 35			11 16		11 45			12 57	13 19		13 37	
	d				08 40	09 25		10 10	10 25		10 40			11 25		11 45	12 25		13 00	13 23		13 44	
Ivybridge	d																						
Totnes	d				09 07	09 50		10 40	10 50		11 07			11 50		12 16	12 52		13 28	13 49		14 10	
Paignton	d						09 49			10 50			11 00		11 49			12 57			13 51		14 19
Torquay	d						09 54			10 56			11 05		11 54			13 02			13 56		14 24
Torre	d						09 57						11 08		11 57			13 05			13 59		14 27
Newton Abbot	a				09 19	10 01	10 05	10 52	11 01	11 06	11 19		11 16	12 01	12 05	12 28	13 04	13 13	13 39	14 01	14 07	14 23	14 35
	d				09 20	10 03	10 07	10 54	11 03	11 08	11 21		11 26	12 03	12 07	12 30	13 05	13 15	13 41	14 03	14 08	14 24	14 37
Teignmouth	d				09 27		10 14			11 15			11 33		12 14			13 22			14 15		14 44
Dawlish	d				09 33		10 19			11 20			11 38		12 19			13 27			14 20		14 49
Dawlish Warren	d						10 24								12 24						14 25		14 54
Starcross	d						10 28								12 28						14 29		14 58
Exeter St Thomas	d						10 37								12 37						14 38		15 07
Exeter St Davids [6]	a				09 47	10 21	10 42	11 14	11 21	11 30	11 41		11 52	12 21	12 43	12 50	13 25	13 41	14 01	14 23	14 43	14 46	15 12
Exeter Central	a						10 50						11 58		12 51			13 51			14 51		15 17
Exmouth	a						11 17						12 25		13 20			14 18			15 18		
Exeter St Davids [6]	d	08 01	08 38	09 35	09 48	10 23		11 18	11 23	11 32	11 43			12 23		12 51	13 27		14 03	14 25		14 47	
Tiverton Parkway	d	08 18	08 53	09 53		10 37		11 33	11 37	11 46	11 58			12 37					14 17	14 39			
Taunton	d	08 35	09 07	10 11	10 14	10 51		11 48	11 51	12 00	12 13			12 51		13 16	13 53		14 32	14 54		15 12	
Bridgwater	a	08 46		10 23																			
Weston-super-Mare	a	09 06		10 41						12 20													
Bristol Temple Meads [10]	a	09 38		11 14		11 24		12 23	12 27	12 46				13 26			14 26			15 27			
Bath Spa [7]	a							12 41															
Filton Abbey Wood	a	09 55																					
Bristol Parkway [7]	a					11 38			12 38					13 41			14 40			15 38			
Swindon	a							13 10															
Newport (South Wales)	a	10 26				12 09			13 11					14 10			15 11			16 10			
Cardiff Central [7]	a	10 42																					
Birmingham New Street [12]	a					13 50			14 50					15 50			16 51			17 49			
Castle Cary	d		09 29								12 34											15 34	
Westbury	d		09 49		10 51						12 53					13b59						15 52	
Pewsey	d		10 06								13 10											16 10	
Hungerford	a																						
Newbury	a		10 26		11 26						13 30											16 31	
Thatcham	a																						
Theale	a																						
Reading [7]	a		10 47		11 47			13 44			13 48					14 49			15 47			16 48	
Slough [3]	a																						
London Paddington [15] ⊖	a		11 27		12 27			14 22			14 29					15 27			16 26			17 27	

A 🛒 from Plymouth

b Arr. 1352

For connections to Oxford, Gatwick Airport and Heathrow Airport please refer to Tables 116, 148 and 125A

Table 135

Sundays

26 June to 31 July

Cornwall and Devon - Birmingham and London

		GW	XC ◇[1] 🛒	XC ◇[1] A 🛒	GW	GW ◇[1] ☕		GW ◇[1] ☕	XC ◇[1] B 🛒	GW ◇[1] ☕	GW	GW ◇[1] ☕	GW	GW	GW ◇[1] ☕	XC ◇[1] B 🛒		GW	GW ◇	GW ◇[1] ☕	XC ◇[1]	XC ◇[1] B 🛒	GW	GW ◇[1] ☕	GW ◇[1] ☕
Penzance	d	12 05		12 30		12 56							13 40						14 40	15 00	15 25			15 50	
St Erth	d	12 14		12 40		13 05							13 50						14 49	15 10	15 33			16 00	
Hayle	d			12 44									13 53						14 52		15 37				
Camborne	d	12 25		12 56		13 19							14 02						15 01	15 22	15 46			16 12	
Redruth	d	12 31		13 02		13 25							14 08						15 07	15 29	15 53			16 19	
Truro	d	12 42		13 14		13 38							14 19						15 18	15 41	16 04			16 32	
St Austell	d	12 59		13 30		13 56							14 36						15 35	15 59	16 20			16 49	
Newquay	d																								16 15
Par	d	13 06		13 38		14 03							14 44						15 43	16 07	16 28			16 56	17 15
Lostwithiel	d	13 13		13 45									14 50						15 49		16 34				17 25
Bodmin Parkway	d	13 19		13 52		14 16							14 56						15 55	16 18	16 41			17 08	17 30
Liskeard [6]	d	13 33		14 04		14 29							15 09						16 08	16 31	16 53			17 21	17 43
Menheniot	d												15x14												
St Germans	d	13 44											15 21						16 19						
Saltash	d	13 52											15 29						16 27						
St Budeaux Ferry Road	d																								
Keyham	d																								
Dockyard	d																								
Devonport	d																								
Plymouth	a	14 01		14 28		14 55							15 38						16 37	16 57	17 16			17 43	18 10
	d	14 06	14 23	14 35		14 55		15 05	15 25			15 43	15 49		16 10	16 25			16 38	17 00		17 23		17 45	18 10
Ivybridge	d	14 21											16 07						16 53						
Totnes	d	14 35	14 49	15 00		15 25		15 35	15 50			16 11	16 21		16 42	16 51			17 07	17 27		17 49		18 13	18 41
Paignton	d				14 57					15 45	15 54			16 22				16 55					17 49		
Torquay	d				15 02					15 51	15 59			16 27				17 00					17 54		
Torre	d				15 05					15 56	16 02			16 30				17 03					17 57		
Newton Abbot	a	14 47	15 01	15 11	15 13	15 37		15 47	16 01	16 04	16 10	16 22	16 33	16 38	16 53	17 03		17 11	17 19	17 39		18 01	18 05	18 25	18 53
	d	14 48	15 03	15 12	15 15	15 38		15 48	16 03	16 05	16 11	16 24	16 34	16 39	16 55	17 04		17 12	17 20	17 40		18 03	18 07	18 26	18 53
Teignmouth	d	14 55			15 22					16 13	16 18			16 47				17 19	17 27				18 14		
Dawlish	d	15 00			15 27					16 18	16 23			16 52				17 24	17 32				18 19		
Dawlish Warren	d										16 28			16 56				17 29					18 24		
Starcross	d													17 00									18 28		
Exeter St Thomas	d													17 10									18 37		
Exeter St Davids [6]	a	15 16	15 23	15 31	15 41	15 58		16 08	16 21	16 32	16 41	16 44	16 55	17 14	17 17	17 23		17 42	17 46	18 00		18 23	18 40	18 47	19 15
Exeter Central	a				15 51						16 51			17 21				17 51					18 51		
Exmouth	a				16 18						17 18							18 18					19 18		
Exeter St Davids [6]	d		15 25	15 33		16 01		16 10	16 23	16 34		16 45			17 19	17 25			17 51	18 02		18 25		18 49	19 17
Tiverton Parkway	d		15 38	15 46		16 16		16 25	16 37			17 01			17 34	17 41				18 17		18 38			19 32
Taunton	d		15 54	16 01		16 31		16 40	16 51	16 59		17 15			17 48	17 54			18 22	18 32		18 54		19 10	19 46
Bridgwater	a									17 09									18 33						
Weston-super-Mare	a			16 20				17 01		17 28									18 52						
Bristol Temple Meads [10]	a		16 28	16 53				17 22	17 26	17 57					18 23	18 27			19 22			19 27			
Bath Spa [7]	a							17 41		18 12					18 41										
Filton Abbey Wood	a																								
Bristol Parkway [7]	a		16 38						17 38							18 41						19 38			
Swindon	a							18 10		18 39					19 10										
Newport (South Wales)	a		17 09						18 03							19 11						20 12			
Cardiff Central [7]	a																								
Birmingham New Street [12]	a		18 51						19 50							20 51						21 52			
Castle Cary	d											17 37													20 08
Westbury	d											17 57								19 09					20 27
Pewsey	d											18 14													
Hungerford	a																								
Newbury	a											18 34												20 17	
Thatcham	a																								
Theale	a																								
Reading [7]	a					17 47		18 42		19 12		18 54			19 42					19 54				20 35	21 13
Slough [8]	a																								
London Paddington [15] ⊖	a					18 27		19 26		19 54		19 37			20 22					20 37				21 20	21 52

A 🛒 from Plymouth

B 🛒 to Newport (South Wales)

For connections to Oxford, Gatwick Airport and Heathrow Airport please refer to Tables 116, 148 and 125A

Table 135

Sundays
26 June to 31 July

Cornwall and Devon - Birmingham and London

		XC		GW	GW	GW	GW	GW	GW	GW	GW	GW		GW	GW
															B
		◇1			◇1			◇1							
															🛏
		⊥			⊏	⊥		⊏			⊥				⊏
Penzance	d				17 20	17 50				19 00	20 05				21 15
St Erth	d				17 29	17 59				19 09	20 14				21 25
Hayle	d					18 02					20 17				
Camborne	d				17 42	18 12				19 20	20 26				21 38
Redruth	d				17 49	18 18				19 26	20 32				21 45
Truro	d				18 01	18 30				19 38	20 44				22 00
St Austell	d				18 19	18 47				19 55	21 01				22 18
Newquay	d														
Par	d				18 27	18 54				20 02	21 08				
Lostwithiel	d					19 01				20 09					
Bodmin Parkway	d				18 39	19 08				20 15	21 20				22 35
Liskeard 6	d				18 52	19 22				20 28	21 34				22 50
Menheniot	d									20x33					
St Germans	d									20 40					
Saltash	d									20 47					
St Budeaux Ferry Road	d					19 43									
Keyham	d														
Dockyard	d														
Devonport	d					19 47				20 55					
Plymouth	a				19 16	19 50				20 59	22 00				23 15
	d	18 23			19 21			19 55		21 15					23 20
Ivybridge	d														
Totnes	d	18 49			19 48					21 42					23 48
Paignton	d			18 55			19 55		20 55			21 52		23 00	
Torquay	d			19 00			20 00		21 00			21 57		23 05	
Torre	d			19 03			20 03		21 03			22 00		23 08	
Newton Abbot	a	19 01		19 11	20 00		20 11	20 31	21 11	21 54		22 08		23 16	23 59
	d	19 03		19 13	20 01		20 13	20 32	21 13	21 55		22 10		23 18	00 01
Teignmouth	d			19 20			20 20		21 20	22 02		22 17		23 25	
Dawlish	d			19 25			20 25		21 25	22 07		22 22		23 30	
Dawlish Warren	d			19 30			20 30					22 27		23 35	
Starcross	d			19 34			20 34					22 31		23 39	
Exeter St Thomas	d			19 43			20 43					22 40		23 48	
Exeter St Davids 6	a	19 23		19 48	20 21		20 48	20 53	21 40	22 21		22 43		23 52	00 40
Exeter Central	a			19 54			20 54		21 51			22 51			
Exmouth	a			20 21			21 21		22 18			23 18			
Exeter St Davids 6	d	19 25			20 22			20 55							00 57
Tiverton Parkway	d	19 38			20 38			21 10							
Taunton	d	19 54			20 53			21 23							
Bridgwater	a														
Weston-super-Mare	a														
Bristol Temple Meads 10	a	20 27						22 00							02 08
Bath Spa 7	a							22 22							
Filton Abbey Wood	a														
Bristol Parkway 7	a	20 38													
Swindon	a							22 50							03 21
Newport (South Wales)	a	21 09													
Cardiff Central 7	a														
Birmingham New Street 12	a	22 50													
Castle Cary	d				21 15										
Westbury	d				21 34										
Pewsey	d				21 52										
Hungerford	a														
Newbury	a				22 12										
Thatcham	a														
Theale	a														
Reading 7	a				22 30			23 27							04s02
Slough 3	a														
London Paddington 15 ⊖	a				23 15			00 16							05 05

For connections to Oxford, Gatwick Airport and Heathrow Airport please refer to Tables 116, 148 and 125A

Table 135

Sundays

7 August to 11 September

Cornwall and Devon - Birmingham and London

		GW	GW	GW	GW	XC	GW	GW	XC	XC		GW	GW	GW	XC	GW	GW	XC	XC	GW		XC	GW	XC	GW
		◇	◇1		◇1	◇1		◇1	◇1	◇1		◇1			◇1		◇1	◇1	◇1			◇1	◇1	◇1	
															A									A	
			☕		☕	🛒		☕	🛒	🛒		☕			🛒		☕	🛒	🛒			🛒	☕	🛒	
Penzance	d											08 35	08 45		09 30		09 47						11 00		
St Erth	d											08 44	08a53		09 38		09 57						11 09		
Hayle	d											08 49													
Camborne	d											09 00			09 48		10 09						11 22		
Redruth	d											09 06			09 54		10 15						11 28		
Truro	d											09 20			10 06		10 28						11 41		
St Austell	d											09 36			10 22		10 45						11 58		
Newquay	d																							11 35	
Par	d											09 45			10 30		10 53						12 06		
Lostwithiel	d																								
Bodmin Parkway	d											09 57			10 41		11 06						12 18	12 41	
Liskeard 6	d											10 10			10 53		11 19						12 32	12 54	
Menheniot	d																								
St Germans	d																11 30								
Saltash	d											10 28													
St Budeaux Ferry Road	d																								
Keyham	d																								
Dockyard	d																								
Devonport	d																								
Plymouth	a											10 35			11 17		11 45						12 57	13 19	
	d				08 40	09 25		10 10	10 25			10 40			11 25		11 45	12 00	12 25			12 52	13 00	13 23	
Ivybridge	d																								
Totnes	d				09 07	09 50		10 40	10 50			11 07			11 50		12 16		12 50				13 27	13 49	
Paignton	d						09 49			10 50				11 00		11 49				12 57					13 51
Torquay	d						09 54			10 56				11 05		11 54				13 02					13 56
Torre	d						09 57							11 08		11 57				13 05					13 59
Newton Abbot	a				09 19	10 01	10 05	10 52	11 01	11 06		11 19		11 16	12 01	12 05	12 28	12 34	13 01	13 13		13 26	13 39	14 01	14 07
	d				09 20	10 03	10 07	10 54	11 03	11 08		11 21		11 26	12 03	12 07	12 30	12 36	13 03	13 15		13 27	13 40	14 03	14 08
Teignmouth	d				09 27		10 14			11 15				11 33		12 14				13 22					14 15
Dawlish	d				09 33		10 19			11 20				11 38		12 19				13 27					14 20
Dawlish Warren	d						10 24									12 24									14 25
Starcross	d						10 28									12 28									14 29
Exeter St Thomas	d						10 37									12 37									14 38
Exeter St Davids 6	a				09 47	10 21	10 42	11 14	11 21	11 30		11 41		11 52	12 21	12 43	12 50	12 55	13 21	13 41		13 46	14 00	14 23	14 43
Exeter Central	a						10 50							11 58		12 51				13 51					14 51
Exmouth	a						11 17							12 25		13 20				14 18					15 18
Exeter St Davids 6	d	08 01	08 30	09 35	09 48	10 23		11 18	11 23	11 32		11 43			12 23		12 51	12 57	13 23			13 48	14 03	14 25	
Tiverton Parkway	d	08 18	08 45	09 53		10 37		11 33	11 37	11 46		11 58			12 37			13 10	13 37				14 17	14 39	
Taunton	d	08 35	08 59	10 11	10 14	10 51		11 48	11 51	12 00		12 13			12 51		13 16	13 25	13 51				14 32	14 54	
Bridgwater	a	08 46		10 23																					
Weston-super-Mare	a	09 06		10 41						12 20															
Bristol Temple Meads 10	a	09 38		11 14		11 27		12 23	12 27	12 46					13 24			13 57	14 26			14 41		15 27	
Bath Spa 7	a							12 41																	
Filton Abbey Wood	a	09 55																							
Bristol Parkway 7	a					11 38			12 38	13 08					13 38			14 08	14 38			15 08		15 38	
Swindon	a							13 10																	
Newport (South Wales)	a	10 26																							
Cardiff Central 7	a	10 42																							
Birmingham New Street 12	a					12 50			13 50	14 26					14 50			15 27	15 50			16 26		16 50	
Castle Cary	d		09 21									12 34													
Westbury	d		09 41		10 51							12b59					13c59								
Pewsey	d																								
Hungerford	a																								
Newbury	a																								
Thatcham	a																								
Theale	a																								
Reading 7	a		10 50		11 52			13 44				14 04					15 04						16 05		
Slough 3	a																								
London Paddington 15 ⊖	a		11 35		12 35			14 21				14 44					15 43						16 44		

A 🛒 from Plymouth

b Arr. 1252

c Arr. 1352

For connections to Oxford, Gatwick Airport and Heathrow Airport please refer to Tables 116, 148 and 125A

Table 135

Sundays

7 August to 11 September

Cornwall and Devon - Birmingham and London

		GW	GW	GW	XC	XC	GW	GW	GW	XC	GW	GW	GW	GW	GW	GW	XC	GW	GW	GW	XC	GW	GW
		◇1			◇1	◇1		◇1	◇1	◇1	◇1		◇1			◇1	◇1		◇	◇1	◇1		◇1
						A											B				A		
		☕			🍴	🍴		☕	☕	🍴	☕		☕			☕	🍴			☕	🍴		☕
Penzance	d	11 40		12 05		12 30		12 56						13 40					14 40	15 00	15 30		15 50
St Erth	d	11 50		12 14		12 40		13 05						13 50					14 49	15 10	15 38		16 00
Hayle	d					12 44								13 53					14 52				
Camborne	d	12 02		12 25		12 56		13 19						14 02					15 01	15 22	15 51		16 12
Redruth	d	12 09		12 31		13 02		13 25						14 08					15 07	15 29	15 57		16 19
Truro	d	12 22		12 42		13 14		13 38						14 19					15 18	15 41	16 09		16 32
St Austell	d	12 39		12 59		13 30		13 56						14 36					15 35	15 59	16 25		16 49
Newquay	d																						
Par	d	12 47		13 06		13 38		14 03						14 44					15 43	16 07	16 33		16 56
Lostwithiel	d			13 13		13 45								14 50					15 49				
Bodmin Parkway	d	12 59		13 19		13 52		14 16						14 56					15 55	16 18	16 44		17 08
Liskeard 6	d	13 12		13 33		14 04		14 29						15 09					16 08	16 31	16 56		17 21
Menheniot	d													15x14									
St Germans	d			13 44										15 21					16 19				
Saltash	d			13 52										15 29					16 27				
St Budeaux Ferry Road	d																						
Keyham	d																						
Dockyard	d																						
Devonport	d																						
Plymouth	a	13 37		14 01		14 28		14 55						15 38					16 37	16 57	17 20		17 43
	d	13 44		14 06	14 23	14 35		14 55	15 05	15 23			15 43	15 49		16 10	16 25		16 38	17 00	17 26		17 46
Ivybridge	d			14 21										16 07					16 53				
Totnes	d	14 10		14 35	14 49	15 00		15 26	15 35	15 49			16 11	16 21		16 42	16 50		17 07	17 27	17 52		18 13
Paignton	d		14 19				14 57				15 45	15 54			16 22			16 55				17 49	
Torquay	d		14 24				15 02				15 51	15 59			16 27			17 00				17 54	
Torre	d		14 27				15 05				15 56	16 02			16 30			17 03				17 57	
Newton Abbot	a	14 23	14 35	14 47	15 01	15 11	15 13	15 37	15 47	16 01	16 04	16 10	16 22	16 33	16 38	16 53	17 01	17 11	17 19	17 39	18 02	18 05	18 25
	d	14 24	14 37	14 48	15 03	15 12	15 15	15 39	15 48	16 03	16 05	16 11	16 24	16 34	16 39	16 55	17 03	17 12	17 20	17 40	18 04	18 07	18 26
Teignmouth	d		14 44	14 55			15 22				16 13	16 18			16 47			17 19	17 27			18 14	
Dawlish	d		14 49	15 00			15 27				16 18	16 23			16 52			17 24	17 32			18 19	
Dawlish Warren	d		14 54									16 28			16 56			17 29				18 24	
Starcross	d		14 58												17 00							18 28	
Exeter St Thomas	d		15 07												17 10							18 37	
Exeter St Davids 6	a	14 46	15 12	15 16	15 23	15 31	15 41	15 59	16 08	16 23	16 32	16 41	16 44	16 55	17 14	17 17	17 21	17 42	17 46	18 00	18 21	18 40	18 47
Exeter Central	a		15 17				15 51					16 51			17 21			17 51				18 51	
Exmouth	a						16 18					17 18						18 18				19 18	
Exeter St Davids 6	d	14 47			15 25	15 33		16 01	16 10	16 25	16 34		16 45			17 20	17 23		17 51	18 02	18 23		18 49
Tiverton Parkway	d				15 38	15 46		16 16	16 25	16 38			17 01			17 35	17 37			18 17	18 38		
Taunton	d	15 12			15 54	16 01		16 31	16 40	16 54	16 59		17 15			17 49	17 51		18 22	18 32	18 52		19 10
Bridgwater	a										17 09								18 33				
Weston-super-Mare	a					16 20			17 01		17 28								18 52				
Bristol Temple Meads 10	a				16 27	16 53			17 22	17 27	17 57					18 25	18 27		19 22		19 27		
Bath Spa 7	a								17 41		18 12					18 41							
Filton Abbey Wood	a																						
Bristol Parkway 7	a				16 38	17 08				17 38							18 38				19 38		
Swindon	a								18 10		18 39					19 10							
Newport (South Wales)	a																						
Cardiff Central 7	a																						
Birmingham New Street 12	a				17 49	18 27				18 51							19 50				20 50		
Castle Cary	d	15 34											17 37										
Westbury	d	15 52											17 57							19 09			
Pewsey	d	16 10											18 14										
Hungerford	a																						
Newbury	a	16 31											18 34										20 17
Thatcham	a																						
Theale	a																						
Reading 7	a	16 51						17 46	18 42		19 12		18 52			19 42				19 54			20 35
Slough 3	a																						
London Paddington 15 ⊖	a	17 36						18 24	19 23		19 53		19 35			20 23				20 36			21 13

A 🍴 from Plymouth to Bristol Parkway

B 🍴 to Bristol Parkway

For connections to Oxford, Gatwick Airport and Heathrow Airport please refer to Tables 116, 148 and 125A

Table 135

Sundays

7 August to 11 September

Cornwall and Devon - Birmingham and London

		XC		GW	XC	GW	GW	GW	GW	GW	GW	GW		GW	GW	GW	GW
		◇1		◇1	◇1 A		◇1			◇1							R
		trolley		buffet	trolley		buffet	trolley		buffet				trolley			sleeper buffet
Penzance	d						17 20	17 50				19 00		20 05			21 15
St Erth	d						17 29	17 59				19 09		20 14			21 25
Hayle	d							18 02						20 17			
Camborne	d						17 42	18 12				19 20		20 26			21 38
Redruth	d						17 49	18 18				19 26		20 32			21 45
Truro	d						18 01	18 30				19 38		20 44			22 00
St Austell	d						18 19	18 47				19 55		21 01			22 18
Newquay	d			16 15													
Par	d			17 15			18 27	18 54				20 02		21 08			
Lostwithiel	d			17 25				19 01				20 09					
Bodmin Parkway	d			17 30			18 39	19 08				20 15		21 20			22 35
Liskeard 6	d			17 43			18 52	19 22				20 28		21 34			22 50
Menheniot	d											20x33					
St Germans	d											20 40					
Saltash	d											20 47					
St Budeaux Ferry Road	d							19 43									
Keyham	d																
Dockyard	d																
Devonport	d							19 47				20 55					
Plymouth	a			18 10			19 16	19 50				20 59		22 00			23 15
	d			18 10	18 23		19 21			19 55		21 15					23 20
Ivybridge	d																
Totnes	d			18 41	18 49		19 48					21 42					23 48
Paignton	d	18 18				18 55			19 55		20 55				21 52	23 00	
Torquay	d	18 24				19 00			20 00		21 00				21 57	23 05	
Torre	d					19 03			20 03		21 03				22 00	23 08	
Newton Abbot	a	18 34		18 53	19 01	19 11	20 00		20 11	20 31	21 11	21 54			22 08	23 16	23 59
	d	18 35		18 53	19 03	19 13	20 01		20 13	20 32	21 13	21 55			22 10	23 18	00 01
Teignmouth	d					19 20			20 20		21 20	22 02			22 17	23 25	
Dawlish	d					19 25			20 25		21 25	22 07			22 22	23 30	
Dawlish Warren	d					19 30			20 30						22 27	23 35	
Starcross	d					19 34			20 34						22 31	23 39	
Exeter St Thomas	d					19 43			20 43						22 40	23 48	
Exeter St Davids 6	a	18 54		19 15	19 23	19 48	20 21		20 48	20 53	21 40	22 21			22 43	23 52	00 40
Exeter Central	a					19 54			20 54		21 51				22 51		
Exmouth	a					20 21			21 21		22 18				23 18		
Exeter St Davids 6	d	18 56		19 17	19 25		20 22			20 55							00 57
Tiverton Parkway	d	19 09		19 32	19 38		20 38			21 10							
Taunton	d	19 23		19 46	19 54		20 53			21 23							
Bridgwater	a																
Weston-super-Mare	a																
Bristol Temple Meads 10	a	19 57			20 27					22 00							02 08
Bath Spa 7	a									22 22							
Filton Abbey Wood	a																
Bristol Parkway 7	a	20 08			20 38												
Swindon	a									22 50							03 21
Newport (South Wales)	a																
Cardiff Central 7	a																
Birmingham New Street 12	a	21 20			21 51												
Castle Cary	d			20 08			21 15										
Westbury	d			20 28			21 34										
Pewsey	d						21 52										
Hungerford	a																
Newbury	a						22 12										
Thatcham	a																
Theale	a																
Reading 7	a			21 15			22 30			23 27							04s02
Slough 3	a																
London Paddington 15 ⊖	a			21 54			23 12			00 11							05 05

A trolley to Bristol Parkway

For connections to Oxford, Gatwick Airport and Heathrow Airport please refer to Tables 116, 148 and 125A

Table 135

Sundays

18 September to 23 October

Cornwall and Devon - Birmingham and London

		GW	GW	XC	GW	GW	XC	GW	GW	XC		GW	GW	XC	GW	GW	XC	GW	GW	XC		GW	GW	GW	GW
		◇	◇1	◇1		◇1	◇1		◇1	◇1		◇1		◇1		◇1	◇1		◇1	◇1				◇1	
														A						A					
			🍽	🛒		🍽	🛒		🍽	🛒		🍽		🛒		🍽	🛒		🍽	🛒				🍽	
Penzance	d											08 35		09 30		09 47			11 00	11 30		11 45			
St Erth	d											08 44		09 38		09 57			11 09	11 38		11a53			
Hayle	d											08 49													
Camborne	d											09 00		09 48		10 09			11 22	11 48					
Redruth	d											09 06		09 54		10 15			11 28	11 54					
Truro	d											09 20		10 06		10 28			11 41	12 06					
St Austell	d											09 36		10 22		10 45			11 58	12 22					
Newquay	d																								
Par	d											09 45		10 30		10 53			12 06	12 30					
Lostwithiel	d													10 37						12 37					
Bodmin Parkway	d											09 57		10 44		11 06			12 18	12 44					
Liskeard 6	d											10 10		10 56		11 19			12 32	12 56					
Menheniot	d																								
St Germans	d															11 30									
Saltash	d											10 28													
St Budeaux Ferry Road	d																								
Keyham	d																								
Dockyard	d																								
Devonport	d																								
Plymouth	a											10 35		11 20		11 45			12 57	13 20					
	d			08 30		08 40	09 25		10 10	10 30		10 40		11 25		11 45	12 32		13 00	13 25				13 44	
Ivybridge	d																								
Totnes	d			08 55		09 07	09 50		10 40	10 55		11 07		11 50		12 16	12 57		13 27	13 50				14 11	
Paignton	d							09 49					11 00		11 49			12 57					13 51		14 19
Torquay	d							09 54					11 05		11 54			13 02					13 56		14 24
Torre	d							09 57					11 08		11 57			13 05					13 59		14 27
Newton Abbot	a			09 06		09 19	10 01	10 05	10 52	11 06		11 19	11 16	12 01	12 05	12 28	13 08	13 13	13 39	14 01			14 07	14 23	14 35
	d			09 07		09 20	10 02	10 07	10 54	11 07		11 21	11 26	12 02	12 07	12 30	13 09	13 15	13 40	14 02			14 08	14 25	14 37
Teignmouth	d					09 27		10 14					11 33		12 14			13 22					14 15		14 44
Dawlish	d					09 33		10 19					11 38		12 19			13 27					14 20		14 49
Dawlish Warren	d							10 24							12 24								14 25		14 54
Starcross	d							10 28							12 28								14 29		14 58
Exeter St Thomas	d							10 37							12 37								14 38		15 07
Exeter St Davids 6	a			09 25		09 47	10 20	10 42	11 14	11 26		11 41	11 52	12 21	12 43	12 50	13 27	13 41	14 00	14 21			14 43	14 46	15 12
Exeter Central	a							10 50					11 58		12 51			13 51					14 51		15 17
Exmouth	a							11 17					12 25		13 19			14 18					15 18		
Exeter St Davids 6	d	07 50	08 30	09 30	09 35	09 48	10 35		11 18	11 32		11 43		12 35		12 51	13 34		14 02	14 31				14 47	
Tiverton Parkway	d	08 07	08 45	09 44	09 53		10 49		11 33	11 45		11 58		12 48			13 48		14 16	14 44					
Taunton	d	08 24	08 59	09 58	10b19	10 14	11 03		11 48	11 59		12 13		13 03		13 16	14 02		14 31	14 59				15 12	
Bridgwater	a	08 35			10 31																				
Weston-super-Mare	a	08 53			10 49																				
Bristol Temple Meads 10	a	09 27		10 32	11 20		11 36		12 23	12 43				13 37			14 39			15 33					
Bath Spa 7	a								12 41																
Filton Abbey Wood	a																								
Bristol Parkway 7	a																								
Swindon	a								13 10																
Newport (South Wales)	a																								
Cardiff Central 7	a																								
Birmingham New Street 12	a																								
Castle Cary	d		09 21									12 34												15 34	
Westbury	d		09 41			10 51						13c00				13e59								15 52	
Pewsey	d																								
Hungerford	a																								
Newbury	a																								
Thatcham	a																								
Theale	a																								
Reading 7	a		10 50			11 52			13 44			14 05				15 04			16 05					16 52	
Slough 3	a																								
London Paddington 15 ⊖	a		11 35			12 35			14 21			14 43				15 43			16 44					17 34	

A 🛒 from Plymouth

b Arr. 1009

c Arr. 1252

e Arr. 1352

For connections to Oxford, Gatwick Airport and Heathrow Airport please refer to Tables 116, 148 and 125A

Table 135

Sundays

18 September to 23 October

Cornwall and Devon - Birmingham and London

		GW	XC	GW	GW	GW		XC	GW	GW	GW	GW	GW	GW	XC	GW		GW	GW	XC	GW	GW	GW	XC	GW
			◇1		◇1	◇1		◇1	◇1		◇1			◇1	◇1			◇	◇1	◇1		◇1	◇1	◇1	
			A																						
			[trolley]		[buffet]	[buffet]		[trolley]	[buffet]		[buffet]			[buffet]	[trolley]				[buffet]	[trolley]		[buffet]	[buffet]	[trolley]	
Penzance	d	12 05	12 20		12 40							13 40						14 40	15 10				16 10		
St Erth	d	12 14	12 28		12 49							13 50						14 49	15 20				16 21		
Hayle	d		12 32									13 53						14 52							
Camborne	d	12 25	12 41		13 03							14 02						15 01	15 32				16 33		
Redruth	d	12 31	12 48		13 09							14 08						15 07	15 39				16 40		
Truro	d	12 42	12 59		13 22							14 19						15 18	15 51				16 53		
St Austell	d	12 59	13 16		13 40							14 36						15 35	16 09				17 10		
Newquay	d																								
Par	d	13 06	13 23		13 47							14 44						15 43	16 17				17 17		
Lostwithiel	d	13 13	13 30									14 50						15 49							
Bodmin Parkway	d	13 19	13 37		14 00							14 56						15 55	16 28				17 29		
Liskeard 6	d	13 33	13 50		14 13							15 09						16 08	16 41				17 42		
Menheniot	d											15x14													
St Germans	d	13 44										15 21						16 19							
Saltash	d	13 52										15 29						16 27							
St Budeaux Ferry Road	d																								
Keyham	d																								
Dockyard	d																								
Devonport	d																								
Plymouth	a	14 01	14 14		14 39							15 38						16 37	17 07				18 08		
	d	14 06	14 27		14 45	15 05		15 25			15 43	15 49		16 10	16 30			16 38	17 10	17 25		17 45	18 10	18 30	
Ivybridge	d	14 21										16 07						16 53							
Totnes	d	14 35	14 52		15 12	15 35		15 50			16 11	16 21		16 42	16 55			17 07	17 38	17 50		18 13	18 38	18 55	
Paignton	d			14 57					15 45	15 54			16 22			16 55					17 49				18 55
Torquay	d			15 02					15 51	15 59			16 27			17 00					17 54				19 00
Torre	d			15 05					15 56	16 02			16 30			17 03					17 57				19 03
Newton Abbot	a	14 47	15 03	15 13	15 24	15 47		16 01	16 04	16 10	16 22	16 33	16 38	16 53	17 06	17 11		17 19	17 49	18 01	18 05	18 25	18 50	19 06	19 11
	d	14 48	15 04	15 15	15 25	15 48		16 03	16 05	16 11	16 24	16 34	16 39	16 55	17 07	17 12		17 20	17 51	18 02	18 07	18 26	18 50	19 07	19 13
Teignmouth	d	14 55		15 22					16 13	16 18			16 47			17 19		17 27			18 14				19 20
Dawlish	d	15 00		15 27					16 18	16 23			16 52			17 24		17 32			18 19				19 25
Dawlish Warren	d									16 28			16 56			17 29					18 24				19 30
Starcross	d												17 00								18 28				19 34
Exeter St Thomas	d												17 10								18 37				19 43
Exeter St Davids 6	a	15 16	15 23	15 41	15 45	16 08		16 20	16 32	16 41	16 44	16 55	17 14	17 17	17 25	17 42		17 46	18 11	18 20	18 40	18 47	19 11	19 25	19 48
Exeter Central	a			15 51						16 51			17 21			17 51					18 51				19 54
Exmouth	a			16 18						17 18						18 18					19 18				20 21
Exeter St Davids 6	d		15 29		15 48	16 10		16 22	16 34		16 45			17 20	17 29			17 51	18 13	18 31		18 49	19 13	19 29	
Tiverton Parkway	d		15 42		16 03	16 25		16 37			17 01			17 35	17 43				18 28	18 45			19 28	19 43	
Taunton	d		15 57		16 18	16 40		16 50	16 59		17 15			17 49	17 57			18 22	18 43	19 00		19 11	19 42	19 57	
Bridgwater	a								17 09									18 33							
Weston-super-Mare	a					17 01			17 28									18 54							
Bristol Temple Meads 10	a		16 31			17 22		17 26	17 57					18 25	18 30			19 32		19 42				20 35	
Bath Spa 7	a					17 41			18 12					18 41											
Filton Abbey Wood	a																								
Bristol Parkway 7	a																								
Swindon	a					18 10			18 39					19 10											
Newport (South Wales)	a																								
Cardiff Central 7	a																								
Birmingham New Street 12	a																								
Castle Cary	d										17 37											19 36			
Westbury	d										17 57											19 56			
Pewsey	d																								
Hungerford	a																								
Newbury	a																								
Thatcham	a																								
Theale	a																								
Reading 7	a				17 46	18 42			19 12		19 06			19 42					20 17			21 00	21 18		
Slough 3	a																								
London Paddington 15 ⊖	a				18 24	19 23			19 53		19 43			20 23					20 55			21 38	21 57		

A [trolley] from Plymouth

For connections to Oxford, Gatwick Airport and Heathrow Airport please refer to Tables 116, 148 and 125A

Table 135

Sundays

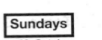

18 September to 23 October

Cornwall and Devon - Birmingham and London

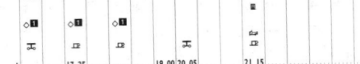

		XC	(blank)	GW	GW	GW	GW	GW	GW	GW	GW	GW
												R
		◇1		◇1		◇1						
												🛏
		🛒		☕		☕			🛒			☕
Penzance	d			17 25				19 00	20 05			21 15
St Erth	d			17 34				19 09	20 14			21 25
Hayle	d								20 17			
Camborne	d			17 47				19 20	20 26			21 38
Redruth	d			17 54				19 26	20 32			21 45
Truro	d			18 06				19 38	20 44			22 00
St Austell	d			18 24				19 55	21 01			22 18
Newquay	d											
Par	d			18 32				20 02	21 08			
Lostwithiel	d							20 09				
Bodmin Parkway	d			18 44				20 15	21 20			22 35
Liskeard 6	d			18 57				20 28	21 34			22 50
Menheniot	d							20x33				
St Germans	d							20 40				
Saltash	d							20 47				
St Budeaux Ferry Road	d											
Keyham	d											
Dockyard	d											
Devonport	d							20 55				
Plymouth	a			19 21				20 59	22 00			23 15
	d	18 55		19 25		19 55		21 15				23 20
Ivybridge	d											
Totnes	d	19 20		19 52				21 42				23 48
Paignton	d				19 55		20 55			21 52	23 00	
Torquay	d				20 00		21 00			21 57	23 05	
Torre	d				20 03		21 03			22 00	23 08	
Newton Abbot	a	19 31		20 04	20 11	20 31	21 11	21 54		22 08	23 16	23 59
	d	19 32		20 05	20 13	20 32	21 13	21 55		22 10	23 18	00 01
Teignmouth	d				20 20		21 20	22 02		22 17	23 25	
Dawlish	d				20 25		21 25	22 07		22 22	23 30	
Dawlish Warren	d				20 30					22 27	23 35	
Starcross	d				20 34					22 31	23 39	
Exeter St Thomas	d				20 43					22 40	23 48	
Exeter St Davids 6	a	19 52		20 25	20 48	20 53	21 40	22 21		22 43	23 52	00 40
Exeter Central	a				20 54		21 51			22 51		
Exmouth	a				21 21		22 18			23 18		
Exeter St Davids 6	d	19 54		20 26		20 55						00 57
Tiverton Parkway	d	20 08		20 42		21 10						
Taunton	d	20 20		20 57		21 23						
Bridgwater	a											
Weston-super-Mare	a											
Bristol Temple Meads 10	a	21 02				22 00						02 08
Bath Spa 7	a					22 22						
Filton Abbey Wood	a											
Bristol Parkway 7	a											
Swindon	a					22 50						03 21
Newport (South Wales)	a											
Cardiff Central 7	a											
Birmingham New Street 12	a											
Castle Cary	d			21 19								
Westbury	d			21 41								
Pewsey	d											
Hungerford	a											
Newbury	a											
Thatcham	a											
Theale	a											
Reading 7	a			22 54		23 27						04s02
Slough 3	a											
London Paddington 15 ⊖	a			23 31		00 11						05 05

For connections to Oxford, Gatwick Airport and Heathrow Airport please refer to Tables 116, 148 and 125A

Table 135

Sundays

from 30 October

Cornwall and Devon - Birmingham and London

		GW	GW	GW	GW	XC	GW	GW	XC	XC		GW	GW	XC	GW	GW	XC	XC	GW	XC		GW	XC	GW	GW
		◇	◇[1]	◇	◇[1]	◇[1]		[1]	◇[1]	◇[1]		◇[1]		◇[1]		◇[1]	◇[1]	◇[1]		◇[1]		◇[1]	◇[1]		
														A									A		
			🍽		🍽	🛒		🍽	🛒	🛒		🍽		🛒		🍽	🛒	🛒		🛒		🍽	🛒		
Penzance	d											08 35		09 30		09 47						11 00	11 25	11 45	
St Erth	d											08 44		09 38		09 58						11 09	11 35	11a53	
Hayle	d											08 49													
Camborne	d											09 00		09 48		10 10						11 22	11 46		
Redruth	d											09 06		09 54		10 16						11 28	11 53		
Truro	d											09 20		10 06		10 29						11 41	12 06		
St Austell	d											09 36		10 22		10 46						11 58	12 23		
Newquay	d																								
Par	d											09 45		10 30		10 54						12 06	12 31		
Lostwithiel	d																								
Bodmin Parkway	d											09 57		10 41		11 07						12 18	12 42		
Liskeard [6]	d											10 10		10 53		11 20						12 32	12 55		
Menheniot	d																								
St Germans	d																								
Saltash	d											10 28													
St Budeaux Ferry Road	d																								
Keyham	d																								
Dockyard	d																								
Devonport	d																								
Plymouth	a											10 35		11 17		11 43						12 57	13 20		
	d				08 40	09 25		10 10	10 25			10 40		11 25		11 46	12 00	12 25		12 52		13 00	13 23		
Ivybridge	d																								
Totnes	d				09 07	09 50		10 40	10 50			11 07		11 50		12 15		12 50				13 27	13 49		
Paignton	d						09 49			10 50			11 00		11 49				12 57						13 51
Torquay	d						09 54			10 56			11 05		11 54				13 02						13 56
Torre	d						09 57						11 08		11 57				13 05						13 59
Newton Abbot	a				09 19	10 01	10 05	10 52	11 01	11 06		11 19	11 16	12 01	12 05	12 28	12 34	13 01	13 13	13 26		13 39	14 01		14 07
	d				09 20	10 03	10 07	10 54	11 03	11 08		11 21	11 24	12 03	12 07	12 29	12 36	13 03	13 15	13 27		13 40	14 03		14 08
Teignmouth	d				09 27		10 14			11 15			11 31		12 14				13 22						14 15
Dawlish	d				09 33		10 19			11 20			11 36		12 19				13 27						14 20
Dawlish Warren	d						10 24								12 24										14 25
Starcross	d						10 28								12 28										14 29
Exeter St Thomas	d						10 37								12 37										14 38
Exeter St Davids [6]	a				09 47	10 21	10 40	11 14	11 21	11 30		11 41	11 50	12 21	12 42	12 49	12 55	13 21	13 40	13 46		14 00	14 23		14 43
Exeter Central	a																								
Exmouth	a																								
Exeter St Davids [6]	d	07 42	08 38	09 35	09 48	10 23		11 18	11 23	11 32		11 43		12 23		12 50	12 57	13 23		13 48		14 02	14 25		
Tiverton Parkway	d	07 59	08 53	09 53		10 37		11 33	11 37	11 46		11 58		12 37			13 10	13 37				14 16	14 39		
Taunton	d	08 16	09 07	10b19	10 14	10 51		11 48	11 53	12 00		12 13		12 51		13 16	13 25	13 51				14 31	14 54		
Bridgwater	a	08 27		10 31																					
Weston-super-Mare	a	08 46		10 49						12 20															
Bristol Temple Meads [10]	a			11 20		11 27		12 22	12 27	12 46				13 24			13 57	14 26		14 41			15 27		
Bath Spa [7]	a							12 37																	
Filton Abbey Wood	a																								
Bristol Parkway [7]	a					11 38			12 38	13 08				13 38			14 08	14 38		15 08			15 38		
Swindon	a							13 05																	
Newport (South Wales)	a																								
Cardiff Central [7]	a																								
Birmingham New Street [12]	a					12 50			13 50	14 26				14 50			15 27	15 50		16 26			16 50		
Castle Cary	d		09 29									12 34													
Westbury	d		09 49		10 53							12 53				13c59									
Pewsey	d		10 06									13 10													
Hungerford	a																								
Newbury	a		10 26		11 26							13 30													
Thatcham	a																								
Theale	a																								
Reading [7]	a		10 43		11 43							13 48				14 50						15 47			
Slough [3]	a																								
London Paddington [15] ⊖	a		11 28		12 29							14 28				15 29						16 30			

A 🛒 from Plymouth

b Arr. 1008

c Arr. 1352

For connections to Oxford, Gatwick Airport and Heathrow Airport please refer to Tables 116, 148 and 125A

Table 135

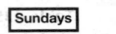

Sundays
from 30 October

Cornwall and Devon - Birmingham and London

		GW	GW	GW	XC	XC	GW	GW	GW	XC	GW	GW	GW	GW	GW	XC	GW	GW	GW	XC	GW	GW	XC
		◇1			◇1	◇1		◇1	◇1	◇1		◇1			◇1	◇1		◇	◇1	◇1		◇1	◇1
						A										B				A			
		buffet			trolley	trolley		buffet	buffet	trolley		buffet			buffet	trolley			buffet	trolley		buffet	trolley
Penzance	d			12 05		12 30		12 55					13 40					14 40	15 05	15 30			
St Erth	d			12 14		12 40		13 06					13 50					14 49	15 17	15 38			
Hayle	d					12 44							13 53					14 52					
Camborne	d			12 25		12 56		13 17					14 02					15 01	15 28	15 51			
Redruth	d			12 31		13 02		13 23					14 08					15 07	15 35	15 57			
Truro	d			12 42		13 14		13 35					14 19					15 18	15 48	16 09			
St Austell	d			12 59		13 30		13 54					14 36					15 35	16 05	16 25			
Newquay	d																						
Par	d			13 06		13 38		14 01					14 44					15 43	16 13	16 33			
Lostwithiel	d			13 13		13 45							14 50					15 49					
Bodmin Parkway	d			13 19		13 52		14 13					14 56					15 55	16 25	16 44			
Liskeard 6	d			13 33		14 04		14 26					15 09					16 08	16 38	16 56			
Menheniot	d												15x14										
St Germans	d			13 44									15 21					16 19					
Saltash	d			13 52									15 29					16 27					
St Budeaux Ferry Road	d																						
Keyham	d																						
Dockyard	d																						
Devonport	d																						
Plymouth	a			14 01		14 28		14 52					15 38					16 37	17 03	17 20			
	d	13 43		14 06	14 23	14 35		14 52		15 23		15 43	15 49		16 01	16 25		16 38	17 05	17 26		17 45	
Ivybridge	d			14 21									16 07					16 53					
Totnes	d	14 09		14 35	14 49	15 00		15 22		15 49		16 11	16 21		16 31	16 50		17 07	17 33	17 52		18 13	
Paignton	d		14 19				14 54		15 22		15 54			16 22			16 55				17 49		18 18
Torquay	d		14 24				15 02		15 28		15 59			16 27			17 00				17 54		18 24
Torre	d		14 27				15 05		15 33		16 02			16 30			17 03				17 57		
Newton Abbot	a	14 22	14 35	14 47	15 01	15 11	15 13	15 34	15 41	16 01	16 10	16 22	16 33	16 38	16 42	17 01	17 11	17 19	17 45	18 02	18 05	18 25	18 34
	d	14 23	14 37	14 48	15 03	15 12	15 15	15 35	15 42	16 03	16 11	16 24	16 34	16 39	16 44	17 03	17 12	17 20	17 46	18 04	18 07	18 26	18 35
Teignmouth	d		14 44	14 55			15 22				16 18			16 46	16 51		17 19	17 27			18 14		
Dawlish	d		14 49	15 00			15 27				16 23			16 51	16 57		17 24	17 32			18 19		
Dawlish Warren	d		14 54								16 28			17b03			17 29				18 24		
Starcross	d		14 58											17 07							18 28		
Exeter St Thomas	d		15 07											17 16							18 37		
Exeter St Davids 6	a	14 46	15 10	15 16	15 23	15 31	15 41	15 55	16 03	16 23	16 40	16 44	16 55	17 21	17 10	17 21	17 41	17 46	18 06	18 21	18 40	18 47	18 54
Exeter Central	a																						
Exmouth	a																						
Exeter St Davids 6	d	14 47			15 25	15 33		15 58	16 05	16 25		16 45			17 12	17 23		17 51	18 08	18 23		18 49	18 56
Tiverton Parkway	d				15 38	15 46		16 13	16 20	16 38		17 01			17 27	17 37			18 23	18 38			19 09
Taunton	d	15 13			15 54	16 01		16 28	16 34	16 54		17 15			17 41	17 51		18 22	18 38	18 52		19 12	19 23
Bridgwater	a														17 52			18 33					
Weston-super-Mare	a					16 20			16 55									18 52					
Bristol Temple Meads 10	a				16 27	16 53			17 24	17 27					18 24	18 27		19 22		19 27			19 57
Bath Spa 7	a								17 41						18 41								
Filton Abbey Wood	a																						
Bristol Parkway 7	a				16 38	17 08				17 38						18 38				19 38			20 08
Swindon	a																						
Newport (South Wales)	a																						
Cardiff Central 7	a																						
Birmingham New Street 12	a				17 49	18 27				18 51						19 50				20 50			21 20
Castle Cary	d	15 35										17 37											
Westbury	d	15 52										17 56							19 14				
Pewsey	d	16 10										18 13											
Hungerford	a																						
Newbury	a	16 31										18 33										20 23	
Thatcham	a																						
Theale	a																						
Reading 7	a	16 48						17 43	18 56			18 52			19 50				19 59			20 42	
Slough 3	a																						
London Paddington 15 ⊖	a	17 29						18 28	19 43			19 29			20 27				20 43			21 28	

A trolley from Plymouth to Bristol Parkway

B trolley to Bristol Parkway

b Arr. 1655

For connections to Oxford, Gatwick Airport and Heathrow Airport please refer to Tables 116, 148 and 125A

Table 135

Sundays
from 30 October

Cornwall and Devon - Birmingham and London

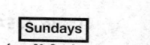

		GW		XC	GW	GW	GW	GW	GW	GW	GW	GW		GW	GW
		◇1		◇1		◇1		1							R
				A											
		⊐		⊤o		⊐		⊐			⊤o				⊐
Penzance	d	16 10				17 25				19 00	20 05				21 15
St Erth	d	16 20				17 34				19 09	20 14				21 25
Hayle	d										20 17				
Camborne	d	16 32				17 47				19 20	20 26				21 38
Redruth	d	16 39				17 54				19 26	20 32				21 45
Truro	d	16 52				18 06				19 38	20 44				22 00
St Austell	d	17 09				18 24				19 55	21 01				22 18
Newquay	d														
Par	d	17 16				18 32				20 02	21 08				
Lostwithiel	d									20 09					
Bodmin Parkway	d	17 28				18 44				20 15	21 20				22 35
Liskeard 6	d	17 41				18 57				20 28	21 34				22 50
Menheniot	d									20x33					
St Germans	d									20 40					
Saltash	d	17 59								20 47					
St Budeaux Ferry Road	d														
Keyham	d														
Dockyard	d														
Devonport	d									20 55					
Plymouth	a	18 09				19 21				20 59	22 00				23 15
	d	18 10		18 23		19 25		19 55		21 15					23 20
Ivybridge	d														
Totnes	d	18 40		18 49		19 52				21 42					23 48
Paignton	d				18 55		19 55		20 55			21 52		23 00	
Torquay	d				19 00		20 00		21 00			21 57		23 05	
Torre	d				19 03		20 03		21 03			22 00		23 08	
Newton Abbot	a	18 52		19 01	19 11	20 04	20 11	20 31	21 11	21 54		22 08		23 16	23 59
	d	18 52		19 03	19 13	20 05	20 13	20 33	21 13	21 55		22 10		23 18	00 01
Teignmouth	d				19 20		20 20		21 20	22 02		22 17		23 25	
Dawlish	d				19 25		20 25		21 25	22 07		22 22		23 30	
Dawlish Warren	d				19 30		20 30					22 27		23 35	
Starcross	d				19 34		20 34					22 31		23 39	
Exeter St Thomas	d				19 43		20 43					22 40		23 48	
Exeter St Davids 6	a	19 13		19 23	19 46	20 25	20 46	20 53	21 39	22 21		22 43		23 52	00 40
Exeter Central	a														
Exmouth	a														
Exeter St Davids 6	d	19 15		19 25		20 26		20 55							00 57
Tiverton Parkway	d	19 30		19 38		20 42		21 10							
Taunton	d	19 44		19 54		20 57		21 25							
Bridgwater	a														
Weston-super-Mare	a														
Bristol Temple Meads 10	a			20 27				21 58							02 08
Bath Spa 7	a							22 26							
Filton Abbey Wood	a														
Bristol Parkway 7	a			20 38											
Swindon	a							22 55							
Newport (South Wales)	a														
Cardiff Central 7	a														
Birmingham New Street 12	a			21 51											
Castle Cary	d	20 06				21 19									
Westbury	d	20 26				21b44									
Pewsey	d					22 02									
Hungerford	a														
Newbury	a					22 22									
Thatcham	a														
Theale	a														
Reading 7	a	21 11				22 40									04s18
Slough 3	a														
London Paddington 15 ⊖	a	22 01				23 17									05 05

A ⊤o to Bristol Parkway

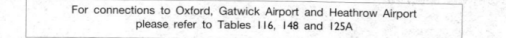

b Arr. 2137

For connections to Oxford, Gatwick Airport and Heathrow Airport please refer to Tables 116, 148 and 125A

Table 135A

Mondays to Fridays

Redruth - Helston

Bus Service

		GW BHX A	GW BHX	GW BHX	GW BHX	GW BHX	GW BHX	GW BHX	GW BHX	GW BHX	GW BHX	GW BHX	GW BHX	GW BHX	GW BHX
Redruth	d	08 00	09 05	10 15	11 05	12 05	13 05	14 05	15 05	16 05	17 00	18 15	19 15	21 15	23 25
Helston Coinagehall St	a	08 38	09 37	10 47	11 37	12 37	13 37	14 37	15 37	16 37	17 42	18 47	19 47	21 47	23 51

Saturdays

		GW A	GW A	GW	GW	GW	GW	GW	GW	GW	GW	GW	GW	GW	GW
Redruth	d	08 00	09 05	10 15	11 05	12 05	13 05	14 05	15 05	16 05	17 10	18 15	19 15	21 15	23 25
Helston Coinagehall St	a	08 29	09 37	10 47	11 37	12 37	13 37	14 37	15 37	16 37	17 42	18 47	19 47	21 47	23 51

Sundays

		GW	GW	GW	GW	GW
Redruth	d	09 50	11 50	13 50	15 50	17 50
Helston Coinagehall St	a	10 19	12 19	14 19	16 19	18 19

A Operates on School Holidays only

Table 135A

Mondays to Fridays

Helston - Redruth

Bus Service

		GW BHX	GW BHX	GW BHX	GW BHX	GW BHX	GW BHX	GW BHX	GW BHX A	GW BHX	GW BHX A	GW BHX	GW BHX	GW BHX	GW BHX
Helston Coinagehall St	d	07 05	08 06	09 35	10 27	11 27	12 27	13 27	14 27	15 15	16 30	17 30	18 30	19 50	21 50
Redruth	a	07 39	08 55	10 09	11 01	12 01	13 01	14 01	15 01	16 01	17 04	18 04	19 02	20 22	22 22

Saturdays

		GW	GW	GW	GW	GW	GW	GW	GW	GW	GW	GW	GW	GW	GW
Helston Coinagehall St	d	07 05	08 13	09 35	10 27	11 27	12 27	13 27	14 27	15 27	16 30	17 30	18 30	19 50	21 50
Redruth	a	07 39	08 47	10 09	11 01	12 01	13 01	14 01	15 01	16 01	17 04	18 04	19 02	20 22	22 22

Sundays

		GW	GW	GW	GW	GW
Helston Coinagehall St	d	08 50	10 50	12 50	14 50	16 50
Redruth	a	09 21	11 21	13 21	15 21	17 21

A Operates during School Holidays only

Table 135B

Mondays to Fridays

St. Austell - Eden Project

Bus Service

		GW	GW BHX	GW BHX	GW	GW	GW BHX	GW	GW BHX	GW BHX	GW	GW	GW BHX	GW	GW BHX	GW	GW BHX	GW	GW BHX	GW
St Austell	d	08 35	08 50	09 30	09 35	10 35	10 40	11 35	11 50	12 30	12 35	13 35	13 55	14 35	15 02	15 35	16 10	16 35	17 05	17 35
Eden Project	a	08 57	09 09	09 49	09 57	10 57	10 59	11 57	12 09	12 49	12 57	13 57	14 14	14 57	15 21	15 57	16 29	16 57	17 24	17 57

Saturdays

		GW	GW	GW	GW	GW	GW	GW	GW	GW	GW	GW	GW	GW	GW	GW	GW	GW	GW
St Austell	d	08 35	08 50	09 30	09 35	10 35	10 40	11 35	12 05	12 35	13 35	13 55	14 35	15 02	15 35	15 50	16 35	17 00	17 35
Eden Project	a	08 57	09 09	09 49	09 57	10 57	10 59	11 57	12 24	12 57	13 57	14 14	14 57	15 21	15 57	16 09	16 57	17 19	17 57

Sundays

		GW	GW	GW	GW	GW	GW	GW	GW	GW	GW	GW	GW
St Austell	d	08 50	10 35	11 35	11 40	12 30	12 35	13 35	14 35	14 45	15 35	16 25	17 10
Eden Project	a	09 09	10 57	11 57	11 59	12 49	12 57	13 54	14 57	15 04	15 57	16 44	17 29

Table 135B

Mondays to Fridays

Eden Project - St. Austell

Bus Service

		GW	GW BHX	GW BHX	GW	GW	GW BHX	GW	GW BHX	GW	GW	GW BHX	GW	GW BHX	GW	GW BHX	GW	GW
Eden Project	d	09 00	09 10	09 55	10 00	11 00	11 15	12 00	12 10	13 00	14 00	14 25	15 00	15 22	16 00	16 30	17 00	18 00
St Austell	a	09 24	09 29	10 14	10 24	11 24	11 34	12 24	12 29	13 24	14 24	14 44	15 24	15 41	16 24	16 49	17 24	18 24

Saturdays

		GW	GW	GW	GW	GW	GW	GW	GW	GW	GW	GW	GW	GW	GW	GW	GW	GW	GW
Eden Project	d	09 00	09 10	09 55	10 00	11 00	11 15	12 00	13 00	13 15	14 00	14 25	15 00	15 22	16 00	16 25	17 00	17 55	18 00
St Austell	a	09 24	09 29	10 14	10 24	11 24	11 34	12 24	13 24	13 34	14 24	14 44	15 24	15 41	16 24	16 44	17 24	18 14	18 24

Sundays

		GW	GW	GW	GW	GW	GW	GW	GW	GW	GW	GW	GW
Eden Project	d	09 50	11 00	12 00	13 05	14 00	14 25	15 00	15 15	16 00	16 05	16 50	18 00
St Austell	a	10 09	11 20	12 20	13 24	14 20	14 44	15 20	15 34	16 24	16 24	17 09	18 19

Table 135C

Mondays to Saturdays

Bodmin - Wadebridge and Padstow

Bus Service

		GW	GW	GW	GW	GW	GW BHX	GW	GW	GW	GW BHX	GW	GW	GW	GW
Bodmin Parkway	d	07 25	08 30	09 30	10 30	11 30	12 30	13 30	14 30	15 30	16 30	17 30	18 30	19 30	22 00
Bodmin Mount Folly	a	07 35	08 40	09 40	10 40	11 40	12 40	13 40	14 40	15 40	16 40	17 40	18 40	19 40	22 10
Wadebridge Bus Station	a	07 55	09 00	10 00	11 00	12 00	13 00	14 00	15 00	16 00	17 00	18 00	19 00	20 00	22 30
Padstow Old Rly Station	a	08 27	09 27	10 27	11 27	12 27	13 27	14 27	15 27	16 27	17 27	18 27	19 27	20 27	22 57

Sundays

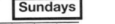

		GW	GW	GW	GW	GW	GW A
Bodmin Parkway	d	09 30	11 30	13 30	15 30	17 30	19 30
Bodmin Mount Folly	a	09 40	11 40	13 40	15 40	17 40	19 40
Wadebridge Bus Station	a	10 00	12 00	14 00	16 00	18 00	20 00
Padstow Old Rly Station	a	10 27	12 27	14 27	16 27	18 27	20 27

A until 23 October

Table 135C

Mondays to Saturdays

Padstow and Wadebridge - Bodmin

Bus Service

		GW BHX	GW BHX	GW BHX	GW BHX	GW BHX	GW BHX	GW BHX	GW BHX	GW BHX	GW BHX	GW BHX	GW	GW BHX	GW BHX
Padstow Old Rly Station	d	06 30	07 30	08 30	09 30	10 30	11 30	12 30	13 30	14 30	15 30	16 30	17 30	18 30	20 30
Wadebridge Bus Station	d	06 55	07 55	08 55	09 55	10 55	11 55	12 55	13 55	14 55	15 55	16 55	17 55	18 55	20 55
Bodmin Mount Folly	d	07 15	08 15	09 15	10 15	11 15	12 15	13 15	14 15	15 15	16 15	17 15	18 15	19 15	21 15
Bodmin Parkway	a	07 25	08 25	09 25	10 25	11 25	12 25	13 25	14 25	15 25	16 25	17 25	18 25	19 25	21 25

Sundays

		GW	GW	GW	GW	GW	GW A
Padstow Old Rly Station	d	08 30	10 30	12 30	14 30	16 30	18 30
Wadebridge Bus Station	d	08 55	10 55	12 55	14 55	16 55	18 55
Bodmin Mount Folly	d	09 15	11 15	13 15	15 15	17 15	19 15
Bodmin Parkway	a	09 25	11 25	13 25	15 25	17 25	19 25

A until 23 October

Exeter - Okehampton, Holsworthy and Bude

Bus Service

		GW	GW	GW	GW	GW	GW	GW BHX	GW BHX	GW	GW	GW	GW	GW BHX	GW BHX	GW	GW
Exeter St Davids	d	08 00	08 50	09 45	10 20	10 45	11 20	11 45	12 20	13 20	13 20	13 45	14 20	15 20	15 45	16 20	17 55
Okehampton West Street	a	08 45	09 40	10 25	11 05	11 25	12 10	12 25	13 05	14 00	14 05	14 25	15 10	16 10	16 25	17 00	18 35
Holsworthy Library	a																
Holsworthy Cattle Market	a																
Bude Strand	a			11 25				13 25		15 00		15 25			17 25		19 35

		GW	GW FSO
Exeter St Davids	d	18 35	20 40
Okehampton West Street	a	19 20	21 30
Holsworthy Library	a		
Holsworthy Cattle Market	a		
Bude Strand	a	20 15	22 29

Sundays

		GW	GW	GW
Exeter St Davids	d	11 50	16 50	17 50
Okehampton West Street	a	12 40	17 30	18 40
Holsworthy Library	a			
Holsworthy Cattle Market	a			
Bude Strand	a	13 40		19 40

Table 135D

Mondays to Saturdays

Bude, Holsworthy and Okehampton - Exeter

Bus Service

		GW BHX	GW BHX	GW	GW BHX	GW BHX	GW	GW	GW	GW BHX	GW BHX	GW	GW	GW BHX	GW	GW BHX	GW SX BHX
Bude Strand	d	06 40				08 40		09 00			11 30			13 30			15 27
Holsworthy Church	d	07 02				09 05		09 22			11 52			13 52			15 57
Holsworthy Cattle Market	d																
Okehampton West Street	d	07 45	09 10	09 25	09 35	09 45	09 55	10 05	11 10	11 40	12 35	13 10	14 10	14 35	15 10	15 40	16 40
Exeter St Davids	a	08 25	09 55	10 00	10 15	10 20	10 40	10 45	11 45	12 25	13 15	13 55	14 50	15 15	15 45	16 25	17 25

		GW BHX	GW SO	GW FSO BHX
Bude Strand	d	15 30	15 30	17 30
Holsworthy Church	d	15 55	15 57	17 52
Holsworthy Cattle Market	d			
Okehampton West Street	d	16 40	16 40	18 29
Exeter St Davids	a	17x25	17 25	19 11

Sundays

		GW	GW	GW
Bude Strand	d	09 45		15 45
Holsworthy Church	d	10 05		16 05
Holsworthy Cattle Market	d			
Okehampton West Street	d	10 40	14 45	16 40
Exeter St Davids	a	11 30	15 30	17 30

Table 135E

Mondays to Saturdays

Taunton - Watchet, Dunster and Minehead

Bus Service

		GW MX BHX A	GW SX BHX	GW	GW	GW	GW	GW B	GW C	GW D	GW E	GW BHX F	GW G	GW H	GW I	GW J	GW K	GW L	GW M	GW N	GW O
Taunton	d	23p16	05 41	06 21	07 17	07 47	08 17	08 47	09 17	09 47	10 17	10 47	11 17	11 47	12 17	12 47	13 17	13 47	14 17	14 47	15 17
Bishops Lydeard Hithermead	a	23p31	05 56	06 36	07 32	08 02	08 32	09 02	09 32	10 02	10 32	11 02	11 32	12 02	12 32	13 02	13 32	14 02	14 32	15 02	15 32
Watchet (West Somerset Ry)	a	23p59	06 25	07 05	08 01	08 31	09 01	09 35	10 07	10 35	11 07	11 35	12 07	12 35	13 07	13 35	14 07	14 35	15 07	15 35	16 07
Dunster Steep	a	00 14	06 39	07 19	08 19	08 49	09 19	09 53	10 25	10 53	11 25	11 53	12 25	12 53	13 25	13 53	14 25	14 53	15 25	15 53	16 25
Minehead Parade	a	00 22	06 47	07 27	08 27	08 57	09 27	10 01	10 33	11 01	11 33	12 01	12 33	13 01	13 33	14 01	14 33	15 01	15 33	16 01	16 33
Minehead Butlins	a	.	06 52	07 32	08 32	09 02	09 32	10 06	10 38	11 06	11 38	12 06	12 38	13 06	13 38	14 06	14 38	15 06	15 38	16 06	16 38

		GW P	GW Q	GW	GW SO	GW	GW	GW BHX	GW	GW	GW	GW	GW A
Taunton	d	15 47	16 17	16 47	17 12	17 37	18 07	18 37	19 16	20 16	21 16	22 16	23 16
Bishops Lydeard Hithermead	a	16 02	16 32	17 02	17 27	17 52	18 22	18 52	19 31	20 31	21 31	22 31	23 31
Watchet (West Somerset Ry)	a	16 35	17 07	17 31	17 56	18 21	18 51	19 21	20 00	21 00	22 00	23 00	23 59
Dunster Steep	a	16 53	17 25	17 49	18 14	18 39	19 09	19 39	20 14	21 14	22 14	23 14	00 14
Minehead Parade	a	17 01	17 33	17 57	18 22	18 47	19 17	19 47	20 22	21 22	22 22	23 22	00 22
Minehead Butlins	a	17 06	17 38	18 02	18 27	18 52	19 22	19 52	20 27	21 27	22 27	23 27	.

Sundays

		GW R	GW S	GW T	GW BHX	GW U	GW	GW V	GW	GW	GW
Taunton	d	23p16	09 35	11 35	12 35	13 35	14 35	15 35	16 35	17 35	19 35
Bishops Lydeard Hithermead	a	23p31	09 49	11 49	12 49	13 49	14 49	15 49	16 49	17 49	19 49
Watchet (West Somerset Ry)	a	23p59	10 18	12 18	13 18	14 18	15 18	16 18	17 18	18 18	20 18
Dunster Steep	a	00 14	10 32	12 32	13 32	14 32	15 32	16 32	17 32	18 32	20 32
Minehead Parade	a	00 22	10 40	12 40	13 40	14 40	15 40	16 40	17 40	18 40	20 40
Minehead Butlins	a	.	10 45	12 45	13 45	14 45	15 45	16 45	17 45	18 45	20 45

A Continues to Minehead West Som Rly Stn
B Also stops at WSR stn at 0906 on railway operating days
C Also stops at WSR stn at 0936 on railway operating days
D Also stops at WSR stn at 1006 on railway operating days
E Also stops at WSR stn at 1036 on railway operating days
F Also stops at WSR stn at 1106 on railway operating days
G Also stops at WSR stn at 1136 on railway operating days
H Also stops at WSR stn at 1206 on railway operating days
I Also stops at WSR stn at 1236 on railway operating days
J Also stops at WSR stn at 1306 on railway operating days
K Also stops at WSR stn at 1336 on railway operating days
L Also stops at WSR stn at 1406 on railway operating days
M Also stops at WSR stn at 1436 on railway operating days
N Also stops at WSR stn at 1506 on railway operating days
O Also stops at WSR stn at 1536 on railway operating days
P Also stops WSR stn at 1606 on railway operating days
Q Also stops at WSR stn at 1636 on railway operating days
R not 22 May. Continues to Minehead West Som Rly Stn
S Also stops at WSR stn at 0952 on railway operating days
T Also stops at WSR stn at 1152 on railway operating days
U Also stops at WSR stn at 1352 on railway operating days
V Also stops at WSR stn at 1552 on railway operating days

Table 135E

Mondays to Saturdays

Minehead, Dunster and Watchet - Taunton

Bus Service

		GW BHX	GW BHX	GW SX BHX	GW SO	GW BHX	GW BHX	GW BHX	GW	GW BHX	GW BHX	GW BHX A	GW BHX B	GW BHX C	GW D	GW BHX E	GW BHX F	GW G	GW H	GW BHX I	GW BHX J
Minehead Butlins	d	05 45	06 30	06 50	07 00	07 50	08 20	08 50	09 20	09 50	10 20	10 50	11 20	11 50	12 20	12 50	13 20	13 50	14 20	14 50	15 20
Minehead Bancks Street	d	05 50	06 35	06 58	07 10	08 00	08 30	09 00	09 30	10 00	10 30	11 00	11 30	12 00	12 30	13 00	13 30	14 00	14 30	15 00	15 30
Dunster Steep	d	05 58	06 43	07 06	07 18	08 08	08 38	09 08	09 38	10 08	10 38	11 08	11 38	12 08	12 38	13 08	13 38	14 08	14 38	15 08	15 38
Watchet (West Somerset Ry)	d	06 13	06 58	07 25	07 37	08 27	08 57	09 27	09 57	10 27	10 57	11 27	11 57	12 27	12 57	13 27	13 57	14 27	14 57	15 27	15 57
Bishops Lydeard Hithermead	d	06 41	07 26	07 54	08 06	08 56	09 26	09 57	10 26	10 57	11 26	12 01	12 30	13 01	13 30	14 01	14 30	15 01	15 30	16 01	16 30
Taunton	a	06 55	07 40	08 16	08 20	09 10	09 40	10 11	10 40	11 11	11 40	12 15	12 44	13 15	13 44	14 15	14 44	15 15	15 44	16 15	16 44

		GW BHX K	GW BHX L	GW BHX M	GW N	GW BHX O	GW BHX	GW BHX	GW BHX	GW BHX	GW BHX
Minehead Butlins	d	15 50	16 20	16 50	17 20	17 50	18 40	19 40	20 30	21 30	22 30
Minehead Bancks Street	d	16 00	16 30	17 00	17 30	18 00	18 45	19 45	20 35	21 35	22 35
Dunster Steep	d	16 08	16 38	17 08	17 38	18 08	18 53	19 53	20 43	21 43	22 43
Watchet (West Somerset Ry)	d	16 27	16 57	17 27	17 57	18 27	19 08	20 08	20 58	21 58	22 58
Bishops Lydeard Hithermead	d	17 01	17 30	18 00	18 30	19 00	19 36	20 36	21 26	22 26	23 26
Taunton	a	17 15	17 44	18 14	18 44	19 14	19 50	20 50	21 40	22 40	23 40

Sundays

		GW	GW P	GW Q	GW	GW R	GW	GW S	GW	GW
Minehead Butlins	d	08 50	10 50	12 50	13 50	14 50	15 50	16 50	17 50	18 50
Minehead Bancks Street	d	08 55	10 55	12 55	13 55	14 55	15 55	16 55	17 55	18 55
Dunster Steep	d	09 03	11 03	13 03	14 03	15 03	16 03	17 03	18 03	19 03
Watchet (West Somerset Ry)	d	09 18	11 18	13 18	14 18	15 18	16 18	17 18	18 18	19 18
Bishops Lydeard Hithermead	d	09 48	11 48	13 48	14 48	15 48	16 48	17 48	18 48	19 48
Taunton	a	10 00	12 00	14 00	15 00	16 00	17 00	18 00	19 00	20 00

A Also stops at WSR stn at 1157 on railway operating days
B Also stops WSR stn at 1226 on railway operating days
C Also stops at WSR stn at 1257 on railway operating days
D Also stops WSR stn at 1326 on railway operating days
E Also stops at WSR stn at 1357 on railway operating days
F Also stops WSR stn at 1426 on railway operating days
G Also stops at WSR stn at 1457 on railway operating days
H Also stops WSR stn at 1526 on railway operating days
I Also stops at WSR stn at 1557 on railway operating days
J Also stops WSR stn at 1626 on railway operating days
K Also stops at WSR stn at 1657 on railway operating days
L Also stops WSR stn at 1726 on railway operating days
M Also stops at WSR stn at 1756 on railway operating days
N Also stops WSR stn at 1826 on railway operating days
O Also stops at WSR stn at 1856 on railway operating days
P Also stops at WSR stn at 1145 on railway operating days
Q Also stops at WSR stn at 1345 on railway operating days
R Also stops at WSR stn at 1545 on railway operating days
S Also stops at WSR stn at 1745 on railway operating days

Exmouth - Exeter - Barnstaple

Miles	Miles			SW MX ◇1 ☕	GW MO	GW MX	GW	SW 1	GW	GW	SW 1	GW	SW 1	GW	GW	GW	GW	GW	SW ◇1	GW	GW	SW ◇1 ☕	GW
0	—	**Exmouth**	d		23p59	00 02			06 12	06 45		07 14		07 53		08 23		08 53		09 23	09 53		10 23
2	—	Lympstone Village	d		00 03	00 06			06 16	06 49		07 18		07 57		08 27		08 57		09 27	09 57		10 27
3	—	Lympstone Commando	d		00x04	00x07			06x17	06x52		07x20		07x58		08x29		08x58		09x28			10x28
3½	—	Exton	d		00x06	00x09			06x19	06x53		07x21		08x00		08x30		09x00		09x30			10x30
5	—	Topsham	d		00 11	00 14			06 24	06 58		07 29		08 05		08 35		09 05		09 35	10 05		10 35
7	—	Digby & Sowton	d		00 16	00 19			06 29	07 03		07 33		08 10		08 40		09 10		09 40	10 10		10 40
9	—	Polsloe Bridge	d		00 19	00 22			06 32	07 06		07 37		08 14		08 44		09 14		09 44			10 44
10	—	St James' Park	d		00 22	00 25			06 35	07 09		07 40		08 17	08 34	08 47		09 17		09 47			10 47
10½	—	**Exeter Central**	a		00 24	00s27			06 37	07 11		07 42		08 20	08 36	08 49		09 19		09 50	10 16		10 49
—	—		d	23p57	00 25			06 32	06 38	07 12	07 39	07 43	08 14	08 24	08 37	08 50	09 06	09 20	09 39	09 50	10 17	10 39	10 50
11¼	—	**Exeter St Davids** 6	a	00 01	00 28	00 31		06 35	06 41	07 15	07 42	07 46	08 17	08 26	08 42	08 54	09 11	09 24	09 42	09 54	10 21	10 42	10 54
—	—		d				05 54		06 47					08 31				09 27			10 27		
15½	—	Newton St Cyres	d																				
18¼	0	Crediton	d				06 05		06 58					08 42				09 38			10 38		
21¾	3½	Yeoford	d				06x11		07x04					08x48				09x44			10x44		
—	14¼	Sampford Courtenay	d																				
—	18	Okehampton	a																				
24½	—	Copplestone	d				06x16		07x09					08x53				09x49			10x49		
26¼	—	Morchard Road	d						07x12					08x56				09x52			10x52		
28¾	—	Lapford	d						07x16														
32½	—	Eggesford	d				06 31		07 33					09 11				10 08			11 08		
36½	—	Kings Nympton	d						07x38					09x17									
39¼	—	Portsmouth Arms	d						07x43														
43½	—	Umberleigh	d				06x45		07x49					09x27				10x23			11x23		
45¾	—	Chapelton	d						07x53														
50¼	—	**Barnstaple**	a				06 59		08 01					09 39				10 35			11 35		

		GW	SW ◇1 ☕	GW	GW	SW ◇1 ☕	GW	GW	SW ◇1 ☕	GW	GW	SW ◇1 ☕	GW	GW	SW ◇1 ☕	GW	GW	SW ◇1 ☕	GW	GW	GW	SW ◇1 ☕	GW
Exmouth	d	10 53		11 23	11 53		12 23	12 53		13 23	13 53		14 23	14 53		15 23	15 53			16 25	16 55		
Lympstone Village	d	10 57		11 27	11 57		12 27	12 57		13 27	13 57		14 27	14 57		15 27	15 57			16 29	16 59		
Lympstone Commando	d			11x28			12x28			13x28			14x28			15x28	15x58			16x30	17x00		
Exton	d			11x30			12x30			13x30			14x30			15x30	16x00			16x32	17x02		
Topsham	d	11 05		11 35	12 05		12 35	13 05		13 35	14 05		14 35	15 05		15 35	16 05			16 37	17 07		
Digby & Sowton	d	11 10		11 40	12 10		12 40	13 10		13 40	14 10		14 40	15 10		15 40	16 10			16 42	17 12		
Polsloe Bridge	d			11 44			12 44			13 44			14 44			15 44	16 14			16 46	17 15		
St James' Park	d			11 47			12 47			13 47			14 47			15 47	16 17		16 43	16 48	17 18		17 40
Exeter Central	a	11 16		11 49	12 16		12 49	13 16		13 49	14 16		14 49	15 16		15 49	16 19		16 45	16 51	17 20		17 42
	d	11 17	11 39	11 50	12 17	12 39	12 50	13 17	13 39	13 50	14 17	14 39	14 50	15 17	15 39	15 50	16 20	16 37	16 46	16 53	17 21	17 36	17 45
Exeter St Davids 6	a	11 21	11 42	11 54	12 21	12 42	12 54	13 21	13 42	13 54	14 21	14 42	14 54	15 21	15 42	15 54	16 25	16 42	16 49	16 56	17 24	17 42	17 48
	d	11 27			12 27			13 27			14 27			15 27						16 57			
Newton St Cyres	d																						
Crediton	d	11 38			12 38			13 38			14 38			15 38						17 08			
Yeoford	d	11x44			12x44			13x44			14x44			15x44						17x15			
Sampford Courtenay	d																						
Okehampton	a																						
Copplestone	d	11x49			12x49			13x49			14x49			15x49						17x19			
Morchard Road	d	11x52			12x52			13x52			14x52			15x52						17x22			
Lapford	d																			17x27			
Eggesford	d	12 08			13 08			14 08			15 08			16 08						17 37			
Kings Nympton	d							14x15												17x44			
Portsmouth Arms	d																						
Umberleigh	d	12x23			13x23			14x23			15x23			16x23						17x54			
Chapelton	d																						
Barnstaple	a	12 35			13 37			14 37			15 35			16 35						18 07			

		GW	GW	SW ◇1 ☕	GW	GW	GW	SW ◇1 ☕	GW	GW	SW ◇1 ☕	GW	GW	GW	SW ◇1 ☕	GW	GW	SW ◇1 ☕	GW FO	GW	SW ◇1 ☕
Exmouth	d	17 25	17 55		18 27		18 55		19 35	20 08				21 04			22 05			23 10	
Lympstone Village	d	17 29	17 59		18 31		18 59		19 42	20 12				21 08			22 09			23 14	
Lympstone Commando	d	17x30	18x01				19x00			20x13				21x09			22x10			23x15	
Exton	d	17x32	18x03				19x02			20x15				21x11			22x12			23x17	
Topsham	d	17 37	18 07		18 37		19 07		19 49	20 20				21 16			22 17			23 22	
Digby & Sowton	d	17 42	18 12		18 42		19 12		19 54	20 25				21 21			22 22			23 27	
Polsloe Bridge	d	17 45	18 15				19 15			20 28				21 24			22 25			23 30	
St James' Park	d	17 48	18 18				19 18			20 31				21 27			22 28			23 33	
Exeter Central	a	17 50	18 20		18 49		19 20		20 00	20 34				21 29			22 30			23 36	
	d	17 51	18 21	18 39	18 49	18 58	19 21	19 40	20 01	20 35	20 40	20 55	21 21	21 30	21 39	21 55	22 31	22 42	22 48	23 37	23 57
Exeter St Davids 6	a	17 55	18 26	18 42	18 53	19 02	19 25	19 45	20 05	20 38	20 44	20 58	21 25	21 34	21 44	22 00	22 34	22 45	22 51	23 41	00 01
	d	17 57			18 57							21 00							22 52		
Newton St Cyres	d	18x04			19x04							21x07									
Crediton	d	18 11			19 11							21 14							23 05		
Yeoford	d	18x17			19x17							21x20							23x11		
Sampford Courtenay	d																				
Okehampton	a																				
Copplestone	d	18x22			19x22							21x26							23x16		
Morchard Road	d	18x25			19x25							21x29							23x19		
Lapford	d	18x29										21x33							23x23		
Eggesford	d	18 41			19 42							21 43							23 33		
Kings Nympton	d	18x48										21x48							23x39		
Portsmouth Arms	d	18x52										21x53									
Umberleigh	d	18x59			19x56							21x59							23x49		
Chapelton	d	19x03										22x03									
Barnstaple	a	19 13			20 08							22 13							23 59		

For connections at Exeter St Davids please refer to Table 135

Table 136

Saturdays

Exmouth - Exeter - Barnstaple

		SW	GW	GW	SW	GW	SW	GW	SW	GW		GW	GW	SW	GW	GW	GW	GW	SW	GW		GW	GW	SW	GW
		◇1			1		1		1					◇1					◇1					◇1	
																A	B					A	B		
		⚲																	⚲					⚲	
Exmouth	d		00 02			06 12		07 15		07 53		08 23	08 53		09 23	09 53	09 53			10 23		10 53	10 53		11 23
Lympstone Village	d		00 06			06 16		07 19		07 57		08 27	08 57		09 27	09 57	09 57			10 27		10 57	10 57		11 27
Lympstone Commando	d		00x07			06x17		07x21		07x58		08x29	08x58		09x28	09x58	09x58			10x28		10x58	10x58		11x28
Exton	d		00x09			06x19		07x22		08x00		08x30	09x00		09x30					10x30					11x30
Topsham	d		00 14			06 24		07 29		08 05		08 35	09 05		09 35	10 05	10 05			10 35		11 05	11 05		11 35
Digby & Sowton	d		00 19			06 29		07 33		08 10		08 40	09 10		09 40	10 10	10 10			10 40		11 10	11 10		11 40
Polsloe Bridge	d		00 22			06 32		07 37		08 14		08 44	09 14		09 44					10 44					11 44
St James' Park	d		00 25			06 35		07 40		08 17		08 47	09 17		09 47					10 47					11 47
Exeter Central	a		00s27			06 37		07 42		08 20		08 49	09 19		09 50	10 16	10 16			10 49		11 16	11 17		11 49
	d	23p57			06 32	06 38	07 39	07 43	08 15	08 24		08 50	09 20	09 39	09 52	10 17	10 17	10 30	10 39	10 50		11 17	11 17	11 39	11 50
Exeter St Davids 6	a	00 01	00 31		06 35	06 41	07 42	07 46	08 18	08 26		08 54	09 24	09 42	09 54	10 21	10 21	10 33	10 42	10 54		11 21	11 21	11 42	11 54
	d			05 54		06 55				08 31			09 27			10 27	10 30					11 27	11 27		
Newton St Cyres	d																								
Crediton	d			06 05		07 06				08 42			09 38			10 38	10 41					11 38	11 38		
Yeoford	d			06x11		07x12				08x48			09x44			10x44	10x47					11x44	11x44		
Sampford Courtenay	d																								
Okehampton	a																								
Copplestone	d			06x16		07x18				08x53			09x49			10x49	10x53					11x49	11x49		
Morchard Road	d					07x21				08x56			09x52			10x52	10x56					11x52	11x52		
Lapford	d					07x25																			
Eggesford	d			06 31		07 38				09 11			10 08			11 08	11 09					12 08	12 08		
Kings Nympton	d					07x43				09x17															
Portsmouth Arms	d					07x48																			
Umberleigh	d			06x45		07x54				09x27			10x23			11x23	11x24					12x23	12x23		
Chapelton	d					07x58																			
Barnstaple	a			06 59		08 07				09 39			10 35			11 35	11 36					12 35	12 35		

		GW	SW	GW	GW	SW		GW	GW	SW	GW	GW	SW	GW	GW	SW		GW	GW	GW	GW	SW	GW	GW	SW
			◇1			◇1				◇1			◇1			◇1						◇1			◇1
			⚲			⚲				⚲			⚲			⚲						⚲			⚲
Exmouth	d	11 53		12 23	12 53			13 23	13 53		14 23	14 53		15 23	15 53				16 25		16 55		17 25	17 55	
Lympstone Village	d	11 57		12 27	12 57			13 27	13 57		14 27	14 57		15 27	15 57				16 29		16 59		17 29	17 59	
Lympstone Commando	d	11x58		12x28	12x58			13x28	13x58		14x28	14x58		15x28	15x58				16x30		17x00		17x30	18x01	
Exton	d			12x30				13x30			14x30			15x30	16x00				16x32		17x02		17x32	18x03	
Topsham	d	12 05		12 35	13 05			13 35	14 05		14 35	15 05		15 35	16 05				16 37		17 07		17 37	18 07	
Digby & Sowton	d	12 10		12 40	13 10			13 40	14 10		14 40	15 10		15 40	16 10				16 42		17 12		17 42	18 12	
Polsloe Bridge	d			12 44				13 44			14 44			15 44	16 14				16 46		17 15		17 45	18 15	
St James' Park	d			12 47				13 47			14 47			15 47	16 17				16 48	17 05	17 18		17 48	18 18	
Exeter Central	a	12 16		12 49	13 16			13 49	14 16		14 49	15 16		15 49	16 19				16 51	17 07	17 20		17 50	18 20	
	d	12 17	12 39	12 50	13 17	13 39		13 50	14 17	14 39	14 50	15 17	15 39	15 50	16 20	16 37		16 48	16 53	17 08	17 21	17 39	17 51	18 21	18 37
Exeter St Davids 6	a	12 21	12 42	12 54	13 21	13 42		13 54	14 22	14 42	14 54	15 21	15 42	15 54	16 25	16 42		16 51	16 56	17 11	17 24	17 42	17 55	18 26	18 42
	d	12 27			13 27				14 27			15 27							16 57				17 57		
Newton St Cyres	d																						18x04		
Crediton	d	12 38			13 38				14 38			15 38							17 08				18 11		
Yeoford	d	12x44			13x44				14x44			15x44							17x15				18x17		
Sampford Courtenay	d																								
Okehampton	a																								
Copplestone	d	12x49			13x49				14x49			15x49							17x19				18x22		
Morchard Road	d	12x52			13x52				14x52			15x52							17x22				18x25		
Lapford	d																		17x27				18x29		
Eggesford	d	13 08			14 08				15 08			16 08							17 37				18 41		
Kings Nympton	d				14x15														17x44				18x48		
Portsmouth Arms	d																						18x52		
Umberleigh	d	13x23			14x23				15x23			16x23							17x54				18x59		
Chapelton	d																						19x03		
Barnstaple	a	13 37			14 37				15 35			16 35							18 07				19 13		

		GW		GW	SW	GW	GW	SW	GW	GW	SW	GW		SW	GW	GW
					◇1			◇1			◇1			◇1		
					⚲			⚲			⚲			⚲		
Exmouth	d	18 27		18 55		19 38	20 08			21 04		22 11			23 10	23 43
Lympstone Village	d	18 31		18 59		19 42	20 12			21 08		22 15			23 14	23 47
Lympstone Commando	d			19x00			20x13			21x09		22x16			23x15	23x48
Exton	d			19x02			20x15			21x11		22x18			23x17	23x50
Topsham	d	18 37		19 07		19 49	20 20			21 16		22 23			23 22	23 55
Digby & Sowton	d	18 42		19 12		19 54	20 25			21 21		22 28			23 27	23 59
Polsloe Bridge	d			19 15			20 28			21 24		22 31			23 30	00 03
St James' Park	d			19 18			20 31			21 27		22 34			23 33	00 06
Exeter Central	a	18 49		19 20		20 00	20 34			21 29		22 36			23 36	00 08
	d	18 49		19 21	19 39	20 01	20 35	20 40	20 52	21 30	21 39	22 37		22 42	23 37	00 09
Exeter St Davids 6	a	18 53		19 25	19 42	20 05	20 38	20 43	20 55	21 34	21 42	22 40		22 45	23 41	00 14
	d	18 57							21 00							
Newton St Cyres	d	19x04							21x07							
Crediton	d	19 11							21 14							
Yeoford	d	19x18							21x20							
Sampford Courtenay	d															
Okehampton	a															
Copplestone	d	19x22							21x26							
Morchard Road	d	19x25							21x29							
Lapford	d								21x33							
Eggesford	d	19 42							21 43							
Kings Nympton	d								21x48							
Portsmouth Arms	d								21x53							
Umberleigh	d	19x56							21x59							
Chapelton	d								22x03							
Barnstaple	a	20 08							22 13							

A from 17 September **B** until 10 September

For connections at Exeter St Davids please refer to Table 135

Table 136

Sundays

Exmouth - Exeter - Barnstaple

		GW	GW	SW	GW	GW	GW	SW	GW	GW	SW	GW	GW	GW	SW	GW	GW	GW	SW	GW	GW	GW	SW
				1				◇1			◇1				◇1				◇1				◇1
		A			B	C			C	B		C	C	D		C	B	C		C	C	D	
											🚲				🚲				🚲				🚲
Exmouth	d	23p43				09 10			10 21			11 24				12 29				13 24			
Lympstone Village	d	23p47				09 14			10 25			11 28				12 33				13 28			
Lympstone Commando	d	23b48				09x15			10x26			11x29				12x34				13x29			
Exton	d	23b50				09x17			10x28			11x31				12x36				13x31			
Topsham	d	23p55				09 22			10 33			11 36				12 41				13 36			
Digby & Sowton	d	23p59				09 27			10 38			11 41				12 46				13 41			
Polsloe Bridge	d	00 03				09 30			10 41			11 44				12 49				13 44			
St James' Park	d	00 06			09 03	09 33			10 44	11 00		11 47				12 52	13 03			13 47			
Exeter Central	a	00 08			09 05	09 36			10 46	11 02		11 49				12 54	13 05			13 49			
	d	00 09		08 58	09 06	09 36		10 42	10 48	11 03	11 42	11 53	11 59		12 42	12 55	13 06	13 20	13 42	13 50	13 55		14 42
Exeter St Davids 6	a	00 14		09 01	09 09	09 40		10 45	10 51	11 06	11 45	11 56	12 02		12 45	12 58	13 10	13 23	13 45	13 53	13 58		14 45
	d		08 41		09 14		09 53			11 07			12 03	12 03			13 10				13 59	13 59	
Newton St Cyres	d		08x49		⌇					⌇			12x11	12x11			⌇				⌇	⌇	
Crediton	d		08 55		09 24		10 04			11 17			12 17	12 17			13 21				14 20	14 21	
Yeoford	d		09x02		⌇		10x11			⌇			12x24	12x24			⌇				14x27	14x28	
Sampford Courtenay	d				09 45					11 38			⌇	⌇			13 42				⌇	⌇	
Okehampton	a				09 52					11 45			⌇	⌇			13 49				⌇	⌇	
Copplestone	d		09x07				10x16						12x30	12x30							14x33	14x33	
Morchard Road	d		09x10				10x19						12x33	12x33							14x36	14x36	
Lapford	d		09x14										12 37	12 37							⌇	⌇	
Eggesford	d		09 24				10 31						12 46	12 46							14 48	14 48	
Kings Nympton	d		09x31										12 52	12 52							14 54	14 55	
Portsmouth Arms	d		09 35										12 57	12 57							14 59	14 59	
Umberleigh	d		09x42				10x46						13x03	13x03							15x05	15x06	
Chapelton	d		09 46										13 07	13 07							⌇	⌇	
Barnstaple	a		09 54				10 57						13 14	13 14							15 15	15 15	

		GW	GW	GW	SW	GW	GW	GW	SW	GW	GW	SW	GW	GW	GW	SW	GW	SW	GW	GW	GW	SW	GW
					◇1				◇1			◇1				◇1		◇1				◇1	
		C	B	C		C	D	C		C	B		C	C	D		C		C	C	D		C
					🚲				🚲			🚲				🚲		🚲				🚲	
Exmouth	d	14 31				15 24				16 24			17 24				18 24		19 24				20 24
Lympstone Village	d	14 35				15 28				16 28			17 28				18 28		19 28				20 28
Lympstone Commando	d	14x36				15x29				16x29			17x29				18x29		19x29				20x29
Exton	d	14x38				15x31				16x31			17x31				18x31		19x31				20x31
Topsham	d	14 43				15 36				16 36			17 36				18 35		19 36				20 36
Digby & Sowton	d	14 48				15 41				16 41			17 41				18 40		19 41				20 41
Polsloe Bridge	d	14 51				15 44				16 44			17 44				18 43		19 44				20 44
St James' Park	d	14 54	15 03			15 47				16 47	17 02		17 47				18 46		19 47				20 47
Exeter Central	a	14 56	15 05			15 49				16 49	17 04		17 49				18 48		19 49				20 49
	d	14 57	15 06	15 20	15 42	15 50		15 59	16 42	16 50	17 05	17 42	17 50	17 56		18 42	18 49	19 42	19 50	19 56		20 42	20 50
Exeter St Davids 6	a	15 01	15 09	15 23	15 45	15 53		16 02	16 45	16 53	17 08	17 45	17 53	17 59		18 45	18 53	19 45	19 53	19 59		20 45	20 53
	d		15 09				16 01	16 04			17 08			18 04	18 04					20 01	20 01		
Newton St Cyres	d		⌇				16x09	16x12			⌇			⌇	⌇					20x08	20x08		
Crediton	d		15 20				16 18	16 19			17 19			18 17	18 17					20 18	20 18		
Yeoford	d		⌇				16x25	16x26			⌇			18x24	18x24					20x24	20x24		
Sampford Courtenay	d		15 40				⌇	⌇			17 39			⌇	⌇					⌇	⌇		
Okehampton	a		15 48				⌇	⌇			17 47			⌇	⌇					⌇	⌇		
Copplestone	d						16x30	16x31						18x29	18x29					20x30	20x30		
Morchard Road	d						16x33	16x34						18x32	18x32					20x33	20x33		
Lapford	d						16x37	16x38						⌇	⌇					20x37	20x37		
Eggesford	d						16 44	16 45						18 45	18 45					20 47	20 47		
Kings Nympton	d						16x52	16x53						⌇	⌇					20x52	20x52		
Portsmouth Arms	d						16x55	16x56						⌇	⌇					20x57	20x57		
Umberleigh	d						17x03	17x04						18x59	18x59					21x03	21x03		
Chapelton	d						17x07	17x08						⌇	⌇					21x07	21x07		
Barnstaple	a						17 16	17 17						19 09	19 09					21 15	21 15		

A not 22 May
B until 18 September
C until 23 October
D from 30 October
b Previous night, stops on request

For connections at Exeter St Davids please refer to Table 135

Table 136

Exmouth - Exeter - Barnstaple

		SW		GW	SW	GW	GW	GW
		◇1			◇1			
				A		A	A	
		⚮			⚮			
Exmouth	d			21§25		22§29	23§29	23 59
Lympstone Village	d			21§28		22§33	23§33	00 03
Lympstone Commando	d			21x30		22x34	23x34	00x04
Exton	d			21x32		22x37	23x36	00x06
Topsham	d			21§36		22§42	23§42	00 11
Digby & Sowton	d			21§41		22§46	23§47	00 16
Polsloe Bridge	d			21§44		22§49	23§50	00 19
St James' Park	d			21§47		22§54	23§53	00 22
Exeter Central	a			21§49		22§56	23§55	00 24
	d	21 42		21§50	22 42	22§56	23§56	00 25
Exeter St Davids 6	a	21 45		21§53	22 45	23§01	23§59	00 28
	d							
Newton St Cyres	d							
Crediton	d							
Yeoford	d							
Sampford Courtenay	d							
Okehampton	a							
Copplestone	d							
Morchard Road	d							
Lapford	d							
Eggesford	d							
Kings Nympton	d							
Portsmouth Arms	d							
Umberleigh	d							
Chapelton	d							
Barnstaple	a							

A until 23 October

For connections at Exeter St Davids please refer to Table 135

Barnstaple - Exeter - Exmouth

Miles	Miles			SW ◇1 🛒	GW	GW	GW	SW ◇1 🛒	GW	SW ◇1 🛒	GW	GW	GW	SW ◇1 🛒	GW	GW	GW	SW ◇1 🛒	GW	GW	SW ◇1 🛒	GW	GW
0	—	**Barnstaple**	d										07 00						08 43			09 43	
4¼	—	Chapelton	d										07x05										
6¾	—	Umberleigh	d										07x09						08x51			09x51	
10¾	—	Portsmouth Arms	d										07x16										
13¾	—	Kings Nympton	d										07x21						09x03				
17½	—	Eggesford	d										07 30						09 07			10 07	
21½	—	Lapford	d										07x35						09x14				
23¾	—	Morchard Road	d										07x40						09x17			10x16	
25½	—	Copplestone	d										07x43						09x22			10x20	
—	0	Okehampton	d																				
—	3¾	Sampford Courtenay	d																				
28½	14½	Yeoford	d										07x48						09x25			10x24	
32	18	Crediton	d										07 55						09 37			10 37	
34¾	—	Newton St Cyres	d										07x58										
39	—	**Exeter St Davids** 6	a										08 07						09 48			10 48	
—	—		d	05 10	05 44	06 06	06 29	06 41	07 11	07 26	07 36	08 13	08 16	08 26	08 48	08 59	09 18	09 26	09 48	10 18	10 26	10 48	11 18
39¾	—	**Exeter Central**	a	05 13	05 47	06 09	06 32	06 44	07 14	07 29	07 39	08 16	08 20	08 29	08 51	09 04	09 21	09 29	09 51	10 21	10 29	10 51	11 21
—	—		d		05 48	06 10	06 39		07 15		07 52	08 17	08 21		08 52		09 22		09 52	10 22		10 52	11 22
40¼	—	St James' Park	d			06 12	06 41		07 17		07 54	08a21	08 23		08 54		09 24			10 24			11 24
41¼	—	Polsloe Bridge	d			06 15	06 44		07 20		07 57		08 27		08 57		09 27			10 27			11 27
43¼	—	Digby & Sowton	d		05 54	06 19	06 48		07 24		08 01		08 31		09 01		09 31		10 01	10 31		11 01	11 31
45¼	—	Topsham	d		05 58	06 25	06 57		07 28		08 05		08 35		09 05		09 35		10 05	10 35		11 05	11 35
46¾	—	Exton	d			06x27	07x00		07x31		08x08		08x38		09x08		09x38			10x38			11x38
47¼	—	Lympstone Commando	d			06x29	07x02		07x33		08x10		08x40		09x10		09x40			10x40			11x40
48¼	—	Lympstone Village	d		06 03	06 31	07 05		07 36		08 13		08 43		09 13		09 43		10 11	10 43		11 11	11 43
50¼	—	**Exmouth**	a		06 10	06 38	07 10		07 43		08 18		08 48		09 20		09 50		10 19	10 50		11 19	11 50

		SW ◇1 🛒	GW	GW	SW ◇1 🛒	GW	GW	SW ◇1 🛒	GW	GW	SW ◇1 🛒	GW	GW	SW ◇1 🛒	GW	GW	GW	SW ◇1 🛒	GW	GW	GW	SW ◇1 🛒	SW 1
Barnstaple	d		10 43			11 43			12 43			13 43			14 43				15 43				
Chapelton	d																						
Umberleigh	d		10x51			11x51			12x51			13x51			14x51				15x51				
Portsmouth Arms	d																						
Kings Nympton	d								13x02														
Eggesford	d		11 07			12 07			13 07			14 07			15 07				16 07				
Lapford	d																						
Morchard Road	d		11x16			12x16			13x16			14x16			15x16				16x16				
Copplestone	d		11x20			12x20			13x20			14x20			15x20				16x20				
Okehampton	d																						
Sampford Courtenay	d																						
Yeoford	d		11x24			12x24			13x24			14x24			15x24				16x24				
Crediton	d		11 37			12 37			13 37			14 37			15 37				16 37				
Newton St Cyres	d																						
Exeter St Davids 6	a		11 48			12 48			13 48			14 48			15 48				16 48				
	d	11 26	11 48	12 18	12 26	12 48	13 18	13 26	13 48	14 18	14 26	14 48	15 18	15 26	15 48	16 08	16 18	16 26	16 50	17 10	17 18	17 26	17 46
Exeter Central	a	11 29	11 51	12 21	12 29	12 51	13 21	13 29	13 51	14 21	14 29	14 51	15 21	15 29	15 51	16 11	16 21	16 29	16 53	17 13	17 21	17 29	17 49
	d		11 52	12 22		12 52	13 22		13 52	14 22		14 52	15 22		15 52	16 12	16 22		16 54	17 14	17 22		
St James' Park	d			12 24			13 24			14 24			15 24			16a16	16 24		16 56	17a18	17 24		
Polsloe Bridge	d			12 27			13 27			14 27			15 27				16 27		16 59		17 27		
Digby & Sowton	d		12 01	12 31		13 01	13 31		14 01	14 31		15 01	15 31		16 01		16 31		17 03		17 31		
Topsham	d		12 05	12 35		13 05	13 35		14 05	14 35		15 05	15 35		16 05		16 37		17 07		17 37		
Exton	d			12x38			13x38			14x38			15x38				16x38		17x10		17x38		
Lympstone Commando	d			12x40			13x40			14x40			15x40				16x40		17x12		17x40		
Lympstone Village	d		12 11	12 43		13 11	13 43		14 11	14 43		15 11	15 43		16 11		16 43		17 15		17 43		
Exmouth	a		12 19	12 50		13 19	13 50		14 19	14 50		15 19	15 50		16 19		16 50		17 22		17 51		

		GW	GW	SW ◇1 🛒	GW	GW	SW ◇1	GW	GW	SW ◇1 🛒	GW	GW	SW 1	GW	GW	GW	SW 1	GW
Barnstaple	d				17 08			18 13	19 16						20 24			22 16
Chapelton	d				17x14													
Umberleigh	d				17x18			18x21	19x24						20x32			22x24
Portsmouth Arms	d							18x28										
Kings Nympton	d				17 29			18x33										
Eggesford	d				17 37			18 40	19 40						20 49			22 40
Lapford	d				17 43			18x47										
Morchard Road	d				17x46			18x51	19x49						20x58			22x48
Copplestone	d				17x50			18x55	19x53						21x01			22x52
Okehampton	d																	
Sampford Courtenay	d																	
Yeoford	d				17x54			18x59	19x57						21x05			22x56
Crediton	d				18 13			19 11	20 06						21 16			23 05
Newton St Cyres	d							19x16	20x09						21x19			23x08
Exeter St Davids 6	a				18 30			19 25	20 18						21 34			23 16
	d	17 52	18 20	18 26	18 32	18 50	19 26	19 32	20 20	20 26	20 30	21 14	21 23	21 32	21 38	22 36	22 57	23 28
Exeter Central	a	17 55	18 23	18 29	18 37	18 53	19 29	19 35	20 25	20 29	20 33	21 19	21 26	21 35	21 41	22 39	23 00	23 31
	d	17 56	18 24			18 54		19 36			20 34			21 35		22 40		23 32
St James' Park	d	17 58	18 26			18 56		19 38			20 36			21 37		22 42		23 34
Polsloe Bridge	d	18 01	18 29			18 59		19 41			20 39			21 40		22 45		23 37
Digby & Sowton	d	18 05	18 33			19 03		19 45			20 43			21 44		22 49		23 41
Topsham	d	18 09	18 37			19 07		19 49			20 47			21 49		22 53		23 45
Exton	d	18x12	18x38			19x10		19x52			20x49			21x51		22x56		23x47
Lympstone Commando	d	18x14	18x40			19x12		19x54			20x51			21x53		22x58		23x49
Lympstone Village	d	18 17	18 43			19 15		19 57			20 54			21 56		23 01		23 52
Exmouth	a	18 25	18 52			19 23		20 03			21 01			22 02		23 08		23 59

For connections at Exeter St Davids please refer to Table 135

Table 136

Saturdays

Barnstaple - Exeter - Exmouth

		GW	SW	GW	GW	SW	GW	SW	GW	GW		SW	GW	GW	SW	GW	GW	SW	GW	GW		GW	SW	GW	GW
			◇1 ⌶			◇1 ⌶		◇1 ⌶				◇1 ⌶			◇1 ⌶			◇1 ⌶	A	B			◇1 ⌶		
Barnstaple	d	00 05								07 08						08 43			09 43	09 43				10 43	
Chapelton	d									07x13															
Umberleigh	d									07x17						08x51			09x51	09x51				10x51	
Portsmouth Arms	d									07x24															
Kings Nympton	d									07x29						09x02									
Eggesford	d	00 29								07 38						09 07			10 07	10 07				11 07	
Lapford	d									07x43						09x14									
Morchard Road	d									07x48						09x17			10x16	10x16				11x16	
Copplestone	d									07x51						09x22			10x20	10x20				11x20	
Okehampton	d																								
Sampford Courtenay	d																								
Yeoford	d									07x57						09x25			10x24	10x24				11x24	
Crediton	d	00 47								08 04						09 37			10 37	10 39				11 37	
Newton St Cyres	d									08x07															
Exeter St Davids 6	a	01 00								08 16						09 48			10 48	10 49				11 48	
	d		05 10	05 44	06 29	06 41	07 11	07 26	07 36	08 16		08 26	08 48	09 18	09 26	09 48	10 18	10 26	10 48	10 49		11 18	11 26	11 48	12 18
Exeter Central	a		05 13	05 47	06 32	06 44	07 14	07 29	07 39	08 19		08 29	08 51	09 21	09 29	09 51	10 21	10 29	10 51	10 52		11 21	11 29	11 51	12 21
	d			05 48	06 39		07 15		07 52	08 20			08 52	09 22		09 52	10 22		10 52	10 53		11 22		11 52	12 22
St James' Park	d				06 41		07 17		07 54	08 23			08 54	09 24		09 54	10 24					11 24			12 24
Polsloe Bridge	d				06 44		07 20		07 57	08 27			08 57	09 27		09 57	10 27					11 27			12 27
Digby & Sowton	d			05 54	06 48		07 24		08 01	08 31			09 01	09 31		10 01	10 31		11 01	11 01		11 31		12 01	12 31
Topsham	d			05 58	06 52		07 28		08 05	08 35			09 05	09 35		10 05	10 35		11 05	11 05		11 35		12 05	12 35
Exton	d				06x54		07x31		08x08	08x38			09x08	09x38		10x08	10x38					11x38			12x38
Lympstone Commando	d				06x56		07x33		08x10	08x40			09x10	09x40		10x10	10x40		11x09	11x09		11x40		12x09	12x40
Lympstone Village	d			06 03	06 59		07 36		08 13	08 43			09 13	09 43		10 11	10 43		11 11	11 11		11 43		12 11	12 43
Exmouth	a			06 10	07 04		07 43		08 18	08 48			09 20	09 50		10 19	10 50		11 19	11 19		11 50		12 19	12 50

		SW	GW	GW	SW	GW		GW	SW	GW	GW	SW	GW	GW	SW	GW		GW	GW	GW	SW	GW	GW	SW	GW
		◇1 ⌶			◇1 ⌶				◇1 ⌶			◇1 ⌶			◇1 ⌶						◇1 ⌶			◇1 ⌶	
Barnstaple	d		11 43			12 43				13 43			14 43					15 43	17 08						
Chapelton	d																		17x14						
Umberleigh	d		11x51			12x51				13x51			14x51					15x51	17x18						
Portsmouth Arms	d																								
Kings Nympton	d					13x02													17x29						
Eggesford	d		12 07			13 07				14 07			15 07					16 07	17 37						
Lapford	d																		17x43						
Morchard Road	d		12x16			13x16				14x16			15x16					16x16	17x46						
Copplestone	d		12x20			13x20				14x20			15x20					16x20	17x50						
Okehampton	d																								
Sampford Courtenay	d																								
Yeoford	d		12x24			13x24				14x24			15x24					16x24	17x54						
Crediton	d		12 37			13 37				14 37			15 37					16 37	18 10						
Newton St Cyres	d																								
Exeter St Davids 6	a		12 48			13 48				14 48			15 48					16 48	18 22						
	d	12 26	12 48	13 18	13 26	13 48		14 18	14 26	14 48	15 18	15 26	15 48	16 18	16 26	16 41		16 50		17 18	17 26	17 50	18 20	18 26	18 50
Exeter Central	a	12 29	12 51	13 21	13 29	13 51		14 21	14 29	14 51	15 21	15 29	15 51	16 21	16 29	16 44		16 53		17 21	17 29	17 53	18 23	18 29	18 53
	d		12 52	13 22		13 52		14 22		14 52	15 22		15 52	16 22				16 54		17 22		17 54	18 24		18 54
St James' Park	d			13 24		13 54		14 24			15 24		15 57	16 24				16 56		17 24		17 56	18 26		18 56
Polsloe Bridge	d			13 27				14 27			15 27			16 27				16 59		17 27		17 59	18 29		18 59
Digby & Sowton	d		13 01	13 31		14 01		14 31		15 01	15 31		16 01	16 31				17 03		17 31		18 03	18 33		19 03
Topsham	d		13 05	13 35		14 05		14 35		15 05	15 35		16 05	16 37				17 07		17 37		18 07	18 37		19 07
Exton	d			13x38				14x38			15x38			16x38				17x10		17x38		18x10	18x38		19x10
Lympstone Commando	d		13x09	13x40		14x09		14x40		15x09	15x40		16x09	16x40				17x12		17x40		18x12	18x40		19x12
Lympstone Village	d		13 11	13 43		14 11		14 43		15 11	15 43		16 11	16 43				17 15		17 43		18 15	18 43		19 15
Exmouth	a		13 19	13 50		14 19		14 50		15 19	15 50		16 19	16 50				17 22		17 50		18 22	18 52		19 22

		SW		GW	GW	SW	GW	SW	GW	GW	GW	GW		SW	GW
		◇1				◇1 ⌶		1						1	
Barnstaple	d			18 13	19 16				20 24		22 18				
Chapelton	d										22x23				
Umberleigh	d			18x21	19x24				20x32		22x27				
Portsmouth Arms	d			18x28							22x34				
Kings Nympton	d			18x33							22x39				
Eggesford	d			18 40	19 40				20 49		22 47				
Lapford	d			18x47							22x52				
Morchard Road	d			18x51	19x49				20x58		22x57				
Copplestone	d			18x55	19x53				21x01		23x00				
Okehampton	d														
Sampford Courtenay	d														
Yeoford	d			18x59	19x58				21x06		23x05				
Crediton	d			19 11	20 06				21 16		23 13				
Newton St Cyres	d			19x16	20x09				21x19		23x16				
Exeter St Davids 6	a			19 25	20 18				21 30		23 26				
	d	19 26		19 32	20 20	20 26	20 30	21 26	21 32	21 38		22 36		22 57	23 06
Exeter Central	a	19 29		19 35	20 25	20 29	20 33	21 29	21 37	21 41		22 39		23 00	23 09
	d			19 36			20 34			21 42		22 40			23 10
St James' Park	d			19 38			20 36			21 44		22 42			23 12
Polsloe Bridge	d			19 41			20 39			21 47		22 45			23 15
Digby & Sowton	d			19 45			20 43			21 51		22 49			23 19
Topsham	d			19 49			20 47			21 55		22 53			23 23
Exton	d			19x52			20x49			21x57		22x56			23x25
Lympstone Commando	d			19x54			20x51			21x59		22x58			23x27
Lympstone Village	d			19 57			20 54			22 03		23 01			23 31
Exmouth	a			20 03			21 01			22 09		23 08			23 36

A from 17 September

B until 10 September

For connections at Exeter St Davids please refer to Table 135

Table 136

Barnstaple - Exeter - Exmouth

		GW	SW	GW	SW	GW	GW	GW	GW	GW		SW	GW	SW	GW	GW	GW	GW	GW	SW		GW	SW	GW	GW
			◇1		◇1							◇1		◇1						◇1			◇1		
		A		A		B	C	A	A	C			A		A	B	D	E	C			A		A	B
			🛒		🛒							🛒		🛒						🛒			🛒		
Barnstaple	d						10 00		10 00	11 26					11 26				13 24					13 24	
Chapelton	d						10 06		10 06	⌇					⌇				13 30					13 30	
Umberleigh	d						10x10		10x10	11x34					11x34				13x33					13x33	
Portsmouth Arms	d						10 17		10 17	⌇					⌇				13 41					13 41	
Kings Nympton	d						10 22		10 22	⌇					⌇				13 46					13 46	
Eggesford	d						10 32		10 32	11 52					11 52				13 54					13 54	
Lapford	d						10x37		10x37	⌇					⌇				14 00					14 00	
Morchard Road	d						10x41		10x41	12x00					12x00				14x04					14x04	
Copplestone	d						10x45		10x45	12x04					12x04				14x07					14x07	
Okehampton	d					10 00	⌇		⌇	⌇					⌇	12 00			⌇					⌇	14 00
Sampford Courtenay	d					10 08	⌇		⌇	⌇					⌇	12 08			⌇					⌇	14 08
Yeoford	d					⌇	10x50		10x50	12x09					12x09	⌇			14x13					14x13	⌇
Crediton	d					10 28	10 58		10 58	12 18					12 18	12 28			14 21					14 21	14 31
Newton St Cyres	d					⌇	11x01		11x01	12x21					12x21	⌇			14 25					14 25	⌇
Exeter St Davids 6	a					10 38	11 10		11 11	12 33					12 32	12 38			14 33					14 33	14 41
	d	08 30	09 26	09 45	10 26	10 38		10 47	11 13			11 26	11 55	12 26	12 32	12 38	12 48	12 48		13 26		13 48	14 26	14 35	14 41
Exeter Central	a	08 33	09 29	09 48	10 29	10 41		10 50	11 16			11 29	11 58	12 29	12 35	12 41	12 51	12 51		13 29		13 51	14 29	14 38	14 44
	d	08 34		09 49		10 42		10 51					11 59			12 42	12 52	12 53				13 52			14 45
St James' Park	d	08 36		09 51		10a44		10 53					12 01			12a44	12 54	12 55				13 54			14a47
Polsloe Bridge	d	08 39		09 54				10 56					12 04				12 57	12 58				13 57			
Digby & Sowton	d	08 43		09 58				11 00					12 08				13 01	13 02				14 01			
Topsham	d	08 47		10 03				11 04					12 12				13 06	13 07				14 06			
Exton	d	08x49		10x05				11x06					12x14				13x08	13x09				14x08			
Lympstone Commando	d	08x51		10x07				11x08					12x16				13x10	13x11				14x10			
Lympstone Village	d	08 55		10 10				11 12					12 20				13 13	13 14				14 13			
Exmouth	a	09 00		10 15				11 17					12 25				13 19	13 20				14 18			

		GW	GW	SW	GW	SW		GW	GW	GW	GW	GW	SW	GW	SW	GW		GW	GW	GW	SW	GW	SW	GW	SW
				◇1		◇1							◇1		◇1						◇1		◇1		1
		A	A		A			A	B	A	A	C		A		A		B	A			A		A	
				🛒		🛒							🛒		🛒										
Barnstaple	d							15 23				17 20				17 20				19 20					
Chapelton	d							⌇				17x25				17x25									
Umberleigh	d							15x31				17x29				17x29				19x28					
Portsmouth Arms	d							15x38				17x36				17x36									
Kings Nympton	d							15x43				17x41				17x41									
Eggesford	d							15 52				17 50				17 50				19 45					
Lapford	d							⌇				17x55				17x55									
Morchard Road	d							16x00				18x00				18x00				19x53					
Copplestone	d							16x03				18x03				18x03				19x57					
Okehampton	d							⌇	16 00			⌇				⌇		18 00							
Sampford Courtenay	d							⌇	16 08			⌇				⌇		18 08							
Yeoford	d							16x09	⌇			18x09				18x09		⌇		20x02					
Crediton	d							16 18	16 28			18 18				18 18		18 28		20 15					
Newton St Cyres	d							16x22	⌇			18x22				18x22		⌇		20x18					
Exeter St Davids 6	a							16 31	16 38			18 32				18 33		18 40		20 27					
	d	14 48	15 14	15 26	15 48	16 26		16 31	16 38	16 48	17 18		17 26	17 48	18 26	18 34		18 41	18 48		19 26	19 51	20 26	20 51	21 26
Exeter Central	a	14 51	15 17	15 29	15 51	16 29		16 34	16 41	16 51	17 21		17 29	17 51	18 29	18 37		18 44	18 51		19 29	19 54	20 29	20 54	21 29
	d	14 52			15 51				16 42	16 51				17 51				18 45	18 52			19 55		20 55	
St James' Park	d	14 54			15 53				16a44	16 53				17 53				18a47	18 54			19 57		20 57	
Polsloe Bridge	d	14 57			15 56					16 56				17 56					18 57			20 00		21 00	
Digby & Sowton	d	15 01			16 00					17 00				18 00					19 01			20 04		21 04	
Topsham	d	15 06			16 05					17 05				18 05					19 06			20 08		21 08	
Exton	d	15x08			16x07					17x07				18x07					19x08			20x10		21x10	
Lympstone Commando	d	15x10			16x09					17x09				18x09					19x11			20x12		21x12	
Lympstone Village	d	15 13			16 13					17 13				18 13					19 13			20 16		21 16	
Exmouth	a	15 18			16 18					17 18				18 18					19 18			20 21		21 21	

		GW		GW	GW	SW	GW
						1	
				A	A		A
Barnstaple	d	21 30					
Chapelton	d	21 36					
Umberleigh	d	21x39					
Portsmouth Arms	d	21 47					
Kings Nympton	d	21 52					
Eggesford	d	22 00					
Lapford	d	22 06					
Morchard Road	d	22x10					
Copplestone	d	22x13					
Okehampton	d						
Sampford Courtenay	d						
Yeoford	d	22x19					
Crediton	d	22 28					
Newton St Cyres	d	22x31					
Exeter St Davids 6	a	22 42					
	d			21 48	22 48	23 15	23 25
Exeter Central	a			21 51	22 51	23 18	23 28
	d			21 51	22 52		23 29
St James' Park	d			21 53	22 54		23 31
Polsloe Bridge	d			21 56	22 57		23 34
Digby & Sowton	d			22 00	23 01		23 38
Topsham	d			22 05	23 06		23 42
Exton	d			22x07	23x08		23x44
Lympstone Commando	d			22x09	23x11		23x46
Lympstone Village	d			22 13	23 13		23 50
Exmouth	a			22 18	23 18		23 54

A until 23 October
B until 18 September
C from 30 October
D from 18 September until 23 October
E until 11 September

For connections at Exeter St Davids please refer to Table 135

Table 139

Plymouth - Gunnislake

Miles			GW	GW	GW	GW	GW	GW	GW	GW	GW	GW	GW	GW	GW	GW	GW	GW	GW
					1	◇	1		◇										
						A	B							B	A				
					[cup]		[cup]												
0	**Plymouth**	d	05 06	06 40	07 02	08 15	08 20	08 54	09 21	10 42	10 54	12 54	14 54	15 53	15 57	16 38	17 04	18 23	21 31
1¼	Devonport	d		06 43	07a06	08a18	08a24	08 57	09a24		10 57	12 57	14 57	15 56	16 00	16 41	17 07	18 26	21 34
1¾	Dockyard	d		06x44				08x58			10x58	12x58	14x58	15x57	16x01	16x42	17x08	18x27	21x35
2¼	Keyham	d		06 46				09 00			11 00	13 00	15 00	15 59	16 03	16 44	17 10	18 29	21 37
—	St Budeaux Ferry Road	a								10 48				16 02	16 06		17 13		
3¼	St Budeaux Victoria Road	d	05 12	06 50				09 04			11 04	13 04	15 04			16 48		18 33	21 41
7½	Bere Ferrers	d		06 57				09 11			11 11	13 11	15 11			16 55		18 40	21 48
10¼	Bere Alston	a	05 24	07 04				09 18			11 18	13 19	15 18			17 02		18 47	21 55
—		d	05 26	07 06				09 20			11 20	13 20	15 20			17 04		18 49	21 57
12	Calstock	d	05 33	07 13				09 27			11 27	13 27	15 27			17 11		18 56	22 04
15	**Gunnislake**	a	05 49	07 26				09 40			11 40	13 41	15 40			17 24		19 09	22 17

Saturdays

		GW	GW	GW	GW	GW	GW	GW	GW	GW	GW	GW	GW	GW	GW	GW
			◇													
				C	D	C	D		C	D						
Plymouth	d	06 40	08 15	08 54	09 02	09 51	09 58	10 33	10 54	10 59	12 54	14 48	16 38	17 52	18 23	21 31
Devonport	d	06 43	08a18	08 57	09 05	09a54	10a01		10 57	11 02	12 57	14 51	16 41	17 55	18 26	21 34
Dockyard	d	06x44		08x58	09x06				10x58	11x03	12x58	14x52	16x42	17x57	18x27	21x35
Keyham	d	06 46		09 00	09 08				11 00	11 05	13 00	14 54	16 44	17 59	18 29	21 37
St Budeaux Ferry Road	a							10 39						18 00		
St Budeaux Victoria Road	d	06 50		09 04	09 12				11 04	11 09	13 04	14 58	16 48		18 33	21 41
Bere Ferrers	d	06 57		09 11	09 19				11 11	11 16	13 11	15 05	16 55		18 40	21 48
Bere Alston	a	07 04		09 18	09 26				11 18	11 23	13 18	15 12	17 02		18 47	21 55
	d	07 06		09 20	09 28				11 20	11 25	13 20	15 14	17 04		18 49	21 57
Calstock	d	07 13		09 27	09 35				11 27	11 32	13 27	15 21	17 11		18 56	22 04
Gunnislake	a	07 26		09 40	09 48				11 40	11 45	13 40	15 34	17 25		19 09	22 17

Sundays

		GW	GW	GW	GW	GW	GW	GW	GW	GW	GW	GW	GW	GW
					◇	◇								
		E	F	G	H	I	E	G	E	G	E	G	E	G
			[vehicle]											
Plymouth	d	09 09	09 15	09 30	10 22	10 24	11 15	11 40	13 13	13 45	15 17	15 40	17 41	17 45
Devonport	d	09 12		09 33	10a28	10a29	11 18	11 43	13 16	13 48	15 20	15 43	17 44	17 48
Dockyard	d	09x14		09x35			11x20	11x45	13x18	13x50	15x22	15x45	17x46	17x50
Keyham	d	09x16		09x37			11x22	11x47	13x20	13x52	15x24	15x47	17x48	17x52
St Budeaux Ferry Road	a		09 21											
St Budeaux Victoria Road	d	09 19		09 40			11 25	11 50	13 23	13 55	15 27	15 50	17 51	17 55
Bere Ferrers	d	09x27		09x48			11x33	11x58	13x31	14x03	15x35	15x58	17x59	18x03
Bere Alston	a	09 33		09 54			11 39	12 04	13 37	14 09	15 41	16 04	18 05	18 09
	d	09 36		09 57			11 42	12 07	13 40	14 12	15 44	16 07	18 08	18 12
Calstock	d	09x43		10x04			11x49	12x14	13x47	14x19	15x51	16x14	18x15	18x19
Gunnislake	a	09 55		10 16			12 01	12 26	13 59	14 31	16 03	16 26	18 27	18 31

A until 1 July, from 5 September
B from 4 July until 2 September
C from 17 September
D until 10 September
E until 25 September
F until 11 September
G from 2 October
H until 23 October
I from 30 October

Gunnislake - Plymouth

Miles			GW	GW	GW	GW	GW	GW	GW	GW A	GW B	GW	GW	GW C	GW B	GW
0	**Gunnislake**	d	05 50		07 31	09 45	11 45	13 45	15 45			17 29	19 13			22 21
3	Calstock	d	06 01		07 42	09 56	11 56	13 56	15 56			17 40	19 24			22 32
4¾	Bere Alston	a	06 08		07 49	10 03	12 03	14 03	16 03			17 47	19 31			22 39
—		d	06 10		07 51	10 05	12 05	14 05	16 05			17 49	19 33			22 41
7½	Bere Ferrers	d	06 15		07 56	10 10	12 10	14 10	16 10			17 54	19 38			22 46
11¾	St Budeaux Victoria Road	d	06 24		08 05	10 19	12 19	14 19	16 19			18 03	19 47			22 55
—	St Budeaux Ferry Road	d		07 52						16⟆41	17⟆06			21⟆09	21⟆34	
12¾	Keyham	d	06 26	07 54	08 07	10 21	12 21	14 21	16 21	16⟆43	17⟆08	18 05	19 49	21⟆11	21⟆36	22 57
13¼	Dockyard	d	06x28	07x56	08x09	10x23	12x23	14x23	16x23	16x45	17x10	18x07	19x51	21x13	21x38	22x59
13¾	Devonport	d	06 31	07 58	08 11	10 25	12 25	14 25	16 25	16⟆47	17⟆12	18 09	19 53	21⟆15	21⟆40	23 01
15	**Plymouth**	a	06 35	08 04	08 17	10 30	12 30	14 30	16 30	16⟆52	17⟆18	18 14	19 58	21⟆20	21⟆46	23 06

Saturdays

		GW	GW	GW D	GW E	GW D	GW E	GW	GW D	GW E	GW	GW	GW	GW	GW	GW
Gunnislake	d		07 31	09⟆45	09⟆51	11⟆45	11⟆52	13 45			15 45	17 29	19 17		22 21	
Calstock	d		07 42	09⟆56	10⟆02	11⟆56	12⟆03	13 56			15 56	17 40	19 28		22 32	
Bere Alston	a		07 49	10⟆03	10⟆09	12⟆03	12⟆10	14 03			16 03	17 47	19 35		22 39	
	d		07 51	10⟆05	10⟆11	12⟆05	12⟆12	14 05			16 05	17 49	19 37		22 41	
Bere Ferrers	d		07 56	10⟆10	10⟆16	12⟆10	12⟆17	14 10			16 10	17 54	19 42		22 46	
St Budeaux Victoria Road	d		08 05	10⟆19	10⟆25	12⟆19	12⟆26	14 19			16 19	18 03	19 52		22 55	
St Budeaux Ferry Road	d	07 28		⟆	⟆	⟆	⟆							20 58		22 59
Keyham	d	07 30	08 07	10⟆21	10⟆27	12⟆21	12⟆28	14 21			16 21	18 05	19 54	21 00	22 57	23 01
Dockyard	d	07x32	08x09	10x23	10x29	12x23	12x30	14x23			16x23	18x07	19x56	21x02	22x59	23x03
Devonport	d	07 34	08 11	10⟆25	10⟆31	12⟆25	12⟆32	14 25	14⟆51	15⟆14	16 25	18 09	19 58	21 04	23 01	23 05
Plymouth	a	07 41	08 17	10⟆30	10⟆36	12⟆30	12⟆37	14 30	14⟆58	15⟆20	16 30	18 14	20 02	21 10	23 06	23 12

Sundays

		GW F	GW G	GW F	GW G	GW F	GW G	GW F	GW G	GW H	GW I	GW J	GW H ⚲	GW
Gunnislake	d	10⟆18	10⟆25	12⟆07	12⟆45	14⟆04	14⟆05	16⟆07	16⟆54	18⟆39	18⟆39	18⟆44		
Calstock	d	10x30	10x37	12x19	12x57	14x16	14x17	16x19	17x06	18x51	18x51	18x56		
Bere Alston	a	10⟆36	10⟆43	12⟆25	13⟆03	14⟆22	14⟆23	16⟆25	17⟆12	18⟆57	18⟆57	19⟆02		
	d	10⟆38	10⟆45	12⟆27	13⟆05	14⟆24	14⟆25	16⟆27	17⟆14	18⟆59	18⟆59	19⟆04		
Bere Ferrers	d	10x44	10x51	12x33	13x11	14x30	14x31	16x33	17x20	19x05	19x05	19x10		
St Budeaux Victoria Road	d	10⟆52	10⟆59	12⟆41	13⟆19	14⟆38	14⟆39	16⟆41	17⟆28	19⟆13	19⟆13	19⟆18		
St Budeaux Ferry Road	d	⟆	⟆	⟆	⟆	⟆	⟆	⟆	⟆	⟆	⟆	⟆	19⟆43	
Keyham	d	10x55	11x02	12x44	13x22	14x41	14x42	16x44	17x31	19x16	19x21	19x21	⟆	
Dockyard	d	10x57	11x04	12x46	13x24	14x43	14x44	16x46	17x33	19x18	19x23	19x23	⟆	
Devonport	d	10⟆59	11⟆06	12⟆48	13⟆26	14⟆45	14⟆46	16⟆48	17⟆35	19⟆20	19⟆25	19⟆25	19⟆47	20 55
Plymouth	a	11⟆03	11⟆10	12⟆52	13⟆30	14⟆49	14⟆50	16⟆52	17⟆39	19⟆24	19⟆29	19⟆29	19⟆50	20 59

A until 1 July, from 5 September
B from 4 July until 2 September
C until 1 July, from 5 September until 8 December
D from 17 September
E until 10 September
F until 25 September
G from 2 October
H until 11 September
I from 18 September until 23 October
J from 30 October

Table 140

Mondays to Fridays

Liskeard - Looe

Miles			GW	GW	GW	GW	GW	GW	GW	GW	GW	GW	GW	GW
0	**Liskeard** 6	d	06 05	07 14	08 33	09 58	11 17	12 14	13 19	14 28	15 40	16 40	18 01	19 18
2	Coombe Junction Halt	a			08 39	10 04								
—		d			08 42	10 07								
3¾	St Keyne Wishing Well Halt	d	06x17	07x26	08x48	10x13		12x26	13x31		15x52	16x52	18x13	19x31
5	Causeland	d	06x21	07x30	08x52	10x17		12x30	13x35		15x56	16x56	18x17	19x33
6½	Sandplace	d	06x24	07x33	08x56	10x20		12x33	13x38		15x59	16x59	18x20	19x38
8¾	**Looe**	a	06 36	07 45	09 04	10 29	11 45	12 45	13 50	14 56	16 11	17 11	18 32	19 49

Saturdays

		GW	GW	GW	GW	GW	GW	GW	GW	GW	GW	GW	GW	GW A
Liskeard 6	d	06 01	07 12	08 35	09 58	11 08	12 12	13 24	14 28	15 42	16 56	18 01	19 28	20 40
Coombe Junction Halt	a			08 41	10 04									
	d			08 44	10 06									
St Keyne Wishing Well Halt	d	06x13	07x24	08x50	10x13		12x24	13x37		15x54	17x09	18x13	19x41	20x53
Causeland	d	06x17	07x28	08x54	10x17		12x28	13x40		15x58	17x12	18x17	19x43	20x55
Sandplace	d	06x20	07x31	08x58	10x20		12x31	13x44		16x01	17x16	18x20	19x48	21x00
Looe	a	06 32	07 43	09 06	10 29	11 36	12 43	13 55	14 56	16 13	17 27	18 32	19 59	21 11

Sundays
until 11 September

		GW	GW	GW	GW	GW	GW	GW	GW
Liskeard 6	d	10 12	11 26	12 50	14 04	15 07	16 14	17 35	20 15
Coombe Junction Halt	a								
	d								
St Keyne Wishing Well Halt	d	10x25	11x39	13x03	14x17	15x20	16x27	17x48	20x28
Causeland	d	10x28	11x42	13x06	14x20	15x23	16x30	17x51	20x31
Sandplace	d	10x32	11x46	13x10	14x24	15x27	16x34	17x55	20x35
Looe	a	10 41	11 55	13 19	14 33	15 36	16 43	18 04	20 44

A until 10 September

For connections at Liskeard please refer to Table 135

Table 140

Mondays to Fridays

Looe - Liskeard

Miles			GW	GW	GW	GW	GW	GW	GW	GW	GW		GW	GW	GW
0	**Looe**	d	06 37	07 46	09 09	10 32	11 46	12 46	13 51	14 57	16 12		17 15	18 33	19 52
2¼	Sandplace	d	06x42	07x51	09x14	10x37		12x51		15x02			17x20	18x38	19x57
3¾	Causeland	d	06x46	07x55	09x18	10x41		12x55		15x06			17x24	18x42	20x01
5	St Keyne Wishing Well Halt	d	06x49	07x58	09x21	10x44		12x58		15x09			17x27	18x45	20x04
6¾	Coombe Junction Halt	a			09 27	10 50									
—		d			09 29	10 52									
8¾	**Liskeard 6**	a	07 05	08 14	09 40	11 03	12 10	13 16	14 15	15 25	16 38		17 43	19 01	20 22

Saturdays

		GW	GW	GW	GW	GW	GW	GW	GW	GW		GW	GW	GW	GW A
Looe	d	06 33	07 47	09 09	10 32	11 37	12 44	13 56	14 56	16 14		17 28	18 33	20 00	21 12
Sandplace	d	06x38	07x52	09x14	10x37		12x49		15x01	16x19		17x33	18x38	20x05	21x17
Causeland	d	06x42	07x56	09x18	10x41		12x53		15x05	16x23		17x37	18x42	20x09	21x21
St Keyne Wishing Well Halt	d	06x45	07x59	09x21	10x45		12x56		15x08	16x27		17x41	18x45	20x13	21x25
Coombe Junction Halt	a			09 27	10 50										
	d			09 29	10 52										
Liskeard 6	a	07 01	08 15	09 40	11 03	12 01	13 12	14 20	15 25	16 44		17 58	19 01	20 28	21 40

Sundays

until 11 September

		GW	GW	GW	GW	GW	GW	GW	GW
Looe	d	10 45	11 58	13 22	14 36	15 39	16 46	18 15	20 50
Sandplace	d	10x50	12x03	13x27	14x41	15x44	16x51	18x20	20x55
Causeland	d	10x54	12x07	13x31	14x45	15x48	16x55	18x24	20x59
St Keyne Wishing Well Halt	d	10x58	12x11	13x35	14x49	15x52	16x59	18x28	21x03
Coombe Junction Halt	a								
	d								
Liskeard 6	a	11 13	12 26	13 50	15 04	16 07	17 14	18 43	21 18

A until 10 September

For connections at Liskeard please refer to Table 135

Table 142

Mondays to Fridays

Par - Newquay

Miles			GW	GW	GW	GW	GW	GW	GW	GW	GW	GW
				◇				◇[1]				
				A	B	A	B	C	B			
								☕				
0	**Par**	d	06 47	09 17	09 17	11 42	12 13	13 29	14 08	16 10	18 29	20 28
4¼	Luxulyan	d		09x28	09x28	11x53	⌇	⌇	⌇	16x21	18x40	20x39
6¼	Bugle	d	07x04	09x34	09x34	11x59	12x30	⌇	14x25	16x27	18x46	20x45
8¾	Roche	d		09x39	09x39	12x04	⌇	⌇	⌇	16x32	18x51	20x50
14½	St Columb Road	d		09x50	09x50	12x15	⌇	⌇	⌇	16x43	19x02	21x01
18¼	Quintrell Downs	d		09 58	09 58	12 23	⌇	⌇	⌇	16 51	19 10	21 09
20¾	**Newquay**	a	07 34	10 09	10 09	12 34	13 01	14 29	14 56	17 02	19 21	21 20

Saturdays
until 10 September

		XC	GW	GW	XC	GW	XC	GW
		◇[1]	◇[1]	◇[1]	◇[1]	[1]	◇[1]	
			☕	☕	🛒	☕	🛒	
Par	d	07 28	09 46	11 41	13 33	15 43	17 41	20 21
Luxulyan	d							
Bugle	d							
Roche	d							
St Columb Road	d							
Quintrell Downs	d							
Newquay	a	08 27	10 55	12 44	14 41	16 52	18 45	21 10

Saturdays
from 17 September

		GW	GW	GW	GW	GW	GW	GW
Par	d	06 52	09 18	12 15	14 08	16 15	18 21	20 15
Luxulyan	d	07x03	09x29	12x26		16x26	18x32	20x26
Bugle	d	07x09	09x35	12x32	14x25	16x32	18x38	20x32
Roche	d	07x14	09x40	12x37		16x37	18x43	20x37
St Columb Road	d	07x25	09x51	12x48		16x48	18x54	20x48
Quintrell Downs	d	07 33	09 59	12 56		16 56	19 02	20 56
Newquay	a	07 44	10 10	13 07	14 55	17 07	19 13	21 07

A from 4 July until 2 September
B until 1 July, from 5 September
C from 4 July until 2 September. The Atlantic Coast Express

For connections at Par please refer to Table 135

No Sunday Service

Table 142

Mondays to Fridays

Newquay - Par

Miles			GW	GW	GW	GW	GW	GW	GW	GW	GW
					A	B	B	◇1 C ☕			
0	**Newquay**	d	07 36	10 13	12§40	13§03	14§58	15§00	17 22	19 25	21 26
2½	Quintrell Downs	d	07 42	10 19	12§46	13§09	15§04	§	17 28	19 31	21 32
6½	St Columb Road	d	07x50	10x27	12x54	13x17	15x12	§	17x36		21x40
12	Roche	d	08x01	10x38	13x05	13x28	15x23	§	17x47		21x51
14½	Bugle	d	08x06	10x43	13x10	13x33	15x28	§	17x52	19x54	21x56
16½	Luxulyan	d	08x11	10x48	13x17	13x38	15x33	§	17x57		22x01
20¾	**Par**	a	08 31	11 02	13§34	13§52	15§47	15§59	18 13	20 13	22 16

Saturdays
until 10 September

		XC	GW	GW	XC	GW	XC	GW
		◇1	R 1 ☕	R 1 ☕	◇1 trolley	R 1 ☕	◇1	
Newquay	d	09 27	11 22	13 14	15 25	17 18	19 55	21 21
Quintrell Downs	d		11 28	13 20		17 24		
St Columb Road	d							
Roche	d							
Bugle	d							
Luxulyan	d							
Par	a	10 24	12 24	14 15	16 24	18 20	20 55	22 07

Saturdays
from 17 September

		GW	GW	GW	GW	GW	GW	GW
Newquay	d	07 48	10 12	13 09	14 59	17 21	19 17	21 18
Quintrell Downs	d	07 54	10 18	13 15	15 05	17 27	19 23	21 24
St Columb Road	d	08x02	10x26	13x23	15x13	17x35		21x32
Roche	d	08x13	10x37	13x34	15x24	17x46		21x43
Bugle	d	08x18	10x42	13x39	15x29	17x51	19x46	21x48
Luxulyan	d	08x23	10x47	13x44	15x34	17x56		21x53
Par	a	08 39	11 01	13 59	15 48	18 10	20 03	22 07

A from 4 July until 2 September
B until 1 July, from 5 September
C from 4 July until 2 September. The Atlantic Coast Express

For connections at Par please refer to Table 135

No Sunday Service

Table 143

Mondays to Fridays

Truro - Falmouth

Miles			GW	GW	GW	GW	GW	GW	GW	GW	GW		GW	GW	GW	GW	GW	GW	GW	GW	GW		GW	GW	GW
0	**Truro**	d	06 04	06 31	07 14	07 47	08 20	08 50	09 20	09 50	10 20		10 50	11 20	11 50	12 20	12 50	13 20	13 50	14 20	14 50		15 20	15 50	16 20
4¼	Perranwell	d	06x10	06x37	07x20	07x53	08x26		09x26		10x26			11x26		12x26		13x26		14x26			15x26		16x26
8¼	Penryn	d	06 18	06 45	07 28	08 01	08 34	09 04	09 34	10 04	10 34		11 04	11 34	12 04	12 34	13 04	13 34	14 04	14 34	15 04		15 34	16 04	16 34
10¼	Penmere	d	06 23	06 50	07 33	08 06	08 39	09 09	09 39	10 09	10 39		11 09	11 39	12 09	12 39	13 09	13 39	14 09	14 39	15 09		15 39	16 09	16 39
11¾	Falmouth Town	d	06 26	06 53	07 36	08 09	08 42	09 12	09 42	10 12	10 42		11 12	11 42	12 12	12 42	13 12	13 42	14 12	14 42	15 12		15 42	16 12	16 42
12¼	**Falmouth Docks**	a	06 28	06 55	07 38	08 11	08 44	09 14	09 44	10 14	10 44		11 14	11 44	12 14	12 44	13 14	13 44	14 14	14 44	15 14		15 44	16 14	16 44

		GW	GW	GW	GW	GW	GW		GW	GW
Truro	d	16 51	17 27	17 59	18 31	19 02	20 04		21 05	22 08
Perranwell	d	16x57	17x33	18x05	18x37	19x08	20x10		21x11	22x14
Penryn	d	17 05	17 41	18 13	18 45	19 16	20 18		21 19	22 22
Penmere	d	17 10	17 46	18 18	18 50	19 21	20 23		21 24	22 27
Falmouth Town	d	17 13	17 49	18 21	18 53	19 24	20 26		21 27	22 30
Falmouth Docks	a	17 15	17 51	18 23	18 55	19 26	20 28		21 29	22 32

Saturdays

		GW	GW	GW	GW	GW	GW	GW	GW	GW		GW	GW	GW	GW	GW	GW	GW	GW	GW		GW	GW	GW	GW
Truro	d	06 10	06 37	07 14	07 47	08 20	08 50	09 20	09 50	10 20		10 50	11 20	11 50	12 20	12 50	13 20	13 50	14 20	14 50		15 20	15 50	16 20	16 51
Perranwell	d	06x16	06x43	07x19	07x53	08x26		09x26		10x26			11x26		12x26		13x26		14x26			15x26		16x26	16x57
Penryn	d	06 24	06 51	07 27	08 01	08 34	09 04	09 34	10 04	10 34		11 04	11 34	12 04	12 34	13 04	13 34	14 04	14 34	15 04		15 34	16 04	16 34	17 05
Penmere	d	06 29	06 56	07 32	08 06	08 39	09 09	09 39	10 09	10 39		11 09	11 39	12 09	12 39	13 09	13 39	14 09	14 39	15 09		15 39	16 09	16 39	17 10
Falmouth Town	d	06 32	06 59	07 35	08 09	08 42	09 12	09 42	10 12	10 42		11 12	11 42	12 12	12 42	13 12	13 42	14 12	14 42	15 12		15 42	16 12	16 42	17 13
Falmouth Docks	a	06 34	07 01	07 38	08 11	08 44	09 14	09 44	10 14	10 44		11 14	11 44	12 14	12 44	13 14	13 44	14 14	14 44	15 14		15 44	16 14	16 44	17 15

		GW	GW	GW	GW	GW		GW	GW
Truro	d	17 27	17 59	18 31	19 02	20 04		21 05	22 06
Perranwell	d	17x33	18x05	18x37	19x08	20x10		21x11	22x12
Penryn	d	17 41	18 13	18 45	19 16	20 18		21 19	22 20
Penmere	d	17 46	18 18	18 50	19 21	20 23		21 24	22 25
Falmouth Town	d	17 49	18 21	18 53	19 24	20 26		21 27	22 28
Falmouth Docks	a	17 51	18 23	18 55	19 26	20 28		21 29	22 30

Sundays
until 11 September

		GW	GW	GW	GW	GW	GW	GW	GW	GW		GW
Truro	d	10 43	12 09	13 07	14 10	15 36	17 00	18 10	19 46	21 03		22 04
Perranwell	d	10x50	12x16	13x14	14x17	15x43	17x07	18x17	19x53	21x10		22x11
Penryn	d	10 57	12 23	13 21	14 24	15 50	17 14	18 24	20 00	21 17		22 18
Penmere	d	11 02	12 28	13 26	14 29	15 54	17 19	18 29	20 05	21 22		22 23
Falmouth Town	d	11 05	12 31	13 29	14 32	15 57	17 22	18 32	20 08	21 25		22 26
Falmouth Docks	a	11 07	12 33	13 31	14 34	16 00	17 24	18 34	20 10	21 27		22 28

Sundays
from 18 September

		GW	GW	GW	GW	GW	GW	GW	GW	GW		GW
Truro	d	10 38	12 09	13 07	14 10	15 36	17 00	18 10	19 46	21 03		22 04
Perranwell	d	10x45	12x16	13x14	14x17	15x43	17x07	18x17	19x53	21x10		22x11
Penryn	d	10 52	12 23	13 21	14 24	15 50	17 14	18 24	20 00	21 17		22 18
Penmere	d	10 57	12 28	13 26	14 29	15 54	17 19	18 29	20 05	21 22		22 23
Falmouth Town	d	11 00	12 31	13 29	14 32	15 57	17 22	18 32	20 08	21 25		22 26
Falmouth Docks	a	11 02	12 33	13 31	14 34	16 00	17 24	18 34	20 10	21 27		22 28

For connections at Truro please refer to Table 135

Falmouth - Truro

Mondays to Fridays

Miles			GW	GW	GW	GW	GW	GW	GW	GW	GW		GW	GW	GW	GW	GW	GW	GW	GW	GW		GW	GW	GW
0	**Falmouth Docks**	d	06 31	07 15	07 47	08 20	08 50	09 20	09 50	10 20	10 50		11 20	11 50	12 20	12 50	13 20	13 50	14 20	14 50	15 20		15 50	16 20	16 50
0½	Falmouth Town	d	06 34	07 18	07 50	08 23	08 53	09 23	09 53	10 23	10 53		11 23	11 53	12 23	12 53	13 23	13 53	14 23	14 53	15 23		15 53	16 23	16 53
2	Penmere	d	06 37	07 21	07 53	08 26	08 56	09 26	09 56	10 26	10 56		11 26	11 56	12 26	12 56	13 26	13 56	14 26	14 56	15 26		15 56	16 26	16 56
4	Penryn	d	06 45	07 29	08 01	08 34	09 04	09 34	10 04	10 34	11 04		11 34	12 04	12 34	13 04	13 34	14 04	14 34	15 04	15 34		16 04	16 34	17 04
8	Perranwell	d	06x51	07x35	08x07	08x40		09x40		10x40			11x40		12x40		13x40		14x40		15x40			16x40	17x11
12¼	**Truro**	a	06 59	07 43	08 15	08 48	09 18	09 48	10 18	10 48	11 18		11 48	12 17	12 48	13 18	13 48	14 18	14 48	15 18	15 48		16 18	16 48	17 19

		GW	GW	GW	GW	GW	GW		GW	GW
Falmouth Docks	d	17 27	17 59	18 31	19 02	19 29	20 31		21 32	22 35
Falmouth Town	d	17 30	18 02	18 34	19 05	19 32	20 34		21 35	22 38
Penmere	d	17 33	18 05	18 37	19 08	19 35	20 37		21 38	22 41
Penryn	d	17 40	18 13	18 45	19 16	19 40	20 42		21 43	22 46
Perranwell	d	17x48	18x19	18x51	19x22	19x46	20x48		21x49	22x52
Truro	a	17 55	18 27	18 59	19 30	19 55	20 57		21 59	23 02

Saturdays

		GW	GW	GW	GW	GW	GW	GW	GW	GW		GW	GW	GW	GW	GW	GW	GW	GW	GW		GW	GW	GW	GW
Falmouth Docks	d	06 37	07 15	07 47	08 20	08 50	09 20	09 50	10 20	10 50		11 20	11 50	12 20	12 50	13 20	13 50	14 20	14 50	15 20		15 50	16 20	16 51	17 27
Falmouth Town	d	06 40	07 18	07 50	08 23	08 53	09 23	09 53	10 23	10 53		11 23	11 53	12 23	12 53	13 23	13 53	14 23	14 53	15 23		15 53	16 23	16 53	17 30
Penmere	d	06 43	07 21	07 53	08 26	08 56	09 26	09 56	10 26	10 56		11 26	11 56	12 26	12 56	13 26	13 56	14 26	14 56	15 26		15 56	16 26	16 56	17 33
Penryn	d	06 51	07 29	08 01	08 34	09 04	09 34	10 04	10 34	11 04		11 34	12 04	12 34	13 04	13 34	14 04	14 34	15 04	15 34		16 04	16 34	17 04	17 40
Perranwell	d	06x57	07x35	08x07	08x40		09x40		10x40			11x40		12x40		13x40		14x40		15x40			16x40	17x11	17x48
Truro	a	07 05	07 43	08 15	08 48	09 18	09 48	10 18	10 48	11 18		11 48	12 18	12 48	13 18	13 48	14 18	14 48	15 18	15 48		16 18	16 48	17 19	17 55

		GW	GW	GW	GW	GW		GW	GW
Falmouth Docks	d	17 59	18 31	19 02	19 29	20 31		21 32	22 33
Falmouth Town	d	18 02	18 34	19 05	19 32	20 34		21 35	22 36
Penmere	d	18 05	18 37	19 08	19 35	20 37		21 38	22 39
Penryn	d	18 13	18 45	19 16	19 40	20 42		21 43	22 44
Perranwell	d	18x19	18x51	19x22	19x46	20x48		21x49	22x50
Truro	a	18 27	18 59	19 30	19 55	20 57		21 58	23 00

Sundays

until 11 September

		GW	GW	GW	GW	GW	GW	GW	GW	GW		GW
Falmouth Docks	d	11 10	12 35	13 34	14 59	16 02	17 30	18 37	20 13	21 30		22 35
Falmouth Town	d	11 13	12 39	13 37	15 02	16 05	17 33	18 40	20 16	21 33		22 38
Penmere	d	11 16	12 42	13 40	15 05	16 08	17 36	18 43	20 19	21 36		22 41
Penryn	d	11 21	12 47	13 45	15 10	16 13	17 41	18 48	20 24	21 40		22 46
Perranwell	d	11x28	12x54	13x52	15x17	16x20	17x48	18x55	20x31	21x47		22x53
Truro	a	11 36	13 02	14 00	15 25	16 27	17 56	19 03	20 39	21 55		23 04

Sundays

18 September to 23 October

		GW	GW	GW	GW	GW	GW	GW	GW	GW		GW
Falmouth Docks	d	11 10	12 35	13 34	14 59	16 19	17 30	18 37	20 13	21 30		22 32
Falmouth Town	d	11 13	12 39	13 37	15 02	16 22	17 33	18 40	20 16	21 33		22 35
Penmere	d	11 16	12 42	13 40	15 05	16 25	17 36	18 43	20 19	21 36		22 38
Penryn	d	11 21	12 47	13 45	15 10	16 30	17 41	18 48	20 24	21 40		22 43
Perranwell	d	11x28	12x54	13x52	15x17	16x37	17x48	18x55	20x31	21x47		22x50
Truro	a	11 36	13 02	14 00	15 25	16 44	17 56	19 03	20 39	21 55		23 01

Sundays

from 30 October

		GW	GW	GW	GW	GW	GW	GW	GW	GW		GW
Falmouth Docks	d	11 10	12 35	13 34	14 59	16 19	17 30	18 37	20 13	21 30		22 35
Falmouth Town	d	11 13	12 39	13 37	15 02	16 22	17 33	18 40	20 16	21 33		22 38
Penmere	d	11 16	12 42	13 40	15 05	16 25	17 36	18 43	20 19	21 36		22 41
Penryn	d	11 21	12 47	13 45	15 10	16 30	17 41	18 48	20 24	21 40		22 46
Perranwell	d	11x28	12x54	13x52	15x17	16x37	17x48	18x55	20x31	21x47		22x53
Truro	a	11 36	13 02	14 00	15 25	16 44	17 56	19 03	20 39	21 55		23 04

For connections at Truro please refer to Table 135

Table 144

Mondays to Fridays

St. Erth - St. Ives

Miles			GW	GW	GW	GW	GW	GW	GW	GW	GW	GW	GW	GW	GW	GW	GW	GW	GW	GW	GW	GW	GW
—	Penzance	d	06 55		08 57																		
0	**St Erth**	d	07 03	08 01	09 05	09 38	10 18	10 48	11 18	11 48	12 18	12 48	13 18	13 48	14 18	14 48	15 18	15 48	16 18	16 48	17 17	17 48	18 18
0¾	Lelant Saltings	d			09 09	09 41	10 21	10 51	11 21	11 51	12 21	12 51	13 21	13 51	14 21	14 51	15 21	15 51	16 21		17 20		18 21
1	Lelant	d	07x07	08x03	09x10															16x50		17x50	18x22
3	Carbis Bay	d	07 12	08 09	09 16	09 47		10 57		11 57		12 57		13 57		14 57		15 57		16 56		17 56	18 27
4¼	**St Ives**	a	07 15	08 14	09 19	09 52	10 31	11 02	11 31	12 02	12 31	13 02	13 31	14 02	14 31	15 02	15 31	16 02	16 31	17 01	17 30	18 01	18 33

		GW	GW	GW	GW	GW	GW	GW
Penzance	d							
St Erth	d	18 48	19 18	19 48	20 18	20 48	21 23	21 58
Lelant Saltings	d		19 21		20 21			22 01
Lelant	d	18x51		19x51		20x51	21x25	22x02
Carbis Bay	d	18 56		19 56		20 56	21 31	22 08
St Ives	a	19 03	19 31	20 01	20 31	21 02	21 36	22 13

Saturdays

		GW	GW	GW	GW	GW	GW	GW	GW	GW	GW	GW	GW	GW	GW	GW	GW	GW	GW	GW	GW	GW	GW
Penzance	d	06 41		08 54																		18 50	
St Erth	d	06 50	08 00	09 02	09 35	10 13	10 48	11 18	11 48	12 18	12 48	13 18	13 48	14 18	14 48	15 18	15 48	16 18	16 48	17 16	17 59	18 58	19 53
Lelant Saltings	d			09 06	09 38	10 16	10 51	11 21	11 51	12 21	12 51	13 21	13 51	14 21	14 51	15 21	15 51	16 21		17 19	18 02	19 02	19 56
Lelant	d	06x53	08x03	09x08															16x51		18x04	19x04	19x58
Carbis Bay	d	06 58	08 08	09 13	09 44		10 57		11 57		12 57		13 57		14 57		15 57		16 56	17 26	18 09	19 09	20 03
St Ives	a	07 03	08 13	09 18	09 49	10 26	11 02	11 31	12 02	12 31	13 02	13 31	14 02	14 31	15 02	15 31	16 02	16 31	17 00	17 31	18 13	19 14	20 07

		GW	GW	GW
Penzance	d			
St Erth	d	20 33	21 06	21 47
Lelant Saltings	d	20 36	21 07	21 48
Lelant	d	20x38	21x09	21x50
Carbis Bay	d	20 43	21 14	21 55
St Ives	a	20 47	21 19	22 01

Sundays

until 11 September

		GW	GW	GW	GW	GW	GW	GW	GW	GW	GW	GW	GW	GW	GW	GW	GW	GW	GW	GW
Penzance	d	08 45																		
St Erth	d	08 53	09 26	10 00	10 30	11 13	11 43	12 12	12 42	13 11	13 41	14 11	14 41	15 11	15 41	16 11	16 41	17 25	18 24	19 30
Lelant Saltings	d	08 56	09 30	10 04	10 33	11 16	11 46	12 15	12 45	13 14	13 44	14 14	14 44	15 14	15 44	16 14	16 44	17 28	18 27	19 33
Lelant	d	08x58																17x30	18x29	19 35
Carbis Bay	d	09 03			10 39		11 52		12 51		13 50		14 50		15 50		16 50	17 35	18 34	19 40
St Ives	a	09 09	09 40	10 14	10 44	11 26	11 57	12 25	12 56	13 24	13 55	14 24	14 55	15 24	15 55	16 24	16 55	17 40	18 39	19 45

Sundays

from 18 September

		GW	GW	GW	GW	GW	GW	GW	GW	GW	GW	GW	GW	GW	GW
Penzance	d	11 45													
St Erth	d	11 56	12 34	13 18	13 48	14 18	14 48	15 18	15 48	16 18	16 48	17 18	17 48	18 30	19 30
Lelant Saltings	d	11 59	12 37	13 21	13 51	14 21	14 51	15 21	15 51	16 21	16 51	17 21	17 51	18 33	19 33
Lelant	d	12x01											17x53	18x35	19x35
Carbis Bay	d	12 06	12 43		13 57		14 57		15 57		16 57		17 58	18 40	19 40
St Ives	a	12 12	12 48	13 31	14 02	14 31	15 02	15 31	16 02	16 31	17 02	17 31	18 02	18 45	19 45

For connections at St Erth please refer to Table 135

Table 144

Mondays to Fridays

St. Ives - St. Erth

Miles			GW	GW	GW	GW	GW	GW	GW	GW	GW	GW	GW	GW	GW	GW	GW	GW	GW	GW	GW	GW	GW
0	**St Ives**	d	07 25	08 15	09 22	09 53	10 33	11 03	11 33	12 03	12 33	13 03	13 33	14 03	14 33	15 03	15 33	16 03	16 33	17 03	17 31	18 03	18 33
1¼	Carbis Bay	d	07 28	08 18	09 25		10 36		11 36		12 36		13 36		14 36		15 36		16 36		17 34		18 36
3¼	Lelant	d	07x33	08x23	09x30																17x39		18x41
3½	Lelant Saltings	d			09 33		10 43		11 43		12 43		13 43	14 13	14 43	15 13	15 43	16 13	16 43	17 12	17 42	18 13	18 44
4¼	**St Erth**	a	07 37	08 28	09 37	10 05	10 47	11 16	11 47	12 16	12 47	13 16	13 47	14 17	14 47	15 17	15 47	16 17	16 47	17 16	17 45	18 17	18 48
—	Penzance	a		08 40																			

		GW	GW	GW	GW	GW	GW	GW
St Ives	d	19 03	19 32	20 03	20 33	21 03	21 37	22 31
Carbis Bay	d		19 35		20 36	21 06	21 40	22 34
Lelant	d		19x40		20x41	21x11	21x45	22x39
Lelant Saltings	d		19 43	20 12	20 44	21 14		22 41
St Erth	a	19 16	19 47	20 16	20 47	21 18	21 51	22 45
Penzance	a							22 57

Saturdays

		GW	GW	GW	GW	GW	GW	GW	GW	GW	GW	GW	GW	GW	GW	GW	GW	GW	GW	GW	GW	GW	GW
St Ives	d	07 12	08 15	09 20	09 50	10 27	11 02	11 33	12 02	12 33	13 02	13 33	14 02	14 33	15 02	15 33	16 02	16 33	17 02	17 32	18 17	19 26	20 10
Carbis Bay	d	07 15	08 18	09 23		10 30		11 36		12 36		13 36		14 36		15 36		16 36		17 35	18 20	19 29	20 13
Lelant	d	07x20	08x23			10x35														17x40	18x25	19x34	20x18
Lelant Saltings	d			09 30		10 38		11 43		12 43		13 43	14 12	14 43	15 12	15 43	16 12	16 43	17 11	17 43	18 28	19 37	20 21
St Erth	a	07 24	08 27	09 33	10 00	10 40	11 14	11 47	12 15	12 47	13 15	13 47	14 14	14 47	15 16	15 47	16 16	16 47	17 14	17 46	18 31	19 41	20 23
Penzance	a		08 40																		18 44		

		GW	GW	GW
St Ives	d	20 49	21 24	22 05
Carbis Bay	d	20 52	21 27	22 08
Lelant	d	20x57	21x32	22x13
Lelant Saltings	d	21 00	21 35	22 16
St Erth	a	21 02	21 37	22 19
Penzance	a			22 32

Sundays

until 11 September

		GW	GW	GW	GW	GW	GW	GW	GW	GW	GW	GW	GW	GW	GW	GW	GW	GW	GW	GW
St Ives	d	09 10	09 41	10 15	10 50	11 28	11 56	12 27	12 57	13 26	13 56	14 25	14 56	15 25	15 56	16 25	16 56	17 41	18 40	19 50
Carbis Bay	d	09 13				11 31		12 30		13 29		14 28		15 28		16 28		17 44	18 43	19 53
Lelant	d	09x18																17x49	18x48	19x58
Lelant Saltings	d	09 21	09 50	10 24	10 59	11 38	12 07	12 37	13 06	13 36	14 05	14 35	15 05	15 35	16 05	16 35	17 05	17 52	18 51	20 01
St Erth	a	09 24	09 52	10 28	11 03	11 42	12 09	12 41	13 10	13 40	14 09	14 39	15 09	15 37	16 07	16 37	17 07	17 54	18 53	20 04
Penzance	a																			20 14

Sundays

from 18 September

		GW	GW	GW	GW	GW	GW	GW	GW	GW A	GW B	GW	GW	GW	GW	GW
St Ives	d	12 12	12 49	13 33	14 03	14 33	15 03	15 33	16 03	16 33	16 33	17 03	17 33	18 03	18 50	19 50
Carbis Bay	d	12 15	12 52	13 36		14 36		15 36		16 36	16 36		17 36		18 52	19 53
Lelant	d	12x20												18x10	18x59	19x58
Lelant Saltings	d	12 23	12 59	13 43	14 12	14 43	15 12	15 43	16 12	16 43	16 43	17 12	17 43	18 13	19 02	20 01
St Erth	a	12 26	13 01	13 45	14 16	14 45	15 14	15 45	16 16	16 45	16 47	17 16	17 47	18 17	19 04	20 04
Penzance	a															20 14

A from 30 October

B from 18 September until 23 October

For connections at St Erth please refer to Table 135

Network Diagram for Tables 148, 149

DM-11/09
Design BAJS

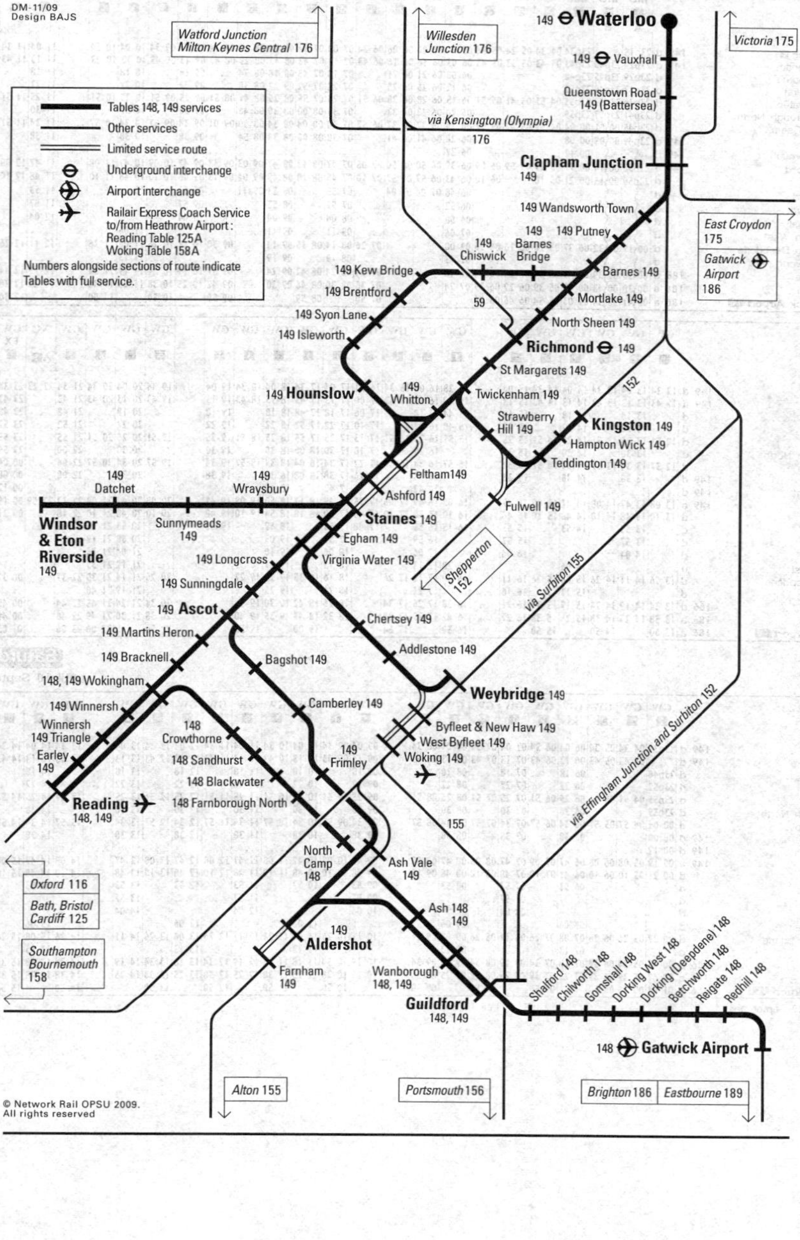

© Network Rail OPSU 2009.
All rights reserved

Reading - Guildford, Redhill and Gatwick Airport

Miles				GW MO 1 A	GW MO 1 B	GW MX 1	GW 1	GW 1	GW 1	GW 1	GW MO 1	GW MX 1	GW 1	GW 1	GW 1	GW 1	GW 1	GW 1	GW 1	GW 1	GW 1	GW 1		GW 1	GW 1	GW 1
0	**Reading** 7	149	d	23p15		23p34	04 34	05 24	05 34	05 54	06 06	06 06	06 34	07 04	07 34	08 04	08 20	08 34	09 04	09 34	10 04	10 34		11 04	11 34	12 04
6¾	Wokingham	149	d	23p24	23p40	23p43	04 43	05 33	05 43	06 03	06 16	06 16	06 43	07 13	07 43	08 13	08 29	08 43	09 13	09 43	10 13	10 43		11 13	11 43	12 13
10	Crowthorne		d	23p29	23p45	23p48				06 08	06 21	06 21		07 18	07 48	08 18	08 34		09 18		10 18			11 18		12 18
11½	Sandhurst		d	23p33	23p49	23p52				06 12	06 25	06 25		07 22	07 52	08 22	08 38		09 22		10 22			11 22		12 22
13½	Blackwater		d	23p36	23p52	23p55	04 51	05 41	05 51	06 15	06 28	06 28	06 51	07 25	07 55	08 25	08 41	08 51	09 25	09 51	10 25	10 51		11 25	11 51	12 25
15½	Farnborough North		d	23p41	23p57	23p59				06 20	06 33	06 33		07 30	08 00	08 30	08 46		09 30		10 30			11 30		12 30
17½	North Camp		d	23p45	00 01	00 04	04 57	05 47	05 57	06 24	06 37	06 37	06 57	07 34	08 04	08 34	08 50	09 01	09 34	09 57	10 34	10 57		11 34	11 57	12 34
19½	Ash 5	149	d	23p49	00 05	00 08				06 28	06 41	06 41		07 38	08 08	08 38	08 54		09 38		10 38			11 38		12 38
21½	Wanborough	149	d			00 12				06 32																
25¾	**Guildford**	149	a	23p58	00 14	00 19	05 09	05 59	06 09	06 39	06 50	06 50	07 08	07 47	08 17	08 47	09 03	09 13	09 47	10 09	10 47	11 08		11 47	12 08	12 47
—			d	23p59	00 15	00 21	05 10		06 10	06 43	06 57	06 57	07 10	07 48	08 18	08 48	09 04	09 13	09 48	10 10	10 48	11 10		11 48	12 10	12 48
27¾	Shalford		d							06 48	07 04	07 04		07 53		08 53	09a11		09 53		10 53			11 53		12 53
29¾	Chilworth		d							06 52				07 57		08 57			09 57					11 57		
33½	Gomshall		d							06 58				08 04		09 04			10 04					12 04		
38¼	Dorking West		d							07 06				08 11		09 11					11 06					13 06
39	Dorking Deepdene		d	00 19	00 32	00 37	05 26	06 16	06 26	07 08			07 26	08 14	08 35	09 14		09 30	10 11	10 26	11 08	11 26		12 11	12 26	13 08
41¾	Betchworth		d							07 13				08 19		09 19					11 13					13 13
44½	Reigate	186	d	00 26	00 39	00 45	05 34	06 24	06 34	07 18			07 34	08 24	08 42	09 24		09 37	10 19	10 34	11 19	11 34		12 19	12 34	13 19
46½	**Redhill**	186	a	00 30	00 43	00 49	05 39	06 29	06 39	07 24			07 38	08 30	08 46	09 30		09 42	10 25	10 38	11 25	11 38		12 25	12 38	13 25
52¼	**Gatwick Airport** 10	186	a	00 41	00 54	01 03	05 54	06 46	06 56				07 50		08 59			09 59		10 50		11 50			12 50	

			GW 1	GW 1	GW 1	GW 1	GW 1	GW 1		GW 1	GW 1	GW 1	GW 1	GW 1	GW 1	GW 1	GW 1	GW 1		GW 1	GW 1	GW 1	GW 1	XC ◇1	GW FX 1	GW FO 1
Reading 7	149	d	12 34	13 04	13 34	14 04	14 34	15 04		15 28	16 04	16 34	16 51	17 04	17 34	18 04	18 34	19 04		19 34	20 04	20 34	21 34	22 23	23 34	23 34
Wokingham	149	d	12 43	13 13	13 43	14 13	14 43	15 13		15 39	16 13	16 43	17 00	17 13	17 43	18 13	18 43	19 13		19 43	20 13	20 43	21 43		23 43	
Crowthorne		d		13 18		14 18		15 18		15 44	16 18		17 06	17 18	17 48	18 18		19 18			20 18		21 48		23 48	23 48
Sandhurst		d		13 22		14 22		15 22		15 48	16 22		17 10	17 22	17 52	18 22		19 22			20 22		21 52		23 52	23 52
Blackwater		d	12 51	13 25	13 51	14 25	14 51	15 25		15 51	16 25	16 51	17 13	17 25	17 55	18 25	18 51	19 25		19 51	20 25	20 51	21 55		23 55	23 55
Farnborough North		d		13 30		14 30		15 30			16 30		17 18	17 30	18 00	18 30		19 30			20 30		22 00		23 59	23 59
North Camp		d	12 57	13 34	13 57	14 34	14 57	15 34		15 57	16 34	16 57	17 22	17 34	18 04	18 34	18 57	19 34		19 57	20 34	20 57	22 04		00 04	00 04
Ash 5	149	d		13 38		14 38		15 38			16 38		17 26	17 38	18 08	18 38		19 38			20 38		22 08		00 08	00 08
Wanborough	149	d									16 42			17 42		18 42									00 12	00 12
Guildford	149	a	13 08	13 47	14 08	14 47	15 08	15 47		16 08	16 49	17 08	17 35	17 49	18 17	18 50	19 08	19 47		20 08	20 47	21 08	22 17	22 59	00 19	00 19
		d	13 10	13 48	14 10	14 48	15 10	15 48		16 10	16 50	17 10	17 40	17 50	18 18	18 54	19 10	19 48		20 10	20 48	21 10	22 18		00 21	00 21
Shalford		d		13 53		14 53		15 53		16 15	16 55		17a48	17 55		18 59		19a55			20 53	21 15	22 23			
Chilworth		d		13 57				15 57			16 59			17 59		19 03					20 58	21 19				
Gomshall		d		14 04				16 04			17 06			18 06		19 10					21 04	21 25				
Dorking West		d				15 06				16 28	17 13			18 13		19 17					21 12	21 33				
Dorking Deepdene		d	13 26	14 11	14 26	15 08	15 26	16 11		16 30	17 16	17 26		18 16	18 35	19 20	19 27			20 26	21 14	21 35	22 37		00 37	00 37
Betchworth		d				15 13		16 16			17 21			18 21		19 25					21 19	21 40				
Reigate	186	d	13 34	14 19	14 34	15 19	15 34	16 21		16 38	17 26	17 34		18 26	18 42	19 30	19 36			20 34	21 24	21 45	22 44		00 45	00 45
Redhill	186	a	13 38	14 25	14 38	15 25	15 38	16 27		16 42	17 32	17 38		18 32	18 47	19 35	19 40			20 38	21 30	21 49	22 48		00 49	00 49
Gatwick Airport 10	186	a	13 50		14 50		15 50			16 59		17 54			19 00		19 55			20 50		22 06	23 06		01 03	01 03

Saturdays
until 10 September

			GW 1	GW 1	GW 1	GW 1	GW 1	GW 1	GW 1	GW 1	GW 1		GW 1	GW 1	GW 1	GW 1	GW 1	GW 1	GW 1	GW 1	GW 1		GW 1	GW 1	GW 1	GW 1
Reading 7	149	d	23p34	04 34	05 34	06 04	06 34	07 04	07 34	08 04	08 34		09 04	09 34	10 04	10 34	11 04	11 34	12 04	12 34	13 04		13 34	14 04	14 34	15 04
Wokingham	149	d		04 43	05 43	06 13	06 43	07 13	07 43	08 13	08 43		09 13	09 43	10 13	10 43	11 13	11 43	12 13	12 43	13 13		13 43	14 13	14 43	15 13
Crowthorne		d	23p48			06 18		07 18		08 18			09 18		10 18		11 18		12 18		13 18			14 18		15 18
Sandhurst		d	23p52			06 22		07 22		08 22			09 22		10 22		11 22		12 22		13 22			14 22		15 22
Blackwater		d	23p55	04 51	05 51	06 25	06 51	07 25	07 51	08 25	08 51		09 25	09 51	10 25	10 51	11 25	11 51	12 25	12 51	13 25		13 51	14 25	14 51	15 25
Farnborough North		d	23p59			06 30		07 30		08 30			09 30		10 30		11 30		12 30		13 30			14 30		15 30
North Camp		d	00 04	04 57	05 57	06 34	06 57	07 34	07 57	08 34	08 57		09 34	09 57	10 34	10 57	11 34	11 57	12 34	12 57	13 34		13 57	14 34	14 57	15 34
Ash 5	149	d	00 08			06 38		07 38		08 38			09 38		10 38		11 38		12 38		13 38			14 38		15 38
Wanborough	149	d	00 12																							
Guildford	149	a	00 19	05 08	06 08	06 47	07 09	07 47	08 08	08 47	09 08		09 47	10 08	10 47	11 08	11 47	12 08	12 47	13 08	13 47		14 08	14 47	15 08	15 47
		d	00 21	05 10	06 10	06 48	07 10	07 48	08 10	08 48	09 10		09 48	10 10	10 48	11 10	11 48	12 10	12 48	13 10	13 48		14 10	14 48	15 10	15 48
Shalford		d				06 53		07 53		08 53			09 53		10 53		11 53		12 53		13 53			14 53		15 53
Chilworth		d						07 57					09 57				11 57				13 57					15 57
Gomshall		d						08 04					10 04				12 04				14 04					16 04
Dorking West		d				07 06				09 06					11 06				13 06					15 06		
Dorking Deepdene		d	00 37	05 26	06 26	07 08	07 26	08 11	08 26	09 08	09 26		10 11	10 26	11 08	11 26	12 11	12 26	13 08	13 26	14 11		14 26	15 08	15 26	16 11
Betchworth		d				07 13				09 13					11 13				13 13					15 13		
Reigate	186	d	00 45	05 34	06 34	07 18	07 34	08 19	08 34	09 18	09 34		10 19	10 34	11 18	11 34	12 19	12 34	13 18	13 34	14 19		14 34	15 18	15 34	16 19
Redhill	186	a	00 49	05 39	06 39	07 25	07 39	08 25	08 38	09 25	09 38		10 25	10 38	11 25	11 38	12 25	12 38	13 25	13 38	14 25		14 38	15 25	15 38	16 25
Gatwick Airport 10	186	a	01 03	05 58	06 50		07 50		08 50		09 50			10 50		11 50		12 50		13 50			14 50		15 50	

A From 19 September **B** Until 12 September

Table 148

Saturdays
until 10 September

Reading - Guildford, Redhill and Gatwick Airport

			GW 1	GW 1	GW 1	GW 1	GW 1	GW 1	GW 1	GW 1	GW 1	GW 1	GW 1	GW (bus)	GW 1	GW (bus)	GW 1	GW (bus)
Reading 7	149	d	15 34	16 04	16 34	17 04	17 34	18 04	18 34	19 04	19 33	20 03	20 33	21 15		22 13		23 35
Wokingham	149	d	15 43	16 13	16 43	17 13	17 43	18 13	18 43	19 13	19 43	20 13	20 43	21a35	21 45	22a33	22 43	23a55
Crowthorne		d		16 18		17 18		18 18		19 18		20 18			21 50		22 48	
Sandhurst		d		16 22		17 22		18 22		19 22		20 22			21 54		22 52	
Blackwater		d	15 51	16 25	16 51	17 25	17 51	18 25	18 51	19 25	19 51	20 25	20 51		21 57		22 55	
Farnborough North		d		16 30		17 30		18 30		19 30		20 30			22 02		23 00	
North Camp		d	15 57	16 34	16 57	17 34	17 57	18 34	18 57	19 34	19 57	20 34	20 57		22 06		23 04	
Ash 5	149	d		16 38		17 38		18 38		19 38		20 38			22 10		23 08	
Wanborough	149	d																
Guildford	149	a	16 08	16 47	17 08	17 47	18 08	18 47	19 08	19 47	20 08	20 47	21 08		22 19		23 17	
		d	16 10	16 48	17 10	17 48	18 10	18 48	19 10	19 48	20 10	20 48	21 10		22 20		23 18	
Shalford		d		16 53		17 53		18 53		19 53		20 53	21 15		22 25		23 23	
Chilworth		d				17 57				19 57			21 19				23 27	
Gomshall		d				18 04				20 04			21 25				23 34	
Dorking West		d		17 06				19 06				21 06			22 38		23 41	
Dorking Deepdene		d	16 26	17 08	17 26	18 11	18 26	19 08	19 26	20 11	20 26	21 08	21 33		22 40		23 44	
Betchworth		d		17 13				19 13				21 13			22 45		23 49	
Reigate	186	d	16 34	17 18	17 34	18 19	18 34	19 18	19 34	20 19	20 34	21 18	21 40		22 50		23 54	
Redhill	186	a	16 38	17 25	17 38	18 25	18 38	19 25	19 38	20 25	20 38	21 25	21 44		22 54		23 58	
Gatwick Airport 10	186	a	16 50		17 50		18 50		19 50		20 50		21 59		23 05		00 10	

Saturdays
from 17 September

			GW 1	GW 1	GW 1	GW 1	GW 1	GW 1	GW 1	GW 1	GW 1	GW 1	GW 1	GW 1	GW 1	GW 1	GW 1	GW 1	GW 1	GW 1	GW 1	GW 1	GW 1	GW 1
Reading 7	149	d	23p34	04 34	05 34	06 04	06 34	07 04	07 34	08 04	08 34	09 04	09 34	10 04	10 34	11 04	11 34	12 04	12 34	13 04	13 34	14 04	14 34	15 04
Wokingham	149	d		04 43	05 43	06 13	06 43	07 13	07 43	08 13	08 43	09 13	09 43	10 13	10 43	11 13	11 43	12 13	12 43	13 13	13 43	14 13	14 43	15 13
Crowthorne		d	23p48			06 18		07 18		08 18		09 18		10 18		11 18		12 18		13 18		14 18		15 18
Sandhurst		d	23p52			06 22		07 22		08 22		09 22		10 22		11 22		12 22		13 22		14 22		15 22
Blackwater		d	23p55	04 51	05 51	06 25	06 51	07 25	07 51	08 25	08 51	09 25	09 51	10 25	10 51	11 25	11 51	12 25	12 51	13 25	13 51	14 25	14 51	15 25
Farnborough North		d	23p59			06 30		07 30		08 30		09 30		10 30		11 30		12 30		13 30		14 30		15 30
North Camp		d	00 04	04 57	05 57	06 34	06 57	07 34	07 57	08 34	08 57	09 34	09 57	10 34	10 57	11 34	11 57	12 34	12 57	13 34	13 57	14 34	14 57	15 34
Ash 5	149	d	00 08			06 38		07 38		08 38		09 38		10 38		11 38		12 38		13 38		14 38		15 38
Wanborough	149	d	00 12																					
Guildford	149	a	00 19	05 08	06 08	06 47	07 09	07 47	08 08	08 47	09 08	09 47	10 08	10 47	11 08	11 47	12 08	12 47	13 08	13 47	14 08	14 47	15 08	15 47
		d	00 21	05 10	06 10	06 48	07 10	07 48	08 10	08 48	09 10	09 48	10 10	10 48	11 10	11 48	12 10	12 48	13 10	13 48	14 10	14 48	15 10	15 48
Shalford		d				06 53		07 53		08 53		09 53		10 53		11 53		12 53		13 53		14 53		15 53
Chilworth		d						07 57				09 57				11 57				13 57				15 57
Gomshall		d						08 04				10 04				12 04				14 04				16 04
Dorking West		d				07 06				09 06				11 06				13 06				15 06		
Dorking Deepdene		d	00 37	05 26	06 26	07 08	07 26	08 11	08 26	09 08	09 26	10 11	10 26	11 08	11 26	12 11	12 26	13 08	13 26	14 11	14 26	15 08	15 26	16 11
Betchworth		d				07 13				09 13				11 13				13 13				15 13		
Reigate	186	d	00 45	05 34	06 34	07 18	07 34	08 19	08 34	09 18	09 34	10 19	10 34	11 18	11 34	12 19	12 34	13 18	13 34	14 19	14 34	15 18	15 34	16 19
Redhill	186	a	00 49	05 39	06 39	07 25	07 39	08 25	08 38	09 25	09 38	10 25	10 38	11 25	11 38	12 25	12 38	13 25	13 38	14 25	14 38	15 25	15 38	16 25
Gatwick Airport 10	186	a	01 03	05 58	06 50		07 50		08 50		09 50		10 50		11 50		12 50		13 50		14 50		15 50	

			GW 1	GW 1	GW 1	GW 1	GW 1	GW 1	GW 1	GW 1	GW 1	GW 1	GW 1	GW 1	XC ◇1	GW 1	GW 1
Reading 7	149	d	15 34	16 04	16 34	17 04	17 34	18 04	18 34	19 04	19 34	20 04	20 34	21 34	22 15	22 34	23 34
Wokingham	149	d	15 43	16 13	16 43	17 13	17 43	18 13	18 43	19 13	19 43	20 13	20 43	21 43		22 43	
Crowthorne		d		16 18		17 18		18 18		19 18		20 18		21 48		22 48	23 48
Sandhurst		d		16 22		17 22		18 22		19 22		20 22		21 52		22 52	23 52
Blackwater		d	15 51	16 25	16 51	17 25	17 51	18 25	18 51	19 25	19 51	20 25	20 51	21 55		22 55	23 55
Farnborough North		d		16 30		17 30		18 30		19 30		20 30		22 00		23 00	23 59
North Camp		d	15 57	16 34	16 57	17 34	17 57	18 34	18 57	19 34	19 57	20 34	20 57	22 04		23 04	00 04
Ash 5	149	d		16 38		17 38		18 38		19 38		20 38		22 08		23 08	00 08
Wanborough	149	d															00 12
Guildford	149	a	16 08	16 47	17 08	17 47	18 08	18 47	19 08	19 47	20 08	20 47	21 08	22 17	22 59	23 17	00 19
		d	16 10	16 48	17 10	17 48	18 10	18 48	19 10	19 48	20 10	20 48	21 10	22 18		23 18	00 21
Shalford		d		16 53		17 53		18 53		19 53		20 53	21 15	22 23		23 23	
Chilworth		d				17 57				19 57			21 19			23 27	
Gomshall		d				18 04				20 04			21 25			23 34	
Dorking West		d		17 06				19 06				21 06		22 36		23 41	
Dorking Deepdene		d	16 26	17 08	17 26	18 11	18 26	19 08	19 26	20 11	20 26	21 08	21 33	22 38		23 44	00 37
Betchworth		d		17 13				19 13				21 13		22 43		23 49	
Reigate	186	d	16 34	17 18	17 34	18 19	18 34	19 18	19 34	20 19	20 34	21 18	21 40	22 48		23 54	00 45
Redhill	186	a	16 38	17 25	17 38	18 25	18 38	19 25	19 38	20 25	20 38	21 25	21 44	22 52		23 58	00 49
Gatwick Airport 10	186	a	16 50		17 50		18 50		19 50		20 50		21 59	23 05		00 10	01 02

Table 148

Sundays
until 11 September

Reading - Guildford, Redhill and Gatwick Airport

		GW	GW	GW	GW	GW	GW	GW	GW	GW	GW	GW	GW	GW	GW	GW	GW	GW	GW	GW	GW	GW	GW
		[1] A	[1]	🚌	[1]	🚌	[1]	🚌	[1]	🚌	[1]	🚌	[1]	🚌	[1]	🚌	[1]	🚌	[1]	🚌	[1]	🚌	[1]
Reading [7]	149 d			05 42		07 12		08 02		09 10		10 02		11 02		12 02		13 02		14 02		15 02	
Wokingham	149 d	22p43	00 07	06 02		07a32	07 42	08a22	08 34	09a30	09 42	10a22	10 34	11a22	11 34	12a22	12 34	13a22	13 34	14a22	14 34	15a22	15 34
Crowthorne	d	22p48	00 12				07 47				09 47				11 39				13 39				15 39
Sandhurst	d	22p52	00 16				07 51				09 51				11 43				13 43				15 43
Blackwater	d	22p55	00 19	06 27			07 54		08 42		09 54		10 42		11 46		12 42		13 46		14 42		15 46
Farnborough North	d	23p00	00 23				07 59				09 59				11 51				13 51				15 51
North Camp	d	23p04	00 28	06 39			08 03		08 48		10 03		10 48		11 55		12 48		13 55		14 48		15 55
Ash [5]	149 d	23p08	00 32				08 07				10 07				11 59				13 59				15 59
Wanborough	149 d	(	00 36																				
Guildford	149 a	23p17	00 43	06 59			08 16		08 59		10 16		10 59		12 08		12 59		14 08		14 59		16 08
	d	23p18	00 45		07 08		08 17		09 01		10 17		11 01		12 10		13 01		14 10		15 01		16 10
Shalford	d	23p23							09 06				11 06				13 06				15 06		
Chilworth	d	23p27							09 10				11 10				13 10				15 10		
Gomshall	d	23p34							09 16				11 16				13 16				15 16		
Dorking West	d	23p41							09 24				11 24				13 24				15 24		
Dorking Deepdene	d	23p44	01 01		07 25		08 34		09 26		10 34		11 26		12 26		13 26		14 26		15 26		16 26
Betchworth	d	23p49							09 31				11 31				13 31				15 31		
Reigate	186 d	23p54	01 09		07 33		08 42		09 36		10 42		11 36		12 34		13 36		14 34		15 36		16 34
Redhill	186 a	23p58	01 13		07 37		08 46		09 40		10 46		11 40		12 38		13 40		14 38		15 40		16 39
Gatwick Airport [10]	186 a	00 10	01 26		07 55		08 57		09 56		10 57		11 54		12 54		13 54		14 54		15 54		16 54

		GW	GW	GW	GW	GW	GW	GW	GW	GW	GW	GW	GW	GW	GW	GW	GW
		🚌	[1]	🚌	[1]	🚌	[1]	🚌	[1]	🚌	[1]	🚌	[1]	🚌	[1]	🚌	[1]
Reading [7]	149 d	16 02		17 02		18 02		19 02		20 02		21 02		22 02		23 15	
Wokingham	149 d	16a22	16 34	17a22	17 34	18a22	18 34	19a22	19 34	20a22	20 34	21a22	21 34	22a22	22 34	23a35	23 40
Crowthorne	d				17 39				19 39				21 39				23 45
Sandhurst	d				17 43				19 43				21 43				23 49
Blackwater	d		16 42		17 46		18 42		19 46		20 42		21 46		22 42		23 52
Farnborough North	d				17 51				19 51				21 51				23 57
North Camp	d		16 48		17 55		18 48		19 55		20 48		21 55		22 48		00 01
Ash [5]	149 d				17 59				19 59				21 59				00 05
Wanborough	149 d																
Guildford	149 a		16 59		18 08		18 59		20 08		20 59		22 08		22 59		00 14
	d		17 01		18 10		19 01		20 10		21 01		22 10		23 01		00 15
Shalford	d		17 06				19 06				21 06				23 06		
Chilworth	d		17 10				19 10				21 10				23 10		
Gomshall	d		17 16				19 16				21 16				23 16		
Dorking West	d		17 24				19 24				21 24				23 24		
Dorking Deepdene	d		17 26		18 26		19 26		20 26		21 26		22 26		23 26		00 32
Betchworth	d		17 31				19 31				21 31				23 31		
Reigate	186 d		17 36		18 34		19 36		20 34		21 36		22 34		23 36		00 39
Redhill	186 a		17 40		18 41		19 40		20 39		21 40		22 39		23 40		00 43
Gatwick Airport [10]	186 a		17 54		18 55		19 55		20 55		21 55		22 54		23 56		00 54

Sundays
from 18 September

		GW	GW	GW	GW	GW	GW	GW	GW	GW	GW	GW	GW	GW	GW	GW	GW	GW	GW	GW	XC	GW
		[1]	[1]	[1]	[1]	[1]	[1]	[1]	[1]	[1]	[1]	[1]	[1]	[1]	[1]	[1]	[1]	[1]	[1]	[1]	◇[1]	[1]
Reading [7]	149 d	22p34	23p34	06 03	07 03	08 03	09 03	10 03	11 03	12 03	13 03	14 03	15 03	16 03	17 03	18 03	19 03	20 03	21 03	22 03	22 14	23 15
Wokingham	149 d	22p43		06 11	07 11	08 11	09 11	10 11	11 11	12 11	13 11	14 11	15 11	16 11	17 11	18 11	19 11	20 11	21 11	22 11		23 24
Crowthorne	d	22p48	23p48		07 17		09 17		11 17		13 17		15 17		17 17		19 17		21 17			23 29
Sandhurst	d	22p52	23p52		07 21		09 21		11 21		13 21		15 21		17 21		19 21		21 21			23 33
Blackwater	d	22p55	23p55	06 19	07 24	08 19	09 24	10 19	11 24	12 19	13 24	14 19	15 24	16 19	17 24	18 19	19 24	20 19	21 24	22 19		23 36
Farnborough North	d	23p00	23p59		07 29		09 29		11 29		13 29		15 29		17 29		19 29		21 29			23 41
North Camp	d	23p04	00 04	06 26	07 33	08 26	09 33	10 26	11 33	12 26	13 33	14 26	15 33	16 26	17 33	18 26	19 33	20 26	21 33	22 26		23 45
Ash [5]	149 d	23p08	00 08		07 37		09 37		11 37		13 37		15 37		17 37		19 37		21 37			23 49
Wanborough	149 d		00 12																			
Guildford	149 a	23p17	00 19	06 37	07 46	08 37	09 46	10 37	11 46	12 37	13 46	14 37	15 46	16 37	17 46	18 37	19 46	20 37	21 46	22 37	22 42	23 58
	d	23p18	00 21	06 39	07 47	08 39	09 47	10 39	11 47	12 39	13 47	14 39	15 47	16 39	17 47	18 39	19 47	20 39	21 47	22 39		23 59
Shalford	d	23p23				08 44		10 44		12 44		14 44		16 44		18 44		20 44		22 44		
Chilworth	d	23p27				08 48		10 48		12 48		14 48		16 48		18 48		20 48		22 48		
Gomshall	d	23p34				08 54		10 54		12 54		14 54		16 54		18 54		20 54		22 54		
Dorking West	d	23p41				09 02		11 02		13 02		15 02		17 02		19 02		21 02		23 02		
Dorking Deepdene	d	23p44	00 37	06 57	08 04	09 04	10 04	11 04	12 04	13 04	14 04	15 04	16 04	17 04	18 04	19 04	20 04	21 04	22 04	23 04		00 19
Betchworth	d	23p49				09 09		11 09		13 09		15 09		17 09		19 09		21 09		23 09		
Reigate	186 d	23p54	00 45	07 05	08 13	09 13	10 13	11 13	12 13	13 13	14 13	15 13	16 13	17 13	18 13	19 13	20 13	21 13	22 13	23 13		00 26
Redhill	186 a	23p58	00 49	07 09	08 18	09 18	10 18	11 18	12 18	13 18	14 18	15 18	16 18	17 18	18 18	19 18	20 18	21 18	22 18	23 18		00 30
Gatwick Airport [10]	186 a	00 10	01 02	07 27	08 31	09 30	10 30	11 30	12 30	13 30	14 30	15 30	16 30	17 30	18 30	19 30	20 30	21 30	22 30	23 30		00 41

A not 22 May

Table 148

Mondays to Fridays

Gatwick Airport, Redhill and Guildford - Reading

Miles	Station			GW MX 1	GW MO 1 A	GW MO 1 B	GW MX 1	GW MO C 🚌	XC ◇1	GW 1	GW 1	GW 1
0	**Gatwick Airport 10**	186	d	22p22	23p08	23p09	23p18			05 31	05 56	
5¾	**Redhill**	186	d	22p33	23p19	23p20	23p28			05 43	06 13	06 24
—	Reigate	186	d	22p38	23p23	23p24	23p33			05 49	06 18	06 28
10½	Betchworth		d	22p43								06 33
13¼	Dorking Deepdene		d	22p47	23p32	23p32	23p40			05 56	06 25	06 37
14	Dorking West		d	22p50								06 40
18¾	Gomshall		d	22p58								06 48
22½	Chilworth		d	23p04								06 54
24½	Shalford		d	23p08								06 58
26½	**Guildford**		a	23p12	23p50	23p48	00 01			06 12	06 41	07 03
—			d	23p14	23p52	23p49	00 02		06 02	06 13	06 43	07 04
30¾	Wanborough	149	d	23p21						06 20		07 12
32¾	Ash 5	149	d	23p26	00 01	23p58				06 25	06 52	07 16
34¾	North Camp		d	23p30	00 05	00 03	00 14			06 29	06 56	07 20
36¾	Farnborough North		d	23p34	00 09	00 07				06 33	07 00	07 24
38¾	Blackwater		d	23p38	00 14	00 12	00 20			06 37	07 05	07 29
40¾	Sandhurst		d	23p42	00 16	00 15				06 41	07 08	07 32
42¼	Crowthorne		d	23p46	00 20	00 19				06 45	07 12	07 36
45½	Wokingham	149	d	23p51	00 26	00a24	00 29	00 33		06 50	07 17	07 41
52¼	**Reading 7**	149	a	00 01	00 37		00 39	00 53	06 31	06 58	07 29	07 52

Station			GW 1	GW 1	GW 1	GW 1	GW 1	GW 1	GW 1	GW 1	GW 1	GW 1	GW 1	GW 1
Gatwick Airport 10	186	d		07 00		07 58			09 07		10 03		11 03	
Redhill	186	d		07 10	07 28	08 08	08 33		09 23	09 34	10 13	10 34	11 13	11 34
Reigate	186	d		07 15	07 32	08 13	08 37		09 28	09 38	10 18	10 38	11 18	11 38
Betchworth		d			07 37		08 42			09 43		10 43		
Dorking Deepdene		d		07 22	07 41	08 20	08 46		09 35	09 47	10 25	10 47	11 25	11 45
Dorking West		d			07 44		08 49			09 50		10 50		
Gomshall		d		07 30	07 52		08 57			09 58				11 53
Chilworth		d			07 58		09 03			10 04				11 59
Shalford		d	07 21		08 02		09 07	09 31		10 08		11 03		12 03
Guildford		a	07 25	07 41	08 06	08 36	09 11	09 36	09 53	10 12	10 42	11 08	11 42	12 08
		d	07 27	07 43	08 13	08 38	09 13	09 38	09 54	10 14	10 44	11 09	11 44	12 09
Wanborough	149	d			08 20		09 20							
Ash 5	149	d	07 36	07 52	08 25		09 25	09 47		10 23		11 19		12 19
North Camp		d	07 41	07 56	08 29	08 50	09 29	09 51		10 27	10 56	11 23	11 56	12 23
Farnborough North		d	07 45	08 00	08 33		09 33			10 31		11 27		12 27
Blackwater		d	07 49	08 05	08 37	08 56	09 37	09 58		10 36	11 02	11 31	12 02	12 31
Sandhurst		d	07 53	08 08	08 41		09 41			10 39		11 35		12 35
Crowthorne		d	07 57	08 12	08 45		09 45			10 43		11 39		12 39
Wokingham	149	d	08 02	08 17	08 50	09 04	09 51	10 06		10 48	11 10	11 44	12 10	12 44
Reading 7	149	a	08 17	08 30	09 00	09 17	10 01	10 17	10 23	10 59	11 19	11 54	12 19	12 54

Station			GW 1	GW 1	GW 1	GW 1	GW 1	GW 1	GW 1	GW 1	GW 1	GW 1	GW 1	GW 1
Gatwick Airport 10	186	d	12 03		13 03		14 03		15 03		16 03		17 03	
Redhill	186	d	12 13	12 34	13 13	13 34	14 13	14 34	15 13	15 29	16 13	16 32	17 13	
Reigate	186	d	12 18	12 38	13 18	13 38	14 18	14 38	15 18	15 34	16 18	16 36	17 18	
Betchworth		d		12 43				14 43		15 38		16 41		
Dorking Deepdene		d	12 25	12 47	13 25	13 45	14 25	14 47	15 25	15 43	16 25	16 45	17 25	
Dorking West		d		12 50				14 50		15 45				
Gomshall		d				13 53				15 53		16 53		
Chilworth		d				13 59				15 59		16 59		
Shalford		d		13 03		14 03		15 03		16 03		17 03		18 05
Guildford		a	12 42	13 08	13 42	14 08	14 42	15 08	15 42	16 08	16 42	17 08	17 43	18 12
		d	12 44	13 09	13 44	14 09	14 44	15 09	15 44	16 14	16 44	17 09	17 44	18 14
Wanborough	149	d												
Ash 5	149	d		13 19		14 19		15 19		16 24		17 19	17 54	18 23
North Camp		d	12 56	13 23	13 56	14 23	14 56	15 23	15 56	16 28	16 56	17 23	17 58	18 27
Farnborough North		d		13 27		14 27		15 27		16 32		17 27	18 02	18 31
Blackwater		d	13 02	13 31	14 02	14 31	15 02	15 31	16 02	16 36	17 02	17 31	18 07	18 36
Sandhurst		d		13 35		14 35		15 35		16 40		17 35		18 39
Crowthorne		d		13 39		14 39		15 39		16 44		17 39		18 43
Wokingham	149	d	13 10	13 44	14 10	14 44	15 10	15 43	16 10	16 48	17 10	17 44	18 15	18 51
Reading 7	149	a	13 19	13 54	14 19	14 54	15 19	15 54	16 24	17 00	17 19	17 54	18 24	19 02

Station			GW 1	GW 1	GW 1	GW 1	GW 1	GW 1	GW 1	GW 1	GW 1	GW 1	GW 1
Gatwick Airport 10	186	d		18 03		19 16		20 03		21 03		22 22	23 18
Redhill	186	d	17 43	18 13	18 43	19 26		20 13	20 34	21 13	21 35	22 33	23 28
Reigate	186	d	17 48	18 18	18 47	19 30		20 18	20 40	21 18	21 39	22 38	23 33
Betchworth		d	17 52		18 52				20 45		21 44	22 43	
Dorking Deepdene		d	17 57	18 25	18 56	19 37		20 25	20 49	21 25	21 48	22 47	23 40
Dorking West		d	17 59		18 59				20 52		21 51	22 50	
Gomshall		d	18 07		19 07				21 00		21 59	22 58	
Chilworth		d	18 13		19 13				21 06		22 05	23 04	
Shalford		d	18 17		19 17		20 02		21 10		22 09	23 08	
Guildford		a	18 22	18 41	19 22	19 54	20 06	20 42	21 14	21 42	22 13	23 12	00 01
		d	18 24	18 47	19 36	19 55	20 10	20 44	21 16	21 44	22 15	23 14	00 02
Wanborough	149	d										23 21	
Ash 5	149	d	18 33		19 46		20 19		21 25		22 23	23 26	
North Camp		d	18 38	19 01	19 50	20 07	20 23	20 56	21 29	21 56	22 27	23 30	00 14
Farnborough North		d	18 42		19 54		20 27		21 33		22 31	23 34	
Blackwater		d	18 47	19 07	19 58	20 14	20 31	21 02	21 38	22 02	22 36	23 38	00 20
Sandhurst		d	18 51		20 02		20 35		21 41		22 39	23 42	
Crowthorne		d	18 59		20 06		20 39		21 45		22 43	23 46	
Wokingham	149	d	19 04	19 15	20 11	20 22	20 43	21 10	21 50	22 10	22 48	23 51	00 29
Reading 7	149	a	19 17	19 25	20 21	20 32	20 55	21 19	22 01	22 19	23 01	00 01	00 39

A From 19 September **B** Until 12 September **C** Until 5 September

Saturdays

until 10 September

Station			GW 1	GW 1	XC ◇1	GW 1	GW 1	GW 1	GW 1	GW 1	GW 1
Gatwick Airport 10	186	d	22p22	23p18		05 31	06 03		07 03		08 03
Redhill	186	d	22p33	23p28		05 41	06 13	06 34	07 13	07 34	08 13
Reigate	186	d	22p38	23p33		05 47	06 18	06 38	07 18	07 38	08 18
Betchworth		d	22p43					06 43			
Dorking Deepdene		d	22p47	23p40		05 54	06 25	06 47	07 25	07 45	08 25
Dorking West		d	22p50					06 50			
Gomshall		d	22p58							07 53	
Chilworth		d	23p04							07 59	
Shalford		d	23p08					07 03		08 03	
Guildford		a	23p12	00 01		06 12	06 43	07 08	07 41	08 08	08 42
		d	23p14	00 02	06 09	06 12	06 44	07 09	07 44	08 09	08 44
Wanborough	149	d	23p21			06 21					
Ash 5	149	d	23p26			06 24		07 19		08 19	
North Camp		d	23p30	00 14		06 28	06 56	07 23	07 56	08 23	08 56
Farnborough North		d	23p34			06 32		07 27		08 27	
Blackwater		d	23p38	00 20		06 38	07 02	07 31	08 02	08 31	09 02
Sandhurst		d	23p42			06 40		07 35		08 35	
Crowthorne		d	23p46			06 44		07 39		08 39	
Wokingham	149	d	23p51	00 29		06 49	07 10	07 44	08 10	08 44	09 10
Reading 7	149	a	00 01	00 39	06 44	07 03	07 19	07 54	08 19	08 54	09 19

Station			GW 1	GW 1	GW 1	GW 1	GW 1	GW 1	GW 1	GW 1	GW 1	GW 1	GW 1	GW 1	GW 1
Gatwick Airport 10	186	d		09 03		10 03		11 03		12 03		13 03		14 03	
Redhill	186	d	08 34	09 13	09 34	10 13	10 34	11 13	11 34	12 13	12 34	13 13	13 34	14 13	14 34
Reigate	186	d	08 38	09 18	09 38	10 18	10 38	11 18	11 38	12 18	12 38	13 18	13 38	14 18	14 38
Betchworth		d	08 43				10 43				12 43				14 43
Dorking Deepdene		d	08 47	09 25	09 45	10 25	10 47	11 25	11 45	12 25	12 47	13 25	13 45	14 25	14 47
Dorking West		d	08 50				10 50				12 50				14 50
Gomshall		d			09 53				11 53				13 53		
Chilworth		d			09 59				11 59				13 59		
Shalford		d	09 03		10 03		11 03		12 03		13 03		14 03		15 03
Guildford		a	09 08	09 42	10 08	10 42	11 08	11 42	12 08	12 42	13 08	13 42	14 08	14 42	15 08
		d	09 09	09 44	10 09	10 44	11 09	11 44	12 09	12 44	13 09	13 44	14 09	14 44	15 09
Wanborough	149	d													
Ash 5	149	d	09 19		10 19		11 19		12 19		13 19		14 19		15 19
North Camp		d	09 23	09 56	10 23	10 56	11 23	11 56	12 23	12 56	13 23	13 56	14 23	14 56	15 23
Farnborough North		d	09 27		10 27		11 27		12 27		13 27		14 27		15 27
Blackwater		d	09 31	10 02	10 31	11 02	11 31	12 02	12 31	13 02	13 31	14 02	14 31	15 02	15 31
Sandhurst		d	09 35		10 35		11 35		12 35		13 35		14 35		15 35
Crowthorne		d	09 39		10 39		11 39		12 39		13 39		14 39		15 39
Wokingham	149	d	09 44	10 10	10 44	11 10	11 44	12 10	12 44	13 10	13 44	14 10	14 44	15 10	15 44
Reading 7	149	a	09 54	10 19	10 54	11 19	11 54	12 19	12 54	13 19	13 54	14 19	14 54	15 19	15 54

Table 148

Saturdays
until 10 September

Gatwick Airport, Redhill and Guildford - Reading

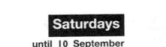

			GW	GW	GW	GW	GW	GW	GW	GW	GW	GW	GW	GW	GW	GW	GW	GW	GW	GW	GW
			1	1	1	1	1	1	1	1	1	1	1	Bus	1	Bus	1	Bus	1	1	Bus
Gatwick Airport 10	186	d	15 03		16 03		17 03		18 03		19 03		20 03		21 03				22 22	23 18	
Redhill	186	d	15 13	15 34	16 13	16 34	17 13	17 34	18 13	18 34	19 13	19 34	20 13		21 13		21 36		22 33	23 28	
Reigate	186	d	15 18	15 38	16 18	16 38	17 18	17 38	18 18	18 38	19 18	19 38	20 18		21 18		21 40		22 38	23 33	
Betchworth		d				16 43				18 43			20 23						22 43		
Dorking Deepdene		d	15 25	15 45	16 25	16 47	17 25	17 45	18 25	18 47	19 25	19 45	20 27		21 25		21 47		22 47	23 40	
Dorking West		d				16 50				18 50			20 30						22 50		
Gomshall		d		15 53				17 53				19 53					21 55		22 58		
Chilworth		d		15 59				17 59				19 59					22 01		23 04		
Shalford		d		16 03		17 03		18 03		19 03		20 03	20 43				22 05		23 08		
Guildford		a	15 42	16 08	16 42	17 08	17 42	18 08	18 42	19 08	19 42	20 08	20 48		21 43		22 13		23 13	00 01	
		d	15 44	16 09	16 44	17 09	17 44	18 09	18 44	19 09	19 44	20 09	20 49		21 43		22 14		23 14		
Wanborough	149	d																	23 22		
Ash 5	149	d		16 19		17 19		18 19		19 19	19 53		20 59		21 54		22 24		23 26		
North Camp		d	15 56	16 23	16 56	17 23	17 56	18 23	18 56	19 23	19 57	20 21	21 03		21 57		22 28		23 30		
Farnborough North		d		16 27		17 27		18 27		19 27	20 01		21 07		22 02		22 32		23 34		
Blackwater		d	16 02	16 31	17 02	17 31	18 02	18 31	19 02	19 31	20 06	20 28	21 11		22 06		22 36		23 39		
Sandhurst		d		16 35		17 35		18 35		19 35	20 09		21 15		22 10		22 40		23 42		
Crowthorne		d		16 39		17 39		18 39		19 39	20 13		21 19		22 14		22 44		23 46		
Wokingham	149	d	16 10	16 44	17 10	17 44	18 10	18 44	19 10	19 44	20 18	20 36	21a23	21 30	22a18	22 25	22a48	22 55	23a51		23 58
Reading 7	149	a	16 19	16 54	17 19	17 54	18 19	18 54	19 20	19 56	20 29	20 45		21 50		22 45		23 15			00 18

Saturdays
from 17 September

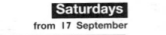

			GW	GW	XC	GW	GW	GW	GW	GW	GW	GW	GW	GW	GW	GW	GW	GW	GW	GW	GW	GW	GW	GW
			1	1	◇1	1	1	1	1	1	1	1	1	1	1	1	1	1	1	1	1	1	1	1
Gatwick Airport 10	186	d	22p22	23p18		05 31	06 03		07 03		08 03		09 03		10 03		11 03		12 03		13 03		14 03	
Redhill	186	d	22p33	23p28		05 41	06 13	06 34	07 13	07 34	08 13	08 34	09 13	09 34	10 13	10 34	11 13	11 34	12 13	12 34	13 13	13 34	14 13	14 34
Reigate	186	d	22p38	23p33		05 47	06 18	06 38	07 18	07 38	08 18	08 38	09 18	09 38	10 18	10 38	11 18	11 38	12 18	12 38	13 18	13 38	14 18	14 38
Betchworth		d	22p43					06 43				08 43				10 43				12 43				14 43
Dorking Deepdene		d	22p47	23p40		05 54	06 25	06 47	07 25	07 45	08 25	08 47	09 25	09 45	10 25	10 47	11 25	11 45	12 25	12 47	13 25	13 45	14 25	14 47
Dorking West		d	22p50					06 50				08 50				10 50				12 50				14 50
Gomshall		d	22p58							07 53				09 53				11 53				13 53		
Chilworth		d	23p04							07 59				09 59				11 59				13 59		
Shalford		d	23p08					07 03		08 03		09 03		10 03		11 03		12 03		13 03		14 03		15 03
Guildford		a	23p12	00 01		06 12	06 43	07 08	07 41	08 08	08 42	09 08	09 42	10 08	10 42	11 08	11 42	12 08	12 42	13 08	13 42	14 08	14 42	15 08
		d	23p14	00 02	06 09	06 12	06 44	07 09	07 44	08 09	08 44	09 09	09 44	10 09	10 44	11 09	11 44	12 09	12 44	13 09	13 44	14 09	14 44	15 09
Wanborough	149	d	23p21			06 21																		
Ash 5	149	d	23p26			06 24		07 19		08 19		09 19		10 19		11 19		12 19		13 19		14 19		15 19
North Camp		d	23p30	00 14		06 28	06 56	07 23	07 56	08 23	08 56	09 23	09 56	10 23	10 56	11 23	11 56	12 23	12 56	13 23	13 56	14 23	14 56	15 23
Farnborough North		d	23p34			06 32		07 27		08 27		09 27		10 27		11 27		12 27		13 27		14 27		15 27
Blackwater		d	23p38	00 20		06 38	07 02	07 31	08 02	08 31	09 02	09 31	10 02	10 31	11 02	11 31	12 02	12 31	13 02	13 31	14 02	14 31	15 02	15 31
Sandhurst		d	23p42			06 40		07 35		08 35		09 35		10 35		11 35		12 35		13 35		14 35		15 35
Crowthorne		d	23p46			06 44		07 39		08 39		09 39		10 39		11 39		12 39		13 39		14 39		15 39
Wokingham	149	d	23p51	00 29		06 49	07 10	07 44	08 10	08 44	09 10	09 44	10 10	10 44	11 10	11 44	12 10	12 44	13 10	13 44	14 10	14 44	15 10	15 44
Reading 7	149	a	00 01	00 39	06 44	07 03	07 19	07 54	08 19	08 54	09 19	09 54	10 19	10 54	11 19	11 54	12 19	12 54	13 19	13 54	14 19	14 54	15 19	15 54

			GW	GW	GW	GW	GW	GW	GW	GW	GW	GW	GW	GW	GW	GW	GW	GW
			1	1	1	1	1	1	1	1	1	1	1	1	1	1	1	1
Gatwick Airport 10	186	d	15 03		16 03		17 03		18 03		19 03		20 03		21 03		22 22	23 18
Redhill	186	d	15 13	15 34	16 13	16 34	17 13	17 34	18 13	18 34	19 13	19 34	20 13	20 34	21 13	21 36	22 33	23 28
Reigate	186	d	15 18	15 38	16 18	16 38	17 18	17 38	18 18	18 38	19 18	19 38	20 18	20 38	21 18	21 40	22 38	23 33
Betchworth		d				16 43				18 43				20 43			22 43	
Dorking Deepdene		d	15 25	15 45	16 25	16 47	17 25	17 45	18 25	18 47	19 25	19 45	20 25	20 47	21 25	21 47	22 47	23 40
Dorking West		d				16 50				18 50				20 50			22 50	
Gomshall		d		15 53				17 53				19 53				21 55	22 58	
Chilworth		d		15 59				17 59				19 59				22 01	23 04	
Shalford		d		16 03		17 03		18 03		19 03		20 03		21 03		22 05	23 08	
Guildford		a	15 42	16 08	16 42	17 08	17 42	18 08	18 42	19 08	19 42	20 08	20 42	21 08	21 42	22 13	23 13	00 01
		d	15 44	16 09	16 44	17 09	17 44	18 09	18 44	19 09	19 44	20 09	20 44	21 09	21 44	22 14	23 14	00 02
Wanborough	149	d															23 22	
Ash 5	149	d		16 19		17 19		18 19		19 19		20 19		21 19		22 24	23 26	
North Camp		d	15 56	16 23	16 56	17 23	17 56	18 23	18 56	19 23	19 56	20 23	20 56	21 23	21 56	22 28	23 30	00 14
Farnborough North		d		16 27		17 27		18 27		19 27		20 27		21 27		22 32	23 34	
Blackwater		d	16 02	16 31	17 02	17 31	18 02	18 31	19 02	19 31	20 02	20 31	21 02	21 31	22 02	22 36	23 39	00 20
Sandhurst		d		16 35		17 35		18 35		19 35		20 35		21 35		22 40	23 42	
Crowthorne		d		16 39		17 39		18 39		19 39		20 39		21 39		22 44	23 46	
Wokingham	149	d	16 10	16 44	17 10	17 44	18 10	18 44	19 10	19 44	20 10	20 44	21 10	21 44	22 10	22 49	23 51	00 29
Reading 7	149	a	16 19	16 54	17 19	17 54	18 19	18 54	19 19	19 54	20 19	20 53	21 19	21 54	22 19	22 57	00 01	00 38

Gatwick Airport, Redhill and Guildford - Reading

Sundays
until 11 September

			GW	GW	GW	GW	GW	GW	GW	GW	GW	GW	GW	GW	GW	GW	GW	GW	GW	GW	GW	GW	GW	GW
			1			1		1		1		1		1		1		1		1			1		1
			A	A																				
				🚌	🚌		🚌		🚌		🚌		🚌		🚌		🚌		🚌		🚌		🚌	
Gatwick Airport 10	186	d	23p18			06 08		07 08		08 08		09 08		10 08		11 08		12 08		13 08		14 08		15 08
Redhill	186	d	23p28			06 19		07 21		08 19		09 19		10 19		11 19		12 19		13 19		14 19		15 19
Reigate	186	d	23p33			06 23		07 26		08 23		09 23		10 23		11 23		12 23		13 23		14 23		15 23
Betchworth		d								08 28				10 28				12 28				14 28		
Dorking Deepdene		d	23p40			06 32		07 32		08 32		09 32		10 32		11 32		12 32		13 32		14 32		15 32
Dorking West		d								08 35				10 35				12 35				14 35		
Gomshall		d								08 43				10 43				12 43				14 43		
Chilworth		d								08 49				10 49				12 49				14 49		
Shalford		d								08 53				10 53				12 53				14 53		
Guildford		a	00 01			06 49		07 50		08 57		09 50		10 57		11 50		12 57		13 51		14 57		15 50
		d			00 11	06 50		07 52		08 59		09 52		10 59		11 52		12 59		13 52		14 59		15 52
Wanborough	149	d																						
Ash 5	149	d						08 02				10 02				12 02				14 02				16 02
North Camp		d			00 36	07 02		08 06		09 11		10 06		11 11		12 06		13 11		14 06		15 11		16 06
Farnborough North		d						08 10				10 10				12 10				14 10				16 10
Blackwater		d			00 56	07 09		08 14		09 17		10 14		11 17		12 14		13 17		14 14		15 17		16 14
Sandhurst		d						08 18				10 18				12 18				14 18				16 18
Crowthorne		d						08 22				10 22				12 22				14 22				16 22
Wokingham	149	d		23p58	01 21	07a16	07 23	08a26	08 33	09a26	09 40	10a26	10 33	11a26	11 33	12a26	12 33	13a26	13 33	14a26	14 33	15a25	15 33	16a26
Reading 7	149	a		00 18	01 41		07 43		08 53		10 00		10 53		11 53		12 53		13 53		14 53		15 53	

			GW	GW	GW	GW	GW	GW	GW	GW	GW	GW	GW	GW	GW	GW	GW	GW
				1		1		1		1		1		1		1		1
			🚌		🚌		🚌		🚌		🚌		🚌		🚌		🚌	
Gatwick Airport 10	186	d		16 08		17 08		18 08		19 08		20 08		21 08		22 08		23 09
Redhill	186	d		16 19		17 19		18 19		19 19		20 19		21 19		22 19		23 20
Reigate	186	d		16 23		17 23		18 23		19 23		20 23		21 23		22 23		23 24
Betchworth		d		16 28				18 28				20 28				22 28		
Dorking Deepdene		d		16 32		17 32		18 32		19 32		20 32		21 32		22 32		23 32
Dorking West		d		16 35				18 35				20 35				22 35		
Gomshall		d		16 43				18 43				20 43				22 43		
Chilworth		d		16 49				18 49				20 49				22 49		
Shalford		d		16 53				18 53				20 53				22 53		
Guildford		a		16 57		17 50		18 57		19 50		20 57		21 50		22 57		23 48
		d		16 59		17 52		18 59		19 52		20 59		21 52		22 59		23 49
Wanborough	149	d																
Ash 5	149	d				18 02				20 02				22 02				23 58
North Camp		d		17 11		18 06		19 11		20 06		21 11		22 06		23 11		00 03
Farnborough North		d				18 10				20 10				22 10				00 07
Blackwater		d		17 18		18 14		19 17		20 14		21 17		22 13		23 17		00 12
Sandhurst		d				18 18				20 18				22 18				00 15
Crowthorne		d				18 22				20 22				22 22				00 19
Wokingham	149	d	16 33	17a25	17 33	18a26	18 33	19a25	19 33	20a26	20 33	21a25	21 33	22a26	22 33	23a26	23 33	00a24
Reading 7	149	a	16 53		17 53		18 53		19 53		20 53		21 53		22 53		23 53	

A not 22 May

Sundays
from 18 September

			GW	GW	GW	GW	GW	GW	GW	GW	GW	GW	GW	GW	GW	GW	GW	GW	GW	GW	GW	GW
			1	1	1	1	1	1	1	1	1	1	1	1	1	1	1	1	1	1	1	1
Gatwick Airport 10	186	d	22p22	23p18	06 08	07 08	08 08	09 08	10 08	11 08	12 08	13 08	14 08	15 08	16 08	17 08	18 08	19 08	20 08	21 08	22 08	23 08
Redhill	186	d	22p33	23p28	06 20	07 20	08 19	09 19	10 19	11 19	12 19	13 19	14 19	15 19	16 19	17 19	18 19	19 19	20 19	21 19	22 19	23 19
Reigate	186	d	22p38	23p33	06 24	07 24	08 23	09 23	10 23	11 23	12 23	13 23	14 23	15 23	16 23	17 23	18 23	19 23	20 23	21 23	22 23	23 23
Betchworth		d	22p43				08 28		10 28		12 28		14 28		16 28		18 28		20 28		22 28	
Dorking Deepdene		d	22p47	23p40	06 32	07 32	08 32	09 32	10 32	11 32	12 32	13 32	14 32	15 32	16 32	17 32	18 32	19 32	20 32	21 32	22 32	23 32
Dorking West		d	22p50				08 35		10 35		12 35		14 35		16 35		18 35		20 35		22 35	
Gomshall		d	22p58				08 43		10 43		12 43		14 43		16 43		18 43		20 43		22 43	
Chilworth		d	23p04				08 49		10 49		12 49		14 49		16 49		18 49		20 49		22 49	
Shalford		d	23p08				08 53		10 53		12 53		14 53		16 53		18 53		20 53		22 53	
Guildford		a	23p13	00 01	06 49	07 50	08 57	09 50	10 57	11 50	12 57	13 52	14 57	15 50	16 57	17 50	18 57	19 50	20 57	21 50	22 57	23 50
		d	23p14	00 02	06 50	07 52	08 59	09 52	10 59	11 52	12 59	13 52	14 59	15 52	16 59	17 52	18 59	19 52	20 59	21 52	22 59	23 52
Wanborough	149	d	23p22																			
Ash 5	149	d	23p26			08 02		10 02		12 02		14 02		16 02		18 02		20 02		22 02		00 01
North Camp		d	23p30	00 14	07 02	08 06	09 11	10 06	11 11	12 06	13 11	14 06	15 11	16 06	17 11	18 06	19 11	20 06	21 11	22 06	23 11	00 05
Farnborough North		d	23p34			08 10		10 10		12 10		14 10		16 10		18 10		20 10		22 10		00 09
Blackwater		d	23p39	00 20	07 09	08 14	09 17	10 14	11 17	12 14	13 17	14 14	15 17	16 14	17 18	18 14	19 17	20 14	21 17	22 14	23 17	00 14
Sandhurst		d	23p42			08 18		10 18		12 18		14 18		16 18		18 18		20 18		22 18		00 16
Crowthorne		d	23p46			08 22		10 22		12 22		14 22		16 22		18 22		20 22		22 22		00 20
Wokingham	149	d	23p51	00 29	07 17	08 26	09 26	10 26	11 26	12 26	13 26	14 26	15 26	16 26	17 26	18 26	19 26	20 26	21 26	22 26	23 26	00 26
Reading 7	149	a	00 01	00 38	07 25	08 35	09 35	10 35	11 35	12 35	13 35	14 35	15 35	16 35	17 35	18 35	19 35	20 35	21 35	22 38	23 37	00 37

Table 149

Mondays to Fridays

until 30 September

London - Hounslow, Richmond, Kingston, Windsor, Weybridge, Ascot, Guildford and Reading

Miles	Miles	Miles			SW MO 1	SW MX 1	SW MO	SW MX	SW MO 1	SW MX	SW MX 1	SW MX	SW MX	SW MX	SW MX	SW MX 1	SW MO 1	SW MX	SW MO	SW MO	SW 1	SW 1	SW MX
0	—	0	**London Waterloo** 15	⊖ d	22p39	22p50	22p50	22p52	23p09	23p13	23p20	23p22	23p33	23p38			23p39			23p44			23p52
1¼	—	1¼	Vauxhall	⊖ d	22p43		22p54	22p56	23p13	23p17		23p26	23p37				23p43			23p48			23p56
2¾	—	2¾	Queenstown Rd.(Battersea)	d			22p57	22p59				23p29	23p40							23p51			23p59
4	—	4	**Clapham Junction** 10	d	22p49	22p58	23p00	23p02	23p19	23p23	23p28	23p32	23p43	23p46			23p49			23p54			00 02
4¾	—	4¾	Wandsworth Town	d			23p03	23p05				23p35	23p46							23p57			00 05
5¾	—	5¾	Putney	d	22p53		23p06	23p08	23p23	23p27		23p38	23p49				23p53			23p59			00 08
7	0	7	Barnes	d			23p09	23p12				23p42	23p52							00 03			00 12
—	0½	—	Barnes Bridge	d			23p11	23p14				23p44											00 14
—	1½	—	Chiswick	d			23p13	23p17				23p47											00 17
—	2½	—	Kew Bridge	d			23p16	23p20				23p50											00 20
—	3½	—	Brentford	d			23p19	23p23				23p53											00 23
—	4¼	—	Syon Lane	d			23p21	23p25				23p55											00 25
—	5	—	Isleworth	d			23p23	23p27				23p57											00 27
—	6½	—	**Hounslow**	d			23p26	23p31				00 01											00 31
8¼	—	8¼	Mortlake	d									23p54							00 05			
9	—	9	North Sheen	d									23p56					←		00 07			
9¾	—	9¾	**Richmond**	⊖ d	22p59	23p06			23p29	23p33	23p37		23p59	23p54			23p59	23p59		00 10			
10¾	—	10¾	St Margarets	d									→					00 01		00 12			
11¼	—	11¼	Twickenham	a	23p02	23p10			23p32	23p36	23p41			23p58			00 02	00 03		00 14			
—	—	—		d	23p03	23p10			23p33	23p37	23p41			23p58			00 03	00 04		00 15			
12¼	—	—	Strawberry Hill	d														00 07					
12½	—	—	Fulwell	a																			
13½	—	—	Teddington	a														00 11					
14¾	—	—	Hampton Wick	a														00 14					
15¾	—	—	**Kingston**	a														00 16					
—	—	12½	Whitton	d						23p40					←					00 18			
—	—	14¾	Feltham	d	23p09	23p16	23p32	23p36	23p39	23p44	23p48	00 06		00 04	00 06		00 09			00 22			00 37
—	—	17½	Ashford (Surrey)	d			23p36	23p40		23p48		→			00 10					00 26			→
0	—	19	**Staines**	d	23p15	23p23	23p40	23p44	23p45	23p52	23p56			00 11	00 14		00 15		00 21	00a30			
2½	—	—	Wraysbury	d						23p56													
3¾	—	—	Sunnymeads	d						23p59													
4¾	—	—	Datchet	d						00 02													
6¼	—	—	**Windsor & Eton Riverside**	a						00 06													
—	—	21	Egham	d	23p20	23p27	23p45	23p49	23p50		00 01			00 15	00 19		00 20		00s25				
0	—	23¾	Virginia Water	a	23p24	23p31	23p49	23p53	23p54		00 05			00 19	00 23		00 24		00s30				
—	—	—		d	23p24	23p31	23p49	23p53	23p54		00 05			00 19	00 23		00 24						
2½	—	—	Chertsey	d			23p55	23p59							00 29				00s35				
4	—	—	Addlestone	d			23p58	00 02							00a32				00s38				
5	—	—	**Weybridge**	a																			
7¼	—	—	Byfleet & New Haw	d			00 02	00 06											00s42				
8½	—	—	West Byfleet	d			00 05	00 09											00s45				
11	—	—	Woking	a			00 11	00 15											00 51				
—	—	25¼	Longcross	d																			
—	—	27	Sunningdale	d	23p29	23p37			23p59		00 11			00 25			00 29						
—	0	29	**Ascot** 3	d	23p34	23p43			00 04		00 15			00 30		00 32	00 34						
—	3¼	—	Bagshot	d												00 38							
—	6½	—	Camberley	a												00 44							
—	8¾	—	Frimley	d												00 48							
—	12	—	Ash Vale	d												00 57							
—	14½	—	**Aldershot**	a												01s02							
—	—	—		d																	06 08	06 38	
—	17¼	—	Ash 5	d																	06 15	06 45	
—	19¼	—	Wanborough	d																	06 18	06 48	
—	23½	—	**Guildford**	a																	06 25	06 55	
—	—	31¼	Martins Heron	d	23p38	23p47			00 08		00 19			00 34			00 38						
—	—	32¼	Bracknell	d	23p41	23p50			00 11		00 23			00 37			00 41						
—	—	36¾	**Wokingham**	d	23p48	23p57			00 18		00 32			00 44			00 48						
—	—	38¾	Winnersh	d	23p51	23p59			00 21		00 36						00 51						
—	—	39¼	Winnersh Triangle	d	23p53	00 02			00 23		00 38						00 53						
—	—	40½	Earley	d	23p56	00 05			00 26		00 40						00 56						
—	—	43½	**Reading** 7	a	00 01	00 10			00 31		00 45			00 52			01 01						

Table 149

Mondays to Fridays

until 30 September

London - Hounslow, Richmond, Kingston, Windsor, Weybridge, Ascot, Guildford and Reading

		SW MX	SW MX	SW	SW 1	SW	SW 1	SW	SW	SW	SW 1	SW 1	SW	SW	SW	SW 1	SW	SW 1	SW	SW 1	SW	SW	SW
London Waterloo 15	⊖ d	23p58		00 18			05 05		05 33			05 50	05 58	06 03			06 15	06 20			06 22	06 28	
Vauxhall	⊖ d	00 02		00 22			05 09		05 37				06 02	06 07			06 19				06 26	06 32	
Queenstown Rd.(Battersea)	d			00 25			05 12		05 40					06 10			06 22				06 29		
Clapham Junction 10	d	00 08		00 29			05 15		05 43			05 58	06 08	06 13			06 25	06 28			06 32	06 38	
Wandsworth Town	d			00 32			05 18		05 46					06 16			06 28				06 35		
Putney	d	00 12		00 35			05 21		05 49				06 12	06 19			06 31				06 38	06 42	
Barnes	d			00 38			05 24		05 52					06 22			06 35				06 42		
Barnes Bridge	d																				06 44		
Chiswick	d																				06 47		
Kew Bridge	d																				06 50		
Brentford	d																				06 53		
Syon Lane	d																				06 55		
Isleworth	d																				06 57		
Hounslow	d																				07 01		
Mortlake	d			00 40			05 26		05 54					06 24			06 37						
North Sheen	d			00 42			05 28		05 56					06 26			06 39		←				
Richmond	⊖ d	00 18		00 45			05 31		05 59			06 06	06 18	06 29			06 42	06 36	06 42			06 48	
St Margarets	d			00 47			05 33		06 01					06 31			→		06 44				
Twickenham	a	00 21		00 49			05 35		06 03			06 10	06 21	06 33				06 40	06 46			06 51	
	d	00 22		00 50			05 36	05 53	06 05			06 10	06 22	06 34				06 40	06 47			06 52	
Strawberry Hill	d			00s53					06 08					06 37									
Fulwell	a																						
Teddington	a			00s56					06 11					06 40									
Hampton Wick	a			00s59					06 14					06 44									
Kingston	a			01 01					06 16					06 46									
Whitton	d	00 25	←				05 39	05 56					06 25						06a50			06 55	←
Feltham	d	00 29	00 37				05 43	06 00				06 16	06 29					06 46			07 06	06 59	07 06
Ashford (Surrey)	d	00 33	00 41				05 47	06 04					06 33								→	07 03	07 10
Staines	d	00a37	00a46		05 23	05 44	05 53	06 08		06 14		06 23	06 37		06 44			06 53				07 07	07 14
Wraysbury	d							06 12					06 41									07 11	
Sunnymeads	d							06 15					06 44									07 14	
Datchet	d							06 18					06 47									07 17	
Windsor & Eton Riverside	a							06 22					06 51									07 21	
Egham	d				05 27	05 49	05 57			06 19		06 27			06 49			06 57					07 19
Virginia Water	a				05 31	05 53	06 01			06 23		06 31			06 53			07 01					07 23
	d				05 31	05 53	06 01			06 23		06 31			06 53			07 01					07 23
Chertsey	d					05 59				06 29					06 59								07 29
Addlestone	d					06 02				06 32					07 02								07 32
Weybridge	a					06 07				06 37					07 07								07 37
Byfleet & New Haw	d																						
West Byfleet	d																						
Woking	a																						
Longcross	d											06 35						07 05					
Sunningdale	d				05 37		06 07					06 37						07 07					
Ascot 3	d				05 43		06 13				06 23	06 43				06 53		07 13		07 23			
Bagshot	d										06 29					06 59				07 29			
Camberley	a										06 35					07 05				07 35			
Frimley	d										06 43					07 13				07 43			
Ash Vale	d										06 49					07 19				07 49			
Aldershot	a										06 56					07 26				07 54			
	d										07 08					07 38				08 08			
Ash 5	d										07 15					07 45				08 15			
Wanborough	d										07 18					07 48				08 18			
Guildford	a										07 25					07 55				08 25			
Martins Heron	d				05 47		06 17					06 47						07 17					
Bracknell	d				05 50		06 20					06 50						07 20					
Wokingham	d				05 57		06 27					06 57						07 27					
Winnersh	d				06 00		06 30					07 00						07 30					
Winnersh Triangle	d				06 02		06 32					07 02						07 32					
Earley	d				06 05		06 35					07 05						07 35					
Reading 7	a				06 10		06 40					07 10						07 40					

London - Hounslow, Richmond, Kingston, Windsor, Weybridge, Ascot, Guildford and Reading

		SW	SW	SW 1	SW		SW 1	SW	SW	SW	SW	SW	SW 1	SW	SW		SW	SW 1	SW	SW	SW	SW	SW 1	SW	SW 1
London Waterloo 15 ⊖	d	06 33	06 45	06 50				06 52	06 58		07 03	07 15	07 20		07 22		07 28			07 33	07 37	07 45	07 50		
Vauxhall ⊖	d	06 37	06 49					06 56	07 02		07 07	07 19			07 26		07 32			07 37	07 41	07 49			
Queenstown Rd.(Battersea)	d	06 40	06 52					06 59			07 10	07 22			07 29					07 40	07 44	07 52			
Clapham Junction 10	d	06 43	06 55	06 58				07 02	07 08		07 13	07 25	07 28		07 32		07 38			07 43	07 47	07 55	07 58		
Wandsworth Town	d	06 46	06 58					07 05			07 16	07 28			07 35					07 46	07 50	07 58			
Putney	d	06 49	07 01					07 08	07 12		07 19	07 31			07 38		07 42			07 49	07 53	08 01			
Barnes	d	06 52	07 05					07 12			07 22	07 35			07 42					07 52	07 57	08 05			
Barnes Bridge	d							07 14							07 44						07 59				
Chiswick	d							07 17							07 47						08 02				
Kew Bridge	d							07 20							07 50						08 05				
Brentford	d							07 23							07 53						08 08				
Syon Lane	d							07 25							07 55						08 10				
Isleworth	d							07 27							07 57						08 12				
Hounslow	d							07 31							08 01						08a18				
Mortlake	d	06 54	07 07								07 24	07 37								07 54		08 07			
North Sheen	d	06 56	07 09		←						07 26	07 39		←						07 56		08 09		←	
Richmond ⊖	d	06 59	07 12	07 06	07 12				07 18		07 29	07 42	07 36	07 42			07 48	07 54		07 59		08 12	08 06	08 12	
St Margarets	d	07 01	→		07 14						07 31	→		07 44						08 01		→		08 14	
Twickenham	a	07 03		07 10	07 16				07 21		07 33		07 40	07 46			07 51	07 57		08 03			08 10	08 16	
	d	07 04		07 10	07 17				07 22		07 34		07 40	07 47			07 52	07 58		08 04			08 10	08 17	
Strawberry Hill	d	07 07									07 37									08 07					
Fulwell	a																								
Teddington	a	07 10									07 40									08 10					
Hampton Wick	a	07 14									07 44									08 14					
Kingston	a	07 16									07 46									08 16					
Whitton	d				07a20				07 25	←				07a50			07 55		←					08a20	
Feltham	d			07 16				07 36	07 29	07 36			07 46		08 06		07 59	08 04	08 06				08 16		
Ashford (Surrey)	d							→	07 33	07 40					→		08 03	08 08	08 10						
Staines	d			07 23					07 37	07 44			07 53				08 07	08 12	08 14				08 23		
Wraysbury	d								07 41								08 11								
Sunnymeads	d								07 44								08 14								
Datchet	d								07 47								08 17								
Windsor & Eton Riverside	a								07 51								08 21								
Egham	d			07 27						07 49			07 57					08 16	08 19				08 27		
Virginia Water	a			07 31						07 53			08 01						08 23				08 31		
	d			07 31						07 53			08 01						08 23				08 31		
Chertsey	d									07 59									08 29						
Addlestone	d									08 02									08 32						
Weybridge	a									08 07									08 38						
Byfleet & New Haw	d																								
West Byfleet	d																								
Woking	a																								
Longcross	d			07 35									08 05										08 35		
Sunningdale	d			07 37									08 07										08 37		
Ascot 3	d			07 43			07 53						08 13					08 26					08 43		08 53
Bagshot	d						07 59											08 32							08 59
Camberley	a						08 05											08 38							09 05
Frimley	d						08 13											08 43							09 13
Ash Vale	d						08 19											08 49							09 19
Aldershot	a						08 24											08 54							09 25
	d						08 38											09 08							09 38
Ash 5	d						08 45											09 15							09 45
Wanborough	d						08 48											09 18							09 48
Guildford	a						08 55											09 25							09 55
Martins Heron	d			07 47									08 17										08 47		
Bracknell	d			07 50									08 20										08 50		
Wokingham	d			07 57									08 27										08 57		
Winnersh	d			08 00									08 30										09 00		
Winnersh Triangle	d			08 02									08 32										09 02		
Earley	d			08 05									08 35										09 05		
Reading 7	a			08 10									08 40										09 10		

London - Hounslow, Richmond, Kingston, Windsor, Weybridge, Ascot, Guildford and Reading

		SW	SW	SW	SW 1	SW	SW	SW	SW	SW 1		SW	SW 1	SW	SW	SW	SW 1	SW	SW	SW		SW	SW 1	SW
London Waterloo 15 ⊖	d	07 52	07 58	08 03	08 07			08 10	08 15	08 20				08 22	08 28	08 33	08 37			08 40		08 43	08 50	
Vauxhall ⊖	d	07 56	08 02	08 07				08 14	08 19					08 26	08 32	08 37				08 44		08 47		
Queenstown Rd.(Battersea)	d	07 59		08 10				08 17	08 22					08 29		08 40				08 47		08 50		
Clapham Junction 10	d	08 02	08 08	08 13	08 16			08 20	08 25	08 28				08 32	08 38	08 43	08 45			08 50		08 55	08 58	
Wandsworth Town	d	08 05		08 16				08 23	08 28					08 35		08 46				08 53		08 58		
Putney	d	08 08	08 12	08 19				08 26	08 31					08 38	08 42	08 49				08 56		09 01		
Barnes	d	08 12		08 23				08 27	08 35					08 42		08 52				08 57		09 05		
Barnes Bridge	d	08 14						08 29						08 44						08 59				
Chiswick	d	08 17						08 32						08 47						09 02				
Kew Bridge	d	08 20						08 35						08 50						09 05				
Brentford	d	08 23						08 38						08 53						09 08				
Syon Lane	d	08 25						08 40						08 55						09 10				
Isleworth	d	08 27						08 42						08 57						09 12				
Hounslow	d	08 31						08 48						09 01						09 18				
Mortlake	d			08 25					08 37							08 54						09 07		
North Sheen	d			08 27			←		08 39			←				08 56			←			09 09		←
Richmond ⊖	d		08 18	08 30	08 24		08 30		08 42	08 36		08 42			08 48	08 59	08 54		08 59			09 12	09 06	09 12
St Margarets	d			→			08 32		→			08 44				→			09 01			→		09 14
Twickenham	a		08 21		08 28		08 34			08 40		08 46			08 51		08 57		09 03				09 10	09 16
	d		08 22		08 28		08 35			08 40		08 47			08 52		08 58		09 04				09 10	09 17
Strawberry Hill	d						08 38												09 07					
Fulwell	a																							
Teddington	a						08 41												09 10					
Hampton Wick	a						08 44												09 14					
Kingston	a						08 46												09 16					
Whitton	d		08 25			←		08a53				08a50			08 55			←		09a23				09a20
Feltham	d	08 36	08 29		08 34	08 36				08 46				09 06	08 59		09 04	09 06					09 16	
Ashford (Surrey)	d	→	08 33		08 38	08 40								→	09 03		09 08	09 10						
Staines	d		08 37		08 42	08 44				08 53					09 07		09 12	09 14					09 23	
Wraysbury	d		08 41												09 11									
Sunnymeads	d		08 44												09 14									
Datchet	d		08 47												09 17									
Windsor & Eton Riverside	a		08 51												09 21									
Egham	d				08 47	08 49				08 57							09 16	09 19					09 27	
Virginia Water	a				08 51	08 53				09 01							09 20	09 23					09 31	
	d				08 51	08 53				09 01							09 20	09 23					09 31	
Chertsey	d					08 59												09 29						
Addlestone	d					09 02												09 32						
Weybridge	a					09 08												09 37						
Byfleet & New Haw	d																							
West Byfleet	d																							
Woking	a																							
Longcross	d				08 54																			
Sunningdale	d				08 58					09 07							09 26						09 37	
Ascot 3	d				09 02					09 13			09 23				09 30						09 43	
Bagshot	d												09 29											
Camberley	a												09 35											
Frimley	d												09 43											
Ash Vale	d												09 49											
Aldershot	a												09 54											
	d												10 08											
Ash 5	d												10 15											
Wanborough	d												10 18											
Guildford	a												10 25											
Martins Heron	d				09 06					09 17							09 34						09 47	
Bracknell	d				09 10					09 20							09 38						09 50	
Wokingham	d				09 17					09 27							09 47						09 57	
Winnersh	d				09 20					09 30													10 00	
Winnersh Triangle	d				09 22					09 32													10 02	
Earley	d				09 25					09 35													10 05	
Reading 7	a				09 30					09 40							09 55						10 10	

Table 149

Mondays to Fridays
until 30 September

London - Hounslow, Richmond, Kingston, Windsor, Weybridge, Ascot, Guildford and Reading

		SW 1	SW	SW	SW	SW	SW		SW	SW 1	SW	SW 1	SW	SW	SW	SW	SW		SW	SW 1	SW	SW 1	SW	SW	SW
London Waterloo [15] ⊖	d		08 52	08 58		09 03	09 07		09 15	09 20			09 22	09 28		09 33	09 37		09 45	09 50			09 52	09 58	
Vauxhall ⊖	d		08 56	09 02		09 07	09 11		09 19				09 26	09 32		09 37	09 41		09 49				09 56	10 02	
Queenstown Rd.(Battersea)	d		08 59			09 10	09 14		09 22				09 29			09 40	09 44		09 52				09 59		
Clapham Junction [10]	d		09 02	09 08		09 13	09 17		09 25	09 28			09 32	09 38		09 43	09 47		09 55	09 58			10 02	10 08	
Wandsworth Town	d		09 05			09 16	09 20		09 28				09 35			09 46	09 50		09 58				10 05		
Putney	d		09 08	09 12		09 19	09 23		09 31				09 38	09 42		09 49	09 53		10 01				10 08	10 12	
Barnes	d		09 12			09 22	09 27		09 35				09 42			09 52	09 57		10 05				10 12		
Barnes Bridge	d		09 14				09 29						09 44				09 59						10 14		
Chiswick	d		09 17				09 32						09 47				10 02						10 17		
Kew Bridge	d		09 20				09 35						09 50				10 05						10 20		
Brentford	d		09 23				09 38						09 53				10 08						10 23		
Syon Lane	d		09 25				09 40						09 55				10 10						10 25		
Isleworth	d		09 27				09 42						09 57				10 12						10 27		
Hounslow	d		09 31				09 48						10 01				10 18						10 31		
Mortlake	d					09 24			09 37							09 54			10 07						
North Sheen	d					09 26			09 39		←					09 56			10 09		←				
Richmond ⊖	d			09 18		09 29			09 42	09 36	09 42			09 48		09 59			10 12	10 06	10 12			10 18	
St Margarets	d					09 31			→		09 44					10 01			→		10 14				
Twickenham	a			09 21		09 33				09 40	09 46			09 51		10 03				10 10	10 16			10 21	
	d			09 22		09 34				09 40	09 47			09 52		10 04				10 10	10 17			10 22	
Strawberry Hill	d					09 37										10 07									
Fulwell	a																								
Teddington	a					09 40										10 10									
Hampton Wick	a					09 44										10 14									
Kingston	a					09 46										10 16									
Whitton	d			09 25	←		09a53				09a50			09 55	←		10a26				10a20			10 25	←
Feltham	d		09 36	09 29	09 36					09 46			10 06	09 59	10 06					10 16			10 36	10 29	10 36
Ashford (Surrey)	d		→	09 33	09 40								→	10 03	10 10								→	10 33	10 40
Staines	d			09 37	09 44					09 53				10 07	10 14					10 23				10 37	10 44
Wraysbury	d			09 41										10 11										10 41	
Sunnymeads	d			09 44										10 14										10 44	
Datchet	d			09 47										10 17										10 47	
Windsor & Eton Riverside	a			09 51										10 21										10 51	
Egham	d				09 49					09 57					10 19					10 27					10 49
Virginia Water	a				09 53					10 01					10 23					10 31					10 53
	d				09 53					10 01					10 23					10 31					10 53
Chertsey	d				09 59										10 29										10 59
Addlestone	d				10 02										10 32										11 02
Weybridge	a				10 07										10 37										11 07
Byfleet & New Haw	d																								
West Byfleet	d																								
Woking	a																								
Longcross	d																								
Sunningdale	d									10 07										10 37					
Ascot [8]	d	09 53								10 13		10 23								10 43		10 53			
Bagshot	d	09 59										10 29										10 59			
Camberley	a	10 05										10 35										11 05			
Frimley	d	10 13										10 43										11 13			
Ash Vale	d	10 19										10 49										11 19			
Aldershot	a	10 24										10 54										11 24			
	d	10 38										11 08										11 38			
Ash [5]	d	10 45										11 15										11 45			
Wanborough	d	10 48										11 18										11 48			
Guildford	a	10 55										11 25										11 55			
Martins Heron	d									10 17										10 47					
Bracknell	d									10 20										10 50					
Wokingham	d									10 27										10 57					
Winnersh	d									10 30										11 00					
Winnersh Triangle	d									10 32										11 02					
Earley	d									10 35										11 05					
Reading [7]	a									10 40										11 10					

Table 149

Mondays to Fridays
until 30 September

London - Hounslow, Richmond, Kingston, Windsor, Weybridge, Ascot, Guildford and Reading

		SW	SW		SW	SW 1	SW	SW 1	SW	SW	SW	SW	SW		SW	SW 1	SW	SW 1	SW	SW	SW	SW	SW		SW
London Waterloo [15] ⊖	d	10 03	10 07		10 15	10 20			10 22	10 28		10 33	10 37		10 45	10 50			10 52	10 58		11 03	11 07		11 15
Vauxhall ⊖	d	10 07	10 11		10 19				10 26	10 32		10 37	10 41		10 49				10 56	11 02		11 07	11 11		11 19
Queenstown Rd.(Battersea)	d	10 10	10 14		10 22				10 29			10 40	10 44		10 52				10 59			11 10	11 14		11 22
Clapham Junction [10]	d	10 13	10 17		10 25	10 28			10 32	10 38		10 43	10 47		10 55	10 58			11 02	11 08		11 13	11 17		11 25
Wandsworth Town	d	10 16	10 20		10 28				10 35			10 46	10 50		10 58				11 05			11 16	11 20		11 28
Putney	d	10 19	10 23		10 31				10 38	10 42		10 49	10 53		11 01				11 08	11 12		11 19	11 23		11 31
Barnes	d	10 22	10 27		10 35				10 42			10 52	10 57		11 05				11 12			11 22	11 27		11 35
Barnes Bridge	d		10 29						10 44				10 59						11 14				11 29		
Chiswick	d		10 32						10 47				11 02						11 17				11 32		
Kew Bridge	d		10 35						10 50				11 05						11 20				11 35		
Brentford	d		10 38						10 53				11 08						11 23				11 38		
Syon Lane	d		10 40						10 55				11 10						11 25				11 40		
Isleworth	d		10 42						10 57				11 12						11 27				11 42		
Hounslow	d		10 48						11 01				11 18						11 31				11 48		
Mortlake	d	10 24			10 37							10 54			11 07							11 24			11 37
North Sheen	d	10 26			10 39		←					10 56			11 09		←					11 26			11 39
Richmond ⊖	d	10 29			10 42	10 36	10 42			10 48		10 59			11 12	11 06	11 12			11 18		11 29			11 42
St Margarets	d	10 31			→		10 44					11 01			→		11 14					11 31			→
Twickenham	a	10 33				10 40	10 46			10 51		11 03				11 10	11 16			11 21		11 33			
	d	10 34				10 40	10 47			10 52		11 04				11 10	11 17			11 22		11 34			
Strawberry Hill	d	10 37										11 07										11 37			
Fulwell	a																								
Teddington	a	10 40										11 10										11 40			
Hampton Wick	a	10 44										11 14										11 44			
Kingston	a	10 46										11 16										11 46			
Whitton	d		10a56				10a50			10 55	←		11a23				11a20			11 25	←		11a53		
Feltham	d					10 46			11 06	10 59	11 06					11 16			11 36	11 29	11 36				
Ashford (Surrey)	d								→	11 03	11 10								→	11 33	11 40				
Staines	d					10 53				11 07	11 14					11 23				11 37	11 44				
Wraysbury	d									11 11										11 41					
Sunnymeads	d									11 14										11 44					
Datchet	d									11 17										11 47					
Windsor & Eton Riverside	a									11 21										11 51					
Egham	d					10 57					11 19					11 27					11 49				
Virginia Water	a					11 01					11 23					11 31					11 53				
	d					11 01					11 23					11 31					11 53				
Chertsey	d										11 29										11 59				
Addlestone	d										11 32										12 02				
Weybridge	a										11 37										12 07				
Byfleet & New Haw	d																								
West Byfleet	d																								
Woking	a																								
Longcross	d																								
Sunningdale	d					11 07										11 37									
Ascot [8]	d					11 13		11 23								11 43		11 53							
Bagshot	d							11 29										11 59							
Camberley	a							11 35										12 05							
Frimley	d							11 43										12 13							
Ash Vale	d							11 49										12 19							
Aldershot	a							11 54										12 24							
	d							12 08										12 38							
Ash [5]	d							12 15										12 45							
Wanborough	d							12 18										12 48							
Guildford	a							12 25										12 55							
Martins Heron	d					11 17										11 47									
Bracknell	d					11 20										11 50									
Wokingham	d					11 27										11 57									
Winnersh	d					11 30										12 00									
Winnersh Triangle	d					11 32										12 02									
Earley	d					11 35										12 05									
Reading [7]	a					11 40										12 10									

London - Hounslow, Richmond, Kingston, Windsor, Weybridge, Ascot, Guildford and Reading

		SW [1]	SW	SW [1]	SW	SW	SW	SW	SW	SW	SW [1]	SW	SW [1]	SW	SW	SW	SW	SW	SW	SW [1]	SW	SW [1]	SW
London Waterloo [15] ⊖	d	11 20			11 22	11 28		11 33	11 37	11 45	11 50			11 52	11 58		12 03	12 07	12 15	12 20			12 22
Vauxhall ⊖	d				11 26	11 32		11 37	11 41	11 49				11 56	12 02		12 07	12 11	12 19				12 26
Queenstown Rd.(Battersea)	d				11 29			11 40	11 44	11 52				11 59			12 10	12 14	12 22				12 29
Clapham Junction [10]	d	11 28			11 32	11 38		11 43	11 47	11 55	11 58			12 02	12 08		12 13	12 17	12 25	12 28			12 32
Wandsworth Town	d				11 35			11 46	11 50	11 58				12 05			12 16	12 20	12 28				12 35
Putney	d				11 38	11 42		11 49	11 53	12 01				12 08	12 12		12 19	12 23	12 31				12 38
Barnes	d				11 42			11 52	11 57	12 05				12 12			12 22	12 27	12 35				12 42
Barnes Bridge	d				11 44				11 59					12 14				12 29					12 44
Chiswick	d				11 47				12 02					12 17				12 32					12 47
Kew Bridge	d				11 50				12 05					12 20				12 35					12 50
Brentford	d				11 53				12 08					12 23				12 38					12 53
Syon Lane	d				11 55				12 10					12 25				12 40					12 55
Isleworth	d				11 57				12 12					12 27				12 42					12 57
Hounslow	d				12 01				12 18					12 31				12 48					13 01
Mortlake	d							11 54		12 07							12 24		12 37				
North Sheen	d		←					11 56		12 09		←					12 26		12 39		←		
Richmond ⊖	d	11 36	11 42			11 48		11 59		12 12	12 06	12 12			12 18		12 29		12 42	12 36	12 42		
St Margarets	d		11 44					12 01		→		12 14					12 31		→		12 44		
Twickenham	a	11 40	11 46			11 51		12 03			12 10	12 16			12 21		12 33			12 40	12 46		
	d	11 40	11 47			11 52		12 04			12 10	12 17			12 22		12 34			12 40	12 47		
Strawberry Hill	d							12 07									12 37						
Fulwell	a																						
Teddington	a							12 10									12 40						
Hampton Wick	a							12 14									12 44						
Kingston	a							12 16									12 46						
Whitton	d		11a50			11 55	←		12a23			12a20			12 25	←		12a53			12a50		
Feltham	d	11 46			12 06	11 59	12 06				12 16			12 36	12 29	12 36				12 46			13 06
Ashford (Surrey)	d				→	12 03	12 10							→	12 33	12 40							→
Staines	d	11 53				12 07	12 14				12 23				12 37	12 44				12 53			
Wraysbury	d					12 11									12 41								
Sunnymeads	d					12 14									12 44								
Datchet	d					12 17									12 47								
Windsor & Eton Riverside	a					12 21									12 51								
Egham	d	11 57					12 19				12 27					12 49				12 57			
Virginia Water	a	12 01					12 23				12 31					12 53				13 01			
	d	12 01					12 23				12 31					12 53				13 01			
Chertsey	d						12 29									12 59							
Addlestone	d						12 32									13 02							
Weybridge	a						12 37									13 07							
Byfleet & New Haw	d																						
West Byfleet	d																						
Woking	a																						
Longcross	d																						
Sunningdale	d	12 07									12 37									13 07			
Ascot [3]	d	12 13		12 23							12 43		12 53							13 13		13 23	
Bagshot	d			12 29									12 59									13 29	
Camberley	a			12 35									13 05									13 35	
Frimley	d			12 43									13 13									13 43	
Ash Vale	d			12 49									13 19									13 49	
Aldershot	a			12 54									13 24									13 54	
	d			13 08									13 38									14 08	
Ash [5]	d			13 15									13 45									14 15	
Wanborough	d			13 18									13 48									14 18	
Guildford	a			13 25									13 55									14 25	
Martins Heron	d	12 17									12 47									13 17			
Bracknell	d	12 20									12 50									13 20			
Wokingham	d	12 27									12 57									13 27			
Winnersh	d	12 30									13 00									13 30			
Winnersh Triangle	d	12 32									13 02									13 32			
Earley	d	12 35									13 05									13 35			
Reading [7]	a	12 40									13 10									13 40			

Table 149

Mondays to Fridays
until 30 September

London - Hounslow, Richmond, Kingston, Windsor, Weybridge, Ascot, Guildford and Reading

		SW	SW	SW	SW	SW	SW [1]	SW	SW [1]	SW	SW	SW	SW	SW	SW	SW [1]	SW	SW [1]	SW	SW	SW	SW	SW
London Waterloo [15] ⊖	d	12 28		12 33	12 37	12 45	12 50			12 52	12 58		13 03	13 07	13 15	13 20			13 22	13 28		13 33	13 37
Vauxhall ⊖	d	12 32		12 37	12 41	12 49				12 56	13 02		13 07	13 11	13 19				13 26	13 32		13 37	13 41
Queenstown Rd.(Battersea)	d			12 40	12 44	12 52				12 59			13 10	13 14	13 22				13 29			13 40	13 44
Clapham Junction [10]	d	12 38		12 43	12 47	12 55	12 58			13 02	13 08		13 13	13 17	13 25	13 28			13 32	13 38		13 43	13 47
Wandsworth Town	d			12 46	12 50	12 58				13 05			13 16	13 20	13 28				13 35			13 46	13 50
Putney	d	12 42		12 49	12 53	13 01				13 08	13 12		13 19	13 23	13 31				13 38	13 42		13 49	13 53
Barnes	d			12 52	12 57	13 05				13 12			13 22	13 27	13 35				13 42			13 52	13 57
Barnes Bridge	d				12 59					13 14				13 29					13 44				13 59
Chiswick	d				13 02					13 17				13 32					13 47				14 02
Kew Bridge	d				13 05					13 20				13 35					13 50				14 05
Brentford	d				13 08					13 23				13 38					13 53				14 08
Syon Lane	d				13 10					13 25				13 40					13 55				14 10
Isleworth	d				13 12					13 27				13 42					13 57				14 12
Hounslow	d				13 18					13 31				13 48					14 01				14 18
Mortlake	d			12 54		13 07							13 24		13 37							13 54	
North Sheen	d			12 56		13 09		←					13 26		13 39		←					13 56	
Richmond ⊖	d	12 48		12 59		13 12	13 06	13 12			13 18		13 29		13 42	13 36	13 42			13 48		13 59	
St Margarets	d			13 01		→		13 14					13 31		→		13 44					14 01	
Twickenham	a	12 51		13 03			13 10	13 16			13 21		13 33			13 40	13 46			13 51		14 03	
	d	12 52		13 04			13 10	13 17			13 22		13 34			13 40	13 47			13 52		14 04	
Strawberry Hill	d			13 07									13 37									14 07	
Fulwell	a																						
Teddington	a			13 10									13 40									14 10	
Hampton Wick	a			13 14									13 44									14 14	
Kingston	a			13 16									13 46									14 16	
Whitton	d	12 55	←		13a23			13a20			13 25	←		13a53			13a50			13 55	←		14a23
Feltham	d	12 59	13 06				13 16			13 36	13 29	13 36				13 46			14 06	13 59	14 06		
Ashford (Surrey)	d	13 03	13 10							→	13 33	13 40							→	14 03	14 10		
Staines	d	13 07	13 14				13 23				13 37	13 44				13 53				14 07	14 14		
Wraysbury	d	13 11									13 41									14 11			
Sunnymeads	d	13 14									13 44									14 14			
Datchet	d	13 17									13 47									14 17			
Windsor & Eton Riverside	a	13 21									13 51									14 21			
Egham	d		13 19				13 27					13 49				13 57					14 19		
Virginia Water	a		13 23				13 31					13 53				14 01					14 23		
	d		13 23				13 31					13 53				14 01					14 23		
Chertsey	d		13 29									13 59									14 29		
Addlestone	d		13 32									14 02									14 32		
Weybridge	a		13 37									14 07									14 37		
Byfleet & New Haw	d																						
West Byfleet	d																						
Woking	a																						
Longcross	d						13 35																
Sunningdale	d						13 37									14 07							
Ascot [3]	d						13 43		13 53							14 13		14 23					
Bagshot	d								13 59									14 29					
Camberley	a								14 05									14 35					
Frimley	d								14 13									14 43					
Ash Vale	d								14 19									14 49					
Aldershot	a								14 24									14 54					
	d								14 38									15 08					
Ash [5]	d								14 45									15 15					
Wanborough	d								14 48									15 18					
Guildford	a								14 55									15 25					
Martins Heron	d						13 47									14 17							
Bracknell	d						13 50									14 20							
Wokingham	d						13 57									14 27							
Winnersh	d						14 00									14 30							
Winnersh Triangle	d						14 02									14 32							
Earley	d						14 05									14 35							
Reading [7]	a						14 10									14 40							

Table 149

Mondays to Fridays
until 30 September

London - Hounslow, Richmond, Kingston, Windsor, Weybridge, Ascot, Guildford and Reading

		SW	SW 1	SW	SW 1	SW	SW	SW	SW	SW	SW	SW 1	SW	SW 1	SW	SW	SW	SW	SW	SW	SW 1	SW
London Waterloo 15 ⊖	d	13 45	13 50			13 52	13 58		14 03	14 07	14 15	14 20			14 22	14 28		14 33	14 37	14 45	14 50	
Vauxhall ⊖	d	13 49				13 56	14 02		14 07	14 11	14 19				14 26	14 32		14 37	14 41	14 49		
Queenstown Rd.(Battersea)	d	13 52				13 59			14 10	14 14	14 22				14 29			14 40	14 44	14 52		
Clapham Junction 10	d	13 55	13 58			14 02	14 08		14 13	14 17	14 25	14 28			14 32	14 38		14 43	14 47	14 55	14 58	
Wandsworth Town	d	13 58				14 05			14 16	14 20	14 28				14 35			14 46	14 50	14 58		
Putney	d	14 01				14 08	14 12		14 19	14 23	14 31				14 38	14 42		14 49	14 53	15 01		
Barnes	d	14 05				14 12			14 22	14 27	14 35				14 42			14 52	14 57	15 05		
Barnes Bridge	d					14 14				14 29					14 44				14 59			
Chiswick	d					14 17				14 32					14 47				15 02			
Kew Bridge	d					14 20				14 35					14 50				15 05			
Brentford	d					14 23				14 38					14 53				15 08			
Syon Lane	d					14 25				14 40					14 55				15 10			
Isleworth	d					14 27				14 42					14 57				15 12			
Hounslow	d					14 31				14 48					15 01				15 18			
Mortlake	d	14 07							14 24		14 37							14 54		15 07		
North Sheen	d	14 09		←					14 26		14 39		←					14 56		15 09		←
Richmond ⊖	d	14 12	14 06	14 12			14 18		14 29		14 42	14 36	14 42			14 48		14 59		15 12	15 06	15 12
St Margarets	d	→		14 14					14 31		→		14 44					15 01		→		15 14
Twickenham	a		14 10	14 16			14 21		14 33			14 40	14 46			14 51		15 03			15 10	15 16
	d		14 10	14 17			14 22		14 34			14 40	14 47			14 52		15 04			15 10	15 17
Strawberry Hill	d								14 37									15 07				
Fulwell	a																					
Teddington	a								14 40									15 10				
Hampton Wick	a								14 44									15 14				
Kingston	a								14 46									15 16				
Whitton	d			14a20			14 25	←		14a53			14a50			14 55	←		15a23			15a20
Feltham	d		14 16			14 36	14 29	14 36				14 46			15 06	14 59	15 06				15 16	
Ashford (Surrey)	d					→	14 33	14 40							→	15 03	15 10					
Staines	d		14 23				14 37	14 44				14 53				15 07	15 14				15 23	
Wraysbury	d						14 41									15 11						
Sunnymeads	d						14 44									15 14						
Datchet	d						14 47									15 17						
Windsor & Eton Riverside	a						14 51									15 21						
Egham	d		14 27					14 49				14 57					15 19				15 27	
Virginia Water	a		14 31					14 53				15 01					15 23				15 31	
	d		14 31					14 53				15 01					15 23				15 31	
Chertsey	d							14 59									15 29					
Addlestone	d							15 02									15 32					
Weybridge	a							15 07									15 37					
Byfleet & New Haw	d																					
West Byfleet	d																					
Woking	a																					
Longcross	d																					
Sunningdale	d		14 37									15 07									15 37	
Ascot 8	d		14 43		14 53							15 13		15 23							15 43	
Bagshot	d				14 59									15 29								
Camberley	a				15 05									15 35								
Frimley	d				15 13									15 43								
Ash Vale	d				15 19									15 49								
Aldershot	a				15 24									15 54								
	d				15 38									16 08								
Ash 5	d				15 45									16 15								
Wanborough	d				15 48									16 18								
Guildford	a				15 55									16 25								
Martins Heron	d		14 47									15 17									15 47	
Bracknell	d		14 50									15 20									15 50	
Wokingham	d		14 57									15 27									15 57	
Winnersh	d		15 00									15 30									16 00	
Winnersh Triangle	d		15 02									15 32									16 02	
Earley	d		15 05									15 35									16 05	
Reading 7	a		15 10									15 40									16 10	

Table 149

Mondays to Fridays
until 30 September

London - Hounslow, Richmond, Kingston, Windsor, Weybridge, Ascot, Guildford and Reading

		SW 1	SW	SW	SW	SW	SW	SW	SW 1	SW	SW 1	SW	SW	SW	SW	SW	SW	SW 1	SW	SW 1	SW	SW	SW
London Waterloo 15 ⊖	d		14 52	14 58		15 03	15 07	15 15	15 20			15 22	15 28		15 33	15 37	15 45	15 50			15 52	15 58	16 01
Vauxhall ⊖	d		14 56	15 02		15 07	15 11	15 19				15 26	15 32		15 37	15 41	15 49				15 56	16 02	16 05
Queenstown Rd.(Battersea)	d		14 59			15 10	15 14	15 22				15 29			15 40	15 44	15 52				15 59		16 08
Clapham Junction 10	d		15 02	15 08		15 13	15 17	15 25	15 28			15 32	15 38		15 43	15 47	15 55	15 58			16 02	16 08	16 11
Wandsworth Town	d		15 05			15 16	15 20	15 28				15 35			15 46	15 50	15 58				16 05		16 14
Putney	d		15 08	15 12		15 19	15 23	15 31				15 38	15 42		15 49	15 53	16 01				16 08	16 12	16 17
Barnes	d		15 12			15 22	15 27	15 35				15 42			15 52	15 57	16 05				16 12		16 22
Barnes Bridge	d		15 14				15 29					15 44				15 59					16 14		
Chiswick	d		15 17				15 32					15 47				16 02					16 17		
Kew Bridge	d		15 20				15 35					15 50				16 05					16 20		
Brentford	d		15 23				15 38					15 53				16 08					16 23		
Syon Lane	d		15 25				15 40					15 55				16 10					16 25		
Isleworth	d		15 27				15 42					15 57				16 12					16 27		
Hounslow	d		15 31				15 48					16 01				16 18					16 31		
Mortlake	d					15 24		15 37							15 54		16 07						16 24
North Sheen	d					15 26		15 39		←					15 56		16 09		←				16 26
Richmond ⊖	d			15 18		15 29		15 42	15 36	15 42			15 48		15 59		16 12	16 06	16 12			16 18	16 29
St Margarets	d					15 31		→		15 44					16 01		→		16 14				→
Twickenham	a			15 21		15 33			15 40	15 46			15 51		16 03			16 10	16 16			16 21	
	d			15 22		15 34			15 40	15 47			15 52		16 04			16 10	16 17			16 22	
Strawberry Hill	d					15 37									16 07								
Fulwell	a																						
Teddington	a					15 40									16 10								
Hampton Wick	a					15 44									16 14								
Kingston	a					15 46									16 16								
Whitton	d			15 25	←		15a53			15a50			15 55	←		16a23			16a20			16 25	
Feltham	d		15 36	15 29	15 36				15 46			16 06	15 59	16 06				16 16			16 36	16 29	
Ashford (Surrey)	d		→	15 33	15 40							→	16 03	16 10							→	16 33	
Staines	d			15 37	15 44				15 53				16 07	16 14				16 23				16 37	
Wraysbury	d			15 41									16 11									16 41	
Sunnymeads	d			15 44									16 14									16 44	
Datchet	d			15 47									16 17									16 47	
Windsor & Eton Riverside	a			15 51									16 21									16 51	
Egham	d				15 49				15 57					16 19				16 27					
Virginia Water	a				15 53				16 01					16 23				16 31					
	d				15 53				16 01					16 23				16 31					
Chertsey	d				15 59									16 29									
Addlestone	d				16 02									16 32									
Weybridge	a				16 07									16 37									
Byfleet & New Haw	d																						
West Byfleet	d																						
Woking	a																						
Longcross	d																						
Sunningdale	d								16 07									16 37					
Ascot 8	d	15 53							16 13		16 23							16 43		16 53			
Bagshot	d	15 59									16 29									16 59			
Camberley	a	16 05									16 35									17 05			
Frimley	d	16 13									16 43									17 13			
Ash Vale	d	16 19									16 49									17 19			
Aldershot	a	16 24									16 54									17 24			
	d	16 38									17 09									17 38			
Ash 5	d	16 45									17 15									17 45			
Wanborough	d	16 48									17 18									17 48			
Guildford	a	16 55									17 25									17 55			
Martins Heron	d								16 17									16 47					
Bracknell	d								16 20									16 50					
Wokingham	d								16 27									16 57					
Winnersh	d								16 30									17 00					
Winnersh Triangle	d								16 32									17 02					
Earley	d								16 35									17 05					
Reading 7	a								16 40									17 10					

London - Hounslow, Richmond, Kingston, Windsor, Weybridge, Ascot, Guildford and Reading

		SW	SW		SW	SW	SW	SW	SW	SW	SW	SW	SW		SW	SW	SW	SW	SW	SW	SW	SW	SW		SW
		◇ 1						◇ 1		1	◇	◇			◇ 1	◇				◇ 1		◇	◇		
London Waterloo 15 ⊖	d	16 05				16 07	16 15	16 20			16 22	16 28	16 31		16 35			16 37	16 45	16 50		16 52	16 58		17 01
Vauxhall ⊖	d	16 09				16 11	16 19				16 26	16 32	16 35		16 39			16 41	16 49			16 56	17 02		17 05
Queenstown Rd.(Battersea)	d					16 14	16 22				16 29		16 38					16 44	16 52			16 59			17 08
Clapham Junction 10	d	16 15				16 17	16 25	16 28			16 32	16 38	16 41		16 45			16 47	16 55	16 58		17 02	17 08		17 11
Wandsworth Town	d					16 20	16 28				16 35		16 44					16 50	16 58			17 05			17 14
Putney	d					16 23	16 31				16 38	16 42	16 47					16 53	17 01			17 08	17 12		17 17
Barnes	d					16 27	16 35				16 42		16 52					16 57	17 05			17 12			17 22
Barnes Bridge	d					16 29					16 44							16 59				17 14			
Chiswick	d					16 32					16 47							17 02				17 17			
Kew Bridge	d					16 35					16 50							17 05				17 20			
Brentford	d					16 38					16 53							17 08				17 23			
Syon Lane	d					16 40					16 55							17 10				17 25			
Isleworth	d					16 42					16 57							17 12				17 27			
Hounslow	d					16 48					17 01							17 18				17 31			
Mortlake	d						16 37						16 54						17 07						17 24
North Sheen	d				←		16 39		←				16 56				←		17 09		←				17 26
Richmond ⊖	d	16 23			16 29		16 42	16 36	16 42			16 48	16 59		16 53		16 59		17 12	17 06	17 12		17 18		17 29
St Margarets	d				16 31		→		16 44				→				17 01		→		17 14				→
Twickenham	a	16 27			16 33			16 40	16 46			16 51			16 57		17 03			17 10	17 16		17 21		
	d	16 27			16 34			16 40	16 47			16 52			16 57		17 04			17 10	17 17		17 22		
Strawberry Hill	d				16 37												17 07								
Fulwell	a																								
Teddington	a				16 42												17 12								
Hampton Wick	a				16 46												17 16								
Kingston	a				16 48												17 18								
Whitton	d		←			16a53			16a50			16 55				←		17a23			17a20		17 25		
Feltham	d	16 33	16 36					16 46			17 06	16 59			17 03	17 06				17 16		17 36	17 29		
Ashford (Surrey)	d	16 37	16 40								→	17 03			17 07	17 10						→	17 33		
Staines	d	16 41	16 44					16 53				17 07			17 11	17 14				17 23			17 37		
Wraysbury	d											17 11											17 41		
Sunnymeads	d											17 14											17 44		
Datchet	d											17 17											17 47		
Windsor & Eton Riverside	a											17 23											17 53		
Egham	d	16 46	16 49					16 57							17 16	17 19				17 27					
Virginia Water	a	16 50	16 53					17 01							17 20	17 23				17 31					
	d	16 50	16 53					17 01							17 20	17 23				17 31					
Chertsey	d		16 59													17 29									
Addlestone	d		17 02													17 32									
Weybridge	a		17 07													17 40									
Byfleet & New Haw	d																								
West Byfleet	d																								
Woking	a																								
Longcross	d														17 23										
Sunningdale	d	16 55						17 07							17 27					17 37					
Ascot 3	d	17 00						17 13		17 23					17 31					17 43					
Bagshot	d									17 29															
Camberley	a									17 35															
Frimley	d									17 43															
Ash Vale	d									17 49															
Aldershot	a									17 54															
	d									18 08															
Ash 5	d									18 15															
Wanborough	d									18 18															
Guildford	a									18 25															
Martins Heron	d	17 04						17 17							17 35					17 47					
Bracknell	d	17 07						17 20							17 39					17 50					
Wokingham	d	17 17						17 27							17 47					17 57					
Winnersh	d							17 30												18 00					
Winnersh Triangle	d							17 32												18 02					
Earley	d							17 35												18 05					
Reading 7	a	17 27						17 42							17 58					18 12					

London - Hounslow, Richmond, Kingston, Windsor, Weybridge, Ascot, Guildford and Reading

		SW	SW	SW	SW	SW	SW	SW	SW		SW	SW	SW	SW	SW	SW	SW	SW	SW		SW	SW	SW	SW	SW
		◇ 1	◇					◇ 1			◇	1	◇	1	1		◇ 1	◇						◇ 1	
London Waterloo 15 ⊖	d	17 05			17 07	17 13	17 15	17 20			17 22	17 25	17 28			17 31	17 35				17 37	17 43	17 45	17 50	
Vauxhall ⊖	d	17 09			17 11	17 17	17 19				17 26		17 32			17 35	17 39				17 41	17 47	17 49		
Queenstown Rd.(Battersea)	d				17 14		17 22				17 29					17 38					17 44		17 52		
Clapham Junction 10	d	17 15			17 17	17 23	17 25	17 28			17 32		17 38			17 41	17 45				17 47	17 53	17 55	17 58	
Wandsworth Town	d				17 20		17 28				17 35					17 44					17 50		17 58		
Putney	d				17 23	17 27	17 31				17 38		17 42			17 47					17 53	17 57	18 01		
Barnes	d				17 27		17 35				17 42					17 52					17 57		18 05		
Barnes Bridge	d				17 29						17 44										17 59				
Chiswick	d				17 32						17 47										18 02				
Kew Bridge	d				17 35						17 50										18 05				
Brentford	d				17 38						17 53										18 08				
Syon Lane	d				17 40						17 55										18 10				
Isleworth	d				17 42						17 57										18 12				
Hounslow	d				17 48						18 01										18 18				
Mortlake	d						17 37									17 54							18 07		
North Sheen	d			←			17 39		←							17 56			←				18 09		←
Richmond ⊖	d	17 23		17 29		17 33	17 42	17 36	17 42				17 48			17 59	17 53		17 59			18 03	18 12	18 06	18 12
St Margarets	d			17 31			→		17 44							→			18 01				→		18 14
Twickenham	a	17 27		17 33		17 37		17 40	17 46				17 51				17 57		18 03			18 07		18 10	18 16
	d	17 27		17 34		17 37		17 40	17 47				17 52				17 57		18 04			18 07		18 10	18 17
Strawberry Hill	d			17 37		17 41													18 07			18 11			
Fulwell	a																					18 13			
Teddington	a			17 42		17 46													18 12						
Hampton Wick	a			17 46		17 54													18 16						
Kingston	a			17 48		17 56													18 18						
Whitton	d		←		17a53				17a50				17 55					←			18a23				18a20
Feltham	d	17 33	17 36					17 46			18 06		17 59				18 03	18 06						18 16	
Ashford (Surrey)	d	17 37	17 40								→		18 03				18 07	18 10							
Staines	d	17 41	17 44					17 53					18 07				18 11	18 14						18 23	
Wraysbury	d												18 11												
Sunnymeads	d												18 14												
Datchet	d												18 17												
Windsor & Eton Riverside	a												18 23												
Egham	d	17 46	17 49					17 57									18 16	18 19						18 27	
Virginia Water	a	17 50	17 53					18 01									18 20	18 23						18 31	
	d	17 50	17 53					18 01									18 20	18 23						18 31	
Chertsey	d		17 59															18 29							
Addlestone	d		18 02															18 32							
Weybridge	a		18 10															18 40							
Byfleet & New Haw	d																								
West Byfleet	d																								
Woking	a											17 50													
Longcross	d																							18 35	
Sunningdale	d	17 55						18 07									18 25							18 37	
Ascot 3	d	18 00						18 13							18 23		18 30							18 43	
Bagshot	d	18 06													18 29										
Camberley	a	18 12													18 35										
Frimley	d	18 17													18 43										
Ash Vale	d	18 24										18 03			18 49										
Aldershot	a	18 31										18 08			18 54										
	d													18 38	19 08										
Ash 5	d													18 45	19 15										
Wanborough	d													18 48	19 18										
Guildford	a													18 55	19 25										
Martins Heron	d							18 17									18 34							18 47	
Bracknell	d							18 20									18 37							18 50	
Wokingham	d							18 27									18 47							18 57	
Winnersh	d							18 30																19 00	
Winnersh Triangle	d							18 32																19 02	
Earley	d							18 35																19 05	
Reading 7	a							18 42									18 57							19 12	

Table 149

Mondays to Fridays

until 30 September

London - Hounslow, Richmond, Kingston, Windsor, Weybridge, Ascot, Guildford and Reading

Station		SW ◇	SW ◇	SW	SW ◇ 1	SW ◇	SW	SW	SW	SW	SW ◇ 1	SW	SW ◇	SW 1	SW ◇	SW 1	SW 1	SW	SW ◇ 1	SW ◇	SW	SW	SW
London Waterloo 15 ⊖	d	17 52	17 58	18 01	18 05			18 07	18 13	18 15	18 20		18 22	18 25	18 28			18 31	18 35			18 37	18 43
Vauxhall ⊖	d	17 56	18 02	18 05	18 09			18 11	18 17	18 19			18 26		18 32			18 35	18 39			18 41	18 47
Queenstown Rd.(Battersea)	d	17 59		18 08				18 14		18 22			18 29					18 38				18 44	
Clapham Junction 10	d	18 02	18 08	18 11	18 15			18 17	18 23	18 25	18 28		18 32		18 38			18 41	18 45			18 47	18 53
Wandsworth Town	d	18 05		18 14				18 20		18 28			18 35					18 44				18 50	
Putney	d	18 08	18 12	18 17				18 23	18 27	18 31			18 38		18 42			18 47				18 53	18 57
Barnes	d	18 12		18 22				18 27		18 35			18 42					18 52				18 57	
Barnes Bridge	d	18 14						18 29					18 44									18 59	
Chiswick	d	18 17						18 32					18 47									19 02	
Kew Bridge	d	18 20						18 35					18 50									19 05	
Brentford	d	18 23						18 38					18 53									19 08	
Syon Lane	d	18 25						18 40					18 55									19 10	
Isleworth	d	18 27						18 42					18 57									19 12	
Hounslow	d	18 31						18 48					19 01									19 18	
Mortlake	d			18 24						18 37								18 54					
North Sheen	d			18 26			←			18 39		←						18 56			←		
Richmond ⊖	d		18 18	18 29	18 23		18 29		18 33	18 42	18 36	18 42			18 48			18 59	18 53		18 59		19 03
St Margarets	d			→			18 31			→		18 44						→			19 01		
Twickenham	a		18 21		18 27		18 33		18 37		18 40	18 46			18 51				18 57		19 03		19 07
	d		18 22		18 27		18 34		18 37		18 40	18 47			18 52				18 57		19 04		19 07
Strawberry Hill	d						18 37		18 41												19 07		19 11
Fulwell	a								18 43														19 13
Teddington	a						18 42														19 12		
Hampton Wick	a						18 46														19 16		
Kingston	a						18 48														19 18		
Whitton	d		18 25			←		18a53				18a50			18 55					←		19a23	
Feltham	d	18 36	18 29		18 33	18 36					18 46		19 06		18 59				19 03	19 06			
Ashford (Surrey)	d	→	18 33		18 37	18 40							→		19 03				19 07	19 10			
Staines	d		18 37		18 41	18 44					18 53				19 07				19 11	19 14			
Wraysbury	d		18 41												19 11								
Sunnymeads	d		18 44												19 14								
Datchet	d		18 47												19 17								
Windsor & Eton Riverside	a		18 53												19 23								
Egham	d				18 46	18 49					18 57								19 16	19 19			
Virginia Water	a				18 50	18 53					19 01								19 20	19 23			
	d				18 50	18 53					19 01								19 20	19 23			
Chertsey	d					18 59														19 29			
Addlestone	d					19 02														19 32			
Weybridge	a					19 10														19 40			
Byfleet & New Haw	d																						
West Byfleet	d																						
Woking	a													18 52									
Longcross	d																						
Sunningdale	d				18 55						19 07								19 25				
Ascot 3	d				19 02						19 13						19 23		19 30				
Bagshot	d				19 08												19 29						
Camberley	a				19 14												19 35						
Frimley	d				19 19												19 43						
Ash Vale	d				19 26									19 05			19 49						
Aldershot	a				19 34									19 10			19 54						
	d															19 38	20 08						
Ash 5	d															19 45	20 15						
Wanborough	d															19 48	20 18						
Guildford	a															19 55	20 25						
Martins Heron	d										19 17								19 34				
Bracknell	d										19 20								19 37				
Wokingham	d										19 27								19 47				
Winnersh	d										19 30												
Winnersh Triangle	d										19 32												
Earley	d										19 35												
Reading 7	a										19 42								19 57				

Table 149

Mondays to Fridays

until 30 September

London - Hounslow, Richmond, Kingston, Windsor, Weybridge, Ascot, Guildford and Reading

Station		SW	SW ◇ 1	SW	SW 1	SW ◇	SW ◇	SW	SW 1	SW ◇	SW	SW	SW	SW 1	SW	SW 1	SW	SW	SW	SW	SW	SW
London Waterloo 15 ⊖	d	18 45	18 50			18 52	18 58	19 01	19 05			19 07	19 15	19 20			19 22	19 28		19 33	19 37	19 45
Vauxhall ⊖	d	18 49				18 56	19 02	19 05	19 09			19 11	19 19				19 26	19 32		19 37	19 41	19 49
Queenstown Rd.(Battersea)	d	18 52				18 59		19 08				19 14	19 22				19 29			19 40	19 44	19 52
Clapham Junction 10	d	18 55	18 58			19 02	19 08	19 11	19 15			19 17	19 25	19 28			19 32	19 38		19 43	19 47	19 55
Wandsworth Town	d	18 58				19 05		19 14				19 20	19 28				19 35			19 46	19 50	19 58
Putney	d	19 01				19 08	19 12	19 17				19 23	19 31				19 38	19 42		19 49	19 53	20 01
Barnes	d	19 05				19 12		19 22				19 27	19 35				19 42			19 52	19 57	20 05
Barnes Bridge	d					19 14						19 29					19 44				19 59	
Chiswick	d					19 17						19 32					19 47				20 02	
Kew Bridge	d					19 20						19 35					19 50				20 05	
Brentford	d					19 23						19 38					19 53				20 08	
Syon Lane	d					19 25						19 40					19 55				20 10	
Isleworth	d					19 27						19 42					19 57				20 12	
Hounslow	d					19 31						19 48					20 01				20 18	
Mortlake	d	19 07						19 24					19 37							19 54		20 07
North Sheen	d	19 09		←				19 26			←		19 39		←					19 56		20 09
Richmond ⊖	d	19 12	19 06	19 12			19 18	19 29	19 23		19 29		19 42	19 36	19 42			19 48		19 59		20 12
St Margarets	d	→		19 14				→			19 31		→		19 44					20 01		→
Twickenham	a		19 10	19 16			19 21		19 27		19 33			19 40	19 46			19 51		20 03		
	d		19 10	19 17			19 22		19 27		19 34			19 40	19 47			19 52		20 04		
Strawberry Hill	d										19 37									20 07		
Fulwell	a																					
Teddington	a										19 42									20 10		
Hampton Wick	a										19 46									20 14		
Kingston	a										19 48									20 16		
Whitton	d			19a20			19 25			←		19a53			19a50			19 55	←		20a23	
Feltham	d		19 16			19 36	19 29		19 33	19 36				19 46			20 06	19 59	20 06			
Ashford (Surrey)	d					→	19 33		19 37	19 40							→	20 03	20 10			
Staines	d		19 23				19 37		19 41	19 44				19 53				20 07	20 14			
Wraysbury	d						19 41											20 11				
Sunnymeads	d						19 44											20 14				
Datchet	d						19 47											20 17				
Windsor & Eton Riverside	a						19 53											20 21				
Egham	d		19 27						19 46	19 49				19 57					20 19			
Virginia Water	a		19 31						19 50	19 53				20 01					20 23			
	d		19 31						19 50	19 53				20 01					20 23			
Chertsey	d									19 59									20 29			
Addlestone	d									20 02									20 32			
Weybridge	a									20 10									20 37			
Byfleet & New Haw	d																					
West Byfleet	d																					
Woking	a																					
Longcross	d																					
Sunningdale	d		19 37						19 55					20 07								
Ascot 3	d		19 43		19 53				20 00					20 13		20 23						
Bagshot	d				19 59											20 29						
Camberley	a				20 05											20 35						
Frimley	d				20 13											20 43						
Ash Vale	d				20 19											20 49						
Aldershot	a				20 24											20 54						
	d				20 38											21 08						
Ash 5	d				20 45											21 15						
Wanborough	d				20 48											21 18						
Guildford	a				20 55											21 25						
Martins Heron	d		19 47						20 04					20 17								
Bracknell	d		19 50						20 07					20 20								
Wokingham	d		19 57						20 17					20 27								
Winnersh	d		20 00											20 30								
Winnersh Triangle	d		20 02											20 32								
Earley	d		20 05											20 35								
Reading 7	a		20 12						20 25					20 40								

London - Hounslow, Richmond, Kingston, Windsor, Weybridge, Ascot, Guildford and Reading

		SW ■	SW	SW ■	SW	SW	SW	SW	SW	SW	SW ■	SW	SW ■	SW ■	SW	SW	SW	SW	SW	SW ■	SW	SW
London Waterloo [15]	⊖ d	19 50			19 52	19 58		20 03	20 07	20 15	20 20				20 22	20 28	20 33	20 37	20 45	20 50		20 52
Vauxhall	⊖ d				19 56	20 02		20 07	20 11	20 19					20 26	20 32	20 37	20 41	20 49			20 56
Queenstown Rd.(Battersea)	d				19 59			20 10	20 14	20 22					20 29		20 40	20 44	20 52			20 59
Clapham Junction [10]	d	19 58			20 02	20 08		20 13	20 17	20 25	20 28				20 32	20 38	20 43	20 47	20 55	20 58		21 02
Wandsworth Town	d				20 05			20 16	20 20	20 28					20 35		20 46	20 50	20 58			21 05
Putney	d				20 08	20 12		20 19	20 23	20 31					20 38	20 42	20 49	20 53	21 01			21 08
Barnes	d				20 12			20 22	20 27	20 35					20 42		20 52	20 57	21 05			21 12
Barnes Bridge	d				20 14				20 29						20 44			20 59				21 14
Chiswick	d				20 17				20 32						20 47			21 02				21 17
Kew Bridge	d				20 20				20 35						20 50			21 05				21 20
Brentford	d				20 23				20 38						20 53			21 08				21 23
Syon Lane	d				20 25				20 40						20 55			21 10				21 25
Isleworth	d				20 27				20 42						20 57			21 12				21 27
Hounslow	d				20 31				20 48						21 01			21 18				21 31
Mortlake	d							20 24		20 37							20 54		21 07			
North Sheen	d		←					20 26		20 39		←					20 56		21 09		←	
Richmond	⊖ d	20 06	20 12			20 18		20 29		20 42	20 36	20 42				20 48	20 59		21 12	21 06	21 12	
St Margarets	d		20 14					20 31		→		20 44					21 01		→		21 14	
Twickenham	a	20 10	20 16			20 21		20 33			20 40	20 46				20 51	21 03			21 10	21 16	
	d	20 10	20 17			20 22		20 34			20 40	20 47				20 52	21 04			21 10	21 17	
Strawberry Hill	d							20 37									21 07					
Fulwell	a																					
Teddington	a							20 40									21 10					
Hampton Wick	a							20 44									21 14					
Kingston	a							20 46									21 16					
Whitton	d		20a20			20 25	←		20a53			20a50				20 55	←	21a23			21a20	
Feltham	d	20 16			20 36	20 29	20 36				20 46				21 06	20 59	21 06			21 16		21 36
Ashford (Surrey)	d				→	20 33	20 40								→	21 03	21 10					→
Staines	d	20 23				20 37	20 44				20 53					21 07	21 14			21 23		
Wraysbury	d					20 41										21 11						
Sunnymeads	d					20 44										21 14						
Datchet	d					20 47										21 17						
Windsor & Eton Riverside	a					20 51										21 21						
Egham	d	20 27					20 49				20 57						21 19			21 27		
Virginia Water	a	20 31					20 53				21 01						21 23			21 31		
	d	20 31					20 53				21 01						21 23			21 31		
Chertsey	d						20 59										21 29					
Addlestone	d						21 02										21 32					
Weybridge	a						21 07										21 37					
Byfleet & New Haw	d																					
West Byfleet	d																					
Woking	a																					
Longcross	d																					
Sunningdale	d	20 37									21 07									21 37		
Ascot [3]	d	20 43		20 53							21 13		21 23							21 43		
Bagshot	d			20 59									21 29									
Camberley	a			21 05									21 35									
Frimley	d			21 13									21 43									
Ash Vale	d			21 19									21 49									
Aldershot	a			21 24									21 54									
	d			21 38									22 08	22 38								
Ash [8]	d			21 45									22 15	22 45								
Wanborough	d			21 48									22 18	22 48								
Guildford	a			21 55									22 25	22 55								
Martins Heron	d	20 47									21 17									21 47		
Bracknell	d	20 50									21 20									21 50		
Wokingham	d	20 57									21 27									21 57		
Winnersh	d	21 00									21 30									22 00		
Winnersh Triangle	d	21 02									21 32									22 02		
Earley	d	21 05									21 35									22 05		
Reading [7]	a	21 10									21 40									22 10		

London - Hounslow, Richmond, Kingston, Windsor, Weybridge, Ascot, Guildford and Reading

		SW	SW	SW	SW	SW	SW ■	SW	SW ■	SW	SW	SW	SW	SW	SW	SW ■	SW	SW	SW	SW	SW	SW ■
London Waterloo [15]	⊖ d	20 58		21 03	21 07	21 15	21 20			21 22	21 28		21 33	21 37	21 45	21 50		21 52	21 58		22 03	22 20
Vauxhall	⊖ d	21 02		21 07	21 11	21 19				21 26	21 32		21 37	21 41	21 49			21 56	22 02		22 07	
Queenstown Rd.(Battersea)	d			21 10	21 14	21 22				21 29			21 40	21 44	21 52			21 59			22 10	
Clapham Junction [10]	d	21 08		21 13	21 17	21 25	21 28			21 32	21 38		21 43	21 47	21 55	21 58		22 02	22 08		22 13	22 28
Wandsworth Town	d			21 16	21 20	21 28				21 35			21 46	21 50	21 58			22 05			22 16	
Putney	d	21 12		21 19	21 23	21 31				21 38	21 42		21 49	21 53	22 01			22 08	22 12		22 19	
Barnes	d			21 22	21 27	21 35				21 42			21 52	21 57	22 05			22 12			22 22	
Barnes Bridge	d				21 29					21 44				21 59				22 14				
Chiswick	d				21 32					21 47				22 02				22 17				
Kew Bridge	d				21 35					21 50				22 05				22 20				
Brentford	d				21 38					21 53				22 08				22 23				
Syon Lane	d				21 40					21 55				22 10				22 25				
Isleworth	d				21 42					21 57				22 12				22 27				
Hounslow	d				21 48					22 01				22 18				22 31				
Mortlake	d			21 24		21 37							21 54		22 07						22 24	
North Sheen	d			21 26		21 39		←					21 56		22 09		←				22 26	
Richmond	⊖ d	21 18		21 29		21 42	21 36	21 42			21 48		21 59		22 12	22 06	22 12		22 18		22 29	22 36
St Margarets	d			21 31		→		21 44					22 01		→		22 14				22 31	
Twickenham	a	21 21		21 33			21 40	21 46			21 51		22 03			22 10	22 16		22 21		22 33	22 40
	d	21 22		21 34			21 40	21 47			21 52		22 04			22 10			22 22		22 34	22 40
Strawberry Hill	d			21 37									22 07								22 37	
Fulwell	a																					
Teddington	a			21 40									22 10								22 40	
Hampton Wick	a			21 44									22 14								22 44	
Kingston	a			21 46									22 16								22 46	
Whitton	d	21 25	←		21a53			21a50			21 55	←		22a23					22 25	←		
Feltham	d	21 29	21 36				21 46			22 06	21 59	22 06				22 16		22 36	22 29	22 36		22 46
Ashford (Surrey)	d	21 33	21 40							→	22 03	22 10						→	22 33	22 40		
Staines	d	21 37	21 44				21 53				22 07	22 14				22 23			22 37	22 44		22 53
Wraysbury	d	21 41									22 11								22 41			
Sunnymeads	d	21 44									22 14								22 44			
Datchet	d	21 47									22 17								22 47			
Windsor & Eton Riverside	a	21 51									22 21								22 51			
Egham	d		21 49				21 57					22 19				22 27				22 49		22 57
Virginia Water	a		21 53				22 01					22 23				22 31				22 53		23 01
	d		21 53				22 01					22 23				22 31				22 53		23 01
Chertsey	d		21 59									22 29								22 59		
Addlestone	d		22 02									22 32								23 02		
Weybridge	a		22 07									22 37								23 07		
Byfleet & New Haw	d																					
West Byfleet	d																					
Woking	a																					
Longcross	d																					
Sunningdale	d						22 07									22 37						23 07
Ascot [3]	d						22 13		22 23							22 43						23 13
Bagshot	d								22 29													
Camberley	a								22 35													
Frimley	d								22 43													
Ash Vale	d								22 49													
Aldershot	a								22 54													
	d								23 08													
Ash [8]	d								23 15													
Wanborough	d								23 18													
Guildford	a								23 25													
Martins Heron	d						22 17									22 47						23 17
Bracknell	d						22 20									22 50						23 20
Wokingham	d						22 27									22 57						23 27
Winnersh	d						22 30									23 00						23 30
Winnersh Triangle	d						22 32									23 02						23 32
Earley	d						22 35									23 05						23 35
Reading [7]	a						22 40									23 10						23 40

Table 149

Mondays to Fridays
until 30 September

London - Hounslow, Richmond, Kingston, Windsor, Weybridge, Ascot, Guildford and Reading

		SW ■	SW	SW	SW	SW	SW ■	SW	SW	SW	SW	SW	SW ■	SW	SW	SW	SW	SW	SW	SW	SW
London Waterloo 15 ⊖	d		22 22	22 28		22 33	22 50	22 52	22 58		23 03	23 13	23 20	23 22	23 33	23 38			23 52	23 58	
Vauxhall ⊖	d		22 26	22 32		22 37		22 56	23 02		23 07	23 17		23 26	23 37				23 56	00 02	
Queenstown Rd.(Battersea)	d		22 29			22 40		22 59			23 10			23 29	23 40				23 59		
Clapham Junction 10	d		22 32	22 38		22 43	22 58	23 02	23 08		23 13	23 23	23 28	23 32	23 43	23 46			00 02	00 08	
Wandsworth Town	d		22 35			22 46		23 05			23 16			23 35	23 46				00 05		
Putney	d		22 38	22 42		22 49		23 08	23 12		23 19	23 27		23 38	23 49				00 08	00 12	
Barnes	d		22 42			22 52		23 12			23 22			23 42	23 52				00 12		
Barnes Bridge	d		22 44					23 14						23 44					00 14		
Chiswick	d		22 47					23 17						23 47					00 17		
Kew Bridge	d		22 50					23 20						23 50					00 20		
Brentford	d		22 53					23 23						23 53					00 23		
Syon Lane	d		22 55					23 25						23 55					00 25		
Isleworth	d		22 57					23 27						23 57					00 27		
Hounslow	d		23 01					23 31						00 01					00 31		
Mortlake	d					22 54					23 24				23 54						
North Sheen	d					22 56					23 26				23 56			←			
Richmond ⊖	d			22 48		22 59	23 06		23 18		23 29	23 33	23 37		23 59	23 54		23 59		00 18	
St Margarets	d					23 01					23 31				→			00 01			
Twickenham	a			22 51		23 03	23 10		23 21		23 33	23 36	23 41			23 58		00 03		00 21	
	d			22 52		23 04	23 10		23 22		23 34	23 37	23 41			23 58		00 04		00 22	
Strawberry Hill	d					23 07					23 37							00 07			
Fulwell	a																				
Teddington	a					23 10					23 40							00 11			
Hampton Wick	a					23 14					23 44							00 14			
Kingston	a					23 16					23 46							00 16			
Whitton	d			22 55	←				23 25	←		23 40					←			00 25	←
Feltham	d		23 06	22 59	23 06		23 16	23 36	23 29	23 36		23 44	23 48	00 06		00 04	00 06		00 37	00 29	00 37
Ashford (Surrey)	d		→	23 03	23 10			→	23 33	23 40		23 48		→			00 10		→	00 33	00 41
Staines	d			23 07	23 14		23 23		23 37	23 44		23 52	23 56			00 11	00 14			00a37	00a46
Wraysbury	d			23 11					23 41			23 56									
Sunnymeads	d			23 14					23 44			23 59									
Datchet	d			23 17					23 47			00 02									
Windsor & Eton Riverside	a			23 21					23 51			00 06									
Egham	d				23 19		23 27			23 49			00 01			00 15	00 19				
Virginia Water	a				23 23		23 31			23 53			00 05			00 19	00 23				
	d				23 23		23 31			23 53			00 05			00 19	00 23				
Chertsey	d				23 29					23 59							00 29				
Addlestone	d				23a32					00 02							00a32				
Weybridge	a																				
Byfleet & New Haw	d									00 06											
West Byfleet	d									00 09											
Woking	a									00 15											
Longcross	d																				
Sunningdale	d						23 37						00 11			00 25					
Ascot 3	d	23 23					23 43						00 15			00 30					
Bagshot	d	23 29																			
Camberley	a	23 35																			
Frimley	d	23 43																			
Ash Vale	d	23 49																			
Aldershot	a	23 54																			
	d																				
Ash 5	d																				
Wanborough	d																				
Guildford	a																				
Martins Heron	d						23 47						00 19			00 34					
Bracknell	d						23 50						00 23			00 37					
Wokingham	d						23 57						00 32			00 44					
Winnersh	d						23 59						00 36								
Winnersh Triangle	d						00 02						00 38								
Earley	d						00 05						00 40								
Reading 7	a						00 10						00 45			00 52					

Table 149

Mondays to Fridays
from 3 October

London - Hounslow, Richmond, Kingston, Windsor, Weybridge, Ascot, Guildford and Reading

		SW MO ■	SW MX ■	SW MO	SW MX	SW MO ■	SW MX	SW MX ■	SW MX	SW MX	SW MX	SW MX	SW MX ■	SW MO ■	SW MX	SW MO	SW MO	SW ■	SW ■	SW MX	SW MX	SW MX	SW
London Waterloo 15 ⊖	d	22p39	22p50	22p50	22p52	23p09	23p13	23p20	23p22	23p33	23p38			23p39			23p44			23p52	23p58		00 18
Vauxhall ⊖	d	22p43		22p54	22p56	23p13	23p17		23p26	23p37				23p43			23p48			23p56	00 02		00 22
Queenstown Rd.(Battersea)	d			22p57	22p59				23p29	23p40							23p51			23p59			00 25
Clapham Junction 10	d	22p49	22p58	23p00	23p02	23p19	23p23	23p28	23p32	23p43	23p46			23p49			23p54			00 02	00 08		00 29
Wandsworth Town	d			23p03	23p05				23p35	23p46							23p57			00 05			00 32
Putney	d	22p53		23p06	23p08	23p23	23p27		23p38	23p49				23p53			23p59			00 08	00 12		00 35
Barnes	d			23p09	23p12				23p42	23p52							00 03			00 12			00 38
Barnes Bridge	d			23p11	23p14				23p44											00 14			
Chiswick	d			23p13	23p17				23p47											00 17			
Kew Bridge	d			23p16	23p20				23p50											00 20			
Brentford	d			23p19	23p23				23p53											00 23			
Syon Lane	d			23p21	23p25				23p55											00 25			
Isleworth	d			23p23	23p27				23p57											00 27			
Hounslow	d			23p26	23p31				00 01											00 31			
Mortlake	d									23p54							00 05						00 40
North Sheen	d									23p56					←		00 07						00 42
Richmond ⊖	d	22p59	23p06			23p29	23p33	23p37		23p59	23p54			23p59	23p59		00 10				00 18		00 45
St Margarets	d									→					00 01		00 12						00 47
Twickenham	a	23p02	23p10			23p32	23p36	23p41			23p58			00 02	00 03		00 14				00 21		00 49
	d	23p03	23p10			23p33	23p37	23p41			23p58			00 03	00 04		00 15				00 22		00 50
Strawberry Hill	d														00 07								00s53
Fulwell	a																						00s56
Teddington	a														00 11								00s59
Hampton Wick	a														00 14								01 01
Kingston	a														00 16								
Whitton	d						23p40					←					00 18				00 25	←	
Feltham	d	23p09	23p16	23p32	23p36	23p39	23p44	23p48	00 06		00 04	00 06		00 09			00 22			00 37	00 29	00 37	
Ashford (Surrey)	d			23p36	23p40		23p48		→			00 10					00 26			→	00 33	00 41	
Staines	d	23p15	23p23	23p40	23p44	23p45	23p52	23p56			00 11	00 14		00 15		00 21	00a30				00a37	00a46	
Wraysbury	d						23p56																
Sunnymeads	d						23p59																
Datchet	d						00 04																
Windsor & Eton Riverside	a						00 09																
Egham	d	23p20	23p27	23p45	23p49	23p50		00 01			00 15	00 19		00 20		00s25							
Virginia Water	a	23p24	23p31	23p49	23p53	23p54		00 05			00 19	00 23		00 24		00s30							
	d	23p24	23p31	23p49	23p53	23p54		00 05			00 19	00 23		00 24									
Chertsey	d			23p55	23p59							00 29				00s35							
Addlestone	d			23p58	00 02							00a32				00s38							
Weybridge	a																						
Byfleet & New Haw	d			00 02	00 06											00s42							
West Byfleet	d			00 05	00 09											00s45							
Woking	a			00 11	00 15											00 51							
Longcross	d																						
Sunningdale	d	23p29	23p37			23p59		00 11			00 25			00 29									
Ascot 3	d	23p34	23p43			00 04		00 15			00 30		00 32	00 34									
Bagshot	d												00 38										
Camberley	a												00 44										
Frimley	d												00 48										
Ash Vale	d												00 57										
Aldershot	a												01s02										
	d																	06 08	06 38				
Ash 5	d																	06 15	06 45				
Wanborough	d																	06 18	06 48				
Guildford	a																	06 25	06 55				
Martins Heron	d	23p38	23p47			00 08		00 19			00 34			00 38									
Bracknell	d	23p41	23p50			00 11		00 23			00 37			00 41									
Wokingham	d	23p48	23p57			00 18		00 32			00 44			00 48									
Winnersh	d	23p51	23p59			00 21		00 36						00 51									
Winnersh Triangle	d	23p53	00 02			00 23		00 38						00 53									
Earley	d	23p56	00 05			00 26		00 40						00 56									
Reading 7	a	00 04	00 13			00 34		00 48			00 55			01 04									

London - Hounslow, Richmond, Kingston, Windsor, Weybridge, Ascot, Guildford and Reading

		SW 1	SW	SW 1	SW	SW		SW	SW 1	SW 1	SW	SW	SW	SW 1	SW	SW 1		SW	SW 1	SW	SW	SW	SW	SW	SW 1
London Waterloo 15 ⊖	d			05 05		05 33				05 50	05 58	06 03			06 15	06 20				06 22	06 28		06 33	06 45	06 50
Vauxhall ⊖	d			05 09		05 37					06 02	06 07			06 19					06 26	06 32		06 37	06 49	
Queenstown Rd.(Battersea)	d			05 12		05 40						06 10			06 22					06 29			06 40	06 52	
Clapham Junction 10	d			05 15		05 43				05 58	06 08	06 13			06 25	06 28				06 32	06 38		06 43	06 55	06 58
Wandsworth Town	d			05 18		05 46						06 16			06 28					06 35			06 46	06 58	
Putney	d			05 21		05 49					06 12	06 19			06 31					06 38	06 42		06 49	07 01	
Barnes	d			05 24		05 52						06 22			06 35					06 42			06 52	07 05	
Barnes Bridge	d																			06 44					
Chiswick	d																			06 47					
Kew Bridge	d																			06 50					
Brentford	d																			06 53					
Syon Lane	d																			06 55					
Isleworth	d																			06 57					
Hounslow	d																			07 01					
Mortlake	d			05 26		05 54						06 24			06 37								06 54	07 07	
North Sheen	d			05 28		05 56						06 26			06 39			←					06 56	07 09	
Richmond ⊖	d			05 31		05 59				06 06	06 18	06 29			06 42	06 36		06 42			06 48		06 59	07 12	07 06
St Margarets	d			05 33		06 01						06 31			→			06 44					07 01	→	
Twickenham	a			05 35		06 03				06 10	06 21	06 33				06 40		06 46			06 51		07 03		07 10
	d			05 36	05 53	06 05				06 10	06 22	06 34				06 40		06 47			06 52		07 04		07 10
Strawberry Hill	d					06 08						06 37											07 07		
Fulwell	a																								
Teddington	a					06 11						06 40											07 10		
Hampton Wick	a					06 14						06 44											07 14		
Kingston	a					06 16						06 46											07 16		
Whitton	d			05 39	05 56						06 25							06a50			06 55	←			
Feltham	d			05 43	06 00					06 16	06 29					06 46				07 06	06 59	07 06			07 16
Ashford (Surrey)	d			05 47	06 04						06 33									→	07 03	07 10			
Staines	d	05 23	05 44	05 53	06 08			06 14		06 23	06 37		06 44			06 53					07 07	07 14			07 23
Wraysbury	d				06 13						06 42										07 12				
Sunnymeads	d				06 16						06 45										07 15				
Datchet	d				06 20						06 49										07 19				
Windsor & Eton Riverside	a				06 24						06 54										07 24				
Egham	d	05 27	05 49	05 57				06 19		06 27			06 49			06 57						07 19			07 27
Virginia Water	a	05 31	05 53	06 01				06 23		06 31			06 53			07 01						07 23			07 31
	d	05 31	05 53	06 01				06 23		06 31			06 53			07 01						07 23			07 31
Chertsey	d		05 59					06 29					06 59									07 29			
Addlestone	d		06 02					06 32					07 02									07 32			
Weybridge	a		06 07					06 37					07 07									07 37			
Byfleet & New Haw	d																								
West Byfleet	d																								
Woking	a																								
Longcross	d									06 35						07 05									07 35
Sunningdale	d	05 37		06 07						06 37						07 07									07 37
Ascot 3	d	05 43		06 13					06 23	06 43				06 53		07 13			07 23						07 43
Bagshot	d								06 29					06 59					07 29						
Camberley	a								06 35					07 05					07 35						
Frimley	d								06 43					07 13					07 43						
Ash Vale	d								06 49					07 19					07 49						
Aldershot	a								06 56					07 26					07 54						
	d								07 08					07 38					08 08						
Ash 5	d								07 15					07 45					08 15						
Wanborough	d								07 18					07 48					08 18						
Guildford	a								07 25					07 55					08 25						
Martins Heron	d	05 47		06 17						06 47						07 17									07 47
Bracknell	d	05 50		06 20						06 50						07 20									07 50
Wokingham	d	05 57		06 27						06 57						07 27									07 57
Winnersh	d	06 00		06 30						07 00						07 30									08 00
Winnersh Triangle	d	06 02		06 32						07 02						07 32									08 02
Earley	d	06 05		06 37						07 07						07 37									08 07
Reading 7	a	06 13		06 43						07 13						07 43									08 13

London - Hounslow, Richmond, Kingston, Windsor, Weybridge, Ascot, Guildford and Reading

		SW		SW 1	SW	SW	SW	SW	SW	SW 1	SW	SW		SW	SW 1	SW	SW	SW	SW	SW 1	SW	SW 1		SW	SW
London Waterloo 15 ⊖	d				06 52	06 58		07 03	07 15	07 20		07 22		07 28			07 33	07 37	07 45	07 50				07 52	07 58
Vauxhall ⊖	d				06 56	07 02		07 07	07 19			07 26		07 32			07 37	07 41	07 49					07 56	08 02
Queenstown Rd.(Battersea)	d				06 59			07 10	07 22			07 29					07 40	07 44	07 52					07 59	
Clapham Junction 10	d				07 02	07 08		07 13	07 25	07 28		07 32		07 38			07 43	07 47	07 55	07 58				08 02	08 08
Wandsworth Town	d				07 05			07 16	07 28			07 35					07 46	07 50	07 58					08 05	
Putney	d				07 08	07 12		07 19	07 31			07 38		07 42			07 49	07 53	08 01					08 08	08 12
Barnes	d				07 12			07 22	07 35			07 42					07 52	07 57	08 05					08 12	
Barnes Bridge	d				07 14							07 44						07 59						08 14	
Chiswick	d				07 17							07 47						08 02						08 17	
Kew Bridge	d				07 20							07 50						08 05						08 20	
Brentford	d				07 23							07 53						08 08						08 23	
Syon Lane	d				07 25							07 55						08 10						08 25	
Isleworth	d				07 27							07 57						08 12						08 27	
Hounslow	d				07 31							08 01						08a18						08 31	
Mortlake	d							07 24	07 37								07 54		08 07						
North Sheen	d	←						07 26	07 39		←						07 56		08 09		←				
Richmond ⊖	d	07 12				07 18		07 29	07 42	07 36	07 42			07 48	07 54		07 59		08 12	08 06	08 12				08 18
St Margarets	d	07 14						07 31	→		07 44						08 01		→		08 14				
Twickenham	a	07 16				07 21		07 33		07 40	07 46			07 51	07 57		08 03			08 10	08 16				08 21
	d	07 17				07 22		07 34		07 40	07 47			07 52	07 58		08 04			08 10	08 17				08 22
Strawberry Hill	d							07 37									08 07								
Fulwell	a																								
Teddington	a							07 40									08 10								
Hampton Wick	a							07 44									08 14								
Kingston	a							07 46									08 16								
Whitton	d	07a20				07 25	←				07a50			07 55		←					08a20				08 25
Feltham	d				07 36	07 29	07 36			07 46		08 06		07 59	08 04	08 06				08 16				08 36	08 29
Ashford (Surrey)	d				→	07 33	07 40					→		08 03	08 08	08 10								→	08 33
Staines	d					07 37	07 44			07 53				08 07	08 12	08 14				08 23					08 37
Wraysbury	d					07 42								08 12											08 42
Sunnymeads	d					07 45								08 15											08 45
Datchet	d					07 49								08 19											08 49
Windsor & Eton Riverside	a					07 54								08 24											08 54
Egham	d						07 49			07 57					08 16	08 19				08 27					
Virginia Water	a						07 53			08 01						08 23				08 31					
	d						07 53			08 01						08 23				08 31					
Chertsey	d						07 59									08 29									
Addlestone	d						08 02									08 32									
Weybridge	a						08 07									08 38									
Byfleet & New Haw	d																								
West Byfleet	d																								
Woking	a																								
Longcross	d									08 05										08 35					
Sunningdale	d									08 07										08 37					
Ascot 3	d			07 53						08 13					08 26					08 43		08 53			
Bagshot	d			07 59											08 32							08 59			
Camberley	a			08 05											08 38							09 05			
Frimley	d			08 13											08 43							09 13			
Ash Vale	d			08 19											08 49							09 19			
Aldershot	a			08 24											08 54							09 25			
	d			08 38											09 08							09 38			
Ash 5	d			08 45											09 15							09 45			
Wanborough	d			08 48											09 18							09 48			
Guildford	a			08 55											09 25							09 55			
Martins Heron	d									08 17										08 47					
Bracknell	d									08 20										08 50					
Wokingham	d									08 27										08 57					
Winnersh	d									08 30										09 00					
Winnersh Triangle	d									08 32										09 02					
Earley	d									08 37										09 07					
Reading 7	a									08 43										09 13					

Table 149

London - Hounslow, Richmond, Kingston, Windsor, Weybridge, Ascot, Guildford and Reading

Station		SW	SW ■	SW	SW	SW	SW	SW ■	SW	SW ■	SW	SW	SW	SW ■	SW	SW	SW	SW	SW ■	SW	SW ■	SW	SW
London Waterloo ■ ⊖	d	08 03	08 07			08 10	08 15	08 20			08 22	08 28	08 33	08 37			08 40	08 43	08 50			08 52	08 58
Vauxhall ⊖	d	08 07				08 14	08 19				08 26	08 32	08 37				08 44	08 47				08 56	09 02
Queenstown Rd.(Battersea)	d	08 10				08 17	08 22				08 29		08 40				08 47	08 50				08 59	
Clapham Junction ■	d	08 13	08 16			08 20	08 25	08 28			08 32	08 38	08 43	08 45			08 50	08 55	08 58			09 02	09 08
Wandsworth Town	d	08 16				08 23	08 28				08 35		08 46				08 53	08 58				09 05	
Putney	d	08 19				08 26	08 31				08 38	08 42	08 49				08 56	09 01				09 08	09 12
Barnes	d	08 23				08 27	08 35				08 42		08 52				08 57	09 05				09 12	
Barnes Bridge	d					08 29					08 44						08 59					09 14	
Chiswick	d					08 32					08 47						09 02					09 17	
Kew Bridge	d					08 35					08 50						09 05					09 20	
Brentford	d					08 38					08 53						09 08					09 23	
Syon Lane	d					08 40					08 55						09 10					09 25	
Isleworth	d					08 42					08 57						09 12					09 27	
Hounslow	d					08 48					09 01						09 18					09 31	
Mortlake	d	08 25					08 37						08 54					09 07					
North Sheen	d	08 27			←		08 39		←				08 56			←		09 09		←			
Richmond ⊖	d	08 30	08 24		08 30		08 42	08 36	08 42			08 48	08 59	08 54		08 59		09 12	09 06	09 12			09 18
St Margarets	d	→			08 32		→		08 44				→			09 01		→		09 14			
Twickenham	a		08 28		08 34			08 40	08 46			08 51		08 57		09 03			09 10	09 16			09 21
	d		08 28		08 35			08 40	08 47			08 52		08 58		09 04			09 10	09 17			09 22
Strawberry Hill	d				08 38											09 07							
Fulwell	a																						
Teddington	a				08 41											09 10							
Hampton Wick	a				08 44											09 14							
Kingston	a				08 46											09 16							
Whitton	d			←		08a53			08a50			08 55			←		09a23			09a20			09 25
Feltham	d		08 34	08 36				08 46			09 06	08 59		09 04	09 06				09 16			09 36	09 29
Ashford (Surrey)	d		08 38	08 40							→	09 03		09 08	09 10							→	09 33
Staines	d		08 42	08 44				08 53				09 07		09 12	09 14				09 23				09 37
Wraysbury	d											09 12											09 42
Sunnymeads	d											09 15											09 45
Datchet	d											09 19											09 49
Windsor & Eton Riverside	a											09 24											09 54
Egham	d		08 47	08 49				08 57						09 16	09 19				09 27				
Virginia Water	a		08 51	08 53				09 01						09 20	09 23				09 31				
	d		08 51	08 53				09 01						09 20	09 23				09 31				
Chertsey	d			08 59											09 29								
Addlestone	d			09 02											09 32								
Weybridge	a			09 08											09 37								
Byfleet & New Haw	d																						
West Byfleet	d																						
Woking	a																						
Longcross	d		08 54																				
Sunningdale	d		08 58					09 07						09 26					09 37				
Ascot ■	d		09 02					09 13		09 23				09 30					09 43		09 53		
Bagshot	d									09 29											09 59		
Camberley	a									09 35											10 05		
Frimley	d									09 43											10 13		
Ash Vale	d									09 49											10 19		
Aldershot	a									09 54											10 24		
	d									10 08											10 38		
Ash ■	d									10 15											10 45		
Wanborough	d									10 18											10 48		
Guildford	a									10 25											10 55		
Martins Heron	d		09 06					09 17						09 34					09 47				
Bracknell	d		09 10					09 20						09 38					09 50				
Wokingham	d		09 17					09 27						09 47					09 57				
Winnersh	d		09 20					09 30											10 00				
Winnersh Triangle	d		09 22					09 32											10 02				
Earley	d		09 27					09 37											10 07				
Reading ■	a		09 33					09 43						09 58					10 13				

Table 149

London - Hounslow, Richmond, Kingston, Windsor, Weybridge, Ascot, Guildford and Reading

Station		SW	SW	SW	SW	SW ■	SW	SW ■	SW	SW	SW	SW	SW	SW	SW ■	SW	SW ■	SW	SW	SW	SW	SW
London Waterloo ■ ⊖	d		09 03	09 07	09 15	09 20			09 22	09 28		09 33	09 37	09 45	09 50			09 52	09 58		10 03	10 07
Vauxhall ⊖	d		09 07	09 11	09 19				09 26	09 32		09 37	09 41	09 49				09 56	10 02		10 07	10 11
Queenstown Rd.(Battersea)	d		09 10	09 14	09 22				09 29			09 40	09 44	09 52				09 59			10 10	10 14
Clapham Junction ■	d		09 13	09 17	09 25	09 28			09 32	09 38		09 43	09 47	09 55	09 58			10 02	10 08		10 13	10 17
Wandsworth Town	d		09 16	09 20	09 28				09 35			09 46	09 50	09 58				10 05			10 16	10 20
Putney	d		09 19	09 23	09 31				09 38	09 42		09 49	09 53	10 01				10 08	10 12		10 19	10 23
Barnes	d		09 22	09 27	09 35				09 42			09 52	09 57	10 05				10 12			10 22	10 27
Barnes Bridge	d			09 29					09 44				09 59					10 14				10 29
Chiswick	d			09 32					09 47				10 02					10 17				10 32
Kew Bridge	d			09 35					09 50				10 05					10 20				10 35
Brentford	d			09 38					09 53				10 08					10 23				10 38
Syon Lane	d			09 40					09 55				10 10					10 25				10 40
Isleworth	d			09 42					09 57				10 12					10 27				10 42
Hounslow	d			09 48					10 01				10 18					10 31				10 48
Mortlake	d		09 24		09 37							09 54		10 07							10 24	
North Sheen	d		09 26		09 39		←					09 56		10 09		←					10 26	
Richmond ⊖	d		09 29		09 42	09 36	09 42			09 48		09 59		10 12	10 06	10 12			10 18		10 29	
St Margarets	d		09 31		→		09 44					10 01		→		10 14					10 31	
Twickenham	a		09 33			09 40	09 46			09 51		10 03			10 10	10 16			10 21		10 33	
	d		09 34			09 40	09 47			09 52		10 04			10 10	10 17			10 22		10 34	
Strawberry Hill	d		09 37									10 07									10 37	
Fulwell	a																					
Teddington	a		09 40									10 10									10 40	
Hampton Wick	a		09 44									10 14									10 44	
Kingston	a		09 46									10 16									10 46	
Whitton	d	←		09a53				09a50		09 55	←		10a26			10a20			10 25	←		10a56
Feltham	d	09 36				09 46			10 06	09 59	10 06				10 16			10 36	10 29	10 36		
Ashford (Surrey)	d	09 40							→	10 03	10 10							→	10 33	10 40		
Staines	d	09 44				09 53				10 07	10 14				10 23				10 37	10 44		
Wraysbury	d									10 12									10 42			
Sunnymeads	d									10 15									10 45			
Datchet	d									10 19									10 49			
Windsor & Eton Riverside	a									10 24									10 54			
Egham	d	09 49				09 57					10 19				10 27					10 49		
Virginia Water	a	09 53				10 01					10 23				10 31					10 53		
	d	09 53				10 01					10 23				10 31					10 53		
Chertsey	d	09 59									10 29									10 59		
Addlestone	d	10 02									10 32									11 02		
Weybridge	a	10 07									10 37									11 07		
Byfleet & New Haw	d																					
West Byfleet	d																					
Woking	a																					
Longcross	d																					
Sunningdale	d					10 07									10 37							
Ascot ■	d					10 13		10 23							10 43		10 53					
Bagshot	d							10 29									10 59					
Camberley	a							10 35									11 05					
Frimley	d							10 43									11 13					
Ash Vale	d							10 49									11 19					
Aldershot	a							10 54									11 24					
	d							11 08									11 38					
Ash ■	d							11 15									11 45					
Wanborough	d							11 18									11 48					
Guildford	a							11 25									11 55					
Martins Heron	d					10 17									10 47							
Bracknell	d					10 20									10 50							
Wokingham	d					10 27									10 57							
Winnersh	d					10 30									11 00							
Winnersh Triangle	d					10 32									11 02							
Earley	d					10 37									11 07							
Reading ■	a					10 43									11 13							

London - Hounslow, Richmond, Kingston, Windsor, Weybridge, Ascot, Guildford and Reading

		SW	SW 1	SW	SW 1	SW	SW	SW	SW	SW	SW	SW 1	SW	SW 1	SW	SW	SW	SW	SW	SW	SW 1	SW	SW 1
London Waterloo 15 ⊖	d	10 15	10 20			10 22	10 28		10 33	10 37	10 45	10 50			10 52	10 58		11 03	11 07	11 15	11 20		
Vauxhall ⊖	d	10 19				10 26	10 32		10 37	10 41	10 49				10 56	11 02		11 07	11 11	11 19			
Queenstown Rd.(Battersea)	d	10 22				10 29			10 40	10 44	10 52				10 59			11 10	11 14	11 22			
Clapham Junction 10	d	10 25	10 28			10 32	10 38		10 43	10 47	10 55	10 58			11 02	11 08		11 13	11 17	11 25	11 28		
Wandsworth Town	d	10 28				10 35			10 46	10 50	10 58				11 05			11 16	11 20	11 28			
Putney	d	10 31				10 38	10 42		10 49	10 53	11 01				11 08	11 12		11 19	11 23	11 31			
Barnes	d	10 35				10 42			10 52	10 57	11 05				11 12			11 22	11 27	11 35			
Barnes Bridge	d					10 44				10 59					11 14				11 29				
Chiswick	d					10 47				11 02					11 17				11 32				
Kew Bridge	d					10 50				11 05					11 20				11 35				
Brentford	d					10 53				11 08					11 23				11 38				
Syon Lane	d					10 55				11 10					11 25				11 40				
Isleworth	d					10 57				11 12					11 27				11 42				
Hounslow	d					11 01				11 18					11 31				11 48				
Mortlake	d	10 37							10 54		11 07							11 24		11 37			
North Sheen	d	10 39		←					10 56		11 09		←					11 26		11 39		←	
Richmond ⊖	d	10 42	10 36	10 42			10 48		10 59		11 12	11 06	11 12			11 18		11 29		11 42	11 36	11 42	
St Margarets	d	→		10 44					11 01		→		11 14					11 31		→		11 44	
Twickenham	a		10 40	10 46			10 51		11 03			11 10	11 16			11 21		11 33			11 40	11 46	
	d		10 40	10 47			10 52		11 04			11 10	11 17			11 22		11 34			11 40	11 47	
Strawberry Hill	d								11 07									11 37					
Fulwell	a																						
Teddington	a								11 10									11 40					
Hampton Wick	a								11 14									11 44					
Kingston	a								11 16									11 46					
Whitton	d			10a50			10 55	←		11a23			11a20			11 25	←		11a53			11a50	
Feltham	d		10 46			11 06	10 59	11 06				11 16			11 36	11 29	11 36				11 46		
Ashford (Surrey)	d					→	11 03	11 10							→	11 33	11 40						
Staines	d		10 53				11 07	11 14				11 23				11 37	11 44				11 53		
Wraysbury	d						11 12									11 42							
Sunnymeads	d						11 15									11 45							
Datchet	d						11 19									11 49							
Windsor & Eton Riverside	a						11 24									11 54							
Egham	d		10 57					11 19				11 27					11 49				11 57		
Virginia Water	a		11 01					11 23				11 31					11 53				12 01		
	d		11 01					11 23				11 31					11 53				12 01		
Chertsey	d							11 29									11 59						
Addlestone	d							11 32									12 02						
Weybridge	a							11 37									12 07						
Byfleet & New Haw	d																						
West Byfleet	d																						
Woking	a																						
Longcross	d																						
Sunningdale	d		11 07									11 37									12 07		
Ascot 3	d		11 13		11 23							11 43		11 53							12 13		12 23
Bagshot	d				11 29									11 59									12 29
Camberley	a				11 35									12 05									12 35
Frimley	d				11 43									12 13									12 43
Ash Vale	d				11 49									12 19									12 49
Aldershot	a				11 54									12 24									12 54
	d				12 08									12 38									13 08
Ash 5	d				12 15									12 45									13 15
Wanborough	d				12 18									12 48									13 18
Guildford	a				12 25									12 55									13 25
Martins Heron	d		11 17									11 47									12 17		
Bracknell	d		11 20									11 50									12 20		
Wokingham	d		11 27									11 57									12 27		
Winnersh	d		11 30									12 00									12 30		
Winnersh Triangle	d		11 32									12 02									12 32		
Earley	d		11 37									12 07									12 37		
Reading 7	a		11 43									12 13									12 43		

London - Hounslow, Richmond, Kingston, Windsor, Weybridge, Ascot, Guildford and Reading

		SW	SW	SW	SW	SW	SW	SW 1	SW	SW 1	SW	SW	SW	SW	SW	SW	SW 1	SW	SW 1	SW	SW	SW	SW
London Waterloo 15 ⊖	d	11 22	11 28		11 33	11 37	11 45	11 50			11 52	11 58		12 03	12 07	12 15	12 20			12 22	12 28		12 33
Vauxhall ⊖	d	11 26	11 32		11 37	11 41	11 49				11 56	12 02		12 07	12 11	12 19				12 26	12 32		12 37
Queenstown Rd.(Battersea)	d	11 29			11 40	11 44	11 52				11 59			12 10	12 14	12 22				12 29			12 40
Clapham Junction 10	d	11 32	11 38		11 43	11 47	11 55	11 58			12 02	12 08		12 13	12 17	12 25	12 28			12 32	12 38		12 43
Wandsworth Town	d	11 35			11 46	11 50	11 58				12 05			12 16	12 20	12 28				12 35			12 46
Putney	d	11 38	11 42		11 49	11 53	12 01				12 08	12 12		12 19	12 23	12 31				12 38	12 42		12 49
Barnes	d	11 42			11 52	11 57	12 05				12 12			12 22	12 27	12 35				12 42			12 52
Barnes Bridge	d	11 44				11 59					12 14				12 29					12 44			
Chiswick	d	11 47				12 02					12 17				12 32					12 47			
Kew Bridge	d	11 50				12 05					12 20				12 35					12 50			
Brentford	d	11 53				12 08					12 23				12 38					12 53			
Syon Lane	d	11 55				12 10					12 25				12 40					12 55			
Isleworth	d	11 57				12 12					12 27				12 42					12 57			
Hounslow	d	12 01				12 18					12 31				12 48					13 01			
Mortlake	d				11 54		12 07							12 24		12 37							12 54
North Sheen	d				11 56		12 09		←					12 26		12 39		←					12 56
Richmond ⊖	d		11 48		11 59		12 12	12 06	12 12			12 18		12 29		12 42	12 36	12 42			12 48		12 59
St Margarets	d				12 01		→		12 14					12 31		→		12 44					13 01
Twickenham	a		11 51		12 03			12 10	12 16			12 21		12 33			12 40	12 46			12 51		13 03
	d		11 52		12 04			12 10	12 17			12 22		12 34			12 40	12 47			12 52		13 04
Strawberry Hill	d				12 07									12 37									13 07
Fulwell	a																						
Teddington	a				12 10									12 40									13 10
Hampton Wick	a				12 14									12 44									13 14
Kingston	a				12 16									12 46									13 16
Whitton	d		11 55	←		12a23			12a20			12 25	←		12a53			12a50			12 55	←	
Feltham	d	12 06	11 59	12 06				12 16			12 36	12 29	12 36				12 46			13 06	12 59	13 06	
Ashford (Surrey)	d	→	12 03	12 10							→	12 33	12 40							→	13 03	13 10	
Staines	d		12 07	12 14				12 23				12 37	12 44				12 53				13 07	13 14	
Wraysbury	d		12 12									12 42									13 12		
Sunnymeads	d		12 15									12 45									13 15		
Datchet	d		12 19									12 49									13 19		
Windsor & Eton Riverside	a		12 24									12 54									13 24		
Egham	d			12 19				12 27					12 49				12 57					13 19	
Virginia Water	a			12 23				12 31					12 53				13 01					13 23	
	d			12 23				12 31					12 53				13 01					13 23	
Chertsey	d			12 29									12 59									13 29	
Addlestone	d			12 32									13 02									13 32	
Weybridge	a			12 37									13 07									13 37	
Byfleet & New Haw	d																						
West Byfleet	d																						
Woking	a																						
Longcross	d																						
Sunningdale	d							12 37									13 07						
Ascot 3	d							12 43		12 53							13 13		13 23				
Bagshot	d									12 59									13 29				
Camberley	a									13 05									13 35				
Frimley	d									13 13									13 43				
Ash Vale	d									13 19									13 49				
Aldershot	a									13 24									13 54				
	d									13 38									14 08				
Ash 5	d									13 45									14 15				
Wanborough	d									13 48									14 18				
Guildford	a									13 55									14 25				
Martins Heron	d							12 47									13 17						
Bracknell	d							12 50									13 20						
Wokingham	d							12 57									13 27						
Winnersh	d							13 00									13 30						
Winnersh Triangle	d							13 02									13 32						
Earley	d							13 07									13 37						
Reading 7	a							13 13									13 43						

Table 149

Mondays to Fridays
from 3 October

London - Hounslow, Richmond, Kingston, Windsor, Weybridge, Ascot, Guildford and Reading

Station		SW	SW	SW 1	SW	SW 1	SW	SW	SW	SW	SW	SW	SW 1	SW	SW 1	SW	SW	SW	SW	SW	SW	SW 1
London Waterloo 15 ⊖	d	12 37	12 45	12 50			12 52	12 58		13 03	13 07	13 15	13 20			13 22	13 28		13 33	13 37	13 45	13 50
Vauxhall ⊖	d	12 41	12 49				12 56	13 02		13 07	13 11	13 19				13 26	13 32		13 37	13 41	13 49	
Queenstown Rd.(Battersea)	d	12 44	12 52				12 59			13 10	13 14	13 22				13 29			13 40	13 44	13 52	
Clapham Junction 10	d	12 47	12 55	12 58			13 02	13 08		13 13	13 17	13 25	13 28			13 32	13 38		13 43	13 47	13 55	13 58
Wandsworth Town	d	12 50	12 58				13 05			13 16	13 20	13 28				13 35			13 46	13 50	13 58	
Putney	d	12 53	13 01				13 08	13 12		13 19	13 23	13 31				13 38	13 42		13 49	13 53	14 01	
Barnes	d	12 57	13 05				13 12			13 22	13 27	13 35				13 42			13 52	13 57	14 05	
Barnes Bridge	d	12 59					13 14				13 29					13 44				13 59		
Chiswick	d	13 02					13 17				13 32					13 47				14 02		
Kew Bridge	d	13 05					13 20				13 35					13 50				14 05		
Brentford	d	13 08					13 23				13 38					13 53				14 08		
Syon Lane	d	13 10					13 25				13 40					13 55				14 10		
Isleworth	d	13 12					13 27				13 42					13 57				14 12		
Hounslow	d	13 18					13 31				13 48					14 01				14 18		
Mortlake	d		13 07							13 24		13 37							13 54		14 07	
North Sheen	d		13 09		←					13 26		13 39		←					13 56		14 09	
Richmond ⊖	d		13 12	13 06	13 12			13 18		13 29		13 42	13 36	13 42			13 48		13 59		14 12	14 06
St Margarets	d		→		13 14					13 31		→		13 44					14 01		→	
Twickenham	a			13 10	13 16			13 21		13 33			13 40	13 46			13 51		14 03			14 10
	d			13 10	13 17			13 22		13 34			13 40	13 47			13 52		14 04			14 10
Strawberry Hill	d									13 37									14 07			
Fulwell	a																					
Teddington	a									13 40									14 10			
Hampton Wick	a									13 44									14 14			
Kingston	a									13 46									14 16			
Whitton	d	13a23			13a20			13 25	←		13a53			13a50			13 55	←		14a23		
Feltham	d			13 16			13 36	13 29	13 36				13 46			14 06	13 59	14 06				14 16
Ashford (Surrey)	d						→	13 33	13 40							→	14 03	14 10				
Staines	d			13 23				13 37	13 44				13 53				14 07	14 14				14 23
Wraysbury	d							13 42									14 12					
Sunnymeads	d							13 45									14 15					
Datchet	d							13 49									14 19					
Windsor & Eton Riverside	a							13 54									14 24					
Egham	d			13 27					13 49				13 57					14 19				14 27
Virginia Water	a			13 31					13 53				14 01					14 23				14 31
	d			13 31					13 53				14 01					14 23				14 31
Chertsey	d								13 59									14 29				
Addlestone	d								14 02									14 32				
Weybridge	a								14 07									14 37				
Byfleet & New Haw	d																					
West Byfleet	d																					
Woking	a																					
Longcross	d			13 35																		
Sunningdale	d			13 37									14 07									14 37
Ascot 3	d			13 43		13 53							14 13		14 23							14 43
Bagshot	d					13 59									14 29							
Camberley	a					14 05									14 35							
Frimley	d					14 13									14 43							
Ash Vale	d					14 19									14 49							
Aldershot	a					14 24									14 54							
	d					14 38									15 08							
Ash 5	d					14 45									15 15							
Wanborough	d					14 48									15 18							
Guildford	a					14 55									15 25							
Martins Heron	d			13 47									14 17									14 47
Bracknell	d			13 50									14 20									14 50
Wokingham	d			13 57									14 27									14 57
Winnersh	d			14 00									14 30									15 00
Winnersh Triangle	d			14 02									14 32									15 02
Earley	d			14 07									14 37									15 07
Reading 7	a			14 13									14 43									15 13

Table 149

Mondays to Fridays
from 3 October

London - Hounslow, Richmond, Kingston, Windsor, Weybridge, Ascot, Guildford and Reading

Station		SW	SW 1	SW	SW	SW	SW	SW	SW	SW 1	SW	SW 1	SW	SW	SW	SW	SW	SW	SW 1	SW	SW 1	SW	SW
London Waterloo 15 ⊖	d			13 52	13 58		14 03	14 07	14 15	14 20			14 22	14 28		14 33	14 37	14 45	14 50			14 52	14 58
Vauxhall ⊖	d			13 56	14 02		14 07	14 11	14 19				14 26	14 32		14 37	14 41	14 49				14 56	15 02
Queenstown Rd.(Battersea)	d			13 59			14 10	14 14	14 22				14 29			14 40	14 44	14 52				14 59	
Clapham Junction 10	d			14 02	14 08		14 13	14 17	14 25	14 28			14 32	14 38		14 43	14 47	14 55	14 58			15 02	15 08
Wandsworth Town	d			14 05			14 16	14 20	14 28				14 35			14 46	14 50	14 58				15 05	
Putney	d			14 08	14 12		14 19	14 23	14 31				14 38	14 42		14 49	14 53	15 01				15 08	15 12
Barnes	d			14 12			14 22	14 27	14 35				14 42			14 52	14 57	15 05				15 12	
Barnes Bridge	d			14 14				14 29					14 44				14 59					15 14	
Chiswick	d			14 17				14 32					14 47				15 02					15 17	
Kew Bridge	d			14 20				14 35					14 50				15 05					15 20	
Brentford	d			14 23				14 38					14 53				15 08					15 23	
Syon Lane	d			14 25				14 40					14 55				15 10					15 25	
Isleworth	d			14 27				14 42					14 57				15 12					15 27	
Hounslow	d			14 31				14 48					15 01				15 18					15 31	
Mortlake	d						14 24		14 37							14 54		15 07					
North Sheen	d	←					14 26		14 39		←					14 56		15 09		←			
Richmond ⊖	d	14 12			14 18		14 29		14 42	14 36	14 42			14 48		14 59		15 12	15 06	15 12			15 18
St Margarets	d	14 14					14 31		→		14 44					15 01		→		15 14			
Twickenham	a	14 16			14 21		14 33			14 40	14 46			14 51		15 03			15 10	15 16			15 21
	d	14 17			14 22		14 34			14 40	14 47			14 52		15 04			15 10	15 17			15 22
Strawberry Hill	d						14 37									15 07							
Fulwell	a																						
Teddington	a						14 40									15 10							
Hampton Wick	a						14 44									15 14							
Kingston	a						14 46									15 16							
Whitton	d	14a20			14 25	←		14a53			14a50			14 55	←		15a23			15a20			15 25
Feltham	d			14 36	14 29	14 36				14 46			15 06	14 59	15 06				15 16			15 36	15 29
Ashford (Surrey)	d			→	14 33	14 40							→	15 03	15 10							→	15 33
Staines	d				14 37	14 44				14 53				15 07	15 14				15 23				15 37
Wraysbury	d				14 42									15 12									15 42
Sunnymeads	d				14 45									15 15									15 45
Datchet	d				14 49									15 19									15 49
Windsor & Eton Riverside	a				14 54									15 24									15 54
Egham	d					14 49				14 57					15 19				15 27				
Virginia Water	a					14 53				15 01					15 23				15 31				
	d					14 53				15 01					15 23				15 31				
Chertsey	d					14 59									15 29								
Addlestone	d					15 02									15 32								
Weybridge	a					15 07									15 37								
Byfleet & New Haw	d																						
West Byfleet	d																						
Woking	a																						
Longcross	d																						
Sunningdale	d									15 07									15 37				
Ascot 3	d		14 53							15 13		15 23							15 43		15 53		
Bagshot	d		14 59									15 29									15 59		
Camberley	a		15 05									15 35									16 05		
Frimley	d		15 13									15 43									16 13		
Ash Vale	d		15 19									15 49									16 19		
Aldershot	a		15 24									15 54									16 24		
	d		15 38									16 08									16 38		
Ash 5	d		15 45									16 15									16 45		
Wanborough	d		15 48									16 18									16 48		
Guildford	a		15 55									16 25									16 55		
Martins Heron	d									15 17									15 47				
Bracknell	d									15 20									15 50				
Wokingham	d									15 27									15 57				
Winnersh	d									15 30									16 00				
Winnersh Triangle	d									15 32									16 02				
Earley	d									15 37									16 07				
Reading 7	a									15 43									16 13				

from 3 October

London - Hounslow, Richmond, Kingston, Windsor, Weybridge, Ascot, Guildford and Reading

		SW	SW	SW		SW	SW ■	SW	SW ■	SW	SW	SW	SW	SW		SW	SW ■	SW	SW ■	SW	SW	SW	SW ◇■	SW
London Waterloo [15] ⊖	d		15 03	15 07		15 15	15 20			15 22	15 28		15 33	15 37		15 45	15 50			15 52	15 58	16 01	16 05	
Vauxhall ⊖	d		15 07	15 11		15 19				15 26	15 32		15 37	15 41		15 49				15 56	16 02	16 05	16 09	
Queenstown Rd.(Battersea)	d		15 10	15 14		15 22				15 29			15 40	15 44		15 52				15 59		16 08		
Clapham Junction [10]	d		15 13	15 17		15 25	15 28			15 32	15 38		15 43	15 47		15 55	15 58			16 02	16 08	16 11	16 15	
Wandsworth Town	d		15 16	15 20		15 28				15 35			15 46	15 50		15 58				16 05		16 14		
Putney	d		15 19	15 23		15 31				15 38	15 42		15 49	15 53		16 01				16 08	16 12	16 17		
Barnes	d		15 22	15 27		15 35				15 42			15 52	15 57		16 05				16 12		16 22		
Barnes Bridge	d			15 29						15 44				15 59						16 14				
Chiswick	d			15 32						15 47				16 02						16 17				
Kew Bridge	d			15 35						15 50				16 05						16 20				
Brentford	d			15 38						15 53				16 08						16 23				
Syon Lane	d			15 40						15 55				16 10						16 25				
Isleworth	d			15 42						15 57				16 12						16 27				
Hounslow	d			15 48						16 01				16 18						16 31				
Mortlake	d		15 24			15 37							15 54			16 07						16 24		
North Sheen	d		15 26			15 39		←					15 56			16 09		←				16 26		
Richmond ⊖	d		15 29			15 42	15 36	15 42			15 48		15 59			16 12	16 06	16 12			16 18	16 29	16 23	
St Margarets	d		15 31			→		15 44					16 01			→		16 14				→		
Twickenham	a		15 33				15 40	15 46			15 51		16 03				16 10	16 16			16 21		16 27	
	d		15 34				15 40	15 47			15 52		16 04				16 10	16 17			16 22		16 27	
Strawberry Hill	d		15 37										16 07											
Fulwell	a																							
Teddington	a		15 40										16 10											
Hampton Wick	a		15 44										16 14											
Kingston	a		15 46										16 16											
Whitton	d	←		15a53				15a50			15 55	←		16a23				16a20			16 25			←
Feltham	d	15 36					15 46			16 06	15 59	16 06					16 16			16 36	16 29		16 33	16 36
Ashford (Surrey)	d	15 40								→	16 03	16 10								→	16 33		16 37	16 40
Staines	d	15 44					15 53				16 07	16 14					16 23				16 37		16 41	16 44
Wraysbury	d										16 12										16 42			
Sunnymeads	d										16 15										16 45			
Datchet	d										16 19										16 49			
Windsor & Eton Riverside	a										16 24										16 54			
Egham	d	15 49					15 57					16 19					16 27						16 46	16 49
Virginia Water	a	15 53					16 01					16 23					16 31						16 50	16 53
	d	15 53					16 01					16 23					16 31						16 50	16 53
Chertsey	d	15 59										16 29												16 59
Addlestone	d	16 02										16 32												17 02
Weybridge	a	16 07										16 37												17 07
Byfleet & New Haw	d																							
West Byfleet	d																							
Woking	a																							
Longcross	d																							
Sunningdale	d						16 07										16 37						16 55	
Ascot [3]	d						16 13		16 23								16 43		16 53				17 00	
Bagshot	d								16 29										16 59					
Camberley	a								16 35										17 05					
Frimley	d								16 43										17 13					
Ash Vale	d								16 49										17 19					
Aldershot	a								16 54										17 24					
	d								17 09										17 38					
Ash [6]	d								17 15										17 45					
Wanborough	d								17 18										17 48					
Guildford	a								17 25										17 55					
Martins Heron	d						16 17										16 47						17 04	
Bracknell	d						16 20										16 50						17 07	
Wokingham	d						16 27										16 57						17 17	
Winnersh	d						16 30										17 00							
Winnersh Triangle	d						16 32										17 02							
Earley	d						16 35										17 07							
Reading [7]	a						16 43										17 13						17 30	

London - Hounslow, Richmond, Kingston, Windsor, Weybridge, Ascot, Guildford and Reading

		SW	SW	SW	SW ◇■	SW	SW ■	SW ◇	SW ◇	SW		SW ◇■	SW ◇	SW	SW	SW	SW ◇■	SW	SW ◇	SW ◇		SW	SW ◇■	SW ◇	SW
London Waterloo [15] ⊖	d		16 07	16 15	16 20			16 22	16 28	16 31		16 35			16 37	16 45	16 50		16 52	16 58		17 01	17 05		
Vauxhall ⊖	d		16 11	16 19				16 26	16 32	16 35		16 39			16 41	16 49			16 56	17 02		17 05	17 09		
Queenstown Rd.(Battersea)	d		16 14	16 22				16 29		16 38					16 44	16 52			16 59			17 08			
Clapham Junction [10]	d		16 17	16 25	16 28			16 32	16 38	16 41		16 45			16 47	16 55	16 58		17 02	17 08		17 11	17 15		
Wandsworth Town	d		16 20	16 28				16 35		16 44					16 50	16 58			17 05			17 14			
Putney	d		16 23	16 31				16 38	16 42	16 47					16 53	17 01			17 08	17 12		17 17			
Barnes	d		16 27	16 35				16 42		16 52					16 57	17 05			17 12			17 22			
Barnes Bridge	d		16 29					16 44							16 59				17 14						
Chiswick	d		16 32					16 47							17 02				17 17						
Kew Bridge	d		16 35					16 50							17 05				17 20						
Brentford	d		16 38					16 53							17 08				17 23						
Syon Lane	d		16 40					16 55							17 10				17 25						
Isleworth	d		16 42					16 57							17 12				17 27						
Hounslow	d		16 48					17 01							17 18				17 31						
Mortlake	d			16 37						16 54						17 07						17 24			
North Sheen	d	←		16 39		←				16 56				←		17 09		←				17 26			←
Richmond ⊖	d	16 29		16 42	16 36	16 42			16 48	16 59		16 53		16 59		17 12	17 06	17 12		17 18		17 29	17 23		17 29
St Margarets	d	16 31		→		16 44				→				17 01		→		17 14				→			17 31
Twickenham	a	16 33			16 40	16 46			16 51			16 57		17 03			17 10	17 16		17 21			17 27		17 33
	d	16 34			16 40	16 47			16 52			16 57		17 04			17 10	17 17		17 22			17 27		17 34
Strawberry Hill	d	16 37												17 07											17 37
Fulwell	a																								
Teddington	a	16 42												17 12											17 42
Hampton Wick	a	16 46												17 16											17 46
Kingston	a	16 48												17 18											17 48
Whitton	d		16a53			16a50			16 55				←		17a23			17a20		17 25				←	
Feltham	d				16 46			17 06	16 59			17 03	17 06				17 16		17 36	17 29			17 33	17 36	
Ashford (Surrey)	d							→	17 03			17 07	17 10						→	17 33			17 37	17 40	
Staines	d				16 53				17 07			17 11	17 14				17 23			17 37			17 41	17 44	
Wraysbury	d								17 12											17 42					
Sunnymeads	d								17 15											17 45					
Datchet	d								17 19											17 49					
Windsor & Eton Riverside	a								17 26											17 56					
Egham	d				16 57							17 16	17 19				17 27						17 46	17 49	
Virginia Water	a				17 01							17 20	17 23				17 31						17 50	17 53	
	d				17 01							17 20	17 23				17 31						17 50	17 53	
Chertsey	d												17 29											17 59	
Addlestone	d												17 32											18 02	
Weybridge	a												17 40											18 10	
Byfleet & New Haw	d																								
West Byfleet	d																								
Woking	a																								
Longcross	d											17 23													
Sunningdale	d				17 07							17 27					17 37						17 55		
Ascot [3]	d				17 13		17 23					17 31					17 43						18 00		
Bagshot	d						17 29																18 06		
Camberley	a						17 35																18 12		
Frimley	d						17 43																18 17		
Ash Vale	d						17 49																18 24		
Aldershot	a						17 54																18 34		
	d						18 08																		
Ash [6]	d						18 15																		
Wanborough	d						18 18																		
Guildford	a						18 25																		
Martins Heron	d				17 17							17 35					17 47								
Bracknell	d				17 20							17 39					17 50								
Wokingham	d				17 27							17 47					17 57								
Winnersh	d				17 30												18 00								
Winnersh Triangle	d				17 32												18 02								
Earley	d				17 37												18 07								
Reading [7]	a				17 45							18 01					18 15								

London - Hounslow, Richmond, Kingston, Windsor, Weybridge, Ascot, Guildford and Reading

		SW	SW	SW	SW	SW	SW	SW	SW	SW	SW	SW	SW	SW	SW	SW	SW	SW	SW	SW	SW	SW	SW
					◇[1]		◇	[1]	◇	[1]	[1]		◇[1]	◇					◇[1]		◇	◇	
London Waterloo [15] ⊖	d	17 07	17 13	17 15	17 20		17 22	17 25	17 28			17 31	17 35			17 37	17 43	17 45	17 50		17 52	17 58	18 01
Vauxhall ⊖	d	17 11	17 17	17 19			17 26		17 32			17 35	17 39			17 41	17 47	17 49			17 56	18 02	18 05
Queenstown Rd.(Battersea)	d	17 14		17 22			17 29					17 38				17 44		17 52			17 59		18 08
Clapham Junction [10]	d	17 17	17 23	17 25	17 28		17 32		17 38			17 41	17 45			17 47	17 53	17 55	17 58		18 02	18 08	18 11
Wandsworth Town	d	17 20		17 28			17 35					17 44				17 50		17 58			18 05		18 14
Putney	d	17 23	17 27	17 31			17 38		17 42			17 47				17 53	17 57	18 01			18 08	18 12	18 17
Barnes	d	17 27		17 35			17 42					17 52				17 57		18 05			18 12		18 22
Barnes Bridge	d	17 29					17 44									17 59					18 14		
Chiswick	d	17 32					17 47									18 02					18 17		
Kew Bridge	d	17 35					17 50									18 05					18 20		
Brentford	d	17 38					17 53									18 08					18 23		
Syon Lane	d	17 40					17 55									18 10					18 25		
Isleworth	d	17 42					17 57									18 12					18 27		
Hounslow	d	17 48					18 01									18 18					18 31		
Mortlake	d			17 37								17 54						18 07					18 24
North Sheen	d			17 39		←						17 56			←			18 09		←			18 26
Richmond ⊖	d		17 33	17 42	17 36	17 42			17 48			17 59	17 53		17 59		18 03	18 12	18 06	18 12		18 18	18 29
St Margarets	d			→		17 44						→			18 01			→		18 14			→
Twickenham	a		17 37		17 40	17 46			17 51				17 57		18 03		18 07		18 10	18 16		18 21	
	d		17 37		17 40	17 47			17 52				17 57		18 04		18 07		18 10	18 17		18 22	
Strawberry Hill	d		17 41												18 07		18 11						
Fulwell	a																18 13						
Teddington	a		17 46												18 12								
Hampton Wick	a		17 54												18 16								
Kingston	a		17 56												18 18								
Whitton	d	17a53				17a50			17 55					←		18a23				18a20		18 25	
Feltham	d				17 46		18 06		17 59				18 03	18 06					18 16		18 36	18 29	
Ashford (Surrey)	d						→		18 03				18 07	18 10							→	18 33	
Staines	d				17 53				18 07				18 11	18 14					18 23			18 37	
Wraysbury	d								18 12													18 42	
Sunnymeads	d								18 15													18 45	
Datchet	d								18 19													18 49	
Windsor & Eton Riverside	a								18 26													18 56	
Egham	d				17 57								18 16	18 19					18 27				
Virginia Water	a				18 01								18 20	18 23					18 31				
	d				18 01								18 20	18 23					18 31				
Chertsey	d													18 29									
Addlestone	d													18 32									
Weybridge	a													18 40									
Byfleet & New Haw	d																						
West Byfleet	d																						
Woking	a							17 50															
Longcross	d																		18 35				
Sunningdale	d				18 07								18 25						18 37				
Ascot [3]	d				18 13						18 23		18 30						18 43				
Bagshot	d										18 29												
Camberley	a										18 35												
Frimley	d										18 43												
Ash Vale	d							18 03			18 49												
Aldershot	a							18 08			18 54												
	d									18 38	19 08												
Ash [6]	d									18 45	19 15												
Wanborough	d									18 48	19 18												
Guildford	a									18 55	19 25												
Martins Heron	d				18 17								18 34						18 47				
Bracknell	d				18 20								18 37						18 50				
Wokingham	d				18 27								18 47						18 57				
Winnersh	d				18 30														19 00				
Winnersh Triangle	d				18 32														19 02				
Earley	d				18 37														19 07				
Reading [7]	a				18 45								19 00						19 15				

London - Hounslow, Richmond, Kingston, Windsor, Weybridge, Ascot, Guildford and Reading

		SW	SW	SW	SW	SW	SW	SW	SW	SW	SW	SW	SW	SW	SW	SW	SW	SW	SW	SW	SW	SW
		◇[1]	◇					◇[1]		◇	[1]	◇	[1]	[1]		◇[1]	◇					◇[1]
London Waterloo [15] ⊖	d	18 05			18 07	18 13	18 15	18 20		18 22	18 25	18 28			18 31	18 35			18 37	18 43	18 45	18 50
Vauxhall ⊖	d	18 09			18 11	18 17	18 19			18 26		18 32			18 35	18 39			18 41	18 47	18 49	
Queenstown Rd.(Battersea)	d				18 14		18 22			18 29					18 38				18 44		18 52	
Clapham Junction [10]	d	18 15			18 17	18 23	18 25	18 28		18 32		18 38			18 41	18 45			18 47	18 53	18 55	18 58
Wandsworth Town	d				18 20		18 28			18 35					18 44				18 50		18 58	
Putney	d				18 23	18 27	18 31			18 38		18 42			18 47				18 53	18 57	19 01	
Barnes	d				18 27		18 35			18 42					18 52				18 57		19 05	
Barnes Bridge	d				18 29					18 44									18 59			
Chiswick	d				18 32					18 47									19 02			
Kew Bridge	d				18 35					18 50									19 05			
Brentford	d				18 38					18 53									19 08			
Syon Lane	d				18 40					18 55									19 10			
Isleworth	d				18 42					18 57									19 12			
Hounslow	d				18 48					19 01									19 18			
Mortlake	d						18 37								18 54						19 07	
North Sheen	d			←			18 39		←						18 56			←			19 09	
Richmond ⊖	d	18 23		18 29		18 33	18 42	18 36	18 42			18 48			18 59	18 53		18 59		19 03	19 12	19 06
St Margarets	d			18 31			→		18 44						→			19 01			→	
Twickenham	a	18 27		18 33		18 37		18 40	18 46			18 51				18 57		19 03		19 07		19 10
	d	18 27		18 34		18 37		18 40	18 47			18 52				18 57		19 04		19 07		19 10
Strawberry Hill	d			18 37		18 41												19 07		19 11		
Fulwell	a					18 43														19 13		
Teddington	a			18 42														19 12				
Hampton Wick	a			18 46														19 16				
Kingston	a			18 48														19 18				
Whitton	d		←		18a53				18a50			18 55					←		19a23			
Feltham	d	18 33	18 36					18 46		19 06		18 59				19 03	19 06					19 16
Ashford (Surrey)	d	18 37	18 40							→		19 03				19 07	19 10					
Staines	d	18 41	18 44					18 53				19 07				19 11	19 14					19 23
Wraysbury	d											19 12										
Sunnymeads	d											19 15										
Datchet	d											19 19										
Windsor & Eton Riverside	a											19 26										
Egham	d	18 46	18 49					18 57								19 16	19 19					19 27
Virginia Water	a	18 50	18 53					19 01								19 20	19 23					19 31
	d	18 50	18 53					19 01								19 20	19 23					19 31
Chertsey	d		18 59														19 29					
Addlestone	d		19 02														19 32					
Weybridge	a		19 10														19 40					
Byfleet & New Haw	d																					
West Byfleet	d																					
Woking	a										18 52											
Longcross	d																					
Sunningdale	d	18 55						19 07								19 25						19 37
Ascot [3]	d	19 02						19 13						19 23		19 30						19 43
Bagshot	d	19 08												19 29								
Camberley	a	19 14												19 35								
Frimley	d	19 19												19 43								
Ash Vale	d	19 26									19 05			19 49								
Aldershot	a	19 34									19 10			19 54								
	d												19 38	20 08								
Ash [6]	d												19 45	20 15								
Wanborough	d												19 48	20 18								
Guildford	a												19 55	20 25								
Martins Heron	d							19 17								19 34						19 47
Bracknell	d							19 20								19 37						19 50
Wokingham	d							19 27								19 47						19 57
Winnersh	d							19 30														20 00
Winnersh Triangle	d							19 32														20 02
Earley	d							19 37														20 07
Reading [7]	a							19 45								20 00						20 15

London - Hounslow, Richmond, Kingston, Windsor, Weybridge, Ascot, Guildford and Reading

		SW	SW 1	SW ◇	SW ◇	SW	SW 1	SW ◇	SW	SW	SW	SW 1	SW	SW 1	SW	SW	SW	SW	SW	SW	SW 1	SW	SW 1
London Waterloo 15 ⊖	d			18 52	18 58	19 01	19 05			19 07	19 15	19 20			19 22	19 28		19 33	19 37	19 45	19 50		
Vauxhall ⊖	d			18 56	19 02	19 05	19 09			19 11	19 19				19 26	19 32		19 37	19 41	19 49			
Queenstown Rd.(Battersea)	d			18 59		19 08				19 14	19 22				19 29			19 40	19 44	19 52			
Clapham Junction 10	d			19 02	19 08	19 11	19 15			19 17	19 25	19 28			19 32	19 38		19 43	19 47	19 55	19 58		
Wandsworth Town	d			19 05		19 14				19 20	19 28				19 35			19 46	19 50	19 58			
Putney	d			19 08	19 12	19 17				19 23	19 31				19 38	19 42		19 49	19 53	20 01			
Barnes	d			19 12		19 22				19 27	19 35				19 42			19 52	19 57	20 05			
Barnes Bridge	d			19 14						19 29					19 44				19 59				
Chiswick	d			19 17						19 32					19 47				20 02				
Kew Bridge	d			19 20						19 35					19 50				20 05				
Brentford	d			19 23						19 38					19 53				20 08				
Syon Lane	d			19 25						19 40					19 55				20 10				
Isleworth	d			19 27						19 42					19 57				20 12				
Hounslow	d			19 31						19 48					20 01				20 18				
Mortlake	d					19 24					19 37							19 54		20 07			
North Sheen	d	←				19 26			←		19 39		←					19 56		20 09		←	
Richmond ⊖	d	19 12			19 18	19 29	19 23		19 29		19 42	19 36	19 42			19 48		19 59		20 12	20 06	20 12	
St Margarets	d	19 14				→			19 31		→		19 44					20 01		→		20 14	
Twickenham	a	19 16			19 21		19 27		19 33			19 40	19 46			19 51		20 03			20 10	20 16	
	d	19 17			19 22		19 27		19 34			19 40	19 47			19 52		20 04			20 10	20 17	
Strawberry Hill	d								19 37									20 07					
Fulwell	a																						
Teddington	a								19 42									20 10					
Hampton Wick	a								19 46									20 14					
Kingston	a								19 48									20 16					
Whitton	d	19a20			19 25			←		19a53			19a50			19 55	←		20a23			20a20	
Feltham	d			19 36	19 29		19 33	19 36				19 46			20 06	19 59	20 06				20 16		
Ashford (Surrey)	d			→	19 33		19 37	19 40							→	20 03	20 10						
Staines	d				19 37		19 41	19 44				19 53				20 07	20 14				20 23		
Wraysbury	d				19 42											20 12							
Sunnymeads	d				19 45											20 15							
Datchet	d				19 49											20 19							
Windsor & Eton Riverside	a				19 56											20 24							
Egham	d						19 46	19 49				19 57					20 19				20 27		
Virginia Water	a						19 50	19 53				20 01					20 23				20 31		
	d						19 50	19 53				20 01					20 23				20 31		
Chertsey	d							19 59									20 29						
Addlestone	d							20 02									20 32						
Weybridge	a							20 10									20 37						
Byfleet & New Haw	d																						
West Byfleet	d																						
Woking	a																						
Longcross	d																						
Sunningdale	d						19 55					20 07									20 37		
Ascot 3	d		19 53				20 00					20 13		20 23							20 43		20 53
Bagshot	d		19 59											20 29									20 59
Camberley	a		20 05											20 35									21 05
Frimley	d		20 13											20 43									21 13
Ash Vale	d		20 19											20 49									21 19
Aldershot	a		20 24											20 54									21 24
	d		20 38											21 08									21 38
Ash 5	d		20 45											21 15									21 45
Wanborough	d		20 48											21 18									21 48
Guildford	a		20 55											21 25									21 55
Martins Heron	d						20 04					20 17									20 47		
Bracknell	d						20 07					20 20									20 50		
Wokingham	d						20 17					20 27									20 57		
Winnersh	d											20 30									21 00		
Winnersh Triangle	d											20 32									21 02		
Earley	d											20 37									21 07		
Reading 7	a						20 28					20 43									21 13		

London - Hounslow, Richmond, Kingston, Windsor, Weybridge, Ascot, Guildford and Reading

		SW	SW	SW	SW	SW	SW	SW 1	SW	SW 1	SW 1	SW	SW	SW	SW	SW	SW	SW 1	SW	SW	SW	SW
London Waterloo 15 ⊖	d	19 52	19 58		20 03	20 07	20 15	20 20				20 22	20 28		20 33	20 37	20 45	20 50		20 52	20 58	
Vauxhall ⊖	d	19 56	20 02		20 07	20 11	20 19					20 26	20 32		20 37	20 41	20 49			20 56	21 02	
Queenstown Rd.(Battersea)	d	19 59			20 10	20 14	20 22					20 29			20 40	20 44	20 52			20 59		
Clapham Junction 10	d	20 02	20 08		20 13	20 17	20 25	20 28				20 32	20 38		20 43	20 47	20 55	20 58		21 02	21 08	
Wandsworth Town	d	20 05			20 16	20 20	20 28					20 35			20 46	20 50	20 58			21 05		
Putney	d	20 08	20 12		20 19	20 23	20 31					20 38	20 42		20 49	20 53	21 01			21 08	21 12	
Barnes	d	20 12			20 22	20 27	20 35					20 42			20 52	20 57	21 05			21 12		
Barnes Bridge	d	20 14				20 29						20 44				20 59				21 14		
Chiswick	d	20 17				20 32						20 47				21 02				21 17		
Kew Bridge	d	20 20				20 35						20 50				21 05				21 20		
Brentford	d	20 23				20 38						20 53				21 08				21 23		
Syon Lane	d	20 25				20 40						20 55				21 10				21 25		
Isleworth	d	20 27				20 42						20 57				21 12				21 27		
Hounslow	d	20 31				20 48						21 01				21 18				21 31		
Mortlake	d				20 24		20 37								20 54		21 07					
North Sheen	d				20 26		20 39		←						20 56		21 09		←			
Richmond ⊖	d		20 18		20 29		20 42	20 36	20 42				20 48		20 59		21 12	21 06	21 12		21 18	
St Margarets	d				20 31		→		20 44						21 01		→		21 14			
Twickenham	a		20 21		20 33			20 40	20 46				20 51		21 03			21 10	21 16		21 21	
	d		20 22		20 34			20 40	20 47				20 52		21 04			21 10	21 17		21 22	
Strawberry Hill	d				20 37										21 07							
Fulwell	a																					
Teddington	a				20 40										21 10							
Hampton Wick	a				20 44										21 14							
Kingston	a				20 46										21 16							
Whitton	d		20 25	←		20a53			20a50				20 55	←		21a23			21a20		21 25	←
Feltham	d	20 36	20 29	20 36				20 46				21 06	20 59	21 06				21 16		21 36	21 29	21 36
Ashford (Surrey)	d	→	20 33	20 40								→	21 03	21 10						→	21 33	21 40
Staines	d		20 37	20 44				20 53					21 07	21 14				21 23			21 37	21 44
Wraysbury	d		20 42										21 12								21 42	
Sunnymeads	d		20 45										21 15								21 45	
Datchet	d		20 49										21 19								21 49	
Windsor & Eton Riverside	a		20 54										21 24								21 54	
Egham	d			20 49				20 57						21 19				21 27				21 49
Virginia Water	a			20 53				21 01						21 23				21 31				21 53
	d			20 53				21 01						21 23				21 31				21 53
Chertsey	d			20 59										21 29								21 59
Addlestone	d			21 02										21 32								22 02
Weybridge	a			21 07										21 37								22 07
Byfleet & New Haw	d																					
West Byfleet	d																					
Woking	a																					
Longcross	d																					
Sunningdale	d							21 07										21 37				
Ascot 3	d							21 13		21 23								21 43				
Bagshot	d									21 29												
Camberley	a									21 35												
Frimley	d									21 43												
Ash Vale	d									21 49												
Aldershot	a									21 54												
	d									22 08	22 38											
Ash 5	d									22 15	22 45											
Wanborough	d									22 18	22 48											
Guildford	a									22 25	22 55											
Martins Heron	d							21 17										21 47				
Bracknell	d							21 20										21 50				
Wokingham	d							21 27										21 57				
Winnersh	d							21 30										22 00				
Winnersh Triangle	d							21 32										22 02				
Earley	d							21 37										22 07				
Reading 7	a							21 43										22 13				

Table 149

Mondays to Fridays
from 3 October

London - Hounslow, Richmond, Kingston, Windsor, Weybridge, Ascot, Guildford and Reading

		SW	SW	SW	SW 1	SW	SW 1	SW	SW	SW	SW	SW	SW	SW 1	SW	SW	SW	SW	SW	SW 1	SW 1	SW	SW
London Waterloo 15 ⊖	d	21 03	21 07	21 15	21 20			21 22	21 28		21 33	21 37	21 45	21 50		21 52	21 58		22 03	22 20		22 22	22 28
Vauxhall ⊖	d	21 07	21 11	21 19				21 26	21 32		21 37	21 41	21 49			21 56	22 02		22 07			22 26	22 32
Queenstown Rd.(Battersea)	d	21 10	21 14	21 22				21 29			21 40	21 44	21 52			21 59			22 10			22 29	
Clapham Junction 10	d	21 13	21 17	21 25	21 28			21 32	21 38		21 43	21 47	21 55	21 58		22 02	22 08		22 13	22 28		22 32	22 38
Wandsworth Town	d	21 16	21 20	21 28				21 35			21 46	21 50	21 58			22 05			22 16			22 35	
Putney	d	21 19	21 23	21 31				21 38	21 42		21 49	21 53	22 01			22 08	22 12		22 19			22 38	22 42
Barnes	d	21 22	21 27	21 35				21 42			21 52	21 57	22 05			22 12			22 22			22 42	
Barnes Bridge	d		21 29					21 44				21 59				22 14						22 44	
Chiswick	d		21 32					21 47				22 02				22 17						22 47	
Kew Bridge	d		21 35					21 50				22 05				22 20						22 50	
Brentford	d		21 38					21 53				22 08				22 23						22 53	
Syon Lane	d		21 40					21 55				22 10				22 25						22 55	
Isleworth	d		21 42					21 57				22 12				22 27						22 57	
Hounslow	d		21 48					22 01				22 18				22 31						23 01	
Mortlake	d	21 24		21 37							21 54		22 07						22 24				
North Sheen	d	21 26		21 39		←					21 56		22 09		←				22 26				
Richmond ⊖	d	21 29		21 42	21 36	21 42			21 48		21 59		22 12	22 06	22 12		22 18		22 29	22 36			22 48
St Margarets	d	21 31		→		21 44					22 01		→		22 14				22 31				
Twickenham	a	21 33			21 40	21 46			21 51		22 03			22 10	22 16		22 21		22 33	22 40			22 51
	d	21 34			21 40	21 47			21 52		22 04			22 10			22 22		22 34	22 40			22 52
Strawberry Hill	d	21 37									22 07								22 37				
Fulwell	a																						
Teddington	a	21 40									22 10								22 40				
Hampton Wick	a	21 44									22 14								22 44				
Kingston	a	21 46									22 16								22 46				
Whitton	d		21a53			21a50			21 55	←		22a23					22 25	←					22 55
Feltham	d				21 46			22 06	21 59	22 06				22 16		22 36	22 29	22 36		22 46		23 06	22 59
Ashford (Surrey)	d							→	22 03	22 10						→	22 33	22 40				→	23 03
Staines	d				21 53				22 07	22 14				22 23			22 37	22 44		22 53			23 07
Wraysbury	d								22 12								22 42						23 11
Sunnymeads	d								22 15								22 45						23 14
Datchet	d								22 19								22 49						23 17
Windsor & Eton Riverside	a								22 24								22 56						23 24
Egham	d				21 57					22 19				22 27				22 49		22 57			
Virginia Water	a				22 01					22 23				22 31				22 53		23 01			
	d				22 01					22 23				22 31				22 53		23 01			
Chertsey	d									22 29								22 59					
Addlestone	d									22 32								23 02					
Weybridge	a									22 37								23 07					
Byfleet & New Haw	d																						
West Byfleet	d																						
Woking	a																						
Longcross	d																						
Sunningdale	d				22 07									22 37						23 07			
Ascot 3	d				22 13		22 23							22 43						23 13	23 23		
Bagshot	d						22 29														23 29		
Camberley	a						22 35														23 35		
Frimley	d						22 43														23 43		
Ash Vale	d						22 49														23 49		
Aldershot	a						22 54														23 54		
	d						23 08																
Ash 5	d						23 15																
Wanborough	d						23 18																
Guildford	a						23 25																
Martins Heron	d				22 17									22 47						23 17			
Bracknell	d				22 20									22 50						23 20			
Wokingham	d				22 27									22 57						23 27			
Winnersh	d				22 30									23 00						23 30			
Winnersh Triangle	d				22 32									23 02						23 32			
Earley	d				22 37									23 06						23 37			
Reading 7	a				22 43									23 13						23 43			

Table 149

Mondays to Fridays
from 3 October

London - Hounslow, Richmond, Kingston, Windsor, Weybridge, Ascot, Guildford and Reading

		SW	SW	SW 1	SW	SW	SW	SW	SW	SW 1	SW	SW	SW	SW	SW	SW	SW	SW
London Waterloo 15 ⊖	d		22 33	22 50	22 52	22 58		23 03	23 13	23 20	23 22	23 33	23 38			23 52	23 58	
Vauxhall ⊖	d		22 37		22 56	23 02		23 07	23 17		23 26	23 37				23 56	00 02	
Queenstown Rd.(Battersea)	d		22 40		22 59			23 10			23 29	23 40				23 59		
Clapham Junction 10	d		22 43	22 58	23 02	23 08		23 13	23 23	23 28	23 32	23 43	23 46			00 02	00 08	
Wandsworth Town	d		22 46		23 05			23 16			23 35	23 46				00 05		
Putney	d		22 49		23 08	23 12		23 19	23 27		23 38	23 49				00 08	00 12	
Barnes	d		22 52		23 12			23 22			23 42	23 52				00 12		
Barnes Bridge	d				23 14						23 44					00 14		
Chiswick	d				23 17						23 47					00 17		
Kew Bridge	d				23 20						23 50					00 20		
Brentford	d				23 23						23 53					00 23		
Syon Lane	d				23 25						23 55					00 25		
Isleworth	d				23 27						23 57					00 27		
Hounslow	d				23 31						00 01					00 31		
Mortlake	d		22 54					23 24				23 54						
North Sheen	d		22 56					23 26				23 56			←			
Richmond ⊖	d		22 59	23 06		23 18		23 29	23 33	23 37		23 59	23 54		23 59		00 18	
St Margarets	d		23 01					23 31				→			00 01			
Twickenham	a		23 03	23 10		23 21		23 33	23 36	23 41			23 58		00 03		00 21	
	d		23 04	23 10		23 22		23 34	23 37	23 41			23 58		00 04		00 22	
Strawberry Hill	d		23 07					23 37							00 07			
Fulwell	a																	
Teddington	a		23 10					23 40							00 11			
Hampton Wick	a		23 14					23 44							00 14			
Kingston	a		23 16					23 46							00 16			
Whitton	d	←				23 25	←		23 40					←			00 25	←
Feltham	d	23 06		23 16	23 36	23 29	23 36		23 44	23 48	00 06		00 04	00 06		00 37	00 29	00 37
Ashford (Surrey)	d	23 10			→	23 33	23 40		23 48		→			00 10		→	00 33	00 41
Staines	d	23 14		23 23		23 37	23 44		23 52	23 56			00 11	00 14			00a37	00a46
Wraysbury	d					23 42			23 56									
Sunnymeads	d					23 45			23 59									
Datchet	d					23 49			00 04									
Windsor & Eton Riverside	a					23 54			00 09									
Egham	d	23 19		23 27			23 49			00 01			00 15	00 19				
Virginia Water	a	23 23		23 31			23 53			00 05			00 19	00 23				
	d	23 23		23 31			23 53			00 05			00 19	00 23				
Chertsey	d	23 29					23 59							00 29				
Addlestone	d	23a32					00 02							00a32				
Weybridge	a																	
Byfleet & New Haw	d						00 06											
West Byfleet	d						00 09											
Woking	a						00 15											
Longcross	d																	
Sunningdale	d			23 37						00 11			00 25					
Ascot 3	d			23 43						00 15			00 30					
Bagshot	d																	
Camberley	a																	
Frimley	d																	
Ash Vale	d																	
Aldershot	a																	
	d																	
Ash 5	d																	
Wanborough	d																	
Guildford	a																	
Martins Heron	d			23 47						00 19			00 34					
Bracknell	d			23 50						00 23			00 37					
Wokingham	d			23 57						00 32			00 44					
Winnersh	d			23 59						00 36								
Winnersh Triangle	d			00 02						00 38								
Earley	d			00 05						00 40								
Reading 7	a			00 13						00 48			00 55					

London - Hounslow, Richmond, Kingston, Windsor, Weybridge, Ascot, Guildford and Reading

		SW ■	SW	SW	SW ■	SW	SW	SW	SW	SW		SW ■	SW ■	SW ■	SW ■	SW	SW	SW	SW	SW ■		SW	SW ■	SW	SW
London Waterloo [15] ⊖	d	22p50	22p52	23p13	23p20	23p22	23p33	23p38								23p52	23p58		00 18				05 05		05 33
Vauxhall ⊖	d		22p56	23p17		23p26	23p37									23p56	00 02		00 22				05 09		05 37
Queenstown Rd.(Battersea)	d		22p59			23p29	23p40									23p59			00 25				05 12		05 40
Clapham Junction [10]	d	22p58	23p02	23p23	23p28	23p32	23p43	23p46								00 02	00 08		00 29				05 15		05 43
Wandsworth Town	d		23p05			23p35	23p46									00 05			00 32				05 18		05 46
Putney	d		23p08	23p27		23p38	23p49									00 08	00 12		00 35				05 21		05 49
Barnes	d		23p12			23p42	23p52									00 12			00 38				05 24		05 52
Barnes Bridge	d		23p14			23p44										00 14									
Chiswick	d		23p17			23p47										00 17									
Kew Bridge	d		23p20			23p50										00 20									
Brentford	d		23p23			23p53										00 23									
Syon Lane	d		23p25			23p55										00 25									
Isleworth	d		23p27			23p57										00 27									
Hounslow	d		23p31			00 01										00 31									
Mortlake	d						23p54												00 40				05 26		05 54
North Sheen	d						23p56			←									00 42				05 28		05 56
Richmond ⊖	d	23p06		23p33	23p37		23p59	23p54		23p59							00 18		00 45				05 31		05 59
St Margarets	d						→			00 01									00 47				05 33		06 01
Twickenham	a	23p10		23p36	23p41			23p58		00 03							00 21		00 49				05 35		06 03
	d	23p10		23p37	23p41			23p58		00 04							00 22		00 50				05 36	05 53	06 04
Strawberry Hill	d									00 07									00s53						06 07
Fulwell	a																								
Teddington	a									00 11									00s56						06 10
Hampton Wick	a									00 14									00s59						06 14
Kingston	a									00 16									01 01						06 16
Whitton	d			23p40					←								00 25	←					05 39	05 56	
Feltham	d	23p16	23p36	23p44	23p48	00 06		00 04	00 06							00 37	00 29	00 37					05 43	06 00	
Ashford (Surrey)	d		23p40	23p48		→			00 10							→	00 33	00 41					05 47	06 04	
Staines	d	23p23	23p44	23p52	23p56			00 11	00 14								00a37	00a46		05 23		05 44	05 53	06 08	
Wraysbury	d			23p56																				06 12	
Sunnymeads	d			23p59																				06 15	
Datchet	d			00 02																				06 18	
Windsor & Eton Riverside	a			00 06																				06 22	
Egham	d	23p27	23p49		00 01			00 15	00 19											05 27		05 49	05 57		
Virginia Water	a	23p31	23p53		00 05			00 19	00 23											05 31		05 53	06 01		
	d	23p31	23p53		00 05			00 19	00 23											05 31		05 53	06 01		
Chertsey	d		23p59						00 29													05 59			
Addlestone	d		00 02						00a32													06 02			
Weybridge	a																					06 07			
Byfleet & New Haw	d		00 06																						
West Byfleet	d		00 09																						
Woking	a		00 15																						
Longcross	d																								
Sunningdale	d	23p37			00 11			00 25												05 37			06 07		
Ascot [3]	d	23p43			00 15			00 30				00 32								05 43			06 13		
Bagshot	d											00 38													
Camberley	a											00 44													
Frimley	d											00 48													
Ash Vale	d											00 57													
Aldershot	a											01s02													
	d												06 08	06 38	07 08										
Ash [5]	d												06 15	06 45	07 15										
Wanborough	d												06 18	06 48	07 18										
Guildford	a												06 25	06 55	07 25										
Martins Heron	d	23p47			00 19			00 34												05 47			06 17		
Bracknell	d	23p50			00 23			00 37												05 50			06 20		
Wokingham	d	23p57			00 32			00 44												05 57			06 27		
Winnersh	d	23p59			00 36															06 00			06 30		
Winnersh Triangle	d	00 02			00 38															06 02			06 32		
Earley	d	00 05			00 40															06 05			06 35		
Reading [7]	a	00 10			00 45			00 52												06 10			06 40		

London - Hounslow, Richmond, Kingston, Windsor, Weybridge, Ascot, Guildford and Reading

		SW	SW ■	SW	SW	SW		SW ■	SW ■	SW ■	SW	SW	SW	SW	SW ■	SW ■		SW	SW	SW	SW	SW	SW ■	SW	SW ■
London Waterloo [15] ⊖	d		05 50	05 58	06 03				06 20		06 22	06 28		06 33	06 50			06 52	06 58		07 03	07 15	07 20		
Vauxhall ⊖	d			06 02	06 07						06 26	06 32		06 37				06 56	07 02		07 07	07 19			
Queenstown Rd.(Battersea)	d				06 10						06 29			06 40				06 59			07 10	07 22			
Clapham Junction [10]	d		05 58	06 08	06 13				06 28		06 32	06 38		06 43	06 58			07 02	07 08		07 13	07 25	07 28		
Wandsworth Town	d				06 16						06 35			06 46				07 05			07 16	07 28			
Putney	d			06 12	06 19						06 38	06 42		06 49				07 08	07 12		07 19	07 31			
Barnes	d				06 22						06 42			06 52				07 12			07 22	07 35			
Barnes Bridge	d										06 44							07 14							
Chiswick	d										06 47							07 17							
Kew Bridge	d										06 50							07 20							
Brentford	d										06 53							07 23							
Syon Lane	d										06 55							07 25							
Isleworth	d										06 57							07 27							
Hounslow	d										07 01							07 31							
Mortlake	d				06 24									06 54							07 24	07 37			
North Sheen	d				06 26									06 56							07 26	07 39		←	
Richmond ⊖	d		06 06	06 18	06 29				06 36			06 48		06 59	07 06				07 18		07 29	07 42	07 36	07 42	
St Margarets	d				06 31									07 01							07 31	→		07 44	
Twickenham	a		06 10	06 21	06 33				06 40			06 51		07 03	07 10				07 21		07 33		07 40	07 46	
	d		06 10	06 22	06 34				06 40			06 52		07 04	07 10				07 22		07 34		07 40	07 47	
Strawberry Hill	d				06 37									07 07							07 37				
Fulwell	a																								
Teddington	a				06 40									07 10							07 40				
Hampton Wick	a				06 44									07 14							07 44				
Kingston	a				06 46									07 16							07 46				
Whitton	d			06 25								06 55	←						07 25	←				07a50	
Feltham	d		06 16	06 29					06 46		07 06	06 59	07 06		07 16			07 36	07 29	07 36			07 46		
Ashford (Surrey)	d			06 33							→	07 03	07 10					→	07 33	07 40					
Staines	d	06 16	06 23	06 37		06 44			06 53			07 07	07 14		07 23				07 37	07 44			07 53		
Wraysbury	d			06 41								07 11							07 41						
Sunnymeads	d			06 44								07 14							07 44						
Datchet	d			06 47								07 17							07 47						
Windsor & Eton Riverside	a			06 51								07 21							07 51						
Egham	d	06 20	06 27			06 49			06 57				07 19		07 27					07 49			07 57		
Virginia Water	a	06 25	06 31			06 53			07 01				07 23		07 31					07 53			08 01		
	d	06 25	06 31			06 53			07 01				07 23		07 31					07 53			08 01		
Chertsey	d	06 30				06 59							07 29							07 59					
Addlestone	d	06 33				07 02							07 32							08 02					
Weybridge	a	06 38				07 07							07 37							08 07					
Byfleet & New Haw	d																								
West Byfleet	d																								
Woking	a																								
Longcross	d																								
Sunningdale	d		06 37						07 07						07 37								08 07		
Ascot [3]	d		06 43					06 53	07 13						07 43	07 53							08 13		08 23
Bagshot	d							06 59								07 59									08 29
Camberley	a							07 05								08 05									08 35
Frimley	d							07 13								08 13									08 43
Ash Vale	d							07 19								08 19									08 49
Aldershot	a							07 24								08 24									08 54
	d							07 38		08 08						08 38									09 08
Ash [5]	d							07 45		08 15						08 45									09 15
Wanborough	d							07 48		08 18						08 48									09 18
Guildford	a							07 55		08 25						08 55									09 25
Martins Heron	d		06 47						07 17						07 47								08 17		
Bracknell	d		06 50						07 20						07 50								08 20		
Wokingham	d		06 57						07 27						07 57								08 27		
Winnersh	d		07 00						07 30						08 00								08 30		
Winnersh Triangle	d		07 02						07 32						08 02								08 32		
Earley	d		07 05						07 35						08 05								08 35		
Reading [7]	a		07 10						07 40						08 10								08 40		

Table 149

Saturdays
until 1 October

London - Hounslow, Richmond, Kingston, Windsor, Weybridge, Ascot, Guildford and Reading

Station		SW	SW	SW	SW	SW	SW	SW 1	SW	SW 1	SW	SW	SW	SW	SW	SW	SW 1	SW	SW 1	SW	SW	SW
London Waterloo 15 ⊖	d	07 22	07 28		07 33	07 37	07 45	07 50			07 52	07 58		08 03	08 07	08 15	08 20			08 22	08 28	
Vauxhall ⊖	d	07 26	07 32		07 37	07 41	07 49				07 56	08 02		08 07	08 11	08 19				08 26	08 32	
Queenstown Rd.(Battersea)	d	07 29			07 40	07 44	07 52				07 59			08 10	08 14	08 22				08 29		
Clapham Junction 10	d	07 32	07 38		07 43	07 47	07 55	07 58			08 02	08 08		08 13	08 17	08 25	08 28			08 32	08 38	
Wandsworth Town	d	07 35			07 46	07 50	07 58				08 05			08 16	08 20	08 28				08 35		
Putney	d	07 38	07 42		07 49	07 53	08 01				08 08	08 12		08 19	08 23	08 31				08 38	08 42	
Barnes	d	07 42			07 52	07 57	08 05				08 12			08 22	08 27	08 35				08 42		
Barnes Bridge	d	07 44				07 59					08 14				08 29					08 44		
Chiswick	d	07 47				08 02					08 17				08 32					08 47		
Kew Bridge	d	07 50				08 05					08 20				08 35					08 50		
Brentford	d	07 53				08 08					08 23				08 38					08 53		
Syon Lane	d	07 55				08 10					08 25				08 40					08 55		
Isleworth	d	07 57				08 12					08 27				08 42					08 57		
Hounslow	d	08 01				08 18					08 31				08 48					09 01		
Mortlake	d				07 54		08 07							08 24		08 37						
North Sheen	d				07 56		08 09		←					08 26		08 39		←				
Richmond ⊖	d		07 48		07 59		08 12	08 06	08 12			08 18		08 29		08 42	08 36	08 42			08 48	
St Margarets	d				08 01		↪		08 14					08 31		↪		08 44				
Twickenham	a		07 51		08 03			08 10	08 16			08 21		08 33			08 40	08 46			08 51	
	d		07 52		08 04			08 10	08 17			08 22		08 34			08 40	08 47			08 52	
Strawberry Hill	d				08 07									08 37								
Fulwell	a																					
Teddington	a				08 10									08 40								
Hampton Wick	a				08 14									08 44								
Kingston	a				08 16									08 46								
Whitton	d		07 55	←		08a23			08a20			08 25	←		08a53			08a50			08 55	←
Feltham	d	08 06	07 59	08 06				08 16			08 36	08 29	08 36				08 46			09 06	08 59	09 06
Ashford (Surrey)	d	↪	08 03	08 10							↪	08 33	08 40							↪	09 03	09 10
Staines	d		08 07	08 14				08 23				08 37	08 44				08 53				09 07	09 14
Wraysbury	d		08 11									08 41									09 11	
Sunnymeads	d		08 14									08 44									09 14	
Datchet	d		08 17									08 47									09 17	
Windsor & Eton Riverside	a		08 21									08 51									09 21	
Egham	d			08 19				08 27					08 49				08 57					09 19
Virginia Water	a			08 23				08 31					08 53				09 01					09 23
	d			08 23				08 31					08 53				09 01					09 23
Chertsey	d			08 29									08 59									09 29
Addlestone	d			08 32									09 02									09 32
Weybridge	a			08 37									09 07									09 37
Byfleet & New Haw	d																					
West Byfleet	d																					
Woking	a																					
Longcross	d																					
Sunningdale	d							08 37									09 07					
Ascot 3	d							08 43		08 53							09 13		09 23			
Bagshot	d									08 59									09 29			
Camberley	a									09 05									09 35			
Frimley	d									09 13									09 43			
Ash Vale	d									09 19									09 49			
Aldershot	a									09 24									09 54			
	d									09 38									10 08			
Ash 5	d									09 45									10 15			
Wanborough	d									09 48									10 18			
Guildford	a									09 55									10 25			
Martins Heron	d							08 47									09 17					
Bracknell	d							08 50									09 20					
Wokingham	d							08 57									09 27					
Winnersh	d							09 00									09 30					
Winnersh Triangle	d							09 02									09 32					
Earley	d							09 05									09 35					
Reading 7	a							09 10									09 40					

Table 149

Saturdays
until 1 October

London - Hounslow, Richmond, Kingston, Windsor, Weybridge, Ascot, Guildford and Reading

Station		SW	SW	SW	SW 1	SW	SW 1	SW	SW	SW	SW	SW	SW	SW 1	SW	SW 1	SW	SW	SW	SW	SW	SW	SW 1
London Waterloo 15 ⊖	d	08 33	08 37	08 45	08 50			08 52	08 58		09 03	09 07	09 15	09 20			09 22	09 28		09 33	09 37	09 45	09 50
Vauxhall ⊖	d	08 37	08 41	08 49				08 56	09 02		09 07	09 11	09 19				09 26	09 32		09 37	09 41	09 49	
Queenstown Rd.(Battersea)	d	08 40	08 44	08 52				08 59			09 10	09 14	09 22				09 29			09 40	09 44	09 52	
Clapham Junction 10	d	08 43	08 47	08 55	08 58			09 02	09 08		09 13	09 17	09 25	09 28			09 32	09 38		09 43	09 47	09 55	09 58
Wandsworth Town	d	08 46	08 50	08 58				09 05			09 16	09 20	09 28				09 35			09 46	09 50	09 58	
Putney	d	08 49	08 53	09 01				09 08	09 12		09 19	09 23	09 31				09 38	09 42		09 49	09 53	10 01	
Barnes	d	08 52	08 57	09 05				09 12			09 22	09 27	09 35				09 42			09 52	09 57	10 05	
Barnes Bridge	d		08 59					09 14				09 29					09 44				09 59		
Chiswick	d		09 02					09 17				09 32					09 47				10 02		
Kew Bridge	d		09 05					09 20				09 35					09 50				10 05		
Brentford	d		09 08					09 23				09 38					09 53				10 08		
Syon Lane	d		09 10					09 25				09 40					09 55				10 10		
Isleworth	d		09 12					09 27				09 42					09 57				10 12		
Hounslow	d		09 18					09 31				09 48					10 01				10 18		
Mortlake	d	08 54		09 07							09 24		09 37							09 54		10 07	
North Sheen	d	08 56		09 09		←					09 26		09 39		←					09 56		10 09	
Richmond ⊖	d	08 59		09 12	09 06	09 12			09 18		09 29		09 42	09 36	09 42			09 48		09 59		10 12	10 06
St Margarets	d	09 01		↪		09 14					09 31		↪		09 44					10 01		↪	
Twickenham	a	09 03			09 10	09 16			09 21		09 33			09 40	09 46			09 51		10 03			10 10
	d	09 04			09 10	09 17			09 22		09 34			09 40	09 47			09 52		10 04			10 10
Strawberry Hill	d	09 07									09 37									10 07			
Fulwell	a																						
Teddington	a	09 10									09 40									10 10			
Hampton Wick	a	09 14									09 44									10 14			
Kingston	a	09 16									09 46									10 16			
Whitton	d		09a23			09a20			09 25	←		09a53			09a50			09 55	←		10a23		
Feltham	d				09 16			09 36	09 29	09 36				09 46			10 06	09 59	10 06				10 16
Ashford (Surrey)	d							↪	09 33	09 40							↪	10 03	10 10				
Staines	d				09 23				09 37	09 44				09 53				10 07	10 14				10 23
Wraysbury	d								09 41									10 11					
Sunnymeads	d								09 44									10 14					
Datchet	d								09 47									10 17					
Windsor & Eton Riverside	a								09 51									10 21					
Egham	d				09 27					09 49				09 57					10 19				10 27
Virginia Water	a				09 31					09 53				10 01					10 23				10 31
	d				09 31					09 53				10 01					10 23				10 31
Chertsey	d									09 59									10 29				
Addlestone	d									10 02									10 32				
Weybridge	a									10 07									10 37				
Byfleet & New Haw	d																						
West Byfleet	d																						
Woking	a																						
Longcross	d																						
Sunningdale	d				09 37									10 07									10 37
Ascot 3	d				09 43		09 53							10 13		10 23							10 43
Bagshot	d						09 59									10 29							
Camberley	a						10 05									10 35							
Frimley	d						10 13									10 43							
Ash Vale	d						10 19									10 49							
Aldershot	a						10 24									10 54							
	d						10 38									11 08							
Ash 5	d						10 45									11 15							
Wanborough	d						10 48									11 18							
Guildford	a						10 55									11 25							
Martins Heron	d				09 47									10 17									10 47
Bracknell	d				09 50									10 20									10 50
Wokingham	d				09 57									10 27									10 57
Winnersh	d				10 00									10 30									11 00
Winnersh Triangle	d				10 02									10 32									11 02
Earley	d				10 05									10 35									11 05
Reading 7	a				10 10									10 40									11 10

London - Hounslow, Richmond, Kingston, Windsor, Weybridge, Ascot, Guildford and Reading

		SW	SW 1	SW	SW	SW	SW	SW	SW	SW 1	SW	SW 1	SW	SW	SW	SW	SW	SW	SW 1	SW	SW 1	SW
London Waterloo 15 ⊖	d			09 52	09 58		10 03	10 07	10 15	10 20			10 22	10 28		10 33	10 37	10 45	10 50			10 52
Vauxhall ⊖	d			09 56	10 02		10 07	10 11	10 19				10 26	10 32		10 37	10 41	10 49				10 56
Queenstown Rd.(Battersea)	d			09 59			10 10	10 14	10 22				10 29			10 40	10 44	10 52				10 59
Clapham Junction 10	d			10 02	10 08		10 13	10 17	10 25	10 28			10 32	10 38		10 43	10 47	10 55	10 58			11 02
Wandsworth Town	d			10 05			10 16	10 20	10 28				10 35			10 46	10 50	10 58				11 05
Putney	d			10 08	10 12		10 19	10 23	10 31				10 38	10 42		10 49	10 53	11 01				11 08
Barnes	d			10 12			10 22	10 27	10 35				10 42			10 52	10 57	11 05				11 12
Barnes Bridge	d			10 14				10 29					10 44				10 59					11 14
Chiswick	d			10 17				10 32					10 47				11 02					11 17
Kew Bridge	d			10 20				10 35					10 50				11 05					11 20
Brentford	d			10 23				10 38					10 53				11 08					11 23
Syon Lane	d			10 25				10 40					10 55				11 10					11 25
Isleworth	d			10 27				10 42					10 57				11 12					11 27
Hounslow	d			10 31				10 48					11 01				11 18					11 31
Mortlake	d						10 24		10 37							10 54		11 07				
North Sheen	d	←					10 26		10 39		←					10 56		11 09		←		
Richmond ⊖	d	10 12			10 18		10 29		10 42	10 36	10 42			10 48		10 59		11 12	11 06	11 12		
St Margarets	d	10 14					10 31		→		10 44					11 01		→		11 14		
Twickenham	a	10 16			10 21		10 33			10 40	10 46			10 51		11 03			11 10	11 16		
	d	10 17			10 22		10 34			10 40	10 47			10 52		11 04			11 10	11 17		
Strawberry Hill	d						10 37									11 07						
Fulwell	a																					
Teddington	a						10 40									11 10						
Hampton Wick	a						10 44									11 14						
Kingston	a						10 46									11 16						
Whitton	d	10a20			10 25	←		10a53			10a50			10 55	←		11a23			11a20		
Feltham	d			10 36	10 29	10 36				10 46			11 06	10 59	11 06				11 16			11 36
Ashford (Surrey)	d			→	10 33	10 40							→	11 03	11 10							→
Staines	d				10 37	10 44				10 53				11 07	11 14				11 23			
Wraysbury	d				10 41									11 11								
Sunnymeads	d				10 44									11 14								
Datchet	d				10 47									11 17								
Windsor & Eton Riverside	a				10 51									11 21								
Egham	d					10 49				10 57					11 19				11 27			
Virginia Water	a					10 53				11 01					11 23				11 31			
	d					10 53				11 01					11 23				11 31			
Chertsey	d					10 59									11 29							
Addlestone	d					11 02									11 32							
Weybridge	a					11 07									11 37							
Byfleet & New Haw	d																					
West Byfleet	d																					
Woking	a																					
Longcross	d																					
Sunningdale	d									11 07									11 37			
Ascot 3	d		10 53							11 13		11 23							11 43		11 53	
Bagshot	d		10 59									11 29									11 59	
Camberley	a		11 05									11 35									12 05	
Frimley	d		11 13									11 43									12 13	
Ash Vale	d		11 19									11 49									12 19	
Aldershot	a		11 24									11 54									12 24	
	d		11 38									12 08									12 38	
Ash 5	d		11 45									12 15									12 45	
Wanborough	d		11 48									12 18									12 48	
Guildford	a		11 55									12 25									12 55	
Martins Heron	d									11 17									11 47			
Bracknell	d									11 20									11 50			
Wokingham	d									11 27									11 57			
Winnersh	d									11 30									12 00			
Winnersh Triangle	d									11 32									12 02			
Earley	d									11 35									12 05			
Reading 7	a									11 40									12 10			

London - Hounslow, Richmond, Kingston, Windsor, Weybridge, Ascot, Guildford and Reading

		SW	SW	SW	SW	SW	SW 1	SW	SW 1	SW	SW	SW	SW	SW	SW	SW 1	SW	SW 1	SW	SW	SW	SW	SW
London Waterloo 15 ⊖	d	10 58		11 03	11 07	11 15	11 20			11 22	11 28		11 33	11 37	11 45	11 50			11 52	11 58		12 03	12 07
Vauxhall ⊖	d	11 02		11 07	11 11	11 19				11 26	11 32		11 37	11 41	11 49				11 56	12 02		12 07	12 11
Queenstown Rd.(Battersea)	d			11 10	11 14	11 22				11 29			11 40	11 44	11 52				11 59			12 10	12 14
Clapham Junction 10	d	11 08		11 13	11 17	11 25	11 28			11 32	11 38		11 43	11 47	11 55	11 58			12 02	12 08		12 13	12 17
Wandsworth Town	d			11 16	11 20	11 28				11 35			11 46	11 50	11 58				12 05			12 16	12 20
Putney	d	11 12		11 19	11 23	11 31				11 38	11 42		11 49	11 53	12 01				12 08	12 12		12 19	12 23
Barnes	d			11 22	11 27	11 35				11 42			11 52	11 57	12 05				12 12			12 22	12 27
Barnes Bridge	d				11 29					11 44				11 59					12 14				12 29
Chiswick	d				11 32					11 47				12 02					12 17				12 32
Kew Bridge	d				11 35					11 50				12 05					12 20				12 35
Brentford	d				11 38					11 53				12 08					12 23				12 38
Syon Lane	d				11 40					11 55				12 10					12 25				12 40
Isleworth	d				11 42					11 57				12 12					12 27				12 42
Hounslow	d				11 48					12 01				12 18					12 31				12 48
Mortlake	d			11 24		11 37							11 54		12 07							12 24	
North Sheen	d			11 26		11 39		←					11 56		12 09		←					12 26	
Richmond ⊖	d	11 18		11 29		11 42	11 36	11 42			11 48		11 59		12 12	12 06	12 12			12 18		12 29	
St Margarets	d			11 31		→		11 44					12 01		→		12 14					12 31	
Twickenham	a	11 21		11 33			11 40	11 46			11 51		12 03			12 10	12 16			12 21		12 33	
	d	11 22		11 34			11 40	11 47			11 52		12 04			12 10	12 17			12 22		12 34	
Strawberry Hill	d			11 37									12 07									12 37	
Fulwell	a																						
Teddington	a			11 40									12 10									12 40	
Hampton Wick	a			11 44									12 14									12 44	
Kingston	a			11 46									12 16									12 46	
Whitton	d	11 25	←		11a53			11a50			11 55	←		12a23			12a20			12 25	←		12a53
Feltham	d	11 29	11 36				11 46			12 06	11 59	12 06				12 16			12 36	12 29	12 36		
Ashford (Surrey)	d	11 33	11 40							→	12 03	12 10							→	12 33	12 40		
Staines	d	11 37	11 44				11 53				12 07	12 14				12 23				12 37	12 44		
Wraysbury	d	11 41									12 11									12 41			
Sunnymeads	d	11 44									12 14									12 44			
Datchet	d	11 47									12 17									12 47			
Windsor & Eton Riverside	a	11 51									12 21									12 51			
Egham	d		11 49				11 57					12 19				12 27					12 49		
Virginia Water	a		11 53				12 01					12 23				12 31					12 53		
	d		11 53				12 01					12 23				12 31					12 53		
Chertsey	d		11 59									12 29									12 59		
Addlestone	d		12 02									12 32									13 02		
Weybridge	a		12 07									12 37									13 07		
Byfleet & New Haw	d																						
West Byfleet	d																						
Woking	a																						
Longcross	d																						
Sunningdale	d						12 07									12 37							
Ascot 3	d						12 13		12 23							12 43		12 53					
Bagshot	d								12 29									12 59					
Camberley	a								12 35									13 05					
Frimley	d								12 43									13 13					
Ash Vale	d								12 49									13 19					
Aldershot	a								12 54									13 24					
	d								13 08									13 38					
Ash 5	d								13 15									13 45					
Wanborough	d								13 18									13 48					
Guildford	a								13 25									13 55					
Martins Heron	d						12 17									12 47							
Bracknell	d						12 20									12 50							
Wokingham	d						12 27									12 57							
Winnersh	d						12 30									13 00							
Winnersh Triangle	d						12 32									13 02							
Earley	d						12 35									13 05							
Reading 7	a						12 40									13 10							

Table 149

Saturdays
until 1 October

London - Hounslow, Richmond, Kingston, Windsor, Weybridge, Ascot, Guildford and Reading

		SW	SW 1	SW	SW 1	SW	SW	SW	SW	SW	SW	SW 1	SW	SW 1	SW	SW	SW	SW	SW	SW	SW 1	SW	SW 1
London Waterloo 15 ⊖	d	12 15	12 20			12 22	12 28		12 33	12 37	12 45	12 50			12 52	12 58		13 03	13 07	13 15	13 20		
Vauxhall ⊖	d	12 19				12 26	12 32		12 37	12 41	12 49				12 56	13 02		13 07	13 11	13 19			
Queenstown Rd.(Battersea)	d	12 22				12 29			12 40	12 44	12 52				12 59			13 10	13 14	13 22			
Clapham Junction 10	d	12 25	12 28			12 32	12 38		12 43	12 47	12 55	12 58			13 02	13 08		13 13	13 17	13 25	13 28		
Wandsworth Town	d	12 28				12 35			12 46	12 50	12 58				13 05			13 16	13 20	13 28			
Putney	d	12 31				12 38	12 42		12 49	12 53	13 01				13 08	13 12		13 19	13 23	13 31			
Barnes	d	12 35				12 42			12 52	12 57	13 05				13 12			13 22	13 27	13 35			
Barnes Bridge	d					12 44				12 59					13 14				13 29				
Chiswick	d					12 47				13 02					13 17				13 32				
Kew Bridge	d					12 50				13 05					13 20				13 35				
Brentford	d					12 53				13 08					13 23				13 38				
Syon Lane	d					12 55				13 10					13 25				13 40				
Isleworth	d					12 57				13 12					13 27				13 42				
Hounslow	d					13 01				13 18					13 31				13 48				
Mortlake	d	12 37							12 54		13 07							13 24		13 37			
North Sheen	d	12 39		←					12 56		13 09		←					13 26		13 39		←	
Richmond ⊖	d	12 42	12 36	12 42			12 48		12 59		13 12	13 06	13 12			13 18		13 29		13 42	13 36	13 42	
St Margarets	d	→		12 44					13 01		→		13 14					13 31		→		13 44	
Twickenham	a		12 40	12 46			12 51		13 03			13 10	13 16			13 21		13 33			13 40	13 46	
	d		12 40	12 47			12 52		13 04			13 10	13 17			13 22		13 34			13 40	13 47	
Strawberry Hill	d								13 07									13 37					
Fulwell	a																						
Teddington	a								13 10									13 40					
Hampton Wick	a								13 14									13 44					
Kingston	a								13 16									13 46					
Whitton	d			12a50			12 55	←		13a23			13a20			13 25	←		13a53			13a50	
Feltham	d		12 46			13 06	12 59	13 06				13 16			13 36	13 29	13 36				13 46		
Ashford (Surrey)	d					→	13 03	13 10							→	13 33	13 40						
Staines	d		12 53				13 07	13 14				13 23				13 37	13 44				13 53		
Wraysbury	d						13 11									13 41							
Sunnymeads	d						13 14									13 44							
Datchet	d						13 17									13 47							
Windsor & Eton Riverside	a						13 21									13 51							
Egham	d		12 57					13 19				13 27					13 49				13 57		
Virginia Water	a		13 01					13 23				13 31					13 53				14 01		
	d		13 01					13 23				13 31					13 53				14 01		
Chertsey	d							13 29									13 59						
Addlestone	d							13 32									14 02						
Weybridge	a							13 37									14 07						
Byfleet & New Haw	d																						
West Byfleet	d																						
Woking	a																						
Longcross	d																						
Sunningdale	d		13 07									13 37									14 07		
Ascot 8	d		13 13		13 23							13 43		13 53							14 13		14 23
Bagshot	d				13 29									13 59									14 29
Camberley	a				13 35									14 05									14 35
Frimley	d				13 43									14 13									14 43
Ash Vale	d				13 49									14 19									14 49
Aldershot	a				13 54									14 24									14 54
	d				14 08									14 38									15 08
Ash 5	d				14 15									14 45									15 15
Wanborough	d				14 18									14 48									15 18
Guildford	a				14 25									14 55									15 25
Martins Heron	d		13 17									13 47									14 17		
Bracknell	d		13 20									13 50									14 20		
Wokingham	d		13 27									13 57									14 27		
Winnersh	d		13 30									14 00									14 30		
Winnersh Triangle	d		13 32									14 02									14 32		
Earley	d		13 35									14 05									14 35		
Reading 7	a		13 40									14 10									14 40		

Table 149

Saturdays
until 1 October

London - Hounslow, Richmond, Kingston, Windsor, Weybridge, Ascot, Guildford and Reading

		SW	SW	SW	SW	SW	SW	SW 1	SW	SW 1	SW	SW	SW	SW	SW	SW	SW 1	SW	SW 1	SW	SW	SW
London Waterloo 15 ⊖	d	13 22	13 28		13 33	13 37	13 45	13 50			13 52	13 58		14 03	14 07	14 15	14 20			14 22	14 28	
Vauxhall ⊖	d	13 26	13 32		13 37	13 41	13 49				13 56	14 02		14 07	14 11	14 19				14 26	14 32	
Queenstown Rd.(Battersea)	d	13 29			13 40	13 44	13 52				13 59			14 10	14 14	14 22				14 29		
Clapham Junction 10	d	13 32	13 38		13 43	13 47	13 55	13 58			14 02	14 08		14 13	14 17	14 25	14 28			14 32	14 38	
Wandsworth Town	d	13 35			13 46	13 50	13 58				14 05			14 16	14 20	14 28				14 35		
Putney	d	13 38	13 42		13 49	13 53	14 01				14 08	14 12		14 19	14 23	14 31				14 38	14 42	
Barnes	d	13 42			13 52	13 57	14 05				14 12			14 22	14 27	14 35				14 42		
Barnes Bridge	d	13 44				13 59					14 14				14 29					14 44		
Chiswick	d	13 47				14 02					14 17				14 32					14 47		
Kew Bridge	d	13 50				14 05					14 20				14 35					14 50		
Brentford	d	13 53				14 08					14 23				14 38					14 53		
Syon Lane	d	13 55				14 10					14 25				14 40					14 55		
Isleworth	d	13 57				14 12					14 27				14 42					14 57		
Hounslow	d	14 01				14 18					14 31				14 48					15 01		
Mortlake	d				13 54		14 07							14 24		14 37						
North Sheen	d				13 56		14 09		←					14 26		14 39		←				
Richmond ⊖	d		13 48		13 59		14 12	14 06	14 12			14 18		14 29		14 42	14 36	14 42			14 48	
St Margarets	d				14 01		→		14 14					14 31		→		14 44				
Twickenham	a		13 51		14 03			14 10	14 16			14 21		14 33			14 40	14 46			14 51	
	d		13 52		14 04			14 10	14 17			14 22		14 34			14 40	14 47			14 52	
Strawberry Hill	d				14 07									14 37								
Fulwell	a																					
Teddington	a				14 10									14 40								
Hampton Wick	a				14 14									14 44								
Kingston	a				14 16									14 46								
Whitton	d		13 55	←		14a23			14a20			14 25	←		14a53			14a50			14 55	←
Feltham	d	14 06	13 59	14 06				14 16			14 36	14 29	14 36				14 46			15 06	14 59	15 06
Ashford (Surrey)	d	→	14 03	14 10							→	14 33	14 40							→	15 03	15 10
Staines	d		14 07	14 14				14 23				14 37	14 44				14 53				15 07	15 14
Wraysbury	d		14 11									14 41									15 11	
Sunnymeads	d		14 14									14 44									15 14	
Datchet	d		14 17									14 47									15 17	
Windsor & Eton Riverside	a		14 21									14 51									15 22	
Egham	d			14 19				14 27					14 49				14 57					15 19
Virginia Water	a			14 23				14 31					14 53				15 01					15 23
	d			14 23				14 31					14 53				15 01					15 23
Chertsey	d			14 29									14 59									15 29
Addlestone	d			14 32									15 02									15 32
Weybridge	a			14 37									15 07									15 37
Byfleet & New Haw	d																					
West Byfleet	d																					
Woking	a																					
Longcross	d																					
Sunningdale	d							14 37									15 07					
Ascot 8	d							14 43		14 53							15 13		15 23			
Bagshot	d									14 59									15 29			
Camberley	a									15 05									15 35			
Frimley	d									15 13									15 43			
Ash Vale	d									15 19									15 49			
Aldershot	a									15 24									15 54			
	d									15 38									16 08			
Ash 5	d									15 45									16 15			
Wanborough	d									15 48									16 18			
Guildford	a									15 55									16 25			
Martins Heron	d							14 47									15 17					
Bracknell	d							14 50									15 20					
Wokingham	d							14 57									15 27					
Winnersh	d							15 00									15 30					
Winnersh Triangle	d							15 02									15 32					
Earley	d							15 05									15 35					
Reading 7	a							15 10									15 40					

London - Hounslow, Richmond, Kingston, Windsor, Weybridge, Ascot, Guildford and Reading

		SW	SW	SW	SW 1	SW	SW 1	SW	SW	SW	SW	SW	SW	SW 1	SW	SW 1	SW	SW	SW	SW	SW	SW	SW 1
London Waterloo 15 ⊖	d	14 33	14 37	14 45	14 50			14 52	14 58		15 03	15 07	15 15	15 20			15 22	15 28		15 33	15 37	15 45	15 50
Vauxhall ⊖	d	14 37	14 41	14 49				14 56	15 02		15 07	15 11	15 19				15 26	15 32		15 37	15 41	15 49	
Queenstown Rd.(Battersea)	d	14 40	14 44	14 52				14 59			15 10	15 14	15 22				15 29			15 40	15 44	15 52	
Clapham Junction 10	d	14 43	14 47	14 55	14 58			15 02	15 08		15 13	15 17	15 25	15 28			15 32	15 38		15 43	15 47	15 55	15 58
Wandsworth Town	d	14 46	14 50	14 58				15 05			15 16	15 20	15 28				15 35			15 46	15 50	15 58	
Putney	d	14 49	14 53	15 01				15 08	15 12		15 19	15 23	15 31				15 38	15 42		15 49	15 53	16 01	
Barnes	d	14 52	14 57	15 05				15 12			15 22	15 27	15 35				15 42			15 52	15 57	16 05	
Barnes Bridge	d		14 59					15 14				15 29					15 44				15 59		
Chiswick	d		15 02					15 17				15 32					15 47				16 02		
Kew Bridge	d		15 05					15 20				15 35					15 50				16 05		
Brentford	d		15 08					15 23				15 38					15 53				16 08		
Syon Lane	d		15 10					15 25				15 40					15 55				16 10		
Isleworth	d		15 12					15 27				15 42					15 57				16 12		
Hounslow	d		15 18					15 31				15 48					16 01				16 18		
Mortlake	d	14 54		15 07							15 24		15 37							15 54		16 07	
North Sheen	d	14 56		15 09		←					15 26		15 39		←					15 56		16 09	
Richmond ⊖	d	14 59		15 12	15 06	15 12			15 18		15 29		15 42	15 36	15 42			15 48		15 59		16 12	16 06
St Margarets	d	15 01		→		15 14					15 31		→		15 44					16 01		→	
Twickenham	a	15 03			15 10	15 16			15 21		15 33			15 40	15 46			15 51		16 03			16 10
	d	15 04			15 10	15 17			15 22		15 34			15 40	15 47			15 52		16 04			16 10
Strawberry Hill	d	15 07									15 37									16 07			
Fulwell	a																						
Teddington	a	15 10									15 40									16 10			
Hampton Wick	a	15 14									15 44									16 14			
Kingston	a	15 16									15 46									16 16			
Whitton	d		15a23			15a20			15 25	←		15a53			15a50			15 55	←		16a23		
Feltham	d				15 16			15 36	15 29	15 36				15 46			16 06	15 59	16 06				16 16
Ashford (Surrey)	d							→	15 33	15 40							→	16 03	16 10				
Staines	d				15 23				15 37	15 44				15 53				16 07	16 14				16 23
Wraysbury	d								15 41									16 11					
Sunnymeads	d								15 44									16 14					
Datchet	d								15 47									16 17					
Windsor & Eton Riverside	a								15 51									16 21					
Egham	d				15 27					15 49				15 57					16 19				16 27
Virginia Water	a				15 31					15 53				16 01					16 23				16 31
	d				15 31					15 53				16 01					16 23				16 31
Chertsey	d									15 59									16 29				
Addlestone	d									16 02									16 32				
Weybridge	a									16 07									16 42				
Byfleet & New Haw	d																						
West Byfleet	d																						
Woking	a																						
Longcross	d																						
Sunningdale	d				15 37									16 07									16 37
Ascot 3	d				15 43		15 53							16 13		16 23							16 43
Bagshot	d						15 59									16 29							
Camberley	a						16 05									16 35							
Frimley	d						16 13									16 43							
Ash Vale	d						16 19									16 49							
Aldershot	a						16 24									16 54							
	d						16 38									17 08							
Ash 5	d						16 45									17 15							
Wanborough	d						16 48									17 18							
Guildford	a						16 55									17 25							
Martins Heron	d				15 47									16 17									16 47
Bracknell	d				15 50									16 20									16 50
Wokingham	d				15 57									16 27									16 57
Winnersh	d				16 00									16 30									17 00
Winnersh Triangle	d				16 02									16 32									17 02
Earley	d				16 05									16 35									17 05
Reading 7	a				16 10									16 40									17 10

London - Hounslow, Richmond, Kingston, Windsor, Weybridge, Ascot, Guildford and Reading

		SW	SW 1	SW	SW	SW	SW	SW	SW	SW 1	SW	SW 1	SW	SW	SW	SW	SW	SW	SW 1	SW	SW 1	SW
London Waterloo 15 ⊖	d			15 52	15 58		16 03	16 07	16 15	16 20			16 22	16 28		16 33	16 37	16 45	16 50			16 52
Vauxhall ⊖	d			15 56	16 02		16 07	16 11	16 19				16 26	16 32		16 37	16 41	16 49				16 56
Queenstown Rd.(Battersea)	d			15 59			16 10	16 14	16 22				16 29			16 40	16 44	16 52				16 59
Clapham Junction 10	d			16 02	16 08		16 13	16 17	16 25	16 28			16 32	16 38		16 43	16 47	16 55	16 58			17 02
Wandsworth Town	d			16 05			16 16	16 20	16 28				16 35			16 46	16 50	16 58				17 05
Putney	d			16 08	16 12		16 19	16 23	16 31				16 38	16 42		16 49	16 53	17 01				17 08
Barnes	d			16 12			16 22	16 27	16 35				16 42			16 52	16 57	17 05				17 12
Barnes Bridge	d			16 14				16 29					16 44				16 59					17 14
Chiswick	d			16 17				16 32					16 47				17 02					17 17
Kew Bridge	d			16 20				16 35					16 50				17 05					17 20
Brentford	d			16 23				16 38					16 53				17 08					17 23
Syon Lane	d			16 25				16 40					16 55				17 10					17 25
Isleworth	d			16 27				16 42					16 57				17 12					17 27
Hounslow	d			16 31				16 48					17 01				17 18					17 31
Mortlake	d						16 24		16 37							16 54		17 07				
North Sheen	d	←					16 26		16 39		←					16 56		17 09		←		
Richmond ⊖	d	16 12			16 18		16 29		16 42	16 36	16 42			16 48		16 59		17 12	17 06	17 12		
St Margarets	d	16 14					16 31		→		16 44					17 01		→		17 14		
Twickenham	a	16 16			16 21		16 33			16 40	16 46			16 51		17 03			17 10	17 16		
	d	16 17			16 22		16 34			16 40	16 47			16 52		17 04			17 10	17 17		
Strawberry Hill	d						16 37									17 07						
Fulwell	a																					
Teddington	a						16 40									17 10						
Hampton Wick	a						16 44									17 14						
Kingston	a						16 46									17 16						
Whitton	d	16a20			16 25	←		16a53			16a50			16 55	←		17a23			17a20		
Feltham	d			16 36	16 29	16 36				16 46			17 06	16 59	17 06				17 16			17 36
Ashford (Surrey)	d			→	16 33	16 40							→	17 03	17 10							→
Staines	d				16 37	16 44				16 53				17 07	17 14				17 23			
Wraysbury	d				16 41									17 11								
Sunnymeads	d				16 44									17 14								
Datchet	d				16 47									17 17								
Windsor & Eton Riverside	a				16 51									17 21								
Egham	d					16 49				16 57					17 19				17 27			
Virginia Water	a					16 53				17 01					17 23				17 31			
	d					16 53				17 01					17 23				17 31			
Chertsey	d					16 59									17 29							
Addlestone	d					17 02									17 32							
Weybridge	a					17 07									17 37							
Byfleet & New Haw	d																					
West Byfleet	d																					
Woking	a																					
Longcross	d																					
Sunningdale	d									17 07									17 37			
Ascot 3	d		16 53							17 13		17 23							17 43		17 53	
Bagshot	d		16 59									17 29									17 59	
Camberley	a		17 05									17 35									18 05	
Frimley	d		17 13									17 43									18 13	
Ash Vale	d		17 19									17 49									18 19	
Aldershot	a		17 24									17 54									18 24	
	d		17 38									18 08									18 38	
Ash 5	d		17 45									18 15									18 45	
Wanborough	d		17 48									18 18									18 48	
Guildford	a		17 55									18 25									18 55	
Martins Heron	d									17 17									17 47			
Bracknell	d									17 20									17 50			
Wokingham	d									17 27									17 57			
Winnersh	d									17 30									18 00			
Winnersh Triangle	d									17 32									18 02			
Earley	d									17 35									18 05			
Reading 7	a									17 40									18 10			

Table 149

Saturdays until 1 October

London - Hounslow, Richmond, Kingston, Windsor, Weybridge, Ascot, Guildford and Reading

		SW	SW	SW	SW	SW	SW 1	SW	SW 1	SW		SW	SW	SW	SW	SW	SW 1	SW	SW 1	SW		SW	SW	SW	SW
London Waterloo [15] ⊖	d	16 58		17 03	17 07	17 15	17 20			17 22		17 28		17 33	17 37	17 45	17 50			17 52		17 58		18 03	18 07
Vauxhall ⊖	d	17 02		17 07	17 11	17 19				17 26		17 32		17 37	17 41	17 49				17 56		18 02		18 07	18 11
Queenstown Rd.(Battersea)	d			17 10	17 14	17 22				17 29				17 40	17 44	17 52				17 59				18 10	18 14
Clapham Junction [10]	d	17 08		17 13	17 17	17 25	17 28			17 32		17 38		17 43	17 47	17 55	17 58			18 02		18 08		18 13	18 17
Wandsworth Town	d			17 16	17 20	17 28				17 35				17 46	17 50	17 58				18 05				18 16	18 20
Putney	d	17 12		17 19	17 23	17 31				17 38		17 42		17 49	17 53	18 01				18 08		18 12		18 19	18 23
Barnes	d			17 22	17 27	17 35				17 42				17 52	17 57	18 05				18 12				18 22	18 27
Barnes Bridge	d				17 29					17 44					17 59					18 14					18 29
Chiswick	d				17 32					17 47					18 02					18 17					18 32
Kew Bridge	d				17 35					17 50					18 05					18 20					18 35
Brentford	d				17 38					17 53					18 08					18 23					18 38
Syon Lane	d				17 40					17 55					18 10					18 25					18 40
Isleworth	d				17 42					17 57					18 12					18 27					18 42
Hounslow	d				17 48					18 01					18 18					18 31					18 48
Mortlake	d			17 24		17 37								17 54		18 07								18 24	
North Sheen	d			17 26		17 39		←						17 56		18 09		←						18 26	
Richmond ⊖	d	17 18		17 29		17 42	17 36	17 42				17 48		17 59		18 12	18 06	18 12				18 18		18 29	
St Margarets	d			17 31		→		17 44						18 01		→		18 14						18 31	
Twickenham	a	17 21		17 33			17 40	17 46				17 51		18 03			18 10	18 16				18 21		18 33	
	d	17 22		17 34			17 40	17 47				17 52		18 04			18 10	18 17				18 22		18 34	
Strawberry Hill	d			17 37										18 07										18 37	
Fulwell	a																								
Teddington	a			17 40										18 10										18 40	
Hampton Wick	a			17 44										18 14										18 44	
Kingston	a			17 46										18 16										18 46	
Whitton	d	17 25	←		17a53			17a50				17 55	←		18a23			18a20				18 25	←		18a53
Feltham	d	17 29	17 36				17 46			18 06		17 59	18 06				18 16			18 36		18 29	18 36		
Ashford (Surrey)	d	17 33	17 40							→		18 03	18 10							→		18 33	18 40		
Staines	d	17 37	17 44				17 53					18 07	18 14				18 23					18 37	18 44		
Wraysbury	d	17 41										18 11										18 41			
Sunnymeads	d	17 44										18 14										18 44			
Datchet	d	17 47										18 17										18 47			
Windsor & Eton Riverside	a	17 51										18 21										18 51			
Egham	d		17 49				17 57						18 19				18 27						18 49		
Virginia Water	a		17 53				18 01						18 23				18 31						18 53		
	d		17 53				18 01						18 23				18 31						18 53		
Chertsey	d		17 59										18 29										18 59		
Addlestone	d		18 02										18 32										19 02		
Weybridge	a		18 07										18 37										19 07		
Byfleet & New Haw	d																								
West Byfleet	d																								
Woking	a																								
Longcross	d																								
Sunningdale	d						18 07										18 37								
Ascot [3]	d						18 13		18 23								18 43		18 53						
Bagshot	d								18 29										18 59						
Camberley	a								18 35										19 05						
Frimley	d								18 43										19 13						
Ash Vale	d								18 49										19 19						
Aldershot	a								18 54										19 24						
	d								19 08										19 38						
Ash [5]	d								19 15										19 45						
Wanborough	d								19 18										19 48						
Guildford	a								19 25										19 55						
Martins Heron	d						18 17										18 47								
Bracknell	d						18 20										18 50								
Wokingham	d						18 27										18 57								
Winnersh	d						18 30										19 00								
Winnersh Triangle	d						18 32										19 02								
Earley	d						18 35										19 05								
Reading [7]	a						18 40										19 10								

Table 149

Saturdays until 1 October

London - Hounslow, Richmond, Kingston, Windsor, Weybridge, Ascot, Guildford and Reading

		SW	SW 1	SW	SW 1	SW		SW	SW	SW	SW	SW	SW 1	SW	SW 1	SW		SW	SW	SW	SW	SW	SW 1	SW	SW 1
London Waterloo [15] ⊖	d	18 15	18 20			18 22		18 28		18 33	18 37	18 45	18 50			18 52		18 58		19 03	19 07	19 15	19 20		
Vauxhall ⊖	d	18 19				18 26		18 32		18 37	18 41	18 49				18 56		19 02		19 07	19 11	19 19			
Queenstown Rd.(Battersea)	d	18 22				18 29				18 40	18 44	18 52				18 59				19 10	19 14	19 22			
Clapham Junction [10]	d	18 25	18 28			18 32		18 38		18 43	18 47	18 55	18 58			19 02		19 08		19 13	19 17	19 25	19 28		
Wandsworth Town	d	18 28				18 35				18 46	18 50	18 58				19 05				19 16	19 20	19 28			
Putney	d	18 31				18 38		18 42		18 49	18 53	19 01				19 08		19 12		19 19	19 23	19 31			
Barnes	d	18 35				18 42				18 52	18 57	19 05				19 12				19 22	19 27	19 35			
Barnes Bridge	d					18 44					18 59					19 14					19 29				
Chiswick	d					18 47					19 02					19 17					19 32				
Kew Bridge	d					18 50					19 05					19 20					19 35				
Brentford	d					18 53					19 08					19 23					19 38				
Syon Lane	d					18 55					19 10					19 25					19 40				
Isleworth	d					18 57					19 12					19 27					19 42				
Hounslow	d					19 01					19 18					19 31					19 48				
Mortlake	d	18 37								18 54		19 07								19 24		19 37			
North Sheen	d	18 39		←						18 56		19 09		←						19 26		19 39		←	
Richmond ⊖	d	18 42	18 36	18 42				18 48		18 59		19 12	19 06	19 12				19 18		19 29		19 42	19 36	19 42	
St Margarets	d	→		18 44						19 01		→		19 14						19 31		→		19 44	
Twickenham	a		18 40	18 46				18 51		19 03			19 10	19 16				19 21		19 33			19 40	19 46	
	d		18 40	18 47				18 52		19 04			19 10	19 17				19 22		19 34			19 40	19 47	
Strawberry Hill	d									19 07										19 37					
Fulwell	a																								
Teddington	a									19 10										19 40					
Hampton Wick	a									19 14										19 44					
Kingston	a									19 16										19 46					
Whitton	d			18a50				18 55	←		19a23			19a20				19 25	←		19a53			19a50	
Feltham	d		18 46			19 06		18 59	19 06				19 16			19 36		19 29	19 36				19 46		
Ashford (Surrey)	d					→		19 03	19 10							→		19 33	19 40						
Staines	d		18 53					19 07	19 14				19 23					19 37	19 44				19 53		
Wraysbury	d							19 11										19 41							
Sunnymeads	d							19 14										19 44							
Datchet	d							19 17										19 47							
Windsor & Eton Riverside	a							19 21										19 51							
Egham	d		18 57						19 19				19 27						19 49				19 57		
Virginia Water	a		19 01						19 23				19 31						19 53				20 01		
	d		19 01						19 23				19 31						19 53				20 01		
Chertsey	d								19 29										19 59						
Addlestone	d								19 32										20 02						
Weybridge	a								19 37										20 07						
Byfleet & New Haw	d																								
West Byfleet	d																								
Woking	a																								
Longcross	d																								
Sunningdale	d		19 07										19 37										20 07		
Ascot [3]	d		19 13		19 23								19 43		19 53								20 13		20 23
Bagshot	d				19 29										19 59										20 29
Camberley	a				19 35										20 05										20 35
Frimley	d				19 43										20 13										20 43
Ash Vale	d				19 49										20 19										20 49
Aldershot	a				19 54										20 24										20 54
	d				20 08										20 38										21 08
Ash [5]	d				20 15										20 45										21 15
Wanborough	d				20 18										20 48										21 18
Guildford	a				20 25										20 55										21 25
Martins Heron	d		19 17										19 47										20 17		
Bracknell	d		19 20										19 50										20 20		
Wokingham	d		19 27										19 57										20 27		
Winnersh	d		19 30										20 00										20 30		
Winnersh Triangle	d		19 32										20 02										20 32		
Earley	d		19 35										20 05										20 35		
Reading [7]	a		19 40										20 10										20 40		

London - Hounslow, Richmond, Kingston, Windsor, Weybridge, Ascot, Guildford and Reading

Station		SW		SW	SW	SW	SW	SW	SW 1	SW	SW 1	SW		SW	SW	SW	SW	SW	SW 1	SW	SW 1	SW 1		SW	SW
London Waterloo 15 ⊖	d	19 22		19 28		19 33	19 37	19 45	19 50			19 52		19 58		20 03	20 07	20 15	20 20					20 22	20 28
Vauxhall ⊖	d	19 26		19 32		19 37	19 41	19 49				19 56		20 02		20 07	20 11	20 19						20 26	20 32
Queenstown Rd.(Battersea)	d	19 29				19 40	19 44	19 52				19 59				20 10	20 14	20 22						20 29	
Clapham Junction 10	d	19 32		19 38		19 43	19 47	19 55	19 58			20 02		20 08		20 13	20 17	20 25	20 28					20 32	20 38
Wandsworth Town	d	19 35				19 46	19 50	19 58				20 05				20 16	20 20	20 28						20 35	
Putney	d	19 38		19 42		19 49	19 53	20 01				20 08		20 12		20 19	20 23	20 31						20 38	20 42
Barnes	d	19 42				19 52	19 57	20 05				20 12				20 22	20 27	20 35						20 42	
Barnes Bridge	d	19 44					19 59					20 14					20 29							20 44	
Chiswick	d	19 47					20 02					20 17					20 32							20 47	
Kew Bridge	d	19 50					20 05					20 20					20 35							20 50	
Brentford	d	19 53					20 08					20 23					20 38							20 53	
Syon Lane	d	19 55					20 10					20 25					20 40							20 55	
Isleworth	d	19 57					20 12					20 27					20 42							20 57	
Hounslow	d	20 01					20 18					20 31					20 48							21 01	
Mortlake	d					19 54		20 07								20 24		20 37							
North Sheen	d					19 56		20 09		←						20 26		20 39		←					
Richmond ⊖	d			19 48		19 59		20 12	20 06	20 12				20 18		20 29		20 42	20 36	20 42					20 48
St Margarets	d					20 01		→		20 14						20 31		→		20 44					
Twickenham	a			19 51		20 03			20 10	20 16				20 21		20 33			20 40	20 46					20 51
	d			19 52		20 04			20 10	20 17				20 22		20 34			20 40	20 47					20 52
Strawberry Hill	d					20 07										20 37									
Fulwell	a																								
Teddington	a					20 10										20 40									
Hampton Wick	a					20 14										20 44									
Kingston	a					20 16										20 46									
Whitton	d			19 55	←		20a23			20a20				20 25	←		20a53			20a50					20 55
Feltham	d	20 06		19 59	20 06				20 16			20 36		20 29	20 36				20 46					21 06	20 59
Ashford (Surrey)	d	→		20 03	20 10							→		20 33	20 40									→	21 03
Staines	d			20 07	20 14				20 23					20 37	20 44				20 53						21 07
Wraysbury	d			20 11										20 41											21 11
Sunnymeads	d			20 14										20 44											21 14
Datchet	d			20 17										20 47											21 17
Windsor & Eton Riverside	a			20 21										20 51											21 21
Egham	d				20 19				20 27						20 49				20 57						
Virginia Water	a				20 23				20 31						20 53				21 01						
	d				20 23				20 31						20 53				21 01						
Chertsey	d				20 29										20 59										
Addlestone	d				20 32										21 02										
Weybridge	a				20 37										21 07										
Byfleet & New Haw	d																								
West Byfleet	d																								
Woking	a																								
Longcross	d																								
Sunningdale	d								20 37										21 07						
Ascot 3	d								20 43		20 53								21 13		21 23				
Bagshot	d										20 59										21 29				
Camberley	a										21 05										21 35				
Frimley	d										21 13										21 43				
Ash Vale	d										21 19										21 49				
Aldershot	a										21 24										21 54				
	d										21 38										22 08	22 38			
Ash 5	d										21 45										22 15	22 45			
Wanborough	d										21 48										22 18	22 48			
Guildford	a										21 55										22 25	22 55			
Martins Heron	d								20 47										21 17						
Bracknell	d								20 50										21 20						
Wokingham	d								20 57										21 27						
Winnersh	d								21 00										21 30						
Winnersh Triangle	d								21 02										21 32						
Earley	d								21 05										21 35						
Reading 7	a								21 10										21 40						

London - Hounslow, Richmond, Kingston, Windsor, Weybridge, Ascot, Guildford and Reading

Station		SW	SW	SW	SW	SW 1	SW	SW		SW	SW	SW	SW	SW	SW 1	SW	SW 1	SW		SW	SW	SW	SW	SW	SW 1
London Waterloo 15 ⊖	d		20 33	20 37	20 45	20 50		20 52		20 58		21 03	21 07	21 15	21 20			21 22		21 28		21 33	21 37	21 45	21 50
Vauxhall ⊖	d		20 37	20 41	20 49			20 56		21 02		21 07	21 11	21 19				21 26		21 32		21 37	21 41	21 49	
Queenstown Rd.(Battersea)	d		20 40	20 44	20 52			20 59				21 10	21 14	21 22				21 29				21 40	21 44	21 52	
Clapham Junction 10	d		20 43	20 47	20 55	20 58		21 02		21 08		21 13	21 17	21 25	21 28			21 32		21 38		21 43	21 47	21 55	21 58
Wandsworth Town	d		20 46	20 50	20 58			21 05				21 16	21 20	21 28				21 35				21 46	21 50	21 58	
Putney	d		20 49	20 53	21 01			21 08		21 12		21 19	21 23	21 31				21 38		21 42		21 49	21 53	22 01	
Barnes	d		20 52	20 57	21 05			21 12				21 22	21 27	21 35				21 42				21 52	21 57	22 05	
Barnes Bridge	d			20 59				21 14					21 29					21 44					21 59		
Chiswick	d			21 02				21 17					21 32					21 47					22 02		
Kew Bridge	d			21 05				21 20					21 35					21 50					22 05		
Brentford	d			21 08				21 23					21 38					21 53					22 08		
Syon Lane	d			21 10				21 25					21 40					21 55					22 10		
Isleworth	d			21 12				21 27					21 42					21 57					22 12		
Hounslow	d			21 18				21 31					21 48					22 01					22 18		
Mortlake	d		20 54		21 07							21 24		21 37								21 54		22 07	
North Sheen	d		20 56		21 09		←					21 26		21 39		←						21 56		22 09	
Richmond ⊖	d		20 59		21 12	21 06	21 12			21 18		21 29		21 42	21 36	21 42				21 48		21 59		22 12	22 06
St Margarets	d		21 01		→		21 14					21 31		→		21 44						22 01		→	
Twickenham	a		21 03			21 10	21 16			21 21		21 33			21 40	21 46				21 51		22 03			22 10
	d		21 04			21 10	21 17			21 22		21 34			21 40	21 47				21 52		22 04			22 10
Strawberry Hill	d		21 07									21 37										22 07			
Fulwell	a																								
Teddington	a		21 10									21 40										22 10			
Hampton Wick	a		21 14									21 44										22 14			
Kingston	a		21 16									21 46										22 16			
Whitton	d	←		21a23			21a20			21 25	←		21a53			21a50				21 55	←		22a23		
Feltham	d	21 06				21 16		21 36		21 29	21 36				21 46			22 06		21 59	22 06				22 16
Ashford (Surrey)	d	21 10						→		21 33	21 40							→		22 03	22 10				
Staines	d	21 14				21 23				21 37	21 44				21 53					22 07	22 14				22 23
Wraysbury	d									21 41										22 11					
Sunnymeads	d									21 44										22 14					
Datchet	d									21 47										22 17					
Windsor & Eton Riverside	a									21 51										22 21					
Egham	d	21 19				21 27					21 49				21 57						22 19				22 27
Virginia Water	a	21 23				21 31					21 53				22 01						22 23				22 31
	d	21 23				21 31					21 53				22 01						22 23				22 31
Chertsey	d	21 29									21 59										22 29				
Addlestone	d	21 32									22 02										22 32				
Weybridge	a	21 37									22 07										22 37				
Byfleet & New Haw	d																								
West Byfleet	d																								
Woking	a																								
Longcross	d																								
Sunningdale	d					21 37									22 07										22 37
Ascot 3	d					21 43									22 13		22 23								22 43
Bagshot	d																22 29								
Camberley	a																22 35								
Frimley	d																22 43								
Ash Vale	d																22 49								
Aldershot	a																22 54								
	d																23 08								
Ash 5	d																23 15								
Wanborough	d																23 18								
Guildford	a																23 25								
Martins Heron	d					21 47									22 17										22 47
Bracknell	d					21 50									22 20										22 50
Wokingham	d					21 57									22 27										22 57
Winnersh	d					22 00									22 30										23 00
Winnersh Triangle	d					22 02									22 32										23 02
Earley	d					22 05									22 35										23 05
Reading 7	a					22 10									22 40										23 10

Table 149

Saturdays
until 1 October

London - Hounslow, Richmond, Kingston, Windsor, Weybridge, Ascot, Guildford and Reading

		SW	SW	SW	SW	SW	SW 1	SW 1	SW	SW	SW	SW	SW 1	SW	SW	SW	SW	SW	SW 1	SW	SW	SW
London Waterloo 15 ⊖	d		21 52	21 58		22 03	22 20		22 22	22 28		22 33	22 50	22 52	22 58		23 03	23 13	23 20	23 22	23 33	23 38
Vauxhall ⊖	d		21 56	22 02		22 07			22 26	22 32		22 37		22 56	23 02		23 07	23 17		23 26	23 37	
Queenstown Rd.(Battersea)	d		21 59			22 10			22 29			22 40		22 59			23 10			23 29	23 40	
Clapham Junction 10	d		22 02	22 08		22 13	22 28		22 32	22 38		22 43	22 58	23 02	23 08		23 13	23 23	23 28	23 32	23 43	23 46
Wandsworth Town	d		22 05			22 16			22 35			22 46		23 05			23 16			23 35	23 46	
Putney	d		22 08	22 12		22 19			22 38	22 42		22 49		23 08	23 12		23 19	23 27		23 38	23 49	
Barnes	d		22 12			22 22			22 42			22 52		23 12			23 22			23 42	23 52	
Barnes Bridge	d		22 14						22 44					23 14						23 44		
Chiswick	d		22 17						22 47					23 17						23 47		
Kew Bridge	d		22 20						22 50					23 20						23 50		
Brentford	d		22 23						22 53					23 23						23 53		
Syon Lane	d		22 25						22 55					23 25						23 55		
Isleworth	d		22 27						22 57					23 27						23 57		
Hounslow	d		22 31						23 01					23 31						00 01		
Mortlake	d					22 24						22 54					23 24				23 54	
North Sheen	d	←				22 26						22 56					23 26				23 56	
Richmond ⊖	d	22 12		22 18		22 29	22 36			22 48		22 59	23 06		23 18		23 29	23 33	23 37		23 59	23 54
St Margarets	d	22 14				22 31						23 01					23 31				→	
Twickenham	a	22 16		22 21		22 33	22 40			22 51		23 03	23 10		23 21		23 33	23 37	23 41			23 58
	d			22 22		22 34	22 40			22 52		23 04	23 10		23 22		23 34	23 37	23 41			23 58
Strawberry Hill	d					22 37						23 07					23 37					
Fulwell	a																					
Teddington	a					22 40						23 10					23 40					
Hampton Wick	a					22 44						23 14					23 44					
Kingston	a					22 46						23 16					23 46					
Whitton	d			22 25	←					22 55	←				23 25	←		23 40				
Feltham	d		22 36	22 29	22 36		22 46		23 06	22 59	23 06		23 16	23 36	23 29	23 36		23 44	23 48	00 06		00 04
Ashford (Surrey)	d		→	22 33	22 40				→	23 03	23 10			→	23 33	23 40		23 48		→		
Staines	d			22 37	22 44		22 53			23 07	23 14		23 23		23 37	23 44		23 52	23 56			00 11
Wraysbury	d			22 41						23 11					23 41			23 56				
Sunnymeads	d			22 44						23 14					23 44			23 59				
Datchet	d			22 47						23 17					23 47			00 02				
Windsor & Eton Riverside	a			22 51						23 21					23 51			00 06				
Egham	d				22 49		22 57				23 19		23 27			23 49			00 01			00 15
Virginia Water	a				22 53		23 01				23 23		23 31			23 53			00 05			00 19
	d				22 53		23 01				23 23		23 31			23 53			00 05			00 19
Chertsey	d				22 59						23 29					23 59						
Addlestone	d				23 02						23a32					00 02						
Weybridge	a				23 07																	
Byfleet & New Haw	d															00 06						
West Byfleet	d															00 09						
Woking	a															00 15						
Longcross	d																					
Sunningdale	d						23 07						23 37						00 11			00 25
Ascot 3	d						23 13	23 23					23 43						00 15			00 30
Bagshot	d							23 29														
Camberley	a							23 35														
Frimley	d							23 43														
Ash Vale	d							23 49														
Aldershot	a							23 54														
	d																					
Ash 5	d																					
Wanborough	d																					
Guildford	a																					
Martins Heron	d						23 17						23 47						00 19			00 34
Bracknell	d						23 20						23 50						00 23			00 37
Wokingham	d						23 27						23 57						00 32			00 44
Winnersh	d						23 30						23 59						00 36			
Winnersh Triangle	d						23 32						00 02						00 38			
Earley	d						23 35						00 05						00 40			
Reading 7	a						23 40						00 10						00 45			00 52

Table 149

Saturdays
until 1 October

London - Hounslow, Richmond, Kingston, Windsor, Weybridge, Ascot, Guildford and Reading

		SW	SW	SW	SW	SW
London Waterloo 15 ⊖	d			23 52	23 58	
Vauxhall ⊖	d			23 56	00 02	
Queenstown Rd.(Battersea)	d			23 59		
Clapham Junction 10	d			00 02	00 08	
Wandsworth Town	d			00 05		
Putney	d			00 08	00 12	
Barnes	d			00 12		
Barnes Bridge	d			00 14		
Chiswick	d			00 17		
Kew Bridge	d			00 20		
Brentford	d			00 23		
Syon Lane	d			00 25		
Isleworth	d			00 27		
Hounslow	d			00 31		
Mortlake	d					
North Sheen	d		←			
Richmond ⊖	d		23 59		00 18	
St Margarets	d		00 01			
Twickenham	a		00 04		00 21	
	d		00 04		00 22	
Strawberry Hill	d		00 07			
Fulwell	a					
Teddington	a		00 11			
Hampton Wick	a		00 14			
Kingston	a		00 16			
Whitton	d	←			00 25	←
Feltham	d	00 06		00 36	00 29	00 36
Ashford (Surrey)	d	00 10		→	00 33	00 40
Staines	d	00 14			00a37	00a46
Wraysbury	d					
Sunnymeads	d					
Datchet	d					
Windsor & Eton Riverside	a					
Egham	d	00 19				
Virginia Water	a	00 23				
	d	00 23				
Chertsey	d	00 29				
Addlestone	d	00a32				
Weybridge	a					
Byfleet & New Haw	d					
West Byfleet	d					
Woking	a					
Longcross	d					
Sunningdale	d					
Ascot 3	d					
Bagshot	d					
Camberley	a					
Frimley	d					
Ash Vale	d					
Aldershot	a					
	d					
Ash 5	d					
Wanborough	d					
Guildford	a					
Martins Heron	d					
Bracknell	d					
Wokingham	d					
Winnersh	d					
Winnersh Triangle	d					
Earley	d					
Reading 7	a					

London - Hounslow, Richmond, Kingston, Windsor, Weybridge, Ascot, Guildford and Reading

		SW [1]	SW	SW	SW [1]	SW	SW	SW	SW	SW	SW [1]	SW [1]	SW [1]	SW [1]	SW	SW	SW	SW	SW [1]	SW	SW [1]	SW	SW
London Waterloo [15] ⊖	d	22p50	22p52	23p13	23p20	23p22	23p33	23p38							23p52	23p58		00 18			05 05		05 33
Vauxhall ⊖	d		22p56	23p17		23p26	23p37								23p56	00 02		00 22			05 09		05 37
Queenstown Rd.(Battersea)	d		22p59			23p29	23p40								23p59			00 25			05 12		05 40
Clapham Junction [10]	d	22p58	23p02	23p23	23p28	23p32	23p43	23p46							00 02	00 08		00 29			05 15		05 43
Wandsworth Town	d		23p05			23p35	23p46								00 05			00 32			05 18		05 46
Putney	d		23p08	23p27		23p38	23p49								00 08	00 12		00 35			05 21		05 49
Barnes	d		23p12			23p42	23p52								00 12			00 38			05 24		05 52
Barnes Bridge	d		23p14			23p44									00 14								
Chiswick	d		23p17			23p47									00 17								
Kew Bridge	d		23p20			23p50									00 20								
Brentford	d		23p23			23p53									00 23								
Syon Lane	d		23p25			23p55									00 25								
Isleworth	d		23p27			23p57									00 27								
Hounslow	d		23p31			00 01									00 31								
Mortlake	d						23p54											00 40			05 26		05 54
North Sheen	d						23p56			←								00 42			05 28		05 56
Richmond ⊖	d	23p06		23p33	23p37		23p59	23p54		23p59						00 18		00 45			05 31		05 59
St Margarets	d						→			00 01								00 47			05 33		06 01
Twickenham	a	23p10		23p36	23p41			23p58		00 03						00 21		00 49			05 35		06 03
	d	23p10		23p37	23p41			23p58		00 04						00 22		00 50			05 36	05 53	06 04
Strawberry Hill	d									00 07								00s53					06 07
Fulwell	a																						
Teddington	a									00 11								00s56					06 10
Hampton Wick	a									00 14								00s59					06 14
Kingston	a									00 16								01 01					06 16
Whitton	d			23p40					←							00 25	←				05 39	05 56	
Feltham	d	23p16	23p36	23p44	23p48	00 06		00 04	00 06						00 37	00 29	00 37				05 43	06 00	
Ashford (Surrey)	d		23p40	23p48		→			00 10						→	00 33	00 41				05 47	06 04	
Staines	d	23p23	23p44	23p52	23p56			00 11	00 14							00a37	00a46		05 23	05 44	05 53	06 08	
Wraysbury	d			23p56																		06 13	
Sunnymeads	d			23p59																		06 16	
Datchet	d			00 04																		06 20	
Windsor & Eton Riverside	a			00 09																		06 24	
Egham	d	23p27	23p49		00 01			00 15	00 19										05 27	05 49	05 57		
Virginia Water	a	23p31	23p53		00 05			00 19	00 23										05 31	05 53	06 01		
	d	23p31	23p53		00 05			00 19	00 23										05 31	05 53	06 01		
Chertsey	d		23p59						00 29											05 59			
Addlestone	d		00 02						00a32											06 02			
Weybridge	a																			06 07			
Byfleet & New Haw	d		00 06																				
West Byfleet	d		00 09																				
Woking	a		00 15																				
Longcross	d																						
Sunningdale	d	23p37			00 11			00 25											05 37		06 07		
Ascot [3]	d	23p43			00 15			00 30			00 32								05 43		06 13		
Bagshot	d										00 38												
Camberley	a										00 44												
Frimley	d										00 48												
Ash Vale	d										00 57												
Aldershot	a										01s02												
	d											06 08	06 38	07 08									
Ash [5]	d											06 15	06 45	07 15									
Wanborough	d											06 18	06 48	07 18									
Guildford	a											06 25	06 55	07 25									
Martins Heron	d	23p47			00 19			00 34											05 47		06 17		
Bracknell	d	23p50			00 23			00 37											05 50		06 20		
Wokingham	d	23p57			00 32			00 44											05 57		06 27		
Winnersh	d	23p59			00 36														06 00		06 30		
Winnersh Triangle	d	00 02			00 38														06 02		06 32		
Earley	d	00 05			00 40														06 07		06 35		
Reading [7]	a	00 13			00 48			00 55											06 13		06 43		

London - Hounslow, Richmond, Kingston, Windsor, Weybridge, Ascot, Guildford and Reading

		SW	SW [1]	SW	SW	SW	SW [1]	SW [1]	SW [1]	SW	SW	SW	SW	SW [1]	SW [1]	SW	SW	SW	SW	SW	SW [1]	SW	SW [1]
London Waterloo [15] ⊖	d		05 50	05 58	06 03			06 20		06 22	06 28		06 33	06 50		06 52	06 58		07 03	07 15	07 20		
Vauxhall ⊖	d			06 02	06 07					06 26	06 32		06 37			06 56	07 02		07 07	07 19			
Queenstown Rd.(Battersea)	d				06 10					06 29			06 40			06 59			07 10	07 22			
Clapham Junction [10]	d		05 58	06 08	06 13			06 28		06 32	06 38		06 43	06 58		07 02	07 08		07 13	07 25	07 28		
Wandsworth Town	d				06 16					06 35			06 46			07 05			07 16	07 28			
Putney	d			06 12	06 19					06 38	06 42		06 49			07 08	07 12		07 19	07 31			
Barnes	d				06 22					06 42			06 52			07 12			07 22	07 35			
Barnes Bridge	d									06 44						07 14							
Chiswick	d									06 47						07 17							
Kew Bridge	d									06 50						07 20							
Brentford	d									06 53						07 23							
Syon Lane	d									06 55						07 25							
Isleworth	d									06 57						07 27							
Hounslow	d									07 01						07 31							
Mortlake	d				06 24								06 54						07 24	07 37			
North Sheen	d				06 26								06 56						07 26	07 39		←	
Richmond ⊖	d		06 06	06 18	06 29			06 36			06 48		06 59	07 06			07 18		07 29	07 42	07 36	07 42	
St Margarets	d				06 31								07 01						07 31	→		07 44	
Twickenham	a		06 10	06 21	06 33			06 40			06 51		07 03	07 10			07 21		07 33		07 40	07 46	
	d		06 10	06 22	06 34			06 40			06 52		07 04	07 10			07 22		07 34		07 40	07 47	
Strawberry Hill	d				06 37								07 07						07 37				
Fulwell	a																						
Teddington	a				06 40								07 10						07 40				
Hampton Wick	a				06 44								07 14						07 44				
Kingston	a				06 46								07 16						07 46				
Whitton	d			06 25							06 55	←					07 25	←				07a50	
Feltham	d		06 16	06 29				06 46		07 06	06 59	07 06		07 16		07 36	07 29	07 36			07 46		
Ashford (Surrey)	d			06 33						→	07 03	07 10				→	07 33	07 40					
Staines	d	06 16	06 23	06 37		06 44		06 53			07 07	07 14		07 23			07 37	07 44			07 53		
Wraysbury	d			06 42							07 12						07 42						
Sunnymeads	d			06 45							07 15						07 45						
Datchet	d			06 49							07 19						07 49						
Windsor & Eton Riverside	a			06 54							07 24						07 54						
Egham	d	06 20	06 27			06 49		06 57				07 19		07 27				07 49			07 57		
Virginia Water	a	06 25	06 31			06 53		07 01				07 23		07 31				07 53			08 01		
	d	06 25	06 31			06 53		07 01				07 23		07 31				07 53			08 01		
Chertsey	d	06 30				06 59						07 29						07 59					
Addlestone	d	06 33				07 02						07 32						08 02					
Weybridge	a	06 38				07 07						07 37						08 07					
Byfleet & New Haw	d																						
West Byfleet	d																						
Woking	a																						
Longcross	d																						
Sunningdale	d		06 37					07 07						07 37							08 07		
Ascot [3]	d		06 43				06 53	07 13						07 43	07 53						08 13		08 23
Bagshot	d						06 59								07 59								08 29
Camberley	a						07 05								08 05								08 35
Frimley	d						07 13								08 13								08 43
Ash Vale	d						07 19								08 19								08 49
Aldershot	a						07 24								08 24								08 54
	d						07 38		08 08						08 38								09 08
Ash [5]	d						07 45		08 15						08 45								09 15
Wanborough	d						07 48		08 18						08 48								09 18
Guildford	a						07 55		08 25						08 55								09 25
Martins Heron	d		06 47					07 17						07 47							08 17		
Bracknell	d		06 50					07 20						07 50							08 20		
Wokingham	d		06 57					07 27						07 57							08 27		
Winnersh	d		07 00					07 30						08 00							08 30		
Winnersh Triangle	d		07 02					07 32						08 02							08 32		
Earley	d		07 07					07 37						08 07							08 37		
Reading [7]	a		07 13					07 43						08 13							08 43		

Table 149

Saturdays
from 8 October

London - Hounslow, Richmond, Kingston, Windsor, Weybridge, Ascot, Guildford and Reading

		SW	SW	SW	SW	SW	SW	SW ■	SW	SW ■	SW	SW	SW	SW	SW	SW	SW ■	SW	SW ■	SW	SW	SW
London Waterloo ■15 ⊖	d	07 22	07 28		07 33	07 37	07 45	07 50			07 52	07 58		08 03	08 07	08 15	08 20			08 22	08 28	
Vauxhall ⊖	d	07 26	07 32		07 37	07 41	07 49				07 56	08 02		08 07	08 11	08 19				08 26	08 32	
Queenstown Rd.(Battersea)	d	07 29			07 40	07 44	07 52				07 59			08 10	08 14	08 22				08 29		
Clapham Junction ■10	d	07 32	07 38		07 43	07 47	07 55	07 58			08 02	08 08		08 13	08 17	08 25	08 28			08 32	08 38	
Wandsworth Town	d	07 35			07 46	07 50	07 58				08 05			08 16	08 20	08 28				08 35		
Putney	d	07 38	07 42		07 49	07 53	08 01				08 08	08 12		08 19	08 23	08 31				08 38	08 42	
Barnes	d	07 42			07 52	07 57	08 05				08 12			08 22	08 27	08 35				08 42		
Barnes Bridge	d	07 44				07 59					08 14				08 29					08 44		
Chiswick	d	07 47				08 02					08 17				08 32					08 47		
Kew Bridge	d	07 50				08 05					08 20				08 35					08 50		
Brentford	d	07 53				08 08					08 23				08 38					08 53		
Syon Lane	d	07 55				08 10					08 25				08 40					08 55		
Isleworth	d	07 57				08 12					08 27				08 42					08 57		
Hounslow	d	08 01				08 18					08 31				08 48					09 01		
Mortlake	d				07 54		08 07							08 24		08 37						
North Sheen	d				07 56		08 09		←					08 26		08 39		←				
Richmond ⊖	d		07 48		07 59		08 12	08 06	08 12			08 18		08 29		08 42	08 36	08 42			08 48	
St Margarets	d				08 01		→		08 14					08 31		→		08 44				
Twickenham	a		07 51		08 03			08 10	08 16			08 21		08 33			08 40	08 46			08 51	
	d		07 52		08 04			08 10	08 17			08 22		08 34			08 40	08 47			08 52	
Strawberry Hill	d				08 07									08 37								
Fulwell	a																					
Teddington	a				08 10									08 40								
Hampton Wick	a				08 14									08 44								
Kingston	a				08 16									08 46								
Whitton	d		07 55	←		08a23			08a20			08 25	←		08a53			08a50			08 55	←
Feltham	d	08 06	07 59	08 06				08 16			08 36	08 29	08 36				08 46			09 06	08 59	09 06
Ashford (Surrey)	d	→	08 03	08 10							→	08 33	08 40							→	09 03	09 10
Staines	d		08 07	08 14				08 23				08 37	08 44				08 53				09 07	09 14
Wraysbury	d		08 12									08 42									09 12	
Sunnymeads	d		08 15									08 45									09 15	
Datchet	d		08 19									08 49									09 19	
Windsor & Eton Riverside	a		08 24									08 54									09 24	
Egham	d			08 19				08 27					08 49				08 57					09 19
Virginia Water	a			08 23				08 31					08 53				09 01					09 23
	d			08 23				08 31					08 53				09 01					09 23
Chertsey	d			08 29									08 59									09 29
Addlestone	d			08 32									09 02									09 32
Weybridge	a			08 37									09 07									09 37
Byfleet & New Haw	d																					
West Byfleet	d																					
Woking	a																					
Longcross	d																					
Sunningdale	d							08 37									09 07					
Ascot ■3	d							08 43		08 53							09 13		09 23			
Bagshot	d									08 59									09 29			
Camberley	a									09 05									09 35			
Frimley	d									09 13									09 43			
Ash Vale	d									09 19									09 49			
Aldershot	a									09 24									09 54			
	d									09 38									10 08			
Ash ■5	d									09 45									10 15			
Wanborough	d									09 48									10 18			
Guildford	a									09 55									10 25			
Martins Heron	d							08 47									09 17					
Bracknell	d							08 50									09 20					
Wokingham	d							08 57									09 27					
Winnersh	d							09 00									09 30					
Winnersh Triangle	d							09 02									09 32					
Earley	d							09 07									09 37					
Reading ■7	a							09 13									09 43					

Table 149

Saturdays
from 8 October

London - Hounslow, Richmond, Kingston, Windsor, Weybridge, Ascot, Guildford and Reading

		SW	SW	SW	SW ■	SW	SW ■	SW	SW	SW	SW	SW	SW	SW ■	SW	SW ■	SW	SW	SW	SW	SW	SW	SW ■
London Waterloo ■15 ⊖	d	08 33	08 37	08 45	08 50			08 52	08 58		09 03	09 07	09 15	09 20			09 22	09 28		09 33	09 37	09 45	09 50
Vauxhall ⊖	d	08 37	08 41	08 49				08 56	09 02		09 07	09 11	09 19				09 26	09 32		09 37	09 41	09 49	
Queenstown Rd.(Battersea)	d	08 40	08 44	08 52				08 59			09 10	09 14	09 22				09 29			09 40	09 44	09 52	
Clapham Junction ■10	d	08 43	08 47	08 55	08 58			09 02	09 08		09 13	09 17	09 25	09 28			09 32	09 38		09 43	09 47	09 55	09 58
Wandsworth Town	d	08 46	08 50	08 58				09 05			09 16	09 20	09 28				09 35			09 46	09 50	09 58	
Putney	d	08 49	08 53	09 01				09 08	09 12		09 19	09 23	09 31				09 38	09 42		09 49	09 53	10 01	
Barnes	d	08 52	08 57	09 05				09 12			09 22	09 27	09 35				09 42			09 52	09 57	10 05	
Barnes Bridge	d		08 59					09 14				09 29					09 44				09 59		
Chiswick	d		09 02					09 17				09 32					09 47				10 02		
Kew Bridge	d		09 05					09 20				09 35					09 50				10 05		
Brentford	d		09 08					09 23				09 38					09 53				10 08		
Syon Lane	d		09 10					09 25				09 40					09 55				10 10		
Isleworth	d		09 12					09 27				09 42					09 57				10 12		
Hounslow	d		09 18					09 31				09 48					10 01				10 18		
Mortlake	d	08 54		09 07							09 24		09 37							09 54		10 07	
North Sheen	d	08 56		09 09		←					09 26		09 39		←					09 56		10 09	
Richmond ⊖	d	08 59		09 12	09 06	09 12			09 18		09 29		09 42	09 36	09 42			09 48		09 59		10 12	10 06
St Margarets	d	09 01		→		09 14					09 31		→		09 44					10 01		→	
Twickenham	a	09 03			09 10	09 16			09 21		09 33			09 40	09 46			09 51		10 03			10 10
	d	09 04			09 10	09 17			09 22		09 34			09 40	09 47			09 52		10 04			10 10
Strawberry Hill	d	09 07									09 37									10 07			
Fulwell	a																						
Teddington	a	09 10									09 40									10 10			
Hampton Wick	a	09 14									09 44									10 14			
Kingston	a	09 16									09 46									10 16			
Whitton	d		09a23			09a20			09 25	←		09a53			09a50			09 55	←		10a23		
Feltham	d				09 16			09 36	09 29	09 36				09 46			10 06	09 59	10 06				10 16
Ashford (Surrey)	d							→	09 33	09 40							→	10 03	10 10				
Staines	d				09 23				09 37	09 44				09 53				10 07	10 14				10 23
Wraysbury	d								09 42									10 12					
Sunnymeads	d								09 45									10 15					
Datchet	d								09 49									10 19					
Windsor & Eton Riverside	a								09 54									10 24					
Egham	d				09 27					09 49				09 57					10 19				10 27
Virginia Water	a				09 31					09 53				10 01					10 23				10 31
	d				09 31					09 53				10 01					10 23				10 31
Chertsey	d									09 59									10 29				
Addlestone	d									10 02									10 32				
Weybridge	a									10 07									10 37				
Byfleet & New Haw	d																						
West Byfleet	d																						
Woking	a																						
Longcross	d																						
Sunningdale	d				09 37									10 07									10 37
Ascot ■3	d				09 43		09 53							10 13		10 23							10 43
Bagshot	d						09 59									10 29							
Camberley	a						10 05									10 35							
Frimley	d						10 13									10 43							
Ash Vale	d						10 19									10 49							
Aldershot	a						10 24									10 54							
	d						10 38									11 08							
Ash ■5	d						10 45									11 15							
Wanborough	d						10 48									11 18							
Guildford	a						10 55									11 25							
Martins Heron	d				09 47									10 17									10 47
Bracknell	d				09 50									10 20									10 50
Wokingham	d				09 57									10 27									10 57
Winnersh	d				10 00									10 30									11 00
Winnersh Triangle	d				10 02									10 32									11 02
Earley	d				10 07									10 37									11 07
Reading ■7	a				10 13									10 43									11 13

London - Hounslow, Richmond, Kingston, Windsor, Weybridge, Ascot, Guildford and Reading

		SW	SW ■	SW	SW	SW	SW	SW	SW	SW ■	SW	SW ■	SW	SW	SW	SW	SW	SW	SW ■	SW	SW ■	SW
London Waterloo 15 ⊖	d			09 52	09 58		10 03	10 07	10 15	10 20			10 22	10 28		10 33	10 37	10 45	10 50			10 52
Vauxhall ⊖	d			09 56	10 02		10 07	10 11	10 19				10 26	10 32		10 37	10 41	10 49				10 56
Queenstown Rd.(Battersea)	d			09 59			10 10	10 14	10 22				10 29			10 40	10 44	10 52				10 59
Clapham Junction 10	d			10 02	10 08		10 13	10 17	10 25	10 28			10 32	10 38		10 43	10 47	10 55	10 58			11 02
Wandsworth Town	d			10 05			10 16	10 20	10 28				10 35			10 46	10 50	10 58				11 05
Putney	d			10 08	10 12		10 19	10 23	10 31				10 38	10 42		10 49	10 53	11 01				11 08
Barnes	d			10 12			10 22	10 27	10 35				10 42			10 52	10 57	11 05				11 12
Barnes Bridge	d			10 14				10 29					10 44				10 59					11 14
Chiswick	d			10 17				10 32					10 47				11 02					11 17
Kew Bridge	d			10 20				10 35					10 50				11 05					11 20
Brentford	d			10 23				10 38					10 53				11 08					11 23
Syon Lane	d			10 25				10 40					10 55				11 10					11 25
Isleworth	d			10 27				10 42					10 57				11 12					11 27
Hounslow	d			10 31				10 48					11 01				11 18					11 31
Mortlake	d						10 24		10 37							10 54		11 07				
North Sheen	d	←					10 26		10 39		←					10 56		11 09		←		
Richmond ⊖	d	10 12			10 18		10 29		10 42	10 36	10 42			10 48		10 59		11 12	11 06	11 12		
St Margarets	d	10 14					10 31		→		10 44					11 01		→		11 14		
Twickenham	a	10 16			10 21		10 33			10 40	10 46			10 51		11 03			11 10	11 16		
	d	10 17			10 22		10 34			10 40	10 47			10 52		11 04			11 10	11 17		
Strawberry Hill	d						10 37									11 07						
Fulwell	a																					
Teddington	a						10 40									11 10						
Hampton Wick	a						10 44									11 14						
Kingston	a						10 46									11 16						
Whitton	d	10a20			10 25	←		10a53			10a50			10 55	←		11a23			11a20		
Feltham	d			10 36	10 29	10 36				10 46			11 06	10 59	11 06				11 16			11 36
Ashford (Surrey)	d			→	10 33	10 40							→	11 03	11 10							→
Staines	d				10 37	10 44				10 53				11 07	11 14				11 23			
Wraysbury	d				10 42									11 12								
Sunnymeads	d				10 45									11 15								
Datchet	d				10 49									11 19								
Windsor & Eton Riverside	a				10 54									11 24								
Egham	d					10 49				10 57					11 19				11 27			
Virginia Water	a					10 53				11 01					11 23				11 31			
	d					10 53				11 01					11 23				11 31			
Chertsey	d					10 59									11 29							
Addlestone	d					11 02									11 32							
Weybridge	a					11 07									11 37							
Byfleet & New Haw	d																					
West Byfleet	d																					
Woking	a																					
Longcross	d																					
Sunningdale	d									11 07									11 37			
Ascot 3	d		10 53							11 13		11 23							11 43		11 53	
Bagshot	d		10 59									11 29									11 59	
Camberley	a		11 05									11 35									12 05	
Frimley	d		11 13									11 43									12 13	
Ash Vale	d		11 19									11 49									12 19	
Aldershot	a		11 24									11 54									12 24	
	d		11 38									12 08									12 38	
Ash 6	d		11 45									12 15									12 45	
Wanborough	d		11 48									12 18									12 48	
Guildford	a		11 55									12 25									12 55	
Martins Heron	d									11 17									11 47			
Bracknell	d									11 20									11 50			
Wokingham	d									11 27									11 57			
Winnersh	d									11 30									12 00			
Winnersh Triangle	d									11 32									12 02			
Earley	d									11 37									12 07			
Reading 7	a									11 43									12 13			

London - Hounslow, Richmond, Kingston, Windsor, Weybridge, Ascot, Guildford and Reading

		SW	SW	SW	SW	SW	SW ■	SW	SW ■	SW	SW	SW	SW	SW	SW	SW ■	SW	SW ■	SW	SW	SW	SW	SW
London Waterloo 15 ⊖	d	10 58		11 03	11 07	11 15	11 20			11 22	11 28		11 33	11 37	11 45	11 50			11 52	11 58		12 03	12 07
Vauxhall ⊖	d	11 02		11 07	11 11	11 19				11 26	11 32		11 37	11 41	11 49				11 56	12 02		12 07	12 11
Queenstown Rd.(Battersea)	d			11 10	11 14	11 22				11 29			11 40	11 44	11 52				11 59			12 10	12 14
Clapham Junction 10	d	11 08		11 13	11 17	11 25	11 28			11 32	11 38		11 43	11 47	11 55	11 58			12 02	12 08		12 13	12 17
Wandsworth Town	d			11 16	11 20	11 28				11 35			11 46	11 50	11 58				12 05			12 16	12 20
Putney	d	11 12		11 19	11 23	11 31				11 38	11 42		11 49	11 53	12 01				12 08	12 12		12 19	12 23
Barnes	d			11 22	11 27	11 35				11 42			11 52	11 57	12 05				12 12			12 22	12 27
Barnes Bridge	d				11 29					11 44				11 59					12 14				12 29
Chiswick	d				11 32					11 47				12 02					12 17				12 32
Kew Bridge	d				11 35					11 50				12 05					12 20				12 35
Brentford	d				11 38					11 53				12 08					12 23				12 38
Syon Lane	d				11 40					11 55				12 10					12 25				12 40
Isleworth	d				11 42					11 57				12 12					12 27				12 42
Hounslow	d				11 48					12 01				12 18					12 31				12 48
Mortlake	d			11 24		11 37							11 54		12 07							12 24	
North Sheen	d			11 26		11 39		←					11 56		12 09		←					12 26	
Richmond ⊖	d	11 18		11 29		11 42	11 36	11 42			11 48		11 59		12 12	12 06	12 12			12 18		12 29	
St Margarets	d			11 31		→		11 44					12 01		→		12 14					12 31	
Twickenham	a	11 21		11 33			11 40	11 46			11 51		12 03			12 10	12 16			12 21		12 33	
	d	11 22		11 34			11 40	11 47			11 52		12 04			12 10	12 17			12 22		12 34	
Strawberry Hill	d			11 37									12 07									12 37	
Fulwell	a																						
Teddington	a			11 40									12 10									12 40	
Hampton Wick	a			11 44									12 14									12 44	
Kingston	a			11 46									12 16									12 46	
Whitton	d	11 25	←		11a53			11a50			11 55	←		12a23			12a20			12 25	←		12a53
Feltham	d	11 29	11 36				11 46			12 06	11 59	12 06				12 16			12 36	12 29	12 36		
Ashford (Surrey)	d	11 33	11 40							→	12 03	12 10							→	12 33	12 40		
Staines	d	11 37	11 44				11 53				12 07	12 14				12 23				12 37	12 44		
Wraysbury	d	11 42									12 12									12 42			
Sunnymeads	d	11 45									12 15									12 45			
Datchet	d	11 49									12 19									12 49			
Windsor & Eton Riverside	a	11 54									12 24									12 54			
Egham	d		11 49				11 57					12 19				12 27					12 49		
Virginia Water	a		11 53				12 01					12 23				12 31					12 53		
	d		11 53				12 01					12 23				12 31					12 53		
Chertsey	d		11 59									12 29									12 59		
Addlestone	d		12 02									12 32									13 02		
Weybridge	a		12 07									12 37									13 07		
Byfleet & New Haw	d																						
West Byfleet	d																						
Woking	a																						
Longcross	d																						
Sunningdale	d						12 07									12 37							
Ascot 3	d						12 13		12 23							12 43		12 53					
Bagshot	d								12 29									12 59					
Camberley	a								12 35									13 05					
Frimley	d								12 43									13 13					
Ash Vale	d								12 49									13 19					
Aldershot	a								12 54									13 24					
	d								13 08									13 38					
Ash 6	d								13 15									13 45					
Wanborough	d								13 18									13 48					
Guildford	a								13 25									13 55					
Martins Heron	d						12 17									12 47							
Bracknell	d						12 20									12 50							
Wokingham	d						12 27									12 57							
Winnersh	d						12 30									13 00							
Winnersh Triangle	d						12 32									13 02							
Earley	d						12 37									13 07							
Reading 7	a						12 43									13 13							

Table 149

Saturdays from 8 October

London - Hounslow, Richmond, Kingston, Windsor, Weybridge, Ascot, Guildford and Reading

		SW	SW 1	SW	SW 1	SW	SW	SW	SW	SW	SW	SW 1	SW	SW 1	SW	SW	SW	SW	SW	SW	SW 1	SW	SW 1
London Waterloo 15 ⊖	d	12 15	12 20			12 22	12 28		12 33	12 37	12 45	12 50			12 52	12 58		13 03	13 07	13 15	13 20		
Vauxhall ⊖	d	12 19				12 26	12 32		12 37	12 41	12 49				12 56	13 02		13 07	13 11	13 19			
Queenstown Rd.(Battersea)	d	12 22				12 29			12 40	12 44	12 52				12 59			13 10	13 14	13 22			
Clapham Junction 10	d	12 25	12 28			12 32	12 38		12 43	12 47	12 55	12 58			13 02	13 08		13 13	13 17	13 25	13 28		
Wandsworth Town	d	12 28				12 35			12 46	12 50	12 58				13 05			13 16	13 20	13 28			
Putney	d	12 31				12 38	12 42		12 49	12 53	13 01				13 08	13 12		13 19	13 23	13 31			
Barnes	d	12 35				12 42			12 52	12 57	13 05				13 12			13 22	13 27	13 35			
Barnes Bridge	d					12 44				12 59					13 14				13 29				
Chiswick	d					12 47				13 02					13 17				13 32				
Kew Bridge	d					12 50				13 05					13 20				13 35				
Brentford	d					12 53				13 08					13 23				13 38				
Syon Lane	d					12 55				13 10					13 25				13 40				
Isleworth	d					12 57				13 12					13 27				13 42				
Hounslow	d					13 01				13 18					13 31				13 48				
Mortlake	d	12 37							12 54		13 07							13 24		13 37			
North Sheen	d	12 39		←					12 56		13 09		←					13 26		13 39		←	
Richmond ⊖	d	12 42	12 36	12 42			12 48		12 59		13 12	13 06	13 12			13 18		13 29		13 42	13 36	13 42	
St Margarets	d	→		12 44					13 01		→		13 14					13 31		→		13 44	
Twickenham	a		12 40	12 46			12 51		13 03			13 10	13 16			13 21		13 33			13 40	13 46	
	d		12 40	12 47			12 52		13 04			13 10	13 17			13 22		13 34			13 40	13 47	
Strawberry Hill	d								13 07									13 37					
Fulwell	a																						
Teddington	a								13 10									13 40					
Hampton Wick	a								13 14									13 44					
Kingston	a								13 16									13 46					
Whitton	d			12a50			12 55	←		13a23			13a20			13 25	←		13a53			13a50	
Feltham	d		12 46			13 06	12 59	13 06				13 16			13 36	13 29	13 36				13 46		
Ashford (Surrey)	d					→	13 03	13 10							→	13 33	13 40						
Staines	d		12 53				13 07	13 14				13 23				13 37	13 44				13 53		
Wraysbury	d						13 12									13 42							
Sunnymeads	d						13 15									13 45							
Datchet	d						13 19									13 49							
Windsor & Eton Riverside	a						13 24									13 54							
Egham	d		12 57					13 19				13 27					13 49				13 57		
Virginia Water	a		13 01					13 23				13 31					13 53				14 01		
	d		13 01					13 23				13 31					13 53				14 01		
Chertsey	d							13 29									13 59						
Addlestone	d							13 32									14 02						
Weybridge	a							13 37									14 07						
Byfleet & New Haw	d																						
West Byfleet	d																						
Woking	a																						
Longcross	d																						
Sunningdale	d		13 07									13 37									14 07		
Ascot 3	d		13 13		13 23							13 43		13 53							14 13		14 23
Bagshot	d				13 29									13 59									14 29
Camberley	a				13 35									14 05									14 35
Frimley	d				13 43									14 13									14 43
Ash Vale	d				13 49									14 19									14 49
Aldershot	a				13 54									14 24									14 54
	d				14 08									14 38									15 08
Ash 5	d				14 15									14 45									15 15
Wanborough	d				14 18									14 48									15 18
Guildford	a				14 25									14 55									15 25
Martins Heron	d		13 17									13 47									14 17		
Bracknell	d		13 20									13 50									14 20		
Wokingham	d		13 27									13 57									14 27		
Winnersh	d		13 30									14 00									14 30		
Winnersh Triangle	d		13 32									14 02									14 32		
Earley	d		13 37									14 07									14 37		
Reading 7	a		13 43									14 13									14 43		

Table 149

Saturdays from 8 October

London - Hounslow, Richmond, Kingston, Windsor, Weybridge, Ascot, Guildford and Reading

		SW	SW	SW	SW	SW	SW	SW 1	SW	SW 1	SW	SW	SW	SW	SW	SW	SW 1	SW	SW 1	SW	SW	SW
London Waterloo 15 ⊖	d	13 22	13 28		13 33	13 37	13 45	13 50			13 52	13 58		14 03	14 07	14 15	14 20			14 22	14 28	
Vauxhall ⊖	d	13 26	13 32		13 37	13 41	13 49				13 56	14 02		14 07	14 11	14 19				14 26	14 32	
Queenstown Rd.(Battersea)	d	13 29			13 40	13 44	13 52				13 59			14 10	14 14	14 22				14 29		
Clapham Junction 10	d	13 32	13 38		13 43	13 47	13 55	13 58			14 02	14 08		14 13	14 17	14 25	14 28			14 32	14 38	
Wandsworth Town	d	13 35			13 46	13 50	13 58				14 05			14 16	14 20	14 28				14 35		
Putney	d	13 38	13 42		13 49	13 53	14 01				14 08	14 12		14 19	14 23	14 31				14 38	14 42	
Barnes	d	13 42			13 52	13 57	14 05				14 12			14 22	14 27	14 35				14 42		
Barnes Bridge	d	13 44				13 59					14 14				14 29					14 44		
Chiswick	d	13 47				14 02					14 17				14 32					14 47		
Kew Bridge	d	13 50				14 05					14 20				14 35					14 50		
Brentford	d	13 53				14 08					14 23				14 38					14 53		
Syon Lane	d	13 55				14 10					14 25				14 40					14 55		
Isleworth	d	13 57				14 12					14 27				14 42					14 57		
Hounslow	d	14 01				14 18					14 31				14 48					15 01		
Mortlake	d				13 54		14 07							14 24		14 37						
North Sheen	d				13 56		14 09		←					14 26		14 39		←				
Richmond ⊖	d		13 48		13 59		14 12	14 06	14 12			14 18		14 29		14 42	14 36	14 42			14 48	
St Margarets	d				14 01		→		14 14					14 31		→		14 44				
Twickenham	a		13 51		14 03			14 10	14 16			14 21		14 33			14 40	14 46			14 51	
	d		13 52		14 04			14 10	14 17			14 22		14 34			14 40	14 47			14 52	
Strawberry Hill	d				14 07									14 37								
Fulwell	a																					
Teddington	a				14 10									14 40								
Hampton Wick	a				14 14									14 44								
Kingston	a				14 16									14 46								
Whitton	d		13 55	←		14a23			14a20			14 25	←		14a53			14a50			14 55	←
Feltham	d	14 06	13 59	14 06				14 16			14 36	14 29	14 36				14 46			15 06	14 59	15 06
Ashford (Surrey)	d	→	14 03	14 10							→	14 33	14 40							→	15 03	15 10
Staines	d		14 07	14 14				14 23				14 37	14 44				14 53				15 07	15 14
Wraysbury	d		14 12									14 42									15 12	
Sunnymeads	d		14 15									14 45									15 15	
Datchet	d		14 19									14 49									15 19	
Windsor & Eton Riverside	a		14 24									14 54									15 24	
Egham	d			14 19				14 27					14 49				14 57					15 19
Virginia Water	a			14 23				14 31					14 53				15 01					15 23
	d			14 23				14 31					14 53				15 01					15 23
Chertsey	d			14 29									14 59									15 29
Addlestone	d			14 32									15 02									15 32
Weybridge	a			14 37									15 07									15 37
Byfleet & New Haw	d																					
West Byfleet	d																					
Woking	a																					
Longcross	d																					
Sunningdale	d							14 37									15 07					
Ascot 3	d							14 43		14 53							15 13		15 23			
Bagshot	d									14 59									15 29			
Camberley	a									15 05									15 35			
Frimley	d									15 13									15 43			
Ash Vale	d									15 19									15 49			
Aldershot	a									15 24									15 54			
	d									15 38									16 08			
Ash 5	d									15 45									16 15			
Wanborough	d									15 48									16 18			
Guildford	a									15 55									16 25			
Martins Heron	d							14 47									15 17					
Bracknell	d							14 50									15 20					
Wokingham	d							14 57									15 27					
Winnersh	d							15 00									15 30					
Winnersh Triangle	d							15 02									15 32					
Earley	d							15 07									15 37					
Reading 7	a							15 13									15 43					

London - Hounslow, Richmond, Kingston, Windsor, Weybridge, Ascot, Guildford and Reading

		SW	SW	SW	SW 1	SW	SW 1	SW	SW	SW	SW	SW	SW	SW 1	SW	SW 1	SW	SW	SW	SW	SW	SW	SW 1
London Waterloo 15 ⊖	d	14 33	14 37	14 45	14 50			14 52	14 58		15 03	15 07	15 15	15 20			15 22	15 28		15 33	15 37	15 45	15 50
Vauxhall ⊖	d	14 37	14 41	14 49				14 56	15 02		15 07	15 11	15 19				15 26	15 32		15 37	15 41	15 49	
Queenstown Rd.(Battersea)	d	14 40	14 44	14 52				14 59			15 10	15 14	15 22				15 29			15 40	15 44	15 52	
Clapham Junction 10	d	14 43	14 47	14 55	14 58			15 02	15 08		15 13	15 17	15 25	15 28			15 32	15 38		15 43	15 47	15 55	15 58
Wandsworth Town	d	14 46	14 50	14 58				15 05			15 16	15 20	15 28				15 35			15 46	15 50	15 58	
Putney	d	14 49	14 53	15 01				15 08	15 12		15 19	15 23	15 31				15 38	15 42		15 49	15 53	16 01	
Barnes	d	14 52	14 57	15 05				15 12			15 22	15 27	15 35				15 42			15 52	15 57	16 05	
Barnes Bridge	d		14 59					15 14				15 29					15 44				15 59		
Chiswick	d		15 02					15 17				15 32					15 47				16 02		
Kew Bridge	d		15 05					15 20				15 35					15 50				16 05		
Brentford	d		15 08					15 23				15 38					15 53				16 08		
Syon Lane	d		15 10					15 25				15 40					15 55				16 10		
Isleworth	d		15 12					15 27				15 42					15 57				16 12		
Hounslow	d		15 18					15 31				15 48					16 01				16 18		
Mortlake	d	14 54		15 07							15 24		15 37							15 54		16 07	
North Sheen	d	14 56		15 09		←					15 26		15 39		←					15 56		16 09	
Richmond ⊖	d	14 59		15 12	15 06	15 12			15 18		15 29		15 42	15 36	15 42			15 48		15 59		16 12	16 06
St Margarets	d	15 01		→		15 14					15 31		→		15 44					16 01		→	
Twickenham	a	15 03			15 10	15 16			15 21		15 33			15 40	15 46			15 51		16 03			16 10
	d	15 04			15 10	15 17			15 22		15 34			15 40	15 47			15 52		16 04			16 10
Strawberry Hill	d	15 07									15 37									16 07			
Fulwell	a																						
Teddington	a	15 10									15 40									16 10			
Hampton Wick	a	15 14									15 44									16 14			
Kingston	a	15 16									15 46									16 16			
Whitton	d		15a23			15a20			15 25	←		15a53			15a50			15 55	←		16a23		
Feltham	d				15 16			15 36	15 29	15 36				15 46			16 06	15 59	16 06				16 16
Ashford (Surrey)	d							→	15 33	15 40							→	16 03	16 10				
Staines	d				15 23				15 37	15 44				15 53				16 07	16 14				16 23
Wraysbury	d								15 42									16 12					
Sunnymeads	d								15 45									16 15					
Datchet	d								15 49									16 19					
Windsor & Eton Riverside	a								15 54									16 24					
Egham	d				15 27					15 49				15 57					16 19				16 27
Virginia Water	a				15 31					15 53				16 01					16 23				16 31
	d				15 31					15 53				16 01					16 23				16 31
Chertsey	d									15 59									16 29				
Addlestone	d									16 02									16 32				
Weybridge	a									16 07									16 42				
Byfleet & New Haw	d																						
West Byfleet	d																						
Woking	a																						
Longcross	d																						
Sunningdale	d				15 37									16 07									16 37
Ascot 3	d				15 43		15 53							16 13		16 23							16 43
Bagshot	d						15 59									16 29							
Camberley	a						16 05									16 35							
Frimley	d						16 13									16 43							
Ash Vale	d						16 19									16 49							
Aldershot	a						16 24									16 54							
	d						16 38									17 08							
Ash 5	d						16 45									17 15							
Wanborough	d						16 48									17 18							
Guildford	a						16 55									17 25							
Martins Heron	d				15 47									16 17									16 47
Bracknell	d				15 50									16 20									16 50
Wokingham	d				15 57									16 27									16 57
Winnersh	d				16 00									16 30									17 00
Winnersh Triangle	d				16 02									16 32									17 02
Earley	d				16 07									16 37									17 07
Reading 7	a				16 13									16 43									17 13

London - Hounslow, Richmond, Kingston, Windsor, Weybridge, Ascot, Guildford and Reading

		SW	SW 1	SW	SW	SW	SW	SW	SW	SW 1	SW	SW 1	SW	SW	SW	SW	SW	SW	SW 1	SW	SW 1	SW
London Waterloo 15 ⊖	d			15 52	15 58		16 03	16 07	16 15	16 20			16 22	16 28		16 33	16 37	16 45	16 50			16 52
Vauxhall ⊖	d			15 56	16 02		16 07	16 11	16 19				16 26	16 32		16 37	16 41	16 49				16 56
Queenstown Rd.(Battersea)	d			15 59			16 10	16 14	16 22				16 29			16 40	16 44	16 52				16 59
Clapham Junction 10	d			16 02	16 08		16 13	16 17	16 25	16 28			16 32	16 38		16 43	16 47	16 55	16 58			17 02
Wandsworth Town	d			16 05			16 16	16 20	16 28				16 35			16 46	16 50	16 58				17 05
Putney	d			16 08	16 12		16 19	16 23	16 31				16 38	16 42		16 49	16 53	17 01				17 08
Barnes	d			16 12			16 22	16 27	16 35				16 42			16 52	16 57	17 05				17 12
Barnes Bridge	d			16 14				16 29					16 44				16 59					17 14
Chiswick	d			16 17				16 32					16 47				17 02					17 17
Kew Bridge	d			16 20				16 35					16 50				17 05					17 20
Brentford	d			16 23				16 38					16 53				17 08					17 23
Syon Lane	d			16 25				16 40					16 55				17 10					17 25
Isleworth	d			16 27				16 42					16 57				17 12					17 27
Hounslow	d			16 31				16 48					17 01				17 18					17 31
Mortlake	d						16 24		16 37							16 54		17 07				
North Sheen	d	←					16 26		16 39		←					16 56		17 09		←		
Richmond ⊖	d	16 12			16 18		16 29		16 42	16 36	16 42			16 48		16 59		17 12	17 06	17 12		
St Margarets	d	16 14					16 31		→		16 44					17 01		→		17 14		
Twickenham	a	16 16			16 21		16 33			16 40	16 46			16 51		17 03			17 10	17 16		
	d	16 17			16 22		16 34			16 40	16 47			16 52		17 04			17 10	17 17		
Strawberry Hill	d						16 37									17 07						
Fulwell	a																					
Teddington	a						16 40									17 10						
Hampton Wick	a						16 44									17 14						
Kingston	a						16 46									17 16						
Whitton	d	16a20			16 25	←		16a53			16a50			16 55	←		17a23			17a20		
Feltham	d			16 36	16 29	16 36				16 46			17 06	16 59	17 06				17 16			17 36
Ashford (Surrey)	d			→	16 33	16 40							→	17 03	17 10							→
Staines	d				16 37	16 44				16 53				17 07	17 14				17 23			
Wraysbury	d				16 42									17 12								
Sunnymeads	d				16 45									17 15								
Datchet	d				16 49									17 19								
Windsor & Eton Riverside	a				16 54									17 24								
Egham	d					16 49				16 57					17 19				17 27			
Virginia Water	a					16 53				17 01					17 23				17 31			
	d					16 53				17 01					17 23				17 31			
Chertsey	d					16 59									17 29							
Addlestone	d					17 02									17 32							
Weybridge	a					17 07									17 37							
Byfleet & New Haw	d																					
West Byfleet	d																					
Woking	a																					
Longcross	d																					
Sunningdale	d									17 07									17 37			
Ascot 3	d		16 53							17 13		17 23							17 43		17 53	
Bagshot	d		16 59									17 29									17 59	
Camberley	a		17 05									17 35									18 05	
Frimley	d		17 13									17 43									18 13	
Ash Vale	d		17 19									17 49									18 19	
Aldershot	a		17 24									17 54									18 24	
	d		17 38									18 08									18 38	
Ash 5	d		17 45									18 15									18 45	
Wanborough	d		17 48									18 18									18 48	
Guildford	a		17 55									18 25									18 55	
Martins Heron	d									17 17									17 47			
Bracknell	d									17 20									17 50			
Wokingham	d									17 27									17 57			
Winnersh	d									17 30									18 00			
Winnersh Triangle	d									17 32									18 02			
Earley	d									17 37									18 07			
Reading 7	a									17 43									18 13			

Table 149

Saturdays
from 8 October

London - Hounslow, Richmond, Kingston, Windsor, Weybridge, Ascot, Guildford and Reading

		SW	SW	SW	SW	SW	SW ■	SW	SW ■	SW	SW	SW	SW	SW	SW	SW ■	SW	SW ■	SW	SW	SW	SW	SW
London Waterloo ■ ⊖	d	16 58		17 03	17 07	17 15	17 20			17 22	17 28		17 33	17 37	17 45	17 50			17 52	17 58		18 03	18 07
Vauxhall ⊖	d	17 02		17 07	17 11	17 19				17 26	17 32		17 37	17 41	17 49				17 56	18 02		18 07	18 11
Queenstown Rd.(Battersea)	d			17 10	17 14	17 22				17 29			17 40	17 44	17 52				17 59			18 10	18 14
Clapham Junction ■	d	17 08		17 13	17 17	17 25	17 28			17 32	17 38		17 43	17 47	17 55	17 58			18 02	18 08		18 13	18 17
Wandsworth Town	d			17 16	17 20	17 28				17 35			17 46	17 50	17 58				18 05			18 16	18 20
Putney	d	17 12		17 19	17 23	17 31				17 38	17 42		17 49	17 53	18 01				18 08	18 12		18 19	18 23
Barnes	d			17 22	17 27	17 35				17 42			17 52	17 57	18 05				18 12			18 22	18 27
Barnes Bridge	d				17 29					17 44				17 59					18 14				18 29
Chiswick	d				17 32					17 47				18 02					18 17				18 32
Kew Bridge	d				17 35					17 50				18 05					18 20				18 35
Brentford	d				17 38					17 53				18 08					18 23				18 38
Syon Lane	d				17 40					17 55				18 10					18 25				18 40
Isleworth	d				17 42					17 57				18 12					18 27				18 42
Hounslow	d				17 48					18 01				18 18					18 31				18 48
Mortlake	d			17 24		17 37							17 54		18 07							18 24	
North Sheen	d			17 26		17 39		←					17 56		18 09		←					18 26	
Richmond ⊖	d	17 18		17 29		17 42	17 36	17 42			17 48		17 59		18 12	18 06	18 12			18 18		18 29	
St Margarets	d			17 31		→		17 44					18 01		→		18 14					18 31	
Twickenham	a	17 21		17 33			17 40	17 46			17 51		18 03			18 10	18 16			18 21		18 33	
	d	17 22		17 34			17 40	17 47			17 52		18 04			18 10	18 17			18 22		18 34	
Strawberry Hill	d			17 37									18 07									18 37	
Fulwell	a																						
Teddington	a			17 40									18 10									18 40	
Hampton Wick	a			17 44									18 14									18 44	
Kingston	a			17 46									18 16									18 46	
Whitton	d	17 25	←		17a53			17a50			17 55	←		18a23			18a20			18 25	←		18a53
Feltham	d	17 29	17 36				17 46			18 06	17 59	18 06				18 16			18 36	18 29	18 36		
Ashford (Surrey)	d	17 33	17 40							→	18 03	18 10							→	18 33	18 40		
Staines	d	17 37	17 44				17 53				18 07	18 14				18 23				18 37	18 44		
Wraysbury	d	17 42									18 12									18 42			
Sunnymeads	d	17 45									18 15									18 45			
Datchet	d	17 49									18 19									18 49			
Windsor & Eton Riverside	a	17 54									18 24									18 54			
Egham	d		17 49				17 57					18 19				18 27					18 49		
Virginia Water	a		17 53				18 01					18 23				18 31					18 53		
	d		17 53				18 01					18 23				18 31					18 53		
Chertsey	d		17 59									18 29									18 59		
Addlestone	d		18 02									18 32									19 02		
Weybridge	a		18 07									18 37									19 07		
Byfleet & New Haw	d																						
West Byfleet	d																						
Woking	a																						
Longcross	d																						
Sunningdale	d						18 07									18 37							
Ascot ■	d						18 13		18 23							18 43		18 53					
Bagshot	d								18 29									18 59					
Camberley	a								18 35									19 05					
Frimley	d								18 43									19 13					
Ash Vale	d								18 49									19 19					
Aldershot	a								18 54									19 24					
	d								19 08									19 38					
Ash ■	d								19 15									19 45					
Wanborough	d								19 18									19 48					
Guildford	a								19 25									19 55					
Martins Heron	d						18 17									18 47							
Bracknell	d						18 20									18 50							
Wokingham	d						18 27									18 57							
Winnersh	d						18 30									19 00							
Winnersh Triangle	d						18 32									19 02							
Earley	d						18 37									19 07							
Reading ■	a						18 43									19 13							

Table 149

Saturdays
from 8 October

London - Hounslow, Richmond, Kingston, Windsor, Weybridge, Ascot, Guildford and Reading

		SW	SW ■	SW	SW ■	SW	SW	SW	SW	SW	SW	SW ■	SW	SW ■	SW	SW	SW	SW	SW	SW	SW ■	SW	SW ■
London Waterloo ■ ⊖	d	18 15	18 20			18 22	18 28		18 33	18 37	18 45	18 50			18 52	18 58		19 03	19 07	19 15	19 20		
Vauxhall ⊖	d	18 19				18 26	18 32		18 37	18 41	18 49				18 56	19 02		19 07	19 11	19 19			
Queenstown Rd.(Battersea)	d	18 22				18 29			18 40	18 44	18 52				18 59			19 10	19 14	19 22			
Clapham Junction ■	d	18 25	18 28			18 32	18 38		18 43	18 47	18 55	18 58			19 02	19 08		19 13	19 17	19 25	19 28		
Wandsworth Town	d	18 28				18 35			18 46	18 50	18 58				19 05			19 16	19 20	19 28			
Putney	d	18 31				18 38	18 42		18 49	18 53	19 01				19 08	19 12		19 19	19 23	19 31			
Barnes	d	18 35				18 42			18 52	18 57	19 05				19 12			19 22	19 27	19 35			
Barnes Bridge	d					18 44				18 59					19 14				19 29				
Chiswick	d					18 47				19 02					19 17				19 32				
Kew Bridge	d					18 50				19 05					19 20				19 35				
Brentford	d					18 53				19 08					19 23				19 38				
Syon Lane	d					18 55				19 10					19 25				19 40				
Isleworth	d					18 57				19 12					19 27				19 42				
Hounslow	d					19 01				19 18					19 31				19 48				
Mortlake	d	18 37							18 54		19 07							19 24		19 37			
North Sheen	d	18 39		←					18 56		19 09		←					19 26		19 39		←	
Richmond ⊖	d	18 42	18 36	18 42			18 48		18 59		19 12	19 06	19 12			19 18		19 29		19 42	19 36	19 42	
St Margarets	d	→		18 44					19 01		→		19 14					19 31		→		19 44	
Twickenham	a		18 40	18 46			18 51		19 03			19 10	19 16			19 21		19 33			19 40	19 46	
	d		18 40	18 47			18 52		19 04			19 10	19 17			19 22		19 34			19 40	19 47	
Strawberry Hill	d								19 07									19 37					
Fulwell	a																						
Teddington	a								19 10									19 40					
Hampton Wick	a								19 14									19 44					
Kingston	a								19 16									19 46					
Whitton	d			18a50			18 55	←		19a23			19a20			19 25	←		19a53			19a50	
Feltham	d		18 46			19 06	18 59	19 06				19 16			19 36	19 29	19 36				19 46		
Ashford (Surrey)	d					→	19 03	19 10							→	19 33	19 40						
Staines	d		18 53				19 07	19 14				19 23				19 37	19 44				19 53		
Wraysbury	d						19 12									19 42							
Sunnymeads	d						19 15									19 45							
Datchet	d						19 19									19 49							
Windsor & Eton Riverside	a						19 24									19 54							
Egham	d		18 57					19 19				19 27					19 49				19 57		
Virginia Water	a		19 01					19 23				19 31					19 53				20 01		
	d		19 01					19 23				19 31					19 53				20 01		
Chertsey	d							19 29									19 59						
Addlestone	d							19 32									20 02						
Weybridge	a							19 37									20 07						
Byfleet & New Haw	d																						
West Byfleet	d																						
Woking	a																						
Longcross	d																						
Sunningdale	d		19 07									19 37									20 07		
Ascot ■	d		19 13		19 23							19 43		19 53							20 13		20 23
Bagshot	d				19 29									19 59									20 29
Camberley	a				19 35									20 05									20 35
Frimley	d				19 43									20 13									20 43
Ash Vale	d				19 49									20 19									20 49
Aldershot	a				19 54									20 24									20 54
	d				20 08									20 38									21 08
Ash ■	d				20 15									20 45									21 15
Wanborough	d				20 18									20 48									21 18
Guildford	a				20 25									20 55									21 25
Martins Heron	d		19 17									19 47									20 17		
Bracknell	d		19 20									19 50									20 20		
Wokingham	d		19 27									19 57									20 27		
Winnersh	d		19 30									20 00									20 30		
Winnersh Triangle	d		19 32									20 02									20 32		
Earley	d		19 37									20 07									20 37		
Reading ■	a		19 43									20 13									20 43		

London - Hounslow, Richmond, Kingston, Windsor, Weybridge, Ascot, Guildford and Reading

		SW	SW	SW	SW	SW	SW	SW 1	SW	SW 1	SW	SW	SW	SW	SW	SW	SW 1	SW	SW 1	SW 1	SW	SW
London Waterloo 15 ⊖	d	19 22	19 28		19 33	19 37	19 45	19 50			19 52	19 58		20 03	20 07	20 15	20 20				20 22	20 28
Vauxhall ⊖	d	19 26	19 32		19 37	19 41	19 49				19 56	20 02		20 07	20 11	20 19					20 26	20 32
Queenstown Rd.(Battersea)	d	19 29			19 40	19 44	19 52				19 59			20 10	20 14	20 22					20 29	
Clapham Junction 10	d	19 32	19 38		19 43	19 47	19 55	19 58			20 02	20 08		20 13	20 17	20 25	20 28				20 32	20 38
Wandsworth Town	d	19 35			19 46	19 50	19 58				20 05			20 16	20 20	20 28					20 35	
Putney	d	19 38	19 42		19 49	19 53	20 01				20 08	20 12		20 19	20 23	20 31					20 38	20 42
Barnes	d	19 42			19 52	19 57	20 05				20 12			20 22	20 27	20 35					20 42	
Barnes Bridge	d	19 44				19 59					20 14				20 29						20 44	
Chiswick	d	19 47				20 02					20 17				20 32						20 47	
Kew Bridge	d	19 50				20 05					20 20				20 35						20 50	
Brentford	d	19 53				20 08					20 23				20 38						20 53	
Syon Lane	d	19 55				20 10					20 25				20 40						20 55	
Isleworth	d	19 57				20 12					20 27				20 42						20 57	
Hounslow	d	20 01				20 18					20 31				20 48						21 01	
Mortlake	d				19 54		20 07							20 24		20 37						
North Sheen	d				19 56		20 09		←					20 26		20 39		←				
Richmond ⊖	d		19 48		19 59		20 12	20 06	20 12			20 18		20 29		20 42	20 36	20 42				20 48
St Margarets	d				20 01		→		20 14					20 31		→		20 44				
Twickenham	a		19 51		20 03			20 10	20 16			20 21		20 33			20 40	20 46				20 51
	d		19 52		20 04			20 10	20 17			20 22		20 34			20 40	20 47				20 52
Strawberry Hill	d				20 07									20 37								
Fulwell	a																					
Teddington	a				20 10									20 40								
Hampton Wick	a				20 14									20 44								
Kingston	a				20 16									20 46								
Whitton	d		19 55	←		20a23			20a20			20 25	←		20a53			20a50				20 55
Feltham	d	20 06	19 59	20 06				20 16			20 36	20 29	20 36				20 46				21 06	20 59
Ashford (Surrey)	d	→	20 03	20 10							→	20 33	20 40								→	21 03
Staines	d		20 07	20 14				20 23				20 37	20 44				20 53					21 07
Wraysbury	d		20 12									20 42										21 12
Sunnymeads	d		20 15									20 45										21 15
Datchet	d		20 19									20 49										21 19
Windsor & Eton Riverside	a		20 24									20 54										21 24
Egham	d			20 19				20 27					20 49				20 57					
Virginia Water	a			20 23				20 31					20 53				21 01					
	d			20 23				20 31					20 53				21 01					
Chertsey	d			20 29									20 59									
Addlestone	d			20 32									21 02									
Weybridge	a			20 37									21 07									
Byfleet & New Haw	d																					
West Byfleet	d																					
Woking	a																					
Longcross	d																					
Sunningdale	d							20 37									21 07					
Ascot 3	d							20 43		20 53							21 13		21 23			
Bagshot	d									20 59									21 29			
Camberley	a									21 05									21 35			
Frimley	d									21 13									21 43			
Ash Vale	d									21 19									21 49			
Aldershot	a									21 24									21 54			
	d									21 38									22 08	22 38		
Ash 5	d									21 45									22 15	22 45		
Wanborough	d									21 48									22 18	22 48		
Guildford	a									21 55									22 25	22 55		
Martins Heron	d							20 47									21 17					
Bracknell	d							20 50									21 20					
Wokingham	d							20 57									21 27					
Winnersh	d							21 00									21 30					
Winnersh Triangle	d							21 02									21 32					
Earley	d							21 07									21 37					
Reading 7	a							21 13									21 43					

London - Hounslow, Richmond, Kingston, Windsor, Weybridge, Ascot, Guildford and Reading

		SW	SW	SW	SW	SW 1	SW	SW	SW	SW	SW	SW	SW	SW 1	SW	SW 1	SW	SW	SW	SW	SW	SW	SW 1
London Waterloo 15 ⊖	d		20 33	20 37	20 45	20 50		20 52	20 58		21 03	21 07	21 15	21 20			21 22	21 28		21 33	21 37	21 45	21 50
Vauxhall ⊖	d		20 37	20 41	20 49			20 56	21 02		21 07	21 11	21 19				21 26	21 32		21 37	21 41	21 49	
Queenstown Rd.(Battersea)	d		20 40	20 44	20 52			20 59			21 10	21 14	21 22				21 29			21 40	21 44	21 52	
Clapham Junction 10	d		20 43	20 47	20 55	20 58		21 02	21 08		21 13	21 17	21 25	21 28			21 32	21 38		21 43	21 47	21 55	21 58
Wandsworth Town	d		20 46	20 50	20 58			21 05			21 16	21 20	21 28				21 35			21 46	21 50	21 58	
Putney	d		20 49	20 53	21 01			21 08	21 12		21 19	21 23	21 31				21 38	21 42		21 49	21 53	22 01	
Barnes	d		20 52	20 57	21 05			21 12			21 22	21 27	21 35				21 42			21 52	21 57	22 05	
Barnes Bridge	d			20 59				21 14				21 29					21 44				21 59		
Chiswick	d			21 02				21 17				21 32					21 47				22 02		
Kew Bridge	d			21 05				21 20				21 35					21 50				22 05		
Brentford	d			21 08				21 23				21 38					21 53				22 08		
Syon Lane	d			21 10				21 25				21 40					21 55				22 10		
Isleworth	d			21 12				21 27				21 42					21 57				22 12		
Hounslow	d			21 18				21 31				21 48					22 01				22 18		
Mortlake	d		20 54		21 07						21 24		21 37							21 54		22 07	
North Sheen	d		20 56		21 09		←				21 26		21 39		←					21 56		22 09	
Richmond ⊖	d		20 59		21 12	21 06	21 12		21 18		21 29		21 42	21 36	21 42			21 48		21 59		22 12	22 06
St Margarets	d		21 01		→		21 14				21 31		→		21 44					22 01		→	
Twickenham	a		21 03			21 10	21 16		21 21		21 33			21 40	21 46			21 51		22 03			22 10
	d		21 04			21 10	21 17		21 22		21 34			21 40	21 47			21 52		22 04			22 10
Strawberry Hill	d		21 07								21 37									22 07			
Fulwell	a																						
Teddington	a		21 10								21 40									22 10			
Hampton Wick	a		21 14								21 44									22 14			
Kingston	a		21 16								21 46									22 16			
Whitton	d	←		21a23			21a20		21 25	←		21a53			21a50			21 55	←		22a23		
Feltham	d	21 06				21 16		21 36	21 29	21 36				21 46			22 06	21 59	22 06				22 16
Ashford (Surrey)	d	21 10						→	21 33	21 40							→	22 03	22 10				
Staines	d	21 14				21 23			21 37	21 44				21 53				22 07	22 14				22 23
Wraysbury	d								21 42									22 12					
Sunnymeads	d								21 45									22 15					
Datchet	d								21 49									22 19					
Windsor & Eton Riverside	a								21 54									22 24					
Egham	d	21 19				21 27				21 49				21 57					22 19				22 27
Virginia Water	a	21 23				21 31				21 53				22 01					22 23				22 31
	d	21 23				21 31				21 53				22 01					22 23				22 31
Chertsey	d	21 29								21 59									22 29				
Addlestone	d	21 32								22 02									22 32				
Weybridge	a	21 37								22 07									22 37				
Byfleet & New Haw	d																						
West Byfleet	d																						
Woking	a																						
Longcross	d																						
Sunningdale	d					21 37								22 07									22 37
Ascot 3	d					21 43								22 13		22 23							22 43
Bagshot	d															22 29							
Camberley	a															22 35							
Frimley	d															22 43							
Ash Vale	d															22 49							
Aldershot	a															22 54							
	d															23 08							
Ash 5	d															23 15							
Wanborough	d															23 18							
Guildford	a															23 25							
Martins Heron	d					21 47								22 17									22 47
Bracknell	d					21 50								22 20									22 50
Wokingham	d					21 57								22 27									22 57
Winnersh	d					22 00								22 30									23 00
Winnersh Triangle	d					22 02								22 32									23 02
Earley	d					22 07								22 37									23 05
Reading 7	a					22 13								22 42									23 13

Table 149

Saturdays
from 8 October

London - Hounslow, Richmond, Kingston, Windsor, Weybridge, Ascot, Guildford and Reading

		SW	SW	SW	SW	SW	SW ■1	SW ■1	SW	SW	SW	SW	SW ■1	SW	SW	SW	SW	SW	SW ■1	SW	SW	SW
London Waterloo ■15 ⊖	d		21 52	21 58		22 03	22 20		22 22	22 28		22 33	22 50	22 52	22 58		23 03	23 13	23 20	23 22	23 33	23 38
Vauxhall ⊖	d		21 56	22 02		22 07			22 26	22 32		22 37		22 56	23 02		23 07	23 17		23 26	23 37	
Queenstown Rd.(Battersea)	d		21 59			22 10			22 29			22 40		22 59			23 10			23 29	23 40	
Clapham Junction ■10	d		22 02	22 08		22 13	22 28		22 32	22 38		22 43	22 58	23 02	23 08		23 13	23 23	23 28	23 32	23 43	23 46
Wandsworth Town	d		22 05			22 16			22 35			22 46		23 05			23 16			23 35	23 46	
Putney	d		22 08	22 12		22 19			22 38	22 42		22 49		23 08	23 12		23 19	23 27		23 38	23 49	
Barnes	d		22 12			22 22			22 42			22 52		23 12			23 22			23 42	23 52	
Barnes Bridge	d		22 14						22 44					23 14						23 44		
Chiswick	d		22 17						22 47					23 17						23 47		
Kew Bridge	d		22 20						22 50					23 20						23 50		
Brentford	d		22 23						22 53					23 23						23 53		
Syon Lane	d		22 25						22 55					23 25						23 55		
Isleworth	d		22 27						22 57					23 27						23 57		
Hounslow	d		22 31						23 01					23 31						00 01		
Mortlake	d					22 24						22 54					23 24				23 54	
North Sheen	d	←				22 26						22 56					23 26				23 56	
Richmond ⊖	d	22 12		22 18		22 29	22 36			22 48		22 59	23 06		23 18		23 29	23 33	23 37		23 59	23 54
St Margarets	d	22 14				22 31						23 01					23 31				→	
Twickenham	a	22 16		22 21		22 33	22 40			22 51		23 03	23 10		23 21		23 33	23 37	23 41			23 58
	d			22 22		22 34	22 40			22 52		23 04	23 10		23 22		23 34	23 37	23 41			23 58
Strawberry Hill	d					22 37						23 07					23 37					
Fulwell	a																					
Teddington	a					22 40						23 10					23 40					
Hampton Wick	a					22 44						23 14					23 44					
Kingston	a					22 46						23 16					23 46					
Whitton	d			22 25	←					22 55	←				23 25	←		23 40				
Feltham	d		22 36	22 29	22 36		22 46		23 06	22 59	23 06		23 16	23 36	23 29	23 36		23 44	23 48	00 06		00 04
Ashford (Surrey)	d		→	22 33	22 40				→	23 03	23 10			→	23 33	23 40		23 48		→		
Staines	d			22 37	22 44		22 53			23 07	23 14		23 23		23 37	23 44		23 52	23 56			00 11
Wraysbury	d			22 42						23 11					23 42			23 57				
Sunnymeads	d			22 45						23 14					23 45			23 59				
Datchet	d			22 49						23 17					23 49			00 04				
Windsor & Eton Riverside	a			22 56						23 24					23 54			00 09				
Egham	d				22 49		22 57				23 19		23 27			23 49			00 01			00 15
Virginia Water	a				22 53		23 01				23 23		23 31			23 53			00 05			00 19
	d				22 53		23 01				23 23		23 31			23 53			00 05			00 19
Chertsey	d				22 59						23 29					23 59						
Addlestone	d				23 02						23a32					00 02						
Weybridge	a				23 07																	
Byfleet & New Haw	d															00 06						
West Byfleet	d															00 09						
Woking	a															00 15						
Longcross	d																					
Sunningdale	d						23 07						23 37						00 11			00 25
Ascot ■3	d						23 13	23 23					23 43						00 15			00 30
Bagshot	d							23 29														
Camberley	a							23 35														
Frimley	d							23 43														
Ash Vale	d							23 49														
Aldershot	a							23 54														
	d																					
Ash ■5	d																					
Wanborough	d																					
Guildford	a																					
Martins Heron	d						23 17						23 47						00 19			00 34
Bracknell	d						23 20						23 50						00 23			00 37
Wokingham	d						23 27						23 57						00 32			00 44
Winnersh	d						23 30						23 59						00 36			
Winnersh Triangle	d						23 32						00 02						00 38			
Earley	d						23 37						00 05						00 40			
Reading ■7	a						23 43						00 13						00 48			00 55

Table 149

Saturdays
from 8 October

London - Hounslow, Richmond, Kingston, Windsor, Weybridge, Ascot, Guildford and Reading

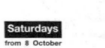

		SW	SW	SW	SW	SW
London Waterloo ■15 ⊖	d			23 52	23 58	
Vauxhall ⊖	d			23 56	00 02	
Queenstown Rd.(Battersea)	d			23 59		
Clapham Junction ■10	d			00 02	00 08	
Wandsworth Town	d			00 05		
Putney	d			00 08	00 12	
Barnes	d			00 12		
Barnes Bridge	d			00 14		
Chiswick	d			00 17		
Kew Bridge	d			00 20		
Brentford	d			00 23		
Syon Lane	d			00 25		
Isleworth	d			00 27		
Hounslow	d			00 31		
Mortlake	d					
North Sheen	d		←			
Richmond ⊖	d		23 59		00 18	
St Margarets	d		00 01			
Twickenham	a		00 04		00 21	
	d		00 04		00 22	
Strawberry Hill	d		00 07			
Fulwell	a					
Teddington	a		00 11			
Hampton Wick	a		00 14			
Kingston	a		00 16			
Whitton	d	←			00 25	←
Feltham	d	00 06		00 36	00 29	00 36
Ashford (Surrey)	d	00 10		→	00 33	00 40
Staines	d	00 14			00a37	00a46
Wraysbury	d					
Sunnymeads	d					
Datchet	d					
Windsor & Eton Riverside	a					
Egham	d	00 19				
Virginia Water	a	00 23				
	d	00 23				
Chertsey	d	00 29				
Addlestone	d	00a32				
Weybridge	a					
Byfleet & New Haw	d					
West Byfleet	d					
Woking	a					
Longcross	d					
Sunningdale	d					
Ascot ■3	d					
Bagshot	d					
Camberley	a					
Frimley	d					
Ash Vale	d					
Aldershot	a					
	d					
Ash ■5	d					
Wanborough	d					
Guildford	a					
Martins Heron	d					
Bracknell	d					
Wokingham	d					
Winnersh	d					
Winnersh Triangle	d					
Earley	d					
Reading ■7	a					

London - Hounslow, Richmond, Kingston, Windsor, Weybridge, Ascot, Guildford and Reading

		SW 1 A	SW A	SW A	SW 1 A	SW A	SW A	SW A	SW A	SW A	SW 1	SW 1	SW A	SW A	SW A	SW	SW	SW	SW	SW	SW	SW	SW 1
London Waterloo 15 ⊖	d	22p50	22p52	23p13	23p20	23p22	23p33	23p38					23p52	23p58		00 18	01 42	06 14	06 18		06 44		07 09
Vauxhall ⊖	d		22p56	23p17		23p26	23p37						23p56	00 02		00 22	01 46	06 18	06 22		06 48		07 13
Queenstown Rd.(Battersea)	d		22p59			23p29	23p40						23p59			00 26		06 21			06 51		
Clapham Junction 10	d	22p58	23p02	23p23	23p28	23p32	23p43	23p46					00 02	00 08		00 29		06 24			06 54		07 19
Wandsworth Town	d		23p05			23p35	23p46						00 05			00 32		06 27			06 57		
Putney	d		23p08	23p27		23p38	23p49						00 08	00 12		00 35		06 30			07 00		07 23
Barnes	d		23p12			23p42	23p52						00 12			00 38		06 33			07 03		
Barnes Bridge	d		23p14			23p44							00 14										
Chiswick	d		23p17			23p47							00 17										
Kew Bridge	d		23p20			23p50							00 20										
Brentford	d		23p23			23p53							00 23										
Syon Lane	d		23p25			23p55							00 25										
Isleworth	d		23p27			23p57							00 27										
Hounslow	d		23p31			00 01							00 31										
Mortlake	d						23p54									00 40		06 35			07 05		
North Sheen	d						23p56			←						00 42		06 37			07 07		
Richmond ⊖	d	23p06		23p33	23p37		23p59	23p54		23p59				00 18		00 45		06 40			07 10		07 29
St Margarets	d						→			00 01						00 47		06 42			07 12		
Twickenham	a	23p10		23p37	23p41			23p58		00 04				00 21		00 49	02 22	06 44	07 02		07 14		07 32
	d	23p10		23p37	23p41			23p58		00 04				00 22		00 50		06 45			07 15		07 33
Strawberry Hill	d									00 07						00s53		06 49					
Fulwell	a																						
Teddington	a									00 11						00s56		06 52					
Hampton Wick	a									00 14						00s59		06 57					
Kingston	a									00 16						01 01		06 59					
Whitton	d			23p40					←					00 25	←						07 18		
Feltham	d	23p16	23p36	23p44	23p48	00 06		00 04	00 06				00 36	00 29	00 36						07 22		07 39
Ashford (Surrey)	d		23p40	23p48		→			00 10				→	00 33	00 40						07 26		
Staines	d	23p23	23p44	23p52	23p56			00 11	00 14					00a37	00a46					06 32	07 30	07 40	07 45
Wraysbury	d			23p56																	07 34		
Sunnymeads	d			23p59																	07 37		
Datchet	d			00 02																	07 40		
Windsor & Eton Riverside	a			00 06																	07 44		
Egham	d	23p27	23p49		00 01			00 15	00 19											06 36		07 45	07 50
Virginia Water	a	23p31	23p53		00 05			00 19	00 23											06 41		07 49	07 54
	d	23p31	23p53		00 05			00 19	00 23											06 41		07 49	07 54
Chertsey	d		23p59						00 29											06 46		07 55	
Addlestone	d		00 02						00a32											06 49		07 58	
Weybridge	a																			06 53			
Byfleet & New Haw	d		00 06																			08 02	
West Byfleet	d		00 09																			08 05	
Woking	a		00 15																			08 11	
Longcross	d																						
Sunningdale	d	23p37			00 11			00 25															07 59
Ascot 3	d	23p43			00 15			00 30			00 32												08 04
Bagshot	d										00 38												
Camberley	a										00 44												
Frimley	d										00 48												
Ash Vale	d										00 57												
Aldershot	a										01s02												
	d											07 48											
Ash 5	d											07 55											
Wanborough	d											07 58											
Guildford	a											08 05											
Martins Heron	d	23p47			00 19			00 34															08 08
Bracknell	d	23p50			00 23			00 37															08 11
Wokingham	d	23p57			00 32			00 44															08 18
Winnersh	d	23p59			00 36																		08 21
Winnersh Triangle	d	00 02			00 38																		08 23
Earley	d	00 05			00 40																		08 26
Reading 7	a	00 10			00 45			00 52															08 31

A not 22 May

London - Hounslow, Richmond, Kingston, Windsor, Weybridge, Ascot, Guildford and Reading

		SW	SW 1	SW 1	SW	SW	SW 1	SW	SW 1	SW 1	SW	SW	SW 1	SW	SW	SW 1	SW 1	SW	SW	SW 1	SW	SW	SW 1
London Waterloo 15 ⊖	d	07 14			07 44	07 50	08 09	08 14		08 39	08 44	08 50	09 09	09 14	09 25		09 39	09 44	09 50	10 09	10 14	10 25	
Vauxhall ⊖	d	07 18			07 48	07 54	08 13	08 18		08 43	08 48	08 54	09 13	09 18	09 29		09 43	09 48	09 54	10 13	10 18	10 29	
Queenstown Rd.(Battersea)	d	07 21			07 51	07 57		08 21			08 51	08 57		09 21				09 51	09 57		10 21		
Clapham Junction 10	d	07 24			07 54	08 00	08 19	08 24		08 49	08 54	09 00	09 19	09 24	09 35		09 49	09 54	10 00	10 19	10 24	10 35	
Wandsworth Town	d	07 27			07 57	08 03		08 27			08 57	09 03		09 27				09 57	10 03		10 27		
Putney	d	07 30			08 00	08 06	08 23	08 30		08 53	09 00	09 06	09 23	09 30	09 39		09 53	10 00	10 06	10 23	10 30	10 39	
Barnes	d	07 33			08 03	08 09		08 33			09 03	09 09		09 33				10 03	10 09		10 33		
Barnes Bridge	d					08 11						09 11							10 11				
Chiswick	d					08 13						09 13							10 13				
Kew Bridge	d					08 16						09 16							10 16				
Brentford	d					08 19						09 19							10 19				
Syon Lane	d					08 21						09 21							10 21				
Isleworth	d					08 23						09 23							10 23				
Hounslow	d					08 26						09 26							10 26				
Mortlake	d	07 35			08 05			08 35			09 05			09 35				10 05			10 35		
North Sheen	d	07 37			08 07			08 37			09 07			09 37				10 07			10 37		
Richmond ⊖	d	07 40			08 10		08 29	08 40		08 59	09 10		09 29	09 40	09 45		09 59	10 10		10 29	10 40	10 45	
St Margarets	d	07 42			08 12			08 42			09 12			09 42				10 12			10 42		
Twickenham	a	07 44			08 14		08 32	08 44		09 02	09 14		09 32	09 44	09 48		10 02	10 14		10 32	10 44	10 48	
	d	07 45			08 15		08 33	08 45		09 03	09 15		09 33	09 45	09 49		10 03	10 15		10 33	10 45	10 49	
Strawberry Hill	d	07 49						08 49						09 49							10 49		
Fulwell	a																						
Teddington	a	07 52						08 52						09 52							10 52		
Hampton Wick	a	07 57						08 57						09 57							10 57		
Kingston	a	07 59						08 59						09 59							10 59		
Whitton	d				08 18						09 18				09 52			10 18				10 52	
Feltham	d				08 22	08 32	08 39			09 09	09 22	09 32	09 39		09 56		10 09	10 22	10 32	10 39		10 56	
Ashford (Surrey)	d				08 26	08 36					09 26	09 36			10 00			10 26	10 36			11 00	
Staines	d			08 15	08 30	08 40	08 45			09 15	09 30	09 40	09 45		10 04		10 15	10 30	10 40	10 45		11 04	
Wraysbury	d				08 34						09 34							10 34					
Sunnymeads	d				08 37						09 37							10 37					
Datchet	d				08 40						09 40				10 12			10 40				11 12	
Windsor & Eton Riverside	a				08 44						09 44				10 16			10 44				11 16	
Egham	d			08 20		08 45	08 50			09 20		09 45	09 50				10 20		10 45	10 50			
Virginia Water	a			08 24		08 49	08 54			09 24		09 49	09 54				10 24		10 49	10 54			
	d			08 24		08 49	08 54			09 24		09 49	09 54				10 24		10 49	10 54			
Chertsey	d					08 55						09 55							10 55				
Addlestone	d					08 58						09 58							10 58				
Weybridge	a																						
Byfleet & New Haw	d					09 02						10 02							11 02				
West Byfleet	d					09 05						10 05							11 05				
Woking	a					09 11						10 11							11 11				
Longcross	d																						
Sunningdale	d			08 29			08 59			09 29			09 59				10 29			10 59			
Ascot 3	d		08 13	08 34			09 04		09 13	09 34			10 04			10 13	10 34			11 04			11 13
Bagshot	d		08 19						09 19							10 19							11 19
Camberley	a		08 25						09 25							10 25							11 25
Frimley	d		08 29						09 29							10 29							11 29
Ash Vale	d		08 36						09 36							10 36							11 36
Aldershot	a		08 41						09 41							10 41							11 41
	d		08 48						09 48							10 48							11 48
Ash 5	d		08 55						09 55							10 55							11 55
Wanborough	d		08 58						09 58							10 58							11 58
Guildford	a		09 05						10 05							11 05							12 05
Martins Heron	d			08 38			09 08			09 38			10 08				10 38			11 08			
Bracknell	d			08 41			09 11			09 41			10 11				10 41			11 11			
Wokingham	d			08 48			09 18			09 48			10 18				10 48			11 18			
Winnersh	d			08 51			09 21			09 51			10 21				10 51			11 21			
Winnersh Triangle	d			08 53			09 23			09 53			10 23				10 53			11 23			
Earley	d			08 56			09 26			09 56			10 26				10 56			11 26			
Reading 7	a			09 01			09 31			10 01			10 31				11 01			11 31			

Table 149

Sundays until 25 September

London - Hounslow, Richmond, Kingston, Windsor, Weybridge, Ascot, Guildford and Reading

		SW ■1		SW	SW	SW ■1	SW	SW	SW ■1	SW ■1	SW	SW		SW ■1	SW	SW	SW ■1	SW ■1	SW	SW	SW ■1	SW		SW	SW ■1
London Waterloo ■15 ⊖	d	10 39		10 44	10 50	11 09	11 14	11 25		11 39	11 44	11 50		12 09	12 14	12 25		12 39	12 44	12 50	13 09	13 14		13 25	
Vauxhall ⊖	d	10 43		10 48	10 54	11 13	11 19	11 29		11 43	11 48	11 54		12 13	12 19	12 29		12 43	12 48	12 54	13 13	13 18		13 29	
Queenstown Rd.(Battersea)	d			10 51	10 57		11 22				11 51	11 57			12 22				12 51	12 57		13 21			
Clapham Junction ■10	d	10 49		10 54	11 00	11 19	11 25	11 35		11 49	11 54	12 00		12 19	12 25	12 35		12 49	12 54	13 00	13 19	13 24		13 35	
Wandsworth Town	d			10 57	11 03		11 28				11 57	12 03			12 28				12 57	13 03		13 27			
Putney	d	10 53		11 00	11 06	11 23	11 31	11 39		11 53	12 00	12 06		12 23	12 31	12 39		12 53	13 00	13 06	13 23	13 30		13 39	
Barnes	d			11 03	11 09		11 34				12 03	12 09			12 34				13 03	13 09		13 33			
Barnes Bridge	d				11 11							12 11								13 11					
Chiswick	d				11 13							12 13								13 13					
Kew Bridge	d				11 16							12 16								13 16					
Brentford	d				11 19							12 19								13 19					
Syon Lane	d				11 21							12 21								13 21					
Isleworth	d				11 23							12 23								13 23					
Hounslow	d				11 26							12 26								13 26					
Mortlake	d			11 05			11 36				12 05				12 36				13 05			13 35			
North Sheen	d			11 07			11 38				12 07				12 38				13 07			13 37			
Richmond ⊖	d	10 59		11 10		11 29	11 41	11 45		11 59	12 10			12 29	12 41	12 45		12 59	13 10		13 29	13 40		13 45	
St Margarets	d			11 12			11 43				12 12				12 43				13 12			13 42			
Twickenham	a	11 02		11 14		11 32	11 45	11 48		12 02	12 14			12 32	12 45	12 48		13 02	13 14		13 32	13 44		13 48	
	d	11 03		11 15		11 33	11 46	11 49		12 03	12 15			12 33	12 46	12 49		13 03	13 15		13 33	13 45		13 49	
Strawberry Hill	d						11 50								12 50							13 49			
Fulwell	a																								
Teddington	a						11 53								12 53							13 52			
Hampton Wick	a						11 57								12 57							13 57			
Kingston	a						11 59								12 59							13 59			
Whitton	d			11 18				11 52			12 18					12 52			13 18					13 52	
Feltham	d	11 09		11 22	11 32	11 39		11 56		12 09	12 22	12 32		12 39		12 56		13 09	13 22	13 32	13 39			13 56	
Ashford (Surrey)	d			11 26	11 36			12 00			12 26	12 36				13 00			13 26	13 36				14 00	
Staines	d	11 15		11 30	11 40	11 45		12 04		12 15	12 30	12 40		12 45		13 04		13 15	13 30	13 40	13 45			14 04	
Wraysbury	d			11 34							12 34								13 34						
Sunnymeads	d			11 37							12 37								13 37						
Datchet	d			11 40				12 12			12 40					13 12			13 40					14 12	
Windsor & Eton Riverside	a			11 44				12 16			12 44					13 16			13 44					14 16	
Egham	d	11 20			11 45	11 50				12 20		12 45		12 50				13 20		13 45	13 50				
Virginia Water	a	11 24			11 49	11 54				12 24		12 49		12 54				13 24		13 49	13 54				
	d	11 24			11 49	11 54				12 24		12 49		12 54				13 24		13 49	13 54				
Chertsey	d				11 55							12 55								13 55					
Addlestone	d				11 58							12 58								13 58					
Weybridge	a																								
Byfleet & New Haw	d				12 02							13 02								14 02					
West Byfleet	d				12 05							13 05								14 05					
Woking	a				12 11							13 11								14 11					
Longcross	d																								
Sunningdale	d	11 29				11 59				12 29				12 59				13 29			13 59				
Ascot ■8	d	11 34				12 04			12 13	12 34				13 04			13 13	13 34			14 04				14 13
Bagshot	d								12 19								13 19								14 19
Camberley	a								12 25								13 25								14 25
Frimley	d								12 29								13 29								14 29
Ash Vale	d								12 36								13 36								14 36
Aldershot	a								12 41								13 41								14 41
	d								12 48								13 48								14 48
Ash ■5	d								12 55								13 55								14 55
Wanborough	d								12 58								13 58								14 58
Guildford	a								13 05								14 05								15 05
Martins Heron	d	11 38				12 08				12 38				13 08				13 38			14 08				
Bracknell	d	11 41				12 11				12 41				13 11				13 41			14 11				
Wokingham	d	11 48				12 18				12 48				13 18				13 48			14 18				
Winnersh	d	11 51				12 21				12 51				13 21				13 51			14 21				
Winnersh Triangle	d	11 53				12 23				12 53				13 23				13 53			14 23				
Earley	d	11 56				12 26				12 56				13 26				13 56			14 26				
Reading ■7	a	12 01				12 31				13 01				13 31				14 01			14 31				

Table 149

Sundays until 25 September

London - Hounslow, Richmond, Kingston, Windsor, Weybridge, Ascot, Guildford and Reading

		SW ■1	SW	SW	SW		SW		SW ■1	SW	SW ■1	SW ■1	SW	SW	SW	SW ■1	SW		SW ■1	SW ■1	SW	SW	SW	SW ■1
London Waterloo ■15 ⊖	d	13 39	13 44	13 50	13 56		19 56		20 09	20 14		20 39	20 44	20 50	20 56	21 09	21 14			21 39	21 44	21 50	21 56	22 09
Vauxhall ⊖	d	13 43	13 48	13 54	14 00		20 00		20 13	20 18		20 43	20 48	20 54	21 00	21 13	21 18			21 43	21 48	21 54	22 00	22 13
Queenstown Rd.(Battersea)	d		13 51	13 57	14 03		20 03			20 21			20 51	20 57	21 03		21 21				21 51	21 57	22 03	
Clapham Junction ■10	d	13 49	13 54	14 00	14 06		20 06		20 19	20 24		20 49	20 54	21 00	21 06	21 19	21 24			21 49	21 54	22 00	22 06	22 19
Wandsworth Town	d		13 57	14 03	14 09		20 09			20 27			20 57	21 03	21 09		21 27				21 57	22 03	22 09	
Putney	d	13 53	14 00	14 06	14 12		20 12		20 23	20 30		20 53	21 00	21 06	21 12	21 23	21 30			21 53	22 00	22 06	22 12	22 23
Barnes	d		14 03	14 09	14 15		20 15			20 33			21 03	21 09	21 15		21 33				22 03	22 09	22 15	
Barnes Bridge	d			14 11										21 11								22 11		
Chiswick	d			14 13										21 13								22 13		
Kew Bridge	d			14 16										21 16								22 16		
Brentford	d			14 19										21 19								22 19		
Syon Lane	d			14 21										21 21								22 21		
Isleworth	d			14 23										21 23								22 23		
Hounslow	d			14 26										21 26								22 26		
Mortlake	d		14 05		14 17		20 17			20 35			21 05		21 17		21 35				22 05		22 17	
North Sheen	d		14 07		14 19		20 19			20 37			21 07		21 19		21 37				22 07		22 19	
Richmond ⊖	d	13 59	14 10		14 22		20 22		20 29	20 40		20 59	21 10		21 22	21 29	21 40			21 59	22 10		22 22	22 29
St Margarets	d		14 12		14 24		20 24			20 42			21 12		21 24		21 42				22 12		22 24	
Twickenham	a	14 02	14 14		14 26		20 26		20 32	20 44		21 02	21 14		21 26	21 32	21 44			22 02	22 14		22 26	22 32
	d	14 03	14 15		14 27		20 27		20 33	20 45		21 03	21 15		21 27	21 33	21 45			22 03	22 15		22 27	22 33
Strawberry Hill	d				14 30		20 30			20 49					21 30		21 49						22 30	
Fulwell	a																							
Teddington	a				14 33		20 33			20 52					21 33		21 52						22 33	
Hampton Wick	a				14 36		20 36			20 57					21 36		21 57						22 36	
Kingston	a				14 38		20 38			20 59					21 38		21 59						22 38	
Whitton	d		14 18										21 18								22 18			
Feltham	d	14 09	14 22	14 32		and at the same minutes past each hour until			20 39			21 09	21 22	21 32		21 39				22 09	22 22	22 32		22 39
Ashford (Surrey)	d		14 26	14 36									21 26	21 36							22 26	22 36		
Staines	d	14 15	14 30	14 40					20 45			21 15	21 30	21 40		21 45				22 15	22 30	22 40		22 45
Wraysbury	d		14 34										21 34								22 34			
Sunnymeads	d		14 37										21 37								22 37			
Datchet	d		14 40										21 40								22 40			
Windsor & Eton Riverside	a		14 44										21 44								22 44			
Egham	d	14 20		14 45					20 50			21 20		21 45		21 50				22 20		22 45		22 50
Virginia Water	a	14 24		14 49					20 54			21 24		21 49		21 54				22 24		22 49		22 54
	d	14 24		14 49					20 54			21 24		21 49		21 54				22 24		22 49		22 54
Chertsey	d			14 55										21 55								22 55		
Addlestone	d			14 58										21 58								22 58		
Weybridge	a																							
Byfleet & New Haw	d			15 02										22 02								23 02		
West Byfleet	d			15 05										22 05								23 05		
Woking	a			15 11										22 11								23 11		
Longcross	d																							
Sunningdale	d	14 29							20 59			21 29				21 59				22 29				22 59
Ascot ■8	d	14 34							21 04		21 13	21 34				22 04			22 13	22 34				23 04
Bagshot	d										21 19								22 19					
Camberley	a										21 25								22 25					
Frimley	d										21 29								22 29					
Ash Vale	d										21 36								22 36					
Aldershot	a										21 41								22 45					
	d										21 48								22 49					
Ash ■5	d										21 55								22 55					
Wanborough	d										21 58								22 58					
Guildford	a										22 05								23 05					
Martins Heron	d	14 38							21 08			21 38				22 08				22 38				23 08
Bracknell	d	14 41							21 11			21 41				22 11				22 41				23 11
Wokingham	d	14 48							21 18			21 48				22 18				22 48				23 18
Winnersh	d	14 51							21 21			21 51				22 21				22 51				23 21
Winnersh Triangle	d	14 53							21 23			21 53				22 23				22 53				23 23
Earley	d	14 56							21 26			21 56				22 26				22 56				23 26
Reading ■7	a	15 01							21 31			22 01				22 31				23 01				23 31

London - Hounslow, Richmond, Kingston, Windsor, Weybridge, Ascot, Guildford and Reading

Sundays until 25 September

		SW	SW 1	SW 1	SW	SW	SW	SW 1	SW	SW 1	SW
London Waterloo 15 ⊖	d	22 14		22 39	22 44	22 50	22 56	23 09	23 14	23 39	23 44
Vauxhall ⊖	d	22 18		22 43	22 48	22 54	23 00	23 13	23 18	23 43	23 48
Queenstown Rd.(Battersea)	d	22 21			22 51	22 57	23 03		23 21		23 51
Clapham Junction 10	d	22 24		22 49	22 54	23 00	23 06	23 19	23 24	23 49	23 54
Wandsworth Town	d	22 27			22 57	23 03	23 09		23 27		23 57
Putney	d	22 30		22 53	23 00	23 06	23 12	23 23	23 30	23 53	23 59
Barnes	d	22 33			23 03	23 09	23 15		23 33		00 03
Barnes Bridge	d					23 11					
Chiswick	d					23 13					
Kew Bridge	d					23 16					
Brentford	d					23 19					
Syon Lane	d					23 21					
Isleworth	d					23 23					
Hounslow	d					23 26					
Mortlake	d	22 35			23 05		23 17		23 35		00 05
North Sheen	d	22 37			23 07		23 19		23 37		00 07
Richmond ⊖	d	22 40		22 59	23 10		23 22	23 29	23 40	23 59	00 10
St Margarets	d	22 42			23 12		23 24		23 42		00 12
Twickenham	a	22 44		23 02	23 14		23 26	23 32	23 44	00 02	00 14
	d	22 45		23 03	23 15		23 27	23 33	23 45	00 03	00 15
Strawberry Hill	d	22 49					23 30		23 48		
Fulwell	a										
Teddington	a	22 52					23 33		23 51		
Hampton Wick	a	22 57					23 36		23 54		
Kingston	a	22 59					23 38		23 56		
Whitton	d				23 18						00 18
Feltham	d			23 09	23 22	23 32		23 39		00 09	00 22
Ashford (Surrey)	d				23 26	23 36					00 26
Staines	d			23 15	23 30	23 40		23 45		00 15	00a30
Wraysbury	d				23 34						
Sunnymeads	d				23 37						
Datchet	d				23 40						
Windsor & Eton Riverside	a				23 44						
Egham	d			23 20		23 45		23 50		00 20	
Virginia Water	a			23 24		23 49		23 54		00 24	
	d			23 24		23 49		23 54		00 24	
Chertsey	d					23 55					
Addlestone	d					23 58					
Weybridge	a										
Byfleet & New Haw	d					00 02					
West Byfleet	d					00 05					
Woking	a					00 11					
Longcross	d										
Sunningdale	d			23 29				23 59		00 29	
Ascot 3	d		23 13	23 34				00 04		00 34	
Bagshot	d		23 19								
Camberley	a		23 25								
Frimley	d		23 29								
Ash Vale	d		23 36								
Aldershot	a		23 41								
	d										
Ash 5	d										
Wanborough	d										
Guildford	a										
Martins Heron	d			23 38				00 08		00 38	
Bracknell	d			23 41				00 11		00 41	
Wokingham	d			23 48				00 18		00 48	
Winnersh	d			23 51				00 21		00 51	
Winnersh Triangle	d			23 53				00 23		00 53	
Earley	d			23 56				00 26		00 56	
Reading 7	a			00 01				00 31		01 01	

London - Hounslow, Richmond, Kingston, Windsor, Weybridge, Ascot, Guildford and Reading

Sundays from 2 October

		SW 1 A	SW 1 B	SW	SW A	SW B	SW 1 A	SW 1 B	SW	SW	SW A	SW B	SW	SW	SW 1	SW 1	SW	SW	SW	SW	SW	SW	SW
London Waterloo 15 ⊖	d	22p50	22p50	22p52	23p13	23p13	23p20	23p20	23p22	23p33	23p38	23p38					23p52	23p58		00 18	01 42	06 14	06 18
Vauxhall ⊖	d			22p56	23p17	23p17			23p26	23p37							23p56	00 02		00 22	01 46	06 18	06 22
Queenstown Rd.(Battersea)	d			22p59					23p29	23p40							23p59			00 26		06 21	
Clapham Junction 10	d	22p58	22p58	23p02	23p23	23p23	23p28	23p28	23p32	23p43	23p46	23p46					00 02	00 08		00 29		06 24	
Wandsworth Town	d			23p05					23p35	23p46							00 05			00 32		06 27	
Putney	d			23p08	23p27	23p27			23p38	23p49							00 08	00 12		00 35		06 30	
Barnes	d			23p12					23p42	23p52							00 12			00 38		06 33	
Barnes Bridge	d			23p14					23p44								00 14						
Chiswick	d			23p17					23p47								00 17						
Kew Bridge	d			23p20					23p50								00 20						
Brentford	d			23p23					23p53								00 23						
Syon Lane	d			23p25					23p55								00 25						
Isleworth	d			23p27					23p57								00 27						
Hounslow	d			23p31					00 01								00 31						
Mortlake	d									23p54										00 40		06 35	
North Sheen	d									23p56				←						00 42		06 37	
Richmond ⊖	d	23p06	23p06		23p33	23p33	23p37	23p37		23p59	23p54	23p54		23p59				00 18		00 45		06 40	
St Margarets	d									→				00 01						00 47		06 42	
Twickenham	a	23p10	23p10		23p37	23p37	23p41	23p41			23p58	23p58		00 04				00 21		00 49	02 22	06 44	07 02
	d	23p10	23p10		23p37	23p37	23p41	23p41			23p58	23p58		00 04				00 22		00 50		06 45	
Strawberry Hill	d													00 07						00s53		06 49	
Fulwell	a																						
Teddington	a													00 11						00s56		06 52	
Hampton Wick	a													00 14						00s59		06 57	
Kingston	a													00 16						01 01		06 59	
Whitton	d				23p40	23p40							←					00 25	←				
Feltham	d	23p16	23p16	23p36	23p44	23p44	23p48	23p48	00 06		00 04	00 04	00 06				00 36	00 29	00 36				
Ashford (Surrey)	d			23p40	23p48	23p48			→				00 10				→	00 33	00 40				
Staines	d	23p23	23p23	23p44	23p52	23p52	23p56	23p56			00 11	00 11	00 14					00a37	00a46				
Wraysbury	d				23p56	23p57																	
Sunnymeads	d				23p59	23p59																	
Datchet	d				00 02	00 04																	
Windsor & Eton Riverside	a				00 06	00 09																	
Egham	d	23p27	23p27	23p49			00 01	00 01			00 15	00 15	00 19										
Virginia Water	a	23p31	23p31	23p53			00 05	00 05			00 19	00 19	00 23										
	d	23p31	23p31	23p53			00 05	00 05			00 19	00 19	00 23										
Chertsey	d			23p59									00 29										
Addlestone	d			00 02									00a32										
Weybridge	a																						
Byfleet & New Haw	d			00 06																			
West Byfleet	d			00 09																			
Woking	a			00 15																			
Longcross	d																						
Sunningdale	d	23p37	23p37				00 11	00 11			00 25	00 25											
Ascot 3	d	23p43	23p43				00 15	00 15			00 30	00 30			00 32								
Bagshot	d														00 38								
Camberley	a														00 44								
Frimley	d														00 48								
Ash Vale	d														00 57								
Aldershot	a														01s02								
	d															07 48							
Ash 5	d															07 55							
Wanborough	d															07 58							
Guildford	a															08 05							
Martins Heron	d	23p47	23p47				00 19	00 19			00 34	00 34											
Bracknell	d	23p50	23p50				00 23	00 23			00 37	00 37											
Wokingham	d	23p57	23p57				00 32	00 32			00 44	00 44											
Winnersh	d	23p59	23p59				00 36	00 36															
Winnersh Triangle	d	00 02	00 02				00 38	00 38															
Earley	d	00 05	00 05				00 40	00 40															
Reading 7	a	00 10	00 13				00 45	00 48			00 52	00 55											

A 2 October

B not 2 October

Table 149

Sundays from 2 October

London - Hounslow, Richmond, Kingston, Windsor, Weybridge, Ascot, Guildford and Reading

		SW	SW	SW	SW 1	SW	SW 1	SW 1	SW	SW	SW 1	SW	SW 1	SW 1	SW	SW	SW 1	SW	SW	SW 1	SW 1	SW	SW
London Waterloo [15] ⊖	d		06 44		07 09	07 14			07 44	07 50	08 09	08 14		08 39	08 44	08 50	09 09	09 14	09 25		09 39	09 44	09 50
Vauxhall ⊖	d		06 48		07 13	07 18			07 48	07 54	08 13	08 18		08 43	08 48	08 54	09 13	09 18	09 29		09 43	09 48	09 54
Queenstown Rd.(Battersea)	d		06 51			07 21			07 51	07 57		08 21			08 51	08 57		09 21				09 51	09 57
Clapham Junction [10]	d		06 54		07 19	07 24			07 54	08 00	08 19	08 24		08 49	08 54	09 00	09 19	09 24	09 35		09 49	09 54	10 00
Wandsworth Town	d		06 57			07 27			07 57	08 03		08 27			08 57	09 03		09 27				09 57	10 03
Putney	d		07 00		07 23	07 30			08 00	08 06	08 23	08 30		08 53	09 00	09 06	09 23	09 30	09 39		09 53	10 00	10 06
Barnes	d		07 03			07 33			08 03	08 09		08 33			09 03	09 09		09 33				10 03	10 09
Barnes Bridge	d									08 11						09 11							10 11
Chiswick	d									08 13						09 13							10 13
Kew Bridge	d									08 16						09 16							10 16
Brentford	d									08 19						09 19							10 19
Syon Lane	d									08 21						09 21							10 21
Isleworth	d									08 23						09 23							10 23
Hounslow	d									08 26						09 26							10 26
Mortlake	d		07 05			07 35			08 05			08 35			09 05			09 35				10 05	
North Sheen	d		07 07			07 37			08 07			08 37			09 07			09 37				10 07	
Richmond ⊖	d		07 10		07 29	07 40			08 10		08 29	08 40		08 59	09 10		09 29	09 40	09 45		09 59	10 10	
St Margarets	d		07 12			07 42			08 12			08 42			09 12			09 42				10 12	
Twickenham	a		07 14		07 32	07 44			08 14		08 32	08 44		09 02	09 14		09 32	09 44	09 48		10 02	10 14	
	d		07 15		07 33	07 45			08 15		08 33	08 45		09 03	09 15		09 33	09 45	09 49		10 03	10 15	
Strawberry Hill	d					07 49						08 49						09 49					
Fulwell	a																						
Teddington	a					07 52						08 52						09 52					
Hampton Wick	a					07 57						08 57						09 57					
Kingston	a					07 59						08 59						09 59					
Whitton	d		07 18						08 18						09 18				09 52			10 18	
Feltham	d		07 22		07 39				08 22	08 32	08 39			09 09	09 22	09 32	09 39		09 56		10 09	10 22	10 32
Ashford (Surrey)	d		07 26						08 26	08 36					09 26	09 36			10 00			10 26	10 36
Staines	d	06 32	07 30	07 40	07 45			08 15	08 30	08 40	08 45			09 15	09 30	09 40	09 45		10 04		10 15	10 30	10 40
Wraysbury	d		07 35						08 35						09 35							10 35	
Sunnymeads	d		07 38						08 38						09 38							10 38	
Datchet	d		07 42						08 42						09 42				10 13			10 42	
Windsor & Eton Riverside	a		07 46						08 46						09 46				10 18			10 46	
Egham	d	06 36		07 45	07 50			08 20		08 45	08 50			09 20		09 45	09 50				10 20		10 45
Virginia Water	a	06 41		07 49	07 54			08 24		08 49	08 54			09 24		09 49	09 54				10 24		10 49
	d	06 41		07 49	07 54			08 24		08 49	08 54			09 24		09 49	09 54				10 24		10 49
Chertsey	d	06 46		07 55						08 55						09 55							10 55
Addlestone	d	06 49		07 58						08 58						09 58							10 58
Weybridge	a	06 53																					
Byfleet & New Haw	d			08 02						09 02						10 02							11 02
West Byfleet	d			08 05						09 05						10 05							11 05
Woking	a			08 11						09 11						10 11							11 11
Longcross	d																						
Sunningdale	d				07 59			08 29			08 59			09 29			09 59				10 29		
Ascot [8]	d				08 04		08 13	08 34			09 04		09 13	09 34			10 04			10 13	10 34		
Bagshot	d						08 19						09 19							10 19			
Camberley	a						08 25						09 25							10 25			
Frimley	d						08 29						09 29							10 29			
Ash Vale	d						08 36						09 36							10 36			
Aldershot	a						08 41						09 41							10 41			
	d						08 48						09 48							10 48			
Ash [5]	d						08 55						09 55							10 55			
Wanborough	d						08 58						09 58							10 58			
Guildford	a						09 05						10 05							11 05			
Martins Heron	d				08 08			08 38			09 08			09 38			10 08				10 38		
Bracknell	d				08 11			08 41			09 11			09 41			10 11				10 41		
Wokingham	d				08 18			08 48			09 18			09 48			10 18				10 48		
Winnersh	d				08 21			08 51			09 21			09 51			10 21				10 51		
Winnersh Triangle	d				08 23			08 53			09 23			09 53			10 23				10 53		
Earley	d				08 26			08 56			09 26			09 56			10 26				10 56		
Reading [7]	a				08 34			09 04			09 34			10 04			10 34				11 04		

Table 149

Sundays from 2 October

London - Hounslow, Richmond, Kingston, Windsor, Weybridge, Ascot, Guildford and Reading

		SW 1	SW	SW	SW 1	SW 1	SW	SW	SW 1	SW	SW	SW 1	SW 1	SW	SW	SW 1	SW	SW	SW 1	SW 1	SW	SW
London Waterloo [15] ⊖	d	10 09	10 14	10 25		10 39	10 44	10 50	11 09	11 14	11 25		11 39	11 44	11 50	12 09	12 14	12 25		12 39	12 44	12 50
Vauxhall ⊖	d	10 13	10 18	10 29		10 43	10 48	10 54	11 13	11 19	11 29		11 43	11 48	11 54	12 13	12 19	12 29		12 43	12 48	12 54
Queenstown Rd.(Battersea)	d		10 21				10 51	10 57		11 22				11 51	11 57		12 22				12 51	12 57
Clapham Junction [10]	d	10 19	10 24	10 35		10 49	10 54	11 00	11 19	11 25	11 35		11 49	11 54	12 00	12 19	12 25	12 35		12 49	12 54	13 00
Wandsworth Town	d		10 27				10 57	11 03		11 28				11 57	12 03		12 28				12 57	13 03
Putney	d	10 23	10 30	10 39		10 53	11 00	11 06	11 23	11 31	11 39		11 53	12 00	12 06	12 23	12 31	12 39		12 53	13 00	13 06
Barnes	d		10 33				11 03	11 09		11 34				12 03	12 09		12 34				13 03	13 09
Barnes Bridge	d							11 11							12 11							13 11
Chiswick	d							11 13							12 13							13 13
Kew Bridge	d							11 16							12 16							13 16
Brentford	d							11 19							12 19							13 19
Syon Lane	d							11 21							12 21							13 21
Isleworth	d							11 23							12 23							13 23
Hounslow	d							11 26							12 26							13 26
Mortlake	d		10 35				11 05			11 36				12 05			12 36				13 05	
North Sheen	d		10 37				11 07			11 38				12 07			12 38				13 07	
Richmond ⊖	d	10 29	10 40	10 45		10 59	11 10		11 29	11 41	11 45		11 59	12 10		12 29	12 41	12 45		12 59	13 10	
St Margarets	d		10 42				11 12			11 43				12 12			12 43				13 12	
Twickenham	a	10 32	10 44	10 48		11 02	11 14		11 32	11 45	11 48		12 02	12 14		12 32	12 45	12 48		13 02	13 14	
	d	10 33	10 45	10 49		11 03	11 15		11 33	11 46	11 49		12 03	12 15		12 33	12 46	12 49		13 03	13 15	
Strawberry Hill	d		10 49							11 50							12 50					
Fulwell	a																					
Teddington	a		10 52							11 53							12 53					
Hampton Wick	a		10 57							11 57							12 57					
Kingston	a		10 59							11 59							12 59					
Whitton	d			10 52			11 18				11 52			12 18				12 52			13 18	
Feltham	d	10 39		10 56		11 09	11 22	11 32	11 39		11 56		12 09	12 22	12 32	12 39		12 56		13 09	13 22	13 32
Ashford (Surrey)	d			11 00			11 26	11 36			12 00			12 26	12 36			13 00			13 26	13 36
Staines	d	10 45		11 04		11 15	11 30	11 40	11 45		12 04		12 15	12 30	12 40	12 45		13 04		13 15	13 30	13 40
Wraysbury	d						11 35							12 35							13 35	
Sunnymeads	d						11 38							12 38							13 38	
Datchet	d			11 13			11 42				12 13			12 42				13 13			13 42	
Windsor & Eton Riverside	a			11 18			11 46				12 18			12 46				13 18			13 46	
Egham	d	10 50				11 20		11 45	11 50				12 20		12 45	12 50				13 20		13 45
Virginia Water	a	10 54				11 24		11 49	11 54				12 24		12 49	12 54				13 24		13 49
	d	10 54				11 24		11 49	11 54				12 24		12 49	12 54				13 24		13 49
Chertsey	d							11 55							12 55							13 55
Addlestone	d							11 58							12 58							13 58
Weybridge	a																					
Byfleet & New Haw	d							12 02							13 02							14 02
West Byfleet	d							12 05							13 05							14 05
Woking	a							12 11							13 11							14 11
Longcross	d																					
Sunningdale	d	10 59				11 29			11 59				12 29			12 59				13 29		
Ascot [8]	d	11 04			11 13	11 34			12 04			12 13	12 34			13 04			13 13	13 34		
Bagshot	d				11 19							12 19							13 19			
Camberley	a				11 25							12 25							13 25			
Frimley	d				11 29							12 29							13 29			
Ash Vale	d				11 36							12 36							13 36			
Aldershot	a				11 41							12 41							13 41			
	d				11 48							12 48							13 48			
Ash [5]	d				11 55							12 55							13 55			
Wanborough	d				11 58							12 58							13 58			
Guildford	a				12 05							13 05							14 05			
Martins Heron	d	11 08				11 38			12 08				12 38			13 08				13 38		
Bracknell	d	11 11				11 41			12 11				12 41			13 11				13 41		
Wokingham	d	11 18				11 48			12 18				12 48			13 18				13 48		
Winnersh	d	11 21				11 51			12 21				12 51			13 21				13 51		
Winnersh Triangle	d	11 23				11 53			12 23				12 53			13 23				13 53		
Earley	d	11 26				11 56			12 26				12 56			13 26				13 56		
Reading [7]	a	11 34				12 04			12 34				13 04			13 34				14 04		

London - Hounslow, Richmond, Kingston, Windsor, Weybridge, Ascot, Guildford and Reading

		SW 1	SW	SW	SW 1	SW 1	SW	SW		SW		SW	SW 1	SW	SW 1	SW 1	SW		SW	SW	SW 1	SW	SW 1	SW 1
London Waterloo 15 ⊖	d	13 09	13 14	13 25		13 39	13 44	13 50		13 56		19 56	20 09	20 14		20 39	20 44		20 50	20 56	21 09	21 14		21 39
Vauxhall ⊖	d	13 13	13 18	13 29		13 43	13 48	13 54		14 00		20 00	20 13	20 18		20 43	20 48		20 54	21 00	21 13	21 18		21 43
Queenstown Rd.(Battersea)	d		13 21				13 51	13 57		14 03		20 03		20 21			20 51		20 57	21 03		21 21		
Clapham Junction 10	d	13 19	13 24	13 35		13 49	13 54	14 00		14 06		20 06	20 19	20 24		20 49	20 54		21 00	21 06	21 19	21 24		21 49
Wandsworth Town	d		13 27				13 57	14 03		14 09		20 09		20 27			20 57		21 03	21 09		21 27		
Putney	d	13 23	13 30	13 39		13 53	14 00	14 06		14 12		20 12	20 23	20 30		20 53	21 00		21 06	21 12	21 23	21 30		21 53
Barnes	d		13 33				14 03	14 09		14 15		20 15		20 33			21 03		21 09	21 15		21 33		
Barnes Bridge	d							14 11											21 11					
Chiswick	d							14 13											21 13					
Kew Bridge	d							14 16											21 16					
Brentford	d							14 19											21 19					
Syon Lane	d							14 21											21 21					
Isleworth	d							14 23											21 23					
Hounslow	d							14 26											21 26					
Mortlake	d		13 35				14 05			14 17		20 17		20 35			21 05			21 17		21 35		
North Sheen	d		13 37				14 07			14 19		20 19		20 37			21 07			21 19		21 37		
Richmond ⊖	d	13 29	13 40	13 45		13 59	14 10			14 22		20 22	20 29	20 40		20 59	21 10			21 22	21 29	21 40		21 59
St Margarets	d		13 42				14 12			14 24		20 24		20 42			21 12			21 24		21 42		
Twickenham	a	13 32	13 44	13 48		14 02	14 14			14 26		20 26	20 32	20 44		21 02	21 14			21 26	21 32	21 44		22 02
	d	13 33	13 45	13 49		14 03	14 15			14 27		20 27	20 33	20 45		21 03	21 15			21 27	21 33	21 45		22 03
Strawberry Hill	d		13 49							14 30		20 30		20 49						21 30		21 49		
Fulwell	a																							
Teddington	a		13 52							14 33		20 33		20 52						21 33		21 52		
Hampton Wick	a		13 57							14 36		20 36		20 57						21 36		21 57		
Kingston	a		13 59							14 38		20 38		20 59						21 38		21 59		
Whitton	d			13 52			14 18				and at the same minutes past each hour until						21 18							
Feltham	d	13 39		13 56		14 09	14 22	14 32					20 39			21 09	21 22		21 32		21 39			22 09
Ashford (Surrey)	d			14 00			14 26	14 36									21 26		21 36					
Staines	d	13 45		14 04		14 15	14 30	14 40					20 45			21 15	21 30		21 40		21 45			22 15
Wraysbury	d						14 35										21 35							
Sunnymeads	d						14 38										21 38							
Datchet	d			14 13			14 42										21 42							
Windsor & Eton Riverside	a			14 18			14 46										21 46							
Egham	d	13 50				14 20		14 45					20 50			21 20			21 45		21 50			22 20
Virginia Water	a	13 54				14 24		14 49					20 54			21 24			21 49		21 54			22 24
	d	13 54				14 24		14 49					20 54			21 24			21 49		21 54			22 24
Chertsey	d							14 55											21 55					
Addlestone	d							14 58											21 58					
Weybridge	a																							
Byfleet & New Haw	d							15 02											22 02					
West Byfleet	d							15 05											22 05					
Woking	a							15 11											22 11					
Longcross	d																							
Sunningdale	d	13 59				14 29							20 59			21 29					21 59			22 29
Ascot 3	d	14 04			14 13	14 34							21 04		21 13	21 34					22 04		22 13	22 34
Bagshot	d				14 19										21 19								22 19	
Camberley	a				14 25										21 25								22 25	
Frimley	d				14 29										21 29								22 29	
Ash Vale	d				14 36										21 36								22 36	
Aldershot	a				14 41										21 41								22 45	
	d				14 48										21 48								22 49	
Ash 5	d				14 55										21 55								22 55	
Wanborough	d				14 58										21 58								22 58	
Guildford	a				15 05										22 05								23 05	
Martins Heron	d	14 08				14 38							21 08			21 38					22 08			22 38
Bracknell	d	14 11				14 41							21 11			21 41					22 11			22 41
Wokingham	d	14 18				14 48							21 18			21 48					22 18			22 48
Winnersh	d	14 21				14 51							21 21			21 51					22 21			22 51
Winnersh Triangle	d	14 23				14 53							21 23			21 53					22 23			22 53
Earley	d	14 26				14 56							21 26			21 56					22 26			22 56
Reading 7	a	14 34				15 04							21 34			22 04					22 34			23 04

London - Hounslow, Richmond, Kingston, Windsor, Weybridge, Ascot, Guildford and Reading

		SW	SW	SW		SW 1	SW	SW 1	SW 1	SW	SW	SW	SW 1	SW		SW 1	SW
London Waterloo 15 ⊖	d	21 44	21 50	21 56		22 09	22 14		22 39	22 44	22 50	22 56	23 09	23 14		23 39	23 44
Vauxhall ⊖	d	21 48	21 54	22 00		22 13	22 18		22 43	22 48	22 54	23 00	23 13	23 18		23 43	23 48
Queenstown Rd.(Battersea)	d	21 51	21 57	22 03			22 21			22 51	22 57	23 03		23 21			23 51
Clapham Junction 10	d	21 54	22 00	22 06		22 19	22 24		22 49	22 54	23 00	23 06	23 19	23 24		23 49	23 54
Wandsworth Town	d	21 57	22 03	22 09			22 27			22 57	23 03	23 09		23 27			23 57
Putney	d	22 00	22 06	22 12		22 23	22 30		22 53	23 00	23 06	23 12	23 23	23 30		23 53	23 59
Barnes	d	22 03	22 09	22 15			22 33			23 03	23 09	23 15		23 33			00 03
Barnes Bridge	d		22 11								23 11						
Chiswick	d		22 13								23 13						
Kew Bridge	d		22 16								23 16						
Brentford	d		22 19								23 19						
Syon Lane	d		22 21								23 21						
Isleworth	d		22 23								23 23						
Hounslow	d		22 26								23 26						
Mortlake	d	22 05		22 17			22 35			23 05		23 17		23 35			00 05
North Sheen	d	22 07		22 19			22 37			23 07		23 19		23 37			00 07
Richmond ⊖	d	22 10		22 22		22 29	22 40		22 59	23 10		23 22	23 29	23 40		23 59	00 10
St Margarets	d	22 12		22 24			22 42			23 12		23 24		23 42			00 12
Twickenham	a	22 14		22 26		22 32	22 44		23 02	23 14		23 26	23 32	23 44		00 02	00 14
	d	22 15		22 27		22 33	22 45		23 03	23 15		23 27	23 33	23 45		00 03	00 15
Strawberry Hill	d			22 30			22 49					23 30		23 48			
Fulwell	a																
Teddington	a			22 33			22 52					23 33		23 51			
Hampton Wick	a			22 36			22 57					23 36		23 54			
Kingston	a			22 38			22 59					23 38		23 56			
Whitton	d	22 18								23 18							00 18
Feltham	d	22 22	22 32			22 39			23 09	23 22	23 32		23 39			00 09	00 22
Ashford (Surrey)	d	22 26	22 36							23 26	23 36						00 26
Staines	d	22 30	22 40			22 45			23 15	23 30	23 40		23 45			00 15	00a30
Wraysbury	d	22 35								23 35							
Sunnymeads	d	22 38								23 38							
Datchet	d	22 42								23 42							
Windsor & Eton Riverside	a	22 46								23 46							
Egham	d		22 45			22 50			23 20		23 45		23 50			00 20	
Virginia Water	a		22 49			22 54			23 24		23 49		23 54			00 24	
	d		22 49			22 54			23 24		23 49		23 54			00 24	
Chertsey	d		22 55								23 55						
Addlestone	d		22 58								23 58						
Weybridge	a																
Byfleet & New Haw	d		23 02								00 02						
West Byfleet	d		23 05								00 05						
Woking	a		23 11								00 11						
Longcross	d																
Sunningdale	d					22 59			23 29				23 59			00 29	
Ascot 3	d					23 04		23 13	23 34				00 04			00 34	
Bagshot	d							23 19									
Camberley	a							23 25									
Frimley	d							23 29									
Ash Vale	d							23 36									
Aldershot	a							23 41									
	d																
Ash 5	d																
Wanborough	d																
Guildford	a																
Martins Heron	d					23 08			23 38				00 08			00 38	
Bracknell	d					23 11			23 41				00 11			00 41	
Wokingham	d					23 18			23 48				00 18			00 48	
Winnersh	d					23 21			23 51				00 21			00 51	
Winnersh Triangle	d					23 23			23 53				00 23			00 53	
Earley	d					23 26			23 56				00 26			00 56	
Reading 7	a					23 34			00 04				00 34			01 04	

Table 149

Sundays
from 9 October

London - Hounslow, Richmond, Kingston, Windsor, Weybridge, Ascot, Guildford and Reading

		SW [1]	SW	SW	SW [1]	SW	SW	SW	SW	SW	SW [1]	SW [1]	SW	SW	SW	SW	SW	SW	SW	SW	SW	SW	SW [1]
London Waterloo [15] ⊖	d	22p50	22p52	23p13	23p20	23p22	23p33	23p38					23p52	23p58		00 18	01 42	06 14	06 18		06 44		07 09
Vauxhall ⊖	d		22p56	23p17		23p26	23p37						23p56	00 02		00 22	01 46	06 18	06 22		06 48		07 13
Queenstown Rd.(Battersea)	d		22p59			23p29	23p40						23p59			00 26		06 21			06 51		
Clapham Junction [10]	d	22p58	23p02	23p23	23p28	23p32	23p43	23p46					00 02	00 08		00 29		06 24			06 54		07 19
Wandsworth Town	d		23p05			23p35	23p46						00 05			00 32		06 27			06 57		
Putney	d		23p08	23p27		23p38	23p49						00 08	00 12		00 35		06 30			07 00		07 23
Barnes	d		23p12			23p42	23p52						00 12			00 38		06 33			07 03		
Barnes Bridge	d		23p14			23p44							00 14										
Chiswick	d		23p17			23p47							00 17										
Kew Bridge	d		23p20			23p50							00 20										
Brentford	d		23p23			23p53							00 23										
Syon Lane	d		23p25			23p55							00 25										
Isleworth	d		23p27			23p57							00 27										
Hounslow	d		23p31			00 01							00 31										
Mortlake	d						23p54									00 40		06 35			07 05		
North Sheen	d						23p56			←						00 42		06 37			07 07		
Richmond ⊖	d	23p06		23p33	23p37		23p59	23p54		23p59				00 18		00 45		06 40			07 10		07 29
St Margarets	d						→			00 01						00 47		06 42			07 12		
Twickenham	a	23p10		23p37	23p41			23p58		00 04				00 21		00 49	02 22	06 44	07 02		07 14		07 32
	d	23p10		23p37	23p41			23p58		00 04				00 22		00 50		06 45			07 15		07 33
Strawberry Hill	d									00 07						00s53		06 49					
Fulwell	a																						
Teddington	a									00 11						00s56		06 52					
Hampton Wick	a									00 14						00s59		06 57					
Kingston	a									00 16						01 01		06 59					
Whitton	d			23p40					←					00 25	←						07 18		
Feltham	d	23p16	23p36	23p44	23p48	00 06		00 04	00 06				00 36	00 29	00 36						07 22		07 39
Ashford (Surrey)	d		23p40	23p48		→			00 10				→	00 33	00 40						07 26		
Staines	d	23p23	23p44	23p52	23p56			00 11	00 14					00a37	00a46					06 32	07 30	07 40	07 45
Wraysbury	d			23p57																	07 35		
Sunnymeads	d			23p59																	07 38		
Datchet	d			00 04																	07 42		
Windsor & Eton Riverside	a			00 09																	07 46		
Egham	d	23p27	23p49		00 01			00 15	00 19											06 36		07 45	07 50
Virginia Water	a	23p31	23p53		00 05			00 19	00 23											06 41		07 49	07 54
	d	23p31	23p53		00 05			00 19	00 23											06 41		07 49	07 54
Chertsey	d		23p59						00 29											06 46		07 55	
Addlestone	d		00 02						00a32											06 49		07 58	
Weybridge	a																			06 53			
Byfleet & New Haw	d		00 06																			08 02	
West Byfleet	d		00 09																			08 05	
Woking	a		00 15																			08 11	
Longcross	d																						
Sunningdale	d	23p37			00 11			00 25															07 59
Ascot [3]	d	23p43			00 15			00 30			00 32												08 04
Bagshot	d										00 38												
Camberley	a										00 44												
Frimley	d										00 48												
Ash Vale	d										00 57												
Aldershot	a										01s02												
	d											07 48											
Ash [6]	d											07 55											
Wanborough	d											07 58											
Guildford	a											08 05											
Martins Heron	d	23p47			00 19			00 34															08 08
Bracknell	d	23p50			00 23			00 37															08 11
Wokingham	d	23p57			00 32			00 44															08 18
Winnersh	d	23p59			00 36																		08 21
Winnersh Triangle	d	00 02			00 38																		08 23
Earley	d	00 05			00 40																		08 26
Reading [7]	a	00 13			00 48			00 55															08 34

Table 149

Sundays
from 9 October

London - Hounslow, Richmond, Kingston, Windsor, Weybridge, Ascot, Guildford and Reading

		SW	SW [1]	SW [1]	SW	SW	SW [1]	SW	SW [1]	SW [1]	SW	SW	SW [1]	SW	SW	SW [1]	SW [1]	SW	SW	SW [1]	SW	SW	SW [1]
London Waterloo [15] ⊖	d	07 14			07 44	07 50	08 09	08 14		08 39	08 44	08 50	09 09	09 14	09 25		09 39	09 44	09 50	10 09	10 14	10 25	
Vauxhall ⊖	d	07 18			07 48	07 54	08 13	08 18		08 43	08 48	08 54	09 13	09 18	09 29		09 43	09 48	09 54	10 13	10 18	10 29	
Queenstown Rd.(Battersea)	d	07 21			07 51	07 57		08 21			08 51	08 57		09 21				09 51	09 57		10 21		
Clapham Junction [10]	d	07 24			07 54	08 00	08 19	08 24		08 49	08 54	09 00	09 19	09 24	09 35		09 49	09 54	10 00	10 19	10 24	10 35	
Wandsworth Town	d	07 27			07 57	08 03		08 27			08 57	09 03		09 27				09 57	10 03		10 27		
Putney	d	07 30			08 00	08 06	08 23	08 30		08 53	09 00	09 06	09 23	09 30	09 39		09 53	10 00	10 06	10 23	10 30	10 39	
Barnes	d	07 33			08 03	08 09		08 33			09 03	09 09		09 33				10 03	10 09		10 33		
Barnes Bridge	d					08 11						09 11							10 11				
Chiswick	d					08 13						09 13							10 13				
Kew Bridge	d					08 16						09 16							10 16				
Brentford	d					08 19						09 19							10 19				
Syon Lane	d					08 21						09 21							10 21				
Isleworth	d					08 23						09 23							10 23				
Hounslow	d					08 26						09 26							10 26				
Mortlake	d	07 35			08 05			08 35			09 05			09 35				10 05			10 35		
North Sheen	d	07 37			08 07			08 37			09 07			09 37				10 07			10 37		
Richmond ⊖	d	07 40			08 10		08 29	08 40		08 59	09 10		09 29	09 40	09 45		09 59	10 10		10 29	10 40	10 45	
St Margarets	d	07 42			08 12			08 42			09 12			09 42				10 12			10 42		
Twickenham	a	07 44			08 14		08 32	08 44		09 02	09 14		09 32	09 44	09 48		10 02	10 14		10 32	10 44	10 48	
	d	07 45			08 15		08 33	08 45		09 03	09 15		09 33	09 45	09 49		10 03	10 15		10 33	10 45	10 49	
Strawberry Hill	d	07 49						08 49						09 49							10 49		
Fulwell	a																						
Teddington	a	07 52						08 52						09 52							10 52		
Hampton Wick	a	07 57						08 57						09 57							10 57		
Kingston	a	07 59						08 59						09 59							10 59		
Whitton	d				08 18						09 18				09 52			10 18				10 52	
Feltham	d				08 22	08 32	08 39			09 09	09 22	09 32	09 39		09 56		10 09	10 22	10 32	10 39		10 56	
Ashford (Surrey)	d				08 26	08 36					09 26	09 36			10 00			10 26	10 36			11 00	
Staines	d			08 15	08 30	08 40	08 45			09 15	09 30	09 40	09 45		10 04		10 15	10 30	10 40	10 45		11 04	
Wraysbury	d				08 35						09 35							10 35					
Sunnymeads	d				08 38						09 38							10 38					
Datchet	d				08 42						09 42				10 13			10 42				11 13	
Windsor & Eton Riverside	a				08 46						09 46				10 18			10 46				11 18	
Egham	d			08 20		08 45	08 50			09 20		09 45	09 50				10 20		10 45	10 50			
Virginia Water	a			08 24		08 49	08 54			09 24		09 49	09 54				10 24		10 49	10 54			
	d			08 24		08 49	08 54			09 24		09 49	09 54				10 24		10 49	10 54			
Chertsey	d					08 55						09 55							10 55				
Addlestone	d					08 58						09 58							10 58				
Weybridge	a																						
Byfleet & New Haw	d					09 02						10 02							11 02				
West Byfleet	d					09 05						10 05							11 05				
Woking	a					09 11						10 11							11 11				
Longcross	d																						
Sunningdale	d			08 29			08 59			09 29			09 59				10 29			10 59			
Ascot [3]	d		08 13	08 34			09 04		09 13	09 34			10 04			10 13	10 34			11 04			11 13
Bagshot	d		08 19						09 19							10 19							11 19
Camberley	a		08 25						09 25							10 25							11 25
Frimley	d		08 29						09 29							10 29							11 29
Ash Vale	d		08 36						09 36							10 36							11 36
Aldershot	a		08 41						09 41							10 41							11 41
	d		08 48						09 48							10 48							11 48
Ash [6]	d		08 55						09 55							10 55							11 55
Wanborough	d		08 58						09 58							10 58							11 58
Guildford	a		09 05						10 05							11 05							12 05
Martins Heron	d			08 38			09 08			09 38			10 08				10 38			11 08			
Bracknell	d			08 41			09 11			09 41			10 11				10 41			11 11			
Wokingham	d			08 48			09 18			09 48			10 18				10 48			11 18			
Winnersh	d			08 51			09 21			09 51			10 21				10 51			11 21			
Winnersh Triangle	d			08 53			09 23			09 53			10 23				10 53			11 23			
Earley	d			08 56			09 26			09 56			10 26				10 56			11 26			
Reading [7]	a			09 04			09 34			10 04			10 34				11 04			11 34			

London - Hounslow, Richmond, Kingston, Windsor, Weybridge, Ascot, Guildford and Reading

Sundays from 9 October

		SW 1	SW	SW	SW 1	SW	SW	SW 1	SW 1	SW	SW	SW 1	SW	SW	SW 1	SW 1	SW	SW	SW 1	SW	SW	SW 1
London Waterloo 15 ⊖	d	10 39	10 44	10 50	11 09	11 14	11 25		11 39	11 44	11 50	12 09	12 14	12 25		12 39	12 44	12 50	13 09	13 14	13 25	
Vauxhall ⊖	d	10 43	10 48	10 54	11 13	11 19	11 29		11 43	11 48	11 54	12 13	12 19	12 29		12 43	12 48	12 54	13 13	13 18	13 29	
Queenstown Rd.(Battersea)	d		10 51	10 57		11 22				11 51	11 57		12 22				12 51	12 57		13 21		
Clapham Junction 10	d	10 49	10 54	11 00	11 19	11 25	11 35		11 49	11 54	12 00	12 19	12 25	12 35		12 49	12 54	13 00	13 19	13 24	13 35	
Wandsworth Town	d		10 57	11 03		11 28				11 57	12 03		12 28				12 57	13 03		13 27		
Putney	d	10 53	11 00	11 06	11 23	11 31	11 39		11 53	12 00	12 06	12 23	12 31	12 39		12 53	13 00	13 06	13 23	13 30	13 39	
Barnes	d		11 03	11 09		11 34				12 03	12 09		12 34				13 03	13 09		13 33		
Barnes Bridge	d			11 11							12 11							13 11				
Chiswick	d			11 13							12 13							13 13				
Kew Bridge	d			11 16							12 16							13 16				
Brentford	d			11 19							12 19							13 19				
Syon Lane	d			11 21							12 21							13 21				
Isleworth	d			11 23							12 23							13 23				
Hounslow	d			11 26							12 26							13 26				
Mortlake	d		11 05			11 36				12 05			12 36				13 05			13 35		
North Sheen	d		11 07			11 38				12 07			12 38				13 07			13 37		
Richmond ⊖	d	10 59	11 10		11 29	11 41	11 45		11 59	12 10		12 29	12 41	12 45		12 59	13 10		13 29	13 40	13 45	
St Margarets	d		11 12			11 43				12 12			12 43				13 12			13 42		
Twickenham	a	11 02	11 14		11 32	11 45	11 48		12 02	12 14		12 32	12 45	12 48		13 02	13 14		13 32	13 44	13 48	
	d	11 03	11 15		11 33	11 46	11 49		12 03	12 15		12 33	12 46	12 49		13 03	13 15		13 33	13 45	13 49	
Strawberry Hill	d					11 50							12 50							13 49		
Fulwell	a																					
Teddington	a					11 53							12 53							13 52		
Hampton Wick	a					11 57							12 57							13 57		
Kingston	a					11 59							12 59							13 59		
Whitton	d		11 18				11 52			12 18				12 52			13 18				13 52	
Feltham	d	11 09	11 22	11 32	11 39		11 56		12 09	12 22	12 32	12 39		12 56		13 09	13 22	13 32	13 39		13 56	
Ashford (Surrey)	d		11 26	11 36			12 00			12 26	12 36			13 00			13 26	13 36			14 00	
Staines	d	11 15	11 30	11 40	11 45		12 04		12 15	12 30	12 40	12 45		13 04		13 15	13 30	13 40	13 45		14 04	
Wraysbury	d		11 35							12 35							13 35					
Sunnymeads	d		11 38							12 38							13 38					
Datchet	d		11 42				12 13			12 42				13 13			13 42				14 13	
Windsor & Eton Riverside	a		11 46				12 18			12 46				13 18			13 46				14 18	
Egham	d	11 20		11 45	11 50				12 20		12 45	12 50				13 20		13 45	13 50			
Virginia Water	a	11 24		11 49	11 54				12 24		12 49	12 54				13 24		13 49	13 54			
	d	11 24		11 49	11 54				12 24		12 49	12 54				13 24		13 49	13 54			
Chertsey	d			11 55							12 55							13 55				
Addlestone	d			11 58							12 58							13 58				
Weybridge	a																					
Byfleet & New Haw	d			12 02							13 02							14 02				
West Byfleet	d			12 05							13 05							14 05				
Woking	a			12 11							13 11							14 11				
Longcross	d																					
Sunningdale	d	11 29			11 59				12 29			12 59				13 29			13 59			
Ascot 3	d	11 34			12 04			12 13	12 34			13 04			13 13	13 34			14 04			14 13
Bagshot	d							12 19							13 19							14 19
Camberley	a							12 25							13 25							14 25
Frimley	d							12 29							13 29							14 29
Ash Vale	d							12 36							13 36							14 36
Aldershot	a							12 41							13 41							14 41
	d							12 48							13 48							14 48
Ash 5	d							12 55							13 55							14 55
Wanborough	d							12 58							13 58							14 58
Guildford	a							13 05							14 05							15 05
Martins Heron	d	11 38			12 08				12 38			13 08				13 38			14 08			
Bracknell	d	11 41			12 11				12 41			13 11				13 41			14 11			
Wokingham	d	11 48			12 18				12 48			13 18				13 48			14 18			
Winnersh	d	11 51			12 21				12 51			13 21				13 51			14 21			
Winnersh Triangle	d	11 53			12 23				12 53			13 23				13 53			14 23			
Earley	d	11 56			12 26				12 56			13 26				13 56			14 26			
Reading 7	a	12 04			12 34				13 04			13 34				14 04			14 34			

London - Hounslow, Richmond, Kingston, Windsor, Weybridge, Ascot, Guildford and Reading

Sundays from 9 October

		SW 1	SW	SW	SW		SW	SW 1	SW	SW 1	SW 1	SW	SW	SW	SW 1	SW	SW 1	SW 1	SW	SW	SW	SW 1
London Waterloo 15 ⊖	d	13 39	13 44	13 50	13 56		19 56	20 09	20 14		20 39	20 44	20 50	20 56	21 09	21 14		21 39	21 44	21 50	21 56	22 09
Vauxhall ⊖	d	13 43	13 48	13 54	14 00		20 00	20 13	20 18		20 43	20 48	20 54	21 00	21 13	21 18		21 43	21 48	21 54	22 00	22 13
Queenstown Rd.(Battersea)	d		13 51	13 57	14 03		20 03		20 21			20 51	20 57	21 03		21 21			21 51	21 57	22 03	
Clapham Junction 10	d	13 49	13 54	14 00	14 06		20 06	20 19	20 24		20 49	20 54	21 00	21 06	21 19	21 24		21 49	21 54	22 00	22 06	22 19
Wandsworth Town	d		13 57	14 03	14 09		20 09		20 27			20 57	21 03	21 09		21 27			21 57	22 03	22 09	
Putney	d	13 53	14 00	14 06	14 12		20 12	20 23	20 30		20 53	21 00	21 06	21 12	21 23	21 30		21 53	22 00	22 06	22 12	22 23
Barnes	d		14 03	14 09	14 15		20 15		20 33			21 03	21 09	21 15		21 33			22 03	22 09	22 15	
Barnes Bridge	d			14 11									21 11							22 11		
Chiswick	d			14 13									21 13							22 13		
Kew Bridge	d			14 16									21 16							22 16		
Brentford	d			14 19									21 19							22 19		
Syon Lane	d			14 21									21 21							22 21		
Isleworth	d			14 23									21 23							22 23		
Hounslow	d			14 26									21 26							22 26		
Mortlake	d		14 05		14 17		20 17		20 35			21 05		21 17		21 35			22 05		22 17	
North Sheen	d		14 07		14 19		20 19		20 37			21 07		21 19		21 37			22 07		22 19	
Richmond ⊖	d	13 59	14 10		14 22		20 22	20 29	20 40		20 59	21 10		21 22	21 29	21 40		21 59	22 10		22 22	22 29
St Margarets	d		14 12		14 24		20 24		20 42			21 12		21 24		21 42			22 12		22 24	
Twickenham	a	14 02	14 14		14 26		20 26	20 32	20 44		21 02	21 14		21 26	21 32	21 44		22 02	22 14		22 26	22 32
	d	14 03	14 15		14 27		20 27	20 33	20 45		21 03	21 15		21 27	21 33	21 45		22 03	22 15		22 27	22 33
Strawberry Hill	d				14 30		20 30		20 49					21 30		21 49					22 30	
Fulwell	a																					
Teddington	a				14 33		20 33		20 52					21 33		21 52					22 33	
Hampton Wick	a				14 36		20 36		20 57					21 36		21 57					22 36	
Kingston	a				14 38		20 38		20 59					21 38		21 59					22 38	
Whitton	d		14 18									21 18							22 18			
Feltham	d	14 09	14 22	14 32		and at the same minutes past each hour until		20 39			21 09	21 22	21 32		21 39			22 09	22 22	22 32		22 39
Ashford (Surrey)	d		14 26	14 36								21 26	21 36						22 26	22 36		
Staines	d	14 15	14 30	14 40				20 45			21 15	21 30	21 40		21 45			22 15	22 30	22 40		22 45
Wraysbury	d		14 35									21 35							22 35			
Sunnymeads	d		14 38									21 38							22 38			
Datchet	d		14 42									21 42							22 42			
Windsor & Eton Riverside	a		14 46									21 46							22 46			
Egham	d	14 20		14 45				20 50			21 20		21 45		21 50			22 20		22 45		22 50
Virginia Water	a	14 24		14 49				20 54			21 24		21 49		21 54			22 24		22 49		22 54
	d	14 24		14 49				20 54			21 24		21 49		21 54			22 24		22 49		22 54
Chertsey	d			14 55									21 55							22 55		
Addlestone	d			14 58									21 58							22 58		
Weybridge	a																					
Byfleet & New Haw	d			15 02									22 02							23 02		
West Byfleet	d			15 05									22 05							23 05		
Woking	a			15 11									22 11							23 11		
Longcross	d																					
Sunningdale	d	14 29						20 59			21 29				21 59			22 29				22 59
Ascot 3	d	14 34						21 04		21 13	21 34				22 04		22 13	22 34				23 04
Bagshot	d									21 19							22 19					
Camberley	a									21 25							22 25					
Frimley	d									21 29							22 29					
Ash Vale	d									21 36							22 36					
Aldershot	a									21 41							22 45					
	d									21 48							22 49					
Ash 5	d									21 55							22 55					
Wanborough	d									21 58							22 58					
Guildford	a									22 05							23 05					
Martins Heron	d	14 38						21 08			21 38				22 08			22 38				23 08
Bracknell	d	14 41						21 11			21 41				22 11			22 41				23 11
Wokingham	d	14 48						21 18			21 48				22 18			22 48				23 18
Winnersh	d	14 51						21 21			21 51				22 21			22 51				23 21
Winnersh Triangle	d	14 53						21 23			21 53				22 23			22 53				23 23
Earley	d	14 56						21 26			21 56				22 26			22 56				23 26
Reading 7	a	15 04						21 34			22 04				22 34			23 04				23 34

Table 149

Sundays from 9 October

London - Hounslow, Richmond, Kingston, Windsor, Weybridge, Ascot, Guildford and Reading

Station		SW	SW 1	SW 1	SW	SW	SW	SW 1	SW	SW 1	SW
London Waterloo 15 ⊖	d	22 14		22 39	22 44	22 50	22 56	23 09	23 14	23 39	23 44
Vauxhall ⊖	d	22 18		22 43	22 48	22 54	23 00	23 13	23 18	23 43	23 48
Queenstown Rd.(Battersea)	d	22 21			22 51	22 57	23 03		23 21		23 51
Clapham Junction 10	d	22 24		22 49	22 54	23 00	23 06	23 19	23 24	23 49	23 54
Wandsworth Town	d	22 27			22 57	23 03	23 09		23 27		23 57
Putney	d	22 30		22 53	23 00	23 06	23 12	23 23	23 30	23 53	23 59
Barnes	d	22 33			23 03	23 09	23 15		23 33		00 03
Barnes Bridge	d					23 11					
Chiswick	d					23 13					
Kew Bridge	d					23 16					
Brentford	d					23 19					
Syon Lane	d					23 21					
Isleworth	d					23 23					
Hounslow	d					23 26					
Mortlake	d	22 35			23 05		23 17		23 35		00 05
North Sheen	d	22 37			23 07		23 19		23 37		00 07
Richmond ⊖	d	22 40		22 59	23 10		23 22	23 29	23 40	23 59	00 10
St Margarets	d	22 42			23 12		23 24		23 42		00 12
Twickenham	a	22 44		23 02	23 14		23 26	23 32	23 44	00 02	00 14
	d	22 45		23 03	23 15		23 27	23 33	23 45	00 03	00 15
Strawberry Hill	d	22 49					23 30		23 48		
Fulwell	a										
Teddington	a	22 52					23 33		23 51		
Hampton Wick	a	22 57					23 36		23 54		
Kingston	a	22 59					23 38		23 56		
Whitton	d				23 18						00 18
Feltham	d			23 09	23 22	23 32		23 39		00 09	00 22
Ashford (Surrey)	d				23 26	23 36					00 26
Staines	d			23 15	23 30	23 40		23 45		00 15	00a30
Wraysbury	d				23 35						
Sunnymeads	d				23 38						
Datchet	d				23 42						
Windsor & Eton Riverside	a				23 46						
Egham	d			23 20		23 45		23 50		00 20	
Virginia Water	a			23 24		23 49		23 54		00 24	
	d			23 24		23 49		23 54		00 24	
Chertsey	d					23 55					
Addlestone	d					23 58					
Weybridge	a										
Byfleet & New Haw	d					00 02					
West Byfleet	d					00 05					
Woking	a					00 11					
Longcross	d										
Sunningdale	d			23 29				23 59		00 29	
Ascot 5	d		23 13	23 34				00 04		00 34	
Bagshot	d		23 19								
Camberley	a		23 25								
Frimley	d		23 29								
Ash Vale	d		23 36								
Aldershot	a		23 41								
	d										
Ash 5	d										
Wanborough	d										
Guildford	a										
Martins Heron	d			23 38				00 08		00 38	
Bracknell	d			23 41				00 11		00 41	
Wokingham	d			23 48				00 18		00 48	
Winnersh	d			23 51				00 21		00 51	
Winnersh Triangle	d			23 53				00 23		00 53	
Earley	d			23 56				00 26		00 56	
Reading 7	a			00 04				00 34		01 04	

Table 149

Mondays to Fridays until 30 September

Reading, Guildford, Ascot, Weybridge, Windsor, Kingston, Richmond and Hounslow - London

Miles	Miles	Miles	Miles	Station		SW MO	SW MO	SW MX 1	SW MX	SW MO 1	SW MX 1	SW	SW	SW	SW	SW	SW	SW ◇	SW ◇	SW ◇	SW ◇ 1	SW 1	SW
—	—	0	—	**Reading 7**	d			22p42		22p54	23p12										05 42		
—	—	3	—	Earley	d			22p47		22p59	23p17										05 47		
—	—	4¼	—	Winnersh Triangle	d			22p49		23p01	23p19										05 49		
—	—	4¾	—	Winnersh	d			22p51		23p03	23p21										05 51		
—	—	6¾	—	**Wokingham**	d			22p56		23p08	23p26										05 56		
—	—	11¼	—	Bracknell	d			23p02		23p14	23p32										06 02		
—	—	12¼	—	Martins Heron	d			23p05		23p17	23p35										06 05		
—	0	—	—	**Guildford**	d																		
—	4¼	—	—	Wanborough	d																		
—	6¼	—	—	Ash 5	d																		
—	9	—	—	**Aldershot**	a																		
—	—	—	—		d																	05 58	
—	11½	—	—	Ash Vale	d																	06 02	
—	14¾	—	—	Frimley	d																	06 10	
—	17	—	—	Camberley	a																	06 14	
—	—	—	—		d																	06 18	
—	20¼	—	—	Bagshot	d																	06 23	
—	23½	14½	—	**Ascot 5**	d			23p10		23p22	23p40										06 10	06a30	
—	—	16½	—	Sunningdale	d			23p13		23p25	23p43										06 13		
—	—	18¼	—	Longcross	d																		
0	—	—	—	Woking	d		22p52											05 27					
2½	—	—	—	West Byfleet	d		22p56											05 32					
3¾	—	—	—	Byfleet & New Haw	d		23p00											05 35					
5¼	—	—	—	**Weybridge**	d																		
7	—	—	—	Addlestone	d		23p04											05 39					
8½	—	—	—	Chertsey	d		23p07											05 42					
11	—	20¼	—	Virginia Water	a		23p12	23p19		23p30	23p49							05 47			06 19		
—	—	—	—		d		23p12	23p19		23p30	23p49							05 54			06 19		
—	—	22½	—	Egham	d		23p16	23p23		23p34	23p53							05 57			06 23		
—	—	—	0	**Windsor & Eton Riverside**	d	23p01													05 53				
—	—	—	2	Datchet	d	23p04													05 56				
—	—	—	3	Sunnymeads	d	23p07													05 59				
—	—	—	4¼	Wraysbury	d	23p10													06 02				
—	—	24½	6¾	**Staines**	d	23p16	23p21	23p29		23p39	23p59	04 58			05 37			06 03	06 08		06 29		
—	—	26	—	Ashford (Surrey)	d	23p19	23p24					05 01			05 40			06 06	06 11				
—	—	28¾	—	Feltham	d	23p24	23p29	23p35		23p46	00 05	05 06			05 45			06 11	06 16		06 35		
—	—	31	—	Whitton	d	23p28						05 10			05 49				06 20				06 20
0	—	—	—	**Kingston**	d				23p29								05 59						
0½	—	—	—	Hampton Wick	d				23p31								06 01						
1¾	—	—	—	Teddington	d				23p35								06 05						
2¼	—	—	—	Fulwell	d									05 36									
3	—	—	—	Strawberry Hill	d				23p38					05 38			06 08						
4	—	32¼	—	Twickenham	a	23p31		23p40	23p42	23p51	00 10	05 13		05 42	05 52		06 12		06 23		06 40		
—	—	—	—		d	23p32		23p41	23p43	23p51	00 11	05 13		05 43	05 53		06 13		06 23		06 41		
4½	—	32¾	—	St Margarets	d	23p34			23p45			05 15		05 45			06 15						
5½	—	33¾	—	**Richmond** ⊖	d	23p37		23p45	23p49	23p56	00 15	05 19		05 49	05 58		06 19		06 28		06 45		
6¼	—	34½	—	North Sheen	d	23p39			23p51			05 21		05 51			06 21						
7	—	35¼	—	Mortlake	d	23p42			23p53			05 23		05 53			06 23						
—	0	—	—	**Hounslow**	d		23p35						05 31			06 01		06 16					06 31
—	—	—	—	Isleworth	d		23p38						05 34			06 04		06 19					06 34
—	2¼	—	—	Syon Lane	d		23p40						05 36			06 06		06 21					06 36
—	3	—	—	Brentford	d		23p42						05 39			06 09		06 24					06 39
—	4	—	—	Kew Bridge	d		23p45						05 41			06 11		06 26					06 41
—	5	—	—	Chiswick	d		23p47						05 44			06 14		06 29					06 44
—	6	—	—	Barnes Bridge	d		23p50						05 46			06 16		06 31					06 46
8¼	6½	36½	—	Barnes	d	23p45	23p53		23p56			05 26	05 49	05 56		06 19	06 26	06 34		←			06 49
9½	—	37¾	—	Putney	d	23p48	23p56		23p59	00 02		05 29	05 52	05 59	06 04	06 22	06 29	06 37	06 34	06 37	06 52		06 52
10½	—	38¾	—	Wandsworth Town	d	23p51	23p59		00 02			05 32	05 55	06 02		06 25	06 32	→		06 40			06 55
11¼	—	39½	—	Clapham Junction 10	d	23p54	00 02	23p54	00 05	00 07	00 24	05 35	05 58	06 05	06 09	06 28	06 35		06 39	06 43	06 56		06 58
12½	—	41¼	—	Queenstown Rd.(Battersea)	d	23p57	00 05		00 08			05 38	06 01	06 08		06 31	06 38			06 46			07 01
14	—	42¼	—	Vauxhall ⊖	d		00 08		00 12	00 12		05 42	06 05	06 12	06 15	06 35	06 42		06 45	06 50			07 05
15¼	—	43½	—	**London Waterloo 15** ⊖	a	00 04	00 13	00 04	00 16	00 17	00 37	05 46	06 09	06 16	06 19	06 39	06 46		06 49	06 56	07 07		07 11

Reading, Guildford, Ascot, Weybridge, Windsor, Kingston, Richmond and Hounslow - London

until 30 September

		SW	SW	SW	SW	SW	SW	SW	SW	SW	SW	SW	SW	SW	SW	SW	SW	SW	SW	SW	SW	SW	SW
				◇				◇ 1			◇	◇	◇			◇ 1	1	◇ 1		◇	◇	◇	
Reading [7]	d							06 12										06 42					
Earley	d							06 17										06 47					
Winnersh Triangle	d							06 19										06 49					
Winnersh	d							06 21										06 51					
Wokingham	d							06 26										06 56					
Bracknell	d							06 32										07 02					
Martins Heron	d							06 35										07 05					
Guildford	d																06 30						
Wanborough	d																06 36						
Ash [5]	d																06 40						
Aldershot	a																06 47						
	d															06 28							
Ash Vale	d															06 32							
Frimley	d															06 40							
Camberley	a															06 44							
	d															06 47							
Bagshot	d															06 52							
Ascot [3]	d							06 40								06 59		07 10					
Sunningdale	d							06 43								07 02		07 13					
Longcross	d																						
Woking	d																						
West Byfleet	d																						
Byfleet & New Haw	d																						
Weybridge	d										06 33									07 03			
Addlestone	d										06 37									07 07			
Chertsey	d										06 40									07 10			
Virginia Water	a							06 49			06 45					07 08		07 19		07 15			
	d							06 49			06 54					07 08		07 19		07 24			
Egham	d							06 53			06 57					07 12		07 23		07 27			
Windsor & Eton Riverside	d			06 23								06 53									07 23		
Datchet	d			06 26								06 56									07 26		
Sunnymeads	d			06 29								06 59									07 29		
Wraysbury	d			06 32								07 02									07 32		
Staines	d		06 33	06 38				06 59			07 03	07 08				07 18		07 29		07 33	07 38		
Ashford (Surrey)	d		06 36	06 41							07 06	07 11				07 21				07 36	07 41		
Feltham	d		06 41	06 46				07 05			07 11	07 16				07 26		07 35		07 41	07 46		
Whitton	d			06 50		06 50	06 53					07 20			07 20	07 30					07 50		
Kingston	d	06 29								06 59									07 29				
Hampton Wick	d	06 31								07 01									07 31				
Teddington	d	06 35								07 05									07 35				
Fulwell	d													07 12									07 42
Strawberry Hill	d	06 38								07 08				07 14					07 38				07 44
Twickenham	a	06 42		06 53			06 56	07 10		07 12		07 23		07 18		07 33		07 40	07 42		07 53		07 48
	d	06 43		06 53			06 58	07 11		07 13		07 23		07 27		07 33		07 41	07 43		07 53		07 57
St Margarets	d	06 45					07 00			07 15				07 29					07 45				07 59
Richmond ⊖	d	06 49		06 58			07 04	07 15		07 19		07 28		07 32		07 38		07 45	07 49		07 58		08 02
North Sheen	d	06 51					07 06			07 21				07 34					07 51				08 04
Mortlake	d	06 53					07 08			07 23				07 37					07 53				08 07
Hounslow	d		06 46			07 01					07 16				07 31					07 46			
Isleworth	d		06 49			07 04					07 19				07 34					07 49			
Syon Lane	d		06 51			07 06					07 21				07 36					07 51			
Brentford	d		06 54			07 09					07 24				07 39					07 54			
Kew Bridge	d		06 56			07 11					07 26				07 41					07 56			
Chiswick	d		06 59			07 14					07 29				07 44					07 59			
Barnes Bridge	d		07 01			07 16			←		07 31				07 46					08 01			
Barnes	d	06 56	07 04		←	07 19	07 11		07 19	07 26	07 34		←	07 40	07 49				07 56	08 04		←	08 10
Putney	d	06 59	07 07	07 04	07 07	→	07 14	07 22	07 22	07 29	07 37	07 34	07 37	07 43	07 52				07 59	08 07	08 04	08 07	08 13
Wandsworth Town	d	07 02	→		07 10		07 17		07 25	07 32	→		07 40	07 46	07 55				08 02	→		08 10	08 16
Clapham Junction [10]	d	07 05		07 09	07 13		07 20	07 26	07 28	07 35		07 39	07 43	07 49	07 58	07 47		07 54	08 05		08 09	08 13	08 19
Queenstown Rd.(Battersea)	d	07 08			07 16		07 23		07 31	07 38			07 46	07 52	08 01				08 08			08 16	08 22
Vauxhall ⊖	d	07 12		07 15	07 20		07 27		07 35	07 42		07 45	07 50	07 56	08 05	07 53			08 12		08 15	08 20	08 26
London Waterloo [15] ⊖	a	07 18		07 21	07 28		07 34	07 37	07 43	07 48		07 51	07 58	08 04	08 11	07 59		08 06	08 18		08 21	08 28	08 34

Reading, Guildford, Ascot, Weybridge, Windsor, Kingston, Richmond and Hounslow - London

until 30 September

		SW	SW	SW	SW	SW	SW	SW	SW	SW	SW	SW	SW	SW	SW	SW	SW	SW	SW	SW	SW	SW	SW
			◇ 1	1	◇ 1		◇	◇ 1	◇	◇			◇ 1	◇ 1	1		◇	◇	◇			◇ 1	
Reading [7]	d				07 12			07 24						07 42								08 12	
Earley	d				07 17									07 47								08 17	
Winnersh Triangle	d				07 19									07 49								08 19	
Winnersh	d				07 21									07 51								08 21	
Wokingham	d				07 26			07 33						07 56								08 26	
Bracknell	d				07 32			07 39						08 02								08 32	
Martins Heron	d				07 35			07 42						08 05								08 35	
Guildford	d			07 00											07 30								
Wanborough	d			07 06											07 36								
Ash [5]	d			07 10											07 40								
Aldershot	a			07 17											07 47								
	d		07 00										07 30		08 00								
Ash Vale	d		07 04										07 34		08 04								
Frimley	d		07 10										07 40		08 10								
Camberley	a		07 14										07 44		08 14								
	d		07 17										07 47		08 18								
Bagshot	d		07 22										07 52		08 23								
Ascot [3]	d		07 29		07 40			07 47					07 59	08 10	08a30							08 40	
Sunningdale	d		07 32		07 43			07 50					08 02	08 13								08 43	
Longcross	d													08 16								08 46	
Woking	d																						
West Byfleet	d																						
Byfleet & New Haw	d																						
Weybridge	d						07 33										08 03						
Addlestone	d						07 37										08 07						
Chertsey	d						07 40										08 10						
Virginia Water	a		07 38				07 45	07 55					08 08	08 19			08 15					08 49	
	d		07 38				07 51	07 55					08 08	08 19			08 24					08 49	
Egham	d		07 42		07 50		07 54	07 58					08 12	08 23			08 27					08 53	
Windsor & Eton Riverside	d								07 53									08 23					
Datchet	d								07 56									08 26					
Sunnymeads	d								07 59									08 29					
Wraysbury	d								08 02									08 32					
Staines	d		07 48		07 56		08 00	08 04	08 08				08 18	08 29			08 33	08 38				08 59	
Ashford (Surrey)	d		07 51				08 03		08 11				08 21				08 36	08 41					
Feltham	d		07 56		08 02		08 08	08 12	08 16				08 26	08 35			08 41	08 46				09 05	
Whitton	d	07 50	08 00						08 20			08 20	08 30					08 50		08 50	08 53		
Kingston	d					07 59										08 29							
Hampton Wick	d					08 01										08 31							
Teddington	d					08 05										08 35							
Fulwell	d										08 12												
Strawberry Hill	d					08 08					08 14					08 38							
Twickenham	a		08 03		08 09	08 12		08 17	08 23		08 18		08 33	08 40		08 42		08 53			08 56	09 10	
	d		08 03		08 09	08 13		08 18	08 23		08 27		08 33	08 41		08 43		08 53			08 58	09 11	
St Margarets	d					08 15					08 29					08 45					09 00		
Richmond ⊖	d		08 08		08 14	08 19		08 24	08 28		08 32		08 38	08 45		08 49		08 58			09 04	09 15	
North Sheen	d					08 21					08 34					08 51					09 06		
Mortlake	d					08 23					08 37					08 53					09 08		
Hounslow	d	08 01					08 16					08 31					08 46			09 01			
Isleworth	d	08 04					08 19					08 34					08 49			09 04			
Syon Lane	d	08 06					08 21					08 36					08 51			09 06			
Brentford	d	08 09					08 24					08 39					08 54			09 09			
Kew Bridge	d	08 11					08 26					08 41					08 56			09 11			
Chiswick	d	08 14					08 29					08 44					08 59			09 14			
Barnes Bridge	d	08 16					08 31					08 46					09 01			09 16			←
Barnes	d	08 19				08 26	08 34			←	08 40	08 49				08 56	09 04		←	09 19	09 11		09 19
Putney	d	08 22				08 29	08 37		08 34	08 37	08 43	08 52				08 59	09 07	09 04	09 07	→	09 14		09 22
Wandsworth Town	d	08 25				08 32	→			08 40	08 46	08 55				09 02	→		09 10		09 17		09 25
Clapham Junction [10]	d	08 28	08 17		08 22	08 35		08 33	08 39	08 43	08 49	08 58	08 47	08 54		09 05		09 09	09 13		09 20	09 24	09 28
Queenstown Rd.(Battersea)	d	08 31				08 38				08 46	08 52	09 01				09 08			09 16		09 23		09 31
Vauxhall ⊖	d	08 35	08 23			08 42		08 38	08 45	08 50	08 56	09 05	08 53			09 12		09 15	09 20		09 27		09 35
London Waterloo [15] ⊖	a	08 43	08 29		08 38	08 49		08 46	08 51	08 58	09 04	09 13	09 00	09 06		09 18		09 21	09 28		09 34	09 34	09 43

Table 149

Mondays to Fridays
until 30 September

Reading, Guildford, Ascot, Weybridge, Windsor, Kingston, Richmond and Hounslow - London

		SW ■	SW	SW ◇	SW ◇	SW ◇	SW	SW	SW ■	SW	SW ■	SW	SW	SW	SW	SW	SW	SW ■	SW	SW	SW	SW
Reading 7	d								08 42									09 12				
Earley	d								08 47									09 17				
Winnersh Triangle	d								08 49									09 19				
Winnersh	d								08 51									09 21				
Wokingham	d								08 56									09 26				
Bracknell	d								09 02									09 32				
Martins Heron	d								09 05									09 35				
Guildford	d	08 00									08 30											
Wanborough	d	08 06									08 36											
Ash 5	d	08 10									08 40											
Aldershot	a	08 17									08 47											
	d	08 30									09 00											
Ash Vale	d	08 34									09 04											
Frimley	d	08 40									09 10											
Camberley	a	08 44									09 14											
	d	08 48									09 18											
Bagshot	d	08 53									09 23											
Ascot 3	d	09a00							09 10		09a30							09 40				
Sunningdale	d								09 13									09 43				
Longcross	d								09 16													
Woking	d																					
West Byfleet	d																					
Byfleet & New Haw	d																					
Weybridge	d			08 33									09 03								09 33	
Addlestone	d			08 37									09 07								09 37	
Chertsey	d			08 40									09 10								09 40	
Virginia Water	a			08 45					09 19				09 15					09 49			09 45	
	d			08 54					09 19				09 24					09 49			09 54	
Egham	d			08 57					09 23				09 27					09 53			09 57	
Windsor & Eton Riverside	d				08 53									09 23								09 53
Datchet	d				08 56									09 26								09 56
Sunnymeads	d				08 59									09 29								09 59
Wraysbury	d				09 02									09 32								10 02
Staines	d			09 03	09 08				09 29				09 33	09 38				09 59			10 03	10 08
Ashford (Surrey)	d			09 06	09 11								09 36	09 41							10 06	10 11
Feltham	d			09 11	09 16				09 35				09 41	09 46				10 05			10 11	10 16
Whitton	d				09 20		09 20	09 23						09 50		09 50	09 53					10 20
Kingston	d		08 59									09 29								09 59		
Hampton Wick	d		09 01									09 31								10 01		
Teddington	d		09 05									09 35								10 05		
Fulwell	d																					
Strawberry Hill	d		09 08									09 38								10 08		
Twickenham	a		09 12		09 23			09 26	09 40			09 42		09 53			09 56	10 10		10 12		10 23
	d		09 13		09 23			09 28	09 41			09 43		09 53			09 58	10 11		10 13		10 23
St Margarets	d		09 15					09 30				09 45					10 00			10 15		
Richmond ⊖	d		09 19		09 28			09 34	09 45			09 49		09 58			10 04	10 15		10 19		10 28
North Sheen	d		09 21					09 36				09 51					10 06			10 21		
Mortlake	d		09 23					09 38				09 53					10 08			10 23		
Hounslow	d			09 16			09 31						09 46			10 01					10 16	
Isleworth	d			09 19			09 34						09 49			10 04					10 19	
Syon Lane	d			09 21			09 36						09 51			10 06					10 21	
Brentford	d			09 24			09 39						09 54			10 09					10 24	
Kew Bridge	d			09 26			09 41						09 56			10 11					10 26	
Chiswick	d			09 29			09 44						09 59			10 14					10 29	
Barnes Bridge	d			09 31			09 46			←			10 01			10 16			←		10 31	
Barnes	d		09 26	09 34		←	09 49	09 41		09 49		09 56	10 04		←	10 19	10 11		10 19	10 26	10 34	
Putney	d		09 29	09 37	09 34	09 37	→	09 44		09 52		09 59	10 07	10 04	10 07	→	10 14		10 22	10 29	10 37	10 34
Wandsworth Town	d		09 32	→		09 40		09 47		09 55		10 02	→		10 10		10 17		10 25	10 32	→	
Clapham Junction 10	d		09 35		09 39	09 43		09 50	09 54	09 58		10 05		10 09	10 13		10 20	10 24	10 28	10 35		10 39
Queenstown Rd.(Battersea)	d		09 38			09 46		09 53		10 01		10 08			10 16		10 23		10 31	10 38		
Vauxhall ⊖	d		09 42		09 45	09 50		09 57		10 05		10 12		10 15	10 20		10 27		10 35	10 42		10 45
London Waterloo 15 ⊖	a		09 48		09 51	09 58		10 02	10 04	10 11		10 16		10 19	10 26		10 32	10 34	10 41	10 46		10 49

Table 149

Mondays to Fridays
until 30 September

Reading, Guildford, Ascot, Weybridge, Windsor, Kingston, Richmond and Hounslow - London

		SW ■	SW	SW ■	SW	SW	SW ■	SW	SW	SW	SW	SW ■	SW	SW ■	SW	SW	SW ■	SW	SW ■	SW	SW	SW	SW
Reading 7	d	09 25					09 42					09 56					10 12						
Earley	d	09 30					09 47					10 01					10 17						
Winnersh Triangle	d	09 32					09 49					10 03					10 19						
Winnersh	d	09 34					09 51					10 05					10 21						
Wokingham	d	09 39					09 56					10 10					10 26						
Bracknell	d	09 46					10 02					10 16					10 32						
Martins Heron	d	09 49					10 05					10 19					10 35						
Guildford	d			09 00										09 30					10 00				
Wanborough	d			09 06										09 36					10 06				
Ash 5	d			09 10										09 40					10 10				
Aldershot	a			09 17										09 47					10 17				
	d			09 30										10 00					10 30				
Ash Vale	d			09 34										10 04					10 34				
Frimley	d			09 40										10 10					10 40				
Camberley	a			09 44										10 14					10 44				
	d			09 48										10 18					10 48				
Bagshot	d			09 53										10 23					10 53				
Ascot 3	d	09 55		10a00			10 10					10 25		10a30			10 40		11a00				
Sunningdale	d	09 58					10 13					10 28					10 43						
Longcross	d																						
Woking	d																						
West Byfleet	d																						
Byfleet & New Haw	d																						
Weybridge	d									10 03											10 33		
Addlestone	d									10 07											10 37		
Chertsey	d									10 10											10 40		
Virginia Water	a	10 03					10 19			10 15		10 33					10 49				10 45		
	d	10 03					10 19			10 24		10 33					10 49				10 54		
Egham	d	10 06					10 23			10 27		10 36					10 53				10 57		
Windsor & Eton Riverside	d										10 23											10 53	
Datchet	d										10 26											10 56	
Sunnymeads	d										10 29											10 59	
Wraysbury	d										10 32											11 02	
Staines	d	10 14					10 29			10 33	10 38	10 44					10 59				11 03	11 08	
Ashford (Surrey)	d									10 36	10 41										11 06	11 11	
Feltham	d	10 20					10 35			10 41	10 46	10 50					11 05				11 11	11 16	
Whitton	d				10 20	10 26					10 50				10 50	10 56						11 20	
Kingston	d								10 29											10 59			
Hampton Wick	d								10 31											11 01			
Teddington	d								10 35											11 05			
Fulwell	d																						
Strawberry Hill	d								10 38											11 08			
Twickenham	a	10 27				10 28	10 40		10 42		10 53	10 57				10 58	11 10			11 12		11 23	
	d	10 27				10 28	10 41		10 43		10 53	10 57				10 58	11 11			11 13		11 23	
St Margarets	d					10 30			10 45							11 00				11 15			
Richmond ⊖	d	10 32				10 34	10 45		10 49		10 58	11 02				11 04	11 15			11 19		11 28	
North Sheen	d					10 36			10 51							11 06				11 21			
Mortlake	d					10 38			10 53							11 08				11 23			
Hounslow	d				10 31					10 46					11 01						11 16		
Isleworth	d				10 34					10 49					11 04						11 19		
Syon Lane	d				10 36					10 51					11 06						11 21		
Brentford	d				10 39					10 54					11 09						11 24		
Kew Bridge	d				10 41					10 56					11 11						11 26		
Chiswick	d				10 44					10 59					11 14						11 29		
Barnes Bridge	d				10 46			←		11 01					11 16			←			11 31		
Barnes	d		←		10 49	10 41		10 49	10 56	11 04			←		11 19	11 11		11 19		11 26	11 34		←
Putney	d		10 37		→	10 44		10 52	10 59	11 07	11 04		11 07		→	11 14		11 22		11 29	11 37	11 34	11 37
Wandsworth Town	d		10 40			10 47		10 55	11 02	→			11 10			11 17		11 25		11 32	→		11 40
Clapham Junction 10	d	10 42	10 43			10 50	10 54	10 58	11 05		11 09	11 12	11 13			11 20	11 24	11 28		11 35		11 39	11 43
Queenstown Rd.(Battersea)	d		10 47			10 53		11 01	11 08				11 17			11 23		11 31		11 38			11 46
Vauxhall ⊖	d		10 50			10 57		11 05	11 12		11 15		11 20			11 27		11 35		11 42		11 45	11 50
London Waterloo 15 ⊖	a	10 53	10 56			11 02	11 04	11 11	11 16		11 19	11 25	11 27			11 32	11 34	11 41		11 46		11 49	11 56

Reading, Guildford, Ascot, Weybridge, Windsor, Kingston, Richmond and Hounslow - London

		SW	SW	SW 1	SW	SW 1	SW	SW	SW	SW	SW	SW	SW 1	SW	SW 1	SW	SW	SW	SW	SW	SW	SW 1
Reading 7	d			10 42									11 12									11 42
Earley	d			10 47									11 17									11 47
Winnersh Triangle	d			10 49									11 19									11 49
Winnersh	d			10 51									11 21									11 51
Wokingham	d			10 56									11 26									11 56
Bracknell	d			11 02									11 32									12 02
Martins Heron	d			11 05									11 35									12 05
Guildford	d					10 30									11 00							
Wanborough	d					10 36									11 06							
Ash 5	d					10 40									11 10							
Aldershot	a					10 47									11 17							
	d					11 00									11 30							
Ash Vale	d					11 04									11 34							
Frimley	d					11 10									11 40							
Camberley	a					11 14									11 44							
	d					11 18									11 48							
Bagshot	d					11 23									11 53							
Ascot 3	d			11 10		11a30							11 40		12a00							12 10
Sunningdale	d			11 13									11 43									12 13
Longcross	d																					
Woking	d																					
West Byfleet	d																					
Byfleet & New Haw	d																					
Weybridge	d							11 03									11 33					
Addlestone	d							11 07									11 37					
Chertsey	d							11 10									11 40					
Virginia Water	a			11 19				11 15					11 49				11 45					12 19
	d			11 19				11 24					11 49				11 54					12 19
Egham	d			11 23				11 27					11 53				11 57					12 23
Windsor & Eton Riverside	d								11 23									11 53				
Datchet	d								11 26									11 56				
Sunnymeads	d								11 29									11 59				
Wraysbury	d								11 32									12 02				
Staines	d			11 29				11 33	11 38				11 59				12 03	12 08				12 29
Ashford (Surrey)	d							11 36	11 41								12 06	12 11				
Feltham	d			11 35				11 41	11 46				12 05				12 11	12 16				12 35
Whitton	d	11 20	11 23						11 50		11 50	11 53						12 20		12 20	12 23	
Kingston	d						11 29									11 59						
Hampton Wick	d						11 31									12 01						
Teddington	d						11 35									12 05						
Fulwell	d																					
Strawberry Hill	d						11 38									12 08						
Twickenham	a		11 26	11 40			11 42		11 53			11 56	12 10			12 12		12 23			12 26	12 40
	d		11 28	11 41			11 43		11 53			11 58	12 11			12 13		12 23			12 28	12 41
St Margarets	d		11 30				11 45					12 00				12 15					12 30	
Richmond ⊖	d		11 34	11 45			11 49		11 58			12 04	12 15			12 19		12 28			12 34	12 45
North Sheen	d		11 36				11 51					12 06				12 21					12 36	
Mortlake	d		11 38				11 53					12 08				12 23					12 38	
Hounslow	d	11 31						11 46			12 01						12 16			12 31		
Isleworth	d	11 34						11 49			12 04						12 19			12 34		
Syon Lane	d	11 36						11 51			12 06						12 21			12 36		
Brentford	d	11 39						11 54			12 09						12 24			12 39		
Kew Bridge	d	11 41						11 56			12 11						12 26			12 41		
Chiswick	d	11 44						11 59			12 14						12 29			12 44		
Barnes Bridge	d	11 46			←			12 01			12 16			←			12 31			12 46		
Barnes	d	11 49	11 41		11 49		11 56	12 04		←	12 19	12 11		12 19		12 26	12 34		←	12 49	12 41	
Putney	d	→	11 44		11 52		11 59	12 07	12 04	12 07	→	12 14		12 22		12 29	12 37	12 34	12 37	→	12 44	
Wandsworth Town	d		11 47		11 55		12 02	→		12 10		12 17		12 25		12 32	→		12 40		12 47	
Clapham Junction 10	d		11 50	11 54	11 58		12 05		12 09	12 13		12 20	12 25	12 28		12 35		12 39	12 43		12 50	12 54
Queenstown Rd.(Battersea)	d		11 53		12 01		12 08			12 16		12 23		12 31		12 38			12 46		12 53	
Vauxhall ⊖	d		11 57		12 05		12 12		12 15	12 20		12 27		12 35		12 42		12 45	12 50		12 57	
London Waterloo 15 ⊖	a		12 02	12 04	12 11		12 16		12 19	12 26		12 32	12 34	12 41		12 46		12 49	12 56		13 02	13 04

Reading, Guildford, Ascot, Weybridge, Windsor, Kingston, Richmond and Hounslow - London

		SW	SW 1	SW	SW	SW	SW	SW	SW	SW 1	SW	SW 1	SW	SW	SW	SW	SW	SW	SW 1	SW	SW 1	SW	SW
Reading 7	d									12 12									12 42				
Earley	d									12 17									12 47				
Winnersh Triangle	d									12 19									12 49				
Winnersh	d									12 21									12 51				
Wokingham	d									12 26									12 56				
Bracknell	d									12 32									13 02				
Martins Heron	d									12 35									13 05				
Guildford	d		11 30									12 00									12 30		
Wanborough	d		11 36									12 06									12 36		
Ash 5	d		11 40									12 10									12 40		
Aldershot	a		11 47									12 17									12 47		
	d		12 00									12 30									13 00		
Ash Vale	d		12 04									12 34									13 04		
Frimley	d		12 10									12 40									13 10		
Camberley	a		12 14									12 44									13 14		
	d		12 18									12 48									13 18		
Bagshot	d		12 23									12 53									13 23		
Ascot 3	d		12a30							12 40		13a00							13 10		13a30		
Sunningdale	d									12 43									13 13				
Longcross	d																		13 16				
Woking	d																						
West Byfleet	d																						
Byfleet & New Haw	d																						
Weybridge	d				12 03									12 33									13 03
Addlestone	d				12 07									12 37									13 07
Chertsey	d				12 10									12 40									13 10
Virginia Water	a				12 15					12 49				12 45					13 19				13 15
	d				12 24					12 49				12 54					13 19				13 24
Egham	d				12 27					12 53				12 57					13 23				13 27
Windsor & Eton Riverside	d					12 23									12 53								
Datchet	d					12 26									12 56								
Sunnymeads	d					12 29									12 59								
Wraysbury	d					12 32									13 02								
Staines	d				12 33	12 38				12 59				13 03	13 08				13 29				13 33
Ashford (Surrey)	d				12 36	12 41								13 06	13 11								13 36
Feltham	d				12 41	12 46				13 05				13 11	13 16				13 35				13 41
Whitton	d					12 50		12 50	12 53						13 20		13 20	13 23					
Kingston	d			12 29									12 59									13 29	
Hampton Wick	d			12 31									13 01									13 31	
Teddington	d			12 35									13 05									13 35	
Fulwell	d																						
Strawberry Hill	d			12 38									13 08									13 38	
Twickenham	a			12 42		12 53			12 56	13 10			13 12		13 23			13 26	13 40			13 42	
	d			12 43		12 53			12 58	13 11			13 13		13 23			13 28	13 41			13 43	
St Margarets	d			12 45					13 00				13 15					13 30				13 45	
Richmond ⊖	d			12 49		12 58			13 04	13 15			13 19		13 28			13 34	13 45			13 49	
North Sheen	d			12 51					13 06				13 21					13 36				13 51	
Mortlake	d			12 53					13 08				13 23					13 38				13 53	
Hounslow	d				12 46			13 01						13 16			13 31						13 46
Isleworth	d				12 49			13 04						13 19			13 34						13 49
Syon Lane	d				12 51			13 06						13 21			13 36						13 51
Brentford	d				12 54			13 09						13 24			13 39						13 54
Kew Bridge	d				12 56			13 11						13 26			13 41						13 56
Chiswick	d				12 59			13 14						13 29			13 44						13 59
Barnes Bridge	d	←			13 01			13 16			←			13 31			13 46			←			14 01
Barnes	d	12 49		12 56	13 04		←	13 19	13 11		13 19		13 26	13 34		←	13 49	13 41		13 49		13 56	14 04
Putney	d	12 52		12 59	13 07	13 04	13 07	→	13 14		13 22		13 29	13 37	13 34	13 37	→	13 44		13 52		13 59	14 07
Wandsworth Town	d	12 55		13 02	→		13 10		13 17		13 25		13 32	→		13 40		13 47		13 55		14 02	→
Clapham Junction 10	d	12 58		13 05		13 09	13 13		13 20	13 24	13 28		13 35		13 39	13 43		13 50	13 54	13 58		14 05	
Queenstown Rd.(Battersea)	d	13 01		13 08			13 16		13 23		13 31		13 38			13 46		13 53		14 01		14 08	
Vauxhall ⊖	d	13 05		13 12		13 15	13 20		13 27		13 35		13 42		13 45	13 50		13 57		14 05		14 12	
London Waterloo 15 ⊖	a	13 11		13 16		13 19	13 26		13 32	13 34	13 41		13 46		13 49	13 56		14 02	14 04	14 11		14 16	

Table 149

Mondays to Fridays

until 30 September

Reading, Guildford, Ascot, Weybridge, Windsor, Kingston, Richmond and Hounslow - London

		SW	SW	SW	SW	SW 1	SW	SW 1	SW	SW	SW	SW	SW	SW	SW 1	SW	SW 1	SW	SW	SW	SW	SW	SW
Reading 7	d					13 12									13 42								
Earley	d					13 17									13 47								
Winnersh Triangle	d					13 19									13 49								
Winnersh	d					13 21									13 51								
Wokingham	d					13 26									13 56								
Bracknell	d					13 32									14 02								
Martins Heron	d					13 35									14 05								
Guildford	d							13 00									13 30						
Wanborough	d							13 06									13 36						
Ash 5	d							13 10									13 40						
Aldershot	a							13 17									13 47						
	d							13 30									14 00						
Ash Vale	d							13 34									14 04						
Frimley	d							13 40									14 10						
Camberley	a							13 44									14 14						
	d							13 48									14 18						
Bagshot	d							13 53									14 23						
Ascot 3	d					13 40		14a00							14 10		14a30						
Sunningdale	d					13 43									14 13								
Longcross	d																						
Woking	d																						
West Byfleet	d																						
Byfleet & New Haw	d																						
Weybridge	d									13 33									14 03				
Addlestone	d									13 37									14 07				
Chertsey	d									13 40									14 10				
Virginia Water	a					13 49				13 45					14 19				14 15				
	d					13 49				13 54					14 19				14 24				
Egham	d					13 53				13 57					14 23				14 27				
Windsor & Eton Riverside	d	13 23									13 53									14 23			
Datchet	d	13 26									13 56									14 26			
Sunnymeads	d	13 29									13 59									14 29			
Wraysbury	d	13 32									14 02									14 32			
Staines	d	13 38				13 59				14 03	14 08				14 29				14 33	14 38			
Ashford (Surrey)	d	13 41								14 06	14 11								14 36	14 41			
Feltham	d	13 46				14 05				14 11	14 16				14 35				14 41	14 46			
Whitton	d	13 50		13 50	13 53						14 20		14 20	14 23						14 50		14 50	14 53
Kingston	d								13 59									14 29					
Hampton Wick	d								14 01									14 31					
Teddington	d								14 05									14 35					
Fulwell	d																						
Strawberry Hill	d								14 08									14 38					
Twickenham	a	13 53			13 56	14 10			14 12		14 23			14 26	14 40			14 42		14 53			14 56
	d	13 53			13 58	14 11			14 13		14 23			14 28	14 41			14 43		14 53			14 58
St Margarets	d				14 00				14 15					14 30				14 45					15 00
Richmond ⊖	d	13 58			14 04	14 15			14 19		14 28			14 34	14 45			14 49		14 58			15 04
North Sheen	d				14 06				14 21					14 36				14 51					15 06
Mortlake	d				14 08				14 23					14 38				14 53					15 08
Hounslow	d			14 01						14 16			14 31						14 46			15 01	
Isleworth	d			14 04						14 19			14 34						14 49			15 04	
Syon Lane	d			14 06						14 21			14 36						14 51			15 06	
Brentford	d			14 09						14 24			14 39						14 54			15 09	
Kew Bridge	d			14 11						14 26			14 41						14 56			15 11	
Chiswick	d			14 14						14 29			14 44						14 59			15 14	
Barnes Bridge	d			14 16			←			14 31			14 46			←			15 01			15 16	
Barnes	d		←	14 19	14 11		14 19		14 26	14 34		←	14 49	14 41		14 49		14 56	15 04		←	15 19	15 11
Putney	d	14 04	14 07	→	14 14		14 22		14 29	14 37	14 34	14 37	→	14 44		14 52		14 59	15 07	15 04	15 07	→	15 14
Wandsworth Town	d		14 10		14 17		14 25		14 32	→		14 40		14 47		14 55		15 02	→		15 10		15 17
Clapham Junction 10	d	14 09	14 13		14 20	14 24	14 28		14 35		14 39	14 43		14 50	14 54	14 58		15 05		15 09	15 13		15 20
Queenstown Rd.(Battersea)	d		14 16		14 23		14 31		14 38			14 46		14 53		15 01		15 08			15 16		15 23
Vauxhall ⊖	d	14 15	14 20		14 27		14 35		14 42		14 45	14 50		14 57		15 05		15 12		15 15	15 20		15 27
London Waterloo 15 ⊖	a	14 19	14 26		14 32	14 34	14 41		14 46		14 49	14 56		15 02	15 04	15 11		15 16		15 19	15 26		15 32

Table 149

Mondays to Fridays

until 30 September

Reading, Guildford, Ascot, Weybridge, Windsor, Kingston, Richmond and Hounslow - London

		SW 1	SW	SW 1	SW	SW	SW	SW	SW	SW	SW 1	SW	SW 1	SW	SW	SW	SW	SW	SW	SW 1	SW	SW 1
Reading 7	d	14 12									14 42									15 12		
Earley	d	14 17									14 47									15 17		
Winnersh Triangle	d	14 19									14 49									15 19		
Winnersh	d	14 21									14 51									15 21		
Wokingham	d	14 26									14 56									15 26		
Bracknell	d	14 32									15 02									15 32		
Martins Heron	d	14 35									15 05									15 35		
Guildford	d			14 00									14 30									15 00
Wanborough	d			14 06									14 36									15 06
Ash 5	d			14 10									14 40									15 10
Aldershot	a			14 17									14 47									15 17
	d			14 30									15 00									15 30
Ash Vale	d			14 34									15 04									15 34
Frimley	d			14 40									15 10									15 40
Camberley	a			14 44									15 14									15 44
	d			14 48									15 18									15 48
Bagshot	d			14 53									15 23									15 53
Ascot 3	d	14 40		15a00							15 10		15a30							15 40		16a00
Sunningdale	d	14 43									15 13									15 43		
Longcross	d																					
Woking	d																					
West Byfleet	d																					
Byfleet & New Haw	d																					
Weybridge	d					14 33									15 03							
Addlestone	d					14 37									15 07							
Chertsey	d					14 40									15 10							
Virginia Water	a	14 49				14 45					15 19				15 15					15 49		
	d	14 49				14 54					15 19				15 24					15 49		
Egham	d	14 53				14 57					15 23				15 27					15 53		
Windsor & Eton Riverside	d						14 53									15 23						
Datchet	d						14 56									15 26						
Sunnymeads	d						14 59									15 29						
Wraysbury	d						15 02									15 32						
Staines	d	14 59				15 03	15 08				15 29				15 33	15 38				15 59		
Ashford (Surrey)	d					15 06	15 11								15 36	15 41						
Feltham	d	15 05				15 11	15 16				15 35				15 41	15 46				16 05		
Whitton	d						15 20		15 20	15 23						15 50		15 50	15 53			
Kingston	d				14 59									15 29								
Hampton Wick	d				15 01									15 31								
Teddington	d				15 05									15 35								
Fulwell	d																					
Strawberry Hill	d				15 08									15 38								
Twickenham	a	15 10			15 12		15 23			15 26	15 40			15 42		15 53			15 56	16 10		
	d	15 11			15 13		15 23			15 28	15 41			15 43		15 53			15 58	16 11		
St Margarets	d				15 15					15 30				15 45					16 00			
Richmond ⊖	d	15 15			15 19		15 28			15 34	15 45			15 49		15 58			16 04	16 15		
North Sheen	d				15 21					15 36				15 51					16 06			
Mortlake	d				15 23					15 38				15 53					16 08			
Hounslow	d					15 16			15 31						15 46			16 01				
Isleworth	d					15 19			15 34						15 49			16 04				
Syon Lane	d					15 21			15 36						15 51			16 06				
Brentford	d					15 24			15 39						15 54			16 09				
Kew Bridge	d					15 26			15 41						15 56			16 11				
Chiswick	d					15 29			15 44						15 59			16 14				
Barnes Bridge	d		←			15 31			15 46			←			16 01			16 16			←	
Barnes	d		15 19		15 26	15 34		←	15 49	15 41		15 49		15 56	16 04		←	16 19	16 11		16 19	
Putney	d		15 22		15 29	15 37	15 34	15 37	→	15 44		15 52		15 59	16 07	16 04	16 07	→	16 14		16 22	
Wandsworth Town	d		15 25		15 32	→		15 40		15 47		15 55		16 02	→		16 10		16 17		16 25	
Clapham Junction 10	d	15 24	15 28		15 35		15 39	15 43		15 50	15 54	15 58		16 05		16 09	16 13		16 20	16 24	16 28	
Queenstown Rd.(Battersea)	d		15 31		15 38			15 46		15 53		16 01		16 08			16 16		16 23		16 31	
Vauxhall ⊖	d		15 35		15 42		15 45	15 50		15 57		16 05		16 12		16 15	16 20		16 27		16 35	
London Waterloo 15 ⊖	a	15 34	15 41		15 46		15 49	15 56		16 02	16 05	16 11		16 19		16 19	16 26		16 32	16 34	16 41	

Reading, Guildford, Ascot, Weybridge, Windsor, Kingston, Richmond and Hounslow - London

until 30 September

		SW	SW	SW	SW	SW	SW	SW 1	SW	SW 1	SW	SW	SW	SW	SW	SW	SW	SW 1	SW	SW 1	SW	SW	SW
Reading 7	d							15 42										16 12					
Earley	d							15 47										16 17					
Winnersh Triangle	d							15 49										16 19					
Winnersh	d							15 51										16 21					
Wokingham	d							15 56										16 26					
Bracknell	d							16 02										16 32					
Martins Heron	d							16 05										16 35					
Guildford	d									15 30										16 00			
Wanborough	d									15 36										16 06			
Ash 5	d									15 40										16 10			
Aldershot	a									15 47										16 17			
	d									16 00										16 30			
Ash Vale	d									16 04										16 34			
Frimley	d									16 10										16 40			
Camberley	a									16 14										16 44			
	d									16 18										16 48			
Bagshot	d									16 23										16 53			
Ascot 8	d							16 10		16a30								16 40		17a00			
Sunningdale	d							16 13										16 43					
Longcross	d																						
Woking	d																						
West Byfleet	d																						
Byfleet & New Haw	d																						
Weybridge	d		15 33										16 03									16 33	
Addlestone	d		15 37										16 07									16 37	
Chertsey	d		15 40										16 10									16 40	
Virginia Water	a		15 45					16 19					16 15					16 49				16 45	
	d		15 54					16 19					16 24					16 49				16 54	
Egham	d		15 57					16 23					16 27					16 53				16 57	
Windsor & Eton Riverside	d			15 53										16 23									16 53
Datchet	d			15 56										16 26									16 56
Sunnymeads	d			15 59										16 29									16 59
Wraysbury	d			16 02										16 32									17 02
Staines	d		16 03	16 08				16 29					16 33	16 38				16 59				17 03	17 08
Ashford (Surrey)	d		16 06	16 11									16 36	16 41								17 06	17 11
Feltham	d		16 11	16 16				16 35					16 41	16 46				17 05				17 11	17 16
Whitton	d			16 20		16 20	16 23							16 50		16 50	16 53						17 20
Kingston	d	15 59									16 29										16 59		
Hampton Wick	d	16 01									16 31										17 01		
Teddington	d	16 05									16 35										17 05		
Fulwell	d																						
Strawberry Hill	d	16 08									16 38										17 08		
Twickenham	a	16 12		16 23			16 26	16 40			16 42			16 53			16 56	17 10			17 12		17 23
	d	16 13		16 23			16 28	16 41			16 43	16 50		16 53			16 58	17 11			17 13		17 23
St Margarets	d	16 15					16 30				16 45						17 00				17 15		
Richmond ⊖	d	16 19		16 28			16 34	16 45			16 49			16 58			17 04	17 15			17 19		17 28
North Sheen	d	16 21					16 36				16 51						17 06				17 21		
Mortlake	d	16 23					16 38				16 53						17 08				17 23		
Hounslow	d		16 16			16 31							16 46			17 01						17 16	
Isleworth	d		16 19			16 34							16 49			17 04						17 19	
Syon Lane	d		16 21			16 36							16 51			17 06						17 21	
Brentford	d		16 24			16 39							16 54			17 09						17 24	
Kew Bridge	d		16 26			16 41							16 56			17 11						17 26	
Chiswick	d		16 29			16 44							16 59			17 14						17 29	
Barnes Bridge	d		16 31			16 46			←				17 01			17 16			←			17 31	
Barnes	d	16 26	16 34		←	16 49	16 41		16 49		16 56		17 04		←	17 19	17 11		17 19		17 26	17 34	
Putney	d	16 29	16 37	16 34	16 37	→	16 44		16 52		16 59		17 07	17 05	17 07	→	17 14		17 22		17 29	17 37	17 34
Wandsworth Town	d	16 32	→		16 40		16 47		16 55		17 02		→		17 10		17 17		17 25		17 32	→	
Clapham Junction 10	d	16 35		16 39	16 43		16 50	16 54	16 58		17 05	17 09		17 09	17 13		17 20	17 24	17 28		17 35		17 39
Queenstown Rd.(Battersea)	d	16 38			16 46		16 53		17 01		17 08				17 16		17 23		17 31		17 38		
Vauxhall ⊖	d	16 42		16 45	16 50		16 57		17 05		17 12			17 15	17 20		17 27		17 35		17 42		17 45
London Waterloo 15 ⊖	a	16 49		16 49	16 56		17 02	17 04	17 11		17 19	17 24		17 19	17 26		17 32	17 35	17 41		17 49		17 49

Mondays to Fridays

Reading, Guildford, Ascot, Weybridge, Windsor, Kingston, Richmond and Hounslow - London

until 30 September

		SW	SW	SW	SW 1	SW	SW 1	SW	SW	SW	SW	SW	SW	SW 1	SW	SW	SW	SW	SW	SW 1	SW 1	SW
Reading 7	d				16 42									17 12						17 22		
Earley	d				16 47									17 17						17 27		
Winnersh Triangle	d				16 49									17 19						17 29		
Winnersh	d				16 51									17 21						17 31		
Wokingham	d				16 56									17 26						17 36		
Bracknell	d				17 02									17 32						17 42		
Martins Heron	d				17 05									17 35						17 45		
Guildford	d						16 30														17 00	
Wanborough	d						16 36														17 06	
Ash 5	d						16 40														17 10	
Aldershot	a						16 47														17 17	
	d						17 00														17 30	
Ash Vale	d						17 04														17 34	
Frimley	d						17 10														17 40	
Camberley	a						17 14														17 44	
	d						17 18														17 48	
Bagshot	d						17 23														17 53	
Ascot 8	d				17 10		17a30							17 40						17b55	18a00	
Sunningdale	d				17 13									17 43						17 58		
Longcross	d				17 16																	
Woking	d																					
West Byfleet	d																					
Byfleet & New Haw	d																					
Weybridge	d								17 03								17 37					
Addlestone	d								17 07								17 41					
Chertsey	d								17 10								17 44					
Virginia Water	a				17 19				17 15					17 49			17 49			18 03		
	d				17 19				17 24					17 49			17 54			18 03		
Egham	d				17 23				17 27					17 53			17 57			18 06		
Windsor & Eton Riverside	d									17 23								17 53				
Datchet	d									17 26								17 56				
Sunnymeads	d									17 29								17 59				
Wraysbury	d									17 32								18 02				
Staines	d				17 29				17 33	17 38				17 59			18 03	18 08		18 14		
Ashford (Surrey)	d								17 36	17 41							18 06	18 11				
Feltham	d				17 35				17 41	17 46				18 05			18 11	18 16		18 20		
Whitton	d		17 20	17 23						17 50		17 50	17 53					18 20				18 20
Kingston	d							17 29								17 59						
Hampton Wick	d							17 31								18 01						
Teddington	d							17 35								18 05						
Fulwell	d																					
Strawberry Hill	d							17 38								18 08						
Twickenham	a			17 26	17 40			17 42		17 53			17 56	18 10		18 12		18 23				
	d			17 28	17 41			17 43		17 53			17 58	18 11		18 13		18 23				
St Margarets	d			17 30				17 45					18 00			18 15						
Richmond ⊖	d			17 34	17 45			17 49		17 58			18 04	18 15		18 19		18 28				
North Sheen	d			17 36				17 51					18 06			18 21						
Mortlake	d			17 38				17 53					18 08			18 23						
Hounslow	d		17 31						17 46			18 01					18 16			18 26		18 31
Isleworth	d		17 34						17 49			18 04					18 19					18 34
Syon Lane	d		17 36						17 51			18 06					18 21					18 36
Brentford	d		17 39						17 54			18 09					18 24			18 31		18 39
Kew Bridge	d		17 41						17 56			18 11					18 26					18 41
Chiswick	d		17 44						17 59			18 14					18 29					18 44
Barnes Bridge	d		17 46			←			18 01			18 16			←		18 31					18 46
Barnes	d	←	17 49	17 41		17 49		17 56	18 04		←	18 19	18 11		18 19	18 26	18 34		←			18 49
Putney	d	17 37	→	17 44		17 52		17 59	18 07	18 04	18 07	→	18 14		18 22	18 29	18 37	18 34	18 37	18 39		→
Wandsworth Town	d	17 40		17 47		17 55		18 02	→		18 10		18 17		18 25	18 32	→		18 40			
Clapham Junction 10	d	17 43		17 50	17 54	17 58		18 05		18 09	18 13		18 20	18 24	18 28	18 35		18 39	18 43	18 44		
Queenstown Rd.(Battersea)	d	17 46		17 53		18 01		18 08			18 16		18 23		18 31	18 38			18 46			
Vauxhall ⊖	d	17 50		17 57		18 05		18 12		18 15	18 20		18 27		18 35	18 42		18 45	18 50			
London Waterloo 15 ⊖	a	17 56		18 02	18 04	18 11		18 19		18 19	18 26		18 32	18 34	18 41	18 49		18 49	18 56	18 56		

b Arr. 1749

Table 149

Mondays to Fridays
until 30 September

Reading, Guildford, Ascot, Weybridge, Windsor, Kingston, Richmond and Hounslow - London

		SW	SW ■	SW	SW	SW	SW	SW	SW ■	SW ■		SW	SW	SW ■	SW	SW ■	SW	SW	SW	SW		SW	SW	SW ■	SW
Reading 7	d		17 42						17 53					18 12										18 42	
Earley	d		17 47						17 58					18 17										18 47	
Winnersh Triangle	d		17 49						18 00					18 19										18 49	
Winnersh	d		17 51						18 02					18 21										18 51	
Wokingham	d		17 56						18 07					18 26										18 56	
Bracknell	d		18 02						18 13					18 32										19 02	
Martins Heron	d		18 05						18 16					18 35										19 05	
Guildford	d									17 30						18 00									
Wanborough	d									17 36						18 06									
Ash 5	d									17 40						18 10									
Aldershot	a									17 47						18 17									
	d									18 00						18 30									
Ash Vale	d									18 04						18 34									
Frimley	d									18 10						18 40									
Camberley	a									18 14						18 44									
	d									18 18						18 48									
Bagshot	d									18 23						18 53									
Ascot 3	d		18 10						18 25	18a30				18 40		19a00								19 10	
Sunningdale	d		18 13						18 28					18 43										19 13	
Longcross	d		18 16											18 46										19 16	
Woking	d																								
West Byfleet	d																								
Byfleet & New Haw	d																								
Weybridge	d					18 07												18 37							
Addlestone	d					18 11												18 41							
Chertsey	d					18 14												18 44							
Virginia Water	a		18 19			18 19			18 33					18 49				18 49						19 19	
	d		18 19			18 24			18 33					18 49				18 54						19 19	
Egham	d		18 23			18 27			18 37					18 53				18 57						19 23	
Windsor & Eton Riverside	d						18 23												18 53						
Datchet	d						18 26												18 56						
Sunnymeads	d						18 29												18 59						
Wraysbury	d						18 32												19 02						
Staines	d		18 29			18 33	18 38		18 44					18 59				19 03	19 08					19 29	
Ashford (Surrey)	d					18 36	18 41											19 06	19 11						
Feltham	d		18 35			18 41	18 46		18 50					19 05				19 11	19 16					19 35	
Whitton	d	18 23					18 50					18 50	18 53						19 20			19 20	19 23		
Kingston	d				18 29												18 59								
Hampton Wick	d				18 31												19 01								
Teddington	d				18 35												19 05								
Fulwell	d																								
Strawberry Hill	d				18 38												19 08								
Twickenham	a	18 26	18 40		18 42		18 53						18 56	19 10			19 12		19 23				19 26	19 40	
	d	18 28	18 41		18 43		18 53						18 58	19 11			19 13		19 23				19 28	19 41	
St Margarets	d	18 30			18 45								19 00				19 15						19 30		
Richmond ⊖	d	18 34	18 45		18 49		18 58						19 04	19 15			19 19		19 28				19 34	19 45	
North Sheen	d	18 36			18 51								19 06				19 21						19 36		
Mortlake	d	18 38			18 53								19 08				19 23						19 38		
Hounslow	d					18 46			18 56			19 01						19 16				19 31			
Isleworth	d					18 49						19 04						19 19				19 34			
Syon Lane	d					18 51						19 06						19 21				19 36			
Brentford	d					18 54			19 01			19 09						19 24				19 39			
Kew Bridge	d					18 56						19 11						19 26				19 41			
Chiswick	d					18 59						19 14						19 29				19 44			
Barnes Bridge	d			←		19 01						19 16			←			19 31				19 46			←
Barnes	d	18 41		18 49	18 56	19 04		←				19 19	19 11		19 19		19 26	19 34		←		19 49	19 41		19 49
Putney	d	18 44		18 52	18 59	19 07	19 04	19 07	19 09			→	19 14		19 22		19 29	19 37	19 34	19 37		→	19 44		19 52
Wandsworth Town	d	18 47		18 55	19 02	→		19 10					19 17		19 25		19 32	→		19 40			19 47		19 55
Clapham Junction 10	d	18 50	18 54	18 58	19 05		19 09	19 13	19 14				19 20	19 24	19 28		19 35		19 39	19 43			19 50	19 54	19 58
Queenstown Rd.(Battersea)	d	18 53		19 01	19 08			19 16					19 23		19 31		19 38			19 46			19 53		20 01
Vauxhall ⊖	d	18 57		19 05	19 12		19 15	19 20					19 27		19 35		19 42		19 45	19 50			19 57		20 05
London Waterloo 15 ⊖	a	19 02	19 04	19 11	19 16		19 19	19 26	19 28				19 32	19 34	19 41		19 46		19 49	19 56			20 02	20 04	20 09

Table 149

Mondays to Fridays
until 30 September

Reading, Guildford, Ascot, Weybridge, Windsor, Kingston, Richmond and Hounslow - London

		SW ■	SW ■	SW	SW	SW		SW	SW	SW	SW ■	SW	SW ■	SW	SW	SW		SW	SW	SW	SW ■	SW	SW ■	SW	SW
Reading 7	d	18 52									19 12										19 42				
Earley	d	18 57									19 17										19 47				
Winnersh Triangle	d	18 59									19 19										19 49				
Winnersh	d	19 01									19 21										19 51				
Wokingham	d	19 06									19 26										19 56				
Bracknell	d	19 12									19 32										20 02				
Martins Heron	d	19 15									19 35										20 05				
Guildford	d		18 30										19 00										19 30		
Wanborough	d		18 36										19 06										19 36		
Ash 5	d		18 40										19 10										19 40		
Aldershot	a		18 47										19 17										19 47		
	d		19 00										19 30										20 00		
Ash Vale	d		19 04										19 34										20 04		
Frimley	d		19 10										19 40										20 10		
Camberley	a		19 14										19 44										20 14		
	d		19 18										19 48										20 18		
Bagshot	d		19 23										19 53										20 23		
Ascot 3	d	19a19	19a30								19 40		20a00								20 10		20a30		
Sunningdale	d										19 43										20 13				
Longcross	d										19 46										20 16				
Woking	d																								
West Byfleet	d																								
Byfleet & New Haw	d																								
Weybridge	d				19 07										19 37										20 03
Addlestone	d				19 11										19 41										20 07
Chertsey	d				19 14										19 44										20 10
Virginia Water	a				19 19						19 49				19 49						20 19				20 15
	d				19 24						19 49				19 54						20 19				20 24
Egham	d				19 27						19 53				19 57						20 23				20 27
Windsor & Eton Riverside	d					19 23										19 53									
Datchet	d					19 26										19 56									
Sunnymeads	d					19 29										19 59									
Wraysbury	d					19 32										20 02									
Staines	d				19 33	19 38					19 59				20 03	20 08					20 29				20 33
Ashford (Surrey)	d				19 36	19 41									20 06	20 11									20 36
Feltham	d				19 41	19 46					20 05				20 11	20 16					20 35				20 41
Whitton	d					19 50			19 50	19 53						20 20			20 20	20 23					
Kingston	d			19 29										19 59										20 29	
Hampton Wick	d			19 31										20 01										20 31	
Teddington	d			19 35										20 05										20 35	
Fulwell	d																								
Strawberry Hill	d			19 38										20 08										20 38	
Twickenham	a			19 42		19 53				19 56	20 10			20 12		20 23				20 26	20 40			20 42	
	d			19 43		19 53				19 58	20 11			20 13		20 23				20 28	20 41			20 43	
St Margarets	d			19 45						20 00				20 15						20 30				20 45	
Richmond ⊖	d			19 49		19 58				20 04	20 15			20 19		20 28				20 34	20 45			20 49	
North Sheen	d			19 51						20 06				20 21						20 36				20 51	
Mortlake	d			19 53						20 08				20 23						20 38				20 53	
Hounslow	d				19 46				20 01						20 16				20 31						20 46
Isleworth	d				19 49				20 04						20 19				20 34						20 49
Syon Lane	d				19 51				20 06						20 21				20 36						20 51
Brentford	d				19 54				20 09						20 24				20 39						20 54
Kew Bridge	d				19 56				20 11						20 26				20 41						20 56
Chiswick	d				19 59				20 14						20 29				20 44						20 59
Barnes Bridge	d				20 01				20 16			←			20 31				20 46			←			21 01
Barnes	d			19 56	20 04			←	20 19	20 11		20 19		20 26	20 34			←	20 49	20 41		20 49		20 56	21 04
Putney	d			19 59	20 07	20 04		20 07	→	20 14		20 22		20 29	20 37	20 34		20 37	→	20 44		20 52		20 59	21 07
Wandsworth Town	d			20 02	→			20 10		20 17		20 25		20 32	→			20 40		20 47		20 55		21 02	→
Clapham Junction 10	d			20 05		20 09		20 13		20 20	20 24	20 28		20 35		20 39		20 43		20 50	20 54	20 58		21 05	
Queenstown Rd.(Battersea)	d			20 08				20 16		20 23		20 31		20 38				20 46		20 53		21 01		21 08	
Vauxhall ⊖	d			20 12		20 15		20 20		20 27		20 35		20 42		20 45		20 50		20 57		21 05		21 12	
London Waterloo 15 ⊖	a			20 16		20 19		20 26		20 32	20 34	20 41		20 46		20 49		20 56		21 02	21 04	21 11		21 16	

Reading, Guildford, Ascot, Weybridge, Windsor, Kingston, Richmond and Hounslow - London

until 30 September

Station		SW	SW	SW	SW	SW 1	SW	SW 1	SW 1	SW	SW	SW	SW	SW	SW	SW 1	SW	SW	SW	SW	SW	SW
Reading 7	d					20 12										20 42						
Earley	d					20 17										20 47						
Winnersh Triangle	d					20 19										20 49						
Winnersh	d					20 21										20 51						
Wokingham	d					20 26										20 56						
Bracknell	d					20 32										21 02						
Martins Heron	d					20 35										21 05						
Guildford	d							20 00	20 30													
Wanborough	d							20 06	20 36													
Ash 5	d							20 10	20 40													
Aldershot	a							20 17	20 47													
	d							20 30														
Ash Vale	d							20 34														
Frimley	d							20 40														
Camberley	a							20 44														
	d							20 48														
Bagshot	d							20 53														
Ascot 3	d					20 40		21a00								21 10						
Sunningdale	d					20 43										21 13						
Longcross	d					20 46																
Woking	d																					
West Byfleet	d																					
Byfleet & New Haw	d																					
Weybridge	d										20 33								21 03			
Addlestone	d										20 37								21 07			
Chertsey	d										20 40								21 10			
Virginia Water	a					20 49					20 45					21 19			21 15			
	d					20 49					20 54					21 19			21 24			
Egham	d					20 53					20 57					21 23			21 27			
Windsor & Eton Riverside	d	20 23										20 53								21 23		
Datchet	d	20 26										20 56								21 26		
Sunnymeads	d	20 29										20 59								21 29		
Wraysbury	d	20 32										21 02								21 32		
Staines	d	20 38				20 59					21 03	21 08				21 29			21 33	21 38		
Ashford (Surrey)	d	20 41									21 06	21 11							21 36	21 41		
Feltham	d	20 46				21 05					21 11	21 16				21 35			21 41	21 46		
Whitton	d	20 50		20 50	20 53							21 20		21 20	21 23					21 50		21 50
Kingston	d									20 59								21 29				
Hampton Wick	d									21 01								21 31				
Teddington	d									21 05								21 35				
Fulwell	d																					
Strawberry Hill	d									21 08								21 38				
Twickenham	a	20 53			20 56	21 10				21 12		21 23			21 26	21 40		21 42		21 53		
	d	20 53			20 58	21 11				21 13		21 23			21 28	21 41		21 43		21 53		
St Margarets	d				21 00					21 15					21 30			21 45				
Richmond ⊖	d	20 58			21 04	21 15				21 19		21 28			21 34	21 45		21 49		21 58		
North Sheen	d				21 06					21 21					21 36			21 51				
Mortlake	d				21 08					21 23					21 38			21 53				
Hounslow	d			21 01							21 16			21 31					21 46			22 01
Isleworth	d			21 04							21 19			21 34					21 49			22 04
Syon Lane	d			21 06							21 21			21 36					21 51			22 06
Brentford	d			21 09							21 24			21 39					21 54			22 09
Kew Bridge	d			21 11							21 26			21 41					21 56			22 11
Chiswick	d			21 14							21 29			21 44					21 59			22 14
Barnes Bridge	d			21 16			←				21 31			21 46			←		22 01			22 16
Barnes	d		←	21 19	21 11		21 19			21 26	21 34		←	21 49	21 41		21 49	21 56	22 04		←	22 19
Putney	d	21 04	21 07	→	21 14		21 22			21 29	21 37	21 34	21 37	→	21 44		21 52	21 59	22 07	22 04	22 07	→
Wandsworth Town	d		21 10		21 17		21 25			21 32	→		21 40		21 47		21 55	22 02	→		22 10	
Clapham Junction 10	d	21 09	21 13		21 20	21 24	21 28			21 35		21 39	21 43		21 50	21 54	21 58	22 05		22 09	22 13	
Queenstown Rd.(Battersea)	d		21 16		21 23		21 31			21 38			21 46		21 53		22 01	22 08			22 16	
Vauxhall ⊖	d	21 15	21 20		21 27		21 35			21 42		21 45	21 50		21 57		22 05	22 12		22 15	22 20	
London Waterloo 15 ⊖	a	21 19	21 26		21 32	21 34	21 41			21 46		21 49	21 56		22 02	22 04	22 11	22 16		22 19	22 26	

Mondays to Fridays

until 30 September

Reading, Guildford, Ascot, Weybridge, Windsor, Kingston, Richmond and Hounslow - London

Station		SW	SW 1	SW	SW 1	SW 1	SW	SW	SW	SW	SW	SW 1	SW	SW	SW	SW	SW 1	SW 1	SW 1	SW	SW	SW	SW
Reading 7	d		21 12									21 42					22 12						
Earley	d		21 17									21 47					22 17						
Winnersh Triangle	d		21 19									21 49					22 19						
Winnersh	d		21 21									21 51					22 21						
Wokingham	d		21 26									21 56					22 26						
Bracknell	d		21 32									22 02					22 32						
Martins Heron	d		21 35									22 05					22 35						
Guildford	d				21 00	21 30												22 00	22 30				
Wanborough	d				21 06	21 36												22 06	22 36				
Ash 5	d				21 10	21 40												22 10	22 40				
Aldershot	a				21 17	21 47												22 17	22 47				
	d				21 30													22 30					
Ash Vale	d				21 34													22 34					
Frimley	d				21 40													22 40					
Camberley	a				21 44													22 44					
	d				21 48													22 48					
Bagshot	d				21 53													22 53					
Ascot 3	d		21 40		22a00							22 10					22 40	23a00					
Sunningdale	d		21 43									22 13					22 43						
Longcross	d																						
Woking	d																						
West Byfleet	d																						
Byfleet & New Haw	d																						
Weybridge	d							21 33						22 03							22 33		
Addlestone	d							21 37						22 07							22 37		
Chertsey	d							21 40						22 10							22 40		
Virginia Water	a		21 49					21 45				22 19		22 15			22 49				22 45		
	d		21 49					21 54				22 19		22 24			22 49				22 54		
Egham	d		21 53					21 57				22 23		22 27			22 53				22 57		
Windsor & Eton Riverside	d								21 53						22 23							22 53	
Datchet	d								21 56						22 26							22 56	
Sunnymeads	d								21 59						22 29							22 59	
Wraysbury	d								22 02						22 32							23 02	
Staines	d		21 59					22 03	22 08			22 29		22 33	22 38		22 59				23 03	23 08	
Ashford (Surrey)	d							22 06	22 11					22 36	22 41						23 06	23 11	
Feltham	d		22 05					22 11	22 16			22 35		22 41	22 46		23 05				23 11	23 16	
Whitton	d	21 53							22 20		22 23				22 50							23 20	
Kingston	d						21 59						22 29							22 59			
Hampton Wick	d						22 01						22 31							23 01			
Teddington	d						22 05						22 35							23 05			
Fulwell	d																						
Strawberry Hill	d						22 08						22 38							23 08			
Twickenham	a	21 56	22 10				22 12		22 23		22 26	22 40	22 42		22 53		23 10			23 12		23 23	
	d	21 58	22 11				22 13		22 23		22 28	22 41	22 43		22 53		23 11			23 13		23 23	
St Margarets	d	22 00					22 15				22 30		22 45							23 15			
Richmond ⊖	d	22 04	22 15				22 19		22 28		22 34	22 45	22 49		22 58		23 15			23 19		23 28	
North Sheen	d	22 06					22 21				22 36		22 51							23 21			
Mortlake	d	22 08					22 23				22 38		22 53							23 23			
Hounslow	d							22 16						22 46							23 16		
Isleworth	d							22 19						22 49							23 19		
Syon Lane	d							22 21						22 51							23 21		
Brentford	d							22 24						22 54							23 24		
Kew Bridge	d							22 26						22 56							23 26		
Chiswick	d							22 29						22 59							23 29		
Barnes Bridge	d			←				22 31						23 01							23 31		
Barnes	d	22 11		22 19			22 26	22 34		←	22 41		22 56	23 04		←				23 26	23 34		←
Putney	d	22 14		22 22			22 29	22 37	22 34	22 37	22 44		22 59	23 07	23 04	23 07				23 29	23 37	23 34	23 37
Wandsworth Town	d	22 17		22 25			22 32	→		22 40	22 47		23 02	→		23 10				23 32	→		23 40
Clapham Junction 10	d	22 20	22 24	22 28			22 35		22 39	22 43	22 50	22 54	23 05		23 09	23 13	23 24			23 35		23 39	23 43
Queenstown Rd.(Battersea)	d	22 23		22 31			22 38			22 46	22 53		23 08			23 16				23 38			23 46
Vauxhall ⊖	d	22 27		22 35			22 42		22 45	22 50	22 57		23 12		23 15	23 20				23 42		23 45	23 50
London Waterloo 15 ⊖	a	22 32	22 34	22 41			22 46		22 49	22 56	23 02	23 04	23 16		23 19	23 26	23 34			23 46		23 49	23 56

Table 149

Mondays to Fridays
until 30 September

Reading, Guildford, Ascot, Weybridge, Windsor, Kingston, Richmond and Hounslow - London

		SW	SW	SW	SW	SW	SW	SW	SW
		1				1	1	1	
Reading 7	d	22 42				23 12			
Earley	d	22 47				23 17			
Winnersh Triangle	d	22 49				23 19			
Winnersh	d	22 51				23 21			
Wokingham	d	22 56				23 26			
Bracknell	d	23 02				23 32			
Martins Heron	d	23 05				23 35			
Guildford	d						23 00	23 30	
Wanborough	d						23 06	23 36	
Ash 5	d						23 10	23 40	
Aldershot	a						23 17	23 47	
	d						23 30		
Ash Vale	d						23 34		
Frimley	d						23 40		
Camberley	a						23 44		
	d						23 48		
Bagshot	d						23 53		
Ascot 3	d	23 10				23 40	00a01		
Sunningdale	d	23 13				23 43			
Longcross	d								
Woking	d								
West Byfleet	d								
Byfleet & New Haw	d								
Weybridge	d		23 03						23 33
Addlestone	d		23 07						23 37
Chertsey	d		23 10						23 40
Virginia Water	a	23 19	23 15			23 49			23 45
	d	23 19	23 24			23 49			23 54
Egham	d	23 23	23 27			23 53			23 57
Windsor & Eton Riverside	d			23 28					
Datchet	d			23 31					
Sunnymeads	d			23 34					
Wraysbury	d			23 37					
Staines	d	23 29	23a32	23a42		23 59			00a02
Ashford (Surrey)	d								
Feltham	d	23 35				00 05			
Whitton	d								
Kingston	d				23 29				
Hampton Wick	d				23 31				
Teddington	d				23 35				
Fulwell	d								
Strawberry Hill	d				23 38				
Twickenham	a	23 40			23 42	00 10			
	d	23 41			23 43	00 11			
St Margarets	d				23 45				
Richmond ⊖	d	23 45			23 49	00 15			
North Sheen	d				23 51				
Mortlake	d				23 53				
Hounslow	d								
Isleworth	d								
Syon Lane	d								
Brentford	d								
Kew Bridge	d								
Chiswick	d								
Barnes Bridge	d								
Barnes	d				23 56				
Putney	d				23 59				
Wandsworth Town	d				00 02				
Clapham Junction 10	d	23 54			00 05	00 24			
Queenstown Rd.(Battersea)	d				00 08				
Vauxhall ⊖	d				00 12				
London Waterloo 15 ⊖	a	00 04			00 16	00 37			

Table 149

Mondays to Fridays
from 3 October

Reading, Guildford, Ascot, Weybridge, Windsor, Kingston, Richmond and Hounslow - London

		SW	SW	SW	SW	SW	SW	SW	SW	SW	SW	SW	SW	SW	SW	SW	SW	SW	SW	SW	SW	SW	SW
		MO	MO	MX	MX	MO	MX																
				1		1	1							◇	◇	◇	◇1	1				◇	
Reading 7	d			22p39		22p54	23p12										05 39						
Earley	d			22p44		22p59	23p17										05 44						
Winnersh Triangle	d			22p46		23p01	23p19										05 46						
Winnersh	d			22p48		23p03	23p21										05 48						
Wokingham	d			22p53		23p08	23p26										05 53						
Bracknell	d			22p59		23p14	23p32										05 59						
Martins Heron	d			23p02		23p17	23p35										06 02						
Guildford	d																						
Wanborough	d																						
Ash 5	d																						
Aldershot	a																						
	d																	05 58					
Ash Vale	d																	06 02					
Frimley	d																	06 10					
Camberley	a																	06 14					
	d																	06 18					
Bagshot	d																	06 23					
Ascot 3	d			23p07		23p22	23p40										06 07	06a30					
Sunningdale	d			23p10		23p25	23p43										06 10						
Longcross	d																						
Woking	d		22p52											05 27									
West Byfleet	d		22p56											05 32									
Byfleet & New Haw	d		23p00											05 35									
Weybridge	d																						
Addlestone	d		23p04											05 39									
Chertsey	d		23p07											05 42									
Virginia Water	a		23p12	23p19		23p30	23p49							05 47			06 19						
	d		23p12	23p19		23p30	23p49							05 54			06 19						
Egham	d		23p16	23p23		23p34	23p53							05 57			06 23						
Windsor & Eton Riverside	d	23p01													05 51							06 21	
Datchet	d	23p04													05 55							06 25	
Sunnymeads	d	23p07													05 58							06 28	
Wraysbury	d	23p10													06 02							06 32	
Staines	d	23p16	23p21	23p29		23p39	23p59	04 58			05 37			06 03	06 08		06 29				06 33	06 38	
Ashford (Surrey)	d	23p19	23p24					05 01			05 40			06 06	06 11						06 36	06 41	
Feltham	d	23p24	23p29	23p35		23p46	00 05	05 06			05 45			06 11	06 16		06 35				06 41	06 46	
Whitton	d	23p28						05 10			05 49				06 20				06 20			06 50	
Kingston	d				23p29								05 59							06 29			
Hampton Wick	d				23p31								06 01							06 31			
Teddington	d				23p35								06 05							06 35			
Fulwell	d									05 36													
Strawberry Hill	d				23p38					05 38			06 08							06 38			
Twickenham	a	23p31		23p40	23p42	23p51	00 10	05 13		05 42	05 52		06 12		06 23		06 40			06 42		06 53	
	d	23p32		23p41	23p43	23p51	00 11	05 13		05 43	05 53		06 13		06 23		06 41			06 43		06 53	
St Margarets	d	23p34			23p45			05 15		05 45			06 15							06 45			
Richmond ⊖	d	23p37		23p45	23p49	23p56	00 15	05 19		05 49	05 58		06 19		06 28		06 45			06 49		06 58	
North Sheen	d	23p39			23p51			05 21		05 51			06 21							06 51			
Mortlake	d	23p42			23p53			05 23		05 53			06 23							06 53			
Hounslow	d		23p35						05 31			06 01		06 16					06 31		06 46		
Isleworth	d		23p38						05 34			06 04		06 19					06 34		06 49		
Syon Lane	d		23p40						05 36			06 06		06 21					06 36		06 51		
Brentford	d		23p42						05 39			06 09		06 24					06 39		06 54		
Kew Bridge	d		23p45						05 41			06 11		06 26					06 41		06 56		
Chiswick	d		23p47						05 44			06 14		06 29					06 44		06 59		
Barnes Bridge	d		23p50						05 46			06 16		06 31					06 46		07 01		
Barnes	d	23p45	23p53		23p56			05 26	05 49	05 56		06 19	06 26	06 34		←			06 49	06 56	07 04		←
Putney	d	23p48	23p56		23p59	00 02		05 29	05 52	05 59	06 04	06 22	06 29	06 37	06 34	06 37	06 52		06 52	06 59	07 07	07 04	07 07
Wandsworth Town	d	23p51	23p59		00 02			05 32	05 55	06 02		06 25	06 32	→		06 40			06 55	07 02	→		07 10
Clapham Junction 10	d	23p54	00 02	23p54	00 05	00 07	00 24	05 35	05 58	06 05	06 09	06 28	06 35		06 39	06 43	06 56		06 58	07 05		07 09	07 13
Queenstown Rd.(Battersea)	d	23p57	00 05		00 08			05 38	06 01	06 08		06 31	06 38			06 46			07 01	07 08			07 16
Vauxhall ⊖	d		00 08		00 12	00 12		05 42	06 05	06 12	06 15	06 35	06 42		06 45	06 50			07 05	07 12		07 15	07 20
London Waterloo 15 ⊖	a	00 04	00 13	00 04	00 16	00 17	00 37	05 46	06 09	06 16	06 19	06 39	06 46		06 49	06 56	07 07		07 11	07 18		07 21	07 28

Reading, Guildford, Ascot, Weybridge, Windsor, Kingston, Richmond and Hounslow - London

		SW	SW	SW	SW	SW	SW	SW	SW	SW	SW	SW	SW	SW	SW	SW	SW	SW	SW	SW	SW	SW	SW
				◇1			◇	◇	◇			◇1	1	◇1		◇	◇	◇			◇1	1	◇1
Reading 7	d			06 12										06 39									07 09
Earley	d			06 17										06 44									07 14
Winnersh Triangle	d			06 19										06 46									07 16
Winnersh	d			06 21										06 48									07 18
Wokingham	d			06 26										06 53									07 23
Bracknell	d			06 32										06 59									07 29
Martins Heron	d			06 35										07 02									07 32
Guildford	d												06 30									07 00	
Wanborough	d												06 36									07 06	
Ash 5	d												06 40									07 10	
Aldershot	a												06 47									07 17	
	d											06 28									06 59		
Ash Vale	d											06 32									07 03		
Frimley	d											06 39									07 09		
Camberley	a											06 43									07 13		
	d											06 44									07 14		
Bagshot	d											06 49									07 19		
Ascot 3	d			06 40								06 56		07 07							07 26		07 37
Sunningdale	d			06 43								06 59		07 10							07 29		07 40
Longcross	d																						
Woking	d																						
West Byfleet	d																						
Byfleet & New Haw	d																						
Weybridge	d						06 33									07 03							
Addlestone	d						06 37									07 07							
Chertsey	d						06 40									07 10							
Virginia Water	a			06 49			06 45					07 08		07 19		07 15					07 38		
	d			06 49			06 54					07 08		07 19		07 24					07 38		
Egham	d			06 53			06 57					07 12		07 23		07 27					07 42		07 50
Windsor & Eton Riverside	d							06 51									07 21						
Datchet	d							06 55									07 25						
Sunnymeads	d							06 58									07 28						
Wraysbury	d							07 02									07 32						
Staines	d			06 59			07 03	07 08				07 18		07 29		07 33	07 38				07 48		07 56
Ashford (Surrey)	d						07 06	07 11				07 21				07 36	07 41				07 51		
Feltham	d			07 05			07 11	07 16				07 26		07 35		07 41	07 46				07 56		08 02
Whitton	d	06 50	06 53					07 20			07 20	07 30					07 50			07 50	08 00		
Kingston	d					06 59									07 29								
Hampton Wick	d					07 01									07 31								
Teddington	d					07 05									07 35								
Fulwell	d									07 12									07 42				
Strawberry Hill	d					07 08				07 14					07 38				07 44				
Twickenham	a		06 56	07 10		07 12		07 23		07 18		07 33		07 40	07 42		07 53		07 48		08 03		08 09
	d		06 58	07 11		07 13		07 23		07 27		07 33		07 41	07 43		07 53		07 57		08 03		08 09
St Margarets	d		07 00			07 15				07 29					07 45				07 59				
Richmond ⊖	d		07 04	07 15		07 19		07 28		07 32		07 38		07 45	07 49		07 58		08 02		08 08		08 14
North Sheen	d		07 06			07 21				07 34					07 51				08 04				
Mortlake	d		07 08			07 23				07 37					07 53				08 07				
Hounslow	d	07 01					07 16				07 31					07 46				08 01			
Isleworth	d	07 04					07 19				07 34					07 49				08 04			
Syon Lane	d	07 06					07 21				07 36					07 51				08 06			
Brentford	d	07 09					07 24				07 39					07 54				08 09			
Kew Bridge	d	07 11					07 26				07 41					07 56				08 11			
Chiswick	d	07 14					07 29				07 44					07 59				08 14			
Barnes Bridge	d	07 16			←		07 31				07 46					08 01				08 16			
Barnes	d	07 19	07 11		07 19	07 26	07 34		←	07 40	07 49				07 56	08 04		←	08 10	08 19			
Putney	d	→	07 14	07 22	07 22	07 29	07 37	07 34	07 37	07 43	07 52				07 59	08 07	08 04	08 07	08 13	08 22			
Wandsworth Town	d		07 17		07 25	07 32	→		07 40	07 46	07 55				08 02	→		08 10	08 16	08 25			
Clapham Junction 10	d		07 20	07 26	07 28	07 35		07 39	07 43	07 49	07 58	07 47		07 54	08 05		08 09	08 13	08 19	08 28	08 17		08 22
Queenstown Rd.(Battersea)	d		07 23		07 31	07 38			07 46	07 52	08 01				08 08			08 16	08 22	08 31			
Vauxhall ⊖	d		07 27		07 35	07 42		07 45	07 50	07 56	08 05	07 53			08 12		08 15	08 20	08 26	08 35	08 23		
London Waterloo 15 ⊖	a		07 34	07 37	07 43	07 48		07 51	07 58	08 04	08 11	07 59		08 06	08 18		08 21	08 28	08 34	08 43	08 29		08 38

Reading, Guildford, Ascot, Weybridge, Windsor, Kingston, Richmond and Hounslow - London

		SW	SW	SW	SW	SW	SW	SW	SW	SW	SW	SW	SW	SW	SW	SW	SW	SW	SW	SW	SW	SW
			◇	◇1	◇	◇			◇1	◇1	1		◇	◇	◇			◇1		1		◇
Reading 7	d			07 24						07 39								08 09				
Earley	d									07 44								08 14				
Winnersh Triangle	d									07 46								08 16				
Winnersh	d									07 48								08 18				
Wokingham	d			07 33						07 53								08 23				
Bracknell	d			07 39						07 59								08 29				
Martins Heron	d			07 42						08 02								08 32				
Guildford	d										07 30									08 00		
Wanborough	d										07 36									08 06		
Ash 5	d										07 40									08 10		
Aldershot	a										07 47									08 17		
	d								07 29		08 00									08 30		
Ash Vale	d								07 33		08 04									08 34		
Frimley	d								07 39		08 10									08 40		
Camberley	a								07 43		08 14									08 44		
	d								07 44		08 18									08 48		
Bagshot	d								07 49		08 23									08 53		
Ascot 3	d			07 47					07 56	08 07	08a30							08 37		09a00		
Sunningdale	d			07 50					07 59	08 10								08 40				
Longcross	d									08 13								08 43				
Woking	d																					
West Byfleet	d																					
Byfleet & New Haw	d																					
Weybridge	d		07 33										08 03									08 33
Addlestone	d		07 37										08 07									08 37
Chertsey	d		07 40										08 10									08 40
Virginia Water	a		07 45	07 55					08 08	08 19			08 15					08 49				08 45
	d		07 51	07 55					08 08	08 19			08 24					08 49				08 54
Egham	d		07 54	07 58					08 12	08 23			08 27					08 53				08 57
Windsor & Eton Riverside	d				07 51									08 21								
Datchet	d				07 55									08 25								
Sunnymeads	d				07 58									08 28								
Wraysbury	d				08 02									08 32								
Staines	d		08 00	08 04	08 08				08 18	08 29			08 33	08 38				08 59				09 03
Ashford (Surrey)	d		08 03		08 11				08 21				08 36	08 41								09 06
Feltham	d		08 08	08 12	08 16				08 26	08 35			08 41	08 46				09 05				09 11
Whitton	d				08 20			08 20	08 30					08 50		08 50	08 53					
Kingston	d	07 59										08 29									08 59	
Hampton Wick	d	08 01										08 31									09 01	
Teddington	d	08 05										08 35									09 05	
Fulwell	d						08 12															
Strawberry Hill	d	08 08					08 14					08 38									09 08	
Twickenham	a	08 12		08 17	08 23		08 18		08 33	08 40		08 42		08 53			08 56	09 10			09 12	
	d	08 13		08 18	08 23		08 27		08 33	08 41		08 43		08 53			08 58	09 11			09 13	
St Margarets	d	08 15					08 29					08 45					09 00				09 15	
Richmond ⊖	d	08 19		08 24	08 28		08 32		08 38	08 45		08 49		08 58			09 04	09 15			09 19	
North Sheen	d	08 21					08 34					08 51					09 06				09 21	
Mortlake	d	08 23					08 37					08 53					09 08				09 23	
Hounslow	d		08 16					08 31					08 46			09 01						09 16
Isleworth	d		08 19					08 34					08 49			09 04						09 19
Syon Lane	d		08 21					08 36					08 51			09 06						09 21
Brentford	d		08 24					08 39					08 54			09 09						09 24
Kew Bridge	d		08 26					08 41					08 56			09 11						09 26
Chiswick	d		08 29					08 44					08 59			09 14						09 29
Barnes Bridge	d		08 31					08 46					09 01			09 16			←			09 31
Barnes	d	08 26	08 34			←	08 40	08 49				08 56	09 04		←	09 19	09 11		09 19		09 26	09 34
Putney	d	08 29	08 37		08 34	08 37	08 43	08 52				08 59	09 07	09 04	09 07	→	09 14		09 22		09 29	09 37
Wandsworth Town	d	08 32	→			08 40	08 46	08 55				09 02	→		09 10		09 17		09 25		09 32	→
Clapham Junction 10	d	08 35		08 33	08 39	08 43	08 49	08 58	08 47	08 54		09 05		09 09	09 13		09 20	09 24	09 28		09 35	
Queenstown Rd.(Battersea)	d	08 38				08 46	08 52	09 01				09 08			09 16		09 23		09 31		09 38	
Vauxhall ⊖	d	08 42		08 38	08 45	08 50	08 56	09 05	08 53			09 12		09 15	09 20		09 27		09 35		09 42	
London Waterloo 15 ⊖	a	08 49		08 46	08 51	08 58	09 04	09 13	09 00	09 06		09 18		09 21	09 28		09 34	09 34	09 43		09 48	

Table 149

Mondays to Fridays
from 3 October

Reading, Guildford, Ascot, Weybridge, Windsor, Kingston, Richmond and Hounslow - London

		SW ◇	SW ◇	SW	SW	SW 1	SW	SW 1	SW	SW	SW	SW	SW	SW	SW 1	SW	SW	SW	SW	SW 1	SW	SW 1	SW
Reading 7	d					08 39									09 09					09 22			
Earley	d					08 44									09 14					09 27			
Winnersh Triangle	d					08 46									09 16					09 29			
Winnersh	d					08 48									09 18					09 31			
Wokingham	d					08 53									09 23					09 36			
Bracknell	d					08 59									09 29					09 43			
Martins Heron	d					09 02									09 32					09 46			
Guildford	d							08 30														09 00	
Wanborough	d							08 36														09 06	
Ash 5	d							08 40														09 10	
Aldershot	a							08 47														09 17	
	d							09 00														09 30	
Ash Vale	d							09 04														09 34	
Frimley	d							09 10														09 40	
Camberley	a							09 14														09 44	
	d							09 18														09 48	
Bagshot	d							09 23														09 53	
Ascot 3	d					09 07		09a30							09 37					09 52		10a00	
Sunningdale	d					09 10									09 40					09 55			
Longcross	d					09 13																	
Woking	d																						
West Byfleet	d																						
Byfleet & New Haw	d																						
Weybridge	d									09 03								09 33					
Addlestone	d									09 07								09 37					
Chertsey	d									09 10								09 40					
Virginia Water	a					09 19				09 15					09 49			09 45		10 03			
	d					09 19				09 24					09 49			09 54		10 03			
Egham	d					09 23				09 27					09 53			09 57		10 06			
Windsor & Eton Riverside	d	08 51									09 21								09 51				
Datchet	d	08 55									09 25								09 55				
Sunnymeads	d	08 58									09 28								09 58				
Wraysbury	d	09 02									09 32								10 02				
Staines	d	09 08				09 29				09 33	09 38				09 59			10 03	10 08	10 14			
Ashford (Surrey)	d	09 11								09 36	09 41							10 06	10 11				
Feltham	d	09 16				09 35				09 41	09 46				10 05			10 11	10 16	10 20			
Whitton	d	09 20		09 20	09 23						09 50		09 50	09 53					10 20				10 20
Kingston	d								09 29								09 59						
Hampton Wick	d								09 31								10 01						
Teddington	d								09 35								10 05						
Fulwell	d																						
Strawberry Hill	d								09 38								10 08						
Twickenham	a	09 23			09 26	09 40			09 42		09 53			09 56	10 10		10 12		10 23	10 27			
	d	09 23			09 28	09 41			09 43		09 53			09 58	10 11		10 13		10 23	10 27			
St Margarets	d				09 30				09 45					10 00			10 15						
Richmond ⊖	d	09 28			09 34	09 45			09 49		09 58			10 04	10 15		10 19		10 28	10 32			
North Sheen	d				09 36				09 51					10 06			10 21						
Mortlake	d				09 38				09 53					10 08			10 23						
Hounslow	d			09 31						09 46			10 01					10 16					10 31
Isleworth	d			09 34						09 49			10 04					10 19					10 34
Syon Lane	d			09 36						09 51			10 06					10 21					10 36
Brentford	d			09 39						09 54			10 09					10 24					10 39
Kew Bridge	d			09 41						09 56			10 11					10 26					10 41
Chiswick	d			09 44						09 59			10 14					10 29					10 44
Barnes Bridge	d			09 46			←			10 01			10 16			←		10 31					10 46
Barnes	d		←	09 49	09 41		09 49		09 56	10 04		←	10 19	10 11		10 19	10 26	10 34			←		10 49
Putney	d	09 34	09 37	→	09 44		09 52		09 59	10 07	10 04	10 07	→	10 14		10 22	10 29	10 37	10 34		10 37		→
Wandsworth Town	d		09 40		09 47		09 55		10 02	→		10 10		10 17		10 25	10 32	→			10 40		
Clapham Junction 10	d	09 39	09 43		09 50	09 54	09 58		10 05		10 09	10 13		10 20	10 24	10 28	10 35		10 39	10 42	10 43		
Queenstown Rd.(Battersea)	d		09 46		09 53		10 01		10 08			10 16		10 23		10 31	10 38				10 47		
Vauxhall ⊖	d	09 45	09 50		09 57		10 05		10 12		10 15	10 20		10 27		10 35	10 42		10 45		10 50		
London Waterloo 15 ⊖	a	09 51	09 58		10 02	10 04	10 11		10 16		10 19	10 26		10 32	10 34	10 41	10 46		10 49	10 53	10 56		

Table 149

Mondays to Fridays
from 3 October

Reading, Guildford, Ascot, Weybridge, Windsor, Kingston, Richmond and Hounslow - London

		SW	SW 1	SW	SW	SW	SW	SW 1	SW	SW 1	SW	SW	SW 1	SW	SW 1	SW	SW	SW	SW	SW	SW	SW 1
Reading 7	d		09 39					09 53					10 09									10 39
Earley	d		09 44					09 58					10 14									10 44
Winnersh Triangle	d		09 46					10 00					10 16									10 46
Winnersh	d		09 48					10 02					10 18									10 48
Wokingham	d		09 53					10 07					10 23									10 53
Bracknell	d		09 59					10 13					10 29									10 59
Martins Heron	d		10 02					10 16					10 32									11 02
Guildford	d									09 30					10 00							
Wanborough	d									09 36					10 06							
Ash 5	d									09 40					10 10							
Aldershot	a									09 47					10 17							
	d									10 00					10 30							
Ash Vale	d									10 04					10 34							
Frimley	d									10 10					10 40							
Camberley	a									10 14					10 44							
	d									10 18					10 48							
Bagshot	d									10 23					10 53							
Ascot 3	d		10 07					10 22		10a30			10 37		11a00							11 07
Sunningdale	d		10 10					10 25					10 40									11 10
Longcross	d																					
Woking	d																					
West Byfleet	d																					
Byfleet & New Haw	d																					
Weybridge	d					10 03											10 33					
Addlestone	d					10 07											10 37					
Chertsey	d					10 10											10 40					
Virginia Water	a		10 19			10 15		10 33					10 49				10 45					11 19
	d		10 19			10 24		10 33					10 49				10 54					11 19
Egham	d		10 23			10 27		10 36					10 53				10 57					11 23
Windsor & Eton Riverside	d						10 21											10 51				
Datchet	d						10 25											10 55				
Sunnymeads	d						10 28											10 58				
Wraysbury	d						10 32											11 02				
Staines	d		10 29			10 33	10 38	10 44					10 59				11 03	11 08				11 29
Ashford (Surrey)	d					10 36	10 41										11 06	11 11				
Feltham	d		10 35			10 41	10 46	10 50					11 05				11 11	11 16				11 35
Whitton	d	10 26					10 50				10 50	10 56						11 20		11 20	11 23	
Kingston	d				10 29											10 59						
Hampton Wick	d				10 31											11 01						
Teddington	d				10 35											11 05						
Fulwell	d																					
Strawberry Hill	d				10 38											11 08						
Twickenham	a	10 28	10 40		10 42		10 53	10 57				10 58	11 10			11 12		11 23			11 26	11 40
	d	10 28	10 41		10 43		10 53	10 57				10 58	11 11			11 13		11 23			11 28	11 41
St Margarets	d	10 30			10 45							11 00				11 15					11 30	
Richmond ⊖	d	10 34	10 45		10 49		10 58	11 02				11 04	11 15			11 19		11 28			11 34	11 45
North Sheen	d	10 36			10 51							11 06				11 21					11 36	
Mortlake	d	10 38			10 53							11 08				11 23					11 38	
Hounslow	d					10 46					11 01						11 16			11 31		
Isleworth	d					10 49					11 04						11 19			11 34		
Syon Lane	d					10 51					11 06						11 21			11 36		
Brentford	d					10 54					11 09						11 24			11 39		
Kew Bridge	d					10 56					11 11						11 26			11 41		
Chiswick	d					10 59					11 14						11 29			11 44		
Barnes Bridge	d			←		11 01					11 16			←			11 31			11 46		
Barnes	d	10 41		10 49	10 56	11 04			←		11 19	11 11		11 19		11 26	11 34		←	11 49	11 41	
Putney	d	10 44		10 52	10 59	11 07	11 04		11 07		→	11 14		11 22		11 29	11 37	11 34	11 37	→	11 44	
Wandsworth Town	d	10 47		10 55	11 02	→			11 10			11 17		11 25		11 32	→		11 40		11 47	
Clapham Junction 10	d	10 50	10 54	10 58	11 05		11 09	11 12	11 13			11 20	11 24	11 28		11 35		11 39	11 43		11 50	11 54
Queenstown Rd.(Battersea)	d	10 53		11 01	11 08				11 17			11 23		11 31		11 38			11 46		11 53	
Vauxhall ⊖	d	10 57		11 05	11 12		11 15		11 20			11 27		11 35		11 42		11 45	11 50		11 57	
London Waterloo 15 ⊖	a	11 02	11 04	11 11	11 16		11 19	11 25	11 27			11 32	11 34	11 41		11 46		11 49	11 56		12 02	12 04

Reading, Guildford, Ascot, Weybridge, Windsor, Kingston, Richmond and Hounslow - London

		SW	SW 1	SW	SW	SW	SW	SW	SW	SW 1		SW	SW 1	SW	SW	SW	SW	SW	SW	SW 1		SW	SW 1	SW	SW
Reading 7	d									11 09										11 39					
Earley	d									11 14										11 44					
Winnersh Triangle	d									11 16										11 46					
Winnersh	d									11 18										11 48					
Wokingham	d									11 23										11 53					
Bracknell	d									11 29										11 59					
Martins Heron	d									11 32										12 02					
Guildford	d		10 30										11 00										11 30		
Wanborough	d		10 36										11 06										11 36		
Ash 5	d		10 40										11 10										11 40		
Aldershot	a		10 47										11 17										11 47		
	d		11 00										11 30										12 00		
Ash Vale	d		11 04										11 34										12 04		
Frimley	d		11 10										11 40										12 10		
Camberley	a		11 14										11 44										12 14		
	d		11 18										11 48										12 18		
Bagshot	d		11 23										11 53										12 23		
Ascot 3	d		11a30							11 37			12a00							12 07			12a30		
Sunningdale	d									11 40										12 10					
Longcross	d																								
Woking	d																								
West Byfleet	d																								
Byfleet & New Haw	d																								
Weybridge	d				11 03										11 33										12 03
Addlestone	d				11 07										11 37										12 07
Chertsey	d				11 10										11 40										12 10
Virginia Water	a				11 15					11 49					11 45					12 19					12 15
	d				11 24					11 49					11 54					12 19					12 24
Egham	d				11 27					11 53					11 57					12 23					12 27
Windsor & Eton Riverside	d					11 21										11 51									
Datchet	d					11 25										11 55									
Sunnymeads	d					11 28										11 58									
Wraysbury	d					11 32										12 02									
Staines	d				11 33	11 38				11 59					12 03	12 08				12 29					12 33
Ashford (Surrey)	d				11 36	11 41									12 06	12 11									12 36
Feltham	d				11 41	11 46				12 05					12 11	12 16				12 35					12 41
Whitton	d					11 50		11 50	11 53							12 20		12 20	12 23						
Kingston	d			11 29										11 59										12 29	
Hampton Wick	d			11 31										12 01										12 31	
Teddington	d			11 35										12 05										12 35	
Fulwell	d																								
Strawberry Hill	d			11 38										12 08										12 38	
Twickenham	a			11 42		11 53			11 56	12 10				12 12		12 23			12 26	12 40				12 42	
	d			11 43		11 53			11 58	12 11				12 13		12 23			12 28	12 41				12 43	
St Margarets	d			11 45					12 00					12 15					12 30					12 45	
Richmond ⊖	d			11 49		11 58			12 04	12 15				12 19		12 28			12 34	12 45				12 49	
North Sheen	d			11 51					12 06					12 21					12 36					12 51	
Mortlake	d			11 53					12 08					12 23					12 38					12 53	
Hounslow	d				11 46			12 01							12 16			12 31							12 46
Isleworth	d				11 49			12 04							12 19			12 34							12 49
Syon Lane	d				11 51			12 06							12 21			12 36							12 51
Brentford	d				11 54			12 09							12 24			12 39							12 54
Kew Bridge	d				11 56			12 11							12 26			12 41							12 56
Chiswick	d				11 59			12 14							12 29			12 44							12 59
Barnes Bridge	d	←			12 01			12 16				←			12 31			12 46				←			13 01
Barnes	d	11 49		11 56	12 04		←	12 19	12 11			12 19		12 26	12 34		←	12 49	12 41			12 49		12 56	13 04
Putney	d	11 52		11 59	12 07	12 04	12 07	→	12 14			12 22		12 29	12 37	12 34	12 37	→	12 44			12 52		12 59	13 07
Wandsworth Town	d	11 55		12 02	→		12 10		12 17			12 25		12 32	→		12 40		12 47			12 55		13 02	→
Clapham Junction 10	d	11 58		12 05		12 09	12 13		12 20	12 25		12 28		12 35		12 39	12 43		12 50	12 54		12 58		13 05	
Queenstown Rd.(Battersea)	d	12 01		12 08			12 16		12 23			12 31		12 38			12 46		12 53			13 01		13 08	
Vauxhall ⊖	d	12 05		12 12		12 15	12 20		12 27			12 35		12 42		12 45	12 50		12 57			13 05		13 12	
London Waterloo 15 ⊖	a	12 11		12 16		12 19	12 26		12 32	12 34		12 41		12 46		12 49	12 56		13 02	13 04		13 11		13 16	

Reading, Guildford, Ascot, Weybridge, Windsor, Kingston, Richmond and Hounslow - London

		SW	SW	SW	SW	SW 1		SW	SW 1	SW	SW	SW	SW	SW	SW	SW 1		SW	SW 1	SW	SW	SW	SW	SW	SW
Reading 7	d					12 09										12 39									
Earley	d					12 14										12 44									
Winnersh Triangle	d					12 16										12 46									
Winnersh	d					12 18										12 48									
Wokingham	d					12 23										12 53									
Bracknell	d					12 29										12 59									
Martins Heron	d					12 32										13 02									
Guildford	d								12 00										12 30						
Wanborough	d								12 06										12 36						
Ash 5	d								12 10										12 40						
Aldershot	a								12 17										12 47						
	d								12 30										13 00						
Ash Vale	d								12 34										13 04						
Frimley	d								12 40										13 10						
Camberley	a								12 44										13 14						
	d								12 48										13 18						
Bagshot	d								12 53										13 23						
Ascot 3	d					12 37			13a00							13 07			13a30						
Sunningdale	d					12 40										13 10									
Longcross	d															13 13									
Woking	d																								
West Byfleet	d																								
Byfleet & New Haw	d																								
Weybridge	d										12 33										13 03				
Addlestone	d										12 37										13 07				
Chertsey	d										12 40										13 10				
Virginia Water	a					12 49					12 45					13 19					13 15				
	d					12 49					12 54					13 19					13 24				
Egham	d					12 53					12 57					13 23					13 27				
Windsor & Eton Riverside	d	12 21										12 51										13 21			
Datchet	d	12 25										12 55										13 25			
Sunnymeads	d	12 28										12 58										13 28			
Wraysbury	d	12 32										13 02										13 32			
Staines	d	12 38				12 59					13 03	13 08				13 29					13 33	13 38			
Ashford (Surrey)	d	12 41									13 06	13 11									13 36	13 41			
Feltham	d	12 46				13 05					13 11	13 16				13 35					13 41	13 46			
Whitton	d	12 50		12 50	12 53							13 20		13 20	13 23							13 50		13 50	13 53
Kingston	d									12 59										13 29					
Hampton Wick	d									13 01										13 31					
Teddington	d									13 05										13 35					
Fulwell	d																								
Strawberry Hill	d									13 08										13 38					
Twickenham	a	12 53			12 56	13 10				13 12		13 23			13 26	13 40				13 42		13 53			13 56
	d	12 53			12 58	13 11				13 13		13 23			13 28	13 41				13 43		13 53			13 58
St Margarets	d				13 00					13 15					13 30					13 45					14 00
Richmond ⊖	d	12 58			13 04	13 15				13 19		13 28			13 34	13 45				13 49		13 58			14 04
North Sheen	d				13 06					13 21					13 36					13 51					14 06
Mortlake	d				13 08					13 23					13 38					13 53					14 08
Hounslow	d			13 01							13 16			13 31							13 46			14 01	
Isleworth	d			13 04							13 19			13 34							13 49			14 04	
Syon Lane	d			13 06							13 21			13 36							13 51			14 06	
Brentford	d			13 09							13 24			13 39							13 54			14 09	
Kew Bridge	d			13 11							13 26			13 41							13 56			14 11	
Chiswick	d			13 14							13 29			13 44							13 59			14 14	
Barnes Bridge	d			13 16				←			13 31			13 46				←			14 01			14 16	
Barnes	d		←	13 19	13 11			13 19		13 26	13 34		←	13 49	13 41			13 49		13 56	14 04		←	14 19	14 11
Putney	d	13 04	13 07	→	13 14			13 22		13 29	13 37	13 34	13 37	→	13 44			13 52		13 59	14 07	14 04	14 07	→	14 14
Wandsworth Town	d		13 10		13 17			13 25		13 32	→		13 40		13 47			13 55		14 02	→		14 10		14 17
Clapham Junction 10	d	13 09	13 13		13 20	13 24		13 28		13 35		13 39	13 43		13 50	13 54		13 58		14 05		14 09	14 13		14 20
Queenstown Rd.(Battersea)	d		13 16		13 23			13 31		13 38			13 46		13 53			14 01		14 08			14 16		14 23
Vauxhall ⊖	d	13 15	13 20		13 27			13 35		13 42		13 45	13 50		13 57			14 05		14 12		14 15	14 20		14 27
London Waterloo 15 ⊖	a	13 19	13 26		13 32	13 34		13 41		13 46		13 49	13 56		14 02	14 04		14 11		14 16		14 19	14 26		14 32

Table 149

Mondays to Fridays from 3 October

Reading, Guildford, Ascot, Weybridge, Windsor, Kingston, Richmond and Hounslow - London

Station		SW ■1	SW	SW ■1	SW	SW	SW	SW	SW	SW	SW ■1	SW	SW ■1	SW	SW	SW	SW	SW	SW	SW ■1	SW	SW ■1
Reading ■7	d	13 09									13 39									14 09		
Earley	d	13 14									13 44									14 14		
Winnersh Triangle	d	13 16									13 46									14 16		
Winnersh	d	13 18									13 48									14 18		
Wokingham	d	13 23									13 53									14 23		
Bracknell	d	13 29									13 59									14 29		
Martins Heron	d	13 32									14 02									14 32		
Guildford	d			13 00									13 30									14 00
Wanborough	d			13 06									13 36									14 06
Ash ■5	d			13 10									13 40									14 10
Aldershot	a			13 17									13 47									14 17
	d			13 30									14 00									14 30
Ash Vale	d			13 34									14 04									14 34
Frimley	d			13 40									14 10									14 40
Camberley	a			13 44									14 14									14 44
	d			13 48									14 18									14 48
Bagshot	d			13 53									14 23									14 53
Ascot ■3	d	13 37		14a00							14 07		14a30							14 37		15a00
Sunningdale	d	13 40									14 10									14 40		
Longcross	d																					
Woking	d																					
West Byfleet	d																					
Byfleet & New Haw	d																					
Weybridge	d					13 33									14 03							
Addlestone	d					13 37									14 07							
Chertsey	d					13 40									14 10							
Virginia Water	a	13 49				13 45					14 19				14 15					14 49		
	d	13 49				13 54					14 19				14 24					14 49		
Egham	d	13 53				13 57					14 23				14 27					14 53		
Windsor & Eton Riverside	d						13 51									14 21						
Datchet	d						13 55									14 25						
Sunnymeads	d						13 58									14 28						
Wraysbury	d						14 02									14 32						
Staines	d	13 59				14 03	14 08				14 29				14 33	14 38				14 59		
Ashford (Surrey)	d					14 06	14 11								14 36	14 41						
Feltham	d	14 05				14 11	14 16				14 35				14 41	14 46				15 05		
Whitton	d						14 20		14 20	14 23						14 50		14 50	14 53			
Kingston	d				13 59									14 29								
Hampton Wick	d				14 01									14 31								
Teddington	d				14 05									14 35								
Fulwell	d																					
Strawberry Hill	d				14 08									14 38								
Twickenham	a	14 10			14 12		14 23			14 26	14 40			14 42		14 53			14 56	15 10		
	d	14 11			14 13		14 23			14 28	14 41			14 43		14 53			14 58	15 11		
St Margarets	d				14 15					14 30				14 45					15 00			
Richmond ⊖	d	14 15			14 19		14 28			14 34	14 45			14 49		14 58			15 04	15 15		
North Sheen	d				14 21					14 36				14 51					15 06			
Mortlake	d				14 23					14 38				14 53					15 08			
Hounslow	d					14 16			14 31						14 46			15 01				
Isleworth	d					14 19			14 34						14 49			15 04				
Syon Lane	d					14 21			14 36						14 51			15 06				
Brentford	d					14 24			14 39						14 54			15 09				
Kew Bridge	d					14 26			14 41						14 56			15 11				
Chiswick	d					14 29			14 44						14 59			15 14				
Barnes Bridge	d		←			14 31			14 46			←			15 01			15 16			←	
Barnes	d		14 19		14 26	14 34		←	14 49	14 41		14 49		14 56	15 04		←	15 19	15 11		15 19	
Putney	d		14 22		14 29	14 37	14 34	14 37	→	14 44		14 52		14 59	15 07	15 04	15 07	→	15 14		15 22	
Wandsworth Town	d		14 25		14 32	→		14 40		14 47		14 55		15 02	→		15 10		15 17		15 25	
Clapham Junction ■10	d	14 24	14 28		14 35		14 39	14 43		14 50	14 54	14 58		15 05		15 09	15 13		15 20	15 24	15 28	
Queenstown Rd.(Battersea)	d		14 31		14 38			14 46		14 53		15 01		15 08			15 16		15 23		15 31	
Vauxhall ⊖	d		14 35		14 42		14 45	14 50		14 57		15 05		15 12		15 15	15 20		15 27		15 35	
London Waterloo ■15 ⊖	a	14 34	14 41		14 46		14 49	14 56		15 02	15 04	15 11		15 16		15 19	15 26		15 32	15 34	15 41	

Table 149

Mondays to Fridays from 3 October

Reading, Guildford, Ascot, Weybridge, Windsor, Kingston, Richmond and Hounslow - London

Station		SW	SW	SW	SW	SW	SW	SW ■1	SW	SW ■1	SW	SW	SW	SW	SW	SW	SW ■1	SW	SW ■1	SW	SW	SW	SW
Reading ■7	d							14 39									15 09						
Earley	d							14 44									15 14						
Winnersh Triangle	d							14 46									15 16						
Winnersh	d							14 48									15 18						
Wokingham	d							14 53									15 23						
Bracknell	d							14 59									15 29						
Martins Heron	d							15 02									15 32						
Guildford	d									14 30									15 00				
Wanborough	d									14 36									15 06				
Ash ■5	d									14 40									15 10				
Aldershot	a									14 47									15 17				
	d									15 00									15 30				
Ash Vale	d									15 04									15 34				
Frimley	d									15 10									15 40				
Camberley	a									15 14									15 44				
	d									15 18									15 48				
Bagshot	d									15 23									15 53				
Ascot ■3	d							15 07		15a30							15 37		16a00				
Sunningdale	d							15 10									15 40						
Longcross	d																						
Woking	d																						
West Byfleet	d																						
Byfleet & New Haw	d																						
Weybridge	d		14 33									15 03									15 33		
Addlestone	d		14 37									15 07									15 37		
Chertsey	d		14 40									15 10									15 40		
Virginia Water	a		14 45					15 19				15 15					15 49				15 45		
	d		14 54					15 19				15 24					15 49				15 54		
Egham	d		14 57					15 23				15 27					15 53				15 57		
Windsor & Eton Riverside	d			14 51									15 21									15 51	
Datchet	d			14 55									15 25									15 55	
Sunnymeads	d			14 58									15 28									15 58	
Wraysbury	d			15 02									15 32									16 02	
Staines	d		15 03	15 08				15 29				15 33	15 38				15 59				16 03	16 08	
Ashford (Surrey)	d		15 06	15 11								15 36	15 41								16 06	16 11	
Feltham	d		15 11	15 16				15 35				15 41	15 46				16 05				16 11	16 16	
Whitton	d			15 20		15 20	15 23						15 50		15 50	15 53						16 20	
Kingston	d	14 59									15 29									15 59			
Hampton Wick	d	15 01									15 31									16 01			
Teddington	d	15 05									15 35									16 05			
Fulwell	d																						
Strawberry Hill	d	15 08									15 38									16 08			
Twickenham	a	15 12		15 23			15 26	15 40			15 42		15 53			15 56	16 10			16 12		16 23	
	d	15 13		15 23			15 28	15 41			15 43		15 53			15 58	16 11			16 13		16 23	
St Margarets	d	15 15					15 30				15 45					16 00				16 15			
Richmond ⊖	d	15 19		15 28			15 34	15 45			15 49		15 58			16 04	16 15			16 19		16 28	
North Sheen	d	15 21					15 36				15 51					16 06				16 21			
Mortlake	d	15 23					15 38				15 53					16 08				16 23			
Hounslow	d		15 16			15 31						15 46			16 01						16 16		
Isleworth	d		15 19			15 34						15 49			16 04						16 19		
Syon Lane	d		15 21			15 36						15 51			16 06						16 21		
Brentford	d		15 24			15 39						15 54			16 09						16 24		
Kew Bridge	d		15 26			15 41						15 56			16 11						16 26		
Chiswick	d		15 29			15 44						15 59			16 14						16 29		
Barnes Bridge	d		15 31			15 46			←			16 01			16 16			←			16 31		
Barnes	d	15 26	15 34		←	15 49	15 41		15 49		15 56	16 04		←	16 19	16 11		16 19		16 26	16 34		←
Putney	d	15 29	15 37	15 34	15 37	→	15 44		15 52		15 59	16 07	16 04	16 07	→	16 14		16 22		16 29	16 37	16 34	16 37
Wandsworth Town	d	15 32	→		15 40		15 47		15 55		16 02	→		16 10		16 17		16 25		16 32	→		16 40
Clapham Junction ■10	d	15 35		15 39	15 43		15 50	15 54	15 58		16 05		16 09	16 13		16 20	16 24	16 28		16 35		16 39	16 43
Queenstown Rd.(Battersea)	d	15 38			15 46		15 53		16 01		16 08			16 16		16 23		16 31		16 38			16 46
Vauxhall ⊖	d	15 42		15 45	15 50		15 57		16 05		16 12		16 15	16 20		16 27		16 35		16 42		16 45	16 50
London Waterloo ■15 ⊖	a	15 46		15 49	15 56		16 02	16 05	16 11		16 19		16 19	16 26		16 32	16 34	16 41		16 49		16 49	16 56

Reading, Guildford, Ascot, Weybridge, Windsor, Kingston, Richmond and Hounslow - London

from 3 October

		SW	SW	SW [1]	SW	SW [1]	SW	SW	SW	SW	SW	SW	SW	SW [1]	SW	SW [1]	SW	SW	SW	SW	SW	SW
Reading [7]	d			15 39										16 09								
Earley	d			15 44										16 14								
Winnersh Triangle	d			15 46										16 16								
Winnersh	d			15 48										16 18								
Wokingham	d			15 53										16 23								
Bracknell	d			15 59										16 29								
Martins Heron	d			16 02										16 32								
Guildford	d					15 30										16 00						
Wanborough	d					15 36										16 06						
Ash [5]	d					15 40										16 10						
Aldershot	a					15 47										16 17						
	d					16 00										16 30						
Ash Vale	d					16 04										16 34						
Frimley	d					16 10										16 40						
Camberley	a					16 14										16 44						
	d					16 18										16 48						
Bagshot	d					16 23										16 53						
Ascot [3]	d			16 07		16a30								16 37		17a00						
Sunningdale	d			16 10										16 40								
Longcross	d																					
Woking	d																					
West Byfleet	d																					
Byfleet & New Haw	d																					
Weybridge	d								16 03									16 33				
Addlestone	d								16 07									16 37				
Chertsey	d								16 10									16 40				
Virginia Water	a			16 19					16 15					16 49				16 45				
	d			16 19					16 24					16 49				16 54				
Egham	d			16 23					16 27					16 53				16 57				
Windsor & Eton Riverside	d									16 21									16 51			
Datchet	d									16 25									16 55			
Sunnymeads	d									16 28									16 58			
Wraysbury	d									16 32									17 02			
Staines	d			16 29					16 33	16 38				16 59				17 03	17 08			
Ashford (Surrey)	d								16 36	16 41								17 06	17 11			
Feltham	d			16 35					16 41	16 46				17 05				17 11	17 16			
Whitton	d	16 20	16 23							16 50		16 50	16 53						17 20		17 20	17 23
Kingston	d						16 29										16 59					
Hampton Wick	d						16 31										17 01					
Teddington	d						16 35										17 05					
Fulwell	d																					
Strawberry Hill	d						16 38										17 08					
Twickenham	a		16 26	16 40			16 42			16 53			16 56	17 10			17 12		17 23			17 26
	d		16 28	16 41			16 43	16 50		16 53			16 58	17 11			17 13		17 23			17 28
St Margarets	d		16 30				16 45						17 00				17 15					17 30
Richmond ⊖	d		16 34	16 45			16 49			16 58			17 04	17 15			17 19		17 28			17 34
North Sheen	d		16 36				16 51						17 06				17 21					17 36
Mortlake	d		16 38				16 53						17 08				17 23					17 38
Hounslow	d	16 31							16 46			17 01						17 16			17 31	
Isleworth	d	16 34							16 49			17 04						17 19			17 34	
Syon Lane	d	16 36							16 51			17 06						17 21			17 36	
Brentford	d	16 39							16 54			17 09						17 24			17 39	
Kew Bridge	d	16 41							16 56			17 11						17 26			17 41	
Chiswick	d	16 44							16 59			17 14						17 29			17 44	
Barnes Bridge	d	16 46			←				17 01			17 16			←			17 31			17 46	
Barnes	d	16 49	16 41		16 49		16 56		17 04		←	17 19	17 11		17 19		17 26	17 34		←	17 49	17 41
Putney	d	→	16 44		16 52		16 59		17 07	17 05	17 07	→	17 14		17 22		17 29	17 37	17 34	17 37	→	17 44
Wandsworth Town	d		16 47		16 55		17 02		→		17 10		17 17		17 25		17 32	→		17 40		17 47
Clapham Junction [10]	d		16 50	16 54	16 58		17 05	17 09		17 09	17 13		17 20	17 24	17 28		17 35		17 39	17 43		17 50
Queenstown Rd.(Battersea)	d		16 53		17 01		17 08				17 16		17 23		17 31		17 38			17 46		17 53
Vauxhall ⊖	d		16 57		17 05		17 12			17 15	17 20		17 27		17 35		17 42		17 45	17 50		17 57
London Waterloo [15] ⊖	a		17 02	17 04	17 11		17 19	17 24		17 19	17 26		17 32	17 35	17 41		17 49		17 49	17 56		18 02

Reading, Guildford, Ascot, Weybridge, Windsor, Kingston, Richmond and Hounslow - London

from 3 October

		SW [1]	SW	SW [1]	SW	SW	SW	SW	SW	SW	SW [1]	SW	SW	SW	SW	SW	SW [1]	SW [1]	SW	SW	SW [1]	SW	SW
Reading [7]	d	16 41									17 09						17 22				17 39		
Earley	d	16 46									17 14						17 27				17 44		
Winnersh Triangle	d	16 48									17 16						17 29				17 46		
Winnersh	d	16 50									17 18						17 31				17 48		
Wokingham	d	16 55									17 23						17 36				17 53		
Bracknell	d	17 01									17 29						17 42				17 59		
Martins Heron	d	17 04									17 32						17 45				18 02		
Guildford	d			16 30														17 00					
Wanborough	d			16 36														17 06					
Ash [5]	d			16 40														17 10					
Aldershot	a			16 47														17 17					
	d			17 00														17 30					
Ash Vale	d			17 04														17 34					
Frimley	d			17 10														17 40					
Camberley	a			17 14														17 44					
	d			17 18														17 48					
Bagshot	d			17 23														17 53					
Ascot [3]	d	17 09		17a30							17 37						17b55	18a00			18 07		
Sunningdale	d	17 12									17 40						17 58				18 10		
Longcross	d	17 15																			18 13		
Woking	d																						
West Byfleet	d																						
Byfleet & New Haw	d																						
Weybridge	d					17 03								17 37									
Addlestone	d					17 07								17 41									
Chertsey	d					17 10								17 44									
Virginia Water	a	17 19				17 15					17 49			17 49			18 03				18 19		
	d	17 19				17 24					17 49			17 54			18 03				18 19		
Egham	d	17 23				17 27					17 53			17 57			18 06				18 23		
Windsor & Eton Riverside	d						17 21								17 51								
Datchet	d						17 25								17 55								
Sunnymeads	d						17 28								17 58								
Wraysbury	d						17 32								18 02								
Staines	d	17 29				17 33	17 38				17 59			18 03	18 08		18 14				18 29		
Ashford (Surrey)	d					17 36	17 41							18 06	18 11								
Feltham	d	17 35				17 41	17 46				18 05			18 11	18 16		18 20				18 35		
Whitton	d						17 50		17 50	17 53					18 20				18 20	18 23			
Kingston	d				17 29								17 59										18 29
Hampton Wick	d				17 31								18 01										18 31
Teddington	d				17 35								18 05										18 35
Fulwell	d																						
Strawberry Hill	d				17 38								18 08										18 38
Twickenham	a	17 40			17 42		17 53			17 56	18 10		18 12		18 23					18 26	18 40		18 42
	d	17 41			17 43		17 53			17 58	18 11		18 13		18 23					18 28	18 41		18 43
St Margarets	d				17 45					18 00			18 15							18 30			18 45
Richmond ⊖	d	17 45			17 49		17 58			18 04	18 15		18 19		18 28					18 34	18 45		18 49
North Sheen	d				17 51					18 06			18 21							18 36			18 51
Mortlake	d				17 53					18 08			18 23							18 38			18 53
Hounslow	d					17 46			18 01					18 16			18 26		18 31				
Isleworth	d					17 49			18 04					18 19					18 34				
Syon Lane	d					17 51			18 06					18 21					18 36				
Brentford	d					17 54			18 09					18 24			18 31		18 39				
Kew Bridge	d					17 56			18 11					18 26					18 41				
Chiswick	d					17 59			18 14					18 29					18 44				
Barnes Bridge	d		←			18 01			18 16			←		18 31					18 46			←	
Barnes	d		17 49		17 56	18 04		←	18 19	18 11		18 19	18 26	18 34		←			18 49	18 41		18 49	18 56
Putney	d		17 52		17 59	18 07	18 04	18 07	→	18 14		18 22	18 29	18 37	18 34	18 37	18 39		→	18 44		18 52	18 59
Wandsworth Town	d		17 55		18 02	→		18 10		18 17		18 25	18 32	→		18 40				18 47		18 55	19 02
Clapham Junction [10]	d	17 54	17 58		18 05		18 09	18 13		18 20	18 24	18 28	18 35		18 39	18 43	18 44			18 50	18 54	18 58	19 05
Queenstown Rd.(Battersea)	d		18 01		18 08			18 16		18 23		18 31	18 38			18 46				18 53		19 01	19 08
Vauxhall ⊖	d		18 05		18 12		18 15	18 20		18 27		18 35	18 42		18 45	18 50				18 57		19 05	19 12
London Waterloo [15] ⊖	a	18 04	18 11		18 19		18 19	18 26		18 32	18 34	18 41	18 49		18 49	18 56	18 56			19 02	19 04	19 11	19 16

b Arr. 1749

Table 149

Mondays to Fridays
from 3 October

Reading, Guildford, Ascot, Weybridge, Windsor, Kingston, Richmond and Hounslow - London

		SW	SW	SW	SW [1]	SW [1]		SW	SW	SW [1]	SW	SW [1]	SW	SW	SW	SW		SW	SW	SW [1]	SW	SW [1]	SW [1]	SW	SW
Reading [7]	d				17 53					18 09										18 39		18 52			
Earley	d				17 58					18 14										18 44		18 57			
Winnersh Triangle	d				18 00					18 16										18 46		18 59			
Winnersh	d				18 02					18 18										18 48		19 01			
Wokingham	d				18 07					18 23										18 53		19 06			
Bracknell	d				18 13					18 29										18 59		19 12			
Martins Heron	d				18 16					18 32										19 02		19 15			
Guildford	d					17 30						18 00											18 30		
Wanborough	d					17 36						18 06											18 36		
Ash [5]	d					17 40						18 10											18 40		
Aldershot	a					17 47						18 17											18 47		
	d					18 00						18 30											19 00		
Ash Vale	d					18 04						18 34											19 04		
Frimley	d					18 10						18 40											19 10		
Camberley	a					18 14						18 44											19 14		
	d					18 18						18 48											19 18		
Bagshot	d					18 23						18 53											19 23		
Ascot [3]	d				18 25	18a30				18 37		19a00								19 07		19a19	19a30		
Sunningdale	d				18 28					18 40										19 10					
Longcross	d									18 43										19 13					
Woking	d																								
West Byfleet	d																								
Byfleet & New Haw	d																								
Weybridge	d	18 07												18 37											19 07
Addlestone	d	18 11												18 41											19 11
Chertsey	d	18 14												18 44											19 14
Virginia Water	a	18 19			18 33					18 49				18 49						19 19					19 19
	d	18 24			18 33					18 49				18 54						19 19					19 24
Egham	d	18 27			18 37					18 53				18 57						19 23					19 27
Windsor & Eton Riverside	d		18 21												18 51										
Datchet	d		18 25												18 55										
Sunnymeads	d		18 28												18 58										
Wraysbury	d		18 32												19 02										
Staines	d	18 33	18 38		18 44					18 59				19 03	19 08					19 29					19 33
Ashford (Surrey)	d	18 36	18 41											19 06	19 11										19 36
Feltham	d	18 41	18 46		18 50					19 05				19 11	19 16					19 35					19 41
Whitton	d		18 50					18 50	18 53						19 20			19 20	19 23						
Kingston	d												18 59											19 29	
Hampton Wick	d												19 01											19 31	
Teddington	d												19 05											19 35	
Fulwell	d																								
Strawberry Hill	d												19 08											19 38	
Twickenham	a		18 53						18 56	19 10			19 12		19 23				19 26	19 40				19 42	
	d		18 53						18 58	19 11			19 13		19 23				19 28	19 41				19 43	
St Margarets	d								19 00				19 15						19 30					19 45	
Richmond ⊖	d		18 58						19 04	19 15			19 19		19 28				19 34	19 45				19 49	
North Sheen	d								19 06				19 21						19 36					19 51	
Mortlake	d								19 08				19 23						19 38					19 53	
Hounslow	d	18 46			18 56			19 01						19 16				19 31							19 46
Isleworth	d	18 49						19 04						19 19				19 34							19 49
Syon Lane	d	18 51						19 06						19 21				19 36							19 51
Brentford	d	18 54			19 01			19 09						19 24				19 39							19 54
Kew Bridge	d	18 56						19 11						19 26				19 41							19 56
Chiswick	d	18 59						19 14						19 29				19 44							19 59
Barnes Bridge	d	19 01						19 16			←			19 31				19 46			←				20 01
Barnes	d	19 04		←				19 19	19 11		19 19		19 26	19 34		←		19 49	19 41		19 49			19 56	20 04
Putney	d	19 07	19 04	19 07	19 09			→	19 14		19 22		19 29	19 37	19 34	19 37		→	19 44		19 52			19 59	20 07
Wandsworth Town	d	→		19 10					19 17		19 25		19 32	→		19 40			19 47		19 55			20 02	→
Clapham Junction [10]	d		19 09	19 13	19 14				19 20	19 24	19 28		19 35		19 39	19 43			19 50	19 54	19 58			20 05	
Queenstown Rd.(Battersea)	d			19 16					19 23		19 31		19 38			19 46			19 53		20 01			20 08	
Vauxhall ⊖	d		19 15	19 20					19 27		19 35		19 42		19 45	19 50			19 57		20 05			20 12	
London Waterloo [15] ⊖	a		19 19	19 26	19 28				19 32	19 34	19 41		19 46		19 49	19 56			20 02	20 04	20 09			20 16	

Table 149

Mondays to Fridays
from 3 October

Reading, Guildford, Ascot, Weybridge, Windsor, Kingston, Richmond and Hounslow - London

		SW		SW	SW	SW	SW [1]	SW	SW [1]	SW	SW	SW		SW	SW	SW	SW [1]	SW	SW [1]	SW	SW	SW		SW	SW
Reading [7]	d						19 09										19 39								
Earley	d						19 14										19 44								
Winnersh Triangle	d						19 16										19 46								
Winnersh	d						19 18										19 48								
Wokingham	d						19 23										19 53								
Bracknell	d						19 29										19 59								
Martins Heron	d						19 32										20 02								
Guildford	d								19 00										19 30						
Wanborough	d								19 06										19 36						
Ash [5]	d								19 10										19 40						
Aldershot	a								19 17										19 47						
	d								19 30										20 00						
Ash Vale	d								19 34										20 04						
Frimley	d								19 40										20 10						
Camberley	a								19 44										20 14						
	d								19 48										20 18						
Bagshot	d								19 53										20 23						
Ascot [3]	d						19 37		20a00								20 07		20a30						
Sunningdale	d						19 40										20 10								
Longcross	d						19 43										20 13								
Woking	d																								
West Byfleet	d																								
Byfleet & New Haw	d																								
Weybridge	d										19 37										20 03				
Addlestone	d										19 41										20 07				
Chertsey	d										19 44										20 10				
Virginia Water	a						19 49				19 49						20 19				20 15				
	d						19 49				19 54						20 19				20 24				
Egham	d						19 53				19 57						20 23				20 27				
Windsor & Eton Riverside	d	19 21										19 51										20 21			
Datchet	d	19 25										19 55										20 25			
Sunnymeads	d	19 28										19 58										20 28			
Wraysbury	d	19 32										20 02										20 32			
Staines	d	19 38					19 59				20 03	20 08					20 29				20 33	20 38			
Ashford (Surrey)	d	19 41									20 06	20 11									20 36	20 41			
Feltham	d	19 46					20 05				20 11	20 16					20 35				20 41	20 46			
Whitton	d	19 50			19 50	19 53						20 20			20 20	20 23						20 50			20 50
Kingston	d									19 59										20 29					
Hampton Wick	d									20 01										20 31					
Teddington	d									20 05										20 35					
Fulwell	d																								
Strawberry Hill	d									20 08										20 38					
Twickenham	a	19 53				19 56	20 10			20 12		20 23				20 26	20 40			20 42		20 53			
	d	19 53				19 58	20 11			20 13		20 23				20 28	20 41			20 43		20 53			
St Margarets	d					20 00				20 15						20 30				20 45					
Richmond ⊖	d	19 58				20 04	20 15			20 19		20 28				20 34	20 45			20 49		20 58			
North Sheen	d					20 06				20 21						20 36				20 51					
Mortlake	d					20 08				20 23						20 38				20 53					
Hounslow	d				20 01						20 16				20 31						20 46				21 01
Isleworth	d				20 04						20 19				20 34						20 49				21 04
Syon Lane	d				20 06						20 21				20 36						20 51				21 06
Brentford	d				20 09						20 24				20 39						20 54				21 09
Kew Bridge	d				20 11						20 26				20 41						20 56				21 11
Chiswick	d				20 14						20 29				20 44						20 59				21 14
Barnes Bridge	d				20 16			←			20 31				20 46			←			21 01				21 16
Barnes	d			←	20 19	20 11		20 19		20 26	20 34			←	20 49	20 41		20 49		20 56	21 04			←	21 19
Putney	d	20 04		20 07	→	20 14		20 22		20 29	20 37	20 34		20 37	→	20 44		20 52		20 59	21 07	21 04		21 07	→
Wandsworth Town	d			20 10		20 17		20 25		20 32	→			20 40		20 47		20 55		21 02	→			21 10	
Clapham Junction [10]	d	20 09		20 13		20 20	20 24	20 28		20 35		20 39		20 43		20 50	20 54	20 58		21 05		21 09		21 13	
Queenstown Rd.(Battersea)	d			20 16		20 23		20 31		20 38				20 46		20 53		21 01		21 08				21 16	
Vauxhall ⊖	d	20 15		20 20		20 27		20 35		20 42		20 45		20 50		20 57		21 05		21 12		21 15		21 20	
London Waterloo [15] ⊖	a	20 19		20 26		20 32	20 34	20 41		20 46		20 49		20 56		21 02	21 04	21 11		21 16		21 19		21 26	

Reading, Guildford, Ascot, Weybridge, Windsor, Kingston, Richmond and Hounslow - London

from 3 October

		SW	SW 1	SW	SW 1	SW 1	SW	SW	SW	SW	SW	SW	SW 1	SW	SW	SW	SW	SW	SW	SW	SW 1	SW	SW 1
Reading 7	d		20 09										20 39								21 09		
Earley	d		20 14										20 44								21 14		
Winnersh Triangle	d		20 16										20 46								21 16		
Winnersh	d		20 18										20 48								21 18		
Wokingham	d		20 23										20 53								21 23		
Bracknell	d		20 29										20 59								21 29		
Martins Heron	d		20 32										21 02								21 32		
Guildford	d				20 00	20 30																	21 00
Wanborough	d				20 06	20 36																	21 06
Ash 5	d				20 10	20 40																	21 10
Aldershot	a				20 17	20 47																	21 17
	d				20 30																		21 30
Ash Vale	d				20 34																		21 34
Frimley	d				20 40																		21 40
Camberley	a				20 44																		21 44
	d				20 48																		21 48
Bagshot	d				20 53																		21 53
Ascot 3	d		20 37		21a00								21 07								21 37		22a00
Sunningdale	d		20 40										21 10								21 40		
Longcross	d		20 43																				
Woking	d																						
West Byfleet	d																						
Byfleet & New Haw	d																						
Weybridge	d							20 33								21 03							
Addlestone	d							20 37								21 07							
Chertsey	d							20 40								21 10							
Virginia Water	a		20 49					20 45					21 19			21 15					21 49		
	d		20 49					20 54					21 19			21 24					21 49		
Egham	d		20 53					20 57					21 23			21 27					21 53		
Windsor & Eton Riverside	d								20 51								21 21						
Datchet	d								20 55								21 25						
Sunnymeads	d								20 58								21 28						
Wraysbury	d								21 02								21 32						
Staines	d		20 59					21 03	21 08				21 29			21 33	21 38				21 59		
Ashford (Surrey)	d							21 06	21 11							21 36	21 41						
Feltham	d		21 05					21 11	21 16				21 35			21 41	21 46				22 05		
Whitton	d	20 53							21 20		21 20	21 23					21 50		21 50	21 53			
Kingston	d						20 59								21 29								
Hampton Wick	d						21 01								21 31								
Teddington	d						21 05								21 35								
Fulwell	d																						
Strawberry Hill	d						21 08								21 38								
Twickenham	a	20 56	21 10				21 12		21 23			21 26	21 40		21 42		21 53			21 56	22 10		
	d	20 58	21 11				21 13		21 23			21 28	21 41		21 43		21 53			21 58	22 11		
St Margarets	d	21 00					21 15					21 30			21 45					22 00			
Richmond ⊖	d	21 04	21 15				21 19		21 28			21 34	21 45		21 49		21 58			22 04	22 15		
North Sheen	d	21 06					21 21					21 36			21 51					22 06			
Mortlake	d	21 08					21 23					21 38			21 53					22 08			
Hounslow	d							21 16			21 31					21 46			22 01				
Isleworth	d							21 19			21 34					21 49			22 04				
Syon Lane	d							21 21			21 36					21 51			22 06				
Brentford	d							21 24			21 39					21 54			22 09				
Kew Bridge	d							21 26			21 41					21 56			22 11				
Chiswick	d							21 29			21 44					21 59			22 14				
Barnes Bridge	d			←				21 31			21 46			←		22 01			22 16			←	
Barnes	d	21 11		21 19			21 26	21 34		←	21 49	21 41		21 49	21 56	22 04		←	22 19	22 11		22 19	
Putney	d	21 14		21 22			21 29	21 37	21 34	21 37	→	21 44		21 52	21 59	22 07	22 04	22 07	→	22 14		22 22	
Wandsworth Town	d	21 17		21 25			21 32	→		21 40		21 47		21 55	22 02	→		22 10		22 17		22 25	
Clapham Junction 10	d	21 20	21 24	21 28			21 35		21 39	21 43		21 50	21 54	21 58	22 05		22 09	22 13		22 20	22 24	22 28	
Queenstown Rd.(Battersea)	d	21 23		21 31			21 38			21 46		21 53		22 01	22 08			22 16		22 23		22 31	
Vauxhall ⊖	d	21 27		21 35			21 42		21 45	21 50		21 57		22 05	22 12		22 15	22 20		22 27		22 35	
London Waterloo 15 ⊖	a	21 32	21 34	21 41			21 46		21 49	21 56		22 02	22 04	22 11	22 16		22 19	22 26		22 32	22 34	22 41	

Mondays to Fridays

from 3 October

Reading, Guildford, Ascot, Weybridge, Windsor, Kingston, Richmond and Hounslow - London

		SW 1	SW	SW	SW	SW	SW	SW 1	SW	SW	SW	SW	SW 1	SW 1	SW 1	SW	SW	SW	SW	SW 1	SW	SW
Reading 7	d							21 39					22 09							22 39		
Earley	d							21 44					22 14							22 44		
Winnersh Triangle	d							21 46					22 16							22 46		
Winnersh	d							21 48					22 18							22 48		
Wokingham	d							21 53					22 23							22 53		
Bracknell	d							21 59					22 29							22 59		
Martins Heron	d							22 02					22 32							23 02		
Guildford	d	21 30												22 00	22 30							
Wanborough	d	21 36												22 06	22 36							
Ash 5	d	21 40												22 10	22 40							
Aldershot	a	21 47												22 17	22 47							
	d													22 30								
Ash Vale	d													22 34								
Frimley	d													22 40								
Camberley	a													22 44								
	d													22 48								
Bagshot	d													22 53								
Ascot 3	d							22 07					22 37	23a00						23 07		
Sunningdale	d							22 10					22 40							23 10		
Longcross	d																					
Woking	d																					
West Byfleet	d																					
Byfleet & New Haw	d																					
Weybridge	d			21 33						22 03							22 33				23 03	
Addlestone	d			21 37						22 07							22 37				23 07	
Chertsey	d			21 40						22 10							22 40				23 10	
Virginia Water	a			21 45				22 19		22 15			22 49				22 45			23 19	23 15	
	d			21 54				22 19		22 24			22 49				22 54			23 19	23 24	
Egham	d			21 57				22 23		22 27			22 53				22 57			23 23	23 27	
Windsor & Eton Riverside	d				21 51						22 21							22 53				23 28
Datchet	d				21 55						22 25							22 56				23 31
Sunnymeads	d				21 58						22 28							22 59				23 34
Wraysbury	d				22 02						22 32							23 02				23 37
Staines	d			22 03	22 08			22 29		22 33	22 38		22 59				23 03	23 08		23 29	23a32	23a42
Ashford (Surrey)	d			22 06	22 11					22 36	22 41						23 06	23 11				
Feltham	d			22 11	22 16			22 35		22 41	22 46		23 05				23 11	23 16		23 35		
Whitton	d				22 20		22 23				22 50							23 20				
Kingston	d		21 59						22 29							22 59						
Hampton Wick	d		22 01						22 31							23 01						
Teddington	d		22 05						22 35							23 05						
Fulwell	d																					
Strawberry Hill	d		22 08						22 38							23 08						
Twickenham	a		22 12		22 23		22 26	22 40	22 42		22 53		23 10			23 12		23 23		23 40		
	d		22 13		22 23		22 28	22 41	22 43		22 53		23 11			23 13		23 23		23 41		
St Margarets	d		22 15				22 30		22 45							23 15						
Richmond ⊖	d		22 19		22 28		22 34	22 45	22 49		22 58		23 15			23 19		23 28		23 45		
North Sheen	d		22 21				22 36		22 51							23 21						
Mortlake	d		22 23				22 38		22 53							23 23						
Hounslow	d			22 16						22 46							23 16					
Isleworth	d			22 19						22 49							23 19					
Syon Lane	d			22 21						22 51							23 21					
Brentford	d			22 24						22 54							23 24					
Kew Bridge	d			22 26						22 56							23 26					
Chiswick	d			22 29						22 59							23 29					
Barnes Bridge	d			22 31						23 01							23 31					
Barnes	d		22 26	22 34		←	22 41		22 56	23 04		←				23 26	23 34		←			
Putney	d		22 29	22 37	22 34	22 37	22 44		22 59	23 07	23 04	23 07				23 29	23 37	23 34	23 37			
Wandsworth Town	d		22 32	→		22 40	22 47		23 02	→		23 10				23 32	→		23 40			
Clapham Junction 10	d		22 35		22 39	22 43	22 50	22 54	23 05		23 09	23 13	23 24			23 35		23 39	23 43	23 54		
Queenstown Rd.(Battersea)	d		22 38			22 46	22 53		23 08			23 16				23 38			23 46			
Vauxhall ⊖	d		22 42		22 45	22 50	22 57		23 12		23 15	23 20				23 42		23 45	23 50			
London Waterloo 15 ⊖	a		22 46		22 49	22 56	23 02	23 04	23 16		23 19	23 26	23 34			23 46		23 49	23 56	00 04		

Table 149

Mondays to Fridays
from 3 October

Reading, Guildford, Ascot, Weybridge, Windsor, Kingston, Richmond and Hounslow - London

		SW	SW ■	SW ■	SW ■	SW
Reading [7]	d		23 12			
Earley	d		23 17			
Winnersh Triangle	d		23 19			
Winnersh	d		23 21			
Wokingham	d		23 26			
Bracknell	d		23 32			
Martins Heron	d		23 35			
Guildford	d			23 00	23 30	
Wanborough	d			23 06	23 36	
Ash [5]	d			23 10	23 40	
Aldershot	a			23 17	23 47	
	d			23 30		
Ash Vale	d			23 34		
Frimley	d			23 40		
Camberley	a			23 44		
	d			23 48		
Bagshot	d			23 53		
Ascot [3]	d		23 40	00a01		
Sunningdale	d		23 43			
Longcross	d					
Woking	d					
West Byfleet	d					
Byfleet & New Haw	d					
Weybridge	d					23 33
Addlestone	d					23 37
Chertsey	d					23 40
Virginia Water	a		23 49			23 45
	d		23 49			23 54
Egham	d		23 53			23 57
Windsor & Eton Riverside	d					
Datchet	d					
Sunnymeads	d					
Wraysbury	d					
Staines	d		23 59			00a02
Ashford (Surrey)	d					
Feltham	d		00 05			
Whitton	d					
Kingston	d	23 29				
Hampton Wick	d	23 31				
Teddington	d	23 35				
Fulwell	d					
Strawberry Hill	d	23 38				
Twickenham	a	23 42	00 10			
	d	23 43	00 11			
St Margarets	d	23 45				
Richmond ⊖	d	23 49	00 15			
North Sheen	d	23 51				
Mortlake	d	23 53				
Hounslow	d					
Isleworth	d					
Syon Lane	d					
Brentford	d					
Kew Bridge	d					
Chiswick	d					
Barnes Bridge	d					
Barnes	d	23 56				
Putney	d	23 59				
Wandsworth Town	d	00 02				
Clapham Junction [10]	d	00 05	00 24			
Queenstown Rd.(Battersea)	d	00 08				
Vauxhall ⊖	d	00 12				
London Waterloo [15] ⊖	a	00 16	00 37			

Table 149

Saturdays
until 1 October

Reading, Guildford, Ascot, Weybridge, Windsor, Kingston, Richmond and Hounslow - London

		SW ■	SW	SW ■	SW	SW	SW	SW	SW	SW	SW	SW	SW	SW ■	SW ■	SW	SW	SW	SW	SW ■	SW	SW	SW
Reading [7]	d	22p42		23p12										05 42						06 12			
Earley	d	22p47		23p17										05 47						06 17			
Winnersh Triangle	d	22p49		23p19										05 49						06 19			
Winnersh	d	22p51		23p21										05 51						06 21			
Wokingham	d	22p56		23p26										05 56						06 26			
Bracknell	d	23p02		23p32										06 02						06 32			
Martins Heron	d	23p05		23p35										06 05						06 35			
Guildford	d																						
Wanborough	d																						
Ash [5]	d																						
Aldershot	a																						
	d														06 00								
Ash Vale	d														06 04								
Frimley	d														06 10								
Camberley	a														06 14								
	d														06 18								
Bagshot	d														06 23								
Ascot [3]	d	23p10		23p40										06 10	06a30					06 40			
Sunningdale	d	23p13		23p43										06 13						06 43			
Longcross	d																						
Woking	d										05 27												
West Byfleet	d										05 32												
Byfleet & New Haw	d										05 35												
Weybridge	d																					06 33	
Addlestone	d										05 39											06 37	
Chertsey	d										05 42											06 40	
Virginia Water	a	23p19		23p49							05 47			06 19						06 49		06 45	
	d	23p19		23p49							05 54			06 19						06 49		06 54	
Egham	d	23p23		23p53							05 57			06 23						06 53		06 57	
Windsor & Eton Riverside	d											05 53						06 23					06 53
Datchet	d											05 56						06 26					06 56
Sunnymeads	d											05 59						06 29					06 59
Wraysbury	d											06 02						06 32					07 02
Staines	d	23p29		23p59	04 58			05 37			06 03	06 08		06 29			06 33	06 38		06 59		07 03	07 08
Ashford (Surrey)	d				05 01			05 40			06 06	06 11					06 36	06 41				07 06	07 11
Feltham	d	23p35		00 05	05 06			05 45			06 11	06 16		06 35			06 41	06 46		07 05		07 11	07 16
Whitton	d				05 10		05 41	05 49				06 20						06 50					07 20
Kingston	d		23p29							05 59						06 29					06 59		
Hampton Wick	d		23p31							06 01						06 31					07 01		
Teddington	d		23p35							06 05						06 35					07 05		
Fulwell	d																						
Strawberry Hill	d		23p38			05 38				06 08						06 38					07 08		
Twickenham	a	23p40	23p42	00 10	05 13	05 41		05 52		06 12		06 23		06 40		06 42		06 53		07 10	07 12		07 23
	d	23p41	23p43	00 11	05 13	05 43		05 53		06 13		06 23		06 41		06 43		06 53		07 11	07 13		07 23
St Margarets	d		23p45		05 15	05 45				06 15						06 45					07 15		
Richmond ⊖	d	23p45	23p49	00 15	05 19	05 49		05 58		06 19		06 28		06 45		06 49		06 58		07 15	07 19		07 28
North Sheen	d		23p51		05 21	05 51				06 21						06 51					07 21		
Mortlake	d		23p53		05 23	05 53				06 23						06 53					07 23		
Hounslow	d						05 46				06 16						06 46					07 16	
Isleworth	d						05 49				06 19						06 49					07 19	
Syon Lane	d						05 51				06 21						06 51					07 21	
Brentford	d						05 54				06 24						06 54					07 24	
Kew Bridge	d						05 56				06 26						06 56					07 26	
Chiswick	d						05 59				06 29						06 59					07 29	
Barnes Bridge	d						06 01				06 31						07 01					07 31	
Barnes	d		23p56		05 26	05 56	06 04		←	06 26	06 34		←			06 56	07 04		←		07 26	07 34	
Putney	d		23p59		05 29	05 59	06 07	06 04	06 07	06 29	06 37	06 34	06 37			06 59	07 07	07 04	07 07		07 29	07 37	07 34
Wandsworth Town	d		00 02		05 32	06 02	→		06 10	06 32	→		06 40			07 02	→		07 10		07 32	→	
Clapham Junction [10]	d	23p54	00 05	00 24	05 35	06 05		06 09	06 13	06 35		06 39	06 43	06 54		07 05		07 09	07 13	07 24	07 35		07 39
Queenstown Rd.(Battersea)	d		00 08		05 38	06 08			06 16	06 38			06 46			07 08			07 16		07 38		
Vauxhall ⊖	d		00 12		05 42	06 12		06 15	06 20	06 42		06 45	06 50			07 12		07 15	07 20		07 42		07 45
London Waterloo [15] ⊖	a	00 04	00 16	00 37	05 46	06 16		06 19	06 26	06 46		06 49	06 56	07 04		07 16		07 19	07 26	07 34	07 46		07 49

Reading, Guildford, Ascot, Weybridge, Windsor, Kingston, Richmond and Hounslow - London

		SW	SW 1	SW 1	SW	SW		SW	SW	SW	SW	SW 1	SW 1	SW	SW	SW		SW	SW	SW	SW	SW 1	SW	SW 1	SW
Reading 7	d		06 42									07 12										07 42			
Earley	d		06 47									07 17										07 47			
Winnersh Triangle	d		06 49									07 19										07 49			
Winnersh	d		06 51									07 21										07 51			
Wokingham	d		06 56									07 26										07 56			
Bracknell	d		07 02									07 32										08 02			
Martins Heron	d		07 05									07 35										08 05			
Guildford	d			06 30									07 00											07 30	
Wanborough	d			06 36									07 06											07 36	
Ash 5	d			06 40									07 10											07 40	
Aldershot	a			06 47									07 17											07 47	
	d			07 00									07 30											08 00	
Ash Vale	d			07 04									07 34											08 04	
Frimley	d			07 10									07 40											08 10	
Camberley	a			07 14									07 44											08 14	
	d			07 18									07 48											08 18	
Bagshot	d			07 23									07 53											08 23	
Ascot 3	d		07 10	07a30								07 40	08a00									08 10		08a30	
Sunningdale	d		07 13									07 43										08 13			
Longcross	d																								
Woking	d																								
West Byfleet	d																								
Byfleet & New Haw	d																								
Weybridge	d							07 03								07 33									
Addlestone	d							07 07								07 37									
Chertsey	d							07 10								07 40									
Virginia Water	a		07 19					07 15				07 49				07 45						08 19			
	d		07 19					07 24				07 49				07 54						08 19			
Egham	d		07 23					07 27				07 53				07 57						08 23			
Windsor & Eton Riverside	d								07 23									07 53							
Datchet	d								07 26									07 56							
Sunnymeads	d								07 29									07 59							
Wraysbury	d								07 32									08 02							
Staines	d		07 29					07 33	07 38			07 59				08 03		08 08				08 29			
Ashford (Surrey)	d							07 36	07 41							08 06		08 11							
Feltham	d		07 35					07 41	07 46			08 05				08 11		08 16				08 35			
Whitton	d								07 50					07 50				08 20		08 20	08 23				
Kingston	d					07 29									07 59										08 29
Hampton Wick	d					07 31									08 01										08 31
Teddington	d					07 35									08 05										08 35
Fulwell	d																								
Strawberry Hill	d					07 38									08 08										08 38
Twickenham	a		07 40			07 42			07 53			08 10			08 12			08 23			08 26	08 40			08 42
	d		07 41			07 43			07 53		07 58	08 11			08 13			08 23			08 28	08 41			08 43
St Margarets	d					07 45					08 00				08 15						08 30				08 45
Richmond ⊖	d		07 45			07 49			07 58		08 04	08 15			08 19			08 28			08 34	08 45			08 49
North Sheen	d					07 51					08 06				08 21						08 36				08 51
Mortlake	d					07 53					08 08				08 23						08 38				08 53
Hounslow	d				07 31			07 46						08 01		08 16				08 31					
Isleworth	d				07 34			07 49						08 04		08 19				08 34					
Syon Lane	d				07 36			07 51						08 06		08 21				08 36					
Brentford	d				07 39			07 54						08 09		08 24				08 39					
Kew Bridge	d				07 41			07 56						08 11		08 26				08 41					
Chiswick	d				07 44			07 59						08 14		08 29				08 44					
Barnes Bridge	d				07 46			08 01						08 16		08 31				08 46			←		
Barnes	d	←			07 49	07 56		08 04		←	08 11			08 19	08 26	08 34			←	08 49	08 41		08 49		08 56
Putney	d	07 37			07 52	07 59		08 07	08 04	08 07	08 14			08 22	08 29	08 37		08 34	08 37	→	08 44		08 52		08 59
Wandsworth Town	d	07 40			07 55	08 02		→		08 10	08 17			08 25	08 32	→			08 40		08 47		08 55		09 02
Clapham Junction 10	d	07 43	07 54		07 58	08 05			08 09	08 13	08 20	08 24		08 28	08 35			08 39	08 43		08 50	08 54	08 58		09 05
Queenstown Rd.(Battersea)	d	07 46			08 01	08 08				08 16	08 23			08 31	08 38				08 46		08 53		09 01		09 08
Vauxhall ⊖	d	07 50			08 05	08 12			08 15	08 20	08 27			08 35	08 42			08 45	08 50		08 57		09 05		09 12
London Waterloo 15 ⊖	a	07 56	08 04		08 11	08 16			08 19	08 26	08 32	08 34		08 41	08 46			08 49	08 56		09 02	09 04	09 11		09 16

Reading, Guildford, Ascot, Weybridge, Windsor, Kingston, Richmond and Hounslow - London

		SW		SW	SW	SW	SW	SW 1	SW	SW 1	SW	SW		SW	SW	SW	SW	SW 1	SW	SW 1	SW	SW		SW	SW
Reading 7	d							08 12										08 42							
Earley	d							08 17										08 47							
Winnersh Triangle	d							08 19										08 49							
Winnersh	d							08 21										08 51							
Wokingham	d							08 26										08 56							
Bracknell	d							08 32										09 02							
Martins Heron	d							08 35										09 05							
Guildford	d									08 00										08 30					
Wanborough	d									08 06										08 36					
Ash 5	d									08 10										08 40					
Aldershot	a									08 17										08 47					
	d									08 30										09 00					
Ash Vale	d									08 34										09 04					
Frimley	d									08 40										09 10					
Camberley	a									08 44										09 14					
	d									08 48										09 18					
Bagshot	d									08 53										09 23					
Ascot 3	d							08 40		09a00								09 10		09a30					
Sunningdale	d							08 43										09 13							
Longcross	d																								
Woking	d																								
West Byfleet	d																								
Byfleet & New Haw	d																								
Weybridge	d	08 03										08 33										09 03			
Addlestone	d	08 07										08 37										09 07			
Chertsey	d	08 10										08 40										09 10			
Virginia Water	a	08 15						08 49				08 45						09 19				09 15			
	d	08 24						08 49				08 54						09 19				09 24			
Egham	d	08 27						08 53				08 57						09 23				09 27			
Windsor & Eton Riverside	d			08 23										08 53										09 23	
Datchet	d			08 26										08 56										09 26	
Sunnymeads	d			08 29										08 59										09 29	
Wraysbury	d			08 32										09 02										09 32	
Staines	d	08 33		08 38				08 59				09 03		09 08				09 29				09 33		09 38	
Ashford (Surrey)	d	08 36		08 41								09 06		09 11								09 36		09 41	
Feltham	d	08 41		08 46				09 05				09 11		09 16				09 35				09 41		09 46	
Whitton	d			08 50		08 50	08 53							09 20		09 20	09 23							09 50	
Kingston	d										08 59										09 29				
Hampton Wick	d										09 01										09 31				
Teddington	d										09 05										09 35				
Fulwell	d																								
Strawberry Hill	d										09 08										09 38				
Twickenham	a			08 53			08 56	09 10			09 12			09 23			09 26	09 40			09 42			09 53	
	d			08 53			08 58	09 11			09 13			09 23			09 28	09 41			09 43			09 53	
St Margarets	d						09 00				09 15						09 30				09 45				
Richmond ⊖	d			08 58			09 04	09 15			09 19			09 28			09 34	09 45			09 49			09 58	
North Sheen	d						09 06				09 21						09 36				09 51				
Mortlake	d						09 08				09 23						09 38				09 53				
Hounslow	d	08 46				09 01						09 16				09 31						09 46			
Isleworth	d	08 49				09 04						09 19				09 34						09 49			
Syon Lane	d	08 51				09 06						09 21				09 36						09 51			
Brentford	d	08 54				09 09						09 24				09 39						09 54			
Kew Bridge	d	08 56				09 11						09 26				09 41						09 56			
Chiswick	d	08 59				09 14						09 29				09 44						09 59			
Barnes Bridge	d	09 01				09 16			←			09 31				09 46			←			10 01			
Barnes	d	09 04			←	09 19	09 11		09 19		09 26	09 34			←	09 49	09 41		09 49		09 56	10 04			←
Putney	d	09 07		09 04	09 07	→	09 14		09 22		09 29	09 37		09 34	09 37	→	09 44		09 52		09 59	10 07		10 04	10 07
Wandsworth Town	d	→			09 10		09 17		09 25		09 32	→			09 40		09 47		09 55		10 02	→			10 10
Clapham Junction 10	d			09 09	09 13		09 20	09 24	09 28		09 35			09 39	09 43		09 50	09 54	09 58		10 05			10 09	10 13
Queenstown Rd.(Battersea)	d				09 16		09 23		09 31		09 38				09 46		09 53		10 01		10 08				10 16
Vauxhall ⊖	d			09 15	09 20		09 27		09 35		09 42			09 45	09 50		09 57		10 05		10 12			10 15	10 20
London Waterloo 15 ⊖	a			09 19	09 26		09 32	09 34	09 41		09 46			09 49	09 56		10 02	10 04	10 11		10 16			10 19	10 26

Table 149

Saturdays until 1 October

Reading, Guildford, Ascot, Weybridge, Windsor, Kingston, Richmond and Hounslow - London

		SW	SW	SW 1	SW	SW 1	SW	SW		SW	SW	SW	SW	SW 1	SW	SW 1	SW	SW		SW	SW	SW	SW	SW 1	SW
Reading 7	d			09 12										09 42										10 12	
Earley	d			09 17										09 47										10 17	
Winnersh Triangle	d			09 19										09 49										10 19	
Winnersh	d			09 21										09 51										10 21	
Wokingham	d			09 26										09 56										10 26	
Bracknell	d			09 32										10 02										10 32	
Martins Heron	d			09 35										10 05										10 35	
Guildford	d					09 00										09 30									
Wanborough	d					09 06										09 36									
Ash 5	d					09 10										09 40									
Aldershot	a					09 17										09 47									
	d					09 30										10 00									
Ash Vale	d					09 34										10 04									
Frimley	d					09 40										10 10									
Camberley	a					09 44										10 14									
	d					09 48										10 18									
Bagshot	d					09 53										10 23									
Ascot 3	d			09 40		10a00								10 10		10a30								10 40	
Sunningdale	d			09 43										10 13										10 43	
Longcross	d																								
Woking	d																								
West Byfleet	d																								
Byfleet & New Haw	d																								
Weybridge	d							09 33										10 03							
Addlestone	d							09 37										10 07							
Chertsey	d							09 40										10 10							
Virginia Water	a			09 49				09 45						10 19				10 15						10 49	
	d			09 49				09 54						10 19				10 24						10 49	
Egham	d			09 53				09 57						10 23				10 27						10 53	
Windsor & Eton Riverside	d									09 53										10 23					
Datchet	d									09 56										10 26					
Sunnymeads	d									09 59										10 29					
Wraysbury	d									10 02										10 32					
Staines	d			09 59				10 03		10 08				10 29				10 33		10 38				10 59	
Ashford (Surrey)	d							10 06		10 11								10 36		10 41					
Feltham	d			10 05				10 11		10 16				10 35				10 41		10 46				11 05	
Whitton	d	09 50	09 53							10 20		10 20	10 23							10 50		10 50	10 53		
Kingston	d						09 59										10 29								
Hampton Wick	d						10 01										10 31								
Teddington	d						10 05										10 35								
Fulwell	d																								
Strawberry Hill	d						10 08										10 38								
Twickenham	a		09 56	10 10			10 12			10 23			10 26	10 40			10 42			10 53			10 56	11 10	
	d		09 58	10 11			10 13			10 23			10 28	10 41			10 43			10 53			10 58	11 11	
St Margarets	d		10 00				10 15						10 30				10 45						11 00		
Richmond ⊖	d		10 04	10 15			10 19			10 28			10 34	10 45			10 49			10 58			11 04	11 15	
North Sheen	d		10 06				10 21						10 36				10 51						11 06		
Mortlake	d		10 08				10 23						10 38				10 53						11 08		
Hounslow	d	10 01						10 16				10 31						10 46				11 01			
Isleworth	d	10 04						10 19				10 34						10 49				11 04			
Syon Lane	d	10 06						10 21				10 36						10 51				11 06			
Brentford	d	10 09						10 24				10 39						10 54				11 09			
Kew Bridge	d	10 11						10 26				10 41						10 56				11 11			
Chiswick	d	10 14						10 29				10 44						10 59				11 14			
Barnes Bridge	d	10 16			←			10 31				10 46			←			11 01				11 16			←
Barnes	d	10 19	10 11		10 19		10 26	10 34			←	10 49	10 41		10 49		10 56	11 04			←	11 19	11 11		11 19
Putney	d	→	10 14		10 22		10 29	10 37		10 34	10 37	→	10 44		10 52		10 59	11 07		11 04	11 07	→	11 14		11 22
Wandsworth Town	d		10 17		10 25		10 32	→			10 40		10 47		10 55		11 02	→			11 10		11 17		11 25
Clapham Junction 10	d		10 20	10 24	10 28		10 35			10 39	10 43		10 50	10 54	10 58		11 05			11 09	11 13		11 20	11 24	11 28
Queenstown Rd.(Battersea)	d		10 23		10 31		10 38				10 46		10 53		11 01		11 08				11 16		11 23		11 31
Vauxhall ⊖	d		10 27		10 35		10 42			10 45	10 50		10 57		11 05		11 12			11 15	11 20		11 27		11 35
London Waterloo 15 ⊖	a		10 32	10 34	10 41		10 46			10 49	10 56		11 02	11 04	11 11		11 16			11 19	11 26		11 32	11 34	11 41

Table 149

Saturdays until 1 October

Reading, Guildford, Ascot, Weybridge, Windsor, Kingston, Richmond and Hounslow - London

		SW 1	SW	SW		SW	SW	SW	SW	SW 1	SW	SW 1	SW	SW		SW	SW	SW	SW	SW 1	SW	SW 1	SW	SW
Reading 7	d									10 42										11 12				
Earley	d									10 47										11 17				
Winnersh Triangle	d									10 49										11 19				
Winnersh	d									10 51										11 21				
Wokingham	d									10 56										11 26				
Bracknell	d									11 02										11 32				
Martins Heron	d									11 05										11 35				
Guildford	d	10 00										10 30										11 00		
Wanborough	d	10 06										10 36										11 06		
Ash 5	d	10 10										10 40										11 10		
Aldershot	a	10 17										10 47										11 17		
	d	10 30										11 00										11 30		
Ash Vale	d	10 34										11 04										11 34		
Frimley	d	10 40										11 10										11 40		
Camberley	a	10 44										11 14										11 44		
	d	10 48										11 18										11 48		
Bagshot	d	10 53										11 23										11 53		
Ascot 3	d	11a00								11 10		11a30								11 40		12a00		
Sunningdale	d									11 13										11 43				
Longcross	d																							
Woking	d																							
West Byfleet	d																							
Byfleet & New Haw	d																							
Weybridge	d			10 33										11 03										11 33
Addlestone	d			10 37										11 07										11 37
Chertsey	d			10 40										11 10										11 40
Virginia Water	a			10 45						11 19				11 15						11 49				11 45
	d			10 54						11 19				11 24						11 49				11 54
Egham	d			10 57						11 23				11 27						11 53				11 57
Windsor & Eton Riverside	d					10 53										11 23								
Datchet	d					10 56										11 26								
Sunnymeads	d					10 59										11 29								
Wraysbury	d					11 02										11 32								
Staines	d			11 03		11 08				11 29				11 33		11 38				11 59				12 03
Ashford (Surrey)	d			11 06		11 11								11 36		11 41								12 06
Feltham	d			11 11		11 16				11 35				11 41		11 46				12 05				12 11
Whitton	d					11 20		11 20	11 23							11 50		11 50	11 53					
Kingston	d		10 59										11 29										11 59	
Hampton Wick	d		11 01										11 31										12 01	
Teddington	d		11 05										11 35										12 05	
Fulwell	d																							
Strawberry Hill	d		11 08										11 38										12 08	
Twickenham	a		11 12			11 23			11 26	11 40			11 42			11 53			11 56	12 10			12 12	
	d		11 13			11 23			11 28	11 41			11 43			11 53			11 58	12 11			12 13	
St Margarets	d		11 15						11 30				11 45						12 00				12 15	
Richmond ⊖	d		11 19			11 28			11 34	11 45			11 49			11 58			12 04	12 15			12 19	
North Sheen	d		11 21						11 36				11 51						12 06				12 21	
Mortlake	d		11 23						11 38				11 53						12 08				12 23	
Hounslow	d			11 16				11 31						11 46				12 01						12 16
Isleworth	d			11 19				11 34						11 49				12 04						12 19
Syon Lane	d			11 21				11 36						11 51				12 06						12 21
Brentford	d			11 24				11 39						11 54				12 09						12 24
Kew Bridge	d			11 26				11 41						11 56				12 11						12 26
Chiswick	d			11 29				11 44						11 59				12 14						12 29
Barnes Bridge	d			11 31				11 46			←			12 01				12 16			←			12 31
Barnes	d		11 26	11 34			←	11 49	11 41		11 49		11 56	12 04			←	12 19	12 11		12 19		12 26	12 34
Putney	d		11 29	11 37		11 34	11 37	→	11 44		11 52		11 59	12 07		12 04	12 07	→	12 14		12 22		12 29	12 37
Wandsworth Town	d		11 32	→			11 40		11 47		11 55		12 02	→			12 10		12 17		12 25		12 32	→
Clapham Junction 10	d		11 35			11 39	11 43		11 50	11 54	11 58		12 05			12 09	12 13		12 20	12 24	12 28		12 35	
Queenstown Rd.(Battersea)	d		11 38				11 46		11 53		12 01		12 08				12 16		12 23		12 31		12 38	
Vauxhall ⊖	d		11 42			11 45	11 50		11 57		12 05		12 12			12 15	12 20		12 27		12 35		12 42	
London Waterloo 15 ⊖	a		11 46			11 49	11 56		12 02	12 04	12 11		12 16			12 19	12 26		12 32	12 34	12 41		12 46	

Reading, Guildford, Ascot, Weybridge, Windsor, Kingston, Richmond and Hounslow - London

		SW	SW	SW	SW	SW 1	SW	SW 1	SW	SW		SW	SW	SW	SW	SW 1	SW	SW 1	SW	SW		SW	SW	SW	SW
Reading 7	d					11 42										12 12									
Earley	d					11 47										12 17									
Winnersh Triangle	d					11 49										12 19									
Winnersh	d					11 51										12 21									
Wokingham	d					11 56										12 26									
Bracknell	d					12 02										12 32									
Martins Heron	d					12 05										12 35									
Guildford	d							11 30										12 00							
Wanborough	d							11 36										12 06							
Ash 5	d							11 40										12 10							
Aldershot	a							11 47										12 17							
	d							12 00										12 30							
Ash Vale	d							12 04										12 34							
Frimley	d							12 10										12 40							
Camberley	a							12 14										12 44							
	d							12 18										12 48							
Bagshot	d							12 23										12 53							
Ascot 3	d					12 10		12a30								12 40		13a00							
Sunningdale	d					12 13										12 43									
Longcross	d																								
Woking	d																								
West Byfleet	d																								
Byfleet & New Haw	d																								
Weybridge	d									12 03										12 33					
Addlestone	d									12 07										12 37					
Chertsey	d									12 10										12 40					
Virginia Water	a					12 19				12 15						12 49				12 45					
	d					12 19				12 24						12 49				12 54					
Egham	d					12 23				12 27						12 53				12 57					
Windsor & Eton Riverside	d	11 53										12 23										12 53			
Datchet	d	11 56										12 26										12 56			
Sunnymeads	d	11 59										12 29										12 59			
Wraysbury	d	12 02										12 32										13 02			
Staines	d	12 08				12 29				12 33		12 38				12 59				13 03		13 08			
Ashford (Surrey)	d	12 11								12 36		12 41								13 06		13 11			
Feltham	d	12 16				12 35				12 41		12 46				13 05				13 11		13 16			
Whitton	d	12 20		12 20	12 23							12 50		12 50	12 53							13 20		13 20	13 23
Kingston	d								12 29										12 59						
Hampton Wick	d								12 31										13 01						
Teddington	d								12 35										13 05						
Fulwell	d																								
Strawberry Hill	d								12 38										13 08						
Twickenham	a	12 23			12 27	12 40			12 42			12 53			12 56	13 10			13 12			13 23			13 26
	d	12 23			12 28	12 41			12 43			12 53			12 58	13 11			13 13			13 23			13 28
St Margarets	d				12 30				12 45						13 00				13 15						13 30
Richmond ⊖	d	12 28			12 34	12 45			12 49			12 58			13 04	13 15			13 19			13 28			13 34
North Sheen	d				12 36				12 51						13 06				13 21						13 36
Mortlake	d				12 38				12 53						13 08				13 23						13 38
Hounslow	d			12 31						12 46				13 01						13 16				13 31	
Isleworth	d			12 34						12 49				13 04						13 19				13 34	
Syon Lane	d			12 36						12 51				13 06						13 21				13 36	
Brentford	d			12 39						12 54				13 09						13 24				13 39	
Kew Bridge	d			12 41						12 56				13 11						13 26				13 41	
Chiswick	d			12 44						12 59				13 14						13 29				13 44	
Barnes Bridge	d			12 46			←			13 01				13 16			←			13 31				13 46	
Barnes	d		←	12 49	12 41		12 49		12 56	13 04			←	13 19	13 11		13 19		13 26	13 34			←	13 49	13 41
Putney	d	12 34	12 37	→	12 44		12 52		12 59	13 07		13 04	13 07	→	13 14		13 22		13 29	13 37		13 34	13 37	→	13 44
Wandsworth Town	d		12 40		12 47		12 55		13 02	→			13 10		13 17		13 25		13 32	→			13 40		13 47
Clapham Junction 10	d	12 39	12 43		12 50	12 54	12 58		13 05			13 09	13 13		13 20	13 24	13 28		13 35			13 39	13 43		13 50
Queenstown Rd.(Battersea)	d		12 46		12 53		13 01		13 08				13 16		13 23		13 31		13 38				13 46		13 53
Vauxhall ⊖	d	12 45	12 50		12 57		13 05		13 12			13 15	13 20		13 27		13 35		13 42			13 45	13 50		13 57
London Waterloo 15 ⊖	a	12 49	12 56		13 02	13 04	13 11		13 16			13 19	13 26		13 32	13 34	13 41		13 46			13 49	13 56		14 02

until 1 October

Reading, Guildford, Ascot, Weybridge, Windsor, Kingston, Richmond and Hounslow - London

		SW 1	SW	SW 1	SW	SW		SW	SW	SW	SW	SW 1	SW	SW 1	SW	SW		SW	SW	SW	SW	SW 1	SW	SW 1	SW
Reading 7	d	12 42										13 12										13 42			
Earley	d	12 47										13 17										13 47			
Winnersh Triangle	d	12 49										13 19										13 49			
Winnersh	d	12 51										13 21										13 51			
Wokingham	d	12 56										13 26										13 56			
Bracknell	d	13 02										13 32										14 02			
Martins Heron	d	13 05										13 35										14 05			
Guildford	d			12 30										13 00										13 30	
Wanborough	d			12 36										13 06										13 36	
Ash 5	d			12 40										13 10										13 40	
Aldershot	a			12 47										13 17										13 47	
	d			13 00										13 30										14 00	
Ash Vale	d			13 04										13 34										14 04	
Frimley	d			13 10										13 40										14 10	
Camberley	a			13 14										13 44										14 14	
	d			13 18										13 48										14 18	
Bagshot	d			13 23										13 53										14 23	
Ascot 3	d	13 10		13a30								13 40		14a00								14 10		14a30	
Sunningdale	d	13 13										13 43										14 13			
Longcross	d																								
Woking	d																								
West Byfleet	d																								
Byfleet & New Haw	d																								
Weybridge	d					13 03										13 33									
Addlestone	d					13 07										13 37									
Chertsey	d					13 10										13 40									
Virginia Water	a	13 19				13 15						13 49				13 45						14 19			
	d	13 19				13 24						13 49				13 54						14 19			
Egham	d	13 23				13 27						13 53				13 57						14 23			
Windsor & Eton Riverside	d							13 23										13 53							
Datchet	d							13 26										13 56							
Sunnymeads	d							13 29										13 59							
Wraysbury	d							13 32										14 02							
Staines	d	13 29				13 33		13 38				13 59				14 03		14 08				14 29			
Ashford (Surrey)	d					13 36		13 41								14 06		14 11							
Feltham	d	13 35				13 41		13 46				14 05				14 11		14 16				14 35			
Whitton	d							13 50		13 50	13 53							14 20		14 20	14 23				
Kingston	d				13 29										13 59										14 29
Hampton Wick	d				13 31										14 01										14 31
Teddington	d				13 35										14 05										14 35
Fulwell	d																								
Strawberry Hill	d				13 38										14 08										14 38
Twickenham	a	13 40			13 42			13 53			13 56	14 10			14 12			14 23			14 26	14 40			14 42
	d	13 41			13 43			13 53			13 58	14 11			14 13			14 23			14 28	14 41			14 43
St Margarets	d				13 45						14 00				14 15						14 30				14 45
Richmond ⊖	d	13 45			13 49			13 58			14 04	14 15			14 19			14 28			14 34	14 45			14 49
North Sheen	d				13 51						14 06				14 21						14 36				14 51
Mortlake	d				13 53						14 08				14 23						14 38				14 53
Hounslow	d					13 46				14 01						14 16				14 31					
Isleworth	d					13 49				14 04						14 19				14 34					
Syon Lane	d					13 51				14 06						14 21				14 36					
Brentford	d					13 54				14 09						14 24				14 39					
Kew Bridge	d					13 56				14 11						14 26				14 41					
Chiswick	d					13 59				14 14						14 29				14 44					
Barnes Bridge	d		←			14 01				14 16			←			14 31				14 46			←		
Barnes	d		13 49		13 56	14 04			←	14 19	14 11		14 19		14 26	14 34			←	14 49	14 41		14 49		14 56
Putney	d		13 52		13 59	14 07		14 04	14 07	→	14 14		14 22		14 29	14 37		14 34	14 37	→	14 44		14 52		14 59
Wandsworth Town	d		13 55		14 02	→			14 10		14 17		14 25		14 32	→			14 40		14 47		14 55		15 02
Clapham Junction 10	d	13 54	13 58		14 05			14 09	14 13		14 20	14 24	14 28		14 35			14 39	14 43		14 50	14 54	14 58		15 05
Queenstown Rd.(Battersea)	d		14 01		14 08				14 16		14 23		14 31		14 38				14 46		14 53		15 01		15 08
Vauxhall ⊖	d		14 05		14 12			14 15	14 20		14 27		14 35		14 42			14 45	14 50		14 57		15 05		15 12
London Waterloo 15 ⊖	a	14 04	14 11		14 16			14 19	14 26		14 32	14 34	14 41		14 46			14 49	14 56		15 02	15 04	15 11		15 16

Saturdays until 1 October

Reading, Guildford, Ascot, Weybridge, Windsor, Kingston, Richmond and Hounslow - London

		SW	SW	SW	SW	SW	SW ■1	SW	SW ■1	SW	SW	SW	SW	SW	SW	SW ■1	SW	SW ■1	SW	SW	SW	SW
Reading 7	d						14 12									14 42						
Earley	d						14 17									14 47						
Winnersh Triangle	d						14 19									14 49						
Winnersh	d						14 21									14 51						
Wokingham	d						14 26									14 56						
Bracknell	d						14 32									15 02						
Martins Heron	d						14 35									15 05						
Guildford	d								14 00									14 30				
Wanborough	d								14 06									14 36				
Ash 5	d								14 10									14 40				
Aldershot	a								14 17									14 47				
	d								14 30									15 00				
Ash Vale	d								14 34									15 04				
Frimley	d								14 40									15 10				
Camberley	a								14 44									15 14				
	d								14 48									15 18				
Bagshot	d								14 53									15 23				
Ascot 3	d						14 40		15a00							15 10		15a30				
Sunningdale	d						14 43									15 13						
Longcross	d																					
Woking	d																					
West Byfleet	d																					
Byfleet & New Haw	d																					
Weybridge	d	14 03									14 33									15 03		
Addlestone	d	14 07									14 37									15 07		
Chertsey	d	14 10									14 40									15 10		
Virginia Water	a	14 15					14 49				14 45					15 19				15 15		
	d	14 24					14 49				14 54					15 19				15 24		
Egham	d	14 27					14 53				14 57					15 23				15 27		
Windsor & Eton Riverside	d		14 23									14 53									15 23	
Datchet	d		14 26									14 56									15 26	
Sunnymeads	d		14 29									14 59									15 29	
Wraysbury	d		14 32									15 02									15 32	
Staines	d	14 33	14 38				14 59				15 03	15 08				15 29				15 33	15 38	
Ashford (Surrey)	d	14 36	14 41								15 06	15 11								15 36	15 41	
Feltham	d	14 41	14 46				15 05				15 11	15 16				15 35				15 41	15 46	
Whitton	d		14 50		14 50	14 53						15 20		15 20	15 23						15 50	
Kingston	d									14 59									15 29			
Hampton Wick	d									15 01									15 31			
Teddington	d									15 05									15 35			
Fulwell	d																					
Strawberry Hill	d									15 08									15 38			
Twickenham	a		14 53			14 56	15 10			15 12		15 23			15 26	15 40			15 42		15 53	
	d		14 53			14 58	15 11			15 13		15 23			15 28	15 41			15 43		15 53	
St Margarets	d					15 00				15 15					15 30				15 45			
Richmond ⊖	d		14 58			15 04	15 15			15 19		15 28			15 34	15 45			15 49		15 58	
North Sheen	d					15 06				15 21					15 36				15 51			
Mortlake	d					15 08				15 23					15 38				15 53			
Hounslow	d	14 46			15 01						15 16			15 31						15 46		
Isleworth	d	14 49			15 04						15 19			15 34						15 49		
Syon Lane	d	14 51			15 06						15 21			15 36						15 51		
Brentford	d	14 54			15 09						15 24			15 39						15 54		
Kew Bridge	d	14 56			15 11						15 26			15 41						15 56		
Chiswick	d	14 59			15 14						15 29			15 44						15 59		
Barnes Bridge	d	15 01			15 16			←			15 31			15 46			←			16 01		
Barnes	d	15 04		←	15 19	15 11		15 19		15 26	15 34		←	15 49	15 41		15 49		15 56	16 04		←
Putney	d	15 07	15 04	15 07	→	15 14		15 22		15 29	15 37	15 34	15 37	→	15 44		15 52		15 59	16 07	16 04	16 07
Wandsworth Town	d	→		15 10		15 17		15 25		15 32	→		15 40		15 47		15 55		16 02	→		16 10
Clapham Junction 10	d		15 09	15 13		15 20	15 24	15 28		15 35		15 39	15 43		15 50	15 54	15 58		16 05		16 09	16 13
Queenstown Rd.(Battersea)	d			15 16		15 23		15 31		15 38			15 46		15 53		16 01		16 08			16 16
Vauxhall ⊖	d		15 15	15 20		15 27		15 35		15 42		15 45	15 50		15 57		16 05		16 12		16 15	16 20
London Waterloo 15 ⊖	a		15 19	15 26		15 32	15 34	15 41		15 46		15 49	15 56		16 02	16 04	16 11		16 16		16 19	16 26

Saturdays until 1 October

Reading, Guildford, Ascot, Weybridge, Windsor, Kingston, Richmond and Hounslow - London

		SW	SW	SW ■1	SW	SW ■1	SW	SW	SW	SW	SW	SW	SW ■1	SW	SW ■1	SW	SW	SW	SW	SW	SW	SW ■1	SW
Reading 7	d			15 12									15 42									16 12	
Earley	d			15 17									15 47									16 17	
Winnersh Triangle	d			15 19									15 49									16 19	
Winnersh	d			15 21									15 51									16 21	
Wokingham	d			15 26									15 56									16 26	
Bracknell	d			15 32									16 02									16 32	
Martins Heron	d			15 35									16 05									16 35	
Guildford	d					15 00									15 30								
Wanborough	d					15 06									15 36								
Ash 5	d					15 10									15 40								
Aldershot	a					15 17									15 47								
	d					15 30									16 00								
Ash Vale	d					15 34									16 04								
Frimley	d					15 40									16 10								
Camberley	a					15 44									16 14								
	d					15 48									16 18								
Bagshot	d					15 53									16 23								
Ascot 3	d			15 40		16a00							16 10		16a30							16 40	
Sunningdale	d			15 43									16 13									16 43	
Longcross	d																						
Woking	d																						
West Byfleet	d																						
Byfleet & New Haw	d																						
Weybridge	d							15 33									16 03						
Addlestone	d							15 37									16 07						
Chertsey	d							15 40									16 10						
Virginia Water	a			15 49				15 45					16 19				16 15					16 49	
	d			15 49				15 54					16 19				16 24					16 49	
Egham	d			15 53				15 57					16 23				16 27					16 53	
Windsor & Eton Riverside	d								15 53									16 23					
Datchet	d								15 56									16 26					
Sunnymeads	d								15 59									16 29					
Wraysbury	d								16 02									16 32					
Staines	d			15 59				16 03	16 08				16 29				16 33	16 38				16 59	
Ashford (Surrey)	d							16 06	16 11								16 36	16 41					
Feltham	d			16 05				16 11	16 16				16 35				16 41	16 46				17 05	
Whitton	d	15 50	15 53						16 20		16 20	16 23						16 50		16 50	16 53		
Kingston	d						15 59									16 29							
Hampton Wick	d						16 01									16 31							
Teddington	d						16 05									16 35							
Fulwell	d																						
Strawberry Hill	d						16 08									16 38							
Twickenham	a		15 56	16 10			16 12		16 23			16 26	16 40			16 42		16 53			16 56	17 10	
	d		15 58	16 11			16 13		16 23			16 28	16 41			16 43		16 53			16 58	17 11	
St Margarets	d		16 00				16 15					16 30				16 45					17 00		
Richmond ⊖	d		16 04	16 15			16 19		16 28			16 34	16 45			16 49		16 58			17 04	17 15	
North Sheen	d		16 06				16 21					16 36				16 51					17 06		
Mortlake	d		16 08				16 23					16 38				16 53					17 08		
Hounslow	d	16 01						16 16			16 31						16 46			17 01			
Isleworth	d	16 04						16 19			16 34						16 49			17 04			
Syon Lane	d	16 06						16 21			16 36						16 51			17 06			
Brentford	d	16 09						16 24			16 39						16 54			17 09			
Kew Bridge	d	16 11						16 26			16 41						16 56			17 11			
Chiswick	d	16 14						16 29			16 44						16 59			17 14			
Barnes Bridge	d	16 16			←			16 31			16 46			←			17 01			17 16			←
Barnes	d	16 19	16 11		16 19		16 26	16 34		←	16 49	16 41		16 49		16 56	17 04		←	17 19	17 11		17 19
Putney	d	→	16 14		16 22		16 29	16 37	16 34	16 37	→	16 44		16 52		16 59	17 07	17 04	17 07	→	17 14		17 22
Wandsworth Town	d		16 17		16 25		16 32	→		16 40		16 47		16 55		17 02	→		17 10		17 17		17 25
Clapham Junction 10	d		16 20	16 24	16 28		16 35		16 39	16 43		16 50	16 54	16 58		17 05		17 09	17 13		17 20	17 24	17 28
Queenstown Rd.(Battersea)	d		16 23		16 31		16 38			16 46		16 53		17 01		17 08			17 16		17 23		17 31
Vauxhall ⊖	d		16 27		16 35		16 42		16 45	16 50		16 57		17 05		17 12		17 15	17 20		17 27		17 35
London Waterloo 15 ⊖	a		16 32	16 34	16 41		16 46		16 49	16 56		17 02	17 04	17 11		17 16		17 19	17 26		17 32	17 34	17 41

Reading, Guildford, Ascot, Weybridge, Windsor, Kingston, Richmond and Hounslow - London

		SW 1	SW	SW	SW	SW	SW	SW	SW 1	SW	SW 1	SW	SW	SW	SW	SW	SW	SW 1	SW	SW 1	SW	SW
Reading 7	d								16 42									17 12				
Earley	d								16 47									17 17				
Winnersh Triangle	d								16 49									17 19				
Winnersh	d								16 51									17 21				
Wokingham	d								16 56									17 26				
Bracknell	d								17 02									17 32				
Martins Heron	d								17 05									17 35				
Guildford	d	16 00									16 30									17 00		
Wanborough	d	16 06									16 36									17 06		
Ash 5	d	16 10									16 40									17 10		
Aldershot	a	16 17									16 47									17 17		
	d	16 30									17 00									17 30		
Ash Vale	d	16 34									17 04									17 34		
Frimley	d	16 40									17 10									17 40		
Camberley	a	16 44									17 14									17 44		
	d	16 48									17 18									17 48		
Bagshot	d	16 53									17 23									17 53		
Ascot 8	d	17a00							17 10		17a30							17 40		18a00		
Sunningdale	d								17 13									17 43				
Longcross	d																					
Woking	d																					
West Byfleet	d																					
Byfleet & New Haw	d																					
Weybridge	d			16 33									17 03									17 33
Addlestone	d			16 37									17 07									17 37
Chertsey	d			16 40									17 10									17 40
Virginia Water	a			16 45					17 19				17 15					17 49				17 45
	d			16 54					17 19				17 24					17 49				17 54
Egham	d			16 57					17 23				17 27					17 53				17 57
Windsor & Eton Riverside	d				16 53									17 23								
Datchet	d				16 56									17 26								
Sunnymeads	d				16 59									17 29								
Wraysbury	d				17 02									17 32								
Staines	d			17 03	17 08				17 29				17 33	17 38				17 59				18 03
Ashford (Surrey)	d			17 06	17 11								17 36	17 41								18 06
Feltham	d			17 11	17 16				17 35				17 41	17 46				18 05				18 11
Whitton	d				17 20		17 20	17 23						17 50		17 50	17 53					
Kingston	d		16 59									17 29									17 59	
Hampton Wick	d		17 01									17 31									18 01	
Teddington	d		17 05									17 35									18 05	
Fulwell	d																					
Strawberry Hill	d		17 08									17 38									18 08	
Twickenham	a		17 12		17 23			17 26	17 40			17 42		17 53			17 56	18 10			18 12	
	d		17 13		17 23			17 28	17 41			17 43		17 53			17 58	18 11			18 13	
St Margarets	d		17 15					17 30				17 45					18 00				18 15	
Richmond ⊖	d		17 19		17 28			17 34	17 45			17 49		17 58			18 04	18 15			18 19	
North Sheen	d		17 21					17 36				17 51					18 06				18 21	
Mortlake	d		17 23					17 38				17 53					18 08				18 23	
Hounslow	d			17 16			17 31						17 46			18 01						18 16
Isleworth	d			17 19			17 34						17 49			18 04						18 19
Syon Lane	d			17 21			17 36						17 51			18 06						18 21
Brentford	d			17 24			17 39						17 54			18 09						18 24
Kew Bridge	d			17 26			17 41						17 56			18 11						18 26
Chiswick	d			17 29			17 44						17 59			18 14						18 29
Barnes Bridge	d			17 31			17 46			←			18 01			18 16			←			18 31
Barnes	d		17 26	17 34		←	17 49	17 41		17 49		17 56	18 04		←	18 19	18 11		18 19		18 26	18 34
Putney	d		17 29	17 37	17 34	17 37	→	17 44		17 52		17 59	18 07	18 04	18 07	→	18 14		18 22		18 29	18 37
Wandsworth Town	d		17 32	→		17 40		17 47		17 55		18 02	→		18 10		18 17		18 25		18 32	→
Clapham Junction 10	d		17 35		17 39	17 43		17 50	17 54	17 58		18 05		18 09	18 13		18 20	18 24	18 28		18 35	
Queenstown Rd.(Battersea)	d		17 38			17 46		17 53		18 01		18 08			18 16		18 23		18 31		18 38	
Vauxhall ⊖	d		17 42		17 45	17 50		17 57		18 05		18 12		18 15	18 20		18 27		18 35		18 42	
London Waterloo 15 ⊖	a		17 46		17 49	17 56		18 02	18 04	18 11		18 16		18 19	18 26		18 32	18 34	18 41		18 46	

Reading, Guildford, Ascot, Weybridge, Windsor, Kingston, Richmond and Hounslow - London

		SW	SW	SW	SW	SW 1	SW	SW 1	SW	SW	SW	SW	SW	SW	SW 1	SW	SW 1	SW	SW	SW	SW	SW	SW
Reading 7	d					17 42									18 12								
Earley	d					17 47									18 17								
Winnersh Triangle	d					17 49									18 19								
Winnersh	d					17 51									18 21								
Wokingham	d					17 56									18 26								
Bracknell	d					18 02									18 32								
Martins Heron	d					18 05									18 35								
Guildford	d							17 30									18 00						
Wanborough	d							17 36									18 06						
Ash 5	d							17 40									18 10						
Aldershot	a							17 47									18 17						
	d							18 00									18 30						
Ash Vale	d							18 04									18 34						
Frimley	d							18 10									18 40						
Camberley	a							18 14									18 44						
	d							18 18									18 48						
Bagshot	d							18 23									18 53						
Ascot 8	d					18 10		18a30							18 40		19a00						
Sunningdale	d					18 13									18 43								
Longcross	d																						
Woking	d																						
West Byfleet	d																						
Byfleet & New Haw	d																						
Weybridge	d									18 03									18 33				
Addlestone	d									18 07									18 37				
Chertsey	d									18 10									18 40				
Virginia Water	a					18 19				18 15					18 49				18 45				
	d					18 19				18 24					18 49				18 54				
Egham	d					18 23				18 27					18 53				18 57				
Windsor & Eton Riverside	d	17 53									18 23									18 53			
Datchet	d	17 56									18 26									18 56			
Sunnymeads	d	17 59									18 29									18 59			
Wraysbury	d	18 02									18 32									19 02			
Staines	d	18 08				18 29				18 33	18 38				18 59				19 03	19 08			
Ashford (Surrey)	d	18 11								18 36	18 41								19 06	19 11			
Feltham	d	18 16				18 35				18 41	18 46				19 05				19 11	19 16			
Whitton	d	18 20		18 20	18 23						18 50		18 50	18 53						19 20		19 20	19 23
Kingston	d								18 29									18 59					
Hampton Wick	d								18 31									19 01					
Teddington	d								18 35									19 05					
Fulwell	d																						
Strawberry Hill	d								18 38									19 08					
Twickenham	a	18 23			18 26	18 40			18 42		18 53			18 56	19 10			19 12		19 23			19 26
	d	18 23			18 28	18 41			18 43		18 53			18 58	19 11			19 13		19 23			19 28
St Margarets	d				18 30				18 45					19 00				19 15					19 30
Richmond ⊖	d	18 28			18 34	18 45			18 49		18 58			19 04	19 15			19 19		19 28			19 34
North Sheen	d				18 36				18 51					19 06				19 21					19 36
Mortlake	d				18 38				18 53					19 08				19 23					19 38
Hounslow	d			18 31						18 46			19 01						19 16			19 31	
Isleworth	d			18 34						18 49			19 04						19 19			19 34	
Syon Lane	d			18 36						18 51			19 06						19 21			19 36	
Brentford	d			18 39						18 54			19 09						19 24			19 39	
Kew Bridge	d			18 41						18 56			19 11						19 26			19 41	
Chiswick	d			18 44						18 59			19 14						19 29			19 44	
Barnes Bridge	d			18 46			←			19 01			19 16			←			19 31			19 46	
Barnes	d		←	18 49	18 41		18 49		18 56	19 04		←	19 19	19 11		19 19		19 26	19 34		←	19 49	19 41
Putney	d	18 34	18 37	→	18 44		18 52		18 59	19 07	19 04	19 07	→	19 14		19 22		19 29	19 37	19 34	19 37	→	19 44
Wandsworth Town	d		18 40		18 47		18 55		19 02	→		19 10		19 17		19 25		19 32	→		19 40		19 47
Clapham Junction 10	d	18 39	18 43		18 50	18 54	18 58		19 05		19 09	19 13		19 20	19 24	19 28		19 35		19 39	19 43		19 50
Queenstown Rd.(Battersea)	d		18 46		18 53		19 01		19 08			19 16		19 23		19 31		19 38			19 46		19 53
Vauxhall ⊖	d	18 45	18 50		18 57		19 05		19 12		19 15	19 20		19 27		19 35		19 42		19 45	19 50		19 57
London Waterloo 15 ⊖	a	18 49	18 56		19 02	19 04	19 11		19 16		19 19	19 26		19 32	19 34	19 41		19 46		19 49	19 56		20 02

Table 149

Saturdays
until 1 October

Reading, Guildford, Ascot, Weybridge, Windsor, Kingston, Richmond and Hounslow - London

		SW 1	SW	SW 1	SW	SW		SW	SW	SW	SW	SW 1	SW	SW 1	SW	SW		SW	SW	SW	SW	SW 1	SW	SW 1	SW
Reading 7	d	18 42										19 12										19 42			
Earley	d	18 47										19 17										19 47			
Winnersh Triangle	d	18 49										19 19										19 49			
Winnersh	d	18 51										19 21										19 51			
Wokingham	d	18 56										19 26										19 56			
Bracknell	d	19 02										19 32										20 02			
Martins Heron	d	19 05										19 35										20 05			
Guildford	d			18 30										19 00										19 30	
Wanborough	d			18 36										19 06										19 36	
Ash 5	d			18 40										19 10										19 40	
Aldershot	a			18 47										19 17										19 47	
	d			19 00										19 30										20 00	
Ash Vale	d			19 04										19 34										20 04	
Frimley	d			19 10										19 40										20 10	
Camberley	a			19 14										19 44										20 14	
	d			19 18										19 48										20 18	
Bagshot	d			19 23										19 53										20 23	
Ascot 3	d	19 10		19a30								19 40		20a00								20 10		20a30	
Sunningdale	d	19 13										19 43										20 13			
Longcross	d																								
Woking	d																								
West Byfleet	d																								
Byfleet & New Haw	d																								
Weybridge	d					19 03										19 33									
Addlestone	d					19 07										19 37									
Chertsey	d					19 10										19 40									
Virginia Water	a	19 19				19 15						19 49				19 45						20 19			
	d	19 19				19 24						19 49				19 54						20 19			
Egham	d	19 23				19 27						19 53				19 57						20 23			
Windsor & Eton Riverside	d							19 23										19 53							
Datchet	d							19 26										19 56							
Sunnymeads	d							19 29										19 59							
Wraysbury	d							19 32										20 02							
Staines	d	19 29				19 33		19 38				19 59				20 03		20 08				20 29			
Ashford (Surrey)	d					19 36		19 41								20 06		20 11							
Feltham	d	19 35				19 41		19 46				20 05				20 11		20 16				20 35			
Whitton	d							19 50		19 50	19 53							20 20		20 20	20 23				
Kingston	d				19 29										19 59										20 29
Hampton Wick	d				19 31										20 01										20 31
Teddington	d				19 35										20 05										20 35
Fulwell	d																								
Strawberry Hill	d				19 38										20 08										20 38
Twickenham	a	19 40			19 42			19 53			19 56	20 10			20 12			20 23			20 26	20 40			20 42
	d	19 41			19 43			19 53			19 58	20 11			20 13			20 23			20 28	20 41			20 43
St Margarets	d				19 45						20 00				20 15						20 30				20 45
Richmond ⊖	d	19 45			19 49			19 58			20 04	20 15			20 19			20 28			20 34	20 45			20 49
North Sheen	d				19 51						20 06				20 21						20 36				20 51
Mortlake	d				19 53						20 08				20 23						20 38				20 53
Hounslow	d					19 46				20 01						20 16				20 31					
Isleworth	d					19 49				20 04						20 19				20 34					
Syon Lane	d					19 51				20 06						20 21				20 36					
Brentford	d					19 54				20 09						20 24				20 39					
Kew Bridge	d					19 56				20 11						20 26				20 41					
Chiswick	d					19 59				20 14						20 29				20 44					
Barnes Bridge	d		←			20 01				20 16			←			20 31				20 46			←		
Barnes	d		19 49		19 56	20 04			←	20 19	20 11		20 19		20 26	20 34			←	20 49	20 41		20 49		20 56
Putney	d		19 52		19 59	20 07		20 04	20 07	→	20 14		20 22		20 29	20 37		20 34	20 37	→	20 44		20 52		20 59
Wandsworth Town	d		19 55		20 02	→			20 10		20 17		20 25		20 32	→			20 40		20 47		20 55		21 02
Clapham Junction 10	d	19 54	19 58		20 05			20 09	20 13		20 20	20 24	20 28		20 35			20 39	20 43		20 50	20 54	20 58		21 05
Queenstown Rd.(Battersea)	d		20 01		20 08				20 16		20 23		20 31		20 38				20 46		20 53		21 01		21 08
Vauxhall ⊖	d		20 05		20 12			20 15	20 20		20 27		20 35		20 42			20 45	20 50		20 57		21 05		21 12
London Waterloo 15 ⊖	a	20 04	20 11		20 16			20 19	20 26		20 32	20 34	20 41		20 46			20 49	20 56		21 02	21 04	21 11		21 16

Table 149

Saturdays
until 1 October

Reading, Guildford, Ascot, Weybridge, Windsor, Kingston, Richmond and Hounslow - London

		SW		SW	SW	SW	SW	SW 1	SW	SW 1	SW 1	SW		SW	SW	SW	SW	SW	SW 1	SW	SW	SW		SW	SW
Reading 7	d							20 12											20 42						
Earley	d							20 17											20 47						
Winnersh Triangle	d							20 19											20 49						
Winnersh	d							20 21											20 51						
Wokingham	d							20 26											20 56						
Bracknell	d							20 32											21 02						
Martins Heron	d							20 35											21 05						
Guildford	d									20 00	20 30														
Wanborough	d									20 06	20 36														
Ash 5	d									20 10	20 40														
Aldershot	a									20 17	20 47														
	d									20 30															
Ash Vale	d									20 34															
Frimley	d									20 40															
Camberley	a									20 44															
	d									20 48															
Bagshot	d									20 53															
Ascot 3	d							20 40		21a00									21 10						
Sunningdale	d							20 43											21 13						
Longcross	d																								
Woking	d																								
West Byfleet	d																								
Byfleet & New Haw	d																								
Weybridge	d	20 03												20 33								21 03			
Addlestone	d	20 07												20 37								21 07			
Chertsey	d	20 10												20 40								21 10			
Virginia Water	a	20 15						20 49						20 45					21 19			21 15			
	d	20 24						20 49						20 54					21 19			21 24			
Egham	d	20 27						20 53						20 57					21 23			21 27			
Windsor & Eton Riverside	d			20 23											20 53									21 23	
Datchet	d			20 26											20 56									21 26	
Sunnymeads	d			20 29											20 59									21 29	
Wraysbury	d			20 32											21 02									21 32	
Staines	d	20 33		20 38				20 59						21 03	21 08				21 29			21 33		21 38	
Ashford (Surrey)	d	20 36		20 41										21 06	21 11							21 36		21 41	
Feltham	d	20 41		20 46				21 05						21 11	21 16				21 35			21 41		21 46	
Whitton	d			20 50		20 50	20 53								21 20		21 20	21 23						21 50	
Kingston	d											20 59									21 29				
Hampton Wick	d											21 01									21 31				
Teddington	d											21 05									21 35				
Fulwell	d																								
Strawberry Hill	d											21 08									21 38				
Twickenham	a			20 53			20 56	21 10				21 12			21 23			21 26	21 40		21 42			21 53	
	d			20 53			20 58	21 11				21 13			21 23			21 28	21 41		21 43			21 53	
St Margarets	d						21 00					21 15						21 30			21 45				
Richmond ⊖	d			20 58			21 04	21 15				21 19			21 28			21 34	21 45		21 49			21 58	
North Sheen	d						21 06					21 21						21 36			21 51				
Mortlake	d						21 08					21 23						21 38			21 53				
Hounslow	d	20 46				21 01								21 16			21 31					21 46			
Isleworth	d	20 49				21 04								21 19			21 34					21 49			
Syon Lane	d	20 51				21 06								21 21			21 36					21 51			
Brentford	d	20 54				21 09								21 24			21 39					21 54			
Kew Bridge	d	20 56				21 11								21 26			21 41					21 56			
Chiswick	d	20 59				21 14								21 29			21 44					21 59			
Barnes Bridge	d	21 01				21 16			←					21 31			21 46			←		22 01			
Barnes	d	21 04			←	21 19	21 11		21 19			21 26		21 34		←	21 49	21 41		21 49	21 56	22 04			←
Putney	d	21 07		21 04	21 07	→	21 14		21 22			21 29		21 37	21 34	21 37	→	21 44		21 52	21 59	22 07		22 04	22 07
Wandsworth Town	d	→			21 10		21 17		21 25			21 32		→		21 40		21 47		21 55	22 02	→			22 10
Clapham Junction 10	d			21 09	21 13		21 20	21 24	21 28			21 35			21 39	21 43		21 50	21 54	21 58	22 05			22 09	22 13
Queenstown Rd.(Battersea)	d				21 16		21 23		21 31			21 38				21 46		21 53		22 01	22 08				22 16
Vauxhall ⊖	d			21 15	21 20		21 27		21 35			21 42			21 45	21 50		21 57		22 05	22 12			22 15	22 20
London Waterloo 15 ⊖	a			21 19	21 26		21 32	21 34	21 41			21 46			21 49	21 56		22 02	22 04	22 11	22 16			22 19	22 26

Reading, Guildford, Ascot, Weybridge, Windsor, Kingston, Richmond and Hounslow - London

		SW	SW	SW 1	SW	SW 1	SW 1	SW	SW	SW	SW	SW	SW 1	SW	SW	SW	SW	SW 1	SW 1	SW 1	SW	SW	SW
Reading 7	d			21 12									21 42					22 12					
Earley	d			21 17									21 47					22 17					
Winnersh Triangle	d			21 19									21 49					22 19					
Winnersh	d			21 21									21 51					22 21					
Wokingham	d			21 26									21 56					22 26					
Bracknell	d			21 32									22 02					22 32					
Martins Heron	d			21 35									22 05					22 35					
Guildford	d					21 00	21 30												22 00	22 30			
Wanborough	d					21 06	21 36												22 06	22 36			
Ash 5	d					21 10	21 40												22 10	22 40			
Aldershot	a					21 17	21 47												22 17	22 47			
	d					21 30													22 30				
Ash Vale	d					21 34													22 34				
Frimley	d					21 40													22 40				
Camberley	a					21 44													22 44				
	d					21 48													22 48				
Bagshot	d					21 53													22 53				
Ascot 3	d			21 40		22a00							22 10					22 40	23a00				
Sunningdale	d			21 43									22 13					22 43					
Longcross	d																						
Woking	d																						
West Byfleet	d																						
Byfleet & New Haw	d																						
Weybridge	d								21 33						22 03							22 33	
Addlestone	d								21 37						22 07							22 37	
Chertsey	d								21 40						22 10							22 40	
Virginia Water	a			21 49					21 45				22 19		22 15			22 49				22 45	
	d			21 49					21 54				22 19		22 24			22 49				22 54	
Egham	d			21 53					21 57				22 23		22 27			22 53				22 57	
Windsor & Eton Riverside	d									21 53						22 23							22 53
Datchet	d									21 56						22 26							22 56
Sunnymeads	d									21 59						22 29							22 59
Wraysbury	d									22 02						22 32							23 02
Staines	d			21 59					22 03	22 08			22 29		22 33	22 38		22 59				23 03	23 08
Ashford (Surrey)	d								22 06	22 11					22 36	22 41						23 06	23 11
Feltham	d			22 05					22 11	22 16			22 35		22 41	22 46		23 05				23 11	23 16
Whitton	d	21 50	21 53							22 20		22 23				22 50							23 20
Kingston	d							21 59						22 29							22 59		
Hampton Wick	d							22 01						22 31							23 01		
Teddington	d							22 05						22 35							23 05		
Fulwell	d																						
Strawberry Hill	d							22 08						22 38							23 08		
Twickenham	a		21 56	22 10				22 12		22 23		22 26	22 40	22 42		22 53		23 10			23 12		23 23
	d		21 58	22 11				22 13		22 23		22 28	22 41	22 43		22 53		23 11			23 13		23 23
St Margarets	d		22 00					22 15				22 30		22 45							23 15		
Richmond ⊖	d		22 04	22 15				22 19		22 28		22 34	22 45	22 49		22 58		23 15			23 19		23 28
North Sheen	d		22 06					22 21				22 36		22 51							23 21		
Mortlake	d		22 08					22 23				22 38		22 53							23 23		
Hounslow	d	22 01							22 16						22 46							23 16	
Isleworth	d	22 04							22 19						22 49							23 19	
Syon Lane	d	22 06							22 21						22 51							23 21	
Brentford	d	22 09							22 24						22 54							23 24	
Kew Bridge	d	22 11							22 26						22 56							23 26	
Chiswick	d	22 14							22 29						22 59							23 29	
Barnes Bridge	d	22 16			←				22 31						23 01							23 31	
Barnes	d	22 19	22 11		22 19			22 26	22 34		←	22 41		22 56	23 04		←				23 26	23 34	
Putney	d	→	22 14		22 22			22 29	22 37	22 34	22 37	22 44		22 59	23 07	23 04	23 07				23 29	23 37	23 34
Wandsworth Town	d		22 17		22 25			22 32	→		22 40	22 47		23 02	→		23 10				23 32	→	
Clapham Junction 10	d		22 20	22 24	22 28			22 35		22 39	22 43	22 50	22 54	23 05		23 09	23 13	23 24			23 35		23 39
Queenstown Rd.(Battersea)	d		22 23		22 31			22 38			22 46	22 53		23 08			23 16				23 38		
Vauxhall ⊖	d		22 27		22 35			22 42		22 45	22 50	22 57		23 12		23 15	23 20				23 42		23 45
London Waterloo 15 ⊖	a		22 32	22 34	22 41			22 46		22 49	22 56	23 02	23 04	23 17		23 19	23 26	23 34			23 46		23 49

Reading, Guildford, Ascot, Weybridge, Windsor, Kingston, Richmond and Hounslow - London

		SW	SW 1	SW	SW	SW	SW 1	SW 1	SW 1	SW
Reading 7	d		22 42				23 12			
Earley	d		22 47				23 17			
Winnersh Triangle	d		22 49				23 19			
Winnersh	d		22 51				23 21			
Wokingham	d		22 56				23 26			
Bracknell	d		23 02				23 32			
Martins Heron	d		23 05				23 35			
Guildford	d							23 00	23 30	
Wanborough	d							23 06	23 36	
Ash 5	d							23 10	23 40	
Aldershot	a							23 17	23 47	
	d							23 30		
Ash Vale	d							23 34		
Frimley	d							23 40		
Camberley	a							23 44		
	d							23 48		
Bagshot	d							23 53		
Ascot 3	d		23 10				23 40	00a01		
Sunningdale	d		23 13				23 43			
Longcross	d									
Woking	d									
West Byfleet	d									
Byfleet & New Haw	d									
Weybridge	d			23 03						23 33
Addlestone	d			23 07						23 37
Chertsey	d			23 10						23 40
Virginia Water	a		23 19	23 15			23 49			23 45
	d		23 19	23 24			23 49			23 54
Egham	d		23 23	23 27			23 53			23 57
Windsor & Eton Riverside	d				23 28					
Datchet	d				23 31					
Sunnymeads	d				23 34					
Wraysbury	d				23 37					
Staines	d		23 29	23a32	23a42		23 59			00a02
Ashford (Surrey)	d									
Feltham	d		23 35				00 05			
Whitton	d									
Kingston	d					23 29				
Hampton Wick	d					23 31				
Teddington	d					23 35				
Fulwell	d									
Strawberry Hill	d					23 38				
Twickenham	a		23 40			23 42	00 10			
	d		23 41			23 43	00 11			
St Margarets	d					23 45				
Richmond ⊖	d		23 45			23 49	00 15			
North Sheen	d					23 51				
Mortlake	d					23 53				
Hounslow	d									
Isleworth	d									
Syon Lane	d									
Brentford	d									
Kew Bridge	d									
Chiswick	d									
Barnes Bridge	d									
Barnes	d	←				23 56				
Putney	d	23 37				23 59				
Wandsworth Town	d	23 40				00 02				
Clapham Junction 10	d	23 43	23 54			00 05	00 24			
Queenstown Rd.(Battersea)	d	23 46				00 08				
Vauxhall ⊖	d	23 50				00 12				
London Waterloo 15 ⊖	a	23 56	00 02			00 16	00 37			

Table 149

Saturdays from 8 October

Reading, Guildford, Ascot, Weybridge, Windsor, Kingston, Richmond and Hounslow - London

		SW ■1	SW	SW ■1	SW	SW	SW	SW	SW	SW	SW	SW	SW	SW ■1	SW ■1	SW	SW	SW	SW	SW ■1	SW	SW	SW
Reading ■7	d	22p39		23p12										05 39						06 09			
Earley	d	22p44		23p17										05 44						06 14			
Winnersh Triangle	d	22p46		23p19										05 46						06 16			
Winnersh	d	22p48		23p21										05 48						06 18			
Wokingham	d	22p53		23p26										05 53						06 23			
Bracknell	d	22p59		23p32										05 59						06 29			
Martins Heron	d	23p02		23p35										06 02						06 32			
Guildford	d																						
Wanborough	d																						
Ash ■5	d																						
Aldershot	a																						
	d														06 00								
Ash Vale	d														06 04								
Frimley	d														06 10								
Camberley	a														06 14								
	d														06 18								
Bagshot	d														06 23								
Ascot ■3	d	23p07		23p40										06 07	06a30					06 37			
Sunningdale	d	23p10		23p43										06 10						06 40			
Longcross	d																						
Woking	d										05 27												
West Byfleet	d										05 32												
Byfleet & New Haw	d										05 35												
Weybridge	d																					06 33	
Addlestone	d										05 39											06 37	
Chertsey	d										05 42											06 40	
Virginia Water	a	23p19		23p49							05 47			06 19						06 49		06 45	
	d	23p19		23p49							05 54			06 19						06 49		06 54	
Egham	d	23p23		23p53							05 57			06 23						06 53		06 57	
Windsor & Eton Riverside	d											05 51						06 21					06 51
Datchet	d											05 55						06 25					06 55
Sunnymeads	d											05 58						06 28					06 58
Wraysbury	d											06 02						06 32					07 02
Staines	d	23p29		23p59	04 58			05 37			06 03	06 08		06 29			06 33	06 38		06 59		07 03	07 08
Ashford (Surrey)	d				05 01			05 40			06 06	06 11					06 36	06 41				07 06	07 11
Feltham	d	23p35		00 05	05 06			05 45			06 11	06 16		06 35			06 41	06 46		07 05		07 11	07 16
Whitton	d				05 10		05 41	05 49				06 20						06 50					07 20
Kingston	d		23p29							05 59						06 29					06 59		
Hampton Wick	d		23p31							06 01						06 31					07 01		
Teddington	d		23p35							06 05						06 35					07 05		
Fulwell	d																						
Strawberry Hill	d		23p38			05 38				06 08						06 38					07 08		
Twickenham	a	23p40	23p42	00 10	05 13	05 41		05 52		06 12		06 23		06 40		06 42		06 53		07 10	07 12		07 23
	d	23p41	23p43	00 11	05 13	05 43		05 53		06 13		06 23		06 41		06 43		06 53		07 11	07 13		07 23
St Margarets	d		23p45		05 15	05 45				06 15						06 45					07 15		
Richmond ⊖	d	23p45	23p49	00 15	05 19	05 49		05 58		06 19		06 28		06 45		06 49		06 58		07 15	07 19		07 28
North Sheen	d		23p51		05 21	05 51				06 21						06 51					07 21		
Mortlake	d		23p53		05 23	05 53				06 23						06 53					07 23		
Hounslow	d						05 46				06 16						06 46					07 16	
Isleworth	d						05 49				06 19						06 49					07 19	
Syon Lane	d						05 51				06 21						06 51					07 21	
Brentford	d						05 54				06 24						06 54					07 24	
Kew Bridge	d						05 56				06 26						06 56					07 26	
Chiswick	d						05 59				06 29						06 59					07 29	
Barnes Bridge	d						06 01				06 31						07 01					07 31	
Barnes	d		23p56		05 26	05 56	06 04		←	06 26	06 34		←			06 56	07 04		←		07 26	07 34	
Putney	d		23p59		05 29	05 59	06 07	06 04	06 07	06 29	06 37	06 34	06 37			06 59	07 07	07 04	07 07		07 29	07 37	07 34
Wandsworth Town	d		00 02		05 32	06 02	→		06 10	06 32	→		06 40			07 02	→		07 10		07 32	→	
Clapham Junction ■10	d	23p54	00 05	00 24	05 35	06 05		06 09	06 13	06 35		06 39	06 43	06 54		07 05		07 09	07 13	07 24	07 35		07 39
Queenstown Rd.(Battersea)	d		00 08		05 38	06 08			06 16	06 38			06 46			07 08			07 16		07 38		
Vauxhall ⊖	d		00 12		05 42	06 12		06 15	06 20	06 42		06 45	06 50			07 12		07 15	07 20		07 42		07 45
London Waterloo ■15 ⊖	a	00 04	00 16	00 37	05 46	06 16		06 19	06 26	06 46		06 49	06 56	07 04		07 16		07 19	07 26	07 34	07 46		07 49

Table 149

Saturdays from 8 October

Reading, Guildford, Ascot, Weybridge, Windsor, Kingston, Richmond and Hounslow - London

		SW	SW ■1	SW ■1	SW	SW	SW	SW	SW	SW	SW ■1	SW ■1	SW	SW	SW	SW	SW	SW	SW	SW ■1	SW	SW ■1	SW
Reading ■7	d		06 39								07 09									07 39			
Earley	d		06 44								07 14									07 44			
Winnersh Triangle	d		06 46								07 16									07 46			
Winnersh	d		06 48								07 18									07 48			
Wokingham	d		06 53								07 23									07 53			
Bracknell	d		06 59								07 29									07 59			
Martins Heron	d		07 02								07 32									08 02			
Guildford	d			06 30								07 00										07 30	
Wanborough	d			06 36								07 06										07 36	
Ash ■5	d			06 40								07 10										07 40	
Aldershot	a			06 47								07 17										07 47	
	d			07 00								07 30										08 00	
Ash Vale	d			07 04								07 34										08 04	
Frimley	d			07 10								07 40										08 10	
Camberley	a			07 14								07 44										08 14	
	d			07 18								07 48										08 18	
Bagshot	d			07 23								07 53										08 23	
Ascot ■3	d		07 07	07a30							07 37	08a00								08 07		08a30	
Sunningdale	d		07 10								07 40									08 10			
Longcross	d																						
Woking	d																						
West Byfleet	d																						
Byfleet & New Haw	d																						
Weybridge	d						07 03								07 33								
Addlestone	d						07 07								07 37								
Chertsey	d						07 10								07 40								
Virginia Water	a		07 19				07 15				07 49				07 45					08 19			
	d		07 19				07 24				07 49				07 54					08 19			
Egham	d		07 23				07 27				07 53				07 57					08 23			
Windsor & Eton Riverside	d							07 21								07 51							
Datchet	d							07 25								07 55							
Sunnymeads	d							07 28								07 58							
Wraysbury	d							07 32								08 02							
Staines	d		07 29				07 33	07 38			07 59				08 03	08 08				08 29			
Ashford (Surrey)	d						07 36	07 41							08 06	08 11							
Feltham	d		07 35				07 41	07 46			08 05				08 11	08 16				08 35			
Whitton	d							07 50					07 50			08 20		08 20	08 23				
Kingston	d					07 29								07 59									08 29
Hampton Wick	d					07 31								08 01									08 31
Teddington	d					07 35								08 05									08 35
Fulwell	d																						
Strawberry Hill	d					07 38								08 08									08 38
Twickenham	a		07 40			07 42		07 53			08 10			08 12		08 23			08 26	08 40			08 42
	d		07 41			07 43		07 53		07 58	08 11			08 13		08 23			08 28	08 41			08 43
St Margarets	d					07 45				08 00				08 15					08 30				08 45
Richmond ⊖	d		07 45			07 49		07 58		08 04	08 15			08 19		08 28			08 34	08 45			08 49
North Sheen	d					07 51				08 06				08 21					08 36				08 51
Mortlake	d					07 53				08 08				08 23					08 38				08 53
Hounslow	d				07 31		07 46						08 01		08 16			08 31					
Isleworth	d				07 34		07 49						08 04		08 19			08 34					
Syon Lane	d				07 36		07 51						08 06		08 21			08 36					
Brentford	d				07 39		07 54						08 09		08 24			08 39					
Kew Bridge	d				07 41		07 56						08 11		08 26			08 41					
Chiswick	d				07 44		07 59						08 14		08 29			08 44					
Barnes Bridge	d				07 46		08 01						08 16		08 31			08 46			←		
Barnes	d	←			07 49	07 56	08 04		←	08 11			08 19	08 26	08 34		←	08 49	08 41		08 49		08 56
Putney	d	07 37			07 52	07 59	08 07	08 04	08 07	08 14			08 22	08 29	08 37	08 34	08 37	→	08 44		08 52		08 59
Wandsworth Town	d	07 40			07 55	08 02	→		08 10	08 17			08 25	08 32	→		08 40		08 47		08 55		09 02
Clapham Junction ■10	d	07 43	07 54		07 58	08 05		08 09	08 13	08 20	08 24		08 28	08 35		08 39	08 43		08 50	08 54	08 58		09 05
Queenstown Rd.(Battersea)	d	07 46			08 01	08 08			08 16	08 23			08 31	08 38			08 46		08 53		09 01		09 08
Vauxhall ⊖	d	07 50			08 05	08 12		08 15	08 20	08 27			08 35	08 42		08 45	08 50		08 57		09 05		09 12
London Waterloo ■15 ⊖	a	07 56	08 04		08 11	08 16		08 19	08 26	08 32	08 34		08 41	08 46		08 49	08 56		09 02	09 04	09 11		09 16

Reading, Guildford, Ascot, Weybridge, Windsor, Kingston, Richmond and Hounslow - London

		SW		SW	SW	SW	SW	SW [1]	SW	SW [1]	SW	SW		SW	SW	SW	SW	SW [1]	SW	SW [1]	SW	SW		SW	SW
Reading [7]	d							08 09										08 39							
Earley	d							08 14										08 44							
Winnersh Triangle	d							08 16										08 46							
Winnersh	d							08 18										08 48							
Wokingham	d							08 23										08 53							
Bracknell	d							08 29										08 59							
Martins Heron	d							08 32										09 02							
Guildford	d									08 00										08 30					
Wanborough	d									08 06										08 36					
Ash [5]	d									08 10										08 40					
Aldershot	a									08 17										08 47					
	d									08 30										09 00					
Ash Vale	d									08 34										09 04					
Frimley	d									08 40										09 10					
Camberley	a									08 44										09 14					
	d									08 48										09 18					
Bagshot	d									08 53										09 23					
Ascot [3]	d							08 37		09a00								09 07		09a30					
Sunningdale	d							08 40										09 10							
Longcross	d																								
Woking	d																								
West Byfleet	d																								
Byfleet & New Haw	d																								
Weybridge	d	08 03										08 33										09 03			
Addlestone	d	08 07										08 37										09 07			
Chertsey	d	08 10										08 40										09 10			
Virginia Water	a	08 15						08 49				08 45						09 19				09 15			
	d	08 24						08 49				08 54						09 19				09 24			
Egham	d	08 27						08 53				08 57						09 23				09 27			
Windsor & Eton Riverside	d			08 21										08 51										09 21	
Datchet	d			08 25										08 55										09 25	
Sunnymeads	d			08 28										08 58										09 28	
Wraysbury	d			08 32										09 02										09 32	
Staines	d	08 33		08 38				08 59				09 03		09 08				09 29				09 33		09 38	
Ashford (Surrey)	d	08 36		08 41								09 06		09 11								09 36		09 41	
Feltham	d	08 41		08 46				09 05				09 11		09 16				09 35				09 41		09 46	
Whitton	d			08 50		08 50	08 53							09 20		09 20	09 23							09 50	
Kingston	d										08 59										09 29				
Hampton Wick	d										09 01										09 31				
Teddington	d										09 05										09 35				
Fulwell	d																								
Strawberry Hill	d										09 08										09 38				
Twickenham	a			08 53			08 56	09 10			09 12			09 23			09 26	09 40			09 42			09 53	
	d			08 53			08 58	09 11			09 13			09 23			09 28	09 41			09 43			09 53	
St Margarets	d						09 00				09 15						09 30				09 45				
Richmond ⊖	d			08 58			09 04	09 15			09 19			09 28			09 34	09 45			09 49			09 58	
North Sheen	d						09 06				09 21						09 36				09 51				
Mortlake	d						09 08				09 23						09 38				09 53				
Hounslow	d	08 46				09 01						09 16				09 31						09 46			
Isleworth	d	08 49				09 04						09 19				09 34						09 49			
Syon Lane	d	08 51				09 06						09 21				09 36						09 51			
Brentford	d	08 54				09 09						09 24				09 39						09 54			
Kew Bridge	d	08 56				09 11						09 26				09 41						09 56			
Chiswick	d	08 59				09 14						09 29				09 44						09 59			
Barnes Bridge	d	09 01				09 16			←			09 31				09 46			←			10 01			
Barnes	d	09 04			←	09 19	09 11		09 19		09 26	09 34			←	09 49	09 41		09 49		09 56	10 04			←
Putney	d	09 07		09 04	09 07	→	09 14		09 22		09 29	09 37		09 34	09 37	→	09 44		09 52		09 59	10 07		10 04	10 07
Wandsworth Town	d	→			09 10		09 17		09 25		09 32	→			09 40		09 47		09 55		10 02	→			10 10
Clapham Junction [10]	d			09 09	09 13		09 20	09 24	09 28		09 35			09 39	09 43		09 50	09 54	09 58		10 05			10 09	10 13
Queenstown Rd.(Battersea)	d				09 16		09 23		09 31		09 38				09 46		09 53		10 01		10 08				10 16
Vauxhall ⊖	d			09 15	09 20		09 27		09 35		09 42			09 45	09 50		09 57		10 05		10 12			10 15	10 20
London Waterloo [15] ⊖	a			09 19	09 26		09 32	09 34	09 41		09 46			09 49	09 56		10 02	10 04	10 11		10 16			10 19	10 26

Reading, Guildford, Ascot, Weybridge, Windsor, Kingston, Richmond and Hounslow - London

		SW	SW	SW [1]	SW	SW [1]	SW	SW		SW	SW	SW	SW	SW [1]	SW	SW [1]	SW	SW		SW	SW	SW	SW	SW [1]	SW
Reading [7]	d			09 09										09 39										10 09	
Earley	d			09 14										09 44										10 14	
Winnersh Triangle	d			09 16										09 46										10 16	
Winnersh	d			09 18										09 48										10 18	
Wokingham	d			09 23										09 53										10 23	
Bracknell	d			09 29										09 59										10 29	
Martins Heron	d			09 32										10 02										10 32	
Guildford	d					09 00										09 30									
Wanborough	d					09 06										09 36									
Ash [5]	d					09 10										09 40									
Aldershot	a					09 17										09 47									
	d					09 30										10 00									
Ash Vale	d					09 34										10 04									
Frimley	d					09 40										10 10									
Camberley	a					09 44										10 14									
	d					09 48										10 18									
Bagshot	d					09 53										10 23									
Ascot [3]	d			09 37		10a00								10 07		10a30								10 37	
Sunningdale	d			09 40										10 10										10 40	
Longcross	d																								
Woking	d																								
West Byfleet	d																								
Byfleet & New Haw	d																								
Weybridge	d							09 33										10 03							
Addlestone	d							09 37										10 07							
Chertsey	d							09 40										10 10							
Virginia Water	a			09 49				09 45						10 19				10 15						10 49	
	d			09 49				09 54						10 19				10 24						10 49	
Egham	d			09 53				09 57						10 23				10 27						10 53	
Windsor & Eton Riverside	d									09 51										10 21					
Datchet	d									09 55										10 25					
Sunnymeads	d									09 58										10 28					
Wraysbury	d									10 02										10 32					
Staines	d			09 59				10 03		10 08				10 29				10 33		10 38				10 59	
Ashford (Surrey)	d							10 06		10 11								10 36		10 41					
Feltham	d			10 05				10 11		10 16				10 35				10 41		10 46				11 05	
Whitton	d	09 50	09 53							10 20		10 20	10 23							10 50		10 50	10 53		
Kingston	d						09 59										10 29								
Hampton Wick	d						10 01										10 31								
Teddington	d						10 05										10 35								
Fulwell	d																								
Strawberry Hill	d						10 08										10 38								
Twickenham	a		09 56	10 10			10 12			10 23			10 26	10 40			10 42			10 53			10 56	11 10	
	d		09 58	10 11			10 13			10 23			10 28	10 41			10 43			10 53			10 58	11 11	
St Margarets	d		10 00				10 15						10 30				10 45						11 00		
Richmond ⊖	d		10 04	10 15			10 19			10 28			10 34	10 45			10 49			10 58			11 04	11 15	
North Sheen	d		10 06				10 21						10 36				10 51						11 06		
Mortlake	d		10 08				10 23						10 38				10 53						11 08		
Hounslow	d	10 01						10 16				10 31						10 46				11 01			
Isleworth	d	10 04						10 19				10 34						10 49				11 04			
Syon Lane	d	10 06						10 21				10 36						10 51				11 06			
Brentford	d	10 09						10 24				10 39						10 54				11 09			
Kew Bridge	d	10 11						10 26				10 41						10 56				11 11			
Chiswick	d	10 14						10 29				10 44						10 59				11 14			
Barnes Bridge	d	10 16			←			10 31				10 46			←			11 01				11 16			←
Barnes	d	10 19	10 11		10 19		10 26	10 34			←	10 49	10 41		10 49		10 56	11 04			←	11 19	11 11		11 19
Putney	d	→	10 14		10 22		10 29	10 37		10 34	10 37	→	10 44		10 52		10 59	11 07		11 04	11 07	→	11 14		11 22
Wandsworth Town	d		10 17		10 25		10 32	→			10 40		10 47		10 55		11 02	→			11 10		11 17		11 25
Clapham Junction [10]	d		10 20	10 24	10 28		10 35			10 39	10 43		10 50	10 54	10 58		11 05			11 09	11 13		11 20	11 24	11 28
Queenstown Rd.(Battersea)	d		10 23		10 31		10 38				10 46		10 53		11 01		11 08				11 16		11 23		11 31
Vauxhall ⊖	d		10 27		10 35		10 42			10 45	10 50		10 57		11 05		11 12			11 15	11 20		11 27		11 35
London Waterloo [15] ⊖	a		10 32	10 34	10 41		10 46			10 49	10 56		11 02	11 04	11 11		11 16			11 19	11 26		11 32	11 34	11 41

Reading, Guildford, Ascot, Weybridge, Windsor, Kingston, Richmond and Hounslow - London

		SW 1	SW	SW		SW	SW	SW	SW	SW 1	SW	SW 1	SW	SW		SW	SW	SW	SW	SW 1	SW	SW 1	SW	SW
Reading 7	d									10 39										11 09				
Earley	d									10 44										11 14				
Winnersh Triangle	d									10 46										11 16				
Winnersh	d									10 48										11 18				
Wokingham	d									10 53										11 23				
Bracknell	d									10 59										11 29				
Martins Heron	d									11 02										11 32				
Guildford	d	10 00										10 30										11 00		
Wanborough	d	10 06										10 36										11 06		
Ash 5	d	10 10										10 40										11 10		
Aldershot	a	10 17										10 47										11 17		
	d	10 30										11 00										11 30		
Ash Vale	d	10 34										11 04										11 34		
Frimley	d	10 40										11 10										11 40		
Camberley	a	10 44										11 14										11 44		
	d	10 48										11 18										11 48		
Bagshot	d	10 53										11 23										11 53		
Ascot 3	d	11a00								11 07		11a30								11 37		12a00		
Sunningdale	d									11 10										11 40				
Longcross	d																							
Woking	d																							
West Byfleet	d																							
Byfleet & New Haw	d																							
Weybridge	d			10 33										11 03										11 33
Addlestone	d			10 37										11 07										11 37
Chertsey	d			10 40										11 10										11 40
Virginia Water	a			10 45						11 19				11 15						11 49				11 45
	d			10 54						11 19				11 24						11 49				11 54
Egham	d			10 57						11 23				11 27						11 53				11 57
Windsor & Eton Riverside	d					10 51										11 21								
Datchet	d					10 55										11 25								
Sunnymeads	d					10 58										11 28								
Wraysbury	d					11 02										11 32								
Staines	d			11 03		11 08				11 29				11 33		11 38				11 59				12 03
Ashford (Surrey)	d			11 06		11 11								11 36		11 41								12 06
Feltham	d			11 11		11 16				11 35				11 41		11 46				12 05				12 11
Whitton	d					11 20		11 20	11 23							11 50		11 50	11 53					
Kingston	d		10 59										11 29										11 59	
Hampton Wick	d		11 01										11 31										12 01	
Teddington	d		11 05										11 35										12 05	
Fulwell	d																							
Strawberry Hill	d		11 08										11 38										12 08	
Twickenham	a		11 12			11 23			11 26	11 40			11 42			11 53			11 56	12 10			12 12	
	d		11 13			11 23			11 28	11 41			11 43			11 53			11 58	12 11			12 13	
St Margarets	d		11 15						11 30				11 45						12 00				12 15	
Richmond ⊖	d		11 19			11 28			11 34	11 45			11 49			11 58			12 04	12 15			12 19	
North Sheen	d		11 21						11 36				11 51						12 06				12 21	
Mortlake	d		11 23						11 38				11 53						12 08				12 23	
Hounslow	d			11 16				11 31						11 46				12 01						12 16
Isleworth	d			11 19				11 34						11 49				12 04						12 19
Syon Lane	d			11 21				11 36						11 51				12 06						12 21
Brentford	d			11 24				11 39						11 54				12 09						12 24
Kew Bridge	d			11 26				11 41						11 56				12 11						12 26
Chiswick	d			11 29				11 44						11 59				12 14						12 29
Barnes Bridge	d			11 31				11 46			←			12 01				12 16			←			12 31
Barnes	d		11 26	11 34			←	11 49	11 41		11 49		11 56	12 04			←	12 19	12 11		12 19		12 26	12 34
Putney	d		11 29	11 37		11 34	11 37	→	11 44		11 52		11 59	12 07		12 04	12 07	→	12 14		12 22		12 29	12 37
Wandsworth Town	d		11 32	→			11 40		11 47		11 55		12 02	→			12 10		12 17		12 25		12 32	→
Clapham Junction 10	d		11 35			11 39	11 43		11 50	11 54	11 58		12 05			12 09	12 13		12 20	12 24	12 28		12 35	
Queenstown Rd.(Battersea)	d		11 38				11 46		11 53		12 01		12 08				12 16		12 23		12 31		12 38	
Vauxhall ⊖	d		11 42			11 45	11 50		11 57		12 05		12 12			12 15	12 20		12 27		12 35		12 42	
London Waterloo 15 ⊖	a		11 46			11 49	11 56		12 02	12 04	12 11		12 16			12 19	12 26		12 32	12 34	12 41		12 46	

Reading, Guildford, Ascot, Weybridge, Windsor, Kingston, Richmond and Hounslow - London

		SW	SW	SW	SW	SW 1	SW	SW 1	SW	SW		SW	SW	SW	SW	SW 1	SW	SW 1	SW	SW		SW	SW	SW	SW
Reading 7	d					11 39										12 09									
Earley	d					11 44										12 14									
Winnersh Triangle	d					11 46										12 16									
Winnersh	d					11 48										12 18									
Wokingham	d					11 53										12 23									
Bracknell	d					11 59										12 29									
Martins Heron	d					12 02										12 32									
Guildford	d							11 30										12 00							
Wanborough	d							11 36										12 06							
Ash 5	d							11 40										12 10							
Aldershot	a							11 47										12 17							
	d							12 00										12 30							
Ash Vale	d							12 04										12 34							
Frimley	d							12 10										12 40							
Camberley	a							12 14										12 44							
	d							12 18										12 48							
Bagshot	d							12 23										12 53							
Ascot 3	d					12 07		12a30								12 37		13a00							
Sunningdale	d					12 10										12 40									
Longcross	d																								
Woking	d																								
West Byfleet	d																								
Byfleet & New Haw	d																								
Weybridge	d									12 03										12 33					
Addlestone	d									12 07										12 37					
Chertsey	d									12 10										12 40					
Virginia Water	a					12 19				12 15						12 49				12 45					
	d					12 19				12 24						12 49				12 54					
Egham	d					12 23				12 27						12 53				12 57					
Windsor & Eton Riverside	d	11 51										12 21										12 51			
Datchet	d	11 55										12 25										12 55			
Sunnymeads	d	11 58										12 28										12 58			
Wraysbury	d	12 02										12 32										13 02			
Staines	d	12 08				12 29				12 33		12 38				12 59				13 03		13 08			
Ashford (Surrey)	d	12 11								12 36		12 41								13 06		13 11			
Feltham	d	12 16				12 35				12 41		12 46				13 05				13 11		13 16			
Whitton	d	12 20		12 20	12 23							12 50		12 50	12 53							13 20		13 20	13 23
Kingston	d								12 29										12 59						
Hampton Wick	d								12 31										13 01						
Teddington	d								12 35										13 05						
Fulwell	d																								
Strawberry Hill	d								12 38										13 08						
Twickenham	a	12 23			12 27	12 40			12 42			12 53			12 56	13 10			13 12			13 23			13 26
	d	12 23			12 28	12 41			12 43			12 53			12 58	13 11			13 13			13 23			13 28
St Margarets	d				12 30				12 45						13 00				13 15						13 30
Richmond ⊖	d	12 28			12 34	12 45			12 49			12 58			13 04	13 15			13 19			13 28			13 34
North Sheen	d				12 36				12 51						13 06				13 21						13 36
Mortlake	d				12 38				12 53						13 08				13 23						13 38
Hounslow	d			12 31						12 46				13 01						13 16				13 31	
Isleworth	d			12 34						12 49				13 04						13 19				13 34	
Syon Lane	d			12 36						12 51				13 06						13 21				13 36	
Brentford	d			12 39						12 54				13 09						13 24				13 39	
Kew Bridge	d			12 41						12 56				13 11						13 26				13 41	
Chiswick	d			12 44						12 59				13 14						13 29				13 44	
Barnes Bridge	d			12 46			←			13 01				13 16			←			13 31				13 46	
Barnes	d		←	12 49	12 41		12 49		12 56	13 04			←	13 19	13 11		13 19		13 26	13 34			←	13 49	13 41
Putney	d	12 34	12 37	→	12 44		12 52		12 59	13 07		13 04	13 07	→	13 14		13 22		13 29	13 37		13 34	13 37	→	13 44
Wandsworth Town	d		12 40		12 47		12 55		13 02	→			13 10		13 17		13 25		13 32	→			13 40		13 47
Clapham Junction 10	d	12 39	12 43		12 50	12 54	12 58		13 05			13 09	13 13		13 20	13 24	13 28		13 35			13 39	13 43		13 50
Queenstown Rd.(Battersea)	d		12 46		12 53		13 01		13 08				13 16		13 23		13 31		13 38				13 46		13 53
Vauxhall ⊖	d	12 45	12 50		12 57		13 05		13 12			13 15	13 20		13 27		13 35		13 42			13 45	13 50		13 57
London Waterloo 15 ⊖	a	12 49	12 56		13 02	13 04	13 11		13 16			13 19	13 26		13 32	13 34	13 41		13 46			13 49	13 56		14 02

Reading, Guildford, Ascot, Weybridge, Windsor, Kingston, Richmond and Hounslow - London

		SW ■	SW	SW ■	SW	SW		SW	SW	SW	SW	SW ■	SW	SW ■	SW	SW		SW	SW	SW	SW	SW ■	SW	SW ■	SW
Reading ■7	d	12 39										13 09										13 39			
Earley	d	12 44										13 14										13 44			
Winnersh Triangle	d	12 46										13 16										13 46			
Winnersh	d	12 48										13 18										13 48			
Wokingham	d	12 53										13 23										13 53			
Bracknell	d	12 59										13 29										13 59			
Martins Heron	d	13 02										13 32										14 02			
Guildford	d			12 30										13 00										13 30	
Wanborough	d			12 36										13 06										13 36	
Ash ■5	d			12 40										13 10										13 40	
Aldershot	a			12 47										13 17										13 47	
	d			13 00										13 30										14 00	
Ash Vale	d			13 04										13 34										14 04	
Frimley	d			13 10										13 40										14 10	
Camberley	a			13 14										13 44										14 14	
	d			13 18										13 48										14 18	
Bagshot	d			13 23										13 53										14 23	
Ascot ■3	d	13 07		13a30								13 37		14a00								14 07		14a30	
Sunningdale	d	13 10										13 40										14 10			
Longcross	d																								
Woking	d																								
West Byfleet	d																								
Byfleet & New Haw	d																								
Weybridge	d					13 03										13 33									
Addlestone	d					13 07										13 37									
Chertsey	d					13 10										13 40									
Virginia Water	a	13 19				13 15						13 49				13 45						14 19			
	d	13 19				13 24						13 49				13 54						14 19			
Egham	d	13 23				13 27						13 53				13 57						14 23			
Windsor & Eton Riverside	d							13 21										13 51							
Datchet	d							13 25										13 55							
Sunnymeads	d							13 28										13 58							
Wraysbury	d							13 32										14 02							
Staines	d	13 29				13 33		13 38				13 59				14 03		14 08				14 29			
Ashford (Surrey)	d					13 36		13 41								14 06		14 11							
Feltham	d	13 35				13 41		13 46				14 05				14 11		14 16				14 35			
Whitton	d							13 50		13 50	13 53							14 20		14 20	14 23				
Kingston	d				13 29										13 59										14 29
Hampton Wick	d				13 31										14 01										14 31
Teddington	d				13 35										14 05										14 35
Fulwell	d																								
Strawberry Hill	d				13 38										14 08										14 38
Twickenham	a	13 40			13 42			13 53			13 56	14 10			14 12			14 23			14 26	14 40			14 42
	d	13 41			13 43			13 53			13 58	14 11			14 13			14 23			14 28	14 41			14 43
St Margarets	d				13 45						14 00				14 15						14 30				14 45
Richmond ⊖	d	13 45			13 49			13 58			14 04	14 15			14 19			14 28			14 34	14 45			14 49
North Sheen	d				13 51						14 06				14 21						14 36				14 51
Mortlake	d				13 53						14 08				14 23						14 38				14 53
Hounslow	d					13 46				14 01						14 16				14 31					
Isleworth	d					13 49				14 04						14 19				14 34					
Syon Lane	d					13 51				14 06						14 21				14 36					
Brentford	d					13 54				14 09						14 24				14 39					
Kew Bridge	d					13 56				14 11						14 26				14 41					
Chiswick	d					13 59				14 14						14 29				14 44					
Barnes Bridge	d		←			14 01				14 16			←			14 31				14 46			←		
Barnes	d		13 49		13 56	14 04			←	14 19	14 11		14 19		14 26	14 34			←	14 49	14 41		14 49		14 56
Putney	d		13 52		13 59	14 07		14 04	14 07	→	14 14		14 22		14 29	14 37		14 34	14 37	→	14 44		14 52		14 59
Wandsworth Town	d		13 55		14 02	→			14 10		14 17		14 25		14 32	→			14 40		14 47		14 55		15 02
Clapham Junction ■10	d	13 54	13 58		14 05			14 09	14 13		14 20	14 24	14 28		14 35			14 39	14 43		14 50	14 54	14 58		15 05
Queenstown Rd.(Battersea)	d		14 01		14 08				14 16		14 23		14 31		14 38				14 46		14 53		15 01		15 08
Vauxhall ⊖	d		14 05		14 12			14 15	14 20		14 27		14 35		14 42			14 45	14 50		14 57		15 05		15 12
London Waterloo ■15 ⊖	a	14 04	14 11		14 16			14 19	14 26		14 32	14 34	14 41		14 46			14 49	14 56		15 02	15 04	15 11		15 16

Reading, Guildford, Ascot, Weybridge, Windsor, Kingston, Richmond and Hounslow - London

		SW		SW	SW	SW	SW	SW ■	SW	SW ■	SW	SW		SW	SW	SW	SW	SW ■	SW	SW ■	SW	SW		SW	SW
Reading ■7	d							14 09										14 39							
Earley	d							14 14										14 44							
Winnersh Triangle	d							14 16										14 46							
Winnersh	d							14 18										14 48							
Wokingham	d							14 23										14 53							
Bracknell	d							14 29										14 59							
Martins Heron	d							14 32										15 02							
Guildford	d									14 00										14 30					
Wanborough	d									14 06										14 36					
Ash ■5	d									14 10										14 40					
Aldershot	a									14 17										14 47					
	d									14 30										15 00					
Ash Vale	d									14 34										15 04					
Frimley	d									14 40										15 10					
Camberley	a									14 44										15 14					
	d									14 48										15 18					
Bagshot	d									14 53										15 23					
Ascot ■3	d							14 37		15a00								15 07		15a30					
Sunningdale	d							14 40										15 10							
Longcross	d																								
Woking	d																								
West Byfleet	d																								
Byfleet & New Haw	d																								
Weybridge	d	14 03										14 33										15 03			
Addlestone	d	14 07										14 37										15 07			
Chertsey	d	14 10										14 40										15 10			
Virginia Water	a	14 15						14 49				14 45						15 19				15 15			
	d	14 24						14 49				14 54						15 19				15 24			
Egham	d	14 27						14 53				14 57						15 23				15 27			
Windsor & Eton Riverside	d			14 21										14 51										15 21	
Datchet	d			14 25										14 55										15 25	
Sunnymeads	d			14 28										14 58										15 28	
Wraysbury	d			14 32										15 02										15 32	
Staines	d	14 33		14 38				14 59				15 03		15 08				15 29				15 33		15 38	
Ashford (Surrey)	d	14 36		14 41								15 06		15 11								15 36		15 41	
Feltham	d	14 41		14 46				15 05				15 11		15 16				15 35				15 41		15 46	
Whitton	d			14 50		14 50	14 53							15 20		15 20	15 23							15 50	
Kingston	d										14 59										15 29				
Hampton Wick	d										15 01										15 31				
Teddington	d										15 05										15 35				
Fulwell	d																								
Strawberry Hill	d										15 08										15 38				
Twickenham	a			14 53			14 56	15 10			15 12			15 23			15 26	15 40			15 42			15 53	
	d			14 53			14 58	15 11			15 13			15 23			15 28	15 41			15 43			15 53	
St Margarets	d						15 00				15 15						15 30				15 45				
Richmond ⊖	d			14 58			15 04	15 15			15 19			15 28			15 34	15 45			15 49			15 58	
North Sheen	d						15 06				15 21						15 36				15 51				
Mortlake	d						15 08				15 23						15 38				15 53				
Hounslow	d	14 46				15 01						15 16				15 31						15 46			
Isleworth	d	14 49				15 04						15 19				15 34						15 49			
Syon Lane	d	14 51				15 06						15 21				15 36						15 51			
Brentford	d	14 54				15 09						15 24				15 39						15 54			
Kew Bridge	d	14 56				15 11						15 26				15 41						15 56			
Chiswick	d	14 59				15 14						15 29				15 44						15 59			
Barnes Bridge	d	15 01				15 16			←			15 31				15 46			←			16 01			
Barnes	d	15 04			←	15 19	15 11		15 19		15 26	15 34			←	15 49	15 41		15 49		15 56	16 04			←
Putney	d	15 07		15 04	15 07	→	15 14		15 22		15 29	15 37		15 34	15 37	→	15 44		15 52		15 59	16 07		16 04	16 07
Wandsworth Town	d	→			15 10		15 17		15 25		15 32	→			15 40		15 47		15 55		16 02	→			16 10
Clapham Junction ■10	d			15 09	15 13		15 20	15 24	15 28		15 35			15 39	15 43		15 50	15 54	15 58		16 05			16 09	16 13
Queenstown Rd.(Battersea)	d				15 16		15 23		15 31		15 38				15 46		15 53		16 01		16 08				16 16
Vauxhall ⊖	d			15 15	15 20		15 27		15 35		15 42			15 45	15 50		15 57		16 05		16 12			16 15	16 20
London Waterloo ■15 ⊖	a			15 19	15 26		15 32	15 34	15 41		15 46			15 49	15 56		16 02	16 04	16 11		16 16			16 19	16 26

Table 149

Saturdays from 8 October

Reading, Guildford, Ascot, Weybridge, Windsor, Kingston, Richmond and Hounslow - London

		SW	SW	SW 1	SW	SW 1	SW	SW	SW	SW	SW	SW	SW 1	SW	SW 1	SW	SW	SW	SW	SW	SW	SW 1	SW
Reading 7	d			15 09									15 39									16 09	
Earley	d			15 14									15 44									16 14	
Winnersh Triangle	d			15 16									15 46									16 16	
Winnersh	d			15 18									15 48									16 18	
Wokingham	d			15 23									15 53									16 23	
Bracknell	d			15 29									15 59									16 29	
Martins Heron	d			15 32									16 02									16 32	
Guildford	d					15 00									15 30								
Wanborough	d					15 06									15 36								
Ash 5	d					15 10									15 40								
Aldershot	a					15 17									15 47								
	d					15 30									16 00								
Ash Vale	d					15 34									16 04								
Frimley	d					15 40									16 10								
Camberley	a					15 44									16 14								
	d					15 48									16 18								
Bagshot	d					15 53									16 23								
Ascot 3	d			15 37		16a00							16 07		16a30							16 37	
Sunningdale	d			15 40									16 10									16 40	
Longcross	d																						
Woking	d																						
West Byfleet	d																						
Byfleet & New Haw	d																						
Weybridge	d							15 33									16 03						
Addlestone	d							15 37									16 07						
Chertsey	d							15 40									16 10						
Virginia Water	a			15 49				15 45					16 19				16 15					16 49	
	d			15 49				15 54					16 19				16 24					16 49	
Egham	d			15 53				15 57					16 23				16 27					16 53	
Windsor & Eton Riverside	d								15 51									16 21					
Datchet	d								15 55									16 25					
Sunnymeads	d								15 58									16 28					
Wraysbury	d								16 02									16 32					
Staines	d			15 59				16 03	16 08				16 29				16 33	16 38				16 59	
Ashford (Surrey)	d							16 06	16 11								16 36	16 41					
Feltham	d			16 05				16 11	16 16				16 35				16 41	16 46				17 05	
Whitton	d	15 50	15 53						16 20		16 20	16 23						16 50		16 50	16 53		
Kingston	d						15 59									16 29							
Hampton Wick	d						16 01									16 31							
Teddington	d						16 05									16 35							
Fulwell	d																						
Strawberry Hill	d						16 08									16 38							
Twickenham	a		15 56	16 10			16 12		16 23			16 26	16 40			16 42		16 53			16 56	17 10	
	d		15 58	16 11			16 13		16 23			16 28	16 41			16 43		16 53			16 58	17 11	
St Margarets	d		16 00				16 15					16 30				16 45					17 00		
Richmond ⊖	d		16 04	16 15			16 19		16 28			16 34	16 45			16 49		16 58			17 04	17 15	
North Sheen	d		16 06				16 21					16 36				16 51					17 06		
Mortlake	d		16 08				16 23					16 38				16 53					17 08		
Hounslow	d	16 01						16 16			16 31						16 46			17 01			
Isleworth	d	16 04						16 19			16 34						16 49			17 04			
Syon Lane	d	16 06						16 21			16 36						16 51			17 06			
Brentford	d	16 09						16 24			16 39						16 54			17 09			
Kew Bridge	d	16 11						16 26			16 41						16 56			17 11			
Chiswick	d	16 14						16 29			16 44						16 59			17 14			
Barnes Bridge	d	16 16			←			16 31			16 46			←			17 01			17 16			←
Barnes	d	16 19	16 11		16 19		16 26	16 34		←	16 49	16 41		16 49		16 56	17 04		←	17 19	17 11		17 19
Putney	d	→	16 14		16 22		16 29	16 37	16 34	16 37	→	16 44		16 52		16 59	17 07	17 04	17 07	→	17 14		17 22
Wandsworth Town	d		16 17		16 25		16 32	→		16 40		16 47		16 55		17 02	→		17 10		17 17		17 25
Clapham Junction 10	d		16 20	16 24	16 28		16 35		16 39	16 43		16 50	16 54	16 58		17 05		17 09	17 13		17 20	17 24	17 28
Queenstown Rd.(Battersea)	d		16 23		16 31		16 38			16 46		16 53		17 01		17 08			17 16		17 23		17 31
Vauxhall ⊖	d		16 27		16 35		16 42		16 45	16 50		16 57		17 05		17 12		17 15	17 20		17 27		17 35
London Waterloo 15 ⊖	a		16 32	16 34	16 41		16 46		16 49	16 56		17 02	17 04	17 11		17 16		17 19	17 26		17 32	17 34	17 41

Table 149

Saturdays from 8 October

Reading, Guildford, Ascot, Weybridge, Windsor, Kingston, Richmond and Hounslow - London

		SW 1	SW	SW	SW	SW	SW	SW	SW 1	SW	SW 1	SW	SW	SW	SW	SW	SW	SW 1	SW	SW 1	SW	SW
Reading 7	d								16 39									17 09				
Earley	d								16 44									17 14				
Winnersh Triangle	d								16 46									17 16				
Winnersh	d								16 48									17 18				
Wokingham	d								16 53									17 23				
Bracknell	d								16 59									17 29				
Martins Heron	d								17 02									17 32				
Guildford	d	16 00									16 30									17 00		
Wanborough	d	16 06									16 36									17 06		
Ash 5	d	16 10									16 40									17 10		
Aldershot	a	16 17									16 47									17 17		
	d	16 30									17 00									17 30		
Ash Vale	d	16 34									17 04									17 34		
Frimley	d	16 40									17 10									17 40		
Camberley	a	16 44									17 14									17 44		
	d	16 48									17 18									17 48		
Bagshot	d	16 53									17 23									17 53		
Ascot 3	d	17a00							17 07		17a30							17 37		18a00		
Sunningdale	d								17 10									17 40				
Longcross	d																					
Woking	d																					
West Byfleet	d																					
Byfleet & New Haw	d																					
Weybridge	d			16 33									17 03									17 33
Addlestone	d			16 37									17 07									17 37
Chertsey	d			16 40									17 10									17 40
Virginia Water	a			16 45					17 19				17 15					17 49				17 45
	d			16 54					17 19				17 24					17 49				17 54
Egham	d			16 57					17 23				17 27					17 53				17 57
Windsor & Eton Riverside	d				16 51									17 21								
Datchet	d				16 55									17 25								
Sunnymeads	d				16 58									17 28								
Wraysbury	d				17 02									17 32								
Staines	d			17 03	17 08				17 29				17 33	17 38				17 59				18 03
Ashford (Surrey)	d			17 06	17 11								17 36	17 41								18 06
Feltham	d			17 11	17 16				17 35				17 41	17 46				18 05				18 11
Whitton	d				17 20		17 20	17 23						17 50		17 50	17 53					
Kingston	d		16 59									17 29									17 59	
Hampton Wick	d		17 01									17 31									18 01	
Teddington	d		17 05									17 35									18 05	
Fulwell	d																					
Strawberry Hill	d		17 08									17 38									18 08	
Twickenham	a		17 12		17 23			17 26	17 40			17 42		17 53			17 56	18 10			18 12	
	d		17 13		17 23			17 28	17 41			17 43		17 53			17 58	18 11			18 13	
St Margarets	d		17 15					17 30				17 45					18 00				18 15	
Richmond ⊖	d		17 19		17 28			17 34	17 45			17 49		17 58			18 04	18 15			18 19	
North Sheen	d		17 21					17 36				17 51					18 06				18 21	
Mortlake	d		17 23					17 38				17 53					18 08				18 23	
Hounslow	d			17 16			17 31						17 46			18 01						18 16
Isleworth	d			17 19			17 34						17 49			18 04						18 19
Syon Lane	d			17 21			17 36						17 51			18 06						18 21
Brentford	d			17 24			17 39						17 54			18 09						18 24
Kew Bridge	d			17 26			17 41						17 56			18 11						18 26
Chiswick	d			17 29			17 44						17 59			18 14						18 29
Barnes Bridge	d			17 31			17 46			←			18 01			18 16			←			18 31
Barnes	d		17 26	17 34		←	17 49	17 41		17 49		17 56	18 04		←	18 19	18 11		18 19		18 26	18 34
Putney	d		17 29	17 37	17 34	17 37	→	17 44		17 52		17 59	18 07	18 04	18 07	→	18 14		18 22		18 29	18 37
Wandsworth Town	d		17 32	→		17 40		17 47		17 55		18 02	→		18 10		18 17		18 25		18 32	→
Clapham Junction 10	d		17 35		17 39	17 43		17 50	17 54	17 58		18 05		18 09	18 13		18 20	18 24	18 28		18 35	
Queenstown Rd.(Battersea)	d		17 38			17 46		17 53		18 01		18 08			18 16		18 23		18 31		18 38	
Vauxhall ⊖	d		17 42		17 45	17 50		17 57		18 05		18 12		18 15	18 20		18 27		18 35		18 42	
London Waterloo 15 ⊖	a		17 46		17 49	17 56		18 02	18 04	18 11		18 16		18 19	18 26		18 32	18 34	18 41		18 46	

Reading, Guildford, Ascot, Weybridge, Windsor, Kingston, Richmond and Hounslow - London

		SW	SW	SW	SW	SW 1	SW	SW 1	SW	SW		SW	SW	SW	SW	SW 1	SW	SW 1	SW	SW		SW	SW	SW	SW
Reading 7	d					17 39										18 09									
Earley	d					17 44										18 14									
Winnersh Triangle	d					17 46										18 16									
Winnersh	d					17 48										18 18									
Wokingham	d					17 53										18 23									
Bracknell	d					17 59										18 29									
Martins Heron	d					18 02										18 32									
Guildford	d							17 30										18 00							
Wanborough	d							17 36										18 06							
Ash 5	d							17 40										18 10							
Aldershot	a							17 47										18 17							
	d							18 00										18 30							
Ash Vale	d							18 04										18 34							
Frimley	d							18 10										18 40							
Camberley	a							18 14										18 44							
	d							18 18										18 48							
Bagshot	d							18 23										18 53							
Ascot 3	d					18 07		18a30								18 37		19a00							
Sunningdale	d					18 10										18 40									
Longcross	d																								
Woking	d																								
West Byfleet	d																								
Byfleet & New Haw	d																								
Weybridge	d									18 03										18 33					
Addlestone	d									18 07										18 37					
Chertsey	d									18 10										18 40					
Virginia Water	a					18 19				18 15						18 49				18 45					
	d					18 19				18 24						18 49				18 54					
Egham	d					18 23				18 27						18 53				18 57					
Windsor & Eton Riverside	d	17 51										18 21										18 51			
Datchet	d	17 55										18 25										18 55			
Sunnymeads	d	17 58										18 28										18 58			
Wraysbury	d	18 02										18 32										19 02			
Staines	d	18 08				18 29				18 33		18 38				18 59				19 03		19 08			
Ashford (Surrey)	d	18 11								18 36		18 41								19 06		19 11			
Feltham	d	18 16				18 35				18 41		18 46				19 05				19 11		19 16			
Whitton	d	18 20		18 20	18 23							18 50		18 50	18 53							19 20		19 20	19 23
Kingston	d								18 29										18 59						
Hampton Wick	d								18 31										19 01						
Teddington	d								18 35										19 05						
Fulwell	d																								
Strawberry Hill	d								18 38										19 08						
Twickenham	a	18 23			18 26	18 40			18 42			18 53			18 56	19 10			19 12			19 23			19 26
	d	18 23			18 28	18 41			18 43			18 53			18 58	19 11			19 13			19 23			19 28
St Margarets	d				18 30				18 45						19 00				19 15						19 30
Richmond ⊖	d	18 28			18 34	18 45			18 49			18 58			19 04	19 15			19 19			19 28			19 34
North Sheen	d				18 36				18 51						19 06				19 21						19 36
Mortlake	d				18 38				18 53						19 08				19 23						19 38
Hounslow	d			18 31						18 46				19 01						19 16				19 31	
Isleworth	d			18 34						18 49				19 04						19 19				19 34	
Syon Lane	d			18 36						18 51				19 06						19 21				19 36	
Brentford	d			18 39						18 54				19 09						19 24				19 39	
Kew Bridge	d			18 41						18 56				19 11						19 26				19 41	
Chiswick	d			18 44						18 59				19 14						19 29				19 44	
Barnes Bridge	d			18 46			←			19 01				19 16			←			19 31				19 46	
Barnes	d		←	18 49	18 41		18 49		18 56	19 04			←	19 19	19 11		19 19		19 26	19 34			←	19 49	19 41
Putney	d	18 34	18 37	→	18 44		18 52		18 59	19 07		19 04	19 07	→	19 14		19 22		19 29	19 37		19 34	19 37	→	19 44
Wandsworth Town	d		18 40		18 47		18 55		19 02	→			19 10		19 17		19 25		19 32	→			19 40		19 47
Clapham Junction 10	d	18 39	18 43		18 50	18 54	18 58		19 05			19 09	19 13		19 20	19 24	19 28		19 35			19 39	19 43		19 50
Queenstown Rd.(Battersea)	d		18 46		18 53		19 01		19 08				19 16		19 23		19 31		19 38				19 46		19 53
Vauxhall ⊖	d	18 45	18 50		18 57		19 05		19 12			19 15	19 20		19 27		19 35		19 42			19 45	19 50		19 57
London Waterloo 15 ⊖	a	18 49	18 56		19 02	19 04	19 11		19 16			19 19	19 26		19 32	19 34	19 41		19 46			19 49	19 56		20 02

Reading, Guildford, Ascot, Weybridge, Windsor, Kingston, Richmond and Hounslow - London

		SW 1	SW	SW 1	SW	SW		SW	SW	SW	SW	SW 1	SW	SW 1	SW	SW		SW	SW	SW	SW	SW 1	SW	SW 1	SW
Reading 7	d	18 39										19 09										19 39			
Earley	d	18 44										19 14										19 44			
Winnersh Triangle	d	18 46										19 16										19 46			
Winnersh	d	18 48										19 18										19 48			
Wokingham	d	18 53										19 23										19 53			
Bracknell	d	18 59										19 29										19 59			
Martins Heron	d	19 02										19 32										20 02			
Guildford	d			18 30										19 00										19 30	
Wanborough	d			18 36										19 06										19 36	
Ash 5	d			18 40										19 10										19 40	
Aldershot	a			18 47										19 17										19 47	
	d			19 00										19 30										20 00	
Ash Vale	d			19 04										19 34										20 04	
Frimley	d			19 10										19 40										20 10	
Camberley	a			19 14										19 44										20 14	
	d			19 18										19 48										20 18	
Bagshot	d			19 23										19 53										20 23	
Ascot 3	d	19 07		19a30								19 37		20a00								20 07		20a30	
Sunningdale	d	19 10										19 40										20 10			
Longcross	d																								
Woking	d																								
West Byfleet	d																								
Byfleet & New Haw	d																								
Weybridge	d					19 03										19 33									
Addlestone	d					19 07										19 37									
Chertsey	d					19 10										19 40									
Virginia Water	a	19 19				19 15						19 49				19 45						20 19			
	d	19 19				19 24						19 49				19 54						20 19			
Egham	d	19 23				19 27						19 53				19 57						20 23			
Windsor & Eton Riverside	d							19 21										19 51							
Datchet	d							19 25										19 55							
Sunnymeads	d							19 28										19 58							
Wraysbury	d							19 32										20 02							
Staines	d	19 29				19 33		19 38				19 59				20 03		20 08				20 29			
Ashford (Surrey)	d					19 36		19 41								20 06		20 11							
Feltham	d	19 35				19 41		19 46				20 05				20 11		20 16				20 35			
Whitton	d							19 50		19 50	19 53							20 20		20 20	20 23				
Kingston	d				19 29										19 59										20 29
Hampton Wick	d				19 31										20 01										20 31
Teddington	d				19 35										20 05										20 35
Fulwell	d																								
Strawberry Hill	d				19 38										20 08										20 38
Twickenham	a	19 40			19 42			19 53			19 56	20 10			20 12			20 23			20 26	20 40			20 42
	d	19 41			19 43			19 53			19 58	20 11			20 13			20 23			20 28	20 41			20 43
St Margarets	d				19 45						20 00				20 15						20 30				20 45
Richmond ⊖	d	19 45			19 49			19 58			20 04	20 15			20 19			20 28			20 34	20 45			20 49
North Sheen	d				19 51						20 06				20 21						20 36				20 51
Mortlake	d				19 53						20 08				20 23						20 38				20 53
Hounslow	d					19 46				20 01						20 16				20 31					
Isleworth	d					19 49				20 04						20 19				20 34					
Syon Lane	d					19 51				20 06						20 21				20 36					
Brentford	d					19 54				20 09						20 24				20 39					
Kew Bridge	d					19 56				20 11						20 26				20 41					
Chiswick	d					19 59				20 14						20 29				20 44					
Barnes Bridge	d		←			20 01				20 16			←			20 31				20 46			←		
Barnes	d		19 49		19 56	20 04			←	20 19	20 11		20 19		20 26	20 34			←	20 49	20 41		20 49		20 56
Putney	d		19 52		19 59	20 07		20 04	20 07	→	20 14		20 22		20 29	20 37		20 34	20 37	→	20 44		20 52		20 59
Wandsworth Town	d		19 55		20 02	→			20 10		20 17		20 25		20 32	→			20 40		20 47		20 55		21 02
Clapham Junction 10	d	19 54	19 58		20 05			20 09	20 13		20 20	20 24	20 28		20 35			20 39	20 43		20 50	20 54	20 58		21 05
Queenstown Rd.(Battersea)	d		20 01		20 08				20 16		20 23		20 31		20 38				20 46		20 53		21 01		21 08
Vauxhall ⊖	d		20 05		20 12			20 15	20 20		20 27		20 35		20 42			20 45	20 50		20 57		21 05		21 12
London Waterloo 15 ⊖	a	20 04	20 11		20 16			20 19	20 26		20 32	20 34	20 41		20 46			20 49	20 56		21 02	21 04	21 11		21 16

Table 149

Saturdays
from 8 October

Reading, Guildford, Ascot, Weybridge, Windsor, Kingston, Richmond and Hounslow - London

		SW		SW	SW	SW	SW	SW ■	SW	SW ■	SW ■	SW		SW	SW	SW	SW	SW	SW ■	SW	SW	SW		SW	SW
Reading ■	d							20 09											20 39						
Earley	d							20 14											20 44						
Winnersh Triangle	d							20 16											20 46						
Winnersh	d							20 18											20 48						
Wokingham	d							20 23											20 53						
Bracknell	d							20 29											20 59						
Martins Heron	d							20 32											21 02						
Guildford	d									20 00	20 30														
Wanborough	d									20 06	20 36														
Ash ■	d									20 10	20 40														
Aldershot	a									20 17	20 47														
	d									20 30															
Ash Vale	d									20 34															
Frimley	d									20 40															
Camberley	a									20 44															
	d									20 48															
Bagshot	d									20 53															
Ascot ■	d							20 37		21a00									21 07						
Sunningdale	d							20 40											21 10						
Longcross	d																								
Woking	d																								
West Byfleet	d																								
Byfleet & New Haw	d																								
Weybridge	d	20 03												20 33								21 03			
Addlestone	d	20 07												20 37								21 07			
Chertsey	d	20 10												20 40								21 10			
Virginia Water	a	20 15						20 49						20 45					21 19			21 15			
	d	20 24						20 49						20 54					21 19			21 24			
Egham	d	20 27						20 53						20 57					21 23			21 27			
Windsor & Eton Riverside	d			20 21											20 51									21 21	
Datchet	d			20 25											20 55									21 25	
Sunnymeads	d			20 28											20 58									21 28	
Wraysbury	d			20 32											21 02									21 32	
Staines	d	20 33		20 38				20 59						21 03	21 08				21 29			21 33		21 38	
Ashford (Surrey)	d	20 36		20 41										21 06	21 11							21 36		21 41	
Feltham	d	20 41		20 46				21 05						21 11	21 16				21 35			21 41		21 46	
Whitton	d			20 50		20 50	20 53								21 20		21 20	21 23						21 50	
Kingston	d											20 59									21 29				
Hampton Wick	d											21 01									21 31				
Teddington	d											21 05									21 35				
Fulwell	d																								
Strawberry Hill	d											21 08									21 38				
Twickenham	a			20 53			20 56	21 10				21 12			21 23			21 26	21 40		21 42			21 53	
	d			20 53			20 58	21 11				21 13			21 23			21 28	21 41		21 43			21 53	
St Margarets	d						21 00					21 15						21 30			21 45				
Richmond ⊖	d			20 58			21 04	21 15				21 19			21 28			21 34	21 45		21 49			21 58	
North Sheen	d						21 06					21 21						21 36			21 51				
Mortlake	d						21 08					21 23						21 38			21 53				
Hounslow	d	20 46				21 01								21 16			21 31					21 46			
Isleworth	d	20 49				21 04								21 19			21 34					21 49			
Syon Lane	d	20 51				21 06								21 21			21 36					21 51			
Brentford	d	20 54				21 09								21 24			21 39					21 54			
Kew Bridge	d	20 56				21 11								21 26			21 41					21 56			
Chiswick	d	20 59				21 14								21 29			21 44					21 59			
Barnes Bridge	d	21 01				21 16			←					21 31			21 46			←		22 01			
Barnes	d	21 04			←	21 19	21 11		21 19			21 26		21 34		←	21 49	21 41		21 49	21 56	22 04			←
Putney	d	21 07		21 04	21 07	→	21 14		21 22			21 29		21 37	21 34	21 37	→	21 44		21 52	21 59	22 07		22 04	22 07
Wandsworth Town	d	→			21 10		21 17		21 25			21 32		→		21 40		21 47		21 55	22 02	→			22 10
Clapham Junction ■	d			21 09	21 13		21 20	21 24	21 28			21 35			21 39	21 43		21 50	21 54	21 58	22 05			22 09	22 13
Queenstown Rd.(Battersea)	d				21 16		21 23		21 31			21 38				21 46		21 53		22 01	22 08				22 16
Vauxhall ⊖	d			21 15	21 20		21 27		21 35			21 42			21 45	21 50		21 57		22 05	22 12			22 15	22 20
London Waterloo ■ ⊖	a			21 19	21 26		21 32	21 34	21 41			21 46			21 49	21 56		22 02	22 04	22 11	22 16			22 19	22 26

Table 149

Saturdays
from 8 October

Reading, Guildford, Ascot, Weybridge, Windsor, Kingston, Richmond and Hounslow - London

		SW	SW	SW ■	SW	SW ■	SW ■	SW		SW	SW	SW	SW	SW ■	SW	SW	SW	SW		SW ■	SW ■	SW ■	SW	SW	SW
Reading ■	d			21 09										21 39						22 09					
Earley	d			21 14										21 44						22 14					
Winnersh Triangle	d			21 16										21 46						22 16					
Winnersh	d			21 18										21 48						22 18					
Wokingham	d			21 23										21 53						22 23					
Bracknell	d			21 29										21 59						22 29					
Martins Heron	d			21 32										22 02						22 32					
Guildford	d					21 00	21 30														22 00	22 30			
Wanborough	d					21 06	21 36														22 06	22 36			
Ash ■	d					21 10	21 40														22 10	22 40			
Aldershot	a					21 17	21 47														22 17	22 47			
	d					21 30															22 30				
Ash Vale	d					21 34															22 34				
Frimley	d					21 40															22 40				
Camberley	a					21 44															22 44				
	d					21 48															22 48				
Bagshot	d					21 53															22 53				
Ascot ■	d			21 37		22a00								22 07						22 37	23a00				
Sunningdale	d			21 40										22 10						22 40					
Longcross	d																								
Woking	d																								
West Byfleet	d																								
Byfleet & New Haw	d																								
Weybridge	d									21 33						22 03								22 33	
Addlestone	d									21 37						22 07								22 37	
Chertsey	d									21 40						22 10								22 40	
Virginia Water	a			21 49						21 45				22 19		22 15				22 49				22 45	
	d			21 49						21 54				22 19		22 24				22 49				22 54	
Egham	d			21 53						21 57				22 23		22 27				22 53				22 57	
Windsor & Eton Riverside	d										21 51						22 21								22 53
Datchet	d										21 55						22 25								22 56
Sunnymeads	d										21 58						22 28								22 59
Wraysbury	d										22 02						22 32								23 02
Staines	d			21 59						22 03	22 08			22 29		22 33	22 38			22 59				23 03	23 08
Ashford (Surrey)	d									22 06	22 11					22 36	22 41							23 06	23 11
Feltham	d			22 05						22 11	22 16			22 35		22 41	22 46			23 05				23 11	23 16
Whitton	d	21 50	21 53								22 20		22 23				22 50								23 20
Kingston	d							21 59							22 29								22 59		
Hampton Wick	d							22 01							22 31								23 01		
Teddington	d							22 05							22 35								23 05		
Fulwell	d																								
Strawberry Hill	d							22 08							22 38								23 08		
Twickenham	a		21 56	22 10				22 12			22 23		22 26	22 40	22 42		22 53			23 10			23 12		23 23
	d		21 58	22 11				22 13			22 23		22 28	22 41	22 43		22 53			23 11			23 13		23 23
St Margarets	d		22 00					22 15					22 30		22 45								23 15		
Richmond ⊖	d		22 04	22 15				22 19			22 28		22 34	22 45	22 49		22 58			23 15			23 19		23 28
North Sheen	d		22 06					22 21					22 36		22 51								23 21		
Mortlake	d		22 08					22 23					22 38		22 53								23 23		
Hounslow	d	22 01								22 16						22 46								23 16	
Isleworth	d	22 04								22 19						22 49								23 19	
Syon Lane	d	22 06								22 21						22 51								23 21	
Brentford	d	22 09								22 24						22 54								23 24	
Kew Bridge	d	22 11								22 26						22 56								23 26	
Chiswick	d	22 14								22 29						22 59								23 29	
Barnes Bridge	d	22 16			←					22 31						23 01								23 31	
Barnes	d	22 19	22 11		22 19			22 26		22 34		←	22 41		22 56	23 04		←					23 26	23 34	
Putney	d	→	22 14		22 22			22 29		22 37	22 34	22 37	22 44		22 59	23 07	23 04	23 07					23 29	23 37	23 34
Wandsworth Town	d		22 17		22 25			22 32		→		22 40	22 47		23 02	→		23 10					23 32	→	
Clapham Junction ■	d		22 20	22 24	22 28			22 35			22 39	22 43	22 50	22 54	23 05		23 09	23 13		23 24			23 35		23 39
Queenstown Rd.(Battersea)	d		22 23		22 31			22 38				22 46	22 53		23 08			23 16					23 38		
Vauxhall ⊖	d		22 27		22 35			22 42			22 45	22 50	22 57		23 12		23 15	23 20					23 42		23 45
London Waterloo ■ ⊖	a		22 32	22 34	22 41			22 46			22 49	22 56	23 02	23 04	23 17		23 19	23 26		23 34			23 46		23 49

from 8 October

Reading, Guildford, Ascot, Weybridge, Windsor, Kingston, Richmond and Hounslow - London

		SW	SW 1	SW		SW	SW	SW 1	SW 1	SW 1	SW
Reading 7	d		22 39					23 12			
Earley	d		22 44					23 17			
Winnersh Triangle	d		22 46					23 19			
Winnersh	d		22 48					23 21			
Wokingham	d		22 53					23 26			
Bracknell	d		22 59					23 32			
Martins Heron	d		23 02					23 35			
Guildford	d								23 00	23 30	
Wanborough	d								23 06	23 36	
Ash 5	d								23 10	23 40	
Aldershot	a								23 17	23 47	
	d								23 30		
Ash Vale	d								23 34		
Frimley	d								23 40		
Camberley	a								23 44		
	d								23 48		
Bagshot	d								23 53		
Ascot 3	d		23 07					23 40	00a01		
Sunningdale	d		23 10					23 43			
Longcross	d										
Woking	d										
West Byfleet	d										
Byfleet & New Haw	d										
Weybridge	d			23 03							23 33
Addlestone	d			23 07							23 37
Chertsey	d			23 10							23 40
Virginia Water	a		23 19	23 15				23 49			23 45
	d		23 19	23 24				23 49			23 54
Egham	d		23 23	23 27				23 53			23 57
Windsor & Eton Riverside	d					23 28					
Datchet	d					23 31					
Sunnymeads	d					23 34					
Wraysbury	d					23 37					
Staines	d		23 29	23a32		23a42		23 59			00a02
Ashford (Surrey)	d										
Feltham	d		23 35					00 05			
Whitton	d										
Kingston	d						23 29				
Hampton Wick	d						23 31				
Teddington	d						23 35				
Fulwell	d										
Strawberry Hill	d						23 38				
Twickenham	a		23 40				23 42	00 10			
	d		23 41				23 43	00 11			
St Margarets	d						23 45				
Richmond ⊖	d		23 45				23 49	00 15			
North Sheen	d						23 51				
Mortlake	d						23 53				
Hounslow	d										
Isleworth	d										
Syon Lane	d										
Brentford	d										
Kew Bridge	d										
Chiswick	d										
Barnes Bridge	d										
Barnes	d	←					23 56				
Putney	d	23 37					23 59				
Wandsworth Town	d	23 40					00 02				
Clapham Junction 10	d	23 43	23 54				00 05	00 24			
Queenstown Rd.(Battersea)	d	23 46					00 08				
Vauxhall ⊖	d	23 50					00 12				
London Waterloo 15 ⊖	a	23 56	00 02				00 16	00 37			

Sundays

until 25 September

Reading, Guildford, Ascot, Weybridge, Windsor, Kingston, Richmond and Hounslow - London

		SW 1 A	SW A	SW 1 A	SW	SW	SW	SW 1	SW	SW		SW	SW 1	SW	SW 1	SW 1	SW	SW	SW 1	SW		SW 1	SW 1	SW	SW
Reading 7	d	22p42		23p12									07 54		08 24				08 54			09 24			
Earley	d	22p47		23p17									07 59		08 29				08 59			09 29			
Winnersh Triangle	d	22p49		23p19									08 01		08 31				09 01			09 31			
Winnersh	d	22p51		23p21									08 03		08 33				09 03			09 33			
Wokingham	d	22p56		23p26									08 08		08 38				09 08			09 38			
Bracknell	d	23p02		23p32									08 14		08 44				09 14			09 44			
Martins Heron	d	23p05		23p35									08 17		08 47				09 17			09 47			
Guildford	d							07 17								08 17							09 17		
Wanborough	d							07 23								08 23							09 23		
Ash 5	d							07 27								08 27							09 27		
Aldershot	a							07 34								08 34							09 34		
	d							07 40								08 40							09 40		
Ash Vale	d							07 45								08 45							09 45		
Frimley	d							07 51								08 51							09 51		
Camberley	a							07 55								08 55							09 55		
	d							07 55								08 55							09 55		
Bagshot	d							08 01								09 01							10 01		
Ascot 3	d	23p10		23p40				08a07					08 22		08 52	09a07			09 22			09 52	10a07		
Sunningdale	d	23p13		23p43									08 25		08 55				09 25			09 55			
Longcross	d																								
Woking	d											07 52						08 52							09 52
West Byfleet	d											07 56						08 56							09 56
Byfleet & New Haw	d											08 00						09 00							10 00
Weybridge	d						07 00																		
Addlestone	d						07 04					08 04						09 04							10 04
Chertsey	d						07 07					08 07						09 07							10 07
Virginia Water	a	23p19		23p49			07 12					08 12	08 30		09 00			09 12	09 30			10 00			10 12
	d	23p19		23p49			07 12					08 12	08 30		09 00			09 12	09 30			10 00			10 12
Egham	d	23p23		23p53			07 16					08 16	08 34		09 04			09 16	09 34			10 04			10 16
Windsor & Eton Riverside	d					07 01				08 01							09 01							10 01	
Datchet	d					07 04				08 04							09 04							10 04	
Sunnymeads	d					07 07				08 07							09 07							10 07	
Wraysbury	d					07 10				08 10							09 10							10 10	
Staines	d	23p29		23p59		07 16	07 21			08 16		08 21	08 39		09 09		09 16	09 21	09 39			10 09		10 16	10 21
Ashford (Surrey)	d					07 19	07 24			08 19		08 24					09 19	09 24						10 19	10 24
Feltham	d	23p35		00 05		07 24	07 29			08 24		08 29	08 46		09 16		09 24	09 29	09 46			10 16		10 24	10 29
Whitton	d					07 28				08 28							09 28							10 28	
Kingston	d		23p29		06 49				07 49					08 49						09 49					
Hampton Wick	d		23p31		06 51				07 51					08 51						09 51					
Teddington	d		23p35		06 56				07 56					08 56						09 56					
Fulwell	d																								
Strawberry Hill	d		23p38		06 59				07 59					08 59						09 59					
Twickenham	a	23p40	23p42	00 10	07 02	07 31			08 02	08 31			08 51	09 02	09 21		09 31		09 51	10 02		10 21		10 31	
	d	23p41	23p43	00 11	07 03	07 32			08 03	08 32			08 51	09 03	09 21		09 32		09 51	10 03		10 21		10 32	
St Margarets	d		23p45		07 05	07 34			08 05	08 34				09 05			09 34			10 05				10 34	
Richmond ⊖	d	23p45	23p49	00 15	07 09	07 37			08 09	08 37			08 56	09 09	09 26		09 37		09 56	10 09		10 26		10 37	
North Sheen	d		23p51		07 11	07 39			08 11	08 39				09 11			09 39			10 11				10 39	
Mortlake	d		23p53		07 13	07 42			08 13	08 42				09 13			09 42			10 13				10 42	
Hounslow	d						07 35					08 35						09 35							10 35
Isleworth	d						07 38					08 38						09 38							10 38
Syon Lane	d						07 40					08 40						09 40							10 40
Brentford	d						07 42					08 42						09 42							10 42
Kew Bridge	d						07 45					08 45						09 45							10 45
Chiswick	d						07 47					08 47						09 47							10 47
Barnes Bridge	d						07 50					08 50						09 50							10 50
Barnes	d		23p56		07 16	07 45	07 53		08 16	08 45		08 53		09 16			09 45	09 53		10 16				10 45	10 53
Putney	d		23p59		07 19	07 48	07 56		08 19	08 48		08 56	09 02	09 19	09 32		09 48	09 56	10 02	10 19		10 32		10 48	10 56
Wandsworth Town	d		00 02		07 22	07 51	07 59		08 22	08 51		08 59		09 22			09 51	09 59		10 22				10 51	10 59
Clapham Junction 10	d	23p54	00 05	00 24	07 25	07 54	08 02		08 25	08 54		09 02	09 07	09 25	09 37		09 54	10 02	10 07	10 25		10 37		10 53	11 02
Queenstown Rd.(Battersea)	d		00 08		07 28	07 57	08 05		08 28	08 57		09 05		09 28			09 57	10 05		10 28				10 57	11 05
Vauxhall ⊖	d		00 12		07 32	08 00	08 08		08 32	09 00		09 08	09 12	09 32	09 42		10 00	10 08	10 12	10 32		10 42		11 00	11 08
London Waterloo 15 ⊖	a	00 02	00 16	00 37	07 41	08 10	08 13		08 41	09 10		09 13	09 23	09 41	09 53		10 10	10 13	10 23	10 41		10 53		11 10	11 13

A not 22 May

Table 149

Sundays until 25 September

Reading, Guildford, Ascot, Weybridge, Windsor, Kingston, Richmond and Hounslow - London

		SW 1	SW	SW	SW 1	SW 1	SW	SW	SW 1	SW	SW	SW 1	SW 1	SW	SW	SW 1	SW	SW	SW 1	SW 1	SW	SW	SW
Reading 7	d	09 54			10 24				10 54			11 24				11 54			12 24				
Earley	d	09 59			10 29				10 59			11 29				11 59			12 29				
Winnersh Triangle	d	10 01			10 31				11 01			11 31				12 01			12 31				
Winnersh	d	10 03			10 33				11 03			11 33				12 03			12 33				
Wokingham	d	10 08			10 38				11 08			11 38				12 08			12 38				
Bracknell	d	10 14			10 44				11 14			11 44				12 14			12 44				
Martins Heron	d	10 17			10 47				11 17			11 47				12 17			12 47				
Guildford	d					10 17							11 17							12 17			
Wanborough	d					10 23							11 23							12 23			
Ash 5	d					10 27							11 27							12 27			
Aldershot	a					10 34							11 34							12 34			
	d					10 40							11 40							12 40			
Ash Vale	d					10 45							11 45							12 45			
Frimley	d					10 51							11 51							12 51			
Camberley	a					10 55							11 55							12 55			
	d					10 55							11 55							12 55			
Bagshot	d					11 01							12 01							13 01			
Ascot 8	d	10 22			10 52	11a07			11 22			11 52	12a07			12 22			12 52	13a07			
Sunningdale	d	10 25			10 55				11 25			11 55				12 25			12 55				
Longcross	d																						
Woking	d							10 52							11 52								12 52
West Byfleet	d							10 56							11 56								12 56
Byfleet & New Haw	d							11 00							12 00								13 00
Weybridge	d																						
Addlestone	d							11 04							12 04								13 04
Chertsey	d							11 07							12 07								13 07
Virginia Water	a	10 30			11 00			11 12	11 30			12 00			12 12	12 30			13 00				13 12
	d	10 30			11 00			11 12	11 30			12 00			12 12	12 30			13 00				13 12
Egham	d	10 34			11 04			11 16	11 34			12 04			12 16	12 34			13 04				13 16
Windsor & Eton Riverside	d		10 34				11 01			11 34				12 01			12 34					13 01	
Datchet	d		10 37				11 04			11 37				12 04			12 37					13 04	
Sunnymeads	d						11 07							12 07								13 07	
Wraysbury	d						11 10							12 10								13 10	
Staines	d	10 39	10 45		11 09		11 16	11 21	11 39	11 45		12 09		12 16	12 21	12 39	12 45		13 09			13 16	13 21
Ashford (Surrey)	d		10 48				11 19	11 24		11 48				12 19	12 24		12 48					13 19	13 24
Feltham	d	10 46	10 53		11 16		11 24	11 29	11 46	11 53		12 16		12 24	12 29	12 46	12 53		13 16			13 24	13 29
Whitton	d		10 57				11 28			11 57				12 28			12 57					13 28	
Kingston	d			10 49							11 49							12 49			13 11		
Hampton Wick	d			10 51							11 51							12 51			13 13		
Teddington	d			10 56							11 56							12 56			13 16		
Fulwell	d																						
Strawberry Hill	d			10 59							11 59							12 59			13 19		
Twickenham	a	10 51	11 00	11 02	11 21		11 31		11 51	12 00	12 02	12 21		12 31		12 51	13 00	13 02	13 21		13 22	13 31	
	d	10 51	11 01	11 03	11 21		11 32		11 51	12 01	12 03	12 21		12 32		12 51	13 01	13 03	13 21		13 23	13 32	
St Margarets	d			11 05			11 34				12 05			12 34				13 05			13 25	13 34	
Richmond ⊖	d	10 56	11 05	11 09	11 26		11 37		11 56	12 05	12 09	12 26		12 37		12 56	13 05	13 09	13 26		13 29	13 37	
North Sheen	d			11 11			11 39				12 11			12 39				13 11			13 31	13 39	
Mortlake	d			11 13			11 42				12 13			12 42				13 13			13 33	13 42	
Hounslow	d							11 35							12 35								13 35
Isleworth	d							11 38							12 38								13 38
Syon Lane	d							11 40							12 40								13 40
Brentford	d							11 42							12 42								13 42
Kew Bridge	d							11 45							12 45								13 45
Chiswick	d							11 47							12 47								13 47
Barnes Bridge	d							11 50							12 50								13 50
Barnes	d			11 16			11 45	11 53			12 16			12 45	12 53			13 16			13 36	13 45	13 53
Putney	d	11 02	11 14	11 19	11 32		11 48	11 56	12 02	12 14	12 19	12 32		12 48	12 56	13 02	13 14	13 19	13 32		13 39	13 48	13 56
Wandsworth Town	d			11 22			11 51	11 59			12 22			12 51	12 59			13 22			13 42	13 51	13 59
Clapham Junction 10	d	11 07	11 18	11 25	11 37		11 53	12 02	12 07	12 18	12 25	12 37		12 53	13 02	13 07	13 18	13 25	13 37		13 45	13 54	14 02
Queenstown Rd.(Battersea)	d			11 28			11 57	12 05			12 28			12 57	13 05			13 28			13 48	13 57	14 05
Vauxhall ⊖	d	11 12	11 24	11 32	11 42		12 00	12 08	12 12	12 24	12 32	12 42		13 00	13 08	13 12	13 24	13 32	13 42		13 52	14 00	14 08
London Waterloo 15 ⊖	a	11 23	11 34	11 41	11 53		12 10	12 13	12 23	12 34	12 41	12 53		13 10	13 13	13 23	13 34	13 41	13 53		14 00	14 10	14 13

Table 149

Sundays until 25 September

Reading, Guildford, Ascot, Weybridge, Windsor, Kingston, Richmond and Hounslow - London

		SW 1	SW	SW	SW 1	SW 1	SW	SW	SW	SW 1	SW	SW	SW 1		SW 1	SW 1	SW	SW	SW	SW 1	SW
Reading 7	d	12 54			13 24					13 54			14 24		20 24					20 54	
Earley	d	12 59			13 29					13 59			14 29		20 29					20 59	
Winnersh Triangle	d	13 01			13 31					14 01			14 31		20 31					21 01	
Winnersh	d	13 03			13 33					14 03			14 33		20 33					21 03	
Wokingham	d	13 08			13 38					14 08			14 38		20 38					21 08	
Bracknell	d	13 14			13 44					14 14			14 44		20 44					21 14	
Martins Heron	d	13 17			13 47					14 17			14 47		20 47					21 17	
Guildford	d					13 17										20 17					
Wanborough	d					13 23										20 23					
Ash 5	d					13 27										20 27					
Aldershot	a					13 34										20 34					
	d					13 40										20 40					
Ash Vale	d					13 45										20 45					
Frimley	d					13 51										20 51					
Camberley	a					13 55										20 55					
	d					13 55										20 55					
Bagshot	d					14 01										21 01					
Ascot 8	d	13 22			13 52	14a07				14 22			14 52		20 52	21a07				21 22	
Sunningdale	d	13 25			13 55					14 25			14 55		20 55					21 25	
Longcross	d																				
Woking	d								13 52										20 52		
West Byfleet	d								13 56										20 56		
Byfleet & New Haw	d								14 00										21 00		
Weybridge	d																				
Addlestone	d								14 04										21 04		
Chertsey	d								14 07										21 07		
Virginia Water	a	13 30			14 00				14 12	14 30			15 00	and at the same minutes past each hour until	21 00				21 12	21 30	
	d	13 30			14 00				14 12	14 30			15 00		21 00				21 12	21 30	
Egham	d	13 34			14 04				14 16	14 34			15 04		21 04				21 16	21 34	
Windsor & Eton Riverside	d		13 34					14 01			14 34							21 01			
Datchet	d		13 37					14 04			14 37							21 04			
Sunnymeads	d							14 07										21 07			
Wraysbury	d							14 10										21 10			
Staines	d	13 39	13 45		14 09			14 16	14 21	14 39	14 45		15 09		21 09			21 16	21 21	21 39	
Ashford (Surrey)	d		13 48					14 19	14 24		14 48							21 19	21 24		
Feltham	d	13 46	13 53		14 16			14 24	14 29	14 46	14 53		15 16		21 16			21 24	21 29	21 46	
Whitton	d		13 57					14 28			14 57							21 28			
Kingston	d			13 49			14 11					14 49					21 11				21 49
Hampton Wick	d			13 51			14 13					14 51					21 13				21 51
Teddington	d			13 56			14 16					14 56					21 16				21 56
Fulwell	d																				
Strawberry Hill	d			13 59			14 19					14 59					21 19				21 59
Twickenham	a	13 51	14 00	14 02	14 21		14 22	14 31		14 51	15 00	15 02	15 21		21 21		21 22	21 31		21 51	22 02
	d	13 51	14 01	14 03	14 21		14 23	14 32		14 51	15 01	15 03	15 21		21 21		21 23	21 32		21 51	22 03
St Margarets	d			14 05			14 25	14 34				15 05					21 25	21 34			22 05
Richmond ⊖	d	13 56	14 05	14 09	14 26		14 29	14 37		14 56	15 05	15 09	15 26		21 26		21 29	21 37		21 56	22 09
North Sheen	d			14 11			14 31	14 39				15 11					21 31	21 39			22 11
Mortlake	d			14 13			14 33	14 42				15 13					21 33	21 42			22 13
Hounslow	d								14 35										21 35		
Isleworth	d								14 38										21 38		
Syon Lane	d								14 40										21 40		
Brentford	d								14 42										21 42		
Kew Bridge	d								14 45										21 45		
Chiswick	d								14 47										21 47		
Barnes Bridge	d								14 50										21 50		
Barnes	d			14 16			14 36	14 45	14 53			15 16					21 36	21 45	21 53		22 16
Putney	d	14 02	14 14	14 19	14 32		14 39	14 48	14 56	15 02	15 14	15 19	15 32		21 32		21 39	21 48	21 56	22 02	22 19
Wandsworth Town	d			14 22			14 42	14 51	14 59			15 22					21 42	21 51	21 59		22 22
Clapham Junction 10	d	14 07	14 18	14 25	14 37		14 45	14 54	15 02	15 07	15 18	15 25	15 37		21 37		21 45	21 54	22 02	22 07	22 25
Queenstown Rd.(Battersea)	d			14 28			14 48	14 57	15 05			15 28					21 48	21 57	22 05		22 28
Vauxhall ⊖	d	14 12	14 24	14 32	14 42		14 52	15 00	15 08	15 12	15 24	15 32	15 42		21 42		21 52	22 00	22 08	22 12	22 32
London Waterloo 15 ⊖	a	14 23	14 34	14 41	14 53		15 00	15 05	15 13	15 18	15 29	15 36	15 48		21 48		22 00	22 05	22 13	22 18	22 36

Reading, Guildford, Ascot, Weybridge, Windsor, Kingston, Richmond and Hounslow - London

Sundays until 25 September

		SW 1	SW 1	SW	SW	SW	SW 1	SW	SW 1	SW 1	SW	SW	SW	SW 1	SW 1
Reading 7	d	21 24					21 54		22 24					22 54	
Earley	d	21 29					21 59		22 29					22 59	
Winnersh Triangle	d	21 31					22 01		22 31					23 01	
Winnersh	d	21 33					22 03		22 33					23 03	
Wokingham	d	21 38					22 08		22 38					23 08	
Bracknell	d	21 44					22 14		22 44					23 14	
Martins Heron	d	21 47					22 17		22 47					23 17	
Guildford	d		21 17							22 17					23 17
Wanborough	d		21 23							22 23					23 23
Ash 5	d		21 27							22 27					23 27
Aldershot	a		21 34							22 34					23 34
	d		21 40							22 40					
Ash Vale	d		21 45							22 45					
Frimley	d		21 51							22 51					
Camberley	a		21 55							22 55					
	d		21 55							22 55					
Bagshot	d		22 01							23 01					
Ascot 3	d	21 52	22a07				22 22		22 52	23a07				23 22	
Sunningdale	d	21 55					22 25		22 55					23 25	
Longcross	d														
Woking	d					21 52							22 52		
West Byfleet	d					21 56							22 56		
Byfleet & New Haw	d					22 00							23 00		
Weybridge	d														
Addlestone	d					22 04							23 04		
Chertsey	d					22 07							23 07		
Virginia Water	a	22 00				22 12	22 30		23 00				23 12	23 30	
	d	22 00				22 12	22 30		23 00				23 12	23 30	
Egham	d	22 04				22 16	22 34		23 04				23 16	23 34	
Windsor & Eton Riverside	d				22 01							23 01			
Datchet	d				22 04							23 04			
Sunnymeads	d				22 07							23 07			
Wraysbury	d				22 10							23 10			
Staines	d	22 09			22 16	22 21	22 39		23 09			23 16	23 21	23 39	
Ashford (Surrey)	d				22 19	22 24						23 19	23 24		
Feltham	d	22 16			22 24	22 29	22 46		23 16			23 24	23 29	23 46	
Whitton	d				22 28							23 28			
Kingston	d			22 11				22 49			23 11				
Hampton Wick	d			22 13				22 51			23 13				
Teddington	d			22 16				22 56			23 16				
Fulwell	d														
Strawberry Hill	d			22 19				22 59			23 19				
Twickenham	a	22 21		22 22	22 31		22 51	23 02	23 21		23 22	23 31		23 51	
	d	22 21		22 23	22 32		22 51	23 03	23 21		23 23	23 32		23 51	
St Margarets	d			22 25	22 34			23 05			23 25	23 34			
Richmond ⊖	d	22 26		22 29	22 37		22 56	23 09	23 26		23 29	23 37		23 56	
North Sheen	d			22 31	22 39			23 11			23 31	23 39			
Mortlake	d			22 33	22 42			23 13			23 33	23 42			
Hounslow	d					22 35							23 35		
Isleworth	d					22 38							23 38		
Syon Lane	d					22 40							23 40		
Brentford	d					22 42							23 42		
Kew Bridge	d					22 45							23 45		
Chiswick	d					22 47							23 47		
Barnes Bridge	d					22 50							23 50		
Barnes	d			22 36	22 45	22 53		23 16			23 36	23 45	23 53		
Putney	d	22 32		22 39	22 48	22 56	23 02	23 19	23 32		23 39	23 48	23 56	00 02	
Wandsworth Town	d			22 42	22 51	22 59		23 22			23 42	23 51	23 59		
Clapham Junction 10	d	22 37		22 45	22 54	23 02	23 07	23 25	23 37		23 45	23 54	00 02	00 07	
Queenstown Rd.(Battersea)	d			22 48	22 57	23 05		23 28			23 48	23 57	00 05		
Vauxhall ⊖	d	22 42		22 52	23 00	23 08	23 12	23 32	23 42		23 52		00 08	00 12	
London Waterloo 15 ⊖	a	22 48		23 00	23 05	23 13	23 18	23 36	23 48		23 59	00 04	00 13	00 17	

Table 149

Reading, Guildford, Ascot, Weybridge, Windsor, Kingston, Richmond and Hounslow - London

Sundays from 2 October

		SW 1 A	SW 1 B	SW	SW 1	SW	SW	SW	SW 1	SW	SW	SW	SW 1	SW	SW 1	SW 1	SW	SW	SW 1	SW	SW 1	SW 1	SW
Reading 7	d	22p39	22p42		23p12								07 51		08 21				08 51		09 21		
Earley	d	22p44	22p47		23p17								07 56		08 26				08 56		09 26		
Winnersh Triangle	d	22p46	22p49		23p19								07 58		08 28				08 58		09 28		
Winnersh	d	22p48	22p51		23p21								08 00		08 30				09 00		09 30		
Wokingham	d	22p53	22p56		23p26								08 05		08 35				09 05		09 35		
Bracknell	d	22p59	23p02		23p32								08 11		08 41				09 11		09 41		
Martins Heron	d	23p02	23p05		23p35								08 14		08 44				09 14		09 44		
Guildford	d								07 17							08 17						09 17	
Wanborough	d								07 23							08 23						09 23	
Ash 5	d								07 27							08 27						09 27	
Aldershot	a								07 34							08 34						09 34	
	d								07 40							08 40						09 40	
Ash Vale	d								07 45							08 45						09 45	
Frimley	d								07 51							08 51						09 51	
Camberley	a								07 55							08 55						09 55	
	d								07 55							08 55						09 55	
Bagshot	d								08 01							09 01						10 01	
Ascot 3	d	23p07	23p10		23p40				08a07				08 19		08 49	09a07			09 19		09 49	10a07	
Sunningdale	d	23p10	23p13		23p43								08 22		08 52				09 22		09 52		
Longcross	d																						
Woking	d											07 52						08 52					
West Byfleet	d											07 56						08 56					
Byfleet & New Haw	d											08 00						09 00					
Weybridge	d							07 00															
Addlestone	d							07 04				08 04						09 04					
Chertsey	d							07 07				08 07						09 07					
Virginia Water	a	23p19	23p19		23p49			07 12				08 12	08 30		09 00			09 12	09 30		10 00		
	d	23p19	23p19		23p49			07 12				08 12	08 30		09 00			09 12	09 30		10 00		
Egham	d	23p23	23p23		23p53			07 16				08 16	08 34		09 04			09 16	09 34		10 04		
Windsor & Eton Riverside	d						06 59				07 59						08 59						09 59
Datchet	d						07 03				08 03						09 03						10 03
Sunnymeads	d						07 06				08 06						09 06						10 06
Wraysbury	d						07 10				08 10						09 10						10 10
Staines	d	23p29	23p29		23p59		07 16	07 21			08 16	08 21	08 39		09 09		09 16	09 21	09 39		10 09		10 16
Ashford (Surrey)	d						07 19	07 24			08 19	08 24					09 19	09 24					10 19
Feltham	d	23p35	23p35		00 05		07 24	07 29			08 24	08 29	08 46		09 16		09 24	09 29	09 46		10 16		10 24
Whitton	d						07 28				08 28						09 28						10 28
Kingston	d			23p29		06 49				07 49				08 49						09 49			
Hampton Wick	d			23p31		06 51				07 51				08 51						09 51			
Teddington	d			23p35		06 56				07 56				08 56						09 56			
Fulwell	d																						
Strawberry Hill	d			23p38		06 59				07 59				08 59						09 59			
Twickenham	a	23p40	23p40	23p42	00 10	07 02	07 31			08 02	08 31		08 51	09 02	09 21		09 31		09 51	10 02	10 21		10 31
	d	23p41	23p41	23p43	00 11	07 03	07 32			08 03	08 32		08 51	09 03	09 21		09 32		09 51	10 03	10 21		10 32
St Margarets	d			23p45		07 05	07 34			08 05	08 34			09 05			09 34			10 05			10 34
Richmond ⊖	d	23p45	23p45	23p49	00 15	07 09	07 37			08 09	08 37		08 56	09 09	09 26		09 37		09 56	10 09	10 26		10 37
North Sheen	d			23p51		07 11	07 39			08 11	08 39			09 11			09 39			10 11			10 39
Mortlake	d			23p53		07 13	07 42			08 13	08 42			09 13			09 42			10 13			10 42
Hounslow	d							07 35				08 35						09 35					
Isleworth	d							07 38				08 38						09 38					
Syon Lane	d							07 40				08 40						09 40					
Brentford	d							07 42				08 42						09 42					
Kew Bridge	d							07 45				08 45						09 45					
Chiswick	d							07 47				08 47						09 47					
Barnes Bridge	d							07 50				08 50						09 50					
Barnes	d			23p56		07 16	07 45	07 53		08 16	08 45	08 53		09 16			09 45	09 53		10 16			10 45
Putney	d			23p59		07 19	07 48	07 56		08 19	08 48	08 56	09 02	09 19	09 32		09 48	09 56	10 02	10 19	10 32		10 48
Wandsworth Town	d			00 02		07 22	07 51	07 59		08 22	08 51	08 59		09 22			09 51	09 59		10 22			10 51
Clapham Junction 10	d	23p54	23p54	00 05	00 24	07 25	07 54	08 02		08 25	08 54	09 02	09 07	09 25	09 37		09 54	10 02	10 07	10 25	10 37		10 53
Queenstown Rd.(Battersea)	d			00 08		07 28	07 57	08 05		08 28	08 57	09 05		09 28			09 57	10 05		10 28			10 57
Vauxhall ⊖	d			00 12		07 32	08 00	08 08		08 32	09 00	09 08	09 12	09 32	09 42		10 00	10 08	10 12	10 32	10 42		11 00
London Waterloo 15 ⊖	a	00 02	00 02	00 16	00 37	07 41	08 10	08 13		08 41	09 10	09 13	09 23	09 41	09 53		10 10	10 13	10 23	10 41	10 53		11 10

A not 2 October

B 2 October

Table 149

Sundays
from 2 October

Reading, Guildford, Ascot, Weybridge, Windsor, Kingston, Richmond and Hounslow - London

		SW	SW ■	SW	SW	SW ■	SW ■	SW	SW	SW ■	SW	SW	SW ■	SW ■	SW	SW	SW ■	SW	SW	SW ■	SW ■	SW	SW
Reading ■	d		09 51			10 21				10 51			11 21				11 51			12 21			
Earley	d		09 56			10 26				10 56			11 26				11 56			12 26			
Winnersh Triangle	d		09 58			10 28				10 58			11 28				11 58			12 28			
Winnersh	d		10 00			10 30				11 00			11 30				12 00			12 30			
Wokingham	d		10 05			10 35				11 05			11 35				12 05			12 35			
Bracknell	d		10 11			10 41				11 11			11 41				12 11			12 41			
Martins Heron	d		10 14			10 44				11 14			11 44				12 14			12 44			
Guildford	d						10 17							11 17							12 17		
Wanborough	d						10 23							11 23							12 23		
Ash ■	d						10 27							11 27							12 27		
Aldershot	a						10 34							11 34							12 34		
	d						10 40							11 40							12 40		
Ash Vale	d						10 45							11 45							12 45		
Frimley	d						10 51							11 51							12 51		
Camberley	a						10 55							11 55							12 55		
	d						10 55							11 55							12 55		
Bagshot	d						11 01							12 01							13 01		
Ascot ■	d		10 19			10 49	11a07			11 19			11 49	12a07			12 19			12 49	13a07		
Sunningdale	d		10 22			10 52				11 22			11 52				12 22			12 52			
Longcross	d																						
Woking	d	09 52							10 52							11 52							
West Byfleet	d	09 56							10 56							11 56							
Byfleet & New Haw	d	10 00							11 00							12 00							
Weybridge	d																						
Addlestone	d	10 04							11 04							12 04							
Chertsey	d	10 07							11 07							12 07							
Virginia Water	a	10 12	10 30			11 00			11 12	11 30			12 00			12 12	12 30			13 00			
	d	10 12	10 30			11 00			11 12	11 30			12 00			12 12	12 30			13 00			
Egham	d	10 16	10 34			11 04			11 16	11 34			12 04			12 16	12 34			13 04			
Windsor & Eton Riverside	d			10 32				10 59			11 32				11 59			12 32					12 59
Datchet	d			10 36				11 03			11 36				12 03			12 36					13 03
Sunnymeads	d							11 06							12 06								13 06
Wraysbury	d							11 10							12 10								13 10
Staines	d	10 21	10 39	10 45		11 09		11 16	11 21	11 39	11 45		12 09		12 16	12 21	12 39	12 45		13 09			13 16
Ashford (Surrey)	d	10 24		10 48				11 19	11 24		11 48				12 19	12 24		12 48					13 19
Feltham	d	10 29	10 46	10 53		11 16		11 24	11 29	11 46	11 53		12 16		12 24	12 29	12 46	12 53		13 16			13 24
Whitton	d			10 57				11 28			11 57				12 28			12 57					13 28
Kingston	d				10 49							11 49							12 49			13 11	
Hampton Wick	d				10 51							11 51							12 51			13 13	
Teddington	d				10 56							11 56							12 56			13 16	
Fulwell	d																						
Strawberry Hill	d				10 59							11 59							12 59			13 19	
Twickenham	a		10 51	11 00	11 02	11 21		11 31		11 51	12 00	12 02	12 21		12 31		12 51	13 00	13 02	13 21		13 22	13 31
	d		10 51	11 01	11 03	11 21		11 32		11 51	12 01	12 03	12 21		12 32		12 51	13 01	13 03	13 21		13 23	13 32
St Margarets	d				11 05			11 34				12 05			12 34				13 05			13 25	13 34
Richmond ⊖	d		10 56	11 05	11 09	11 26		11 37		11 56	12 05	12 09	12 26		12 37		12 56	13 05	13 09	13 26		13 29	13 37
North Sheen	d				11 11			11 39				12 11			12 39				13 11			13 31	13 39
Mortlake	d				11 13			11 42				12 13			12 42				13 13			13 33	13 42
Hounslow	d	10 35							11 35							12 35							
Isleworth	d	10 38							11 38							12 38							
Syon Lane	d	10 40							11 40							12 40							
Brentford	d	10 42							11 42							12 42							
Kew Bridge	d	10 45							11 45							12 45							
Chiswick	d	10 47							11 47							12 47							
Barnes Bridge	d	10 50							11 50							12 50							
Barnes	d	10 53			11 16			11 45	11 53			12 16			12 45	12 53			13 16			13 36	13 45
Putney	d	10 56	11 02	11 14	11 19	11 32		11 48	11 56	12 02	12 14	12 19	12 32		12 48	12 56	13 02	13 14	13 19	13 32		13 39	13 48
Wandsworth Town	d	10 59			11 22			11 51	11 59			12 22			12 51	12 59			13 22			13 42	13 51
Clapham Junction ■	d	11 02	11 07	11 18	11 25	11 37		11 53	12 02	12 07	12 18	12 25	12 37		12 53	13 02	13 07	13 18	13 25	13 37		13 45	13 54
Queenstown Rd.(Battersea)	d	11 05			11 28			11 57	12 05			12 28			12 57	13 05			13 28			13 48	13 57
Vauxhall ⊖	d	11 08	11 12	11 24	11 32	11 42		12 00	12 08	12 12	12 24	12 32	12 42		13 00	13 08	13 12	13 24	13 32	13 42		13 52	14 00
London Waterloo ■ ⊖	a	11 13	11 23	11 34	11 41	11 53		12 10	12 13	12 23	12 34	12 41	12 53		13 10	13 13	13 23	13 34	13 41	13 53		14 00	14 10

Table 149

Sundays
from 2 October

Reading, Guildford, Ascot, Weybridge, Windsor, Kingston, Richmond and Hounslow - London

		SW	SW ■	SW	SW	SW ■	SW ■	SW	SW	SW	SW ■	SW	SW	SW ■		SW ■	SW ■	SW	SW	SW	SW ■
Reading ■	d		12 51			13 21					13 51			14 21		20 21					20 51
Earley	d		12 56			13 26					13 56			14 26		20 26					20 56
Winnersh Triangle	d		12 58			13 28					13 58			14 28		20 28					20 58
Winnersh	d		13 00			13 30					14 00			14 30		20 30					21 00
Wokingham	d		13 05			13 35					14 05			14 35		20 35					21 05
Bracknell	d		13 11			13 41					14 11			14 41		20 41					21 11
Martins Heron	d		13 14			13 44					14 14			14 44		20 44					21 14
Guildford	d						13 17										20 17				
Wanborough	d						13 23										20 23				
Ash ■	d						13 27										20 27				
Aldershot	a						13 34										20 34				
	d						13 40										20 40				
Ash Vale	d						13 45										20 45				
Frimley	d						13 51										20 51				
Camberley	a						13 55										20 55				
	d						13 55										20 55				
Bagshot	d						14 01										21 01				
Ascot ■	d		13 19			13 49	14a07				14 19			14 49		20 49	21a07				21 19
Sunningdale	d		13 22			13 52					14 22			14 52		20 52					21 22
Longcross	d																				
Woking	d	12 52								13 52										20 52	
West Byfleet	d	12 56								13 56										20 56	
Byfleet & New Haw	d	13 00								14 00										21 00	
Weybridge	d																				
Addlestone	d	13 04								14 04										21 04	
Chertsey	d	13 07								14 07										21 07	
Virginia Water	a	13 12	13 30			14 00				14 12	14 30			15 00	and at	21 00				21 12	21 30
	d	13 12	13 30			14 00				14 12	14 30			15 00	the same	21 00				21 12	21 30
Egham	d	13 16	13 34			14 04				14 16	14 34			15 04	minutes	21 04				21 16	21 34
Windsor & Eton Riverside	d			13 32					13 59			14 32			past				20 59		
Datchet	d			13 36					14 03			14 36			each				21 03		
Sunnymeads	d								14 06						hour until				21 06		
Wraysbury	d								14 10										21 10		
Staines	d	13 21	13 39	13 45		14 09			14 16	14 21	14 39	14 45		15 09		21 09			21 16	21 21	21 39
Ashford (Surrey)	d	13 24		13 48					14 19	14 24		14 48							21 19	21 24	
Feltham	d	13 29	13 46	13 53		14 16			14 24	14 29	14 46	14 53		15 16		21 16			21 24	21 29	21 46
Whitton	d			13 57					14 28			14 57							21 28		
Kingston	d				13 49			14 11					14 49					21 11			
Hampton Wick	d				13 51			14 13					14 51					21 13			
Teddington	d				13 56			14 16					14 56					21 16			
Fulwell	d																				
Strawberry Hill	d				13 59			14 19					14 59					21 19			
Twickenham	a		13 51	14 00	14 02	14 21		14 22	14 31		14 51	15 00	15 02	15 21		21 21		21 22	21 31		21 51
	d		13 51	14 01	14 03	14 21		14 23	14 32		14 51	15 01	15 03	15 21		21 21		21 23	21 32		21 51
St Margarets	d				14 05			14 25	14 34				15 05					21 25	21 34		
Richmond ⊖	d		13 56	14 05	14 09	14 26		14 29	14 37		14 56	15 05	15 09	15 26		21 26		21 29	21 37		21 56
North Sheen	d				14 11			14 31	14 39				15 11					21 31	21 39		
Mortlake	d				14 13			14 33	14 42				15 13					21 33	21 42		
Hounslow	d	13 35								14 35										21 35	
Isleworth	d	13 38								14 38										21 38	
Syon Lane	d	13 40								14 40										21 40	
Brentford	d	13 42								14 42										21 42	
Kew Bridge	d	13 45								14 45										21 45	
Chiswick	d	13 47								14 47										21 47	
Barnes Bridge	d	13 50								14 50										21 50	
Barnes	d	13 53			14 16			14 36	14 45	14 53			15 16					21 36	21 45	21 53	
Putney	d	13 56	14 02	14 14	14 19	14 32		14 39	14 48	14 56	15 02	15 14	15 19	15 32		21 32		21 39	21 48	21 56	22 02
Wandsworth Town	d	13 59			14 22			14 42	14 51	14 59			15 22					21 42	21 51	21 59	
Clapham Junction ■	d	14 02	14 07	14 18	14 25	14 37		14 45	14 54	15 02	15 07	15 18	15 25	15 37		21 37		21 45	21 54	22 02	22 07
Queenstown Rd.(Battersea)	d	14 05			14 28			14 48	14 57	15 05			15 28					21 48	21 57	22 05	
Vauxhall ⊖	d	14 08	14 12	14 24	14 32	14 42		14 52	15 00	15 08	15 12	15 24	15 32	15 42		21 42		21 52	22 00	22 08	22 12
London Waterloo ■ ⊖	a	14 13	14 23	14 34	14 41	14 53		15 00	15 05	15 13	15 18	15 29	15 36	15 48		21 48		22 00	22 05	22 13	22 18

Sundays

from 2 October

Reading, Guildford, Ascot, Weybridge, Windsor, Kingston, Richmond and Hounslow - London

		SW	SW 1	SW 1	SW	SW	SW	SW 1	SW	SW 1	SW 1	SW	SW	SW	SW 1	SW 1
Reading 7	d		21 21					21 51		22 21					22 54	
Earley	d		21 26					21 56		22 26					22 59	
Winnersh Triangle	d		21 28					21 58		22 28					23 01	
Winnersh	d		21 30					22 00		22 30					23 03	
Wokingham	d		21 35					22 05		22 35					23 08	
Bracknell	d		21 41					22 11		22 41					23 14	
Martins Heron	d		21 44					22 14		22 44					23 17	
Guildford	d			21 17							22 17					23 17
Wanborough	d			21 23							22 23					23 23
Ash 5	d			21 27							22 27					23 27
Aldershot	a			21 34							22 34					23 34
	d			21 40							22 40					
Ash Vale	d			21 45							22 45					
Frimley	d			21 51							22 51					
Camberley	a			21 55							22 55					
	d			21 55							22 55					
Bagshot	d			22 01							23 01					
Ascot 8	d		21 49	22a07				22 19		22 49	23a07				23 22	
Sunningdale	d		21 52					22 22		22 52					23 25	
Longcross	d															
Woking	d						21 52							22 52		
West Byfleet	d						21 56							22 56		
Byfleet & New Haw	d						22 00							23 00		
Weybridge	d															
Addlestone	d						22 04							23 04		
Chertsey	d						22 07							23 07		
Virginia Water	a		22 00				22 12	22 30		23 00				23 12	23 30	
	d		22 00				22 12	22 30		23 00				23 12	23 30	
Egham	d		22 04				22 16	22 34		23 04				23 16	23 34	
Windsor & Eton Riverside	d					21 59							23 01			
Datchet	d					22 03							23 04			
Sunnymeads	d					22 06							23 07			
Wraysbury	d					22 10							23 10			
Staines	d		22 09			22 16	22 21	22 39		23 09			23 16	23 21	23 39	
Ashford (Surrey)	d					22 19	22 24						23 19	23 24		
Feltham	d		22 16			22 24	22 29	22 46		23 16			23 24	23 29	23 46	
Whitton	d					22 28							23 28			
Kingston	d	21 49			22 11				22 49			23 11				
Hampton Wick	d	21 51			22 13				22 51			23 13				
Teddington	d	21 56			22 16				22 56			23 16				
Fulwell	d															
Strawberry Hill	d	21 59			22 19				22 59			23 19				
Twickenham	a	22 02	22 21		22 22	22 31		22 51	23 02	23 21		23 22	23 31		23 51	
	d	22 03	22 21		22 23	22 32		22 51	23 03	23 21		23 23	23 32		23 51	
St Margarets	d	22 05			22 25	22 34			23 05			23 25	23 34			
Richmond ⊖	d	22 09	22 26		22 29	22 37		22 56	23 09	23 26		23 29	23 37		23 56	
North Sheen	d	22 11			22 31	22 39			23 11			23 31	23 39			
Mortlake	d	22 13			22 33	22 42			23 13			23 33	23 42			
Hounslow	d						22 35							23 35		
Isleworth	d						22 38							23 38		
Syon Lane	d						22 40							23 40		
Brentford	d						22 42							23 42		
Kew Bridge	d						22 45							23 45		
Chiswick	d						22 47							23 47		
Barnes Bridge	d						22 50							23 50		
Barnes	d	22 16			22 36	22 45	22 53		23 16			23 36	23 45	23 53		
Putney	d	22 19	22 32		22 39	22 48	22 56	23 02	23 19	23 32		23 39	23 48	23 56	00 02	
Wandsworth Town	d	22 22			22 42	22 51	22 59		23 22			23 42	23 51	23 59		
Clapham Junction 10	d	22 25	22 37		22 45	22 54	23 02	23 07	23 25	23 37		23 45	23 54	00 02	00 07	
Queenstown Rd.(Battersea)	d	22 28			22 48	22 57	23 05		23 28			23 48	23 57	00 05		
Vauxhall ⊖	d	22 32	22 42		22 52	23 00	23 08	23 12	23 32	23 42		23 52		00 08	00 12	
London Waterloo 15 ⊖	a	22 36	22 48		23 00	23 05	23 13	23 18	23 36	23 48		23 59	00 04	00 13	00 17	

Sundays

from 9 October

Reading, Guildford, Ascot, Weybridge, Windsor, Kingston, Richmond and Hounslow - London

		SW 1	SW	SW 1	SW	SW	SW	SW 1	SW	SW	SW	SW 1	SW	SW 1	SW 1	SW	SW	SW 1	SW	SW 1	SW 1	SW	SW
Reading 7	d	22p39		23p12								07 51		08 21				08 51		09 21			
Earley	d	22p44		23p17								07 56		08 26				08 56		09 26			
Winnersh Triangle	d	22p46		23p19								07 58		08 28				08 58		09 28			
Winnersh	d	22p48		23p21								08 00		08 30				09 00		09 30			
Wokingham	d	22p53		23p26								08 05		08 35				09 05		09 35			
Bracknell	d	22p59		23p32								08 11		08 41				09 11		09 41			
Martins Heron	d	23p02		23p35								08 14		08 44				09 14		09 44			
Guildford	d							07 17							08 17						09 17		
Wanborough	d							07 23							08 23						09 23		
Ash 5	d							07 27							08 27						09 27		
Aldershot	a							07 34							08 34						09 34		
	d							07 40							08 40						09 40		
Ash Vale	d							07 45							08 45						09 45		
Frimley	d							07 51							08 51						09 51		
Camberley	a							07 55							08 55						09 55		
	d							07 55							08 55						09 55		
Bagshot	d							08 01							09 01						10 01		
Ascot 8	d	23p07		23p40				08a07				08 19		08 49	09a07			09 19		09 49	10a07		
Sunningdale	d	23p10		23p43								08 22		08 52				09 22		09 52			
Longcross	d																						
Woking	d										07 52						08 52						09 52
West Byfleet	d										07 56						08 56						09 56
Byfleet & New Haw	d										08 00						09 00						10 00
Weybridge	d						07 00																
Addlestone	d						07 04				08 04						09 04						10 04
Chertsey	d						07 07				08 07						09 07						10 07
Virginia Water	a	23p19		23p49			07 12				08 12	08 30		09 00			09 12	09 30		10 00			10 12
	d	23p19		23p49			07 12				08 12	08 30		09 00			09 12	09 30		10 00			10 12
Egham	d	23p23		23p53			07 16				08 16	08 34		09 04			09 16	09 34		10 04			10 16
Windsor & Eton Riverside	d					06 59				07 59						08 59						09 59	
Datchet	d					07 03				08 03						09 03						10 03	
Sunnymeads	d					07 06				08 06						09 06						10 06	
Wraysbury	d					07 10				08 10						09 10						10 10	
Staines	d	23p29		23p59		07 16	07 21			08 16	08 21	08 39		09 09		09 16	09 21	09 39		10 09		10 16	10 21
Ashford (Surrey)	d					07 19	07 24			08 19	08 24					09 19	09 24					10 19	10 24
Feltham	d	23p35		00 05		07 24	07 29			08 24	08 29	08 46		09 16		09 24	09 29	09 46		10 16		10 24	10 29
Whitton	d					07 28				08 28						09 28						10 28	
Kingston	d		23p29		06 49				07 49				08 49						09 49				
Hampton Wick	d		23p31		06 51				07 51				08 51						09 51				
Teddington	d		23p35		06 56				07 56				08 56						09 56				
Fulwell	d																						
Strawberry Hill	d		23p38		06 59				07 59				08 59						09 59				
Twickenham	a	23p40	23p42	00 10	07 02	07 31			08 02	08 31		08 51	09 02	09 21		09 31		09 51	10 02	10 21		10 31	
	d	23p41	23p43	00 11	07 03	07 32			08 03	08 32		08 51	09 03	09 21		09 32		09 51	10 03	10 21		10 32	
St Margarets	d		23p45		07 05	07 34			08 05	08 34			09 05			09 34			10 05			10 34	
Richmond ⊖	d	23p45	23p49	00 15	07 09	07 37			08 09	08 37		08 56	09 09	09 26		09 37		09 56	10 09	10 26		10 37	
North Sheen	d		23p51		07 11	07 39			08 11	08 39			09 11			09 39			10 11			10 39	
Mortlake	d		23p53		07 13	07 42			08 13	08 42			09 13			09 42			10 13			10 42	
Hounslow	d						07 35				08 35						09 35						10 35
Isleworth	d						07 38				08 38						09 38						10 38
Syon Lane	d						07 40				08 40						09 40						10 40
Brentford	d						07 42				08 42						09 42						10 42
Kew Bridge	d						07 45				08 45						09 45						10 45
Chiswick	d						07 47				08 47						09 47						10 47
Barnes Bridge	d						07 50				08 50						09 50						10 50
Barnes	d		23p56		07 16	07 45	07 53		08 16	08 45	08 53		09 16			09 45	09 53		10 16			10 45	10 53
Putney	d		23p59		07 19	07 48	07 56		08 19	08 48	08 56	09 02	09 19	09 32		09 48	09 56	10 02	10 19	10 32		10 48	10 56
Wandsworth Town	d		00 02		07 22	07 51	07 59		08 22	08 51	08 59		09 22			09 51	09 59		10 22			10 51	10 59
Clapham Junction 10	d	23p54	00 05	00 24	07 25	07 54	08 02		08 25	08 54	09 02	09 07	09 25	09 37		09 54	10 02	10 07	10 25	10 37		10 53	11 02
Queenstown Rd.(Battersea)	d		00 08		07 28	07 57	08 05		08 28	08 57	09 05		09 28			09 57	10 05		10 28			10 57	11 05
Vauxhall ⊖	d		00 12		07 32	08 00	08 08		08 32	09 00	09 08	09 12	09 32	09 42		10 00	10 08	10 12	10 32	10 42		11 00	11 08
London Waterloo 15 ⊖	a	00 02	00 16	00 37	07 41	08 10	08 13		08 41	09 10	09 13	09 23	09 41	09 53		10 10	10 13	10 23	10 41	10 53		11 10	11 13

Table 149

Sundays from 9 October

Reading, Guildford, Ascot, Weybridge, Windsor, Kingston, Richmond and Hounslow - London

		SW 1	SW	SW	SW 1	SW 1	SW	SW	SW 1	SW	SW	SW 1	SW 1	SW	SW	SW 1	SW	SW	SW 1	SW 1	SW	SW	SW
Reading 7	d	09 51			10 21				10 51			11 21				11 51			12 21				
Earley	d	09 56			10 26				10 56			11 26				11 56			12 26				
Winnersh Triangle	d	09 58			10 28				10 58			11 28				11 58			12 28				
Winnersh	d	10 00			10 30				11 00			11 30				12 00			12 30				
Wokingham	d	10 05			10 35				11 05			11 35				12 05			12 35				
Bracknell	d	10 11			10 41				11 11			11 41				12 11			12 41				
Martins Heron	d	10 14			10 44				11 14			11 44				12 14			12 44				
Guildford	d					10 17							11 17							12 17			
Wanborough	d					10 23							11 23							12 23			
Ash 5	d					10 27							11 27							12 27			
Aldershot	a					10 34							11 34							12 34			
	d					10 40							11 40							12 40			
Ash Vale	d					10 45							11 45							12 45			
Frimley	d					10 51							11 51							12 51			
Camberley	a					10 55							11 55							12 55			
	d					10 55							11 55							12 55			
Bagshot	d					11 01							12 01							13 01			
Ascot 3	d	10 19			10 49	11a07			11 19			11 49	12a07			12 19			12 49	13a07			
Sunningdale	d	10 22			10 52				11 22			11 52				12 22			12 52				
Longcross	d																						
Woking	d							10 52							11 52								12 52
West Byfleet	d							10 56							11 56								12 56
Byfleet & New Haw	d							11 00							12 00								13 00
Weybridge	d																						
Addlestone	d							11 04							12 04								13 04
Chertsey	d							11 07							12 07								13 07
Virginia Water	a	10 30			11 00			11 12	11 30			12 00			12 12	12 30			13 00				13 12
	d	10 30			11 00			11 12	11 30			12 00			12 12	12 30			13 00				13 12
Egham	d	10 34			11 04			11 16	11 34			12 04			12 16	12 34			13 04				13 16
Windsor & Eton Riverside	d		10 32				10 59			11 32				11 59			12 32					12 59	
Datchet	d		10 36				11 03			11 36				12 03			12 36					13 03	
Sunnymeads	d						11 06							12 06								13 06	
Wraysbury	d						11 10							12 10								13 10	
Staines	d	10 39	10 45		11 09		11 16	11 21	11 39	11 45		12 09		12 16	12 21	12 39	12 45		13 09			13 16	13 21
Ashford (Surrey)	d		10 48				11 19	11 24		11 48				12 19	12 24		12 48					13 19	13 24
Feltham	d	10 46	10 53		11 16		11 24	11 29	11 46	11 53		12 16		12 24	12 29	12 46	12 53		13 16			13 24	13 29
Whitton	d		10 57				11 28			11 57				12 28			12 57					13 28	
Kingston	d			10 49							11 49							12 49			13 11		
Hampton Wick	d			10 51							11 51							12 51			13 13		
Teddington	d			10 56							11 56							12 56			13 16		
Fulwell	d																						
Strawberry Hill	d			10 59							11 59							12 59			13 19		
Twickenham	a	10 51	11 00	11 02	11 21		11 31		11 51	12 00	12 02	12 21		12 31		12 51	13 00	13 02	13 21		13 22	13 31	
	d	10 51	11 01	11 03	11 21		11 32		11 51	12 01	12 03	12 21		12 32		12 51	13 01	13 03	13 21		13 23	13 32	
St Margarets	d			11 05			11 34				12 05			12 34				13 05			13 25	13 34	
Richmond ⊖	d	10 56	11 05	11 09	11 26		11 37		11 56	12 05	12 09	12 26		12 37		12 56	13 05	13 09	13 26		13 29	13 37	
North Sheen	d			11 11			11 39				12 11			12 39				13 11			13 31	13 39	
Mortlake	d			11 13			11 42				12 13			12 42				13 13			13 33	13 42	
Hounslow	d							11 35							12 35								13 35
Isleworth	d							11 38							12 38								13 38
Syon Lane	d							11 40							12 40								13 40
Brentford	d							11 42							12 42								13 42
Kew Bridge	d							11 45							12 45								13 45
Chiswick	d							11 47							12 47								13 47
Barnes Bridge	d							11 50							12 50								13 50
Barnes	d			11 16			11 45	11 53			12 16			12 45	12 53			13 16			13 36	13 45	13 53
Putney	d	11 02	11 14	11 19	11 32		11 48	11 56	12 02	12 14	12 19	12 32		12 48	12 56	13 02	13 14	13 19	13 32		13 39	13 48	13 56
Wandsworth Town	d			11 22			11 51	11 59			12 22			12 51	12 59			13 22			13 42	13 51	13 59
Clapham Junction 10	d	11 07	11 18	11 25	11 37		11 53	12 02	12 07	12 18	12 25	12 37		12 53	13 02	13 07	13 18	13 25	13 37		13 45	13 54	14 02
Queenstown Rd.(Battersea)	d			11 28			11 57	12 05			12 28			12 57	13 05			13 28			13 48	13 57	14 05
Vauxhall ⊖	d	11 12	11 24	11 32	11 42		12 00	12 08	12 12	12 24	12 32	12 42		13 00	13 08	13 12	13 24	13 32	13 42		13 52	14 00	14 08
London Waterloo 15 ⊖	a	11 23	11 34	11 41	11 53		12 10	12 13	12 23	12 34	12 41	12 53		13 10	13 13	13 23	13 34	13 41	13 53		14 00	14 10	14 13

Table 149

Sundays from 9 October

Reading, Guildford, Ascot, Weybridge, Windsor, Kingston, Richmond and Hounslow - London

		SW 1	SW	SW	SW 1	SW 1	SW	SW	SW	SW 1	SW	SW	SW 1		SW 1	SW 1	SW	SW	SW	SW 1	SW
Reading 7	d	12 51			13 21					13 51			14 21		20 21					20 51	
Earley	d	12 56			13 26					13 56			14 26		20 26					20 56	
Winnersh Triangle	d	12 58			13 28					13 58			14 28		20 28					20 58	
Winnersh	d	13 00			13 30					14 00			14 30		20 30					21 00	
Wokingham	d	13 05			13 35					14 05			14 35		20 35					21 05	
Bracknell	d	13 11			13 41					14 11			14 41		20 41					21 11	
Martins Heron	d	13 14			13 44					14 14			14 44		20 44					21 14	
Guildford	d					13 17										20 17					
Wanborough	d					13 23										20 23					
Ash 5	d					13 27										20 27					
Aldershot	a					13 34										20 34					
	d					13 40										20 40					
Ash Vale	d					13 45										20 45					
Frimley	d					13 51										20 51					
Camberley	a					13 55										20 55					
	d					13 55										20 55					
Bagshot	d					14 01										21 01					
Ascot 3	d	13 19			13 49	14a07				14 19			14 49		20 49	21a07				21 19	
Sunningdale	d	13 22			13 52					14 22			14 52		20 52					21 22	
Longcross	d																				
Woking	d								13 52										20 52		
West Byfleet	d								13 56										20 56		
Byfleet & New Haw	d								14 00										21 00		
Weybridge	d																				
Addlestone	d								14 04										21 04		
Chertsey	d								14 07										21 07		
Virginia Water	a	13 30			14 00				14 12	14 30			15 00	and at	21 00				21 12	21 30	
	d	13 30			14 00				14 12	14 30			15 00	the same	21 00				21 12	21 30	
Egham	d	13 34			14 04				14 16	14 34			15 04	minutes	21 04				21 16	21 34	
Windsor & Eton Riverside	d		13 32					13 59			14 32			past				20 59			
Datchet	d		13 36					14 03			14 36			each				21 03			
Sunnymeads	d							14 06						hour until				21 06			
Wraysbury	d							14 10										21 10			
Staines	d	13 39	13 45		14 09			14 16	14 21	14 39	14 45		15 09		21 09			21 16	21 21	21 39	
Ashford (Surrey)	d		13 48					14 19	14 24		14 48							21 19	21 24		
Feltham	d	13 46	13 53		14 16			14 24	14 29	14 46	14 53		15 16		21 16			21 24	21 29	21 46	
Whitton	d		13 57					14 28			14 57							21 28			
Kingston	d			13 49			14 11					14 49					21 11				21 49
Hampton Wick	d			13 51			14 13					14 51					21 13				21 51
Teddington	d			13 56			14 16					14 56					21 16				21 56
Fulwell	d																				
Strawberry Hill	d			13 59			14 19					14 59					21 19				21 59
Twickenham	a	13 51	14 00	14 02	14 21		14 22	14 31		14 51	15 00	15 02	15 21		21 21		21 22	21 31		21 51	22 02
	d	13 51	14 01	14 03	14 21		14 23	14 32		14 51	15 01	15 03	15 21		21 21		21 23	21 32		21 51	22 03
St Margarets	d			14 05			14 25	14 34				15 05					21 25	21 34			22 05
Richmond ⊖	d	13 56	14 05	14 09	14 26		14 29	14 37		14 56	15 05	15 09	15 26		21 26		21 29	21 37		21 56	22 09
North Sheen	d			14 11			14 31	14 39				15 11					21 31	21 39			22 11
Mortlake	d			14 13			14 33	14 42				15 13					21 33	21 42			22 13
Hounslow	d								14 35										21 35		
Isleworth	d								14 38										21 38		
Syon Lane	d								14 40										21 40		
Brentford	d								14 42										21 42		
Kew Bridge	d								14 45										21 45		
Chiswick	d								14 47										21 47		
Barnes Bridge	d								14 50										21 50		
Barnes	d			14 16			14 36	14 45	14 53			15 16					21 36	21 45	21 53		22 16
Putney	d	14 02	14 14	14 19	14 32		14 39	14 48	14 56	15 02	15 14	15 19	15 32		21 32		21 39	21 48	21 56	22 02	22 19
Wandsworth Town	d			14 22			14 42	14 51	14 59			15 22					21 42	21 51	21 59		22 22
Clapham Junction 10	d	14 07	14 18	14 25	14 37		14 45	14 54	15 02	15 07	15 18	15 25	15 37		21 37		21 45	21 54	22 02	22 07	22 25
Queenstown Rd.(Battersea)	d			14 28			14 48	14 57	15 05			15 28					21 48	21 57	22 05		22 28
Vauxhall ⊖	d	14 12	14 24	14 32	14 42		14 52	15 00	15 08	15 12	15 24	15 32	15 42		21 42		21 52	22 00	22 08	22 12	22 32
London Waterloo 15 ⊖	a	14 23	14 34	14 41	14 53		15 00	15 05	15 13	15 18	15 29	15 36	15 48		21 48		22 00	22 05	22 13	22 18	22 36

from 9 October

Reading, Guildford, Ascot, Weybridge, Windsor, Kingston, Richmond and Hounslow - London

		SW 1	SW 1	SW	SW	SW	SW 1	SW	SW 1	SW 1	SW	SW	SW	SW 1	SW 1
Reading 7	d	21 21					21 51		22 21					22 54	
Earley	d	21 26					21 56		22 26					22 59	
Winnersh Triangle	d	21 28					21 58		22 28					23 01	
Winnersh	d	21 30					22 00		22 30					23 03	
Wokingham	d	21 35					22 05		22 35					23 08	
Bracknell	d	21 41					22 11		22 41					23 14	
Martins Heron	d	21 44					22 14		22 44					23 17	
Guildford	d		21 17							22 17					23 17
Wanborough	d		21 23							22 23					23 23
Ash 5	d		21 27							22 27					23 27
Aldershot	a		21 34							22 34					23 34
	d		21 40							22 40					
Ash Vale	d		21 45							22 45					
Frimley	d		21 51							22 51					
Camberley	a		21 55							22 55					
	d		21 55							22 55					
Bagshot	d		22 01							23 01					
Ascot 8	d	21 49	22a07				22 19		22 49	23a07				23 22	
Sunningdale	d	21 52					22 22		22 52					23 25	
Longcross	d														
Woking	d					21 52							22 52		
West Byfleet	d					21 56							22 56		
Byfleet & New Haw	d					22 00							23 00		
Weybridge	d														
Addlestone	d					22 04							23 04		
Chertsey	d					22 07							23 07		
Virginia Water	a	22 00				22 12	22 30		23 00				23 12	23 30	
	d	22 00				22 12	22 30		23 00				23 12	23 30	
Egham	d	22 04				22 16	22 34		23 04				23 16	23 34	
Windsor & Eton Riverside	d				21 59							23 01			
Datchet	d				22 03							23 04			
Sunnymeads	d				22 06							23 07			
Wraysbury	d				22 10							23 10			
Staines	d	22 09			22 16	22 21	22 39		23 09			23 16	23 21	23 39	
Ashford (Surrey)	d				22 19	22 24						23 19	23 24		
Feltham	d	22 16			22 24	22 29	22 46		23 16			23 24	23 29	23 46	
Whitton	d				22 28							23 28			
Kingston	d			22 11				22 49			23 11				
Hampton Wick	d			22 13				22 51			23 13				
Teddington	d			22 16				22 56			23 16				
Fulwell	d														
Strawberry Hill	d			22 19				22 59			23 19				
Twickenham	a	22 21		22 22	22 31		22 51	23 02	23 21		23 22	23 31		23 51	
	d	22 21		22 23	22 32		22 51	23 03	23 21		23 23	23 32		23 51	
St Margarets	d			22 25	22 34			23 05			23 25	23 34			
Richmond ⊖	d	22 26		22 29	22 37		22 56	23 09	23 26		23 29	23 37		23 56	
North Sheen	d			22 31	22 39			23 11			23 31	23 39			
Mortlake	d			22 33	22 42			23 13			23 33	23 42			
Hounslow	d					22 35							23 35		
Isleworth	d					22 38							23 38		
Syon Lane	d					22 40							23 40		
Brentford	d					22 42							23 42		
Kew Bridge	d					22 45							23 45		
Chiswick	d					22 47							23 47		
Barnes Bridge	d					22 50							23 50		
Barnes	d			22 36	22 45	22 53		23 16			23 36	23 45	23 53		
Putney	d	22 32		22 39	22 48	22 56	23 02	23 19	23 32		23 39	23 48	23 56	00 02	
Wandsworth Town	d			22 42	22 51	22 59		23 22			23 42	23 51	23 59		
Clapham Junction 10	d	22 37		22 45	22 54	23 02	23 07	23 25	23 37		23 45	23 54	00 02	00 07	
Queenstown Rd.(Battersea)	d			22 48	22 57	23 05		23 28			23 48	23 57	00 05		
Vauxhall ⊖	d	22 42		22 52	23 00	23 08	23 12	23 32	23 42		23 52		00 08	00 12	
London Waterloo 15 ⊖	a	22 48		23 00	23 05	23 13	23 18	23 36	23 48		23 59	00 04	00 13	00 17	

Network Diagram for Table 152

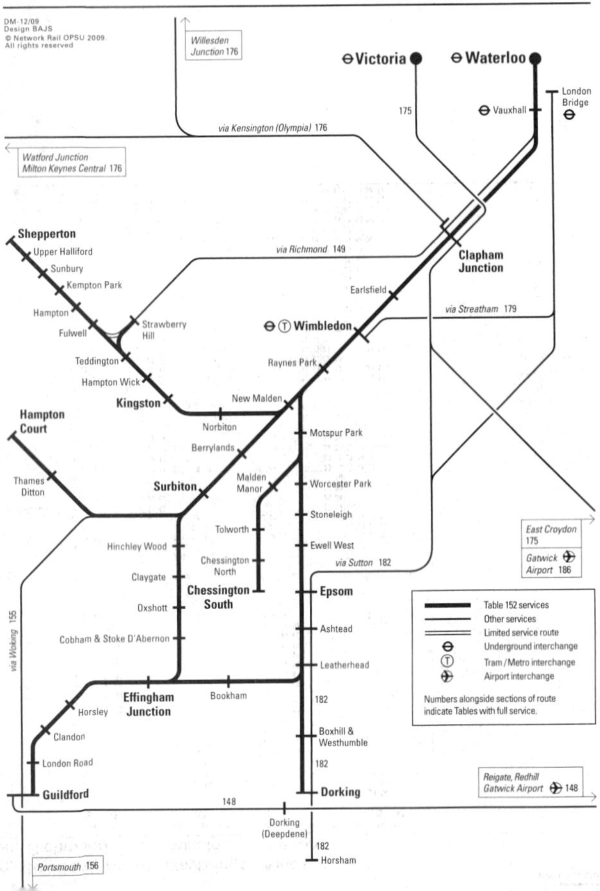

Table 152

Mondays to Fridays

until 30 September

London - Chessington South, Dorking, Guildford, Shepperton and Hampton Court

Miles	Miles	Miles	Miles	Miles			SW MX	SW MO	SW MO	SW MX	SW MX	SW MO	SW MX	SW MX	SW MX	SW MX	SW MX	SW MO	SW MX	SW MX	SW	SW MX	SW	SW 1
0	—	—	—	0	London Waterloo 15 ⊖	d	23p03	23p00	23p10	23p12	23p27	23p32	23p33	23p36	23p42	23p50	23p57	00 01	00 09	00 15	00 18	00 27	00 42	05 00
1¼	—	—	—	1¼	Vauxhall ⊖	d	23p07	23p04	23p14	23p16	23p31	23p36	23p37	23p40	23p46	23p54	00 01	00 04	00 13	00 19	00 22	00 31	00 46	05 04
4	—	—	—	4	Clapham Junction 10	d	23p12	23p09	23p19	23p21	23p36	23p41		23p45	23p51	23p59	00 06	00 09	00 20	00 25		00 37		05 11
5½	—	—	—	5½	Earlsfield	d	23p15	23p12	23p22	23p24	23p39	23p44		23p48	23p54	00 02	00 09	00 12	00 23	00 29		00s41		05 14
7¼	—	—	—	7¼	Wimbledon 6 ⊖	d	23p19	23p16	23p26	23p28	23p43	23p48		23p52	23p58	00 06	00 13	00 16	00 27	00 33		00 45	01 05	05 18
8¾	—	0	0	8¾	Raynes Park 6	d				23p31	23p46	23p52		23p55	00 01		00 16	00 19		00 36		00 48	01 08	
—	—	1	1	—	Motspur Park	d						23p55			00 04					00 38				
—	—	—	2½	—	Malden Manor	d																		
—	—	—	3½	—	Tolworth	d																		
—	—	—	4½	—	Chessington North	d																		
—	—	—	5¼	—	**Chessington South**	a																		
—	—	2	—	—	Worcester Park	d						23p57			00 06					00 41				
—	—	3¼	—	—	Stoneleigh	d						23p59			00 09					00 44				
—	—	4¼	—	—	Ewell West	d						00 03			00 12					00 46				
—	—	5½	—	—	**Epsom 3**	a						00 06			00 15					00 50				
—	—	—	—	—		d									00 19									
—	—	7½	—	—	Ashtead	d									00 23									
—	0	9¼	—	—	Leatherhead	d									00 26									
—	—	12½	—	—	Boxhill & Westhumble	d																		
—	—	13¼	—	—	**Dorking 4**	a																		
9¾	—	—	—	9¾	New Malden 6	d				23p34	23p49			23p58			00 19	00 22				00 50	01 11	
—	—	—	—	11¼	Norbiton	d				23p37	23p52						00 22						01 14	
—	—	—	—	12	Kingston	a				23p40	23p55		00 16				00 25				01 01		01 17	
—	—	—	—	—		d				23p40	23p55						00 25						01 17	
—	—	—	—	12½	Hampton Wick	d				23p42	23p57						00 27						01s22	
—	—	—	—	13¾	Teddington	d				23p45	23p59						00 30						01s25	
—	—	—	—	—	Strawberry Hill	a					00 03												01 28	
—	—	—	—	14¾	Fulwell	d				23p49							00 34							
—	—	—	—	16½	Hampton	d				23p53							00 38							
—	—	—	—	18¼	Kempton Park	d				23p56							00 41							
—	—	—	—	18¾	Sunbury	d				23p58							00 43							
—	—	—	—	19¼	Upper Halliford	d				23p59							00 45							
—	—	—	—	20¼	**Shepperton**	a				00 03							00 48							
11	—	—	—	—	Berrylands	d								23p59				00 25				00s53		
12	—	—	0	—	**Surbiton 6**	d	23p27	23p32	23p35					00 05		00 14		00 31	00 35			00a56		05 26
—	—	—	2	—	Thames Ditton	d								00 09										
—	—	—	3	—	**Hampton Court**	a								00 12										
14	—	—	—	—	Hinchley Wood	d	23p31	23p36								00 18		00 35						
15¼	—	—	—	—	Claygate	d	23p34	23p39								00 20		00 38						
17	—	—	—	—	Oxshott	d	23p37	23p42								00 24		00 41						
19	—	—	—	—	Cobham & Stoke D'abernon	d	23p41	23p46								00 27		00 45						
—	2½	—	—	—	Bookham	d									00 31									
21¼	4¼	—	—	—	Effingham Junction 6	d	23p45	23p50							00 36	00 32		00 49						
22¼	—	—	—	—	Horsley	d	23p48	23p53							00 39	00 34		00 52						
25½	—	—	—	—	Clandon	d	23p53	23p58							00 44	00 39		00 57						
28¾	—	—	—	—	London Road (Guildford)	d	23p58	00 03							00 49	00 44		01 02						
30	—	—	—	—	**Guildford**	a	00 02	00 07	00 13						00 53	00 48		01 06	01 07					06 00

London - Chessington South, Dorking, Guildford, Shepperton and Hampton Court

	SW	SW 1	SW	SW	SW	SW	SW	SW	SW	SW	SW	SW	SW	SW	SW	SW	SW	SW	SW	SW	SW
London Waterloo 15 ⊖ d	05 12	05 20	05 33		05 47	05 50	06 03		06 03	06 06	06 12	06 16	06 20	06 24	06 27	06 33	06 33	06 36	06 39	06 42	06 46
Vauxhall ⊖ d	05 16	05 24	05 37		05 51	05 54	06 07		06 07	06 10	06 16	06 20	06 24	06 28	06 31	06 37	06 37	06 40	06 43	06 46	06 50
Clapham Junction 10 d	05 21	05 29			05 56	05 59			06 12	06 15	06 21	06 25	06 29	06 33	06 36	06 42		06 45	06 48	06 51	06 55
Earlsfield d	05 24	05 32			05 59	06 02			06 15	06 18	06 24	06 28	06 32	06 36	06 39	06 45		06 48	06 51	06 54	06 58
Wimbledon 6 ⊖ ⇌ d	05 28	05 36		05 49	06 03	06 06		06 16	06 19	06 22	06 28	06 32	06 36	06 40	06 43	06 49		06 52	06 55	06 58	07 02
Raynes Park 6 d	05 31				06 06			06 19		06 25	06 31	06 35		06 43	06 46			06 55	06 58	07 01	07 05
Motspur Park d					06 09			06 21				06 38		06 46							07 08
Malden Manor d								06 25				06 41									07 11
Tolworth d								06 27				06 44									07 14
Chessington North d								06 30				06 47									07 17
Chessington South a								06 32				06 49									07 19
Worcester Park d					06 11									06 48					07 02		
Stoneleigh d					06 14									06 51					07 05		
Ewell West d					06 17									06 54					07 08		
Epsom 3 a					06 20									06 57					07 11		
d					06 21									06 58					07 12		
Ashtead d					06 25									07 02					07 16		
Leatherhead d					06 28									07 05					07 19		
Boxhill & Westhumble d																					
Dorking 4 a														07 11							
New Malden 6 d	05 34									06 28	06 34				06 49			06 58		07 04	
Norbiton d	05 37										06 37				06 52					07 07	
Kingston a	05 40		06 16				06 46				06 40				06 55		07 16			07 10	
d	05 40										06 40				06 59					07 10	
Hampton Wick d	05 42										06 42				07 01					07 12	
Teddington d	05 45										06 45				07 05					07 15	
Strawberry Hill a															07 08						
Fulwell d	05 49										06 49									07 19	
Hampton d	05 53										06 53									07 23	
Kempton Park d																					
Sunbury d	05 58										06 58									07 28	
Upper Halliford d	06 00										07 00									07 30	
Shepperton a	06 03										07 03									07 33	
Berrylands d										06 30								07 00			
Surbiton 6 d		05 44		05 57		06a13			06 27	06 35			06 44			06 57		07 05			
Thames Ditton d										06 39								07 09			
Hampton Court a										06 42								07 12			
Hinchley Wood d				06 01					06 31							07 01					
Claygate d				06 04					06 34							07 04					
Oxshott d				06 07					06 37							07 07					
Cobham & Stoke D'abernon d				06 11					06 41							07 11					
Bookham d					06 33														07 24		
Effingham Junction 6 d				06 15	06 37				06 45							07 15			07a28		
Horsley d				06 18					06 48							07 18					
Clandon d				06 23					06 53							07 23					
London Road (Guildford) d				06 28	06 46				06 58							07 28					
Guildford a		06 21		06 32	06 50				07 02				07 20			07 32					

London - Chessington South, Dorking, Guildford, Shepperton and Hampton Court

	SW	SW	SW	SW	SW	SW	SW	SW	SW	SW	SW	SW	SW	SW	SW	SW	SW	SW	SW	SW	SW	SW
London Waterloo 15 ⊖ d	06 50	06 54	06 57	07 03	07 03	07 06	07 09	07 12	07 16	07 20	07 24	07 27	07 33	07 33	07 36	07 39	07 42	07 46	07 50	07 54	07 57	08 03
Vauxhall ⊖ d	06 54	06 58	07 01	07 07	07 07	07 10	07 13	07 16	07 20	07 24	07 28	07 31	07 37	07 37	07 40	07 43	07 46	07 50	07 54	07 58	08 01	08 07
Clapham Junction 10 d	06 59	07 03	07 06	07 12		07 15	07 18	07 21	07 25	07 29	07 33	07 36	07 42		07 45	07 48	07 51	07 55	07 59	08 03	08 06	08 12
Earlsfield d	07 02	07 06	07 09	07 15		07 18	07 21	07 24	07 28	07 32	07 36	07 39	07 45		07 48	07 51	07 54	07 58	08 02	08 06	08 09	08 15
Wimbledon 6 ⊖ ⇌ d	07 06	07 10	07 13	07 19		07 22	07 25	07 28	07 32	07 36	07 40	07 43	07 49		07 52	07 55	07 58	08 02	08 06	08 10	08 13	08 19
Raynes Park 6 d		07 13	07 16			07 25	07 28	07 31	07 35		07 43	07 46			07 55	07 58	08 01	08 05		08 13	08 16	
Motspur Park d		07 16					07 31		07 38		07 46					08 01		08 08		08 16		
Malden Manor d									07 41									08 11				
Tolworth d									07 44									08 14				
Chessington North d									07 47									08 17				
Chessington South a									07 49									08 19				
Worcester Park d		07 18					07 33				07 48					08 03				08 18		
Stoneleigh d		07 21					07 36				07 51					08 06				08 21		
Ewell West d		07 24					07 39				07 54					08 09				08 24		
Epsom 3 a		07 27					07 42				07 58					08 13				08 27		
d		07 28									07 58					08 17				08 28		
Ashtead d		07 32									08 02					08 21				08 32		
Leatherhead d		07 35									08 05					08 24				08 35		
Boxhill & Westhumble d																						
Dorking 4 a		07 41									08 12									08 41		
New Malden 6 d			07 19			07 28		07 34				07 49			07 58		08 04				08 19	
Norbiton d			07 22					07 37				07 52					08 07				08 22	
Kingston a			07 25		07 46			07 40				07 55		08 16			08 10				08 25	
d			07 29					07 40				07 59					08 10				08 29	
Hampton Wick d			07 31					07 42				08 01					08 12				08 31	
Teddington d			07 35					07 45				08 05					08 15				08 35	
Strawberry Hill a			07 38									08 08									08 38	
Fulwell d								07 49									08 19					
Hampton d								07 53									08 23					
Kempton Park d								07 56									08 26					
Sunbury d								07 58									08 28					
Upper Halliford d								08 00									08 30					
Shepperton a								08 03									08 33					
Berrylands d						07 30									08 00							
Surbiton 6 d	07 14			07 27		07 35				07a43			07 57		08 05				08 14			08 27
Thames Ditton d						07 39									08 09							
Hampton Court a						07 42									08 12							
Hinchley Wood d				07 31									08 01									08 31
Claygate d				07 34									08 04									08 34
Oxshott d				07 37									08 07									08 37
Cobham & Stoke D'abernon d				07 41									08 11									08 41
Bookham d																08 29						
Effingham Junction 6 d				07 45									08 15			08 33						08 45
Horsley d				07 48									08 18			08 36						08 48
Clandon d				07 53									08 23			08 41						08 53
London Road (Guildford) d				07 58									08 28			08 46						08 58
Guildford a	07 47			08 02									08 32			08 50			08 50			09 04

	SW	SW	SW	SW	SW	SW	SW	SW	SW	SW	SW	SW	SW	SW	SW	SW	SW	SW	SW	SW	SW
London Waterloo 15 ⊖ d	08 03	08 06	08 09	08 12	08 16	08 20	08 24	08 27	08 33	08 33	08 36	08 39	08 42	08 46	08 50	08 54	08 57	09 03	09 03	09 06	09 09
Vauxhall ⊖ d	08 07	08 10	08 13	08 16	08 20	08 24	08 28	08 31	08 37	08 37	08 40	08 43	08 46	08 50	08 54	08 58	09 01	09 07	09 07	09 10	09 13
Clapham Junction 10 d		08 15	08 18	08 21	08 25	08 29	08 33	08 36	08 42		08 45	08 48	08 51	08 55	08 59	09 03	09 06	09 12		09 15	09 18
Earlsfield d		08 18	08 21	08 24	08 28	08 32	08 36	08 39	08 45		08 48	08 51	08 54	08 58	09 02	09 06	09 09	09 15		09 18	09 21
Wimbledon 6 ⊖ ⇌ d		08 22	08 25	08 28	08 32	08 36	08 40	08 43	08 49		08 52	08 55	08 58	09 02	09 06	09 10	09 13	09 19		09 22	09 25
Raynes Park 6 d		08 25	08 28	08 31	08 35		08 43	08 46			08 55	08 58	09 01	09 05		09 13	09 16			09 25	09 28
Motspur Park d			08 31		08 38		08 46					09 01		09 08		09 16					09 31
Malden Manor d					08 41									09 11							
Tolworth d					08 44									09 14							
Chessington North d					08 47									09 17							
Chessington South a					08 49									09 19							
Worcester Park d			08 33				08 48					09 03				09 18					09 33
Stoneleigh d			08 36				08 51					09 06				09 21					09 36
Ewell West d			08 39				08 54					09 09				09 24					09 39
Epsom 3 a			08 42				08 57					09 16				09 27					09 42
d			08 47				08 58					09 17				09 28					09 47
Ashtead d			08 51				09 02					09 21				09 32					09 51
Leatherhead d			08 54				09 05					09 24				09 35					09 54
Boxhill & Westhumble d																					
Dorking 4 a							09 11									09 41					
New Malden 6 d		08 28		08 34				08 49			08 58		09 04				09 19			09 28	
Norbiton d				08 37				08 52					09 07				09 22				
Kingston a	08 46			08 39				08 55		09 16			09 10				09 25		09 46		
d				08 40				08 59					09 10				09 29				
Hampton Wick d				08 42				09 01					09 12				09 31				
Teddington d				08 45				09 05					09 15				09 35				
Strawberry Hill a								09 08									09 38				
Fulwell d				08 49									09 19								
Hampton d				08 53									09 23								
Kempton Park d				08 56									09 26								
Sunbury d				08 58									09 28								
Upper Halliford d				09 00									09 30								
Shepperton a				09 04									09 33								
Berrylands d		08 30									09 00									09 30	
Surbiton 6 d		08 35				08a43			08 57		09 05				09a13			09 27		09 35	
Thames Ditton d		08 39									09 09									09 39	
Hampton Court a		08 42									09 12									09 42	
Hinchley Wood d									09 01									09 31			
Claygate d									09 04									09 34			
Oxshott d									09 07									09 37			
Cobham & Stoke D'abernon d									09 11									09 41			
Bookham d			08 59									09 29									09 59
Effingham Junction 6 d			09 03						09 15			09 33						09 45			10 03
Horsley d			09 06						09 18			09 36						09 48			10 06
Clandon d			09 11						09 23			09 41						09 53			10 11
London Road (Guildford) d			09 16						09 28			09 46						09 58			10 16
Guildford a			09 20						09 32			09 50						10 02			10 20

London - Chessington South, Dorking, Guildford, Shepperton and Hampton Court

Station		SW	SW	SW	SW	SW	SW	SW	SW	SW	SW	SW	SW	SW	SW	SW	SW	SW	SW	SW	SW	SW
London Waterloo 15 ⊖	d	09 12	09 16	09 20	09 24	09 27	09 33	09 33	09 36	09 39	09 42	09 46	09 50	09 54	09 57	10 03	10 03	10 06	10 09	10 12	10 16	10 20
Vauxhall ⊖	d	09 16	09 20	09 24	09 28	09 31	09 37	09 37	09 40	09 43	09 46	09 50	09 54	09 58	10 01	10 07	10 07	10 10	10 13	10 16	10 20	10 24
Clapham Junction 10	d	09 21	09 25	09 29	09 33	09 36	09 42		09 45	09 48	09 51	09 55	09 59	10 03	10 06	10 12		10 15	10 18	10 21	10 25	10 29
Earlsfield	d	09 24	09 28	09 32	09 36	09 39	09 45		09 48	09 51	09 54	09 58	10 02	10 06	10 09	10 15		10 18	10 21	10 24	10 28	10 32
Wimbledon 6 ⊖	d	09 28	09 32	09 36	09 40	09 43	09 49		09 52	09 55	09 58	10 02	10 06	10 10	10 13	10 19		10 22	10 25	10 28	10 32	10 36
Raynes Park 6	d	09 31	09 35		09 43	09 46			09 55	09 58	10 01	10 05		10 13	10 16			10 25	10 28	10 31	10 35	
Motspur Park	d		09 38		09 46					10 01		10 08		10 16					10 31		10 38	
Malden Manor	d		09 41									10 11									10 41	
Tolworth	d		09 44									10 14									10 44	
Chessington North	d		09 47									10 17									10 47	
Chessington South	a		09 49									10 19									10 49	
Worcester Park	d				09 48					10 03				10 18					10 33			
Stoneleigh	d				09 51					10 06				10 21					10 36			
Ewell West	d				09 54					10 09				10 24					10 39			
Epsom 3	a				09 57					10 16				10 27					10 46			
	d				09 58					10 17				10 28					10 47			
Ashtead	d				10 02					10 21				10 32					10 51			
Leatherhead	d				10 05					10 24				10 35					10 54			
Boxhill & Westhumble	d																					
Dorking 4	a				10 11									10 41								
New Malden 6	d	09 34				09 49			09 58		10 04				10 19			10 28		10 34		
Norbiton	d	09 37				09 52					10 07				10 22					10 37		
Kingston	a	09 40				09 55		10 16			10 10				10 25		10 46			10 40		
	d	09 40				09 59					10 10				10 29					10 40		
Hampton Wick	d	09 42				10 01					10 12				10 31					10 42		
Teddington	d	09 45				10 05					10 15				10 35					10 45		
Strawberry Hill	a					10 08									10 38							
Fulwell	d	09 49									10 19									10 49		
Hampton	d	09 53									10 23									10 53		
Kempton Park	d	09 56									10 26									10 56		
Sunbury	d	09 58									10 28									10 58		
Upper Halliford	d	10 00									10 30									11 00		
Shepperton	a	10 03									10 33									11 03		
Berrylands	d								10 00									10 30				
Surbiton 6	d			09a43			09 57		10 05				10a13			10 27		10 35				10a43
Thames Ditton	d								10 09									10 39				
Hampton Court	a								10 12									10 42				
Hinchley Wood	d						10 01									10 31						
Claygate	d						10 04									10 34						
Oxshott	d						10 07									10 37						
Cobham & Stoke D'abernon	d						10 11									10 41						
Bookham	d									10 29									10 59			
Effingham Junction 6	d						10 15			10 33						10 45			11 03			
Horsley	d						10 18			10 36						10 48			11 06			
Clandon	d						10 23			10 41						10 53			11 11			
London Road (Guildford)	d						10 28			10 46						10 58			11 16			
Guildford	a						10 32			10 50						11 02			11 20			

London - Chessington South, Dorking, Guildford, Shepperton and Hampton Court

Station		SW	SW	SW	SW	SW	SW	SW	SW	SW	SW	SW	SW	SW	SW	SW	SW	SW	SW	SW	SW	SW	SW
London Waterloo 15 ⊖	d	10 24	10 27	10 33	10 33	10 36	10 39	10 42	10 46	10 50	10 54	10 57	11 03	11 03	11 06	11 09	11 12	11 16	11 20	11 24	11 27	11 33	11 33
Vauxhall ⊖	d	10 28	10 31	10 37	10 37	10 40	10 43	10 46	10 50	10 54	10 58	11 01	11 07	11 07	11 10	11 13	11 16	11 20	11 24	11 28	11 31	11 37	11 37
Clapham Junction 10	d	10 33	10 36	10 42		10 45	10 48	10 51	10 55	10 59	11 03	11 06	11 12		11 15	11 18	11 21	11 25	11 29	11 33	11 36	11 42	
Earlsfield	d	10 36	10 39	10 45		10 48	10 51	10 54	10 58	11 02	11 06	11 09	11 15		11 18	11 21	11 24	11 28	11 32	11 36	11 39	11 45	
Wimbledon 6 ⊖	d	10 40	10 43	10 49		10 52	10 55	10 58	11 02	11 06	11 10	11 13	11 19		11 22	11 25	11 28	11 32	11 36	11 40	11 43	11 49	
Raynes Park 6	d	10 43	10 46			10 55	10 58	11 01	11 05		11 13	11 16			11 25	11 28	11 31	11 35		11 43	11 46		
Motspur Park	d	10 46					11 01		11 08		11 16					11 31		11 38		11 46			
Malden Manor	d								11 11									11 41					
Tolworth	d								11 14									11 44					
Chessington North	d								11 17									11 47					
Chessington South	a								11 19									11 49					
Worcester Park	d	10 48					11 03				11 18					11 33				11 48			
Stoneleigh	d	10 51					11 06				11 21					11 36				11 51			
Ewell West	d	10 54					11 09				11 24					11 39				11 54			
Epsom 3	a	10 57					11 16				11 27					11 46				11 57			
	d	10 58					11 17				11 28					11 47				11 58			
Ashtead	d	11 02					11 21				11 32					11 51				12 02			
Leatherhead	d	11 05					11 24				11 35					11 54				12 05			
Boxhill & Westhumble	d																						
Dorking 4	a	11 11									11 41									12 11			
New Malden 6	d		10 49			10 58		11 04				11 19			11 28		11 34				11 49		
Norbiton	d		10 52					11 07				11 22					11 37				11 52		
Kingston	a		10 55		11 16			11 10				11 25		11 46			11 40				11 55		12 16
	d		10 59					11 10				11 29					11 40				11 59		
Hampton Wick	d		11 01					11 12				11 31					11 42				12 01		
Teddington	d		11 05					11 15				11 35					11 45				12 05		
Strawberry Hill	a		11 08									11 38									12 08		
Fulwell	d							11 19									11 49						
Hampton	d							11 23									11 53						
Kempton Park	d							11 26									11 56						
Sunbury	d							11 28									11 58						
Upper Halliford	d							11 30									12 00						
Shepperton	a							11 33									12 03						
Berrylands	d					11 00									11 30								
Surbiton 6	d			10 57		11 05				11a13			11 27		11 35				11a43			11 57	
Thames Ditton	d					11 09									11 39								
Hampton Court	a					11 12									11 42								
Hinchley Wood	d			11 01									11 31									12 01	
Claygate	d			11 04									11 34									12 04	
Oxshott	d			11 07									11 37									12 07	
Cobham & Stoke D'abernon	d			11 11									11 41									12 11	
Bookham	d						11 29									11 59							
Effingham Junction 6	d			11 15			11 33						11 45			12 03						12 15	
Horsley	d			11 18			11 36						11 48			12 06						12 18	
Clandon	d			11 23			11 41						11 53			12 11						12 23	
London Road (Guildford)	d			11 28			11 46						11 58			12 16						12 28	
Guildford	a			11 32			11 50						12 02			12 20						12 32	

Station		SW	SW	SW	SW	SW	SW	SW	SW	SW	SW	SW	SW	SW	SW	SW	SW	SW	SW	SW	SW	SW
London Waterloo 15 ⊖	d	11 36	11 39	11 42	11 46	11 50	11 54	11 57	12 03	12 03	12 06	12 09	12 12	12 16	12 20	12 24	12 27	12 33	12 33	12 36	12 39	12 42
Vauxhall ⊖	d	11 40	11 43	11 46	11 50	11 54	11 58	12 01	12 07	12 07	12 10	12 13	12 16	12 20	12 24	12 28	12 31	12 37	12 37	12 40	12 43	12 46
Clapham Junction 10	d	11 45	11 48	11 51	11 55	11 59	12 03	12 06	12 12		12 15	12 18	12 21	12 25	12 29	12 33	12 36	12 42		12 45	12 48	12 51
Earlsfield	d	11 48	11 51	11 54	11 58	12 02	12 06	12 09	12 15		12 18	12 21	12 24	12 28	12 32	12 36	12 39	12 45		12 48	12 51	12 54
Wimbledon 6 ⊖	d	11 52	11 55	11 58	12 02	12 06	12 10	12 13	12 19		12 22	12 25	12 28	12 32	12 36	12 40	12 43	12 49		12 52	12 55	12 58
Raynes Park 6	d	11 55	11 58	12 01	12 05		12 13	12 16			12 25	12 28	12 31	12 35		12 43	12 46			12 55	12 58	13 01
Motspur Park	d		12 01		12 08		12 16					12 31		12 38		12 46					13 01	
Malden Manor	d				12 11									12 41								
Tolworth	d				12 14									12 44								
Chessington North	d				12 17									12 47								
Chessington South	a				12 19									12 49								
Worcester Park	d		12 03				12 18					12 33				12 48					13 03	
Stoneleigh	d		12 06				12 21					12 36				12 51					13 06	
Ewell West	d		12 09				12 24					12 39				12 54					13 09	
Epsom 3	a		12 16				12 27					12 46				12 57					13 16	
	d		12 17				12 28					12 47				12 58					13 17	
Ashtead	d		12 21				12 32					12 51				13 02					13 21	
Leatherhead	d		12 24				12 35					12 54				13 05					13 24	
Boxhill & Westhumble	d																					
Dorking 4	a						12 41									13 11						
New Malden 6	d	11 58		12 04				12 19			12 28		12 34				12 49			12 58		13 04
Norbiton	d			12 07				12 22					12 37				12 52					13 07
Kingston	a			12 10				12 25		12 46			12 40				12 55		13 16			13 10
	d			12 10				12 29					12 40				12 59					13 10
Hampton Wick	d			12 12				12 31					12 42				13 01					13 12
Teddington	d			12 15				12 35					12 45				13 05					13 15
Strawberry Hill	a							12 38									13 08					
Fulwell	d			12 19									12 49									13 19
Hampton	d			12 23									12 53									13 23
Kempton Park	d			12 26									12 56									13 26
Sunbury	d			12 28									12 58									13 28
Upper Halliford	d			12 30									13 00									13 30
Shepperton	a			12 33									13 03									13 33
Berrylands	d	12 00									12 30									13 00		
Surbiton 6	d	12 05				12a13			12 27		12 35				12a43			12 57		13 05		
Thames Ditton	d	12 09									12 39									13 09		
Hampton Court	a	12 12									12 42									13 12		
Hinchley Wood	d								12 31									13 01				
Claygate	d								12 34									13 04				
Oxshott	d								12 37									13 07				
Cobham & Stoke D'abernon	d								12 41									13 11				
Bookham	d		12 29									12 59									13 29	
Effingham Junction 6	d		12 33						12 45			13 03						13 15			13 33	
Horsley	d		12 36						12 48			13 06						13 18			13 36	
Clandon	d		12 41						12 53			13 11						13 23			13 41	
London Road (Guildford)	d		12 46						12 58			13 16						13 28			13 46	
Guildford	a		12 50						13 02			13 20						13 32			13 50	

London - Chessington South, Dorking, Guildford, Shepperton and Hampton Court

		SW	SW	SW	SW	SW	SW		SW	SW	SW	SW	SW	SW	SW	SW	SW		SW	SW	SW	SW	SW	SW	SW
London Waterloo 15 ⊖	d	12 46	12 50	12 54	12 57	13 03	13 03		13 06	13 09	13 12	13 16	13 20	13 24	13 27	13 33	13 33		13 36	13 39	13 42	13 46	13 50	13 54	13 57
Vauxhall ⊖	d	12 50	12 54	12 58	13 01	13 07	13 07		13 10	13 13	13 16	13 20	13 24	13 28	13 31	13 37	13 37		13 40	13 43	13 46	13 50	13 54	13 58	14 01
Clapham Junction 10	d	12 55	12 59	13 03	13 06	13 12			13 15	13 18	13 21	13 25	13 29	13 33	13 36	13 42			13 45	13 48	13 51	13 55	13 59	14 03	14 06
Earlsfield	d	12 58	13 02	13 06	13 09	13 15			13 18	13 21	13 24	13 28	13 32	13 36	13 39	13 45			13 48	13 51	13 54	13 58	14 02	14 06	14 09
Wimbledon 6 ⊖	d	13 02	13 06	13 10	13 13	13 19			13 22	13 25	13 28	13 32	13 36	13 40	13 43	13 49			13 52	13 55	13 58	14 02	14 06	14 10	14 13
Raynes Park 6	d	13 05		13 13	13 16				13 25	13 28	13 31	13 35		13 43	13 46				13 55	13 58	14 01	14 05		14 13	14 16
Motspur Park	d	13 08		13 16						13 31		13 38		13 46						14 01		14 08		14 16	
Malden Manor	d	13 11										13 41										14 11			
Tolworth	d	13 14										13 44										14 14			
Chessington North	d	13 17										13 47										14 17			
Chessington South	a	13 19										13 49										14 19			
Worcester Park	d			13 18						13 33				13 48						14 03				14 18	
Stoneleigh	d			13 21						13 36				13 51						14 06				14 21	
Ewell West	d			13 24						13 39				13 54						14 09				14 24	
Epsom 3	a			13 27						13 46				13 57						14 16				14 27	
	d			13 28						13 47				13 58						14 17				14 28	
Ashtead	d			13 32						13 51				14 02						14 21				14 32	
Leatherhead	d			13 35						13 54				14 05						14 24				14 35	
Boxhill & Westhumble	d																								
Dorking 4	a			13 41										14 11										14 41	
New Malden 6	d				13 19				13 28		13 34				13 49				13 58		14 04				14 19
Norbiton	d				13 22						13 37				13 52						14 07				14 22
Kingston	a				13 25		13 46				13 40				13 55		14 16				14 10				14 25
	d				13 29						13 40				13 59						14 10				14 29
Hampton Wick	d				13 31						13 42				14 01						14 12				14 31
Teddington	d				13 35						13 45				14 05						14 15				14 35
Strawberry Hill	a				13 38										14 08										14 38
Fulwell	d										13 49										14 19				
Hampton	d										13 53										14 23				
Kempton Park	d										13 56										14 26				
Sunbury	d										13 58										14 28				
Upper Halliford	d										14 00										14 30				
Shepperton	a										14 03										14 33				
Berrylands	d								13 30										14 00						
Surbiton 6	d		13a13			13 27			13 35				13a43			13 57			14 05				14a13		
Thames Ditton	d								13 39										14 09						
Hampton Court	a								13 42										14 12						
Hinchley Wood	d					13 31										14 01									
Claygate	d					13 34										14 04									
Oxshott	d					13 37										14 07									
Cobham & Stoke D'abernon	d					13 41										14 11									
Bookham	d									13 59										14 29					
Effingham Junction 6	d					13 45				14 03						14 15				14 33					
Horsley	d					13 48				14 06						14 18				14 36					
Clandon	d					13 53				14 11						14 23				14 41					
London Road (Guildford)	d					13 58				14 16						14 28				14 46					
Guildford	a					14 02				14 20						14 32				14 50					

		SW	SW		SW	SW	SW	SW	SW	SW	SW	SW	SW		SW	SW	SW	SW	SW	SW	SW	SW	SW		SW
London Waterloo 15 ⊖	d	14 03	14 03		14 06	14 09	14 12	14 16	14 20	14 24	14 27	14 33	14 33		14 36	14 39	14 42	14 46	14 50	14 54	14 57	15 03	15 03		15 06
Vauxhall ⊖	d	14 07	14 07		14 10	14 13	14 16	14 20	14 24	14 28	14 31	14 37	14 37		14 40	14 43	14 46	14 50	14 54	14 58	15 01	15 07	15 07		15 10
Clapham Junction 10	d	14 12			14 15	14 18	14 21	14 25	14 29	14 33	14 36	14 42			14 45	14 48	14 51	14 55	14 59	15 03	15 06	15 12			15 15
Earlsfield	d	14 15			14 18	14 21	14 24	14 28	14 32	14 36	14 39	14 45			14 48	14 51	14 54	14 58	15 02	15 06	15 09	15 15			15 18
Wimbledon 6 ⊖	d	14 19			14 22	14 25	14 28	14 32	14 36	14 40	14 43	14 49			14 52	14 55	14 58	15 02	15 06	15 10	15 13	15 19			15 22
Raynes Park 6	d				14 25	14 28	14 31	14 35		14 43	14 46				14 55	14 58	15 01	15 05		15 13	15 16				15 25
Motspur Park	d					14 31		14 38		14 46						15 01		15 08		15 16					
Malden Manor	d							14 41										15 11							
Tolworth	d							14 44										15 14							
Chessington North	d							14 47										15 17							
Chessington South	a							14 49										15 19							
Worcester Park	d					14 33				14 48						15 03				15 18					
Stoneleigh	d					14 36				14 51						15 06				15 21					
Ewell West	d					14 39				14 54						15 09				15 24					
Epsom 3	a					14 46				14 57						15 16				15 27					
	d					14 47				14 58						15 17				15 28					
Ashtead	d					14 51				15 02						15 21				15 32					
Leatherhead	d					14 54				15 05						15 24				15 35					
Boxhill & Westhumble	d																								
Dorking 4	a									15 11										15 41					
New Malden 6	d				14 28		14 34				14 49				14 58		15 04				15 19				15 28
Norbiton	d						14 37				14 52						15 07				15 22				
Kingston	a		14 46				14 40				14 55		15 16				15 10				15 25		15 46		
	d						14 40				14 59						15 10				15 29				
Hampton Wick	d						14 42				15 01						15 12				15 31				
Teddington	d						14 45				15 05						15 15				15 35				
Strawberry Hill	a										15 08										15 38				
Fulwell	d						14 49										15 19								
Hampton	d						14 53										15 23								
Kempton Park	d						14 56										15 26								
Sunbury	d						14 58										15 28								
Upper Halliford	d						15 00										15 30								
Shepperton	a						15 03										15 33								
Berrylands	d				14 30										15 00										15 30
Surbiton 6	d	14 27			14 35				14a43			14 57			15 05				15a13			15 27			15 35
Thames Ditton	d				14 39										15 09										15 39
Hampton Court	a				14 42										15 12										15 42
Hinchley Wood	d	14 31										15 01										15 31			
Claygate	d	14 34										15 04										15 34			
Oxshott	d	14 37										15 07										15 37			
Cobham & Stoke D'abernon	d	14 41										15 11										15 41			
Bookham	d					14 59										15 29									
Effingham Junction 6	d	14 45				15 03						15 15				15 33						15 45			
Horsley	d	14 48				15 06						15 18				15 36						15 48			
Clandon	d	14 53				15 11						15 23				15 41						15 53			
London Road (Guildford)	d	14 58				15 16						15 28				15 46						15 58			
Guildford	a	15 02				15 20						15 32				15 50						16 02			

London - Chessington South, Dorking, Guildford, Shepperton and Hampton Court

		SW	SW	SW	SW	SW	SW	SW	SW		SW	SW	SW	SW	SW	SW	SW	SW	SW		SW	SW	SW	SW	SW
London Waterloo 15 ⊖	d	15 09	15 12	15 16	15 20	15 24	15 27	15 33	15 33		15 36	15 39	15 42	15 46	15 50	15 54	15 57	16 01	16 03		16 06	16 09	16 12	16 16	16 20
Vauxhall ⊖	d	15 13	15 16	15 20	15 24	15 28	15 31	15 37	15 37		15 40	15 43	15 46	15 50	15 54	15 58	16 01	16 05	16 07		16 10	16 13	16 16	16 20	16 24
Clapham Junction 10	d	15 18	15 21	15 25	15 29	15 33	15 36	15 42			15 45	15 48	15 51	15 55	15 59	16 03	16 06		16 12		16 15	16 18	16 21	16 25	16 29
Earlsfield	d	15 21	15 24	15 28	15 32	15 36	15 39	15 45			15 48	15 51	15 54	15 58	16 02	16 06	16 09		16 15		16 18	16 21	16 24	16 28	16 32
Wimbledon 6 ⊖	d	15 25	15 28	15 32	15 36	15 40	15 43	15 49			15 52	15 55	15 58	16 02	16 06	16 10	16 13		16 19		16 22	16 25	16 28	16 32	16 36
Raynes Park 6	d	15 28	15 31	15 35		15 43	15 46				15 55	15 58	16 01	16 05		16 13	16 16				16 25	16 28	16 31	16 35	
Motspur Park	d	15 31		15 38		15 46						16 01		16 08		16 16						16 31		16 38	
Malden Manor	d			15 41										16 11										16 41	
Tolworth	d			15 44										16 14										16 44	
Chessington North	d			15 47										16 17										16 47	
Chessington South	a			15 49										16 19										16 51	
Worcester Park	d	15 33				15 48						16 03				16 18						16 33			
Stoneleigh	d	15 36				15 51						16 06				16 21						16 36			
Ewell West	d	15 39				15 54						16 09				16 24						16 39			
Epsom 3	a	15 46				15 57						16 15				16 27						16 46			
	d	15 47				15 58						16 17				16 28						16 47			
Ashtead	d	15 51				16 02						16 21				16 32						16 51			
Leatherhead	d	15 54				16 05						16 24				16 35						16 54			
Boxhill & Westhumble	d																								
Dorking 4	a					16 11										16 41									
New Malden 6	d		15 34				15 49				15 58		16 04				16 19				16 28		16 34		
Norbiton	d		15 37				15 52						16 07				16 22						16 37		
Kingston	a		15 40				15 55		16 16				16 10				16 25	16 48					16 40		
	d		15 40				15 59						16 10				16 29						16 40		
Hampton Wick	d		15 42				16 01						16 12				16 31						16 42		
Teddington	d		15 45				16 05						16 15				16 35						16 45		
Strawberry Hill	a						16 08										16 38								
Fulwell	d		15 49										16 19										16 49		
Hampton	d		15 53										16 23										16 53		
Kempton Park	d		15 56										16 26										16 56		
Sunbury	d		15 58										16 28										16 58		
Upper Halliford	d		16 00										16 30										17 00		
Shepperton	a		16 03										16 33										17 05		
Berrylands	d										16 00										16 30				
Surbiton 6	d				15a43			15 57			16 05				16a13				16 27		16 35				16a43
Thames Ditton	d										16 09										16 39				
Hampton Court	a										16 12										16 44				
Hinchley Wood	d							16 01											16 31						
Claygate	d							16 04											16 34						
Oxshott	d							16 07											16 37						
Cobham & Stoke D'abernon	d							16 11											16 41						
Bookham	d	15 59										16 29										16 59			
Effingham Junction 6	d	16 03						16 15				16 33							16 45			17 03			
Horsley	d	16 06						16 18				16 36							16 48			17 06			
Clandon	d	16 11						16 23				16 41							16 53			17 11			
London Road (Guildford)	d	16 16						16 28				16 46							16 58			17 16			
Guildford	a	16 20						16 32				16 50							17 04			17 22			

Table 152

Mondays to Fridays
until 30 September

London - Chessington South, Dorking, Guildford, Shepperton and Hampton Court

		SW	SW	SW	SW	SW	SW	SW	SW	SW	SW	SW	SW	SW [1]	SW	SW	SW	SW	SW	SW	SW	SW	SW
London Waterloo [15] ⊖	d	16 24	16 27	16 31	16 33	16 36	16 39	16 42	16 46	16 50	16 54	16 57	17 01	17 02	17 02	17 06	17 09	17 12	17 13	17 16	17 20	17 24	17 27
Vauxhall ⊖	d	16 28	16 31	16 35	16 37	16 40	16 43	16 46	16 50	16 54	16 58	17 01	17 05		17 07	17 10	17 13	17 16	17 17	17 20	17 24	17 28	17 31
Clapham Junction [10]	d	16 33	16 36		16 42	16 45	16 48	16 51	16 55	16 59	17 03	17 06			17 12	17 15	17 18	17 21		17 25	17 29	17 33	17 36
Earlsfield	d	16 36	16 39		16 45	16 48	16 51	16 54	16 58	17 02	17 06	17 09			17 15	17 18	17 21	17 24		17 28	17 32	17 36	17 39
Wimbledon [6] ⊖ ⛴	d	16 40	16 43		16 49	16 52	16 55	16 58	17 02	17 06	17 10	17 13			17 19	17 22	17 25	17 28		17 32	17 36	17 40	17 43
Raynes Park [6]	d	16 43	16 46			16 55	16 58	17 01	17 05		17 13	17 16				17 25	17 28	17 31		17 35		17 43	17 46
Motspur Park	d	16 46					17 01		17 08		17 16						17 31			17 38			
Malden Manor	d								17 11											17 41			
Tolworth	d								17 14											17 44			
Chessington North	d								17 17											17 47			
Chessington South	a								17 21											17 51			
Worcester Park	d	16 48					17 03				17 18						17 33					17 47	
Stoneleigh	d	16 51					17 06				17 21						17 36						
Ewell West	d	16 54					17 09				17 24						17 39						
Epsom [3]	a	16 57					17 12				17 27						17 42					17 54	
	d	16 58					17 17				17 28						17 47					17 54	
Ashtead	d	17 02					17 21				17 32						17 51					17 58	
Leatherhead	d	17 05					17 24				17 35						17 54					18 01	
Boxhill & Westhumble	d	17 10									17 40											18 06	
Dorking [4]	a	17 14									17 44											18 11	
New Malden [6]	d		16 49			16 58		17 04				17 19				17 28		17 34					17 49
Norbiton	d		16 52					17 07				17 22						17 37					17 52
Kingston	a		16 55	17 18				17 10				17 25	17 48					17 40	17 56				17 55
	d		16 59					17 10				17 29						17 40					17 59
Hampton Wick	d		17 01					17 12				17 31						17 42					18 01
Teddington	d		17 05					17 15				17 35						17 45					18 05
Strawberry Hill	a		17 08									17 38											18 08
Fulwell	d							17 19										17 49					
Hampton	d							17 23										17 53					
Kempton Park	d							17 26										17 56					
Sunbury	d							17 28										17 58					
Upper Halliford	d							17 30										18 00					
Shepperton	a							17 35										18 06					
Berrylands	d					17 00										17 30							
Surbiton [6]	d				16 57	17 05				17a13				17 18	17 27	17 35					17a43		
Thames Ditton	d					17 09										17 39							
Hampton Court	a					17 14										17 44							
Hinchley Wood	d				17 01										17 31								
Claygate	d				17 04										17 34								
Oxshott	d				17 07										17 37								
Cobham & Stoke D'abernon	d				17 11										17 41								
Bookham	d						17 29										17 59						
Effingham Junction [6]	d				17 15		17 33								17 45		18a05						
Horsley	d				17 18		17 36								17 48								
Clandon	d				17 23		17 41								17 53								
London Road (Guildford)	d				17 28		17 46								17 58								
Guildford	a				17 34		17 52							17 56	18 04								

Table 152

Mondays to Fridays
until 30 September

London - Chessington South, Dorking, Guildford, Shepperton and Hampton Court

		SW	SW	SW [1]	SW	SW	SW	SW	SW	SW	SW	SW	SW	SW	SW	SW [1]	SW	SW	SW	SW	SW	SW
London Waterloo [15] ⊖	d	17 30	17 31	17 32	17 32	17 36	17 39	17 43	17 42	17 46	17 50	17 54	17 57	18 00	18 01	18 02	18 02	18 06	18 09	18 13	18 12	18 16
Vauxhall ⊖	d	17 34	17 35		17 37	17 40	17 43	17 47	17 46	17 50	17 54	17 58	18 01	18 04	18 05		18 07	18 10	18 13	18 17	18 16	18 20
Clapham Junction [10]	d	17 39			17 42	17 45	17 48		17 51	17 55	17 59	18 03	18 06	18 09			18 12	18 15	18 18		18 21	18 25
Earlsfield	d	17 42			17 45	17 48	17 51		17 54	17 58	18 02	18 06	18 09	18 12			18 15	18 18	18 21		18 24	18 28
Wimbledon [6] ⊖ ⛴	d	17 46			17 49	17 52	17 55		17 58	18 02	18 06	18 10	18 13	18 16			18 19	18 22	18 25		18 28	18 32
Raynes Park [6]	d	17 49				17 55	17 58		18 01	18 05		18 13	18 16	18 19				18 25	18 28		18 31	18 35
Motspur Park	d	17 52					18 01			18 08				18 22					18 31			18 38
Malden Manor	d									18 11												18 41
Tolworth	d									18 14												18 44
Chessington North	d									18 17												18 47
Chessington South	a									18 21												18 51
Worcester Park	d	17 54					18 03					18 17		18 24					18 33			
Stoneleigh	d	17 57					18 06							18 27					18 36			
Ewell West	d	18 00					18 09							18 30					18 39			
Epsom [3]	a	18 07					18 15					18 24		18 35					18 46			
	d						18 17					18 24							18 47			
Ashtead	d						18 21					18 28							18 51			
Leatherhead	d						18 24					18 31							18 54			
Boxhill & Westhumble	d											18 36										
Dorking [4]	a											18 41										
New Malden [6]	d					17 58			18 04				18 19					18 28			18 34	
Norbiton	d								18 07				18 22								18 37	
Kingston	a		18 18						18 10				18 25		18 48						18 40	
	d								18 10				18 29								18 40	
Hampton Wick	d								18 12				18 31								18 42	
Teddington	d								18 15				18 35								18 45	
Strawberry Hill	a							18 11					18 38							18 41		
Fulwell	d							18 13	18 19											18 43	18 49	
Hampton	d							18 17	18 23											18 47	18 53	
Kempton Park	d								18 26												18 56	
Sunbury	d							18 21	18 28											18 51	18 58	
Upper Halliford	d							18 23	18 30											18 53	19 00	
Shepperton	a							18 28	18 40											18 58	19 10	
Berrylands	d					18 00												18 30				
Surbiton [6]	d			17 48	17 57	18 05					18a13					18a17	18 27	18 35				
Thames Ditton	d					18 09												18 39				
Hampton Court	a					18 14												18 44				
Hinchley Wood	d				18 05												18 35					
Claygate	d				18 08												18 38					
Oxshott	d				18 11												18 41					
Cobham & Stoke D'abernon	d				18 15												18 45					
Bookham	d						18 29												18 59			
Effingham Junction [6]	d				18 20		18a42										18 50		19 03			
Horsley	d				18 22												18 52		19 06			
Clandon	d				18 27												18 57		19 11			
London Road (Guildford)	d				18 32												19 02		19 16			
Guildford	a			18 29	18 38												19 09		19 22			

London - Chessington South, Dorking, Guildford, Shepperton and Hampton Court

Station		SW	SW	SW	SW	SW	SW	SW	SW	SW	SW	SW	SW	SW	SW	SW	SW	SW	SW 1	SW	SW	SW	SW
London Waterloo 15 ⊖	d	18 20	18 24	18 27	18 30	18 31	18 32	18 36	18 39	18 43	18 42	18 46	18 48	18 50	18 54	18 57	19 00	19 01	19 02	19 02	19 06	19 09	19 12
Vauxhall ⊖	d	18 24	18 28	18 31	18 34	18 35	18 37	18 40	18 43	18 47	18 46	18 50		18 54	18 58	19 01	19 04	19 05		19 07	19 10	19 13	19 16
Clapham Junction 10	d	18 29	18 33	18 36	18 39		18 42	18 45	18 48		18 51	18 55		18 59	19 03	19 06	19 09			19 12	19 15	19 18	19 21
Earlsfield	d	18 32	18 36	18 39	18 42		18 45	18 48	18 51		18 54	18 58		19 02	19 06	19 09	19 12			19 15	19 18	19 21	19 24
Wimbledon 6 ⊖	d	18 36	18 40	18 43	18 46		18 49	18 52	18 55		18 58	19 02		19 06	19 10	19 13	19 16			19 19	19 22	19 25	19 28
Raynes Park 6	d		18 43	18 46	18 49			18 55	18 58		19 01	19 05			19 13	19 16	19 19				19 25	19 28	19 31
Motspur Park	d				18 52				19 01			19 08					19 22					19 31	
Malden Manor	d											19 11											
Tolworth	d											19 14											
Chessington North	d											19 17											
Chessington South	a											19 21											
Worcester Park	d		18 47		18 54				19 03						19 17		19 24					19 33	
Stoneleigh	d				18 57				19 06								19 27					19 36	
Ewell West	d				19 00				19 09								19 30					19 39	
Epsom 3	a		18 54		19 07				19 16						19 24		19 35					19 44	
	d		18 54						19 17						19 24							19 47	
Ashtead	d		18 58						19 21						19 28							19 51	
Leatherhead	d		19 01						19 24						19 31							19 54	
Boxhill & Westhumble	d		19 06												19 36								
Dorking 4	a		19 11												19 41								
New Malden 6	d			18 49				18 58			19 04					19 19					19 28		19 34
Norbiton	d			18 52							19 07					19 22							19 37
Kingston	a			18 55		19 18					19 10					19 25		19 48					19 40
	d			18 59							19 10					19 29							19 40
Hampton Wick	d			19 01							19 12					19 31							19 42
Teddington	d			19 05							19 15					19 35							19 45
Strawberry Hill	a			19 08						19 11						19 38							
Fulwell	d									19 13	19 19												19 49
Hampton	d									19 17	19 23												19 53
Kempton Park	d										19 26												19 56
Sunbury	d									19 21	19 28												19 58
Upper Halliford	d									19 23	19 30												20 00
Shepperton	a									19 28	19 36												20 03
Berrylands	d							19 00													19 30		
Surbiton 6	d	18a43					18 57	19 05					19 06	19a13					19a17	19 27	19 35		
Thames Ditton	d							19 09													19 39		
Hampton Court	a							19 14													19 42		
Hinchley Wood	d						19 01						19 10							19 31			
Claygate	d						19 04						19 13							19 34			
Oxshott	d						19 07						19 16							19 37			
Cobham & Stoke D'abernon	d						19 11						19 20							19 41			
Bookham	d								19 29													19 59	
Effingham Junction 6	d						19 15		19 33				19 24							19 45		20 03	
Horsley	d						19 18		19 36				19 27							19 48		20 06	
Clandon	d						19 23		19 41				19 32							19 53		20 11	
London Road (Guildford)	d						19 28		19 46				19 37							19 58		20 16	
Guildford	a						19 34		19 52				19 43							20 02		20 20	

London - Chessington South, Dorking, Guildford, Shepperton and Hampton Court

Station		SW	SW	SW	SW	SW	SW	SW	SW	SW	SW	SW	SW	SW	SW	SW	SW	SW	SW	SW	SW	SW
London Waterloo 15 ⊖	d	19 16	19 20	19 23	19 24	19 27	19 33	19 33	19 36	19 39	19 42	19 46	19 50	19 54	19 57	20 03	20 03	20 06	20 09	20 12	20 16	20 20
Vauxhall ⊖	d	19 20	19 24		19 28	19 31	19 37	19 37	19 40	19 43	19 46	19 50	19 54	19 58	20 01	20 07	20 07	20 10	20 13	20 16	20 20	20 24
Clapham Junction 10	d	19 25	19 29		19 33	19 36	19 42		19 45	19 48	19 51	19 55	19 59	20 03	20 06	20 12		20 15	20 18	20 21	20 25	20 29
Earlsfield	d	19 28	19 32		19 36	19 39	19 45		19 48	19 51	19 54	19 58	20 02	20 06	20 09	20 15		20 18	20 21	20 24	20 28	20 32
Wimbledon 6 ⊖	d	19 32	19 36		19 40	19 43	19 49		19 52	19 55	19 58	20 02	20 06	20 10	20 13	20 19		20 22	20 25	20 28	20 32	20 36
Raynes Park 6	d	19 35			19 43	19 46			19 55	19 58	20 01	20 05		20 13	20 16			20 25	20 28	20 31	20 35	
Motspur Park	d	19 38			19 46					20 01		20 08		20 16					20 31		20 38	
Malden Manor	d	19 41										20 11									20 41	
Tolworth	d	19 44										20 14									20 44	
Chessington North	d	19 47										20 17									20 47	
Chessington South	a	19 49										20 19									20 49	
Worcester Park	d				19 48					20 03				20 18					20 33			
Stoneleigh	d				19 51					20 06				20 21					20 36			
Ewell West	d				19 54					20 09				20 24					20 39			
Epsom 3	a				19 57					20 16				20 27					20 42			
	d				19 58					20 17									20 43			
Ashtead	d				20 02					20 21									20 47			
Leatherhead	d				20 05					20 24									20 50			
Boxhill & Westhumble	d				20 10														20 55			
Dorking 4	a				20 12														20 57			
New Malden 6	d					19 49			19 58		20 04				20 19			20 28		20 34		
Norbiton	d					19 52					20 07				20 22					20 37		
Kingston	a					19 55		20 16			20 10				20 25		20 46			20 40		
	d					19 59					20 10				20 29					20 40		
Hampton Wick	d					20 01					20 12				20 31					20 42		
Teddington	d					20 05					20 15				20 35					20 45		
Strawberry Hill	a					20 08									20 38							
Fulwell	d										20 19									20 49		
Hampton	d										20 23									20 53		
Kempton Park	d										20 26									20 56		
Sunbury	d										20 28									20 58		
Upper Halliford	d										20 30									21 00		
Shepperton	a										20 33									21 03		
Berrylands	d								20 00									20 30				
Surbiton 6	d		19a43	19a39			19 57		20 05				20a13			20 27		20 35				20a43
Thames Ditton	d								20 09									20 39				
Hampton Court	a								20 12									20 42				
Hinchley Wood	d						20 01									20 31						
Claygate	d						20 04									20 34						
Oxshott	d						20 07									20 37						
Cobham & Stoke D'abernon	d						20 11									20 41						
Bookham	d									20 29												
Effingham Junction 6	d						20 15			20 33						20 45						
Horsley	d						20 18			20 36						20 48						
Clandon	d						20 23			20 41						20 53						
London Road (Guildford)	d						20 28			20 46						20 58						
Guildford	a						20 32			20 50						21 02						

Station		SW	SW	SW	SW	SW	SW	SW	SW	SW	SW	SW	SW	SW	SW	SW	SW	SW	SW	SW	SW	SW	SW
London Waterloo 15 ⊖	d	20 24	20 27	20 33	20 33	20 36	20 39	20 42	20 46	20 50	20 54	20 57	21 03	21 03	21 09	21 12	21 20	21 24	21 27	21 33	21 33	21 36	21 39
Vauxhall ⊖	d	20 28	20 31	20 37	20 37	20 40	20 43	20 46	20 50	20 54	20 58	21 01	21 07	21 07	21 13	21 16	21 24	21 28	21 31	21 37	21 37	21 40	21 43
Clapham Junction 10	d	20 33	20 36	20 42		20 45	20 48	20 51	20 55	20 59	21 03	21 06	21 12		21 18	21 21	21 29	21 33	21 36	21 42		21 45	21 48
Earlsfield	d	20 36	20 39	20 45		20 48	20 51	20 54	20 58	21 02	21 06	21 09	21 15		21 21	21 24	21 32	21 36	21 39	21 45		21 48	21 51
Wimbledon 6 ⊖	d	20 40	20 43	20 49		20 52	20 55	20 58	21 02	21 06	21 10	21 13	21 19		21 25	21 28	21 36	21 40	21 43	21 49		21 52	21 55
Raynes Park 6	d	20 43	20 46			20 55	20 58	21 01	21 05		21 13	21 16			21 28	21 31		21 43	21 46			21 55	21 58
Motspur Park	d	20 46					21 01		21 08		21 16				21 31			21 46					22 01
Malden Manor	d								21 11														
Tolworth	d								21 14														
Chessington North	d								21 17														
Chessington South	a								21 19														
Worcester Park	d	20 48					21 03				21 18				21 33			21 48					22 03
Stoneleigh	d	20 51					21 06				21 21				21 36			21 51					22 06
Ewell West	d	20 54					21 09				21 24				21 39			21 54					22 09
Epsom 3	a	20 57					21 12				21 27				21 42			21 57					22 12
	d						21 13								21 43								22 13
Ashtead	d						21 17								21 47								22 17
Leatherhead	d						21 20								21 50								22 20
Boxhill & Westhumble	d														21 55								
Dorking 4	a														21 57								
New Malden 6	d		20 49			20 58		21 04				21 19				21 34			21 49			21 58	
Norbiton	d		20 52					21 07				21 22				21 37			21 52				
Kingston	a		20 55		21 16			21 10				21 25		21 46		21 40			21 55		22 16		
	d		20 59					21 10				21 29				21 40			21 59				
Hampton Wick	d		21 01					21 12				21 31				21 42			22 01				
Teddington	d		21 05					21 15				21 35				21 45			22 05				
Strawberry Hill	a		21 08									21 38							22 08				
Fulwell	d							21 19								21 49							
Hampton	d							21 23								21 53							
Kempton Park	d							21 26								21 56							
Sunbury	d							21 28								21 58							
Upper Halliford	d							21 30								22 00							
Shepperton	a							21 33								22 03							
Berrylands	d					21 00																22 00	
Surbiton 6	d			20 57		21 05				21a13			21 27				21a43			21 57		22 05	
Thames Ditton	d					21 09																22 09	
Hampton Court	a					21 12																22 12	
Hinchley Wood	d			21 01									21 31							22 01			
Claygate	d			21 04									21 34							22 04			
Oxshott	d			21 07									21 37							22 07			
Cobham & Stoke D'abernon	d			21 11									21 41							22 11			
Bookham	d						21 25																22 25
Effingham Junction 6	d			21 15			21 29						21 45							22 15			22 29
Horsley	d			21 18			21 32						21 48							22 18			22 32
Clandon	d			21 23			21 37						21 53							22 23			22 37
London Road (Guildford)	d			21 28			21 42						21 58							22 28			22 42
Guildford	a			21 32			21 46						22 02							22 32			22 46

Table 152

Mondays to Fridays
until 30 September

London - Chessington South, Dorking, Guildford, Shepperton and Hampton Court

		SW	SW	SW	SW	SW	SW	SW	SW	SW	SW	SW	SW	SW	SW	SW	SW	SW	SW	SW	SW	SW	SW
London Waterloo 15 ⊖	d	21 42	21 46	21 50	21 54	21 57	22 03	22 03	22 09	22 12	22 20	22 27	22 33	22 33	22 36	22 39	22 42	22 50	22 57	23 00	23 03	23 03	23 09
Vauxhall ⊖	d	21 46	21 50	21 54	21 58	22 01	22 07	22 07	22 13	22 16	22 24	22 31	22 37	22 37	22 40	22 43	22 46	22 54	23 01	23 04	23 07	23 07	23 13
Clapham Junction 10	d	21 51	21 55	21 59	22 03	22 06	22 12		22 18	22 21	22 29	22 36	22 42		22 45	22 48	22 51	22 59	23 06	23 09	23 12		23 18
Earlsfield	d	21 54	21 58	22 02	22 06	22 09	22 15		22 21	22 24	22 32	22 39	22 45		22 48	22 51	22 54	23 02	23 09	23 12	23 15		23 21
Wimbledon 6 ⊖ ⇌	d	21 58	22 02	22 06	22 10	22 13	22 19		22 25	22 28	22 36	22 43	22 49		22 52	22 55	22 58	23 06	23 13	23 16	23 19		23 25
Raynes Park 6	d	22 01	22 05		22 13	22 16			22 28	22 31		22 46			22 55	22 58	23 01		23 16	23 19			23 28
Motspur Park	d		22 08		22 16				22 31							23 01				23 22			23 31
Malden Manor	d		22 11																	23 25			
Tolworth	d		22 14																	23 28			
Chessington North	d		22 17																	23 31			
Chessington South	a		22 19																	23 33			
Worcester Park	d				22 18				22 33							23 03							23 33
Stoneleigh	d				22 21				22 36							23 06							23 36
Ewell West	d				22 24				22 39							23 09							23 39
Epsom 3	a				22 27				22 42							23 12							23 42
	d								22 43							23 13							23 43
Ashtead	d								22 47							23 17							23 47
Leatherhead	d								22 50							23 20							23 50
Boxhill & Westhumble	d								22 55														23 55
Dorking 4	a								22 57														23 57
New Malden 6	d	22 04				22 19				22 34		22 49			22 58		23 04		23 19				
Norbiton	d	22 07				22 22				22 37		22 52					23 07		23 22				
Kingston	a	22 10				22 25		22 46		22 40		22 55		23 16			23 10		23 25			23 46	
	d	22 10				22 29				22 40		22 59					23 10		23 29				
Hampton Wick	d	22 12				22 31				22 42		23 01					23 12		23 31				
Teddington	d	22 15				22 35				22 45		23 05					23 15		23 35				
Strawberry Hill	a					22 38						23 08							23 38				
Fulwell	d	22 19								22 49							23 19						
Hampton	d	22 23								22 53							23 23						
Kempton Park	d	22 26								22 56							23 26						
Sunbury	d	22 28								22 58							23 28						
Upper Halliford	d	22 30								23 00							23 30						
Shepperton	a	22 33								23 03							23 33						
Berrylands	d														23 00								
Surbiton 6	d			22 14			22 27				22a43		22 57		23 05			23a13			23 27		
Thames Ditton	d														23 09								
Hampton Court	a														23 12								
Hinchley Wood	d						22 31						23 01								23 31		
Claygate	d						22 34						23 04								23 34		
Oxshott	d						22 37						23 07								23 37		
Cobham & Stoke D'abernon	d						22 41						23 11								23 41		
Bookham	d															23 25							
Effingham Junction 6	d						22 45						23 15			23 29					23 45		
Horsley	d						22 48						23 18			23 32					23 48		
Clandon	d						22 53						23 23			23 37					23 53		
London Road (Guildford)	d						22 58						23 28			23 42					23 58		
Guildford	a			22 47			23 02						23 32			23 46					00 02		

		SW	SW	SW	SW	SW	SW	SW	SW
London Waterloo 15 ⊖	d	23 12	23 20	23 27	23 33	23 36	23 42	23 50	23 57
Vauxhall ⊖	d	23 16	23 24	23 31	23 37	23 40	23 46	23 54	00 01
Clapham Junction 10	d	23 21	23 29	23 36		23 45	23 51	23 59	00 06
Earlsfield	d	23 24	23 32	23 39		23 48	23 54	00 02	00 09
Wimbledon 6 ⊖ ⇌	d	23 28	23 36	23 43		23 52	23 58	00 06	00 13
Raynes Park 6	d	23 31		23 46		23 55	00 01		00 16
Motspur Park	d						00 04		
Malden Manor	d								
Tolworth	d								
Chessington North	d								
Chessington South	a								
Worcester Park	d						00 06		
Stoneleigh	d						00 09		
Ewell West	d						00 12		
Epsom 3	a						00 15		
	d						00 19		
Ashtead	d						00 23		
Leatherhead	d						00 26		
Boxhill & Westhumble	d								
Dorking 4	a								
New Malden 6	d	23 34		23 49		23 58			00 19
Norbiton	d	23 37		23 52					00 22
Kingston	a	23 40		23 55	00 16				00 25
	d	23 40		23 55					00 25
Hampton Wick	d	23 42		23 57					00 27
Teddington	d	23 45		23 59					00 30
Strawberry Hill	a			00 03					
Fulwell	d	23 49							00 34
Hampton	d	23 53							00 38
Kempton Park	d	23 56							00 41
Sunbury	d	23 58							00 43
Upper Halliford	d	23 59							00 45
Shepperton	a	00 03							00 48
Berrylands	d					23 59			
Surbiton 6	d		23a43			00 05		00 14	
Thames Ditton	d					00 09			
Hampton Court	a					00 12			
Hinchley Wood	d							00 18	
Claygate	d							00 20	
Oxshott	d							00 24	
Cobham & Stoke D'abernon	d							00 27	
Bookham	d						00 31		
Effingham Junction 6	d						00 36	00 32	
Horsley	d						00 39	00 34	
Clandon	d						00 44	00 39	
London Road (Guildford)	d						00 49	00 44	

Table 152

Mondays to Fridays
from 3 October

London - Chessington South, Dorking, Guildford, Shepperton and Hampton Court

		SW MX	SW MO	SW MO	SW MX	SW MX	SW MO	SW MX	SW MX	SW MX	SW MX	SW MX	SW MO	SW MX	SW MX	SW	SW MX	SW	SW [1]	SW	SW [1]	SW	SW
London Waterloo 15 ⊖	d	23p03	23p00	23p10	23p12	23p27	23p32	23p33	23p36	23p42	23p50	23p57	00 01	00 09	00 15	00 18	00 27	00 42	05 00	05 12	05 20	05 33	
Vauxhall ⊖	d	23p07	23p04	23p14	23p16	23p31	23p36	23p37	23p40	23p46	23p54	00 01	00 04	00 13	00 19	00 22	00 31	00 46	05 04	05 16	05 24	05 37	
Clapham Junction 10	d	23p12	23p09	23p19	23p21	23p36	23p41		23p45	23p51	23p59	00 06	00 09	00 20	00 25		00 37		05 11	05 21	05 29		
Earlsfield	d	23p15	23p12	23p22	23p24	23p39	23p44		23p48	23p54	00 02	00 09	00 12	00 23	00 29		00s41		05 14	05 24	05 32		
Wimbledon 6 ⊖ ⇌	d	23p19	23p16	23p26	23p28	23p43	23p48		23p52	23p58	00 06	00 13	00 16	00 27	00 33		00 45	01 05	05 18	05 28	05 36		05 49
Raynes Park 6	d				23p31	23p46	23p52		23p55	00 01		00 16	00 19		00 36		00 48	01 08		05 31			
Motspur Park	d						23p55			00 04					00 38								
Malden Manor	d																						
Tolworth	d																						
Chessington North	d																						
Chessington South	a																						
Worcester Park	d						23p57			00 06					00 41								
Stoneleigh	d						23p59			00 09					00 44								
Ewell West	d						00 03			00 12					00 46								
Epsom 3	a						00 06			00 15					00 50								
	d									00 19													
Ashtead	d									00 23													
Leatherhead	d									00 26													
Boxhill & Westhumble	d																						
Dorking 4	a																						
New Malden 6	d				23p34	23p49			23p58			00 19	00 22				00 50	01 11		05 34			
Norbiton	d				23p37	23p52						00 22						01 14		05 37			
Kingston	a				23p40	23p55		00 16				00 25				01 01		01 17		05 40		06 16	
	d				23p40	23p55						00 25						01 17		05 40			
Hampton Wick	d				23p42	23p57						00 27						01s22		05 42			
Teddington	d				23p45	23p59						00 30						01s25		05 45			
Strawberry Hill	a					00 03												01 28					
Fulwell	d				23p49							00 34								05 49			
Hampton	d				23p53							00 38								05 53			
Kempton Park	d				23p56							00 41											
Sunbury	d				23p58							00 43								05 58			
Upper Halliford	d				23p59							00 45								06 00			
Shepperton	a				00 05							00 50								06 05			
Berrylands	d								23p59				00 25				00s53						
Surbiton 6	d	23p27	23p32	23p35					00 05		00 14		00 31	00 35			00a56		05 26		05 44		05 57
Thames Ditton	d								00 09														
Hampton Court	a								00 12														
Hinchley Wood	d	23p31	23p36								00 18		00 35										06 01
Claygate	d	23p34	23p39								00 20		00 38										06 04
Oxshott	d	23p37	23p42								00 24		00 41										06 07
Cobham & Stoke D'abernon	d	23p41	23p46								00 27		00 45										06 11
Bookham	d									00 31													
Effingham Junction 6	d	23p45	23p50							00 36	00 32		00 49										06 15
Horsley	d	23p48	23p53							00 39	00 34		00 52										06 18
Clandon	d	23p53	23p58							00 44	00 39		00 57										06 23
London Road (Guildford)	d	23p58	00 03							00 49	00 44		01 02										06 28
Guildford	a	00 05	00 10	00 13						00 56	00 51		01 09	01 07					06 00		06 21		06 35

London - Chessington South, Dorking, Guildford, Shepperton and Hampton Court

from 3 October

		SW	SW	SW	SW	SW		SW	SW	SW	SW	SW	SW	SW	SW	SW		SW	SW	SW	SW	SW	SW	SW	SW
London Waterloo [15] ⊖	d	05 47	05 50	06 03		06 03		06 06	06 12	06 16	06 20	06 24	06 27	06 33	06 33	06 36		06 39	06 42	06 46	06 50	06 54	06 57	07 03	07 03
Vauxhall ⊖	d	05 51	05 54	06 07		06 07		06 10	06 16	06 20	06 24	06 28	06 31	06 37	06 37	06 40		06 43	06 46	06 50	06 54	06 58	07 01	07 07	07 07
Clapham Junction [10]	d	05 56	05 59			06 12		06 15	06 21	06 25	06 29	06 33	06 36	06 42		06 45		06 48	06 51	06 55	06 59	07 03	07 06	07 12	
Earlsfield	d	05 59	06 02			06 15		06 18	06 24	06 28	06 32	06 36	06 39	06 45		06 48		06 51	06 54	06 58	07 02	07 06	07 09	07 15	
Wimbledon [6] ⊖	d	06 03	06 06		06 16	06 19		06 22	06 28	06 32	06 36	06 40	06 43	06 49		06 52		06 55	06 58	07 02	07 06	07 10	07 13	07 19	
Raynes Park [6]	d	06 06			06 19			06 25	06 31	06 35		06 43	06 46			06 55		06 58	07 01	07 05		07 13	07 16		
Motspur Park	d	06 09			06 21					06 38		06 46								07 08		07 16			
Malden Manor	d				06 25					06 41										07 11					
Tolworth	d				06 27					06 44										07 14					
Chessington North	d				06 30					06 47										07 17					
Chessington South	a				06 32					06 49										07 19					
Worcester Park	d	06 11										06 48						07 02				07 18			
Stoneleigh	d	06 14										06 51						07 05				07 21			
Ewell West	d	06 17										06 54						07 08				07 24			
Epsom [3]	a	06 20										06 57						07 11				07 27			
	d	06 21										06 58						07 12				07 28			
Ashtead	d	06 25										07 02						07 16				07 32			
Leatherhead	d	06 28										07 05						07 19				07 35			
Boxhill & Westhumble	d																								
Dorking [4]	a											07 13										07 43			
New Malden [6]	d							06 28	06 34				06 49			06 58			07 04				07 19		
Norbiton	d								06 37				06 52						07 07				07 22		
Kingston	a			06 46					06 40				06 55		07 16				07 10				07 25		07 46
	d								06 40				06 59						07 10				07 29		
Hampton Wick	d								06 42				07 01						07 12				07 31		
Teddington	d								06 45				07 05						07 15				07 35		
Strawberry Hill	a												07 08										07 38		
Fulwell	d								06 49										07 19						
Hampton	d								06 53										07 23						
Kempton Park	d																								
Sunbury	d								06 58										07 28						
Upper Halliford	d								07 00										07 30						
Shepperton	a								07 05										07 35						
Berrylands	d							06 30								07 00									
Surbiton [6]	d		06a13			06 27		06 35			06 44			06 57		07 05					07 14			07 27	
Thames Ditton	d							06 39								07 09									
Hampton Court	a							06 42								07 12									
Hinchley Wood	d					06 31								07 01										07 31	
Claygate	d					06 34								07 04										07 34	
Oxshott	d					06 37								07 07										07 37	
Cobham & Stoke D'abernon	d					06 41								07 11										07 41	
Bookham	d	06 33																07 24							
Effingham Junction [6]	d	06 37				06 45								07 15				07a28						07 45	
Horsley	d					06 48								07 18										07 48	
Clandon	d					06 53								07 23										07 53	
London Road (Guildford)	d	06 46				06 58								07 28										07 58	
Guildford	a	06 53				07 05					07 20			07 35							07 47			08 05	

		SW		SW	SW	SW	SW	SW	SW	SW	SW	SW		SW	SW	SW	SW	SW	SW	SW	SW	SW		SW	SW
London Waterloo [15] ⊖	d	07 06		07 09	07 12	07 16	07 20	07 24	07 27	07 33	07 33	07 36		07 39	07 42	07 46	07 50	07 54	07 57	08 03	08 03	08 06		08 09	08 12
Vauxhall ⊖	d	07 10		07 13	07 16	07 20	07 24	07 28	07 31	07 37	07 37	07 40		07 43	07 46	07 50	07 54	07 58	08 01	08 07	08 07	08 10		08 13	08 16
Clapham Junction [10]	d	07 15		07 18	07 21	07 25	07 29	07 33	07 36	07 42		07 45		07 48	07 51	07 55	07 59	08 03	08 06	08 12		08 15		08 18	08 21
Earlsfield	d	07 18		07 21	07 24	07 28	07 32	07 36	07 39	07 45		07 48		07 51	07 54	07 58	08 02	08 06	08 09	08 15		08 18		08 21	08 24
Wimbledon [6] ⊖	d	07 22		07 25	07 28	07 32	07 36	07 40	07 43	07 49		07 52		07 55	07 58	08 02	08 06	08 10	08 13	08 19		08 22		08 25	08 28
Raynes Park [6]	d	07 25		07 28	07 31	07 35		07 43	07 46			07 55		07 58	08 01	08 05		08 13	08 16			08 25		08 28	08 31
Motspur Park	d			07 31		07 38		07 46						08 01		08 08		08 16						08 31	
Malden Manor	d					07 41										08 11									
Tolworth	d					07 44										08 14									
Chessington North	d					07 47										08 17									
Chessington South	a					07 49										08 19									
Worcester Park	d			07 33				07 48						08 03				08 18						08 33	
Stoneleigh	d			07 36				07 51						08 06				08 21						08 36	
Ewell West	d			07 39				07 54						08 09				08 24						08 39	
Epsom [3]	a			07 42				07 58						08 13				08 27						08 42	
	d							07 58						08 17				08 28						08 47	
Ashtead	d							08 02						08 21				08 32						08 51	
Leatherhead	d							08 05						08 24				08 35						08 54	
Boxhill & Westhumble	d																								
Dorking [4]	a							08 14										08 43							
New Malden [6]	d	07 28			07 34				07 49			07 58			08 04				08 19			08 28			08 34
Norbiton	d				07 37				07 52						08 07				08 22						08 37
Kingston	a				07 40				07 55		08 16				08 10				08 25		08 46				08 39
	d				07 40				07 59						08 10				08 29						08 40
Hampton Wick	d				07 42				08 01						08 12				08 31						08 42
Teddington	d				07 45				08 05						08 15				08 35						08 45
Strawberry Hill	a								08 08										08 38						
Fulwell	d				07 49										08 19										08 49
Hampton	d				07 53										08 23										08 53
Kempton Park	d				07 56										08 26										08 56
Sunbury	d				07 58										08 28										08 58
Upper Halliford	d				08 00										08 30										09 00
Shepperton	a				08 05										08 35										09 06
Berrylands	d	07 30										08 00										08 30			
Surbiton [6]	d	07 35					07a43			07 57		08 05					08 14			08 27		08 35			
Thames Ditton	d	07 39										08 09										08 39			
Hampton Court	a	07 42										08 12										08 42			
Hinchley Wood	d									08 01										08 31					
Claygate	d									08 04										08 34					
Oxshott	d									08 07										08 37					
Cobham & Stoke D'abernon	d									08 11										08 41					
Bookham	d													08 29										08 59	
Effingham Junction [6]	d									08 15				08 33						08 45				09 03	
Horsley	d									08 18				08 36						08 48				09 06	
Clandon	d									08 23				08 41						08 53				09 11	
London Road (Guildford)	d									08 28				08 46						08 58				09 16	
Guildford	a									08 35				08 53			08 50			09 07				09 23	

Mondays to Fridays

London - Chessington South, Dorking, Guildford, Shepperton and Hampton Court

from 3 October

		SW	SW	SW	SW	SW	SW	SW		SW	SW	SW	SW	SW	SW	SW	SW	SW		SW	SW	SW	SW	SW	SW
London Waterloo [15] ⊖	d	08 16	08 20	08 24	08 27	08 33	08 33	08 36		08 39	08 42	08 46	08 50	08 54	08 57	09 03	09 03	09 06		09 09	09 12	09 16	09 20	09 24	09 27
Vauxhall ⊖	d	08 20	08 24	08 28	08 31	08 37	08 37	08 40		08 43	08 46	08 50	08 54	08 58	09 01	09 07	09 07	09 10		09 13	09 16	09 20	09 24	09 28	09 31
Clapham Junction [10]	d	08 25	08 29	08 33	08 36	08 42		08 45		08 48	08 51	08 55	08 59	09 03	09 06	09 12		09 15		09 18	09 21	09 25	09 29	09 33	09 36
Earlsfield	d	08 28	08 32	08 36	08 39	08 45		08 48		08 51	08 54	08 58	09 02	09 06	09 09	09 15		09 18		09 21	09 24	09 28	09 32	09 36	09 39
Wimbledon [6] ⊖	d	08 32	08 36	08 40	08 43	08 49		08 52		08 55	08 58	09 02	09 06	09 10	09 13	09 19		09 22		09 25	09 28	09 32	09 36	09 40	09 43
Raynes Park [6]	d	08 35		08 43	08 46			08 55		08 58	09 01	09 05		09 13	09 16			09 25		09 28	09 31	09 35		09 43	09 46
Motspur Park	d	08 38		08 46						09 01		09 08		09 16						09 31		09 38		09 46	
Malden Manor	d	08 41										09 11										09 41			
Tolworth	d	08 44										09 14										09 44			
Chessington North	d	08 47										09 17										09 47			
Chessington South	a	08 49										09 19										09 49			
Worcester Park	d			08 48						09 03				09 18						09 33				09 48	
Stoneleigh	d			08 51						09 06				09 21						09 36				09 51	
Ewell West	d			08 54						09 09				09 24						09 39				09 54	
Epsom [3]	a			08 57						09 16				09 27						09 42				09 57	
	d			08 58						09 17				09 28						09 47				09 58	
Ashtead	d			09 02						09 21				09 32						09 51				10 02	
Leatherhead	d			09 05						09 24				09 35						09 54				10 05	
Boxhill & Westhumble	d																								
Dorking [4]	a			09 13										09 43										10 13	
New Malden [6]	d				08 49			08 58			09 04				09 19			09 28			09 34				09 49
Norbiton	d				08 52						09 07				09 22						09 37				09 52
Kingston	a				08 55		09 16				09 10				09 25		09 46				09 40				09 55
	d				08 59						09 10				09 29						09 40				09 59
Hampton Wick	d				09 01						09 12				09 31						09 42				10 01
Teddington	d				09 05						09 15				09 35						09 45				10 05
Strawberry Hill	a				09 08										09 38										10 08
Fulwell	d										09 19										09 49				
Hampton	d										09 23										09 53				
Kempton Park	d										09 26										09 56				
Sunbury	d										09 28										09 58				
Upper Halliford	d										09 30										10 00				
Shepperton	a										09 35										10 05				
Berrylands	d							09 00										09 30							
Surbiton [6]	d		08a43			08 57		09 05					09a13			09 27		09 35					09a43		
Thames Ditton	d							09 09										09 39							
Hampton Court	a							09 12										09 42							
Hinchley Wood	d					09 01										09 31									
Claygate	d					09 04										09 34									
Oxshott	d					09 07										09 37									
Cobham & Stoke D'abernon	d					09 11										09 41									
Bookham	d									09 29										09 59					
Effingham Junction [6]	d					09 15				09 33						09 45				10 03					
Horsley	d					09 18				09 36						09 48				10 06					
Clandon	d					09 23				09 41						09 53				10 11					
London Road (Guildford)	d					09 28				09 46						09 58				10 16					
Guildford	a					09 35				09 53						10 05				10 23					

Table 152

Mondays to Fridays
from 3 October

London - Chessington South, Dorking, Guildford, Shepperton and Hampton Court

		SW	SW	SW	SW	SW	SW	SW	SW	SW	SW	SW	SW	SW	SW	SW	SW	SW [1]	SW	SW	SW	SW
London Waterloo ⊖	d	09 33	09 33	09 36	09 39	09 42	09 46	09 50	09 54	09 57	10 03	10 03	10 06	10 09	10 12	10 16	10 20	10 23	10 24	10 27	10 33	10 33
Vauxhall ⊖	d	09 37	09 37	09 40	09 43	09 46	09 50	09 54	09 58	10 01	10 07	10 07	10 10	10 13	10 16	10 20	10 24		10 28	10 31	10 37	10 37
Clapham Junction	d	09 42		09 45	09 48	09 51	09 55	09 59	10 03	10 06	10 12		10 15	10 18	10 21	10 25	10 29		10 33	10 36	10 42	
Earlsfield	d	09 45		09 48	09 51	09 54	09 58	10 02	10 06	10 09	10 15		10 18	10 21	10 24	10 28	10 32		10 36	10 39	10 45	
Wimbledon ⊖	d	09 49		09 52	09 55	09 58	10 02	10 06	10 10	10 13	10 19		10 22	10 25	10 28	10 32	10 36		10 40	10 43	10 49	
Raynes Park	d			09 55	09 58	10 01	10 05		10 13	10 16			10 25	10 28	10 31	10 35			10 43	10 46		
Motspur Park	d				10 01		10 08		10 16					10 31		10 38			10 46			
Malden Manor	d						10 11									10 41						
Tolworth	d						10 14									10 44						
Chessington North	d						10 17									10 47						
Chessington South	a						10 19									10 49						
Worcester Park	d				10 03				10 18					10 33					10 48			
Stoneleigh	d				10 06				10 21					10 36					10 51			
Ewell West	d				10 09				10 24					10 39					10 54			
Epsom	a				10 16				10 27					10 46					10 57			
	d				10 17				10 28					10 47					10 58			
Ashtead	d				10 21				10 32					10 51					11 02			
Leatherhead	d				10 24				10 35					10 54					11 05			
Boxhill & Westhumble	d																					
Dorking	a								10 43										11 13			
New Malden	d			09 58		10 04				10 19			10 28		10 34					10 49		
Norbiton	d					10 07				10 22					10 37					10 52		
Kingston	a		10 16			10 10				10 25		10 46			10 40					10 55		11 16
	d					10 10				10 29					10 40					10 59		
Hampton Wick	d					10 12				10 31					10 42					11 01		
Teddington	d					10 15				10 35					10 45					11 05		
Strawberry Hill	a									10 38										11 08		
Fulwell	d					10 19									10 49							
Hampton	d					10 23									10 53							
Kempton Park	d					10 26									10 56							
Sunbury	d					10 28									10 58							
Upper Halliford	d					10 30									11 00							
Shepperton	a					10 35									11 05							
Berrylands	d			10 00									10 30									
Surbiton	d	09 57		10 05				10a13			10 27		10 35				10a43	10a39			10 57	
Thames Ditton	d			10 09									10 39									
Hampton Court	a			10 12									10 42									
Hinchley Wood	d	10 01									10 31										11 01	
Claygate	d	10 04									10 34										11 04	
Oxshott	d	10 07									10 37										11 07	
Cobham & Stoke D'abernon	d	10 11									10 41										11 11	
Bookham	d				10 29									10 59								
Effingham Junction	d	10 15			10 33						10 45			11 03							11 15	
Horsley	d	10 18			10 36						10 48			11 06							11 18	
Clandon	d	10 23			10 41						10 53			11 11							11 23	
London Road (Guildford)	d	10 28			10 46						10 58			11 16							11 28	
Guildford	a	10 35			10 53						11 05			11 23							11 35	

Table 152

Mondays to Fridays
from 3 October

London - Chessington South, Dorking, Guildford, Shepperton and Hampton Court

		SW	SW	SW	SW	SW	SW	SW	SW	SW	SW	SW	SW	SW	SW	SW	SW	SW	SW	SW	SW	SW	SW
London Waterloo ⊖	d	10 36	10 39	10 42	10 46	10 50	10 54	10 57	11 03	11 03	11 06	11 09	11 12	11 16	11 20	11 24	11 27	11 33	11 33	11 36	11 39	11 42	11 46
Vauxhall ⊖	d	10 40	10 43	10 46	10 50	10 54	10 58	11 01	11 07	11 07	11 10	11 13	11 16	11 20	11 24	11 28	11 31	11 37	11 37	11 40	11 43	11 46	11 50
Clapham Junction	d	10 45	10 48	10 51	10 55	10 59	11 03	11 06	11 12		11 15	11 18	11 21	11 25	11 29	11 33	11 36	11 42		11 45	11 48	11 51	11 55
Earlsfield	d	10 48	10 51	10 54	10 58	11 02	11 06	11 09	11 15		11 18	11 21	11 24	11 28	11 32	11 36	11 39	11 45		11 48	11 51	11 54	11 58
Wimbledon ⊖	d	10 52	10 55	10 58	11 02	11 06	11 10	11 13	11 19		11 22	11 25	11 28	11 32	11 36	11 40	11 43	11 49		11 52	11 55	11 58	12 02
Raynes Park	d	10 55	10 58	11 01	11 05		11 13	11 16			11 25	11 28	11 31	11 35		11 43	11 46			11 55	11 58	12 01	12 05
Motspur Park	d		11 01		11 08		11 16					11 31		11 38		11 46					12 01		12 08
Malden Manor	d				11 11									11 41									12 11
Tolworth	d				11 14									11 44									12 14
Chessington North	d				11 17									11 47									12 17
Chessington South	a				11 19									11 49									12 19
Worcester Park	d		11 03				11 18					11 33				11 48					12 03		
Stoneleigh	d		11 06				11 21					11 36				11 51					12 06		
Ewell West	d		11 09				11 24					11 39				11 54					12 09		
Epsom	a		11 16				11 27					11 46				11 57					12 16		
	d		11 17				11 28					11 47				11 58					12 17		
Ashtead	d		11 21				11 32					11 51				12 02					12 21		
Leatherhead	d		11 24				11 35					11 54				12 05					12 24		
Boxhill & Westhumble	d																						
Dorking	a						11 43									12 13							
New Malden	d	10 58		11 04				11 19			11 28		11 34				11 49			11 58		12 04	
Norbiton	d			11 07				11 22					11 37				11 52					12 07	
Kingston	a			11 10				11 25		11 46			11 40				11 55		12 16			12 10	
	d			11 10				11 29					11 40				11 59					12 10	
Hampton Wick	d			11 12				11 31					11 42				12 01					12 12	
Teddington	d			11 15				11 35					11 45				12 05					12 15	
Strawberry Hill	a							11 38									12 08						
Fulwell	d			11 19									11 49									12 19	
Hampton	d			11 23									11 53									12 23	
Kempton Park	d			11 26									11 56									12 26	
Sunbury	d			11 28									11 58									12 28	
Upper Halliford	d			11 30									12 00									12 30	
Shepperton	a			11 35									12 05									12 35	
Berrylands	d	11 00									11 30									12 00			
Surbiton	d	11 05				11a13			11 27		11 35				11a43			11 57		12 05			
Thames Ditton	d	11 09									11 39									12 09			
Hampton Court	a	11 12									11 42									12 12			
Hinchley Wood	d								11 31									12 01					
Claygate	d								11 34									12 04					
Oxshott	d								11 37									12 07					
Cobham & Stoke D'abernon	d								11 41									12 11					
Bookham	d		11 29									11 59									12 29		
Effingham Junction	d		11 33						11 45			12 03						12 15			12 33		
Horsley	d		11 36						11 48			12 06						12 18			12 36		
Clandon	d		11 41						11 53			12 11						12 23			12 41		
London Road (Guildford)	d		11 46						11 58			12 16						12 28			12 46		
Guildford	a		11 53						12 05			12 23						12 35			12 53		

		SW	SW	SW	SW	SW	SW	SW	SW	SW	SW	SW	SW	SW	SW	SW	SW	SW	SW	SW	SW	SW	SW
London Waterloo ⊖	d	11 50	11 54	11 57	12 03	12 03	12 06	12 09	12 12	12 16	12 20	12 24	12 27	12 33	12 33	12 36	12 39	12 42	12 46	12 50	12 54	12 57	13 03
Vauxhall ⊖	d	11 54	11 58	12 01	12 07	12 07	12 10	12 13	12 16	12 20	12 24	12 28	12 31	12 37	12 37	12 40	12 43	12 46	12 50	12 54	12 58	13 01	13 07
Clapham Junction	d	11 59	12 03	12 06	12 12		12 15	12 18	12 21	12 25	12 29	12 33	12 36	12 42		12 45	12 48	12 51	12 55	12 59	13 03	13 06	13 12
Earlsfield	d	12 02	12 06	12 09	12 15		12 18	12 21	12 24	12 28	12 32	12 36	12 39	12 45		12 48	12 51	12 54	12 58	13 02	13 06	13 09	13 15
Wimbledon ⊖	d	12 06	12 10	12 13	12 19		12 22	12 25	12 28	12 32	12 36	12 40	12 43	12 49		12 52	12 55	12 58	13 02	13 06	13 10	13 13	13 19
Raynes Park	d		12 13	12 16			12 25	12 28	12 31	12 35		12 43	12 46			12 55	12 58	13 01	13 05		13 13	13 16	
Motspur Park	d		12 16					12 31		12 38		12 46					13 01		13 08		13 16		
Malden Manor	d									12 41									13 11				
Tolworth	d									12 44									13 14				
Chessington North	d									12 47									13 17				
Chessington South	a									12 49									13 19				
Worcester Park	d		12 18					12 33				12 48					13 03				13 18		
Stoneleigh	d		12 21					12 36				12 51					13 06				13 21		
Ewell West	d		12 24					12 39				12 54					13 09				13 24		
Epsom	a		12 27					12 46				12 57					13 16				13 27		
	d		12 28					12 47				12 58					13 17				13 28		
Ashtead	d		12 32					12 51				13 02					13 21				13 32		
Leatherhead	d		12 35					12 54				13 05					13 24				13 35		
Boxhill & Westhumble	d																						
Dorking	a		12 43									13 13									13 43		
New Malden	d			12 19			12 28		12 34				12 49			12 58		13 04				13 19	
Norbiton	d			12 22					12 37				12 52					13 07				13 22	
Kingston	a			12 25		12 46			12 40				12 55		13 16			13 10				13 25	
	d			12 29					12 40				12 59					13 10				13 29	
Hampton Wick	d			12 31					12 42				13 01					13 12				13 31	
Teddington	d			12 35					12 45				13 05					13 15				13 35	
Strawberry Hill	a			12 38									13 08									13 38	
Fulwell	d								12 49									13 19					
Hampton	d								12 53									13 23					
Kempton Park	d								12 56									13 26					
Sunbury	d								12 58									13 28					
Upper Halliford	d								13 00									13 30					
Shepperton	a								13 05									13 35					
Berrylands	d						12 30									13 00							
Surbiton	d	12a13			12 27		12 35				12a43			12 57		13 05				13a13			13 27
Thames Ditton	d						12 39									13 09							
Hampton Court	a						12 42									13 12							
Hinchley Wood	d				12 31									13 01									13 31
Claygate	d				12 34									13 04									13 34
Oxshott	d				12 37									13 07									13 37
Cobham & Stoke D'abernon	d				12 41									13 11									13 41
Bookham	d							12 59									13 29						
Effingham Junction	d				12 45			13 03						13 15			13 33						13 45
Horsley	d				12 48			13 06						13 18			13 36						13 48
Clandon	d				12 53			13 11						13 23			13 41						13 53
London Road (Guildford)	d				12 58			13 16						13 28			13 46						13 58
Guildford	a				13 05			13 23						13 35			13 53						14 05

London - Chessington South, Dorking, Guildford, Shepperton and Hampton Court

from 3 October

		SW		SW	SW	SW	SW	SW	SW	SW	SW	SW		SW	SW	SW	SW	SW	SW	SW	SW	SW		SW	SW
London Waterloo 15	⊖ d	13 03		13 06	13 09	13 12	13 16	13 20	13 24	13 27	13 33	13 33		13 36	13 39	13 42	13 46	13 50	13 54	13 57	14 03	14 03		14 06	14 09
Vauxhall	⊖ d	13 07		13 10	13 13	13 16	13 20	13 24	13 28	13 31	13 37	13 37		13 40	13 43	13 46	13 50	13 54	13 58	14 01	14 07	14 07		14 10	14 13
Clapham Junction 10	d			13 15	13 18	13 21	13 25	13 29	13 33	13 36	13 42			13 45	13 48	13 51	13 55	13 59	14 03	14 06	14 12			14 15	14 18
Earlsfield	d			13 18	13 21	13 24	13 28	13 32	13 36	13 39	13 45			13 48	13 51	13 54	13 58	14 02	14 06	14 09	14 15			14 18	14 21
Wimbledon 6	⊖ d			13 22	13 25	13 28	13 32	13 36	13 40	13 43	13 49			13 52	13 55	13 58	14 02	14 06	14 10	14 13	14 19			14 22	14 25
Raynes Park 6	d			13 25	13 28	13 31	13 35		13 43	13 46				13 55	13 58	14 01	14 05		14 13	14 16				14 25	14 28
Motspur Park	d				13 31		13 38		13 46						14 01		14 08		14 16						14 31
Malden Manor	d						13 41										14 11								
Tolworth	d						13 44										14 14								
Chessington North	d						13 47										14 17								
Chessington South	a						13 49										14 19								
Worcester Park	d				13 33				13 48						14 03				14 18						14 33
Stoneleigh	d				13 36				13 51						14 06				14 21						14 36
Ewell West	d				13 39				13 54						14 09				14 24						14 39
Epsom 3	a				13 46				13 57						14 16				14 27						14 46
	d				13 47				13 58						14 17				14 28						14 47
Ashtead	d				13 51				14 02						14 21				14 32						14 51
Leatherhead	d				13 54				14 05						14 24				14 35						14 54
Boxhill & Westhumble	d																								
Dorking 4	a								14 13										14 43						
New Malden 6	d			13 28		13 34				13 49				13 58		14 04				14 19				14 28	
Norbiton	d					13 37				13 52						14 07				14 22					
Kingston	a	13 46				13 40				13 55		14 16				14 10				14 25		14 46			
	d					13 40				13 59						14 10				14 29					
Hampton Wick	d					13 42				14 01						14 12				14 31					
Teddington	d					13 45				14 05						14 15				14 35					
Strawberry Hill	a									14 08										14 38					
Fulwell	d					13 49										14 19									
Hampton	d					13 53										14 23									
Kempton Park	d					13 56										14 26									
Sunbury	d					13 58										14 28									
Upper Halliford	d					14 00										14 30									
Shepperton	a					14 05										14 35									
Berrylands	d			13 30										14 00										14 30	
Surbiton 6	d			13 35				13a43			13 57			14 05				14a13			14 27			14 35	
Thames Ditton	d			13 39										14 09										14 39	
Hampton Court	a			13 42										14 12										14 42	
Hinchley Wood	d										14 01										14 31				
Claygate	d										14 04										14 34				
Oxshott	d										14 07										14 37				
Cobham & Stoke D'abernon	d										14 11										14 41				
Bookham	d				13 59										14 29										14 59
Effingham Junction 6	d				14 03						14 15				14 33						14 45				15 03
Horsley	d				14 06						14 18				14 36						14 48				15 06
Clandon	d				14 11						14 23				14 41						14 53				15 11
London Road (Guildford)	d				14 16						14 28				14 46						14 58				15 16
Guildford	a				14 23						14 35				14 53						15 05				15 23

		SW	SW	SW	SW	SW	SW	SW		SW	SW	SW	SW	SW	SW	SW	SW	SW		SW	SW	SW	SW	SW	SW
London Waterloo 15	⊖ d	14 12	14 16	14 20	14 24	14 27	14 33	14 33		14 36	14 39	14 42	14 46	14 50	14 54	14 57	15 03	15 03		15 06	15 09	15 12	15 16	15 20	15 24
Vauxhall	⊖ d	14 16	14 20	14 24	14 28	14 31	14 37	14 37		14 40	14 43	14 46	14 50	14 54	14 58	15 01	15 07	15 07		15 10	15 13	15 16	15 20	15 24	15 28
Clapham Junction 10	d	14 21	14 25	14 29	14 33	14 36	14 42			14 45	14 48	14 51	14 55	14 59	15 03	15 06	15 12			15 15	15 18	15 21	15 25	15 29	15 33
Earlsfield	d	14 24	14 28	14 32	14 36	14 39	14 45			14 48	14 51	14 54	14 58	15 02	15 06	15 09	15 15			15 18	15 21	15 24	15 28	15 32	15 36
Wimbledon 6	⊖ d	14 28	14 32	14 36	14 40	14 43	14 49			14 52	14 55	14 58	15 02	15 06	15 10	15 13	15 19			15 22	15 25	15 28	15 32	15 36	15 40
Raynes Park 6	d	14 31	14 35		14 43	14 46				14 55	14 58	15 01	15 05		15 13	15 16				15 25	15 28	15 31	15 35		15 43
Motspur Park	d		14 38		14 46						15 01		15 08		15 16						15 31		15 38		15 46
Malden Manor	d		14 41										15 11										15 41		
Tolworth	d		14 44										15 14										15 44		
Chessington North	d		14 47										15 17										15 47		
Chessington South	a		14 49										15 19										15 49		
Worcester Park	d				14 48						15 03				15 18						15 33				15 48
Stoneleigh	d				14 51						15 06				15 21						15 36				15 51
Ewell West	d				14 54						15 09				15 24						15 39				15 54
Epsom 3	a				14 57						15 16				15 27						15 46				15 57
	d				14 58						15 17				15 28						15 47				15 58
Ashtead	d				15 02						15 21				15 32						15 51				16 02
Leatherhead	d				15 05						15 24				15 35						15 54				16 05
Boxhill & Westhumble	d																								
Dorking 4	a				15 13										15 43										16 13
New Malden 6	d	14 34				14 49				14 58		15 04				15 19				15 28		15 34			
Norbiton	d	14 37				14 52						15 07				15 22						15 37			
Kingston	a	14 40				14 55		15 16				15 10				15 25		15 46				15 40			
	d	14 40				14 59						15 10				15 29						15 40			
Hampton Wick	d	14 42				15 01						15 12				15 31						15 42			
Teddington	d	14 45				15 05						15 15				15 35						15 45			
Strawberry Hill	a					15 08										15 38									
Fulwell	d	14 49										15 19										15 49			
Hampton	d	14 53										15 23										15 53			
Kempton Park	d	14 56										15 26										15 56			
Sunbury	d	14 58										15 28										15 58			
Upper Halliford	d	15 00										15 30										16 00			
Shepperton	a	15 05										15 35										16 05			
Berrylands	d									15 00										15 30					
Surbiton 6	d			14a43			14 57			15 05				15a13			15 27			15 35				15a43	
Thames Ditton	d									15 09										15 39					
Hampton Court	a									15 12										15 42					
Hinchley Wood	d						15 01										15 31								
Claygate	d						15 04										15 34								
Oxshott	d						15 07										15 37								
Cobham & Stoke D'abernon	d						15 11										15 41								
Bookham	d										15 29										15 59				
Effingham Junction 6	d						15 15				15 33						15 45				16 03				
Horsley	d						15 18				15 36						15 48				16 06				
Clandon	d						15 23				15 41						15 53				16 11				
London Road (Guildford)	d						15 28				15 46						15 58				16 16				
Guildford	a						15 35				15 53						16 05				16 23				

London - Chessington South, Dorking, Guildford, Shepperton and Hampton Court

from 3 October

		SW	SW	SW		SW	SW	SW	SW	SW	SW	SW	SW	SW		SW	SW	SW	SW	SW	SW	SW	SW	SW	
London Waterloo 15	⊖ d	15 27	15 33	15 33		15 36	15 39	15 42	15 46	15 50	15 54	15 57	16 01	16 03		16 06	16 09	16 12	16 16	16 20	16 24	16 27	16 31	16 33	
Vauxhall	⊖ d	15 31	15 37	15 37		15 40	15 43	15 46	15 50	15 54	15 58	16 01	16 05	16 07		16 10	16 13	16 16	16 20	16 24	16 28	16 31	16 35	16 37	
Clapham Junction 10	d	15 36	15 42			15 45	15 48	15 51	15 55	15 59	16 03	16 06		16 12		16 15	16 18	16 21	16 25	16 29	16 33	16 36		16 42	
Earlsfield	d	15 39	15 45			15 48	15 51	15 54	15 58	16 02	16 06	16 09		16 15		16 18	16 21	16 24	16 28	16 32	16 36	16 39		16 45	
Wimbledon 6	⊖ d	15 43	15 49			15 52	15 55	15 58	16 02	16 06	16 10	16 13		16 19		16 22	16 25	16 28	16 32	16 36	16 40	16 43		16 49	
Raynes Park 6	d	15 46				15 55	15 58	16 01	16 05		16 13	16 16				16 25	16 28	16 31	16 35		16 43	16 46			
Motspur Park	d						16 01		16 08		16 16						16 31		16 38		16 46				
Malden Manor	d								16 11										16 41						
Tolworth	d								16 14										16 44						
Chessington North	d								16 17										16 47						
Chessington South	a								16 19										16 51						
Worcester Park	d						16 03				16 18						16 33				16 48				
Stoneleigh	d						16 06				16 21						16 36				16 51				
Ewell West	d						16 09				16 24						16 39				16 54				
Epsom 3	a						16 15				16 27						16 46				16 57				
	d						16 17				16 28						16 47				16 58				
Ashtead	d						16 21				16 32						16 51				17 02				
Leatherhead	d						16 24				16 35						16 54				17 05				
Boxhill & Westhumble	d																				17 10				
Dorking 4	a										16 43										17 16				
New Malden 6	d	15 49				15 58		16 04				16 19				16 28		16 34				16 49			
Norbiton	d	15 52						16 07				16 22						16 37				16 52			
Kingston	a	15 55		16 16				16 10				16 25	16 48					16 40				16 55	17 18		
	d	15 59						16 10				16 29						16 40				16 59			
Hampton Wick	d	16 01						16 12				16 31						16 42				17 01			
Teddington	d	16 05						16 15				16 35						16 45				17 05			
Strawberry Hill	a	16 08										16 38										17 08			
Fulwell	d							16 19										16 49							
Hampton	d							16 23										16 53							
Kempton Park	d							16 26										16 56							
Sunbury	d							16 28										16 58							
Upper Halliford	d							16 30										17 00							
Shepperton	a							16 35										17 07							
Berrylands	d					16 00										16 30									
Surbiton 6	d		15 57			16 05				16a13				16 27		16 35				16a43				16 57	
Thames Ditton	d					16 09										16 39									
Hampton Court	a					16 12										16 44									
Hinchley Wood	d		16 01											16 31										17 01	
Claygate	d		16 04											16 34										17 04	
Oxshott	d		16 07											16 37										17 07	
Cobham & Stoke D'abernon	d		16 11											16 41										17 11	
Bookham	d						16 29										16 59								
Effingham Junction 6	d		16 15				16 33							16 45			17 03							17 15	
Horsley	d		16 18				16 36							16 48			17 06							17 18	
Clandon	d		16 23				16 41							16 53			17 11							17 23	
London Road (Guildford)	d		16 28				16 46							16 58			17 16							17 28	
Guildford	a		16 35				16 53							17 07			17 25							17 37	

London - Chessington South, Dorking, Guildford, Shepperton and Hampton Court

		SW	SW	SW	SW	SW	SW	SW	SW	SW 1	SW	SW	SW	SW	SW	SW	SW	SW	SW	SW	SW	SW 1	SW
London Waterloo 15 ⊖	d	16 36	16 39	16 42	16 46	16 50	16 54	16 57	17 01	17 02	17 02	17 06	17 09	17 12	17 13	17 16	17 20	17 24	17 27	17 30	17 31	17 32	17 32
Vauxhall ⊖	d	16 40	16 43	16 46	16 50	16 54	16 58	17 01	17 05		17 07	17 10	17 13	17 16	17 17	17 20	17 24	17 28	17 31	17 34	17 35		17 37
Clapham Junction 10	d	16 45	16 48	16 51	16 55	16 59	17 03	17 06			17 12	17 15	17 18	17 21		17 25	17 29	17 33	17 36	17 39			17 42
Earlsfield	d	16 48	16 51	16 54	16 58	17 02	17 06	17 09			17 15	17 18	17 21	17 24		17 28	17 32	17 36	17 39	17 42			17 45
Wimbledon 6 ⊖ 🚊	d	16 52	16 55	16 58	17 02	17 06	17 10	17 13			17 19	17 22	17 25	17 28		17 32	17 36	17 40	17 43	17 46			17 49
Raynes Park 6	d	16 55	16 58	17 01	17 05		17 13	17 16				17 25	17 28	17 31		17 35		17 43	17 46	17 49			
Motspur Park	d		17 01		17 08		17 16						17 31			17 38				17 52			
Malden Manor	d				17 11											17 41							
Tolworth	d				17 14											17 44							
Chessington North	d				17 17											17 47							
Chessington South	a				17 21											17 51							
Worcester Park	d		17 03				17 18						17 33					17 47		17 54			
Stoneleigh	d		17 06				17 21						17 36							17 57			
Ewell West	d		17 09				17 24						17 39							18 00			
Epsom 3	a		17 12				17 27						17 42					17 54		18 07			
	d		17 17				17 28						17 47					17 54					
Ashtead	d		17 21				17 32						17 51					17 58					
Leatherhead	d		17 24				17 35						17 54					18 01					
Boxhill & Westhumble	d						17 40											18 06					
Dorking 4	a						17 46											18 13					
New Malden 6	d	16 58		17 04				17 19				17 28		17 34					17 49				
Norbiton	d			17 07				17 22						17 37					17 52				
Kingston	a			17 10				17 25	17 48					17 40	17 56				17 55		18 18		
	d			17 10				17 29						17 40					17 59				
Hampton Wick	d			17 12				17 31						17 42					18 01				
Teddington	d			17 15				17 35						17 45					18 05				
Strawberry Hill	a							17 38											18 08				
Fulwell	d			17 19										17 49									
Hampton	d			17 23										17 53									
Kempton Park	d			17 26										17 56									
Sunbury	d			17 28										17 58									
Upper Halliford	d			17 30										18 00									
Shepperton	a			17 37										18 08									
Berrylands	d	17 00										17 30											
Surbiton 6	d	17 05				17a13				17 18	17 27	17 35					17a43					17 48	17 57
Thames Ditton	d	17 09										17 39											
Hampton Court	a	17 14										17 44											
Hinchley Wood	d										17 31												18 05
Claygate	d										17 34												18 08
Oxshott	d										17 37												18 11
Cobham & Stoke D'abernon	d										17 41												18 15
Bookham	d		17 29										17 59										
Effingham Junction 6	d		17 33								17 45		18a05										18 20
Horsley	d		17 36								17 48												18 22
Clandon	d		17 41								17 53												18 27
London Road (Guildford)	d		17 46								17 58												18 32
Guildford	a		17 55							17 56	18 07											18 29	18 41

London - Chessington South, Dorking, Guildford, Shepperton and Hampton Court

		SW	SW	SW	SW	SW	SW	SW	SW	SW	SW	SW 1	SW	SW	SW	SW	SW	SW	SW	SW	SW	SW	SW
London Waterloo 15 ⊖	d	17 36	17 39	17 43	17 42	17 46	17 50	17 54	17 57	18 00	18 01	18 02	18 02	18 06	18 09	18 13	18 12	18 16	18 20	18 24	18 27	18 30	18 31
Vauxhall ⊖	d	17 40	17 43	17 47	17 46	17 50	17 54	17 58	18 01	18 04	18 05		18 07	18 10	18 13	18 17	18 16	18 20	18 24	18 28	18 31	18 34	18 35
Clapham Junction 10	d	17 45	17 48		17 51	17 55	17 59	18 03	18 06	18 09			18 12	18 15	18 18		18 21	18 25	18 29	18 33	18 36	18 39	
Earlsfield	d	17 48	17 51		17 54	17 58	18 02	18 06	18 09	18 12			18 15	18 18	18 21		18 24	18 28	18 32	18 36	18 39	18 42	
Wimbledon 6 ⊖ 🚊	d	17 52	17 55		17 58	18 02	18 06	18 10	18 13	18 16			18 19	18 22	18 25		18 28	18 32	18 36	18 40	18 43	18 46	
Raynes Park 6	d	17 55	17 58		18 01	18 05		18 13	18 16	18 19				18 25	18 28		18 31	18 35		18 43	18 46	18 49	
Motspur Park	d		18 01			18 08				18 22					18 31			18 38				18 52	
Malden Manor	d					18 11												18 41					
Tolworth	d					18 14												18 44					
Chessington North	d					18 17												18 47					
Chessington South	a					18 21												18 51					
Worcester Park	d		18 03					18 17		18 24					18 33					18 47		18 54	
Stoneleigh	d		18 06							18 27					18 36							18 57	
Ewell West	d		18 09							18 30					18 39							19 00	
Epsom 3	a		18 15					18 24		18 35					18 46					18 54		19 07	
	d		18 17					18 24							18 47					18 54			
Ashtead	d		18 21					18 28							18 51					18 58			
Leatherhead	d		18 24					18 31							18 54					19 01			
Boxhill & Westhumble	d							18 36												19 06			
Dorking 4	a							18 43												19 13			
New Malden 6	d	17 58			18 04				18 19					18 28			18 34				18 49		
Norbiton	d				18 07				18 22								18 37				18 52		
Kingston	a				18 10				18 25		18 48						18 40				18 55		19 18
	d				18 10				18 29								18 40				18 59		
Hampton Wick	d				18 12				18 31								18 42				19 01		
Teddington	d				18 15				18 35								18 45				19 05		
Strawberry Hill	a			18 11					18 38							18 41					19 08		
Fulwell	d			18 13	18 19											18 43	18 49						
Hampton	d			18 17	18 23											18 47	18 53						
Kempton Park	d				18 26												18 56						
Sunbury	d			18 21	18 28											18 51	18 58						
Upper Halliford	d			18 23	18 30											18 53	19 00						
Shepperton	a			18 30	18 40											19 00	19 10						
Berrylands	d	18 00												18 30									
Surbiton 6	d	18 05					18a13					18a17	18 27	18 35					18a43				
Thames Ditton	d	18 09												18 39									
Hampton Court	a	18 14												18 44									
Hinchley Wood	d												18 35										
Claygate	d												18 38										
Oxshott	d												18 41										
Cobham & Stoke D'abernon	d												18 45										
Bookham	d		18 29												18 59								
Effingham Junction 6	d		18a42										18 50		19 03								
Horsley	d												18 52		19 06								
Clandon	d												18 57		19 11								
London Road (Guildford)	d												19 02		19 16								
Guildford	a												19 12		19 25								

London - Chessington South, Dorking, Guildford, Shepperton and Hampton Court

from 3 October

		SW	SW	SW	SW	SW	SW	SW	SW	SW	SW	SW	SW	SW [1]	SW	SW	SW	SW	SW	SW	SW	SW
London Waterloo [15] ⊖	d	18 32	18 36	18 39	18 43	18 42	18 46	18 48	18 50	18 54	18 57	19 00	19 01	19 02	19 02	19 06	19 09	19 12	19 16	19 20	19 23	19 24
Vauxhall ⊖	d	18 37	18 40	18 43	18 47	18 46	18 50		18 54	18 58	19 01	19 04	19 05		19 07	19 10	19 13	19 16	19 20	19 24		19 28
Clapham Junction [10]	d	18 42	18 45	18 48		18 51	18 55		18 59	19 03	19 06	19 09			19 12	19 15	19 18	19 21	19 25	19 29		19 33
Earlsfield	d	18 45	18 48	18 51		18 54	18 58		19 02	19 06	19 09	19 12			19 15	19 18	19 21	19 24	19 28	19 32		19 36
Wimbledon [6] ⊖	d	18 49	18 52	18 55		18 58	19 02		19 06	19 10	19 13	19 16			19 19	19 22	19 25	19 28	19 32	19 36		19 40
Raynes Park [6]	d		18 55	18 58		19 01	19 05			19 13	19 16	19 19				19 25	19 28	19 31	19 35			19 43
Motspur Park	d			19 01			19 08					19 22					19 31		19 38			19 46
Malden Manor	d						19 11												19 41			
Tolworth	d						19 14												19 44			
Chessington North	d						19 17												19 47			
Chessington South	a						19 21												19 49			
Worcester Park	d			19 03						19 17		19 24					19 33					19 48
Stoneleigh	d			19 06								19 27					19 36					19 51
Ewell West	d			19 09								19 30					19 39					19 54
Epsom [3]	a			19 16						19 24		19 35					19 44					19 57
	d			19 17						19 24							19 47					19 58
Ashtead	d			19 21						19 28							19 51					20 02
Leatherhead	d			19 24						19 31							19 54					20 05
Boxhill & Westhumble	d									19 36												20 10
Dorking [4]	a									19 43												20 14
New Malden [6]	d		18 58			19 04					19 19					19 28		19 34				
Norbiton	d					19 07					19 22							19 37				
Kingston	a					19 10					19 25		19 48					19 40				
	d					19 10					19 29							19 40				
Hampton Wick	d					19 12					19 31							19 42				
Teddington	d					19 15					19 35							19 45				
Strawberry Hill	a				19 11						19 38											
Fulwell	d				19 13	19 19												19 49				
Hampton	d				19 17	19 23												19 53				
Kempton Park	d					19 26												19 56				
Sunbury	d				19 21	19 28												19 58				
Upper Halliford	d				19 23	19 30												20 00				
Shepperton	a				19 30	19 39												20 06				
Berrylands	d		19 00													19 30						
Surbiton [6]	d	18 57	19 05					19 06	19a13					19a17	19 27	19 35				19a43	19a39	
Thames Ditton	d		19 09													19 39						
Hampton Court	a		19 14													19 42						
Hinchley Wood	d	19 01						19 10							19 31							
Claygate	d	19 04						19 13							19 34							
Oxshott	d	19 07						19 16							19 37							
Cobham & Stoke D'abernon	d	19 11						19 20							19 41							
Bookham	d			19 29													19 59					
Effingham Junction [6]	d	19 15		19 33				19 24							19 45		20 03					
Horsley	d	19 18		19 36				19 27							19 48		20 06					
Clandon	d	19 23		19 41				19 32							19 53		20 11					
London Road (Guildford)	d	19 28		19 46				19 37							19 58		20 16					
Guildford	a	19 37		19 55				19 46							20 05		20 23					

London - Chessington South, Dorking, Guildford, Shepperton and Hampton Court

from 3 October

		SW	SW	SW	SW	SW	SW	SW	SW	SW	SW	SW	SW	SW	SW	SW	SW	SW	SW	SW	SW	SW	SW
London Waterloo [15] ⊖	d	19 27	19 33	19 33	19 36	19 39	19 42	19 46	19 50	19 54	19 57	20 03	20 03	20 06	20 09	20 12	20 16	20 20	20 24	20 27	20 33	20 33	20 36
Vauxhall ⊖	d	19 31	19 37	19 37	19 40	19 43	19 46	19 50	19 54	19 58	20 01	20 07	20 07	20 10	20 13	20 16	20 20	20 24	20 28	20 31	20 37	20 37	20 40
Clapham Junction [10]	d	19 36	19 42		19 45	19 48	19 51	19 55	19 59	20 03	20 06	20 12		20 15	20 18	20 21	20 25	20 29	20 33	20 36	20 42		20 45
Earlsfield	d	19 39	19 45		19 48	19 51	19 54	19 58	20 02	20 06	20 09	20 15		20 18	20 21	20 24	20 28	20 32	20 36	20 39	20 45		20 48
Wimbledon [6] ⊖	d	19 43	19 49		19 52	19 55	19 58	20 02	20 06	20 10	20 13	20 19		20 22	20 25	20 28	20 32	20 36	20 40	20 43	20 49		20 52
Raynes Park [6]	d	19 46			19 55	19 58	20 01	20 05		20 13	20 16			20 25	20 28	20 31	20 35		20 43	20 46			20 55
Motspur Park	d					20 01		20 08		20 16					20 31		20 38		20 46				
Malden Manor	d							20 11									20 41						
Tolworth	d							20 14									20 44						
Chessington North	d							20 17									20 47						
Chessington South	a							20 19									20 49						
Worcester Park	d					20 03				20 18					20 33				20 48				
Stoneleigh	d					20 06				20 21					20 36				20 51				
Ewell West	d					20 09				20 24					20 39				20 54				
Epsom [3]	a					20 16				20 27					20 42				20 57				
	d					20 17									20 43								
Ashtead	d					20 21									20 47								
Leatherhead	d					20 24									20 50								
Boxhill & Westhumble	d														20 55								
Dorking [4]	a														20 59								
New Malden [6]	d	19 49			19 58		20 04				20 19			20 28		20 34				20 49			20 58
Norbiton	d	19 52					20 07				20 22					20 37				20 52			
Kingston	a	19 55		20 16			20 10				20 25		20 46			20 40				20 55		21 16	
	d	19 59					20 10				20 29					20 40				20 59			
Hampton Wick	d	20 01					20 12				20 31					20 42				21 01			
Teddington	d	20 05					20 15				20 35					20 45				21 05			
Strawberry Hill	a	20 08									20 38									21 08			
Fulwell	d						20 19									20 49							
Hampton	d						20 23									20 53							
Kempton Park	d						20 26									20 56							
Sunbury	d						20 28									20 58							
Upper Halliford	d						20 30									21 00							
Shepperton	a						20 35									21 05							
Berrylands	d				20 00									20 30									21 00
Surbiton [6]	d		19 57		20 05				20a13			20 27		20 35				20a43			20 57		21 05
Thames Ditton	d				20 09									20 39									21 09
Hampton Court	a				20 12									20 42									21 12
Hinchley Wood	d		20 01									20 31									21 01		
Claygate	d		20 04									20 34									21 04		
Oxshott	d		20 07									20 37									21 07		
Cobham & Stoke D'abernon	d		20 11									20 41									21 11		
Bookham	d					20 29																	
Effingham Junction [6]	d		20 15			20 33						20 45									21 15		
Horsley	d		20 18			20 36						20 48									21 18		
Clandon	d		20 23			20 41						20 53									21 23		
London Road (Guildford)	d		20 28			20 46						20 58									21 28		
Guildford	a		20 35			20 53						21 05									21 35		

		SW	SW	SW	SW	SW	SW	SW	SW	SW	SW	SW	SW	SW	SW	SW	SW	SW	SW	SW	SW	SW
London Waterloo [15] ⊖	d	20 39	20 42	20 46	20 50	20 54	20 57	21 03	21 03	21 09	21 12	21 20	21 24	21 27	21 33	21 33	21 36	21 39	21 42	21 46	21 50	21 54
Vauxhall ⊖	d	20 43	20 46	20 50	20 54	20 58	21 01	21 07	21 07	21 13	21 16	21 24	21 28	21 31	21 37	21 37	21 40	21 43	21 46	21 50	21 54	21 58
Clapham Junction [10]	d	20 48	20 51	20 55	20 59	21 03	21 06	21 12		21 18	21 21	21 29	21 33	21 36	21 42		21 45	21 48	21 51	21 55	21 59	22 03
Earlsfield	d	20 51	20 54	20 58	21 02	21 06	21 09	21 15		21 21	21 24	21 32	21 36	21 39	21 45		21 48	21 51	21 54	21 58	22 02	22 06
Wimbledon [6] ⊖	d	20 55	20 58	21 02	21 06	21 10	21 13	21 19		21 25	21 28	21 36	21 40	21 43	21 49		21 52	21 55	21 58	22 02	22 06	22 10
Raynes Park [6]	d	20 58	21 01	21 05		21 13	21 16			21 28	21 31		21 43	21 46			21 55	21 58	22 01	22 05		22 13
Motspur Park	d	21 01		21 08		21 16				21 31			21 46					22 01		22 08		22 16
Malden Manor	d			21 11																22 11		
Tolworth	d			21 14																22 14		
Chessington North	d			21 17																22 17		
Chessington South	a			21 19																22 19		
Worcester Park	d	21 03				21 18				21 33			21 48					22 03				22 18
Stoneleigh	d	21 06				21 21				21 36			21 51					22 06				22 21
Ewell West	d	21 09				21 24				21 39			21 54					22 09				22 24
Epsom [3]	a	21 12				21 27				21 42			21 57					22 12				22 27
	d	21 13								21 43								22 13				
Ashtead	d	21 17								21 47								22 17				
Leatherhead	d	21 20								21 50								22 20				
Boxhill & Westhumble	d									21 55												
Dorking [4]	a									21 59												
New Malden [6]	d		21 04				21 19				21 34			21 49			21 58		22 04			
Norbiton	d		21 07				21 22				21 37			21 52					22 07			
Kingston	a		21 10				21 25		21 46		21 40			21 55		22 16			22 10			
	d		21 10				21 29				21 40			21 59					22 10			
Hampton Wick	d		21 12				21 31				21 42			22 01					22 12			
Teddington	d		21 15				21 35				21 45			22 05					22 15			
Strawberry Hill	a						21 38							22 08								
Fulwell	d		21 19								21 49								22 19			
Hampton	d		21 23								21 53								22 23			
Kempton Park	d		21 26								21 56								22 26			
Sunbury	d		21 28								21 58								22 28			
Upper Halliford	d		21 30								22 00								22 30			
Shepperton	a		21 35								22 05								22 35			
Berrylands	d																22 00					
Surbiton [6]	d				21a13			21 27				21a43			21 57		22 05				22 14	
Thames Ditton	d																22 09					
Hampton Court	a																22 12					
Hinchley Wood	d							21 31							22 01							
Claygate	d							21 34							22 04							
Oxshott	d							21 37							22 07							
Cobham & Stoke D'abernon	d							21 41							22 11							
Bookham	d	21 25																22 25				
Effingham Junction [6]	d	21 29						21 45							22 15			22 29				
Horsley	d	21 32						21 48							22 18			22 32				
Clandon	d	21 37						21 53							22 23			22 37				
London Road (Guildford)	d	21 42						21 58							22 28			22 42				
Guildford	a	21 49						22 05							22 35			22 49			22 47	

Table 152

Mondays to Fridays
from 3 October

London - Chessington South, Dorking, Guildford, Shepperton and Hampton Court

		SW	SW	SW	SW	SW	SW	SW	SW	SW	SW	SW	SW	SW	SW	SW	SW	SW	SW	SW	SW	SW	SW
London Waterloo 15 ⊖	d	21 57	22 03	22 03	22 09	22 12	22 20	22 27	22 33	22 33	22 36	22 39	22 42	22 50	22 57	23 00	23 03	23 03	23 09	23 12	23 20	23 27	23 33
Vauxhall ⊖	d	22 01	22 07	22 07	22 13	22 16	22 24	22 31	22 37	22 37	22 40	22 43	22 46	22 54	23 01	23 04	23 07	23 07	23 13	23 16	23 24	23 31	23 37
Clapham Junction 10	d	22 06	22 12		22 18	22 21	22 29	22 36	22 42		22 45	22 48	22 51	22 59	23 06	23 09	23 12		23 18	23 21	23 29	23 36	
Earlsfield	d	22 09	22 15		22 21	22 24	22 32	22 39	22 45		22 48	22 51	22 54	23 02	23 09	23 12	23 15		23 21	23 24	23 32	23 39	
Wimbledon 6 ⊖	d	22 13	22 19		22 25	22 28	22 36	22 43	22 49		22 52	22 55	22 58	23 06	23 13	23 16	23 19		23 25	23 28	23 36	23 43	
Raynes Park 6	d	22 16			22 28	22 31		22 46			22 55	22 58	23 01		23 16	23 19			23 28	23 31		23 46	
Motspur Park	d				22 31							23 01				23 22			23 31				
Malden Manor	d															23 25							
Tolworth	d															23 28							
Chessington North	d															23 31							
Chessington South	a															23 33							
Worcester Park	d				22 33							23 03							23 33				
Stoneleigh	d				22 36							23 06							23 36				
Ewell West	d				22 39							23 09							23 39				
Epsom 3	a				22 42							23 12							23 42				
	d				22 43							23 13							23 43				
Ashtead	d				22 47							23 17							23 47				
Leatherhead	d				22 50							23 20							23 50				
Boxhill & Westhumble	d				22 55														23 55				
Dorking 4	a				22 59														23 59				
New Malden 6	d	22 19				22 34		22 49			22 58		23 04		23 19					23 34		23 49	
Norbiton	d	22 22				22 37		22 52					23 07		23 22					23 37		23 52	
Kingston	a	22 25		22 46		22 40		22 55		23 16			23 10		23 25			23 46		23 40		23 55	00 16
	d	22 29				22 40		22 59					23 10		23 29					23 40		23 55	
Hampton Wick	d	22 31				22 42		23 01					23 12		23 31					23 42		23 57	
Teddington	d	22 35				22 45		23 05					23 15		23 35					23 45		23 59	
Strawberry Hill	a	22 38						23 08							23 38							00 03	
Fulwell	d					22 49							23 19							23 49			
Hampton	d					22 53							23 23							23 53			
Kempton Park	d					22 56							23 26							23 56			
Sunbury	d					22 58							23 28							23 58			
Upper Halliford	d					23 00							23 30							23 59			
Shepperton	a					23 05							23 35							00 05			
Berrylands	d										23 00												
Surbiton 6	d		22 27				22a43		22 57		23 05			23a13			23 27				23a43		
Thames Ditton	d										23 09												
Hampton Court	a										23 12												
Hinchley Wood	d		22 31						23 01								23 31						
Claygate	d		22 34						23 04								23 34						
Oxshott	d		22 37						23 07								23 37						
Cobham & Stoke D'abernon	d		22 41						23 11								23 41						
Bookham	d											23 25											
Effingham Junction 6	d		22 45						23 15			23 29					23 45						
Horsley	d		22 48						23 18			23 32					23 48						
Clandon	d		22 53						23 23			23 37					23 53						
London Road (Guildford)	d		22 58						23 28			23 42					23 58						
Guildford	a		23 05						23 35			23 49					00 05						

		SW	SW	SW	SW
London Waterloo 15 ⊖	d	23 36	23 42	23 50	23 57
Vauxhall ⊖	d	23 40	23 46	23 54	00 01
Clapham Junction 10	d	23 45	23 51	23 59	00 06
Earlsfield	d	23 48	23 54	00 02	00 09
Wimbledon 6 ⊖	d	23 52	23 58	00 06	00 13
Raynes Park 6	d	23 55	00 01		00 16
Motspur Park	d		00 04		
Malden Manor	d				
Tolworth	d				
Chessington North	d				
Chessington South	a				
Worcester Park	d		00 06		
Stoneleigh	d		00 09		
Ewell West	d		00 12		
Epsom 3	a		00 15		
	d		00 19		
Ashtead	d		00 23		
Leatherhead	d		00 26		
Boxhill & Westhumble	d				
Dorking 4	a				
New Malden 6	d	23 58			00 19
Norbiton	d				00 22
Kingston	a				00 25
	d				00 25
Hampton Wick	d				00 27
Teddington	d				00 30
Strawberry Hill	a				
Fulwell	d				00 34
Hampton	d				00 38
Kempton Park	d				00 41
Sunbury	d				00 43
Upper Halliford	d				00 45
Shepperton	a				00 50
Berrylands	d	23 59			
Surbiton 6	d	00 05		00 14	
Thames Ditton	d	00 09			
Hampton Court	a	00 12			
Hinchley Wood	d			00 18	
Claygate	d			00 20	
Oxshott	d			00 24	
Cobham & Stoke D'abernon	d			00 27	
Bookham	d		00 31		
Effingham Junction 6	d		00 36	00 32	
Horsley	d		00 39	00 34	
Clandon	d		00 44	00 39	
London Road (Guildford)	d		00 49	00 44	

Table 152

Saturdays
until 1 October

London - Chessington South, Dorking, Guildford, Shepperton and Hampton Court

		SW	SW	SW	SW	SW	SW	SW	SW	SW	SW	SW	SW	SW	SW	SW	SW	SW	SW	SW	SW	SW	SW
															1		1						
London Waterloo 15 ⊖	d	23p03	23p12	23p27	23p33	23p36	23p42	23p50	23p57	00 09	00 15	00 18	00 27	00 42	05 00	05 12	05 20	05 33	05 50	06 03	06 06	06 12	06 16
Vauxhall ⊖	d	23p07	23p16	23p31	23p37	23p40	23p46	23p54	00 01	00 13	00 19	00 22	00 31	00 46	05 04	05 16	05 24	05 37	05 54	06 07	06 10	06 16	06 20
Clapham Junction 10	d	23p12	23p21	23p36		23p45	23p51	23p59	00 06	00 20	00 25		00 37	00 51	05 11	05 21	05 29		05 59		06 15	06 21	06 25
Earlsfield	d	23p15	23p24	23p39		23p48	23p54	00 02	00 09	00 23	00 29		00s41		05 14	05 24	05 32		06 02		06 18	06 24	06 28
Wimbledon 6 ⊖	d	23p19	23p28	23p43		23p52	23p58	00 06	00 13	00 27	00 33		00 45	01b05	05 18	05 28	05 36		06 06		06 22	06 28	06 32
Raynes Park 6	d		23p31	23p46		23p55	00 01		00 16		00 36		00 48	01 08		05 31					06 25	06 31	06 35
Motspur Park	d						00 04				00 38												06 38
Malden Manor	d																						06 41
Tolworth	d																						06 44
Chessington North	d																						06 47
Chessington South	a																						06 49
Worcester Park	d						00 06				00 41												
Stoneleigh	d						00 09				00 44												
Ewell West	d						00 12				00 46												
Epsom 3	a						00 15				00 50												
	d						00 19																
Ashtead	d						00 23																
Leatherhead	d						00 26																
Boxhill & Westhumble	d																						
Dorking 4	a																						
New Malden 6	d		23p34	23p49		23p58			00 19				00 50	01 11		05 34					06 28	06 34	
Norbiton	d		23p37	23p52					00 22					01 14		05 37						06 37	
Kingston	a		23p40	23p55	00 16				00 25			01 01		01 17		05 40		06 16		06 46		06 40	
	d		23p40	23p55					00 25					01 17		05 40						06 40	
Hampton Wick	d		23p42	23p57					00 27					01s19		05 42						06 42	
Teddington	d		23p45	23p59					00 30					01s22		05 45						06 45	
Strawberry Hill	a			00 03										01 28									
Fulwell	d		23p49						00 34							05 49						06 49	
Hampton	d		23p53						00 38							05 53						06 53	
Kempton Park	d		23p56						00 41							05 56						06 56	
Sunbury	d		23p58						00 43							05 58						06 58	
Upper Halliford	d		23p59						00 45							06 00						07 00	
Shepperton	a		00 03						00 48							06 03						07 03	
Berrylands	d					23p59							00s53								06 30		
Surbiton 6	d	23p27				00 05		00 14		00 35			00a56		05 26		05 44		06a13		06 35		
Thames Ditton	d					00 09															06 39		
Hampton Court	a					00 12															06 42		
Hinchley Wood	d	23p31						00 18															
Claygate	d	23p34						00 20															
Oxshott	d	23p37						00 24															
Cobham & Stoke D'abernon	d	23p41						00 27															
Bookham	d						00 31																
Effingham Junction 6	d	23p45					00 36	00 32															
Horsley	d	23p48					00 39	00 34															
Clandon	d	23p53					00 44	00 39															
London Road (Guildford)	d	23p58					00 49	00 44															
Guildford	a	00 02					00 53	00 48		01 07					06 00		06 23						

b Arr. 0056

London - Chessington South, Dorking, Guildford, Shepperton and Hampton Court

		SW	SW	SW	SW	SW	SW	SW	SW	SW	SW	SW	SW	SW	SW	SW	SW	SW	SW	SW	SW	SW	SW
London Waterloo 15 ⊖	d	06 20	06 27	06 33	06 33	06 36	06 39	06 42	06 46	06 50	06 57	07 03	07 03	07 06	07 09	07 12	07 16	07 20	07 24	07 27	07 33	07 33	07 36
Vauxhall ⊖	d	06 24	06 31	06 37	06 37	06 40	06 43	06 46	06 50	06 54	07 01	07 07	07 07	07 10	07 13	07 16	07 20	07 24	07 28	07 31	07 37	07 37	07 40
Clapham Junction 10	d	06 29	06 36	06 42		06 45	06 48	06 51	06 55	06 59	07 06	07 12		07 15	07 18	07 21	07 25	07 29	07 33	07 36	07 42		07 45
Earlsfield	d	06 32	06 39	06 45		06 48	06 51	06 54	06 58	07 02	07 09	07 15		07 18	07 21	07 24	07 28	07 32	07 36	07 39	07 45		07 48
Wimbledon 6 ⊖	d	06 36	06 43	06 49		06 52	06 55	06 58	07 02	07 06	07 13	07 19		07 22	07 25	07 28	07 32	07 36	07 40	07 43	07 49		07 52
Raynes Park 6	d		06 46			06 55	06 58	07 01	07 05		07 16			07 25	07 28	07 31	07 35		07 43	07 46			07 55
Motspur Park	d						07 01		07 08						07 31		07 38		07 46				
Malden Manor	d								07 11								07 41						
Tolworth	d								07 14								07 44						
Chessington North	d								07 17								07 47						
Chessington South	a								07 19								07 49						
Worcester Park	d						07 03								07 33				07 48				
Stoneleigh	d						07 06								07 36				07 51				
Ewell West	d						07 09								07 39				07 54				
Epsom 3	a						07 16								07 46				07 57				
	d						07 17								07 47				07 58				
Ashtead	d						07 21								07 51				08 02				
Leatherhead	d						07 24								07 54				08 05				
Boxhill & Westhumble	d																						
Dorking 4	a																		08 11				
New Malden 6	d		06 49			06 58		07 04			07 19			07 28		07 34				07 49			07 58
Norbiton	d		06 52					07 07			07 22					07 37				07 52			
Kingston	a		06 55		07 16			07 10			07 25		07 46			07 40				07 55		08 16	
	d		06 59					07 10			07 29					07 40				07 59			
Hampton Wick	d		07 01					07 12			07 31					07 42				08 01			
Teddington	d		07 05					07 15			07 35					07 45				08 05			
Strawberry Hill	a		07 08								07 38									08 08			
Fulwell	d							07 19								07 49							
Hampton	d							07 23								07 53							
Kempton Park	d							07 26								07 56							
Sunbury	d							07 28								07 58							
Upper Halliford	d							07 30								08 00							
Shepperton	a							07 33								08 03							
Berrylands	d					07 00								07 30									08 00
Surbiton 6	d	06a43		06 57		07 05				07a13		07 27		07 35				07a43			07 57		08 05
Thames Ditton	d					07 09								07 39									08 09
Hampton Court	a					07 12								07 42									08 12
Hinchley Wood	d			07 01								07 31									08 01		
Claygate	d			07 04								07 34									08 04		
Oxshott	d			07 07								07 37									08 07		
Cobham & Stoke D'abernon	d			07 11								07 41									08 11		
Bookham	d						07 29								07 59								
Effingham Junction 6	d			07 15			07 33					07 45			08 03						08 15		
Horsley	d			07 18			07 36					07 48			08 06						08 18		
Clandon	d			07 23			07 41					07 53			08 11						08 23		
London Road (Guildford)	d			07 28			07 46					07 58			08 16						08 28		
Guildford	a			07 32			07 50					08 02			08 20						08 32		

		SW	SW	SW	SW	SW	SW	SW	SW	SW	SW	SW	SW	SW	SW	SW	SW	SW	SW	SW	SW	SW
London Waterloo 15 ⊖	d	07 39	07 42	07 46	07 50	07 54	07 57	08 03	08 03	08 06	08 09	08 12	08 16	08 20	08 24	08 27	08 33	08 33	08 36	08 39	08 42	08 46
Vauxhall ⊖	d	07 43	07 46	07 50	07 54	07 58	08 01	08 07	08 07	08 10	08 13	08 16	08 20	08 24	08 28	08 31	08 37	08 37	08 40	08 43	08 46	08 50
Clapham Junction 10	d	07 48	07 51	07 55	07 59	08 03	08 06	08 12		08 15	08 18	08 21	08 25	08 29	08 33	08 36	08 42		08 45	08 48	08 51	08 55
Earlsfield	d	07 51	07 54	07 58	08 02	08 06	08 09	08 15		08 18	08 21	08 24	08 28	08 32	08 36	08 39	08 45		08 48	08 51	08 54	08 58
Wimbledon 6 ⊖	d	07 55	07 58	08 02	08 06	08 10	08 13	08 19		08 22	08 25	08 28	08 32	08 36	08 40	08 43	08 49		08 52	08 55	08 58	09 02
Raynes Park 6	d	07 58	08 01	08 05		08 13	08 16			08 25	08 28	08 31	08 35		08 43	08 46			08 55	08 58	09 01	09 05
Motspur Park	d	08 01		08 08		08 16					08 31		08 38		08 46					09 01		09 08
Malden Manor	d			08 11									08 41									09 11
Tolworth	d			08 14									08 44									09 14
Chessington North	d			08 17									08 47									09 17
Chessington South	a			08 19									08 49									09 19
Worcester Park	d	08 03				08 18					08 33				08 48					09 03		
Stoneleigh	d	08 06				08 21					08 36				08 51					09 06		
Ewell West	d	08 09				08 24					08 39				08 54					09 09		
Epsom 3	a	08 16				08 27					08 46				08 57					09 16		
	d	08 17				08 28					08 47				08 58					09 17		
Ashtead	d	08 21				08 32					08 51				09 02					09 21		
Leatherhead	d	08 24				08 35					08 54				09 05					09 24		
Boxhill & Westhumble	d																					
Dorking 4	a					08 41									09 11							
New Malden 6	d		08 04				08 19			08 28		08 34				08 49			08 58		09 04	
Norbiton	d		08 07				08 22					08 37				08 52					09 07	
Kingston	a		08 10				08 25		08 46			08 40				08 55		09 16			09 10	
	d		08 10				08 29					08 40				08 59					09 10	
Hampton Wick	d		08 12				08 31					08 42				09 01					09 12	
Teddington	d		08 15				08 35					08 45				09 05					09 15	
Strawberry Hill	a						08 38									09 08						
Fulwell	d		08 19									08 49									09 19	
Hampton	d		08 23									08 53									09 23	
Kempton Park	d		08 26									08 56									09 26	
Sunbury	d		08 28									08 58									09 28	
Upper Halliford	d		08 30									09 00									09 30	
Shepperton	a		08 33									09 03									09 33	
Berrylands	d									08 30									09 00			
Surbiton 6	d				08a13			08 27		08 35				08a43			08 57		09 05			
Thames Ditton	d									08 39									09 09			
Hampton Court	a									08 42									09 12			
Hinchley Wood	d							08 31									09 01					
Claygate	d							08 34									09 04					
Oxshott	d							08 37									09 07					
Cobham & Stoke D'abernon	d							08 41									09 11					
Bookham	d	08 29									08 59									09 29		
Effingham Junction 6	d	08 33						08 45			09 03						09 15			09 33		
Horsley	d	08 36						08 48			09 06						09 18			09 36		
Clandon	d	08 41						08 53			09 11						09 23			09 41		
London Road (Guildford)	d	08 46						08 58			09 16						09 28			09 46		
Guildford	a	08 50						09 02			09 20						09 32			09 50		

London - Chessington South, Dorking, Guildford, Shepperton and Hampton Court

		SW	SW	SW	SW	SW	SW	SW	SW	SW	SW	SW	SW	SW	SW	SW	SW	SW	SW	SW	SW	SW	SW
London Waterloo 15 ⊖	d	08 50	08 54	08 57	09 03	09 03	09 06	09 09	09 12	09 16	09 20	09 24	09 27	09 33	09 33	09 36	09 39	09 42	09 46	09 50	09 54	09 57	10 03
Vauxhall ⊖	d	08 54	08 58	09 01	09 07	09 07	09 10	09 13	09 16	09 20	09 24	09 28	09 31	09 37	09 37	09 40	09 43	09 46	09 50	09 54	09 58	10 01	10 07
Clapham Junction 10	d	08 59	09 03	09 06	09 12		09 15	09 18	09 21	09 25	09 29	09 33	09 36	09 42		09 45	09 48	09 51	09 55	09 59	10 03	10 06	10 12
Earlsfield	d	09 02	09 06	09 09	09 15		09 18	09 21	09 24	09 28	09 32	09 36	09 39	09 45		09 48	09 51	09 54	09 58	10 02	10 06	10 09	10 15
Wimbledon 6 ⊖	d	09 06	09 10	09 13	09 19		09 22	09 25	09 28	09 32	09 36	09 40	09 43	09 49		09 52	09 55	09 58	10 02	10 06	10 10	10 13	10 19
Raynes Park 6	d		09 13	09 16			09 25	09 28	09 31	09 35		09 43	09 46			09 55	09 58	10 01	10 05		10 13	10 16	
Motspur Park	d		09 16					09 31		09 38		09 46					10 01		10 08		10 16		
Malden Manor	d									09 41									10 11				
Tolworth	d									09 44									10 14				
Chessington North	d									09 47									10 17				
Chessington South	a									09 49									10 19				
Worcester Park	d		09 18					09 33				09 48					10 03				10 18		
Stoneleigh	d		09 21					09 36				09 51					10 06				10 21		
Ewell West	d		09 24					09 39				09 54					10 09				10 24		
Epsom 3	a		09 27					09 46				09 57					10 16				10 27		
	d		09 28					09 47				09 58					10 17				10 28		
Ashtead	d		09 32					09 51				10 02					10 21				10 32		
Leatherhead	d		09 35					09 54				10 05					10 24				10 35		
Boxhill & Westhumble	d																						
Dorking 4	a		09 41									10 11									10 41		
New Malden 6	d			09 19			09 28		09 34				09 49			09 58		10 04				10 19	
Norbiton	d			09 22					09 37				09 52					10 07				10 22	
Kingston	a			09 25		09 46			09 40				09 55		10 16			10 10				10 25	
	d			09 29					09 40				09 59					10 10				10 29	
Hampton Wick	d			09 31					09 42				10 01					10 12				10 31	
Teddington	d			09 35					09 45				10 05					10 15				10 35	
Strawberry Hill	a			09 38									10 08									10 38	
Fulwell	d								09 49									10 19					
Hampton	d								09 53									10 23					
Kempton Park	d								09 56									10 26					
Sunbury	d								09 58									10 28					
Upper Halliford	d								10 00									10 30					
Shepperton	a								10 03									10 33					
Berrylands	d						09 30									10 00							
Surbiton 6	d	09a13			09 27		09 35				09a43			09 57		10 05				10a13			10 27
Thames Ditton	d						09 39									10 09							
Hampton Court	a						09 42									10 12							
Hinchley Wood	d				09 31									10 01									10 31
Claygate	d				09 34									10 04									10 34
Oxshott	d				09 37									10 07									10 37
Cobham & Stoke D'abernon	d				09 41									10 11									10 41
Bookham	d							09 59									10 29						
Effingham Junction 6	d				09 45			10 03						10 15			10 33						10 45
Horsley	d				09 48			10 06						10 18			10 36						10 48
Clandon	d				09 53			10 11						10 23			10 41						10 53
London Road (Guildford)	d				09 58			10 16						10 28			10 46						10 58
Guildford	a				10 02			10 20						10 32			10 50						11 02

		SW	SW	SW	SW	SW	SW	SW	SW	SW	SW	SW	SW	SW	SW	SW	SW	SW	SW	SW	SW	SW
London Waterloo 15 ⊖	d	10 03	10 06	10 09	10 12	10 16	10 20	10 24	10 27	10 33	10 33	10 36	10 39	10 42	10 46	10 50	10 54	10 57	11 03	11 03	11 06	11 09
Vauxhall ⊖	d	10 07	10 10	10 13	10 16	10 20	10 24	10 28	10 31	10 37	10 37	10 40	10 43	10 46	10 50	10 54	10 58	11 01	11 07	11 07	11 10	11 13
Clapham Junction 10	d		10 15	10 18	10 21	10 25	10 29	10 33	10 36	10 42		10 45	10 48	10 51	10 55	10 59	11 03	11 06	11 12		11 15	11 18
Earlsfield	d		10 18	10 21	10 24	10 28	10 32	10 36	10 39	10 45		10 48	10 51	10 54	10 58	11 02	11 06	11 09	11 15		11 18	11 21
Wimbledon 6 ⊖	d		10 22	10 25	10 28	10 32	10 36	10 40	10 43	10 49		10 52	10 55	10 58	11 02	11 06	11 10	11 13	11 19		11 22	11 25
Raynes Park 6	d		10 25	10 28	10 31	10 35		10 43	10 46			10 55	10 58	11 01	11 05		11 13	11 16			11 25	11 28
Motspur Park	d			10 31		10 38		10 46					11 01		11 08		11 16					11 31
Malden Manor	d					10 41									11 11							
Tolworth	d					10 44									11 14							
Chessington North	d					10 47									11 17							
Chessington South	a					10 49									11 19							
Worcester Park	d			10 33				10 48					11 03				11 18					11 33
Stoneleigh	d			10 36				10 51					11 06				11 21					11 36
Ewell West	d			10 39				10 54					11 09				11 24					11 39
Epsom 3	a			10 46				10 57					11 16				11 27					11 46
	d			10 47				10 58					11 17				11 28					11 47
Ashtead	d			10 51				11 02					11 21				11 32					11 51
Leatherhead	d			10 54				11 05					11 24				11 35					11 54
Boxhill & Westhumble	d																					
Dorking 4	a							11 11									11 41					
New Malden 6	d		10 28		10 34				10 49			10 58		11 04				11 19			11 28	
Norbiton	d				10 37				10 52					11 07				11 22				
Kingston	a	10 46			10 40				10 55		11 16			11 10				11 25		11 46		
	d				10 40				10 59					11 10				11 29				
Hampton Wick	d				10 42				11 01					11 12				11 31				
Teddington	d				10 45				11 05					11 15				11 35				
Strawberry Hill	a								11 08									11 38				
Fulwell	d				10 49									11 19								
Hampton	d				10 53									11 23								
Kempton Park	d				10 56									11 26								
Sunbury	d				10 58									11 28								
Upper Halliford	d				11 00									11 30								
Shepperton	a				11 03									11 33								
Berrylands	d		10 30									11 00									11 30	
Surbiton 6	d		10 35				10a43			10 57		11 05				11a13			11 27		11 35	
Thames Ditton	d		10 39									11 09									11 39	
Hampton Court	a		10 42									11 12									11 42	
Hinchley Wood	d									11 01									11 31			
Claygate	d									11 04									11 34			
Oxshott	d									11 07									11 37			
Cobham & Stoke D'abernon	d									11 11									11 41			
Bookham	d			10 59									11 29									11 59
Effingham Junction 6	d			11 03						11 15			11 33						11 45			12 03
Horsley	d			11 06						11 18			11 36						11 48			12 06
Clandon	d			11 11						11 23			11 41						11 53			12 11
London Road (Guildford)	d			11 16						11 28			11 46						11 58			12 16
Guildford	a			11 20						11 32			11 50						12 02			12 20

Table 152

Saturdays
until 1 October

London - Chessington South, Dorking, Guildford, Shepperton and Hampton Court

Station		SW	SW	SW	SW	SW	SW	SW	SW	SW	SW	SW	SW	SW	SW	SW	SW	SW	SW	SW	SW	SW	SW
London Waterloo ⊖	d	11 12	11 16	11 20	11 24	11 27	11 33	11 33	11 36	11 39	11 42	11 46	11 50	11 54	11 57	12 03	12 03	12 06	12 09	12 12	12 16	12 20	12 24
Vauxhall ⊖	d	11 16	11 20	11 24	11 28	11 31	11 37	11 37	11 40	11 43	11 46	11 50	11 54	11 58	12 01	12 07	12 07	12 10	12 13	12 16	12 20	12 24	12 28
Clapham Junction	d	11 21	11 25	11 29	11 33	11 36	11 42		11 45	11 48	11 51	11 55	11 59	12 03	12 06	12 12		12 15	12 18	12 21	12 25	12 29	12 33
Earlsfield	d	11 24	11 28	11 32	11 36	11 39	11 45		11 48	11 51	11 54	11 58	12 02	12 06	12 09	12 15		12 18	12 21	12 24	12 28	12 32	12 36
Wimbledon ⊖	d	11 28	11 32	11 36	11 40	11 43	11 49		11 52	11 55	11 58	12 02	12 06	12 10	12 13	12 19		12 22	12 25	12 28	12 32	12 36	12 40
Raynes Park	d	11 31	11 35		11 43	11 46			11 55	11 58	12 01	12 05		12 13	12 16			12 25	12 28	12 31	12 35		12 43
Motspur Park	d		11 38		11 46					12 01		12 08		12 16					12 31		12 38		12 46
Malden Manor	d		11 41									12 11									12 41		
Tolworth	d		11 44									12 14									12 44		
Chessington North	d		11 47									12 17									12 47		
Chessington South	a		11 49									12 19									12 49		
Worcester Park	d				11 48					12 03				12 18					12 33				12 48
Stoneleigh	d				11 51					12 06				12 21					12 36				12 51
Ewell West	d				11 54					12 09				12 24					12 39				12 54
Epsom	a				11 57					12 16				12 27					12 46				12 57
	d				11 58					12 17				12 28					12 47				12 58
Ashtead	d				12 02					12 21				12 32					12 51				13 02
Leatherhead	d				12 05					12 24				12 35					12 54				13 05
Boxhill & Westhumble	d																						
Dorking	a				12 11									12 41									13 11
New Malden	d	11 34				11 49			11 58		12 04				12 19			12 28		12 34			
Norbiton	d	11 37				11 52					12 07				12 22					12 37			
Kingston	a	11 40				11 55		12 16			12 10				12 25		12 46			12 40			
	d	11 40				11 59					12 10				12 29					12 40			
Hampton Wick	d	11 42				12 01					12 12				12 31					12 42			
Teddington	d	11 45				12 05					12 15				12 35					12 45			
Strawberry Hill	a					12 08									12 38								
Fulwell	d	11 49									12 19									12 49			
Hampton	d	11 53									12 23									12 53			
Kempton Park	d	11 56									12 26									12 56			
Sunbury	d	11 58									12 28									12 58			
Upper Halliford	d	12 00									12 30									13 00			
Shepperton	a	12 03									12 33									13 03			
Berrylands	d								12 00									12 30					
Surbiton	d			11a43			11 57		12 05				12a13			12 27		12 35				12a43	
Thames Ditton	d								12 09									12 39					
Hampton Court	a								12 12									12 42					
Hinchley Wood	d						12 01									12 31							
Claygate	d						12 04									12 34							
Oxshott	d						12 07									12 37							
Cobham & Stoke D'abernon	d						12 11									12 41							
Bookham	d									12 29									12 59				
Effingham Junction	d						12 15			12 33						12 45			13 03				
Horsley	d						12 18			12 36						12 48			13 06				
Clandon	d						12 23			12 41						12 53			13 11				
London Road (Guildford)	d						12 28			12 46						12 58			13 16				
Guildford	a						12 32			12 50						13 02			13 20				

Station		SW	SW	SW	SW	SW	SW	SW	SW	SW	SW	SW	SW	SW	SW	SW	SW	SW	SW	SW	SW	SW	SW
London Waterloo ⊖	d	12 27	12 33	12 33	12 36	12 39	12 42	12 46	12 50	12 54	12 57	13 03	13 03	13 06	13 09	13 12	13 16	13 20	13 24	13 27	13 33	13 33	13 36
Vauxhall ⊖	d	12 31	12 37	12 37	12 40	12 43	12 46	12 50	12 54	12 58	13 01	13 07	13 07	13 10	13 13	13 16	13 20	13 24	13 28	13 31	13 37	13 37	13 40
Clapham Junction	d	12 36	12 42		12 45	12 48	12 51	12 55	12 59	13 03	13 06	13 12		13 15	13 18	13 21	13 25	13 29	13 33	13 36	13 42		13 45
Earlsfield	d	12 39	12 45		12 48	12 51	12 54	12 58	13 02	13 06	13 09	13 15		13 18	13 21	13 24	13 28	13 32	13 36	13 39	13 45		13 48
Wimbledon ⊖	d	12 43	12 49		12 52	12 55	12 58	13 02	13 06	13 10	13 13	13 19		13 22	13 25	13 28	13 32	13 36	13 40	13 43	13 49		13 52
Raynes Park	d	12 46			12 55	12 58	13 01	13 05		13 13	13 16			13 25	13 28	13 31	13 35		13 43	13 46			13 55
Motspur Park	d					13 01		13 08		13 16					13 31		13 38		13 46				
Malden Manor	d							13 11									13 41						
Tolworth	d							13 14									13 44						
Chessington North	d							13 17									13 47						
Chessington South	a							13 19									13 49						
Worcester Park	d					13 03				13 18					13 33				13 48				
Stoneleigh	d					13 06				13 21					13 36				13 51				
Ewell West	d					13 09				13 24					13 39				13 54				
Epsom	a					13 16				13 27					13 46				13 57				
	d					13 17				13 28					13 47				13 58				
Ashtead	d					13 21				13 32					13 51				14 02				
Leatherhead	d					13 24				13 35					13 54				14 05				
Boxhill & Westhumble	d																						
Dorking	a									13 41									14 11				
New Malden	d	12 49			12 58		13 04				13 19			13 28		13 34				13 49			13 58
Norbiton	d	12 52					13 07				13 22					13 37				13 52			
Kingston	a	12 55		13 16			13 10				13 25		13 46			13 40				13 55		14 16	
	d	12 59					13 10				13 29					13 40				13 59			
Hampton Wick	d	13 01					13 12				13 31					13 42				14 01			
Teddington	d	13 05					13 15				13 35					13 45				14 05			
Strawberry Hill	a	13 08									13 38									14 08			
Fulwell	d						13 19									13 49							
Hampton	d						13 23									13 53							
Kempton Park	d						13 26									13 56							
Sunbury	d						13 28									13 58							
Upper Halliford	d						13 30									14 00							
Shepperton	a						13 33									14 03							
Berrylands	d				13 00									13 30									14 00
Surbiton	d		12 57		13 05				13a13			13 27		13 35				13a43			13 57		14 05
Thames Ditton	d				13 09									13 39									14 09
Hampton Court	a				13 12									13 42									14 12
Hinchley Wood	d		13 01									13 31									14 01		
Claygate	d		13 04									13 34									14 04		
Oxshott	d		13 07									13 37									14 07		
Cobham & Stoke D'abernon	d		13 11									13 41									14 11		
Bookham	d					13 29									13 59								
Effingham Junction	d		13 15			13 33						13 45			14 03						14 15		
Horsley	d		13 18			13 36						13 48			14 06						14 18		
Clandon	d		13 23			13 41						13 53			14 11						14 23		
London Road (Guildford)	d		13 28			13 46						13 58			14 16						14 28		

Table 152

Saturdays
until 1 October

London - Chessington South, Dorking, Guildford, Shepperton and Hampton Court

Station		SW	SW	SW	SW	SW	SW	SW	SW	SW	SW	SW	SW	SW	SW	SW	SW	SW	SW	SW	SW	SW
London Waterloo ⊖	d	13 39	13 42	13 46	13 50	13 54	13 57	14 03	14 03	14 06	14 09	14 12	14 16	14 20	14 24	14 27	14 33	14 33	14 36	14 39	14 42	14 46
Vauxhall ⊖	d	13 43	13 46	13 50	13 54	13 58	14 01	14 07	14 07	14 10	14 13	14 16	14 20	14 24	14 28	14 31	14 37	14 37	14 40	14 43	14 46	14 50
Clapham Junction	d	13 48	13 51	13 55	13 59	14 03	14 06	14 12		14 15	14 18	14 21	14 25	14 29	14 33	14 36	14 42		14 45	14 48	14 51	14 55
Earlsfield	d	13 51	13 54	13 58	14 02	14 06	14 09	14 15		14 18	14 21	14 24	14 28	14 32	14 36	14 39	14 45		14 48	14 51	14 54	14 58
Wimbledon ⊖	d	13 55	13 58	14 02	14 06	14 10	14 13	14 19		14 22	14 25	14 28	14 32	14 36	14 40	14 43	14 49		14 52	14 55	14 58	15 02
Raynes Park	d	13 58	14 01	14 05		14 13	14 16			14 25	14 28	14 31	14 35		14 43	14 46			14 55	14 58	15 01	15 05
Motspur Park	d	14 01		14 08		14 16					14 31		14 38		14 46					15 01		15 08
Malden Manor	d			14 11									14 41									15 11
Tolworth	d			14 14									14 44									15 14
Chessington North	d			14 17									14 47									15 17
Chessington South	a			14 19									14 49									15 19
Worcester Park	d	14 03				14 18					14 33				14 48					15 03		
Stoneleigh	d	14 06				14 21					14 36				14 51					15 06		
Ewell West	d	14 09				14 24					14 39				14 54					15 09		
Epsom	a	14 16				14 27					14 46				14 57					15 16		
	d	14 17				14 28					14 47				14 58					15 17		
Ashtead	d	14 21				14 32					14 51				15 02					15 21		
Leatherhead	d	14 24				14 35					14 54				15 05					15 24		
Boxhill & Westhumble	d																					
Dorking	a					14 41									15 11							
New Malden	d		14 04				14 19			14 28		14 34				14 49			14 58		15 04	
Norbiton	d		14 07				14 22					14 37				14 52					15 07	
Kingston	a		14 10				14 25		14 46			14 40				14 55		15 16			15 10	
	d		14 10				14 29					14 40				14 59					15 10	
Hampton Wick	d		14 12				14 31					14 42				15 01					15 12	
Teddington	d		14 15				14 35					14 45				15 05					15 15	
Strawberry Hill	a						14 38									15 08						
Fulwell	d		14 19									14 49									15 19	
Hampton	d		14 23									14 53									15 23	
Kempton Park	d		14 26									14 56									15 26	
Sunbury	d		14 28									14 58									15 28	
Upper Halliford	d		14 30									15 00									15 30	
Shepperton	a		14 33									15 03									15 33	
Berrylands	d									14 30									15 00			
Surbiton	d				14a13			14 27		14 35				14a43			14 57		15 05			
Thames Ditton	d									14 39									15 09			
Hampton Court	a									14 42									15 12			
Hinchley Wood	d							14 31									15 01					
Claygate	d							14 34									15 04					
Oxshott	d							14 37									15 07					
Cobham & Stoke D'abernon	d							14 41									15 11					
Bookham	d	14 29									14 59									15 29		
Effingham Junction	d	14 33						14 45			15 03						15 15			15 33		
Horsley	d	14 36						14 48			15 06						15 18			15 36		
Clandon	d	14 41						14 53			15 11						15 23			15 41		
London Road (Guildford)	d	14 46						14 58			15 16						15 28			15 46		
Guildford	a	14 50						15 02			15 20						15 32			15 50		

Station		SW	SW	SW	SW	SW	SW	SW	SW	SW	SW	SW	SW	SW	SW	SW	SW	SW	SW	SW	SW	SW	SW
London Waterloo ⊖	d	14 50	14 54	14 57	15 03	15 03	15 06	15 09	15 12	15 16	15 20	15 24	15 27	15 33	15 33	15 36	15 39	15 42	15 46	15 50	15 54	15 57	16 03
Vauxhall ⊖	d	14 54	14 58	15 01	15 07	15 07	15 10	15 13	15 16	15 20	15 24	15 28	15 31	15 37	15 37	15 40	15 43	15 46	15 50	15 54	15 58	16 01	16 07
Clapham Junction	d	14 59	15 03	15 06	15 12		15 15	15 18	15 21	15 25	15 29	15 33	15 36	15 42		15 45	15 48	15 51	15 55	15 59	16 03	16 06	16 12
Earlsfield	d	15 02	15 06	15 09	15 15		15 18	15 21	15 24	15 28	15 32	15 36	15 39	15 45		15 48	15 51	15 54	15 58	16 02	16 06	16 09	16 15
Wimbledon ⊖	d	15 06	15 10	15 13	15 19		15 22	15 25	15 28	15 32	15 36	15 40	15 43	15 49		15 52	15 55	15 58	16 02	16 06	16 10	16 13	16 19
Raynes Park	d		15 13	15 16			15 25	15 28	15 31	15 35		15 43	15 46			15 55	15 58	16 01	16 05		16 13	16 16	
Motspur Park	d		15 16					15 31		15 38		15 46					16 01		16 08		16 16		
Malden Manor	d									15 41									16 11				
Tolworth	d									15 44									16 14				
Chessington North	d									15 47									16 17				
Chessington South	a									15 49									16 19				
Worcester Park	d		15 18					15 33				15 48					16 03				16 18		
Stoneleigh	d		15 21					15 36				15 51					16 06				16 21		
Ewell West	d		15 24					15 39				15 54					16 09				16 24		
Epsom	a		15 27					15 46				15 57					16 16				16 27		
	d		15 28					15 47				15 58					16 17				16 28		
Ashtead	d		15 32					15 51				16 02					16 21				16 32		
Leatherhead	d		15 35					15 54				16 05					16 24				16 35		
Boxhill & Westhumble	d																						
Dorking	a		15 41									16 11									16 41		
New Malden	d			15 19			15 28		15 34				15 49			15 58		16 04				16 19	
Norbiton	d			15 22					15 37				15 52					16 07				16 22	
Kingston	a			15 25		15 46			15 40				15 55		16 16			16 10				16 25	
	d			15 29					15 40				15 59					16 10				16 29	
Hampton Wick	d			15 31					15 42				16 01					16 12				16 31	
Teddington	d			15 35					15 45				16 05					16 15				16 35	
Strawberry Hill	a			15 38									16 08									16 38	
Fulwell	d								15 49									16 19					
Hampton	d								15 53									16 23					
Kempton Park	d								15 56									16 26					
Sunbury	d								15 58									16 28					
Upper Halliford	d								16 00									16 30					
Shepperton	a								16 03									16 33					
Berrylands	d						15 30									16 00							
Surbiton	d	15a13			15 27		15 35				15a43			15 57		16 05				16a13			16 27
Thames Ditton	d						15 39									16 09							
Hampton Court	a						15 42									16 12							
Hinchley Wood	d				15 31									16 01									16 31
Claygate	d				15 34									16 04									16 34
Oxshott	d				15 37									16 07									16 37
Cobham & Stoke D'abernon	d				15 41									16 11									16 41
Bookham	d							15 59									16 29						
Effingham Junction	d				15 45			16 03						16 15			16 33						16 45
Horsley	d				15 48			16 06						16 18			16 36						16 48
Clandon	d				15 53			16 11						16 23			16 41						16 53
London Road (Guildford)	d				15 58			16 16						16 28			16 46						16 58
Guildford	a				16 02			16 20						16 32			16 50						17 02

London - Chessington South, Dorking, Guildford, Shepperton and Hampton Court

until 1 October

		SW	SW	SW	SW	SW	SW	SW	SW	SW	SW	SW	SW	SW	SW	SW	SW	SW	SW	SW	SW	SW
London Waterloo 15 ⊖	d	16 03	16 06	16 09	16 12	16 16	16 20	16 24	16 27	16 33	16 33	16 36	16 39	16 42	16 46	16 50	16 54	16 57	17 03	17 03	17 06	17 09
Vauxhall ⊖	d	16 07	16 10	16 13	16 16	16 20	16 24	16 28	16 31	16 37	16 37	16 40	16 43	16 46	16 50	16 54	16 58	17 01	17 07	17 07	17 10	17 13
Clapham Junction 10	d		16 15	16 18	16 21	16 25	16 29	16 33	16 36	16 42		16 45	16 48	16 51	16 55	16 59	17 03	17 06	17 12		17 15	17 18
Earlsfield	d		16 18	16 21	16 24	16 28	16 32	16 36	16 39	16 45		16 48	16 51	16 54	16 58	17 02	17 06	17 09	17 15		17 18	17 21
Wimbledon 6 ⊖	d		16 22	16 25	16 28	16 32	16 36	16 40	16 43	16 49		16 52	16 55	16 58	17 02	17 06	17 10	17 13	17 19		17 22	17 25
Raynes Park 6	d		16 25	16 28	16 31	16 35		16 43	16 46			16 55	16 58	17 01	17 05		17 13	17 16			17 25	17 28
Motspur Park	d			16 31		16 38		16 46					17 01		17 08		17 16					17 31
Malden Manor	d					16 41									17 11							
Tolworth	d					16 44									17 14							
Chessington North	d					16 47									17 17							
Chessington South	a					16 49									17 19							
Worcester Park	d			16 33				16 48					17 03				17 18					17 33
Stoneleigh	d			16 36				16 51					17 06				17 21					17 36
Ewell West	d			16 39				16 54					17 09				17 24					17 39
Epsom 3	a			16 46				16 57					17 16				17 27					17 46
	d			16 47				16 58					17 17				17 28					17 47
Ashtead	d			16 51				17 02					17 21				17 32					17 51
Leatherhead	d			16 54				17 05					17 24				17 35					17 54
Boxhill & Westhumble	d																					
Dorking 4	a							17 11									17 41					
New Malden 6	d		16 28		16 34				16 49			16 58		17 04				17 19			17 28	
Norbiton	d				16 37				16 52					17 07				17 22				
Kingston	a	16 46			16 40				16 55		17 16			17 10				17 25		17 46		
	d				16 40				16 59					17 10				17 29				
Hampton Wick	d				16 42				17 01					17 12				17 31				
Teddington	d				16 45				17 05					17 15				17 35				
Strawberry Hill	a								17 08									17 38				
Fulwell	d				16 49									17 19								
Hampton	d				16 53									17 23								
Kempton Park	d				16 56									17 26								
Sunbury	d				16 58									17 28								
Upper Halliford	d				17 00									17 30								
Shepperton	a				17 03									17 33								
Berrylands	d		16 30									17 00									17 30	
Surbiton 6	d		16 35				16a43			16 57		17 05				17a13			17 27		17 35	
Thames Ditton	d		16 39									17 09									17 39	
Hampton Court	a		16 42									17 12									17 42	
Hinchley Wood	d									17 01									17 31			
Claygate	d									17 04									17 34			
Oxshott	d									17 07									17 37			
Cobham & Stoke D'abernon	d									17 11									17 41			
Bookham	d			16 59									17 29									17 59
Effingham Junction 6	d			17 03						17 15			17 33						17 45			18 03
Horsley	d			17 06						17 18			17 36						17 48			18 06
Clandon	d			17 11						17 23			17 41						17 53			18 11
London Road (Guildford)	d			17 16						17 28			17 46						17 58			18 16
Guildford	a			17 20						17 32			17 50						18 02			18 20

		SW	SW	SW	SW	SW	SW	SW	SW	SW	SW	SW	SW	SW	SW	SW	SW	SW	SW	SW	SW	SW	SW
London Waterloo 15 ⊖	d	17 12	17 16	17 20	17 24	17 27	17 33	17 33	17 36	17 39	17 42	17 46	17 50	17 54	17 57	18 03	18 03	18 06	18 09	18 12	18 16	18 20	18 24
Vauxhall ⊖	d	17 16	17 20	17 24	17 28	17 31	17 37	17 37	17 40	17 43	17 46	17 50	17 54	17 58	18 01	18 07	18 07	18 10	18 13	18 16	18 20	18 24	18 28
Clapham Junction 10	d	17 21	17 25	17 29	17 33	17 36	17 42		17 45	17 48	17 51	17 55	17 59	18 03	18 06	18 12		18 15	18 18	18 21	18 25	18 29	18 33
Earlsfield	d	17 24	17 28	17 32	17 36	17 39	17 45		17 48	17 51	17 54	17 58	18 02	18 06	18 09	18 15		18 18	18 21	18 24	18 28	18 32	18 36
Wimbledon 6 ⊖	d	17 28	17 32	17 36	17 40	17 43	17 49		17 52	17 55	17 58	18 02	18 06	18 10	18 13	18 19		18 22	18 25	18 28	18 32	18 36	18 40
Raynes Park 6	d	17 31	17 35		17 43	17 46			17 55	17 58	18 01	18 05		18 13	18 16			18 25	18 28	18 31	18 35		18 43
Motspur Park	d		17 38		17 46					18 01		18 08		18 16					18 31		18 38		18 46
Malden Manor	d		17 41									18 11									18 41		
Tolworth	d		17 44									18 14									18 44		
Chessington North	d		17 47									18 17									18 47		
Chessington South	a		17 49									18 19									18 49		
Worcester Park	d				17 48					18 03				18 18					18 33				18 48
Stoneleigh	d				17 51					18 06				18 21					18 36				18 51
Ewell West	d				17 54					18 09				18 24					18 39				18 54
Epsom 3	a				17 57					18 16				18 27					18 46				18 57
	d				17 58					18 17				18 28					18 47				18 58
Ashtead	d				18 02					18 21				18 32					18 51				19 02
Leatherhead	d				18 05					18 24				18 35					18 54				19 05
Boxhill & Westhumble	d																						
Dorking 4	a				18 11									18 41									19 11
New Malden 6	d	17 34				17 49			17 58		18 04				18 19			18 28		18 34			
Norbiton	d	17 37				17 52					18 07				18 22					18 37			
Kingston	a	17 40				17 55		18 16			18 10				18 25		18 46			18 40			
	d	17 40				17 59					18 10				18 29					18 40			
Hampton Wick	d	17 42				18 01					18 12				18 31					18 42			
Teddington	d	17 45				18 05					18 15				18 35					18 45			
Strawberry Hill	a					18 08									18 38								
Fulwell	d	17 49									18 19									18 49			
Hampton	d	17 53									18 23									18 53			
Kempton Park	d	17 56									18 26									18 56			
Sunbury	d	17 58									18 28									18 58			
Upper Halliford	d	18 00									18 30									19 00			
Shepperton	a	18 03									18 33									19 03			
Berrylands	d								18 00									18 30					
Surbiton 6	d			17a43			17 57		18 05				18a13			18 27		18 35				18a43	
Thames Ditton	d								18 09									18 39					
Hampton Court	a								18 12									18 42					
Hinchley Wood	d						18 01									18 31							
Claygate	d						18 04									18 34							
Oxshott	d						18 07									18 37							
Cobham & Stoke D'abernon	d						18 11									18 41							
Bookham	d									18 29									18 59				
Effingham Junction 6	d						18 15			18 33						18 45			19 03				
Horsley	d						18 18			18 36						18 48			19 06				
Clandon	d						18 23			18 41						18 53			19 11				
London Road (Guildford)	d						18 28			18 46						18 58			19 16				
Guildford	a						18 32			18 50						19 02			19 20				

London - Chessington South, Dorking, Guildford, Shepperton and Hampton Court

		SW	SW	SW	SW	SW	SW	SW	SW	SW	SW	SW	SW	SW	SW	SW	SW	SW	SW	SW	SW	SW	SW
London Waterloo 15 ⊖	d	18 27	18 33	18 33	18 36	18 39	18 42	18 46	18 50	18 54	18 57	19 03	19 03	19 06	19 09	19 12	19 16	19 20	19 24	19 27	19 33	19 33	19 36
Vauxhall ⊖	d	18 31	18 37	18 37	18 40	18 43	18 46	18 50	18 54	18 58	19 01	19 07	19 07	19 10	19 13	19 16	19 20	19 24	19 28	19 31	19 37	19 37	19 40
Clapham Junction 10	d	18 36	18 42		18 45	18 48	18 51	18 55	18 59	19 03	19 06	19 12		19 15	19 18	19 21	19 25	19 29	19 33	19 36	19 42		19 45
Earlsfield	d	18 39	18 45		18 48	18 51	18 54	18 58	19 02	19 06	19 09	19 15		19 18	19 21	19 24	19 28	19 32	19 36	19 39	19 45		19 48
Wimbledon 6 ⊖	d	18 43	18 49		18 52	18 55	18 58	19 02	19 06	19 10	19 13	19 19		19 22	19 25	19 28	19 32	19 36	19 40	19 43	19 49		19 52
Raynes Park 6	d	18 46			18 55	18 58	19 01	19 05		19 13	19 16			19 25	19 28	19 31	19 35		19 43	19 46			19 55
Motspur Park	d					19 01		19 08		19 16					19 31		19 38		19 46				
Malden Manor	d							19 11									19 41						
Tolworth	d							19 14									19 44						
Chessington North	d							19 17									19 47						
Chessington South	a							19 19									19 49						
Worcester Park	d					19 03				19 18					19 33				19 48				
Stoneleigh	d					19 06				19 21					19 36				19 51				
Ewell West	d					19 09				19 24					19 39				19 54				
Epsom 3	a					19 16				19 27					19 46				19 57				
	d					19 17				19 28					19 47				19 58				
Ashtead	d					19 21				19 32					19 51				20 02				
Leatherhead	d					19 24				19 35					19 54				20 05				
Boxhill & Westhumble	d																						
Dorking 4	a									19 41									20 11				
New Malden 6	d	18 49			18 58		19 04				19 19			19 28		19 34				19 49			19 58
Norbiton	d	18 52					19 07				19 22					19 37				19 52			
Kingston	a	18 55		19 16			19 10				19 25		19 46			19 40				19 55		20 16	
	d	18 59					19 10				19 29					19 40				19 59			
Hampton Wick	d	19 01					19 12				19 31					19 42				20 01			
Teddington	d	19 05					19 15				19 35					19 45				20 05			
Strawberry Hill	a	19 08									19 38									20 08			
Fulwell	d						19 19									19 49							
Hampton	d						19 23									19 53							
Kempton Park	d						19 26									19 56							
Sunbury	d						19 28									19 58							
Upper Halliford	d						19 30									20 00							
Shepperton	a						19 33									20 03							
Berrylands	d				19 00									19 30									20 00
Surbiton 6	d		18 57		19 05				19a13			19 27		19 35				19a43			19 57		20 05
Thames Ditton	d				19 09									19 39									20 09
Hampton Court	a				19 12									19 42									20 12
Hinchley Wood	d		19 01									19 31									20 01		
Claygate	d		19 04									19 34									20 04		
Oxshott	d		19 07									19 37									20 07		
Cobham & Stoke D'abernon	d		19 11									19 41									20 11		
Bookham	d					19 29									19 59								
Effingham Junction 6	d		19 15			19 33						19 45			20 03						20 15		
Horsley	d		19 18			19 36						19 48			20 06						20 18		
Clandon	d		19 23			19 41						19 53			20 11						20 23		
London Road (Guildford)	d		19 28			19 46						19 58			20 16						20 28		
Guildford	a		19 32			19 50						20 02			20 20						20 32		

		SW	SW	SW	SW	SW	SW	SW	SW	SW	SW	SW	SW	SW	SW	SW	SW	SW	SW	SW	SW	SW
London Waterloo 15 ⊖	d	19 39	19 42	19 46	19 50	19 54	19 57	20 03	20 03	20 06	20 09	20 12	20 16	20 20	20 24	20 27	20 33	20 33	20 36	20 39	20 42	20 46
Vauxhall ⊖	d	19 43	19 46	19 50	19 54	19 58	20 01	20 07	20 07	20 10	20 13	20 16	20 20	20 24	20 28	20 31	20 37	20 37	20 40	20 43	20 46	20 50
Clapham Junction 10	d	19 48	19 51	19 55	19 59	20 03	20 06	20 12		20 15	20 18	20 21	20 25	20 29	20 33	20 36	20 42		20 45	20 48	20 51	20 55
Earlsfield	d	19 51	19 54	19 58	20 02	20 06	20 09	20 15		20 18	20 21	20 24	20 28	20 32	20 36	20 39	20 45		20 48	20 51	20 54	20 58
Wimbledon 6 ⊖	d	19 55	19 58	20 02	20 06	20 10	20 13	20 19		20 22	20 25	20 28	20 32	20 36	20 40	20 43	20 49		20 52	20 55	20 58	21 02
Raynes Park 6	d	19 58	20 01	20 05		20 13	20 16			20 25	20 28	20 31	20 35		20 43	20 46			20 55	20 58	21 01	21 05
Motspur Park	d	20 01		20 08		20 16					20 31		20 38		20 46					21 01		21 08
Malden Manor	d			20 11									20 41									21 11
Tolworth	d			20 14									20 44									21 14
Chessington North	d			20 17									20 47									21 17
Chessington South	a			20 19									20 49									21 19
Worcester Park	d	20 03				20 18					20 33				20 48					21 03		
Stoneleigh	d	20 06				20 21					20 36				20 51					21 06		
Ewell West	d	20 09				20 24					20 39				20 54					21 09		
Epsom 3	a	20 16				20 27					20 46				20 57					21 16		
	d	20 17									20 47									21 17		
Ashtead	d	20 21									20 51									21 21		
Leatherhead	d	20 24									20 54									21 24		
Boxhill & Westhumble	d																					
Dorking 4	a										21 00											
New Malden 6	d		20 04				20 19			20 28		20 34				20 49			20 58		21 04	
Norbiton	d		20 07				20 22					20 37				20 52					21 07	
Kingston	a		20 10				20 25		20 46			20 40				20 55		21 16			21 10	
	d		20 10				20 29					20 40				20 59					21 10	
Hampton Wick	d		20 12				20 31					20 42				21 01					21 12	
Teddington	d		20 15				20 35					20 45				21 05					21 15	
Strawberry Hill	a						20 38									21 08						
Fulwell	d		20 19									20 49									21 19	
Hampton	d		20 23									20 53									21 23	
Kempton Park	d		20 26									20 56									21 26	
Sunbury	d		20 28									20 58									21 28	
Upper Halliford	d		20 30									21 00									21 30	
Shepperton	a		20 33									21 03									21 33	
Berrylands	d									20 30									21 00			
Surbiton 6	d				20a13			20 27		20 35				20a43			20 57		21 05			
Thames Ditton	d									20 39									21 09			
Hampton Court	a									20 42									21 12			
Hinchley Wood	d							20 31									21 01					
Claygate	d							20 34									21 04					
Oxshott	d							20 37									21 07					
Cobham & Stoke D'abernon	d							20 41									21 11					
Bookham	d	20 29																		21 29		
Effingham Junction 6	d	20 33						20 45									21 15			21 33		
Horsley	d	20 36						20 48									21 18			21 36		
Clandon	d	20 41						20 53									21 23			21 41		
London Road (Guildford)	d	20 46						20 58									21 28			21 46		
Guildford	a	20 50						21 02									21 32			21 50		

Table 152

London - Chessington South, Dorking, Guildford, Shepperton and Hampton Court

Saturdays
until 1 October

Station		SW	SW	SW	SW	SW	SW	SW	SW	SW	SW	SW	SW	SW	SW	SW	SW	SW	SW	SW	SW	SW	SW
London Waterloo ⊖	d	20 50	20 54	20 57	21 03	21 03	21 09	21 12	21 20	21 24	21 27	21 33	21 33	21 36	21 39	21 42	21 46	21 50	21 54	21 57	22 03	22 03	22 09
Vauxhall ⊖	d	20 54	20 58	21 01	21 07	21 07	21 13	21 16	21 24	21 28	21 31	21 37	21 37	21 40	21 43	21 46	21 50	21 54	21 58	22 01	22 07	22 07	22 13
Clapham Junction	d	20 59	21 03	21 06	21 12		21 18	21 21	21 29	21 33	21 36	21 42		21 45	21 48	21 51	21 55	21 59	22 03	22 06	22 12		22 18
Earlsfield	d	21 02	21 06	21 09	21 15		21 21	21 24	21 32	21 36	21 39	21 45		21 48	21 51	21 54	21 58	22 02	22 06	22 09	22 15		22 21
Wimbledon ⊖	d	21 06	21 10	21 13	21 19		21 25	21 28	21 36	21 40	21 43	21 49		21 52	21 55	21 58	22 02	22 06	22 10	22 13	22 19		22 25
Raynes Park	d		21 13	21 16			21 28	21 31		21 43	21 46			21 55	21 58	22 01	22 05		22 13	22 16			22 28
Motspur Park	d		21 16				21 31			21 46					22 01		22 08		22 16				22 31
Malden Manor	d																22 11						
Tolworth	d																22 14						
Chessington North	d																22 17						
Chessington South	a																22 19						
Worcester Park	d		21 18				21 33			21 48					22 03				22 18				22 33
Stoneleigh	d		21 21				21 36			21 51					22 06				22 21				22 36
Ewell West	d		21 24				21 39			21 54					22 09				22 24				22 39
Epsom	a		21 27				21 46			21 57					22 16				22 27				22 46
	d						21 47								22 17								22 47
Ashtead	d						21 51								22 21								22 51
Leatherhead	d						21 54								22 24								22 54
Boxhill & Westhumble	d																						
Dorking	a						22 00																23 00
New Malden	d			21 19				21 34			21 49			21 58		22 04				22 19			
Norbiton	d			21 22				21 37			21 52					22 07				22 22			
Kingston	a			21 25		21 46		21 40			21 55		22 16			22 10				22 25		22 46	
	d			21 29				21 40			21 59					22 10				22 29			
Hampton Wick	d			21 31				21 42			22 01					22 12				22 31			
Teddington	d			21 35				21 45			22 05					22 15				22 35			
Strawberry Hill	a			21 38							22 08									22 38			
Fulwell	d							21 49								22 19							
Hampton	d							21 53								22 23							
Kempton Park	d							21 56								22 26							
Sunbury	d							21 58								22 28							
Upper Halliford	d							22 00								22 30							
Shepperton	a							22 03								22 33							
Berrylands	d													22 00									
Surbiton	d	21a13			21 27				21a43			21 57		22 05				22 14			22 27		
Thames Ditton	d													22 09									
Hampton Court	a													22 12									
Hinchley Wood	d				21 31							22 01									22 31		
Claygate	d				21 34							22 04									22 34		
Oxshott	d				21 37							22 07									22 37		
Cobham & Stoke D'abernon	d				21 41							22 11									22 41		
Bookham	d														22 29								
Effingham Junction	d				21 45							22 15			22 33						22 45		
Horsley	d				21 48							22 18			22 36						22 48		
Clandon	d				21 53							22 23			22 41						22 53		
London Road (Guildford)	d				21 58							22 28			22 46						22 58		
Guildford	a				22 02							22 32			22 50			22 47			23 02		

Station		SW	SW	SW	SW	SW	SW	SW	SW	SW	SW	SW	SW	SW	SW	SW	SW	SW	SW	SW	SW	SW
London Waterloo ⊖	d	22 12	22 20	22 27	22 33	22 33	22 36	22 39	22 42	22 50	22 57	23 00	23 03	23 03	23 09	23 12	23 20	23 27	23 33	23 36	23 42	23 50
Vauxhall ⊖	d	22 16	22 24	22 31	22 37	22 37	22 40	22 43	22 46	22 54	23 01	23 04	23 07	23 07	23 13	23 16	23 24	23 31	23 37	23 40	23 46	23 54
Clapham Junction	d	22 21	22 29	22 36	22 42		22 45	22 48	22 51	22 59	23 06	23 09	23 12		23 18	23 21	23 29	23 36		23 45	23 51	23 59
Earlsfield	d	22 24	22 32	22 39	22 45		22 48	22 51	22 54	23 02	23 09	23 12	23 15		23 21	23 24	23 32	23 39		23 48	23 54	00 02
Wimbledon ⊖	d	22 28	22 36	22 43	22 49		22 52	22 55	22 58	23 06	23 13	23 16	23 19		23 25	23 28	23 36	23 43		23 52	23 58	00 06
Raynes Park	d	22 31		22 46			22 55	22 58	23 01		23 16	23 19			23 28	23 31		23 46		23 55	00 01	
Motspur Park	d							23 01				23 22			23 31						00 04	
Malden Manor	d											23 25										
Tolworth	d											23 28										
Chessington North	d											23 31										
Chessington South	a											23 33										
Worcester Park	d							23 03							23 33						00 06	
Stoneleigh	d							23 06							23 36						00 09	
Ewell West	d							23 09							23 39						00 12	
Epsom	a							23 12							23 42						00 15	
	d							23 17							23 47						00 19	
Ashtead	d							23 21							23 51						00 23	
Leatherhead	d							23 24							23 54						00 26	
Boxhill & Westhumble	d																					
Dorking	a														00 01							
New Malden	d	22 34		22 49			22 58		23 04		23 19					23 34		23 49		23 58		
Norbiton	d	22 37		22 52					23 07		23 22					23 37		23 52				
Kingston	a	22 40		22 55		23 16			23 10		23 25			23 46		23 40		23 55	00 16			
	d	22 40		22 59					23 10		23 29					23 40		23 55				
Hampton Wick	d	22 42		23 01					23 12		23 31					23 42		23 57				
Teddington	d	22 45		23 05					23 15		23 35					23 45		23 59				
Strawberry Hill	a			23 08							23 38							00 03				
Fulwell	d	22 49							23 19							23 49						
Hampton	d	22 53							23 23							23 53						
Kempton Park	d	22 56							23 26							23 56						
Sunbury	d	22 58							23 28							23 58						
Upper Halliford	d	23 00							23 30							23 59						
Shepperton	a	23 03							23 33							00 03						
Berrylands	d						23 00													23 59		
Surbiton	d		22a43		22 57		23 05			23a13			23 27				23a43			00 05		00 14
Thames Ditton	d						23 09													00 09		
Hampton Court	a						23 12													00 12		
Hinchley Wood	d				23 01								23 31									00 18
Claygate	d				23 04								23 34									00 20
Oxshott	d				23 07								23 37									00 24
Cobham & Stoke D'abernon	d				23 11								23 41									00 27
Bookham	d							23 29													00 31	
Effingham Junction	d				23 15			23 33					23 45								00 36	00 32
Horsley	d				23 18			23 36					23 48								00 39	00 34
Clandon	d				23 23			23 41					23 53								00 44	00 39
London Road (Guildford)	d				23 28			23 46					23 58								00 49	00 44
Guildford	a				[illegible]			23 50					00 02								00 53	00 48

Table 152

London - Chessington South, Dorking, Guildford, Shepperton and Hampton Court

Saturdays
until 1 October

Station		SW
London Waterloo ⊖	d	23 57
Vauxhall ⊖	d	00 01
Clapham Junction	d	00 06
Earlsfield	d	00 09
Wimbledon ⊖	d	00 13
Raynes Park	d	00 16
Motspur Park	d	
Malden Manor	d	
Tolworth	d	
Chessington North	d	
Chessington South	a	
Worcester Park	d	
Stoneleigh	d	
Ewell West	d	
Epsom	a	
	d	
Ashtead	d	
Leatherhead	d	
Boxhill & Westhumble	d	
Dorking	a	
New Malden	d	00 19
Norbiton	d	00 22
Kingston	a	00 25
	d	00 25
Hampton Wick	d	00 27
Teddington	d	00 30
Strawberry Hill	a	
Fulwell	d	00 34
Hampton	d	00 38
Kempton Park	d	00 41
Sunbury	d	00 43
Upper Halliford	d	00 45
Shepperton	a	00 48
Berrylands	d	
Surbiton	d	
Thames Ditton	d	
Hampton Court	a	
Hinchley Wood	d	
Claygate	d	
Oxshott	d	
Cobham & Stoke D'abernon	d	
Bookham	d	
Effingham Junction	d	
Horsley	d	
Clandon	d	
London Road (Guildford)	d	
Guildford	a	

London - Chessington South, Dorking, Guildford, Shepperton and Hampton Court

		SW	SW	SW	SW	SW	SW	SW	SW	SW	SW	SW	SW	SW	SW 1	SW	SW 1	SW	SW	SW	SW	SW	SW
London Waterloo 15 ⊖	d	23p03	23p12	23p27	23p33	23p36	23p42	23p50	23p57	00 09	00 15	00 18	00 27	00 42	05 00	05 12	05 20	05 33	05 50	06 03	06 06	06 12	06 16
Vauxhall ⊖	d	23p07	23p16	23p31	23p37	23p40	23p46	23p54	00 01	00 13	00 19	00 22	00 31	00 46	05 04	05 16	05 24	05 37	05 54	06 07	06 10	06 16	06 20
Clapham Junction 10	d	23p12	23p21	23p36		23p45	23p51	23p59	00 06	00 20	00 25		00 37	00 51	05 11	05 21	05 29		05 59		06 15	06 21	06 25
Earlsfield	d	23p15	23p24	23p39		23p48	23p54	00 02	00 09	00 23	00 29		00s41		05 14	05 24	05 32		06 02		06 18	06 24	06 28
Wimbledon 6 ⊖	d	23p19	23p28	23p43		23p52	23p58	00 06	00 13	00 27	00 33		00 45	01b05	05 18	05 28	05 36		06 06		06 22	06 28	06 32
Raynes Park 6	d		23p31	23p46		23p55	00 01		00 16		00 36		00 48	01 08		05 31					06 25	06 31	06 35
Motspur Park	d						00 04				00 38												06 38
Malden Manor	d																						06 41
Tolworth	d																						06 44
Chessington North	d																						06 47
Chessington South	a																						06 49
Worcester Park	d						00 06				00 41												
Stoneleigh	d						00 09				00 44												
Ewell West	d						00 12				00 46												
Epsom 3	a						00 15				00 50												
	d						00 19																
Ashtead	d						00 23																
Leatherhead	d						00 26																
Boxhill & Westhumble	d																						
Dorking 4	a																						
New Malden 6	d		23p34	23p49		23p58			00 19				00 50	01 11		05 34					06 28	06 34	
Norbiton	d		23p37	23p52					00 22					01 14		05 37						06 37	
Kingston	a		23p40	23p55	00 16				00 25			01 01		01 17		05 40		06 16		06 46		06 40	
	d		23p40	23p55					00 25					01 17		05 40						06 40	
Hampton Wick	d		23p42	23p57					00 27					01s19		05 42						06 42	
Teddington	d		23p45	23p59					00 30					01s22		05 45						06 45	
Strawberry Hill	a			00 03										01 28									
Fulwell	d		23p49						00 34							05 49						06 49	
Hampton	d		23p53						00 38							05 53						06 53	
Kempton Park	d		23p56						00 41							05 56						06 56	
Sunbury	d		23p58						00 43							05 58						06 58	
Upper Halliford	d		23p59						00 45							06 00						07 00	
Shepperton	a		00 05						00 50							06 05						07 05	
Berrylands	d					23p59							00s53								06 30		
Surbiton 6	d	23p27				00 05		00 14		00 35			00a56		05 26		05 44		06a13		06 35		
Thames Ditton	d					00 09															06 39		
Hampton Court	a					00 12															06 42		
Hinchley Wood	d	23p31						00 18															
Claygate	d	23p34						00 20															
Oxshott	d	23p37						00 24															
Cobham & Stoke D'abernon	d	23p41						00 27															
Bookham	d						00 31																
Effingham Junction 6	d	23p45					00 36	00 32															
Horsley	d	23p48					00 39	00 34															
Clandon	d	23p53					00 44	00 39															
London Road (Guildford)	d	23p58					00 49	00 44															
Guildford	a	00 05					00 56	00 51		01 07					06 00		06 23						

b Arr. 0056

London - Chessington South, Dorking, Guildford, Shepperton and Hampton Court

		SW	SW	SW	SW	SW	SW	SW	SW	SW	SW	SW	SW	SW	SW	SW	SW	SW	SW	SW	SW	SW	SW
London Waterloo 15 ⊖	d	06 20	06 27	06 33	06 33	06 36	06 39	06 42	06 46	06 50	06 57	07 03	07 03	07 06	07 09	07 12	07 16	07 20	07 24	07 27	07 33	07 33	07 36
Vauxhall ⊖	d	06 24	06 31	06 37	06 37	06 40	06 43	06 46	06 50	06 54	07 01	07 07	07 07	07 10	07 13	07 16	07 20	07 24	07 28	07 31	07 37	07 37	07 40
Clapham Junction 10	d	06 29	06 36	06 42		06 45	06 48	06 51	06 55	06 59	07 06	07 12		07 15	07 18	07 21	07 25	07 29	07 33	07 36	07 42		07 45
Earlsfield	d	06 32	06 39	06 45		06 48	06 51	06 54	06 58	07 02	07 09	07 15		07 18	07 21	07 24	07 28	07 32	07 36	07 39	07 45		07 48
Wimbledon 6 ⊖	d	06 36	06 43	06 49		06 52	06 55	06 58	07 02	07 06	07 13	07 19		07 22	07 25	07 28	07 32	07 36	07 40	07 43	07 49		07 52
Raynes Park 6	d		06 46			06 55	06 58	07 01	07 05		07 16			07 25	07 28	07 31	07 35		07 43	07 46			07 55
Motspur Park	d						07 01		07 08						07 31		07 38		07 46				
Malden Manor	d								07 11								07 41						
Tolworth	d								07 14								07 44						
Chessington North	d								07 17								07 47						
Chessington South	a								07 19								07 49						
Worcester Park	d						07 03								07 33				07 48				
Stoneleigh	d						07 06								07 36				07 51				
Ewell West	d						07 09								07 39				07 54				
Epsom 3	a						07 16								07 46				07 57				
	d						07 17								07 47				07 58				
Ashtead	d						07 21								07 51				08 02				
Leatherhead	d						07 24								07 54				08 05				
Boxhill & Westhumble	d																						
Dorking 4	a																		08 13				
New Malden 6	d		06 49			06 58		07 04			07 19			07 28		07 34				07 49			07 58
Norbiton	d		06 52					07 07			07 22					07 37				07 52			
Kingston	a		06 55		07 16			07 10			07 25		07 46			07 40				07 55		08 16	
	d		06 59					07 10			07 29					07 40				07 59			
Hampton Wick	d		07 01					07 12			07 31					07 42				08 01			
Teddington	d		07 05					07 15			07 35					07 45				08 05			
Strawberry Hill	a		07 08								07 38									08 08			
Fulwell	d							07 19								07 49							
Hampton	d							07 23								07 53							
Kempton Park	d							07 26								07 56							
Sunbury	d							07 28								07 58							
Upper Halliford	d							07 30								08 00							
Shepperton	a							07 35								08 05							
Berrylands	d					07 00								07 30									08 00
Surbiton 6	d	06a43		06 57		07 05				07a13		07 27		07 35				07a43			07 57		08 05
Thames Ditton	d					07 09								07 39									08 09
Hampton Court	a					07 12								07 42									08 12
Hinchley Wood	d			07 01								07 31									08 01		
Claygate	d			07 04								07 34									08 04		
Oxshott	d			07 07								07 37									08 07		
Cobham & Stoke D'abernon	d			07 11								07 41									08 11		
Bookham	d						07 29								07 59								
Effingham Junction 6	d			07 15			07 33					07 45			08 03						08 15		
Horsley	d			07 18			07 36					07 48			08 06						08 18		
Clandon	d			07 23			07 41					07 53			08 11						08 23		
London Road (Guildford)	d			07 28			07 46					07 58			08 16						08 28		
Guildford	a			07 35			07 53					08 05			08 23						08 35		

		SW	SW	SW	SW	SW	SW	SW	SW	SW	SW	SW	SW	SW	SW	SW	SW	SW	SW	SW	SW	SW
London Waterloo 15 ⊖	d	07 39	07 42	07 46	07 50	07 54	07 57	08 03	08 03	08 06	08 09	08 12	08 16	08 20	08 24	08 27	08 33	08 33	08 36	08 39	08 42	08 46
Vauxhall ⊖	d	07 43	07 46	07 50	07 54	07 58	08 01	08 07	08 07	08 10	08 13	08 16	08 20	08 24	08 28	08 31	08 37	08 37	08 40	08 43	08 46	08 50
Clapham Junction 10	d	07 48	07 51	07 55	07 59	08 03	08 06	08 12		08 15	08 18	08 21	08 25	08 29	08 33	08 36	08 42		08 45	08 48	08 51	08 55
Earlsfield	d	07 51	07 54	07 58	08 02	08 06	08 09	08 15		08 18	08 21	08 24	08 28	08 32	08 36	08 39	08 45		08 48	08 51	08 54	08 58
Wimbledon 6 ⊖	d	07 55	07 58	08 02	08 06	08 10	08 13	08 19		08 22	08 25	08 28	08 32	08 36	08 40	08 43	08 49		08 52	08 55	08 58	09 02
Raynes Park 6	d	07 58	08 01	08 05		08 13	08 16			08 25	08 28	08 31	08 35		08 43	08 46			08 55	08 58	09 01	09 05
Motspur Park	d	08 01		08 08		08 16					08 31		08 38		08 46					09 01		09 08
Malden Manor	d			08 11									08 41									09 11
Tolworth	d			08 14									08 44									09 14
Chessington North	d			08 17									08 47									09 17
Chessington South	a			08 19									08 49									09 19
Worcester Park	d	08 03				08 18					08 33				08 48					09 03		
Stoneleigh	d	08 06				08 21					08 36				08 51					09 06		
Ewell West	d	08 09				08 24					08 39				08 54					09 09		
Epsom 3	a	08 16				08 27					08 46				08 57					09 16		
	d	08 17				08 28					08 47				08 58					09 17		
Ashtead	d	08 21				08 32					08 51				09 02					09 21		
Leatherhead	d	08 24				08 35					08 54				09 05					09 24		
Boxhill & Westhumble	d																					
Dorking 4	a					08 43									09 13							
New Malden 6	d		08 04				08 19			08 28		08 34				08 49			08 58		09 04	
Norbiton	d		08 07				08 22					08 37				08 52					09 07	
Kingston	a		08 10				08 25		08 46			08 40				08 55		09 16			09 10	
	d		08 10				08 29					08 40				08 59					09 10	
Hampton Wick	d		08 12				08 31					08 42				09 01					09 12	
Teddington	d		08 15				08 35					08 45				09 05					09 15	
Strawberry Hill	a						08 38									09 08						
Fulwell	d		08 19									08 49									09 19	
Hampton	d		08 23									08 53									09 23	
Kempton Park	d		08 26									08 56									09 26	
Sunbury	d		08 28									08 58									09 28	
Upper Halliford	d		08 30									09 00									09 30	
Shepperton	a		08 35									09 05									09 35	
Berrylands	d									08 30									09 00			
Surbiton 6	d				08a13			08 27		08 35				08a43			08 57		09 05			
Thames Ditton	d									08 39									09 09			
Hampton Court	a									08 42									09 12			
Hinchley Wood	d							08 31									09 01					
Claygate	d							08 34									09 04					
Oxshott	d							08 37									09 07					
Cobham & Stoke D'abernon	d							08 41									09 11					
Bookham	d	08 29									08 59									09 29		
Effingham Junction 6	d	08 33						08 45			09 03						09 15			09 33		
Horsley	d	08 36						08 48			09 06						09 18			09 36		
Clandon	d	08 41						08 53			09 11						09 23			09 41		
London Road (Guildford)	d	08 46						08 58			09 16						09 28			09 46		
Guildford	a	08 53						09 05			09 23						09 35			09 53		

Table 152

Saturdays
from 8 October

London - Chessington South, Dorking, Guildford, Shepperton and Hampton Court

		SW	SW	SW	SW	SW	SW	SW	SW	SW	SW	SW	SW	SW	SW	SW	SW	SW	SW	SW	SW	SW	SW
London Waterloo 15 ⊖	d	08 50	08 54	08 57	09 03	09 03	09 06	09 09	09 12	09 16	09 20	09 24	09 27	09 33	09 33	09 36	09 39	09 42	09 46	09 50	09 54	09 57	10 03
Vauxhall ⊖	d	08 54	08 58	09 01	09 07	09 07	09 10	09 13	09 16	09 20	09 24	09 28	09 31	09 37	09 37	09 40	09 43	09 46	09 50	09 54	09 58	10 01	10 07
Clapham Junction 10	d	08 59	09 03	09 06	09 12		09 15	09 18	09 21	09 25	09 29	09 33	09 36	09 42		09 45	09 48	09 51	09 55	09 59	10 03	10 06	10 12
Earlsfield	d	09 02	09 06	09 09	09 15		09 18	09 21	09 24	09 28	09 32	09 36	09 39	09 45		09 48	09 51	09 54	09 58	10 02	10 06	10 09	10 15
Wimbledon 6 ⊖	d	09 06	09 10	09 13	09 19		09 22	09 25	09 28	09 32	09 36	09 40	09 43	09 49		09 52	09 55	09 58	10 02	10 06	10 10	10 13	10 19
Raynes Park 6	d		09 13	09 16			09 25	09 28	09 31	09 35		09 43	09 46			09 55	09 58	10 01	10 05		10 13	10 16	
Motspur Park	d		09 16					09 31		09 38		09 46					10 01		10 08		10 16		
Malden Manor	d									09 41									10 11				
Tolworth	d									09 44									10 14				
Chessington North	d									09 47									10 17				
Chessington South	a									09 49									10 19				
Worcester Park	d		09 18					09 33				09 48					10 03				10 18		
Stoneleigh	d		09 21					09 36				09 51					10 06				10 21		
Ewell West	d		09 24					09 39				09 54					10 09				10 24		
Epsom 3	a		09 27					09 46				09 57					10 16				10 27		
	d		09 28					09 47				09 58					10 17				10 28		
Ashtead	d		09 32					09 51				10 02					10 21				10 32		
Leatherhead	d		09 35					09 54				10 05					10 24				10 35		
Boxhill & Westhumble	d																						
Dorking 4	a		09 43									10 13									10 43		
New Malden 6	d			09 19			09 28		09 34				09 49			09 58		10 04				10 19	
Norbiton	d			09 22					09 37				09 52					10 07				10 22	
Kingston	a			09 25		09 46			09 40				09 55		10 16			10 10				10 25	
	d			09 29					09 40				09 59					10 10				10 29	
Hampton Wick	d			09 31					09 42				10 01					10 12				10 31	
Teddington	d			09 35					09 45				10 05					10 15				10 35	
Strawberry Hill	a			09 38									10 08									10 38	
Fulwell	d								09 49									10 19					
Hampton	d								09 53									10 23					
Kempton Park	d								09 56									10 26					
Sunbury	d								09 58									10 28					
Upper Halliford	d								10 00									10 30					
Shepperton	a								10 05									10 35					
Berrylands	d						09 30									10 00							
Surbiton 6	d	09a13			09 27		09 35				09a43			09 57		10 05				10a13			10 27
Thames Ditton	d						09 39									10 09							
Hampton Court	a						09 42									10 12							
Hinchley Wood	d				09 31									10 01									10 31
Claygate	d				09 34									10 04									10 34
Oxshott	d				09 37									10 07									10 37
Cobham & Stoke D'abernon	d				09 41									10 11									10 41
Bookham	d							09 59									10 29						
Effingham Junction 6	d				09 45			10 03						10 15			10 33						10 45
Horsley	d				09 48			10 06						10 18			10 36						10 48
Clandon	d				09 53			10 11						10 23			10 41						10 53
London Road (Guildford)	d				09 58			10 16						10 28			10 46						10 58
Guildford	a				10 05			10 23						10 35			10 53						11 05

		SW	SW	SW	SW	SW	SW	SW	SW	SW	SW	SW	SW	SW	SW	SW	SW	SW	SW	SW	SW	SW
London Waterloo 15 ⊖	d	10 03	10 06	10 09	10 12	10 16	10 20	10 24	10 27	10 33	10 33	10 36	10 39	10 42	10 46	10 50	10 54	10 57	11 03	11 03	11 06	11 09
Vauxhall ⊖	d	10 07	10 10	10 13	10 16	10 20	10 24	10 28	10 31	10 37	10 37	10 40	10 43	10 46	10 50	10 54	10 58	11 01	11 07	11 07	11 10	11 13
Clapham Junction 10	d		10 15	10 18	10 21	10 25	10 29	10 33	10 36	10 42		10 45	10 48	10 51	10 55	10 59	11 03	11 06	11 12		11 15	11 18
Earlsfield	d		10 18	10 21	10 24	10 28	10 32	10 36	10 39	10 45		10 48	10 51	10 54	10 58	11 02	11 06	11 09	11 15		11 18	11 21
Wimbledon 6 ⊖	d		10 22	10 25	10 28	10 32	10 36	10 40	10 43	10 49		10 52	10 55	10 58	11 02	11 06	11 10	11 13	11 19		11 22	11 25
Raynes Park 6	d		10 25	10 28	10 31	10 35		10 43	10 46			10 55	10 58	11 01	11 05		11 13	11 16			11 25	11 28
Motspur Park	d			10 31		10 38		10 46					11 01		11 08		11 16					11 31
Malden Manor	d					10 41									11 11							
Tolworth	d					10 44									11 14							
Chessington North	d					10 47									11 17							
Chessington South	a					10 49									11 19							
Worcester Park	d			10 33				10 48					11 03				11 18					11 33
Stoneleigh	d			10 36				10 51					11 06				11 21					11 36
Ewell West	d			10 39				10 54					11 09				11 24					11 39
Epsom 3	a			10 46				10 57					11 16				11 27					11 46
	d			10 47				10 58					11 17				11 28					11 47
Ashtead	d			10 51				11 02					11 21				11 32					11 51
Leatherhead	d			10 54				11 05					11 24				11 35					11 54
Boxhill & Westhumble	d																					
Dorking 4	a							11 13									11 43					
New Malden 6	d		10 28		10 34				10 49			10 58		11 04				11 19			11 28	
Norbiton	d				10 37				10 52					11 07				11 22				
Kingston	a	10 46			10 40				10 55		11 16			11 10				11 25		11 46		
	d				10 40				10 59					11 10				11 29				
Hampton Wick	d				10 42				11 01					11 12				11 31				
Teddington	d				10 45				11 05					11 15				11 35				
Strawberry Hill	a								11 08									11 38				
Fulwell	d				10 49									11 19								
Hampton	d				10 53									11 23								
Kempton Park	d				10 56									11 26								
Sunbury	d				10 58									11 28								
Upper Halliford	d				11 00									11 30								
Shepperton	a				11 05									11 35								
Berrylands	d		10 30									11 00									11 30	
Surbiton 6	d		10 35				10a43			10 57		11 05				11a13			11 27		11 35	
Thames Ditton	d		10 39									11 09									11 39	
Hampton Court	a		10 42									11 12									11 42	
Hinchley Wood	d									11 01									11 31			
Claygate	d									11 04									11 34			
Oxshott	d									11 07									11 37			
Cobham & Stoke D'abernon	d									11 11									11 41			
Bookham	d			10 59									11 29									11 59
Effingham Junction 6	d			11 03						11 15			11 33						11 45			12 03
Horsley	d			11 06						11 18			11 36						11 48			12 06
Clandon	d			11 11						11 23			11 41						11 53			12 11
London Road (Guildford)	d			11 16						11 28			11 46						11 58			12 16
[illegible]				[illegible]						[illegible]			[illegible]						12 05			[illegible]

Table 152

Saturdays
from 8 October

London - Chessington South, Dorking, Guildford, Shepperton and Hampton Court

		SW	SW	SW	SW	SW	SW	SW	SW	SW	SW	SW	SW	SW	SW	SW	SW	SW	SW	SW	SW	SW	SW
London Waterloo 15 ⊖	d	11 12	11 16	11 20	11 24	11 27	11 33	11 33	11 36	11 39	11 42	11 46	11 50	11 54	11 57	12 03	12 03	12 06	12 09	12 12	12 16	12 20	12 24
Vauxhall ⊖	d	11 16	11 20	11 24	11 28	11 31	11 37	11 37	11 40	11 43	11 46	11 50	11 54	11 58	12 01	12 07	12 07	12 10	12 13	12 16	12 20	12 24	12 28
Clapham Junction 10	d	11 21	11 25	11 29	11 33	11 36	11 42		11 45	11 48	11 51	11 55	11 59	12 03	12 06	12 12		12 15	12 18	12 21	12 25	12 29	12 33
Earlsfield	d	11 24	11 28	11 32	11 36	11 39	11 45		11 48	11 51	11 54	11 58	12 02	12 06	12 09	12 15		12 18	12 21	12 24	12 28	12 32	12 36
Wimbledon 6 ⊖	d	11 28	11 32	11 36	11 40	11 43	11 49		11 52	11 55	11 58	12 02	12 06	12 10	12 13	12 19		12 22	12 25	12 28	12 32	12 36	12 40
Raynes Park 6	d	11 31	11 35		11 43	11 46			11 55	11 58	12 01	12 05		12 13	12 16			12 25	12 28	12 31	12 35		12 43
Motspur Park	d		11 38		11 46					12 01		12 08		12 16					12 31		12 38		12 46
Malden Manor	d		11 41									12 11									12 41		
Tolworth	d		11 44									12 14									12 44		
Chessington North	d		11 47									12 17									12 47		
Chessington South	a		11 49									12 19									12 49		
Worcester Park	d				11 48					12 03				12 18					12 33				12 48
Stoneleigh	d				11 51					12 06				12 21					12 36				12 51
Ewell West	d				11 54					12 09				12 24					12 39				12 54
Epsom 3	a				11 57					12 16				12 27					12 46				12 57
	d				11 58					12 17				12 28					12 47				12 58
Ashtead	d				12 02					12 21				12 32					12 51				13 02
Leatherhead	d				12 05					12 24				12 35					12 54				13 05
Boxhill & Westhumble	d																						
Dorking 4	a				12 13									12 43									13 13
New Malden 6	d	11 34				11 49			11 58		12 04				12 19			12 28		12 34			
Norbiton	d	11 37				11 52					12 07				12 22					12 37			
Kingston	a	11 40				11 55		12 16			12 10				12 25		12 46			12 40			
	d	11 40				11 59					12 10				12 29					12 40			
Hampton Wick	d	11 42				12 01					12 12				12 31					12 42			
Teddington	d	11 45				12 05					12 15				12 35					12 45			
Strawberry Hill	a					12 08									12 38								
Fulwell	d	11 49									12 19									12 49			
Hampton	d	11 53									12 23									12 53			
Kempton Park	d	11 56									12 26									12 56			
Sunbury	d	11 58									12 28									12 58			
Upper Halliford	d	12 00									12 30									13 00			
Shepperton	a	12 05									12 35									13 05			
Berrylands	d								12 00									12 30					
Surbiton 6	d			11a43			11 57		12 05				12a13			12 27		12 35				12a43	
Thames Ditton	d								12 09									12 39					
Hampton Court	a								12 12									12 42					
Hinchley Wood	d						12 01									12 31							
Claygate	d						12 04									12 34							
Oxshott	d						12 07									12 37							
Cobham & Stoke D'abernon	d						12 11									12 41							
Bookham	d									12 29									12 59				
Effingham Junction 6	d						12 15			12 33						12 45			13 03				
Horsley	d						12 18			12 36						12 48			13 06				
Clandon	d						12 23			12 41						12 53			13 11				
London Road (Guildford)	d						12 28			12 46						12 58			13 16				
Guildford	a						12 35			12 53						13 05			13 23				

		SW	SW	SW	SW	SW	SW	SW	SW	SW	SW	SW	SW	SW	SW	SW	SW	SW	SW	SW	SW	SW	SW
London Waterloo 15 ⊖	d	12 27	12 33	12 33	12 36	12 39	12 42	12 46	12 50	12 54	12 57	13 03	13 03	13 06	13 09	13 12	13 16	13 20	13 24	13 27	13 33	13 33	13 36
Vauxhall ⊖	d	12 31	12 37	12 37	12 40	12 43	12 46	12 50	12 54	12 58	13 01	13 07	13 07	13 10	13 13	13 16	13 20	13 24	13 28	13 31	13 37	13 37	13 40
Clapham Junction 10	d	12 36	12 42		12 45	12 48	12 51	12 55	12 59	13 03	13 06	13 12		13 15	13 18	13 21	13 25	13 29	13 33	13 36	13 42		13 45
Earlsfield	d	12 39	12 45		12 48	12 51	12 54	12 58	13 02	13 06	13 09	13 15		13 18	13 21	13 24	13 28	13 32	13 36	13 39	13 45		13 48
Wimbledon 6 ⊖	d	12 43	12 49		12 52	12 55	12 58	13 02	13 06	13 10	13 13	13 19		13 22	13 25	13 28	13 32	13 36	13 40	13 43	13 49		13 52
Raynes Park 6	d	12 46			12 55	12 58	13 01	13 05		13 13	13 16			13 25	13 28	13 31	13 35		13 43	13 46			13 55
Motspur Park	d					13 01		13 08		13 16					13 31		13 38		13 46				
Malden Manor	d							13 11									13 41						
Tolworth	d							13 14									13 44						
Chessington North	d							13 17									13 47						
Chessington South	a							13 19									13 49						
Worcester Park	d					13 03				13 18					13 33				13 48				
Stoneleigh	d					13 06				13 21					13 36				13 51				
Ewell West	d					13 09				13 24					13 39				13 54				
Epsom 3	a					13 16				13 27					13 46				13 57				
	d					13 17				13 28					13 47				13 58				
Ashtead	d					13 21				13 32					13 51				14 02				
Leatherhead	d					13 24				13 35					13 54				14 05				
Boxhill & Westhumble	d																						
Dorking 4	a									13 43									14 13				
New Malden 6	d	12 49			12 58		13 04				13 19			13 28		13 34				13 49			13 58
Norbiton	d	12 52					13 07				13 22					13 37				13 52			
Kingston	a	12 55		13 16			13 10				13 25		13 46			13 40				13 55		14 16	
	d	12 59					13 10				13 29					13 40				13 59			
Hampton Wick	d	13 01					13 12				13 31					13 42				14 01			
Teddington	d	13 05					13 15				13 35					13 45				14 05			
Strawberry Hill	a	13 08									13 38									14 08			
Fulwell	d						13 19									13 49							
Hampton	d						13 23									13 53							
Kempton Park	d						13 26									13 56							
Sunbury	d						13 28									13 58							
Upper Halliford	d						13 30									14 00							
Shepperton	a						13 35									14 05							
Berrylands	d				13 00									13 30									14 00
Surbiton 6	d		12 57		13 05				13a13			13 27		13 35				13a43			13 57		14 05
Thames Ditton	d				13 09									13 39									14 09
Hampton Court	a				13 12									13 42									14 12
Hinchley Wood	d		13 01									13 31									14 01		
Claygate	d		13 04									13 34									14 04		
Oxshott	d		13 07									13 37									14 07		
Cobham & Stoke D'abernon	d		13 11									13 41									14 11		
Bookham	d					13 29									13 59								
Effingham Junction 6	d		13 15			13 33						13 45			14 03						14 15		
Horsley	d		13 18			13 36						13 48			14 06						14 18		
Clandon	d		13 23			13 41						13 53			14 11						14 23		
London Road (Guildford)	d		13 28			13 46						13 58			14 16						14 28		
Guildford	a		13 35			13 53						14 05			14 23						14 35		

London - Chessington South, Dorking, Guildford, Shepperton and Hampton Court

from 8 October

		SW		SW	SW	SW	SW	SW	SW	SW	SW	SW		SW	SW	SW	SW	SW	SW	SW	SW	SW		SW	SW
London Waterloo ⊖	d	13 39		13 42	13 46	13 50	13 54	13 57	14 03	14 03	14 06	14 09		14 12	14 16	14 20	14 24	14 27	14 33	14 33	14 36	14 39		14 42	14 46
Vauxhall ⊖	d	13 43		13 46	13 50	13 54	13 58	14 01	14 07	14 07	14 10	14 13		14 16	14 20	14 24	14 28	14 31	14 37	14 37	14 40	14 43		14 46	14 50
Clapham Junction	d	13 48		13 51	13 55	13 59	14 03	14 06	14 12		14 15	14 18		14 21	14 25	14 29	14 33	14 36	14 42		14 45	14 48		14 51	14 55
Earlsfield	d	13 51		13 54	13 58	14 02	14 06	14 09	14 15		14 18	14 21		14 24	14 28	14 32	14 36	14 39	14 45		14 48	14 51		14 54	14 58
Wimbledon ⊖	d	13 55		13 58	14 02	14 06	14 10	14 13	14 19		14 22	14 25		14 28	14 32	14 36	14 40	14 43	14 49		14 52	14 55		14 58	15 02
Raynes Park	d	13 58		14 01	14 05		14 13	14 16			14 25	14 28		14 31	14 35		14 43	14 46			14 55	14 58		15 01	15 05
Motspur Park	d	14 01			14 08		14 16					14 31			14 38		14 46					15 01			15 08
Malden Manor	d				14 11										14 41										15 11
Tolworth	d				14 14										14 44										15 14
Chessington North	d				14 17										14 47										15 17
Chessington South	a				14 19										14 49										15 19
Worcester Park	d	14 03					14 18					14 33					14 48					15 03			
Stoneleigh	d	14 06					14 21					14 36					14 51					15 06			
Ewell West	d	14 09					14 24					14 39					14 54					15 09			
Epsom	a	14 16					14 27					14 46					14 57					15 16			
	d	14 17					14 28					14 47					14 58					15 17			
Ashtead	d	14 21					14 32					14 51					15 02					15 21			
Leatherhead	d	14 24					14 35					14 54					15 05					15 24			
Boxhill & Westhumble	d																								
Dorking	a						14 43										15 13								
New Malden	d			14 04				14 19			14 28			14 34				14 49			14 58			15 04	
Norbiton	d			14 07				14 22						14 37				14 52						15 07	
Kingston	a			14 10				14 25		14 46				14 40				14 55		15 16				15 10	
	d			14 10				14 29						14 40				14 59						15 10	
Hampton Wick	d			14 12				14 31						14 42				15 01						15 12	
Teddington	d			14 15				14 35						14 45				15 05						15 15	
Strawberry Hill	a							14 38										15 08							
Fulwell	d			14 19										14 49										15 19	
Hampton	d			14 23										14 53										15 23	
Kempton Park	d			14 26										14 56										15 26	
Sunbury	d			14 28										14 58										15 28	
Upper Halliford	d			14 30										15 00										15 30	
Shepperton	a			14 35										15 05										15 35	
Berrylands	d										14 30										15 00				
Surbiton	d					14a13			14 27		14 35					14a43			14 57		15 05				
Thames Ditton	d										14 39										15 09				
Hampton Court	a										14 42										15 12				
Hinchley Wood	d								14 31										15 01						
Claygate	d								14 34										15 04						
Oxshott	d								14 37										15 07						
Cobham & Stoke D'abernon	d								14 41										15 11						
Bookham	d	14 29										14 59										15 29			
Effingham Junction	d	14 33							14 45			15 03							15 15			15 33			
Horsley	d	14 36							14 48			15 06							15 18			15 36			
Clandon	d	14 41							14 53			15 11							15 23			15 41			
London Road (Guildford)	d	14 46							14 58			15 16							15 28			15 46			
Guildford	a	14 53							15 05			15 23							15 35			15 53			

		SW	SW	SW	SW	SW	SW	SW		SW	SW	SW	SW	SW	SW	SW	SW	SW		SW	SW	SW	SW	SW	SW
London Waterloo ⊖	d	14 50	14 54	14 57	15 03	15 03	15 06	15 09		15 12	15 16	15 20	15 24	15 27	15 33	15 33	15 36	15 39		15 42	15 46	15 50	15 54	15 57	16 03
Vauxhall ⊖	d	14 54	14 58	15 01	15 07	15 07	15 10	15 13		15 16	15 20	15 24	15 28	15 31	15 37	15 37	15 40	15 43		15 46	15 50	15 54	15 58	16 01	16 07
Clapham Junction	d	14 59	15 03	15 06	15 12		15 15	15 18		15 21	15 25	15 29	15 33	15 36	15 42		15 45	15 48		15 51	15 55	15 59	16 03	16 06	16 12
Earlsfield	d	15 02	15 06	15 09	15 15		15 18	15 21		15 24	15 28	15 32	15 36	15 39	15 45		15 48	15 51		15 54	15 58	16 02	16 06	16 09	16 15
Wimbledon ⊖	d	15 06	15 10	15 13	15 19		15 22	15 25		15 28	15 32	15 36	15 40	15 43	15 49		15 52	15 55		15 58	16 02	16 06	16 10	16 13	16 19
Raynes Park	d		15 13	15 16			15 25	15 28		15 31	15 35		15 43	15 46			15 55	15 58		16 01	16 05		16 13	16 16	
Motspur Park	d		15 16					15 31			15 38		15 46					16 01			16 08		16 16		
Malden Manor	d										15 41										16 11				
Tolworth	d										15 44										16 14				
Chessington North	d										15 47										16 17				
Chessington South	a										15 49										16 19				
Worcester Park	d		15 18					15 33					15 48					16 03					16 18		
Stoneleigh	d		15 21					15 36					15 51					16 06					16 21		
Ewell West	d		15 24					15 39					15 54					16 09					16 24		
Epsom	a		15 27					15 46					15 57					16 16					16 27		
	d		15 28					15 47					15 58					16 17					16 28		
Ashtead	d		15 32					15 51					16 02					16 21					16 32		
Leatherhead	d		15 35					15 54					16 05					16 24					16 35		
Boxhill & Westhumble	d																								
Dorking	a		15 43										16 13										16 43		
New Malden	d			15 19			15 28			15 34				15 49			15 58			16 04				16 19	
Norbiton	d			15 22						15 37				15 52						16 07				16 22	
Kingston	a			15 25		15 46				15 40				15 55		16 16				16 10				16 25	
	d			15 29						15 40				15 59						16 10				16 29	
Hampton Wick	d			15 31						15 42				16 01						16 12				16 31	
Teddington	d			15 35						15 45				16 05						16 15				16 35	
Strawberry Hill	a			15 38										16 08										16 38	
Fulwell	d									15 49										16 19					
Hampton	d									15 53										16 23					
Kempton Park	d									15 56										16 26					
Sunbury	d									15 58										16 28					
Upper Halliford	d									16 00										16 30					
Shepperton	a									16 05										16 35					
Berrylands	d						15 30										16 00								
Surbiton	d	15a13			15 27		15 35					15a43			15 57		16 05					16a13			16 27
Thames Ditton	d						15 39										16 09								
Hampton Court	a						15 42										16 12								
Hinchley Wood	d				15 31										16 01										16 31
Claygate	d				15 34										16 04										16 34
Oxshott	d				15 37										16 07										16 37
Cobham & Stoke D'abernon	d				15 41										16 11										16 41
Bookham	d							15 59										16 29							
Effingham Junction	d				15 45			16 03							16 15			16 33							16 45
Horsley	d				15 48			16 06							16 18			16 36							16 48
Clandon	d				15 53			16 11							16 23			16 41							16 53
London Road (Guildford)	d				15 58			16 16							16 28			16 46							16 58
Guildford	a				16 05			16 23							16 35			16 53							17 05

London - Chessington South, Dorking, Guildford, Shepperton and Hampton Court

Saturdays
from 8 October

		SW	SW	SW		SW	SW	SW	SW	SW	SW	SW	SW	SW		SW	SW	SW	SW	SW	SW	SW	SW	SW	
London Waterloo ⊖	d	16 03	16 06	16 09		16 12	16 16	16 20	16 24	16 27	16 33	16 33	16 36	16 39		16 42	16 46	16 50	16 54	16 57	17 03	17 03	17 06	17 09	
Vauxhall ⊖	d	16 07	16 10	16 13		16 16	16 20	16 24	16 28	16 31	16 37	16 37	16 40	16 43		16 46	16 50	16 54	16 58	17 01	17 07	17 07	17 10	17 13	
Clapham Junction	d		16 15	16 18		16 21	16 25	16 29	16 33	16 36	16 42		16 45	16 48		16 51	16 55	16 59	17 03	17 06	17 12		17 15	17 18	
Earlsfield	d		16 18	16 21		16 24	16 28	16 32	16 36	16 39	16 45		16 48	16 51		16 54	16 58	17 02	17 06	17 09	17 15		17 18	17 21	
Wimbledon ⊖	d		16 22	16 25		16 28	16 32	16 36	16 40	16 43	16 49		16 52	16 55		16 58	17 02	17 06	17 10	17 13	17 19		17 22	17 25	
Raynes Park	d		16 25	16 28		16 31	16 35		16 43	16 46			16 55	16 58		17 01	17 05		17 13	17 16			17 25	17 28	
Motspur Park	d			16 31			16 38		16 46					17 01			17 08		17 16					17 31	
Malden Manor	d						16 41										17 11								
Tolworth	d						16 44										17 14								
Chessington North	d						16 47										17 17								
Chessington South	a						16 49										17 19								
Worcester Park	d			16 33					16 48					17 03					17 18					17 33	
Stoneleigh	d			16 36					16 51					17 06					17 21					17 36	
Ewell West	d			16 39					16 54					17 09					17 24					17 39	
Epsom	a			16 46					16 57					17 16					17 27					17 46	
	d			16 47					16 58					17 17					17 28					17 47	
Ashtead	d			16 51					17 02					17 21					17 32					17 51	
Leatherhead	d			16 54					17 05					17 24					17 35					17 54	
Boxhill & Westhumble	d																								
Dorking	a								17 13										17 43						
New Malden	d		16 28			16 34				16 49			16 58			17 04				17 19			17 28		
Norbiton	d					16 37				16 52						17 07				17 22					
Kingston	a	16 46				16 40				16 55		17 16				17 10				17 25		17 46			
	d					16 40				16 59						17 10				17 29					
Hampton Wick	d					16 42				17 01						17 12				17 31					
Teddington	d					16 45				17 05						17 15				17 35					
Strawberry Hill	a									17 08										17 38					
Fulwell	d					16 49										17 19									
Hampton	d					16 53										17 23									
Kempton Park	d					16 56										17 26									
Sunbury	d					16 58										17 28									
Upper Halliford	d					17 00										17 30									
Shepperton	a					17 05										17 35									
Berrylands	d		16 30										17 00										17 30		
Surbiton	d		16 35					16a43			16 57		17 05					17a13			17 27		17 35		
Thames Ditton	d		16 39										17 09										17 39		
Hampton Court	a		16 42										17 12										17 42		
Hinchley Wood	d										17 01										17 31				
Claygate	d										17 04										17 34				
Oxshott	d										17 07										17 37				
Cobham & Stoke D'abernon	d										17 11										17 41				
Bookham	d			16 59										17 29										17 59	
Effingham Junction	d			17 03							17 15			17 33							17 45			18 03	
Horsley	d			17 06							17 18			17 36							17 48			18 06	
Clandon	d			17 11							17 23			17 41							17 53			18 11	
London Road (Guildford)	d			17 16							17 28			17 46							17 58			18 16	
Guildford	a			17 23							17 35			17 53							18 05			18 23	

		SW	SW	SW	SW	SW	SW	SW	SW	SW		SW	SW	SW	SW	SW	SW	SW	SW	SW		SW	SW	SW	SW
London Waterloo ⊖	d	17 12	17 16	17 20	17 24	17 27	17 33	17 33	17 36	17 39		17 42	17 46	17 50	17 54	17 57	18 03	18 03	18 06	18 09		18 12	18 16	18 20	18 24
Vauxhall ⊖	d	17 16	17 20	17 24	17 28	17 31	17 37	17 37	17 40	17 43		17 46	17 50	17 54	17 58	18 01	18 07	18 07	18 10	18 13		18 16	18 20	18 24	18 28
Clapham Junction	d	17 21	17 25	17 29	17 33	17 36	17 42		17 45	17 48		17 51	17 55	17 59	18 03	18 06	18 12		18 15	18 18		18 21	18 25	18 29	18 33
Earlsfield	d	17 24	17 28	17 32	17 36	17 39	17 45		17 48	17 51		17 54	17 58	18 02	18 06	18 09	18 15		18 18	18 21		18 24	18 28	18 32	18 36
Wimbledon ⊖	d	17 28	17 32	17 36	17 40	17 43	17 49		17 52	17 55		17 58	18 02	18 06	18 10	18 13	18 19		18 22	18 25		18 28	18 32	18 36	18 40
Raynes Park	d	17 31	17 35		17 43	17 46			17 55	17 58		18 01	18 05		18 13	18 16			18 25	18 28		18 31	18 35		18 43
Motspur Park	d		17 38		17 46					18 01			18 08		18 16					18 31			18 38		18 46
Malden Manor	d		17 41										18 11										18 41		
Tolworth	d		17 44										18 14										18 44		
Chessington North	d		17 47										18 17										18 47		
Chessington South	a		17 49										18 19										18 49		
Worcester Park	d				17 48					18 03					18 18					18 33					18 48
Stoneleigh	d				17 51					18 06					18 21					18 36					18 51
Ewell West	d				17 54					18 09					18 24					18 39					18 54
Epsom	a				17 57					18 16					18 27					18 46					18 57
	d				17 58					18 17					18 28					18 47					18 58
Ashtead	d				18 02					18 21					18 32					18 51					19 02
Leatherhead	d				18 05					18 24					18 35					18 54					19 05
Boxhill & Westhumble	d																								
Dorking	a				18 13										18 43										19 13
New Malden	d	17 34				17 49			17 58			18 04				18 19			18 28			18 34			
Norbiton	d	17 37				17 52						18 07				18 22						18 37			
Kingston	a	17 40				17 55		18 16				18 10				18 25		18 46				18 40			
	d	17 40				17 59						18 10				18 29						18 40			
Hampton Wick	d	17 42				18 01						18 12				18 31						18 42			
Teddington	d	17 45				18 05						18 15				18 35						18 45			
Strawberry Hill	a					18 08										18 38									
Fulwell	d	17 49										18 19										18 49			
Hampton	d	17 53										18 23										18 53			
Kempton Park	d	17 56										18 26										18 56			
Sunbury	d	17 58										18 28										18 58			
Upper Halliford	d	18 00										18 30										19 00			
Shepperton	a	18 05										18 35										19 05			
Berrylands	d								18 00										18 30						
Surbiton	d			17a43			17 57		18 05					18a13			18 27		18 35					18a43	
Thames Ditton	d								18 09										18 39						
Hampton Court	a								18 12										18 42						
Hinchley Wood	d						18 01										18 31								
Claygate	d						18 04										18 34								
Oxshott	d						18 07										18 37								
Cobham & Stoke D'abernon	d						18 11										18 41								
Bookham	d									18 29										18 59					
Effingham Junction	d						18 15			18 33							18 45			19 03					
Horsley	d						18 18			18 36							18 48			19 06					
Clandon	d						18 23			18 41							18 53			19 11					
London Road (Guildford)	d						18 28			18 46							18 58			19 16					
Guildford	a						18 35			18 53							19 05			19 23					

Table 152

Saturdays from 8 October

London - Chessington South, Dorking, Guildford, Shepperton and Hampton Court

Station		SW	SW	SW	SW	SW	SW	SW	SW	SW	SW	SW	SW	SW	SW	SW	SW	SW	SW	SW	SW	SW	SW
London Waterloo 15 ⊖	d	18 27	18 33	18 33	18 36	18 39	18 42	18 46	18 50	18 54	18 57	19 03	19 03	19 06	19 09	19 12	19 16	19 20	19 24	19 27	19 33	19 33	19 36
Vauxhall ⊖	d	18 31	18 37	18 37	18 40	18 43	18 46	18 50	18 54	18 58	19 01	19 07	19 07	19 10	19 13	19 16	19 20	19 24	19 28	19 31	19 37	19 37	19 40
Clapham Junction 10	d	18 36	18 42		18 45	18 48	18 51	18 55	18 59	19 03	19 06	19 12		19 15	19 18	19 21	19 25	19 29	19 33	19 36	19 42		19 45
Earlsfield	d	18 39	18 45		18 48	18 51	18 54	18 58	19 02	19 06	19 09	19 15		19 18	19 21	19 24	19 28	19 32	19 36	19 39	19 45		19 48
Wimbledon 6 ⊖	d	18 43	18 49		18 52	18 55	18 58	19 02	19 06	19 10	19 13	19 19		19 22	19 25	19 28	19 32	19 36	19 40	19 43	19 49		19 52
Raynes Park 6	d	18 46			18 55	18 58	19 01	19 05		19 13	19 16			19 25	19 28	19 31	19 35		19 43	19 46			19 55
Motspur Park	d					19 01		19 08		19 16					19 31		19 38		19 46				
Malden Manor	d							19 11									19 41						
Tolworth	d							19 14									19 44						
Chessington North	d							19 17									19 47						
Chessington South	a							19 19									19 49						
Worcester Park	d					19 03				19 18					19 33				19 48				
Stoneleigh	d					19 06				19 21					19 36				19 51				
Ewell West	d					19 09				19 24					19 39				19 54				
Epsom 3	a					19 16				19 27					19 46				19 57				
	d					19 17				19 28					19 47				19 58				
Ashtead	d					19 21				19 32					19 51				20 02				
Leatherhead	d					19 24				19 35					19 54				20 05				
Boxhill & Westhumble	d																						
Dorking 4	a									19 43									20 13				
New Malden 6	d	18 49			18 58		19 04				19 19			19 28		19 34				19 49			19 58
Norbiton	d	18 52					19 07				19 22					19 37				19 52			
Kingston	a	18 55		19 16			19 10				19 25		19 46			19 40				19 55		20 16	
	d	18 59					19 10				19 29					19 40				19 59			
Hampton Wick	d	19 01					19 12				19 31					19 42				20 01			
Teddington	d	19 05					19 15				19 35					19 45				20 05			
Strawberry Hill	a	19 08									19 38									20 08			
Fulwell	d						19 19									19 49							
Hampton	d						19 23									19 53							
Kempton Park	d						19 26									19 56							
Sunbury	d						19 28									19 58							
Upper Halliford	d						19 30									20 00							
Shepperton	a						19 35									20 05							
Berrylands	d				19 00									19 30									20 00
Surbiton 6	d		18 57		19 05				19a13			19 27		19 35				19a43			19 57		20 05
Thames Ditton	d				19 09									19 39									20 09
Hampton Court	a				19 12									19 42									20 12
Hinchley Wood	d		19 01									19 31									20 01		
Claygate	d		19 04									19 34									20 04		
Oxshott	d		19 07									19 37									20 07		
Cobham & Stoke D'abernon	d		19 11									19 41									20 11		
Bookham	d					19 29									19 59								
Effingham Junction 6	d		19 15			19 33						19 45			20 03						20 15		
Horsley	d		19 18			19 36						19 48			20 06						20 18		
Clandon	d		19 23			19 41						19 53			20 11						20 23		
London Road (Guildford)	d		19 28			19 46						19 58			20 16						20 28		
Guildford	a		19 35			19 53						20 05			20 23						20 35		

Station		SW	SW	SW	SW	SW	SW	SW	SW	SW	SW	SW	SW	SW	SW	SW	SW	SW	SW	SW	SW	SW
London Waterloo 15 ⊖	d	19 39	19 42	19 46	19 50	19 54	19 57	20 03	20 03	20 06	20 09	20 12	20 16	20 20	20 24	20 27	20 33	20 33	20 36	20 39	20 42	20 46
Vauxhall ⊖	d	19 43	19 46	19 50	19 54	19 58	20 01	20 07	20 07	20 10	20 13	20 16	20 20	20 24	20 28	20 31	20 37	20 37	20 40	20 43	20 46	20 50
Clapham Junction 10	d	19 48	19 51	19 55	19 59	20 03	20 06	20 12		20 15	20 18	20 21	20 25	20 29	20 33	20 36	20 42		20 45	20 48	20 51	20 55
Earlsfield	d	19 51	19 54	19 58	20 02	20 06	20 09	20 15		20 18	20 21	20 24	20 28	20 32	20 36	20 39	20 45		20 48	20 51	20 54	20 58
Wimbledon 6 ⊖	d	19 55	19 58	20 02	20 06	20 10	20 13	20 19		20 22	20 25	20 28	20 32	20 36	20 40	20 43	20 49		20 52	20 55	20 58	21 02
Raynes Park 6	d	19 58	20 01	20 05		20 13	20 16			20 25	20 28	20 31	20 35		20 43	20 46			20 55	20 58	21 01	21 05
Motspur Park	d	20 01		20 08		20 16					20 31		20 38		20 46					21 01		21 08
Malden Manor	d			20 11									20 41									21 11
Tolworth	d			20 14									20 44									21 14
Chessington North	d			20 17									20 47									21 17
Chessington South	a			20 19									20 49									21 19
Worcester Park	d	20 03				20 18					20 33				20 48					21 03		
Stoneleigh	d	20 06				20 21					20 36				20 51					21 06		
Ewell West	d	20 09				20 24					20 39				20 54					21 09		
Epsom 3	a	20 16				20 27					20 46				20 57					21 16		
	d	20 17									20 47									21 17		
Ashtead	d	20 21									20 51									21 21		
Leatherhead	d	20 24									20 54									21 24		
Boxhill & Westhumble	d																					
Dorking 4	a										21 02											
New Malden 6	d		20 04				20 19			20 28		20 34				20 49			20 58		21 04	
Norbiton	d		20 07				20 22					20 37				20 52					21 07	
Kingston	a		20 10				20 25		20 46			20 40				20 55		21 16			21 10	
	d		20 10				20 29					20 40				20 59					21 10	
Hampton Wick	d		20 12				20 31					20 42				21 01					21 12	
Teddington	d		20 15				20 35					20 45				21 05					21 15	
Strawberry Hill	a						20 38									21 08						
Fulwell	d		20 19									20 49									21 19	
Hampton	d		20 23									20 53									21 23	
Kempton Park	d		20 26									20 56									21 26	
Sunbury	d		20 28									20 58									21 28	
Upper Halliford	d		20 30									21 00									21 30	
Shepperton	a		20 35									21 05									21 35	
Berrylands	d									20 30									21 00			
Surbiton 6	d				20a13			20 27		20 35				20a43			20 57		21 05			
Thames Ditton	d									20 39									21 09			
Hampton Court	a									20 42									21 12			
Hinchley Wood	d							20 31									21 01					
Claygate	d							20 34									21 04					
Oxshott	d							20 37									21 07					
Cobham & Stoke D'abernon	d							20 41									21 11					
Bookham	d	20 29																		21 29		
Effingham Junction 6	d	20 33						20 45									21 15			21 33		
Horsley	d	20 36						20 48									21 18			21 36		
Clandon	d	20 41						20 53									21 23			21 41		
London Road (Guildford)	d	20 46						20 58									21 28			21 46		

Table 152

Saturdays from 8 October

London - Chessington South, Dorking, Guildford, Shepperton and Hampton Court

Station		SW	SW	SW	SW	SW	SW	SW	SW	SW	SW	SW	SW	SW	SW	SW	SW	SW	SW	SW	SW	SW	SW
London Waterloo 15 ⊖	d	20 50	20 54	20 57	21 03	21 03	21 09	21 12	21 20	21 24	21 27	21 33	21 33	21 36	21 39	21 42	21 46	21 50	21 54	21 57	22 03	22 03	22 09
Vauxhall ⊖	d	20 54	20 58	21 01	21 07	21 07	21 13	21 16	21 24	21 28	21 31	21 37	21 37	21 40	21 43	21 46	21 50	21 54	21 58	22 01	22 07	22 07	22 13
Clapham Junction 10	d	20 59	21 03	21 06	21 12		21 18	21 21	21 29	21 33	21 36	21 42		21 45	21 48	21 51	21 55	21 59	22 03	22 06	22 12		22 18
Earlsfield	d	21 02	21 06	21 09	21 15		21 21	21 24	21 32	21 36	21 39	21 45		21 48	21 51	21 54	21 58	22 02	22 06	22 09	22 15		22 21
Wimbledon 6 ⊖	d	21 06	21 10	21 13	21 19		21 25	21 28	21 36	21 40	21 43	21 49		21 52	21 55	21 58	22 02	22 06	22 10	22 13	22 19		22 25
Raynes Park 6	d		21 13	21 16			21 28	21 31		21 43	21 46			21 55	21 58	22 01	22 05		22 13	22 16			22 28
Motspur Park	d		21 16				21 31			21 46					22 01		22 08		22 16				22 31
Malden Manor	d																22 11						
Tolworth	d																22 14						
Chessington North	d																22 17						
Chessington South	a																22 19						
Worcester Park	d		21 18				21 33			21 48					22 03				22 18				22 33
Stoneleigh	d		21 21				21 36			21 51					22 06				22 21				22 36
Ewell West	d		21 24				21 39			21 54					22 09				22 24				22 39
Epsom 3	a		21 27				21 46			21 57					22 16				22 27				22 46
	d						21 47								22 17								22 47
Ashtead	d						21 51								22 21								22 51
Leatherhead	d						21 54								22 24								22 54
Boxhill & Westhumble	d																						
Dorking 4	a						22 02																23 02
New Malden 6	d			21 19				21 34			21 49			21 58		22 04				22 19			
Norbiton	d			21 22				21 37			21 52					22 07				22 22			
Kingston	a			21 25		21 46		21 40			21 55		22 16			22 10				22 25		22 46	
	d			21 29				21 40			21 59					22 10				22 29			
Hampton Wick	d			21 31				21 42			22 01					22 12				22 31			
Teddington	d			21 35				21 45			22 05					22 15				22 35			
Strawberry Hill	a			21 38							22 08									22 38			
Fulwell	d							21 49								22 19							
Hampton	d							21 53								22 23							
Kempton Park	d							21 56								22 26							
Sunbury	d							21 58								22 28							
Upper Halliford	d							22 00								22 30							
Shepperton	a							22 05								22 35							
Berrylands	d													22 00									
Surbiton 6	d	21a13			21 27				21a43			21 57		22 05				22 14			22 27		
Thames Ditton	d													22 09									
Hampton Court	a													22 12									
Hinchley Wood	d				21 31							22 01									22 31		
Claygate	d				21 34							22 04									22 34		
Oxshott	d				21 37							22 07									22 37		
Cobham & Stoke D'abernon	d				21 41							22 11									22 41		
Bookham	d														22 29								
Effingham Junction 6	d				21 45							22 15			22 33						22 45		
Horsley	d				21 48							22 18			22 36						22 48		
Clandon	d				21 53							22 23			22 41						22 53		
London Road (Guildford)	d				21 58							22 28			22 46						22 58		
Guildford	a				22 05							22 35			22 53			22 47			23 05		

Station		SW	SW	SW	SW	SW	SW	SW	SW	SW	SW	SW	SW	SW	SW	SW	SW	SW	SW	SW	SW	SW
London Waterloo 15 ⊖	d	22 12	22 20	22 27	22 33	22 33	22 36	22 39	22 42	22 50	22 57	23 00	23 03	23 03	23 09	23 12	23 20	23 27	23 33	23 36	23 42	23 50
Vauxhall ⊖	d	22 16	22 24	22 31	22 37	22 37	22 40	22 43	22 46	22 54	23 01	23 04	23 07	23 07	23 13	23 16	23 24	23 31	23 37	23 40	23 46	23 54
Clapham Junction 10	d	22 21	22 29	22 36	22 42		22 45	22 48	22 51	22 59	23 06	23 09	23 12		23 18	23 21	23 29	23 36		23 45	23 51	23 59
Earlsfield	d	22 24	22 32	22 39	22 45		22 48	22 51	22 54	23 02	23 09	23 12	23 15		23 21	23 24	23 32	23 39		23 48	23 54	00 02
Wimbledon 6 ⊖	d	22 28	22 36	22 43	22 49		22 52	22 55	22 58	23 06	23 13	23 16	23 19		23 25	23 28	23 36	23 43		23 52	23 58	00 06
Raynes Park 6	d	22 31		22 46			22 55	22 58	23 01		23 16	23 19			23 28	23 31		23 46		23 55	00 01	
Motspur Park	d							23 01				23 22			23 31						00 04	
Malden Manor	d											23 25										
Tolworth	d											23 28										
Chessington North	d											23 31										
Chessington South	a											23 33										
Worcester Park	d							23 03							23 33						00 06	
Stoneleigh	d							23 06							23 36						00 09	
Ewell West	d							23 09							23 39						00 12	
Epsom 3	a							23 12							23 42						00 15	
	d							23 17							23 47						00 19	
Ashtead	d							23 21							23 51						00 23	
Leatherhead	d							23 24							23 54						00 26	
Boxhill & Westhumble	d																					
Dorking 4	a														00 03							
New Malden 6	d	22 34		22 49			22 58		23 04		23 19					23 34		23 49		23 58		
Norbiton	d	22 37		22 52					23 07		23 22					23 37		23 52				
Kingston	a	22 40		22 55		23 16			23 10		23 25			23 46		23 40		23 55	00 16			
	d	22 40		22 59					23 10		23 29					23 40		23 55				
Hampton Wick	d	22 42		23 01					23 12		23 31					23 42		23 57				
Teddington	d	22 45		23 05					23 15		23 35					23 45		23 59				
Strawberry Hill	a			23 08							23 38							00 03				
Fulwell	d	22 49							23 19							23 49						
Hampton	d	22 53							23 23							23 53						
Kempton Park	d	22 56							23 26							23 56						
Sunbury	d	22 58							23 28							23 58						
Upper Halliford	d	23 00							23 30							23 59						
Shepperton	a	23 05							23 35							00 05						
Berrylands	d						23 00													23 59		
Surbiton 6	d		22a43		22 57		23 05			23a13			23 27				23a43			00 05		00 14
Thames Ditton	d						23 09													00 09		
Hampton Court	a						23 12													00 12		
Hinchley Wood	d				23 01								23 31									00 18
Claygate	d				23 04								23 34									00 20
Oxshott	d				23 07								23 37									00 24
Cobham & Stoke D'abernon	d				23 11								23 41									00 27
Bookham	d							23 29													00 31	
Effingham Junction 6	d				23 15			23 33					23 45								00 36	00 32
Horsley	d				23 18			23 36					23 48								00 39	00 34
Clandon	d				23 23			23 41					23 53								00 44	00 39
London Road (Guildford)	d				23 28			23 46					23 58								00 49	00 44
Guildford	a				23 35			23 53					00 05								00 56	00 51

London - Chessington South, Dorking, Guildford, Shepperton and Hampton Court

Sundays from 8 October

		SW
London Waterloo	d	23 57
Vauxhall	d	00 01
Clapham Junction	d	00 06
Earlsfield	d	00 09
Wimbledon	d	00 13
Raynes Park	d	00 16
Motspur Park	d	
Malden Manor	d	
Tolworth	d	
Chessington North	d	
Chessington South	a	
Worcester Park	d	
Stoneleigh	d	
Ewell West	d	
Epsom	a	
	d	
Ashtead	d	
Leatherhead	d	
Boxhill & Westhumble	d	
Dorking	a	
New Malden	d	00 19
Norbiton	d	00 22
Kingston	a	00 25
	d	00 25
Hampton Wick	d	00 27
Teddington	d	00 30
Strawberry Hill	a	
Fulwell	d	00 34
Hampton	d	00 38
Kempton Park	d	00 41
Sunbury	d	00 43
Upper Halliford	d	00 45
Shepperton	a	00 50
Berrylands	d	
Surbiton	d	
Thames Ditton	d	
Hampton Court	a	
Hinchley Wood	d	
Claygate	d	
Oxshott	d	
Cobham & Stoke D'abernon	d	
Bookham	d	
Effingham Junction	d	
Horsley	d	
Clandon	d	
London Road (Guildford)	d	
Guildford	a	

London - Chessington South, Dorking, Guildford, Shepperton and Hampton Court

Sundays until 25 September

		SW A	SW A	SW A	SW A	SW A	SW A	SW A	SW A	SW A	SW	SW	SW	SW	SW	SW	SW	SW	SW	SW	SW	SW	SW
London Waterloo	d	23p03	23p09	23p12	23p27	23p33	23p36	23p42	23p50	23p57	00 09	00 15	00 18	00 27	00 42	01 42	06 14	06 18		06 57			07 10
Vauxhall	d	23p07	23p13	23p16	23p31	23p37	23p40	23p46	23p54	00 01	00 13	00 19	00 22	00 31	00 46	01 46	06 18	06 22		07 01			07 14
Clapham Junction	d	23p12	23p18	23p21	23p36		23p45	23p51	23p59	00 06	00 20	00 25		00 37		01 53		06 27		07 06			07 19
Earlsfield	d	23p15	23p21	23p24	23p39		23p48	23p54	00 02	00 09	00 23	00 29		00s41						07 09			07 22
Wimbledon	d	23p19	23p25	23p28	23p43		23p52	23p58	00 06	00 13	00 27	00 33		00 45	01 05	01 59		06 34	06 48	07 13	07 16	07 20	07 26
Raynes Park	d		23p28	23p31	23p46		23p55	00 01		00 16		00 36		00 48	01 08	02 02		06 37	06 52	07 16		07 23	
Motspur Park	d		23p31					00 04				00 38							06 55			07 26	
Malden Manor	d																						
Tolworth	d																						
Chessington North	d																						
Chessington South	a																						
Worcester Park	d		23p33					00 06				00 41							06 57			07 28	
Stoneleigh	d		23p36					00 09				00 44							07 00			07 31	
Ewell West	d		23p39					00 12				00 46							07 03			07 34	
Epsom	a		23p42					00 15				00 50							07 06			07 37	
	d		23p47					00 19															
Ashtead	d		23p51					00 23															
Leatherhead	d		23p54					00 26															
Boxhill & Westhumble	d																						
Dorking	a		00 01																				
New Malden	d			23p34	23p49		23p58			00 19				00 50	01 11	02 04		06 40		07 19			
Norbiton	d			23p37	23p52					00 22					01 14	02 08		06 43					
Kingston	a			23p40	23p55	00 16				00 25			01 01		01 17	02 10	06 59	06 46					
	d			23p40	23p55					00 25					01 17	02 11		06 49					
Hampton Wick	d			23p42	23p57					00 27					01s22	02s13		06 51					
Teddington	d			23p45	23p59					00 30					01s25	02s15		06 56					
Strawberry Hill	a				00 03										01 28	02s18		06 59					
Fulwell	d			23p49						00 34													
Hampton	d			23p53						00 38													
Kempton Park	d			23p56						00 41													
Sunbury	d			23p58						00 43													
Upper Halliford	d			23p59						00 45													
Shepperton	a			00 03						00 48													
Berrylands	d						23p59							00s53						07 21			
Surbiton	d	23p27					00 05		00 14		00 35			00a56						07 25	07 32		07 35
Thames Ditton	d						00 09													07 30			
Hampton Court	a						00 12													07 33			
Hinchley Wood	d	23p31							00 18												07 36		
Claygate	d	23p34							00 20												07 39		
Oxshott	d	23p37							00 24												07 42		
Cobham & Stoke D'abernon	d	23p41							00 27												07 46		
Bookham	d							00 31															
Effingham Junction	d	23p45						00 36	00 32												07 50		
Horsley	d	23p48						00 39	00 34												07 53		
Clandon	d	23p53						00 44	00 39												07 58		
London Road (Guildford)	d	23p58						00 49	00 44												08 03		
Guildford	a	00 02						00 53	00 48		01 07										08 07		08 14

A not 22 May

Table 152

Sundays until 25 September

London - Chessington South, Dorking, Guildford, Shepperton and Hampton Court

		SW	SW	SW	SW	SW	SW	SW	SW	SW	SW	SW	SW	SW	SW	SW	SW	SW	SW	SW	SW	SW	SW
London Waterloo ⊖	d	07 14	07 18		07 27		07 40	07 48		07 57		08 02	08 10	08 14	08 18	08 21	08 27	08 32	08 40	08 48	08 51	08 57	
Vauxhall ⊖	d	07 18	07 22		07 31		07 44	07 52		08 01		08 06	08 14	08 18	08 22	08 25	08 31	08 36	08 44	08 52	08 55	09 01	
Clapham Junction	d		07 27		07 36		07 49	07 57		08 06		08 11	08 19		08 27	08 30	08 36	08 41	08 49	08 57	09 00	09 06	
Earlsfield	d		07 30		07 39		07 52	08 00		08 09		08 14	08 22		08 30	08 33	08 39	08 44	08 52	09 00	09 03	09 09	
Wimbledon ⊖	d		07 34	07 37	07 43	07 48	07 56	08 04	08 07	08 13	08 16	08 18	08 26		08 34	08 37	08 43	08 48	08 56	09 04	09 07	09 13	09 16
Raynes Park	d		07 37	07 40	07 46	07 52		08 07	08 10	08 16		08 22			08 37	08 40	08 46	08 52		09 07	09 10	09 16	
Motspur Park	d			07 43		07 55			08 13			08 25				08 43		08 55			09 13		
Malden Manor	d			07 46					08 16							08 46					09 16		
Tolworth	d			07 49					08 19							08 49					09 19		
Chessington North	d			07 52					08 22							08 52					09 22		
Chessington South	a			07 54					08 24							08 54					09 24		
Worcester Park	d					07 57						08 27						08 57					
Stoneleigh	d					08 00						08 30						09 00					
Ewell West	d					08 03						08 33						09 03					
Epsom	a					08 06						08 36						09 06					
	d					08 08						08 38						09 08					
Ashtead	d					08 12						08 42						09 12					
Leatherhead	d					08 15						08 45						09 15					
Boxhill & Westhumble	d																						
Dorking	a											08 51											
New Malden	d		07 40		07 49			08 10		08 19					08 40		08 49			09 10		09 19	
Norbiton	d		07 43					08 13							08 43					09 13			
Kingston	a	07 59	07 46					08 16						08 59	08 46					09 16			
	d		07 49					08 16							08 49					09 16			
Hampton Wick	d		07 51					08 18							08 51					09 18			
Teddington	d		07 56					08 21							08 56					09 21			
Strawberry Hill	a		07 59												08 59								
Fulwell	d							08 25												09 25			
Hampton	d							08 29												09 29			
Kempton Park	d							08 32												09 32			
Sunbury	d							08 34												09 34			
Upper Halliford	d							08 36												09 36			
Shepperton	a							08 39												09 39			
Berrylands	d				07 51					08 21							08 51					09 21	
Surbiton	d				07 55		08 05			08 25	08 32		08 35				08 55		09 05			09 25	09 32
Thames Ditton	d				08 00					08 30							09 00					09 30	
Hampton Court	a				08 03					08 33							09 03					09 33	
Hinchley Wood	d										08 36												09 36
Claygate	d										08 39												09 39
Oxshott	d										08 42												09 42
Cobham & Stoke D'abernon	d										08 46												09 46
Bookham	d					08 21												09 21					
Effingham Junction	d					08 25					08 50							09 25					09 50
Horsley	d					08 27					08 53							09 27					09 53
Clandon	d					08 32					08 58							09 32					09 58
London Road (Guildford)	d					08 37					09 03							09 37					10 03
Guildford	a					08 41	08 40				09 07		09 10					09 41	09 40				10 07

		SW	SW	SW	SW	SW	SW	SW	SW	SW	SW	SW	SW	SW	SW	SW	SW	SW	SW	SW	SW	SW
London Waterloo ⊖	d	09 02	09 10	09 14	09 18	09 21	09 27	09 32	09 40	09 48	09 51	09 57		10 02	10 10	10 14	10 18	10 21	10 27	10 32	10 40	10 48
Vauxhall ⊖	d	09 06	09 14	09 18	09 22	09 25	09 31	09 36	09 44	09 52	09 55	10 01		10 06	10 14	10 18	10 22	10 25	10 31	10 36	10 44	10 52
Clapham Junction	d	09 11	09 19		09 27	09 30	09 36	09 41	09 49	09 57	10 00	10 06		10 11	10 19		10 27	10 30	10 36	10 41	10 49	10 57
Earlsfield	d	09 14	09 22		09 30	09 33	09 39	09 44	09 52	10 00	10 03	10 09		10 14	10 22		10 30	10 33	10 39	10 44	10 52	11 00
Wimbledon ⊖	d	09 18	09 26		09 34	09 37	09 43	09 48	09 56	10 04	10 07	10 13	10 16	10 18	10 26		10 34	10 37	10 43	10 48	10 56	11 04
Raynes Park	d	09 22			09 37	09 40	09 46	09 52		10 07	10 10	10 16		10 22			10 37	10 40	10 46	10 52		11 07
Motspur Park	d	09 25				09 43		09 55			10 13			10 25				10 43		10 55		
Malden Manor	d					09 46					10 16							10 46				
Tolworth	d					09 49					10 19							10 49				
Chessington North	d					09 52					10 22							10 52				
Chessington South	a					09 54					10 24							10 54				
Worcester Park	d	09 27						09 57						10 27						10 57		
Stoneleigh	d	09 30						10 00						10 30						11 00		
Ewell West	d	09 33						10 03						10 33						11 03		
Epsom	a	09 36						10 06						10 36						11 06		
	d	09 38						10 08						10 38						11 08		
Ashtead	d	09 42						10 12						10 42						11 12		
Leatherhead	d	09 45						10 15						10 45						11 15		
Boxhill & Westhumble	d																					
Dorking	a	09 51												10 51								
New Malden	d				09 40		09 49			10 10		10 19					10 40		10 49			11 10
Norbiton	d				09 43					10 13							10 43					11 13
Kingston	a			09 59	09 46					10 16						10 59	10 46					11 16
	d				09 49					10 16							10 49					11 16
Hampton Wick	d				09 51					10 18							10 51					11 18
Teddington	d				09 56					10 21							10 56					11 21
Strawberry Hill	a				09 59												10 59					
Fulwell	d									10 25												11 25
Hampton	d									10 29												11 29
Kempton Park	d									10 32												11 32
Sunbury	d									10 34												11 34
Upper Halliford	d									10 36												11 36
Shepperton	a									10 39												11 39
Berrylands	d						09 51					10 21							10 51			
Surbiton	d		09 35				09 55		10 05			10 25	10 32		10 35				10 55		11 05	
Thames Ditton	d						10 00					10 30							11 00			
Hampton Court	a						10 03					10 33							11 03			
Hinchley Wood	d												10 36									
Claygate	d												10 39									
Oxshott	d												10 42									
Cobham & Stoke D'abernon	d												10 46									
Bookham	d							10 21												11 21		
Effingham Junction	d							10 25					10 50							11 25		
Horsley	d							10 27					10 53							11 27		
Clandon	d							10 32					10 58							11 32		
London Road (Guildford)	d							10 37					11 03							11 37		
Guildford	a		10 10					10 41	10 44				11 07		11 14					11 41	11 44	

Table 152

Sundays until 25 September

London - Chessington South, Dorking, Guildford, Shepperton and Hampton Court

		SW	SW	SW	SW	SW	SW	SW	SW	SW	SW	SW	SW	SW	SW	SW	SW	SW	SW	SW	SW	SW	SW
London Waterloo ⊖	d	10 51	10 57		11 02	11 10	11 14	11 18	11 21	11 27	11 32	11 40	11 48	11 51	11 57		12 02	12 10	12 14	12 18	12 21	12 27	12 32
Vauxhall ⊖	d	10 55	11 01		11 06	11 14	11 19	11 22	11 25	11 31	11 36	11 44	11 52	11 55	12 01		12 06	12 14	12 19	12 22	12 25	12 31	12 36
Clapham Junction	d	11 00	11 06		11 11	11 19		11 27	11 30	11 36	11 41	11 49	11 57	12 00	12 06		12 11	12 19		12 27	12 30	12 36	12 41
Earlsfield	d	11 03	11 09		11 14	11 22		11 30	11 33	11 39	11 44	11 52	12 00	12 03	12 09		12 14	12 22		12 30	12 33	12 39	12 44
Wimbledon ⊖	d	11 07	11 13	11 16	11 18	11 26		11 34	11 37	11 43	11 48	11 56	12 04	12 07	12 13	12 16	12 18	12 26		12 34	12 37	12 43	12 48
Raynes Park	d	11 10	11 16		11 22			11 37	11 40	11 46	11 52		12 07	12 10	12 16		12 22			12 37	12 40	12 46	12 52
Motspur Park	d	11 13			11 25				11 43		11 55			12 13			12 25				12 43		12 55
Malden Manor	d	11 16							11 46					12 16							12 46		
Tolworth	d	11 19							11 49					12 19							12 49		
Chessington North	d	11 22							11 52					12 22							12 52		
Chessington South	a	11 24							11 54					12 24							12 54		
Worcester Park	d				11 27						11 57						12 27						12 57
Stoneleigh	d				11 30						12 00						12 30						13 00
Ewell West	d				11 33						12 03						12 33						13 03
Epsom	a				11 36						12 06						12 36						13 06
	d				11 38						12 08						12 38						13 08
Ashtead	d				11 42						12 12						12 42						13 12
Leatherhead	d				11 45						12 15						12 45						13 15
Boxhill & Westhumble	d																						
Dorking	a				11 51												12 51						
New Malden	d		11 19					11 40		11 49			12 10		12 19					12 40		12 49	
Norbiton	d							11 43					12 13							12 43			
Kingston	a						11 59	11 46					12 16						12 59	12 46			
	d							11 49					12 16							12 49			
Hampton Wick	d							11 51					12 18							12 51			
Teddington	d							11 56					12 21							12 56			
Strawberry Hill	a							11 59												12 59			
Fulwell	d												12 25										
Hampton	d												12 29										
Kempton Park	d												12 32										
Sunbury	d												12 34										
Upper Halliford	d												12 36										
Shepperton	a												12 39										
Berrylands	d		11 21							11 51					12 21							12 51	
Surbiton	d		11 25	11 32		11 35				11 55		12 05			12 25	12 32		12 35				12 55	
Thames Ditton	d		11 30							12 00					12 30							13 00	
Hampton Court	a		11 33							12 03					12 33							13 03	
Hinchley Wood	d			11 36												12 36							
Claygate	d			11 39												12 39							
Oxshott	d			11 42												12 42							
Cobham & Stoke D'abernon	d			11 46												12 46							
Bookham	d										12 21												13 21
Effingham Junction	d			11 50							12 25					12 50							13 25
Horsley	d			11 53							12 27					12 53							13 27
Clandon	d			11 58							12 32					12 58							13 32
London Road (Guildford)	d			12 03							12 37					13 03							13 37
Guildford	a			12 07		12 14					12 41	12 44				13 07		13 14					13 41

		SW	SW	SW	SW	SW	SW	SW	SW	SW	SW	SW	SW	SW	SW	SW	SW	SW	SW	SW	SW	SW
London Waterloo ⊖	d	12 40	12 48	12 51	12 57	13 00	13 02	13 10	13 14	13 18	13 21	13 27	13 32	13 40	13 48	13 51	13 56	13 57	14 00	14 02	14 10	14 14
Vauxhall ⊖	d	12 44	12 52	12 55	13 01	13 04	13 06	13 14	13 18	13 22	13 25	13 31	13 36	13 44	13 52	13 55	14 00	14 01	14 04	14 06	14 14	14 18
Clapham Junction	d	12 49	12 57	13 00	13 06	13 09	13 11	13 19		13 27	13 30	13 36	13 41	13 49	13 57	14 00		14 06	14 09	14 11	14 19	
Earlsfield	d	12 52	13 00	13 03	13 09	13 12	13 14	13 22		13 30	13 33	13 39	13 44	13 52	14 00	14 03		14 09	14 12	14 14	14 22	
Wimbledon ⊖	d	12 56	13 04	13 07	13 13	13 16	13 18	13 26		13 34	13 37	13 43	13 48	13 56	14 04	14 07		14 13	14 16	14 18	14 26	
Raynes Park	d		13 07	13 10	13 16		13 22			13 37	13 40	13 46	13 52		14 07	14 10		14 16		14 22		
Motspur Park	d			13 13			13 25				13 43		13 55			14 13				14 25		
Malden Manor	d			13 16							13 46					14 16						
Tolworth	d			13 19							13 49					14 19						
Chessington North	d			13 22							13 52					14 22						
Chessington South	a			13 24							13 54					14 24						
Worcester Park	d						13 27						13 57							14 27		
Stoneleigh	d						13 30						14 00							14 30		
Ewell West	d						13 33						14 03							14 33		
Epsom	a						13 36						14 06							14 36		
	d						13 38						14 08							14 38		
Ashtead	d						13 42						14 12							14 42		
Leatherhead	d						13 45						14 15							14 45		
Boxhill & Westhumble	d																					
Dorking	a						13 51													14 51		
New Malden	d		13 10		13 19					13 40		13 49			14 10			14 19				
Norbiton	d		13 13							13 43					14 13							
Kingston	a		13 16						13 59	13 46					14 16		14 38					14 59
	d		13 16							13 49					14 16							
Hampton Wick	d		13 18							13 51					14 18							
Teddington	d		13 21							13 56					14 21							
Strawberry Hill	a									13 59												
Fulwell	d		13 25												14 25							
Hampton	d		13 29												14 29							
Kempton Park	d		13 32												14 32							
Sunbury	d		13 34												14 34							
Upper Halliford	d		13 36												14 36							
Shepperton	a		13 39												14 39							
Berrylands	d				13 21							13 51						14 21				
Surbiton	d	13 05			13 25	13 32		13 35				13 55		14 05				14 25	14 32		14 35	
Thames Ditton	d				13 30							14 00						14 30				
Hampton Court	a				13 33							14 03						14 33				
Hinchley Wood	d					13 36													14 36			
Claygate	d					13 39													14 39			
Oxshott	d					13 42													14 42			
Cobham & Stoke D'abernon	d					13 46													14 46			
Bookham	d												14 21									
Effingham Junction	d					13 50							14 25						14 50			
Horsley	d					13 53							14 27						14 53			
Clandon	d					13 58							14 32						14 58			
London Road (Guildford)	d					14 03							14 37						15 03			
Guildford	a	13 44				14 07		14 14					14 41	14 44					15 07		15 14	

London - Chessington South, Dorking, Guildford, Shepperton and Hampton Court

		SW	SW	SW	SW	SW	SW	SW	SW	SW	SW	SW	SW	SW	SW	SW	SW	SW	SW	SW	SW	SW	SW
London Waterloo 15 ⊖	d	14 18	14 21	14 27	14 32	14 40	14 48	14 51	14 56	14 57	15 00	15 02	15 10	15 14	15 18	15 21	15 27	15 32	15 40	15 48	15 51	15 56	15 57
Vauxhall ⊖	d	14 22	14 25	14 31	14 36	14 44	14 52	14 55	15 00	15 01	15 04	15 06	15 14	15 18	15 22	15 25	15 31	15 36	15 44	15 52	15 55	16 00	16 01
Clapham Junction 10	d	14 27	14 30	14 36	14 41	14 49	14 57	15 00		15 06	15 09	15 11	15 19		15 27	15 30	15 36	15 41	15 49	15 57	16 00		16 06
Earlsfield	d	14 30	14 33	14 39	14 44	14 52	15 00	15 03		15 09	15 12	15 14	15 22		15 30	15 33	15 39	15 44	15 52	16 00	16 03		16 09
Wimbledon 6 ⊖	d	14 34	14 37	14 43	14 48	14 56	15 04	15 07		15 13	15 16	15 18	15 26		15 34	15 37	15 43	15 48	15 56	16 04	16 07		16 13
Raynes Park 6	d	14 37	14 40	14 46	14 52		15 07	15 10		15 16		15 22			15 37	15 40	15 46	15 52		16 07	16 10		16 16
Motspur Park	d		14 43		14 55			15 13				15 25				15 43		15 55			16 13		
Malden Manor	d		14 46					15 16								15 46					16 16		
Tolworth	d		14 49					15 19								15 49					16 19		
Chessington North	d		14 52					15 22								15 52					16 22		
Chessington South	a		14 54					15 24								15 54					16 24		
Worcester Park	d				14 57							15 27						15 57					
Stoneleigh	d				15 00							15 30						16 00					
Ewell West	d				15 03							15 33						16 03					
Epsom 3	a				15 06							15 36						16 06					
	d				15 08							15 38						16 08					
Ashtead	d				15 12							15 42						16 12					
Leatherhead	d				15 15							15 45						16 15					
Boxhill & Westhumble	d																						
Dorking 4	a											15 51											
New Malden 6	d	14 40		14 49			15 10			15 19					15 40		15 49			16 10			16 19
Norbiton	d	14 43					15 13								15 43					16 13			
Kingston	a	14 46					15 16		15 38					15 59	15 46					16 16		16 38	
	d	14 49					15 16								15 49					16 16			
Hampton Wick	d	14 51					15 18								15 51					16 18			
Teddington	d	14 56					15 21								15 56					16 21			
Strawberry Hill	a	14 59													15 59								
Fulwell	d						15 25													16 25			
Hampton	d						15 29													16 29			
Kempton Park	d						15 32													16 32			
Sunbury	d						15 34													16 34			
Upper Halliford	d						15 36													16 36			
Shepperton	a						15 39													16 39			
Berrylands	d			14 51						15 21							15 51						16 21
Surbiton 6	d			14 55		15 05				15 25	15 32		15 35				15 55		16 05				16 25
Thames Ditton	d			15 00						15 30							16 00						16 30
Hampton Court	a			15 03						15 33							16 03						16 33
Hinchley Wood	d										15 36												
Claygate	d										15 39												
Oxshott	d										15 42												
Cobham & Stoke D'abernon	d										15 46												
Bookham	d				15 21													16 21					
Effingham Junction 6	d				15 25						15 50							16 25					
Horsley	d				15 27						15 53							16 27					
Clandon	d				15 32						15 58							16 32					
London Road (Guildford)	d				15 37						16 03							16 37					
Guildford	a				15 41	15 44					16 07		16 14					16 41	16 44				

		SW	SW	SW	SW	SW	SW	SW	SW	SW	SW	SW	SW	SW	SW	SW	SW	SW	SW	SW	SW	SW	SW
London Waterloo 15 ⊖	d	16 00	16 02	16 10	16 14	16 18	16 21	16 27	16 32	16 40	16 48	16 51	16 56	16 57	17 00	17 02	17 10	17 14	17 18	17 21	17 27	17 32	17 40
Vauxhall ⊖	d	16 04	16 06	16 14	16 18	16 22	16 25	16 31	16 36	16 44	16 52	16 55	17 00	17 01	17 04	17 06	17 14	17 18	17 22	17 25	17 31	17 36	17 44
Clapham Junction 10	d	16 09	16 11	16 19		16 27	16 30	16 36	16 41	16 49	16 57	17 00		17 06	17 09	17 11	17 19		17 27	17 30	17 36	17 41	17 49
Earlsfield	d	16 12	16 14	16 22		16 30	16 33	16 39	16 44	16 52	17 00	17 03		17 09	17 12	17 14	17 22		17 30	17 33	17 39	17 44	17 52
Wimbledon 6 ⊖	d	16 16	16 18	16 26		16 34	16 37	16 43	16 48	16 56	17 04	17 07		17 13	17 16	17 18	17 26		17 34	17 37	17 43	17 48	17 56
Raynes Park 6	d		16 22			16 37	16 40	16 46	16 52		17 07	17 10		17 16		17 22			17 37	17 40	17 46	17 52	
Motspur Park	d		16 25				16 43		16 55			17 13				17 25				17 43		17 55	
Malden Manor	d						16 46					17 16								17 46			
Tolworth	d						16 49					17 19								17 49			
Chessington North	d						16 52					17 22								17 52			
Chessington South	a						16 54					17 24								17 54			
Worcester Park	d		16 27						16 57							17 27						17 57	
Stoneleigh	d		16 30						17 00							17 30						18 00	
Ewell West	d		16 33						17 03							17 33						18 03	
Epsom 3	a		16 36						17 06							17 36						18 06	
	d		16 38						17 08							17 38						18 08	
Ashtead	d		16 42						17 12							17 42						18 12	
Leatherhead	d		16 45						17 15							17 45						18 15	
Boxhill & Westhumble	d																						
Dorking 4	a		16 51													17 51							
New Malden 6	d					16 40		16 49			17 10			17 19					17 40		17 49		
Norbiton	d					16 43					17 13								17 43				
Kingston	a				16 59	16 46					17 16		17 38					17 59	17 46				
	d					16 49					17 16								17 49				
Hampton Wick	d					16 51					17 18								17 51				
Teddington	d					16 56					17 21								17 56				
Strawberry Hill	a					16 59													17 59				
Fulwell	d										17 25												
Hampton	d										17 29												
Kempton Park	d										17 32												
Sunbury	d										17 34												
Upper Halliford	d										17 36												
Shepperton	a										17 39												
Berrylands	d							16 51						17 21							17 51		
Surbiton 6	d	16 32		16 35				16 55		17 05				17 25	17 32		17 35				17 55		18 05
Thames Ditton	d							17 00						17 30							18 00		
Hampton Court	a							17 03						17 33							18 03		
Hinchley Wood	d	16 36													17 36								
Claygate	d	16 39													17 39								
Oxshott	d	16 42													17 42								
Cobham & Stoke D'abernon	d	16 46													17 46								
Bookham	d								17 21													18 21	
Effingham Junction 6	d	16 50							17 25						17 50							18 25	
Horsley	d	16 53							17 27						17 53							18 27	
Clandon	d	16 58							17 32						17 58							18 32	
London Road (Guildford)	d	17 03							17 37						18 03							18 37	
Guildford	a	17 07		17 14					17 41	17 44					18 07		18 14					18 41	18 44

London - Chessington South, Dorking, Guildford, Shepperton and Hampton Court

		SW	SW	SW	SW	SW	SW	SW	SW	SW	SW	SW	SW	SW	SW	SW	SW	SW	SW	SW	SW	SW
London Waterloo 15 ⊖	d	17 48	17 51	17 56	17 57	18 00	18 02	18 10	18 14	18 18	18 21	18 27	18 32	18 40	18 48	18 51	18 56	18 57	19 00	19 02	19 10	19 14
Vauxhall ⊖	d	17 52	17 55	18 00	18 01	18 04	18 06	18 14	18 18	18 22	18 25	18 31	18 36	18 44	18 52	18 55	19 00	19 01	19 04	19 06	19 14	19 18
Clapham Junction 10	d	17 57	18 00		18 06	18 09	18 11	18 19		18 27	18 30	18 36	18 41	18 49	18 57	19 00		19 06	19 09	19 11	19 19	
Earlsfield	d	18 00	18 03		18 09	18 12	18 14	18 22		18 30	18 33	18 39	18 44	18 52	19 00	19 03		19 09	19 12	19 14	19 22	
Wimbledon 6 ⊖	d	18 04	18 07		18 13	18 16	18 18	18 26		18 34	18 37	18 43	18 48	18 56	19 04	19 07		19 13	19 16	19 18	19 26	
Raynes Park 6	d	18 07	18 10		18 16		18 22			18 37	18 40	18 46	18 52		19 07	19 10		19 16		19 22		
Motspur Park	d		18 13				18 25				18 43		18 55			19 13				19 25		
Malden Manor	d		18 16								18 46					19 16						
Tolworth	d		18 19								18 49					19 19						
Chessington North	d		18 22								18 52					19 22						
Chessington South	a		18 24								18 54					19 24						
Worcester Park	d						18 27						18 57							19 27		
Stoneleigh	d						18 30						19 00							19 30		
Ewell West	d						18 33						19 03							19 33		
Epsom 3	a						18 36						19 06							19 36		
	d						18 38						19 08							19 38		
Ashtead	d						18 42						19 12							19 42		
Leatherhead	d						18 45						19 15							19 45		
Boxhill & Westhumble	d																					
Dorking 4	a						18 51													19 51		
New Malden 6	d	18 10			18 19					18 40		18 49			19 10			19 19				
Norbiton	d	18 13								18 43					19 13							
Kingston	a	18 16		18 38					18 59	18 46					19 16		19 38					19 59
	d	18 16								18 49					19 16							
Hampton Wick	d	18 18								18 51					19 18							
Teddington	d	18 21								18 56					19 21							
Strawberry Hill	a									18 59												
Fulwell	d	18 25													19 25							
Hampton	d	18 29													19 29							
Kempton Park	d	18 32													19 32							
Sunbury	d	18 34													19 34							
Upper Halliford	d	18 36													19 36							
Shepperton	a	18 39													19 39							
Berrylands	d				18 21							18 51						19 21				
Surbiton 6	d				18 25	18 32		18 35				18 55		19 05				19 25	19 32		19 35	
Thames Ditton	d				18 30							19 00						19 30				
Hampton Court	a				18 33							19 03						19 33				
Hinchley Wood	d					18 36													19 36			
Claygate	d					18 39													19 39			
Oxshott	d					18 42													19 42			
Cobham & Stoke D'abernon	d					18 46													19 46			
Bookham	d												19 21									
Effingham Junction 6	d					18 50							19 25						19 50			
Horsley	d					18 53							19 27						19 53			
Clandon	d					18 58							19 32						19 58			
London Road (Guildford)	d					19 03							19 37						20 03			
Guildford	a					19 07		19 14					19 41	19 44					20 07		20 14	

		SW	SW	SW	SW	SW	SW	SW	SW	SW	SW	SW	SW	SW	SW	SW	SW	SW	SW	SW	SW	SW	SW
London Waterloo 15 ⊖	d	19 18	19 21	19 27	19 32	19 40	19 48	19 56	19 57	20 00	20 02	20 10	20 14	20 18	20 21	20 27	20 32	20 40	20 48	20 56	20 57	21 00	21 02
Vauxhall ⊖	d	19 22	19 25	19 31	19 36	19 44	19 52	20 00	20 01	20 04	20 06	20 14	20 18	20 22	20 25	20 31	20 36	20 44	20 52	21 00	21 01	21 04	21 06
Clapham Junction 10	d	19 27	19 30	19 36	19 41	19 49	19 57		20 06	20 09	20 11	20 19		20 27	20 30	20 36	20 41	20 49	20 57		21 06	21 09	21 11
Earlsfield	d	19 30	19 33	19 39	19 44	19 52	20 00		20 09	20 12	20 14	20 22		20 30	20 33	20 39	20 44	20 52	21 00		21 09	21 12	21 14
Wimbledon 6 ⊖	d	19 34	19 37	19 43	19 48	19 56	20 04		20 13	20 16	20 18	20 26		20 34	20 37	20 43	20 48	20 56	21 04		21 13	21 16	21 18
Raynes Park 6	d	19 37	19 40	19 46	19 52		20 07		20 16		20 22			20 37	20 40	20 46	20 52		21 07		21 16		21 22
Motspur Park	d		19 43		19 55						20 25				20 43		20 55						21 25
Malden Manor	d		19 46												20 46								
Tolworth	d		19 49												20 49								
Chessington North	d		19 52												20 52								
Chessington South	a		19 54												20 54								
Worcester Park	d				19 57						20 27						20 57						21 27
Stoneleigh	d				20 00						20 30						21 00						21 30
Ewell West	d				20 03						20 33						21 03						21 33
Epsom 3	a				20 06						20 36						21 06						21 36
	d				20 08						20 38						21 08						21 38
Ashtead	d				20 12						20 42						21 12						21 42
Leatherhead	d				20 15						20 45						21 15						21 45
Boxhill & Westhumble	d																						
Dorking 4	a										20 51												21 51
New Malden 6	d	19 40		19 49			20 10		20 19					20 40		20 49			21 10		21 19		
Norbiton	d	19 43					20 13							20 43					21 13				
Kingston	a	19 46					20 16	20 38					20 59	20 46					21 16	21 38			
	d	19 49					20 16							20 49					21 16				
Hampton Wick	d	19 51					20 18							20 51					21 18				
Teddington	d	19 56					20 21							20 56					21 21				
Strawberry Hill	a	19 59												20 59									
Fulwell	d						20 25												21 25				
Hampton	d						20 29												21 29				
Kempton Park	d						20 32												21 32				
Sunbury	d						20 34												21 34				
Upper Halliford	d						20 36												21 36				
Shepperton	a						20 39												21 39				
Berrylands	d			19 51					20 21							20 51					21 21		
Surbiton 6	d			19 55		20 05			20 25	20 32		20 35				20 55		21 05			21 25	21 32	
Thames Ditton	d			20 00					20 30							21 00					21 30		
Hampton Court	a			20 03					20 33							21 03					21 33		
Hinchley Wood	d									20 36												21 36	
Claygate	d									20 39												21 39	
Oxshott	d									20 42												21 42	
Cobham & Stoke D'abernon	d									20 46												21 46	
Bookham	d				20 21												21 21						
Effingham Junction 6	d				20 25					20 50							21 25					21 50	
Horsley	d				20 27					20 53							21 27					21 53	
Clandon	d				20 32					20 58							21 32					21 58	
London Road (Guildford)	d				20 37					21 03							21 37					22 03	
Guildford	a				20 41	20 44				21 07		21 14					21 41	21 44				22 07	

Table 152

Sundays
until 25 September

London - Chessington South, Dorking, Guildford, Shepperton and Hampton Court

		SW	SW	SW	SW	SW	SW	SW	SW	SW	SW	SW	SW	SW	SW	SW	SW	SW	SW	SW	SW	SW
London Waterloo 15 ⊖	d	21 10	21 14	21 18	21 21	21 32	21 40	21 48	21 56	21 57	22 00	22 02	22 10	22 14	22 18	22 21	22 32	22 40	22 48	22 51	22 56	22 57
Vauxhall ⊖	d	21 14	21 18	21 22	21 25	21 36	21 44	21 52	22 00	22 01	22 04	22 06	22 14	22 18	22 22	22 25	22 36	22 44	22 52	22 55	23 00	23 01
Clapham Junction 10	d	21 19		21 27	21 30	21 41	21 49	21 57		22 06	22 09	22 11	22 19		22 27	22 30	22 41	22 49	22 57	23 00		23 06
Earlsfield	d	21 22		21 30	21 33	21 44	21 52	22 00		22 09	22 12	22 14	22 22		22 30	22 33	22 44	22 52	23 00	23 03		23 09
Wimbledon 6 ⊖	d	21 26		21 34	21 37	21 48	21 56	22 04		22 13	22 16	22 18	22 26		22 34	22 37	22 48	22 56	23 04	23 07		23 13
Raynes Park 6	d			21 37	21 40	21 52		22 07		22 16		22 22			22 37	22 40	22 52		23 07	23 10		23 16
Motspur Park	d				21 43	21 55						22 25				22 43	22 55			23 13		
Malden Manor	d				21 46											22 46				23 16		
Tolworth	d				21 49											22 49				23 19		
Chessington North	d				21 52											22 52				23 22		
Chessington South	a				21 54											22 54				23 24		
Worcester Park	d					21 57						22 27					22 57					
Stoneleigh	d					22 00						22 30					23 00					
Ewell West	d					22 03						22 33					23 03					
Epsom 3	a					22 06						22 36					23 06					
	d					22 08						22 38					23 08					
Ashtead	d					22 12						22 42					23 12					
Leatherhead	d					22 15						22 45					23 15					
Boxhill & Westhumble	d																					
Dorking 4	a											22 51										
New Malden 6	d			21 40				22 10		22 19					22 40				23 10			23 19
Norbiton	d			21 43				22 13							22 43				23 13			
Kingston	a		21 59	21 46				22 16	22 38					22 59	22 46				23 16		23 38	
	d			21 49				22 16							22 49				23 16			
Hampton Wick	d			21 51				22 18							22 51				23 18			
Teddington	d			21 56				22 21							22 56				23 21			
Strawberry Hill	a			21 59											22 59							
Fulwell	d							22 25											23 25			
Hampton	d							22 29											23 29			
Kempton Park	d							22 32											23 32			
Sunbury	d							22 34											23 34			
Upper Halliford	d							22 36											23 36			
Shepperton	a							22 39											23 39			
Berrylands	d									22 21												23 21
Surbiton 6	d	21 35					22 05			22 25	22 32		22 35					23 05				23 25
Thames Ditton	d									22 30												23 30
Hampton Court	a									22 33												23 33
Hinchley Wood	d										22 36											
Claygate	d										22 39											
Oxshott	d										22 42											
Cobham & Stoke D'abernon	d										22 46											
Bookham	d					22 21											23 21					
Effingham Junction 6	d					22 25					22 50						23 25					
Horsley	d					22 27					22 53						23 27					
Clandon	d					22 32					22 58						23 32					
London Road (Guildford)	d					22 37					23 03						23 37					
Guildford	a	22 14				22 41	22 44				23 07		23 13				23 41	23 45				

Table 152

Sundays
until 25 September

London - Chessington South, Dorking, Guildford, Shepperton and Hampton Court

		SW	SW	SW	SW	SW	SW	SW 1
London Waterloo 15 ⊖	d	23 00	23 02	23 10	23 14	23 18	23 32	23 40
Vauxhall ⊖	d	23 04	23 06	23 14	23 18	23 22	23 36	23 44
Clapham Junction 10	d	23 09	23 11	23 19		23 27	23 41	23 49
Earlsfield	d	23 12	23 14	23 22		23 30	23 44	23 52
Wimbledon 6 ⊖	d	23 16	23 18	23 26		23 34	23 48	23 56
Raynes Park 6	d		23 22			23 37	23 52	
Motspur Park	d		23 25				23 55	
Malden Manor	d							
Tolworth	d							
Chessington North	d							
Chessington South	a							
Worcester Park	d		23 27				23 57	
Stoneleigh	d		23 30				23 59	
Ewell West	d		23 33				00 03	
Epsom 3	a		23 36				00 06	
	d							
Ashtead	d							
Leatherhead	d							
Boxhill & Westhumble	d							
Dorking 4	a							
New Malden 6	d					23 40		
Norbiton	d					23 43		
Kingston	a				23 56	23 46		
	d					23 47		
Hampton Wick	d					23 49		
Teddington	d					23 51		
Strawberry Hill	a					23 54		
Fulwell	d							
Hampton	d							
Kempton Park	d							
Sunbury	d							
Upper Halliford	d							
Shepperton	a							
Berrylands	d							
Surbiton 6	d	23 32		23 35				00a04
Thames Ditton	d							
Hampton Court	a							
Hinchley Wood	d	23 36						
Claygate	d	23 39						
Oxshott	d	23 42						
Cobham & Stoke D'abernon	d	23 46						
Bookham	d							
Effingham Junction 6	d	23 50						
Horsley	d	23 53						
Clandon	d	23 58						
London Road (Guildford)	d	00 03						
Guildford	a	00 07		00 13				

London - Chessington South, Dorking, Guildford, Shepperton and Hampton Court

		SW A	SW B	SW A	SW B	SW A	SW B	SW	SW	SW	SW A	SW B	SW A	SW B	SW A	SW B	SW	SW	SW	SW	SW	SW	SW
London Waterloo 15 ⊖	d	23p03	23p03	23p09	23p09	23p12	23p12	23p27	23p33	23p36	23p42	23p42	23p50	23p50	23p57	23p57	00 09	00 15	00 18	00 27	00 42	01 42	06 14
Vauxhall ⊖	d	23p07	23p07	23p13	23p13	23p16	23p16	23p31	23p37	23p40	23p46	23p46	23p54	23p54	00 01	00 01	00 13	00 19	00 22	00 31	00 46	01 46	06 18
Clapham Junction 10	d	23p12	23p12	23p18	23p18	23p21	23p21	23p36		23p45	23p51	23p51	23p59	23p59	00 06	00 06	00 20	00 25		00 37		01 53	
Earlsfield	d	23p15	23p15	23p21	23p21	23p24	23p24	23p39		23p48	23p54	23p54	00 02	00 02	00 09	00 09	00 23	00 29		00s41			
Wimbledon 6 ⊖	d	23p19	23p19	23p25	23p25	23p28	23p28	23p43		23p52	23p58	23p58	00 06	00 06	00 13	00 13	00 27	00 33		00 45	01 05	01 59	
Raynes Park 6	d			23p28	23p28	23p31	23p31	23p46		23p55	00 01	00 01			00 16	00 16		00 36		00 48	01 08	02 02	
Motspur Park	d			23p31	23p31						00 04	00 04						00 38					
Malden Manor	d																						
Tolworth	d																						
Chessington North	d																						
Chessington South	a																						
Worcester Park	d			23p33	23p33						00 06	00 06						00 41					
Stoneleigh	d			23p36	23p36						00 09	00 09						00 44					
Ewell West	d			23p39	23p39						00 12	00 12						00 46					
Epsom 3	a			23p42	23p42						00 15	00 15						00 50					
	d			23p47	23p47						00 19	00 19											
Ashtead	d			23p51	23p51						00 23	00 23											
Leatherhead	d			23p54	23p54						00 26	00 26											
Boxhill & Westhumble	d																						
Dorking 4	a			00 01	00 03																		
New Malden 6	d					23p34	23p34	23p49		23p58					00 19	00 19				00 50	01 11	02 04	
Norbiton	d					23p37	23p37	23p52							00 22	00 22					01 14	02 08	
Kingston	a					23p40	23p40	23p55	00 16						00 25	00 25			01 01		01 17	02 10	06 59
	d					23p40	23p40	23p55							00 25	00 25					01 17	02 11	
Hampton Wick	d					23p42	23p42	23p57							00 27	00 27					01s22	02s13	
Teddington	d					23p45	23p45	23p59							00 30	00 30					01s25	02s15	
Strawberry Hill	a							00 03													01 28	02s18	
Fulwell	d					23p49	23p49								00 34	00 34							
Hampton	d					23p53	23p53								00 38	00 38							
Kempton Park	d					23p56	23p56								00 41	00 41							
Sunbury	d					23p58	23p58								00 43	00 43							
Upper Halliford	d					23p59	23p59								00 45	00 45							
Shepperton	a					00 03	00 05								00 48	00 50							
Berrylands	d									23p59										00s53			
Surbiton 6	d	23p27	23p27							00 05			00 14	00 14			00 35			00a56			
Thames Ditton	d									00 09													
Hampton Court	a									00 12													
Hinchley Wood	d	23p31	23p31										00 18	00 18									
Claygate	d	23p34	23p34										00 20	00 20									
Oxshott	d	23p37	23p37										00 24	00 24									
Cobham & Stoke D'abernon	d	23p41	23p41										00 27	00 27									
Bookham	d										00 31	00 31											
Effingham Junction 6	d	23p45	23p45								00 36	00 36	00 32	00 32									
Horsley	d	23p48	23p48								00 39	00 39	00 34	00 34									
Clandon	d	23p53	23p53								00 44	00 44	00 39	00 39									
London Road (Guildford)	d	23p58	23p58								00 49	00 49	00 44	00 44									
Guildford	a	00 02	00 05								00 53	00 56	00 48	00 51			01 07						

A 2 October

B not 2 October

London - Chessington South, Dorking, Guildford, Shepperton and Hampton Court

		SW	SW	SW	SW	SW	SW	SW	SW	SW	SW	SW	SW	SW	SW	SW	SW	SW	SW	SW	SW	SW	SW
London Waterloo 15 ⊖	d	06 18		06 57			07 10	07 14	07 18		07 27		07 40	07 48		07 57		08 02	08 10	08 14	08 18	08 21	08 27
Vauxhall ⊖	d	06 22		07 01			07 14	07 18	07 22		07 31		07 44	07 52		08 01		08 06	08 14	08 18	08 22	08 25	08 31
Clapham Junction 10	d	06 27		07 06			07 19		07 27		07 36		07 49	07 57		08 06		08 11	08 19		08 27	08 30	08 36
Earlsfield	d			07 09			07 22		07 30		07 39		07 52	08 00		08 09		08 14	08 22		08 30	08 33	08 39
Wimbledon 6 ⊖	d	06 34	06 48	07 13	07 16	07 20	07 26		07 34	07 37	07 43	07 48	07 56	08 04	08 07	08 13	08 16	08 18	08 26		08 34	08 37	08 43
Raynes Park 6	d	06 37	06 52	07 16		07 23			07 37	07 40	07 46	07 52		08 07	08 10	08 16		08 22			08 37	08 40	08 46
Motspur Park	d		06 55			07 26				07 43		07 55			08 13			08 25				08 43	
Malden Manor	d									07 46					08 16							08 46	
Tolworth	d									07 49					08 19							08 49	
Chessington North	d									07 52					08 22							08 52	
Chessington South	a									07 54					08 24							08 54	
Worcester Park	d		06 57			07 28						07 57						08 27					
Stoneleigh	d		07 00			07 31						08 00						08 30					
Ewell West	d		07 03			07 34						08 03						08 33					
Epsom 3	a		07 06			07 37						08 06						08 36					
	d											08 08						08 38					
Ashtead	d											08 12						08 42					
Leatherhead	d											08 15						08 45					
Boxhill & Westhumble	d																						
Dorking 4	a																	08 53					
New Malden 6	d	06 40		07 19					07 40		07 49			08 10		08 19					08 40		08 49
Norbiton	d	06 43							07 43					08 13							08 43		
Kingston	a	06 46						07 59	07 46					08 16						08 59	08 46		
	d	06 49							07 49					08 16							08 49		
Hampton Wick	d	06 51							07 51					08 18							08 51		
Teddington	d	06 56							07 56					08 21							08 56		
Strawberry Hill	a	06 59							07 59												08 59		
Fulwell	d													08 25									
Hampton	d													08 29									
Kempton Park	d													08 32									
Sunbury	d													08 34									
Upper Halliford	d													08 36									
Shepperton	a													08 41									
Berrylands	d			07 21							07 51					08 21							08 51
Surbiton 6	d			07 25	07 32		07 35				07 55		08 05			08 25	08 32		08 35				08 55
Thames Ditton	d			07 30							08 00					08 30							09 00
Hampton Court	a			07 33							08 03					08 33							09 03
Hinchley Wood	d				07 36												08 36						
Claygate	d				07 39												08 39						
Oxshott	d				07 42												08 42						
Cobham & Stoke D'abernon	d				07 46												08 46						
Bookham	d											08 21											
Effingham Junction 6	d				07 50							08 25					08 50						
Horsley	d				07 53							08 27					08 53						
Clandon	d				07 58							08 32					08 58						
London Road (Guildford)	d				08 03							08 37					09 03						
Guildford	a				08 10		08 14					08 44	08 40				09 10		09 10				

		SW	SW	SW	SW	SW	SW	SW	SW	SW	SW	SW	SW	SW	SW	SW	SW	SW	SW	SW	SW	SW
London Waterloo 15 ⊖	d	08 32	08 40	08 48	08 51	08 57		09 02	09 10	09 14	09 18	09 21	09 27	09 32	09 40	09 48	09 51	09 57		10 02	10 10	10 14
Vauxhall ⊖	d	08 36	08 44	08 52	08 55	09 01		09 06	09 14	09 18	09 22	09 25	09 31	09 36	09 44	09 52	09 55	10 01		10 06	10 14	10 18
Clapham Junction 10	d	08 41	08 49	08 57	09 00	09 06		09 11	09 19		09 27	09 30	09 36	09 41	09 49	09 57	10 00	10 06		10 11	10 19	
Earlsfield	d	08 44	08 52	09 00	09 03	09 09		09 14	09 22		09 30	09 33	09 39	09 44	09 52	10 00	10 03	10 09		10 14	10 22	
Wimbledon 6 ⊖	d	08 48	08 56	09 04	09 07	09 13	09 16	09 18	09 26		09 34	09 37	09 43	09 48	09 56	10 04	10 07	10 13	10 16	10 18	10 26	
Raynes Park 6	d	08 52		09 07	09 10	09 16		09 22			09 37	09 40	09 46	09 52		10 07	10 10	10 16		10 22		
Motspur Park	d	08 55			09 13			09 25				09 43		09 55			10 13			10 25		
Malden Manor	d				09 16							09 46					10 16					
Tolworth	d				09 19							09 49					10 19					
Chessington North	d				09 22							09 52					10 22					
Chessington South	a				09 24							09 54					10 24					
Worcester Park	d	08 57						09 27						09 57						10 27		
Stoneleigh	d	09 00						09 30						10 00						10 30		
Ewell West	d	09 03						09 33						10 03						10 33		
Epsom 3	a	09 06						09 36						10 06						10 36		
	d	09 08						09 38						10 08						10 38		
Ashtead	d	09 12						09 42						10 12						10 42		
Leatherhead	d	09 15						09 45						10 15						10 45		
Boxhill & Westhumble	d																					
Dorking 4	a							09 53												10 53		
New Malden 6	d			09 10		09 19					09 40		09 49			10 10		10 19				
Norbiton	d			09 13							09 43					10 13						
Kingston	a			09 16						09 59	09 46					10 16						10 59
	d			09 16							09 49					10 16						
Hampton Wick	d			09 18							09 51					10 18						
Teddington	d			09 21							09 56					10 21						
Strawberry Hill	a										09 59											
Fulwell	d			09 25												10 25						
Hampton	d			09 29												10 29						
Kempton Park	d			09 32												10 32						
Sunbury	d			09 34												10 34						
Upper Halliford	d			09 36												10 36						
Shepperton	a			09 41												10 41						
Berrylands	d					09 21							09 51					10 21				
Surbiton 6	d		09 05			09 25	09 32		09 35				09 55		10 05			10 25	10 32		10 35	
Thames Ditton	d					09 30							10 00					10 30				
Hampton Court	a					09 33							10 03					10 33				
Hinchley Wood	d						09 36												10 36			
Claygate	d						09 39												10 39			
Oxshott	d						09 42												10 42			
Cobham & Stoke D'abernon	d						09 46												10 46			
Bookham	d	09 21												10 21								
Effingham Junction 6	d	09 25					09 50							10 25					10 50			
Horsley	d	09 27					09 53							10 27					10 53			
Clandon	d	09 32					09 58							10 32					10 58			
London Road (Guildford)	d	09 37					10 03							10 37					11 03			
Guildford	a	09 44	09 40				10 10		10 10					10 44	10 44				11 10		11 14	

Table 152

Sundays
from 2 October

London - Chessington South, Dorking, Guildford, Shepperton and Hampton Court

Station		SW	SW	SW	SW	SW	SW	SW	SW	SW	SW	SW	SW	SW	SW	SW	SW	SW	SW	SW	SW	SW	SW
London Waterloo ⊖	d	10 18	10 21	10 27	10 32	10 40	10 48	10 51	10 57		11 02	11 10	11 14	11 18	11 21	11 27	11 32	11 40	11 48	11 51	11 57		12 02
Vauxhall ⊖	d	10 22	10 25	10 31	10 36	10 44	10 52	10 55	11 01		11 06	11 14	11 19	11 22	11 25	11 31	11 36	11 44	11 52	11 55	12 01		12 06
Clapham Junction	d	10 27	10 30	10 36	10 41	10 49	10 57	11 00	11 06		11 11	11 19		11 27	11 30	11 36	11 41	11 49	11 57	12 00	12 06		12 11
Earlsfield	d	10 30	10 33	10 39	10 44	10 52	11 00	11 03	11 09		11 14	11 22		11 30	11 33	11 39	11 44	11 52	12 00	12 03	12 09		12 14
Wimbledon ⊖	d	10 34	10 37	10 43	10 48	10 56	11 04	11 07	11 13	11 16	11 18	11 26		11 34	11 37	11 43	11 48	11 56	12 04	12 07	12 13	12 16	12 18
Raynes Park	d	10 37	10 40	10 46	10 52		11 07	11 10	11 16		11 22			11 37	11 40	11 46	11 52		12 07	12 10	12 16		12 22
Motspur Park	d		10 43		10 55			11 13			11 25				11 43		11 55			12 13			12 25
Malden Manor	d		10 46					11 16							11 46					12 16			
Tolworth	d		10 49					11 19							11 49					12 19			
Chessington North	d		10 52					11 22							11 52					12 22			
Chessington South	a		10 54					11 24							11 54					12 24			
Worcester Park	d				10 57						11 27						11 57						12 27
Stoneleigh	d				11 00						11 30						12 00						12 30
Ewell West	d				11 03						11 33						12 03						12 33
Epsom	a				11 06						11 36						12 06						12 36
	d				11 08						11 38						12 08						12 38
Ashtead	d				11 12						11 42						12 12						12 42
Leatherhead	d				11 15						11 45						12 15						12 45
Boxhill & Westhumble	d																						
Dorking	a										11 53												12 53
New Malden	d	10 40		10 49			11 10		11 19					11 40		11 49			12 10		12 19		
Norbiton	d	10 43					11 13							11 43					12 13				
Kingston	a	10 46					11 16						11 59	11 46					12 16				
	d	10 49					11 16							11 49					12 16				
Hampton Wick	d	10 51					11 18							11 51					12 18				
Teddington	d	10 56					11 21							11 56					12 21				
Strawberry Hill	a	10 59												11 59									
Fulwell	d						11 25												12 25				
Hampton	d						11 29												12 29				
Kempton Park	d						11 32												12 32				
Sunbury	d						11 34												12 34				
Upper Halliford	d						11 36												12 36				
Shepperton	a						11 41												12 41				
Berrylands	d			10 51					11 21							11 51					12 21		
Surbiton	d			10 55		11 05			11 25	11 32		11 35				11 55		12 05			12 25	12 32	
Thames Ditton	d			11 00					11 30							12 00					12 30		
Hampton Court	a			11 03					11 33							12 03					12 33		
Hinchley Wood	d									11 36												12 36	
Claygate	d									11 39												12 39	
Oxshott	d									11 42												12 42	
Cobham & Stoke D'abernon	d									11 46												12 46	
Bookham	d				11 21												12 21						
Effingham Junction	d				11 25					11 50							12 25					12 50	
Horsley	d				11 27					11 53							12 27					12 53	
Clandon	d				11 32					11 58							12 32					12 58	
London Road (Guildford)	d				11 37					12 03							12 37					13 03	
Guildford	a				11 44	11 44				12 10		12 14					12 44	12 44				13 10	

Station		SW	SW	SW	SW	SW	SW	SW	SW	SW	SW	SW	SW	SW	SW	SW	SW	SW	SW	SW	SW	SW
London Waterloo ⊖	d	12 10	12 14	12 18	12 21	12 27	12 32	12 40	12 48	12 51	12 57	13 00	13 02	13 10	13 14	13 18	13 21	13 27	13 32	13 40	13 48	13 51
Vauxhall ⊖	d	12 14	12 19	12 22	12 25	12 31	12 36	12 44	12 52	12 55	13 01	13 04	13 06	13 14	13 18	13 22	13 25	13 31	13 36	13 44	13 52	13 55
Clapham Junction	d	12 19		12 27	12 30	12 36	12 41	12 49	12 57	13 00	13 06	13 09	13 11	13 19		13 27	13 30	13 36	13 41	13 49	13 57	14 00
Earlsfield	d	12 22		12 30	12 33	12 39	12 44	12 52	13 00	13 03	13 09	13 12	13 14	13 22		13 30	13 33	13 39	13 44	13 52	14 00	14 03
Wimbledon ⊖	d	12 26		12 34	12 37	12 43	12 48	12 56	13 04	13 07	13 13	13 16	13 18	13 26		13 34	13 37	13 43	13 48	13 56	14 04	14 07
Raynes Park	d			12 37	12 40	12 46	12 52		13 07	13 10	13 16		13 22			13 37	13 40	13 46	13 52		14 07	14 10
Motspur Park	d				12 43		12 55			13 13			13 25				13 43		13 55			14 13
Malden Manor	d				12 46					13 16							13 46					14 16
Tolworth	d				12 49					13 19							13 49					14 19
Chessington North	d				12 52					13 22							13 52					14 22
Chessington South	a				12 54					13 24							13 54					14 24
Worcester Park	d						12 57						13 27						13 57			
Stoneleigh	d						13 00						13 30						14 00			
Ewell West	d						13 03						13 33						14 03			
Epsom	a						13 06						13 36						14 06			
	d						13 08						13 38						14 08			
Ashtead	d						13 12						13 42						14 12			
Leatherhead	d						13 15						13 45						14 15			
Boxhill & Westhumble	d																					
Dorking	a												13 53									
New Malden	d			12 40		12 49			13 10		13 19					13 40		13 49			14 10	
Norbiton	d			12 43					13 13							13 43					14 13	
Kingston	a		12 59	12 46					13 16						13 59	13 46					14 16	
	d			12 49					13 16							13 49					14 16	
Hampton Wick	d			12 51					13 18							13 51					14 18	
Teddington	d			12 56					13 21							13 56					14 21	
Strawberry Hill	a			12 59												13 59						
Fulwell	d								13 25												14 25	
Hampton	d								13 29												14 29	
Kempton Park	d								13 32												14 32	
Sunbury	d								13 34												14 34	
Upper Halliford	d								13 36												14 36	
Shepperton	a								13 41												14 41	
Berrylands	d					12 51					13 21							13 51				
Surbiton	d	12 35				12 55		13 05			13 25	13 32		13 35				13 55		14 05		
Thames Ditton	d					13 00					13 30							14 00				
Hampton Court	a					13 03					13 33							14 03				
Hinchley Wood	d											13 36										
Claygate	d											13 39										
Oxshott	d											13 42										
Cobham & Stoke D'abernon	d											13 46										
Bookham	d						13 21												14 21			
Effingham Junction	d						13 25					13 50							14 25			
Horsley	d						13 27					13 53							14 27			
Clandon	d						13 32					13 58							14 32			
London Road (Guildford)	d						13 37					14 03							14 37			
[illegible]							[illegible]	[illegible]				[illegible]		[illegible]					14 44	14 44		

Table 152

Sundays
from 2 October

London - Chessington South, Dorking, Guildford, Shepperton and Hampton Court

Station		SW	SW	SW	SW	SW	SW	SW	SW	SW	SW	SW	SW	SW	SW	SW	SW	SW	SW	SW	SW	SW	SW
London Waterloo ⊖	d	13 56	13 57	14 00	14 02	14 10	14 14	14 18	14 21	14 27	14 32	14 40	14 48	14 51	14 56	14 57	15 00	15 02	15 10	15 14	15 18	15 21	15 27
Vauxhall ⊖	d	14 00	14 01	14 04	14 06	14 14	14 18	14 22	14 25	14 31	14 36	14 44	14 52	14 55	15 00	15 01	15 04	15 06	15 14	15 18	15 22	15 25	15 31
Clapham Junction	d		14 06	14 09	14 11	14 19		14 27	14 30	14 36	14 41	14 49	14 57	15 00		15 06	15 09	15 11	15 19		15 27	15 30	15 36
Earlsfield	d		14 09	14 12	14 14	14 22		14 30	14 33	14 39	14 44	14 52	15 00	15 03		15 09	15 12	15 14	15 22		15 30	15 33	15 39
Wimbledon ⊖	d		14 13	14 16	14 18	14 26		14 34	14 37	14 43	14 48	14 56	15 04	15 07		15 13	15 16	15 18	15 26		15 34	15 37	15 43
Raynes Park	d		14 16		14 22			14 37	14 40	14 46	14 52		15 07	15 10		15 16		15 22			15 37	15 40	15 46
Motspur Park	d				14 25				14 43		14 55			15 13				15 25				15 43	
Malden Manor	d								14 46					15 16								15 46	
Tolworth	d								14 49					15 19								15 49	
Chessington North	d								14 52					15 22								15 52	
Chessington South	a								14 54					15 24								15 54	
Worcester Park	d				14 27						14 57							15 27					
Stoneleigh	d				14 30						15 00							15 30					
Ewell West	d				14 33						15 03							15 33					
Epsom	a				14 36						15 06							15 36					
	d				14 38						15 08							15 38					
Ashtead	d				14 42						15 12							15 42					
Leatherhead	d				14 45						15 15							15 45					
Boxhill & Westhumble	d																						
Dorking	a				14 53													15 53					
New Malden	d		14 19					14 40		14 49			15 10			15 19					15 40		15 49
Norbiton	d							14 43					15 13								15 43		
Kingston	a	14 38					14 59	14 46					15 16		15 38					15 59	15 46		
	d							14 49					15 16								15 49		
Hampton Wick	d							14 51					15 18								15 51		
Teddington	d							14 56					15 21								15 56		
Strawberry Hill	a							14 59													15 59		
Fulwell	d												15 25										
Hampton	d												15 29										
Kempton Park	d												15 32										
Sunbury	d												15 34										
Upper Halliford	d												15 36										
Shepperton	a												15 41										
Berrylands	d		14 21							14 51						15 21							15 51
Surbiton	d		14 25	14 32		14 35				14 55		15 05				15 25	15 32		15 35				15 55
Thames Ditton	d		14 30							15 00						15 30							16 00
Hampton Court	a		14 33							15 03						15 33							16 03
Hinchley Wood	d			14 36													15 36						
Claygate	d			14 39													15 39						
Oxshott	d			14 42													15 42						
Cobham & Stoke D'abernon	d			14 46													15 46						
Bookham	d										15 21												
Effingham Junction	d			14 50							15 25						15 50						
Horsley	d			14 53							15 27						15 53						
Clandon	d			14 58							15 32						15 58						
London Road (Guildford)	d			15 03							15 37						16 03						
Guildford	a			15 10		15 14					15 44	15 44					16 10		16 14				

Station		SW	SW	SW	SW	SW	SW	SW	SW	SW	SW	SW	SW	SW	SW	SW	SW	SW	SW	SW	SW	SW	SW
London Waterloo ⊖	d	15 32	15 40	15 48	15 51	15 56	15 57	16 00	16 02	16 10	16 14	16 18	16 21	16 27	16 32	16 40	16 48	16 51	16 56	16 57	17 00	17 02	17 10
Vauxhall ⊖	d	15 36	15 44	15 52	15 55	16 00	16 01	16 04	16 06	16 14	16 18	16 22	16 25	16 31	16 36	16 44	16 52	16 55	17 00	17 01	17 04	17 06	17 14
Clapham Junction	d	15 41	15 49	15 57	16 00		16 06	16 09	16 11	16 19		16 27	16 30	16 36	16 41	16 49	16 57	17 00		17 06	17 09	17 11	17 19
Earlsfield	d	15 44	15 52	16 00	16 03		16 09	16 12	16 14	16 22		16 30	16 33	16 39	16 44	16 52	17 00	17 03		17 09	17 12	17 14	17 22
Wimbledon ⊖	d	15 48	15 56	16 04	16 07		16 13	16 16	16 18	16 26		16 34	16 37	16 43	16 48	16 56	17 04	17 07		17 13	17 16	17 18	17 26
Raynes Park	d	15 52		16 07	16 10		16 16		16 22			16 37	16 40	16 46	16 52		17 07	17 10		17 16		17 22	
Motspur Park	d	15 55			16 13				16 25				16 43		16 55			17 13				17 25	
Malden Manor	d				16 16								16 46					17 16					
Tolworth	d				16 19								16 49					17 19					
Chessington North	d				16 22								16 52					17 22					
Chessington South	a				16 24								16 54					17 24					
Worcester Park	d	15 57							16 27						16 57							17 27	
Stoneleigh	d	16 00							16 30						17 00							17 30	
Ewell West	d	16 03							16 33						17 03							17 33	
Epsom	a	16 06							16 36						17 06							17 36	
	d	16 08							16 38						17 08							17 38	
Ashtead	d	16 12							16 42						17 12							17 42	
Leatherhead	d	16 15							16 45						17 15							17 45	
Boxhill & Westhumble	d																						
Dorking	a								16 53													17 53	
New Malden	d			16 10			16 19					16 40		16 49			17 10			17 19			
Norbiton	d			16 13								16 43					17 13						
Kingston	a			16 16		16 38					16 59	16 46					17 16		17 38				
	d			16 16								16 49					17 16						
Hampton Wick	d			16 18								16 51					17 18						
Teddington	d			16 21								16 56					17 21						
Strawberry Hill	a											16 59											
Fulwell	d			16 25													17 25						
Hampton	d			16 29													17 29						
Kempton Park	d			16 32													17 32						
Sunbury	d			16 34													17 34						
Upper Halliford	d			16 36													17 36						
Shepperton	a			16 41													17 41						
Berrylands	d						16 21							16 51						17 21			
Surbiton	d		16 05				16 25	16 32		16 35				16 55		17 05				17 25	17 32		17 35
Thames Ditton	d						16 30							17 00						17 30			
Hampton Court	a						16 33							17 03						17 33			
Hinchley Wood	d							16 36													17 36		
Claygate	d							16 39													17 39		
Oxshott	d							16 42													17 42		
Cobham & Stoke D'abernon	d							16 46													17 46		
Bookham	d	16 21													17 21								
Effingham Junction	d	16 25						16 50							17 25						17 50		
Horsley	d	16 27						16 53							17 27						17 53		
Clandon	d	16 32						16 58							17 32						17 58		
London Road (Guildford)	d	16 37						17 03							17 37						18 03		
Guildford	a	16 44	16 44					17 10		17 14					17 44	17 44					18 10		18 14

London - Chessington South, Dorking, Guildford, Shepperton and Hampton Court

Station		SW		SW	SW	SW	SW	SW	SW	SW	SW	SW		SW	SW	SW	SW	SW	SW	SW	SW	SW		SW	SW
London Waterloo 15 ⊖	d	17 14		17 18	17 21	17 27	17 32	17 40	17 48	17 51	17 56	17 57		18 00	18 02	18 10	18 14	18 18	18 21	18 27	18 32	18 40		18 48	18 51
Vauxhall ⊖	d	17 18		17 22	17 25	17 31	17 36	17 44	17 52	17 55	18 00	18 01		18 04	18 06	18 14	18 18	18 22	18 25	18 31	18 36	18 44		18 52	18 55
Clapham Junction 10	d			17 27	17 30	17 36	17 41	17 49	17 57	18 00		18 06		18 09	18 11	18 19		18 27	18 30	18 36	18 41	18 49		18 57	19 00
Earlsfield	d			17 30	17 33	17 39	17 44	17 52	18 00	18 03		18 09		18 12	18 14	18 22		18 30	18 33	18 39	18 44	18 52		19 00	19 03
Wimbledon 6 ⊖	d			17 34	17 37	17 43	17 48	17 56	18 04	18 07		18 13		18 16	18 18	18 26		18 34	18 37	18 43	18 48	18 56		19 04	19 07
Raynes Park 6	d			17 37	17 40	17 46	17 52		18 07	18 10		18 16			18 22			18 37	18 40	18 46	18 52			19 07	19 10
Motspur Park	d				17 43		17 55			18 13					18 25				18 43		18 55				19 13
Malden Manor	d				17 46					18 16									18 46						19 16
Tolworth	d				17 49					18 19									18 49						19 19
Chessington North	d				17 52					18 22									18 52						19 22
Chessington South	a				17 54					18 24									18 54						19 24
Worcester Park	d						17 57								18 27						18 57				
Stoneleigh	d						18 00								18 30						19 00				
Ewell West	d						18 03								18 33						19 03				
Epsom 3	a						18 06								18 36						19 06				
	d						18 08								18 38						19 08				
Ashtead	d						18 12								18 42						19 12				
Leatherhead	d						18 15								18 45						19 15				
Boxhill & Westhumble	d																								
Dorking 4	a														18 53										
New Malden 6	d			17 40		17 49			18 10			18 19						18 40		18 49				19 10	
Norbiton	d			17 43					18 13									18 43						19 13	
Kingston	a	17 59		17 46					18 16		18 38						18 59	18 46						19 16	
	d			17 49					18 16									18 49						19 16	
Hampton Wick	d			17 51					18 18									18 51						19 18	
Teddington	d			17 56					18 21									18 56						19 21	
Strawberry Hill	a			17 59														18 59							
Fulwell	d								18 25															19 25	
Hampton	d								18 29															19 29	
Kempton Park	d								18 32															19 32	
Sunbury	d								18 34															19 34	
Upper Halliford	d								18 36															19 36	
Shepperton	a								18 41															19 41	
Berrylands	d					17 51						18 21								18 51					
Surbiton 6	d					17 55		18 05				18 25		18 32		18 35				18 55		19 05			
Thames Ditton	d					18 00						18 30								19 00					
Hampton Court	a					18 03						18 33								19 03					
Hinchley Wood	d													18 36											
Claygate	d													18 39											
Oxshott	d													18 42											
Cobham & Stoke D'abernon	d													18 46											
Bookham	d						18 21														19 21				
Effingham Junction 6	d						18 25							18 50							19 25				
Horsley	d						18 27							18 53							19 27				
Clandon	d						18 32							18 58							19 32				
London Road (Guildford)	d						18 37							19 03							19 37				
Guildford	a						18 44	18 44						19 10		19 14					19 44	19 44			

Station		SW	SW	SW	SW	SW	SW	SW		SW	SW	SW	SW	SW	SW	SW	SW	SW		SW	SW	SW	SW	SW	SW
London Waterloo 15 ⊖	d	18 56	18 57	19 00	19 02	19 10	19 14	19 18		19 21	19 27	19 32	19 40	19 48	19 56	19 57	20 00	20 02		20 10	20 14	20 18	20 21	20 27	20 32
Vauxhall ⊖	d	19 00	19 01	19 04	19 06	19 14	19 18	19 22		19 25	19 31	19 36	19 44	19 52	20 00	20 01	20 04	20 06		20 14	20 18	20 22	20 25	20 31	20 36
Clapham Junction 10	d		19 06	19 09	19 11	19 19		19 27		19 30	19 36	19 41	19 49	19 57		20 06	20 09	20 11		20 19		20 27	20 30	20 36	20 41
Earlsfield	d		19 09	19 12	19 14	19 22		19 30		19 33	19 39	19 44	19 52	20 00		20 09	20 12	20 14		20 22		20 30	20 33	20 39	20 44
Wimbledon 6 ⊖	d		19 13	19 16	19 18	19 26		19 34		19 37	19 43	19 48	19 56	20 04		20 13	20 16	20 18		20 26		20 34	20 37	20 43	20 48
Raynes Park 6	d		19 16		19 22			19 37		19 40	19 46	19 52		20 07		20 16		20 22				20 37	20 40	20 46	20 52
Motspur Park	d				19 25					19 43		19 55						20 25					20 43		20 55
Malden Manor	d									19 46													20 46		
Tolworth	d									19 49													20 49		
Chessington North	d									19 52													20 52		
Chessington South	a									19 54													20 54		
Worcester Park	d				19 27							19 57						20 27							20 57
Stoneleigh	d				19 30							20 00						20 30							21 00
Ewell West	d				19 33							20 03						20 33							21 03
Epsom 3	a				19 36							20 06						20 36							21 06
	d				19 38							20 08						20 38							21 08
Ashtead	d				19 42							20 12						20 42							21 12
Leatherhead	d				19 45							20 15						20 45							21 15
Boxhill & Westhumble	d																								
Dorking 4	a				19 53													20 53							
New Malden 6	d		19 19					19 40			19 49			20 10		20 19						20 40		20 49	
Norbiton	d							19 43						20 13								20 43			
Kingston	a	19 38					19 59	19 46						20 16	20 38						20 59	20 46			
	d							19 49						20 16								20 49			
Hampton Wick	d							19 51						20 18								20 51			
Teddington	d							19 56						20 21								20 56			
Strawberry Hill	a							19 59														20 59			
Fulwell	d													20 25											
Hampton	d													20 29											
Kempton Park	d													20 32											
Sunbury	d													20 34											
Upper Halliford	d													20 36											
Shepperton	a													20 41											
Berrylands	d		19 21								19 51					20 21								20 51	
Surbiton 6	d		19 25	19 32		19 35					19 55		20 05			20 25	20 32			20 35				20 55	
Thames Ditton	d		19 30								20 00					20 30								21 00	
Hampton Court	a		19 33								20 03					20 33								21 03	
Hinchley Wood	d			19 36													20 36								
Claygate	d			19 39													20 39								
Oxshott	d			19 42													20 42								
Cobham & Stoke D'abernon	d			19 46													20 46								
Bookham	d											20 21													21 21
Effingham Junction 6	d			19 50								20 25					20 50								21 25
Horsley	d			19 53								20 27					20 53								21 27
Clandon	d			19 58								20 32					20 58								21 32
London Road (Guildford)	d			20 03								20 37					21 03								21 37
Guildford	a			20 10		20 14						20 44	20 44				21 10			21 14					21 44

London - Chessington South, Dorking, Guildford, Shepperton and Hampton Court

Station		SW	SW	SW		SW	SW	SW	SW	SW	SW	SW	SW	SW		SW	SW	SW	SW	SW	SW	SW	SW	SW	
London Waterloo 15 ⊖	d	20 40	20 48	20 56		20 57	21 00	21 02	21 10	21 14	21 18	21 21	21 32	21 40		21 48	21 56	21 57	22 00	22 02	22 10	22 14	22 18	22 21	
Vauxhall ⊖	d	20 44	20 52	21 00		21 01	21 04	21 06	21 14	21 18	21 22	21 25	21 36	21 44		21 52	22 00	22 01	22 04	22 06	22 14	22 18	22 22	22 25	
Clapham Junction 10	d	20 49	20 57			21 06	21 09	21 11	21 19		21 27	21 30	21 41	21 49		21 57		22 06	22 09	22 11	22 19		22 27	22 30	
Earlsfield	d	20 52	21 00			21 09	21 12	21 14	21 22		21 30	21 33	21 44	21 52		22 00		22 09	22 12	22 14	22 22		22 30	22 33	
Wimbledon 6 ⊖	d	20 56	21 04			21 13	21 16	21 18	21 26		21 34	21 37	21 48	21 56		22 04		22 13	22 16	22 18	22 26		22 34	22 37	
Raynes Park 6	d		21 07			21 16		21 22			21 37	21 40	21 52			22 07		22 16		22 22			22 37	22 40	
Motspur Park	d							21 25				21 43	21 55							22 25				22 43	
Malden Manor	d											21 46												22 46	
Tolworth	d											21 49												22 49	
Chessington North	d											21 52												22 52	
Chessington South	a											21 54												22 54	
Worcester Park	d							21 27					21 57							22 27					
Stoneleigh	d							21 30					22 00							22 30					
Ewell West	d							21 33					22 03							22 33					
Epsom 3	a							21 36					22 06							22 36					
	d							21 38					22 08							22 38					
Ashtead	d							21 42					22 12							22 42					
Leatherhead	d							21 45					22 15							22 45					
Boxhill & Westhumble	d																								
Dorking 4	a							21 53												22 53					
New Malden 6	d		21 10			21 19					21 40					22 10		22 19					22 40		
Norbiton	d		21 13								21 43					22 13							22 43		
Kingston	a		21 16	21 38						21 59	21 46					22 16	22 38					22 59	22 46		
	d		21 16								21 49					22 16							22 49		
Hampton Wick	d		21 18								21 51					22 18							22 51		
Teddington	d		21 21								21 56					22 21							22 56		
Strawberry Hill	a										21 59												22 59		
Fulwell	d		21 25													22 25									
Hampton	d		21 29													22 29									
Kempton Park	d		21 32													22 32									
Sunbury	d		21 34													22 34									
Upper Halliford	d		21 36													22 36									
Shepperton	a		21 41													22 41									
Berrylands	d					21 21												22 21							
Surbiton 6	d	21 05				21 25	21 32		21 35					22 05				22 25	22 32		22 35				
Thames Ditton	d					21 30												22 30							
Hampton Court	a					21 33												22 33							
Hinchley Wood	d						21 36												22 36						
Claygate	d						21 39												22 39						
Oxshott	d						21 42												22 42						
Cobham & Stoke D'abernon	d						21 46												22 46						
Bookham	d												22 21												
Effingham Junction 6	d						21 50						22 25						22 50						
Horsley	d						21 53						22 27						22 53						
Clandon	d						21 58						22 32						22 58						
London Road (Guildford)	d						22 03						22 37						23 03						
Guildford	a	21 44					22 10		22 14				22 44	22 44					23 10		23 13				

Table 152

Sundays from 2 October

London - Chessington South, Dorking, Guildford, Shepperton and Hampton Court

Station		SW	SW	SW	SW	SW	SW	SW	SW	SW	SW	SW	SW	SW 1
London Waterloo 15 ⊖	d	22 32	22 40	22 48	22 51	22 56	22 57	23 00	23 02	23 10	23 14	23 18	23 32	23 40
Vauxhall ⊖	d	22 36	22 44	22 52	22 55	23 00	23 01	23 04	23 06	23 14	23 18	23 22	23 36	23 44
Clapham Junction 10	d	22 41	22 49	22 57	23 00		23 06	23 09	23 11	23 19		23 27	23 41	23 49
Earlsfield	d	22 44	22 52	23 00	23 03		23 09	23 12	23 14	23 22		23 30	23 44	23 52
Wimbledon 6 ⊖	d	22 48	22 56	23 04	23 07		23 13	23 16	23 18	23 26		23 34	23 48	23 56
Raynes Park 6	d	22 52		23 07	23 10		23 16		23 22			23 37	23 52	
Motspur Park	d	22 55			23 13				23 25				23 55	
Malden Manor	d				23 16									
Tolworth	d				23 19									
Chessington North	d				23 22									
Chessington South	a				23 24									
Worcester Park	d	22 57							23 27				23 57	
Stoneleigh	d	23 00							23 30				23 59	
Ewell West	d	23 03							23 33				00 03	
Epsom 3	a	23 06							23 36				00 06	
	d	23 08												
Ashtead	d	23 12												
Leatherhead	d	23 15												
Boxhill & Westhumble	d													
Dorking 4	a													
New Malden 6	d			23 10			23 19					23 40		
Norbiton	d			23 13								23 43		
Kingston	a			23 16		23 38					23 56	23 46		
	d			23 16								23 47		
Hampton Wick	d			23 18								23 49		
Teddington	d			23 21								23 51		
Strawberry Hill	a											23 54		
Fulwell	d			23 25										
Hampton	d			23 29										
Kempton Park	d			23 32										
Sunbury	d			23 34										
Upper Halliford	d			23 36										
Shepperton	a			23 41										
Berrylands	d						23 21							
Surbiton 6	d		23 05				23 25	23 32		23 35				00a04
Thames Ditton	d						23 30							
Hampton Court	a						23 33							
Hinchley Wood	d							23 36						
Claygate	d							23 39						
Oxshott	d							23 42						
Cobham & Stoke D'abernon	d							23 46						
Bookham	d	23 21												
Effingham Junction 6	d	23 25						23 50						
Horsley	d	23 27						23 53						
Clandon	d	23 32						23 58						
London Road (Guildford)	d	23 37						00 03						
Guildford	a	23 44	23 45					00 10		00 13				

Table 152

Sundays from 9 October

London - Chessington South, Dorking, Guildford, Shepperton and Hampton Court

Station		SW	SW	SW	SW	SW	SW	SW	SW	SW	SW	SW	SW	SW	SW	SW	SW	SW	SW	SW	SW	SW	SW
London Waterloo 15 ⊖	d	23p03	23p09	23p12	23p27	23p33	23p36	23p42	23p50	23p57	00 09	00 15	00 18	00 27	00 42	01 42	06 14	06 18		06 57			07 10
Vauxhall ⊖	d	23p07	23p13	23p16	23p31	23p37	23p40	23p46	23p54	00 01	00 13	00 19	00 22	00 31	00 46	01 46	06 18	06 22		07 01			07 14
Clapham Junction 10	d	23p12	23p18	23p21	23p36		23p45	23p51	23p59	00 06	00 20	00 25		00 37		01 53		06 27		07 06			07 19
Earlsfield	d	23p15	23p21	23p24	23p39		23p48	23p54	00 02	00 09	00 23	00 29		00s41						07 09			07 22
Wimbledon 6 ⊖	d	23p19	23p25	23p28	23p43		23p52	23p58	00 06	00 13	00 27	00 33		00 45	01 05	01 59		06 34	06 48	07 13	07 16	07 20	07 26
Raynes Park 6	d		23p28	23p31	23p46		23p55	00 01		00 16		00 36		00 48	01 08	02 02		06 37	06 52	07 16		07 23	
Motspur Park	d		23p31					00 04				00 38							06 55			07 26	
Malden Manor	d																						
Tolworth	d																						
Chessington North	d																						
Chessington South	a																						
Worcester Park	d		23p33					00 06				00 41							06 57			07 28	
Stoneleigh	d		23p36					00 09				00 44							07 00			07 31	
Ewell West	d		23p39					00 12				00 46							07 03			07 34	
Epsom 3	a		23p42					00 15				00 50							07 06			07 37	
	d		23p47					00 19															
Ashtead	d		23p51					00 23															
Leatherhead	d		23p54					00 26															
Boxhill & Westhumble	d																						
Dorking 4	a		00 03																				
New Malden 6	d			23p34	23p49		23p58			00 19				00 50	01 11	02 04		06 40		07 19			
Norbiton	d			23p37	23p52					00 22					01 14	02 08		06 43					
Kingston	a			23p40	23p55	00 16				00 25			01 01		01 17	02 10	06 59	06 46					
	d			23p40	23p55					00 25					01 17	02 11		06 49					
Hampton Wick	d			23p42	23p57					00 27					01s22	02s13		06 51					
Teddington	d			23p45	23p59					00 30					01s25	02s15		06 56					
Strawberry Hill	a				00 03										01 28	02s18		06 59					
Fulwell	d			23p49						00 34													
Hampton	d			23p53						00 38													
Kempton Park	d			23p56						00 41													
Sunbury	d			23p58						00 43													
Upper Halliford	d			23p59						00 45													
Shepperton	a			00 05						00 50													
Berrylands	d						23p59							00s53						07 21			
Surbiton 6	d	23p27					00 05		00 14		00 35			00a56						07 25	07 32		07 35
Thames Ditton	d						00 09													07 30			
Hampton Court	a						00 12													07 33			
Hinchley Wood	d	23p31							00 18												07 36		
Claygate	d	23p34							00 20												07 39		
Oxshott	d	23p37							00 24												07 42		
Cobham & Stoke D'abernon	d	23p41							00 27												07 46		
Bookham	d							00 31															
Effingham Junction 6	d	23p45						00 36	00 32												07 50		
Horsley	d	23p48						00 39	00 34												07 53		
Clandon	d	23p53						00 44	00 39												07 58		
London Road (Guildford)	d	23p58						00 49	00 44												08 03		
Guildford	a	00 05						00 56	00 51		01 07										08 10		08 14

Station		SW	SW	SW	SW	SW	SW	SW	SW	SW	SW	SW	SW	SW	SW	SW	SW	SW	SW	SW	SW	SW	SW
London Waterloo 15 ⊖	d	07 14	07 18		07 27		07 40	07 48		07 57		08 02	08 10	08 14	08 18	08 21	08 27	08 32	08 40	08 48	08 51	08 57	
Vauxhall ⊖	d	07 18	07 22		07 31		07 44	07 52		08 01		08 06	08 14	08 18	08 22	08 25	08 31	08 36	08 44	08 52	08 55	09 01	
Clapham Junction 10	d		07 27		07 36		07 49	07 57		08 06		08 11	08 19		08 27	08 30	08 36	08 41	08 49	08 57	09 00	09 06	
Earlsfield	d		07 30		07 39		07 52	08 00		08 09		08 14	08 22		08 30	08 33	08 39	08 44	08 52	09 00	09 03	09 09	
Wimbledon 6 ⊖	d		07 34	07 37	07 43	07 48	07 56	08 04	08 07	08 13	08 16	08 18	08 26		08 34	08 37	08 43	08 48	08 56	09 04	09 07	09 13	09 16
Raynes Park 6	d		07 37	07 40	07 46	07 52		08 07	08 10	08 16		08 22			08 37	08 40	08 46	08 52		09 07	09 10	09 16	
Motspur Park	d			07 43		07 55			08 13			08 25				08 43		08 55			09 13		
Malden Manor	d			07 46					08 16							08 46					09 16		
Tolworth	d			07 49					08 19							08 49					09 19		
Chessington North	d			07 52					08 22							08 52					09 22		
Chessington South	a			07 54					08 24							08 54					09 24		
Worcester Park	d					07 57						08 27						08 57					
Stoneleigh	d					08 00						08 30						09 00					
Ewell West	d					08 03						08 33						09 03					
Epsom 3	a					08 06						08 36						09 06					
	d					08 08						08 38						09 08					
Ashtead	d					08 12						08 42						09 12					
Leatherhead	d					08 15						08 45						09 15					
Boxhill & Westhumble	d																						
Dorking 4	a											08 53											
New Malden 6	d		07 40		07 49			08 10		08 19					08 40		08 49			09 10		09 19	
Norbiton	d		07 43					08 13							08 43					09 13			
Kingston	a	07 59	07 46					08 16						08 59	08 46					09 16			
	d		07 49					08 16							08 49					09 16			
Hampton Wick	d		07 51					08 18							08 51					09 18			
Teddington	d		07 56					08 21							08 56					09 21			
Strawberry Hill	a		07 59												08 59								
Fulwell	d							08 25												09 25			
Hampton	d							08 29												09 29			
Kempton Park	d							08 32												09 32			
Sunbury	d							08 34												09 34			
Upper Halliford	d							08 36												09 36			
Shepperton	a							08 41												09 41			
Berrylands	d				07 51					08 21							08 51					09 21	
Surbiton 6	d				07 55		08 05			08 25	08 32		08 35				08 55		09 05			09 25	09 32
Thames Ditton	d				08 00					08 30							09 00					09 30	
Hampton Court	a				08 03					08 33							09 03					09 33	
Hinchley Wood	d										08 36												09 36
Claygate	d										08 39												09 39
Oxshott	d										08 42												09 42
Cobham & Stoke D'abernon	d										08 46												09 46
Bookham	d					08 21												09 21					
Effingham Junction 6	d					08 25					08 50							09 25					09 50
Horsley	d					08 27					08 53							09 27					09 53
Clandon	d					08 32					08 58							09 32					09 58
London Road (Guildford)	d					08 37					09 03							09 37					10 03
Guildford	a					08 44	08 40				09 10		09 10					09 44	09 40				10 10

London - Chessington South, Dorking, Guildford, Shepperton and Hampton Court

		SW		SW	SW	SW	SW	SW	SW	SW	SW	SW		SW	SW	SW	SW	SW	SW	SW	SW	SW		SW	SW
London Waterloo	d	09 02		09 10	09 14	09 18	09 21	09 27	09 32	09 40	09 48	09 51		09 57		10 02	10 10	10 14	10 18	10 21	10 27	10 32		10 40	10 48
Vauxhall	d	09 06		09 14	09 18	09 22	09 25	09 31	09 36	09 44	09 52	09 55		10 01		10 06	10 14	10 18	10 22	10 25	10 31	10 36		10 44	10 52
Clapham Junction	d	09 11		09 19		09 27	09 30	09 36	09 41	09 49	09 57	10 00		10 06		10 11	10 19		10 27	10 30	10 36	10 41		10 49	10 57
Earlsfield	d	09 14		09 22		09 30	09 33	09 39	09 44	09 52	10 00	10 03		10 09		10 14	10 22		10 30	10 33	10 39	10 44		10 52	11 00
Wimbledon	d	09 18		09 26		09 34	09 37	09 43	09 48	09 56	10 04	10 07		10 13	10 16	10 18	10 26		10 34	10 37	10 43	10 48		10 56	11 04
Raynes Park	d	09 22				09 37	09 40	09 46	09 52		10 07	10 10		10 16		10 22			10 37	10 40	10 46	10 52			11 07
Motspur Park	d	09 25					09 43		09 55			10 13				10 25				10 43		10 55			
Malden Manor	d						09 46					10 16								10 46					
Tolworth	d						09 49					10 19								10 49					
Chessington North	d						09 52					10 22								10 52					
Chessington South	a						09 54					10 24								10 54					
Worcester Park	d	09 27							09 57							10 27						10 57			
Stoneleigh	d	09 30							10 00							10 30						11 00			
Ewell West	d	09 33							10 03							10 33						11 03			
Epsom	a	09 36							10 06							10 36						11 06			
	d	09 38							10 08							10 38						11 08			
Ashtead	d	09 42							10 12							10 42						11 12			
Leatherhead	d	09 45							10 15							10 45						11 15			
Boxhill & Westhumble	d																								
Dorking	a	09 53														10 53									
New Malden	d					09 40		09 49			10 10			10 19					10 40		10 49				11 10
Norbiton	d					09 43					10 13								10 43						11 13
Kingston	a				09 59	09 46					10 16							10 59	10 46						11 16
	d					09 49					10 16								10 49						11 16
Hampton Wick	d					09 51					10 18								10 51						11 18
Teddington	d					09 56					10 21								10 56						11 21
Strawberry Hill	a					09 59													10 59						
Fulwell	d										10 25														11 25
Hampton	d										10 29														11 29
Kempton Park	d										10 32														11 32
Sunbury	d										10 34														11 34
Upper Halliford	d										10 36														11 36
Shepperton	a										10 41														11 41
Berrylands	d							09 51						10 21							10 51				
Surbiton	d			09 35				09 55		10 05				10 25	10 32		10 35				10 55			11 05	
Thames Ditton	d							10 00						10 30							11 00				
Hampton Court	a							10 03						10 33							11 03				
Hinchley Wood	d														10 36										
Claygate	d														10 39										
Oxshott	d														10 42										
Cobham & Stoke D'abernon	d														10 46										
Bookham	d								10 21													11 21			
Effingham Junction	d								10 25						10 50							11 25			
Horsley	d								10 27						10 53							11 27			
Clandon	d								10 32						10 58							11 32			
London Road (Guildford)	d								10 37						11 03							11 37			
Guildford	a			10 10					10 44	10 44					11 10		11 14					11 44		11 44	

		SW	SW	SW	SW	SW	SW	SW		SW	SW	SW	SW	SW	SW	SW	SW	SW		SW	SW	SW	SW	SW	SW
London Waterloo	d	10 51	10 57		11 02	11 10	11 14	11 18		11 21	11 27	11 32	11 40	11 48	11 51	11 57		12 02		12 10	12 14	12 18	12 21	12 27	12 32
Vauxhall	d	10 55	11 01		11 06	11 14	11 19	11 22		11 25	11 31	11 36	11 44	11 52	11 55	12 01		12 06		12 14	12 19	12 22	12 25	12 31	12 36
Clapham Junction	d	11 00	11 06		11 11	11 19		11 27		11 30	11 36	11 41	11 49	11 57	12 00	12 06		12 11		12 19		12 27	12 30	12 36	12 41
Earlsfield	d	11 03	11 09		11 14	11 22		11 30		11 33	11 39	11 44	11 52	12 00	12 03	12 09		12 14		12 22		12 30	12 33	12 39	12 44
Wimbledon	d	11 07	11 13	11 16	11 18	11 26		11 34		11 37	11 43	11 48	11 56	12 04	12 07	12 13	12 16	12 18		12 26		12 34	12 37	12 43	12 48
Raynes Park	d	11 10	11 16		11 22			11 37		11 40	11 46	11 52		12 07	12 10	12 16		12 22				12 37	12 40	12 46	12 52
Motspur Park	d	11 13			11 25					11 43		11 55			12 13			12 25					12 43		12 55
Malden Manor	d	11 16								11 46					12 16								12 46		
Tolworth	d	11 19								11 49					12 19								12 49		
Chessington North	d	11 22								11 52					12 22								12 52		
Chessington South	a	11 24								11 54					12 24								12 54		
Worcester Park	d				11 27							11 57						12 27							12 57
Stoneleigh	d				11 30							12 00						12 30							13 00
Ewell West	d				11 33							12 03						12 33							13 03
Epsom	a				11 36							12 06						12 36							13 06
	d				11 38							12 08						12 38							13 08
Ashtead	d				11 42							12 12						12 42							13 12
Leatherhead	d				11 45							12 15						12 45							13 15
Boxhill & Westhumble	d																								
Dorking	a				11 53													12 53							
New Malden	d		11 19					11 40			11 49			12 10		12 19						12 40		12 49	
Norbiton	d							11 43						12 13								12 43			
Kingston	a						11 59	11 46						12 16							12 59	12 46			
	d							11 49						12 16								12 49			
Hampton Wick	d							11 51						12 18								12 51			
Teddington	d							11 56						12 21								12 56			
Strawberry Hill	a							11 59														12 59			
Fulwell	d													12 25											
Hampton	d													12 29											
Kempton Park	d													12 32											
Sunbury	d													12 34											
Upper Halliford	d													12 36											
Shepperton	a													12 41											
Berrylands	d		11 21								11 51					12 21								12 51	
Surbiton	d		11 25	11 32		11 35					11 55		12 05			12 25	12 32			12 35				12 55	
Thames Ditton	d		11 30								12 00					12 30								13 00	
Hampton Court	a		11 33								12 03					12 33								13 03	
Hinchley Wood	d			11 36													12 36								
Claygate	d			11 39													12 39								
Oxshott	d			11 42													12 42								
Cobham & Stoke D'abernon	d			11 46													12 46								
Bookham	d											12 21													13 21
Effingham Junction	d			11 50								12 25					12 50								13 25
Horsley	d			11 53								12 27					12 53								13 27
Clandon	d			11 58								12 32					12 58								13 32
London Road (Guildford)	d			12 03								12 37					13 03								13 37
Guildford	a			12 10		12 14						12 44	12 44				13 10			13 14					13 44

London - Chessington South, Dorking, Guildford, Shepperton and Hampton Court

		SW	SW	SW		SW	SW	SW	SW	SW	SW	SW	SW	SW		SW	SW	SW	SW	SW	SW	SW	SW	SW	
London Waterloo	d	12 40	12 48	12 51		12 57	13 00	13 02	13 10	13 14	13 18	13 21	13 27	13 32		13 40	13 48	13 51	13 56	13 57	14 00	14 02	14 10	14 14	
Vauxhall	d	12 44	12 52	12 55		13 01	13 04	13 06	13 14	13 18	13 22	13 25	13 31	13 36		13 44	13 52	13 55	14 00	14 01	14 04	14 06	14 14	14 18	
Clapham Junction	d	12 49	12 57	13 00		13 06	13 09	13 11	13 19		13 27	13 30	13 36	13 41		13 49	13 57	14 00		14 06	14 09	14 11	14 19		
Earlsfield	d	12 52	13 00	13 03		13 09	13 12	13 14	13 22		13 30	13 33	13 39	13 44		13 52	14 00	14 03		14 09	14 12	14 14	14 22		
Wimbledon	d	12 56	13 04	13 07		13 13	13 16	13 18	13 26		13 34	13 37	13 43	13 48		13 56	14 04	14 07		14 13	14 16	14 18	14 26		
Raynes Park	d		13 07	13 10		13 16		13 22			13 37	13 40	13 46	13 52			14 07	14 10		14 16		14 22			
Motspur Park	d			13 13				13 25				13 43		13 55				14 13				14 25			
Malden Manor	d			13 16								13 46						14 16							
Tolworth	d			13 19								13 49						14 19							
Chessington North	d			13 22								13 52						14 22							
Chessington South	a			13 24								13 54						14 24							
Worcester Park	d							13 27						13 57								14 27			
Stoneleigh	d							13 30						14 00								14 30			
Ewell West	d							13 33						14 03								14 33			
Epsom	a							13 36						14 06								14 36			
	d							13 38						14 08								14 38			
Ashtead	d							13 42						14 12								14 42			
Leatherhead	d							13 45						14 15								14 45			
Boxhill & Westhumble	d																								
Dorking	a							13 53														14 53			
New Malden	d		13 10			13 19					13 40		13 49				14 10			14 19					
Norbiton	d		13 13								13 43						14 13								
Kingston	a		13 16							13 59	13 46						14 16		14 38					14 59	
	d		13 16								13 49						14 16								
Hampton Wick	d		13 18								13 51						14 18								
Teddington	d		13 21								13 56						14 21								
Strawberry Hill	a										13 59														
Fulwell	d		13 25														14 25								
Hampton	d		13 29														14 29								
Kempton Park	d		13 32														14 32								
Sunbury	d		13 34														14 34								
Upper Halliford	d		13 36														14 36								
Shepperton	a		13 41														14 41								
Berrylands	d					13 21							13 51							14 21					
Surbiton	d	13 05				13 25	13 32		13 35				13 55			14 05				14 25	14 32		14 35		
Thames Ditton	d					13 30							14 00							14 30					
Hampton Court	a					13 33							14 03							14 33					
Hinchley Wood	d						13 36														14 36				
Claygate	d						13 39														14 39				
Oxshott	d						13 42														14 42				
Cobham & Stoke D'abernon	d						13 46														14 46				
Bookham	d													14 21											
Effingham Junction	d						13 50							14 25							14 50				
Horsley	d						13 53							14 27							14 53				
Clandon	d						13 58							14 32							14 58				
London Road (Guildford)	d						14 03							14 37							15 03				
Guildford	a	13 44					14 10		14 14					14 44		14 44					15 10		15 14		

		SW	SW	SW	SW	SW	SW	SW	SW	SW		SW	SW	SW	SW	SW	SW	SW	SW	SW		SW	SW	SW	SW
London Waterloo	d	14 18	14 21	14 27	14 32	14 40	14 48	14 51	14 56	14 57		15 00	15 02	15 10	15 14	15 18	15 21	15 27	15 32	15 40		15 48	15 51	15 56	15 57
Vauxhall	d	14 22	14 25	14 31	14 36	14 44	14 52	14 55	15 00	15 01		15 04	15 06	15 14	15 18	15 22	15 25	15 31	15 36	15 44		15 52	15 55	16 00	16 01
Clapham Junction	d	14 27	14 30	14 36	14 41	14 49	14 57	15 00		15 06		15 09	15 11	15 19		15 27	15 30	15 36	15 41	15 49		15 57	16 00		16 06
Earlsfield	d	14 30	14 33	14 39	14 44	14 52	15 00	15 03		15 09		15 12	15 14	15 22		15 30	15 33	15 39	15 44	15 52		16 00	16 03		16 09
Wimbledon	d	14 34	14 37	14 43	14 48	14 56	15 04	15 07		15 13		15 16	15 18	15 26		15 34	15 37	15 43	15 48	15 56		16 04	16 07		16 13
Raynes Park	d	14 37	14 40	14 46	14 52		15 07	15 10		15 16			15 22			15 37	15 40	15 46	15 52			16 07	16 10		16 16
Motspur Park	d		14 43		14 55			15 13					15 25				15 43		15 55				16 13		
Malden Manor	d		14 46					15 16									15 46						16 16		
Tolworth	d		14 49					15 19									15 49						16 19		
Chessington North	d		14 52					15 22									15 52						16 22		
Chessington South	a		14 54					15 24									15 54						16 24		
Worcester Park	d				14 57								15 27						15 57						
Stoneleigh	d				15 00								15 30						16 00						
Ewell West	d				15 03								15 33						16 03						
Epsom	a				15 06								15 36						16 06						
	d				15 08								15 38						16 08						
Ashtead	d				15 12								15 42						16 12						
Leatherhead	d				15 15								15 45						16 15						
Boxhill & Westhumble	d																								
Dorking	a												15 53												
New Malden	d	14 40		14 49			15 10			15 19						15 40		15 49				16 10			16 19
Norbiton	d	14 43					15 13									15 43						16 13			
Kingston	a	14 46					15 16		15 38						15 59	15 46						16 16		16 38	
	d	14 49					15 16									15 49						16 16			
Hampton Wick	d	14 51					15 18									15 51						16 18			
Teddington	d	14 56					15 21									15 56						16 21			
Strawberry Hill	a	14 59														15 59									
Fulwell	d						15 25															16 25			
Hampton	d						15 29															16 29			
Kempton Park	d						15 32															16 32			
Sunbury	d						15 34															16 34			
Upper Halliford	d						15 36															16 36			
Shepperton	a						15 41															16 41			
Berrylands	d			14 51						15 21								15 51							16 21
Surbiton	d			14 55		15 05				15 25		15 32		15 35				15 55		16 05					16 25
Thames Ditton	d			15 00						15 30								16 00							16 30
Hampton Court	a			15 03						15 33								16 03							16 33
Hinchley Wood	d											15 36													
Claygate	d											15 39													
Oxshott	d											15 42													
Cobham & Stoke D'abernon	d											15 46													
Bookham	d				15 21														16 21						
Effingham Junction	d				15 25							15 50							16 25						
Horsley	d				15 27							15 53							16 27						
Clandon	d				15 32							15 58							16 32						
London Road (Guildford)	d				15 37							16 03							16 37						
Guildford	a				15 44	15 44						16 10		16 14					16 44	16 44					

Sundays
from 9 October

London - Chessington South, Dorking, Guildford, Shepperton and Hampton Court

		SW	SW	SW	SW	SW	SW	SW	SW	SW	SW	SW	SW	SW	SW	SW	SW	SW	SW	SW	SW	SW	SW
London Waterloo 15 ⊖	d	16 00	16 02	16 10	16 14	16 18	16 21	16 27	16 32	16 40	16 48	16 51	16 56	16 57	17 00	17 02	17 10	17 14	17 18	17 21	17 27	17 32	17 40
Vauxhall ⊖	d	16 04	16 06	16 14	16 18	16 22	16 25	16 31	16 36	16 44	16 52	16 55	17 00	17 01	17 04	17 06	17 14	17 18	17 22	17 25	17 31	17 36	17 44
Clapham Junction 10	d	16 09	16 11	16 19		16 27	16 30	16 36	16 41	16 49	16 57	17 00		17 06	17 09	17 11	17 19		17 27	17 30	17 36	17 41	17 49
Earlsfield	d	16 12	16 14	16 22		16 30	16 33	16 39	16 44	16 52	17 00	17 03		17 09	17 12	17 14	17 22		17 30	17 33	17 39	17 44	17 52
Wimbledon 6 ⊖	d	16 16	16 18	16 26		16 34	16 37	16 43	16 48	16 56	17 04	17 07		17 13	17 16	17 18	17 26		17 34	17 37	17 43	17 48	17 56
Raynes Park 6	d		16 22			16 37	16 40	16 46	16 52		17 07	17 10		17 16		17 22			17 37	17 40	17 46	17 52	
Motspur Park	d		16 25				16 43		16 55			17 13				17 25				17 43		17 55	
Malden Manor	d						16 46					17 16								17 46			
Tolworth	d						16 49					17 19								17 49			
Chessington North	d						16 52					17 22								17 52			
Chessington South	a						16 54					17 24								17 54			
Worcester Park	d		16 27						16 57							17 27						17 57	
Stoneleigh	d		16 30						17 00							17 30						18 00	
Ewell West	d		16 33						17 03							17 33						18 03	
Epsom 3	a		16 36						17 06							17 36						18 06	
	d		16 38						17 08							17 38						18 08	
Ashtead	d		16 42						17 12							17 42						18 12	
Leatherhead	d		16 45						17 15							17 45						18 15	
Boxhill & Westhumble	d																						
Dorking 4	a		16 53													17 53							
New Malden 6	d					16 40		16 49			17 10			17 19					17 40		17 49		
Norbiton	d					16 43					17 13								17 43				
Kingston	a				16 59	16 46					17 16		17 38					17 59	17 46				
	d					16 49					17 16								17 49				
Hampton Wick	d					16 51					17 18								17 51				
Teddington	d					16 56					17 21								17 56				
Strawberry Hill	a					16 59													17 59				
Fulwell	d										17 25												
Hampton	d										17 29												
Kempton Park	d										17 32												
Sunbury	d										17 34												
Upper Halliford	d										17 36												
Shepperton	a										17 41												
Berrylands	d							16 51						17 21							17 51		
Surbiton 6	d	16 32		16 35				16 55		17 05				17 25	17 32		17 35				17 55		18 05
Thames Ditton	d							17 00						17 30							18 00		
Hampton Court	a							17 03						17 33							18 03		
Hinchley Wood	d	16 36													17 36								
Claygate	d	16 39													17 39								
Oxshott	d	16 42													17 42								
Cobham & Stoke D'abernon	d	16 46													17 46								
Bookham	d								17 21													18 21	
Effingham Junction 6	d	16 50							17 25						17 50							18 25	
Horsley	d	16 53							17 27						17 53							18 27	
Clandon	d	16 58							17 32						17 58							18 32	
London Road (Guildford)	d	17 03							17 37						18 03							18 37	
Guildford	a	17 10		17 14					17 44	17 44					18 10		18 14					18 44	18 44

		SW	SW	SW	SW	SW	SW	SW	SW	SW	SW	SW	SW	SW	SW	SW	SW	SW	SW	SW	SW	SW
London Waterloo 15 ⊖	d	17 48	17 51	17 56	17 57	18 00	18 02	18 10	18 14	18 18	18 21	18 27	18 32	18 40	18 48	18 51	18 56	18 57	19 00	19 02	19 10	19 14
Vauxhall ⊖	d	17 52	17 55	18 00	18 01	18 04	18 06	18 14	18 18	18 22	18 25	18 31	18 36	18 44	18 52	18 55	19 00	19 01	19 04	19 06	19 14	19 18
Clapham Junction 10	d	17 57	18 00		18 06	18 09	18 11	18 19		18 27	18 30	18 36	18 41	18 49	18 57	19 00		19 06	19 09	19 11	19 19	
Earlsfield	d	18 00	18 03		18 09	18 12	18 14	18 22		18 30	18 33	18 39	18 44	18 52	19 00	19 03		19 09	19 12	19 14	19 22	
Wimbledon 6 ⊖	d	18 04	18 07		18 13	18 16	18 18	18 26		18 34	18 37	18 43	18 48	18 56	19 04	19 07		19 13	19 16	19 18	19 26	
Raynes Park 6	d	18 07	18 10		18 16		18 22			18 37	18 40	18 46	18 52		19 07	19 10		19 16		19 22		
Motspur Park	d		18 13				18 25				18 43		18 55			19 13				19 25		
Malden Manor	d		18 16								18 46					19 16						
Tolworth	d		18 19								18 49					19 19						
Chessington North	d		18 22								18 52					19 22						
Chessington South	a		18 24								18 54					19 24						
Worcester Park	d						18 27						18 57							19 27		
Stoneleigh	d						18 30						19 00							19 30		
Ewell West	d						18 33						19 03							19 33		
Epsom 3	a						18 36						19 06							19 36		
	d						18 38						19 08							19 38		
Ashtead	d						18 42						19 12							19 42		
Leatherhead	d						18 45						19 15							19 45		
Boxhill & Westhumble	d																					
Dorking 4	a						18 53													19 53		
New Malden 6	d	18 10			18 19					18 40		18 49			19 10			19 19				
Norbiton	d	18 13								18 43					19 13							
Kingston	a	18 16		18 38					18 59	18 46					19 16		19 38					19 59
	d	18 16								18 49					19 16							
Hampton Wick	d	18 18								18 51					19 18							
Teddington	d	18 21								18 56					19 21							
Strawberry Hill	a									18 59												
Fulwell	d	18 25													19 25							
Hampton	d	18 29													19 29							
Kempton Park	d	18 32													19 32							
Sunbury	d	18 34													19 34							
Upper Halliford	d	18 36													19 36							
Shepperton	a	18 41													19 41							
Berrylands	d				18 21							18 51						19 21				
Surbiton 6	d				18 25	18 32		18 35				18 55		19 05				19 25	19 32		19 35	
Thames Ditton	d				18 30							19 00						19 30				
Hampton Court	a				18 33							19 03						19 33				
Hinchley Wood	d					18 36													19 36			
Claygate	d					18 39													19 39			
Oxshott	d					18 42													19 42			
Cobham & Stoke D'abernon	d					18 46													19 46			
Bookham	d												19 21									
Effingham Junction 6	d					18 50							19 25						19 50			
Horsley	d					18 53							19 27						19 53			
Clandon	d					18 58							19 32						19 58			

Table 152

Sundays
from 9 October

London - Chessington South, Dorking, Guildford, Shepperton and Hampton Court

		SW	SW	SW	SW	SW	SW	SW	SW	SW	SW	SW	SW	SW	SW	SW	SW	SW	SW	SW	SW	SW	SW
London Waterloo 15 ⊖	d	19 18	19 21	19 27	19 32	19 40	19 48	19 56	19 57	20 00	20 02	20 10	20 14	20 18	20 21	20 27	20 32	20 40	20 48	20 56	20 57	21 00	21 02
Vauxhall ⊖	d	19 22	19 25	19 31	19 36	19 44	19 52	20 00	20 01	20 04	20 06	20 14	20 18	20 22	20 25	20 31	20 36	20 44	20 52	21 00	21 01	21 04	21 06
Clapham Junction 10	d	19 27	19 30	19 36	19 41	19 49	19 57		20 06	20 09	20 11	20 19		20 27	20 30	20 36	20 41	20 49	20 57		21 06	21 09	21 11
Earlsfield	d	19 30	19 33	19 39	19 44	19 52	20 00		20 09	20 12	20 14	20 22		20 30	20 33	20 39	20 44	20 52	21 00		21 09	21 12	21 14
Wimbledon 6 ⊖	d	19 34	19 37	19 43	19 48	19 56	20 04		20 13	20 16	20 18	20 26		20 34	20 37	20 43	20 48	20 56	21 04		21 13	21 16	21 18
Raynes Park 6	d	19 37	19 40	19 46	19 52		20 07		20 16		20 22			20 37	20 40	20 46	20 52		21 07		21 16		21 22
Motspur Park	d		19 43		19 55						20 25				20 43		20 55						21 25
Malden Manor	d		19 46												20 46								
Tolworth	d		19 49												20 49								
Chessington North	d		19 52												20 52								
Chessington South	a		19 54												20 54								
Worcester Park	d				19 57						20 27						20 57						21 27
Stoneleigh	d				20 00						20 30						21 00						21 30
Ewell West	d				20 03						20 33						21 03						21 33
Epsom 3	a				20 06						20 36						21 06						21 36
	d				20 08						20 38						21 08						21 38
Ashtead	d				20 12						20 42						21 12						21 42
Leatherhead	d				20 15						20 45						21 15						21 45
Boxhill & Westhumble	d																						
Dorking 4	a										20 53												21 53
New Malden 6	d	19 40		19 49			20 10		20 19					20 40		20 49			21 10		21 19		
Norbiton	d	19 43					20 13							20 43					21 13				
Kingston	a	19 46					20 16	20 38					20 59	20 46					21 16	21 38			
	d	19 49					20 16							20 49					21 16				
Hampton Wick	d	19 51					20 18							20 51					21 18				
Teddington	d	19 56					20 21							20 56					21 21				
Strawberry Hill	a	19 59												20 59									
Fulwell	d						20 25												21 25				
Hampton	d						20 29												21 29				
Kempton Park	d						20 32												21 32				
Sunbury	d						20 34												21 34				
Upper Halliford	d						20 36												21 36				
Shepperton	a						20 41												21 41				
Berrylands	d			19 51					20 21							20 51					21 21		
Surbiton 6	d			19 55		20 05			20 25	20 32		20 35				20 55		21 05			21 25	21 32	
Thames Ditton	d			20 00					20 30							21 00					21 30		
Hampton Court	a			20 03					20 33							21 03					21 33		
Hinchley Wood	d									20 36												21 36	
Claygate	d									20 39												21 39	
Oxshott	d									20 42												21 42	
Cobham & Stoke D'abernon	d									20 46												21 46	
Bookham	d				20 21												21 21						
Effingham Junction 6	d				20 25					20 50							21 25					21 50	
Horsley	d				20 27					20 53							21 27					21 53	
Clandon	d				20 32					20 58							21 32					21 58	
London Road (Guildford)	d				20 37					21 03							21 37					22 03	
Guildford	a				20 44	20 44				21 10		21 14					21 44	21 44				22 10	

		SW	SW	SW	SW	SW	SW	SW	SW	SW	SW	SW	SW	SW	SW	SW	SW	SW	SW	SW	SW	SW
London Waterloo 15 ⊖	d	21 10	21 14	21 18	21 21	21 32	21 40	21 48	21 56	21 57	22 00	22 02	22 10	22 14	22 18	22 21	22 32	22 40	22 48	22 51	22 56	22 57
Vauxhall ⊖	d	21 14	21 18	21 22	21 25	21 36	21 44	21 52	22 00	22 01	22 04	22 06	22 14	22 18	22 22	22 25	22 36	22 44	22 52	22 55	23 00	23 01
Clapham Junction 10	d	21 19		21 27	21 30	21 41	21 49	21 57		22 06	22 09	22 11	22 19		22 27	22 30	22 41	22 49	22 57	23 00		23 06
Earlsfield	d	21 22		21 30	21 33	21 44	21 52	22 00		22 09	22 12	22 14	22 22		22 30	22 33	22 44	22 52	23 00	23 03		23 09
Wimbledon 6 ⊖	d	21 26		21 34	21 37	21 48	21 56	22 04		22 13	22 16	22 18	22 26		22 34	22 37	22 48	22 56	23 04	23 07		23 13
Raynes Park 6	d			21 37	21 40	21 52		22 07		22 16		22 22			22 37	22 40	22 52		23 07	23 10		23 16
Motspur Park	d				21 43	21 55						22 25				22 43	22 55			23 13		
Malden Manor	d				21 46											22 46				23 16		
Tolworth	d				21 49											22 49				23 19		
Chessington North	d				21 52											22 52				23 22		
Chessington South	a				21 54											22 54				23 24		
Worcester Park	d					21 57						22 27					22 57					
Stoneleigh	d					22 00						22 30					23 00					
Ewell West	d					22 03						22 33					23 03					
Epsom 3	a					22 06						22 36					23 06					
	d					22 08						22 38					23 08					
Ashtead	d					22 12						22 42					23 12					
Leatherhead	d					22 15						22 45					23 15					
Boxhill & Westhumble	d																					
Dorking 4	a											22 53										
New Malden 6	d			21 40				22 10		22 19					22 40				23 10			23 19
Norbiton	d			21 43				22 13							22 43				23 13			
Kingston	a		21 59	21 46				22 16	22 38					22 59	22 46				23 16		23 38	
	d			21 49				22 16							22 49				23 16			
Hampton Wick	d			21 51				22 18							22 51				23 18			
Teddington	d			21 56				22 21							22 56				23 21			
Strawberry Hill	a			21 59											22 59							
Fulwell	d							22 25											23 25			
Hampton	d							22 29											23 29			
Kempton Park	d							22 32											23 32			
Sunbury	d							22 34											23 34			
Upper Halliford	d							22 36											23 36			
Shepperton	a							22 41											23 41			
Berrylands	d									22 21												23 21
Surbiton 6	d	21 35					22 05			22 25	22 32		22 35					23 05				23 25
Thames Ditton	d									22 30												23 30
Hampton Court	a									22 33												23 33
Hinchley Wood	d										22 36											
Claygate	d										22 39											
Oxshott	d										22 42											
Cobham & Stoke D'abernon	d										22 46											
Bookham	d					22 21											23 21					
Effingham Junction 6	d					22 25					22 50						23 25					
Horsley	d					22 27					22 53						23 27					
Clandon	d					22 32					22 58						23 32					
London Road (Guildford)	d					22 37					23 03						23 37					
Guildford	a																23 44	23 45				

London - Chessington South, Dorking, Guildford, Shepperton and Hampton Court

		SW	SW	SW	SW	SW	SW	SW 1
London Waterloo 15 ⊖	d	23 00	23 02	23 10	23 14	23 18	23 32	23 40
Vauxhall ⊖	d	23 04	23 06	23 14	23 18	23 22	23 36	23 44
Clapham Junction 10	d	23 09	23 11	23 19		23 27	23 41	23 49
Earlsfield	d	23 12	23 14	23 22		23 30	23 44	23 52
Wimbledon 6 ⊖	d	23 16	23 18	23 26		23 34	23 48	23 56
Raynes Park 6	d		23 22			23 37	23 52	
Motspur Park	d		23 25				23 55	
Malden Manor	d							
Tolworth	d							
Chessington North	d							
Chessington South	a							
Worcester Park	d		23 27				23 57	
Stoneleigh	d		23 30				23 59	
Ewell West	d		23 33				00 03	
Epsom 3	a		23 36				00 06	
	d							
Ashtead	d							
Leatherhead	d							
Boxhill & Westhumble	d							
Dorking 4	a							
New Malden 6	d					23 40		
Norbiton	d					23 43		
Kingston	a				23 56	23 46		
	d					23 47		
Hampton Wick	d					23 49		
Teddington	d					23 51		
Strawberry Hill	a					23 54		
Fulwell	d							
Hampton	d							
Kempton Park	d							
Sunbury	d							
Upper Halliford	d							
Shepperton	a							
Berrylands	d							
Surbiton 6	d	23 32		23 35				00a04
Thames Ditton	d							
Hampton Court	a							
Hinchley Wood	d	23 36						
Claygate	d	23 39						
Oxshott	d	23 42						
Cobham & Stoke D'abernon	d	23 46						
Bookham	d							
Effingham Junction 6	d	23 50						
Horsley	d	23 53						
Clandon	d	23 58						
London Road (Guildford)	d	00 03						
Guildford	a	00 10		00 13				

Hampton Court, Shepperton, Guildford, Dorking and Chessington South - London

Miles	Miles	Miles	Miles	Miles			SW MO	SW MX	SW MX	SW MX	SW MX	SW MO	SW	SW	SW		SW	SW	SW	SW	SW	SW	SW	SW	SW
0	—	—	—	—	**Guildford**	d			23p08				04 00		04 58				05 14			05 38			
1¼	—	—	—	—	London Road (Guildford)	d			23p12						05 02							05 42			
4½	—	—	—	—	Clandon	d			23p17						05 07							05 47			
7¾	—	—	—	—	Horsley	d			23p21						05 11							05 51			
8¾	0	—	—	—	Effingham Junction 6	d			23p24						05 16							05 54			
—	1¾	—	—	—	Bookham	d									05 19										
11	—	—	—	—	Cobham & Stoke d'Abernon	d			23p28													05 58			
13	—	—	—	—	Oxshott	d			23p31													06 01			
14¾	—	—	—	—	Claygate	d			23p34													06 04			
16	—	—	—	—	Hinchley Wood	d			23p37													06 07			
—	—	—	0	—	**Hampton Court**	d						23p45									05 54				
—	—	—	1	—	Thames Ditton	d						23p47									05 56				
18	—	—	3	—	**Surbiton** 6	d			23p42			23p53	04 24						05 57	06 01	06 02	06 12			
19	—	—	—	—	Berrylands	d						23p55									06 04				
—	—	—	—	0	**Shepperton**	d	23p11	23p11									05 23								
—	—	—	—	1½	Upper Halliford	d	23p14	23p14									05 26								
—	—	—	—	2	Sunbury	d	23p16	23p16									05 28								
—	—	—	—	2½	Kempton Park	d	23p18	23p18																	
—	—	—	—	4¼	Hampton	d	23p21	23p21									05 33								
—	—	—	—	6	Fulwell	d	23p24	23p24									05 36								
—	—	—	0	—	Strawberry Hill	d				23p37	23p38			04 55			05 38							06 08	06 08
—	—	—	1¼	7	Teddington	d	23p29	23p29		23p41				04 59				05 44							06 11
—	—	—	—	8¼	Hampton Wick	d	23p31	23p31		23p44				05 01				05 46							06 14
—	—	—	—	8¾	Kingston	a	23p33	23p33		23p46				05 03				05 48							06 16
—	—	—	—	—		d	23p34	23p34		23p49				05 04				05 49							06 19
—	—	—	—	9½	Norbiton	d	23p36	23p36		23p51				05 06				05 51							06 21
20	—	—	—	11	New Malden 6	d	23p40	23p41		23p55		23p58		05 10				05 55			06 07				06 25
—	—	0	—	—	**Dorking** 4	d																	05 48		
—	—	0¾	—	—	Boxhill & Westhumble	d																	05 50		
—	4½	4	—	—	Leatherhead	d									05 24								05 56		
—	—	5¾	—	—	Ashtead	d									05 28								05 59		
—	—	7¾	—	—	**Epsom** 3	a									05 32								06 04		
—	—	—	—	—		d									05 34								06 04		
—	—	9	—	—	Ewell West	d									05 37								06 07		
—	—	10	—	—	Stoneleigh	d									05 40								06 10		
—	—	11¼	—	—	Worcester Park	d									05 42								06 12		
—	0	—	—	—	**Chessington South**	d																			
—	0¾	—	—	—	Chessington North	d																			
—	1¾	—	—	—	Tolworth	d																			
—	2¾	—	—	—	Malden Manor	d																			
—	3¾	12¼	—	—	Motspur Park	d									05 46								06 16		
21¼	5¼	13¼	—	12	Raynes Park 6	d	23p43	23p43		23p58		00 01		05 13	05 49			05 58			06 10		06 19		06 28
22¾	6¾	14¾	—	13½	**Wimbledon** 6 ⊖	d	23p47	23p50	23p53	00 02		00a04	04 32	05 17	05 53			06 02	06 05		06 14	06 20	06 23		06 32
24½	8½	16½	—	15¼	Earlsfield	d	23p50	23p53	23p56	00 05				05 21	05 57			06 05	06 08		06 17	06 24	06 27		06 35
26	10	18	—	16¾	**Clapham Junction** 10	d	23p54	23p57	23p59	00 09			04 44	05 25	06 01			06 09	06 12		06 21	06 28	06 31		06 39
28¾	12¾	20¾	—	19½	Vauxhall ⊖	d	23p59	00 02	00 05	00 14	00 12			05 30	06 06		06 12	06 14	06 17		06 26	06 33	06 36	06 42	06 44
30	14	22	—	20¾	**London Waterloo** 15 ⊖	a	00 04	00 10	00 14	00 22	00 16		04 53	05 35	06 11		06 16	06 19	06 22	06 20	06 31	06 37	06 40	06 46	06 49

Table 152

Mondays to Fridays
until 30 September

Hampton Court, Shepperton, Guildford, Dorking and Chessington South - London

		SW	SW	SW	SW	SW	SW	SW	SW	SW	SW	SW	SW	SW 1	SW	SW	SW	SW	SW	SW	SW 1	SW
Guildford	d					05 58	06 07									06 28	06 37					
London Road (Guildford)	d					06 02	06 11									06 32	06 41					
Clandon	d					06 07	06 16									06 37	06 46					
Horsley	d					06 11	06 20									06 41	06 50					
Effingham Junction 6	d					06 16	06 24									06 48	06 54					
Bookham	d					06 19										06 51						
Cobham & Stoke d'Abernon	d						06 27										06 57					
Oxshott	d						06 31										07 01					
Claygate	d						06 34										07 04					
Hinchley Wood	d						06 37										07 07					
Hampton Court	d			06 24									06 54									
Thames Ditton	d			06 26									06 56									
Surbiton 6	d	06 28		06 32			06 42				06 57		07 02	07 08			07 12				07 27	
Berrylands	d			06 34									07 04									
Shepperton	d				06 11										06 41							
Upper Halliford	d				06 14										06 44							
Sunbury	d				06 16										06 46							
Kempton Park	d																					
Hampton	d				06 21										06 51							
Fulwell	d				06 24										06 54							
Strawberry Hill	d								06 37	06 38									07 07	07 08		
Teddington	d				06 29				06 41						06 59				07 11			
Hampton Wick	d				06 31				06 44						07 01				07 14			
Kingston	a				06 33				06 46						07 03				07 16			
	d				06 34				06 49						07 04				07 19			
Norbiton	d				06 36				06 51						07 06				07 21			
New Malden 6	d			06 37	06 40				06 55				07 07		07 10				07 25			
Dorking 4	d											06 32										07 02
Boxhill & Westhumble	d											06 34										07 04
Leatherhead	d					06 24						06 39				06 56						07 09
Ashtead	d					06 28						06 43				06 59						07 13
Epsom 3	a					06 32						06 47				07 04						07 17
	d		06 18			06 34						06 48				07 04						07 18
Ewell West	d		06 21			06 37						06 51				07 07						
Stoneleigh	d		06 24			06 40						06 53				07 10						
Worcester Park	d		06 27			06 42						06 56				07 12						07 25
Chessington South	d							06 40										07 10				
Chessington North	d							06 42										07 12				
Tolworth	d							06 44										07 14				
Malden Manor	d							06 47										07 17				
Motspur Park	d		06 30			06 46		06 50				07 00				07 16		07 20				
Raynes Park 6	d		06 34	06 40	06 43	06 49		06 54	06 58			07 04	07 10		07 13	07 19		07 24	07 28			07 31
Wimbledon 6 ⊖	d	06 35	06 38	06 44	06 47	06 53	06 50	06 58	07 02		07 05	07 08	07 14		07 17	07 23	07 20	07 28	07 32			07 35
Earlsfield	d	06 39	06 42	06 47	06 50	06 57	06 54	07 01	07 05		07 08	07 11	07 17		07 20	07 27	07 24	07 31	07 35			07 38
Clapham Junction 10	d	06 43	06 46	06 51	06 54	07 01	06 58	07 05	07 09		07 12	07 15	07 21		07 24	07 31	07 28	07 35	07 39			07 42
Vauxhall ⊖	d	06 48	06 51	06 56	06 59	07 06	07 03	07 10	07 14	07 12	07 17	07 20	07 26		07 29	07 36	07 33	07 40	07 44	07 42		07 47
London Waterloo 15 ⊖	a	06 52	06 55	07 03	07 06	07 12	07 09	07 17	07 21	07 18	07 24	07 27	07 33	07 26	07 36	07 42	07 39	07 47	07 51	07 48	07 49	07 54

Table 152

Mondays to Fridays
until 30 September

Hampton Court, Shepperton, Guildford, Dorking and Chessington South - London

		SW	SW	SW	SW	SW 1	SW	SW	SW	SW	SW	SW	SW	SW 1	SW	SW	SW	SW	SW	SW 1	SW	SW	SW
Guildford	d							06 58	07 07	07 17													07 37
London Road (Guildford)	d							07 02	07 11	07 21													07 41
Clandon	d							07 07	07 16	07 26													07 46
Horsley	d							07 11	07 20	07 30													07 50
Effingham Junction 6	d							07 16	07 24	07 34												07 46	07 54
Bookham	d							07 19														07 49	
Cobham & Stoke d'Abernon	d								07 27	07 37													07 57
Oxshott	d								07 31	07 41													08 01
Claygate	d								07 34	07 44													08 04
Hinchley Wood	d								07 37	07 47													08 07
Hampton Court	d				07 24														07 54				
Thames Ditton	d				07 26														07 56				
Surbiton 6	d				07 32	07 38			07 42	07 53				07 57					08 02	08 08			08 12
Berrylands	d				07 34														08 04				
Shepperton	d			07 00			07 11									07 30					07 41		
Upper Halliford	d			07 03			07 14									07 33					07 44		
Sunbury	d			07 05			07 16									07 35					07 46		
Kempton Park	d																						
Hampton	d			07 09			07 21									07 39					07 51		
Fulwell	d			07 12			07 24									07 42					07 54		
Strawberry Hill	d			07 14								07 37	07 38			07 44	07 47						
Teddington	d	07 20					07 29					07 41					07 50				07 59		
Hampton Wick	d	07 22					07 31					07 44					07 52				08 01		
Kingston	a	07 24					07 33					07 46					07 54				08 03		
	d	07 26					07 34					07 49					07 56				08 04		
Norbiton	d	07 28					07 36					07 51					07 58				08 06		
New Malden 6	d	07 32			07 37		07 40		07 46			07 55					08 02		08 07		08 10		08 16
Dorking 4	d														07 32								
Boxhill & Westhumble	d														07 34								
Leatherhead	d							07 26							07 39							07 56	
Ashtead	d							07 29							07 43							07 59	
Epsom 3	a							07 34							07 47							08 04	
	d		07 22					07 34							07 48			07 52				08 04	
Ewell West	d		07 25					07 37										07 55				08 07	
Stoneleigh	d		07 27					07 40										07 57				08 10	
Worcester Park	d		07 30					07 43							07 55			08 00				08 13	
Chessington South	d										07 40												
Chessington North	d										07 42												
Tolworth	d										07 44												
Malden Manor	d										07 47												
Motspur Park	d		07 34					07 46			07 50							08 04				08 16	
Raynes Park 6	d	07 34	07 37		07 40		07 43	07 50			07 54	07 58			08 01		08 04	08 07	08 10		08 13	08 20	
Wimbledon 6 ⊖	d	07 38	07 41		07 44		07 47	07 54	07 51		07 58	08 02			08 05		08 08	08 11	08 14		08 17	08 24	08 21
Earlsfield	d	07 42	07 45		07 48		07 51	07 58	07 54		08 01	08 05			08 08		08 12	08 15	08 18		08 21	08 28	08 24
Clapham Junction 10	d	07 46	07 49		07 52		07 55	08 02	07 58		08 05	08 09			08 12		08 16	08 19	08 22		08 25	08 32	08 28
Vauxhall ⊖	d	07 51	07 54	07 56	07 57		08 00	08 07	08 03		08 10	08 14	08 12		08 17	08 26	08 21	08 24	08 27		08 30	08 37	08 33
London Waterloo 15 ⊖	a	07 57	08 00	08 04	08 04	07 56	08 06	08 13	08 11	08 13	08 17	08 21	08 18	08 19	08 24	08 34	08 27	08 30	08 33	08 26	08 36	08 43	08 40

Hampton Court, Shepperton, Guildford, Dorking and Chessington South - London

		SW 1	SW 1		SW	SW	SW	SW	SW	SW	SW	SW	SW 1		SW	SW	SW	SW	SW	SW	SW	SW	SW		SW
Guildford	d															07 58	08 07					08 20			
London Road (Guildford)	d															08 02	08 11								
Clandon	d															08 07	08 16								
Horsley	d															08 11	08 20								
Effingham Junction 6	d															08 16	08 24								
Bookham	d															08 19									
Cobham & Stoke d'Abernon	d																08 27								
Oxshott	d																08 31								
Claygate	d																08 34								
Hinchley Wood	d																08 37								
Hampton Court	d											08 24													08 54
Thames Ditton	d											08 26													08 56
Surbiton 6	d	08 19	08 25									08 32	08 38				08 42	08 48				08 57			09 02
Berrylands	d											08 34													09 04
Shepperton	d								08 00						08 11										
Upper Halliford	d								08 03						08 14										
Sunbury	d								08 05						08 16										
Kempton Park	d																								
Hampton	d								08 09						08 21										
Fulwell	d								08 12						08 24										
Strawberry Hill	d					08 07	08 08		08 14	08 17										08 38	08 38				
Teddington	d					08 11				08 20					08 29						08 41				
Hampton Wick	d					08 14				08 22					08 31						08 44				
Kingston	a					08 16				08 24					08 33						08 46				
	d					08 19				08 26					08 34						08 49				
Norbiton	d					08 21				08 28					08 36						08 51				
New Malden 6	d					08 25				08 32		08 37			08 40						08 55				09 07
Dorking 4	d							08 02															08 31		
Boxhill & Westhumble	d							08 04															08 33		
Leatherhead	d							08 09								08 25							08 38		
Ashtead	d							08 13								08 28							08 42		
Epsom 3	a							08 17								08 33							08 46		
	d							08 18			08 22					08 34							08 48		
Ewell West	d										08 25					08 37							08 51		
Stoneleigh	d										08 27					08 40							08 54		
Worcester Park	d							08 25			08 30					08 42							08 57		
Chessington South	d				08 10														08 40						
Chessington North	d				08 12														08 42						
Tolworth	d				08 14														08 44						
Malden Manor	d				08 17														08 47						
Motspur Park	d				08 20						08 34					08 46			08 50				09 00		
Raynes Park 6	d				08 24	08 28		08 31		08 34	08 37	08 40			08 43	08 49			08 54		08 58		09 04		09 10
Wimbledon 6 ⊖	d				08 28	08 32		08 35		08 38	08 41	08 44			08 47	08 53			08 58		09 02	09 05	09 08		09 14
Earlsfield	d				08 31	08 35		08 38		08 42	08 45	08 48			08 51	08 57			09 01		09 05	09 08	09 12		09 17
Clapham Junction 10	d				08 35	08 39		08 42		08 46	08 49	08 52			08 55	09 01			09 05		09 09	09 12	09 16		09 21
Vauxhall ⊖	d				08 40	08 44	08 42	08 47	08 56	08 51	08 54	08 57			09 00	09 06			09 10	09 12	09 14	09 17	09 21		09 26
London Waterloo 15 ⊖	a	08 36	08 46		08 47	08 51	08 49	08 54	09 04	08 57	09 00	09 03	08 59		09 06	09 12	09 01	09 06	09 17	09 18	09 21	09 24	09 27		09 33

until 30 September

Hampton Court, Shepperton, Guildford, Dorking and Chessington South - London

		SW	SW	SW	SW 1	SW	SW	SW	SW		SW	SW	SW	SW	SW	SW	SW	SW	SW		SW	SW	SW	SW	SW
Guildford	d			08 37					08 46					08 58	09 08									09 28	09 38
London Road (Guildford)	d			08 41										09 02	09 12									09 32	09 42
Clandon	d			08 46										09 07	09 17									09 37	09 47
Horsley	d			08 50										09 11	09 21									09 41	09 51
Effingham Junction 6	d		08 48	08 54										09 16	09 24									09 46	09 54
Bookham	d		08 51											09 19										09 49	
Cobham & Stoke d'Abernon	d			08 57											09 28										09 58
Oxshott	d			09 01											09 31										10 01
Claygate	d			09 04											09 34										10 04
Hinchley Wood	d			09 07											09 37										10 07
Hampton Court	d											09 24										09 54			
Thames Ditton	d											09 26										09 56			
Surbiton 6	d			09 12	09 19				09 27			09 32			09 42				09 57			10 02			10 12
Berrylands	d											09 34										10 04			
Shepperton	d	08 41											09 11										09 41		
Upper Halliford	d	08 44											09 14										09 44		
Sunbury	d	08 46											09 16										09 46		
Kempton Park	d												09 18										09 48		
Hampton	d	08 51											09 21										09 51		
Fulwell	d	08 54											09 24										09 54		
Strawberry Hill	d						09 07	09 08									09 37	09 38							
Teddington	d	08 59					09 11						09 29				09 41						09 59		
Hampton Wick	d	09 01					09 14						09 31				09 44						10 01		
Kingston	a	09 03					09 16						09 33				09 46						10 03		
	d	09 04					09 19						09 34				09 49						10 04		
Norbiton	d	09 06					09 21						09 36				09 51						10 06		
New Malden 6	d	09 10					09 25					09 37	09 40				09 55					10 07	10 10		
Dorking 4	d										09 02										09 35				
Boxhill & Westhumble	d										09 04														
Leatherhead	d		08 56								09 09			09 24							09 41			09 54	
Ashtead	d		08 59								09 13			09 28							09 45			09 58	
Epsom 3	a		09 04								09 17			09 32							09 49			10 02	
	d		09 04								09 18			09 35							09 50			10 05	
Ewell West	d		09 07								09 21			09 38							09 53			10 08	
Stoneleigh	d		09 10								09 24			09 40							09 55			10 10	
Worcester Park	d		09 12								09 27			09 43							09 58			10 13	
Chessington South	d					09 10										09 40									
Chessington North	d					09 12										09 42									
Tolworth	d					09 14										09 44									
Malden Manor	d					09 17										09 47									
Motspur Park	d		09 16			09 20					09 30			09 46		09 50					10 01			10 16	
Raynes Park 6	d	09 13	09 19			09 24	09 28				09 34	09 40	09 43	09 49		09 53	09 58				10 04	10 10	10 13	10 19	
Wimbledon 6 ⊖	d	09 17	09 23	09 20		09 28	09 32		09 35		09 38	09 44	09 47	09 53	09 50	09 57	10 02		10 05		10 08	10 14	10 17	10 23	10 20
Earlsfield	d	09 20	09 27	09 24		09 31	09 35		09 38		09 42	09 47	09 50	09 57	09 54	10 01	10 05		10 08		10 12	10 17	10 20	10 27	10 24
Clapham Junction 10	d	09 24	09 31	09 28		09 35	09 39		09 42		09 46	09 51	09 54	10 01	09 58	10 05	10 09		10 12		10 16	10 21	10 24	10 31	10 28
Vauxhall ⊖	d	09 29	09 36	09 33		09 40	09 44	09 42	09 47		09 51	09 56	09 59	10 06	10 03	10 10	10 14	10 12	10 17		10 21	10 26	10 29	10 36	10 33
London Waterloo 15 ⊖	a	09 36	09 42	09 39	09 40	09 47	09 51	09 48	09 54		09 57	10 01	10 04	10 10	10 07	10 15	10 19	10 16	10 22		10 25	10 31	10 34	10 40	10 37

Table 152

Mondays to Fridays
until 30 September

Hampton Court, Shepperton, Guildford, Dorking and Chessington South - London

		SW	SW	SW	SW		SW	SW	SW	SW	SW	SW	SW	SW	SW		SW	SW	SW	SW	SW	SW	SW	SW	SW
Guildford	d									09 58	10 08									10 28	10 38				
London Road (Guildford)	d									10 02	10 12									10 32	10 42				
Clandon	d									10 07	10 17									10 37	10 47				
Horsley	d									10 11	10 21									10 41	10 51				
Effingham Junction	d									10 16	10 24									10 46	10 54				
Bookham	d									10 19										10 49					
Cobham & Stoke d'Abernon	d										10 28										10 58				
Oxshott	d										10 31										11 01				
Claygate	d										10 34										11 04				
Hinchley Wood	d										10 37										11 07				
Hampton Court	d							10 24										10 54							
Thames Ditton	d							10 26										10 56							
Surbiton	d				10 27			10 32			10 42				10 57			11 02			11 12				11 27
Berrylands	d							10 34										11 04							
Shepperton	d								10 11										10 41						
Upper Halliford	d								10 14										10 44						
Sunbury	d								10 16										10 46						
Kempton Park	d								10 18										10 48						
Hampton	d								10 21										10 51						
Fulwell	d								10 24										10 54						
Strawberry Hill	d		10 07	10 08									10 37	10 38									11 07	11 08	
Teddington	d		10 11						10 29				10 41						10 59				11 11		
Hampton Wick	d		10 14						10 31				10 44						11 01				11 14		
Kingston	a		10 16						10 33				10 46						11 03				11 16		
	d		10 19						10 34				10 49						11 04				11 19		
Norbiton	d		10 21						10 36				10 51						11 06				11 21		
New Malden	d		10 25					10 37	10 40				10 55					11 07	11 10				11 25		
Dorking	d						10 05										10 35								
Boxhill & Westhumble	d																								
Leatherhead	d						10 11			10 24							10 41			10 54					
Ashtead	d						10 14			10 28							10 44			10 58					
Epsom	a						10 19			10 32							10 49			11 02					
	d						10 20			10 35							10 50			11 05					
Ewell West	d						10 23			10 38							10 53			11 08					
Stoneleigh	d						10 25			10 40							10 55			11 10					
Worcester Park	d						10 28			10 43							10 58			11 13					
Chessington South	d	10 10										10 40										11 10			
Chessington North	d	10 12										10 42										11 12			
Tolworth	d	10 14										10 44										11 14			
Malden Manor	d	10 17										10 47										11 17			
Motspur Park	d	10 20					10 31			10 46		10 50					11 01			11 16		11 20			
Raynes Park	d	10 23	10 28				10 34	10 40	10 43	10 49		10 53	10 58				11 04	11 10	11 13	11 19		11 23	11 28		
Wimbledon	d	10 27	10 32		10 35		10 38	10 44	10 47	10 53	10 50	10 57	11 02		11 05		11 08	11 14	11 17	11 23	11 20	11 27	11 32		11 35
Earlsfield	d	10 31	10 35		10 38		10 42	10 47	10 50	10 57	10 54	11 01	11 05		11 08		11 12	11 17	11 20	11 27	11 24	11 31	11 35		11 38
Clapham Junction	d	10 35	10 39		10 42		10 46	10 51	10 54	11 01	10 58	11 05	11 09		11 12		11 16	11 21	11 24	11 31	11 28	11 35	11 39		11 42
Vauxhall	d	10 40	10 44	10 42	10 47		10 51	10 56	10 59	11 06	11 03	11 10	11 14	11 12	11 17		11 21	11 26	11 29	11 36	11 33	11 40	11 44	11 42	11 47
London Waterloo	a	10 45	10 49	10 46	10 52		10 55	11 01	11 04	11 10	11 07	11 15	11 19	11 16	11 22		11 25	11 31	11 34	11 40	11 37	11 45	11 49	11 46	11 52

			SW	SW	SW	SW	SW	SW	SW	SW	SW		SW	SW	SW	SW	SW	SW	SW	SW	SW		SW	SW	SW
Guildford	d					10 58	11 08									11 28	11 38								
London Road (Guildford)	d					11 02	11 12									11 32	11 42								
Clandon	d					11 07	11 17									11 37	11 47								
Horsley	d					11 11	11 21									11 41	11 51								
Effingham Junction	d					11 16	11 24									11 46	11 54								
Bookham	d					11 19										11 49									
Cobham & Stoke d'Abernon	d						11 28										11 58								
Oxshott	d						11 31										12 01								
Claygate	d						11 34										12 04								
Hinchley Wood	d						11 37										12 07								
Hampton Court	d			11 24										11 54										12 24	
Thames Ditton	d			11 26										11 56										12 26	
Surbiton	d			11 32			11 42				11 57			12 02			12 12				12 27			12 32	
Berrylands	d			11 34										12 04										12 34	
Shepperton	d				11 11										11 41										12 11
Upper Halliford	d				11 14										11 44										12 14
Sunbury	d				11 16										11 46										12 16
Kempton Park	d				11 18										11 48										12 18
Hampton	d				11 21										11 51										12 21
Fulwell	d				11 24										11 54										12 24
Strawberry Hill	d								11 37	11 38									12 07	12 08					
Teddington	d				11 29				11 41						11 59				12 11						12 29
Hampton Wick	d				11 31				11 44						12 01				12 14						12 31
Kingston	a				11 33				11 46						12 03				12 16						12 33
	d				11 34				11 49						12 04				12 19						12 34
Norbiton	d				11 36				11 51						12 06				12 21						12 36
New Malden	d			11 37	11 40				11 55					12 07	12 10				12 25					12 37	12 40
Dorking	d		11 05										11 35										12 05		
Boxhill & Westhumble	d																								
Leatherhead	d		11 11			11 24							11 41			11 54							12 11		
Ashtead	d		11 14			11 28							11 44			11 58							12 14		
Epsom	a		11 19			11 32							11 49			12 02							12 19		
	d		11 20			11 35							11 50			12 05							12 20		
Ewell West	d		11 23			11 38							11 53			12 08							12 23		
Stoneleigh	d		11 25			11 40							11 55			12 10							12 25		
Worcester Park	d		11 28			11 43							11 58			12 13							12 28		
Chessington South	d							11 40										12 10							
Chessington North	d							11 42										12 12							
Tolworth	d							11 44										12 14							
Malden Manor	d							11 47										12 17							
Motspur Park	d		11 31			11 46		11 50					12 01			12 16		12 20					12 31		
Raynes Park	d		11 34	11 40	11 43	11 49		11 53	11 58				12 04	12 10	12 13	12 19		12 23	12 28				12 34	12 40	12 43
Wimbledon	d		11 38	11 44	11 47	11 53	11 50	11 57	12 02		12 05		12 08	12 14	12 17	12 23	12 20	12 27	12 32		12 35		12 38	12 44	12 47
Earlsfield	d		11 42	11 47	11 50	11 57	11 54	12 01	12 05		12 08		12 12	12 17	12 20	12 27	12 24	12 31	12 35		12 38		12 42	12 47	12 50
Clapham Junction	d		11 46	11 51	11 54	12 01	11 58	12 05	12 09		12 12		12 16	12 21	12 24	12 31	12 28	12 35	12 39		12 42		12 46	12 51	12 54
Vauxhall	d		11 51	11 56	11 59	12 06	12 03	12 10	12 14	12 12	12 17		12 21	12 26	12 29	12 36	12 33	12 40	12 44	12 42	12 47		12 51	12 56	12 59

Table 152

Mondays to Fridays
until 30 September

Hampton Court, Shepperton, Guildford, Dorking and Chessington South - London

		SW	SW	SW	SW	SW	SW		SW	SW	SW 1	SW	SW	SW	SW	SW	SW		SW	SW	SW	SW	SW	SW	SW
Guildford	d	11 58	12 08										12 28	12 38									12 58	13 08	
London Road (Guildford)	d	12 02	12 12										12 32	12 42									13 02	13 12	
Clandon	d	12 07	12 17										12 37	12 47									13 07	13 17	
Horsley	d	12 11	12 21										12 41	12 51									13 11	13 21	
Effingham Junction	d	12 16	12 24										12 46	12 54									13 16	13 24	
Bookham	d	12 19											12 49										13 19		
Cobham & Stoke d'Abernon	d		12 28											12 58										13 28	
Oxshott	d		12 31											13 01										13 31	
Claygate	d		12 34											13 04										13 34	
Hinchley Wood	d		12 37											13 07										13 37	
Hampton Court	d									12 54											13 24				
Thames Ditton	d									12 56											13 26				
Surbiton	d		12 42				12 57			13 02	13 08			13 12					13 27		13 32			13 42	
Berrylands	d									13 04											13 34				
Shepperton	d											12 41										13 11			
Upper Halliford	d											12 44										13 14			
Sunbury	d											12 46										13 16			
Kempton Park	d											12 48										13 18			
Hampton	d											12 51										13 21			
Fulwell	d											12 54										13 24			
Strawberry Hill	d				12 37	12 38										13 07	13 08								
Teddington	d				12 41							12 59				13 11						13 29			
Hampton Wick	d				12 44							13 01				13 14						13 31			
Kingston	a				12 46							13 03				13 16						13 33			
	d				12 49							13 04				13 19						13 34			
Norbiton	d				12 51							13 06				13 21						13 36			
New Malden	d				12 55					13 07		13 10				13 25					13 37	13 40			
Dorking	d								12 35											13 05					
Boxhill & Westhumble	d																								
Leatherhead	d	12 24							12 41				12 54							13 11			13 24		
Ashtead	d	12 28							12 44				12 58							13 14			13 28		
Epsom	a	12 32							12 49				13 02							13 19			13 32		
	d	12 35							12 50				13 05							13 20			13 35		
Ewell West	d	12 38							12 53				13 08							13 23			13 38		
Stoneleigh	d	12 40							12 55				13 10							13 25			13 40		
Worcester Park	d	12 43							12 58				13 13							13 28			13 43		
Chessington South	d			12 40											13 10										13 40
Chessington North	d			12 42											13 12										13 42
Tolworth	d			12 44											13 14										13 44
Malden Manor	d			12 47											13 17										13 47
Motspur Park	d	12 46		12 50					13 01				13 16		13 20					13 31			13 46		13 50
Raynes Park	d	12 49		12 53	12 58				13 04	13 10		13 13	13 19		13 23	13 28				13 34	13 40	13 43	13 49		13 53
Wimbledon	d	12 53	12 50	12 57	13 02		13 05		13 08	13 14		13 17	13 23	13 20	13 27	13 32			13 35	13 38	13 44	13 47	13 53	13 50	13 57
Earlsfield	d	12 57	12 54	13 01	13 05		13 08		13 12	13 17		13 20	13 27	13 24	13 31	13 35			13 38	13 42	13 47	13 50	13 57	13 54	14 01
Clapham Junction	d	13 01	12 58	13 05	13 09		13 12		13 16	13 21		13 24	13 31	13 28	13 35	13 39			13 42	13 46	13 51	13 54	14 01	13 58	14 05
Vauxhall	d	13 06	13 03	13 10	13 14	13 12	13 17		13 21	13 26		13 29	13 36	13 33	13 40	13 44	13 42		13 47	13 51	13 56	13 59	14 06	14 03	14 10
London Waterloo	a	13 10	13 07	13 15	13 19	13 16	13 22		13 25	13 31	13 25	13 34	13 40	13 37	13 45	13 49	13 46		13 52	13 55	14 01	14 04	14 10	14 07	14 15

Hampton Court, Shepperton, Guildford, Dorking and Chessington South - London

		SW	SW		SW	SW	SW	SW	SW	SW	SW	SW	SW		SW	SW	SW	SW	SW	SW	SW	SW	SW		SW
Guildford	d								13 28	13 38									13 58	14 08					
London Road (Guildford)	d								13 32	13 42									14 02	14 12					
Clandon	d								13 37	13 47									14 07	14 17					
Horsley	d								13 41	13 51									14 11	14 21					
Effingham Junction 6	d								13 46	13 54									14 16	14 24					
Bookham	d								13 49										14 19						
Cobham & Stoke d'Abernon	d									13 58										14 28					
Oxshott	d									14 01										14 31					
Claygate	d									14 04										14 34					
Hinchley Wood	d									14 07										14 37					
Hampton Court	d						13 54										14 24								
Thames Ditton	d						13 56										14 26								
Surbiton 6	d				13 57		14 02			14 12					14 27		14 32			14 42					14 57
Berrylands	d						14 04										14 34								
Shepperton	d							13 41										14 11							
Upper Halliford	d							13 44										14 14							
Sunbury	d							13 46										14 16							
Kempton Park	d							13 48										14 18							
Hampton	d							13 51										14 21							
Fulwell	d							13 54										14 24							
Strawberry Hill	d	13 37	13 38									14 07	14 08									14 37	14 38		
Teddington	d	13 41						13 59				14 11						14 29				14 41			
Hampton Wick	d	13 44						14 01				14 14						14 31				14 44			
Kingston	a	13 46						14 03				14 16						14 33				14 46			
	d	13 49						14 04				14 19						14 34				14 49			
Norbiton	d	13 51						14 06				14 21						14 36				14 51			
New Malden 6	d	13 55					14 07	14 10				14 25					14 37	14 40				14 55			
Dorking 4	d					13 35										14 05									
Boxhill & Westhumble	d																								
Leatherhead	d					13 41			13 54							14 11			14 24						
Ashtead	d					13 44			13 58							14 14			14 28						
Epsom 3	a					13 49			14 02							14 19			14 32						
	d					13 50			14 05							14 20			14 35						
Ewell West	d					13 53			14 08							14 23			14 38						
Stoneleigh	d					13 55			14 10							14 25			14 40						
Worcester Park	d					13 58			14 13							14 28			14 43						
Chessington South	d										14 10										14 40				
Chessington North	d										14 12										14 42				
Tolworth	d										14 14										14 44				
Malden Manor	d										14 17										14 47				
Motspur Park	d					14 01			14 16		14 20					14 31			14 46		14 50				
Raynes Park 6	d	13 58				14 04	14 10	14 13	14 19		14 23	14 28				14 34	14 40	14 43	14 49		14 53	14 58			
Wimbledon 6 ⊖	d	14 02			14 05	14 08	14 14	14 17	14 23	14 20	14 27	14 32			14 35	14 38	14 44	14 47	14 53	14 50	14 57	15 02			15 05
Earlsfield	d	14 05			14 08	14 12	14 17	14 20	14 27	14 24	14 31	14 35			14 38	14 42	14 47	14 50	14 57	14 54	15 01	15 05			15 08
Clapham Junction 10	d	14 09			14 12	14 16	14 21	14 24	14 31	14 28	14 35	14 39			14 42	14 46	14 51	14 54	15 01	14 58	15 05	15 09			15 12
Vauxhall ⊖	d	14 14	14 12		14 17	14 21	14 26	14 29	14 36	14 33	14 40	14 44	14 42		14 47	14 51	14 56	14 59	15 06	15 03	15 10	15 14	15 12		15 17
London Waterloo 15 ⊖	a	14 19	14 16		14 22	14 25	14 31	14 34	14 40	14 37	14 45	14 49	14 46		14 52	14 55	15 01	15 04	15 10	15 07	15 15	15 19	15 16		15 22

		SW	SW	SW	SW	SW	SW	SW	SW		SW	SW	SW	SW	SW	SW	SW	SW	SW		SW	SW	SW	SW	SW
Guildford	d				14 28	14 38									14 58	15 08									15 28
London Road (Guildford)	d				14 32	14 42									15 02	15 12									15 32
Clandon	d				14 37	14 47									15 07	15 17									15 37
Horsley	d				14 41	14 51									15 11	15 21									15 41
Effingham Junction 6	d				14 46	14 54									15 16	15 24									15 46
Bookham	d				14 49										15 19										15 49
Cobham & Stoke d'Abernon	d					14 58										15 28									
Oxshott	d					15 01										15 31									
Claygate	d					15 04										15 34									
Hinchley Wood	d					15 07										15 37									
Hampton Court	d		14 54										15 24										15 54		
Thames Ditton	d		14 56										15 26										15 56		
Surbiton 6	d		15 02			15 12					15 27		15 32			15 42					15 57		16 02		
Berrylands	d		15 04										15 34										16 04		
Shepperton	d			14 41										15 11										15 41	
Upper Halliford	d			14 44										15 14										15 44	
Sunbury	d			14 46										15 16										15 46	
Kempton Park	d			14 48										15 18										15 48	
Hampton	d			14 51										15 21										15 51	
Fulwell	d			14 54										15 24										15 54	
Strawberry Hill	d							15 07	15 08									15 37	15 38						
Teddington	d			14 59				15 11						15 29				15 41						15 59	
Hampton Wick	d			15 01				15 14						15 31				15 44						16 01	
Kingston	a			15 03				15 16						15 33				15 46						16 03	
	d			15 04				15 19						15 34				15 49						16 04	
Norbiton	d			15 06				15 21						15 36				15 51						16 06	
New Malden 6	d		15 07	15 10				15 25					15 37	15 40				15 55					16 07	16 10	
Dorking 4	d	14 35										15 05										15 35			
Boxhill & Westhumble	d																								
Leatherhead	d	14 41			14 54							15 11			15 24							15 41			15 54
Ashtead	d	14 44			14 58							15 14			15 28							15 44			15 58
Epsom 3	a	14 49			15 02							15 19			15 32							15 49			16 02
	d	14 50			15 05							15 20			15 35							15 50			16 05
Ewell West	d	14 53			15 08							15 23			15 38							15 53			16 08
Stoneleigh	d	14 55			15 10							15 25			15 40							15 55			16 10
Worcester Park	d	14 58			15 13							15 28			15 43							15 58			16 13
Chessington South	d						15 10										15 40								
Chessington North	d						15 12										15 42								
Tolworth	d						15 14										15 44								
Malden Manor	d						15 17										15 47								
Motspur Park	d	15 01			15 16		15 20					15 31			15 46		15 50					16 01			16 16
Raynes Park 6	d	15 04	15 10	15 13	15 19		15 23	15 28				15 34	15 40	15 43	15 49		15 53	15 58				16 04	16 10	16 13	16 19
Wimbledon 6 ⊖	d	15 08	15 14	15 17	15 23	15 20	15 27	15 32			15 35	15 38	15 44	15 47	15 53	15 50	15 57	16 02			16 05	16 08	16 14	16 17	16 23
Earlsfield	d	15 12	15 17	15 20	15 27	15 24	15 31	15 35			15 38	15 42	15 47	15 50	15 57	15 54	16 01	16 05			16 08	16 12	16 17	16 20	16 27
Clapham Junction 10	d	15 16	15 21	15 24	15 31	15 28	15 35	15 39			15 42	15 46	15 51	15 54	16 01	15 58	16 05	16 09			16 12	16 16	16 21	16 24	16 31
Vauxhall ⊖	d	15 21	15 26	15 29	15 36	15 33	15 40	15 44	15 42		15 47	15 51	15 56	15 59	16 06	16 03	16 10	16 14	16 12		16 17	16 21	16 26	16 29	16 36
London Waterloo 15 ⊖	a	15 25	15 31	15 34	15 40	15 37	15 45	15 49	15 46		15 52	15 55	16 01	16 04	16 10	16 07	16 15	16 19	16 19		16 22	16 25	16 31	16 34	16 40

Hampton Court, Shepperton, Guildford, Dorking and Chessington South - London

		SW	SW	SW	SW		SW	SW	SW	SW	SW	SW	SW	SW	SW		SW	SW	SW	SW	SW	SW	SW	SW	SW
Guildford	d	15 38									15 58	16 08									16 28	16 38			
London Road (Guildford)	d	15 42									16 02	16 12									16 32	16 42			
Clandon	d	15 47									16 07	16 17									16 37	16 47			
Horsley	d	15 51									16 11	16 21									16 41	16 51			
Effingham Junction 6	d	15 54									16 16	16 24									16 46	16 54			
Bookham	d										16 19										16 49				
Cobham & Stoke d'Abernon	d	15 58										16 28										16 58			
Oxshott	d	16 01										16 31										17 01			
Claygate	d	16 04										16 34										17 04			
Hinchley Wood	d	16 07										16 37										17 07			
Hampton Court	d								16 24										16 54						
Thames Ditton	d								16 26										16 56						
Surbiton 6	d	16 12					16 27		16 32			16 42					16 57		17 02			17 12			
Berrylands	d								16 34										17 04						
Shepperton	d									16 11										16 41					
Upper Halliford	d									16 14										16 44					
Sunbury	d									16 16										16 46					
Kempton Park	d									16 18										16 48					
Hampton	d									16 21										16 51					
Fulwell	d									16 24										16 54					
Strawberry Hill	d			16 07	16 08									16 37	16 38									17 07	17 08
Teddington	d			16 11						16 29				16 43						16 59				17 13	
Hampton Wick	d			16 14						16 31				16 46						17 01				17 16	
Kingston	a			16 16						16 33				16 48						17 03				17 18	
	d			16 19						16 34				16 49						17 04				17 19	
Norbiton	d			16 21						16 36				16 51						17 06				17 21	
New Malden 6	d			16 25					16 37	16 40				16 55					17 07	17 10				17 25	
Dorking 4	d							16 05										16 35							
Boxhill & Westhumble	d																								
Leatherhead	d							16 11			16 24							16 41			16 54				
Ashtead	d							16 14			16 28							16 44			16 58				
Epsom 3	a							16 19			16 32							16 49			17 02				
	d							16 20			16 35							16 50			17 05				
Ewell West	d							16 23			16 38							16 53			17 08				
Stoneleigh	d							16 25			16 40							16 55			17 10				
Worcester Park	d							16 28			16 43							16 58			17 13				
Chessington South	d		16 10										16 40										17 10		
Chessington North	d		16 12										16 42										17 12		
Tolworth	d		16 14										16 44										17 14		
Malden Manor	d		16 17										16 47										17 17		
Motspur Park	d		16 20					16 31			16 46		16 50					17 01			17 16		17 20		
Raynes Park 6	d		16 23	16 28				16 34	16 40	16 43	16 49		16 53	16 58				17 04	17 10	17 13	17 19		17 23	17 28	
Wimbledon 6 ⊖	d	16 20	16 27	16 32			16 35	16 38	16 44	16 47	16 53	16 50	16 57	17 02			17 05	17 08	17 14	17 17	17 23	17 20	17 27	17 32	
Earlsfield	d	16 24	16 31	16 35			16 38	16 42	16 47	16 50	16 57	16 54	17 01	17 05			17 08	17 12	17 17	17 20	17 27	17 24	17 31	17 35	
Clapham Junction 10	d	16 28	16 35	16 39			16 42	16 46	16 51	16 54	17 01	16 58	17 05	17 09			17 12	17 16	17 21	17 24	17 31	17 28	17 35	17 39	
Vauxhall ⊖	d	16 33	16 40	16 44	16 42		16 47	16 51	16 56	16 59	17 06	17 03	17 10	17 14	17 12		17 17	17 21	17 26	17 29	17 36	17 33	17 40	17 44	17 42
London Waterloo 15 ⊖	a	16 37	16 45	16 49	16 49		16 52	16 55	17 01	17 05	17 10	17 07	17 16	17 19	17 19		17 22	17 25	17 31	17 35	17 40	17 37	17 45	17 49	17 49

Table 152

Mondays to Fridays

until 30 September

Hampton Court, Shepperton, Guildford, Dorking and Chessington South - London

		SW	SW	SW	SW	SW	SW	SW	SW	SW	SW	SW	SW	SW	SW	SW	SW	SW	SW	SW	SW	SW
Guildford	d					16 58	17 08									17 28	17 38					
London Road (Guildford)	d					17 02	17 12									17 32	17 42					
Clandon	d					17 07	17 17									17 37	17 47					
Horsley	d					17 11	17 21									17 41	17 51					
Effingham Junction ■	d					17 16	17 24									17 46	17 54					
Bookham	d					17 19										17 49						
Cobham & Stoke d'Abernon	d						17 28										17 58					
Oxshott	d						17 31										18 01					
Claygate	d						17 34										18 04					
Hinchley Wood	d						17 37										18 07					
Hampton Court	d			17 24										17 54								
Thames Ditton	d			17 26										17 56								
Surbiton ■	d	17 27		17 32			17 42				17 57			18 02			18 12				18 27	
Berrylands	d			17 34										18 04								
Shepperton	d				17 11										17 41							
Upper Halliford	d				17 14										17 44							
Sunbury	d				17 16										17 46							
Kempton Park	d				17 18										17 48							
Hampton	d				17 21										17 51							
Fulwell	d				17 24										17 54							
Strawberry Hill	d								17 37	17 38			17 41						18 07	18 08		
Teddington	d				17 29				17 43				17b52		17 59				18 13			
Hampton Wick	d				17 31				17 46				17 54		18 01				18 16			
Kingston	a				17 33				17 48				17 56		18 03				18 18			
	d				17 34				17 49				17 58		18 04				18 19			
Norbiton	d				17 36				17 51				18 00		18 06				18 21			
New Malden ■	d			17 37	17 40				17 55				18 04	18 07	18 10				18 25			
Dorking ■	d		17 05									17 35										18 05
Boxhill & Westhumble	d																					
Leatherhead	d		17 11			17 24						17 41				17 54						18 11
Ashtead	d		17 14			17 28						17 45				17 58						18 14
Epsom ■	a		17 19			17 32						17 49				18 02						18 19
	d		17 20			17 35						17 50				18 05						18 20
Ewell West	d		17 23			17 38						17 53				18 08						18 23
Stoneleigh	d		17 25			17 40						17 55				18 10						18 25
Worcester Park	d		17 28			17 43						17 58				18 13						18 28
Chessington South	d							17 40										18 10				
Chessington North	d							17 42										18 12				
Tolworth	d							17 44										18 14				
Malden Manor	d							17 47										18 17				
Motspur Park	d		17 31			17 46		17 50				18 01				18 16		18 20				18 31
Raynes Park ■	d		17 34	17 40	17 43	17 49		17 53	17 58			18 04	18 07	18 10	18 13	18 19		18 23	18 28			18 34
Wimbledon ■ ⊖ ⛴	d	17 35	17 38	17 44	17 47	17 53	17 50	17 57	18 02		18 05	18 08	18 11	18 14	18 17	18 23	18 20	18 27	18 32		18 35	18 38
Earlsfield	d	17 38	17 42	17 47	17 50	17 57	17 54	18 01	18 05		18 08	18 12	18 15	18 17	18 20	18 27	18 24	18 31	18 35		18 38	18 42
Clapham Junction ■	d	17 42	17 46	17 51	17 54	18 01	17 58	18 05	18 09		18 12	18 16	18 19	18 21	18 24	18 31	18 28	18 35	18 39		18 42	18 46
Vauxhall ⊖	d	17 47	17 51	17 56	17 59	18 06	18 03	18 10	18 14	18 12	18 17	18 21	18 24	18 26	18 29	18 36	18 33	18 40	18 44	18 42	18 47	18 51
London Waterloo ■ ⊖	a	17 52	17 55	18 01	18 05	18 10	18 07	18 15	18 19	18 19	18 23	18 25	18 29	18 31	18 35	18 40	18 37	18 47	18 49	18 49	18 52	18 55

b Arr. 1746

Table 152

Mondays to Fridays

until 30 September

Hampton Court, Shepperton, Guildford, Dorking and Chessington South - London

		SW	SW	SW	SW	SW	SW	SW	SW	SW	SW	SW	SW	SW	SW	SW	SW	SW	SW	SW	SW	SW	SW
Guildford	d			17 58	18 08								18 38									19 08	
London Road (Guildford)	d			18 02	18 12								18 42									19 12	
Clandon	d			18 07	18 17								18 47									19 17	
Horsley	d			18 11	18 21								18 51									19 21	
Effingham Junction ■	d			18 16	18 24								18 54						18 59			19 25	
Bookham	d			18 19															19 02				
Cobham & Stoke d'Abernon	d				18 28								18 58									19 28	
Oxshott	d				18 31								19 01									19 32	
Claygate	d				18 34								19 04									19 35	
Hinchley Wood	d				18 37								19 07									19 37	
Hampton Court	d	18 24									18 54									19 24			
Thames Ditton	d	18 26									18 56									19 26			
Surbiton ■	d	18 32			18 42				18 57		19 02		19 12					19 27		19 32		19 42	
Berrylands	d	18 34									19 04									19 34			
Shepperton	d		18 11									18 36									19 06		
Upper Halliford	d		18 14									18 39									19 09		
Sunbury	d		18 16									18 41									19 11		
Kempton Park	d		18 18									18 43									19 13		
Hampton	d		18 21									18b51									19c21		
Fulwell	d		18 24									18 54									19 24		
Strawberry Hill	d						18 37	18 38								19 07	19 08						
Teddington	d		18 29				18 43					18 59				19 13					19 29		
Hampton Wick	d		18 31				18 46					19 01				19 16					19 31		
Kingston	a		18 33				18 48					19 03				19 18					19 33		
	d		18 34				18 49					19 04				19 19					19 34		
Norbiton	d		18 36				18 51					19 06				19 21					19 36		
New Malden ■	d	18 37	18 40				18 55				19 07	19 10				19 25				19 37	19 40		
Dorking ■	d									18 35				18 50									
Boxhill & Westhumble	d																						
Leatherhead	d			18 24						18 41				18 56					19 08				
Ashtead	d			18 28						18 45				18 59					19 12				
Epsom ■	a			18 32						18 49				19 04					19 16				
	d			18 35						18 50				19 05					19 20				19 35
Ewell West	d			18 38						18 53				19 08					19 23				19 38
Stoneleigh	d			18 40						18 55				19 10					19 25				19 40
Worcester Park	d			18 43						18 58				19 13					19 28				19 43
Chessington South	d					18 40									19 10								
Chessington North	d					18 42									19 12								
Tolworth	d					18 44									19 14								
Malden Manor	d					18 47									19 17								
Motspur Park	d			18 46		18 50				19 01				19 16	19 20				19 31				19 46
Raynes Park ■	d	18 40	18 43	18 49		18 53	18 58			19 04	19 10	19 13		19 19	19 23	19 28			19 34	19 40	19 43		19 49
Wimbledon ■ ⊖ ⛴	d	18 44	18 47	18 53	18 50	18 57	19 02		19 05	19 08	19 14	19 17	19 20	19 23	19 27	19 32		19 35	19 38	19 44	19 47	19 50	19 53
Earlsfield	d	18 47	18 50	18 57	18 54	19 01	19 05		19 08	19 12	19 17	19 20	19 24	19 27	19 31	19 35		19 38	19 42	19 47	19 50	19 54	19 57
Clapham Junction ■	d	18 51	18 54	19 01	18 58	19 05	19 09		19 12	19 16	19 21	19 24	19 28	19 31	19 35	19 39		19 42	19 46	19 51	19 54	19 58	20 01
Vauxhall ⊖	d	18 56	18 59	19 06	19 03	19 10	19 14	19 12	19 17	19 21	19 26	19 29	19 33	19 36	19 40	19 44	19 42	19 47	19 51	19 56	19 59	20 03	20 06
London Waterloo ■ ⊖	a	19 01	19 05	19 10	19 07	19 14	19 19	19 16	19 23	19 27	19 31	19 34	19 37	19 41	19 45	19 49	19 46	19 52	19 55	20 01	20 04	20 07	20 10

b Arr. 1846 c Arr. 1916

Hampton Court, Shepperton, Guildford, Dorking and Chessington South - London

		SW	SW		SW	SW	SW	SW	SW	SW	SW	SW	SW		SW	SW	SW	SW	SW	SW	SW	SW	SW		SW
Guildford	d									19 28	19 38									19 58	20 08				
London Road (Guildford)	d									19 32	19 42									20 02	20 12				
Clandon	d									19 37	19 47									20 07	20 17				
Horsley	d									19 41	19 51									20 11	20 21				
Effingham Junction 6	d									19 46	19 54									20 16	20 24				
Bookham	d									19 49										20 19					
Cobham & Stoke d'Abernon	d										19 58										20 28				
Oxshott	d										20 01										20 31				
Claygate	d										20 04										20 34				
Hinchley Wood	d										20 07										20 37				
Hampton Court	d							19 54										20 24							
Thames Ditton	d							19 56										20 26							
Surbiton 6	d					19 57		20 02			20 12					20 27		20 32			20 42				
Berrylands	d							20 04										20 34							
Shepperton	d								19 41										20 11						
Upper Halliford	d								19 44										20 14						
Sunbury	d								19 46										20 16						
Kempton Park	d								19 48										20 18						
Hampton	d								19 51										20 21						
Fulwell	d								19 54										20 24						
Strawberry Hill	d		19 37		19 38								20 07		20 08								20 37		20 38
Teddington	d		19 43						19 59				20 11						20 29				20 41		
Hampton Wick	d		19 46						20 01				20 14						20 31				20 44		
Kingston	a		19 48						20 04				20 16						20 33				20 46		
	d		19 49						20 04				20 19						20 34				20 49		
Norbiton	d		19 51						20 06				20 21						20 36				20 51		
New Malden 6	d		19 55					20 07	20 10				20 25					20 37	20 40				20 55		
Dorking 4	d						19 33										20 05								
Boxhill & Westhumble	d																								
Leatherhead	d						19 39			19 54							20 11			20 24					
Ashtead	d						19 42			19 58							20 14			20 28					
Epsom 3	a						19 47			20 02							20 19			20 32					
	d						19 50			20 05							20 20			20 35					
Ewell West	d						19 53			20 08							20 23			20 38					
Stoneleigh	d						19 55			20 10							20 25			20 40					
Worcester Park	d						19 58			20 13							20 28			20 43					
Chessington South	d	19 40										20 10										20 40			
Chessington North	d	19 42										20 12										20 42			
Tolworth	d	19 44										20 14										20 44			
Malden Manor	d	19 47										20 17										20 47			
Motspur Park	d	19 50					20 01			20 16		20 20					20 31			20 46		20 50			
Raynes Park 6	d	19 53	19 58				20 04	20 10	20 13	20 19		20 23	20 28				20 34	20 40	20 43	20 49		20 53	20 58		
Wimbledon 6 ⊖	d	19 57	20 02			20 05	20 08	20 14	20 17	20 23	20 20	20 27	20 32			20 35	20 38	20 44	20 47	20 53	20 50	20 57	21 02		
Earlsfield	d	20 01	20 05			20 08	20 12	20 17	20 20	20 27	20 24	20 31	20 35			20 38	20 42	20 47	20 50	20 57	20 54	21 01	21 05		
Clapham Junction 10	d	20 05	20 09			20 12	20 16	20 21	20 24	20 31	20 28	20 35	20 39			20 42	20 46	20 51	20 54	21 01	20 58	21 05	21 09		
Vauxhall ⊖	d	20 10	20 14		20 12	20 17	20 21	20 26	20 29	20 36	20 33	20 40	20 44		20 42	20 47	20 51	20 56	20 59	21 06	21 03	21 10	21 14		21 12
London Waterloo 15 ⊖	a	20 15	20 19		20 16	20 22	20 25	20 31	20 35	20 41	20 38	20 46	20 49		20 46	20 52	20 55	21 01	21 04	21 10	21 07	21 15	21 19		21 16

		SW	SW	SW	SW	SW	SW	SW	SW		SW	SW	SW	SW	SW	SW	SW	SW	SW		SW	SW	SW	SW	SW
Guildford	d					20 38							20 46			21 08									21 38
London Road (Guildford)	d					20 42							20 50			21 12									21 42
Clandon	d					20 47							20 55			21 17									21 47
Horsley	d					20 51							20 59			21 21									21 51
Effingham Junction 6	d					20 54							21 03			21 24									21 54
Bookham	d												21 06												
Cobham & Stoke d'Abernon	d					20 58										21 28									21 58
Oxshott	d					21 01										21 31									22 01
Claygate	d					21 04										21 34									22 04
Hinchley Wood	d					21 07										21 37									22 07
Hampton Court	d			20 54										21 24											
Thames Ditton	d			20 56										21 26											
Surbiton 6	d	20 57		21 02		21 12						21 27		21 32		21 42						21 57			22 12
Berrylands	d			21 04										21 34											
Shepperton	d				20 41										21 11									21 41	
Upper Halliford	d				20 44										21 14									21 44	
Sunbury	d				20 46										21 16									21 46	
Kempton Park	d				20 48										21 18									21 48	
Hampton	d				20 51										21 21									21 51	
Fulwell	d				20 54										21 24									21 54	
Strawberry Hill	d								21 07		21 08								21 37		21 38				
Teddington	d				20 59				21 11						21 29				21 41					21 59	
Hampton Wick	d				21 01				21 14						21 31				21 44					22 01	
Kingston	a				21 03				21 16						21 33				21 46					22 03	
	d				21 04				21 19						21 34				21 49					22 04	
Norbiton	d				21 06				21 21						21 36				21 51					22 06	
New Malden 6	d			21 07	21 10				21 25					21 37	21 40				21 55					22 10	
Dorking 4	d		20 35																				21 35		
Boxhill & Westhumble	d																								
Leatherhead	d		20 41										21 11										21 41		
Ashtead	d		20 44										21 14										21 44		
Epsom 3	a		20 49										21 19										21 49		
	d		20 50				21 05						21 20				21 35						21 50		
Ewell West	d		20 53				21 08						21 23				21 38						21 53		
Stoneleigh	d		20 55				21 10						21 25				21 40						21 55		
Worcester Park	d		20 58				21 13						21 28				21 43						21 58		
Chessington South	d							21 10										21 40							
Chessington North	d							21 12										21 42							
Tolworth	d							21 14										21 44							
Malden Manor	d							21 17										21 47							
Motspur Park	d		21 01				21 16	21 20					21 31				21 46	21 50					22 01		
Raynes Park 6	d		21 04	21 10	21 13		21 19	21 23	21 28				21 34	21 40	21 43		21 49	21 53	21 58				22 04	22 13	
Wimbledon 6 ⊖	d	21 05	21 08	21 14	21 17	21 20	21 23	21 27	21 32			21 35	21 38	21 44	21 47	21 50	21 53	21 57	22 02			22 05	22 08	22 17	22 20
Earlsfield	d	21 08	21 12	21 17	21 20	21 24	21 27	21 31	21 35			21 38	21 42	21 47	21 50	21 54	21 57	22 01	22 05			22 08	22 12	22 20	22 24
Clapham Junction 10	d	21 12	21 16	21 21	21 24	21 28	21 31	21 35	21 39			21 42	21 46	21 51	21 54	21 58	22 01	22 05	22 09			22 12	22 16	22 24	22 28
Vauxhall ⊖	d	21 17	21 21	21 26	21 29	21 33	21 36	21 40	21 44		21 42	21 47	21 51	21 56	21 59	22 03	22 06	22 10	22 14		22 12	22 17	22 21	22 29	22 33
London Waterloo 15 ⊖	a	21 22	21 25	21 31	21 34	21 37	21 40	21 45	21 49		21 46	21 52	21 55	22 01	22 04	22 07	22 10	22 16	22 19		22 16	22 22	22 25	22 34	22 39

Hampton Court, Shepperton, Guildford, Dorking and Chessington South - London

		SW	SW	SW	SW		SW	SW	SW	SW	SW	SW	SW	SW	SW		SW	SW	SW	SW	SW	SW	SW	SW	SN
Guildford	d				21 46				22 08				22 20				22 38			22 46	22 55			23 08	
London Road (Guildford)	d				21 50				22 12								22 42			22 50				23 12	
Clandon	d				21 55				22 17								22 47			22 55				23 17	
Horsley	d				21 59				22 21								22 51			22 59				23 21	
Effingham Junction 6	d				22 03				22 24								22 54			23 03				23 24	
Bookham	d				22 06															23 06					
Cobham & Stoke d'Abernon	d								22 28								22 58							23 28	
Oxshott	d								22 31								23 01							23 31	
Claygate	d								22 34								23 04							23 34	
Hinchley Wood	d								22 37								23 07							23 37	
Hampton Court	d						22 24															23 24			
Thames Ditton	d						22 26															23 26			
Surbiton 6	d			22 27			22 32		22 42				22 57				23 12				23 30	23 33		23 42	
Berrylands	d						22 34															23 35			
Shepperton	d							22 11							22 41								23 11		
Upper Halliford	d							22 14							22 44								23 14		
Sunbury	d							22 16							22 46								23 16		
Kempton Park	d							22 18							22 48								23 18		
Hampton	d							22 21							22 51								23 21		
Fulwell	d							22 24							22 54								23 24		
Strawberry Hill	d	22 07	22 08								22 37	22 38						23 07	23 08						
Teddington	d	22 11						22 29			22 41				22 59			23 11					23 29		
Hampton Wick	d	22 14						22 31			22 44				23 01			23 14					23 31		
Kingston	a	22 16						22 33			22 46				23 03			23 16					23 33		
	d	22 19						22 34			22 49				23 04			23 19					23 34		
Norbiton	d	22 21						22 36			22 51				23 06			23 21					23 36		
New Malden 6	d	22 25					22 37	22 40			22 55				23 10			23 25				23 38	23 41		
Dorking 4	d													22 35											23 30
Boxhill & Westhumble	d																								
Leatherhead	d				22 11									22 41						23 11					23 36
Ashtead	d				22 14									22 44						23 14					23 39
Epsom 3	a				22 19									22 49						23 19					23 45
	d				22 20									22 50						23 20					
Ewell West	d				22 23									22 53						23 23					
Stoneleigh	d				22 25									22 55						23 25					
Worcester Park	d				22 28									22 58						23 28					
Chessington South	d									22 40															
Chessington North	d									22 42															
Tolworth	d									22 44															
Malden Manor	d									22 47															
Motspur Park	d				22 31					22 50				23 01						23 31					
Raynes Park 6	d	22 28			22 34		22 40	22 43		22 53	22 58			23 04	23 13			23 28		23 37		23 41	23 43		
Wimbledon 6 ⊖	d	22 32		22 35	22 38		22 44	22 47	22 50	22 57	23 02		23 05	23 08	23 17		23 20	23 32		23 41	23 37	23a45	23 50	23 53	
Earlsfield	d	22 35		22 38	22 42		22 47	22 50	22 54	23 01	23 05		23 08	23 12	23 20		23 24	23 36		23 44	23 41		23 53	23 56	
Clapham Junction 10	d	22 39		22 42	22 46		22 51	22 54	22 58	23 05	23 09		23 12	23 16	23 24		23 28	23 40		23 48	23 45		23 57	23 59	
Vauxhall ⊖	d	22 44	22 42	22 47	22 51		22 56	22 59	23 03	23 10	23 14	23 12	23 17	23 21	23 29		23 33	23 45	23 42	23 53	23 50		00 02	00 05	
London Waterloo 15 ⊖	a	22 49	22 46	22 52	22 55		23 01	23 04	23 07	23 15	23 19	23 16	23 23	23 27	23 34		23 37	23 49	23 46	23 58	23 54		00 10	00 14	

			SW	SW	SW
Guildford	d				
London Road (Guildford)	d				
Clandon	d				
Horsley	d				
Effingham Junction 6	d				
Bookham	d				
Cobham & Stoke d'Abernon	d				
Oxshott	d				
Claygate	d				
Hinchley Wood	d				
Hampton Court	d				
Thames Ditton	d				
Surbiton 6	d				
Berrylands	d				
Shepperton	d				
Upper Halliford	d				
Sunbury	d				
Kempton Park	d				
Hampton	d				
Fulwell	d				
Strawberry Hill	d			23 37	23 38
Teddington	d			23 41	
Hampton Wick	d			23 44	
Kingston	a			23 46	
	d			23 49	
Norbiton	d			23 51	
New Malden 6	d			23 55	
Dorking 4	d				
Boxhill & Westhumble	d				
Leatherhead	d				
Ashtead	d				
Epsom 3	a				
	d				
Ewell West	d				
Stoneleigh	d				
Worcester Park	d				
Chessington South	d		23 40		
Chessington North	d		23 42		
Tolworth	d		23 44		
Malden Manor	d		23 47		
Motspur Park	d		23 50		
Raynes Park 6	d		23 54	23 58	
Wimbledon 6 ⊖	d		23a57	00 02	
Earlsfield	d			00 05	
Clapham Junction 10	d			00 09	
Vauxhall ⊖	d			00 14	00 12
London Waterloo 15 ⊖	a			00 22	00 16

Table 152

Mondays to Fridays
from 3 October

Hampton Court, Shepperton, Guildford, Dorking and Chessington South - London

		SW MO	SW MX	SW MX	SW MX	SW MX	SW MO	SW	SW	SW		SW	SW	SW	SW	SW	SW	SW	SW	SW		SW	SW	SW	SW
Guildford	d			23p08				04 00		04 58				05 14			05 35								
London Road (Guildford)	d			23p12						05 02							05 39								
Clandon	d			23p17						05 07							05 44								
Horsley	d			23p21						05 11							05 48								
Effingham Junction 6	d			23p24						05 16							05 51								
Bookham	d									05 19															
Cobham & Stoke d'Abernon	d			23p28													05 55								
Oxshott	d			23p31													05 58								
Claygate	d			23p34													06 01								
Hinchley Wood	d			23p37													06 04								
Hampton Court	d						23p45									05 54								06 24	
Thames Ditton	d						23p47									05 56								06 26	
Surbiton 6	d			23p42			23p53	04 24						05 57	06 01	06 02	06 12					06 28		06 32	
Berrylands	d						23p55									06 04								06 34	
Shepperton	d	23p11	23p11									05 23													06 11
Upper Halliford	d	23p14	23p14									05 26													06 14
Sunbury	d	23p16	23p16									05 28													06 16
Kempton Park	d	23p18	23p18																						
Hampton	d	23p21	23p21									05 33													06 21
Fulwell	d	23p24	23p24									05 36													06 24
Strawberry Hill	d				23p37	23p38			04 55			05 38							06 08	06 08					
Teddington	d	23p29	23p29		23p41				04 59				05 44							06 11					06 29
Hampton Wick	d	23p31	23p31		23p44				05 01				05 46							06 14					06 31
Kingston	a	23p33	23p33		23p46				05 03				05 48							06 16					06 33
	d	23p34	23p34		23p49				05 04				05 49							06 19					06 34
Norbiton	d	23p36	23p36		23p51				05 06				05 51							06 21					06 36
New Malden 6	d	23p40	23p41		23p55		23p58		05 10				05 55			06 07				06 25				06 37	06 40
Dorking 4	d																	05 48							
Boxhill & Westhumble	d																	05 50							
Leatherhead	d									05 24								05 56							
Ashtead	d									05 28								05 59							
Epsom 3	a									05 32								06 04							
	d									05 34								06 04					06 18		
Ewell West	d									05 37								06 07					06 21		
Stoneleigh	d									05 40								06 10					06 24		
Worcester Park	d									05 42								06 12					06 27		
Chessington South	d																								
Chessington North	d																								
Tolworth	d																								
Malden Manor	d																								
Motspur Park	d									05 46								06 16					06 30		
Raynes Park 6	d	23p43	23p43		23p58		00 01		05 13	05 49			05 58			06 10		06 19		06 28			06 34	06 40	06 43
Wimbledon 6 ⊖ ⇌	d	23p47	23p50	23p53	00 02		00a04	04 32	05 17	05 53			06 02	06 05		06 14	06 20	06 23		06 32		06 35	06 38	06 44	06 47
Earlsfield	d	23p50	23p53	23p56	00 05				05 21	05 57			06 05	06 08		06 17	06 24	06 27		06 35		06 39	06 42	06 47	06 50
Clapham Junction 10	d	23p54	23p57	23p59	00 09			04 44	05 25	06 01			06 09	06 12		06 21	06 28	06 31		06 39		06 43	06 46	06 51	06 54
Vauxhall ⊖	d	23p59	00 02	00 05	00 14	00 12			05 30	06 06		06 12	06 14	06 17		06 26	06 33	06 36	06 42	06 44		06 48	06 51	06 56	06 59
London Waterloo 15 ⊖	a	00 04	00 10	00 14	00 22	00 16		04 53	05 35	06 11		06 16	06 19	06 22	06 20	06 31	06 37	06 40	06 46	06 49		06 52	06 55	07 03	07 06

Table 152

Mondays to Fridays
from 3 October

Hampton Court, Shepperton, Guildford, Dorking and Chessington South - London

		SW	SW	SW	SW	SW		SW	SW	SW	SW 1	SW	SW	SW	SW	SW		SW	SW 1	SW	SW	SW	SW	SW	SW 1
Guildford	d	05 58	06 04										06 28	06 34											
London Road (Guildford)	d	06 02	06 08										06 32	06 38											
Clandon	d	06 07	06 13										06 37	06 43											
Horsley	d	06 11	06 17										06 41	06 47											
Effingham Junction 6	d	06 16	06 21										06 48	06 51											
Bookham	d	06 19											06 51												
Cobham & Stoke d'Abernon	d		06 24											06 54											
Oxshott	d		06 28											06 58											
Claygate	d		06 31											07 01											
Hinchley Wood	d		06 34											07 04											
Hampton Court	d									06 54														07 24	
Thames Ditton	d									06 56														07 26	
Surbiton 6	d		06 42					06 57		07 02	07 08			07 12					07 27					07 32	07 38
Berrylands	d									07 04														07 34	
Shepperton	d											06 41											07 00		
Upper Halliford	d											06 44											07 03		
Sunbury	d											06 46											07 05		
Kempton Park	d																								
Hampton	d											06 51											07 09		
Fulwell	d											06 54											07 12		
Strawberry Hill	d				06 37	06 38										07 07		07 08					07 14		
Teddington	d				06 41							06 59				07 11					07 20				
Hampton Wick	d				06 44							07 01				07 14					07 22				
Kingston	a				06 46							07 03				07 16					07 24				
	d				06 49							07 04				07 19					07 26				
Norbiton	d				06 51							07 06				07 21					07 28				
New Malden 6	d				06 55					07 07		07 10				07 25					07 32			07 37	
Dorking 4	d								06 32											07 02					
Boxhill & Westhumble	d								06 34											07 04					
Leatherhead	d	06 24							06 39				06 56							07 09					
Ashtead	d	06 28							06 43				06 59							07 13					
Epsom 3	a	06 32							06 47				07 04							07 17					
	d	06 34							06 48				07 04							07 18		07 22			
Ewell West	d	06 37							06 51				07 07									07 25			
Stoneleigh	d	06 40							06 53				07 10									07 27			
Worcester Park	d	06 42							06 56				07 12							07 25		07 30			
Chessington South	d			06 40											07 10										
Chessington North	d			06 42											07 12										
Tolworth	d			06 44											07 14										
Malden Manor	d			06 47											07 17										
Motspur Park	d	06 46		06 50					07 00				07 16		07 20							07 34			
Raynes Park 6	d	06 49		06 54	06 58				07 04	07 10		07 13	07 19		07 24	07 28				07 31	07 34	07 37		07 40	
Wimbledon 6 ⊖ ⇌	d	06 53	06 50	06 58	07 02			07 05	07 08	07 14		07 17	07 23	07 20	07 28	07 32				07 35	07 38	07 41		07 44	
Earlsfield	d	06 57	06 54	07 01	07 05			07 08	07 11	07 17		07 20	07 27	07 24	07 31	07 35				07 38	07 42	07 45		07 48	
Clapham Junction 10	d	07 01	06 58	07 05	07 09			07 12	07 15	07 21		07 24	07 31	07 28	07 35	07 39				07 42	07 46	07 49		07 52	
Vauxhall ⊖	d	07 06	07 03	07 10	07 14	07 12		07 17	07 20	07 26		07 29	07 36	07 33	07 40	07 44		07 42		07 47	07 51	07 54	07 56	07 57	
London Waterloo 15 ⊖	a	07 12	07 09	07 17	07 21	07 18		07 24	07 27	07 33	07 26	07 36	07 42	07 39	07 47	07 51		07 48	07 49	07 54	07 57	08 00	08 04	08 04	07 56

Hampton Court, Shepperton, Guildford, Dorking and Chessington South - London

from 3 October

		SW		SW	SW	SW	SW	SW	SW	SW 1	SW	SW		SW	SW	SW	SW 1	SW	SW	SW	SW 1	SW 1		SW	SW
Guildford	d			06 58	07 04	07 14														07 34					
London Road (Guildford)	d			07 02	07 08	07 18														07 38					
Clandon	d			07 07	07 13	07 23														07 43					
Horsley	d			07 11	07 17	07 27														07 47					
Effingham Junction 6	d			07 16	07 21	07 31													07 46	07 51					
Bookham	d			07 19															07 49						
Cobham & Stoke d'Abernon	d				07 24	07 34														07 54					
Oxshott	d				07 28	07 38														07 58					
Claygate	d				07 31	07 41														08 01					
Hinchley Wood	d				07 34	07 44														08 04					
Hampton Court	d															07 54									
Thames Ditton	d															07 56									
Surbiton 6	d				07 42	07 53				07 57						08 02	08 08			08 12	08 19	08 25			
Berrylands	d															08 04									
Shepperton	d	07 11										07 30						07 41							
Upper Halliford	d	07 14										07 33						07 44							
Sunbury	d	07 16										07 35						07 46							
Kempton Park	d																								
Hampton	d	07 21										07 39						07 51							
Fulwell	d	07 24										07 42						07 54							
Strawberry Hill	d							07 37	07 38			07 44		07 47											08 07
Teddington	d	07 29						07 41						07 50				07 59							08 11
Hampton Wick	d	07 31						07 44						07 52				08 01							08 14
Kingston	a	07 33						07 46						07 54				08 03							08 16
	d	07 34						07 49						07 56				08 04							08 19
Norbiton	d	07 36						07 51						07 58				08 06							08 21
New Malden 6	d	07 40			07 46			07 55						08 02		08 07		08 10		08 16					08 25
Dorking 4	d										07 32														
Boxhill & Westhumble	d										07 34														
Leatherhead	d			07 26							07 39								07 56						
Ashtead	d			07 29							07 43								07 59						
Epsom 3	a			07 34							07 47								08 04						
	d			07 34							07 48				07 52				08 04						
Ewell West	d			07 37											07 55				08 07						
Stoneleigh	d			07 40											07 57				08 10						
Worcester Park	d			07 43							07 55				08 00				08 13						
Chessington South	d						07 40																	08 10	
Chessington North	d						07 42																	08 12	
Tolworth	d						07 44																	08 14	
Malden Manor	d						07 47																	08 17	
Motspur Park	d			07 46			07 50								08 04				08 16					08 20	
Raynes Park 6	d	07 43		07 50			07 54	07 58			08 01			08 04	08 07	08 10		08 13	08 20					08 24	08 28
Wimbledon 6 ⊖	d	07 47		07 54	07 51		07 58	08 02			08 05			08 08	08 11	08 14		08 17	08 24	08 21				08 28	08 32
Earlsfield	d	07 51		07 58	07 54		08 01	08 05			08 08			08 12	08 15	08 18		08 21	08 28	08 24				08 31	08 35
Clapham Junction 10	d	07 55		08 02	07 58		08 05	08 09			08 12			08 16	08 19	08 22		08 25	08 32	08 28				08 35	08 39
Vauxhall ⊖	d	08 00		08 07	08 03		08 10	08 14	08 12		08 17	08 26		08 21	08 24	08 27		08 30	08 37	08 33				08 40	08 44
London Waterloo 15 ⊖	a	08 06		08 13	08 11	08 13	08 17	08 21	08 18	08 19	08 24	08 34		08 27	08 30	08 33	08 26	08 36	08 43	08 40	08 36	08 46		08 47	08 51

Hampton Court, Shepperton, Guildford, Dorking and Chessington South - London

from 3 October

		SW	SW	SW	SW	SW	SW	SW 1		SW	SW	SW	SW	SW	SW	SW	SW	SW		SW	SW	SW	SW	SW 1	SW
Guildford	d										07 58	08 04					08 20						08 34		
London Road (Guildford)	d										08 02	08 08											08 38		
Clandon	d										08 07	08 13											08 43		
Horsley	d										08 11	08 17											08 47		
Effingham Junction 6	d										08 16	08 21										08 48	08 51		
Bookham	d										08 19											08 51			
Cobham & Stoke d'Abernon	d											08 24											08 54		
Oxshott	d											08 28											08 58		
Claygate	d											08 31											09 01		
Hinchley Wood	d											08 34											09 04		
Hampton Court	d						08 24													08 54					
Thames Ditton	d						08 26													08 56					
Surbiton 6	d						08 32	08 38				08 42	08 48				08 57			09 02			09 12	09 19	
Berrylands	d						08 34													09 04					
Shepperton	d			08 00						08 11											08 41				
Upper Halliford	d			08 03						08 14											08 44				
Sunbury	d			08 05						08 16											08 46				
Kempton Park	d																								
Hampton	d			08 09						08 21											08 51				
Fulwell	d			08 12						08 24											08 54				
Strawberry Hill	d	08 08		08 14	08 17										08 38	08 38									
Teddington	d				08 20					08 29						08 41					08 59				
Hampton Wick	d				08 22					08 31						08 44					09 01				
Kingston	a				08 24					08 33						08 46					09 03				
	d				08 26					08 34						08 49					09 04				
Norbiton	d				08 28					08 36						08 51					09 06				
New Malden 6	d				08 32		08 37			08 40						08 55				09 07	09 10				
Dorking 4	d		08 02															08 31							
Boxhill & Westhumble	d		08 04															08 33							
Leatherhead	d		08 09								08 25							08 38				08 56			
Ashtead	d		08 13								08 28							08 42				08 59			
Epsom 3	a		08 17								08 33							08 46				09 04			
	d		08 18			08 22					08 34							08 48				09 04			
Ewell West	d					08 25					08 37							08 51				09 07			
Stoneleigh	d					08 27					08 40							08 54				09 10			
Worcester Park	d		08 25			08 30					08 42							08 57				09 12			
Chessington South	d													08 40											09 10
Chessington North	d													08 42											09 12
Tolworth	d													08 44											09 14
Malden Manor	d													08 47											09 17
Motspur Park	d					08 34					08 46			08 50				09 00				09 16			09 20
Raynes Park 6	d		08 31		08 34	08 37	08 40			08 43	08 49			08 54		08 58		09 04		09 10	09 13	09 19			09 24
Wimbledon 6 ⊖	d		08 35		08 38	08 41	08 44			08 47	08 53			08 58		09 02	09 05	09 08		09 14	09 17	09 23	09 20		09 28
Earlsfield	d		08 38		08 42	08 45	08 48			08 51	08 57			09 01		09 05	09 08	09 12		09 17	09 20	09 27	09 24		09 31
Clapham Junction 10	d		08 42		08 46	08 49	08 52			08 55	09 01			09 05		09 09	09 12	09 16		09 21	09 24	09 31	09 28		09 35
Vauxhall ⊖	d	08 42	08 47	08 56	08 51	08 54	08 57			09 00	09 06			09 10	09 12	09 14	09 17	09 21		09 26	09 29	09 36	09 33		09 40
London Waterloo 15 ⊖	a	08 49	08 54	09 04	08 57	09 00	09 03	08 59		09 06	09 12	09 01	09 06	09 17	09 18	09 21	09 24	09 27		09 33	09 36	09 42	09 39	09 40	09 47

Table 152

Mondays to Fridays

from 3 October

Hampton Court, Shepperton, Guildford, Dorking and Chessington South - London

		SW	SW	SW		SW	SW	SW	SW	SW	SW	SW	SW	SW		SW	SW	SW	SW	SW	SW	SW	SW	SW	
Guildford	d			08 46					08 58	09 05									09 28	09 35					
London Road (Guildford)	d								09 02	09 09									09 32	09 39					
Clandon	d								09 07	09 14									09 37	09 44					
Horsley	d								09 11	09 18									09 41	09 48					
Effingham Junction 6	d								09 16	09 21									09 46	09 51					
Bookham	d								09 19										09 49						
Cobham & Stoke d'Abernon	d									09 25										09 55					
Oxshott	d									09 28										09 58					
Claygate	d									09 31										10 01					
Hinchley Wood	d									09 34										10 04					
Hampton Court	d						09 24										09 54								
Thames Ditton	d						09 26										09 56								
Surbiton 6	d			09 27			09 32			09 42				09 57			10 02			10 12				10 27	
Berrylands	d						09 34										10 04								
Shepperton	d							09 11										09 41							
Upper Halliford	d							09 14										09 44							
Sunbury	d							09 16										09 46							
Kempton Park	d							09 18										09 48							
Hampton	d							09 21										09 51							
Fulwell	d							09 24										09 54							
Strawberry Hill	d	09 07	09 08									09 37	09 38									10 07	10 08		
Teddington	d	09 11						09 29				09 41						09 59				10 11			
Hampton Wick	d	09 14						09 31				09 44						10 01				10 14			
Kingston	a	09 16						09 33				09 46						10 03				10 16			
	d	09 19						09 34				09 49						10 04				10 19			
Norbiton	d	09 21						09 36				09 51						10 06				10 21			
New Malden 6	d	09 25					09 37	09 40				09 55					10 07	10 10				10 25			
Dorking 4	d					09 02										09 35									
Boxhill & Westhumble	d					09 04																			
Leatherhead	d					09 09			09 24							09 41			09 54						
Ashtead	d					09 13			09 28							09 45			09 58						
Epsom 3	a					09 17			09 32							09 49			10 02						
	d					09 18			09 35							09 50			10 05						
Ewell West	d					09 21			09 38							09 53			10 08						
Stoneleigh	d					09 24			09 40							09 55			10 10						
Worcester Park	d					09 27			09 43							09 58			10 13						
Chessington South	d										09 40										10 10				
Chessington North	d										09 42										10 12				
Tolworth	d										09 44										10 14				
Malden Manor	d										09 47										10 17				
Motspur Park	d					09 30			09 46		09 50					10 01			10 16		10 20				
Raynes Park 6	d	09 28				09 34	09 40	09 43	09 49		09 53	09 58				10 04	10 10	10 13	10 19		10 23	10 28			
Wimbledon 6 ⊖	d	09 32		09 35		09 38	09 44	09 47	09 53	09 50	09 57	10 02		10 05		10 08	10 14	10 17	10 23	10 20	10 27	10 32		10 35	
Earlsfield	d	09 35		09 38		09 42	09 47	09 50	09 57	09 54	10 01	10 05		10 08		10 12	10 17	10 20	10 27	10 24	10 31	10 35		10 38	
Clapham Junction 10	d	09 39		09 42		09 46	09 51	09 54	10 01	09 58	10 05	10 09		10 12		10 16	10 21	10 24	10 31	10 28	10 35	10 39		10 42	
Vauxhall ⊖	d	09 44	09 42	09 47		09 51	09 56	09 59	10 06	10 03	10 10	10 14	10 12	10 17		10 21	10 26	10 29	10 36	10 33	10 40	10 44	10 42	10 47	
London Waterloo 15 ⊖	a	09 51	09 48	09 54		09 57	10 01	10 04	10 10	10 07	10 15	10 19	10 16	10 22		10 25	10 31	10 34	10 40	10 37	10 45	10 49	10 46	10 52	

		SW	SW	SW	SW	SW	SW	SW	SW	SW		SW	SW	SW	SW	SW	SW	SW	SW	SW		SW	SW	SW	SW
Guildford	d				09 58	10 05									10 28	10 35									10 58
London Road (Guildford)	d				10 02	10 09									10 32	10 39									11 02
Clandon	d				10 07	10 14									10 37	10 44									11 07
Horsley	d				10 11	10 18									10 41	10 48									11 11
Effingham Junction 6	d				10 16	10 21									10 46	10 51									11 16
Bookham	d				10 19										10 49										11 19
Cobham & Stoke d'Abernon	d					10 25										10 55									
Oxshott	d					10 28										10 58									
Claygate	d					10 31										11 01									
Hinchley Wood	d					10 34										11 04									
Hampton Court	d		10 24										10 54										11 24		
Thames Ditton	d		10 26										10 56										11 26		
Surbiton 6	d		10 32			10 42				10 57			11 02			11 12				11 27			11 32		
Berrylands	d		10 34										11 04										11 34		
Shepperton	d			10 11										10 41										11 11	
Upper Halliford	d			10 14										10 44										11 14	
Sunbury	d			10 16										10 46										11 16	
Kempton Park	d			10 18										10 48										11 18	
Hampton	d			10 21										10 51										11 21	
Fulwell	d			10 24										10 54										11 24	
Strawberry Hill	d							10 37	10 38									11 07	11 08						
Teddington	d			10 29				10 41						10 59				11 11						11 29	
Hampton Wick	d			10 31				10 44						11 01				11 14						11 31	
Kingston	a			10 33				10 46						11 03				11 16						11 33	
	d			10 34				10 49						11 04				11 19						11 34	
Norbiton	d			10 36				10 51						11 06				11 21						11 36	
New Malden 6	d		10 37	10 40				10 55					11 07	11 10				11 25					11 37	11 40	
Dorking 4	d	10 05										10 35										11 05			
Boxhill & Westhumble	d																								
Leatherhead	d	10 11			10 24							10 41			10 54							11 11			11 24
Ashtead	d	10 14			10 28							10 44			10 58							11 14			11 28
Epsom 3	a	10 19			10 32							10 49			11 02							11 19			11 32
	d	10 20			10 35							10 50			11 05							11 20			11 35
Ewell West	d	10 23			10 38							10 53			11 08							11 23			11 38
Stoneleigh	d	10 25			10 40							10 55			11 10							11 25			11 40
Worcester Park	d	10 28			10 43							10 58			11 13							11 28			11 43
Chessington South	d						10 40										11 10								
Chessington North	d						10 42										11 12								
Tolworth	d						10 44										11 14								
Malden Manor	d						10 47										11 17								
Motspur Park	d	10 31			10 46		10 50					11 01			11 16		11 20					11 31			11 46
Raynes Park 6	d	10 34	10 40	10 43	10 49		10 53	10 58				11 04	11 10	11 13	11 19		11 23	11 28				11 34	11 40	11 43	11 49
Wimbledon 6 ⊖	d	10 38	10 44	10 47	10 53	10 50	10 57	11 02		11 05		11 08	11 14	11 17	11 23	11 20	11 27	11 32		11 35		11 38	11 44	11 47	11 53
Earlsfield	d	10 42	10 47	10 50	10 57	10 54	11 01	11 05		11 08		11 12	11 17	11 20	11 27	11 24	11 31	11 35		11 38		11 42	11 47	11 50	11 57
Clapham Junction 10	d	10 46	10 51	10 54	11 01	10 58	11 05	11 09		11 12		11 16	11 21	11 24	11 31	11 28	11 35	11 39		11 42		11 46	11 51	11 54	12 01
Vauxhall ⊖	d	10 51	10 56	10 59	11 06	11 03	11 10	11 14	11 12	11 17		11 21	11 26	11 29	11 36	11 33	11 40	11 44	11 42	11 47		11 51	11 56	11 59	12 06

Table 152

Mondays to Fridays

from 3 October

Hampton Court, Shepperton, Guildford, Dorking and Chessington South - London

		SW	SW	SW	SW	SW		SW	SW	SW	SW	SW	SW	SW	SW	SW		SW	SW	SW	SW	SW	SW	SW	SW
Guildford	d	11 05									11 28	11 35									11 58	12 05			
London Road (Guildford)	d	11 09									11 32	11 39									12 02	12 09			
Clandon	d	11 14									11 37	11 44									12 07	12 14			
Horsley	d	11 18									11 41	11 48									12 11	12 18			
Effingham Junction 6	d	11 21									11 46	11 51									12 16	12 21			
Bookham	d										11 49										12 19				
Cobham & Stoke d'Abernon	d	11 25										11 55										12 25			
Oxshott	d	11 28										11 58										12 28			
Claygate	d	11 31										12 01										12 31			
Hinchley Wood	d	11 34										12 04										12 34			
Hampton Court	d								11 54										12 24						
Thames Ditton	d								11 56										12 26						
Surbiton 6	d	11 42				11 57			12 02			12 12				12 27			12 32			12 42			
Berrylands	d								12 04										12 34						
Shepperton	d									11 41										12 11					
Upper Halliford	d									11 44										12 14					
Sunbury	d									11 46										12 16					
Kempton Park	d									11 48										12 18					
Hampton	d									11 51										12 21					
Fulwell	d									11 54										12 24					
Strawberry Hill	d			11 37	11 38									12 07	12 08									12 37	12 38
Teddington	d			11 41						11 59				12 11						12 29				12 41	
Hampton Wick	d			11 44						12 01				12 14						12 31				12 44	
Kingston	a			11 46						12 03				12 16						12 33				12 46	
	d			11 49						12 04				12 19						12 34				12 49	
Norbiton	d			11 51						12 06				12 21						12 36				12 51	
New Malden 6	d			11 55					12 07	12 10				12 25					12 37	12 40				12 55	
Dorking 4	d							11 35										12 05							
Boxhill & Westhumble	d																								
Leatherhead	d							11 41			11 54							12 11			12 24				
Ashtead	d							11 44			11 58							12 14			12 28				
Epsom 3	a							11 49			12 02							12 19			12 32				
	d							11 50			12 05							12 20			12 35				
Ewell West	d							11 53			12 08							12 23			12 38				
Stoneleigh	d							11 55			12 10							12 25			12 40				
Worcester Park	d							11 58			12 13							12 28			12 43				
Chessington South	d		11 40										12 10										12 40		
Chessington North	d		11 42										12 12										12 42		
Tolworth	d		11 44										12 14										12 44		
Malden Manor	d		11 47										12 17										12 47		
Motspur Park	d		11 50					12 01			12 16		12 20					12 31			12 46		12 50		
Raynes Park 6	d		11 53	11 58				12 04	12 10	12 13	12 19		12 23	12 28				12 34	12 40	12 43	12 49		12 53	12 58	
Wimbledon 6 ⊖	d	11 50	11 57	12 02		12 05		12 08	12 14	12 17	12 23	12 20	12 27	12 32		12 35		12 38	12 44	12 47	12 53	12 50	12 57	13 02	
Earlsfield	d	11 54	12 01	12 05		12 08		12 12	12 17	12 20	12 27	12 24	12 31	12 35		12 38		12 42	12 47	12 50	12 57	12 54	13 01	13 05	
Clapham Junction 10	d	11 58	12 05	12 09		12 12		12 16	12 21	12 24	12 31	12 28	12 35	12 39		12 42		12 46	12 51	12 54	13 01	12 58	13 05	13 09	
Vauxhall ⊖	d	12 03	12 10	12 14	12 12	12 17		12 21	12 26	12 29	12 36	12 33	12 40	12 44	12 42	12 47		12 51	12 56	12 59	13 06	13 03	13 10	13 14	13 12
London Waterloo 15 ⊖	a	12 07	12 15	12 19	12 16	12 22		12 25	12 31	12 34	12 40	12 37	12 45	12 49	12 46	12 52		12 55	13 01	13 04	13 10	13 07	13 15	13 19	13 16

Hampton Court, Shepperton, Guildford, Dorking and Chessington South - London

from 3 October

		SW	SW	SW	SW 1	SW	SW	SW	SW	SW	SW	SW	SW	SW	SW	SW	SW	SW	SW	SW	SW	SW
Guildford	d						12 28	12 35								12 58	13 05					
London Road (Guildford)	d						12 32	12 39								13 02	13 09					
Clandon	d						12 37	12 44								13 07	13 14					
Horsley	d						12 41	12 48								13 11	13 18					
Effingham Junction	d						12 46	12 51								13 16	13 21					
Bookham	d						12 49									13 19						
Cobham & Stoke d'Abernon	d							12 55									13 25					
Oxshott	d							12 58									13 28					
Claygate	d							13 01									13 31					
Hinchley Wood	d							13 04									13 34					
Hampton Court	d			12 54										13 24								
Thames Ditton	d			12 56										13 26								
Surbiton	d	12 57		13 02	13 08			13 12				13 27		13 32			13 42				13 57	
Berrylands	d			13 04										13 34								
Shepperton	d					12 41									13 11							
Upper Halliford	d					12 44									13 14							
Sunbury	d					12 46									13 16							
Kempton Park	d					12 48									13 18							
Hampton	d					12 51									13 21							
Fulwell	d					12 54									13 24							
Strawberry Hill	d									13 07	13 08								13 37	13 38		
Teddington	d					12 59				13 11					13 29				13 41			
Hampton Wick	d					13 01				13 14					13 31				13 44			
Kingston	a					13 03				13 16					13 33				13 46			
	d					13 04				13 19					13 34				13 49			
Norbiton	d					13 06				13 21					13 36				13 51			
New Malden	d			13 07		13 10				13 25				13 37	13 40				13 55			
Dorking	d		12 35										13 05									13 35
Boxhill & Westhumble	d																					
Leatherhead	d		12 41				12 54						13 11			13 24						13 41
Ashtead	d		12 44				12 58						13 14			13 28						13 44
Epsom	a		12 49				13 02						13 19			13 32						13 49
	d		12 50				13 05						13 20			13 35						13 50
Ewell West	d		12 53				13 08						13 23			13 38						13 53
Stoneleigh	d		12 55				13 10						13 25			13 40						13 55
Worcester Park	d		12 58				13 13						13 28			13 43						13 58
Chessington South	d								13 10									13 40				
Chessington North	d								13 12									13 42				
Tolworth	d								13 14									13 44				
Malden Manor	d								13 17									13 47				
Motspur Park	d		13 01				13 16		13 20				13 31			13 46		13 50				14 01
Raynes Park	d		13 04	13 10		13 13	13 19		13 23	13 28			13 34	13 40	13 43	13 49		13 53	13 58			14 04
Wimbledon ⊖	d	13 05	13 08	13 14		13 17	13 23	13 20	13 27	13 32		13 35	13 38	13 44	13 47	13 53	13 50	13 57	14 02		14 05	14 08
Earlsfield	d	13 08	13 12	13 17		13 20	13 27	13 24	13 31	13 35		13 38	13 42	13 47	13 50	13 57	13 54	14 01	14 05		14 08	14 12
Clapham Junction	d	13 12	13 16	13 21		13 24	13 31	13 28	13 35	13 39		13 42	13 46	13 51	13 54	14 01	13 58	14 05	14 09		14 12	14 16
Vauxhall ⊖	d	13 17	13 21	13 26		13 29	13 36	13 33	13 40	13 44	13 42	13 47	13 51	13 56	13 59	14 06	14 03	14 10	14 14	14 12	14 17	14 21
London Waterloo ⊖	a	13 22	13 25	13 31	13 25	13 34	13 40	13 37	13 45	13 49	13 46	13 52	13 55	14 01	14 04	14 10	14 07	14 15	14 19	14 16	14 22	14 25

Hampton Court, Shepperton, Guildford, Dorking and Chessington South - London

from 3 October

		SW	SW	SW	SW	SW	SW	SW	SW	SW	SW	SW	SW	SW	SW	SW	SW	SW	SW	SW	SW	SW	SW
Guildford	d			13 28	13 35								13 58	14 05								14 28	14 35
London Road (Guildford)	d			13 32	13 39								14 02	14 09								14 32	14 39
Clandon	d			13 37	13 44								14 07	14 14								14 37	14 44
Horsley	d			13 41	13 48								14 11	14 18								14 41	14 48
Effingham Junction	d			13 46	13 51								14 16	14 21								14 46	14 51
Bookham	d			13 49									14 19									14 49	
Cobham & Stoke d'Abernon	d				13 55									14 25									14 55
Oxshott	d				13 58									14 28									14 58
Claygate	d				14 01									14 31									15 01
Hinchley Wood	d				14 04									14 34									15 04
Hampton Court	d	13 54									14 24									14 54			
Thames Ditton	d	13 56									14 26									14 56			
Surbiton	d	14 02			14 12				14 27		14 32			14 42				14 57		15 02			15 12
Berrylands	d	14 04									14 34									15 04			
Shepperton	d		13 41									14 11									14 41		
Upper Halliford	d		13 44									14 14									14 44		
Sunbury	d		13 46									14 16									14 46		
Kempton Park	d		13 48									14 18									14 48		
Hampton	d		13 51									14 21									14 51		
Fulwell	d		13 54									14 24									14 54		
Strawberry Hill	d						14 07	14 08								14 37	14 38						
Teddington	d		13 59				14 11					14 29				14 41					14 59		
Hampton Wick	d		14 01				14 14					14 31				14 44					15 01		
Kingston	a		14 03				14 16					14 33				14 46					15 03		
	d		14 04				14 19					14 34				14 49					15 04		
Norbiton	d		14 06				14 21					14 36				14 51					15 06		
New Malden	d	14 07	14 10				14 25				14 37	14 40				14 55				15 07	15 10		
Dorking	d									14 05									14 35				
Boxhill & Westhumble	d																						
Leatherhead	d			13 54						14 11			14 24						14 41			14 54	
Ashtead	d			13 58						14 14			14 28						14 44			14 58	
Epsom	a			14 02						14 19			14 32						14 49			15 02	
	d			14 05						14 20			14 35						14 50			15 05	
Ewell West	d			14 08						14 23			14 38						14 53			15 08	
Stoneleigh	d			14 10						14 25			14 40						14 55			15 10	
Worcester Park	d			14 13						14 28			14 43						14 58			15 13	
Chessington South	d					14 10									14 40								
Chessington North	d					14 12									14 42								
Tolworth	d					14 14									14 44								
Malden Manor	d					14 17									14 47								
Motspur Park	d			14 16		14 20				14 31			14 46		14 50				15 01			15 16	
Raynes Park	d	14 10	14 13	14 19		14 23	14 28			14 34	14 40	14 43	14 49		14 53	14 58			15 04	15 10	15 13	15 19	
Wimbledon ⊖	d	14 14	14 17	14 23	14 20	14 27	14 32		14 35	14 38	14 44	14 47	14 53	14 50	14 57	15 02		15 05	15 08	15 14	15 17	15 23	15 20
Earlsfield	d	14 17	14 20	14 27	14 24	14 31	14 35		14 38	14 42	14 47	14 50	14 57	14 54	15 01	15 05		15 08	15 12	15 17	15 20	15 27	15 24
Clapham Junction	d	14 21	14 24	14 31	14 28	14 35	14 39		14 42	14 46	14 51	14 54	15 01	14 58	15 05	15 09		15 12	15 16	15 21	15 24	15 31	15 28
Vauxhall ⊖	d	14 26	14 29	14 36	14 33	14 40	14 44	14 42	14 47	14 51	14 56	14 59	15 06	15 03	15 10	15 14	15 12	15 17	15 21	15 26	15 29	15 36	15 33
London Waterloo ⊖	a	14 31	14 34	14 40	14 37	14 45	14 49	14 46	14 52	14 55	15 01	15 04	15 10	15 07	15 15	15 19	15 16	15 22	15 25	15 31	15 34	15 40	15 37

		SW	SW	SW	SW	SW	SW	SW	SW	SW	SW	SW	SW	SW	SW	SW	SW	SW	SW	SW	SW	SW
Guildford	d								14 58	15 05								15 28	15 35			
London Road (Guildford)	d								15 02	15 09								15 32	15 39			
Clandon	d								15 07	15 14								15 37	15 44			
Horsley	d								15 11	15 18								15 41	15 48			
Effingham Junction	d								15 16	15 21								15 46	15 51			
Bookham	d								15 19									15 49				
Cobham & Stoke d'Abernon	d									15 25									15 55			
Oxshott	d									15 28									15 58			
Claygate	d									15 31									16 01			
Hinchley Wood	d									15 34									16 04			
Hampton Court	d						15 24									15 54						
Thames Ditton	d						15 26									15 56						
Surbiton	d				15 27		15 32			15 42				15 57		16 02			16 12			
Berrylands	d						15 34									16 04						
Shepperton	d							15 11									15 41					
Upper Halliford	d							15 14									15 44					
Sunbury	d							15 16									15 46					
Kempton Park	d							15 18									15 48					
Hampton	d							15 21									15 51					
Fulwell	d							15 24									15 54					
Strawberry Hill	d		15 07	15 08								15 37	15 38								16 07	16 08
Teddington	d		15 11					15 29				15 41					15 59				16 11	
Hampton Wick	d		15 14					15 31				15 44					16 01				16 14	
Kingston	a		15 16					15 33				15 46					16 03				16 16	
	d		15 19					15 34				15 49					16 04				16 19	
Norbiton	d		15 21					15 36				15 51					16 06				16 21	
New Malden	d		15 25				15 37	15 40				15 55				16 07	16 10				16 25	
Dorking	d					15 05									15 35							
Boxhill & Westhumble	d																					
Leatherhead	d					15 11			15 24						15 41			15 54				
Ashtead	d					15 14			15 28						15 44			15 58				
Epsom	a					15 19			15 32						15 49			16 02				
	d					15 20			15 35						15 50			16 05				
Ewell West	d					15 23			15 38						15 53			16 08				
Stoneleigh	d					15 25			15 40						15 55			16 10				
Worcester Park	d					15 28			15 43						15 58			16 13				
Chessington South	d	15 10									15 40									16 10		
Chessington North	d	15 12									15 42									16 12		
Tolworth	d	15 14									15 44									16 14		
Malden Manor	d	15 17									15 47									16 17		
Motspur Park	d	15 20				15 31			15 46		15 50				16 01			16 16		16 20		
Raynes Park	d	15 23	15 28			15 34	15 40	15 43	15 49		15 53	15 58			16 04	16 10	16 13	16 19		16 23	16 28	
Wimbledon ⊖	d	15 27	15 32		15 35	15 38	15 44	15 47	15 53	15 50	15 57	16 02		16 05	16 08	16 14	16 17	16 23	16 20	16 27	16 32	
Earlsfield	d	15 31	15 35		15 38	15 42	15 47	15 50	15 57	15 54	16 01	16 05		16 08	16 12	16 17	16 20	16 27	16 24	16 31	16 35	
Clapham Junction	d	15 35	15 39		15 42	15 46	15 51	15 54	16 01	15 58	16 05	16 09		16 12	16 16	16 21	16 24	16 31	16 28	16 35	16 39	
Vauxhall ⊖	d	15 40	15 44	15 42	15 47	15 51	15 56	15 59	16 06	16 03	16 10	16 14	16 12	16 17	16 21	16 26	16 29	16 36	16 33	16 40	16 44	16 42
London Waterloo ⊖	a	15 45	15 49	15 46	15 52	15 55	16 01	16 04	16 10	16 07	16 15	16 19	16 19	16 22	16 25	16 31	16 34	16 40	16 37	16 45	16 49	16 49

Table 152

Mondays to Fridays

from 3 October

Hampton Court, Shepperton, Guildford, Dorking and Chessington South - London

		SW	SW	SW	SW	SW	SW	SW	SW	SW	SW	SW	SW	SW	SW	SW	SW	SW	SW	SW	SW	SW	SW
Guildford	d					15 58	16 05								16 28	16 35							
London Road (Guildford)	d					16 02	16 09								16 32	16 39							
Clandon	d					16 07	16 14								16 37	16 44							
Horsley	d					16 11	16 18								16 41	16 48							
Effingham Junction 6	d					16 16	16 21								16 46	16 51							
Bookham	d					16 19									16 49								
Cobham & Stoke d'Abernon	d						16 25									16 55							
Oxshott	d						16 28									16 58							
Claygate	d						16 31									17 01							
Hinchley Wood	d						16 34									17 04							
Hampton Court	d			16 24									16 54									17 24	
Thames Ditton	d			16 26									16 56									17 26	
Surbiton 6	d	16 27		16 32			16 42				16 57		17 02			17 12				17 27		17 32	
Berrylands	d			16 34									17 04									17 34	
Shepperton	d				16 11									16 41									17 11
Upper Halliford	d				16 14									16 44									17 14
Sunbury	d				16 16									16 46									17 16
Kempton Park	d				16 18									16 48									17 18
Hampton	d				16 21									16 51									17 21
Fulwell	d				16 24									16 54									17 24
Strawberry Hill	d								16 37	16 38								17 07	17 08				
Teddington	d				16 29				16 43					16 59				17 13					17 29
Hampton Wick	d				16 31				16 46					17 01				17 16					17 31
Kingston	a				16 33				16 48					17 03				17 18					17 33
	d				16 34				16 49					17 04				17 19					17 34
Norbiton	d				16 36				16 51					17 06				17 21					17 36
New Malden 6	d			16 37	16 40				16 55				17 07	17 10				17 25				17 37	17 40
Dorking 4	d		16 05									16 35									17 05		
Boxhill & Westhumble	d																						
Leatherhead	d		16 11			16 24						16 41			16 54						17 11		
Ashtead	d		16 14			16 28						16 44			16 58						17 14		
Epsom 3	a		16 19			16 32						16 49			17 02						17 19		
	d		16 20			16 35						16 50			17 05						17 20		
Ewell West	d		16 23			16 38						16 53			17 08						17 23		
Stoneleigh	d		16 25			16 40						16 55			17 10						17 25		
Worcester Park	d		16 28			16 43						16 58			17 13						17 28		
Chessington South	d							16 40									17 10						
Chessington North	d							16 42									17 12						
Tolworth	d							16 44									17 14						
Malden Manor	d							16 47									17 17						
Motspur Park	d		16 31			16 46		16 50				17 01			17 16		17 20				17 31		
Raynes Park 6	d		16 34	16 40	16 43	16 49		16 53	16 58			17 04	17 10	17 13	17 19		17 23	17 28			17 34	17 40	17 43
Wimbledon 6 ⊖	d	16 35	16 38	16 44	16 47	16 53	16 50	16 57	17 02		17 05	17 08	17 14	17 17	17 23	17 20	17 27	17 32		17 35	17 38	17 44	17 47
Earlsfield	d	16 38	16 42	16 47	16 50	16 57	16 54	17 01	17 05		17 08	17 12	17 17	17 20	17 27	17 24	17 31	17 35		17 38	17 42	17 47	17 50
Clapham Junction 10	d	16 42	16 46	16 51	16 54	17 01	16 58	17 05	17 09		17 12	17 16	17 21	17 24	17 31	17 28	17 35	17 39		17 42	17 46	17 51	17 54
Vauxhall ⊖	d	16 47	16 51	16 56	16 59	17 06	17 03	17 10	17 14	17 12	17 17	17 21	17 26	17 29	17 36	17 33	17 40	17 44	17 42	17 47	17 51	17 56	17 59
London Waterloo 15 ⊖	a	16 52	16 55	17 01	17 05	17 10	17 07	17 16	17 19	17 19	17 22	17 25	17 31	17 35	17 40	17 37	17 45	17 49	17 49	17 52	17 55	18 01	18 05

Table 152

Mondays to Fridays

from 3 October

Hampton Court, Shepperton, Guildford, Dorking and Chessington South - London

		SW	SW	SW	SW	SW	SW	SW	SW	SW	SW	SW	SW	SW	SW	SW	SW	SW	SW	SW	SW	SW	SW
Guildford	d	16 58	17 05									17 28	17 35								17 58	18 05	
London Road (Guildford)	d	17 02	17 09									17 32	17 39								18 02	18 09	
Clandon	d	17 07	17 14									17 37	17 44								18 07	18 14	
Horsley	d	17 11	17 18									17 41	17 48								18 11	18 20	
Effingham Junction 6	d	17 16	17 21									17 46	17 51								18 16	18 23	
Bookham	d	17 19										17 49									18 19		
Cobham & Stoke d'Abernon	d		17 25										17 55									18 27	
Oxshott	d		17 28										17 58									18 30	
Claygate	d		17 31										18 01									18 33	
Hinchley Wood	d		17 34										18 04									18 36	
Hampton Court	d									17 54									18 24				
Thames Ditton	d									17 56									18 26				
Surbiton 6	d		17 42				17 57			18 02			18 12				18 27		18 32			18 42	
Berrylands	d									18 04									18 34				
Shepperton	d										17 41									18 11			
Upper Halliford	d										17 44									18 14			
Sunbury	d										17 46									18 16			
Kempton Park	d										17 48									18 18			
Hampton	d										17 51									18 21			
Fulwell	d										17 54									18 24			
Strawberry Hill	d				17 37	17 38			17 41						18 07	18 08							
Teddington	d				17 43				17b52		17 59				18 13					18 29			
Hampton Wick	d				17 46				17 54		18 01				18 16					18 31			
Kingston	a				17 48				17 56		18 03				18 18					18 33			
	d				17 49				17 58		18 04				18 19					18 34			
Norbiton	d				17 51				18 00		18 06				18 21					18 36			
New Malden 6	d				17 55				18 04	18 07	18 10				18 25				18 37	18 40			
Dorking 4	d							17 35										18 05					
Boxhill & Westhumble	d																						
Leatherhead	d	17 24						17 41				17 54						18 11			18 24		
Ashtead	d	17 28						17 45				17 58						18 14			18 28		
Epsom 3	a	17 32						17 49				18 02						18 19			18 32		
	d	17 35						17 50				18 05						18 20			18 35		
Ewell West	d	17 38						17 53				18 08						18 23			18 38		
Stoneleigh	d	17 40						17 55				18 10						18 25			18 40		
Worcester Park	d	17 43						17 58				18 13						18 28			18 43		
Chessington South	d			17 40										18 10									18 40
Chessington North	d			17 42										18 12									18 42
Tolworth	d			17 44										18 14									18 44
Malden Manor	d			17 47										18 17									18 47
Motspur Park	d	17 46		17 50				18 01				18 16		18 20				18 31			18 46		18 50
Raynes Park 6	d	17 49		17 53	17 58			18 04	18 07	18 10	18 13	18 19		18 23	18 28			18 34	18 40	18 43	18 49		18 53
Wimbledon 6 ⊖	d	17 53	17 50	17 57	18 02		18 05	18 08	18 11	18 14	18 17	18 23	18 20	18 27	18 32		18 35	18 38	18 44	18 47	18 53	18 50	18 57
Earlsfield	d	17 57	17 54	18 01	18 05		18 08	18 12	18 15	18 17	18 20	18 27	18 24	18 31	18 35		18 38	18 42	18 47	18 50	18 57	18 54	19 01
Clapham Junction 10	d	18 01	17 58	18 05	18 09		18 12	18 16	18 19	18 21	18 24	18 31	18 28	18 35	18 39		18 42	18 46	18 51	18 54	19 01	18 58	19 05
Vauxhall ⊖	d	18 06	18 03	18 10	18 14	18 12	18 17	18 21	18 24	18 26	18 29	18 36	18 33	18 40	18 44	18 42	18 47	18 51	18 56	18 59	19 06	19 03	19 10
London Waterloo 15 ⊖	a	18 10	18 07	18 15	18 19	18 19	18 23	18 25	18 29	18 31	18 35	18 40	18 37	18 47	18 49	18 49	18 52	18 55	19 01	19 05	19 10	19 07	19 14

b Arr. 1746

Hampton Court, Shepperton, Guildford, Dorking and Chessington South - London

from 3 October

		SW		SW	SW	SW	SW	SW	SW	SW	SW	SW		SW	SW	SW	SW	SW	SW	SW	SW	SW		SW	SW
Guildford	d								18 35										19 08						
London Road (Guildford)	d								18 39										19 12						
Clandon	d								18 44										19 17						
Horsley	d								18 48										19 21						
Effingham Junction [6]	d								18 51							18 59			19 25						
Bookham	d															19 02									
Cobham & Stoke d'Abernon	d								18 55										19 28						
Oxshott	d								18 58										19 32						
Claygate	d								19 01										19 35						
Hinchley Wood	d								19 04										19 37						
Hampton Court	d						18 54										19 24								
Thames Ditton	d						18 56										19 26								
Surbiton [6]	d				18 57		19 02		19 12						19 27		19 32		19 42						19 57
Berrylands	d						19 04										19 34								
Shepperton	d							18 36										19 06							
Upper Halliford	d							18 39										19 09							
Sunbury	d							18 41										19 11							
Kempton Park	d							18 43										19 13							
Hampton	d							18b51										19c21							
Fulwell	d							18 54										19 24							
Strawberry Hill	d	18 37		18 38								19 07		19 08								19 37		19 38	
Teddington	d	18 43						18 59				19 13						19 29				19 43			
Hampton Wick	d	18 46						19 01				19 16						19 31				19 46			
Kingston	a	18 48						19 03				19 18						19 33				19 48			
	d	18 49						19 04				19 19						19 34				19 49			
Norbiton	d	18 51						19 06				19 21						19 36				19 51			
New Malden [6]	d	18 55					19 07	19 10				19 25					19 37	19 40				19 55			
Dorking [4]	d					18 35				18 50															
Boxhill & Westhumble	d																								
Leatherhead	d					18 41				18 56						19 08									
Ashtead	d					18 45				18 59						19 12									
Epsom [3]	a					18 49				19 04						19 16									
	d					18 50				19 05						19 20				19 35					
Ewell West	d					18 53				19 08						19 23				19 38					
Stoneleigh	d					18 55				19 10						19 25				19 40					
Worcester Park	d					18 58				19 13						19 28				19 43					
Chessington South	d										19 10										19 40				
Chessington North	d										19 12										19 42				
Tolworth	d										19 14										19 44				
Malden Manor	d										19 17										19 47				
Motspur Park	d					19 01				19 16	19 20					19 31				19 46	19 50				
Raynes Park [6]	d	18 58				19 04	19 10	19 13		19 19	19 23	19 28				19 34	19 40	19 43		19 49	19 53	19 58			
Wimbledon [6] ⊖ ⇌	d	19 02			19 05	19 08	19 14	19 17	19 20	19 23	19 27	19 32			19 35	19 38	19 44	19 47	19 50	19 53	19 57	20 02			20 05
Earlsfield	d	19 05			19 08	19 12	19 17	19 20	19 24	19 27	19 31	19 35			19 38	19 42	19 47	19 50	19 54	19 57	20 01	20 05			20 08
Clapham Junction [10]	d	19 09			19 12	19 16	19 21	19 24	19 28	19 31	19 35	19 39			19 42	19 46	19 51	19 54	19 58	20 01	20 05	20 09			20 12
Vauxhall ⊖	d	19 14		19 12	19 17	19 21	19 26	19 29	19 33	19 36	19 40	19 44		19 42	19 47	19 51	19 56	19 59	20 03	20 06	20 10	20 14		20 12	20 17
London Waterloo [15] ⊖	a	19 19		19 16	19 23	19 27	19 31	19 34	19 37	19 41	19 45	19 49		19 46	19 52	19 55	20 01	20 04	20 07	20 10	20 15	20 19		20 16	20 22

b Arr. 1846 c Arr. 1916

Hampton Court, Shepperton, Guildford, Dorking and Chessington South - London

from 3 October

		SW	SW	SW	SW	SW	SW	SW		SW	SW	SW	SW	SW	SW	SW	SW	SW		SW	SW	SW	SW	SW	SW
Guildford	d				19 28	19 35									19 58	20 05									20 35
London Road (Guildford)	d				19 32	19 39									20 02	20 09									20 39
Clandon	d				19 37	19 44									20 07	20 14									20 44
Horsley	d				19 41	19 48									20 11	20 18									20 48
Effingham Junction [6]	d				19 46	19 51									20 16	20 21									20 51
Bookham	d				19 49										20 19										
Cobham & Stoke d'Abernon	d					19 55										20 25									20 55
Oxshott	d					19 58										20 28									20 58
Claygate	d					20 01										20 31									21 01
Hinchley Wood	d					20 04										20 34									21 04
Hampton Court	d		19 54										20 24										20 54		
Thames Ditton	d		19 56										20 26										20 56		
Surbiton [6]	d		20 02			20 12					20 27		20 32			20 42					20 57		21 02		21 12
Berrylands	d		20 04										20 34										21 04		
Shepperton	d			19 41										20 11										20 41	
Upper Halliford	d			19 44										20 14										20 44	
Sunbury	d			19 46										20 16										20 46	
Kempton Park	d			19 48										20 18										20 48	
Hampton	d			19 51										20 21										20 51	
Fulwell	d			19 54										20 24										20 54	
Strawberry Hill	d							20 07		20 08								20 37		20 38					
Teddington	d			19 59				20 11						20 29				20 41						20 59	
Hampton Wick	d			20 01				20 14						20 31				20 44						21 01	
Kingston	a			20 04				20 16						20 33				20 46						21 03	
	d			20 04				20 19						20 34				20 49						21 04	
Norbiton	d			20 06				20 21						20 36				20 51						21 06	
New Malden [6]	d		20 07	20 10				20 25					20 37	20 40				20 55					21 07	21 10	
Dorking [4]	d	19 33										20 05										20 35			
Boxhill & Westhumble	d																								
Leatherhead	d	19 39			19 54							20 11			20 24							20 41			
Ashtead	d	19 42			19 58							20 14			20 28							20 44			
Epsom [3]	a	19 47			20 02							20 19			20 32							20 49			
	d	19 50			20 05							20 20			20 35							20 50			
Ewell West	d	19 53			20 08							20 23			20 38							20 53			
Stoneleigh	d	19 55			20 10							20 25			20 40							20 55			
Worcester Park	d	19 58			20 13							20 28			20 43							20 58			
Chessington South	d						20 10										20 40								
Chessington North	d						20 12										20 42								
Tolworth	d						20 14										20 44								
Malden Manor	d						20 17										20 47								
Motspur Park	d	20 01			20 16		20 20					20 31			20 46		20 50					21 01			
Raynes Park [6]	d	20 04	20 10	20 13	20 19		20 23	20 28				20 34	20 40	20 43	20 49		20 53	20 58				21 04	21 10	21 13	
Wimbledon [6] ⊖ ⇌	d	20 08	20 14	20 17	20 23	20 20	20 27	20 32			20 35	20 38	20 44	20 47	20 53	20 50	20 57	21 02			21 05	21 08	21 14	21 17	21 20
Earlsfield	d	20 12	20 17	20 20	20 27	20 24	20 31	20 35			20 38	20 42	20 47	20 50	20 57	20 54	21 01	21 05			21 08	21 12	21 17	21 20	21 24
Clapham Junction [10]	d	20 16	20 21	20 24	20 31	20 28	20 35	20 39			20 42	20 46	20 51	20 54	21 01	20 58	21 05	21 09			21 12	21 16	21 21	21 24	21 28
Vauxhall ⊖	d	20 21	20 26	20 29	20 36	20 33	20 40	20 44		20 42	20 47	20 51	20 56	20 59	21 06	21 03	21 10	21 14		21 12	21 17	21 21	21 26	21 29	21 33
London Waterloo [15] ⊖	a	20 25	20 31	20 35	20 41	20 38	20 46	20 49		20 46	20 52	20 55	21 01	21 04	21 10	21 07	21 15	21 19		21 16	21 22	21 25	21 31	21 34	21 37

		SW	SW	SW		SW	SW	SW	SW	SW	SW	SW	SW	SW		SW	SW	SW	SW	SW	SW	SW	SW	SW
Guildford	d							20 46			21 05									21 35				21 46
London Road (Guildford)	d							20 50			21 09									21 39				21 50
Clandon	d							20 55			21 14									21 44				21 55
Horsley	d							20 59			21 18									21 48				21 59
Effingham Junction [6]	d							21 03			21 21									21 51				22 03
Bookham	d							21 06																22 06
Cobham & Stoke d'Abernon	d										21 25									21 55				
Oxshott	d										21 28									21 58				
Claygate	d										21 31									22 01				
Hinchley Wood	d										21 34									22 04				
Hampton Court	d								21 24															
Thames Ditton	d								21 26															
Surbiton [6]	d						21 27		21 32		21 42						21 57			22 12			22 27	
Berrylands	d								21 34															
Shepperton	d									21 11									21 41					
Upper Halliford	d									21 14									21 44					
Sunbury	d									21 16									21 46					
Kempton Park	d									21 18									21 48					
Hampton	d									21 21									21 51					
Fulwell	d									21 24									21 54					
Strawberry Hill	d			21 07		21 08								21 37		21 38					22 07	22 08		
Teddington	d			21 11						21 29				21 41					21 59		22 11			
Hampton Wick	d			21 14						21 31				21 44					22 01		22 14			
Kingston	a			21 16						21 33				21 46					22 03		22 16			
	d			21 19						21 34				21 49					22 04		22 19			
Norbiton	d			21 21						21 36				21 51					22 06		22 21			
New Malden [6]	d			21 25					21 37	21 40				21 55					22 10		22 25			
Dorking [4]	d																	21 35						
Boxhill & Westhumble	d																							
Leatherhead	d							21 11										21 41						22 11
Ashtead	d							21 14										21 44						22 14
Epsom [3]	a							21 19										21 49						22 19
	d	21 05						21 20				21 35						21 50						22 20
Ewell West	d	21 08						21 23				21 38						21 53						22 23
Stoneleigh	d	21 10						21 25				21 40						21 55						22 25
Worcester Park	d	21 13						21 28				21 43						21 58						22 28
Chessington South	d		21 10										21 40											
Chessington North	d		21 12										21 42											
Tolworth	d		21 14										21 44											
Malden Manor	d		21 17										21 47											
Motspur Park	d	21 16	21 20					21 31				21 46	21 50					22 01						22 31
Raynes Park [6]	d	21 19	21 23	21 28				21 34	21 40	21 43		21 49	21 53	21 58				22 04	22 13		22 28			22 34
Wimbledon [6] ⊖ ⇌	d	21 23	21 27	21 32			21 35	21 38	21 44	21 47	21 50	21 53	21 57	22 02			22 05	22 08	22 17	22 20	22 32		22 35	22 38
Earlsfield	d	21 27	21 31	21 35			21 38	21 42	21 47	21 50	21 54	21 57	22 01	22 05			22 08	22 12	22 20	22 24	22 35		22 38	22 42
Clapham Junction [10]	d	21 31	21 35	21 39			21 42	21 46	21 51	21 54	21 58	22 01	22 05	22 09			22 12	22 16	22 24	22 28	22 39		22 42	22 46
Vauxhall ⊖	d	21 36	21 40	21 44		21 42	21 47	21 51	21 56	21 59	22 03	22 06	22 10	22 14		22 12	22 17	22 21	22 29	22 33	22 44	22 42	22 47	22 51
London Waterloo [15] ⊖	a	21 40	21 45	21 49		21 46	21 52	21 55	22 01	22 04	22 07	22 10	22 16	22 19		22 16	22 22	22 25	22 34	22 39	22 49	22 46	22 52	22 55

Table 152

Mondays to Fridays
from 3 October

Hampton Court, Shepperton, Guildford, Dorking and Chessington South - London

		SW	SW	SW	SW	SW	SW	SW	SW	SW	SW	SW	SW	SW	SW	SW	SW	SW	SN	SW	SW	SW
Guildford	d			22 05				22 20			22 35			22 46	22 55			23 08				
London Road (Guildford)	d			22 09							22 39			22 50				23 12				
Clandon	d			22 14							22 44			22 55				23 17				
Horsley	d			22 18							22 48			22 59				23 21				
Effingham Junction 6	d			22 21							22 51			23 03				23 24				
Bookham	d													23 06								
Cobham & Stoke d'Abernon	d			22 25							22 55							23 28				
Oxshott	d			22 28							22 58							23 31				
Claygate	d			22 31							23 01							23 34				
Hinchley Wood	d			22 34							23 04							23 37				
Hampton Court	d	22 24														23 24						
Thames Ditton	d	22 26														23 26						
Surbiton 6	d	22 32		22 42				22 57			23 12				23 30	23 33		23 42				
Berrylands	d	22 34														23 35						
Shepperton	d		22 11							22 41							23 11					
Upper Halliford	d		22 14							22 44							23 14					
Sunbury	d		22 16							22 46							23 16					
Kempton Park	d		22 18							22 48							23 18					
Hampton	d		22 21							22 51							23 21					
Fulwell	d		22 24							22 54							23 24					
Strawberry Hill	d					22 37	22 38					23 07	23 08								23 37	23 38
Teddington	d		22 29			22 41				22 59		23 11					23 29				23 41	
Hampton Wick	d		22 31			22 44				23 01		23 14					23 31				23 44	
Kingston	a		22 33			22 46				23 03		23 16					23 33				23 46	
	d		22 34			22 49				23 04		23 19					23 34				23 49	
Norbiton	d		22 36			22 51				23 06		23 21					23 36				23 51	
New Malden 6	d	22 37	22 40			22 55				23 10		23 25				23 38	23 41				23 55	
Dorking 4	d								22 35										23 30			
Boxhill & Westhumble	d																					
Leatherhead	d								22 41					23 11					23 36			
Ashtead	d								22 44					23 14					23 39			
Epsom 3	a								22 49					23 19					23 45			
	d								22 50					23 20								
Ewell West	d								22 53					23 23								
Stoneleigh	d								22 55					23 25								
Worcester Park	d								22 58					23 28								
Chessington South	d				22 40															23 40		
Chessington North	d				22 42															23 42		
Tolworth	d				22 44															23 44		
Malden Manor	d				22 47															23 47		
Motspur Park	d				22 50				23 01					23 31						23 50		
Raynes Park 6	d	22 40	22 43		22 53	22 58			23 04	23 13		23 28		23 37		23 41	23 43			23 54	23 58	
Wimbledon 6 ⊖ ⇌	d	22 44	22 47	22 50	22 57	23 02		23 05	23 08	23 17	23 20	23 32		23 41	23 37	23a45	23 50	23 53		23a57	00 02	
Earlsfield	d	22 47	22 50	22 54	23 01	23 05		23 08	23 12	23 20	23 24	23 36		23 44	23 41		23 53	23 56			00 05	
Clapham Junction 10	d	22 51	22 54	22 58	23 05	23 09		23 12	23 16	23 24	23 28	23 40		23 48	23 45		23 57	23 59			00 09	
Vauxhall ⊖	d	22 56	22 59	23 03	23 10	23 14	23 12	23 17	23 21	23 29	23 33	23 45	23 42	23 53	23 50		00 02	00 05			00 14	00 12
London Waterloo 15 ⊖	a	23 01	23 04	23 07	23 15	23 19	23 16	23 23	23 27	23 34	23 37	23 49	23 46	23 58	23 54		00 10	00 14			00 22	00 16

Table 152

Saturdays
until 1 October

Hampton Court, Shepperton, Guildford, Dorking and Chessington South - London

		SW	SW	SW	SW	SW	SW	SW	SW	SW	SW	SW	SW	SW	SW	SW	SW	SW	SW	SW	SW	SW	SW
Guildford	d		23p08			04 00					05 14												
London Road (Guildford)	d		23p12																				
Clandon	d		23p17																				
Horsley	d		23p21																				
Effingham Junction 6	d		23p24																				
Bookham	d																						
Cobham & Stoke d'Abernon	d		23p28																				
Oxshott	d		23p31																				
Claygate	d		23p34																				
Hinchley Wood	d		23p37																				
Hampton Court	d											05 54					06 24						
Thames Ditton	d											05 56					06 26						
Surbiton 6	d		23p42			04 24					05 57	06 02				06 27	06 32						06 57
Berrylands	d											06 04					06 34						
Shepperton	d	23p11																06 11					
Upper Halliford	d	23p14																06 14					
Sunbury	d	23p16																06 16					
Kempton Park	d	23p18																06 18					
Hampton	d	23p21																06 21					
Fulwell	d	23p24																06 24					
Strawberry Hill	d			23p37	23p38		04 55		05 38					06 07	06 08						06 37	06 38	
Teddington	d	23p29		23p41			04 59			05 44				06 11				06 29			06 41		
Hampton Wick	d	23p31		23p44			05 01			05 46				06 14				06 31			06 44		
Kingston	a	23p33		23p46			05 03			05 48				06 16				06 33			06 46		
	d	23p34		23p49			05 04			05 49				06 19				06 34			06 49		
Norbiton	d	23p36		23p51			05 06			05 51				06 21				06 36			06 51		
New Malden 6	d	23p41		23p55			05 10			05 55		06 07		06 25			06 37	06 40			06 55		
Dorking 4	d																						
Boxhill & Westhumble	d																						
Leatherhead	d																						
Ashtead	d																						
Epsom 3	a																						
	d							05 35					06 05						06 35				
Ewell West	d							05 38					06 08						06 38				
Stoneleigh	d							05 40					06 10						06 40				
Worcester Park	d							05 43					06 13						06 43				
Chessington South	d																			06 40			
Chessington North	d																			06 42			
Tolworth	d																			06 44			
Malden Manor	d																			06 47			
Motspur Park	d							05 46					06 16						06 46	06 50			
Raynes Park 6	d	23p43		23p58			05 13	05 49		05 58		06 10	06 19	06 28			06 40	06 43	06 49	06 53	06 58		
Wimbledon 6 ⊖ ⇌	d	23p50	23p53	00 02		04 32	05 17	05 53		06 02	06 05	06 14	06 23	06 32		06 35	06 44	06 47	06 53	06 57	07 02		07 05
Earlsfield	d	23p53	23p56	00 05			05 21	05 57		06 05	06 08	06 17	06 27	06 35		06 38	06 47	06 50	06 57	07 01	07 05		07 08
Clapham Junction 10	d	23p57	23p59	00 09		04 44	05 25	06 01		06 09	06 12	06 21	06 31	06 39		06 42	06 51	06 54	07 01	07 05	07 09		07 12
Vauxhall ⊖	d	00 02	00 05	00 14	00 12		05 30	06 06	06 12	06 14	06 17	06 26	06 36	06 44	06 42	06 47	06 56	06 59	07 06	07 10	07 14	07 12	07 17
London Waterloo 15 ⊖	a	00 10	00 14	00 22	00 16	04 53	05 35	06 11	06 16	06 19	06 22	06 31	06 40	06 49	06 46	06 52	07 01	07 04	07 10	07 15	07 19	07 16	07 22

		SW	SW	SW	SW	SW	SW	SW	SW	SW	SW	SW	SW	SW	SW	SW	SW	SW	SW	SW	SW	SW	SW
Guildford	d			06 28	06 38							06 58	07 08							07 28	07 38		
London Road (Guildford)	d			06 32	06 42							07 02	07 12							07 32	07 42		
Clandon	d			06 37	06 47							07 07	07 17							07 37	07 47		
Horsley	d			06 41	06 51							07 11	07 21							07 41	07 51		
Effingham Junction 6	d			06 46	06 54							07 16	07 24							07 46	07 54		
Bookham	d			06 49								07 19								07 49			
Cobham & Stoke d'Abernon	d				06 58								07 28								07 58		
Oxshott	d				07 01								07 31								08 01		
Claygate	d				07 04								07 34								08 04		
Hinchley Wood	d				07 07								07 37								08 07		
Hampton Court	d	06 54								07 24								07 54					
Thames Ditton	d	06 56								07 26								07 56					
Surbiton 6	d	07 02			07 12				07 27	07 32			07 42				07 57	08 02			08 12		
Berrylands	d	07 04								07 34								08 04					
Shepperton	d		06 41								07 11								07 41				
Upper Halliford	d		06 44								07 14								07 44				
Sunbury	d		06 46								07 16								07 46				
Kempton Park	d		06 48								07 18								07 48				
Hampton	d		06 51								07 21								07 51				
Fulwell	d		06 54								07 24								07 54				
Strawberry Hill	d						07 07	07 08							07 37	07 38							08 07
Teddington	d		06 59				07 11				07 29				07 41				07 59				08 11
Hampton Wick	d		07 01				07 14				07 31				07 44				08 01				08 14
Kingston	a		07 03				07 16				07 33				07 46				08 03				08 16
	d		07 04				07 19				07 34				07 49				08 04				08 19
Norbiton	d		07 06				07 21				07 36				07 51				08 06				08 21
New Malden 6	d	07 07	07 10				07 25			07 37	07 40				07 55			08 07	08 10				08 25
Dorking 4	d																						
Boxhill & Westhumble	d																						
Leatherhead	d			06 54								07 24								07 54			
Ashtead	d			06 58								07 28								07 58			
Epsom 3	a			07 02								07 32								08 02			
	d			07 05								07 35								08 05			
Ewell West	d			07 08								07 38								08 08			
Stoneleigh	d			07 10								07 40								08 10			
Worcester Park	d			07 13								07 43								08 13			
Chessington South	d					07 10								07 40								08 10	
Chessington North	d					07 12								07 42								08 12	
Tolworth	d					07 14								07 44								08 14	
Malden Manor	d					07 17								07 47								08 17	
Motspur Park	d			07 16		07 20						07 46		07 50						08 16		08 20	
Raynes Park 6	d	07 10	07 13	07 19		07 23	07 28			07 40	07 43	07 49		07 53	07 58			08 10	08 13	08 19		08 23	08 28
Wimbledon 6 ⊖ ⇌	d	07 14	07 17	07 23	07 20	07 27	07 32		07 35	07 44	07 47	07 53	07 50	07 57	08 02		08 05	08 14	08 17	08 23	08 20	08 27	08 32
Earlsfield	d	07 17	07 20	07 27	07 24	07 31	07 35		07 38	07 47	07 50	07 57	07 54	08 01	08 05		08 08	08 17	08 20	08 27	08 24	08 31	08 35
Clapham Junction 10	d	07 21	07 24	07 31	07 28	07 35	07 39		07 42	07 51	07 54	08 01	07 58	08 05	08 09		08 12	08 21	08 24	08 31	08 28	08 35	08 39
Vauxhall ⊖	d	07 26	07 29	07 36	07 33	07 40	07 44	07 42	07 47	07 56	07 59	08 06	08 03	08 10	08 14	08 12	08 17	08 26	08 29	08 36	08 33	08 40	08 44
London Waterloo 15 ⊖	a	07 31	07 34	07 40	07 37	07 45	07 49	07 46	07 52	08 01	08 04	08 10	08 07	08 15	08 19	08 16	08 22	08 31	08 34	08 40	08 37	08 45	08 49

Hampton Court, Shepperton, Guildford, Dorking and Chessington South - London

until 1 October

		SW		SW	SW	SW	SW	SW	SW	SW	SW	SW		SW	SW	SW	SW	SW	SW	SW	SW	SW		SW	SW
Guildford	d							07 58	08 08									08 28	08 38						
London Road (Guildford)	d							08 02	08 12									08 32	08 42						
Clandon	d							08 07	08 17									08 37	08 47						
Horsley	d							08 11	08 21									08 41	08 51						
Effingham Junction 6	d							08 16	08 24									08 46	08 54						
Bookham	d							08 19										08 49							
Cobham & Stoke d'Abernon	d								08 28										08 58						
Oxshott	d								08 31										09 01						
Claygate	d								08 34										09 04						
Hinchley Wood	d								08 37										09 07						
Hampton Court	d					08 24										08 54									
Thames Ditton	d					08 26										08 56									
Surbiton 6	d			08 27		08 32			08 42					08 57		09 02			09 12					09 27	
Berrylands	d					08 34										09 04									
Shepperton	d						08 11										08 41								
Upper Halliford	d						08 14										08 44								
Sunbury	d						08 16										08 46								
Kempton Park	d						08 18										08 48								
Hampton	d						08 21										08 51								
Fulwell	d						08 24										08 54								
Strawberry Hill	d	08 08									08 37	08 38									09 07	09 08			
Teddington	d						08 29				08 41						08 59				09 11				
Hampton Wick	d						08 31				08 44						09 01				09 14				
Kingston	a						08 33				08 46						09 03				09 16				
	d						08 34				08 49						09 04				09 19				
Norbiton	d						08 36				08 51						09 06				09 21				
New Malden 6	d					08 37	08 40				08 55					09 07	09 10				09 25				
Dorking 4	d				08 05										08 35										09 05
Boxhill & Westhumble	d																								
Leatherhead	d				08 11			08 24							08 41			08 54							09 11
Ashtead	d				08 14			08 28							08 44			08 58							09 14
Epsom 3	a				08 19			08 32							08 49			09 02							09 19
	d				08 20			08 35							08 50			09 05							09 20
Ewell West	d				08 23			08 38							08 53			09 08							09 23
Stoneleigh	d				08 25			08 40							08 55			09 10							09 25
Worcester Park	d				08 28			08 43							08 58			09 13							09 28
Chessington South	d									08 40										09 10					
Chessington North	d									08 42										09 12					
Tolworth	d									08 44										09 14					
Malden Manor	d									08 47										09 17					
Motspur Park	d				08 31			08 46		08 50					09 01			09 16		09 20					09 31
Raynes Park 6	d				08 34	08 40	08 43	08 49		08 53	08 58				09 04	09 10	09 13	09 19		09 23	09 28				09 34
Wimbledon 6 ⊖	d			08 35	08 38	08 44	08 47	08 53	08 50	08 57	09 02			09 05	09 08	09 14	09 17	09 23	09 20	09 27	09 32			09 35	09 38
Earlsfield	d			08 38	08 42	08 47	08 50	08 57	08 54	09 01	09 05			09 08	09 12	09 17	09 20	09 27	09 24	09 31	09 35			09 38	09 42
Clapham Junction 10	d			08 42	08 46	08 51	08 54	09 01	08 58	09 05	09 09			09 12	09 16	09 21	09 24	09 31	09 28	09 35	09 39			09 42	09 46
Vauxhall ⊖	d	08 42		08 47	08 51	08 56	08 59	09 06	09 03	09 10	09 14	09 12		09 17	09 21	09 26	09 29	09 36	09 33	09 40	09 44	09 42		09 47	09 51
London Waterloo 15 ⊖	a	08 46		08 52	08 55	09 01	09 04	09 10	09 07	09 15	09 19	09 16		09 22	09 25	09 31	09 34	09 40	09 37	09 45	09 49	09 46		09 52	09 55

		SW	SW	SW	SW	SW	SW	SW		SW	SW	SW	SW	SW	SW	SW	SW	SW		SW	SW	SW	SW	SW	SW
Guildford	d			08 58	09 08									09 28	09 38									09 58	10 08
London Road (Guildford)	d			09 02	09 12									09 32	09 42									10 02	10 12
Clandon	d			09 07	09 17									09 37	09 47									10 07	10 17
Horsley	d			09 11	09 21									09 41	09 51									10 11	10 21
Effingham Junction 6	d			09 16	09 24									09 46	09 54									10 16	10 24
Bookham	d			09 19										09 49										10 19	
Cobham & Stoke d'Abernon	d				09 28										09 58										10 28
Oxshott	d				09 31										10 01										10 31
Claygate	d				09 34										10 04										10 34
Hinchley Wood	d				09 37										10 07										10 37
Hampton Court	d	09 24										09 54										10 24			
Thames Ditton	d	09 26										09 56										10 26			
Surbiton 6	d	09 32			09 42					09 57		10 02			10 12					10 27		10 32			10 42
Berrylands	d	09 34										10 04										10 34			
Shepperton	d		09 11										09 41										10 11		
Upper Halliford	d		09 14										09 44										10 14		
Sunbury	d		09 16										09 46										10 16		
Kempton Park	d		09 18										09 48										10 18		
Hampton	d		09 21										09 51										10 21		
Fulwell	d		09 24										09 54										10 24		
Strawberry Hill	d						09 37	09 38									10 07	10 08							
Teddington	d		09 29				09 41						09 59				10 11						10 29		
Hampton Wick	d		09 31				09 44						10 01				10 14						10 31		
Kingston	a		09 33				09 46						10 03				10 16						10 33		
	d		09 34				09 49						10 04				10 19						10 34		
Norbiton	d		09 36				09 51						10 06				10 21						10 36		
New Malden 6	d	09 37	09 40				09 55					10 07	10 10				10 25					10 37	10 40		
Dorking 4	d										09 35										10 05				
Boxhill & Westhumble	d																								
Leatherhead	d			09 24							09 41			09 54							10 11			10 24	
Ashtead	d			09 28							09 44			09 58							10 14			10 28	
Epsom 3	a			09 32							09 49			10 02							10 19			10 32	
	d			09 35							09 50			10 05							10 20			10 35	
Ewell West	d			09 38							09 53			10 08							10 23			10 38	
Stoneleigh	d			09 40							09 55			10 10							10 25			10 40	
Worcester Park	d			09 43							09 58			10 13							10 28			10 43	
Chessington South	d					09 40										10 10									
Chessington North	d					09 42										10 12									
Tolworth	d					09 44										10 14									
Malden Manor	d					09 47										10 17									
Motspur Park	d			09 46		09 50					10 01			10 16		10 20					10 31			10 46	
Raynes Park 6	d	09 40	09 43	09 49		09 53	09 58				10 04	10 10	10 13	10 19		10 23	10 28				10 34	10 40	10 43	10 49	
Wimbledon 6 ⊖	d	09 44	09 47	09 53	09 50	09 57	10 02			10 05	10 08	10 14	10 17	10 23	10 20	10 27	10 32			10 35	10 38	10 44	10 47	10 53	10 50
Earlsfield	d	09 47	09 50	09 57	09 54	10 01	10 05			10 08	10 12	10 17	10 20	10 27	10 24	10 31	10 35			10 38	10 42	10 47	10 50	10 57	10 54
Clapham Junction 10	d	09 51	09 54	10 01	09 58	10 05	10 09			10 12	10 16	10 21	10 24	10 31	10 28	10 35	10 39			10 42	10 46	10 51	10 54	11 01	10 58
Vauxhall ⊖	d	09 56	09 59	10 06	10 03	10 10	10 14	10 12		10 17	10 21	10 26	10 29	10 36	10 33	10 40	10 44	10 42		10 47	10 51	10 56	10 59	11 06	11 03
London Waterloo 15 ⊖	a	10 01	10 04	10 10	10 07	10 15	10 19	10 16		10 22	10 25	10 31	10 34	10 40	10 37	10 45	10 49	10 46		10 52	10 55	11 01	11 04	11 10	11 07

Hampton Court, Shepperton, Guildford, Dorking and Chessington South - London

		SW	SW	SW		SW	SW	SW	SW	SW	SW	SW	SW	SW		SW	SW	SW	SW	SW	SW	SW	SW	SW	
Guildford	d									10 28	10 38									10 58	11 08				
London Road (Guildford)	d									10 32	10 42									11 02	11 12				
Clandon	d									10 37	10 47									11 07	11 17				
Horsley	d									10 41	10 51									11 11	11 21				
Effingham Junction 6	d									10 46	10 54									11 16	11 24				
Bookham	d									10 49										11 19					
Cobham & Stoke d'Abernon	d										10 58										11 28				
Oxshott	d										11 01										11 31				
Claygate	d										11 04										11 34				
Hinchley Wood	d										11 07										11 37				
Hampton Court	d							10 54										11 24							
Thames Ditton	d							10 56										11 26							
Surbiton 6	d					10 57		11 02			11 12					11 27		11 32			11 42				
Berrylands	d							11 04										11 34							
Shepperton	d								10 41										11 11						
Upper Halliford	d								10 44										11 14						
Sunbury	d								10 46										11 16						
Kempton Park	d								10 48										11 18						
Hampton	d								10 51										11 21						
Fulwell	d								10 54										11 24						
Strawberry Hill	d		10 37	10 38									11 07	11 08									11 37	11 38	
Teddington	d		10 41						10 59				11 11						11 29				11 41		
Hampton Wick	d		10 44						11 01				11 14						11 31				11 44		
Kingston	a		10 46						11 03				11 16						11 33				11 46		
	d		10 49						11 04				11 19						11 34				11 49		
Norbiton	d		10 51						11 06				11 21						11 36				11 51		
New Malden 6	d		10 55					11 07	11 10				11 25					11 37	11 40				11 55		
Dorking 4	d						10 35										11 05								
Boxhill & Westhumble	d																								
Leatherhead	d						10 41			10 54							11 11			11 24					
Ashtead	d						10 44			10 58							11 14			11 28					
Epsom 3	a						10 49			11 02							11 19			11 32					
	d						10 50			11 05							11 20			11 35					
Ewell West	d						10 53			11 08							11 23			11 38					
Stoneleigh	d						10 55			11 10							11 25			11 40					
Worcester Park	d						10 58			11 13							11 28			11 43					
Chessington South	d	10 40										11 10										11 40			
Chessington North	d	10 42										11 12										11 42			
Tolworth	d	10 44										11 14										11 44			
Malden Manor	d	10 47										11 17										11 47			
Motspur Park	d	10 50					11 01			11 16		11 20					11 31			11 46		11 50			
Raynes Park 6	d	10 53	10 58				11 04	11 10	11 13	11 19		11 23	11 28				11 34	11 40	11 43	11 49		11 53	11 58		
Wimbledon 6 ⊖	d	10 57	11 02			11 05	11 08	11 14	11 17	11 23	11 20	11 27	11 32			11 35	11 38	11 44	11 47	11 53	11 50	11 57	12 02		
Earlsfield	d	11 01	11 05			11 08	11 12	11 17	11 20	11 27	11 24	11 31	11 35			11 38	11 42	11 47	11 50	11 57	11 54	12 01	12 05		
Clapham Junction 10	d	11 05	11 09			11 12	11 16	11 21	11 24	11 31	11 28	11 35	11 39			11 42	11 46	11 51	11 54	12 01	11 58	12 05	12 09		
Vauxhall ⊖	d	11 10	11 14	11 12		11 17	11 21	11 26	11 29	11 36	11 33	11 40	11 44	11 42		11 47	11 51	11 56	11 59	12 06	12 03	12 10	12 14	12 12	
London Waterloo 15 ⊖	a	11 15	11 19	11 16		11 22	11 25	11 31	11 34	11 40	11 37	11 45	11 49	11 46		11 52	11 55	12 01	12 04	12 10	12 07	12 15	12 19	12 16	

		SW	SW	SW	SW	SW	SW	SW	SW	SW		SW	SW	SW	SW	SW	SW	SW	SW	SW		SW	SW	SW	SW
Guildford	d					11 28	11 38									11 58	12 08								
London Road (Guildford)	d					11 32	11 42									12 02	12 12								
Clandon	d					11 37	11 47									12 07	12 17								
Horsley	d					11 41	11 51									12 11	12 21								
Effingham Junction 6	d					11 46	11 54									12 16	12 24								
Bookham	d					11 49										12 19									
Cobham & Stoke d'Abernon	d						11 58										12 28								
Oxshott	d						12 01										12 31								
Claygate	d						12 04										12 34								
Hinchley Wood	d						12 07										12 37								
Hampton Court	d			11 54										12 24										12 54	
Thames Ditton	d			11 56										12 26										12 56	
Surbiton 6	d	11 57		12 02			12 12					12 27		12 32			12 42					12 57		13 02	
Berrylands	d			12 04										12 34										13 04	
Shepperton	d				11 41										12 11										12 41
Upper Halliford	d				11 44										12 14										12 44
Sunbury	d				11 46										12 16										12 46
Kempton Park	d				11 48										12 18										12 48
Hampton	d				11 51										12 21										12 51
Fulwell	d				11 54										12 24										12 54
Strawberry Hill	d								12 07	12 08									12 37	12 38					
Teddington	d				11 59				12 11						12 29				12 41						12 59
Hampton Wick	d				12 01				12 14						12 31				12 44						13 01
Kingston	a				12 03				12 16						12 33				12 46						13 03
	d				12 04				12 19						12 34				12 49						13 04
Norbiton	d				12 06				12 21						12 36				12 51						13 06
New Malden 6	d			12 07	12 10				12 25					12 37	12 40				12 55					13 07	13 10
Dorking 4	d		11 35										12 05										12 35		
Boxhill & Westhumble	d																								
Leatherhead	d		11 41			11 54							12 11			12 24							12 41		
Ashtead	d		11 44			11 58							12 14			12 28							12 44		
Epsom 3	a		11 49			12 02							12 19			12 32							12 49		
	d		11 50			12 05							12 20			12 35							12 50		
Ewell West	d		11 53			12 08							12 23			12 38							12 53		
Stoneleigh	d		11 55			12 10							12 25			12 40							12 55		
Worcester Park	d		11 58			12 13							12 28			12 43							12 58		
Chessington South	d							12 10										12 40							
Chessington North	d							12 12										12 42							
Tolworth	d							12 14										12 44							
Malden Manor	d							12 17										12 47							
Motspur Park	d		12 01			12 16		12 20					12 31			12 46		12 50					13 01		
Raynes Park 6	d		12 04	12 10	12 13	12 19		12 23	12 28				12 34	12 40	12 43	12 49		12 53	12 58				13 04	13 10	13 13
Wimbledon 6 ⊖	d	12 05	12 08	12 14	12 17	12 23	12 20	12 27	12 32			12 35	12 38	12 44	12 47	12 53	12 50	12 57	13 02			13 05	13 08	13 14	13 17
Earlsfield	d	12 08	12 12	12 17	12 20	12 27	12 24	12 31	12 35			12 38	12 42	12 47	12 50	12 57	12 54	13 01	13 05			13 08	13 12	13 17	13 20
Clapham Junction 10	d	12 12	12 16	12 21	12 24	12 31	12 28	12 35	12 39			12 42	12 46	12 51	12 54	13 01	12 58	13 05	13 09			13 12	13 16	13 21	13 24
Vauxhall ⊖	d	12 17	12 21	12 26	12 29	12 36	12 33	12 40	12 44	12 42		12 47	12 51	12 56	12 59	13 06	13 03	13 10	13 14	13 12		13 17	13 21	13 26	13 29
London Waterloo 15 ⊖	a	12 22	12 25	12 31	12 34	12 40	12 37	12 45	12 49	12 46		12 52	12 55	13 01	13 04	13 10	13 07	13 15	13 19	13 16		13 22	13 25	13 31	13 34

Table 152

Saturdays
until 1 October

Hampton Court, Shepperton, Guildford, Dorking and Chessington South - London

		SW	SW	SW	SW	SW	SW	SW	SW	SW	SW	SW	SW	SW	SW	SW	SW	SW	SW	SW	SW	SW	SW
Guildford	d	12 28	12 38								12 58	13 08								13 28	13 38		
London Road (Guildford)	d	12 32	12 42								13 02	13 12								13 32	13 42		
Clandon	d	12 37	12 47								13 07	13 17								13 37	13 47		
Horsley	d	12 41	12 51								13 11	13 21								13 41	13 51		
Effingham Junction	d	12 46	12 54								13 16	13 24								13 46	13 54		
Bookham	d	12 49									13 19									13 49			
Cobham & Stoke d'Abernon	d		12 58									13 28									13 58		
Oxshott	d		13 01									13 31									14 01		
Claygate	d		13 04									13 34									14 04		
Hinchley Wood	d		13 07									13 37									14 07		
Hampton Court	d								13 24									13 54					
Thames Ditton	d								13 26									13 56					
Surbiton	d		13 12				13 27		13 32			13 42				13 57		14 02			14 12		
Berrylands	d								13 34									14 04					
Shepperton	d									13 11									13 41				
Upper Halliford	d									13 14									13 44				
Sunbury	d									13 16									13 46				
Kempton Park	d									13 18									13 48				
Hampton	d									13 21									13 51				
Fulwell	d									13 24									13 54				
Strawberry Hill	d				13 07	13 08								13 37	13 38								14 07
Teddington	d				13 11					13 29				13 41					13 59				14 11
Hampton Wick	d				13 14					13 31				13 44					14 01				14 14
Kingston	a				13 16					13 33				13 46					14 03				14 16
	d				13 19					13 34				13 49					14 04				14 19
Norbiton	d				13 21					13 36				13 51					14 06				14 21
New Malden	d				13 25				13 37	13 40				13 55				14 07	14 10				14 25
Dorking	d							13 05									13 35						
Boxhill & Westhumble	d																						
Leatherhead	d	12 54						13 11			13 24						13 41			13 54			
Ashtead	d	12 58						13 14			13 28						13 44			13 58			
Epsom	a	13 02						13 19			13 32						13 49			14 02			
	d	13 05						13 20			13 35						13 50			14 05			
Ewell West	d	13 08						13 23			13 38						13 53			14 08			
Stoneleigh	d	13 10						13 25			13 40						13 55			14 10			
Worcester Park	d	13 13						13 28			13 43						13 58			14 13			
Chessington South	d			13 10									13 40									14 10	
Chessington North	d			13 12									13 42									14 12	
Tolworth	d			13 14									13 44									14 14	
Malden Manor	d			13 17									13 47									14 17	
Motspur Park	d	13 16		13 20				13 31			13 46		13 50				14 01			14 16		14 20	
Raynes Park	d	13 19		13 23	13 28			13 34	13 40	13 43	13 49		13 53	13 58			14 04	14 10	14 13	14 19		14 23	14 28
Wimbledon	d	13 23	13 20	13 27	13 32		13 35	13 38	13 44	13 47	13 53	13 50	13 57	14 02		14 05	14 08	14 14	14 17	14 23	14 20	14 27	14 32
Earlsfield	d	13 27	13 24	13 31	13 35		13 38	13 42	13 47	13 50	13 57	13 54	14 01	14 05		14 08	14 12	14 17	14 20	14 27	14 24	14 31	14 35
Clapham Junction	d	13 31	13 28	13 35	13 39		13 42	13 46	13 51	13 54	14 01	13 58	14 05	14 09		14 12	14 16	14 21	14 24	14 31	14 28	14 35	14 39
Vauxhall	d	13 36	13 33	13 40	13 44	13 42	13 47	13 51	13 56	13 59	14 06	14 03	14 10	14 14	14 12	14 17	14 21	14 26	14 29	14 36	14 33	14 40	14 44
London Waterloo	a	13 40	13 37	13 45	13 49	13 46	13 52	13 55	14 01	14 04	14 10	14 07	14 15	14 19	14 16	14 22	14 25	14 31	14 34	14 40	14 37	14 45	14 49

		SW	SW	SW	SW	SW	SW	SW	SW	SW	SW	SW	SW	SW	SW	SW	SW	SW	SW	SW	SW	SW
Guildford	d						13 58	14 08								14 28	14 38					
London Road (Guildford)	d						14 02	14 12								14 32	14 42					
Clandon	d						14 07	14 17								14 37	14 47					
Horsley	d						14 11	14 21								14 41	14 51					
Effingham Junction	d						14 16	14 24								14 46	14 54					
Bookham	d						14 19									14 49						
Cobham & Stoke d'Abernon	d							14 28									14 58					
Oxshott	d							14 31									15 01					
Claygate	d							14 34									15 04					
Hinchley Wood	d							14 37									15 07					
Hampton Court	d				14 24									14 54								
Thames Ditton	d				14 26									14 56								
Surbiton	d		14 27		14 32			14 42				14 57		15 02			15 12				15 27	
Berrylands	d				14 34									15 04								
Shepperton	d					14 11									14 41							
Upper Halliford	d					14 14									14 44							
Sunbury	d					14 16									14 46							
Kempton Park	d					14 18									14 48							
Hampton	d					14 21									14 51							
Fulwell	d					14 24									14 54							
Strawberry Hill	d	14 08								14 37	14 38								15 07	15 08		
Teddington	d					14 29				14 41					14 59				15 11			
Hampton Wick	d					14 31				14 44					15 01				15 14			
Kingston	a					14 33				14 46					15 03				15 16			
	d					14 34				14 49					15 04				15 19			
Norbiton	d					14 36				14 51					15 06				15 21			
New Malden	d				14 37	14 40				14 55				15 07	15 10				15 25			
Dorking	d			14 05									14 35									15 05
Boxhill & Westhumble	d																					
Leatherhead	d			14 11			14 24						14 41			14 54						15 11
Ashtead	d			14 14			14 28						14 44			14 58						15 14
Epsom	a			14 19			14 32						14 49			15 02						15 19
	d			14 20			14 35						14 50			15 05						15 20
Ewell West	d			14 23			14 38						14 53			15 08						15 23
Stoneleigh	d			14 25			14 40						14 55			15 10						15 25
Worcester Park	d			14 28			14 43						14 58			15 13						15 28
Chessington South	d								14 40									15 10				
Chessington North	d								14 42									15 12				
Tolworth	d								14 44									15 14				
Malden Manor	d								14 47									15 17				
Motspur Park	d			14 31			14 46		14 50				15 01			15 16		15 20				15 31
Raynes Park	d			14 34	14 40	14 43	14 49		14 53	14 58			15 04	15 10	15 13	15 19		15 23	15 28			15 34
Wimbledon	d		14 35	14 38	14 44	14 47	14 53	14 50	14 57	15 02		15 05	15 08	15 14	15 17	15 23	15 20	15 27	15 32		15 35	15 38
Earlsfield	d		14 38	14 42	14 47	14 50	14 57	14 54	15 01	15 05		15 08	15 12	15 17	15 20	15 27	15 24	15 31	15 35		15 38	15 42
Clapham Junction	d		14 42	14 46	14 51	14 54	15 01	14 58	15 05	15 09		15 12	15 16	15 21	15 24	15 31	15 28	15 35	15 39		15 42	15 46
Vauxhall	d	14 42	14 47	14 51	14 56	14 59	15 06	15 03	15 10	15 14	15 12	15 17	15 21	15 26	15 29	15 36	15 33	15 40	15 44	15 42	15 47	15 51
[illegible]	[illegible]	[illegible]	[illegible]	[illegible]	[illegible]	[illegible]	[illegible]	[illegible]	[illegible]	[illegible]	[illegible]	15 22	15 25	15 31	15 34	15 40	15 37	15 45	15 49	15 46	15 52	15 55

Table 152

Saturdays
until 1 October

Hampton Court, Shepperton, Guildford, Dorking and Chessington South - London

		SW	SW	SW	SW	SW	SW	SW	SW	SW	SW	SW	SW	SW	SW	SW	SW	SW	SW	SW	SW	SW	SW
Guildford	d			14 58	15 08								15 28	15 38								15 58	16 08
London Road (Guildford)	d			15 02	15 12								15 32	15 42								16 02	16 12
Clandon	d			15 07	15 17								15 37	15 47								16 07	16 17
Horsley	d			15 11	15 21								15 41	15 51								16 11	16 21
Effingham Junction	d			15 16	15 24								15 46	15 54								16 16	16 24
Bookham	d			15 19									15 49									16 19	
Cobham & Stoke d'Abernon	d				15 28									15 58									16 28
Oxshott	d				15 31									16 01									16 31
Claygate	d				15 34									16 04									16 34
Hinchley Wood	d				15 37									16 07									16 37
Hampton Court	d	15 24									15 54									16 24			
Thames Ditton	d	15 26									15 56									16 26			
Surbiton	d	15 32			15 42				15 57		16 02			16 12				16 27		16 32			16 42
Berrylands	d	15 34									16 04									16 34			
Shepperton	d		15 11									15 41									16 11		
Upper Halliford	d		15 14									15 44									16 14		
Sunbury	d		15 16									15 46									16 16		
Kempton Park	d		15 18									15 48									16 18		
Hampton	d		15 21									15 51									16 21		
Fulwell	d		15 24									15 54									16 24		
Strawberry Hill	d						15 37	15 38								16 07	16 08						
Teddington	d		15 29				15 41					15 59				16 11					16 29		
Hampton Wick	d		15 31				15 44					16 01				16 14					16 31		
Kingston	a		15 33				15 46					16 03				16 16					16 33		
	d		15 34				15 49					16 04				16 19					16 34		
Norbiton	d		15 36				15 51					16 06				16 21					16 36		
New Malden	d	15 37	15 40				15 55				16 07	16 10				16 25				16 37	16 40		
Dorking	d									15 35									16 05				
Boxhill & Westhumble	d																						
Leatherhead	d			15 24						15 41			15 54						16 11			16 24	
Ashtead	d			15 28						15 44			15 58						16 14			16 28	
Epsom	a			15 32						15 49			16 02						16 19			16 32	
	d			15 35						15 50			16 05						16 20			16 35	
Ewell West	d			15 38						15 53			16 08						16 23			16 38	
Stoneleigh	d			15 40						15 55			16 10						16 25			16 40	
Worcester Park	d			15 43						15 58			16 13						16 28			16 43	
Chessington South	d					15 40									16 10								
Chessington North	d					15 42									16 12								
Tolworth	d					15 44									16 14								
Malden Manor	d					15 47									16 17								
Motspur Park	d			15 46		15 50				16 01			16 16		16 20				16 31			16 46	
Raynes Park	d	15 40	15 43	15 49		15 53	15 58			16 04	16 10	16 13	16 19		16 23	16 28			16 34	16 40	16 43	16 49	
Wimbledon	d	15 44	15 47	15 53	15 50	15 57	16 02		16 05	16 08	16 14	16 17	16 23	16 20	16 27	16 32		16 35	16 38	16 44	16 47	16 53	16 50
Earlsfield	d	15 47	15 50	15 57	15 54	16 01	16 05		16 08	16 12	16 17	16 20	16 27	16 24	16 31	16 35		16 38	16 42	16 47	16 50	16 57	16 54
Clapham Junction	d	15 51	15 54	16 01	15 58	16 05	16 09		16 12	16 16	16 21	16 24	16 31	16 28	16 35	16 39		16 42	16 46	16 51	16 54	17 01	16 58
Vauxhall	d	15 56	15 59	16 06	16 03	16 10	16 14	16 12	16 17	16 21	16 26	16 29	16 36	16 33	16 40	16 44	16 42	16 47	16 51	16 56	16 59	17 06	17 03
London Waterloo	a	16 01	16 04	16 10	16 07	16 15	16 19	16 16	16 22	16 25	16 31	16 34	16 40	16 37	16 45	16 49	16 46	16 52	16 55	17 01	17 04	17 10	17 07

		SW	SW	SW	SW	SW	SW	SW	SW	SW	SW	SW	SW	SW	SW	SW	SW	SW	SW	SW	SW	SW
Guildford	d								16 28	16 38								16 58	17 08			
London Road (Guildford)	d								16 32	16 42								17 02	17 12			
Clandon	d								16 37	16 47								17 07	17 17			
Horsley	d								16 41	16 51								17 11	17 21			
Effingham Junction	d								16 46	16 54								17 16	17 24			
Bookham	d								16 49									17 19				
Cobham & Stoke d'Abernon	d									16 58									17 28			
Oxshott	d									17 01									17 31			
Claygate	d									17 04									17 34			
Hinchley Wood	d									17 07									17 37			
Hampton Court	d						16 54									17 24						
Thames Ditton	d						16 56									17 26						
Surbiton	d				16 57		17 02			17 12				17 27		17 32			17 42			
Berrylands	d						17 04									17 34						
Shepperton	d							16 41									17 11					
Upper Halliford	d							16 44									17 14					
Sunbury	d							16 46									17 16					
Kempton Park	d							16 48									17 18					
Hampton	d							16 51									17 21					
Fulwell	d							16 54									17 24					
Strawberry Hill	d		16 37	16 38								17 07	17 08								17 37	17 38
Teddington	d		16 41					16 59				17 11					17 29				17 41	
Hampton Wick	d		16 44					17 01				17 14					17 31				17 44	
Kingston	a		16 46					17 03				17 16					17 33				17 46	
	d		16 49					17 04				17 19					17 34				17 49	
Norbiton	d		16 51					17 06				17 21					17 36				17 51	
New Malden	d		16 55				17 07	17 10				17 25				17 37	17 40				17 55	
Dorking	d					16 35									17 05							
Boxhill & Westhumble	d																					
Leatherhead	d					16 41			16 54						17 11			17 24				
Ashtead	d					16 44			16 58						17 14			17 28				
Epsom	a					16 49			17 02						17 19			17 32				
	d					16 50			17 05						17 20			17 35				
Ewell West	d					16 53			17 08						17 23			17 38				
Stoneleigh	d					16 55			17 10						17 25			17 40				
Worcester Park	d					16 58			17 13						17 28			17 43				
Chessington South	d	16 40									17 10									17 40		
Chessington North	d	16 42									17 12									17 42		
Tolworth	d	16 44									17 14									17 44		
Malden Manor	d	16 47									17 17									17 47		
Motspur Park	d	16 50				17 01			17 16		17 20				17 31			17 46		17 50		
Raynes Park	d	16 53	16 58			17 04	17 10	17 13	17 19		17 23	17 28			17 34	17 40	17 43	17 49		17 53	17 58	
Wimbledon	d	16 57	17 02		17 05	17 08	17 14	17 17	17 23	17 20	17 27	17 32		17 35	17 38	17 44	17 47	17 53	17 50	17 57	18 02	
Earlsfield	d	17 01	17 05		17 08	17 12	17 17	17 20	17 27	17 24	17 31	17 35		17 38	17 42	17 47	17 50	17 57	17 54	18 01	18 05	
Clapham Junction	d	17 05	17 09		17 12	17 16	17 21	17 24	17 31	17 28	17 35	17 39		17 42	17 46	17 51	17 54	18 01	17 58	18 05	18 09	
Vauxhall	d	17 10	17 14	17 12	17 17	17 21	17 26	17 29	17 36	17 33	17 40	17 44	17 42	17 47	17 51	17 56	17 59	18 06	18 03	18 10	18 14	18 12
London Waterloo	a	17 15	17 19	17 16	17 22	17 25	17 31	17 34	17 40	17 37	17 45	17 49	17 46	17 52	17 55	18 01	18 04	18 10	18 07	18 15	18 19	18 16

Hampton Court, Shepperton, Guildford, Dorking and Chessington South - London

		SW	SW	SW	SW	SW	SW	SW	SW	SW	SW	SW	SW	SW	SW	SW	SW	SW	SW	SW	SW	SW	SW
Guildford	d					17 28	17 38								17 58	18 08							
London Road (Guildford)	d					17 32	17 42								18 02	18 12							
Clandon	d					17 37	17 47								18 07	18 17							
Horsley	d					17 41	17 51								18 11	18 21							
Effingham Junction ■	d					17 46	17 54								18 16	18 24							
Bookham	d					17 49									18 19								
Cobham & Stoke d'Abernon	d						17 58									18 28							
Oxshott	d						18 01									18 31							
Claygate	d						18 04									18 34							
Hinchley Wood	d						18 07									18 37							
Hampton Court	d			17 54									18 24									18 54	
Thames Ditton	d			17 56									18 26									18 56	
Surbiton ■	d	17 57		18 02			18 12				18 27		18 32			18 42				18 57		19 02	
Berrylands	d			18 04									18 34									19 04	
Shepperton	d				17 41									18 11									18 41
Upper Halliford	d				17 44									18 14									18 44
Sunbury	d				17 46									18 16									18 46
Kempton Park	d				17 48									18 18									18 48
Hampton	d				17 51									18 21									18 51
Fulwell	d				17 54									18 24									18 54
Strawberry Hill	d								18 07	18 08								18 37	18 38				
Teddington	d				17 59				18 11					18 29				18 41					18 59
Hampton Wick	d				18 01				18 14					18 31				18 44					19 01
Kingston	a				18 03				18 16					18 33				18 46					19 03
	d				18 04				18 19					18 34				18 49					19 04
Norbiton	d				18 06				18 21					18 36				18 51					19 06
New Malden ■	d			18 07	18 10				18 25				18 37	18 40				18 55				19 07	19 10
Dorking ■	d		17 35									18 05									18 35		
Boxhill & Westhumble	d																						
Leatherhead	d		17 41			17 54						18 11			18 24						18 41		
Ashtead	d		17 44			17 58						18 14			18 28						18 44		
Epsom ■	a		17 49			18 02						18 19			18 32						18 49		
	d		17 50			18 05						18 20			18 35						18 50		
Ewell West	d		17 53			18 08						18 23			18 38						18 53		
Stoneleigh	d		17 55			18 10						18 25			18 40						18 55		
Worcester Park	d		17 58			18 13						18 28			18 43						18 58		
Chessington South	d							18 10									18 40						
Chessington North	d							18 12									18 42						
Tolworth	d							18 14									18 44						
Malden Manor	d							18 17									18 47						
Motspur Park	d		18 01			18 16		18 20				18 31			18 46		18 50				19 01		
Raynes Park ■	d		18 04	18 10	18 13	18 19		18 23	18 28			18 34	18 40	18 43	18 49		18 53	18 58			19 04	19 10	19 13
Wimbledon ■ ⊖	d	18 05	18 08	18 14	18 17	18 23	18 20	18 27	18 32		18 35	18 38	18 44	18 47	18 53	18 50	18 57	19 02		19 05	19 08	19 14	19 17
Earlsfield	d	18 08	18 12	18 17	18 20	18 27	18 24	18 31	18 35		18 38	18 42	18 47	18 50	18 57	18 54	19 01	19 05		19 08	19 12	19 17	19 20
Clapham Junction ■	d	18 12	18 16	18 21	18 24	18 31	18 28	18 35	18 39		18 42	18 46	18 51	18 54	19 01	18 58	19 05	19 09		19 12	19 16	19 21	19 24
Vauxhall ⊖	d	18 17	18 21	18 26	18 29	18 36	18 33	18 40	18 44	18 42	18 47	18 51	18 56	18 59	19 06	19 03	19 10	19 14	19 12	19 17	19 21	19 26	19 29
London Waterloo ■ ⊖	a	18 22	18 25	18 31	18 34	18 40	18 37	18 45	18 49	18 46	18 52	18 55	19 01	19 04	19 10	19 07	19 15	19 19	19 16	19 22	19 25	19 31	19 34

		SW	SW	SW	SW	SW	SW	SW	SW	SW	SW	SW	SW	SW	SW	SW	SW	SW	SW	SW	SW	SW	SW
Guildford	d	18 28	18 38								18 58	19 08								19 28	19 38		
London Road (Guildford)	d	18 32	18 42								19 02	19 12								19 32	19 42		
Clandon	d	18 37	18 47								19 07	19 17								19 37	19 47		
Horsley	d	18 41	18 51								19 11	19 21								19 41	19 51		
Effingham Junction ■	d	18 46	18 54								19 16	19 24								19 46	19 54		
Bookham	d	18 49									19 19									19 49			
Cobham & Stoke d'Abernon	d		18 58									19 28									19 58		
Oxshott	d		19 01									19 31									20 01		
Claygate	d		19 04									19 34									20 04		
Hinchley Wood	d		19 07									19 37									20 07		
Hampton Court	d								19 24									19 54					
Thames Ditton	d								19 26									19 56					
Surbiton ■	d		19 12				19 27		19 32			19 42				19 57		20 02			20 12		
Berrylands	d								19 34									20 04					
Shepperton	d									19 11									19 41				
Upper Halliford	d									19 14									19 44				
Sunbury	d									19 16									19 46				
Kempton Park	d									19 18									19 48				
Hampton	d									19 21									19 51				
Fulwell	d									19 24									19 54				
Strawberry Hill	d				19 07	19 08								19 37	19 38								20 07
Teddington	d				19 11					19 29				19 41					19 59				20 11
Hampton Wick	d				19 14					19 31				19 44					20 01				20 14
Kingston	a				19 16					19 33				19 46					20 03				20 16
	d				19 19					19 34				19 49					20 04				20 19
Norbiton	d				19 21					19 36				19 51					20 06				20 21
New Malden ■	d				19 25				19 37	19 40				19 55				20 07	20 10				20 25
Dorking ■	d							19 05									19 35						
Boxhill & Westhumble	d																						
Leatherhead	d	18 54						19 11			19 24						19 41			19 54			
Ashtead	d	18 58						19 14			19 28						19 44			19 58			
Epsom ■	a	19 02						19 19			19 32						19 49			20 02			
	d	19 05						19 20			19 35						19 50			20 05			
Ewell West	d	19 08						19 23			19 38						19 53			20 08			
Stoneleigh	d	19 10						19 25			19 40						19 55			20 10			
Worcester Park	d	19 13						19 28			19 43						19 58			20 13			
Chessington South	d			19 10									19 40									20 10	
Chessington North	d			19 12									19 42									20 12	
Tolworth	d			19 14									19 44									20 14	
Malden Manor	d			19 17									19 47									20 17	
Motspur Park	d	19 16		19 20				19 31			19 46		19 50				20 01			20 16		20 20	
Raynes Park ■	d	19 19		19 23	19 28			19 34	19 40	19 43	19 49		19 53	19 58			20 04	20 10	20 13	20 19		20 23	20 28
Wimbledon ■ ⊖	d	19 23	19 20	19 27	19 32		19 35	19 38	19 44	19 47	19 53	19 50	19 57	20 02		20 05	20 08	20 14	20 17	20 23	20 20	20 27	20 32
Earlsfield	d	19 27	19 24	19 31	19 35		19 38	19 42	19 47	19 50	19 57	19 54	20 01	20 05		20 08	20 12	20 17	20 20	20 27	20 24	20 31	20 35
Clapham Junction ■	d	19 31	19 28	19 35	19 39		19 42	19 46	19 51	19 54	20 01	19 58	20 05	20 09		20 12	20 16	20 21	20 24	20 31	20 28	20 35	20 39
Vauxhall ⊖	d	19 36	19 33	19 40	19 44	19 42	19 47	19 51	19 56	19 59	20 06	20 03	20 10	20 14	20 12	20 17	20 21	20 26	20 29	20 36	20 33	20 40	20 44
London Waterloo ■ ⊖	a	19 40	19 37	19 45	19 49	19 46	19 52	19 55	20 01	20 04	20 10	20 07	20 15	20 19	20 16	20 22	20 25	20 31	20 34	20 40	20 37	20 45	20 49

Hampton Court, Shepperton, Guildford, Dorking and Chessington South - London

		SW	SW	SW	SW	SW	SW	SW	SW	SW	SW	SW	SW	SW	SW	SW	SW	SW	SW	SW	SW	SW
Guildford	d						19 58	20 08								20 38						20 46
London Road (Guildford)	d						20 02	20 12								20 42						20 50
Clandon	d						20 07	20 17								20 47						20 55
Horsley	d						20 11	20 21								20 51						20 59
Effingham Junction ■	d						20 16	20 24								20 54						21 03
Bookham	d						20 19															21 06
Cobham & Stoke d'Abernon	d							20 28								20 58						
Oxshott	d							20 31								21 01						
Claygate	d							20 34								21 04						
Hinchley Wood	d							20 37								21 07						
Hampton Court	d				20 24									20 54								
Thames Ditton	d				20 26									20 56								
Surbiton ■	d		20 27		20 32			20 42				20 57		21 02		21 12					21 27	
Berrylands	d				20 34									21 04								
Shepperton	d					20 11									20 41							
Upper Halliford	d					20 14									20 44							
Sunbury	d					20 16									20 46							
Kempton Park	d					20 18									20 48							
Hampton	d					20 21									20 51							
Fulwell	d					20 24									20 54							
Strawberry Hill	d	20 08								20 37	20 38								21 07	21 08		
Teddington	d					20 29				20 41					20 59				21 11			
Hampton Wick	d					20 31				20 44					21 01				21 14			
Kingston	a					20 33				20 46					21 03				21 16			
	d					20 34				20 49					21 04				21 19			
Norbiton	d					20 36				20 51					21 06				21 21			
New Malden ■	d				20 37	20 40				20 55				21 07	21 10				21 25			
Dorking ■	d			20 05									20 35									
Boxhill & Westhumble	d																					
Leatherhead	d			20 11			20 24						20 41									21 11
Ashtead	d			20 14			20 28						20 44									21 14
Epsom ■	a			20 19			20 32						20 49									21 19
	d			20 20			20 35						20 50				21 05					21 20
Ewell West	d			20 23			20 38						20 53				21 08					21 23
Stoneleigh	d			20 25			20 40						20 55				21 10					21 25
Worcester Park	d			20 28			20 43						20 58				21 13					21 28
Chessington South	d								20 40									21 10				
Chessington North	d								20 42									21 12				
Tolworth	d								20 44									21 14				
Malden Manor	d								20 47									21 17				
Motspur Park	d			20 31			20 46		20 50				21 01				21 16	21 20				21 31
Raynes Park ■	d			20 34	20 40	20 43	20 49		20 53	20 58			21 04	21 10	21 13		21 19	21 23	21 28			21 34
Wimbledon ■ ⊖	d		20 35	20 38	20 44	20 47	20 53	20 50	20 57	21 02		21 05	21 08	21 14	21 17	21 20	21 23	21 27	21 32		21 35	21 38
Earlsfield	d		20 38	20 42	20 47	20 50	20 57	20 54	21 01	21 05		21 08	21 12	21 17	21 20	21 24	21 27	21 31	21 35		21 38	21 42
Clapham Junction ■	d		20 42	20 46	20 51	20 54	21 01	20 58	21 05	21 09		21 12	21 16	21 21	21 24	21 28	21 31	21 35	21 39		21 42	21 46
Vauxhall ⊖	d	20 42	20 47	20 51	20 56	20 59	21 06	21 03	21 10	21 14	21 12	21 17	21 21	21 26	21 29	21 33	21 36	21 40	21 44	21 42	21 47	21 51
London Waterloo ■ ⊖	a	20 46	20 52	20 55	21 01	21 04	21 10	21 07	21 15	21 19	21 16	21 23	21 25	21 31	21 34	21 37	21 40	21 45	21 49	21 46	21 52	21 55

		SW	SW	SW	SW	SW	SW	SW	SW	SW	SW	SW	SW	SW	SW	SW	SW	SW	SW	SW	SW	SW	SW
Guildford	d			21 08								21 38				21 46			22 08				22 20
London Road (Guildford)	d			21 12								21 42				21 50			22 12				
Clandon	d			21 17								21 47				21 55			22 17				
Horsley	d			21 21								21 51				21 59			22 21				
Effingham Junction ■	d			21 24								21 54				22 03			22 24				
Bookham	d															22 06							
Cobham & Stoke d'Abernon	d			21 28								21 58							22 28				
Oxshott	d			21 31								22 01							22 31				
Claygate	d			21 34								22 04							22 34				
Hinchley Wood	d			21 37								22 07							22 37				
Hampton Court	d	21 24															22 24						
Thames Ditton	d	21 26															22 26						
Surbiton ■	d	21 32		21 42					21 57			22 12			22 27		22 32		22 42				22 57
Berrylands	d	21 34															22 34						
Shepperton	d		21 11								21 41							22 11					
Upper Halliford	d		21 14								21 44							22 14					
Sunbury	d		21 16								21 46							22 16					
Kempton Park	d		21 18								21 48							22 18					
Hampton	d		21 21								21 51							22 21					
Fulwell	d		21 24								21 54							22 24					
Strawberry Hill	d						21 37	21 38					22 07	22 08							22 37	22 38	
Teddington	d		21 29				21 41				21 59		22 11					22 29			22 41		
Hampton Wick	d		21 31				21 44				22 01		22 14					22 31			22 44		
Kingston	a		21 33				21 46				22 03		22 16					22 33			22 46		
	d		21 34				21 49				22 04		22 19					22 34			22 49		
Norbiton	d		21 36				21 51				22 06		22 21					22 36			22 51		
New Malden ■	d	21 37	21 40				21 55				22 10		22 25				22 37	22 40			22 55		
Dorking ■	d									21 35													
Boxhill & Westhumble	d																						
Leatherhead	d									21 41						22 11							
Ashtead	d									21 44						22 14							
Epsom ■	a									21 49						22 19							
	d				21 35					21 50						22 20							
Ewell West	d				21 38					21 53						22 23							
Stoneleigh	d				21 40					21 55						22 25							
Worcester Park	d				21 43					21 58						22 28							
Chessington South	d					21 40														22 40			
Chessington North	d					21 42														22 42			
Tolworth	d					21 44														22 44			
Malden Manor	d					21 47														22 47			
Motspur Park	d				21 46	21 50				22 01						22 31				22 50			
Raynes Park ■	d	21 40	21 43		21 49	21 53	21 58			22 04	22 13		22 28			22 34	22 40	22 43		22 53	22 58		
Wimbledon ■ ⊖	d	21 44	21 47	21 50	21 53	21 57	22 02		22 05	22 08	22 17	22 20	22 32		22 35	22 38	22 44	22 47	22 50	22 57	23 02		23 05
Earlsfield	d	21 47	21 50	21 54	21 57	22 01	22 05		22 08	22 12	22 20	22 24	22 35		22 38	22 42	22 47	22 50	22 54	23 01	23 05		23 08
Clapham Junction ■	d	21 51	21 54	21 58	22 01	22 05	22 09		22 12	22 16	22 24	22 28	22 39		22 42	22 46	22 51	22 54	22 58	23 05	23 09		23 12
Vauxhall ⊖	d	21 56	21 59	22 03	22 06	22 10	22 14	22 12	22 17	22 21	22 29	22 33	22 44	22 42	22 47	22 51	22 56	22 59	23 03	23 10	23 14	23 12	23 17
London Waterloo ■ ⊖	a	22 01	22 04	22 07	22 10	22 15	22 19	22 16	22 22	22 25	22 34	22 39	22 49	22 46	22 52	22 55	23 01	23 04	23 07	23 15	23 19	23 17	23 22

Table 152

Saturdays
until 1 October

Hampton Court, Shepperton, Guildford, Dorking and Chessington South - London

		SW	SW	SW		SW	SW	SW	SW	SW	SW	SW	SN	SW		SW	SW
Guildford	d			22 38				22 46	22 55			23 08					
London Road (Guildford)	d			22 42				22 50				23 12					
Clandon	d			22 47				22 55				23 17					
Horsley	d			22 51				22 59				23 21					
Effingham Junction ■	d			22 54				23 03				23 24					
Bookham	d							23 06									
Cobham & Stoke d'Abernon	d			22 58								23 28					
Oxshott	d			23 01								23 31					
Claygate	d			23 04								23 34					
Hinchley Wood	d			23 07								23 37					
Hampton Court	d									23 24							
Thames Ditton	d									23 26							
Surbiton ■	d			23 12					23 30	23 33		23 42					
Berrylands	d									23 35							
Shepperton	d		22 41								23 11						
Upper Halliford	d		22 44								23 14						
Sunbury	d		22 46								23 16						
Kempton Park	d		22 48								23 18						
Hampton	d		22 51								23 21						
Fulwell	d		22 54								23 24						
Strawberry Hill	d					23 07	23 08									23 37	23 38
Teddington	d		22 59			23 11					23 29					23 41	
Hampton Wick	d		23 01			23 14					23 31					23 44	
Kingston	a		23 03			23 16					23 33					23 46	
	d		23 04			23 19					23 34					23 49	
Norbiton	d		23 06			23 21					23 36					23 51	
New Malden ■	d		23 10			23 25				23 38	23 41					23 55	
Dorking ■	d	22 35											23 30				
Boxhill & Westhumble	d																
Leatherhead	d	22 41						23 11					23 36				
Ashtead	d	22 44						23 14					23 39				
Epsom ■	a	22 49						23 19					23 45				
	d	22 50						23 20									
Ewell West	d	22 53						23 23									
Stoneleigh	d	22 55						23 25									
Worcester Park	d	22 58						23 28									
Chessington South	d													23 40			
Chessington North	d													23 42			
Tolworth	d													23 44			
Malden Manor	d													23 47			
Motspur Park	d	23 01						23 31						23 50			
Raynes Park ■	d	23 04	23 13			23 28		23 37		23 41	23 43			23 54		23 58	
Wimbledon ■ ⊖ tram	d	23 08	23 17	23 20		23 32		23 41	23 37	23 46	23 49	23 52		23a57		00 02	
Earlsfield	d	23 12	23 20	23 24		23 35		23 44	23 41	23 50	23 53	23 56				00 05	
Clapham Junction ■	d	23 16	23 24	23 28		23 39		23 48	23 45	23 53	23 56	23 58				00 09	
Vauxhall ⊖	d	23 21	23 29	23 33		23 44	23 42	23 53	23 50	23 58	00 01	00 04				00 15	00 12
London Waterloo ■ ⊖	a	23 25	23 34	23 37		23 49	23 46	23 58	23 54	00 03	00 05	00 14				00 22	00 16

Table 152

Saturdays
from 8 October

Hampton Court, Shepperton, Guildford, Dorking and Chessington South - London

		SW	SW	SW	SW	SW	SW	SW	SW	SW		SW	SW	SW	SW	SW	SW	SW	SW	SW		SW	SW	SW	SW
Guildford	d		23p08			04 00						05 14													
London Road (Guildford)	d		23p12																						
Clandon	d		23p17																						
Horsley	d		23p21																						
Effingham Junction ■	d		23p24																						
Bookham	d																								
Cobham & Stoke d'Abernon	d		23p28																						
Oxshott	d		23p31																						
Claygate	d		23p34																						
Hinchley Wood	d		23p37																						
Hampton Court	d												05 54					06 24							
Thames Ditton	d												05 56					06 26							
Surbiton ■	d		23p42			04 24						05 57	06 02				06 27	06 32							06 57
Berrylands	d												06 04					06 34							
Shepperton	d	23p11																	06 11						
Upper Halliford	d	23p14																	06 14						
Sunbury	d	23p16																	06 16						
Kempton Park	d	23p18																	06 18						
Hampton	d	23p21																	06 21						
Fulwell	d	23p24																	06 24						
Strawberry Hill	d			23p37	23p38		04 55		05 38						06 07	06 08							06 37	06 38	
Teddington	d	23p29		23p41			04 59			05 44					06 11				06 29				06 41		
Hampton Wick	d	23p31		23p44			05 01			05 46					06 14				06 31				06 44		
Kingston	a	23p33		23p46			05 03			05 48					06 16				06 33				06 46		
	d	23p34		23p49			05 04			05 49					06 19				06 34				06 49		
Norbiton	d	23p36		23p51			05 06			05 51					06 21				06 36				06 51		
New Malden ■	d	23p41		23p55			05 10			05 55			06 07		06 25			06 37	06 40				06 55		
Dorking ■	d																								
Boxhill & Westhumble	d																								
Leatherhead	d																								
Ashtead	d																								
Epsom ■	a																								
	d							05 35						06 05						06 35					
Ewell West	d							05 38						06 08						06 38					
Stoneleigh	d							05 40						06 10						06 40					
Worcester Park	d							05 43						06 13						06 43					
Chessington South	d																					06 40			
Chessington North	d																					06 42			
Tolworth	d																					06 44			
Malden Manor	d																					06 47			
Motspur Park	d							05 46						06 16						06 46		06 50			
Raynes Park ■	d	23p43		23p58			05 13	05 49		05 58			06 10	06 19	06 28			06 40	06 43	06 49		06 53	06 58		
Wimbledon ■ ⊖ tram	d	23p50	23p53	00 02		04 32	05 17	05 53		06 02		06 05	06 14	06 23	06 32		06 35	06 44	06 47	06 53		06 57	07 02		07 05
Earlsfield	d	23p53	23p56	00 05			05 21	05 57		06 05		06 08	06 17	06 27	06 35		06 38	06 47	06 50	06 57		07 01	07 05		07 08
Clapham Junction ■	d	23p57	23p59	00 09		04 44	05 25	06 01		06 09		06 12	06 21	06 31	06 39		06 42	06 51	06 54	07 01		07 05	07 09		07 12
Vauxhall ⊖	d	00 02	00 05	00 14	00 12		05 30	06 06	06 12	06 14		06 17	06 26	06 36	06 44	06 42	06 47	06 56	06 59	07 06		07 10	07 14	07 12	07 17
London Waterloo ■ ⊖	a	00 10	00 14	00 22	00 16	04 53	05 35	06 11	06 16	06 19		06 22	06 31	06 40	06 49	06 46	06 52	07 01	07 04	07 10		07 15	07 19	07 16	07 22

		SW	SW	SW	SW	SW		SW	SW	SW	SW	SW	SW	SW	SW	SW		SW	SW	SW	SW	SW	SW	SW	SW
Guildford	d			06 28	06 35								06 58	07 05								07 28	07 35		
London Road (Guildford)	d			06 32	06 39								07 02	07 09								07 32	07 39		
Clandon	d			06 37	06 44								07 07	07 14								07 37	07 44		
Horsley	d			06 41	06 48								07 11	07 18								07 41	07 48		
Effingham Junction ■	d			06 46	06 51								07 16	07 21								07 46	07 51		
Bookham	d			06 49									07 19									07 49			
Cobham & Stoke d'Abernon	d				06 55									07 25									07 55		
Oxshott	d				06 58									07 28									07 58		
Claygate	d				07 01									07 31									08 01		
Hinchley Wood	d				07 04									07 34									08 04		
Hampton Court	d	06 54									07 24									07 54					
Thames Ditton	d	06 56									07 26									07 56					
Surbiton ■	d	07 02			07 12					07 27	07 32			07 42					07 57	08 02			08 12		
Berrylands	d	07 04									07 34									08 04					
Shepperton	d		06 41									07 11									07 41				
Upper Halliford	d		06 44									07 14									07 44				
Sunbury	d		06 46									07 16									07 46				
Kempton Park	d		06 48									07 18									07 48				
Hampton	d		06 51									07 21									07 51				
Fulwell	d		06 54									07 24									07 54				
Strawberry Hill	d							07 07	07 08							07 37		07 38							08 07
Teddington	d		06 59					07 11				07 29				07 41					07 59				08 11
Hampton Wick	d		07 01					07 14				07 31				07 44					08 01				08 14
Kingston	a		07 03					07 16				07 33				07 46					08 03				08 16
	d		07 04					07 19				07 34				07 49					08 04				08 19
Norbiton	d		07 06					07 21				07 36				07 51					08 06				08 21
New Malden ■	d	07 07	07 10					07 25			07 37	07 40				07 55				08 07	08 10				08 25
Dorking ■	d																								
Boxhill & Westhumble	d																								
Leatherhead	d			06 54									07 24									07 54			
Ashtead	d			06 58									07 28									07 58			
Epsom ■	a			07 02									07 32									08 02			
	d			07 05									07 35									08 05			
Ewell West	d			07 08									07 38									08 08			
Stoneleigh	d			07 10									07 40									08 10			
Worcester Park	d			07 13									07 43									08 13			
Chessington South	d					07 10									07 40									08 10	
Chessington North	d					07 12									07 42									08 12	
Tolworth	d					07 14									07 44									08 14	
Malden Manor	d					07 17									07 47									08 17	
Motspur Park	d			07 16		07 20							07 46		07 50							08 16		08 20	
Raynes Park ■	d	07 10	07 13	07 19		07 23		07 28			07 40	07 43	07 49		07 53	07 58				08 10	08 13	08 19		08 23	08 28
Wimbledon ■ ⊖ tram	d	07 14	07 17	07 23	07 20	07 27		07 32		07 35	07 44	07 47	07 53	07 50	07 57	08 02			08 05	08 14	08 17	08 23	08 20	08 27	08 32
Earlsfield	d	07 17	07 20	07 27	07 24	07 31		07 35		07 38	07 47	07 50	07 57	07 54	08 01	08 05			08 08	08 17	08 20	08 27	08 24	08 31	08 35
Clapham Junction ■	d	07 21	07 24	07 31	07 28	07 35		07 39		07 42	07 51	07 54	08 01	07 58	08 05	08 09			08 12	08 21	08 24	08 31	08 28	08 35	08 39
Vauxhall ⊖	d	07 26	07 29	07 36	07 33	07 40		07 44	07 42	07 47	07 56	07 59	08 06	08 03	08 10	08 14		08 12	08 17	08 26	08 29	08 36	08 33	08 40	08 44
London Waterloo ■ ⊖	a	07 31	07 34	07 40	07 37	07 45		07 49	07 46	07 52	08 01	08 04	08 10	08 07	08 15	08 19		08 16	08 22	08 31	08 34	08 40	08 37	08 45	08 49

Hampton Court, Shepperton, Guildford, Dorking and Chessington South - London

		SW		SW	SW	SW	SW	SW	SW	SW	SW	SW		SW	SW	SW	SW	SW	SW	SW	SW	SW		SW	SW
Guildford	d							07 58	08 05									08 28	08 35						
London Road (Guildford)	d							08 02	08 09									08 32	08 39						
Clandon	d							08 07	08 14									08 37	08 44						
Horsley	d							08 11	08 18									08 41	08 48						
Effingham Junction 6	d							08 16	08 21									08 46	08 51						
Bookham	d							08 19										08 49							
Cobham & Stoke d'Abernon	d								08 25										08 55						
Oxshott	d								08 28										08 58						
Claygate	d								08 31										09 01						
Hinchley Wood	d								08 34										09 04						
Hampton Court	d					08 24										08 54									
Thames Ditton	d					08 26										08 56									
Surbiton 6	d			08 27		08 32			08 42					08 57		09 02			09 12					09 27	
Berrylands	d					08 34										09 04									
Shepperton	d						08 11										08 41								
Upper Halliford	d						08 14										08 44								
Sunbury	d						08 16										08 46								
Kempton Park	d						08 18										08 48								
Hampton	d						08 21										08 51								
Fulwell	d						08 24										08 54								
Strawberry Hill	d	08 08									08 37	08 38									09 07	09 08			
Teddington	d						08 29				08 41						08 59				09 11				
Hampton Wick	d						08 31				08 44						09 01				09 14				
Kingston	a						08 33				08 46						09 03				09 16				
	d						08 34				08 49						09 04				09 19				
Norbiton	d						08 36				08 51						09 06				09 21				
New Malden 6	d					08 37	08 40				08 55					09 07	09 10				09 25				
Dorking 4	d				08 05										08 35										09 05
Boxhill & Westhumble	d																								
Leatherhead	d				08 11			08 24							08 41			08 54							09 11
Ashtead	d				08 14			08 28							08 44			08 58							09 14
Epsom 3	a				08 19			08 32							08 49			09 02							09 19
	d				08 20			08 35							08 50			09 05							09 20
Ewell West	d				08 23			08 38							08 53			09 08							09 23
Stoneleigh	d				08 25			08 40							08 55			09 10							09 25
Worcester Park	d				08 28			08 43							08 58			09 13							09 28
Chessington South	d									08 40										09 10					
Chessington North	d									08 42										09 12					
Tolworth	d									08 44										09 14					
Malden Manor	d									08 47										09 17					
Motspur Park	d				08 31			08 46		08 50					09 01			09 16		09 20					09 31
Raynes Park 6	d				08 34	08 40	08 43	08 49		08 53	08 58				09 04	09 10	09 13	09 19		09 23	09 28				09 34
Wimbledon 6 ⊖	d			08 35	08 38	08 44	08 47	08 53	08 50	08 57	09 02			09 05	09 08	09 14	09 17	09 23	09 20	09 27	09 32			09 35	09 38
Earlsfield	d			08 38	08 42	08 47	08 50	08 57	08 54	09 01	09 05			09 08	09 12	09 17	09 20	09 27	09 24	09 31	09 35			09 38	09 42
Clapham Junction 10	d			08 42	08 46	08 51	08 54	09 01	08 58	09 05	09 09			09 12	09 16	09 21	09 24	09 31	09 28	09 35	09 39			09 42	09 46
Vauxhall ⊖	d	08 42		08 47	08 51	08 56	08 59	09 06	09 03	09 10	09 14	09 12		09 17	09 21	09 26	09 29	09 36	09 33	09 40	09 44	09 42		09 47	09 51
London Waterloo 15 ⊖	a	08 46		08 52	08 55	09 01	09 04	09 10	09 07	09 15	09 19	09 16		09 22	09 25	09 31	09 34	09 40	09 37	09 45	09 49	09 46		09 52	09 55

		SW	SW	SW	SW	SW	SW	SW		SW	SW	SW	SW	SW	SW	SW	SW	SW	SW	SW	SW	SW	SW	SW	SW
Guildford	d			08 58	09 05									09 28	09 35									09 58	10 05
London Road (Guildford)	d			09 02	09 09									09 32	09 39									10 02	10 09
Clandon	d			09 07	09 14									09 37	09 44									10 07	10 14
Horsley	d			09 11	09 18									09 41	09 48									10 11	10 18
Effingham Junction 6	d			09 16	09 21									09 46	09 51									10 16	10 21
Bookham	d			09 19										09 49										10 19	
Cobham & Stoke d'Abernon	d				09 25										09 55										10 25
Oxshott	d				09 28										09 58										10 28
Claygate	d				09 31										10 01										10 31
Hinchley Wood	d				09 34										10 04										10 34
Hampton Court	d	09 24										09 54										10 24			
Thames Ditton	d	09 26										09 56										10 26			
Surbiton 6	d	09 32			09 42					09 57		10 02			10 12					10 27		10 32			10 42
Berrylands	d	09 34										10 04										10 34			
Shepperton	d		09 11										09 41										10 11		
Upper Halliford	d		09 14										09 44										10 14		
Sunbury	d		09 16										09 46										10 16		
Kempton Park	d		09 18										09 48										10 18		
Hampton	d		09 21										09 51										10 21		
Fulwell	d		09 24										09 54										10 24		
Strawberry Hill	d						09 37	09 38									10 07	10 08							
Teddington	d		09 29				09 41						09 59				10 11						10 29		
Hampton Wick	d		09 31				09 44						10 01				10 14						10 31		
Kingston	a		09 33				09 46						10 03				10 16						10 33		
	d		09 34				09 49						10 04				10 19						10 34		
Norbiton	d		09 36				09 51						10 06				10 21						10 36		
New Malden 6	d	09 37	09 40				09 55					10 07	10 10				10 25					10 37	10 40		
Dorking 4	d										09 35										10 05				
Boxhill & Westhumble	d																								
Leatherhead	d			09 24							09 41			09 54							10 11			10 24	
Ashtead	d			09 28							09 44			09 58							10 14			10 28	
Epsom 3	a			09 32							09 49			10 02							10 19			10 32	
	d			09 35							09 50			10 05							10 20			10 35	
Ewell West	d			09 38							09 53			10 08							10 23			10 38	
Stoneleigh	d			09 40							09 55			10 10							10 25			10 40	
Worcester Park	d			09 43							09 58			10 13							10 28			10 43	
Chessington South	d					09 40										10 10									
Chessington North	d					09 42										10 12									
Tolworth	d					09 44										10 14									
Malden Manor	d					09 47										10 17									
Motspur Park	d			09 46		09 50					10 01			10 16		10 20					10 31			10 46	
Raynes Park 6	d	09 40	09 43	09 49		09 53	09 58				10 04	10 10	10 13	10 19		10 23	10 28				10 34	10 40	10 43	10 49	
Wimbledon 6 ⊖	d	09 44	09 47	09 53	09 50	09 57	10 02			10 05	10 08	10 14	10 17	10 23	10 20	10 27	10 32			10 35	10 38	10 44	10 47	10 53	10 50
Earlsfield	d	09 47	09 50	09 57	09 54	10 01	10 05			10 08	10 12	10 17	10 20	10 27	10 24	10 31	10 35			10 38	10 42	10 47	10 50	10 57	10 54
Clapham Junction 10	d	09 51	09 54	10 01	09 58	10 05	10 09			10 12	10 16	10 21	10 24	10 31	10 28	10 35	10 39			10 42	10 46	10 51	10 54	11 01	10 58
Vauxhall ⊖	d	09 56	09 59	10 06	10 03	10 10	10 14	10 12		10 17	10 21	10 26	10 29	10 36	10 33	10 40	10 44	10 42		10 47	10 51	10 56	10 59	11 06	11 03
London Waterloo 15 ⊖	a	10 01	10 04	10 10	10 07	10 15	10 19	10 16		10 22	10 25	10 31	10 34	10 40	10 37	10 45	10 49	10 46		10 52	10 55	11 01	11 04	11 10	11 07

Hampton Court, Shepperton, Guildford, Dorking and Chessington South - London

		SW	SW	SW		SW	SW	SW	SW	SW	SW	SW	SW	SW		SW	SW	SW	SW	SW	SW	SW	SW	SW	
Guildford	d									10 28	10 35									10 58	11 05				
London Road (Guildford)	d									10 32	10 39									11 02	11 09				
Clandon	d									10 37	10 44									11 07	11 14				
Horsley	d									10 41	10 48									11 11	11 18				
Effingham Junction 6	d									10 46	10 51									11 16	11 21				
Bookham	d									10 49										11 19					
Cobham & Stoke d'Abernon	d										10 55										11 25				
Oxshott	d										10 58										11 28				
Claygate	d										11 01										11 31				
Hinchley Wood	d										11 04										11 34				
Hampton Court	d							10 54										11 24							
Thames Ditton	d							10 56										11 26							
Surbiton 6	d					10 57		11 02			11 12					11 27		11 32			11 42				
Berrylands	d							11 04										11 34							
Shepperton	d								10 41										11 11						
Upper Halliford	d								10 44										11 14						
Sunbury	d								10 46										11 16						
Kempton Park	d								10 48										11 18						
Hampton	d								10 51										11 21						
Fulwell	d								10 54										11 24						
Strawberry Hill	d		10 37	10 38									11 07	11 08									11 37	11 38	
Teddington	d		10 41						10 59				11 11						11 29				11 41		
Hampton Wick	d		10 44						11 01				11 14						11 31				11 44		
Kingston	a		10 46						11 03				11 16						11 33				11 46		
	d		10 49						11 04				11 19						11 34				11 49		
Norbiton	d		10 51						11 06				11 21						11 36				11 51		
New Malden 6	d		10 55					11 07	11 10				11 25					11 37	11 40				11 55		
Dorking 4	d						10 35										11 05								
Boxhill & Westhumble	d																								
Leatherhead	d						10 41			10 54							11 11			11 24					
Ashtead	d						10 44			10 58							11 14			11 28					
Epsom 3	a						10 49			11 02							11 19			11 32					
	d						10 50			11 05							11 20			11 35					
Ewell West	d						10 53			11 08							11 23			11 38					
Stoneleigh	d						10 55			11 10							11 25			11 40					
Worcester Park	d						10 58			11 13							11 28			11 43					
Chessington South	d	10 40										11 10										11 40			
Chessington North	d	10 42										11 12										11 42			
Tolworth	d	10 44										11 14										11 44			
Malden Manor	d	10 47										11 17										11 47			
Motspur Park	d	10 50					11 01			11 16		11 20					11 31			11 46		11 50			
Raynes Park 6	d	10 53	10 58				11 04	11 10	11 13	11 19		11 23	11 28				11 34	11 40	11 43	11 49		11 53	11 58		
Wimbledon 6 ⊖	d	10 57	11 02			11 05	11 08	11 14	11 17	11 23	11 20	11 27	11 32			11 35	11 38	11 44	11 47	11 53	11 50	11 57	12 02		
Earlsfield	d	11 01	11 05			11 08	11 12	11 17	11 20	11 27	11 24	11 31	11 35			11 38	11 42	11 47	11 50	11 57	11 54	12 01	12 05		
Clapham Junction 10	d	11 05	11 09			11 12	11 16	11 21	11 24	11 31	11 28	11 35	11 39			11 42	11 46	11 51	11 54	12 01	11 58	12 05	12 09		
Vauxhall ⊖	d	11 10	11 14	11 12		11 17	11 21	11 26	11 29	11 36	11 33	11 40	11 44	11 42		11 47	11 51	11 56	11 59	12 06	12 03	12 10	12 14	12 12	
London Waterloo 15 ⊖	a	11 15	11 19	11 16		11 22	11 25	11 31	11 34	11 40	11 37	11 45	11 49	11 46		11 52	11 55	12 01	12 04	12 10	12 07	12 15	12 19	12 16	

		SW	SW	SW	SW	SW	SW	SW	SW	SW		SW	SW	SW	SW	SW	SW	SW	SW	SW		SW	SW	SW	SW
Guildford	d					11 28	11 35									11 58	12 05								
London Road (Guildford)	d					11 32	11 39									12 02	12 09								
Clandon	d					11 37	11 44									12 07	12 14								
Horsley	d					11 41	11 48									12 11	12 18								
Effingham Junction 6	d					11 46	11 51									12 16	12 21								
Bookham	d					11 49										12 19									
Cobham & Stoke d'Abernon	d						11 55										12 25								
Oxshott	d						11 58										12 28								
Claygate	d						12 01										12 31								
Hinchley Wood	d						12 04										12 34								
Hampton Court	d			11 54										12 24										12 54	
Thames Ditton	d			11 56										12 26										12 56	
Surbiton 6	d	11 57		12 02			12 12					12 27		12 32			12 42					12 57		13 02	
Berrylands	d			12 04										12 34										13 04	
Shepperton	d				11 41										12 11										12 41
Upper Halliford	d				11 44										12 14										12 44
Sunbury	d				11 46										12 16										12 46
Kempton Park	d				11 48										12 18										12 48
Hampton	d				11 51										12 21										12 51
Fulwell	d				11 54										12 24										12 54
Strawberry Hill	d								12 07	12 08									12 37	12 38					
Teddington	d				11 59				12 11						12 29				12 41						12 59
Hampton Wick	d				12 01				12 14						12 31				12 44						13 01
Kingston	a				12 03				12 16						12 33				12 46						13 03
	d				12 04				12 19						12 34				12 49						13 04
Norbiton	d				12 06				12 21						12 36				12 51						13 06
New Malden 6	d			12 07	12 10				12 25					12 37	12 40				12 55					13 07	13 10
Dorking 4	d		11 35										12 05										12 35		
Boxhill & Westhumble	d																								
Leatherhead	d		11 41			11 54							12 11			12 24							12 41		
Ashtead	d		11 44			11 58							12 14			12 28							12 44		
Epsom 3	a		11 49			12 02							12 19			12 32							12 49		
	d		11 50			12 05							12 20			12 35							12 50		
Ewell West	d		11 53			12 08							12 23			12 38							12 53		
Stoneleigh	d		11 55			12 10							12 25			12 40							12 55		
Worcester Park	d		11 58			12 13							12 28			12 43							12 58		
Chessington South	d							12 10										12 40							
Chessington North	d							12 12										12 42							
Tolworth	d							12 14										12 44							
Malden Manor	d							12 17										12 47							
Motspur Park	d		12 01			12 16		12 20					12 31			12 46		12 50					13 01		
Raynes Park 6	d		12 04	12 10	12 13	12 19		12 23	12 28				12 34	12 40	12 43	12 49		12 53	12 58				13 04	13 10	13 13
Wimbledon 6 ⊖	d	12 05	12 08	12 14	12 17	12 23	12 20	12 27	12 32			12 35	12 38	12 44	12 47	12 53	12 50	12 57	13 02			13 05	13 08	13 14	13 17
Earlsfield	d	12 08	12 12	12 17	12 20	12 27	12 24	12 31	12 35			12 38	12 42	12 47	12 50	12 57	12 54	13 01	13 05			13 08	13 12	13 17	13 20
Clapham Junction 10	d	12 12	12 16	12 21	12 24	12 31	12 28	12 35	12 39			12 42	12 46	12 51	12 54	13 01	12 58	13 05	13 09			13 12	13 16	13 21	13 24
Vauxhall ⊖	d	12 17	12 21	12 26	12 29	12 36	12 33	12 40	12 44	12 42		12 47	12 51	12 56	12 59	13 06	13 03	13 10	13 14	13 12		13 17	13 21	13 26	13 29
London Waterloo 15 ⊖	a	12 22	12 25	12 31	12 34	12 40	12 37	12 45	12 49	12 46		12 52	12 55	13 01	13 04	13 10	13 07	13 15	13 19	13 16		13 22	13 25	13 31	13 34

Table 152

Saturdays from 8 October

Hampton Court, Shepperton, Guildford, Dorking and Chessington South - London

		SW	SW	SW	SW	SW		SW	SW	SW	SW	SW	SW	SW	SW	SW		SW	SW	SW	SW	SW	SW	SW	SW
Guildford	d	12 28	12 35									12 58	13 05									13 28	13 35		
London Road (Guildford)	d	12 32	12 39									13 02	13 09									13 32	13 39		
Clandon	d	12 37	12 44									13 07	13 14									13 37	13 44		
Horsley	d	12 41	12 48									13 11	13 18									13 41	13 48		
Effingham Junction	d	12 46	12 51									13 16	13 21									13 46	13 51		
Bookham	d	12 49										13 19										13 49			
Cobham & Stoke d'Abernon	d		12 55										13 25										13 55		
Oxshott	d		12 58										13 28										13 58		
Claygate	d		13 01										13 31										14 01		
Hinchley Wood	d		13 04										13 34										14 04		
Hampton Court	d									13 24										13 54					
Thames Ditton	d									13 26										13 56					
Surbiton	d		13 12					13 27		13 32			13 42					13 57		14 02			14 12		
Berrylands	d									13 34										14 04					
Shepperton	d										13 11										13 41				
Upper Halliford	d										13 14										13 44				
Sunbury	d										13 16										13 46				
Kempton Park	d										13 18										13 48				
Hampton	d										13 21										13 51				
Fulwell	d										13 24										13 54				
Strawberry Hill	d				13 07	13 08									13 37	13 38									14 07
Teddington	d				13 11						13 29				13 41						13 59				14 11
Hampton Wick	d				13 14						13 31				13 44						14 01				14 14
Kingston	a				13 16						13 33				13 46						14 03				14 16
	d				13 19						13 34				13 49						14 04				14 19
Norbiton	d				13 21						13 36				13 51						14 06				14 21
New Malden	d				13 25					13 37	13 40				13 55					14 07	14 10				14 25
Dorking	d								13 05										13 35						
Boxhill & Westhumble	d																								
Leatherhead	d	12 54							13 11			13 24							13 41			13 54			
Ashtead	d	12 58							13 14			13 28							13 44			13 58			
Epsom	a	13 02							13 19			13 32							13 49			14 02			
	d	13 05							13 20			13 35							13 50			14 05			
Ewell West	d	13 08							13 23			13 38							13 53			14 08			
Stoneleigh	d	13 10							13 25			13 40							13 55			14 10			
Worcester Park	d	13 13							13 28			13 43							13 58			14 13			
Chessington South	d			13 10										13 40										14 10	
Chessington North	d			13 12										13 42										14 12	
Tolworth	d			13 14										13 44										14 14	
Malden Manor	d			13 17										13 47										14 17	
Motspur Park	d	13 16		13 20					13 31			13 46		13 50					14 01			14 16		14 20	
Raynes Park	d	13 19		13 23	13 28				13 34	13 40	13 43	13 49		13 53	13 58				14 04	14 10	14 13	14 19		14 23	14 28
Wimbledon	d	13 23	13 20	13 27	13 32			13 35	13 38	13 44	13 47	13 53	13 50	13 57	14 02			14 05	14 08	14 14	14 17	14 23	14 20	14 27	14 32
Earlsfield	d	13 27	13 24	13 31	13 35			13 38	13 42	13 47	13 50	13 57	13 54	14 01	14 05			14 08	14 12	14 17	14 20	14 27	14 24	14 31	14 35
Clapham Junction	d	13 31	13 28	13 35	13 39			13 42	13 46	13 51	13 54	14 01	13 58	14 05	14 09			14 12	14 16	14 21	14 24	14 31	14 28	14 35	14 39
Vauxhall	d	13 36	13 33	13 40	13 44	13 42		13 47	13 51	13 56	13 59	14 06	14 03	14 10	14 14	14 12		14 17	14 21	14 26	14 29	14 36	14 33	14 40	14 44
London Waterloo	a	13 40	13 37	13 45	13 49	13 46		13 52	13 55	14 01	14 04	14 10	14 07	14 15	14 19	14 16		14 22	14 25	14 31	14 34	14 40	14 37	14 45	14 49

		SW		SW	SW	SW	SW	SW	SW	SW	SW	SW		SW	SW	SW	SW	SW	SW	SW	SW	SW		SW	SW
Guildford	d							13 58	14 05									14 28	14 35						
London Road (Guildford)	d							14 02	14 09									14 32	14 39						
Clandon	d							14 07	14 14									14 37	14 44						
Horsley	d							14 11	14 18									14 41	14 48						
Effingham Junction	d							14 16	14 21									14 46	14 51						
Bookham	d							14 19										14 49							
Cobham & Stoke d'Abernon	d								14 25										14 55						
Oxshott	d								14 28										14 58						
Claygate	d								14 31										15 01						
Hinchley Wood	d								14 34										15 04						
Hampton Court	d					14 24										14 54									
Thames Ditton	d					14 26										14 56									
Surbiton	d			14 27		14 32			14 42					14 57		15 02			15 12					15 27	
Berrylands	d					14 34										15 04									
Shepperton	d						14 11										14 41								
Upper Halliford	d						14 14										14 44								
Sunbury	d						14 16										14 46								
Kempton Park	d						14 18										14 48								
Hampton	d						14 21										14 51								
Fulwell	d						14 24										14 54								
Strawberry Hill	d	14 08									14 37	14 38									15 07	15 08			
Teddington	d						14 29				14 41						14 59				15 11				
Hampton Wick	d						14 31				14 44						15 01				15 14				
Kingston	a						14 33				14 46						15 03				15 16				
	d						14 34				14 49						15 04				15 19				
Norbiton	d						14 36				14 51						15 06				15 21				
New Malden	d					14 37	14 40				14 55					15 07	15 10				15 25				
Dorking	d				14 05										14 35										15 05
Boxhill & Westhumble	d																								
Leatherhead	d				14 11			14 24							14 41			14 54							15 11
Ashtead	d				14 14			14 28							14 44			14 58							15 14
Epsom	a				14 19			14 32							14 49			15 02							15 19
	d				14 20			14 35							14 50			15 05							15 20
Ewell West	d				14 23			14 38							14 53			15 08							15 23
Stoneleigh	d				14 25			14 40							14 55			15 10							15 25
Worcester Park	d				14 28			14 43							14 58			15 13							15 28
Chessington South	d									14 40										15 10					
Chessington North	d									14 42										15 12					
Tolworth	d									14 44										15 14					
Malden Manor	d									14 47										15 17					
Motspur Park	d				14 31			14 46		14 50					15 01			15 16		15 20					15 31
Raynes Park	d				14 34	14 40	14 43	14 49		14 53	14 58				15 04	15 10	15 13	15 19		15 23	15 28				15 34
Wimbledon	d			14 35	14 38	14 44	14 47	14 53	14 50	14 57	15 02			15 05	15 08	15 14	15 17	15 23	15 20	15 27	15 32			15 35	15 38
Earlsfield	d			14 38	14 42	14 47	14 50	14 57	14 54	15 01	15 05			15 08	15 12	15 17	15 20	15 27	15 24	15 31	15 35			15 38	15 42
Clapham Junction	d			14 42	14 46	14 51	14 54	15 01	14 58	15 05	15 09			15 12	15 16	15 21	15 24	15 31	15 28	15 35	15 39			15 42	15 46
Vauxhall	d	14 42		14 47	14 51	14 56	14 59	15 06	15 03	15 10	15 14	15 12		15 17	15 21	15 26	15 29	15 36	15 33	15 40	15 44	15 42		15 47	15 51
London Waterloo	a	[illegible]		[illegible]	14 55	15 01	15 04	15 10	15 07	15 15	15 19	15 16		15 22	15 25	15 31	15 34	15 40	15 37	15 45	15 49	15 46		15 52	15 55

Table 152

Saturdays from 8 October

Hampton Court, Shepperton, Guildford, Dorking and Chessington South - London

		SW	SW	SW	SW	SW	SW	SW		SW	SW	SW	SW	SW	SW	SW	SW	SW		SW	SW	SW	SW	SW	SW
Guildford	d			14 58	15 05									15 28	15 35									15 58	16 05
London Road (Guildford)	d			15 02	15 09									15 32	15 39									16 02	16 09
Clandon	d			15 07	15 14									15 37	15 44									16 07	16 14
Horsley	d			15 11	15 18									15 41	15 48									16 11	16 18
Effingham Junction	d			15 16	15 21									15 46	15 51									16 16	16 21
Bookham	d			15 19										15 49										16 19	
Cobham & Stoke d'Abernon	d				15 25										15 55										16 25
Oxshott	d				15 28										15 58										16 28
Claygate	d				15 31										16 01										16 31
Hinchley Wood	d				15 34										16 04										16 34
Hampton Court	d	15 24										15 54										16 24			
Thames Ditton	d	15 26										15 56										16 26			
Surbiton	d	15 32			15 42					15 57		16 02			16 12					16 27		16 32			16 42
Berrylands	d	15 34										16 04										16 34			
Shepperton	d		15 11										15 41										16 11		
Upper Halliford	d		15 14										15 44										16 14		
Sunbury	d		15 16										15 46										16 16		
Kempton Park	d		15 18										15 48										16 18		
Hampton	d		15 21										15 51										16 21		
Fulwell	d		15 24										15 54										16 24		
Strawberry Hill	d						15 37	15 38									16 07	16 08							
Teddington	d		15 29				15 41						15 59				16 11						16 29		
Hampton Wick	d		15 31				15 44						16 01				16 14						16 31		
Kingston	a		15 33				15 46						16 03				16 16						16 33		
	d		15 34				15 49						16 04				16 19						16 34		
Norbiton	d		15 36				15 51						16 06				16 21						16 36		
New Malden	d	15 37	15 40				15 55					16 07	16 10				16 25					16 37	16 40		
Dorking	d										15 35										16 05				
Boxhill & Westhumble	d																								
Leatherhead	d			15 24							15 41			15 54							16 11			16 24	
Ashtead	d			15 28							15 44			15 58							16 14			16 28	
Epsom	a			15 32							15 49			16 02							16 19			16 32	
	d			15 35							15 50			16 05							16 20			16 35	
Ewell West	d			15 38							15 53			16 08							16 23			16 38	
Stoneleigh	d			15 40							15 55			16 10							16 25			16 40	
Worcester Park	d			15 43							15 58			16 13							16 28			16 43	
Chessington South	d					15 40										16 10									
Chessington North	d					15 42										16 12									
Tolworth	d					15 44										16 14									
Malden Manor	d					15 47										16 17									
Motspur Park	d			15 46		15 50					16 01			16 16		16 20					16 31			16 46	
Raynes Park	d	15 40	15 43	15 49		15 53	15 58				16 04	16 10	16 13	16 19		16 23	16 28				16 34	16 40	16 43	16 49	
Wimbledon	d	15 44	15 47	15 53	15 50	15 57	16 02			16 05	16 08	16 14	16 17	16 23	16 20	16 27	16 32			16 35	16 38	16 44	16 47	16 53	16 50
Earlsfield	d	15 47	15 50	15 57	15 54	16 01	16 05			16 08	16 12	16 17	16 20	16 27	16 24	16 31	16 35			16 38	16 42	16 47	16 50	16 57	16 54
Clapham Junction	d	15 51	15 54	16 01	15 58	16 05	16 09			16 12	16 16	16 21	16 24	16 31	16 28	16 35	16 39			16 42	16 46	16 51	16 54	17 01	16 58
Vauxhall	d	15 56	15 59	16 06	16 03	16 10	16 14	16 12		16 17	16 21	16 26	16 29	16 36	16 33	16 40	16 44	16 42		16 47	16 51	16 56	16 59	17 06	17 03
London Waterloo	a	16 01	16 04	16 10	16 07	16 15	16 19	16 16		16 22	16 25	16 31	16 34	16 40	16 37	16 45	16 49	16 46		16 52	16 55	17 01	17 04	17 10	17 07

		SW	SW	SW		SW	SW	SW	SW	SW	SW	SW	SW	SW		SW	SW	SW	SW	SW	SW	SW	SW	SW	
Guildford	d									16 28	16 35									16 58	17 05				
London Road (Guildford)	d									16 32	16 39									17 02	17 09				
Clandon	d									16 37	16 44									17 07	17 14				
Horsley	d									16 41	16 48									17 11	17 18				
Effingham Junction	d									16 46	16 51									17 16	17 21				
Bookham	d									16 49										17 19					
Cobham & Stoke d'Abernon	d										16 55										17 25				
Oxshott	d										16 58										17 28				
Claygate	d										17 01										17 31				
Hinchley Wood	d										17 04										17 34				
Hampton Court	d							16 54										17 24							
Thames Ditton	d							16 56										17 26							
Surbiton	d					16 57		17 02			17 12					17 27		17 32			17 42				
Berrylands	d							17 04										17 34							
Shepperton	d								16 41										17 11						
Upper Halliford	d								16 44										17 14						
Sunbury	d								16 46										17 16						
Kempton Park	d								16 48										17 18						
Hampton	d								16 51										17 21						
Fulwell	d								16 54										17 24						
Strawberry Hill	d		16 37	16 38									17 07	17 08									17 37	17 38	
Teddington	d		16 41						16 59				17 11						17 29				17 41		
Hampton Wick	d		16 44						17 01				17 14						17 31				17 44		
Kingston	a		16 46						17 03				17 16						17 33				17 46		
	d		16 49						17 04				17 19						17 34				17 49		
Norbiton	d		16 51						17 06				17 21						17 36				17 51		
New Malden	d		16 55					17 07	17 10				17 25					17 37	17 40				17 55		
Dorking	d						16 35										17 05								
Boxhill & Westhumble	d																								
Leatherhead	d						16 41			16 54							17 11			17 24					
Ashtead	d						16 44			16 58							17 14			17 28					
Epsom	a						16 49			17 02							17 19			17 32					
	d						16 50			17 05							17 20			17 35					
Ewell West	d						16 53			17 08							17 23			17 38					
Stoneleigh	d						16 55			17 10							17 25			17 40					
Worcester Park	d						16 58			17 13							17 28			17 43					
Chessington South	d	16 40										17 10										17 40			
Chessington North	d	16 42										17 12										17 42			
Tolworth	d	16 44										17 14										17 44			
Malden Manor	d	16 47										17 17										17 47			
Motspur Park	d	16 50					17 01			17 16		17 20					17 31			17 46		17 50			
Raynes Park	d	16 53	16 58				17 04	17 10	17 13	17 19		17 23	17 28				17 34	17 40	17 43	17 49		17 53	17 58		
Wimbledon	d	16 57	17 02			17 05	17 08	17 14	17 17	17 23	17 20	17 27	17 32			17 35	17 38	17 44	17 47	17 53	17 50	17 57	18 02		
Earlsfield	d	17 01	17 05			17 08	17 12	17 17	17 20	17 27	17 24	17 31	17 35			17 38	17 42	17 47	17 50	17 57	17 54	18 01	18 05		
Clapham Junction	d	17 05	17 09			17 12	17 16	17 21	17 24	17 31	17 28	17 35	17 39			17 42	17 46	17 51	17 54	18 01	17 58	18 05	18 09		
Vauxhall	d	17 10	17 14	17 12		17 17	17 21	17 26	17 29	17 36	17 33	17 40	17 44	17 42		17 47	17 51	17 56	17 59	18 06	18 03	18 10	18 14	18 12	
London Waterloo	a	17 15	17 19	17 16		17 22	17 25	17 31	17 34	17 40	17 37	17 45	17 49	17 46		17 52	17 55	18 01	18 04	18 10	18 07	18 15	18 19	18 16	

Hampton Court, Shepperton, Guildford, Dorking and Chessington South - London

		SW	SW	SW	SW	SW	SW	SW	SW	SW		SW	SW	SW	SW	SW	SW	SW	SW	SW		SW	SW	SW	SW
Guildford	d					17 28	17 35									17 58	18 05								
London Road (Guildford)	d					17 32	17 39									18 02	18 09								
Clandon	d					17 37	17 44									18 07	18 14								
Horsley	d					17 41	17 48									18 11	18 18								
Effingham Junction 6	d					17 46	17 51									18 16	18 21								
Bookham	d					17 49										18 19									
Cobham & Stoke d'Abernon	d						17 55										18 25								
Oxshott	d						17 58										18 28								
Claygate	d						18 01										18 31								
Hinchley Wood	d						18 04										18 34								
Hampton Court	d			17 54										18 24										18 54	
Thames Ditton	d			17 56										18 26										18 56	
Surbiton 6	d	17 57		18 02			18 12					18 27		18 32			18 42					18 57		19 02	
Berrylands	d			18 04										18 34										19 04	
Shepperton	d				17 41										18 11										18 41
Upper Halliford	d				17 44										18 14										18 44
Sunbury	d				17 46										18 16										18 46
Kempton Park	d				17 48										18 18										18 48
Hampton	d				17 51										18 21										18 51
Fulwell	d				17 54										18 24										18 54
Strawberry Hill	d								18 07	18 08									18 37	18 38					
Teddington	d				17 59				18 11						18 29				18 41						18 59
Hampton Wick	d				18 01				18 14						18 31				18 44						19 01
Kingston	a				18 03				18 16						18 33				18 46						19 03
	d				18 04				18 19						18 34				18 49						19 04
Norbiton	d				18 06				18 21						18 36				18 51						19 06
New Malden 6	d			18 07	18 10				18 25					18 37	18 40				18 55					19 07	19 10
Dorking 4	d		17 35										18 05										18 35		
Boxhill & Westhumble	d																								
Leatherhead	d		17 41			17 54							18 11			18 24							18 41		
Ashtead	d		17 44			17 58							18 14			18 28							18 44		
Epsom 3	a		17 49			18 02							18 19			18 32							18 49		
	d		17 50			18 05							18 20			18 35							18 50		
Ewell West	d		17 53			18 08							18 23			18 38							18 53		
Stoneleigh	d		17 55			18 10							18 25			18 40							18 55		
Worcester Park	d		17 58			18 13							18 28			18 43							18 58		
Chessington South	d							18 10										18 40							
Chessington North	d							18 12										18 42							
Tolworth	d							18 14										18 44							
Malden Manor	d							18 17										18 47							
Motspur Park	d		18 01			18 16		18 20					18 31			18 46		18 50					19 01		
Raynes Park 6	d		18 04	18 10	18 13	18 19		18 23	18 28				18 34	18 40	18 43	18 49		18 53	18 58				19 04	19 10	19 13
Wimbledon 6 ⊖	d	18 05	18 08	18 14	18 17	18 23	18 20	18 27	18 32			18 35	18 38	18 44	18 47	18 53	18 50	18 57	19 02			19 05	19 08	19 14	19 17
Earlsfield	d	18 08	18 12	18 17	18 20	18 27	18 24	18 31	18 35			18 38	18 42	18 47	18 50	18 57	18 54	19 01	19 05			19 08	19 12	19 17	19 20
Clapham Junction 10	d	18 12	18 16	18 21	18 24	18 31	18 28	18 35	18 39			18 42	18 46	18 51	18 54	19 01	18 58	19 05	19 09			19 12	19 16	19 21	19 24
Vauxhall ⊖	d	18 17	18 21	18 26	18 29	18 36	18 33	18 40	18 44	18 42		18 47	18 51	18 56	18 59	19 06	19 03	19 10	19 14	19 12		19 17	19 21	19 26	19 29
London Waterloo 15 ⊖	a	18 22	18 25	18 31	18 34	18 40	18 37	18 45	18 49	18 46		18 52	18 55	19 01	19 04	19 10	19 07	19 15	19 19	19 16		19 22	19 25	19 31	19 34

		SW	SW	SW	SW	SW		SW	SW	SW	SW	SW	SW	SW	SW	SW		SW	SW	SW	SW	SW	SW	SW	SW
Guildford	d	18 28	18 35									18 58	19 05									19 28	19 35		
London Road (Guildford)	d	18 32	18 39									19 02	19 09									19 32	19 39		
Clandon	d	18 37	18 44									19 07	19 14									19 37	19 44		
Horsley	d	18 41	18 48									19 11	19 18									19 41	19 48		
Effingham Junction 6	d	18 46	18 51									19 16	19 21									19 46	19 51		
Bookham	d	18 49										19 19										19 49			
Cobham & Stoke d'Abernon	d		18 55										19 25										19 55		
Oxshott	d		18 58										19 28										19 58		
Claygate	d		19 01										19 31										20 01		
Hinchley Wood	d		19 04										19 34										20 04		
Hampton Court	d									19 24										19 54					
Thames Ditton	d									19 26										19 56					
Surbiton 6	d		19 12					19 27		19 32			19 42					19 57		20 02			20 12		
Berrylands	d									19 34										20 04					
Shepperton	d										19 11										19 41				
Upper Halliford	d										19 14										19 44				
Sunbury	d										19 16										19 46				
Kempton Park	d										19 18										19 48				
Hampton	d										19 21										19 51				
Fulwell	d										19 24										19 54				
Strawberry Hill	d				19 07	19 08									19 37	19 38									20 07
Teddington	d				19 11						19 29				19 41						19 59				20 11
Hampton Wick	d				19 14						19 31				19 44						20 01				20 14
Kingston	a				19 16						19 33				19 46						20 03				20 16
	d				19 19						19 34				19 49						20 04				20 19
Norbiton	d				19 21						19 36				19 51						20 06				20 21
New Malden 6	d				19 25					19 37	19 40				19 55					20 07	20 10				20 25
Dorking 4	d								19 05										19 35						
Boxhill & Westhumble	d																								
Leatherhead	d	18 54							19 11			19 24							19 41			19 54			
Ashtead	d	18 58							19 14			19 28							19 44			19 58			
Epsom 3	a	19 02							19 19			19 32							19 49			20 02			
	d	19 05							19 20			19 35							19 50			20 05			
Ewell West	d	19 08							19 23			19 38							19 53			20 08			
Stoneleigh	d	19 10							19 25			19 40							19 55			20 10			
Worcester Park	d	19 13							19 28			19 43							19 58			20 13			
Chessington South	d			19 10										19 40										20 10	
Chessington North	d			19 12										19 42										20 12	
Tolworth	d			19 14										19 44										20 14	
Malden Manor	d			19 17										19 47										20 17	
Motspur Park	d	19 16		19 20					19 31			19 46		19 50					20 01			20 16		20 20	
Raynes Park 6	d	19 19		19 23	19 28				19 34	19 40	19 43	19 49		19 53	19 58				20 04	20 10	20 13	20 19		20 23	20 28
Wimbledon 6 ⊖	d	19 23	19 20	19 27	19 32			19 35	19 38	19 44	19 47	19 53	19 50	19 57	20 02			20 05	20 08	20 14	20 17	20 23	20 20	20 27	20 32
Earlsfield	d	19 27	19 24	19 31	19 35			19 38	19 42	19 47	19 50	19 57	19 54	20 01	20 05			20 08	20 12	20 17	20 20	20 27	20 24	20 31	20 35
Clapham Junction 10	d	19 31	19 28	19 35	19 39			19 42	19 46	19 51	19 54	20 01	19 58	20 05	20 09			20 12	20 16	20 21	20 24	20 31	20 28	20 35	20 39
Vauxhall ⊖	d	19 36	19 33	19 40	19 44	19 42		19 47	19 51	19 56	19 59	20 06	20 03	20 10	20 14	20 12		20 17	20 21	20 26	20 29	20 36	20 33	20 40	20 44
London Waterloo 15 ⊖	a	19 40	19 37	19 45	19 49	19 46		19 52	19 55	20 01	20 04	20 10	20 07	20 15	20 19	20 16		20 22	20 25	20 31	20 34	20 40	20 37	20 45	20 49

Hampton Court, Shepperton, Guildford, Dorking and Chessington South - London

		SW		SW	SW	SW	SW	SW	SW	SW	SW	SW		SW	SW	SW	SW	SW	SW	SW	SW	SW		SW	SW
Guildford	d							19 58	20 05									20 35							20 46
London Road (Guildford)	d							20 02	20 09									20 39							20 50
Clandon	d							20 07	20 14									20 44							20 55
Horsley	d							20 11	20 18									20 48							20 59
Effingham Junction 6	d							20 16	20 21									20 51							21 03
Bookham	d							20 19																	21 06
Cobham & Stoke d'Abernon	d								20 25									20 55							
Oxshott	d								20 28									20 58							
Claygate	d								20 31									21 01							
Hinchley Wood	d								20 34									21 04							
Hampton Court	d					20 24										20 54									
Thames Ditton	d					20 26										20 56									
Surbiton 6	d			20 27		20 32			20 42					20 57		21 02		21 12						21 27	
Berrylands	d					20 34										21 04									
Shepperton	d						20 11										20 41								
Upper Halliford	d						20 14										20 44								
Sunbury	d						20 16										20 46								
Kempton Park	d						20 18										20 48								
Hampton	d						20 21										20 51								
Fulwell	d						20 24										20 54								
Strawberry Hill	d	20 08									20 37	20 38									21 07	21 08			
Teddington	d						20 29				20 41						20 59				21 11				
Hampton Wick	d						20 31				20 44						21 01				21 14				
Kingston	a						20 33				20 46						21 03				21 16				
	d						20 34				20 49						21 04				21 19				
Norbiton	d						20 36				20 51						21 06				21 21				
New Malden 6	d					20 37	20 40				20 55					21 07	21 10				21 25				
Dorking 4	d				20 05										20 35										
Boxhill & Westhumble	d																								
Leatherhead	d				20 11			20 24							20 41										21 11
Ashtead	d				20 14			20 28							20 44										21 14
Epsom 3	a				20 19			20 32							20 49										21 19
	d				20 20			20 35							20 50				21 05						21 20
Ewell West	d				20 23			20 38							20 53				21 08						21 23
Stoneleigh	d				20 25			20 40							20 55				21 10						21 25
Worcester Park	d				20 28			20 43							20 58				21 13						21 28
Chessington South	d									20 40										21 10					
Chessington North	d									20 42										21 12					
Tolworth	d									20 44										21 14					
Malden Manor	d									20 47										21 17					
Motspur Park	d				20 31			20 46		20 50					21 01				21 16	21 20					21 31
Raynes Park 6	d				20 34	20 40	20 43	20 49		20 53	20 58				21 04	21 10	21 13		21 19	21 23	21 28				21 34
Wimbledon 6 ⊖	d			20 35	20 38	20 44	20 47	20 53	20 50	20 57	21 02			21 05	21 08	21 14	21 17	21 20	21 23	21 27	21 32			21 35	21 38
Earlsfield	d			20 38	20 42	20 47	20 50	20 57	20 54	21 01	21 05			21 08	21 12	21 17	21 20	21 24	21 27	21 31	21 35			21 38	21 42
Clapham Junction 10	d			20 42	20 46	20 51	20 54	21 01	20 58	21 05	21 09			21 12	21 16	21 21	21 24	21 28	21 31	21 35	21 39			21 42	21 46
Vauxhall ⊖	d	20 42		20 47	20 51	20 56	20 59	21 06	21 03	21 10	21 14	21 12		21 17	21 21	21 26	21 29	21 33	21 36	21 40	21 44	21 42		21 47	21 51
London Waterloo 15 ⊖	a	20 46		20 52	20 55	21 01	21 04	21 10	21 07	21 15	21 19	21 16		21 23	21 25	21 31	21 34	21 37	21 40	21 45	21 49	21 46		21 52	21 55

		SW	SW	SW	SW	SW	SW	SW		SW	SW	SW	SW	SW	SW	SW	SW	SW		SW	SW	SW	SW	SW	SW
Guildford	d			21 05									21 35				21 46				22 05				22 20
London Road (Guildford)	d			21 09									21 39				21 50				22 09				
Clandon	d			21 14									21 44				21 55				22 14				
Horsley	d			21 18									21 48				21 59				22 18				
Effingham Junction 6	d			21 21									21 51				22 03				22 21				
Bookham	d																22 06								
Cobham & Stoke d'Abernon	d			21 25									21 55								22 25				
Oxshott	d			21 28									21 58								22 28				
Claygate	d			21 31									22 01								22 31				
Hinchley Wood	d			21 34									22 04								22 34				
Hampton Court	d	21 24																22 24							
Thames Ditton	d	21 26																22 26							
Surbiton 6	d	21 32		21 42						21 57			22 12			22 27		22 32			22 42				22 57
Berrylands	d	21 34																22 34							
Shepperton	d		21 11									21 41								22 11					
Upper Halliford	d		21 14									21 44								22 14					
Sunbury	d		21 16									21 46								22 16					
Kempton Park	d		21 18									21 48								22 18					
Hampton	d		21 21									21 51								22 21					
Fulwell	d		21 24									21 54								22 24					
Strawberry Hill	d						21 37	21 38						22 07	22 08								22 37	22 38	
Teddington	d		21 29				21 41					21 59		22 11						22 29			22 41		
Hampton Wick	d		21 31				21 44					22 01		22 14						22 31			22 44		
Kingston	a		21 33				21 46					22 03		22 16						22 33			22 46		
	d		21 34				21 49					22 04		22 19						22 34			22 49		
Norbiton	d		21 36				21 51					22 06		22 21						22 36			22 51		
New Malden 6	d	21 37	21 40				21 55					22 10		22 25				22 37		22 40			22 55		
Dorking 4	d										21 35														
Boxhill & Westhumble	d																								
Leatherhead	d										21 41						22 11								
Ashtead	d										21 44						22 14								
Epsom 3	a										21 49						22 19								
	d				21 35						21 50						22 20								
Ewell West	d				21 38						21 53						22 23								
Stoneleigh	d				21 40						21 55						22 25								
Worcester Park	d				21 43						21 58						22 28								
Chessington South	d					21 40																22 40			
Chessington North	d					21 42																22 42			
Tolworth	d					21 44																22 44			
Malden Manor	d					21 47																22 47			
Motspur Park	d				21 46	21 50					22 01						22 31					22 50			
Raynes Park 6	d	21 40	21 43		21 49	21 53	21 58				22 04	22 13		22 28			22 34	22 40		22 43		22 53	22 58		
Wimbledon 6 ⊖	d	21 44	21 47	21 50	21 53	21 57	22 02			22 05	22 08	22 17	22 20	22 32		22 35	22 38	22 44		22 47	22 50	22 57	23 02		23 05
Earlsfield	d	21 47	21 50	21 54	21 57	22 01	22 05			22 08	22 12	22 20	22 24	22 35		22 38	22 42	22 47		22 50	22 54	23 01	23 05		23 08
Clapham Junction 10	d	21 51	21 54	21 58	22 01	22 05	22 09			22 12	22 16	22 24	22 28	22 39		22 42	22 46	22 51		22 54	22 58	23 05	23 09		23 12
Vauxhall ⊖	d	21 56	21 59	22 03	22 06	22 10	22 14	22 12		22 17	22 21	22 29	22 33	22 44	22 42	22 47	22 51	22 56		22 59	23 03	23 10	23 14	23 12	23 17
London Waterloo 15 ⊖	a	22 01	22 04	22 07	22 10	22 15	22 19	22 16		22 22	22 25	22 34	22 39	22 49	22 46	22 52	22 55	23 01		23 04	23 07	23 15	23 19	23 17	23 22

Table 152

Saturdays from 8 October

Hampton Court, Shepperton, Guildford, Dorking and Chessington South - London

		SW	SW	SW	SW	SW	SW	SW	SW	SW	SW	SN	SW	SW	SW
Guildford	d			22 35			22 46	22 55			23 08				
London Road (Guildford)	d			22 39			22 50				23 12				
Clandon	d			22 44			22 55				23 17				
Horsley	d			22 48			22 59				23 21				
Effingham Junction 6	d			22 51			23 03				23 24				
Bookham	d						23 06								
Cobham & Stoke d'Abernon	d			22 55							23 28				
Oxshott	d			22 58							23 31				
Claygate	d			23 01							23 34				
Hinchley Wood	d			23 04							23 37				
Hampton Court	d								23 24						
Thames Ditton	d								23 26						
Surbiton 6	d			23 12				23 30	23 33		23 42				
Berrylands	d								23 35						
Shepperton	d		22 41							23 11					
Upper Halliford	d		22 44							23 14					
Sunbury	d		22 46							23 16					
Kempton Park	d		22 48							23 18					
Hampton	d		22 51							23 21					
Fulwell	d		22 54							23 24					
Strawberry Hill	d				23 07	23 08								23 37	23 38
Teddington	d		22 59		23 11					23 29				23 41	
Hampton Wick	d		23 01		23 14					23 31				23 44	
Kingston	a		23 03		23 16					23 33				23 46	
	d		23 04		23 19					23 34				23 49	
Norbiton	d		23 06		23 21					23 36				23 51	
New Malden 6	d		23 10		23 25				23 38	23 41				23 55	
Dorking 4	d	22 35										23 30			
Boxhill & Westhumble	d														
Leatherhead	d	22 41					23 11					23 36			
Ashtead	d	22 44					23 14					23 39			
Epsom 3	a	22 49					23 19					23 45			
	d	22 50					23 20								
Ewell West	d	22 53					23 23								
Stoneleigh	d	22 55					23 25								
Worcester Park	d	22 58					23 28								
Chessington South	d												23 40		
Chessington North	d												23 42		
Tolworth	d												23 44		
Malden Manor	d												23 47		
Motspur Park	d	23 01					23 31						23 50		
Raynes Park 6	d	23 04	23 13		23 28		23 37		23 41	23 43			23 54	23 58	
Wimbledon 6 ⊖	d	23 08	23 17	23 20	23 32		23 41	23 37	23 46	23 49	23 52		23a57	00 02	
Earlsfield	d	23 12	23 20	23 24	23 35		23 44	23 41	23 50	23 53	23 56			00 05	
Clapham Junction 10	d	23 16	23 24	23 28	23 39		23 48	23 45	23 53	23 56	23 58			00 09	
Vauxhall ⊖	d	23 21	23 29	23 33	23 44	23 42	23 53	23 50	23 58	00 01	00 04			00 15	00 12
London Waterloo 15 ⊖	a	23 25	23 34	23 37	23 49	23 46	23 58	23 54	00 03	00 05	00 14			00 22	00 16

Table 152

Sundays until 25 September

Hampton Court, Shepperton, Guildford, Dorking and Chessington South - London

		SW A	SW A	SW A	SW A	SW A	SW	SW	SW	SW	SW	SW	SW	SW	SW	SW	SW	SW	SW	SW	SW	SW	SW
Guildford	d			23p08						06 57				07 27						07 50	07 57		
London Road (Guildford)	d			23p12																07 54			
Clandon	d			23p17																07 59			
Horsley	d			23p21																08 03			
Effingham Junction 6	d			23p24																08 06			
Bookham	d																						
Cobham & Stoke d'Abernon	d			23p28																08 10			
Oxshott	d			23p31																08 13			
Claygate	d			23p34																08 16			
Hinchley Wood	d			23p37																08 19			
Hampton Court	d	23p24											07 35					08 05					
Thames Ditton	d	23p26											07 37					08 07					
Surbiton 6	d	23p33		23p42			07 00			07 30			07 43	08 00				08 13		08 24	08 30		
Berrylands	d	23p35											07 45					08 15					
Shepperton	d		23p11									07 11											08 11
Upper Halliford	d		23p14									07 14											08 14
Sunbury	d		23p16									07 16											08 16
Kempton Park	d		23p18									07 18											08 18
Hampton	d		23p21									07 21											08 21
Fulwell	d		23p24									07 24											08 24
Strawberry Hill	d				23p37	23p38		06 49	06 59							07 49	07 59						
Teddington	d		23p29		23p41			06 55				07 29				07 55							08 29
Hampton Wick	d		23p31		23p44			06 57				07 31				07 57							08 31
Kingston	a		23p33		23p46			06 59				07 33				07 59							08 33
	d		23p34		23p49			07 04				07 34				08 04							08 34
Norbiton	d		23p36		23p51			07 06				07 36				08 06							08 36
New Malden 6	d	23p38	23p41		23p55			07 10				07 40	07 48			08 10		08 18					08 40
Dorking 4	d																						
Boxhill & Westhumble	d																						
Leatherhead	d																						
Ashtead	d																						
Epsom 3	a																						
	d										07 24				07 54							08 24	
Ewell West	d										07 27				07 57							08 27	
Stoneleigh	d										07 29				07 59							08 29	
Worcester Park	d										07 32				08 02							08 32	
Chessington South	d																		08 10				
Chessington North	d																		08 12				
Tolworth	d																		08 14				
Malden Manor	d																		08 17				
Motspur Park	d										07 35				08 05				08 20			08 35	
Raynes Park 6	d	23p41	23p43		23p58			07 13			07 38	07 43	07 51		08 08	08 13		08 21	08 24			08 38	08 43
Wimbledon 6 ⊖	d	23p46	23p49	23p52	00 02		07 08	07 19		07 38	07 42	07 47	07 55	08 08	08 12	08 17		08 25	08 28	08a33	08 38	08 42	08 47
Earlsfield	d	23p50	23p53	23p56	00 05		07 11	07 22		07 41	07 46	07 50	07 58	08 11	08 16	08 20		08 28	08 31		08 41	08 46	08 50
Clapham Junction 10	d	23p53	23p56	23p58	00 09		07 15	07 26		07 45	07 50	07 54	08 02	08 15	08 20	08 24		08 34	08 37		08 45	08 50	08 54
Vauxhall ⊖	d	23p58	00 01	00 04	00 15	00 12	07 20	07 31	07 32	07 50	07 55	07 59	08 07	08 20	08 25	08 29	08 32	08 39	08 42		08 50	08 55	08 59
London Waterloo 15 ⊖	a	00 03	00 05	00 14	00 22	00 16	07 30	07 41	07 41	08 00	08 04	08 07	08 17	08 30	08 34	08 39	08 41	08 47	08 50		09 00	09 04	09 07

A not 22 May

Hampton Court, Shepperton, Guildford, Dorking and Chessington South - London

until 25 September

		SW	SW	SW	SW	SW	SW	SW	SW	SW	SW	SW	SW	SW	SW	SW	SW	SW	SW	SW	SW	SW	SW
Guildford	d			08 20	08 27					08 50	08 57					09 20	09 27					09 50	09 57
London Road (Guildford)	d			08 24						08 54						09 24						09 54	
Clandon	d			08 29						08 59						09 29						09 59	
Horsley	d			08 33						09 03						09 33						10 03	
Effingham Junction 6	d			08 36						09 06						09 36						10 06	
Bookham	d			08 39												09 39							
Cobham & Stoke d'Abernon	d									09 10												10 10	
Oxshott	d									09 13												10 13	
Claygate	d									09 16												10 16	
Hinchley Wood	d									09 19												10 19	
Hampton Court	d	08 35						09 05						09 35						10 05			
Thames Ditton	d	08 37						09 07						09 37						10 07			
Surbiton 6	d	08 43			09 00			09 13		09 24	09 30			09 43			10 00			10 13		10 24	10 30
Berrylands	d	08 45						09 15						09 45						10 15			
Shepperton	d												09 11										
Upper Halliford	d												09 14										
Sunbury	d												09 16										
Kempton Park	d												09 18										
Hampton	d												09 21										
Fulwell	d												09 24										
Strawberry Hill	d					08 49	08 59											09 49	09 59				
Teddington	d					08 55							09 29					09 55					
Hampton Wick	d					08 57							09 31					09 57					
Kingston	a					08 59							09 33					09 59					
	d					09 04							09 34					10 04					
Norbiton	d					09 06							09 36					10 06					
New Malden 6	d	08 48				09 10		09 18					09 40	09 48				10 10		10 18			
Dorking 4	d											09 08											
Boxhill & Westhumble	d																						
Leatherhead	d			08 45								09 15				09 45							
Ashtead	d			08 48								09 18				09 48							
Epsom 3	a			08 53								09 23				09 53							
	d			08 54								09 24				09 54							
Ewell West	d			08 57								09 27				09 57							
Stoneleigh	d			08 59								09 29				09 59							
Worcester Park	d			09 02								09 32				10 02							
Chessington South	d		08 40						09 10						09 40						10 10		
Chessington North	d		08 42						09 12						09 42						10 12		
Tolworth	d		08 44						09 14						09 44						10 14		
Malden Manor	d		08 47						09 17						09 47						10 17		
Motspur Park	d		08 50	09 05					09 20			09 35			09 50	10 05					10 20		
Raynes Park 6	d	08 51	08 54	09 08		09 13		09 21	09 24			09 38	09 43	09 51	09 54	10 08		10 13		10 21	10 24		
Wimbledon 6 ⊖	d	08 55	08 58	09 12	09 08	09 17		09 25	09 28	09a33	09 38	09 42	09 47	09 55	09 58	10 12	10 08	10 17		10 25	10 28	10a33	10 38
Earlsfield	d	08 58	09 01	09 16	09 11	09 20		09 28	09 31		09 41	09 46	09 50	09 58	10 01	10 16	10 11	10 20		10 28	10 31		10 41
Clapham Junction 10	d	09 02	09 09	09 20	09 15	09 24		09 33	09 36		09 45	09 50	09 54	10 06	10 09	10 20	10 15	10 24		10 32	10 36		10 45
Vauxhall ⊖	d	09 07	09 14	09 25	09 20	09 29	09 32	09 38	09 41		09 50	09 55	09 59	10 11	10 14	10 25	10 20	10 32	10 32	10 37	10 41		10 50
London Waterloo 15 ⊖	a	09 17	09 20	09 34	09 30	09 39	09 41	09 47	09 50		10 00	10 04	10 07	10 17	10 20	10 34	10 30	10 39	10 41	10 45	10 50		11 00

		SW	SW	SW	SW	SW	SW	SW	SW	SW	SW	SW	SW	SW	SW	SW	SW	SW	SW	SW	SW	SW
Guildford	d					10 20	10 27					10 50	10 57					11 20	11 27			
London Road (Guildford)	d					10 24						10 54						11 24				
Clandon	d					10 29						10 59						11 29				
Horsley	d					10 33						11 03						11 33				
Effingham Junction 6	d					10 36						11 06						11 36				
Bookham	d					10 39												11 39				
Cobham & Stoke d'Abernon	d											11 10										
Oxshott	d											11 13										
Claygate	d											11 16										
Hinchley Wood	d											11 19										
Hampton Court	d			10 35						11 05						11 35						12 05
Thames Ditton	d			10 37						11 07						11 37						12 07
Surbiton 6	d			10 43			11 00			11 13		11 24	11 30			11 43			12 00			12 13
Berrylands	d			10 45						11 15						11 45						12 15
Shepperton	d		10 11												11 11							
Upper Halliford	d		10 14												11 14							
Sunbury	d		10 16												11 16							
Kempton Park	d		10 18												11 18							
Hampton	d		10 21												11 21							
Fulwell	d		10 24												11 24							
Strawberry Hill	d							10 49	10 59											11 50	11 59	
Teddington	d		10 29					10 55							11 29					11 55		
Hampton Wick	d		10 31					10 57							11 31					11 57		
Kingston	a		10 33					10 59							11 33					11 59		
	d		10 34					11 04							11 34					12 04		
Norbiton	d		10 36					11 06							11 36					12 06		
New Malden 6	d		10 40	10 48				11 10		11 18					11 40	11 48				12 10		12 18
Dorking 4	d	10 08												11 08								
Boxhill & Westhumble	d																					
Leatherhead	d	10 15				10 45								11 15				11 45				
Ashtead	d	10 18				10 48								11 18				11 48				
Epsom 3	a	10 23				10 53								11 23				11 53				
	d	10 24				10 54								11 24				11 54				
Ewell West	d	10 27				10 57								11 27				11 57				
Stoneleigh	d	10 29				10 59								11 29				11 59				
Worcester Park	d	10 32				11 02								11 32				12 02				
Chessington South	d				10 40						11 10						11 40					
Chessington North	d				10 42						11 12						11 42					
Tolworth	d				10 44						11 14						11 44					
Malden Manor	d				10 47						11 17						11 47					
Motspur Park	d	10 35			10 50	11 05					11 20			11 35			11 50	12 05				
Raynes Park 6	d	10 38	10 43	10 51	10 54	11 08		11 13		11 21	11 24			11 38	11 43	11 51	11 54	12 08		12 13		12 21
Wimbledon 6 ⊖	d	10 42	10 47	10 55	10 58	11 12	11 08	11 17		11 25	11 28	11a33	11 38	11 42	11 47	11 55	11 58	12 12	12 08	12 17		12 25
Earlsfield	d	10 46	10 50	10 58	11 01	11 16	11 11	11 20		11 28	11 31		11 41	11 46	11 50	11 58	12 01	12 16	12 11	12 20		12 28
Clapham Junction 10	d	10 50	10 54	11 02	11 05	11 20	11 15	11 24		11 32	11 35		11 45	11 50	11 54	12 02	12 05	12 20	12 15	12 24		12 32
Vauxhall ⊖	d	10 55	10 59	11 07	11 13	11 25	11 20	11 32	11 32	11 37	11 40		11 50	11 55	11 59	12 07	12 13	12 25	12 20	12 29	12 32	12 37
London Waterloo 15 ⊖	a	11 04	11 07	11 17	11 20	11 34	11 30	11 39	11 41	11 47	11 50		12 00	12 04	12 07	12 17	12 22	12 34	12 30	12 39	12 41	12 47

Hampton Court, Shepperton, Guildford, Dorking and Chessington South - London

Sundays until 25 September

		SW	SW	SW	SW	SW	SW	SW	SW	SW	SW	SW	SW	SW	SW	SW	SW	SW	SW	SW	SW	SW	SW
Guildford	d		11 50	11 57					12 20	12 27					12 50	12 57						13 20	13 27
London Road (Guildford)	d		11 54						12 24						12 54							13 24	
Clandon	d		11 59						12 29						12 59							13 29	
Horsley	d		12 03						12 33						13 03							13 33	
Effingham Junction 6	d		12 06						12 36						13 06							13 36	
Bookham	d								12 39													13 39	
Cobham & Stoke d'Abernon	d		12 10												13 10								
Oxshott	d		12 13												13 13								
Claygate	d		12 16												13 16								
Hinchley Wood	d		12 19												13 19								
Hampton Court	d						12 35						13 05							13 35			
Thames Ditton	d						12 37						13 07							13 37			
Surbiton 6	d		12 24	12 30			12 43			13 00			13 13		13 24	13 30				13 43			14 00
Berrylands	d						12 45						13 15							13 45			
Shepperton	d					12 11													13 11				
Upper Halliford	d					12 14													13 14				
Sunbury	d					12 16													13 16				
Kempton Park	d					12 18													13 18				
Hampton	d					12 21													13 21				
Fulwell	d					12 24													13 24				
Strawberry Hill	d										12 50	12 59					13 19						
Teddington	d					12 29					12 55								13 29				
Hampton Wick	d					12 31					12 57								13 31				
Kingston	a					12 33					12 59								13 33				
	d					12 34					13 04								13 34				
Norbiton	d					12 36					13 06								13 36				
New Malden 6	d					12 40	12 48				13 10		13 18						13 40	13 48			
Dorking 4	d				12 08													13 08					
Boxhill & Westhumble	d																						
Leatherhead	d				12 15				12 45									13 15				13 45	
Ashtead	d				12 18				12 48									13 18				13 48	
Epsom 3	a				12 23				12 53									13 23				13 53	
	d				12 24				12 54									13 24				13 54	
Ewell West	d				12 27				12 57									13 27				13 57	
Stoneleigh	d				12 29				12 59									13 29				13 59	
Worcester Park	d				12 32				13 02									13 32				14 02	
Chessington South	d	12 10						12 40						13 10							13 40		
Chessington North	d	12 12						12 42						13 12							13 42		
Tolworth	d	12 14						12 44						13 14							13 44		
Malden Manor	d	12 17						12 47						13 17							13 47		
Motspur Park	d	12 20			12 35			12 50	13 05					13 20				13 35			13 50	14 05	
Raynes Park 6	d	12 24			12 38	12 43	12 51	12 54	13 08		13 13		13 21	13 24				13 38	13 43	13 51	13 54	14 08	
Wimbledon 6 ⊖	d	12 28	12 31	12 38	12 42	12 47	12 55	12 58	13 12	13 08	13 17		13 25	13 28	13 31	13 38		13 42	13 47	13 55	13 58	14 12	14 08
Earlsfield	d	12 31	12 35	12 41	12 46	12 50	12 58	13 01	13 16	13 11	13 20		13 28	13 31	13 35	13 41		13 46	13 50	13 58	14 01	14 16	14 11
Clapham Junction 10	d	12 35	12 39	12 45	12 50	12 54	13 02	13 05	13 20	13 15	13 24		13 32	13 35	13 39	13 45		13 50	13 54	14 02	14 05	14 20	14 15
Vauxhall ⊖	d	12 40	12 44	12 50	12 55	12 59	13 07	13 10	13 25	13 20	13 29	13 32	13 37	13 40	13 44	13 50	13 52	13 55	13 59	14 07	14 10	14 25	14 20
London Waterloo 15 ⊖	a	12 50	12 53	13 00	13 04	13 07	13 17	13 20	13 34	13 30	13 39	13 41	13 47	13 50	13 53	14 00	14 00	14 04	14 07	14 17	14 20	14 34	14 30

		SW	SW	SW	SW	SW	SW	SW	SW	SW	SW	SW	SW	SW	SW	SW	SW	SW	SW	SW	SW	SW
Guildford	d					13 50	13 57						14 20	14 27					14 50	14 57		
London Road (Guildford)	d					13 54							14 24						14 54			
Clandon	d					13 59							14 29						14 59			
Horsley	d					14 03							14 33						15 03			
Effingham Junction 6	d					14 06							14 36						15 06			
Bookham	d												14 39									
Cobham & Stoke d'Abernon	d					14 10													15 10			
Oxshott	d					14 13													15 13			
Claygate	d					14 16													15 16			
Hinchley Wood	d					14 19													15 19			
Hampton Court	d			14 05							14 35						15 05					
Thames Ditton	d			14 07							14 37						15 07					
Surbiton 6	d			14 13		14 24	14 30				14 43			15 00			15 13		15 24	15 30		
Berrylands	d			14 15							14 45						15 15					
Shepperton	d									14 11												
Upper Halliford	d									14 14												
Sunbury	d									14 16												
Kempton Park	d									14 18												
Hampton	d									14 21												
Fulwell	d									14 24												
Strawberry Hill	d	13 49	13 59					14 19							14 49	14 59					15 19	
Teddington	d	13 55								14 29					14 55							
Hampton Wick	d	13 57								14 31					14 57							
Kingston	a	13 59								14 33					14 59							
	d	14 04								14 34					15 04							
Norbiton	d	14 06								14 36					15 06							
New Malden 6	d	14 10		14 18						14 40	14 48				15 10		15 18					
Dorking 4	d								14 08													15 08
Boxhill & Westhumble	d																					
Leatherhead	d								14 15				14 45									15 15
Ashtead	d								14 18				14 48									15 18
Epsom 3	a								14 23				14 53									15 23
	d								14 24				14 54									15 24
Ewell West	d								14 27				14 57									15 27
Stoneleigh	d								14 29				14 59									15 29
Worcester Park	d								14 32				15 02									15 32
Chessington South	d				14 10							14 40						15 10				
Chessington North	d				14 12							14 42						15 12				
Tolworth	d				14 14							14 44						15 14				
Malden Manor	d				14 17							14 47						15 17				
Motspur Park	d				14 20				14 35			14 50	15 05					15 20				15 35
Raynes Park 6	d	14 13		14 21	14 24				14 38	14 43	14 51	14 54	15 08		15 13		15 21	15 24				15 38
Wimbledon 6 ⊖	d	14 17		14 25	14 28	14 31	14 38		14 42	14 47	14 55	14 58	15 12	15 08	15 17		15 25	15 28	15 31	15 38		15 42
Earlsfield	d	14 20		14 28	14 31	14 35	14 41		14 46	14 50	14 58	15 01	15 16	15 11	15 20		15 28	15 31	15 35	15 41		15 46
Clapham Junction 10	d	14 24		14 32	14 35	14 39	14 45		14 50	14 54	15 02	15 05	15 20	15 15	15 24		15 32	15 35	15 39	15 45		15 50
Vauxhall ⊖	d	14 29	14 32	14 37	14 40	14 44	14 50	14 52	14 55	14 59	15 07	15 10	15 25	15 20	15 29	15 32	15 37	15 40	15 44	15 50	15 52	15 55
London Waterloo 15 ⊖	a	14 34	14 41	14 42	14 45	14 48	14 55	15 00	14 59	15 04	15 12	15 15	15 29	15 25	15 34	15 36	15 42	15 45	15 48	15 55	16 00	15 59

Hampton Court, Shepperton, Guildford, Dorking and Chessington South - London

		SW	SW	SW	SW	SW	SW	SW	SW	SW		SW	SW	SW	SW	SW	SW	SW	SW	SW		SW	SW	SW	SW
Guildford	d				15 20	15 27						15 50	15 57						16 20	16 27					
London Road (Guildford)	d				15 24							15 54							16 24						
Clandon	d				15 29							15 59							16 29						
Horsley	d				15 33							16 03							16 33						
Effingham Junction 6	d				15 36							16 06							16 36						
Bookham	d				15 39														16 39						
Cobham & Stoke d'Abernon	d											16 10													
Oxshott	d											16 13													
Claygate	d											16 16													
Hinchley Wood	d											16 19													
Hampton Court	d		15 35						16 05								16 35							17 05	
Thames Ditton	d		15 37						16 07								16 37							17 07	
Surbiton 6	d		15 43			16 00			16 13			16 24	16 30				16 43			17 00				17 13	
Berrylands	d		15 45						16 15								16 45							17 15	
Shepperton	d	15 11														16 11									
Upper Halliford	d	15 14														16 14									
Sunbury	d	15 16														16 16									
Kempton Park	d	15 18														16 18									
Hampton	d	15 21														16 21									
Fulwell	d	15 24														16 24									
Strawberry Hill	d						15 49	15 59						16 19								16 49	16 59		
Teddington	d	15 29					15 55									16 29						16 55			
Hampton Wick	d	15 31					15 57									16 31						16 57			
Kingston	a	15 33					15 59									16 33						16 59			
	d	15 34					16 04									16 34						17 04			
Norbiton	d	15 36					16 06									16 36						17 06			
New Malden 6	d	15 40	15 48				16 10		16 18							16 40	16 48					17 10		17 18	
Dorking 4	d														16 08										
Boxhill & Westhumble	d																								
Leatherhead	d				15 45										16 15				16 45						
Ashtead	d				15 48										16 18				16 48						
Epsom 3	a				15 53										16 23				16 53						
	d				15 54										16 24				16 54						
Ewell West	d				15 57										16 27				16 57						
Stoneleigh	d				15 59										16 29				16 59						
Worcester Park	d				16 02										16 32				17 02						
Chessington South	d			15 40						16 10								16 40							17 10
Chessington North	d			15 42						16 12								16 42							17 12
Tolworth	d			15 44						16 14								16 44							17 14
Malden Manor	d			15 47						16 17								16 47							17 17
Motspur Park	d			15 50	16 05					16 20					16 35			16 50	17 05						17 20
Raynes Park 6	d	15 43	15 51	15 54	16 08		16 13		16 21	16 24					16 38	16 43	16 51	16 54	17 08			17 13		17 21	17 24
Wimbledon 6	d	15 47	15 55	15 58	16 12	16 08	16 17		16 25	16 28		16 31	16 38		16 42	16 47	16 55	16 58	17 12	17 08		17 17		17 25	17 28
Earlsfield	d	15 50	15 58	16 01	16 16	16 11	16 20		16 28	16 31		16 35	16 41		16 46	16 50	16 58	17 01	17 16	17 11		17 20		17 28	17 31
Clapham Junction 10	d	15 54	16 02	16 05	16 20	16 15	16 24		16 32	16 35		16 39	16 45		16 50	16 54	17 02	17 05	17 20	17 15		17 24		17 32	17 35
Vauxhall	d	15 59	16 07	16 10	16 25	16 20	16 29	16 32	16 37	16 40		16 44	16 50	16 52	16 55	16 59	17 07	17 10	17 25	17 20		17 29	17 32	17 37	17 40
London Waterloo 15	a	16 04	16 12	16 15	16 29	16 25	16 34	16 36	16 42	16 45		16 48	16 55	17 00	16 59	17 04	17 12	17 15	17 29	17 25		17 34	17 36	17 42	17 45

		SW	SW	SW	SW	SW		SW	SW	SW	SW	SW	SW	SW	SW	SW		SW	SW	SW	SW	SW	SW	SW	SW
Guildford	d	16 50	16 57							17 20	17 27					17 50		17 57						18 20	18 27
London Road (Guildford)	d	16 54								17 24						17 54								18 24	
Clandon	d	16 59								17 29						17 59								18 29	
Horsley	d	17 03								17 33						18 03								18 33	
Effingham Junction 6	d	17 06								17 36						18 06								18 36	
Bookham	d									17 39														18 39	
Cobham & Stoke d'Abernon	d	17 10														18 10									
Oxshott	d	17 13														18 13									
Claygate	d	17 16														18 16									
Hinchley Wood	d	17 19														18 19									
Hampton Court	d							17 35						18 05								18 35			
Thames Ditton	d							17 37						18 07								18 37			
Surbiton 6	d	17 24	17 30					17 43			18 00			18 13		18 24		18 30				18 43			19 00
Berrylands	d							17 45						18 15								18 45			
Shepperton	d					17 11															18 11				
Upper Halliford	d					17 14															18 14				
Sunbury	d					17 16															18 16				
Kempton Park	d					17 18															18 18				
Hampton	d					17 21															18 21				
Fulwell	d					17 24															18 24				
Strawberry Hill	d			17 19								17 49	17 59						18 19						
Teddington	d					17 29						17 55									18 29				
Hampton Wick	d					17 31						17 57									18 31				
Kingston	a					17 33						17 59									18 33				
	d					17 34						18 04									18 34				
Norbiton	d					17 36						18 06									18 36				
New Malden 6	d					17 40		17 48				18 10		18 18							18 40	18 48			
Dorking 4	d				17 08															18 08					
Boxhill & Westhumble	d																								
Leatherhead	d				17 15					17 45										18 15				18 45	
Ashtead	d				17 18					17 48										18 18				18 48	
Epsom 3	a				17 23					17 53										18 23				18 53	
	d				17 24					17 54										18 24				18 54	
Ewell West	d				17 27					17 57										18 27				18 57	
Stoneleigh	d				17 29					17 59										18 29				18 59	
Worcester Park	d				17 32					18 02										18 32				19 02	
Chessington South	d								17 40						18 10								18 40		
Chessington North	d								17 42						18 12								18 42		
Tolworth	d								17 44						18 14								18 44		
Malden Manor	d								17 47						18 17								18 47		
Motspur Park	d				17 35				17 50	18 05					18 20					18 35			18 50	19 05	
Raynes Park 6	d				17 38	17 43		17 51	17 54	18 08		18 13		18 21	18 24					18 38	18 43	18 51	18 54	19 08	
Wimbledon 6	d	17 31	17 38		17 42	17 47		17 55	17 58	18 12	18 08	18 17		18 25	18 28	18 31		18 38		18 42	18 47	18 55	18 58	19 12	19 08
Earlsfield	d	17 35	17 41		17 46	17 50		17 58	18 01	18 16	18 11	18 20		18 28	18 31	18 35		18 41		18 46	18 50	18 58	19 01	19 16	19 11
Clapham Junction 10	d	17 39	17 45		17 50	17 54		18 02	18 05	18 20	18 15	18 24		18 32	18 35	18 39		18 45		18 50	18 54	19 02	19 05	19 20	19 15
[illegible]		[illegible]	[illegible]	[illegible]	[illegible]	[illegible]		[illegible]	[illegible]	[illegible]	[illegible]	[illegible]	[illegible]	[illegible]	[illegible]	[illegible]		18 50	18 52	18 55	18 59	19 07	19 10	19 25	19 20

Table 152

Sundays
until 25 September

Hampton Court, Shepperton, Guildford, Dorking and Chessington South - London

		SW		SW	SW	SW	SW	SW	SW	SW	SW	SW		SW	SW	SW	SW	SW	SW	SW	SW	SW		SW	SW
Guildford	d						18 50	18 57							19 20	19 27					19 50	19 57			
London Road (Guildford)	d						18 54								19 24						19 54				
Clandon	d						18 59								19 29						19 59				
Horsley	d						19 03								19 33						20 03				
Effingham Junction 6	d						19 06								19 36						20 06				
Bookham	d														19 39										
Cobham & Stoke d'Abernon	d						19 10														20 10				
Oxshott	d						19 13														20 13				
Claygate	d						19 16														20 16				
Hinchley Wood	d						19 19														20 19				
Hampton Court	d				19 05							19 35							20 05						
Thames Ditton	d				19 07							19 37							20 07						
Surbiton 6	d				19 13		19 24	19 30				19 43				20 00			20 13		20 24	20 30			
Berrylands	d				19 15							19 45							20 15						
Shepperton	d										19 11														
Upper Halliford	d										19 14														
Sunbury	d										19 16														
Kempton Park	d										19 18														
Hampton	d										19 21														
Fulwell	d										19 24														
Strawberry Hill	d	18 49		18 59					19 19								19 49	19 59						20 19	
Teddington	d	18 55									19 29						19 55								
Hampton Wick	d	18 57									19 31						19 57								
Kingston	a	18 59									19 33						19 59								
	d	19 04									19 34						20 04								
Norbiton	d	19 06									19 36						20 06								
New Malden 6	d	19 10			19 18						19 40	19 48					20 10		20 18						
Dorking 4	d									19 08															20 08
Boxhill & Westhumble	d																								
Leatherhead	d									19 15					19 45										20 15
Ashtead	d									19 18					19 48										20 18
Epsom 3	a									19 23					19 53										20 23
	d									19 24					19 54										20 24
Ewell West	d									19 27					19 57										20 27
Stoneleigh	d									19 29					19 59										20 29
Worcester Park	d									19 32					20 02										20 32
Chessington South	d					19 10								19 40						20 10					
Chessington North	d					19 12								19 42						20 12					
Tolworth	d					19 14								19 44						20 14					
Malden Manor	d					19 17								19 47						20 17					
Motspur Park	d					19 20				19 35				19 50	20 05					20 20					20 35
Raynes Park 6	d	19 13			19 21	19 24				19 38	19 43	19 51		19 54	20 08		20 13		20 21	20 24					20 38
Wimbledon 6	d	19 17			19 25	19 28	19 31	19 38		19 42	19 47	19 55		19 58	20 12	20 08	20 17		20 25	20 28	20 31	20 38			20 42
Earlsfield	d	19 20			19 28	19 31	19 35	19 41		19 46	19 50	19 58		20 01	20 16	20 11	20 20		20 28	20 31	20 35	20 41			20 46
Clapham Junction 10	d	19 24			19 32	19 35	19 39	19 45		19 50	19 54	20 02		20 05	20 20	20 15	20 24		20 32	20 35	20 39	20 45			20 50
Vauxhall	d	19 29		19 32	19 37	19 40	19 44	19 50	19 52	19 55	19 59	20 07		20 10	20 25	20 20	20 29	20 32	20 37	20 40	20 44	20 50		20 52	20 55
London Waterloo 15	a	19 34		19 36	19 42	19 45	19 48	19 55	20 00	19 59	20 04	20 12		20 15	20 29	20 25	20 34	20 36	20 42	20 45	20 48	20 55		21 00	21 00

		SW	SW	SW	SW	SW	SW	SW		SW	SW	SW	SW	SW	SW	SW	SW	SW		SW	SW	SW	SW	SW	SW
Guildford	d			20 20	20 27						20 50	20 57					21 20	21 27						21 50	21 57
London Road (Guildford)	d			20 24							20 54						21 24							21 54	
Clandon	d			20 29							20 59						21 29							21 59	
Horsley	d			20 33							21 03						21 33							22 03	
Effingham Junction 6	d			20 36							21 06						21 36							22 06	
Bookham	d			20 39													21 39								
Cobham & Stoke d'Abernon	d										21 10													22 10	
Oxshott	d										21 13													22 13	
Claygate	d										21 16													22 16	
Hinchley Wood	d										21 19													22 19	
Hampton Court	d		20 35					21 05								21 35						22 05			
Thames Ditton	d		20 37					21 07								21 37						22 07			
Surbiton 6	d		20 43		21 00			21 13			21 24	21 30				21 43		22 00				22 13		22 24	22 30
Berrylands	d		20 45					21 15								21 45						22 15			
Shepperton	d	20 11													21 11										
Upper Halliford	d	20 14													21 14										
Sunbury	d	20 16													21 16										
Kempton Park	d	20 18													21 18										
Hampton	d	20 21													21 21										
Fulwell	d	20 24													21 24										
Strawberry Hill	d					20 49	20 59						21 19							21 49	21 59				
Teddington	d	20 29				20 55									21 29					21 55					
Hampton Wick	d	20 31				20 57									21 31					21 57					
Kingston	a	20 33				20 59									21 33					21 59					
	d	20 34				21 04									21 34					22 04					
Norbiton	d	20 36				21 06									21 36					22 06					
New Malden 6	d	20 40	20 48			21 10		21 18							21 40	21 48				22 10		22 18			
Dorking 4	d													21 08											
Boxhill & Westhumble	d																								
Leatherhead	d			20 45										21 15			21 45								
Ashtead	d			20 48										21 18			21 48								
Epsom 3	a			20 53										21 23			21 53								
	d			20 54										21 24			21 54								
Ewell West	d			20 57										21 27			21 57								
Stoneleigh	d			20 59										21 29			21 59								
Worcester Park	d			21 02										21 32			22 02								
Chessington South	d									21 10													22 10		
Chessington North	d									21 12													22 12		
Tolworth	d									21 14													22 14		
Malden Manor	d									21 17													22 17		
Motspur Park	d			21 05						21 20				21 35			22 05						22 20		
Raynes Park 6	d	20 43	20 51	21 08		21 13		21 21		21 24				21 38	21 43	21 51	22 08			22 13		22 21	22 24		
Wimbledon 6	d	20 47	20 55	21 12	21 08	21 17		21 25		21 28	21 31	21 38		21 42	21 47	21 55	22 12	22 08		22 17		22 25	22 28	22 31	22 38
Earlsfield	d	20 50	20 58	21 16	21 11	21 20		21 28		21 31	21 35	21 41		21 46	21 50	21 58	22 16	22 11		22 20		22 28	22 31	22 35	22 41
Clapham Junction 10	d	20 54	21 02	21 20	21 15	21 24		21 32		21 35	21 39	21 45		21 50	21 54	22 02	22 20	22 15		22 24		22 32	22 35	22 39	22 45
Vauxhall	d	20 59	21 07	21 25	21 20	21 29	21 32	21 37		21 40	21 44	21 50	21 52	21 55	21 59	22 07	22 25	22 20		22 29	22 32	22 37	22 40	22 44	22 50
[illegible]		[illegible]	[illegible]	[illegible]	[illegible]	[illegible]	[illegible]	[illegible]		21 45	21 49	21 55	22 00	22 00	22 04	22 12	22 29	22 25		22 35	22 36	22 42	22 45	22 48	22 55

Hampton Court, Shepperton, Guildford, Dorking and Chessington South - London

until 25 September

Station		SW	SW	SW		SW	SW	SW	SW	SW	SW	SW	SW	SW		SW	SW	SW	SW
Guildford	d					22 20	22 27					22 50	22 57						
London Road (Guildford)	d					22 24						22 54							
Clandon	d					22 29						22 59							
Horsley	d					22 33						23 03							
Effingham Junction 6	d					22 36						23 06							
Bookham	d					22 39													
Cobham & Stoke d'Abernon	d											23 10							
Oxshott	d											23 13							
Claygate	d											23 16							
Hinchley Wood	d											23 19							
Hampton Court	d									23 05									23 45
Thames Ditton	d									23 07									23 47
Surbiton 6	d						23 00			23 13		23 24	23 30						23 53
Berrylands	d									23 15									23 55
Shepperton	d			22 11													23 11		
Upper Halliford	d			22 14													23 14		
Sunbury	d			22 16													23 16		
Kempton Park	d			22 18													23 18		
Hampton	d			22 21													23 21		
Fulwell	d			22 24													23 24		
Strawberry Hill	d	22 19						22 49	22 59					23 19					
Teddington	d			22 29				22 55									23 29		
Hampton Wick	d			22 31				22 57									23 31		
Kingston	a			22 33				22 59									23 33		
	d			22 34				23 04									23 34		
Norbiton	d			22 36				23 06									23 36		
New Malden 6	d			22 40				23 10		23 18							23 40		23 58
Dorking 4	d		22 08													23 08			
Boxhill & Westhumble	d																		
Leatherhead	d		22 15			22 45										23 15			
Ashtead	d		22 18			22 48										23 18			
Epsom 3	a		22 23			22 53										23 23			
	d		22 24			22 54										23 24			
Ewell West	d		22 27			22 57										23 27			
Stoneleigh	d		22 29			22 59										23 29			
Worcester Park	d		22 32			23 02										23 32			
Chessington South	d										23 10							23 40	
Chessington North	d										23 12							23 42	
Tolworth	d										23 14							23 44	
Malden Manor	d										23 17							23 47	
Motspur Park	d		22 35			23 05					23 20					23 35		23 50	
Raynes Park 6	d		22 38	22 43		23 08		23 13		23 21	23 24					23 38	23 43	23 54	00 01
Wimbledon 6 ⊖	d		22 42	22 47		23 12	23 08	23 17		23 25	23 28	23 31	23 38			23 42	23 47	23a59	00a04
Earlsfield	d		22 46	22 50		23 16	23 11	23 20		23 28	23 31	23 35	23 41			23 46	23 50		
Clapham Junction 10	d		22 50	22 54		23 20	23 15	23 24		23 32	23 35	23 39	23 45			23 50	23 54		
Vauxhall ⊖	d	22 52	22 55	22 59		23 25	23 20	23 29	23 32	23 37	23 40	23 44	23 50	23 52		23 55	23 59		
London Waterloo 15 ⊖	a	23 00	23 00	23 04		23 29	23 25	23 35	23 36	23 42	23 45	23 48	23 55	23 59		23 59	00 04		

Hampton Court, Shepperton, Guildford, Dorking and Chessington South - London

Sundays

from 2 October

Station		SW	SW	SW	SW	SW	SW	SW	SW	SW		SW	SW	SW	SW	SW	SW	SW	SW 1	SW		SW	SW	SW	SW
Guildford	d			23p08						06 57					07 27								07 48	07 57	
London Road (Guildford)	d			23p12																			07 52		
Clandon	d			23p17																			07 57		
Horsley	d			23p21																			08 01		
Effingham Junction 6	d			23p24																			08 04		
Bookham	d																								
Cobham & Stoke d'Abernon	d			23p28																			08 08		
Oxshott	d			23p31																			08 11		
Claygate	d			23p34																			08 14		
Hinchley Wood	d			23p37																			08 17		
Hampton Court	d	23p24												07 35						08 05					
Thames Ditton	d	23p26												07 37						08 07					
Surbiton 6	d	23p33		23p42			07 00			07 30				07 43	08 00				08 10	08 13			08 24	08 30	
Berrylands	d	23p35												07 45						08 15					
Shepperton	d		23p11										07 11												
Upper Halliford	d		23p14										07 14												
Sunbury	d		23p16										07 16												
Kempton Park	d		23p18										07 18												
Hampton	d		23p21										07 21												
Fulwell	d		23p24										07 24												
Strawberry Hill	d				23p37	23p38		06 49	06 59								07 49	07 59							
Teddington	d		23p29		23p41			06 55					07 29				07 55								
Hampton Wick	d		23p31		23p44			06 57					07 31				07 57								
Kingston	a		23p33		23p46			06 59					07 33				07 59								
	d		23p34		23p49			07 04					07 34				08 04								
Norbiton	d		23p36		23p51			07 06					07 36				08 06								
New Malden 6	d	23p38	23p41		23p55			07 10					07 40	07 48			08 10			08 18					
Dorking 4	d																								
Boxhill & Westhumble	d																								
Leatherhead	d																								
Ashtead	d																								
Epsom 3	a																								
	d											07 24				07 54									08 24
Ewell West	d											07 27				07 57									08 27
Stoneleigh	d											07 29				07 59									08 29
Worcester Park	d											07 32				08 02									08 32
Chessington South	d																					08 10			
Chessington North	d																					08 12			
Tolworth	d																					08 14			
Malden Manor	d																					08 17			
Motspur Park	d											07 35				08 05						08 20			08 35
Raynes Park 6	d	23p41	23p43		23p58			07 13				07 38	07 43	07 51		08 08	08 13			08 21		08 24			08 38
Wimbledon 6 ⊖	d	23p46	23p49	23p52	00 02		07 08	07 19		07 38		07 42	07 47	07 55	08 08	08 12	08 17		08 20	08 25		08 28	08a33	08 38	08 42
Earlsfield	d	23p50	23p53	23p56	00 05		07 11	07 22		07 41		07 46	07 50	07 58	08 11	08 16	08 20			08 28		08 31		08 41	08 46
Clapham Junction 10	d	23p53	23p56	23p58	00 09		07 15	07 26		07 45		07 50	07 54	08 02	08 15	08 20	08 24		08 28	08 34		08 37		08 45	08 50
Vauxhall ⊖	d	23p58	00 01	00 04	00 15	00 12	07 20	07 31	07 32	07 50		07 55	07 59	08 07	08 20	08 25	08 29	08 32		08 39		08 42		08 50	08 55
London Waterloo 15 ⊖	a	00 03	00 05	00 14	00 22	00 16	07 30	07 41	07 41	08 00		08 04	08 07	08 17	08 30	08 34	08 39	08 41	08 42	08 47		08 50		09 00	09 04

Hampton Court, Shepperton, Guildford, Dorking and Chessington South - London

		SW	SW	SW	SW	SW		SW	SW	SW	SW	SW	SW	SW	SW	SW		SW	SW	SW	SW	SW	SW	SW	SW
Guildford	d				08 18	08 27						08 48	08 57						09 18	09 27					09 48
London Road (Guildford)	d				08 22							08 52							09 22						09 52
Clandon	d				08 27							08 57							09 27						09 57
Horsley	d				08 31							09 01							09 31						10 01
Effingham Junction 6	d				08 34							09 04							09 34						10 04
Bookham	d				08 37														09 37						
Cobham & Stoke d'Abernon	d											09 08													10 08
Oxshott	d											09 11													10 11
Claygate	d											09 14													10 14
Hinchley Wood	d											09 17													10 17
Hampton Court	d		08 35							09 05						09 35							10 05		
Thames Ditton	d		08 37							09 07						09 37							10 07		
Surbiton 6	d		08 43			09 00				09 13		09 24	09 30			09 43				10 00			10 13		10 24
Berrylands	d		08 45							09 15						09 45							10 15		
Shepperton	d	08 11													09 11										
Upper Halliford	d	08 14													09 14										
Sunbury	d	08 16													09 16										
Kempton Park	d	08 18													09 18										
Hampton	d	08 21													09 21										
Fulwell	d	08 24													09 24										
Strawberry Hill	d							08 49	08 59												09 49	09 59			
Teddington	d	08 29						08 55							09 29						09 55				
Hampton Wick	d	08 31						08 57							09 31						09 57				
Kingston	a	08 33						08 59							09 33						09 59				
	d	08 34						09 04							09 34						10 04				
Norbiton	d	08 36						09 06							09 36						10 06				
New Malden 6	d	08 40	08 48					09 10		09 18					09 40	09 48					10 10		10 18		
Dorking 4	d													09 08											
Boxhill & Westhumble	d																								
Leatherhead	d				08 45									09 15					09 45						
Ashtead	d				08 48									09 18					09 48						
Epsom 3	a				08 53									09 23					09 53						
	d				08 54									09 24					09 54						
Ewell West	d				08 57									09 27					09 57						
Stoneleigh	d				08 59									09 29					09 59						
Worcester Park	d				09 02									09 32					10 02						
Chessington South	d			08 40							09 10							09 40						10 10	
Chessington North	d			08 42							09 12							09 42						10 12	
Tolworth	d			08 44							09 14							09 44						10 14	
Malden Manor	d			08 47							09 17							09 47						10 17	
Motspur Park	d			08 50	09 05						09 20			09 35				09 50	10 05					10 20	
Raynes Park 6	d	08 43	08 51	08 54	09 08			09 13		09 21	09 24			09 38	09 43	09 51		09 54	10 08		10 13		10 21	10 24	
Wimbledon 6	d	08 47	08 55	08 58	09 12	09 08		09 17		09 25	09 28	09a33	09 38	09 42	09 47	09 55		09 58	10 12	10 08	10 17		10 25	10 28	10a33
Earlsfield	d	08 50	08 58	09 01	09 16	09 11		09 20		09 28	09 31		09 41	09 46	09 50	09 58		10 01	10 16	10 11	10 20		10 28	10 31	
Clapham Junction 10	d	08 54	09 02	09 09	09 20	09 15		09 24		09 33	09 36		09 45	09 50	09 54	10 06		10 09	10 20	10 15	10 24		10 32	10 36	
Vauxhall	d	08 59	09 07	09 14	09 25	09 20		09 29	09 32	09 38	09 41		09 50	09 55	09 59	10 11		10 14	10 25	10 20	10 32	10 32	10 37	10 41	
London Waterloo 15	a	09 07	09 17	09 20	09 34	09 30		09 39	09 41	09 47	09 50		10 00	10 04	10 07	10 17		10 20	10 34	10 30	10 39	10 41	10 45	10 50	

		SW		SW	SW	SW	SW	SW	SW	SW	SW	SW		SW	SW	SW	SW	SW	SW	SW	SW	SW		SW	SW
Guildford	d	09 57						10 18	10 27						10 48	10 57					11 18	11 27			
London Road (Guildford)	d							10 22							10 52						11 22				
Clandon	d							10 27							10 57						11 27				
Horsley	d							10 31							11 01						11 31				
Effingham Junction 6	d							10 34							11 04						11 34				
Bookham	d							10 37													11 37				
Cobham & Stoke d'Abernon	d														11 08										
Oxshott	d														11 11										
Claygate	d														11 14										
Hinchley Wood	d														11 17										
Hampton Court	d					10 35						11 05							11 35						
Thames Ditton	d					10 37						11 07							11 37						
Surbiton 6	d	10 30				10 43			11 00			11 13			11 24	11 30			11 43			12 00			
Berrylands	d					10 45						11 15							11 45						
Shepperton	d				10 11													11 11							
Upper Halliford	d				10 14													11 14							
Sunbury	d				10 16													11 16							
Kempton Park	d				10 18													11 18							
Hampton	d				10 21													11 21							
Fulwell	d				10 24													11 24							
Strawberry Hill	d									10 49	10 59													11 50	11 59
Teddington	d				10 29					10 55								11 29						11 55	
Hampton Wick	d				10 31					10 57								11 31						11 57	
Kingston	a				10 33					10 59								11 33						11 59	
	d				10 34					11 04								11 34						12 04	
Norbiton	d				10 36					11 06								11 36						12 06	
New Malden 6	d				10 40	10 48				11 10		11 18						11 40	11 48					12 10	
Dorking 4	d			10 08													11 08								
Boxhill & Westhumble	d																								
Leatherhead	d			10 15				10 45									11 15				11 45				
Ashtead	d			10 18				10 48									11 18				11 48				
Epsom 3	a			10 23				10 53									11 23				11 53				
	d			10 24				10 54									11 24				11 54				
Ewell West	d			10 27				10 57									11 27				11 57				
Stoneleigh	d			10 29				10 59									11 29				11 59				
Worcester Park	d			10 32				11 02									11 32				12 02				
Chessington South	d						10 40							11 10						11 40					
Chessington North	d						10 42							11 12						11 42					
Tolworth	d						10 44							11 14						11 44					
Malden Manor	d						10 47							11 17						11 47					
Motspur Park	d			10 35			10 50	11 05						11 20			11 35			11 50	12 05				
Raynes Park 6	d			10 38	10 43	10 51	10 54	11 08		11 13		11 21		11 24			11 38	11 43	11 51	11 54	12 08			12 13	
Wimbledon 6	d	10 38		10 42	10 47	10 55	10 58	11 12	11 08	11 17		11 25		11 28	11a33	11 38	11 42	11 47	11 55	11 58	12 12	12 08		12 17	
Earlsfield	d	10 41		10 46	10 50	10 58	11 01	11 16	11 11	11 20		11 28		11 31		11 41	11 46	11 50	11 58	12 01	12 16	12 11		12 20	
Clapham Junction 10	d	10 45		10 50	10 54	11 02	11 05	11 20	11 15	11 24		11 32		11 35		11 45	11 50	11 54	12 02	12 05	12 20	12 15		12 24	
Vauxhall	d	10 50		10 55	10 59	11 07	11 13	11 25	11 20	11 32	11 32	11 37		11 40		11 50	11 55	11 59	12 07	12 13	12 25	12 20		12 29	12 32
London Waterloo 15	a	[illegible]		[illegible]	[illegible]	[illegible]	[illegible]	[illegible]	[illegible]	[illegible]	[illegible]	[illegible]		[illegible]		[illegible]	[illegible]	[illegible]	[illegible]	[illegible]	[illegible]	[illegible]		12 39	12 41

Table 152

Sundays
from 2 October

Hampton Court, Shepperton, Guildford, Dorking and Chessington South - London

		SW	SW	SW	SW	SW	SW	SW		SW	SW	SW	SW	SW	SW	SW	SW	SW		SW	SW	SW	SW	SW	SW
Guildford	d			11 48	11 57						12 18	12 27					12 48	12 57							13 18
London Road (Guildford)	d			11 52							12 22						12 52								13 22
Clandon	d			11 57							12 27						12 57								13 27
Horsley	d			12 01							12 31						13 01								13 31
Effingham Junction 6	d			12 04							12 34						13 04								13 34
Bookham	d										12 37														13 37
Cobham & Stoke d'Abernon	d			12 08													13 08								
Oxshott	d			12 11													13 11								
Claygate	d			12 14													13 14								
Hinchley Wood	d			12 17													13 17								
Hampton Court	d	12 05						12 35							13 05								13 35		
Thames Ditton	d	12 07						12 37							13 07								13 37		
Surbiton 6	d	12 13		12 24	12 30			12 43				13 00			13 13		13 24	13 30					13 43		
Berrylands	d	12 15						12 45							13 15								13 45		
Shepperton	d						12 11															13 11			
Upper Halliford	d						12 14															13 14			
Sunbury	d						12 16															13 16			
Kempton Park	d						12 18															13 18			
Hampton	d						12 21															13 21			
Fulwell	d						12 24															13 24			
Strawberry Hill	d												12 50	12 59						13 19					
Teddington	d						12 29						12 55									13 29			
Hampton Wick	d						12 31						12 57									13 31			
Kingston	a						12 33						12 59									13 33			
	d						12 34						13 04									13 34			
Norbiton	d						12 36						13 06									13 36			
New Malden 6	d	12 18					12 40	12 48					13 10		13 18							13 40	13 48		
Dorking 4	d					12 08															13 08				
Boxhill & Westhumble	d																								
Leatherhead	d					12 15					12 45										13 15				13 45
Ashtead	d					12 18					12 48										13 18				13 48
Epsom 3	a					12 23					12 53										13 23				13 53
	d					12 24					12 54										13 24				13 54
Ewell West	d					12 27					12 57										13 27				13 57
Stoneleigh	d					12 29					12 59										13 29				13 59
Worcester Park	d					12 32					13 02										13 32				14 02
Chessington South	d		12 10							12 40						13 10								13 40	
Chessington North	d		12 12							12 42						13 12								13 42	
Tolworth	d		12 14							12 44						13 14								13 44	
Malden Manor	d		12 17							12 47						13 17								13 47	
Motspur Park	d		12 20			12 35				12 50	13 05					13 20					13 35			13 50	14 05
Raynes Park 6	d	12 21	12 24			12 38	12 43	12 51		12 54	13 08		13 13		13 21	13 24					13 38	13 43	13 51	13 54	14 08
Wimbledon 6	d	12 25	12 28	12 31	12 38	12 42	12 47	12 55		12 58	13 12	13 08	13 17		13 25	13 28	13 31	13 38			13 42	13 47	13 55	13 58	14 12
Earlsfield	d	12 28	12 31	12 35	12 41	12 46	12 50	12 58		13 01	13 16	13 11	13 20		13 28	13 31	13 35	13 41			13 46	13 50	13 58	14 01	14 16
Clapham Junction 10	d	12 32	12 35	12 39	12 45	12 50	12 54	13 02		13 05	13 20	13 15	13 24		13 32	13 35	13 39	13 45			13 50	13 54	14 02	14 05	14 20
Vauxhall	d	12 37	12 40	12 44	12 50	12 55	12 59	13 07		13 10	13 25	13 20	13 29	13 32	13 37	13 40	13 44	13 50		13 52	13 55	13 59	14 07	14 10	14 25
London Waterloo 15	a	12 47	12 50	12 53	13 00	13 04	13 07	13 17		13 20	13 34	13 30	13 39	13 41	13 47	13 50	13 53	14 00		14 00	14 04	14 07	14 17	14 20	14 34

		SW	SW	SW		SW	SW	SW	SW	SW	SW	SW	SW	SW		SW	SW	SW	SW	SW	SW	SW	SW	SW	
Guildford	d	13 27						13 48	13 57							14 18	14 27					14 48	14 57		
London Road (Guildford)	d							13 52								14 22						14 52			
Clandon	d							13 57								14 27						14 57			
Horsley	d							14 01								14 31						15 01			
Effingham Junction 6	d							14 04								14 34						15 04			
Bookham	d															14 37									
Cobham & Stoke d'Abernon	d							14 08														15 08			
Oxshott	d							14 11														15 11			
Claygate	d							14 14														15 14			
Hinchley Wood	d							14 17														15 17			
Hampton Court	d					14 05							14 35							15 05					
Thames Ditton	d					14 07							14 37							15 07					
Surbiton 6	d	14 00				14 13		14 24	14 30				14 43				15 00			15 13		15 24	15 30		
Berrylands	d					14 15							14 45							15 15					
Shepperton	d											14 11													
Upper Halliford	d											14 14													
Sunbury	d											14 16													
Kempton Park	d											14 18													
Hampton	d											14 21													
Fulwell	d											14 24													
Strawberry Hill	d		13 49	13 59						14 19								14 49	14 59					15 19	
Teddington	d		13 55									14 29						14 55							
Hampton Wick	d		13 57									14 31						14 57							
Kingston	a		13 59									14 33						14 59							
	d		14 04									14 34						15 04							
Norbiton	d		14 06									14 36						15 06							
New Malden 6	d		14 10			14 18						14 40	14 48					15 10		15 18					
Dorking 4	d										14 08														
Boxhill & Westhumble	d																								
Leatherhead	d										14 15					14 45									
Ashtead	d										14 18					14 48									
Epsom 3	a										14 23					14 53									
	d										14 24					14 54									
Ewell West	d										14 27					14 57									
Stoneleigh	d										14 29					14 59									
Worcester Park	d										14 32					15 02									
Chessington South	d						14 10							14 40							15 10				
Chessington North	d						14 12							14 42							15 12				
Tolworth	d						14 14							14 44							15 14				
Malden Manor	d						14 17							14 47							15 17				
Motspur Park	d						14 20				14 35			14 50		15 05					15 20				
Raynes Park 6	d		14 13			14 21	14 24				14 38	14 43	14 51	14 54		15 08		15 13		15 21	15 24				
Wimbledon 6	d	14 08	14 17			14 25	14 28	14 31	14 38		14 42	14 47	14 55	14 58		15 12	15 08	15 17		15 25	15 28	15 31	15 38		
Earlsfield	d	14 11	14 20			14 28	14 31	14 35	14 41		14 46	14 50	14 58	15 01		15 16	15 11	15 20		15 28	15 31	15 35	15 41		
Clapham Junction 10	d	14 15	14 24			14 32	14 35	14 39	14 45		14 50	14 54	15 02	15 05		15 20	15 15	15 24		15 32	15 35	15 39	15 45		
Vauxhall	d	14 20	14 29	14 32		14 37	14 40	14 44	14 50	14 52	14 55	14 59	15 07	15 10		15 25	15 20	15 29	15 32	15 37	15 40	15 44	15 50	15 52	
London Waterloo 15	a	14 30	14 34	14 41		14 42	14 45	14 48	14 55	15 00	14 59	15 04	15 12	15 15		15 29	15 25	15 34	15 36	15 42	15 45	15 48	15 55	16 00	

Hampton Court, Shepperton, Guildford, Dorking and Chessington South - London

		SW	SW	SW	SW	SW	SW	SW	SW	SW		SW	SW	SW	SW	SW	SW	SW	SW	SW		SW	SW	SW	SW
Guildford	d					15 18	15 27						15 48	15 57						16 18		16 27			
London Road (Guildford)	d					15 22							15 52							16 22					
Clandon	d					15 27							15 57							16 27					
Horsley	d					15 31							16 01							16 31					
Effingham Junction	d					15 34							16 04							16 34					
Bookham	d					15 37														16 37					
Cobham & Stoke d'Abernon	d												16 08												
Oxshott	d												16 11												
Claygate	d												16 14												
Hinchley Wood	d												16 17												
Hampton Court	d			15 35						16 05								16 35							17 05
Thames Ditton	d			15 37						16 07								16 37							17 07
Surbiton	d			15 43			16 00			16 13			16 24	16 30				16 43				17 00			17 13
Berrylands	d			15 45						16 15								16 45							17 15
Shepperton	d		15 11														16 11								
Upper Halliford	d		15 14														16 14								
Sunbury	d		15 16														16 16								
Kempton Park	d		15 18														16 18								
Hampton	d		15 21														16 21								
Fulwell	d		15 24														16 24								
Strawberry Hill	d							15 49	15 59						16 19								16 49	16 59	
Teddington	d		15 29					15 55									16 29						16 55		
Hampton Wick	d		15 31					15 57									16 31						16 57		
Kingston	a		15 33					15 59									16 33						16 59		
	d		15 34					16 04									16 34						17 04		
Norbiton	d		15 36					16 06									16 36						17 06		
New Malden	d		15 40	15 48				16 10		16 18							16 40	16 48					17 10		17 18
Dorking	d	15 08														16 08									
Boxhill & Westhumble	d																								
Leatherhead	d	15 15				15 45										16 15				16 45					
Ashtead	d	15 18				15 48										16 18				16 48					
Epsom	a	15 23				15 53										16 23				16 53					
	d	15 24				15 54										16 24				16 54					
Ewell West	d	15 27				15 57										16 27				16 57					
Stoneleigh	d	15 29				15 59										16 29				16 59					
Worcester Park	d	15 32				16 02										16 32				17 02					
Chessington South	d				15 40							16 10							16 40						
Chessington North	d				15 42							16 12							16 42						
Tolworth	d				15 44							16 14							16 44						
Malden Manor	d				15 47							16 17							16 47						
Motspur Park	d	15 35			15 50	16 05						16 20				16 35			16 50	17 05					
Raynes Park	d	15 38	15 43	15 51	15 54	16 08		16 13		16 21		16 24				16 38	16 43	16 51	16 54	17 08			17 13		17 21
Wimbledon	d	15 42	15 47	15 55	15 58	16 12	16 08	16 17		16 25		16 28	16 31	16 38		16 42	16 47	16 55	16 58	17 12		17 08	17 17		17 25
Earlsfield	d	15 46	15 50	15 58	16 01	16 16	16 11	16 20		16 28		16 31	16 35	16 41		16 46	16 50	16 58	17 01	17 16		17 11	17 20		17 28
Clapham Junction	d	15 50	15 54	16 02	16 05	16 20	16 15	16 24		16 32		16 35	16 39	16 45		16 50	16 54	17 02	17 05	17 20		17 15	17 24		17 32
Vauxhall	d	15 55	15 59	16 07	16 10	16 25	16 20	16 29	16 32	16 37		16 40	16 44	16 50	16 52	16 55	16 59	17 07	17 10	17 25		17 20	17 29	17 32	17 37
London Waterloo	a	15 59	16 04	16 12	16 15	16 29	16 25	16 34	16 36	16 42		16 45	16 48	16 55	17 00	16 59	17 04	17 12	17 15	17 29		17 25	17 34	17 36	17 42

		SW	SW	SW	SW	SW		SW	SW	SW	SW	SW	SW	SW	SW	SW		SW	SW	SW	SW	SW	SW	SW	SW
Guildford	d		16 48	16 57							17 18	17 27						17 48	17 57						18 18
London Road (Guildford)	d		16 52								17 22							17 52							18 22
Clandon	d		16 57								17 27							17 57							18 27
Horsley	d		17 01								17 31							18 01							18 31
Effingham Junction	d		17 04								17 34							18 04							18 34
Bookham	d										17 37														18 37
Cobham & Stoke d'Abernon	d		17 08															18 08							
Oxshott	d		17 11															18 11							
Claygate	d		17 14															18 14							
Hinchley Wood	d		17 17															18 17							
Hampton Court	d								17 35						18 05								18 35		
Thames Ditton	d								17 37						18 07								18 37		
Surbiton	d		17 24	17 30					17 43			18 00			18 13			18 24	18 30				18 43		
Berrylands	d								17 45						18 15								18 45		
Shepperton	d							17 11														18 11			
Upper Halliford	d							17 14														18 14			
Sunbury	d							17 16														18 16			
Kempton Park	d							17 18														18 18			
Hampton	d							17 21														18 21			
Fulwell	d							17 24														18 24			
Strawberry Hill	d				17 19								17 49	17 59						18 19					
Teddington	d							17 29					17 55									18 29			
Hampton Wick	d							17 31					17 57									18 31			
Kingston	a							17 33					17 59									18 33			
	d							17 34					18 04									18 34			
Norbiton	d							17 36					18 06									18 36			
New Malden	d							17 40	17 48				18 10		18 18							18 40	18 48		
Dorking	d					17 08															18 08				
Boxhill & Westhumble	d																								
Leatherhead	d					17 15					17 45										18 15				18 45
Ashtead	d					17 18					17 48										18 18				18 48
Epsom	a					17 23					17 53										18 23				18 53
	d					17 24					17 54										18 24				18 54
Ewell West	d					17 27					17 57										18 27				18 57
Stoneleigh	d					17 29					17 59										18 29				18 59
Worcester Park	d					17 32					18 02										18 32				19 02
Chessington South	d	17 10								17 40						18 10								18 40	
Chessington North	d	17 12								17 42						18 12								18 42	
Tolworth	d	17 14								17 44						18 14								18 44	
Malden Manor	d	17 17								17 47						18 17								18 47	
Motspur Park	d	17 20				17 35				17 50	18 05					18 20					18 35			18 50	19 05
Raynes Park	d	17 24				17 38		17 43	17 51	17 54	18 08		18 13		18 21	18 24					18 38	18 43	18 51	18 54	19 08
Wimbledon	d	17 28	17 31	17 38		17 42		17 47	17 55	17 58	18 12	18 08	18 17		18 25	18 28		18 31	18 38		18 42	18 47	18 55	18 58	19 12
Earlsfield	d	17 31	17 35	17 41		17 46		17 50	17 58	18 01	18 16	18 11	18 20		18 28	18 31		18 35	18 41		18 46	18 50	18 58	19 01	19 16
Clapham Junction	d	17 35	17 39	17 45		17 50		17 54	18 02	18 05	18 20	18 15	18 24		18 32	18 35		18 39	18 45		18 50	18 54	19 02	19 05	19 20
Vauxhall	d	17 40	17 44	17 50	17 52	17 55		17 59	18 07	18 10	18 25	18 20	18 29	18 32	18 37	18 40		18 44	18 50	18 52	18 55	18 59	19 07	19 10	19 25
London Waterloo	a	17 45	17 48	17 55	18 00	17 59		18 04	18 12	18 15	18 29	18 25	18 34	18 36	18 42	18 45		18 48	18 55	19 00	18 59	19 04	19 12	19 15	19 29

Hampton Court, Shepperton, Guildford, Dorking and Chessington South - London

		SW		SW	SW	SW	SW	SW	SW	SW	SW	SW		SW	SW	SW	SW	SW	SW	SW	SW	SW		SW	SW
Guildford	d	18 27						18 48	18 57							19 18	19 27					19 48		19 57	
London Road (Guildford)	d							18 52								19 22						19 52			
Clandon	d							18 57								19 27						19 57			
Horsley	d							19 01								19 31						20 01			
Effingham Junction	d							19 04								19 34						20 04			
Bookham	d															19 37									
Cobham & Stoke d'Abernon	d							19 08														20 08			
Oxshott	d							19 11														20 11			
Claygate	d							19 14														20 14			
Hinchley Wood	d							19 17														20 17			
Hampton Court	d					19 05								19 35						20 05					
Thames Ditton	d					19 07								19 37						20 07					
Surbiton	d	19 00				19 13		19 24	19 30					19 43			20 00			20 13		20 24		20 30	
Berrylands	d					19 15								19 45						20 15					
Shepperton	d											19 11													
Upper Halliford	d											19 14													
Sunbury	d											19 16													
Kempton Park	d											19 18													
Hampton	d											19 21													
Fulwell	d											19 24													
Strawberry Hill	d			18 49	18 59					19 19								19 49	19 59						20 19
Teddington	d			18 55								19 29						19 55							
Hampton Wick	d			18 57								19 31						19 57							
Kingston	a			18 59								19 33						19 59							
	d			19 04								19 34						20 04							
Norbiton	d			19 06								19 36						20 06							
New Malden	d			19 10		19 18						19 40		19 48				20 10		20 18					
Dorking	d										19 08														
Boxhill & Westhumble	d																								
Leatherhead	d										19 15					19 45									
Ashtead	d										19 18					19 48									
Epsom	a										19 23					19 53									
	d										19 24					19 54									
Ewell West	d										19 27					19 57									
Stoneleigh	d										19 29					19 59									
Worcester Park	d										19 32					20 02									
Chessington South	d						19 10								19 40						20 10				
Chessington North	d						19 12								19 42						20 12				
Tolworth	d						19 14								19 44						20 14				
Malden Manor	d						19 17								19 47						20 17				
Motspur Park	d						19 20				19 35				19 50	20 05					20 20				
Raynes Park	d			19 13		19 21	19 24				19 38	19 43		19 51	19 54	20 08		20 13		20 21	20 24				
Wimbledon	d	19 08		19 17		19 25	19 28	19 31	19 38		19 42	19 47		19 55	19 58	20 12	20 08	20 17		20 25	20 28	20 31		20 38	
Earlsfield	d	19 11		19 20		19 28	19 31	19 35	19 41		19 46	19 50		19 58	20 01	20 16	20 11	20 20		20 28	20 31	20 35		20 41	
Clapham Junction	d	19 15		19 24		19 32	19 35	19 39	19 45		19 50	19 54		20 02	20 05	20 20	20 15	20 24		20 32	20 35	20 39		20 45	
Vauxhall	d	19 20		19 29	19 32	19 37	19 40	19 44	19 50	19 52	19 55	19 59		20 07	20 10	20 25	20 20	20 29	20 32	20 37	20 40	20 44		20 50	20 52
London Waterloo	a	19 25		19 34	19 36	19 42	19 45	19 48	19 55	20 00	19 59	20 04		20 12	20 15	20 29	20 25	20 34	20 36	20 42	20 45	20 48		20 55	21 00

		SW	SW	SW	SW	SW	SW	SW		SW	SW	SW	SW	SW	SW	SW	SW	SW		SW	SW	SW	SW	SW	SW
Guildford	d				20 18	20 27						20 48	20 57					21 18		21 27					21 48
London Road (Guildford)	d				20 22							20 52						21 22							21 52
Clandon	d				20 27							20 57						21 27							21 57
Horsley	d				20 31							21 01						21 31							22 01
Effingham Junction	d				20 34							21 04						21 34							22 04
Bookham	d				20 37													21 37							
Cobham & Stoke d'Abernon	d											21 08													22 08
Oxshott	d											21 11													22 11
Claygate	d											21 14													22 14
Hinchley Wood	d											21 17													22 17
Hampton Court	d			20 35						21 05							21 35						22 05		
Thames Ditton	d			20 37						21 07							21 37						22 07		
Surbiton	d			20 43		21 00				21 13		21 24	21 30				21 43			22 00			22 13		22 24
Berrylands	d			20 45						21 15							21 45						22 15		
Shepperton	d		20 11													21 11									
Upper Halliford	d		20 14													21 14									
Sunbury	d		20 16													21 16									
Kempton Park	d		20 18													21 18									
Hampton	d		20 21													21 21									
Fulwell	d		20 24													21 24									
Strawberry Hill	d						20 49	20 59						21 19							21 49	21 59			
Teddington	d		20 29				20 55									21 29					21 55				
Hampton Wick	d		20 31				20 57									21 31					21 57				
Kingston	a		20 33				20 59									21 33					21 59				
	d		20 34				21 04									21 34					22 04				
Norbiton	d		20 36				21 06									21 36					22 06				
New Malden	d		20 40	20 48			21 10			21 18						21 40	21 48				22 10		22 18		
Dorking	d	20 08													21 08										
Boxhill & Westhumble	d																								
Leatherhead	d	20 15			20 45										21 15			21 45							
Ashtead	d	20 18			20 48										21 18			21 48							
Epsom	a	20 23			20 53										21 23			21 53							
	d	20 24			20 54										21 24			21 54							
Ewell West	d	20 27			20 57										21 27			21 57							
Stoneleigh	d	20 29			20 59										21 29			21 59							
Worcester Park	d	20 32			21 02										21 32			22 02							
Chessington South	d										21 10													22 10	
Chessington North	d										21 12													22 12	
Tolworth	d										21 14													22 14	
Malden Manor	d										21 17													22 17	
Motspur Park	d	20 35			21 05						21 20				21 35			22 05						22 20	
Raynes Park	d	20 38	20 43	20 51	21 08		21 13			21 21	21 24				21 38	21 43	21 51	22 08			22 13		22 21	22 24	
Wimbledon	d	20 42	20 47	20 55	21 12	21 08	21 17			21 25	21 28	21 31	21 38		21 42	21 47	21 55	22 12		22 08	22 17		22 25	22 28	22 31
Earlsfield	d	20 46	20 50	20 58	21 16	21 11	21 20			21 28	21 31	21 35	21 41		21 46	21 50	21 58	22 16		22 11	22 20		22 28	22 31	22 35
Clapham Junction	d	20 50	20 54	21 02	21 20	21 15	21 24			21 32	21 35	21 39	21 45		21 50	21 54	22 02	22 20		22 15	22 24		22 32	22 35	22 39
Vauxhall	d	20 55	20 59	21 07	21 25	21 20	21 29	21 32		21 37	21 40	21 44	21 50	21 52	21 55	21 59	22 07	22 25		22 20	22 29	22 32	22 37	22 40	22 44
London Waterloo	a	21 00	21 04	21 13	21 29	21 25	21 35	21 36		21 42	21 45	21 48	21 55	22 00	22 00	22 04	22 12	22 29		22 25	22 35	22 36	22 42	22 45	22 48

Table 152

Sundays from 2 October

Hampton Court, Shepperton, Guildford, Dorking and Chessington South - London

		SW	SW	SW		SW	SW	SW	SW	SW	SW	SW	SW	SW		SW	SW	SW	SW	SW
Guildford	d	21 57					22 20	22 27					22 50	22 57						
London Road (Guildford)	d						22 24						22 54							
Clandon	d						22 29						22 59							
Horsley	d						22 33						23 03							
Effingham Junction 6	d						22 36						23 06							
Bookham	d						22 39													
Cobham & Stoke d'Abernon	d												23 10							
Oxshott	d												23 13							
Claygate	d												23 16							
Hinchley Wood	d												23 19							
Hampton Court	d										23 05									23 45
Thames Ditton	d										23 07									23 47
Surbiton 6	d	22 30						23 00			23 13		23 24	23 30						23 53
Berrylands	d										23 15									23 55
Shepperton	d					22 11												23 11		
Upper Halliford	d					22 14												23 14		
Sunbury	d					22 16												23 16		
Kempton Park	d					22 18												23 18		
Hampton	d					22 21												23 21		
Fulwell	d					22 24												23 24		
Strawberry Hill	d		22 19						22 49	22 59						23 19				
Teddington	d					22 29			22 55									23 29		
Hampton Wick	d					22 31			22 57									23 31		
Kingston	a					22 33			22 59									23 33		
	d					22 34			23 04									23 34		
Norbiton	d					22 36			23 06									23 36		
New Malden 6	d					22 40			23 10		23 18							23 40		23 58
Dorking 4	d			22 08													23 08			
Boxhill & Westhumble	d																			
Leatherhead	d			22 15			22 45										23 15			
Ashtead	d			22 18			22 48										23 18			
Epsom 3	a			22 23			22 53										23 23			
	d			22 24			22 54										23 24			
Ewell West	d			22 27			22 57										23 27			
Stoneleigh	d			22 29			22 59										23 29			
Worcester Park	d			22 32			23 02										23 32			
Chessington South	d											23 10							23 40	
Chessington North	d											23 12							23 42	
Tolworth	d											23 14							23 44	
Malden Manor	d											23 17							23 47	
Motspur Park	d			22 35			23 05					23 20					23 35		23 50	
Raynes Park 6	d			22 38		22 43	23 08		23 13		23 21	23 24					23 38	23 43	23 54	00 01
Wimbledon 6 ⊖ ⛴	d	22 38		22 42		22 47	23 12	23 08	23 17		23 25	23 28	23 31	23 38			23 42	23 47	23a59	00a04
Earlsfield	d	22 41		22 46		22 50	23 16	23 11	23 20		23 28	23 31	23 35	23 41			23 46	23 50		
Clapham Junction 10	d	22 45		22 50		22 54	23 20	23 15	23 24		23 32	23 35	23 39	23 45			23 50	23 54		
Vauxhall ⊖	d	22 50	22 52	22 55		22 59	23 25	23 20	23 29	23 32	23 37	23 40	23 44	23 50		23 52	23 55	23 59		
London Waterloo 15 ⊖	a	22 55	23 00	23 00		23 04	23 29	23 25	23 35	23 36	23 42	23 45	23 48	23 55		23 59	23 59	00 04		

Table 152

Sundays from 9 October

Hampton Court, Shepperton, Guildford, Dorking and Chessington South - London

		SW	SW	SW	SW	SW	SW	SW	SW	SW		SW	SW	SW	SW	SW	SW	SW	SW 1	SW		SW	SW	SW	SW
Guildford	d			23p08						06 57					07 27								07 48	07 57	
London Road (Guildford)	d			23p12																			07 52		
Clandon	d			23p17																			07 57		
Horsley	d			23p21																			08 01		
Effingham Junction 6	d			23p24																			08 04		
Bookham	d																								
Cobham & Stoke d'Abernon	d			23p28																			08 08		
Oxshott	d			23p31																			08 11		
Claygate	d			23p34																			08 14		
Hinchley Wood	d			23p37																			08 17		
Hampton Court	d	23p24												07 35						08 05					
Thames Ditton	d	23p26												07 37						08 07					
Surbiton 6	d	23p33		23p42			07 00			07 30				07 43	08 00				08 10	08 13			08 24	08 30	
Berrylands	d	23p35												07 45						08 15					
Shepperton	d		23p11										07 11												
Upper Halliford	d		23p14										07 14												
Sunbury	d		23p16										07 16												
Kempton Park	d		23p18										07 18												
Hampton	d		23p21										07 21												
Fulwell	d		23p24										07 24												
Strawberry Hill	d				23p37	23p38		06 49	06 59								07 49	07 59							
Teddington	d		23p29		23p41			06 55					07 29				07 55								
Hampton Wick	d		23p31		23p44			06 57					07 31				07 57								
Kingston	a		23p33		23p46			06 59					07 33				07 59								
	d		23p34		23p49			07 04					07 34				08 04								
Norbiton	d		23p36		23p51			07 06					07 36				08 06								
New Malden 6	d	23p38	23p41		23p55			07 10					07 40	07 48			08 10			08 18					
Dorking 4	d																								
Boxhill & Westhumble	d																								
Leatherhead	d																								
Ashtead	d																								
Epsom 3	a																								
	d											07 24				07 54									08 24
Ewell West	d											07 27				07 57									08 27
Stoneleigh	d											07 29				07 59									08 29
Worcester Park	d											07 32				08 02									08 32
Chessington South	d																					08 10			
Chessington North	d																					08 12			
Tolworth	d																					08 14			
Malden Manor	d																					08 17			
Motspur Park	d											07 35				08 05						08 20			08 35
Raynes Park 6	d	23p41	23p43		23p58			07 13				07 38	07 43	07 51		08 08	08 13			08 21		08 24			08 38
Wimbledon 6 ⊖ ⛴	d	23p46	23p49	23p52	00 02		07 08	07 19		07 38		07 42	07 47	07 55	08 08	08 12	08 17		08 20	08 25		08 28	08a33	08 38	08 42
Earlsfield	d	23p50	23p53	23p56	00 05		07 11	07 22		07 41		07 46	07 50	07 58	08 11	08 16	08 20			08 28		08 31		08 41	08 46
Clapham Junction 10	d	23p53	23p56	23p58	00 09		07 15	07 26		07 45		07 50	07 54	08 02	08 15	08 20	08 24		08 28	08 34		08 37		08 45	08 50
Vauxhall ⊖	d	23p58	00 01	00 04	00 15	00 12	07 20	07 31	07 32	07 50		07 55	07 59	08 07	08 20	08 25	08 29	08 32		08 39		08 42		08 50	08 55
London Waterloo 15 ⊖	a	00 03	00 05	00 14	00 22	00 16	07 30	07 41	07 41	08 00		08 04	08 07	08 17	08 30	08 34	08 39	08 41	08 42	08 47		08 50		09 00	09 04

Hampton Court, Shepperton, Guildford, Dorking and Chessington South - London

from 9 October

		SW	SW	SW	SW	SW		SW	SW	SW	SW	SW	SW	SW	SW	SW		SW	SW	SW	SW	SW	SW	SW	SW
Guildford	d				08 18	08 27						08 48	08 57						09 18	09 27					09 48
London Road (Guildford)	d				08 22							08 52							09 22						09 52
Clandon	d				08 27							08 57							09 27						09 57
Horsley	d				08 31							09 01							09 31						10 01
Effingham Junction	d				08 34							09 04							09 34						10 04
Bookham	d				08 37														09 37						
Cobham & Stoke d'Abernon	d											09 08													10 08
Oxshott	d											09 11													10 11
Claygate	d											09 14													10 14
Hinchley Wood	d											09 17													10 17
Hampton Court	d		08 35							09 05						09 35							10 05		
Thames Ditton	d		08 37							09 07						09 37							10 07		
Surbiton	d		08 43			09 00				09 13		09 24	09 30			09 43				10 00			10 13		10 24
Berrylands	d		08 45							09 15						09 45							10 15		
Shepperton	d	08 11													09 11										
Upper Halliford	d	08 14													09 14										
Sunbury	d	08 16													09 16										
Kempton Park	d	08 18													09 18										
Hampton	d	08 21													09 21										
Fulwell	d	08 24													09 24										
Strawberry Hill	d							08 49	08 59												09 49	09 59			
Teddington	d	08 29						08 55							09 29						09 55				
Hampton Wick	d	08 31						08 57							09 31						09 57				
Kingston	a	08 33						08 59							09 33						09 59				
	d	08 34						09 04							09 34						10 04				
Norbiton	d	08 36						09 06							09 36						10 06				
New Malden	d	08 40	08 48					09 10		09 18					09 40	09 48					10 10		10 18		
Dorking	d													09 08											
Boxhill & Westhumble	d																								
Leatherhead	d				08 45									09 15					09 45						
Ashtead	d				08 48									09 18					09 48						
Epsom	a				08 53									09 23					09 53						
	d				08 54									09 24					09 54						
Ewell West	d				08 57									09 27					09 57						
Stoneleigh	d				08 59									09 29					09 59						
Worcester Park	d				09 02									09 32					10 02						
Chessington South	d			08 40							09 10							09 40						10 10	
Chessington North	d			08 42							09 12							09 42						10 12	
Tolworth	d			08 44							09 14							09 44						10 14	
Malden Manor	d			08 47							09 17							09 47						10 17	
Motspur Park	d			08 50	09 05						09 20			09 35				09 50	10 05					10 20	
Raynes Park	d	08 43	08 51	08 54	09 08			09 13		09 21	09 24			09 38	09 43	09 51		09 54	10 08		10 13		10 21	10 24	
Wimbledon	d	08 47	08 55	08 58	09 12	09 08		09 17		09 25	09 28	09a33	09 38	09 42	09 47	09 55		09 58	10 12	10 08	10 17		10 25	10 28	10a33
Earlsfield	d	08 50	08 58	09 01	09 16	09 11		09 20		09 28	09 31		09 41	09 46	09 50	09 58		10 01	10 16	10 11	10 20		10 28	10 31	
Clapham Junction	d	08 54	09 02	09 09	09 20	09 15		09 24		09 33	09 36		09 45	09 50	09 54	10 06		10 09	10 20	10 15	10 24		10 32	10 36	
Vauxhall	d	08 59	09 07	09 14	09 25	09 20		09 29	09 32	09 38	09 41		09 50	09 55	09 59	10 11		10 14	10 25	10 20	10 32	10 32	10 37	10 41	
London Waterloo	a	09 07	09 17	09 20	09 34	09 30		09 39	09 41	09 47	09 50		10 00	10 04	10 07	10 17		10 20	10 34	10 30	10 39	10 41	10 45	10 50	

		SW		SW	SW	SW	SW	SW	SW	SW	SW	SW		SW	SW	SW	SW	SW	SW	SW	SW	SW		SW	SW
Guildford	d	09 57						10 18	10 27						10 48	10 57					11 18	11 27			
London Road (Guildford)	d							10 22							10 52						11 22				
Clandon	d							10 27							10 57						11 27				
Horsley	d							10 31							11 01						11 31				
Effingham Junction	d							10 34							11 04						11 34				
Bookham	d							10 37													11 37				
Cobham & Stoke d'Abernon	d														11 08										
Oxshott	d														11 11										
Claygate	d														11 14										
Hinchley Wood	d														11 17										
Hampton Court	d					10 35						11 05							11 35						
Thames Ditton	d					10 37						11 07							11 37						
Surbiton	d	10 30				10 43			11 00			11 13			11 24	11 30			11 43			12 00			
Berrylands	d					10 45						11 15							11 45						
Shepperton	d				10 11													11 11							
Upper Halliford	d				10 14													11 14							
Sunbury	d				10 16													11 16							
Kempton Park	d				10 18													11 18							
Hampton	d				10 21													11 21							
Fulwell	d				10 24													11 24							
Strawberry Hill	d									10 49	10 59													11 50	11 59
Teddington	d				10 29					10 55								11 29						11 55	
Hampton Wick	d				10 31					10 57								11 31						11 57	
Kingston	a				10 33					10 59								11 33						11 59	
	d				10 34					11 04								11 34						12 04	
Norbiton	d				10 36					11 06								11 36						12 06	
New Malden	d				10 40	10 48				11 10		11 18						11 40	11 48					12 10	
Dorking	d			10 08													11 08								
Boxhill & Westhumble	d																								
Leatherhead	d			10 15				10 45									11 15				11 45				
Ashtead	d			10 18				10 48									11 18				11 48				
Epsom	a			10 23				10 53									11 23				11 53				
	d			10 24				10 54									11 24				11 54				
Ewell West	d			10 27				10 57									11 27				11 57				
Stoneleigh	d			10 29				10 59									11 29				11 59				
Worcester Park	d			10 32				11 02									11 32				12 02				
Chessington South	d						10 40							11 10						11 40					
Chessington North	d						10 42							11 12						11 42					
Tolworth	d						10 44							11 14						11 44					
Malden Manor	d						10 47							11 17						11 47					
Motspur Park	d			10 35			10 50	11 05						11 20			11 35			11 50	12 05				
Raynes Park	d			10 38	10 43	10 51	10 54	11 08		11 13		11 21		11 24			11 38	11 43	11 51	11 54	12 08			12 13	
Wimbledon	d	10 38		10 42	10 47	10 55	10 58	11 12	11 08	11 17		11 25		11 28	11a33	11 38	11 42	11 47	11 55	11 58	12 12	12 08		12 17	
Earlsfield	d	10 41		10 46	10 50	10 58	11 01	11 16	11 11	11 20		11 28		11 31		11 41	11 46	11 50	11 58	12 01	12 16	12 11		12 20	
Clapham Junction	d	10 45		10 50	10 54	11 02	11 05	11 20	11 15	11 24		11 32		11 35		11 45	11 50	11 54	12 02	12 05	12 20	12 15		12 24	
Vauxhall	d	10 50		10 55	10 59	11 07	11 13	11 25	11 20	11 32	11 32	11 37		11 40		11 50	11 55	11 59	12 07	12 13	12 25	12 20		12 29	12 32
London Waterloo	a	11 00		11 04	11 07	11 17	11 20	11 34	11 30	11 39	11 41	11 47		11 50		12 00	12 04	12 07	12 17	12 22	12 34	12 30		12 39	12 41

Hampton Court, Shepperton, Guildford, Dorking and Chessington South - London

from 9 October

		SW	SW	SW	SW	SW	SW	SW		SW	SW	SW	SW	SW	SW	SW	SW	SW		SW	SW	SW	SW	SW	SW
Guildford	d			11 48	11 57						12 18	12 27					12 48	12 57							13 18
London Road (Guildford)	d			11 52							12 22						12 52								13 22
Clandon	d			11 57							12 27						12 57								13 27
Horsley	d			12 01							12 31						13 01								13 31
Effingham Junction	d			12 04							12 34						13 04								13 34
Bookham	d										12 37														13 37
Cobham & Stoke d'Abernon	d			12 08													13 08								
Oxshott	d			12 11													13 11								
Claygate	d			12 14													13 14								
Hinchley Wood	d			12 17													13 17								
Hampton Court	d	12 05						12 35							13 05								13 35		
Thames Ditton	d	12 07						12 37							13 07								13 37		
Surbiton	d	12 13		12 24	12 30			12 43				13 00			13 13		13 24	13 30					13 43		
Berrylands	d	12 15						12 45							13 15								13 45		
Shepperton	d						12 11															13 11			
Upper Halliford	d						12 14															13 14			
Sunbury	d						12 16															13 16			
Kempton Park	d						12 18															13 18			
Hampton	d						12 21															13 21			
Fulwell	d						12 24															13 24			
Strawberry Hill	d												12 50	12 59						13 19					
Teddington	d						12 29						12 55									13 29			
Hampton Wick	d						12 31						12 57									13 31			
Kingston	a						12 33						12 59									13 33			
	d						12 34						13 04									13 34			
Norbiton	d						12 36						13 06									13 36			
New Malden	d	12 18					12 40	12 48					13 10		13 18							13 40	13 48		
Dorking	d					12 08															13 08				
Boxhill & Westhumble	d																								
Leatherhead	d					12 15					12 45										13 15				13 45
Ashtead	d					12 18					12 48										13 18				13 48
Epsom	a					12 23					12 53										13 23				13 53
	d					12 24					12 54										13 24				13 54
Ewell West	d					12 27					12 57										13 27				13 57
Stoneleigh	d					12 29					12 59										13 29				13 59
Worcester Park	d					12 32					13 02										13 32				14 02
Chessington South	d		12 10							12 40						13 10								13 40	
Chessington North	d		12 12							12 42						13 12								13 42	
Tolworth	d		12 14							12 44						13 14								13 44	
Malden Manor	d		12 17							12 47						13 17								13 47	
Motspur Park	d		12 20			12 35				12 50	13 05					13 20					13 35			13 50	14 05
Raynes Park	d	12 21	12 24			12 38	12 43	12 51		12 54	13 08		13 13		13 21	13 24					13 38	13 43	13 51	13 54	14 08
Wimbledon	d	12 25	12 28	12 31	12 38	12 42	12 47	12 55		12 58	13 12	13 08	13 17		13 25	13 28	13 31	13 38			13 42	13 47	13 55	13 58	14 12
Earlsfield	d	12 28	12 31	12 35	12 41	12 46	12 50	12 58		13 01	13 16	13 11	13 20		13 28	13 31	13 35	13 41			13 46	13 50	13 58	14 01	14 16
Clapham Junction	d	12 32	12 35	12 39	12 45	12 50	12 54	13 02		13 05	13 20	13 15	13 24		13 32	13 35	13 39	13 45			13 50	13 54	14 02	14 05	14 20
Vauxhall	d	12 37	12 40	12 44	12 50	12 55	12 59	13 07		13 10	13 25	13 20	13 29	13 32	13 37	13 40	13 44	13 50		13 52	13 55	13 59	14 07	14 10	14 25
London Waterloo	a	12 47	12 50	12 53	13 00	13 04	13 07	13 17		13 20	13 34	13 30	13 39	13 41	13 47	13 50	13 53	14 00		14 00	14 04	14 07	14 17	14 20	14 34

		SW	SW	SW		SW	SW	SW	SW	SW	SW	SW	SW	SW		SW	SW	SW	SW	SW	SW	SW	SW	SW	
Guildford	d	13 27						13 48	13 57							14 18	14 27					14 48	14 57		
London Road (Guildford)	d							13 52								14 22						14 52			
Clandon	d							13 57								14 27						14 57			
Horsley	d							14 01								14 31						15 01			
Effingham Junction	d							14 04								14 34						15 04			
Bookham	d															14 37									
Cobham & Stoke d'Abernon	d							14 08														15 08			
Oxshott	d							14 11														15 11			
Claygate	d							14 14														15 14			
Hinchley Wood	d							14 17														15 17			
Hampton Court	d					14 05							14 35							15 05					
Thames Ditton	d					14 07							14 37							15 07					
Surbiton	d	14 00				14 13		14 24	14 30				14 43				15 00			15 13		15 24	15 30		
Berrylands	d					14 15							14 45							15 15					
Shepperton	d											14 11													
Upper Halliford	d											14 14													
Sunbury	d											14 16													
Kempton Park	d											14 18													
Hampton	d											14 21													
Fulwell	d											14 24													
Strawberry Hill	d		13 49	13 59						14 19								14 49	14 59					15 19	
Teddington	d		13 55									14 29						14 55							
Hampton Wick	d		13 57									14 31						14 57							
Kingston	a		13 59									14 33						14 59							
	d		14 04									14 34						15 04							
Norbiton	d		14 06									14 36						15 06							
New Malden	d		14 10			14 18						14 40	14 48					15 10		15 18					
Dorking	d										14 08														
Boxhill & Westhumble	d																								
Leatherhead	d										14 15					14 45									
Ashtead	d										14 18					14 48									
Epsom	a										14 23					14 53									
	d										14 24					14 54									
Ewell West	d										14 27					14 57									
Stoneleigh	d										14 29					14 59									
Worcester Park	d										14 32					15 02									
Chessington South	d						14 10							14 40							15 10				
Chessington North	d						14 12							14 42							15 12				
Tolworth	d						14 14							14 44							15 14				
Malden Manor	d						14 17							14 47							15 17				
Motspur Park	d						14 20				14 35			14 50		15 05					15 20				
Raynes Park	d		14 13			14 21	14 24				14 38	14 43	14 51	14 54		15 08		15 13		15 21	15 24				
Wimbledon	d	14 08	14 17			14 25	14 28	14 31	14 38		14 42	14 47	14 55	14 58		15 12	15 08	15 17		15 25	15 28	15 31	15 38		
Earlsfield	d	14 11	14 20			14 28	14 31	14 35	14 41		14 46	14 50	14 58	15 01		15 16	15 11	15 20		15 28	15 31	15 35	15 41		
Clapham Junction	d	14 15	14 24			14 32	14 35	14 39	14 45		14 50	14 54	15 02	15 05		15 20	15 15	15 24		15 32	15 35	15 39	15 45		
Vauxhall	d	14 20	14 29	14 32		14 37	14 40	14 44	14 50	14 52	14 55	14 59	15 07	15 10		15 25	15 20	15 29	15 32	15 37	15 40	15 44	15 50	15 52	
London Waterloo	a	14 30	14 34	14 41		14 42	14 45	14 48	14 55	15 00	14 59	15 04	15 12	15 15		15 29	15 25	15 34	15 36	15 42	15 45	15 48	15 55	16 00	

Table 152

Sundays from 9 October

Hampton Court, Shepperton, Guildford, Dorking and Chessington South - London

		SW	SW	SW	SW	SW	SW	SW	SW	SW	SW	SW	SW	SW	SW	SW	SW	SW	SW	SW	SW	SW	SW
Guildford	d					15 18	15 27					15 48	15 57						16 18	16 27			
London Road (Guildford)	d					15 22						15 52							16 22				
Clandon	d					15 27						15 57							16 27				
Horsley	d					15 31						16 01							16 31				
Effingham Junction 6	d					15 34						16 04							16 34				
Bookham	d					15 37													16 37				
Cobham & Stoke d'Abernon	d											16 08											
Oxshott	d											16 11											
Claygate	d											16 14											
Hinchley Wood	d											16 17											
Hampton Court	d			15 35						16 05							16 35						17 05
Thames Ditton	d			15 37						16 07							16 37						17 07
Surbiton 6	d			15 43			16 00			16 13		16 24	16 30				16 43			17 00			17 13
Berrylands	d			15 45						16 15							16 45						17 15
Shepperton	d		15 11													16 11							
Upper Halliford	d		15 14													16 14							
Sunbury	d		15 16													16 16							
Kempton Park	d		15 18													16 18							
Hampton	d		15 21													16 21							
Fulwell	d		15 24													16 24							
Strawberry Hill	d							15 49	15 59					16 19							16 49	16 59	
Teddington	d		15 29					15 55								16 29					16 55		
Hampton Wick	d		15 31					15 57								16 31					16 57		
Kingston	a		15 33					15 59								16 33					16 59		
	d		15 34					16 04								16 34					17 04		
Norbiton	d		15 36					16 06								16 36					17 06		
New Malden 6	d		15 40	15 48				16 10		16 18						16 40	16 48				17 10		17 18
Dorking 4	d	15 08													16 08								
Boxhill & Westhumble	d																						
Leatherhead	d	15 15				15 45									16 15				16 45				
Ashtead	d	15 18				15 48									16 18				16 48				
Epsom 3	a	15 23				15 53									16 23				16 53				
	d	15 24				15 54									16 24				16 54				
Ewell West	d	15 27				15 57									16 27				16 57				
Stoneleigh	d	15 29				15 59									16 29				16 59				
Worcester Park	d	15 32				16 02									16 32				17 02				
Chessington South	d				15 40						16 10							16 40					
Chessington North	d				15 42						16 12							16 42					
Tolworth	d				15 44						16 14							16 44					
Malden Manor	d				15 47						16 17							16 47					
Motspur Park	d	15 35			15 50	16 05					16 20				16 35			16 50	17 05				
Raynes Park 6	d	15 38	15 43	15 51	15 54	16 08		16 13		16 21	16 24				16 38	16 43	16 51	16 54	17 08		17 13		17 21
Wimbledon 6 ⊖	d	15 42	15 47	15 55	15 58	16 12	16 08	16 17		16 25	16 28	16 31	16 38		16 42	16 47	16 55	16 58	17 12	17 08	17 17		17 25
Earlsfield	d	15 46	15 50	15 58	16 01	16 16	16 11	16 20		16 28	16 31	16 35	16 41		16 46	16 50	16 58	17 01	17 16	17 11	17 20		17 28
Clapham Junction 10	d	15 50	15 54	16 02	16 05	16 20	16 15	16 24		16 32	16 35	16 39	16 45		16 50	16 54	17 02	17 05	17 20	17 15	17 24		17 32
Vauxhall ⊖	d	15 55	15 59	16 07	16 10	16 25	16 20	16 29	16 32	16 37	16 40	16 44	16 50	16 52	16 55	16 59	17 07	17 10	17 25	17 20	17 29	17 32	17 37
London Waterloo 15 ⊖	a	15 59	16 04	16 12	16 15	16 29	16 25	16 34	16 36	16 42	16 45	16 48	16 55	17 00	16 59	17 04	17 12	17 15	17 29	17 25	17 34	17 36	17 42

		SW	SW	SW	SW	SW	SW	SW	SW	SW	SW	SW	SW	SW	SW	SW	SW	SW	SW	SW	SW	SW	SW
Guildford	d		16 48	16 57						17 18	17 27					17 48	17 57						18 18
London Road (Guildford)	d		16 52							17 22						17 52							18 22
Clandon	d		16 57							17 27						17 57							18 27
Horsley	d		17 01							17 31						18 01							18 31
Effingham Junction 6	d		17 04							17 34						18 04							18 34
Bookham	d									17 37													18 37
Cobham & Stoke d'Abernon	d		17 08													18 08							
Oxshott	d		17 11													18 11							
Claygate	d		17 14													18 14							
Hinchley Wood	d		17 17													18 17							
Hampton Court	d							17 35						18 05							18 35		
Thames Ditton	d							17 37						18 07							18 37		
Surbiton 6	d		17 24	17 30				17 43			18 00			18 13		18 24	18 30				18 43		
Berrylands	d							17 45						18 15							18 45		
Shepperton	d						17 11													18 11			
Upper Halliford	d						17 14													18 14			
Sunbury	d						17 16													18 16			
Kempton Park	d						17 18													18 18			
Hampton	d						17 21													18 21			
Fulwell	d						17 24													18 24			
Strawberry Hill	d				17 19							17 49	17 59					18 19					
Teddington	d						17 29					17 55								18 29			
Hampton Wick	d						17 31					17 57								18 31			
Kingston	a						17 33					17 59								18 33			
	d						17 34					18 04								18 34			
Norbiton	d						17 36					18 06								18 36			
New Malden 6	d						17 40	17 48				18 10		18 18						18 40	18 48		
Dorking 4	d					17 08													18 08				
Boxhill & Westhumble	d																						
Leatherhead	d					17 15				17 45									18 15				18 45
Ashtead	d					17 18				17 48									18 18				18 48
Epsom 3	a					17 23				17 53									18 23				18 53
	d					17 24				17 54									18 24				18 54
Ewell West	d					17 27				17 57									18 27				18 57
Stoneleigh	d					17 29				17 59									18 29				18 59
Worcester Park	d					17 32				18 02									18 32				19 02
Chessington South	d	17 10							17 40						18 10							18 40	
Chessington North	d	17 12							17 42						18 12							18 42	
Tolworth	d	17 14							17 44						18 14							18 44	
Malden Manor	d	17 17							17 47						18 17							18 47	
Motspur Park	d	17 20				17 35			17 50	18 05					18 20				18 35			18 50	19 05
Raynes Park 6	d	17 24				17 38	17 43	17 51	17 54	18 08		18 13		18 21	18 24				18 38	18 43	18 51	18 54	19 08
Wimbledon 6 ⊖	d	17 28	17 31	17 38		17 42	17 47	17 55	17 58	18 12	18 08	18 17		18 25	18 28	18 31	18 38		18 42	18 47	18 55	18 58	19 12
Earlsfield	d	17 31	17 35	17 41		17 46	17 50	17 58	18 01	18 16	18 11	18 20		18 28	18 31	18 35	18 41		18 46	18 50	18 58	19 01	19 16
Clapham Junction 10	d	17 35	17 39	17 45		17 50	17 54	18 02	18 05	18 20	18 15	18 24		18 32	18 35	18 39	18 45		18 50	18 54	19 02	19 05	19 20

Hampton Court, Shepperton, Guildford, Dorking and Chessington South - London

		SW	SW	SW	SW	SW	SW	SW	SW	SW	SW	SW	SW	SW	SW	SW	SW	SW	SW	SW	SW	SW
Guildford	d	18 27					18 48	18 57						19 18	19 27					19 48	19 57	
London Road (Guildford)	d						18 52							19 22						19 52		
Clandon	d						18 57							19 27						19 57		
Horsley	d						19 01							19 31						20 01		
Effingham Junction 6	d						19 04							19 34						20 04		
Bookham	d													19 37								
Cobham & Stoke d'Abernon	d						19 08													20 08		
Oxshott	d						19 11													20 11		
Claygate	d						19 14													20 14		
Hinchley Wood	d						19 17													20 17		
Hampton Court	d				19 05							19 35						20 05				
Thames Ditton	d				19 07							19 37						20 07				
Surbiton 6	d	19 00			19 13		19 24	19 30				19 43			20 00			20 13		20 24	20 30	
Berrylands	d				19 15							19 45						20 15				
Shepperton	d										19 11											
Upper Halliford	d										19 14											
Sunbury	d										19 16											
Kempton Park	d										19 18											
Hampton	d										19 21											
Fulwell	d										19 24											
Strawberry Hill	d		18 49	18 59					19 19							19 49	19 59					20 19
Teddington	d		18 55								19 29					19 55						
Hampton Wick	d		18 57								19 31					19 57						
Kingston	a		18 59								19 33					19 59						
	d		19 04								19 34					20 04						
Norbiton	d		19 06								19 36					20 06						
New Malden 6	d		19 10		19 18						19 40	19 48				20 10		20 18				
Dorking 4	d									19 08												
Boxhill & Westhumble	d																					
Leatherhead	d									19 15				19 45								
Ashtead	d									19 18				19 48								
Epsom 3	a									19 23				19 53								
	d									19 24				19 54								
Ewell West	d									19 27				19 57								
Stoneleigh	d									19 29				19 59								
Worcester Park	d									19 32				20 02								
Chessington South	d					19 10							19 40						20 10			
Chessington North	d					19 12							19 42						20 12			
Tolworth	d					19 14							19 44						20 14			
Malden Manor	d					19 17							19 47						20 17			
Motspur Park	d					19 20				19 35			19 50	20 05					20 20			
Raynes Park 6	d		19 13		19 21	19 24				19 38	19 43	19 51	19 54	20 08		20 13		20 21	20 24			
Wimbledon 6 ⊖	d	19 08	19 17		19 25	19 28	19 31	19 38		19 42	19 47	19 55	19 58	20 12	20 08	20 17		20 25	20 28	20 31	20 38	
Earlsfield	d	19 11	19 20		19 28	19 31	19 35	19 41		19 46	19 50	19 58	20 01	20 16	20 11	20 20		20 28	20 31	20 35	20 41	
Clapham Junction 10	d	19 15	19 24		19 32	19 35	19 39	19 45		19 50	19 54	20 02	20 05	20 20	20 15	20 24		20 32	20 35	20 39	20 45	
Vauxhall ⊖	d	19 20	19 29	19 32	19 37	19 40	19 44	19 50	19 52	19 55	19 59	20 07	20 10	20 25	20 20	20 29	20 32	20 37	20 40	20 44	20 50	20 52
London Waterloo 15 ⊖	a	19 25	19 34	19 36	19 42	19 45	19 48	19 55	20 00	19 59	20 04	20 12	20 15	20 29	20 25	20 34	20 36	20 42	20 45	20 48	20 55	21 00

		SW	SW	SW	SW	SW	SW	SW	SW	SW	SW	SW	SW	SW	SW	SW	SW	SW	SW	SW	SW	SW	SW
Guildford	d				20 18	20 27					20 48	20 57					21 18	21 27					21 48
London Road (Guildford)	d				20 22						20 52						21 22						21 52
Clandon	d				20 27						20 57						21 27						21 57
Horsley	d				20 31						21 01						21 31						22 01
Effingham Junction 6	d				20 34						21 04						21 34						22 04
Bookham	d				20 37												21 37						
Cobham & Stoke d'Abernon	d										21 08												22 08
Oxshott	d										21 11												22 11
Claygate	d										21 14												22 14
Hinchley Wood	d										21 17												22 17
Hampton Court	d			20 35					21 05							21 35					22 05		
Thames Ditton	d			20 37					21 07							21 37					22 07		
Surbiton 6	d			20 43		21 00			21 13		21 24	21 30				21 43		22 00			22 13		22 24
Berrylands	d			20 45					21 15							21 45					22 15		
Shepperton	d		20 11												21 11								
Upper Halliford	d		20 14												21 14								
Sunbury	d		20 16												21 16								
Kempton Park	d		20 18												21 18								
Hampton	d		20 21												21 21								
Fulwell	d		20 24												21 24								
Strawberry Hill	d						20 49	20 59					21 19						21 49	21 59			
Teddington	d		20 29				20 55								21 29				21 55				
Hampton Wick	d		20 31				20 57								21 31				21 57				
Kingston	a		20 33				20 59								21 33				21 59				
	d		20 34				21 04								21 34				22 04				
Norbiton	d		20 36				21 06								21 36				22 06				
New Malden 6	d		20 40	20 48			21 10		21 18						21 40	21 48			22 10		22 18		
Dorking 4	d	20 08												21 08									
Boxhill & Westhumble	d																						
Leatherhead	d	20 15			20 45									21 15			21 45						
Ashtead	d	20 18			20 48									21 18			21 48						
Epsom 3	a	20 23			20 53									21 23			21 53						
	d	20 24			20 54									21 24			21 54						
Ewell West	d	20 27			20 57									21 27			21 57						
Stoneleigh	d	20 29			20 59									21 29			21 59						
Worcester Park	d	20 32			21 02									21 32			22 02						
Chessington South	d									21 10												22 10	
Chessington North	d									21 12												22 12	
Tolworth	d									21 14												22 14	
Malden Manor	d									21 17												22 17	
Motspur Park	d	20 35			21 05					21 20				21 35			22 05					22 20	
Raynes Park 6	d	20 38	20 43	20 51	21 08		21 13		21 21	21 24				21 38	21 43	21 51	22 08		22 13		22 21	22 24	
Wimbledon 6 ⊖	d	20 42	20 47	20 55	21 12	21 08	21 17		21 25	21 28	21 31	21 38		21 42	21 47	21 55	22 12	22 08	22 17		22 25	22 28	22 31
Earlsfield	d	20 46	20 50	20 58	21 16	21 11	21 20		21 28	21 31	21 35	21 41		21 46	21 50	21 58	22 16	22 11	22 20		22 28	22 31	22 35
Clapham Junction 10	d	20 50	20 54	21 02	21 20	21 15	21 24		21 32	21 35	21 39	21 45		21 50	21 54	22 02	22 20	22 15	22 24		22 32	22 35	22 39
Vauxhall ⊖	d	20 55	20 59	21 07	21 25	21 20	21 29	21 32	21 37	21 40	21 44	21 50	21 52	21 55	21 59	22 07	22 25	22 20	22 29	22 32	22 37	22 40	22 44

Hampton Court, Shepperton, Guildford, Dorking and Chessington South - London

		SW	SW	SW		SW	SW	SW	SW	SW	SW	SW	SW	SW		SW	SW	SW	SW	SW
Guildford	d	21 57					22 20	22 27					22 50	22 57						
London Road (Guildford)	d						22 24						22 54							
Clandon	d						22 29						22 59							
Horsley	d						22 33						23 03							
Effingham Junction 6	d						22 36						23 06							
Bookham	d						22 39													
Cobham & Stoke d'Abernon	d												23 10							
Oxshott	d												23 13							
Claygate	d												23 16							
Hinchley Wood	d												23 19							
Hampton Court	d										23 05									23 45
Thames Ditton	d										23 07									23 47
Surbiton 6	d	22 30						23 00			23 13		23 24	23 30						23 53
Berrylands	d										23 15									23 55
Shepperton	d					22 11												23 11		
Upper Halliford	d					22 14												23 14		
Sunbury	d					22 16												23 16		
Kempton Park	d					22 18												23 18		
Hampton	d					22 21												23 21		
Fulwell	d					22 24												23 24		
Strawberry Hill	d		22 19						22 49	22 59						23 19				
Teddington	d					22 29			22 55									23 29		
Hampton Wick	d					22 31			22 57									23 31		
Kingston	a					22 33			22 59									23 33		
	d					22 34			23 04									23 34		
Norbiton	d					22 36			23 06									23 36		
New Malden 6	d					22 40			23 10		23 18							23 40		23 58
Dorking 4	d			22 08													23 08			
Boxhill & Westhumble	d																			
Leatherhead	d			22 15			22 45										23 15			
Ashtead	d			22 18			22 48										23 18			
Epsom 3	a			22 23			22 53										23 23			
	d			22 24			22 54										23 24			
Ewell West	d			22 27			22 57										23 27			
Stoneleigh	d			22 29			22 59										23 29			
Worcester Park	d			22 32			23 02										23 32			
Chessington South	d											23 10							23 40	
Chessington North	d											23 12							23 42	
Tolworth	d											23 14							23 44	
Malden Manor	d											23 17							23 47	
Motspur Park	d			22 35			23 05					23 20					23 35		23 50	
Raynes Park 6	d			22 38		22 43	23 08		23 13		23 21	23 24					23 38	23 43	23 54	00 01
Wimbledon 6 ⊖ ⇌	d	22 38		22 42		22 47	23 12	23 08	23 17		23 25	23 28	23 31	23 38			23 42	23 47	23a59	00a04
Earlsfield	d	22 41		22 46		22 50	23 16	23 11	23 20		23 28	23 31	23 35	23 41			23 46	23 50		
Clapham Junction 10	d	22 45		22 50		22 54	23 20	23 15	23 24		23 32	23 35	23 39	23 45			23 50	23 54		
Vauxhall ⊖	d	22 50	22 52	22 55		22 59	23 25	23 20	23 29	23 32	23 37	23 40	23 44	23 50		23 52	23 55	23 59		
London Waterloo 15 ⊖	a	22 55	23 00	23 00		23 04	23 29	23 25	23 35	23 36	23 42	23 45	23 48	23 55		23 59	23 59	00 04		

Network Diagram for Tables 155, 156, 157

DM-13/09(2)
Design BAJS

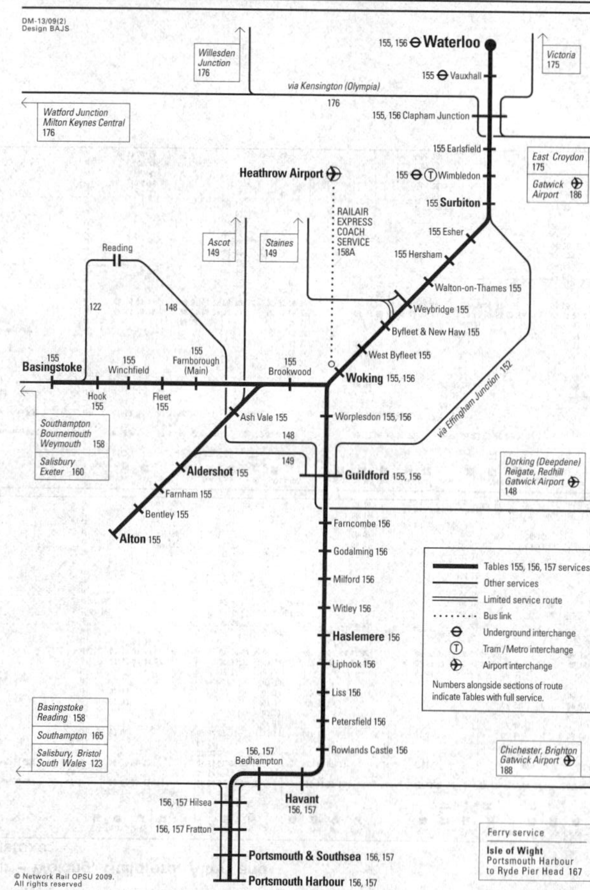

© Network Rail OPSU 2009.
All rights reserved

Table 155

Mondays to Fridays

London - Woking, Guildford, Alton and Basingstoke

Miles	Miles	Miles			SW MO 1	SW MX 1	SW MX 1	SW MO 1		SW MO	SW MX 1	SW MX	SW MX 1	SW MO 1	SW MX 1	SW MO	SW MX	SW MO 1	SW MX 1	SW MO 1	SW MX 1	SW MX 1	SW MO 1
0	—	—	**London Waterloo** [15] ⊖	d	22p37	22p53		23p07		23p10	23p12	23p20	23p23	23p30	23p35			23p35	23p40	23p40	23p45	23p48	
1¼	—	—	Vauxhall ⊖	d						23p14		23p24								23p44			
4	—	—	Clapham Junction [10]	d	22p46	23b00		23p15		23p19		23p29	23b30	23b39	23b42			23b44	23b47	23p49	23b52	23b55	
5½	—	—	Earlsfield	d						23p22		23p32								23p52			
7¼	—	—	Wimbledon [6] ⊖	d	22p53			23p22		23p26		23p36					←			23p56			
12	—	—	**Surbiton** [6]	d	23p02	23p11		23p30		23p35	23p38	23p44	23p41				23p44			00 05		00 09	
14½	—	—	Esher	d						23p39		→					23p48			00 09			
16	—	—	Hersham	d						23p42							23p51			00 12			
17	—	—	Walton-on-Thames	d	23p09					23p45	23p45						23p54			00 15		00 16	
19	—	—	Weybridge	d	23p13					23p49	23p49						23p57			00 19		00 20	
20½	—	—	Byfleet & New Haw	d						23p51							00 01			00 21			
21¾	—	—	West Byfleet	d		23p21				23p54			23p55			←	00 03			00 24			←
24½	0	—	**Woking**	a	23p19	23p29		23p42		23p59	23p55		23p59	00 01	00 01	23p59	00 08	00 07	00 06	00 30	00 11	00 26	00 30
—	—	—																					
—	—	—		d	23p26	23p30		23p46	23p49	00 05	23p57		00 01	00 03	00 03	00 05		00 08	00 08	00 35	00 13	00 28	00 35
—	2½	—	Worplesdon	d						→										→	00 18		
—	6	—	**Guildford**	a										00 10		00 13					00 24		
28	—	0	Brookwood	d	23p32	23p36		23p51	23p55		00 03		00 07									00 34	00 41
—	—	4½	Ash Vale	d	23p40	23p44	23p49		00 03				00 15										00 48
—	—	7	**Aldershot**	a	23p45	23p49	23p54		00 07				00 19										00 53
—	—	—		d	23p48	23p50	23p55		00 08				00 20										00 54
—	—	10	Farnham	a	23p54	23p55	00 03		00 13				00 25										00 59
—	—	—		d	23p55	23p57			00 14				00 26										
—	—	14	Bentley	d		00 03			00 24				00 33										
—	—	18¾	**Alton**	a	00 07	00 11			00 31				00 40										
33¼	—	—	Farnborough (Main)	d				23p59			00 10				00 14			00 18				00 41	
36½	—	—	Fleet	d				00 04			00 16				00 20			00 24				00 47	
40	—	—	Winchfield	d				00 10			00 21											00s52	
42¼	—	—	Hook	d				00 14			00 26											00s57	
47¼	—	—	**Basingstoke**	a				00 21			00 33				00 33			00 39	00 27			01 06	

		SW MX 1	SW MX 1	SW MX	SW MO 1	SW MX 1	SW 1	SW 1	SW 1	SW ◇1	SW 1	SW 1	SW 1	SW 1	SW	SW 1	SW 1	SW 1	SW 1	SW	SW ◇1	SW 1	SW
London Waterloo [15] ⊖	d	00 05		00 09	00 50		01 05	05 00	05 20	05 30					05 50		06 12	06 15		06 20	06 30		
Vauxhall ⊖	d			00 13			01 09	05 04	05 24						05 54					06 24			
Clapham Junction [10]	d	00u12		00 20	00 57			05 11	05 29	05u37					05 59		06u19	06u22		06 29	06u37		
Earlsfield	d			00 23				05 14	05 32						06 02					06 32			
Wimbledon [6] ⊖	d	00u18		00 27			01s27	05 18	05 36	05 43					06 06					06 36			
Surbiton [6]	d			00 35			01s35	05 26	05 44						06 14		06 30			06 44			
Esher	d			00s39				05 30	05 48						06 18					06 48			
Hersham	d			00s42				05 33	05 51						06 21					06 51			
Walton-on-Thames	d			00s44				05 37	05 54						06 24		06 37			06 54			
Weybridge	d			00s48				05 41	05 57						06 27		06 41			06 57			
Byfleet & New Haw	d			00s51				05 44	06 00						06 30					07 00			
West Byfleet	d			00s54				05 47	06 03			←			06 33				←	07 03			←
Woking	a	00 35		00 58	01 16		01 42	05 51	06 08	05 59		06 08			06 38		06 48	06 41	06 48	07 07	06 56		07 07
	d	00 37	00 40	01 00	01 18		01 42	05 53	06 11	06 01	06 02	06 11	06 19	06 30			06 50	06 43	06 50	07 10	06 57	06 58	07 10
Worplesdon	d								→			06 16					→	06 48		→			
Guildford	a			01 07	01s26			06 00				06 21						06 53					07 20
Brookwood	d		00 45								06 08		06 25	06 36					06 56			07 06	
Ash Vale	d		00 53			00 57					06 16			06 44		06 49						07 14	
Aldershot	a		00 58			01s02					06 21			06 49		06 56						07 19	
	d		00 59								06 21			06 50								07 20	
Farnham	a		01 04			01 11					06 27			06 55								07 25	
	d		01 05								06 27			06 56								07 26	
Bentley	d		01s11								06 34			07 02								07 32	
Alton	a		01 18								06 41			07 10								07 40	
Farnborough (Main)	d						01s58						06 33						07 04				
Fleet	d						02s04						06 38						07 09				
Winchfield	d												06 44						07 15				
Hook	d												06 48						07 19				
Basingstoke	a	00 55					02s16			06 20			06 58						07 28		07 16		

b Previous night, stops to pick up only

Table 155

Mondays to Fridays

London - Woking, Guildford, Alton and Basingstoke

		SW 1	SW 1	SW 1	SW 1	SW	SW 1	SW ◇1 🛒	SW	SW 1	SW 1	SW 1	SW 1	SW	SW 1	SW 1 🛒	SW 1	SW ◇1 🛒	SW	SW 1 🛒	SW 1	SW 1	SW 1
London Waterloo [15] ⊖	d		06 42	06 45		06 50	06 53	07 10			07 12	07 15		07 20	07 23	07 30		07 35		07 39		07 42	07 45
Vauxhall ⊖	d					06 54								07 24									
Clapham Junction [10]	d		06u49	06u52		06 59	07u00	07u17			07u20	07u23		07 29	07u30					07u46			07u52
Earlsfield	d					07 02								07 32									
Wimbledon [6] ⊖	d					07 06			←					07 36					←				
Surbiton [6]	d		07 00			07 14	07 11		07 14		07 31			07 44	07 41				07 44			08 00	
Esher	d					→			07 18					→					07 48				
Hersham	d								07 21										07 51				
Walton-on-Thames	d		07 07						07 24		07 38								07 54			08 07	
Weybridge	d		07 11						07 27		07 42								07 57			08 11	
Byfleet & New Haw	d								07 30										08 00				
West Byfleet	d				←		07 21		07 33				←		07 51		←		08 03				
Woking	a		07 18	07 11	07 18		07 26	07 35	07 37		07 48	07 42	07 48		07 59	07 54	07 59	07 58	08 08			08 18	08 12
	d		07 19	07 13	07 19		07 30	07 36	07 39		07 50	07 44	07 50		08 00	07 55	08 00	08 00				08 19	08 14
Worplesdon	d		→	07 18							→	07 49			→							→	08 19
Guildford	a			07 23					07 47			07 54				08 03							08 24
Brookwood	d				07 25		07 36						07 56				08 06						
Ash Vale	d	07 19					07 44			07 49							08 14				08 19		
Aldershot	a	07 26					07 49			07 54							08 19				08 24		
	d						07 50										08 20						
Farnham	a						07 55										08 25						
	d						07 56										08 26						
Bentley	d						08 02										08 32						
Alton	a						08 10										08 39						
Farnborough (Main)	d				07 33								08 03							08 13			
Fleet	d				07 38								08 09							08 19			
Winchfield	d				07 44								08 14										
Hook	d				07 48								08 19										
Basingstoke	a				07 56			07 55					08 26					08 19		08 32			

		SW ◇1 🛒	SW 1	SW	SW 1	SW 1 🛒	SW 1	SW ◇1 🛒	SW 1	SW	SW 1	SW 1	SW 1	SW ◇1 🛒	SW 1	SW	SW 1	SW 1 🛒	SW ◇1 🛒	SW 1	SW	SW 1
London Waterloo [15] ⊖	d	07 50		07 50	07 53	08 00		08 05	08 09			08 12	08 15	08 20		08 20	08 23	08 30	08 35			08 39
Vauxhall ⊖	d			07 54												08 24						
Clapham Junction [10]	d	07u57		07 59	08u00			08u12				08u19	08u22	08u27		08 29						08u46
Earlsfield	d			08 02												08 32						
Wimbledon [6] ⊖	d			08 06						←						08 36					←	
Surbiton [6]	d			08 14	08 11					08 14		08 30				08 44	08 41				08 44	
Esher	d			→						08 18						→					08 48	
Hersham	d									08 21											08 51	
Walton-on-Thames	d									08 24		08 37									08 54	
Weybridge	d									08 27		08 41									08 57	
Byfleet & New Haw	d									08 30											09 00	
West Byfleet	d		←		08 21		←			08 33					←		08 51			←	09 03	
Woking	a	08 15	08 18		08 29	08 24	08 29		08 33	08 37		08 49	08 42	08 46	08 49		09 00	08 55	08 58	09 00	09 08	
	d	08 16	08 19		08 30	08 25	08 30		08 35	08 39		08 49	08 44	08 46	08 49		09 00	08 55		09 00		
Worplesdon	d				→							→	08 49				→					
Guildford	a					08 35				08 50			08 54					09 05				
Brookwood	d		08 25				08 36								08 55					09 06		
Ash Vale	d						08 44				08 49									09 14		
Aldershot	a						08 49				08 54									09 20		
	d						08 50													09 20		
Farnham	a						08 55													09 26		
	d						08 56													09 26		
Bentley	d						09 02															
Alton	a						09 10													09 39		
Farnborough (Main)	d		08 33						08 45						09 03							09 13
Fleet	d		08 38												09 08							09 19
Winchfield	d		08 44												09 14							
Hook	d		08 48												09 18							
Basingstoke	a	08 37	08 58					08 47	08 58					09 05	09 28							09 31

London - Woking, Guildford, Alton and Basingstoke

		SW ■1	SW ■1	SW ■1	SW ◇■1 ⊼	SW ■1	SW		SW ■1	SW ■1 ⊼	SW ■1	SW ◇■1 ⊼	SW ■1	SW	SW ■1	SW ■1	SW ■1		SW ◇■1 ⊼	SW ■1	SW	SW ■1 A	SW ■1 B	SW ■1 ⊼	SW ◇■1 ⊼
London Waterloo 15 ⊖	d		08 42	08 45	08 50		08 50		08 53	09 00		09 05	09 09			09 12	09 15		09 20		09 20	09 23	09 23	09 30	09 35
Vauxhall ⊖	d						08 54														09 24				
Clapham Junction 10	d			08u52			08 59		09u00			09u12				09u19	09u22		09u27		09 29				
Earlsfield	d						09 02														09 32				
Wimbledon 6 ⊖	d						09 06							←							09 36				
Surbiton 6	d		09 00				09 14		09 11					09 14		09 30					09 44	09 41	09 41		
Esher	d						→							09 18							→				
Hersham	d													09 21											
Walton-on-Thames	d		09 07											09 24		09 37									
Weybridge	d		09 11											09 27		09 41									
Byfleet & New Haw	d													09 30											
West Byfleet	d					←			09 21		←			09 33						←		09 51	09 51		
Woking	a		09 18	09 11	09 15	09 18			09 29	09 24	09 29		09 33	09 38		09 48	09 42		09 45	09 48		09 59	09 59	09 54	09 58
	d		09 19	09 13	09 16	09 19			09 30	09 25	09 30		09 35			09 49	09 43		09 46	09 49		10 00	10 00	09 55	
Worplesdon	d		→	09 18					→							→						→	→		
Guildford	a			09 23						09 33							09 52							10 03	
Brookwood	d					09 25					09 36									09 55					
Ash Vale	d	09 19									09 44				09 49										
Aldershot	a	09 25									09 49				09 54										
	d										09 50														
Farnham	a										09 55														
	d										09 56														
Bentley	d										10 02														
Alton	a										10 10														
Farnborough (Main)	d					09 33							09 45							10 03					
Fleet	d					09 38														10 08					
Winchfield	d					09 44														10 14					
Hook	d					09 48														10 18					
Basingstoke	a				09 36	09 58						09 47	09 58						10 05	10 28					

		SW ■1 A	SW ■1 B		SW	SW ■1	SW ■1	SW ■1	SW ■1	SW ◇■1 ⊼	SW ■1	SW	SW ■1		SW ■1 ⊼	SW ■1	SW ◇■1 ⊼	SW ■1	SW	SW ■1	SW ■1	SW ■1	SW ◇■1 ⊼		SW ■1
London Waterloo 15 ⊖	d					09 39		09 42	09 45	09 50		09 50	09 53		10 00		10 05	10 09			10 12	10 15	10 20		
Vauxhall ⊖	d											09 54													
Clapham Junction 10	d					09u46			09u52			09 59	10u00				10u12				10u19	10u22	10u27		
Earlsfield	d											10 02													
Wimbledon 6 ⊖	d				←							10 06							←						
Surbiton 6	d				09 44			10 00				10 14	10 11						10 14		10 30				
Esher	d				09 48							→							10 18						
Hersham	d				09 51														10 21						
Walton-on-Thames	d				09 54			10 07											10 24		10 37				
Weybridge	d				09 57			10 11											10 27		10 41				
Byfleet & New Haw	d				10 00														10 30						
West Byfleet	d	←	←		10 03						←		10 21			←			10 33						←
Woking	a	09 59	09 59		10 08			10 18	10 11	10 14	10 18		10 29		10 24	10 29		10 33	10 38		10 48	10 41	10 45		10 48
	d	10 00	10 00					10 19	10 13	10 16	10 19		10 30		10 25	10 30		10 35			10 49	10 43	10 46		10 49
Worplesdon	d							→	10 18				→								→				
Guildford	a								10 23						10 33							10 50			
Brookwood	d	10 06	10 06								10 25					10 36									10 55
Ash Vale	d	10 14	10 14				10 19									10 44				10 49					
Aldershot	a	10 19	10 19				10 24									10 49				10 54					
	d	10 20	10 20													10 50									
Farnham	a	10 25	10 25													10 55									
	d	10 26	10 26													10 56									
Bentley	d		10b52													11 02									
Alton	a	10 37	10 59													11 10									
Farnborough (Main)	d					10 13					10 33							10 45							11 03
Fleet	d					10 19					10 38														11 08
Winchfield	d										10 44														11 14
Hook	d										10 48														11 18
Basingstoke	a					10 31				10 36	10 58						10 47	10 58					11 05		11 28

A until 30 September

B from 3 October

b Arr. 1032

London - Woking, Guildford, Alton and Basingstoke

		SW	SW ■1	SW ■1 ⊼	SW ◇■1 ⊼	SW ■1	SW	SW ■1	SW ■1		SW ■1	SW ■1	SW ◇■1 ⊼	SW ■1	SW	SW ■1	SW ■1 ⊼	SW ■1	SW ◇■1 ⊼		SW ■1	SW	SW ■1	SW ■1	SW ■1
London Waterloo 15 ⊖	d	10 20	10 23	10 30	10 35			10 39			10 42	10 45	10 50		10 50	10 53	11 00		11 05		11 09			11 12	11 15
Vauxhall ⊖	d	10 24													10 54										
Clapham Junction 10	d	10 29						10u46				10u52			10 59	11u00			11u12					11u19	11u22
Earlsfield	d	10 32													11 02										
Wimbledon 6 ⊖	d	10 36					←								11 06							←			
Surbiton 6	d	10 44	10 41				10 44				11 00				11 14	11 11						11 14		11 30	
Esher	d	→					10 48								→							11 18			
Hersham	d						10 51															11 21			
Walton-on-Thames	d						10 54				11 07											11 24		11 37	
Weybridge	d						10 57				11 11											11 27		11 41	
Byfleet & New Haw	d						11 00															11 30			
West Byfleet	d		10 51			←	11 03							←		11 21		←				11 33			
Woking	a		10 59	10 54	10 58	10 59	11 08				11 18	11 11	11 14	11 18		11 29	11 24	11 29			11 33	11 38		11 48	11 41
	d		11 00	10 55		11 00					11 19	11 13	11 16	11 19		11 30	11 25	11 30			11 35			11 49	11 43
Worplesdon	d		→								→	11 18				→								→	
Guildford	a			11 03								11 23					11 33								11 50
Brookwood	d					11 06								11 25				11 36							
Ash Vale	d					11 14			11 19									11 44					11 49		
Aldershot	a					11 19			11 24									11 49					11 54		
	d					11 20												11 50							
Farnham	a					11 25												11 55							
	d																	11 56							
Bentley	d																	12 02							
Alton	a																	12 10							
Farnborough (Main)	d							11 13						11 33							11 45				
Fleet	d							11 19						11 38											
Winchfield	d													11 44											
Hook	d													11 48											
Basingstoke	a							11 31					11 36	11 58					11 47		11 58				

		SW ◇■1 ⊼	SW ■1	SW	SW ■1		SW ■1 ⊼	SW ◇■1 ⊼	SW ■1	SW	SW ■1	SW ■1	SW ■1	SW ■1	SW ◇■1 ⊼		SW ■1	SW	SW ■1	SW ■1 ⊼	SW ■1	SW ◇■1 ⊼	SW ■1	SW	SW ■1
London Waterloo 15 ⊖	d	11 20		11 20	11 23		11 30	11 35			11 39		11 42	11 45	11 50			11 50	11 53	12 00		12 05	12 09		
Vauxhall ⊖	d			11 24														11 54							
Clapham Junction 10	d	11u27		11 29							11u46			11u52				11 59	12u00			12u12			
Earlsfield	d			11 32														12 02							
Wimbledon 6 ⊖	d			11 36						←								12 06						←	
Surbiton 6	d			11 44	11 41					11 44			12 00					12 14	12 11					12 14	
Esher	d			→						11 48								→						12 18	
Hersham	d									11 51														12 21	
Walton-on-Thames	d									11 54			12 07											12 24	
Weybridge	d									11 57			12 11											12 27	
Byfleet & New Haw	d									12 00														12 30	
West Byfleet	d		←		11 51				←	12 03							←		12 21		←			12 33	
Woking	a	11 45	11 48		11 59		11 54	11 58	11 59	12 08			12 18	12 11	12 14		12 18		12 29	12 24	12 29		12 33	12 38	
	d	11 46	11 49		12 00		11 55		12 00				12 19	12 13	12 16		12 19		12 30	12 25	12 30		12 35		
Worplesdon	d				→								→	12 18					→						
Guildford	a						12 03							12 23						12 33					
Brookwood	d		11 55						12 06								12 25				12 36				
Ash Vale	d								12 14			12 19									12 44				12 49
Aldershot	a								12 19			12 24									12 49				12 54
	d								12 20												12 50				
Farnham	a								12 25												12 55				
	d								12 26												12 56				
Bentley	d																				13 02				
Alton	a								12 37												13 10				
Farnborough (Main)	d		12 03								12 13						12 33						12 45		
Fleet	d		12 08								12 19						12 38								
Winchfield	d		12 14														12 44								
Hook	d		12 18														12 48								
Basingstoke	a	12 05	12 28								12 31				12 36		12 58					12 47	12 58		

London - Woking, Guildford, Alton and Basingstoke

	SW 1	SW 1	SW ◇1 🛒	SW 1	SW	SW 1	SW 1 🛒	SW ◇1 🛒	SW 1	SW	SW 1	SW 1	SW 1	SW 1	SW ◇1 🛒	SW 1	SW	SW 1	SW 1 🛒	SW 1	SW ◇1 🛒
London Waterloo 15 ⊖ d	12 12	12 15	12 20		12 20	12 23	12 30	12 35			12 39		12 42	12 45	12 50		12 50	12 53	13 00		13 05
Vauxhall ⊖ d					12 24												12 54				
Clapham Junction 10 d	12u19	12u22	12u27		12 29						12u46			12u52			12 59	13u00			13u12
Earlsfield d					12 32												13 02				
Wimbledon 8 ⊖ d					12 36					←							13 06				
Surbiton 8 d	12 30				12 44	12 41				12 44			13 00				13 14	13 11			
Esher d					→					12 48							→				
Hersham d										12 51											
Walton-on-Thames d	12 37									12 54			13 07								
Weybridge d	12 41									12 57			13 11								
Byfleet & New Haw d										13 00											
West Byfleet d				←		12 51			←	13 03						←		13 21		←	
Woking a	12 48	12 41	12 45	12 48		12 59	12 54	12 58	12 59	13 08			13 18	13 11	13 14	13 18		13 29	13 24	13 29	
d	12 49	12 43	12 46	12 49		13 00	12 55		13 00				13 19	13 13	13 16	13 19		13 30	13 25	13 30	
Worplesdon d	→					→							→	13 18				→			
Guildford a		12 50					13 03							13 23					13 33		
Brookwood d				12 55					13 06							13 25				13 36	
Ash Vale d									13 14			13 19								13 44	
Aldershot a									13 19			13 24								13 49	
d									13 20											13 50	
Farnham a									13 25											13 55	
d									13 26											13 56	
Bentley d																				14 02	
Alton a									13 37											14 11	
Farnborough (Main) d				13 03							13 13					13 33					
Fleet d				13 08							13 19					13 38					
Winchfield d				13 14												13 44					
Hook d				13 18												13 48					
Basingstoke a			13 05	13 28							13 31				13 36	13 58					13 47

	SW 1	SW	SW 1	SW 1	SW 1	SW ◇1 🛒	SW 1	SW	SW 1	SW 1 🛒	SW ◇1 🛒	SW 1	SW	SW 1	SW 1	SW 1	SW 1	SW ◇1 🛒	SW 1	SW	SW 1	SW 1 🛒
London Waterloo 15 ⊖ d	13 09			13 12	13 15	13 20		13 20	13 23	13 30	13 35			13 39		13 42	13 45	13 50		13 50	13 53	14 00
Vauxhall ⊖ d								13 24												13 54		
Clapham Junction 10 d				13u19	13u22	13u27		13 29						13u46			13u52			13 59	14u00	
Earlsfield d								13 32												14 02		
Wimbledon 8 ⊖ d		←						13 36					←							14 06		
Surbiton 8 d		13 14		13 30				13 44	13 41				13 44			14 00				14 14	14 11	
Esher d		13 18						→					13 48							→		
Hersham d		13 21											13 51									
Walton-on-Thames d		13 24		13 37									13 54			14 07						
Weybridge d		13 27		13 41									13 57			14 11						
Byfleet & New Haw d		13 30											14 00									
West Byfleet d		13 33					←		13 51			←	14 03						←		14 21	
Woking a	13 33	13 38		13 48	13 41	13 45	13 48		13 59	13 54	13 58	13 59	14 08			14 18	14 11	14 14	14 18		14 29	14 24
d	13 35			13 49	13 43	13 46	13 49		14 00	13 55		14 00				14 19	14 13	14 16	14 19		14 30	14 25
Worplesdon d				→					→							→	14 18				→	
Guildford a					13 50					14 03							14 23					14 33
Brookwood d							13 55					14 06							14 25			
Ash Vale d			13 49									14 14			14 19							
Aldershot a			13 54									14 19			14 24							
d												14 20										
Farnham a												14 25										
d												14 26										
Bentley d																						
Alton a												14 37										
Farnborough (Main) d	13 45						14 03							14 13					14 33			
Fleet d							14 08							14 19					14 38			
Winchfield d							14 14												14 44			
Hook d							14 18												14 48			
Basingstoke a	13 58					14 05	14 28							14 31				14 36	14 58			

London - Woking, Guildford, Alton and Basingstoke

	SW 1	SW ◇1 🛒	SW 1	SW	SW 1	SW 1	SW 1	SW ◇1 🛒	SW 1	SW	SW 1	SW 1 🛒	SW ◇1 🛒	SW 1	SW	SW 1	SW 1	SW 1	SW 1	SW ◇1 🛒	SW 1
London Waterloo 15 ⊖ d		14 05	14 09			14 12	14 15	14 20		14 20	14 23	14 30	14 35			14 39		14 42	14 45	14 50	
Vauxhall ⊖ d										14 24											
Clapham Junction 10 d		14u12				14u19	14u22	14u27		14 29						14u46			14u52		
Earlsfield d										14 32											
Wimbledon 8 ⊖ d				←						14 36					←						
Surbiton 8 d				14 14		14 30				14 44	14 41				14 44			15 00			
Esher d				14 18						→					14 48						
Hersham d				14 21											14 51						
Walton-on-Thames d				14 24		14 37									14 54			15 07			
Weybridge d				14 27		14 41									14 57			15 11			
Byfleet & New Haw d				14 30											15 00						
West Byfleet d	←			14 33					←		14 51			←	15 03						←
Woking a	14 29		14 33	14 38		14 48	14 41	14 45	14 48		14 59	14 54	14 58	14 59	15 08			15 18	15 11	15 14	15 18
d	14 30		14 35			14 49	14 43	14 46	14 49		15 00	14 55		15 00				15 19	15 13	15 16	15 19
Worplesdon d						→					→							→	15 18		
Guildford a							14 50					15 03							15 23		
Brookwood d	14 36								14 55					15 06							15 25
Ash Vale d	14 44				14 49									15 14			15 19				
Aldershot a	14 49				14 54									15 19			15 24				
d	14 50													15 20							
Farnham a	14 55													15 25							
d	14 56													15 26							
Bentley d	15 02																				
Alton a	15 10													15 37							
Farnborough (Main) d			14 45						15 03							15 13					15 33
Fleet d									15 08							15 19					15 38
Winchfield d									15 14												15 44
Hook d									15 18												15 48
Basingstoke a		14 47	14 58					15 05	15 28							15 31				15 36	15 58

	SW	SW 1	SW 1 🛒	SW 1	SW ◇1 🛒	SW 1	SW	SW 1	SW 1	SW 1	SW ◇1 🛒	SW 1	SW	SW 1	SW 1 🛒	SW ◇1 🛒	SW 1	SW	SW 1	SW 1	SW 1	SW 1
London Waterloo 15 ⊖ d	14 50	14 53	15 00		15 05	15 09			15 12	15 15	15 20		15 20	15 23	15 30	15 35			15 39		15 42	15 45
Vauxhall ⊖ d	14 54												15 24									
Clapham Junction 10 d	14 59	15u00			15u12				15u19	15u22	15u27		15 29						15u46			15u52
Earlsfield d	15 02												15 32									
Wimbledon 8 ⊖ d	15 06						←						15 36					←				
Surbiton 8 d	15 14	15 11					15 14		15 30				15 44	15 41				15 44			16 00	
Esher d	→						15 18						→					15 48				
Hersham d							15 21											15 51				
Walton-on-Thames d							15 24		15 37									15 54			16 07	
Weybridge d							15 27		15 41									15 57			16 11	
Byfleet & New Haw d							15 30											16 00				
West Byfleet d		15 21		←			15 33					←		15 51			←	16 03				
Woking a		15 29	15 24	15 29		15 33	15 38		15 48	15 41	15 45	15 48		15 59	15 54	15 58	15 59	16 08			16 18	16 11
d		15 30	15 25	15 30		15 35			15 49	15 43	15 46	15 49		16 00	15 55		16 00				16 19	16 13
Worplesdon d		→							→	15 48				→							→	
Guildford a			15 33							15 53					16 03							16 20
Brookwood d				15 36								15 55					16 06					
Ash Vale d				15 44				15 49									16 14			16 19		
Aldershot a				15 49				15 54									16 19			16 24		
d				15 50													16 20					
Farnham a				15 55													16 25					
d				15 56													16 26					
Bentley d				16 02																		
Alton a				16 10													16 37					
Farnborough (Main) d						15 45						16 03							16 13			
Fleet d												16 08							16 19			
Winchfield d												16 14										
Hook d												16 18										
Basingstoke a					15 47	15 58					16 05	16 28							16 31			

London - Woking, Guildford, Alton and Basingstoke

		SW ◇1 ⌶	SW 1	SW	SW 1	SW 1 ⌶	SW 1	SW ◇1 ⌶	SW 1	SW	SW 1	SW 1	SW 1	SW ◇1 ⌶	SW 1	SW	SW 1	SW 1 ⌶	SW 1	SW	SW ◇1 ⌶	SW 1	SW 1
London Waterloo 15 ⊖	d	15 50		15 50	15 53	16 00		16 05	16 09			16 12	16 15	16 20		16 20	16 25	16 30			16 35	16 39	
Vauxhall ⊖	d			15 54												16 24							
Clapham Junction 10	d	15u57		15 59	16u00			16u12				16u19	16u22	16u27		16 29						16u46	
Earlsfield	d			16 02												16 32							
Wimbledon 6 ⊖	d			16 06						←						16 36				←			
Surbiton 6	d			16 14	16 11					16 14		16 30				16 44	16 41			16 44			
Esher	d			→						16 18						→				16 48			
Hersham	d									16 21										16 51			
Walton-on-Thames	d									16 24		16 37								16 54			
Weybridge	d									16 27		16 41								16 57			
Byfleet & New Haw	d									16 30										17 00			
West Byfleet	d		←		16 21		←			16 33					←		16 51		←	17 03			
Woking	a	16 15	16 18		16 29	16 24	16 29		16 33	16 38		16 48	16 41	16 45	16 48		16 59	16 54	16 59	17 10			
	d	16 16	16 19		16 30	16 25	16 30		16 35			16 49	16 43	16 46	16 49		17 00	16 55	17 00				
Worplesdon	d				→							→	16 48				→						
Guildford	a					16 33							16 53					17 03					
Brookwood	d		16 25				16 36								16 55				17 06				
Ash Vale	d						16 44				16 49								17 14				17 19
Aldershot	a						16 49				16 54								17 19				17 24
	d						16 50												17 20				
Farnham	a						16 55												17 25				
	d						16 56												17 26				
Bentley	d						17 02												17 32				
Alton	a						17 10												17 41				
Farnborough (Main)	d		16 33						16 45						17 03							17 13	
Fleet	d		16 38												17 08							17 19	
Winchfield	d		16 44												17 14								
Hook	d		16 48												17 18								
Basingstoke	a	16 36	16 58					16 47	16 58					17 05	17 30							17 31	

		SW 1	SW 1	SW ◇1 ⌶	SW 1	SW	SW 1	SW 1 ⌶	SW 1	SW 1	SW 1	SW 1	SW 1	SW 1	SW 1	SW ◇1 ⌶	SW	SW 1	SW 1	SW 1	SW 1 ⌶	SW
London Waterloo 15 ⊖	d	16 42	16 45	16 50		16 50	16 55	17 00			17 02	17 09	17 12	17 15		17 20	17 20	17 23	17 25		17 30	
Vauxhall ⊖	d					16 54											17 24					
Clapham Junction 10	d		16u52	16u57		16 59	17u02										17 29					
Earlsfield	d					17 02											17 32					
Wimbledon 6 ⊖	d					17 06											17 36					←
Surbiton 6	d	17 00				17 14					17 18						17 44	17 39				17 44
Esher	d					17 18					17 22						→					17 48
Hersham	d					17 21					17 25											17 51
Walton-on-Thames	d	17 07				17 24					17 29											17 54
Weybridge	d	17 11				17 27					17 33											17 57
Byfleet & New Haw	d					17 30					17 36											18 00
West Byfleet	d				←	17 33	17 21		←		17 39				←					←		18 03
Woking	a	17 18	17 11		17 18	17 43	17 29	17 24	17 29		17 44	17 32	17 36	17 38	17 44			17 51	17 50	17 51	17 54	18 10
	d	17 19	17 13	17u16	17 19		17 30	17 25	17 30		17 46	17 34	17 37	17 40	17 46	17u46		17 52	17 51	17 52	17 56	
Worplesdon	d	→					→	17 30			→			17 45				→			18 00	
Guildford	a		17 20					17 36						17 51	17 56						18 06	
Brookwood	d				17 25				17 36				17 43							18 00		
Ash Vale	d								17 44	17 49									18 03			
Aldershot	a								17 49	17 54									18 08			
	d								17 50										18 09			
Farnham	a								17 55										18 14			
	d								17 56										18 15			
Bentley	d								18 02										18 24			
Alton	a								18 11										18 32			
Farnborough (Main)	d				17 33								17 51							18 08		
Fleet	d				17 38								17 56							18 13		
Winchfield	d				17 44								18 02							18 19		
Hook	d				17 48								18 06							18 23		
Basingstoke	a			17 36	18 00							17 52	18 16			18 05				18 32		

London - Woking, Guildford, Alton and Basingstoke

		SW 1	SW 1	SW 1	SW 1	SW 1	SW ◇1 ⌶	SW	SW 1	SW 1	SW 1	SW	SW 1	SW 1	SW 1	SW 1	SW ◇1 ⌶	SW 1	SW	SW 1	SW 1	SW 1 ⌶	SW
London Waterloo 15 ⊖	d	17 32	17 39	17 41	17 48		17 50	17 50	17 53	17 55			18 02	18 09	18 12	18 18	18 20		18 20	18 23	18 25	18 30	
Vauxhall ⊖	d							17 54											18 24				
Clapham Junction 10	d							17 59									18u27		18 29		18u33		
Earlsfield	d							18 02											18 32				
Wimbledon 6 ⊖	d							18 06				←							18 36				←
Surbiton 6	d	17 48						18 14	18 09			18 14	18 18						18 44	18 40			18 44
Esher	d	17 52						→				18 18	18 22						→				18 48
Hersham	d	17 55										18 21	18 25										18 51
Walton-on-Thames	d	17 59										18 24	18 29										18 54
Weybridge	d	18 03										18 27	18 33										18 57
Byfleet & New Haw	d	18 06										18 30	18 36										19 00
West Byfleet	d	18 09				←			18 19		←	18 33	18 39										19 03
Woking	a	18 14	18 02		18 11	18 14			18 23	18 20	18 23	18 40	18 48	18 33		18 42	18 45			18 52	18 52	18 57	19 12
	d	18 16	18 04		18 13	18 16			18 25	18 21	18 25			18 35		18 43	18 46			18 54	18 53	18 58	
Worplesdon	d	→				18 21			→							18 48							
Guildford	a					18 29										18 54						19 06	
Brookwood	d			18 11						18 27					18 41					19 02			
Ash Vale	d									18 35								18 49			19 05		
Aldershot	a									18 40								18 54			19 10		
	d									18 41											19 11		
Farnham	a									18 46											19 16		
	d									18 48											19 18		
Bentley	d									18 54											19 24		
Alton	a									19 03											19 33		
Farnborough (Main)	d			18 19							18 39				18 48					19 10			
Fleet	d			18 24							18 44				18 54					19 15			
Winchfield	d			18 30							18 50				18 59					19 21			
Hook	d			18 34							18 54				19 04					19 25			
Basingstoke	a		18 22	18 45	18 31		18 37				19 03			18 53	19 16		19 05			19 34			

		SW 1	SW 1	SW 1	SW 1	SW ◇1 ⌶	SW 1	SW	SW 1	SW 1 ⌶	SW 1	SW ◇1 ⌶	SW 1	SW 1	SW 1	SW ◇1 ⌶	SW	SW 1	SW 1	SW 1 ⌶	SW ◇1 ⌶	SW 1
London Waterloo 15 ⊖	d	18 32	18 39	18 41	18 45	18 50		18 50	18 55	19 00	19 02	19 05	19 09	19 12	19 15	19 20	19 20		19 25	19 30	19 35	
Vauxhall ⊖	d							18 54									19 24					
Clapham Junction 10	d		18u46					18 59	19u02			19u12		19u19	19u22	19u27	19 29		19u32			
Earlsfield	d							19 02									19 32					
Wimbledon 6 ⊖	d							19 06									19 36					
Surbiton 6	d	18 48						19 14			19 18						19 44					
Esher	d	18 52						19 18			19 22						19 48					
Hersham	d	18 55						19 21			19 25						19 51					
Walton-on-Thames	d	18 59						19 24			19 29						19 54					
Weybridge	d	19 03						19 27			19 33						19 57					
Byfleet & New Haw	d	19 06						19 30			19 36						20 00					
West Byfleet	d	19 09			19 08		←	19 33			19 39						20 03		19 51			←
Woking	a	19 18	19 05		19 13	19 17	19 18	19 42	19 21	19 24	19 48		19 33	19 38	19 43	19 45	20 08		19 59	19 54	19 58	19 59
	d	19 20	19 06		19 14	19 18	19 20		19 23	19 25			19 35	19 39	19 45	19 46			20 00	19 55		20 00
Worplesdon	d	→								19 30									→			
Guildford	a				19 23					19 36					19 52					20 03		
Brookwood	d			19 13					19 30					19 45								20 06
Ash Vale	d								19 37									19 49				20 14
Aldershot	a								19 42									19 54				20 19
	d								19 43													20 20
Farnham	a								19 48													20 25
	d								19 49													20 26
Bentley	d								19 55													20 32
Alton	a								20 04													20 39
Farnborough (Main)	d			19 20			19 31						19 45	19 53								
Fleet	d			19 26			19 37							19 58								
Winchfield	d			19 31			19 42							20 04								
Hook	d			19 36			19 47							20 09								
Basingstoke	a		19 28	19 47		19 37	19 59					19 47	19 58	20 16		20 06						

Table 155

Mondays to Fridays

London - Woking, Guildford, Alton and Basingstoke

	SW [1]	SW [1]	SW [1]	SW [1]	SW ◇[1] 🍴	SW [1]	SW	SW [1]	SW [1] 🍴	SW [1]	SW ◇[1] 🍴	SW [1]	SW	SW [1]	SW [1]	SW [1]	SW ◇[1] 🍴	SW [1]	SW	SW [1]	SW [1] 🍴	SW ◇[1] 🍴
London Waterloo [15] ⊖ d	19 39		19 42	19 45	19 50		19 50	19 53	20 00		20 05	20 09			20 12	20 15	20 20		20 20	20 23	20 30	20 35
Vauxhall ⊖ d							19 54												20 24			
Clapham Junction [10] d	19u46			19u52			19 59	20u00			20u12				20u19	20u22	20u27		20 29			
Earlsfield d							20 02												20 32			
Wimbledon [8] ⊖ d							20 06						←						20 36			
Surbiton [8] d			20 00				20 14	20 11					20 14		20 30				20 44	20 41		
Esher d							→						20 18						→			
Hersham d													20 21									
Walton-on-Thames d			20 07										20 24		20 37							
Weybridge d			20 11										20 27		20 41							
Byfleet & New Haw d													20 30									
West Byfleet d						←		20 21		←			20 33					←		20 51		
Woking a			20 18	20 11	20 14	20 18		20 29	20 24	20 29		20 33	20 38		20 48	20 41	20 45	20 48		20 59	20 54	20 58
Woking d			20 19	20 13	20 16	20 19		20 30	20 25	20 30		20 35			20 49	20 43	20 46	20 49		21 00	20 55	
Worplesdon d			→	20 18				→							→					→		
Guildford a				20 23					20 33							20 50					21 03	
Brookwood d						20 25				20 36								20 55				
Ash Vale d		20 19								20 44				20 49								
Aldershot a		20 24								20 49				20 54								
Aldershot d										20 50												
Farnham a										20 55												
Farnham d										20 56												
Bentley d										21 02												
Alton a										21 10												
Farnborough (Main) d	20 13					20 33						20 45						21 03				
Fleet d	20 19					20 38												21 08				
Winchfield d						20 44												21 14				
Hook d						20 48												21 18				
Basingstoke a	20 31				20 36	20 58					20 47	20 58					21 05	21 28				

	SW [1]	SW	SW [1]	SW [1]	SW [1]	SW [1]	SW [1]	SW	SW [1]	SW [1] 🍴	SW [1]	SW ◇[1] 🍴	SW	SW [1]	SW ◇[1] 🍴	SW [1]	SW	SW [1]	SW [1] 🍴	SW ◇[1] 🍴	SW [1]	SW
London Waterloo [15] ⊖ d			20 39		20 42	20 45		20 50	20 53	21 00		21 05		21 12	21 20		21 20	21 23	21 30	21 35		
Vauxhall ⊖ d								20 54									21 24					
Clapham Junction [10] d			20u46			20u52		20 59	21u00			21u12		21u19	21u27		21 29					
Earlsfield d								21 02									21 32					
Wimbledon [8] ⊖ d		←						21 06					←				21 36					←
Surbiton [8] d		20 44			21 00			21 14	21 11				21 14	21 30			21 44	21 41				21 44
Esher d		20 48						→					21 18				→					21 48
Hersham d		20 51											21 21									21 51
Walton-on-Thames d		20 54			21 07								21 24	21 37								21 54
Weybridge d		20 57			21 11								21 27	21 41								21 57
Byfleet & New Haw d		21 00											21 30									22 00
West Byfleet d	←	21 03					←		21 21		←		21 33					21 51			←	22 03
Woking a	20 59	21 08			21 18	21 11	21 18		21 29	21 24	21 29	21 31	21 38	21 48	21 45			21 59	21 54	21 58	21 59	22 08
Woking d	21 00				21 19	21 13	21 19		21 30	21 25	21 30	21 32		21 49	21 49			22 00	21 55		22 00	
Worplesdon d					→	21 18			→									→				
Guildford a						21 23				21 33									22 03			
Brookwood d	21 06						21 25				21 36			21 55							22 06	
Ash Vale d	21 14			21 19							21 44					21 49					22 14	
Aldershot a	21 19			21 24							21 49					21 54					22 19	
Aldershot d	21 20										21 50										22 20	
Farnham a	21 25										21 55										22 25	
Farnham d	21 26										21 56										22 26	
Bentley d	21 32										22 02										22 32	
Alton a	21 39										22 10										22 39	
Farnborough (Main) d			21 13				21 33							22 03								
Fleet d			21 19				21 38							22 08								
Winchfield d							21 44							22 14								
Hook d							21 48							22 18								
Basingstoke a			21 31				21 58					21 51		22 28	22 08							

Table 155

Mondays to Fridays

London - Woking, Guildford, Alton and Basingstoke

	SW [1]	SW [1]	SW [1]	SW [1]	SW	SW [1]	SW [1]	SW [1]	SW ◇[1] 🍴	SW	SW [1]	SW [1] 🍴	SW [1]	SW	SW [1]	SW [1]	SW ◇[1] 🍴	SW [1]	SW	SW [1]	SW [1]
London Waterloo [15] ⊖ d	21 39	21 42	21 45		21 50	21 53	22 00		22 05		22 12	22 20		22 20	22 23	22 30	22 35			22 39	22 42
Vauxhall ⊖ d					21 54									22 24							
Clapham Junction [10] d	21u46		21u52		21 59	22u00			22u12		22u19	22u27		22 29	22u30					22u46	22u49
Earlsfield d					22 02									22 32							
Wimbledon [8] ⊖ d					22 06					←				22 36					←		
Surbiton [8] d		22 00			22 14	22 11				22 14	22 30			22 44	22 41				22 44		23 00
Esher d					→					22 18				→					22 48		
Hersham d										22 21									22 51		
Walton-on-Thames d		22 07								22 24	22 37								22 54		23 07
Weybridge d		22 11								22 27	22 41								22 57		23 11
Byfleet & New Haw d										22 30									23 00		
West Byfleet d				←		22 21		←		22 33					22 51			←	23 03		
Woking a		22 18	22 11	22 18		22 29	22 24	22 29	22 31	22 37	22 48	22 45			22 59	22 54	22 58	22 59	23 08		23 18
Woking d		22 19	22 13	22 19		22 30	22 25	22 30	22 32	22 39	22 49	22 49			23 00	22 55		23 00			23 19
Worplesdon d		→	22 18			→									→						→
Guildford a			22 23				22 33			22 47						23 03					
Brookwood d				22 25				22 36			22 55							23 06			
Ash Vale d								22 44					22 49					23 14			
Aldershot a								22 50					22 54					23 19			
Aldershot d								22 50										23 20			
Farnham a								22 56										23 25			
Farnham d								22 56										23 26			
Bentley d								23 02										23 32			
Alton a								23 10										23 39			
Farnborough (Main) d	22 13			22 33							23 03									23 16	
Fleet d	22 19			22 38							23 08									23 21	
Winchfield d				22 44							23 14										
Hook d				22 48							23 18										
Basingstoke a	22 31			22 58					22 51		23 27	23 09								23 33	

	SW [1]	SW [1]	SW	SW [1]	SW ◇[1]	SW	SW [1]	SW [1]	SW [1]	SW [1]	SW	SW [1]	SW [1]	SW	SW [1]	SW [1]	SW [1]
London Waterloo [15] ⊖ d	22 45		22 50	22 53	23 05			23 12	23 15		23 20	23 23	23 35		23 40	23 45	23 48
Vauxhall ⊖ d			22 54								23 24						
Clapham Junction [10] d	22u52		22 59	23u00	23u12				23u22		23 29	23u30	23u42		23u47	23u52	23u55
Earlsfield d			23 02								23 32						
Wimbledon [8] ⊖ d			23 06			←					23 36			←			
Surbiton [8] d			23 14	23 11		23 14		23 38			23 44	23 41		23 44			00 09
Esher d			→			23 18					→			23 48			
Hersham d						23 21								23 51			
Walton-on-Thames d						23 24		23 45						23 54			00 16
Weybridge d						23 27		23 49						23 57			00 20
Byfleet & New Haw d						23 30								00 01			
West Byfleet d		←		23 21		23 33				←		23 55		00 03			
Woking a	23 11	23 18		23 29	23 31	23 38		23 55	23 41	23 55		23 59	00 01	00 08	00 06	00 11	00 26
Woking d	23 13	23 19		23 30	23 32			23 57	23 43	23 57		00 01	00 03		00 08	00 13	00 28
Worplesdon d	23 18							→								00 18	
Guildford a	23 23								23 51							00 24	
Brookwood d		23 25		23 36						00 03		00 07					00 34
Ash Vale d				23 44			23 49					00 15					
Aldershot a				23 49			23 54					00 19					
Aldershot d				23 50			23 55					00 20					
Farnham a				23 55			00 03					00 25					
Farnham d				23 57								00 26					
Bentley d				00 03								00 33					
Alton a				00 11								00 40					
Farnborough (Main) d		23 33								00 10			00 14				00 41
Fleet d		23 38								00 16			00 20				00 47
Winchfield d		23 44								00 21							00s52
Hook d		23 48								00 26							00s57
Basingstoke a		23 57			23 53					00 33			00 33		00 27		01 06

London - Woking, Guildford, Alton and Basingstoke

		SW ■	SW ■	SW ■	SW	SW ■	SW ■	SW	SW ■	SW ■		SW ■	SW ■	SW ■	SW	SW ■	SW ■	SW ■	SW ■	SW ◇■		SW ■	SW ■	SW ■	SW ■
London Waterloo [15] ⊖	d	22p53	23p12		23p20	23p23	23p35		23p40	23p45		23p48	00 05		00 09		01 05	05 00	05 20	05 30					
Vauxhall ⊖	d				23p24										00 13		01 09	05 04	05 24						
Clapham Junction [10]	d	23b00			23p29	23b30	23b42		23b47	23b52		23b55	00u12		00 20		01 15	05 11	05 29	05u37					
Earlsfield	d				23p32										00 23			05 14	05 32						
Wimbledon [6] ⊖	d				23p36			←					00u18		00 27		01s20	05 18	05 36	05 43					
Surbiton [6]	d	23p11	23p38		23p44	23p41		23p44				00 09			00 35		01s28	05 26	05 44						
Esher	d				→			23p48							00s39			05 30	05 48						
Hersham	d							23p51							00s42			05 33	05 51						
Walton-on-Thames	d		23p45					23p54				00 16			00s44			05 37	05 54						
Weybridge	d		23p49					23p57				00 20			00s48			05 41	05 57						
Byfleet & New Haw	d							00 01							00s51			05 44	06 00						
West Byfleet	d	23p21				23p55		00 03							00s54			05 47	06 03				←		
Woking	a	23p29	23p55			23p59	00 01	00 08	00 06	00 11		00 26	00 35		00 58		01 41	05 51	06 08	05 59			06 08		
	d	23p30	23p57			00 01	00 03		00 08	00 13		00 28	00 37	00 40	01 00		01 42	05 53	06 13	06 01		06 02	06 13	06 19	06 30
Worplesdon	d									00 18									→				06 18		
Guildford	a									00 24					01 07			06 00					06 23		
Brookwood	d	23p36	00 03			00 07						00 34		00 45								06 08		06 25	06 36
Ash Vale	d	23p44		23p49		00 15								00 53		00 57						06 16			06 44
Aldershot	a	23p49		23p54		00 19								00 58		01s02						06 21			06 49
	d	23p50		23p55		00 20								00 59								06 21			06 50
Farnham	a	23p55		00 03		00 25								01 04		01 11						06 27			06 55
	d	23p57				00 26								01 05								06 27			06 56
Bentley	d	00 03				00 33								01s11								06 34			07 02
Alton	a	00 11				00 40								01 18								06 41			07 10
Farnborough (Main)	d		00 10				00 14					00 41					01s51							06 33	
Fleet	d		00 16				00 20					00 47					01s57							06 38	
Winchfield	d		00 21									00s52												06 43	
Hook	d		00 26									00s57												06 48	
Basingstoke	a		00 33				00 33		00 27			01 06	00 55				02s09			06 20				06 58	

		SW	SW ■	SW ■	SW ■	SW		SW ◇■	SW ■	SW ■	SW ■	SW ■	SW ■	SW	SW ■	SW ◇■ ⊼		SW	SW ■	SW ■	SW ■	SW	SW ■	SW ■	SW ■
London Waterloo [15] ⊖	d	05 50	06 12	06 15		06 20		06 30			06 42	06 45		06 50	06 53	07 10			07 12	07 15		07 20	07 23	07 30	
Vauxhall ⊖	d	05 54				06 24								06 54								07 24			
Clapham Junction [10]	d	05 59	06u19	06u22		06 29		06u37			06u49	06u52		06 59	07u00	07u17			07u20	07u23		07 29	07u30		
Earlsfield	d	06 02				06 32								07 02								07 32			
Wimbledon [6] ⊖	d	06 06				06 36								07 06				←				07 36			
Surbiton [6]	d	06 14	06 30			06 44					07 00			07 14	07 11			07 14	07 31			07 44	07 41		
Esher	d	06 18				06 48								→				07 18				→			
Hersham	d	06 21				06 51												07 21							
Walton-on-Thames	d	06 24	06 37			06 54					07 07							07 24	07 38						
Weybridge	d	06 27	06 41			06 57					07 11							07 27	07 42						
Byfleet & New Haw	d	06 30				07 00												07 30							
West Byfleet	d	06 33			←	07 03							←		07 21			07 33			←		07 51		←
Woking	a	06 38	06 48	06 41	06 48	07 08		06 56			07 18	07 11	07 18		07 26	07 35		07 38	07 48	07 42	07 48		07 59	07 54	07 59
	d		06 49	06 43	06 49			06 57	07 00		07 19	07 13	07 19		07 30	07 36			07 50	07 44	07 50		08 00	07 55	08 00
Worplesdon	d		→								→	07 18							→				→		
Guildford	a			06 51								07 23								07 51				08 03	
Brookwood	d				06 55				07 06				07 25		07 36						07 56				08 06
Ash Vale	d								07 14	07 19					07 44										08 14
Aldershot	a								07 19	07 24					07 49										08 19
	d								07 20						07 50										08 20
Farnham	a								07 25						07 55										08 25
	d								07 26						07 56										08 26
Bentley	d								07 32						08 02										08 32
Alton	a								07 40						08 10										08 39
Farnborough (Main)	d				07 03								07 33								08 03				
Fleet	d				07 08								07 38								08 09				
Winchfield	d				07 14								07 44								08 14				
Hook	d				07 18								07 48								08 19				
Basingstoke	a				07 28			07 16					07 58			07 57					08 28				

b Previous night, stops to pick up only

London - Woking, Guildford, Alton and Basingstoke

		SW ◇■		SW	SW ■	SW ■	SW ■	SW ■	SW ◇■ ⊼	SW ■	SW	SW ■		SW ■	SW ■	SW ◇■	SW ■	SW	SW ■	SW ■	SW ■	SW ◇■ ⊼		SW ■	SW
London Waterloo [15] ⊖	d	07 35			07 39		07 42	07 45	07 50		07 50	07 53		08 00		08 05	08 09			08 12	08 15	08 20			08 20
Vauxhall ⊖	d										07 54														08 24
Clapham Junction [10]	d				07u46			07u52	07u57		07 59	08u00				08u12				08u19	08u22	08u27			08 29
Earlsfield	d										08 02														08 32
Wimbledon [6] ⊖	d			←							08 06							←							08 36
Surbiton [6]	d			07 44			08 00				08 14	08 11						08 14		08 30					08 44
Esher	d			07 48							→							08 18							→
Hersham	d			07 51														08 21							
Walton-on-Thames	d			07 54			08 07											08 24		08 37					
Weybridge	d			07 57			08 11											08 27		08 41					
Byfleet & New Haw	d			08 00														08 30							
West Byfleet	d			08 03						←		08 21			←			08 33						←	
Woking	a	07 58		08 08			08 18	08 11	08 15	08 18		08 29		08 24	08 29		08 33	08 38		08 48	08 41	08 45		08 48	
	d	08 00					08 19	08 13	08 16	08 19		08 30		08 25	08 30		08 35			08 49	08 43	08 46		08 49	
Worplesdon	d						→	08 18				→								→					
Guildford	a							08 23						08 33							08 50				
Brookwood	d									08 25					08 36									08 55	
Ash Vale	d					08 19									08 44				08 49						
Aldershot	a					08 24									08 49				08 54						
	d														08 50										
Farnham	a														08 55										
	d														08 56										
Bentley	d														09 02										
Alton	a														09 10										
Farnborough (Main)	d				08 13					08 33							08 45							09 03	
Fleet	d				08 19					08 38														09 08	
Winchfield	d									08 44														09 14	
Hook	d									08 48														09 18	
Basingstoke	a	08 20			08 31				08 36	08 58						08 47	08 58					09 05		09 28	

		SW ■	SW ■	SW ◇■ ⊼	SW ■	SW	SW ■	SW ■		SW ■	SW ■	SW ◇■ ⊼	SW ■	SW	SW ■ A	SW ■ B	SW ■ ⊼	SW ■ A		SW ■ B	SW ◇■ ⊼	SW ■	SW	SW ■	SW ■
London Waterloo [15] ⊖	d	08 23	08 30	08 35			08 39			08 42	08 45	08 50		08 50	08 53	08 53	09 00				09 05	09 09			09 12
Vauxhall ⊖	d													08 54											
Clapham Junction [10]	d						08u46				08u52			08 59	09u00	09u00					09u12				09u19
Earlsfield	d													09 02											
Wimbledon [6] ⊖	d					←								09 06									←		
Surbiton [6]	d	08 41				08 44				09 00				09 14	09 11	09 11							09 14		09 30
Esher	d					08 48								→									09 18		
Hersham	d					08 51																	09 21		
Walton-on-Thames	d					08 54				09 07													09 24		09 37
Weybridge	d					08 57				09 11													09 27		09 41
Byfleet & New Haw	d					09 00																	09 30		
West Byfleet	d	08 51			←	09 03							←		09 21	09 21		←		←			09 33		
Woking	a	08 59	08 54	08 58	08 59	09 08				09 18	09 11	09 14	09 18		09 29	09 29	09 24	09 29		09 29		09 33	09 38		09 48
	d	09 00	08 55		09 00					09 19	09 13	09 16	09 19		09 30	09 30	09 25	09 30		09 30		09 35			09 49
Worplesdon	d	→								→	09 18				→	→									→
Guildford	a		09 03								09 23						09 33								
Brookwood	d				09 06								09 25					09 36		09 36					
Ash Vale	d				09 14			09 19										09 44		09 44				09 49	
Aldershot	a				09 19			09 24										09 49		09 49				09 54	
	d				09 20													09 50		09 50					
Farnham	a				09 25													09 55		09 55					
	d				09 26													09 56		09 56					
Bentley	d																	10 02		10 02					
Alton	a				09 37													10 10		10 29					
Farnborough (Main)	d						09 13						09 33									09 45			
Fleet	d						09 19						09 38												
Winchfield	d												09 44												
Hook	d												09 48												
Basingstoke	a						09 31					09 36	09 58								09 47	09 58			

A until 1 October

B from 8 October

Table 155

London - Woking, Guildford, Alton and Basingstoke

		SW 1	SW ◇1 ⌶	SW 1	SW	SW 1	SW 1 ⌶	SW ◇1 ⌶	SW 1	SW	SW 1	SW 1	SW 1	SW 1	SW ◇1 ⌶	SW 1	SW	SW 1	SW 1 ⌶	SW 1	SW ◇1 ⌶	SW 1
London Waterloo 15 ⊖	d	09 15	09 20		09 20	09 23	09 30	09 35			09 39		09 42	09 45	09 50		09 50	09 53	10 00		10 05	10 09
Vauxhall ⊖	d				09 24												09 54					
Clapham Junction 10	d	09u22	09u27		09 29						09u46			09u52			09 59	10u00			10u12	
Earlsfield	d				09 32												10 02					
Wimbledon 6 ⊖	d				09 36					←							10 06					
Surbiton 6	d				09 44	09 41				09 44			10 00				10 14	10 11				
Esher	d				→					09 48							→					
Hersham	d									09 51												
Walton-on-Thames	d									09 54			10 07									
Weybridge	d									09 57			10 11									
Byfleet & New Haw	d									10 00												
West Byfleet	d			←		09 51			←	10 03						←		10 21		←		
Woking	a	09 41	09 45	09 48		09 59	09 54	09 58	09 59	10 08			10 18	10 11	10 14	10 18		10 29	10 24	10 29		10 33
	d	09 43	09 46	09 49		10 00	09 55		10 00				10 19	10 13	10 16	10 19		10 30	10 25	10 30		10 35
Worplesdon	d					→							→	10 18				→				
Guildford	a	09 50					10 03							10 23					10 33			
Brookwood	d			09 55					10 06							10 25				10 36		
Ash Vale	d								10 14			10 19								10 44		
Aldershot	a								10 19			10 24								10 49		
	d								10 20											10 50		
Farnham	a								10 25											10 55		
	d								10 26											10 56		
Bentley	d																			11 02		
Alton	a								10 37											11 10		
Farnborough (Main)	d			10 03							10 13					10 33						10 45
Fleet	d			10 08							10 19					10 38						
Winchfield	d			10 14												10 44						
Hook	d			10 18												10 48						
Basingstoke	a		10 05	10 28							10 31				10 36	10 58					10 47	10 58

		SW	SW 1	SW 1	SW 1	SW ◇1 ⌶	SW 1	SW	SW 1	SW 1 ⌶	SW ◇1 ⌶	SW 1	SW	SW 1	SW 1	SW 1	SW 1	SW ◇1 ⌶	SW 1	SW	SW 1	SW 1 ⌶	SW 1
London Waterloo 15 ⊖	d			10 12	10 15	10 20		10 20	10 23	10 30	10 35			10 39		10 42	10 45	10 50		10 50	10 53	11 00	
Vauxhall ⊖	d							10 24												10 54			
Clapham Junction 10	d			10u19	10u22	10u27		10 29						10u46			10u52			10 59	11u00		
Earlsfield	d							10 32												11 02			
Wimbledon 6 ⊖	d	←						10 36					←							11 06			
Surbiton 6	d	10 14		10 30				10 44	10 41				10 44			11 00				11 14	11 11		
Esher	d	10 18						→					10 48							→			
Hersham	d	10 21											10 51										
Walton-on-Thames	d	10 24		10 37									10 54			11 07							
Weybridge	d	10 27		10 41									10 57			11 11							
Byfleet & New Haw	d	10 30											11 00										
West Byfleet	d	10 33					←		10 51			←	11 03						←		11 21		←
Woking	a	10 38		10 48	10 41	10 45	10 48		10 59	10 54	10 58	10 59	11 08			11 18	11 11	11 14	11 18		11 29	11 24	11 29
	d			10 49	10 43	10 46	10 49		11 00	10 55		11 00				11 19	11 13	11 16	11 19		11 30	11 25	11 30
Worplesdon	d			→					→							→	11 18				→		
Guildford	a				10 50					11 03							11 23					11 33	
Brookwood	d						10 55					11 06							11 25				11 36
Ash Vale	d		10 49									11 14			11 19								11 44
Aldershot	a		10 54									11 19			11 24								11 49
	d											11 20											11 50
Farnham	a											11 25											11 55
	d											11 26											11 56
Bentley	d																						12 02
Alton	a											11 37											12 10
Farnborough (Main)	d						11 03							11 13					11 33				
Fleet	d						11 08							11 19					11 38				
Winchfield	d						11 14												11 44				
Hook	d						11 18												11 48				
Basingstoke	a					11 05	11 28							11 31				11 36	11 58				

Table 155

London - Woking, Guildford, Alton and Basingstoke

		SW ◇1 ⌶	SW 1	SW	SW 1	SW 1	SW 1	SW ◇1 ⌶	SW 1	SW	SW 1	SW 1 ⌶	SW ◇1 ⌶	SW 1	SW	SW 1	SW 1	SW 1	SW 1	SW ◇1 ⌶	SW 1	SW	SW 1
London Waterloo 15 ⊖	d	11 05	11 09			11 12	11 15	11 20		11 20	11 23	11 30	11 35			11 39		11 42	11 45	11 50		11 50	11 53
Vauxhall ⊖	d									11 24												11 54	
Clapham Junction 10	d	11u12				11u19	11u22	11u27		11 29						11u46			11u52			11 59	12u00
Earlsfield	d									11 32												12 02	
Wimbledon 6 ⊖	d			←						11 36					←							12 06	
Surbiton 6	d			11 14		11 30				11 44	11 41				11 44			12 00				12 14	12 11
Esher	d			11 18						→					11 48							→	
Hersham	d			11 21											11 51								
Walton-on-Thames	d			11 24		11 37									11 54			12 07					
Weybridge	d			11 27		11 41									11 57			12 11					
Byfleet & New Haw	d			11 30											12 00								
West Byfleet	d			11 33					←		11 51			←	12 03						←		12 21
Woking	a		11 33	11 38		11 48	11 41	11 45	11 48		11 59	11 54	11 58	11 59	12 08			12 18	12 11	12 14	12 18		12 29
	d		11 35			11 49	11 43	11 46	11 49		12 00	11 55		12 00				12 19	12 13	12 16	12 19		12 30
Worplesdon	d					→					→							→	12 18				→
Guildford	a						11 50					12 03							12 23				
Brookwood	d								11 55					12 06							12 25		
Ash Vale	d				11 49									12 14			12 19						
Aldershot	a				11 54									12 19			12 24						
	d													12 20									
Farnham	a													12 25									
	d													12 26									
Bentley	d																						
Alton	a													12 37									
Farnborough (Main)	d		11 45						12 03							12 13					12 33		
Fleet	d								12 08							12 19					12 38		
Winchfield	d								12 14												12 44		
Hook	d								12 18												12 48		
Basingstoke	a	11 47	11 58					12 05	12 28							12 31				12 36	12 58		

		SW 1 ⌶	SW 1	SW ◇1 ⌶	SW 1	SW	SW 1	SW 1	SW 1	SW ◇1 ⌶	SW 1	SW	SW 1	SW 1 ⌶	SW ◇1 ⌶	SW 1	SW	SW 1	SW 1	SW 1	SW 1	SW ◇1 ⌶
London Waterloo 15 ⊖	d	12 00		12 05	12 09			12 12	12 15	12 20		12 20	12 23	12 30	12 35			12 39		12 42	12 45	12 50
Vauxhall ⊖	d											12 24										
Clapham Junction 10	d			12u12				12u19	12u22	12u27		12 29						12u46			12u52	
Earlsfield	d											12 32										
Wimbledon 6 ⊖	d					←						12 36					←					
Surbiton 6	d					12 14		12 30				12 44	12 41				12 44			13 00		
Esher	d					12 18						→					12 48					
Hersham	d					12 21											12 51					
Walton-on-Thames	d					12 24		12 37									12 54			13 07		
Weybridge	d					12 27		12 41									12 57			13 11		
Byfleet & New Haw	d					12 30											13 00					
West Byfleet	d		←			12 33					←		12 51			←	13 03					
Woking	a	12 24	12 29		12 33	12 38		12 48	12 41	12 45	12 48		12 59	12 54	12 58	12 59	13 08			13 18	13 11	13 14
	d	12 25	12 30		12 35			12 49	12 43	12 46	12 49		13 00	12 55		13 00				13 19	13 13	13 16
Worplesdon	d							→					→							→	13 18	
Guildford	a	12 33							12 50					13 03							13 23	
Brookwood	d		12 36								12 55					13 06						
Ash Vale	d		12 44				12 49									13 14			13 19			
Aldershot	a		12 49				12 54									13 19			13 24			
	d		12 50													13 20						
Farnham	a		12 55													13 25						
	d		12 56													13 26						
Bentley	d		13 02																			
Alton	a		13 10													13 37						
Farnborough (Main)	d				12 45						13 03							13 13				
Fleet	d										13 08							13 19				
Winchfield	d										13 14											
Hook	d										13 18											
Basingstoke	a			12 47	12 58					13 05	13 28							13 31				13 36

London - Woking, Guildford, Alton and Basingstoke

	SW [1]	SW	SW [1]	SW [1] ⚲	SW [1]	SW ◇[1] ⚲	SW [1]		SW	SW [1]	SW [1]	SW [1]	SW ◇[1] ⚲	SW [1]	SW	SW [1]	SW [1] ⚲		SW ◇[1] ⚲	SW [1]	SW	SW [1]	SW [1]	SW [1]
London Waterloo [15] ⊖ d		12 50	12 53	13 00		13 05	13 09				13 12	13 15	13 20		13 20	13 23	13 30		13 35			13 39		13 42
Vauxhall ⊖ d		12 54													13 24									
Clapham Junction [10] d		12 59	13u00			13u12					13u19	13u22	13u27		13 29							13u46		
Earlsfield d		13 02													13 32									
Wimbledon [6] ⊖ d		13 06							←						13 36						←			
Surbiton [6] d		13 14	13 11						13 14		13 30				13 44	13 41					13 44			14 00
Esher d		→							13 18						→						13 48			
Hersham d									13 21												13 51			
Walton-on-Thames d									13 24		13 37										13 54			14 07
Weybridge d									13 27		13 41										13 57			14 11
Byfleet & New Haw d									13 30												14 00			
West Byfleet d	←		13 21		←				13 33					←		13 51				←	14 03			
Woking a	13 18		13 29	13 24	13 29		13 33		13 38		13 48	13 41	13 45	13 48		13 59	13 54		13 58	13 59	14 08			14 18
d	13 19		13 30	13 25	13 30		13 35				13 49	13 43	13 46	13 49		14 00	13 55			14 00				14 19
Worplesdon d			→								→					→								→
Guildford a				13 33								13 50					14 03							
Brookwood d	13 25				13 36									13 55						14 06				
Ash Vale d					13 44					13 49										14 14			14 19	
Aldershot a					13 49					13 54										14 19			14 24	
d					13 50															14 20				
Farnham a					13 55															14 25				
d					13 56															14 26				
Bentley d					14 02																			
Alton a					14 10															14 37				
Farnborough (Main) d	13 33						13 45							14 03								14 13		
Fleet d	13 38													14 08								14 19		
Winchfield d	13 44													14 14										
Hook d	13 48													14 18										
Basingstoke a	13 58					13 47	13 58						14 05	14 28								14 31		

	SW [1]	SW ◇[1] ⚲	SW [1]		SW	SW [1]	SW [1] ⚲	SW [1]	SW ◇[1] ⚲	SW [1]	SW	SW [1]	SW [1]		SW [1]	SW ◇[1] ⚲	SW [1]	SW	SW [1]	SW [1] ⚲	SW ◇[1] ⚲	SW [1]	SW	
London Waterloo [15] ⊖ d	13 45	13 50			13 50	13 53	14 00		14 05	14 09			14 12		14 15	14 20		14 20	14 23	14 30	14 35			
Vauxhall ⊖ d					13 54													14 24						
Clapham Junction [10] d	13u52				13 59	14u00			14u12				14u19		14u22	14u27		14 29						
Earlsfield d					14 02													14 32						
Wimbledon [6] ⊖ d					14 06						←							14 36					←	
Surbiton [6] d					14 14	14 11					14 14		14 30					14 44	14 41				14 44	
Esher d					→						14 18							→					14 48	
Hersham d											14 21												14 51	
Walton-on-Thames d											14 24		14 37										14 54	
Weybridge d											14 27		14 41										14 57	
Byfleet & New Haw d											14 30												15 00	
West Byfleet d			←			14 21		←			14 33						←		14 51			←	15 03	
Woking a	14 11	14 14	14 18			14 29	14 24	14 29		14 33	14 38		14 48		14 41	14 45	14 48		14 59	14 54	14 58	14 59	15 08	
d	14 13	14 16	14 19			14 30	14 25	14 30		14 35			14 49		14 43	14 46	14 49		15 00	14 55		15 00		
Worplesdon d	14 18					→							→						→					
Guildford a	14 23						14 33								14 50					15 03				
Brookwood d			14 25					14 36									14 55					15 06		
Ash Vale d								14 44				14 49										15 14		
Aldershot a								14 49				14 54										15 19		
d								14 50														15 20		
Farnham a								14 55														15 25		
d								14 56														15 26		
Bentley d								15 02																
Alton a								15 10														15 37		
Farnborough (Main) d			14 33							14 45							15 03							
Fleet d			14 38														15 08							
Winchfield d			14 44														15 14							
Hook d			14 48														15 18							
Basingstoke a		14 36	14 58						14 47	14 58						15 05	15 28							

London - Woking, Guildford, Alton and Basingstoke

	SW [1]	SW [1]	SW [1]	SW [1]	SW ◇[1] ⚲	SW [1]	SW	SW [1]	SW [1] ⚲		SW [1]	SW ◇[1] ⚲	SW [1]	SW	SW [1]	SW [1]	SW [1]	SW ◇[1] ⚲	SW [1]		SW	SW [1]	SW [1] ⚲	SW ◇[1] ⚲
London Waterloo [15] ⊖ d	14 39		14 42	14 45	14 50		14 50	14 53	15 00			15 05	15 09			15 12	15 15	15 20			15 20	15 23	15 30	15 35
Vauxhall ⊖ d							14 54														15 24			
Clapham Junction [10] d	14u46			14u52			14 59	15u00				15u12				15u19	15u22	15u27			15 29			
Earlsfield d							15 02														15 32			
Wimbledon [6] ⊖ d							15 06							←							15 36			
Surbiton [6] d			15 00				15 14	15 11						15 14		15 30					15 44	15 41		
Esher d							→							15 18							→			
Hersham d														15 21										
Walton-on-Thames d			15 07											15 24		15 37								
Weybridge d			15 11											15 27		15 41								
Byfleet & New Haw d														15 30										
West Byfleet d						←		15 21			←			15 33					←			15 51		
Woking a			15 18	15 11	15 14	15 18		15 29	15 24		15 29		15 33	15 38		15 48	15 41	15 45	15 48			15 59	15 54	15 58
d			15 19	15 13	15 16	15 19		15 30	15 25		15 30		15 35			15 49	15 43	15 46	15 49			16 00	15 55	
Worplesdon d			→	15 18				→								→						→		
Guildford a				15 23					15 33								15 50						16 03	
Brookwood d						15 25					15 36								15 55					
Ash Vale d		15 19									15 44				15 49									
Aldershot a		15 24									15 49				15 54									
d											15 50													
Farnham a											15 55													
d											15 56													
Bentley d											16 02													
Alton a											16 10													
Farnborough (Main) d	15 13					15 33							15 45						16 03					
Fleet d	15 19					15 38													16 08					
Winchfield d						15 44													16 14					
Hook d						15 48													16 18					
Basingstoke a	15 31				15 36	15 58						15 47	15 58					16 05	16 28					

	SW [1]	SW	SW [1]	SW [1]	SW [1]		SW [1]	SW ◇[1] ⚲	SW [1]	SW	SW [1]	SW [1] ⚲	SW [1]	SW ◇[1] ⚲	SW [1]		SW	SW [1]	SW [1]	SW [1]	SW ◇[1] ⚲	SW [1]	SW	SW [1]
London Waterloo [15] ⊖ d			15 39		15 42		15 45	15 50		15 50	15 53	16 00		16 05	16 09				16 12	16 15	16 20		16 20	16 23
Vauxhall ⊖ d										15 54													16 24	
Clapham Junction [10] d			15u46				15u52			15 59	16u00			16u12					16u19	16u22	16u27		16 29	
Earlsfield d										16 02													16 32	
Wimbledon [6] ⊖ d		←								16 06							←						16 36	
Surbiton [6] d		15 44			16 00					16 14	16 11						16 14		16 30				16 44	16 41
Esher d		15 48								→							16 18						→	
Hersham d		15 51															16 21							
Walton-on-Thames d		15 54			16 07												16 24		16 37					
Weybridge d		15 57			16 11												16 27		16 41					
Byfleet & New Haw d		16 00															16 30							
West Byfleet d	←	16 03							←		16 21		←				16 33					←		16 51
Woking a	15 59	16 08			16 18		16 11	16 14	16 18		16 29	16 24	16 29		16 33		16 38		16 48	16 41	16 45	16 48		16 59
d	16 00				16 19		16 13	16 16	16 19		16 30	16 25	16 30		16 35				16 49	16 43	16 46	16 49		17 00
Worplesdon d					→		16 18				→								→					→
Guildford a							16 23					16 33								16 50				
Brookwood d	16 06								16 25				16 36									16 55		
Ash Vale d	16 14			16 19									16 44					16 49						
Aldershot a	16 19			16 24									16 49					16 54						
d	16 20												16 50											
Farnham a	16 25												16 55											
d	16 26												16 56											
Bentley d													17 02											
Alton a	16 37												17 10											
Farnborough (Main) d			16 13						16 33						16 45							17 03		
Fleet d			16 19						16 38													17 08		
Winchfield d									16 44													17 14		
Hook d									16 48													17 18		
Basingstoke a			16 31					16 36	16 58					16 47	16 58						17 05	17 28		

Table 155

London - Woking, Guildford, Alton and Basingstoke

		SW 1 🍴	SW ◇1 🍴	SW 1	SW	SW 1	SW 1	SW 1	SW 1	SW ◇1 🍴	SW 1	SW	SW 1	SW 1 🍴	SW 1	SW ◇1 🍽	SW 1	SW	SW 1	SW 1	SW 1	SW ◇1 🍴
London Waterloo 15 ⊖	d	16 30	16 35			16 39		16 42	16 45	16 50		16 50	16 53	17 00		17 05	17 09			17 12	17 15	17 20
Vauxhall ⊖	d											16 54										
Clapham Junction 10	d					16u46			16u52			16 59	17u00			17u12				17u19	17u22	17u27
Earlsfield	d											17 02										
Wimbledon 6 ⊖	d				←							17 06						←				
Surbiton 6	d				16 44			17 00				17 14	17 11					17 14		17 30		
Esher	d				16 48							→						17 18				
Hersham	d				16 51													17 21				
Walton-on-Thames	d				16 54			17 07										17 24		17 37		
Weybridge	d				16 57			17 11										17 27		17 41		
Byfleet & New Haw	d				17 00													17 30				
West Byfleet	d			←	17 03						←		17 21		←			17 33				
Woking	a	16 54	16 58	16 59	17 08			17 18	17 11	17 14	17 18		17 29	17 24	17 29		17 33	17 38		17 48	17 41	17 45
	d	16 55		17 00				17 19	17 13	17 16	17 19		17 30	17 25	17 30		17 35			17 49	17 43	17 46
Worplesdon	d							→	17 18				→							→		
Guildford	a	17 03							17 23					17 33							17 50	
Brookwood	d			17 06							17 25				17 36							
Ash Vale	d			17 14			17 19								17 44				17 49			
Aldershot	a			17 19			17 24								17 49				17 54			
	d			17 20											17 50							
Farnham	a			17 25											17 55							
	d			17 26											17 56							
Bentley	d			17 32											18 02							
Alton	a			17 39											18 10							
Farnborough (Main)	d					17 13					17 33						17 45					
Fleet	d					17 19					17 38											
Winchfield	d										17 44											
Hook	d										17 48											
Basingstoke	a					17 31				17 36	17 58					17 47	17 58					18 05

		SW 1	SW	SW 1	SW 1 🍴	SW ◇1 🍴	SW 1	SW	SW 1	SW 1	SW 1	SW 1	SW ◇1 🍴	SW 1	SW	SW 1	SW 1 🍴	SW 1	SW ◇1 🍴	SW 1	SW	SW 1	SW 1
London Waterloo 15 ⊖	d		17 20	17 23	17 30	17 35			17 39		17 42	17 45	17 50		17 50	17 53	18 00		18 05	18 09			18 12
Vauxhall ⊖	d		17 24												17 54								
Clapham Junction 10	d		17 29						17u46			17u52			17 59	18u00			18u12				18u19
Earlsfield	d		17 32												18 02								
Wimbledon 6 ⊖	d		17 36					←							18 06						←		
Surbiton 6	d		17 44	17 41				17 44			18 00				18 14	18 11					18 14		18 30
Esher	d		→					17 48							→						18 18		
Hersham	d							17 51													18 21		
Walton-on-Thames	d							17 54			18 07										18 24		18 37
Weybridge	d							17 57			18 11										18 27		18 41
Byfleet & New Haw	d							18 00													18 30		
West Byfleet	d	←		17 51			←	18 03						←		18 21		←			18 33		
Woking	a	17 48		17 59	17 54	17 58	17 59	18 08			18 18	18 11	18 14	18 18		18 29	18 24	18 29		18 33	18 38		18 48
	d	17 49		18 00	17 55		18 00				18 19	18 13	18 16	18 19		18 30	18 25	18 30		18 35			18 49
Worplesdon	d			→							→	18 18				→							→
Guildford	a				18 03							18 23					18 33						
Brookwood	d	17 55					18 06							18 25				18 36					
Ash Vale	d						18 14			18 19								18 44				18 49	
Aldershot	a						18 19			18 24								18 49				18 54	
	d						18 20											18 50					
Farnham	a						18 25											18 55					
	d						18 26											18 56					
Bentley	d						18 32											19 02					
Alton	a						18 39											19 10					
Farnborough (Main)	d	18 03							18 13					18 33						18 45			
Fleet	d	18 08							18 19					18 38									
Winchfield	d	18 14												18 44									
Hook	d	18 18												18 48									
Basingstoke	a	18 28							18 31				18 36	18 58					18 47	18 58			

Table 155

London - Woking, Guildford, Alton and Basingstoke

		SW 1	SW ◇1 🍴	SW 1	SW	SW 1	SW 1 🍴	SW ◇1 🍴	SW 1	SW	SW 1	SW 1	SW 1	SW 1	SW ◇1 🍴	SW 1	SW	SW 1	SW 1 🍴	SW 1	SW ◇1 🍴	SW 1
London Waterloo 15 ⊖	d	18 15	18 20		18 20	18 23	18 30	18 35			18 39		18 42	18 45	18 50		18 50	18 53	19 00		19 05	19 09
Vauxhall ⊖	d				18 24												18 54					
Clapham Junction 10	d	18u22	18u27		18 29						18u46			18u52			18 59	19u00			19u12	
Earlsfield	d				18 32												19 02					
Wimbledon 6 ⊖	d				18 36					←							19 06					
Surbiton 6	d				18 44	18 41				18 44			19 00				19 14	19 11				
Esher	d				→					18 48							→					
Hersham	d									18 51												
Walton-on-Thames	d									18 54			19 07									
Weybridge	d									18 57			19 11									
Byfleet & New Haw	d									19 00												
West Byfleet	d			←		18 51			←	19 03						←		19 21		←		
Woking	a	18 41	18 45	18 48		18 59	18 54	18 58	18 59	19 08			19 18	19 11	19 15	19 18		19 29	19 24	19 29		19 33
	d	18 43	18 46	18 49		19 00	18 55		19 00				19 19	19 13	19 16	19 19		19 30	19 25	19 30		19 35
Worplesdon	d					→							→	19 18				→				
Guildford	a	18 50					19 03							19 23					19 33			
Brookwood	d			18 55					19 06							19 25				19 36		
Ash Vale	d								19 14			19 19								19 44		
Aldershot	a								19 19			19 24								19 49		
	d								19 20											19 50		
Farnham	a								19 25											19 55		
	d								19 26											19 56		
Bentley	d								19 32											20 02		
Alton	a								19 39											20 10		
Farnborough (Main)	d			19 03							19 13					19 33						19 45
Fleet	d			19 08							19 19					19 38						
Winchfield	d			19 14												19 44						
Hook	d			19 18												19 48						
Basingstoke	a		19 05	19 28							19 31				19 36	19 58					19 47	19 58

		SW	SW 1	SW 1	SW 1	SW ◇1 🍴	SW 1	SW	SW 1	SW 1 🍴	SW ◇1 🍴	SW 1	SW	SW 1	SW 1	SW 1	SW 1	SW ◇1 🍴	SW 1	SW	SW 1	SW 1	SW 1
London Waterloo 15 ⊖	d			19 12	19 15	19 20		19 20	19 23	19 30	19 35			19 39		19 42	19 45	19 50		19 50	19 53	20 00	
Vauxhall ⊖	d							19 24												19 54			
Clapham Junction 10	d			19u19	19u22	19u27		19 29						19u46			19u52			19 59	20u00		
Earlsfield	d							19 32												20 02			
Wimbledon 6 ⊖	d	←						19 36					←							20 06			
Surbiton 6	d	19 14		19 30				19 44	19 41				19 44			20 00				20 14	20 11		
Esher	d	19 18						→					19 48							→			
Hersham	d	19 21											19 51										
Walton-on-Thames	d	19 24		19 37									19 54			20 07							
Weybridge	d	19 27		19 41									19 57			20 11							
Byfleet & New Haw	d	19 30											20 00										
West Byfleet	d	19 33					←		19 51			←	20 03						←		20 21		←
Woking	a	19 38		19 48	19 41	19 45	19 48		19 59	19 54	19 58	19 59	20 08			20 18	20 11	20 14	20 18		20 29	20 24	20 29
	d			19 49	19 43	19 46	19 49		20 00	19 55		20 00				20 19	20 13	20 16	20 19		20 30	20 25	20 30
Worplesdon	d			→					→							→	20 18				→		
Guildford	a				19 50					20 03							20 23					20 33	
Brookwood	d						19 55					20 06							20 25				20 36
Ash Vale	d		19 49									20 14			20 19								20 44
Aldershot	a		19 54									20 19			20 24								20 49
	d											20 20											20 50
Farnham	a											20 25											20 55
	d											20 26											20 56
Bentley	d											20 32											21 02
Alton	a											20 39											21 10
Farnborough (Main)	d						20 03							20 13					20 33				
Fleet	d						20 08							20 19					20 38				
Winchfield	d						20 14												20 44				
Hook	d						20 18												20 48				
Basingstoke	a					20 05	20 28							20 31				20 36	20 58				

London - Woking, Guildford, Alton and Basingstoke

Station		SW ◇1 ⌶	SW 1	SW	SW 1	SW 1	SW 1	SW ◇1 ⌶	SW 1	SW	SW 1	SW 1
London Waterloo 15 ⊖	d	20 05	20 09			20 12	20 15	20 20		20 20	20 23	20 30
Vauxhall ⊖	d									20 24		
Clapham Junction 10	d	20u12				20u19	20u22	20u27		20 29		
Earlsfield	d									20 32		
Wimbledon 6 ⊖	d			←						20 36		
Surbiton 6	d			20 14		20 30				20 44	20 41	
Esher	d			20 18						→		
Hersham	d			20 21								
Walton-on-Thames	d			20 24		20 37						
Weybridge	d			20 27		20 41						
Byfleet & New Haw	d			20 30								
West Byfleet	d			20 33					←		20 51	
Woking	a		20 33	20 38		20 48	20 41	20 45	20 48		20 59	20 54
	d		20 35			20 49	20 43	20 46	20 49		21 00	20 55
Worplesdon	d					→					→	
Guildford	a						20 50					21 03
Brookwood	d								20 55			
Ash Vale	d				20 49							
Aldershot	a				20 54							
	d											
Farnham	a											
	d											
Bentley	d											
Alton	a											
Farnborough (Main)	d		20 45						21 03			
Fleet	d								21 08			
Winchfield	d								21 14			
Hook	d								21 18			
Basingstoke	a	20 47	20 58					21 05	21 28			

Station		SW ◇1 ⌶	SW 1	SW	SW 1	SW 1	SW 1	SW 1	SW 1	SW	SW 1	SW 1
London Waterloo 15 ⊖	d	20 35			20 39		20 42	20 45		20 50	20 53	21 00
Vauxhall ⊖	d									20 54		
Clapham Junction 10	d				20u46			20u52		20 59	21u00	
Earlsfield	d									21 02		
Wimbledon 6 ⊖	d			←						21 06		
Surbiton 6	d			20 44			21 00			21 14	21 11	
Esher	d			20 48						→		
Hersham	d			20 51								
Walton-on-Thames	d			20 54			21 07					
Weybridge	d			20 57			21 11					
Byfleet & New Haw	d			21 00								
West Byfleet	d		←	21 03					←		21 21	
Woking	a	20 58	20 59	21 08			21 18	21 11	21 18		21 29	21 24
	d		21 00				21 19	21 13	21 19		21 30	21 25
Worplesdon	d						→	21 18			→	
Guildford	a							21 23				21 33
Brookwood	d		21 06						21 25			
Ash Vale	d		21 14			21 19						
Aldershot	a		21 19			21 24						
	d		21 20									
Farnham	a		21 25									
	d		21 26									
Bentley	d		21 32									
Alton	a		21 39									
Farnborough (Main)	d				21 13				21 33			
Fleet	d				21 19				21 38			
Winchfield	d								21 44			
Hook	d								21 48			
Basingstoke	a				21 31				21 58			

Station		SW 1	SW ◇1 ⌶	SW	SW 1	SW ◇1 ⌶	SW 1	SW	SW 1	SW 1	SW ◇1 ⌶
London Waterloo 15 ⊖	d		21 05		21 12	21 20		21 20	21 23	21 30	21 35
Vauxhall ⊖	d							21 24			
Clapham Junction 10	d		21u12		21u19	21u27		21 29			
Earlsfield	d							21 32			
Wimbledon 6 ⊖	d			←				21 36			
Surbiton 6	d			21 14	21 30			21 44	21 41		
Esher	d			21 18				→			
Hersham	d			21 21							
Walton-on-Thames	d			21 24	21 37						
Weybridge	d			21 27	21 41						
Byfleet & New Haw	d			21 30							
West Byfleet	d	←		21 33					21 51		
Woking	a	21 29	21 31	21 38	21 48	21 45			21 59	21 54	21 58
	d	21 30	21 32		21 49	21 49			22 00	21 55	
Worplesdon	d								→		
Guildford	a									22 03	
Brookwood	d	21 36			21 55						
Ash Vale	d	21 44					21 49				
Aldershot	a	21 49					21 54				
	d	21 50									
Farnham	a	21 55									
	d	21 56									
Bentley	d	22 02									
Alton	a	22 10									
Farnborough (Main)	d				22 03						
Fleet	d				22 08						
Winchfield	d				22 14						
Hook	d				22 18						
Basingstoke	a		21 51		22 25	22 09					

Station		SW 1	SW	SW 1	SW 1	SW 1	SW 1	SW	SW 1	SW 1	SW 1	SW ◇1 ⌶
London Waterloo 15 ⊖	d			21 39	21 42	21 45		21 50	21 53	22 00		22 05
Vauxhall ⊖	d							21 54				
Clapham Junction 10	d			21u46		21u52		21 59	22u00			22u12
Earlsfield	d							22 02				
Wimbledon 6 ⊖	d		←					22 06				
Surbiton 6	d		21 44		22 00			22 14	22 11			
Esher	d		21 48					→				
Hersham	d		21 51									
Walton-on-Thames	d		21 54		22 07							
Weybridge	d		21 57		22 11							
Byfleet & New Haw	d		22 00									
West Byfleet	d	←	22 03				←		22 21		←	
Woking	a	21 59	22 08		22 18	22 11	22 18		22 29	22 24	22 29	22 31
	d	22 00			22 19	22 13	22 19		22 30	22 25	22 30	22 32
Worplesdon	d				→	22 18			→			
Guildford	a					22 23				22 33		
Brookwood	d	22 06					22 25				22 36	
Ash Vale	d	22 14									22 44	
Aldershot	a	22 19									22 50	
	d	22 20									22 50	
Farnham	a	22 25									22 56	
	d	22 26									22 56	
Bentley	d	22 32									23 02	
Alton	a	22 39									23 10	
Farnborough (Main)	d			22 13			22 33					
Fleet	d			22 19			22 38					
Winchfield	d						22 44					
Hook	d						22 48					
Basingstoke	a			22 31			22 58					22 51

London - Woking, Guildford, Alton and Basingstoke

Station		SW	SW 1	SW 1 ⌶	SW 1	SW	SW 1	SW 1	SW ◇1 ⌶	SW 1	SW	SW 1
London Waterloo 15 ⊖	d		22 12	22 20		22 20	22 23	22 30	22 35			22 39
Vauxhall ⊖	d					22 24						
Clapham Junction 10	d		22u19	22u27		22 29	22u30					22u46
Earlsfield	d					22 32						
Wimbledon 6 ⊖	d	←				22 36					←	
Surbiton 6	d	22 14	22 30			22 44	22 41				22 44	
Esher	d	22 18				→					22 48	
Hersham	d	22 21									22 51	
Walton-on-Thames	d	22 24	22 37								22 54	
Weybridge	d	22 27	22 41								22 57	
Byfleet & New Haw	d	22 30									23 00	
West Byfleet	d	22 33					22 51			←	23 03	
Woking	a	22 37	22 48	22 45			22 59	22 54	22 58	22 59	23 08	
	d	22 39	22 49	22 49			23 00	22 55		23 00		
Worplesdon	d						→					
Guildford	a	22 47						23 03				
Brookwood	d		22 55							23 06		
Ash Vale	d				22 49					23 14		
Aldershot	a				22 54					23 19		
	d									23 20		
Farnham	a									23 25		
	d									23 26		
Bentley	d									23 32		
Alton	a									23 39		
Farnborough (Main)	d		23 03									23 16
Fleet	d		23 08									23 21
Winchfield	d		23 14									
Hook	d		23 18									
Basingstoke	a		23 25	23 10								23 34

Station		SW 1	SW 1	SW 1	SW	SW 1	SW ◇1	SW	SW 1	SW 1	SW 1	SW 1
London Waterloo 15 ⊖	d	22 42	22 45		22 50	22 53	23 05			23 12	23 15	
Vauxhall ⊖	d				22 54							
Clapham Junction 10	d	22u49	22u52		22 59	23u00	23u12				23u22	
Earlsfield	d				23 02							
Wimbledon 6 ⊖	d				23 06			←				
Surbiton 6	d	23 00			23 14	23 11		23 14		23 38		
Esher	d				→			23 18				
Hersham	d							23 21				
Walton-on-Thames	d	23 07						23 24		23 45		
Weybridge	d	23 11						23 27		23 49		
Byfleet & New Haw	d							23 30				
West Byfleet	d			←		23 21		23 33				←
Woking	a	23 18	23 11	23 18		23 29	23 31	23 38		23 55	23 41	23 55
	d	23 19	23 13	23 19		23 30	23 32			23 57	23 43	23 57
Worplesdon	d	→	23 18							→		
Guildford	a		23 23								23 51	
Brookwood	d			23 25		23 36						00 03
Ash Vale	d					23 44						
Aldershot	a					23 49						
	d					23 50			23 58			
Farnham	a					23 55			00 03			
	d					23 57						
Bentley	d					00 03						
Alton	a					00 11						
Farnborough (Main)	d			23 33								00 10
Fleet	d			23 38								00 16
Winchfield	d			23 44								00 21
Hook	d			23 48								00 26
Basingstoke	a			23 55			23 51					00 33

Station		SW	SW 1	SW 1	SW	SW 1	SW 1	SW 1
London Waterloo 15 ⊖	d	23 20	23 23	23 35		23 40	23 45	23 48
Vauxhall ⊖	d	23 24						
Clapham Junction 10	d	23 29	23u30	23u42		23u47	23u52	23u54
Earlsfield	d	23 32						
Wimbledon 6 ⊖	d	23 36			←			
Surbiton 6	d	23 44	23 41		23 44			00 09
Esher	d	→			23 48			
Hersham	d				23 51			
Walton-on-Thames	d				23 54			00 16
Weybridge	d				23 57			00 20
Byfleet & New Haw	d				23 59			
West Byfleet	d		23 55		00 03			
Woking	a		23 59	00 01	00 08	00 06	00 11	00 26
	d		00 01	00 03		00 08	00 13	00 28
Worplesdon	d						00 18	
Guildford	a						00 24	
Brookwood	d		00 07					00 34
Ash Vale	d		00 15					
Aldershot	a		00 19					
	d		00 20					
Farnham	a		00 25					
	d		00 26					
Bentley	d		00 33					
Alton	a		00 40					
Farnborough (Main)	d			00 14				00 41
Fleet	d			00 20				00 47
Winchfield	d							00s52
Hook	d							00s57
Basingstoke	a			00 33		00 27		01 06

London - Woking, Guildford, Alton and Basingstoke

Station		SW ■ A	SW ■ A	SW ■ A	SW A	SW ■ A	SW ■ A	SW A	SW ■ A	SW ■ A	SW ■ A	SW ■	SW ■	SW	SW ■	SW ■	SW ■	SW ■	SW ■	SW	SW ■	SW	SW ◇■
London Waterloo 15 ⊖	d	22p53	23p12		23p20	23p23	23p35		23p40	23p45	23p48	00 05		00 09		01 05				07 10		07 40	07 54
Vauxhall ⊖	d				23p24									00 13		01 09				07 14		07 44	
Clapham Junction 10	d	23b00			23p29	23b30	23b42		23b47	23b52	23b54	00u12		00 20						07 19		07 49	08u03
Earlsfield	d				23p32									00 23						07 22		07 52	
Wimbledon 6 ⊖	d				23p36			←				00u18		00 27		01s27				07 26		07 56	
Surbiton 6	d	23p11	23p38		23p44	23p41		23p44			00 09			00 35		01s35				07 35		08 05	
Esher	d				→			23p48						00s39						07 39		08 09	
Hersham	d							23p51						00s42						07 42		08 12	
Walton-on-Thames	d		23p45					23p54			00 16			00s44						07 45		08 15	
Weybridge	d		23p49					23p57			00 20			00s48						07 49		08 19	
Byfleet & New Haw	d							23p59						00s51						07 51		08 21	
West Byfleet	d	23p21				23p55		00 03						00s54						07 54		08 24	
Woking	a	23p29	23p55			23p59	00 01	00 08	00 06	00 11	00 26	00 35		00 58		01 42				07 59		08 29	08 27
	d	23p30	23p57			00 01	00 03		00 08	00 13	00 28	00 37	00 40	01 00		01 42	07 32	07 46	07 49	08 05		08 32	08 28
Worplesdon	d									00 18												→	
Guildford	a									00 24				01 07			07 39			08 14			
Brookwood	d	23p36	00 03			00 07					00 34		00 45					07 51	07 55				
Ash Vale	d	23p44				00 15							00 53		00 57				08 03		08 36		
Aldershot	a	23p49				00 19							00 58		01s02				08 07		08 41		
	d	23p50		23p58		00 20							00 59						08 08				
Farnham	a	23p55		00 03		00 25							01 04		01 11				08 13				
	d	23p57				00 26							01 05						08 14				
Bentley	d	00 03				00 33							01s11						08 24				
Alton	a	00 11				00 40							01 18						08 31				
Farnborough (Main)	d		00 10				00 14				00 41					01s58		07 59					
Fleet	d		00 16				00 20				00 47					02s04		08 04					
Winchfield	d		00 21								00s52							08 10					
Hook	d		00 26								00s57							08 14					
Basingstoke	a		00 33				00 33		00 27		01 06	00 55				02s16		08 21					08 46

Station		SW	SW ■	SW ■	SW ■	SW	SW ◇■ ⌶	SW ■	SW ■	SW	SW ■	SW ◇■	SW ■	SW	SW ◇■	SW	SW ■	SW ■	SW ■	SW	SW ◇■ ⌶	SW ■	SW ■
London Waterloo 15 ⊖	d		08 00	08 07	08 07	08 10	08 15				08 30	08 35		08 40	08 54		09 00	09 07	09 07	09 10	09 15		
Vauxhall ⊖	d					08 14								08 44						09 14			
Clapham Junction 10	d		08u09	08 15	08 15	08 19	08u22				08u39	08u45		08 49	09u03		09u09	09 15	09 15	09 19	09u22		
Earlsfield	d					08 22								08 52						09 22			
Wimbledon 6 ⊖	d			08 22	08 22	08 26								08 56				09 22	09 22	09 26			
Surbiton 6	d			08 30	08 30	08 35								09 05				09 30	09 30	09 35			
Esher	d					08 39								09 09						09 39			
Hersham	d					08 42								09 12						09 42			
Walton-on-Thames	d					08 45								09 15						09 45			
Weybridge	d					08 49								09 19						09 49			
Byfleet & New Haw	d					08 51								09 21						09 51			
West Byfleet	d	←				08 54		←		←				09 24		←				09 54		←	
Woking	a	08 29	08 34	08 42	08 42	08 59	08 46	08 42		08 59	09 03	09 08		09 29	09 27	09 29	09 34	09 42	09 42	09 59	09 46	09 42	
	d	08 32	08 35	08 46	08 49	09 02	08 47	08 49	08 49	09 02	09 04	09 09		09 32	09 28	09 32	09 35	09 46	09 49	10 02	09 47	09 49	09 49
Worplesdon	d				→	→								→					→	→			
Guildford	a	08 40	08 43							09 10	09 12					09 40	09 43						
Brookwood	d			08 51				08 55	08 55									09 51				09 55	09 55
Ash Vale	d							09 03	09 03				09 36									10 03	10 03
Aldershot	a							09 07	09 07				09 41									10 07	10 07
	d							09 08	09 08													10 08	10 08
Farnham	a							09 13	09 13													10 13	10 13
	d							09 14	09 14													10 14	10 14
Bentley	d							09 24	09 24													10 24	10 24
Alton	a							09 31	09 31													10 31	10 31
Farnborough (Main)	d			08 59														09 59					
Fleet	d			09 04														10 04					
Winchfield	d			09 10														10 10					
Hook	d			09 14														10 14					
Basingstoke	a			09 21			09 06					09 28			09 46			10 21			10 06		

A not 22 May

b Previous night, stops to pick up only

London - Woking, Guildford, Alton and Basingstoke

Station		SW	SW ■	SW ◇■	SW ■	SW	SW ◇■	SW ■	SW	SW ■	SW ■	SW	SW ◇■ ⌶	SW ■	SW ■	SW ■	SW	SW ◇■ ⌶	SW ■	SW	SW ◇■	SW ■
London Waterloo 15 ⊖	d		09 30	09 35		09 40	09 54	10 00		10 07	10 07	10 10	10 15			10 30		10 35		10 40	10 54	11 00
Vauxhall ⊖	d					09 44						10 14								10 44		
Clapham Junction 10	d		09u39	09u45		09 49	10u03	10u09		10 15	10 15	10 19	10u22			10u39		10u45		10 49	11u04	11u09
Earlsfield	d					09 52						10 22								10 52		
Wimbledon 6 ⊖	d					09 56				10 22	10 22	10 26								10 56		
Surbiton 6	d					10 05				10 30	10 30	10 35								11 05		
Esher	d					10 09						10 39								11 09		
Hersham	d					10 12						10 42								11 12		
Walton-on-Thames	d					10 15						10 45								11 15		
Weybridge	d					10 19						10 49								11 19		
Byfleet & New Haw	d					10 21						10 51								11 21		
West Byfleet	d	←				10 24			←			10 54		←			←			11 24		
Woking	a	09 59	10 03	10 08		10 29	10 26	10 31	10 29	10 42	10 42	10 59	10 45	10 42		11 01	10 59	11 06		11 29	11 26	11 31
	d	10 02	10 04	10 09		10 35	10 28	10 32	10 35	10 46	10 49	11 05	10 46	10 49	10 49	11 02	11 05	11 07		11 35	11 28	11 32
Worplesdon	d					→					→	→								→		
Guildford	a	10 10	10 12					10 40	10 44							11 10	11 14					11 40
Brookwood	d									10 51				10 55	10 55							
Ash Vale	d				10 36									11 03	11 03				11 36			
Aldershot	a				10 41									11 07	11 07				11 41			
	d													11 08	11 08							
Farnham	a													11 13	11 13							
	d													11 14	11 14							
Bentley	d													11 24	11 24							
Alton	a													11 31	11 31							
Farnborough (Main)	d									10 59												
Fleet	d									11 04												
Winchfield	d									11 10												
Hook	d									11 14												
Basingstoke	a			10 28			10 46			11 21			11 05					11 26			11 46	

Station		SW	SW ■	SW ■	SW	SW ◇■ ⌶	SW ■	SW ■	SW ■ ⌶	SW	SW ◇■ ⌶	SW ■	SW	SW ◇■ ⌶	SW ■	SW	SW ■	SW ■	SW	SW ◇■ ⌶	SW ■	SW ■	SW ■ ⌶
London Waterloo 15 ⊖	d		11 07	11 07	11 10	11 15			11 30		11 35		11 40	11 54	12 00		12 07	12 07	12 10	12 15			12 30
Vauxhall ⊖	d				11 14								11 44						12 14				
Clapham Junction 10	d		11 15	11 15	11 19	11u22			11u39		11u45		11 49	12u04	12u09		12 15	12 15	12 19	12u22			12u39
Earlsfield	d				11 22								11 52						12 22				
Wimbledon 6 ⊖	d		11 22	11 22	11 26								11 56				12 22	12 22	12 26				
Surbiton 6	d		11 30	11 30	11 35								12 05				12 30	12 30	12 35				
Esher	d				11 39								12 09						12 39				
Hersham	d				11 42								12 12						12 42				
Walton-on-Thames	d				11 45								12 15						12 45				
Weybridge	d				11 49								12 19						12 49				
Byfleet & New Haw	d				11 51								12 21						12 51				
West Byfleet	d	←			11 54		←			←			12 24			←			12 54		←		
Woking	a	11 29	11 42	11 42	11 59	11 45	11 42		12 01	11 59	12 06		12 29	12 26	12 31	12 29	12 42	12 42	12 59	12 45	12 42		13 01
	d	11 35	11 46	11 49	12 05	11 46	11 49	11 49	12 02	12 05	12 07		12 35	12 28	12 32	12 35	12 46	12 49	13 05	12 46	12 49	12 49	13 02
Worplesdon	d			→	→								→					→	→				
Guildford	a	11 44							12 10	12 14					12 40	12 44							13 10
Brookwood	d		11 51				11 55	11 55									12 51				12 55	12 55	
Ash Vale	d						12 03	12 03				12 36									13 03	13 03	
Aldershot	a						12 07	12 07				12 41									13 07	13 07	
	d						12 08	12 08													13 08	13 08	
Farnham	a						12 13	12 13													13 13	13 13	
	d						12 14	12 14													13 14	13 14	
Bentley	d						12 24	12 24													13 24	13 24	
Alton	a						12 31	12 31													13 31	13 31	
Farnborough (Main)	d		11 59														12 59						
Fleet	d		12 04														13 04						
Winchfield	d		12 10														13 10						
Hook	d		12 14														13 14						
Basingstoke	a		12 21			12 05					12 26			12 46			13 21			13 05			

London - Woking, Guildford, Alton and Basingstoke

		SW	SW ◇1 ╤	SW 1	SW	SW ◇1 ╤	SW 1	SW	SW 1	SW 1	SW	SW ◇1 ╤	SW 1	SW 1	SW 1 ╤	SW	SW ◇1 ╤	SW 1	SW	SW ◇1 ╤	SW 1	SW
London Waterloo 15 ⊖	d		12 35		12 40	12 54	13 00		13 07	13 07	13 10	13 15			13 30		13 35		13 40	13 54	14 00	
Vauxhall ⊖	d				12 44						13 14								13 44			
Clapham Junction 10	d		12u42		12 49	13u03	13u09		13 15	13 15	13 19	13u22			13u39		13u42		13 49	14u03	14u09	
Earlsfield	d				12 52						13 22								13 52			
Wimbledon 6 ⊖	d				12 56				13 22	13 22	13 26								13 56			
Surbiton 6	d				13 05				13 30	13 30	13 35								14 05			
Esher	d				13 09						13 39								14 09			
Hersham	d				13 12						13 42								14 12			
Walton-on-Thames	d				13 15						13 45								14 15			
Weybridge	d				13 19						13 49								14 19			
Byfleet & New Haw	d				13 21						13 51								14 21			
West Byfleet	d	←			13 24			←			13 54		←			←			14 24			←
Woking	a	12 59	13 06		13 29	13 26	13 31	13 29	13 42	13 42	13 59	13 45	13 42		14 01	13 59	14 06		14 29	14 26	14 31	14 29
	d	13 05	13 07		13 35	13 28	13 32	13 35	13 46	13 49	14 05	13 46	13 49	13 49	14 02	14 05	14 07		14 35	14 28	14 32	14 35
Worplesdon	d				→					→	→								→			
Guildford	a	13 14					13 40	13 44							14 10	14 14					14 40	14 44
Brookwood	d								13 51				13 55	13 55								
Ash Vale	d			13 36									14 03	14 03				14 36				
Aldershot	a			13 41									14 07	14 07				14 41				
	d												14 08	14 08								
Farnham	a												14 13	14 13								
	d												14 14	14 14								
Bentley	d												14 24	14 24								
Alton	a												14 31	14 31								
Farnborough (Main)	d								13 59													
Fleet	d								14 04													
Winchfield	d								14 10													
Hook	d								14 14													
Basingstoke	a		13 26			13 46			14 21			14 05					14 26			14 46		

		SW 1	SW 1	SW	SW ◇1 ╤	SW 1	SW 1	SW 1 ╤	SW	SW ◇1 ╤	SW 1	SW	SW ◇1 ╤	SW 1	SW	SW 1	SW 1	SW	SW ◇1 ╤	SW 1	SW 1	SW 1 ╤	SW
London Waterloo 15 ⊖	d	14 07	14 07	14 10	14 15			14 30		14 35		14 40	14 54	15 00		15 07	15 07	15 10	15 15			15 30	
Vauxhall ⊖	d			14 14								14 44						15 14					
Clapham Junction 10	d	14 15	14 15	14 19	14u22			14u39		14u42		14 49	15u03	15u09		15 15	15 15	15 19	15u22			15u39	
Earlsfield	d			14 22								14 52						15 22					
Wimbledon 6 ⊖	d	14 22	14 22	14 26								14 56				15 22	15 22	15 26					
Surbiton 6	d	14 30	14 30	14 35								15 05				15 30	15 30	15 35					
Esher	d			14 39								15 09						15 39					
Hersham	d			14 42								15 12						15 42					
Walton-on-Thames	d			14 45								15 15						15 45					
Weybridge	d			14 49								15 19						15 49					
Byfleet & New Haw	d			14 51								15 21						15 51					
West Byfleet	d			14 54		←			←			15 24			←			15 54		←			←
Woking	a	14 42	14 42	14 59	14 45	14 42		15 01	14 59	15 06		15 29	15 26	15 31	15 29	15 42	15 42	15 59	15 45	15 42		16 01	15 59
	d	14 46	14 49	15 05	14 46	14 49	14 49	15 02	15 05	15 07		15 35	15 28	15 32	15 35	15 46	15 49	16 05	15 46	15 49	15 49	16 02	16 05
Worplesdon	d		→	→								→					→	→					
Guildford	a							15 10	15 14					15 40	15 44							16 10	16 14
Brookwood	d	14 51				14 55	14 55									15 51				15 55	15 55		
Ash Vale	d					15 03	15 03				15 36									16 03	16 03		
Aldershot	a					15 07	15 07				15 41									16 07	16 07		
	d					15 08	15 08													16 08	16 08		
Farnham	a					15 13	15 13													16 13	16 13		
	d					15 14	15 14													16 14	16 14		
Bentley	d					15 24	15 24													16 24	16 24		
Alton	a					15 31	15 31													16 31	16 31		
Farnborough (Main)	d	14 59														15 59							
Fleet	d	15 04														16 04							
Winchfield	d	15 10														16 10							
Hook	d	15 14														16 14							
Basingstoke	a	15 21			15 05					15 26			15 46			16 21			16 05				

London - Woking, Guildford, Alton and Basingstoke

		SW ◇1 ╤	SW 1	SW 1		SW	SW ◇1 ╤	SW 1	SW	SW 1	SW 1	SW	SW ◇1 ╤	SW 1	SW 1	SW 1 ╤	SW	SW ◇1 ╤	SW 1	SW 1		SW	SW ◇1 ╤
London Waterloo 15 ⊖	d	15 35		15 37		15 40	15 54	16 00		16 07	16 07	16 10	16 15			16 30		16 35		16 37		16 40	16 54
Vauxhall ⊖	d					15 44						16 14										16 44	
Clapham Junction 10	d	15u42		15 46		15 49	16u03	16u09		16 15	16 15	16 19	16u22			16u39		16u42		16 46		16 49	17u03
Earlsfield	d					15 52						16 22										16 52	
Wimbledon 6 ⊖	d			15 53		15 56				16 22	16 22	16 26								16 53		16 56	
Surbiton 6	d			16 02		16 05				16 30	16 30	16 35								17 02		17 05	
Esher	d					16 09						16 39										17 09	
Hersham	d					16 12						16 42										17 12	
Walton-on-Thames	d			16 09		16 15						16 45								17 09		17 15	
Weybridge	d			16 13		16 19						16 49								17 13		17 19	
Byfleet & New Haw	d					16 21						16 51										17 21	
West Byfleet	d					16 24			←			16 54		←			←					17 24	
Woking	a	16 06		16 19		16 29	16 26	16 31	16 29	16 42	16 42	16 59	16 45	16 42		17 01	16 59	17 06		17 19		17 29	17 26
	d	16 07		16 23	16 26	16 35	16 28	16 32	16 35	16 46	16 49	17 05	16 46	16 49	16 49	17 02	17 05	17 07		17 23	17 26	17 35	17 28
Worplesdon	d					→					→	→										→	
Guildford	a							16 40	16 44							17 10	17 14						
Brookwood	d			16 28	16 32					16 51				16 55	16 55					17 28	17 32		
Ash Vale	d		16 36		16 40									17 03	17 03				17 36		17 40		
Aldershot	a		16 41		16 45									17 07	17 07				17 41		17 45		
	d				16 46									17 08	17 08						17 46		
Farnham	a				16 51									17 13	17 13						17 51		
	d				16 55									17 14	17 14						17 55		
Bentley	d													17 24	17 24								
Alton	a				17 07									17 31	17 31						18 07		
Farnborough (Main)	d			16 36						16 59										17 36			
Fleet	d			16 41						17 04										17 41			
Winchfield	d									17 10													
Hook	d									17 14													
Basingstoke	a	16 26		16 54			16 46			17 21			17 05					17 26		17 54			17 46

		SW 1	SW	SW 1	SW 1	SW	SW ◇1 ╤	SW 1	SW 1	SW 1 ╤	SW	SW ◇1 ╤	SW 1	SW 1		SW	SW ◇1 ╤	SW 1	SW	SW 1	SW 1	SW
London Waterloo 15 ⊖	d	17 00		17 07	17 07	17 10	17 15			17 30		17 35		17 37		17 40	17 54	18 00		18 07	18 07	18 10
Vauxhall ⊖	d					17 14										17 44						18 14
Clapham Junction 10	d	17u09		17 15	17 15	17 19	17u22			17u39		17u42		17 46		17 49	18u03	18u09		18 15	18 15	18 19
Earlsfield	d					17 22										17 52						18 22
Wimbledon 6 ⊖	d			17 22	17 22	17 26								17 53		17 56				18 22	18 22	18 26
Surbiton 6	d			17 30	17 30	17 35								18 02		18 05				18 30	18 30	18 35
Esher	d					17 39										18 09						18 39
Hersham	d					17 42										18 12						18 42
Walton-on-Thames	d					17 45								18 09		18 15						18 45
Weybridge	d					17 49								18 13		18 19						18 49
Byfleet & New Haw	d					17 51										18 21						18 51
West Byfleet	d		←			17 54		←			←					18 24			←			18 54
Woking	a	17 31	17 29	17 42	17 42	17 59	17 45	17 42		18 01	17 59	18 06		18 19		18 29	18 26	18 31	18 29	18 42	18 42	18 59
	d	17 32	17 35	17 46	17 49	18 05	17 46	17 49	17 49	18 02	18 05	18 07		18 23	18 26	18 35	18 28	18 32	18 35	18 46	18 49	19 05
Worplesdon	d				→	→										→					→	→
Guildford	a	17 40	17 44							18 10	18 14							18 40	18 44			
Brookwood	d			17 51				17 55	17 55					18 28	18 32					18 51		
Ash Vale	d							18 03	18 03				18 36		18 40							
Aldershot	a							18 07	18 07				18 41		18 45							
	d							18 08	18 08						18 46							
Farnham	a							18 13	18 13						18 51							
	d							18 14	18 14						18 55							
Bentley	d							18 24	18 24													
Alton	a							18 31	18 31						19 07							
Farnborough (Main)	d			17 59										18 36						18 59		
Fleet	d			18 04										18 41						19 04		
Winchfield	d			18 10																19 10		
Hook	d			18 14																19 14		
Basingstoke	a			18 21			18 05					18 26		18 54			18 46			19 21		

Table 155

Sundays

London - Woking, Guildford, Alton and Basingstoke

		SW ◇1 ✠	SW 1	SW 1	SW 1 ✠	SW	SW ◇1 ✠	SW 1	SW 1		SW	SW ◇1 ✠	SW 1	SW	SW 1	SW 1	SW	SW ◇1 ✠	SW 1	SW 1	SW 1 ✠	SW	SW ◇1 ✠
London Waterloo 15 ⊖	d	18 15			18 30		18 35		18 37		18 40	18 54	19 00		19 07	19 07	19 10	19 15			19 30		19 35
Vauxhall ⊖	d										18 44						19 14						
Clapham Junction 10	d	18u22			18u39		18u42		18 46		18 49	19u03	19u09		19 15	19 15	19 19	19u22			19u39		19u42
Earlsfield	d										18 52						19 22						
Wimbledon 6 ⊖	d								18 53		18 56				19 22	19 22	19 26						
Surbiton 6	d								19 02		19 05				19 30	19 30	19 35						
Esher	d										19 09						19 39						
Hersham	d										19 12						19 42						
Walton-on-Thames	d								19 09		19 15						19 45						
Weybridge	d								19 13		19 19						19 49						
Byfleet & New Haw	d										19 21						19 51						
West Byfleet	d		←			←					19 24			←			19 54		←			←	
Woking	a	18 45	18 42		19 01	18 59	19 06		19 19		19 29	19 26	19 31	19 29	19 42	19 42	19 59	19 45	19 42		20 01	19 59	20 06
	d	18 46	18 49	18 49	19 02	19 05	19 07		19 23	19 26	19 35 →	19 28	19 32	19 35	19 46	19 49 →	20 05 →	19 46	19 49	19 49	20 02	20 05	20 07
Worplesdon	d																						
Guildford	a				19 10	19 14							19 40	19 44							20 10	20 14	
Brookwood	d		18 55	18 55					19 28	19 32					19 51				19 55	19 55			
Ash Vale	d		19 03	19 03				19 36		19 40									20 03	20 03			
Aldershot	a		19 07	19 07				19 41		19 45									20 07	20 07			
	d		19 08	19 08						19 46									20 08	20 08			
Farnham	a		19 13	19 13						19 51									20 13	20 13			
	d		19 14	19 14						19 55									20 14	20 14			
Bentley	d		19 24	19 24															20 24	20 24			
Alton	a		19 31	19 31						20 07									20 31	20 31			
Farnborough (Main)	d								19 36						19 59								
Fleet	d								19 41						20 04								
Winchfield	d														20 10								
Hook	d														20 14								
Basingstoke	a	19 05					19 26		19 54			19 46			20 21			20 05					20 26

		SW 1	SW 1		SW	SW ◇1	SW 1	SW	SW 1	SW 1	SW	SW ◇1 ✠	SW 1	SW 1	SW 1 ✠	SW	SW ◇1 ✠	SW 1	SW 1		SW	SW ◇1
London Waterloo 15 ⊖	d		19 37		19 40	19 54	20 00		20 07	20 07	20 10	20 15			20 30		20 35		20 37		20 40	20 54
Vauxhall ⊖	d				19 44						20 14										20 44	
Clapham Junction 10	d		19 46		19 49	20u03	20u09		20 15	20 15	20 19	20u22			20u39		20u42		20 46		20 49	21u03
Earlsfield	d				19 52						20 22										20 52	
Wimbledon 6 ⊖	d		19 53		19 56				20 22	20 22	20 26								20 53		20 56	
Surbiton 6	d		20 02		20 05				20 30	20 30	20 35								21 02		21 05	
Esher	d				20 09						20 39										21 09	
Hersham	d				20 12						20 42										21 12	
Walton-on-Thames	d		20 09		20 15						20 45								21 09		21 15	
Weybridge	d		20 13		20 19						20 49								21 13		21 19	
Byfleet & New Haw	d				20 21						20 51										21 21	
West Byfleet	d				20 24			←			20 54		←			←					21 24	
Woking	a		20 19		20 29	20 26	20 31	20 29	20 42	20 42	20 59	20 45	20 42		21 01	20 59	21 06		21 19		21 29	21 26
	d		20 23	20 26	20 35 →	20 28	20 32	20 35	20 46	20 49 →	21 05 →	20 46	20 49	20 49	21 02	21 05	21 07		21 23	21 26	21 35 →	21 28
Worplesdon	d																					
Guildford	a						20 40	20 44							21 10	21 14						
Brookwood	d		20 28	20 32					20 51				20 55	20 55					21 28	21 32		
Ash Vale	d	20 36		20 40									21 03	21 03				21 36		21 40		
Aldershot	a	20 41		20 45									21 07	21 07				21 41		21 45		
	d			20 46									21 08	21 08						21 46		
Farnham	a			20 51									21 13	21 13						21 51		
	d			20 55									21 14	21 14						21 55		
Bentley	d												21 24	21 24								
Alton	a			21 07									21 31	21 31						22 07		
Farnborough (Main)	d		20 36						20 59										21 36			
Fleet	d		20 41						21 04										21 41			
Winchfield	d								21 10													
Hook	d								21 14													
Basingstoke	a		20 54			20 46			21 21			21 05					21 26		21 54			21 46

Table 155

Sundays

London - Woking, Guildford, Alton and Basingstoke

		SW 1	SW	SW 1	SW 1	SW	SW ◇1 ✠	SW 1	SW 1	SW 1	SW	SW ◇1 ✠	SW 1	SW 1		SW	SW ◇1	SW 1	SW	SW 1	SW 1	SW	SW 1 ✠
London Waterloo 15 ⊖	d	21 00		21 07	21 07	21 10	21 15			21 30		21 35		21 37		21 40	21 54	22 00		22 07	22 07	22 10	22 15
Vauxhall ⊖	d					21 14										21 44						22 14	
Clapham Junction 10	d	21u09		21 15	21 15	21 19	21u22			21u39		21u42		21 46		21 49	22u03	22u09		22 15	22 15	22 19	22u22
Earlsfield	d					21 22										21 52						22 22	
Wimbledon 6 ⊖	d			21 22	21 22	21 26								21 53		21 56				22 22	22 22	22 26	
Surbiton 6	d			21 30	21 30	21 35								22 02		22 05				22 30	22 30	22 35	
Esher	d					21 39										22 09						22 39	
Hersham	d					21 42										22 12						22 42	
Walton-on-Thames	d					21 45								22 09		22 15						22 45	
Weybridge	d					21 49								22 13		22 19						22 49	
Byfleet & New Haw	d					21 51										22 21						22 51	
West Byfleet	d		←			21 54		←			←					22 24			←			22 54	
Woking	a	21 31	21 29	21 42	21 42	21 59	21 45	21 42		22 01	21 59	22 06		22 19		22 29	22 26	22 31	22 29	22 42	22 42	22 59	22 45
	d	21 32	21 35	21 46	21 49 →	22 05 →	21 46	21 49	21 49	22 02	22 05	22 07		22 23	22 26	22 35 →	22 28	22 32	22 35	22 46	22 49 →	23 05 →	22 46
Worplesdon	d																						
Guildford	a	21 40	21 44							22 10	22 14							22 40	22 44				
Brookwood	d			21 51				21 55	21 55					22 28	22 32					22 51			
Ash Vale	d							22 03	22 03				22 36		22 40								
Aldershot	a							22 07	22 07				22 45		22 47								
	d							22 08	22 08						22 48								
Farnham	a							22 13	22 13						22 53								
	d							22 14	22 14						22 55								
Bentley	d							22 24	22 24														
Alton	a							22 31	22 31						23 07								
Farnborough (Main)	d			21 59										22 36						22 59			
Fleet	d			22 04										22 41						23 04			
Winchfield	d			22 10																23 10			
Hook	d			22 14																23 14			
Basingstoke	a			22 21			22 05					22 26		22 54			22 46			23 21			23 05

		SW 1	SW 1	SW 1	SW	SW 1	SW 1		SW	SW ◇1 ✠	SW 1	SW	SW 1		SW	SW 1	SW	SW 1	SW 1
London Waterloo 15 ⊖	d			22 30			22 37		22 40	22 54	23 00		23 07		23 10	23 30		23 35	23 40
Vauxhall ⊖	d								22 44						23 14				23 44
Clapham Junction 10	d			22u39			22 46		22 49	23u03	23u09		23 15		23 19	23u39		23u44	23 49
Earlsfield	d								22 52						23 22				23 52
Wimbledon 6 ⊖	d						22 53		22 56				23 22		23 26				23 56
Surbiton 6	d						23 02		23 05				23 30		23 35				00 05
Esher	d								23 09						23 39				00 09
Hersham	d								23 12						23 42				00 12
Walton-on-Thames	d						23 09		23 15						23 45				00 15
Weybridge	d						23 13		23 19						23 49				00 19
Byfleet & New Haw	d								23 21						23 51				00 21
West Byfleet	d	←			←				23 24			←			23 54		←		00 24
Woking	a	22 42		23 01	22 59		23 19		23 29	23 26	23 31	23 29	23 42		23 59	00 01	23 59	00 07	00 30
	d	22 49	22 49	23 02	23 05		23 23	23 26	23 35 →	23 28	23 32	23 35	23 46	23 49	00 05 →	00 03	00 05	00 08	00 35
Worplesdon	d																		
Guildford	a			23 10	23 13						23 40	23 45				00 10	00 13		
Brookwood	d	22 55	22 55				23 28	23 32					23 51	23 55					00 41
Ash Vale	d	23 03	23 03			23 36		23 40						00 03					00 48
Aldershot	a	23 07	23 07			23 41		23 45						00 07					00 53
	d	23 08	23 08			23 42		23 48						00 08					00 54
Farnham	a	23 13	23 13			23 47		23 54						00 13					00 59
	d	23 14	23 14					23 55						00 14					
Bentley	d	23 24	23 24											00 24					
Alton	a	23 31	23 31					00 07						00 31					
Farnborough (Main)	d						23 36						23 59					00 18	
Fleet	d						23 41						00 04					00 24	
Winchfield	d												00 10						
Hook	d												00 14						
Basingstoke	a						23 54			23 46			00 21					00 39	

Basingstoke, Alton, Guildford and Woking - Waterloo

Miles	Miles	Miles			SW MO	SW MX 1	SW MO 1	SW 1	SW MX 1	SW MX 1	SW MO 1	SW MX 1	SW MO 1		SW MX 1	SW MO ◇1	SW MX 1	SW	SW ◇	SW 1 A	SW 1 B	SW	SW		SW 1
0	—	—	**Basingstoke**	d					22p54	23p13						23p44	23p44			04 54	04 54				
5½	—	—	Hook	d					23p01								23p51			05 01	05 01				
7¾	—	—	Winchfield	d					23p05								23p55			05 05	05 05				
11¼	—	—	Fleet	d					23p10								00 01			05 10	05 10				
14½	—	—	Farnborough (Main)	d					23p16								00 06			05 16	05 16				
—	0	—	**Alton**	d		22p44	22p45																		
—	4¾	—	Bentley	d		22p51																			
—	8¾	—	Farnham	a		22p56	22p55																		
—	—	—		d		22p58	23p00																		
—	11¾	—	**Aldershot**	d		23p04	23p06	05 58																	
—	14¾	—	Ash Vale	d		23p09	23p11	06a02																	
19¾	18¾	—	Brookwood	d		23p16	23p18		23p23								00 13			05 23	05 23				
—	—	0	**Guildford**	d									23p35		23p39			04 00				05 14			05 50
—	—	3½	Worplesdon	d								←			23p44							05 19			05 55
23½	—	6	**Woking**	a		23p21	23p24		23p28	23p31		23p28	23p42		23p49	00 02	00 18	04 08		05 28	05 28	05 24			06 00
—	—	—		d	22p52	23p22	23p28		23p33	23p32		23p33	23p45		23p56	00 04	00 20	04 10	05 27	05 29	05 29	05 33	05 43		06 01
26	—	—	West Byfleet	d	22p56	23p27			→			23p37					00 25		05 32			05 37	05 47		
27¼	—	—	Byfleet & New Haw	d	23p00							23p40							05 35			05 40			
28¾	—	—	Weybridge	d			23p34					23p43					00 29					05 43	05 51		
30¾	—	—	Walton-on-Thames	d			23p38					23p47					00 33					05 47	05 55		
31¾	—	—	Hersham	d								23p49										05 49			
33¼	—	—	Esher	d								23p52										05 52			
35¾	—	—	**Surbiton** 6	a		23p37	23p45					23p57					00 39	04 24		05 40	05 40	05 56	06 01		
40½	—	—	Wimbledon 6 ⊖	a			23p53					00 06					00 47	04 31		05 48	05 48	06 04			
42¼	—	—	Earlsfield	a							←											06 08			
43¾	—	—	Clapham Junction 10	a		23p51	23p59			23p55	23p59		00 04		00 19	00 23	00 53	04 43				06 12			06 20
46½	—	—	Vauxhall ⊖	a	00 08		→					00 28							06 49	06 07	06 07	06 17			
47¾	—	—	**London Waterloo** 15 ⊖	a	00 13	00 02				00 09	00 10	00 35	00 14		00 33	00 33	01 04	04 53	06 56	06 12	06 15	06 22	06 20		06 29

		SW	SW 1	SW 1	SW ◇1 ⊥	SW	SW 1 A	SW 1 B	SW 1		SW 1	SW	SW 1	SW 1	SW 1 ⊥	SW 1	SW ◇1 ⊥	SW ◇1	SW 1		SW	SW ◇1 ⊥	SW 1	SW 1	SW 1
Basingstoke	d		05 39	05 54	05 59						06 23						06 27					06 35			
Hook	d			06 01							06 31														
Winchfield	d			06 05							06 35														
Fleet	d		05 50	06 10							06 40														
Farnborough (Main)	d		05 56	06 16							06 46														
Alton	d						05 42	05 42											06 12						
Bentley	d						05 49	05 49											06 19						
Farnham	a						05 54	05 54											06 24						
	d						05 56	05 56											06 26						
Aldershot	d						06 02	06 02						06 08				06 28	06 32						
Ash Vale	d						06 07	06 07										06 32	06 37						
Brookwood	d			06 23			06 14	06 14			06 53								06 44						
Guildford	d												06 24	06a25	06 31										06 53
Worplesdon	d								←				06 30										←		06 59
Woking	a		06 05	06 28	06 18		06 19	06 19	06 28		06 58		06 35		06 39		06 46		06 49			06 53	06 58		07 03
	d	06 04	06 06	06 29	06 19		06 20	06 20	06 29		06 59	06 32	06 37		06 41	06 41	06 47		06 50			06 55	06 59	07 02	07 05
West Byfleet	d	06 08		→			06 25	06 25			→	06 36				06 46								07 07	
Byfleet & New Haw	d	06 11										06 39				06 49									
Weybridge	d	06 14										06 43				06 52								07 11	
Walton-on-Thames	d	06 18										06 47				06 57								07 16	
Hersham	d	06 20										06 49				07 00								07 19	
Esher	d	06 23										06 52				07 03								07 22	
Surbiton 6	a	06 27					06 35	06 35	06 40			06 56				07 07								07 26	
Wimbledon 6 ⊖	a	06 35							06 47			07 04													
Earlsfield	a	06 39				←						07 08									←				
Clapham Junction 10	a	06 42	06 25		06 38	06 42	06 46	06 46	06 54			07 12	06 58		07 02				07 10		07 12	07 14	07 20		07 24
Vauxhall ⊖	a	→				06 47						→						07 52			07 17				
London Waterloo 15 ⊖	a		06 34		06 49	06 52	06 54	06 56	07 04				07 08		07 12	07 26	07 14	07 59	07 20		07 24	07 24	07 31	07 49	07 36

A until 30 September

B from 3 October

Basingstoke, Alton, Guildford and Woking - Waterloo

		SW 1	SW 1	SW 1	SW ◇1 ⊥		SW 1	SW ◇1 A	SW ◇1 B	SW 1	SW 1 ⊥	SW 1	SW 1	SW 1	SW 1		SW ◇1	SW 1	SW 1	SW ◇1 A	SW ◇1 B	SW 1	SW 1	SW 1	SW ◇1 ⊥
Basingstoke	d			06 42	06 51							06 54	07 06	07 17										07 24	07 29
Hook	d											07 01	07 13											07 31	
Winchfield	d											07 05	07 17											07 35	
Fleet	d			06 54								07 10	07 22											07 40	
Farnborough (Main)	d			07 00								07 16	07 28											07 46	
Alton	d									06 44												07 14			
Bentley	d									06 51												07 21			
Farnham	a									06 56												07 26			
	d									06 58												07 28			
Aldershot	d	06 38						06 59	07 00	07 04										07 29	07 30	07 34			
Ash Vale	d							07 03	07 04	07 09										07 33	07 34	07 39			
Brookwood	d									07 16		07 23										07 46		07 53	
Guildford	d	06a55					07 07				07 17												07 45		
Worplesdon	d																						07 50		
Woking	a			07 10			07 15			07 21	07 25	07 28										07 51	07 54	07 58	
	d		07 07	07 11			07 17			07 22	07 26	07 29			07 32		07 40		07 47			07 52	07 56	07 59	
West Byfleet	d		07 16												07 37			07 46	07 54						
Byfleet & New Haw	d		07 19															07 49	07 57						
Weybridge	d		07 22												07 41			07 52	08 01						
Walton-on-Thames	d		07 27												07 46			07 57	08 06						
Hersham	d		07 30												07 49			08 00	08 09						
Esher	d		07 33												07 52			08 03	08 13						
Surbiton 6	a		07 37												07 56			08 07	08 18						
Wimbledon 6 ⊖	a																								
Earlsfield	a																								
Clapham Junction 10	a				07 28																				
Vauxhall ⊖	a							08 22	08 22											08 52	08 52				
London Waterloo 15 ⊖	a		07 56	07 41	07 39		07 45	08 29	08 29	07 51	07 54	07 59	08 06	08 01	08 19		08 08	08 26	08 36	09 00	09 00	08 22	08 24	08 29	08 14

			SW 1	SW 1	SW 1	SW 1	SW 1	SW 1	SW 1	SW	SW 1		SW ◇1 ⊥	SW 1	SW 1 ⊥	SW 1	SW 1	SW 1	SW	SW 1	SW 1		SW 1	SW 1	SW 1
Basingstoke	d					07 36	07 47				07 52		07 59					08 05		08 16				08 24	
Hook	d					07 43					07 59							08 12						08 31	
Winchfield	d					07 47					08 04							08 16						08 35	
Fleet	d					07 52					08 09							08 22						08 40	
Farnborough (Main)	d					07 58					08 16							08 28						08 46	
Alton	d													07 44											
Bentley	d													07 51											
Farnham	a													07 56											
	d			07 39										07 58											
Aldershot	d			07 46	08 00									08 04			08 30								
Ash Vale	d			07 50	08a04									08 09			08a34								
Brookwood	d			07 57							08 23			08 16										08 53	
Guildford	d								08 03						08 15				08 20				08 31		
Worplesdon	d							←							08 20	←					←		08 37		
Woking	a			08 03		08 08	08 05	08 08	08 11		08 28		08 18	08 21	08 26	08 28		08 38	08 30	08 34	08 38		08 41	08 58	
	d		08 02	08 05		08 09	08 06	08 09	08 12	08 17	08 29		08 19	08 23	08 27	08 29		08 39	08 32	08 36	08 39		08 43	08 59	08 47
West Byfleet	d		08 06	08b16		→				08 26	→							→	08 36					→	08 54
Byfleet & New Haw	d			08 19						08 29									08 39						08 57
Weybridge	d		08 11	08 22						08 32									08 43						09 02
Walton-on-Thames	d		08 15	08 27						08 36									08 47						09 07
Hersham	d		08 17	08 30						08 39									08 49						09 10
Esher	d		08 20	08 33						08 43									08 52						09 13
Surbiton 6	a		08 24	08 37						08 47									08 56						09 18
Wimbledon 6 ⊖	a																		09 04						→
Earlsfield	a																		09 08						
Clapham Junction 10	a																		09 12				09 03		
Vauxhall ⊖	a																		→						
London Waterloo 15 ⊖	a		08 46	08 59			08 34	08 39	08 41	09 06			08 46	08 52	08 55	09 00				09 03	09 10		09 13		

A from 3 October

B until 30 September

b Arr. 0810

Table 155

Mondays to Fridays

Basingstoke, Alton, Guildford and Woking - Waterloo

		SW ◇1 ✠	SW 1	SW	SW ◇1 ✠	SW 1	SW 1		SW 1	SW 1	SW	SW 1	SW 1	SW ◇1 ✠	SW	SW 1	SW ◇1 ✠		SW 1 ✠	SW 1	SW 1	SW 1	SW	SW 1	SW 1
Basingstoke	d	08 29			08 35		08 43						08 54	08 59										09 17	
Hook	d												09 01												
Winchfield	d												09 05												
Fleet	d						08 54						09 10												
Farnborough (Main)	d						09 00						09 16											09 30	
Alton	d		08 14													08 44									
Bentley	d		08 21													08 51									
Farnham	a		08 26													08 56									
	d		08 28													08 58									
Aldershot	d		08 34							09 00						09 04						09 30			
Ash Vale	d		08 39							09a04						09 09						09a34			
Brookwood	d		08 46										09 23			09 16									
Guildford	d										08 46	09 03							09 17						09 34
Worplesdon	d					←					08 51										←				09 40
Woking	a	08 48	08 51		08 53	08 58					08 59	09 11	09 28	09 18		09 21			09 27		09 28			09 39	09 44
	d	08 49	08 52		08 55	08 59					09 02	09 13	09 29	09 19		09 22	09 24		09 28		09 29		09 33	09 41	09 46
West Byfleet	d										09 06		→			09 27							09 37		
Byfleet & New Haw	d										09 09												09 40		
Weybridge	d										09 13										09 36		09 43		
Walton-on-Thames	d										09 17										09 40		09 47		
Hersham	d										09 19												09 49		
Esher	d								←		09 22												09 52		
Surbiton 6	a					09 10			09 18		09 26					09 37					09 46		09 56		
Wimbledon 6	⊖ a										09 34												10 04		
Earlsfield	a			←							09 38				←					←			10 08		
Clapham Junction 10	a			09 12	09 14		09 26				09 42	09 32		09 38	09 42	09 50	09 43			09 50	09 57		10 12		10 05
Vauxhall	⊖ a			09 17							→				09 47	→							→		
London Waterloo 15	⊖ a	09 17	09 21	09 24	09 25	09 29	09 38		09 40			09 43		09 51	09 54		09 53		09 55	09 59	10 05			10 08	10 13

		SW 1	SW ◇1 ✠		SW	SW 1	SW ◇1 ✠	SW 1 ✠	SW 1 ✠	SW 1	SW 1	SW 1	SW		SW 1	SW ◇1 ✠	SW ◇1 ✠	SW	SW 1	SW 1 ✠	SW 1	SW 1	SW		SW 1
Basingstoke	d	09 24	09 30				09 36		09 43			09 54				09 57									10 17
Hook	d	09 31										10 01													
Winchfield	d	09 35										10 05													
Fleet	d	09 40							09 54			10 10													
Farnborough (Main)	d	09 46							10 00			10 16													10 30
Alton	d					09 14													09 44						
Bentley	d					09 21													09 51						
Farnham	a					09 26													09 56						
	d					09 28													09 58						
Aldershot	d					09 34					10 00								10 04			10 30			
Ash Vale	d					09 39					10a04								10 09			10a34			
Brookwood	d	09 53				09 46						10 23							10 16						
Guildford	d							09 47							10 02					10 17					
Worplesdon	d									←											←				
Woking	a	09 58	09 49			09 51	09 54	09 59		09 58		10 28			10 11	10 15			10 21	10 25	10 28				10 39
	d	09 59	09 50			09 52	09 56	09 59		09 59		10 29	10 03		10 12	10 17	10 21		10 22	10 26	10 29		10 33		10 41
West Byfleet	d	→				09 57						→	10 07						10 27				10 37		
Byfleet & New Haw	d												10 10										10 40		
Weybridge	d									10 06			10 13								10 36		10 43		
Walton-on-Thames	d									10 10			10 17								10 40		10 47		
Hersham	d												10 19										10 49		
Esher	d												10 22										10 52		
Surbiton 6	a					10 07				10 16			10 26						10 37		10 46		10 56		
Wimbledon 6	⊖ a												10 34										11 04		
Earlsfield	a				←								10 38					←					11 08		
Clapham Junction 10	a		10 09		10 12		10 15		10 25				10 42		10 31	10 36		10 42	10 48		10 57		11 12		
Vauxhall	⊖ a				10 17								→					10 47					→		
London Waterloo 15	⊖ a		10 19		10 22	10 25	10 23	10 27	10 34	10 36					10 40	10 49	10 49	10 52	10 57	10 51	11 05				11 08

Table 155

Mondays to Fridays

Basingstoke, Alton, Guildford and Woking - Waterloo

		SW 1	SW 1	SW ◇1 ✠	SW ◇1 ✠	SW	SW 1	SW 1 ✠	SW 1		SW 1	SW 1	SW 1	SW	SW 1	SW ◇1 ✠	SW ◇1 ✠	SW	SW 1		SW 1 ✠	SW 1	SW 1	SW	SW 1
Basingstoke	d		10 24	10 30	10 35				10 43				10 54			10 57									11 17
Hook	d		10 31										11 01												
Winchfield	d		10 35										11 05												
Fleet	d		10 40						10 54				11 10												
Farnborough (Main)	d		10 46						11 00				11 16												11 30
Alton	d						10 14												10 44						
Bentley	d						10 21												10 51						
Farnham	a						10 26												10 56						
	d						10 28												10 58						
Aldershot	d						10 34					11 00							11 04				11 30		
Ash Vale	d						10 39					11a04							11 09				11a34		
Brookwood	d		10 53				10 46						11 23						11 16						
Guildford	d	10 34						10 47							11 02						11 17				
Worplesdon	d	10 40									←											←			
Woking	a	10 44	10 58	10 49			10 51	10 57			10 58		11 28		11 11	11 15			11 21		11 25	11 28			11 39
	d	10 46	10 59	10 50			10 52	10 59			10 59		11 29	11 03	11 12	11 17	11 21		11 22		11 26	11 29		11 33	11 41
West Byfleet	d		→				10 57						→	11 07					11 27					11 37	
Byfleet & New Haw	d													11 10										11 40	
Weybridge	d										11 06			11 13								11 36		11 43	
Walton-on-Thames	d										11 10			11 17								11 40		11 47	
Hersham	d													11 19										11 49	
Esher	d													11 22										11 52	
Surbiton 6	a						11 07				11 16			11 26					11 37			11 46		11 56	
Wimbledon 6	⊖ a													11 34										12 04	
Earlsfield	a					←								11 38				←						12 08	
Clapham Junction 10	a	11 05			11 12	11 12			11 25					11 42	11 31	11 36		11 42	11 49			11 57		12 12	
Vauxhall	⊖ a					11 17								→				11 47						→	
London Waterloo 15	⊖ a	11 13		11 19	11 20	11 22	11 27	11 24	11 34		11 36				11 40	11 49	11 49	11 52	11 57		11 51	12 06			12 08

		SW 1	SW 1	SW ◇1 ✠	SW ◇1 ✠		SW	SW 1	SW 1 ✠	SW 1	SW 1	SW 1	SW 1	SW	SW 1		SW ◇1 ✠	SW ◇1 ✠	SW	SW 1	SW 1 ✠	SW 1	SW 1	SW	SW 1
Basingstoke	d		11 24	11 30	11 35					11 43			11 54				11 57								12 17
Hook	d		11 31										12 01												
Winchfield	d		11 35										12 05												
Fleet	d		11 40							11 54			12 10												
Farnborough (Main)	d		11 46							12 00			12 16												12 30
Alton	d							11 15												11 44					
Bentley	d																			11 51					
Farnham	a							11 25												11 56					
	d							11 28												11 58					
Aldershot	d							11 34				12 00								12 04			12 30		
Ash Vale	d							11 39				12a04								12 09			12a34		
Brookwood	d		11 53					11 46					12 23							12 16					
Guildford	d	11 34							11 47						12 02						12 17				
Worplesdon	d	11 40									←											←			
Woking	a	11 44	11 58	11 49				11 51	11 57		11 58		12 28		12 11		12 15			12 21	12 25	12 28			12 39
	d	11 46	11 59	11 50				11 52	11 59		11 59		12 29	12 03	12 12		12 17	12 21		12 22	12 26	12 29		12 33	12 41
West Byfleet	d		→					11 57					→	12 07						12 27				12 37	
Byfleet & New Haw	d													12 10										12 40	
Weybridge	d										12 06			12 13								12 36		12 43	
Walton-on-Thames	d										12 10			12 17								12 40		12 47	
Hersham	d													12 19										12 49	
Esher	d													12 22										12 52	
Surbiton 6	a							12 07			12 16			12 26						12 37		12 46		12 56	
Wimbledon 6	⊖ a													12 34										13 04	
Earlsfield	a						←							12 38					←					13 08	
Clapham Junction 10	a	12 05			12 12		12 12			12 25				12 42	12 31		12 36		12 42	12 48		12 57		13 12	
Vauxhall	⊖ a						12 17							→					12 47					→	
London Waterloo 15	⊖ a	12 13		12 19	12 20		12 22	12 27	12 23	12 34	12 36				12 40		12 49	12 49	12 52	12 57	12 51	13 05			13 07

Basingstoke, Alton, Guildford and Woking - Waterloo

			SW 1	SW 1	SW ◇1 ⌶	SW ◇1 ⌶	SW	SW 1	SW 1 ⌶	SW 1	SW 1		SW 1	SW 1	SW	SW 1	SW ◇1 ⌶	SW ◇1 ⌶	SW	SW 1	SW 1 ⌶		SW 1	SW 1	SW
Basingstoke	d			12 24	12 30	12 35				12 43				12 54			12 57								
Hook	d			12 31										13 01											
Winchfield	d			12 35										13 05											
Fleet	d			12 40						12 54				13 10											
Farnborough (Main)	d			12 46						13 00				13 16											
Alton	d																			12 44					
Bentley	d																			12 51					
Farnham	a																			12 56					
	d							12 28												12 58					
Aldershot	d							12 34					13 00							13 04				13 30	
Ash Vale	d							12 39					13a04							13 09				13a34	
Brookwood	d			12 53				12 46						13 23						13 16					
Guildford	d		12 34						12 47							13 02					13 17				
Worplesdon	d		12 40								←												←		
Woking	a		12 44	12 58	12 49			12 51	12 57		12 58			13 28		13 11	13 15			13 21	13 25		13 28		
	d		12 46	12 59	12 50			12 52	12 59		12 59			13 29	13 03	13 12	13 17	13 21		13 22	13 26		13 29		13 33
West Byfleet	d			→				12 57						→	13 07					13 27					13 37
Byfleet & New Haw	d														13 10										13 40
Weybridge	d										13 06				13 13								13 36		13 43
Walton-on-Thames	d										13 10				13 17								13 40		13 47
Hersham	d														13 19										13 49
Esher	d														13 22										13 52
Surbiton 6	a							13 07			13 16				13 26					13 37			13 46		13 56
Wimbledon 6 ⊖	a														13 34										14 04
Earlsfield	a						←								13 38				←						14 08
Clapham Junction 10	a		13 05			13 12	13 12			13 25					13 42	13 31	13 38		13 42	13 48			13 57		14 12
Vauxhall ⊖	a						13 17								→				13 47						→
London Waterloo 15 ⊖	a		13 13		13 19	13 20	13 22	13 25	13 23	13 34	13 36					13 40	13 49	13 49	13 52	13 57	13 51		14 05		

		SW 1	SW 1	SW 1	SW ◇1 ⌶	SW ◇1 ⌶	SW		SW 1	SW 1 ⌶	SW 1	SW 1	SW 1	SW 1	SW	SW 1	SW ◇1 ⌶		SW ◇1 ⌶	SW	SW 1	SW 1 ⌶	SW 1	SW 1	SW
Basingstoke	d	13 17		13 24	13 30	13 35					13 43			13 54			13 57								
Hook	d			13 31										14 01											
Winchfield	d			13 35										14 05											
Fleet	d			13 40							13 54			14 10											
Farnborough (Main)	d	13 30		13 46							14 00			14 16											
Alton	d								13 15												13 44				
Bentley	d																				13 51				
Farnham	a								13 25												13 56				
	d								13 28												13 58				
Aldershot	d								13 34				14 00								14 04			14 30	
Ash Vale	d								13 39				14a04								14 09			14a34	
Brookwood	d			13 53					13 46					14 23							14 16				
Guildford	d		13 34							13 47						14 02						14 17			
Worplesdon	d		13 40									←											←		
Woking	a	13 39	13 44	13 58	13 49				13 51	13 57		13 58		14 28		14 11	14 15				14 21	14 25	14 28		
	d	13 41	13 46	13 59	13 50				13 52	13 59		13 59		14 29	14 03	14 12	14 17		14 21		14 22	14 26	14 29		14 33
West Byfleet	d			→					13 57					→	14 07						14 27				14 37
Byfleet & New Haw	d														14 10										14 40
Weybridge	d											14 06			14 13								14 36		14 43
Walton-on-Thames	d											14 10			14 17								14 40		14 47
Hersham	d														14 19										14 49
Esher	d														14 22										14 52
Surbiton 6	a								14 07			14 16			14 26						14 37		14 46		14 56
Wimbledon 6 ⊖	a														14 34										15 04
Earlsfield	a						←								14 38					←					15 08
Clapham Junction 10	a		14 05			14 12	14 12				14 25				14 42	14 31	14 36			14 42	14 48		14 57		15 12
Vauxhall ⊖	a						14 17								→					14 47					→
London Waterloo 15 ⊖	a	14 07	14 13		14 19	14 20	14 22		14 25	14 23	14 34	14 36				14 40	14 49		14 49	14 52	14 57	14 51	15 05		

Basingstoke, Alton, Guildford and Woking - Waterloo

		SW 1	SW 1		SW 1	SW ◇1 ⌶	SW ◇1 ⌶	SW	SW 1	SW 1 ⌶	SW 1	SW 1	SW 1		SW 1	SW	SW 1	SW ◇1 ⌶	SW ◇1 ⌶	SW	SW 1	SW 1 ⌶	SW 1		SW 1
Basingstoke	d	14 17			14 24	14 30	14 35				14 43				14 54			14 57							
Hook	d				14 31										15 01										
Winchfield	d				14 35										15 05										
Fleet	d				14 40						14 54				15 10										
Farnborough (Main)	d	14 30			14 46						15 00				15 16										
Alton	d								14 15												14 44				
Bentley	d																				14 51				
Farnham	a								14 25												14 56				
	d								14 28												14 58				
Aldershot	d								14 34				15 00								15 04				15 30
Ash Vale	d								14 39				15a04								15 09				15a34
Brookwood	d				14 53				14 46						15 23						15 16				
Guildford	d		14 34							14 47							15 02					15 17			
Worplesdon	d		14 40									←											←		
Woking	a	14 39	14 44		14 58	14 49			14 51	14 57		14 58			15 28		15 11	15 15			15 21	15 25	15 28		
	d	14 41	14 46		14 59	14 50			14 52	14 59		14 59			15 29	15 03	15 12	15 17	15 21		15 22	15 26	15 29		
West Byfleet	d				→				14 57						→	15 07					15 27				
Byfleet & New Haw	d															15 10									
Weybridge	d											15 06				15 13							15 36		
Walton-on-Thames	d											15 10				15 17							15 40		
Hersham	d															15 19									
Esher	d															15 22									
Surbiton 6	a								15 07			15 16				15 26					15 37		15 46		
Wimbledon 6 ⊖	a															15 34									
Earlsfield	a							←								15 38				←					
Clapham Junction 10	a		15 05				15 12	15 12			15 25					15 42	15 31	15 36		15 42	15 50		15 57		
Vauxhall ⊖	a							15 17								→				15 47					
London Waterloo 15 ⊖	a	15 08	15 13			15 19	15 20	15 22	15 25	15 23	15 34	15 37					15 43	15 49	15 49	15 52	15 58	15 51	16 05		

		SW	SW 1	SW 1	SW 1	SW ◇1 ⌶	SW ◇1 ⌶	SW	SW 1		SW 1 ⌶	SW 1	SW 1	SW 1	SW 1	SW	SW 1	SW ◇1 ⌶	SW ◇1 ⌶		SW	SW 1	SW 1 ⌶	SW 1	SW 1
Basingstoke	d		15 17		15 24	15 30	15 35					15 43			15 54			15 57							
Hook	d				15 31										16 01										
Winchfield	d				15 35										16 05										
Fleet	d				15 40							15 54			16 10										
Farnborough (Main)	d		15 30		15 46							16 00			16 16										
Alton	d								15 15													15 44			
Bentley	d																					15 51			
Farnham	a								15 25													15 56			
	d								15 28													15 58			
Aldershot	d								15 34					16 00								16 04			16 30
Ash Vale	d								15 39					16a04								16 09			16a34
Brookwood	d				15 53				15 46						16 23							16 16			
Guildford	d			15 34							15 47						16 00						16 17		
Worplesdon	d			15 40									←				16 06							←	
Woking	a		15 39	15 44	15 58	15 49			15 51		15 57		15 58		16 28		16 11	16 15				16 21	16 25	16 28	
	d	15 33	15 41	15 46	15 59	15 50			15 52		15 59		15 59		16 29	16 03	16 12	16 17	16 21			16 22	16 26	16 29	
West Byfleet	d	15 37			→				15 57						→	16 07						16 27			
Byfleet & New Haw	d	15 40														16 10									
Weybridge	d	15 43											16 06			16 13								16 36	
Walton-on-Thames	d	15 47											16 10			16 17								16 40	
Hersham	d	15 49														16 19									
Esher	d	15 52														16 22									
Surbiton 6	a	15 56							16 07				16 16			16 26						16 37		16 46	
Wimbledon 6 ⊖	a	16 04														16 34									
Earlsfield	a	16 08						←								16 38					←				
Clapham Junction 10	a	16 12		16 05			16 12	16 12				16 25				16 42	16 31	16 36			16 42	16 48		16 57	
Vauxhall ⊖	a	→						16 17								→					16 47				
London Waterloo 15 ⊖	a		16 07	16 13		16 19	16 20	16 22	16 29		16 24	16 34	16 36				16 40	16 49	16 49		16 52	16 59	16 51	17 08	

Table 155

Basingstoke, Alton, Guildford and Woking - Waterloo

		SW	SW 1	SW 1	SW 1		SW ◇1 [trolley]	SW ◇1 [trolley]	SW	SW 1	SW 1	SW 1	SW 1	SW 1	SW 1		SW	SW 1 [trolley]	SW ◇1 [trolley]	SW ◇1 [trolley]	SW	SW 1	SW 1 [trolley]	SW 1	SW 1
Basingstoke	d		16 17		16 24		16 30	16 35					16 43		16 54				16 57						
Hook	d				16 31										17 01										
Winchfield	d				16 35										17 05										
Fleet	d				16 40								16 54		17 10										
Farnborough (Main)	d		16 30		16 46								17 00		17 16										
Alton	d									16 15												16 44			
Bentley	d																					16 51			
Farnham	a									16 25												16 56			
	d									16 28												16 58			
Aldershot	d									16 34				17 00								17 04			17 30
Ash Vale	d									16 39				17a04								17 09			17a34
Brookwood	d				16 53					16 46					17 23							17 16			
Guildford	d			16 34							16 47							17 00					17 17		
Worplesdon	d			16 40								←						17 06						←	
Woking	a		16 39	16 44	16 58		16 49			16 51	16 57	16 58			17 28			17 11	17 15			17 21	17 25	17 28	
	d	16 33	16 41	16 46	16 59		16 50			16 52	16 59	16 59			17 29		17 03	17 12	17 17	17 21		17 22	17 26	17 29	
West Byfleet	d	16 37			→					16 57					→		17 07					17 27			
Byfleet & New Haw	d	16 40															17 10								
Weybridge	d	16 43										17 06					17 13							17 36	
Walton-on-Thames	d	16 47										17 10					17 17							17 40	
Hersham	d	16 49															17 19								
Esher	d	16 52															17 22								
Surbiton 6	a	16 56								17 07		17 16					17 26					17 37		17 46	
Wimbledon 6 ⊖	a	17 04															17 34								
Earlsfield	a	17 08							←								17 38				←				
Clapham Junction 10	a	17 12		17 05				17 12	17 12				17 25				17 42	17 31	17 36		17 42	17 48		17 57	
Vauxhall ⊖	a	→							17 17								→				17 47				
London Waterloo 15 ⊖	a		17 08	17 14			17 19	17 20	17 22	17 29	17 27	17 35	17 36					17 43	17 44	17 50	17 52	17 59	17 54	18 09	

			SW	SW 1	SW 1	SW 1	SW ◇1 [trolley]	SW	SW ◇1 [trolley]	SW 1	SW 1		SW 1	SW 1	SW 1	SW 1	SW	SW 1 [trolley]	SW ◇1 [trolley]	SW ◇1 [trolley]	SW		SW 1	SW 1	SW 1
Basingstoke	d			17 17		17 24	17 30		17 36				17 43			17 54			17 57						
Hook	d					17 31										18 01									
Winchfield	d					17 35										18 05									
Fleet	d					17 40							17 54			18 10									
Farnborough (Main)	d			17 30		17 46							18 00			18 16									
Alton	d									17 14													17 44		
Bentley	d									17 21													17 51		
Farnham	a									17 26													17 56		
	d									17 28													17 58		
Aldershot	d									17 34					18 00								18 04		18 30
Ash Vale	d									17 39					18a04								18 09		18a34
Brookwood	d					17 53				17 46						18 23							18 16		
Guildford	d				17 34						17 47							18 00							
Worplesdon	d				17 40									←				18 06						←	
Woking	a			17 39	17 44	17 58	17 49			17 51	17 58			17 58		18 28		18 11	18 15				18 21	18 28	
	d		17 33	17 41	17 46	17 59	17 51			17 52	17 59			17 59		18 29	18 03	18 12	18 17	18 21			18 22	18 29	
West Byfleet	d		17 37			→				17 57						→	18 07						18 27		
Byfleet & New Haw	d		17 40														18 10								
Weybridge	d		17 43											18 06			18 13							18 36	
Walton-on-Thames	d		17 47											18 10			18 17							18 40	
Hersham	d		17 49														18 19								
Esher	d		17 52														18 22								
Surbiton 6	a		17 56							18 07				18 16			18 26						18 37	18 47	
Wimbledon 6 ⊖	a		18 04														18 34								
Earlsfield	a		18 08					←									18 38				←				
Clapham Junction 10	a		18 12		18 05			18 12	18 12				18 25				18 42	18 31	18 36		18 42		18 48	18 58	
Vauxhall ⊖	a		→					18 17									→				18 47				
London Waterloo 15 ⊖	a			18 08	18 14		18 21	18 23	18 23	18 29	18 27		18 34	18 38				18 43	18 45	18 47	18 52		18 57	19 06	

Table 155

Basingstoke, Alton, Guildford and Woking - Waterloo

		SW	SW 1	SW 1	SW 1	SW ◇1 [trolley]	SW		SW ◇1 [trolley]	SW 1	SW 1	SW 1	SW 1 [trolley]	SW 1	SW 1	SW	SW 1		SW ◇1 [trolley]	SW 1	SW ◇1 [trolley]	SW 1 [trolley]	SW 1	SW 1	SW
Basingstoke	d		18 17		18 24	18 30			18 35					18 43			18 54		19 02						
Hook	d				18 31												19 01								
Winchfield	d				18 35												19 05								
Fleet	d				18 40									18 54			19 10								
Farnborough (Main)	d		18 30		18 46									19 00			19 16								
Alton	d									18 14										18 35					
Bentley	d									18 23										18 42					
Farnham	a									18 27										18 47					
	d									18 28										18 58					
Aldershot	d									18 34		18 38			19 00					19 04				19 30	
Ash Vale	d									18 39					19a04					19 09				19a34	
Brookwood	d				18 53					18 46							19 23			19 16					
Guildford	d			18 34								18a55	18 55									19 21			
Worplesdon	d			18 40							←												←		
Woking	a		18 39	18 44	18 58	18 49				18 52	18 58		19 03				19 28		19 20	19 21		19 28	19 28		
	d	18 33	18 41	18 46	18 59	18 50				18 52	18 59		19 05			19 03	19 29		19 22	19 22	19 25	19 30	19 29		19 33
West Byfleet	d	18 37			→					18 57						19 07	→			19 27					19 37
Byfleet & New Haw	d	18 40														19 10									19 40
Weybridge	d	18 43									19 06					19 13							19 36		19 43
Walton-on-Thames	d	18 47									19 10					19 17							19 40		19 47
Hersham	d	18 49														19 19									19 49
Esher	d	18 52														19 22									19 52
Surbiton 6	a	18 56								19 07	19 16					19 26				19 37			19 46		19 56
Wimbledon 6 ⊖	a	19 04														19 34									20 04
Earlsfield	a	19 08					←									19 38									20 08
Clapham Junction 10	a	19 11		19 05			19 11		19 12					19 26		19 41			19 41	19 48			19 57		20 11
Vauxhall ⊖	a	→					19 16									19 46									→
London Waterloo 15 ⊖	a		19 08	19 13		19 19	19 23		19 20	19 25	19 39		19 29	19 34		19 52			19 50	19 57	19 51	19 59	20 05		

		SW 1	SW 1		SW 1	SW ◇1 [trolley]	SW	SW ◇1 [trolley]	SW 1	SW 1 [trolley]	SW 1	SW 1	SW 1		SW 1	SW	SW 1	SW ◇1 [trolley]	SW	SW 1	SW 1 [trolley]	SW 1	SW 1		SW ◇1 [trolley]
Basingstoke	d	19 17			19 24	19 30		19 35				19 43											19 54		20 09
Hook	d				19 31																		20 01		
Winchfield	d				19 35																		20 05		
Fleet	d				19 40							19 54											20 10		
Farnborough (Main)	d	19 30			19 46							20 00											20 16		
Alton	d								19 07											19 35					
Bentley	d																			19 42					
Farnham	a								19 17											19 47					
	d								19 28											19 58					
Aldershot	d								19 34		19 38				20 00					20 04		20 30			
Ash Vale	d								19 39						20a04					20 09		20a34			
Brookwood	d				19 53				19 46											20 16			20 23		
Guildford	d		19 34							19 47	19a55						20 02				20 17				
Worplesdon	d		19 40										←												
Woking	a	19 39	19 45		19 58	19 49			19 51	19 57			19 58				20 11			20 21	20 25		20 28		20 29
	d	19 41	19 46		19 59	19 50			19 52	19 59			19 59			20 03	20 12	20 21		20 22	20 26		20 29		20 30
West Byfleet	d				→				19 57							20 07				20 27					
Byfleet & New Haw	d															20 10									
Weybridge	d												20 06			20 13							20 36		
Walton-on-Thames	d												20 10			20 17							20 40		
Hersham	d															20 19									
Esher	d															20 22									
Surbiton 6	a								20 07				20 16			20 26				20 37			20 46		
Wimbledon 6 ⊖	a															20 35									
Earlsfield	a						←									20 38			←						
Clapham Junction 10	a		20 05				20 11	20 12				20 25				20 41	20 31		20 41	20 48			20 57		20 52
Vauxhall ⊖	a						20 16									→			20 46				→		
London Waterloo 15 ⊖	a	20 08	20 14			20 19	20 22	20 20	20 26	20 24		20 34	20 36				20 40	20 49	20 52	20 57	20 50				21 00

Basingstoke, Alton, Guildford and Woking - Waterloo

		SW 1	SW	SW 1	SW 1	SW 1	SW 1	SW ◇1 (trolley)	SW 1	SW	SW 1	SW ◇1 (trolley)	SW	SW 1	SW 1	SW 1	SW 1	SW ◇1 (trolley)	SW 1	SW	SW 1	SW	SW 1
Basingstoke	d			20 17			20 24	20 36			20 43						20 54	21 09					
Hook	d						20 31										21 01						
Winchfield	d						20 35										21 05						
Fleet	d						20 40				20 54						21 10						
Farnborough (Main)	d			20 30			20 46				21 00						21 16						
Alton	d				20 15									20 44									21 15
Bentley	d													20 51									
Farnham	a				20 25									20 56									21 25
	d				20 28									20 58									21 28
Aldershot	d				20 34									21 04		21 30							21 34
Ash Vale	d				20 39									21 09		21a34							21 39
Brookwood	d				20 46		20 53							21 16			21 23						21 46
Guildford	d					20 39			20 47						21 17						21 39		
Worplesdon	d					20 44															21 44		
Woking	a			20 39	20 51	20 52	20 58		20 56		21 09			21 21	21 25		21 28	21 29			21 49		21 51
	d		20 33	20 41	20 52	20 53	20 59		20 59	21 03	21 10	21 21		21 22	21 26		21 29	21 30		21 33	21 50		21 52
West Byfleet	d		20 37		20 57					21 07				21 27						21 37			21 57
Byfleet & New Haw	d		20 40							21 10										21 40			
Weybridge	d		20 43				21 06			21 13							21 36			21 43			
Walton-on-Thames	d		20 47				21 10			21 17							21 40			21 47			
Hersham	d		20 49							21 19										21 49			
Esher	d		20 52							21 22										21 52			
Surbiton 5	a		20 56		21 07		21 16			21 26				21 37			21 46			21 56			22 07
Wimbledon 5 ⊖	a		21 05							21 34										22 04			
Earlsfield	a	←	21 08							21 38			←						←	22 08		←	
Clapham Junction 10	a	20 57	21 11			21 12		21 16		21 42	21 29		21 42	21 48			21 57	21 52	21 57	22 12	22 09	22 12	
Vauxhall ⊖	a		21 16							→			21 47				→			→		22 17	
London Waterloo 15 ⊖	a	21 05	21 22	21 07	21 29	21 21	21 34	21 24	21 27		21 38	21 49	21 52	21 57	21 50			22 04	22 06		22 18	22 22	22 27

		SW 1	SW ◇1	SW 1	SW	SW 1	SW 1	SW	SW 1	SW 1	SW 1	SW ◇1 (trolley)	SW 1	SW 1	SW	SW 1	SW	SW 1	SW 1	SW 1	SW ◇1	SW 1	SW
Basingstoke	d	21 24	21 35			21 43					21 54	22 09								22 24	22 36		
Hook	d	21 31									22 01									22 31			
Winchfield	d	21 35									22 05									22 35			
Fleet	d	21 40				21 54					22 10									22 40			
Farnborough (Main)	d	21 46				22 00					22 16									22 46			
Alton	d								21 44									22 15					
Bentley	d								21 51														
Farnham	a								21 56									22 25					
	d								21 58									22 28					
Aldershot	d								22 04	22 30								22 34	22 38				
Ash Vale	d								22 09	22a34								22 39					
Brookwood	d	21 53							22 16		22 23							22 46		22 53			
Guildford	d			21 47											22 20	22 39			22a55				22 55
Worplesdon	d															22 44						←	
Woking	a	21 58		21 57		22 09			22 21		22 28	22 28			22 32	22 49		22 51		22 58	22 54	22 58	23 05
	d	21 59		21 59	22 03	22 10	22 21		22 22		22 29	22 29			22 33	22 50		22 52		22 59	22 55	22 59	23 06
West Byfleet	d				22 07				22 27						22 37			22 57		→			23 10
Byfleet & New Haw	d				22 10										22 40								23 13
Weybridge	d	22 06			22 13						22 36				22 43							23 06	23 16
Walton-on-Thames	d	22 10			22 17						22 40				22 47							23 10	23 20
Hersham	d				22 19										22 49								23 22
Esher	d				22 22										22 52								23 25
Surbiton 5	a	22 16			22 26				22 37		22 46				22 56			23 07				23 16	23 29
Wimbledon 5 ⊖	a				22 34										23 04								23 37
Earlsfield	a				22 38			←					←	←	23 08		←						23 41
Clapham Junction 10	a		22 14		22 42	22 29		22 42	22 52		22 57	22 48	22 52	22 57	23 12	23 09	23 12				23 14		23 44
Vauxhall ⊖	a				→			22 47	→		→				→		23 17						→
London Waterloo 15 ⊖	a	22 34	22 22	22 27		22 38	22 49	22 52				22 58	23 01	23 08		23 19	23 23	23 27			23 23	23 32	

Basingstoke, Alton, Guildford and Woking - Waterloo

		SW 1	SW	SW 1	SW 1	SW FX 1	SW FO 1	SW 1	SW FX 1	SW FO 1	SW 1	SW FO 1	SW FX 1	SW 1	SW 1
Basingstoke	d	22 43				22 54	22 54	23 13						23 44	
Hook	d					23 01	23 01							23 51	
Winchfield	d					23 05	23 05							23 55	
Fleet	d	22 54				23 10	23 10							00 01	
Farnborough (Main)	d	23 00				23 16	23 16							00 06	
Alton	d			22 44							23 15				23 45
Bentley	d			22 51											23 52
Farnham	a			22 56							23 25				23 57
	d			22 58							23 28				
Aldershot	d			23 04	23 30						23 34				
Ash Vale	d			23 09	23a34						23 39				
Brookwood	d			23 16		23 23	23 23				23 46			00 13	
Guildford	d											23 39	23 39		
Worplesdon	d								←	←		23 44	23 44		
Woking	a	23 09		23 21		23 28	23 28	23 31	23 28	23 28	23 51	23 49	23 49	00 18	
	d	23 10		23 22		23 33	23 33	23 32	23 33	23 33		23 56	23 56	00 20	
West Byfleet	d			23 27		→	→		23 37	23 37				00 25	
Byfleet & New Haw	d								23 40	23 40					
Weybridge	d								23 43	23 43				00 29	
Walton-on-Thames	d								23 47	23 47				00 33	
Hersham	d								23 49	23 49					
Esher	d								23 52	23 52					
Surbiton 5	a			23 37					23 57	23 57				00 39	
Wimbledon 5 ⊖	a								00 06	00 06				00 47	
Earlsfield	a		←												
Clapham Junction 10	a	23 29	23 44	23 51				23 55				00 19	00 19	00 53	
Vauxhall ⊖	a		23 49						00 28	00 30					
London Waterloo 15 ⊖	a	23 42	23 54	00 02				00 09	00 35	00 35		00 32	00 33	01 04	

Saturdays
until 1 October

		SW 1	SW 1	SW 1	SW 1	SW 1	SW 1	SW 1	SW	SW	SW 1	SW	SW 1	SW	SW 1	SW ◇1 (trolley)	SW	SW 1	SW 1	SW 1	SW	SW 1	SW ◇1 (trolley)
Basingstoke	d			22p54	23p13			23p44			04 54		05 54			05 59				06 24			06 30
Hook	d			23p01				23p51			05 01		06 01							06 31			
Winchfield	d			23p05				23p55			05 05		06 05							06 35			
Fleet	d			23p10				00 01			05 10		06 10							06 40			
Farnborough (Main)	d			23p16				00 06			05 16		06 16							06 46			
Alton	d	22p44																					
Bentley	d	22p51																					
Farnham	a	22p56																					
	d	22p58																					
Aldershot	d	23p04	06 00																06 00				
Ash Vale	d	23p09	06a04																06 08				
Brookwood	d	23p16		23p23				00 13			05 23		06 23							06 53			
Guildford	d						23p39		04 00			05 14			06 02				06a25			06 34	
Worplesdon	d					←	23p44					05 19						←				06 40	
Woking	a	23p21		23p28	23p31	23p28	23p49	00 18	04 08		05 28	05 24	06 28		06 11	06 18		06 28		06 58		06 44	06 49
	d	23p22		23p33	23p32	23p33	23p56	00 20	04 10	05 27	05 29	05 33	06 29	06 03	06 13	06 19		06 29		06 59	06 33	06 46	06 50
West Byfleet	d	23p27		→		23p37		00 25		05 32		05 37	→	06 07						→	06 37		
Byfleet & New Haw	d					23p40				05 35		05 40		06 10							06 40		
Weybridge	d					23p43		00 29				05 43		06 13				06 36			06 43		
Walton-on-Thames	d					23p47		00 33				05 47		06 17				06 40			06 47		
Hersham	d					23p49						05 49		06 19							06 49		
Esher	d					23p52						05 52		06 22							06 52		
Surbiton 5	a	23p37				23p57		00 39	04 24		05 40	05 56		06 26				06 46			06 56		
Wimbledon 5 ⊖	a					00 06		00 47	04 31		05 48	06 04		06 34							07 04		
Earlsfield	a											06 08		06 38			←				07 08		
Clapham Junction 10	a	23p51			23p55		00 19	00 53	04 43			06 12		06 42	06 32	06 38	06 42	06 57			07 12	07 05	
Vauxhall ⊖	a					00 30				06 49	06 07	06 17		→			06 47				→		
London Waterloo 15 ⊖	a	00 02			00 09	00 35	00 32	01 04	04 53	06 56	06 12	06 22			06 40	06 49	06 52	07 05				07 13	07 19

Table 155

Saturdays
until 1 October

Basingstoke, Alton, Guildford and Woking - Waterloo

	SW	SW 1	SW 1	SW 1	SW 1	SW 1	SW 1	SW	SW 1	SW ◇1 ✕	SW	SW 1	SW 1	SW ◇1 ✕	SW 1	SW 1	SW 1	SW	SW 1	SW ◇1 ✕	SW	SW 1
Basingstoke d				06 40			06 54			06 57				07 09			07 24			07 30		
Hook d							07 01										07 31					
Winchfield d							07 05										07 35					
Fleet d							07 10										07 40					
Farnborough (Main) d							07 16										07 46					
Alton d		06 14										06 44										07 14
Bentley d		06 21										06 51										07 21
Farnham a		06 26										06 56										07 26
d		06 28										06 58										07 28
Aldershot d		06 34	06 38			07 00						07 04	07 08			07 30						07 34
Ash Vale d		06 39				07a04						07 09				07a34						07 39
Brookwood d		06 46					07 23					07 16					07 53					07 46
Guildford d			06a55						07 02				07a25						07 34			
Worplesdon d					←										←				07 40			
Woking a		06 51		06 58	06 58		07 28		07 11	07 15		07 21		07 27	07 28		07 58		07 44	07 49		07 51
d		06 52		07 00	06 59		07 29	07 03	07 12	07 17		07 22		07 29	07 29		07 59	07 33	07 46	07 50		07 52
West Byfleet d		06 57					→	07 07				07 27					→	07 37				07 57
Byfleet & New Haw d								07 10										07 40				
Weybridge d					07 06			07 13							07 36			07 43				
Walton-on-Thames d					07 10			07 17							07 40			07 47				
Hersham d								07 19										07 49				
Esher d								07 22										07 52				
Surbiton 6 a		07 07			07 16			07 26				07 37			07 46			07 56				08 07
Wimbledon 6 ⊖ a								07 34										08 04				
Earlsfield a	←							07 38			←							08 08			←	
Clapham Junction 10 a	07 12	07 18		07 23				07 42	07 31	07 36	07 42	07 50			07 57			08 12	08 05		08 12	
Vauxhall ⊖ a	07 17							→			07 47							→			08 17	
London Waterloo 15 ⊖ a	07 22	07 27		07 31	07 33				07 40	07 49	07 52	07 58		07 53	08 05				08 13	08 19	08 22	08 25

	SW 1 ✕	SW 1	SW 1	SW	SW 1	SW 1	SW 1	SW ◇1 ✕	SW	SW 1	SW ◇1 ✕	SW 1 ✕	SW 1	SW 1	SW 1	SW	SW 1	SW 1	SW 1	SW ◇1 ✕	SW ◇1 ✕
Basingstoke d					07 43		07 54	07 57									08 17		08 24	08 30	08 35
Hook d							08 01												08 31		
Winchfield d							08 05												08 35		
Fleet d					07 54		08 10												08 40		
Farnborough (Main) d					08 00		08 16										08 30		08 46		
Alton d										07 44											
Bentley d										07 51											
Farnham a										07 56											
d										07 58											
Aldershot d			08 00							08 04				08 08	08 30						
Ash Vale d			08a04							08 09					08a34						
Brookwood d							08 23			08 16									08 53		
Guildford d	07 47					08 02						08 17		08a25				08 34			
Worplesdon d		←											←					08 40			
Woking a	07 57	07 58			08 09	08 10	08 28	08 17		08 21		08 26	08 28				08 39	08 44	08 58	08 49	
d	07 59	07 59		08 03	08 11	08 13	08 29	08 18		08 22	08 23	08 27	08 29			08 33	08 41	08 46	08 59	08 50	
West Byfleet d				08 07			→			08 27						08 37			→		
Byfleet & New Haw d				08 10												08 40					
Weybridge d		08 06		08 13									08 36			08 43					
Walton-on-Thames d		08 10		08 17									08 40			08 47					
Hersham d				08 19												08 49					
Esher d				08 22												08 52					
Surbiton 6 a		08 16		08 26						08 37			08 46			08 56					
Wimbledon 6 ⊖ a				08 34												09 04					
Earlsfield a				08 38					←							09 08					
Clapham Junction 10 a				08 42	08 30	08 33		08 37	08 42	08 49			08 57			09 12		09 05			09 12
Vauxhall ⊖ a				→					08 47							→					
London Waterloo 15 ⊖ a	08 23	08 34			08 39	08 42		08 49	08 52	08 58	08 49	08 51	09 05				09 08	09 13		09 19	09 20

Table 155

Saturdays
until 1 October

Basingstoke, Alton, Guildford and Woking - Waterloo

	SW	SW 1	SW 1 ✕	SW 1	SW 1	SW 1	SW 1	SW	SW 1	SW ◇1 ✕	SW ◇1 ✕	SW	SW 1	SW 1 ✕	SW 1	SW 1	SW	SW 1	SW 1	SW 1	SW ◇1 ✕	SW ◇1 ✕
Basingstoke d				08 43			08 54			08 57								09 17		09 24	09 30	09 35
Hook d							09 01													09 31		
Winchfield d							09 05													09 35		
Fleet d				08 54			09 10													09 40		
Farnborough (Main) d				09 00			09 16											09 30		09 46		
Alton d		08 14											08 44									
Bentley d		08 21											08 51									
Farnham a		08 26											08 56									
d		08 28											08 58									
Aldershot d		08 34				09 00							09 04			09 30						
Ash Vale d		08 39				09a04							09 09			09a34						
Brookwood d		08 46					09 23						09 16							09 53		
Guildford d			08 47						09 02					09 17					09 34			
Worplesdon d					←										←				09 40			
Woking a		08 51	08 57		08 58		09 28		09 11	09 15			09 21	09 25	09 28			09 39	09 44	09 58	09 49	
d		08 52	08 59		08 59		09 29	09 03	09 12	09 17	09 21		09 22	09 26	09 29		09 33	09 41	09 46	09 59	09 50	
West Byfleet d		08 57					→	09 07					09 27				09 37			→		
Byfleet & New Haw d								09 10									09 40					
Weybridge d					09 06			09 13							09 36		09 43					
Walton-on-Thames d					09 10			09 17							09 40		09 47					
Hersham d								09 19									09 49					
Esher d								09 22									09 52					
Surbiton 6 a		09 07			09 16			09 26					09 37		09 46		09 56					
Wimbledon 6 ⊖ a								09 34									10 04					
Earlsfield a	←							09 38				←					10 08					
Clapham Junction 10 a	09 12			09 25				09 42	09 31	09 36		09 42	09 48		09 57		10 12		10 05			10 12
Vauxhall ⊖ a	09 17							→				09 47					→					
London Waterloo 15 ⊖ a	09 22	09 25	09 23	09 34	09 36				09 40	09 49	09 49	09 52	09 57	09 51	10 05			10 07	10 13		10 19	10 20

	SW	SW 1	SW 1 ✕	SW 1	SW 1	SW 1	SW 1	SW	SW 1	SW ◇1 ✕	SW ◇1 ✕	SW	SW 1	SW 1 ✕	SW 1	SW 1	SW	SW 1	SW 1	SW 1	SW ◇1 ✕
Basingstoke d				09 43			09 54			09 57								10 17		10 24	10 30
Hook d							10 01													10 31	
Winchfield d							10 05													10 35	
Fleet d				09 54			10 10													10 40	
Farnborough (Main) d				10 00			10 16											10 30		10 46	
Alton d		09 14											09 44								
Bentley d		09 21											09 51								
Farnham a		09 26											09 56								
d		09 28											09 58								
Aldershot d		09 34				10 00							10 04			10 30					
Ash Vale d		09 39				10a04							10 09			10a34					
Brookwood d		09 46					10 23						10 16							10 53	
Guildford d			09 47						10 02					10 17					10 34		
Worplesdon d					←										←				10 40		
Woking a		09 51	09 57		09 58		10 28		10 11	10 15			10 21	10 25	10 28			10 39	10 44	10 58	10 49
d		09 52	09 59		09 59		10 29	10 03	10 12	10 17	10 21		10 22	10 26	10 29		10 33	10 41	10 46	10 59	10 50
West Byfleet d		09 57					→	10 07					10 27				10 37			→	
Byfleet & New Haw d								10 10									10 40				
Weybridge d					10 06			10 13							10 36		10 43				
Walton-on-Thames d					10 10			10 17							10 40		10 47				
Hersham d								10 19									10 49				
Esher d								10 22									10 52				
Surbiton 6 a		10 07			10 16			10 26					10 37		10 46		10 56				
Wimbledon 6 ⊖ a								10 34									11 04				
Earlsfield a	←							10 38				←					11 08				
Clapham Junction 10 a	10 12			10 25				10 42	10 31	10 36		10 42	10 48		10 57		11 12		11 05		
Vauxhall ⊖ a	10 17							→				10 47					→				
London Waterloo 15 ⊖ a	10 22	10 25	10 23	10 34	10 36				10 40	10 49	10 49	10 52	10 57	10 51	11 05			11 07	11 13		11 19

Basingstoke, Alton, Guildford and Woking - Waterloo

		SW	SW	SW	SW	SW	SW	SW	SW	SW		SW	SW	SW	SW	SW	SW	SW	SW	SW		SW	SW	SW	SW
		◇1 ✠		1	1 ✠	1	1	1	1			1	◇1 ✠	◇1 ✠		1	1 ✠	1	1			1	1	1	◇1 ✠
Basingstoke	d	10 35				10 43			10 54				10 57									11 17		11 24	11 30
Hook	d								11 01															11 31	
Winchfield	d								11 05															11 35	
Fleet	d					10 54			11 10															11 40	
Farnborough (Main)	d					11 00			11 16													11 30		11 46	
Alton	d			10 14												10 44									
Bentley	d			10 21												10 51									
Farnham	a			10 26												10 56									
	d			10 28												10 58									
Aldershot	d			10 34				11 00								11 04			11 30						
Ash Vale	d			10 39				11a04								11 09			11a34						
Brookwood	d			10 46					11 23							11 16								11 53	
Guildford	d				10 47							11 02					11 17						11 34		
Worplesdon	d						←											←					11 40		
Woking	a			10 51	10 57		10 58		11 28			11 11	11 15			11 21	11 25	11 28				11 39	11 44	11 58	11 49
	d			10 52	10 59		10 59		11 29	11 03		11 12	11 17	11 21		11 22	11 26	11 29		11 33		11 41	11 46	11 59	11 50
West Byfleet	d			10 57					→	11 07						11 27				11 37				→	
Byfleet & New Haw	d									11 10										11 40					
Weybridge	d						11 06			11 13								11 36		11 43					
Walton-on-Thames	d						11 10			11 17								11 40		11 47					
Hersham	d									11 19										11 49					
Esher	d									11 22										11 52					
Surbiton 6	a			11 07			11 16			11 26						11 37		11 46		11 56					
Wimbledon 6 ⊖	a									11 34										12 04					
Earlsfield	a		←							11 38					←					12 08					
Clapham Junction 10	a	11 12	11 12			11 25				11 42		11 31	11 36		11 42	11 48		11 57		12 12			12 05		
Vauxhall ⊖	a		11 17							→					11 47					→					
London Waterloo 15 ⊖	a	11 20	11 22	11 25	11 23	11 34	11 36					11 40	11 49	11 49	11 52	11 57	11 51	12 05				12 07	12 13		12 19

		SW	SW	SW	SW	SW		SW	SW	SW	SW	SW	SW	SW	SW	SW		SW	SW	SW	SW	SW	SW	SW	SW
		◇1 ✠		1	1 ✠	1		1	1	1		1	◇1 ✠	◇1 ✠		1		1 ✠	1	1		1	1	1	◇1 ✠
Basingstoke	d	11 35				11 43				11 54			11 57									12 17		12 24	12 30
Hook	d									12 01														12 31	
Winchfield	d									12 05														12 35	
Fleet	d					11 54				12 10														12 40	
Farnborough (Main)	d					12 00				12 16												12 30		12 46	
Alton	d			11 15												11 44									
Bentley	d															11 51									
Farnham	a			11 25												11 56									
	d			11 28												11 58									
Aldershot	d			11 34					12 00							12 04				12 30					
Ash Vale	d			11 39					12a04							12 09				12a34					
Brookwood	d			11 46						12 23						12 16								12 53	
Guildford	d				11 47							12 02						12 17					12 34		
Worplesdon	d							←											←				12 40		
Woking	a			11 51	11 57			11 58		12 28		12 11	12 15			12 21		12 25	12 28			12 39	12 44	12 58	12 49
	d			11 52	11 59			11 59		12 29	12 03	12 12	12 17	12 21		12 22		12 26	12 29		12 33	12 41	12 46	12 59	12 50
West Byfleet	d			11 57						→	12 07					12 27					12 37			→	
Byfleet & New Haw	d										12 10										12 40				
Weybridge	d							12 06			12 13								12 36		12 43				
Walton-on-Thames	d							12 10			12 17								12 40		12 47				
Hersham	d										12 19										12 49				
Esher	d										12 22										12 52				
Surbiton 6	a			12 07				12 16			12 26					12 37			12 46		12 56				
Wimbledon 6 ⊖	a										12 34										13 04				
Earlsfield	a		←								12 38				←						13 08				
Clapham Junction 10	a	12 12	12 12			12 25					12 42	12 31	12 36		12 42	12 48			12 57		13 12		13 05		
Vauxhall ⊖	a		12 17								→				12 47						→				
London Waterloo 15 ⊖	a	12 21	12 22	12 29	12 27	12 34		12 36				12 43	12 49	12 51	12 52	12 59		12 57	13 05			13 07	13 13		13 19

Basingstoke, Alton, Guildford and Woking - Waterloo

		SW		SW	SW	SW	SW	SW	SW	SW	SW	SW		SW	SW	SW	SW	SW	SW	SW	SW	SW		SW	SW
		◇1 ✠			1	1 ✠	1	1	1	1		1		◇1 ✠	◇1 ✠		1	1 ✠	1	1		1		1	1
Basingstoke	d	12 35					12 43			12 54				12 57								13 17			13 24
Hook	d									13 01															13 31
Winchfield	d									13 05															13 35
Fleet	d						12 54			13 10															13 40
Farnborough (Main)	d						13 00			13 16												13 30			13 46
Alton	d				12 15												12 44								
Bentley	d																12 51								
Farnham	a				12 25												12 56								
	d				12 28												12 58								
Aldershot	d				12 34				13 00								13 04			13 30					
Ash Vale	d				12 39				13a04								13 09			13a34					
Brookwood	d				12 46					13 23							13 16								13 53
Guildford	d					12 47						13 02						13 17						13 34	
Worplesdon	d							←											←					13 40	
Woking	a				12 51	12 57		12 58		13 28		13 11		13 15			13 21	13 25	13 28			13 39		13 44	13 58
	d				12 52	12 59		12 59		13 29	13 03	13 12		13 17	13 21		13 22	13 26	13 29		13 33	13 41		13 46	13 59
West Byfleet	d				12 57					→	13 07						13 27				13 37				→
Byfleet & New Haw	d										13 10										13 40				
Weybridge	d							13 06			13 13								13 36		13 43				
Walton-on-Thames	d							13 10			13 17								13 40		13 47				
Hersham	d										13 19										13 49				
Esher	d										13 22										13 52				
Surbiton 6	a				13 07			13 16			13 26						13 37		13 46		13 56				
Wimbledon 6 ⊖	a										13 34										14 04				
Earlsfield	a			←							13 38					←					14 08				
Clapham Junction 10	a	13 12		13 12			13 25				13 42	13 31		13 36		13 42	13 48		13 57		14 12			14 05	
Vauxhall ⊖	a			13 17							→					13 47					→				
London Waterloo 15 ⊖	a	13 21		13 22	13 29	13 27	13 34	13 36				13 43		13 49	13 51	13 52	13 59	13 57	14 05			14 07		14 14	

		SW	SW	SW	SW	SW	SW	SW		SW	SW	SW	SW	SW	SW	SW	SW	SW		SW	SW	SW	SW	SW	SW
		◇1 ✠	◇1 ✠		1	1 ✠	1	1		1	1		1	◇1 ✠	◇1 ✠		1	1 ✠		1	1		1	1	1
Basingstoke	d	13 30	13 35				13 43				13 54			13 57									14 17		14 24
Hook	d										14 01														14 31
Winchfield	d										14 05														14 35
Fleet	d						13 54				14 10														14 40
Farnborough (Main)	d						14 00				14 16												14 30		14 46
Alton	d				13 15												13 44								
Bentley	d																13 51								
Farnham	a				13 25												13 56								
	d				13 28												13 58								
Aldershot	d				13 34					14 00							14 04				14 30				
Ash Vale	d				13 39					14a04							14 09				14a34				
Brookwood	d				13 46						14 23						14 16								14 53
Guildford	d					13 47							14 02					14 17						14 34	
Worplesdon	d							←												←				14 40	
Woking	a	13 49			13 51	13 57		13 58			14 28		14 11	14 15			14 21	14 25		14 28			14 39	14 44	14 58
	d	13 50			13 52	13 59		13 59			14 29	14 03	14 12	14 17	14 21		14 22	14 26		14 29		14 33	14 41	14 46	14 59
West Byfleet	d				13 57						→	14 07					14 27					14 37			→
Byfleet & New Haw	d											14 10										14 40			
Weybridge	d							14 06				14 13								14 36		14 43			
Walton-on-Thames	d							14 10				14 17								14 40		14 47			
Hersham	d											14 19										14 49			
Esher	d											14 22										14 52			
Surbiton 6	a				14 07			14 16				14 26					14 37			14 46		14 56			
Wimbledon 6 ⊖	a											14 34										15 04			
Earlsfield	a			←								14 38				←						15 08			
Clapham Junction 10	a		14 12	14 12			14 25					14 42	14 31	14 36		14 42	14 48			14 57		15 12		15 05	
Vauxhall ⊖	a			14 17								→				14 47						→			
London Waterloo 15 ⊖	a	14 19	14 21	14 22	14 29	14 27	14 34	14 36					14 41	14 49	14 51	14 52	14 59	14 57		15 05			15 07	15 14	

Table 155

Saturdays
until 1 October

Basingstoke, Alton, Guildford and Woking - Waterloo

		SW	SW	SW	SW	SW	SW	SW	SW	SW	SW	SW	SW	SW	SW	SW	SW	SW	SW	SW	SW	SW
		◇1 ⌶	◇1 ⌶		1	1 ⌶	1	1	1	1		1	◇1 ⌶	◇1 ⌶		1	1 ⌶	1	1		1	1
Basingstoke	d	14 30	14 35				14 43			14 54			14 57								15 17	
Hook	d									15 01												
Winchfield	d									15 05												
Fleet	d						14 54			15 10												
Farnborough (Main)	d						15 00			15 16											15 30	
Alton	d				14 15											14 44						
Bentley	d															14 51						
Farnham	a				14 25											14 56						
	d				14 28											14 58						
Aldershot	d				14 34				15 00							15 04			15 30			
Ash Vale	d				14 39				15a04							15 09			15a34			
Brookwood	d				14 46					15 23						15 16						
Guildford	d					14 47						15 02					15 17					15 34
Worplesdon	d							←										←				15 40
Woking	a	14 49			14 51	14 57		14 58		15 28		15 11	15 15			15 21	15 25	15 28			15 39	15 44
	d	14 50			14 52	14 59		14 59		15 29	15 03	15 12	15 17	15 21		15 22	15 26	15 29		15 33	15 41	15 46
West Byfleet	d				14 57					→	15 07					15 27				15 37		
Byfleet & New Haw	d										15 10									15 40		
Weybridge	d							15 06			15 13							15 36		15 43		
Walton-on-Thames	d							15 10			15 17							15 40		15 47		
Hersham	d										15 19									15 49		
Esher	d										15 22									15 52		
Surbiton 6	a				15 07			15 16			15 26					15 37		15 46		15 56		
Wimbledon 6 ⊖	a										15 34									16 04		
Earlsfield	a			←							15 38				←					16 08		
Clapham Junction 10	a		15 12	15 12			15 25				15 42	15 31	15 36		15 42	15 48		15 57		16 12		16 05
Vauxhall ⊖	a			15 17							→				15 47					→		
London Waterloo 15 ⊖	a	15 19	15 21	15 22	15 29	15 27	15 34	15 36				15 41	15 49	15 51	15 52	15 59	15 57	16 05			16 07	16 13

		SW	SW	SW	SW	SW	SW	SW	SW	SW	SW	SW	SW	SW	SW	SW	SW	SW	SW	SW	SW	SW	SW
		1	◇1 ⌶	◇1 ⌶		1	1 ⌶	1	1	1	1		1	◇1 ⌶	◇1 ⌶		1	1 ⌶	1	1		1	1
Basingstoke	d	15 24	15 30	15 35				15 43			15 54			15 57								16 17	
Hook	d	15 31									16 01												
Winchfield	d	15 35									16 05												
Fleet	d	15 40						15 54			16 10												
Farnborough (Main)	d	15 46						16 00			16 16											16 30	
Alton	d					15 15											15 44						
Bentley	d																15 51						
Farnham	a					15 25											15 56						
	d					15 28											15 58						
Aldershot	d					15 34				16 00							16 04			16 30			
Ash Vale	d					15 39				16a04							16 09			16a34			
Brookwood	d	15 53				15 46					16 23						16 16						
Guildford	d						15 47						16 02					16 17					16 34
Worplesdon	d								←										←				16 40
Woking	a	15 58	15 49			15 51	15 57		15 58		16 28		16 11	16 15			16 21	16 25	16 28			16 39	16 44
	d	15 59	15 50			15 52	15 59		15 59		16 29	16 03	16 12	16 17	16 21		16 22	16 26	16 29		16 33	16 41	16 46
West Byfleet	d	→				15 57					→	16 07					16 27				16 37		
Byfleet & New Haw	d											16 10									16 40		
Weybridge	d								16 06			16 13							16 36		16 43		
Walton-on-Thames	d								16 10			16 17							16 40		16 47		
Hersham	d											16 19									16 49		
Esher	d											16 22									16 52		
Surbiton 6	a					16 07			16 16			16 26					16 37		16 46		16 56		
Wimbledon 6 ⊖	a											16 34									17 04		
Earlsfield	a				←							16 38				←					17 08		
Clapham Junction 10	a			16 12	16 12			16 25				16 42	16 31	16 36		16 42	16 48		16 57		17 12		17 05
Vauxhall ⊖	a				16 17							→				16 47					→		
London Waterloo 15 ⊖	a		16 19	16 20	16 22	16 25	16 23	16 34	16 36				16 40	16 49	16 49	16 52	16 57	16 51	17 05			17 07	17 13

Table 155

Saturdays
until 1 October

Basingstoke, Alton, Guildford and Woking - Waterloo

		SW	SW	SW	SW	SW	SW	SW	SW	SW	SW	SW	SW	SW	SW	SW	SW	SW	SW	SW	SW	SW	SW
		1	◇1 ⌶	◇1 ⌶		1	1 ⌶	1	1	1	1		1	◇1 ⌶	◇1 ⌶		1	1 ⌶	1	1		1	1
Basingstoke	d	16 24	16 30	16 35				16 43			16 54			16 57								17 17	
Hook	d	16 31									17 01												
Winchfield	d	16 35									17 05												
Fleet	d	16 40						16 54			17 10												
Farnborough (Main)	d	16 46						17 00			17 16											17 30	
Alton	d					16 15											16 44						
Bentley	d																16 51						
Farnham	a					16 25											16 56						
	d					16 28											16 58						
Aldershot	d					16 34				17 00							17 04			17 30			
Ash Vale	d					16 39				17a04							17 09			17a34			
Brookwood	d	16 53				16 46					17 23						17 16						
Guildford	d						16 47						17 02					17 17					17 34
Worplesdon	d								←										←				17 40
Woking	a	16 58	16 49			16 51	16 57		16 58		17 28		17 11	17 15			17 21	17 25	17 28			17 39	17 44
	d	16 59	16 50			16 52	16 59		16 59		17 29	17 03	17 12	17 17	17 21		17 22	17 26	17 29		17 33	17 41	17 46
West Byfleet	d	→				16 57					→	17 07					17 27				17 37		
Byfleet & New Haw	d											17 10									17 40		
Weybridge	d								17 06			17 13							17 36		17 43		
Walton-on-Thames	d								17 10			17 17							17 40		17 47		
Hersham	d											17 19									17 49		
Esher	d											17 22									17 52		
Surbiton 6	a					17 07			17 16			17 26					17 37		17 46		17 56		
Wimbledon 6 ⊖	a											17 34									18 04		
Earlsfield	a				←							17 38				←					18 08		
Clapham Junction 10	a			17 12	17 12			17 25				17 42	17 31	17 36		17 42	17 48		17 57		18 12		18 05
Vauxhall ⊖	a				17 17							→				17 47					→		
London Waterloo 15 ⊖	a		17 19	17 20	17 22	17 25	17 23	17 34	17 36				17 40	17 49	17 49	17 52	17 57	17 51	18 05			18 07	18 13

		SW	SW	SW	SW	SW	SW	SW	SW	SW	SW	SW	SW	SW	SW	SW	SW	SW	SW	SW	SW	SW
		1	◇1 ⌶	◇1 ⌶		1	1 ⌶	1	1	1	1		1	◇1 ⌶	◇1 ⌶		1	1	1	1		1
Basingstoke	d	17 24	17 30	17 35				17 43			17 54			17 57								18 17
Hook	d	17 31									18 01											
Winchfield	d	17 35									18 05											
Fleet	d	17 40						17 54			18 10											
Farnborough (Main)	d	17 46						18 00			18 16											18 30
Alton	d					17 15											17 44					
Bentley	d																17 51					
Farnham	a					17 25											17 56					
	d					17 28											17 58					
Aldershot	d					17 34				18 00							18 04			18 30		
Ash Vale	d					17 39				18a04							18 09			18a34		
Brookwood	d	17 53				17 46					18 23						18 16					
Guildford	d						17 47						18 02					18 17				
Worplesdon	d								←										←			
Woking	a	17 58	17 49			17 51	17 57		17 58		18 28		18 11	18 15			18 21	18 25	18 28			18 39
	d	17 59	17 50			17 52	17 59		17 59		18 29	18 03	18 12	18 17	18 21		18 22	18 26	18 29		18 33	18 41
West Byfleet	d	→				17 57					→	18 07					18 27				18 37	
Byfleet & New Haw	d											18 10									18 40	
Weybridge	d								18 06			18 13							18 36		18 43	
Walton-on-Thames	d								18 10			18 17							18 40		18 47	
Hersham	d											18 19									18 49	
Esher	d											18 22									18 52	
Surbiton 6	a					18 07			18 16			18 26					18 37		18 46		18 56	
Wimbledon 6 ⊖	a											18 34									19 04	
Earlsfield	a				←							18 38				←					19 08	
Clapham Junction 10	a			18 12	18 12			18 25				18 42	18 31	18 36		18 42	18 48		18 57		19 12	
Vauxhall ⊖	a				18 17							→				18 47					→	
London Waterloo 15 ⊖	a		18 19	18 20	18 22	18 25	18 23	18 34	18 36				18 40	18 49	18 49	18 52	18 57	18 51	19 05			19 07

Basingstoke, Alton, Guildford and Woking - Waterloo

		SW 1	SW 1	SW ◇1 🛒	SW ◇1 🛒	SW	SW 1	SW 1 🛒	SW 1	SW 1	SW 1	SW 1	SW	SW 1	SW ◇1 🛒	SW ◇1 🛒	SW	SW 1	SW 1	SW 1	SW 1	SW	SW 1
Basingstoke	d		18 24	18 30	18 35				18 43			18 54			18 57								19 17
Hook	d		18 31									19 01											
Winchfield	d		18 35									19 05											
Fleet	d		18 40						18 54			19 10											
Farnborough (Main)	d		18 46						19 00			19 16											19 30
Alton	d						18 15											18 44					
Bentley	d																	18 51					
Farnham	a						18 25											18 56					
	d						18 28											18 58					
Aldershot	d						18 34				19 00							19 04			19 30		
Ash Vale	d						18 39				19a04							19 09			19a34		
Brookwood	d		18 53				18 46					19 23						19 16					
Guildford	d	18 34						18 47						19 02					19 17				
Worplesdon	d	18 40								←										←			
Woking	a	18 44	18 58	18 49			18 51	18 57		18 58		19 28		19 11	19 15			19 21	19 25	19 28			19 39
	d	18 46	18 59	18 50			18 52	18 59		18 59		19 29	19 03	19 12	19 17	19 21		19 22	19 26	19 29		19 33	19 41
West Byfleet	d		→				18 57					→	19 07					19 27				19 37	
Byfleet & New Haw	d												19 10									19 40	
Weybridge	d									19 06			19 13							19 36		19 43	
Walton-on-Thames	d									19 10			19 17							19 40		19 47	
Hersham	d												19 19									19 49	
Esher	d												19 22									19 52	
Surbiton 6	a						19 07			19 16			19 26					19 37		19 46		19 56	
Wimbledon 6 ⊖	a												19 34									20 04	
Earlsfield	a					←							19 38				←					20 08	
Clapham Junction 10	a	19 05			19 12	19 12			19 25				19 42	19 31	19 36		19 42	19 48		19 57		20 12	
Vauxhall ⊖	a					19 17							→				19 47					→	
London Waterloo 15 ⊖	a	19 13		19 19	19 20	19 22	19 25	19 23	19 34	19 36				19 40	19 49	19 49	19 52	19 57	19 51	20 05			20 07

		SW 1	SW 1	SW ◇1 🛒	SW ◇1 🛒	SW	SW 1	SW 1	SW 1	SW 1	SW 1	SW	SW 1	SW ◇1 🛒	SW	SW 1	SW 1	SW 1	SW 1	SW ◇1 🛒	SW 1	SW
Basingstoke	d		19 24	19 30	19 35				19 43										19 54	20 09		
Hook	d		19 31																20 01			
Winchfield	d		19 35																20 05			
Fleet	d		19 40						19 54										20 10			
Farnborough (Main)	d		19 46						20 00										20 16			
Alton	d						19 15									19 44						
Bentley	d															19 51						
Farnham	a						19 25									19 56						
	d						19 28									19 58						
Aldershot	d						19 34				20 00					20 04		20 30				
Ash Vale	d						19 39				20a04					20 09		20a34				
Brookwood	d		19 53				19 46									20 16			20 23			
Guildford	d	19 34						19 47					20 02				20 17					
Worplesdon	d	19 40								←												
Woking	a	19 44	19 58	19 49			19 51	19 57		19 58			20 11			20 21	20 25		20 28	20 29		
	d	19 46	19 59	19 50			19 52	19 59		19 59		20 03	20 12	20 21		20 22	20 26		20 29	20 30		20 33
West Byfleet	d		→				19 57					20 07				20 27						20 37
Byfleet & New Haw	d											20 10										20 40
Weybridge	d									20 06		20 13							20 36			20 43
Walton-on-Thames	d									20 10		20 17							20 40			20 47
Hersham	d											20 19										20 49
Esher	d											20 22										20 52
Surbiton 6	a						20 07			20 16		20 26				20 37			20 46			20 56
Wimbledon 6 ⊖	a											20 34										21 04
Earlsfield	a					←						20 38			←						←	21 08
Clapham Junction 10	a	20 05			20 12	20 12			20 25			20 42	20 31		20 42	20 48			20 57	20 52	20 57	21 12
Vauxhall ⊖	a					20 17						→			20 47				→			21 17
London Waterloo 15 ⊖	a	20 13		20 19	20 20	20 22	20 25	20 23	20 34	20 36			20 40	20 49	20 52	20 57	20 50			21 04	21 05	21 23

Basingstoke, Alton, Guildford and Woking - Waterloo

		SW 1	SW 1	SW 1	SW 1	SW ◇1 🛒	SW 1	SW	SW 1	SW ◇1 🛒	SW	SW 1	SW 1	SW 1	SW 1	SW ◇1 🛒	SW 1	SW	SW 1	SW	SW 1	SW 1	SW ◇1
Basingstoke	d	20 17			20 24	20 35			20 43						20 54	21 09						21 24	21 35
Hook	d				20 31										21 01							21 31	
Winchfield	d				20 35										21 05							21 35	
Fleet	d				20 40				20 54						21 10							21 40	
Farnborough (Main)	d	20 30			20 46				21 00						21 16							21 46	
Alton	d		20 15									20 44									21 15		
Bentley	d											20 51											
Farnham	a		20 25									20 56									21 25		
	d		20 28									20 58									21 28		
Aldershot	d		20 34									21 04		21 30							21 34		
Ash Vale	d		20 39									21 09		21a34							21 39		
Brookwood	d		20 46		20 53							21 16			21 23						21 46	21 53	
Guildford	d			20 39			20 47						21 17						21 39				
Worplesdon	d			20 44															21 44				
Woking	a	20 39	20 51	20 52	20 58		20 57		21 09			21 21	21 25		21 28	21 29			21 49		21 51	21 58	
	d	20 41	20 52	20 53	20 59		20 59	21 03	21 10	21 21		21 22	21 26		21 29	21 30		21 33	21 50		21 52	21 59	
West Byfleet	d		20 57					21 07				21 27						21 37			21 57		
Byfleet & New Haw	d							21 10										21 40					
Weybridge	d				21 06			21 13							21 36			21 43				22 06	
Walton-on-Thames	d				21 10			21 17							21 40			21 47				22 10	
Hersham	d							21 19										21 49					
Esher	d							21 22										21 52					
Surbiton 6	a		21 07		21 16			21 26				21 37			21 46			21 56			22 07	22 16	
Wimbledon 6 ⊖	a							21 34										22 04					
Earlsfield	a							21 38			←						←	22 08		←			
Clapham Junction 10	a			21 12		21 16		21 42	21 29		21 42	21 48			21 57	21 52	21 57	22 12	22 09	22 12			22 14
Vauxhall ⊖	a							→			21 47				→			→		22 17			
London Waterloo 15 ⊖	a	21 07	21 29	21 21	21 34	21 24	21 27		21 38	21 49	21 52	21 57	21 50			22 04	22 07		22 18	22 22	22 27	22 34	22 22

		SW 1	SW	SW 1	SW 1	SW	SW 1	SW 1	SW 1	SW ◇1 🛒	SW 1	SW 1	SW	SW 1	SW	SW 1	SW 1	SW 1	SW ◇1	SW 1	SW	SW 1	SW
Basingstoke	d			21 43					21 54	22 09								22 24	22 35			22 43	
Hook	d								22 01									22 31					
Winchfield	d								22 05									22 35					
Fleet	d			21 54					22 10									22 40				22 54	
Farnborough (Main)	d			22 00					22 16									22 46				23 00	
Alton	d						21 44									22 15							
Bentley	d						21 51																
Farnham	a						21 56									22 25							
	d						21 58									22 28							
Aldershot	d						22 04	22 30								22 34	22 38						
Ash Vale	d						22 09	22a34								22 39							
Brookwood	d						22 16		22 23							22 46		22 53					
Guildford	d	21 49											22 20	22 39			22a55				22 55		
Worplesdon	d													22 44						←			
Woking	a	21 57		22 09			22 21		22 28	22 28			22 32	22 49		22 51		22 58	22 53	22 58	23 05	23 09	
	d	21 59	22 03	22 10	22 21		22 22		22 29	22 29			22 33	22 50		22 52		22 59	22 55	22 59	23 06	23 10	
West Byfleet	d		22 07				22 27						22 37			22 57		→			23 10		
Byfleet & New Haw	d		22 10										22 40								23 13		
Weybridge	d		22 13						22 36				22 43							23 06	23 16		
Walton-on-Thames	d		22 17						22 40				22 47							23 10	23 20		
Hersham	d		22 19										22 49								23 22		
Esher	d		22 22										22 52								23 25		
Surbiton 6	a		22 26				22 37		22 46				22 56			23 07				23 16	23 29		
Wimbledon 6 ⊖	a		22 34										23 04								23 37		
Earlsfield	a		22 38			←					←	←	23 08		←						23 41		←
Clapham Junction 10	a		22 42	22 29		22 42	22 52		22 57	22 48	22 52	22 57	23 12	23 09	23 12				23 14		23 44	23 29	23 44
Vauxhall ⊖	a		→			22 47	→		→				→		23 17						→		23 49
London Waterloo 15 ⊖	a	22 24		22 38	22 49	22 52				22 57	23 01	23 05		23 18	23 22	23 28			23 22	23 32		23 39	23 54

Table 155

Basingstoke, Alton, Guildford and Woking - Waterloo

Saturdays until 1 October

	SW ■		SW ■	SW ■	SW ■	SW ■	SW ■	SW ■	SW ■	SW ■
Basingstoke d				22 54	23 13				23 44	
Hook d				23 01					23 51	
Winchfield d				23 05					23 55	
Fleet d				23 10					00 01	
Farnborough (Main) d				23 16					00 06	
Alton d	22 44						23 15			23 45
Bentley d	22 51									23 52
Farnham a	22 56						23 25			23 57
d	22 58						23 28			
Aldershot d	23 04		23 30				23 34			
Ash Vale d	23 09		23a34				23 39			
Brookwood d	23 16			23 23			23 46		00 13	
Guildford d								23 39		
Worplesdon d						←		23 44		
Woking a	23 21			23 28	23 31	23 28	23 51	23 49	00 18	
d	23 22			23 33	23 32	23 33		23 56	00 20	
West Byfleet d	23 27			→		23 37			00 25	
Byfleet & New Haw d						23 40				
Weybridge d						23 43			00 29	
Walton-on-Thames d						23 47			00 33	
Hersham d						23 49				
Esher d						23 52				
Surbiton 6 a	23 37					23 57			00 39	
Wimbledon 6 ⊖ a						00 06			00 47	
Earlsfield a										
Clapham Junction 10 a	23 48				23 52			00 18	00 53	
Vauxhall ⊖ a						00 30				
London Waterloo 15 ⊖ a	00 01				00 03	00 35		00 32	01 04	

Saturdays from 8 October

	SW ■	SW ■	SW ■	SW ■	SW ■	SW ■	SW ■	SW	SW		SW ■	SW	SW ■	SW	SW ■	SW ◇■ ⌶	SW	SW ■	SW ■		SW ■	SW	SW ■	SW ◇■ ⌶
Basingstoke d			22p54	23p13			23p44				04 54		05 54			05 59					06 24			06 30
Hook d			23p01				23p51				05 01		06 01								06 31			
Winchfield d			23p05				23p55				05 05		06 05								06 35			
Fleet d			23p10				00 01				05 10		06 10								06 40			
Farnborough (Main) d			23p16				00 06				05 16		06 16								06 46			
Alton d	22p44																							
Bentley d	22p51																							
Farnham a	22p56																							
d	22p58																							
Aldershot d	23p04	06 00																	06 00					
Ash Vale d	23p09	06a04																	06 08					
Brookwood d	23p16		23p23				00 13				05 23		06 23								06 53			
Guildford d						23p39		04 00				05 14			06 02				06a25				06 34	
Worplesdon d					←	23p44						05 19						←					06 40	
Woking a	23p21		23p28	23p31	23p28	23p49	00 18	04 08			05 28	05 24	06 28		06 11	06 18		06 28			06 58		06 44	06 49
d	23p22		23p33	23p32	23p33	23p56	00 20	04 10	05 27		05 29	05 33	06 29	06 03	06 13	06 19		06 29			06 59	06 33	06 46	06 50
West Byfleet d	23p27		→		23p37		00 25		05 32			05 37	→	06 07							→	06 37		
Byfleet & New Haw d					23p40				05 35			05 40		06 10								06 40		
Weybridge d					23p43		00 29					05 43		06 13				06 36				06 43		
Walton-on-Thames d					23p47		00 33					05 47		06 17				06 40				06 47		
Hersham d					23p49							05 49		06 19								06 49		
Esher d					23p52							05 52		06 22								06 52		
Surbiton 6 a	23p37				23p57		00 39	04 24			05 40	05 56		06 26				06 46				06 56		
Wimbledon 6 ⊖ a					00 06		00 47	04 31			05 48	06 04		06 34								07 04		
Earlsfield a												06 08		06 38			←					07 08		
Clapham Junction 10 a	23p51			23p55		00 19	00 53	04 43				06 12		06 42	06 32	06 38	06 42	06 57				07 12	07 05	
Vauxhall ⊖ a					00 30				06 49		06 07	06 17		→			06 47					→		
London Waterloo 15 ⊖ a	00 02			00 09	00 35	00 32	01 04	04 53	06 56		06 15	06 22			06 40	06 49	06 52	07 08					07 13	07 19

Table 155

Basingstoke, Alton, Guildford and Woking - Waterloo

Saturdays from 8 October

	SW	SW ■	SW ■	SW ■	SW ■		SW ■	SW ■	SW	SW ■	SW ◇■ ⌶	SW	SW ■	SW ■	SW ◇■ ⌶		SW ■	SW ■	SW ■	SW	SW ■	SW ◇■ ⌶	SW	SW ■
Basingstoke d				06 40				06 54			06 57				07 09				07 24			07 30		
Hook d								07 01											07 31					
Winchfield d								07 05											07 35					
Fleet d								07 10											07 40					
Farnborough (Main) d								07 16											07 46					
Alton d		06 14											06 44											07 14
Bentley d		06 21											06 51											07 21
Farnham a		06 26											06 56											07 26
d		06 28											06 58											07 28
Aldershot d		06 34	06 38				07 00						07 04	07 08				07 30						07 34
Ash Vale d		06 39					07a04						07 09					07a34						07 39
Brookwood d		06 46						07 23					07 16						07 53					07 46
Guildford d			06a55							07 02				07a25							07 34			
Worplesdon d					←												←				07 40			
Woking a		06 51		06 58	06 58			07 28		07 11	07 15		07 21		07 27		07 28		07 58		07 44	07 49		07 51
d		06 52		07 00	06 59			07 29	07 03	07 12	07 17		07 22		07 29		07 29		07 59	07 33	07 46	07 50		07 52
West Byfleet d		06 57						→	07 07				07 27						→	07 37				07 57
Byfleet & New Haw d									07 10											07 40				
Weybridge d					07 06				07 13								07 36			07 43				
Walton-on-Thames d					07 10				07 17								07 40			07 47				
Hersham d									07 19											07 49				
Esher d									07 22											07 52				
Surbiton 6 a		07 07			07 16				07 26				07 37				07 46			07 56				08 07
Wimbledon 6 ⊖ a									07 34											08 04				
Earlsfield a	←								07 38			←								08 08			←	
Clapham Junction 10 a	07 12	07 18		07 23					07 42	07 31	07 36	07 42	07 50				07 57			08 12	08 05		08 12	
Vauxhall ⊖ a	07 17								→			07 47								→			08 17	
London Waterloo 15 ⊖ a	07 22	07 30		07 31	07 33					07 40	07 49	07 52	07 58		07 53		08 05				08 13	08 19	08 22	08 25

	SW ■ ⌶		SW ■	SW ■	SW	SW ■	SW ■	SW ■	SW ◇■ ⌶	SW	SW ■		SW ◇■ ⌶	SW ■ ⌶	SW ■	SW ■	SW ■	SW	SW ■	SW ■	SW ■		SW ◇■ ⌶	SW ◇■ ⌶
Basingstoke d						07 43		07 54	07 57										08 17		08 24		08 30	08 35
Hook d								08 01													08 31			
Winchfield d								08 05													08 35			
Fleet d						07 54		08 10													08 40			
Farnborough (Main) d						08 00		08 16											08 30		08 46			
Alton d											07 44													
Bentley d											07 51													
Farnham a											07 56													
d											07 58													
Aldershot d				08 00							08 04					08 08	08 30							
Ash Vale d				08a04							08 09						08a34							
Brookwood d								08 23			08 16										08 53			
Guildford d	07 47						08 02							08 17		08a25				08 34				
Worplesdon d			←												←					08 40				
Woking a	07 57		07 58			08 09	08 10	08 28	08 17		08 21			08 26	08 28				08 39	08 44	08 58		08 49	
d	07 59		07 59		08 03	08 11	08 13	08 29	08 18		08 22		08 23	08 27	08 29			08 33	08 41	08 46	08 59		08 50	
West Byfleet d					08 07			→			08 27							08 37			→			
Byfleet & New Haw d					08 10													08 40						
Weybridge d			08 06		08 13										08 36			08 43						
Walton-on-Thames d			08 10		08 17										08 40			08 47						
Hersham d					08 19													08 49						
Esher d					08 22													08 52						
Surbiton 6 a			08 16		08 26						08 37				08 46			08 56						
Wimbledon 6 ⊖ a					08 34													09 04						
Earlsfield a					08 38					←								09 08						
Clapham Junction 10 a					08 42	08 30	08 33		08 37	08 42	08 49				08 57			09 12		09 05				09 12
Vauxhall ⊖ a					→					08 47								→						
London Waterloo 15 ⊖ a	08 23		08 34			08 39	08 42		08 49	08 52	08 58		08 49	08 51	09 05				09 08	09 13			09 19	09 20

Basingstoke, Alton, Guildford and Woking - Waterloo

		SW	SW [1]	SW [1] 🛒	SW [1]	SW [1]	SW [1]	SW [1]		SW	SW [1]	SW ◇[1] 🛒	SW ◇[1] 🛒	SW	SW [1]	SW [1] 🛒	SW [1]	SW [1]		SW	SW [1]	SW [1]	SW [1]	SW ◇[1] 🛒	SW ◇[1] 🛒
Basingstoke	d				08 43			08 54				08 57									09 17		09 24	09 30	09 35
Hook	d							09 01															09 31		
Winchfield	d							09 05															09 35		
Fleet	d				08 54			09 10															09 40		
Farnborough (Main)	d				09 00			09 16													09 30		09 46		
Alton	d		08 14												08 44										
Bentley	d		08 21												08 51										
Farnham	a		08 26												08 56										
	d		08 28												08 58										
Aldershot	d		08 34				09 00								09 04			09 30							
Ash Vale	d		08 39				09a04								09 09			09a34							
Brookwood	d		08 46					09 23							09 16								09 53		
Guildford	d			08 47							09 02					09 17						09 34			
Worplesdon	d					←											←					09 40			
Woking	a		08 51	08 57		08 58		09 28			09 11	09 15			09 21	09 25	09 28				09 39	09 44	09 58	09 49	
	d		08 52	08 59		08 59		09 29		09 03	09 12	09 17	09 21		09 22	09 26	09 29			09 33	09 41	09 46	09 59	09 50	
West Byfleet	d		08 57					→		09 07					09 27					09 37			→		
Byfleet & New Haw	d									09 10										09 40					
Weybridge	d					09 06				09 13							09 36			09 43					
Walton-on-Thames	d					09 10				09 17							09 40			09 47					
Hersham	d									09 19										09 49					
Esher	d									09 22										09 52					
Surbiton [6]	a		09 07			09 16				09 26					09 37		09 46			09 56					
Wimbledon [6] ⊖	a									09 34										10 04					
Earlsfield	a	←								09 38				←						10 08					
Clapham Junction [10]	a	09 12			09 25					09 42	09 31	09 36		09 42	09 48		09 57			10 12		10 05			10 12
Vauxhall ⊖	a	09 17								→				09 47						→					
London Waterloo [15] ⊖	a	09 22	09 25	09 23	09 34	09 36					09 40	09 49	09 49	09 52	09 57	09 51	10 05				10 07	10 13		10 19	10 20

		SW	SW [1]	SW [1] 🛒		SW [1]	SW [1]	SW [1]	SW [1]	SW	SW [1]	SW ◇[1] 🛒	SW ◇[1] 🛒	SW		SW [1]	SW [1] 🛒	SW [1]	SW [1]	SW	SW [1]	SW [1]	SW [1]	SW ◇[1] 🛒	
Basingstoke	d					09 43			09 54			09 57									10 17		10 24	10 30	
Hook	d								10 01														10 31		
Winchfield	d								10 05														10 35		
Fleet	d					09 54			10 10														10 40		
Farnborough (Main)	d					10 00			10 16												10 30		10 46		
Alton	d		09 14													09 44									
Bentley	d		09 21													09 51									
Farnham	a		09 26													09 56									
	d		09 28													09 58									
Aldershot	d		09 34					10 00								10 04			10 30						
Ash Vale	d		09 39					10a04								10 09			10a34						
Brookwood	d		09 46						10 23							10 16							10 53		
Guildford	d			09 47							10 02						10 17					10 34			
Worplesdon	d						←											←				10 40			
Woking	a		09 51	09 57			09 58		10 28		10 11	10 15				10 21	10 25	10 28			10 39	10 44	10 58	10 49	
	d		09 52	09 59			09 59		10 29	10 03	10 12	10 17	10 21			10 22	10 26	10 29		10 33	10 41	10 46	10 59	10 50	
West Byfleet	d		09 57						→	10 07						10 27				10 37			→		
Byfleet & New Haw	d									10 10										10 40					
Weybridge	d						10 06			10 13								10 36		10 43					
Walton-on-Thames	d						10 10			10 17								10 40		10 47					
Hersham	d									10 19										10 49					
Esher	d									10 22										10 52					
Surbiton [6]	a		10 07				10 16			10 26						10 37		10 46		10 56					
Wimbledon [6] ⊖	a									10 34										11 04					
Earlsfield	a	←								10 38				←						11 08					
Clapham Junction [10]	a	10 12				10 25				10 42	10 31	10 36		10 42		10 48		10 57		11 12		11 05			
Vauxhall ⊖	a	10 17								→				10 47						→					
London Waterloo [15] ⊖	a	10 22	10 25	10 23		10 34	10 36				10 40	10 49	10 49	10 52		10 57	10 51	11 05			11 07	11 13		11 19	

Basingstoke, Alton, Guildford and Woking - Waterloo

		SW ◇[1] 🛒	SW	SW [1]	SW [1] 🛒	SW [1]	SW [1]	SW [1]	SW [1]	SW		SW [1]	SW ◇[1] 🛒	SW ◇[1] 🛒	SW	SW [1]	SW [1] 🛒	SW [1]	SW [1]	SW		SW [1]	SW [1]	SW [1]	SW ◇[1] 🛒
Basingstoke	d	10 35				10 43			10 54				10 57									11 17		11 24	11 30
Hook	d								11 01															11 31	
Winchfield	d								11 05															11 35	
Fleet	d					10 54			11 10															11 40	
Farnborough (Main)	d					11 00			11 16													11 30		11 46	
Alton	d			10 14												10 44									
Bentley	d			10 21												10 51									
Farnham	a			10 26												10 56									
	d			10 28												10 58									
Aldershot	d			10 34				11 00								11 04			11 30						
Ash Vale	d			10 39				11a04								11 09			11a34						
Brookwood	d			10 46					11 23							11 16								11 53	
Guildford	d				10 47							11 02					11 17						11 34		
Worplesdon	d						←											←					11 40		
Woking	a			10 51	10 57		10 58		11 28			11 11	11 15			11 21	11 25	11 28				11 39	11 44	11 58	11 49
	d			10 52	10 59		10 59		11 29	11 03		11 12	11 17	11 21		11 22	11 26	11 29		11 33		11 41	11 46	11 59	11 50
West Byfleet	d			10 57					→	11 07						11 27				11 37				→	
Byfleet & New Haw	d									11 10										11 40					
Weybridge	d						11 06			11 13								11 36		11 43					
Walton-on-Thames	d						11 10			11 17								11 40		11 47					
Hersham	d									11 19										11 49					
Esher	d									11 22										11 52					
Surbiton [6]	a			11 07			11 16			11 26						11 37		11 46		11 56					
Wimbledon [6] ⊖	a									11 34										12 04					
Earlsfield	a		←							11 38					←					12 08					
Clapham Junction [10]	a	11 12	11 12			11 25				11 42		11 31	11 36		11 42	11 48		11 57		12 12			12 05		
Vauxhall ⊖	a		11 17							→					11 47					→					
London Waterloo [15] ⊖	a	11 20	11 22	11 25	11 23	11 34	11 36					11 40	11 49	11 49	11 52	11 57	11 51	12 05				12 07	12 13		12 19

		SW ◇[1] 🛒	SW	SW [1]	SW [1] 🛒	SW [1]		SW [1]	SW [1]	SW [1]	SW	SW [1]	SW ◇[1] 🛒	SW ◇[1] 🛒	SW	SW [1]		SW [1] 🛒	SW [1]	SW [1]	SW	SW [1]	SW [1]	SW [1]	SW ◇[1] 🛒
Basingstoke	d	11 35				11 43				11 54			11 57									12 17		12 24	12 30
Hook	d									12 01														12 31	
Winchfield	d									12 05														12 35	
Fleet	d					11 54				12 10														12 40	
Farnborough (Main)	d					12 00				12 16												12 30		12 46	
Alton	d			11 15												11 44									
Bentley	d															11 51									
Farnham	a			11 25												11 56									
	d			11 28												11 58									
Aldershot	d			11 34					12 00							12 04				12 30					
Ash Vale	d			11 39					12a04							12 09				12a34					
Brookwood	d			11 46						12 23						12 16								12 53	
Guildford	d				11 47							12 02						12 17					12 34		
Worplesdon	d							←											←				12 40		
Woking	a			11 51	11 57			11 58		12 28		12 11	12 15			12 21		12 25	12 28			12 39	12 44	12 58	12 49
	d			11 52	11 59			11 59		12 29	12 03	12 12	12 17	12 21		12 22		12 26	12 29		12 33	12 41	12 46	12 59	12 50
West Byfleet	d			11 57						→	12 07					12 27					12 37			→	
Byfleet & New Haw	d										12 10										12 40				
Weybridge	d							12 06			12 13								12 36		12 43				
Walton-on-Thames	d							12 10			12 17								12 40		12 47				
Hersham	d										12 19										12 49				
Esher	d										12 22										12 52				
Surbiton [6]	a			12 07				12 16			12 26					12 37			12 46		12 56				
Wimbledon [6] ⊖	a										12 34										13 04				
Earlsfield	a		←								12 38				←						13 08				
Clapham Junction [10]	a	12 12	12 12			12 25					12 42	12 31	12 36		12 42	12 48			12 57		13 12		13 05		
Vauxhall ⊖	a		12 17								→				12 47						→				
London Waterloo [15] ⊖	a	12 21	12 22	12 29	12 27	12 34		12 36				12 43	12 49	12 51	12 52	12 59		12 57	13 05			13 07	13 13		13 19

Table 155

Saturdays
from 8 October

Basingstoke, Alton, Guildford and Woking - Waterloo

		SW ◇1 H	SW	SW 1	SW 1 H	SW 1	SW 1	SW 1	SW 1	SW	SW 1	SW ◇1 H	SW ◇1 H	SW	SW 1	SW 1 H	SW 1	SW 1	SW	SW 1	SW 1	SW 1
Basingstoke	d	12 35				12 43			12 54			12 57								13 17		13 24
Hook	d								13 01													13 31
Winchfield	d								13 05													13 35
Fleet	d					12 54			13 10													13 40
Farnborough (Main)	d					13 00			13 16											13 30		13 46
Alton	d			12 15											12 44							
Bentley	d														12 51							
Farnham	a			12 25											12 56							
	d			12 28											12 58							
Aldershot	d			12 34				13 00							13 04			13 30				
Ash Vale	d			12 39				13a04							13 09			13a34				
Brookwood	d			12 46					13 23						13 16							13 53
Guildford	d				12 47						13 02					13 17					13 34	
Worplesdon	d						←										←				13 40	
Woking	a			12 51	12 57		12 58		13 28		13 11	13 15			13 21	13 25	13 28			13 39	13 44	13 58
	d			12 52	12 59		12 59		13 29	13 03	13 12	13 17	13 21		13 22	13 26	13 29		13 33	13 41	13 46	13 59
West Byfleet	d			12 57					→	13 07					13 27				13 37			→
Byfleet & New Haw	d									13 10									13 40			
Weybridge	d						13 06			13 13							13 36		13 43			
Walton-on-Thames	d						13 10			13 17							13 40		13 47			
Hersham	d									13 19									13 49			
Esher	d									13 22									13 52			
Surbiton 6	a			13 07			13 16			13 26					13 37		13 46		13 56			
Wimbledon 6 ⊖	a									13 34									14 04			
Earlsfield	a		←							13 38				←					14 08			
Clapham Junction 10	a	13 12	13 12			13 25				13 42	13 31	13 36		13 42	13 48		13 57		14 12		14 05	
Vauxhall ⊖	a		13 17							→				13 47					→			
London Waterloo 15 ⊖	a	13 21	13 22	13 29	13 27	13 34	13 36				13 43	13 49	13 51	13 52	13 59	13 57	14 05			14 07	14 14	

		SW ◇1 H	SW ◇1 H	SW	SW 1	SW 1 H	SW 1	SW 1	SW 1	SW 1	SW	SW 1	SW ◇1 H	SW ◇1 H	SW	SW 1	SW 1 H	SW 1	SW 1	SW	SW 1	SW 1	SW 1
Basingstoke	d	13 30	13 35				13 43			13 54			13 57								14 17		14 24
Hook	d									14 01													14 31
Winchfield	d									14 05													14 35
Fleet	d						13 54			14 10													14 40
Farnborough (Main)	d						14 00			14 16											14 30		14 46
Alton	d				13 15											13 44							
Bentley	d															13 51							
Farnham	a				13 25											13 56							
	d				13 28											13 58							
Aldershot	d				13 34				14 00							14 04			14 30				
Ash Vale	d				13 39				14a04							14 09			14a34				
Brookwood	d				13 46					14 23						14 16							14 53
Guildford	d					13 47						14 02					14 17					14 34	
Worplesdon	d							←										←				14 40	
Woking	a	13 49			13 51	13 57		13 58		14 28		14 11	14 15			14 21	14 25	14 28			14 39	14 44	14 58
	d	13 50			13 52	13 59		13 59		14 29	14 03	14 12	14 17	14 21		14 22	14 26	14 29		14 33	14 41	14 46	14 59
West Byfleet	d				13 57					→	14 07					14 27				14 37			→
Byfleet & New Haw	d										14 10									14 40			
Weybridge	d							14 06			14 13							14 36		14 43			
Walton-on-Thames	d							14 10			14 17							14 40		14 47			
Hersham	d										14 19									14 49			
Esher	d										14 22									14 52			
Surbiton 6	a				14 07			14 16			14 26					14 37		14 46		14 56			
Wimbledon 6 ⊖	a										14 34									15 04			
Earlsfield	a			←							14 38				←					15 08			
Clapham Junction 10	a		14 12	14 12			14 25				14 42	14 31	14 36		14 42	14 48		14 57		15 12		15 05	
Vauxhall ⊖	a			14 17							→				14 47					→			
London Waterloo 15 ⊖	a	14 19	14 21	14 22	14 29	14 27	14 34	14 36				14 41	14 49	14 51	14 52	14 59	14 57	15 05			15 07	15 14	

Table 155

Saturdays
from 8 October

Basingstoke, Alton, Guildford and Woking - Waterloo

		SW ◇1 H	SW ◇1 H	SW	SW 1	SW 1 H	SW 1	SW 1	SW 1	SW 1	SW	SW 1	SW ◇1 H	SW ◇1 H	SW	SW 1	SW 1 H	SW 1	SW 1	SW	SW 1	SW 1
Basingstoke	d	14 30	14 35				14 43			14 54			14 57								15 17	
Hook	d									15 01												
Winchfield	d									15 05												
Fleet	d						14 54			15 10												
Farnborough (Main)	d						15 00			15 16											15 30	
Alton	d				14 15											14 44						
Bentley	d															14 51						
Farnham	a				14 25											14 56						
	d				14 28											14 58						
Aldershot	d				14 34				15 00							15 04			15 30			
Ash Vale	d				14 39				15a04							15 09			15a34			
Brookwood	d				14 46					15 23						15 16						
Guildford	d					14 47						15 02					15 17					15 34
Worplesdon	d							←										←				15 40
Woking	a	14 49			14 51	14 57		14 58		15 28		15 11	15 15			15 21	15 25	15 28			15 39	15 44
	d	14 50			14 52	14 59		14 59		15 29	15 03	15 12	15 17	15 21		15 22	15 26	15 29		15 33	15 41	15 46
West Byfleet	d				14 57					→	15 07					15 27				15 37		
Byfleet & New Haw	d										15 10									15 40		
Weybridge	d							15 06			15 13							15 36		15 43		
Walton-on-Thames	d							15 10			15 17							15 40		15 47		
Hersham	d										15 19									15 49		
Esher	d										15 22									15 52		
Surbiton 6	a				15 07			15 16			15 26					15 37		15 46		15 56		
Wimbledon 6 ⊖	a										15 34									16 04		
Earlsfield	a			←							15 38				←					16 08		
Clapham Junction 10	a		15 12	15 12			15 25				15 42	15 31	15 36		15 42	15 48		15 57		16 12		16 05
Vauxhall ⊖	a			15 17							→				15 47					→		
London Waterloo 15 ⊖	a	15 19	15 21	15 22	15 29	15 27	15 34	15 36				15 41	15 49	15 51	15 52	15 59	15 57	16 05			16 07	16 13

		SW 1	SW ◇1 H	SW ◇1 H	SW	SW 1	SW 1 H	SW 1	SW 1	SW 1	SW 1	SW	SW 1	SW ◇1 H	SW ◇1 H	SW	SW 1	SW 1 H	SW 1	SW 1	SW	SW 1	SW 1
Basingstoke	d	15 24	15 30	15 35				15 43			15 54			15 57								16 17	
Hook	d	15 31									16 01												
Winchfield	d	15 35									16 05												
Fleet	d	15 40						15 54			16 10												
Farnborough (Main)	d	15 46						16 00			16 16											16 30	
Alton	d					15 15											15 44						
Bentley	d																15 51						
Farnham	a					15 25											15 56						
	d					15 28											15 58						
Aldershot	d					15 34				16 00							16 04			16 30			
Ash Vale	d					15 39				16a04							16 09			16a34			
Brookwood	d	15 53				15 46					16 23						16 16						
Guildford	d						15 47						16 02					16 17					16 34
Worplesdon	d								←										←				16 40
Woking	a	15 58	15 49			15 51	15 57		15 58		16 28		16 11	16 15			16 21	16 25	16 28			16 39	16 44
	d	15 59	15 50			15 52	15 59		15 59		16 29	16 03	16 12	16 17	16 21		16 22	16 26	16 29		16 33	16 41	16 46
West Byfleet	d	→				15 57					→	16 07					16 27				16 37		
Byfleet & New Haw	d											16 10									16 40		
Weybridge	d								16 06			16 13							16 36		16 43		
Walton-on-Thames	d								16 10			16 17							16 40		16 47		
Hersham	d											16 19									16 49		
Esher	d											16 22									16 52		
Surbiton 6	a					16 07			16 16			16 26					16 37		16 46		16 56		
Wimbledon 6 ⊖	a											16 34									17 04		
Earlsfield	a				←							16 38				←					17 08		
Clapham Junction 10	a			16 12	16 12			16 25				16 42	16 31	16 36		16 42	16 48		16 57		17 12		17 05
Vauxhall ⊖	a				16 17							→				16 47					→		
London Waterloo 15 ⊖	a		16 19	16 20	16 22	16 25	16 23	16 34	16 36				16 40	16 49	16 49	16 52	16 57	16 51	17 05			17 07	17 13

Basingstoke, Alton, Guildford and Woking - Waterloo

		SW 1	SW ◇1 ⌶	SW ◇1 ⌶	SW	SW 1	SW 1 ⌶	SW 1	SW 1	SW 1	SW 1	SW	SW 1	SW ◇1 ⌶	SW ◇1 ⌶	SW	SW 1	SW 1 ⌶	SW 1	SW 1	SW	SW 1	SW 1
Basingstoke	d	16 24	16 30	16 35				16 43			16 54			16 57								17 17	
Hook	d	16 31									17 01												
Winchfield	d	16 35									17 05												
Fleet	d	16 40						16 54			17 10												
Farnborough (Main)	d	16 46						17 00			17 16											17 30	
Alton	d					16 15											16 44						
Bentley	d																16 51						
Farnham	a					16 25											16 56						
	d					16 28											16 58						
Aldershot	d					16 34				17 00							17 04			17 30			
Ash Vale	d					16 39				17a04							17 09			17a34			
Brookwood	d	16 53				16 46					17 23						17 16						
Guildford	d						16 47						17 02					17 17					17 34
Worplesdon	d								←										←				17 40
Woking	a	16 58	16 49			16 51	16 57		16 58		17 28		17 11	17 15			17 21	17 25	17 28			17 39	17 44
	d	16 59	16 50			16 52	16 59		16 59		17 29	17 03	17 12	17 17	17 21		17 22	17 26	17 29		17 33	17 41	17 46
West Byfleet	d	→				16 57					→	17 07					17 27				17 37		
Byfleet & New Haw	d											17 10									17 40		
Weybridge	d								17 06			17 13							17 36		17 43		
Walton-on-Thames	d								17 10			17 17							17 40		17 47		
Hersham	d											17 19									17 49		
Esher	d											17 22									17 52		
Surbiton 6	a					17 07			17 16			17 26					17 37		17 46		17 56		
Wimbledon 6 ⊖	a											17 34									18 04		
Earlsfield	a				←							17 38				←					18 08		
Clapham Junction 10	a			17 12	17 12			17 25				17 42	17 31	17 36		17 42	17 48		17 57		18 12		18 05
Vauxhall ⊖	a				17 17							→				17 47					→		
London Waterloo 15 ⊖	a		17 19	17 20	17 22	17 25	17 23	17 34	17 36				17 40	17 49	17 49	17 52	17 57	17 51	18 05			18 07	18 13

		SW 1	SW ◇1 ⌶	SW ◇1 ⌶	SW	SW 1	SW 1 ⌶	SW 1	SW 1	SW 1	SW 1	SW	SW 1	SW ◇1 ⌶	SW ◇1 ⌶	SW	SW 1	SW 1	SW 1	SW 1	SW	SW 1
Basingstoke	d	17 24	17 30	17 35				17 43			17 54			17 57								18 17
Hook	d	17 31									18 01											
Winchfield	d	17 35									18 05											
Fleet	d	17 40						17 54			18 10											
Farnborough (Main)	d	17 46						18 00			18 16											18 30
Alton	d					17 15											17 44					
Bentley	d																17 51					
Farnham	a					17 25											17 56					
	d					17 28											17 58					
Aldershot	d					17 34				18 00							18 04			18 30		
Ash Vale	d					17 39				18a04							18 09			18a34		
Brookwood	d	17 53				17 46					18 23						18 16					
Guildford	d						17 47						18 02					18 17				
Worplesdon	d								←										←			
Woking	a	17 58	17 49			17 51	17 57		17 58		18 28		18 11	18 15			18 21	18 25	18 28			18 39
	d	17 59	17 50			17 52	17 59		17 59		18 29	18 03	18 12	18 17	18 21		18 22	18 26	18 29		18 33	18 41
West Byfleet	d	→				17 57					→	18 07					18 27				18 37	
Byfleet & New Haw	d											18 10									18 40	
Weybridge	d								18 06			18 13							18 36		18 43	
Walton-on-Thames	d								18 10			18 17							18 40		18 47	
Hersham	d											18 19									18 49	
Esher	d											18 22									18 52	
Surbiton 6	a					18 07			18 16			18 26					18 37		18 46		18 56	
Wimbledon 6 ⊖	a											18 34									19 04	
Earlsfield	a				←							18 38				←					19 08	
Clapham Junction 10	a			18 12	18 12			18 25				18 42	18 31	18 36		18 42	18 48		18 57		19 12	
Vauxhall ⊖	a				18 17							→				18 47					→	
London Waterloo 15 ⊖	a		18 19	18 20	18 22	18 25	18 23	18 34	18 36				18 40	18 49	18 49	18 52	18 57	18 51	19 05			19 07

Basingstoke, Alton, Guildford and Woking - Waterloo

		SW 1	SW 1	SW ◇1 ⌶	SW ◇1 ⌶	SW	SW 1	SW 1 ⌶	SW 1	SW 1	SW 1	SW 1	SW	SW 1	SW ◇1 ⌶	SW ◇1 ⌶	SW	SW 1	SW 1	SW 1	SW 1	SW	SW 1
Basingstoke	d		18 24	18 30	18 35				18 43			18 54			18 57								19 17
Hook	d		18 31									19 01											
Winchfield	d		18 35									19 05											
Fleet	d		18 40						18 54			19 10											
Farnborough (Main)	d		18 46						19 00			19 16											19 30
Alton	d						18 15											18 44					
Bentley	d																	18 51					
Farnham	a						18 25											18 56					
	d						18 28											18 58					
Aldershot	d						18 34				19 00							19 04			19 30		
Ash Vale	d						18 39				19a04							19 09			19a34		
Brookwood	d		18 53				18 46					19 23						19 16					
Guildford	d	18 34						18 47						19 02					19 17				
Worplesdon	d	18 40								←										←			
Woking	a	18 44	18 58	18 49			18 51	18 57		18 58		19 28		19 11	19 15			19 21	19 25	19 28			19 39
	d	18 46	18 59	18 50			18 52	18 59		18 59		19 29	19 03	19 12	19 17	19 21		19 22	19 26	19 29		19 33	19 41
West Byfleet	d		→				18 57					→	19 07					19 27				19 37	
Byfleet & New Haw	d												19 10									19 40	
Weybridge	d									19 06			19 13							19 36		19 43	
Walton-on-Thames	d									19 10			19 17							19 40		19 47	
Hersham	d												19 19									19 49	
Esher	d												19 22									19 52	
Surbiton 6	a						19 07			19 16			19 26					19 37		19 46		19 56	
Wimbledon 6 ⊖	a												19 34									20 04	
Earlsfield	a					←							19 38				←					20 08	
Clapham Junction 10	a	19 05			19 12	19 12			19 25				19 42	19 31	19 36		19 42	19 48		19 57		20 12	
Vauxhall ⊖	a					19 17							→				19 47					→	
London Waterloo 15 ⊖	a	19 13		19 19	19 20	19 22	19 25	19 23	19 34	19 36				19 40	19 49	19 49	19 52	19 57	19 51	20 05			20 07

		SW 1	SW 1	SW ◇1 ⌶	SW ◇1 ⌶	SW	SW 1	SW 1	SW 1	SW 1	SW 1	SW	SW 1	SW ◇1 ⌶	SW	SW 1	SW 1	SW 1	SW 1	SW ◇1 ⌶	SW 1	SW
Basingstoke	d		19 24	19 30	19 35				19 43										19 54	20 09		
Hook	d		19 31																20 01			
Winchfield	d		19 35																20 05			
Fleet	d		19 40						19 54										20 10			
Farnborough (Main)	d		19 46						20 00										20 16			
Alton	d						19 15									19 44						
Bentley	d															19 51						
Farnham	a						19 25									19 56						
	d						19 28									19 58						
Aldershot	d						19 34				20 00					20 04		20 30				
Ash Vale	d						19 39				20a04					20 09		20a34				
Brookwood	d		19 53				19 46									20 16			20 23			
Guildford	d	19 34						19 47					20 02				20 17					
Worplesdon	d	19 40								←												
Woking	a	19 44	19 58	19 49			19 51	19 57		19 58			20 11			20 21	20 25		20 28	20 29		
	d	19 46	19 59	19 50			19 52	19 59		19 59		20 03	20 12	20 21		20 22	20 26		20 29	20 30		20 33
West Byfleet	d		→				19 57					20 07				20 27						20 37
Byfleet & New Haw	d											20 10										20 40
Weybridge	d									20 06		20 13							20 36			20 43
Walton-on-Thames	d									20 10		20 17							20 40			20 47
Hersham	d											20 19										20 49
Esher	d											20 22										20 52
Surbiton 6	a						20 07			20 16		20 26				20 37			20 46			20 56
Wimbledon 6 ⊖	a											20 34										21 04
Earlsfield	a					←						20 38			←						←	21 08
Clapham Junction 10	a	20 05			20 12	20 12			20 25			20 42	20 31		20 42	20 48			20 57	20 52	20 57	21 12
Vauxhall ⊖	a					20 17						→			20 47				→			21 17
London Waterloo 15 ⊖	a	20 13		20 19	20 20	20 22	20 25	20 23	20 34	20 36			20 40	20 49	20 52	20 57	20 50			21 04	21 05	21 23

Basingstoke, Alton, Guildford and Woking - Waterloo

		SW 1	SW 1	SW 1	SW 1	SW ◇1 H	SW 1	SW	SW 1	SW ◇1 H		SW	SW 1	SW 1	SW 1	SW 1	SW ◇1 H	SW 1	SW	SW 1		SW	SW 1	SW 1	SW ◇1
Basingstoke	d	20 17			20 24	20 35			20 43							20 54	21 09							21 24	21 35
Hook	d				20 31											21 01								21 31	
Winchfield	d				20 35											21 05								21 35	
Fleet	d				20 40				20 54							21 10								21 40	
Farnborough (Main)	d	20 30			20 46				21 00							21 16								21 46	
Alton	d		20 15										20 44										21 15		
Bentley	d												20 51												
Farnham	a		20 25										20 56										21 25		
	d		20 28										20 58										21 28		
Aldershot	d		20 34										21 04		21 30								21 34		
Ash Vale	d		20 39										21 09		21a34								21 39		
Brookwood	d		20 46		20 53								21 16			21 23							21 46	21 53	
Guildford	d			20 39			20 47							21 17						21 39					
Worplesdon	d			20 44																21 44					
Woking	a	20 39	20 51	20 52	20 58		20 57		21 09				21 21	21 25		21 28	21 29			21 49			21 51	21 58	
	d	20 41	20 52	20 53	20 59		20 59	21 03	21 10	21 21			21 22	21 26		21 29	21 30		21 33	21 50			21 52	21 59	
West Byfleet	d		20 57					21 07					21 27						21 37				21 57		
Byfleet & New Haw	d							21 10											21 40						
Weybridge	d				21 06			21 13								21 36			21 43					22 06	
Walton-on-Thames	d				21 10			21 17								21 40			21 47					22 10	
Hersham	d							21 19											21 49						
Esher	d							21 22											21 52						
Surbiton 6	a		21 07		21 16			21 26					21 37			21 46			21 56				22 07	22 16	
Wimbledon 6 ⊖	a							21 34											22 04						
Earlsfield	a							21 38				←						←	22 08			←			
Clapham Junction 10	a			21 12		21 16		21 42	21 29			21 42	21 48			21 57	21 52	21 57	22 12	22 09		22 12			22 14
Vauxhall ⊖	a							→				21 47				→			→			22 17			
London Waterloo 15 ⊖	a	21 07	21 29	21 21	21 34	21 24	21 27		21 38	21 49		21 52	21 57	21 50			22 04	22 07		22 18		22 22	22 27	22 34	22 22

		SW 1	SW	SW 1	SW 1	SW		SW 1	SW 1	SW 1	SW ◇1 H	SW 1	SW 1	SW	SW 1	SW		SW 1	SW 1	SW 1	SW ◇1	SW 1	SW	SW 1	SW
Basingstoke	d			21 43						21 54	22 09									22 24	22 35			22 43	
Hook	d									22 01										22 31					
Winchfield	d									22 05										22 35					
Fleet	d			21 54						22 10										22 40				22 54	
Farnborough (Main)	d			22 00						22 16										22 46				23 00	
Alton	d							21 44										22 15							
Bentley	d							21 51																	
Farnham	a							21 56										22 25							
	d							21 58										22 28							
Aldershot	d							22 04	22 30									22 34	22 38						
Ash Vale	d							22 09	22a34									22 39							
Brookwood	d							22 16		22 23								22 46		22 53					
Guildford	d	21 49												22 20	22 39				22a55				22 55		
Worplesdon	d														22 44							←			
Woking	a	21 57		22 09				22 21		22 28	22 28			22 32	22 49			22 51		22 58	22 53	22 58	23 05	23 09	
	d	21 59	22 03	22 10	22 21			22 22		22 29	22 29			22 33	22 50			22 52		22 59	22 55	22 59	23 06	23 10	
West Byfleet	d		22 07					22 27						22 37				22 57		→			23 10		
Byfleet & New Haw	d		22 10											22 40									23 13		
Weybridge	d		22 13							22 36				22 43								23 06	23 16		
Walton-on-Thames	d		22 17							22 40				22 47								23 10	23 20		
Hersham	d		22 19											22 49									23 22		
Esher	d		22 22											22 52									23 25		
Surbiton 6	a		22 26					22 37		22 46				22 56				23 07				23 16	23 29		
Wimbledon 6 ⊖	a		22 34											23 04									23 37		
Earlsfield	a		22 38			←						←	←	23 08		←							23 41		←
Clapham Junction 10	a		22 42	22 29		22 42		22 52		22 57	22 48	22 52	22 57	23 12	23 09	23 12					23 14		23 44	23 29	23 44
Vauxhall ⊖	a		→			22 47		→		→				→		23 17							→		23 49
London Waterloo 15 ⊖	a	22 24		22 38	22 49	22 52					22 57	23 01	23 05		23 18	23 22		23 28			23 22	23 32		23 39	23 54

Basingstoke, Alton, Guildford and Woking - Waterloo

		SW 1		SW 1	SW 1	SW 1	SW 1	SW 1	SW 1	SW 1	SW 1
Basingstoke	d				22 54	23 13				23 44	
Hook	d				23 01					23 51	
Winchfield	d				23 05					23 55	
Fleet	d				23 10					00 01	
Farnborough (Main)	d				23 16					00 06	
Alton	d	22 44						23 15			23 45
Bentley	d	22 51									23 52
Farnham	a	22 56						23 25			23 57
	d	22 58						23 28			
Aldershot	d	23 04		23 30				23 34			
Ash Vale	d	23 09		23a34				23 39			
Brookwood	d	23 16			23 23			23 46		00 13	
Guildford	d								23 39		
Worplesdon	d						←		23 44		
Woking	a	23 21			23 28	23 31	23 28	23 51	23 49	00 18	
	d	23 22			23 33	23 32	23 33		23 56	00 20	
West Byfleet	d	23 27			→		23 37			00 25	
Byfleet & New Haw	d						23 40				
Weybridge	d						23 43			00 29	
Walton-on-Thames	d						23 47			00 33	
Hersham	d						23 49				
Esher	d						23 52				
Surbiton 6	a	23 37					23 57			00 39	
Wimbledon 6 ⊖	a						00 06			00 47	
Earlsfield	a										
Clapham Junction 10	a	23 48				23 52			00 18	00 53	
Vauxhall ⊖	a						00 30				
London Waterloo 15 ⊖	a	00 01				00 03	00 35		00 32	01 04	

Sundays
until 25 September

		SW 1 A	SW 1 A	SW 1 A	SW 1 A	SW 1 A	SW 1 A	SW	SW	SW 1		SW	SW ◇1 H	SW	SW 1	SW	SW 1	SW 1	SW 1	SW		SW 1	SW 1	SW	SW ◇1 H
Basingstoke	d		22p54	23p13			23p44			07 16			07 20						07 44						08 10
Hook	d		23p01				23p51			07 23															
Winchfield	d		23p05				23p55			07 27															
Fleet	d		23p10				00 01			07 32															
Farnborough (Main)	d		23p16				00 06			07 38															
Alton	d	22p44																							
Bentley	d	22p51																							
Farnham	a	22p56																							
	d	22p58															07 30								
Aldershot	d	23p04															07 36	07 40				07 48			
Ash Vale	d	23p09															07 41	07a44							
Brookwood	d	23p16	23p23				00 13			07 45							07 48								
Guildford	d					23p39			06 57			07 27								07 57		08a05	08 05		
Worplesdon	d				←	23p44									←										
Woking	a	23p21	23p28	23p31	23p28	23p49	00 18		07 05	07 50		07 35	07 39		07 50		07 54		08 02	08 05			08 13		08 28
	d	23p22	23p33	23p32	23p33	23p56	00 20	06 36	07 06	07 58		07 36	07 40		07 58	07 52			08 04	08 06			08 15		08 30
West Byfleet	d	23p27	→		23p37		00 25	06 40	07 10	→		07 40				07 56				08 10					
Byfleet & New Haw	d				23p40			06 43	07 13			07 43				08 00				08 13					
Weybridge	d				23p43		00 29	06 46	07 16			07 46								08 16					
Walton-on-Thames	d				23p47		00 33	06 50	07 20			07 50								08 20					
Hersham	d				23p49			06 52	07 22			07 52								08 22					
Esher	d				23p52			06 55	07 25			07 55								08 25					
Surbiton 6	a	23p37			23p57		00 39	06 59	07 29			07 59			08 09					08 29					
Wimbledon 6 ⊖	a				00 06		00 47	07 07	07 37			08 07			08 19					08 37					
Earlsfield	a							07 11	07 41			08 11		←						08 41				←	
Clapham Junction 10	a	23p48		23p52		00 18	00 53	07 15	07 45			08 15	08 05	08 15	08 27				08 30	08 45			08 40	08 45	08 57
Vauxhall ⊖	a				00 30			07 20	07 50			→		08 20		09 08				→				08 50	
London Waterloo 15 ⊖	a	00 01		00 03	00 35	00 32	01 04	07 30	08 00				08 19	08 30	08 39	09 13			08 42				08 49	09 00	09 09

A not 22 May

Basingstoke, Alton, Guildford and Woking - Waterloo

Station		SW	SW 1	SW	SW	SW 1	SW 1	SW 1	SW 1	SW	SW 1	SW	SW ◇1 🍴	SW	SW 1	SW	SW	SW 1	SW 1	SW 1	SW 1	SW	SW 1
Basingstoke	d					08 16			08 44				09 10					09 16			09 44		
Hook	d					08 23												09 23					
Winchfield	d					08 27												09 27					
Fleet	d					08 32												09 32					
Farnborough (Main)	d					08 38												09 38					
Alton	d						08 15												09 15				
Bentley	d						08 23												09 23				
Farnham	a						08 28												09 28				
	d						08 30												09 30				
Aldershot	d						08 36	08 40											09 36	09 40			
Ash Vale	d						08 41	08a44											09 41	09a44			
Brookwood	d					08 45	08 48											09 45	09 48				
Guildford	d	08 27	08 35							08 57	09 05			09 27	09 35							09 57	10 05
Worplesdon	d																						
Woking	a	08 35	08 42			08 50	08 54		09 02	09 05	09 15		09 28	09 35	09 42			09 50	09 54		10 02	10 05	10 15
	d	08 36	08 45		08 52	08 58			09 04	09 06	09 15		09 30	09 36	09 45		09 52	09 58			10 04	10 06	10 15
West Byfleet	d	08 40			08 56					09 10				09 40			09 56					10 10	
Byfleet & New Haw	d	08 43			09 00					09 13				09 43			10 00					10 13	
Weybridge	d	08 46								09 16				09 46								10 16	
Walton-on-Thames	d	08 50								09 20				09 50								10 20	
Hersham	d	08 52								09 22				09 52								10 22	
Esher	d	08 55								09 25				09 55								10 25	
Surbiton ■	a	08 59				09 09				09 29				09 59				10 09				10 29	
Wimbledon ■ ⊖	a	09 07				09 19				09 37				10 07				10 17				10 37	
Earlsfield	a	09 11		←						09 41		←		10 11		←						10 41	
Clapham Junction 10	a	09 15	09 06	09 15		09 26			09 30	09 45	09 38	09 45	09 57	10 15	10 04	10 15		10 23			10 27	10 45	10 35
Vauxhall ⊖	a	→		09 20	10 08					→		09 50		→		10 20	11 08					→	
London Waterloo 15 ⊖	a		09 19	09 30	10 13	09 39			09 43		09 49	10 00	10 08		10 19	10 30	11 13	10 38			10 42		10 49

Station		SW ◇1 🍴	SW	SW ◇1 🍴	SW	SW 1 🍴	SW	SW	SW 1	SW 1	SW 1	SW 1 🍴	SW	SW 1	SW ◇1 🍴	SW	SW ◇1 🍴	SW	SW 1 🍴	SW	SW
Basingstoke	d	10 00		10 10					10 16			10 44			11 00		11 10				
Hook	d								10 23												
Winchfield	d								10 27												
Fleet	d								10 32												
Farnborough (Main)	d								10 38												
Alton	d									10 15											
Bentley	d									10 23											
Farnham	a									10 28											
	d									10 30											
Aldershot	d									10 36	10 40										
Ash Vale	d									10 41	10a44										
Brookwood	d								10 45	10 48											
Guildford	d				10 27	10 35							10 57	11 06				11 27	11 35		
Worplesdon	d																				
Woking	a	10 19		10 28	10 35	10 42			10 50	10 54		11 02	11 05	11 13	11 18		11 28	11 35	11 42		
	d	10 20		10 30	10 36	10 45		10 52	10 58			11 04	11 06	11 15	11 20		11 30	11 36	11 45		11 52
West Byfleet	d				10 40			10 56					11 10					11 40			11 56
Byfleet & New Haw	d				10 43			11 00					11 13					11 43			12 00
Weybridge	d				10 46								11 16					11 46			
Walton-on-Thames	d				10 50								11 20					11 50			
Hersham	d				10 52								11 22					11 52			
Esher	d				10 55								11 25					11 55			
Surbiton ■	a				10 59				11 09				11 29					11 59			
Wimbledon ■ ⊖	a				11 07				11 17				11 37					12 07			
Earlsfield	a		←		11 11		←						11 41			←		12 11		←	
Clapham Junction 10	a	10 40	10 45	10 49	11 15	11 04	11 15		11 23			11 27	11 45	11 34	11 39	11 45	11 49	12 15	12 04	12 15	
Vauxhall ⊖	a		10 50		→		11 20	12 08					→			11 50		→		12 20	13 08
London Waterloo 15 ⊖	a	10 54	11 00	11 04		11 19	11 30	12 13	11 38			11 42		11 49	11 54	12 00	12 03		12 19	12 30	13 13

Basingstoke, Alton, Guildford and Woking - Waterloo

Station		SW 1	SW 1	SW 1	SW 1 🍴	SW	SW 1	SW ◇1 🍴	SW	SW ◇1 🍴	SW	SW 1 🍴	SW	SW	SW 1	SW 1	SW 1	SW 1 🍴	SW	SW 1	SW ◇1 🍴	SW	SW ◇1 🍴
Basingstoke	d	11 16			11 44			12 00		12 10					12 16			12 44			13 00		13 10
Hook	d	11 23													12 23								
Winchfield	d	11 27													12 27								
Fleet	d	11 32													12 32								
Farnborough (Main)	d	11 38													12 38								
Alton	d		11 15													12 15							
Bentley	d		11 23													12 23							
Farnham	a		11 28													12 28							
	d		11 30													12 30							
Aldershot	d		11 36	11 40												12 36	12 40						
Ash Vale	d		11 41	11a44												12 41	12a44						
Brookwood	d	11 45	11 48												12 45	12 48							
Guildford	d					11 57	12 06				12 27	12 35							12 57	13 05			
Worplesdon	d																						
Woking	a	11 50	11 54		12 02	12 05	12 13	12 18		12 28	12 35	12 42			12 50	12 54		13 02	13 05	13 13	13 18		13 28
	d	11 58			12 04	12 06	12 15	12 20		12 30	12 36	12 45		12 52	12 58			13 04	13 06	13 15	13 20		13 30
West Byfleet	d					12 10					12 40			12 56					13 10				
Byfleet & New Haw	d					12 13					12 43			13 00					13 13				
Weybridge	d					12 16					12 46								13 16				
Walton-on-Thames	d					12 20					12 50								13 20				
Hersham	d					12 22					12 52								13 22				
Esher	d					12 25					12 55								13 25				
Surbiton ■	a	12 09				12 29					12 59				13 09				13 29				
Wimbledon ■ ⊖	a	12 17				12 37					13 07				13 17				13 37				
Earlsfield	a					12 41			←		13 11		←						13 41			←	
Clapham Junction 10	a	12 23			12 27	12 45	12 34	12 39	12 45	12 49	13 15	13 04	13 15		13 23			13 27	13 45	13 34	13 39	13 45	13 49
Vauxhall ⊖	a					→			12 50		→		13 20	14 08					→			13 50	
London Waterloo 15 ⊖	a	12 39			12 42		12 49	12 49	13 00	13 04		13 14	13 30	14 13	13 39			13 37		13 44	13 49	14 00	13 59

Station		SW	SW 1 🍴	SW	SW	SW 1	SW 1	SW 1	SW 1 🍴	SW	SW 1	SW ◇1 🍴	SW 1	SW	SW 1	SW 1	SW ◇1 🍴	SW 1	SW 1	SW	SW 1 🍴	SW	SW
Basingstoke	d					13 16			13 44			14 00			13 50		14 10						
Hook	d					13 23																	
Winchfield	d					13 27																	
Fleet	d					13 32									14 02								
Farnborough (Main)	d					13 38									14 08								
Alton	d						13 15									13 45							
Bentley	d						13 23																
Farnham	a						13 28									13 55							
	d						13 30									14 00							
Aldershot	d						13 36	13 40								14 06							
Ash Vale	d						13 41	13a44								14 11							
Brookwood	d					13 45	13 48								14 15	14 18							
Guildford	d	13 27	13 35							13 57	14 05									14 27	14 35		
Worplesdon	d												←										
Woking	a	13 35	13 42			13 50	13 54		14 02	14 05	14 13	14 18	14 20		14 20	14 24	14 28			14 35	14 42		
	d	13 36	13 45		13 52	13 58			14 04	14 06	14 15	14 20	14 28		14 28		14 30			14 36	14 45		14 52
West Byfleet	d	13 40			13 56					14 10					→					14 40			14 56
Byfleet & New Haw	d	13 43			14 00					14 13										14 43			15 00
Weybridge	d	13 46								14 16			14 34							14 46			
Walton-on-Thames	d	13 50								14 20			14 38							14 50			
Hersham	d	13 52								14 22										14 52			
Esher	d	13 55								14 25										14 55			
Surbiton ■	a	13 59				14 09				14 29			14 45							14 59			
Wimbledon ■ ⊖	a	14 07				14 17				14 37			14 53							15 07			
Earlsfield	a	14 11		←						14 41				←				←	←	15 11		←	
Clapham Junction 10	a	14 15	14 04	14 15		14 23			14 27	14 45	14 34	14 39	14 59	14 45			14 49	14 59	14 59	15 15	15 04	15 15	
Vauxhall ⊖	a	→		14 20	15 08					→			→	14 50						→		15 20	16 08
London Waterloo 15 ⊖	a		14 14	14 30	15 13	14 34			14 37		14 44	14 49		14 55			14 59	15 10	15 10		15 14	15 25	16 13

Table 155

Sundays until 25 September

Basingstoke, Alton, Guildford and Woking - Waterloo

		SW 1	SW 1		SW 1	SW 1 ⊥	SW	SW 1	SW ◇1 ⊥	SW 1	SW	SW 1	SW 1		SW ◇1 ⊥	SW 1	SW 1	SW	SW 1 ⊥	SW	SW	SW 1	SW 1		SW 1
Basingstoke	d	14 16				14 44			15 00			14 50			15 10							15 16			
Hook	d	14 23																				15 23			
Winchfield	d	14 27																				15 27			
Fleet	d	14 32										15 02										15 32			
Farnborough (Main)	d	14 38										15 08										15 38			
Alton	d		14 15										14 45										15 15		
Bentley	d		14 23																				15 23		
Farnham	a		14 28										14 55										15 28		
	d		14 30										15 00										15 30		
Aldershot	d		14 36		14 40								15 06										15 36		15 40
Ash Vale	d		14 41		14a44								15 11										15 41		15a44
Brookwood	d	14 45	14 48									15 15	15 18									15 45	15 48		
Guildford	d						14 57	15 05										15 27	15 35						
Worplesdon	d									←															
Woking	a	14 50	14 54			15 02	15 05	15 13	15 18	15 20		15 20	15 24		15 28			15 35	15 42			15 50	15 54		
	d	14 58				15 04	15 06	15 15	15 20	15 28		15 28 →			15 30			15 36	15 45		15 52	15 58			
West Byfleet	d						15 10											15 40			15 56				
Byfleet & New Haw	d						15 13											15 43			16 00				
Weybridge	d						15 16			15 34								15 46							
Walton-on-Thames	d						15 20			15 38								15 50							
Hersham	d						15 22											15 52							
Esher	d						15 25											15 55							
Surbiton 6	a	15 09					15 29			15 45								15 59				16 09			
Wimbledon 6 ⊖	a	15 17					15 37			15 53								16 07				16 17			
Earlsfield	a						15 41				←					←	←	16 11		←					
Clapham Junction 10	a	15 23				15 27	15 45	15 34	15 39	15 59	15 45				15 49	15 59	15 59	16 15	16 04	16 15		16 23			
Vauxhall ⊖	a						→			→	15 50							→		16 20	17 08				
London Waterloo 15 ⊖	a	15 34				15 37		15 44	15 49		15 55				15 59	16 10	16 10		16 14	16 25	17 13	16 34			

		SW 1 ⊥	SW	SW 1	SW ◇1 ⊥	SW 1	SW	SW 1	SW 1		SW ◇1 ⊥	SW 1	SW 1	SW	SW 1 ⊥	SW	SW	SW 1	SW 1		SW 1	SW 1 ⊥	SW	SW 1	SW ◇1 ⊥
Basingstoke	d	15 44			16 00			15 50			16 10							16 16				16 44			17 00
Hook	d																	16 23							
Winchfield	d																	16 27							
Fleet	d							16 02										16 32							
Farnborough (Main)	d							16 08										16 38							
Alton	d								15 45										16 15						
Bentley	d																		16 23						
Farnham	a								15 55										16 28						
	d								16 00										16 30						
Aldershot	d								16 06										16 36		16 40				
Ash Vale	d								16 11										16 41		16a44				
Brookwood	d							16 15	16 18									16 45	16 48						
Guildford	d		15 57	16 05										16 27	16 35								16 57	17 05	
Worplesdon	d					←																			
Woking	a	16 02	16 05	16 13	16 18	16 20		16 20	16 24		16 28			16 35	16 42			16 50	16 54			17 02	17 05	17 13	17 18
	d	16 04	16 06	16 15	16 20	16 28		16 28 →			16 30			16 36	16 45		16 52	16 58				17 04	17 06	17 15	17 20
West Byfleet	d		16 10											16 40			16 56						17 10		
Byfleet & New Haw	d		16 13											16 43			17 00						17 13		
Weybridge	d		16 16			16 34								16 46									17 16		
Walton-on-Thames	d		16 20			16 38								16 50									17 20		
Hersham	d		16 22											16 52									17 22		
Esher	d		16 25											16 55									17 25		
Surbiton 6	a		16 29			16 45								16 59				17 09					17 29		
Wimbledon 6 ⊖	a		16 37			16 53								17 07				17 17					17 37		
Earlsfield	a		16 41				←					←	←	17 11		←							17 41		
Clapham Junction 10	a	16 27	16 45	16 34	16 39	16 59	16 45				16 49	16 59	16 59	17 15	17 04	17 15		17 23				17 27	17 45	17 34	17 39
Vauxhall ⊖	a		→			→	16 50							→		17 20	18 08						→		
London Waterloo 15 ⊖	a	16 37		16 44	16 49		16 55				16 59	17 10	17 10		17 14	17 25	18 13	17 34				17 37		17 44	17 49

Table 155

Sundays until 25 September

Basingstoke, Alton, Guildford and Woking - Waterloo

		SW 1	SW	SW 1	SW 1		SW ◇1 ⊥	SW 1	SW 1	SW	SW 1 ⊥	SW	SW	SW 1	SW 1		SW 1	SW 1 ⊥	SW	SW 1	SW ◇1 ⊥	SW 1	SW	SW 1	SW 1
Basingstoke	d			16 50			17 10							17 16				17 44			18 00			17 50	
Hook	d													17 23											
Winchfield	d													17 27											
Fleet	d			17 02										17 32										18 02	
Farnborough (Main)	d			17 08										17 38										18 08	
Alton	d				16 45										17 15										17 45
Bentley	d														17 23										
Farnham	a				16 55										17 28										17 55
	d				17 00										17 30										18 00
Aldershot	d				17 06										17 36		17 40								18 06
Ash Vale	d				17 11										17 41		17a44								18 11
Brookwood	d			17 15	17 18									17 45	17 48									18 15	18 18
Guildford	d									17 27	17 35								17 57	18 05					
Worplesdon	d	←																				←			
Woking	a	17 20		17 20	17 24		17 28			17 35	17 42			17 50	17 54			18 02	18 05	18 13	18 18	18 20		18 20	18 24
	d	17 28		17 28 →			17 30			17 36	17 45		17 52	17 58				18 04	18 06	18 15	18 20	18 28		18 28 →	
West Byfleet	d									17 40			17 56						18 10						
Byfleet & New Haw	d									17 43			18 00						18 13						
Weybridge	d	17 34								17 46									18 16			18 34			
Walton-on-Thames	d	17 38								17 50									18 20			18 38			
Hersham	d									17 52									18 22						
Esher	d									17 55									18 25						
Surbiton 6	a	17 45								17 59				18 09					18 29			18 45			
Wimbledon 6 ⊖	a	17 53								18 07				18 17					18 37			18 53			
Earlsfield	a		←					←	←	18 11		←							18 41				←		
Clapham Junction 10	a	17 59	17 45				17 49	17 59	17 59	18 15	18 04	18 15		18 23				18 27	18 45	18 34	18 39	18 59	18 45		
Vauxhall ⊖	a	→	17 50							→		18 20	19 08						→			→	18 50		
London Waterloo 15 ⊖	a		17 55				17 59	18 10	18 10		18 14	18 25	19 13	18 34				18 37		18 44	18 49		18 55		

			SW ◇1 ⊥	SW 1	SW 1	SW	SW 1 ⊥	SW	SW	SW 1	SW 1		SW 1	SW 1	SW	SW 1	SW ◇1 ⊥	SW 1	SW	SW 1	SW 1		SW ◇1 ⊥	SW 1	SW 1
Basingstoke	d		18 10							18 16				18 44			19 00			18 50			19 10		
Hook	d									18 23															
Winchfield	d									18 27															
Fleet	d									18 32										19 02					
Farnborough (Main)	d									18 38										19 08					
Alton	d										18 15										18 45				
Bentley	d										18 23														
Farnham	a										18 28										18 55				
	d										18 30										19 00				
Aldershot	d										18 36		18 40								19 06				
Ash Vale	d										18 41		18a44								19 11				
Brookwood	d									18 45	18 48									19 15	19 18				
Guildford	d					18 27	18 35								18 57	19 05									
Worplesdon	d																	←							
Woking	a		18 28			18 35	18 42			18 50	18 54			19 02	19 05	19 13	19 18	19 20		19 20	19 24		19 28		
	d		18 30			18 36	18 45		18 52	18 58				19 04	19 06	19 15	19 20	19 28		19 28 →			19 30		
West Byfleet	d					18 40			18 56						19 10										
Byfleet & New Haw	d					18 43			19 00						19 13										
Weybridge	d					18 46									19 16			19 34							
Walton-on-Thames	d					18 50									19 20			19 38							
Hersham	d					18 52									19 22										
Esher	d					18 55									19 25										
Surbiton 6	a					18 59				19 09					19 29			19 45							
Wimbledon 6 ⊖	a					19 07				19 17					19 37			19 53							
Earlsfield	a			←	←	19 11		←							19 41				←					←	←
Clapham Junction 10	a		18 49	18 59	18 59	19 15	19 04	19 15		19 23				19 27	19 45	19 34	19 39	19 59	19 45				19 49	19 59	19 59
Vauxhall ⊖	a					→		19 20	20 08						→			→	19 50						
London Waterloo 15 ⊖	a		18 59	19 10	19 10		19 14	19 25	20 13	19 34				19 37		19 44	19 49		19 55				19 59	20 10	20 10

Basingstoke, Alton, Guildford and Woking - Waterloo

		SW	SW	SW	SW	SW	SW		SW	SW	SW	SW	SW	SW	SW	SW	SW		SW	SW	SW	SW	SW	SW	SW
			1 trolley			1	1		1	1		1	◇1 trolley	1		1	1		◇1 trolley	1	1		1		
Basingstoke	d					19 16				19 44			20 00			19 50			20 10						
Hook	d					19 23																			
Winchfield	d					19 27																			
Fleet	d					19 32										20 02									
Farnborough (Main)	d					19 38										20 08									
Alton	d						19 15										19 45								
Bentley	d						19 23																		
Farnham	a						19 28										19 55								
	d						19 30										20 00								
Aldershot	d						19 36		19 40								20 06								
Ash Vale	d						19 41		19a44								20 11								
Brookwood	d					19 45	19 48									20 15	20 18								
Guildford	d	19 27	19 35								19 57	20 05										20 27	20 35		
Worplesdon	d													←											
Woking	a	19 35	19 42			19 50	19 54			20 02	20 05	20 13	20 18	20 20		20 20	20 24		20 28			20 35	20 42		
	d	19 36	19 45		19 52	19 58				20 04	20 06	20 15	20 20	20 28		20 28			20 30			20 36	20 45		20 52
West Byfleet	d	19 40			19 56						20 10						→					20 40			20 56
Byfleet & New Haw	d	19 43			20 00						20 13											20 43			21 00
Weybridge	d	19 46									20 16			20 34								20 46			
Walton-on-Thames	d	19 50									20 20			20 38								20 50			
Hersham	d	19 52									20 22											20 52			
Esher	d	19 55									20 25											20 55			
Surbiton 6	a	19 59				20 09					20 29			20 45								20 59			
Wimbledon 6 ⊖	a	20 07				20 17					20 37			20 53								21 07			
Earlsfield	a	20 11		←							20 41				←					←	←	21 11		←	
Clapham Junction 10	a	20 15	20 04	20 15		20 23				20 27	20 45	20 34	20 39	20 59	20 45				20 49	20 59	20 59	21 15	21 04	21 15	
Vauxhall ⊖	a	→		20 20	21 08						→			→	20 50							→		21 20	22 08
London Waterloo 15 ⊖	a		20 14	20 25	21 13	20 34				20 37		20 44	20 49		20 55				20 59	21 10	21 10		21 14	21 25	22 13

		SW	SW		SW	SW	SW	SW	SW	SW	SW	SW	SW		SW	SW	SW	SW	SW	SW	SW	SW	SW		SW
		1	1		1	1		1	◇1 trolley	1		1	1		◇1 trolley	1	1		1			1	1		1
Basingstoke	d	20 16				20 44			21 00			20 50			21 10							21 16			
Hook	d	20 23																				21 23			
Winchfield	d	20 27																				21 27			
Fleet	d	20 32										21 02										21 32			
Farnborough (Main)	d	20 38										21 08										21 38			
Alton	d		20 15										20 45										21 15		
Bentley	d		20 23																				21 23		
Farnham	a		20 28										20 55										21 28		
	d		20 30										21 00										21 30		
Aldershot	d		20 36		20 40								21 06										21 36		21 40
Ash Vale	d		20 41		20a44								21 11										21 41		21a44
Brookwood	d	20 45	20 48									21 15	21 18									21 45	21 48		
Guildford	d						20 57	21 05										21 27	21 35						
Worplesdon	d									←															
Woking	a	20 50	20 54			21 02	21 05	21 13	21 18	21 20		21 20	21 24		21 28			21 35	21 42			21 50	21 54		
	d	20 58				21 04	21 06	21 15	21 20	21 28		21 28			21 30			21 36	21 45		21 52	21 58			
West Byfleet	d						21 10						→					21 40			21 56				
Byfleet & New Haw	d						21 13											21 43			22 00				
Weybridge	d						21 16			21 34								21 46							
Walton-on-Thames	d						21 20			21 38								21 50							
Hersham	d						21 22											21 52							
Esher	d						21 25											21 55							
Surbiton 6	a	21 09					21 29			21 45								21 59				22 09			
Wimbledon 6 ⊖	a	21 17					21 37			21 53								22 07				22 17			
Earlsfield	a						21 41				←					←	←	22 11		←					
Clapham Junction 10	a	21 23				21 27	21 45	21 34	21 39	21 59	21 45				21 49	21 59	21 59	22 15	22 04	22 15		22 23			
Vauxhall ⊖	a						→			→	21 50							→		22 20	23 08				
London Waterloo 15 ⊖	a	21 34				21 37		21 44	21 49		21 55				21 59	22 10	22 10		22 14	22 25	23 13	22 34			

Basingstoke, Alton, Guildford and Woking - Waterloo

		SW	SW	SW	SW	SW	SW	SW	SW		SW	SW	SW	SW	SW	SW	SW	SW	SW		SW	SW	SW	SW	SW
		1		1		1	1	◇1 trolley	1		1		1			1	1	1	1			1		1	1
Basingstoke	d	21 44				21 50		22 10								22 16			22 44						
Hook	d															22 23									
Winchfield	d															22 27									
Fleet	d					22 02										22 32									
Farnborough (Main)	d					22 08										22 38									
Alton	d						21 45										22 15							22 45	
Bentley	d																22 23								
Farnham	a						21 55										22 28							22 55	
	d						22 00										22 30							23 00	
Aldershot	d						22 06										22 36	22 40						23 06	
Ash Vale	d						22 11										22 41	22a44						23 11	
Brookwood	d					22 15	22 18									22 45	22 48							23 18	
Guildford	d		21 57	22 05								22 27	22 35								22 57	23 05			23 35
Worplesdon	d																								
Woking	a	22 02	22 05	22 13		22 21	22 24	22 28				22 35	22 42			22 50	22 54		23 02		23 05	23 13		23 24	23 42
	d	22 04	22 06	22 15		22 28		22 30				22 36	22 45		22 52	22 58			23 04		23 06	23 15		23 28	23 45
West Byfleet	d		22 10									22 40			22 56						23 10				
Byfleet & New Haw	d		22 13									22 43			23 00						23 13				
Weybridge	d		22 16			22 34						22 46									23 16			23 34	
Walton-on-Thames	d		22 20			22 38						22 50									23 20			23 38	
Hersham	d		22 22									22 52									23 22				
Esher	d		22 25									22 55									23 25				
Surbiton 6	a		22 29			22 45						22 59				23 09					23 29			23 45	
Wimbledon 6 ⊖	a		22 37			22 53						23 07				23 17					23 37			23 53	
Earlsfield	a		22 41		←				←		←	23 11		←							23 41		←		
Clapham Junction 10	a	22 27	22 45	22 34	22 45	22 59		22 49	22 59		22 59	23 15	23 04	23 15		23 23			23 27		23 45	23 34	23 45	23 59	00 04
Vauxhall ⊖	a		→		22 50	→						→		23 20	00 08						→		23 50		
London Waterloo 15 ⊖	a	22 37		22 44	22 55			22 59	23 10		23 10		23 14	23 25	00 13	23 34			23 37			23 44	23 55	00 10	00 14

		SW	SW	SW
		1	1	◇1
Basingstoke	d	23 16		23 44
Hook	d	23 23		
Winchfield	d	23 27		
Fleet	d	23 32		
Farnborough (Main)	d	23 38		
Alton	d		23 15	
Bentley	d		23 23	
Farnham	a		23 28	
	d		23 30	
Aldershot	d		23 36	
Ash Vale	d		23 41	
Brookwood	d	23 45	23 48	
Guildford	d			
Worplesdon	d			
Woking	a	23 50	23 54	00 02
	d			00 04
West Byfleet	d			
Byfleet & New Haw	d			
Weybridge	d			
Walton-on-Thames	d			
Hersham	d			
Esher	d			
Surbiton 6	a			
Wimbledon 6 ⊖	a			
Earlsfield	a			
Clapham Junction 10	a			00 23
Vauxhall ⊖	a			
London Waterloo 15 ⊖	a			00 33

Table 155

Sundays from 2 October

Basingstoke, Alton, Guildford and Woking - Waterloo

		SW 1	SW 1	SW 1	SW 1	SW 1	SW 1	SW	SW	SW		SW ◇1 ✠	SW	SW 1	SW	SW 1	SW 1	SW 1	SW 1	SW		SW 1	SW 1	SW	SW ◇1 ✠
Basingstoke	d		22p54	23p13			23p44					07 20				07 16			07 44						08 10
Hook	d		23p01				23p51									07 23									
Winchfield	d		23p05				23p55									07 27									
Fleet	d		23p10				00 01									07 32									
Farnborough (Main)	d		23p16				00 06									07 38									
Alton	d	22p44																							
Bentley	d	22p51																							
Farnham	a	22p56																							
	d	22p58															07 30								
Aldershot	d	23p04															07 36	07 40				07 48			
Ash Vale	d	23p09															07 41	07a44							
Brookwood	d	23p16	23p23				00 13									07 45	07 48								
Guildford	d					23p39			06 57	07 27										07 57		08a05	08 05		
Worplesdon	d				←	23p44								←											
Woking	a	23p21	23p28	23p31	23p28	23p49	00 18		07 05	07 35		07 39		07 50		07 50	07 54		08 02	08 05			08 13		08 28
	d	23p22	23p33	23p32	23p33	23p56	00 20	06 36	07 06	07 36		07 40		07 58	07 52	07 58			08 04	08 06			08 15		08 30
West Byfleet	d	23p27	→		23p37		00 25	06 40	07 10	07 40					07 56	→				08 10					
Byfleet & New Haw	d				23p40			06 43	07 13	07 43					08 00					08 13					
Weybridge	d				23p43		00 29	06 46	07 16	07 46										08 16					
Walton-on-Thames	d				23p47		00 33	06 50	07 20	07 50										08 20					
Hersham	d				23p49			06 52	07 22	07 52										08 22					
Esher	d				23p52			06 55	07 25	07 55										08 25					
Surbiton 6	a	23p37			23p57		00 39	06 59	07 29	07 59				08 09						08 29					
Wimbledon 6 ⊖	a				00 06		00 47	07 07	07 37	08 07				08 19						08 37					
Earlsfield	a							07 11	07 41	08 11			←							08 41				←	
Clapham Junction 10	a	23p48		23p52		00 18	00 53	07 15	07 45	08 15		08 05	08 15	08 27					08 30	08 45			08 40	08 45	08 57
Vauxhall ⊖	a				00 30			07 20	07 50	→			08 20		09 08					→				08 50	
London Waterloo 15 ⊖	a	00 01		00 03	00 35	00 32	01 04	07 30	08 00			08 19	08 30	08 42	09 13				08 42				08 49	09 00	09 09

		SW	SW 1	SW	SW 1	SW		SW 1	SW 1	SW 1	SW	SW 1	SW	SW ◇1 ✠	SW	SW 1		SW	SW	SW 1	SW 1	SW 1	SW 1	SW	SW 1
Basingstoke	d				08 16					08 44				09 10						09 16			09 44		
Hook	d				08 23															09 23					
Winchfield	d				08 27															09 27					
Fleet	d				08 32															09 32					
Farnborough (Main)	d				08 38															09 38					
Alton	d							08 15													09 15				
Bentley	d							08 23													09 23				
Farnham	a							08 28													09 28				
	d							08 30													09 30				
Aldershot	d							08 36	08 40												09 36	09 40			
Ash Vale	d							08 41	08a44												09 41	09a44			
Brookwood	d				08 45			08 48												09 45	09 48				
Guildford	d	08 27	08 35								08 57	09 05			09 27	09 35								09 57	10 05
Worplesdon	d																								
Woking	a	08 35	08 42		08 50			08 54		09 02	09 05	09 15		09 28	09 35	09 42				09 50	09 54		10 02	10 05	10 15
	d	08 36	08 45		08 58	08 52				09 04	09 06	09 15		09 30	09 36	09 45			09 52	09 58			10 04	10 06	10 15
West Byfleet	d	08 40				08 56					09 10				09 40				09 56					10 10	
Byfleet & New Haw	d	08 43				09 00					09 13				09 43				10 00					10 13	
Weybridge	d	08 46									09 16				09 46									10 16	
Walton-on-Thames	d	08 50									09 20				09 50									10 20	
Hersham	d	08 52									09 22				09 52									10 22	
Esher	d	08 55									09 25				09 55									10 25	
Surbiton 6	a	08 59			09 09						09 29				09 59					10 09				10 29	
Wimbledon 6 ⊖	a	09 07			09 19						09 37				10 07					10 17				10 37	
Earlsfield	a	09 11		←							09 41		←		10 11			←						10 41	
Clapham Junction 10	a	09 15	09 06	09 15	09 26					09 30	09 45	09 38	09 45	09 57	10 15	10 04		10 15		10 23			10 27	10 45	10 35
Vauxhall ⊖	a	→		09 20		10 08					→		09 50		→			10 20	11 08					→	
London Waterloo 15 ⊖	a		09 19	09 30	09 42	10 13				09 43		09 49	10 00	10 08		10 19		10 30	11 13	10 38			10 42		10 49

Table 155

Sundays from 2 October

Basingstoke, Alton, Guildford and Woking - Waterloo

		SW ◇1 ✠		SW	SW ◇1 ✠	SW	SW 1 ✠	SW	SW	SW 1	SW 1	SW 1		SW 1 ✠	SW	SW 1	SW ◇1 ✠	SW	SW ◇1 ✠	SW	SW 1 ✠	SW		SW	
Basingstoke	d	10 00			10 10					10 16				10 44			11 00		11 10						
Hook	d									10 23															
Winchfield	d									10 27															
Fleet	d									10 32															
Farnborough (Main)	d									10 38															
Alton	d										10 15														
Bentley	d										10 23														
Farnham	a										10 28														
	d										10 30														
Aldershot	d										10 36	10 40													
Ash Vale	d										10 41	10a44													
Brookwood	d									10 45	10 48														
Guildford	d					10 27	10 35								10 57	11 06				11 27	11 35				
Worplesdon	d																								
Woking	a	10 19			10 28	10 35	10 42			10 50	10 54			11 02	11 05	11 13	11 18		11 28	11 35	11 42				
	d	10 20			10 30	10 36	10 45		10 52	10 58				11 04	11 06	11 15	11 20		11 30	11 36	11 45			11 52	
West Byfleet	d					10 40			10 56						11 10					11 40				11 56	
Byfleet & New Haw	d					10 43			11 00						11 13					11 43				12 00	
Weybridge	d					10 46									11 16					11 46					
Walton-on-Thames	d					10 50									11 20					11 50					
Hersham	d					10 52									11 22					11 52					
Esher	d					10 55									11 25					11 55					
Surbiton 6	a					10 59				11 09					11 29					11 59					
Wimbledon 6 ⊖	a					11 07				11 17					11 37					12 07					
Earlsfield	a			←		11 11		←							11 41			←		12 11		←			
Clapham Junction 10	a	10 40		10 45	10 49	11 15	11 04	11 15		11 23				11 27	11 45	11 34	11 39	11 45	11 49	12 15	12 04	12 15			
Vauxhall ⊖	a			10 50		→		11 20	12 08						→			11 50		→		12 20		13 08	
London Waterloo 15 ⊖	a	10 54		11 00	11 04		11 19	11 30	12 13	11 38				11 42		11 49	11 54	12 00	12 03		12 19	12 30		13 13	

		SW 1	SW 1	SW 1	SW 1 ✠	SW	SW 1	SW ◇1 ✠	SW		SW ◇1 ✠	SW	SW 1 ✠	SW	SW	SW 1	SW 1	SW 1	SW 1 ✠		SW	SW 1	SW ◇1 ✠	SW	SW ◇1 ✠
Basingstoke	d	11 16			11 44			12 00			12 10					12 16			12 44				13 00		13 10
Hook	d	11 23														12 23									
Winchfield	d	11 27														12 27									
Fleet	d	11 32														12 32									
Farnborough (Main)	d	11 38														12 38									
Alton	d		11 15														12 15								
Bentley	d		11 23														12 23								
Farnham	a		11 28														12 28								
	d		11 30														12 30								
Aldershot	d		11 36	11 40													12 36	12 40							
Ash Vale	d		11 41	11a44													12 41	12a44							
Brookwood	d	11 45	11 48													12 45	12 48								
Guildford	d					11 57	12 06					12 27	12 35								12 57	13 05			
Worplesdon	d																								
Woking	a	11 50	11 54		12 02	12 05	12 13	12 18			12 28	12 35	12 42			12 50	12 54		13 02		13 05	13 13	13 18		13 28
	d	11 58			12 04	12 06	12 15	12 20			12 30	12 36	12 45		12 52	12 58			13 04		13 06	13 15	13 20		13 30
West Byfleet	d					12 10						12 40			12 56						13 10				
Byfleet & New Haw	d					12 13						12 43			13 00						13 13				
Weybridge	d					12 16						12 46									13 16				
Walton-on-Thames	d					12 20						12 50									13 20				
Hersham	d					12 22						12 52									13 22				
Esher	d					12 25						12 55									13 25				
Surbiton 6	a	12 09				12 29						12 59				13 09					13 29				
Wimbledon 6 ⊖	a	12 17				12 37						13 07				13 17					13 37				
Earlsfield	a					12 41			←			13 11		←							13 41			←	
Clapham Junction 10	a	12 23			12 27	12 45	12 34	12 39	12 45		12 49	13 15	13 04	13 15		13 23			13 27		13 45	13 34	13 39	13 45	13 49
Vauxhall ⊖	a					→			12 50			→		13 20	14 08						→			13 50	
London Waterloo 15 ⊖	a	12 39			12 42		12 49	12 49	13 00		13 04		13 14	13 30	14 13	13 39			13 37			13 44	13 49	14 00	13 59

Sundays
from 2 October

Basingstoke, Alton, Guildford and Woking - Waterloo

		SW	SW 1 ⌶	SW	SW	SW 1	SW 1	SW 1	SW 1 ⌶	SW	SW 1	SW ◇1 ⌶	SW 1	SW	SW 1	SW 1	SW ◇1 ⌶	SW 1	SW 1	SW	SW 1 ⌶	SW	SW
Basingstoke	d					13 16			13 44			14 00			13 50		14 10						
Hook	d					13 23																	
Winchfield	d					13 27																	
Fleet	d					13 32									14 02								
Farnborough (Main)	d					13 38									14 08								
Alton	d						13 15									13 45							
Bentley	d						13 23																
Farnham	a						13 28									13 55							
	d						13 30									14 00							
Aldershot	d						13 36	13 40								14 06							
Ash Vale	d						13 41	13a44								14 11							
Brookwood	d					13 45	13 48								14 15	14 18							
Guildford	d	13 27	13 35							13 57	14 05									14 27	14 35		
Worplesdon	d												←										
Woking	a	13 35	13 42			13 50	13 54		14 02	14 05	14 13	14 18	14 20		14 20	14 24	14 28			14 35	14 42		
	d	13 36	13 45		13 52	13 58			14 04	14 06	14 15	14 20	14 28		14 28		14 30			14 36	14 45		14 52
West Byfleet	d	13 40			13 56					14 10					→					14 40			14 56
Byfleet & New Haw	d	13 43			14 00					14 13										14 43			15 00
Weybridge	d	13 46								14 16			14 34							14 46			
Walton-on-Thames	d	13 50								14 20			14 38							14 50			
Hersham	d	13 52								14 22										14 52			
Esher	d	13 55								14 25										14 55			
Surbiton 6	a	13 59				14 09				14 29			14 45							14 59			
Wimbledon 6 ⊖	a	14 07				14 17				14 37			14 53							15 07			
Earlsfield	a	14 11		←						14 41				←				←	←	15 11		←	
Clapham Junction 10	a	14 15	14 04	14 15		14 23			14 27	14 45	14 34	14 39	14 59	14 45			14 49	14 59	14 59	15 15	15 04	15 15	
Vauxhall ⊖	a	→		14 20	15 08					→			→	14 50						→		15 20	16 08
London Waterloo 15 ⊖	a		14 14	14 30	15 13	14 34			14 37		14 44	14 49		14 55			14 59	15 10	15 10		15 14	15 25	16 13

		SW 1	SW 1	SW 1	SW 1 ⌶	SW	SW 1	SW ◇1 ⌶	SW 1	SW	SW 1	SW 1	SW ◇1 ⌶	SW 1	SW 1	SW	SW 1 ⌶	SW	SW	SW 1	SW 1	SW 1
Basingstoke	d	14 16			14 44			15 00			14 50		15 10							15 16		
Hook	d	14 23																		15 23		
Winchfield	d	14 27																		15 27		
Fleet	d	14 32									15 02									15 32		
Farnborough (Main)	d	14 38									15 08									15 38		
Alton	d		14 15									14 45									15 15	
Bentley	d		14 23																		15 23	
Farnham	a		14 28									14 55									15 28	
	d		14 30									15 00									15 30	
Aldershot	d		14 36	14 40								15 06									15 36	15 40
Ash Vale	d		14 41	14a44								15 11									15 41	15a44
Brookwood	d	14 45	14 48								15 15	15 18								15 45	15 48	
Guildford	d					14 57	15 05									15 27	15 35					
Worplesdon	d								←													
Woking	a	14 50	14 54		15 02	15 05	15 13	15 18	15 20		15 20	15 24	15 28			15 35	15 42			15 50	15 54	
	d	14 58			15 04	15 06	15 15	15 20	15 28		15 28		15 30			15 36	15 45		15 52	15 58		
West Byfleet	d					15 10					→					15 40			15 56			
Byfleet & New Haw	d					15 13										15 43			16 00			
Weybridge	d					15 16			15 34							15 46						
Walton-on-Thames	d					15 20			15 38							15 50						
Hersham	d					15 22										15 52						
Esher	d					15 25										15 55						
Surbiton 6	a	15 09				15 29			15 45							15 59				16 09		
Wimbledon 6 ⊖	a	15 17				15 37			15 53							16 07				16 17		
Earlsfield	a					15 41				←				←	←	16 11		←				
Clapham Junction 10	a	15 23			15 27	15 45	15 34	15 39	15 59	15 45			15 49	15 59	15 59	16 15	16 04	16 15		16 23		
Vauxhall ⊖	a					→			→	15 50						→		16 20	17 08			
London Waterloo 15 ⊖	a	15 34			15 37		15 44	15 49		15 55			15 59	16 10	16 10		16 14	16 25	17 13	16 34		

Sundays
from 2 October

Basingstoke, Alton, Guildford and Woking - Waterloo

		SW 1 ⌶	SW	SW 1	SW ◇1 ⌶	SW 1	SW	SW 1	SW 1	SW ◇1 ⌶	SW 1	SW 1	SW	SW 1 ⌶	SW	SW	SW 1	SW 1	SW 1	SW 1 ⌶	SW	SW 1	SW ◇1 ⌶
Basingstoke	d	15 44			16 00			15 50		16 10							16 16			16 44			17 00
Hook	d																16 23						
Winchfield	d																16 27						
Fleet	d							16 02									16 32						
Farnborough (Main)	d							16 08									16 38						
Alton	d								15 45									16 15					
Bentley	d																	16 23					
Farnham	a								15 55									16 28					
	d								16 00									16 30					
Aldershot	d								16 06									16 36	16 40				
Ash Vale	d								16 11									16 41	16a44				
Brookwood	d							16 15	16 18								16 45	16 48					
Guildford	d		15 57	16 05									16 27	16 35							16 57	17 05	
Worplesdon	d					←																	
Woking	a	16 02	16 05	16 13	16 18	16 20		16 20	16 24	16 28			16 35	16 42			16 50	16 54		17 02	17 05	17 13	17 18
	d	16 04	16 06	16 15	16 20	16 28		16 28		16 30			16 36	16 45		16 52	16 58			17 04	17 06	17 15	17 20
West Byfleet	d		16 10					→					16 40			16 56					17 10		
Byfleet & New Haw	d		16 13										16 43			17 00					17 13		
Weybridge	d		16 16			16 34							16 46								17 16		
Walton-on-Thames	d		16 20			16 38							16 50								17 20		
Hersham	d		16 22										16 52								17 22		
Esher	d		16 25										16 55								17 25		
Surbiton 6	a		16 29			16 45							16 59				17 09				17 29		
Wimbledon 6 ⊖	a		16 37			16 53							17 07				17 17				17 37		
Earlsfield	a		16 41				←				←	←	17 11		←						17 41		
Clapham Junction 10	a	16 27	16 45	16 34	16 39	16 59	16 45			16 49	16 59	16 59	17 15	17 04	17 15		17 23			17 27	17 45	17 34	17 39
Vauxhall ⊖	a		→			→	16 50						→		17 20	18 08					→		
London Waterloo 15 ⊖	a	16 37		16 44	16 49		16 55			16 59	17 10	17 10		17 14	17 25	18 13	17 34			17 37		17 44	17 49

		SW 1	SW	SW 1	SW 1	SW ◇1 ⌶	SW 1	SW 1	SW	SW 1 ⌶	SW	SW	SW 1	SW 1	SW 1	SW 1 ⌶	SW	SW 1	SW ◇1 ⌶	SW 1	SW
Basingstoke	d			16 50		17 10							17 16			17 44			18 00		
Hook	d												17 23								
Winchfield	d												17 27								
Fleet	d			17 02									17 32								
Farnborough (Main)	d			17 08									17 38								
Alton	d				16 45									17 15							
Bentley	d													17 23							
Farnham	a				16 55									17 28							
	d				17 00									17 30							
Aldershot	d				17 06									17 36	17 40						
Ash Vale	d				17 11									17 41	17a44						
Brookwood	d			17 15	17 18								17 45	17 48							
Guildford	d								17 27	17 35							17 57	18 05			
Worplesdon	d	←																		←	
Woking	a	17 20		17 20	17 24	17 28			17 35	17 42			17 50	17 54		18 02	18 05	18 13	18 18	18 20	
	d	17 28		17 28		17 30			17 36	17 45		17 52	17 58			18 04	18 06	18 15	18 20	18 28	
West Byfleet	d			→					17 40			17 56					18 10				
Byfleet & New Haw	d								17 43			18 00					18 13				
Weybridge	d	17 34							17 46								18 16			18 34	
Walton-on-Thames	d	17 38							17 50								18 20			18 38	
Hersham	d								17 52								18 22				
Esher	d								17 55								18 25				
Surbiton 6	a	17 45							17 59				18 09				18 29			18 45	
Wimbledon 6 ⊖	a	17 53							18 07				18 17				18 37			18 53	
Earlsfield	a		←				←	←	18 11		←						18 41				←
Clapham Junction 10	a	17 59	17 45			17 49	17 59	17 59	18 15	18 04	18 15		18 23			18 27	18 45	18 34	18 39	18 59	18 45
Vauxhall ⊖	a	→	17 50						→		18 20	19 08					→			→	18 50
London Waterloo 15 ⊖	a		17 55			17 59	18 10	18 10		18 14	18 25	19 13	18 34			18 37		18 44	18 49		18 55

Table 155

Sundays
from 2 October

Basingstoke, Alton, Guildford and Woking - Waterloo

		SW [1]	SW [1]	SW ◇[1] 🛒	SW [1]	SW [1]	SW	SW [1] 🛒	SW	SW		SW [1]	SW [1]	SW [1]	SW [1]	SW	SW [1]	SW ◇[1] 🛒	SW [1]	SW		SW [1]	SW [1]	SW ◇[1] 🛒	SW [1]
Basingstoke	d	17 50		18 10								18 16			18 44			19 00				18 50		19 10	
Hook	d											18 23													
Winchfield	d											18 27													
Fleet	d	18 02										18 32										19 02			
Farnborough (Main)	d	18 08										18 38										19 08			
Alton	d		17 45										18 15										18 45		
Bentley	d												18 23												
Farnham	a		17 55										18 28										18 55		
	d		18 00										18 30										19 00		
Aldershot	d		18 06										18 36	18 40									19 06		
Ash Vale	d		18 11										18 41	18a44									19 11		
Brookwood	d	18 15	18 18									18 45	18 48									19 15	19 18		
Guildford	d						18 27	18 35								18 57	19 05								
Worplesdon	d																		←						
Woking	a	18 20	18 24	18 28			18 35	18 42				18 50	18 54		19 02	19 05	19 13	19 18	19 20			19 20	19 24	19 28	
	d	18 28		18 30			18 36	18 45		18 52		18 58			19 04	19 06	19 15	19 20	19 28			19 28		19 30	
West Byfleet	d	→					18 40			18 56						19 10						→			
Byfleet & New Haw	d						18 43			19 00						19 13									
Weybridge	d						18 46									19 16			19 34						
Walton-on-Thames	d						18 50									19 20			19 38						
Hersham	d						18 52									19 22									
Esher	d						18 55									19 25									
Surbiton [6]	a						18 59					19 09				19 29			19 45						
Wimbledon [6] ⊖	a						19 07					19 17				19 37			19 53						
Earlsfield	a				←	←	19 11		←							19 41				←					←
Clapham Junction [10]	a			18 49	18 59	18 59	19 15	19 04	19 15			19 23			19 27	19 45	19 34	19 39	19 59	19 45				19 49	19 59
Vauxhall ⊖	a						→		19 20	20 08						→			→	19 50					
London Waterloo [15] ⊖	a			18 59	19 10	19 10		19 14	19 25	20 13		19 34			19 37		19 44	19 49		19 55				19 59	20 10

		SW [1]	SW	SW [1] 🛒	SW	SW		SW [1]	SW [1]	SW [1]	SW [1]	SW	SW [1]	SW ◇[1] 🛒	SW [1]	SW		SW [1]	SW [1]	SW ◇[1] 🛒	SW [1]	SW [1]	SW	SW [1]	SW
Basingstoke	d							19 16			19 44			20 00				19 50		20 10					
Hook	d							19 23																	
Winchfield	d							19 27																	
Fleet	d							19 32										20 02							
Farnborough (Main)	d							19 38										20 08							
Alton	d								19 15										19 45						
Bentley	d								19 23																
Farnham	a								19 28										19 55						
	d								19 30										20 00						
Aldershot	d								19 36	19 40									20 06						
Ash Vale	d								19 41	19a44									20 11						
Brookwood	d							19 45	19 48									20 15	20 18						
Guildford	d		19 27	19 35								19 57	20 05									20 27	20 35		
Worplesdon	d														←										
Woking	a		19 35	19 42				19 50	19 54		20 02	20 05	20 13	20 18	20 20			20 20	20 24	20 28			20 35	20 42	
	d		19 36	19 45		19 52		19 58			20 04	20 06	20 15	20 20	20 28			20 28		20 30			20 36	20 45	
West Byfleet	d		19 40			19 56						20 10						→					20 40		
Byfleet & New Haw	d		19 43			20 00						20 13											20 43		
Weybridge	d		19 46									20 16			20 34								20 46		
Walton-on-Thames	d		19 50									20 20			20 38								20 50		
Hersham	d		19 52									20 22											20 52		
Esher	d		19 55									20 25											20 55		
Surbiton [6]	a		19 59					20 09				20 29			20 45								20 59		
Wimbledon [6] ⊖	a		20 07					20 17				20 37			20 53								21 07		
Earlsfield	a	←	20 11		←							20 41				←					←	←	21 11		←
Clapham Junction [10]	a	19 59	20 15	20 04	20 15			20 23			20 27	20 45	20 34	20 39	20 59	20 45				20 49	20 59	20 59	21 15	21 04	21 15
Vauxhall ⊖	a		→		20 20	21 08						→			→	20 50							→		21 20
London Waterloo [15] ⊖	a	20 10		20 14	20 25	21 13		20 34			20 37		20 44	20 49		20 55				20 59	21 10	21 10		21 14	21 25

Table 155

Sundays
from 2 October

Basingstoke, Alton, Guildford and Woking - Waterloo

		SW		SW [1]	SW [1]	SW [1]	SW [1]	SW	SW [1]	SW ◇[1] 🛒	SW [1]	SW		SW [1]	SW [1]	SW ◇[1] 🛒	SW [1]	SW [1]	SW	SW [1]	SW	SW		SW [1]	SW [1]
Basingstoke	d			20 16			20 44			21 00				20 50		21 10								21 16	
Hook	d			20 23																				21 23	
Winchfield	d			20 27																				21 27	
Fleet	d			20 32										21 02										21 32	
Farnborough (Main)	d			20 38										21 08										21 38	
Alton	d				20 15										20 45										21 15
Bentley	d				20 23																				21 23
Farnham	a				20 28										20 55										21 28
	d				20 30										21 00										21 30
Aldershot	d				20 36	20 40									21 06										21 36
Ash Vale	d				20 41	20a44									21 11										21 41
Brookwood	d			20 45	20 48									21 15	21 18									21 45	21 48
Guildford	d							20 57	21 05										21 27	21 35					
Worplesdon	d										←														
Woking	a			20 50	20 54		21 02	21 05	21 13	21 18	21 20			21 20	21 24	21 28			21 35	21 42				21 50	21 54
	d	20 52		20 58			21 04	21 06	21 15	21 20	21 28			21 28		21 30			21 36	21 45		21 52		21 58	
West Byfleet	d	20 56						21 10						→					21 40			21 56			
Byfleet & New Haw	d	21 00						21 13											21 43			22 00			
Weybridge	d							21 16			21 34								21 46						
Walton-on-Thames	d							21 20			21 38								21 50						
Hersham	d							21 22											21 52						
Esher	d							21 25											21 55						
Surbiton [6]	a			21 09				21 29			21 45								21 59					22 09	
Wimbledon [6] ⊖	a			21 17				21 37			21 53								22 07					22 17	
Earlsfield	a							21 41				←					←	←	22 11		←				
Clapham Junction [10]	a			21 23			21 27	21 45	21 34	21 39	21 59	21 45				21 49	21 59	21 59	22 15	22 04	22 15			22 23	
Vauxhall ⊖	a	22 08						→			→	21 50							→		22 20	23 08			
London Waterloo [15] ⊖	a	22 13		21 34			21 37		21 44	21 49		21 55				21 59	22 10	22 10		22 14	22 25	23 13		22 34	

		SW [1]	SW [1]	SW	SW [1]	SW	SW [1]	SW [1]		SW ◇[1] 🛒	SW [1]	SW [1]	SW	SW [1]	SW	SW	SW [1]	SW [1]		SW [1]	SW [1]	SW	SW [1]	SW	SW [1]
Basingstoke	d		21 44				21 50			22 10							22 16				22 44				
Hook	d																22 23								
Winchfield	d																22 27								
Fleet	d						22 02										22 32								
Farnborough (Main)	d						22 08										22 38								
Alton	d							21 45										22 15							22 45
Bentley	d																	22 23							
Farnham	a							21 55										22 28							22 55
	d							22 00										22 30							23 00
Aldershot	d	21 40						22 06										22 36		22 40					23 06
Ash Vale	d	21a44						22 11										22 41		22a44					23 11
Brookwood	d						22 15	22 18									22 45	22 48							23 18
Guildford	d			21 57	22 05								22 27	22 35								22 57	23 05		
Worplesdon	d																								
Woking	a		22 02	22 05	22 13		22 21	22 24		22 28			22 35	22 42			22 50	22 54			23 02	23 05	23 13		23 24
	d		22 04	22 06	22 15		22 28			22 30			22 36	22 45		22 52	22 58				23 04	23 06	23 15		23 28
West Byfleet	d			22 10									22 40			22 56						23 10			
Byfleet & New Haw	d			22 13									22 43			23 00						23 13			
Weybridge	d			22 16			22 34						22 46									23 16			23 34
Walton-on-Thames	d			22 20			22 38						22 50									23 20			23 38
Hersham	d			22 22									22 52									23 22			
Esher	d			22 25									22 55									23 25			
Surbiton [6]	a			22 29			22 45						22 59				23 09					23 29			23 45
Wimbledon [6] ⊖	a			22 37			22 53						23 07				23 17					23 37			23 53
Earlsfield	a			22 41		←					←	←	23 11		←							23 41		←	
Clapham Junction [10]	a		22 27	22 45	22 34	22 45	22 59			22 49	22 59	22 59	23 15	23 04	23 15		23 23				23 27	23 45	23 34	23 45	23 59
Vauxhall ⊖	a			→		22 50	→						→		23 20	00 08						→		23 50	
London Waterloo [15] ⊖	a		22 37		22 44	22 55				22 59	23 10	23 10			23 25	00 13	23 34				23 37		23 44	23 55	00 10

Basingstoke, Alton, Guildford and Woking - Waterloo

from 2 October

		SW 1	SW 1	SW 1	SW ◇1
Basingstoke	d		23 16		23 44
Hook	d		23 23		
Winchfield	d		23 27		
Fleet	d		23 32		
Farnborough (Main)	d		23 38		
Alton	d			23 15	
Bentley	d			23 23	
Farnham	a			23 28	
	d			23 30	
Aldershot	d			23 36	
Ash Vale	d			23 41	
Brookwood	d		23 45	23 48	
Guildford	d	23 35			
Worplesdon	d				
Woking	a	23 42	23 50	23 54	00 02
	d	23 45			00 04
West Byfleet	d				
Byfleet & New Haw	d				
Weybridge	d				
Walton-on-Thames	d				
Hersham	d				
Esher	d				
Surbiton 6	a				
Wimbledon 6 ⊖	a				
Earlsfield	a				
Clapham Junction 10	a	00 04			00 23
Vauxhall ⊖	a				
London Waterloo 15 ⊖	a	00 14			00 33

London - Guildford, Haslemere and Portsmouth

Miles			SW MX 1	SW MO 1	SW MX 1	SW MO 1	SW MX 1	SW MO 1	SW MX 1	SW MO 1	SW 1		SW 1	SW 1	SW 1	SW 1	SW 1	SW 1	SW 1 🍴	SW 1	SW 1		SW 1 🍴	SW 1	SW 1
0	London Waterloo 15 ⊖	d	22p30	22p30	22p45	23p00	23p15	23p30	23p45	00 50				05 00	05 20	06 15	06 45	07 15	07 30		07 45		08 00		08 15
4	Clapham Junction 10	d		22b39	22b52	23b09	23b22	23b39	23b52	00 57				05 11	05 29	06u22	06u52	07u23			07u52				08u22
24½	Woking	a	22p54	23p01	23p11	23p31	23p41	00 01	00 11	01 16				05 51	06 08	06 41	07 11	07 42	07 54		08 12		08 24		08 42
—		d	22p55	23p02	23p13	23p32	23p43	00 03	00 13	01 18				05 53	06 11	06 43	07 13	07 44	07 55		08 14		08 25		08 44
26¾	Worplesdon	d			23p18				00 18						06 16	06 48	07 18	07 49			08 19				08 49
30¼	Guildford	a	23p03	23p10	23p23	23p40	23p51	00 10	00 24	01s26				06 00	06 21	06 53	07 23	07 54	08 03		08 24		08 35		08 54
—		d	23p04	23p12	23p25	23p42	23p52	00 12	00 25				05 15	06 04	06 25	06 55	07 25	07 56	08 04		08 26		08 39		08 56
33½	Farncombe	d	23p10		23p31	23p48	23p58		00 31					06 10	06 31	07 01	07 31	08 02			08 32				09 02
34½	Godalming	d	23p13		23p34	23p51	00 02		00 34					06 13	06 34	07 04	07 34	08 05	08 11		08 35				09 05
36¼	Milford (Surrey)	d			23p38	23p55			00s38					06 17	06 38	07 08	07 38	08 09			08 39				09 09
38½	Witley	d			23p42	23p59			00s43					06 21	06 42	07 12	07 42	08 13		←	08 43			←	09 13
43	Haslemere 4	a	23p24	23p26	23p49	00 06	00 12	00 26	00 49				05 29	06 28	06 49	07 19	07 49	08 20	08 24	08 20	08 50		08 54	08 50	09 20
—		d	23p25	23p27	23p50	00 07	00 13	00 27	00 50				05 30	06 28	06 55	07 20	07 53	08 30	08 25	08 30	08 58		08 55	08 58	
46¾	Liphook	d			23p55	00 12			00s55				05 35	06 33	07 00	07 25	07 59	→		08 35	→			09 03	
51½	Liss	d			00 01	00 18			01s01				05 41	06 39	07 06	07 31	08 05			08 41				09 09	
55	Petersfield	d	23p36	23p38	00 06	00 23	00 24	00 38	01 06				05 46	06 45	07 11	07 36	08 11		08 36	08 46			09 06	09 15	
63¼	Rowlands Castle	d			00 16	00 33			01s16				05 56	06 54	07 21	07 46	08 21			08 56				09 24	
66½	Havant	a	23p48	23p50	00 21	00 38	00 36	00 50	01 21	02s00			06 01	06 59	07 27	07 51	08 26		08 49	09 04			09 19	09 29	
—		d	23p49	23p51	00 22	00 39	00 37	00 51	01 21		04 40		06 02	07 00	07 28	07 52	08 27		08 50	09 05			09 20	09 30	
67¼	Bedhampton	a			00 24	00 41			01s24		04 42		06 04	07 02	07 30	07 54	08 29			09 07				09 32	
70½	Hilsea	a			00 30				01s29		04 48		06 10	07 08	07 37	08 00	08 35			09 13				09 38	
72¾	Fratton	a	23p58	23p59	00 34	00 49	00 46	01 00	01s33	02s10	04 52		06 14	07 12	07 41	08 04	08 39		08 58	09 17			09 28	09 42	
73¾	Portsmouth & Southsea	a	00 02	00 04	00 38	00 53	00 50	01 04	01 37	02s14	04 55		06 18	07 16	07 46	08 07	08 43		09 02	09 20			09 32	09 46	
74½	Portsmouth Harbour ⛴	a	00 07	00 09		00 58	00 55	01 09		02 19	04 59		06 22	07 20		08 12	08 48		09 07	09 26			09 37		

		SW 1 🍴	SW 1	SW 1 🍴	SW 1	SW 1	SW 1 🍴		SW 1	SW 1 🍴	SW 1	SW 1	SW 1 🍴	SW 1	SW 1 🍴	SW 1	SW 1		SW 1 🍴	SW 1	SW 1 🍴	SW 1	SW 1	SW 1 🍴	SW 1
London Waterloo 15 ⊖	d	08 30	08 45	09 00		09 15	09 30		09 45	10 00		10 15	10 30	10 45	11 00		11 15		11 30	11 45	12 00		12 15	12 30	12 45
Clapham Junction 10	d		08u52			09u22			09u52			10u22		10u52			11u22			11u52			12u22		12u52
Woking	a	08 55	09 11	09 24		09 42	09 54		10 11	10 24		10 41	10 54	11 11	11 24		11 41		11 54	12 11	12 24		12 41	12 54	13 11
	d	08 55	09 13	09 25		09 43	09 55		10 13	10 25		10 43	10 55	11 13	11 25		11 43		11 55	12 13	12 25		12 43	12 55	13 13
Worplesdon	d		09 18						10 18					11 18						12 18					13 18
Guildford	a	09 05	09 23	09 33		09 52	10 03		10 23	10 33		10 50	11 03	11 23	11 33		11 50		12 03	12 23	12 33		12 50	13 03	13 23
	d	09 07	09 25	09 34		09 54	10 04		10 25	10 34		10 52	11 04	11 25	11 34		11 52		12 04	12 25	12 34		12 52	13 04	13 25
Farncombe	d		09 31			10 00			10 31			10 58		11 31			11 58			12 31			12 58		13 31
Godalming	d		09 34			10 03			10 34			11 01		11 34			12 01			12 34			13 01		13 34
Milford (Surrey)	d					10 07						11 05					12 05						13 05		
Witley	d				←	10 11					←	11 09				←	12 09					←	13 09		
Haslemere 4	a	09 24	09 45	09 49	09 45	10 19	10 22		10 45	10 49	10 45	11 16	11 20	11 45	11 49	11 45	12 16		12 20	12 45	12 49	12 45	13 16	13 20	13 45
	d	09 25	09 55	09 50	09 55		10 23		10 55	10 50	10 55		11 21	11 55	11 50	11 55			12 21	12 55	12 50	12 55		13 21	13 55
Liphook	d		→		10 00				→		11 00			→		12 00				→		13 00			→
Liss	d				10 06						11 06					12 06						13 06			
Petersfield	d	09 36		10 01	10 11		10 34			11 01	11 11		11 32		12 01	12 11			12 32		13 01	13 11		13 32	
Rowlands Castle	d				10 21						11 21					12 21						13 21			
Havant	a	09 49		10 15	10 26		10 49			11 15	11 26		11 49		12 15	12 26			12 49		13 15	13 26		13 49	
	d	09 50		10 16	10 27		10 50			11 16	11 27		11 50		12 16	12 27			12 50		13 16	13 27		13 50	
Bedhampton	a				10 29						11 29					12 29						13 29			
Hilsea	a				10 36						11 36					12 36						13 36			
Fratton	a	09 59		10 24	10 40		10 59			11 24	11 40		11 59		12 24	12 40			12 59		13 24	13 40		13 59	
Portsmouth & Southsea	a	10 02		10 28	10 44		11 02			11 28	11 44		12 02		12 28	12 44			13 02		13 28	13 44		14 02	
Portsmouth Harbour ⛴	a	10 07		10 33			11 07			11 33			12 07		12 33				13 07		13 33			14 07	

		SW 1 🍴	SW 1		SW 1	SW 1 🍴	SW 1	SW 1 🍴	SW 1	SW 1	SW 1 🍴	SW 1	SW 1 🍴		SW 1	SW 1	SW 1 🍴	SW 1	SW 1	SW 1 🍴	SW 1	SW 1	SW 1 🍴		SW 1
London Waterloo 15 ⊖	d	13 00			13 15	13 30	13 45	14 00		14 15	14 30	14 45	15 00			15 15	15 30		15 45	16 00		16 15	16 30		
Clapham Junction 10	d				13u22		13u52			14u22		14u52				15u22			15u52			16u22			
Woking	a	13 24			13 41	13 54	14 11	14 24		14 41	14 54	15 11	15 24			15 41	15 54		16 11	16 24		16 41	16 54		
	d	13 25			13 43	13 55	14 13	14 25		14 43	14 55	15 13	15 25			15 43	15 55		16 13	16 25		16 43	16 55		
Worplesdon	d						14 18					15 18				15 48						16 48			
Guildford	a	13 33			13 50	14 03	14 23	14 33		14 50	15 03	15 23	15 33			15 53	16 03		16 20	16 33		16 53	17 03		
	d	13 34			13 52	14 04	14 25	14 34		14 52	15 04	15 25	15 34			15 55	16 04		16 22	16 34		16 55	17 04		
Farncombe	d				13 58		14 31			14 58		15 31				16 01			16 28			17 01			
Godalming	d				14 01		14 34			15 01		15 34				16 04			16 31			17 04			
Milford (Surrey)	d				14 05					15 05						16 08			16 35			17 08			
Witley	d		←		14 09				←	15 09					←	16 12		←	16 39		←	17 12			←
Haslemere 4	a	13 49	13 45		14 16	14 20	14 45	14 49	14 45	15 16	15 20	15 45	15 49		15 45	16 19	16 23	16 19	16 46	16 50	16 46	17 19	17 23		17 19
	d	13 50	13 55			14 21	14 55	14 50	14 55		15 21	15 55	15 50		15 55	16 29	16 24	16 29	16 55	16 51	16 55	17 29	17 24		17 29
Liphook	d		14 00				→		15 00			→			16 00	→		16 34	→		17 00	→			17 34
Liss	d		14 06						15 06						16 06			16 40			17 06				17 40
Petersfield	d	14 01	14 11			14 32		15 01	15 11		15 32		16 01		16 11		16 35	16 45		17 02	17 11		17 35		17 45
Rowlands Castle	d		14 21						15 21						16 21			16 55			17 21				17 55
Havant	a	14 15	14 26			14 49		15 14	15 26		15 49		16 15		16 26		16 49	17 03		17 15	17 26		17 49		18 03
	d	14 16	14 27			14 50		15 16	15 27		15 50		16 16		16 27		16 50	17 04		17 16	17 27		17 50		18 04
Bedhampton	a		14 29						15 29						16 29			17 06			17 29				18 07
Hilsea	a		14 36						15 36						16 36			17 11			17 36				18 12
Fratton	a	14 24	14 40			14 58		15 24	15 40		15 59		16 24		16 40		16 59	17 15		17 24	17 40		17 59		18 16
Portsmouth & Southsea	a	14 28	14 44			15 02		15 28	15 44		16 02		16 28		16 44		17 02	17 20		17 28	17 44		18 02		18 20
Portsmouth Harbour ⛴	a	14 33				15 07		15 33			16 07		16 33		16 49		17 07	17 26		17 35			18 09		18 28

b Previous night, stops to pick up only

Table 156

Mondays to Fridays

until 30 September

London - Guildford, Haslemere and Portsmouth

		SW 1	SW 1 ⚲	SW 1	SW 1	SW 1 ⚲	SW 1	SW 1	SW 1 ⚲
London Waterloo 15 ⊖	d	16 45	17 00		17 15	17 30		17 45	18 00
Clapham Junction 10	d	16u52							
Woking	a	17 11	17 24		17 38	17 54			
	d	17 13	17 25		17 40	17 56			
Worplesdon	d		17 30		17 45	18 00			
Guildford	a	17 20	17 36		17 51	18 06		18 21	18 32
	d	17 22	17 37		17 54	18 08		18 23	18 33
Farncombe	d	17 28			18 00			18 29	
Godalming	d	17 31			18 03	18 15		18 32	18 40
Milford (Surrey)	d	17 35			18 07			18 36	
Witley	d	17 39		←	18 11		←	18 40	
Haslemere 4	a	17 46	17 51	17 46	18 18	18 25	18 18	18 49	18 51
	d	17 56	17 52	17 56	18 31	18 26	18 31	18 56	18 52
Liphook	d	→		18 01	→		18 36	→	
Liss	d			18 07			18 42		
Petersfield	d		18 03	18 12		18 37	18 47		19 03
Rowlands Castle	d			18 22			18 57		
Havant	a		18 19	18 29		18 50	19 02		19 16
	d		18 20	18 30		18 51	19 03		19 17
Bedhampton	a			18 32			19 06		
Hilsea	a			18 39			19 11		
Fratton	a		18 28	18 43		18 59	19 15		19 25
Portsmouth & Southsea	a		18 32	18 46		19 03			19 29
Portsmouth Harbour ⛴	a		18 39			19 10			19 36

		SW 1	SW 1	SW 1	SW 1 ⚲	SW 1	SW 1 ⚲	SW 1	SW 1	SW 1 ⚲
London Waterloo 15 ⊖	d		18 15	18 18	18 30	18 45	19 00		19 15	19 30
Clapham Junction 10	d								19u22	
Woking	a			18 42	18 57	19 13	19 24		19 43	19 54
	d			18 43	18 58	19 14	19 25		19 45	19 55
Worplesdon	d			18 48			19 30			
Guildford	a		18 50	18 54	19 06	19 23	19 36		19 52	20 03
	d		18 51	18 57	19 08	19 24	19 37		19 54	20 04
Farncombe	d			19 03		19 30			20 00	
Godalming	d			19 06	19 14	19 33			20 03	20 11
Milford (Surrey)	d			19 10		19 37			20 07	
Witley	d	←		19 14		19 41		←	20 11	
Haslemere 4	a	18 49	19 05	19 23	19 25	19 49	19 52	19 49	20 18	20 22
	d	18 56	19 06		19 26	19 57	19 53	19 57	20 27	20 22
Liphook	d	19 01	19 11			→		20 02	→	
Liss	d	19 07	19 17					20 08		
Petersfield	d	19 12	19 23		19 37		20 04	20 13		20 33
Rowlands Castle	d	19 22	19 32					20 23		
Havant	a	19 29	19 40		19 50		20 16	20 28		20 48
	d		19 41		19 51		20 17	20 29		20 49
Bedhampton	a		19 44					20 31		
Hilsea	a		19 49					20 37		
Fratton	a		19 55		19 59		20 25	20 41		20 57
Portsmouth & Southsea	a				20 03		20 29	20 44		21 01
Portsmouth Harbour ⛴	a				20 10		20 34	20 52		21 06

		SW 1	SW 1	SW 1 ⚲	SW 1	SW 1
London Waterloo 15 ⊖	d		19 45	20 00		20 15
Clapham Junction 10	d		19u52			20u22
Woking	a		20 11	20 24		20 41
	d		20 13	20 25		20 43
Worplesdon	d		20 18			
Guildford	a		20 23	20 33		20 50
	d		20 25	20 34		20 52
Farncombe	d		20 31	20 40		20 58
Godalming	d		20 34	20 43		21 01
Milford (Surrey)	d		20 38			21 05
Witley	d	←	20 42		←	21 09
Haslemere 4	a	20 18	20 49	20 54	20 49	21 16
	d	20 27	20 59	20 55	20 59	
Liphook	d	20 32	→		21 04	
Liss	d	20 38			21 10	
Petersfield	d	20 43		21 06	21 16	
Rowlands Castle	d	20 53			21 25	
Havant	a	21 00		21 18	21 30	
	d			21 19	21 31	
Bedhampton	a				21 34	
Hilsea	a				21 41	
Fratton	a			21 28	21 45	
Portsmouth & Southsea	a			21 32	21 48	
Portsmouth Harbour ⛴	a			21 37		

		SW 1 ⚲	SW 1	SW 1 ⚲	SW 1	SW 1 ⚲	SW 1	SW 1	SW 1	SW 1	SW 1	SW 1	SW 1
London Waterloo 15 ⊖	d	20 30	20 45	21 00		21 30	21 45	22 00		22 30	22 45	23 15	23 45
Clapham Junction 10	d		20u52				21u52				22u52	23u22	23u52
Woking	a	20 54	21 11	21 24		21 54	22 11	22 24		22 54	23 11	23 41	00 11
	d	20 55	21 13	21 25		21 55	22 13	22 25		22 55	23 13	23 43	00 13
Worplesdon	d		21 18				22 18				23 18		00 18
Guildford	a	21 03	21 23	21 33		22 03	22 23	22 33		23 03	23 23	23 51	00 24
	d	21 04	21 25	21 34		22 04	22 25	22 34		23 04	23 25	23 52	00 25
Farncombe	d		21 31	21 40		22 10	22 31	22 40		23 10	23 31	23 58	00 31
Godalming	d	21 11	21 34	21 43		22 13	22 34	22 43		23 13	23 34	00 02	00 34
Milford (Surrey)	d		21 38				22 38				23 38		00s38
Witley	d		21 42		←		22 42		←		23 42		00s43
Haslemere 4	a	21 21	21 49	21 54	21 49	22 24	22 49	22 54	22 49	23 24	23 49	00 12	00 49
	d	21 22	21 59	21 55	21 59	22 25	22 59	22 55	22 59	23 25	23 50	00 13	00 50
Liphook	d		→		22 04		→		23 04		23 55		00s55
Liss	d				22 10				23 10		00 01		01s01
Petersfield	d	21 33		22 06	22 16	22 36		23 06	23 15	23 36	00 06	00 24	01 06
Rowlands Castle	d				22 25				23 25		00 16		01s16
Havant	a	21 45		22 18	22 30	22 48		23 18	23 30	23 48	00 21	00 36	01 21
	d	21 46		22 19	22 31	22 49		23 19	23 31	23 49	00 22	00 37	01 21
Bedhampton	a				22 34				23 33		00 24		01s24
Hilsea	a				22 39				23 39		00 30		01s29
Fratton	a	21 54		22 28	22 43	22 59		23 28	23 43	23 58	00 34	00 46	01s33
Portsmouth & Southsea	a	21 58		22 32	22 47	23 04		23 32	23 47	00 02	00 38	00 50	01 37
Portsmouth Harbour ⛴	a	22 02		22 37		23 08		23 37		00 07		00 55	

Mondays to Fridays

from 3 October

		SW MX 1	SW MO 1	SW MX 1	SW MO 1	SW MX 1	SW MO 1	SW MX 1	SW MO 1	SW 1	SW 1	SW 1
London Waterloo 15 ⊖	d	22p30	22p30	22p45	23p00	23p15	23p30	23p45	00 50			05 00
Clapham Junction 10	d		22b39	22b52	23b09	23b22	23b39	23b52	00 57			05 11
Woking	a	22p54	23p01	23p11	23p31	23p41	00 01	00 11	01 16			05 51
	d	22p55	23p02	23p13	23p32	23p43	00 03	00 13	01 18			05 53
Worplesdon	d			23p18				00 18				
Guildford	a	23p03	23p10	23p23	23p40	23p51	00 10	00 24	01s26			06 00
	d	23p04	23p12	23p25	23p42	23p52	00 12	00 25			05 15	06 04
Farncombe	d	23p10		23p31	23p48	23p58		00 31				06 10
Godalming	d	23p13		23p34	23p51	00 02		00 34				06 13
Milford (Surrey)	d			23p38	23p55			00s38				06 17
Witley	d			23p42	23p59			00s43				06 21
Haslemere 4	a	23p24	23p26	23p49	00 06	00 12	00 26	00 49			05 29	06 28
	d	23p25	23p27	23p50	00 07	00 13	00 27	00 50			05 30	06 28
Liphook	d			23p55	00 12			00s55			05 35	06 33
Liss	d			00 01	00 18			01s01			05 41	06 39
Petersfield	d	23p36	23p38	00 06	00 23	00 24	00 38	01 06			05 46	06 45
Rowlands Castle	d			00 16	00 33			01s16			05 56	06 54
Havant	a	23p48	23p50	00 21	00 38	00 36	00 50	01 21	02s00		06 01	06 59
	d	23p49	23p51	00 22	00 39	00 37	00 51	01 21		04 40	06 02	07 00
Bedhampton	a			00 24	00 41			01s24		04 42	06 04	07 02
Hilsea	a			00 30				01s29		04 48	06 10	07 08
Fratton	a	23p58	23p59	00 34	00 49	00 46	01 00	01s33	02s10	04 52	06 14	07 12
Portsmouth & Southsea	a	00 02	00 04	00 38	00 53	00 50	01 04	01 37	02s14	04 55	06 18	07 16
Portsmouth Harbour ⛴	a	00 07	00 09		00 58	00 55	01 09		02 19	04 59	06 22	07 20

		SW 1	SW 1	SW 1	SW 1	SW 1 ⚲	SW 1	SW 1	SW 1 ⚲	SW 1	SW 1	SW 1 ⚲
London Waterloo 15 ⊖	d	05 20	06 15	06 45	07 15	07 30		07 45	08 00		08 15	08 30
Clapham Junction 10	d	05 29	06u22	06u52	07u23			07u52			08u22	
Woking	a	06 08	06 41	07 11	07 42	07 54		08 12	08 24		08 42	08 55
	d	06 11	06 43	07 13	07 44	07 55		08 14	08 25		08 44	08 55
Worplesdon	d	06 16	06 48	07 18	07 49			08 19			08 49	
Guildford	a	06 21	06 53	07 23	07 54	08 03		08 24	08 35		08 54	09 05
	d	06 25	06 55	07 25	07 56	08 04		08 26	08 39		08 56	09 07
Farncombe	d	06 31	07 01	07 31	08 02			08 32			09 02	
Godalming	d	06 34	07 04	07 34	08 05	08 11		08 35			09 05	
Milford (Surrey)	d	06 38	07 08	07 38	08 09			08 39			09 09	
Witley	d	06 42	07 12	07 42	08 13		←	08 43		←	09 13	
Haslemere 4	a	06 49	07 19	07 49	08 20	08 24	08 20	08 50	08 54	08 50	09 20	09 24
	d	06 55	07 20	07 53	08 30	08 25	08 30	08 58	08 55	08 58		09 25
Liphook	d	07 00	07 25	07 59	→		08 35	→		09 03		
Liss	d	07 06	07 31	08 05			08 41			09 09		
Petersfield	d	07 11	07 36	08 11		08 36	08 46		09 06	09 15		09 36
Rowlands Castle	d	07 21	07 46	08 21			08 56			09 24		
Havant	a	07 27	07 51	08 26		08 49	09 04		09 19	09 29		09 49
	d	07 28	07 52	08 27		08 50	09 05		09 20	09 30		09 50
Bedhampton	a	07 30	07 54	08 29			09 07			09 32		
Hilsea	a	07 37	08 00	08 35			09 13			09 38		
Fratton	a	07 41	08 04	08 39		08 58	09 17		09 28	09 42		09 59
Portsmouth & Southsea	a	07 46	08 07	08 43		09 02	09 20		09 32	09 46		10 02
Portsmouth Harbour ⛴	a		08 12	08 48		09 07	09 26		09 37			10 07

b Previous night, stops to pick up only

Table 156

Mondays to Fridays

from 3 October

London - Guildford, Haslemere and Portsmouth

		SW 1	SW 1 🍴	SW 1	SW 1	SW 1 🍴		SW 1	SW 1 🍴	SW 1	SW 1	SW 1 🍴	SW 1	SW 1 🍴	SW 1	SW 1		SW 1 🍴	SW 1	SW 1 🍴	SW 1	SW 1	SW 1 🍴	SW 1	SW 1 🍴
London Waterloo 15 ⊖	d	08 45	09 00		09 15	09 30		09 45	10 00		10 15	10 30	10 45	11 00		11 15		11 30	11 45	12 00		12 15	12 30	12 45	13 00
Clapham Junction 10	d	08u52			09u22			09u52			10u22		10u52			11u22			11u52			12u22		12u52	
Woking	a	09 11	09 24		09 42	09 54		10 11	10 24		10 41	10 54	11 11	11 24		11 41		11 54	12 11	12 24		12 41	12 54	13 11	13 24
	d	09 13	09 25		09 43	09 55		10 13	10 25		10 43	10 55	11 13	11 25		11 43		11 55	12 13	12 25		12 43	12 55	13 13	13 25
Worplesdon	d	09 18						10 18					11 18						12 18					13 18	
Guildford	a	09 23	09 33		09 52	10 03		10 23	10 33		10 50	11 03	11 23	11 33		11 50		12 03	12 23	12 33		12 50	13 03	13 23	13 33
	d	09 25	09 34		09 54	10 04		10 25	10 34		10 52	11 04	11 25	11 34		11 52		12 04	12 25	12 34		12 52	13 04	13 25	13 34
Farncombe	d	09 31			10 00			10 31			10 58		11 31			11 58			12 31			12 58		13 31	
Godalming	d	09 34			10 03			10 34			11 01		11 34			12 01			12 34			13 01		13 34	
Milford (Surrey)	d				10 07						11 05					12 05						13 05			
Witley	d			←	10 11					←	11 09				←	12 09					←	13 09			
Haslemere 4	a	09 45	09 49	09 45	10 19	10 22		10 45	10 49	10 45	11 16	11 20	11 45	11 49	11 45	12 16		12 20	12 45	12 49	12 45	13 16	13 20	13 45	13 49
	d	09 55	09 50	09 55		10 23		10 55	10 50	10 55		11 21	11 55	11 50	11 55			12 21	12 55	12 50	12 55		13 21	13 55	13 50
Liphook	d	→		10 00				→		11 00			→		12 00				→		13 00			→	
Liss	d			10 06						11 06					12 06						13 06				
Petersfield	d		10 01	10 11		10 34			11 01	11 11		11 32		12 01	12 11			12 32		13 01	13 11		13 32		14 01
Rowlands Castle	d			10 21						11 21					12 21						13 21				
Havant	a		10 15	10 26		10 49			11 15	11 26		11 49		12 15	12 26			12 49		13 15	13 26		13 49		14 15
	d		10 16	10 27		10 50			11 16	11 27		11 50		12 16	12 27			12 50		13 16	13 27		13 50		14 16
Bedhampton	a			10 29						11 29					12 29						13 29				
Hilsea	a			10 36						11 36					12 36						13 36				
Fratton	a		10 24	10 40		10 59			11 24	11 40		11 59		12 24	12 40			12 59		13 24	13 40		13 59		14 24
Portsmouth & Southsea	a		10 28	10 44		11 02			11 28	11 44		12 02		12 28	12 44			13 02		13 28	13 44		14 02		14 28
Portsmouth Harbour ⛴	a		10 33			11 07			11 33			12 07		12 33				13 07		13 33			14 07		14 33

		SW 1		SW 1	SW 1 🍴	SW 1	SW 1 🍴	SW 1	SW 1	SW 1 🍴	SW 1	SW 1 🍴		SW 1	SW 1	SW 1 🍴	SW 1	SW 1	SW 1 🍴	SW 1	SW 1	SW 1 🍴		SW 1	SW 1
London Waterloo 15 ⊖	d			13 15	13 30	13 45	14 00		14 15	14 30	14 45	15 00			15 15	15 30		15 45	16 00		16 15	16 30			16 45
Clapham Junction 10	d			13u22		13u52			14u22		14u52				15u22			15u52			16u22				16u52
Woking	a			13 41	13 54	14 11	14 24		14 41	14 54	15 11	15 24			15 41	15 54		16 11	16 24		16 41	16 54			17 11
	d			13 43	13 55	14 13	14 25		14 43	14 55	15 13	15 25			15 43	15 55		16 13	16 25		16 43	16 55			17 13
Worplesdon	d					14 18					15 18				15 48						16 48				
Guildford	a			13 50	14 03	14 23	14 33		14 50	15 03	15 23	15 33			15 53	16 03		16 20	16 33		16 53	17 03			17 20
	d			13 52	14 04	14 25	14 34		14 52	15 04	15 25	15 34			15 55	16 04		16 22	16 34		16 55	17 04			17 22
Farncombe	d			13 58		14 31			14 58		15 31				16 01			16 28			17 01				17 28
Godalming	d			14 01		14 34			15 01		15 34				16 04			16 31			17 04				17 31
Milford (Surrey)	d			14 05					15 05						16 08			16 35			17 08				17 35
Witley	d	←		14 09				←	15 09					←	16 12		←	16 39		←	17 12			←	17 39
Haslemere 4	a	13 45		14 16	14 20	14 45	14 49	14 45	15 16	15 20	15 45	15 49		15 45	16 19	16 23	16 19	16 46	16 50	16 46	17 19	17 23		17 19	17 46
	d	13 55			14 21	14 55	14 50	14 55		15 21	15 55	15 50		15 55	16 29	16 24	16 29	16 55	16 51	16 55	17 29	17 24		17 29	17 56
Liphook	d	14 00				→		15 00			→			16 00	→		16 34	→		17 00	→			17 34	→
Liss	d	14 06						15 06						16 06			16 40			17 06				17 40	
Petersfield	d	14 11			14 32		15 01	15 11		15 32		16 01		16 11		16 35	16 45		17 02	17 11		17 35		17 45	
Rowlands Castle	d	14 21						15 21						16 21			16 55			17 21				17 55	
Havant	a	14 26			14 49		15 14	15 26		15 49		16 15		16 26		16 49	17 03		17 15	17 26		17 49		18 03	
	d	14 27			14 50		15 16	15 27		15 50		16 16		16 27		16 50	17 04		17 16	17 27		17 50		18 04	
Bedhampton	a	14 29						15 29						16 29			17 06			17 29				18 07	
Hilsea	a	14 36						15 36						16 36			17 11			17 36				18 12	
Fratton	a	14 40			14 58		15 24	15 40		15 59		16 24		16 40		16 59	17 15		17 24	17 40		17 59		18 16	
Portsmouth & Southsea	a	14 44			15 02		15 28	15 44		16 02		16 28		16 44		17 02	17 20		17 28	17 44		18 02		18 20	
Portsmouth Harbour ⛴	a				15 07		15 33			16 07		16 33		16 49		17 07	17 26		17 35			18 09		18 28	

		SW 1 🍴	SW 1	SW 1	SW 1 🍴	SW 1	SW 1	SW 1 🍴		SW 1	SW 1	SW 1	SW 1 🍴	SW 1	SW 1 🍴	SW 1	SW 1	SW 1 🍴		SW 1	SW 1	SW 1 🍴	SW 1	SW 1	SW 1 🍴
London Waterloo 15 ⊖	d	17 00		17 15	17 30		17 45	18 00			18 15	18 18	18 30	18 45	19 00		19 15	19 30			19 45	20 00		20 15	20 30
Clapham Junction 10	d																19u22				19u52			20u22	
Woking	a	17 24		17 38	17 54							18 42	18 57	19 13	19 24		19 43	19 54			20 11	20 24		20 41	20 54
	d	17 25		17 40	17 56							18 43	18 58	19 14	19 25		19 45	19 55			20 13	20 25		20 43	20 55
Worplesdon	d	17 30		17 45	18 00							18 48			19 30						20 18				
Guildford	a	17 36		17 51	18 06		18 21	18 32			18 50	18 54	19 06	19 23	19 36		19 52	20 03			20 23	20 33		20 50	21 03
	d	17 37		17 54	18 08		18 23	18 33			18 51	18 57	19 08	19 24	19 37		19 54	20 04			20 25	20 34		20 52	21 04
Farncombe	d			18 00			18 29					19 03		19 30			20 00				20 31	20 40		20 58	
Godalming	d			18 03	18 15		18 32	18 40				19 06	19 14	19 33			20 03	20 11			20 34	20 43		21 01	21 11
Milford (Surrey)	d			18 07			18 36					19 10		19 37			20 07				20 38			21 05	
Witley	d		←	18 11		←	18 40			←		19 14		19 41		←	20 11			←	20 42		←	21 09	
Haslemere 4	a	17 51	17 46	18 18	18 25	18 18	18 49	18 51		18 49	19 05	19 23	19 25	19 49	19 52	19 49	20 18	20 22		20 18	20 49	20 54	20 49	21 16	21 21
	d	17 52	17 56	18 31	18 26	18 31	18 56	18 52		18 56	19 06		19 26	19 57	19 53	19 57	20 27	20 22		20 27	20 59	20 55	20 59		21 22
Liphook	d		18 01	→		18 36	→			19 01	19 11			→		20 02	→			20 32	→		21 04		
Liss	d		18 07			18 42				19 07	19 17					20 08				20 38			21 10		
Petersfield	d	18 03	18 12		18 37	18 47		19 03		19 12	19 23		19 37		20 04	20 13		20 33		20 43		21 06	21 16		21 33
Rowlands Castle	d		18 22			18 57				19 22	19 32					20 23				20 53			21 25		
Havant	a	18 19	18 29		18 50	19 02		19 16		19 29	19 40		19 50		20 16	20 28		20 48		21 00		21 18	21 30		21 45
	d	18 20	18 30		18 51	19 03		19 17			19 41		19 51		20 17	20 29		20 49				21 19	21 31		21 46
Bedhampton	a		18 32			19 06					19 44					20 31							21 34		
Hilsea	a		18 39			19 11					19 49					20 37							21 41		
Fratton	a	18 28	18 43		18 59	19 15		19 25			19 55		19 59		20 25	20 41		20 57				21 28	21 45		21 54
Portsmouth & Southsea	a	18 32	18 46		19 03			19 29					20 03		20 29	20 44		21 01				21 32	21 48		21 58
Portsmouth Harbour ⛴	a	18 39			19 10			19 36					20 10		20 34	20 52		21 06				21 37			22 02

Table 156

London - Guildford, Haslemere and Portsmouth

Mondays to Fridays

from 3 October

		SW 1	SW 1 ⚲	SW 1		SW 1 ⚲	SW 1	SW 1	SW 1	SW 1	SW 1	SW 1	SW 1
London Waterloo 15 ⊖	d	20 45	21 00			21 30	21 45	22 00		22 30	22 45	23 15	23 45
Clapham Junction 10	d	20u52					21u52				22u52	23u22	23u52
Woking	a	21 11	21 24			21 54	22 11	22 24		22 54	23 11	23 41	00 11
	d	21 13	21 25			21 55	22 13	22 25		22 55	23 13	23 43	00 13
Worplesdon	d	21 18					22 18				23 18		00 18
Guildford	a	21 23	21 33			22 03	22 23	22 33		23 03	23 23	23 51	00 24
	d	21 25	21 34			22 04	22 25	22 34		23 04	23 25	23 52	00 25
Farncombe	d	21 31	21 40			22 10	22 31	22 40		23 10	23 31	23 58	00 31
Godalming	d	21 34	21 43			22 13	22 34	22 43		23 13	23 34	00 02	00 34
Milford (Surrey)	d	21 38					22 38				23 38		00s38
Witley	d	21 42		←			22 42		←		23 42		00s43
Haslemere 4	a	21 49	21 54	21 49		22 24	22 49	22 54	22 49	23 24	23 49	00 12	00 49
	d	21 59	21 55	21 59		22 25	22 59	22 55	22 59	23 25	23 50	00 13	00 50
Liphook	d	→		22 04			→		23 04		23 55		00s55
Liss	d			22 10					23 10		00 01		01s01
Petersfield	d		22 06	22 16		22 36		23 06	23 15	23 36	00 06	00 24	01 06
Rowlands Castle	d			22 25					23 25		00 16		01s16
Havant	a		22 18	22 30		22 48		23 18	23 30	23 48	00 21	00 36	01 21
	d		22 19	22 31		22 49		23 19	23 31	23 49	00 22	00 37	01 21
Bedhampton	a			22 34					23 33		00 24		01s24
Hilsea	a			22 39					23 39		00 30		01s29
Fratton	a		22 28	22 43		22 59		23 28	23 43	23 58	00 34	00 46	01s33
Portsmouth & Southsea	a		22 32	22 47		23 04		23 32	23 47	00 02	00 38	00 50	01 37
Portsmouth Harbour ⛴	a		22 37			23 08		23 37		00 07		00 55	

Saturdays

until 1 October

		SW 1	SW 1	SW 1	SW 1	SW 1	SW 1	SW 1	SW 1	SW 1		SW 1	SW 1	SW 1	SW 1	SW 1	SW 1	SW 1	SW 1	SW 1		SW 1 ⚲	SW 1	SW 1	SW 1 ⚲
London Waterloo 15 ⊖	d	22p30	22p45	23p15	23p45			05 00	05 20	06 15		06 45	07 15	07 30	07 45	08 00		08 15	08 30	08 45		09 00		09 15	09 30
Clapham Junction 10	d		22b52	23b22	23b52			05 11	05 29	06u22		06u52	07u23		07u52			08u22		08u52				09u22	
Woking	a	22p54	23p11	23p41	00 11			05 51	06 08	06 41		07 11	07 42	07 54	08 11	08 24		08 41	08 54	09 11		09 24		09 41	09 54
	d	22p55	23p13	23p43	00 13			05 53	06 13	06 43		07 13	07 44	07 55	08 13	08 25		08 43	08 55	09 13		09 25		09 43	09 55
Worplesdon	d		23p18		00 18				06 18			07 18			08 18					09 18					
Guildford	a	23p03	23p23	23p51	00 24			06 00	06 23	06 51		07 23	07 51	08 03	08 23	08 33		08 50	09 03	09 23		09 33		09 50	10 03
	d	23p04	23p25	23p52	00 25		05 15	06 02	06 25	06 53		07 25	07 53	08 04	08 25	08 34		08 52	09 04	09 25		09 34		09 52	10 04
Farncombe	d	23p10	23p31	23p58	00 31			06 08	06 31	06 59		07 31	07 59		08 31			08 58		09 31				09 58	
Godalming	d	23p13	23p34	00 02	00 34			06 11	06 34	07 02		07 34	08 02		08 34			09 01		09 34				10 01	
Milford (Surrey)	d		23p38		00s38			06 15		07 06			08 06					09 05						10 05	
Witley	d		23p42		00s43			06 19		07 10			08 10				←	09 09					←	10 09	
Haslemere 4	a	23p24	23p49	00 12	00 49		05 29	06 26	06 44	07 17		07 44	08 17	08 20	08 45	08 49	08 45	09 16	09 20	09 45		09 49	09 45	10 16	10 20
	d	23p25	23p50	00 13	00 50		05 30		06 45			07 45		08 21	08 55	08 50	08 55		09 21	09 55		09 50	09 55		10 21
Liphook	d		23p55		00s55		05 35		06 50			07 50			→		09 00			→			10 00		
Liss	d		00 01		01s01		05 41		06 56			07 56					09 06						10 06		
Petersfield	d	23p36	00 06	00 24	01 06		05 46		07 01			08 01		08 32		09 01	09 11		09 32			10 01	10 11		10 32
Rowlands Castle	d		00 16		01s16		05 56		07 11			08 11					09 21						10 21		
Havant	a	23p48	00 21	00 36	01 21		06 01		07 19			08 16		08 49		09 15	09 26		09 49			10 15	10 26		10 49
	d	23p49	00 22	00 37	01 21	04 40	06 02		07 20			08 17		08 50		09 16	09 27		09 50			10 16	10 27		10 50
Bedhampton	a		00 24		01s24	04 42	06 04		07 22			08 19					09 29						10 29		
Hilsea	a		00 30		01s29	04 48	06 10		07 27			08 25					09 36						10 36		
Fratton	a	23p58	00 34	00 46	01s33	04 52	06 14		07 31			08 29		08 59		09 24	09 40		09 59			10 24	10 40		10 59
Portsmouth & Southsea	a	00 02	00 38	00 50	01 37	04 55	06 18		07 35			08 32		09 02		09 28	09 44		10 02			10 28	10 44		11 02
Portsmouth Harbour ⛴	a	00 07		00 55		05 00	06 22		07 40			08 37		09 07		09 33			10 07			10 33			11 07

		SW 1	SW 1 ⚲	SW 1	SW 1	SW 1 ⚲		SW 1	SW 1 ⚲	SW 1	SW 1	SW 1 ⚲	SW 1	SW 1 ⚲	SW 1	SW 1		SW 1 ⚲	SW 1	SW 1 ⚲	SW 1	SW 1	SW 1 ⚲	SW 1	SW 1 ⚲
London Waterloo 15 ⊖	d	09 45	10 00		10 15	10 30		10 45	11 00		11 15	11 30	11 45	12 00		12 15		12 30	12 45	13 00		13 15	13 30	13 45	14 00
Clapham Junction 10	d	09u52			10u22			10u52			11u22		11u52			12u22			12u52			13u22		13u52	
Woking	a	10 11	10 24		10 41	10 54		11 11	11 24		11 41	11 54	12 11	12 24		12 41		12 54	13 11	13 24		13 41	13 54	14 11	14 24
	d	10 13	10 25		10 43	10 55		11 13	11 25		11 43	11 55	12 13	12 25		12 43		12 55	13 13	13 25		13 43	13 55	14 13	14 25
Worplesdon	d	10 18						11 18					12 18						13 18					14 18	
Guildford	a	10 23	10 33		10 50	11 03		11 23	11 33		11 50	12 03	12 23	12 33		12 50		13 03	13 23	13 33		13 50	14 03	14 23	14 33
	d	10 25	10 34		10 52	11 04		11 25	11 34		11 52	12 04	12 25	12 34		12 52		13 04	13 25	13 34		13 52	14 04	14 25	14 34
Farncombe	d	10 31			10 58			11 31			11 58		12 31			12 58			13 31			13 58		14 31	
Godalming	d	10 34			11 01			11 34			12 01		12 34			13 01			13 34			14 01		14 34	
Milford (Surrey)	d				11 05						12 05					13 05						14 05			
Witley	d			←	11 09					←	12 09				←	13 09					←	14 09			
Haslemere 4	a	10 45	10 49	10 45	11 16	11 20		11 45	11 49	11 45	12 16	12 20	12 45	12 49	12 45	13 16		13 20	13 45	13 49	13 45	14 16	14 20	14 45	14 49
	d	10 55	10 50	10 55		11 21		11 55	11 50	11 55		12 21	12 55	12 50	12 55			13 21	13 55	13 50	13 55		14 21	14 55	14 50
Liphook	d	→		11 00				→		12 00			→		13 00				→		14 00			→	
Liss	d			11 06						12 06					13 06						14 06				
Petersfield	d		11 01	11 11		11 32			12 01	12 11		12 32		13 01	13 11			13 32		14 01	14 11		14 32		15 01
Rowlands Castle	d			11 21						12 21					13 21						14 21				
Havant	a		11 15	11 26		11 49			12 15	12 26		12 49		13 15	13 26			13 49		14 15	14 26		14 49		15 14
	d		11 16	11 27		11 50			12 16	12 27		12 50		13 16	13 27			13 50		14 16	14 27		14 50		15 16
Bedhampton	a			11 29						12 29					13 29						14 29				
Hilsea	a			11 36						12 36					13 36						14 36				
Fratton	a		11 24	11 40		11 59			12 24	12 40		12 59		13 24	13 40			13 59		14 24	14 40		14 59		15 24
Portsmouth & Southsea	a		11 28	11 44		12 02			12 28	12 44		13 02		13 28	13 44			14 02		14 28	14 44		15 02		15 28
Portsmouth Harbour ⛴	a		11 33			12 07			12 33			13 07		13 33				14 07		14 33			15 07		15 33

b Previous night, stops to pick up only

London - Guildford, Haslemere and Portsmouth

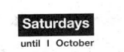

		SW		SW	SW	SW	SW	SW	SW	SW	SW	SW		SW	SW	SW	SW	SW	SW	SW	SW	SW		SW	SW
		1		1	1	1	1	1	1	1	1	1		1	1	1	1	1	1	1	1	1		1	1
					🛒		🛒			🛒		🛒				🛒		🛒			🛒			🛒	
London Waterloo 15 ⊖	d			14 15	14 30	14 45	15 00		15 15	15 30	15 45	16 00			16 15	16 30	16 45	17 00		17 15	17 30	17 45		18 00	
Clapham Junction 10	d			14u22		14u52			15u22		15u52				16u22		16u52			17u22		17u52			
Woking	a			14 41	14 54	15 11	15 24		15 41	15 54	16 11	16 24			16 41	16 54	17 11	17 24		17 41	17 54	18 11		18 24	
	d			14 43	14 55	15 13	15 25		15 43	15 55	16 13	16 25			16 43	16 55	17 13	17 25		17 43	17 55	18 13		18 25	
Worplesdon	d					15 18					16 18						17 18					18 18			
Guildford	a			14 50	15 03	15 23	15 33		15 50	16 03	16 23	16 33			16 50	17 03	17 23	17 33		17 50	18 03	18 23		18 33	
	d			14 52	15 04	15 25	15 34		15 52	16 04	16 25	16 34			16 52	17 04	17 25	17 34		17 52	18 04	18 25		18 34	
Farncombe	d			14 58		15 31			15 58		16 31				16 58		17 31			17 58		18 31			
Godalming	d			15 01		15 34			16 01		16 34				17 01		17 34			18 01		18 34			
Milford (Surrey)	d			15 05					16 05						17 05					18 05					
Witley	d	←		15 09				←	16 09					←	17 09				←	18 09					←
Haslemere 4	a	14 45		15 16	15 20	15 45	15 49	15 45	16 16	16 20	16 45	16 49		16 45	17 16	17 20	17 45	17 49	17 45	18 16	18 20	18 45		18 49	18 45
	d	14 55			15 21	15 55	15 50	15 55		16 21	16 55	16 50		16 55		17 21	17 55	17 50	17 55		18 21	18 55		18 50	18 55
Liphook	d	15 00				→		16 00			→			17 00			→		18 00			→			19 00
Liss	d	15 06						16 06						17 06					18 06						19 06
Petersfield	d	15 11			15 32		16 01	16 11		16 32		17 01		17 11		17 32		18 01	18 11		18 32			19 01	19 11
Rowlands Castle	d	15 21						16 21						17 21					18 21						19 21
Havant	a	15 26			15 49		16 15	16 26		16 49		17 15		17 26		17 49		18 15	18 26		18 49			19 15	19 26
	d	15 27			15 50		16 16	16 27		16 50		17 16		17 27		17 50		18 16	18 27		18 50			19 16	19 27
Bedhampton	a	15 29						16 29						17 29					18 29						19 29
Hilsea	a	15 36						16 36						17 36					18 36						19 36
Fratton	a	15 40			15 59		16 24	16 40		16 59		17 24		17 40		17 59		18 24	18 40		18 59			19 24	19 40
Portsmouth & Southsea	a	15 44			16 02		16 28	16 44		17 02		17 28		17 44		18 02		18 28	18 44		19 02			19 28	19 44
Portsmouth Harbour ⛴	a				16 07		16 33			17 07		17 33				18 07		18 33			19 07			19 33	

		SW	SW	SW	SW	SW	SW	SW		SW	SW	SW	SW	SW	SW	SW	SW	SW		SW	SW	SW	SW	SW	SW
		1	1	1	1	1	1	1		1	1	1	1	1	1	1	1	1		1	1	1	1	1	1
			🛒		🛒			🛒																	
London Waterloo 15 ⊖	d	18 15	18 30	18 45	19 00		19 15	19 30		19 45	20 00		20 15	20 30	20 45	21 00		21 30		21 45	22 00		22 30	22 45	23 15
Clapham Junction 10	d	18u22		18u52			19u22			19u52			20u22		20u52					21u52				22u52	23u22
Woking	a	18 41	18 54	19 11	19 24		19 41	19 54		20 11	20 24		20 41	20 54	21 11	21 24		21 54		22 11	22 24		22 54	23 11	23 41
	d	18 43	18 55	19 13	19 25		19 43	19 55		20 13	20 25		20 43	20 55	21 13	21 25		21 55		22 13	22 25		22 55	23 13	23 43
Worplesdon	d			19 18						20 18					21 18					22 18				23 18	
Guildford	a	18 50	19 03	19 23	19 33		19 50	20 03		20 23	20 33		20 50	21 03	21 23	21 33		22 03		22 23	22 33		23 03	23 23	23 51
	d	18 52	19 04	19 25	19 34		19 52	20 04		20 25	20 34		20 52	21 04	21 25	21 34		22 04		22 25	22 34		23 04	23 25	23 52
Farncombe	d	18 58		19 31			19 58			20 31			20 58		21 31	21 40		22 10		22 31	22 40		23 10	23 31	23 58
Godalming	d	19 01		19 34			20 01			20 34			21 01		21 34	21 43		22 13		22 34	22 43		23 13	23 34	00 02
Milford (Surrey)	d	19 05					20 05						21 05		21 38					22 38				23 38	
Witley	d	19 09				←	20 09					←	21 09		21 42		←			22 42		←		23 42	
Haslemere 4	a	19 16	19 20	19 45	19 49	19 45	20 16	20 20		20 45	20 49	20 45	21 16	21 20	21 49	21 54	21 49	22 24		22 49	22 54	22 49	23 24	23 49	00 12
	d		19 21	19 55	19 50	19 55		20 21		20 55	20 50	20 55		21 21	21 59	21 55	21 59	22 25		22 59	22 55	22 59	23 25	23 50	00 13
Liphook	d			→		20 00				→		21 00			→		22 04			→		23 04		23 55	
Liss	d					20 06						21 06					22 10					23 10		00 01	
Petersfield	d		19 32		20 01	20 11		20 32			21 01	21 11		21 32		22 06	22 15	22 36			23 06	23 15	23 36	00 06	00 24
Rowlands Castle	d					20 21						21 21					22 25					23 25		00 16	
Havant	a		19 49		20 15	20 29		20 49			21 15	21 26		21 45		22 18	22 30	22 48			23 18	23 30	23 48	00 21	00 36
	d		19 50		20 16	20 30		20 50			21 16	21 27		21 46		22 19	22 31	22 49			23 19	23 31	23 49	00 22	00 37
Bedhampton	a					20 32						21 29					22 33					23 33		00 24	
Hilsea	a					20 41						21 36					22 41					23 41		00 30	
Fratton	a		19 59		20 24	20 45		20 59			21 24	21 40		21 54		22 28	22 45	22 58			23 28	23 45	23 58	00 34	00 46
Portsmouth & Southsea	a		20 02		20 28	20 48		21 02			21 28	21 43		21 58		22 32	22 49	23 02			23 32	23 48	00 02	00 38	00 50
Portsmouth Harbour ⛴	a		20 07		20 33			21 07			21 33			22 03		22 36	22 53	23 08			23 37	23 53	00 07		00 55

		SW
		1
London Waterloo 15 ⊖	d	23 45
Clapham Junction 10	d	23u52
Woking	a	00 11
	d	00 13
Worplesdon	d	00 18
Guildford	a	00 24
	d	00 25
Farncombe	d	00 31
Godalming	d	00 34
Milford (Surrey)	d	00s38
Witley	d	00s43
Haslemere 4	a	00 49
	d	00 50
Liphook	d	00s55
Liss	d	01s01
Petersfield	d	01 06
Rowlands Castle	d	01s16
Havant	a	01 21
	d	01 21
Bedhampton	a	01s24
Hilsea	a	01s29
Fratton	a	01s33
Portsmouth & Southsea	a	01 37
Portsmouth Harbour ⛴	a	

Table 156

Saturdays
from 8 October

London - Guildford, Haslemere and Portsmouth

		SW 1	SW 1	SW 1	SW 1	SW 1	SW 1	SW 1	SW 1	SW 1		SW 1	SW 1	SW 1	SW 1	SW 1	SW 1	SW 1	SW 1	SW 1		SW 1 🛒	SW 1	SW 1	SW 1 🛒
London Waterloo 15 ⊖	d	22p30	22p45	23p15	23p45			05 00	05 20	06 15		06 45	07 15	07 30	07 45	08 00		08 15	08 30	08 45		09 00		09 15	09 30
Clapham Junction 10	d		22b52	23b22	23b52			05 11	05 29	06u22		06u52	07u23		07u52			08u22		08u52				09u22	
Woking	a	22p54	23p11	23p41	00 11			05 51	06 08	06 41		07 11	07 42	07 54	08 11	08 24		08 41	08 54	09 11		09 24		09 41	09 54
	d	22p55	23p13	23p43	00 13			05 53	06 13	06 43		07 13	07 44	07 55	08 13	08 25		08 43	08 55	09 13		09 25		09 43	09 55
Worplesdon	d		23p18		00 18				06 18			07 18			08 18					09 18					
Guildford	a	23p03	23p23	23p51	00 24			06 00	06 23	06 51		07 23	07 51	08 03	08 23	08 33		08 50	09 03	09 23		09 33		09 50	10 03
	d	23p04	23p25	23p52	00 25		05 15	06 02	06 25	06 53		07 25	07 53	08 04	08 25	08 34		08 52	09 04	09 25		09 34		09 52	10 04
Farncombe	d	23p10	23p31	23p58	00 31			06 08	06 31	06 59		07 31	07 59		08 31			08 58		09 31				09 58	
Godalming	d	23p13	23p34	00 02	00 34			06 11	06 34	07 02		07 34	08 02		08 34			09 01		09 34				10 01	
Milford (Surrey)	d		23p38		00s38			06 15		07 06			08 06					09 05						10 05	
Witley	d		23p42		00s43			06 19		07 10			08 10				←	09 09					←	10 09	
Haslemere 4	a	23p24	23p49	00 12	00 49		05 29	06 26	06 44	07 17		07 44	08 17	08 20	08 45	08 49	08 45	09 16	09 20	09 45		09 49	09 45	10 16	10 20
	d	23p25	23p50	00 13	00 50		05 30		06 45			07 45		08 21	08 55	08 50	08 55		09 21	09 55		09 50	09 55		10 21
Liphook	d		23p55		00s55		05 35		06 50			07 50			→		09 00			→			10 00		
Liss	d		00 01		01s01		05 41		06 56			07 56					09 06						10 06		
Petersfield	d	23p36	00 06	00 24	01 06		05 46		07 01			08 01		08 32		09 01	09 11		09 32			10 01	10 11		10 32
Rowlands Castle	d		00 16		01s16		05 56		07 11			08 11					09 21						10 21		
Havant	a	23p48	00 21	00 36	01 21		06 01		07 19			08 16		08 49		09 15	09 26		09 49			10 15	10 26		10 49
	d	23p49	00 22	00 37	01 21	04 40	06 02		07 20			08 17		08 50		09 16	09 27		09 50			10 16	10 27		10 50
Bedhampton	a		00 24		01s24	04 42	06 04		07 22			08 19					09 29						10 29		
Hilsea	a		00 30		01s29	04 48	06 10		07 27			08 25					09 36						10 36		
Fratton	a	23p58	00 34	00 46	01s33	04 52	06 14		07 31			08 29		08 59		09 24	09 40		09 59			10 24	10 40		10 59
Portsmouth & Southsea	a	00 02	00 38	00 50	01 37	04 55	06 18		07 35			08 32		09 02		09 28	09 44		10 02			10 28	10 44		11 02
Portsmouth Harbour ⛴	a	00 07		00 55		05 00	06 22		07 40			08 37		09 07		09 33			10 07			10 33			11 07

		SW 1	SW 1 🛒	SW 1	SW 1	SW 1 🛒		SW 1	SW 1 🛒	SW 1	SW 1	SW 1 🛒	SW 1	SW 1 🛒	SW 1	SW 1		SW 1 🛒	SW 1	SW 1 🛒	SW 1	SW 1	SW 1 🛒	SW 1	SW 1 🛒
London Waterloo 15 ⊖	d	09 45	10 00		10 15	10 30		10 45	11 00		11 15	11 30	11 45	12 00		12 15		12 30	12 45	13 00		13 15	13 30	13 45	14 00
Clapham Junction 10	d	09u52			10u22			10u52			11u22		11u52			12u22			12u52			13u22		13u52	
Woking	a	10 11	10 24		10 41	10 54		11 11	11 24		11 41	11 54	12 11	12 24		12 41		12 54	13 11	13 24		13 41	13 54	14 11	14 24
	d	10 13	10 25		10 43	10 55		11 13	11 25		11 43	11 55	12 13	12 25		12 43		12 55	13 13	13 25		13 43	13 55	14 13	14 25
Worplesdon	d	10 18						11 18					12 18						13 18					14 18	
Guildford	a	10 23	10 33		10 50	11 03		11 23	11 33		11 50	12 03	12 23	12 33		12 50		13 03	13 23	13 33		13 50	14 03	14 23	14 33
	d	10 25	10 34		10 52	11 04		11 25	11 34		11 52	12 04	12 25	12 34		12 52		13 04	13 25	13 34		13 52	14 04	14 25	14 34
Farncombe	d	10 31			10 58			11 31			11 58		12 31			12 58			13 31			13 58		14 31	
Godalming	d	10 34			11 01			11 34			12 01		12 34			13 01			13 34			14 01		14 34	
Milford (Surrey)	d				11 05						12 05					13 05						14 05			
Witley	d			←	11 09					←	12 09				←	13 09					←	14 09			
Haslemere 4	a	10 45	10 49	10 45	11 16	11 20		11 45	11 49	11 45	12 16	12 20	12 45	12 49	12 45	13 16		13 20	13 45	13 49	13 45	14 16	14 20	14 45	14 49
	d	10 55	10 50	10 55		11 21		11 55	11 50	11 55		12 21	12 55	12 50	12 55			13 21	13 55	13 50	13 55		14 21	14 55	14 50
Liphook	d	→		11 00				→		12 00			→		13 00				→		14 00			→	
Liss	d			11 06						12 06					13 06						14 06				
Petersfield	d		11 01	11 11		11 32			12 01	12 11		12 32		13 01	13 11			13 32		14 01	14 11		14 32		15 01
Rowlands Castle	d			11 21						12 21					13 21						14 21				
Havant	a		11 15	11 26		11 49			12 15	12 26		12 49		13 15	13 26			13 49		14 15	14 26		14 49		15 14
	d		11 16	11 27		11 50			12 16	12 27		12 50		13 16	13 27			13 50		14 16	14 27		14 50		15 16
Bedhampton	a			11 29						12 29					13 29						14 29				
Hilsea	a			11 36						12 36					13 36						14 36				
Fratton	a		11 24	11 40		11 59			12 24	12 40		12 59		13 24	13 40			13 59		14 24	14 40		14 59		15 24
Portsmouth & Southsea	a		11 28	11 44		12 02			12 28	12 44		13 02		13 28	13 44			14 02		14 28	14 44		15 02		15 28
Portsmouth Harbour ⛴	a		11 33			12 07			12 33			13 07		13 33				14 07		14 33			15 07		15 33

		SW 1		SW 1	SW 1 🛒	SW 1	SW 1 🛒	SW 1	SW 1	SW 1 🛒	SW 1	SW 1 🛒		SW 1	SW 1	SW 1 🛒	SW 1	SW 1 🛒	SW 1	SW 1	SW 1 🛒	SW 1		SW 1 🛒	SW 1
London Waterloo 15 ⊖	d			14 15	14 30	14 45	15 00		15 15	15 30	15 45	16 00			16 15	16 30	16 45	17 00		17 15	17 30	17 45		18 00	
Clapham Junction 10	d			14u22		14u52			15u22		15u52				16u22		16u52			17u22		17u52			
Woking	a			14 41	14 54	15 11	15 24		15 41	15 54	16 11	16 24			16 41	16 54	17 11	17 24		17 41	17 54	18 11		18 24	
	d			14 43	14 55	15 13	15 25		15 43	15 55	16 13	16 25			16 43	16 55	17 13	17 25		17 43	17 55	18 13		18 25	
Worplesdon	d					15 18					16 18						17 18					18 18			
Guildford	a			14 50	15 03	15 23	15 33		15 50	16 03	16 23	16 33			16 50	17 03	17 23	17 33		17 50	18 03	18 23		18 33	
	d			14 52	15 04	15 25	15 34		15 52	16 04	16 25	16 34			16 52	17 04	17 25	17 34		17 52	18 04	18 25		18 34	
Farncombe	d			14 58		15 31			15 58		16 31				16 58		17 31			17 58		18 31			
Godalming	d			15 01		15 34			16 01		16 34				17 01		17 34			18 01		18 34			
Milford (Surrey)	d			15 05					16 05						17 05					18 05					
Witley	d	←		15 09				←	16 09					←	17 09				←	18 09					←
Haslemere 4	a	14 45		15 16	15 20	15 45	15 49	15 45	16 16	16 20	16 45	16 49		16 45	17 16	17 20	17 45	17 49	17 45	18 16	18 20	18 45		18 49	18 45
	d	14 55			15 21	15 55	15 50	15 55		16 21	16 55	16 50		16 55		17 21	17 55	17 50	17 55		18 21	18 55		18 50	18 55
Liphook	d	15 00				→		16 00			→			17 00			→		18 00			→			19 00
Liss	d	15 06						16 06						17 06					18 06						19 06
Petersfield	d	15 11			15 32		16 01	16 11		16 32		17 01		17 11		17 32		18 01	18 11		18 32			19 01	19 11
Rowlands Castle	d	15 21						16 21						17 21					18 21						19 21
Havant	a	15 26			15 49		16 15	16 26		16 49		17 15		17 26		17 49		18 15	18 26		18 49			19 15	19 26
	d	15 27			15 50		16 16	16 27		16 50		17 16		17 27		17 50		18 16	18 27		18 50			19 16	19 27
Bedhampton	a	15 29						16 29						17 29					18 29						19 29
Hilsea	a	15 36						16 36						17 36					18 36						19 36
Fratton	a	15 40			15 59		16 24	16 40		16 59		17 24		17 40		17 59		18 24	18 40		18 59			19 24	19 40
Portsmouth & Southsea	a	15 44			16 02		16 28	16 44		17 02		17 28		17 44		18 02		18 28	18 44		19 02			19 28	19 44
Portsmouth Harbour ⛴	a				16 07		16 33			17 07		17 33				18 07		18 33			19 07			19 33	

b Previous night, stops to pick up only

Table 156

Saturdays
from 8 October

London - Guildford, Haslemere and Portsmouth

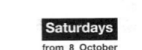

		SW 1	SW 1	SW 1	SW 1	SW 1	SW 1	SW 1	SW 1	SW 1	SW 1	SW 1	SW 1	SW 1	SW 1	SW 1	SW 1	SW 1	SW 1	SW 1	SW 1	SW 1	SW 1
			⊥		⊥			⊥															
London Waterloo 15 ⊖	d	18 15	18 30	18 45	19 00		19 15	19 30	19 45	20 00		20 15	20 30	20 45	21 00		21 30	21 45	22 00		22 30	22 45	23 15
Clapham Junction 10	d	18u22		18u52			19u22		19u52			20u22		20u52				21u52				22u52	23u22
Woking	a	18 41	18 54	19 11	19 24		19 41	19 54	20 11	20 24		20 41	20 54	21 11	21 24		21 54	22 11	22 24		22 54	23 11	23 41
	d	18 43	18 55	19 13	19 25		19 43	19 55	20 13	20 25		20 43	20 55	21 13	21 25		21 55	22 13	22 25		22 55	23 13	23 43
Worplesdon	d			19 18					20 18					21 18				22 18				23 18	
Guildford	a	18 50	19 03	19 23	19 33		19 50	20 03	20 23	20 33		20 50	21 03	21 23	21 33		22 03	22 23	22 33		23 03	23 23	23 51
	d	18 52	19 04	19 25	19 34		19 52	20 04	20 25	20 34		20 52	21 04	21 25	21 34		22 04	22 25	22 34		23 04	23 25	23 52
Farncombe	d	18 58		19 31			19 58		20 31			20 58		21 31	21 40		22 10	22 31	22 40		23 10	23 31	23 58
Godalming	d	19 01		19 34			20 01		20 34			21 01		21 34	21 43		22 13	22 34	22 43		23 13	23 34	00 02
Milford (Surrey)	d	19 05					20 05					21 05		21 38				22 38				23 38	
Witley	d	19 09				←	20 09				←	21 09		21 42		←		22 42		←		23 42	
Haslemere 4	a	19 16	19 20	19 45	19 49	19 45	20 16	20 20	20 45	20 49	20 45	21 16	21 20	21 49	21 54	21 49	22 24	22 49	22 54	22 49	23 24	23 49	00 12
	d		19 21	19 55	19 50	19 55		20 21	20 55	20 50	20 55		21 21	21 59	21 55	21 59	22 25	22 59	22 55	22 59	23 25	23 50	00 13
Liphook	d			→		20 00			→		21 00			→		22 04		→		23 04		23 55	
Liss	d					20 06					21 06					22 10				23 10		00 01	
Petersfield	d		19 32		20 01	20 11		20 32		21 01	21 11		21 32		22 06	22 15	22 36		23 06	23 15	23 36	00 06	00 24
Rowlands Castle	d					20 21					21 21					22 25				23 25		00 16	
Havant	a		19 49		20 15	20 29		20 49		21 15	21 26		21 45		22 18	22 30	22 48		23 18	23 30	23 48	00 21	00 36
	d		19 50		20 16	20 30		20 50		21 16	21 27		21 46		22 19	22 31	22 49		23 19	23 31	23 49	00 22	00 37
Bedhampton	a					20 32					21 29					22 33				23 33		00 24	
Hilsea	a					20 41					21 36					22 41				23 41		00 30	
Fratton	a		19 59		20 24	20 45		20 59		21 24	21 40		21 54		22 28	22 45	22 58		23 28	23 45	23 58	00 34	00 46
Portsmouth & Southsea	a		20 02		20 28	20 48		21 02		21 28	21 43		21 58		22 32	22 49	23 02		23 32	23 48	00 02	00 38	00 50
Portsmouth Harbour ⛴	a		20 07		20 33			21 07		21 33			22 03		22 36	22 53	23 08		23 37	23 53	00 07		00 55

		SW 1
London Waterloo 15 ⊖	d	23 45
Clapham Junction 10	d	23u52
Woking	a	00 11
	d	00 13
Worplesdon	d	00 18
Guildford	a	00 24
	d	00 25
Farncombe	d	00 31
Godalming	d	00 34
Milford (Surrey)	d	00s38
Witley	d	00s43
Haslemere 4	a	00 49
	d	00 50
Liphook	d	00s55
Liss	d	01s01
Petersfield	d	01 06
Rowlands Castle	d	01s16
Havant	a	01 21
	d	01 21
Bedhampton	a	01s24
Hilsea	a	01s29
Fratton	a	01s33
Portsmouth & Southsea	a	01 37
Portsmouth Harbour ⛴	a	

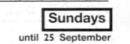

Sundays
until 25 September

		SW 1	SW 1	SW 1	SW 1	SW 1	SW 1	SW 1	SW 1	SW 1	SW 1	SW 1	SW 1	SW 1	SW 1	SW 1	SW 1	SW 1	SW 1	SW 1	SW 1	SW 1	SW 1
		A	A	A	A									⊥		⊥		⊥		⊥		⊥	
London Waterloo 15 ⊖	d	22p30	22p45	23p15	23p45		08 00	08 30	09 00	09 30	10 00	10 30	11 00	11 30	12 00	12 30	13 00	13 30	14 00	14 30	15 00	15 30	16 00
Clapham Junction 10	d	∫	22b52	23b22	23b52		08u09	08u39	09u09	09u39	10u09	10u39	11u09	11u39	12u09	12u39	13u09	13u39	14u09	14u39	15u09	15u39	16u09
Woking	a	22p54	23p11	23p41	00∫11		08 34	09 03	09 34	10 03	10 31	11 01	11 31	12 01	12 31	13 01	13 31	14 01	14 31	15 01	15 31	16 01	16 31
	d	22p55	23p13	23p43	00∫13	07 32	08 35	09 04	09 35	10 04	10 32	11 02	11 32	12 02	12 32	13 02	13 32	14 02	14 32	15 02	15 32	16 02	16 32
Worplesdon	d	∫	23p18	∫	00∫18																		
Guildford	a	23p03	23p23	23p51	00∫24	07 39	08 43	09 12	09 43	10 12	10 40	11 10	11 40	12 10	12 40	13 10	13 40	14 10	14 40	15 10	15 40	16 10	16 40
	d	23p04	23p25	23p52	00∫25	07 41	08 45	09 14	09 45	10 14	10 42	11 12	11 42	12 12	12 42	13 12	13 42	14 12	14 42	15 12	15 42	16 12	16 42
Farncombe	d	23p10	23p31	23p58	00∫31	07 48	08 53		09 53		10 48		11 48		12 48		13 48		14 48		15 48		16 48
Godalming	d	23p13	23p34	00∫02	00∫34	07 51	08 56		09 56		10 51		11 51		12 51		13 51		14 51		15 51		16 51
Milford (Surrey)	d	∫	23p38	∫	00s38	07 55	09 00		10 00		10 55		11 55		12 55		13 55		14 55		15 55		16 55
Witley	d	∫	23p42	∫	00s43	07 59	09 04		10 04		10 59		11 59		12 59		13 59		14 59		15 59		16 59
Haslemere 4	a	23p24	23p49	00∫12	00∫49	08 06	09 11	09 28	10 11	10 28	11 06	11 26	12 06	12 26	13 06	13 26	14 06	14 26	15 06	15 26	16 06	16 26	17 06
	d	23p25	23p50	00∫13	00∫50	08 07	09 12	09 29	10 12	10 29	11 07	11 27	12 07	12 27	13 07	13 27	14 07	14 27	15 07	15 27	16 07	16 27	17 07
Liphook	d	∫	23p55	∫	00s55	08 12	09 17		10 17		11 12		12 12		13 12		14 12		15 12		16 12		17 12
Liss	d	∫	00∫01	∫	01s01	08 18	09 23		10 23		11 18		12 18		13 18		14 18		15 18		16 18		17 18
Petersfield	d	23p36	00∫06	00∫24	01∫06	08 23	09 28	09 40	10 28	10 40	11 23	11 38	12 23	12 38	13 23	13 38	14 23	14 38	15 23	15 38	16 23	16 38	17 23
Rowlands Castle	d	∫	00∫16	∫	01s16	08 33	09 38		10 38		11 33		12 33		13 33		14 33		15 33		16 33		17 33
Havant	a	23p48	00∫21	00∫36	01∫21	08 38	09 44	09 52	10 44	10 52	11 38	11 50	12 38	12 50	13 38	13 50	14 38	14 50	15 38	15 50	16 38	16 50	17 38
	d	23p49	00∫22	00∫37	01∫21	08 39	09 45	09 53	10 45	10 53	11 39	11 51	12 39	12 51	13 39	13 51	14 39	14 51	15 39	15 51	16 39	16 51	17 39
Bedhampton	a	∫	00∫24	∫	01s24	08 41	09 47		10 47		11 41		12 41		13 41		14 41		15 41		16 41		17 41
Hilsea	a	∫	00∫30	∫	01s29																		
Fratton	a	23p58	00∫34	00∫46	01s33	08 49	09 55	10 01	10 55	11 01	11 49	12 00	12 49	13 00	13 49	14 00	14 49	15 00	15 49	16 00	16 49	17 00	17 49
Portsmouth & Southsea	a	00∫02	00∫38	00∫50	01∫37	08 53	09 59	10 06	10 59	11 05	11 53	12 04	12 53	13 04	13 53	14 04	14 53	15 04	15 54	16 04	16 53	17 04	17 53
Portsmouth Harbour ⛴	a	00∫07		00∫55		08 57	10 04	10 11	11 04	11 11	11 58	12 09	12 58	13 11	13 58	14 11	14 58	15 11	15 58	16 11	16 58	17 11	17 58

A not 22 May

b Previous night, stops to pick up only

Table 156

Sundays
until 25 September

London - Guildford, Haslemere and Portsmouth

		SW 1 (trolley)	SW 1	SW 1 (trolley)	SW 1	SW 1 (trolley)	SW 1	SW 1 (trolley)	SW 1	SW 1 (trolley)	SW 1	SW 1	SW 1	SW 1	SW 1	SW 1
London Waterloo 15 ⊖	d	16 30	17 00	17 30	18 00	18 30	19 00	19 30	20 00	20 30	21 00	21 30	22 00	22 30	23 00	23 30
Clapham Junction 10	d	16u39	17u09	17u39	18u09	18u39	19u09	19u39	20u09	20u39	21u09	21u39	22u09	22u39	23u09	23u39
Woking	a	17 01	17 31	18 01	18 31	19 01	19 31	20 01	20 31	21 01	21 31	22 01	22 31	23 01	23 31	00 01
	d	17 02	17 32	18 02	18 32	19 02	19 32	20 02	20 32	21 02	21 32	22 02	22 32	23 02	23 32	00 03
Worplesdon	d															
Guildford	a	17 10	17 40	18 10	18 40	19 10	19 40	20 10	20 40	21 10	21 40	22 10	22 40	23 10	23 40	00 10
	d	17 12	17 42	18 12	18 42	19 12	19 42	20 12	20 42	21 12	21 42	22 12	22 42	23 12	23 42	00 12
Farncombe	d		17 48		18 48		19 48		20 48		21 48		22 48		23 48	
Godalming	d		17 51		18 51		19 51		20 51		21 51		22 51		23 51	
Milford (Surrey)	d		17 55		18 55		19 55		20 55		21 55		22 55		23 55	
Witley	d		17 59		18 59		19 59		20 59		21 59		22 59		23 59	
Haslemere 4	a	17 26	18 06	18 26	19 06	19 26	20 06	20 26	21 06	21 26	22 06	22 26	23 06	23 26	00 06	00 26
	d	17 27	18 07	18 27	19 07	19 27	20 07	20 27	21 07	21 27	22 07	22 27	23 07	23 27	00 07	00 27
Liphook	d		18 12		19 12		20 12		21 12		22 12		23 12		00 12	
Liss	d		18 18		19 18		20 18		21 18		22 18		23 18		00 18	
Petersfield	d	17 38	18 23	18 38	19 23	19 38	20 23	20 38	21 23	21 38	22 23	22 38	23 23	23 38	00 23	00 38
Rowlands Castle	d		18 33		19 33		20 33		21 33		22 33		23 33		00 33	
Havant	a	17 50	18 38	18 50	19 38	19 50	20 38	20 50	21 39	21 50	22 38	22 50	23 38	23 50	00 38	00 50
	d	17 51	18 39	18 51	19 39	19 51	20 39	20 51	21 39	21 51	22 39	22 51	23 39	23 51	00 39	00 51
Bedhampton	a		18 41		19 41		20 41		21 42		22 41		23 41		00 41	
Hilsea	a															
Fratton	a	18 00	18 49	19 00	19 49	20 00	20 49	21 00	21 49	22 00	22 49	23 00	23 49	23 59	00 49	01 00
Portsmouth & Southsea	a	18 04	18 53	19 04	19 53	20 04	20 53	21 04	21 53	22 04	22 53	23 04	23 53	00 04	00 53	01 04
Portsmouth Harbour ⛴	a	18 11	18 58	19 11	19 58	20 11	20 58	21 09	21 58	22 11	22 58	23 09	23 58	00 09	00 58	01 09

Sundays
from 2 October

		SW 1	SW 1	SW 1	SW 1	SW 1	SW 1	SW 1	SW 1	SW 1	SW 1	SW 1	SW 1	SW 1 (trolley)	SW 1	SW 1 (trolley)	SW 1	SW 1 (trolley)	SW 1	SW 1 (trolley)	SW 1	SW 1 (trolley)	SW 1
London Waterloo 15 ⊖	d	22p30	22p45	23p15	23p45		08 00	08 30	09 00	09 30	10 00	10 30	11 00	11 30	12 00	12 30	13 00	13 30	14 00	14 30	15 00	15 30	16 00
Clapham Junction 10	d		22b52	23b22	23b52		08u09	08u39	09u09	09u39	10u09	10u39	11u09	11u39	12u09	12u39	13u09	13u39	14u09	14u39	15u09	15u39	16u09
Woking	a	22p54	23p11	23p41	00 11		08 34	09 03	09 34	10 03	10 31	11 01	11 31	12 01	12 31	13 01	13 31	14 01	14 31	15 01	15 31	16 01	16 31
	d	22p55	23p13	23p43	00 13	07 32	08 35	09 04	09 35	10 04	10 32	11 02	11 32	12 02	12 32	13 02	13 32	14 02	14 32	15 02	15 32	16 02	16 32
Worplesdon	d		23p18		00 18																		
Guildford	a	23p03	23p23	23p51	00 24	07 39	08 43	09 12	09 43	10 12	10 40	11 10	11 40	12 10	12 40	13 10	13 40	14 10	14 40	15 10	15 40	16 10	16 40
	d	23p04	23p25	23p52	00 25	07 41	08 45	09 14	09 45	10 14	10 42	11 12	11 42	12 12	12 42	13 12	13 42	14 12	14 42	15 12	15 42	16 12	16 42
Farncombe	d	23p10	23p31	23p58	00 31	07 48	08 53		09 53		10 48		11 48		12 48		13 48		14 48		15 48		16 48
Godalming	d	23p13	23p34	00 02	00 34	07 51	08 56		09 56		10 51		11 51		12 51		13 51		14 51		15 51		16 51
Milford (Surrey)	d		23p38		00s38	07 55	09 00		10 00		10 55		11 55		12 55		13 55		14 55		15 55		16 55
Witley	d		23p42		00s43	07 59	09 04		10 04		10 59		11 59		12 59		13 59		14 59		15 59		16 59
Haslemere 4	a	23p24	23p49	00 12	00 49	08 06	09 11	09 28	10 11	10 28	11 06	11 26	12 06	12 26	13 06	13 26	14 06	14 26	15 06	15 26	16 06	16 26	17 06
	d	23p25	23p50	00 13	00 50	08 07	09 12	09 29	10 12	10 29	11 07	11 27	12 07	12 27	13 07	13 27	14 07	14 27	15 07	15 27	16 07	16 27	17 07
Liphook	d		23p55		00s55	08 12	09 17		10 17		11 12		12 12		13 12		14 12		15 12		16 12		17 12
Liss	d		00 01		01s01	08 18	09 23		10 23		11 18		12 18		13 18		14 18		15 18		16 18		17 18
Petersfield	d	23p36	00 06	00 24	01 06	08 23	09 28	09 40	10 28	10 40	11 23	11 38	12 23	12 38	13 23	13 38	14 23	14 38	15 23	15 38	16 23	16 38	17 23
Rowlands Castle	d		00 16		01s16	08 33	09 38		10 38		11 33		12 33		13 33		14 33		15 33		16 33		17 33
Havant	a	23p48	00 21	00 36	01 21	08 38	09 44	09 52	10 44	10 52	11 38	11 50	12 38	12 50	13 38	13 50	14 38	14 50	15 38	15 50	16 38	16 50	17 38
	d	23p49	00 22	00 37	01 21	08 39	09 45	09 53	10 45	10 53	11 39	11 51	12 39	12 51	13 39	13 51	14 39	14 51	15 39	15 51	16 39	16 51	17 39
Bedhampton	a		00 24		01s24	08 41	09 47		10 47		11 41		12 41		13 41		14 41		15 41		16 41		17 41
Hilsea	a		00 30		01s29																		
Fratton	a	23p58	00 34	00 46	01s33	08 49	09 55	10 01	10 55	11 01	11 49	12 00	12 49	13 00	13 49	14 00	14 49	15 00	15 49	16 00	16 49	17 00	17 49
Portsmouth & Southsea	a	00 02	00 38	00 50	01 37	08 53	09 59	10 06	10 59	11 05	11 53	12 04	12 53	13 04	13 53	14 04	14 53	15 04	15 54	16 04	16 53	17 04	17 53
Portsmouth Harbour ⛴	a	00 07		00 55		08 57	10 04	10 11	11 04	11 11	11 58	12 09	12 58	13 11	13 58	14 11	14 58	15 11	15 58	16 11	16 58	17 11	17 58

		SW 1 (trolley)	SW 1	SW 1 (trolley)	SW 1	SW 1 (trolley)	SW 1	SW 1 (trolley)	SW 1	SW 1 (trolley)	SW 1	SW 1	SW 1	SW 1	SW 1	SW 1
London Waterloo 15 ⊖	d	16 30	17 00	17 30	18 00	18 30	19 00	19 30	20 00	20 30	21 00	21 30	22 00	22 30	23 00	23 30
Clapham Junction 10	d	16u39	17u09	17u39	18u09	18u39	19u09	19u39	20u09	20u39	21u09	21u39	22u09	22u39	23u09	23u39
Woking	a	17 01	17 31	18 01	18 31	19 01	19 31	20 01	20 31	21 01	21 31	22 01	22 31	23 01	23 31	00 01
	d	17 02	17 32	18 02	18 32	19 02	19 32	20 02	20 32	21 02	21 32	22 02	22 32	23 02	23 32	00 03
Worplesdon	d															
Guildford	a	17 10	17 40	18 10	18 40	19 10	19 40	20 10	20 40	21 10	21 40	22 10	22 40	23 10	23 40	00 10
	d	17 12	17 42	18 12	18 42	19 12	19 42	20 12	20 42	21 12	21 42	22 12	22 42	23 12	23 42	00 12
Farncombe	d		17 48		18 48		19 48		20 48		21 48		22 48		23 48	
Godalming	d		17 51		18 51		19 51		20 51		21 51		22 51		23 51	
Milford (Surrey)	d		17 55		18 55		19 55		20 55		21 55		22 55		23 55	
Witley	d		17 59		18 59		19 59		20 59		21 59		22 59		23 59	
Haslemere 4	a	17 26	18 06	18 26	19 06	19 26	20 06	20 26	21 06	21 26	22 06	22 26	23 06	23 26	00 06	00 26
	d	17 27	18 07	18 27	19 07	19 27	20 07	20 27	21 07	21 27	22 07	22 27	23 07	23 27	00 07	00 27
Liphook	d		18 12		19 12		20 12		21 12		22 12		23 12		00 12	
Liss	d		18 18		19 18		20 18		21 18		22 18		23 18		00 18	
Petersfield	d	17 38	18 23	18 38	19 23	19 38	20 23	20 38	21 23	21 38	22 23	22 38	23 23	23 38	00 23	00 38
Rowlands Castle	d		18 33		19 33		20 33		21 33		22 33		23 33		00 33	
Havant	a	17 50	18 38	18 50	19 38	19 50	20 38	20 50	21 39	21 50	22 38	22 50	23 38	23 50	00 38	00 50
	d	17 51	18 39	18 51	19 39	19 51	20 39	20 51	21 39	21 51	22 39	22 51	23 39	23 51	00 39	00 51
Bedhampton	a		18 41		19 41		20 41		21 42		22 41		23 41		00 41	
Hilsea	a															
Fratton	a	18 00	18 49	19 00	19 49	20 00	20 49	21 00	21 49	22 00	22 49	23 00	23 49	23 59	00 49	01 00
Portsmouth & Southsea	a	18 04	18 53	19 04	19 53	20 04	20 53	21 04	21 53	22 04	22 53	23 04	23 53	00 04	00 53	01 04
Portsmouth Harbour ⛴	a	18 11	18 58	19 11	19 58	20 11	20 58	21 09	21 58	22 11	22 58	23 09	23 58	00 09	00 58	01 09

b Previous night, stops to pick up only

Table 156

Mondays to Fridays

until 30 September

Portsmouth, Haslemere and Guildford - London

Miles	Station		SW MX 1	SW MO 1	SW MO 1	SW MX 1	SW 1	SW 1	SW 1 (trolley)	SW 1	SW 1		SW 1 (trolley)	SW 1	SW 1	SW 1 (trolley)	SW 1	SW 1	SW 1 (trolley)	SW 1	SW 1		SW 1 (trolley)	SW 1	SW 1 (trolley)
0	**Portsmouth Harbour** ⛴	d	22p18	22p32	22p48	23p19	04 30		05 19		05 50		06 15			06 42		06 55	07 13		07 29		07 45		08 15
0¾	**Portsmouth & Southsea**	d	22p24	22p37	22p53	23p24	04 35		05 24		05 55		06 20			06 47		07 00	07 18		07 33		07 50		08 20
1¾	Fratton	d	22p28	22p41	22p57	23p28	04 39		05 28		05 59		06 24			06 51		07 04	07 22		07 37		07 54		08 24
4	Hilsea	d	22p32			23p32	04 43		05 32		06 03				06 42			07 08			07 41				
7¼	Bedhampton	d	22p37		23p04	23p37	04 48		05 37		06 08				06 47			07 13			07 48				
8	**Havant**	a	22p39	22p49	23p07	23p39	04 50		05 40		06 10		06 33		06 49	06 59		07 15	07 30		07 50		08 03		08 32
—		d	22p40	22p50	23p07	23p40	04 51		05 41		06 11		06 34		06 50	07 00	07 11	07 16	07 32		07 52		08 04		08 34
11¼	Rowlands Castle	d	22p46		23p13	23p46	04 57		05 46		06 16				06 56			07 22			07 57				
19½	Petersfield	d	22p57	23p04	23p24	23p57	05 08		05 57		06 29		06 48		07 07	07 14	07 25	07 33	07 46		08 08		08 18		08 48
23	Liss	d	23p02		23p29	00 02	05 13		06 02		06 34				07 12	07 20		07 38			08 13				
27¾	Liphook	d	23p09		23p36	00 09	05 20		06 09		06 41				07 19	07 27		07 45		←	08 20			←	
31½	**Haslemere** 4	a	23p15	23p16	23p41	00 15	05 25		06 15		06 46		07 01		07 25	07 33	07 38	07 51	07 59	07 51	08 26		08 31	08 26	09 01
—		d	23p15	23p17	23p42	00 15	05 26	06 00	06 16	06 30	06 47		07 02	07 10	07 26	07 35	07 40	08 07	08 00	08 07	08 39		08 32	08 39	09 02
36	Witley	d	23p21		23p48	00 21	05 32	06 06		06 36				07 16			07 46	→		08 13	→			08 45	
38¼	Milford (Surrey)	d	23p25		23p52	00 25	05 36	06 11		06 40				07 21			07 50			08 17				08 49	
40	Godalming	d	23p29		23p56	00 29	05 40	06 15		06 44	06 57			07 25	07 35	07 45	07 54			08 21				08 53	
41	Farncombe	d	23p32		23p59	00 32	05 43	06 18		06 47	07 00			07 28	07 38		07 57			08 25				08 57	
44¼	**Guildford**	a	23p37	23p31	00 04	00 37	05 48	06 23	06 29	06 52	07 06		07 15	07 33	07 43	07 52	08 02		08 13	08 30			08 46	09 02	09 15
—		d	23p39	23p35	00 05		05 50	06 24	06 31	06 53	07 07		07 17	07 34	07 45	07 54	08 03		08 15	08 31			08 54	09 03	09 17
47¾	Worplesdon	d	23p44				05 55	06 30		06 59				07 40	07 50				08 20	08 37					
50½	**Woking**	a	23p49	23p42	00 13		06 00	06 35	06 39	07 03	07 15		07 25		07 54		08 11		08 26	08 41				09 11	09 27
—		d	23p56	23p45			06 01	06 37	06 41	07 05	07 17		07 26		07 56		08 12		08 27	08 43				09 13	09 28
70½	Clapham Junction 10	a	00 19	00 04			06 20	06 58	07 02	07 24										09 03				09 32	
74½	**London Waterloo** 15 ⊖	a	00 33	00 14			06 29	07 08	07 12	07 36	07 45		07 54	08 11	08 24	08 32	08 41		08 55	09 13			09 31	09 43	09 55

Station		SW 1	SW 1 (trolley)	SW 1	SW 1 (trolley)	SW 1	SW 1 (trolley)		SW 1	SW 1 (trolley)	SW 1	SW 1 (trolley)	SW 1	SW 1 (trolley)	SW 1	SW 1 (trolley)	SW 1		SW 1 (trolley)	SW 1	SW 1 (trolley)	SW 1	SW 1 (trolley)	SW 1	SW 1 (trolley)
Portsmouth Harbour ⛴	d		08 45		09 15	09 18	09 45			10 15		10 45		11 15		11 45			12 15		12 45		13 15		13 45
Portsmouth & Southsea	d	08 24	08 50		09 20	09 24	09 50			10 20	10 24	10 50		11 20	11 24	11 50			12 20	12 24	12 50		13 20	13 24	13 50
Fratton	d	08 28	08 54		09 24	09 28	09 54			10 24	10 28	10 54		11 24	11 28	11 54			12 24	12 28	12 54		13 24	13 28	13 54
Hilsea	d	08 32				09 32					10 32				11 32					12 32				13 32	
Bedhampton	d	08 37				09 37					10 37				11 37					12 37				13 37	
Havant	a	08 40	09 03		09 33	09 39	10 03			10 33	10 39	11 03		11 33	11 39	12 03			12 33	12 39	13 03		13 33	13 39	14 03
	d	08 40	09 04		09 34	09 40	10 04			10 34	10 40	11 04		11 34	11 40	12 04			12 34	12 40	13 04		13 34	13 40	14 04
Rowlands Castle	d	08 46				09 46					10 46				11 46					12 46				13 46	
Petersfield	d	08 57	09 18		09 48	09 57	10 18			10 48	10 57	11 18		11 48	11 57	12 18			12 48	12 57	13 18		13 48	13 57	14 18
Liss	d	09 02				10 02					11 02				12 02					13 02				14 02	
Liphook	d	09 09				10 09					11 09				12 09					13 09				14 09	
Haslemere 4	a	09 15	09 31		10 01	10 15	10 31			11 01	11 15	11 31		12 01	12 15	12 31			13 01	13 15	13 31		14 01	14 15	14 31
	d	09 15	09 32	09 39	10 02	10 15	10 32		10 39	11 02	11 15	11 32	11 39	12 02	12 15	12 32	12 39		13 02	13 15	13 32	13 39	14 02	14 15	14 32
Witley	d			09 45					10 45				11 45				12 45					13 45			
Milford (Surrey)	d			09 49					10 49				11 49				12 49					13 49			
Godalming	d	09 25		09 53		10 25			10 53		11 25		11 53		12 25		12 53			13 25		13 53		14 25	
Farncombe	d	09 28		09 56		10 28			10 56		11 28		11 56		12 28		12 56			13 28		13 56		14 28	
Guildford	a	09 33	09 45	10 01	10 15	10 33	10 46		11 01	11 15	11 33	11 45	12 01	12 15	12 33	12 45	13 01		13 15	13 33	13 45	14 01	14 15	14 33	14 45
	d	09 34	09 47	10 02	10 17	10 34	10 47		11 02	11 17	11 34	11 47	12 02	12 17	12 34	12 47	13 02		13 17	13 34	13 47	14 02	14 17	14 34	14 47
Worplesdon	d	09 40				10 40					11 40				12 40					13 40				14 40	
Woking	a	09 44	09 59	10 11	10 25	10 44	10 57		11 11	11 25	11 44	11 57	12 11	12 25	12 44	12 57	13 11		13 25	13 44	13 57	14 11	14 25	14 44	14 57
	d	09 46	09 59	10 12	10 26	10 46	10 59		11 12	11 26	11 46	11 59	12 12	12 26	12 46	12 59	13 12		13 26	13 46	13 59	14 12	14 26	14 46	14 59
Clapham Junction 10	a	10 05		10 31		11 05			11 31		12 05		12 31		13 05		13 31			14 05		14 31		15 05	
London Waterloo 15 ⊖	a	10 13	10 27	10 40	10 51	11 13	11 24		11 40	11 51	12 13	12 23	12 40	12 51	13 13	13 23	13 40		13 51	14 13	14 23	14 40	14 51	15 13	15 23

Station		SW 1	SW 1 (trolley)		SW 1	SW 1 (trolley)	SW 1	SW 1 (trolley)	SW 1	SW 1	SW 1 (trolley)	SW 1 (trolley)	SW 1		SW 1 (trolley)	SW 1 (trolley)	SW 1	SW 1 (trolley)	SW 1 (trolley)	SW 1	SW 1 (trolley)	SW 1	SW 1 (trolley)		SW 1
Portsmouth Harbour ⛴	d		14 15			14 45		15 15			15 45	16 15			16 45	17 15	17 18	17 45	18 15		18 45		19 15		
Portsmouth & Southsea	d		14 20		14 24	14 50		15 20	15 24		15 50	16 20	16 24		16 50	17 20	17 24	17 50	18 20	18 24	18 50		19 20		19 24
Fratton	d		14 24		14 28	14 54		15 24	15 28		15 54	16 24	16 28		16 54	17 24	17 28	17 54	18 24	18 28	18 54		19 24		19 28
Hilsea	d				14 32				15 32				16 32				17 32			18 32					19 32
Bedhampton	d				14 37				15 37				16 37				17 37			18 37					19 37
Havant	a		14 33		14 39	15 03		15 33	15 39		16 03	16 33	16 39		17 03	17 33	17 39	18 03	18 33	18 39	19 03		19 33		19 39
	d		14 34		14 40	15 04		15 34	15 40	15 54	16 04	16 34	16 40		17 04	17 34	17 40	18 04	18 34	18 40	19 04		19 34		19 40
Rowlands Castle	d				14 46				15 46				16 46				17 46			18 46					19 46
Petersfield	d		14 48		14 57	15 18		15 48	15 57	16 10	16 18	16 48	16 57		17 18	17 48	17 57	18 18	18 48	18 57	19 18		19 48		19 57
Liss	d				15 02				16 02		16 23		17 02		17 23		18 02			19 02					20 02
Liphook	d				15 09				16 09		16 30		17 09		17 30		18 09			19 09					20 09
Haslemere 4	a		15 01		15 15	15 31		16 01	16 15	16 23	16 36	17 01	17 15		17 36	18 01	18 15	18 31	19 01	19 15	19 31		20 01		20 15
	d	14 39	15 02		15 15	15 32	15 37	16 02	16 15	16 24	16 37	17 02	17 15		17 37	18 02	18 15	18 32	19 02	19 15	19 32	19 39	20 02		20 15
Witley	d	14 45					15 43			16 30	16 43				17 43			18 38				19 45			20 21
Milford (Surrey)	d	14 49					15 47			16 34	16 47				17 47			18 42				19 49			20 25
Godalming	d	14 53			15 25		15 51		16 25	16 38	16 51		17 25		17 51		18 25	18 46	19 11	19 25		19 53			20 29
Farncombe	d	14 56			15 28		15 54		16 28	16 41	16 54		17 28		17 54		18 28	18 49	19 14	19 28		19 56			20 32
Guildford	a	15 01	15 15		15 33	15 45	15 59	16 15	16 33	16 46	16 59	17 15	17 33		17 59	18 15	18 33	18 54	19 19	19 33	19 45	20 01	20 15		20 37
	d	15 02	15 17		15 34	15 47	16 00	16 17	16 34	16 47	17 00	17 17	17 34		18 00	18 17	18 34	18 55	19 21	19 34	19 47	20 02	20 17		20 39
Worplesdon	d				15 40		16 06		16 40		17 06		17 40		18 06		18 40			19 40					20 44
Woking	a	15 11	15 25		15 44	15 57	16 11	16 25	16 44	16 57	17 11	17 25	17 44		18 11		18 44	19 03	19 28	19 45	19 57	20 11	20 25		20 52
	d	15 12	15 26		15 46	15 59	16 12	16 26	16 46	16 59	17 12	17 26	17 46		18 12		18 46	19 05	19 30	19 46	19 59	20 12	20 26		20 53
Clapham Junction 10	a	15 31			16 05		16 31		17 05		17 31		18 05		18 31		19 05			20 05		20 31			21 12
London Waterloo 15 ⊖	a	15 43	15 51		16 13	16 24	16 40	16 51	17 14	17 27	17 43	17 54	18 14		18 43	18 59	19 13	19 29	19 59	20 14	20 24	20 40	20 50		21 21

Table 156

Mondays to Fridays

until 30 September

Portsmouth, Haslemere and Guildford - London

		SW 1	SW 1	SW 1	SW 1	SW 1	SW 1	SW FO 1	SW FX 1	SW 1	SW 1
Portsmouth Harbour ⛴	d	19 45	20 15	20 18	20 45	21 18	21 28	22 18	22 18	22 28	23 19
Portsmouth & Southsea	d	19 50	20 20	20 24	20 50	21 24	21 33	22 24	22 24	22 33	23 24
Fratton	d	19 54	20 24	20 28	20 54	21 28	21 37	22 28	22 28	22 37	23 28
Hilsea	d			20 32		21 32	21 41	22 32	22 32	22 41	23 32
Bedhampton	d			20 37		21 37	21 47	22 37	22 37	22 46	23 37
Havant	a	20 03	20 33	20 39	21 03	21 40	21 52	22 39	22 39	22 53	23 39
	d	20 04	20 34	20 40	21 04	21 40		22 40	22 40		23 40
Rowlands Castle	d			20 46		21 46		22 46	22 46		23 46
Petersfield	d	20 18	20 48	20 57	21 18	21 57		22 57	22 57		23 57
Liss	d			21 02		22 02		23 02	23 02		00 02
Liphook	d			21 09		22 09		23 09	23 09		00 09
Haslemere 4	a	20 31	21 01	21 15	21 31	22 15		23 15	23 15		00 15
	d	20 32	21 02	21 15	21 32	22 15		23 15	23 15		00 15
Witley	d			21 21		22 21		23 21	23 21		00 21
Milford (Surrey)	d			21 25		22 25		23 25	23 25		00 25
Godalming	d			21 29		22 29		23 29	23 29		00 29
Farncombe	d			21 32		22 32		23 32	23 32		00 32
Guildford	a	20 45	21 16	21 37	21 45	22 37		23 37	23 37		00 37
	d	20 47	21 17	21 39	21 47	22 39		23 39	23 39		
Worplesdon	d			21 44		22 44		23 44	23 44		
Woking	a	20 56	21 25	21 49	21 57	22 49		23 49	23 49		
	d	20 59	21 26	21 50	21 59	22 50		23 56	23 56		
Clapham Junction 10	a			22 09		23 09		00 19	00 19		
London Waterloo 15 ⊖	a	21 27	21 50	22 18	22 27	23 19		00 32	00 33		

Mondays to Fridays

from 3 October

		SW MX 1	SW MO 1	SW MO 1	SW MX 1	SW 1	SW 1	SW 1 Trolley	SW 1	SW 1
Portsmouth Harbour ⛴	d	22p18	22p32	22p48	23p19	04 25		05 14		05 50
Portsmouth & Southsea	d	22p24	22p37	22p53	23p24	04 30		05 19		05 55
Fratton	d	22p28	22p41	22p57	23p28	04 34		05 23		05 59
Hilsea	d	22p32			23p32	04 38		05 27		06 03
Bedhampton	d	22p37		23p04	23p37	04 43		05 32		06 08
Havant	a	22p39	22p49	23p07	23p39	04 45		05 35		06 10
	d	22p40	22p50	23p07	23p40	04 46		05 36		06 11
Rowlands Castle	d	22p46		23p13	23p46	04 52		05 41		06 16
Petersfield	d	22p57	23p04	23p24	23p57	05 03		05 52		06 29
Liss	d	23p02		23p29	00 02	05 08		05 57		06 34
Liphook	d	23p09		23p36	00 09	05 15		06 04		06 41
Haslemere 4	a	23p15	23p16	23p41	00 15	05 20		06 10		06 46
	d	23p15	23p17	23p42	00 15	05 21	05 57	06 11	06 27	06 47
Witley	d	23p21		23p48	00 21	05 27	06 03		06 33	
Milford (Surrey)	d	23p25		23p52	00 25	05 31	06 08		06 37	
Godalming	d	23p29		23p56	00 29	05 35	06 12		06 41	06 57
Farncombe	d	23p32		23p59	00 32	05 38	06 15		06 44	07 00
Guildford	a	23p37	23p31	00 04	00 37	05 48	06 23	06 29	06 52	07 06
	d	23p39	23p35	00 05		05 50	06 24	06 31	06 53	07 07
Worplesdon	d	23p44				05 55	06 30		06 59	
Woking	a	23p49	23p42	00 13		06 00	06 35	06 39	07 03	07 15
	d	23p56	23p45			06 01	06 37	06 41	07 05	07 17
Clapham Junction 10	a	00 19	00 04			06 20	06 58	07 02	07 24	
London Waterloo 15 ⊖	a	00 33	00 14			06 29	07 08	07 12	07 36	07 45

		SW 1 Trolley	SW 1	SW 1	SW 1 Trolley	SW 1	SW 1	SW 1 Trolley	SW 1	SW 1	SW 1 Trolley	SW 1	SW 1 Trolley	SW 1
Portsmouth Harbour ⛴	d	06 15			06 42		06 55	07 13		07 29	07 45		08 15	
Portsmouth & Southsea	d	06 20			06 47		07 00	07 18		07 33	07 50		08 20	08 24
Fratton	d	06 24			06 51		07 04	07 22		07 37	07 54		08 24	08 28
Hilsea	d			06 42			07 08			07 41				08 32
Bedhampton	d			06 47			07 13			07 48				08 37
Havant	a	06 33		06 49	06 59		07 15	07 30		07 50	08 03		08 32	08 40
	d	06 34		06 50	07 00	07 11	07 16	07 32		07 52	08 04		08 34	08 40
Rowlands Castle	d			06 56			07 22			07 57				08 46
Petersfield	d	06 48		07 07	07 14	07 25	07 33	07 46		08 08	08 18		08 48	08 57
Liss	d			07 12	07 20		07 38			08 13				09 02
Liphook	d			07 19	07 27		07 45		←	08 20		←		09 09
Haslemere 4	a	07 01		07 25	07 33	07 38	07 51	07 59	07 51	08 26	08 31	08 26	09 01	09 15
	d	07 02	07 10	07 26	07 35	07 40	08 07	08 00	08 07	08 39	08 32	08 39	09 02	09 15
Witley	d		07 16			07 46	→		08 13	→		08 45		
Milford (Surrey)	d		07 21			07 50			08 17			08 49		
Godalming	d		07 25	07 35	07 45	07 54			08 21			08 53		09 25
Farncombe	d		07 28	07 38		07 57			08 25			08 57		09 28
Guildford	a	07 15	07 33	07 43	07 52	08 02		08 13	08 30		08 46	09 02	09 15	09 33
	d	07 17	07 34	07 45	07 54	08 03		08 15	08 31		08 54	09 03	09 17	09 34
Worplesdon	d		07 40	07 50				08 20	08 37					09 40
Woking	a	07 25		07 54		08 11		08 26	08 41			09 11	09 27	09 44
	d	07 26		07 56		08 12		08 27	08 43			09 13	09 28	09 46
Clapham Junction 10	a								09 03			09 32		10 05
London Waterloo 15 ⊖	a	07 54	08 11	08 24	08 32	08 41		08 55	09 13		09 31	09 43	09 55	10 13

		SW 1 Trolley	SW 1	SW 1 Trolley	SW 1	SW 1 Trolley
Portsmouth Harbour ⛴	d	08 45		09 15	09 18	09 45
Portsmouth & Southsea	d	08 50		09 20	09 24	09 50
Fratton	d	08 54		09 24	09 28	09 54
Hilsea	d				09 32	
Bedhampton	d				09 37	
Havant	a	09 03		09 33	09 39	10 03
	d	09 04		09 34	09 40	10 04
Rowlands Castle	d				09 46	
Petersfield	d	09 18		09 48	09 57	10 18
Liss	d				10 02	
Liphook	d				10 09	
Haslemere 4	a	09 31		10 01	10 15	10 31
	d	09 32	09 39	10 02	10 15	10 32
Witley	d		09 45			
Milford (Surrey)	d		09 49			
Godalming	d		09 53		10 25	
Farncombe	d		09 56		10 28	
Guildford	a	09 45	10 01	10 15	10 33	10 46
	d	09 47	10 02	10 17	10 34	10 47
Worplesdon	d				10 40	
Woking	a	09 59	10 11	10 25	10 44	10 57
	d	09 59	10 12	10 26	10 46	10 59
Clapham Junction 10	a		10 31		11 05	
London Waterloo 15 ⊖	a	10 27	10 40	10 51	11 13	11 24

		SW 1	SW 1 Trolley	SW 1	SW 1 Trolley	SW 1	SW 1 Trolley	SW 1	SW 1 Trolley	SW 1
Portsmouth Harbour ⛴	d		10 15		10 45		11 15		11 45	
Portsmouth & Southsea	d		10 20	10 24	10 50		11 20	11 24	11 50	
Fratton	d		10 24	10 28	10 54		11 24	11 28	11 54	
Hilsea	d			10 32				11 32		
Bedhampton	d			10 37				11 37		
Havant	a		10 33	10 39	11 03		11 33	11 39	12 03	
	d		10 34	10 40	11 04		11 34	11 40	12 04	
Rowlands Castle	d			10 46				11 46		
Petersfield	d		10 48	10 57	11 18		11 48	11 57	12 18	
Liss	d			11 02				12 02		
Liphook	d			11 09				12 09		
Haslemere 4	a		11 01	11 15	11 31		12 01	12 15	12 31	
	d	10 39	11 02	11 15	11 32	11 39	12 02	12 15	12 32	12 39
Witley	d	10 45				11 45				12 45
Milford (Surrey)	d	10 49				11 49				12 49
Godalming	d	10 53		11 25		11 53		12 25		12 53
Farncombe	d	10 56		11 28		11 56		12 28		12 56
Guildford	a	11 01	11 15	11 33	11 45	12 01	12 15	12 33	12 45	13 01
	d	11 02	11 17	11 34	11 47	12 02	12 17	12 34	12 47	13 02
Worplesdon	d			11 40				12 40		
Woking	a	11 11	11 25	11 44	11 57	12 11	12 25	12 44	12 57	13 11
	d	11 12	11 26	11 46	11 59	12 12	12 26	12 46	12 59	13 12
Clapham Junction 10	a	11 31		12 05		12 31		13 05		13 31
London Waterloo 15 ⊖	a	11 40	11 51	12 13	12 23	12 40	12 51	13 13	13 23	13 40

		SW 1 Trolley	SW 1	SW 1 Trolley	SW 1	SW 1 Trolley	SW 1	SW 1 Trolley	SW 1
Portsmouth Harbour ⛴	d	12 15		12 45		13 15		13 45	
Portsmouth & Southsea	d	12 20	12 24	12 50		13 20	13 24	13 50	
Fratton	d	12 24	12 28	12 54		13 24	13 28	13 54	
Hilsea	d		12 32				13 32		
Bedhampton	d		12 37				13 37		
Havant	a	12 33	12 39	13 03		13 33	13 39	14 03	
	d	12 34	12 40	13 04		13 34	13 40	14 04	
Rowlands Castle	d		12 46				13 46		
Petersfield	d	12 48	12 57	13 18		13 48	13 57	14 18	
Liss	d		13 02				14 02		
Liphook	d		13 09				14 09		
Haslemere 4	a	13 01	13 15	13 31		14 01	14 15	14 31	
	d	13 02	13 15	13 32	13 39	14 02	14 15	14 32	14 39
Witley	d				13 45				14 45
Milford (Surrey)	d				13 49				14 49
Godalming	d		13 25		13 53		14 25		14 53
Farncombe	d		13 28		13 56		14 28		14 56
Guildford	a	13 15	13 33	13 45	14 01	14 15	14 33	14 45	15 01
	d	13 17	13 34	13 47	14 02	14 17	14 34	14 47	15 02
Worplesdon	d		13 40				14 40		
Woking	a	13 25	13 44	13 57	14 11	14 25	14 44	14 57	15 11
	d	13 26	13 46	13 59	14 12	14 26	14 46	14 59	15 12
Clapham Junction 10	a		14 05		14 31		15 05		15 31
London Waterloo 15 ⊖	a	13 51	14 13	14 23	14 40	14 51	15 13	15 23	15 43

Table 156

Mondays to Fridays
from 3 October

Portsmouth, Haslemere and Guildford - London

		SW	SW	SW	SW	SW	SW	SW	SW	SW	SW
		1	1	1	1	1	1	1	1	1	1
		🍴		🍴		🍴			🍴	🍴	
Portsmouth Harbour ⛴	d	14 15		14 45		15 15			15 45	16 15	
Portsmouth & Southsea	d	14 20	14 24	14 50		15 20	15 24		15 50	16 20	16 24
Fratton	d	14 24	14 28	14 54		15 24	15 28		15 54	16 24	16 28
Hilsea	d		14 32				15 32				16 32
Bedhampton	d		14 37				15 37				16 37
Havant	a	14 33	14 39	15 03		15 33	15 39		16 03	16 33	16 39
	d	14 34	14 40	15 04		15 34	15 40	15 54	16 04	16 34	16 40
Rowlands Castle	d		14 46				15 46				16 46
Petersfield	d	14 48	14 57	15 18		15 48	15 57	16 10	16 18	16 48	16 57
Liss	d		15 02				16 02		16 23		17 02
Liphook	d		15 09				16 09		16 30		17 09
Haslemere 4	a	15 01	15 15	15 31		16 01	16 15	16 23	16 36	17 01	17 15
	d	15 02	15 15	15 32	15 37	16 02	16 15	16 24	16 37	17 02	17 15
Witley	d				15 43			16 30	16 43		
Milford (Surrey)	d				15 47			16 34	16 47		
Godalming	d		15 25		15 51		16 25	16 38	16 51		17 25
Farncombe	d		15 28		15 54		16 28	16 41	16 54		17 28
Guildford	a	15 15	15 33	15 45	15 59	16 15	16 33	16 46	16 59	17 15	17 33
	d	15 17	15 34	15 47	16 00	16 17	16 34	16 47	17 00	17 17	17 34
Worplesdon	d		15 40		16 06		16 40		17 06		17 40
Woking	a	15 25	15 44	15 57	16 11	16 25	16 44	16 57	17 11	17 25	17 44
	d	15 26	15 46	15 59	16 12	16 26	16 46	16 59	17 12	17 26	17 46
Clapham Junction 10	a		16 05		16 31		17 05		17 31		18 05
London Waterloo 15 ⊖	a	15 51	16 13	16 24	16 40	16 51	17 14	17 27	17 43	17 54	18 14

		SW	SW	SW	SW	SW	SW	SW	SW	SW	SW	SW
		1	1	1	1	1	1	1	1	1	1	1
		🍴	🍴		🍴	🍴		🍴		🍴		
Portsmouth Harbour ⛴	d	16 45	17 15	17 18	17 45	18 15		18 45		19 15		19 45
Portsmouth & Southsea	d	16 50	17 20	17 24	17 50	18 20	18 24	18 50		19 20	19 24	19 50
Fratton	d	16 54	17 24	17 28	17 54	18 24	18 28	18 54		19 24	19 28	19 54
Hilsea	d			17 32			18 32				19 32	
Bedhampton	d			17 37			18 37				19 37	
Havant	a	17 03	17 33	17 39	18 03	18 33	18 39	19 03		19 33	19 39	20 03
	d	17 04	17 34	17 40	18 04	18 34	18 40	19 04		19 34	19 40	20 04
Rowlands Castle	d			17 46			18 46				19 46	
Petersfield	d	17 18	17 48	17 57	18 18	18 48	18 57	19 18		19 48	19 57	20 18
Liss	d	17 23		18 02			19 02				20 02	
Liphook	d	17 30		18 09			19 09				20 09	
Haslemere 4	a	17 36	18 01	18 15	18 31	19 01	19 15	19 31		20 01	20 15	20 31
	d	17 37	18 02	18 15	18 32	19 02	19 15	19 32	19 39	20 02	20 15	20 32
Witley	d	17 43			18 38				19 45		20 21	
Milford (Surrey)	d	17 47			18 42				19 49		20 25	
Godalming	d	17 51		18 25	18 46	19 11	19 25		19 53		20 29	
Farncombe	d	17 54		18 28	18 49	19 14	19 28		19 56		20 32	
Guildford	a	17 59	18 15	18 33	18 54	19 19	19 33	19 45	20 01	20 15	20 37	20 45
	d	18 00	18 17	18 34	18 55	19 21	19 34	19 47	20 02	20 17	20 39	20 47
Worplesdon	d	18 06		18 40			19 40				20 44	
Woking	a	18 11		18 44	19 03	19 28	19 45	19 57	20 11	20 25	20 52	20 56
	d	18 12		18 46	19 05	19 30	19 46	19 59	20 12	20 26	20 53	20 59
Clapham Junction 10	a	18 31		19 05			20 05		20 31		21 12	
London Waterloo 15 ⊖	a	18 43	18 59	19 13	19 29	19 59	20 14	20 24	20 40	20 50	21 21	21 27

		SW	SW	SW	SW	SW	SW FO	SW FX	SW	SW
		1	1	1	1	1	1	1	1	1
Portsmouth Harbour ⛴	d	20 15	20 18	20 45	21 18	21 28	22 18	22 18	22 28	23 19
Portsmouth & Southsea	d	20 20	20 24	20 50	21 24	21 33	22 24	22 24	22 33	23 24
Fratton	d	20 24	20 28	20 54	21 28	21 37	22 28	22 28	22 37	23 28
Hilsea	d		20 32		21 32	21 41	22 32	22 32	22 41	23 32
Bedhampton	d		20 37		21 37	21 47	22 37	22 37	22 46	23 37
Havant	a	20 33	20 39	21 03	21 40	21 52	22 39	22 39	22 53	23 39
	d	20 34	20 40	21 04	21 40		22 40	22 40		23 40
Rowlands Castle	d		20 46		21 46		22 46	22 46		23 46
Petersfield	d	20 48	20 57	21 18	21 57		22 57	22 57		23 57
Liss	d		21 02		22 02		23 02	23 02		00 02
Liphook	d		21 09		22 09		23 09	23 09		00 09
Haslemere 4	a	21 01	21 15	21 31	22 15		23 15	23 15		00 15
	d	21 02	21 15	21 32	22 15		23 15	23 15		00 15
Witley	d		21 21		22 21		23 21	23 21		00 21
Milford (Surrey)	d		21 25		22 25		23 25	23 25		00 25
Godalming	d		21 29		22 29		23 29	23 29		00 29
Farncombe	d		21 32		22 32		23 32	23 32		00 32
Guildford	a	21 16	21 37	21 45	22 37		23 37	23 37		00 37
	d	21 17	21 39	21 47	22 39		23 39	23 39		
Worplesdon	d		21 44		22 44		23 44	23 44		
Woking	a	21 25	21 49	21 57	22 49		23 49	23 49		
	d	21 26	21 50	21 59	22 50		23 56	23 56		
Clapham Junction 10	a		22 09		23 09		00 19	00 19		
London Waterloo 15 ⊖	a	21 50	22 18	22 27	23 19		00 32	00 33		

Saturdays
until 1 October

		SW	SW	SW	SW	SW	SW	SW	SW	SW
		1	1	1	1	1	1	1	1	1
								🍴		🍴
Portsmouth Harbour ⛴	d	22p18	23p19	04 43	05 19		06 19	06 45		07 15
Portsmouth & Southsea	d	22p24	23p24	04 48	05 24		06 24	06 50		07 20
Fratton	d	22p28	23p28	04 52	05 28		06 28	06 54		07 24
Hilsea	d	22p32	23p32	04 56	05 32		06 32			
Bedhampton	d	22p37	23p37	05 01	05 37		06 37			
Havant	a	22p39	23p39	05 03	05 39		06 40	07 03		07 33
	d	22p40	23p40	05 04	05 40		06 41	07 04		07 34
Rowlands Castle	d	22p46	23p46	05 09	05 46		06 46			
Petersfield	d	22p57	23p57	05 20	05 57		06 57	07 18		07 48
Liss	d	23p02	00 02	05 25	06 02		07 02			
Liphook	d	23p09	00 09	05 32	06 09		07 09			
Haslemere 4	a	23p15	00 15	05 38	06 14		07 14	07 31		08 01
	d	23p15	00 15	05 39	06 15	06 39	07 15	07 32	07 39	08 02
Witley	d	23p21	00 21	05 45		06 45			07 45	
Milford (Surrey)	d	23p25	00 25	05 49		06 49			07 49	
Godalming	d	23p29	00 29	05 53	06 25	06 53	07 25		07 53	
Farncombe	d	23p32	00 32	05 56	06 28	06 56	07 28		07 56	
Guildford	a	23p37	00 37	06 01	06 33	07 01	07 33	07 45	08 01	08 15
	d	23p39		06 02	06 34	07 02	07 34	07 47	08 02	08 17
Worplesdon	d	23p44			06 40		07 40			
Woking	a	23p49		06 11	06 44	07 11	07 44	07 57	08 10	08 26
	d	23p56		06 13	06 46	07 12	07 46	07 59	08 13	08 27
Clapham Junction 10	a	00 19		06 32	07 05	07 31	08 05		08 33	
London Waterloo 15 ⊖	a	00 32		06 40	07 13	07 40	08 13	08 23	08 42	08 51

		SW	SW	SW	SW	SW	SW	SW	SW	SW
		1	1	1	1	1	1	1	1	1
			🍴		🍴		🍴		🍴	
Portsmouth Harbour ⛴	d		07 45		08 15		08 45		09 15	
Portsmouth & Southsea	d	07 24	07 50		08 20	08 24	08 50		09 20	09 24
Fratton	d	07 28	07 54		08 24	08 28	08 54		09 24	09 28
Hilsea	d	07 32				08 32				09 32
Bedhampton	d	07 37				08 37				09 37
Havant	a	07 39	08 03		08 33	08 39	09 03		09 33	09 39
	d	07 40	08 04		08 34	08 40	09 04		09 34	09 40
Rowlands Castle	d	07 46				08 46				09 46
Petersfield	d	07 57	08 18		08 48	08 57	09 18		09 48	09 57
Liss	d	08 02				09 02				10 02
Liphook	d	08 09				09 09				10 09
Haslemere 4	a	08 14	08 31		09 01	09 15	09 31		10 01	10 15
	d	08 15	08 32	08 39	09 02	09 15	09 32	09 39	10 02	10 15
Witley	d			08 45				09 45		
Milford (Surrey)	d			08 49				09 49		
Godalming	d	08 25		08 53		09 25		09 53		10 25
Farncombe	d	08 28		08 56		09 28		09 56		10 28
Guildford	a	08 33	08 45	09 01	09 15	09 33	09 45	10 01	10 15	10 33
	d	08 34	08 47	09 02	09 17	09 34	09 47	10 02	10 17	10 34
Worplesdon	d	08 40				09 40				10 40
Woking	a	08 44	08 57	09 11	09 25	09 44	09 57	10 11	10 25	10 44
	d	08 46	08 59	09 12	09 26	09 46	09 59	10 12	10 26	10 46
Clapham Junction 10	a	09 05		09 31		10 05		10 31		11 05
London Waterloo 15 ⊖	a	09 13	09 23	09 40	09 51	10 13	10 23	10 40	10 51	11 13

		SW	SW	SW	SW
		1	1	1	1
		🍴		🍴	
Portsmouth Harbour ⛴	d	09 45		10 15	
Portsmouth & Southsea	d	09 50		10 20	10 24
Fratton	d	09 54		10 24	10 28
Hilsea	d				10 32
Bedhampton	d				10 37
Havant	a	10 03		10 33	10 39
	d	10 04		10 34	10 40
Rowlands Castle	d				10 46
Petersfield	d	10 18		10 48	10 57
Liss	d				11 02
Liphook	d				11 09
Haslemere 4	a	10 31		11 01	11 15
	d	10 32	10 39	11 02	11 15
Witley	d		10 45		
Milford (Surrey)	d		10 49		
Godalming	d		10 53		11 25
Farncombe	d		10 56		11 28
Guildford	a	10 45	11 01	11 15	11 33
	d	10 47	11 02	11 17	11 34
Worplesdon	d				11 40
Woking	a	10 57	11 11	11 25	11 44
	d	10 59	11 12	11 26	11 46
Clapham Junction 10	a		11 31		12 05
London Waterloo 15 ⊖	a	11 23	11 40	11 51	12 13

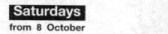

Table 156

Saturdays
until 1 October

Portsmouth, Haslemere and Guildford - London

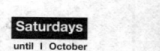

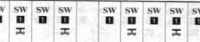

		SW	SW	SW	SW	SW		SW	SW	SW	SW	SW	SW	SW	SW	SW		SW	SW	SW	SW	SW	SW	SW	SW
		1 trolley	1	1 trolley	1	1 trolley		1	1 trolley	1	1 trolley	1	1 trolley	1	1 trolley	1		1 trolley	1	1 trolley	1	1 trolley	1	1 trolley	1
Portsmouth Harbour ⛴	d	10 45		11 15		11 45			12 15		12 45		13 15		13 45			14 15		14 45		15 15		15 45	
Portsmouth & Southsea	d	10 50		11 20	11 24	11 50			12 20	12 24	12 50		13 20	13 24	13 50			14 20	14 24	14 50		15 20	15 24	15 50	
Fratton	d	10 54		11 24	11 28	11 54			12 24	12 28	12 54		13 24	13 28	13 54			14 24	14 28	14 54		15 24	15 28	15 54	
Hilsea	d				11 32					12 32				13 32					14 32				15 32		
Bedhampton	d				11 37					12 37				13 37					14 37				15 37		
Havant	a	11 03		11 33	11 39	12 03			12 33	12 39	13 03		13 33	13 39	14 03			14 33	14 39	15 03		15 33	15 39	16 03	
	d	11 04		11 34	11 40	12 04			12 34	12 40	13 04		13 34	13 40	14 04			14 34	14 40	15 04		15 34	15 40	16 04	
Rowlands Castle	d				11 46					12 46				13 46					14 46				15 46		
Petersfield	d	11 18		11 48	11 57	12 18			12 48	12 57	13 18		13 48	13 57	14 18			14 48	14 57	15 18		15 48	15 57	16 18	
Liss	d				12 02					13 02				14 02					15 02				16 02		
Liphook	d				12 09					13 09				14 09					15 09				16 09		
Haslemere 4	a	11 31		12 01	12 15	12 31			13 01	13 15	13 31		14 01	14 15	14 31			15 01	15 15	15 31		16 01	16 15	16 31	
	d	11 32	11 39	12 02	12 15	12 32		12 39	13 02	13 15	13 32	13 39	14 02	14 15	14 32	14 39		15 02	15 15	15 32	15 39	16 02	16 15	16 32	16 39
Witley	d		11 45					12 45				13 45				14 45					15 45				16 45
Milford (Surrey)	d		11 49					12 49				13 49				14 49					15 49				16 49
Godalming	d		11 53		12 25			12 53		13 25		13 53		14 25		14 53			15 25		15 53		16 25		16 53
Farncombe	d		11 56		12 28			12 56		13 28		13 56		14 28		14 56			15 28		15 56		16 28		16 56
Guildford	a	11 45	12 01	12 15	12 33	12 45		13 01	13 15	13 33	13 45	14 01	14 15	14 33	14 45	15 01		15 15	15 33	15 45	16 01	16 15	16 33	16 45	17 01
	d	11 47	12 02	12 17	12 34	12 47		13 02	13 17	13 34	13 47	14 02	14 17	14 34	14 47	15 02		15 17	15 34	15 47	16 02	16 17	16 34	16 47	17 02
Worplesdon	d				12 40					13 40				14 40					15 40				16 40		
Woking	a	11 57	12 11	12 25	12 44	12 57		13 11	13 25	13 44	13 57	14 11	14 25	14 44	14 57	15 11		15 25	15 44	15 57	16 11	16 25	16 44	16 57	17 11
	d	11 59	12 12	12 26	12 46	12 59		13 12	13 26	13 46	13 59	14 12	14 26	14 46	14 59	15 12		15 26	15 46	15 59	16 12	16 26	16 46	16 59	17 12
Clapham Junction 10	a		12 31		13 05			13 31		14 05		14 31		15 05		15 31			16 05		16 31		17 05		17 31
London Waterloo 15 ⊖	a	12 27	12 43	12 57	13 13	13 27		13 43	13 57	14 14	14 27	14 41	14 57	15 14	15 27	15 41		15 57	16 13	16 23	16 40	16 51	17 13	17 23	17 40

		SW		SW	SW	SW	SW	SW	SW	SW	SW	SW		SW	SW	SW	SW	SW	SW	SW	SW	SW		SW	SW
		1 trolley		1	1 trolley	1	1	1	1 trolley	1	1	1		1	1	1	1	1	1	1	1	1		1	1
Portsmouth Harbour ⛴	d	16 15			16 45			17 18	17 45		18 15			18 45		19 15		19 45	20 15		20 45	21 18		22 18	23 19
Portsmouth & Southsea	d	16 20		16 24	16 50		17 10	17 24	17 50		18 20	18 24		18 50		19 20	19 24	19 50	20 20	20 24	20 50	21 24		22 24	23 24
Fratton	d	16 24		16 28	16 54		17 14	17 28	17 54		18 24	18 28		18 54		19 24	19 28	19 54	20 24	20 28	20 54	21 28		22 28	23 28
Hilsea	d			16 32			17 18	17 32				18 32					19 32			20 32		21 32		22 32	23 32
Bedhampton	d			16 37			17 23	17 37				18 37					19 37			20 37		21 37		22 37	23 37
Havant	a	16 33		16 39	17 03		17 25	17 39	18 03		18 33	18 39		19 03		19 33	19 39	20 03	20 33	20 39	21 03	21 39		22 39	23 39
	d	16 34		16 40	17 04		17 26	17 40	18 04		18 34	18 40		19 04		19 34	19 40	20 04	20 34	20 40	21 04	21 40		22 40	23 40
Rowlands Castle	d			16 46			17 32	17 46				18 46					19 46			20 46		21 46		22 46	23 46
Petersfield	d	16 48		16 57	17 18		17 43	17 57	18 18		18 48	18 57		19 18		19 48	19 57	20 18	20 48	20 57	21 18	21 57		22 57	23 57
Liss	d			17 02			17 48	18 02				19 02					20 02			21 02		22 02		23 02	00 02
Liphook	d			17 09			17 55	18 09				19 09					20 09			21 09		22 09		23 09	00 09
Haslemere 4	a	17 01		17 15	17 31		18 01	18 15	18 31		19 01	19 15		19 31		20 01	20 15	20 31	21 01	21 15	21 31	22 15		23 15	00 15
	d	17 02		17 15	17 32	17 39	18 02	18 15	18 32	18 39	19 02	19 15		19 32	19 39	20 02	20 15	20 32	21 02	21 15	21 32	22 15		23 15	00 15
Witley	d					17 45				18 45					19 45		20 21			21 21		22 21		23 21	00 21
Milford (Surrey)	d					17 49				18 49					19 49		20 25			21 25		22 25		23 25	00 25
Godalming	d			17 25		17 53		18 25		18 53		19 25			19 53		20 29			21 29		22 29		23 29	00 29
Farncombe	d			17 28		17 56		18 28		18 56		19 28			19 56		20 32			21 32		22 32		23 32	00 32
Guildford	a	17 15		17 33	17 45	18 01	18 15	18 33	18 45	19 01	19 15	19 33		19 45	20 01	20 15	20 37	20 45	21 15	21 37	21 47	22 37		23 37	00 37
	d	17 17		17 34	17 47	18 02	18 17	18 34	18 47	19 02	19 17	19 34		19 47	20 02	20 17	20 39	20 47	21 17	21 39	21 49	22 39		23 39	
Worplesdon	d			17 40				18 40				19 40					20 44			21 44		22 44		23 44	
Woking	a	17 25		17 44	17 57	18 11	18 25	18 44	18 57	19 11	19 25	19 44		19 57	20 11	20 25	20 52	20 57	21 25	21 49	21 57	22 49		23 49	
	d	17 26		17 46	17 59	18 12	18 26	18 46	18 59	19 12	19 26	19 46		19 59	20 12	20 26	20 53	20 59	21 26	21 50	21 59	22 50		23 56	
Clapham Junction 10	a			18 05		18 31		19 05		19 31		20 05			20 31		21 12			22 09		23 09		00 18	
London Waterloo 15 ⊖	a	17 51		18 13	18 23	18 40	18 51	19 13	19 23	19 40	19 51	20 13		20 23	20 40	20 50	21 21	21 27	21 50	22 18	22 24	23 18		00 32	

Saturdays
from 8 October

		SW	SW	SW	SW	SW	SW	SW	SW	SW		SW	SW	SW	SW	SW	SW	SW	SW	SW		SW	SW	SW	SW
		1	1	1	1	1	1	1 trolley	1	1 trolley		1	1 trolley	1	1 trolley	1	1 trolley	1	1 trolley	1		1 trolley	1	1 trolley	1
Portsmouth Harbour ⛴	d	22p18	23p19	04 38	05 14		06 19	06 45		07 15			07 45		08 15		08 45		09 15			09 45		10 15	
Portsmouth & Southsea	d	22p24	23p24	04 43	05 19		06 24	06 50		07 20		07 24	07 50		08 20	08 24	08 50		09 20	09 24		09 50		10 20	10 24
Fratton	d	22p28	23p28	04 47	05 23		06 28	06 54		07 24		07 28	07 54		08 24	08 28	08 54		09 24	09 28		09 54		10 24	10 28
Hilsea	d	22p32	23p32	04 51	05 27		06 32					07 32				08 32				09 32					10 32
Bedhampton	d	22p37	23p37	04 56	05 32		06 37					07 37				08 37				09 37					10 37
Havant	a	22p39	23p39	04 58	05 34		06 40	07 03		07 33		07 39	08 03		08 33	08 39	09 03		09 33	09 39		10 03		10 33	10 39
	d	22p40	23p40	04 59	05 35		06 41	07 04		07 34		07 40	08 04		08 34	08 40	09 04		09 34	09 40		10 04		10 34	10 40
Rowlands Castle	d	22p46	23p46	05 04	05 41		06 46					07 46				08 46				09 46					10 46
Petersfield	d	22p57	23p57	05 15	05 52		06 57	07 18		07 48		07 57	08 18		08 48	08 57	09 18		09 48	09 57		10 18		10 48	10 57
Liss	d	23p02	00 02	05 20	05 57		07 02					08 02				09 02				10 02					11 02
Liphook	d	23p09	00 09	05 27	06 04		07 09					08 09				09 09				10 09					11 09
Haslemere 4	a	23p15	00 15	05 33	06 09		07 14	07 31		08 01		08 14	08 31		09 01	09 15	09 31		10 01	10 15		10 31		11 01	11 15
	d	23p15	00 15	05 34	06 10	06 39	07 15	07 32	07 39	08 02		08 15	08 32	08 39	09 02	09 15	09 32	09 39	10 02	10 15		10 32	10 39	11 02	11 15
Witley	d	23p21	00 21	05 40		06 45			07 45					08 45				09 45					10 45		
Milford (Surrey)	d	23p25	00 25	05 44		06 49			07 49					08 49				09 49					10 49		
Godalming	d	23p29	00 29	05 48	06 20	06 53	07 25		07 53			08 25		08 53		09 25		09 53		10 25			10 53		11 25
Farncombe	d	23p32	00 32	05 51	06 23	06 56	07 28		07 56			08 28		08 56		09 28		09 56		10 28			10 56		11 28
Guildford	a	23p37	00 37	06 01	06 33	07 01	07 33	07 45	08 01	08 15		08 33	08 45	09 01	09 15	09 33	09 45	10 01	10 15	10 33		10 45	11 01	11 15	11 33
	d	23p39		06 02	06 34	07 02	07 34	07 47	08 02	08 17		08 34	08 47	09 02	09 17	09 34	09 47	10 02	10 17	10 34		10 47	11 02	11 17	11 34
Worplesdon	d	23p44			06 40		07 40					08 40				09 40				10 40					11 40
Woking	a	23p49		06 11	06 44	07 11	07 44	07 57	08 10	08 26		08 44	08 57	09 11	09 25	09 44	09 57	10 11	10 25	10 44		10 57	11 11	11 25	11 44
	d	23p56		06 13	06 46	07 12	07 46	07 59	08 13	08 27		08 46	08 59	09 12	09 26	09 46	09 59	10 12	10 26	10 46		10 59	11 12	11 26	11 46
Clapham Junction 10	a	00 19		06 32	07 05	07 31	08 05		08 33			09 05		09 31		10 05		10 31		11 05			11 31		12 05
London Waterloo 15 ⊖	a	00 32		06 40	07 13	07 40	08 13	08 23	08 42	08 51		09 13	09 23	09 40	09 51	10 13	10 23	10 40	10 51	11 13		11 23	11 40	11 51	12 13

Table 156

Saturdays
from 8 October

Portsmouth, Haslemere and Guildford - London

		SW	SW	SW	SW	SW	SW	SW	SW	SW	SW	SW	SW	SW	SW	SW	SW	SW	SW	SW	SW	SW	SW
		1	1	1	1	1	1	1	1	1	1	1	1	1	1	1	1	1	1	1	1	1	1
		🛒		🛒		🛒		🛒		🛒		🛒		🛒		🛒		🛒		🛒		🛒	
Portsmouth Harbour ⛴	d	10 45		11 15		11 45		12 15		12 45		13 15		13 45		14 15		14 45		15 15		15 45	
Portsmouth & Southsea	d	10 50		11 20	11 24	11 50		12 20	12 24	12 50		13 20	13 24	13 50		14 20	14 24	14 50		15 20	15 24	15 50	
Fratton	d	10 54		11 24	11 28	11 54		12 24	12 28	12 54		13 24	13 28	13 54		14 24	14 28	14 54		15 24	15 28	15 54	
Hilsea	d				11 32				12 32				13 32				14 32				15 32		
Bedhampton	d				11 37				12 37				13 37				14 37				15 37		
Havant	a	11 03		11 33	11 39	12 03		12 33	12 39	13 03		13 33	13 39	14 03		14 33	14 39	15 03		15 33	15 39	16 03	
	d	11 04		11 34	11 40	12 04		12 34	12 40	13 04		13 34	13 40	14 04		14 34	14 40	15 04		15 34	15 40	16 04	
Rowlands Castle	d				11 46				12 46				13 46				14 46				15 46		
Petersfield	d	11 18		11 48	11 57	12 18		12 48	12 57	13 18		13 48	13 57	14 18		14 48	14 57	15 18		15 48	15 57	16 18	
Liss	d				12 02				13 02				14 02				15 02				16 02		
Liphook	d				12 09				13 09				14 09				15 09				16 09		
Haslemere 4	a	11 31		12 01	12 15	12 31		13 01	13 15	13 31		14 01	14 15	14 31		15 01	15 15	15 31		16 01	16 15	16 31	
	d	11 32	11 39	12 02	12 15	12 32	12 39	13 02	13 15	13 32	13 39	14 02	14 15	14 32	14 39	15 02	15 15	15 32	15 39	16 02	16 15	16 32	16 39
Witley	d		11 45				12 45				13 45				14 45				15 45				16 45
Milford (Surrey)	d		11 49				12 49				13 49				14 49				15 49				16 49
Godalming	d		11 53		12 25		12 53		13 25		13 53		14 25		14 53		15 25		15 53		16 25		16 53
Farncombe	d		11 56		12 28		12 56		13 28		13 56		14 28		14 56		15 28		15 56		16 28		16 56
Guildford	a	11 45	12 01	12 15	12 33	12 45	13 01	13 15	13 33	13 45	14 01	14 15	14 33	14 45	15 01	15 15	15 33	15 45	16 01	16 15	16 33	16 45	17 01
	d	11 47	12 02	12 17	12 34	12 47	13 02	13 17	13 34	13 47	14 02	14 17	14 34	14 47	15 02	15 17	15 34	15 47	16 02	16 17	16 34	16 47	17 02
Worplesdon	d				12 40				13 40				14 40				15 40				16 40		
Woking	a	11 57	12 11	12 25	12 44	12 57	13 11	13 25	13 44	13 57	14 11	14 25	14 44	14 57	15 11	15 25	15 44	15 57	16 11	16 25	16 44	16 57	17 11
	d	11 59	12 12	12 26	12 46	12 59	13 12	13 26	13 46	13 59	14 12	14 26	14 46	14 59	15 12	15 26	15 46	15 59	16 12	16 26	16 46	16 59	17 12
Clapham Junction 10	a		12 31		13 05		13 31		14 05		14 31		15 05		15 31		16 05		16 31		17 05		17 31
London Waterloo 15 ⊖	a	12 27	12 43	12 57	13 13	13 27	13 43	13 57	14 14	14 27	14 41	14 57	15 14	15 27	15 41	15 57	16 13	16 23	16 40	16 51	17 13	17 23	17 40

		SW	SW	SW	SW	SW	SW	SW	SW	SW	SW	SW	SW	SW	SW	SW	SW	SW	SW	SW	SW	SW
		1	1	1	1	1	1	1	1	1	1	1	1	1	1	1	1	1	1	1	1	1
		🛒		🛒				🛒														
Portsmouth Harbour ⛴	d	16 15		16 45			17 18	17 45		18 15		18 45		19 15		19 45	20 15		20 45	21 18	22 18	23 19
Portsmouth & Southsea	d	16 20	16 24	16 50		17 10	17 24	17 50		18 20	18 24	18 50		19 20	19 24	19 50	20 20	20 24	20 50	21 24	22 24	23 24
Fratton	d	16 24	16 28	16 54		17 14	17 28	17 54		18 24	18 28	18 54		19 24	19 28	19 54	20 24	20 28	20 54	21 28	22 28	23 28
Hilsea	d		16 32			17 18	17 32				18 32				19 32			20 32		21 32	22 32	23 32
Bedhampton	d		16 37			17 23	17 37				18 37				19 37			20 37		21 37	22 37	23 37
Havant	a	16 33	16 39	17 03		17 25	17 39	18 03		18 33	18 39	19 03		19 33	19 39	20 03	20 33	20 39	21 03	21 39	22 39	23 39
	d	16 34	16 40	17 04		17 26	17 40	18 04		18 34	18 40	19 04		19 34	19 40	20 04	20 34	20 40	21 04	21 40	22 40	23 40
Rowlands Castle	d		16 46			17 32	17 46				18 46				19 46			20 46		21 46	22 46	23 46
Petersfield	d	16 48	16 57	17 18		17 43	17 57	18 18		18 48	18 57	19 18		19 48	19 57	20 18	20 48	20 57	21 18	21 57	22 57	23 57
Liss	d		17 02			17 48	18 02				19 02				20 02			21 02		22 02	23 02	00 02
Liphook	d		17 09			17 55	18 09				19 09				20 09			21 09		22 09	23 09	00 09
Haslemere 4	a	17 01	17 15	17 31		18 01	18 15	18 31		19 01	19 15	19 31		20 01	20 15	20 31	21 01	21 15	21 31	22 15	23 15	00 15
	d	17 02	17 15	17 32	17 39	18 02	18 15	18 32	18 39	19 02	19 15	19 32	19 39	20 02	20 15	20 32	21 02	21 15	21 32	22 15	23 15	00 15
Witley	d				17 45				18 45				19 45		20 21			21 21		22 21	23 21	00 21
Milford (Surrey)	d				17 49				18 49				19 49		20 25			21 25		22 25	23 25	00 25
Godalming	d		17 25		17 53		18 25		18 53		19 25		19 53		20 29			21 29		22 29	23 29	00 29
Farncombe	d		17 28		17 56		18 28		18 56		19 28		19 56		20 32			21 32		22 32	23 32	00 32
Guildford	a	17 15	17 33	17 45	18 01	18 15	18 33	18 45	19 01	19 15	19 33	19 45	20 01	20 15	20 37	20 45	21 15	21 37	21 47	22 37	23 37	00 37
	d	17 17	17 34	17 47	18 02	18 17	18 34	18 47	19 02	19 17	19 34	19 47	20 02	20 17	20 39	20 47	21 17	21 39	21 49	22 39	23 39	
Worplesdon	d		17 40				18 40				19 40				20 44			21 44		22 44	23 44	
Woking	a	17 25	17 44	17 57	18 11	18 25	18 44	18 57	19 11	19 25	19 44	19 57	20 11	20 25	20 52	20 57	21 25	21 49	21 57	22 49	23 49	
	d	17 26	17 46	17 59	18 12	18 26	18 46	18 59	19 12	19 26	19 46	19 59	20 12	20 26	20 53	20 59	21 26	21 50	21 59	22 50	23 56	
Clapham Junction 10	a		18 05		18 31		19 05		19 31		20 05		20 31		21 12			22 09		23 09	00 18	
London Waterloo 15 ⊖	a	17 51	18 13	18 23	18 40	18 51	19 13	19 23	19 40	19 51	20 13	20 23	20 40	20 50	21 21	21 27	21 50	22 18	22 24	23 18	00 32	

Sundays
until 25 September

		SW	SW	SW	SW	SW	SW	SW	SW	SW	SW	SW	SW	SW	SW	SW	SW	SW	SW	SW	SW	SW	SW
		1	1	1	1	1	1	1	1	1	1	1	1	1	1	1	1	1	1	1	1	1	1
		A	A																				
									🛒		🛒		🛒		🛒		🛒		🛒		🛒		🛒
Portsmouth Harbour ⛴	d	22p18	23p19	06 48	07 32	07 48	08 32	08 48	09 32	09 48	10 32	10 48	11 32	11 48	12 32	12 48	13 32	13 48	14 32	14 48	15 32	15 48	16 32
Portsmouth & Southsea	d	22p24	23p24	06 53	07 37	07 53	08 37	08 53	09 37	09 53	10 37	10 53	11 37	11 53	12 37	12 53	13 37	13 53	14 37	14 53	15 37	15 53	16 37
Fratton	d	22p28	23p28	06 57	07 41	07 57	08 41	08 57	09 41	09 57	10 41	10 57	11 41	11 57	12 41	12 57	13 41	13 57	14 41	14 57	15 41	15 57	16 41
Hilsea	d	22p32	23p32																				
Bedhampton	d	22p37	23p37	07 04		08 04		09 04		10 04		11 04		12 04		13 04		14 04		15 04		16 04	
Havant	a	22p39	23p39	07 07	07 49	08 07	08 49	09 07	09 49	10 07	10 49	11 07	11 49	12 07	12 49	13 07	13 49	14 07	14 49	15 07	15 49	16 07	16 49
	d	22p40	23p40	07 07	07 50	08 07	08 50	09 07	09 50	10 07	10 50	11 07	11 50	12 07	12 50	13 07	13 50	14 07	14 50	15 07	15 50	16 07	16 50
Rowlands Castle	d	22p46	23p46	07 13		08 13		09 13		10 13		11 13		12 13		13 13		14 13		15 13		16 13	
Petersfield	d	22p57	23p57	07 24	08 04	08 24	09 04	09 24	10 04	10 24	11 04	11 24	12 04	12 24	13 04	13 24	14 04	14 24	15 04	15 24	16 04	16 24	17 04
Liss	d	23p02	00 02	07 29		08 29		09 29		10 29		11 29		12 29		13 29		14 29		15 29		16 29	
Liphook	d	23p09	00 09	07 36		08 36		09 36		10 36		11 36		12 36		13 36		14 36		15 36		16 36	
Haslemere 4	a	23p15	00 15	07 41	08 16	08 41	09 16	09 41	10 16	10 41	11 16	11 41	12 16	12 41	13 16	13 41	14 16	14 41	15 16	15 41	16 16	16 41	17 16
	d	23p15	00 15	07 42	08 17	08 42	09 17	09 42	10 17	10 42	11 17	11 42	12 17	12 42	13 17	13 42	14 17	14 42	15 17	15 42	16 17	16 42	17 17
Witley	d	23p21	00 21	07 48		08 48		09 48		10 48		11 48		12 48		13 48		14 48		15 48		16 48	
Milford (Surrey)	d	23p25	00 25	07 52		08 52		09 52		10 52		11 52		12 52		13 52		14 52		15 52		16 52	
Godalming	d	23p29	00 29	07 56		08 56		09 56		10 56		11 56		12 56		13 56		14 56		15 56		16 56	
Farncombe	d	23p32	00 32	07 59		08 59		09 59		10 59		11 59		12 59		13 59		14 59		15 59		16 59	
Guildford	a	23p37	00 37	08 04	08 31	09 04	09 31	10 04	10 31	11 04	11 31	12 04	12 31	13 04	13 31	14 04	14 31	15 04	15 31	16 04	16 31	17 04	17 31
	d	23p39		08 05	08 35	09 05	09 35	10 05	10 35	11 06	11 35	12 06	12 35	13 05	13 35	14 05	14 35	15 05	15 35	16 05	16 35	17 05	17 35
Worplesdon	d	23p44																					
Woking	a	23p49		08 13	08 42	09 15	09 42	10 15	10 42	11 13	11 42	12 13	12 42	13 13	13 42	14 13	14 42	15 13	15 42	16 13	16 42	17 13	17 42
	d	23p56		08 15	08 45	09 15	09 45	10 15	10 45	11 15	11 45	12 15	12 45	13 15	13 45	14 15	14 45	15 15	15 45	16 15	16 45	17 15	17 45
Clapham Junction 10	a	00 18		08 40	09 06	09 38	10 04	10 35	11 04	11 34	12 04	12 34	13 04	13 34	14 04	14 34	15 04	15 34	16 04	16 34	17 04	17 34	18 04
London Waterloo 15 ⊖	a	00 32		08 49	09 19	09 49	10 19	10 49	11 19	11 49	12 19	12 49	13 14	13 44	14 14	14 44	15 14	15 44	16 14	16 44	17 14	17 44	18 14

A not 22 May

Table 156

Portsmouth, Haslemere and Guildford - London

Sundays
until 25 September

		SW 1	SW 1 🚲	SW 1	SW 1 🚲	SW 1		SW 1	SW 1	SW 1	SW 1	SW 1	SW 1	SW 1	SW 1
Portsmouth Harbour ⛴	d	16 48	17 32	17 48	18 32	18 48		19 32	19 48	20 32	20 48	21 32	21 48	22 32	22 48
Portsmouth & Southsea	d	16 53	17 37	17 53	18 37	18 53		19 37	19 53	20 37	20 53	21 37	21 53	22 37	22 53
Fratton	d	16 57	17 41	17 57	18 41	18 57		19 41	19 57	20 41	20 57	21 41	21 57	22 41	22 57
Hilsea	d														
Bedhampton	d	17 04		18 04		19 04			20 04		21 04		22 04		23 04
Havant	a	17 07	17 49	18 07	18 49	19 07		19 49	20 07	20 49	21 07	21 49	22 07	22 49	23 07
	d	17 07	17 50	18 07	18 50	19 07		19 50	20 07	20 50	21 07	21 50	22 07	22 50	23 07
Rowlands Castle	d	17 13		18 13		19 13			20 13		21 13		22 13		23 13
Petersfield	d	17 24	18 04	18 24	19 04	19 24		20 04	20 24	21 04	21 24	22 04	22 24	23 04	23 24
Liss	d	17 29		18 29		19 29			20 29		21 29		22 29		23 29
Liphook	d	17 36		18 36		19 36			20 36		21 36		22 36		23 36
Haslemere 4	a	17 41	18 16	18 41	19 16	19 41		20 16	20 41	21 16	21 41	22 16	22 41	23 16	23 41
	d	17 42	18 17	18 42	19 17	19 42		20 17	20 42	21 17	21 42	22 17	22 42	23 17	23 42
Witley	d	17 48		18 48		19 48			20 48		21 48		22 48		23 48
Milford (Surrey)	d	17 52		18 52		19 52			20 52		21 52		22 52		23 52
Godalming	d	17 56		18 56		19 56			20 56		21 56		22 56		23 56
Farncombe	d	17 59		18 59		19 59			20 59		21 59		22 59		23 59
Guildford	a	18 04	18 31	19 04	19 31	20 04		20 31	21 04	21 31	22 04	22 31	23 04	23 31	00 04
	d	18 05	18 35	19 05	19 35	20 05		20 35	21 05	21 35	22 05	22 35	23 05	23 35	00 05
Worplesdon	d														
Woking	a	18 13	18 42	19 13	19 42	20 13		20 42	21 13	21 42	22 13	22 42	23 13	23 42	00 13
	d	18 15	18 45	19 15	19 45	20 15		20 45	21 15	21 45	22 15	22 45	23 15	23 45	
Clapham Junction 10	a	18 34	19 04	19 34	20 04	20 34		21 04	21 34	22 04	22 34	23 04	23 34	00 04	
London Waterloo 15 ⊖	a	18 44	19 14	19 44	20 14	20 44		21 14	21 44	22 14	22 44	23 14	23 44	00 14	

Sundays
from 2 October

		SW 1	SW 1	SW 1	SW 1	SW 1	SW 1	SW 1	SW 1 🚲	SW 1
Portsmouth Harbour ⛴	d	22p18	23p19	06 43	07 29	07 48	08 29	08 48	09 32	09 48
Portsmouth & Southsea	d	22p24	23p24	06 48	07 34	07 53	08 34	08 53	09 37	09 53
Fratton	d	22p28	23p28	06 52	07 38	07 57	08 38	08 57	09 41	09 57
Hilsea	d	22p32	23p32							
Bedhampton	d	22p37	23p37	06 59		08 04		09 04		10 04
Havant	a	22p39	23p39	07 02	07 46	08 07	08 46	09 07	09 49	10 07
	d	22p40	23p40	07 02	07 47	08 07	08 47	09 07	09 50	10 07
Rowlands Castle	d	22p46	23p46	07 08		08 13		09 13		10 13
Petersfield	d	22p57	23p57	07 19	08 01	08 24	09 01	09 24	10 04	10 24
Liss	d	23p02	00 02	07 24		08 29		09 29		10 29
Liphook	d	23p09	00 09	07 31		08 36		09 36		10 36
Haslemere 4	a	23p15	00 15	07 36	08 13	08 41	09 13	09 41	10 16	10 41
	d	23p15	00 15	07 37	08 14	08 42	09 14	09 42	10 17	10 42
Witley	d	23p21	00 21	07 43		08 48		09 48		10 48
Milford (Surrey)	d	23p25	00 25	07 47		08 52		09 52		10 52
Godalming	d	23p29	00 29	07 51		08 56		09 56		10 56
Farncombe	d	23p32	00 32	07 54		08 59		09 59		10 59
Guildford	a	23p37	00 37	08 04	08 31	09 04	09 31	10 04	10 31	11 04
	d	23p39		08 05	08 35	09 05	09 35	10 05	10 35	11 06
Worplesdon	d	23p44								
Woking	a	23p49		08 13	08 42	09 15	09 42	10 15	10 42	11 13
	d	23p56		08 15	08 45	09 15	09 45	10 15	10 45	11 15
Clapham Junction 10	a	00 18		08 40	09 06	09 38	10 04	10 35	11 04	11 34
London Waterloo 15 ⊖	a	00 32		08 49	09 19	09 49	10 19	10 49	11 19	11 49

		SW 1 🚲	SW 1	SW 1 🚲	SW 1	SW 1 🚲	SW 1	SW 1 🚲	SW 1	SW 1 🚲		SW 1	SW 1 🚲	SW 1	SW 1 🚲
Portsmouth Harbour ⛴	d	10 32	10 48	11 32	11 48	12 32	12 48	13 32	13 48	14 32		14 48	15 32	15 48	16 32
Portsmouth & Southsea	d	10 37	10 53	11 37	11 53	12 37	12 53	13 37	13 53	14 37		14 53	15 37	15 53	16 37
Fratton	d	10 41	10 57	11 41	11 57	12 41	12 57	13 41	13 57	14 41		14 57	15 41	15 57	16 41
Hilsea	d														
Bedhampton	d		11 04		12 04		13 04		14 04			15 04		16 04	
Havant	a	10 49	11 07	11 49	12 07	12 49	13 07	13 49	14 07	14 49		15 07	15 49	16 07	16 49
	d	10 50	11 07	11 50	12 07	12 50	13 07	13 50	14 07	14 50		15 07	15 50	16 07	16 50
Rowlands Castle	d		11 13		12 13		13 13		14 13			15 13		16 13	
Petersfield	d	11 04	11 24	12 04	12 24	13 04	13 24	14 04	14 24	15 04		15 24	16 04	16 24	17 04
Liss	d		11 29		12 29		13 29		14 29			15 29		16 29	
Liphook	d		11 36		12 36		13 36		14 36			15 36		16 36	
Haslemere 4	a	11 16	11 41	12 16	12 41	13 16	13 41	14 16	14 41	15 16		15 41	16 16	16 41	17 16
	d	11 17	11 42	12 17	12 42	13 17	13 42	14 17	14 42	15 17		15 42	16 17	16 42	17 17
Witley	d		11 48		12 48		13 48		14 48			15 48		16 48	
Milford (Surrey)	d		11 52		12 52		13 52		14 52			15 52		16 52	
Godalming	d		11 56		12 56		13 56		14 56			15 56		16 56	
Farncombe	d		11 59		12 59		13 59		14 59			15 59		16 59	
Guildford	a	11 31	12 04	12 31	13 04	13 31	14 04	14 31	15 04	15 31		16 04	16 31	17 04	17 31
	d	11 35	12 06	12 35	13 05	13 35	14 05	14 35	15 05	15 35		16 05	16 35	17 05	17 35
Worplesdon	d														
Woking	a	11 42	12 13	12 42	13 13	13 42	14 13	14 42	15 13	15 42		16 13	16 42	17 13	17 42
	d	11 45	12 15	12 45	13 15	13 45	14 15	14 45	15 15	15 45		16 15	16 45	17 15	17 45
Clapham Junction 10	a	12 04	12 34	13 04	13 34	14 04	14 34	15 04	15 34	16 04		16 34	17 04	17 34	18 04
London Waterloo 15 ⊖	a	12 19	12 49	13 14	13 44	14 14	14 44	15 14	15 44	16 14		16 44	17 14	17 44	18 14

		SW 1	SW 1 🚲	SW 1	SW 1 🚲	SW 1		SW 1	SW 1	SW 1	SW 1	SW 1	SW 1	SW 1	SW 1
Portsmouth Harbour ⛴	d	16 48	17 32	17 48	18 32	18 48		19 32	19 48	20 32	20 48	21 32	21 48	22 32	22 48
Portsmouth & Southsea	d	16 53	17 37	17 53	18 37	18 53		19 37	19 53	20 37	20 53	21 37	21 53	22 37	22 53
Fratton	d	16 57	17 41	17 57	18 41	18 57		19 41	19 57	20 41	20 57	21 41	21 57	22 41	22 57
Hilsea	d														
Bedhampton	d	17 04		18 04		19 04			20 04		21 04		22 04		23 04
Havant	a	17 07	17 49	18 07	18 49	19 07		19 49	20 07	20 49	21 07	21 49	22 07	22 49	23 07
	d	17 07	17 50	18 07	18 50	19 07		19 50	20 07	20 50	21 07	21 50	22 07	22 50	23 07
Rowlands Castle	d	17 13		18 13		19 13			20 13		21 13		22 13		23 13
Petersfield	d	17 24	18 04	18 24	19 04	19 24		20 04	20 24	21 04	21 24	22 04	22 24	23 04	23 24
Liss	d	17 29		18 29		19 29			20 29		21 29		22 29		23 29
Liphook	d	17 36		18 36		19 36			20 36		21 36		22 36		23 36
Haslemere 4	a	17 41	18 16	18 41	19 16	19 41		20 16	20 41	21 16	21 41	22 16	22 41	23 16	23 41
	d	17 42	18 17	18 42	19 17	19 42		20 17	20 42	21 17	21 42	22 17	22 42	23 17	23 42
Witley	d	17 48		18 48		19 48			20 48		21 48		22 48		23 48
Milford (Surrey)	d	17 52		18 52		19 52			20 52		21 52		22 52		23 52
Godalming	d	17 56		18 56		19 56			20 56		21 56		22 56		23 56
Farncombe	d	17 59		18 59		19 59			20 59		21 59		22 59		23 59
Guildford	a	18 04	18 31	19 04	19 31	20 04		20 31	21 04	21 31	22 04	22 31	23 04	23 31	00 04
	d	18 05	18 35	19 05	19 35	20 05		20 35	21 05	21 35	22 05	22 35	23 05	23 35	00 05
Worplesdon	d														
Woking	a	18 13	18 42	19 13	19 42	20 13		20 42	21 13	21 42	22 13	22 42	23 13	23 42	00 13
	d	18 15	18 45	19 15	19 45	20 15		20 45	21 15	21 45	22 15	22 45	23 15	23 45	
Clapham Junction 10	a	18 34	19 04	19 34	20 04	20 34		21 04	21 34	22 04	22 34	23 04	23 34	00 04	
London Waterloo 15 ⊖	a	18 44	19 14	19 44	20 14	20 44		21 14	21 44	22 14	22 44	23 14	23 44	00 14	

Table 157

Mondays to Fridays

until 30 September

Havant - Portsmouth Harbour

(Complete service)

	SW	SW	SW	SW	SW	SW	SW	SW	SW		SW	SW	SW	SN	SN	SW	SN	SW	SN		SW	SW	SW	GW
	MX	MO	MO	MX	MX	MX	MO	MO			MX	MO												
	1	1	1	1	1	1	1	1	1		1	1	1	◇	◇	1	◇1	1	◇1		1	1	1	
Havant d	23p49	23p51			00 22	00 37	00 39	00 51			01 21		04 40	05 21	05 40	06 02	06 13		06 53			07 00		
Bedhampton d					00 25		00 41				01s24		04 43			06 05	06 15		06 56			07 03		
Hilsea d			23p59	00 03	00 30						01s29		04 48			06 10	06 20	06 33	07 01		07 05	07 08	07 13	
Fratton d	23p59	00 01	00 04	00 08	00 34	00 47	00 50	01 01			01s33	02s10	04 52	05 30	05 49	06 15	06 25	06 38	07 05		07 09	07 12	07 17	07 35
Portsmouth & Southsea a	00 02	00 04	00 08	00 11	00 38	00 50	00 53	01 04	01s08		01 37	02s14	04 55	05 33	05 52	06 18	06 28	06 44	07 08		07 12	07 16	07 22	07 38
d	00 03	00 05	00 09	00 13		00 51	00 54	01 05					04 56	05 33	05 52	06 19	06 28	06 45	07 09		07 13	07 17		07 39
Portsmouth Harbour ⛴ a	00 07	00 09	00 13	00 16		00 55	00 58	01 09	01 12			02 19	04 59	05 37	05 56	06 22	06 32	06 49	07 12		07 17	07 20		07 45

	SW	SW	SN	SN	SW		SW	SN	SW	GW	SN	SW	SW	SN	SW		SW	SN	SW	SW	SW	SW	GW	SN
	1	1	◇1	◇1	1		1	◇	1	◇	◇	1	1	◇1	1		1	◇1	1	1	1	1	◇	◇
															⊥					⊥			⊥	
Havant d		07 28	07 35	07 41	07 52			07 58			08 22	08 27		08 44	08 50			09 01	09 05	09 20		09 30		09 33
Bedhampton d		07 31	07 37		07 55			08 00			08 25	08 30							09 08			09 33		09 36
Hilsea d	07 35	07 37	07 42		08 00		08 03	08 05	08 09		08 30	08 35	08 45				09 05		09 13		09 33	09 38		09 42
Fratton d	07 39	07 42	07 47	07 50	08 04		08 07	08 10	08 13	08 21	08 34	08 40	08 49	08 53	08 59		09 10	09 13	09 17	09 29	09 37	09 43	09 42	09 47
Portsmouth & Southsea a	07 42	07 46	07 50	07 53	08 07		08 11	08 15	08 19	08 24	08 37	08 43	08 52	08 56	09 02		09 13	09 17	09 20	09 32	09 42	09 46	09 46	09 50
d	07 43			07 53	08 09		08 13	08 17	08 21	08 25	08 38	08 45	08 54	08 57	09 04		09 14	09 18	09 22	09 34			09 46	
Portsmouth Harbour ⛴ a	07 48			07 58	08 12		08 16	08 20	08 24	08 30	08 41	08 48	08 57	09 02	09 07		09 18	09 21	09 26	09 37			09 55	

	SN		SW	SW	SN	SW	SW	SW	GW	SN	SN		SW	SW	SN	SW	SW	SW	GW	SN	SN		SW	SW
									R															
	◇1		1	1	◇1	1	1	1		◇1	◇1		1	1	◇	1	1	1	◇	◇	◇1		1	1
			⊥			⊥			⊥				⊥			⊥			⊥				⊥	
Havant d	09 46		09 50		10 07	10 16		10 27		10 32	10 46		10 50		11 05	11 16		11 27		11 32	11 46		11 50	
Bedhampton d								10 30		10 34								11 30		11 34				
Hilsea d				10 03			10 33	10 36		10 42				11 03			11 33	11 36		11 42				12 03
Fratton d	09 55		09 59	10 08	10 16	10 25	10 37	10 40	10 42	10 47	10 55		10 59	11 08	11 14	11 25	11 37	11 40	11 42	11 47	11 55		11 59	12 08
Portsmouth & Southsea a	09 58		10 02	10 11	10 19	10 28	10 42	10 44	10 46	10 50	10 58		11 02	11 11	11 17	11 28	11 42	11 44	11 46	11 50	11 58		12 02	12 11
d	09 58		10 04	10 12	10 20	10 29			10 46		10 58		11 04	11 12	11 17	11 29			11 46		11 58		12 04	12 12
Portsmouth Harbour ⛴ a	10 02		10 07	10 18	10 23	10 33			10 54		11 02		11 07	11 18	11 21	11 33			11 54		12 02		12 07	12 18

	SN	SW	SW	SW	GW	SN	SN		SW	SW	SN	SW	SW	SW	GW	SN	SN		SW	SW	SN	SW	SW	SW
	◇	1	1	1	◇	◇	◇1		1	1	◇1	1	1	1	◇	◇	◇1		1	1	◇	1	1	1
		⊥			⊥				⊥			⊥			⊥				⊥			⊥		
Havant d	12 05	12 16		12 27		12 32	12 46		12 50		13 05	13 16		13 27		13 32	13 46		13 50		14 05	14 16		14 27
Bedhampton d				12 30		12 34								13 30		13 34								14 30
Hilsea d			12 33	12 36		12 42				13 03			13 33	13 36		13 42				14 03			14 33	14 36
Fratton d	12 14	12 25	12 37	12 40	12 42	12 47	12 55		12 59	13 08	13 14	13 25	13 37	13 40	13 42	13 47	13 55		13 59	14 08	14 14	14 25	14 37	14 40
Portsmouth & Southsea a	12 17	12 28	12 42	12 44	12 46	12 50	12 58		13 02	13 11	13 17	13 28	13 42	13 44	13 46	13 50	13 58		14 02	14 11	14 17	14 28	14 42	14 44
d	12 17	12 29			12 46		12 58		13 04	13 12	13 17	13 29			13 46		13 58		14 04	14 12	14 17	14 29		
Portsmouth Harbour ⛴ a	12 21	12 33			12 54		13 02		13 07	13 18	13 21	13 33			13 54		14 02		14 07	14 18	14 21	14 33		

	GW	SN	SN		SW	SW	SN	SW	SW	SW	GW	SN	SN		SW	SW	SN	SN	SW	SW	SW	GW	SN	
	◇	◇1	◇1		1	1	◇	1	1	1	◇	◇1	◇1		1	1	◇	◇1	1	1	1	◇	◇	
	⊥				⊥			⊥			⊥				⊥				⊥			⊥		
Havant d		14 32	14 47		14 50		15 05	15 16		15 27		15 32	15 46		15 50		16 02	16 09	16 16		16 27		16 32	
Bedhampton d		14 34								15 30		15 34					16 04				16 30		16 34	
Hilsea d		14 42				15 03			15 33	15 36		15 42				16 03				16 33	16 36		16 42	
Fratton d	14 42	14 47	14 56		14 59	15 08	15 14	15 25	15 37	15 40	15 42	15 47	15 55		15 59	16 08	16 12	16 18	16 25	16 37	16 40	16 42	16 47	
Portsmouth & Southsea a	14 46	14 50	14 59		15 02	15 11	15 17	15 28	15 42	15 44	15 46	15 50	15 58		16 02	16 11	16 15	16 21	16 28	16 40	16 44	16 46	16 50	
d	14 46		14 59		15 04	15 12	15 17	15 29			15 46		15 58		16 04	16 12	16 16	16 22	16 29	16 41	16 45	16 46		
Portsmouth Harbour ⛴ a	14 54		15 03		15 07	15 18	15 21	15 33			15 54		16 02		16 07	16 18	16 21	16 26	16 33	16 44	16 49	16 54		

	SN	SW	SW	SN	SW	SN	SW	SW	SW		SW	GW	SN	SW	SN	SW	SW	SN	SW		SW	SW	SW	SN
	◇1	1	1	◇	1	◇	1	1	1		1	◇	◇1	1	◇1	1	1	◇	1		1	1	1	◇
		⊥					⊥					⊥		⊥					⊥					
Havant d	16 46	16 50		17 00	17 04	17 09	17 16				17 27		17 32	17 50	17 54		18 04	18 13	18 20				18 30	18 34
Bedhampton d				17 02	17 06						17 30		17 34		17 56		18 07						18 33	18 36
Hilsea d			17 03	17 07	17 11				17 33		17 36		17 42		18 01	18 04	18 12				18 33		18 39	18 42
Fratton d	16 55	16 59	17 08	17 12	17 16	17 19	17 25	17 32	17 37		17 40	17 42	17 47	17 59	18 06	18 09	18 17	18 22	18 29		18 37	18 40	18 43	18 46
Portsmouth & Southsea a	16 58	17 02	17 11	17 16	17 20	17 22	17 28	17 35	17 42		17 44	17 46	17 50	18 02	18 09	18 12	18 20	18 25	18 32		18 41	18 43	18 46	18 49
d	16 58	17 04	17 12	17 16	17 21		17 30	17 36				17 46		18 04	18 09	18 14	18 22	18 26	18 33			18 45		
Portsmouth Harbour ⛴ a	17 02	17 07	17 18	17 20	17 26		17 35	17 40				17 54		18 09	18 15	18 20	18 28	18 31	18 39			18 51		

	GW	SW	SN	SW	SN		SW	SW	SW	GW	SN	SN	SW	SW	SN		SW	SW	SW	GW	SW	SN	SW	SN
										R										R				
	◇	1	◇1	1	◇		1	1	1		◇	◇1	1	1	◇		1	1	1		1	◇1	1	◇1
	⊥	⊥					⊥			⊥			⊥				⊥			⊥	⊥			
Havant d		18 51	18 54		19 08		19 17				19 33	19 46	19 51		20 07		20 17		20 29		20 49	20 52		21 10
Bedhampton d			18 57								19 35								20 32					
Hilsea d			19 02	19 05				19 28	19 33		19 43			20 02				20 33	20 37				21 03	
Fratton d	18 48	19 00	19 06	19 09	19 18		19 26	19 33	19 37	19 42	19 47	19 57	20 00	20 08	20 16		20 26	20 37	20 41	20 42	20 58	21 02	21 08	21 19
Portsmouth & Southsea a	18 52	19 03	19 09	19 12	19 21		19 29	19 36	19 42	19 46	19 50	20 01	20 03	20 11	20 19		20 29	20 42	20 44	20 46	21 01	21 06	21 11	21 23
d	18 52	19 05		19 14	19 21		19 31	19 38		19 46		20 01	20 05	20 12			20 31		20 46	20 46	21 03		21 13	21 23
Portsmouth Harbour ⛴ a	19 00	19 10		19 20	19 26		19 36	19 43		19 54		20 07	20 10	20 20			20 34		20 52	20 54	21 06		21 16	21 27

Table 157

Mondays to Fridays
until 30 September

Havant - Portsmouth Harbour

(Complete service)

		SW		SW	GW	SW	SW	SN	SW	SN	SW	SW		SW	SN	GW	SW	SN	SW	SW	SW	SW		GW	SN
		■1 trolley		■1	◇ trolley	■1	■1 trolley	◇■1 trolley	■1	◇■1	■1 trolley	■1		■1	◇■1	◇	■1 trolley	◇	■1	■1	■1	■1		◇	■1
Havant	d	21 19				21 31	21 46	21 49		22 10	22 19			22 31	22 43		22 49	23 11	23 19			23 31			23 34
Bedhampton	d					21 34								22 34								23 34			
Hilsea	d			21 33		21 41			22 03			22 33		22 39						23 24	23 33	23 39			
Fratton	d	21 29		21 37	21 42	21 45	21 55	21 58	22 08	22 19	22 29	22 37		22 44	22 52	22 56	23 00	23 20	23 29	23 33	23 37	23 44		23 44	23 47
Portsmouth & Southsea	a	21 32		21 40	21 45	21 48	21 58	22 01	22 11	22 22	22 32	22 42		22 47	22 55	22 59	23 04	23 23	23 32	23 36	23 40	23 47		23 48	23 54
	d	21 33		21 41	21 46		21 58	22 02	22 13	22 22	22 33				22 56	22 59	23 05	23 24	23 33	23 36				23 48	
Portsmouth Harbour ⛴	a	21 37		21 45	21 52		22 02	22 05	22 16	22 26	22 37				22 59	23 04	23 08	23 27	23 37	23 40				23 54	

		SW
		■1
Havant	d	23 49
Bedhampton	d	
Hilsea	d	
Fratton	d	23 59
Portsmouth & Southsea	a	00 02
	d	00 03
Portsmouth Harbour ⛴	a	00 07

Mondays to Fridays
from 3 October

		SW	SW	SW	SW	SW	SW	SW	SW	SW		SW	SW	SW	SN	SN	SW	SN	SW	SN		SW	SW	SW	GW
		MX	MO	MO	MX	MX	MX	MO	MO			MX	MO												
		■1	■1	■1	■1	■1	■1	■1	■1	■1		■1	■1	■1	◇	◇	■1	◇■1	■1	◇■1		■1	■1	■1	
Havant	d	23p49	23p51			00 22	00 37	00 39	00 51			01 21		04 40	05 21	05 40	06 02	06 13		06 53			07 00		
Bedhampton	d					00 25		00 41				01s24		04 43			06 05	06 15		06 56			07 03		
Hilsea	d			23p59	00 03	00 30						01s29		04 48			06 10	06 20	06 33	07 01		07 05	07 08	07 13	
Fratton	d	23p59	00 01	00 04	00 08	00 34	00 47	00 50	01 01			01s33	02s10	04 52	05 30	05 49	06 15	06 25	06 38	07 05		07 09	07 12	07 17	07 35
Portsmouth & Southsea	a	00 02	00 04	00 08	00 11	00 38	00 50	00 53	01 04	01s08		01 37	02s14	04 55	05 33	05 52	06 18	06 28	06 44	07 08		07 12	07 16	07 22	07 38
	d	00 03	00 05	00 09	00 13		00 51	00 54	01 05					04 56	05 33	05 52	06 19	06 28	06 45	07 09		07 13	07 17		07 39
Portsmouth Harbour ⛴	a	00 07	00 09	00 13	00 16		00 55	00 58	01 09	01 12			02 19	04 59	05 37	05 56	06 22	06 32	06 49	07 12		07 17	07 20		07 45

		SW	SW	SN	SN	SW		SW	SN	SW	GW	SN	SW	SW	SN	SW		SW	SN	SW	SW	SW	SW	GW	SN
		■1	■1	◇■1	◇■1	■1		■1	◇	■1	◇	◇	■1	■1	◇■1	■1 trolley		■1	◇■1	■1	■1 trolley	■1	■1	◇ trolley	◇
Havant	d		07 28	07 35	07 41	07 52			07 58			08 22	08 27		08 44	08 50			09 01	09 05	09 20		09 30		09 33
Bedhampton	d		07 31	07 37		07 55			08 00			08 25	08 30							09 08			09 33		09 36
Hilsea	d	07 35	07 37	07 42		08 00		08 03	08 05	08 09		08 30	08 35	08 45				09 05		09 13		09 33	09 38		09 42
Fratton	d	07 39	07 42	07 47	07 50	08 04		08 07	08 10	08 13	08 21	08 34	08 40	08 49	08 53	08 59		09 10	09 13	09 17	09 29	09 37	09 43	09 42	09 47
Portsmouth & Southsea	a	07 42	07 46	07 50	07 53	08 07		08 11	08 15	08 19	08 24	08 37	08 43	08 52	08 56	09 02		09 13	09 17	09 20	09 32	09 42	09 46	09 46	09 50
	d	07 43			07 53	08 09		08 13	08 17	08 21	08 25	08 38	08 45	08 54	08 57	09 04		09 14	09 18	09 22	09 34			09 46	
Portsmouth Harbour ⛴	a	07 48			07 58	08 12		08 16	08 20	08 24	08 30	08 41	08 48	08 57	09 02	09 07		09 18	09 21	09 26	09 37			09 55	

		SN		SW	SW	SN	SW	SW	SW	GW	SN	SN		SW	SW	SN	SW	SW	SW	GW	SN	SN		SW	SW
		◇■1		■1 trolley	■1	◇■1	■1 trolley	■1	■1	R trolley	◇■1	◇■1		■1 trolley	■1	◇	■1 trolley	■1	■1	◇ trolley	◇	◇■1		■1 trolley	■1
Havant	d	09 46		09 50		10 07	10 16		10 27		10 32	10 46		10 50		11 05	11 16		11 27		11 32	11 46		11 50	
Bedhampton	d								10 30		10 34								11 30		11 34				
Hilsea	d				10 03			10 33	10 36		10 42				11 03			11 33	11 36		11 42				12 03
Fratton	d	09 55		09 59	10 08	10 16	10 25	10 37	10 40	10 42	10 47	10 55		10 59	11 08	11 14	11 25	11 37	11 40	11 42	11 47	11 55		11 59	12 08
Portsmouth & Southsea	a	09 58		10 02	10 11	10 19	10 28	10 42	10 44	10 46	10 50	10 58		11 02	11 11	11 17	11 28	11 42	11 44	11 46	11 50	11 58		12 02	12 11
	d	09 58		10 04	10 12	10 20	10 29			10 46		10 58		11 04	11 12	11 17	11 29			11 46		11 58		12 04	12 12
Portsmouth Harbour ⛴	a	10 02		10 07	10 18	10 23	10 33			10 54		11 02		11 07	11 18	11 21	11 33			11 54		12 02		12 07	12 18

		SN	SW	SW	SW	GW	SN	SN		SW	SW	SN	SW	SW	SW	GW	SN	SN		SW	SW	SN	SW	SW	SW
		◇	■1 trolley	■1	■1	◇ trolley	◇	◇■1		■1 trolley	■1	◇■1	■1 trolley	■1	■1	◇ trolley	◇	◇■1		■1 trolley	■1	◇	■1 trolley	■1	■1
Havant	d	12 05	12 16		12 27		12 32	12 46		12 50		13 05	13 16		13 27		13 32	13 46		13 50		14 05	14 16		14 27
Bedhampton	d				12 30		12 34								13 30		13 34								14 30
Hilsea	d			12 33	12 36		12 42				13 03			13 33	13 36		13 42				14 03			14 33	14 36
Fratton	d	12 14	12 25	12 37	12 40	12 42	12 47	12 55		12 59	13 08	13 14	13 25	13 37	13 40	13 42	13 47	13 55		13 59	14 08	14 14	14 25	14 37	14 40
Portsmouth & Southsea	a	12 17	12 28	12 42	12 44	12 46	12 50	12 58		13 02	13 11	13 17	13 28	13 42	13 44	13 46	13 50	13 58		14 02	14 11	14 17	14 28	14 42	14 44
	d	12 17	12 29			12 46		12 58		13 04	13 12	13 17	13 29			13 46		13 58		14 04	14 12	14 17	14 29		
Portsmouth Harbour ⛴	a	12 21	12 33			12 54		13 02		13 07	13 18	13 21	13 33			13 54		14 02		14 07	14 18	14 21	14 33		

		GW	SN	SN		SW	SW	SN	SW	SW	SW	GW	SN	SN		SW	SW	SN	SN	SW	SW	SW	GW	SN
		◇ trolley	◇■1	◇■1		■1 trolley	■1	◇	■1 trolley	■1	■1	◇ trolley	◇■1	◇■1		■1 trolley	■1	◇	◇■1	■1 trolley	■1	■1	◇ trolley	◇
Havant	d		14 32	14 47		14 50		15 05	15 16		15 27		15 32	15 46		15 50		16 02	16 09	16 16		16 27		16 32
Bedhampton	d		14 34								15 30		15 34					16 04				16 30		16 34
Hilsea	d		14 42				15 03			15 33	15 36		15 42				16 03				16 33	16 36		16 42
Fratton	d	14 42	14 47	14 56		14 59	15 08	15 14	15 25	15 37	15 40	15 42	15 47	15 55		15 59	16 08	16 12	16 18	16 25	16 37	16 40	16 42	16 47
Portsmouth & Southsea	a	14 46	14 50	14 59		15 02	15 11	15 17	15 28	15 42	15 44	15 46	15 50	15 58		16 02	16 11	16 15	16 21	16 28	16 40	16 44	16 46	16 50
	d	14 46		14 59		15 04	15 12	15 17	15 29			15 46		15 58		16 04	16 12	16 16	16 22	16 29	16 41	16 45	16 46	
Portsmouth Harbour ⛴	a	14 54		15 03		15 07	15 18	15 21	15 33			15 54		16 02		16 07	16 18	16 21	16 26	16 33	16 44	16 49	16 54	

Table 157

Mondays to Fridays

from 3 October

Havant - Portsmouth Harbour

(Complete service)

		SN	SW	SW	SN	SW	SN	SW	SW	SW		SW	GW	SN	SW	SN	SW	SW	SN	SW		SW	SW	SW	SN
		◇1	1 🍴	1	◇	1	◇	1 🍴	1	1		1	◇ 🍴	◇1	1 🍴	◇1	1	1	◇	1 🍴		1	1	1	◇
Havant	d	16 46	16 50		17 00	17 04	17 09	17 16				17 27		17 32	17 50	17 54		18 04	18 13	18 20				18 30	18 34
Bedhampton	d				17 02	17 06						17 30		17 34		17 56		18 07						18 33	18 36
Hilsea	d			17 03	17 07	17 11				17 33		17 36		17 42		18 01	18 04	18 12				18 33		18 39	18 42
Fratton	d	16 55	16 59	17 08	17 12	17 16	17 19	17 25	17 32	17 37		17 40	17 42	17 47	17 59	18 06	18 09	18 17	18 22	18 29		18 37	18 40	18 43	18 46
Portsmouth & Southsea	a	16 58	17 02	17 11	17 16	17 20	17 22	17 28	17 35	17 42		17 44	17 46	17 50	18 02	18 09	18 12	18 20	18 25	18 32		18 41	18 43	18 46	18 49
	d	16 58	17 04	17 12	17 16	17 21		17 30	17 36				17 46		18 04	18 09	18 14	18 22	18 26	18 33			18 45		
Portsmouth Harbour ⛴	a	17 02	17 07	17 18	17 20	17 26		17 35	17 40				17 54		18 09	18 15	18 20	18 28	18 31	18 39			18 51		

		GW	SW	SN	SW	SN		SW	SW	SW	GW	SN	SN	SW	SW	SN		SW	SW	SW	GW	SW	SN	SW	SN
		◇ 🍴	1 🍴	◇1	1	◇		1 🍴	1	1	R 🍴	◇	◇1	1 🍴	1	◇		1 🍴	1	1	R 🍴	1 🍴	◇1	1	◇1
Havant	d		18 51	18 54		19 08		19 17				19 33	19 46	19 51		20 07		20 17		20 29		20 49	20 52		21 10
Bedhampton	d			18 57								19 35								20 32					
Hilsea	d			19 02	19 05				19 28	19 33		19 43			20 02				20 33	20 37				21 03	
Fratton	d	18 48	19 00	19 06	19 09	19 18		19 26	19 33	19 37	19 42	19 47	19 57	20 00	20 08	20 16		20 26	20 37	20 41	20 42	20 58	21 02	21 08	21 19
Portsmouth & Southsea	a	18 52	19 03	19 09	19 12	19 21		19 29	19 36	19 42	19 46	19 50	20 01	20 03	20 11	20 19		20 29	20 42	20 44	20 46	21 01	21 06	21 11	21 23
	d	18 52	19 05		19 14	19 21		19 31	19 38		19 46		20 01	20 05	20 12			20 31		20 46	20 46	21 03		21 13	21 23
Portsmouth Harbour ⛴	a	19 00	19 10		19 20	19 26		19 36	19 43		19 54		20 07	20 10	20 20			20 34		20 52	20 54	21 06		21 16	21 27

		SW		SW	GW	SW	SW	SN	SW	SN	SW	SW		SW	SN	GW	SW	SN	SW	SW	SW	SW		GW	SN
		1 🍴		1	◇ 🍴	1	1 🍴	◇1 🍴	1	◇1	1 🍴	1		1	◇1	◇	1 🍴	◇	1	1	1	1		◇	1
Havant	d	21 19				21 31	21 46	21 49		22 10	22 19			22 31	22 43		22 49	23 11	23 19			23 31			23 34
Bedhampton	d					21 34								22 34								23 34			
Hilsea	d			21 33		21 41			22 03			22 33		22 39						23 24	23 33	23 39			
Fratton	d	21 29		21 37	21 42	21 45	21 55	21 58	22 08	22 19	22 29	22 37		22 44	22 52	22 56	23 00	23 20	23 29	23 33	23 37	23 44		23 44	23 47
Portsmouth & Southsea	a	21 32		21 40	21 45	21 48	21 58	22 01	22 11	22 22	22 32	22 42		22 47	22 55	22 59	23 04	23 23	23 32	23 36	23 40	23 47		23 48	23 54
	d	21 33		21 41	21 46		21 58	22 02	22 13	22 22	22 33				22 56	22 59	23 05	23 24	23 33	23 36				23 48	
Portsmouth Harbour ⛴	a	21 37		21 45	21 52		22 02	22 05	22 16	22 26	22 37				22 59	23 04	23 08	23 27	23 37	23 40				23 54	

		SW
		1
Havant	d	23 49
Bedhampton	d	
Hilsea	d	
Fratton	d	23 59
Portsmouth & Southsea	a	00 02
	d	00 03
Portsmouth Harbour ⛴	a	00 07

Saturdays

until 1 October

		SW	SW	SW	SW	SW	SW	SW	SN	SN		SN	SW	SW	SN	SN	SW	SN	SW	SW		GW	SN	SN	SW
		1	1	1	1	1	1	1	◇1	◇1		◇1	1	1	◇	◇1	1	◇1	1	1			◇	1	1
Havant	d	23p49		00 22	00 37		01 21	04 40	05 34	05 49		05 57	06 02		06 32	06 46		07 04	07 20				07 32	07 46	
Bedhampton	d			00 25			01s24	04 43					06 05		06 34				07 22				07 34		
Hilsea	d		00 03	00 30			01s29	04 48					06 10	06 33	06 42		07 03		07 27	07 33			07 42		08 03
Fratton	d	23p59	00 08	00 34	00 47		01s33	04 52	05 43	05 58		06 06	06 15	06 37	06 47	06 55	07 08	07 13	07 32	07 37		07 42	07 47	07 55	08 08
Portsmouth & Southsea	a	00 02	00 11	00 38	00 50	01s08	01 37	04 55	05 46	06 01		06 09	06 18	06 42	06 50	06 58	07 11	07 16	07 35	07 42		07 46	07 50	07 58	08 11
	d	00 03	00 13		00 51			04 57		06 01		06 09	06 19			06 58	07 12	07 16	07 36			07 46		07 59	08 13
Portsmouth Harbour ⛴	a	00 07	00 16		00 55	01 12		05 00		06 05		06 16	06 22			07 02	07 16	07 20	07 40			07 52		08 02	08 18

		SN	SW	SW	GW	SN		SN	SW	SW	SN	SW	SW	SW	GW	SN		SN	SW	SW	SN	SW	SW	SW	GW
		◇1	1	1	◇	◇		1	1	1	◇1	1	1	1	◇	◇		◇1	1	1	◇1	1 🍴	1	1	◇
Havant	d	08 04	08 17			08 32		08 46	08 50		09 04	09 16		09 27		09 32		09 46	09 50		10 07	10 16		10 27	
Bedhampton	d		08 20			08 34								09 30		09 34								10 30	
Hilsea	d		08 25	08 33		08 42				09 04			09 33	09 36		09 42				10 03			10 33	10 36	
Fratton	d	08 13	08 29	08 37	08 42	08 47		08 55	08 59	09 09	09 13	09 25	09 37	09 40	09 42	09 47		09 55	09 59	10 08	10 16	10 25	10 37	10 40	10 42
Portsmouth & Southsea	a	08 16	08 32	08 42	08 46	08 50		08 58	09 02	09 12	09 16	09 28	09 42	09 44	09 46	09 50		09 58	10 02	10 11	10 19	10 28	10 42	10 44	10 46
	d	08 16	08 34		08 46			08 59	09 04	09 13	09 16	09 29			09 47			09 58	10 04	10 12	10 20	10 29			10 46
Portsmouth Harbour ⛴	a	08 20	08 37		08 52			09 02	09 07	09 18	09 20	09 33			09 52			10 02	10 07	10 18	10 23	10 33			10 52

		SN		SN	SW	SW	SN	SW	SW	SW	GW	SN		SN	SW	SW	SN	SW	SW	SW	GW	SN		SN	SW
		◇		◇1	1 🍴	1	◇1	1 🍴	1	1	◇	◇		◇1	1 🍴	1	◇1	1 🍴	1	1	◇ 🍴	◇		◇1	1 🍴
Havant	d	10 32		10 46	10 50		11 05	11 16		11 27		11 32		11 46	11 50		12 05	12 16		12 27		12 32		12 46	12 50
Bedhampton	d	10 34								11 30		11 34								12 30		12 34			
Hilsea	d	10 43				11 03			11 33	11 36		11 42				12 03			12 33	12 36		12 42			
Fratton	d	10 47		10 55	10 59	11 08	11 14	11 25	11 37	11 40	11 42	11 47		11 55	11 59	12 08	12 14	12 25	12 37	12 40	12 42	12 47		12 55	12 59
Portsmouth & Southsea	a	10 50		10 58	11 02	11 11	11 17	11 28	11 42	11 44	11 46	11 50		11 58	12 02	12 11	12 17	12 28	12 42	12 44	12 46	12 50		12 58	13 02
	d			10 58	11 04	11 12	11 17	11 29			11 47			11 58	12 04	12 12	12 17	12 29			12 47			12 58	13 04
Portsmouth Harbour ⛴	a			11 02	11 07	11 18	11 21	11 33			11 52			12 02	12 07	12 18	12 21	12 33			12 51			13 02	13 07

Table 157

Saturdays until 1 October

Havant - Portsmouth Harbour

(Complete service)

		SW	SN	SW	SW	SW	GW	SN	SN	SW	SW	SN	SW	SW	SW	GW	SN	SN	SW	SW	SN	SW	SW
		1	◇1	1 (catering)	1	1	◇ (catering)	◇	◇1	1 (catering)	1	◇1	1 (catering)	1	1	◇ (catering)	◇	◇1	1 (catering)	1	◇1	1 (catering)	1
Havant	d		13 05	13 16		13 27		13 32	13 46	13 50		14 05	14 16		14 27		14 32	14 46	14 50		15 05	15 16	
Bedhampton	d					13 30		13 34							14 30		14 34						
Hilsea	d	13 03			13 33	13 36		13 42			14 03			14 33	14 36		14 42			15 03			15 33
Fratton	d	13 08	13 14	13 25	13 37	13 40	13 42	13 47	13 55	13 59	14 08	14 14	14 25	14 37	14 40	14 42	14 47	14 55	14 59	15 08	15 14	15 25	15 37
Portsmouth & Southsea	a	13 11	13 17	13 28	13 42	13 44	13 46	13 50	13 58	14 02	14 11	14 17	14 28	14 42	14 44	14 46	14 50	14 58	15 02	15 11	15 17	15 28	15 42
	d	13 12	13 17	13 29			13 47		13 58	14 04	14 12	14 17	14 29			14 47		14 58	15 04	15 12	15 17	15 29	
Portsmouth Harbour ⛴	a	13 18	13 21	13 33			13 51		14 02	14 07	14 18	14 21	14 33			14 51		15 02	15 07	15 18	15 21	15 33	

		SW	GW	SN	SN	SW	SW	SN	SW	SW	SW	GW	SN	SN	SW	SW	SN	SW	SW	SW	GW	SN
		1	◇	◇	◇1	1 (catering)	1	◇1	1 (catering)	1	1	◇	◇	◇1	1 (catering)	1	◇1	1 (catering)	1	1	◇	◇
Havant	d	15 27		15 32	15 46	15 50		16 05	16 16		16 27		16 32	16 46	16 50		17 05	17 16		17 27		17 32
Bedhampton	d	15 30		15 34							16 30		16 34							17 30		17 34
Hilsea	d	15 36		15 42			16 03			16 33	16 36		16 42			17 03			17 33	17 36		17 42
Fratton	d	15 40	15 42	15 47	15 55	15 59	16 08	16 14	16 25	16 37	16 40	16 42	16 47	16 55	16 59	17 08	17 14	17 25	17 37	17 40	17 44	17 47
Portsmouth & Southsea	a	15 44	15 46	15 50	15 58	16 02	16 11	16 17	16 28	16 40	16 44	16 46	16 50	16 58	17 02	17 11	17 17	17 28	17 42	17 44	17 48	17 50
	d		15 47		15 58	16 04	16 12	16 17	16 29	16 41		16 47		16 58	17 04	17 12	17 17	17 29			17 49	
Portsmouth Harbour ⛴	a		15 51		16 02	16 07	16 18	16 21	16 33	16 44		16 51		17 02	17 07	17 16	17 21	17 33			17 53	

		SN	SW	SW	SN	SW	SW	SW	GW	SN	SN	SW	SW	SN	SW	SW	SW	GW	SN	SN	SW	SW	SN
		◇1	1 (catering)	1	◇1	1 (catering)	1	1	◇	◇	◇1	1 (catering)	1	◇1	1 (catering)	1	1		◇	◇1	1 (catering)	1	◇1
Havant	d	17 46	17 50		18 06	18 16		18 27		18 32	18 46	18 50		19 05	19 16		19 27		19 32	19 46	19 50		20 10
Bedhampton	d							18 30		18 34							19 30		19 34				
Hilsea	d			18 03			18 33	18 36		18 42			19 03			19 33	19 36		19 42			20 03	
Fratton	d	17 55	17 59	18 08	18 15	18 25	18 37	18 40	18 42	18 47	18 55	18 59	19 08	19 14	19 25	19 37	19 40	19 42	19 47	19 55	19 59	20 08	20 19
Portsmouth & Southsea	a	17 58	18 02	18 11	18 18	18 28	18 42	18 44	18 46	18 50	18 58	19 02	19 11	19 17	19 28	19 42	19 44	19 46	19 50	19 58	20 02	20 11	20 22
	d	17 58	18 04	18 12	18 19	18 29			18 47		18 58	19 04	19 12	19 17	19 29			19 47		19 58	20 04	20 12	20 22
Portsmouth Harbour ⛴	a	18 02	18 07	18 18	18 22	18 33			18 52		19 02	19 07	19 18	19 21	19 33			19 52		20 02	20 07	20 18	20 26

		SW	SW	GW	SW	SN	SW	SW	SN	SW	SW	SW	GW	SW	SN	SW	SN	SW	SW	GW	SW	SN	SW
		1 (catering)	1	◇	1	◇1	1 (catering)	1	◇1	1	1	1	◇	1	◇1	1	◇1	1	1	◇	1	◇1	1
Havant	d	20 16			20 30	20 46	20 50		21 10	21 16		21 27		21 46	21 49		22 10	22 19			22 31	22 43	22 49
Bedhampton	d				20 33							21 30									22 34		
Hilsea	d		20 37		20 41			21 03			21 33	21 36				22 03			22 33		22 41		
Fratton	d	20 25	20 41	20 42	20 45	20 55	20 59	21 08	21 19	21 25	21 37	21 40	21 42	21 55	21 59	22 08	22 19	22 29	22 37	22 42	22 45	22 52	22 59
Portsmouth & Southsea	a	20 28	20 44	20 46	20 48	20 58	21 02	21 11	21 22	21 28	21 40	21 43	21 46	21 58	22 02	22 11	22 22	22 32	22 40	22 46	22 49	22 55	23 02
	d	20 29		20 47		20 58	21 04	21 12	21 22	21 29	21 41		21 47	22 00	22 03	22 12	22 22	22 33	22 41	22 46	22 50	22 56	23 03
Portsmouth Harbour ⛴	a	20 33		20 52		21 02	21 07	21 18	21 26	21 33	21 45		21 52	22 03	22 06	22 18	22 26	22 36	22 47	22 52	22 53	22 59	23 08

		SW	SN	SW	SW	GW	SW	SN	SW
		1	◇1	1	1	◇	1	1	1
Havant	d		23 10	23 19			23 31	23 36	23 49
Bedhampton	d						23 34		
Hilsea	d	23 03			23 33		23 41		
Fratton	d	23 08	23 19	23 29	23 37	23 41	23 45	23 48	23 59
Portsmouth & Southsea	a	23 11	23 22	23 32	23 40	23 44	23 48	23 51	00 02
	d	23 12	23 22	23 33		23 45	23 50		00 03
Portsmouth Harbour ⛴	a	23 18	23 26	23 37		23 52	23 53		00 07

Saturdays from 8 October

		SW	SW	SW	SW	SW	SW	SW	SN	SN	SN	SW	SW	SN	SN	SW	SN	SW	SW	GW	SN	SN	SW
		1	1	1	1	1	1	1	◇1	◇1	◇1	1	1	◇	◇1	1	◇1	1	1	◇	◇	1	1
Havant	d	23p49		00 22	00 37		01 21	04 40	05 34	05 49	05 57	06 02		06 32	06 46		07 04	07 20			07 32	07 46	
Bedhampton	d			00 25			01s24	04 43				06 05		06 34				07 22			07 34		
Hilsea	d		00 03	00 30			01s29	04 48				06 10	06 33	06 42		07 03		07 27	07 33		07 42		08 03
Fratton	d	23p59	00 08	00 34	00 47		01s33	04 52	05 43	05 58	06 06	06 15	06 37	06 47	06 55	07 08	07 13	07 32	07 37	07 42	07 47	07 55	08 08
Portsmouth & Southsea	a	00 02	00 11	00 38	00 50	01s08	01 37	04 55	05 46	06 01	06 09	06 18	06 42	06 50	06 58	07 11	07 16	07 35	07 42	07 46	07 50	07 58	08 11
	d	00 03	00 13		00 51			04 57		06 01	06 09	06 19			06 58	07 12	07 16	07 36		07 46		07 59	08 13
Portsmouth Harbour ⛴	a	00 07	00 16		00 55	01 12		05 00		06 05	06 16	06 22			07 02	07 16	07 20	07 40		07 52		08 02	08 18

		SN	SW	SW	GW	SN	SN	SW	SW	SN	SW	SW	SW	GW	SN	SN	SW	SW	SN	SW	SW	SW	GW
		◇1	1	1	◇	◇	1	1	1	◇1	1	1	1	◇	◇	◇1	1	1	◇1	1 (catering)	1	1	◇
Havant	d	08 04	08 17			08 32	08 46	08 50		09 04	09 16		09 27		09 32	09 46	09 50		10 07	10 16		10 27	
Bedhampton	d		08 20			08 34							09 30		09 34							10 30	
Hilsea	d		08 25	08 33		08 42			09 04			09 33	09 36		09 42			10 03			10 33	10 36	
Fratton	d	08 13	08 29	08 37	08 42	08 47	08 55	08 59	09 09	09 13	09 25	09 37	09 40	09 42	09 47	09 55	09 59	10 08	10 16	10 25	10 37	10 40	10 42
Portsmouth & Southsea	a	08 16	08 32	08 42	08 46	08 50	08 58	09 02	09 12	09 16	09 28	09 42	09 44	09 46	09 50	09 58	10 02	10 11	10 19	10 28	10 42	10 44	10 46
	d	08 16	08 34		08 46		08 59	09 04	09 13	09 16	09 29			09 47		09 58	10 04	10 12	10 20	10 29			10 46
Portsmouth Harbour ⛴	a	08 20	08 37		08 52		09 02	09 07	09 18	09 20	09 33			09 52		10 02	10 07	10 18	10 23	10 33			10 52

Table 157

Saturdays from 8 October

Havant - Portsmouth Harbour

(Complete service)

		SN ◇		SN ◇■1	SW ■1 ⊼	SW ■1	SN ◇■1	SW ■1 ⊼	SW ■1	SW ■1	GW ◇	SN ◇		SN ◇■1	SW ■1 ⊼	SW ■1	SN ◇■1	SW ■1 ⊼	SW ■1	SW ■1	GW ◇ ⊼	SN ◇		SN ◇■1	SW ■1 ⊼
Havant	d	10 32		10 46	10 50		11 05	11 16		11 27		11 32		11 46	11 50		12 05	12 16		12 27		12 32		12 46	12 50
Bedhampton	d	10 34								11 30		11 34								12 30		12 34			
Hilsea	d	10 43				11 03			11 33	11 36		11 42				12 03			12 33	12 36		12 42			
Fratton	d	10 47		10 55	10 59	11 08	11 14	11 25	11 37	11 40	11 42	11 47		11 55	11 59	12 08	12 14	12 25	12 37	12 40	12 42	12 47		12 55	12 59
Portsmouth & Southsea	a	10 50		10 58	11 02	11 11	11 17	11 28	11 42	11 44	11 46	11 50		11 58	12 02	12 11	12 17	12 28	12 42	12 44	12 46	12 50		12 58	13 02
	d			10 58	11 04	11 12	11 17	11 29			11 47			11 58	12 04	12 12	12 17	12 29			12 47			12 58	13 04
Portsmouth Harbour ⛴	a			11 02	11 07	11 18	11 21	11 33			11 52			12 02	12 07	12 18	12 21	12 33			12 51			13 02	13 07

		SW ■1	SN ◇■1	SW ■1 ⊼	SW ■1	SW ■1	GW ◇ ⊼	SN ◇		SN ◇■1	SW ■1 ⊼	SW ■1	SN ◇■1	SW ■1 ⊼	SW ■1	SW ■1	GW ◇ ⊼	SN ◇		SN ◇■1	SW ■1 ⊼	SW ■1	SN ◇■1	SW ■1 ⊼	SW ■1
Havant	d		13 05	13 16		13 27		13 32		13 46	13 50		14 05	14 16		14 27		14 32		14 46	14 50		15 05	15 16	
Bedhampton	d					13 30		13 34								14 30		14 34							
Hilsea	d	13 03			13 33	13 36		13 42				14 03			14 33	14 36		14 42				15 03			15 33
Fratton	d	13 08	13 14	13 25	13 37	13 40	13 42	13 47		13 55	13 59	14 08	14 14	14 25	14 37	14 40	14 42	14 47		14 55	14 59	15 08	15 14	15 25	15 37
Portsmouth & Southsea	a	13 11	13 17	13 28	13 42	13 44	13 46	13 50		13 58	14 02	14 11	14 17	14 28	14 42	14 44	14 46	14 50		14 58	15 02	15 11	15 17	15 28	15 42
	d	13 12	13 17	13 29			13 47			13 58	14 04	14 12	14 17	14 29			14 47			14 58	15 04	15 12	15 17	15 29	
Portsmouth Harbour ⛴	a	13 18	13 21	13 33			13 51			14 02	14 07	14 18	14 21	14 33			14 51			15 02	15 07	15 18	15 21	15 33	

		SW ■1	GW ◇	SN ◇		SN ◇■1	SW ■1 ⊼	SW ■1	SN ◇■1	SW ■1 ⊼	SW ■1	SW ■1	GW ◇	SN ◇		SN ◇■1	SW ■1 ⊼	SW ■1	SN ◇■1	SW ■1 ⊼	SW ■1	SW ■1	GW ◇	SN ◇	
Havant	d	15 27		15 32		15 46	15 50		16 05	16 16		16 27		16 32		16 46	16 50		17 05	17 16		17 27		17 32	
Bedhampton	d	15 30		15 34								16 30		16 34								17 30		17 34	
Hilsea	d	15 36		15 42				16 03			16 33	16 36		16 42				17 03			17 33	17 36		17 42	
Fratton	d	15 40	15 42	15 47		15 55	15 59	16 08	16 14	16 25	16 37	16 40	16 42	16 47		16 55	16 59	17 08	17 14	17 25	17 37	17 40	17 44	17 47	
Portsmouth & Southsea	a	15 44	15 46	15 50		15 58	16 02	16 11	16 17	16 28	16 40	16 44	16 46	16 50		16 58	17 02	17 11	17 17	17 28	17 42	17 44	17 48	17 50	
	d		15 47			15 58	16 04	16 12	16 17	16 29	16 41		16 47			16 58	17 04	17 12	17 17	17 29			17 49		
Portsmouth Harbour ⛴	a		15 51			16 02	16 07	16 18	16 21	16 33	16 44		16 51			17 02	17 07	17 16	17 21	17 33			17 53		

		SN ◇■1	SW ■1 ⊼	SW ■1	SN ◇■1	SW ■1 ⊼	SW ■1	SW ■1	GW ◇	SN ◇		SN ◇■1	SW ■1 ⊼	SW ■1	SN ◇■1	SW ■1 ⊼	SW ■1	SW ■1	GW R	SN ◇		SN ◇■1	SW ■1 ⊼	SW ■1	SN ◇■1
Havant	d	17 46	17 50		18 06	18 16		18 27		18 32		18 46	18 50		19 05	19 16		19 27		19 32		19 46	19 50		20 10
Bedhampton	d							18 30		18 34								19 30		19 34					
Hilsea	d			18 03			18 33	18 36		18 42				19 03			19 33	19 36		19 42				20 03	
Fratton	d	17 55	17 59	18 08	18 15	18 25	18 37	18 40	18 42	18 47		18 55	18 59	19 08	19 14	19 25	19 37	19 40	19 42	19 47		19 55	19 59	20 08	20 19
Portsmouth & Southsea	a	17 58	18 02	18 11	18 18	18 28	18 42	18 44	18 46	18 50		18 58	19 02	19 11	19 17	19 28	19 42	19 44	19 46	19 50		19 58	20 02	20 11	20 22
	d	17 58	18 04	18 12	18 19	18 29			18 47			18 58	19 04	19 12	19 17	19 29			19 47			19 58	20 04	20 12	20 22
Portsmouth Harbour ⛴	a	18 02	18 07	18 18	18 22	18 33			18 52			19 02	19 07	19 18	19 21	19 33			19 52			20 02	20 07	20 18	20 26

		SW ■1 ⊼	SW ■1	GW ◇	SW ■1	SN ◇■1		SW ■1 ⊼	SW ■1	SN ◇■1	SW ■1	SW ■1	SW ■1	GW ◇	SW ■1	SN ◇■1		SW ■1	SN ◇■1	SW ■1	SW ■1	GW ◇	SW ■1	SN ◇■1	SW ■1
Havant	d	20 16			20 30	20 46		20 50		21 10	21 16		21 27		21 46	21 49			22 10	22 19			22 31	22 43	22 49
Bedhampton	d				20 33								21 30										22 34		
Hilsea	d		20 37		20 41				21 03			21 33	21 36					22 03			22 33		22 41		
Fratton	d	20 25	20 41	20 42	20 45	20 55		20 59	21 08	21 19	21 25	21 37	21 40	21 42	21 55	21 59		22 08	22 19	22 29	22 37	22 42	22 45	22 52	22 59
Portsmouth & Southsea	a	20 28	20 44	20 46	20 48	20 58		21 02	21 11	21 22	21 28	21 40	21 43	21 46	21 58	22 02		22 11	22 22	22 32	22 40	22 46	22 49	22 55	23 02
	d	20 29		20 47		20 58		21 04	21 12	21 22	21 29	21 41		21 47	22 00	22 03		22 12	22 22	22 33	22 41	22 46	22 50	22 56	23 03
Portsmouth Harbour ⛴	a	20 33		20 52		21 02		21 07	21 18	21 26	21 33	21 45		21 52	22 03	22 06		22 18	22 26	22 36	22 47	22 52	22 53	22 59	23 08

		SW ■1		SN ◇■1	SW ■1	SW ■1	GW ◇	SW ■1	SN ■1	SW ■1
Havant	d			23 10	23 19			23 31	23 36	23 49
Bedhampton	d							23 34		
Hilsea	d	23 03				23 33		23 41		
Fratton	d	23 08		23 19	23 29	23 37	23 41	23 45	23 48	23 59
Portsmouth & Southsea	a	23 11		23 22	23 32	23 40	23 44	23 48	23 51	00 02
	d	23 12		23 22	23 33		23 45	23 50		00 03
Portsmouth Harbour ⛴	a	23 18		23 26	23 37		23 52	23 53		00 07

Sundays until 25 September

		SW ■1 A	SW ■1 A	SW ■1 A	SW ■1 A	SW ■1	SW ■1 A	SN ◇■1	SW ■1	SW ■1		SN ◇■1	SW ■1	SN ◇■1 B	SW ■1	SN ◇■1 C	SW ■1	SN ◇■1	SW ■1	SN ◇■1 B		SW ■1	SN ◇■1 C	SW ■1	SW ■1
Havant	d	23p49		00⌇22	00⌇37		01⌇21	07 10				08 11		08⌇35	08 39	08⌇49		09 11		09⌇35		09 45	09⌇49	09 53	
Bedhampton	d	⌇		00⌇25	⌇		01s24							08⌇37	08 41	08⌇51				09⌇37		09 47	09⌇51		
Hilsea	d	⌇	00⌇03	00⌇30	⌇		01s29		07 26	08 00			08 26	⌇		⌇	09 00		09 26	⌇			⌇		10 04
Fratton	d	23p59	00⌇07	00⌇34	00⌇47		01s33	07 19	07 30	08 04		08 20	08 30	08⌇45	08 50	08⌇59	09 04	09 20	09 30	09⌇45		09 56	09⌇59	10 02	10 08
Portsmouth & Southsea	a	00⌇02	00⌇11	00⌇38	00⌇50	01s08	01⌇37	07 22	07 33	08 08		08 23	08 33	08⌇48	08 53	09⌇03	09 08	09 23	09 33	09⌇48		09 59	10⌇03	10 06	10 11
	d	00⌇03	00⌇12		00⌇51			07 22		08 09		08 23		08⌇49	08 54	09⌇04	09 09	09 23		09⌇49		10 00	10⌇04	10 08	10 12
Portsmouth Harbour ⛴	a	00⌇07	00⌇16		00⌇55	01 12		07 26		08 13		08 27		08⌇52	08 57	09⌇07	09 13	09 27		09⌇52		10 04	10⌇07	10 11	10 15

A not 22 May

B until 4 September

C 11 September, 18 September, 25 September

Table 157

Sundays

until 25 September

Havant - Portsmouth Harbour

(Complete service)

		SN ◇1 A	SN ◇1 B	SW 1	SN ◇1 A	SN ◇1 B		SW 1	SW 1	SW 1	SN ◇1 A	SN ◇1 B	SW 1	GW ◇	SN ◇1 A	SW 1		SN ◇1 B	SW 1	SW 1	SN ◇1 A	SN ◇1 B	SW 1	GW ◇	SW 1
Havant	d	10 14	10 17		10 35	10 41		10 45	10 53		11 14	11 17			11 35	11 39		11 44	11 51		12 14	12 17			12 39
Bedhampton	d				10 37	10 43		10 47							11 37	11 41		11 46							12 41
Hilsea	d			10 26						11 04			11 26							12 00			12 26		
Fratton	d	10 23	10 26	10 30	10 45	10 51		10 56	11 02	11 08	11 23	11 26	11 30	11 41	11 45	11 50		11 54	12 01	12 04	12 23	12 26	12 30	12 41	12 50
Portsmouth & Southsea	a	10 26	10 29	10 33	10 50	10 54		10 59	11 05	11 11	11 26	11 29	11 33	11 45	11 49	11 53		11 57	12 04	12 08	12 26	12 29	12 33	12 45	12 53
	d	10 27	10 30		10 51	10 55		11 00	11 07	11 12	11 27	11 30		11 45	11 50	11 54		11 58	12 05	12 09	12 27	12 30		12 45	12 54
Portsmouth Harbour ⛴	a	10 30	10 35		10 54	10 58		11 04	11 11	11 15	11 30	11 35		11 52	11 53	11 58		12 01	12 09	12 13	12 30	12 35		12 52	12 58

		SN ◇1 A		SN ◇1 B	SW 1 ⊤	SW 1	SN ◇1 A	SN ◇1 B	SW 1	SN ◇1 A	SW 1	SN ◇1 B		SW 1 ⊤	SW 1	SN ◇1 A	SN ◇1 B	SW 1	GW ◇ ⊤	SN ◇1 A	SW 1	SN ◇1 B		SW 1 ⊤	SW 1
Havant	d	12 35		12 44	12 51		13 14	13 17		13 35	13 39	13 44		13 51		14 14	14 17			14 35	14 39	14 44		14 51	
Bedhampton	d	12 37		12 46						13 37	13 41	13 46								14 37	14 41	14 46			
Hilsea	d					13 00			13 26						14 00			14 26							15 00
Fratton	d	12 54		12 54	13 01	13 04	13 23	13 26	13 30	13 45	13 50	13 54		14 01	14 04	14 23	14 26	14 30	14 41	14 45	14 50	14 54		15 01	15 04
Portsmouth & Southsea	a	12 57		12 57	13 04	13 08	13 26	13 29	13 33	13 48	13 53	13 57		14 04	14 08	14 26	14 29	14 33	14 45	14 48	14 53	14 57		15 04	15 08
	d	12 58		12 58	13 05	13 09	13 27	13 30		13 49	13 54	13 58		14 05	14 09	14 27	14 30		14 45	14 49	14 54	14 58		15 05	15 09
Portsmouth Harbour ⛴	a	13 01		13 01	13 11	13 13	13 30	13 35		13 52	13 58	14 01		14 11	14 13	14 30	14 35		14 55	14 53	14 58	15 01		15 11	15 13

		SN ◇1 A	SN ◇1 B	SW 1	SN ◇1 A	SW 1	SN ◇1 B	SW 1 ⊤		SW 1	SN ◇1 A	SN ◇1 B	SW 1	GW ◇	SW 1	SN ◇1 A	SN ◇1 B	SW 1 ⊤		SW 1	SN ◇1 A	SN ◇1 B	SW 1	GW ◇	SW 1
Havant	d	15 14	15 17		15 35	15 39	15 44	15 51			16 14	16 17			16 39	16 35	16 44	16 51			17 14	17 17			17 39
Bedhampton	d				15 37	15 41	15 46								16 41	16 37	16 46								17 41
Hilsea	d			15 26						16 00			16 26							17 00			17 26		
Fratton	d	15 23	15 26	15 30	15 45	15 50	15 54	16 01		16 04	16 23	16 26	16 30	16 41	16 50	16 54	16 54	17 01		17 04	17 23	17 26	17 30	17 41	17 50
Portsmouth & Southsea	a	15 26	15 29	15 33	15 48	15 54	15 57	16 04		16 08	16 26	16 29	16 33	16 45	16 53	16 57	16 57	17 04		17 08	17 26	17 29	17 33	17 45	17 53
	d	15 27	15 30		15 49	15 54	15 58	16 05		16 09	16 27	16 30		16 45	16 54	16 58	16 58	17 05		17 09	17 27	17 30		17 45	17 54
Portsmouth Harbour ⛴	a	15 30	15 35		15 52	15 58	16 01	16 11		16 13	16 30	16 35		16 52	16 58	17 01	17 01	17 11		17 13	17 30	17 35		17 52	17 58

		SN ◇1 A	SN ◇1 B	SW 1 ⊤		SW 1	SN ◇1 A	SN ◇1 B	SW 1	GW ◇	SW 1	SN ◇1 A	SN ◇1 B	SW 1 ⊤		SW 1	SN ◇1 A	SN ◇1 B	SW 1	GW ◇	SW 1	SN ◇1 A	SN ◇1 B	SW 1 ⊤	
Havant	d	17 35	17 44	17 51			18 14	18 17			18 39	18 35	18 44	18 51			19 14	19 17			19 39	19 35	19 44	19 51	
Bedhampton	d	17 37	17 46								18 41	18 37	18 46								19 41	19 37	19 46		
Hilsea	d					18 00			18 26							19 00			19 26						
Fratton	d	17 54	17 54	18 01		18 04	18 23	18 26	18 30	18 41	18 50	18 54	18 54	19 01		19 04	19 23	19 26	19 30	19 41	19 50	19 54	19 54	20 01	
Portsmouth & Southsea	a	17 57	17 57	18 04		18 08	18 26	18 29	18 33	18 45	18 53	18 57	18 57	19 04		19 08	19 26	19 29	19 33	19 45	19 53	19 57	19 57	20 04	
	d	17 58	17 58	18 05		18 09	18 27	18 30		18 45	18 54	18 58	18 58	19 05		19 09	19 27	19 30		19 45	19 54	19 58	19 58	20 05	
Portsmouth Harbour ⛴	a	18 01	18 01	18 11		18 13	18 30	18 35		18 52	18 58	19 01	19 01	19 11		19 13	19 30	19 35		19 52	19 58	20 01	20 01	20 11	

		SW 1	SN ◇1 A	SN ◇1 B	SW 1	GW ◇	SN ◇1 A	SW 1	SN ◇1 B	SW 1 ⊤		SW 1	GW R	SN ◇1 A	SN ◇1 B	SW 1	GW ◇ C	GW ◇ D	SN ◇1 A	SW 1		SN ◇1 B	SW 1 ⊤	SW 1	SN ◇1 A
Havant	d		20 14	20 17			20 35	20 39	20 44	20 51				21 15	21 17				21 36	21 39		21 44	21 51		22 14
Bedhampton	d						20 37	20 41	20 46										21 39	21 42		21 46			
Hilsea	d	20 00			20 26							21 00				21 26								22 00	
Fratton	d	20 04	20 23	20 26	20 30	20 41	20 45	20 50	20 54	21 01		21 04	21 10	21 24	21 26	21 30	21 38	21 39	21 47	21 50		21 54	22 01	22 04	22 23
Portsmouth & Southsea	a	20 08	20 26	20 29	20 33	20 45	20 48	20 53	20 57	21 04		21 08	21 15	21 27	21 29	21 33	21 41	21 42	21 50	21 53		21 57	22 04	22 08	22 26
	d	20 09	20 27	20 30		20 45	20 49	20 54	20 58	21 05		21 09	21 15	21 27	21 30		21 41	21 42	21 50	21 54		21 58	22 05	22 09	22 27
Portsmouth Harbour ⛴	a	20 13	20 30	20 35		20 52	20 52	20 58	21 01	21 09		21 13	21 26	21 31	21 35		21 48	21 48	21 53	21 58		22 01	22 11	22 13	22 30

		SN ◇1 B	SW 1	GW ◇	SN ◇1 A	SW 1		SN ◇1 B	GW	SW 1	SW 1	SW 1	SN ◇1	GW ◇ D	GW ◇ C	SW 1		SW 1	SW 1						
Havant	d	22 17			22 35	22 39		22 44	22 47	22 51			23 22			23 39		23 51							
Bedhampton	d				22 37	22 41		22 46								23 41									
Hilsea	d		22 26								23 00	23 24							23 59						
Fratton	d	22 26	22 30	22 40	22 45	22 50		22 54	22 57	23 01	23 04	23 29	23 32	23 41	23 43	23 50		00 01	00 04						
Portsmouth & Southsea	a	22 29	22 33	22 43	22 48	22 53		22 57	23 00	23 04	23 08	23 32	23 35	23 44	23 46	23 53		00 04	00 08						
	d	22 30		22 44	22 49	22 54		22 58	23 00	23 05	23 09		23 36	23 45	23 46	23 54		00 05	00 09						
Portsmouth Harbour ⛴	a	22 35		22 49	22 52	22 58		23 01	23 04	23 09	23 13		23 39	23 53	23 52	23 58		00 09	00 13						

A until 4 September

B 11 September, 18 September, 25 September

C not from 18 September until 25 September

D 18 September, 25 September

Table 157

Sundays
2 October to 23 October

Havant - Portsmouth Harbour
(Complete service)

		SW	SW	SW	SW	SW	SW	SN	SW	SW		SN	SW	SW	SN	SW	SN	SW	SW	SN		SW	SW	SN	SW
		1	1	1	1	1	1	◇1	1	1		◇1	1	1	◇1	1	◇1	1	1	◇1		1	1	◇1	1
Havant	d	23p49		00 22	00 37		01 21	07 10				08 11		08 39	08 49		09 11		09 45	09 49		09 53		10 17	
Bedhampton	d			00 25			01s24							08 41	08 51				09 47	09 51					
Hilsea	d		00 03	00 30			01s29		07 26	08 00			08 26			09 00		09 26					10 04		10 26
Fratton	d	23p59	00 07	00 34	00 47		01s33	07 19	07 30	08 04		08 20	08 30	08 50	08 59	09 04	09 20	09 30	09 56	09 59		10 02	10 08	10 26	10 30
Portsmouth & Southsea	a	00 02	00 11	00 38	00 50	01s08	01 37	07 22	07 33	08 08		08 23	08 33	08 53	09 03	09 08	09 23	09 33	09 59	10 03		10 06	10 11	10 29	10 33
	d	00 03	00 12		00 51			07 22		08 09		08 23		08 54	09 04	09 09	09 23		10 00	10 04		10 08	10 12	10 30	
Portsmouth Harbour ⛴	a	00 07	00 16		00 55	01 12		07 26		08 13		08 27		08 57	09 07	09 13	09 27		10 04	10 07		10 11	10 15	10 35	

		SN	SW	SW	SW	SN		SW	GW	SW	SN	SW	SW	SN	SW	GW		SW	SN	SW	SW	SN	SW	SW	SN
		◇1	1	1	1	◇1		1	◇	1	◇1	1	1	◇1	1	◇		1	◇1	1	1	◇1	1	1	◇1
																				⊼					
Havant	d	10 41	10 45	10 53		11 17				11 39	11 44	11 51		12 17				12 39	12 44	12 51		13 17		13 39	13 44
Bedhampton	d	10 43	10 47							11 41	11 46							12 41	12 46					13 41	13 46
Hilsea	d				11 04			11 26					12 00		12 26						13 00		13 26		
Fratton	d	10 51	10 56	11 02	11 08	11 26		11 30	11 41	11 50	11 54	12 01	12 04	12 26	12 30	12 41		12 50	12 54	13 01	13 04	13 26	13 30	13 50	13 54
Portsmouth & Southsea	a	10 54	10 59	11 05	11 11	11 29		11 33	11 45	11 53	11 57	12 04	12 08	12 29	12 33	12 45		12 53	12 57	13 04	13 08	13 29	13 33	13 53	13 57
	d	10 55	11 00	11 07	11 12	11 30			11 45	11 54	11 58	12 05	12 09	12 30		12 45		12 54	12 58	13 05	13 09	13 30		13 54	13 58
Portsmouth Harbour ⛴	a	10 58	11 04	11 11	11 15	11 35			11 52	11 58	12 01	12 09	12 13	12 35		12 52		12 58	13 01	13 11	13 13	13 35		13 58	14 01

		SW		SW	SN	SW	GW	SW	SN	SW	SW	SN		SW	SW	SN	SW	SW	SN	SW	GW	SW		SN	SW
		1		1	◇1	1	◇	1	◇1	1	1	◇1		1	1	◇1	1	1	◇1	1	◇	1		◇1	1
		⊼					⊼			⊼							⊼								⊼
Havant	d	13 51			14 17			14 39	14 44	14 51		15 17			15 39	15 44	15 51		16 17			16 39		16 44	16 51
Bedhampton	d							14 41	14 46						15 41	15 46						16 41		16 46	
Hilsea	d			14 00		14 26					15 00			15 26				16 00		16 26					
Fratton	d	14 01		14 04	14 26	14 30	14 41	14 50	14 54	15 01	15 04	15 26		15 30	15 50	15 54	16 01	16 04	16 26	16 30	16 41	16 50		16 54	17 01
Portsmouth & Southsea	a	14 04		14 08	14 29	14 33	14 45	14 53	14 57	15 04	15 08	15 29		15 33	15 54	15 57	16 04	16 08	16 29	16 33	16 45	16 53		16 57	17 04
	d	14 05		14 09	14 30		14 45	14 54	14 58	15 05	15 09	15 30			15 54	15 58	16 05	16 09	16 30		16 45	16 54		16 58	17 05
Portsmouth Harbour ⛴	a	14 11		14 13	14 35		14 55	14 58	15 01	15 11	15 13	15 35			15 58	16 01	16 11	16 13	16 35		16 52	16 58		17 01	17 11

		SW	SN	SW	GW	SW	SN	SW		SW	SN	SW	GW	SW	SN	SW	SW	SN		SW	GW	SW	SN	SW	SW
		1	◇1	1	◇	1	◇1	1		1	◇1	1	◇	1	◇1	1	1	◇1		1	◇	1	◇1	1	1
								⊼								⊼								⊼	
Havant	d		17 17			17 39	17 44	17 51			18 17			18 39	18 44	18 51		19 17				19 39	19 44	19 51	
Bedhampton	d					17 41	17 46							18 41	18 46							19 41	19 46		
Hilsea	d	17 00		17 26						18 00		18 26					19 00			19 26					20 00
Fratton	d	17 04	17 26	17 30	17 41	17 50	17 54	18 01		18 04	18 26	18 30	18 41	18 50	18 54	19 01	19 04	19 26		19 30	19 41	19 50	19 54	20 01	20 04
Portsmouth & Southsea	a	17 08	17 29	17 33	17 45	17 53	17 57	18 04		18 08	18 29	18 33	18 45	18 53	18 57	19 04	19 08	19 29		19 33	19 45	19 53	19 57	20 04	20 08
	d	17 09	17 30		17 45	17 54	17 58	18 05		18 09	18 30		18 45	18 54	18 58	19 05	19 09	19 30			19 45	19 54	19 58	20 05	20 09
Portsmouth Harbour ⛴	a	17 13	17 35		17 52	17 58	18 01	18 11		18 13	18 35		18 52	18 58	19 01	19 11	19 13	19 35			19 52	19 58	20 01	20 11	20 13

		SN	SW	GW		SW	SN	SW	SW	GW	SN	SW	GW	SW		SN	SW	SW	SN	SW	GW	SW	SN	GW	
										R															
		◇1	1	◇		1	◇1	1	1		◇1	1	◇	1		◇1	1	1	◇1	1	◇	1	◇1		
								⊼									⊼								
Havant	d	20 17				20 39	20 44	20 51			21 17			21 39		21 44	21 51		22 17			22 39	22 44	22 47	
Bedhampton	d					20 41	20 46							21 42		21 46						22 41	22 46		
Hilsea	d		20 26						21 00			21 26						22 00		22 26					
Fratton	d	20 26	20 30	20 41		20 50	20 54	21 01	21 04	21 10	21 26	21 30	21 39	21 50		21 54	22 01	22 04	22 26	22 30	22 40	22 50	22 54	22 57	
Portsmouth & Southsea	a	20 29	20 33	20 45		20 53	20 57	21 04	21 08	21 15	21 29	21 33	21 42	21 53		21 57	22 04	22 08	22 29	22 33	22 43	22 53	22 57	23 00	
	d	20 30		20 45		20 54	20 58	21 05	21 09	21 15	21 30		21 42	21 54		21 58	22 05	22 09	22 30		22 44	22 54	22 58	23 00	
Portsmouth Harbour ⛴	a	20 35		20 52		20 58	21 01	21 09	21 13	21 26	21 35		21 48	21 58		22 01	22 11	22 13	22 35		22 49	22 58	23 01	23 04	

		SW	SW	SW	SN	GW	SW	SW	SW
		1	1	1	◇1	◇	1	1	1
Havant	d	22 51			23 22		23 39	23 51	
Bedhampton	d						23 41		
Hilsea	d		23 00	23 24					23 59
Fratton	d	23 01	23 04	23 29	23 32	23 41	23 50	00 01	00 04
Portsmouth & Southsea	a	23 04	23 08	23 32	23 35	23 44	23 53	00 04	00 08
	d	23 05	23 09		23 36	23 45	23 54	00 05	00 09
Portsmouth Harbour ⛴	a	23 09	23 13		23 39	23 53	23 58	00 09	00 13

Sundays
from 30 October

		SW	SW	SW	SW	SW	SW	SN	SW	SW		SN	SW	SW	SN	SW	SN	SW	SW	SN		SW	SW	SN	SW
		1	1	1	1	1	1	◇1	1	1		◇1	1	1	◇1	1	◇1	1	1	◇1		1	1	◇1	1
Havant	d	23p49		00 22	00 37		01 21	07 10				08 11		08 39	08 49		09 11		09 45	09 49		09 53		10 17	
Bedhampton	d			00 25			01s24							08 41	08 51				09 47	09 51					
Hilsea	d		00 03	00 30			01s29		07 26	08 00			08 26			09 00		09 26					10 04		10 26
Fratton	d	23p59	00 07	00 34	00 47		01s33	07 19	07 30	08 04		08 20	08 30	08 50	08 59	09 04	09 20	09 30	09 56	09 59		10 02	10 08	10 26	10 30
Portsmouth & Southsea	a	00 02	00 11	00 38	00 50	01s08	01 37	07 22	07 33	08 08		08 23	08 33	08 53	09 03	09 08	09 23	09 33	09 59	10 03		10 06	10 11	10 29	10 33
	d	00 03	00 12		00 51			07 22		08 09		08 23		08 54	09 04	09 09	09 23		10 00	10 04		10 08	10 12	10 30	
Portsmouth Harbour ⛴	a	00 07	00 16		00 55	01 12		07 26		08 13		08 27		08 57	09 07	09 13	09 27		10 04	10 07		10 11	10 15	10 35	

Table 157

Sundays

from 30 October

Havant - Portsmouth Harbour

(Complete service)

		SN ◇1	SW 1	SW 1	SW 1	SN ◇1		SW 1	GW ◇	SW 1	SN ◇1	SW 1	SW 1	SN ◇1	SW 1	GW ◇		SW 1	SN ◇1	SW 1 (trolley)	SW 1	SN ◇1	SW 1	SW 1	SN ◇1
Havant	d	10 41	10 45	10 53		11 17				11 39	11 44	11 51		12 17				12 39	12 44	12 51		13 17		13 39	13 44
Bedhampton	d	10 43	10 47							11 41	11 46							12 41	12 46					13 41	13 46
Hilsea	d				11 04			11 26					12 00		12 26						13 00		13 26		
Fratton	d	10 51	10 56	11 02	11 08	11 26		11 30	11 41	11 50	11 54	12 01	12 04	12 26	12 30	12 41		12 50	12 54	13 01	13 04	13 26	13 30	13 50	13 54
Portsmouth & Southsea	a	10 54	10 59	11 05	11 11	11 29		11 33	11 45	11 53	11 57	12 04	12 08	12 29	12 33	12 45		12 53	12 57	13 04	13 08	13 29	13 33	13 53	13 57
	d	10 55	11 00	11 07	11 12	11 30			11 45	11 54	11 58	12 05	12 09	12 30		12 45		12 54	12 58	13 05	13 09	13 30		13 54	13 58
Portsmouth Harbour ⛴	a	10 58	11 04	11 11	11 15	11 35			11 52	11 58	12 01	12 09	12 13	12 35		12 52		12 58	13 01	13 11	13 13	13 35		13 58	14 01

		SW 1 (trolley)		SW 1	SN ◇1	SW 1	GW ◇ (trolley)	SW 1	SN ◇1	SW 1 (trolley)	SW 1	SN ◇1		SW 1	SW 1	SN ◇1	SW 1 (trolley)	SW 1	SN ◇1	SW 1	GW ◇	SW 1		SN ◇1	SW 1 (trolley)
Havant	d	13 51			14 17			14 39	14 44	14 51		15 17			15 39	15 44	15 51		16 17			16 39		16 44	16 51
Bedhampton	d							14 41	14 46						15 41	15 46						16 41		16 46	
Hilsea	d			14 00		14 26					15 00			15 26				16 00		16 26					
Fratton	d	14 01		14 04	14 26	14 30	14 41	14 50	14 54	15 01	15 04	15 26		15 30	15 50	15 54	16 01	16 04	16 26	16 30	16 41	16 50		16 54	17 01
Portsmouth & Southsea	a	14 04		14 08	14 29	14 33	14 45	14 53	14 57	15 04	15 08	15 29		15 33	15 54	15 57	16 04	16 08	16 29	16 33	16 45	16 53		16 57	17 04
	d	14 05		14 09	14 30		14 45	14 54	14 58	15 05	15 09	15 30			15 54	15 58	16 05	16 09	16 30		16 45	16 54		16 58	17 05
Portsmouth Harbour ⛴	a	14 11		14 13	14 35		14 55	14 58	15 01	15 11	15 13	15 35			15 58	16 01	16 11	16 13	16 35		16 52	16 58		17 01	17 11

		SW 1	SN ◇1	SW 1	GW ◇	SW 1	SN ◇1	SW 1 (trolley)		SW 1	SN ◇1	SW 1	GW ◇	SW 1	SN ◇1	SW 1 (trolley)	SW 1	SN ◇1		SW 1	GW ◇	SW 1	SN ◇1	SW 1 (trolley)	SW 1
Havant	d		17 17			17 39	17 44	17 51			18 17			18 39	18 44	18 51		19 17				19 39	19 44	19 51	
Bedhampton	d					17 41	17 46							18 41	18 46							19 41	19 46		
Hilsea	d	17 00		17 26						18 00		18 26					19 00			19 26					20 00
Fratton	d	17 04	17 26	17 30	17 41	17 50	17 54	18 01		18 04	18 26	18 30	18 41	18 50	18 54	19 01	19 04	19 26		19 30	19 41	19 50	19 54	20 01	20 04
Portsmouth & Southsea	a	17 08	17 29	17 33	17 45	17 53	17 57	18 04		18 08	18 29	18 33	18 45	18 53	18 57	19 04	19 08	19 29		19 33	19 45	19 53	19 57	20 04	20 08
	d	17 09	17 30		17 45	17 54	17 58	18 05		18 09	18 30		18 45	18 54	18 58	19 05	19 09	19 30			19 45	19 54	19 58	20 05	20 09
Portsmouth Harbour ⛴	a	17 13	17 35		17 52	17 58	18 01	18 11		18 13	18 35		18 52	18 58	19 01	19 11	19 13	19 35			19 52	19 58	20 01	20 11	20 13

		SN ◇1	SW 1	GW ◇		SW 1	SN ◇1	SW 1 (trolley)	SW 1	GW ■	SN ◇1	SW 1	GW ◇	SW 1		SN ◇1	SW 1 (trolley)	SW 1	SN ◇1	SW 1	GW ◇	SW 1	SN ◇1	GW	
Havant	d	20 17				20 39	20 44	20 51			21 17			21 39		21 44	21 51		22 17			22 39	22 44	22 47	
Bedhampton	d					20 41	20 46							21 42		21 46						22 41	22 46		
Hilsea	d		20 26						21 00			21 26						22 00		22 26					
Fratton	d	20 26	20 30	20 41		20 50	20 54	21 01	21 04	21 10	21 26	21 30	21 38	21 50		21 54	22 01	22 04	22 26	22 30	22 40	22 50	22 54	22 57	
Portsmouth & Southsea	a	20 29	20 33	20 45		20 53	20 57	21 04	21 08	21 15	21 29	21 33	21 41	21 53		21 57	22 04	22 08	22 29	22 33	22 43	22 53	22 57	23 00	
	d	20 30		20 45		20 54	20 58	21 05	21 09	21 15	21 30		21 41	21 54		21 58	22 05	22 09	22 30		22 44	22 54	22 58	23 00	
Portsmouth Harbour ⛴	a	20 35		20 52		20 58	21 01	21 09	21 13	21 26	21 35		21 48	21 58		22 01	22 11	22 13	22 35		22 49	22 58	23 01	23 04	

		SW 1	SW 1	SW 1	SN ◇1	GW ◇	SW 1	SW 1	SW 1
Havant	d	22 51			23 22		23 39	23 51	
Bedhampton	d						23 41		
Hilsea	d		23 00	23 24					23 59
Fratton	d	23 01	23 04	23 29	23 32	23 41	23 50	00 01	00 04
Portsmouth & Southsea	a	23 04	23 08	23 32	23 35	23 44	23 53	00 04	00 08
	d	23 05	23 09		23 36	23 44	23 54	00 05	00 09
Portsmouth Harbour ⛴	a	23 09	23 13		23 39	23 52	23 58	00 09	00 13

Table 157

Mondays to Fridays

until 30 September

Portsmouth Harbour - Havant

(Complete service)

		SW [1]	SW [1]	SW [1]	SW [1] 🍴	SN ◇[1]	SW [1]	SN ◇[1]	SW [1]	GW ■ 🍴		SN ◇[1] 🍴	SW [1]	SW [1]	SW [1]	SW [1] 🍴	SN ◇[1]	SW [1]	SW [1]	GW 🍴		GW ◇ 🍴	SW [1] 🍴	SN ◇[1]	SW [1]
Portsmouth Harbour ⛴	d	04 30	05 00		05 19	05 33	05 43	05 47	05 50	06 00		06 04	06 15		06 23	06 42	06 46	06 50	06 55	07 01		07 05	07 13	07 20	07 24
Portsmouth & Southsea	a	04 33	05 03		05 22	05 36	05 46	05 50	05 53	06 03		06 07	06 18		06 26	06 45	06 49	06 53	06 58	07 04		07 08	07 16	07 23	07 27
	d	04 35	05 05	05 16	05 24	05 37	05 48	05 51	05 55	06 04		06 08	06 20	06 23	06 28	06 47	06 50	06 55	07 00	07 05		07 09	07 18	07 24	07 29
Fratton	d	04 39	05 09	05 20	05 28	05 41	05 52	05 55	05 59	06a07		06 12	06 24	06 27	06 32	06 51	06 54	06 59	07 04	07 10		07a13	07 22	07 28	07 33
Hilsea	d	04 43	05a13	05a24	05 32	05 45	05a56	05 59	06 03					06a31	06a36		06 58	07a03	07 08						07a37
Bedhampton	d	04 48			05 37	05 50		06 04	06 08								07 03		07 13						
Havant	a	04 50			05 40	05 52		06 06	06 10			06 20	06 33			06 59	07 05		07 15	07 19			07 30	07 36	

		SW [1]	SW [1]	SW [1] 🍴	SW [1]	SN ◇[1]		SW [1]	SN ◇[1]	SW [1] 🍴	SW [1]	GW ◇ 🍴	SN ◇	SW [1]	SW [1] 🍴	SN ◇		SW [1]	SN ◇[1]	SW [1] 🍴	SW [1]	GW ◇ 🍴	SN ◇	SW [1]	SW [1] 🍴
Portsmouth Harbour ⛴	d	07 29		07 45	07 55			08 05	08 10	08 15		08 23	08 29	08 33	08 45	08 51		08 59	09 12	09 15	09 18	09 23	09 29	09 33	09 45
Portsmouth & Southsea	a	07 32		07 48	07 58			08 08	08 13	08 18		08 26	08 32	08 36	08 48	08 54		09 01	09 15	09 18	09 22	09 26	09 32	09 36	09 48
	d	07 33	07 38	07 50	08 00	08 03		08 10	08 14	08 20	08 24	08 27	08 33	08 38	08 50	08 55		09 03	09 16	09 20	09 24	09 27	09 33	09 38	09 50
Fratton	d	07 37	07 42	07 54	08 04	08 07		08 13	08 18	08 24	08 28	08a31	08 37	08 42	08 54	08 59		09 07	09 20	09 24	09 28	09a31	09 37	09 42	09 54
Hilsea	d	07 41	07a46		08a08	08 11		08a17			08 32			08a46		09 04		09a11			09 32			09a46	
Bedhampton	d	07 48				08 16					08 37					09 13					09 37				
Havant	a	07 50		08 03		08 18			08 26	08 32	08 40		08 45		09 03	09 15			09 29	09 33	09 39		09 45		10 03

		SN ◇		SW [1]	SN ◇[1]	SW [1] 🍴	SW [1]	GW ◇ 🍴	SN ◇[1]	SW [1]	SW [1] 🍴	SN ◇[1]		SW [1]	SN ◇[1]	SW [1] 🍴	SW [1]	GW ◇ 🍴	SN ◇	SW [1]	SW [1] 🍴	SN ◇		SW [1]	SN ◇[1]
Portsmouth Harbour ⛴	d			09 59	10 12	10 15		10 23	10 29	10 33	10 45			10 59	11 12	11 15		11 23	11 29		11 45			11 59	12 12
Portsmouth & Southsea	a			10 02	10 15	10 18		10 26	10 32	10 36	10 48			11 02	11 15	11 18		11 26	11 32		11 48			12 02	12 15
	d	09 59		10 03	10 16	10 20	10 24	10 27	10 33	10 38	10 50	10 59		11 03	11 16	11 20	11 24	11 27	11 33	11 38	11 50	11 59		12 03	12 16
Fratton	d	10 04		10 07	10 20	10 24	10 28	10a31	10 37	10 42	10 54	11 04		11 07	11 20	11 24	11 28	11a31	11 37	11 42	11 54	12 04		12 07	12 20
Hilsea	d	10 08		10a11			10 32			10a46		11 08		11a11			11 32			11a46		12 08		12a11	
Bedhampton	d	10 13					10 37					11 13					11 37					12 13			
Havant	a	10 15			10 29	10 33	10 39		10 45		11 03	11 15			11 29	11 33	11 39		11 45		12 03	12 15			12 29

		SW [1] 🍴	SW [1]	GW ◇ 🍴	SN ◇	SW [1]	SW [1] 🍴	SN ◇		SW [1]	SN ◇[1]	SW [1] 🍴	SW [1]	GW ◇ 🍴	SN ◇[1]	SW [1]	SW [1] 🍴	SN ◇		SW [1]	SN ◇[1]	SW [1] 🍴	SW [1]	GW ■ 🍴	SN ◇
Portsmouth Harbour ⛴	d	12 15		12 23	12 29		12 45			12 59	13 12	13 15		13 23	13 29		13 45			13 59	14 12	14 15		14 23	14 29
Portsmouth & Southsea	a	12 18		12 26	12 32		12 48			13 02	13 15	13 18		13 26	13 32		13 48			14 02	14 15	14 18		14 26	14 32
	d	12 20	12 24	12 27	12 33	12 38	12 50	12 59		13 03	13 16	13 20	13 24	13 27	13 33	13 38	13 50	13 59		14 03	14 16	14 20	14 24	14 27	14 33
Fratton	d	12 24	12 28	12a31	12 37	12 42	12 54	13 04		13 07	13 20	13 24	13 28	13a31	13 37	13 42	13 54	14 04		14 07	14 20	14 24	14 28	14a31	14 37
Hilsea	d		12 32			12a46		13 08		13a11			13 32			13a46		14 08		14a11			14 32		
Bedhampton	d		12 37					13 13					13 37					14 13					14 37		
Havant	a	12 33	12 39		12 45		13 03	13 15			13 29	13 33	13 39		13 45		14 03	14 15			14 29	14 33	14 39		14 45

		SW [1]	SW [1] 🍴	SN ◇[1]		SW [1]	SN ◇[1]	SW [1] 🍴	SW [1]	GW ■ 🍴	SN ◇	SW [1]	SW [1] 🍴	SN ◇[1]		SW [1]	SN ◇[1]	SW [1] 🍴	SW [1]	GW ■ 🍴	SN ◇	SW [1]	SN ◇	SW [1] 🍴	
Portsmouth Harbour ⛴	d		14 45			14 59	15 12	15 15		15 23	15 29		15 45			15 59	16 12	16 15		16 23	16 29		16 40	16 45	
Portsmouth & Southsea	a		14 48			15 02	15 15	15 18		15 26	15 32		15 48			16 02	16 15	16 18		16 26	16 32		16 44	16 48	
	d	14 38	14 50	14 59		15 03	15 16	15 20	15 24	15 27	15 33	15 38	15 50	15 59		16 03	16 16	16 20	16 24	16 27	16 33	16 38	16 46	16 50	
Fratton	d	14 42	14 54	15 04		15 07	15 20	15 24	15 28	15a31	15 37	15 42	15 54	16 04		16 07	16 20	16 24	16 28	16a31	16 37	16 42	16 50	16 54	
Hilsea	d	14a46		15 08		15a11			15 32			15a46		16 08		16a11			16 32			16a46	16 54		
Bedhampton	d			15 14					15 37					16 13					16 37						
Havant	a		15 03	15 17			15 29	15 33	15 39		15 45		16 03	16 15			16 29	16 33	16 39		16 45		16 59	17 03	

		SW [1]	SN ◇	SW [1]	SN ◇[1]	SW [1] 🍴	SW [1]	GW ◇ 🍴	SN ◇	SW [1]		SN ◇	SW [1] 🍴	SN [1]	SW [1]	SW [1] 🍴	SW [1]	GW ◇ 🍴	SN ◇[1]	SW [1]		SN ◇[1]	SW [1] 🍴	SN ◇	SW [1]
Portsmouth Harbour ⛴	d	16 49		16 59	17 12	17 15	17 18	17 23	17 29	17 33			17 45		17 59	18 15		18 23	18 28			18 37	18 45		18 59
Portsmouth & Southsea	a	16 53		17 02	17 15	17 18	17 22	17 26	17 32	17 36			17 48		18 02	18 18		18 26	18 31			18 40	18 48		19 02
	d	16 55	17 00	17 03	17 16	17 20	17 24	17 27	17 33	17 38		17 46	17 50	17 59	18 03	18 20	18 24	18 27	18 32	18 38		18 42	18 50	18 59	19 03
Fratton	d	16 59	17 04	17 07	17 20	17 24	17 28	17a31	17 37	17 42		17 50	17 54	18 04	18 07	18 24	18 28	18a31	18 36	18 42		18 46	18 54	19 04	19 07
Hilsea	d	17a03	17 08	17a11			17 32			17a46		17 54		18 08	18a11		18 32			18a46		18 50		19 08	19a11
Bedhampton	d		17 14				17 37							18 13			18 37							19 13	
Havant	a		17 17		17 29	17 33	17 39		17 45			17 59	18 03	18 15		18 33	18 39		18 44			18 56	19 03	19 15	

		SW [1] 🍴	SW [1]	GW ◇	SN ◇[1]	SW [1]		SN ◇[1]	SW [1]	SN ◇	SW [1]	SW [1]	SW [1]	GW ◇	SN ◇	SW [1]		SN ◇[1]	SW [1]	SW [1]	SN ◇[1]	SW [1]	GW	SW [1]	SW [1]
Portsmouth Harbour ⛴	d	19 15		19 23				19 40	19 45		19 59	20 15	20 18	20 23				20 40	20 45	20 59		21 18	21 23	21 28	
Portsmouth & Southsea	a	19 18		19 26				19 43	19 48		20 02	20 18	20 22	20 26				20 43	20 48	21 02		21 21	21 26	21 31	
	d	19 20	19 24	19 27	19 32	19 38		19 44	19 50	19 59	20 03	20 20	20 24	20 27	20 32	20 38		20 44	20 50	21 03	21 15	21 24	21 27	21 33	21 38
Fratton	d	19 24	19 28	19a31	19 36	19 42		19 48	19 54	20 04	20 07	20 24	20 28	20a31	20 36	20 42		20 48	20 54	21 07	21 19	21 28	21a31	21 37	21 42
Hilsea	d		19 32			19a46				20 08	20a11		20 32			20a46				21a11	21 23	21 32		21 41	21a46
Bedhampton	d		19 37							20 14			20 37								21 28	21 37		21 47	
Havant	a	19 33	19 39		19 46			19 56	20 03	20 16		20 33	20 39		20 44			20 56	21 03		21 30	21 40		21 52	

Table 157

Mondays to Fridays

until 30 September

Portsmouth Harbour - Havant

(Complete service)

		SN		SW	SN	SW	SW	SW	SN	SN	SW	SW
		1		1	◇1	1	1	1	◇1	◇1	1	1
Portsmouth Harbour ⛴	d	21 40		21 54	22 15	22 18	22 28	22 33	22 44	23 15	23 19	23 24
Portsmouth & Southsea	a	21 43		21 57	22 18	22 21	22 31	22 37	22 47	23 18	23 22	23 27
	d	21 44		21 59	22 19	22 24	22 33	22 38	22 48	23 19	23 24	23 29
Fratton	d	21 48		22 03	22 23	22 28	22 37	22 42	22 52	23 23	23 28	23 33
Hilsea	d	21 52		22a07	22 27	22 32	22 41	22a46	22 56	23 27	23 32	23a37
Bedhampton	d	21 57			22 32	22 37	22 46		23 01	23 33	23 37	
Havant	a	21 59			22 34	22 39	22 53		23 05	23 36	23 39	

Mondays to Fridays

from 3 October

		SW	SW	SW	SW	SN	SW	SN	SW	GW		SN	SW	SW	SW	SW	SN	SW	SW	GW		GW	SW	SN	SW
		1	1	1	1 🛒	◇1	1	◇1	1	R 🛒		◇1	1 🛒	1	1	1 🛒	◇1	1	1	🛒		◇ 🛒	1 🛒	◇1	1
Portsmouth Harbour ⛴	d	04 25	04 55		05 14	05 33	05 43	05 47	05 50	06 00		06 04	06 15		06 23	06 42	06 46	06 50	06 55	07 01		07 05	07 13	07 20	07 24
Portsmouth & Southsea	a	04 28	04 58		05 17	05 36	05 46	05 50	05 53	06 03		06 07	06 18		06 26	06 45	06 49	06 53	06 58	07 04		07 08	07 16	07 23	07 27
	d	04 30	05 00	05 16	05 19	05 37	05 48	05 51	05 55	06 04		06 08	06 20	06 23	06 28	06 47	06 50	06 55	07 00	07 05		07 09	07 18	07 24	07 29
Fratton	d	04 34	05 04	05 20	05 23	05 41	05 52	05 55	05 59	06a07		06 12	06 24	06 27	06 32	06 51	06 54	06 59	07 04	07 10		07a13	07 22	07 28	07 33
Hilsea	d	04 38	05a08	05a24	05 27	05 45	05a56	05 59	06 03					06a31	06a36		06 58	07a03	07 08						07a37
Bedhampton	d	04 43			05 32	05 50		06 04	06 08								07 03		07 13						
Havant	a	04 45			05 35	05 52		06 06	06 10			06 20	06 33			06 59	07 05		07 15	07 19			07 30	07 36	

		SW	SW	SW	SW	SN		SW	SN	SW	SW	GW	SN	SW	SW	SN		SW	SN	SW	SW	GW	SN	SW	SW
		1	1	1 🛒	1	◇1		1	◇1	1 🛒	1	◇ 🛒	◇	1	1 🛒	◇		1	◇1	1 🛒	1	◇ 🛒	◇	1	1 🛒
Portsmouth Harbour ⛴	d	07 29		07 45	07 55			08 05	08 10	08 15		08 23	08 29	08 33	08 45	08 51		08 59	09 12	09 15	09 18	09 23	09 29	09 33	09 45
Portsmouth & Southsea	a	07 32		07 48	07 58			08 08	08 13	08 18		08 26	08 32	08 36	08 48	08 54		09 01	09 15	09 18	09 22	09 26	09 32	09 36	09 48
	d	07 33	07 38	07 50	08 00	08 03		08 10	08 14	08 20	08 24	08 27	08 33	08 38	08 50	08 55		09 03	09 16	09 20	09 24	09 27	09 33	09 38	09 50
Fratton	d	07 37	07 42	07 54	08 04	08 07		08 13	08 18	08 24	08 28	08a31	08 37	08 42	08 54	08 59		09 07	09 20	09 24	09 28	09a31	09 37	09 42	09 54
Hilsea	d	07 41	07a46		08a08	08 11		08a17			08 32			08a46		09 04		09a11			09 32			09a46	
Bedhampton	d	07 48				08 16					08 37					09 13					09 37				
Havant	a	07 50		08 03		08 18			08 26	08 32	08 40		08 45		09 03	09 15			09 29	09 33	09 39		09 45		10 03

		SN		SW	SN	SW	SW	GW	SN	SW	SW	SN		SW	SN	SW	SW	GW	SN	SW	SW	SN		SW	SN
		◇		1	◇1	1 🛒	1	◇ 🛒	◇1	1	1 🛒	◇1		1	◇1	1 🛒	1	◇ 🛒	◇	1	1 🛒	◇		1	◇1
Portsmouth Harbour ⛴	d			09 59	10 12	10 15		10 23	10 29	10 33	10 45			10 59	11 12	11 15		11 23	11 29		11 45			11 59	12 12
Portsmouth & Southsea	a			10 02	10 15	10 18		10 26	10 32	10 36	10 48			11 02	11 15	11 18		11 26	11 32		11 48			12 02	12 15
	d	09 59		10 03	10 16	10 20	10 24	10 27	10 33	10 38	10 50	10 59		11 03	11 16	11 20	11 24	11 27	11 33	11 38	11 50	11 59		12 03	12 16
Fratton	d	10 04		10 07	10 20	10 24	10 28	10a31	10 37	10 42	10 54	11 04		11 07	11 20	11 24	11 28	11a31	11 37	11 42	11 54	12 04		12 07	12 20
Hilsea	d	10 08		10a11			10 32			10a46		11 08		11a11			11 32			11a46		12 08		12a11	
Bedhampton	d	10 13					10 37					11 13					11 37					12 13			
Havant	a	10 15			10 29	10 33	10 39		10 45		11 03	11 15			11 29	11 33	11 39		11 45		12 03	12 15			12 29

		SW	SW	GW	SN	SW	SW	SN		SW	SN	SW	SW	GW	SN	SW	SW	SN		SW	SN	SW	SW	GW	SN
		1 🛒	1	◇ 🛒	◇	1	1 🛒	◇		1	◇1	1 🛒	1	◇ 🛒	◇1	1	1 🛒	◇		1	◇1	1 🛒	1	R 🛒	◇
Portsmouth Harbour ⛴	d	12 15		12 23	12 29		12 45			12 59	13 12	13 15		13 23	13 29		13 45			13 59	14 12	14 15		14 23	14 29
Portsmouth & Southsea	a	12 18		12 26	12 32		12 48			13 02	13 15	13 18		13 26	13 32		13 48			14 02	14 15	14 18		14 26	14 32
	d	12 20	12 24	12 27	12 33	12 38	12 50	12 59		13 03	13 16	13 20	13 24	13 27	13 33	13 38	13 50	13 59		14 03	14 16	14 20	14 24	14 27	14 33
Fratton	d	12 24	12 28	12a31	12 37	12 42	12 54	13 04		13 07	13 20	13 24	13 28	13a31	13 37	13 42	13 54	14 04		14 07	14 20	14 24	14 28	14a31	14 37
Hilsea	d		12 32			12a46		13 08		13a11			13 32			13a46		14 08		14a11			14 32		
Bedhampton	d		12 37					13 13					13 37					14 13					14 37		
Havant	a	12 33	12 39		12 45		13 03	13 15			13 29	13 33	13 39		13 45		14 03	14 15			14 29	14 33	14 39		14 45

		SW	SW	SN		SW	SN	SW	SW	GW	SN	SW	SW	SN		SW	SN	SW	SW	GW	SN	SW	SN	SW	
		1	1 🛒	◇1		1	◇1	1 🛒	1	R 🛒	◇	1	1 🛒	◇1		1	◇1	1 🛒	1	R 🛒	◇	1	◇	1 🛒	
Portsmouth Harbour ⛴	d		14 45			14 59	15 12	15 15		15 23	15 29		15 45			15 59	16 12	16 15		16 23	16 29		16 40	16 45	
Portsmouth & Southsea	a		14 48			15 02	15 15	15 18		15 26	15 32		15 48			16 02	16 15	16 18		16 26	16 32		16 44	16 48	
	d	14 38	14 50	14 59		15 03	15 16	15 20	15 24	15 27	15 33	15 38	15 50	15 59		16 03	16 16	16 20	16 24	16 27	16 33	16 38	16 46	16 50	
Fratton	d	14 42	14 54	15 04		15 07	15 20	15 24	15 28	15a31	15 37	15 42	15 54	16 04		16 07	16 20	16 24	16 28	16a31	16 37	16 42	16 50	16 54	
Hilsea	d	14a46		15 08		15a11			15 32			15a46		16 08		16a11			16 32			16a46	16 54		
Bedhampton	d			15 14					15 37					16 13					16 37						
Havant	a		15 03	15 17			15 29	15 33	15 39		15 45		16 03	16 15			16 29	16 33	16 39		16 45		16 59	17 03	

		SW	SN	SW	SN	SW	SW	GW	SN	SW		SN	SW	SN	SW	SW	SW	GW	SN	SW		SN	SW	SN	SW
		1	◇	1	◇1	1 🛒	1	◇ 🛒	◇	1		◇	1 🛒	1	1	1 🛒	1	◇ 🛒	◇1	1		◇1	1 🛒	◇	1
Portsmouth Harbour ⛴	d	16 49		16 59	17 12	17 15	17 18	17 23	17 29	17 33			17 45		17 59	18 15		18 23	18 28			18 37	18 45		18 59
Portsmouth & Southsea	a	16 53		17 02	17 15	17 18	17 22	17 26	17 32	17 36			17 48		18 02	18 18		18 26	18 31			18 40	18 48		19 02
	d	16 55	17 00	17 03	17 16	17 20	17 24	17 27	17 33	17 38		17 46	17 50	17 59	18 03	18 20	18 24	18 27	18 32	18 38		18 42	18 50	18 59	19 03
Fratton	d	16 59	17 04	17 07	17 20	17 24	17 28	17a31	17 37	17 42		17 50	17 54	18 04	18 07	18 24	18 28	18a31	18 36	18 42		18 46	18 54	19 04	19 07
Hilsea	d	17a03	17 08	17a11			17 32			17a46		17 54		18 08	18a11		18 32			18a46		18 50		19 08	19a11
Bedhampton	d		17 14				17 37							18 13			18 37							19 13	
Havant	a		17 17		17 29	17 33	17 39		17 45			17 59	18 03	18 15		18 33	18 39		18 44			18 56	19 03	19 15	

Table 157

Mondays to Fridays

from 3 October

Portsmouth Harbour - Havant

(Complete service)

		SW 1 🚲	SW 1	GW ◇	SN ◇1	SW 1		SN ◇1	SW 1	SN ◇	SW 1	SW 1	SW 1	GW ◇	SN ◇	SW 1		SN ◇1	SW 1	SW 1	SN ◇1	SW 1	GW	SW 1	SW 1
Portsmouth Harbour ⛴	d	19 15		19 23				19 40	19 45		19 59	20 15	20 18	20 23				20 40	20 45	20 59		21 18	21 23	21 28	
Portsmouth & Southsea	a	19 18		19 26				19 43	19 48		20 02	20 18	20 22	20 26				20 43	20 48	21 02		21 21	21 26	21 31	
	d	19 20	19 24	19 27	19 32	19 38		19 44	19 50	19 59	20 03	20 20	20 24	20 27	20 32	20 38		20 44	20 50	21 03	21 15	21 24	21 27	21 33	21 38
Fratton	d	19 24	19 28	19a31	19 36	19 42		19 48	19 54	20 04	20 07	20 24	20 28	20a31	20 36	20 42		20 48	20 54	21 07	21 19	21 28	21a31	21 37	21 42
Hilsea	d		19 32			19a46				20 08	20a11		20 32			20a46				21a11	21 23	21 32		21 41	21a46
Bedhampton	d		19 37							20 14			20 37								21 28	21 37		21 47	
Havant	a	19 33	19 39		19 46			19 56	20 03	20 16		20 33	20 39		20 44			20 56	21 03		21 30	21 40		21 52	

		SN 1		SW 1	SN ◇1	SW 1	SW 1	SW 1	SN ◇1	SN ◇1	SW 1	SW 1
Portsmouth Harbour ⛴	d	21 40		21 54	22 15	22 18	22 28	22 33	22 44	23 15	23 19	23 24
Portsmouth & Southsea	a	21 43		21 57	22 18	22 21	22 31	22 37	22 47	23 18	23 22	23 27
	d	21 44		21 59	22 19	22 24	22 33	22 38	22 48	23 19	23 24	23 29
Fratton	d	21 48		22 03	22 23	22 28	22 37	22 42	22 52	23 23	23 28	23 33
Hilsea	d	21 52		22a07	22 27	22 32	22 41	22a46	22 56	23 27	23 32	23a37
Bedhampton	d	21 57			22 32	22 37	22 46		23 01	23 33	23 37	
Havant	a	21 59			22 34	22 39	22 53		23 05	23 36	23 39	

Saturdays

until 1 October

		SW 1	SN ◇1	SW 1	SW 1	SW 1	SN ◇	GW ◇	SN ◇1	SW 1		SN ◇1	SW 1	SW 1 🚲	GW	SN ◇	SW 1	GW ◇ 🚲	SN ◇1	SW 1 🚲		SW 1	SN ◇1	SW 1	SW 1 🚲
Portsmouth Harbour ⛴	d	04 43			05 19	05 50		06 00	06 12	06 19		06 29		06 45	06 48		06 55	07 05	07 12	07 15			07 29		07 45
Portsmouth & Southsea	a	04 46			05 22	05 53		06 03	06 15	06 22		06 32		06 48	06 53		06 58	07 08	07 15	07 18			07 32		07 48
	d	04 48	04 56	05 16	05 24	05 55	05 59	06 04	06 16	06 24		06 33	06 38	06 50	06 54	06 56	07 00	07 09	07 16	07 20		07 24	07 33	07 38	07 50
Fratton	d	04 52	05 00	05 20	05 28	05 59	06 04	06a07	06 20	06 28		06 37	06 42	06 54	06 58	07 01	07 04	07a13	07 20	07 24		07 28	07 37	07 42	07 54
Hilsea	d	04 56		05a24	05 32	06a03	06 08			06 32			06a46			07 05	07a08					07 32		07a46	
Bedhampton	d	05 01			05 37		06 13			06 37						07 13						07 37			
Havant	a	05 03	05 08		05 39		06 15		06 29	06 40		06 45		07 03	07 08	07 15			07 29	07 33		07 39	07 45		08 03

		SN ◇	SW 1	SN ◇1	SW 1 🚲	SW 1		GW ◇ 🚲	SN ◇1	SW 1	SW 1 🚲	SN ◇	SW 1	SN ◇1	SW 1 🚲	SW 1		GW ◇ 🚲	SN ◇1	SW 1	SW 1 🚲	SN ◇	SW 1	SN ◇1	SW 1 🚲
Portsmouth Harbour ⛴	d		07 59	08 12	08 15			08 23	08 29		08 45		08 59	09 12	09 15			09 23	09 29		09 45		09 59	10 12	10 15
Portsmouth & Southsea	a		08 02	08 15	08 18			08 26	08 32		08 48		09 02	09 15	09 18			09 26	09 32		09 48		10 02	10 15	10 18
	d	07 59	08 03	08 16	08 20	08 24		08 27	08 33	08 38	08 50	08 59	09 03	09 16	09 20	09 24		09 27	09 33	09 38	09 50	09 59	10 03	10 16	10 20
Fratton	d	08 04	08 07	08 20	08 24	08 28		08a30	08 37	08 42	08 54	09 04	09 07	09 20	09 24	09 28		09a30	09 37	09 42	09 54	10 04	10 07	10 20	10 24
Hilsea	d	08 08	08a11			08 32				08a46		09 08	09a11			09 32				09a46		10 08	10a11		
Bedhampton	d	08 13				08 37						09 13				09 37						10 13			
Havant	a	08 15		08 29	08 33	08 39			08 45		09 03	09 15		09 29	09 33	09 39			09 45		10 03	10 15		10 29	10 33

		SW 1		GW ◇	SN ◇1	SW 1	SW 1 🚲	SN ◇	SW 1	SN ◇1	SW 1 🚲	SW 1		GW ◇	SN ◇1	SW 1	SW 1 🚲	SN ◇	SW 1	SN ◇1	SW 1 🚲	SW 1		GW ◇	SN ◇1
Portsmouth Harbour ⛴	d			10 23	10 29		10 45		10 59	11 12	11 15			11 23	11 29		11 45		11 59	12 12	12 15			12 23	12 29
Portsmouth & Southsea	a			10 26	10 32		10 48		11 02	11 15	11 18			11 26	11 32		11 48		12 02	12 15	12 18			12 26	12 32
	d	10 24		10 27	10 33	10 38	10 50	10 59	11 03	11 16	11 20	11 24		11 27	11 33	11 38	11 50	11 59	12 03	12 16	12 20	12 24		12 27	12 33
Fratton	d	10 28		10a30	10 37	10 42	10 54	11 04	11 07	11 20	11 24	11 28		11a30	11 37	11 42	11 54	12 04	12 07	12 20	12 24	12 28		12a30	12 37
Hilsea	d	10 32				10a46		11 08	11a11			11 32				11a46		12 08	12a11			12 32			
Bedhampton	d	10 37						11 13				11 37						12 13				12 37			
Havant	a	10 39			10 45		11 03	11 15		11 29	11 33	11 39			11 45		12 03	12 15		12 29	12 33	12 39			12 45

		SW 1	SW 1 🚲	SN ◇	SW 1	SN ◇1	SW 1 🚲	SW 1		GW ◇	SN ◇1	SW 1	SW 1 🚲	SN ◇	SW 1	SN ◇1	SW 1 🚲	SW 1		GW ◇	SN ◇1	SW 1	SW 1 🚲	SN ◇	SW 1
Portsmouth Harbour ⛴	d		12 45		12 59	13 12	13 15			13 23	13 29		13 45		13 59	14 12	14 15			14 23	14 29		14 45		14 59
Portsmouth & Southsea	a		12 48		13 02	13 15	13 18			13 26	13 32		13 48		14 02	14 15	14 18			14 26	14 32		14 48		15 02
	d	12 38	12 50	12 59	13 03	13 16	13 20	13 24		13 27	13 33	13 38	13 50	13 59	14 03	14 16	14 20	14 24		14 27	14 33	14 38	14 50	14 59	15 03
Fratton	d	12 42	12 54	13 04	13 07	13 20	13 24	13 28		13a30	13 37	13 42	13 54	14 04	14 07	14 20	14 24	14 28		14a30	14 37	14 42	14 54	15 04	15 07
Hilsea	d	12a46		13 08	13a11			13 32				13a46		14 08	14a11			14 32				14a46		15 08	15a11
Bedhampton	d			13 13				13 37						14 13				14 37						15 14	
Havant	a		13 03	13 15		13 29	13 33	13 39			13 45		14 03	14 15		14 29	14 33	14 39			14 45		15 03	15 17	

		SN ◇1	SW 1 🚲	SW 1		GW ◇	SN ◇1	SW 1	SW 1 🚲	SN ◇	SW 1	SN ◇1	SW 1 🚲	SW 1		GW R	SN ◇1	SW 1	SW 1 🚲	SN ◇	SW 1	SW 1	SN ◇1	SW 1	
Portsmouth Harbour ⛴	d	15 12	15 15			15 23	15 29		15 45		15 59	16 12	16 15			16 23	16 29		16 45		16 59		17 12	17 18	
Portsmouth & Southsea	a	15 15	15 18			15 26	15 32		15 48		16 02	16 15	16 18			16 26	16 32		16 48		17 02		17 15	17 22	
	d	15 16	15 20	15 24		15 27	15 33	15 38	15 50	15 59	16 03	16 16	16 20	16 24		16 27	16 33	16 38	16 50	16 59	17 03	17 10	17 16	17 24	
Fratton	d	15 20	15 24	15 28		15a30	15 37	15 42	15 54	16 04	16 07	16 20	16 24	16 28		16a31	16 37	16 42	16 54	17 04	17 07	17 14	17 20	17 28	
Hilsea	d			15 32				15a46		16 08	16a11			16 32				16a46		17 08	17a11	17 18		17 32	
Bedhampton	d			15 37						16 13				16 37						17 13		17 23		17 37	
Havant	a	15 29	15 33	15 39			15 45		16 03	16 15		16 29	16 33	16 39			16 45		17 03	17 15		17 25	17 29	17 39	

Table 157

Saturdays
until 1 October

Portsmouth Harbour - Havant

(Complete service)

		GW	SN	SW	SW	SN	SW	SN	SW	SW		GW	SN	SW	SW	SN	SW	SN	SW	SW		GW	SN	SW	SW
		◇	◇[1]	[1]	[1] 🛒	[1]	[1]	◇	[1]	[1]		◇	◇[1]	[1]	[1]	◇	[1]	◇[1]	[1]	[1]		◇	◇[1]	[1]	[1]
Portsmouth Harbour ⛴	d	17 23	17 29	17 33	17 45		17 59	18 12	18 15			18 23	18 29		18 45		18 59	19 12	19 15			19 23	19 29		19 45
Portsmouth & Southsea	a	17 26	17 32	17 36	17 48		18 02	18 15	18 18			18 27	18 32		18 48		19 02	19 15	19 18			19 26	19 32		19 48
	d	17 27	17 33	17 38	17 50	17 59	18 03	18 16	18 20	18 24		18 27	18 33	18 38	18 50	18 59	19 03	19 16	19 20	19 24		19 27	19 33	19 38	19 50
Fratton	d	17a31	17 37	17 42	17 54	18 04	18 07	18 20	18 24	18 28		18a31	18 37	18 42	18 54	19 04	19 07	19 20	19 24	19 28		19a30	19 37	19 42	19 54
Hilsea	d			17a46		18 08	18a11			18 32				18a46		19 08	19a11			19 32				19a46	
Bedhampton	d					18 13				18 37						19 13				19 37					
Havant	a		17 45		18 03	18 15		18 29	18 33	18 39			18 45		19 03	19 15		19 29	19 33	19 39			19 45		20 03

		SN	SW	SW	SW	GW		SN	SW	SN	SW	SW	SN	SW	SW	SN		SW	SN	SW	SW	SN	SN	SW	SW
		◇	[1]	[1]	[1]	◇		◇[1]	[1]		[1]	[1]	◇[1]	[1]	[1]	[1]		[1]	◇[1]	[1]	[1]	◇[1]	◇[1]	[1]	[1]
Portsmouth Harbour ⛴	d		19 59	20 15		20 23		20 28		20 40	20 45	20 59	21 11	21 18		21 40		21 54	22 15	22 18	22 33	22 44	23 15	23 19	23 24
Portsmouth & Southsea	a		20 02	20 18		20 26		20 31		20 43	20 48	21 02	21 14	21 21		21 43		21 57	22 18	22 21	22 37	22 47	23 18	23 22	23 28
	d	19 59	20 03	20 20	20 24	20 27		20 32	20 38	20 44	20 50	21 03	21 15	21 24	21 38	21 44		21 59	22 19	22 24	22 38	22 48	23 19	23 24	23 29
Fratton	d	20 04	20 07	20 24	20 28	20a30		20 36	20 42	20 48	20 54	21 07	21 19	21 28	21 42	21 48		22 03	22 23	22 28	22 42	22 52	23 23	23 28	23 33
Hilsea	d	20 08	20a11		20 32				20a46	20 52		21a11	21 23	21 32	21a46	21 52		22a07	22 27	22 32	22a46	22 56	23 27	23 32	23a37
Bedhampton	d	20 13			20 37								21 28	21 37		21 57			22 32	22 37		23 01	23 33	23 37	
Havant	a	20 15		20 33	20 39			20 44		20 58	21 03		21 30	21 39		21 59			22 34	22 39		23 05	23 36	23 39	

Saturdays
from 8 October

		SW	SN	SW	SW	SW	SN	GW	SN	SW		SN	SW	SW	GW	SN	SW	GW	SN	SW		SW	SN	SW	SW
		[1]	◇[1]	[1]	[1]	[1]	◇	◇	◇[1]	[1]		◇[1]	[1]	[1] 🛒		◇	[1]	◇ 🛒	◇[1]	[1] 🛒		[1]	◇[1]	[1]	[1] 🛒
Portsmouth Harbour ⛴	d	04 38			05 14	05 50		06 00	06 12	06 19		06 29		06 45	06 48		06 55	07 05	07 12	07 15			07 29		07 45
Portsmouth & Southsea	a	04 41			05 17	05 53		06 03	06 15	06 22		06 32		06 48	06 53		06 58	07 08	07 15	07 18			07 32		07 48
	d	04 43	04 56	05 16	05 19	05 55	05 59	06 04	06 16	06 24		06 33	06 38	06 50	06 54	06 56	07 00	07 09	07 16	07 20		07 24	07 33	07 38	07 50
Fratton	d	04 47	05 00	05 20	05 23	05 59	06 04	06a07	06 20	06 28		06 37	06 42	06 54	06 58	07 01	07 04	07a13	07 20	07 24		07 28	07 37	07 42	07 54
Hilsea	d	04 51		05a24	05 27	06a03	06 08			06 32			06a46			07 05	07a08					07 32		07a46	
Bedhampton	d	04 56			05 32		06 13			06 37						07 13						07 37			
Havant	a	04 58	05 08		05 34		06 15		06 29	06 40		06 45		07 03	07 08	07 15			07 29	07 33		07 39	07 45		08 03

		SN	SW	SN	SW	SW		GW	SN	SW	SW	SN	SW	SN	SW	SW		GW	SN	SW	SW	SN	SW	SN	SW
		◇	[1]	◇[1]	[1] 🛒	[1]		◇ 🛒	◇[1]	[1]	[1] 🛒	◇	[1]	◇[1]	[1] 🛒	[1]		◇ 🛒	◇[1]	[1]	[1] 🛒	◇	[1]	◇[1]	[1] 🛒
Portsmouth Harbour ⛴	d		07 59	08 12	08 15			08 23	08 29		08 45		08 59	09 12	09 15			09 23	09 29		09 45		09 59	10 12	10 15
Portsmouth & Southsea	a		08 02	08 15	08 18			08 26	08 32		08 48		09 02	09 15	09 18			09 26	09 32		09 48		10 02	10 15	10 18
	d	07 59	08 03	08 16	08 20	08 24		08 27	08 33	08 38	08 50	08 59	09 03	09 16	09 20	09 24		09 27	09 33	09 38	09 50	09 59	10 03	10 16	10 20
Fratton	d	08 04	08 07	08 20	08 24	08 28		08a30	08 37	08 42	08 54	09 04	09 07	09 20	09 24	09 28		09a30	09 37	09 42	09 54	10 04	10 07	10 20	10 24
Hilsea	d	08 08	08a11			08 32				08a46		09 08	09a11			09 32				09a46		10 08	10a11		
Bedhampton	d	08 13				08 37						09 13				09 37						10 13			
Havant	a	08 15		08 29	08 33	08 39			08 45		09 03	09 15		09 29	09 33	09 39			09 45		10 03	10 15		10 29	10 33

		SW		GW	SN	SW	SW	SN	SW	SN	SW	SW		GW	SN	SW	SW	SN	SW	SN	SW	SW		GW	SN
		[1]		◇	◇[1]	[1]	[1] 🛒	◇	[1]	◇[1]	[1] 🛒	[1]		◇	◇[1]	[1]	[1] 🛒	◇	[1]	◇[1]	[1] 🛒	[1]		◇	◇[1]
Portsmouth Harbour ⛴	d			10 23	10 29		10 45		10 59	11 12	11 15			11 23	11 29		11 45		11 59	12 12	12 15			12 23	12 29
Portsmouth & Southsea	a			10 26	10 32		10 48		11 02	11 15	11 18			11 26	11 32		11 48		12 02	12 15	12 18			12 26	12 32
	d	10 24		10 27	10 33	10 38	10 50	10 59	11 03	11 16	11 20	11 24		11 27	11 33	11 38	11 50	11 59	12 03	12 16	12 20	12 24		12 27	12 33
Fratton	d	10 28		10a30	10 37	10 42	10 54	11 04	11 07	11 20	11 24	11 28		11a30	11 37	11 42	11 54	12 04	12 07	12 20	12 24	12 28		12a30	12 37
Hilsea	d	10 32				10a46		11 08	11a11			11 32				11a46		12 08	12a11			12 32			
Bedhampton	d	10 37						11 13				11 37						12 13				12 37			
Havant	a	10 39			10 45		11 03	11 15		11 29	11 33	11 39			11 45		12 03	12 15		12 29	12 33	12 39			12 45

		SW	SW	SN	SW	SN	SW	SW		GW	SN	SW	SW	SN	SW	SN	SW	SW		GW	SN	SW	SW	SN	SW
		[1]	[1] 🛒	◇	[1]	◇[1]	[1] 🛒	[1]		◇	◇[1]	[1]	[1] 🛒	◇	[1]	◇[1]	[1] 🛒	[1]		◇	◇[1]	[1]	[1] 🛒	◇	[1]
Portsmouth Harbour ⛴	d		12 45		12 59	13 12	13 15			13 23	13 29		13 45		13 59	14 12	14 15			14 23	14 29		14 45		14 59
Portsmouth & Southsea	a		12 48		13 02	13 15	13 18			13 26	13 32		13 48		14 02	14 15	14 18			14 26	14 32		14 48		15 02
	d	12 38	12 50	12 59	13 03	13 16	13 20	13 24		13 27	13 33	13 38	13 50	13 59	14 03	14 16	14 20	14 24		14 27	14 33	14 38	14 50	14 59	15 03
Fratton	d	12 42	12 54	13 04	13 07	13 20	13 24	13 28		13a30	13 37	13 42	13 54	14 04	14 07	14 20	14 24	14 28		14a30	14 37	14 42	14 54	15 04	15 07
Hilsea	d	12a46		13 08	13a11			13 32				13a46		14 08	14a11			14 32				14a46		15 08	15a11
Bedhampton	d			13 13				13 37						14 13				14 37						15 14	
Havant	a		13 03	13 15		13 29	13 33	13 39			13 45		14 03	14 15		14 29	14 33	14 39			14 45		15 03	15 17	

		SN	SW	SW		GW	SN	SW	SW	SN	SW	SN	SW	SW		GW	SN	SW	SW	SN	SW	SW	SN	SW	
		◇[1]	[1] 🛒	[1]		◇	◇[1]	[1]	[1] 🛒	◇	[1]	◇[1]	[1] 🛒	[1]		[R]	◇[1]	[1]	[1] 🛒	◇	[1]	[1]	◇[1]	[1]	
Portsmouth Harbour ⛴	d	15 12	15 15			15 23	15 29		15 45		15 59	16 12	16 15			16 23	16 29		16 45		16 59		17 12	17 18	
Portsmouth & Southsea	a	15 15	15 18			15 26	15 32		15 48		16 02	16 15	16 18			16 26	16 32		16 48		17 02		17 15	17 22	
	d	15 16	15 20	15 24		15 27	15 33	15 38	15 50	15 59	16 03	16 16	16 20	16 24		16 27	16 33	16 38	16 50	16 59	17 03	17 10	17 16	17 24	
Fratton	d	15 20	15 24	15 28		15a30	15 37	15 42	15 54	16 04	16 07	16 20	16 24	16 28		16a31	16 37	16 42	16 54	17 04	17 07	17 14	17 20	17 28	
Hilsea	d			15 32				15a46		16 08	16a11			16 32				16a46		17 08	17a11	17 18		17 32	
Bedhampton	d			15 37						16 13				16 37						17 13		17 23		17 37	
Havant	a	15 29	15 33	15 39			15 45		16 03	16 15		16 29	16 33	16 39			16 45		17 03	17 15		17 25	17 29	17 39	

Table 157

Saturdays
from 8 October

Portsmouth Harbour - Havant

(Complete service)

		GW ◇	SN ◇1	SW 1	SW 1 🛒	SN 1	SW 1	SN ◇	SW 1	SW 1		GW ◇	SN ◇1	SW 1	SW 1	SN ◇	SW 1	SN ◇1	SW 1	SW 1		GW ◇	SN ◇1	SW 1	SW 1
Portsmouth Harbour ⛴	d	17 23	17 29	17 33	17 45		17 59	18 12	18 15			18 23	18 29		18 45		18 59	19 12	19 15			19 23	19 29		19 45
Portsmouth & Southsea	a	17 26	17 32	17 36	17 48		18 02	18 15	18 18			18 27	18 32		18 48		19 02	19 15	19 18			19 26	19 32		19 48
	d	17 27	17 33	17 38	17 50	17 59	18 03	18 16	18 20	18 24		18 27	18 33	18 38	18 50	18 59	19 03	19 16	19 20	19 24		19 27	19 33	19 38	19 50
Fratton	d	17a31	17 37	17 42	17 54	18 04	18 07	18 20	18 24	18 28		18a31	18 37	18 42	18 54	19 04	19 07	19 20	19 24	19 28		19a30	19 37	19 42	19 54
Hilsea	d			17a46		18 08	18a11			18 32				18a46		19 08	19a11			19 32				19a46	
Bedhampton	d					18 13				18 37						19 13				19 37					
Havant	a		17 45		18 03	18 15		18 29	18 33	18 39			18 45		19 03	19 15		19 29	19 33	19 39			19 45		20 03

		SN ◇	SW 1	SW 1	SW 1	GW ◇		SN ◇1	SW 1	SN	SW 1	SW 1	SN ◇1	SW 1	SW 1	SN 1		SW 1	SN ◇1	SW 1	SW 1	SN ◇1	SN ◇1	SW 1	SW 1
Portsmouth Harbour ⛴	d		19 59	20 15		20 23		20 28		20 40	20 45	20 59	21 11	21 18		21 40		21 54	22 15	22 18	22 33	22 44	23 15	23 19	23 24
Portsmouth & Southsea	a		20 02	20 18		20 26		20 31		20 43	20 48	21 02	21 14	21 21		21 43		21 57	22 18	22 21	22 37	22 47	23 18	23 22	23 28
	d	19 59	20 03	20 20	20 24	20 27		20 32	20 38	20 44	20 50	21 03	21 15	21 24	21 38	21 44		21 59	22 19	22 24	22 38	22 48	23 19	23 24	23 29
Fratton	d	20 04	20 07	20 24	20 28	20a30		20 36	20 42	20 48	20 54	21 07	21 19	21 28	21 42	21 48		22 03	22 23	22 28	22 42	22 52	23 23	23 28	23 33
Hilsea	d	20 08	20a11		20 32				20a46	20 52		21a11	21 23	21 32	21a46	21 52		22a07	22 27	22 32	22a46	22 56	23 27	23 32	23a37
Bedhampton	d	20 13			20 37								21 28	21 37		21 57			22 32	22 37		23 01	23 33	23 37	
Havant	a	20 15		20 33	20 39			20 44		20 58	21 03		21 30	21 39		21 59			22 34	22 39		23 05	23 36	23 39	

Sundays
until 25 September

		SW 1	SW 1	SN ◇1 A	SN ◇1 B	SW 1	SW 1	SW 1	SN ◇1	SW 1		SN ◇1 A	SN ◇1 B	SW 1	SW 1	SW 1	SN ◇1	SW 1	SN ◇1 A	GW R		SN ◇1 B	SW 1 🛒	SW 1 🛒	SW 1
Portsmouth Harbour ⛴	d	06 37	06 48	07 05	07 14	07 17	07 32		07 43	07 48		08 05	08 14	08 17	08 32		08 43	08 48	09 05	09 08		09 14	09 17	09 32	
Portsmouth & Southsea	a	06 40	06 51	07 08	07 17	07 20	07 35		07 46	07 51		08 08	08 17	08 20	08 35		08 46	08 51	09 08	09 11		09 17	09 20	09 35	
	d	06 42	06 53	07 09	07 18	07 22	07 37	07 42	07 47	07 53		08 09	08 18	08 22	08 37	08 42	08 47	08 53	09 09	09 12		09 18	09 22	09 37	09 42
Fratton	d	06 46	06 57	07 13	07 22	07 26	07 41	07 46	07 51	07 57		08 13	08 22	08 26	08 41	08 46	08 51	08 57	09 13	09a15		09 22	09 26	09 41	09 46
Hilsea	d	06a50				07a30		07a50						08a30		08a50							09a30		09a50
Bedhampton	d		07 04	07 21	07 30					08 04		08 20	08 30					09 04	09 20			09 30			
Havant	a		07 07	07 24	07 32		07 49		07 59	08 07		08 23	08 32		08 49		08 59	09 07	09 23			09 32		09 49	

		SN ◇1	SW 1	SN ◇1 A	SN ◇1 B	SW 1 🛒		SW 1 🛒	SW 1	SN ◇1	SW 1	SN ◇1 A	GW ◇	SN ◇1 B	SW 1 🛒	SW 1 🛒		SW 1	SN ◇1	SW 1	SN ◇1 A	SN ◇1 B	SW 1 🛒	SW 1 🛒	SW 1
Portsmouth Harbour ⛴	d	09 43	09 48	10 05	10 14	10 17		10 32		10 43	10 48	11 05	11 08	11 14	11 17	11 32			11 43	11 48	12 05	12 14	12 17	12 32	
Portsmouth & Southsea	a	09 46	09 51	10 08	10 17	10 20		10 35		10 46	10 51	11 08	11 11	11 17	11 20	11 35			11 46	11 51	12 08	12 17	12 20	12 35	
	d	09 47	09 53	10 09	10 18	10 22		10 37	10 42	10 47	10 53	11 09	11 12	11 18	11 22	11 37		11 42	11 47	11 53	12 09	12 18	12 22	12 37	12 42
Fratton	d	09 51	09 57	10 13	10 22	10 26		10 41	10 46	10 51	10 57	11 13	11a15	11 22	11 26	11 41		11 46	11 51	11 57	12 13	12 22	12 26	12 41	12 46
Hilsea	d					10a30			10a50						11a30			11a50					12a30		12a50
Bedhampton	d		10 04	10 20	10 30						11 04	11 20		11 30						12 04	12 20	12 30			
Havant	a	09 59	10 07	10 23	10 32			10 49		10 59	11 07	11 23		11 32		11 49			11 59	12 07	12 23	12 32		12 49	

		SN ◇1		SW 1	SN ◇1 A	GW ◇	SN ◇1 B	SW 1 🛒	SW 1 🛒	SW 1	SN ◇1	SW 1		SN ◇1 A	GW ◇	SN ◇1 B	SW 1 🛒	SW 1 🛒	SW 1	SN ◇1	SW 1	SN ◇1 A		GW R	SN ◇1 B
Portsmouth Harbour ⛴	d	12 43		12 48	13 05	13 08	13 14	13 17	13 32		13 43	13 48		14 05	14 08	14 14	14 17	14 32		14 43	14 48	15 05		15 08	15 14
Portsmouth & Southsea	a	12 46		12 51	13 08	13 11	13 17	13 20	13 35		13 46	13 51		14 08	14 11	14 17	14 20	14 35		14 46	14 51	15 08		15 11	15 17
	d	12 47		12 53	13 09	13 12	13 18	13 22	13 37	13 42	13 47	13 53		14 09	14 12	14 18	14 22	14 37	14 42	14 47	14 53	15 09		15 12	15 18
Fratton	d	12 51		12 57	13 13	13a15	13 22	13 26	13 41	13 46	13 51	13 57		14 13	14a15	14 22	14 26	14 41	14 46	14 51	14 57	15 13		15a15	15 22
Hilsea	d							13a30		13a50							14a30		14a50						
Bedhampton	d			13 04	13 20		13 30					14 04		14 20		14 30					15 04	15 20			15 30
Havant	a	12 59		13 07	13 23		13 32		13 49		13 59	14 07		14 23		14 32		14 49		14 59	15 07	15 23			15 32

		SW 1 🛒	SW 1 🛒	SW 1	SN ◇1	SW 1	SN ◇1 A	GW ◇		SN ◇1 B	SW 1 🛒	SW 1 🛒	SW 1	SN ◇1	SW 1	SN ◇1 A	GW ◇	SN ◇1 B		SW 1	SW 1 🛒	SW 1	SN ◇1	SW 1	SN ◇1 A
Portsmouth Harbour ⛴	d	15 17	15 32		15 43	15 48	16 05	16 08		16 14	16 17	16 32		16 43	16 48	17 05	17 08	17 14		17 17	17 32		17 43	17 48	18 05
Portsmouth & Southsea	a	15 20	15 35		15 46	15 51	16 08	16 11		16 17	16 20	16 35		16 46	16 51	17 08	17 11	17 17		17 20	17 35		17 46	17 51	18 08
	d	15 22	15 37	15 42	15 47	15 53	16 09	16 12		16 18	16 22	16 37	16 42	16 47	16 53	17 09	17 12	17 18		17 22	17 37	17 42	17 47	17 53	18 09
Fratton	d	15 26	15 41	15 46	15 51	15 57	16 13	16a15		16 22	16 26	16 41	16 46	16 51	16 57	17 13	17a15	17 22		17 26	17 41	17 46	17 51	17 57	18 13
Hilsea	d	15a30		15a50							16a30		16a50							17a30		17a50			
Bedhampton	d					16 04	16 20			16 30					17 04	17 20		17 30						18 04	18 20
Havant	a		15 49		15 59	16 07	16 23			16 32		16 49		16 59	17 07	17 23		17 32			17 49		17 59	18 07	18 23

A until 4 September

B 11 September, 18 September, 25 September

Table 157

Portsmouth Harbour - Havant

(Complete service)

Sundays

until 25 September

		GW	SN	SW		SW	SW	SN	SW	SN	GW	SN	SW	SW		SW	SN	SW	SN	GW	SN	SW	SW	SW	
		◇	◇1	1		1	1	◇1	1	◇1	◇	◇1	1	1		1	◇1	1	◇1	◇	◇1	1	1	1	
			A			🛒				B		A							B		A				
Portsmouth Harbour ⛴	d	18 08	18 14	18 17		18 32		18 43	18 48	19 05	19 08	19 14	19 17	19 32			19 43	19 48	20 05	20 08	20 14	20 17	20 32		
Portsmouth & Southsea	a	18 11	18 17	18 20		18 35		18 46	18 51	19 08	19 11	19 17	19 20	19 35			19 46	19 51	20 08	20 11	20 17	20 20	20 35		
	d	18 12	18 18	18 22		18 37	18 42	18 47	18 53	19 09	19 12	19 18	19 22	19 37		19 42	19 47	19 53	20 09	20 12	20 18	20 22	20 37	20 42	
Fratton	d	18a15	18 22	18 26		18 41	18 46	18 51	18 57	19 13	19a15	19 22	19 26	19 41		19 46	19 51	19 57	20 13	20a15	20 22	20 26	20 41	20 46	
Hilsea	d			18a30			18a50						19a30			19a50						20a30		20a50	
Bedhampton	d		18 30						19 04	19 20		19 30						20 04	20 20		20 30				
Havant	a		18 32			18 49		18 59	19 07	19 23		19 32		19 49			19 59	20 07	20 23		20 32		20 49		

		SN	SW	SN	SN	SW	SW	SW	SN	SW		GW	SN	SW	SW	SW	SN	SW	SW
		◇1	1	◇1	◇1	1	1	1	◇1	1			◇1	1	1	1	◇1	1	1
				B	A														
Portsmouth Harbour ⛴	d	20 43	20 48	21 05	21 14	21 17	21 32		21 43	21 48		22 03	22 14	22 17	22 32		22 43	22 48	23 17
Portsmouth & Southsea	a	20 46	20 51	21 08	21 17	21 20	21 35		21 46	21 51		22 11	22 17	22 20	22 35		22 46	22 51	23 20
	d	20 47	20 53	21 09	21 18	21 22	21 37	21 42	21 47	21 53		22 12	22 18	22 22	22 37	22 42	22 47	22 53	23 22
Fratton	d	20 51	20 57	21 13	21 22	21 26	21 41	21 46	21 51	21 57		22a15	22 22	22 26	22 41	22 46	22 51	22 57	23 26
Hilsea	d					21a30		21a50						22a30		22a50			23a30
Bedhampton	d		21 04	21 20	21 30					22 04			22 32					23 04	
Havant	a	20 59	21 07	21 23	21 32		21 49		21 59	22 07			22 35		22 49		22 59	23 07	

Sundays

2 October to 23 October

		SW	SW	SN	SW	SW	SW	SN	SW	SN		SW	SW	SW	SN	SW	GW	SN	SW	SW		SW	SN	SW	SN
		1	1	◇1	1	1	1	◇1	1	◇1		1	1	1	◇1	1	R	◇1	1 🛒	1 🛒		1	◇1	1	◇1
Portsmouth Harbour ⛴	d	06 37	06 43	07 14	07 17	07 29		07 43	07 48	08 14		08 17	08 29		08 43	08 48	09 08	09 14	09 17	09 32			09 43	09 48	10 14
Portsmouth & Southsea	a	06 40	06 46	07 17	07 20	07 32		07 46	07 51	08 17		08 20	08 32		08 46	08 51	09 11	09 17	09 20	09 35			09 46	09 51	10 17
	d	06 42	06 48	07 18	07 22	07 34	07 42	07 47	07 53	08 18		08 22	08 34	08 42	08 47	08 53	09 12	09 18	09 22	09 37		09 42	09 47	09 53	10 18
Fratton	d	06 46	06 52	07 22	07 26	07 38	07 46	07 51	07 57	08 22		08 26	08 38	08 46	08 51	08 57	09a15	09 22	09 26	09 41		09 46	09 51	09 57	10 22
Hilsea	d	06a50			07a30		07a50					08a30		08a50					09a30			09a50			
Bedhampton	d		06 59	07 30					08 04	08 30						09 04		09 30						10 04	10 30
Havant	a		07 02	07 32		07 46		07 59	08 07	08 32			08 46		08 59	09 07		09 32		09 49			09 59	10 07	10 32

		SW	SW	SW	SN	SW		GW	SN	SW	SW	SW	SN	SW	SN	SW		SW	SW	SN	SW	GW	SN	SW	SW
		1 🛒	1 🛒	1	◇1	1		◇	◇1	1 🛒	1 🛒	1	◇1	1	◇1	1 🛒		1 🛒	1	◇1	1	◇	◇1	1 🛒	1 🛒
Portsmouth Harbour ⛴	d	10 17	10 32		10 43	10 48		11 08	11 14	11 17	11 32		11 43	11 48	12 14	12 17		12 32		12 43	12 48	13 08	13 14	13 17	13 32
Portsmouth & Southsea	a	10 20	10 35		10 46	10 51		11 11	11 17	11 20	11 35		11 46	11 51	12 17	12 20		12 35		12 46	12 51	13 11	13 17	13 20	13 35
	d	10 22	10 37	10 42	10 47	10 53		11 12	11 18	11 22	11 37	11 42	11 47	11 53	12 18	12 22		12 37	12 42	12 47	12 53	13 12	13 18	13 22	13 37
Fratton	d	10 26	10 41	10 46	10 51	10 57		11a15	11 22	11 26	11 41	11 46	11 51	11 57	12 22	12 26		12 41	12 46	12 51	12 57	13a15	13 22	13 26	13 41
Hilsea	d	10a30		10a50						11a30		11a50				12a30			12a50					13a30	
Bedhampton	d					11 04			11 30					12 04	12 30						13 04		13 30		
Havant	a		10 49		10 59	11 07			11 32		11 49		11 59	12 07	12 32			12 49		12 59	13 07		13 32		13 49

		SW		SN	SW	GW	SN	SW	SW	SW	SN	SW		GW	SN	SW	SW	SW	SN	SW	GW	SN		SW	SW
		1		◇1	1	◇	◇1	1 🛒	1 🛒	1	◇1	1		R	◇1	1 🛒	1 🛒	1	◇1	1	◇	◇1		1 🛒	1 🛒
Portsmouth Harbour ⛴	d			13 43	13 48	14 08	14 14	14 17	14 32		14 43	14 48		15 08	15 14	15 17	15 32		15 43	15 48	16 08	16 14		16 17	16 32
Portsmouth & Southsea	a			13 46	13 51	14 11	14 17	14 20	14 35		14 46	14 51		15 11	15 17	15 20	15 35		15 46	15 51	16 11	16 17		16 20	16 35
	d	13 42		13 47	13 53	14 12	14 18	14 22	14 37	14 42	14 47	14 53		15 12	15 18	15 22	15 37	15 42	15 47	15 53	16 12	16 18		16 22	16 37
Fratton	d	13 46		13 51	13 57	14a15	14 22	14 26	14 41	14 46	14 51	14 57		15a15	15 22	15 26	15 41	15 46	15 51	15 57	16a15	16 22		16 26	16 41
Hilsea	d	13a50						14a30		14a50						15a30		15a50						16a30	
Bedhampton	d				14 04		14 30					15 04			15 30					16 04		16 30			
Havant	a			13 59	14 07		14 32		14 49		14 59	15 07			15 32		15 49		15 59	16 07		16 32			16 49

		SW	SN	SW	GW	SN	SW	SW		SW	SN	SW	GW	SN	SW	SW	SW	SN		SW	GW	SN	SW	SW	SW
		1	◇1	1	◇	◇1	1	1 🛒		1	◇1	1	◇	◇1	1	1 🛒	1	◇1		1	◇	◇1	1	1	1
Portsmouth Harbour ⛴	d		16 43	16 48	17 08	17 14	17 17	17 32			17 43	17 48	18 08	18 14	18 17	18 32		18 43		18 48	19 08	19 14	19 17	19 32	
Portsmouth & Southsea	a		16 46	16 51	17 11	17 17	17 20	17 35			17 46	17 51	18 11	18 17	18 20	18 35		18 46		18 51	19 11	19 17	19 20	19 35	
	d	16 42	16 47	16 53	17 12	17 18	17 22	17 37		17 42	17 47	17 53	18 12	18 18	18 22	18 37	18 42	18 47		18 53	19 12	19 18	19 22	19 37	19 42
Fratton	d	16 46	16 51	16 57	17a15	17 22	17 26	17 41		17 46	17 51	17 57	18a15	18 22	18 26	18 41	18 46	18 51		18 57	19a15	19 22	19 26	19 41	19 46
Hilsea	d	16a50					17a30			17a50					18a30		18a50						19a30		19a50
Bedhampton	d			17 04		17 30						18 04		18 30						19 04		19 30			
Havant	a		16 59	17 07		17 32		17 49			17 59	18 07		18 32		18 49		18 59		19 07		19 32		19 49	

		SN	SW	GW		SN	SW	SW	SW	SN	SW	SN	SW	SW		SW	SN	SW	GW	SN	SW	SW	SW	SN	
		◇1	1	◇		◇1	1	1	1	◇1	1	◇1	1	1		1	◇1	1		◇1	1	1	1	◇1	
Portsmouth Harbour ⛴	d	19 43	19 48	20 08		20 14	20 17	20 32		20 43	20 48	21 14	21 17	21 32			21 43	21 48	22 03	22 14	22 17	22 32		22 43	
Portsmouth & Southsea	a	19 46	19 51	20 11		20 17	20 20	20 35		20 46	20 51	21 17	21 20	21 35			21 46	21 51	22 11	22 17	22 20	22 35		22 46	
	d	19 47	19 53	20 12		20 18	20 22	20 37	20 42	20 47	20 53	21 18	21 22	21 37		21 42	21 47	21 53	22 12	22 18	22 22	22 37	22 42	22 47	
Fratton	d	19 51	19 57	20a15		20 22	20 26	20 41	20 46	20 51	20 57	21 22	21 26	21 41		21 46	21 51	21 57	22a15	22 22	22 26	22 41	22 46	22 51	
Hilsea	d						20a30		20a50				21a30			21a50					22a30		22a50		
Bedhampton	d		20 04			20 30					21 04	21 30						22 04		22 32					
Havant	a	19 59	20 07			20 32		20 49		20 59	21 07	21 32		21 49			21 59	22 07		22 35		22 49		22 59	

A 11 September, 18 September, 25 September

B until 4 September

Table 157

Sundays
2 October to 23 October

Portsmouth Harbour - Havant

(Complete service)

		SW	SW
		1	1
Portsmouth Harbour ⛴	d	22 48	23 17
Portsmouth & Southsea	a	22 51	23 20
	d	22 53	23 22
Fratton	d	22 57	23 26
Hilsea	d		23a30
Bedhampton	d	23 04	
Havant	a	23 07	

Sundays
from 30 October

		SW	SW	SN	SW	SW	SW	SN	SW	SN		SW	SW	SW	SN	SW	GW	SN	SW	SW		SW	SN	SW	SN
		1	1	◇1	1	1	1	◇1	1	◇1		1	1	1	◇1	1	R	◇1	1 🛒	1 🛒		1	◇1	1	◇1
Portsmouth Harbour ⛴	d	06 37	06 43	07 14	07 17	07 29		07 43	07 48	08 14		08 17	08 29		08 43	08 48	09 08	09 14	09 17	09 32			09 43	09 48	10 14
Portsmouth & Southsea	a	06 40	06 46	07 17	07 20	07 32		07 46	07 51	08 17		08 20	08 32		08 46	08 51	09 11	09 17	09 20	09 35			09 46	09 51	10 17
	d	06 42	06 48	07 18	07 22	07 34	07 42	07 47	07 53	08 18		08 22	08 34	08 42	08 47	08 53	09 12	09 18	09 22	09 37		09 42	09 47	09 53	10 18
Fratton	d	06 46	06 52	07 22	07 26	07 38	07 46	07 51	07 57	08 22		08 26	08 38	08 46	08 51	08 57	09a15	09 22	09 26	09 41		09 46	09 51	09 57	10 22
Hilsea	d	06a50			07a30		07a50					08a30		08a50					09a30			09a50			
Bedhampton	d		06 59	07 30					08 04	08 30						09 04		09 30						10 04	10 30
Havant	a		07 02	07 32		07 46		07 59	08 07	08 32			08 46		08 59	09 07		09 32		09 49			09 59	10 07	10 32

		SW	SW	SW	SN	SW		GW	SN	SW	SW	SW	SN	SW	SN	SW		SW	SW	SN	SW	GW	SN	SW	SW
		1 🛒	1 🛒	1	◇1	1		◇	◇1	1 🛒	1 🛒	1	◇1	1	◇1	1 🛒		1 🛒	1	◇1	1	◇	◇1	1 🛒	1 🛒
Portsmouth Harbour ⛴	d	10 17	10 32		10 43	10 48		11 08	11 14	11 17	11 32		11 43	11 48	12 14	12 17		12 32		12 43	12 48	13 08	13 14	13 17	13 32
Portsmouth & Southsea	a	10 20	10 35		10 46	10 51		11 11	11 17	11 20	11 35		11 46	11 51	12 17	12 20		12 35		12 46	12 51	13 11	13 17	13 20	13 35
	d	10 22	10 37	10 42	10 47	10 53		11 12	11 18	11 22	11 37	11 42	11 47	11 53	12 18	12 22		12 37	12 42	12 47	12 53	13 12	13 18	13 22	13 37
Fratton	d	10 26	10 41	10 46	10 51	10 57		11a15	11 22	11 26	11 41	11 46	11 51	11 57	12 22	12 26		12 41	12 46	12 51	12 57	13a15	13 22	13 26	13 41
Hilsea	d	10a30		10a50						11a30		11a50				12a30			12a50					13a30	
Bedhampton	d					11 04			11 30					12 04	12 30						13 04		13 30		
Havant	a		10 49		10 59	11 07			11 32		11 49		11 59	12 07	12 32			12 49		12 59	13 07		13 32		13 49

		SW		SN	SW	GW	SN	SW	SW	SW	SN	SW		GW	SN	SW	SW	SW	SN	SW	GW	SN		SW	SW
		1		◇1	1	◇	◇1	1 🛒	1 🛒	1	◇1	1		R	◇1	1 🛒	1 🛒	1	◇1	1	◇	◇1		1 🛒	1 🛒
Portsmouth Harbour ⛴	d			13 43	13 48	14 08	14 14	14 17	14 32		14 43	14 48		15 08	15 14	15 17	15 32		15 43	15 48	16 08	16 14		16 17	16 32
Portsmouth & Southsea	a			13 46	13 51	14 11	14 17	14 20	14 35		14 46	14 51		15 11	15 17	15 20	15 35		15 46	15 51	16 11	16 17		16 20	16 35
	d	13 42		13 47	13 53	14 12	14 18	14 22	14 37	14 42	14 47	14 53		15 12	15 18	15 22	15 37	15 42	15 47	15 53	16 12	16 18		16 22	16 37
Fratton	d	13 46		13 51	13 57	14a15	14 22	14 26	14 41	14 46	14 51	14 57		15a15	15 22	15 26	15 41	15 46	15 51	15 57	16a15	16 22		16 26	16 41
Hilsea	d	13a50						14a30		14a50						15a30		15a50						16a30	
Bedhampton	d				14 04		14 30					15 04			15 30					16 04		16 30			
Havant	a			13 59	14 07		14 32		14 49		14 59	15 07			15 32		15 49		15 59	16 07		16 32			16 49

		SW	SN	SW	GW	SN	SW	SW		SW	SN	SW	GW	SN	SW	SW	SW	SN		SW	GW	SN	SW	SW	SW
		1	◇1	1	◇	◇1	1	1 🛒		1	◇1	1	◇	◇1	1	1 🛒	1	◇1		1	◇	◇1	1	1	1
Portsmouth Harbour ⛴	d		16 43	16 48	17 08	17 14	17 17	17 32			17 43	17 48	18 08	18 14	18 17	18 32		18 43		18 48	19 08	19 14	19 17	19 32	
Portsmouth & Southsea	a		16 46	16 51	17 11	17 17	17 20	17 35			17 46	17 51	18 11	18 17	18 20	18 35		18 46		18 51	19 11	19 17	19 20	19 35	
	d	16 42	16 47	16 53	17 12	17 18	17 22	17 37		17 42	17 47	17 53	18 12	18 18	18 22	18 37	18 42	18 47		18 53	19 12	19 18	19 22	19 37	19 42
Fratton	d	16 46	16 51	16 57	17a15	17 22	17 26	17 41		17 46	17 51	17 57	18a15	18 22	18 26	18 41	18 46	18 51		18 57	19a15	19 22	19 26	19 41	19 46
Hilsea	d	16a50					17a30			17a50					18a30		18a50						19a30		19a50
Bedhampton	d			17 04		17 30						18 04		18 30						19 04		19 30			
Havant	a		16 59	17 07		17 32		17 49			17 59	18 07		18 32		18 49		18 59		19 07		19 32		19 49	

		SN	SW	GW		SN	SW	SW	SW	SN	SW	SN	SW	SW		SW	SN	SW	GW	SN	SW	SW	SW	SN	
		◇1	1	◇		◇1	1	1	1	◇1	1	◇1	1	1		1	◇1	1		◇1	1	1	1	◇1	
Portsmouth Harbour ⛴	d	19 43	19 48	20 08		20 14	20 17	20 32		20 43	20 48	21 14	21 17	21 32			21 43	21 48	22 03	22 14	22 17	22 32		22 43	
Portsmouth & Southsea	a	19 46	19 51	20 11		20 17	20 20	20 35		20 46	20 51	21 17	21 20	21 35			21 46	21 51	22 11	22 17	22 20	22 35		22 46	
	d	19 47	19 53	20 12		20 18	20 22	20 37	20 42	20 47	20 53	21 18	21 22	21 37		21 42	21 47	21 53	22 12	22 18	22 22	22 37	22 42	22 47	
Fratton	d	19 51	19 57	20a15		20 22	20 26	20 41	20 46	20 51	20 57	21 22	21 26	21 41		21 46	21 51	21 57	22a15	22 22	22 26	22 41	22 46	22 51	
Hilsea	d						20a30		20a50				21a30			21a50					22a30		22a50		
Bedhampton	d		20 04			20 30					21 04	21 30						22 04		22 32					
Havant	a	19 59	20 07			20 32		20 49		20 59	21 07	21 32		21 49			21 59	22 07		22 35		22 49		22 59	

		SW	SW
		1	1
Portsmouth Harbour ⛴	d	22 48	23 17
Portsmouth & Southsea	a	22 51	23 20
	d	22 53	23 22
Fratton	d	22 57	23 26
Hilsea	d		23a30
Bedhampton	d	23 04	
Havant	a	23 07	

Network Diagram for Table 158

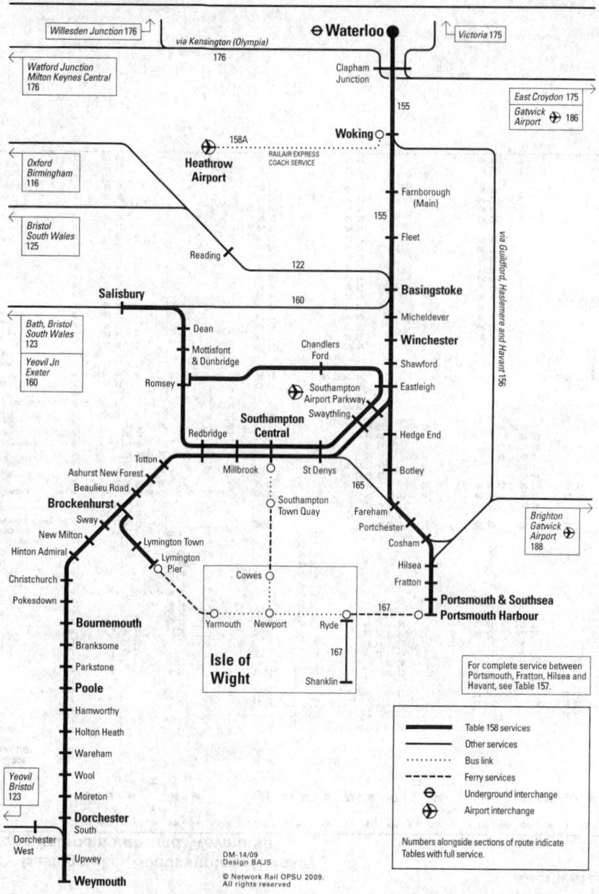

London - Basingstoke, Southampton, Romsey Lymington, Bournemouth and Weymouth

until 30 September

Miles	Miles			SW MX ◇1 A 🚌	SW MO ◇1 B 🚌	SW MO ◇1		SW MX ◇1 🚌	SW MO ◇1	SW MX 1	SW MX ◇1 🚌	SW MX 1	SW MO ◇1 🚌	SW MX ◇1	SW 1	SW MX 1	SW MX 1	SW MO 1	SW 1	SW 1	SW 1	SW 1	SW 1
0	—	**London Waterloo** 15 ⊖	d	21p35	21p35	21p54		22p05			22p35	22p39	22p54	23p05		23p35	00 05	00 50	01 05				
4	—	**Clapham Junction** 10	d		21b42	22b03		22b12				22b46	23b03	23b12		23b42	00u12	00 57					
24¼	—	**Woking**	d	22p00	22p07	22p28		22p32			23p00		23p28	23p32		00 03	00 37	01 18	01 42				
33¼	—	Farnborough (Main)	d									23p16				00 14			01s58				
36½	—	Fleet	d									23p21				00 20			02s04				
—	—	Reading 7	d																				
47¾	—	**Basingstoke**	a		22p26	22p46		22p51				23p33	23p46	23p53		00 33	00 55		02s16				
—	—		d		22p28	22p48		22p52				23p34	23p48	23p53		00 35	00 56						
58	—	Micheldever	d			22p58							23p58	00 03									
66½	—	**Winchester**	d	22p33	22p44	23p08		23p09			23p33	23p51	00 08	00 14		00 51	01 13		02s33				
69¾	—	Shawford	d									23p55											
—	0	**Romsey**	d							23p07													
—	5¼	Chandlers Ford	d							23p14													
73½	0	Eastleigh 8	a			23p17		23p17		23p22		00 01	00 18	00 22		00 59	01 21		02s42				
—	—		d			23p22	23p26	23p18		23p22		00 02	00 22	00 23	00 30	01 00	01 22				06 00		
—	4½	Hedge End	d				23p32								00s36						06 06		
—	5½	Botley	d				23p36								00s39						06 10		
—	11	Fareham	d				23p44								00s47						06 18		
—	14¼	Portchester	d				23p49								00s53						06 23		
—	16¾	Cosham	d				23p54								00s57						06 28		
—	18¾	Hilsea	a				23p59														06 33		
—	20½	Fratton	a				00 04								01s05			02s10			06 38		
—	21½	**Portsmouth & Southsea**	a				00 08								01s08			02s14			06 44		
—	22¼	**Portsmouth Harbour** ⛴	a				00 13								01 12			02 19			06 49		
75	—	**Southampton Airport Pkwy** ✈	d	22p42	22p53	23p27		23p22		23p26	23p42	00 06	00 27	00 28		01 05	01 26		02s46				
75¾	—	Swaythling	d							23p28													
77¼	—	St Denys	d						⟵	23p31			00s31	00s32					02s51				
79¼	—	**Southampton Central** ⛴	a	22p49	23p00	23p34		23p29	23p34	23p36	23p49	00 13	00 36	00 37		01 12	01 35		02 56				
—	—		d	22p51	23p03	23p35		23p31	23p35	23p38	23p51		00 37	00 38			01 37						
80¼	—	Millbrook (Hants)	d			⟶				23p40													
82	0	Redbridge	d							23p44													
—	6	**Romsey**	d							23p56													
—	9¾	Mottisfont & Dunbridge	d							00 01													
—	13½	Dean	d							00 07													
—	22½	**Salisbury**	a							00 19													
82½	—	Totton	d					23p36	23p41				00s42	00s43			01s42						
85½	—	Ashurst New Forest	d					23p41	23p45														
88	—	Beaulieu Road	d																				
92¾	0	**Brockenhurst** 3	a	23p04	23p16			23p49	23p53		00 04		00s53	00s54			01s53						
—	—		d	23p05	23p17			23p50	23p54		00 05									05 59			06 16
—	4¾	Lymington Town	d																	06 07			
—	5¼	**Lymington Pier**	a																	06 10			
95½	—	Sway	d					23p54	23p59														06 20
98½	—	New Milton	d		23p24			23p59	00 04				01s01	01s02			02s00						06 25
101	—	Hinton Admiral	d					00 03	00 08														06 29
104¼	—	Christchurch	d					00 08	00 13				01s08	01s09			02s07						06 34
106¼	—	Pokesdown	d					00 11	00 16				01s12	01s13			02s11						06 38
108	—	**Bournemouth**	a	23p25	23p34			00 15	00 20		00 21		01 16	01 17			02 15						06 42
—	—		d	23p29	23p39			00 17	00 22		00 22		01 17	01 18								06 11	06 44
110¾	—	Branksome	d	23p35	23p44			00 22	00 27		00 27		01s22	01s23								06 16	06 49
112	—	Parkstone (Dorset)	d	23p38	23p47			00 25	00 30		00 30		01s25	01s26								06 19	06 52
113¾	—	**Poole** 4	a	23p41	23p50			00 29	00 34		00 35		01 29	01 30								06 23	06 55
—	—		d	23p42	23p51																	06 24	06 57
116	—	Hamworthy	d	23p47	23p56																	06 29	07 02
118¾	—	Holton Heath	d																			06 33	07 06
120¾	—	Wareham	d	23p54	00 03																	06 38	07 11
125¾	—	Wool	d	00 01	00 10																	06 44	07 17
130¼	—	Moreton (Dorset)	d	00 07	00 16																	06 50	07 23
135¾	—	**Dorchester South**	d	00 15	00 24																	06 58	07 31
—	—	Dorchester West	d																				
140½	—	Upwey	d	00 21	00 31																	07 05	07 38
142¾	—	**Weymouth**	a	00 26	00 35																	07 09	07 42

A 🚌 to Brockenhurst

B 🚌 to New Milton

b Previous night, stops to pick up only

London - Basingstoke, Southampton, Romsey Lymington, Bournemouth and Weymouth

Station		SW	SW	SW	GW	SW	SW	GW	SW	SW	SW	SW	SW	SW	SW	GW	SW	SW	GW	SW	SW	XC	SW
		1	1	1	■ ⌶	1	1		◇1	1	1	1	1	1	1	◇ ⌶	1	◇1	◇	1	1	◇1 ⌶	1
London Waterloo 15 ⊖	d								05 30									06 30					
Clapham Junction 10	d								05u37									06u37					
Woking	d								06 01									06 57					
Farnborough (Main)	d																						
Fleet	d																						
Reading 7	d																					07 46	
Basingstoke	a								06 20									07 16				08 08	
	d		05 40						06 21						06 55			07 18				08 10	
Micheldever	d		05 50																				
Winchester	d		05 59			06 18			06 38						07 11			07 34				08 25	
Shawford	d					06 23									07 16								
Romsey	d			05 58										07 07						08 07			
Chandlers Ford	d			06 06										07 14						08 14			
Eastleigh 8	a		06 07	06 11		06 28			06 47					07 20	07 22			07 43		08 20			
	d		06 08	06 13		06 29			06 48	06 50	07 02			07 21	07 24			07 44		08 21			
Hedge End	d					06 35					07 08												
Botley	d					06 39					07 12												
Fareham	d				06 24	06 50					07 20					07 29							
Portchester	d					06 55					07 25												
Cosham	d					07 00					07 29												
Hilsea	a					07 05					07 35												
Fratton	a					07 09					07 39												
Portsmouth & Southsea	a					07 12					07 42												
Portsmouth Harbour ⛴	a					07 17					07 48												
Southampton Airport Pkwy ✈	d		06 13	06 17					06 53					07 25	07 29			07 49		08 25		08 33	
Swaythling	d		06 15	06 20										07 27	07 31					08 27			
St Denys	d		06 18	06 24										07 30	07 34					08 30			
Southampton Central ⛴	a		06 23	06 29	06 45				07 00					07 35	07 39	07 50		07 57		08 35		08 44	
	d		06 25	06 30	06 46				07 01				07 19	07 37		07 52		08 00	08 23	08 37		08 46	
Millbrook (Hants)	d			06 33									07 21	07 40						08 40			
Redbridge	d			06 36									07 25	07 43						08 43			
Romsey	d			06 44	07 00					07a03				07 51		08 11			08 35	08 51			
Mottisfont & Dunbridge	d			06 49										07 56						08 56			
Dean	d			06 55										08 02						09 02			
Salisbury	a			07 07	07 18									08 15		08 29			09 00	09 15			
Totton	d		06 30						07 07				07 28					08 05					
Ashurst New Forest	d		06 35										07 32										
Beaulieu Road	d												07 37										
Brockenhurst 3	a		06 43						07 17				07 43					08 16				08 59	
	d	06 29	06 44				06 59		07 18			07 29	07 44				07 59	08 17			08 29	09 00	08 59
Lymington Town	d	06 37					07 07					07 37					08 07				08 37		09 07
Lymington Pier	a	06 40					07 10					07 40					08 10				08 40		09 10
Sway	d		06 48						07 23				07 48					08 21					
New Milton	d		06 53						07 28				07 53					08 26					
Hinton Admiral	d		06 57						07 32				07 57					08 30					
Christchurch	d		07 02						07 37				08 02					08 35					
Pokesdown	d		07 06						07 40				08 06					08 39					
Bournemouth	a		07 10						07 44				08 10					08 43				09 15	
	d		07 11						07 46				08 11					08 44					
Branksome	d		07 16						07 51				08 16					08 49					
Parkstone (Dorset)	d		07 19						07 54				08 19					08 52					
Poole 4	a		07 23						07 57				08 23					08 56					
	d		07 24						07 58				08 24					08 57					
Hamworthy	d		07 29						08 03				08 29					09 02					
Holton Heath	d		07 33						08 07				08 33										
Wareham	d		07 38						08 12				08 38					09 09					
Wool	d		07 44						08 19				08 44					09 15					
Moreton (Dorset)	d		07 50						08 25				08 50					09 21					
Dorchester South	d		07 58						08 33				08 58					09 29					
Dorchester West	d							08 09															
Upwey	d		08 05					08 17	08 40				09 05					09 36					
Weymouth	a		08 09					08 24	08 44				09 09					09 40					

London - Basingstoke, Southampton, Romsey Lymington, Bournemouth and Weymouth

Station		SW	GW	SW	GW	SW	XC	SW	SW	SW	SW	XC	SW	SW	GW	SW	SW	SW	SW	GW	SW	SW
		◇1 A ⌶	◇ ⌶	1		1 ⌶	◇1 ⌶	◇1 A ⌶	1 ⌶	1	1	◇1 ⌶	◇1 B ⌶	1 ⌶	◇ ⌶	1	1	◇1 A ⌶	1	◇	1	1
London Waterloo 15 ⊖	d	07 35				07 39		08 05			08 09		08 35				08 39	09 05				09 09
Clapham Junction 10	d					07u46		08u12									08u46	09u12				
Woking	d	08 00									08 35		09 00									09 35
Farnborough (Main)	d					08 13					08 45						09 13					09 45
Fleet	d					08 19											09 19					
Reading 7	d						08 15					08 46										
Basingstoke	a	08 19				08 32	08 40	08 47			08 58	09 08					09 31	09 47				09 58
	d	08 20				08 33	08 42	08 49			09 00	09 10					09 33	09 49				10 00
Micheldever	d										09 10											10 10
Winchester	d	08 37				08 50	08 57	09 05			09 19	09 25	09 33				09 49	10 05				10 19
Shawford	d					08 54											09 54					
Romsey	d									09 07											10 07	
Chandlers Ford	d									09 14											10 14	
Eastleigh 8	a	08 47				09 00				09 20	09 27						10 02				10 20	10 27
	d	08 48				09 01				09 21	09 28						10 03				10 21	10 28
Hedge End	d										09 34											10 34
Botley	d										09 38											10 38
Fareham	d		08 47								09 48				09 47					10 14		10 48
Portchester	d										09 53											10 53
Cosham	d										09 58											10 58
Hilsea	a										10 03											11 03
Fratton	a										10 07											11 07
Portsmouth & Southsea	a										10 11											11 11
Portsmouth Harbour ⛴	a										10 18											11 18
Southampton Airport Pkwy ✈	d	08 52				09 05	09 09	09 14		09 25		09 33	09 42				10 08	10 14			10 25	
Swaythling	d									09 27											10 27	
St Denys	d								←	09 30									←		10 30	
Southampton Central ⛴	a	08 59	09 08			09 15	09 17	09 22	09 15	09 35		09 41	09 49		10 08		10 18	10 22	10 18	10 41	10 35	
	d	09 01	09 10			09 30		09 24	09 30	09 37		09 43	09 51		10 10		10 30	10 24	10 30	10 42	10 44	
Millbrook (Hants)	d					→				09 40							→				10 48	
Redbridge	d									09 43											10 51	
Romsey	d		09 21							09 51					10 21					10 54	10 59	
Mottisfont & Dunbridge	d									09 56											11 04	
Dean	d									10 02											11 10	
Salisbury	a		09 40							10 15					10 40					11 13	11 22	
Totton	d	09 06							09 35										10 35			
Ashurst New Forest	d								09 40										10 40			
Beaulieu Road	d													←					10 44			
Brockenhurst 3	a	09 17						09 37	09 49			09 56	10 04	09 49				10 37	10 51			
	d	09 18		09 29				09 38	10 16			09 57	10 05	10 16		10 12		10 38	11 16			
Lymington Town	d			09 37					→							10 20			→			
Lymington Pier	a			09 40												10 23						
Sway	d	09 22												10 20								
New Milton	d	09 27						09 45						10 25				10 45				
Hinton Admiral	d	09 31												10 29								
Christchurch	d	09 36						09 52						10 34				10 52				
Pokesdown	d	09 40						09 56						10 38				10 56				
Bournemouth	a	09 44						10 00				10 12	10 20	10 42				11 00				
	d	09 45						10 04					10 24	10 43				11 04				
Branksome	d	09 50											10 29	10 48								
Parkstone (Dorset)	d	09 53											10 32	10 51								
Poole 4	a	09 57						10 13					10 36	10 55				11 13				
	d	09 58						10 14					10 37					11 14				
Hamworthy	d	10 03						10 19					10 42					11 19				
Holton Heath	d							10 23										11 23				
Wareham	d	10 10						10 28					10 49					11 28				
Wool	d							10 35										11 35				
Moreton (Dorset)	d							10 41										11 41				
Dorchester South	d	10 26						10 54					11 05					11 49				
Dorchester West	d				10 48																	
Upwey	d				10 55			11 01										11 55				
Weymouth	a	10 34			11 03			11 06					11 13					12 00				

A ⌶ to Pokesdown

B ⌶ to Brockenhurst

London - Basingstoke, Southampton, Romsey Lymington, Bournemouth and Weymouth

		SW	XC	GW	SW	SW	GW	SW	SW	XC	SW	SW	SW	SW	SW	XC	SW	SW	GW	SW	SW	SW	SW
		1	◇1		◇1	1	◇	1	1	◇1	◇1	1	1	1	1	◇1	◇1	1	◇	1	1	◇1	1
					A						B						A					B	
			⌶		⌶		⌶			⌶	⌶					⌶	⌶		⌶			⌶	
London Waterloo 15 ⊖	d				09 35				09 39		10 05			10 09			10 35				10 39	11 05	
Clapham Junction 10	d								09u46		10u12										10u46	11u12	
Woking	d				10 00									10 35			11 00						
Farnborough (Main)	d								10 13					10 45							11 13		
Fleet	d								10 19												11 19		
Reading 7	d		09 46							10 15						10 46							
Basingstoke	a		10 08						10 31	10 39	10 47			10 58		11 08					11 31	11 47	
	d		10 10						10 33	10 40	10 49			11 00		11 10					11 33	11 49	
Micheldever	d													11 10									
Winchester	d		10 25		10 33				10 49	10 55	11 05			11 19		11 25	11 33				11 49	12 05	
Shawford	d								10 54												11 54		
Romsey	d												11 07										
Chandlers Ford	d												11 14										
Eastleigh 3	a								10 59				11 20	11 27							11 59		
	d								11 00				11 21	11 28							12 00		
Hedge End	d													11 34									
Botley	d													11 38									
Fareham	d						10 47							11 48					11 47				
Portchester	d													11 53									
Cosham	d													11 58									
Hilsea	a													12 03									
Fratton	a													12 07									
Portsmouth & Southsea	a													12 11									
Portsmouth Harbour ⛴	a													12 18									
Southampton Airport Pkwy ✈	d		10 33		10 42				11 05	11 09	11 14		11 25			11 33	11 42				12 05	12 14	
Swaythling	d												11 27										
St Denys	d											←	11 30										←
Southampton Central ⛴	a		10 43		10 49		11 08		11 12	11 16	11 22	11 12	11 35			11 43	11 49		12 08		12 15	12 22	12 15
	d		10 45		10 51		11 10		11 30		11 24	11 30	11 37			11 45	11 51		12 10		12 30	12 24	12 30
Millbrook (Hants)	d								→				11 40								→		
Redbridge	d												11 43										
Romsey	d						11 21						11 51						12 21				
Mottisfont & Dunbridge	d												11 56										
Dean	d												12 02										
Salisbury	a						11 40						12 15						12 40				
Totton	d											11 35											12 35
Ashurst New Forest	d											11 40											12 40
Beaulieu Road	d					←						11 44						←					
Brockenhurst 3	a		10 58		11 04	10 51					11 37	11 51				11 58	12 04	11 51				12 37	12 51
	d	10 42	10 59		11 05	11 16		11 12			11 38	12 16			11 42	11 59	12 05	12 16		12 12		12 38	13 16
Lymington Town	d	10 50						11 20				→			11 50					12 20			→
Lymington Pier	a	10 53						11 23							11 53					12 23			
Sway	d					11 20												12 20					
New Milton	d					11 25					11 45							12 25				12 45	
Hinton Admiral	d					11 29												12 29					
Christchurch	d					11 34					11 52							12 34				12 52	
Pokesdown	d					11 38					11 56							12 38				12 56	
Bournemouth	a		11 12		11 20	11 42					12 00					12 12	12 20	12 42				13 00	
	d				11 24	11 43					12 04						12 24	12 43				13 04	
Branksome	d				11 29	11 48											12 29	12 48					
Parkstone (Dorset)	d				11 32	11 51											12 32	12 51					
Poole 4	a				11 36	11 55					12 13						12 36	12 55				13 13	
	d				11 37						12 14						12 37					13 14	
Hamworthy	d				11 42						12 19						12 42					13 19	
Holton Heath	d										12 23											13 23	
Wareham	d				11 49						12 28						12 49					13 28	
Wool	d										12 35											13 35	
Moreton (Dorset)	d										12 41											13 41	
Dorchester South	d				12 05						12 49						13 05					13 49	
Dorchester West	d			11 54																			
Upwey	d			12 02							12 55											13 55	
Weymouth	a			12 09	12 13						13 00						13 13					14 00	

A ⌶ to Brockenhurst

B ⌶ to Pokesdown

London - Basingstoke, Southampton, Romsey Lymington, Bournemouth and Weymouth

		GW	SW	SW	SW	XC	GW	SW	SW	GW	SW	SW	XC	SW	SW	SW	SW	SW	XC	SW	SW	GW	SW
		◇	1	1	1	◇1		◇1	1	◇	1	1	◇1	◇1	1	1	1	1	◇1	◇1	1	◇	1
								A						B						A			
						⌶		⌶		⌶			⌶	⌶					⌶	⌶		⌶	
London Waterloo 15 ⊖	d			11 09				11 35				11 39		12 05			12 09			12 35			
Clapham Junction 10	d											11u46		12u12									
Woking	d			11 35				12 00									12 35			13 00			
Farnborough (Main)	d			11 45								12 13					12 45						
Fleet	d											12 19											
Reading 7	d					11 46							12 15						12 46				
Basingstoke	a			11 58		12 08						12 31	12 39	12 47			12 58		13 08				
	d			12 00		12 10						12 33	12 40	12 49			13 00		13 10				
Micheldever	d			12 10													13 10						
Winchester	d			12 19		12 25		12 33				12 49	12 55	13 05			13 19		13 25	13 33			
Shawford	d											12 54											
Romsey	d		12 07													13 07							
Chandlers Ford	d		12 14													13 14							
Eastleigh 3	a		12 20	12 27								12 59				13 20	13 27						
	d		12 21	12 28								13 00				13 21	13 28						
Hedge End	d			12 34													13 34						
Botley	d			12 38													13 38						
Fareham	d			12 48						12 47							13 48					13 47	
Portchester	d			12 53													13 53						
Cosham	d			12 58													13 58						
Hilsea	a			13 03													14 03						
Fratton	a			13 07													14 07						
Portsmouth & Southsea	a			13 11													14 11						
Portsmouth Harbour ⛴	a			13 18													14 18						
Southampton Airport Pkwy ✈	d		12 25			12 33		12 42				13 05	13 09	13 14		13 25			13 33	13 42			
Swaythling	d		12 27													13 27							
St Denys	d		12 30												←	13 30							
Southampton Central ⛴	a		12 35			12 41		12 49		13 08		13 15	13 17	13 22	13 15	13 35			13 41	13 49		14 08	
	d	12 27	12 37			12 43		12 51		13 10		13 30		13 24	13 30	13 37			13 43	13 51		14 10	
Millbrook (Hants)	d		12 40									→				13 40							
Redbridge	d		12 43													13 43							
Romsey	d	12 39	12 51							13 21						13 51						14 21	
Mottisfont & Dunbridge	d		12 56													13 56							
Dean	d		13 02													14 02							
Salisbury	a	13 02	13 15							13 40						14 15						14 40	
Totton	d														13 35								
Ashurst New Forest	d														13 40								
Beaulieu Road	d								←												←		
Brockenhurst 3	a					12 56		13 04	12 51					13 37	13 51				13 56	14 04	13 51		
	d				12 42	12 57		13 05	13 16		13 12			13 38	14 16			13 42	13 57	14 05	14 16		14 12
Lymington Town	d				12 50						13 20				→			13 50					14 20
Lymington Pier	a				12 53						13 23							13 53					14 23
Sway	d								13 20												14 20		
New Milton	d								13 25					13 45							14 25		
Hinton Admiral	d								13 29												14 29		
Christchurch	d								13 34					13 52							14 34		
Pokesdown	d								13 38					13 56							14 38		
Bournemouth	a					13 10		13 20	13 42					14 00					14 10	14 20	14 42		
	d							13 24	13 43					14 04						14 24	14 43		
Branksome	d							13 29	13 48											14 29	14 48		
Parkstone (Dorset)	d							13 32	13 51											14 32	14 51		
Poole 4	a							13 36	13 55					14 13						14 36	14 55		
	d							13 37						14 14						14 37			
Hamworthy	d							13 42						14 19						14 42			
Holton Heath	d													14 23									
Wareham	d							13 49						14 28						14 49			
Wool	d													14 35									
Moreton (Dorset)	d													14 41									
Dorchester South	d							14 05						14 49						15 05			
Dorchester West	d						13 54																
Upwey	d						14 02							14 55									
Weymouth	a						14 09	14 13						15 00						15 13			

A ⌶ to Brockenhurst

B ⌶ to Pokesdown

Table 158

Mondays to Fridays
until 30 September

London - Basingstoke, Southampton, Romsey Lymington, Bournemouth and Weymouth

		SW	SW	SW	SW	SW	SW	XC	SW	SW	GW	SW	SW	XC	SW	SW	SW	SW	SW	XC	GW	SW
		1	◇1 A ⊼	1	1	1	1	◇1 ⊼	◇1 B ⊼	1	■ ⊼	1	1	◇1 ⊼	◇1 A ⊼	1	1	1	1	◇1 ⊼		◇1 B ⊼
London Waterloo 15 ⊖	d	12 39	13 05			13 09			13 35				13 39		14 05			14 09				14 35
Clapham Junction 10	d	12u46	13u12										13u46		14u12							
Woking	d					13 35			14 00									14 35				15 00
Farnborough (Main)	d	13 13				13 45							14 13					14 45				
Fleet	d	13 19											14 19									
Reading 7	d							13 46						14 15						14 46		
Basingstoke	a	13 31	13 47			13 58		14 08					14 31	14 39	14 47			14 58		15 08		
	d	13 33	13 49			14 00		14 10					14 33	14 40	14 49			15 00		15 10		
Micheldever	d					14 10												15 10				
Winchester	d	13 49	14 05			14 19		14 25	14 33				14 49	14 55	15 05			15 19		15 25		15 33
Shawford	d	13 54											14 54									
Romsey	d				14 07												15 07					
Chandlers Ford	d				14 14												15 14					
Eastleigh 3	a	13 59			14 20	14 27							14 59				15 20	15 27				
	d	14 00			14 21	14 28							15 00				15 21	15 28				
Hedge End	d					14 34												15 34				
Botley	d					14 38												15 38				
Fareham	d					14 48					14 47							15 48				
Portchester	d					14 53												15 53				
Cosham	d					14 58												15 58				
Hilsea	a					15 03												16 03				
Fratton	a					15 07												16 07				
Portsmouth & Southsea	a					15 11												16 11				
Portsmouth Harbour ⛴	a					15 18												16 18				
Southampton Airport Pkwy ✈	d	14 05	14 14		14 25			14 35	14 42				15 05	15 10	15 14		15 25			15 33		15 42
Swaythling	d				14 27												15 27					
St Denys	d			←	14 30											←	15 30					
Southampton Central ⛴	a	14 12	14 22	14 12	14 35			14 42	14 49		15 08		15 12	15 17	15 22	15 12	15 35			15 41		15 49
	d	14 30	14 24	14 30	14 37			14 43	14 51		15 10		15 30		15 24	15 30	15 37			15 43		15 51
Millbrook (Hants)	d	→			14 40								→				15 40					
Redbridge	d				14 43												15 43					
Romsey	d				14 51						15 21						15 51					
Mottisfont & Dunbridge	d				14 56												15 56					
Dean	d				15 02												16 02					
Salisbury	a				15 15						15 40						16 15					
Totton	d			14 35												15 35						
Ashurst New Forest	d			14 40												15 40						
Beaulieu Road	d									←												
Brockenhurst 3	a		14 37	14 51				14 56	15 04	14 51					15 37	15 51				15 56		16 04
	d		14 38	15 16			14 42	14 57	15 05	15 16		15 12			15 38	16 28			15 42	15 57		16 05
Lymington Town	d			→			14 50					15 20				→			15 50			
Lymington Pier	a						14 53					15 23							15 53			
Sway	d									15 20												
New Milton	d		14 45							15 25					15 45							
Hinton Admiral	d									15 29												
Christchurch	d		14 52							15 34					15 52							
Pokesdown	d		14 56							15 38					15 56							
Bournemouth	a		15 00					15 11	15 20	15 42					16 00					16 10		16 20
	d		15 04						15 24	15 43					16 04							16 24
Branksome	d								15 29	15 48												16 29
Parkstone (Dorset)	d								15 32	15 51												16 32
Poole 4	a		15 13						15 36	15 55					16 13							16 36
	d		15 14						15 37						16 14							16 37
Hamworthy	d		15 19						15 42						16 19							16 42
Holton Heath	d		15 23												16 23							
Wareham	d		15 28						15 49						16 28							16 49
Wool	d		15 35												16 35							16 55
Moreton (Dorset)	d		15 41												16 41							
Dorchester South	d		15 49						16 05						16 49							17 06
Dorchester West	d																				16 58	
Upwey	d		15 55												16 55						17 05	
Weymouth	a		16 00						16 13						17 00						17 10	17 15

A ⊼ to Pokesdown
B ⊼ to Brockenhurst

Table 158

Mondays to Fridays
until 30 September

London - Basingstoke, Southampton, Romsey Lymington, Bournemouth and Weymouth

		SW	GW	SW	SW	SW	SW	SW	SW	SW	XC	SW	SW		SW	GW	SW	SW	XC	SW	SN	SW	SW
		1	■ ⊼	1	1	◇1 A ⊼	1	1	1	1	◇1 ⊼	1	◇1 B ⊼		1	■ ⊼	1	1	◇1 ⊼	◇1 A ⊼	◇1	1	1
London Waterloo 15 ⊖	d				14 39	15 05				15 09			15 35					15 39		16 05			
Clapham Junction 10	d				14u46	15u12												15u46		16u12			
Woking	d									15 35			16 00										
Farnborough (Main)	d				15 13					15 45								16 13					
Fleet	d				15 19													16 19					
Reading 7	d										15 46								16 15				
Basingstoke	a				15 31	15 47				15 58	16 08							16 31	16 39	16 47			
	d				15 33	15 49				16 00	16 10						16 24	16 33	16 40	16 49			
Micheldever	d									16 10													
Winchester	d				15 49	16 05				16 19	16 25		16 33		16 38		16 45	16 50	17 00	17 05			
Shawford	d				15 54										16 43			16 54					
Romsey	d								16 07														
Chandlers Ford	d								16 14														
Eastleigh 3	a				15 59				16 20	16 27					16 48		16 53	17 00					
	d				16 00				16 21	16 28					16 49		16 54	17 01			17 16		
Hedge End	d									16 34							17 00						
Botley	d									16 38							17 04						
Fareham	d		15 47							16 48						16 47	17 12						
Portchester	d									16 53							17 17						
Cosham	d									16 58							17 22						
Hilsea	a									17 03													
Fratton	a									17 07							17 31						
Portsmouth & Southsea	a									17 11							17 35						
Portsmouth Harbour ⛴	a									17 18							17 40						
Southampton Airport Pkwy ✈	d				16 05	16 14			16 25		16 33		16 42		16 54			17 05		17 14	17 20		
Swaythling	d								16 27						16 56								
St Denys	d							←	16 30						16 59								←
Southampton Central ⛴	a		16 08		16 15	16 22		16 15	16 35		16 41		16 49		17 04	17 08		17 13	17 17	17 22	17 28		17 13
	d		16 10		16 30	16 24		16 30	16 37		16 43		16 54	16 56	17 06	17 10		17 30		17 24			17 30
Millbrook (Hants)	d				→				16 40									→					
Redbridge	d								16 43														
Romsey	d		16 21						16 51							17 21							
Mottisfont & Dunbridge	d								16 56														
Dean	d								17 02														
Salisbury	a		16 40						17 15							17 40							
Totton	d							16 35						17 01	17a11								17 35
Ashurst New Forest	d							16 40						17 06									17 40
Beaulieu Road	d	←						16 44															17 44
Brockenhurst 3	a	15 51				16 37		16 51			16 56		17 07	17 14						17 37			17 51
	d	16 28		16 12		16 38	16 42				16 57	17 12	17 08	17 16						17 38		17 42	
Lymington Town	d			16 20			16 50					17 20										17 50	
Lymington Pier	a			16 23			16 53					17 23										17 53	
Sway	d	16 32				16 43								17 20						17 43			
New Milton	d	16 37				16 48								17 25						17 48			
Hinton Admiral	d	16 41				16 52								17 29						17 52			
Christchurch	d	16 46				16 57								17 34						17 57			
Pokesdown	d	16 50				17 00								17 38						18 00			
Bournemouth	a	16 54				17 04					17 10		17 23	17 42						18 04			
	d	16 55				17 07							17 24	17 43						18 09			
Branksome	d	17 00											17 29	17 48									
Parkstone (Dorset)	d	17 03											17 32	17 51									
Poole 4	a	17 07				17 16							17 36	17 55						18 18			
	d					17 17							17 37							18 19			
Hamworthy	d					17 22							17 42							18 24			
Holton Heath	d					17 26														18 28			
Wareham	d					17 31							17 49							18 33			
Wool	d					17 37							17 55							18 39			
Moreton (Dorset)	d					17 43														18 45			
Dorchester South	d					17 51							18 06							18 53			
Dorchester West	d																						
Upwey	d					17 58														19 00			
Weymouth	a					18 02							18 15							19 06			

A ⊼ to Pokesdown
B ⊼ to Brockenhurst

London - Basingstoke, Southampton, Romsey Lymington, Bournemouth and Weymouth

		SW 1	SW 1	XC ◇1 ⌶	GW	SW 1	SW ◇1 A ⌶		SW 1	GW ◇ ⌶	SW 1	SW ◇1 ⌶		SW 1	GW ◇ ⌶	SW 1	SW 1	XC ◇1 ⌶	GW	SW ◇1 B ⌶		GW ◇ ⌶
London Waterloo 15 ⊖	d		16 09				16 35				16 39	17 05				17 09				17 35		
Clapham Junction 10	d										16u46											
Woking	d		16 35				17u00									17 34						
Farnborough (Main)	d		16 45								17 13											
Fleet	d										17 19											
Reading 7	d			16 46														17 46				
Basingstoke	a		16 58	17 08							17 31					17 52		18 08				
	d		17 00	17 10					17 24		17 33					17 54		18 10				
Micheldever	d		17 10						17 34							18 04						
Winchester	d		17 19	17 25			17 33		17 44		17 49	18 00				18 14		18 25		18 30		
Shawford	d								17 49		17 54					18 18						
Romsey	d	17 07												18 07								
Chandlers Ford	d	17 14												18 14								
Eastleigh 3	a	17 20	17 27						17 54		17 59			18 20		18 24						
	d	17 21	17 28						17 55		18 01			18 21		18 25						
Hedge End	d		17 34								18 07					18 31						
Botley	d		17 39								18 11					18 36						
Fareham	d		17 48							17 47	18 23				18 13	18 45						18 47
Portchester	d		17 53								18 28					18 50						
Cosham	d		17 58								18 33					18 55						
Hilsea	a		18 04													19 05						
Fratton	a		18 08								18 40					19 09						
Portsmouth & Southsea	a		18 12								18 43					19 12						
Portsmouth Harbour ⛴	a		18 20								18 51					19 20						
Southampton Airport Pkwy ✈	d	17 25		17 33			17 42		18 00			18 09		18 25				18 33		18 39		
Swaythling	d	17 27							18 02					18 27								
St Denys	d	17 30							18 05					18 30								
Southampton Central ⛴	a	17 35		17 41			17 49		18 10	18 08		18 16		18 35	18 41			18 44		18 46		19 08
	d	17 37		17 43			17 53	17 56		18 10		18 21	18 24	18 37	18 42			18 45		18 51	18 54	19 10
Millbrook (Hants)	d	17 40												18 40								
Redbridge	d	17 43												18 44								
Romsey	d	17 51								18 21				19 00	18 54							19 21
Mottisfont & Dunbridge	d	17 56												19 05								
Dean	d	18 02												19 10								
Salisbury	a	18 15								18 40				19 23	19 12							19 40
Totton	d							18 01					18 29								18 59	
Ashurst New Forest	d							18 06					18 34								19 04	
Beaulieu Road	d																					
Brockenhurst 3	a			17 56			18 07	18 14					18 42					18 58			19 12	
	d			17 57		18 12	18 08	18 16					18 43				18 48	18 59			19 13	
Lymington Town	d					18 20											18 56					
Lymington Pier	a					18 23											18 59					
Sway	d							18 20					18 47								19 17	
New Milton	d							18 25					18 52								19 22	
Hinton Admiral	d							18 29					18 57								19 26	
Christchurch	d							18 34					19 01								19 31	
Pokesdown	d							18 38					19 05								19 35	
Bournemouth	a			18 15			18 22	18 42				18 48	19 09					19 13		19 20	19 39	
	d						18 24					18 50	19 10							19 21	19 40	
Branksome	d						18 29					18 55	19 15							19 26	19 45	
Parkstone (Dorset)	d						18 32					18 58	19 18							19 29	19 48	
Poole 4	a						18 36					19 02	19 26							19 33	19 56	
	d						18 37					19 03								19 34		
Hamworthy	d						18 42					19 08								19 39		
Holton Heath	d											19 12										
Wareham	d						18 49					19 17								19 46		
Wool	d											19 23										
Moreton (Dorset)	d											19 29										
Dorchester South	d						19 05					19 37								20 02		
Dorchester West	d				18 58														19 54			
Upwey	d				19 06							19 44							20 01			
Weymouth	a				19 14		19 17					19 50							20 09	20 15		

A ⌶ to Brockenhurst

B ⌶ to Southampton Central

until 30 September

London - Basingstoke, Southampton, Romsey Lymington, Bournemouth and Weymouth

		SW 1	SW 1	SW 1	SW ◇1 A ⌶	SW 1	SW 1	XC ◇1 ⌶	SW 1	SW 1	XC ◇1 ⌶	SW ◇1 B ⌶		GW ◇	SW 1	SW 1	SW 1	SW ◇1 A ⌶	SW 1	SW 1	SW 1	SW 1	XC ◇1 ⌶
London Waterloo 15 ⊖	d	17 39	17 48		18 05				18 09			18 35					18 39	19 05			19 09		
Clapham Junction 10	d																18u46	19u12					
Woking	d	18 04	18 13						18 35								19 06				19 35		
Farnborough (Main)	d																				19 45		
Fleet	d																						
Reading 7	d							18 15			18 46												19 46
Basingstoke	a	18 22	18 31					18 47	18 53		19 08						19 28	19 47			19 58		20 09
	d	18 24	18 33					18 48	18 55		19 10				19 24		19 30	19 49			20 00		20 10
Micheldever	d	18 34							19 05								19 40				20 10		
Winchester	d	18 44	18 50		19 00	19 05			19 14		19 25	19 30			19 40		19 49	20 05			20 19		20 25
Shawford	d	18 49				19 09			19 19						19 45		19 54				20 24		
Romsey	d						19 07													20 07			
Chandlers Ford	d						19 14													20 14			
Eastleigh 3	a	18 54	18 58			19 15	19 20		19 25						19 50		19 59			20 20	20 29		
	d	18 55	18 59			19 16	19 21		19 28						19 51		20 00			20 21	20 30		
Hedge End	d	19 01							19 34						19 57						20 36		
Botley	d	19 05							19 38						20 01						20 40		
Fareham	d	19 14							19 48					19 47	20a09						20 49		
Portchester	d	19 19							19 53												20 54		
Cosham	d	19 24							19 58												20 59		
Hilsea	a	19 28							20 02												21 03		
Fratton	a	19 32							20 06												21 07		
Portsmouth & Southsea	a	19 36							20 11												21 11		
Portsmouth Harbour ⛴	a	19 43							20 20												21 16		
Southampton Airport Pkwy ✈	d		19 03		19 09	19 20	19 25				19 33	19 39					20 05	20 14		20 25			20 33
Swaythling	d		19 06			19 23	19 27													20 27			
St Denys	d		19 09			19 26	19 30												←	20 30			
Southampton Central ⛴	a		19 18		19 18	19 33	19 35	19 53			19 41	19 46		20 08			20 16	20 22	20 16	20 35			20 41
	d				19 19		19 37				19 43	19 51	19 54	20 10			20 30	20 24	20 30	20 37			20 43
Millbrook (Hants)	d						19 40										→			20 40			
Redbridge	d						19 43													20 43			
Romsey	d						19 51							20 21						20 51			
Mottisfont & Dunbridge	d						19 56													20 56			
Dean	d						20 02													21 02			
Salisbury	a						20 15							20 40						21 15			
Totton	d				19 25								19 59						20 35				
Ashurst New Forest	d												20 04						20 40				
Beaulieu Road	d																		20 44				
Brockenhurst 3	a				19 35						19 56		20 12					20 37	20 51				20 58
	d			19 18	19 36					19 48	19 57		20 13			20 18		20 38	21 16			20 48	20 59
Lymington Town	d			19 26						19 56						20 26			→			20 56	
Lymington Pier	a			19 29						19 59						20 29						20 59	
Sway	d				19 41								20 17										
New Milton	d				19 46								20 22					20 45					
Hinton Admiral	d				19 50								20 26										
Christchurch	d				19 55								20 31					20 52					
Pokesdown	d				19 58								20 35					20 56					
Bournemouth	a				20 02						20 12	20 20	20 39					21 00					21 15
	d				20 07							20 21	20 40					21 04					
Branksome	d				20 12							20 26	20 45										
Parkstone (Dorset)	d				20 15							20 29	20 48										
Poole 4	a				20 18							20 33	20 56					21 13					
	d				20 19							20 34						21 15					
Hamworthy	d				20 24							20 39						21 20					
Holton Heath	d				20 28																		
Wareham	d				20 33							20 46						21 27					
Wool	d				20 40													21 33					
Moreton (Dorset)	d				20 46													21 39					
Dorchester South	d				20 54							21 02						21 47					
Dorchester West	d																						
Upwey	d				21 00													21 54					
Weymouth	a				21 07							21 13						21 58					

A ⌶ to Pokesdown

B ⌶ to Southampton Central

London - Basingstoke, Southampton, Romsey Lymington, Bournemouth and Weymouth

		SW	SW	GW	SW	SW		GW	SW	SW	SW	SW	XC	GW	SW	SW		GW	SW	SW	SW	XC	SW	SW	SW
		◇■	■	◇	■	■			◇■	■	■	■	◇■		◇■	■			■	◇■	■	◇■	◇■	■	■
		A 🛒							🛒						A 🛒					🛒			A 🛒		
London Waterloo 15 ⊖	d	19 35			19 39				20 05		20 09				20 35	20 39				21 05			21 35		21 39
Clapham Junction 10	d				19u46				20u12							20u46				21u12					21u46
Woking	d	20 00									20 35				21 00					21 32			22 00		
Farnborough (Main)	d				20 13						20 45					21 13									22 13
Fleet	d				20 19											21 19									22 19
Reading 7	d												20 46									21 46			
Basingstoke	a				20 31				20 47		20 58		21 09			21 31				21 51		22 09			22 31
	d				20 33				20 49		21 00		21 10			21 33				21 52		22 10		22 21	22 33
Micheldever	d										21 10					21 43								22 31	22s43
Winchester	d	20 33			20 49				21 05		21 19		21 25		21 33	21 52				22 09		22 25	22 33	22 40	22 52
Shawford	d				20 54						21 24					21 57								22 45	22 57
Romsey	d									21 07											22 07				
Chandlers Ford	d									21 14											22 14				
Eastleigh 8	a				20 59					21 20	21 30					22 02				22 17	22 21			22 50	23 02
	d				21 00					21 21	21 30					22 03		22 11		22 18	22 22			22 51	23 03
Hedge End	d										21 36													22 57	
Botley	d										21 40													23 01	
Fareham	d			20 47							21 48													23 10	
Portchester	d										21 53													23 15	
Cosham	d										21 58													23 20	
Hilsea	a										22 03													23 24	
Fratton	a										22 08													23 32	
Portsmouth & Southsea	a										22 11													23 36	
Portsmouth Harbour ⛴	a										22 16													23 40	
Southampton Airport Pkwy ✈	d	20 42			21 05				21 15	21 24			21 33		21 42	22 08				22 22	22 26	22 33	22 42		23 08
Swaythling	d									21 27											22 28				
St Denys	d									21 30											22 31				
Southampton Central ⛴	a	20 49		21 08	21 12				21 24	21 35			21 41		21 49	22 18		22 21		22 29	22 36	22 42	22 49		23 17
	d	20 51		21 10				21 20	21 25	21 37			21 43		21 51			22 22		22 31	22 38	22 43	22 51		
Millbrook (Hants)	d									21 40											22 40				
Redbridge	d									21 43											22 44				
Romsey	d			21 21				21 31		21 51								22 34			22a52				
Mottisfont & Dunbridge	d									21 56															
Dean	d									22 02															
Salisbury	a			21 40				21 51		22 15								22 58							
Totton	d	20 56							21 31											22 36					
Ashurst New Forest	d								21 35											22 41					
Beaulieu Road	d		←																						
Brockenhurst 8	a	21 07	20 51						21 43				21 56		22 04					22 49		22 56	23 04		
	d	21 08	21 16			21 18			21 44			21 48	21 57		22 05				22 18	22 50		22 59	23 05		
Lymington Town	d					21 26						21 56							22 26						
Lymington Pier	a					21 29						21 59							22 29						
Sway	d		21 20						21 49											22 54					
New Milton	d		21 25						21 54											22 59					
Hinton Admiral	d		21 29						21 58											23 03					
Christchurch	d		21 34						22 03											23 08					
Pokesdown	d		21 38						22 06											23 12					
Bournemouth	a	21 22	21 42						22 10				22 16		22 20					23 16		23 21	23 25		
	d	21 27	21 43						22 12						22 24					23 17			23 29		
Branksome	d	21 32	21 48						22 17						22 29					23 22			23 35		
Parkstone (Dorset)	d	21 35	21 51						22 20						22 32					23 25			23 38		
Poole 4	a	21 38	21 57						22 23						22 36					23 29			23 41		
	d	21 39													22 37								23 42		
Hamworthy	d	21 44													22 42								23 47		
Holton Heath	d																								
Wareham	d	21 51													22 49								23 54		
Wool	d	21 58													22 55								00 01		
Moreton (Dorset)	d	22 04													23 01								00 07		
Dorchester South	d	22 12													23 09								00 15		
Dorchester West	d													22 54											
Upwey	d	22 18												23 02	23 16								00 21		
Weymouth	a	22 23												23 10	23 20								00 26		

A 🛒 to Brockenhurst

London - Basingstoke, Southampton, Romsey Lymington, Bournemouth and Weymouth

		SW		SW	XC	SW	SW	SW	SW	SW
		◇■		■	◇■	◇■	■	■	◇■	■
		🛒				🛒				
London Waterloo 15 ⊖	d	22 05				22 35		22 39	23 05	23 35
Clapham Junction 10	d	22u12						22u46	23u12	23u42
Woking	d	22 32				23 00			23 32	00 03
Farnborough (Main)	d							23 16		00 14
Fleet	d							23 21		00 20
Reading 7	d				22 48					
Basingstoke	a	22 51			23 06			23 33	23 53	00 33
	d	22 52			23 10			23 34	23 53	00 35
Micheldever	d								00 03	
Winchester	d	23 09			23 25	23 33		23 51	00 14	00 51
Shawford	d							23 55		
Romsey	d			23 07			22 58			
Chandlers Ford	d			23 14						
Eastleigh 8	a	23 17		23 22			23 34	00 01	00 22	00 59
	d	23 18		23 22			23 36	00 02	00 23	01 00
Hedge End	d									
Botley	d									
Fareham	d									
Portchester	d									
Cosham	d									
Hilsea	a									
Fratton	a									
Portsmouth & Southsea	a									
Portsmouth Harbour ⛴	a									
Southampton Airport Pkwy ✈	d	23 22		23 26	23 37	23 42		00 06	00 28	01 05
Swaythling	d			23 28						
St Denys	d			23 31					00s32	
Southampton Central ⛴	a	23 29		23 36	23 43	23 49		00 13	00 37	01 12
	d	23 31		23 38		23 51			00 38	
Millbrook (Hants)	d			23 40						
Redbridge	d			23 44						
Romsey	d			23 56			23a48			
Mottisfont & Dunbridge	d			00 01						
Dean	d			00 07						
Salisbury	a			00 19						
Totton	d	23 36							00s43	
Ashurst New Forest	d	23 41								
Beaulieu Road	d									
Brockenhurst 8	a	23 49				00 04			00s54	
	d	23 50				00 05				
Lymington Town	d									
Lymington Pier	a									
Sway	d	23 54								
New Milton	d	23 59							01s02	
Hinton Admiral	d	00 03								
Christchurch	d	00 08							01s09	
Pokesdown	d	00 11							01s13	
Bournemouth	a	00 15				00 21			01 17	
	d	00 17				00 22			01 18	
Branksome	d	00 22				00 27			01s23	
Parkstone (Dorset)	d	00 25				00 30			01s26	
Poole 4	a	00 29				00 35			01 30	
	d									
Hamworthy	d									
Holton Heath	d									
Wareham	d									
Wool	d									
Moreton (Dorset)	d									
Dorchester South	d									
Dorchester West	d									
Upwey	d									
Weymouth	a									

London - Basingstoke, Southampton, Romsey Lymington, Bournemouth and Weymouth

		SW MX ◇1 A ⊼	SW MO ◇1 B ⊼	SW MO ◇1	SW MO ◇1	SW MX ◇1 ⊼	SW MO ◇1	SW MX 1	SW MX ◇1 ⊼	SW MX 1
London Waterloo 15 ⊖	d	21p35	21p35	21p54		22p05			22p35	22p39
Clapham Junction 10	d		21b42	22b03		22b12				22b46
Woking	d	22p00	22p07	22p28		22p32			23p00	
Farnborough (Main)	d									23p16
Fleet	d									23p21
Reading 7	d									
Basingstoke	a		22p26	22p46		22p51				23p33
	d		22p28	22p48		22p52				23p34
Micheldever	d			22p58						
Winchester	d	22p33	22p44	23p08		23p09			23p33	23p51
Shawford	d									23p55
Romsey	d							23p07		
Chandlers Ford	d							23p14		
Eastleigh 3	a			23p17		23p17		23p22		00 01
	d			23p22	23p26	23p18		23p22		00 02
Hedge End	d				23p32					
Botley	d				23p36					
Fareham	d				23p44					
Portchester	d				23p49					
Cosham	d				23p54					
Hilsea	a				23p59					
Fratton	a				00 04					
Portsmouth & Southsea	a				00 08					
Portsmouth Harbour ⛴	a				00 13					
Southampton Airport Pkwy ✈	d	22p42	22p53	23p27		23p22		23p26	23p42	00 06
Swaythling	d							23p28		
St Denys	d						←	23p31		
Southampton Central ⛴	a	22p49	23p00	23p34		23p29	23p34	23p36	23p49	00 13
	d	22p51	23p03	23p35		23p31	23p35	23p38	23p51	
Millbrook (Hants)	d			→				23p40		
Redbridge	d							23p44		
Romsey	d							23p56		
Mottisfont & Dunbridge	d							00 01		
Dean	d							00 07		
Salisbury	a							00 19		
Totton	d					23p36	23p41			
Ashurst New Forest	d					23p41	23p45			
Beaulieu Road	d									
Brockenhurst 3	a	23p04	23p16			23p49	23p53		00 04	
	d	23p05	23p17			23p50	23p54		00 05	
Lymington Town	d									
Lymington Pier	a									
Sway	d					23p54	23p59			
New Milton	d		23p24			23p59	00 04			
Hinton Admiral	d					00 03	00 08			
Christchurch	d					00 08	00 13			
Pokesdown	d					00 11	00 16			
Bournemouth	a	23p25	23p34			00 15	00 20		00 21	
	d	23p29	23p39			00 17	00 22		00 22	
Branksome	d	23p35	23p44			00 22	00 27		00 27	
Parkstone (Dorset)	d	23p38	23p47			00 25	00 30		00 30	
Poole 4	a	23p41	23p50			00 29	00 34		00 35	
	d	23p42	23p51							
Hamworthy	d	23p47	23p56							
Holton Heath	d									
Wareham	d	23p54	00 03							
Wool	d	00 01	00 10							
Moreton (Dorset)	d	00 07	00 16							
Dorchester South	d	00 15	00 24							
Dorchester West	d									
Upwey	d	00 21	00 31							
Weymouth	a	00 26	00 35							

		SW MO ◇1 ⊼	SW MX ◇1	SW 1	SW MX 1	SW MX 1	SW MO 1	SW 1	SW 1	SW 1	SW 1	SW 1	SW 1	SW 1
London Waterloo 15 ⊖	d	22p54	23p05		23p35	00 05	00 50	01 05						
Clapham Junction 10	d	23b03	23b12		23b42	00u12	00 57							
Woking	d	23p28	23p32		00 03	00 37	01 18	01 42						
Farnborough (Main)	d				00 14			01s58						
Fleet	d				00 20			02s04						
Reading 7	d													
Basingstoke	a	23p46	23p53		00 33	00 55		02s16						
	d	23p48	23p53		00 35	00 56								
Micheldever	d	23p58	00 03											05 40
Winchester	d	00 08	00 14		00 51	01 13		02s33						05 50
Shawford	d													05 59
Romsey	d													
Chandlers Ford	d													
Eastleigh 3	a	00 18	00 22		00 59	01 21		02s42						06 07
	d	00 22	00 23	00 30	01 00	01 22				06 00				06 08
Hedge End	d			00s36						06 06				
Botley	d			00s39						06 10				
Fareham	d			00s47						06 18				
Portchester	d			00s53						06 23				
Cosham	d			00s57						06 28				
Hilsea	a									06 33				
Fratton	a			01s05			02s10			06 38				
Portsmouth & Southsea	a			01s08			02s14			06 44				
Portsmouth Harbour ⛴	a			01 12			02 19			06 49				
Southampton Airport Pkwy ✈	d	00 27	00 28		01 05	01 26		02s46						06 13
Swaythling	d													06 15
St Denys	d	00s31	00s32					02s51						06 18
Southampton Central ⛴	a	00 36	00 37		01 12	01 35		02 56						06 23
	d	00 37	00 38			01 37								06 25
Millbrook (Hants)	d													
Redbridge	d													
Romsey	d													
Mottisfont & Dunbridge	d													
Dean	d													
Salisbury	a													
Totton	d	00s42	00s43			01s42								06 30
Ashurst New Forest	d													06 35
Beaulieu Road	d													
Brockenhurst 3	a	00s53	00s54			01s53								06 43
	d								05 59			06 16	06 29	06 44
Lymington Town	d								06 07				06 37	
Lymington Pier	a								06 10				06 40	
Sway	d											06 20		06 48
New Milton	d	01s01	01s02			02s00						06 25		06 53
Hinton Admiral	d											06 29		06 57
Christchurch	d	01s08	01s09			02s07						06 34		07 02
Pokesdown	d	01s12	01s13			02s11						06 38		07 06
Bournemouth	a	01 16	01 17			02 15						06 42		07 10
	d	01 17	01 18								06 11	06 44		07 11
Branksome	d	01s22	01s23								06 16	06 49		07 16
Parkstone (Dorset)	d	01s25	01s26								06 19	06 52		07 19
Poole 4	a	01 29	01 30								06 23	06 55		07 23
	d										06 24	06 57		07 24
Hamworthy	d										06 29	07 02		07 29
Holton Heath	d										06 33	07 06		07 33
Wareham	d										06 38	07 11		07 38
Wool	d										06 44	07 17		07 44
Moreton (Dorset)	d										06 50	07 23		07 50
Dorchester South	d										06 58	07 31		07 58
Dorchester West	d													
Upwey	d										07 05	07 38		08 05
Weymouth	a										07 14	07 42		08 14

A ⊼ to Brockenhurst

B ⊼ to New Milton

b Previous night, stops to pick up only

London - Basingstoke, Southampton, Romsey Lymington, Bournemouth and Weymouth

		SW 1	GW ⊼	SW 1	SW 1	GW	SW ◇1	SW 1	SW 1	SW 1	SW 1
London Waterloo 15 ⊖	d						05 30				
Clapham Junction 10	d						05u37				
Woking	d						06 01				
Farnborough (Main)	d										
Fleet	d										
Reading 7	d										
Basingstoke	a						06 20				
	d						06 21				
Micheldever	d										
Winchester	d			06 18			06 38				
Shawford	d			06 23							
Romsey	d	05 58									
Chandlers Ford	d	06 06									
Eastleigh 3	a	06 11		06 28			06 47				
	d	06 13		06 29			06 48	06 50	07 02		
Hedge End	d			06 35					07 08		
Botley	d			06 39					07 12		
Fareham	d		06 24	06 50					07 20		
Portchester	d			06 55					07 25		
Cosham	d			07 00					07 29		
Hilsea	a			07 05					07 35		
Fratton	a			07 09					07 39		
Portsmouth & Southsea	a			07 12					07 42		
Portsmouth Harbour ⛴	a			07 17					07 48		
Southampton Airport Pkwy ✈	d	06 17					06 53				
Swaythling	d	06 20									
St Denys	d	06 24									
Southampton Central ⛴	a	06 29	06 45				07 00				
	d	06 30	06 46				07 01				07 19
Millbrook (Hants)	d	06 33									07 21
Redbridge	d	06 36									07 25
Romsey	d	06 44	07 00					07a03			
Mottisfont & Dunbridge	d	06 49									
Dean	d	06 55									
Salisbury	a	07 07	07 18								
Totton	d						07 07				07 28
Ashurst New Forest	d										07 32
Beaulieu Road	d										07 37
Brockenhurst 3	a						07 17				07 43
	d				06 59		07 18			07 29	07 44
Lymington Town	d				07 07					07 37	
Lymington Pier	a				07 10					07 40	
Sway	d						07 23				07 48
New Milton	d						07 28				07 53
Hinton Admiral	d						07 32				07 57
Christchurch	d						07 37				08 02
Pokesdown	d						07 40				08 06
Bournemouth	a						07 44				08 10
	d						07 46				08 11
Branksome	d						07 51				08 16
Parkstone (Dorset)	d						07 54				08 19
Poole 4	a						07 57				08 23
	d						07 58				08 24
Hamworthy	d						08 03				08 29
Holton Heath	d						08 07				08 33
Wareham	d						08 12				08 38
Wool	d						08 19				08 44
Moreton (Dorset)	d						08 25				08 50
Dorchester South	d						08 33				08 58
Dorchester West	d					08 09					
Upwey	d					08 17	08 40				09 05
Weymouth	a					08 24	08 44				09 09

		SW 1	SW 1	GW ◇ ⊼	SW 1	SW ◇1	GW ◇	SW 1	SW 1	XC ◇1 ⊼	SW 1	SW ◇1 A ⊼	GW ◇ ⊼
London Waterloo 15 ⊖	d					06 30						07 35	
Clapham Junction 10	d					06u37							
Woking	d					06 57						08 00	
Farnborough (Main)	d												
Fleet	d												
Reading 7	d									07 46			
Basingstoke	a					07 16				08 08		08 19	
	d					07 18				08 10		08 20	
Micheldever	d		06 55										
Winchester	d		07 11			07 34				08 25		08 37	
Shawford	d		07 16										
Romsey	d	07 07						08 07					
Chandlers Ford	d	07 14						08 14					
Eastleigh 3	a	07 20	07 22			07 43		08 20				08 47	
	d	07 21	07 24			07 44		08 21				08 48	
Hedge End	d												
Botley	d												
Fareham	d			07 29									08 47
Portchester	d												
Cosham	d												
Hilsea	a												
Fratton	a												
Portsmouth & Southsea	a												
Portsmouth Harbour ⛴	a												
Southampton Airport Pkwy ✈	d	07 25	07 29			07 49		08 25		08 33		08 52	
Swaythling	d	07 27	07 31					08 27					
St Denys	d	07 30	07 34					08 30					
Southampton Central ⛴	a	07 35	07 39	07 50		07 57		08 35		08 44		08 59	09 08
	d	07 37		07 52		08 00	08 23	08 37		08 46		09 01	09 10
Millbrook (Hants)	d	07 40						08 40					
Redbridge	d	07 43						08 43					
Romsey	d	07 51		08 11			08 35	08 51					09 21
Mottisfont & Dunbridge	d	07 56						08 56					
Dean	d	08 02						09 02					
Salisbury	a	08 15		08 29			09 00	09 15					09 40
Totton	d					08 05						09 06	
Ashurst New Forest	d												
Beaulieu Road	d												
Brockenhurst 3	a					08 16				08 59		09 17	
	d				07 59	08 17			08 29	09 00	08 59	09 18	
Lymington Town	d				08 07				08 37		09 07		
Lymington Pier	a				08 10				08 40		09 10		
Sway	d					08 21						09 22	
New Milton	d					08 26						09 27	
Hinton Admiral	d					08 30						09 31	
Christchurch	d					08 35						09 36	
Pokesdown	d					08 39						09 40	
Bournemouth	a					08 43				09 15		09 44	
	d					08 44						09 45	
Branksome	d					08 49						09 50	
Parkstone (Dorset)	d					08 52						09 53	
Poole 4	a					08 56						09 57	
	d					08 57						09 58	
Hamworthy	d					09 02						10 03	
Holton Heath	d												
Wareham	d					09 09						10 10	
Wool	d					09 15							
Moreton (Dorset)	d					09 21							
Dorchester South	d					09 29						10 26	
Dorchester West	d												
Upwey	d					09 36							
Weymouth	a					09 40						10 34	

A ⊼ to Pokesdown

Table 158

Mondays to Fridays

from 3 October

London - Basingstoke, Southampton, Romsey Lymington, Bournemouth and Weymouth

		SW ■	GW	SW ■ ✠	XC ◇■ ✠	SW ◇■ A ✠	SW ■ ✠	SW ■	SW ■	XC ◇■ ✠	SW ◇■ B ✠	SW ■ ✠	GW ◇ ✠	SW ■	SW ■	SW ◇■ A ✠	SW ■	GW ◇	SW ■	SW ■	SW ■	XC ◇■ ✠
London Waterloo ■15 ⊖	d			07 39		08 05			08 09		08 35				08 39	09 05				09 09		
Clapham Junction ■10	d			07u46		08u12									08u46	09u12						
Woking	d								08 35		09 00									09 35		
Farnborough (Main)	d			08 13					08 45						09 13					09 45		
Fleet	d			08 19											09 19							
Reading ■7	d				08 15					08 46												09 46
Basingstoke	a			08 32	08 40	08 47			08 58	09 08					09 31	09 47				09 58		10 08
	d			08 33	08 42	08 49			09 00	09 10					09 33	09 49				10 00		10 10
Micheldever	d								09 10											10 10		
Winchester	d			08 50	08 57	09 05			09 19	09 25	09 33				09 49	10 05				10 19		10 25
Shawford	d			08 54											09 54							
Romsey	d							09 07											10 07			
Chandlers Ford	d							09 14											10 14			
Eastleigh ■8	a			09 00				09 20	09 27						10 02				10 20	10 27		
	d			09 01				09 21	09 28						10 03				10 21	10 28		
Hedge End	d								09 34											10 34		
Botley	d								09 38											10 38		
Fareham	d								09 48				09 47					10 14		10 48		
Portchester	d								09 53											10 53		
Cosham	d								09 58											10 58		
Hilsea	a								10 03											11 03		
Fratton	a								10 07											11 07		
Portsmouth & Southsea	a								10 11											11 11		
Portsmouth Harbour ⛴	a								10 18											11 18		
Southampton Airport Pkwy ✈	d			09 05	09 09	09 14		09 25		09 33	09 42				10 08	10 14			10 25			10 33
Swaythling	d							09 27											10 27			
St Denys	d						←	09 30									←		10 30			
Southampton Central ⛴	a			09 15	09 17	09 22	09 15	09 35		09 41	09 49		10 08		10 18	10 22	10 18	10 41	10 35			10 43
	d			09 30		09 24	09 30	09 37		09 43	09 51		10 10		10 30	10 24	10 30	10 42	10 44			10 45
Millbrook (Hants)	d			→				09 40							→				10 48			
Redbridge	d							09 43											10 51			
Romsey	d							09 51					10 21					10 54	10 59			
Mottisfont & Dunbridge	d							09 56											11 04			
Dean	d							10 02											11 10			
Salisbury	a							10 15					10 40					11 13	11 22			
Totton	d						09 35										10 35					
Ashurst New Forest	d						09 40										10 40					
Beaulieu Road	d											←					10 44					
Brockenhurst ■3	a					09 37	09 49			09 56	10 04	09 49				10 37	10 51					10 58
	d	09 29				09 38	10 16			09 57	10 05	10 16		10 12		10 38	11 16				10 42	10 59
Lymington Town	d	09 37					→							10 20			→				10 50	
Lymington Pier	a	09 40												10 23							10 53	
Sway	d											10 20										
New Milton	d					09 45						10 25				10 45						
Hinton Admiral	d											10 29										
Christchurch	d					09 52						10 34				10 52						
Pokesdown	d					09 56						10 38				10 56						
Bournemouth	a					10 00				10 12	10 20	10 42				11 00						11 12
	d					10 04					10 24	10 43				11 04						
Branksome	d										10 29	10 48										
Parkstone (Dorset)	d										10 32	10 51										
Poole ■4	a					10 13					10 36	10 55				11 13						
	d					10 14					10 37					11 14						
Hamworthy	d					10 19					10 42					11 19						
Holton Heath	d					10 23										11 23						
Wareham	d					10 28					10 49					11 28						
Wool	d					10 35										11 35						
Moreton (Dorset)	d					10 41										11 41						
Dorchester South	d					10 54					11 05					11 49						
Dorchester West	d		10 48																			
Upwey	d		10 55			11 01										11 55						
Weymouth	a		11 03			11 06					11 13					12 00						

A ✠ to Pokesdown

B ✠ to Brockenhurst

Table 158

Mondays to Fridays

from 3 October

London - Basingstoke, Southampton, Romsey Lymington, Bournemouth and Weymouth

		GW	SW ◇■ A ✠	SW ■	GW ◇ ✠	SW ■	SW ■	XC ◇■ ✠	SW ◇■ B ✠	SW ■	SW ■	SW ■	SW ■	XC ◇■ ✠	SW ◇■ A ✠	SW ■	GW ◇ ✠	SW ■	SW ■	SW ◇■ B ✠	SW ■	GW ◇	SW ■
London Waterloo ■15 ⊖	d		09 35				09 39		10 05			10 09			10 35				10 39	11 05			
Clapham Junction ■10	d						09u46		10u12										10u46	11u12			
Woking	d		10 00									10 35			11 00								
Farnborough (Main)	d						10 13					10 45							11 13				
Fleet	d						10 19												11 19				
Reading ■7	d							10 15						10 46									
Basingstoke	a						10 31	10 39	10 47			10 58		11 08					11 31	11 47			
	d						10 33	10 40	10 49			11 00		11 10					11 33	11 49			
Micheldever	d											11 10											
Winchester	d		10 33				10 49	10 55	11 05			11 19		11 25	11 33				11 49	12 05			
Shawford	d						10 54												11 54				
Romsey	d										11 07												12 07
Chandlers Ford	d										11 14												12 14
Eastleigh ■8	a						10 59				11 20	11 27							11 59				12 20
	d						11 00				11 21	11 28							12 00				12 21
Hedge End	d											11 34											
Botley	d											11 38											
Fareham	d				10 47							11 48					11 47						
Portchester	d											11 53											
Cosham	d											11 58											
Hilsea	a											12 03											
Fratton	a											12 07											
Portsmouth & Southsea	a											12 11											
Portsmouth Harbour ⛴	a											12 18											
Southampton Airport Pkwy ✈	d		10 42				11 05	11 09	11 14		11 25			11 33	11 42				12 05	12 14			12 25
Swaythling	d										11 27												12 27
St Denys	d									←	11 30										←		12 30
Southampton Central ⛴	a		10 49		11 08		11 12	11 16	11 22	11 12	11 35			11 43	11 49		12 08		12 15	12 22	12 15		12 35
	d		10 51		11 10		11 30		11 24	11 30	11 37			11 45	11 51		12 10		12 30	12 24	12 30	12 27	12 37
Millbrook (Hants)	d						→				11 40								→				12 40
Redbridge	d										11 43												12 43
Romsey	d				11 21						11 51						12 21					12 39	12 51
Mottisfont & Dunbridge	d										11 56												12 56
Dean	d										12 02												13 02
Salisbury	a				11 40						12 15						12 40					13 02	13 15
Totton	d									11 35											12 35		
Ashurst New Forest	d									11 40											12 40		
Beaulieu Road	d			←						11 44						←							
Brockenhurst ■3	a		11 04	10 51					11 37	11 51				11 58	12 04	11 51				12 37	12 51		
	d		11 05	11 16		11 12			11 38	12 16			11 42	11 59	12 05	12 16		12 12		12 38	13 16		
Lymington Town	d					11 20				→			11 50					12 20			→		
Lymington Pier	a					11 23							11 53					12 23					
Sway	d			11 20												12 20							
New Milton	d			11 25					11 45							12 25				12 45			
Hinton Admiral	d			11 29												12 29							
Christchurch	d			11 34					11 52							12 34				12 52			
Pokesdown	d			11 38					11 56							12 38				12 56			
Bournemouth	a		11 20	11 42					12 00					12 12	12 20	12 42				13 00			
	d		11 24	11 43					12 04						12 24	12 43				13 04			
Branksome	d		11 29	11 48											12 29	12 48							
Parkstone (Dorset)	d		11 32	11 51											12 32	12 51							
Poole ■4	a		11 36	11 55					12 13						12 36	12 55				13 13			
	d		11 37						12 14						12 37					13 14			
Hamworthy	d		11 42						12 19						12 42					13 19			
Holton Heath	d								12 23											13 23			
Wareham	d		11 49						12 28						12 49					13 28			
Wool	d								12 35											13 35			
Moreton (Dorset)	d								12 41											13 41			
Dorchester South	d		12 05						12 49						13 05					13 49			
Dorchester West	d	11 54																					
Upwey	d	12 02							12 55											13 55			
Weymouth	a	12 09	12 13						13 00						13 13					14 00			

A ✠ to Brockenhurst

B ✠ to Pokesdown

London - Basingstoke, Southampton, Romsey Lymington, Bournemouth and Weymouth

		SW	SW	XC	GW	SW	SW	GW	SW	SW	XC	SW	SW	SW	SW	SW	XC	SW	SW	GW	SW	SW
		1	1	◇1 🍴		◇1 A 🍴	1	◇ 🍴	1	1	◇1 🍴	◇1 B 🍴	1	1	1	1	◇1 🍴	◇1 A 🍴	1	◇ 🍴	1	1
London Waterloo 15 ⊖	d	11 09				11 35				11 39		12 05			12 09			12 35				12 39
Clapham Junction 10	d									11u46		12u12										12u46
Woking	d	11 35				12 00									12 35			13 00				
Farnborough (Main)	d	11 45								12 13					12 45							13 13
Fleet	d									12 19												13 19
Reading 7	d			11 46							12 15						12 46					
Basingstoke	a	11 58		12 08						12 31	12 39	12 47			12 58		13 08					13 31
	d	12 00		12 10						12 33	12 40	12 49			13 00		13 10					13 33
Micheldever	d	12 10													13 10							
Winchester	d	12 19		12 25		12 33				12 49	12 55	13 05			13 19		13 25	13 33				13 49
Shawford	d									12 54												13 54
Romsey	d													13 07								
Chandlers Ford	d													13 14								
Eastleigh 3	a	12 27								12 59				13 20	13 27							13 59
	d	12 28								13 00				13 21	13 28							14 00
Hedge End	d	12 34													13 34							
Botley	d	12 38													13 38							
Fareham	d	12 48						12 47							13 48					13 47		
Portchester	d	12 53													13 53							
Cosham	d	12 58													13 58							
Hilsea	a	13 03													14 03							
Fratton	a	13 07													14 07							
Portsmouth & Southsea	a	13 11													14 11							
Portsmouth Harbour ⛴	a	13 18													14 18							
Southampton Airport Pkwy ✈	d			12 33		12 42				13 05	13 09	13 14		13 25			13 33	13 42				14 05
Swaythling	d													13 27								
St Denys	d												←	13 30								
Southampton Central ⛴	a			12 41		12 49		13 08		13 15	13 17	13 22	13 15	13 35			13 41	13 49		14 08		14 12
	d			12 43		12 51		13 10		13 30		13 24	13 30	13 37			13 43	13 51		14 10		14 30
Millbrook (Hants)	d									→				13 40								→
Redbridge	d													13 43								
Romsey	d							13 21						13 51						14 21		
Mottisfont & Dunbridge	d													13 56								
Dean	d													14 02								
Salisbury	a							13 40						14 15						14 40		
Totton	d												13 35									
Ashurst New Forest	d												13 40									
Beaulieu Road	d						←												←			
Brockenhurst 3	a			12 56		13 04	12 51					13 37	13 51				13 56	14 04	13 51			
	d		12 42	12 57		13 05	13 16		13 12			13 38	14 16			13 42	13 57	14 05	14 16		14 12	
Lymington Town	d		12 50						13 20				→			13 50					14 20	
Lymington Pier	a		12 53						13 23							13 53					14 23	
Sway	d						13 20												14 20			
New Milton	d						13 25					13 45							14 25			
Hinton Admiral	d						13 29												14 29			
Christchurch	d						13 34					13 52							14 34			
Pokesdown	d						13 38					13 56							14 38			
Bournemouth	a			13 10		13 20	13 42					14 00					14 10	14 20	14 42			
	d					13 24	13 43					14 04						14 24	14 43			
Branksome	d					13 29	13 48											14 29	14 48			
Parkstone (Dorset)	d					13 32	13 51											14 32	14 51			
Poole 4	a					13 36	13 55					14 13						14 36	14 55			
	d					13 37						14 14						14 37				
Hamworthy	d					13 42						14 19						14 42				
Holton Heath	d											14 23										
Wareham	d					13 49						14 28						14 49				
Wool	d											14 35										
Moreton (Dorset)	d											14 41										
Dorchester South	d					14 05						14 49						15 05				
Dorchester West	d				13 54																	
Upwey	d				14 02							14 55										
Weymouth	a				14 09	14 13						15 00						15 13				

A 🍴 to Brockenhurst

B 🍴 to Pokesdown

London - Basingstoke, Southampton, Romsey Lymington, Bournemouth and Weymouth

		SW	SW	SW	SW	SW	XC	SW	SW	GW	SW	SW	XC	SW	SW	SW	SW	SW	XC	GW	SW	SW	GW
		◇1 A 🍴	1	1	1	1	◇1 🍴	◇1 B 🍴	1	■ 🍴	1	1	◇1 🍴	◇1 A 🍴	1	1	1	1	◇1 🍴		◇1 B 🍴	1	■ 🍴
London Waterloo 15 ⊖	d	13 05			13 09			13 35				13 39		14 05			14 09				14 35		
Clapham Junction 10	d	13u12										13u46		14u12									
Woking	d				13 35			14 00									14 35				15 00		
Farnborough (Main)	d				13 45							14 13					14 45						
Fleet	d											14 19											
Reading 7	d						13 46						14 15						14 46				
Basingstoke	a	13 47			13 58		14 08					14 31	14 39	14 47			14 58		15 08				
	d	13 49			14 00		14 10					14 33	14 40	14 49			15 00		15 10				
Micheldever	d				14 10												15 10						
Winchester	d	14 05			14 19		14 25	14 33				14 49	14 55	15 05			15 19		15 25		15 33		
Shawford	d											14 54											
Romsey	d			14 07												15 07							
Chandlers Ford	d			14 14												15 14							
Eastleigh 3	a			14 20	14 27							14 59				15 20	15 27						
	d			14 21	14 28							15 00				15 21	15 28						
Hedge End	d				14 34												15 34						
Botley	d				14 38												15 38						
Fareham	d				14 48					14 47							15 48						15 47
Portchester	d				14 53												15 53						
Cosham	d				14 58												15 58						
Hilsea	a				15 03												16 03						
Fratton	a				15 07												16 07						
Portsmouth & Southsea	a				15 11												16 11						
Portsmouth Harbour ⛴	a				15 18												16 18						
Southampton Airport Pkwy ✈	d	14 14		14 25			14 35	14 42				15 05	15 10	15 14		15 25			15 33		15 42		
Swaythling	d			14 27												15 27							
St Denys	d		←	14 30											←	15 30							
Southampton Central ⛴	a	14 22	14 12	14 35			14 42	14 49		15 08		15 12	15 17	15 22	15 12	15 35			15 41		15 49		16 08
	d	14 24	14 30	14 37			14 43	14 51		15 10		15 30		15 24	15 30	15 37			15 43		15 51		16 10
Millbrook (Hants)	d			14 40								→				15 40							
Redbridge	d			14 43												15 43							
Romsey	d			14 51						15 21						15 51							16 21
Mottisfont & Dunbridge	d			14 56												15 56							
Dean	d			15 02												16 02							
Salisbury	a			15 15						15 40						16 15							16 40
Totton	d		14 35												15 35								
Ashurst New Forest	d		14 40												15 40								
Beaulieu Road	d								←													←	
Brockenhurst 3	a	14 37	14 51				14 56	15 04	14 51					15 37	15 51				15 56		16 04	15 51	
	d	14 38	15 16			14 42	14 57	15 05	15 16		15 12			15 38	16 28			15 42	15 57		16 05	16 28	
Lymington Town	d		→			14 50					15 20				→			15 50					
Lymington Pier	a					14 53					15 23							15 53					
Sway	d								15 20													16 32	
New Milton	d	14 45							15 25					15 45								16 37	
Hinton Admiral	d								15 29													16 41	
Christchurch	d	14 52							15 34					15 52								16 46	
Pokesdown	d	14 56							15 38					15 56								16 50	
Bournemouth	a	15 00					15 11	15 20	15 42					16 00					16 10		16 20	16 54	
	d	15 04						15 24	15 43					16 04							16 24	16 55	
Branksome	d							15 29	15 48												16 29	17 00	
Parkstone (Dorset)	d							15 32	15 51												16 32	17 03	
Poole 4	a	15 13						15 36	15 55					16 13							16 36	17 07	
	d	15 14						15 37						16 14							16 37		
Hamworthy	d	15 19						15 42						16 19							16 42		
Holton Heath	d	15 23												16 23									
Wareham	d	15 28						15 49						16 28							16 49		
Wool	d	15 35												16 35							16 55		
Moreton (Dorset)	d	15 41												16 41									
Dorchester South	d	15 49						16 05						16 49							17 06		
Dorchester West	d																			16 58			
Upwey	d	15 55												16 55						17 05			
Weymouth	a	16 00						16 13						17 00						17 10	17 15		

A 🍴 to Pokesdown

B 🍴 to Brockenhurst

Table 158

Mondays to Fridays
from 3 October

London - Basingstoke, Southampton, Romsey Lymington, Bournemouth and Weymouth

		SW	SW	SW	SW	SW	SW	SW	XC	SW	SW		SW	GW	SW	SW	XC	SW	SN	SW	SW	SW	SW
		1	1	◇1 A ⊼	1	1	1	1	◇1 ⊼	1	◇1 B ⊼		1	⊼	1	1	◇1 ⊼	◇1 A ⊼	◇1	1	1	1	1
London Waterloo 15 ⊖	d		14 39	15 05				15 09			15 35					15 39		16 05					16 09
Clapham Junction 10	d		14u46	15u12												15u46		16u12					
Woking	d							15 35			16 00												16 35
Farnborough (Main)	d		15 13					15 45								16 13							16 45
Fleet	d		15 19													16 19							
Reading 7	d								15 46								16 15						
Basingstoke	a		15 31	15 47				15 58	16 08							16 31	16 39	16 47					16 58
	d		15 33	15 49				16 00	16 10						16 24	16 33	16 40	16 49					17 00
Micheldever	d							16 10															17 10
Winchester	d		15 49	16 05				16 19	16 25		16 33		16 38		16 45	16 50	17 00	17 05					17 19
Shawford	d		15 54										16 43			16 54							
Romsey	d						16 07															17 07	
Chandlers Ford	d						16 14															17 14	
Eastleigh 8	a		15 59				16 20	16 27					16 48		16 53	17 00						17 20	17 27
	d		16 00				16 21	16 28					16 49		16 54	17 01			17 16			17 21	17 28
Hedge End	d							16 34							17 00								17 34
Botley	d							16 38							17 04								17 39
Fareham	d							16 48						16 47	17 12								17 48
Portchester	d							16 53							17 17								17 53
Cosham	d							16 58							17 22								17 58
Hilsea	a							17 03															18 04
Fratton	a							17 07							17 31								18 08
Portsmouth & Southsea	a							17 11							17 35								18 12
Portsmouth Harbour ⛴	a							17 18							17 40								18 20
Southampton Airport Pkwy ✈	d		16 05	16 14			16 25		16 33		16 42		16 54			17 05		17 14	17 20			17 25	
Swaythling	d						16 27						16 56									17 27	
St Denys	d					←	16 30						16 59								←	17 30	
Southampton Central ⛴	a		16 15	16 22		16 15	16 35		16 41		16 49		17 04	17 08		17 13	17 17	17 22	17 28		17 13	17 35	
	d		16 30	16 24		16 30	16 37		16 43		16 54	16 56	17 06	17 10		17 30		17 24			17 30	17 37	
Millbrook (Hants)	d		→				16 40									→						17 40	
Redbridge	d						16 43															17 43	
Romsey	d						16 51							17 21								17 51	
Mottisfont & Dunbridge	d						16 56															17 56	
Dean	d						17 02															18 02	
Salisbury	a						17 15							17 40								18 15	
Totton	d					16 35						17 01	17a11								17 35		
Ashurst New Forest	d					16 40						17 06									17 40		
Beaulieu Road	d					16 44															17 44		
Brockenhurst 3	a			16 37		16 51			16 56		17 07	17 14						17 37			17 51		
	d	16 12		16 38	16 42				16 57	17 12	17 08	17 16						17 38		17 42			
Lymington Town	d	16 20			16 50					17 20										17 50			
Lymington Pier	a	16 23			16 53					17 23										17 53			
Sway	d			16 43								17 20						17 43					
New Milton	d			16 48								17 25						17 48					
Hinton Admiral	d			16 52								17 29						17 52					
Christchurch	d			16 57								17 34						17 57					
Pokesdown	d			17 00								17 38						18 00					
Bournemouth	a			17 04					17 10		17 23	17 42						18 04					
	d			17 07							17 24	17 43						18 09					
Branksome	d										17 29	17 48											
Parkstone (Dorset)	d										17 32	17 51											
Poole 4	a			17 16							17 36	17 55						18 18					
	d			17 17							17 37							18 19					
Hamworthy	d			17 22							17 42							18 24					
Holton Heath	d			17 26														18 28					
Wareham	d			17 31							17 49							18 33					
Wool	d			17 37							17 55							18 39					
Moreton (Dorset)	d			17 43														18 45					
Dorchester South	d			17 51							18 06							18 53					
Dorchester West	d																						
Upwey	d			17 58														19 00					
Weymouth	a			18 02							18 15							19 06					

A ⊼ to Pokesdown

B ⊼ to Brockenhurst

Table 158

Mondays to Fridays
from 3 October

London - Basingstoke, Southampton, Romsey Lymington, Bournemouth and Weymouth

		XC	GW	SW	SW		SW	GW	SW	SW		SW	GW	SW	SW	XC	GW	SW		GW	SW	SW
		◇1 ⊼		1	◇1 A ⊼		1	◇ ⊼	1	◇1 ⊼		1	◇ ⊼	1	1	◇1 ⊼		◇1 B ⊼		◇ ⊼	1	1
London Waterloo 15 ⊖	d				16 35				16 39	17 05				17 09				17 35			17 39	17 48
Clapham Junction 10	d								16u46													
Woking	d				17u00									17 34							18 04	18 13
Farnborough (Main)	d								17 13													
Fleet	d								17 19													
Reading 7	d	16 46														17 46						
Basingstoke	a	17 08							17 31					17 52		18 08					18 22	18 31
	d	17 10					17 24		17 33					17 54		18 10					18 24	18 33
Micheldever	d						17 34							18 04							18 34	
Winchester	d	17 25			17 33		17 44		17 49	18 00				18 14		18 25		18 30			18 44	18 50
Shawford	d						17 49		17 54					18 18							18 49	
Romsey	d											18 07										
Chandlers Ford	d											18 14										
Eastleigh 8	a						17 54		17 59			18 20		18 24							18 54	18 58
	d						17 55		18 01			18 21		18 25							18 55	18 59
Hedge End	d								18 07					18 31							19 01	
Botley	d								18 11					18 36							19 05	
Fareham	d							17 47	18 23				18 13	18 45						18 47	19 14	
Portchester	d								18 28					18 50							19 19	
Cosham	d								18 33					18 55							19 24	
Hilsea	a													19 05							19 28	
Fratton	a								18 40					19 09							19 32	
Portsmouth & Southsea	a								18 43					19 12							19 36	
Portsmouth Harbour ⛴	a								18 51					19 20							19 43	
Southampton Airport Pkwy ✈	d	17 33			17 42		18 00			18 09		18 25				18 33		18 39				19 03
Swaythling	d						18 02					18 27										19 06
St Denys	d						18 05					18 30										19 09
Southampton Central ⛴	a	17 41			17 49		18 10	18 08		18 16		18 35	18 41			18 44		18 46		19 08		19 18
	d	17 43			17 53	17 56		18 10		18 21	18 24	18 37	18 42			18 45		18 51	18 54	19 10		
Millbrook (Hants)	d											18 40										
Redbridge	d											18 44										
Romsey	d							18 21				19 00	18 54							19 21		
Mottisfont & Dunbridge	d											19 05										
Dean	d											19 10										
Salisbury	a							18 40				19 23	19 12							19 40		
Totton	d					18 01					18 29								18 59			
Ashurst New Forest	d					18 06					18 34								19 04			
Beaulieu Road	d																					
Brockenhurst 3	a	17 56			18 07	18 14					18 42					18 58			19 12			
	d	17 57		18 12	18 08	18 16					18 43				18 48	18 59			19 13			
Lymington Town	d			18 20											18 56							
Lymington Pier	a			18 23											18 59							
Sway	d					18 20					18 47								19 17			
New Milton	d					18 25					18 52								19 22			
Hinton Admiral	d					18 29					18 57								19 26			
Christchurch	d					18 34					19 01								19 31			
Pokesdown	d					18 38					19 05								19 35			
Bournemouth	a	18 15			18 22	18 42				18 48	19 09					19 13		19 20	19 39			
	d				18 24					18 50	19 10							19 21	19 40			
Branksome	d				18 29					18 55	19 15							19 26	19 45			
Parkstone (Dorset)	d				18 32					18 58	19 18							19 29	19 48			
Poole 4	a				18 36					19 02	19 26							19 33	19 56			
	d				18 37					19 03								19 34				
Hamworthy	d				18 42					19 08								19 39				
Holton Heath	d									19 12												
Wareham	d				18 49					19 17								19 46				
Wool	d									19 23												
Moreton (Dorset)	d									19 29												
Dorchester South	d				19 05					19 37								20 02				
Dorchester West	d		18 58														19 54					
Upwey	d		19 06							19 44							20 01					
Weymouth	a		19 14		19 17					19 50							20 09	20 15				

A ⊼ to Brockenhurst

B ⊼ to Southampton Central

London - Basingstoke, Southampton, Romsey Lymington, Bournemouth and Weymouth

		SW 1	SW ◇1 A ⌶	SW 1	SW 1	XC ◇1 ⌶	SW 1	SW 1	XC ◇1 ⌶	SW ◇1 B ⌶		GW ◇	SW 1	SW 1	SW 1	SW ◇1 A ⌶	SW 1	SW 1	SW 1	SW 1	XC ◇1 ⌶	SW ◇1 C ⌶	SW 1
London Waterloo 15 ⊖	d		18 05				18 09			18 35					18 39	19 05			19 09			19 35	
Clapham Junction 10	d														18u46	19u12							
Woking	d						18 35								19 06				19 35			20 00	
Farnborough (Main)	d																		19 45				
Fleet	d																						
Reading 7	d					18 15			18 46												19 46		
Basingstoke	a					18 47	18 53		19 08						19 28	19 47			19 58		20 09		
	d					18 48	18 55		19 10				19 24		19 30	19 49			20 00		20 10		
Micheldever	d						19 05								19 40				20 10				
Winchester	d		19 00	19 05			19 14		19 25	19 30			19 40		19 49	20 05			20 19		20 25	20 33	
Shawford	d			19 09			19 19						19 45		19 54				20 24				
Romsey	d				19 07													20 07					
Chandlers Ford	d				19 14													20 14					
Eastleigh 3	a			19 15	19 20		19 25						19 50		19 59			20 20	20 29				
	d			19 16	19 21		19 28						19 51		20 00			20 21	20 30				
Hedge End	d						19 34						19 57						20 36				
Botley	d						19 38						20 01						20 40				
Fareham	d						19 48					19 47	20a09						20 49				
Portchester	d						19 53												20 54				
Cosham	d						19 58												20 59				
Hilsea	a						20 02												21 03				
Fratton	a						20 06												21 07				
Portsmouth & Southsea	a						20 11												21 11				
Portsmouth Harbour ⛴	a						20 20												21 16				
Southampton Airport Pkwy ✈	d		19 09	19 20	19 25				19 33	19 39					20 05	20 14		20 25			20 33	20 42	
Swaythling	d			19 23	19 27													20 27					
St Denys	d			19 26	19 30												←	20 30					
Southampton Central ⛴	a		19 18	19 33	19 35	19 53			19 41	19 46		20 08			20 16	20 22	20 16	20 35			20 41	20 49	
	d		19 19		19 37				19 43	19 51	19 54	20 10			20 30	20 24	20 30	20 37			20 43	20 51	
Millbrook (Hants)	d				19 40										→			20 40					
Redbridge	d				19 43													20 43					
Romsey	d				19 51							20 21						20 51					
Mottisfont & Dunbridge	d				19 56													20 56					
Dean	d				20 02													21 02					
Salisbury	a				20 15							20 40						21 15					
Totton	d		19 25								19 59						20 35					20 56	
Ashurst New Forest	d										20 04						20 40						
Beaulieu Road	d																20 44						←
Brockenhurst 3	a		19 35						19 56		20 12					20 37	20 51				20 58	21 07	20 51
	d	19 18	19 36					19 48	19 57		20 13			20 18		20 38	21 16			20 48	20 59	21 08	21 16
Lymington Town	d	19 26						19 56						20 26			→			20 56			
Lymington Pier	a	19 29						19 59						20 29						20 59			
Sway	d		19 41								20 17												21 20
New Milton	d		19 46								20 22					20 45							21 25
Hinton Admiral	d		19 50								20 26												21 29
Christchurch	d		19 55								20 31					20 52							21 34
Pokesdown	d		19 58								20 35					20 56							21 38
Bournemouth	a		20 02						20 12	20 20	20 39					21 00					21 15	21 22	21 42
	d		20 07							20 21	20 40					21 04						21 27	21 43
Branksome	d		20 12							20 26	20 45											21 32	21 48
Parkstone (Dorset)	d		20 15							20 29	20 48											21 35	21 51
Poole 4	a		20 18							20 33	20 56					21 13						21 38	21 57
	d		20 19							20 34						21 15						21 39	
Hamworthy	d		20 24							20 39						21 20						21 44	
Holton Heath	d		20 28																				
Wareham	d		20 33							20 46						21 27						21 51	
Wool	d		20 40													21 33						21 58	
Moreton (Dorset)	d		20 46													21 39						22 04	
Dorchester South	d		20 54							21 02						21 47						22 12	
Dorchester West	d																						
Upwey	d		21 00													21 54						22 18	
Weymouth	a		21 07							21 13						21 58						22 23	

A ⌶ to Pokesdown
B ⌶ to Southampton Central
C ⌶ to Brockenhurst

London - Basingstoke, Southampton, Romsey Lymington, Bournemouth and Weymouth

		GW ◇	SW 1	SW 1	GW	SW ◇1 ⌶	SW 1	SW 1	SW 1	XC ◇1	GW	SW ◇1 A ⌶	SW 1	GW	SW 1	SW ◇1 ⌶	SW 1	XC ◇1	SW ◇1 A ⌶	SW 1	SW 1	SW ◇1 ⌶
London Waterloo 15 ⊖	d		19 39			20 05		20 09				20 35	20 39			21 05			21 35		21 39	22 05
Clapham Junction 10	d		19u46			20u12							20u46			21u12					21u46	22u12
Woking	d							20 35				21 00				21 32			22 00			22 32
Farnborough (Main)	d		20 13					20 45					21 13								22 13	
Fleet	d		20 19										21 19								22 19	
Reading 7	d									20 46								21 46				
Basingstoke	a		20 31			20 47		20 58		21 09			21 31			21 51		22 09			22 31	22 51
	d		20 33			20 49		21 00		21 10			21 33			21 52		22 10		22 21	22 33	22 52
Micheldever	d							21 10					21 43							22 31	22s43	
Winchester	d		20 49			21 05		21 19		21 25		21 33	21 52			22 09		22 25	22 33	22 40	22 52	23 09
Shawford	d		20 54					21 24					21 57							22 45	22 57	
Romsey	d						21 07										22 07					
Chandlers Ford	d						21 14										22 14					
Eastleigh 3	a		20 59				21 20	21 30					22 02			22 17	22 21			22 50	23 02	23 17
	d		21 00				21 21	21 30					22 03	22 11		22 18	22 22			22 51	23 03	23 18
Hedge End	d							21 36												22 57		
Botley	d							21 40												23 01		
Fareham	d	20 47						21 48												23 10		
Portchester	d							21 53												23 15		
Cosham	d							21 58												23 20		
Hilsea	a							22 03												23 24		
Fratton	a							22 08												23 32		
Portsmouth & Southsea	a							22 11												23 36		
Portsmouth Harbour ⛴	a							22 16												23 40		
Southampton Airport Pkwy ✈	d		21 05			21 15	21 24			21 33		21 42	22 08			22 22	22 26	22 33	22 42		23 08	23 22
Swaythling	d						21 27										22 28					
St Denys	d						21 30										22 31					
Southampton Central ⛴	a	21 08	21 12			21 24	21 35			21 41		21 49	22 18	22 21		22 29	22 36	22 42	22 49		23 17	23 29
	d	21 10			21 20	21 25	21 37			21 43		21 51		22 22		22 31	22 38	22 43	22 51			23 31
Millbrook (Hants)	d						21 40										22 40					
Redbridge	d						21 43										22 44					
Romsey	d	21 21			21 31		21 51							22 34			22a52					
Mottisfont & Dunbridge	d						21 56															
Dean	d						22 02															
Salisbury	a	21 40			21 51		22 15							22 58								
Totton	d					21 31										22 36						23 36
Ashurst New Forest	d					21 35										22 41						23 41
Beaulieu Road	d																					
Brockenhurst 3	a					21 43				21 56		22 04				22 49		22 56	23 04			23 49
	d			21 18		21 44			21 48	21 57		22 05			22 18	22 50		22 59	23 05			23 50
Lymington Town	d			21 26					21 56						22 26							
Lymington Pier	a			21 29					21 59						22 29							
Sway	d					21 49										22 54						23 54
New Milton	d					21 54										22 59						23 59
Hinton Admiral	d					21 58										23 03						00 03
Christchurch	d					22 03										23 08						00 08
Pokesdown	d					22 06										23 12						00 11
Bournemouth	a					22 10				22 16		22 20				23 16		23 21	23 25			00 15
	d					22 12						22 24				23 17			23 29			00 17
Branksome	d					22 17						22 29				23 22			23 35			00 22
Parkstone (Dorset)	d					22 20						22 32				23 25			23 38			00 25
Poole 4	a					22 23						22 36				23 29			23 41			00 29
	d											22 37							23 42			
Hamworthy	d											22 42							23 47			
Holton Heath	d																					
Wareham	d											22 49							23 54			
Wool	d											22 55							00 01			
Moreton (Dorset)	d											23 01							00 07			
Dorchester South	d											23 09							00 15			
Dorchester West	d										22 54											
Upwey	d										23 02	23 16							00 21			
Weymouth	a										23 10	23 20							00 26			

A ⌶ to Brockenhurst

Table 158

Mondays to Fridays
from 3 October

London - Basingstoke, Southampton, Romsey Lymington, Bournemouth and Weymouth

		SW	XC	SW	SW	SW	SW	SW
		1	◇1	◇1 ✠	1	1	◇1	1
London Waterloo [15] ⊖	d			22 35		22 39	23 05	23 35
Clapham Junction [10]	d					22u46	23u12	23u42
Woking	d			23 00			23 32	00 03
Farnborough (Main)	d					23 16		00 14
Fleet	d					23 21		00 20
Reading [7]	d		22 48					
Basingstoke	a		23 06			23 33	23 53	00 33
	d		23 10			23 34	23 53	00 35
Micheldever	d						00 03	
Winchester	d		23 25	23 33		23 51	00 14	00 51
Shawford	d					23 55		
Romsey	d	23 07			22 58			
Chandlers Ford	d	23 14						
Eastleigh [8]	a	23 22			23 34	00 01	00 22	00 59
	d	23 22			23 36	00 02	00 23	01 00
Hedge End	d							
Botley	d							
Fareham	d							
Portchester	d							
Cosham	d							
Hilsea	a							
Fratton	a							
Portsmouth & Southsea	a							
Portsmouth Harbour ⛴	a							
Southampton Airport Pkwy ✈	d	23 26	23 37	23 42		00 06	00 28	01 05
Swaythling	d	23 28						
St Denys	d	23 31					00s32	
Southampton Central ⛴	a	23 36	23 43	23 49		00 13	00 37	01 12
	d	23 38		23 51			00 38	
Millbrook (Hants)	d	23 40						
Redbridge	d	23 44						
Romsey	d	23 56			23a48			
Mottisfont & Dunbridge	d	00 01						
Dean	d	00 07						
Salisbury	a	00 19						
Totton	d						00s43	
Ashurst New Forest	d							
Beaulieu Road	d							
Brockenhurst [5]	a			00 04			00s54	
	d			00 05				
Lymington Town	d							
Lymington Pier	a							
Sway	d							
New Milton	d						01s02	
Hinton Admiral	d							
Christchurch	d						01s09	
Pokesdown	d						01s13	
Bournemouth	a			00 21			01 17	
	d			00 22			01 18	
Branksome	d			00 27			01s23	
Parkstone (Dorset)	d			00 30			01s26	
Poole [4]	a			00 35			01 30	
	d							
Hamworthy	d							
Holton Heath	d							
Wareham	d							
Wool	d							
Moreton (Dorset)	d							
Dorchester South	d							
Dorchester West	d							
Upwey	d							
Weymouth	a							

Table 158

Saturdays

London - Basingstoke, Southampton, Romsey Lymington, Bournemouth and Weymouth

		SW	SW	SW	SW	SW	SW	SW	SW	SW
		◇1 A ✠	◇1 ✠	1	◇1 ✠	1	◇1	1	1	1
London Waterloo [15] ⊖	d	21p35	22p05		22p35	22p39	23p05		23p35	00 05
Clapham Junction [10]	d		22b12			22b46	23b12		23b42	00u12
Woking	d	22p00	22p32		23p00		23p32		00 03	00 37
Farnborough (Main)	d					23p16			00 14	
Fleet	d					23p21			00 20	
Reading [7]	d									
Basingstoke	a		22p51			23p33	23p53		00 33	00 55
	d		22p52			23p34	23p53		00 35	00 56
Micheldever	d						00 03			
Winchester	d	22p33	23p09		23p33	23p51	00 14		00 51	01 13
Shawford	d					23p55				
Romsey	d			23p07						
Chandlers Ford	d			23p14						
Eastleigh [8]	a		23p17	23p22		00 01	00 22		00 59	01 21
	d		23p18	23p22		00 02	00 23	00 30	01 00	01 22
Hedge End	d							00s36		
Botley	d							00s39		
Fareham	d							00s47		
Portchester	d							00s53		
Cosham	d							00s57		
Hilsea	a									
Fratton	a							01s05		
Portsmouth & Southsea	a							01s08		
Portsmouth Harbour ⛴	a							01 12		
Southampton Airport Pkwy ✈	d	22p42	23p22	23p26	23p42	00 06	00 28		01 05	01 26
Swaythling	d			23p28						
St Denys	d			23p31			00s32			
Southampton Central ⛴	a	22p49	23p29	23p36	23p49	00 13	00 37		01 12	01 35
	d	22p51	23p31	23p38	23p51		00 38			01 37
Millbrook (Hants)	d			23p40						
Redbridge	d			23p44						
Romsey	d			23p56						
Mottisfont & Dunbridge	d			00 01						
Dean	d			00 07						
Salisbury	a			00 19						
Totton	d		23p36				00s43			01s42
Ashurst New Forest	d		23p41							
Beaulieu Road	d									
Brockenhurst [5]	a	23p04	23p49		00 04		00s54			01s53
	d	23p05	23p50		00 05					
Lymington Town	d									
Lymington Pier	a									
Sway	d		23p54							
New Milton	d		23p59				01s02			02s00
Hinton Admiral	d		00 03							
Christchurch	d		00 08				01s09			02s07
Pokesdown	d		00 11				01s13			02s11
Bournemouth	a	23p25	00 15		00 21		01 17			02 15
	d	23p29	00 17		00 22		01 18			
Branksome	d	23p35	00 22		00 27		01s23			
Parkstone (Dorset)	d	23p38	00 25		00 30		01s26			
Poole [4]	a	23p41	00 29		00 35		01 30			
	d	23p42								
Hamworthy	d	23p47								
Holton Heath	d									
Wareham	d	23p54								
Wool	d	00 01								
Moreton (Dorset)	d	00 07								
Dorchester South	d	00 15								
Dorchester West	d									
Upwey	d	00 21								
Weymouth	a	00 26								

		SW	SW	SW	SW	SW	SW	GW	SW	SW	SW	SW	GW	SW
		1	1	1	1	1	1	◇	1	1	1	1		◇1
London Waterloo [15] ⊖	d	01 05												05 30
Clapham Junction [10]	d	01 15												05u37
Woking	d	01 42												06 01
Farnborough (Main)	d	01s51												
Fleet	d	01s57												
Reading [7]	d													
Basingstoke	a	02s09												06 20
	d													06 21
Micheldever	d													06 31
Winchester	d	02s26												06 41
Shawford	d													
Romsey	d						05 58							
Chandlers Ford	d						06 06							
Eastleigh [8]	a	02s35					06 11							06 50
	d						06 13		06 28		06 50			06 51
Hedge End	d								06 34					
Botley	d								06 38					
Fareham	d							06 28	06 48					
Portchester	d								06 53					
Cosham	d								06 58					
Hilsea	a								07 03					
Fratton	a								07 07					
Portsmouth & Southsea	a								07 11					
Portsmouth Harbour ⛴	a								07 16					
Southampton Airport Pkwy ✈	d	02s39					06 17							06 56
Swaythling	d						06 20							
St Denys	d	02s44					06 23							
Southampton Central ⛴	a	02 49					06 28	06 49						07 03
	d					06 21	06 30	06 53						07 05
Millbrook (Hants)	d						06 32							
Redbridge	d						06 36							
Romsey	d						06 44	07 11			07a03			
Mottisfont & Dunbridge	d						06 49							
Dean	d						06 54							
Salisbury	a						07 07	07 29						
Totton	d					06 26								07 10
Ashurst New Forest	d					06 31								
Beaulieu Road	d													
Brockenhurst [5]	a					06 39								07 21
	d			06 12	06 16	06 40				06 42		07 12		07 22
Lymington Town	d			06 20						06 50		07 20		
Lymington Pier	a			06 22						06 52		07 22		
Sway	d				06 20	06 44								07 26
New Milton	d				06 25	06 49								07 31
Hinton Admiral	d				06 29	06 53								07 35
Christchurch	d				06 34	06 58								07 40
Pokesdown	d				06 38	07 02								07 44
Bournemouth	a				06 42	07 06								07 48
	d		06 11		06 44	07 11								07 49
Branksome	d		06 16		06 49	07 16								07 54
Parkstone (Dorset)	d		06 19		06 52	07 19								07 57
Poole [4]	a		06 23		06 55	07 23								08 01
	d		06 24		06 57	07 24								08 02
Hamworthy	d		06 29		07 02	07 29								08 07
Holton Heath	d		06 33		07 06	07 33								
Wareham	d		06 38		07 11	07 38								08 14
Wool	d		06 44		07 17	07 44								08 20
Moreton (Dorset)	d		06 50		07 23	07 50								08 26
Dorchester South	d		06 58		07 31	07 58								08 34
Dorchester West	d												08 03	
Upwey	d		07 05		07 38	08 05							08 11	08 41
Weymouth	a		07 09		07 42	08 09							08 17	08 45

A ✠ to Brockenhurst

b Previous night, stops to pick up only

London - Basingstoke, Southampton, Romsey Lymington, Bournemouth and Weymouth

		SW 1	SN ◇1	SW 1	GW ◇ ᅲ	SW 1	SW 1	SW ◇1	SW 1	GW ◇	SN ◇1	SW 1	SW 1	XC ◇1 ᅲ	SW 1	SW ◇1	GW ◇ ᅲ	GW	SW 1	XC ◇1 ᅲ	SW ◇1	SW 1	SW 1
London Waterloo 15 ⊖	d							06 30								07 35			07 39		08 05		
Clapham Junction 10	d							06u37											07u46		08u12		
Woking	d							06 57								08 00							
Farnborough (Main)	d																		08 13				
Fleet	d																		08 19				
Reading 7	d													07 46						08 23			
Basingstoke	a							07 16						08 08		08 20			08 31	08 40	08 47		
	d							07 18						08 10		08 21			08 33	08 41	08 49		
Micheldever	d																						
Winchester	d							07 34						08 25		08 38			08 49	08 56	09 05		
Shawford	d																		08 54				
Romsey	d			07 07								08 07											09 07
Chandlers Ford	d			07 14								08 14											09 14
Eastleigh 3	a			07 20				07 42				08 20				08 46			08 59				09 20
	d		07 14	07 21				07 43			08 14	08 21				08 47			09 00				09 21
Hedge End	d																						
Botley	d																						
Fareham	d				07 30												08 47						
Portchester	d																						
Cosham	d																						
Hilsea	a																						
Fratton	a																						
Portsmouth & Southsea	a																						
Portsmouth Harbour ⛴	a																						
Southampton Airport Pkwy ✈	d		07 18	07 25				07 48			08 18	08 25		08 33		08 51			09 05	09 09	09 14		09 25
Swaythling	d			07 27								08 27											09 27
St Denys	d			07 30								08 30										←	09 30
Southampton Central ⛴	a		07 28	07 36	07 51			07 56			08 28	08 35		08 41		08 58	09 08		09 12	09 17	09 22	09 12	09 35
	d	07 21		07 37	07 54			08 00	08 19	08 27		08 37		08 43		09 00	09 10		09 30		09 24	09 30	09 37
Millbrook (Hants)	d			07 40								08 40							→				09 40
Redbridge	d			07 43								08 43											09 43
Romsey	d			07 51	08 12					08 38		08 51					09 21						09 51
Mottisfont & Dunbridge	d			07 56								08 56											09 56
Dean	d			08 02								09 02											10 02
Salisbury	a			08 15	08 30					09 03		09 15					09 40						10 15
Totton	d	07 26						08 05	08 24							09 05						09 35	
Ashurst New Forest	d	07 31							08 29													09 40	
Beaulieu Road	d								08 33													09 44	
Brockenhurst 5	a	07 39						08 16	08 39					08 56		09 16					09 37	09 51	
	d	07 40				07 42	08 12	08 17	08 40				08 42	08 58	09 12	09 17					09 38	10 16	
Lymington Town	d					07 50	08 20						08 50		09 20							→	
Lymington Pier	a					07 52	08 22						08 52		09 22								
Sway	d	07 44						08 21	08 45							09 21							
New Milton	d	07 49						08 26	08 50							09 26					09 45		
Hinton Admiral	d	07 53						08 30	08 54							09 30							
Christchurch	d	07 58						08 35	08 59							09 35					09 52		
Pokesdown	d	08 02						08 39	09 02							09 39					09 56		
Bournemouth	a	08 06						08 43	09 06					09 14		09 43					10 00		
	d	08 11						08 44	09 11							09 44					10 04		
Branksome	d	08 16						08 49	09 16							09 49							
Parkstone (Dorset)	d	08 19						08 52	09 19							09 52							
Poole 4	a	08 23						08 56	09 23							09 56					10 13		
	d	08 24						08 57	09 24							09 57					10 14		
Hamworthy	d	08 29						09 02	09 29							10 02					10 19		
Holton Heath	d	08 33							09 33												10 23		
Wareham	d	08 38						09 09	09 38							10 09					10 28		
Wool	d	08 44						09 15	09 44												10 35		
Moreton (Dorset)	d	08 50						09 21	09 50												10 41		
Dorchester South	d	08 58						09 29	09 58							10 27					10 49		
Dorchester West	d																	10 38					
Upwey	d	09 05						09 36	10 05									10 49			10 54		
Weymouth	a	09 09						09 40	10 09							10 35		10 57			11 00		

London - Basingstoke, Southampton, Romsey Lymington, Bournemouth and Weymouth

		SW 1	SW 1	XC ◇1 ᅲ	SW ◇1 A ᅲ	SW 1	GW ◇ ᅲ	SW 1	SW 1	SW ◇1 B ᅲ	SW 1	SN ◇1	SW 1	GW ◇	SW 1	SW 1	XC ◇1 ᅲ	GW	SW ◇1 A ᅲ	SW 1	GW ◇	SW 1
London Waterloo 15 ⊖	d	08 09			08 35				08 39	09 05					09 09				09 35			
Clapham Junction 10	d								08u46	09u12												
Woking	d	08 35			09 00										09 35				10 00			
Farnborough (Main)	d	08 45							09 13						09 45							
Fleet	d								09 19													
Reading 7	d			08 46													09 46					
Basingstoke	a	08 58		09 08					09 31	09 47					09 58		10 08					
	d	09 00		09 10					09 33	09 49					10 00		10 10					
Micheldever	d	09 10													10 10							
Winchester	d	09 19		09 25	09 33				09 49	10 05					10 19		10 25		10 33			
Shawford	d								09 54													
Romsey	d												10 07									
Chandlers Ford	d												10 14									
Eastleigh 3	a	09 27							09 59				10 20		10 27							
	d	09 28							10 00			10 14	10 21		10 28							
Hedge End	d	09 34													10 34							
Botley	d	09 38													10 38							
Fareham	d	09 48					09 47							10 16	10 48						10 47	
Portchester	d	09 53													10 53							
Cosham	d	09 58													10 58							
Hilsea	a	10 03													11 03							
Fratton	a	10 07													11 07							
Portsmouth & Southsea	a	10 11													11 11							
Portsmouth Harbour ⛴	a	10 18													11 18							
Southampton Airport Pkwy ✈	d			09 33	09 42				10 05	10 14		10 18	10 25				10 33		10 42			
Swaythling	d												10 27									
St Denys	d										←		10 30									
Southampton Central ⛴	a			09 40	09 49		10 08		10 12	10 22	10 12	10 28	10 35	10 40			10 43		10 49		11 08	
	d			09 42	09 51		10 10		10 30	10 24	10 30		10 37	10 42			10 45		10 51		11 10	
Millbrook (Hants)	d								→				10 40									
Redbridge	d												10 44									
Romsey	d						10 21						10 59	10 53							11 21	
Mottisfont & Dunbridge	d												11 04									
Dean	d												11 10									
Salisbury	a						10 40						11 22	11 13							11 40	
Totton	d										10 35											
Ashurst New Forest	d										10 40											
Beaulieu Road	d					←														←		
Brockenhurst 5	a			09 57	10 04	09 51				10 37	10 51						10 58		11 04	10 51		
	d		09 42	09 58	10 05	10 16		10 12		10 38	11 16					10 42	10 59		11 05	11 16		11 12
Lymington Town	d		09 50					10 20			→					10 50						11 20
Lymington Pier	a		09 52					10 22								10 52						11 22
Sway	d					10 20														11 20		
New Milton	d					10 25				10 45										11 25		
Hinton Admiral	d					10 29														11 29		
Christchurch	d					10 34				10 52										11 34		
Pokesdown	d					10 38				10 56										11 38		
Bournemouth	a			10 11	10 20	10 42				11 00							11 12		11 20	11 42		
	d				10 24	10 43				11 04									11 24	11 43		
Branksome	d				10 29	10 48													11 29	11 48		
Parkstone (Dorset)	d				10 32	10 51													11 32	11 51		
Poole 4	a				10 36	10 55				11 13									11 36	11 55		
	d				10 37					11 14									11 37			
Hamworthy	d				10 42					11 19									11 42			
Holton Heath	d									11 23												
Wareham	d				10 49					11 28									11 49			
Wool	d									11 35												
Moreton (Dorset)	d									11 41												
Dorchester South	d				11 05					11 49									12 05			
Dorchester West	d																	11 54				
Upwey	d									11 55								12 02				
Weymouth	a				11 13					12 00								12 09	12 13			

A ᅲ to Brockenhurst

B ᅲ to Pokesdown

Table 158

Saturdays

London - Basingstoke, Southampton, Romsey Lymington, Bournemouth and Weymouth

		SW	XC	SW	SW	SW	SW	SW	XC	SW	SW	GW	SW	SW	SW	SW	GW	SN	SW	SW	SW	XC	GW
		1	◇1	◇1	1	1	1	1	◇1	◇1	1	◇	1	1	◇1	1	◇	◇1	1	1	1	◇1	
			⌶	A ⌶					⌶	B ⌶					A ⌶							⌶	
London Waterloo 15 ⊖	d	09 39		10 05			10 09			10 35				10 39	11 05					11 09			
Clapham Junction 10	d	09u46		10u12										10u46	11u12								
Woking	d						10 35			11 00										11 35			
Farnborough (Main)	d	10 13					10 45							11 13						11 45			
Fleet	d	10 19												11 19									
Reading 7	d		10 15						10 46													11 46	
Basingstoke	a	10 31	10 39	10 47			10 58		11 08					11 31	11 47					11 58		12 08	
	d	10 33	10 40	10 49			11 00		11 10					11 33	11 49					12 00		12 10	
Micheldever	d						11 10													12 10			
Winchester	d	10 49	10 55	11 06			11 19		11 25	11 33				11 49	12 05					12 19		12 25	
Shawford	d	10 54												11 54									
Romsey	d					11 07													12 07				
Chandlers Ford	d					11 14													12 14				
Eastleigh 8	a	10 59				11 20	11 27							11 59					12 20	12 27			
	d	11 00				11 21	11 28							12 00				12 14	12 21	12 28			
Hedge End	d						11 34													12 34			
Botley	d						11 38													12 38			
Fareham	d						11 48					11 47								12 48			
Portchester	d						11 53													12 53			
Cosham	d						11 58													12 58			
Hilsea	a						12 03													13 03			
Fratton	a						12 07													13 07			
Portsmouth & Southsea	a						12 11													13 11			
Portsmouth Harbour ⛴	a						12 18													13 18			
Southampton Airport Pkwy ✈	d	11 05	11 09	11 15		11 25			11 33	11 42				12 05	12 14			12 19	12 25			12 33	
Swaythling	d					11 27													12 27				
St Denys	d				←	11 30										←			12 30				
Southampton Central ⛴	a	11 12	11 17	11 22	11 12	11 35			11 41	11 49		12 08		12 12	12 22	12 12		12 28	12 35			12 41	
	d	11 30		11 24	11 30	11 37			11 43	11 51		12 10		12 30	12 24	12 30	12 27		12 37			12 43	
Millbrook (Hants)	d	→				11 40								→					12 40				
Redbridge	d					11 43													12 43				
Romsey	d					11 51						12 21					12 38		12 51				
Mottisfont & Dunbridge	d					11 56													12 56				
Dean	d					12 02													13 02				
Salisbury	a					12 15						12 40					13 03		13 15				
Totton	d				11 35											12 35							
Ashurst New Forest	d				11 40											12 40							
Beaulieu Road	d				11 44						←												
Brockenhurst 3	a			11 37	11 51				11 57	12 04	11 51				12 37	12 51						12 57	
	d			11 38	12 16			11 42	11 58	12 05	12 16		12 12		12 38	13 16					12 42	12 58	
Lymington Town	d				→			11 50					12 20			→					12 50		
Lymington Pier	a							11 52					12 22								12 52		
Sway	d										12 20												
New Milton	d			11 45							12 25				12 45								
Hinton Admiral	d										12 29												
Christchurch	d			11 52							12 34				12 52								
Pokesdown	d			11 56							12 38				12 56								
Bournemouth	a			12 00					12 11	12 20	12 42				13 00							13 11	
	d			12 04						12 24	12 43				13 04								
Branksome	d									12 29	12 48												
Parkstone (Dorset)	d									12 32	12 51												
Poole 4	a			12 13						12 36	12 55				13 13								
	d			12 14						12 37					13 14								
Hamworthy	d			12 19						12 42					13 19								
Holton Heath	d			12 23											13 23								
Wareham	d			12 28						12 49					13 28								
Wool	d			12 35											13 35								
Moreton (Dorset)	d			12 41											13 41								
Dorchester South	d			12 49						13 05					13 49								
Dorchester West	d																						13 54
Upwey	d			12 55											13 55								14 02
Weymouth	a			13 00						13 13					14 00								14 08

A ⌶ to Pokesdown

B ⌶ to Brockenhurst

Table 158

Saturdays

London - Basingstoke, Southampton, Romsey Lymington, Bournemouth and Weymouth

		SW	SW	GW	SW	SW	XC	SW	SW	SW	SW	SW	XC	SW	SW	GW	SW	SW	SW	SW	SW	SW
		◇1	1	◇	1	1	◇1	◇1	1	1	1	1	◇1	◇1	1	◇	1	1	◇1	1	1	1
		A ⌶					⌶	B ⌶					⌶	A ⌶					B ⌶			
London Waterloo 15 ⊖	d	11 35				11 39		12 05			12 09			12 35				12 39	13 05			13 09
Clapham Junction 10	d					11u46		12u12										12u46	13u12			
Woking	d	12 00									12 35			13 00								13 35
Farnborough (Main)	d					12 13					12 45							13 13				13 45
Fleet	d					12 19												13 19				
Reading 7	d						12 15						12 46									
Basingstoke	a					12 31	12 40	12 47			12 58		13 08					13 31	13 47			13 58
	d					12 33	12 41	12 49			13 00		13 10					13 33	13 49			14 00
Micheldever	d										13 10											14 10
Winchester	d	12 33				12 49	12 56	13 05			13 19		13 25	13 33				13 49	14 05			14 19
Shawford	d					12 54												13 54				
Romsey	d									13 07											14 07	
Chandlers Ford	d									13 14											14 14	
Eastleigh 8	a					12 59				13 20	13 27							13 59			14 20	14 27
	d					13 00				13 21	13 28							14 00			14 21	14 28
Hedge End	d										13 34											14 34
Botley	d										13 38											14 38
Fareham	d			12 47							13 48					13 47						14 48
Portchester	d										13 53											14 53
Cosham	d										13 58											14 58
Hilsea	a										14 03											15 03
Fratton	a										14 07											15 07
Portsmouth & Southsea	a										14 11											15 11
Portsmouth Harbour ⛴	a										14 18											15 18
Southampton Airport Pkwy ✈	d	12 42				13 05	13 09	13 14		13 25			13 33	13 42				14 05	14 14		14 25	
Swaythling	d									13 27											14 27	
St Denys	d								←	13 30										←	14 30	
Southampton Central ⛴	a	12 49		13 08		13 12	13 17	13 22	13 12	13 35			13 41	13 49		14 08		14 12	14 22	14 12	14 35	
	d	12 51		13 10		13 30		13 24	13 30	13 37			13 43	13 51		14 10		14 30	14 24	14 30	14 37	
Millbrook (Hants)	d					→				13 40								→			14 40	
Redbridge	d									13 43											14 43	
Romsey	d			13 21						13 51						14 21					14 51	
Mottisfont & Dunbridge	d									13 56											14 56	
Dean	d									14 02											15 02	
Salisbury	a			13 40						14 15						14 40					15 15	
Totton	d								13 35											14 35		
Ashurst New Forest	d								13 40											14 40		
Beaulieu Road	d		←						13 44						←							
Brockenhurst 3	a	13 04	12 51					13 37	13 51				13 57	14 04	13 51				14 37	14 51		
	d	13 05	13 16		13 12			13 38	14 16			13 42	13 58	14 05	14 16		14 12		14 38	15 16		
Lymington Town	d				13 20				→			13 50					14 20			→		
Lymington Pier	a				13 22							13 52					14 22					
Sway	d		13 20												14 20							
New Milton	d		13 25					13 45							14 25				14 45			
Hinton Admiral	d		13 29												14 29							
Christchurch	d		13 34					13 52							14 34				14 52			
Pokesdown	d		13 38					13 56							14 38				14 56			
Bournemouth	a	13 20	13 42					14 00					14 11	14 20	14 42				15 00			
	d	13 24	13 43					14 04						14 24	14 43				15 04			
Branksome	d	13 29	13 48											14 29	14 48							
Parkstone (Dorset)	d	13 32	13 51											14 32	14 51							
Poole 4	a	13 36	13 55					14 13						14 36	14 55				15 13			
	d	13 37						14 14						14 37					15 14			
Hamworthy	d	13 42						14 19						14 42					15 19			
Holton Heath	d							14 23											15 23			
Wareham	d	13 49						14 28						14 49					15 28			
Wool	d							14 35											15 35			
Moreton (Dorset)	d							14 41											15 41			
Dorchester South	d	14 05						14 49						15 05					15 49			
Dorchester West	d																					
Upwey	d							14 55											15 55			
Weymouth	a	14 13						15 00						15 13					16 00			

A ⌶ to Brockenhurst

B ⌶ to Pokesdown

London - Basingstoke, Southampton, Romsey Lymington, Bournemouth and Weymouth

		SW	XC	SW	SW	GW	SW	SW	XC	SW		SW	SW	SW	SW	XC	GW	SW	SW	GW		SW	SW	SW	SW
		1	◇1	◇1	1	◇	1	1	◇1	◇1		1	1	1	1	◇1		◇1	1	◇		1	1	◇1	1
			🛒	A 🛒					🛒	🛒						🛒		A 🛒						B 🛒	
London Waterloo 15 ⊖	d			13 35				13 39		14 05				14 09				14 35					14 39	15 05	
Clapham Junction 10	d							13u46		14u12													14u46	15u12	
Woking	d			14 00										14 35				15 00							
Farnborough (Main)	d							14 13						14 45									15 13		
Fleet	d							14 19															15 19		
Reading 7	d		13 46						14 15							14 46									
Basingstoke	a		14 08					14 31	14 40	14 47				14 58		15 08							15 31	15 47	
	d		14 10					14 33	14 41	14 49				15 00		15 10							15 33	15 49	
Micheldever	d													15 10											
Winchester	d		14 25	14 33				14 49	14 56	15 05				15 19		15 25		15 33					15 49	16 05	
Shawford	d							14 54															15 54		
Romsey	d												15 07												
Chandlers Ford	d												15 14												
Eastleigh 8	a							14 59					15 20	15 27									15 59		
	d							15 00					15 21	15 28									16 00		
Hedge End	d													15 34											
Botley	d													15 38											
Fareham	d					14 47								15 48						15 47					
Portchester	d													15 53											
Cosham	d													15 58											
Hilsea	a													16 03											
Fratton	a													16 07											
Portsmouth & Southsea	a													16 11											
Portsmouth Harbour ⛴	a													16 18											
Southampton Airport Pkwy ✈	d		14 34	14 42				15 05	15 09	15 14			15 25			15 33		15 42					16 05	16 14	
Swaythling	d												15 27												
St Denys	d											←	15 30												←
Southampton Central ⛴	a		14 41	14 49		15 08		15 12	15 17	15 22		15 12	15 35			15 41		15 49		16 08			16 12	16 22	16 12
	d		14 43	14 51		15 10		15 30		15 24		15 30	15 37			15 43		15 51		16 10			16 30	16 24	16 30
Millbrook (Hants)	d							→					15 40										→		
Redbridge	d												15 43												
Romsey	d					15 21							15 51							16 21					
Mottisfont & Dunbridge	d												15 56												
Dean	d												16 02												
Salisbury	a					15 40							16 15							16 40					
Totton	d											15 35													16 35
Ashurst New Forest	d											15 40													16 40
Beaulieu Road	d				←							15 44							←						
Brockenhurst 3	a		14 57	15 04	14 51					15 37		15 51				15 57		16 04	15 51					16 37	16 51
	d	14 42	14 58	15 05	15 16		15 12			15 38		16 16			15 42	15 58		16 05	16 16			16 12		16 38	17 16
Lymington Town	d	14 50					15 20					→			15 50							16 20			→
Lymington Pier	a	14 52					15 22								15 52							16 22			
Sway	d				15 20														16 20						
New Milton	d				15 25					15 45									16 25					16 45	
Hinton Admiral	d				15 29														16 29						
Christchurch	d				15 34					15 52									16 34					16 52	
Pokesdown	d				15 38					15 56									16 38					16 56	
Bournemouth	a		15 11	15 20	15 42					16 00						16 11		16 20	16 42					17 00	
	d			15 24	15 43					16 04								16 24	16 43					17 04	
Branksome	d			15 29	15 48													16 29	16 48						
Parkstone (Dorset)	d			15 32	15 51													16 32	16 51						
Poole 4	a			15 36	15 55					16 13								16 36	16 55					17 13	
	d			15 37						16 14								16 37						17 14	
Hamworthy	d			15 42						16 19								16 42						17 19	
Holton Heath	d									16 23														17 23	
Wareham	d			15 49						16 28								16 49						17 28	
Wool	d									16 35														17 35	
Moreton (Dorset)	d									16 41														17 41	
Dorchester South	d			16 05						16 49								17 06						17 49	
Dorchester West	d																16 58								
Upwey	d									16 55							17 05							17 55	
Weymouth	a			16 13						17 00							17 11	17 15						18 00	

A 🛒 to Brockenhurst
B 🛒 to Pokesdown

London - Basingstoke, Southampton, Romsey Lymington, Bournemouth and Weymouth

		SN	SW	SW	SW	XC		SW	SW	GW	SW	SW	XC	SW	SW	SW		SW	SW	XC	GW	SW	SW	SW	GW
		◇1	1	1	1	◇1		◇1	1	■	1	1	◇1	◇1	1	1		1	1	◇1		◇1	1	1	◇
						🛒		A 🛒					🛒	B 🛒						🛒		A 🛒			
London Waterloo 15 ⊖	d			15 09				15 35				15 39		16 05				16 09				16 35			
Clapham Junction 10	d											15u46		16u12											
Woking	d			15 35				16 00										16 35				17 00			
Farnborough (Main)	d			15 45								16 13						16 45							
Fleet	d											16 19													
Reading 7	d					15 46							16 15							16 46					
Basingstoke	a			15 58		16 08						16 31	16 40	16 47				16 58		17 08					
	d			16 00		16 10						16 33	16 41	16 49				17 00		17 10				17 24	
Micheldever	d			16 10														17 10						17 34	
Winchester	d			16 19		16 25		16 33				16 49	16 56	17 05				17 19		17 25		17 33		17 43	
Shawford	d											16 54												17 48	
Romsey	d		16 07													17 07									
Chandlers Ford	d		16 14													17 14									
Eastleigh 8	a		16 20	16 27								16 59				17 20		17 27						17 53	
	d	16 14	16 21	16 28								17 00				17 21		17 28						17 54	
Hedge End	d			16 34														17 34							
Botley	d			16 38														17 38							
Fareham	d			16 48						16 47								17 48							17 47
Portchester	d			16 53														17 53							
Cosham	d			16 58														17 58							
Hilsea	a			17 03														18 03							
Fratton	a			17 07														18 07							
Portsmouth & Southsea	a			17 11														18 11							
Portsmouth Harbour ⛴	a			17 16														18 18							
Southampton Airport Pkwy ✈	d	16 18	16 25			16 33		16 42				17 05	17 09	17 14		17 25				17 33		17 42		17 59	
Swaythling	d		16 27													17 27								18 01	
St Denys	d		16 30												←	17 30								18 04	
Southampton Central ⛴	a	16 28	16 35			16 41		16 49		17 08		17 12	17 17	17 22	17 12	17 35				17 41		17 49		18 10	18 08
	d		16 37			16 43		16 51		17 10		17 30		17 24	17 30	17 37				17 43		17 51			18 10
Millbrook (Hants)	d		16 40									→				17 40									
Redbridge	d		16 43													17 43									
Romsey	d		16 51							17 21						17 51									18 21
Mottisfont & Dunbridge	d		16 56													17 56									
Dean	d		17 02													18 02									
Salisbury	a		17 15							17 40						18 15									18 40
Totton	d														17 35										
Ashurst New Forest	d														17 40										
Beaulieu Road	d								←						17 44								←		
Brockenhurst 3	a					16 57		17 04	16 51					17 37	17 51					17 57		18 04	17 51		
	d				16 42	16 58		17 05	17 16		17 12			17 38	18 16				17 42	17 58		18 05	18 16		
Lymington Town	d				16 50						17 20				→				17 50						
Lymington Pier	a				16 52						17 22								17 52						
Sway	d								17 20														18 20		
New Milton	d								17 25					17 45									18 25		
Hinton Admiral	d								17 29														18 29		
Christchurch	d								17 34					17 52									18 34		
Pokesdown	d								17 38					17 56									18 38		
Bournemouth	a					17 11		17 20	17 42					18 00						18 11		18 20	18 42		
	d							17 24	17 43					18 04								18 24	18 43		
Branksome	d							17 29	17 48													18 29	18 48		
Parkstone (Dorset)	d							17 32	17 51													18 32	18 51		
Poole 4	a							17 36	17 55					18 13								18 36	18 55		
	d							17 37						18 14								18 37			
Hamworthy	d							17 42						18 19								18 42			
Holton Heath	d													18 23											
Wareham	d							17 49						18 28								18 49			
Wool	d													18 35											
Moreton (Dorset)	d													18 41											
Dorchester South	d							18 05						18 49								19 05			
Dorchester West	d																				18 54				
Upwey	d													18 55							19 02				
Weymouth	a							18 13						19 00							19 10	19 13			

A 🛒 to Brockenhurst
B 🛒 to Pokesdown

Table 158

Saturdays

London - Basingstoke, Southampton, Romsey Lymington, Bournemouth and Weymouth

		SW	SW	SW	SW	SN	SW	SW	SW	XC	GW	GW	SW	SW	GW	SW	SW	XC	SW	SW	SW	SW
		1	1	◇1	1	◇1	1	1	1	◇1	◇		◇1	1	◇	1	1	◇1	◇1	1	1	1
				A □						⊼			B ⊼					⊼	C ⊼			
London Waterloo [15] ⊖	d		16 39	17 05				17 09					17 35				17 39		18 05			18 09
Clapham Junction [10]	d		16u46	17u12													17u46		18u12			
Woking	d							17 35					18 00									18 35
Farnborough (Main)	d		17 13					17 45									18 13					18 45
Fleet	d		17 19														18 19					
Reading [7]	d									17 46								18 15				
Basingstoke	a		17 31	17 47				17 58		18 08							18 31	18 40	18 47			18 58
	d		17 33	17 49				18 00		18 10							18 33	18 41	18 49			19 00
Micheldever	d							18 10														19 10
Winchester	d		17 49	18 05				18 19		18 25			18 33				18 49	18 56	19 05			19 19
Shawford	d		17 54														18 54					
Romsey	d						18 07														19 07	
Chandlers Ford	d						18 14														19 14	
Eastleigh [8]	a		17 59				18 20	18 27									18 59				19 20	19 27
	d		18 00			18 14	18 21	18 28									19 00				19 21	19 28
Hedge End	d							18 34														19 34
Botley	d							18 38														19 38
Fareham	d							18 48			18 15				18 47							19 48
Portchester	d							18 53														19 53
Cosham	d							18 58														19 58
Hilsea	a							19 03														20 03
Fratton	a							19 07														20 07
Portsmouth & Southsea	a							19 11														20 11
Portsmouth Harbour ⛴	a							19 18														20 18
Southampton Airport Pkwy ✈	d		18 05	18 14		18 18	18 25			18 33			18 42				19 05	19 09	19 14		19 25	
Swaythling	d						18 27														19 27	
St Denys	d				←		18 30													←	19 30	
Southampton Central ⛴	a		18 14	18 22	18 14	18 28	18 35			18 40	18 43		18 49		19 08		19 12	19 17	19 22	19 12	19 35	
	d		18 30	18 24	18 30		18 37			18 43	18 45		18 51		19 10		19 30		19 24	19 30	19 37	
Millbrook (Hants)	d		→				18 40										→				19 40	
Redbridge	d						18 44														19 43	
Romsey	d						19 00				18 56				19 21						19 51	
Mottisfont & Dunbridge	d						19 05														19 56	
Dean	d						19 10														20 02	
Salisbury	a						19 23				19 15				19 40						20 15	
Totton	d				18 35															19 35		
Ashurst New Forest	d				18 40															19 40		
Beaulieu Road	d													←						19 44		
Brockenhurst [8]	a			18 37	18 51					18 57			19 04	18 51					19 37	19 51		
	d	18 12		18 38	19 16				18 42	18 58			19 05	19 16		19 12			19 38	20 16		
Lymington Town	d	18 20			→				18 50							19 20				→		
Lymington Pier	a	18 22							18 52							19 22						
Sway	d													19 20								
New Milton	d			18 45										19 25					19 45			
Hinton Admiral	d													19 29								
Christchurch	d			18 52										19 34					19 52			
Pokesdown	d			18 56										19 38					19 56			
Bournemouth	a			19 00						19 11			19 20	19 42					20 00			
	d			19 04									19 24	19 43					20 04			
Branksome	d												19 29	19 48								
Parkstone (Dorset)	d												19 32	19 51								
Poole [4]	a			19 13									19 36	19 55					20 13			
	d			19 14									19 37						20 14			
Hamworthy	d			19 19									19 42						20 19			
Holton Heath	d			19 23															20 23			
Wareham	d			19 28									19 49						20 28			
Wool	d			19 35															20 35			
Moreton (Dorset)	d			19 41															20 41			
Dorchester South	d			19 49									20 05						20 49			
Dorchester West	d											19 54										
Upwey	d			19 55								20 01							20 55			
Weymouth	a			20 00								20 09	20 13						21 00			

A □ to Pokesdown B ⊼ to Brockenhurst C ⊼ to Pokesdown

Table 158

Saturdays

London - Basingstoke, Southampton, Romsey Lymington, Bournemouth and Weymouth

		SW	XC	SW	SW	GW	SW	SW	SW	SW	SN	SW	SW	SW	XC	SW	SW	GW	SW	SW	SW	GW	SW
		1	◇1	◇1	1	◇	1	1	◇1	1	◇1	1	1	1	◇1	◇1	1	◇	1	1	◇1		1
			⊼	A ⊼					B ⊼						⊼	A ⊼					⊼		
London Waterloo [15] ⊖	d			18 35				18 39	19 05				19 09			19 35			19 39		20 05		
Clapham Junction [10]	d							18u46	19u12										19u46		20u12		
Woking	d			19 00									19 35			20 00							
Farnborough (Main)	d							19 13					19 45						20 13				
Fleet	d							19 19											20 19				
Reading [7]	d		18 46												19 46								
Basingstoke	a		19 08					19 31	19 47				19 58		20 08				20 31		20 47		
	d		19 10					19 33	19 49				20 00		20 10				20 33		20 49		
Micheldever	d												20 10										
Winchester	d		19 25	19 33				19 49	20 05				20 19		20 25	20 33			20 49		21 05		
Shawford	d							19 54											20 54				
Romsey	d											20 07											21 07
Chandlers Ford	d											20 14											21 14
Eastleigh [8]	a							19 59				20 20	20 27						20 59				21 20
	d							20 00			20 14	20 21	20 28						21 00				21 21
Hedge End	d												20 34										
Botley	d												20 38										
Fareham	d					19 47							20 48					20 47					
Portchester	d												20 53										
Cosham	d												20 58										
Hilsea	a												21 03										
Fratton	a												21 07										
Portsmouth & Southsea	a												21 11										
Portsmouth Harbour ⛴	a												21 18										
Southampton Airport Pkwy ✈	d		19 33	19 42				20 05	20 14		20 18	20 25			20 33	20 42			21 05		21 14		21 25
Swaythling	d											20 27											21 27
St Denys	d									←		20 30											21 30
Southampton Central ⛴	a		19 41	19 49		20 09		20 14	20 22	20 14	20 28	20 35			20 41	20 49		21 10	21 12		21 22		21 35
	d		19 43	19 51		20 10		20 30	20 24	20 30		20 37			20 43	20 51		21 10			21 24	21 27	21 37
Millbrook (Hants)	d							→				20 40											21 40
Redbridge	d											20 43											21 43
Romsey	d					20 21						20 51						21 21				21 38	21 51
Mottisfont & Dunbridge	d											20 56											21 56
Dean	d											21 02											22 02
Salisbury	a					20 40						21 15						21 41				22 03	22 15
Totton	d									20 35											21 29		
Ashurst New Forest	d									20 40											21 34		
Beaulieu Road	d				←												←						
Brockenhurst [8]	a		19 57	20 04	19 51				20 37	20 51					20 57	21 04	20 51				21 42		
	d	19 42	19 58	20 05	20 16		20 12		20 38	21 16				20 42	20 58	21 05	21 16			21 12	21 43		
Lymington Town	d	19 50					20 20			→				20 50						21 20			
Lymington Pier	a	19 52					20 22							20 52						21 22			
Sway	d				20 20												21 20				21 47		
New Milton	d				20 25				20 45								21 25				21 52		
Hinton Admiral	d				20 29												21 29				21 56		
Christchurch	d				20 34				20 52								21 34				22 01		
Pokesdown	d				20 38				20 56								21 38				22 05		
Bournemouth	a		20 11	20 20	20 42				21 00						21 11	21 20	21 42				22 09		
	d			20 24	20 43				21 04							21 24	21 43				22 10		
Branksome	d			20 29	20 48											21 29	21 48				22 15		
Parkstone (Dorset)	d			20 32	20 51											21 32	21 51				22 18		
Poole [4]	a			20 36	20 55				21 13							21 36	21 55				22 23		
	d			20 37					21 14							21 37							
Hamworthy	d			20 42					21 19							21 42							
Holton Heath	d																						
Wareham	d			20 49					21 28							21 49							
Wool	d								21 35							21 55							
Moreton (Dorset)	d								21 41							22 01							
Dorchester South	d			21 05					21 49							22 09							
Dorchester West	d																						
Upwey	d								21 55							22 16							
Weymouth	a			21 13					22 00							22 20							

A ⊼ to Brockenhurst B ⊼ to Pokesdown

London - Basingstoke, Southampton, Romsey Lymington, Bournemouth and Weymouth

		SW	SW	XC	GW	SW	SW	SW	SW	SW	XC	SW	SW	SW	SW	XC	SW	SW	SW	SW	SW
		1	1	◇1		◇1 A ⌶	1	1	◇1 ⌶	1	◇1	◇1 A ⌶	1	◇1 ⌶	1	◇1	◇1 ⌶	1	1	◇1	1
London Waterloo 15 ⊖	d	20 09				20 35	20 39		21 05			21 35	21 39	22 05			22 35		22 39	23 05	23 35
Clapham Junction 10	d						20u46		21u12				21u46	22u12					22u46	23u12	23u42
Woking	d	20 35				21 00			21 32			22 00		22 32			23 00			23 32	00 03
Farnborough (Main)	d	20 45					21 13						22 13						23 16		00 14
Fleet	d						21 19						22 19						23 21		00 20
Reading 7	d			20 46							21 46					22 49					
Basingstoke	a	20 58		21 08			21 31		21 51		22 08		22 31	22 51		23 06			23 34	23 51	00 33
	d	21 00		21 10			21 33		21 52		22 10		22 33	22 52		23 10			23 36	23 52	00 35
Micheldever	d	21 10					21 43						22s43							00 02	
Winchester	d	21 19		21 25		21 33	21 52		22 09		22 25	22 33	22 53	23 09		23 25	23 33		23 52	00 12	00 51
Shawford	d						21 57						22 57						23 57		
Romsey	d									22 07					23 09			23 00			
Chandlers Ford	d									22 14					23 16						
Eastleigh 8	a	21 27					22 02		22 17	22 21			23 03	23 17	23 22			23 35	00 02	00 20	00 59
	d	21 28					22 03		22 18	22 22			23 04	23 18	23 23			23 37	00 03	00 21	01 00
Hedge End	d	21 34																			
Botley	d	21 38																			
Fareham	d	21 48																			
Portchester	d	21 53																			
Cosham	d	21 58																			
Hilsea	a	22 03																			
Fratton	a	22 07																			
Portsmouth & Southsea	a	22 11																			
Portsmouth Harbour ⛴	a	22 18																			
Southampton Airport Pkwy ✈	d			21 34		21 42	22 08		22 22	22 26	22 33	22 42	23 08	23 22	23 27	23 33	23 42		00 08	00 25	01 05
Swaythling	d									22 29					23 30						
St Denys	d									22 32					23 33					00s29	
Southampton Central ⛴	a			21 41		21 49	22 17		22 29	22 36	22 41	22 49	23 17	23 29	23 38	23 41	23 49		00 15	00 34	01 12
	d			21 43		21 51			22 31	22 38	22 43	22 51		23 31	23 40		23 51			00 36	
Millbrook (Hants)	d									22 41					23 42						
Redbridge	d									22 45					23 46						
Romsey	d									22a52					23 57			23a49			
Mottisfont & Dunbridge	d														00 02						
Dean	d														00 08						
Salisbury	a														00 20						
Totton	d								22 36					23 36						00s41	
Ashurst New Forest	d								22 41					23 41							
Beaulieu Road	d																				
Brockenhurst 3	a			21 57		22 04			22 49		22 57	23 04		23 49			00 04			00s52	
	d		21 48	21 58		22 05		22 18	22 50		23 00	23 05		23 50			00 05				
Lymington Town	d		21 56					22 26													
Lymington Pier	a		21 58					22 28													
Sway	d								22 54					23 54							
New Milton	d								22 59					23 59						01s00	
Hinton Admiral	d								23 03					00 03							
Christchurch	d								23 08					00 08						01s07	
Pokesdown	d								23 12					00 11						01s11	
Bournemouth	a			22 15		22 20			23 16		23 21	23 25		00 15			00 21			01 15	
	d					22 24			23 17			23 29		00 17			00 22			01 16	
Branksome	d					22 29			23 22			23 35		00 23			00 27			01s21	
Parkstone (Dorset)	d					22 32			23 25			23 38		00 26			00 30			01s24	
Poole 4	a					22 36			23 29			23 41		00 30			00 35			01 29	
	d					22 37						23 42									
Hamworthy	d					22 42						23 47									
Holton Heath	d																				
Wareham	d					22 49						23 54									
Wool	d					22 55						00 01									
Moreton (Dorset)	d					23 01						00 07									
Dorchester South	d					23 09						00 15									
Dorchester West	d				22 54																
Upwey	d				23 02	23 16						00 21									
Weymouth	a				23 10	23 20						00 26									

A ⌶ to Brockenhurst

London - Basingstoke, Southampton, Romsey Lymington, Bournemouth and Weymouth

until 19 June

		SW	SW	SW	SW	SW	SW	SW	SW	SW	SW	SW	GW	SW	SW		SW	SW	SW	SW	GW	SW	
		◇1 A ⌶	◇1 B ⌶	1 B	◇1 B ⌶	1 B	◇1 B	1	1 B	1	1	1		1	1		1	1	1	1	■	◇1	
London Waterloo 15 ⊖	d	21p35	22p05		22p35	22p39	23p05		23p35	00 05	01 05											07 54	
Clapham Junction 10	d		22b12			22b46	23b12		23b42	00u12												08u03	
Woking	d	22p00	22p32		23p00		23p32		00 03	00 37	01 42											08 28	
Farnborough (Main)	d					23p16			00 14		01s58												
Fleet	d					23p21			00 20		02s04												
Reading 7	d																						
Basingstoke	a		22p51			23p34	23p51		00 33	00 55	02s16											08 46	
	d		22p52			23p36	23p52		00 35	00 56					07 48							08 48	
Micheldever	d						00 02								07 58							08 58	
Winchester	d	22p33	23p09		23p33	23p52	00 12		00 51	01 13	02s33				08 08							09 08	
Shawford	d					23p57									08 12								
Romsey	d			23p09									08 19						08 35				
Chandlers Ford	d			23p16															08 42				
Eastleigh 8	a		23p17	23p22		00 02	00 20		00 59	01 21	02s42				08 18				08 47			09 18	
	d		23p18	23p23		00 03	00 21	00 30	01 00	01 22					08 22	08 26			08 54			09 22	09 26
Hedge End	d							00s36								08 32							09 32
Botley	d							00s39								08 36							09 36
Fareham	d							00s47				07 44				08 44					09 32		09 44
Portchester	d							00s53				07 49				08 49							09 49
Cosham	d							00s57				07 54				08 54							09 54
Hilsea	a											08 00				09 00							10 04
Fratton	a							01s05				08 04				09 04							10 08
Portsmouth & Southsea	a							01s08				08 08				09 08							10 11
Portsmouth Harbour ⛴	a							01 12				08 13				09 13							10 15
Southampton Airport Pkwy ✈	d	22p42	23p22	23p27	23p42	00 08	00 25		01 05	01 26	02s46				08 27				08 58			09 27	
Swaythling	d			23p30															09 01				
St Denys	d			23p33			00s29				02s51								09 04				
Southampton Central ⛴	a	22p49	23p29	23p38	23p49	00 15	00 34		01 12	01 35	02 56		08 29		08 34				09 09		09 53	09 34	
	d	22p51	23p31	23p40	23p51		00 36			01 37					08 35			09 03	09 10		09 54	09 35	
Millbrook (Hants)	d			23p42															09 13				
Redbridge	d			23p46															09 16				
Romsey	d			23p57															09 24		10 06		
Mottisfont & Dunbridge	d			00 02															09 29				
Dean	d			00 08															09 35				
Salisbury	a			00 20															09 49		10 24		
Totton	d		23p36				00s41			01s42					08 41							09 41	
Ashurst New Forest	d		23p41												08 45							09 45	
Beaulieu Road	d														08 50							09 50	
Brockenhurst 3	a	23p04	23p49		00 04		00s52			01s53					08 56			09 16				09 56	
	d	23p05	23p50		00 05										08 57		08 59	09 17		09 29		09 57	
Lymington Town	d																09 07			09 37			
Lymington Pier	a																09 09			09 39			
Sway	d		23p54												09 01							10 01	
New Milton	d		23p59				01s00			02s00					09 06			09 24				10 06	
Hinton Admiral	d		00 03												09 10							10 10	
Christchurch	d		00 08				01s07			02s07					09 15							10 15	
Pokesdown	d		00 11				01s11			02s11					09 19							10 19	
Bournemouth	a	23p25	00 15		00 21		01 15			02 15					09 23			09 34				10 23	
	d	23p29	00 17		00 22		01 16							08 39	09 24			09 39				10 24	
Branksome	d	23p35	00 23		00 27		01s21							08 44				09 44					
Parkstone (Dorset)	d	23p38	00 26		00 30		01s24							08 47				09 47					
Poole 4	a	23p41	00 30		00 35		01 29							08 50	09 33			09 50				10 33	
	d	23p42												08 51				09 51					
Hamworthy	d	23p47												08 56				09 56					
Holton Heath	d																						
Wareham	d	23p54												09 03				10 03					
Wool	d	00 01												09 10				10 10					
Moreton (Dorset)	d	00 07												09 16				10 16					
Dorchester South	d	00 15												09 24				10 24					
Dorchester West	d																						
Upwey	d	00 21												09 31				10 31					
Weymouth	a	00 26												09 35				10 35					

A not 22 May. ⌶ to Brockenhurst

B not 22 May

b Previous night, stops to pick up only

Table 158

Sundays until 19 June

London - Basingstoke, Southampton, Romsey Lymington, Bournemouth and Weymouth

		SW	GW	SW	SW	SW	SW		SW	XC	GW	SW	SW	SW	SW		SW	XC	GW	SW	SW	SW
		1		◇1	1	1	◇1		1	◇1		◇1	1	1	◇1		1	◇1	◇	◇1	1	1
										✠								✠		A ✠		
London Waterloo [15] ⊖	d			08 35			08 54					09 35			09 54					10 35		
Clapham Junction [10]	d			08u45			09u03					09u45			10u03					10u45		
Woking	d			09 09			09 28					10 09			10 28					11 07		
Farnborough (Main)	d																					
Fleet	d																					
Reading [7]	d									09 51								10 51				
Basingstoke	a			09 28			09 46			10 09		10 28			10 46			11 09		11 26		
	d			09 29			09 48			10 10		10 29			10 48			11 10		11 28		
Micheldever	d						09 58								10 58							
Winchester	d			09 46			10 08			10 25		10 46			11 08			11 25		11 44		
Shawford	d						10 12															
Romsey	d				09 35								10 35								11 35	
Chandlers Ford	d				09 42								10 42								11 42	
Eastleigh [8]	a				09 48		10 18						10 48		11 18						11 48	
	d				09 54		10 22	10 26					10 54		11 22	11 26					11 54	
Hedge End	d							10 32								11 32						
Botley	d							10 36								11 36						
Fareham	d							10 44								11 44			11 32			
Portchester	d							10 49								11 49						
Cosham	d							10 54								11 54						
Hilsea	a							11 04								12 00						
Fratton	a							11 08								12 04						
Portsmouth & Southsea	a							11 11								12 08						
Portsmouth Harbour ⛴	a							11 15								12 13						
Southampton Airport Pkwy ✈	d			09 55	09 58		10 27			10 34		10 55	10 58		11 27			11 34		11 53	11 58	
Swaythling	d				10 01								11 01								12 01	
St Denys	d				10 04								11 04								12 04	
Southampton Central ⛴	a			10 02	10 09		10 34			10 42		11 02	11 09		11 34			11 42	11 53	11 59	12 09	
	d			10 03	10 10		10 35			10 45		11 03	11 10		11 35			11 45	11 54	12 03	12 10	
Millbrook (Hants)	d				10 13								11 13								12 13	
Redbridge	d				10 16								11 16								12 16	
Romsey	d				10 24								11 24						12 06		12 24	
Mottisfont & Dunbridge	d												11 29									
Dean	d												11 35									
Salisbury	a				10 42								11 48						12 24		12 42	
Totton	d						10 41								11 41							
Ashurst New Forest	d						10 45								11 45							
Beaulieu Road	d						10 50								11 50							
Brockenhurst [8]	a			10 17			10 56			11 02		11 17			11 56			12 02		12 16		
	d	09 59		10 18		10 29	10 57		10 59	11 02		11 18		11 29	11 57		11 59	12 03		12 17		12 29
Lymington Town	d	10 07				10 37			11 07					11 37			12 07					12 37
Lymington Pier	a	10 09				10 39			11 09					11 39			12 09					12 39
Sway	d						11 01								12 01							
New Milton	d			10 25			11 06					11 25			12 06					12 24		
Hinton Admiral	d						11 10								12 10							
Christchurch	d						11 15								12 15							
Pokesdown	d						11 19								12 19							
Bournemouth	a			10 35			11 23			11 26		11 35			12 23			12 26		12 34		
	d			10 39			11 24					11 39			12 24					12 39		
Branksome	d			10 44								11 44								12 44		
Parkstone (Dorset)	d			10 47								11 47								12 47		
Poole [4]	a			10 50			11 33					11 50			12 33					12 50		
	d			10 51								11 51								12 51		
Hamworthy	d			10 56								11 56								12 56		
Holton Heath	d																					
Wareham	d			11 03								12 03								13 03		
Wool	d			11 10								12 10								13 10		
Moreton (Dorset)	d			11 16								12 16								13 16		
Dorchester South	d			11 24								12 24								13 24		
Dorchester West	d		10 26								11 30											
Upwey	d		10 37	11 31							11 37	12 31								13 31		
Weymouth	a		10 42	11 35							11 43	12 35								13 35		

A ✠ to New Milton

Table 158

Sundays until 19 June

London - Basingstoke, Southampton, Romsey Lymington, Bournemouth and Weymouth

		SW		SW	XC	GW	SW	SW	SW	SW		SW	XC	GW	SW	SW	SW	SW		SW	XC	GW
		◇1		1	◇1	◇	◇1	1	1	◇1		1	◇1	◇	◇1	1	1	◇1		1	◇1	◇
					✠		A ✠			✠			✠		A ✠			✠			✠	
London Waterloo [15] ⊖	d	10 54					11 35			11 54					12 35			12 54				
Clapham Junction [10]	d	11u04					11u45			12u04					12u42			13u03				
Woking	d	11 28					12 07			12 28					13 07			13 28				
Farnborough (Main)	d																					
Fleet	d																					
Reading [7]	d				11 51								12 51								13 51	
Basingstoke	a	11 46			12 09		12 26			12 46			13 09		13 26			13 46			14 09	
	d	11 48			12 10		12 28			12 48			13 10		13 28			13 48			14 10	
Micheldever	d	11 58								12 58								13 58				
Winchester	d	12 08			12 25		12 44			13 08			13 25		13 44			14 08			14 25	
Shawford	d	12 12																14 12				
Romsey	d							12 35								13 35						
Chandlers Ford	d							12 42								13 42						
Eastleigh [8]	a	12 18						12 48		13 18						13 48		14 18				
	d	12 22	12 26					12 54		13 22	13 26					13 54		14 22	14 26			
Hedge End	d		12 32								13 32								14 32			
Botley	d		12 36								13 36								14 36			
Fareham	d		12 44			12 32					13 44			13 32					14 44			14 32
Portchester	d		12 49								13 49								14 49			
Cosham	d		12 54								13 54								14 54			
Hilsea	a		13 00								14 00								15 00			
Fratton	a		13 04								14 04								15 04			
Portsmouth & Southsea	a		13 08								14 08								15 08			
Portsmouth Harbour ⛴	a		13 13								14 13								15 13			
Southampton Airport Pkwy ✈	d	12 27			12 34		12 53	12 58		13 27			13 34		13 53	13 58		14 27			14 34	
Swaythling	d							13 01								14 01						
St Denys	d							13 04								14 04						
Southampton Central ⛴	a	12 34			12 42	12 53	13 00	13 09		13 34			13 42	13 54	14 00	14 09		14 34			14 42	14 53
	d	12 35			12 45	12 54	13 03	13 10		13 35			13 45	13 54	14 03	14 10		14 35			14 45	14 54
Millbrook (Hants)	d							13 13								14 13						
Redbridge	d							13 16								14 16						
Romsey	d					13 06		13 24						14 06		14 24						15 06
Mottisfont & Dunbridge	d							13 29														
Dean	d							13 35														
Salisbury	a					13 24		13 48						14 24		14 42						15 24
Totton	d	12 41								13 41								14 41				
Ashurst New Forest	d	12 45								13 45								14 45				
Beaulieu Road	d	12 50								13 50								14 50				
Brockenhurst [8]	a	12 56			13 02		13 16			13 56			14 01		14 16			14 56			15 02	
	d	12 57		12 59	13 03		13 17		13 29	13 57		13 59	14 02		14 17		14 29	14 57		14 59	15 03	
Lymington Town	d			13 07					13 37			14 07					14 37			15 07		
Lymington Pier	a			13 09					13 39			14 09					14 39			15 09		
Sway	d	13 01								14 01								15 01				
New Milton	d	13 06					13 24			14 06					14 24			15 06				
Hinton Admiral	d	13 10								14 10								15 10				
Christchurch	d	13 15								14 15								15 15				
Pokesdown	d	13 19								14 19								15 19				
Bournemouth	a	13 23			13 26		13 34			14 23			14 26		14 34			15 23			15 26	
	d	13 24					13 39			14 24					14 39			15 24				
Branksome	d						13 44								14 44							
Parkstone (Dorset)	d						13 47								14 47							
Poole [4]	a	13 33					13 50			14 33					14 50			15 33				
	d						13 51								14 51							
Hamworthy	d						13 56								14 56							
Holton Heath	d																					
Wareham	d						14 03								15 03							
Wool	d						14 10								15 10							
Moreton (Dorset)	d						14 16								15 16							
Dorchester South	d						14 24								15 24							
Dorchester West	d																					
Upwey	d						14 31								15 31							
Weymouth	a						14 35								15 35							

A ✠ to New Milton

London - Basingstoke, Southampton, Romsey Lymington, Bournemouth and Weymouth

		GW	SW	SW	SW	SW		SW	XC	GW	SW	SW	SW	SW		SW	XC	GW	SW	SW	SW	GW	SW
			◇1 A 🛒	1	1	◇1 🛒		1	◇1 🛒	■	◇1 A 🛒	1	1	◇1 🛒		1	◇1 🛒	◇	◇1 A 🛒	1	1	◇	1
London Waterloo 15 ⊖	d		13 35			13 54					14 35			14 54					15 35	15 37			
Clapham Junction 10	d		13u42			14u03					14u42			15u03					15u42	15 46			
Woking	d		14 07			14 28					15 07			15 28					16 07	16 23			
Farnborough (Main)	d																			16 36			
Fleet	d																			16 41			
Reading 7	d								14 51								15 51						
Basingstoke	a		14 26			14 46			15 09		15 26			15 46			16 09		16 26	16 54			
	d		14 28			14 48			15 10		15 28			15 48			16 10		16 28				
Micheldever	d					14 58								15 58									
Winchester	d		14 44			15 08			15 25		15 44			16 08			16 25		16 44				
Shawford	d													16 12									
Romsey	d			14 35								15 35									16 35		
Chandlers Ford	d			14 42								15 42									16 42		
Eastleigh 8	a			14 48		15 18						15 48		16 18							16 48		
	d			14 54		15 22	15 26					15 54		16 22	16 26						16 54		
Hedge End	d						15 32								16 32								
Botley	d						15 36								16 36								
Fareham	d						15 44			15 32					16 44			16 32				17 03	
Portchester	d						15 49								16 49								
Cosham	d						15 54								16 54								
Hilsea	a						16 00								17 00								
Fratton	a						16 04								17 03								
Portsmouth & Southsea	a						16 08								17 08								
Portsmouth Harbour ⛴	a						16 13								17 13								
Southampton Airport Pkwy ✈	d		14 53	14 58		15 27			15 34		15 53	15 58		16 27			16 34		16 53		16 58		
Swaythling	d			15 01								16 01									17 01		
St Denys	d			15 04								16 04									17 04		
Southampton Central ⛴	a		15 00	15 09		15 34			15 42	15 53	16 00	16 09		16 34			16 42	16 53	17 00		17 09	17 24	
	d		15 03	15 10		15 35			15 45	15 54	16 03	16 10		16 35			16 45	16 54	17 03		17 10	17 26	
Millbrook (Hants)	d			15 13								16 13									17 13		
Redbridge	d			15 16								16 16									17 16		
Romsey	d			15 24						16 06		16 24						17 06			17 24	17 39	
Mottisfont & Dunbridge	d			15 29																	17 29		
Dean	d			15 35																	17 35		
Salisbury	a			15 48						16 24		16 42						17 24			17 48	18 01	
Totton	d					15 41								16 41									
Ashurst New Forest	d					15 45								16 45									
Beaulieu Road	d					15 50								16 50									
Brockenhurst 3	a		15 16			15 56			16 02		16 16			16 56			17 02		17 16				
	d		15 17		15 29	15 57		15 59	16 03		16 17		16 29	16 57		16 59	17 03		17 17				17 29
Lymington Town	d				15 37			16 07					16 37			17 07							17 37
Lymington Pier	a				15 39			16 09					16 39			17 09							17 39
Sway	d					16 01								17 01									
New Milton	d		15 24			16 06					16 24			17 06					17 24				
Hinton Admiral	d					16 10								17 10									
Christchurch	d					16 15								17 15									
Pokesdown	d					16 19								17 19									
Bournemouth	a		15 34			16 23			16 26		16 34			17 23			17 26		17 34				
	d		15 39			16 24					16 39			17 24					17 39				
Branksome	d		15 44								16 44								17 44				
Parkstone (Dorset)	d		15 47								16 47								17 47				
Poole 4	a		15 50			16 33					16 50			17 33					17 50				
	d		15 51								16 51								17 51				
Hamworthy	d		15 56								16 56								17 56				
Holton Heath	d																						
Wareham	d		16 03								17 03								18 03				
Wool	d		16 10								17 10								18 10				
Moreton (Dorset)	d		16 16								17 16								18 16				
Dorchester South	d		16 24								17 24								18 24				
Dorchester West	d	15 41																					
Upwey	d	15 50	16 31								17 31								18 31				
Weymouth	a	15 55	16 35								17 35								18 35				

A 🛒 to New Milton

London - Basingstoke, Southampton, Romsey Lymington, Bournemouth and Weymouth

		SW		SW	XC	GW	SW	SW	SW	SW	SW		SW	XC	GW	GW	SW	SW	SW	GW	SW	SW	
		◇1 🛒		1	◇1 🛒	◇	◇1 A 🛒	1	1	1	◇1 🛒		1	◇1 🛒	◇		◇1 A 🛒	1	1	◇	1	◇1 🛒	
London Waterloo 15 ⊖	d	15 54					16 35	16 37			16 54						17 35	17 37				17 54	
Clapham Junction 10	d	16u03					16u42	16 46			17u03						17u42	17 46				18u03	
Woking	d	16 28					17 07	17 23			17 28						18 07	18 23				18 28	
Farnborough (Main)	d							17 36										18 36					
Fleet	d							17 41										18 41					
Reading 7	d				16 51									17 51									
Basingstoke	a	16 46			17 09		17 26	17 54			17 46			18 09			18 26	18 54				18 46	
	d	16 48			17 10		17 28				17 48			18 10			18 28					18 48	
Micheldever	d	16 58									17 58											18 58	
Winchester	d	17 08			17 25		17 44				18 08			18 25			18 44					19 08	
Shawford	d										18 12												
Romsey	d								17 35										18 35				
Chandlers Ford	d								17 42										18 42				
Eastleigh 8	a	17 18							17 48		18 18								18 48			19 18	
	d	17 22	17 26						17 54		18 22	18 26							18 54			19 22	19 26
Hedge End	d		17 32									18 32											19 32
Botley	d		17 36									18 36											19 36
Fareham	d		17 44			17 32						18 44			18 32					19 03			19 44
Portchester	d		17 49									18 49											19 49
Cosham	d		17 54									18 54											19 54
Hilsea	a		18 00									19 00											20 00
Fratton	a		18 04									19 03											20 04
Portsmouth & Southsea	a		18 08									19 08											20 08
Portsmouth Harbour ⛴	a		18 13									19 13											20 13
Southampton Airport Pkwy ✈	d	17 27			17 34		17 53		17 58		18 27			18 34			18 53		18 58			19 27	
Swaythling	d								18 01										19 01				
St Denys	d								18 04										19 04				
Southampton Central ⛴	a	17 34			17 40	17 53	18 00		18 09		18 34			18 42	18 53		19 00		19 09	19 24		19 34	
	d	17 35			17 45	17 54	18 03		18 10		18 35			18 45	18 54		19 03		19 10	19 30		19 35	
Millbrook (Hants)	d								18 13										19 13				
Redbridge	d								18 16										19 16				
Romsey	d					18 06			18 24						19 06				19 24	19 42			
Mottisfont & Dunbridge	d																		19 29				
Dean	d																		19 35				
Salisbury	a					18 24			18 42						19 24				19 48	20 00			
Totton	d	17 41									18 41											19 41	
Ashurst New Forest	d	17 45									18 45											19 45	
Beaulieu Road	d	17 50									18 50											19 50	
Brockenhurst 3	a	17 56			18 02		18 16				18 56			19 01			19 16					19 56	
	d	17 57		17 59	18 03		18 17			18 29	18 57		18 59	19 02			19 17				19 29	19 57	
Lymington Town	d			18 07						18 37			19 07								19 37		
Lymington Pier	a			18 09						18 39			19 09								19 39		
Sway	d	18 01									19 01											20 01	
New Milton	d	18 06					18 24				19 06						19 24					20 06	
Hinton Admiral	d	18 10									19 10											20 10	
Christchurch	d	18 15									19 15											20 15	
Pokesdown	d	18 19									19 19											20 19	
Bournemouth	a	18 23			18 26		18 34				19 23			19 26			19 34					20 23	
	d	18 24					18 39				19 24						19 39					20 24	
Branksome	d						18 44										19 44						
Parkstone (Dorset)	d						18 47										19 47						
Poole 4	a	18 33					18 50				19 33						19 50					20 33	
	d						18 51										19 51						
Hamworthy	d						18 56										19 56						
Holton Heath	d																						
Wareham	d						19 03										20 03						
Wool	d						19 10										20 10						
Moreton (Dorset)	d						19 16										20 16						
Dorchester South	d						19 24										20 25						
Dorchester West	d															19 47							
Upwey	d						19 31									19 55	20 32						
Weymouth	a						19 35									20 01	20 36						

A 🛒 to New Milton

Table 158

Sundays until 19 June

London - Basingstoke, Southampton, Romsey Lymington, Bournemouth and Weymouth

		SW	XC	GW	SW	SW	SW	SW	SW		SW	XC	GW	SW	SW	SW	SW	SW		SW	XC	GW
		1	◇1	◇	◇1	1	1	1	◇1		1	◇1	◇	◇1	1	1	1	◇1		1	◇1	
					A									A								
			⌶		⌶				⌶			⌶		⌶								
London Waterloo 15 ⊖	d				18 35	18 37			18 54					19 35	19 37			19 54				
Clapham Junction 10	d				18u42	18 46			19u03					19u42	19 46			20u03				
Woking	d				19 07	19 23			19 28					20 07	20 23			20 28				
Farnborough (Main)	d					19 36									20 36							
Fleet	d					19 41									20 41							
Reading 7	d		18 51									19 51									20 51	
Basingstoke	a		19 09		19 26	19 54			19 46			20 09		20 26	20 54			20 46			21 09	
	d		19 10		19 28				19 48			20 10		20 28				20 48			21 10	
Micheldever	d								19 58									20 58				
Winchester	d		19 25		19 44				20 08			20 25		20 44				21 08			21 25	
Shawford	d								20 12													
Romsey	d						19 35									20 35						
Chandlers Ford	d						19 42									20 42						
Eastleigh 3	a						19 48		20 18							20 48		21 18				
	d						19 54		20 22	20 26						20 54		21 22	21 26			
Hedge End	d									20 32									21 32			
Botley	d									20 36									21 36			
Fareham	d			19 32						20 44			20 32						21 44			
Portchester	d									20 49									21 49			
Cosham	d									20 54									21 54			
Hilsea	a									21 00									22 00			
Fratton	a									21 04									22 04			
Portsmouth & Southsea	a									21 08									22 08			
Portsmouth Harbour ⛴	a									21 13									22 13			
Southampton Airport Pkwy ✈	d		19 34		19 53		19 58		20 27			20 34		20 53		20 58		21 27			21 34	
Swaythling	d						20 01									21 01						
St Denys	d						20 04									21 04						
Southampton Central ⛴	a		19 40	19 53	20 00		20 09		20 34			20 42	20 53	21 00		21 09		21 34			21 43	
	d		19 45	19 54	20 03		20 10		20 35			20 45	20 54	21 03		21 10		21 35			21 45	
Millbrook (Hants)	d						20 13									21 13						
Redbridge	d						20 16									21 16						
Romsey	d			20 06			20 24						21 06			21 24						
Mottisfont & Dunbridge	d															21 29						
Dean	d															21 35						
Salisbury	a			20 24			20 42						21 24			21 48						
Totton	d								20 41									21 41				
Ashurst New Forest	d								20 45									21 45				
Beaulieu Road	d								20 50									21 50				
Brockenhurst 3	a		20 02		20 16				20 56			21 02		21 16				21 56			22 02	
	d	19 59	20 03		20 17			20 29	20 57		20 59	21 03		21 17			21 29	21 57		21 59	22 03	
Lymington Town	d	20 07						20 37			21 07						21 37			22 07		
Lymington Pier	a	20 09						20 39			21 09						21 39			22 09		
Sway	d								21 01									22 01				
New Milton	d				20 24				21 06					21 24				22 06				
Hinton Admiral	d								21 10									22 10				
Christchurch	d								21 15									22 15				
Pokesdown	d								21 19									22 19				
Bournemouth	a		20 26		20 34				21 23			21 26		21 34				22 23			22 26	
	d				20 39				21 24					21 39				22 24				
Branksome	d				20 44									21 44								
Parkstone (Dorset)	d				20 47									21 47								
Poole 4	a				20 50				21 33					21 50				22 33				
	d				20 51									21 51								
Hamworthy	d				20 56									21 56								
Holton Heath	d																					
Wareham	d				21 03									22 03								
Wool	d				21 10									22 10								
Moreton (Dorset)	d				21 16									22 16								
Dorchester South	d				21 25									22 25								
Dorchester West	d																					22 53
Upwey	d				21 32									22 32								23 01
Weymouth	a				21 36									22 36								23 06

A ⌶ to New Milton

Table 158

Sundays until 19 June

London - Basingstoke, Southampton, Romsey Lymington, Bournemouth and Weymouth

		SW	SW	SW	SW		XC	GW	SW	SW	SW	SW	SW		SW	SW
		◇1	1	1	◇1		◇1		◇1	1	1	1	◇1		1	◇1
		A							A							
		⌶							⌶							⌶
London Waterloo 15 ⊖	d	20 35	20 37		20 54				21 35	21 37			21 54		22 37	22 54
Clapham Junction 10	d	20u42	20 46		21u03				21u42	21 46			22u03		22 46	23u03
Woking	d	21 07	21 23		21 28				22 07	22 23			22 28		23 23	23 28
Farnborough (Main)	d		21 36							22 36					23 36	
Fleet	d		21 41							22 41					23 41	
Reading 7	d						21 51									
Basingstoke	a	21 26	21 54		21 46		22 09		22 26	22 54			22 46		23 54	23 46
	d	21 28			21 48		22 10		22 28				22 48			23 48
Micheldever	d				21 58								22 58			23 58
Winchester	d	21 44			22 08		22 26		22 44				23 08			00 08
Shawford	d				22 12											
Romsey	d			21 35							22 35	22 28				
Chandlers Ford	d			21 42							22 42					
Eastleigh 3	a			21 48	22 18						22 48	23 19	23 17			00 18
	d			21 54	22 22	22 26					22 54	23 21	23 22	23 26		00 22
Hedge End	d					22 32								23 32		
Botley	d					22 36								23 36		
Fareham	d					22 44		22 32						23 44		
Portchester	d					22 49								23 49		
Cosham	d					22 54								23 54		
Hilsea	a					23 00								23 59		
Fratton	a					23 04								00 04		
Portsmouth & Southsea	a					23 08								00 08		
Portsmouth Harbour ⛴	a					23 13								00 13		
Southampton Airport Pkwy ✈	d	21 53		21 58	22 27		22 34		22 53		22 58		23 27			00 27
Swaythling	d			22 01							23 01					
St Denys	d			22 04							23 04					00s31
Southampton Central ⛴	a	22 00		22 09	22 34		22 42	22 53	23 00		23 09		23 34			00 36
	d	22 03		22 10	22 35			22 57	23 03		23 10		23 35			00 37
Millbrook (Hants)	d			22 13							23 13					
Redbridge	d			22 16							23 16					
Romsey	d			22a24				23 09			23 24	23a33				
Mottisfont & Dunbridge	d										23 29					
Dean	d										23 35					
Salisbury	a							23 27			23 51					
Totton	d				22 41								23 41			00s42
Ashurst New Forest	d				22 45								23 45			
Beaulieu Road	d				22 50											
Brockenhurst 3	a	22 16			22 56				23 16				23 53			00s53
	d	22 17			22 57				23 17				23 54			
Lymington Town	d															
Lymington Pier	a															
Sway	d				23 01								23 59			
New Milton	d	22 24			23 06				23 24				00 04			01s01
Hinton Admiral	d				23 10								00 08			
Christchurch	d				23 15								00 13			01s08
Pokesdown	d				23 19								00 16			01s12
Bournemouth	a	22 34			23 23				23 34				00 20			01 16
	d	22 39			23 24				23 39				00 22			01 17
Branksome	d	22 44							23 44				00 27			01s22
Parkstone (Dorset)	d	22 47							23 47				00 30			01s25
Poole 4	a	22 50			23 33				23 50				00 34			01 29
	d	22 51							23 51							
Hamworthy	d	22 56							23 56							
Holton Heath	d															
Wareham	d	23 03							00 03							
Wool	d	23 10							00 10							
Moreton (Dorset)	d	23 16							00 16							
Dorchester South	d	23 25							00 24							
Dorchester West	d															
Upwey	d	23 32							00 31							
Weymouth	a	23 36							00 35							

A ⌶ to New Milton

London - Basingstoke, Southampton, Romsey Lymington, Bournemouth and Weymouth

		SW	SW	SW	SW	SW	SW	SW	SW	SW	SW	SW	GW	SW	SW		SW	SW	SW	SW	GW	SW	
		◇1 A [trolley]	◇1 [trolley]	1	◇1 [trolley]	1	◇1	1	1	1	1	1		1	1		1	1	1	1	■	◇1	
London Waterloo 15 ⊖	d	21p35	22p05		22p35	22p39	23p05		23p35	00 05	01 05											07 54	
Clapham Junction 10	d		22b12			22b46	23b12		23b42	00u12												08u03	
Woking	d	22p00	22p32		23p00		23p32		00 03	00 37	01 42											08 28	
Farnborough (Main)	d					23p16			00 14		01s58												
Fleet	d					23p21			00 20		02s04												
Reading 7	d																						
Basingstoke	a		22p51			23p34	23p51		00 33	00 55	02s16											08 46	
	d		22p52			23p36	23p52		00 35	00 56					07 48							08 48	
Micheldever	d						00 02								07 58							08 58	
Winchester	d	22p33	23p09		23p33	23p52	00 12		00 51	01 13	02s33				08 08							09 08	
Shawford	d					23p57									08 12								
Romsey	d			23p09									08 19						08 35				
Chandlers Ford	d			23p16															08 42				
Eastleigh 8	a		23p17	23p22		00 02	00 20		00 59	01 21	02s42				08 18				08 47			09 18	
	d		23p18	23p23		00 03	00 21	00 30	01 00	01 22					08 22	08 26			08 54			09 22	09 26
Hedge End	d							00s36								08 32							09 32
Botley	d							00s39								08 36							09 36
Fareham	d							00s47				07 44				08 44					09 32		09 44
Portchester	d							00s53				07 49				08 49							09 49
Cosham	d							00s57				07 54				08 54							09 54
Hilsea	a											08 00				09 00							10 04
Fratton	a							01s05				08 04				09 04							10 08
Portsmouth & Southsea	a							01s08				08 08				09 08							10 11
Portsmouth Harbour ⛴	a							01 12				08 13				09 13							10 15
Southampton Airport Pkwy ✈	d	22p42	23p22	23p27	23p42	00 08	00 25		01 05	01 26	02s46				08 27				08 58			09 27	
Swaythling	d			23p30															09 01				
St Denys	d			23p33			00s29				02s51								09 04				
Southampton Central ⛴	a	22p49	23p29	23p38	23p49	00 15	00 34		01 12	01 35	02 56		08 29		08 34				09 09		09 53	09 34	
	d	22p51	23p31	23p40	23p51		00 36			01 37					08 35			09 03	09 10		09 54	09 35	
Millbrook (Hants)	d			23p42															09 13				
Redbridge	d			23p46															09 16				
Romsey	d			23p57															09 24		10 06		
Mottisfont & Dunbridge	d			00 02															09 29				
Dean	d			00 08															09 35				
Salisbury	a			00 20															09 49		10 24		
Totton	d		23p36				00s41			01s42					08 41							09 41	
Ashurst New Forest	d		23p41												08 45							09 45	
Beaulieu Road	d														08 50							09 50	
Brockenhurst 8	a	23p04	23p49		00 04		00s52			01s53					08 56			09 16				09 56	
	d	23p05	23p50		00 05										08 57		08 59	09 17		09 29		09 57	
Lymington Town	d																09 07			09 37			
Lymington Pier	a																09 09			09 39			
Sway	d		23p54												09 01							10 01	
New Milton	d		23p59				01s00			02s00					09 06			09 24				10 06	
Hinton Admiral	d		00 03												09 10							10 10	
Christchurch	d		00 08				01s07			02s07					09 15							10 15	
Pokesdown	d		00 11				01s11			02s11					09 19							10 19	
Bournemouth	a	23p25	00 15		00 21		01 15			02 15					09 23			09 34				10 23	
	d	23p29	00 17		00 22		01 16							08 39	09 24			09 39				10 24	
Branksome	d	23p35	00 23		00 27		01s21							08 44				09 44					
Parkstone (Dorset)	d	23p38	00 26		00 30		01s24							08 47				09 47					
Poole 4	a	23p41	00 30		00 35		01 29							08 50	09 33			09 50				10 33	
	d	23p42												08 51				09 51					
Hamworthy	d	23p47												08 56				09 56					
Holton Heath	d																						
Wareham	d	23p54												09 03				10 03					
Wool	d	00 01												09 10				10 10					
Moreton (Dorset)	d	00 07												09 16				10 16					
Dorchester South	d	00 15												09 24				10 24					
Dorchester West	d																						
Upwey	d	00 21												09 31				10 31					
Weymouth	a	00 26												09 35				10 35					

A [trolley] to Brockenhurst

b Previous night, stops to pick up only

London - Basingstoke, Southampton, Romsey Lymington, Bournemouth and Weymouth

		SW	GW	SW	SW	SW	SW		SW	XC	GW	SW	SW	SW	SW		SW	XC	GW	SW	SW	SW
		1		◇1	1	1	◇1		1	◇1 [trolley]		◇1	1	1	◇1		1	◇1 [trolley]	◇	◇1 A [trolley]	1	1
London Waterloo 15 ⊖	d			08 35			08 54					09 35			09 54					10 35		
Clapham Junction 10	d			08u45			09u03					09u45			10u03					10u45		
Woking	d			09 09			09 28					10 09			10 28					11 07		
Farnborough (Main)	d																					
Fleet	d																					
Reading 7	d									09 51								10 51				
Basingstoke	a			09 28			09 46			10 09		10 28			10 46			11 09		11 26		
	d			09 29			09 48			10 10		10 29			10 48			11 10		11 28		
Micheldever	d						09 58								10 58							
Winchester	d			09 46			10 08			10 25		10 46			11 08			11 25		11 44		
Shawford	d						10 12															
Romsey	d				09 35								10 35								11 35	
Chandlers Ford	d				09 42								10 42								11 42	
Eastleigh 8	a				09 48		10 18						10 48		11 18						11 48	
	d				09 54		10 22	10 26					10 54		11 22	11 26					11 54	
Hedge End	d							10 32								11 32						
Botley	d							10 36								11 36						
Fareham	d							10 44								11 44			11 32			
Portchester	d							10 49								11 49						
Cosham	d							10 54								11 54						
Hilsea	a							11 04								12 00						
Fratton	a							11 08								12 04						
Portsmouth & Southsea	a							11 11								12 08						
Portsmouth Harbour ⛴	a							11 15								12 13						
Southampton Airport Pkwy ✈	d			09 55	09 58		10 27			10 34		10 55	10 58		11 27			11 34		11 53	11 58	
Swaythling	d				10 01								11 01								12 01	
St Denys	d				10 04								11 04								12 04	
Southampton Central ⛴	a			10 02	10 09		10 34			10 42		11 02	11 09		11 34			11 42	11 53	11 59	12 09	
	d			10 03	10 10		10 35			10 45		11 03	11 10		11 35			11 45	11 54	12 03	12 10	
Millbrook (Hants)	d				10 13								11 13								12 13	
Redbridge	d				10 16								11 16								12 16	
Romsey	d				10 24								11 24						12 06		12 24	
Mottisfont & Dunbridge	d												11 29									
Dean	d												11 35									
Salisbury	a				10 42								11 48						12 24		12 42	
Totton	d						10 41								11 41							
Ashurst New Forest	d						10 45								11 45							
Beaulieu Road	d						10 50								11 50							
Brockenhurst 8	a			10 17			10 56			11 02		11 17			11 56			12 02		12 16		
	d	09 59		10 18		10 29	10 57		10 59	11 02		11 18		11 29	11 57		11 59	12 03		12 17		12 29
Lymington Town	d	10 07				10 37			11 07					11 37			12 07					12 37
Lymington Pier	a	10 09				10 39			11 09					11 39			12 09					12 39
Sway	d						11 01								12 01							
New Milton	d			10 25			11 06					11 25			12 06					12 24		
Hinton Admiral	d						11 10								12 10							
Christchurch	d						11 15								12 15							
Pokesdown	d						11 19								12 19							
Bournemouth	a			10 35			11 23			11 26		11 35			12 23			12 26		12 34		
	d			10 39			11 24					11 39			12 24					12 39		
Branksome	d			10 44								11 44								12 44		
Parkstone (Dorset)	d			10 47								11 47								12 47		
Poole 4	a			10 50			11 33					11 50			12 33					12 50		
	d			10 51								11 51								12 51		
Hamworthy	d			10 56								11 56								12 56		
Holton Heath	d																					
Wareham	d			11 03								12 03								13 03		
Wool	d			11 10								12 10								13 10		
Moreton (Dorset)	d			11 16								12 16								13 16		
Dorchester South	d			11 24								12 24								13 24		
Dorchester West	d		10 26								11 30											
Upwey	d		10 37	11 31							11 37	12 31								13 31		
Weymouth	a		10 42	11 35							11 43	12 35								13 35		

A [trolley] to New Milton

Table 158

Sundays

26 June to 31 July

London - Basingstoke, Southampton, Romsey Lymington, Bournemouth and Weymouth

	SW ◇1		SW 1	XC ◇1 ⌶	GW ◇	SW ◇1 A ⌶	SW 1	SW 1	SW ◇1 ⌶		SW 1	XC ◇1 ⌶	GW ◇	SW ◇1 A ⌶	SW 1	SW 1	SW ◇1 ⌶		SW 1	XC ◇1 ⌶	GW ◇
London Waterloo 15 ⊖ d	10 54					11 35			11 54					12 35			12 54				
Clapham Junction 10 d	11u04					11u45			12u04					12u42			13u03				
Woking d	11 28					12 07			12 28					13 07			13 28				
Farnborough (Main) d																					
Fleet d																					
Reading 7 d				11 51								12 51								13 51	
Basingstoke a	11 46			12 09		12 26			12 46			13 09		13 26			13 46			14 09	
d	11 48			12 10		12 28			12 48			13 10		13 28			13 48			14 10	
Micheldever d	11 58								12 58								13 58				
Winchester d	12 08			12 25		12 44			13 08			13 25		13 44			14 08			14 25	
Shawford d	12 12																14 12				
Romsey d							12 35								13 35						
Chandlers Ford d							12 42								13 42						
Eastleigh 3 a	12 18						12 48		13 18						13 48		14 18				
d	12 22	12 26					12 54		13 22	13 26					13 54		14 22	14 26			
Hedge End d		12 32								13 32								14 32			
Botley d		12 36								13 36								14 36			
Fareham d		12 44			12 32					13 44			13 32					14 44			14 32
Portchester d		12 49								13 49								14 49			
Cosham d		12 54								13 54								14 54			
Hilsea a		13 00								14 00								15 00			
Fratton a		13 04								14 04								15 04			
Portsmouth & Southsea a		13 08								14 08								15 08			
Portsmouth Harbour ⛴ a		13 13								14 13								15 13			
Southampton Airport Pkwy ✈ d	12 27			12 34		12 53	12 58		13 27			13 34		13 53	13 58		14 27			14 34	
Swaythling d							13 01								14 01						
St Denys d							13 04								14 04						
Southampton Central ⛴ a	12 34			12 42	12 53	13 00	13 09		13 34			13 42	13 54	14 00	14 09		14 34			14 42	14 53
d	12 35			12 45	12 54	13 03	13 10		13 35			13 45	13 54	14 03	14 10		14 35			14 45	14 54
Millbrook (Hants) d							13 13								14 13						
Redbridge d							13 16								14 16						
Romsey d					13 06		13 24						14 06		14 24						15 06
Mottisfont & Dunbridge d							13 29														
Dean d							13 35														
Salisbury a					13 24		13 48						14 24		14 42						15 24
Totton d	12 41								13 41								14 41				
Ashurst New Forest d	12 45								13 45								14 45				
Beaulieu Road d	12 50								13 50								14 50				
Brockenhurst 3 a	12 56			13 02		13 16			13 56			14 01		14 16			14 56			15 02	
d	12 57		12 59	13 03		13 17		13 29	13 57		13 59	14 02		14 17		14 29	14 57		14 59	15 03	
Lymington Town d			13 07					13 37			14 07					14 37			15 07		
Lymington Pier a			13 09					13 39			14 09					14 39			15 09		
Sway d	13 01								14 01								15 01				
New Milton d	13 06					13 24			14 06					14 24			15 06				
Hinton Admiral d	13 10								14 10								15 10				
Christchurch d	13 15								14 15								15 15				
Pokesdown d	13 19								14 19								15 19				
Bournemouth a	13 23			13 26		13 34			14 23			14 26		14 34			15 23			15 26	
d	13 24					13 39			14 24					14 39			15 24				
Branksome d						13 44								14 44							
Parkstone (Dorset) d						13 47								14 47							
Poole 4 a	13 33					13 50			14 33					14 50			15 33				
d						13 51								14 51							
Hamworthy d						13 56								14 56							
Holton Heath d																					
Wareham d						14 03								15 03							
Wool d						14 10								15 10							
Moreton (Dorset) d						14 16								15 16							
Dorchester South d						14 24								15 24							
Dorchester West d																					
Upwey d						14 31								15 31							
Weymouth a						14 35								15 35							

A ⌶ to New Milton

Table 158

Sundays

26 June to 31 July

London - Basingstoke, Southampton, Romsey Lymington, Bournemouth and Weymouth

	GW	SW ◇1 A ⌶	SW 1	SW 1	SW ◇1 ⌶		SW 1	XC ◇1 ⌶	GW ■	SW ◇1 A ⌶	SW 1	SW 1	SW ◇1 ⌶		SW 1	XC ◇1 ⌶	GW ◇	SW ◇1 A ⌶	SW 1	SW 1	GW ◇	SW 1
London Waterloo 15 ⊖ d		13 35			13 54					14 35			14 54					15 35	15 37			
Clapham Junction 10 d		13u42			14u03					14u42			15u03					15u42	15 46			
Woking d		14 07			14 28					15 07			15 28					16 07	16 23			
Farnborough (Main) d																			16 36			
Fleet d																			16 41			
Reading 7 d								14 51								15 51						
Basingstoke a		14 26			14 46			15 09		15 26			15 46			16 09		16 26	16 54			
d		14 28			14 48			15 10		15 28			15 48			16 10		16 28				
Micheldever d					14 58								15 58									
Winchester d		14 44			15 08			15 25		15 44			16 08			16 25		16 44				
Shawford d													16 12									
Romsey d			14 35								15 35									16 35		
Chandlers Ford d			14 42								15 42									16 42		
Eastleigh 3 a			14 48		15 18						15 48		16 18							16 48		
d			14 54		15 22	15 26					15 54		16 22	16 26						16 54		
Hedge End d						15 32								16 32								
Botley d						15 36								16 36								
Fareham d						15 44			15 32					16 44			16 32				17 03	
Portchester d						15 49								16 49								
Cosham d						15 54								16 54								
Hilsea a						16 00								17 00								
Fratton a						16 04								17 03								
Portsmouth & Southsea a						16 08								17 08								
Portsmouth Harbour ⛴ a						16 13								17 13								
Southampton Airport Pkwy ✈ d		14 53	14 58		15 27			15 34		15 53	15 58		16 27			16 34		16 53		16 58		
Swaythling d			15 01								16 01									17 01		
St Denys d			15 04								16 04									17 04		
Southampton Central ⛴ a		15 00	15 09		15 34			15 42	15 53	16 00	16 09		16 34			16 42	16 53	17 00		17 09	17 24	
d		15 03	15 10		15 35			15 45	15 54	16 03	16 10		16 35			16 45	16 54	17 03		17 10	17 26	
Millbrook (Hants) d			15 13								16 13									17 13		
Redbridge d			15 16								16 16									17 16		
Romsey d			15 24						16 06		16 24						17 06			17 24	17 39	
Mottisfont & Dunbridge d			15 29																	17 29		
Dean d			15 35																	17 35		
Salisbury a			15 48						16 24		16 42						17 24			17 48	18 01	
Totton d					15 41								16 41									
Ashurst New Forest d					15 45								16 45									
Beaulieu Road d					15 50								16 50									
Brockenhurst 3 a		15 16			15 56			16 02		16 16			16 56			17 02		17 16				
d		15 17		15 29	15 57		15 59	16 03		16 17		16 29	16 57		16 59	17 03		17 17				17 29
Lymington Town d				15 37			16 07					16 37			17 07							17 37
Lymington Pier a				15 39			16 09					16 39			17 09							17 39
Sway d					16 01								17 01									
New Milton d		15 24			16 06					16 24			17 06					17 24				
Hinton Admiral d					16 10								17 10									
Christchurch d					16 15								17 15									
Pokesdown d					16 19								17 19									
Bournemouth a		15 34			16 23			16 26		16 34			17 23			17 26		17 34				
d		15 39			16 24					16 39			17 24					17 39				
Branksome d		15 44								16 44								17 44				
Parkstone (Dorset) d		15 47								16 47								17 47				
Poole 4 a		15 50			16 33					16 50			17 33					17 50				
d		15 51								16 51								17 51				
Hamworthy d		15 56								16 56								17 56				
Holton Heath d																						
Wareham d		16 03								17 03								18 03				
Wool d		16 10								17 10								18 10				
Moreton (Dorset) d		16 16								17 16								18 16				
Dorchester South d		16 24								17 24								18 24				
Dorchester West d	15 41																					
Upwey d	15 50	16 31								17 31								18 31				
Weymouth a	15 55	16 35								17 35								18 35				

A ⌶ to New Milton

London - Basingstoke, Southampton, Romsey Lymington, Bournemouth and Weymouth

		SW ◇1 ⊤		SW 1	XC ◇1 ⊤	GW ◇		SW ◇1 A ⊤	SW 1	SW 1	SW 1	SW ◇1 ⊤		SW 1	XC ◇1 ⊤	GW ◇		GW	SW ◇1 A ⊤	SW 1	SW 1	GW ◇	SW 1	SW ◇1 ⊤	
London Waterloo 15 ⊖	d	15 54						16 35	16 37			16 54							17 35	17 37				17 54	
Clapham Junction 10	d	16u03						16u42	16 46			17u03							17u42	17 46				18u03	
Woking	d	16 28						17 07	17 23			17 28							18 07	18 23				18 28	
Farnborough (Main)	d								17 36											18 36					
Fleet	d								17 41											18 41					
Reading 7	d				16 51										17 51										
Basingstoke	a	16 46			17 09			17 26	17 54			17 46			18 09				18 26	18 54				18 46	
	d	16 48			17 10			17 28				17 48			18 10				18 28					18 48	
Micheldever	d	16 58										17 58												18 58	
Winchester	d	17 08			17 25			17 44				18 08			18 25				18 44					19 08	
Shawford	d											18 12													
Romsey	d									17 35											18 35				
Chandlers Ford	d									17 42											18 42				
Eastleigh 8	a	17 18								17 48		18 18									18 48			19 18	
	d	17 22	17 26							17 54		18 22	18 26								18 54			19 22	19 26
Hedge End	d		17 32										18 32												19 32
Botley	d		17 36										18 36												19 36
Fareham	d		17 44			17 32							18 44			18 32						19 03			19 44
Portchester	d		17 49										18 49												19 49
Cosham	d		17 54										18 54												19 54
Hilsea	a		18 00										19 00												20 00
Fratton	a		18 04										19 03												20 04
Portsmouth & Southsea	a		18 08										19 08												20 08
Portsmouth Harbour ⛴	a		18 13										19 13												20 13
Southampton Airport Pkwy ✈	d	17 27			17 34			17 53		17 58		18 27			18 34				18 53		18 58			19 27	
Swaythling	d									18 01											19 01				
St Denys	d									18 04											19 04				
Southampton Central ⛴	a	17 34			17 40	17 53		18 00		18 09		18 34			18 42	18 53			19 00		19 09	19 24		19 34	
	d	17 35			17 45	17 54		18 03		18 10		18 35			18 45	18 54			19 03		19 10	19 30		19 35	
Millbrook (Hants)	d									18 13											19 13				
Redbridge	d									18 16											19 16				
Romsey	d					18 06				18 24						19 06					19 24	19 42			
Mottisfont & Dunbridge	d																				19 29				
Dean	d																				19 35				
Salisbury	a					18 24				18 42						19 24					19 48	20 00			
Totton	d	17 41										18 41												19 41	
Ashurst New Forest	d	17 45										18 45												19 45	
Beaulieu Road	d	17 50										18 50												19 50	
Brockenhurst 3	a	17 56			18 02			18 16				18 56			19 01				19 16					19 56	
	d	17 57		17 59	18 03			18 17			18 29	18 57		18 59	19 02				19 17				19 29	19 57	
Lymington Town	d			18 07							18 37			19 07									19 37		
Lymington Pier	a			18 09							18 39			19 09									19 39		
Sway	d	18 01										19 01												20 01	
New Milton	d	18 06						18 24				19 06							19 24					20 06	
Hinton Admiral	d	18 10										19 10												20 10	
Christchurch	d	18 15										19 15												20 15	
Pokesdown	d	18 19										19 19												20 19	
Bournemouth	a	18 23			18 26			18 34				19 23			19 26				19 34					20 23	
	d	18 24						18 39				19 24							19 39					20 24	
Branksome	d							18 44											19 44						
Parkstone (Dorset)	d							18 47											19 47						
Poole 4	a	18 33						18 50				19 33							19 50					20 33	
	d							18 51											19 51						
Hamworthy	d							18 56											19 56						
Holton Heath	d																								
Wareham	d							19 03											20 03						
Wool	d							19 10											20 10						
Moreton (Dorset)	d							19 16											20 16						
Dorchester South	d							19 24											20 25						
Dorchester West	d																	19 47							
Upwey	d							19 31										19 55	20 32						
Weymouth	a							19 35										20 01	20 36						

A ⊤ to New Milton

London - Basingstoke, Southampton, Romsey Lymington, Bournemouth and Weymouth

		SW 1		XC ◇1 ⊤	GW ◇	SW ◇1 A ⊤	SW 1	SW 1	SW 1	SW ◇1 ⊤		SW 1		XC ◇1 ⊤	GW ◇	SW ◇1 A ⊤	SW 1	SW 1	SW 1	SW ◇1		SW 1		XC ◇1	GW
London Waterloo 15 ⊖	d					18 35	18 37			18 54						19 35	19 37			19 54					
Clapham Junction 10	d					18u42	18 46			19u03						19u42	19 46			20u03					
Woking	d					19 07	19 23			19 28						20 07	20 23			20 28					
Farnborough (Main)	d						19 36										20 36								
Fleet	d						19 41										20 41								
Reading 7	d			18 51										19 51										20 51	
Basingstoke	a			19 09		19 26	19 54			19 46				20 09		20 26	20 54			20 46				21 09	
	d			19 10		19 28				19 48				20 10		20 28				20 48				21 10	
Micheldever	d									19 58										20 58					
Winchester	d			19 25		19 44				20 08				20 25		20 44				21 08				21 25	
Shawford	d									20 12															
Romsey	d							19 35										20 35							
Chandlers Ford	d							19 42										20 42							
Eastleigh 8	a							19 48		20 18								20 48		21 18					
	d							19 54		20 22	20 26							20 54		21 22	21 26				
Hedge End	d										20 32										21 32				
Botley	d										20 36										21 36				
Fareham	d				19 32						20 44				20 32						21 44				
Portchester	d										20 49										21 49				
Cosham	d										20 54										21 54				
Hilsea	a										21 00										22 00				
Fratton	a										21 04										22 04				
Portsmouth & Southsea	a										21 08										22 08				
Portsmouth Harbour ⛴	a										21 13										22 13				
Southampton Airport Pkwy ✈	d			19 34		19 53		19 58		20 27				20 34		20 53		20 58		21 27				21 34	
Swaythling	d							20 01										21 01							
St Denys	d							20 04										21 04							
Southampton Central ⛴	a			19 40	19 53	20 00		20 09		20 34				20 42	20 53	21 00		21 09		21 34				21 43	
	d			19 45	19 54	20 03		20 10		20 35				20 45	20 54	21 03		21 10		21 35				21 45	
Millbrook (Hants)	d							20 13										21 13							
Redbridge	d							20 16										21 16							
Romsey	d				20 06			20 24							21 06			21 24							
Mottisfont & Dunbridge	d																	21 29							
Dean	d																	21 35							
Salisbury	a				20 24			20 42							21 24			21 48							
Totton	d									20 41										21 41					
Ashurst New Forest	d									20 45										21 45					
Beaulieu Road	d									20 50										21 50					
Brockenhurst 3	a			20 02		20 16				20 56				21 02		21 16				21 56				22 02	
	d	19 59		20 03		20 17			20 29	20 57		20 59		21 03		21 17			21 29	21 57		21 59		22 03	
Lymington Town	d	20 07							20 37			21 07							21 37			22 07			
Lymington Pier	a	20 09							20 39			21 09							21 39			22 09			
Sway	d									21 01										22 01					
New Milton	d					20 24				21 06						21 24				22 06					
Hinton Admiral	d									21 10										22 10					
Christchurch	d									21 15										22 15					
Pokesdown	d									21 19										22 19					
Bournemouth	a			20 26		20 34				21 23				21 26		21 34				22 23				22 26	
	d					20 39				21 24						21 39				22 24					
Branksome	d					20 44										21 44									
Parkstone (Dorset)	d					20 47										21 47									
Poole 4	a					20 50				21 33						21 50				22 33					
	d					20 51										21 51									
Hamworthy	d					20 56										21 56									
Holton Heath	d																								
Wareham	d					21 03										22 03									
Wool	d					21 10										22 10									
Moreton (Dorset)	d					21 16										22 16									
Dorchester South	d					21 25										22 25									
Dorchester West	d																								22 53
Upwey	d					21 32										22 32									23 01
Weymouth	a					21 36										22 36									23 06

A ⊤ to New Milton

Table 158

Sundays
26 June to 31 July

London - Basingstoke, Southampton, Romsey Lymington, Bournemouth and Weymouth

		SW	SW	SW	SW	XC	GW	SW	SW	SW	SW	SW	SW	SW
		◇1	1	1	◇1	◇1		◇1	1	1	1	◇1	1	◇1
		A 🍴						A 🍴						🍴
London Waterloo 15 ⊖	d	20 35	20 37		20 54			21 35	21 37			21 54	22 37	22 54
Clapham Junction 10	d	20u42	20 46		21u03			21u42	21 46			22u03	22 46	23u03
Woking	d	21 07	21 23		21 28			22 07	22 23			22 28	23 23	23 28
Farnborough (Main)	d		21 36						22 36				23 36	
Fleet	d		21 41						22 41				23 41	
Reading 7	d					21 51								
Basingstoke	a	21 26	21 54		21 46	22 09		22 26	22 54			22 46	23 54	23 46
	d	21 28			21 48	22 10		22 28				22 48		23 48
Micheldever	d				21 58							22 58		23 58
Winchester	d	21 44			22 08	22 26		22 44				23 08		00 08
Shawford	d				22 12									
Romsey	d			21 35						22 35	22 28			
Chandlers Ford	d			21 42						22 42				
Eastleigh 3	a			21 48	22 18					22 48	23 19	23 17		00 18
	d			21 54	22 22 / 22 26					22 54	23 21	23 22 / 23 26		00 22
Hedge End	d				22 32							23 32		
Botley	d				22 36							23 36		
Fareham	d				22 44		22 32					23 44		
Portchester	d				22 49							23 49		
Cosham	d				22 54							23 54		
Hilsea	a				23 00							23 59		
Fratton	a				23 04							00 04		
Portsmouth & Southsea	a				23 08							00 08		
Portsmouth Harbour ⛴	a				23 13							00 13		
Southampton Airport Pkwy ✈	d	21 53		21 58	22 27	22 34		22 53		22 58		23 27		00 27
Swaythling	d			22 01						23 01				
St Denys	d			22 04						23 04				00s31
Southampton Central ⛴	a	22 00		22 09	22 34	22 42	22 53	23 00		23 09		23 34		00 36
	d	22 03		22 10	22 35		22 57	23 03		23 10		23 35		00 37
Millbrook (Hants)	d			22 13						23 13				
Redbridge	d			22 16						23 16				
Romsey	d			22a24			23 09			23 24	23a33			
Mottisfont & Dunbridge	d									23 29				
Dean	d									23 35				
Salisbury	a						23 27			23 51				
Totton	d				22 41							23 41		00s42
Ashurst New Forest	d				22 45							23 45		
Beaulieu Road	d				22 50									
Brockenhurst 3	a	22 16			22 56			23 16				23 53		00s53
	d	22 17			22 57			23 17				23 54		
Lymington Town	d													
Lymington Pier	a													
Sway	d				23 01							23 59		
New Milton	d	22 24			23 06			23 24				00 04		01s01
Hinton Admiral	d				23 10							00 08		
Christchurch	d				23 15							00 13		01s08
Pokesdown	d				23 19							00 16		01s12
Bournemouth	a	22 34			23 23			23 34				00 20		01 16
	d	22 39			23 24			23 39				00 22		01 17
Branksome	d	22 44						23 44				00 27		01s22
Parkstone (Dorset)	d	22 47						23 47				00 30		01s25
Poole 4	a	22 50			23 33			23 50				00 34		01 29
	d	22 51						23 51						
Hamworthy	d	22 56						23 56						
Holton Heath	d													
Wareham	d	23 03						00 03						
Wool	d	23 10						00 10						
Moreton (Dorset)	d	23 16						00 16						
Dorchester South	d	23 25						00 24						
Dorchester West	d													
Upwey	d	23 32						00 31						
Weymouth	a	23 36						00 35						

A 🍴 to New Milton

Table 158

Sundays
7 August to 11 September

London - Basingstoke, Southampton, Romsey Lymington, Bournemouth and Weymouth

		SW	SW	SW	SW	SW	SW	SW	SW	SW	SW	SW	GW	SW	SW	SW	SW	SW	SW	GW	SW
		◇1	◇1	1	◇1	1	◇1	1	1	1	1	1		1	1	1	1	1	1	2	◇1
		A 🍴	🍴		🍴																
London Waterloo 15 ⊖	d	21p35	22p05		22p35	22p39	23p05		23p35	00 05	01 05										07 54
Clapham Junction 10	d		22b12			22b46	23b12		23b42	00u12											08u03
Woking	d	22p00	22p32		23p00		23p32		00 03	00 37	01 42										08 28
Farnborough (Main)	d					23p16			00 14		01s58										
Fleet	d					23p21			00 20		02s04										
Reading 7	d																				
Basingstoke	a		22p51			23p34	23p51		00 33	00 55	02s16										08 46
	d		22p52			23p36	23p52		00 35	00 56					07 48						08 48
Micheldever	d						00 02								07 58						08 58
Winchester	d	22p33	23p09		23p33	23p52	00 12		00 51	01 13	02s33				08 08						09 08
Shawford	d					23p57									08 12						
Romsey	d			23p09									08 19					08 35			
Chandlers Ford	d			23p16														08 42			
Eastleigh 3	a		23p17	23p22		00 02	00 20		00 59	01 21	02s42				08 18			08 47			09 18
	d		23p18	23p23		00 03	00 21	00 30	01 00	01 22					08 22 / 08 26			08 54			09 22 / 09 26
Hedge End	d							00s36							08 32						09 32
Botley	d							00s39							08 36						09 36
Fareham	d							00s47				07 44			08 44					09 32	09 44
Portchester	d							00s53				07 49			08 49						09 49
Cosham	d							00s57				07 54			08 54						09 54
Hilsea	a											08 00			09 00						10 04
Fratton	a							01s05				08 04			09 04						10 08
Portsmouth & Southsea	a							01s08				08 08			09 08						10 11
Portsmouth Harbour ⛴	a							01 12				08 13			09 13						10 15
Southampton Airport Pkwy ✈	d	22p42	23p22	23p27	23p42	00 08	00 25		01 05	01 26	02s46				08 27			08 58			09 27
Swaythling	d			23p30														09 01			
St Denys	d			23p33			00s29				02s51							09 04			
Southampton Central ⛴	a	22p49	23p29	23p38	23p49	00 15	00 34		01 12	01 35	02 56		08 29		08 34			09 09		09 53	09 34
	d	22p51	23p31	23p40	23p51		00 36			01 37					08 35		09 03	09 10		09 54	09 35
Millbrook (Hants)	d			23p42														09 13			
Redbridge	d			23p46														09 16			
Romsey	d			23p57														09 24		10 06	
Mottisfont & Dunbridge	d			00 02														09 29			
Dean	d			00 08														09 35			
Salisbury	a			00 20														09 49		10 24	
Totton	d		23p36				00s41			01s42					08 41						09 41
Ashurst New Forest	d		23p41												08 45						09 45
Beaulieu Road	d														08 50						09 50
Brockenhurst 3	a	23p04	23p49		00 04		00s52			01s53					08 56		09 16				09 56
	d	23p05	23p50		00 05										08 57	08 59	09 17		09 29		09 57
Lymington Town	d															09 07			09 37		
Lymington Pier	a															09 09			09 39		
Sway	d		23p54												09 01						10 01
New Milton	d		23p59				01s00			02s00					09 06		09 24				10 06
Hinton Admiral	d		00 03												09 10						10 10
Christchurch	d		00 08				01s07			02s07					09 15						10 15
Pokesdown	d		00 11				01s11			02s11					09 19						10 19
Bournemouth	a	23p25	00 15		00 21		01 15			02 15					09 23		09 34				10 23
	d	23p29	00 17		00 22		01 16							08 39	09 24		09 39				10 24
Branksome	d	23p35	00 23		00 27		01s21							08 44			09 44				
Parkstone (Dorset)	d	23p38	00 26		00 30		01s24							08 47			09 47				
Poole 4	a	23p41	00 30		00 35		01 29							08 50	09 33		09 50				10 33
	d	23p42												08 51			09 51				
Hamworthy	d	23p47												08 56			09 56				
Holton Heath	d																				
Wareham	d	23p54												09 03			10 03				
Wool	d	00 01												09 10			10 10				
Moreton (Dorset)	d	00 07												09 16			10 16				
Dorchester South	d	00 15												09 24			10 24				
Dorchester West	d																				
Upwey	d	00 21												09 31			10 31				
Weymouth	a	00 26												09 35			10 35				

A 🍴 to Brockenhurst

b Previous night, stops to pick up only

London - Basingstoke, Southampton, Romsey Lymington, Bournemouth and Weymouth

		SW [1]	GW	SW ◇[1]	SW [1]	SW [1]	SW ◇[1]		SW [1]	XC ◇[1] ⊼	GW	SW ◇[1]	SW [1]	SW [1]	SW ◇[1]		SW [1]	XC ◇[1] ⊼	GW ◇	SW ◇[1] A ⊼	SW [1]	SW [1]
London Waterloo [15] ⊖	d			08 35			08 54					09 35			09 54					10 35		
Clapham Junction [10]	d			08u45			09u03					09u45			10u03					10u45		
Woking	d			09 09			09 28					10 09			10 28					11 07		
Farnborough (Main)	d																					
Fleet	d																					
Reading [7]	d									09 51								10 51				
Basingstoke	a			09 28			09 46			10 09		10 28			10 46			11 09		11 26		
	d			09 29			09 48			10 10		10 29			10 48			11 10		11 28		
Micheldever	d						09 58								10 58							
Winchester	d			09 46			10 08			10 25		10 46			11 08			11 25		11 44		
Shawford	d						10 12															
Romsey	d				09 35								10 35								11 35	
Chandlers Ford	d				09 42								10 42								11 42	
Eastleigh [8]	a				09 48		10 18						10 48		11 18						11 48	
	d				09 54		10 22	10 26					10 54		11 22	11 26					11 54	
Hedge End	d							10 32								11 32						
Botley	d							10 36								11 36						
Fareham	d							10 44								11 44			11 32			
Portchester	d							10 49								11 49						
Cosham	d							10 54								11 54						
Hilsea	a							11 04								12 00						
Fratton	a							11 08								12 04						
Portsmouth & Southsea	a							11 11								12 08						
Portsmouth Harbour ⛴	a							11 15								12 13						
Southampton Airport Pkwy ✈	d			09 55	09 58		10 27			10 34		10 55	10 58		11 27			11 34		11 53	11 58	
Swaythling	d				10 01								11 01								12 01	
St Denys	d				10 04								11 04								12 04	
Southampton Central ⛴	a			10 02	10 09		10 34			10 42		11 02	11 09		11 34			11 42	11 53	11 59	12 09	
	d			10 03	10 10		10 35			10 45		11 03	11 10		11 35			11 45	11 54	12 03	12 10	
Millbrook (Hants)	d				10 13								11 13								12 13	
Redbridge	d				10 16								11 16								12 16	
Romsey	d				10 24								11 24						12 06		12 24	
Mottisfont & Dunbridge	d												11 29									
Dean	d												11 35									
Salisbury	a				10 42								11 48						12 24		12 42	
Totton	d						10 41								11 41							
Ashurst New Forest	d						10 45								11 45							
Beaulieu Road	d						10 50								11 50							
Brockenhurst [8]	a			10 17			10 56			11 02		11 17			11 56			12 02		12 16		
	d	09 59		10 18		10 29	10 57		10 59	11 02		11 18		11 29	11 57		11 59	12 03		12 17		12 29
Lymington Town	d	10 07				10 37			11 07					11 37			12 07					12 37
Lymington Pier	a	10 09				10 39			11 09					11 39			12 09					12 39
Sway	d						11 01								12 01							
New Milton	d			10 25			11 06					11 25			12 06					12 24		
Hinton Admiral	d						11 10								12 10							
Christchurch	d						11 15								12 15							
Pokesdown	d						11 19								12 19							
Bournemouth	a			10 35			11 23			11 26		11 35			12 23			12 26		12 34		
	d			10 39			11 24					11 39			12 24					12 39		
Branksome	d			10 44								11 44								12 44		
Parkstone (Dorset)	d			10 47								11 47								12 47		
Poole [4]	a			10 50			11 33					11 50			12 33					12 50		
	d			10 51								11 51								12 51		
Hamworthy	d			10 56								11 56								12 56		
Holton Heath	d																					
Wareham	d			11 03								12 03								13 03		
Wool	d			11 10								12 10								13 10		
Moreton (Dorset)	d			11 16								12 16								13 16		
Dorchester South	d			11 24								12 24								13 24		
Dorchester West	d		10 26								11 30											
Upwey	d		10 37	11 31							11 37	12 31								13 31		
Weymouth	a		10 42	11 35							11 43	12 35								13 35		

A ⊼ to New Milton

London - Basingstoke, Southampton, Romsey Lymington, Bournemouth and Weymouth

		SW ◇[1]		SW [1]	XC ◇[1] ⊼	GW ◇	SW ◇[1] A ⊼	SW [1]	SW [1]	SW ◇[1] ⊼		SW [1]	XC ◇[1] ⊼	GW ◇	SW ◇[1] A ⊼	SW [1]	SW [1]	SW ◇[1] ⊼		SW [1]	XC ◇[1] ⊼	GW ◇
London Waterloo [15] ⊖	d	10 54					11 35			11 54					12 35			12 54				
Clapham Junction [10]	d	11u04					11u45			12u04					12u42			13u03				
Woking	d	11 28					12 07			12 28					13 07			13 28				
Farnborough (Main)	d																					
Fleet	d																					
Reading [7]	d				11 51								12 51								13 51	
Basingstoke	a	11 46			12 09		12 26			12 46			13 09		13 26			13 46			14 09	
	d	11 48			12 10		12 28			12 48			13 10		13 28			13 48			14 10	
Micheldever	d	11 58								12 58								13 58				
Winchester	d	12 08			12 25		12 44			13 08			13 25		13 44			14 08			14 25	
Shawford	d	12 12																14 12				
Romsey	d							12 35								13 35						
Chandlers Ford	d							12 42								13 42						
Eastleigh [8]	a	12 18						12 48		13 18						13 48		14 18				
	d	12 22	12 26					12 54		13 22	13 26					13 54		14 22	14 26			
Hedge End	d		12 32								13 32								14 32			
Botley	d		12 36								13 36								14 36			
Fareham	d		12 44			12 32					13 44			13 32					14 44			14 32
Portchester	d		12 49								13 49								14 49			
Cosham	d		12 54								13 54								14 54			
Hilsea	a		13 00								14 00								15 00			
Fratton	a		13 04								14 04								15 04			
Portsmouth & Southsea	a		13 08								14 08								15 08			
Portsmouth Harbour ⛴	a		13 13								14 13								15 13			
Southampton Airport Pkwy ✈	d	12 27			12 34		12 53	12 58		13 27			13 34		13 53	13 58		14 27			14 34	
Swaythling	d							13 01								14 01						
St Denys	d							13 04								14 04						
Southampton Central ⛴	a	12 34			12 42	12 53	13 00	13 09		13 34			13 42	13 54	14 00	14 09		14 34			14 42	14 53
	d	12 35			12 45	12 54	13 03	13 10		13 35			13 45	13 54	14 03	14 10		14 35			14 45	14 54
Millbrook (Hants)	d							13 13								14 13						
Redbridge	d							13 16								14 16						
Romsey	d					13 06		13 24						14 06		14 24						15 06
Mottisfont & Dunbridge	d							13 29														
Dean	d							13 35														
Salisbury	a					13 24		13 48						14 24		14 42						15 24
Totton	d	12 41								13 41								14 41				
Ashurst New Forest	d	12 45								13 45								14 45				
Beaulieu Road	d	12 50								13 50								14 50				
Brockenhurst [8]	a	12 56			13 02		13 16			13 56			14 01		14 16			14 56			15 02	
	d	12 57		12 59	13 03		13 17		13 29	13 57		13 59	14 02		14 17		14 29	14 57		14 59	15 03	
Lymington Town	d			13 07					13 37			14 07					14 37			15 07		
Lymington Pier	a			13 09					13 39			14 09					14 39			15 09		
Sway	d	13 01								14 01								15 01				
New Milton	d	13 06					13 24			14 06					14 24			15 06				
Hinton Admiral	d	13 10								14 10								15 10				
Christchurch	d	13 15								14 15								15 15				
Pokesdown	d	13 19								14 19								15 19				
Bournemouth	a	13 23			13 26		13 34			14 23			14 26		14 34			15 23			15 26	
	d	13 24					13 39			14 24					14 39			15 24				
Branksome	d						13 44								14 44							
Parkstone (Dorset)	d						13 47								14 47							
Poole [4]	a	13 33					13 50			14 33					14 50			15 33				
	d						13 51								14 51							
Hamworthy	d						13 56								14 56							
Holton Heath	d																					
Wareham	d						14 03								15 03							
Wool	d						14 10								15 10							
Moreton (Dorset)	d						14 16								15 16							
Dorchester South	d						14 24								15 24							
Dorchester West	d																					
Upwey	d						14 31								15 31							
Weymouth	a						14 35								15 35							

A ⊼ to New Milton

Table 158

Sundays

7 August to 11 September

London - Basingstoke, Southampton, Romsey Lymington, Bournemouth and Weymouth

		GW	SW	SW	SW	SW	SW	XC	GW	SW	SW	SW	SW	SW	XC	GW	SW	SW	SW	GW	SW
			◇1 A ✕	1	1	◇1 ✕	1	◇1 ✕	■	◇1 A ✕	1	1	◇1 ✕	1	◇1 ✕	◇	◇1 A ✕	1	1	◇	1
London Waterloo [15] ⊖	d		13 35			13 54				14 35			14 54				15 35	15 37			
Clapham Junction [10]	d		13u42			14u03				14u42			15u03				15u42	15 46			
Woking	d		14 07			14 28				15 07			15 28				16 07	16 23			
Farnborough (Main)	d																	16 36			
Fleet	d																	16 41			
Reading [7]	d							14 51							15 51						
Basingstoke	a		14 26			14 46		15 09		15 26			15 46		16 09		16 26	16 54			
	d		14 28			14 48		15 10		15 28			15 48		16 10		16 28				
Micheldever	d					14 58							15 58								
Winchester	d		14 44			15 08		15 25		15 44			16 08		16 25		16 44				
Shawford	d												16 12								
Romsey	d			14 35							15 35								16 35		
Chandlers Ford	d			14 42							15 42								16 42		
Eastleigh [5]	a			14 48		15 18					15 48		16 18						16 48		
	d			14 54		15 22 / 15 26					15 54		16 22 / 16 26						16 54		
Hedge End	d					15 32							16 32								
Botley	d					15 36							16 36								
Fareham	d					15 44			15 32				16 44			16 32				17 03	
Portchester	d					15 49							16 49								
Cosham	d					15 54							16 54								
Hilsea	a					16 00							17 00								
Fratton	a					16 04							17 03								
Portsmouth & Southsea	a					16 08							17 08								
Portsmouth Harbour ⛴	a					16 13							17 13								
Southampton Airport Pkwy ✈	d		14 53	14 58		15 27		15 34		15 53	15 58		16 27		16 34		16 53		16 58		
Swaythling	d			15 01							16 01								17 01		
St Denys	d			15 04							16 04								17 04		
Southampton Central ⛴	a		15 00	15 09		15 34		15 42	15 53	16 00	16 09		16 34		16 42	16 53	17 00		17 09	17 24	
	d		15 03	15 10		15 35		15 45	15 54	16 03	16 10		16 35		16 45	16 54	17 03		17 10	17 26	
Millbrook (Hants)	d			15 13							16 13								17 13		
Redbridge	d			15 16							16 16								17 16		
Romsey	d			15 24					16 06		16 24					17 06			17 24	17 39	
Mottisfont & Dunbridge	d			15 29															17 29		
Dean	d			15 35															17 35		
Salisbury	a			15 48					16 24		16 42					17 24			17 48	18 01	
Totton	d					15 41							16 41								
Ashurst New Forest	d					15 45							16 45								
Beaulieu Road	d					15 50							16 50								
Brockenhurst [3]	a		15 16			15 56		16 02		16 16			16 56		17 02		17 16				
	d		15 17		15 29	15 57	15 59	16 03		16 17		16 29	16 57	16 59	17 03		17 17				17 29
Lymington Town	d				15 37		16 07					16 37		17 07							17 37
Lymington Pier	a				15 39		16 09					16 39		17 09							17 39
Sway	d					16 01							17 01								
New Milton	d		15 24			16 06				16 24			17 06				17 24				
Hinton Admiral	d					16 10							17 10								
Christchurch	d					16 15							17 15								
Pokesdown	d					16 19							17 19								
Bournemouth	a		15 34			16 23		16 26		16 34			17 23		17 26		17 34				
	d		15 39			16 24				16 39			17 24				17 39				
Branksome	d		15 44							16 44							17 44				
Parkstone (Dorset)	d		15 47							16 47							17 47				
Poole [4]	a		15 50			16 33				16 50			17 33				17 50				
	d		15 51							16 51							17 51				
Hamworthy	d		15 56							16 56							17 56				
Holton Heath	d																				
Wareham	d		16 03							17 03							18 03				
Wool	d		16 10							17 10							18 10				
Moreton (Dorset)	d		16 16							17 16							18 16				
Dorchester South	d		16 24							17 24							18 24				
Dorchester West	d	15 41																			
Upwey	d	15 50	16 31							17 31							18 31				
Weymouth	a	15 55	16 35							17 35							18 35				

A ✕ to New Milton

Table 158

Sundays

7 August to 11 September

London - Basingstoke, Southampton, Romsey Lymington, Bournemouth and Weymouth

		SW	SW	XC	GW	SW	SW	SW	SW	SW	SW	XC	GW	GW	SW	SW	SW	GW	SW	SW
		◇1 ✕	1	◇1 ✕	◇	◇1 A ✕	1	1	1	◇1 ✕	1	◇1 ✕	◇		◇1 A ✕	1	1	◇	1	◇1 ✕
London Waterloo [15] ⊖	d	15 54				16 35	16 37			16 54					17 35	17 37				17 54
Clapham Junction [10]	d	16u03				16u42	16 46			17u03					17u42	17 46				18u03
Woking	d	16 28				17 07	17 23			17 28					18 07	18 23				18 28
Farnborough (Main)	d						17 36									18 36				
Fleet	d						17 41									18 41				
Reading [7]	d			16 51								17 51								
Basingstoke	a	16 46		17 09		17 26	17 54			17 46		18 09			18 26	18 54				18 46
	d	16 48		17 10		17 28				17 48		18 10			18 28					18 48
Micheldever	d	16 58								17 58										18 58
Winchester	d	17 08		17 25		17 44				18 08		18 25			18 44					19 08
Shawford	d									18 12										
Romsey	d							17 35									18 35			
Chandlers Ford	d							17 42									18 42			
Eastleigh [5]	a	17 18						17 48		18 18							18 48			19 18
	d	17 22 / 17 26						17 54		18 22 / 18 26							18 54			19 22 / 19 26
Hedge End	d	17 32								18 32										19 32
Botley	d	17 36								18 36										19 36
Fareham	d	17 44			17 32					18 44			18 32					19 03		19 44
Portchester	d	17 49								18 49										19 49
Cosham	d	17 54								18 54										19 54
Hilsea	a	18 00								19 00										20 00
Fratton	a	18 04								19 03										20 04
Portsmouth & Southsea	a	18 08								19 08										20 08
Portsmouth Harbour ⛴	a	18 13								19 13										20 13
Southampton Airport Pkwy ✈	d	17 27		17 34		17 53		17 58		18 27		18 34			18 53		18 58			19 27
Swaythling	d							18 01									19 01			
St Denys	d							18 04									19 04			
Southampton Central ⛴	a	17 34		17 40	17 53	18 00		18 09		18 34		18 42	18 53		19 00		19 09	19 24		19 34
	d	17 35		17 45	17 54	18 03		18 10		18 35		18 45	18 54		19 03		19 10	19 30		19 35
Millbrook (Hants)	d							18 13									19 13			
Redbridge	d							18 16									19 16			
Romsey	d				18 06			18 24					19 06				19 24	19 42		
Mottisfont & Dunbridge	d																19 29			
Dean	d																19 35			
Salisbury	a				18 24			18 42					19 24				19 48	20 00		
Totton	d	17 41								18 41										19 41
Ashurst New Forest	d	17 45								18 45										19 45
Beaulieu Road	d	17 50								18 50										19 50
Brockenhurst [3]	a	17 56		18 02		18 16				18 56		19 01			19 16					19 56
	d	17 57	17 59	18 03		18 17			18 29	18 57	18 59	19 02			19 17				19 29	19 57
Lymington Town	d		18 07						18 37		19 07								19 37	
Lymington Pier	a		18 09						18 39		19 09								19 39	
Sway	d	18 01								19 01										20 01
New Milton	d	18 06				18 24				19 06					19 24					20 06
Hinton Admiral	d	18 10								19 10										20 10
Christchurch	d	18 15								19 15										20 15
Pokesdown	d	18 19								19 19										20 19
Bournemouth	a	18 23		18 26		18 34				19 23		19 26			19 34					20 23
	d	18 24				18 39				19 24					19 39					20 24
Branksome	d					18 44									19 44					
Parkstone (Dorset)	d					18 47									19 47					
Poole [4]	a	18 33				18 50				19 33					19 50					20 33
	d					18 51									19 51					
Hamworthy	d					18 56									19 56					
Holton Heath	d																			
Wareham	d					19 03									20 03					
Wool	d					19 10									20 10					
Moreton (Dorset)	d					19 16									20 16					
Dorchester South	d					19 24									20 25					
Dorchester West	d													19 47						
Upwey	d					19 31								19 55	20 32					
Weymouth	a					19 35								20 01	20 36					

A ✕ to New Milton

London - Basingstoke, Southampton, Romsey Lymington, Bournemouth and Weymouth

		SW	XC	GW	SW	SW	SW	SW	SW		SW	XC	GW	SW	SW	SW	SW	SW		SW	XC	GW
		1	◇1 ✠	◇	◇1 A ✠	1	1	1	◇1 ✠		1	◇1 ✠	◇	◇1 A ✠	1	1	1	◇1		1	◇1	
London Waterloo 15 ⊖	d				18 35	18 37			18 54					19 35	19 37			19 54				
Clapham Junction 10	d				18u42	18 46			19u03					19u42	19 46			20u03				
Woking	d				19 07	19 23			19 28					20 07	20 23			20 28				
Farnborough (Main)	d					19 36									20 36							
Fleet	d					19 41									20 41							
Reading 7	d		18 51									19 51									20 51	
Basingstoke	a		19 09		19 26	19 54			19 46			20 09		20 26	20 54			20 46			21 09	
	d		19 10		19 28				19 48			20 10		20 28				20 48			21 10	
Micheldever	d								19 58									20 58				
Winchester	d		19 25		19 44				20 08			20 25		20 44				21 08			21 25	
Shawford	d								20 12													
Romsey	d						19 35									20 35						
Chandlers Ford	d						19 42									20 42						
Eastleigh 8	a						19 48		20 18							20 48		21 18				
	d						19 54		20 22	20 26						20 54		21 22	21 26			
Hedge End	d									20 32									21 32			
Botley	d									20 36									21 36			
Fareham	d			19 32						20 44			20 32						21 44			
Portchester	d									20 49									21 49			
Cosham	d									20 54									21 54			
Hilsea	a									21 00									22 00			
Fratton	a									21 04									22 04			
Portsmouth & Southsea	a									21 08									22 08			
Portsmouth Harbour ⛴	a									21 13									22 13			
Southampton Airport Pkwy ✈	d		19 34		19 53		19 58		20 27			20 34		20 53		20 58		21 27			21 34	
Swaythling	d						20 01									21 01						
St Denys	d						20 04									21 04						
Southampton Central ⛴	a		19 40	19 53	20 00		20 09		20 34			20 42	20 53	21 00		21 09		21 34			21 43	
	d		19 45	19 54	20 03		20 10		20 35			20 45	20 54	21 03		21 10		21 35			21 45	
Millbrook (Hants)	d						20 13									21 13						
Redbridge	d						20 16									21 16						
Romsey	d			20 06			20 24						21 06			21 24						
Mottisfont & Dunbridge	d															21 29						
Dean	d															21 35						
Salisbury	a			20 24			20 42						21 24			21 48						
Totton	d								20 41									21 41				
Ashurst New Forest	d								20 45									21 45				
Beaulieu Road	d								20 50									21 50				
Brockenhurst 3	a		20 02		20 16				20 56			21 02		21 16				21 56			22 02	
	d	19 59	20 03		20 17			20 29	20 57		20 59	21 03		21 17			21 29	21 57		21 59	22 03	
Lymington Town	d	20 07						20 37			21 07						21 37			22 07		
Lymington Pier	a	20 09						20 39			21 09						21 39			22 09		
Sway	d								21 01									22 01				
New Milton	d				20 24				21 06					21 24				22 06				
Hinton Admiral	d								21 10									22 10				
Christchurch	d								21 15									22 15				
Pokesdown	d								21 19									22 19				
Bournemouth	a		20 26		20 34				21 23			21 26		21 34				22 23			22 26	
	d				20 39				21 24					21 39				22 24				
Branksome	d				20 44									21 44								
Parkstone (Dorset)	d				20 47									21 47								
Poole 4	a				20 50				21 33					21 50				22 33				
	d				20 51									21 51								
Hamworthy	d				20 56									21 56								
Holton Heath	d																					
Wareham	d				21 03									22 03								
Wool	d				21 10									22 10								
Moreton (Dorset)	d				21 16									22 16								
Dorchester South	d				21 25									22 25								
Dorchester West	d																					22 53
Upwey	d				21 32									22 32								23 01
Weymouth	a				21 36									22 36								23 06

A ✠ to New Milton

7 August to 11 September

London - Basingstoke, Southampton, Romsey Lymington, Bournemouth and Weymouth

		SW	SW	SW	SW		XC	GW	SW	SW	SW	SW	SW		SW	SW
		◇1 A ✠	1	1	◇1		◇1		◇1 A ✠	1	1	1	◇1		1	◇1 ✠
London Waterloo 15 ⊖	d	20 35	20 37		20 54				21 35	21 37			21 54		22 37	22 54
Clapham Junction 10	d	20u42	20 46		21u03				21u42	21 46			22u03		22 46	23u03
Woking	d	21 07	21 23		21 28				22 07	22 23			22 28		23 23	23 28
Farnborough (Main)	d		21 36							22 36					23 36	
Fleet	d		21 41							22 41					23 41	
Reading 7	d						21 51									
Basingstoke	a	21 26	21 54		21 46		22 09		22 26	22 54			22 46		23 54	23 46
	d	21 28			21 48		22 10		22 28				22 48			23 48
Micheldever	d				21 58								22 58			23 58
Winchester	d	21 44			22 08		22 26		22 44				23 08			00 08
Shawford	d				22 12											
Romsey	d			21 35							22 35	22 28				
Chandlers Ford	d			21 42							22 42					
Eastleigh 8	a			21 48	22 18						22 48	23 19	23 17			00 18
	d			21 54	22 22	22 26					22 54	23 21	23 22	23 26		00 22
Hedge End	d					22 32								23 32		
Botley	d					22 36								23 36		
Fareham	d					22 44		22 32						23 44		
Portchester	d					22 49								23 49		
Cosham	d					22 54								23 54		
Hilsea	a					23 00								23 59		
Fratton	a					23 04								00 04		
Portsmouth & Southsea	a					23 08								00 08		
Portsmouth Harbour ⛴	a					23 13								00 13		
Southampton Airport Pkwy ✈	d	21 53		21 58	22 27		22 34		22 53		22 58		23 27			00 27
Swaythling	d			22 01							23 01					
St Denys	d			22 04							23 04					00s31
Southampton Central ⛴	a	22 00		22 09	22 34		22 42	22 53	23 00		23 09		23 34			00 36
	d	22 03		22 10	22 35			22 57	23 03		23 10		23 35			00 37
Millbrook (Hants)	d			22 13							23 13					
Redbridge	d			22 16							23 16					
Romsey	d			22a24				23 09			23 24	23a33				
Mottisfont & Dunbridge	d										23 29					
Dean	d										23 35					
Salisbury	a							23 27			23 51					
Totton	d				22 41								23 41			00s42
Ashurst New Forest	d				22 45								23 45			
Beaulieu Road	d				22 50											
Brockenhurst 3	a	22 16			22 56				23 16				23 53			00s53
	d	22 17			22 57				23 17				23 54			
Lymington Town	d															
Lymington Pier	a															
Sway	d				23 01								23 59			
New Milton	d	22 24			23 06				23 24				00 04			01s01
Hinton Admiral	d				23 10								00 08			
Christchurch	d				23 15								00 13			01s08
Pokesdown	d				23 19								00 16			01s12
Bournemouth	a	22 34			23 23				23 34				00 20			01 16
	d	22 39			23 24				23 39				00 22			01 17
Branksome	d	22 44							23 44				00 27			01s22
Parkstone (Dorset)	d	22 47							23 47				00 30			01s25
Poole 4	a	22 50			23 33				23 50				00 34			01 29
	d	22 51							23 51							
Hamworthy	d	22 56							23 56							
Holton Heath	d															
Wareham	d	23 03							00 03							
Wool	d	23 10							00 10							
Moreton (Dorset)	d	23 16							00 16							
Dorchester South	d	23 25							00 24							
Dorchester West	d															
Upwey	d	23 32							00 31							
Weymouth	a	23 36							00 35							

A ✠ to New Milton

Table 158

Sundays
18 September to 23 October

London - Basingstoke, Southampton, Romsey Lymington, Bournemouth and Weymouth

		SW	SW	SW	SW	SW	SW	SW	SW	SW	SW	SW	GW	SW	SW		SW	SW	SW	SW	GW	SW	
		◇1 A ⊤	◇1 ⊤	1	◇1 ⊤	1	◇1	1	1	1	1	1		1	1		1	1	1	1	■	◇1	
London Waterloo [15] ⊖	d	21p35	22p05		22p35	22p39	23p05		23p35	00 05	01 05											07 54	
Clapham Junction [10]	d		22b12			22b46	23b12		23b42	00u12												08u03	
Woking	d	22p00	22p32		23p00		23p32		00 03	00 37	01 42											08 28	
Farnborough (Main)	d					23p16			00 14		01s58												
Fleet	d					23p21			00 20		02s04												
Reading [7]	d																						
Basingstoke	a		22p51			23p34	23p51		00 33	00 55	02s16											08 46	
	d		22p52			23p36	23p52		00 35	00 56					07 48							08 48	
Micheldever	d						00 02								07 58							08 58	
Winchester	d	22p33	23p09		23p33	23p52	00 12		00 51	01 13	02s33				08 08							09 08	
Shawford	d					23p57									08 12								
Romsey	d			23p09									08 19						08 35				
Chandlers Ford	d			23p16															08 42				
Eastleigh [8]	a		23p17	23p22		00 02	00 20		00 59	01 21	02s42				08 18				08 47			09 18	
	d		23p18	23p23		00 03	00 21	00 30	01 00	01 22					08 22	08 26			08 54			09 22	09 26
Hedge End	d							00s36								08 32							09 32
Botley	d							00s39								08 36							09 36
Fareham	d							00s47				07 44				08 44					09 32		09 44
Portchester	d							00s53				07 49				08 49							09 49
Cosham	d							00s57				07 54				08 54							09 54
Hilsea	a											08 00				09 00							10 04
Fratton	a							01s05				08 04				09 04							10 08
Portsmouth & Southsea	a							01s08				08 08				09 08							10 11
Portsmouth Harbour ⛴	a							01 12				08 13				09 13							10 15
Southampton Airport Pkwy ✈	d	22p42	23p22	23p27	23p42	00 08	00 25		01 05	01 26	02s46				08 27				08 58			09 27	
Swaythling	d			23p30															09 01				
St Denys	d			23p33			00s29				02s51								09 04				
Southampton Central ⛴	a	22p49	23p29	23p38	23p49	00 15	00 34		01 12	01 35	02 56		08 29		08 34				09 09		09 53	09 34	
	d	22p51	23p31	23p40	23p51		00 36			01 37					08 35			09 03	09 10		09 54	09 35	
Millbrook (Hants)	d			23p42															09 13				
Redbridge	d			23p46															09 16				
Romsey	d			23p57															09 24		10 06		
Mottisfont & Dunbridge	d			00 02															09 29				
Dean	d			00 08															09 35				
Salisbury	a			00 20															09 49		10 24		
Totton	d		23p36				00s41			01s42					08 41							09 41	
Ashurst New Forest	d		23p41												08 45							09 45	
Beaulieu Road	d														08 50							09 50	
Brockenhurst [3]	a	23p04	23p49		00 04		00s52			01s53					08 56			09 16				09 56	
	d	23p05	23p50		00 05										08 57		08 59	09 17		09 29		09 57	
Lymington Town	d																09 07			09 37			
Lymington Pier	a																09 09			09 39			
Sway	d		23p54												09 01							10 01	
New Milton	d		23p59				01s00			02s00					09 06			09 24				10 06	
Hinton Admiral	d		00 03												09 10							10 10	
Christchurch	d		00 08				01s07			02s07					09 15							10 15	
Pokesdown	d		00 11				01s11			02s11					09 19							10 19	
Bournemouth	a	23p25	00 15		00 21		01 15			02 15					09 23			09 34				10 23	
	d	23p29	00 17		00 22		01 16							08 39	09 24			09 39				10 24	
Branksome	d	23p35	00 23		00 27		01s21							08 44				09 44					
Parkstone (Dorset)	d	23p38	00 26		00 30		01s24							08 47				09 47					
Poole [4]	a	23p41	00 30		00 35		01 29							08 50	09 33			09 50				10 33	
	d	23p42												08 51				09 51					
Hamworthy	d	23p47												08 56				09 56					
Holton Heath	d																						
Wareham	d	23p54												09 03				10 03					
Wool	d	00 01												09 10				10 10					
Moreton (Dorset)	d	00 07												09 16				10 16					
Dorchester South	d	00 15												09 24				10 24					
Dorchester West	d																						
Upwey	d	00 21												09 31				10 31					
Weymouth	a	00 26												09 35				10 35					

A ⊤ to Brockenhurst

b Previous night, stops to pick up only

Table 158

Sundays
18 September to 23 October

London - Basingstoke, Southampton, Romsey Lymington, Bournemouth and Weymouth

		SW	SW	SW	SW	SW		SW	XC	SW	SW	SW	SW		SW	XC	GW	SW	SW	SW	SW		SW
		1	◇1	1	1	◇1		1	◇1 ⊤	◇1	1	1	◇1		1	◇1 ⊤	◇	◇1 A ⊤	1	1	◇1		1
London Waterloo [15] ⊖	d		08 35			08 54				09 35			09 54					10 35			10 54		
Clapham Junction [10]	d		08u45			09u03				09u45			10u03					10u45			11u04		
Woking	d		09 09			09 28				10 09			10 28					11 07			11 28		
Farnborough (Main)	d																						
Fleet	d																						
Reading [7]	d								09 51							10 51							
Basingstoke	a		09 28			09 46			10 09	10 28			10 46			11 09		11 26			11 46		
	d		09 29			09 48			10 10	10 29			10 48			11 10		11 28			11 48		
Micheldever	d					09 58							10 58								11 58		
Winchester	d		09 46			10 08			10 25	10 46			11 08			11 25		11 44			12 08		
Shawford	d					10 12															12 12		
Romsey	d			09 35							10 35								11 35				
Chandlers Ford	d			09 42							10 42								11 42				
Eastleigh [8]	a			09 48		10 18					10 48		11 18						11 48		12 18		
	d			09 54		10 22	10 26				10 54		11 22	11 26					11 54		12 22	12 26	
Hedge End	d						10 32							11 32								12 32	
Botley	d						10 36							11 36								12 36	
Fareham	d						10 44							11 44			11 32					12 44	
Portchester	d						10 49							11 49								12 49	
Cosham	d						10 54							11 54								12 54	
Hilsea	a						11 04							12 00								13 00	
Fratton	a						11 08							12 04								13 04	
Portsmouth & Southsea	a						11 11							12 08								13 08	
Portsmouth Harbour ⛴	a						11 15							12 13								13 13	
Southampton Airport Pkwy ✈	d		09 55	09 58		10 27			10 34	10 55	10 58		11 27			11 34		11 53	11 58		12 27		
Swaythling	d			10 01							11 01								12 01				
St Denys	d			10 04							11 04								12 04				
Southampton Central ⛴	a		10 02	10 09		10 34			10 42	11 02	11 09		11 34			11 42	11 53	11 59	12 09		12 34		
	d		10 03	10 10		10 35			10 45	11 03	11 10		11 35			11 45	11 54	12 03	12 10		12 35		
Millbrook (Hants)	d			10 13							11 13								12 13				
Redbridge	d			10 16							11 16								12 16				
Romsey	d			10 24							11 24						12 06		12 24				
Mottisfont & Dunbridge	d										11 29												
Dean	d										11 35												
Salisbury	a			10 42							11 48						12 24		12 42				
Totton	d					10 41							11 41								12 41		
Ashurst New Forest	d					10 45							11 45								12 45		
Beaulieu Road	d					10 50							11 50								12 50		
Brockenhurst [3]	a		10 17			10 56			11 02	11 17			11 56			12 02		12 16			12 56		
	d	09 59	10 18		10 29	10 57		10 59	11 02	11 18		11 29	11 57		11 59	12 03		12 17		12 29	12 57		12 59
Lymington Town	d	10 07			10 37			11 07				11 37			12 07					12 37			13 07
Lymington Pier	a	10 09			10 39			11 09				11 39			12 09					12 39			13 09
Sway	d					11 01							12 01								13 01		
New Milton	d		10 25			11 06				11 25			12 06					12 24			13 06		
Hinton Admiral	d					11 10							12 10								13 10		
Christchurch	d					11 15							12 15								13 15		
Pokesdown	d					11 19							12 19								13 19		
Bournemouth	a		10 35			11 23			11 26	11 35			12 23			12 26		12 34			13 23		
	d		10 39			11 24				11 39			12 24					12 39			13 24		
Branksome	d		10 44							11 44								12 44					
Parkstone (Dorset)	d		10 47							11 47								12 47					
Poole [4]	a		10 50			11 33				11 50			12 33					12 50			13 33		
	d		10 51							11 51								12 51					
Hamworthy	d		10 56							11 56								12 56					
Holton Heath	d																						
Wareham	d		11 03							12 03								13 03					
Wool	d		11 10							12 10								13 10					
Moreton (Dorset)	d		11 16							12 16								13 16					
Dorchester South	d		11 24							12 24								13 24					
Dorchester West	d																						
Upwey	d		11 31							12 31								13 31					
Weymouth	a		11 35							12 35								13 35					

A ⊤ to New Milton

London - Basingstoke, Southampton, Romsey Lymington, Bournemouth and Weymouth

		XC	GW		SW	SW	SW	SW		SW	XC	GW	SW		SW	SW	SW		SW	XC	GW	GW	SW		SW
		◇[1]	◇		◇[1]	[1]	[1]	◇[1]		[1]	◇[1]	◇	◇[1]		[1]	[1]	◇[1]		[1]	◇[1]	◇		◇[1]		[1]
					A								A										A		
		⏉			⏉			⏉			⏉		⏉				⏉			⏉			⏉		
London Waterloo [15] ⊖	d				11 35			11 54					12 35				12 54						13 35		
Clapham Junction [10]	d				11u45			12u04					12u42				13u03						13u42		
Woking	d				12 07			12 28					13 07				13 28						14 07		
Farnborough (Main)	d																								
Fleet	d																								
Reading [7]	d	11 51									12 51									13 51					
Basingstoke	a	12 09			12 26			12 46			13 09		13 26				13 46			14 09			14 26		
	d	12 10			12 28			12 48			13 10		13 28				13 48			14 10			14 28		
Micheldever	d							12 58									13 58								
Winchester	d	12 25			12 44			13 08			13 25		13 44				14 08			14 25			14 44		
Shawford	d																14 12								
Romsey	d					12 35									13 35										14 35
Chandlers Ford	d					12 42									13 42										14 42
Eastleigh [8]	a					12 48		13 18							13 48		14 18								14 48
	d					12 54		13 22	13 26						13 54		14 22	14 26							14 54
Hedge End	d								13 32									14 32							
Botley	d								13 36									14 36							
Fareham	d		12 32						13 44			13 32						14 44			14 32				
Portchester	d								13 49									14 49							
Cosham	d								13 54									14 54							
Hilsea	a								14 00									15 00							
Fratton	a								14 04									15 04							
Portsmouth & Southsea	a								14 08									15 08							
Portsmouth Harbour ⛴	a								14 13									15 13							
Southampton Airport Pkwy ✈	d	12 34			12 53	12 58		13 27			13 34		13 53		13 58		14 27			14 34			14 53		14 58
Swaythling	d					13 01									14 01										15 01
St Denys	d					13 04									14 04										15 04
Southampton Central ⛴	a	12 42	12 53		13 00	13 09		13 34			13 42	13 54	14 00		14 09		14 34			14 42	14 53		15 00		15 09
	d	12 45	12 54		13 03	13 10		13 35			13 45	13 54	14 03		14 10		14 35			14 45	14 54		15 03		15 10
Millbrook (Hants)	d					13 13									14 13										15 13
Redbridge	d					13 16									14 16										15 16
Romsey	d		13 06			13 24						14 06			14 24						15 06				15 24
Mottisfont & Dunbridge	d					13 29																			15 29
Dean	d					13 35																			15 35
Salisbury	a		13 24			13 48						14 24			14 42						15 24				15 48
Totton	d							13 41									14 41								
Ashurst New Forest	d							13 45									14 45								
Beaulieu Road	d							13 50									14 50								
Brockenhurst [3]	a	13 02			13 16			13 56			14 01		14 16				14 56			15 02			15 16		
	d	13 03			13 17		13 29	13 57		13 59	14 02		14 17			14 29	14 57		14 59	15 03			15 17		
Lymington Town	d						13 37			14 07						14 37			15 07						
Lymington Pier	a						13 39			14 09						14 39			15 09						
Sway	d							14 01									15 01								
New Milton	d				13 24			14 06					14 24				15 06						15 24		
Hinton Admiral	d							14 10									15 10								
Christchurch	d							14 15									15 15								
Pokesdown	d							14 19									15 19								
Bournemouth	a	13 26			13 34			14 23			14 26		14 34				15 23			15 26			15 34		
	d				13 39			14 24					14 39				15 24						15 39		
Branksome	d				13 44								14 44										15 44		
Parkstone (Dorset)	d				13 47								14 47										15 47		
Poole [4]	a				13 50			14 33					14 50				15 33						15 50		
	d				13 51								14 51										15 51		
Hamworthy	d				13 56								14 56										15 56		
Holton Heath	d																								
Wareham	d				14 03								15 03										16 03		
Wool	d				14 10								15 10										16 10		
Moreton (Dorset)	d				14 16								15 16										16 16		
Dorchester South	d				14 24								15 24										16 24		
Dorchester West	d																					16 01			
Upwey	d				14 31								15 31									16 10	16 31		
Weymouth	a				14 35								15 35									16 15	16 35		

A ⏉ to New Milton

London - Basingstoke, Southampton, Romsey Lymington, Bournemouth and Weymouth

		SW	SW		SW	XC	GW	SW	SW		SW	SW		SW	XC	GW	SW	SW	SW		GW	SW	SW		SW
		[1]	◇[1]		[1]	◇[1]	■	◇[1]	[1]		[1]	◇[1]		[1]	◇[1]	◇	◇[1]	[1]	[1]		◇	[1]	◇[1]		[1]
								A									A								
			⏉			⏉		⏉				⏉			⏉		⏉						⏉		
London Waterloo [15] ⊖	d		13 54					14 35				14 54					15 35	15 37					15 54		
Clapham Junction [10]	d		14u03					14u42				15u03					15u42	15 46					16u03		
Woking	d		14 28					15 07				15 28					16 07	16 23					16 28		
Farnborough (Main)	d																	16 36							
Fleet	d																	16 41							
Reading [7]	d					14 51									15 51										
Basingstoke	a		14 46			15 09		15 26				15 46			16 09		16 26	16 54					16 46		
	d		14 48			15 10		15 28				15 48			16 10		16 28						16 48		
Micheldever	d		14 58									15 58											16 58		
Winchester	d		15 08			15 25		15 44				16 08			16 25		16 44						17 08		
Shawford	d											16 12													
Romsey	d								15 35										16 35						
Chandlers Ford	d								15 42										16 42						
Eastleigh [8]	a		15 18						15 48			16 18							16 48				17 18		
	d		15 22	15 26					15 54			16 22	16 26						16 54				17 22	17 26	
Hedge End	d			15 32									16 32											17 32	
Botley	d			15 36									16 36											17 36	
Fareham	d			15 44			15 32						16 44			16 32					17 03			17 44	
Portchester	d			15 49									16 49											17 49	
Cosham	d			15 54									16 54											17 54	
Hilsea	a			16 00									17 00											18 00	
Fratton	a			16 04									17 03											18 04	
Portsmouth & Southsea	a			16 08									17 08											18 08	
Portsmouth Harbour ⛴	a			16 13									17 13											18 13	
Southampton Airport Pkwy ✈	d		15 27			15 34		15 53	15 58			16 27			16 34		16 53		16 58				17 27		
Swaythling	d								16 01										17 01						
St Denys	d								16 04										17 04						
Southampton Central ⛴	a		15 34			15 42	15 53	16 00	16 09			16 34			16 42	16 53	17 00		17 09		17 24		17 34		
	d		15 35			15 45	15 54	16 03	16 10			16 35			16 45	16 54	17 03		17 10		17 26		17 35		
Millbrook (Hants)	d								16 13										17 13						
Redbridge	d								16 16										17 16						
Romsey	d						16 06		16 24							17 06			17 24		17 39				
Mottisfont & Dunbridge	d																		17 29						
Dean	d																		17 35						
Salisbury	a						16 24		16 42							17 24			17 48		18 01				
Totton	d		15 41									16 41											17 41		
Ashurst New Forest	d		15 45									16 45											17 45		
Beaulieu Road	d		15 50									16 50											17 50		
Brockenhurst [3]	a		15 56			16 02		16 16				16 56			17 02		17 16						17 56		
	d	15 29	15 57		15 59	16 03		16 17			16 29	16 57		16 59	17 03		17 17					17 29	17 57		17 59
Lymington Town	d	15 37			16 07						16 37			17 07								17 37			18 07
Lymington Pier	a	15 39			16 09						16 39			17 09								17 39			18 09
Sway	d		16 01									17 01											18 01		
New Milton	d		16 06					16 24				17 06					17 24						18 06		
Hinton Admiral	d		16 10									17 10											18 10		
Christchurch	d		16 15									17 15											18 15		
Pokesdown	d		16 19									17 19											18 19		
Bournemouth	a		16 23			16 26		16 34				17 23			17 26		17 34						18 23		
	d		16 24					16 39				17 24					17 39						18 24		
Branksome	d							16 44									17 44								
Parkstone (Dorset)	d							16 47									17 47								
Poole [4]	a		16 33					16 50				17 33					17 50						18 33		
	d							16 51									17 51								
Hamworthy	d							16 56									17 56								
Holton Heath	d																								
Wareham	d							17 03									18 03								
Wool	d							17 10									18 10								
Moreton (Dorset)	d							17 16									18 16								
Dorchester South	d							17 24									18 24								
Dorchester West	d																								
Upwey	d							17 31									18 31								
Weymouth	a							17 35									18 35								

A ⏉ to New Milton

Table 158

Sundays

18 September to 23 October

London - Basingstoke, Southampton, Romsey Lymington, Bournemouth and Weymouth

		XC	GW	SW	SW	SW	SW	SW		SW	XC	GW	GW	SW	SW	SW	GW	SW	SW		SW	XC	GW
		◇1	◇	◇1	1	1	1	◇1		1	◇1	◇		◇1	1	1	◇	1	◇1		1	◇1	◇
				A										A									
		✠		✠				✠			✠			✠					✠			✠	
London Waterloo 15 ⊖	d			16 35	16 37			16 54						17 35	17 37				17 54				
Clapham Junction 10	d			16u42	16 46			17u03						17u42	17 46				18u03				
Woking	d			17 07	17 23			17 28						18 07	18 23				18 28				
Farnborough (Main)	d				17 36										18 36								
Fleet	d				17 41										18 41								
Reading 7	d	16 51									17 51											18 51	
Basingstoke	a	17 09		17 26	17 54			17 46			18 09			18 26	18 54				18 46			19 09	
	d	17 10		17 28				17 48			18 10			18 28					18 48			19 10	
Micheldever	d							17 58											18 58				
Winchester	d	17 25		17 44				18 08			18 25			18 44					19 08			19 25	
Shawford	d							18 12															
Romsey	d					17 35										18 35							
Chandlers Ford	d					17 42										18 42							
Eastleigh 3	a					17 48		18 18								18 48			19 18				
	d					17 54		18 22	18 26							18 54			19 22	19 26			
Hedge End	d								18 32											19 32			
Botley	d								18 36											19 36			
Fareham	d		17 32						18 44			18 32					19 03			19 44			19 32
Portchester	d								18 49											19 49			
Cosham	d								18 54											19 54			
Hilsea	a								19 00											20 00			
Fratton	a								19 03											20 04			
Portsmouth & Southsea	a								19 08											20 08			
Portsmouth Harbour ⛴	a								19 13											20 13			
Southampton Airport Pkwy ✈	d	17 34		17 53		17 58		18 27			18 34			18 53		18 58			19 27			19 34	
Swaythling	d					18 01										19 01							
St Denys	d					18 04										19 04							
Southampton Central ⛴	a	17 40	17 53	18 00		18 09		18 34			18 42	18 53		19 00		19 09	19 24		19 34			19 40	19 53
	d	17 45	17 54	18 03		18 10		18 35			18 45	18 54		19 03		19 10	19 30		19 35			19 45	19 54
Millbrook (Hants)	d					18 13										19 13							
Redbridge	d					18 16										19 16							
Romsey	d		18 06			18 24						19 06				19 24	19 42						20 06
Mottisfont & Dunbridge	d															19 29							
Dean	d															19 35							
Salisbury	a		18 24			18 42						19 24				19 48	20 00						20 24
Totton	d							18 41											19 41				
Ashurst New Forest	d							18 45											19 45				
Beaulieu Road	d							18 50											19 50				
Brockenhurst 3	a	18 02		18 16				18 56			19 01			19 16					19 56			20 02	
	d	18 03		18 17			18 29	18 57		18 59	19 02			19 17				19 29	19 57		19 59	20 03	
Lymington Town	d						18 37			19 07								19 37			20 07		
Lymington Pier	a						18 39			19 09								19 39			20 09		
Sway	d							19 01											20 01				
New Milton	d			18 24				19 06						19 24					20 06				
Hinton Admiral	d							19 10											20 10				
Christchurch	d							19 15											20 15				
Pokesdown	d							19 19											20 19				
Bournemouth	a	18 26		18 34				19 23			19 26			19 34					20 23			20 26	
	d			18 39				19 24						19 39					20 24				
Branksome	d			18 44										19 44									
Parkstone (Dorset)	d			18 47										19 47									
Poole 4	a			18 50				19 33						19 50					20 33				
	d			18 51										19 51									
Hamworthy	d			18 56										19 56									
Holton Heath	d																						
Wareham	d			19 03										20 03									
Wool	d			19 10										20 10									
Moreton (Dorset)	d			19 16										20 16									
Dorchester South	d			19 24										20 25									
Dorchester West	d												19 47										
Upwey	d			19 31									19 55	20 32									
Weymouth	a			19 35									20 01	20 36									

A ✠ to New Milton

Table 158

Sundays

18 September to 23 October

London - Basingstoke, Southampton, Romsey Lymington, Bournemouth and Weymouth

		SW	SW	SW	SW	SW		SW	XC	GW	SW	SW	SW	SW	SW		SW	XC	GW	SW	SW	SW
		◇1	1	1	1	◇1		1	◇1	◇	◇1	1	1	1	◇1		1	◇1		◇1	1	1
		A									A									A		
		✠				✠			✠		✠				✠					✠		
London Waterloo 15 ⊖	d	18 35	18 37			18 54					19 35	19 37			19 54					20 35	20 37	
Clapham Junction 10	d	18u42	18 46			19u03					19u42	19 46			20u03					20u42	20 46	
Woking	d	19 07	19 23			19 28					20 07	20 23			20 28					21 07	21 23	
Farnborough (Main)	d		19 36									20 36									21 36	
Fleet	d		19 41									20 41									21 41	
Reading 7	d								19 51									20 51				
Basingstoke	a	19 26	19 54			19 46			20 09		20 26	20 54			20 46			21 09		21 26	21 54	
	d	19 28				19 48			20 10		20 28				20 48			21 10		21 28		
Micheldever	d					19 58									20 58							
Winchester	d	19 44				20 08			20 25		20 44				21 08			21 25		21 44		
Shawford	d					20 12																
Romsey	d			19 35									20 35									21 35
Chandlers Ford	d			19 42									20 42									21 42
Eastleigh 3	a			19 48		20 18							20 48		21 18							21 48
	d			19 54		20 22	20 26						20 54		21 22	21 26						21 54
Hedge End	d						20 32									21 32						
Botley	d						20 36									21 36						
Fareham	d						20 44			20 32						21 44						
Portchester	d						20 49									21 49						
Cosham	d						20 54									21 54						
Hilsea	a						21 00									22 00						
Fratton	a						21 04									22 04						
Portsmouth & Southsea	a						21 08									22 08						
Portsmouth Harbour ⛴	a						21 13									22 13						
Southampton Airport Pkwy ✈	d	19 53		19 58		20 27			20 34		20 53		20 58		21 27			21 34		21 53		21 58
Swaythling	d			20 01									21 01									22 01
St Denys	d			20 04									21 04									22 04
Southampton Central ⛴	a	20 00		20 09		20 34			20 42	20 53	21 00		21 09		21 34			21 43		22 00		22 09
	d	20 03		20 10		20 35			20 45	20 54	21 03		21 10		21 35			21 45		22 03		22 10
Millbrook (Hants)	d			20 13									21 13									22 13
Redbridge	d			20 16									21 16									22 16
Romsey	d			20 24						21 06			21 24									22a24
Mottisfont & Dunbridge	d												21 29									
Dean	d												21 35									
Salisbury	a			20 42						21 24			21 48									
Totton	d					20 41									21 41							
Ashurst New Forest	d					20 45									21 45							
Beaulieu Road	d					20 50									21 50							
Brockenhurst 3	a	20 16				20 56			21 02		21 16				21 56			22 02		22 16		
	d	20 17			20 29	20 57		20 59	21 03		21 17			21 29	21 57		21 59	22 03		22 17		
Lymington Town	d				20 37			21 07						21 37			22 07					
Lymington Pier	a				20 39			21 09						21 39			22 09					
Sway	d					21 01									22 01							
New Milton	d	20 24				21 06					21 24				22 06					22 24		
Hinton Admiral	d					21 10									22 10							
Christchurch	d					21 15									22 15							
Pokesdown	d					21 19									22 19							
Bournemouth	a	20 34				21 23			21 26		21 34				22 23			22 26		22 34		
	d	20 39				21 24					21 39				22 24					22 39		
Branksome	d	20 44									21 44									22 44		
Parkstone (Dorset)	d	20 47									21 47									22 47		
Poole 4	a	20 50				21 33					21 50				22 33					22 50		
	d	20 51									21 51									22 51		
Hamworthy	d	20 56									21 56									22 56		
Holton Heath	d																					
Wareham	d	21 03									22 03									23 03		
Wool	d	21 10									22 10									23 10		
Moreton (Dorset)	d	21 16									22 16									23 16		
Dorchester South	d	21 25									22 25									23 25		
Dorchester West	d																		22 56			
Upwey	d	21 32									22 32								23 04	23 32		
Weymouth	a	21 36									22 36								23 09	23 36		

A ✠ to New Milton

London - Basingstoke, Southampton, Romsey Lymington, Bournemouth and Weymouth

		SW		XC	GW	SW	SW	SW	SW	SW		SW	SW
		◇1		◇1		◇1 A 🛒	1	1	1	◇1		1	◇1 🛒
London Waterloo 15 ⊖	d	20 54				21 35	21 37			21 54		22 37	22 54
Clapham Junction 10	d	21u03				21u42	21 46			22u03		22 46	23u03
Woking	d	21 28				22 07	22 23			22 28		23 23	23 28
Farnborough (Main)	d						22 36					23 36	
Fleet	d						22 41					23 41	
Reading 7	d			21 51									
Basingstoke	a	21 46		22 09		22 26	22 54			22 46		23 54	23 46
	d	21 48		22 10		22 28				22 48			23 48
Micheldever	d	21 58								22 58			23 58
Winchester	d	22 08		22 26		22 44				23 08			00 08
Shawford	d	22 12											
Romsey	d							22 35	22 28				
Chandlers Ford	d							22 42					
Eastleigh 3	a	22 18						22 48	23 19	23 17			00 18
	d	22 22	22 26					22 54	23 21	23 22	23 26		00 22
Hedge End	d		22 32								23 32		
Botley	d		22 36								23 36		
Fareham	d		22 44		22 32						23 44		
Portchester	d		22 49								23 49		
Cosham	d		22 54								23 54		
Hilsea	a		23 00								23 59		
Fratton	a		23 04								00 04		
Portsmouth & Southsea	a		23 08								00 08		
Portsmouth Harbour ⛴	a		23 13								00 13		
Southampton Airport Pkwy ✈	d	22 27		22 34		22 53		22 58		23 27			00 27
Swaythling	d							23 01					
St Denys	d							23 04					00s31
Southampton Central ⛴	a	22 34		22 42	22 53	23 00		23 09		23 34			00 36
	d	22 35			22 57	23 03		23 10		23 35			00 37
Millbrook (Hants)	d							23 13					
Redbridge	d							23 16					
Romsey	d				23 09			23 24	23a33				
Mottisfont & Dunbridge	d							23 29					
Dean	d							23 35					
Salisbury	a				23 27			23 51					
Totton	d	22 41								23 41			00s42
Ashurst New Forest	d	22 45								23 45			
Beaulieu Road	d	22 50											
Brockenhurst 3	a	22 56				23 16				23 53			00s53
	d	22 57				23 17				23 54			
Lymington Town	d												
Lymington Pier	a												
Sway	d	23 01								23 59			
New Milton	d	23 06				23 24				00 04			01s01
Hinton Admiral	d	23 10								00 08			
Christchurch	d	23 15								00 13			01s08
Pokesdown	d	23 19								00 16			01s12
Bournemouth	a	23 23				23 34				00 20			01 16
	d	23 24				23 39				00 22			01 17
Branksome	d					23 44				00 27			01s22
Parkstone (Dorset)	d					23 47				00 30			01s25
Poole 4	a	23 33				23 50				00 34			01 29
	d					23 51							
Hamworthy	d					23 56							
Holton Heath	d												
Wareham	d					00 03							
Wool	d					00 10							
Moreton (Dorset)	d					00 16							
Dorchester South	d					00 24							
Dorchester West	d												
Upwey	d					00 31							
Weymouth	a					00 35							

A 🛒 to New Milton

London - Basingstoke, Southampton, Romsey Lymington, Bournemouth and Weymouth

		SW	SW	SW	SW	SW	SW	SW	SW	SW	SW	SW	GW	SW	SW		SW	SW	SW	SW	GW	SW	
		◇1 A 🛒	◇1 🛒	1	◇1 🛒	1	◇1	1	1	1	1	1		1	1		1	1	1	1	■	◇1	
London Waterloo 15 ⊖	d	21p35	22p05		22p35	22p39	23p05		23p35	00 05	01 05											07 54	
Clapham Junction 10	d		22b12			22b46	23b12		23b42	00u12												08u03	
Woking	d	22p00	22p32		23p00		23p32		00 03	00 37	01 42											08 28	
Farnborough (Main)	d					23p16			00 14		01s58												
Fleet	d					23p21			00 20		02s04												
Reading 7	d																						
Basingstoke	a		22p51			23p34	23p51		00 33	00 55	02s16											08 46	
	d		22p52			23p36	23p52		00 35	00 56					07 48							08 48	
Micheldever	d						00 02								07 58							08 58	
Winchester	d	22p33	23p09		23p33	23p52	00 12		00 51	01 13	02s33				08 08							09 08	
Shawford	d					23p57									08 12								
Romsey	d			23p09									08 19						08 35				
Chandlers Ford	d			23p16															08 42				
Eastleigh 3	a		23p17	23p22		00 02	00 20		00 59	01 21	02s42				08 18				08 47			09 18	
	d		23p18	23p23		00 03	00 21	00 30	01 00	01 22					08 22	08 26			08 54			09 22	09 26
Hedge End	d							00s36								08 32							09 32
Botley	d							00s39								08 36							09 36
Fareham	d							00s47				07 44				08 44					09 32		09 44
Portchester	d							00s53				07 49				08 49							09 49
Cosham	d							00s57				07 54				08 54							09 54
Hilsea	a											08 00				09 00							10 04
Fratton	a							01s05				08 04				09 04							10 08
Portsmouth & Southsea	a							01s08				08 08				09 08							10 11
Portsmouth Harbour ⛴	a							01 12				08 13				09 13							10 15
Southampton Airport Pkwy ✈	d	22p42	23p22	23p27	23p42	00 08	00 25		01 05	01 26	02s46				08 27				08 58			09 27	
Swaythling	d			23p30															09 01				
St Denys	d			23p33			00s29				02s51								09 04				
Southampton Central ⛴	a	22p49	23p29	23p38	23p49	00 15	00 34		01 12	01 35	02 56		08 29		08 34				09 09		09 53	09 34	
	d	22p51	23p31	23p40	23p51		00 36			01 37					08 35			09 03	09 10		09 54	09 35	
Millbrook (Hants)	d			23p42															09 13				
Redbridge	d			23p46															09 16				
Romsey	d			23p57															09 24		10 06		
Mottisfont & Dunbridge	d			00 02															09 29				
Dean	d			00 08															09 35				
Salisbury	a			00 20															09 49		10 24		
Totton	d		23p36				00s41			01s42					08 41							09 41	
Ashurst New Forest	d		23p41												08 45							09 45	
Beaulieu Road	d														08 50							09 50	
Brockenhurst 3	a	23p04	23p49		00 04		00s52			01s53					08 56			09 16				09 56	
	d	23p05	23p50		00 05										08 57		08 59	09 17		09 29		09 57	
Lymington Town	d																09 07			09 37			
Lymington Pier	a																09 09			09 39			
Sway	d		23p54												09 01							10 01	
New Milton	d		23p59				01s00			02s00					09 06			09 24				10 06	
Hinton Admiral	d		00 03												09 10							10 10	
Christchurch	d		00 08				01s07			02s07					09 15							10 15	
Pokesdown	d		00 11				01s11			02s11					09 19							10 19	
Bournemouth	a	23p25	00 15		00 21		01 15			02 15					09 23			09 34				10 23	
	d	23p29	00 17		00 22		01 16							08 39	09 24			09 39				10 24	
Branksome	d	23p35	00 23		00 27		01s21							08 44				09 44					
Parkstone (Dorset)	d	23p38	00 26		00 30		01s24							08 47				09 47					
Poole 4	a	23p41	00 30		00 35		01 29							08 50	09 33			09 50				10 33	
	d	23p42												08 51				09 51					
Hamworthy	d	23p47												08 56				09 56					
Holton Heath	d																						
Wareham	d	23p54												09 03				10 03					
Wool	d	00 01												09 10				10 10					
Moreton (Dorset)	d	00 07												09 16				10 16					
Dorchester South	d	00 15												09 24				10 24					
Dorchester West	d																						
Upwey	d	00 21												09 31				10 31					
Weymouth	a	00 26												09 35				10 35					

A 🛒 to Brockenhurst

b Previous night, stops to pick up only

Table 158

Sundays
from 30 October

London - Basingstoke, Southampton, Romsey Lymington, Bournemouth and Weymouth

		SW	SW	SW	SW	SW		SW	XC	SW	SW	SW	SW		SW	XC	GW	SW	SW	SW	SW		SW
		■	◇■	■	■	◇■		■	◇■	◇■	■	■	◇■		■	◇■	◇	◇■	■	■	◇■		■
									⌶							⌶		A ⌶					
London Waterloo ■ ⊖	d		08 35			08 54				09 35			09 54					10 35			10 54		
Clapham Junction ■	d		08u45			09u03				09u45			10u03					10u45			11u04		
Woking	d		09 09			09 28				10 09			10 28					11 07			11 28		
Farnborough (Main)	d																						
Fleet	d																						
Reading ■	d								09 51							10 51							
Basingstoke	a		09 28			09 46			10 09	10 28			10 46			11 09		11 26			11 46		
	d		09 29			09 48			10 10	10 29			10 48			11 10		11 28			11 48		
Micheldever	d					09 58							10 58								11 58		
Winchester	d		09 46			10 08			10 25	10 46			11 08			11 25		11 44			12 08		
Shawford	d					10 12															12 12		
Romsey	d			09 35							10 35								11 35				
Chandlers Ford	d			09 42							10 42								11 42				
Eastleigh ■	a			09 48		10 18					10 48		11 18						11 48		12 18		
	d			09 54		10 22	10 26				10 54		11 22	11 26					11 54		12 22	12 26	
Hedge End	d						10 32							11 32								12 32	
Botley	d						10 36							11 36								12 36	
Fareham	d						10 44							11 44			11 32					12 44	
Portchester	d						10 49							11 49								12 49	
Cosham	d						10 54							11 54								12 54	
Hilsea	a						11 04							12 00								13 00	
Fratton	a						11 08							12 04								13 04	
Portsmouth & Southsea	a						11 11							12 08								13 08	
Portsmouth Harbour ⛴	a						11 15							12 13								13 13	
Southampton Airport Pkwy ✈	d		09 55	09 58		10 27			10 34	10 55	10 58		11 27			11 34		11 53	11 58		12 27		
Swaythling	d			10 01							11 01								12 01				
St Denys	d			10 04							11 04								12 04				
Southampton Central ⛴	a		10 02	10 09		10 34			10 42	11 02	11 09		11 34			11 42	11 53	11 59	12 09		12 34		
	d		10 03	10 10		10 35			10 45	11 03	11 10		11 35			11 45	11 54	12 03	12 10		12 35		
Millbrook (Hants)	d			10 13							11 13								12 13				
Redbridge	d			10 16							11 16								12 16				
Romsey	d			10 24							11 24						12 06		12 24				
Mottisfont & Dunbridge	d										11 29												
Dean	d										11 35												
Salisbury	a			10 42							11 48						12 24		12 42				
Totton	d					10 41							11 41								12 41		
Ashurst New Forest	d					10 45							11 45								12 45		
Beaulieu Road	d					10 50							11 50								12 50		
Brockenhurst ■	a		10 17			10 56			11 02	11 17			11 56			12 02		12 16			12 56		
	d	09 59	10 18		10 29	10 57		10 59	11 02	11 18		11 29	11 57		11 59	12 03		12 17		12 29	12 57		12 59
Lymington Town	d	10 07			10 37			11 07				11 37			12 07					12 37			13 07
Lymington Pier	a	10 09			10 39			11 09				11 39			12 09					12 39			13 09
Sway	d					11 01							12 01								13 01		
New Milton	d		10 25			11 06				11 25			12 06					12 24			13 06		
Hinton Admiral	d					11 10							12 10								13 10		
Christchurch	d					11 15							12 15								13 15		
Pokesdown	d					11 19							12 19								13 19		
Bournemouth	a		10 35			11 23			11 26	11 35			12 23			12 26		12 34			13 23		
	d		10 39			11 24				11 39			12 24					12 39			13 24		
Branksome	d		10 44							11 44								12 44					
Parkstone (Dorset)	d		10 47							11 47								12 47					
Poole ■	a		10 50			11 33				11 50			12 33					12 50			13 33		
	d		10 51							11 51								12 51					
Hamworthy	d		10 56							11 56								12 56					
Holton Heath	d																						
Wareham	d		11 03							12 03								13 03					
Wool	d		11 10							12 10								13 10					
Moreton (Dorset)	d		11 16							12 16								13 16					
Dorchester South	d		11 24							12 24								13 24					
Dorchester West	d																						
Upwey	d		11 31							12 31								13 31					
Weymouth	a		11 35							12 35								13 35					

A ⌶ to New Milton

Table 158

Sundays
from 30 October

London - Basingstoke, Southampton, Romsey Lymington, Bournemouth and Weymouth

		XC	GW	SW	SW	SW	SW		SW	XC	GW	SW	SW	SW	SW		SW	XC	GW	GW	SW	SW
		◇■	◇	◇■	■	■	◇■		■	◇■	◇	◇■	■	■	◇■		■	◇■	◇		◇■	■
		⌶		A ⌶			⌶			⌶		A ⌶			⌶			⌶			A ⌶	
London Waterloo ■ ⊖	d			11 35			11 54					12 35			12 54						13 35	
Clapham Junction ■	d			11u45			12u04					12u42			13u03						13u42	
Woking	d			12 07			12 28					13 07			13 28						14 07	
Farnborough (Main)	d																					
Fleet	d																					
Reading ■	d	11 51								12 51								13 51				
Basingstoke	a	12 09		12 26			12 46			13 09		13 26			13 46			14 09			14 26	
	d	12 10		12 28			12 48			13 10		13 28			13 48			14 10			14 28	
Micheldever	d						12 58								13 58							
Winchester	d	12 25		12 44			13 08			13 25		13 44			14 08			14 25			14 44	
Shawford	d														14 12							
Romsey	d				12 35								13 35									14 35
Chandlers Ford	d				12 42								13 42									14 42
Eastleigh ■	a				12 48		13 18						13 48		14 18							14 48
	d				12 54		13 22	13 26					13 54		14 22	14 26						14 54
Hedge End	d							13 32								14 32						
Botley	d							13 36								14 36						
Fareham	d		12 32					13 44			13 32					14 44			14 32			
Portchester	d							13 49								14 49						
Cosham	d							13 54								14 54						
Hilsea	a							14 00								15 00						
Fratton	a							14 04								15 04						
Portsmouth & Southsea	a							14 08								15 08						
Portsmouth Harbour ⛴	a							14 13								15 13						
Southampton Airport Pkwy ✈	d	12 34		12 53	12 58		13 27			13 34		13 53	13 58		14 27			14 34			14 53	14 58
Swaythling	d				13 01								14 01									15 01
St Denys	d				13 04								14 04									15 04
Southampton Central ⛴	a	12 42	12 53	13 00	13 09		13 34			13 42	13 54	14 00	14 09		14 34			14 42	14 53		15 00	15 09
	d	12 45	12 54	13 03	13 10		13 35			13 45	13 54	14 03	14 10		14 35			14 45	14 54		15 03	15 10
Millbrook (Hants)	d				13 13								14 13									15 13
Redbridge	d				13 16								14 16									15 16
Romsey	d		13 06		13 24						14 06		14 24						15 06			15 24
Mottisfont & Dunbridge	d				13 29																	15 29
Dean	d				13 35																	15 35
Salisbury	a		13 24		13 48						14 24		14 42						15 24			15 48
Totton	d						13 41								14 41							
Ashurst New Forest	d						13 45								14 45							
Beaulieu Road	d						13 50								14 50							
Brockenhurst ■	a	13 02		13 16			13 56			14 01		14 16			14 56			15 02			15 16	
	d	13 03		13 17		13 29	13 57		13 59	14 02		14 17		14 29	14 57		14 59	15 03			15 17	
Lymington Town	d					13 37			14 07					14 37			15 07					
Lymington Pier	a					13 39			14 09					14 39			15 09					
Sway	d						14 01								15 01							
New Milton	d			13 24			14 06					14 24			15 06						15 24	
Hinton Admiral	d						14 10								15 10							
Christchurch	d						14 15								15 15							
Pokesdown	d						14 19								15 19							
Bournemouth	a	13 26		13 34			14 23			14 26		14 34			15 23			15 26			15 34	
	d			13 39			14 24					14 39			15 24						15 39	
Branksome	d			13 44								14 44									15 44	
Parkstone (Dorset)	d			13 47								14 47									15 47	
Poole ■	a			13 50			14 33					14 50			15 33						15 50	
	d			13 51								14 51									15 51	
Hamworthy	d			13 56								14 56									15 56	
Holton Heath	d																					
Wareham	d			14 03								15 03									16 03	
Wool	d			14 10								15 10									16 10	
Moreton (Dorset)	d			14 16								15 16									16 16	
Dorchester South	d			14 24								15 24									16 24	
Dorchester West	d																			16 10		
Upwey	d			14 31								15 31								16 19	16 31	
Weymouth	a			14 35								15 35								16 24	16 35	

A ⌶ to New Milton

London - Basingstoke, Southampton, Romsey
Lymington, Bournemouth and Weymouth

from 30 October

		SW	SW	SW	XC	GW	SW	SW	SW	SW	SW	XC	GW	SW	SW	SW	GW	SW	SW	SW
		1	◇1 🛒	1	◇1 🛒	■	◇1 A 🛒	1	1	◇1 🛒	1	◇1 🛒	◇	◇1 A 🛒	1	1	◇	1	◇1 🛒	1
London Waterloo 15 ⊖	d		13 54				14 35			14 54				15 35	15 37				15 54	
Clapham Junction 10	d		14u03				14u42			15u03				15u42	15 46				16u03	
Woking	d		14 28				15 07			15 28				16 07	16 23				16 28	
Farnborough (Main)	d														16 36					
Fleet	d														16 41					
Reading 7	d				14 51							15 51								
Basingstoke	a		14 46		15 09		15 26			15 46		16 09		16 26	16 54				16 46	
	d		14 48		15 10		15 28			15 48		16 10		16 28					16 48	
Micheldever	d		14 58							15 58									16 58	
Winchester	d		15 08		15 25		15 44			16 08		16 25		16 44					17 08	
Shawford	d									16 12										
Romsey	d							15 35								16 35				
Chandlers Ford	d							15 42								16 42				
Eastleigh 8	a		15 18					15 48		16 18						16 48			17 18	
	d		15 22 15 26					15 54		16 22 16 26						16 54			17 22 17 26	
Hedge End	d		15 32							16 32									17 32	
Botley	d		15 36							16 36									17 36	
Fareham	d		15 44			15 32				16 44			16 32				17 03		17 44	
Portchester	d		15 49							16 49									17 49	
Cosham	d		15 54							16 54									17 54	
Hilsea	a		16 00							17 00									18 00	
Fratton	a		16 04							17 03									18 04	
Portsmouth & Southsea	a		16 08							17 08									18 08	
Portsmouth Harbour ⛴	a		16 13							17 13									18 13	
Southampton Airport Pkwy ✈	d		15 27		15 34		15 53	15 58		16 27		16 34		16 53		16 58			17 27	
Swaythling	d							16 01								17 01				
St Denys	d							16 04								17 04				
Southampton Central ⛴	a		15 34		15 42	15 53	16 00	16 09		16 34		16 42	16 53	17 00		17 09	17 24		17 34	
	d		15 35		15 45	15 54	16 03	16 10		16 35		16 45	16 54	17 03		17 10	17 26		17 35	
Millbrook (Hants)	d							16 13								17 13				
Redbridge	d							16 16								17 16				
Romsey	d					16 06		16 24					17 06			17 24	17 39			
Mottisfont & Dunbridge	d															17 29				
Dean	d															17 35				
Salisbury	a					16 24		16 42					17 24			17 48	18 01			
Totton	d		15 41							16 41									17 41	
Ashurst New Forest	d		15 45							16 45									17 45	
Beaulieu Road	d		15 50							16 50									17 50	
Brockenhurst 3	a		15 56		16 02		16 16			16 56		17 02		17 16					17 56	
	d	15 29	15 57	15 59	16 03		16 17		16 29	16 57	16 59	17 03		17 17				17 29	17 57	17 59
Lymington Town	d	15 37		16 07					16 37		17 07							17 37		18 07
Lymington Pier	a	15 39		16 09					16 39		17 09							17 39		18 09
Sway	d		16 01							17 01									18 01	
New Milton	d		16 06				16 24			17 06				17 24					18 06	
Hinton Admiral	d		16 10							17 10									18 10	
Christchurch	d		16 15							17 15									18 15	
Pokesdown	d		16 19							17 19									18 19	
Bournemouth	a		16 23		16 26		16 34			17 23		17 26		17 34					18 23	
	d		16 24				16 39			17 24				17 39					18 24	
Branksome	d						16 44							17 44						
Parkstone (Dorset)	d						16 47							17 47						
Poole 4	a		16 33				16 50			17 33				17 50					18 33	
	d						16 51							17 51						
Hamworthy	d						16 56							17 56						
Holton Heath	d																			
Wareham	d						17 03							18 03						
Wool	d						17 10							18 10						
Moreton (Dorset)	d						17 16							18 16						
Dorchester South	d						17 24							18 24						
Dorchester West	d																			
Upwey	d						17 31							18 31						
Weymouth	a						17 35							18 35						

A 🛒 to New Milton

London - Basingstoke, Southampton, Romsey
Lymington, Bournemouth and Weymouth

from 30 October

		XC	GW	SW	SW	SW	SW	SW	SW	XC	GW	GW	SW	SW	SW	GW	SW	SW	SW	XC	GW
		◇1 🛒	◇	◇1 A 🛒	1	1	1	◇1 🛒	1	◇1 🛒	◇		◇1 A 🛒	1	1	◇	1	◇1 🛒	1	◇1 🛒	◇
London Waterloo 15 ⊖	d			16 35	16 37			16 54					17 35	17 37				17 54			
Clapham Junction 10	d			16u42	16 46			17u03					17u42	17 46				18u03			
Woking	d			17 07	17 23			17 28					18 07	18 23				18 28			
Farnborough (Main)	d				17 36									18 36							
Fleet	d				17 41									18 41							
Reading 7	d	16 51								17 51										18 51	
Basingstoke	a	17 09		17 26	17 54			17 46		18 09			18 26	18 54				18 46		19 09	
	d	17 10		17 28				17 48		18 10			18 28					18 48		19 10	
Micheldever	d							17 58										18 58			
Winchester	d	17 25		17 44				18 08		18 25			18 44					19 08		19 25	
Shawford	d							18 12													
Romsey	d					17 35									18 35						
Chandlers Ford	d					17 42									18 42						
Eastleigh 8	a					17 48		18 18							18 48			19 18			
	d					17 54		18 22 18 26							18 54			19 22 19 26			
Hedge End	d							18 32										19 32			
Botley	d							18 36										19 36			
Fareham	d		17 32					18 44			18 32					19 03		19 44			19 32
Portchester	d							18 49										19 49			
Cosham	d							18 54										19 54			
Hilsea	a							19 00										20 00			
Fratton	a							19 03										20 04			
Portsmouth & Southsea	a							19 08										20 08			
Portsmouth Harbour ⛴	a							19 13										20 13			
Southampton Airport Pkwy ✈	d	17 34		17 53		17 58		18 27		18 34			18 53		18 58			19 27		19 34	
Swaythling	d					18 01									19 01						
St Denys	d					18 04									19 04						
Southampton Central ⛴	a	17 40	17 53	18 00		18 09		18 34		18 42	18 53		19 00		19 09	19 24		19 34		19 40	19 53
	d	17 45	17 54	18 03		18 10		18 35		18 45	18 54		19 03		19 10	19 30		19 35		19 45	19 54
Millbrook (Hants)	d					18 13									19 13						
Redbridge	d					18 16									19 16						
Romsey	d		18 06			18 24					19 06				19 24	19 42					20 06
Mottisfont & Dunbridge	d														19 29						
Dean	d														19 35						
Salisbury	a		18 24			18 42					19 24				19 48	20 00					20 24
Totton	d							18 41										19 41			
Ashurst New Forest	d							18 45										19 45			
Beaulieu Road	d							18 50										19 50			
Brockenhurst 3	a	18 02		18 16				18 56		19 01			19 16					19 56		20 02	
	d	18 03		18 17			18 29	18 57	18 59	19 02			19 17				19 29	19 57	19 59	20 03	
Lymington Town	d						18 37		19 07								19 37		20 07		
Lymington Pier	a						18 39		19 09								19 39		20 09		
Sway	d							19 01										20 01			
New Milton	d			18 24				19 06					19 24					20 06			
Hinton Admiral	d							19 10										20 10			
Christchurch	d							19 15										20 15			
Pokesdown	d							19 19										20 19			
Bournemouth	a	18 26		18 34				19 23		19 26			19 34					20 23		20 26	
	d			18 39				19 24					19 39					20 24			
Branksome	d			18 44									19 44								
Parkstone (Dorset)	d			18 47									19 47								
Poole 4	a			18 50				19 33					19 50					20 33			
	d			18 51									19 51								
Hamworthy	d			18 56									19 56								
Holton Heath	d																				
Wareham	d			19 03									20 03								
Wool	d			19 10									20 10								
Moreton (Dorset)	d			19 16									20 16								
Dorchester South	d			19 24									20 25								
Dorchester West	d											19 47									
Upwey	d			19 31								19 55	20 32								
Weymouth	a			19 35								20 01	20 36								

A 🛒 to New Milton

Table 158

Sundays
from 30 October

London - Basingstoke, Southampton, Romsey Lymington, Bournemouth and Weymouth

		SW ◇1 A ⚒	SW 1	SW 1	SW 1	SW ◇1 ⚒		SW 1	XC ◇1 ⚒	GW ◇	SW ◇1 A ⚒	SW 1	SW 1	SW 1	SW ◇1		SW 1	XC ◇1	GW	SW ◇1 A ⚒	SW 1	SW 1
London Waterloo 15 ⊖	d	18 35	18 37			18 54					19 35	19 37			19 54					20 35	20 37	
Clapham Junction 10	d	18u42	18 46			19u03					19u42	19 46			20u03					20u42	20 46	
Woking	d	19 07	19 23			19 28					20 07	20 23			20 28					21 07	21 23	
Farnborough (Main)	d		19 36									20 36									21 36	
Fleet	d		19 41									20 41									21 41	
Reading 7	d								19 51									20 51				
Basingstoke	a	19 26	19 54			19 46			20 09		20 26	20 54			20 46			21 09		21 26	21 54	
	d	19 28				19 48			20 10		20 28				20 48			21 10		21 28		
Micheldever	d					19 58									20 58							
Winchester	d	19 44				20 08			20 25		20 44				21 08			21 25		21 44		
Shawford	d					20 12																
Romsey	d			19 35									20 35									21 35
Chandlers Ford	d			19 42									20 42									21 42
Eastleigh 3	a			19 48		20 18							20 48		21 18							21 48
	d			19 54		20 22	20 26						20 54		21 22	21 26						21 54
Hedge End	d						20 32									21 32						
Botley	d						20 36									21 36						
Fareham	d						20 44			20 32						21 44						
Portchester	d						20 49									21 49						
Cosham	d						20 54									21 54						
Hilsea	a						21 00									22 00						
Fratton	a						21 04									22 04						
Portsmouth & Southsea	a						21 08									22 08						
Portsmouth Harbour ⛴	a						21 13									22 13						
Southampton Airport Pkwy ✈	d	19 53		19 58		20 27			20 34		20 53		20 58		21 27			21 34		21 53		21 58
Swaythling	d			20 01									21 01									22 01
St Denys	d			20 04									21 04									22 04
Southampton Central ⛴	a	20 00		20 09		20 34			20 42	20 53	21 00		21 09		21 34			21 43		22 00		22 09
	d	20 03		20 10		20 35			20 45	20 54	21 03		21 10		21 35			21 45		22 03		22 10
Millbrook (Hants)	d			20 13									21 13									22 13
Redbridge	d			20 16									21 16									22 16
Romsey	d			20 24						21 06			21 24									22a24
Mottisfont & Dunbridge	d												21 29									
Dean	d												21 35									
Salisbury	a			20 42						21 24			21 48									
Totton	d					20 41									21 41							
Ashurst New Forest	d					20 45									21 45							
Beaulieu Road	d					20 50									21 50							
Brockenhurst 3	a	20 16				20 56			21 02		21 16				21 56			22 02		22 16		
	d	20 17			20 29	20 57		20 59	21 03		21 17			21 29	21 57		21 59	22 03		22 17		
Lymington Town	d				20 37			21 07						21 37			22 07					
Lymington Pier	a				20 39			21 09						21 39			22 09					
Sway	d					21 01									22 01							
New Milton	d	20 24				21 06					21 24				22 06					22 24		
Hinton Admiral	d					21 10									22 10							
Christchurch	d					21 15									22 15							
Pokesdown	d					21 19									22 19							
Bournemouth	a	20 34				21 23			21 26		21 34				22 23			22 26		22 34		
	d	20 39				21 24					21 39				22 24					22 39		
Branksome	d	20 44									21 44									22 44		
Parkstone (Dorset)	d	20 47									21 47									22 47		
Poole 4	a	20 50				21 33					21 50				22 33					22 50		
	d	20 51									21 51									22 51		
Hamworthy	d	20 56									21 56									22 56		
Holton Heath	d																					
Wareham	d	21 03									22 03									23 03		
Wool	d	21 10									22 10									23 10		
Moreton (Dorset)	d	21 16									22 16									23 16		
Dorchester South	d	21 25									22 25									23 25		
Dorchester West	d																		22 53			
Upwey	d	21 32									22 32								23 01	23 32		
Weymouth	a	21 36									22 36								23 06	23 36		

A ⚒ to New Milton

Table 158

Sundays
from 30 October

London - Basingstoke, Southampton, Romsey Lymington, Bournemouth and Weymouth

		SW ◇1		XC ◇1	GW	SW ◇1 A ⚒	SW 1	SW 1	SW 1	SW ◇1		SW 1	SW ◇1 ⚒
London Waterloo 15 ⊖	d	20 54				21 35	21 37			21 54		22 37	22 54
Clapham Junction 10	d	21u03				21u42	21 46			22u03		22 46	23u03
Woking	d	21 28				22 07	22 23			22 28		23 23	23 28
Farnborough (Main)	d						22 36					23 36	
Fleet	d						22 41					23 41	
Reading 7	d			21 51									
Basingstoke	a	21 46		22 09		22 26	22 54			22 46		23 54	23 46
	d	21 48		22 10		22 28				22 48			23 48
Micheldever	d	21 58								22 58			23 58
Winchester	d	22 08		22 26		22 44				23 08			00 08
Shawford	d	22 12											
Romsey	d							22 35	22 28				
Chandlers Ford	d							22 42					
Eastleigh 3	a	22 18						22 48	23 19	23 17			00 18
	d	22 22	22 26					22 54	23 21	23 22	23 26		00 22
Hedge End	d		22 32								23 32		
Botley	d		22 36								23 36		
Fareham	d		22 44		22 32						23 44		
Portchester	d		22 49								23 49		
Cosham	d		22 54								23 54		
Hilsea	a		23 00								23 59		
Fratton	a		23 04								00 04		
Portsmouth & Southsea	a		23 08								00 08		
Portsmouth Harbour ⛴	a		23 13								00 13		
Southampton Airport Pkwy ✈	d	22 27		22 34		22 53		22 58		23 27			00 27
Swaythling	d							23 01					
St Denys	d							23 04					00s31
Southampton Central ⛴	a	22 34		22 42	22 53	23 00		23 09		23 34			00 36
	d	22 35			22 57	23 03		23 10		23 35			00 37
Millbrook (Hants)	d							23 13					
Redbridge	d							23 16					
Romsey	d				23 09			23 24	23a33				
Mottisfont & Dunbridge	d							23 29					
Dean	d							23 35					
Salisbury	a				23 27			23 51					
Totton	d	22 41								23 41			00s42
Ashurst New Forest	d	22 45								23 45			
Beaulieu Road	d	22 50											
Brockenhurst 3	a	22 56				23 16				23 53			00s53
	d	22 57				23 17				23 54			
Lymington Town	d												
Lymington Pier	a												
Sway	d	23 01								23 59			
New Milton	d	23 06				23 24				00 04			01s01
Hinton Admiral	d	23 10								00 08			
Christchurch	d	23 15								00 13			01s08
Pokesdown	d	23 19								00 16			01s12
Bournemouth	a	23 23				23 34				00 20			01 16
	d	23 24				23 39				00 22			01 17
Branksome	d					23 44				00 27			01s22
Parkstone (Dorset)	d					23 47				00 30			01s25
Poole 4	a	23 33				23 50				00 34			01 29
	d					23 51							
Hamworthy	d					23 56							
Holton Heath	d												
Wareham	d					00 03							
Wool	d					00 10							
Moreton (Dorset)	d					00 16							
Dorchester South	d					00 24							
Dorchester West	d												
Upwey	d					00 31							
Weymouth	a					00 35							

A ⚒ to New Milton

Weymouth, Bournemouth, Lymington, Romsey, Southampton and Basingstoke - London

Miles	Miles			SW	SW	SW	SW	SW	SW	XC	SW	SW	SW	GW	SW	XC	SW	SW	SW	SW	GW	SW	SW
				MO	MO	MX	MX	MO	MX														
				◇1	1	1	◇1	1	1	◇1	1	◇1 ⊼	1		1	◇1 ⊼	◇1 ⊼	1	1	1		◇1 ⊼	◇1 ⊼
0	—	**Weymouth**	d	20p58			22p10	22p58	23p10					05 33									
2¼	—	Upwey	d	21p02			22p14	23p02	23p14					05 37									
—	—	Dorchester West	a											05 44									
7	—	**Dorchester South**	d	21p10			22p22	23p10	23p22														
12½	—	Moreton (Dorset)	d	21p17			22p28	23p17	23p28														
17	—	Wool	d	21p23			22p34	23p23	23p34														
22	—	Wareham	d	21p30			22p42	23p30	23p42														
24	—	Holton Heath	d																				
26¾	—	Hamworthy	d	21p37			22p48	23p37	23p48														
29	—	**Poole** 4	a	21p41			22p53	23p41	23p53														
—	—		d	21p50			22p54	23p50	23p54			05 00	05 26				05 45						06 11
30¾	—	Parkstone (Dorset)	d	21p54			22p58	23p54				05 04	05 30										06 15
32	—	Branksome	d	21p57			23p01	23p57				05 07	05 33										06 18
34¾	—	**Bournemouth**	a	22p03			23p07	00 03	00 03			05 12	05 38				05 54						06 23
—	—		d	22p06			23p12					05 15	05 40				05 57					06 04	06 25
36½	—	Pokesdown	d	22p10			23p16					05 19	05 44									06 08	
38½	—	Christchurch	d	22p14			23p20					05 23	05 48									06 12	
41¾	—	Hinton Admiral	d	22p19			23p25						05 53									06 17	
44¼	—	New Milton	d	22p23			23p29					05 30	05 57									06 21	
47¼	—	Sway	d	22p28			23p34						06 02									06 26	
—	0	**Lymington Pier**	d																	06 14			
—	0½	Lymington Town	d																	06 16			
50	5¼	**Brockenhurst** 3	a	22p33			23p39					05 37	06 07				06 12			06 25		06 31	
—	—		d	22p34			23p40					05 38					06 14					06 33	
54¾	—	Beaulieu Road	d	22p39																			
57¼	—	Ashurst New Forest	d	22p43			23p47															06 41	
60¼	—	Totton	d	22p48			23p52					05 49							06 12			06 46	
—	0	**Salisbury**	d												05 35						06 20		
—	9	Dean	d												05 47								
—	12¾	Mottisfont & Dunbridge	d												05 53								
—	16½	**Romsey**	d												05 58						06 38		
60¾	22½	Redbridge	d																06 14				
62½	—	Millbrook (Hants)	d																06 17				
63½	—	**Southampton Central** ⛴	a	22p53			23p57					05 54					06 27		06 24		06 49	06 51	06 55
—	—		d	22p55			23p59			05 15		05 55				06 15	06 30		06 35		06 53	07 00	
65½	—	St Denys	d				00 04												06 40				
67	—	Swaythling	d				00 07												06 43				
67¾	—	**Southampton Airport Pkwy** ✈	d	23p03			00 10			05 22		06 03				06 22	06 38		06 46			07 08	
—	0	**Portsmouth Harbour** ⛴	d		23p17	23p24					05 00							05 43					
—	0¾	**Portsmouth & Southsea**	d		23p22	23p29					05 05							05 48					
—	1¾	Fratton	d		23p26	23p33					05 09							05 52					
—	4	Hilsea	d		23p30	23p37					05 13							05 56					
—	5½	Cosham	d		23p35	23p42					05 19							06 03					
—	8	Portchester	d		23p40	23p47					05 23							06 08					
—	11¼	Fareham	d		23p46	23p53					05 29							06 19			07a14		
—	16¾	Botley	d		23p54	23p59					05 37							06 27					
—	17¾	Hedge End	d		23p58	00 05					05 41							06 31					
69¼	22¼	Eastleigh 3	a	23p09	00 04	00 11	00 14				05 49	06 07						06 37	06 49				
—	—		d	23p11		00 19					05 50	06 08						06 43	06 50				
—	24¼	Chandlers Ford	d												06 06				06 55				
—	29½	**Romsey**	a												06 44				07 03				
73	—	Shawford	d								05 56							06 49					
76¼	—	**Winchester**	d	23p23		00a28				05 31	06 02	06 18				06 31	06 48	06 55				07 18	
84¾	—	Micheldever	d	23p32							06 10							07 04					
95	—	**Basingstoke**	a	23p42						05 46	06 20	06 34				06 46		07 14					
—	—		d	23p44						05 47		06 35				06 47		07 17					
—	—	Reading 7	a							06 04						07 04							
106¼	—	Fleet	d																				
109½	—	Farnborough (Main)	d																				
118½	—	**Woking**	a	00 02								06 53											
138¾	—	**Clapham Junction** 10	a	00 23								07 14											
142¾	—	**London Waterloo** 15 ⊖	a	00 33								07 24					07 47	08 01				08 16	

Weymouth, Bournemouth, Lymington, Romsey, Southampton and Basingstoke - London

		SW	XC	SW	SW	SW	SW	SW	GW	SW	XC	SW	SW	GW	SW	XC	GW	SW	SW	SW	SW	SW	SW
		1	◇1	1	◇1	◇1	1	1	◇	1	◇1	◇1	◇1		1	◇1		1	1	◇1	1	1	1
						A							A							A			
			⊼		⊼	⊼					⊼	⊼	⊼			⊼			⊼	⊼			
Weymouth	d					05 55							06 25	06 40						06 55			
Upwey	d					05 59							06 29	06 45						06 59			
Dorchester West	a													06 52									
Dorchester South	d					06 07							06 37							07 07			
Moreton (Dorset)	d					06 14							06 44							07 14			
Wool	d					06 20							06 50							07 20			
Wareham	d					06 27							06 57							07 27			
Holton Heath	d					06 31														07 31			
Hamworthy	d					06 36							07 04							07 36			
Poole 4	a					06 40							07 08							07 40			
	d					06 41							07 11						07 20	07 41			
Parkstone (Dorset)	d					06 45							07 15						07 24	07 45			
Branksome	d					06 49							07 19						07 27	07 49			
Bournemouth	a					06 54							07 24						07 32	07 54			
	d		06 30		06 34	06 56						07 04	07 26			07 30			07 34	07 59			
Pokesdown	d				06 38							07 08							07 38				
Christchurch	d				06 42							07 12							07 42				
Hinton Admiral	d				06 47							07 17							07 47				
New Milton	d				06 51							07 21							07 51				
Sway	d				06 56							07 26							07 56				
Lymington Pier	d			06 44						07 14								07 44					
Lymington Town	d			06 46						07 16								07 46					
Brockenhurst 3	a		06 46	06 55	07 01					07 25		07 31				07 46		07 55	08 01	08 14			
	d		06 49		07 03							07 33				07 49			08 03	08 15			
Beaulieu Road	d																		08 08				
Ashurst New Forest	d				07 11							07 41							08 12				
Totton	d				07 16							07 46							08 17				
Salisbury	d							06 50	07 11								07 36					07 50	
Dean	d							07 02														08 02	
Mottisfont & Dunbridge	d							07 08														08 08	
Romsey	d							07 13	07 30								07 56					08 13	
Redbridge	d							07 23														08 21	
Millbrook (Hants)	d							07 26														08 25	
Southampton Central ⛴	a		07 01		07 21	07 25		07 29	07 41			07 51	07 55			08 03	08 09		08 23	08 28		08 27	
	d		07 15		07 30			07 35	07 42			08 00				08 15			08 48	08 30		08 35	
St Denys	d							07 40											→			08 40	
Swaythling	d							07 43														08 43	
Southampton Airport Pkwy ✈	d		07 22		07 38			07 46				08 08				08 22				08 38		08 46	
Portsmouth Harbour ⛴	d	06 23					06 50								07 24						07 55		08 05
Portsmouth & Southsea	d	06 28					06 55								07 29						08 00		08 10
Fratton	d	06 32					06 59								07 33						08 04		08 13
Hilsea	d	06 36					07 03								07 37						08 08		08 17
Cosham	d	06 42					07 08								07 43						08 13		08 22
Portchester	d	06 46					07 13								07 48						08 18		08 27
Fareham	d	06 53					07 20		08a05						07 54						08 24		08 34
Botley	d	07 01					07 28								08 01						08 30		08 41
Hedge End	d	07 05					07 32								08 06						08 36		08 45
Eastleigh 3	a	07 11					07 38	07 49							08 12						08 42	08 49	08 51
	d	07 13					07 43	07 50							08 13						08 43	08 50	08 53
Chandlers Ford	d							07 55														08 55	
Romsey	a							08 03														09 03	
Shawford	d						07 49								08 20						08 49		
Winchester	d	07 22	07 31		07 48		07 55				08 01	08 18			08 26	08 31				08 48	08 55		09 02
Micheldever	d	07 31					08 02														09 03		
Basingstoke	a	07 41	07 46				08 14				08 16	08 34			08 42	08 46					09 15		09 19
	d	07 47	07 47				08 16				08 18	08 35			08 43	08 47					09 17		
Reading 7	a		08 04								08 36					09 04							
Fleet	d														08 54								
Farnborough (Main)	d														09 00						09 30		
Woking	a	08 05					08 34					08 53								09 22	09 39		
Clapham Junction 10	a											09 14			09 26					09 43			
London Waterloo 15 ⊖	a	08 34			08 50		09 03					09 25			09 38					09 53	10 08		

A ⊼ from Bournemouth

Table 158

Weymouth, Bournemouth, Lymington, Romsey, Southampton and Basingstoke - London

		SW ■ ⚒	SW ■	SW ◇■ ⚒	SW ■ ⚒	SW ■	GW ◇ ⚒	SW ■	XC ◇■ ⚒	SW ◇■ A ⚒	SW ■	SW ■	SW ■	XC ◇■ ⚒	SW ■	SW ◇■ A ⚒	SW ■	GW	GW ■ ⚒	SW ■	SW ■	XC ◇■ ⚒
Weymouth	d					07 25				07 55						08 20		08 53				
Upwey	d					07 29				07 59						08 24		08 58				
Dorchester West	a																	09 05				
Dorchester South	d					07 37				08 07						08 33						
Moreton (Dorset)	d					07 44				08 14						08 39						
Wool	d					07 50				08 20						08 45						
Wareham	d					07 57				08 27						08 53						
Holton Heath	d					08 01				08 31						08 56						
Hamworthy	d					08 06				08 36						09 01						
Poole ■	a					08 10				08 40						09 06						
	d			07 55		08 11				08 41					08 50	09 07				09 13		
Parkstone (Dorset)	d			07 59		08 15				08 45					08 54					09 17		
Branksome	d			08 02		08 19				08 49					08 57					09 20		
Bournemouth	a			08 07		08 24				08 54					09 02	09 16				09 25		
	d			08 10		08 25			08 45	08 59					09 05	09 18				09 27		09 45
Pokesdown	d			08 14		08 29									09 09	09 22				09 30		
Christchurch	d			08 18		08 33									09 13	09 26				09 34		
Hinton Admiral	d			08 24		08 38									09 18					09 39		
New Milton	d			08 29		08 42									09 22	09 33				09 44		
Sway	d			08 34		08 47									09 27					09 48		
Lymington Pier	d		08 14					08 44					09 14								09 44	
Lymington Town	d		08 16					08 46					09 16								09 46	
Brockenhurst ■	a		08 25	08 39		08 52		08 55	08 58	09 14			09 25		09 32	09 40				09 53	09 55	09 59
	d			08 41					09 00	09 15					09 33	09 41				09 54		10 00
Beaulieu Road	d																					
Ashurst New Forest	d			08 48											09 40							
Totton	d			08 53											09 45							
Salisbury	d						08 32					08 56							09 32			
Dean	d											09 08										
Mottisfont & Dunbridge	d											09 14										
Romsey	d						08 50					09 19							09 51			
Redbridge	d											09 27										
Millbrook (Hants)	d	←										09 31										
Southampton Central ⛴	a	08 23		08 58			09 04		09 12	09 28		09 34			09 52	09 55			10 04	10 09		10 12
	d	08 48		09 00			09 05		09 15	09 30		09 35		09 46	09 55	10 00			10 05			10 15
St Denys	d	08 53										09 40										
Swaythling	d	08 56										09 43										
Southampton Airport Pkwy ✈	d	08 59		09 08					09 22	09 38		09 46		09 53	10 03	10 08						10 22
Portsmouth Harbour ⛴	d										08 59											
Portsmouth & Southsea	d										09 03											
Fratton	d										09 07											
Hilsea	d										09 11											
Cosham	d										09 17											
Portchester	d										09 21											
Fareham	d						09a27				09 28								10a27			
Botley	d										09 35											
Hedge End	d										09 40											
Eastleigh ■	a	09 03									09 46	09 49			10 06							
	d	09 14									09 47	09 50			10 14							
Chandlers Ford	d											09 55										
Romsey	a											10 03										
Shawford	d	09 19			←										10 19		←					
Winchester	d	09 25		09 18	09 25				09 31	09 48	09 56			10 03	10 25	10 18	10 25					10 31
Micheldever	d	→									10 05				→							
Basingstoke	a			09 35	09 41				09 46		10 15			10 18		10 34	10 41					10 46
	d			09 36	09 43				09 47		10 17			10 19		10 35	10 43					10 47
Reading ■	a								10 04					10 35								11 04
Fleet	d				09 54												10 54					
Farnborough (Main)	d				10 00						10 30						11 00					
Woking	a			09 54						10 20	10 39											
Clapham Junction ■	a			10 15	10 25											11 12	11 25					
London Waterloo ■ ⊖	a			10 23	10 34					10 49	11 08					11 20	11 34					

A ⚒ from Bournemouth

Table 158

Weymouth, Bournemouth, Lymington, Romsey, Southampton and Basingstoke - London

		SW ◇■ A ⚒	SW ■	SW ■	SW ■	SW ■	SW ◇■ A ⚒	SW ■	GW ◇ ⚒	XC ◇■ ⚒	SW ■	SW ◇■ A ⚒	SW ■	SW ■	XC ◇■ ⚒	SW ■	SW ■	SW ◇■ A ⚒	SW ■	GW ◇ ⚒	XC ◇■ ⚒	GW	SW ■
Weymouth	d	09 03					09 20					10 03						10 20					
Upwey	d						09 24											10 24					
Dorchester West	a																						
Dorchester South	d	09 13					09 33					10 13						10 33					
Moreton (Dorset)	d						09 39											10 39					
Wool	d						09 45											10 45					
Wareham	d	09 28					09 53					10 28						10 53					
Holton Heath	d						09 56											10 56					
Hamworthy	d	09 35					10 01					10 35						11 01					
Poole ■	a	09 39					10 06					10 39						11 06					
	d	09 40			09 50		10 07					10 40				10 50		11 07					
Parkstone (Dorset)	d	09 44			09 54							10 44				10 54							
Branksome	d	09 48			09 57							10 48				10 57							
Bournemouth	a	09 53			10 02		10 17					10 54				11 02		11 17					
	d	09 55			10 05		10 22			10 45		10 59				11 05		11 22			11 45		
Pokesdown	d				10 09		10 26									11 09		11 26					
Christchurch	d				10 13		10 30									11 13		11 30					
Hinton Admiral	d				10 18											11 18							
New Milton	d				10 22		10 37									11 22		11 37					
Sway	d				10 27											11 27							
Lymington Pier	d					10 27					10 57						11 27						11 57
Lymington Town	d					10 29					10 59						11 29						11 59
Brockenhurst ■	a	10 10			10 32	10 38	10 44			10 58	11 08	11 14				11 32	11 38	11 44			11 58		12 08
	d	10 11			10 33		10 45			11 00		11 15				11 33		11 45			12 00		
Beaulieu Road	d															11 38							
Ashurst New Forest	d				10 40											11 42							
Totton	d				10 45											11 47							
Salisbury	d			09 56					10 30					10 56						11 32		11 43	
Dean	d			10 08										11 08									
Mottisfont & Dunbridge	d			10 14										11 14									
Romsey	d			10 19					10 50					11 20						11 51		12 11	
Redbridge	d			10 27										11 27									
Millbrook (Hants)	d			10 31										11 31									
Southampton Central ⛴	a	10 26		10 34	10 53		10 58		11 04	11 12		11 28		11 34		11 53		11 58		12 04	12 12	12 22	
	d	10 30		10 35	10 55		11 00		11 05	11 15		11 30		11 35	11 46	11 55		12 00		12 05	12 15		
St Denys	d			10 40										11 40									
Swaythling	d			10 43										11 43									
Southampton Airport Pkwy ✈	d	10 38		10 46	11 03		11 08			11 22		11 38		11 46	11 53	12 03		12 08			12 22		
Portsmouth Harbour ⛴	d		09 59										10 59										
Portsmouth & Southsea	d		10 03										11 03										
Fratton	d		10 07										11 07										
Hilsea	d		10 11										11 11										
Cosham	d		10 17										11 17										
Portchester	d		10 21										11 21										
Fareham	d		10 28						11a27				11 28							12a27			
Botley	d		10 35										11 35										
Hedge End	d		10 40										11 40										
Eastleigh ■	a		10 46	10 49	11 06								11 46	11 49		12 06							
	d		10 47	10 50	11 14								11 47	11 50		12 14							
Chandlers Ford	d			10 55										11 55									
Romsey	a			11 03										12 03									
Shawford	d				11 19			←								12 19			←				
Winchester	d	10 48	10 56		11 25		11 18	11 25		11 31		11 48	11 56		12 02	12 25		12 18	12 25		12 31		
Micheldever	d		11 05		→								12 05			→							
Basingstoke	a		11 15				11 34	11 41		11 46			12 15		12 17			12 34	12 41		12 46		
	d		11 17				11 35	11 43		11 47			12 17		12 18			12 35	12 43		12 47		
Reading ■	a									12 04					12 35						13 04		
Fleet	d							11 54											12 54				
Farnborough (Main)	d		11 30					12 00					12 30						13 00				
Woking	a	11 19	11 39									12 19	12 39										
Clapham Junction ■	a						12 12	12 25										13 12	13 25				
London Waterloo ■ ⊖	a	11 49	12 08				12 20	12 34				12 49	13 07					13 20	13 34				

A ⚒ from Bournemouth

Weymouth, Bournemouth, Lymington, Romsey, Southampton and Basingstoke - London

until 30 September

		SW	GW	SW	SW	SW	SW	SW	SW	GW	XC	SW	SW	SW	SW	XC	SW	SW	SW	SW	GW	XC	SW
		◇■ A ⚒		■	■	■	■	◇■ A ⚒	■	◇ ⚒	◇■ ⚒	■	◇■ A ⚒	■	■	◇■	■	■	◇■ A ⚒	■	◇ ⚒	◇■ ⚒	■
Weymouth	d	11 03	11 10					11 20					12 03						12 20				
Upwey	d		11 15					11 24											12 24				
Dorchester West	a		11 22																				
Dorchester South	d	11 13						11 33					12 13						12 33				
Moreton (Dorset)	d							11 39											12 39				
Wool	d							11 45											12 45				
Wareham	d	11 28						11 53					12 28						12 53				
Holton Heath	d							11 56											12 56				
Hamworthy	d	11 35						12 01					12 35						13 01				
Poole 4	a	11 39						12 06					12 39						13 06				
	d	11 40				11 50		12 07					12 40				12 50		13 07				
Parkstone (Dorset)	d	11 44				11 54							12 44				12 54						
Branksome	d	11 48				11 57							12 48				12 57						
Bournemouth	a	11 54				12 02		12 17					12 54				13 02		13 17				
	d	11 59				12 05		12 22			12 45		12 59				13 05		13 22			13 45	
Pokesdown	d					12 09		12 26									13 09		13 26				
Christchurch	d					12 13		12 30									13 13		13 30				
Hinton Admiral	d					12 18											13 18						
New Milton	d					12 22		12 37									13 22		13 37				
Sway	d					12 27											13 27						
Lymington Pier	d						12 27					12 57						13 27					13 57
Lymington Town	d						12 29					12 59						13 29					13 59
Brockenhurst 3	a	12 14				12 32	12 38	12 44			12 58	13 08	13 14				13 32	13 38	13 44			13 58	14 08
	d	12 15				12 33		12 45			13 00		13 15				13 33		13 45			14 00	
Beaulieu Road	d																						
Ashurst New Forest	d					12 40											13 40						
Totton	d					12 45											13 45						
Salisbury	d				11 56					12 32					12 56						13 32		
Dean	d				12 08										13 08								
Mottisfont & Dunbridge	d				12 14										13 14								
Romsey	d				12 19					12 51					13 19						13 51		
Redbridge	d				12 27										13 27								
Millbrook (Hants)	d				12 31										13 31								
Southampton Central ⛴	a	12 28			12 34	12 52		12 58		13 04	13 12		13 28		13 34		13 53		13 58		14 04	14 12	
	d	12 30			12 35	12 55		13 00		13 05	13 15		13 30		13 35	13 46	13 55		14 00		14 05	14 15	
St Denys	d				12 40										13 40								
Swaythling	d				12 43										13 43								
Southampton Airport Pkwy ✈	d	12 38			12 46	13 03		13 08			13 22		13 38		13 46		14 03		14 08			14 22	
Portsmouth Harbour ⛴	d			11 59										12 59									
Portsmouth & Southsea	d			12 03										13 03									
Fratton	d			12 07										13 07									
Hilsea	d			12 11										13 11									
Cosham	d			12 17										13 17									
Portchester	d			12 21										13 21									
Fareham	d			12 28						13a27				13 28							14a27		
Botley	d			12 35										13 35									
Hedge End	d			12 40										13 40									
Eastleigh 3	a			12 46	12 49	13 06								13 46	13 49		14 06						
	d			12 47	12 50	13 14								13 47	13 50		14 14						
Chandlers Ford	d				12 55										13 55								
Romsey	a				13 03										14 03								
Shawford	d					13 19			←								14 19			←			
Winchester	d	12 48		12 56		13 25		13 18	13 25		13 31		13 48	13 56			14 25		14 18	14 25		14 31	
Micheldever	d			13 05		→								14 05			→						
Basingstoke	a			13 15				13 34	13 41		13 46			14 15		14 17			14 34	14 41		14 46	
	d			13 17				13 35	13 43		13 47			14 17		14 18			14 35	14 43		14 47	
Reading 7	a										14 04					14 35						15 04	
Fleet	d								13 54											14 54			
Farnborough (Main)	d			13 30					14 00					14 30						15 00			
Woking	a	13 19		13 39									14 19	14 39									
Clapham Junction 10	a							14 12	14 25										15 12	15 25			
London Waterloo 15 ⊖	a	13 49		14 07				14 20	14 34				14 49	15 08					15 20	15 34			

A ⚒ from Bournemouth

Weymouth, Bournemouth, Lymington, Romsey, Southampton and Basingstoke - London

until 30 September

		SW	SW	GW	SW	SW	SW	SW	SW	GW	XC	SW	SW	SW	SW	XC	SW	SW	SW	SW	GW	XC
		◇■ A ⚒	■	■ ⚒	■	■	■	◇■ A ⚒	■	◇ ⚒	◇■ ⚒	■	◇■ A ⚒	■	■	◇■ ⚒	■	■	◇■ A ⚒	■	◇ ⚒	◇■ ⚒
Weymouth	d	13 03						13 20					14 03						14 20			
Upwey	d							13 24											14 24			
Dorchester West	a																					
Dorchester South	d	13 13						13 33					14 13						14 33			
Moreton (Dorset)	d							13 39											14 39			
Wool	d							13 45											14 45			
Wareham	d	13 28						13 53					14 28						14 53			
Holton Heath	d							13 56											14 56			
Hamworthy	d	13 35						14 01					14 35						15 01			
Poole 4	a	13 39						14 06					14 39						15 06			
	d	13 40				13 50		14 07					14 40				14 50		15 07			
Parkstone (Dorset)	d	13 44				13 54							14 44				14 54					
Branksome	d	13 48				13 57							14 48				14 57					
Bournemouth	a	13 54				14 02		14 17					14 54				15 02		15 17			
	d	13 59				14 05		14 22			14 45		14 59				15 05		15 22			15 45
Pokesdown	d					14 09		14 26									15 09		15 26			
Christchurch	d					14 13		14 30									15 13		15 30			
Hinton Admiral	d					14 18											15 18					
New Milton	d					14 22		14 37									15 22		15 37			
Sway	d					14 27											15 27					
Lymington Pier	d						14 27					14 57						15 27				
Lymington Town	d						14 29					14 59						15 29				
Brockenhurst 3	a	14 14				14 32	14 38	14 44			14 58	15 08	15 14				15 32	15 38	15 44			15 58
	d	14 15				14 33		14 45			15 00		15 15				15 33		15 45			16 00
Beaulieu Road	d																					
Ashurst New Forest	d					14 40											15 40					
Totton	d					14 45											15 45					
Salisbury	d			13 59	13 50					14 32					14 56						15 32	
Dean	d				14 02										15 08							
Mottisfont & Dunbridge	d				14 08										15 14							
Romsey	d			14 20	14 13					14 51					15 19						15 51	
Redbridge	d				14 21										15 27							
Millbrook (Hants)	d				14 24										15 31							
Southampton Central ⛴	a	14 28		14 32	14 27	14 53		14 58		15 04	15 12		15 28		15 34		15 51		15 58		16 04	16 12
	d	14 30		14 34	14 35	14 55		15 00		15 05	15 15		15 30		15 35	15 47	15 55		16 00		16 05	16 15
St Denys	d				14 40										15 40							
Swaythling	d				14 43										15 43							
Southampton Airport Pkwy ✈	d	14 38			14 46	15 03		15 08			15 22		15 38		15 46		16 03		16 08			16 22
Portsmouth Harbour ⛴	d		13 59											14 59								
Portsmouth & Southsea	d		14 03											15 03								
Fratton	d		14 07											15 07								
Hilsea	d		14 11											15 11								
Cosham	d		14 17											15 17								
Portchester	d		14 21											15 21								
Fareham	d		14 28	14a55						15a27				15 28							16a27	
Botley	d		14 35											15 35								
Hedge End	d		14 40											15 40								
Eastleigh 3	a		14 46		14 49	15 06								15 46	15 49		16 07					
	d		14 47		14 50	15 14								15 47	15 50		16 14					
Chandlers Ford	d				14 55										15 55							
Romsey	a				15 04										16 03							
Shawford	d					15 19			←								16 19			←		
Winchester	d	14 48	14 56			15 25		15 18	15 25		15 31		15 48	15 56			16 25		16 18	16 25		16 31
Micheldever	d		15 05			→								16 05			→					
Basingstoke	a		15 15					15 34	15 41		15 46			16 15		16 17			16 34	16 41		16 46
	d		15 17					15 35	15 43		15 47			16 17		16 18			16 35	16 43		16 47
Reading 7	a										16 04					16 35						17 04
Fleet	d								15 54											16 54		
Farnborough (Main)	d		15 30						16 00					16 30						17 00		
Woking	a	15 19	15 39										16 19	16 39								
Clapham Junction 10	a							16 12	16 25										17 12	17 25		
London Waterloo 15 ⊖	a	15 49	16 07					16 20	16 34				16 49	17 08					17 20	17 36		

A ⚒ from Bournemouth

Weymouth, Bournemouth, Lymington, Romsey, Southampton and Basingstoke - London

		SW	SW	GW	SW	SW	SW	SW	SW	SW	SW	GW	XC	SW	SW	SW	SW	SW	XC	SW	SW	SW	SW
		1	◇1 A ⊼		1	1	1	1	1	◇1 A ⊼	1	◇ ⊼	◇1 ⊼	1	◇1 A ⊼	1	1	1	◇1 ⊼	1	1	◇1 A ⊼	1
Weymouth	d		15 03	15 08						15 20					16 03							16 20	
Upwey	d			15 13						15 24												16 24	
Dorchester West	a			15 20																			
Dorchester South	d		15 13							15 33					16 13							16 33	
Moreton (Dorset)	d									15 39												16 39	
Wool	d									15 45												16 45	
Wareham	d		15 28							15 53					16 28							16 53	
Holton Heath	d									15 56												16 56	
Hamworthy	d		15 35							16 01					16 35							17 01	
Poole 4	a		15 39							16 06					16 39							17 06	
	d		15 40					15 50		16 07					16 40					16 50		17 07	
Parkstone (Dorset)	d		15 44					15 54							16 44					16 54			
Branksome	d		15 48					15 57							16 48					16 57			
Bournemouth	a		15 54					16 02		16 17					16 54					17 02		17 17	
	d		15 59					16 05		16 22			16 45		16 59					17 05		17 22	
Pokesdown	d							16 09		16 26										17 09		17 26	
Christchurch	d							16 13		16 30										17 13		17 30	
Hinton Admiral	d							16 18												17 18			
New Milton	d							16 22		16 37										17 22		17 37	
Sway	d							16 27												17 27			
Lymington Pier	d	15 57							16 27					16 57							17 27		
Lymington Town	d	15 59							16 29					16 59							17 29		
Brockenhurst 3	a	16 08	16 14					16 32	16 38	16 44			16 58	17 08	17 14					17 32	17 38	17 44	
	d		16 15					16 33		16 45			17 00		17 15			17 20		17 33		17 45	
Beaulieu Road	d																						
Ashurst New Forest	d							16 40										17 27		17 40			
Totton	d							16 45										17 32		17 45			
Salisbury	d					15 56						16 32					16 56						
Dean	d					16 08											17 08						
Mottisfont & Dunbridge	d					16 14											17 14						
Romsey	d					16 19						16 51					17 19						
Redbridge	d					16 27											17 27						
Millbrook (Hants)	d					16 31											17 31						
Southampton Central ⛴	a		16 28			16 34		16 51		16 58		17 04	17 12		17 28		17 34	17 41		17 53		17 58	
	d		16 30			16 35		16 52		17 00		17 05	17 15		17 30		17 35		17 46	17 55		18 00	
St Denys	d					16 40		16 57									17 40						
Swaythling	d					16 43		17 00									17 43						
Southampton Airport Pkwy ✈	d		16 38			16 46		17 04		17 08			17 22		17 38		17 46			18 03		18 08	
Portsmouth Harbour ⛴	d				15 59		16 49									16 59							
Portsmouth & Southsea	d				16 03		16 55									17 03							
Fratton	d				16 07		16 59									17 07							
Hilsea	d				16 11		17 03									17 11							
Cosham	d				16 17		17 08									17 17							
Portchester	d				16 21		17 13									17 21							
Fareham	d				16 28		17a18					17a27				17 28							
Botley	d				16 35											17 35							
Hedge End	d				16 40											17 40							
Eastleigh 3	a				16 46	16 49		17 07								17 46	17 49			18 06			
	d				16 47	16 50		17 14								17 47	17 50			18 14			
Chandlers Ford	d					16 55											17 55						
Romsey	a					17 03											18 03						
Shawford	d							17 19			←									18 19			←
Winchester	d		16 48		16 56			17 25		17 18	17 25		17 31		17 48	17 56			18 01	18 25		18 18	18 25
Micheldever	d				17 05			→								18 05				→			
Basingstoke	a				17 15					17 34	17 42		17 46			18 15			18 17			18 34	18 41
	d				17 17					17 36	17 43		17 47			18 17			18 18			18 35	18 43
Reading 7	a												18 04						18 35				
Fleet	d										17 54												18 54
Farnborough (Main)	d				17 30						18 00					18 30							19 00
Woking	a		17 20		17 39										18 19	18 39							
Clapham Junction 10	a									18 12	18 25											19 12	19 26
London Waterloo 15 ⊖	a		17 50		18 08					18 23	18 34				18 47	19 08						19 20	19 34

A ⊼ from Bournemouth

Table 158 — Mondays to Fridays until 30 September

Weymouth, Bournemouth, Lymington, Romsey, Southampton and Basingstoke - London

		GW	XC	SW	SW	SW	SW	SW	SW	SW	SW	GW	GW	XC	SW	SW	SW	SW	SW	SW	SW	GW
		◇ ⊼	◇1 ⊼	1	◇1 A ⊼	1	1	1	1	◇1 A ⊼	1		■ ⊼	◇1 B ⊼	◇1 A ⊼	1	1	1	1	◇1 A ⊼	1	■ ⊼
Weymouth	d				17 04					17 20		17 30			18 06					18 20		
Upwey	d									17 24		17 35								18 24		
Dorchester West	a											17 42										
Dorchester South	d				17 14					17 33					18 16					18 33		
Moreton (Dorset)	d									17 39										18 39		
Wool	d									17 45										18 45		
Wareham	d				17 29					17 53					18 31					18 53		
Holton Heath	d									17 56										18 56		
Hamworthy	d				17 36					18 01					18 38					19 01		
Poole 4	a				17 40					18 06					18 42					19 06		
	d				17 41			17 50		18 07					18 43				18 50	19 07		
Parkstone (Dorset)	d				17 45			17 54							18 47				18 54			
Branksome	d				17 49			17 57							18 51				18 57			
Bournemouth	a				17 54			18 02		18 17					18 56				19 02	19 17		
	d		17 45		17 59			18 05		18 22				18 45	18 59				19 05	19 22		
Pokesdown	d							18 09		18 26									19 09	19 26		
Christchurch	d							18 13		18 30									19 13	19 30		
Hinton Admiral	d							18 18											19 18			
New Milton	d							18 22		18 37									19 22	19 37		
Sway	d							18 27											19 27			
Lymington Pier	d			17 57					18 27									19 03				
Lymington Town	d			17 59					18 29									19 05				
Brockenhurst 3	a		17 58	18 08	18 14			18 32	18 38	18 44				18 58	19 14			19 14	19 32	19 44		
	d		18 00		18 15			18 33		18 45				19 00	19 15				19 33	19 45		
Beaulieu Road	d							18 38														
Ashurst New Forest	d							18 42											19 41			
Totton	d							18 47											19 46			
Salisbury	d	17 32					17 56						18 35				18 56					19 32
Dean	d						18 08										19 08					
Mottisfont & Dunbridge	d						18 14										19 14					
Romsey	d	17 51					18 19						18 54				19 19					19 51
Redbridge	d						18 27										19 27					
Millbrook (Hants)	d						18 31										19 31					
Southampton Central ⛴	a	18 04	18 12		18 28		18 34	18 53		18 58			19 04	19 12	19 28		19 34		19 52	19 58		20 04
	d	18 05	18 15		18 30		18 35	18 55		19 00			19 05	19 15	19 30		19 35		19 55	20 00		20 05
St Denys	d						18 40										19 40					
Swaythling	d						18 43										19 43					
Southampton Airport Pkwy ✈	d		18 22		18 38		18 46	19 03		19 08				19 22	19 38		19 46		20 03	20 08		
Portsmouth Harbour ⛴	d					17 59										18 59						
Portsmouth & Southsea	d					18 03										19 03						
Fratton	d					18 07										19 07						
Hilsea	d					18 11										19 11						
Cosham	d					18 17										19 17						
Portchester	d					18 21										19 21						
Fareham	d	18a27				18 28							19a27			19 28						20a27
Botley	d					18 35										19 35						
Hedge End	d					18 40										19 40						
Eastleigh 3	a					18 46	18 49	19 06								19 46	19 49		20 06			
	d					18 47	18 50	19 14								19 47	19 50		20 14			
Chandlers Ford	d						18 55										19 55					
Romsey	a						19 04										20 03					
Shawford	d							19 19			←								20 19		←	
Winchester	d		18 31		18 48	18 56		19 25		19 18	19 25			19 31	19 48	19 56			20 25	20 18	20 25	
Micheldever	d					19 05		→								20 05			→			
Basingstoke	a		18 46			19 15				19 34	19 41			19 46		20 15				20 34	20 41	
	d		18 47			19 17				19 35	19 43			19 47		20 17				20 36	20 43	
Reading 7	a		19 04											20 04								
Fleet	d										19 54										20 54	
Farnborough (Main)	d					19 30					20 00					20 30					21 00	
Woking	a				19 24	19 39									20 19	20 39					21 09	
Clapham Junction 10	a									20 12	20 25									21 16	21 29	
London Waterloo 15 ⊖	a				19 51	20 08				20 20	20 34				20 49	21 07				21 24	21 38	

A ⊼ from Bournemouth

B ⊼ to Basingstoke

Weymouth, Bournemouth, Lymington, Romsey, Southampton and Basingstoke - London

until 30 September

		SW	XC	SW	SW	SW	GW	SW	SW	SW		GW	SW	SW	SW	SW	GW	GW	SW	SW		SW	SW	GW	SW
		■	◇■	◇■ A ⌶	■	■		■	◇■	■		◇ ⌶	■	■	■	◇■		◇	■	■		■	■	◇	■
Weymouth	d			19 06					19 20							20 10	20 21								
Upwey	d								19 24							20 14	20 26								
Dorchester West	a																20 33								
Dorchester South	d			19 16					19 37							20 22									
Moreton (Dorset)	d								19 43							20 28									
Wool	d								19 49							20 34									
Wareham	d			19 31					19 57							20 42									
Holton Heath	d																								
Hamworthy	d			19 38					20 03							20 48									
Poole [4]	a			19 42					20 08							20 53									
	d			19 43				19 50	20 09							20 54									
Parkstone (Dorset)	d			19 47				19 54								20 58									
Branksome	d			19 51				19 57								21 01									
Bournemouth	a			19 56				20 02	20 18							21 07									
	d		19 45	19 59				20 05	20 22							21 12									
Pokesdown	d							20 09	20 26							21 16									
Christchurch	d							20 13	20 30							21 20									
Hinton Admiral	d							20 18								21 25									
New Milton	d							20 22	20 37							21 29									
Sway	d							20 27								21 34									
Lymington Pier	d	19 33				20 03							20 33		21 03				21 33				22 03		22 33
Lymington Town	d	19 35				20 05							20 35		21 05				21 35				22 05		22 35
Brockenhurst [3]	a	19 44	19 58	20 14		20 14		20 32	20 44				20 44		21 14	21 39			21 44				22 14		22 44
	d		20 00	20 15				20 33	20 45							21 40									
Beaulieu Road	d																								
Ashurst New Forest	d							20 40								21 47									
Totton	d							20 45								21 52									
Salisbury	d				19 56		20 14					20 32		20 56				21 32				21 56		22 32	
Dean	d				20 08									21 08								22 08			
Mottisfont & Dunbridge	d				20 14									21 14								22 14			
Romsey	d				20 19		20 35					20 51		21 19				21 50				22 19		22 50	
Redbridge	d				20 27									21 27								22 27			
Millbrook (Hants)	d				20 31									21 31								22 31			
Southampton Central ⛴	a		20 12	20 28	20 34		20 48	20 51	20 58			21 04		21 34		21 57		22 02				22 34		23 04	
	d		20 15	20 30	20 35			20 55	21 00			21 05		21 35		22 00		22 04				22 35		23 05	
St Denys	d				20 40									21 40								22 40			
Swaythling	d				20 43									21 43								22 43			
Southampton Airport Pkwy ✈	d		20 22	20 38	20 46			21 03	21 08					21 46		22 08						22 46			
Portsmouth Harbour ⛴	d																			21 54					
Portsmouth & Southsea	d																			21 59					
Fratton	d																			22 03					
Hilsea	d																			22 07					
Cosham	d																			22 12					
Portchester	d																			22 17					
Fareham	d											21a27								22 23				23a27	
Botley	d																			22 30					
Hedge End	d																			22 35					
Eastleigh [8]	a				20 49			21 06						21 49				22 14		22 41		22 49			
	d				20 50			21 14						21 50								22 50			
Chandlers Ford	d				20 55									21 55								22 55			
Romsey	a				21 03									22 03								23 03			
Shawford	d							21 19		←															
Winchester	d		20 31	20 48				21 25	21 18	21 25						22 18									
Micheldever	d							→																	
Basingstoke	a		20 46						21 34	21 41						22 34									
	d		20 47						21 35	21 43						22 36									
Reading [7]	a		21 04																						
Fleet	d									21 54															
Farnborough (Main)	d									22 00															
Woking	a			21 19						22 09						22 54									
Clapham Junction [10]	a								22 14	22 29						23 14									
London Waterloo [15] ⊖	a			21 49					22 22	22 38						23 23									

A ⌶ from Bournemouth

Weymouth, Bournemouth, Lymington, Romsey, Southampton and Basingstoke - London

until 30 September

		SW	SW	SW
		■	◇■	■
Weymouth	d		22 10	23 10
Upwey	d		22 14	23 14
Dorchester West	a			
Dorchester South	d		22 22	23 22
Moreton (Dorset)	d		22 28	23 28
Wool	d		22 34	23 34
Wareham	d		22 42	23 42
Holton Heath	d			
Hamworthy	d		22 48	23 48
Poole [4]	a		22 53	23 53
	d		22 54	23 54
Parkstone (Dorset)	d		22 58	
Branksome	d		23 01	
Bournemouth	a		23 07	00 03
	d		23 12	
Pokesdown	d		23 16	
Christchurch	d		23 20	
Hinton Admiral	d		23 25	
New Milton	d		23 29	
Sway	d		23 34	
Lymington Pier	d			
Lymington Town	d			
Brockenhurst [3]	a		23 39	
	d		23 40	
Beaulieu Road	d			
Ashurst New Forest	d		23 47	
Totton	d		23 52	
Salisbury	d			
Dean	d			
Mottisfont & Dunbridge	d			
Romsey	d			
Redbridge	d			
Millbrook (Hants)	d			
Southampton Central ⛴	a		23 57	
	d		23 59	
St Denys	d		00 04	
Swaythling	d		00 07	
Southampton Airport Pkwy ✈	d		00 10	
Portsmouth Harbour ⛴	d	23 24		
Portsmouth & Southsea	d	23 29		
Fratton	d	23 33		
Hilsea	d	23 37		
Cosham	d	23 42		
Portchester	d	23 47		
Fareham	d	23 53		
Botley	d	23 59		
Hedge End	d	00 05		
Eastleigh [8]	a	00 11	00 14	
	d	00 19		
Chandlers Ford	d			
Romsey	a			
Shawford	d			
Winchester	d	00a28		
Micheldever	d			
Basingstoke	a			
	d			
Reading [7]	a			
Fleet	d			
Farnborough (Main)	d			
Woking	a			
Clapham Junction [10]	a			
London Waterloo [15] ⊖	a			

Table 158

Mondays to Fridays
from 3 October

Weymouth, Bournemouth, Lymington, Romsey, Southampton and Basingstoke - London

		SW MO ◇1	SW MO 1	SW MX 1	SW MX ◇1	SW MO 1	SW MX 1	XC ◇1	SW 1	SW ◇1 🍴	SW 1	GW	SW 1	XC ◇1 🍴	SW ◇1 🍴	SW 1	SW 1	SW 1	GW	SW ◇1 🍴	SW ◇1 🍴	SW 1	XC ◇1 🍴
Weymouth	d	20p58			22p10	22p58	23p10					05 33											
Upwey	d	21p02			22p14	23p02	23p14					05 37											
Dorchester West	a											05 44											
Dorchester South	d	21p10			22p22	23p10	23p22																
Moreton (Dorset)	d	21p17			22p28	23p17	23p28																
Wool	d	21p23			22p34	23p23	23p34																
Wareham	d	21p30			22p42	23p30	23p42																
Holton Heath	d																						
Hamworthy	d	21p37			22p48	23p37	23p48																
Poole 4	a	21p41			22p53	23p41	23p53																
	d	21p50			22p54	23p50	23p54			04 57	05 23				05 42						06 08		
Parkstone (Dorset)	d	21p54			22p58	23p54				05 01	05 27										06 12		
Branksome	d	21p57			23p01	23p57				05 04	05 30										06 15		
Bournemouth	a	22p03			23p07	00 03	00 03			05 09	05 36				05 51						06 23		
	d	22p06			23p12					05 12	05 38				05 54					06 04	06 25		06 30
Pokesdown	d	22p10			23p16					05 16	05 42									06 08			
Christchurch	d	22p14			23p20					05 20	05 46									06 12			
Hinton Admiral	d	22p19			23p25						05 51									06 17			
New Milton	d	22p23			23p29					05 27	05 55									06 21			
Sway	d	22p28			23p34						06 00									06 26			
Lymington Pier	d																	06 14					
Lymington Town	d																	06 16					
Brockenhurst 3	a	22p33			23p39					05 37	06 07				06 12			06 25		06 31			06 46
	d	22p34			23p40					05 38					06 14					06 33			06 49
Beaulieu Road	d	22p39																					
Ashurst New Forest	d	22p43			23p47															06 41			
Totton	d	22p48			23p52					05 49							06 12			06 46			
Salisbury	d												05 35						06 20				
Dean	d												05 47										
Mottisfont & Dunbridge	d												05 53										
Romsey	d												05 58						06 38				
Redbridge	d																06 14						
Millbrook (Hants)	d																06 17						
Southampton Central	a	22p53			23p57					05 54					06 27		06 24		06 49	06 51	06 55		07 01
	d	22p55			23p59			05 15		05 55				06 15	06 30		06 35		06 53	07 00			07 15
St Denys	d				00 04												06 40						
Swaythling	d				00 07												06 43						
Southampton Airport Pkwy	d	23p03			00 10			05 22		06 03				06 22	06 38		06 46			07 08			07 22
Portsmouth Harbour	d		23p17	23p24					04 55							05 43						06 23	
Portsmouth & Southsea	d		23p22	23p29					05 00							05 48						06 28	
Fratton	d		23p26	23p33					05 04							05 52						06 32	
Hilsea	d		23p30	23p37					05 08							05 56						06 36	
Cosham	d		23p35	23p42					05 16							06 03						06 42	
Portchester	d		23p40	23p47					05 20							06 08						06 46	
Fareham	d		23p46	23p53					05 26							06 19			07a14			06 53	
Botley	d		23p54	23p59					05 34							06 27						07 01	
Hedge End	d		23p58	00 05					05 38							06 31						07 05	
Eastleigh 3	a	23p09	00 04	00 11	00 14				05 46	06 07						06 37	06 49					07 11	
	d	23p11		00 19					05 47	06 08						06 43	06 50					07 13	
Chandlers Ford	d												06 06				06 55						
Romsey	a												06 44				07 03						
Shawford	d								05 53							06 49							
Winchester	d	23p23		00a28				05 31	05 59	06 18				06 31	06 48	06 55				07 18		07 22	07 31
Micheldever	d	23p32							06 07							07 04						07 31	
Basingstoke	a	23p42						05 46	06 20	06 34				06 46		07 14						07 41	07 46
	d	23p44						05 47		06 35				06 47		07 17						07 47	07 47
Reading 7	a							06 04						07 04									08 04
Fleet	d																						
Farnborough (Main)	d																						
Woking	a	00 02								06 53												08 05	
Clapham Junction 10	a	00 23								07 14													
London Waterloo 15	a	00 33								07 24					07 47	08 01				08 16		08 34	

Table 158

Mondays to Fridays
from 3 October

Weymouth, Bournemouth, Lymington, Romsey, Southampton and Basingstoke - London

		SW 1	SW ◇1 🍴	SW ◇1 A 🍴	SW 1	SW 1	GW ◇	SW 1	XC ◇1 🍴	SW ◇1 🍴	SW ◇1 A 🍴	GW	SW 1	XC ◇1 🍴	GW	SW 1	SW 1 🍴	SW ◇1 A 🍴	SW 1	SW 1	SW 1	SW 1 🍴	SW 1
Weymouth	d			05 50							06 20	06 40						06 50					
Upwey	d			05 54							06 24	06 45						06 54					
Dorchester West	a											06 52											
Dorchester South	d			06 02							06 32							07 02					
Moreton (Dorset)	d			06 09							06 39							07 09					
Wool	d			06 15							06 45							07 15					
Wareham	d			06 22							06 52							07 22					
Holton Heath	d			06 26														07 26					
Hamworthy	d			06 31							06 59							07 31					
Poole 4	a			06 38							07 06							07 38					
	d			06 39							07 09						07 20	07 39					
Parkstone (Dorset)	d			06 43							07 13						07 24	07 43					
Branksome	d			06 46							07 16						07 27	07 46					
Bournemouth	a			06 54							07 24						07 32	07 54					
	d		06 34	06 56						07 04	07 26			07 30			07 34	07 59					
Pokesdown	d		06 38							07 08							07 38						
Christchurch	d		06 42							07 12							07 42						
Hinton Admiral	d		06 47							07 17							07 47						
New Milton	d		06 51							07 21							07 51						
Sway	d		06 56							07 26							07 56						
Lymington Pier	d	06 44						07 14								07 44							08 14
Lymington Town	d	06 46						07 16								07 46							08 16
Brockenhurst 3	a	06 55	07 01					07 25		07 31				07 46		07 55	08 01	08 14					08 25
	d		07 03							07 33				07 49			08 03	08 15					
Beaulieu Road	d																08 08						
Ashurst New Forest	d		07 11							07 41							08 12						
Totton	d		07 16							07 46							08 17						
Salisbury	d					06 50	07 11								07 36					07 50			
Dean	d					07 02														08 02			
Mottisfont & Dunbridge	d					07 08														08 08			
Romsey	d					07 13	07 30								07 56					08 13			
Redbridge	d					07 23														08 21			
Millbrook (Hants)	d					07 26														08 25		←	
Southampton Central	a		07 21	07 25		07 29	07 41			07 51	07 55			08 03	08 09		08 23	08 28		08 27		08 23	
	d		07 30			07 35	07 42			08 00				08 15			08 48	08 30		08 35		08 48	
St Denys	d					07 40											→			08 40		08 53	
Swaythling	d					07 43														08 43		08 56	
Southampton Airport Pkwy	d		07 38			07 46				08 08				08 22				08 38		08 46		08 59	
Portsmouth Harbour	d				06 50								07 24						07 55		08 05		
Portsmouth & Southsea	d				06 55								07 29						08 00		08 10		
Fratton	d				06 59								07 33						08 04		08 13		
Hilsea	d				07 03								07 37						08 08		08 17		
Cosham	d				07 08								07 43						08 13		08 22		
Portchester	d				07 13								07 48						08 18		08 27		
Fareham	d				07 20		08a05						07 54						08 24		08 34		
Botley	d				07 28								08 01						08 30		08 41		
Hedge End	d				07 32								08 06						08 36		08 45		
Eastleigh 3	a				07 38	07 49							08 12						08 42	08 49	08 51	09 03	
	d				07 43	07 50							08 13						08 43	08 50	08 53	09 14	
Chandlers Ford	d					07 55														08 55			
Romsey	a					08 03														09 03			
Shawford	d				07 49								08 20						08 49			09 19	
Winchester	d		07 48		07 55				08 01	08 18			08 26	08 31				08 48	08 55		09 02	09 25	
Micheldever	d				08 02														09 03			→	
Basingstoke	a				08 14				08 16	08 34			08 42	08 46					09 15		09 19		
	d				08 16				08 18	08 35			08 43	08 47					09 17				
Reading 7	a								08 36					09 04									
Fleet	d												08 54										
Farnborough (Main)	d												09 00						09 30				
Woking	a				08 34					08 53								09 22	09 39				
Clapham Junction 10	a									09 14			09 26					09 43					
London Waterloo 15	a		08 50		09 03					09 25			09 38					09 53	10 08				

A 🍴 from Bournemouth

Weymouth, Bournemouth, Lymington, Romsey, Southampton and Basingstoke - London

from 3 October

		SW	SW	SW	GW	SW	XC	SW	SW	SW	SW	XC	SW	SW	SW	GW	GW	SW	SW	XC	SW	SW
		◇1 ⊼	1 ⊼	1	◇ ⊼	1	◇1 ⊼	◇1 A ⊼	1	1	1	◇1 ⊼	1	◇1 A ⊼	1		■ ⊼	1	1	◇1 ⊼	◇1 A ⊼	1
Weymouth	d			07 25				07 55						08 20		08 53					09 03	
Upwey	d			07 29				07 59						08 24		08 58						
Dorchester West	a															09 05						
Dorchester South	d			07 37				08 07						08 33							09 13	
Moreton (Dorset)	d			07 44				08 14						08 39								
Wool	d			07 50				08 20						08 45								
Wareham	d			07 57				08 27						08 53							09 28	
Holton Heath	d			08 01				08 31						08 56								
Hamworthy	d			08 06				08 36						09 01							09 35	
Poole 4	a			08 10				08 40						09 06							09 39	
	d	07 55		08 11				08 41					08 50	09 07				09 13			09 40	
Parkstone (Dorset)	d	07 59		08 15				08 45					08 54					09 17			09 44	
Branksome	d	08 02		08 19				08 49					08 57					09 20			09 48	
Bournemouth	a	08 07		08 24				08 54					09 02	09 16				09 25			09 53	
	d	08 10		08 25			08 45	08 59					09 05	09 18				09 27		09 45	09 55	
Pokesdown	d	08 14		08 29									09 09	09 22				09 30				
Christchurch	d	08 18		08 33									09 13	09 26				09 34				
Hinton Admiral	d	08 24		08 38									09 18					09 39				
New Milton	d	08 29		08 42									09 22	09 33				09 44				
Sway	d	08 34		08 47									09 27					09 48				
Lymington Pier	d					08 44					09 14								09 44			
Lymington Town	d					08 46					09 16								09 46			
Brockenhurst 3	a	08 39		08 52		08 55	08 58	09 14			09 25		09 32	09 40				09 53	09 55	09 59	10 10	
	d	08 41					09 00	09 15					09 33	09 41				09 54		10 00	10 11	
Beaulieu Road	d																					
Ashurst New Forest	d	08 48											09 40									
Totton	d	08 53											09 45									
Salisbury	d				08 32					08 56							09 32					
Dean	d									09 08												
Mottisfont & Dunbridge	d									09 14												
Romsey	d				08 50					09 19							09 51					
Redbridge	d									09 27												
Millbrook (Hants)	d									09 31												
Southampton Central ⛴	a	08 58			09 04		09 12	09 28		09 34			09 52	09 55			10 04	10 09		10 12	10 26	
	d	09 00			09 05		09 15	09 30		09 35		09 46	09 55	10 00			10 05			10 15	10 30	
St Denys	d									09 40												
Swaythling	d									09 43												
Southampton Airport Pkwy ✈	d	09 08					09 22	09 38		09 46		09 53	10 03	10 08						10 22	10 38	
Portsmouth Harbour ⛴	d								08 59													09 59
Portsmouth & Southsea	d								09 03													10 03
Fratton	d								09 07													10 07
Hilsea	d								09 11													10 11
Cosham	d								09 17													10 17
Portchester	d								09 21													10 21
Fareham	d				09a27				09 28								10a27					10 28
Botley	d								09 35													10 35
Hedge End	d								09 40													10 40
Eastleigh 3	a								09 46	09 49			10 06									10 46
	d								09 47	09 50			10 14									10 47
Chandlers Ford	d									09 55												
Romsey	a									10 03												
Shawford	d		←										10 19		←							
Winchester	d	09 18	09 25				09 31	09 48	09 56			10 03	10 25	10 18	10 25					10 31	10 48	10 56
Micheldever	d								10 05				→									11 05
Basingstoke	a	09 35	09 41				09 46		10 15			10 18		10 34	10 41					10 46		11 15
	d	09 36	09 43				09 47		10 17			10 19		10 35	10 43					10 47		11 17
Reading 7	a						10 04					10 35								11 04		
Fleet	d		09 54												10 54							
Farnborough (Main)	d		10 00						10 30						11 00							11 30
Woking	a	09 54						10 20	10 39												11 19	11 39
Clapham Junction 10	a	10 15	10 25											11 12	11 25							
London Waterloo 15 ⊖	a	10 23	10 34					10 49	11 08					11 20	11 34						11 49	12 08

A ⊼ from Bournemouth

Weymouth, Bournemouth, Lymington, Romsey, Southampton and Basingstoke - London

from 3 October

		SW	SW	SW	SW	SW	GW	XC	SW	SW	SW	SW	XC	SW	SW	SW	SW	GW	XC	GW	SW	SW	GW
		1	1	1	◇1 A ⊼	1	◇ ⊼	◇1 ⊼	1	◇1 A ⊼	1	1	◇1 ⊼	1	1	◇1 A ⊼	1	◇ ⊼	◇1 ⊼		1	◇1 A ⊼	
Weymouth	d				09 20					10 03						10 20						11 03	11 10
Upwey	d				09 24											10 24							11 15
Dorchester West	a																						11 22
Dorchester South	d				09 33					10 13						10 33						11 13	
Moreton (Dorset)	d				09 39											10 39							
Wool	d				09 45											10 45							
Wareham	d				09 53					10 28						10 53						11 28	
Holton Heath	d				09 56											10 56							
Hamworthy	d				10 01					10 35						11 01						11 35	
Poole 4	a				10 06					10 39						11 06						11 39	
	d		09 50		10 07					10 40				10 50		11 07						11 40	
Parkstone (Dorset)	d		09 54							10 44				10 54								11 44	
Branksome	d		09 57							10 48				10 57								11 48	
Bournemouth	a		10 02		10 17					10 54				11 02		11 17						11 54	
	d		10 05		10 22			10 45		10 59				11 05		11 22			11 45			11 59	
Pokesdown	d		10 09		10 26									11 09		11 26							
Christchurch	d		10 13		10 30									11 13		11 30							
Hinton Admiral	d		10 18											11 18									
New Milton	d		10 22		10 37									11 22		11 37							
Sway	d		10 27											11 27									
Lymington Pier	d			10 27					10 57						11 27						11 57		
Lymington Town	d			10 29					10 59						11 29						11 59		
Brockenhurst 3	a		10 32	10 38	10 44			10 58	11 08	11 14				11 32	11 38	11 44			11 58		12 08	12 14	
	d		10 33		10 45			11 00		11 15				11 33		11 45			12 00			12 15	
Beaulieu Road	d													11 38									
Ashurst New Forest	d		10 40											11 42									
Totton	d		10 45											11 47									
Salisbury	d	09 56					10 30					10 56						11 32		11 43			
Dean	d	10 08										11 08											
Mottisfont & Dunbridge	d	10 14										11 14											
Romsey	d	10 19					10 50					11 20						11 51		12 11			
Redbridge	d	10 27										11 27											
Millbrook (Hants)	d	10 31										11 31											
Southampton Central ⛴	a	10 34	10 53		10 58		11 04	11 12		11 28		11 34		11 53		11 58		12 04	12 12	12 22		12 28	
	d	10 35	10 55		11 00		11 05	11 15		11 30		11 35	11 46	11 55		12 00		12 05	12 15			12 30	
St Denys	d	10 40										11 40											
Swaythling	d	10 43										11 43											
Southampton Airport Pkwy ✈	d	10 46	11 03		11 08			11 22		11 38		11 46	11 53	12 03		12 08			12 22			12 38	
Portsmouth Harbour ⛴	d										10 59												
Portsmouth & Southsea	d										11 03												
Fratton	d										11 07												
Hilsea	d										11 11												
Cosham	d										11 17												
Portchester	d										11 21												
Fareham	d						11a27				11 28							12a27					
Botley	d										11 35												
Hedge End	d										11 40												
Eastleigh 3	a	10 49	11 06								11 46	11 49		12 06									
	d	10 50	11 14								11 47	11 50		12 14									
Chandlers Ford	d	10 55										11 55											
Romsey	a	11 03										12 03											
Shawford	d		11 19			←								12 19			←						
Winchester	d		11 25		11 18	11 25		11 31		11 48	11 56		12 02	12 25		12 18	12 25		12 31			12 48	
Micheldever	d		→								12 05			→									
Basingstoke	a				11 34	11 41		11 46			12 15		12 17			12 34	12 41		12 46				
	d				11 35	11 43		11 47			12 17		12 18			12 35	12 43		12 47				
Reading 7	a							12 04					12 35						13 04				
Fleet	d					11 54											12 54						
Farnborough (Main)	d					12 00					12 30						13 00						
Woking	a									12 19	12 39											13 19	
Clapham Junction 10	a				12 12	12 25										13 12	13 25						
London Waterloo 15 ⊖	a				12 20	12 34				12 49	13 07					13 20	13 34					13 49	

A ⊼ from Bournemouth

Table 158

Mondays to Fridays

from 3 October

Weymouth, Bournemouth, Lymington, Romsey, Southampton and Basingstoke - London

		SW	SW	SW	SW	SW	SW	GW	XC	SW	SW	SW	SW	XC	SW	SW	SW	SW	GW	XC	SW	SW
		■	■	■	■	◇■ A ✠	■	◇ ✠	◇■ ✠	■	◇■ A ✠	■	■	◇■	■	■	◇■ A ✠	■	◇ ✠	◇■ ✠	■	◇■ A ✠
Weymouth	d					11 20					12 03						12 20					13 03
Upwey	d					11 24											12 24					
Dorchester West	a																					
Dorchester South	d					11 33					12 13						12 33					13 13
Moreton (Dorset)	d					11 39											12 39					
Wool	d					11 45											12 45					
Wareham	d					11 53					12 28						12 53					13 28
Holton Heath	d					11 56											12 56					
Hamworthy	d					12 01					12 35						13 01					13 35
Poole ■	a					12 06					12 39						13 06					13 39
	d			11 50		12 07					12 40				12 50		13 07					13 40
Parkstone (Dorset)	d			11 54							12 44				12 54							13 44
Branksome	d			11 57							12 48				12 57							13 48
Bournemouth	a			12 02		12 17					12 54				13 02		13 17					13 54
	d			12 05		12 22			12 45		12 59				13 05		13 22			13 45		13 59
Pokesdown	d			12 09		12 26									13 09		13 26					
Christchurch	d			12 13		12 30									13 13		13 30					
Hinton Admiral	d			12 18											13 18							
New Milton	d			12 22		12 37									13 22		13 37					
Sway	d			12 27											13 27							
Lymington Pier	d				12 27					12 57						13 27					13 57	
Lymington Town	d				12 29					12 59						13 29					13 59	
Brockenhurst ■	a			12 32	12 38	12 44			12 58	13 08	13 14				13 32	13 38	13 44			13 58	14 08	14 14
	d			12 33		12 45			13 00		13 15				13 33		13 45			14 00		14 15
Beaulieu Road	d																					
Ashurst New Forest	d			12 40											13 40							
Totton	d			12 45											13 45							
Salisbury	d		11 56					12 32					12 56						13 32			
Dean	d		12 08										13 08									
Mottisfont & Dunbridge	d		12 14										13 14									
Romsey	d		12 19					12 51					13 19						13 51			
Redbridge	d		12 27										13 27									
Millbrook (Hants)	d		12 31										13 31									
Southampton Central	a		12 34	12 52		12 58		13 04	13 12		13 28		13 34		13 53		13 58		14 04	14 12		14 28
	d		12 35	12 55		13 00		13 05	13 15		13 30		13 35	13 46	13 55		14 00		14 05	14 15		14 30
St Denys	d		12 40										13 40									
Swaythling	d		12 43										13 43									
Southampton Airport Pkwy ✈	d		12 46	13 03		13 08			13 22		13 38		13 46		14 03		14 08			14 22		14 38
Portsmouth Harbour	d	11 59										12 59										
Portsmouth & Southsea	d	12 03										13 03										
Fratton	d	12 07										13 07										
Hilsea	d	12 11										13 11										
Cosham	d	12 17										13 17										
Portchester	d	12 21										13 21										
Fareham	d	12 28						13a27				13 28							14a27			
Botley	d	12 35										13 35										
Hedge End	d	12 40										13 40										
Eastleigh ■	a	12 46	12 49	13 06								13 46	13 49		14 06							
	d	12 47	12 50	13 14								13 47	13 50		14 14							
Chandlers Ford	d		12 55										13 55									
Romsey	a		13 03										14 03									
Shawford	d			13 19			←								14 19			←				
Winchester	d	12 56		13 25		13 18	13 25		13 31		13 48	13 56			14 25		14 18	14 25		14 31		14 48
Micheldever	d	13 05		↪								14 05			↪							
Basingstoke	a	13 15				13 34	13 41		13 46			14 15		14 17			14 34	14 41		14 46		
	d	13 17				13 35	13 43		13 47			14 17		14 18			14 35	14 43		14 47		
Reading ■	a								14 04					14 35						15 04		
Fleet	d						13 54											14 54				
Farnborough (Main)	d	13 30					14 00					14 30						15 00				
Woking	a	13 39									14 19	14 39										15 19
Clapham Junction ■	a					14 12	14 25										15 12	15 25				
London Waterloo ■ ⊖	a	14 07				14 20	14 34				14 49	15 08					15 20	15 34				15 49

A ✠ from Bournemouth

Table 158

Mondays to Fridays

from 3 October

Weymouth, Bournemouth, Lymington, Romsey, Southampton and Basingstoke - London

		SW	GW	SW	SW	SW	SW	SW	GW	XC	SW	SW	SW	SW	XC	SW	SW	SW	SW	GW	XC	SW	SW
		■	■ ✠	■	■	■	◇■ A ✠	■	◇ ✠	◇■ ✠	■	◇■ A ✠	■	■	◇■ ✠	■	■	◇■ A ✠	■	◇ ✠	◇■ ✠	■	◇■ A ✠
Weymouth	d						13 20					14 03						14 20					15 03
Upwey	d						13 24											14 24					
Dorchester West	a																						
Dorchester South	d						13 33					14 13						14 33					15 13
Moreton (Dorset)	d						13 39											14 39					
Wool	d						13 45											14 45					
Wareham	d						13 53					14 28						14 53					15 28
Holton Heath	d						13 56											14 56					
Hamworthy	d						14 01					14 35						15 01					15 35
Poole ■	a						14 06					14 39						15 06					15 39
	d				13 50		14 07					14 40				14 50		15 07					15 40
Parkstone (Dorset)	d				13 54							14 44				14 54							15 44
Branksome	d				13 57							14 48				14 57							15 48
Bournemouth	a				14 02		14 17					14 54				15 02		15 17					15 54
	d				14 05		14 22			14 45		14 59				15 05		15 22			15 45		15 59
Pokesdown	d				14 09		14 26									15 09		15 26					
Christchurch	d				14 13		14 30									15 13		15 30					
Hinton Admiral	d				14 18											15 18							
New Milton	d				14 22		14 37									15 22		15 37					
Sway	d				14 27											15 27							
Lymington Pier	d					14 27					14 57						15 27					15 57	
Lymington Town	d					14 29					14 59						15 29					15 59	
Brockenhurst ■	a				14 32	14 38	14 44			14 58	15 08	15 14				15 32	15 38	15 44			15 58	16 08	16 14
	d				14 33		14 45			15 00		15 15				15 33		15 45			16 00		16 15
Beaulieu Road	d																						
Ashurst New Forest	d				14 40											15 40							
Totton	d				14 45											15 45							
Salisbury	d		13 59	13 50					14 32					14 56						15 32			
Dean	d			14 02										15 08									
Mottisfont & Dunbridge	d			14 08										15 14									
Romsey	d		14 20	14 13					14 51					15 19						15 51			
Redbridge	d			14 21										15 27									
Millbrook (Hants)	d			14 24										15 31									
Southampton Central	a		14 32	14 27	14 53		14 58		15 04	15 12		15 28		15 34		15 51		15 58		16 04	16 12		16 28
	d		14 34	14 35	14 55		15 00		15 05	15 15		15 30		15 35	15 47	15 55		16 00		16 05	16 15		16 30
St Denys	d			14 40										15 40									
Swaythling	d			14 43										15 43									
Southampton Airport Pkwy ✈	d			14 46	15 03		15 08			15 22		15 38		15 46		16 03		16 08			16 22		16 38
Portsmouth Harbour	d	13 59											14 59										
Portsmouth & Southsea	d	14 03											15 03										
Fratton	d	14 07											15 07										
Hilsea	d	14 11											15 11										
Cosham	d	14 17											15 17										
Portchester	d	14 21											15 21										
Fareham	d	14 28	14a55						15a27				15 28							16a27			
Botley	d	14 35											15 35										
Hedge End	d	14 40											15 40										
Eastleigh ■	a	14 46		14 49	15 06								15 46	15 49		16 07							
	d	14 47		14 50	15 14								15 47	15 50		16 14							
Chandlers Ford	d			14 55										15 55									
Romsey	a			15 04										16 03									
Shawford	d				15 19			←								16 19			←				
Winchester	d	14 56			15 25		15 18	15 25		15 31		15 48	15 56			16 25		16 18	16 25		16 31		16 48
Micheldever	d	15 05			↪								16 05			↪							
Basingstoke	a	15 15					15 34	15 41		15 46			16 15		16 17			16 34	16 41		16 46		
	d	15 17					15 35	15 43		15 47			16 17		16 18			16 35	16 43		16 47		
Reading ■	a									16 04					16 35						17 04		
Fleet	d							15 54											16 54				
Farnborough (Main)	d	15 30						16 00					16 30						17 00				
Woking	a	15 39										16 19	16 39										17 20
Clapham Junction ■	a						16 12	16 25										17 12	17 25				
London Waterloo ■ ⊖	a	16 07					16 20	16 34				16 49	17 08					17 20	17 36				17 50

A ✠ from Bournemouth

Weymouth, Bournemouth, Lymington, Romsey, Southampton and Basingstoke - London

		GW	SW	SW	SW	SW	SW	SW	SW	GW	XC	SW	SW	SW	SW	SW	XC	SW	SW	SW	SW	GW	XC
			[1]	[1]	[1]	[1]	[1]	◇[1]	[1]	◇	◇[1]	[1]	◇[1]	[1]	[1]	[1]	◇[1]	[1]	[1]	◇[1]	[1]	◇	◇[1]
								A					A							A			
								⌶		⌶	⌶		⌶				⌶			⌶		⌶	⌶
Weymouth	d	15 08						15 20					16 03							16 20			
Upwey	d	15 13						15 24												16 24			
Dorchester West	a	15 20																					
Dorchester South	d							15 33					16 13							16 33			
Moreton (Dorset)	d							15 39												16 39			
Wool	d							15 45												16 45			
Wareham	d							15 53					16 28							16 53			
Holton Heath	d							15 56												16 56			
Hamworthy	d							16 01					16 35							17 01			
Poole [4]	a							16 06					16 39							17 06			
	d					15 50		16 07					16 40					16 50		17 07			
Parkstone (Dorset)	d					15 54							16 44					16 54					
Branksome	d					15 57							16 48					16 57					
Bournemouth	a					16 02		16 17					16 54					17 02		17 17			
	d					16 05		16 22			16 45		16 59					17 05		17 22			17 45
Pokesdown	d					16 09		16 26										17 09		17 26			
Christchurch	d					16 13		16 30										17 13		17 30			
Hinton Admiral	d					16 18												17 18					
New Milton	d					16 22		16 37										17 22		17 37			
Sway	d					16 27												17 27					
Lymington Pier	d						16 27					16 57							17 27				
Lymington Town	d						16 29					16 59							17 29				
Brockenhurst [3]	a					16 32	16 38	16 44			16 58	17 08	17 14					17 32	17 38	17 44			17 58
	d					16 33		16 45			17 00		17 15			17 20		17 33		17 45			18 00
Beaulieu Road	d																						
Ashurst New Forest	d					16 40										17 27		17 40					
Totton	d					16 45										17 32		17 45					
Salisbury	d			15 56						16 32					16 56							17 32	
Dean	d			16 08											17 08								
Mottisfont & Dunbridge	d			16 14											17 14								
Romsey	d			16 19						16 51					17 19							17 51	
Redbridge	d			16 27											17 27								
Millbrook (Hants)	d			16 31											17 31								
Southampton Central ⛴	a			16 34		16 51		16 58		17 04	17 12		17 28		17 34	17 41		17 53		17 58		18 04	18 12
	d			16 35		16 52		17 00		17 05	17 15		17 30		17 35		17 46	17 55		18 00		18 05	18 15
St Denys	d			16 40		16 57									17 40								
Swaythling	d			16 43		17 00									17 43								
Southampton Airport Pkwy ✈	d			16 46		17 04		17 08			17 22		17 38		17 46			18 03		18 08			18 22
Portsmouth Harbour ⛴	d		15 59		16 49									16 59									
Portsmouth & Southsea	d		16 03		16 55									17 03									
Fratton	d		16 07		16 59									17 07									
Hilsea	d		16 11		17 03									17 11									
Cosham	d		16 17		17 08									17 17									
Portchester	d		16 21		17 13									17 21									
Fareham	d		16 28		17a18					17a27				17 28								18a27	
Botley	d		16 35											17 35									
Hedge End	d		16 40											17 40									
Eastleigh [3]	a		16 46	16 49		17 07								17 46	17 49			18 06					
	d		16 47	16 50		17 14								17 47	17 50			18 14					
Chandlers Ford	d			16 55											17 55								
Romsey	a			17 03											18 03								
Shawford	d					17 19			←									18 19			←		
Winchester	d		16 56			17 25		17 18	17 25		17 31		17 48	17 56			18 01	18 25		18 18	18 25		18 31
Micheldever	d		17 05			→								18 05				→					
Basingstoke	a		17 15					17 34	17 42		17 46			18 15			18 17			18 34	18 41		18 46
	d		17 17					17 36	17 43		17 47			18 17			18 18			18 35	18 43		18 47
Reading [7]	a										18 04						18 35						19 04
Fleet	d								17 54												18 54		
Farnborough (Main)	d		17 30						18 00					18 30							19 00		
Woking	a		17 39										18 19	18 39									
Clapham Junction [10]	a							18 12	18 25											19 12	19 26		
London Waterloo [15] ⊖	a		18 08					18 23	18 34				18 47	19 08						19 20	19 34		

A ⌶ from Bournemouth

Weymouth, Bournemouth, Lymington, Romsey, Southampton and Basingstoke - London

		SW	SW	SW	SW	SW	SW	SW	SW	GW	GW	XC	SW	SW	SW	SW	SW	SW	SW	GW	SW	XC
											■									■		
		[1]	◇[1]	[1]	[1]	[1]	[1]	◇[1]	[1]			◇[1]	◇[1]	[1]	[1]	[1]	[1]	◇[1]	[1]		[1]	◇[1]
			A					A				B	A					A				
			⌶					⌶			⌶	⌶	⌶					⌶		⌶		
Weymouth	d		17 04					17 20		17 30			18 06					18 20				
Upwey	d							17 24		17 35								18 24				
Dorchester West	a									17 42												
Dorchester South	d		17 14					17 33					18 16					18 33				
Moreton (Dorset)	d							17 39										18 39				
Wool	d							17 45										18 45				
Wareham	d		17 29					17 53					18 31					18 53				
Holton Heath	d							17 56										18 56				
Hamworthy	d		17 36					18 01					18 38					19 01				
Poole [4]	a		17 40					18 06					18 42					19 06				
	d		17 41			17 50		18 07					18 43				18 50	19 07				
Parkstone (Dorset)	d		17 45			17 54							18 47				18 54					
Branksome	d		17 49			17 57							18 51				18 57					
Bournemouth	a		17 54			18 02		18 17					18 56				19 02	19 17				
	d		17 59			18 05		18 22				18 45	18 59				19 05	19 22				19 45
Pokesdown	d					18 09		18 26									19 09	19 26				
Christchurch	d					18 13		18 30									19 13	19 30				
Hinton Admiral	d					18 18											19 18					
New Milton	d					18 22		18 37									19 22	19 37				
Sway	d					18 27											19 27					
Lymington Pier	d	17 57					18 27									19 03					19 33	
Lymington Town	d	17 59					18 29									19 05					19 35	
Brockenhurst [3]	a	18 08	18 14			18 32	18 38	18 44				18 58	19 14			19 14	19 32	19 44			19 44	19 58
	d		18 15			18 33		18 45				19 00	19 15				19 33	19 45				20 00
Beaulieu Road	d					18 38																
Ashurst New Forest	d					18 42											19 41					
Totton	d					18 47											19 46					
Salisbury	d				17 56						18 35				18 56					19 32		
Dean	d				18 08										19 08							
Mottisfont & Dunbridge	d				18 14										19 14							
Romsey	d				18 19						18 54				19 19					19 51		
Redbridge	d				18 27										19 27							
Millbrook (Hants)	d				18 31										19 31							
Southampton Central ⛴	a		18 28		18 34	18 53		18 58			19 04	19 12	19 28		19 34		19 52	19 58		20 04		20 12
	d		18 30		18 35	18 55		19 00			19 05	19 15	19 30		19 35		19 55	20 00		20 05		20 15
St Denys	d				18 40										19 40							
Swaythling	d				18 43										19 43							
Southampton Airport Pkwy ✈	d		18 38		18 46	19 03		19 08				19 22	19 38		19 46		20 03	20 08				20 22
Portsmouth Harbour ⛴	d			17 59										18 59								
Portsmouth & Southsea	d			18 03										19 03								
Fratton	d			18 07										19 07								
Hilsea	d			18 11										19 11								
Cosham	d			18 17										19 17								
Portchester	d			18 21										19 21								
Fareham	d			18 28							19a27			19 28						20a27		
Botley	d			18 35										19 35								
Hedge End	d			18 40										19 40								
Eastleigh [3]	a			18 46	18 49	19 06								19 46	19 49		20 06					
	d			18 47	18 50	19 14								19 47	19 50		20 14					
Chandlers Ford	d				18 55										19 55							
Romsey	a				19 04										20 03							
Shawford	d					19 19			←								20 19		←			
Winchester	d		18 48	18 56		19 25		19 18	19 25			19 31	19 48	19 56			20 25	20 18	20 25			20 31
Micheldever	d			19 05		→								20 05			→					
Basingstoke	a			19 15				19 34	19 41			19 46		20 15				20 34	20 41			20 46
	d			19 17				19 35	19 43			19 47		20 17				20 36	20 43			20 47
Reading [7]	a											20 04										21 04
Fleet	d								19 54										20 54			
Farnborough (Main)	d			19 30					20 00					20 30					21 00			
Woking	a		19 24	19 39									20 19	20 39					21 09			
Clapham Junction [10]	a							20 12	20 25									21 16	21 29			
London Waterloo [15] ⊖	a		19 51	20 08				20 20	20 34				20 49	21 07				21 24	21 38			

A ⌶ from Bournemouth

B ⌶ to Basingstoke

Table 158

Mondays to Fridays
from 3 October

Weymouth, Bournemouth, Lymington, Romsey, Southampton and Basingstoke - London

		SW ◇1 A 🍴	SW 1	SW 1	GW	SW 1	SW ◇1	SW 1	GW ◇ 🍴	SW 1	SW 1	SW 1	SW ◇1	GW	GW ◇	SW 1	SW 1	SW 1	SW 1	GW ◇	SW 1	SW 1	SW ◇1
Weymouth	d	19 06					19 20						20 10	20 21									22 10
Upwey	d						19 24						20 14	20 26									22 14
Dorchester West	a													20 33									
Dorchester South	d	19 16					19 37						20 22										22 22
Moreton (Dorset)	d						19 43						20 28										22 28
Wool	d						19 49						20 34										22 34
Wareham	d	19 31					19 57						20 42										22 42
Holton Heath	d																						
Hamworthy	d	19 38					20 03						20 48										22 48
Poole 4	a	19 42					20 08						20 53										22 53
	d	19 43				19 50	20 09						20 54										22 54
Parkstone (Dorset)	d	19 47				19 54							20 58										22 58
Branksome	d	19 51				19 57							21 01										23 01
Bournemouth	a	19 56				20 02	20 18						21 07										23 07
	d	19 59				20 05	20 22						21 12										23 12
Pokesdown	d					20 09	20 26						21 16										23 16
Christchurch	d					20 13	20 30						21 20										23 20
Hinton Admiral	d					20 18							21 25										23 25
New Milton	d					20 22	20 37						21 29										23 29
Sway	d					20 27							21 34										23 34
Lymington Pier	d			20 03						20 33		21 03				21 33			22 03		22 33		
Lymington Town	d			20 05						20 35		21 05				21 35			22 05		22 35		
Brockenhurst 3	a	20 14		20 14		20 32	20 44			20 44		21 14	21 39			21 44			22 14		22 44		23 39
	d	20 15				20 33	20 45						21 40										23 40
Beaulieu Road	d																						
Ashurst New Forest	d					20 40							21 47										23 47
Totton	d					20 45							21 52										23 52
Salisbury	d		19 56		20 14				20 32		20 56				21 32			21 56		22 32			
Dean	d		20 08								21 08							22 08					
Mottisfont & Dunbridge	d		20 14								21 14							22 14					
Romsey	d		20 19		20 35				20 51		21 19				21 50			22 19		22 50			
Redbridge	d		20 27								21 27							22 27					
Millbrook (Hants)	d		20 31								21 31							22 31					
Southampton Central ⛴	a	20 28	20 34		20 48	20 51	20 58		21 04		21 34		21 57		22 02			22 34		23 04			23 57
	d	20 30	20 35			20 55	21 00		21 05		21 35		22 00		22 04			22 35		23 05			23 59
St Denys	d		20 40								21 40							22 40					00 04
Swaythling	d		20 43								21 43							22 43					00 07
Southampton Airport Pkwy ✈	d	20 38	20 46			21 03	21 08				21 46		22 08					22 46					00 10
Portsmouth Harbour ⛴	d																21 54					23 24	
Portsmouth & Southsea	d																21 59					23 29	
Fratton	d																22 03					23 33	
Hilsea	d																22 07					23 37	
Cosham	d																22 12					23 42	
Portchester	d																22 17					23 47	
Fareham	d								21a27								22 23			23a27		23 53	
Botley	d																22 30					23 59	
Hedge End	d																22 35					00 05	
Eastleigh 3	a		20 49			21 06					21 49				22 14		22 41	22 49				00 11	00 14
	d		20 50			21 14					21 50							22 50				00 19	
Chandlers Ford	d		20 55								21 55							22 55					
Romsey	a		21 03								22 03							23 03					
Shawford	d					21 19		←															
Winchester	d	20 48				21 25	21 18	21 25					22 18									00a28	
Micheldever	d					→																	
Basingstoke	a						21 34	21 41					22 34										
	d						21 35	21 43					22 36										
Reading 7	a																						
Fleet	d							21 54															
Farnborough (Main)	d							22 00															
Woking	a	21 19						22 09					22 54										
Clapham Junction 10	a						22 14	22 29					23 14										
London Waterloo 15 ⊖	a	21 49					22 22	22 38					23 23										

A 🍴 from Bournemouth

Table 158

Mondays to Fridays
from 3 October

Weymouth, Bournemouth, Lymington, Romsey, Southampton and Basingstoke - London

		SW 1
Weymouth	d	23 10
Upwey	d	23 14
Dorchester West	a	
Dorchester South	d	23 22
Moreton (Dorset)	d	23 28
Wool	d	23 34
Wareham	d	23 42
Holton Heath	d	
Hamworthy	d	23 48
Poole 4	a	23 53
	d	23 54
Parkstone (Dorset)	d	
Branksome	d	
Bournemouth	a	00 03
	d	
Pokesdown	d	
Christchurch	d	
Hinton Admiral	d	
New Milton	d	
Sway	d	
Lymington Pier	d	
Lymington Town	d	
Brockenhurst 3	a	
	d	
Beaulieu Road	d	
Ashurst New Forest	d	
Totton	d	
Salisbury	d	
Dean	d	
Mottisfont & Dunbridge	d	
Romsey	d	
Redbridge	d	
Millbrook (Hants)	d	
Southampton Central ⛴	a	
	d	
St Denys	d	
Swaythling	d	
Southampton Airport Pkwy ✈	d	
Portsmouth Harbour ⛴	d	
Portsmouth & Southsea	d	
Fratton	d	
Hilsea	d	
Cosham	d	
Portchester	d	
Fareham	d	
Botley	d	
Hedge End	d	
Eastleigh 3	a	
	d	
Chandlers Ford	d	
Romsey	a	
Shawford	d	
Winchester	d	
Micheldever	d	
Basingstoke	a	
	d	
Reading 7	a	
Fleet	d	
Farnborough (Main)	d	
Woking	a	
Clapham Junction 10	a	
London Waterloo 15 ⊖	a	

Weymouth, Bournemouth, Lymington, Romsey, Southampton and Basingstoke - London

		SW 1	SW ◇1	SW 1	XC ◇1	SW 1	XC ◇1 ⫪	SW ◇1 ⫪	SW 1	SW 1	XC ◇1 ⫪	GW	XC ◇1 ⫪	GW	SW 1	SW ◇1 A ⫪	SW 1	SW 1	XC ◇1 ⫪	SW 1	SW 1	SW ◇1 ⫪	SW 1
Weymouth	d		22p10	23p10										06 40									
Upwey	d		22p14	23p14										06 45									
Dorchester West	a													06 52									
Dorchester South	d		22p22	23p22																			
Moreton (Dorset)	d		22p28	23p28																			
Wool	d		22p34	23p34																			
Wareham	d		22p42	23p42												06 10							
Holton Heath	d															06 13							
Hamworthy	d		22p48	23p48												06 18							
Poole 4	a		22p53	23p53												06 23							
	d		22p54	23p54				05 28								06 24				06 50		07 07	
Parkstone (Dorset)	d		22p58					05 32								06 28				06 54			
Branksome	d		23p01					05 35								06 31				06 57			
Bournemouth	a		23p07	00 03				05 40								06 37				07 02		07 17	
	d		23p12					05 42			06 25		06 37			06 42				07 05		07 22	
Pokesdown	d		23p16					05 46								06 46				07 09		07 26	
Christchurch	d		23p20					05 50								06 50				07 13		07 30	
Hinton Admiral	d		23p25					05 55								06 55				07 18			
New Milton	d		23p29					05 59								06 59				07 22		07 37	
Sway	d		23p34					06 04								07 04				07 27			
Lymington Pier	d									06 27					06 57						07 27		
Lymington Town	d									06 29					06 59						07 29		
Brockenhurst 3	a		23p39					06 09		06 37	06 38		06 52		07 07	07 09				07 32	07 37	07 44	
	d		23p40					06 10			06 39		06 55			07 10				07 33		07 45	
Beaulieu Road	d																						
Ashurst New Forest	d		23p47					06 17								07 17				07 40			
Totton	d		23p52					06 22	06 12							07 22				07 45			
Salisbury	d					05 35						06 32						06 50					
Dean	d					05 47												07 02					
Mottisfont & Dunbridge	d					05 53												07 08					
Romsey	d					05 58						06 50						07 13					
Redbridge	d								06 14									07 21					
Millbrook (Hants)	d								06 18									07 24					
Southampton Central ⛴	a		23p57					06 27	06 21		06 52	07 02	07 07			07 27		07 27		07 52		07 58	
	d		23p59		05 09		06 15	06 30	06 35		06 53	07 05	07 15			07 30		07 35	07 47	07 55		08 00	
St Denys	d		00 04						06 40									07 40					
Swaythling	d		00 07						06 43									07 43					
Southampton Airport Pkwy ✈	d		00 10		05 16		06 22	06 38	06 46		07 01		07 22			07 38		07 46	07 54	08 03		08 08	
Portsmouth Harbour ⛴	d	23p24															06 55						
Portsmouth & Southsea	d	23p29															07 00						
Fratton	d	23p33															07 04						
Hilsea	d	23p37															07 08						
Cosham	d	23p42															07 13						
Portchester	d	23p47															07 18						
Fareham	d	23p53										07a27					07 24						
Botley	d	23p59															07 31						
Hedge End	d	00 05															07 36						
Eastleigh 3	a	00 11	00 14					06 41	06 49								07 42	07 49		08 06			
	d	00 19						06 42	06 50								07 47	07 50		08 14			
Chandlers Ford	d					06 06			06 55									07 55					
Romsey	a					06 43			07 03									08 03					
Shawford	d																			08 19			←
Winchester	d	00a28			05 25		06 31	06 52			07 09		07 31			07 48	07 56		08 03	08 25		08 18	08 25
Micheldever	d																08 05			→			
Basingstoke	a				05 40		06 46	07 08			07 24		07 46				08 15		08 17			08 34	08 41
	d				05 41		06 47	07 09			07 25		07 47				08 17		08 19			08 35	08 43
Reading 7	a				05 59		07 04				07 42		08 04						08 35				
Fleet	d																						08 54
Farnborough (Main)	d																08 30						09 00
Woking	a							07 27								08 21	08 39						
Clapham Junction 10	a																					09 12	09 25
London Waterloo 15 ⊖	a							07 53								08 49	09 08					09 20	09 34

A ⫪ from Bournemouth

Weymouth, Bournemouth, Lymington, Romsey, Southampton and Basingstoke - London

		GW ◇	GW	XC ◇1 ⫪	SW 1	SW ◇1 A ⫪	SW ◇1 B ⫪	SW 1	SW 1	SW 1	SW 1	SW ◇1 A ⫪	SW ◇1 B ⫪	SW 1	GW ◇	XC ◇1 ⫪	SW 1	SW ◇1 A ⫪	SW ◇1 B ⫪	SW 1	SW 1	XC ◇1 ⫪	SW 1
Weymouth	d					06 50	06 55					07 17	07 20					07 58	08 03				
Upwey	d					06 54	06 59					07 21	07 24										
Dorchester West	a																						
Dorchester South	d					07 02	07 07					07 33	07 33					08 08	08 13				
Moreton (Dorset)	d					07 09	07 14					07 39	07 39										
Wool	d					07 15	07 20					07 45	07 45										
Wareham	d					07 22	07 27					07 53	07 53					08 23	08 28				
Holton Heath	d					07 26	07 31					07 56	07 56										
Hamworthy	d					07 31	07 36					08 01	08 01					08 30	08 35				
Poole 4	a					07 38	07 40					08 06	08 06					08 37	08 39				
	d					07 39	07 41			07 50		08 07	08 07					08 38	08 40				08 50
Parkstone (Dorset)	d					07 43	07 45			07 54								08 42	08 44				08 54
Branksome	d					07 46	07 49			07 57								08 46	08 48				08 57
Bournemouth	a					07 54	07 54			08 02		08 17	08 17					08 54	08 54				09 02
	d			07 45		07 59	07 59			08 05		08 22	08 22			08 45		08 59	08 59				09 05
Pokesdown	d									08 09		08 26	08 26										09 09
Christchurch	d									08 13		08 30	08 30										09 13
Hinton Admiral	d									08 18													09 18
New Milton	d									08 22		08 37	08 37										09 22
Sway	d									08 27													09 27
Lymington Pier	d				07 57						08 27						08 57						
Lymington Town	d				07 59						08 29						08 59						
Brockenhurst 3	a			07 58	08 07	08 14	08 14			08 32	08 37	08 44	08 44			08 58	09 07	09 14	09 14				09 32
	d			08 00		08 15	08 15			08 33		08 45	08 45			09 00		09 15	09 15				09 33
Beaulieu Road	d																						09 38
Ashurst New Forest	d									08 40													09 42
Totton	d									08 45													09 47
Salisbury	d	07 24	07 37						07 56						08 32						08 56		
Dean	d								08 08												09 08		
Mottisfont & Dunbridge	d								08 14												09 14		
Romsey	d	07 44	07 56						08 19						08 51						09 19		
Redbridge	d								08 27												09 27		
Millbrook (Hants)	d								08 31												09 31		
Southampton Central ⛴	a	08 02	08 07	08 12		08 28	08 28		08 34	08 52		08 58	08 58		09 02	09 12		09 28	09 28		09 34		09 53
	d	08 05		08 15		08 30	08 30		08 35	08 55		09 00	09 00		09 04	09 15		09 30	09 30		09 35	09 47	09 55
St Denys	d								08 40												09 40		
Swaythling	d								08 43												09 43		
Southampton Airport Pkwy ✈	d			08 22		08 38	08 38		08 46	09 03		09 08	09 08			09 22		09 38	09 38		09 46	09 54	10 03
Portsmouth Harbour ⛴	d							07 59												08 59			
Portsmouth & Southsea	d							08 03												09 03			
Fratton	d							08 07												09 07			
Hilsea	d							08 11												09 11			
Cosham	d							08 17												09 17			
Portchester	d							08 21												09 21			
Fareham	d	08a27						08 28							09a27					09 28			
Botley	d							08 35												09 35			
Hedge End	d							08 40												09 40			
Eastleigh 3	a							08 46	08 49	09 06										09 46	09 49		10 06
	d							08 47	08 50	09 14										09 47	09 50		10 14
Chandlers Ford	d								08 55												09 55		
Romsey	a								09 03												10 03		
Shawford	d									09 19				←									10 19
Winchester	d			08 31		08 48	08 48	08 56		09 25		09 18	09 18	09 25		09 31		09 48	09 48	09 56		10 03	10 25
Micheldever	d							09 05		→										10 05			→
Basingstoke	a			08 46				09 15				09 34	09 34	09 41		09 46				10 15		10 17	
	d			08 47				09 17				09 35	09 35	09 43		09 47				10 17		10 19	
Reading 7	a			09 04												10 04						10 35	
Fleet	d													09 54									
Farnborough (Main)	d							09 30						10 00						10 30			
Woking	a					09 19	09 19	09 39										10 19	10 19	10 39			
Clapham Junction 10	a											10 12	10 12	10 25									
London Waterloo 15 ⊖	a					09 49	09 49	10 07				10 20	10 20	10 34				10 49	10 49	11 07			

A from 8 October. ⫪ from Bournemouth

B until 1 October. ⫪ from Bournemouth

Weymouth, Bournemouth, Lymington, Romsey, Southampton and Basingstoke - London

		SW 1		SW ◇1 A 🛒	SW 1	GW	GW ◇	XC ◇1 🛒	SW 1	SW ◇1 A 🛒	SW 1	SW 1		SW 1	SW 1	SW ◇1 A 🛒	SW 1	GW ◇	XC ◇1 🛒	SW 1	SW ◇1 A 🛒	SW 1		SW 1	XC ◇1 🛒
Weymouth	d			08 20		08 46				09 03						09 20					10 03				
Upwey	d			08 24		08 51										09 24									
Dorchester West	a					08 58																			
Dorchester South	d			08 33						09 13						09 33					10 13				
Moreton (Dorset)	d			08 39												09 39									
Wool	d			08 45												09 45									
Wareham	d			08 53						09 28						09 53					10 28				
Holton Heath	d			08 56												09 56									
Hamworthy	d			09 01						09 35						10 01					10 35				
Poole 4	a			09 07						09 39						10 06					10 39				
	d			09 07						09 40				09 50		10 07					10 40				
Parkstone (Dorset)	d									09 44				09 54							10 44				
Branksome	d									09 48				09 57							10 48				
Bournemouth	a			09 17						09 54				10 02		10 17					10 54				
	d			09 22				09 45		09 59				10 05		10 22			10 45		10 59				
Pokesdown	d			09 26										10 09		10 26									
Christchurch	d			09 30										10 13		10 30									
Hinton Admiral	d													10 18											
New Milton	d			09 37										10 22		10 37									
Sway	d													10 27											
Lymington Pier	d	09 27							09 57						10 27					10 57					
Lymington Town	d	09 29							09 59						10 29					10 59					
Brockenhurst 3	a	09 37		09 44				09 58	10 07	10 14				10 32	10 37	10 44			10 58	11 07	11 14				
	d			09 45				10 00		10 15				10 33		10 45			11 00		11 15				
Beaulieu Road	d																								
Ashurst New Forest	d													10 40											
Totton	d													10 45											
Salisbury	d						09 32					09 56						10 32						10 56	
Dean	d											10 08												11 08	
Mottisfont & Dunbridge	d											10 14												11 14	
Romsey	d						09 50					10 19						10 51						11 19	
Redbridge	d											10 27												11 27	
Millbrook (Hants)	d											10 31												11 31	
Southampton Central ⛴	a			09 58			10 02	10 12		10 28		10 34		10 53		10 58		11 02	11 12		11 28			11 34	
	d			10 00			10 04	10 15		10 30		10 35		10 55		11 00		11 04	11 15		11 30			11 35	11 47
St Denys	d											10 40												11 40	
Swaythling	d											10 43												11 43	
Southampton Airport Pkwy ✈	d			10 08				10 22		10 38		10 46		11 03		11 08			11 22		11 38			11 46	11 54
Portsmouth Harbour ⛴	d										09 59											10 59			
Portsmouth & Southsea	d										10 03											11 03			
Fratton	d										10 07											11 07			
Hilsea	d										10 11											11 11			
Cosham	d										10 17											11 17			
Portchester	d										10 21											11 21			
Fareham	d						10a27				10 28							11a27				11 28			
Botley	d										10 35											11 35			
Hedge End	d										10 40											11 40			
Eastleigh 8	a										10 46	10 49		11 06								11 46		11 49	
	d										10 47	10 50		11 14								11 47		11 50	
Chandlers Ford	d											10 55												11 55	
Romsey	a											11 03												12 03	
Shawford	d				←									11 19			←								
Winchester	d			10 18	10 25			10 31		10 48	10 56			11 25		11 18	11 25		11 31		11 48	11 56			12 03
Micheldever	d										11 05			→								12 05			
Basingstoke	a			10 34	10 41			10 46			11 15					11 34	11 41		11 46			12 15			12 17
	d			10 35	10 43			10 47			11 17					11 35	11 43		11 47			12 17			12 19
Reading 7	a							11 04											12 04						12 35
Fleet	d				10 54												11 54								
Farnborough (Main)	d				11 00						11 30						12 00					12 30			
Woking	a									11 19	11 39										12 19	12 39			
Clapham Junction 10	a			11 12	11 25											12 12	12 25								
London Waterloo 15 ⊖	a			11 20	11 34					11 49	12 07					12 21	12 34				12 51	13 07			

A 🛒 from Bournemouth

Weymouth, Bournemouth, Lymington, Romsey, Southampton and Basingstoke - London

		SW 1	SW 1	SW ◇1 A 🛒	SW 1	GW ◇ 🛒	XC ◇1 🛒	GW		SW 1	SW ◇1 A 🛒	GW	SW 1	SW 1	SW 1	SW 1	SW ◇1 A 🛒	SW 1		GW ◇ 🛒	XC ◇1 🛒	SW 1	SW ◇1 A 🛒	SW 1	SW 1
Weymouth	d			10 20							11 03	11 10					11 20						12 03		
Upwey	d			10 24								11 15					11 24								
Dorchester West	a											11 23													
Dorchester South	d			10 33							11 13						11 33						12 13		
Moreton (Dorset)	d			10 39													11 39								
Wool	d			10 45													11 45								
Wareham	d			10 53							11 28						11 53						12 28		
Holton Heath	d			10 56													11 56								
Hamworthy	d			11 01							11 35						12 01						12 35		
Poole 4	a			11 06							11 39						12 06						12 39		
	d	10 50		11 07							11 40				11 50		12 07						12 40		
Parkstone (Dorset)	d	10 54									11 44				11 54								12 44		
Branksome	d	10 57									11 48				11 57								12 48		
Bournemouth	a	11 02		11 17							11 54				12 02		12 17						12 54		
	d	11 05		11 22			11 45				11 59				12 05		12 22				12 45		12 59		
Pokesdown	d	11 09		11 26											12 09		12 26								
Christchurch	d	11 13		11 30											12 13		12 30								
Hinton Admiral	d	11 18													12 18										
New Milton	d	11 22		11 37											12 22		12 37								
Sway	d	11 27													12 27										
Lymington Pier	d		11 27							11 57						12 27						12 57			
Lymington Town	d		11 29							11 59						12 29						12 59			
Brockenhurst 3	a	11 32	11 37	11 44			11 58			12 07	12 14				12 32	12 37	12 44				12 58	13 07	13 14		
	d	11 33		11 45			12 00				12 15				12 33		12 45				13 00		13 15		
Beaulieu Road	d	11 38																							
Ashurst New Forest	d	11 42													12 40										
Totton	d	11 47													12 45										
Salisbury	d					11 32		11 43						11 56						12 32					12 56
Dean	d													12 08											13 08
Mottisfont & Dunbridge	d													12 14											13 14
Romsey	d					11 51		12 04						12 19						12 51					13 19
Redbridge	d													12 27											13 27
Millbrook (Hants)	d													12 31											13 31
Southampton Central ⛴	a	11 53		11 58		12 02	12 12	12 20			12 28			12 34	12 51		12 58			13 02	13 12		13 28		13 34
	d	11 55		12 00		12 05	12 15				12 30			12 35	12 55		13 00			13 04	13 15		13 30		13 35
St Denys	d													12 40											13 40
Swaythling	d													12 43											13 43
Southampton Airport Pkwy ✈	d	12 03		12 08			12 22				12 38			12 46	13 03		13 08				13 22		13 38		13 46
Portsmouth Harbour ⛴	d												11 59											12 59	
Portsmouth & Southsea	d												12 03											13 03	
Fratton	d												12 07											13 07	
Hilsea	d												12 11											13 11	
Cosham	d												12 17											13 17	
Portchester	d												12 21											13 21	
Fareham	d					12a27							12 28							13a27				13 28	
Botley	d												12 35											13 35	
Hedge End	d												12 40											13 40	
Eastleigh 8	a	12 06											12 46	12 49	13 06									13 46	13 49
	d	12 14											12 47	12 50	13 14									13 47	13 50
Chandlers Ford	d													12 55											13 55
Romsey	a													13 03											14 03
Shawford	d	12 19			←										13 19			←							
Winchester	d	12 25		12 18	12 25		12 31				12 48		12 56		13 25		13 18	13 25			13 31		13 48	13 56	
Micheldever	d	→											13 05		→									14 05	
Basingstoke	a			12 34	12 41		12 46						13 15				13 34	13 41			13 46			14 15	
	d			12 35	12 43		12 47						13 17				13 35	13 43			13 47			14 17	
Reading 7	a						13 04														14 04				
Fleet	d				12 54													13 54							
Farnborough (Main)	d				13 00								13 30					14 00						14 30	
Woking	a										13 19		13 39										14 19	14 39	
Clapham Junction 10	a			13 12	13 25												14 12	14 25							
London Waterloo 15 ⊖	a			13 21	13 34						13 51		14 07				14 21	14 34					14 51	15 07	

A 🛒 from Bournemouth

Weymouth, Bournemouth, Lymington, Romsey, Southampton and Basingstoke - London

		XC ◇■ ⌶	SW ■	SW ■	SW ◇■ A ⌶	SW ■	GW ◇ ⌶	XC ◇■ ⌶	SW ■	SW ◇■ A ⌶	GW	SW ■	GW ◇	SW ■	SW ■	SW ■	SW ◇■ A ⌶	SW ■	GW ◇	XC ◇■ ⌶	SW ■	SW ◇■ A ⌶
Weymouth	d				12 20					13 03	13 10						13 20					14 03
Upwey	d				12 24						13 15						13 24					
Dorchester West	a										13 22											
Dorchester South	d				12 33					13 13							13 33					14 13
Moreton (Dorset)	d				12 39												13 39					
Wool	d				12 45												13 45					
Wareham	d				12 53					13 28							13 53					14 28
Holton Heath	d				12 56												13 56					
Hamworthy	d				13 01					13 35							14 01					14 35
Poole [4]	a				13 06					13 39							14 06					14 39
	d		12 50		13 07					13 40					13 50		14 07					14 40
Parkstone (Dorset)	d		12 54							13 44					13 54							14 44
Branksome	d		12 57							13 48					13 57							14 48
Bournemouth	a		13 02		13 17					13 54					14 02		14 17					14 54
	d		13 05		13 22			13 45		13 59					14 05		14 22			14 45		14 59
Pokesdown	d		13 09		13 26										14 09		14 26					
Christchurch	d		13 13		13 30										14 13		14 30					
Hinton Admiral	d		13 18												14 18							
New Milton	d		13 22		13 37										14 22		14 37					
Sway	d		13 27												14 27							
Lymington Pier	d			13 27					13 57							14 27					14 57	
Lymington Town	d			13 29					13 59							14 29					14 59	
Brockenhurst [3]	a		13 32	13 37	13 44			13 58	14 07	14 14					14 32	14 37	14 44			14 58	15 07	15 14
	d		13 33		13 45			14 00		14 15					14 33		14 45			15 00		15 15
Beaulieu Road	d		13 38																			
Ashurst New Forest	d		13 42												14 40							
Totton	d		13 47												14 45							
Salisbury	d						13 32						13 59	13 50					14 32			
Dean	d													14 02								
Mottisfont & Dunbridge	d													14 08								
Romsey	d						13 51						14 19	14 13					14 51			
Redbridge	d													14 21								
Millbrook (Hants)	d													14 24								
Southampton Central ⛴	a		13 53		13 58		14 02	14 12		14 28			14 32	14 27	14 51		14 58		15 02	15 12		15 28
	d	13 47	13 55		14 00		14 05	14 15		14 30			14 34	14 35	14 55		15 00		15 04	15 15		15 30
St Denys	d													14 40								
Swaythling	d													14 43								
Southampton Airport Pkwy ✈	d	13 54	14 03		14 08			14 22		14 38				14 46	15 03		15 08			15 22		15 38
Portsmouth Harbour ⛴	d											13 59										
Portsmouth & Southsea	d											14 03										
Fratton	d											14 07										
Hilsea	d											14 11										
Cosham	d											14 17										
Portchester	d											14 21										
Fareham	d						14a27					14 28	14a54						15a27			
Botley	d											14 35										
Hedge End	d											14 40										
Eastleigh [3]	a		14 06									14 46		14 49	15 06							
	d		14 14									14 47		14 50	15 14							
Chandlers Ford	d													14 55								
Romsey	a													15 04								
Shawford	d		14 19			←									15 19			←				
Winchester	d	14 03	14 25		14 18	14 25		14 31		14 48		14 56			15 25		15 18	15 25		15 31		15 48
Micheldever	d		→									15 05			→							
Basingstoke	a	14 17			14 34	14 41		14 46				15 15					15 34	15 41		15 46		
	d	14 19			14 35	14 43		14 47				15 17					15 35	15 43		15 47		
Reading [7]	a	14 35						15 04												16 05		
Fleet	d					14 54												15 54				
Farnborough (Main)	d					15 00						15 30						16 00				
Woking	a									15 19		15 39										16 19
Clapham Junction [10]	a				15 12	15 25											16 12	16 25				
London Waterloo [15] ⊖	a				15 21	15 34				15 51		16 07					16 20	16 34				16 49

A ⌶ from Bournemouth

Weymouth, Bournemouth, Lymington, Romsey, Southampton and Basingstoke - London

		SW ■	SW ■	XC ◇■ ⌶	SW ■	SW ■	SW ◇■ A ⌶	SW ■	GW ◇	XC ◇■ ⌶	SW ■	SW ◇■ A ⌶	GW B	SW ■	SW ■	SW ■	SW ■	SW ◇■ A ⌶	SW ■	GW ◇	XC ◇■ ⌶	SW ■	SW ◇■ A ⌶
Weymouth	d						14 20					15 03	15 08					15 20					16 03
Upwey	d						14 24						15 13					15 24					
Dorchester West	a												15 20										
Dorchester South	d						14 33					15 13						15 33					16 13
Moreton (Dorset)	d						14 39											15 39					
Wool	d						14 45											15 45					
Wareham	d						14 53					15 28						15 53					16 28
Holton Heath	d						14 56											15 56					
Hamworthy	d						15 01					15 35						16 01					16 35
Poole [4]	a						15 06					15 39						16 06					16 39
	d				14 50		15 07					15 40				15 50		16 07					16 40
Parkstone (Dorset)	d				14 54							15 44				15 54							16 44
Branksome	d				14 57							15 48				15 57							16 48
Bournemouth	a				15 02		15 17					15 54				16 02		16 17					16 54
	d				15 05		15 22			15 45		15 59				16 05		16 22			16 45		16 59
Pokesdown	d				15 09		15 26									16 09		16 26					
Christchurch	d				15 13		15 30									16 13		16 30					
Hinton Admiral	d				15 18											16 18							
New Milton	d				15 22		15 37									16 22		16 37					
Sway	d				15 27											16 27							
Lymington Pier	d					15 27					15 57						16 27					16 57	
Lymington Town	d					15 29					15 59						16 29					16 59	
Brockenhurst [3]	a				15 32	15 37	15 44			15 58	16 07	16 14				16 32	16 37	16 44			16 58	17 07	17 14
	d				15 33		15 45			16 00		16 15				16 33		16 45			17 00		17 15
Beaulieu Road	d				15 38																		
Ashurst New Forest	d				15 42											16 40							
Totton	d				15 47											16 45							
Salisbury	d		14 56						15 32						15 56					16 34			
Dean	d		15 08												16 08								
Mottisfont & Dunbridge	d		15 14												16 14								
Romsey	d		15 19						15 51						16 19					16 53			
Redbridge	d		15 27												16 27								
Millbrook (Hants)	d		15 31												16 31								
Southampton Central ⛴	a		15 34		15 53		15 58		16 02	16 12		16 28			16 34	16 51		16 58		17 04	17 12		17 28
	d		15 35	15 47	15 55		16 00		16 05	16 15		16 30			16 35	16 55		17 00		17 06	17 15		17 30
St Denys	d		15 40												16 40								
Swaythling	d		15 43												16 43								
Southampton Airport Pkwy ✈	d		15 46	15 54	16 03		16 08			16 22		16 38			16 46	17 03		17 08			17 22		17 38
Portsmouth Harbour ⛴	d	14 59												15 59									
Portsmouth & Southsea	d	15 03												16 03									
Fratton	d	15 07												16 07									
Hilsea	d	15 11												16 11									
Cosham	d	15 17												16 17									
Portchester	d	15 21												16 21									
Fareham	d	15 28							16a27					16 28						17a29			
Botley	d	15 35												16 35									
Hedge End	d	15 40												16 40									
Eastleigh [3]	a	15 46	15 49		16 06									16 46	16 49	17 06							
	d	15 47	15 50		16 14									16 47	16 50	17 14							
Chandlers Ford	d		15 55												16 55								
Romsey	a		16 03												17 03								
Shawford	d				16 19			←								17 19			←				
Winchester	d	15 56		16 03	16 25		16 18	16 25		16 31		16 48		16 56		17 25		17 18	17 25		17 31		17 48
Micheldever	d	16 05			→									17 05		→							
Basingstoke	a	16 15		16 17			16 34	16 41		16 46				17 15				17 34	17 41		17 46		
	d	16 17		16 19			16 35	16 43		16 47				17 17				17 35	17 43		17 47		
Reading [7]	a			16 35						17 04											18 04		
Fleet	d							16 54											17 54				
Farnborough (Main)	d	16 30						17 00						17 30					18 00				
Woking	a	16 39										17 19		17 39									18 19
Clapham Junction [10]	a						17 12	17 25										18 12	18 25				
London Waterloo [15] ⊖	a	17 07					17 20	17 34				17 49		18 07				18 20	18 34				18 49

A ⌶ from Bournemouth

B from 17 September

Table 158

Weymouth, Bournemouth, Lymington, Romsey, Southampton and Basingstoke - London

		GW	SW	SW	XC	SW	SW	SW	SW	GW	XC	SW	SW	SW	SW	SW	SW	SW	SW	GW	GW	XC	SW
		A	■	■	◇■ 🍴	■	■	◇■ B 🍴	■	◇	◇■ 🍴	■	◇■ B 🍴	■	■	■	■	◇■ B 🍴	■		■	◇■ C 🍴	■
Weymouth	d	16 08						16 20					17 03					17 20		17 28			
Upwey	d	16 13						16 24										17 24		17 33			
Dorchester West	a	16 21																		17 40			
Dorchester South	d							16 33					17 13					17 33					
Moreton (Dorset)	d							16 39										17 39					
Wool	d							16 45										17 45					
Wareham	d							16 53					17 28					17 53					
Holton Heath	d							16 56										17 56					
Hamworthy	d							17 01					17 35					18 01					
Poole 4	a							17 06					17 39					18 06					
	d					16 50		17 07					17 40			17 50		18 07					
Parkstone (Dorset)	d					16 54							17 44			17 54							
Branksome	d					16 57							17 48			17 57							
Bournemouth	a					17 02		17 17					17 54			18 02		18 17					
	d					17 05		17 22			17 45		17 59			18 05		18 22				18 45	
Pokesdown	d					17 09		17 26								18 09		18 26					
Christchurch	d					17 13		17 30								18 13		18 30					
Hinton Admiral	d					17 18										18 18							
New Milton	d					17 22		17 37								18 22		18 37					
Sway	d					17 27										18 27							
Lymington Pier	d						17 27					17 57					18 27						18 57
Lymington Town	d						17 29					17 59					18 29						18 59
Brockenhurst 3	a					17 32	17 37	17 44			17 58	18 07	18 14			18 32	18 37	18 44				18 58	19 07
	d					17 33		17 45			18 00		18 15			18 33		18 45				19 00	
Beaulieu Road	d					17 38																	
Ashurst New Forest	d					17 42										18 40							
Totton	d					17 47										18 45							
Salisbury	d			16 56						17 32					17 56						18 32		
Dean	d			17 08											18 08								
Mottisfont & Dunbridge	d			17 14											18 14								
Romsey	d			17 19						17 51					18 19						18 51		
Redbridge	d			17 27											18 27								
Millbrook (Hants)	d			17 31											18 31								
Southampton Central ⛴	a			17 34		17 53		17 58		18 02	18 12		18 28		18 34	18 51		18 58			19 02	19 12	
	d			17 35	17 47	17 55		18 00		18 05	18 15		18 30		18 35	18 55		19 00			19 05	19 15	
St Denys	d			17 40											18 40								
Swaythling	d			17 43											18 43								
Southampton Airport Pkwy ✈	d			17 46	17 54	18 03		18 08			18 22		18 38		18 46	19 03		19 08				19 22	
Portsmouth Harbour ⛴	d		16 59											17 59									
Portsmouth & Southsea	d		17 03											18 03									
Fratton	d		17 07											18 07									
Hilsea	d		17 11											18 11									
Cosham	d		17 17											18 17									
Portchester	d		17 21											18 21									
Fareham	d		17 28							18a27				18 28							19a27		
Botley	d		17 35											18 35									
Hedge End	d		17 40											18 40									
Eastleigh 8	a		17 46	17 49		18 06								18 46	18 49	19 06							
	d		17 47	17 50		18 14								18 47	18 50	19 14							
Chandlers Ford	d			17 55											18 55								
Romsey	a			18 03											19 04								
Shawford	d					18 19			←							19 19			←				
Winchester	d		17 56		18 03	18 25		18 18	18 25		18 31		18 48	18 56		19 25		19 18	19 25			19 31	
Micheldever	d		18 05			→								19 05		→							
Basingstoke	a		18 15		18 17			18 34	18 41		18 46			19 15				19 34	19 41			19 46	
	d		18 17		18 19			18 35	18 43		18 47			19 17				19 35	19 43			19 47	
Reading 7	a				18 35						19 04											20 04	
Fleet	d								18 54										19 54				
Farnborough (Main)	d		18 30						19 00					19 30					20 00				
Woking	a		18 39										19 19	19 39									
Clapham Junction 10	a							19 12	19 25									20 12	20 25				
London Waterloo 15 ⊖	a		19 07					19 20	19 34				19 49	20 07				20 20	20 34				

A until 10 September

B 🍴 from Bournemouth

C 🍴 to Basingstoke

Table 158

Saturdays

Weymouth, Bournemouth, Lymington, Romsey, Southampton and Basingstoke - London

		SW	SW	SW	SW	SW	SW	SW	GW	XC	GW	SW	SW	SW	SW	SW	SW	SW	GW	SW	SW	SW
		◇■ A 🍴	■	■	■	■	◇■ A 🍴	■	◇	◇■ 🍴		■	◇■ A 🍴	■	■	■	◇■	■	◇	■	■	■
Weymouth	d	18 06					18 20						19 03				19 20					
Upwey	d						18 24										19 24					
Dorchester West	a																					
Dorchester South	d	18 16					18 33						19 13				19 33					
Moreton (Dorset)	d						18 39										19 39					
Wool	d						18 45										19 45					
Wareham	d	18 31					18 53						19 28				19 53					
Holton Heath	d						18 56															
Hamworthy	d	18 38					19 01						19 35				20 01					
Poole 4	a	18 42					19 06						19 39				20 06					
	d	18 43			18 50		19 07						19 40		19 50		20 07					
Parkstone (Dorset)	d	18 47			18 54								19 44		19 54							
Branksome	d	18 51			18 57								19 48		19 57							
Bournemouth	a	18 56			19 02		19 17						19 54		20 02		20 17					
	d	18 59			19 05		19 22			19 45			19 59		20 05		20 22					
Pokesdown	d				19 09		19 26								20 09		20 26					
Christchurch	d				19 13		19 30								20 13		20 30					
Hinton Admiral	d				19 18										20 18							
New Milton	d				19 22		19 37								20 22		20 37					
Sway	d				19 27										20 27							
Lymington Pier	d					19 27						19 57				20 27					20 57	21 27
Lymington Town	d					19 29						19 59				20 29					20 59	21 29
Brockenhurst 3	a	19 14			19 32	19 37	19 44			19 58		20 07	20 14		20 32	20 37	20 44				21 07	21 37
	d	19 15			19 33		19 45			20 00			20 15		20 33		20 45					
Beaulieu Road	d																					
Ashurst New Forest	d				19 40										20 40							
Totton	d				19 45										20 45							
Salisbury	d			18 56					19 32		19 41			19 56					20 32	20 56		
Dean	d			19 08										20 08						21 08		
Mottisfont & Dunbridge	d			19 14										20 14						21 14		
Romsey	d			19 19					19 51		20 04			20 19					20 51	21 19		
Redbridge	d			19 27										20 27						21 27		
Millbrook (Hants)	d			19 31										20 31						21 31		
Southampton Central ⛴	a	19 28		19 34	19 51		19 58		20 02	20 12	20 18		20 28	20 34	20 51		20 58		21 02	21 34		
	d	19 30		19 35	19 55		20 00		20 04	20 15			20 30	20 35	20 55		21 00		21 04	21 35		
St Denys	d			19 40										20 40						21 40		
Swaythling	d			19 43										20 43						21 43		
Southampton Airport Pkwy ✈	d	19 38		19 46	20 03		20 08			20 22			20 38	20 46	21 03		21 08			21 46		
Portsmouth Harbour ⛴	d		18 59																			
Portsmouth & Southsea	d		19 03																			
Fratton	d		19 07																			
Hilsea	d		19 11																			
Cosham	d		19 17																			
Portchester	d		19 21																			
Fareham	d		19 28						20a27										21a27			
Botley	d		19 35																			
Hedge End	d		19 40																			
Eastleigh 8	a		19 46	19 49	20 06									20 49	21 06					21 49		
	d		19 47	19 50	20 14									20 50	21 14					21 50		
Chandlers Ford	d			19 55										20 55						21 55		
Romsey	a			20 03										21 03						22 03		
Shawford	d				20 19			←							21 19			←				
Winchester	d	19 48	19 56		20 25		20 18	20 25		20 31			20 48		21 25		21 18	21 25				
Micheldever	d		20 05		→										→							
Basingstoke	a		20 15				20 34	20 41		20 46							21 34	21 41				
	d		20 17				20 35	20 43		20 47							21 35	21 43				
Reading 7	a									21 04												
Fleet	d							20 54										21 54				
Farnborough (Main)	d		20 30					21 00										22 00				
Woking	a	20 19	20 39					21 09					21 19					22 09				
Clapham Junction 10	a						21 16	21 29									22 14	22 29				
London Waterloo 15 ⊖	a	20 49	21 07				21 24	21 38					21 49				22 22	22 38				

A 🍴 from Bournemouth

Weymouth, Bournemouth, Lymington, Romsey, Southampton and Basingstoke - London

		SW	GW	SW	GW	SW	SW	GW		SW	SW	SW	SW
		◇1		1	◇	1	1	◇		1	1	1	1
Weymouth	d	20 10	20 21									22 10	23 10
Upwey	d	20 14	20 26									22 14	23 14
Dorchester West	a		20 33										
Dorchester South	d	20 22										22 22	23 22
Moreton (Dorset)	d	20 28										22 28	23 28
Wool	d	20 34										22 34	23 34
Wareham	d	20 42										22 42	23 42
Holton Heath	d												
Hamworthy	d	20 48										22 48	23 48
Poole 4	a	20 53										22 53	23 53
	d	20 54										22 54	23 54
Parkstone (Dorset)	d	20 58										22 58	
Branksome	d	21 01										23 01	
Bournemouth	a	21 07										23 07	00 03
	d	21 12										23 12	
Pokesdown	d	21 16										23 16	
Christchurch	d	21 20										23 20	
Hinton Admiral	d	21 25										23 25	
New Milton	d	21 29										23 29	
Sway	d	21 34										23 34	
Lymington Pier	d						22 03			22 33			
Lymington Town	d						22 05			22 35			
Brockenhurst 3	a	21 39					22 13			22 43		23 39	
	d	21 40										23 40	
Beaulieu Road	d												
Ashurst New Forest	d	21 47										23 47	
Totton	d	21 52										23 52	
Salisbury	d				21 32	21 56		22 33					
Dean	d					22 08							
Mottisfont & Dunbridge	d					22 14							
Romsey	d				21 51	22 19		22 51					
Redbridge	d					22 27							
Millbrook (Hants)	d					22 31							
Southampton Central ⛴	a	21 57			22 02	22 34		23 03				23 57	
	d	22 00			22 05	22 35		23 05				23 59	
St Denys	d					22 40						00 04	
Swaythling	d					22 43						00 07	
Southampton Airport Pkwy ✈	d	22 08				22 46						00 10	
Portsmouth Harbour ⛴	d			21 54							23 24		
Portsmouth & Southsea	d			21 59							23 29		
Fratton	d			22 03							23 33		
Hilsea	d			22 07							23 37		
Cosham	d			22 12							23 42		
Portchester	d			22 17							23 47		
Fareham	d			22 23	22a26			23a26			23 53		
Botley	d			22 30							23 59		
Hedge End	d			22 35							00 05		
Eastleigh 3	a			22 41		22 49					00 11	00 14	
	d					22 50					00 21		
Chandlers Ford	d					22 55							
Romsey	a					23 03							
Shawford	d												
Winchester	d	22 18									00a30		
Micheldever	d												
Basingstoke	a	22 34											
	d	22 35											
Reading 7	a												
Fleet	d												
Farnborough (Main)	d												
Woking	a	22 53											
Clapham Junction 10	a	23 14											
London Waterloo 15 ⊖	a	23 22											

Weymouth, Bournemouth, Lymington, Romsey, Southampton and Basingstoke - London

		SW	SW	SW	SW	SW	SW	SW	SW	SW		XC	SW	SW	SW	SW	SW	XC	SW	SW		SW	SW	SW	SW
		1	1	1	1	◇1	1	1	◇1	1		◇1	◇1	1	1	◇1	1	◇1	1	◇1		1	1	◇1	1
		A	A	A		B			C				D			E				D				F	
						🚲						🚲	🚲		🚲	🚲		🚲		🚲			🚲	🚲	
Weymouth	d		22p10	23p10									07 48							08 48					
Upwey	d		22p14	23p14									07 52							08 52					
Dorchester West	a																								
Dorchester South	d		22p22	23p22									08 00							09 00					
Moreton (Dorset)	d		22p28	23p28									08 07							09 07					
Wool	d		22p34	23p34									08 13							09 13					
Wareham	d		22p42	23p42									08 20							09 20					
Holton Heath	d																								
Hamworthy	d		22p48	23p48									08 27							09 27					
Poole 4	a		22p53	23p53									08 31							09 31					
	d		22p54	23p54		06 50			07 50				08 32			08 55				09 32				09 55	
Parkstone (Dorset)	d		22p58			06 54			07 54				08 36							09 36					
Branksome	d		23p01			06 57			07 57				08 40							09 40					
Bournemouth	a		23p07	00 03		07 02			08 02				08 46			09 04				09 46				10 04	
	d		23p12			07 06			08 06				08 50			09 06		09 40		09 50				10 06	
Pokesdown	d		23p16			07 10			08 10							09 10								10 10	
Christchurch	d		23p20			07 14			08 14							09 14								10 14	
Hinton Admiral	d		23p25			07 19			08 19							09 19								10 19	
New Milton	d		23p29			07 23			08 23				09 01			09 23				10 01				10 23	
Sway	d		23p34			07 28			08 28							09 28								10 28	
Lymington Pier	d													09 14					09 44			10 14			
Lymington Town	d													09 16					09 46			10 16			
Brockenhurst 3	a		23p39			07 33			08 33				09 08	09 24		09 33		09 53	09 54	10 08		10 24		10 33	
	d		23p40			07 34			08 34				09 09			09 34		09 57		10 09				10 34	
Beaulieu Road	d								08 39							09 39								10 39	
Ashurst New Forest	d		23p47			07 43			08 43							09 43								10 43	
Totton	d		23p52			07 48			08 48							09 48								10 48	
Salisbury	d						08 08			08 20							09 08								10 13
Dean	d						08 20										09 20								
Mottisfont & Dunbridge	d						08 26										09 26								
Romsey	d						08 35			08 39							09 32								10 32
Redbridge	d									08 46							09 39								10 39
Millbrook (Hants)	d									08 50							09 43								10 43
Southampton Central ⛴	a		23p57			07 53			08 53	08 52			09 23			09 53	09 45	10 10		10 23				10 53	10 45
	d		23p59			07 55			08 55	08 59		09 15	09 25			09 55	09 59	10 15		10 25				10 55	10 59
St Denys	d		00 04							09 04							10 04								11 04
Swaythling	d		00 07							09 07							10 07								11 07
Southampton Airport Pkwy ✈	d		00 10			08 03			09 03	09 10		09 22	09 33			10 03	10 10	10 22		10 33				11 03	11 10
Portsmouth Harbour ⛴	d	23p24			07 17			08 17							09 17								10 17		
Portsmouth & Southsea	d	23p29			07 22			08 22							09 22								10 22		
Fratton	d	23p33			07 26			08 26							09 26								10 26		
Hilsea	d	23p37			07 30			08 30							09 30								10 30		
Cosham	d	23p42			07 35			08 35							09 35								10 35		
Portchester	d	23p47			07 40			08 40							09 40								10 40		
Fareham	d	23p53			07 46			08 46							09 46								10 46		
Botley	d	23p59			07 54			08 54							09 54								10 54		
Hedge End	d	00 05			07 58			08 58							09 58								10 58		
Eastleigh 3	a	00 11	00 14		08 04	08 07		09 04	09 07	09 13					10 04	10 07	10 13						11 04	11 07	11 13
	d	00 21			08 11			09 11		09 15					10 11		10 15						11 11		11 15
Chandlers Ford	d						08 42			09 20							10 20								11 20
Romsey	a						09 24			09 28							10 28								11 28
Shawford	d							09 17															11 17		
Winchester	d	00a30			08 23			09 23				09 31	09 42		10 23			10 31		10 42			11 23		
Micheldever	d				08 32			09 32							10 32								11 32		
Basingstoke	a				08 42			09 42				09 46	09 58		10 42			10 46		10 58			11 42		
	d				08 44			09 44				09 47	10 00		10 44			10 47		11 00			11 44		
Reading 7	a											10 04						11 04							
Fleet	d																								
Farnborough (Main)	d																								
Woking	a				09 02			10 02					10 19		11 02					11 18			12 02		
Clapham Junction 10	a				09 30			10 27					10 40		11 27					11 39			12 27		
London Waterloo 15 ⊖	a				09 43			10 42					10 54		11 42					11 54			12 42		

A not 22 May
B 🚲 to Eastleigh ◇ to Eastleigh
C ◇ to Eastleigh
D 🚲 from Bournemouth
E 🚲 from Eastleigh ◇ to Eastleigh
F 🚲 from Bournemouth ◇ to Eastleigh

Table 158

Sundays
until 19 June

Weymouth, Bournemouth, Lymington, Romsey, Southampton and Basingstoke - London

		GW ◇	XC ◇[1] ✠	SW [1]	SW ◇[1] A ✠	SW [1]	SW [1] ✠	SW ◇[1] B ✠	SW [1]	GW ◇	XC ◇[1] ✠	SW [1]	SW ◇[1] A ✠	GW	SW [1]	SW [1] ✠	SW ◇[1] C ✠	SW [1]	GW ◇	XC ◇[1] ✠	SW [1]	SW ◇[1] A ✠	SW [1]
Weymouth	d				09 48								10 48	11 14								11 48	
Upwey	d				09 52								10 52	11 19								11 52	
Dorchester West	a													11 27									
Dorchester South	d				10 00								11 00									12 00	
Moreton (Dorset)	d				10 07								11 07									12 07	
Wool	d				10 13								11 13									12 13	
Wareham	d				10 20								11 20									12 20	
Holton Heath	d																						
Hamworthy	d				10 27								11 27									12 27	
Poole [4]	a				10 31								11 31									12 31	
	d				10 32			10 55					11 32				11 55					12 32	
Parkstone (Dorset)	d				10 36								11 36									12 36	
Branksome	d				10 40								11 40									12 40	
Bournemouth	a				10 46			11 04					11 46				12 04					12 46	
	d		10 40		10 50			11 06			11 40		11 50				12 06			12 40		12 50	
Pokesdown	d							11 10									12 10						
Christchurch	d							11 14									12 14						
Hinton Admiral	d							11 19									12 19						
New Milton	d				11 01			11 23					12 01				12 23					13 01	
Sway	d							11 28									12 28						
Lymington Pier	d			10 44		11 14						11 44			12 14						12 44		13 14
Lymington Town	d			10 46		11 16						11 46			12 16						12 46		13 16
Brockenhurst [3]	a		10 53	10 54	11 08	11 24		11 33			11 53	11 54	12 08		12 24		12 33			12 53	12 54	13 08	13 24
	d		10 57		11 09			11 34			11 57		12 09				12 34			12 57		13 09	
Beaulieu Road	d							11 39									12 39						
Ashurst New Forest	d							11 43									12 43						
Totton	d							11 48									12 48						
Salisbury	d	10 32							11 08	11 32								12 13	12 36				
Dean	d								11 20														
Mottisfont & Dunbridge	d								11 26														
Romsey	d	10 50							11 32	11 50								12 32	12 54				
Redbridge	d								11 39									12 39					
Millbrook (Hants)	d								11 43									12 43					
Southampton Central ⛴	a	11 02	11 10		11 23			11 53	11 45	12 02	12 10		12 23				12 53	12 45	13 06	13 10		13 23	
	d	11 04	11 15		11 25			11 55	11 59	12 04	12 15		12 25				12 55	12 59	13 08	13 15		13 25	
St Denys	d								12 04									13 04					
Swaythling	d								12 07									13 07					
Southampton Airport Pkwy ✈	d		11 22		11 33			12 03	12 10		12 22		12 33				13 03	13 10		13 22		13 33	
Portsmouth Harbour ⛴	d						11 17									12 17							
Portsmouth & Southsea	d						11 22									12 22							
Fratton	d						11 26									12 26							
Hilsea	d						11 30									12 30							
Cosham	d						11 35									12 35							
Portchester	d						11 40									12 40							
Fareham	d	11a26					11 46			12a26						12 46			13a33				
Botley	d						11 54									12 54							
Hedge End	d						11 58									12 58							
Eastleigh [8]	a						12 04	12 07	12 13							13 04	13 07	13 13					
	d						12 11		12 15							13 11		13 15					
Chandlers Ford	d								12 20									13 20					
Romsey	a								12 28									13 28					
Shawford	d															13 17							
Winchester	d		11 31		11 42		12 23				12 31		12 42			13 23				13 31		13 42	
Micheldever	d						12 32									13 32							
Basingstoke	a		11 46		11 58		12 42				12 46		12 58			13 42				13 46		13 58	
	d		11 47		12 00		12 44				12 47		13 00			13 44				13 47		14 00	
Reading [7]	a		12 04								13 04									14 04			
Fleet	d																						
Farnborough (Main)	d																						
Woking	a				12 18		13 02						13 18			14 02						14 18	
Clapham Junction [10]	a				12 39		13 27						13 39			14 27						14 39	
London Waterloo [15] ⊖	a				12 49		13 37						13 49			14 37						14 49	

A ✠ from Bournemouth

B ✠ from Eastleigh ◇ to Eastleigh

C ✠ from Bournemouth ◇ to Eastleigh

Table 158

Sundays
until 19 June

Weymouth, Bournemouth, Lymington, Romsey, Southampton and Basingstoke - London

		SW [1] ✠	SW ◇[1] A ✠	SW [1]	GW ◇ ✠	XC ◇[1] ✠	SW [1]	SW ◇[1] B ✠	SW [1]	SW [1] ✠	SW ◇[1] A ✠	SW [1]	XC ◇[1] ✠	SW [1]	GW ◇	SW ◇[1] B ✠	GW	SW [1]	SW [1] ✠	SW ◇[1] A ✠	SW [1]	GW ◇
Weymouth	d							12 48								13 48	14 12					
Upwey	d							12 52								13 52	14 17					
Dorchester West	a																14 24					
Dorchester South	d							13 00								14 00						
Moreton (Dorset)	d							13 07								14 07						
Wool	d							13 13								14 13						
Wareham	d							13 20								14 20						
Holton Heath	d																					
Hamworthy	d							13 27								14 27						
Poole [4]	a							13 31								14 31						
	d		12 55					13 32			13 55					14 32				14 55		
Parkstone (Dorset)	d							13 36								14 36						
Branksome	d							13 40								14 40						
Bournemouth	a		13 04					13 46			14 04					14 46				15 04		
	d		13 06			13 40		13 50			14 06		14 40			14 50				15 06		
Pokesdown	d		13 10								14 10									15 10		
Christchurch	d		13 14								14 14									15 14		
Hinton Admiral	d		13 19								14 19									15 19		
New Milton	d		13 23					14 01			14 23					15 01				15 23		
Sway	d		13 28								14 28									15 28		
Lymington Pier	d						13 44		14 14					14 44				15 14				
Lymington Town	d						13 46		14 16					14 46				15 16				
Brockenhurst [3]	a		13 33			13 53	13 54	14 08	14 24		14 33		14 53	14 54		15 08		15 24		15 33		
	d		13 34			13 57		14 09			14 34		14 57			15 09				15 34		
Beaulieu Road	d		13 39								14 39									15 39		
Ashurst New Forest	d		13 43								14 43									15 43		
Totton	d		13 48								14 48									15 48		
Salisbury	d			13 08	13 32							14 13			14 48						15 08	15 32
Dean	d			13 20																	15 20	
Mottisfont & Dunbridge	d			13 26																	15 26	
Romsey	d			13 32	13 50							14 32			15 10						15 32	15 50
Redbridge	d			13 39								14 39									15 39	
Millbrook (Hants)	d			13 43								14 43									15 43	
Southampton Central ⛴	a		13 53	13 45	14 02	14 10		14 23			14 53	14 45	15 10		15 20	15 23				15 53	15 45	16 02
	d		13 55	13 59	14 04	14 15		14 25			14 55	14 59	15 15		15 22	15 25				15 55	15 59	16 04
St Denys	d			14 04								15 04									16 04	
Swaythling	d			14 07								15 07									16 07	
Southampton Airport Pkwy ✈	d		14 03	14 10		14 22		14 33			15 03	15 10	15 22			15 33				16 03	16 10	
Portsmouth Harbour ⛴	d	13 17								14 17									15 17			
Portsmouth & Southsea	d	13 22								14 22									15 22			
Fratton	d	13 26								14 26									15 26			
Hilsea	d	13 30								14 30									15 30			
Cosham	d	13 35								14 35									15 35			
Portchester	d	13 40								14 40									15 40			
Fareham	d	13 46			14a26					14 46					15a50				15 46			16a26
Botley	d	13 54								14 54									15 54			
Hedge End	d	13 58								14 58									15 58			
Eastleigh [8]	a	14 04	14 07	14 13						15 04	15 07	15 13							16 04	16 07	16 13	
	d	14 11		14 15						15 11		15 15							16 11		16 15	
Chandlers Ford	d			14 20								15 20									16 20	
Romsey	a			14 28								15 28									16 28	
Shawford	d									15 17												
Winchester	d	14 23				14 31		14 42		15 23			15 31			15 42			16 23			
Micheldever	d	14 32								15 32									16 32			
Basingstoke	a	14 42				14 46		14 58		15 42			15 46			15 58			16 42			
	d	14 44				14 47		15 00		15 44			15 47			16 00			16 44			
Reading [7]	a					15 04							16 04									
Fleet	d																					
Farnborough (Main)	d																					
Woking	a	15 02						15 18		16 02						16 18			17 02			
Clapham Junction [10]	a	15 27						15 39		16 27						16 39			17 27			
London Waterloo [15] ⊖	a	15 37						15 49		16 37						16 49			17 37			

A ✠ from Eastleigh ◇ to Eastleigh

B ✠ from Bournemouth

Weymouth, Bournemouth, Lymington, Romsey, Southampton and Basingstoke - London

		XC ◇■ ⌶	SW ■	SW ◇■ A ⌶	SW ■	SW ■ ⌶	SW ◇■ B ⌶	SW ■	GW ◇	XC ◇■ ⌶	SW ■	SW ◇■ A ⌶	GW	SW ■	SW ■	SW ◇■ C	SW ■	GW ◇	XC ◇■ ⌶	SW ■	SW ◇■ A ⌶	SW ■
Weymouth	d			14 48								15 48	16 10								16 48	
Upwey	d			14 52								15 52	16 15								16 52	
Dorchester West	a												16 22									
Dorchester South	d			15 00								16 00									17 00	
Moreton (Dorset)	d			15 07								16 07									17 07	
Wool	d			15 13								16 13									17 13	
Wareham	d			15 20								16 20									17 20	
Holton Heath	d																					
Hamworthy	d			15 27								16 27									17 27	
Poole ■	a			15 31								16 31									17 31	
	d			15 32			15 55					16 32				16 55					17 32	
Parkstone (Dorset)	d			15 36								16 36									17 36	
Branksome	d			15 40								16 40									17 40	
Bournemouth	a			15 46			16 04					16 46				17 04					17 46	
	d	15 40		15 50			16 06			16 40		16 50				17 06			17 40		17 50	
Pokesdown	d						16 10									17 10						
Christchurch	d						16 14									17 14						
Hinton Admiral	d						16 19									17 19						
New Milton	d			16 01			16 23					17 01				17 23					18 01	
Sway	d						16 28									17 28						
Lymington Pier	d		15 44		16 14						16 44			17 14						17 44		18 14
Lymington Town	d		15 46		16 16						16 46			17 16						17 46		18 16
Brockenhurst ■	a	15 53	15 54	16 08	16 24		16 33			16 53	16 54	17 08		17 24		17 33			17 53	17 54	18 08	18 24
	d	15 57		16 09			16 34			16 57		17 09				17 34			17 57		18 09	
Beaulieu Road	d						16 39									17 39						
Ashurst New Forest	d						16 43									17 43						
Totton	d						16 48									17 48						
Salisbury	d							16 13	16 32								17 08	17 32				
Dean	d																17 20					
Mottisfont & Dunbridge	d																17 26					
Romsey	d							16 32	16 50								17 32	17 50				
Redbridge	d							16 39									17 39					
Millbrook (Hants)	d							16 43									17 43					
Southampton Central ⛴	a	16 10		16 23			16 53	16 45	17 02	17 10		17 23				17 53	17 45	18 02	18 10		18 23	
	d	16 15		16 25			16 55	16 59	17 04	17 15		17 25				17 55	17 59	18 04	18 15		18 25	
St Denys	d							17 04									18 04					
Swaythling	d							17 07									18 07					
Southampton Airport Pkwy ✈	d	16 22		16 33			17 03	17 10		17 22		17 33				18 03	18 10		18 22		18 33	
Portsmouth Harbour ⛴	d					16 17									17 17							
Portsmouth & Southsea	d					16 22									17 22							
Fratton	d					16 26									17 26							
Hilsea	d					16 30									17 30							
Cosham	d					16 35									17 35							
Portchester	d					16 40									17 40							
Fareham	d					16 46			17a26						17 46			18a26				
Botley	d					16 54									17 54							
Hedge End	d					16 58									17 58							
Eastleigh ■	a					17 04	17 07	17 13							18 04	18 07	18 13					
	d						17 11	17 15								18 11	18 15					
Chandlers Ford	d							17 20									18 20					
Romsey	a							17 28									18 28					
Shawford	d						17 17															
Winchester	d	16 31		16 42			17 23			17 31		17 42				18 23			18 31		18 42	
Micheldever	d						17 32									18 32						
Basingstoke	a	16 46		16 58			17 42			17 46		17 58				18 42			18 46		18 58	
	d	16 47		17 00			17 44			17 47		18 00				18 44			18 47		19 00	
Reading ■	a	17 04								18 04									19 04			
Fleet	d																					
Farnborough (Main)	d																					
Woking	a			17 18			18 02					18 18				19 02					19 18	
Clapham Junction ■	a			17 39			18 27					18 39				19 27					19 39	
London Waterloo ■ ⊖	a			17 49			18 37					18 49				19 37					19 49	

A ⌶ from Bournemouth

B ⌶ from Eastleigh ◇ to Eastleigh

C ◇ to Eastleigh

until 19 June

Weymouth, Bournemouth, Lymington, Romsey, Southampton and Basingstoke - London

		SW ■	SW ◇■ A	SW ■	GW ◇	XC ◇■ B ⌶	SW ■	SW ◇■ C ⌶	GW	SW ■	GW ◇	SW ■	SW ◇■ A	SW ■	GW ◇	XC ◇■	SW ■	SW ◇■ C ⌶	SW ■	GW ■	SW ■	SW ◇■ A	SW ■
Weymouth	d							17 48	17 56									18 48					
Upwey	d							17 52	18 01									18 52					
Dorchester West	a								18 08														
Dorchester South	d							18 00										19 00					
Moreton (Dorset)	d							18 07										19 07					
Wool	d							18 13										19 13					
Wareham	d							18 20										19 20					
Holton Heath	d																						
Hamworthy	d							18 27										19 27					
Poole ■	a							18 31										19 31					
	d		17 55					18 32					18 55					19 32				19 55	
Parkstone (Dorset)	d							18 36										19 36					
Branksome	d							18 40										19 40					
Bournemouth	a		18 04					18 46					19 04					19 46				20 04	
	d		18 06			18 40		18 50					19 06			19 40		19 50				20 06	
Pokesdown	d		18 10										19 10									20 10	
Christchurch	d		18 14										19 14									20 14	
Hinton Admiral	d		18 19										19 19									20 19	
New Milton	d		18 23					19 01					19 23					20 01				20 23	
Sway	d		18 28										19 28									20 28	
Lymington Pier	d						18 44			19 14							19 44		20 14				
Lymington Town	d						18 46			19 16							19 46		20 16				
Brockenhurst ■	a		18 33			18 53	18 54	19 08		19 24			19 33			19 53	19 54	20 08	20 24			20 33	
	d		18 34			18 57		19 09					19 34			19 57		20 09				20 34	
Beaulieu Road	d		18 39										19 39									20 39	
Ashurst New Forest	d		18 43										19 43									20 43	
Totton	d		18 48										19 48									20 48	
Salisbury	d			18 13	18 32						18 57			19 08	19 32					20 00			20 13
Dean	d													19 20									
Mottisfont & Dunbridge	d													19 26									
Romsey	d			18 32	18 50						19 15			19 32	19 50					20 19			20 32
Redbridge	d			18 39										19 39									20 39
Millbrook (Hants)	d			18 43										19 43									20 43
Southampton Central ⛴	a		18 53	18 45	19 02	19 10		19 23			19 26		19 53	19 45	20 02	20 10		20 23		20 29		20 53	20 45
	d		18 55	18 59	19 04	19 15		19 25			19 27		19 55	19 59	20 04	20 15		20 25		20 31		20 55	20 59
St Denys	d			19 04										20 04									21 04
Swaythling	d			19 07										20 07									21 07
Southampton Airport Pkwy ✈	d		19 03	19 10		19 22		19 33					20 03	20 10		20 22		20 33				21 03	21 10
Portsmouth Harbour ⛴	d	18 17										19 17									20 17		
Portsmouth & Southsea	d	18 22										19 22									20 22		
Fratton	d	18 26										19 26									20 26		
Hilsea	d	18 30										19 30									20 30		
Cosham	d	18 35										19 35									20 35		
Portchester	d	18 40										19 40									20 40		
Fareham	d	18 46			19a26						19a49	19 46			20a25					20a54	20 46		
Botley	d	18 54										19 54									20 54		
Hedge End	d	18 58										19 58									20 58		
Eastleigh ■	a	19 04	19 07	19 13								20 04	20 07	20 13							21 04	21 07	21 13
	d		19 11	19 15									20 11	20 15								21 11	21 15
Chandlers Ford	d			19 20										20 20									21 20
Romsey	a			19 28										20 28									21 28
Shawford	d		19 17																			21 17	
Winchester	d		19 23			19 31		19 42					20 23			20 31		20 42				21 23	
Micheldever	d		19 32										20 32									21 32	
Basingstoke	a		19 42			19 46		19 58					20 42			20 46		20 58				21 42	
	d		19 44			19 47		20 00					20 44			20 47		21 00				21 44	
Reading ■	a					20 04										21 04							
Fleet	d																						
Farnborough (Main)	d																						
Woking	a		20 02					20 18					21 02					21 18				22 02	
Clapham Junction ■	a		20 27					20 39					21 27					21 39				22 27	
London Waterloo ■ ⊖	a		20 37					20 49					21 37					21 49				22 37	

A ◇ to Eastleigh

B ⌶ to Basingstoke

C ⌶ from Bournemouth

Table 158

Sundays
until 19 June

Weymouth, Bournemouth, Lymington, Romsey, Southampton and Basingstoke - London

		GW ◇		SW ■	SW ■	SW ■	SW ◇■ A	GW	SW ■	GW ◇	SW ■	SW ■		SW ■	SW ◇■	GW ◇	SW ■	SW ■	SW ■
Weymouth	d						19 58	20 09							20 58		21 58	22 58	
Upwey	d						20 02	20 14							21 02		22 02	23 02	
Dorchester West	a							20 21											
Dorchester South	d						20 10								21 10		22 10	23 10	
Moreton (Dorset)	d						20 17								21 17		22 17	23 17	
Wool	d						20 23								21 23		22 23	23 23	
Wareham	d						20 30								21 30		22 30	23 30	
Holton Heath	d																		
Hamworthy	d						20 37								21 37		22 37	23 37	
Poole [4]	a						20 41								21 41		22 41	23 41	
	d						20 50								21 50		22 50	23 50	
Parkstone (Dorset)	d						20 54								21 54		22 54	23 54	
Branksome	d						20 57								21 57		22 57	23 57	
Bournemouth	a						21 03								22 03		23 03	00 03	
	d						21 06								22 06		23 06		
Pokesdown	d						21 10								22 10		23 10		
Christchurch	d						21 14								22 14		23 14		
Hinton Admiral	d						21 19								22 19		23 19		
New Milton	d						21 23								22 23		23 23		
Sway	d						21 28								22 28		23 28		
Lymington Pier	d			20 44	21 14						21 44	22 14							
Lymington Town	d			20 46	21 16						21 46	22 16							
Brockenhurst [3]	a			20 54	21 24		21 33				21 54	22 24			22 33		23 33		
	d						21 34								22 34		23 34		
Beaulieu Road	d						21 39								22 39				
Ashurst New Forest	d						21 43								22 43		23 43		
Totton	d						21 48								22 48		23 48		
Salisbury	d	20 30							21 08	21 32						22 35			
Dean	d								21 20										
Mottisfont & Dunbridge	d								21 26										
Romsey	d	20 48							21 32	21 50						22 54			
Redbridge	d								21 39										
Millbrook (Hants)	d								21 43										
Southampton Central ⛴	a	20 59					21 53		21 45	22 02					22 53	23 04	23 53		
	d	21 01					21 55		21 59	22 04					22 55	23 07			
St Denys	d								22 04										
Swaythling	d								22 07										
Southampton Airport Pkwy ✈	d						22 03		22 10						23 03				
Portsmouth Harbour ⛴	d					21 17								22 17					23 17
Portsmouth & Southsea	d					21 22								22 22					23 22
Fratton	d					21 26								22 26					23 26
Hilsea	d					21 30								22 30					23 30
Cosham	d					21 35								22 35					23 35
Portchester	d					21 40								22 40					23 40
Fareham	d	21a23				21 46				22a26				22 46		23a28			23 46
Botley	d					21 54								22 54					23 54
Hedge End	d					21 58								22 58					23 58
Eastleigh [3]	a					22 04	22 07		22 13					23 04	23 09				00 04
	d						22 11		22 15						23 11				
Chandlers Ford	d								22 20										
Romsey	a								22 31										
Shawford	d																		
Winchester	d						22 23								23 23				
Micheldever	d						22 32								23 32				
Basingstoke	a						22 42								23 42				
	d						22 44								23 44				
Reading [7]	a																		
Fleet	d																		
Farnborough (Main)	d																		
Woking	a						23 02								00 02				
Clapham Junction [10]	a						23 27								00 23				
London Waterloo [15] ⊖	a						23 37								00 33				

A ◇ to Eastleigh

Table 158

Sundays
26 June to 31 July

Weymouth, Bournemouth, Lymington, Romsey, Southampton and Basingstoke - London

		SW ■	SW ■	SW ■	SW ■	SW ◇■ A ⌶	SW ■	SW ■	SW ◇■ B	SW ■		XC ◇■ ⌶	SW ◇■ C ⌶	SW ■	SW ■ ⌶	SW ◇■ D ⌶	SW ■	XC ◇■ ⌶	SW ■	SW ◇■ C ⌶		SW ■	SW ■ ⌶	SW ◇■ E ⌶	SW ■
Weymouth	d		22p10	23p10									07 48							08 48					
Upwey	d		22p14	23p14									07 52							08 52					
Dorchester West	a																								
Dorchester South	d		22p22	23p22									08 00							09 00					
Moreton (Dorset)	d		22p28	23p28									08 07							09 07					
Wool	d		22p34	23p34									08 13							09 13					
Wareham	d		22p42	23p42									08 20							09 20					
Holton Heath	d																								
Hamworthy	d		22p48	23p48									08 27							09 27					
Poole [4]	a		22p53	23p53									08 31							09 31					
	d		22p54	23p54		06 50			07 50				08 32			08 55				09 32				09 55	
Parkstone (Dorset)	d		22p58			06 54			07 54				08 36							09 36					
Branksome	d		23p01			06 57			07 57				08 40							09 40					
Bournemouth	a		23p07	00 03		07 02			08 02				08 46			09 04				09 46				10 04	
	d		23p12			07 06			08 06				08 50			09 06		09 40		09 50				10 06	
Pokesdown	d		23p16			07 10			08 10							09 10								10 10	
Christchurch	d		23p20			07 14			08 14							09 14								10 14	
Hinton Admiral	d		23p25			07 19			08 19							09 19								10 19	
New Milton	d		23p29			07 23			08 23				09 01			09 23				10 01				10 23	
Sway	d		23p34			07 28			08 28							09 28								10 28	
Lymington Pier	d													09 14					09 44			10 14			
Lymington Town	d													09 16					09 46			10 16			
Brockenhurst [3]	a		23p39			07 33			08 33				09 08	09 24		09 33		09 53	09 54	10 08		10 24		10 33	
	d		23p40			07 34			08 34				09 09			09 34		09 57		10 09				10 34	
Beaulieu Road	d								08 39							09 39								10 39	
Ashurst New Forest	d		23p47			07 43			08 43							09 43								10 43	
Totton	d		23p52			07 48			08 48							09 48								10 48	
Salisbury	d						08 08			08 20							09 08								10 13
Dean	d						08 20										09 20								
Mottisfont & Dunbridge	d						08 26										09 26								
Romsey	d						08 35			08 39							09 32								10 32
Redbridge	d									08 46							09 39								10 39
Millbrook (Hants)	d									08 50							09 43								10 43
Southampton Central ⛴	a		23p57			07 53			08 53	08 52			09 23			09 53	09 45	10 10		10 23				10 53	10 45
	d		23p59			07 55			08 55	08 59		09 15	09 25			09 55	09 59	10 15		10 25				10 55	10 59
St Denys	d		00 04							09 04							10 04								11 04
Swaythling	d		00 07							09 07							10 07								11 07
Southampton Airport Pkwy ✈	d		00 10			08 03			09 03	09 10		09 22	09 33			10 03	10 10	10 22		10 33				11 03	11 10
Portsmouth Harbour ⛴	d	23p24			07 17			08 17							09 17								10 17		
Portsmouth & Southsea	d	23p29			07 22			08 22							09 22								10 22		
Fratton	d	23p33			07 26			08 26							09 26								10 26		
Hilsea	d	23p37			07 30			08 30							09 30								10 30		
Cosham	d	23p42			07 35			08 35							09 35								10 35		
Portchester	d	23p47			07 40			08 40							09 40								10 40		
Fareham	d	23p53			07 46			08 46							09 46								10 46		
Botley	d	23p59			07 54			08 54							09 54								10 54		
Hedge End	d	00 05			07 58			08 58							09 58								10 58		
Eastleigh [3]	a	00 11	00 14		08 04	08 07		09 04	09 07	09 13					10 04	10 07	10 13						11 04	11 07	11 13
	d	00 21				08 11			09 11	09 15						10 11	10 15							11 11	11 15
Chandlers Ford	d						08 42			09 20							10 20								11 20
Romsey	a						09 24			09 28							10 28								11 28
Shawford	d								09 17															11 17	
Winchester	d	00a30				08 23			09 23			09 31	09 42			10 23		10 31		10 42				11 23	
Micheldever	d					08 32			09 32							10 32								11 32	
Basingstoke	a					08 42			09 42			09 46	09 58			10 42		10 46		10 58				11 42	
	d					08 44			09 44			09 47	10 00			10 44		10 47		11 00				11 44	
Reading [7]	a											10 04						11 04							
Fleet	d																								
Farnborough (Main)	d																								
Woking	a					09 02			10 02				10 19			11 02				11 18				12 02	
Clapham Junction [10]	a					09 30			10 27				10 40			11 27				11 39				12 27	
London Waterloo [15] ⊖	a					09 43			10 42				10 54			11 42				11 54				12 42	

A ⌶ to Eastleigh ◇ to Eastleigh
B ◇ to Eastleigh
C ⌶ from Bournemouth
D ⌶ from Eastleigh ◇ to Eastleigh
E ⌶ from Bournemouth ◇ to Eastleigh

Weymouth, Bournemouth, Lymington, Romsey, Southampton and Basingstoke - London

		GW ◇	XC ◇1 ⌶	SW 1	SW ◇1 A ⌶	SW 1	SW 1 ⌶	SW ◇1 B ⌶	SW 1	GW ◇	XC ◇1 ⌶	SW 1	SW ◇1 A ⌶	GW	SW 1	SW 1 ⌶	SW ◇1 C ⌶	SW 1	GW ◇	XC ◇1 ⌶	SW 1	SW ◇1 A ⌶	SW 1
Weymouth	d				09 48								10 48	11 14								11 48	
Upwey	d				09 52								10 52	11 19								11 52	
Dorchester West	a													11 27									
Dorchester South	d				10 00								11 00									12 00	
Moreton (Dorset)	d				10 07								11 07									12 07	
Wool	d				10 13								11 13									12 13	
Wareham	d				10 20								11 20									12 20	
Holton Heath	d																						
Hamworthy	d				10 27								11 27									12 27	
Poole 4	a				10 31								11 31									12 31	
	d				10 32			10 55					11 32				11 55					12 32	
Parkstone (Dorset)	d				10 36								11 36									12 36	
Branksome	d				10 40								11 40									12 40	
Bournemouth	a				10 46			11 04					11 46				12 04					12 46	
	d		10 40		10 50			11 06			11 40		11 50				12 06			12 40		12 50	
Pokesdown	d							11 10									12 10						
Christchurch	d							11 14									12 14						
Hinton Admiral	d							11 19									12 19						
New Milton	d				11 01			11 23					12 01				12 23					13 01	
Sway	d							11 28									12 28						
Lymington Pier	d			10 44		11 14						11 44			12 14						12 44		13 14
Lymington Town	d			10 46		11 16						11 46			12 16						12 46		13 16
Brockenhurst 3	a		10 53	10 54	11 08	11 24		11 33			11 53	11 54	12 08		12 24		12 33			12 53	12 54	13 08	13 24
	d		10 57		11 09			11 34			11 57		12 09				12 34			12 57		13 09	
Beaulieu Road	d							11 39									12 39						
Ashurst New Forest	d							11 43									12 43						
Totton	d							11 48									12 48						
Salisbury	d	10 32							11 08	11 32								12 13	12 36				
Dean	d								11 20														
Mottisfont & Dunbridge	d								11 26														
Romsey	d	10 50							11 32	11 50								12 32	12 54				
Redbridge	d								11 39									12 39					
Millbrook (Hants)	d								11 43									12 43					
Southampton Central	a	11 02	11 10		11 23			11 53	11 45	12 02	12 10		12 23				12 53	12 45	13 06	13 10		13 23	
	d	11 04	11 15		11 25			11 55	11 59	12 04	12 15		12 25				12 55	12 59	13 08	13 15		13 25	
St Denys	d								12 04									13 04					
Swaythling	d								12 07									13 07					
Southampton Airport Pkwy	d		11 22		11 33			12 03	12 10		12 22		12 33				13 03	13 10		13 22		13 33	
Portsmouth Harbour	d						11 17									12 17							
Portsmouth & Southsea	d						11 22									12 22							
Fratton	d						11 26									12 26							
Hilsea	d						11 30									12 30							
Cosham	d						11 35									12 35							
Portchester	d						11 40									12 40							
Fareham	d	11a26					11 46			12a26						12 46			13a33				
Botley	d						11 54									12 54							
Hedge End	d						11 58									12 58							
Eastleigh 3	a						12 04	12 07	12 13							13 04	13 07	13 13					
	d						12 11		12 15							13 11		13 15					
Chandlers Ford	d								12 20									13 20					
Romsey	a								12 28									13 28					
Shawford	d															13 17							
Winchester	d		11 31		11 42		12 23				12 31		12 42			13 23				13 31		13 42	
Micheldever	d						12 32									13 32							
Basingstoke	a		11 46		11 58		12 42				12 46		12 58			13 42				13 46		13 58	
	d		11 47		12 00		12 44				12 47		13 00			13 44				13 47		14 00	
Reading 7	a		12 04								13 04									14 04			
Fleet	d																						
Farnborough (Main)	d																						
Woking	a				12 18		13 02						13 18			14 02						14 18	
Clapham Junction 10	a				12 39		13 27						13 39			14 27						14 39	
London Waterloo 15 ⊖	a				12 49		13 37						13 49			14 37						14 49	

A ⌶ from Bournemouth
B ⌶ from Eastleigh ◇ to Eastleigh
C ⌶ from Bournemouth ◇ to Eastleigh

Weymouth, Bournemouth, Lymington, Romsey, Southampton and Basingstoke - London

		SW 1 ⌶	SW ◇1 A ⌶	SW 1	GW ◇ ⌶	XC ◇1 ⌶	SW 1	SW ◇1 B ⌶	SW 1	SW 1 ⌶	SW ◇1 A ⌶	SW 1	XC ◇1 ⌶	SW 1	GW ◇	SW ◇1 B ⌶	GW	SW 1	SW 1 ⌶	SW ◇1 A ⌶	SW 1	GW ◇
Weymouth	d							12 48								13 48	14 12					
Upwey	d							12 52								13 52	14 17					
Dorchester West	a																14 24					
Dorchester South	d							13 00								14 00						
Moreton (Dorset)	d							13 07								14 07						
Wool	d							13 13								14 13						
Wareham	d							13 20								14 20						
Holton Heath	d																					
Hamworthy	d							13 27								14 27						
Poole 4	a							13 31								14 31						
	d		12 55					13 32			13 55					14 32				14 55		
Parkstone (Dorset)	d							13 36								14 36						
Branksome	d							13 40								14 40						
Bournemouth	a		13 04					13 46			14 04					14 46				15 04		
	d		13 06			13 40		13 50			14 06		14 40			14 50				15 06		
Pokesdown	d		13 10								14 10									15 10		
Christchurch	d		13 14								14 14									15 14		
Hinton Admiral	d		13 19								14 19									15 19		
New Milton	d		13 23					14 01			14 23					15 01				15 23		
Sway	d		13 28								14 28									15 28		
Lymington Pier	d						13 44		14 14					14 44				15 14				
Lymington Town	d						13 46		14 16					14 46				15 16				
Brockenhurst 3	a		13 33			13 53	13 54	14 08	14 24		14 33		14 53	14 54		15 08		15 24		15 33		
	d		13 34			13 57		14 09			14 34		14 57			15 09				15 34		
Beaulieu Road	d		13 39								14 39									15 39		
Ashurst New Forest	d		13 43								14 43									15 43		
Totton	d		13 48								14 48									15 48		
Salisbury	d			13 08	13 32							14 13			14 48						15 08	15 32
Dean	d			13 20																	15 20	
Mottisfont & Dunbridge	d			13 26																	15 26	
Romsey	d			13 32	13 50							14 32			15 10						15 32	15 50
Redbridge	d			13 39								14 39									15 39	
Millbrook (Hants)	d			13 43								14 43									15 43	
Southampton Central	a		13 53	13 45	14 02	14 10		14 23			14 53	14 45	15 10		15 20	15 23				15 53	15 45	16 02
	d		13 55	13 59	14 04	14 15		14 25			14 55	14 59	15 15		15 22	15 25				15 55	15 59	16 04
St Denys	d			14 04								15 04									16 04	
Swaythling	d			14 07								15 07									16 07	
Southampton Airport Pkwy	d		14 03	14 10		14 22		14 33			15 03	15 10	15 22			15 33				16 03	16 10	
Portsmouth Harbour	d	13 17								14 17									15 17			
Portsmouth & Southsea	d	13 22								14 22									15 22			
Fratton	d	13 26								14 26									15 26			
Hilsea	d	13 30								14 30									15 30			
Cosham	d	13 35								14 35									15 35			
Portchester	d	13 40								14 40									15 40			
Fareham	d	13 46			14a26					14 46					15a50				15 46			16a26
Botley	d	13 54								14 54									15 54			
Hedge End	d	13 58								14 58									15 58			
Eastleigh 3	a	14 04	14 07	14 13						15 04	15 07	15 13							16 04	16 07	16 13	
	d	14 11		14 15						15 11		15 15							16 11		16 15	
Chandlers Ford	d			14 20								15 20									16 20	
Romsey	a			14 28								15 28									16 28	
Shawford	d									15 17												
Winchester	d	14 23				14 31		14 42		15 23			15 31			15 42			16 23			
Micheldever	d	14 32								15 32									16 32			
Basingstoke	a	14 42				14 46		14 58		15 42			15 46			15 58			16 42			
	d	14 44				14 47		15 00		15 44			15 47			16 00			16 44			
Reading 7	a					15 04							16 04									
Fleet	d																					
Farnborough (Main)	d																					
Woking	a	15 02						15 18		16 02						16 18			17 02			
Clapham Junction 10	a	15 27						15 39		16 27						16 39			17 27			
London Waterloo 15 ⊖	a	15 37						15 49		16 37						16 49			17 37			

A ⌶ from Eastleigh ◇ to Eastleigh
B ⌶ from Bournemouth

Table 158

Sundays
26 June to 31 July

Weymouth, Bournemouth, Lymington, Romsey, Southampton and Basingstoke - London

		XC	SW	SW	SW	SW	SW	SW	GW	XC	SW	SW	GW	SW	SW	SW	SW	GW	XC	SW	SW	SW
		◇1	1	◇1	1	1	◇1	1	◇	◇1	1	◇1		1	1	◇1	1	◇	◇1	1	◇1	1
				A			B					A				C					A	
		🍴		🍴		🍴	🍴			🍴		🍴							🍴		🍴	
Weymouth	d			14 48								15 48	16 10								16 48	
Upwey	d			14 52								15 52	16 15								16 52	
Dorchester West	a												16 22									
Dorchester South	d			15 00								16 00									17 00	
Moreton (Dorset)	d			15 07								16 07									17 07	
Wool	d			15 13								16 13									17 13	
Wareham	d			15 20								16 20									17 20	
Holton Heath	d																					
Hamworthy	d			15 27								16 27									17 27	
Poole 4	a			15 31								16 31									17 31	
	d			15 32			15 55					16 32				16 55					17 32	
Parkstone (Dorset)	d			15 36								16 36									17 36	
Branksome	d			15 40								16 40									17 40	
Bournemouth	a			15 46			16 04					16 46				17 04					17 46	
	d	15 40		15 50			16 06			16 40		16 50				17 06			17 40		17 50	
Pokesdown	d						16 10									17 10						
Christchurch	d						16 14									17 14						
Hinton Admiral	d						16 19									17 19						
New Milton	d			16 01			16 23					17 01				17 23					18 01	
Sway	d						16 28									17 28						
Lymington Pier	d		15 44		16 14						16 44			17 14						17 44		18 14
Lymington Town	d		15 46		16 16						16 46			17 16						17 46		18 16
Brockenhurst 3	a	15 53	15 54	16 08	16 24		16 33			16 53	16 54	17 08		17 24		17 33			17 53	17 54	18 08	18 24
	d	15 57		16 09			16 34			16 57		17 09				17 34			17 57		18 09	
Beaulieu Road	d						16 39									17 39						
Ashurst New Forest	d						16 43									17 43						
Totton	d						16 48									17 48						
Salisbury	d							16 13	16 32								17 08	17 32				
Dean	d																17 20					
Mottisfont & Dunbridge	d																17 26					
Romsey	d							16 32	16 50								17 32	17 50				
Redbridge	d							16 39									17 39					
Millbrook (Hants)	d							16 43									17 43					
Southampton Central ⛴	a	16 10		16 23			16 53	16 45	17 02	17 10		17 23				17 53	17 45	18 02	18 10		18 23	
	d	16 15		16 25			16 55	16 59	17 04	17 15		17 25				17 55	17 59	18 04	18 15		18 25	
St Denys	d							17 04									18 04					
Swaythling	d							17 07									18 07					
Southampton Airport Pkwy ✈	d	16 22		16 33			17 03	17 10		17 22		17 33				18 03	18 10		18 22		18 33	
Portsmouth Harbour ⛴	d					16 17									17 17							
Portsmouth & Southsea	d					16 22									17 22							
Fratton	d					16 26									17 26							
Hilsea	d					16 30									17 30							
Cosham	d					16 35									17 35							
Portchester	d					16 40									17 40							
Fareham	d					16 46			17a26						17 46			18a26				
Botley	d					16 54									17 54							
Hedge End	d					16 58									17 58							
Eastleigh 3	a					17 04	17 07	17 13							18 04	18 07	18 13					
	d						17 11	17 15								18 11	18 15					
Chandlers Ford	d							17 20									18 20					
Romsey	a							17 28									18 28					
Shawford	d						17 17															
Winchester	d	16 31		16 42			17 23			17 31		17 42				18 23			18 31		18 42	
Micheldever	d						17 32									18 32						
Basingstoke	a	16 46		16 58			17 42			17 46		17 58				18 42			18 46		18 58	
	d	16 47		17 00			17 44			17 47		18 00				18 44			18 47		19 00	
Reading 7	a	17 04								18 04									19 04			
Fleet	d																					
Farnborough (Main)	d																					
Woking	a			17 18			18 02					18 18				19 02					19 18	
Clapham Junction 10	a			17 39			18 27					18 39				19 27					19 39	
London Waterloo 15 ⊖	a			17 49			18 37					18 49				19 37					19 49	

A 🍴 from Bournemouth
B 🍴 from Eastleigh ◇ to Eastleigh
C ◇ to Eastleigh

Table 158

Sundays
26 June to 31 July

Weymouth, Bournemouth, Lymington, Romsey, Southampton and Basingstoke - London

		SW	SW	SW	GW	XC	SW	SW	GW	SW	GW	SW	SW	SW	GW	XC	SW	SW	SW	GW	SW	SW	SW
		1	◇1	1	◇	◇1	1	◇1		1	◇	1	◇1	1	◇	◇1	1	◇1	1	1	1	◇1	1
			A			B		C					A					C				A	
						🍴		🍴										🍴					
Weymouth	d							17 48	17 56									18 48					
Upwey	d							17 52	18 01									18 52					
Dorchester West	a								18 08														
Dorchester South	d							18 00										19 00					
Moreton (Dorset)	d							18 07										19 07					
Wool	d							18 13										19 13					
Wareham	d							18 20										19 20					
Holton Heath	d																						
Hamworthy	d							18 27										19 27					
Poole 4	a							18 31										19 31					
	d		17 55					18 32					18 55					19 32				19 55	
Parkstone (Dorset)	d							18 36										19 36					
Branksome	d							18 40										19 40					
Bournemouth	a		18 04					18 46					19 04					19 46				20 04	
	d		18 06			18 40		18 50					19 06			19 40		19 50				20 06	
Pokesdown	d		18 10										19 10									20 10	
Christchurch	d		18 14										19 14									20 14	
Hinton Admiral	d		18 19										19 19									20 19	
New Milton	d		18 23					19 01					19 23					20 01				20 23	
Sway	d		18 28										19 28									20 28	
Lymington Pier	d						18 44			19 14							19 44		20 14				
Lymington Town	d						18 46			19 16							19 46		20 16				
Brockenhurst 3	a		18 33			18 53	18 54	19 08		19 24			19 33			19 53	19 54	20 08	20 24			20 33	
	d		18 34			18 57		19 09					19 34			19 57		20 09				20 34	
Beaulieu Road	d		18 39										19 39									20 39	
Ashurst New Forest	d		18 43										19 43									20 43	
Totton	d		18 48										19 48									20 48	
Salisbury	d			18 13	18 32						18 57			19 08	19 32					20 00			20 13
Dean	d													19 20									
Mottisfont & Dunbridge	d													19 26									
Romsey	d			18 32	18 50						19 15			19 32	19 50					20 19			20 32
Redbridge	d			18 39										19 39									20 39
Millbrook (Hants)	d			18 43										19 43									20 43
Southampton Central ⛴	a		18 53	18 45	19 02	19 10		19 23			19 26		19 53	19 45	20 02	20 10		20 23		20 29		20 53	20 45
	d		18 55	18 59	19 04	19 15		19 25			19 27		19 55	19 59	20 04	20 15		20 25		20 31		20 55	20 59
St Denys	d			19 04										20 04									21 04
Swaythling	d			19 07										20 07									21 07
Southampton Airport Pkwy ✈	d		19 03	19 10		19 22		19 33					20 03	20 10		20 22		20 33				21 03	21 10
Portsmouth Harbour ⛴	d	18 17										19 17									20 17		
Portsmouth & Southsea	d	18 22										19 22									20 22		
Fratton	d	18 26										19 26									20 26		
Hilsea	d	18 30										19 30									20 30		
Cosham	d	18 35										19 35									20 35		
Portchester	d	18 40										19 40									20 40		
Fareham	d	18 46			19a26						19a49	19 46			20a25					20a54	20 46		
Botley	d	18 54										19 54									20 54		
Hedge End	d	18 58										19 58									20 58		
Eastleigh 3	a	19 04	19 07	19 13								20 04	20 07	20 13							21 04	21 07	21 13
	d		19 11	19 15									20 11	20 15								21 11	21 15
Chandlers Ford	d			19 20										20 20									21 20
Romsey	a			19 28										20 28									21 28
Shawford	d		19 17																			21 17	
Winchester	d		19 23			19 31		19 42					20 23			20 31		20 42				21 23	
Micheldever	d		19 32										20 32									21 32	
Basingstoke	a		19 42			19 46		19 58					20 42			20 46		20 58				21 42	
	d		19 44			19 47		20 00					20 44			20 47		21 00				21 44	
Reading 7	a					20 04										21 04							
Fleet	d																						
Farnborough (Main)	d																						
Woking	a		20 02					20 18					21 02					21 18				22 02	
Clapham Junction 10	a		20 27					20 39					21 27					21 39				22 27	
London Waterloo 15 ⊖	a		20 37					20 49					21 37					21 49				22 37	

A ◇ to Eastleigh
B 🍴 to Basingstoke
C 🍴 from Bournemouth

Weymouth, Bournemouth, Lymington, Romsey, Southampton and Basingstoke - London

		GW ◇		SW ■	SW ■	SW ■	SW ◇■ A	GW	SW ■	GW ◇	SW ■	SW ■		SW ■	SW ◇■	GW ◇	SW ■	SW ■	SW ■
Weymouth	d						19 58	20 09							20 58		21 58	22 58	
Upwey	d						20 02	20 14							21 02		22 02	23 02	
Dorchester West	a							20 21											
Dorchester South	d						20 10								21 10		22 10	23 10	
Moreton (Dorset)	d						20 17								21 17		22 17	23 17	
Wool	d						20 23								21 23		22 23	23 23	
Wareham	d						20 30								21 30		22 30	23 30	
Holton Heath	d																		
Hamworthy	d						20 37								21 37		22 37	23 37	
Poole 4	a						20 41								21 41		22 41	23 41	
	d						20 50								21 50		22 50	23 50	
Parkstone (Dorset)	d						20 54								21 54		22 54	23 54	
Branksome	d						20 57								21 57		22 57	23 57	
Bournemouth	a						21 03								22 03		23 03	00 03	
	d						21 06								22 06		23 06		
Pokesdown	d						21 10								22 10		23 10		
Christchurch	d						21 14								22 14		23 14		
Hinton Admiral	d						21 19								22 19		23 19		
New Milton	d						21 23								22 23		23 23		
Sway	d						21 28								22 28		23 28		
Lymington Pier	d			20 44	21 14						21 44	22 14							
Lymington Town	d			20 46	21 16						21 46	22 16							
Brockenhurst 3	a			20 54	21 24		21 33				21 54	22 24			22 33		23 33		
	d						21 34								22 34		23 34		
Beaulieu Road	d						21 39								22 39				
Ashurst New Forest	d						21 43								22 43		23 43		
Totton	d						21 48								22 48		23 48		
Salisbury	d	20 30							21 08	21 32						22 35			
Dean	d								21 20										
Mottisfont & Dunbridge	d								21 26										
Romsey	d	20 48							21 32	21 50						22 54			
Redbridge	d								21 39										
Millbrook (Hants)	d								21 43										
Southampton Central	a	20 59					21 53		21 45	22 02					22 53	23 04	23 53		
	d	21 01					21 55		21 59	22 04					22 55	23 07			
St Denys	d								22 04										
Swaythling	d								22 07										
Southampton Airport Pkwy	d						22 03		22 10						23 03				
Portsmouth Harbour	d					21 17								22 17					23 17
Portsmouth & Southsea	d					21 22								22 22					23 22
Fratton	d					21 26								22 26					23 26
Hilsea	d					21 30								22 30					23 30
Cosham	d					21 35								22 35					23 35
Portchester	d					21 40								22 40					23 40
Fareham	d	21a23				21 46				22a26				22 46		23a28			23 46
Botley	d					21 54								22 54					23 54
Hedge End	d					21 58								22 58					23 58
Eastleigh 3	a					22 04	22 07		22 13					23 04	23 09				00 04
	d					22 11			22 15						23 11				
Chandlers Ford	d								22 20										
Romsey	a								22 31										
Shawford	d																		
Winchester	d					22 23									23 23				
Micheldever	d					22 32									23 32				
Basingstoke	a					22 42									23 42				
	d					22 44									23 44				
Reading 7	a																		
Fleet	d																		
Farnborough (Main)	d																		
Woking	a					23 02									00 02				
Clapham Junction 10	a					23 27									00 23				
London Waterloo 15 ⊖	a					23 37									00 33				

A ◇ to Eastleigh

Weymouth, Bournemouth, Lymington, Romsey, Southampton and Basingstoke - London

		SW ■	SW ■	SW ■	SW ■	SW ◇■ A 🛒	SW ■	SW ■	SW ◇■ B	SW ■		XC ◇■ 🛒	SW ◇■ C 🛒	SW ■	SW ■ 🛒	SW ◇■ D 🛒	SW ■	XC ◇■ 🛒	SW ■	SW ◇■ C 🛒		SW ■	SW ■ 🛒	SW ◇■ E 🛒	SW ■
Weymouth	d		22p10	23p10									07 48							08 48					
Upwey	d		22p14	23p14									07 52							08 52					
Dorchester West	a																								
Dorchester South	d		22p22	23p22									08 00							09 00					
Moreton (Dorset)	d		22p28	23p28									08 07							09 07					
Wool	d		22p34	23p34									08 13							09 13					
Wareham	d		22p42	23p42									08 20							09 20					
Holton Heath	d																								
Hamworthy	d		22p48	23p48									08 27							09 27					
Poole 4	a		22p53	23p53									08 31							09 31					
	d		22p54	23p54		06 50			07 50				08 32			08 55				09 32				09 55	
Parkstone (Dorset)	d		22p58			06 54			07 54				08 36							09 36					
Branksome	d		23p01			06 57			07 57				08 40							09 40					
Bournemouth	a		23p07	00 03		07 02			08 02				08 46			09 04				09 46				10 04	
	d		23p12			07 06			08 06				08 50			09 06		09 40		09 50				10 06	
Pokesdown	d		23p16			07 10			08 10							09 10								10 10	
Christchurch	d		23p20			07 14			08 14							09 14								10 14	
Hinton Admiral	d		23p25			07 19			08 19							09 19								10 19	
New Milton	d		23p29			07 23			08 23				09 01			09 23				10 01				10 23	
Sway	d		23p34			07 28			08 28							09 28								10 28	
Lymington Pier	d													09 14					09 44			10 14			
Lymington Town	d													09 16					09 46			10 16			
Brockenhurst 3	a		23p39			07 33			08 33				09 08	09 24		09 33		09 53	09 54	10 08		10 24		10 33	
	d		23p40			07 34			08 34				09 09			09 34		09 57		10 09				10 34	
Beaulieu Road	d								08 39							09 39								10 39	
Ashurst New Forest	d		23p47			07 43			08 43							09 43								10 43	
Totton	d		23p52			07 48			08 48							09 48								10 48	
Salisbury	d						08 08			08 20							09 08								10 13
Dean	d						08 20										09 20								
Mottisfont & Dunbridge	d						08 26										09 26								
Romsey	d						08 35			08 39							09 32								10 32
Redbridge	d									08 46							09 39								10 39
Millbrook (Hants)	d									08 50							09 43								10 43
Southampton Central	a		23p57			07 53			08 53	08 52			09 23			09 53	09 45	10 10		10 23				10 53	10 45
	d		23p59			07 55			08 55	08 59		09 15	09 25			09 55	09 59	10 15		10 25				10 55	10 59
St Denys	d		00 04							09 04							10 04								11 04
Swaythling	d		00 07							09 07							10 07								11 07
Southampton Airport Pkwy	d		00 10			08 03			09 03	09 10		09 22	09 33			10 03	10 10	10 22		10 33				11 03	11 10
Portsmouth Harbour	d	23p24			07 17			08 17							09 17								10 17		
Portsmouth & Southsea	d	23p29			07 22			08 22							09 22								10 22		
Fratton	d	23p33			07 26			08 26							09 26								10 26		
Hilsea	d	23p37			07 30			08 30							09 30								10 30		
Cosham	d	23p42			07 35			08 35							09 35								10 35		
Portchester	d	23p47			07 40			08 40							09 40								10 40		
Fareham	d	23p53			07 46			08 46							09 46								10 46		
Botley	d	23p59			07 54			08 54							09 54								10 54		
Hedge End	d	00 05			07 58			08 58							09 58								10 58		
Eastleigh 3	a	00 11	00 14		08 04	08 07		09 04	09 07	09 13					10 04	10 07	10 13						11 04	11 07	11 13
	d	00 21			08 11			09 11		09 15					10 11		10 15						11 11		11 15
Chandlers Ford	d						08 42			09 20							10 20								11 20
Romsey	a						09 24			09 28							10 28								11 28
Shawford	d							09 17															11 17		
Winchester	d	00a30			08 23			09 23				09 31	09 42		10 23			10 31		10 42			11 23		
Micheldever	d				08 32			09 32							10 32								11 32		
Basingstoke	a				08 42			09 42				09 46	09 58		10 42			10 46		10 58			11 42		
	d				08 44			09 44				09 47	10 00		10 44			10 47		11 00			11 44		
Reading 7	a											10 04						11 04							
Fleet	d																								
Farnborough (Main)	d																								
Woking	a				09 02			10 02					10 19		11 02					11 18			12 02		
Clapham Junction 10	a				09 30			10 27					10 40		11 27					11 39			12 27		
London Waterloo 15 ⊖	a				09 43			10 42					10 54		11 42					11 54			12 42		

A 🛒 to Eastleigh ◇ to Eastleigh

B ◇ to Eastleigh

C 🛒 from Bournemouth

D 🛒 from Eastleigh ◇ to Eastleigh

E 🛒 from Bournemouth ◇ to Eastleigh

Table 158

Sundays
7 August to 11 September

Weymouth, Bournemouth, Lymington, Romsey, Southampton and Basingstoke - London

		GW ◇	XC ◇1 ✠	SW 1	SW ◇1 A ✠	SW 1	SW 1 ✠	SW ◇1 B ✠	SW 1	GW ◇	XC ◇1 ✠	SW 1	SW ◇1 A ✠	GW	SW 1	SW 1 ✠	SW ◇1 C ✠	SW 1	GW ◇	XC ◇1 ✠	SW 1	SW ◇1 A ✠	SW 1
Weymouth	d				09 48								10 48	11 14								11 48	
Upwey	d				09 52								10 52	11 19								11 52	
Dorchester West	a													11 27									
Dorchester South	d				10 00								11 00									12 00	
Moreton (Dorset)	d				10 07								11 07									12 07	
Wool	d				10 13								11 13									12 13	
Wareham	d				10 20								11 20									12 20	
Holton Heath	d																						
Hamworthy	d				10 27								11 27									12 27	
Poole 4	a				10 31								11 31									12 31	
	d				10 32			10 55					11 32				11 55					12 32	
Parkstone (Dorset)	d				10 36								11 36									12 36	
Branksome	d				10 40								11 40									12 40	
Bournemouth	a				10 46			11 04					11 46				12 04					12 46	
	d		10 40		10 50			11 06			11 40		11 50				12 06			12 40		12 50	
Pokesdown	d							11 10									12 10						
Christchurch	d							11 14									12 14						
Hinton Admiral	d							11 19									12 19						
New Milton	d				11 01			11 23					12 01				12 23					13 01	
Sway	d							11 28									12 28						
Lymington Pier	d			10 44		11 14						11 44			12 14						12 44		13 14
Lymington Town	d			10 46		11 16						11 46			12 16						12 46		13 16
Brockenhurst 3	a		10 53	10 54	11 08	11 24		11 33			11 53	11 54	12 08		12 24		12 33			12 53	12 54	13 08	13 24
	d		10 57		11 09			11 34			11 57		12 09				12 34			12 57		13 09	
Beaulieu Road	d							11 39									12 39						
Ashurst New Forest	d							11 43									12 43						
Totton	d							11 48									12 48						
Salisbury	d	10 32							11 08	11 32								12 13	12 36				
Dean	d								11 20														
Mottisfont & Dunbridge	d								11 26														
Romsey	d	10 50							11 32	11 50								12 32	12 54				
Redbridge	d								11 39									12 39					
Millbrook (Hants)	d								11 43									12 43					
Southampton Central ⛴	a	11 02	11 10		11 23			11 53	11 45	12 02	12 10		12 23				12 53	12 45	13 06	13 10		13 23	
	d	11 04	11 15		11 25			11 55	11 59	12 04	12 15		12 25				12 55	12 59	13 08	13 15		13 25	
St Denys	d								12 04									13 04					
Swaythling	d								12 07									13 07					
Southampton Airport Pkwy ✈	d		11 22		11 33			12 03	12 10		12 22		12 33				13 03	13 10		13 22		13 33	
Portsmouth Harbour ⛴	d						11 17									12 17							
Portsmouth & Southsea	d						11 22									12 22							
Fratton	d						11 26									12 26							
Hilsea	d						11 30									12 30							
Cosham	d						11 35									12 35							
Portchester	d						11 40									12 40							
Fareham	d	11a26					11 46			12a26						12 46			13a33				
Botley	d						11 54									12 54							
Hedge End	d						11 58									12 58							
Eastleigh 3	a						12 04	12 07	12 13							13 04	13 07	13 13					
	d							12 11	12 15								13 11	13 15					
Chandlers Ford	d								12 20									13 20					
Romsey	a								12 28									13 28					
Shawford	d																13 17						
Winchester	d		11 31		11 42			12 23			12 31		12 42				13 23			13 31		13 42	
Micheldever	d							12 32									13 32						
Basingstoke	a		11 46		11 58			12 42			12 46		12 58				13 42			13 46		13 58	
	d		11 47		12 00			12 44			12 47		13 00				13 44			13 47		14 00	
Reading 7	a		12 04								13 04									14 04			
Fleet	d																						
Farnborough (Main)	d																						
Woking	a				12 18			13 02					13 18				14 02					14 18	
Clapham Junction 10	a				12 39			13 27					13 39				14 27					14 39	
London Waterloo 15 ⊖	a				12 49			13 37					13 49				14 37					14 49	

A ✠ from Bournemouth
B ✠ from Eastleigh ◇ to Eastleigh
C ✠ from Bournemouth ◇ to Eastleigh

Table 158

Sundays
7 August to 11 September

Weymouth, Bournemouth, Lymington, Romsey, Southampton and Basingstoke - London

		SW 1 ✠	SW ◇1 A ✠	SW 1	GW ◇ ✠	XC ◇1 ✠	SW 1	SW ◇1 B ✠	SW 1	SW 1 ✠	SW ◇1 A ✠	SW 1	XC ◇1 ✠	SW 1	GW ◇	SW ◇1 B ✠	GW	SW 1	SW 1 ✠	SW ◇1 A ✠	SW 1	GW ◇
Weymouth	d							12 48								13 48	14 12					
Upwey	d							12 52								13 52	14 17					
Dorchester West	a																14 24					
Dorchester South	d							13 00								14 00						
Moreton (Dorset)	d							13 07								14 07						
Wool	d							13 13								14 13						
Wareham	d							13 20								14 20						
Holton Heath	d																					
Hamworthy	d							13 27								14 27						
Poole 4	a							13 31								14 31						
	d		12 55					13 32			13 55					14 32				14 55		
Parkstone (Dorset)	d							13 36								14 36						
Branksome	d							13 40								14 40						
Bournemouth	a		13 04					13 46			14 04					14 46				15 04		
	d		13 06			13 40		13 50			14 06		14 40			14 50				15 06		
Pokesdown	d		13 10								14 10									15 10		
Christchurch	d		13 14								14 14									15 14		
Hinton Admiral	d		13 19								14 19									15 19		
New Milton	d		13 23					14 01			14 23					15 01				15 23		
Sway	d		13 28								14 28									15 28		
Lymington Pier	d						13 44		14 14					14 44				15 14				
Lymington Town	d						13 46		14 16					14 46				15 16				
Brockenhurst 3	a		13 33			13 53	13 54	14 08	14 24		14 33		14 53	14 54		15 08		15 24		15 33		
	d		13 34			13 57		14 09			14 34		14 57			15 09				15 34		
Beaulieu Road	d		13 39								14 39									15 39		
Ashurst New Forest	d		13 43								14 43									15 43		
Totton	d		13 48								14 48									15 48		
Salisbury	d			13 08	13 32							14 13			14 48						15 08	15 32
Dean	d			13 20																	15 20	
Mottisfont & Dunbridge	d			13 26																	15 26	
Romsey	d			13 32	13 50							14 32			15 10						15 32	15 50
Redbridge	d			13 39								14 39									15 39	
Millbrook (Hants)	d			13 43								14 43									15 43	
Southampton Central ⛴	a		13 53	13 45	14 02	14 10		14 23			14 53	14 45	15 10		15 20	15 23				15 53	15 45	16 02
	d		13 55	13 59	14 04	14 15		14 25			14 55	14 59	15 15		15 22	15 25				15 55	15 59	16 04
St Denys	d			14 04								15 04									16 04	
Swaythling	d			14 07								15 07									16 07	
Southampton Airport Pkwy ✈	d		14 03	14 10		14 22		14 33			15 03	15 10	15 22			15 33				16 03	16 10	
Portsmouth Harbour ⛴	d	13 17								14 17									15 17			
Portsmouth & Southsea	d	13 22								14 22									15 22			
Fratton	d	13 26								14 26									15 26			
Hilsea	d	13 30								14 30									15 30			
Cosham	d	13 35								14 35									15 35			
Portchester	d	13 40								14 40									15 40			
Fareham	d	13 46			14a26					14 46					15a50				15 46			16a26
Botley	d	13 54								14 54									15 54			
Hedge End	d	13 58								14 58									15 58			
Eastleigh 3	a	14 04	14 07	14 13						15 04	15 07	15 13							16 04	16 07	16 13	
	d		14 11	14 15							15 11	15 15								16 11	16 15	
Chandlers Ford	d			14 20								15 20									16 20	
Romsey	a			14 28								15 28									16 28	
Shawford	d										15 17											
Winchester	d		14 23			14 31		14 42			15 23		15 31			15 42				16 23		
Micheldever	d		14 32								15 32									16 32		
Basingstoke	a		14 42			14 46		14 58			15 42		15 46			15 58				16 42		
	d		14 44			14 47		15 00			15 44		15 47			16 00				16 44		
Reading 7	a					15 04							16 04									
Fleet	d																					
Farnborough (Main)	d																					
Woking	a		15 02					15 18			16 02					16 18				17 02		
Clapham Junction 10	a		15 27					15 39			16 27					16 39				17 27		
London Waterloo 15 ⊖	a		15 37					15 49			16 37					16 49				17 37		

A ✠ from Eastleigh ◇ to Eastleigh
B ✠ from Bournemouth

Weymouth, Bournemouth, Lymington, Romsey, Southampton and Basingstoke - London

		XC ◇1 ⌶	SW 1	SW ◇1 A ⌶	SW 1	SW 1 ⌶	SW ◇1 B ⌶	SW 1	GW ◇	XC ◇1 ⌶	SW 1	SW ◇1 A ⌶	GW	SW 1	SW 1	SW ◇1 C	SW 1	GW ◇	XC ◇1 ⌶	SW 1	SW ◇1 A ⌶	SW 1
Weymouth	d			14 48								15 48	16 10								16 48	
Upwey	d			14 52								15 52	16 15								16 52	
Dorchester West	a												16 22									
Dorchester South	d			15 00								16 00									17 00	
Moreton (Dorset)	d			15 07								16 07									17 07	
Wool	d			15 13								16 13									17 13	
Wareham	d			15 20								16 20									17 20	
Holton Heath	d																					
Hamworthy	d			15 27								16 27									17 27	
Poole 4	a			15 31								16 31									17 31	
	d			15 32			15 55					16 32				16 55					17 32	
Parkstone (Dorset)	d			15 36								16 36									17 36	
Branksome	d			15 40								16 40									17 40	
Bournemouth	a			15 46			16 04					16 46				17 04					17 46	
	d	15 40		15 50			16 06			16 40		16 50				17 06			17 40		17 50	
Pokesdown	d						16 10									17 10						
Christchurch	d						16 14									17 14						
Hinton Admiral	d						16 19									17 19						
New Milton	d			16 01			16 23					17 01				17 23					18 01	
Sway	d						16 28									17 28						
Lymington Pier	d		15 44		16 14						16 44			17 14						17 44		18 14
Lymington Town	d		15 46		16 16						16 46			17 16						17 46		18 16
Brockenhurst 3	a	15 53	15 54	16 08	16 24		16 33			16 53	16 54	17 08		17 24		17 33			17 53	17 54	18 08	18 24
	d	15 57		16 09			16 34			16 57		17 09				17 34			17 57		18 09	
Beaulieu Road	d						16 39									17 39						
Ashurst New Forest	d						16 43									17 43						
Totton	d						16 48									17 48						
Salisbury	d							16 13	16 32								17 08	17 32				
Dean	d																17 20					
Mottisfont & Dunbridge	d																17 26					
Romsey	d							16 32	16 50								17 32	17 50				
Redbridge	d							16 39									17 39					
Millbrook (Hants)	d							16 43									17 43					
Southampton Central ⛴	a	16 10		16 23			16 53	16 45	17 02	17 10		17 23				17 53	17 45	18 02	18 10		18 23	
	d	16 15		16 25			16 55	16 59	17 04	17 15		17 25				17 55	17 59	18 04	18 15		18 25	
St Denys	d							17 04									18 04					
Swaythling	d							17 07									18 07					
Southampton Airport Pkwy ✈	d	16 22		16 33			17 03	17 10		17 22		17 33				18 03	18 10		18 22		18 33	
Portsmouth Harbour ⛴	d					16 17									17 17							
Portsmouth & Southsea	d					16 22									17 22							
Fratton	d					16 26									17 26							
Hilsea	d					16 30									17 30							
Cosham	d					16 35									17 35							
Portchester	d					16 40									17 40							
Fareham	d					16 46			17a26						17 46			18a26				
Botley	d					16 54									17 54							
Hedge End	d					16 58									17 58							
Eastleigh 8	a					17 04	17 07	17 13							18 04	18 07	18 13					
	d					17 11		17 15							18 11		18 15					
Chandlers Ford	d							17 20									18 20					
Romsey	a							17 28									18 28					
Shawford	d					17 17																
Winchester	d	16 31		16 42		17 23				17 31		17 42			18 23				18 31		18 42	
Micheldever	d					17 32									18 32							
Basingstoke	a	16 46		16 58		17 42				17 46		17 58			18 42				18 46		18 58	
	d	16 47		17 00		17 44				17 47		18 00			18 44				18 47		19 00	
Reading 7	a	17 04								18 04									19 04			
Fleet	d																					
Farnborough (Main)	d																					
Woking	a			17 18		18 02						18 18			19 02						19 18	
Clapham Junction 10	a			17 39		18 27						18 39			19 27						19 39	
London Waterloo 15 ⊖	a			17 49		18 37						18 49			19 37						19 49	

A ⌶ from Bournemouth
B ⌶ from Eastleigh ◇ to Eastleigh
C ◇ to Eastleigh

Weymouth, Bournemouth, Lymington, Romsey, Southampton and Basingstoke - London

		SW 1	SW ◇1 A	SW 1	GW ◇	XC ◇1 B ⌶	SW 1	SW ◇1 C ⌶	GW	SW 1	GW ◇	SW 1	SW ◇1 A	SW 1	GW ◇	XC ◇1	SW 1	SW ◇1 C ⌶	SW 1	GW 1	SW 1	SW ◇1 A	SW 1
Weymouth	d							17 48	17 56									18 48					
Upwey	d							17 52	18 01									18 52					
Dorchester West	a								18 08														
Dorchester South	d							18 00										19 00					
Moreton (Dorset)	d							18 07										19 07					
Wool	d							18 13										19 13					
Wareham	d							18 20										19 20					
Holton Heath	d																						
Hamworthy	d							18 27										19 27					
Poole 4	a							18 31										19 31					
	d		17 55					18 32					18 55					19 32				19 55	
Parkstone (Dorset)	d							18 36										19 36					
Branksome	d							18 40										19 40					
Bournemouth	a		18 04					18 46					19 04					19 46				20 04	
	d		18 06			18 40		18 50					19 06			19 40		19 50				20 06	
Pokesdown	d		18 10										19 10									20 10	
Christchurch	d		18 14										19 14									20 14	
Hinton Admiral	d		18 19										19 19									20 19	
New Milton	d		18 23					19 01					19 23					20 01				20 23	
Sway	d		18 28										19 28									20 28	
Lymington Pier	d						18 44			19 14							19 44		20 14				
Lymington Town	d						18 46			19 16							19 46		20 16				
Brockenhurst 3	a		18 33			18 53	18 54	19 08		19 24			19 33			19 53	19 54	20 08	20 24			20 33	
	d		18 34			18 57		19 09					19 34			19 57		20 09				20 34	
Beaulieu Road	d		18 39										19 39									20 39	
Ashurst New Forest	d		18 43										19 43									20 43	
Totton	d		18 48										19 48									20 48	
Salisbury	d			18 13	18 32						18 57			19 08	19 32					20 00			20 13
Dean	d													19 20									
Mottisfont & Dunbridge	d													19 26									
Romsey	d			18 32	18 50						19 15			19 32	19 50					20 19			20 32
Redbridge	d			18 39										19 39									20 39
Millbrook (Hants)	d			18 43										19 43									20 43
Southampton Central ⛴	a		18 53	18 45	19 02	19 10		19 23			19 26		19 53	19 45	20 02	20 10		20 23		20 29		20 53	20 45
	d		18 55	18 59	19 04	19 15		19 25			19 27		19 55	19 59	20 04	20 15		20 25		20 31		20 55	20 59
St Denys	d			19 04										20 04									21 04
Swaythling	d			19 07										20 07									21 07
Southampton Airport Pkwy ✈	d		19 03	19 10		19 22		19 33					20 03	20 10		20 22		20 33				21 03	21 10
Portsmouth Harbour ⛴	d	18 17										19 17									20 17		
Portsmouth & Southsea	d	18 22										19 22									20 22		
Fratton	d	18 26										19 26									20 26		
Hilsea	d	18 30										19 30									20 30		
Cosham	d	18 35										19 35									20 35		
Portchester	d	18 40										19 40									20 40		
Fareham	d	18 46			19a26						19a49	19 46			20a25					20a54	20 46		
Botley	d	18 54										19 54									20 54		
Hedge End	d	18 58										19 58									20 58		
Eastleigh 8	a	19 04	19 07	19 13								20 04	20 07	20 13							21 04	21 07	21 13
	d	19 11		19 15								20 11		20 15							21 11		21 15
Chandlers Ford	d			19 20										20 20									21 20
Romsey	a			19 28										20 28									21 28
Shawford	d	19 17																			21 17		
Winchester	d	19 23				19 31		19 42				20 23				20 31		20 42			21 23		
Micheldever	d	19 32										20 32									21 32		
Basingstoke	a	19 42				19 46		19 58				20 42				20 46		20 58			21 42		
	d	19 44				19 47		20 00				20 44				20 47		21 00			21 44		
Reading 7	a					20 04										21 04							
Fleet	d																						
Farnborough (Main)	d																						
Woking	a	20 02						20 18				21 02						21 18			22 02		
Clapham Junction 10	a	20 27						20 39				21 27						21 39			22 27		
London Waterloo 15 ⊖	a	20 37						20 49				21 37						21 49			22 37		

A ◇ to Eastleigh
B ⌶ to Basingstoke
C ⌶ from Bournemouth

Table 158

Sundays
7 August to 11 September

Weymouth, Bournemouth, Lymington, Romsey, Southampton and Basingstoke - London

		GW	SW	SW	SW	SW	GW	SW	GW	SW	SW	SW	SW	GW	SW	SW	SW
		◇	1	1	1	◇1		1	◇	1	1	1	◇1	◇	1	1	1
						A											
Weymouth	d					19 58	20 09						20 58		21 58	22 58	
Upwey	d					20 02	20 14						21 02		22 02	23 02	
Dorchester West	a						20 21										
Dorchester South	d					20 10							21 10		22 10	23 10	
Moreton (Dorset)	d					20 17							21 17		22 17	23 17	
Wool	d					20 23							21 23		22 23	23 23	
Wareham	d					20 30							21 30		22 30	23 30	
Holton Heath	d																
Hamworthy	d					20 37							21 37		22 37	23 37	
Poole 4	a					20 41							21 41		22 41	23 41	
	d					20 50							21 50		22 50	23 50	
Parkstone (Dorset)	d					20 54							21 54		22 54	23 54	
Branksome	d					20 57							21 57		22 57	23 57	
Bournemouth	a					21 03							22 03		23 03	00 03	
	d					21 06							22 06		23 06		
Pokesdown	d					21 10							22 10		23 10		
Christchurch	d					21 14							22 14		23 14		
Hinton Admiral	d					21 19							22 19		23 19		
New Milton	d					21 23							22 23		23 23		
Sway	d					21 28							22 28		23 28		
Lymington Pier	d		20 44	21 14						21 44	22 14						
Lymington Town	d		20 46	21 16						21 46	22 16						
Brockenhurst 3	a		20 54	21 24		21 33				21 54	22 24		22 33		23 33		
	d					21 34							22 34		23 34		
Beaulieu Road	d					21 39							22 39				
Ashurst New Forest	d					21 43							22 43		23 43		
Totton	d					21 48							22 48		23 48		
Salisbury	d	20 30						21 08	21 32					22 35			
Dean	d							21 20									
Mottisfont & Dunbridge	d							21 26									
Romsey	d	20 48						21 32	21 50					22 54			
Redbridge	d							21 39									
Millbrook (Hants)	d							21 43									
Southampton Central	a	20 59				21 53		21 45	22 02				22 53	23 04	23 53		
	d	21 01				21 55		21 59	22 04				22 55	23 07			
St Denys	d							22 04									
Swaythling	d							22 07									
Southampton Airport Pkwy ✈	d					22 03		22 10					23 03				
Portsmouth Harbour	d				21 17							22 17					23 17
Portsmouth & Southsea	d				21 22							22 22					23 22
Fratton	d				21 26							22 26					23 26
Hilsea	d				21 30							22 30					23 30
Cosham	d				21 35							22 35					23 35
Portchester	d				21 40							22 40					23 40
Fareham	d	21a23			21 46				22a26			22 46		23a28			23 46
Botley	d				21 54							22 54					23 54
Hedge End	d				21 58							22 58					23 58
Eastleigh 3	a				22 04	22 07		22 13				23 04	23 09				00 04
	d					22 11		22 15					23 11				
Chandlers Ford	d							22 20									
Romsey	a							22 31									
Shawford	d																
Winchester	d					22 23							23 23				
Micheldever	d					22 32							23 32				
Basingstoke	a					22 42							23 42				
	d					22 44							23 44				
Reading 7	a																
Fleet	d																
Farnborough (Main)	d																
Woking	a					23 02							00 02				
Clapham Junction 10	a					23 27							00 23				
London Waterloo 15 ⊖	a					23 37							00 33				

A ◇ to Eastleigh

Table 158

Sundays
18 September to 23 October

Weymouth, Bournemouth, Lymington, Romsey, Southampton and Basingstoke - London

		SW	SW	SW	SW	SW	SW	SW	SW	SW	XC	SW	SW	SW	SW	SW	SW	XC	SW	SW	SW	SW
		1	1	1	1	◇1	1	1	◇1	1	◇1	◇1	◇1	1	1	◇1	1	◇1	1	◇1	◇1	1
						A			B			C	D			E				C	D	
						⌶					⌶	⌶	⌶		⌶	⌶		⌶		⌶	⌶	
Weymouth	d		22p10	23p10								07 43	07 48							08 43	08 48	
Upwey	d		22p14	23p14								07 47	07 52							08 47	08 52	
Dorchester West	a																					
Dorchester South	d		22p22	23p22								07 55	08 00							08 55	09 00	
Moreton (Dorset)	d		22p28	23p28								08 02	08 07							09 02	09 07	
Wool	d		22p34	23p34								08 08	08 13							09 08	09 13	
Wareham	d		22p42	23p42								08 15	08 20							09 15	09 20	
Holton Heath	d																					
Hamworthy	d		22p48	23p48								08 22	08 27							09 22	09 27	
Poole 4	a		22p53	23p53								08 29	08 31							09 29	09 31	
	d		22p54	23p54		06 50			07 50			08 30	08 32			08 55				09 30	09 32	
Parkstone (Dorset)	d		22p58			06 54			07 54			08 34	08 36							09 34	09 36	
Branksome	d		23p01			06 57			07 57			08 37	08 40							09 37	09 40	
Bournemouth	a		23p07	00 03		07 02			08 02			08 46	08 46			09 04				09 46	09 46	
	d		23p12			07 06			08 06			08 50	08 50			09 06		09 40		09 50	09 50	
Pokesdown	d		23p16			07 10			08 10							09 10						
Christchurch	d		23p20			07 14			08 14							09 14						
Hinton Admiral	d		23p25			07 19			08 19							09 19						
New Milton	d		23p29			07 23			08 23			09 01	09 01			09 23				10 01	10 01	
Sway	d		23p34			07 28			08 28							09 28						
Lymington Pier	d													09 14					09 44			10 14
Lymington Town	d													09 16					09 46			10 16
Brockenhurst 3	a		23p39			07 33			08 33			09 08	09 08	09 24		09 33		09 53	09 54	10 08	10 08	10 24
	d		23p40			07 34			08 34			09 09	09 09			09 34		09 57		10 09	10 09	
Beaulieu Road	d								08 39							09 39						
Ashurst New Forest	d		23p47			07 43			08 43							09 43						
Totton	d		23p52			07 48			08 48							09 48						
Salisbury	d						08 08			08 20							09 08					
Dean	d						08 20										09 20					
Mottisfont & Dunbridge	d						08 26										09 26					
Romsey	d						08 35			08 39							09 32					
Redbridge	d									08 46							09 39					
Millbrook (Hants)	d									08 50							09 43					
Southampton Central	a		23p57			07 53			08 53	08 52		09 23	09 23			09 53	09 45	10 10		10 23	10 23	
	d		23p59			07 55			08 55	08 59	09 15	09 25	09 25			09 55	09 59	10 15		10 25	10 25	
St Denys	d		00 04							09 04							10 04					
Swaythling	d		00 07							09 07							10 07					
Southampton Airport Pkwy ✈	d		00 10			08 03			09 03	09 10	09 22	09 33	09 33			10 03	10 10	10 22		10 33	10 33	
Portsmouth Harbour	d	23p24			07 17			08 17							09 17							
Portsmouth & Southsea	d	23p29			07 22			08 22							09 22							
Fratton	d	23p33			07 26			08 26							09 26							
Hilsea	d	23p37			07 30			08 30							09 30							
Cosham	d	23p42			07 35			08 35							09 35							
Portchester	d	23p47			07 40			08 40							09 40							
Fareham	d	23p53			07 46			08 46							09 46							
Botley	d	23p59			07 54			08 54							09 54							
Hedge End	d	00 05			07 58			08 58							09 58							
Eastleigh 3	a	00 11	00 14		08 04	08 07		09 04	09 07	09 13					10 04	10 07	10 13					
	d	00 21				08 11			09 11	09 15						10 11	10 15					
Chandlers Ford	d						08 42			09 20							10 20					
Romsey	a						09 24			09 28							10 28					
Shawford	d								09 17													
Winchester	d	00a30				08 23			09 23		09 31	09 42	09 42			10 23		10 31		10 42	10 42	
Micheldever	d					08 32			09 32							10 32						
Basingstoke	a					08 42			09 42		09 46	09 58	09 58			10 42		10 46		10 58	10 58	
	d					08 44			09 44		09 47	10 00	10 00			10 44		10 47		11 00	11 00	
Reading 7	a										10 04							11 04				
Fleet	d																					
Farnborough (Main)	d																					
Woking	a					09 02			10 02			10 19	10 19			11 02				11 18	11 18	
Clapham Junction 10	a					09 30			10 27			10 40	10 40			11 27				11 39	11 39	
London Waterloo 15 ⊖	a					09 43			10 42			10 54	10 54			11 42				11 54	11 54	

A ⌶ to Eastleigh ◇ to Eastleigh

B ◇ to Eastleigh

C not from 18 September until 25 September. ⌶ from Bournemouth

D 18 September, 25 September. ⌶ from Bournemouth

E ⌶ from Eastleigh ◇ to Eastleigh

Weymouth, Bournemouth, Lymington, Romsey, Southampton and Basingstoke - London

		SW 1 🛒	SW ◇1 A 🛒	SW 1	GW ◇	XC ◇1 🛒	SW 1	SW ◇1 B 🛒	SW 1	SW 1 🛒	SW ◇1 C 🛒	SW 1	GW ◇	XC ◇1 🛒	SW 1	SW ◇1 B 🛒	SW 1	SW 1 🛒	SW ◇1 A 🛒	SW 1	GW ◇	XC ◇1 🛒	SW 1
Weymouth	d							09 48								10 48							
Upwey	d							09 52								10 52							
Dorchester West	a																						
Dorchester South	d							10 00								11 00							
Moreton (Dorset)	d							10 07								11 07							
Wool	d							10 13								11 13							
Wareham	d							10 20								11 20							
Holton Heath	d																						
Hamworthy	d							10 27								11 27							
Poole 4	a							10 31								11 31							
	d		09 55					10 32			10 55					11 32			11 55				
Parkstone (Dorset)	d							10 36								11 36							
Branksome	d							10 40								11 40							
Bournemouth	a		10 04					10 46			11 04					11 46			12 04				
	d		10 06			10 40		10 50			11 06			11 40		11 50			12 06			12 40	
Pokesdown	d		10 10								11 10								12 10				
Christchurch	d		10 14								11 14								12 14				
Hinton Admiral	d		10 19								11 19								12 19				
New Milton	d		10 23					11 01			11 23					12 01			12 23				
Sway	d		10 28								11 28								12 28				
Lymington Pier	d						10 44		11 14						11 44		12 14						12 44
Lymington Town	d						10 46		11 16						11 46		12 16						12 46
Brockenhurst 3	a		10 33			10 53	10 54	11 08	11 24		11 33			11 53	11 54	12 08	12 24		12 33			12 53	12 54
	d		10 34			10 57		11 09			11 34			11 57		12 09			12 34			12 57	
Beaulieu Road	d		10 39								11 39								12 39				
Ashurst New Forest	d		10 43								11 43								12 43				
Totton	d		10 48								11 48								12 48				
Salisbury	d			10 13	10 32							11 08	11 33							12 13	12 36		
Dean	d											11 20											
Mottisfont & Dunbridge	d											11 26											
Romsey	d			10 32	10 50							11 32	11 52							12 32	12 54		
Redbridge	d			10 39								11 39								12 39			
Millbrook (Hants)	d			10 43								11 43								12 43			
Southampton Central ⛴	a		10 53	10 45	11 02	11 10		11 23			11 53	11 45	12 02	12 10		12 23			12 53	12 45	13 06	13 10	
	d		10 55	10 59	11 04	11 15		11 25			11 55	11 59	12 04	12 15		12 25			12 55	12 59	13 08	13 15	
St Denys	d			11 04								12 04								13 04			
Swaythling	d			11 07								12 07								13 07			
Southampton Airport Pkwy ✈	d		11 03	11 10		11 22		11 33			12 03	12 10		12 22		12 33			13 03	13 10		13 22	
Portsmouth Harbour ⛴	d	10 17								11 17								12 17					
Portsmouth & Southsea	d	10 22								11 22								12 22					
Fratton	d	10 26								11 26								12 26					
Hilsea	d	10 30								11 30								12 30					
Cosham	d	10 35								11 35								12 35					
Portchester	d	10 40								11 40								12 40					
Fareham	d	10 46			11a26					11 46			12a26					12 46			13a33		
Botley	d	10 54								11 54								12 54					
Hedge End	d	10 58								11 58								12 58					
Eastleigh 3	a	11 04	11 07	11 13						12 04	12 07	12 13						13 04	13 07	13 13			
	d		11 11	11 15							12 11	12 15							13 11	13 15			
Chandlers Ford	d			11 20								12 20								13 20			
Romsey	a			11 28								12 28								13 28			
Shawford	d		11 17																13 17				
Winchester	d		11 23			11 31		11 42			12 23			12 31		12 42			13 23			13 31	
Micheldever	d		11 32								12 32								13 32				
Basingstoke	a		11 42			11 46		11 58			12 42			12 46		12 58			13 42			13 46	
	d		11 44			11 47		12 00			12 44			12 47		13 00			13 44			13 47	
Reading 7	a					12 04								13 04								14 04	
Fleet	d																						
Farnborough (Main)	d																						
Woking	a		12 02					12 18			13 02					13 18			14 02				
Clapham Junction 10	a		12 27					12 39			13 27					13 39			14 27				
London Waterloo 15 ⊖	a		12 42					12 49			13 37					13 49			14 37				

A 🛒 from Bournemouth ◇ to Eastleigh

B 🛒 from Bournemouth

C 🛒 from Eastleigh ◇ to Eastleigh

18 September to 23 October

Weymouth, Bournemouth, Lymington, Romsey, Southampton and Basingstoke - London

		SW ◇1 A 🛒	SW 1	SW 1 🛒	SW ◇1 B 🛒	SW 1	GW ◇ 🛒	XC ◇1 🛒	SW 1	SW ◇1 A 🛒	SW 1	SW 1 🛒	SW ◇1 B 🛒	SW 1	XC ◇1 🛒	SW 1	GW ◇	SW ◇1 A 🛒	GW	SW 1	SW 1 🛒	SW ◇1 B 🛒
Weymouth	d	11 48								12 48								13 48	14 00			
Upwey	d	11 52								12 52								13 52	14 05			
Dorchester West	a																		14 12			
Dorchester South	d	12 00								13 00								14 00				
Moreton (Dorset)	d	12 07								13 07								14 07				
Wool	d	12 13								13 13								14 13				
Wareham	d	12 20								13 20								14 20				
Holton Heath	d																					
Hamworthy	d	12 27								13 27								14 27				
Poole 4	a	12 31								13 31								14 31				
	d	12 32			12 55					13 32			13 55					14 32				14 55
Parkstone (Dorset)	d	12 36								13 36								14 36				
Branksome	d	12 40								13 40								14 40				
Bournemouth	a	12 46			13 04					13 46			14 04					14 46				15 04
	d	12 50			13 06			13 40		13 50			14 06		14 40			14 50				15 06
Pokesdown	d				13 10								14 10									15 10
Christchurch	d				13 14								14 14									15 14
Hinton Admiral	d				13 19								14 19									15 19
New Milton	d	13 01			13 23					14 01			14 23					15 01				15 23
Sway	d				13 28								14 28									15 28
Lymington Pier	d		13 14						13 44		14 14					14 44				15 14		
Lymington Town	d		13 16						13 46		14 16					14 46				15 16		
Brockenhurst 3	a	13 08	13 24		13 33			13 53	13 54	14 08	14 24		14 33		14 53	14 54		15 08		15 24		15 33
	d	13 09			13 34			13 57		14 09			14 34		14 57			15 09				15 34
Beaulieu Road	d				13 39								14 39									15 39
Ashurst New Forest	d				13 43								14 43									15 43
Totton	d				13 48								14 48									15 48
Salisbury	d					13 08	13 32							14 13			14 48					
Dean	d					13 20																
Mottisfont & Dunbridge	d					13 26																
Romsey	d					13 32	13 50							14 32			15 10					
Redbridge	d					13 39								14 39								
Millbrook (Hants)	d					13 43								14 43								
Southampton Central ⛴	a	13 23			13 53	13 45	14 02	14 10		14 23			14 53	14 45	15 10		15 20	15 23				15 53
	d	13 25			13 55	13 59	14 04	14 15		14 25			14 55	14 59	15 15		15 22	15 25				15 55
St Denys	d					14 04								15 04								
Swaythling	d					14 07								15 07								
Southampton Airport Pkwy ✈	d	13 33			14 03	14 10		14 22		14 33			15 03	15 10	15 22			15 33				16 03
Portsmouth Harbour ⛴	d			13 17								14 17									15 17	
Portsmouth & Southsea	d			13 22								14 22									15 22	
Fratton	d			13 26								14 26									15 26	
Hilsea	d			13 30								14 30									15 30	
Cosham	d			13 35								14 35									15 35	
Portchester	d			13 40								14 40									15 40	
Fareham	d			13 46			14a26					14 46					15a50				15 46	
Botley	d			13 54								14 54									15 54	
Hedge End	d			13 58								14 58									15 58	
Eastleigh 3	a			14 04	14 07	14 13						15 04	15 07	15 13							16 04	16 07
	d				14 11	14 15							15 11	15 15								16 11
Chandlers Ford	d					14 20								15 20								
Romsey	a					14 28								15 28								
Shawford	d												15 17									
Winchester	d	13 42			14 23			14 31		14 42			15 23		15 31			15 42				16 23
Micheldever	d				14 32								15 32									16 32
Basingstoke	a	13 58			14 42			14 46		14 58			15 42		15 46			15 58				16 42
	d	14 00			14 44			14 47		15 00			15 44		15 47			16 00				16 44
Reading 7	a							15 04							16 04							
Fleet	d																					
Farnborough (Main)	d																					
Woking	a	14 18			15 02					15 18			16 02					16 18				17 02
Clapham Junction 10	a	14 39			15 27					15 39			16 27					16 39				17 27
London Waterloo 15 ⊖	a	14 49			15 37					15 49			16 37					16 49				17 37

A 🛒 from Bournemouth

B 🛒 from Eastleigh ◇ to Eastleigh

Table 158

Sundays

18 September to 23 October

Weymouth, Bournemouth, Lymington, Romsey, Southampton and Basingstoke - London

		SW	GW	XC	SW	SW	SW	SW	SW	SW		GW	XC	SW	SW	SW	SW	SW	SW	GW		XC	SW	SW	SW
		■1	◇	◇■1 🍴	■1	◇■1 A 🍴	■1	■1 🍴	◇■1 B 🍴	■1		◇	◇■1 🍴	■1	◇■1 A 🍴	■1	■1	◇■1 C	■1	◇		◇■1 🍴	■1	◇■1 A 🍴	■1
Weymouth	d					14 48									15 48									16 48	
Upwey	d					14 52									15 52									16 52	
Dorchester West	a																								
Dorchester South	d					15 00									16 00									17 00	
Moreton (Dorset)	d					15 07									16 07									17 07	
Wool	d					15 13									16 13									17 13	
Wareham	d					15 20									16 20									17 20	
Holton Heath	d																								
Hamworthy	d					15 27									16 27									17 27	
Poole ■4	a					15 31									16 31									17 31	
	d					15 32			15 55						16 32			16 55						17 32	
Parkstone (Dorset)	d					15 36									16 36									17 36	
Branksome	d					15 40									16 40									17 40	
Bournemouth	a					15 46			16 04						16 46			17 04						17 46	
	d			15 40		15 50			16 06				16 40		16 50			17 06				17 40		17 50	
Pokesdown	d								16 10									17 10							
Christchurch	d								16 14									17 14							
Hinton Admiral	d								16 19									17 19							
New Milton	d					16 01			16 23						17 01			17 23						18 01	
Sway	d								16 28									17 28							
Lymington Pier	d				15 44		16 14							16 44		17 14							17 44		18 14
Lymington Town	d				15 46		16 16							16 46		17 16							17 46		18 16
Brockenhurst ■3	a			15 53	15 54	16 08	16 24		16 33				16 53	16 54	17 08	17 24		17 33				17 53	17 54	18 08	18 24
	d			15 57		16 09			16 34				16 57		17 09			17 34				17 57		18 09	
Beaulieu Road	d								16 39									17 39							
Ashurst New Forest	d								16 43									17 43							
Totton	d								16 48									17 48							
Salisbury	d	15 08	15 32							16 13		16 32							17 08	17 32					
Dean	d	15 20																	17 20						
Mottisfont & Dunbridge	d	15 26																	17 26						
Romsey	d	15 32	15 50							16 32		16 50							17 32	17 50					
Redbridge	d	15 39								16 39									17 39						
Millbrook (Hants)	d	15 43								16 43									17 43						
Southampton Central ⛴	a	15 45	16 02	16 10		16 23			16 53	16 45		17 02	17 10		17 23			17 53	17 45	18 02		18 10		18 23	
	d	15 59	16 04	16 15		16 25			16 55	16 59		17 04	17 15		17 25			17 55	17 59	18 04		18 15		18 25	
St Denys	d	16 04								17 04									18 04						
Swaythling	d	16 07								17 07									18 07						
Southampton Airport Pkwy ✈	d	16 10		16 22		16 33			17 03	17 10			17 22		17 33			18 03	18 10			18 22		18 33	
Portsmouth Harbour ⛴	d							16 17									17 17								
Portsmouth & Southsea	d							16 22									17 22								
Fratton	d							16 26									17 26								
Hilsea	d							16 30									17 30								
Cosham	d							16 35									17 35								
Portchester	d							16 40									17 40								
Fareham	d		16a26					16 46				17a26					17 46			18a26					
Botley	d							16 54									17 54								
Hedge End	d							16 58									17 58								
Eastleigh ■3	a	16 13						17 04	17 07	17 13							18 04	18 07	18 13						
	d	16 15							17 11	17 15								18 11	18 15						
Chandlers Ford	d	16 20								17 20									18 20						
Romsey	a	16 28								17 28									18 28						
Shawford	d								17 17																
Winchester	d			16 31		16 42			17 23				17 31		17 42			18 23				18 31		18 42	
Micheldever	d								17 32									18 32							
Basingstoke	a			16 46		16 58			17 42				17 46		17 58			18 42				18 46		18 58	
	d			16 47		17 00			17 44				17 47		18 00			18 44				18 47		19 00	
Reading ■7	a			17 04									18 04									19 04			
Fleet	d																								
Farnborough (Main)	d																								
Woking	a					17 18			18 02						18 18			19 02						19 18	
Clapham Junction ■10	a					17 39			18 27						18 39			19 27						19 39	
London Waterloo ■15 ⊖	a					17 49			18 37						18 49			19 37						19 49	

A 🍴 from Bournemouth
B 🍴 from Eastleigh ◇ to Eastleigh
C ◇ to Eastleigh

Table 158

Sundays

18 September to 23 October

Weymouth, Bournemouth, Lymington, Romsey, Southampton and Basingstoke - London

		SW	SW	SW	GW	XC		SW	SW	GW	SW	GW	SW	SW	SW	GW		XC	SW	SW	SW	GW	SW	SW	SW
		■1	◇■1 A	■1	◇	◇■1 B 🍴		■1	◇■1 C 🍴		■1	◇	■1	◇■1 A	■1	◇		◇■1	■1	◇■1 C 🍴	■1	■	■1	◇■1 A	■1
Weymouth	d								17 48	17 56										18 48					
Upwey	d								17 52	18 01										18 52					
Dorchester West	a									18 08															
Dorchester South	d								18 00											19 00					
Moreton (Dorset)	d								18 07											19 07					
Wool	d								18 13											19 13					
Wareham	d								18 20											19 20					
Holton Heath	d																								
Hamworthy	d								18 27											19 27					
Poole ■4	a								18 31											19 31					
	d		17 55						18 32					18 55						19 32				19 55	
Parkstone (Dorset)	d								18 36											19 36					
Branksome	d								18 40											19 40					
Bournemouth	a		18 04						18 46					19 04						19 46				20 04	
	d		18 06			18 40			18 50					19 06				19 40		19 50				20 06	
Pokesdown	d		18 10											19 10										20 10	
Christchurch	d		18 14											19 14										20 14	
Hinton Admiral	d		18 19											19 19										20 19	
New Milton	d		18 23						19 01					19 23						20 01				20 23	
Sway	d		18 28											19 28										20 28	
Lymington Pier	d							18 44			19 14								19 44		20 14				
Lymington Town	d							18 46			19 16								19 46		20 16				
Brockenhurst ■3	a		18 33			18 53		18 54	19 08		19 24			19 33				19 53	19 54	20 08	20 24			20 33	
	d		18 34			18 57			19 09					19 34				19 57		20 09				20 34	
Beaulieu Road	d		18 39											19 39										20 39	
Ashurst New Forest	d		18 43											19 43										20 43	
Totton	d		18 48											19 48										20 48	
Salisbury	d			18 13	18 32							18 57			19 08	19 32						20 00			20 13
Dean	d														19 20										
Mottisfont & Dunbridge	d														19 26										
Romsey	d			18 32	18 50							19 15			19 32	19 50						20 19			20 32
Redbridge	d			18 39											19 39										20 39
Millbrook (Hants)	d			18 43											19 43										20 43
Southampton Central ⛴	a		18 53	18 45	19 02	19 10			19 23			19 26		19 53	19 45	20 02		20 10		20 23		20 29		20 53	20 45
	d		18 55	18 59	19 04	19 15			19 25			19 27		19 55	19 59	20 04		20 15		20 25		20 31		20 55	20 59
St Denys	d			19 04											20 04										21 04
Swaythling	d			19 07											20 07										21 07
Southampton Airport Pkwy ✈	d		19 03	19 10		19 22			19 33					20 03	20 10			20 22		20 33				21 03	21 10
Portsmouth Harbour ⛴	d	18 17											19 17										20 17		
Portsmouth & Southsea	d	18 22											19 22										20 22		
Fratton	d	18 26											19 26										20 26		
Hilsea	d	18 30											19 30										20 30		
Cosham	d	18 35											19 35										20 35		
Portchester	d	18 40											19 40										20 40		
Fareham	d	18 46			19a26							19a49	19 46			20a25						20a54	20 46		
Botley	d	18 54											19 54										20 54		
Hedge End	d	18 58											19 58										20 58		
Eastleigh ■3	a	19 04	19 07	19 13									20 04	20 07	20 13								21 04	21 07	21 13
	d		19 11	19 15										20 11	20 15									21 11	21 15
Chandlers Ford	d			19 20											20 20										21 20
Romsey	a			19 28											20 28										21 28
Shawford	d		19 17																					21 17	
Winchester	d		19 23			19 31			19 42					20 23				20 31		20 42				21 23	
Micheldever	d		19 32											20 32										21 32	
Basingstoke	a		19 42			19 46			19 58					20 42				20 46		20 58				21 42	
	d		19 44			19 47			20 00					20 44				20 47		21 00				21 44	
Reading ■7	a					20 04												21 04							
Fleet	d																								
Farnborough (Main)	d																								
Woking	a		20 02						20 18					21 02						21 18				22 02	
Clapham Junction ■10	a		20 27						20 39					21 27						21 39				22 27	
London Waterloo ■15 ⊖	a		20 37						20 49					21 37						21 49				22 37	

A ◇ to Eastleigh
B 🍴 to Basingstoke
C 🍴 from Bournemouth

Weymouth, Bournemouth, Lymington, Romsey, Southampton and Basingstoke - London

		GW ◇	SW ■	SW ■	SW ■	SW ◇■ A	GW	SW ■	GW ◇	SW ■	SW ■	SW ■	SW ◇■	GW ◇	SW ■	SW ■	SW ■
Weymouth	d					19 58	20 09						20 58		21 58	22 58	
Upwey	d					20 02	20 14						21 02		22 02	23 02	
Dorchester West	a						20 21										
Dorchester South	d					20 10							21 10		22 10	23 10	
Moreton (Dorset)	d					20 17							21 17		22 17	23 17	
Wool	d					20 23							21 23		22 23	23 23	
Wareham	d					20 30							21 30		22 30	23 30	
Holton Heath	d																
Hamworthy	d					20 37							21 37		22 37	23 37	
Poole ■	a					20 41							21 41		22 41	23 41	
	d					20 50							21 50		22 50	23 50	
Parkstone (Dorset)	d					20 54							21 54		22 54	23 54	
Branksome	d					20 57							21 57		22 57	23 57	
Bournemouth	a					21 03							22 03		23 03	00 03	
	d					21 06							22 06		23 06		
Pokesdown	d					21 10							22 10		23 10		
Christchurch	d					21 14							22 14		23 14		
Hinton Admiral	d					21 19							22 19		23 19		
New Milton	d					21 23							22 23		23 23		
Sway	d					21 28							22 28		23 28		
Lymington Pier	d		20 44	21 14						21 44	22 14						
Lymington Town	d		20 46	21 16						21 46	22 16						
Brockenhurst ■	a		20 54	21 24		21 33				21 54	22 24		22 33		23 33		
	d					21 34							22 34		23 34		
Beaulieu Road	d					21 39							22 39				
Ashurst New Forest	d					21 43							22 43		23 43		
Totton	d					21 48							22 48		23 48		
Salisbury	d	20 33						21 08	21 32					22 35			
Dean	d							21 20									
Mottisfont & Dunbridge	d							21 26									
Romsey	d	20 51						21 32	21 50					22 54			
Redbridge	d							21 39									
Millbrook (Hants)	d							21 43									
Southampton Central ⛴	a	21 02				21 53		21 45	22 02				22 53	23 04	23 53		
	d	21 03				21 55		21 59	22 04				22 55	23 06			
St Denys	d							22 04									
Swaythling	d							22 07									
Southampton Airport Pkwy ✈	d					22 03		22 10					23 03				
Portsmouth Harbour ⛴	d				21 17							22 17					23 17
Portsmouth & Southsea	d				21 22							22 22					23 22
Fratton	d				21 26							22 26					23 26
Hilsea	d				21 30							22 30					23 30
Cosham	d				21 35							22 35					23 35
Portchester	d				21 40							22 40					23 40
Fareham	d	21a24			21 46				22a26			22 46		23a27			23 46
Botley	d				21 54							22 54					23 54
Hedge End	d				21 58							22 58					23 58
Eastleigh ■	a				22 04	22 07		22 13				23 04	23 09				00 04
	d				22 11			22 15					23 11				
Chandlers Ford	d							22 20									
Romsey	a							22 31									
Shawford	d																
Winchester	d				22 23								23 23				
Micheldever	d				22 32								23 32				
Basingstoke	a				22 42								23 42				
	d				22 44								23 44				
Reading ■	a																
Fleet	d																
Farnborough (Main)	d																
Woking	a				23 02								00 02				
Clapham Junction ■	a				23 27								00 23				
London Waterloo ■ ⊖	a				23 37								00 33				

A ◇ to Eastleigh

Weymouth, Bournemouth, Lymington, Romsey, Southampton and Basingstoke - London

		SW ■	SW ■	SW ■	SW ■	SW ◇■ A 🍴	SW ■	SW ■	SW ◇■ B	SW ■	XC ◇■ 🍴	SW ◇■ C 🍴	SW ■	SW ■ 🍴	SW ◇■ D 🍴	SW ■	XC ◇■ 🍴	SW ■	SW ◇■ C 🍴	SW ■	SW ■ 🍴	SW ◇■ E 🍴	SW ■
Weymouth	d		22p10	23p10								07 43							08 43				
Upwey	d		22p14	23p14								07 47							08 47				
Dorchester West	a																						
Dorchester South	d		22p22	23p22								07 55							08 55				
Moreton (Dorset)	d		22p28	23p28								08 02							09 02				
Wool	d		22p34	23p34								08 08							09 08				
Wareham	d		22p42	23p42								08 15							09 15				
Holton Heath	d																						
Hamworthy	d		22p48	23p48								08 22							09 22				
Poole ■	a		22p53	23p53								08 29							09 29				
	d		22p54	23p54		06 50			07 50			08 30			08 55				09 30			09 55	
Parkstone (Dorset)	d		22p58			06 54			07 54			08 34							09 34				
Branksome	d		23p01			06 57			07 57			08 37							09 37				
Bournemouth	a		23p07	00 03		07 02			08 02			08 46			09 04				09 46			10 04	
	d		23p12			07 06			08 06			08 50			09 06		09 40		09 50			10 06	
Pokesdown	d		23p16			07 10			08 10						09 10							10 10	
Christchurch	d		23p20			07 14			08 14						09 14							10 14	
Hinton Admiral	d		23p25			07 19			08 19						09 19							10 19	
New Milton	d		23p29			07 23			08 23			09 01			09 23				10 01			10 23	
Sway	d		23p34			07 28			08 28						09 28							10 28	
Lymington Pier	d												09 14					09 44		10 14			
Lymington Town	d												09 16					09 46		10 16			
Brockenhurst ■	a		23p39			07 33			08 33			09 08	09 24		09 33		09 53	09 54	10 08	10 24		10 33	
	d		23p40			07 34			08 34			09 09			09 34		09 57		10 09			10 34	
Beaulieu Road	d								08 39						09 39							10 39	
Ashurst New Forest	d		23p47			07 43			08 43						09 43							10 43	
Totton	d		23p52			07 48			08 48						09 48							10 48	
Salisbury	d						08 08			08 20						09 08							10 13
Dean	d						08 20									09 20							
Mottisfont & Dunbridge	d						08 26									09 26							
Romsey	d						08 35			08 39						09 32							10 32
Redbridge	d									08 46						09 39							10 39
Millbrook (Hants)	d									08 50						09 43							10 43
Southampton Central ⛴	a		23p57			07 53			08 53	08 52		09 23			09 53	09 45	10 10		10 23			10 53	10 45
	d		23p59			07 55			08 55	08 59	09 15	09 25			09 55	09 59	10 15		10 25			10 55	10 59
St Denys	d		00 04							09 04						10 04							11 04
Swaythling	d		00 07							09 07						10 07							11 07
Southampton Airport Pkwy ✈	d		00 10			08 03			09 03	09 10	09 22	09 33			10 03	10 10	10 22		10 33			11 03	11 10
Portsmouth Harbour ⛴	d	23p24			07 17			08 17						09 17							10 17		
Portsmouth & Southsea	d	23p29			07 22			08 22						09 22							10 22		
Fratton	d	23p33			07 26			08 26						09 26							10 26		
Hilsea	d	23p37			07 30			08 30						09 30							10 30		
Cosham	d	23p42			07 35			08 35						09 35							10 35		
Portchester	d	23p47			07 40			08 40						09 40							10 40		
Fareham	d	23p53			07 46			08 46						09 46							10 46		
Botley	d	23p59			07 54			08 54						09 54							10 54		
Hedge End	d	00 05			07 58			08 58						09 58							10 58		
Eastleigh ■	a	00 11	00 14		08 04	08 07		09 04	09 07	09 13				10 04	10 07	10 13					11 04	11 07	11 13
	d	00 21			08 11			09 11		09 15				10 11		10 15					11 11		11 15
Chandlers Ford	d						08 42			09 20						10 20							11 20
Romsey	a						09 24			09 28						10 28							11 28
Shawford	d							09 17													11 17		
Winchester	d	00a30			08 23			09 23			09 31	09 42		10 23			10 31		10 42		11 23		
Micheldever	d				08 32			09 32						10 32							11 32		
Basingstoke	a				08 42			09 42			09 46	09 58		10 42			10 46		10 58		11 42		
	d				08 44			09 44			09 47	10 00		10 44			10 47		11 00		11 44		
Reading ■	a										10 04						11 04						
Fleet	d																						
Farnborough (Main)	d																						
Woking	a				09 02			10 02				10 19		11 02					11 18		12 02		
Clapham Junction ■	a				09 30			10 27				10 40		11 27					11 39		12 27		
London Waterloo ■ ⊖	a				09 43			10 42				10 54		11 42					11 54		12 42		

A 🍴 to Eastleigh ◇ to Eastleigh
B ◇ to Eastleigh
C 🍴 from Bournemouth
D 🍴 from Eastleigh ◇ to Eastleigh
E 🍴 from Bournemouth ◇ to Eastleigh

Table 158

Sundays
from 30 October

Weymouth, Bournemouth, Lymington, Romsey, Southampton and Basingstoke - London

		GW	XC	SW	SW	SW	SW	SW	SW	GW	XC	SW	SW	SW	SW	SW	SW	GW	XC	SW	SW	SW
		◇	◇■ ⌶	■	◇■ A ⌶	■	■ ⌶	◇■ B ⌶	■	◇	◇■ ⌶	■	◇■ A ⌶	■	■ ⌶	◇■ C ⌶	■	◇	◇■ ⌶	■	◇■ A ⌶	■
Weymouth	d				09 48								10 48								11 48	
Upwey	d				09 52								10 52								11 52	
Dorchester West	a																					
Dorchester South	d				10 00								11 00								12 00	
Moreton (Dorset)	d				10 07								11 07								12 07	
Wool	d				10 13								11 13								12 13	
Wareham	d				10 20								11 20								12 20	
Holton Heath	d																					
Hamworthy	d				10 27								11 27								12 27	
Poole ■	a				10 31								11 31								12 31	
	d				10 32			10 55					11 32			11 55					12 32	
Parkstone (Dorset)	d				10 36								11 36								12 36	
Branksome	d				10 40								11 40								12 40	
Bournemouth	a				10 46			11 04					11 46			12 04					12 46	
	d		10 40		10 50			11 06			11 40		11 50			12 06			12 40		12 50	
Pokesdown	d							11 10								12 10						
Christchurch	d							11 14								12 14						
Hinton Admiral	d							11 19								12 19						
New Milton	d				11 01			11 23					12 01			12 23					13 01	
Sway	d							11 28								12 28						
Lymington Pier	d			10 44		11 14						11 44		12 14						12 44		13 14
Lymington Town	d			10 46		11 16						11 46		12 16						12 46		13 16
Brockenhurst ■	a		10 53	10 54	11 08	11 24		11 33			11 53	11 54	12 08	12 24		12 33			12 53	12 54	13 08	13 24
	d		10 57		11 09			11 34			11 57		12 09			12 34			12 57		13 09	
Beaulieu Road	d							11 39								12 39						
Ashurst New Forest	d							11 43								12 43						
Totton	d							11 48								12 48						
Salisbury	d	10 32							11 08	11 32							12 13	12 36				
Dean	d								11 20													
Mottisfont & Dunbridge	d								11 26													
Romsey	d	10 50							11 32	11 50							12 32	12 54				
Redbridge	d								11 39								12 39					
Millbrook (Hants)	d								11 43								12 43					
Southampton Central ⛴	a	11 02	11 10		11 23			11 53	11 45	12 02	12 10		12 23			12 53	12 45	13 06	13 10		13 23	
	d	11 04	11 15		11 25			11 55	11 59	12 04	12 15		12 25			12 55	12 59	13 08	13 15		13 25	
St Denys	d								12 04								13 04					
Swaythling	d								12 07								13 07					
Southampton Airport Pkwy ✈	d		11 22		11 33			12 03	12 10		12 22		12 33			13 03	13 10		13 22		13 33	
Portsmouth Harbour ⛴	d						11 17								12 17							
Portsmouth & Southsea	d						11 22								12 22							
Fratton	d						11 26								12 26							
Hilsea	d						11 30								12 30							
Cosham	d						11 35								12 35							
Portchester	d						11 40								12 40							
Fareham	d	11a26					11 46			12a26					12 46			13a33				
Botley	d						11 54								12 54							
Hedge End	d						11 58								12 58							
Eastleigh ■	a						12 04	12 07	12 13						13 04	13 07	13 13					
	d							12 11	12 15							13 11	13 15					
Chandlers Ford	d								12 20								13 20					
Romsey	a								12 28								13 28					
Shawford	d															13 17						
Winchester	d		11 31		11 42			12 23			12 31		12 42			13 23			13 31		13 42	
Micheldever	d							12 32								13 32						
Basingstoke	a		11 46		11 58			12 42			12 46		12 58			13 42			13 46		13 58	
	d		11 47		12 00			12 44			12 47		13 00			13 44			13 47		14 00	
Reading ■	a		12 04								13 04								14 04			
Fleet	d																					
Farnborough (Main)	d																					
Woking	a				12 18			13 02					13 18			14 02					14 18	
Clapham Junction ■	a				12 39			13 27					13 39			14 27					14 39	
London Waterloo ■ ⊖	a				12 49			13 37					13 49			14 37					14 49	

A ⌶ from Bournemouth

B ⌶ from Eastleigh ◇ to Eastleigh

C ⌶ from Bournemouth ◇ to Eastleigh

Table 158

Sundays
from 30 October

Weymouth, Bournemouth, Lymington, Romsey, Southampton and Basingstoke - London

		SW	SW	SW	GW	XC	SW	SW	SW	SW	SW	SW	XC	SW	GW	SW	GW	SW	SW	SW	SW	GW
		■ ⌶	◇■ A ⌶	■	◇ ⌶	◇■ ⌶	■	◇■ B ⌶	■	■ ⌶	◇■ A ⌶	■	◇■ ⌶	■	◇	◇■ B ⌶		■	■ ⌶	◇■ A ⌶	■	◇
Weymouth	d							12 48								13 48	14 00					
Upwey	d							12 52								13 52	14 05					
Dorchester West	a																14 12					
Dorchester South	d							13 00								14 00						
Moreton (Dorset)	d							13 07								14 07						
Wool	d							13 13								14 13						
Wareham	d							13 20								14 20						
Holton Heath	d																					
Hamworthy	d							13 27								14 27						
Poole ■	a							13 31								14 31						
	d		12 55					13 32			13 55					14 32				14 55		
Parkstone (Dorset)	d							13 36								14 36						
Branksome	d							13 40								14 40						
Bournemouth	a		13 04					13 46			14 04					14 46				15 04		
	d		13 06			13 40		13 50			14 06		14 40			14 50				15 06		
Pokesdown	d		13 10								14 10									15 10		
Christchurch	d		13 14								14 14									15 14		
Hinton Admiral	d		13 19								14 19									15 19		
New Milton	d		13 23					14 01			14 23					15 01				15 23		
Sway	d		13 28								14 28									15 28		
Lymington Pier	d						13 44		14 14					14 44				15 14				
Lymington Town	d						13 46		14 16					14 46				15 16				
Brockenhurst ■	a		13 33			13 53	13 54	14 08	14 24		14 33		14 53	14 54		15 08		15 24		15 33		
	d		13 34			13 57		14 09			14 34		14 57			15 09				15 34		
Beaulieu Road	d		13 39								14 39									15 39		
Ashurst New Forest	d		13 43								14 43									15 43		
Totton	d		13 48								14 48									15 48		
Salisbury	d			13 08	13 32							14 13			14 48						15 08	15 32
Dean	d			13 20																	15 20	
Mottisfont & Dunbridge	d			13 26																	15 26	
Romsey	d			13 32	13 50							14 32			15 10						15 32	15 50
Redbridge	d			13 39								14 39									15 39	
Millbrook (Hants)	d			13 43								14 43									15 43	
Southampton Central ⛴	a		13 53	13 45	14 02	14 10		14 23			14 53	14 45	15 10		15 20	15 23				15 53	15 45	16 02
	d		13 55	13 59	14 04	14 15		14 25			14 55	14 59	15 15		15 22	15 25				15 55	15 59	16 04
St Denys	d			14 04								15 04									16 04	
Swaythling	d			14 07								15 07									16 07	
Southampton Airport Pkwy ✈	d		14 03	14 10		14 22		14 33			15 03	15 10	15 22			15 33				16 03	16 10	
Portsmouth Harbour ⛴	d	13 17								14 17									15 17			
Portsmouth & Southsea	d	13 22								14 22									15 22			
Fratton	d	13 26								14 26									15 26			
Hilsea	d	13 30								14 30									15 30			
Cosham	d	13 35								14 35									15 35			
Portchester	d	13 40								14 40									15 40			
Fareham	d	13 46			14a26					14 46					15a50				15 46			16a26
Botley	d	13 54								14 54									15 54			
Hedge End	d	13 58								14 58									15 58			
Eastleigh ■	a	14 04	14 07	14 13						15 04	15 07	15 13							16 04	16 07	16 13	
	d		14 11	14 15							15 11	15 15								16 11	16 15	
Chandlers Ford	d			14 20								15 20									16 20	
Romsey	a			14 28								15 28									16 28	
Shawford	d										15 17											
Winchester	d		14 23			14 31		14 42			15 23		15 31			15 42				16 23		
Micheldever	d		14 32								15 32									16 32		
Basingstoke	a		14 42			14 46		14 58			15 42		15 46			15 58				16 42		
	d		14 44			14 47		15 00			15 44		15 47			16 00				16 44		
Reading ■	a					15 04							16 04									
Fleet	d																					
Farnborough (Main)	d																					
Woking	a		15 02					15 18			16 02					16 18				17 02		
Clapham Junction ■	a		15 27					15 39			16 27					16 39				17 27		
London Waterloo ■ ⊖	a		15 37					15 49			16 37					16 49				17 37		

A ⌶ from Eastleigh ◇ to Eastleigh

B ⌶ from Bournemouth

Weymouth, Bournemouth, Lymington, Romsey, Southampton and Basingstoke - London

		XC	SW	SW	SW	SW	SW	SW	GW	XC	SW	SW	SW	SW	SW	SW	GW	XC	SW	SW	SW	SW	SW
		◇1 ⌶	1	◇1 A ⌶	1	1 ⌶	◇1 B ⌶	1	◇	◇1 ⌶	1	◇1 A ⌶	1	1	◇1 C	1	◇	◇1 ⌶	1	◇1 A ⌶	1	1	◇1 C
Weymouth	d			14 48								15 48								16 48			
Upwey	d			14 52								15 52								16 52			
Dorchester West	a																						
Dorchester South	d			15 00								16 00								17 00			
Moreton (Dorset)	d			15 07								16 07								17 07			
Wool	d			15 13								16 13								17 13			
Wareham	d			15 20								16 20								17 20			
Holton Heath	d																						
Hamworthy	d			15 27								16 27								17 27			
Poole 4	a			15 31								16 31								17 31			
	d			15 32			15 55					16 32			16 55					17 32			17 55
Parkstone (Dorset)	d			15 36								16 36								17 36			
Branksome	d			15 40								16 40								17 40			
Bournemouth	a			15 46			16 04					16 46			17 04					17 46			18 04
	d	15 40		15 50			16 06			16 40		16 50			17 06			17 40		17 50			18 06
Pokesdown	d						16 10								17 10								18 10
Christchurch	d						16 14								17 14								18 14
Hinton Admiral	d						16 19								17 19								18 19
New Milton	d			16 01			16 23					17 01			17 23					18 01			18 23
Sway	d						16 28								17 28								18 28
Lymington Pier	d		15 44		16 14						16 44		17 14						17 44		18 14		
Lymington Town	d		15 46		16 16						16 46		17 16						17 46		18 16		
Brockenhurst 3	a	15 53	15 54	16 08	16 24		16 33			16 53	16 54	17 08	17 24		17 33			17 53	17 54	18 08	18 24		18 33
	d	15 57		16 09			16 34			16 57		17 09			17 34			17 57		18 09			18 34
Beaulieu Road	d						16 39								17 39								18 39
Ashurst New Forest	d						16 43								17 43								18 43
Totton	d						16 48								17 48								18 48
Salisbury	d							16 13	16 32							17 08	17 32						
Dean	d															17 20							
Mottisfont & Dunbridge	d															17 26							
Romsey	d							16 32	16 50							17 32	17 50						
Redbridge	d							16 39								17 39							
Millbrook (Hants)	d							16 43								17 43							
Southampton Central ⛴	a	16 10		16 23			16 53	16 45	17 02	17 10		17 23			17 53	17 45	18 02	18 10		18 23			18 53
	d	16 15		16 25			16 55	16 59	17 04	17 15		17 25			17 55	17 59	18 04	18 15		18 25			18 55
St Denys	d							17 04								18 04							
Swaythling	d							17 07								18 07							
Southampton Airport Pkwy ✈	d	16 22		16 33			17 03	17 10		17 22		17 33			18 03	18 10		18 22		18 33			19 03
Portsmouth Harbour ⛴	d					16 17								17 17								18 17	
Portsmouth & Southsea	d					16 22								17 22								18 22	
Fratton	d					16 26								17 26								18 26	
Hilsea	d					16 30								17 30								18 30	
Cosham	d					16 35								17 35								18 35	
Portchester	d					16 40								17 40								18 40	
Fareham	d					16 46			17a26					17 46			18a26					18 46	
Botley	d					16 54								17 54								18 54	
Hedge End	d					16 58								17 58								18 58	
Eastleigh 3	a					17 04	17 07	17 13						18 04	18 07	18 13						19 04	19 07
	d					17 11		17 15						18 11		18 15						19 11	
Chandlers Ford	d							17 20								18 20							
Romsey	a							17 28								18 28							
Shawford	d					17 17																19 17	
Winchester	d	16 31		16 42		17 23				17 31		17 42		18 23				18 31		18 42		19 23	
Micheldever	d					17 32								18 32								19 32	
Basingstoke	a	16 46		16 58		17 42				17 46		17 58		18 42				18 46		18 58		19 42	
	d	16 47		17 00		17 44				17 47		18 00		18 44				18 47		19 00		19 44	
Reading 7	a	17 04								18 04								19 04					
Fleet	d																						
Farnborough (Main)	d																						
Woking	a			17 18		18 02						18 18		19 02						19 18		20 02	
Clapham Junction 10	a			17 39		18 27						18 39		19 27						19 39		20 27	
London Waterloo 15 ⊖	a			17 49		18 37						18 49		19 37						19 49		20 37	

A ⌶ from Bournemouth

B ⌶ from Eastleigh ◇ to Eastleigh

C ◇ to Eastleigh

from 30 October

Weymouth, Bournemouth, Lymington, Romsey, Southampton and Basingstoke - London

		SW	GW	XC	SW	SW	GW	SW	GW	SW	SW	SW	GW	XC	SW	SW	SW	GW	SW	SW	SW	GW	SW
		1	◇	◇1 A ⌶	1	◇1 B ⌶		1	◇	1	◇1 C	1	◇	◇1	1	◇1 B ⌶	1	1	1	◇1 C	1	◇	1
Weymouth	d					17 48	17 56									18 48							
Upwey	d					17 52	18 01									18 52							
Dorchester West	a						18 08																
Dorchester South	d					18 00										19 00							
Moreton (Dorset)	d					18 07										19 07							
Wool	d					18 13										19 13							
Wareham	d					18 20										19 20							
Holton Heath	d																						
Hamworthy	d					18 27										19 27							
Poole 4	a					18 31										19 31							
	d					18 32					18 55					19 32				19 55			
Parkstone (Dorset)	d					18 36										19 36							
Branksome	d					18 40										19 40							
Bournemouth	a					18 46					19 04					19 46				20 04			
	d			18 40		18 50					19 06			19 40		19 50				20 06			
Pokesdown	d										19 10									20 10			
Christchurch	d										19 14									20 14			
Hinton Admiral	d										19 19									20 19			
New Milton	d					19 01					19 23					20 01				20 23			
Sway	d										19 28									20 28			
Lymington Pier	d				18 44			19 14							19 44		20 14						20 44
Lymington Town	d				18 46			19 16							19 46		20 16						20 46
Brockenhurst 3	a			18 53	18 54	19 08		19 24			19 33			19 53	19 54	20 08	20 24			20 33			20 54
	d			18 57		19 09					19 34			19 57		20 09				20 34			
Beaulieu Road	d										19 39									20 39			
Ashurst New Forest	d										19 43									20 43			
Totton	d										19 48									20 48			
Salisbury	d	18 13	18 32						18 57			19 08	19 32					20 00			20 13	20 30	
Dean	d											19 20											
Mottisfont & Dunbridge	d											19 26											
Romsey	d	18 32	18 50						19 15			19 32	19 50					20 19			20 32	20 48	
Redbridge	d	18 39										19 39									20 39		
Millbrook (Hants)	d	18 43										19 43									20 43		
Southampton Central ⛴	a	18 45	19 02	19 10		19 23			19 26		19 53	19 45	20 02	20 10		20 23		20 29		20 53	20 45	20 59	
	d	18 59	19 04	19 15		19 25			19 27		19 55	19 59	20 04	20 15		20 25		20 31		20 55	20 59	21 01	
St Denys	d	19 04										20 04									21 04		
Swaythling	d	19 07										20 07									21 07		
Southampton Airport Pkwy ✈	d	19 10		19 22		19 33					20 03	20 10		20 22		20 33				21 03	21 10		
Portsmouth Harbour ⛴	d									19 17									20 17				
Portsmouth & Southsea	d									19 22									20 22				
Fratton	d									19 26									20 26				
Hilsea	d									19 30									20 30				
Cosham	d									19 35									20 35				
Portchester	d									19 40									20 40				
Fareham	d		19a26						19a49	19 46			20a25					20a54	20 46			21a23	
Botley	d									19 54									20 54				
Hedge End	d									19 58									20 58				
Eastleigh 3	a	19 13								20 04	20 07	20 13							21 04	21 07	21 13		
	d	19 15								20 11		20 15							21 11		21 15		
Chandlers Ford	d	19 20										20 20									21 20		
Romsey	a	19 28										20 28									21 28		
Shawford	d																		21 17				
Winchester	d			19 31		19 42				20 23				20 31		20 42			21 23				
Micheldever	d									20 32									21 32				
Basingstoke	a			19 46		19 58				20 42				20 46		20 58			21 42				
	d			19 47		20 00				20 44				20 47		21 00			21 44				
Reading 7	a			20 04										21 04									
Fleet	d																						
Farnborough (Main)	d																						
Woking	a					20 18				21 02						21 18			22 02				
Clapham Junction 10	a					20 39				21 27						21 39			22 27				
London Waterloo 15 ⊖	a					20 49				21 37						21 49			22 37				

A ⌶ to Basingstoke

B ⌶ from Bournemouth

C ◇ to Eastleigh

Table 158

Sundays
from 30 October

Weymouth, Bournemouth, Lymington, Romsey, Southampton and Basingstoke - London

		SW 1	SW 1	SW ◇1 A	GW	SW 1	GW ◇	SW 1	SW 1	SW 1	SW ◇1	GW ◇	SW 1	SW 1	SW 1
Weymouth	d			19 58	20 09						20 58		21 58	22 58	
Upwey	d			20 02	20 14						21 02		22 02	23 02	
Dorchester West	a				20 21										
Dorchester South	d			20 10							21 10		22 10	23 10	
Moreton (Dorset)	d			20 17							21 17		22 17	23 17	
Wool	d			20 23							21 23		22 23	23 23	
Wareham	d			20 30							21 30		22 30	23 30	
Holton Heath	d														
Hamworthy	d			20 37							21 37		22 37	23 37	
Poole 3	a			20 41							21 41		22 41	23 41	
	d			20 50							21 50		22 50	23 50	
Parkstone (Dorset)	d			20 54							21 54		22 54	23 54	
Branksome	d			20 57							21 57		22 57	23 57	
Bournemouth	a			21 03							22 03		23 03	00 03	
	d			21 06							22 06		23 06		
Pokesdown	d			21 10							22 10		23 10		
Christchurch	d			21 14							22 14		23 14		
Hinton Admiral	d			21 19							22 19		23 19		
New Milton	d			21 23							22 23		23 23		
Sway	d			21 28							22 28		23 28		
Lymington Pier	d	21 14						21 44	22 14						
Lymington Town	d	21 16						21 46	22 16						
Brockenhurst 3	a	21 24		21 33				21 54	22 24		22 33		23 33		
	d			21 34							22 34		23 34		
Beaulieu Road	d			21 39							22 39				
Ashurst New Forest	d			21 43							22 43		23 43		
Totton	d			21 48							22 48		23 48		
Salisbury	d					21 08	21 32					22 35			
Dean	d					21 20									
Mottisfont & Dunbridge	d					21 26									
Romsey	d					21 32	21 50					22 53			
Redbridge	d					21 39									
Millbrook (Hants)	d					21 43									
Southampton Central ⛴	a			21 53		21 45	22 02				22 53	23 04	23 53		
	d			21 55		21 59	22 04				22 55	23 05			
St Denys	d					22 04									
Swaythling	d					22 07									
Southampton Airport Pkwy ✈	d			22 03		22 10					23 03				
Portsmouth Harbour ⛴	d		21 17							22 17					23 17
Portsmouth & Southsea	d		21 22							22 22					23 22
Fratton	d		21 26							22 26					23 26
Hilsea	d		21 30							22 30					23 30
Cosham	d		21 35							22 35					23 35
Portchester	d		21 40							22 40					23 40
Fareham	d		21 46				22a26			22 46		23a26			23 46
Botley	d		21 54							22 54					23 54
Hedge End	d		21 58							22 58					23 58
Eastleigh 3	a		22 04	22 07		22 13				23 04	23 09				00 04
	d			22 11		22 15					23 11				
Chandlers Ford	d					22 20									
Romsey	a					22 31									
Shawford	d														
Winchester	d			22 23							23 23				
Micheldever	d			22 32							23 32				
Basingstoke	a			22 42							23 42				
	d			22 44							23 44				
Reading 7	a														
Fleet	d														
Farnborough (Main)	d														
Woking	a			23 02							00 02				
Clapham Junction 10	a			23 27							00 23				
London Waterloo 15 ⊖	a			23 37							00 33				

A ◇ to Eastleigh

Table 158A

Mondays to Saturdays

Woking - Heathrow Railair

Express Coach Service

		SW	SW	SW	SW	SW	SW	SW	SW	SW		SW	SW	SW	SW	SW	SW	SW	SW	SW		SW	SW	SW	SW
		SX	SX	SX	SX				SO	SX			SO	SX	SO		SX	SO		SX		SO		SX	
Woking	d		05 20		05 50		06 20		06 50	06 50			07 20	07 20	07 50		07 50	08 20		08 20		08 50		08 50	
Heathrow Terminal 5 Bus	d		05 45		06 15		06 45		07 15	07 25			07 45	08 05	08 15		08 35	08 45		09 05		09 15		09 35	
Heathrow Central Bus Stn	a		06 00		06 30		07 00		07 30	07 40			08 00	08 20	08 30		08 50	09 00		09 20		09 30		09 50	
	d	05 45		06 15		06 45		07 15				07 45				08 30			09 00				09 30		10 00
Heathrow Terminal 5 Bus	a	06 00		06 30		07 00		07 30				08 00				08 45			09 15				09 45		10 15
Woking	a	06 30		07 00		07 30		08 05				08 40				09 25			09 55				10 25		10 50

		SW	SW	SW	SW	SW		SW	SW	SW	SW	SW	SW	SW	SW	SW		SW	SW	SW	SW	SW	SW	SW	SW
		SO	SX																						
Woking	d	09 35	09 35		10 05			10 35		11 05		11 35		12 05		12 35			13 05		13 35		14 05		14 35
Heathrow Terminal 5 Bus	d	10 00	10 10		10 30			11 00		11 30		12 00		12 30		13 00			13 30		14 00		14 30		15 00
Heathrow Central Bus Stn	a	10 15	10 25		10 45			11 15		11 45		12 15		12 45		13 15			13 45		14 15		14 45		15 15
	d			10 30		11 00			11 30		12 00		12 30		13 00			13 30		14 00		14 30		15 00	
Heathrow Terminal 5 Bus	a			10 45		11 15			11 45		12 15		12 45		13 15			13 45		14 15		14 45		15 15	
Woking	a			11 15		11 45			12 15		12 45		13 15		13 45			14 15		14 45		15 15		15 45	

		SW		SW	SW	SW	SW	SW	SW	SW	SW	SW		SW	SW	SW	SW	SW	SW	SW	SW	SW		SW	SW
								SO	SX		SO	SX			SO	SX		SO	SX		SO	SX			
Woking	d			15 05		15 35		16 05	16 05		16 35	16 35			17 05	17 05		17 35	17 35		18 05	18 05			18 35
Heathrow Terminal 5 Bus	d			15 30		16 00		16 30	16 35		17 00	17 10			17 30	17 40		18 00	18 10		18 30	18 40			19 00
Heathrow Central Bus Stn	a			15 45		16 15		16 45	16 50		17 15	17 25			17 45	17 55		18 15	18 25		18 45	18 55			19 15
	d	15 30			16 00		16 30			17 00				17 30			18 00			18 30				19 00	
Heathrow Terminal 5 Bus	a	15 45			16 15		16 45			17 15				17 45			18 15			18 45				19 15	
Woking	a	16 15			16 45		17 25			18 05				18 35			19 05			19 35				19 55	

		SW	SW	SW	SW	SW	SW	SW		SW	SW	SW	SW	SW	SW	SW	SW	SW		SW	SW	SW	SW		
			SO	SX		SO	SX			SO	SX	SO	SX		SO	SX	SO	SX		SO	SX	SO	SX		
Woking	d		19 05	19 05		19 35	19 35			20 05	20 05	20 35	20 35		21 05	21 05				22 05	22 05				
Heathrow Terminal 5 Bus	d		19 30	19 35		20 00	20 05			20 30	20 35	21 00	21 05		21 30	21 35				22 30	22 35				
Heathrow Central Bus Stn	a		19 45	19 45		20 15	20 15			20 45	20 45	21 15	21 15		21 45	21 45				22 45	22 45				
	d	19 30			20 00			20 30						21 15			22 15	22 15				23 15	23 15		
Heathrow Terminal 5 Bus	a	19 45			20 15			20 45						21 30			22 30	22 30				23 30	23 30		
Woking	a	20 15			20 45			21 15						22 00			22 55	23 00				23 55	23 59		

Sundays

		SW	SW	SW	SW	SW	SW	SW	SW	SW		SW	SW	SW	SW	SW	SW	SW	SW	SW		SW	SW	SW	SW
Woking	d		06 20		06 50		07 20	07 50		08 20			08 50			09 35		10 05		10 35			11 05		11 35
Heathrow Terminal 5 Bus	d		06 45		07 15		07 45	08 15		08 45			09 15			10 00		10 30		11 00			11 30		12 00
Heathrow Central Bus Stn	a		07 00		07 30		08 00	08 30		09 00			09 30			10 15		10 45		11 15			11 45		12 15
	d	06 45		07 15		07 45			08 30			09 00		09 30	10 00		10 30		11 00			11 30		12 00	
Heathrow Terminal 5 Bus	a	07 00		07 30		08 00			08 45			09 15		09 45	10 15		10 45		11 15			11 45		12 15	
Woking	a	07 30		08 00		08 25			09 15			09 45		10 15	10 45		11 15		11 45			12 15		12 45	

		SW	SW	SW	SW	SW		SW	SW	SW	SW	SW	SW	SW	SW	SW		SW	SW	SW	SW	SW	SW	SW	SW
Woking	d		12 05		12 35			13 05		13 35		14 05		14 35		15 05			15 35		16 05		16 35		17 05
Heathrow Terminal 5 Bus	d		12 30		13 00			13 30		14 00		14 30		15 00		15 30			16 00		16 30		17 00		17 30
Heathrow Central Bus Stn	a		12 45		13 15			13 45		14 15		14 45		15 15		15 45			16 15		16 45		17 15		17 45
	d	12 30		13 00		13 30			14 00		14 30		15 00		15 30			16 00		16 30		17 00		17 30	
Heathrow Terminal 5 Bus	a	12 45		13 15		13 45			14 15		14 45		15 15		15 45			16 15		16 45		17 15		17 45	
Woking	a	13 15		13 45		14 15			14 45		15 15		15 45		16 15			16 45		17 15		17 45		18 15	

		SW		SW	SW	SW	SW	SW	SW	SW	SW	SW		SW	SW	SW	SW	SW	SW	SW	SW				
Woking	d			17 35		18 05		18 35		19 05		19 35			20 05	20 35		21 05		22 05					
Heathrow Terminal 5 Bus	d			18 00		18 30		19 00		19 30		20 00			20 30	21 00		21 30		22 30					
Heathrow Central Bus Stn	a			18 15		18 45		19 15		19 45		20 15			20 45	21 15		21 45		22 45					
	d	18 00			18 30		19 00		19 30		20 00			20 30			21 15		22 15		23 15				
Heathrow Terminal 5 Bus	a	18 15			18 45		19 15		19 45		20 15			20 45			21 30		22 30		23 30				
Woking	a	18 45			19 15		19 45		20 15		20 45			21 15			22 00		23 00		23 59				

Network Diagram for Table 160

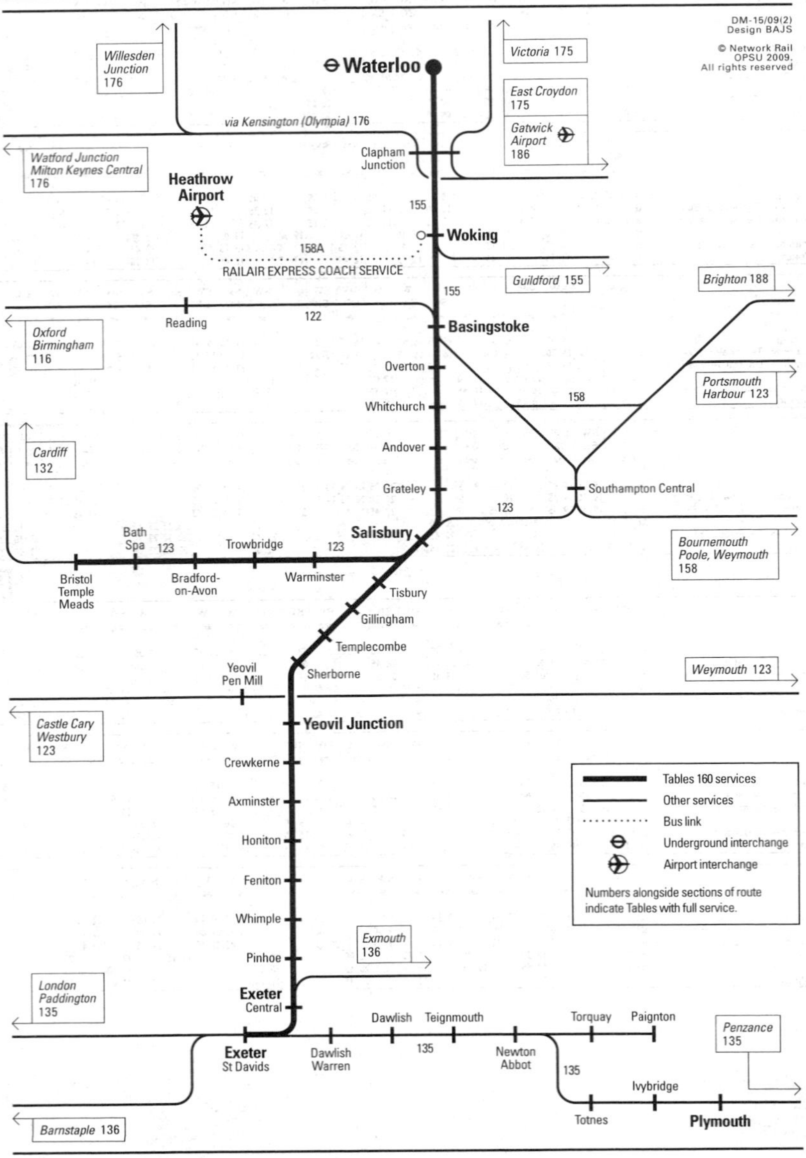

© Network Rail
OPSU 2009.
All rights reserved

Table 160

London - Salisbury and Exeter

Mondays to Fridays

until 30 September

Miles			SW	SW	SW	SW	SW	GW	SW	SW	SW		SW	SW	SW	SW	SW	SW	SW		SW		SW	SW	SW
			MX	MO	MO	MX																			
			◇1 🛒	◇1 🛒	1	1	1		1	1	1		◇1	◇1	◇1 🛒	◇1 🛒	◇1 🛒	◇1 🛒	◇1 🛒		◇1 🛒		◇1 🛒	◇1 🛒	◇1 🛒
0	**London Waterloo** 15 ⊖	d	20p20	21p15	23p35	23p40									07 10	07 50	08 20	08 50	09 20		09 50		10 20	10 50	11 20
4	Clampham Junction 10	d	20b27	21b22	23b44	23b47									07u17	07u57	08u27		09u27				10u27		11u27
24½	Woking	d	20p46	21p46	00 08	00 08									07 36	08 16	08 46	09 16	09 46		10 16		10 46	11 16	11 46
47¾	**Basingstoke**	d	21p07	22p07	00 40	00 28								07 22	07 57	08 38	09 07	09 38	10 07		10 38		11 07	11 38	12 07
55½	Overton	d	21p15		00s49	00s37								07 30	08 05	08 47		09 46			10 46			11 46	
59¼	Whitchurch (Hants)	d	21p20		00s54	00s42								07 35	08 10	08 52		09 51			10 51			11 51	
66½	Andover	d	21p29	22p26	01 02	00 50								07 44	08 19	09 00	09 24	10 00	10 24		11 00		11 24	12 00	12 24
72¾	Grateley	d	21p36	22p33	01s10	00s58								07 51	08 26	09 08		10 07			11 07			12 07	
83¾	**Salisbury**	a	21p48	22p45	01 22	01 10								08 03	08 39	09 20	09 43	10 19	10 42		11 19		11 42	12 19	12 42
—																									
—		d	22p06	22p51				06 04		06 08	06 40		07 40	08 08	08 47		09 47		10 47	10 52			11 47		12 47
—	Warminster	d						06 25			07 00									11 12					
—	Westbury	d						06a33			07 09									11 21					
—	Trowbridge	d									07 15									11 27					
—	Bradford-on-Avon	d									07 21									11 33					
—	Bath Spa 7	a									07 33									11 46					
—	Bristol Temple Meads 10	a									07 52									12 05					
96¼	Tisbury	d	22p24	23p10						06 29			07 59	08 27	09 07		10 07		11 07				12 07		13 07
105¼	Gillingham (Dorset)	a	22p34	23p20						06 39			08 09	08 37	09 17		10 17		11 17				12 17		13 17
—		d	22p35	23p21						06 42			08 11		09 18		10 18		11 18				12 18		13 18
112¼	Templecombe	d	22p42	23p28						06 50			08 19		09 25		10 25		11 25				12 25		13 25
118¼	Sherborne	d	22p50	23p36						06 57			08 26		09 33		10 33		11 33				12 33		13 33
122¾	Yeovil Junction	a	22p55	23p41						07 03			08 32		09 38		10 38		11 38				12 38		13 38
—		d	22p57	23p43					06 15	07 07			08 40		09 40		10 40		11 40				12 40		13 40
131¾	Crewkerne	d	23p06	23p52					06 24	07 16			08 49		09 49		10 49		11 49				12 49		13 49
144¾	Axminster	a	23p19	00 05					06 43	07 35			09 02		10 02		11 02		12 02				13 02		14 02
—		d	23p20	00 06			05 52		06 56	07 36			09 04		10 04		11 04		12 04				13 04		14 04
155	Honiton	a	23p31	00 18			06 03		07 07	07 49			09 15		10 15		11 15		12 15				13 15		14 15
—		d	23p32	00 19			06 08		07 12	07 50			09 16		10 16		11 16		12 16				13 16		14 16
159½	Feniton	d	23p38	00 24			06 13		07 18	07 56			09 21				11 21						13 21		
163¼	Whimple	d	23p43	00 29			06 18		07 23	08 01			09 26				11 26						13 26		
169	Pinhoe	d	23p49				06 25		07 30	08 08			09 33		10 28				12 28						14 28
171¾	**Exeter Central**	a	23p56				06 29		07 37	08 12			09 37		10 37		11 37		12 37				13 37		14 37
172¾	**Exeter St Davids** 6	a	00 01	00 40			06 35		07 42	08 17			09 42		10 42		11 42		12 42				13 42		14 42

		SW	SW		SW	SW	SW		SW	SW	SW	SW	SW	SW	SW	SW	SW		SW	SW		SW	SW	SW	SW
		◇1 🛒	◇1 🛒		◇1 🛒	◇1 🛒	◇1 🛒		◇1 🛒	◇1 🛒	◇1 🛒	◇1 🛒	◇1 🛒	◇1 🛒	◇1 🛒	◇1 🛒	◇1 🛒		◇1 🛒	◇1 🛒		◇1 🛒	◇1 🛒	◇1 🛒	1 🛒
London Waterloo 15 ⊖	d	11 50	12 20		12 50	13 20	13 50		14 20	14 50	15 20	15 50	16 20	16 50	17 20	17 50	18 20		18 50	19 20		19 50	20 20	21 20	22 20
Clampham Junction 10	d		12u27			13u27			14u27		15u27	15u57	16u27	16u57			18u27			19u27			20u27	21u27	22u27
Woking	d	12 16	12 46		13 16	13 46	14 16		14 46	15 16	15 46	16 16	16 46	17u16	17u46		18 46		19 18	19 46		20 16	20 46	21 49	22 49
Basingstoke	d	12 38	13 07		13 38	14 07	14 38		15 07	15 38	16 07	16 38	17 07	17 38	18 07	18 38	19 07		19 39	20 07		20 38	21 07	22 10	23 11
Overton	d	12 46			13 46		14 46			15 46		16 46	17 15	17 46	18 15	18 47	19 15		19 47	20 15		20 46	21 15	22 18	23 19
Whitchurch (Hants)	d	12 51			13 51		14 51			15 51		16 51	17 20	17 51	18 20	18 52	19 20		19 52	20 20		20 51	21 20	22 23	23 24
Andover	d	13 00	13 24		14 00	14 24	15 00		15 24	16 00	16 24	17 00	17 29	18 00	18 29	19 00	19 29		20 01	20 29		21 00	21 29	22 32	23 33
Grateley	d	13 07			14 07		15 07			16 07		17 07	17 36	18 07	18 36	19 08	19 36		20 08	20 36		21 07	21 36	22 39	23 40
Salisbury	a	13 19	13 43		14 19	14 42	15 19		15 42	16 19	16 42	17 19	17 48	18 19	18 48	19 20	19 48		20 22	20 49		21 19	21 48	22 55	23 52
	d		13 47	13 52		14 47	15 23		15 47		16 47	17 23	17 53	18 23	18 53	19 23	19 53			20 53	20 57		22 06	23 03	
Warminster	d			14 12																	21 17				
Westbury	d			14 21																	21 25				
Trowbridge	d			14 27																	21 31				
Bradford-on-Avon	d			14 33																	21 37				
Bath Spa 7	a			14 46																	21 50				
Bristol Temple Meads 10	a			15 05																	22 06				
Tisbury	d		14 07			15 07	15 37		16 07		17 07	17 37	18 08	18 37	19 08	19 37	20 08			21 08			22 24	23s16	
Gillingham (Dorset)	a		14 17			15 17	15 47		16 17		17 17	17 47	18 18	18 47	19 18	19 48	20 18			21 18			22 34	23s27	
	d		14 18			15 18			16 18		17 18		18 19	18 51	19 19	19 51	20 19			21 19			22 35		
Templecombe	d		14 25			15 25			16 25		17 25		18 27	18 58	19 27	19 58	20 27			21 27			22 42	23s35	
Sherborne	d		14 33			15 33			16 33		17 33		18 34	19 06	19 34	20 06	20 34			21 34			22 50	23s42	
Yeovil Junction	a		14 38			15 38			16 38		17 38		18 40	19 14	19 40	20 14	20 40			21 40			22 55	23 49	
	d		14 40			15 40			16 40		17 40		18 41		19 41		20 41			21 41			22 57		
Crewkerne	d		14 49			15 49			16 49		17 49		18 51		19 51		20 51			21 51			23 06		
Axminster	a		15 02			16 02			17 02		18 02		19 04		20 04		21 04			22 04			23 19		
	d		15 04			16 04			17 04		18 04		19 05		20 05		21 05			22 05			23 20		
Honiton	a		15 15			16 15			17 15		18 15		19 16		20 16		21 16			22 16			23 31		
	d		15 16			16 16			17 16		18 18		19 17		20 17		21 17			22 17			23 32		
Feniton	d		15 21						17 21				19 22				21 22			22 22			23 38		
Whimple	d		15 26						17 26				19 27				21 27			22 27			23 43		
Pinhoe	d					16 28					18 31				20 29					22 34			23 49		
Exeter Central	a		15 37			16 35			17 35		18 38		19 38		20 39		21 37			22 40			23 56		
Exeter St Davids 6	a		15 42			16 42			17 42		18 42		19 45		20 44		21 44			22 45			00 01		

b Previous night, stops to pick up only

Table 160

Mondays to Fridays

until 30 September

London - Salisbury and Exeter

		SW
		1
London Waterloo 15 ⊖	d	23 40
Clapham Junction 10	d	23u47
Woking	d	00 08
Basingstoke	d	00 28
Overton	d	00s37
Whitchurch (Hants)	d	00s42
Andover	d	00 50
Grateley	d	00s58
Salisbury	a	01 10
	d	
Warminster	d	
Westbury	d	
Trowbridge	d	
Bradford-on-Avon	d	
Bath Spa 7	a	
Bristol Temple Meads 10	a	
Tisbury	d	
Gillingham (Dorset)	a	
	d	
Templecombe	d	
Sherborne	d	
Yeovil Junction	a	
	d	
Crewkerne	d	
Axminster	a	
	d	
Honiton	a	
	d	
Feniton	d	
Whimple	d	
Pinhoe	d	
Exeter Central	a	
Exeter St Davids 6	a	

Mondays to Fridays

from 3 October

		SW MX	SW MO	SW MO	SW MX	SW	GW	SW	SW	SW	SW	SW	SW	SW	SW	SW	SW		SW	SW	SW	SW	SW
		◇1 ⊥	◇1 ⊥	1	1	1		1	1	1	◇1	◇1	◇1 ⊥	◇1 ⊥	◇1 ⊥	◇1 ⊥	◇1 ⊥		◇1 ⊥	◇1 ⊥	◇1 ⊥	◇1 ⊥	◇1 ⊥
London Waterloo 15 ⊖	d	20p20	21p15	23p35	23p40								07 10	07 50	08 20	08 50	09 20		09 50	10 20	10 50	11 20	11 50
Clapham Junction 10	d	20b27	21b22	23b44	23b47								07u17	07u57	08u27		09u27			10u27		11u27	
Woking	d	20p46	21p46	00 08	00 08								07 36	08 16	08 46	09 16	09 46		10 16	10 46	11 16	11 46	12 16
Basingstoke	d	21p07	22p07	00 40	00 28							07 22	07 57	08 38	09 07	09 38	10 07		10 38	11 07	11 38	12 07	12 38
Overton	d	21p15		00s49	00s37							07 30	08 05	08 47		09 46			10 46		11 46		12 46
Whitchurch (Hants)	d	21p20		00s54	00s42							07 35	08 10	08 52		09 51			10 51		11 51		12 51
Andover	d	21p29	22p26	01 02	00 50							07 44	08 19	09 00	09 24	10 00	10 24		11 00	11 24	12 00	12 24	13 00
Grateley	d	21p36	22p33	01s10	00s58							07 51	08 26	09 08		10 07			11 07		12 07		13 07
Salisbury	a	21p48	22p45	01 22	01 10							08 03	08 39	09 20	09 43	10 19	10 42		11 19	11 42	12 19	12 42	13 19
	d	22p06	22p51				06 04		06 08	06 40	07 40	08 08	08 47		09 47		10 47	10 52		11 47		12 47	
Warminster	d						06 25			07 00								11 12					
Westbury	d						06a33			07 09								11 21					
Trowbridge	d									07 15								11 27					
Bradford-on-Avon	d									07 21								11 33					
Bath Spa 7	a									07 33								11 46					
Bristol Temple Meads 10	a									07 52								12 05					
Tisbury	d	22p24	23p10						06 29		07 59	08 27	09 07		10 07		11 07			12 07		13 07	
Gillingham (Dorset)	a	22p34	23p20						06 39		08 09	08 37	09 17		10 17		11 17			12 17		13 17	
	d	22p35	23p21						06 42		08 11		09 18		10 18		11 18			12 18		13 18	
Templecombe	d	22p42	23p28						06 50		08 19		09 25		10 25		11 25			12 25		13 25	
Sherborne	d	22p50	23p36						06 57		08 26		09 33		10 33		11 33			12 33		13 33	
Yeovil Junction	a	22p55	23p41						07 03		08 32		09 38		10 38		11 38			12 38		13 38	
	d	22p57	23p43					06 15	07 07		08 40		09 40		10 40		11 40			12 40		13 40	
Crewkerne	d	23p06	23p52					06 24	07 16		08 49		09 49		10 49		11 49			12 49		13 49	
Axminster	a	23p19	00 05					06 43	07 35		09 02		10 02		11 02		12 02			13 02		14 02	
	d	23p20	00 06			05 52		06 56	07 36		09 04		10 04		11 04		12 04			13 04		14 04	
Honiton	a	23p31	00 18			06 03		07 07	07 49		09 15		10 15		11 15		12 15			13 15		14 15	
	d	23p32	00 19			06 08		07 12	07 50		09 16		10 16		11 16		12 16			13 16		14 16	
Feniton	d	23p38	00 24			06 13		07 18	07 56		09 21				11 21					13 21			
Whimple	d	23p43	00 29			06 18		07 23	08 01		09 26				11 26					13 26			
Pinhoe	d	23p49				06 25		07 30	08 08		09 33		10 28				12 28					14 28	
Exeter Central	a	23p56				06 29		07 37	08 12		09 37		10 37		11 37		12 37			13 37		14 37	
Exeter St Davids 6	a	00 01	00 40			06 35		07 42	08 17		09 42		10 42		11 42		12 42			13 42		14 42	

b Previous night, stops to pick up only

Table 160

Mondays to Fridays

from 3 October

London - Salisbury and Exeter

		SW		SW	SW	SW		SW	SW	SW	SW	SW	SW	SW	SW	SW		SW	SW		SW	SW	SW	SW	SW
		◇1		◇1	◇1	◇1		◇1	◇1	◇1	◇1	◇1	◇1	◇1	◇1	◇1		◇1	◇1		◇1	◇1	◇1	1	1
		🛒		🛒	🛒	🛒		🛒	🛒	🛒	🛒	🛒	🛒	🛒	🛒	🛒		🛒	🛒		🛒	🛒	🛒	🛒	
London Waterloo 15 ⊖	d	12 20		12 50	13 20	13 50		14 20	14 50	15 20	15 50	16 20	16 50	17 20	17 50	18 20		18 50	19 20		19 50	20 20	21 20	22 20	23 40
Clampham Junction 10	d	12u27			13u27			14u27		15u27	15u57	16u27	16u57			18u27			19u27			20u27	21u27	22u27	23u47
Woking	d	12 46		13 16	13 46	14 16		14 46	15 16	15 46	16 16	16 46	17u16	17u46		18 46		19 18	19 46		20 16	20 46	21 49	22 49	00 08
Basingstoke	d	13 07		13 38	14 07	14 38		15 07	15 38	16 07	16 38	17 07	17 38	18 07	18 38	19 07		19 39	20 07		20 38	21 07	22 10	23 11	00 28
Overton	d			13 46		14 46			15 46		16 46	17 15	17 46	18 15	18 47	19 15		19 47	20 15		20 46	21 15	22 18	23 19	00s37
Whitchurch (Hants)	d			13 51		14 51			15 51		16 51	17 20	17 51	18 20	18 52	19 20		19 52	20 20		20 51	21 20	22 23	23 24	00s42
Andover	d	13 24		14 00	14 24	15 00		15 24	16 00	16 24	17 00	17 29	18 00	18 29	19 00	19 29		20 01	20 29		21 00	21 29	22 32	23 33	00 50
Grateley	d			14 07		15 07			16 07		17 07	17 36	18 07	18 36	19 08	19 36		20 08	20 36		21 07	21 36	22 39	23 40	00s58
Salisbury	a	13 43		14 19	14 42	15 19		15 42	16 19	16 42	17 19	17 48	18 19	18 48	19 20	19 48		20 22	20 49		21 19	21 48	22 55	23 52	01 10
	d	13 47	13 52		14 47	15 23		15 47		16 47	17 23	17 53	18 23	18 53	19 23	19 53			20 53	20 57		22 06	23 03		
Warminster	d		14 12																	21 17					
Westbury	d		14 21																	21 25					
Trowbridge	d		14 27																	21 31					
Bradford-on-Avon	d		14 33																	21 37					
Bath Spa 7	a		14 46																	21 50					
Bristol Temple Meads 10	a		15 05																	22 06					
Tisbury	d	14 07			15 07	15 37		16 07		17 07	17 37	18 08	18 37	19 08	19 37	20 08			21 08			22 24	23s16		
Gillingham (Dorset)	a	14 17			15 17	15 47		16 17		17 17	17 47	18 18	18 47	19 18	19 48	20 18			21 18			22 34	23s27		
	d	14 18			15 18			16 18		17 18		18 19	18 51	19 19	19 51	20 19			21 19			22 35			
Templecombe	d	14 25			15 25			16 25		17 25		18 27	18 58	19 27	19 58	20 27			21 27			22 42	23s35		
Sherborne	d	14 33			15 33			16 33		17 33		18 34	19 06	19 34	20 06	20 34			21 34			22 50	23s42		
Yeovil Junction	a	14 38			15 38			16 38		17 38		18 40	19 14	19 40	20 14	20 40			21 40			22 55	23 49		
	d	14 40			15 40			16 40		17 40		18 41		19 41		20 41			21 41			22 57			
Crewkerne	d	14 49			15 49			16 49		17 49		18 51		19 51		20 51			21 51			23 06			
Axminster	a	15 02			16 02			17 02		18 02		19 04		20 04		21 04			22 04			23 19			
	d	15 04			16 04			17 04		18 04		19 05		20 05		21 05			22 05			23 20			
Honiton	a	15 15			16 15			17 15		18 15		19 16		20 16		21 16			22 16			23 31			
	d	15 16			16 16			17 16		18 18		19 17		20 17		21 17			22 17			23 32			
Feniton	d	15 21						17 21				19 22				21 22			22 22			23 38			
Whimple	d	15 26						17 26				19 27				21 27			22 27			23 43			
Pinhoe	d				16 28					18 31				20 29					22 34			23 49			
Exeter Central	a	15 37			16 35			17 35		18 38		19 38		20 39		21 37			22 40			23 56			
Exeter St Davids 6	a	15 42			16 42			17 42		18 42		19 45		20 44		21 44			22 45			00 01			

Saturdays

until 1 October

		SW	SW	SW	GW	GW	SW	SW	SW	SW		SW	SW	SW	SW	SW	SW		SW	SW		SW	SW	SW	
		◇1	1	1			1	1	1	◇1		◇1	◇1	◇1	◇1	◇1	◇1		◇1	◇1		◇1	◇1	◇1	
		🛒											🛒	🛒	🛒	🛒	🛒		🛒	🛒		🛒	🛒	🛒	
London Waterloo 15 ⊖	d	20p20	23p40										07 10	07 50	08 20	08 50	09 20		09 50	10 20		10 50	11 20	11 50	
Clampham Junction 10	d	20b27	23b47										07u17	07u57	08u27		09u27			10u27			11u27		
Woking	d	20p46	00 08										07 36	08 16	08 46	09 16	09 46		10 16	10 46		11 16	11 46	12 16	
Basingstoke	d	21p07	00 28							07 22			07 59	08 38	09 07	09 38	10 07		10 38	11 07		11 38	12 07	12 38	
Overton	d	21p15	00s37							07 30			08 07	08 46		09 46			10 46			11 46		12 46	
Whitchurch (Hants)	d	21p20	00s42							07 35			08 12	08 51		09 51			10 51			11 51		12 51	
Andover	d	21p29	00 50							07 44			08 21	09 00	09 24	10 00	10 24		11 00	11 24		12 00	12 24	13 00	
Grateley	d	21p36	00s58							07 51			08 28	09 07		10 07			11 07			12 07		13 07	
Salisbury	a	21p48	01 10							08 05			08 42	09 19	09 42	10 19	10 42		11 19	11 42		12 19	12 42	13 19	
	d	22p06			06 03	06 03		06 15	06 40			07 45	08 47		09 47		10 47	10 52		11 47			12 47		
Warminster	d				06 23				07 00									11 12							
Westbury	d				06a31	06 38			07 09									11 21							
Trowbridge	d					06 44			07 15									11 27							
Bradford-on-Avon	d					06 50			07 21									11 33							
Bath Spa 7	a					07 06			07 33									11 46							
Bristol Temple Meads 10	a					07 29			07 53									12 05							
Tisbury	d	22p24						06 29				07 59	09 07		10 07		11 07			12 07			13 07		
Gillingham (Dorset)	a	22p34						06 39				08 09	09 17		10 17		11 17			12 17			13 17		
	d	22p35						06 42				08 11	09 18		10 18		11 18			12 18			13 18		
Templecombe	d	22p42						06 50				08 19	09 25		10 25		11 25			12 25			13 25		
Sherborne	d	22p50						06 57				08 26	09 33		10 33		11 33			12 33			13 33		
Yeovil Junction	a	22p55						07 03				08 32	09 38		10 38		11 38			12 38			13 38		
	d	22p57					06 15	07 07				08 40	09 40		10 40		11 40			12 40			13 40		
Crewkerne	d	23p06					06 24	07 16				08 49	09 49		10 49		11 49			12 49			13 49		
Axminster	a	23p19					06 43	07 36				09 02	10 02		11 02		12 02			13 02			14 02		
	d	23p20		05 52			06 56	07 38				09 04	10 04		11 04		12 04			13 04			14 04		
Honiton	a	23p31		06 03			07 07	07 51				09 15	10 15		11 15		12 15			13 15			14 15		
	d	23p32		06 08			07 12	07 52				09 16	10 16		11 16		12 16			13 16			14 16		
Feniton	d	23p38		06 13			07 18	07 57				09 21			11 21					13 21					
Whimple	d	23p43		06 18			07 23	08 02				09 26			11 26					13 26					
Pinhoe	d	23p49		06 25			07 30	08 09				09 33	10 28				12 28						14 28		
Exeter Central	a	23p56		06 29			07 37	08 13				09 37	10 37		11 37		12 37			13 37			14 37		
Exeter St Davids 6	a	00 01		06 35			07 42	08 18				09 42	10 42		11 42		12 42			13 42			14 42		

b Previous night, stops to pick up only

Table 160

Saturdays
until 1 October

London - Salisbury and Exeter

		SW		SW	SW	SW	SW	SW	SW	SW	SW	SW	SW	SW	SW	SW	SW		SW	SW	SW	SW	SW
		◇1		◇1	◇1	◇1	◇1	◇1	◇1	◇1	◇1	◇1	◇1	◇1	◇1	◇1	◇1		◇1	◇1	◇1	1	1
		🛒		🛒	🛒	🛒	🛒	🛒	🛒	🛒	🛒	🛒	🛒	🛒	🛒	🛒	🛒		🛒	🛒	🛒	🛒	
London Waterloo 15 ⊖	d	12 20		12 50	13 20	13 50	14 20	14 50	15 20	15 50	16 20	16 50	17 20	17 50	18 20	18 50	19 20		19 50	20 20	21 20	22 20	23 40
Clapham Junction 10	d	12u27			13u27		14u27		15u27		16u27		17u27		18u27		19u27			20u27	21u27	22u27	23u47
Woking	d	12 46		13 16	13 46	14 16	14 46	15 16	15 46	16 16	16 46	17 16	17 46	18 16	18 46	19 16	19 46		20 16	20 46	21 49	22 49	00 08
Basingstoke	d	13 07		13 38	14 07	14 38	15 07	15 38	16 07	16 38	17 07	17 38	18 07	18 38	19 07	19 38	20 07		20 38	21 07	22 12	23 11	00 28
Overton	d			13 46		14 46		15 46		16 46		17 46		18 46		19 46			20 46	21 15	22 20	23 20	00s37
Whitchurch (Hants)	d			13 51		14 51		15 51		16 51		17 51		18 51		19 51			20 51	21 20	22 25	23 25	00s42
Andover	d	13 24		14 00	14 24	15 00	15 24	16 00	16 24	17 00	17 24	18 00	18 24	19 00	19 24	20 00	20 24		21 00	21 29	22 34	23 33	00 50
Grateley	d			14 07		15 07		16 07		17 07		18 07		19 07		20 07			21 07	21 36	22 41	23 41	00s58
Salisbury	a	13 42		14 19	14 42	15 19	15 42	16 19	16 42	17 19	17 42	18 19	18 43	19 19	19 43	20 19	20 42		21 19	21 48	22 53	23 53	01 10
	d	13 47	13 52		14 47		15 47		16 47		17 47		18 47		19 47		20 47	20 57		21 53	23 03		
Warminster	d		14 12															21 17					
Westbury	d		14 21															21 25					
Trowbridge	d		14 27															21 31					
Bradford-on-Avon	d		14 33															21 37					
Bath Spa 7	a		14 46															21 50					
Bristol Temple Meads 10	a		15 05															22 06					
Tisbury	d	14 07			15 07		16 07		17 07		18 07		19 07		20 07		21 07			22 07	23s16		
Gillingham (Dorset)	a	14 17			15 17		16 17		17 17		18 17		19 17		20 17		21 17			22 17	23s27		
	d	14 18			15 18		16 18		17 18		18 18		19 18		20 18		21 18			22 18			
Templecombe	d	14 25			15 25		16 25		17 25		18 25		19 25		20 25		21 25			22 25	23s35		
Sherborne	d	14 33			15 33		16 33		17 33		18 33		19 33		20 33		21 33			22 33	23s42		
Yeovil Junction	a	14 38			15 38		16 38		17 38		18 38		19 38		20 38		21 38			22 40	23 49		
	d	14 40			15 40		16 40		17 40		18 40		19 40		20 40		21 40						
Crewkerne	d	14 49			15 49		16 49		17 49		18 49		19 49		20 49		21 49						
Axminster	a	15 02			16 02		17 02		18 02		19 02		20 02		21 02		22 02						
	d	15 04			16 04		17 04		18 04		19 04		20 04		21 04		22 04						
Honiton	a	15 15			16 15		17 15		18 15		19 15		20 15		21 15		22 15						
	d	15 16			16 16		17 16		18 16		19 16		20 16		21 16		22 16						
Feniton	d	15 21					17 21				19 21				21 21		22 21						
Whimple	d	15 26					17 26				19 26				21 26		22 26						
Pinhoe	d				16 28				18 28				20 28				22 33						
Exeter Central	a	15 37			16 35		17 37		18 35		19 37		20 39		21 37		22 41						
Exeter St Davids 6	a	15 42			16 42		17 42		18 42		19 42		20 43		21 42		22 45						

Saturdays
from 8 October

		SW	SW	SW	GW	GW	SW	SW	SW	SW	SW	SW	SW	SW	SW	SW		SW	SW	SW	SW	SW
		◇1	1	1			1	1	1	◇1	◇1	◇1	◇1	◇1	◇1	◇1		◇1	◇1	◇1	◇1	◇1
		🛒										🛒	🛒	🛒	🛒	🛒		🛒	🛒	🛒	🛒	🛒
London Waterloo 15 ⊖	d	20p20	23p40									07 10	07 50	08 20	08 50	09 20		09 50	10 20	10 50	11 20	11 50
Clapham Junction 10	d	20b27	23b47									07u17	07u57	08u27		09u27			10u27		11u27	
Woking	d	20p46	00 08									07 36	08 16	08 46	09 16	09 46		10 16	10 46	11 16	11 46	12 16
Basingstoke	d	21p07	00 28							07 22		07 59	08 38	09 07	09 38	10 07		10 38	11 07	11 38	12 07	12 38
Overton	d	21p15	00s37							07 30		08 07	08 46		09 46			10 46		11 46		12 46
Whitchurch (Hants)	d	21p20	00s42							07 35		08 12	08 51		09 51			10 51		11 51		12 51
Andover	d	21p29	00 50							07 44		08 21	09 00	09 24	10 00	10 24		11 00	11 24	12 00	12 24	13 00
Grateley	d	21p36	00s58							07 51		08 28	09 07		10 07			11 07		12 07		13 07
Salisbury	a	21p48	01 10							08 05		08 42	09 19	09 42	10 19	10 42		11 19	11 42	12 19	12 42	13 19
	d	22p06			06 03	06 03		06 15	06 40		07 45	08 47		09 47		10 47	10 52		11 47		12 47	
Warminster	d				06 23				07 00								11 12					
Westbury	d				06a31	06 38			07 09								11 21					
Trowbridge	d					06 44			07 15								11 27					
Bradford-on-Avon	d					06 50			07 21								11 33					
Bath Spa 7	a					07 06			07 33								11 46					
Bristol Temple Meads 10	a					07 29			07 53								12 05					
Tisbury	d	22p24						06 29			07 59	09 07		10 07		11 07			12 07		13 07	
Gillingham (Dorset)	a	22p34						06 39			08 09	09 17		10 17		11 17			12 17		13 17	
	d	22p35						06 42			08 11	09 18		10 18		11 18			12 18		13 18	
Templecombe	d	22p42						06 50			08 19	09 25		10 25		11 25			12 25		13 25	
Sherborne	d	22p50						06 57			08 26	09 33		10 33		11 33			12 33		13 33	
Yeovil Junction	a	22p55						07 03			08 32	09 38		10 38		11 38			12 38		13 38	
	d	22p57					06 15	07 07			08 40	09 40		10 40		11 40			12 40		13 40	
Crewkerne	d	23p06					06 24	07 16			08 49	09 49		10 49		11 49			12 49		13 49	
Axminster	a	23p19					06 43	07 36			09 02	10 02		11 02		12 02			13 02		14 02	
	d	23p20		05 52			06 56	07 38			09 04	10 04		11 04		12 04			13 04		14 04	
Honiton	a	23p31		06 03			07 07	07 51			09 15	10 15		11 15		12 15			13 15		14 15	
	d	23p32		06 08			07 12	07 52			09 16	10 16		11 16		12 16			13 16		14 16	
Feniton	d	23p38		06 13			07 18	07 57			09 21			11 21					13 21			
Whimple	d	23p43		06 18			07 23	08 02			09 26			11 26					13 26			
Pinhoe	d	23p49		06 25			07 30	08 09			09 33	10 28				12 28					14 28	
Exeter Central	a	23p56		06 29			07 37	08 13			09 37	10 37		11 37		12 37			13 37		14 37	
Exeter St Davids 6	a	00 01		06 35			07 42	08 18			09 42	10 42		11 42		12 42			13 42		14 42	

b Previous night, stops to pick up only

Table 160

Saturdays from 8 October

London - Salisbury and Exeter

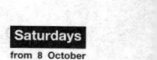

		SW ◇1 🚲		SW ◇1 🚲	SW ◇1 🚲	SW ◇1 🚲	SW ◇1 🚲	SW ◇1 🚲	SW ◇1 🚲	SW ◇1 🚲	SW ◇1 🚲	SW ◇1 🚲	SW ◇1 🚲	SW ◇1 🚲	SW ◇1 🚲	SW ◇1 🚲	SW ◇1 🚲		SW ◇1 🚲	SW ◇1 🚲	SW ◇1 🚲	SW 1 🚲	SW 1
London Waterloo 15 ⊖	d	12 20		12 50	13 20	13 50	14 20	14 50	15 20	15 50	16 20	16 50	17 20	17 50	18 20	18 50	19 20		19 50	20 20	21 20	22 20	23 40
Clampham Junction 10	d	12u27			13u27		14u27		15u27		16u27		17u27		18u27		19u27			20u27	21u27	22u27	23u47
Woking	d	12 46		13 16	13 46	14 16	14 46	15 16	15 46	16 16	16 46	17 16	17 46	18 16	18 46	19 16	19 46		20 16	20 46	21 49	22 49	00 08
Basingstoke	d	13 07		13 38	14 07	14 38	15 07	15 38	16 07	16 38	17 07	17 38	18 07	18 38	19 07	19 38	20 07		20 38	21 07	22 12	23 11	00 28
Overton	d			13 46		14 46		15 46		16 46		17 46		18 46		19 46			20 46	21 15	22 20	23 20	00s37
Whitchurch (Hants)	d			13 51		14 51		15 51		16 51		17 51		18 51		19 51			20 51	21 20	22 25	23 25	00s42
Andover	d	13 24		14 00	14 24	15 00	15 24	16 00	16 24	17 00	17 24	18 00	18 24	19 00	19 24	20 00	20 24		21 00	21 29	22 34	23 33	00 50
Grateley	d			14 07		15 07		16 07		17 07		18 07		19 07		20 07			21 07	21 36	22 41	23 41	00s58
Salisbury	a	13 42		14 19	14 42	15 19	15 42	16 19	16 42	17 19	17 42	18 19	18 43	19 19	19 43	20 19	20 42		21 19	21 48	22 53	23 53	01 10
	d	13 47	13 52		14 47		15 47		16 47		17 47		18 47		19 47		20 47	20 57		21 53	23 03		
Warminster	d		14 12															21 17					
Westbury	d		14 21															21 25					
Trowbridge	d		14 27															21 31					
Bradford-on-Avon	d		14 33															21 37					
Bath Spa 7	a		14 46															21 50					
Bristol Temple Meads 10	a		15 05															22 06					
Tisbury	d	14 07			15 07		16 07		17 07		18 07		19 07		20 07		21 07			22 07	23s16		
Gillingham (Dorset)	a	14 17			15 17		16 17		17 17		18 17		19 17		20 17		21 17			22 17	23s27		
	d	14 18			15 18		16 18		17 18		18 18		19 18		20 18		21 18			22 18			
Templecombe	d	14 25			15 25		16 25		17 25		18 25		19 25		20 25		21 25			22 25	23s35		
Sherborne	d	14 33			15 33		16 33		17 33		18 33		19 33		20 33		21 33			22 33	23s42		
Yeovil Junction	a	14 38			15 38		16 38		17 38		18 38		19 38		20 38		21 38			22 40	23 49		
	d	14 40			15 40		16 40		17 40		18 40		19 40		20 40		21 40						
Crewkerne	d	14 49			15 49		16 49		17 49		18 49		19 49		20 49		21 49						
Axminster	a	15 02			16 02		17 02		18 02		19 02		20 02		21 02		22 02						
	d	15 04			16 04		17 04		18 04		19 04		20 04		21 04		22 04						
Honiton	a	15 15			16 15		17 15		18 15		19 15		20 15		21 15		22 15						
	d	15 16			16 16		17 16		18 16		19 16		20 16		21 16		22 16						
Feniton	d	15 21					17 21				19 21				21 21		22 21						
Whimple	d	15 26					17 26				19 26				21 26		22 26						
Pinhoe	d				16 28				18 28				20 28				22 33						
Exeter Central	a	15 37			16 35		17 37		18 35		19 37		20 39		21 37		22 41						
Exeter St Davids 6	a	15 42			16 42		17 42		18 42		19 42		20 43		21 42		22 45						

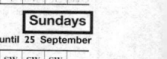

Sundays until 25 September

		SW 1 A	SW 1	SW ◇1	SW ◇1 🚲	SW ◇1 🚲	SW ◇1 🚲	SW ◇1 🚲	SW ◇1 🚲		SW ◇1 🚲	SW ◇1 🚲	SW ◇1 🚲	SW ◇1 🚲	SW ◇1 🚲	SW ◇1 🚲		SW ◇1 🚲	SW ◇1 🚲	SW ◇1 🚲	SW 1 🚲	SW 1
London Waterloo 15 ⊖	d	23p40			08 15	09 15	10 15	11 15	12 15		13 15	14 15	15 15	16 15	17 15	18 15		19 15	20 15	21 15	22 15	23 35
Clampham Junction 10	d	23b47			08u22	09u22	10u22	11u22	12u22		13u22	14u22	15u22	16u22	17u22	18u22		19u22	20u22	21u22	22u22	23u44
Woking	d	00 08			08 47	09 47	10 46	11 46	12 46		13 46	14 46	15 46	16 46	17 46	18 46		19 46	20 46	21 46	22 46	00 08
Basingstoke	d	00 28		08 05	09 08	10 08	11 07	12 07	13 07		14 07	15 07	16 07	17 07	18 07	19 07		20 07	21 07	22 07	23 07	00 40
Overton	d	00s37		08 13	09 16		11 15		13 15			15 15		17 15		19 15			21 15		23 15	00s49
Whitchurch (Hants)	d	00s42		08 18	09 21		11 20		13 20			15 20		17 20		19 20			21 20		23 20	00s54
Andover	d	00 50		08 27	09 30	10 25	11 29	12 24	13 29		14 24	15 29	16 24	17 29	18 24	19 29		20 24	21 29	22 26	23 29	01 02
Grateley	d	00s58		08 34		10 32		12 31			14 31		16 31		18 31			20 31		22 33	23 36	01s10
Salisbury	a	01 10		08 46	09 46	10 45	11 45	12 45	13 45		14 45	15 45	16 45	17 45	18 45	19 45		20 45	21 45	22 45	23 48	01 22
	d		07 10	08 51	09 51	10 51	11 51	12 51	13 51	13 55	14 51	15 51	16 51	17 51	18 51	19 51	19 55	20 51	21 51	22 51		
Warminster	d									14 15							20 15					
Westbury	d									14 24							20 23					
Trowbridge	d									14 30							20 29					
Bradford-on-Avon	d									14 36							20 35					
Bath Spa 7	a									14 49							20 48					
Bristol Temple Meads 10	a									15 05							21 04					
Tisbury	d		07 24	09 10	10 10	11 10	12 10	13 10	14 10		15 10	16 10	17 10	18 10	19 10	20 10		21 10	22 10	23 10		
Gillingham (Dorset)	a		07 34	09 20	10 20	11 20	12 20	13 20	14 20		15 20	16 20	17 20	18 20	19 20	20 20		21 20	22 20	23 20		
	d		07 35	09 21	10 21	11 21	12 21	13 21	14 21		15 21	16 21	17 21	18 21	19 21	20 21		21 21	22 21	23 21		
Templecombe	d		07 42	09 28	10 28	11 28	12 28	13 28	14 28		15 28	16 28	17 28	18 28	19 28	20 28		21 28	22 28	23 28		
Sherborne	d		07 50	09 36	10 36	11 36	12 36	13 36	14 36		15 36	16 36	17 36	18 36	19 36	20 36		21 36	22 36	23 36		
Yeovil Junction	a		07 55	09 41	10 41	11 41	12 41	13 41	14 41		15 41	16 41	17 41	18 41	19 41	20 41		21 41	22 42	23 41		
	d		07 57	09 43	10 43	11 43	12 43	13 43	14 43		15 43	16 43	17 43	18 43	19 43	20 43		21 43		23 43		
Crewkerne	d		08 06	09 52	10 52	11 52	12 52	13 52	14 52		15 52	16 52	17 52	18 52	19 52	20 52		21 52		23 52		
Axminster	a		08 19	10 05	11 05	12 05	13 05	14 05	15 05		16 05	17 05	18 05	19 05	20 05	21 05		22 05		00 05		
	d		08 20	10 06	11 06	12 06	13 06	14 06	15 06		16 06	17 06	18 06	19 06	20 06	21 06		22 06		00 06		
Honiton	a		08 31	10 18	11 18	12 18	13 18	14 18	15 18		16 18	17 18	18 18	19 18	20 18	21 18		22 18		00 18		
	d		08 35	10 19	11 19	12 19	13 19	14 19	15 19		16 19	17 19	18 19	19 19	20 19	21 19		22 19		00 19		
Feniton	d		08 40		11 24		13 24		15 24			17 24		19 24		21 24		22 24		00 24		
Whimple	d		08 45		11 29		13 29		15 29			17 29		19 29		21 29		22 29		00 29		
Pinhoe	d			10 31		12 31		14 31			16 31		18 31		20 31			22 36				
Exeter Central	a		08 56	10 40	11 40	12 40	13 40	14 40	15 40		16 40	17 40	18 40	19 40	20 40	21 40		22 40				
Exeter St Davids 6	a		09 01	10 45	11 45	12 45	13 45	14 45	15 45		16 45	17 45	18 45	19 45	20 45	21 45		22 45		00 40		

A not 22 May

b Previous night, stops to pick up only

Table 160

Sundays

from 2 October

London - Salisbury and Exeter

		SW	SW	SW	SW	SW	SW	SW	SW			SW	SW	SW	SW	SW	SW		SW	SW		SW	SW	SW
		1	1	◇1	◇1	◇1	◇1	◇1	◇1			◇1	◇1	◇1	◇1	◇1	◇1		◇1	◇1		◇1	1	1
					⊥	⊥	⊥	⊥	⊥			⊥	⊥	⊥	⊥	⊥	⊥		⊥	⊥		⊥	⊥	
London Waterloo 15 ⊖	d	23p40			08 15	09 15	10 15	11 15	12 15			13 15	14 15	15 15	16 15	17 15	18 15		19 15	20 15		21 15	22 15	23 35
Clampham Junction 10	d	23b47			08u22	09u22	10u22	11u22	12u22			13u22	14u22	15u22	16u22	17u22	18u22		19u22	20u22		21u22	22u22	23u44
Woking	d	00 08			08 47	09 47	10 46	11 46	12 46			13 46	14 46	15 46	16 46	17 46	18 46		19 46	20 46		21 46	22 46	00 08
Basingstoke	d	00 28		08 05	09 08	10 08	11 07	12 07	13 07			14 07	15 07	16 07	17 07	18 07	19 07		20 07	21 07		22 07	23 07	00 40
Overton	d	00s37		08 13	09 16		11 15		13 15				15 15		17 15		19 15			21 15			23 15	00s49
Whitchurch (Hants)	d	00s42		08 18	09 21		11 20		13 20				15 20		17 20		19 20			21 20			23 20	00s54
Andover	d	00 50		08 27	09 30	10 25	11 29	12 24	13 29			14 24	15 29	16 24	17 29	18 24	19 29		20 24	21 29		22 26	23 29	01 02
Grateley	d	00s58		08 34		10 32		12 31				14 31		16 31		18 31			20 31			22 33	23 36	01s10
Salisbury	a	01 10		08 46	09 46	10 45	11 45	12 45	13 45			14 45	15 45	16 45	17 45	18 45	19 45		20 45	21 45		22 45	23 48	01 22
	d		07 10	08 51	09 51	10 51	11 51	12 51	13 51	13 55		14 51	15 51	16 51	17 51	18 51	19 51	19 55	20 51	21 51		22 51		
Warminster	d									14 15								20 15						
Westbury	d									14 24								20 23						
Trowbridge	d									14 30								20 29						
Bradford-on-Avon	d									14 36								20 35						
Bath Spa 7	a									14 49								20 48						
Bristol Temple Meads 10	a									15 05								21 04						
Tisbury	d		07 24	09 10	10 10	11 10	12 10	13 10	14 10			15 10	16 10	17 10	18 10	19 10	20 10		21 10	22 10		23 10		
Gillingham (Dorset)	a		07 34	09 20	10 20	11 20	12 20	13 20	14 20			15 20	16 20	17 20	18 20	19 20	20 20		21 20	22 20		23 20		
	d		07 35	09 21	10 21	11 21	12 21	13 21	14 21			15 21	16 21	17 21	18 21	19 21	20 21		21 21	22 21		23 21		
Templecombe	d		07 42	09 28	10 28	11 28	12 28	13 28	14 28			15 28	16 28	17 28	18 28	19 28	20 28		21 28	22 28		23 28		
Sherborne	d		07 50	09 36	10 36	11 36	12 36	13 36	14 36			15 36	16 36	17 36	18 36	19 36	20 36		21 36	22 36		23 36		
Yeovil Junction	a		07 55	09 41	10 41	11 41	12 41	13 41	14 41			15 41	16 41	17 41	18 41	19 41	20 41		21 41	22 42		23 41		
	d		07 57	09 43	10 43	11 43	12 43	13 43	14 43			15 43	16 43	17 43	18 43	19 43	20 43		21 43			23 43		
Crewkerne	d		08 06	09 52	10 52	11 52	12 52	13 52	14 52			15 52	16 52	17 52	18 52	19 52	20 52		21 52			23 52		
Axminster	a		08 19	10 05	11 05	12 05	13 05	14 05	15 05			16 05	17 05	18 05	19 05	20 05	21 05		22 05			00 05		
	d		08 20	10 06	11 06	12 06	13 06	14 06	15 06			16 06	17 06	18 06	19 06	20 06	21 06		22 06			00 06		
Honiton	a		08 31	10 18	11 18	12 18	13 18	14 18	15 18			16 18	17 18	18 18	19 18	20 18	21 18		22 18			00 18		
	d		08 35	10 19	11 19	12 19	13 19	14 19	15 19			16 19	17 19	18 19	19 19	20 19	21 19		22 19			00 19		
Feniton	d		08 40		11 24		13 24		15 24				17 24		19 24		21 24		22 24			00 24		
Whimple	d		08 45		11 29		13 29		15 29				17 29		19 29		21 29		22 29			00 29		
Pinhoe	d			10 31		12 31		14 31				16 31		18 31		20 31			22 36					
Exeter Central	a		08 56	10 40	11 40	12 40	13 40	14 40	15 40			16 40	17 40	18 40	19 40	20 40	21 40		22 40					
Exeter St Davids 6	a		09 01	10 45	11 45	12 45	13 45	14 45	15 45			16 45	17 45	18 45	19 45	20 45	21 45		22 45			00 40		

b Previous night, stops to pick up only

Table 160

Exeter and Salisbury - London

Mondays to Fridays

until 30 September

Miles			SW	SW	SW	GW	SW	SW	SW	SW	SW	SW	SW	SW	SW	SW	SW	SW	SW	SW	SW	SW	SW
			MX	MO																			
			1	1	◇1		◇1	◇1	◇1	◇1	◇1	◇1	◇1	◇1	◇1	◇1	◇1	◇1	◇1	◇1	◇1	◇1	◇1
																A							
					🍴		🍴	🍴	🍴	🍴	🍴	🍴	🍴	🍴	🍴	🍴	🍴	🍴	🍴	🍴	🍴	🍴	🍴
0	**Exeter St Davids** 6	d	22p57	23p15						05 10			06 41	07 26			08 26		09 26		10 26		11 26
0¾	**Exeter Central**	d	23p01	23p19						05 14			06 45	07 30			08 30		09 30		10 30		11 30
3½	Pinhoe	d	23p06							05 19			06 50	07 35			08 35		09 35				11 35
9¼	Whimple	d	23p13							05 26			06 57				08 42				10 39		
13	Feniton	d	23p18							05 31			07 02				08 47				10 45		
17½	Honiton	a	23p25	23b34						05 38			07 10	07 47			08 54		09 47		10 51		11 48
—		d	23p32							05 39	06 19		07 11	07 49			08 55		09 53		10 53		11 53
27¾	Axminster	a	23p42	23b45						05 49	06 29		07 21	07 59			09 05		10 03		11 03		12 03
—		d	23p43							05 51	06 30		07 22	08 00			09 06		10 06		11 06		12 06
40¾	Crewkerne	d	23p56	00s11						06 04	06 43		07 35	08 13			09 19		10 19		11 19		12 19
49¾	Yeovil Junction	a	00 04	00s20						06 12	06 52		07 44	08 22			09 27		10 27		11 27		12 27
—		d	00 09					05 15	05 50	06 20	06 53	07 22	07 50	08 29			09 29		10 29		11 29		12 29
54¼	Sherborne	d						05 21	05 56	06 26	07 00	07 28	07 56	08 36			09 36		10 36		11 36		12 36
60¼	Templecombe	d						05 29	06 04	06 34	07 07	07 36	08 04	08 43			09 43		10 43		11 43		12 43
67¾	Gillingham (Dorset)	a						05 36	06 11	06 41	07 14	07 43	08 11	08 50			09 50		10 50		11 50		12 50
—		d						05 37	06 12	06 42	07 15	07 44	08 12	08 51	09 18		09 51		10 51		11 51		12 51
76¼	Tisbury	d						05 47	06 24	06 52	07 26	07 54	08 22	09 02	09 28		10 02		11 02		12 02		13 02
—	Bristol Temple Meads 10	d														08 51							
—	Bath Spa 7	d														09 07							
—	Bradford-on-Avon	d														09 20							
—	Trowbridge	d														09 27							
—	Westbury	d				05 24										09 39							
—	Warminster	d				05 32										09 46							
88¾	**Salisbury**	a	00 43	00 56		05 53		06 02	06 39	07 07	07 40	08 09	08 37	09 16	09 42	10 09	10 16		11 16		12 16		13 16
—																							
—		d			05 15		05 43	06 06	06 45	07 15	07 45	08 15	08 47	09 21	09 47	10 21		10 47	11 21	11 47	12 21	12 47	13 21
99¾	Grateley	d			05 27		05 55	06 19	06 57	07 27	07 57	08 27	08 59		09 59			10 59		11 59		12 59	
106	Andover	d			05 35		06 03	06 26	07 05	07 35	08 05	08 35	09 06	09 38	10 06	10 38		11 06	11 38	12 06	12 38	13 06	13 38
113¼	Whitchurch (Hants)	d			05 43		06 11	06 35	07 13	07 43	08 13	08 43	09 14		10 14			11 14		12 14		13 14	
117	Overton	d			05 49		06 17	06 41	07 19	07 49	08 19	08 49	09 20		10 20			11 20		12 20		13 20	
124¾	**Basingstoke**	a			05 58		06 26	06 49	07 28	07 58	08 28	08 58	09 28	09 55	10 28	10 55		11 28	11 55	12 28	12 55	13 28	13 55
148¼	Woking	a			06 18		06 46			08 18	08 48	09 18	09 49	10 15	10 49	11 15		11 49	12 15	12 49	13 15	13 49	14 15
168¼	Clapham Junction 10	a			06 38			07 28				09 38	10 09	10 36		11 36			12 36		13 38		14 36
172½	**London Waterloo** 15 ⊖	a			06 49		07 14	07 39	08 14	08 46	09 17	09 51	10 19	10 49	11 19	11 49		12 19	12 49	13 19	13 49	14 19	14 49

		SW	SW	SW	SW	SW	SW	SW	SW	SW	SW	SW	SW	SW	SW	SW	SW	SW	SW	SW	SW
		◇1	◇1	◇1	◇1	◇1	◇1	◇1	◇1	◇1	◇1	◇1	◇1	◇1	1	◇1	◇1	◇1	1	1	1
									A												
		🍴	🍴	🍴	🍴	🍴	🍴	🍴	🍴	🍴	🍴	🍴	🍴	🍴		🍴		🍴			
Exeter St Davids 6	d		12 26		13 26		14 26			15 26		16 26		17 26	17 46	18 26	19 26	20 26	21 23		22 57
Exeter Central	d		12 30		13 30		14 30			15 30		16 30		17 30	17 50	18 30	19 30	20 30	21 30		23 01
Pinhoe	d				13 35					15 35				17 35	17 56		19 35		21 35		23 06
Whimple	d		12 39				14 39					16 39			18 02	18 39		20 39			23 13
Feniton	d		12 45				14 45					16 45			18 08	18 45		20 45			23 18
Honiton	a		12 51		13 48		14 51			15 48		16 51		17 48	18 18	18 51	19 48	20 51	21 47		23 25
	d		12 53		13 53		14 53			15 53		16 53		17 53	18 19	18 53	19 53	20 53	21 53		23 32
Axminster	a		13 03		14 03		15 03			16 03		17 03		18 03	18 29	19 03	20 03	21 03	22 03		23 42
	d		13 06		14 06		15 06			16 06		17 06		18 06		19 06	20 06	21 06	22 06		23 43
Crewkerne	d		13 19		14 19		15 19			16 19		17 19		18 19		19 19	20 19	21 19	22 19		23 56
Yeovil Junction	a		13 27		14 27		15 27			16 27		17 27		18 27		19 27	20 27	21 27	22 27		00 04
	d		13 29		14 29		15 29			16 29		17 29		18 29		19 29	20 29	21 29	22 29		00 09
Sherborne	d		13 36		14 36		15 36			16 36		17 36		18 36		19 36	20 36	21 36	22 36		
Templecombe	d		13 43		14 43		15 43			16 43		17 43		18 43		19 43	20 43	21 43	22 47		
Gillingham (Dorset)	a		13 50		14 50		15 50			16 50		17 50		18 50		19 50	20 50	21 50	22 54		
	d		13 51		14 51		15 51	16 18		16 51		17 51		18 51		19 51	20 51	21 51	22 55		
Tisbury	d		14 02		15 02		16 02	16 28		17 02		18 02		19 02		20 02	21 02	22 02	23 05		
Bristol Temple Meads 10	d			13 15					15 51											22 25	
Bath Spa 7	d			13 28					16 07											22 38	
Bradford-on-Avon	d			13 40					16 22											22 51	
Trowbridge	d			13 47					16 28											22 57	
Westbury	d			13 54					16 39											23 08	
Warminster	d			14 02					16 47											23 15	
Salisbury	a		14 16	14 28	15 16		16 16	16 43	17 09	17 16		18 21		19 23		20 21	21 21	22 16	23 29	23 35	00 43
	d	13 47	14 21	14 47	15 21	15 47	16 21	16 47	17 21		17 47	18 26	18 47	19 26		20 26	21 26	22 26			
Grateley	d	13 59		14 59		15 59		16 59			17 59		18 59	19 38		20 38	21 38	22 38			
Andover	d	14 06	14 38	15 06	15 38	16 06	16 38	17 06	17 38		18 06	18 43	19 06	19 45		20 45	21 45	22 45			
Whitchurch (Hants)	d	14 14		15 14		16 14		17 14			18 14		19 14	19 53		20 53	21 53	22 53			
Overton	d	14 20		15 20		16 20		17 20			18 20		19 20	19 59		20 59	21 59	22 59			
Basingstoke	a	14 28	14 55	15 28	15 55	16 28	16 55	17 29	17 55		18 28	19 00	19 28	20 08		21 08	22 07	23 07			
Woking	a	14 49	15 15	15 49	16 15	16 49	17 15	17 49	18 15		18 49	19 20	19 49	20 29		21 29	22 28				
Clapham Junction 10	a		15 36		16 36		17 36		18 36			19 41		20 52		21 52	22 48				
London Waterloo 15 ⊖	a	15 19	15 49	16 19	16 49	17 19	17 44	18 21	18 45		19 19	19 50	20 19	21 00		22 04	22 58				

A 🍴 from Salisbury

b Previous night, stops to set down only

Table 160

Mondays to Fridays

from 3 October

Exeter and Salisbury - London

		SW	SW	SW	GW	SW	SW	SW	SW	SW	SW	SW	SW	SW	SW	SW	SW	SW	SW	SW	SW	SW	SW
		MX 1	MO 1	◇1		◇1	◇1	◇1	◇1	◇1	◇1	◇1	◇1	◇1	◇1 A	◇1	◇1	◇1	◇1	◇1	◇1	◇1	◇1
				[trolley]		[trolley]	[trolley]	[trolley]	[trolley]	[trolley]	[trolley]	[trolley]	[trolley]	[trolley]	[trolley]	[trolley]	[trolley]	[trolley]	[trolley]	[trolley]	[trolley]	[trolley]	[trolley]
Exeter St Davids 6	d	22p57	23p15						05 10			06 41	07 26			08 26		09 26		10 26		11 26	
Exeter Central	d	23p01	23p19						05 14			06 45	07 30			08 30		09 30		10 30		11 30	
Pinhoe	d	23p06							05 19			06 50	07 35			08 35		09 35				11 35	
Whimple	d	23p13							05 26			06 57				08 42				10 39			
Feniton	d	23p18							05 31			07 02				08 47				10 45			
Honiton	a	23p25	23b34						05 38			07 10	07 47			08 54		09 47		10 51		11 48	
	d	23p32							05 39	06 19		07 11	07 49			08 55		09 53		10 53		11 53	
Axminster	a	23p42	23b45						05 49	06 29		07 21	07 59			09 05		10 03		11 03		12 03	
	d	23p43							05 51	06 30		07 22	08 00			09 06		10 06		11 06		12 06	
Crewkerne	d	23p56	00s11						06 04	06 43		07 35	08 13			09 19		10 19		11 19		12 19	
Yeovil Junction	a	00 04	00s20						06 12	06 52		07 44	08 22			09 27		10 27		11 27		12 27	
	d	00 09					05 12	05 50	06 20	06 53	07 22	07 50	08 29			09 29		10 29		11 29		12 29	
Sherborne	d						05 18	05 56	06 26	07 00	07 28	07 56	08 36			09 36		10 36		11 36		12 36	
Templecombe	d						05 26	06 04	06 34	07 07	07 36	08 04	08 43			09 43		10 43		11 43		12 43	
Gillingham (Dorset)	a						05 33	06 11	06 41	07 14	07 43	08 11	08 50			09 50		10 50		11 50		12 50	
	d						05 34	06 12	06 42	07 15	07 44	08 12	08 51	09 18		09 51		10 51		11 51		12 51	
Tisbury	d						05 44	06 24	06 52	07 26	07 54	08 22	09 02	09 28		10 02		11 02		12 02		13 02	
Bristol Temple Meads 10	d														08 51								
Bath Spa 7	d														09 07								
Bradford-on-Avon	d														09 20								
Trowbridge	d														09 27								
Westbury	d				05 24										09c39								
Warminster	d				05 32										09 46								
Salisbury	a	00 43	00 56		05 53		05 59	06 39	07 07	07 40	08 09	08 37	09 16	09 42	10 09	10 16		11 16		12 16		13 16	
	d			05 12		05 40	06 03	06 45	07 15	07 45	08 15	08 47	09 21	09 47		10 21	10 47	11 21	11 47	12 21	12 47	13 21	13 47
Grateley	d			05 24		05 52	06 16	06 57	07 27	07 57	08 27	08 59		09 59			10 59		11 59		12 59		13 59
Andover	d			05 32		06 00	06 23	07 05	07 35	08 05	08 35	09 06	09 38	10 06		10 38	11 06	11 38	12 06	12 38	13 06	13 38	14 06
Whitchurch (Hants)	d			05 40		06 08	06 32	07 13	07 43	08 13	08 43	09 14		10 14			11 14		12 14		13 14		14 14
Overton	d			05 46		06 14	06 38	07 19	07 49	08 19	08 49	09 20		10 20			11 20		12 20		13 20		14 20
Basingstoke	a			05 59		06 26	06 49	07 28	07 58	08 28	08 58	09 28	09 55	10 28		10 55	11 28	11 55	12 28	12 55	13 28	13 55	14 28
Woking	a			06 18		06 46			08 18	08 48	09 18	09 49	10 15	10 49		11 15	11 49	12 15	12 49	13 15	13 49	14 15	14 49
Clapham Junction 10	a			06 39			07 28				09 38	10 09	10 36			11 36		12 36		13 38		14 36	
London Waterloo 15 ⊖	a			06 49		07 14	07 39	08 14	08 46	09 17	09 51	10 19	10 49	11 19		11 49	12 19	12 49	13 19	13 49	14 19	14 49	15 19

		SW	SW	SW	SW	SW	SW	SW	SW	SW	SW	SW	SW	SW	SW	SW	SW	SW	SW	SW
		◇1	◇1	◇1	◇1	◇1	◇1	◇1 A	◇1	◇1	◇1	◇1	◇1	1	◇1	◇1	◇1	1	1	1
		[trolley]	[trolley]	[trolley]	[trolley]	[trolley]	[trolley]	[trolley]	[trolley]	[trolley]	[trolley]	[trolley]	[trolley]		[trolley]		[trolley]			
Exeter St Davids 6	d	12 26		13 26		14 26			15 26		16 26		17 26	17 46	18 26	19 26	20 26	21 23		22 57
Exeter Central	d	12 30		13 30		14 30			15 30		16 30		17 30	17 50	18 30	19 30	20 30	21 30		23 01
Pinhoe	d			13 35					15 35				17 35	17 56		19 35		21 35		23 06
Whimple	d	12 39				14 39					16 39			18 02	18 39		20 39			23 13
Feniton	d	12 45				14 45					16 45			18 08	18 45		20 45			23 18
Honiton	a	12 51		13 48		14 51			15 48		16 51		17 48	18 18	18 51	19 48	20 51	21 47		23 25
	d	12 53		13 53		14 53			15 53		16 53		17 53	18 19	18 53	19 53	20 53	21 53		23 32
Axminster	a	13 03		14 03		15 03			16 03		17 03		18 03	18 29	19 03	20 03	21 03	22 03		23 42
	d	13 06		14 06		15 06			16 06		17 06		18 06		19 06	20 06	21 06	22 06		23 43
Crewkerne	d	13 19		14 19		15 19			16 19		17 19		18 19		19 19	20 19	21 19	22 19		23 56
Yeovil Junction	a	13 27		14 27		15 27			16 27		17 27		18 27		19 27	20 27	21 27	22 27		00 04
	d	13 29		14 29		15 29			16 29		17 29		18 29		19 29	20 29	21 29	22 29		00 09
Sherborne	d	13 36		14 36		15 36			16 36		17 36		18 36		19 36	20 36	21 36	22 36		
Templecombe	d	13 43		14 43		15 43			16 43		17 43		18 43		19 43	20 43	21 43	22 47		
Gillingham (Dorset)	a	13 50		14 50		15 50			16 50		17 50		18 50		19 50	20 50	21 50	22 54		
	d	13 51		14 51		15 51	16 18		16 51		17 51		18 51		19 51	20 51	21 51	22 55		
Tisbury	d	14 02		15 02		16 02	16 28		17 02		18 02		19 02		20 02	21 02	22 02	23 05		
Bristol Temple Meads 10	d		13 15					15 51											22 25	
Bath Spa 7	d		13 28					16 07											22 38	
Bradford-on-Avon	d		13 40					16 22											22 51	
Trowbridge	d		13 47					16 28											22 57	
Westbury	d		13 54					16 39											23 08	
Warminster	d		14 02					16 47											23 15	
Salisbury	a	14 16	14 28	15 16		16 16	16 43	17 09	17 16		18 21		19 23		20 21	21 21	22 16	23 29	23 35	00 43
	d	14 21	14 47	15 21	15 47	16 21	16 47		17 21	17 47	18 26	18 47	19 26		20 26	21 26	22 26			
Grateley	d		14 59		15 59		16 59			17 59		18 59	19 38		20 38	21 38	22 38			
Andover	d	14 38	15 06	15 38	16 06	16 38	17 06		17 38	18 06	18 43	19 06	19 45		20 45	21 45	22 45			
Whitchurch (Hants)	d		15 14		16 14		17 14			18 14		19 14	19 53		20 53	21 53	22 53			
Overton	d		15 20		16 20		17 20			18 20		19 20	19 59		20 59	21 59	22 59			
Basingstoke	a	14 55	15 28	15 55	16 28	16 55	17 29		17 55	18 28	19 00	19 28	20 08		21 08	22 07	23 07			
Woking	a	15 15	15 49	16 15	16 49	17 15	17 49		18 15	18 49	19 20	19 49	20 29		21 29	22 28				
Clapham Junction 10	a	15 36		16 36		17 36			18 36		19 41		20 52		21 52	22 48				
London Waterloo 15 ⊖	a	15 49	16 19	16 49	17 19	17 44	18 21		18 45	19 19	19 50	20 19	21 00		22 04	22 58				

A [trolley] from Salisbury

b Previous night, stops to set down only

Table 160

Exeter and Salisbury - London

Saturdays

until 1 October

		SW	SW	GW	SW	SW	SW	SW	SW	SW	SW	SW	SW	SW	SW	SW	SW	SW	SW	SW	SW	SW	SW
		1	◇1		◇1	◇1	◇1	◇1	◇1	◇1	◇1	◇1	◇1	◇1	◇1	◇1	◇1	◇1	◇1	◇1	◇1	◇1	◇1
														A									
			trolley		trolley	trolley	trolley	trolley	trolley	trolley	trolley	trolley	trolley	trolley	trolley	trolley	trolley	trolley	trolley	trolley	trolley	trolley	trolley
Exeter St Davids 6	d	22p57						05 10			06 41	07 26			08 26		09 26		10 26		11 26		12 26
Exeter Central	d	23p01						05 14			06 45	07 30			08 30		09 30		10 30		11 30		12 30
Pinhoe	d	23p06						05 19			06 50	07 35			08 35		09 35				11 35		
Whimple	d	23p13						05 26			06 57				08 42				10 39				12 39
Feniton	d	23p18						05 31			07 02				08 47				10 45				12 45
Honiton	a	23p25						05 38			07 11	07 48			08 54		09 48		10 51		11 48		12 51
	d	23p32						05 39	06 19		07 13	07 53			08 55		09 53		10 53		11 53		12 53
Axminster	a	23p42						05 49	06 29		07 23	08 03			09 05		10 03		11 03		12 03		13 03
	d	23p43						05 51	06 30		07 24	08 06			09 06		10 06		11 06		12 06		13 06
Crewkerne	d	23p56						06 04	06 43		07 37	08 19			09 19		10 19		11 19		12 19		13 19
Yeovil Junction	a	00 04						06 12	06 52		07 45	08 27			09 27		10 27		11 27		12 27		13 27
	d	00 09						06 20	06 53		07 50	08 29			09 29		10 29		11 29		12 29		13 29
Sherborne	d							06 26	07 00		07 56	08 36			09 36		10 36		11 36		12 36		13 36
Templecombe	d							06 34	07 07		08 04	08 43			09 43		10 43		11 43		12 43		13 43
Gillingham (Dorset)	a							06 41	07 14		08 11	08 50			09 50		10 50		11 50		12 50		13 50
	d							06 42	07 15		08 12	08 51			09 51		10 51		11 51		12 51		13 51
Tisbury	d							06 52	07 26		08 22	09 02			10 02		11 02		12 02		13 02		14 02
Bristol Temple Meads 10	d													08 51									
Bath Spa 7	d													09 07									
Bradford-on-Avon	d													09 20									
Trowbridge	d													09 27									
Westbury	d			05 26										09 39									
Warminster	d			05 34										09 46									
Salisbury	a	00 43		05 58				07 07	07 40		08 37	09 16		10 09	10 16		11 16		12 16		13 16		14 16
	d		05 15		05 47	06 21	06 47	07 21	07 47	08 21	08 47	09 21	09 47	10 21		10 47	11 21	11 47	12 21	12 47	13 21	13 47	14 21
Grateley	d		05 27		05 59		06 59		07 59		08 59		09 59			10 59		11 59		12 59		13 59	
Andover	d		05 35		06 06	06 38	07 06	07 38	08 06	08 38	09 06	09 38	10 06	10 38		11 06	11 38	12 06	12 38	13 06	13 38	14 06	14 38
Whitchurch (Hants)	d		05 43		06 14		07 14		08 14		09 14		10 14			11 14		12 14		13 14		14 14	
Overton	d		05 49		06 20		07 20		08 20		09 20		10 20			11 20		12 20		13 20		14 20	
Basingstoke	a		05 58		06 28	06 55	07 28	07 55	08 28	08 55	09 28	09 55	10 28	10 55		11 28	11 55	12 28	12 55	13 28	13 55	14 28	14 55
Woking	a		06 18		06 49	07 15	07 49	08 17	08 49	09 15	09 49	10 15	10 49	11 15		11 49	12 15	12 49	13 15	13 49	14 15	14 49	15 15
Clapham Junction 10	a		06 38			07 36		08 37		09 36		10 36		11 36			12 36		13 36		14 36		15 36
London Waterloo 15 ⊖	a		06 49		07 19	07 49	08 19	08 49	09 19	09 49	10 19	10 49	11 19	11 49		12 19	12 49	13 19	13 49	14 19	14 49	15 19	15 49

		SW	SW	SW	SW	SW	SW	SW	SW	SW	SW	SW	SW	SW	SW	SW	SW	SW
		◇1	◇1	◇1	◇1	◇1	◇1	◇1	◇1	◇1	◇1	◇1	◇1	◇1	◇1	1	1	1
							A											
		trolley	trolley	trolley	trolley	trolley	trolley	trolley	trolley	trolley	trolley	trolley	trolley		trolley			
Exeter St Davids 6	d		13 26		14 26			15 26		16 26		17 26	18 26	19 26	20 26	21 26		22 57
Exeter Central	d		13 30		14 30			15 30		16 30		17 30	18 30	19 30	20 30	21 30		23 01
Pinhoe	d		13 35					15 35				17 35		19 35		21 35		23 06
Whimple	d				14 39					16 39		17 42	18 39		20 39			23 13
Feniton	d				14 45					16 45		17 47	18 45		20 45			23 18
Honiton	a		13 48		14 51			15 48		16 51		17 54	18 51	19 48	20 51	21 48		23 25
	d		13 53		14 53			15 53		16 53		17 55	18 53	19 53	20 53	21 53		23 32
Axminster	a		14 03		15 03			16 03		17 03		18 05	19 03	20 03	21 03	22 03		23 42
	d		14 06		15 06			16 06		17 06		18 06	19 06	20 06	21 06	22 06		23 43
Crewkerne	d		14 19		15 19			16 19		17 19		18 19	19 19	20 19	21 19	22 19		23 56
Yeovil Junction	a		14 27		15 27			16 27		17 27		18 27	19 27	20 27	21 27	22 27		00 04
	d		14 29		15 29			16 29		17 29		18 29	19 29	20 29	21 29	22 29		00 16
Sherborne	d		14 36		15 36			16 36		17 36		18 36	19 36	20 36	21 36	22 36		
Templecombe	d		14 43		15 43			16 43		17 43		18 43	19 43	20 43	21 43	22 43		
Gillingham (Dorset)	a		14 50		15 50			16 50		17 50		18 50	19 50	20 50	21 50	22 50		
	d		14 51		15 51			16 51		17 51		18 51	19 51	20 51	21 51	22 51		
Tisbury	d		15 02		16 02			17 02		18 02		19 02	20 02	21 02	22 02	23 02		
Bristol Temple Meads 10	d	13 15					15 51										22 23	
Bath Spa 7	d	13 28					16 07										22 36	
Bradford-on-Avon	d	13 40					16 24										22 47	
Trowbridge	d	13 47					16 30										22 53	
Westbury	d	13 54					16 39										23 04	
Warminster	d	14 02					16 47										23 11	
Salisbury	a	14 25	15 16		16 16		17 09	17 16		18 16		19 16	20 16	21 16	22 21	23 29	23 34	00 50
	d	14 47	15 21	15 47	16 21	16 47	17 21		17 47	18 21	18 47	19 26	20 26	21 26	22 26			
Grateley	d	14 59		15 59		16 59			17 59		18 59	19 38	20 38	21 38	22 38			
Andover	d	15 06	15 38	16 06	16 38	17 06	17 38		18 06	18 38	19 06	19 45	20 45	21 45	22 45			
Whitchurch (Hants)	d	15 14		16 14		17 14			18 14		19 14	19 53	20 53	21 53	22 53			
Overton	d	15 20		16 20		17 20			18 20		19 20	19 59	20 59	21 59	22 59			
Basingstoke	a	15 28	15 55	16 28	16 55	17 28	17 55		18 28	18 55	19 28	20 08	21 08	22 07	23 07			
Woking	a	15 49	16 15	16 49	17 15	17 49	18 15		18 49	19 15	19 49	20 29	21 29	22 28				
Clapham Junction 10	a		16 36		17 36		18 36			19 36		20 52	21 52	22 48				
London Waterloo 15 ⊖	a	16 19	16 49	17 19	17 49	18 19	18 49		19 19	19 49	20 19	21 04	22 04	22 57				

A trolley from Salisbury

Table 160

Saturdays
from 8 October

Exeter and Salisbury - London

	SW 1	SW ◇1 🛒	GW	SW ◇1 🛒	SW ◇1 🛒	SW ◇1 🛒	SW ◇1 🛒	SW ◇1 🛒	SW ◇1 🛒	SW ◇1 🛒	SW ◇1 🛒
Exeter St Davids 6 d	22p57						05 10			06 41	07 26
Exeter Central d	23p01						05 14			06 45	07 30
Pinhoe d	23p06						05 19			06 50	07 35
Whimple d	23p13						05 26			06 57	
Feniton d	23p18						05 31			07 02	
Honiton a	23p25						05 38			07 11	07 48
d	23p32						05 39	06 19		07 13	07 53
Axminster a	23p42						05 49	06 29		07 23	08 03
d	23p43						05 51	06 30		07 24	08 06
Crewkerne d	23p56						06 04	06 43		07 37	08 19
Yeovil Junction a	00 04						06 12	06 52		07 45	08 27
d	00 09						06 20	06 53		07 50	08 29
Sherborne d							06 26	07 00		07 56	08 36
Templecombe d							06 34	07 07		08 04	08 43
Gillingham (Dorset) a							06 41	07 14		08 11	08 50
d							06 42	07 15		08 12	08 51
Tisbury d							06 52	07 26		08 22	09 02
Bristol Temple Meads 10 d											
Bath Spa 7 d											
Bradford-on-Avon d											
Trowbridge d											
Westbury d			05 26								
Warminster d			05 34								
Salisbury a	00 43		05 58				07 07	07 40		08 37	09 16
d		05 12		05 44	06 18	06 47	07 21	07 47	08 21	08 47	09 21
Grateley d		05 24		05 56		06 59		07 59		08 59	
Andover d		05 32		06 03	06 35	07 06	07 38	08 06	08 38	09 06	09 38
Whitchurch (Hants) d		05 40		06 11		07 14		08 14		09 14	
Overton d		05 46		06 17		07 20		08 20		09 20	
Basingstoke a		05 58		06 28	06 55	07 28	07 55	08 28	08 55	09 28	09 55
Woking a		06 18		06 49	07 15	07 49	08 17	08 49	09 15	09 49	10 15
Clapham Junction 10 a		06 38			07 36		08 37		09 36		10 36
London Waterloo 15 ⊖ a		06 49		07 19	07 49	08 19	08 49	09 19	09 49	10 19	10 49

	SW ◇1 🛒	SW ◇1 A 🛒	SW ◇1 🛒	SW ◇1 🛒	SW ◇1 🛒	SW ◇1 🛒	SW ◇1 🛒	SW ◇1 🛒	SW ◇1 🛒	SW ◇1 🛒	SW ◇1 🛒
Exeter St Davids 6 d			08 26		09 26		10 26		11 26		12 26
Exeter Central d			08 30		09 30		10 30		11 30		12 30
Pinhoe d			08 35		09 35				11 35		
Whimple d			08 42				10 39				12 39
Feniton d			08 47				10 45				12 45
Honiton a			08 54		09 48		10 51		11 48		12 51
d			08 55		09 53		10 53		11 53		12 53
Axminster a			09 05		10 03		11 03		12 03		13 03
d			09 06		10 06		11 06		12 06		13 06
Crewkerne d			09 19		10 19		11 19		12 19		13 19
Yeovil Junction a			09 27		10 27		11 27		12 27		13 27
d			09 29		10 29		11 29		12 29		13 29
Sherborne d			09 36		10 36		11 36		12 36		13 36
Templecombe d			09 43		10 43		11 43		12 43		13 43
Gillingham (Dorset) a			09 50		10 50		11 50		12 50		13 50
d			09 51		10 51		11 51		12 51		13 51
Tisbury d			10 02		11 02		12 02		13 02		14 02
Bristol Temple Meads 10 d		08 51									
Bath Spa 7 d		09 07									
Bradford-on-Avon d		09 20									
Trowbridge d		09 27									
Westbury d		09 39									
Warminster d		09 46									
Salisbury a		10 09	10 16		11 16		12 16		13 16		14 16
d	09 47		10 21	10 47	11 21	11 47	12 21	12 47	13 21	13 47	14 21
Grateley d	09 59			10 59		11 59		12 59		13 59	
Andover d	10 06		10 38	11 06	11 38	12 06	12 38	13 06	13 38	14 06	14 38
Whitchurch (Hants) d	10 14			11 14		12 14		13 14		14 14	
Overton d	10 20			11 20		12 20		13 20		14 20	
Basingstoke a	10 28		10 55	11 28	11 55	12 28	12 55	13 28	13 55	14 28	14 55
Woking a	10 49		11 15	11 49	12 15	12 49	13 15	13 49	14 15	14 49	15 15
Clapham Junction 10 a			11 36		12 36		13 36		14 36		15 36
London Waterloo 15 ⊖ a	11 19		11 49	12 19	12 49	13 19	13 49	14 19	14 49	15 19	15 49

	SW ◇1 🛒	SW ◇1 🛒	SW ◇1 🛒	SW ◇1 🛒	SW ◇1 🛒	SW ◇1 A 🛒	SW ◇1 🛒	SW ◇1 🛒	SW ◇1 🛒
Exeter St Davids 6 d		13 26		14 26			15 26		16 26
Exeter Central d		13 30		14 30			15 30		16 30
Pinhoe d		13 35					15 35		
Whimple d				14 39					16 39
Feniton d				14 45					16 45
Honiton a		13 48		14 51			15 48		16 51
d		13 53		14 53			15 53		16 53
Axminster a		14 03		15 03			16 03		17 03
d		14 06		15 06			16 06		17 06
Crewkerne d		14 19		15 19			16 19		17 19
Yeovil Junction a		14 27		15 27			16 27		17 27
d		14 29		15 29			16 29		17 29
Sherborne d		14 36		15 36			16 36		17 36
Templecombe d		14 43		15 43			16 43		17 43
Gillingham (Dorset) a		14 50		15 50			16 50		17 50
d		14 51		15 51			16 51		17 51
Tisbury d		15 02		16 02			17 02		18 02
Bristol Temple Meads 10 d	13 15					15 51			
Bath Spa 7 d	13 28					16 07			
Bradford-on-Avon d	13 40					16 24			
Trowbridge d	13 47					16 30			
Westbury d	13 54					16 39			
Warminster d	14 02					16 47			
Salisbury a	14 25	15 16		16 16		17 09	17 16		18 16
d	14 47	15 21	15 47	16 21	16 47		17 21	17 47	18 21
Grateley d	14 59		15 59		16 59			17 59	
Andover d	15 06	15 38	16 06	16 38	17 06		17 38	18 06	18 38
Whitchurch (Hants) d	15 14		16 14		17 14			18 14	
Overton d	15 20		16 20		17 20			18 20	
Basingstoke a	15 28	15 55	16 28	16 55	17 28		17 55	18 28	18 55
Woking a	15 49	16 15	16 49	17 15	17 49		18 15	18 49	19 15
Clapham Junction 10 a		16 36		17 36			18 36		19 36
London Waterloo 15 ⊖ a	16 19	16 49	17 19	17 49	18 19		18 49	19 19	19 49

	SW ◇1 🛒	SW ◇1 🛒	SW ◇1 🛒	SW ◇1	SW ◇1 🛒	SW 1	SW 1	SW 1
Exeter St Davids 6 d		17 26	18 26	19 26	20 26	21 26		22 57
Exeter Central d		17 30	18 30	19 30	20 30	21 30		23 01
Pinhoe d		17 35		19 35		21 35		23 06
Whimple d		17 42	18 39		20 39			23 13
Feniton d		17 47	18 45		20 45			23 18
Honiton a		17 54	18 51	19 48	20 51	21 48		23 25
d		17 55	18 53	19 53	20 53	21 53		23 32
Axminster a		18 05	19 03	20 03	21 03	22 03		23 42
d		18 06	19 06	20 06	21 06	22 06		23 43
Crewkerne d		18 19	19 19	20 19	21 19	22 19		23 56
Yeovil Junction a		18 27	19 27	20 27	21 27	22 27		00 04
d		18 29	19 29	20 29	21 29	22 29		00 16
Sherborne d		18 36	19 36	20 36	21 36	22 36		
Templecombe d		18 43	19 43	20 43	21 43	22 43		
Gillingham (Dorset) a		18 50	19 50	20 50	21 50	22 50		
d		18 51	19 51	20 51	21 51	22 51		
Tisbury d		19 02	20 02	21 02	22 02	23 02		
Bristol Temple Meads 10 d							22 23	
Bath Spa 7 d							22 36	
Bradford-on-Avon d							22 47	
Trowbridge d							22 53	
Westbury d							23 04	
Warminster d							23 11	
Salisbury a		19 16	20 16	21 16	22 21	23 29	23 34	00 50
d	18 47	19 26	20 26	21 26	22 26			
Grateley d	18 59	19 38	20 38	21 38	22 38			
Andover d	19 06	19 45	20 45	21 45	22 45			
Whitchurch (Hants) d	19 14	19 53	20 53	21 53	22 53			
Overton d	19 20	19 59	20 59	21 59	22 59			
Basingstoke a	19 28	20 08	21 08	22 07	23 07			
Woking a	19 49	20 29	21 29	22 28				
Clapham Junction 10 a		20 52	21 52	22 48				
London Waterloo 15 ⊖ a	20 19	21 04	22 04	22 57				

A 🛒 from Salisbury

Table 160

Exeter and Salisbury - London

Sundays until 25 September

		SW	SW	SW	SW	SW	SW	SW	SW	SW	SW	SW	SW	SW	SW	SW	SW	SW	SW	SW	SW	SW	SW
		1	◇1	◇1	◇1	◇1	◇1	◇1	◇1	◇1	◇1	◇1	◇1	◇1	◇1	◇1	◇1	◇1	◇1	◇1	1	1	1
		A												B									
			🛒	🛒	🛒	🛒	🛒	🛒	🛒	🛒	🛒	🛒	🛒	🛒	🛒	🛒	🛒	🛒					
Exeter St Davids 6	d	22p57						09 26	10 26	11 26	12 26	13 26	14 26		15 26	16 26	17 26	18 26	19 26	20 26		21 26	23 15
Exeter Central	d	23p01						09 30	10 30	11 30	12 30	13 30	14 30		15 30	16 30	17 30	18 30	19 30	20 30		21 30	23 19
Pinhoe	d	23p06						09 35		11 35		13 35			15 35		17 35		19 35			21 35	
Whimple	d	23p13						09 42	10 39		12 39		14 39			16 39		18 39		20 39		21 42	
Feniton	d	23p18						09 47	10 45		12 45		14 45			16 45		18 45		20 45		21 47	
Honiton	a	23p25						09 54	10 51	11 48	12 51	13 48	14 51		15 48	16 51	17 48	18 51	19 48	20 51		21 54	23s34
	d	23p32					08 58	09 55	10 53	11 53	12 53	13 53	14 53		15 53	16 53	17 53	18 53	19 53	20 53		21 55	
Axminster	a	23p42					09 08	10 05	11 03	12 03	13 03	14 03	15 03		16 03	17 03	18 03	19 03	20 03	21 03		22 05	23s45
	d	23p43					09 09	10 09	11 09	12 09	13 09	14 09	15 09		16 09	17 09	18 09	19 09	20 09	21 09		22 09	
Crewkerne	d	23p56					09 22	10 22	11 22	12 22	13 22	14 22	15 22		16 22	17 22	18 22	19 22	20 22	21 22		22 22	00s11
Yeovil Junction	a	00 04					09 30	10 30	11 30	12 30	13 30	14 30	15 30		16 30	17 30	18 30	19 30	20 30	21 30		22 30	00s20
	d	00 16			07 32		09 32	10 32	11 32	12 32	13 32	14 32	15 32		16 32	17 32	18 32	19 32	20 32	21 32		22 32	
Sherborne	d				07 39		09 39	10 39	11 39	12 39	13 39	14 39	15 39		16 39	17 39	18 39	19 39	20 39	21 39		22 39	
Templecombe	d				07 46		09 46	10 46	11 46	12 46	13 46	14 46	15 46		16 46	17 46	18 46	19 46	20 46	21 46		22 46	
Gillingham (Dorset)	a				07 53		09 53	10 53	11 53	12 53	13 53	14 53	15 53		16 53	17 53	18 53	19 53	20 53	21 53		22 53	
	d				07 54	08 54	09 54	10 54	11 54	12 54	13 54	14 54	15 54		16 54	17 54	18 54	19 54	20 54	21 54		22 54	
Tisbury	d				08 05	09 05	10 05	11 05	12 05	13 05	14 05	15 05	16 05		17 05	18 05	19 05	20 05	21 05	22 05		23 05	
Bristol Temple Meads 10	d													16 04							21 35		
Bath Spa 7	d													16 20							21 49		
Bradford-on-Avon	d													16 31							22 00		
Trowbridge	d													16 37							22 06		
Westbury	d													16 46							22 15		
Warminster	d													16 53							22 22		
Salisbury	a	00 50			08 20	09 20	10 20	11 20	12 20	13 20	14 20	15 20	16 20	17 16	17 20	18 20	19 20	20 20	21 20	22 20	22 46	23 19	00 56
	d		06 45	07 27	08 27	09 27	10 27	11 27	12 27	13 27	14 27	15 27	16 27		17 27	18 27	19 27	20 27	21 27	22 27			
Grateley	d				08 39	09 39		11 39		13 39		15 39			17 39		19 39		21 39	22 39			
Andover	d		07 02	07 44	08 46	09 46	10 44	11 46	12 44	13 46	14 44	15 46	16 44		17 46	18 44	19 46	20 44	21 46	22 46			
Whitchurch (Hants)	d			07 52	08 54		10 52		12 52		14 52		16 52			18 52		20 52		22 54			
Overton	d			07 58	09 00		10 58		12 58		14 58		16 58			18 58		20 58		23 00			
Basingstoke	a		07 19	08 06	09 08	10 02	11 06	12 02	13 06	14 02	15 06	16 02	17 06		18 02	19 06	20 02	21 06	22 03	23 08			
Woking	a		07 39	08 28	09 28	10 28	11 28	12 28	13 28	14 28	15 28	16 28	17 28		18 28	19 28	20 28	21 28	22 28				
Clapham Junction 10	a		08 05	08 57	09 57	10 49	11 49	12 49	13 49	14 49	15 49	16 49	17 49		18 49	19 49	20 49	21 49	22 49				
London Waterloo 15 ⊖	a		08 19	09 09	10 08	11 04	12 03	13 04	13 59	14 59	15 59	16 59	17 59		18 59	19 59	20 59	21 59	22 59				

Sundays from 2 October

		SW	SW	SW	SW	SW	SW	SW	SW	SW	SW	SW	SW	SW	SW	SW	SW	SW	SW	SW	SW	SW	SW
		1	◇1	◇1	◇1	◇1	◇1	◇1	◇1	◇1	◇1	◇1	◇1	◇1	◇1	◇1	◇1	◇1	◇1	◇1	1	1	1
														B									
			🛒	🛒	🛒	🛒	🛒	🛒	🛒	🛒	🛒	🛒	🛒	🛒	🛒	🛒	🛒	🛒					
Exeter St Davids 6	d	22p57						09 26	10 26	11 26	12 26	13 26	14 26		15 26	16 26	17 26	18 26	19 26	20 26		21 26	23 15
Exeter Central	d	23p01						09 30	10 30	11 30	12 30	13 30	14 30		15 30	16 30	17 30	18 30	19 30	20 30		21 30	23 19
Pinhoe	d	23p06						09 35		11 35		13 35			15 35		17 35		19 35			21 35	
Whimple	d	23p13						09 42	10 39		12 39		14 39			16 39		18 39		20 39		21 42	
Feniton	d	23p18						09 47	10 45		12 45		14 45			16 45		18 45		20 45		21 47	
Honiton	a	23p25						09 54	10 51	11 48	12 51	13 48	14 51		15 48	16 51	17 48	18 51	19 48	20 51		21 54	23s34
	d	23p32					08 58	09 55	10 53	11 53	12 53	13 53	14 53		15 53	16 53	17 53	18 53	19 53	20 53		21 55	
Axminster	a	23p42					09 08	10 05	11 03	12 03	13 03	14 03	15 03		16 03	17 03	18 03	19 03	20 03	21 03		22 05	23s45
	d	23p43					09 09	10 09	11 09	12 09	13 09	14 09	15 09		16 09	17 09	18 09	19 09	20 09	21 09		22 09	
Crewkerne	d	23p56					09 22	10 22	11 22	12 22	13 22	14 22	15 22		16 22	17 22	18 22	19 22	20 22	21 22		22 22	00s11
Yeovil Junction	a	00 04					09 30	10 30	11 30	12 30	13 30	14 30	15 30		16 30	17 30	18 30	19 30	20 30	21 30		22 30	00s20
	d	00 16			07 32		09 32	10 32	11 32	12 32	13 32	14 32	15 32		16 32	17 32	18 32	19 32	20 32	21 32		22 32	
Sherborne	d				07 39		09 39	10 39	11 39	12 39	13 39	14 39	15 39		16 39	17 39	18 39	19 39	20 39	21 39		22 39	
Templecombe	d				07 46		09 46	10 46	11 46	12 46	13 46	14 46	15 46		16 46	17 46	18 46	19 46	20 46	21 46		22 46	
Gillingham (Dorset)	a				07 53		09 53	10 53	11 53	12 53	13 53	14 53	15 53		16 53	17 53	18 53	19 53	20 53	21 53		22 53	
	d				07 54	08 54	09 54	10 54	11 54	12 54	13 54	14 54	15 54		16 54	17 54	18 54	19 54	20 54	21 54		22 54	
Tisbury	d				08 05	09 05	10 05	11 05	12 05	13 05	14 05	15 05	16 05		17 05	18 05	19 05	20 05	21 05	22 05		23 05	
Bristol Temple Meads 10	d													16 04							21 35		
Bath Spa 7	d													16 20							21 49		
Bradford-on-Avon	d													16 31							22 00		
Trowbridge	d													16 37							22 06		
Westbury	d													16 46							22 15		
Warminster	d													16 53							22 22		
Salisbury	a	00 50			08 20	09 20	10 20	11 20	12 20	13 20	14 20	15 20	16 20	17 16	17 20	18 20	19 20	20 20	21 20	22 20	22 46	23 19	00 56
	d		06 42	07 24	08 27	09 27	10 27	11 27	12 27	13 27	14 27	15 27	16 27		17 27	18 27	19 27	20 27	21 27	22 27			
Grateley	d				08 39	09 39		11 39		13 39		15 39			17 39		19 39		21 39	22 39			
Andover	d		06 59	07 41	08 46	09 46	10 44	11 46	12 44	13 46	14 44	15 46	16 44		17 46	18 44	19 46	20 44	21 46	22 46			
Whitchurch (Hants)	d			07 49	08 54		10 52		12 52		14 52		16 52			18 52		20 52		22 54			
Overton	d			07 55	09 00		10 58		12 58		14 58		16 58			18 58		20 58		23 00			
Basingstoke	a		07 19	08 06	09 08	10 02	11 06	12 02	13 06	14 02	15 06	16 02	17 06		18 02	19 06	20 02	21 06	22 03	23 08			
Woking	a		07 39	08 28	09 28	10 28	11 28	12 28	13 28	14 28	15 28	16 28	17 28		18 28	19 28	20 28	21 28	22 28				
Clapham Junction 10	a		08 05	08 57	09 57	10 49	11 49	12 49	13 49	14 49	15 49	16 49	17 49		18 49	19 49	20 49	21 49	22 49				
London Waterloo 15 ⊖	a		08 19	09 09	10 08	11 04	12 03	13 04	13 59	14 59	15 59	16 59	17 59		18 59	19 59	20 59	21 59	22 59				

A not 22 May

B 🛒 from Salisbury

Network Diagram for Tables 165, 167

DM-20/08(2)
Design BAJS

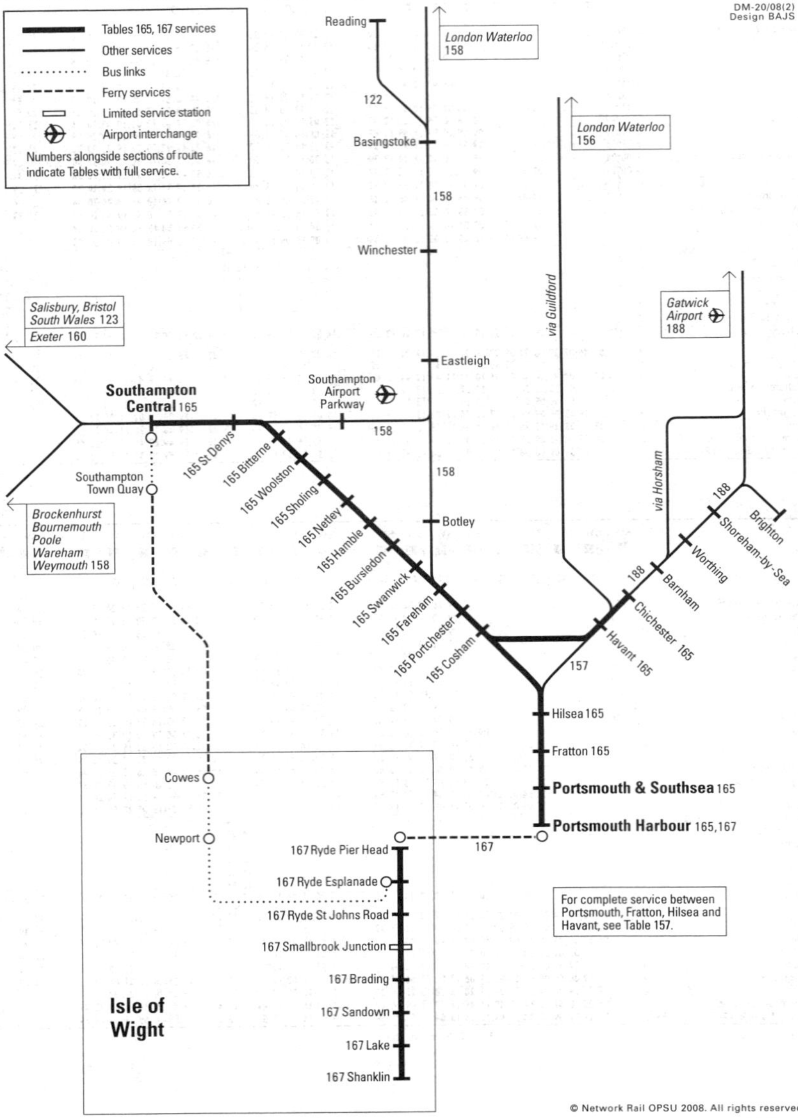

© Network Rail OPSU 2008. All rights reserved

Table 165

Mondays to Fridays

until 30 September

Southampton - Fareham and Portsmouth

Miles	Miles			SW	SW	SW	SW	SN	SW	SN	SW	SW		GW	SW	SN	SW	SW	SN	GW	SW	SN		SW	SN
				MO	MX	MX	MO																		
				1	1	1	1	◇1	1	◇1	1	1			1	◇1	1	1	◇1	◇	1	◇1		1	◇1
0	—	**Southampton Central** ⛴	d					05 48		06 10		06 21		06 53		07 06		07 17	07 33	07 42	07 51	08 10			08 33
2	—	St Denys	d									06 28						07 23			07 57	08 15			
2½	—	Bitterne	d									06 30						07 25			08 00				
4¼	—	Woolston	d					05 57		06 19		06 34				07 15		07 29			08 03				
5	—	Sholing	d									06 36						07 31			08 06				
6¾	—	Netley	d									06 40						07 35			08 10				
7½	—	Hamble	d									06 42						07 37			08 12				
8¾	—	Bursledon	d									06 45						07 40			08 15				
10¾	—	Swanwick	d					06 06		06 27		06 49				07 24		07 44	07 51		08 20	08 28			08 50
14½	—	**Fareham**	a					06 12		06 33		06 57		07 14		07 30		07 52	07 58	08 05	08 27	08 34			08 56
—	—		d	23p44	23p49			06 13	06 18	06 34	06 50	06 58		07 15	07 20	07 31	07 48	07 53	07 58	08 06	08 28	08 35		08 51	08 57
17¾	—	Portchester	d	23p49	23p54	00s53	00s53	06 18	06 23	06 40	06 55	07 03			07 25	07 36	07 53	07 58			08 33	08 40		08 56	
20¼	0	Cosham	d	23p54	23p59	00s57	00s57	06 23	06 28	06 44	07 00	07 08		07 23	07 29	07 40	07 58	08 03	08 07	08 14	08 38	08 44		09 01	09 05
—	4	Havant	a					06 37		06 53						07 46			08 13			08 50			09 11
—	12¾	Chichester 4	a					06 58		07 07						08 08			08 27			09 11			09 24
21¾	—	Hilsea	a	23p59	00 03				06 33		07 05	07 13			07 35		08 03	08 09			08 45			09 05	
24	—	Fratton	a	00 04	00 07	01s05	01s05		06 38		07 09	07 17		07 34	07 39		08 07	08 13		08 21	08 49			09 09	
25	—	**Portsmouth & Southsea**	a	00 08	00 11	01s08	01s08		06 44		07 12	07 22		07 38	07 42		08 11	08 19		08 24	08 52			09 13	
25¾	—	**Portsmouth Harbour** ⛴	a	00 13	00 16	01 12	01 12		06 49		07 17			07 45	07 48		08 16	08 24		08 30	08 57			09 18	

		SW	GW	SN	SW	SN	SW	GW		SN	SW	SN	SW	GW	SN	SW	SN	SW		GW	SN	SW	SN	SW	GW
								R																	
		1	◇ ⊥	◇1	1	◇1	1	⊥		◇1	1	◇1	1	◇ ⊥	◇1	1	◇1	1		◇ ⊥	◇1	1	◇1	1	◇ ⊥
Southampton Central ⛴	d	08 44	09 05	09 10		09 33	09 44	10 05		10 13		10 33	10 44	11 05	11 13		11 33	11 44		12 05	12 13		12 33	12 44	13 05
St Denys	d	08 49					09 49						10 49					11 49						12 49	
Bitterne	d	08 52					09 52						10 52					11 52						12 52	
Woolston	d	08 55					09 55						10 55					11 55						12 55	
Sholing	d	08 58					09 58						10 58					11 58						12 58	
Netley	d	09 02					10 02						11 02					12 02						13 02	
Hamble	d	09 04					10 04						11 04					12 04						13 04	
Bursledon	d	09 07					10 07						11 07					12 07						13 07	
Swanwick	d	09 11		09 28		09 50	10 11			10 32		10 50	11 11		11 33		11 50	12 11			12 33		12 50	13 11	
Fareham	a	09 17	09 27	09 36		09 56	10 17	10 27		10 38		10 56	11 17	11 27	11 39		11 56	12 17		12 27	12 39		12 56	13 17	13 27
	d	09 18	09 27	09 37	09 48	09 56	10 18	10 27		10 39	10 48	10 57	11 18	11 27	11 40	11 48	11 57	12 18		12 27	12 40	12 48	12 56	13 18	13 27
Portchester	d	09 23		09 42	09 53		10 23			10 44	10 53		11 23		11 45	11 53		12 23			12 45	12 53		13 23	
Cosham	d	09 28	09 35	09 46	09 58	10 05	10 28	10 35		10 48	10 58	11 05	11 28	11 35	11 49	11 58	12 05	12 28		12 35	12 49	12 58	13 05	13 28	13 35
Havant	a			09 53		10 11				10 55		11 11			11 55		12 11				12 55		13 11		
Chichester 4	a			10 10		10 23				11 10		11 24			12 10		12 24				13 10		13 23		
Hilsea	a	09 33			10 03		10 33				11 03		11 33			12 03		12 33				13 03		13 33	
Fratton	a	09 37	09 42		10 07		10 37	10 42			11 07		11 37	11 42		12 07		12 37		12 42		13 07		13 37	13 42
Portsmouth & Southsea	a	09 42	09 46		10 11		10 42	10 46			11 11		11 42	11 46		12 11		12 42		12 46		13 11		13 42	13 46
Portsmouth Harbour ⛴	a		09 55		10 18			10 54			11 18			11 54		12 18				12 54		13 18			13 54

		SN	SW	SN		SW	GW	SN	SW	GW	SN	SW	GW	SN		SW	SN	SW	GW	SN	SW	SW	SN	SW
										R														
		◇1	1	◇1		1	◇ ⊥	◇1	1	⊥	◇1	1	◇ ⊥	◇1		1	◇1	1	◇ ⊥	◇1	1	1	◇1	1
Southampton Central ⛴	d	13 13		13 33		13 44	14 05	14 13		14 34	14 26	14 44	15 05	15 13			15 33	15 44	16 05	16 12			16 33	
St Denys	d					13 49						14 49						15 49						
Bitterne	d					13 52						14 52						15 52						
Woolston	d					13 55						14 55						15 55						
Sholing	d					13 58						14 58						15 58						
Netley	d					14 02						15 02						16 02						
Hamble	d					14 04						15 04						16 04						
Bursledon	d					14 07						15 07						16 07						
Swanwick	d	13 33		13 50		14 11		14 33				15 11		15 33			15 50	16 11		16 29			16 50	
Fareham	a	13 39		13 56		14 17	14 27	14 39		14 55	14 59	15 17	15 27	15 39			15 56	16 17	16 27	16 35			16 56	
	d	13 40	13 48	13 56		14 18	14 27	14 40	14 48	14 56	15 00	15 18	15 27	15 40		15 48	15 57	16 18	16 27	16 36	16 43	16 48	16 57	17 12
Portchester	d	13 45	13 53			14 23		14 45	14 53			15 23		15 45		15 53		16 23		16 41		16 53		17 17
Cosham	d	13 49	13 58	14 05		14 28	14 35	14 49	14 58	15 04		15 28	15 35	15 49		15 58	16 05	16 28	16 35	16 45		16 58	17 05	17 22
Havant	a	13 55		14 11				14 55		15 10	15 14			15 57			16 11			16 51	16 55		17 11	
Chichester 4	a	14 10		14 23				15 10		15 21	15 25			16 12			16 24			17 08			17 25	
Hilsea	a		14 03			14 33			15 03			15 33				16 03		16 33				17 03		
Fratton	a		14 07			14 37	14 42		15 07			15 37	15 42			16 07		16 37	16 42			17 07		17 31
Portsmouth & Southsea	a		14 11			14 42	14 46		15 11			15 42	15 46			16 11		16 40	16 46			17 11		17 35
Portsmouth Harbour ⛴	a		14 18				14 54		15 18				15 54			16 18		16 44	16 54			17 18		17 40

Table 165

Southampton - Fareham and Portsmouth

Mondays to Fridays

until 30 September

		SW	GW	SN	SW	SN	SW	SW	GW	SN	SW	SN	SW	SW	GW	SN	SW	SN	SW	SW	GW	SN	SW
		[1]	◇ [trolley]	◇[1]	[1]	◇[1]	[1]	[1]	◇ [trolley]	◇[1]	[1]	◇[1]	[1]	[1]	▣ [trolley]	◇[1]	[1]	◇[1]	[1]	[1]	▣ [trolley]	◇[1]	[1]
Southampton Central ⛴	d	16 44	17 05	17 13		17 33	17 44		18 05	18 11		18 33		18 44	19 05	19 12		19 33		19 44	20 05	20 11	
St Denys	d	16 49					17 49							18 49						19 49			
Bitterne	d	16 52					17 52							18 52						19 52			
Woolston	d	16 55					17 55							18 55						19 55			
Sholing	d	16 58					17 58							18 58						19 58			
Netley	d	17 02					18 02							19 02						20 02			
Hamble	d	17 04					18 04							19 04						20 04			
Bursledon	d	17 07					18 07							19 07						20 07			
Swanwick	d	17 11		17 33		17 50	18 11			18 28		18 50		19 11		19 29		19 51		20 11		20 28	
Fareham	a	17 17	17 27	17 39		17 56	18 17		18 27	18 34		18 56		19 17	19 27	19 35		19 57		20 17	20 27	20 34	
	d	17 18	17 27	17 40	17 48	17 56	18 18	18 23	18 27	18 35	18 45	18 56	19 14	19 18	19 27	19 36	19 48	19 57	20 09	20 18	20 27	20 35	20 49
Portchester	d	17 23		17 45	17 53		18 23	18 28		18 40	18 50		19 19	19 23		19 41	19 53			20 23		20 40	20 54
Cosham	d	17 28	17 35	17 49	17 58	18 05	18 28	18 33	18 35	18 44	18 55	19 05	19 24	19 28	19 35	19 46	19 58	20 06		20 28		20 44	20 59
Havant	a			17 55		18 11				18 50		19 11				19 52		20 12	20 21			20 50	
Chichester [4]	a			18 10		18 24				19 05		19 22				20 06		20 24				21 05	
Hilsea	a	17 33			18 04		18 33				19 05		19 28	19 33			20 02			20 33			21 03
Fratton	a	17 37	17 42		18 08		18 37	18 40	18 48		19 09		19 32	19 37	19 42		20 06			20 37	20 42		21 07
Portsmouth & Southsea	a	17 42	17 46		18 12		18 41	18 43	18 52		19 12		19 36	19 42	19 46		20 11			20 42	20 46		21 11
Portsmouth Harbour ⛴	a		17 54		18 20			18 51	19 00		19 20		19 43		19 54		20 20				20 54		21 16

		SN	SW	GW	SN	SW	SN	SW	SN	GW	SN	SW	SW	GW	SW
		◇[1]	[1]	◇ [trolley]	◇[1]	[1]	◇[1]	[1]	◇[1]	◇	◇[1]	[1]	[1]	◇	[1]
Southampton Central ⛴	d	20 33	20 44	21 05	21 13		21 33	21 44	22 13	22 04	22 33		22 44	23 05	
St Denys	d		20 49					21 49					22 49		
Bitterne	d		20 52					21 52					22 52		
Woolston	d		20 55					21 55					22 55		
Sholing	d		20 58					21 58					22 58		
Netley	d		21 02					22 02					23 02		
Hamble	d		21 04					22 04					23 04		
Bursledon	d		21 07					22 07					23 07		
Swanwick	d	20 50	21 11		21 33		21 51	22 11	22 30		22 50		23 11		
Fareham	a	20 56	21 17	21 27	21 39		21 57	22 17	22 36	22 42	22 56		23 17	23 27	
	d	20 57	21 18	21 27	21 40	21 48	21 58	22 18	22 37	22 42	22 57	23 10	23 18	23 27	23 49
Portchester	d		21 23		21 45	21 53	22 03	22 23	22 42			23 15	23 23		23 54
Cosham	d	21 06	21 28		21 49	21 58	22 07	22 28	22 47		23 05	23 20	23 28		23 59
Havant	a	21 12			21 55		22 13		22 56		23 11				
Chichester [4]	a	21 24			22 06		22 34		23 11		23 22				
Hilsea	a		21 33			22 03		22 33				23 24	23 33		00 03
Fratton	a		21 37	21 41		22 08		22 37		22 56		23 32	23 37	23 44	00 07
Portsmouth & Southsea	a		21 40	21 45		22 11		22 42		22 59		23 36	23 40	23 48	00 11
Portsmouth Harbour ⛴	a		21 45	21 52		22 16				23 04		23 40		23 54	00 16

Mondays to Fridays

from 3 October

		SW MO	SW MX	SW MX	SW MO	SN	SW	SN	SW	SW	GW	SW	SN	SW	SW	SN	GW	SW	SN	SW	SN	SW	GW
		[1]	[1]	[1]	[1]	◇[1]	[1]	◇[1]	[1]	[1]		[1]	◇[1]	[1]	[1]	◇[1]	◇	[1]	◇[1]	[1]	◇[1]	[1]	◇ [trolley]
Southampton Central ⛴	d					05 48		06 10		06 21	06 53		07 06		07 17	07 33	07 42	07 51	08 10		08 33	08 44	09 05
St Denys	d									06 28					07 23			07 57	08 15			08 49	
Bitterne	d									06 30					07 25			08 00				08 52	
Woolston	d					05 57		06 19		06 34			07 15		07 29			08 03				08 55	
Sholing	d									06 36					07 31			08 06				08 58	
Netley	d									06 40					07 35			08 10				09 02	
Hamble	d									06 42					07 37			08 12				09 04	
Bursledon	d									06 45					07 40			08 15				09 07	
Swanwick	d					06 06		06 27		06 49			07 24		07 44	07 51		08 20	08 28		08 50	09 11	
Fareham	a					06 12		06 33		06 57	07 14		07 30		07 52	07 58	08 05	08 27	08 34		08 56	09 17	09 27
	d	23p44	23p49			06 13	06 18	06 34	06 50	06 58	07 15	07 20	07 31	07 48	07 53	07 58	08 06	08 28	08 35	08 51	08 57	09 18	09 27
Portchester	d	23p49	23p54	00s53	00s53	06 18	06 23	06 40	06 55	07 03		07 25	07 36	07 53	07 58			08 33	08 40	08 56		09 23	
Cosham	d	23p54	23p59	00s57	00s57	06 23	06 28	06 44	07 00	07 08	07 23	07 29	07 40	07 58	08 03	08 07	08 14	08 38	08 44	09 01	09 05	09 28	09 35
Havant	a					06 37		06 53					07 46			08 13			08 50		09 11		
Chichester [4]	a					06 58		07 07					08 08			08 27			09 11		09 24		
Hilsea	a	23p59	00 03				06 33		07 05	07 13		07 35		08 03	08 09			08 45		09 05		09 33	
Fratton	a	00 04	00 07	01s05	01s05		06 38		07 09	07 17	07 34	07 39		08 07	08 13		08 21	08 49		09 09		09 37	09 42
Portsmouth & Southsea	a	00 08	00 11	01s08	01s08		06 44		07 12	07 22	07 38	07 42		08 11	08 19		08 24	08 52		09 13		09 42	09 46
Portsmouth Harbour ⛴	a	00 13	00 16	01 12	01 12		06 49		07 17		07 45	07 48		08 16	08 24		08 30	08 57		09 18			09 55

Table 165

Southampton - Fareham and Portsmouth

Mondays to Fridays

from 3 October

		SN	SW	SN	SW	GW		SN	SW	SN	SW	GW	SN	SW	SN	SW		GW	SN	SW	SN	SW	GW	SN	SW
		◇1	1	◇1	1	R ⊼		◇1	1	◇1	1	◇ ⊼	◇1	1	◇1	1		◇ ⊼	◇1	1	◇1	1	◇ ⊼	◇1	1
Southampton Central ⛴	d	09 10		09 33	09 44	10 05		10 13		10 33	10 44	11 05	11 13		11 33	11 44		12 05	12 13		12 33	12 44	13 05	13 13	
St Denys	d				09 49						10 49					11 49						12 49			
Bitterne	d				09 52						10 52					11 52						12 52			
Woolston	d				09 55						10 55					11 55						12 55			
Sholing	d				09 58						10 58					11 58						12 58			
Netley	d				10 02						11 02					12 02						13 02			
Hamble	d				10 04						11 04					12 04						13 04			
Bursledon	d				10 07						11 07					12 07						13 07			
Swanwick	d	09 28		09 50	10 11			10 32		10 50	11 11		11 33		11 50	12 11			12 33		12 50	13 11		13 33	
Fareham	a	09 36		09 56	10 17	10 27		10 38		10 56	11 17	11 27	11 39		11 56	12 17		12 27	12 39		12 56	13 17	13 27	13 39	
	d	09 37	09 48	09 56	10 18	10 27		10 39	10 48	10 57	11 18	11 27	11 40	11 48	11 57	12 18		12 27	12 40	12 48	12 56	13 18	13 27	13 40	13 48
Portchester	d	09 42	09 53		10 23			10 44	10 53		11 23		11 45	11 53		12 23			12 45	12 53		13 23		13 45	13 53
Cosham	d	09 46	09 58	10 05	10 28	10 35		10 48	10 58	11 05	11 28	11 35	11 49	11 58	12 05	12 28		12 35	12 49	12 58	13 05	13 28	13 35	13 49	13 58
Havant	a	09 53		10 11				10 55		11 11			11 55		12 11				12 55		13 11			13 55	
Chichester 4	a	10 10		10 23				11 10		11 24			12 10		12 24				13 10		13 23			14 10	
Hilsea	a		10 03		10 33				11 03		11 33			12 03		12 33				13 03		13 33			14 03
Fratton	a		10 07		10 37	10 42			11 07		11 37	11 42		12 07		12 37		12 42		13 07		13 37	13 42		14 07
Portsmouth & Southsea	a		10 11		10 42	10 46			11 11		11 42	11 46		12 11		12 42		12 46		13 11		13 42	13 46		14 11
Portsmouth Harbour ⛴	a		10 18			10 54			11 18			11 54		12 18				12 54		13 18			13 54		14 18

		SN		SW	GW	SN	SW	GW	SN	SW	GW	SN		SW	SN	SW	GW	SN	SW	SW	SN	SW		SW	GW
		◇1		1	◇ ⊼	◇1	1	R ⊼	◇1	1	◇ ⊼	◇1		1	◇1	1	◇ ⊼	◇1	1	1	◇1	1		1	◇ ⊼
Southampton Central ⛴	d	13 33		13 44	14 05	14 13		14 34	14 26	14 44	15 05	15 13			15 33	15 44	16 05	16 12			16 33			16 44	17 05
St Denys	d			13 49						14 49						15 49								16 49	
Bitterne	d			13 52						14 52						15 52								16 52	
Woolston	d			13 55						14 55						15 55								16 55	
Sholing	d			13 58						14 58						15 58								16 58	
Netley	d			14 02						15 02						16 02								17 02	
Hamble	d			14 04						15 04						16 04								17 04	
Bursledon	d			14 07						15 07						16 07								17 07	
Swanwick	d	13 50		14 11		14 33				15 11		15 33			15 50	16 11		16 29			16 50			17 11	
Fareham	a	13 56		14 17	14 27	14 39		14 55	14 59	15 17	15 27	15 39			15 56	16 17	16 27	16 35			16 56			17 17	17 27
	d	13 56		14 18	14 27	14 40	14 48	14 56	15 00	15 18	15 27	15 40		15 48	15 57	16 18	16 27	16 36	16 43	16 48	16 57	17 12		17 18	17 27
Portchester	d			14 23		14 45	14 53			15 23		15 45		15 53		16 23		16 41		16 53		17 17		17 23	
Cosham	d	14 05		14 28	14 35	14 49	14 58	15 04		15 28	15 35	15 49		15 58	16 05	16 28	16 35	16 45		16 58	17 05	17 22		17 28	17 35
Havant	a	14 11				14 55		15 10	15 14			15 57			16 11			16 51	16 55		17 11				
Chichester 4	a	14 23				15 10		15 21	15 25			16 12			16 24			17 08			17 25				
Hilsea	a			14 33			15 03			15 33				16 03		16 33				17 03				17 33	
Fratton	a			14 37	14 42		15 07			15 37	15 42			16 07		16 37	16 42			17 07		17 31		17 37	17 42
Portsmouth & Southsea	a			14 42	14 46		15 11			15 42	15 46			16 11		16 40	16 46			17 11		17 35		17 42	17 46
Portsmouth Harbour ⛴	a				14 54		15 18				15 54			16 18		16 44	16 54			17 18		17 40			17 54

		SN	SW	SN	SW	SW	GW	SN		SW	SN	SW	SW	GW	SN	SW	SN	SW		SW	GW	SN	SW	SN	SW
		◇1	1	◇1	1	1	◇ ⊼	◇1		1	◇1	1	1	R ⊼	◇1	1	◇1	1		1	R ⊼	◇1	1	◇1	1
Southampton Central ⛴	d	17 13		17 33	17 44		18 05	18 11			18 33		18 44	19 05	19 12		19 33			19 44	20 05	20 11		20 33	20 44
St Denys	d				17 49								18 49							19 49					20 49
Bitterne	d				17 52								18 52							19 52					20 52
Woolston	d				17 55								18 55							19 55					20 55
Sholing	d				17 58								18 58							19 58					20 58
Netley	d				18 02								19 02							20 02					21 02
Hamble	d				18 04								19 04							20 04					21 04
Bursledon	d				18 07								19 07							20 07					21 07
Swanwick	d	17 33		17 50	18 11			18 28			18 50		19 11		19 29		19 51			20 11		20 28		20 50	21 11
Fareham	a	17 39		17 56	18 17		18 27	18 34			18 56		19 17	19 27	19 35		19 57			20 17	20 27	20 34		20 56	21 17
	d	17 40	17 48	17 56	18 18	18 23	18 27	18 35		18 45	18 56	19 14	19 18	19 27	19 36	19 48	19 57	20 09		20 18	20 27	20 35	20 49	20 57	21 18
Portchester	d	17 45	17 53		18 23	18 28		18 40		18 50		19 19	19 23		19 41	19 53				20 23		20 40	20 54		21 23
Cosham	d	17 49	17 58	18 05	18 28	18 33	18 35	18 44		18 55	19 05	19 24	19 28	19 35	19 46	19 58	20 06			20 28		20 44	20 59	21 06	21 28
Havant	a	17 55		18 11				18 50			19 11				19 52		20 12	20 21				20 50		21 12	
Chichester 4	a	18 10		18 24				19 05			19 22				20 06		20 24					21 05		21 24	
Hilsea	a		18 04		18 33					19 05		19 28	19 33			20 02				20 33			21 03		21 33
Fratton	a		18 08		18 37	18 40	18 48			19 09		19 32	19 37	19 42		20 06				20 37	20 42		21 07		21 37
Portsmouth & Southsea	a		18 12		18 41	18 43	18 52			19 12		19 36	19 42	19 46		20 11				20 42	20 46		21 11		21 40
Portsmouth Harbour ⛴	a		18 20			18 51	19 00			19 20		19 43		19 54		20 20					20 54		21 16		21 45

Table 165

Mondays to Fridays

from 3 October

Southampton - Fareham and Portsmouth

		GW ◇ ⊼	SN ◇1	SW 1		SN ◇1	SW 1	SN ◇1	GW ◇	SN ◇1	SW 1	SW 1	GW ◇	SW 1
Southampton Central ⛴	d	21 05	21 13			21 33	21 44	22 13	22 04	22 33		22 44	23 05	
St Denys	d						21 49					22 49		
Bitterne	d						21 52					22 52		
Woolston	d						21 55					22 55		
Sholing	d						21 58					22 58		
Netley	d						22 02					23 02		
Hamble	d						22 04					23 04		
Bursledon	d						22 07					23 07		
Swanwick	d		21 33			21 51	22 11	22 30		22 50		23 11		
Fareham	a	21 27	21 39			21 57	22 17	22 36	22 42	22 56		23 17	23 27	
	d	21 27	21 40	21 48		21 58	22 18	22 37	22 42	22 57	23 10	23 18	23 27	23 49
Portchester	d		21 45	21 53		22 03	22 23	22 42			23 15	23 23		23 54
Cosham	d		21 49	21 58		22 07	22 28	22 47		23 05	23 20	23 28		23 59
Havant	a		21 55			22 13		22 56		23 11				
Chichester 4	a		22 06			22 34		23 11		23 22				
Hilsea	a			22 03			22 33				23 24	23 33		00 03
Fratton	a	21 41		22 08			22 37		22 56		23 32	23 37	23 44	00 07
Portsmouth & Southsea	a	21 45		22 11			22 42		22 59		23 36	23 40	23 48	00 11
Portsmouth Harbour ⛴	a	21 52		22 16					23 04		23 40		23 54	00 16

Saturdays

		SW 1	SW 1	SW 1	SN ◇1	SW 1	SN ◇1	SW 1	GW	SN ◇1		SW 1	SN ◇1	SW 1	GW ◇	SN ◇1	SW 1	SN ◇1	SW 1	GW ◇		SN ◇1	SW 1	SN ◇1	SW 1
Southampton Central ⛴	d			05 44	06 13		06 33	06 44	07 05	07 13			07 33	07 44	08 05	08 13		08 33	08 44	09 04		09 13		09 33	09 44
St Denys	d			05 49				06 49						07 49					08 49						09 49
Bitterne	d			05 52				06 52						07 52					08 52						09 52
Woolston	d			05 55				06 55						07 55					08 55						09 55
Sholing	d			05 58				06 58						07 58					08 58						09 58
Netley	d			06 02				07 02						08 02					09 02						10 02
Hamble	d			06 04				07 04						08 04					09 04						10 04
Bursledon	d			06 07				07 07						08 07					09 07						10 07
Swanwick	d			06 11	06 33		06 50	07 11		07 33			07 50	08 11		08 33		08 50	09 11			09 33		09 50	10 11
Fareham	a			06 17	06 39		06 56	07 17	07 27	07 39			07 56	08 17	08 27	08 39		08 56	09 17	09 27		09 39		09 56	10 17
	d	23p49		06 18	06 40	06 48	06 56	07 18	07 27	07 40		07 49	07 56	08 18	08 27	08 40	08 49	08 56	09 18	09 27		09 40	09 48	09 56	10 18
Portchester	d	23p54	00s53	06 23	06 45	06 53		07 23		07 45		07 54		08 23		08 45	08 54		09 23			09 45	09 53		10 23
Cosham	d	23p59	00s57	06 28	06 49	06 58	07 05	07 28	07 35	07 49		07 59	08 05	08 28	08 35	08 49	08 59	09 05	09 28	09 35		09 49	09 58	10 05	10 28
Havant	a				06 55		07 11			07 55			08 11			08 55		09 11				09 55		10 11	
Chichester 4	a				07 10		07 23			08 10			08 23			09 10		09 23				10 10		10 23	
Hilsea	a	00 03		06 33		07 03		07 33				08 03		08 33			09 04		09 33				10 03		10 33
Fratton	a	00 07	01s05	06 37		07 07		07 37	07 42			08 07		08 37	08 42		09 08		09 37	09 42			10 07		10 37
Portsmouth & Southsea	a	00 11	01s08	06 42		07 11		07 42	07 46			08 11		08 42	08 46		09 12		09 42	09 46			10 11		10 42
Portsmouth Harbour ⛴	a	00 16	01 12			07 16			07 52			08 18			08 52		09 18			09 52			10 18		

		GW ◇	SN ◇1	SW 1	SN ◇1	SW 1		GW ◇	SN ◇1	SW 1	SN ◇1	SW 1	GW ◇ ⊼	SN ◇1	SW 1	SN ◇1		SW 1	GW ◇ ⊼	SN ◇1	SW 1	SN ◇1	SW 1	GW ◇ ⊼	SN ◇1
Southampton Central ⛴	d	10 04	10 13		10 33	10 44		11 04	11 13		11 33	11 44	12 05	12 13		12 33		12 44	13 04	13 13		13 33	13 44	14 05	14 13
St Denys	d					10 49						11 49						12 49					13 49		
Bitterne	d					10 52						11 52						12 52					13 52		
Woolston	d					10 55						11 55						12 55					13 55		
Sholing	d					10 58						11 58						12 58					13 58		
Netley	d					11 02						12 02						13 02					14 02		
Hamble	d					11 04						12 04						13 04					14 04		
Bursledon	d					11 07						12 07						13 07					14 07		
Swanwick	d		10 33		10 50	11 11			11 33		11 50	12 11		12 33		12 50		13 11		13 33		13 50	14 11		14 33
Fareham	a	10 27	10 39		10 56	11 17		11 27	11 39		11 56	12 17	12 27	12 39		12 56		13 17	13 27	13 39		13 56	14 17	14 27	14 39
	d	10 27	10 40	10 48	10 56	11 18		11 27	11 40	11 48	11 56	12 18	12 27	12 40	12 48	12 56		13 18	13 27	13 40	13 48	13 56	14 18	14 27	14 40
Portchester	d		10 45	10 53		11 23			11 45	11 53		12 23		12 45	12 53			13 23		13 45	13 53		14 23		14 45
Cosham	d	10 35	10 49	10 58	11 05	11 28		11 35	11 49	11 58	12 05	12 28	12 35	12 49	12 58	13 05		13 28	13 35	13 49	13 58	14 05	14 28	14 35	14 49
Havant	a		10 55		11 11				11 55		12 11			12 55		13 11				13 55		14 11			14 55
Chichester 4	a		11 10		11 23				12 10		12 23			13 10		13 23				14 10		14 23			15 10
Hilsea	a			11 03		11 33				12 03		12 33			13 03			13 33			14 03		14 33		
Fratton	a	10 42		11 07		11 37		11 42		12 07		12 37	12 42		13 07			13 37	13 42		14 07		14 37	14 42	
Portsmouth & Southsea	a	10 46		11 11		11 42		11 46		12 11		12 42	12 46		13 11			13 42	13 46		14 11		14 42	14 46	
Portsmouth Harbour ⛴	a	10 52		11 18				11 52		12 18			12 51		13 18				13 51		14 18			14 51	

		SW 1		GW ◇	SN ◇1	SW 1	GW ◇	SN ◇1	SW 1	SN ◇1	SW 1	GW ◇		SN ◇1	SW 1	SN ◇1	SW 1	GW ◇	SN ◇1	SW 1	SN ◇1	SW 1		GW ◇	SN ◇1
Southampton Central ⛴	d			14 34	14 26	14 44	15 04	15 13		15 33	15 44	16 05		16 13		16 33	16 44	17 06	17 13		17 33	17 44		18 05	18 11
St Denys	d					14 49					15 49						16 49					17 49			
Bitterne	d					14 52					15 52						16 52					17 52			
Woolston	d					14 55					15 55						16 55					17 55			
Sholing	d					14 58					15 58						16 58					17 58			
Netley	d					15 02					16 02						17 02					18 02			
Hamble	d					15 04					16 04						17 04					18 04			
Bursledon	d					15 07					16 07						17 07					18 07			
Swanwick	d					15 11		15 33		15 50	16 11			16 33		16 50	17 11		17 33		17 50	18 11			18 28
Fareham	a			14 54	14 59	15 17	15 27	15 39		15 56	16 17	16 27		16 39		16 56	17 17	17 29	17 39		17 56	18 17		18 27	18 34
	d	14 48		14 55	15 00	15 18	15 27	15 40	15 48	15 56	16 18	16 27		16 40	16 48	16 56	17 18	17 29	17 40	17 48	17 56	18 18		18 27	18 35
Portchester	d	14 53				15 23		15 45	15 53		16 23			16 45	16 53		17 23		17 45	17 53		18 23			18 40
Cosham	d	14 58		15 03		15 28	15 35	15 49	15 58	16 05	16 28	16 35		16 49	16 58	17 05	17 28	17 37	17 49	17 58	18 05	18 28		18 35	18 44
Havant	a			15 10	15 14			15 55		16 11				16 55		17 11			17 55		18 11				18 50
Chichester 4	a			15 21	15 25			16 10		16 23				17 10		17 23			18 10		18 23				19 05
Hilsea	a	15 03				15 33			16 03		16 33				17 03		17 33			18 03		18 33			
Fratton	a	15 07				15 37	15 42		16 07		16 37	16 42			17 07		17 37	17 44		18 07		18 37		18 42	
Portsmouth & Southsea	a	15 11				15 42	15 46		16 11		16 40	16 46			17 11		17 42	17 48		18 11		18 42		18 46	
Portsmouth Harbour ⛴	a	15 18					15 51		16 18		16 44	16 51			17 16			17 53		18 18				18 52	

Table 165

Saturdays

Southampton - Fareham and Portsmouth

		SW	SN	SW	GW	SN	SW	SN		SW	GW	SN	SW	SN	SW	GW	SN	SW		SN	SW	GW	SN	SW	SN
		■1	◇■1	■1	■	◇■1	■1	◇■1		■1	◇	◇■1	■1	◇■1	■1	◇	◇■1	■1		◇■1	■1	◇	◇■1	■1	◇■1
Southampton Central ⛴	d		18 33	18 44	19 05	19 09		19 33		19 44	20 04	20 11		20 33	20 44	21 04	21 13			21 33	21 44	22 05	22 13		22 33
St Denys	d			18 49						19 49					20 49						21 49				
Bitterne	d			18 52						19 52					20 52						21 52				
Woolston	d			18 55						19 55					20 55						21 55				
Sholing	d			18 58						19 58					20 58						21 58				
Netley	d			19 02						20 02					21 02						22 02				
Hamble	d			19 04						20 04					21 04						22 04				
Bursledon	d			19 07						20 07					21 07						22 07				
Swanwick	d		18 50	19 11		19 28		19 50		20 11		20 28		20 50	21 11		21 33			21 50	22 11		22 31		22 50
Fareham	a		18 56	19 17	19 27	19 34		19 56		20 17	20 27	20 34		20 56	21 17	21 27	21 39			21 56	22 17	22 26	22 38		22 56
	d	18 48	18 56	19 18	19 27	19 35	19 48	19 56		20 18	20 27	20 35	20 48	20 56	21 18	21 27	21 40	21 48		21 57	22 18	22 27	22 39	22 48	23 00
Portchester	d	18 53		19 23		19 40	19 53			20 23		20 40	20 53		21 23		21 45	21 53		22 02	22 23		22 44	22 53	
Cosham	d	18 58	19 05	19 28	19 35	19 44	19 58	20 05		20 28		20 44	20 58	21 05	21 28		21 49	21 58		22 06	22 28		22 48	22 58	23 08
Havant	a		19 11			19 51		20 11				20 50		21 11			21 55			22 12			22 54		23 14
Chichester ■4	a		19 23			20 06		20 23				21 05		21 23			22 06			22 33			23 09		23 25
Hilsea	a	19 03		19 33			20 03			20 37			21 03		21 33			22 03			22 33			23 03	
Fratton	a	19 07		19 37	19 42		20 07			20 41	20 42		21 07		21 37	21 42		22 07			22 37	22 42		23 07	
Portsmouth & Southsea	a	19 11		19 42	19 46		20 11			20 44	20 46		21 11		21 40	21 46		22 11			22 40	22 46		23 11	
Portsmouth Harbour ⛴	a	19 18			19 52		20 18				20 52		21 18		21 45	21 52		22 18			22 47	22 52		23 18	

		SW	GW	SW
		■1	◇	■1
Southampton Central ⛴	d	22 44	23 05	
St Denys	d	22 49		
Bitterne	d	22 52		
Woolston	d	22 55		
Sholing	d	22 58		
Netley	d	23 02		
Hamble	d	23 04		
Bursledon	d	23 07		
Swanwick	d	23 11		
Fareham	a	23 17	23 26	
	d	23 18	23 27	23 48
Portchester	d	23 23		23 53
Cosham	d	23 28		23 58
Havant	a			
Chichester ■4	a			
Hilsea	a	23 33		00 03
Fratton	a	23 37	23 40	00 07
Portsmouth & Southsea	a	23 40	23 44	00 11
Portsmouth Harbour ⛴	a		23 52	00 16

Sundays

until 11 September

		SW	SW	SW	SW	SN	SW	SW	GW	SN		SW	SW	SN	SW	SW	SN	SW	GW	SW		SN	SW	GW	SW
		■1	■1	■1	■1	◇■1	■1	■1		◇■1		■1	■1	◇■1	■1	■1	◇■1	■1	◇	■1		◇■1	■1	◇	■1
		A																							
Southampton Central ⛴	d			06 35		07 29	07 35		08 31	08 27		08 35		09 29	09 35		10 29	10 35	11 04			11 28	11 35	12 04	
St Denys	d			06 41			07 41					08 41			09 41			10 41					11 41		
Bitterne	d			06 43			07 43					08 43			09 43			10 43					11 43		
Woolston	d			06 47			07 47					08 47			09 47			10 47					11 47		
Sholing	d			06 49			07 49					08 49			09 49			10 49					11 49		
Netley	d			06 53			07 53					08 53			09 53			10 53					11 53		
Hamble	d			06 55			07 55					08 55			09 55			10 55					11 55		
Bursledon	d			06 58			07 58					08 58			09 58			10 58					11 58		
Swanwick	d			07 02		07 46	08 02					09 02		09 46	10 02		10 46	11 02				11 46	12 02		
Fareham	a			07 09		07 52	08 09		08 51	09 02		09 09		09 52	10 09		10 52	11 09	11 26			11 52	12 09	12 26	
	d	23p48		07 10	07 44	07 53	08 10	08 44	08 52	09 02		09 10	09 44	09 53	10 10	10 44	10 53	11 10	11 26	11 44		11 53	12 10	12 26	12 44
Portchester	d	23p53	00s53	07 15	07 49		08 15	08 49				09 15	09 49		10 15	10 49		11 15		11 49			12 15		12 49
Cosham	d	23p58	00s57	07 20	07 54	08 02	08 20	08 54	09 00	09 11		09 20	09 54	10 02	10 20	10 54	11 02	11 20	11 34	11 54		12 02	12 20	12 34	12 54
Havant	a					08 10			09 11	09 17				10 10			11 10					12 10			
Chichester ■4	a					08 23			09 22	09 29				10 23			11 23					12 23			
Hilsea	a	00 03		07 26	08 00		08 26	09 00				09 26	10 04		10 26	11 04		11 26		12 00			12 26		13 00
Fratton	a	00 07	01s05	07 30	08 04		08 30	09 04				09 30	10 08		10 30	11 08		11 30	11 41	12 04			12 30	12 41	13 04
Portsmouth & Southsea	a	00 11	01s08	07 33	08 08		08 33	09 08				09 33	10 11		10 33	11 11		11 33	11 45	12 08			12 33	12 45	13 08
Portsmouth Harbour ⛴	a	00 16	01 12		08 13			09 13					10 15			11 15			11 52	12 13				12 52	13 13

A not 22 May

Table 165

Sundays
until 11 September

Southampton - Fareham and Portsmouth

		SN ◇1	SW 1	GW ◇	SW 1	SN ◇1		SW 1	GW ◇	SW 1	SN ◇1	SW 1	SW 1	GW ◇	SN ◇1	SW 1		GW ◇	SW 1	SN ◇1	SW 1	GW ◇	SW 1	SN ◇1	SW 1
Southampton Central	d	12 29	12 35	13 08		13 29		13 35	14 04		14 29	14 35		15 22	15 29	15 35		16 04		16 29	16 35	17 04		17 29	17 35
St Denys	d		12 41					13 41				14 41				15 41					16 41				17 41
Bitterne	d		12 43					13 43				14 43				15 43					16 43				17 43
Woolston	d		12 47					13 47				14 47				15 47					16 47				17 47
Sholing	d		12 49					13 49				14 49				15 49					16 49				17 49
Netley	d		12 53					13 53				14 53				15 53					16 53				17 53
Hamble	d		12 55					13 55				14 55				15 55					16 55				17 55
Bursledon	d		12 58					13 58				14 58				15 58					16 58				17 58
Swanwick	d	12 46	13 02			13 46		14 02			14 46	15 02			15 46	16 02				16 46	17 02			17 46	18 02
Fareham	a	12 52	13 09	13 33		13 52		14 09	14 26		14 52	15 09		15 50	15 57	16 09		16 26		16 52	17 09	17 26		17 52	18 09
	d	12 53	13 10	13 34	13 44	13 53		14 10	14 26	14 44	14 53	15 10	15 44	15 51	15 58	16 10		16 26	16 44	16 53	17 10	17 26	17 44	17 53	18 10
Portchester	d		13 15		13 49			14 15		14 49		15 15	15 49			16 15			16 49		17 15		17 49		18 15
Cosham	d	13 02	13 20	13 42	13 54	14 02		14 20	14 34	14 54	15 02	15 20	15 54	16 01	16 07	16 20		16 34	16 54	17 02	17 20	17 34	17 54	18 02	18 20
Havant	a	13 10		14 03		14 10					15 10			16 11	16 15					17 10				18 10	
Chichester 4	a	13 23		14 19		14 23					15 23			16 22	16 28					17 23				18 23	
Hilsea	a		13 26		14 00			14 26		15 00		15 26	16 00			16 26			17 00		17 26		18 00		18 26
Fratton	a		13 30		14 04			14 30	14 41	15 04		15 30	16 04			16 30		16 41	17 03		17 30	17 41	18 04		18 30
Portsmouth & Southsea	a		13 33		14 08			14 33	14 45	15 08		15 33	16 08			16 33		16 45	17 08		17 33	17 45	18 08		18 33
Portsmouth Harbour	a				14 13				14 55	15 13			16 13					16 52	17 13			17 52	18 13		

		GW ◇		SW 1	SN ◇1	SW 1	GW ◇	SW 1	GW ◇	SN ◇1	SW 1	GW ◇		SW 1	GW	SN ◇1	SW 1	GW ◇	SW 1	SN ◇1	SW 1	GW ◇		SN ◇1	SW 1
Southampton Central	d	18 04			18 29	18 35	19 04		19 27	19 30	19 35	20 04			20 31	20 29	20 35	21 01		21 30	21 35	22 04		22 15	
St Denys	d					18 41					19 41						20 41				21 41				
Bitterne	d					18 43					19 43						20 43				21 43				
Woolston	d					18 47					19 47						20 47				21 47				
Sholing	d					18 49					19 49						20 49				21 49				
Netley	d					18 53					19 53						20 53				21 53				
Hamble	d					18 55					19 55						20 55				21 55				
Bursledon	d					18 58					19 58						20 58				21 58				
Swanwick	d				18 46	19 02					20 02						21 02			21 47	22 02			22 32	
Fareham	a	18 26			18 52	19 09	19 26		19 49	20 02	20 09	20 25			20 54	21 02	21 10	21 23		21 53	22 09	22 26		22 38	
	d	18 26		18 44	18 53	19 10	19 26	19 44	19 50	20 03	20 10	20 26		20 44	20 55	21 02	21 10	21 24	21 44	21 54	22 10	22 26		22 39	22 44
Portchester	d			18 49		19 15		19 49			20 15			20 49			21 15		21 49		22 15				22 49
Cosham	d	18 34		18 54	19 02	19 20	19 34	19 54	19 59	20 12	20 20			20 54		21 11	21 20		21 54	22 03	22 20			22 48	22 54
Havant	a				19 10				20 10	20 18						21 17				22 10				22 54	
Chichester 4	a				19 23				20 21	20 30						21 29				22 23				23 06	
Hilsea	a			19 00		19 26		20 00			20 26			21 00			21 26		22 00		22 26				23 00
Fratton	a	18 41		19 03		19 30	19 41	20 04			20 30	20 41		21 04	21 09		21 30	21 37	22 04		22 30	22 40			23 04
Portsmouth & Southsea	a	18 45		19 08		19 33	19 45	20 08			20 33	20 45		21 08	21 15		21 33	21 41	22 08		22 33	22 43			23 08
Portsmouth Harbour	a	18 52		19 13			19 52	20 13				20 52		21 13	21 26			21 48	22 13			22 49			23 13

		SW 1	SN ◇1	GW ◇	SW 1
Southampton Central	d	22 35	22 52	23 07	
St Denys	d	22 41			
Bitterne	d	22 43			
Woolston	d	22 47			
Sholing	d	22 49			
Netley	d	22 53			
Hamble	d	22 55			
Bursledon	d	22 58			
Swanwick	d	23 02	23 11		
Fareham	a	23 09	23 17	23 28	
	d	23 10	23 17	23 29	23 44
Portchester	d	23 15			23 49
Cosham	d	23 20	23 26		23 54
Havant	a		23 32		
Chichester 4	a		23 44		
Hilsea	a	23 24			23 59
Fratton	a	23 28		23 42	00 04
Portsmouth & Southsea	a	23 32		23 46	00 08
Portsmouth Harbour	a			23 52	00 13

Sundays
18 September to 23 October

		SW 1	SW 1	SW 1	SW 1	SN ◇1	SW 1	SW 1	GW	SN ◇1		SW 1	SW 1	SN ◇1	SW 1	SW 1	SN ◇1	SW 1	GW ◇	SW 1		SN ◇1	SW 1	GW ◇	SW 1
Southampton Central	d			06 35		07 29	07 35		08 31	08 27		08 35		09 29	09 35		10 29	10 35	11 04			11 28	11 35	12 04	
St Denys	d			06 41			07 41					08 41			09 41			10 41					11 41		
Bitterne	d			06 43			07 43					08 43			09 43			10 43					11 43		
Woolston	d			06 47			07 47					08 47			09 47			10 47					11 47		
Sholing	d			06 49			07 49					08 49			09 49			10 49					11 49		
Netley	d			06 53			07 53					08 53			09 53			10 53					11 53		
Hamble	d			06 55			07 55					08 55			09 55			10 55					11 55		
Bursledon	d			06 58			07 58					08 58			09 58			10 58					11 58		
Swanwick	d			07 02		07 46	08 02					09 02		09 46	10 02		10 46	11 02				11 46	12 02		
Fareham	a			07 09		07 52	08 09		08 51	09 02		09 09		09 52	10 09		10 52	11 09	11 26			11 52	12 09	12 26	
	d	23p48		07 10	07 44	07 53	08 10	08 44	08 52	09 02		09 10	09 44	09 53	10 10	10 44	10 53	11 10	11 26	11 44		11 53	12 10	12 26	12 44
Portchester	d	23p53	00s53	07 15	07 49		08 15	08 49				09 15	09 49		10 15	10 49		11 15		11 49			12 15		12 49
Cosham	d	23p58	00s57	07 20	07 54	08 02	08 20	08 54	09 00	09 11		09 20	09 54	10 02	10 20	10 54	11 02	11 20	11 34	11 54		12 02	12 20	12 34	12 54
Havant	a					08 10			09 11	09 17				10 10			11 10					12 10			
Chichester 4	a					08 23			09 22	09 29				10 23			11 23					12 23			
Hilsea	a	00 03		07 26	08 00		08 26	09 00				09 26	10 04		10 26	11 04		11 26		12 00			12 26		13 00
Fratton	a	00 07	01s05	07 30	08 04		08 30	09 04				09 30	10 08		10 30	11 08		11 30	11 41	12 04			12 30	12 41	13 04
Portsmouth & Southsea	a	00 11	01s08	07 33	08 08		08 33	09 08				09 33	10 11		10 33	11 11		11 33	11 45	12 08			12 33	12 45	13 08
Portsmouth Harbour	a	00 16	01 12		08 13			09 13					10 15			11 15			11 52	12 13				12 52	13 13

Table 165

Sundays

18 September to 23 October

Southampton - Fareham and Portsmouth

		SN	SW	GW	SW	SN		SW	GW	SW	SN	SW	SW	GW	SN	SW		GW	SW	SN	SW	GW	SW	SN	SW
		◇1	1	◇	1	◇1		1	◇	1	◇1	1	1	◇	◇1	1		◇	1	◇1	1	◇	1	◇1	1
Southampton Central	d	12 29	12 35	13 08		13 29		13 35	14 04		14 29	14 35		15 22	15 29	15 35		16 04		16 29	16 35	17 04		17 29	17 35
St Denys	d		12 41					13 41				14 41				15 41					16 41				17 41
Bitterne	d		12 43					13 43				14 43				15 43					16 43				17 43
Woolston	d		12 47					13 47				14 47				15 47					16 47				17 47
Sholing	d		12 49					13 49				14 49				15 49					16 49				17 49
Netley	d		12 53					13 53				14 53				15 53					16 53				17 53
Hamble	d		12 55					13 55				14 55				15 55					16 55				17 55
Bursledon	d		12 58					13 58				14 58				15 58					16 58				17 58
Swanwick	d	12 46	13 02			13 46		14 02			14 46	15 02			15 46	16 02				16 46	17 02			17 46	18 02
Fareham	a	12 52	13 09	13 33		13 52		14 09	14 26		14 52	15 09		15 50	15 57	16 09		16 26		16 52	17 09	17 26		17 52	18 09
	d	12 53	13 10	13 34	13 44	13 53		14 10	14 26	14 44	14 53	15 10	15 44	15 51	15 58	16 10		16 26	16 44	16 53	17 10	17 26	17 44	17 53	18 10
Portchester	d		13 15		13 49			14 15		14 49		15 15	15 49			16 15			16 49		17 15		17 49		18 15
Cosham	d	13 02	13 20	13 42	13 54	14 02		14 20	14 34	14 54	15 02	15 20	15 54	16 01	16 07	16 20		16 34	16 54	17 02	17 20	17 34	17 54	18 02	18 20
Havant	a	13 10		14 03		14 10					15 10			16 11	16 15					17 10				18 10	
Chichester 4	a	13 23		14 19		14 23					15 23			16 22	16 28					17 23				18 23	
Hilsea	a		13 26		14 00			14 26		15 00		15 26	16 00			16 26			17 00		17 26		18 00		18 26
Fratton	a		13 30		14 04			14 30	14 41	15 04		15 30	16 04			16 30		16 41	17 03		17 30	17 41	18 04		18 30
Portsmouth & Southsea	a		13 33		14 08			14 33	14 45	15 08		15 33	16 08			16 33		16 45	17 08		17 33	17 45	18 08		18 33
Portsmouth Harbour	a				14 13				14 55	15 13			16 13					16 52	17 13			17 52	18 13		

		GW		SW	SN	SW	GW	SW	GW	SN	SW	GW		SW	GW	SN	SW	GW	SW	SN	SW	GW		SN	SW
		◇		1	◇1	1	◇	1	◇	◇1	1	◇		1	R	◇1	1	◇	1	◇1	1	◇		◇1	1
Southampton Central	d	18 04			18 29	18 35	19 04		19 27	19 30	19 35	20 04			20 31	20 29	20 35	21 03		21 30	21 35	22 04		22 15	
St Denys	d					18 41					19 41						20 41				21 41				
Bitterne	d					18 43					19 43						20 43				21 43				
Woolston	d					18 47					19 47						20 47				21 47				
Sholing	d					18 49					19 49						20 49				21 49				
Netley	d					18 53					19 53						20 53				21 53				
Hamble	d					18 55					19 55						20 55				21 55				
Bursledon	d					18 58					19 58						20 58				21 58				
Swanwick	d				18 46	19 02					20 02						21 02			21 47	22 02			22 32	
Fareham	a	18 26			18 52	19 09	19 26		19 49	20 02	20 09	20 25			20 54	21 02	21 10	21 24		21 53	22 09	22 26		22 38	
	d	18 26		18 44	18 53	19 10	19 26	19 44	19 50	20 03	20 10	20 26		20 44	20 55	21 02	21 10	21 25	21 44	21 54	22 10	22 26		22 39	22 44
Portchester	d			18 49		19 15		19 49			20 15			20 49			21 15		21 49		22 15				22 49
Cosham	d	18 34		18 54	19 02	19 20	19 34	19 54	19 59	20 12	20 20			20 54		21 11	21 20		21 54	22 03	22 20			22 48	22 54
Havant	a				19 10				20 10	20 18						21 17				22 10				22 54	
Chichester 4	a				19 23				20 21	20 30						21 29				22 23				23 06	
Hilsea	a			19 00		19 26		20 00			20 26			21 00			21 26		22 00		22 26				23 00
Fratton	a	18 41		19 03		19 30	19 41	20 04			20 30	20 41		21 04	21 09		21 30	21 38	22 04		22 30	22 40			23 04
Portsmouth & Southsea	a	18 45		19 08		19 33	19 45	20 08			20 33	20 45		21 08	21 15		21 33	21 42	22 08		22 33	22 43			23 08
Portsmouth Harbour	a	18 52		19 13			19 52	20 13				20 52		21 13	21 26			21 48	22 13			22 49			23 13

		SW	SN	GW	SW
		1	◇1	◇	1
Southampton Central	d	22 35	22 52	23 06	
St Denys	d	22 41			
Bitterne	d	22 43			
Woolston	d	22 47			
Sholing	d	22 49			
Netley	d	22 53			
Hamble	d	22 55			
Bursledon	d	22 58			
Swanwick	d	23 02	23 11		
Fareham	a	23 09	23 17	23 27	
	d	23 10	23 17	23 28	23 44
Portchester	d	23 15			23 49
Cosham	d	23 20	23 26		23 54
Havant	a		23 32		
Chichester 4	a		23 44		
Hilsea	a	23 24			23 59
Fratton	a	23 28		23 41	00 04
Portsmouth & Southsea	a	23 32		23 44	00 08
Portsmouth Harbour	a			23 53	00 13

Sundays

from 30 October

		SW	SW	SW	SW	SN	SW	SW	GW	SN		SW	SW	SN	SW	SW	SN	SW	GW	SW		SN	SW	GW	SW
		1	1	1	1	◇1	1	1		◇1		1	1	◇1	1	1	◇1	1	◇	1		◇1	1	◇	1
Southampton Central	d			06 35		07 29	07 35		08 31	08 27		08 35		09 29	09 35		10 29	10 35	11 04			11 28	11 35	12 04	
St Denys	d			06 41			07 41					08 41			09 41			10 41					11 41		
Bitterne	d			06 43			07 43					08 43			09 43			10 43					11 43		
Woolston	d			06 47			07 47					08 47			09 47			10 47					11 47		
Sholing	d			06 49			07 49					08 49			09 49			10 49					11 49		
Netley	d			06 53			07 53					08 53			09 53			10 53					11 53		
Hamble	d			06 55			07 55					08 55			09 55			10 55					11 55		
Bursledon	d			06 58			07 58					08 58			09 58			10 58					11 58		
Swanwick	d			07 02		07 46	08 02					09 02		09 46	10 02		10 46	11 02				11 46	12 02		
Fareham	a			07 09		07 52	08 09		08 51	09 02		09 09		09 52	10 09		10 52	11 09	11 26			11 52	12 09	12 26	
	d	23p48		07 10	07 44	07 53	08 10	08 44	08 52	09 02		09 10	09 44	09 53	10 10	10 44	10 53	11 10	11 26	11 44		11 53	12 10	12 26	12 44
Portchester	d	23p53	00s53	07 15	07 49		08 15	08 49				09 15	09 49		10 15	10 49		11 15		11 49			12 15		12 49
Cosham	d	23p58	00s57	07 20	07 54	08 02	08 20	08 54	09 00	09 11		09 20	09 54	10 02	10 20	10 54	11 02	11 20	11 34	11 54		12 02	12 20	12 34	12 54
Havant	a					08 10			09 11	09 17				10 10			11 10					12 10			
Chichester 4	a					08 23			09 22	09 29				10 23			11 23					12 23			
Hilsea	a	00 03		07 26	08 00		08 26	09 00				09 26	10 04		10 26	11 04		11 26		12 00			12 26		13 00
Fratton	a	00 07	01s05	07 30	08 04		08 30	09 04				09 30	10 08		10 30	11 08		11 30	11 41	12 04			12 30	12 41	13 04
Portsmouth & Southsea	a	00 11	01s08	07 33	08 08		08 33	09 08				09 33	10 11		10 33	11 11		11 33	11 45	12 08			12 33	12 45	13 08
Portsmouth Harbour	a	00 16	01 12		08 13			09 13					10 15			11 15			11 52	12 13				12 52	13 13

Table 165

Sundays
from 30 October

Southampton - Fareham and Portsmouth

		SN	SW	GW	SW	SN		SW	GW	SW	SN	SW	SW	GW	SN	SW		GW	SW	SN	SW	GW	SW	SN	SW
		◇1	1	◇	1	◇1		1	◇	1	◇1	1	1	◇	◇1	1		◇	1	◇1	1	◇	1	◇1	1
Southampton Central ⛴	d	12 29	12 35	13 08		13 29		13 35	14 04		14 29	14 35		15 22	15 29	15 35		16 04		16 29	16 35	17 04		17 29	17 35
St Denys	d		12 41					13 41				14 41				15 41					16 41				17 41
Bitterne	d		12 43					13 43				14 43				15 43					16 43				17 43
Woolston	d		12 47					13 47				14 47				15 47					16 47				17 47
Sholing	d		12 49					13 49				14 49				15 49					16 49				17 49
Netley	d		12 53					13 53				14 53				15 53					16 53				17 53
Hamble	d		12 55					13 55				14 55				15 55					16 55				17 55
Bursledon	d		12 58					13 58				14 58				15 58					16 58				17 58
Swanwick	d	12 46	13 02			13 46		14 02			14 46	15 02			15 46	16 02				16 46	17 02			17 46	18 02
Fareham	a	12 52	13 09	13 33		13 52		14 09	14 26		14 52	15 09		15 50	15 57	16 09		16 26		16 52	17 09	17 26		17 52	18 09
	d	12 53	13 10	13 34	13 44	13 53		14 10	14 26	14 44	14 53	15 10	15 44	15 51	15 58	16 10		16 26	16 44	16 53	17 10	17 26	17 44	17 53	18 10
Portchester	d		13 15		13 49			14 15		14 49		15 15	15 49			16 15			16 49		17 15		17 49		18 15
Cosham	d	13 02	13 20	13 42	13 54	14 02		14 20	14 34	14 54	15 02	15 20	15 54	16 01	16 07	16 20		16 34	16 54	17 02	17 20	17 34	17 54	18 02	18 20
Havant	a	13 10		14 03		14 10					15 10			16 11	16 15					17 10				18 10	
Chichester 4	a	13 23		14 19		14 23					15 23			16 22	16 28					17 23				18 23	
Hilsea	a		13 26		14 00			14 26		15 00		15 26	16 00			16 26			17 00		17 26		18 00		18 26
Fratton	a		13 30		14 04			14 30	14 41	15 04		15 30	16 04			16 30		16 41	17 03		17 30	17 41	18 04		18 30
Portsmouth & Southsea	a		13 33		14 08			14 33	14 45	15 08		15 33	16 08			16 33		16 45	17 08		17 33	17 45	18 08		18 33
Portsmouth Harbour ⛴	a				14 13				14 55	15 13			16 13					16 52	17 13			17 52	18 13		

		GW		SW	SN	SW	GW	SW	GW	SN	SW	GW		SW	GW	SN	SW	GW	SW	SN	SW	GW		SN	SW
		◇		1	◇1	1	◇	1	◇	◇1	1	◇		1	■	◇1	1	◇	1	◇1	1	◇		◇1	1
Southampton Central ⛴	d	18 04			18 29	18 35	19 04		19 27	19 30	19 35	20 04			20 31	20 29	20 35	21 01		21 30	21 35	22 04		22 15	
St Denys	d					18 41					19 41						20 41				21 41				
Bitterne	d					18 43					19 43						20 43				21 43				
Woolston	d					18 47					19 47						20 47				21 47				
Sholing	d					18 49					19 49						20 49				21 49				
Netley	d					18 53					19 53						20 53				21 53				
Hamble	d					18 55					19 55						20 55				21 55				
Bursledon	d					18 58					19 58						20 58				21 58				
Swanwick	d				18 46	19 02					20 02						21 02			21 47	22 02			22 32	
Fareham	a	18 26			18 52	19 09	19 26		19 49	20 02	20 09	20 25			20 54	21 02	21 10	21 23		21 53	22 09	22 26		22 38	
	d	18 26		18 44	18 53	19 10	19 26	19 44	19 50	20 03	20 10	20 26		20 44	20 55	21 02	21 10	21 24	21 44	21 54	22 10	22 26		22 39	22 44
Portchester	d			18 49		19 15		19 49			20 15			20 49			21 15		21 49		22 15				22 49
Cosham	d	18 34		18 54	19 02	19 20	19 34	19 54	19 59	20 12	20 20			20 54		21 11	21 20		21 54	22 03	22 20			22 48	22 54
Havant	a				19 10				20 10	20 18						21 17				22 10				22 54	
Chichester 4	a				19 23				20 21	20 30						21 29				22 23				23 06	
Hilsea	a			19 00		19 26		20 00			20 26			21 00			21 26		22 00		22 26				23 00
Fratton	a	18 41		19 03		19 30	19 41	20 04			20 30	20 41		21 04	21 09		21 30	21 37	22 04		22 30	22 40			23 04
Portsmouth & Southsea	a	18 45		19 08		19 33	19 45	20 08			20 33	20 45		21 08	21 15		21 33	21 41	22 08		22 33	22 43			23 08
Portsmouth Harbour ⛴	a	18 52		19 13			19 52	20 13				20 52		21 13	21 26			21 48	22 13			22 49			23 13

		SW	SN	GW	SW
		1	◇1	◇	1
Southampton Central ⛴	d	22 35	22 52	23 05	
St Denys	d	22 41			
Bitterne	d	22 43			
Woolston	d	22 47			
Sholing	d	22 49			
Netley	d	22 53			
Hamble	d	22 55			
Bursledon	d	22 58			
Swanwick	d	23 02	23 11		
Fareham	a	23 09	23 17	23 26	
	d	23 10	23 17	23 27	23 44
Portchester	d	23 15			23 49
Cosham	d	23 20	23 26		23 54
Havant	a		23 32		
Chichester 4	a		23 44		
Hilsea	a	23 24			23 59
Fratton	a	23 28		23 40	00 04
Portsmouth & Southsea	a	23 32		23 44	00 08
Portsmouth Harbour ⛴	a			23 52	00 13

Table 165

Mondays to Fridays

until 30 September

Portsmouth and Fareham - Southampton

Miles	Miles			SW	SN	SW	SW	GW	SN	SW	SW	SN		SW	GW	SN	SN	SW	SW	SN	SW	SW		GW	SN
				[1]	◇[1]	[1]	[1]	[R] [trolley]	◇[1]	[1]	[1]	◇[1]		[1]	◇ [trolley]	[1]	◇[1]	[1]	[1]	◇[1]	[1]	[1]		◇ [trolley]	[1]
0	—	**Portsmouth Harbour** ⛴	d	05 00			05 43	06 00			06 23			06 50	07 05			07 24			07 55	08 05		08 23	
0¾	—	**Portsmouth & Southsea**	d	05 05		05 16	05 48	06 04		06 23	06 28			06 55	07 09			07 29	07 38		08 00	08 10		08 27	
1¾	—	Fratton	d	05 09		05 20	05 52	06 08		06 27	06 32			06 59	07 13			07 33	07 42		08 04	08 13		08 31	
4	—	Hilsea	d	05 13		05 24	05 56			06 31	06 36			07 03				07 37	07 46		08 08	08 17			
—	0	Chichester [4]	d		05 06				06 09			06 26				07 08	07 13			07 52					08 22
—	8¾	Havant	d		05 17				06 20			06 40				07 19	07 31			08 03					08 37
5½	12¾	Cosham	d	05 19	05 24	05 29	06 03	06 15	06 27	06 36	06 42	06 50		07 08	07 21	07 26	07 38	07 43	07 51	08 09	08 13	08 22		08 39	08 45
8	—	Portchester	d	05 23	05 28	05 34	06 08			06 41	06 46	06 54		07 13		07 30		07 48	07 56	08 13	08 18	08 27			08 49
11¼	—	**Fareham**	a	05 28	05 33	05 39	06 13	06 23	06 36	06 46	06 51	06 59		07 18	07 28	07 35	07 46	07 53	08 01	08 18	08 23	08 32		08 46	08 54
—	—		d		05 34	05 40		06 24	06 37	06 47		07 00			07 29	07 36	07 47		08 03	08 19				08 47	08 55
15	—	Swanwick	d		05 40	05 46			06 43	06 53		07 06				07 42	07 53		08 09	08 26					09 01
17	—	Bursledon	d			05 50				06 57									08 13	08 29					
18¼	—	Hamble	d			05 53				07 00									08 16	08 32					
19	—	Netley	d		05 46	05 55				07 02						07 48	07 59		08 18	08 34					
20¾	—	Sholing	d			05 59				07 06									08 22	08 38					
21½	—	Woolston	d		05 50	06 01				07 08						07 52	08 04		08 24	08 40					
23¼	—	Bitterne	d			06 05				07 12									08 28	08 43					
23¾	—	St Denys	d			06 08				07 15							08 08		08 31	08 46					
25¾	—	**Southampton Central** ⛴	a		05 59	06 13		06 45	07 02	07 21		07 25			07 50	08 01	08 13		08 38	08 52				09 08	09 19

		SW	SW	SN	GW	SN	SW	GW		SW	SN	GW	SN	SW	SW	SN	GW	SN		SW	SW	SN	GW	SN	SW
		[1]	[1]	◇[1]	◇ [trolley]	[1]	[1]	◇ A [trolley]		[1]	◇[1]	◇ [trolley]	[1]	[1]	[1]	◇[1]	◇ [trolley]	[1]		[1]	[1]	◇[1]	◇ [trolley]	[1]	[1]
Portsmouth Harbour ⛴	d	08 33	08 59		09 23		09 33			09 59		10 23		10 33	10 59		11 23				11 59		12 23		
Portsmouth & Southsea	d	08 38	09 03		09 27		09 38			10 03		10 27		10 38	11 03		11 27			11 38	12 03		12 27		12 38
Fratton	d	08 42	09 07		09 31		09 42			10 07		10 31		10 42	11 07		11 31			11 42	12 07		12 31		12 42
Hilsea	d	08 46	09 11				09 46			10 11				10 46	11 11					11 46	12 11				12 46
Chichester [4]	d			09 08		09 24		09 47			10 06		10 25			11 05		11 25				12 05		12 25	
Havant	d			09 23		09 38		09 59			10 20		10 37			11 19		11 37				12 19		12 37	
Cosham	d	08 51	09 17	09 30	09 39	09 46	09 51	10 05		10 17	10 28	10 39	10 46	10 51	11 17	11 26	11 39	11 46		11 51	12 17	12 26	12 39	12 46	12 51
Portchester	d	08 56	09 21				09 56			10 21	10 32			10 56	11 21	11 30				11 56	12 21	12 30			12 56
Fareham	a	09 01	09 26	09 37	09 46	09 53	10 01	10 14		10 26	10 37	10 46	10 53	11 01	11 26	11 35	11 46	11 53		12 01	12 26	12 35	12 46	12 53	13 01
	d	09 03		09 38	09 47	09 54	10 03	10 14			10 38	10 47	10 54	11 03		11 36	11 47	11 54		12 03		12 36	12 47	12 54	13 03
Swanwick	d	09 09		09 44		10 00	10 09				10 44		11 00	11 09		11 42		12 00		12 09		12 42		13 00	13 09
Bursledon	d	09 13					10 13							11 13						12 13					13 13
Hamble	d	09 16					10 16							11 16						12 16					13 16
Netley	d	09 18					10 18							11 18						12 18					13 18
Sholing	d	09 22					10 22							11 22						12 22					13 22
Woolston	d	09 24					10 24							11 24						12 24					13 24
Bitterne	d	09 28					10 28							11 28						12 28					13 28
St Denys	d	09 31					10 31							11 31						12 31					13 31
Southampton Central ⛴	a	09 38		10 01	10 08	10 20	10 38	10 41			11 01	11 08	11 19	11 38		12 01	12 08	12 19		12 38		12 59	13 08	13 19	13 38

		SW	SN	GW		SN	SW	SW	SN	GW	SN	SW	SW	SN		GW	SN	SW	SW	SN	GW	SN	SW	SW	
		[1]	◇[1]	◇ [trolley]		◇[1]	[1]	[1]	◇[1]	[R] [trolley]	[1]	[1]	[1]	◇[1]		[R] [trolley]	[1]	[1]	[1]	◇[1]	[R] [trolley]	◇[1]	[1]	[1]	
Portsmouth Harbour ⛴	d	12 59		13 23				13 59		14 23			14 59			15 23			15 59		16 23			16 49	
Portsmouth & Southsea	d	13 03		13 27			13 38	14 03		14 27		14 38	15 03			15 27		15 38	16 03		16 27		16 38	16 55	
Fratton	d	13 07		13 31			13 42	14 07		14 31		14 42	15 07			15 31		15 42	16 07		16 31		16 42	16 59	
Hilsea	d	13 11					13 46	14 11				14 46	15 11					15 46	16 11				16 46	17 03	
Chichester [4]	d		13 05			13 25			14 05		14 25			15 05			15 25			16 05		16 25			
Havant	d		13 19			13 37			14 19		14 37			15 19			15 37			16 19		16 37			
Cosham	d	13 17	13 26	13 39		13 46	13 51	14 17	14 26	14 39	14 46	14 51	15 17	15 26		15 39	15 46	15 51	16 17	16 26	16 39	16 46	16 51	17 08	
Portchester	d	13 21	13 30				13 56	14 21	14 30			14 56	15 21	15 30				15 56	16 21	16 30			16 56	17 13	
Fareham	a	13 26	13 35	13 46		13 53	14 01	14 26	14 35	14 46	14 53	15 01	15 26	15 35		15 46	15 53	16 01	16 26	16 35	16 46	16 53	17 01	17 18	
	d		13 36	13 47		13 56	14 03		14 36	14 47	14 54	15 03		15 36		15 47	15 54	16 03		16 36	16 47	16 57	17 03		
Swanwick	d		13 42			14 02	14 09		14 42		15 00	15 09		15 42			16 00	16 09		16 42			17 09		
Bursledon	d						14 13					15 13						16 13					17 13		
Hamble	d						14 16					15 16						16 16					17 16		
Netley	d						14 18					15 18						16 18					17 18		
Sholing	d						14 22					15 22						16 22					17 22		
Woolston	d						14 24					15 24						16 24					17 24		
Bitterne	d						14 28					15 28						16 28					17 28		
St Denys	d						14 31					15 31						16 31					17 31		
Southampton Central ⛴	a		13 59	14 08		14 19	14 39		14 59	15 08	15 19	15 38		15 59		16 08	16 20	16 38		17 01	17 08	17 28	17 38		

A [trolley] to Fareham

Table 165

Mondays to Fridays

until 30 September

Portsmouth and Fareham - Southampton

		SW	SN	GW	SN	SW	GW	SW	SN	GW	SN	SW	SW	SN	GW	SN	SW	SW	SN	GW	SN	SW	SW
		[1]	◇[1]	◇ (trolley)	[1]	[1]	◇ (trolley)	[1]	◇[1]	◇ (trolley)	[1]	[1]	[1]	◇[1]	◇	[1]	[1]	[1]	◇[1]	◇	[1]	[1]	[1]
Portsmouth Harbour ⛴	d	16 59		17 23		17 33		17 59		18 23			18 59		19 23			19 59		20 23			20 59
Portsmouth & Southsea	d	17 03		17 27		17 38		18 03		18 27		18 38	19 03		19 27		19 38	20 03		20 27		20 38	21 03
Fratton	d	17 07		17 31		17 42		18 07		18 31		18 42	19 07		19 31		19 42	20 07		20 31		20 42	21 07
Hilsea	d	17 11				17 46		18 11				18 46	19 11				19 46	20 11				20 46	21 11
Chichester [4]	d		17 05		17 25		17 47		18 05		18 25			19 02		19 20			20 01		20 26		
Havant	d		17 19		17 37		17 58		18 23		18 37			19 20		19 37			20 22		20 37		
Cosham	d	17 17	17 27	17 39	17 46	17 51	18 05	18 17	18 30	18 39	18 44	18 51	19 17	19 29	19 39	19 46	19 51	20 17	20 29		20 44	20 51	21 17
Portchester	d	17 21	17 31			17 56		18 21	18 34			18 56	19 21	19 33			19 56	20 21			20 48	20 56	21 21
Fareham	a	17 26	17 36	17 46	17 53	18 01	18 12	18 26	18 39	18 46	18 52	19 01	19 26	19 38	19 46	19 54	20 01	20 26	20 36	20 46	20 53	21 01	21 26
	d		17 37	17 47	17 54	18 03	18 13		18 40	18 47	18 53	19 03		19 39	19 47	19 55	20 03		20 37	20 47	20 54	21 03	
Swanwick	d		17 43		18 00	18 09			18 46		18 59	19 09		19 45		20 01	20 09		20 43		21 00	21 09	
Bursledon	d					18 13						19 13					20 13					21 13	
Hamble	d					18 16						19 16					20 16					21 16	
Netley	d		17 49			18 18						19 18					20 18					21 18	
Sholing	d					18 22						19 22					20 22					21 22	
Woolston	d		17 53			18 24						19 24					20 24					21 24	
Bitterne	d					18 28						19 28					20 28					21 28	
St Denys	d		17 58			18 31						19 31					20 31					21 31	
Southampton Central ⛴	a		18 03	18 08	18 20	18 38	18 41		19 05	19 08	19 20	19 38		20 03	20 08	20 18	20 38		21 01	21 08	21 19	21 38	

		SN	GW	SN	SW	SW	SW	SN	SW	SW	SW
		◇[1]		◇[1]	[1]	[1]	[1]	◇[1]	[1]	[1]	[1]
Portsmouth Harbour ⛴	d		21 23				21 54		22 33		23 24
Portsmouth & Southsea	d		21 27		21 38		21 59		22 38		23 29
Fratton	d		21 31		21 42		22 03		22 42		23 33
Hilsea	d				21 46		22 07		22 46		23 37
Chichester [4]	d	21 05		21 26				22 05			
Havant	d	21 26		21 37		21 58		22 26		22 59	
Cosham	d	21 34		21 44	21 51	22 05	22 12	22 34	22 51	23 08	23 42
Portchester	d	21 38			21 56		22 17		22 56	23 13	23 47
Fareham	a	21 43	21 47	21 51	22 01	22 12	22 22	22 42	23 01	23 18	23 52
	d	21 43	21 48	21 52	22 03			22 43	23 03		
Swanwick	d	21 49		21 58	22 09			22 49	23 09		
Bursledon	d				22 13				23 13		
Hamble	d				22 16				23 16		
Netley	d				22 18				23 18		
Sholing	d				22 22				23 22		
Woolston	d	21 58			22 24				23 24		
Bitterne	d				22 28				23 28		
St Denys	d	22 02			22 31				23 31		
Southampton Central ⛴	a	22 07	22 21	22 16	22 39			23 07	23 39		

Mondays to Fridays

from 3 October

		SW	SN	SW	SW	GW	SN	SW	SW	SN	SW	GW	SN	SN	SW	SW	SN	SW	SW	GW	SN	SW	SW
		[1]	◇[1]	[1]	[1]	■ (trolley)	◇[1]	[1]	[1]	◇[1]	[1]	◇ (trolley)	[1]	◇[1]	[1]	[1]	◇[1]	[1]	[1]	◇ (trolley)	[1]	[1]	[1]
Portsmouth Harbour ⛴	d	04 55			05 43	06 00			06 23		06 50	07 05			07 24			07 55	08 05	08 23		08 33	08 59
Portsmouth & Southsea	d	05 00		05 16	05 48	06 04		06 23	06 28		06 55	07 09			07 29	07 38		08 00	08 10	08 27		08 38	09 03
Fratton	d	05 04		05 20	05 52	06 08		06 27	06 32		06 59	07 13			07 33	07 42		08 04	08 13	08 31		08 42	09 07
Hilsea	d	05 08		05 24	05 56			06 31	06 36		07 03				07 37	07 46		08 08	08 17			08 46	09 11
Chichester [4]	d		05 06				06 09			06 26			07 08	07 13			07 52				08 22		
Havant	d		05 17				06 20			06 40			07 19	07 31			08 03				08 37		
Cosham	d	05 16	05 24	05 29	06 03	06 15	06 27	06 36	06 42	06 50	07 08	07 21	07 26	07 38	07 43	07 51	08 09	08 13	08 22	08 39	08 45	08 51	09 17
Portchester	d	05 20	05 28	05 34	06 08			06 41	06 46	06 54	07 13		07 30		07 48	07 56	08 13	08 18	08 27		08 49	08 56	09 21
Fareham	a	05 25	05 33	05 39	06 13	06 23	06 36	06 46	06 51	06 59	07 18	07 28	07 35	07 46	07 53	08 01	08 18	08 23	08 32	08 46	08 54	09 01	09 26
	d		05 34	05 40		06 24	06 37	06 47		07 00		07 29	07 36	07 47		08 03	08 19			08 47	08 55	09 03	
Swanwick	d		05 40	05 46			06 43	06 53		07 06			07 42	07 53		08 09	08 26				09 01	09 09	
Bursledon	d			05 50				06 57								08 13	08 29					09 13	
Hamble	d			05 53				07 00								08 16	08 32					09 16	
Netley	d		05 46	05 55				07 02					07 48	07 59		08 18	08 34					09 18	
Sholing	d			05 59				07 06								08 22	08 38					09 22	
Woolston	d		05 50	06 01				07 08					07 52	08 04		08 24	08 40					09 24	
Bitterne	d			06 05				07 12								08 28	08 43					09 28	
St Denys	d			06 08				07 15						08 08		08 31	08 46					09 31	
Southampton Central ⛴	a		05 59	06 13		06 45	07 02	07 21		07 25		07 50	08 01	08 13		08 38	08 52			09 08	09 19	09 38	

Table 165

Portsmouth and Fareham - Southampton

Mondays to Fridays

from 3 October

		SN	GW	SN	SW	GW		SW	SN	GW	SN	SW	SW	SN	GW	SN		SW	SW	SN	GW	SN	SW	SW	SN
		◇ 1	◇	1	1	◇		1	◇ 1	◇	1	1	1	◇ 1	◇	1		1	1	◇ 1	◇	1	1	1	◇ 1
						A																			
			[trolley]			[trolley]				[trolley]					[trolley]						[trolley]				
Portsmouth Harbour ⛴	d		09 23		09 33			09 59		10 23		10 33	10 59		11 23				11 59		12 23			12 59	
Portsmouth & Southsea	d		09 27		09 38			10 03		10 27		10 38	11 03		11 27			11 38	12 03		12 27		12 38	13 03	
Fratton	d		09 31		09 42			10 07		10 31		10 42	11 07		11 31			11 42	12 07		12 31		12 42	13 07	
Hilsea	d				09 46			10 11				10 46	11 11					11 46	12 11				12 46	13 11	
Chichester 4	d	09 08		09 24		09 47			10 06		10 25			11 05		11 25				12 05		12 25			13 05
Havant	d	09 23		09 38		09 59			10 20		10 37			11 19		11 37				12 19		12 37			13 19
Cosham	d	09 30	09 39	09 46	09 51	10 05		10 17	10 28	10 39	10 46	10 51	11 17	11 26	11 39	11 46		11 51	12 17	12 26	12 39	12 46	12 51	13 17	13 26
Portchester	d				09 56			10 21	10 32			10 56	11 21	11 30				11 56	12 21	12 30			12 56	13 21	13 30
Fareham	a	09 37	09 46	09 53	10 01	10 14		10 26	10 37	10 46	10 53	11 01	11 26	11 35	11 46	11 53		12 01	12 26	12 35	12 46	12 53	13 01	13 26	13 35
	d	09 38	09 47	09 54	10 03	10 14			10 38	10 47	10 54	11 03		11 36	11 47	11 54		12 03		12 36	12 47	12 54	13 03		13 36
Swanwick	d	09 44		10 00	10 09				10 44		11 00	11 09		11 42		12 00		12 09		12 42		13 00	13 09		13 42
Bursledon	d				10 13							11 13						12 13					13 13		
Hamble	d				10 16							11 16						12 16					13 16		
Netley	d				10 18							11 18						12 18					13 18		
Sholing	d				10 22							11 22						12 22					13 22		
Woolston	d				10 24							11 24						12 24					13 24		
Bitterne	d				10 28							11 28						12 28					13 28		
St Denys	d				10 31							11 31						12 31					13 31		
Southampton Central ⛴	a	10 01	10 08	10 20	10 38	10 41			11 01	11 08	11 19	11 38		12 01	12 08	12 19		12 38		12 59	13 08	13 19	13 38		13 59

		GW		SN	SW	SW	SN	GW	SN	SW	SW	SN		GW	SN	SW	SW	SN	GW	SN	SW	SW		SW	SN
								R						R					R						
		◇		◇ 1	1	1	◇ 1		1	1	1	◇ 1			1	1	1	◇ 1		◇ 1	1	1		1	◇ 1
		[trolley]						[trolley]						[trolley]					[trolley]						
Portsmouth Harbour ⛴	d	13 23				13 59		14 23			14 59			15 23			15 59		16 23			16 49		16 59	
Portsmouth & Southsea	d	13 27			13 38	14 03		14 27		14 38	15 03			15 27		15 38	16 03		16 27		16 38	16 55		17 03	
Fratton	d	13 31			13 42	14 07		14 31		14 42	15 07			15 31		15 42	16 07		16 31		16 42	16 59		17 07	
Hilsea	d				13 46	14 11				14 46	15 11					15 46	16 11				16 46	17 03		17 11	
Chichester 4	d			13 25			14 05		14 25			15 05			15 25			16 05		16 25					17 05
Havant	d			13 37			14 19		14 37			15 19			15 37			16 19		16 37					17 19
Cosham	d	13 39		13 46	13 51	14 17	14 26	14 39	14 46	14 51	15 17	15 26		15 39	15 46	15 51	16 17	16 26	16 39	16 46	16 51	17 08		17 17	17 27
Portchester	d				13 56	14 21	14 30			14 56	15 21	15 30				15 56	16 21	16 30			16 56	17 13		17 21	17 31
Fareham	a	13 46		13 53	14 01	14 26	14 35	14 46	14 53	15 01	15 26	15 35		15 46	15 53	16 01	16 26	16 35	16 46	16 53	17 01	17 18		17 26	17 36
	d	13 47		13 56	14 03		14 36	14 47	14 54	15 03		15 36		15 47	15 54	16 03		16 36	16 47	16 57	17 03				17 37
Swanwick	d			14 02	14 09		14 42		15 00	15 09		15 42			16 00	16 09		16 42			17 09				17 43
Bursledon	d				14 13					15 13						16 13					17 13				
Hamble	d				14 16					15 16						16 16					17 16				
Netley	d				14 18					15 18						16 18					17 18				17 49
Sholing	d				14 22					15 22						16 22					17 22				
Woolston	d				14 24					15 24						16 24					17 24				17 53
Bitterne	d				14 28					15 28						16 28					17 28				
St Denys	d				14 31					15 31						16 31					17 31				17 58
Southampton Central ⛴	a	14 08		14 19	14 39		14 59	15 08	15 19	15 38		15 59		16 08	16 20	16 38		17 01	17 08	17 28	17 38				18 03

		GW	SN	SW	GW	SW	SN	GW		SN	SW	SW	SN	GW	SN	SW	SW	SN		GW	SN	SW	SW	SN	GW
		◇	1	1	◇	1	◇ 1	◇		1	1	1	◇ 1	◇	1	1	1	◇ 1		◇	1	1	1	◇ 1	
		[trolley]			[trolley]			[trolley]																	
Portsmouth Harbour ⛴	d	17 23		17 33		17 59		18 23				18 59		19 23			19 59			20 23			20 59		21 23
Portsmouth & Southsea	d	17 27		17 38		18 03		18 27			18 38	19 03		19 27		19 38	20 03			20 27		20 38	21 03		21 27
Fratton	d	17 31		17 42		18 07		18 31			18 42	19 07		19 31		19 42	20 07			20 31		20 42	21 07		21 31
Hilsea	d			17 46		18 11					18 46	19 11				19 46	20 11					20 46	21 11		
Chichester 4	d		17 25		17 47		18 05			18 25			19 02		19 20			20 01			20 26			21 05	
Havant	d		17 37		17 58		18 23			18 37			19 20		19 37			20 22			20 37			21 26	
Cosham	d	17 39	17 46	17 51	18 05	18 17	18 30	18 39		18 44	18 51	19 17	19 29	19 39	19 46	19 51	20 17	20 29			20 44	20 51	21 17	21 34	
Portchester	d			17 56		18 21	18 34				18 56	19 21	19 33			19 56	20 21				20 48	20 56	21 21	21 38	
Fareham	a	17 46	17 53	18 01	18 12	18 26	18 39	18 46		18 52	19 01	19 26	19 38	19 46	19 54	20 01	20 26	20 36		20 46	20 53	21 01	21 26	21 43	21 47
	d	17 47	17 54	18 03	18 13		18 40	18 47		18 53	19 03		19 39	19 47	19 55	20 03		20 37		20 47	20 54	21 03		21 43	21 48
Swanwick	d		18 00	18 09			18 46			18 59	19 09		19 45		20 01	20 09		20 43			21 00	21 09		21 49	
Bursledon	d			18 13							19 13					20 13						21 13			
Hamble	d			18 16							19 16					20 16						21 16			
Netley	d			18 18							19 18					20 18						21 18			
Sholing	d			18 22							19 22					20 22						21 22			
Woolston	d			18 24							19 24					20 24						21 24		21 58	
Bitterne	d			18 28							19 28					20 28						21 28			
St Denys	d			18 31							19 31					20 31						21 31		22 02	
Southampton Central ⛴	a	18 08	18 20	18 38	18 41		19 05	19 08		19 20	19 38		20 03	20 08	20 18	20 38		21 01		21 08	21 19	21 38		22 07	22 21

		SN	SW	SW		SW	SN	SW	SW	SW
		◇ 1	1	1		1	◇ 1	1	1	1
Portsmouth Harbour ⛴	d					21 54		22 33		23 24
Portsmouth & Southsea	d		21 38			21 59		22 38		23 29
Fratton	d		21 42			22 03		22 42		23 33
Hilsea	d		21 46			22 07		22 46		23 37
Chichester 4	d	21 26					22 05			
Havant	d	21 37		21 58			22 26		22 59	
Cosham	d	21 44	21 51	22 05		22 12	22 34	22 51	23 08	23 42
Portchester	d		21 56			22 17		22 56	23 13	23 47
Fareham	a	21 51	22 01	22 12		22 22	22 42	23 01	23 18	23 52
	d	21 52	22 03				22 43	23 03		
Swanwick	d	21 58	22 09				22 49	23 09		
Bursledon	d		22 13					23 13		
Hamble	d		22 16					23 16		
Netley	d		22 18					23 18		
Sholing	d		22 22					23 22		
Woolston	d		22 24					23 24		
Bitterne	d		22 28					23 28		
St Denys	d		22 31					23 31		
Southampton Central ⛴	a	22 16	22 39				23 07	23 39		

A [trolley] to Fareham

Table 165

Saturdays

Portsmouth and Fareham - Southampton

		SW 1	SN ◇1	SW 1	SN ◇1	SW 1	GW ◇	SN ◇1	SN ◇1	SW 1		SW 1	GW ◇	SN 1	SN ◇1	SW 1	SW 1	SN 1	GW ◇	SN 1		SW 1	SW 1	SN ◇1	GW ◇
Portsmouth Harbour ⛴	d					05 50	06 00					06 55	07 05				07 59		08 23				08 59		09 23
Portsmouth & Southsea	d			05 16		05 55	06 04			06 38		07 00	07 09			07 38	08 03		08 27			08 38	09 03		09 27
Fratton	d			05 20		05 59	06 08			06 42		07 04	07 14			07 42	08 07		08 31			08 42	09 07		09 31
Hilsea	d			05 24		06 03				06 46		07 08				07 46	08 11					08 46	09 11		
Chichester 4	d		05 05		05 28			06 06	06 23					07 07	07 25			08 05		08 25				09 05	
Havant	d		05 16		05 39			06 24	06 37					07 23	07 37			08 20		08 37				09 19	
Cosham	d	05 09	05 23	05 29	05 49	06 08	06 19	06 30	06 46	06 51		07 13	07 21	07 30	07 46	07 51	08 17	08 28	08 39	08 46		08 51	09 17	09 26	09 39
Portchester	d	05 14	05 27	05 34		06 13		06 34		06 56		07 18		07 34		07 56	08 21	08 32				08 56	09 21	09 30	
Fareham	a	05 19	05 32	05 39	05 57	06 18	06 27	06 39	06 53	07 01		07 23	07 29	07 39	07 53	08 01	08 26	08 37	08 46	08 53		09 01	09 26	09 35	09 46
	d		05 33	05 40	05 58		06 28	06 40	06 57	07 03			07 30	07 39	07 57	08 03		08 38	08 47	08 54		09 03		09 36	09 47
Swanwick	d		05 39	05 46	06 04			06 46		07 09				07 45		08 09		08 44		09 00		09 09		09 42	
Bursledon	d			05 50						07 13						08 13						09 13			
Hamble	d			05 53						07 16						08 16						09 16			
Netley	d		05 45	05 55						07 18						08 18						09 18			
Sholing	d			05 59						07 22						08 22						09 22			
Woolston	d		05 49	06 01						07 24						08 24						09 24			
Bitterne	d			06 05						07 28						08 28						09 28			
St Denys	d			06 08						07 31						08 31						09 31			
Southampton Central ⛴	a		05 58	06 13	06 24		06 49	07 05	07 28	07 38			07 51	08 03	08 28	08 38		09 01	09 08	09 19		09 38		09 59	10 08

		SN ◇1	SW 1	GW ◇	SW 1	SN ◇1		GW ◇	SN 1	SW 1	SW 1	SN ◇1	GW ◇	SN ◇1	SW 1	SW 1		SN ◇1	GW ◇	SN 1	SW 1	SW 1	SN ◇1	GW ◇	SN ◇1
Portsmouth Harbour ⛴	d				09 59			10 23			10 59		11 23			11 59			12 23			12 59		13 23	
Portsmouth & Southsea	d		09 38		10 03			10 27		10 38	11 03		11 27		11 38	12 03			12 27		12 38	13 03		13 27	
Fratton	d		09 42		10 07			10 31		10 42	11 07		11 31		11 42	12 07			12 31		12 42	13 07		13 31	
Hilsea	d		09 46		10 11					10 46	11 11				11 46	12 11					12 46	13 11			
Chichester 4	d	09 25		09 49		10 05			10 25			11 05		11 25				12 05		12 25			13 05		13 25
Havant	d	09 37		10 00		10 19			10 37			11 19		11 37				12 19		12 37			13 19		13 37
Cosham	d	09 46	09 51	10 06	10 17	10 26		10 39	10 46	10 51	11 17	11 26	11 39	11 46	11 51	12 17		12 26	12 39	12 46	12 51	13 17	13 26	13 39	13 46
Portchester	d		09 56		10 21	10 30				10 56	11 21	11 30			11 56	12 21		12 30			12 56	13 21	13 30		
Fareham	a	09 53	10 01	10 15	10 26	10 35		10 46	10 53	11 01	11 26	11 35	11 46	11 53	12 01	12 26		12 35	12 46	12 53	13 01	13 26	13 35	13 46	13 53
	d	09 57	10 03	10 16		10 36		10 47	10 54	11 03		11 36	11 47	11 57	12 03			12 36	12 47	12 54	13 03		13 36	13 47	13 56
Swanwick	d		10 09			10 42			11 00	11 09		11 42			12 09			12 42		13 00	13 09		13 42		14 02
Bursledon	d		10 13							11 13					12 13						13 13				
Hamble	d		10 16							11 16					12 16						13 16				
Netley	d		10 18							11 18					12 18						13 18				
Sholing	d		10 22							11 22					12 22						13 22				
Woolston	d		10 24							11 24					12 24						13 24				
Bitterne	d		10 28							11 28					12 28						13 28				
St Denys	d		10 31							11 31					12 31						13 31				
Southampton Central ⛴	a	10 28	10 38	10 40		10 59		11 08	11 19	11 38		11 59	12 08	12 28	12 38			12 59	13 08	13 19	13 38		13 59	14 08	14 19

		SW 1		SW 1	SN ◇1	GW ◇	SN 1	SW 1	SW 1	SN ◇1	GW ◇	SN ◇1		SW 1	SW 1	SN ◇1	GW	SN 1	SW 1	SW 1	SN ◇1	GW ◇		SN ◇1	SW 1
Portsmouth Harbour ⛴	d			13 59		14 23			14 59		15 23				15 59		16 23			16 59		17 23			17 33
Portsmouth & Southsea	d	13 38		14 03		14 27		14 38	15 03		15 27			15 38	16 03		16 27		16 38	17 03		17 27			17 38
Fratton	d	13 42		14 07		14 31		14 42	15 07		15 31			15 42	16 07		16 31		16 42	17 07		17 31			17 42
Hilsea	d	13 46		14 11				14 46	15 11					15 46	16 11				16 46	17 11					17 46
Chichester 4	d				14 05		14 25			15 05		15 25				16 05		16 25			17 05			17 25	
Havant	d				14 19		14 37			15 19		15 37				16 19		16 37			17 19			17 37	
Cosham	d	13 51		14 17	14 26	14 39	14 46	14 51	15 17	15 26	15 39	15 46		15 51	16 17	16 26	16 39	16 46	16 51	17 17	17 26	17 39		17 46	17 51
Portchester	d	13 56		14 21	14 30			14 56	15 21	15 30				15 56	16 21	16 30			16 56	17 21	17 30				17 56
Fareham	a	14 01		14 26	14 35	14 46	14 53	15 01	15 26	15 35	15 46	15 53		16 01	16 26	16 35	16 46	16 53	17 01	17 26	17 35	17 46		17 53	18 01
	d	14 03			14 36	14 47	14 54	15 03		15 36	15 47	15 57		16 03		16 36	16 47	16 54	17 03		17 36	17 47		17 57	18 03
Swanwick	d	14 09			14 42		15 00	15 09		15 42				16 09		16 42		17 00	17 09		17 42				18 09
Bursledon	d	14 13						15 13						16 13					17 13						18 13
Hamble	d	14 16						15 16						16 16					17 16						18 16
Netley	d	14 18						15 18						16 18					17 18						18 18
Sholing	d	14 22						15 22						16 22					17 22						18 22
Woolston	d	14 24						15 24						16 24					17 24						18 24
Bitterne	d	14 28						15 28						16 28					17 28						18 28
St Denys	d	14 31						15 31						16 31					17 31						18 31
Southampton Central ⛴	a	14 39			14 59	15 08	15 19	15 38		15 59	16 08	16 28		16 38		16 59	17 08	17 19	17 38		17 59	18 08		18 28	18 38

		GW ◇	SW 1	SN ◇1	GW ◇	SN 1	SW 1	SW 1		SN ◇1	GW ◇	SN ◇1	SW 1	SW 1	SN ◇1	GW ◇	SN 1	SW 1		SW 1	SN ◇1	SN ◇1	SW 1	SW 1	SN ◇1
Portsmouth Harbour ⛴	d		17 59		18 23			18 59			19 23			19 59		20 23				20 59				21 54	
Portsmouth & Southsea	d		18 03		18 27		18 38	19 03			19 27		19 38	20 03		20 27		20 38		21 03			21 38	21 59	
Fratton	d		18 07		18 31		18 42	19 07			19 31		19 42	20 07		20 31		20 42		21 07			21 42	22 03	
Hilsea	d		18 11				18 46	19 11					19 46	20 11				20 46		21 11			21 46	22 07	
Chichester 4	d	17 46		18 05		18 25				19 05		19 25			20 05		20 25				21 05	21 28			22 05
Havant	d	18 00		18 19		18 37				19 19		19 37			20 26		20 37				21 23	21 40			22 26
Cosham	d	18 06	18 17	18 26	18 39	18 46	18 51	19 17		19 26	19 39	19 46	19 51	20 17	20 32		20 46	20 51		21 17	21 29	21 47	21 51	22 12	22 34
Portchester	d		18 21	18 30			18 56	19 21		19 30			19 56	20 21	20 36			20 56		21 21	21 33		21 56	22 17	
Fareham	a	18 14	18 26	18 35	18 46	18 53	19 01	19 26		19 35	19 46	19 53	20 01	20 26	20 41	20 45	20 53	21 01		21 26	21 38	21 54	22 01	22 22	22 41
	d	18 15		18 36	18 47	18 54	19 03			19 36	19 47	19 57	20 03		20 42	20 47	20 54	21 03			21 39	21 55	22 03		22 42
Swanwick	d			18 42		19 00	19 09			19 42			20 09		20 48		21 00	21 09			21 45	22 01	22 09		22 48
Bursledon	d						19 13						20 13					21 13					22 13		
Hamble	d						19 16						20 16					21 16					22 16		
Netley	d						19 18						20 18					21 18					22 18		
Sholing	d						19 22						20 22					21 22					22 22		
Woolston	d						19 24						20 24					21 24					22 24		
Bitterne	d						19 28						20 28					21 28					22 28		
St Denys	d						19 31						20 31					21 31					22 31		
Southampton Central ⛴	a	18 43		18 59	19 08	19 19	19 38			19 59	20 09	20 28	20 38		21 05	21 10	21 19	21 38			22 02	22 20	22 39		23 05

Saturdays

Portsmouth and Fareham - Southampton

		SW	SW
		1	1
Portsmouth Harbour ⛴	d	22 33	23 24
Portsmouth & Southsea	d	22 38	23 29
Fratton	d	22 42	23 33
Hilsea	d	22 46	23 37
Chichester 4	d		
Havant	d		
Cosham	d	22 51	23 42
Portchester	d	22 56	23 47
Fareham	a	23 01	23 52
	d	23 03	
Swanwick	d	23 09	
Bursledon	d	23 13	
Hamble	d	23 16	
Netley	d	23 18	
Sholing	d	23 22	
Woolston	d	23 24	
Bitterne	d	23 28	
St Denys	d	23 31	
Southampton Central ⛴	a	23 36	

Sundays

until 11 September

		SW	SW	SW	SN	SW	SW	SN	SN	GW		SW	SW	SN	SN	SW	SW	SN	SN	GW		SW	SW	SN	SN
		1	1	1	◇1	1	1	◇1	◇1	R		1	1	◇1	◇1	1	1	◇1	◇1	◇		1	1	◇1	◇1
								A	B					A	B			A	B					A	B
												🛒				🛒						🛒			
Portsmouth Harbour ⛴	d	06 37	07 17			08 17				09 08		09 17				10 17				11 08		11 17			
Portsmouth & Southsea	d	06 42	07 22	07 42		08 22	08 42			09 12		09 22	09 42			10 22	10 42			11 12		11 22	11 42		
Fratton	d	06 46	07 26	07 46		08 26	08 46			09 16		09 26	09 46			10 26	10 46			11 16		11 26	11 46		
Hilsea	d	06 50	07 30	07 50		08 30	08 50					09 30	09 50			10 30	10 50					11 30	11 50		
Chichester 4	d				07 45			08 44	08 45					09 44	09 45			10 44	10 45					11 44	11 45
Havant	d				07 58			08 58	08 58					09 58	09 58			10 58	10 58					11 58	11 58
Cosham	d	06 55	07 35	07 55	08 05	08 35	08 55	09 05	09 05	09 23		09 35	09 55	10 06	10 06	10 35	10 55	11 06	11 06	11 23		11 35	11 55	12 05	12 05
Portchester	d	07 00	07 40	08 00		08 40	09 00					09 40	10 00			10 40	11 00					11 40	12 00		
Fareham	a	07 05	07 45	08 05	08 13	08 45	09 05	09 13	09 13	09 31		09 45	10 05	10 14	10 14	10 45	11 05	11 14	11 14	11 31		11 45	12 05	12 13	12 13
	d	07 06		08 06	08 14		09 06	09 14	09 14	09 32			10 06	10 15	10 15		11 06	11 15	11 15	11 32			12 06	12 14	12 14
Swanwick	d	07 12		08 12	08 20		09 12	09 20	09 20				10 12	10 21	10 21		11 12	11 21	11 21				12 12	12 20	12 20
Bursledon	d	07 16		08 16			09 16						10 16				11 16						12 16		
Hamble	d	07 19		08 19			09 19						10 19				11 19						12 19		
Netley	d	07 21		08 21			09 21						10 21				11 21						12 21		
Sholing	d	07 25		08 25			09 25						10 25				11 25						12 25		
Woolston	d	07 27		08 27			09 27						10 27				11 27						12 27		
Bitterne	d	07 31		08 31			09 31						10 31				11 31						12 31		
St Denys	d	07 34		08 34			09 34						10 34				11 34						12 34		
Southampton Central ⛴	a	07 40		08 40	08 44		09 40	09 44	09 44	09 53			10 40	10 44	10 44		11 40	11 45	11 44	11 53			12 40	12 44	12 44

		GW	SW	SW	SN	SN		GW	SW	SW	SN	SN	GW	SW	SW	SN		SN	GW	SW	SW	SN	SN	GW	SW
		◇	1	1	◇1	◇1		◇	1	1	◇1	◇1	◇	1	1	◇1		◇1	R	1	1	◇1	◇1	◇	1
					A	B					A	B				A		B				A	B		
			🛒						🛒					🛒						🛒					🛒
Portsmouth Harbour ⛴	d		12 17					13 08	13 17				14 08	14 17					15 08	15 17				16 08	16 17
Portsmouth & Southsea	d		12 22	12 42				13 12	13 22	13 42			14 12	14 22	14 42				15 12	15 22	15 42			16 12	16 22
Fratton	d		12 26	12 46				13 16	13 26	13 46			14 16	14 26	14 46				15 16	15 26	15 46			16 16	16 26
Hilsea	d		12 30	12 50					13 30	13 50				14 30	14 50					15 30	15 50				16 30
Chichester 4	d	11 54			12 44	12 45					13 44	13 45				14 44		14 45				15 44	15 45		
Havant	d	12 10			12 58	12 58					13 58	13 58				14 58		14 58				15 56	15 58		
Cosham	d	12 23	12 35	12 55	13 05	13 05		13 23	13 35	13 55	14 05	14 05	14 23	14 35	14 55	15 05		15 05	15 23	15 35	15 55	16 04	16 05	16 23	16 35
Portchester	d		12 40	13 00					13 40	14 00				14 40	15 00					15 40	16 00				16 40
Fareham	a	12 31	12 45	13 05	13 13	13 13		13 31	13 45	14 05	14 13	14 13	14 31	14 45	15 05	15 13		15 13	15 31	15 45	16 05	16 12	16 13	16 31	16 45
	d	12 32		13 06	13 14	13 14		13 32		14 06	14 14	14 14	14 32		15 06	15 14		15 14	15 32		16 06	16 13	16 14	16 32	
Swanwick	d			13 12	13 20	13 20				14 12	14 20	14 20			15 12	15 20		15 20			16 12	16 19	16 20		
Bursledon	d			13 16						14 16					15 16						16 16				
Hamble	d			13 19						14 19					15 19						16 19				
Netley	d			13 21						14 21					15 21						16 21				
Sholing	d			13 25						14 25					15 25						16 25				
Woolston	d			13 27						14 27					15 27						16 27				
Bitterne	d			13 31						14 31					15 31						16 31				
St Denys	d			13 34						14 34					15 34						16 34				
Southampton Central ⛴	a	12 53		13 40	13 45	13 44		13 54		14 40	14 44	14 44	14 53		15 40	15 45		15 44	15 53		16 40	16 44	16 44	16 53	

A not 11 September

B 11 September

Table 165

Sundays

until 11 September

Portsmouth and Fareham - Southampton

		GW ◇		SW 1	SN ◇1 A	SN ◇1 B	GW ◇	SW 1	SW 1	SN ◇1 B	SN ◇1 A	GW ◇		SW 1	GW ◇	SW 1	SN ◇1	GW ◇	SW 1	SW 1	SN ◇1 B	SN ◇1 A		GW ◇	SW 1
Portsmouth Harbour ⛴	d						17 08	17 17				18 08		18 17				19 08	19 17					20 08	20 17
Portsmouth & Southsea	d			16 42			17 12	17 22	17 42			18 12		18 22		18 42		19 12	19 22	19 42				20 12	20 22
Fratton	d			16 46			17 16	17 26	17 46			18 16		18 26		18 46		19 16	19 26	19 46				20 16	20 26
Hilsea	d			16 50				17 30	17 50					18 30		18 50			19 30	19 50					20 30
Chichester 4	d	16 34			16 45	16 45				17 44	17 45				18 34		18 45				19 44	19 45			
Havant	d	16 48			16 58	16 59				17 58	17 58				18 48		18 58				19 58	19 58			
Cosham	d	16 55		16 59	17 05	17 07	17 23	17 35	17 55	18 05	18 05	18 23		18 35	18 55	18 59	19 05	19 23	19 35	19 55	20 05	20 05			20 35
Portchester	d			17 03				17 40	18 00					18 40		19 03			19 40	20 00					20 40
Fareham	a	17 02		17 08	17 14	17 15	17 31	17 45	18 05	18 13	18 13	18 31		18 45	19 02	19 08	19 13	19 31	19 45	20 05	20 13	20 13		20 31	20 45
	d	17 03		17 09	17 15	17 16	17 32		18 06	18 14	18 14	18 32			19 03	19 09	19 14	19 32		20 06	20 14	20 14		20 32	
Swanwick	d			17 16	17 22	17 24			18 12	18 20	18 20					19 16	19 22			20 12	20 20	20 20			
Bursledon	d			17 19					18 16							19 19				20 16					
Hamble	d			17 23					18 19							19 23				20 19					
Netley	d			17 25					18 21							19 25				20 21					
Sholing	d			17 29					18 25							19 29				20 25					
Woolston	d			17 31					18 27							19 31				20 27					
Bitterne	d			17 34					18 31							19 34				20 31					
St Denys	d			17 38					18 34							19 38				20 34					
Southampton Central ⛴	a	17 24		17 43	17 48	17 49	17 53		18 40	18 47	18 44	18 53			19 24	19 43	19 48	19 53		20 40	20 46	20 46		20 53	

		SW 1	SN ◇1 B	SN ◇1 A	SW 1	SW 1	SN ◇1 B	SN ◇1 A		GW	SW 1	SW 1	SW 1
Portsmouth Harbour ⛴	d				21 17					22 03	22 17		23 17
Portsmouth & Southsea	d	20 42			21 22	21 42				22 12	22 22	22 42	23 22
Fratton	d	20 46			21 26	21 46				22 16	22 26	22 46	23 26
Hilsea	d	20 50			21 30	21 50					22 30	22 50	23 30
Chichester 4	d		20 44	20 45			21 44	21 45					
Havant	d		20 58	20 58			21 58	21 58					
Cosham	d	20 55	21 07	21 07	21 35	21 55	22 05	22 05			22 35	22 55	23 35
Portchester	d	21 00			21 40	22 00					22 40	23 00	23 40
Fareham	a	21 05	21 15	21 15	21 45	22 05	22 13	22 13		22 31	22 45	23 05	23 45
	d	21 06	21 16	21 16		22 06	22 14	22 14		22 32		23 06	
Swanwick	d	21 12	21 22	21 22		22 12	22 20	22 20				23 12	
Bursledon	d	21 16				22 16						23 16	
Hamble	d	21 19				22 19						23 19	
Netley	d	21 21				22 21						23 21	
Sholing	d	21 25				22 25						23 25	
Woolston	d	21 27				22 27						23 27	
Bitterne	d	21 31				22 31						23 31	
St Denys	d	21 34				22 34						23 34	
Southampton Central ⛴	a	21 40	21 45	21 45		22 40	22 44	22 44		22 53		23 40	

Sundays

18 September to 23 October

		SW 1	SW 1	SW 1	SN ◇1	SW 1	SW 1	SN ◇1	GW	SW 1 🍴		SW 1	SN ◇1	SW 1 🍴	SW 1	SN ◇1	GW ◇	SW 1 🍴	SW 1	SN ◇1		GW ◇	SW 1 🍴	SW 1	SN ◇1
Portsmouth Harbour ⛴	d	06 37	07 17			08 17			09 08	09 17				10 17			11 08	11 17					12 17		
Portsmouth & Southsea	d	06 42	07 22	07 42		08 22	08 42		09 12	09 22		09 42		10 22	10 42		11 12	11 22	11 42				12 22	12 42	
Fratton	d	06 46	07 26	07 46		08 26	08 46		09 16	09 26		09 46		10 26	10 46		11 16	11 26	11 46				12 26	12 46	
Hilsea	d	06 50	07 30	07 50		08 30	08 50			09 30		09 50		10 30	10 50			11 30	11 50				12 30	12 50	
Chichester 4	d				07 45			08 45					09 45			10 45				11 45		11 54			12 45
Havant	d				07 58			08 58					09 58			10 58				11 58		12 10			12 58
Cosham	d	06 55	07 35	07 55	08 05	08 35	08 55	09 05	09 23	09 35		09 55	10 06	10 35	10 55	11 06	11 23	11 35	11 55	12 05		12 23	12 35	12 55	13 05
Portchester	d	07 00	07 40	08 00		08 40	09 00			09 40		10 00		10 40	11 00			11 40	12 00				12 40	13 00	
Fareham	a	07 05	07 45	08 05	08 13	08 45	09 05	09 13	09 31	09 45		10 05	10 14	10 45	11 05	11 14	11 31	11 45	12 05	12 13		12 31	12 45	13 05	13 13
	d	07 06		08 06	08 14		09 06	09 14	09 32			10 06	10 15		11 06	11 15	11 32		12 06	12 14		12 32		13 06	13 14
Swanwick	d	07 12		08 12	08 20		09 12	09 20				10 12	10 21		11 12	11 21			12 12	12 20				13 12	13 20
Bursledon	d	07 16		08 16			09 16					10 16			11 16				12 16					13 16	
Hamble	d	07 19		08 19			09 19					10 19			11 19				12 19					13 19	
Netley	d	07 21		08 21			09 21					10 21			11 21				12 21					13 21	
Sholing	d	07 25		08 25			09 25					10 25			11 25				12 25					13 25	
Woolston	d	07 27		08 27			09 27					10 27			11 27				12 27					13 27	
Bitterne	d	07 31		08 31			09 31					10 31			11 31				12 31					13 31	
St Denys	d	07 34		08 34			09 34					10 34			11 34				12 34					13 34	
Southampton Central ⛴	a	07 40		08 40	08 44		09 40	09 44	09 53			10 40	10 44		11 40	11 44	11 53		12 40	12 44		12 53		13 40	13 44

A 11 September

B not 11 September

Table 165

Sundays

18 September to 23 October

Portsmouth and Fareham - Southampton

	GW	SW	SW	SN	GW		SW	SW	SN	GW	SW	SW	SN	GW	SW		GW	SW	SN	GW	SW	SW	SN	GW
	◇	1 🚲	1	◇1	◇		1 🚲	1	◇1	R	1 🚲	1	◇1	◇	1 🚲		◇	1	◇1	◇	1	1	◇1	◇
Portsmouth Harbour ⛴ d	13 08	13 17			14 08		14 17			15 08	15 17			16 08	16 17					17 08	17 17			18 08
Portsmouth & Southsea d	13 12	13 22	13 42		14 12		14 22	14 42		15 12	15 22	15 42		16 12	16 22			16 42		17 12	17 22	17 42		18 12
Fratton d	13 16	13 26	13 46		14 16		14 26	14 46		15 16	15 26	15 46		16 16	16 26			16 46		17 16	17 26	17 46		18 16
Hilsea d		13 30	13 50				14 30	14 50			15 30	15 50			16 30			16 50			17 30	17 50		
Chichester 4 d				13 45					14 45				15 45				16 34		16 45				17 45	
Havant d				13 58					14 58				15 58				16 48		16 58				17 58	
Cosham d	13 23	13 35	13 55	14 05	14 23		14 35	14 55	15 05	15 23	15 35	15 55	16 05	16 23	16 35		16 55	16 59	17 05	17 23	17 35	17 55	18 05	18 23
Portchester d		13 40	14 00				14 40	15 00			15 40	16 00			16 40			17 03			17 40	18 00		
Fareham a	13 31	13 45	14 05	14 13	14 31		14 45	15 05	15 13	15 31	15 45	16 05	16 13	16 31	16 45		17 02	17 08	17 14	17 31	17 45	18 05	18 13	18 31
d	13 32		14 06	14 14	14 32			15 06	15 14	15 32		16 06	16 14	16 32			17 03	17 09	17 15	17 32		18 06	18 14	18 32
Swanwick d			14 12	14 20				15 12	15 20			16 12	16 20					17 16	17 22			18 12	18 20	
Bursledon d			14 16					15 16				16 16						17 19				18 16		
Hamble d			14 19					15 19				16 19						17 23				18 19		
Netley d			14 21					15 21				16 21						17 25				18 21		
Sholing d			14 25					15 25				16 25						17 29				18 25		
Woolston d			14 27					15 27				16 27						17 31				18 27		
Bitterne d			14 31					15 31				16 31						17 34				18 31		
St Denys d			14 34					15 34				16 34						17 38				18 34		
Southampton Central ⛴ a	13 54		14 40	14 44	14 53			15 40	15 44	15 53		16 40	16 44	16 53			17 24	17 43	17 48	17 53		18 40	18 44	18 53

	SW		GW	SW	SN	GW	SW	SW	SN	GW	SW		SW	SN	SW	SW	SN	GW	SW	SW	SW			
	1		◇	1	◇1	◇	1	1	◇1	◇	1		1	◇1	1	1	◇1		1	1	1			
Portsmouth Harbour ⛴ d	18 17					19 08	19 17			20 08	20 17				21 17			22 03	22 17		23 17			
Portsmouth & Southsea d	18 22			18 42		19 12	19 22	19 42		20 12	20 22		20 42		21 22	21 42		22 12	22 22	22 42	23 22			
Fratton d	18 26			18 46		19 16	19 26	19 46		20 16	20 26		20 46		21 26	21 46		22 16	22 26	22 46	23 26			
Hilsea d	18 30			18 50			19 30	19 50			20 30		20 50		21 30	21 50			22 30	22 50	23 30			
Chichester 4 d			18 34		18 45				19 45					20 45			21 45							
Havant d			18 48		18 58				19 58					20 58			21 58							
Cosham d	18 35		18 55	18 59	19 05	19 23	19 35	19 55	20 05		20 35		20 55	21 07	21 35	21 55	22 05		22 35	22 55	23 35			
Portchester d	18 40			19 03			19 40	20 00			20 40		21 00		21 40	22 00			22 40	23 00	23 40			
Fareham a	18 45		19 02	19 08	19 13	19 31	19 45	20 05	20 13	20 31	20 45		21 05	21 15	21 45	22 05	22 13	22 31	22 45	23 05	23 45			
d			19 03	19 09	19 14	19 32		20 06	20 14	20 32			21 06	21 16		22 06	22 14	22 32		23 06				
Swanwick d				19 16	19 22			20 12	20 20				21 12	21 22		22 12	22 20			23 12				
Bursledon d				19 19				20 16					21 16			22 16				23 16				
Hamble d				19 23				20 19					21 19			22 19				23 19				
Netley d				19 25				20 21					21 21			22 21				23 21				
Sholing d				19 29				20 25					21 25			22 25				23 25				
Woolston d				19 31				20 27					21 27			22 27				23 27				
Bitterne d				19 34				20 31					21 31			22 31				23 31				
St Denys d				19 38				20 34					21 34			22 34				23 34				
Southampton Central ⛴ a			19 24	19 43	19 48	19 53		20 40	20 46	20 53			21 40	21 45		22 40	22 44	22 53		23 40				

Sundays

from 30 October

	SW	SW	SW	SN	SW	SW	SN	GW	SW		SW	SN	SW	SW	SN	GW	SW	SW	SN		GW	SW	SW	SN
	1	1	1	◇1	1	1	◇1	R	1 🚲		1	◇1	1 🚲	1	◇1	◇	1 🚲	1	◇1		◇	1 🚲	1	◇1
Portsmouth Harbour ⛴ d	06 37	07 17			08 17			09 08	09 17				10 17			11 08	11 17					12 17		
Portsmouth & Southsea d	06 42	07 22	07 42		08 22	08 42		09 12	09 22		09 42		10 22	10 42		11 12	11 22	11 42				12 22	12 42	
Fratton d	06 46	07 26	07 46		08 26	08 46		09 16	09 26		09 46		10 26	10 46		11 16	11 26	11 46				12 26	12 46	
Hilsea d	06 50	07 30	07 50		08 30	08 50			09 30		09 50		10 30	10 50			11 30	11 50				12 30	12 50	
Chichester 4 d				07 45			08 45					09 45			10 45				11 45		11 54			12 45
Havant d				07 58			08 58					09 58			10 58				11 58		12 10			12 58
Cosham d	06 55	07 35	07 55	08 05	08 35	08 55	09 05	09 23	09 35		09 55	10 06	10 35	10 55	11 06	11 23	11 35	11 55	12 05		12 23	12 35	12 55	13 05
Portchester d	07 00	07 40	08 00		08 40	09 00			09 40		10 00		10 40	11 00			11 40	12 00				12 40	13 00	
Fareham a	07 05	07 45	08 05	08 13	08 45	09 05	09 13	09 31	09 45		10 05	10 14	10 45	11 05	11 14	11 31	11 45	12 05	12 13		12 31	12 45	13 05	13 13
d	07 06		08 06	08 14		09 06	09 14	09 32			10 06	10 15		11 06	11 15	11 32		12 06	12 14		12 32		13 06	13 14
Swanwick d	07 12		08 12	08 20		09 12	09 20				10 12	10 21		11 12	11 21			12 12	12 20				13 12	13 20
Bursledon d	07 16		08 16			09 16					10 16			11 16				12 16					13 16	
Hamble d	07 19		08 19			09 19					10 19			11 19				12 19					13 19	
Netley d	07 21		08 21			09 21					10 21			11 21				12 21					13 21	
Sholing d	07 25		08 25			09 25					10 25			11 25				12 25					13 25	
Woolston d	07 27		08 27			09 27					10 27			11 27				12 27					13 27	
Bitterne d	07 31		08 31			09 31					10 31			11 31				12 31					13 31	
St Denys d	07 34		08 34			09 34					10 34			11 34				12 34					13 34	
Southampton Central ⛴ a	07 40		08 40	08 44		09 40	09 44	09 53			10 40	10 44		11 40	11 44	11 53		12 40	12 44		12 53		13 40	13 44

Table 165

Sundays
from 30 October

Portsmouth and Fareham - Southampton

		GW	SW	SW	SN	GW	SW	SW	SN	GW	SW	SW	SN	GW	SW	GW	SW	SN	GW	SW	SW	SN	GW
		◇	[1] 🛒	[1]	◇[1]	◇	[1] 🛒	[1]	◇[1]	[R]	[1] 🛒	[1]	◇[1]	◇	[1] 🛒	◇	[1]	◇[1]	◇	[1]	[1]	◇[1]	◇
Portsmouth Harbour ⛴	d	13 08	13 17			14 08	14 17			15 08	15 17			16 08	16 17				17 08	17 17			18 08
Portsmouth & Southsea	d	13 12	13 22	13 42		14 12	14 22	14 42		15 12	15 22	15 42		16 12	16 22		16 42		17 12	17 22	17 42		18 12
Fratton	d	13 16	13 26	13 46		14 16	14 26	14 46		15 16	15 26	15 46		16 16	16 26		16 46		17 16	17 26	17 46		18 16
Hilsea	d		13 30	13 50			14 30	14 50			15 30	15 50			16 30		16 50			17 30	17 50		
Chichester [4]	d				13 45				14 45				15 45			16 34		16 45				17 45	
Havant	d				13 58				14 58				15 58			16 48		16 58				17 58	
Cosham	d	13 23	13 35	13 55	14 05	14 23	14 35	14 55	15 05	15 23	15 35	15 55	16 05	16 23	16 35	16 55	16 59	17 05	17 23	17 35	17 55	18 05	18 23
Portchester	d		13 40	14 00			14 40	15 00			15 40	16 00			16 40		17 03			17 40	18 00		
Fareham	a	13 31	13 45	14 05	14 13	14 31	14 45	15 05	15 13	15 31	15 45	16 05	16 13	16 31	16 45	17 02	17 08	17 14	17 31	17 45	18 05	18 13	18 31
	d	13 32		14 06	14 14	14 32		15 06	15 14	15 32		16 06	16 14	16 32		17 03	17 09	17 15	17 32		18 06	18 14	18 32
Swanwick	d			14 12	14 20			15 12	15 20			16 12	16 20				17 16	17 22			18 12	18 20	
Bursledon	d			14 16				15 16				16 16					17 19				18 16		
Hamble	d			14 19				15 19				16 19					17 23				18 19		
Netley	d			14 21				15 21				16 21					17 25				18 21		
Sholing	d			14 25				15 25				16 25					17 29				18 25		
Woolston	d			14 27				15 27				16 27					17 31				18 27		
Bitterne	d			14 31				15 31				16 31					17 34				18 31		
St Denys	d			14 34				15 34				16 34					17 38				18 34		
Southampton Central ⛴	a	13 54		14 40	14 44	14 53		15 40	15 44	15 53		16 40	16 44	16 53		17 24	17 43	17 48	17 53		18 40	18 44	18 53

		SW	GW	SW	SN	GW	SW	SW	SN	GW	SW	SW	SN	SW	SW	SN	GW	SW	SW	SW
		[1]	◇	[1]	◇[1]	◇	[1]	[1]	◇[1]	◇	[1]	[1]	◇[1]	[1]	[1]	◇[1]		[1]	[1]	[1]
Portsmouth Harbour ⛴	d	18 17				19 08	19 17			20 08	20 17			21 17			22 03	22 17		23 17
Portsmouth & Southsea	d	18 22		18 42		19 12	19 22	19 42		20 12	20 22	20 42		21 22	21 42		22 12	22 22	22 42	23 22
Fratton	d	18 26		18 46		19 16	19 26	19 46		20 16	20 26	20 46		21 26	21 46		22 16	22 26	22 46	23 26
Hilsea	d	18 30		18 50			19 30	19 50			20 30	20 50		21 30	21 50			22 30	22 50	23 30
Chichester [4]	d		18 34		18 45				19 45				20 45			21 45				
Havant	d		18 48		18 58				19 58				20 58			21 58				
Cosham	d	18 35	18 55	18 59	19 05	19 23	19 35	19 55	20 05		20 35	20 55	21 07	21 35	21 55	22 05		22 35	22 55	23 35
Portchester	d	18 40		19 03			19 40	20 00			20 40	21 00		21 40	22 00			22 40	23 00	23 40
Fareham	a	18 45	19 02	19 08	19 13	19 31	19 45	20 05	20 13	20 31	20 45	21 05	21 15	21 45	22 05	22 13	22 31	22 45	23 05	23 45
	d		19 03	19 09	19 14	19 32		20 06	20 14	20 32		21 06	21 16		22 06	22 14	22 32		23 06	
Swanwick	d			19 16	19 22			20 12	20 20			21 12	21 22		22 12	22 20			23 12	
Bursledon	d			19 19				20 16				21 16			22 16				23 16	
Hamble	d			19 23				20 19				21 19			22 19				23 19	
Netley	d			19 25				20 21				21 21			22 21				23 21	
Sholing	d			19 29				20 25				21 25			22 25				23 25	
Woolston	d			19 31				20 27				21 27			22 27				23 27	
Bitterne	d			19 34				20 31				21 31			22 31				23 31	
St Denys	d			19 38				20 34				21 34			22 34				23 34	
Southampton Central ⛴	a		19 24	19 43	19 48	19 53		20 40	20 46	20 53		21 40	21 45		22 40	22 44	22 53		23 40	

Table 167

Mondays to Fridays

To and from the Isle of Wight via Portsmouth and Ryde

Miles			IL	IL	IL	IL	IL	IL	IL	IL	IL		IL	IL	IL	IL	IL	IL	IL	IL	IL		IL	IL	IL
—	**Portsmouth Harbour**	d																							
0	**Ryde Pier Head**	d	05 49	06 07	06 49	07 07	07 49	08 07	08 49	09 07	09 49		10 07	10 49	11 07	11 49	12 07	12 49	13 07	13 49	14 07		14 49	15 07	15 49
—	**Ryde Esplanade**	d	05 51	06 09	06 52	07 09	07 52	08 09	08 52	09 09	09 52		10 09	10 52	11 09	11 52	12 09	12 52	13 09	13 52	14 09		14 52	15 09	15 52
1¼	Ryde St Johns Road	d	05 55	06 13	06 55	07 13	07 55	08 13	08 55	09 13	09 55		10 13	10 55	11 13	11 55	12 13	12 55	13 13	13 55	14 13		14 55	15 13	15 55
2¼	Smallbrook Junction §	d												10 58		11 58	12 15	12 58	13 15				14 58	15 15	15 58
4¾	Brading	d	06 02	06 20	07 03	07 20	08 03	08 20	09 03	09 20	10 03		10 20	11 03	11 20	12 03	12 20	13 03	13 20	14 03	14 20		15 03	15 20	16 03
6½	Sandown	d	06 07	06 25	07 07	07 25	08 07	08 25	09 07	09 25	10 07		10 25	11 07	11 25	12 07	12 25	13 07	13 25	14 07	14 25		15 07	15 25	16 07
7¼	Lake	d	06 09	06 27	07 10	07 27	08 10	08 27	09 10	09 27	10 10		10 27	11 10	11 27	12 10	12 27	13 10	13 27	14 10	14 27		15 10	15 27	16 10
8½	**Shanklin**	a	06 12	06 30	07 13	07 30	08 13	08 30	09 13	09 30	10 13		10 30	11 13	11 30	12 13	12 30	13 13	13 30	14 13	14 30		15 13	15 30	16 13

		IL	IL	IL	IL	IL	IL		IL	IL	IL	IL	IL	IL
Portsmouth Harbour	d													
Ryde Pier Head	d	16 07	16 49	17 07	17 49	18 07	18 49		19 07	19 49	20 07	20 45	21 45	22 45
Ryde Esplanade	d	16 09	16 52	17 09	17 52	18 09	18 52		19 09	19 52	20 09	20 47	21 47	22 47
Ryde St Johns Road	d	16 13	16 55	17 13	17 55	18 13	18 55		19 13	19 55	20 13	20 51	21 51	22a51
Smallbrook Junction §	d	16 15												
Brading	d	16 20	17 03	17 20	18 03	18 20	19 03		19 20	20 03	20 20	20 57	21 57	
Sandown	d	16 25	17 07	17 25	18 07	18 25	19 07		19 25	20 07	20 25	21 01	22 01	
Lake	d	16 27	17 10	17 27	18 10	18 27	19 10		19 27	20 10	20 27	21 04	22 04	
Shanklin	a	16 30	17 13	17 30	18 13	18 30	19 13		19 30	20 13	20 30	21 07	22 07	

Saturdays

		IL	IL	IL	IL	IL	IL	IL	IL	IL		IL	IL	IL	IL	IL	IL	IL	IL	IL		IL	IL	IL	IL
Portsmouth Harbour	d																								
Ryde Pier Head	d	05 49	06 07	06 49	07 07	07 49	08 07	08 49	09 07	09 49		10 07	10 49	11 07	11 49	12 07	12 49	13 07	13 49	14 07		14 49	15 07	15 49	16 07
Ryde Esplanade	d	05 51	06 09	06 52	07 09	07 52	08 09	08 52	09 09	09 52		10 09	10 52	11 09	11 52	12 09	12 52	13 09	13 52	14 09		14 52	15 09	15 52	16 09
Ryde St Johns Road	d	05 55	06 13	06 55	07 13	07 55	08 13	08 55	09 13	09 55		10 13	10 55	11 13	11 55	12 13	12 55	13 13	13 55	14 13		14 55	15 13	15 55	16 13
Smallbrook Junction §	d												10 58		11 58	12 15	12 58	13 15				14 58	15 15	15 58	16 15
Brading	d	06 02	06 20	07 03	07 20	08 03	08 20	09 03	09 20	10 03		10 20	11 03	11 20	12 03	12 20	13 03	13 20	14 03	14 20		15 03	15 20	16 03	16 20
Sandown	d	06 07	06 25	07 07	07 25	08 07	08 25	09 07	09 25	10 07		10 25	11 07	11 25	12 07	12 25	13 07	13 25	14 07	14 25		15 07	15 25	16 07	16 25
Lake	d	06 09	06 27	07 10	07 27	08 10	08 27	09 10	09 27	10 10		10 27	11 10	11 27	12 10	12 27	13 10	13 27	14 10	14 27		15 10	15 27	16 10	16 27
Shanklin	a	06 12	06 30	07 13	07 30	08 13	08 30	09 13	09 30	10 13		10 30	11 13	11 30	12 13	12 30	13 14	13 30	14 13	14 30		15 13	15 30	16 13	16 30

		IL	IL	IL	IL	IL		IL	IL	IL	IL	IL	IL
Portsmouth Harbour	d												
Ryde Pier Head	d	16 49	17 07	17 49	18 07	18 49		19 07	19 49	20 07	20 45	21 45	22 45
Ryde Esplanade	d	16 52	17 09	17 52	18 09	18 52		19 09	19 52	20 09	20 47	21 47	22 47
Ryde St Johns Road	d	16 55	17 13	17 55	18 13	18 55		19 13	19 55	20 13	20 51	21 51	22a51
Smallbrook Junction §	d												
Brading	d	17 03	17 20	18 03	18 20	19 03		19 20	20 03	20 20	20 57	21 57	
Sandown	d	17 07	17 25	18 07	18 25	19 07		19 25	20 07	20 25	21 01	22 01	
Lake	d	17 10	17 27	18 10	18 27	19 10		19 27	20 10	20 27	21 04	22 04	
Shanklin	a	17 13	17 30	18 13	18 30	19 13		19 30	20 13	20 30	21 07	22 07	

Sundays

until 25 September

		IL	IL	IL	IL	IL	IL	IL	IL	IL		IL	IL	IL	IL	IL	IL	IL	IL	IL		IL	IL	IL	IL
Portsmouth Harbour	d																								
Ryde Pier Head	d	06 49	07 49		08 49	09 07	09 49	10 07	10 49	11 07		11 49	12 07	12 49	13 07	13 49	14 07	14 49	15 07	15 49		16 07	16 49	17 07	17 49
Ryde Esplanade	d	06 52	07 52		08 52	09 09	09 52	10 09	10 52	11 09		11 52	12 09	12 52	13 09	13 52	14 09	14 52	15 09	15 52		16 09	16 52	17 09	17 52
Ryde St Johns Road	d	06 55	07 55	08 13	08 55	09 13	09 55	10 13	10 55	11 13		11 55	12 13	12 55	13 13	13 55	14 13	14 55	15 13	15 55		16 13	16 55	17 13	17 55
Smallbrook Junction §	d								10 58			11 58	12 15	12 58	13 15			14 58	15 15	15 58		16 15			
Brading	d	07 03	08 03	08 20	09 03	09 20	10 03	10 20	11 03	11 20		12 03	12 20	13 03	13 20	14 03	14 20	15 03	15 20	16 03		16 20	17 03	17 20	18 03
Sandown	d	07 07	08 07	08 25	09 07	09 25	10 07	10 25	11 07	11 25		12 07	12 25	13 07	13 25	14 07	14 25	15 07	15 25	16 07		16 25	17 07	17 25	18 07
Lake	d	07 10	08 10	08 27	09 10	09 27	10 10	10 27	11 10	11 27		12 10	12 27	13 10	13 27	14 10	14 27	15 10	15 27	16 10		16 27	17 10	17 27	18 10
Shanklin	a	07 13	08 13	08 30	09 13	09 30	10 13	10 30	11 13	11 30		12 13	12 30	13 13	13 30	14 13	14 30	15 13	15 30	16 13		16 30	17 13	17 30	18 13

		IL	IL	IL	IL	IL		IL	IL	IL
Portsmouth Harbour	d									
Ryde Pier Head	d	18 07	18 49	19 07	19 49	20 07		20 45	21 45	22 45
Ryde Esplanade	d	18 09	18 52	19 09	19 52	20 09		20 47	21 47	22 47
Ryde St Johns Road	d	18 13	18 55	19 13	19 55	20a13		20 51	21 51	22a51
Smallbrook Junction §	d									
Brading	d	18 20	19 03	19 20	20 03			20 57	21 57	
Sandown	d	18 25	19 07	19 25	20 07			21 01	22 01	
Lake	d	18 27	19 10	19 27	20 10			21 04	22 04	
Shanklin	a	18 30	19 13	19 30	20 13			21 07	22 07	

Sundays

from 2 October

		IL	IL	IL	IL	IL	IL	IL	IL	IL		IL	IL	IL	IL	IL	IL	IL	IL	IL		IL	IL	IL	IL
Portsmouth Harbour	d																								
Ryde Pier Head	d	06 49	07 49	08 49	09 49	10 49	11 49	12 49	13 07	13 49		14 07	14 49	15 07	15 49	16 07	16 49	17 07	17 49	18 07		18 49	19 49	20 45	21 45
Ryde Esplanade	d	06 52	07 52	08 52	09 52	10 52	11 52	12 52	13 09	13 52		14 09	14 52	15 09	15 52	16 09	16 52	17 09	17 52	18 09		18 52	19 52	20 47	21 47
Ryde St Johns Road	d	06 55	07 55	08 55	09 55	10 55	11 55	12 55	13 13	13 55		14 13	14 55	15 13	15 55	16 13	16 55	17 13	17 55	18 13		18 55	19 55	20 51	21 51
Smallbrook Junction §	d					10 58	11 58	12 58	13 15				14 58	15 15	15 58	16 15									
Brading	d	07 03	08 03	09 03	10 03	11 03	12 03	13 03	13 20	14 03		14 20	15 03	15 20	16 03	16 20	17 03	17 20	18 03	18 20		19 03	20 03	20 57	21 57
Sandown	d	07 07	08 07	09 07	10 07	11 07	12 07	13 07	13 25	14 07		14 25	15 07	15 25	16 07	16 25	17 07	17 25	18 07	18 25		19 07	20 07	21 01	22 01
Lake	d	07 10	08 10	09 10	10 10	11 10	12 10	13 10	13 27	14 10		14 27	15 10	15 27	16 10	16 27	17 10	17 27	18 10	18 27		19 10	20 10	21 04	22 04
Shanklin	a	07 13	08 13	09 13	10 13	11 13	12 13	13 13	13 30	14 13		14 30	15 13	15 30	16 13	16 30	17 13	17 30	18 13	18 30		19 13	20 13	21 07	22 07

§ Smallbrook Jn. is only open for access to the I.O.W Steam Railway. For days of operation please enquire locally.

Table 167

Sundays
from 2 October

To and from the Isle of Wight via Portsmouth and Ryde

		IL
Portsmouth Harbour ⛴	d	
Ryde Pier Head	d	22 45
Ryde Esplanade	d	22 47
Ryde St Johns Road	d	22a51
Smallbrook Junction §	d	
Brading	d	
Sandown	d	
Lake	d	
Shanklin	a	

Mondays to Fridays

		IL	IL	IL	IL	IL	IL	IL	IL	IL		IL	IL	IL	IL	IL	IL	IL	IL	IL		IL	IL	IL	IL
Shanklin	d			06 18	06 38	07 18	07 38	08 18	08 38	09 18		09 38	10 18	10 38	11 18	11 38	12 18	12 38	13 18	13 38		14 18	14 38	15 18	15 38
Lake	d			06 21	06 41	07 21	07 41	08 21	08 41	09 21		09 41	10 21	10 41	11 21	11 41	12 21	12 41	13 21	13 41		14 21	14 41	15 21	15 41
Sandown	d			06 24	06 44	07 24	07 44	08 24	08 44	09 24		09 44	10 24	10 44	11 24	11 44	12 24	12 44	13 24	13 44		14 24	14 44	15 24	15 44
Brading	d			06 28	06 48	07 28	07 48	08 28	08 48	09 28		09 48	10 28	10 48	11 28	11 48	12 28	12 48	13 28	13 48		14 28	14 48	15 28	15 48
Smallbrook Junction §	d													10 53		11 53	12 33	12 53	13 33				14 53	15 33	15 53
Ryde St Johns Road	d	05 35	05 56	06 35	06 55	07 35	07 55	08 35	08 55	09 35		09 55	10 35	10 55	11 35	11 55	12 35	12 55	13 35	13 55		14 35	14 55	15 35	15 55
Ryde Esplanade	d	05 40	06 00	06 40	07 00	07 40	08 00	08 40	09 00	09 40		10 00	10 40	11 00	11 40	12 00	12 40	13 00	13 40	14 00		14 40	15 00	15 40	16 00
Ryde Pier Head	a	05 42	06 02	06 42	07 02	07 42	08 02	08 42	09 02	09 41		10 02	10 42	11 02	11 42	12 02	12 42	13 02	13 42	14 02		14 42	15 02	15 42	16 02
Portsmouth Harbour ⛴	a																								

		IL	IL	IL	IL	IL		IL	IL	IL	IL	IL	IL	IL
Shanklin	d	16 18	16 38	17 18	17 38	18 18		18 38	19 18	19 38	20 18	20 38	21 18	22 18
Lake	d	16 21	16 41	17 21	17 41	18 21		18 41	19 21	19 41	20 21	20 41	21 21	22 21
Sandown	d	16 24	16 44	17 24	17 44	18 24		18 44	19 24	19 44	20 24	20 44	21 24	22 24
Brading	d	16 28	16 48	17 28	17 48	18 28		18 48	19 28	19 48	20 28	20 48	21 28	22 28
Smallbrook Junction §	d	16 33												
Ryde St Johns Road	d	16 35	16 55	17 35	17 55	18 35		18 55	19 35	19 55	20 35	20a54	21 35	22 35
Ryde Esplanade	d	16 40	17 00	17 40	18 00	18 40		19 00	19 40	20 00	20 40		21 40	22 40
Ryde Pier Head	a	16 42	17 02	17 42	18 02	18 42		19 02	19 42	20 02	20 42		21 42	22 42
Portsmouth Harbour ⛴	a													

Saturdays

		IL	IL	IL	IL	IL	IL	IL	IL	IL		IL	IL	IL	IL	IL	IL	IL	IL	IL		IL	IL	IL	IL
Shanklin	d			06 18	06 38	07 18	07 38	08 18	08 38	09 18		09 38	10 18	10 38	11 18	11 38	12 18	12 38	13 18	13 38		14 18	14 38	15 18	15 38
Lake	d			06 21	06 41	07 21	07 41	08 21	08 41	09 21		09 41	10 21	10 41	11 21	11 41	12 21	12 41	13 21	13 41		14 21	14 41	15 21	15 41
Sandown	d			06 24	06 44	07 24	07 44	08 24	08 44	09 24		09 44	10 24	10 44	11 24	11 44	12 24	12 44	13 24	13 44		14 24	14 44	15 24	15 44
Brading	d			06 28	06 48	07 28	07 48	08 28	08 48	09 28		09 48	10 28	10 48	11 28	11 48	12 28	12 48	13 28	13 48		14 28	14 48	15 28	15 48
Smallbrook Junction §	d													10 53		11 53	12 33	12 53	13 33				14 53	15 33	15 53
Ryde St Johns Road	d	05 35	05 56	06 35	06 55	07 35	07 55	08 35	08 55	09 35		09 55	10 35	10 55	11 35	11 55	12 35	12 55	13 35	13 55		14 35	14 55	15 35	15 55
Ryde Esplanade	d	05 40	06 00	06 40	07 00	07 40	08 00	08 40	09 00	09 40		10 00	10 40	11 00	11 40	12 00	12 40	13 00	13 40	14 00		14 40	15 00	15 40	16 00
Ryde Pier Head	a	05 42	06 02	06 42	07 02	07 42	08 02	08 42	09 02	09 42		10 02	10 42	11 02	11 42	12 02	12 42	13 02	13 42	14 02		14 42	15 02	15 42	16 02
Portsmouth Harbour ⛴	a																								

		IL	IL	IL	IL	IL		IL	IL	IL	IL	IL	IL	IL
Shanklin	d	16 18	16 38	17 18	17 38	18 18		18 38	19 18	19 38	20 18	20 38	21 18	22 18
Lake	d	16 21	16 41	17 21	17 41	18 21		18 41	19 21	19 41	20 21	20 41	21 21	22 21
Sandown	d	16 24	16 44	17 24	17 44	18 24		18 44	19 24	19 44	20 24	20 44	21 24	22 24
Brading	d	16 28	16 48	17 28	17 48	18 28		18 48	19 28	19 48	20 28	20 48	21 28	22 28
Smallbrook Junction §	d	16 33												
Ryde St Johns Road	d	16 35	16 55	17 35	17 55	18 35		18 55	19 35	19 55	20 35	20a54	21 35	22 35
Ryde Esplanade	d	16 40	17 00	17 40	18 00	18 40		19 00	19 40	20 00	20 40		21 40	22 40
Ryde Pier Head	a	16 42	17 02	17 42	18 02	18 42		19 02	19 42	20 02	20 42		21 42	22 42
Portsmouth Harbour ⛴	a													

Sundays
until 25 September

		IL	IL	IL	IL	IL	IL	IL	IL	IL		IL	IL	IL	IL	IL	IL	IL	IL	IL		IL	IL	IL	IL
Shanklin	d		07 18	08 18	08 38	09 18	09 38	10 18	10 38	11 18		11 38	12 18	12 38	13 18	13 38	14 18	14 38	15 18	15 38		16 18	16 38	17 18	17 38
Lake	d		07 21	08 21	08 41	09 21	09 41	10 21	10 41	11 21		11 41	12 21	12 41	13 21	13 41	14 21	14 41	15 21	15 41		16 21	16 41	17 21	17 41
Sandown	d		07 24	08 24	08 44	09 24	09 44	10 24	10 44	11 24		11 44	12 24	12 44	13 24	13 44	14 24	14 44	15 24	15 44		16 24	16 44	17 24	17 44
Brading	d		07 28	08 28	08 48	09 28	09 48	10 28	10 48	11 28		11 48	12 28	12 48	13 28	13 48	14 28	14 48	15 28	15 48		16 28	16 48	17 28	17 48
Smallbrook Junction §	d								10 53			11 53	12 33	12 53	13 33			14 53	15 33	15 53		16 33			
Ryde St Johns Road	d	06 35	07 35	08 35	08 55	09 35	09 55	10 35	10 55	11 35		11 55	12 35	12 55	13 35	13 55	14 35	14 55	15 35	15 55		16 35	16 55	17 35	17 55
Ryde Esplanade	d	06 40	07 40	08 40	09 00	09 40	10 00	10 40	11 00	11 40		12 00	12 40	13 00	13 40	14 00	14 40	15 00	15 40	16 00		16 40	17 00	17 40	18 00
Ryde Pier Head	a	06 42	07 42	08 42	09 02	09 42	10 02	10 42	11 02	11 42		12 02	12 42	13 02	13 42	14 02	14 42	15 02	15 42	16 02		16 42	17 02	17 42	18 02
Portsmouth Harbour ⛴	a																								

		IL	IL	IL	IL	IL		IL	IL
Shanklin	d	18 18	18 38	19 18	19 38	20 18		21 18	22 18
Lake	d	18 21	18 41	19 21	19 41	20 21		21 21	22 21
Sandown	d	18 24	18 44	19 24	19 44	20 24		21 24	22 24
Brading	d	18 28	18 48	19 28	19 48	20 28		21 28	22 28
Smallbrook Junction §	d								
Ryde St Johns Road	d	18 35	18 55	19 35	19 55	20 35		21 35	22 35
Ryde Esplanade	d	18 40	19 00	19 40	20 00	20 40		21 40	22 40
Ryde Pier Head	a	18 42	19 02	19 42	20 02	20 42		21 42	22 42
Portsmouth Harbour ⛴	a								

§ Smallbrook Jn. is only open for access to the I.O.W Steam Railway. For days of operation please enquire locally.

Table 167

Sundays

from 2 October

To and from the Isle of Wight via Portsmouth and Ryde

		IL	IL	IL	IL	IL	IL	IL	IL	IL	
Shanklin	d		07 18	08 18	09 18	10 18	11 18	12 18		13 18	
Lake	d		07 21	08 21	09 21	10 21	11 21	12 21		13 21	
Sandown	d		07 24	08 24	09 24	10 24	11 24	12 24		13 24	
Brading	d		07 28	08 28	09 28	10 28	11 28	12 28		13 28	
Smallbrook Junction §	d							12 33		13 33	
Ryde St Johns Road	d	06 35	07 35	08 35	09 35	10 35	11 35	12 35	12 55	13 35	
Ryde Esplanade	d	06 40	07 40	08 40	09 40	10 40	11 40	12 40	13 00	13 40	
Ryde Pier Head	a	06 42	07 42	08 42	09 42	10 42	11 42	12 42	13 02	13 42	
Portsmouth Harbour ⛴	a										

		IL	IL	IL	IL	IL	IL	IL	IL	IL		IL	IL	IL	IL
Shanklin	d	13 38	14 18	14 38	15 18	15 38	16 18	16 38	17 18	17 38		18 18	18 38	19 18	20 18
Lake	d	13 41	14 21	14 41	15 21	15 41	16 21	16 41	17 21	17 41		18 21	18 41	19 21	20 21
Sandown	d	13 44	14 24	14 44	15 24	15 44	16 24	16 44	17 24	17 44		18 24	18 44	19 24	20 24
Brading	d	13 48	14 28	14 48	15 28	15 48	16 28	16 48	17 28	17 48		18 28	18 48	19 28	20 28
Smallbrook Junction §	d			14 53	15 33	15 53	16 33								
Ryde St Johns Road	d	13 55	14 35	14 55	15 35	15 55	16 35	16 55	17 35	17 55		18 35	18a54	19 35	20 35
Ryde Esplanade	d	14 00	14 40	15 00	15 40	16 00	16 40	17 00	17 40	18 00		18 40		19 40	20 40
Ryde Pier Head	a	14 02	14 42	15 02	15 42	16 02	16 42	17 02	17 42	18 02		18 42		19 42	20 42
Portsmouth Harbour ⛴	a														

		IL	IL
Shanklin	d	21 18	22 18
Lake	d	21 21	22 21
Sandown	d	21 24	22 24
Brading	d	21 28	22 28
Smallbrook Junction §	d		
Ryde St Johns Road	d	21 35	22 35
Ryde Esplanade	d	21 40	22 40
Ryde Pier Head	a	21 42	22 42
Portsmouth Harbour ⛴	a		

§ Smallbrook Jn. is only open for access to the I.O.W Steam Railway. For days of operation please enquire locally.

Table 167A

Mondays to Fridays

Portsmouth Harbour - Ryde Pier Head

		SW A	SW B	SW	SW	SW	SW	SW	SW	SW		SW	SW	SW	SW	SW	SW	SW	SW	SW		SW	SW	SW	SW
Portsmouth Harbour	d			00 15		04 15		05 15		06 15			06 40		07 15		07 40		08 15			08 40		09 15	
Ryde Pier Head	a			00 37		04 37		05 37		06 37			07 02		07 37		08 02		08 37			09 02		09 37	
	d	23p45	23p47		00 47		04 47		05 47			06 47		07 10		07 47		08 10		08 47			09 10		09 47
Portsmouth Harbour	a	00 07	00 09		01 09		05 09		06 09			07 09		07 32		08 09		08 32		09 09			09 32		10 09

		SW	SW	SW	SW	SW		SW	SW	SW	SW	SW	SW	SW	SW C	SW		SW	SW	SW	SW	SW	SW	SW	SW
Portsmouth Harbour	d	09 40		10 40		11 15			12 15		13 15		14 15		15 15			15 40		16 15		16 40		17 15	
Ryde Pier Head	a	10 02		11 02		11 37			12 37		13 37		14 37		15 37			16 02		16 37		17 02		17 37	
	d		10 10		11 10			11 47		12 47		13 47		14 47		15 47			16 10		16 47		17 10		17 47
Portsmouth Harbour	a		10 32		11 32			12 09		13 09		14 09		15 09		16 09			16 32		17 09		17 32		18 09

		SW		SW	SW	SW	SW	SW	SW	SW	SW FO	SW FO		SW	SW	SW	SW	SW	SW	SW	SW				
Portsmouth Harbour	d	17 40			18 15		18 45		19 15		19 45			20 15		21 15		22 15		23 15					
Ryde Pier Head	a	18 02			18 37		19 07		19 37		20 07			20 37		21 37		22 37		23 37					
	d			18 10		18 47		19 15		19 47		20 15			20 47		21 47		22 47		23 47				
Portsmouth Harbour	a			18 32		19 09		19 37		20 09		20 37			21 09		22 09		23 09		00 09				

Saturdays

		SW	SW D	SW E	SW F	SW	SW E	SW F	SW	SW E		SW F	SW	SW E	SW F	SW	SW E	SW F	SW	SW E		SW F	SW	SW	SW
Portsmouth Harbour	d		00 15			04 15			05 15				06 15			07 15			08 15					08 40	09 15
Ryde Pier Head	a		00 37			04 37			05 37				06 37			07 37			08 37					09 12	09 37
	d	23p47		00 45	00 47		04 45	04 47		05 45		05 47		06 45	06 47		07 45	07 47		08 45		08 47	09 10		
Portsmouth Harbour	a	00 09		01 07	01 09		05 07	05 09		06 07		06 09		07 07	07 09		08 07	08 09		09 07		09 09	09 32		

		SW E	SW F	SW	SW	SW		SW E	SW F	SW	SW	SW	SW E	SW F	SW	SW		SW	SW E	SW F	SW	SW	SW G	SW G	SW
Portsmouth Harbour	d			09 40		10 15				10 40		11 15			11 40			12 15			12 40		13 15		13 40
Ryde Pier Head	a			10 02		10 37				11 02		11 37			12 02			12 37			13 02		13 37		14 02
	d	09 45	09 47		10 10			10 45	10 47		11 10		11 45	11 47		12 10			12 45	12 47		13 10		13 47	
Portsmouth Harbour	a	10 07	10 09		10 32			11 07	11 09		11 32		12 07	12 09		12 32			13 07	13 09		13 32		14 09	

		SW		SW G	SW G	SW	SW	SW	SW E	SW F	SW	SW		SW	SW E	SW F	SW	SW	SW	SW E	SW F	SW		SW	SW
Portsmouth Harbour	d			14 15		14 40		15 15			15 40			16 15			16 40		17 15			17 40			18 15
Ryde Pier Head	a			14 37		15 02		15 37			16 02			16 37			17 02		17 37			18 02			18 37
	d	14 10			14 47		15 10		15 45	15 47		16 10			16 45	16 47		17 10		17 45	17 47			18 10	
Portsmouth Harbour	a	14 32			15 09		15 32		16 07	16 09		16 32			17 07	17 09		17 32		18 07	18 09			18 32	

		SW E	SW F	SW	SW	SW	SW E	SW F		SW	SW E	SW F	SW	SW E	SW F	SW	SW E	SW F		SW	SW E	SW F			
Portsmouth Harbour	d			18 45		19 15				20 15			21 15			22 15				23 15					
Ryde Pier Head	a			19 07		19 37				20 37			21 37			22 37				23 37					
	d	18 45	18 47		19 15		19 45	19 47			20 45	20 47		21 45	21 47		22 45	22 47			23 45	23 47			
Portsmouth Harbour	a	19 07	19 09		19 37		20 07	20 09			21 07	21 09		22 07	22 09		23 07	23 09			00 07	00 09			

Sundays

		SW H	SW I	SW	SW J	SW I	SW	SW J	SW I	SW		SW J	SW I	SW	SW J	SW I	SW	SW J	SW I	SW J		SW J	SW	SW J	SW I
Portsmouth Harbour	d			00 15			06 15			07 15				08 15			09 15			09 40			10 15		
Ryde Pier Head	a			00 37			06 37			07 37				08 37			09 37			10 02			10 37		
	d	23p45	23p47		00 45	00 47		06 45	06 47			07 45	07 47		08 45	08 47		09 45	09 47			10 10		10 45	10 47
Portsmouth Harbour	a	00 07	00 09		01 07	01 09		07 07	07 09			08 07	08 09		09 07	09 09		10 07	10 09			10 32		11 07	11 09

		SW K	SW L	SW	SW J	SW I		SW K	SW L	SW	SW J	SW I	SW K	SW K	SW I	SW I		SW K	SW K	SW I	SW I	SW	SW	SW	SW J
Portsmouth Harbour	d	10 40		11 15				11 40		12 15			12 40		13 15			13 40		14 15		14 40		15 15	
Ryde Pier Head	a	11 02		11 37				12 02		12 37			13 02		13 37			14 02		14 37		15 02		15 37	
	d		11 10		11 45	11 47			12 10		12 45	12 47		13 10		13 47			14 10		14 47		15 10		15 45
Portsmouth Harbour	a		11 32		12 07	12 09			12 32		13 07	13 09		13 32		14 09			14 32		15 09		15 32		16 07

		SW I		SW	SW	SW	SW J	SW I	SW	SW	SW	SW J		SW I	SW	SW	SW	SW J	SW I	SW	SW J	SW I		SW	SW J
Portsmouth Harbour	d			15 40		16 15			16 40		17 15				17 40		18 15			19 15				20 15	
Ryde Pier Head	a			16 02		16 37			17 02		17 37				18 02		18 37			19 37				20 37	
	d	15 47			16 10		16 45	16 47		17 10		17 45		17 47		18 10		18 45	18 47		19 45	19 47			20 45
Portsmouth Harbour	a	16 09			16 32		17 07	17 09		17 32		18 07		18 09		18 32		19 07	19 09		20 07	20 09			21 07

		SW M	SW	SW N	SW M	SW	SW N	SW M		SW	SW N	SW M													
Portsmouth Harbour	d		21 15			22 15				23 15															
Ryde Pier Head	a		21 37			22 37				23 37															
	d	20 47		21 45	21 47		22 45	22 47			23 45	23 47													
Portsmouth Harbour	a	21 09		22 07	22 09		23 07	23 09			00 07	00 09													

A 23 May, 30 May
B not 23 May, 30 May
C from 1 June
D not 28 May, 10 December
E 28 May
F not 28 May
G 4 June, from 30 July until 27 August
H 29 May
I not until 29 May
J 22 May, 29 May
K 22 May, 29 May, 5 June, from 31 July until 28 August
L 5 June, from 31 July until 28 August
M not until 29 May
N 22 May, 29 May

London - East Croydon and Purley

COMPLETE SERVICE

	SN	SN	SN	SN	SN	SN	SN	SN	SN		SN	FC	SN	SN	SN	FC	SN	SN	SN		FC	FC	SN	FC
	MX ■1	MO	MX	MX ■1	MO	MO	MX ■1	MO	MO ■1		MX ◇■1		■1	MX			MX		◇■1		■1	■1	■1	■1
London Victoria 15 ⊖ d				23p47	23p47		23p49	23p50			00 05		00 14		00 16			00 42	01 00				02 00	
Clapham Junction 10 d	23p40			23p53	23p53		23p56	23p56	00 05		00 11		00 20		00 24			00 50	01 08				02 08	
St Pancras International 15 ⊖ d																								
Farringdon 3 ⊖ d																								
City Thameslink 3 d																								
London Blackfriars 3 ⊖ d																								
London Bridge 4 ⊖ d		23p21	23p36			23p39						00 12		00 06		00 42	00 36				01 05	01 35		02 05
New Cross Gate d			23p41			23p44								00 11			00 41							
Norwood Junction 2 a			23p59			00 02								00 29			00 59							
East Croydon a	00 01	00 01	00 03	00 05	00 06	00 06	00 09	00 17	00 22		00 24	00 26	00 31	00 33	00 44	00 56	01 03	01 10	01 21		01 32	02 02	02 21	02 30
South Croydon 4 a			00 06			00 09		00 20						00 37										
Purley Oaks a			00 09			00 12		00 23						00 40										
Purley 4 a			00 12	00 11		00 15		00 26					00 37	00 43					01 27				02 27	

	SN	FC	FC	SN	FC		FC	SN	FC	SN	SN	FC	FC	SN	SN		SN	SN	FC	SN	SN	SN	SN	SN
	■1		■1	◇■1	■1		■1	◇■1	■1	■1	◇■1	■1	■1	■1	◇■1		■1		■1		◇■1	■1	■1	◇■1
London Victoria 15 ⊖ d	03 00			04 00				05 02		05 23	05 32			05 53	06 02					06 13	06 21	06 24		06 32
Clapham Junction 10 d	03 08			04 08				05 08		05 33	05 38			05 59	06 08					06 21	06 27	06 30		06 38
St Pancras International 15 ⊖ d									04 54			05 12	05 32						06 02					
Farringdon 3 ⊖ d									04 59			05 17	05 37						06 07					
City Thameslink 3 d												05 21	05 41						06 11					
London Blackfriars 3 ⊖ d									05 04			05 24	05 44						06 14					
London Bridge 4 ⊖ d		03 05	03 35		04 05		04 35					05 30	05 50				06 08	06 06	06 20				06 32	
New Cross Gate d																		06 11						
Norwood Junction 2 a										05 49								06 29						
East Croydon a	03 21	03 30	04 00	04 21	04 30		05 00	05 20	05 30	05 53	05 48	05 51	06 04	06 09	06 17		06 22	06 33	06 35	06 43	06 38	06 40	06 47	06 48
South Croydon 4 a										05 56								06 36						
Purley Oaks a																		06 39						
Purley 4 a	03 27			04 27				05 25			05 54				06 23			06 42		06 51	06 44			06 54

	FC		SN	SN	SN	SN	SN	FC	SN	SN	SN		SN	FC	SN	SN	SN	SN	SN	SN	SN		SN	SN
	■1				◇■1	■1	■1	■1	■1	■1			■1	■1	◇■1	■1		■1			■1		■1	■1
London Victoria 15 ⊖ d				06 44	06 47	06 51	06 54			07 02			07 10		07 17				07 20	07 23				07 32
Clapham Junction 10 d				06 50	06 53	06 57	07 00			07 08			07 16		07 23				07 28	07 30				07 38
St Pancras International 15 ⊖ d	06 22							06 38						06 58										
Farringdon 3 ⊖ d	06 27							06 43						07 03										
City Thameslink 3 d	06 31							06 47						07 05										
London Blackfriars 3 ⊖ d	06 34							06 50						07 08										
London Bridge 4 ⊖ d	06 42		06 36					07 00	07 03		06 54			07 16		07 19	07 06	07 27			07 30		07 33	
New Cross Gate d			06 41								06 59						07 11						07 38	
Norwood Junction 2 a			06 59								07 17					07 30	07 29	07 38			07 41			
East Croydon a	06 55		07 03	07 12	07 03	07 06	07 10	07 14	07 16	07 17	07 21		07 26	07 30	07 33	07 34	07 37	07 42	07 49	07 44	07 45		07 48	07 52
South Croydon 4 a			07 06								07 24						07 40		07 52					
Purley Oaks a			07 09								07 28						07 43		07 55					
Purley 4 a			07 12							07 23	07 31						07 46		07 58	07 52				

	SN	FC	SN	SN	SN	SN	SN		SN	SN	SN	SN	SN	SN	SN	FC	SN		SN	SN	SN	SN	FC	SN
	■1	■1				◇■1	■1		◇■1	■1	■1	◇■1	■1	◇■1	■1	■1	■1					◇■1	■1	■1
London Victoria 15 ⊖ d	07 36				07 45	07 47			07 52			08 02		08 07			08 10				08 15	08 17		
Clapham Junction 10 d	07 42				07 51	07 53			07 58			08 08		08 13			08 16				08 23	08 23		
St Pancras International 15 ⊖ d		07 20														07 48							08 00	
Farringdon 3 ⊖ d		07 25														07 53							08 05	
City Thameslink 3 d		07 29														07 57							08 07	
London Blackfriars 3 ⊖ d		07 32														08 00							08 10	
London Bridge 4 ⊖ d		07 42	07 46	07 36			07 53			07 56	08 00		08 02		08 08				08 14	08 06			08 18	08 23
New Cross Gate d				07 41									08 07							08 11				
Norwood Junction 2 a				07 59						08 07			08 15						08 27	08 29				
East Croydon a	07 52	07 55	08 00	08 03	08 12	08 03	08 06		08 09	08 10	08 15	08 18	08 19	08 22	08 22	08 25	08 26		08 30	08 33	08 44	08 33	08 36	08 37
South Croydon 4 a				08 06	08 15										08 26					08 36	08 47			
Purley Oaks a				08 09	08 18															08 39	08 50			
Purley 4 a	07 57			08 12	08 21								08 24						08 38	08 42	08 53			

	SN	SN	SN		SN	SN	SN	FC	SN	SN	SN	SN	SN		SN	SN	SN	SN	SN	SN	SN	FC	SN	
	◇■1	■1			◇■1 trolley	■1	◇■1 trolley	■1	■1			◇■1 trolley	■1			◇■1	■1	◇■1 trolley	■1	◇■1 trolley	■1	■1	■1	
London Victoria 15 ⊖ d	08 21				08 32		08 36				08 43	08 47				08 51	08 53	09 02		09 06				
Clapham Junction 10 d	08 27				08 38		08 43				08 51	08 53	08 36				08 59	09 08		09 12				
St Pancras International 15 ⊖ d								08 20														08 48		
Farringdon 3 ⊖ d								08 25														08 53		
City Thameslink 3 d								08 29														08 57		
London Blackfriars 3 ⊖ d								08 32														09 00		
London Bridge 4 ⊖ d		08 25	08 27			08 32			08 45	08 47					08 36				09 03		09 08	09 12	09 15	
New Cross Gate d						08 37									08 41				09 08					
Norwood Junction 2 a		08 36				08 45			08 56						08 59				09 16				09 26	
East Croydon a	08 39	08 40	08 42		08 48	08 49	08 52	08 56	08 59	09 02	09 12	09 03	09 04		09 06	09 07	09 09	09 18	09 20	09 22	09 22	09 24	09 30	
South Croydon 4 a											09 15				09 09									
Purley Oaks a											09 18				09 12									
Purley 4 a						08 58			09 05	09 09	09 21				09 15				09 26				09 35	

London - East Croydon and Purley

COMPLETE SERVICE

Station		SN	SN	SN	SN	FC	SN	SN	SN	SN		FC	SN	SN	SN	SN	SN	SN	SN	FC		SN	SN	SN	SN
				◇1 (trolley)		1	1	◇1 (trolley)	1	◇1		1	1	1			◇1 (trolley)		◇1	1		1	◇1 (trolley)	1	◇1 (trolley)
London Victoria 15 ⊖	d		09 13	09 17			09 23	09 32		09 36						09 43	09 47		09 51			09 53	10 02		10 06
Clapham Junction 10	d		09 21	09 23			09 29	09 38		09 42			09 34			09 51	09 53					09 59	10 08		10 12
St Pancras International 15 ⊖	d					09 04						09 24								09 40					
Farringdon 3 ⊖	d					09 09						09 29								09 44					
City Thameslink 3	d					09 13						09 32								09 47					
London Blackfriars 3 ⊖	d					09 16						09 34								09 50					
London Bridge 4 ⊖	d	09 06			09 20	09 27			09 32			09 42		09 45	09 36			09 50		09 57				10 03	
New Cross Gate	d	09 12							09 37						09 41									10 08	
Norwood Junction 2	a	09 30			09 32				09 45					09 56	09 59			10 02						10 16	
East Croydon	a	09 33	09 42	09 33	09 36	09 39	09 39	09 48	09 49	09 52		09 54	09 57	10 00	10 03	10 12	10 03	10 06	10 07	10 09		10 09	10 18	10 20	10 22
South Croydon 4	a	09 36	09 45										10 01		10 06	10 15									
Purley Oaks	a	09 39	09 48												10 09	10 18									
Purley 4	a	09 42	09 51		09 45				09 56					10 05	10 12	10 21		10 15						10 26	

Station		SN	FC	SN	SN	SN		SN	SN	FC	SN	SN	SN	SN	FC	SN		SN	SN	SN	SN	SN	SN	FC	SN
		1	1	1				◇1 (trolley)		1	1	◇1 (trolley)	1	◇1	1	1		1			◇1 (trolley)		◇1	1	1
London Victoria 15 ⊖	d					10 13		10 17			10 23	10 32		10 36						10 43	10 47		10 51		10 53
Clapham Junction 10	d					10 21		10 23			10 29	10 38		10 42		10 34				10 51	10 53				10 59
St Pancras International 15 ⊖	d		09 54							10 10					10 24									10 40	
Farringdon 3 ⊖	d		09 59							10 14					10 29									10 44	
City Thameslink 3	d		10 02							10 17					10 32									10 47	
London Blackfriars 3 ⊖	d		10 05							10 20					10 35									10 50	
London Bridge 4 ⊖	d	10 08	10 12	10 15	10 06				10 20	10 27			10 33		10 42			10 45	10 36			10 50		10 57	
New Cross Gate	d				10 11								10 38						10 41						
Norwood Junction 2	a			10 26	10 29				10 32				10 46					10 56	10 59			11 02			
East Croydon	a	10 22	10 24	10 30	10 33	10 42		10 33	10 36	10 39	10 39	10 48	10 50	10 52	10 54	10 57		11 00	11 03	11 12	11 03	11 06	11 07	11 09	11 09
South Croydon 4	a				10 36	10 45										11 01			11 06	11 15					
Purley Oaks	a				10 39	10 48													11 09	11 18					
Purley 4	a			10 35	10 42	10 51			10 45				10 56					11 05	11 12	11 21		11 15			

Station		SN		SN	SN	SN	FC	SN	SN	SN	SN	SN		FC	SN	SN	SN	SN	FC	SN	SN	SN		SN	SN
		◇1		1	◇1	1	1	1			◇1			1	1	◇1	1	◇1 (trolley)	1	1	1				◇1
London Victoria 15 ⊖	d	11 02			11 06					11 13	11 17				11 23	11 32		11 36						11 43	11 47
Clapham Junction 10	d	11 08			11 12					11 21	11 23				11 29	11 38		11 42		11 34				11 51	11 53
St Pancras International 15 ⊖	d						10 54							11 10					11 24						
Farringdon 3 ⊖	d						10 59							11 14					11 29						
City Thameslink 3	d						11 02							11 17					11 32						
London Blackfriars 3 ⊖	d						11 05							11 20					11 35						
London Bridge 4 ⊖	d			11 03		11 08	11 12	11 15	11 06			11 20		11 27			11 33		11 42		11 45	11 36			
New Cross Gate	d			11 08					11 11								11 38					11 41			
Norwood Junction 2	a			11 16				11 26	11 29			11 32					11 46				11 56	11 59			
East Croydon	a	11 18		11 20	11 22	11 23	11 24	11 30	11 33	11 42	11 33	11 36		11 39	11 39	11 48	11 50	11 52	11 54	11 57	12 00	12 03		12 12	12 03
South Croydon 4	a								11 36	11 45										12 01		12 06		12 15	
Purley Oaks	a								11 39	11 48												12 09		12 18	
Purley 4	a			11 26				11 35	11 42	11 51		11 45					11 56				12 05	12 12		12 21	

Station		SN	SN	FC	SN	SN	SN	SN		SN	FC	SN	SN	SN	SN	SN	FC	SN		SN	SN	SN	FC	SN	SN
			◇1	1	1	◇1	1	◇1 (trolley)		1	1	1			◇1		1	1		◇1	1	◇1 (trolley)	1	1	1
London Victoria 15 ⊖	d		11 51		11 53	12 02		12 06						12 13	12 17			12 23		12 32		12 36			
Clapham Junction 10	d				11 59	12 08		12 12						12 21	12 23			12 29		12 38		12 42		12 34	
St Pancras International 15 ⊖	d			11 40							11 54						12 10						12 24		
Farringdon 3 ⊖	d			11 44							11 59						12 14						12 29		
City Thameslink 3	d			11 47							12 02						12 17						12 32		
London Blackfriars 3 ⊖	d			11 50							12 05						12 20						12 35		
London Bridge 4 ⊖	d	11 50		11 57			12 03			12 08	12 12	12 15	12 06			12 20	12 27				12 33		12 42		12 45
New Cross Gate	d						12 08						12 11								12 38				
Norwood Junction 2	a	12 02					12 16					12 26	12 29			12 32					12 46				12 56
East Croydon	a	12 06	12 07	12 09	12 09	12 18	12 20	12 22		12 22	12 24	12 30	12 33	12 42	12 33	12 36	12 39	12 39		12 48	12 50	12 52	12 54	12 57	13 00
South Croydon 4	a												12 36	12 45										13 01	
Purley Oaks	a												12 39	12 48											
Purley 4	a	12 15					12 26					12 35	12 42	12 51		12 45					12 56				13 05

Station		SN	SN	SN		SN	SN	FC	SN	SN	SN	SN	SN	FC		SN	SN	SN	SN	SN	FC	SN	SN	SN	
				◇1			◇1	1	1	◇1	1	◇1 (trolley)	1	1		1			◇1		1	1	◇1 (trolley)	1	
London Victoria 15 ⊖	d		12 43	12 47			12 51		12 53	13 02		13 06						13 13	13 17			13 23	13 32		
Clapham Junction 10	d		12 51	12 53					12 59	13 08		13 12						13 21	13 23			13 29	13 38		
St Pancras International 15 ⊖	d							12 40						12 54							13 10				
Farringdon 3 ⊖	d							12 44						12 59							13 14				
City Thameslink 3	d							12 47						13 02							13 17				
London Blackfriars 3 ⊖	d							12 50						13 05							13 20				
London Bridge 4 ⊖	d	12 36				12 50		12 57			13 03		13 08	13 12		13 15	13 06			13 20	13 27			13 33	
New Cross Gate	d	12 41									13 08						13 11							13 38	
Norwood Junction 2	a	12 59				13 02					13 16		13 19			13 26	13 29			13 32				13 46	
East Croydon	a	13 03	13 12	13 03		13 06	13 07	13 09	13 09	13 18	13 20	13 22	13 23	13 24		13 30	13 33	13 42	13 33	13 36	13 39	13 39	13 48	13 50	
South Croydon 4	a	13 06	13 15														13 36	13 45							
Purley Oaks	a	13 09	13 18														13 39	13 48							
Purley 4	a	13 12	13 21			13 15					13 26					13 35	13 42	13 51		13 45				13 56	

Table 175

Mondays to Fridays

until 2 September

London - East Croydon and Purley

COMPLETE SERVICE

	SN	FC	SN	SN	SN	SN	SN	SN	SN		FC	SN	SN	SN	SN	SN	FC	SN	SN		SN	SN	SN	FC
	◇1 🛒	1	1	1			◇1		◇1		1	1	◇1	1	◇1 🛒	1	1	1				◇1		1
London Victoria 15 ⊖ d	13 36					13 43	13 47		13 51			13 53	14 02		14 06						14 13	14 17		
Clapham Junction 10 d	13 42		13 34			13 51	13 53					13 59	14 08		14 12						14 21	14 23		
St Pancras International 15 ⊖ d		13 24									13 40						13 54							14 10
Farringdon 3 ⊖ d		13 29									13 44						13 59							14 14
City Thameslink 3 d		13 32									13 47						14 02							14 17
London Blackfriars 3 ⊖ d		13 35									13 50						14 05							14 20
London Bridge 4 ⊖ d		13 42		13 45	13 36			13 50			13 57			14 03		14 08	14 12	14 15	14 06				14 20	14 27
New Cross Gate d					13 41									14 08					14 11					
Norwood Junction 2 a				13 56	13 59			14 02						14 16		14 19		14 26	14 29				14 32	
East Croydon a	13 52	13 54	13 57	14 00	14 03	14 12	14 03	14 06	14 07		14 09	14 09	14 18	14 20	14 22	14 23	14 24	14 30	14 33		14 43	14 33	14 36	14 39
South Croydon 4 a			14 01		14 06	14 15													14 36		14 46			
Purley Oaks a					14 09	14 18													14 39		14 49			
Purley 4 a				14 05	14 12	14 21		14 15						14 26				14 35	14 42		14 52		14 45	

	SN	SN	SN	SN	FC		SN	SN	SN	SN	SN	SN	SN	FC	SN		SN	SN	SN	SN	FC	SN	SN	SN
	1	◇1 🛒	1	◇1 🛒	1		1	1			◇1		◇1	1	1		◇1	1	◇1 🛒	1	1	1		
London Victoria 15 ⊖ d	14 23	14 32		14 36						14 43	14 47		14 51		14 53		15 02		15 06					15 13
Clapham Junction 10 d	14 29	14 38		14 42			14 34			14 51	14 53				14 59		15 08		15 12					15 21
St Pancras International 15 ⊖ d					14 24									14 40							14 54			
Farringdon 3 ⊖ d					14 29									14 44							14 59			
City Thameslink 3 d					14 32									14 47							15 02			
London Blackfriars 3 ⊖ d					14 35									14 50							15 05			
London Bridge 4 ⊖ d			14 33		14 42			14 45	14 36			14 50		14 57				15 03		15 08	15 12	15 15	15 06	
New Cross Gate d			14 38						14 41									15 08					15 11	
Norwood Junction 2 a			14 46					14 56	14 59			15 02						15 16		15 19		15 26	15 29	
East Croydon a	14 40	14 48	14 50	14 52	14 54		14 57	15 00	15 03	15 12	15 03	15 06	15 07	15 09	15 09		15 18	15 20	15 22	15 23	15 24	15 30	15 33	15 43
South Croydon 4 a							15 01		15 06	15 15													15 36	15 46
Purley Oaks a									15 09	15 18													15 39	15 49
Purley 4 a			14 56					15 05	15 12	15 21		15 15						15 26				15 35	15 42	15 52

	SN		SN	FC	SN	SN	SN	SN	SN	FC	SN		SN	SN	SN	SN	SN	SN	FC	SN	SN		SN	SN
	◇1			1	1	◇1	1	◇1 🛒	1	1	1		1			◇1		◇1	1	1	◇1		1	1 🛒
London Victoria 15 ⊖ d	15 17				15 23	15 32		15 36							15 43	15 47		15 51		15 53	16 02			16 06
Clapham Junction 10 d	15 23				15 29	15 38		15 42			15 34				15 51	15 53				15 59	16 08			16 12
St Pancras International 15 ⊖ d				15 10						15 24									15 40					
Farringdon 3 ⊖ d				15 14						15 29									15 44					
City Thameslink 3 d				15 17						15 32									15 47					
London Blackfriars 3 ⊖ d				15 20						15 35									15 50					
London Bridge 4 ⊖ d			15 20	15 27			15 33		15 38	15 42			15 45	15 36			15 50		15 57				16 03	
New Cross Gate d							15 38							15 41									16 08	
Norwood Junction 2 a			15 32				15 46						15 56	15 59			16 02						16 16	
East Croydon a	15 33		15 36	15 39	15 40	15 48	15 50	15 52	15 52	15 54	15 57		16 00	16 03	16 12	16 03	16 06	16 07	16 09	16 09	16 18		16 20	16 22
South Croydon 4 a					15 43						16 01			16 06	16 15					16 12				
Purley Oaks a														16 09	16 18									
Purley 4 a			15 45				15 56						16 05	16 12	16 21		16 15						16 26	

	SN	FC	SN	SN	SN	SN	SN		SN	FC	SN	SN	SN	SN	SN	SN	SN		FC	SN	SN	SN	SN	SN
	1	1	1			◇1 🛒	1		1	1	1	◇1 🛒	1	1 🛒	1		1		1		◇1 🛒		1	1
London Victoria 15 ⊖ d					16 13	16 17	16 19				16 23	16 32		16 36		16 39				16 43	16 47		16 49	16 53
Clapham Junction 10 d					16 21	16 23	16 26				16 29	16 38		16 42		16 45	16 34			16 51	16 53		16 56	16 59
St Pancras International 15 ⊖ d		15 54								16 10									16 24					
Farringdon 3 ⊖ d		15 59								16 14									16 29					
City Thameslink 3 d		16 02								16 17									16 33					
London Blackfriars 3 ⊖ d		16 05								16 20									16 36					
London Bridge 4 ⊖ d	16 08	16 12	16 15	16 06					16 20	16 27			16 33		16 38				16 43			16 48		
New Cross Gate d				16 11																				
Norwood Junction 2 a	16 19		16 26	16 29					16 32				16 44									17 01		
East Croydon a	16 23	16 24	16 30	16 33	16 42	16 33	16 36		16 36	16 39	16 39	16 47	16 48	16 52	16 52	16 55	16 58		16 59	17 12	17 03	17 05	17 06	17 09
South Croydon 4 a				16 36	16 45						16 42					16 58	17 02			17 19		17 08		17 12
Purley Oaks a				16 39	16 48											17 01				17 22		17 11		
Purley 4 a			16 35	16 42	16 51				16 45				16 55			17 04				17 25		17 14		

	SN	SN	SN		SN	SN	FC	SN	SN	SN	SN	SN	SN		SN	FC	SN	SN	SN	SN	SN	SN	SN	
	1	1	◇1 🛒		1	1	1		1	◇1		1	1		1	1	◇1	1	◇1 🛒	1		1	1	
London Victoria 15 ⊖ d			17 02		17 06			17 09		17 17			17 21		17 23		17 32		17 35		17 39			
Clapham Junction 10 d			17 08		17 12			17 15		17 23			17 27		17 30		17 38		17 42		17 45		17 33	
St Pancras International 15 ⊖ d							16 46									17 10								
Farringdon 3 ⊖ d							16 51									17 15								
City Thameslink 3 d							16 55									17 19								
London Blackfriars 3 ⊖ d							17 00									17 22								
London Bridge 4 ⊖ d	16 57	16 59				17 09			17 15		17 17	17 23						17 32		17 42		17 44		
New Cross Gate d																								
Norwood Junction 2 a		17 10									17 30							17 43						
East Croydon a	17 09	17 14	17 17		17 22	17 22	17 25	17 27	17 29	17 32	17 34	17 35	17 36		17 40	17 46	17 48	17 48	17 51	17 54	17 55	17 57	17 59	
South Croydon 4 a								17 30	17 32		17 37										17 58	18 01		
Purley Oaks a								17 33			17 40										18 01			
Purley 4 a		17 20						17 36			17 44							17 54			18 04			

until 2 September

London - East Croydon and Purley

COMPLETE SERVICE

	SN	SN	SN	SN	FC	SN	SN	SN	SN		SN	SN	FC	SN	SN	SN	SN	SN	SN		SN	SN	SN	FC
	[1]	◇[1]	[1]		[1]	[1]	[1]	[1]	◇[1]		[1]	◇[1] (trolley)	[1]	[1]		[1]		◇[1]			[1]	[1]	[1]	[1]
London Victoria [15] ⊖ d		17 47	17 49			17 53			18 02			18 06			18 09			18 17				18 19	18 23	
Clapham Junction [10] d		17 53	17 56			18 00			18 08			18 12			18 15		18 02	18 23				18 26	18 30	
St Pancras International [15] ⊖ d					17 28								17 40											18 08
Farringdon [3] ⊖ d					17 33								17 45											18 13
City Thameslink [3] d					17 37								17 49											18 17
London Blackfriars [3] ⊖ d					17 40								17 52											18 20
London Bridge [4] ⊖ d	17 47			17 49			17 57	17 59			18 08			18 12		18 16			18 18		18 23			18 27
New Cross Gate d																								
Norwood Junction [2] a				18 01				18 11											18 30					
East Croydon (tram) a	17 59	18 02	18 05	18 05	18 08	18 10	18 11	18 15	18 17		18 21	18 22	18 24	18 24	18 27	18 30	18 32	18 33	18 35		18 36	18 37	18 40	18 41
South Croydon [4] a				18 08											18 30	18 33	18 35		18 39					
Purley Oaks a				18 11											18 33		18 38		18 45					
Purley [4] a				18 14				18 20							18 36		18 40		18 48			18 42		

	SN	SN	SN	FC	SN		SN	SN	SN	SN	SN	SN	FC	SN	SN		SN	SN	SN	FC	SN	SN	SN	SN
	[1]	◇[1]	[1]	[1]			[1]	[1]		◇[1] (trolley)		[1]	[1]	[1]	◇[1] (trolley)		[1]	[1] (trolley)	[1]	[1]	[1]			◇[1] (trolley)
London Victoria [15] ⊖ d		18 32	18 36		18 39				18 45	18 47		18 51		18 53	19 02			19 06			19 10		19 15	19 17
Clapham Junction [10] d		18 38	18 42		18 45			18 34	18 53	18 53		18 57		19 00	19 08			19 12			19 16		19 23	19 23
St Pancras International [15] ⊖ d				18 20									18 34							18 54				
Farringdon [3] ⊖ d				18 25									18 39							18 59				
City Thameslink [3] d				18 29									18 43							19 03				
London Blackfriars [3] ⊖ d				18 32									18 46							19 05				
London Bridge [4] ⊖ d	18 30						18 47				18 49		18 57				19 03		19 08	19 12		19 06		
New Cross Gate d																						19 11		
Norwood Junction [2] a	18 41										19 01						19 14					19 29		
East Croydon (tram) a	18 45	18 48	18 52	18 55	18 57		19 00	19 02	19 13	19 02	19 05	19 07	19 10	19 10	19 18		19 18	19 22	19 22	19 24	19 27	19 33	19 44	19 33
South Croydon [4] a					19 00		19 03		19 16		19 08											19 36	19 47	
Purley Oaks a					19 03				19 19		19 11											19 39	19 50	
Purley [4] a	18 50				19 06				19 22		19 14						19 24				19 33	19 42	19 53	

	FC		SN	SN	SN	FC	SN	SN	SN	SN	SN		FC	SN	SN	SN	SN	FC	SN	SN	SN		SN	SN
	[1]		[1]	◇[1] (trolley)	[1]	[1]	[1]			◇[1] (trolley)	[1]		[1]	[1]	◇[1] (trolley)	[1]	◇[1]	[1]	[1]				◇[1]	[1]
London Victoria [15] ⊖ d			19 23	19 32	19 36		19 40		19 45	19 47				19 53	20 02		20 06		20 10		20 15		20 17	20 23
Clapham Junction [10] d			19 29	19 38	19 42		19 46		19 53	19 53				19 59	20 08		20 12		20 16		20 23		20 23	20 29
St Pancras International [15] ⊖ d	19 10					19 24							19 40					19 54						
Farringdon [3] ⊖ d	19 14					19 29							19 44					19 59						
City Thameslink [3] d	19 17					19 32							19 47					20 02						
London Blackfriars [3] ⊖ d	19 20					19 35							19 50					20 05						
London Bridge [4] ⊖ d	19 27					19 42		19 36			19 52		19 57			20 04		20 12		20 06				
New Cross Gate d								19 41												20 11				
Norwood Junction [2] a								19 59			20 03					20 16				20 29				
East Croydon (tram) a	19 39		19 39	19 48	19 52	19 54	19 57	20 03	20 14	20 03	20 06		20 09	20 09	20 19	20 19	20 22	20 24	20 27	20 33	20 44		20 33	20 39
South Croydon [4] a								20 06	20 17											20 36	20 47			
Purley Oaks a								20 09	20 21											20 39	20 50			
Purley [4] a							20 03	20 12	20 24		20 12								20 33	20 42	20 53			

	SN	SN	SN	SN	FC	SN	SN		SN	SN	SN	SN	SN	SN	SN	FC	SN		SN	SN	SN	SN	SN	SN
	[1]	◇[1]	[1]	◇[1]	[1]	[1]				◇[1]	[1]	[1]	[1]	[1]	◇[1]	[1]	[1]				◇[1]	[1]	[1]	[1]
London Victoria [15] ⊖ d		20 32		20 36		20 40			20 45	20 47	20 53		21 02		21 06		21 10			21 15	21 17	21 23		21 32
Clapham Junction [10] d		20 38		20 42		20 46			20 53	20 53	20 59		21 08		21 12		21 16			21 23	21 23	21 29		21 38
St Pancras International [15] ⊖ d					20 24											20 54								
Farringdon [3] ⊖ d					20 29											20 59								
City Thameslink [3] d					20 32											21 02								
London Blackfriars [3] ⊖ d					20 35											21 05								
London Bridge [4] ⊖ d	20 28		20 34		20 42		20 36					20 58		21 04		21 12			21 06				21 26	
New Cross Gate d							20 41												21 11					
Norwood Junction [2] a			20 45				20 59							21 15					21 29				21 37	
East Croydon (tram) a	20 40	20 48	20 49	20 52	20 54	20 57	21 03		21 14	21 03	21 09	21 10	21 18	21 19	21 22	21 24	21 27		21 33	21 44	21 33	21 39	21 41	21 48
South Croydon [4] a							21 06		21 17										21 36	21 47				
Purley Oaks a							21 09		21 20										21 39	21 50				
Purley [4] a						21 03	21 12		21 23								21 33		21 42	21 53				

	SN	FC	SN		SN	SN	SN	SN	SN	SN	SN	FC	SN		SN	SN	SN	SN	SN	SN	SN	FC	SN
	◇[1]	[1]	[1]				◇[1]	[1]	◇[1]	[1]	◇[1]	[1]	[1]			◇[1]		[1]		[1]	[1]	[1]	[1]
London Victoria [15] ⊖ d	21 36		21 40			21 45	21 47	21 53	22 02		22 06		22 10		22 15	22 17		22 23		22 32	22 36		22 40
Clapham Junction [10] d	21 42		21 46			21 53	21 53	21 59	22 08		22 12		22 16		22 23	22 23		22 29		22 38	22 42		22 46
St Pancras International [15] ⊖ d		21 24										21 54											
Farringdon [3] ⊖ d		21 29										21 59											
City Thameslink [3] d		21 32										22 02											
London Blackfriars [3] ⊖ d		21 35										22 05											
London Bridge [4] ⊖ d		21 42			21 36					22 04		22 12					22 08		22 26			22 42	
New Cross Gate d					21 41												22 13						
Norwood Junction [2] a					21 59					22 15							22 31		22 38				
East Croydon (tram) a	21 52	21 54	21 57		22 03	22 14	22 03	22 09	22 18	22 19	22 22	22 24	22 26		22 44	22 33	22 35	22 39	22 42	22 48	22 52	22 54	22 57
South Croydon [4] a					22 06	22 17									22 47		22 38						
Purley Oaks a					22 09	22 20									22 50		22 41						
Purley [4] a			22 03		22 12	22 23							22 33		22 53		22 44						23 03

Table 175

London - East Croydon and Purley

COMPLETE SERVICE

Mondays to Fridays

until 2 September

		SN	SN	SN	SN	SN	SN	SN	SN	FC	SN	SN	SN	SN	SN	SN	FC	SN	SN	SN FO	SN	SN
			◇1		1		◇1	1	◇1	1	1			◇1	1	◇1	1	1			1	1
London Victoria 15 ⊖	d	22 45	22 47		22 53		23 02		23 06		23 10		23 15	23 17	23 24	23 32				23 45	23 47	23 49
Clapham Junction 10	d	22 53	22 53		22 59		23 08		23 12		23 16		23 23	23 23	23 30	23 38		23 40		23 53	23 53	23 56
St Pancras International 15 ⊖	d																					
Farringdon 3 ⊖	d																					
City Thameslink 3	d																					
London Blackfriars 3 ⊖	d																					
London Bridge 4 ⊖	d			22 38		22 56		23 04		23 12		23 06					23 42		23 36			
New Cross Gate	d			22 43								23 11							23 41			
Norwood Junction 2	a			23 01		23 07		23 15				23 29							23 59			
East Croydon	a	23 14	23 03	23 06	23 09	23 11	23 19	23 19	23 22	23 24	23 27	23 33	23 44	23 33	23 40	23 51	23 56	00 01	00 03	00 14	00 05	00 09
South Croydon 4	a	23 17		23 09								23 36	23 47						00 06	00 17		
Purley Oaks	a	23 20		23 12								23 39	23 50						00 09	00 20		
Purley 4	a	23 23		23 15							23 33	23 42	23 54						00 12	00 23	00 11	

Mondays to Fridays

from 5 September

		SN MX	SN MO	SN MX	SN MX	SN MO	SN MO	SN MX	SN MO	SN MO	SN MX	FC	SN	SN MX	SN	FC	SN MX	SN	SN	FC	FC	SN	FC
		1			1			1		1	◇1		1						◇1	1	1	1	1
London Victoria 15 ⊖	d				23p47	23p47		23p49	23p50		00 05		00 14		00 16			00 42	01 00			02 00	
Clapham Junction 10	d	23p40			23p53	23p53		23p56	23p56	00 05	00 11		00 20		00 24			00 50	01 08			02 08	
St Pancras International 15 ⊖	d																						
Farringdon 3 ⊖	d																						
City Thameslink 3	d																						
London Blackfriars 3 ⊖	d																						
London Bridge 4 ⊖	d		23p21	23p36			23p39					00 12		00 06		00 42	00 36			01 05	01 35		02 05
New Cross Gate	d			23p41			23p44							00 11			00 41						
Norwood Junction 2	a			23p59			00 02							00 29			00 59						
East Croydon	a	00 01	00 01	00 03	00 05	00 06	00 06	00 09	00 17	00 22	00 24	00 26	00 31	00 33	00 44	00 56	01 03	01 10	01 21	01 32	02 02	02 21	02 30
South Croydon 4	a			00 06			00 09		00 20					00 37									
Purley Oaks	a			00 09			00 12		00 23					00 40									
Purley 4	a			00 12	00 11		00 15		00 26				00 37	00 43					01 27			02 27	

		SN	FC	FC	SN	FC	FC	SN	FC	SN	SN	FC	FC	SN	SN	SN	SN	FC	SN	SN	SN	SN	SN
		1		1	◇1	1	1	◇1	1	1	◇1	1	1	1	◇1	1		1		◇1	1	1	◇1
London Victoria 15 ⊖	d	03 00			04 00			05 02		05 23	05 32			05 53	06 02				06 13	06 21	06 24		06 32
Clapham Junction 10	d	03 08			04 08			05 08		05 33	05 38			05 59	06 08				06 21	06 27	06 30		06 38
St Pancras International 15 ⊖	d								04 54			05 12	05 32					06 02					
Farringdon 3 ⊖	d								04 59			05 17	05 37					06 07					
City Thameslink 3	d											05 21	05 41					06 11					
London Blackfriars 3 ⊖	d								05 04			05 24	05 44					06 14					
London Bridge 4 ⊖	d		03 05	03 35		04 05	04 35					05 30	05 50			06 08	06 06	06 20				06 32	
New Cross Gate	d																06 11						
Norwood Junction 2	a									05 49							06 29						
East Croydon	a	03 21	03 30	04 00	04 21	04 30	05 00	05 20	05 30	05 53	05 48	05 51	06 04	06 09	06 17	06 22	06 33	06 35	06 43	06 38	06 40	06 47	06 48
South Croydon 4	a									05 56							06 36						
Purley Oaks	a																06 39						
Purley 4	a	03 27			04 27			05 25			05 54				06 23		06 42		06 51	06 44			06 54

		FC	SN	SN	SN	SN	SN	FC	SN	SN	SN	SN	FC	SN	SN	SN	SN	SN	SN	SN	SN	SN
		1			◇1	1	1	1	1	1		1	1	◇1	1		1			1	1	1
London Victoria 15 ⊖	d			06 44	06 47	06 51	06 54			07 02		07 10		07 17				07 20	07 23			07 32
Clapham Junction 10	d			06 50	06 53	06 57	07 00			07 08		07 16		07 23				07 28	07 30			07 38
St Pancras International 15 ⊖	d	06 22						06 38					06 58									
Farringdon 3 ⊖	d	06 27						06 43					07 03									
City Thameslink 3	d	06 31						06 47					07 05									
London Blackfriars 3 ⊖	d	06 34						06 50					07 08									
London Bridge 4 ⊖	d	06 42	06 36					07 00	07 03		06 54		07 16		07 19	07 06	07 27			07 30	07 33	
New Cross Gate	d		06 41								06 59					07 11					07 38	
Norwood Junction 2	a		06 59								07 17				07 30	07 29	07 38			07 41		
East Croydon	a	06 55	07 03	07 12	07 03	07 06	07 10	07 14	07 16	07 17	07 21	07 26	07 30	07 33	07 34	07 37	07 42	07 49	07 44	07 45	07 48	07 52
South Croydon 4	a		07 06								07 24					07 40		07 52				
Purley Oaks	a		07 09								07 28					07 43		07 55				
Purley 4	a		07 12							07 23	07 31					07 46		07 58	07 52			

		SN	FC	SN	SN	SN	SN	SN	SN	SN	SN	SN	SN	SN	SN	FC	SN	SN	SN	SN	SN	FC	SN
		1	1				◇1	1	◇1	1	1	◇1	1	◇1	1	1	1				◇1	1	1
London Victoria 15 ⊖	d	07 36				07 45	07 47		07 52			08 02		08 07			08 10			08 15	08 17		
Clapham Junction 10	d	07 42				07 51	07 53		07 58			08 08		08 13			08 16			08 23	08 23		
St Pancras International 15 ⊖	d		07 20													07 48						08 00	
Farringdon 3 ⊖	d		07 25													07 53						08 05	
City Thameslink 3	d		07 29													07 57						08 07	
London Blackfriars 3 ⊖	d		07 32													08 00						08 10	
London Bridge 4 ⊖	d		07 42	07 46	07 36			07 53		07 56	08 00		08 02		08 08			08 14	08 06			08 18	08 23
New Cross Gate	d				07 41								08 07						08 11				
Norwood Junction 2	a				07 59					08 07			08 15					08 27	08 29				
East Croydon	a	07 52	07 55	08 00	08 03	08 12	08 03	08 06	08 09	08 10	08 15	08 18	08 19	08 22	08 22	08 25	08 26	08 30	08 33	08 44	08 33	08 36	08 37
South Croydon 4	a				08 06	08 15									08 26				08 36	08 47			
Purley Oaks	a				08 09	08 18													08 39	08 50			
Purley 4	a	07 57			08 12	08 21							08 24					08 38	08 42	08 53			

Table 175

Mondays to Fridays

from 5 September

London - East Croydon and Purley

COMPLETE SERVICE

		SN ◇1	SN 1	SN		SN ◇1 ⊼	SN 1	SN ◇1 ⊼	FC 1	SN 1	SN	SN	SN ◇1 ⊼	SN 1		SN	SN ◇1	SN 1	SN ◇1 ⊼	SN 1	SN ◇1 ⊼	SN 1	FC 1	SN 1
London Victoria 15 ⊖	d	08 21				08 32		08 36				08 43	08 47				08 51	08 53	09 02		09 06			
Clapham Junction 10	d	08 27				08 38		08 43				08 51	08 53	08 36				08 59	09 08		09 12			
St Pancras International 15 ⊖	d								08 20														08 48	
Farringdon 3 ⊖	d								08 25														08 53	
City Thameslink 3	d								08 29														08 57	
London Blackfriars 3 ⊖	d								08 32														09 00	
London Bridge 4 ⊖	d		08 25	08 27			08 32			08 45	08 47					08 36				09 03		09 08	09 12	09 15
New Cross Gate	d						08 37									08 41				09 08				
Norwood Junction 2	a		08 36				08 45			08 56						08 59				09 16				09 26
East Croydon	a	08 39	08 40	08 42		08 48	08 49	08 52	08 56	08 59	09 02	09 12	09 03	09 04		09 06	09 07	09 09	09 18	09 20	09 22	09 22	09 24	09 30
South Croydon 4	a											09 15				09 09								
Purley Oaks	a											09 18				09 12								
Purley 4	a						08 58			09 05	09 09	09 21				09 15				09 26				09 35

		SN	SN	SN ◇1 ⊼	SN	FC 1	SN 1	SN ◇1 ⊼	SN 1	SN ◇1		FC 1	SN 1	SN 1	SN	SN	SN ◇1 ⊼	SN	SN ◇1	FC 1		SN 1	SN ◇1 ⊼	SN 1	SN ◇1 ⊼
London Victoria 15 ⊖	d		09 13	09 17			09 23	09 32		09 36						09 43	09 47		09 51			09 53	10 02		10 06
Clapham Junction 10	d		09 21	09 23			09 29	09 38		09 42			09 34			09 51	09 53					09 59	10 08		10 12
St Pancras International 15 ⊖	d					09 04						09 24								09 40					
Farringdon 3 ⊖	d					09 09						09 29								09 44					
City Thameslink 3	d					09 13						09 32								09 47					
London Blackfriars 3 ⊖	d					09 16						09 34								09 50					
London Bridge 4 ⊖	d	09 06			09 20	09 27			09 32			09 42		09 45	09 36			09 50		09 57				10 03	
New Cross Gate	d	09 12							09 37						09 41									10 08	
Norwood Junction 2	a	09 30			09 32				09 45					09 56	09 59			10 02						10 16	
East Croydon	a	09 33	09 42	09 33	09 36	09 39	09 39	09 48	09 49	09 52		09 54	09 57	10 00	10 03	10 12	10 03	10 06	10 07	10 09		10 09	10 18	10 20	10 22
South Croydon 4	a	09 36	09 45										10 01		10 06	10 15									
Purley Oaks	a	09 39	09 48												10 09	10 18									
Purley 4	a	09 42	09 51		09 45				09 56					10 05	10 12	10 21		10 15						10 26	

		SN 1	FC 1	SN 1	SN	SN		SN ◇1 ⊼	SN	FC 1	SN 1	SN ◇1 ⊼	SN 1	SN ◇1	FC 1	SN 1		SN 1	SN	SN	SN ◇1 ⊼	SN	SN ◇1	FC 1	SN 1
London Victoria 15 ⊖	d					10 13		10 17			10 23	10 32		10 36						10 43	10 47		10 51		10 53
Clapham Junction 10	d					10 21		10 23			10 29	10 38		10 42		10 34				10 51	10 53				10 59
St Pancras International 15 ⊖	d		09 54							10 10					10 24									10 40	
Farringdon 3 ⊖	d		09 59							10 14					10 29									10 44	
City Thameslink 3	d		10 02							10 17					10 32									10 47	
London Blackfriars 3 ⊖	d		10 05							10 20					10 35									10 50	
London Bridge 4 ⊖	d	10 08	10 12	10 15	10 06				10 20	10 27			10 33		10 42			10 45	10 36			10 50		10 57	
New Cross Gate	d				10 11								10 38						10 41						
Norwood Junction 2	a			10 26	10 29				10 32				10 46					10 56	10 59			11 02			
East Croydon	a	10 22	10 24	10 30	10 33	10 42		10 33	10 36	10 39	10 39	10 48	10 50	10 52	10 54	10 57		11 00	11 03	11 12	11 03	11 06	11 07	11 09	11 09
South Croydon 4	a				10 36	10 45										11 01			11 06	11 15					
Purley Oaks	a				10 39	10 48													11 09	11 18					
Purley 4	a			10 35	10 42	10 51			10 45				10 56					11 05	11 12	11 21		11 15			

		SN ◇1		SN 1	SN ◇1	SN 1	FC 1	SN 1	SN	SN	SN ◇1	SN		FC 1	SN 1	SN ◇1	SN 1	SN ◇1 ⊼	FC 1	SN 1	SN 1	SN		SN	SN ◇1
London Victoria 15 ⊖	d	11 02			11 06					11 13	11 17				11 23	11 32		11 36						11 43	11 47
Clapham Junction 10	d	11 08			11 12					11 21	11 23				11 29	11 38		11 42		11 34				11 51	11 53
St Pancras International 15 ⊖	d						10 54							11 10					11 24						
Farringdon 3 ⊖	d						10 59							11 14					11 29						
City Thameslink 3	d						11 02							11 17					11 32						
London Blackfriars 3 ⊖	d						11 05							11 20					11 35						
London Bridge 4 ⊖	d			11 03		11 08	11 12	11 15	11 06			11 20		11 27			11 33		11 42		11 45	11 36			
New Cross Gate	d			11 08					11 11								11 38					11 41			
Norwood Junction 2	a			11 16				11 26	11 29			11 32					11 46				11 56	11 59			
East Croydon	a	11 18		11 20	11 22	11 23	11 24	11 30	11 33	11 42	11 33	11 36		11 39	11 39	11 48	11 50	11 52	11 54	11 57	12 00	12 03		12 12	12 03
South Croydon 4	a								11 36	11 45										12 01		12 06		12 15	
Purley Oaks	a								11 39	11 48												12 09		12 18	
Purley 4	a			11 26				11 35	11 42	11 51		11 45					11 56				12 05	12 12		12 21	

		SN	SN ◇1	FC 1	SN 1	SN ◇1	SN 1	SN ◇1 ⊼		SN 1	FC 1	SN 1	SN	SN	SN ◇1	SN	FC 1	SN 1		SN ◇1	SN 1	SN ◇1 ⊼	FC 1	SN 1	SN 1
London Victoria 15 ⊖	d		11 51		11 53	12 02		12 06						12 13	12 17			12 23		12 32		12 36			
Clapham Junction 10	d				11 59	12 08		12 12						12 21	12 23			12 29		12 38		12 42		12 34	
St Pancras International 15 ⊖	d			11 40							11 54						12 10						12 24		
Farringdon 3 ⊖	d			11 44							11 59						12 14						12 29		
City Thameslink 3	d			11 47							12 02						12 17						12 32		
London Blackfriars 3 ⊖	d			11 50							12 05						12 20						12 35		
London Bridge 4 ⊖	d	11 50		11 57			12 03			12 08	12 12	12 15	12 06			12 20	12 27				12 33		12 42		12 45
New Cross Gate	d						12 08						12 11								12 38				
Norwood Junction 2	a	12 02					12 16					12 26	12 29			12 32					12 46				12 56
East Croydon	a	12 06	12 07	12 09	12 09	12 18	12 20	12 22		12 22	12 24	12 30	12 33	12 42	12 33	12 36	12 39	12 39		12 48	12 50	12 52	12 54	12 57	13 00
South Croydon 4	a												12 36	12 45										13 01	
Purley Oaks	a												12 39	12 48											
Purley 4	a	12 15					12 26					12 35	12 42	12 51		12 45					12 56				13 05

Table 175

London - East Croydon and Purley

Mondays to Fridays

from 5 September

COMPLETE SERVICE

		SN	SN	SN ◇1		SN	SN ◇1	FC 1	SN 1	SN ◇1	SN 1	SN ◇1 trolley	SN 1	FC 1		SN 1	SN	SN	SN ◇1	SN	FC 1	SN 1	SN ◇1 trolley	SN 1	
London Victoria 15 ⊖	d		12 43	12 47			12 51		12 53	13 02		13 06						13 13	13 17			13 23	13 32		
Clapham Junction 10	d		12 51	12 53					12 59	13 08		13 12						13 21	13 23			13 29	13 38		
St Pancras International 15 ⊖	d							12 40						12 54							13 10				
Farringdon 3 ⊖	d							12 44						12 59							13 14				
City Thameslink 3	d							12 47						13 02							13 17				
London Blackfriars 3 ⊖	d							12 50						13 05							13 20				
London Bridge 4 ⊖	d	12 36				12 50		12 57			13 03		13 08	13 12		13 15	13 06			13 20	13 27			13 33	
New Cross Gate	d	12 41									13 08						13 11							13 38	
Norwood Junction 2	a	12 59				13 02					13 16		13 19			13 26	13 29			13 32				13 46	
East Croydon (tram)	a	13 03	13 12	13 03		13 06	13 07	13 09	13 09	13 18	13 20	13 22	13 23	13 24		13 30	13 33	13 42	13 33	13 36	13 39	13 39	13 48	13 50	
South Croydon 4	a	13 06	13 15														13 36	13 45							
Purley Oaks	a	13 09	13 18														13 39	13 48							
Purley 4	a	13 12	13 21			13 15					13 26					13 35	13 42	13 51		13 45				13 56	

		SN ◇1 trolley	FC 1	SN 1	SN 1	SN	SN	SN ◇1	SN	SN ◇1		FC 1	SN 1	SN ◇1	SN 1	SN ◇1 trolley	SN 1	FC 1	SN 1	SN		SN	SN ◇1	SN	FC 1
London Victoria 15 ⊖	d	13 36					13 43	13 47		13 51			13 53	14 02		14 06						14 13	14 17		
Clapham Junction 10	d	13 42		13 34			13 51	13 53					13 59	14 08		14 12						14 21	14 23		
St Pancras International 15 ⊖	d		13 24									13 40						13 54							14 10
Farringdon 3 ⊖	d		13 29									13 44						13 59							14 14
City Thameslink 3	d		13 32									13 47						14 02							14 17
London Blackfriars 3 ⊖	d		13 35									13 50						14 05							14 20
London Bridge 4 ⊖	d		13 42		13 45	13 36			13 50			13 57			14 03		14 08	14 12	14 15	14 06				14 20	14 27
New Cross Gate	d					13 41									14 08					14 11					
Norwood Junction 2	a				13 56	13 59			14 02						14 16		14 19		14 26	14 29				14 32	
East Croydon (tram)	a	13 52	13 54	13 57	14 00	14 03	14 12	14 03	14 06	14 07		14 09	14 09	14 18	14 20	14 22	14 23	14 24	14 30	14 33		14 43	14 33	14 36	14 39
South Croydon 4	a			14 01		14 06	14 15													14 36		14 46			
Purley Oaks	a					14 09	14 18													14 39		14 49			
Purley 4	a				14 05	14 12	14 21		14 15						14 26				14 35	14 42		14 52		14 45	

		SN 1	SN ◇1 trolley	SN 1	SN ◇1 trolley	FC 1		SN 1	SN 1	SN	SN	SN ◇1	SN	SN ◇1	FC 1	SN 1		SN ◇1	SN 1	SN ◇1 trolley	SN 1	FC 1	SN 1	SN	SN
London Victoria 15 ⊖	d	14 23	14 32		14 36						14 43	14 47		14 51		14 53		15 02		15 06					15 13
Clapham Junction 10	d	14 29	14 38		14 42			14 34			14 51	14 53				14 59		15 08		15 12					15 21
St Pancras International 15 ⊖	d					14 24									14 40							14 54			
Farringdon 3 ⊖	d					14 29									14 44							14 59			
City Thameslink 3	d					14 32									14 47							15 02			
London Blackfriars 3 ⊖	d					14 35									14 50							15 05			
London Bridge 4 ⊖	d			14 33		14 42			14 45	14 36			14 50		14 57				15 03		15 08	15 12	15 15	15 06	
New Cross Gate	d			14 38						14 41									15 08					15 11	
Norwood Junction 2	a			14 46					14 56	14 59			15 02						15 16		15 19		15 26	15 29	
East Croydon (tram)	a	14 40	14 48	14 50	14 52	14 54		14 57	15 00	15 03	15 12	15 03	15 06	15 07	15 09	15 09		15 18	15 20	15 22	15 23	15 24	15 30	15 33	15 43
South Croydon 4	a							15 01		15 06	15 15													15 36	15 46
Purley Oaks	a									15 09	15 18													15 39	15 49
Purley 4	a			14 56					15 05	15 12	15 21		15 15						15 26				15 35	15 42	15 52

		SN ◇1		SN	FC 1	SN 1	SN ◇1	SN 1	SN ◇1 trolley	SN 1	FC 1	SN 1		SN 1	SN	SN	SN ◇1	SN	SN ◇1	FC 1	SN 1	SN ◇1		SN 1	SN 1 trolley
London Victoria 15 ⊖	d	15 17				15 23	15 32		15 36							15 43	15 47		15 51		15 53	16 02			16 06
Clapham Junction 10	d	15 23				15 29	15 38		15 42			15 34				15 51	15 53				15 59	16 08			16 12
St Pancras International 15 ⊖	d				15 10						15 24									15 40					
Farringdon 3 ⊖	d				15 14						15 29									15 44					
City Thameslink 3	d				15 17						15 32									15 47					
London Blackfriars 3 ⊖	d				15 20						15 35									15 50					
London Bridge 4 ⊖	d			15 20	15 27			15 33		15 38	15 42			15 45	15 36			15 50		15 57				16 03	
New Cross Gate	d							15 38							15 41									16 08	
Norwood Junction 2	a			15 32				15 46						15 56	15 59			16 02						16 16	
East Croydon (tram)	a	15 33		15 36	15 39	15 40	15 48	15 50	15 52	15 52	15 54	15 57		16 00	16 03	16 12	16 03	16 06	16 07	16 09	16 09	16 18		16 20	16 22
South Croydon 4	a					15 43						16 01			16 06	16 15					16 12				
Purley Oaks	a														16 09	16 18									
Purley 4	a			15 45				15 56						16 05	16 12	16 21		16 15						16 26	

		SN 1	FC 1	SN 1	SN	SN	SN ◇1 trolley	SN 1		SN	FC 1	SN 1	SN ◇1 trolley	SN 1	SN 1 trolley	SN 1	SN	SN 1		FC 1	SN	SN ◇1 trolley	SN	SN 1	SN 1
London Victoria 15 ⊖	d					16 13	16 17	16 19				16 23	16 32		16 36		16 39				16 43	16 47		16 49	16 53
Clapham Junction 10	d					16 21	16 23	16 26				16 29	16 38		16 42		16 45	16 34			16 51	16 53		16 56	16 59
St Pancras International 15 ⊖	d		15 54								16 10									16 24					
Farringdon 3 ⊖	d		15 59								16 14									16 29					
City Thameslink 3	d		16 02								16 17									16 33					
London Blackfriars 3 ⊖	d		16 05								16 20									16 36					
London Bridge 4 ⊖	d	16 08	16 12	16 15	16 06					16 20	16 27			16 33		16 38				16 43			16 48		
New Cross Gate	d				16 11																				
Norwood Junction 2	a	16 19		16 26	16 29					16 32				16 44									17 01		
East Croydon (tram)	a	16 23	16 24	16 30	16 33	16 42	16 33	16 36		16 36	16 39	16 39	16 47	16 48	16 52	16 52	16 55	16 58		16 59	17 12	17 03	17 05	17 06	17 09
South Croydon 4	a				16 36	16 45						16 42					16 58	17 02			17 19		17 08		17 12
Purley Oaks	a				16 39	16 48											17 01				17 22		17 11		
Purley 4	a			16 35	16 42	16 51				16 45				16 55			17 04				17 25		17 14		

London - East Croydon and Purley

COMPLETE SERVICE

	SN 1	SN 1	SN ◇1 ⚲		SN 1	SN 1	FC 1	SN	SN 1	SN ◇1	SN	SN 1	SN 1		SN 1	FC 1	SN ◇1	SN 1	SN ◇1 ⚲	SN 1	SN	SN 1	SN 1
London Victoria 15 ⊖ d			17 02		17 06			17 09		17 17			17 21		17 23		17 32		17 35		17 39		
Clapham Junction 10 d			17 08		17 12			17 15		17 23			17 27		17 30		17 38		17 42		17 45		17 33
St Pancras International 15 ⊖ d							16 46									17 10							
Farringdon 3 ⊖ d							16 51									17 15							
City Thameslink 3 d							16 55									17 19							
London Blackfriars 3 ⊖ d							17 00									17 22							
London Bridge 4 ⊖ d	16 57	16 59				17 09			17 15		17 17	17 23						17 32		17 42		17 44	
New Cross Gate d																							
Norwood Junction 2 a		17 10									17 30							17 43					
East Croydon a	17 09	17 14	17 17		17 22	17 22	17 25	17 27	17 29	17 32	17 34	17 35	17 36		17 40	17 46	17 48	17 48	17 51	17 54	17 55	17 57	17 59
South Croydon 4 a								17 30	17 32		17 37										17 58	18 01	
Purley Oaks a								17 33			17 40										18 01		
Purley 4 a		17 20						17 36			17 44							17 54			18 04		

	SN 1	SN ◇1	SN 1	SN	FC 1	SN 1	SN 1	SN 1	SN ◇1		SN 1	SN ◇1 ⚲	FC 1	SN 1	SN	SN 1	SN	SN ◇1	SN		SN 1	SN 1	SN 1	FC 1
London Victoria 15 ⊖ d		17 47	17 49			17 53			18 02			18 06			18 09			18 17				18 19	18 23	
Clapham Junction 10 d		17 53	17 56			18 00			18 08			18 12			18 15		18 02	18 23				18 26	18 30	
St Pancras International 15 ⊖ d					17 28								17 40											18 08
Farringdon 3 ⊖ d					17 33								17 45											18 13
City Thameslink 3 d					17 37								17 49											18 17
London Blackfriars 3 ⊖ d					17 40								17 52											18 20
London Bridge 4 ⊖ d	17 47			17 49			17 57	17 59			18 08			18 12		18 16			18 18		18 23			18 27
New Cross Gate d																								
Norwood Junction 2 a				18 01				18 11											18 30					
East Croydon a	17 59	18 02	18 05	18 05	18 08	18 10	18 11	18 15	18 17		18 21	18 22	18 24	18 24	18 27	18 30	18 32	18 33	18 35		18 36	18 37	18 40	18 41
South Croydon 4 a				18 08											18 30	18 33	18 35		18 39					
Purley Oaks a				18 11											18 33		18 38		18 45					
Purley 4 a				18 14				18 20							18 36		18 40		18 48			18 42		

	SN 1	SN ◇1	SN 1	FC 1	SN		SN 1	SN 1	SN	SN ◇1 ⚲	SN	SN 1	FC 1	SN 1	SN ◇1 ⚲		SN 1	SN 1 ⚲	SN 1	FC 1	SN 1	SN	SN	SN ◇1 ⚲
London Victoria 15 ⊖ d		18 32	18 36		18 39				18 45	18 47		18 51		18 53	19 02			19 06			19 10		19 15	19 17
Clapham Junction 10 d		18 38	18 42		18 45			18 34	18 53	18 53		18 57		19 00	19 08			19 12			19 16		19 23	19 23
St Pancras International 15 ⊖ d				18 20									18 34							18 54				
Farringdon 3 ⊖ d				18 25									18 39							18 59				
City Thameslink 3 d				18 29									18 43							19 03				
London Blackfriars 3 ⊖ d				18 32									18 46							19 05				
London Bridge 4 ⊖ d	18 30						18 47				18 49		18 57				19 03		19 08	19 12		19 06		
New Cross Gate d																						19 11		
Norwood Junction 2 a	18 41										19 01						19 14					19 29		
East Croydon a	18 45	18 48	18 52	18 55	18 57		19 00	19 02	19 13	19 02	19 05	19 07	19 10	19 10	19 18		19 18	19 22	19 22	19 24	19 27	19 33	19 44	19 33
South Croydon 4 a					19 00		19 03		19 16		19 08											19 36	19 47	
Purley Oaks a					19 03				19 19		19 11											19 39	19 50	
Purley 4 a	18 50				19 06				19 22		19 14						19 24				19 33	19 42	19 53	

	FC 1		SN 1	SN ◇1 ⚲	SN 1	FC 1	SN 1	SN	SN	SN ◇1 ⚲	SN 1		FC 1	SN 1	SN ◇1 ⚲	SN 1	SN ◇1	FC 1	SN 1	SN	SN		SN ◇1	SN 1
London Victoria 15 ⊖ d			19 23	19 32	19 36		19 40		19 45	19 47				19 53	20 02		20 06		20 10		20 15		20 17	20 23
Clapham Junction 10 d			19 29	19 38	19 42		19 46		19 53	19 53				19 59	20 08		20 12		20 16		20 23		20 23	20 29
St Pancras International 15 ⊖ d	19 10					19 24							19 40					19 54						
Farringdon 3 ⊖ d	19 14					19 29							19 44					19 59						
City Thameslink 3 d	19 17					19 32							19 47					20 02						
London Blackfriars 3 ⊖ d	19 20					19 35							19 50					20 05						
London Bridge 4 ⊖ d	19 27					19 42		19 36			19 52		19 57			20 04		20 12		20 06				
New Cross Gate d								19 41												20 11				
Norwood Junction 2 a								19 59			20 03					20 16				20 29				
East Croydon a	19 39		19 39	19 48	19 52	19 54	19 57	20 03	20 14	20 03	20 06		20 09	20 09	20 19	20 19	20 22	20 24	20 27	20 33	20 44		20 33	20 39
South Croydon 4 a								20 06	20 17											20 36	20 47			
Purley Oaks a								20 09	20 21											20 39	20 50			
Purley 4 a							20 03	20 12	20 24		20 12								20 33	20 42	20 53			

	SN 1	SN ◇1	SN 1	SN ◇1	FC 1	SN 1	SN		SN	SN ◇1	SN 1	SN 1	SN 1	SN 1	SN ◇1	FC 1	SN 1		SN	SN	SN ◇1	SN 1	SN 1	SN 1
London Victoria 15 ⊖ d		20 32		20 36		20 40			20 45	20 47	20 53		21 02		21 06		21 10			21 15	21 17	21 23		21 32
Clapham Junction 10 d		20 38		20 42		20 46			20 53	20 53	20 59		21 08		21 12		21 16			21 23	21 23	21 29		21 38
St Pancras International 15 ⊖ d					20 24											20 54								
Farringdon 3 ⊖ d					20 29											20 59								
City Thameslink 3 d					20 32											21 02								
London Blackfriars 3 ⊖ d					20 35											21 05								
London Bridge 4 ⊖ d	20 28		20 34		20 42		20 36					20 58		21 04		21 12			21 06				21 26	
New Cross Gate d							20 41												21 11					
Norwood Junction 2 a			20 45				20 59							21 15					21 29				21 37	
East Croydon a	20 40	20 48	20 49	20 52	20 54	20 57	21 03		21 14	21 03	21 09	21 10	21 18	21 19	21 22	21 24	21 27		21 33	21 44	21 33	21 39	21 41	21 48
South Croydon 4 a							21 06		21 17										21 36	21 47				
Purley Oaks a							21 09		21 20										21 39	21 50				
Purley 4 a						21 03	21 12		21 23								21 33		21 42	21 53				

Table 175

Mondays to Fridays

from 5 September

London - East Croydon and Purley

COMPLETE SERVICE

	SN ◇1	FC 1	SN 1		SN	SN	SN ◇1	SN 1	SN ◇1	SN 1	SN ◇1	FC 1	SN 1		SN	SN ◇1	SN	SN 1	SN	SN 1	SN 1	FC 1	SN 1
London Victoria 15 ⊖ d	21 36		21 40			21 45	21 47	21 53	22 02		22 06		22 10		22 15	22 17		22 23		22 32	22 36		22 40
Clapham Junction 10 d	21 42		21 46			21 53	21 53	21 59	22 08		22 12		22 16		22 23	22 23		22 29		22 38	22 42		22 46
St Pancras International 15 ⊖ d		21 24										21 54											
Farringdon 3 ⊖ d		21 29										21 59											
City Thameslink 3 d		21 32										22 02											
London Blackfriars 3 ⊖ d		21 35										22 05											
London Bridge 4 ⊖ d		21 42			21 36					22 04		22 12					22 08		22 26			22 42	
New Cross Gate d					21 41												22 13						
Norwood Junction 2 a					21 59					22 15							22 31		22 38				
East Croydon a	21 52	21 54	21 57		22 03	22 14	22 03	22 09	22 18	22 19	22 22	22 24	22 26		22 44	22 33	22 35	22 39	22 42	22 48	22 52	22 54	22 57
South Croydon 4 a					22 06	22 17									22 47		22 38						
Purley Oaks a					22 09	22 20									22 50		22 41						
Purley 4 a			22 03		22 12	22 23							22 33		22 53		22 44						23 03

	SN	SN ◇1	SN	SN 1	SN	SN ◇1	SN 1	SN ◇1	FC 1		SN 1	SN	SN	SN ◇1	SN 1	SN ◇1	FC 1	SN 1	SN		SN FO	SN 1	SN 1
London Victoria 15 ⊖ d	22 45	22 47		22 53		23 02		23 06			23 10		23 15	23 17	23 24	23 32					23 45	23 47	23 49
Clapham Junction 10 d	22 53	22 53		22 59		23 08		23 12			23 16		23 23	23 23	23 30	23 38		23 40			23 53	23 53	23 56
St Pancras International 15 ⊖ d																							
Farringdon 3 ⊖ d																							
City Thameslink 3 d																							
London Blackfriars 3 ⊖ d																							
London Bridge 4 ⊖ d			22 38		22 56		23 04		23 12			23 06					23 42		23 36				
New Cross Gate d			22 43									23 11							23 41				
Norwood Junction 2 a			23 01		23 07		23 15					23 29							23 59				
East Croydon a	23 14	23 03	23 06	23 09	23 11	23 19	23 19	23 22	23 24		23 27	23 33	23 44	23 33	23 40	23 51	23 56	00 01	00 03		00 14	00 05	00 09
South Croydon 4 a	23 17		23 09									23 36	23 47						00 06		00 17		
Purley Oaks a	23 20		23 12									23 39	23 50						00 09		00 20		
Purley 4 a	23 23		23 15								23 33	23 42	23 54						00 12		00 23	00 11	

Saturdays

until 3 September

	SN 1	SN	SN	SN 1	SN 1	SN ◇1	FC	SN 1	SN		SN	FC	SN	SN	SN ◇1	FC 1	FC 1	SN 1	FC 1		SN 1	FC 1	FC 1	SN ◇1
London Victoria 15 ⊖ d			23p45	23p47	23p49	00 05		00 14			00 16			00 42	01 00			02 00			03 00			04 00
Clapham Junction 10 d	23p40		23p53	23p53	23p56	00 11		00 20			00 24			00 50	01 08			02 08			03 08			04 08
St Pancras International 15 ⊖ d																								
Farringdon 3 ⊖ d																								
City Thameslink 3 d																								
London Blackfriars 3 ⊖ d																								
London Bridge 4 ⊖ d		23p36					00 12		00 06			00 42	00 36			01 05	01 35		02 05			03 05	03 35	
New Cross Gate d		23p41							00 11				00 41											
Norwood Junction 2 a		23p59							00 29				00 59											
East Croydon a	00 01	00 03	00 14	00 05	00 09	00 24	00 26	00 31	00 33		00 44	00 56	01 03	01 10	01 21	01 32	02 02	02 21	02 30		03 21	03 30	04 00	04 21
South Croydon 4 a		00 06	00 17						00 36		00 50													
Purley Oaks a		00 09	00 20						00 39		00 53													
Purley 4 a		00 12	00 23	00 11				00 37	00 42		00 56				01 27			02 27			03 27			04 27

	FC 1	FC 1	SN ◇1	FC 1	SN 1		SN ◇1	FC 1	SN 1	SN 1	SN 1	FC 1	SN 1	FC 1	SN 1		SN	SN	FC 1	SN	SN 1	SN 1	SN ◇1	SN 1
London Victoria 15 ⊖ d			05 02		05 23		05 32		06 02		06 23		06 32							06 43	06 53		07 06	
Clapham Junction 10 d			05 08		05 31		05 38		06 08		06 29		06 38		06 34					06 51	06 59		07 12	
St Pancras International 15 ⊖ d																								
Farringdon 3 ⊖ d																								
City Thameslink 3 d																								
London Blackfriars 3 ⊖ d																								
London Bridge 4 ⊖ d	04 05	04 35		05 05				05 52		06 08		06 27		06 42			06 36	06 50	06 57			07 03		07 08
New Cross Gate d																	06 41					07 08		
Norwood Junction 2 a					05 47												06 59	07 02				07 16		
East Croydon a	04 30	05 00	05 21	05 31	05 51		05 48	06 04	06 18	06 22	06 39	06 39	06 48	06 54	06 57		07 03	07 06	07 09	07 12	07 09	07 20	07 22	07 22
South Croydon 4 a					05 54										07 01		07 06			07 15				
Purley Oaks a																	07 09			07 18				
Purley 4 a			05 26				05 53		06 23				06 53				07 12	07 15		07 21		07 26		

	FC 1		SN	SN	FC 1	SN	SN 1	SN ◇1	SN 1	SN ◇1	FC 1		SN 1	SN 1	SN	SN	SN ◇1	SN	SN ◇1	SN 1	FC 1		SN ◇1	SN 1
London Victoria 15 ⊖ d						07 13	07 23	07 32		07 36						07 43	07 47		07 51	07 53			08 02	
Clapham Junction 10 d						07 21	07 29	07 38		07 42			07 34			07 51	07 53			07 59			08 08	
St Pancras International 15 ⊖ d																								
Farringdon 3 ⊖ d																								
City Thameslink 3 d																								
London Blackfriars 3 ⊖ d																								
London Bridge 4 ⊖ d	07 12		07 06	07 20	07 27				07 33		07 42			07 45	07 36			07 50			07 57			08 03
New Cross Gate d			07 11						07 38						07 41									08 08
Norwood Junction 2 a			07 29	07 32					07 46					07 56	07 59			08 02						08 16
East Croydon a	07 24		07 33	07 36	07 39	07 42	07 39	07 48	07 50	07 52	07 54		07 57	08 00	08 03	08 12	08 03	08 06	08 07	08 09	08 09		08 18	08 20
South Croydon 4 a			07 36			07 45							08 01		08 06	08 15								
Purley Oaks a			07 39			07 48									08 09	08 18								
Purley 4 a			07 42	07 45		07 51			07 56					08 05	08 12	08 21		08 15						08 26

Table 175

Saturdays
until 3 September

London - East Croydon and Purley

COMPLETE SERVICE

	SN ◇1	SN 1	FC 1	SN 1	SN	SN	SN ◇1		SN	SN 1	FC 1		FC 1	SN ◇1	SN 1	SN ◇1 (trolley)		FC 1	SN 1	SN 1	SN	SN	SN ◇1
London Victoria 15 ⊖ d	08 06					08 13	08 17			08 23		and at the same minutes past each hour until		17 32		17 36						17 43	17 47
Clapham Junction 10 d	08 12					08 21	08 23			08 29				17 38		17 42			17 34			17 51	17 53
St Pancras International 15 ⊖ d																							
Farringdon 3 ⊖ d																							
City Thameslink 3 d																							
London Blackfriars 3 ⊖ d																							
London Bridge 4 ⊖ d		08 08	08 12	08 15	08 06				08 20		08 27		17 27		17 33			17 42		17 45	17 36		
New Cross Gate d					08 11										17 38						17 41		
Norwood Junction 2 a				08 26	08 29				08 32						17 46					17 57	17 59		
East Croydon a	08 22	08 22	08 24	08 30	08 33	08 42	08 33		08 36	08 39	08 39		17 39	17 48	17 50	17 52		17 54	17 57	18 00	18 03	18 12	18 03
South Croydon 4 a					08 36	08 45													18 01		18 06	18 15	
Purley Oaks a					08 39	08 48															18 09	18 18	
Purley 4 a				08 35	08 42	08 51			08 45						17 56					18 06	18 12	18 21	

	SN	SN ◇1	SN 1		FC 1	SN ◇1 (trolley)	SN 1	SN ◇1 (trolley)	SN 1	FC 1	SN 1	SN	SN		SN ◇1	SN	SN 1	FC 1	SN ◇1	SN 1	SN ◇1 (trolley)	FC 1	SN 1	
London Victoria 15 ⊖ d		17 51	17 53			18 02		18 06					18 13		18 17		18 23		18 32		18 36			
Clapham Junction 10 d			17 59			18 08		18 12					18 21		18 23		18 29		18 38		18 42		18 34	
St Pancras International 15 ⊖ d																								
Farringdon 3 ⊖ d																								
City Thameslink 3 d																								
London Blackfriars 3 ⊖ d																								
London Bridge 4 ⊖ d	17 50				17 57		18 03		18 08	18 12	18 15	18 06				18 20		18 27		18 33		18 42		
New Cross Gate d							18 08					18 11								18 38				
Norwood Junction 2 a	18 02						18 16				18 26	18 29				18 32				18 46				
East Croydon a	18 06	18 07	18 09		18 09	18 18	18 20	18 22	18 22	18 24	18 30	18 33	18 42		18 33	18 36	18 39	18 39	18 48	18 50	18 52	18 54	18 57	
South Croydon 4 a												18 36	18 45										19 01	
Purley Oaks a												18 39	18 48											
Purley 4 a	18 15						18 26				18 35	18 42	18 51			18 45				18 56				

	SN 1	SN	SN	SN ◇1	SN	SN ◇1	SN 1	FC 1	SN ◇1 (trolley)		SN 1	SN ◇1 (trolley)	SN 1	FC 1	SN	SN	SN ◇1	SN	SN 1		FC 1	SN ◇1	SN 1	SN ◇1
London Victoria 15 ⊖ d			18 43	18 47		18 51	18 53		19 02			19 06				19 13	19 17		19 23			19 32		19 36
Clapham Junction 10 d			18 51	18 53			18 59		19 08			19 12				19 21	19 23		19 29			19 38		19 42
St Pancras International 15 ⊖ d																								
Farringdon 3 ⊖ d																								
City Thameslink 3 d																								
London Blackfriars 3 ⊖ d																								
London Bridge 4 ⊖ d	18 45	18 36			18 50			18 57			19 03		19 08	19 12	19 06			19 20			19 27		19 33	
New Cross Gate d		18 41									19 08				19 11								19 38	
Norwood Junction 2 a	18 56	18 59			19 02						19 16				19 29			19 32					19 46	
East Croydon a	19 00	19 03	19 12	19 03	19 06	19 07	19 09	19 09	19 18		19 20	19 22	19 22	19 24	19 33	19 42	19 33	19 36	19 39		19 39	19 48	19 50	19 52
South Croydon 4 a		19 06	19 15												19 36	19 45								
Purley Oaks a		19 09	19 18												19 39	19 48								
Purley 4 a	19 05	19 12	19 21		19 15						19 26				19 42	19 51		19 45					19 56	

	FC 1	SN 1	SN	SN	SN ◇1		SN	SN ◇1	SN 1	FC 1	SN ◇1	SN ◇1	SN 1	FC 1	SN 1		SN	SN	SN ◇1	SN	SN ◇1	SN 1	SN ◇1	SN ◇1
London Victoria 15 ⊖ d				19 43	19 47			19 51	19 53		20 02	20 06			20 10			20 13	20 17		20 21	20 23	20 32	20 36
Clapham Junction 10 d		19 34		19 51	19 53				19 59		20 08	20 12			20 16			20 21	20 23			20 29	20 38	20 42
St Pancras International 15 ⊖ d																								
Farringdon 3 ⊖ d																								
City Thameslink 3 d																								
London Blackfriars 3 ⊖ d																								
London Bridge 4 ⊖ d	19 42		19 36				19 50			19 57			20 08	20 12			20 06			20 20				
New Cross Gate d			19 41														20 11							
Norwood Junction 2 a			19 59				20 02						20 19				20 29			20 32				
East Croydon a	19 54	19 57	20 03	20 12	20 03		20 06	20 07	20 09	20 09	20 19	20 22	20 22	20 24	20 27		20 33	20 42	20 33	20 36	20 37	20 39	20 48	20 52
South Croydon 4 a			20 06	20 15													20 36	20 45						
Purley Oaks a			20 09	20 18													20 39	20 48						
Purley 4 a			20 12	20 21			20 15								20 33		20 42	20 51		20 45				

	FC 1		SN 1	SN 1	SN	SN	SN ◇1	SN	SN 1	SN ◇1	SN ◇1		SN 1	FC 1	SN 1	SN	SN	SN ◇1	SN	SN 1	SN 1		SN ◇1	FC 1
London Victoria 15 ⊖ d			20 40			20 43	20 47		20 53	21 02	21 06				21 10		21 13	21 17		21 23	21 32		21 36	
Clapham Junction 10 d			20 46	20 34		20 51	20 53		20 59	21 08	21 12				21 16		21 21	21 23		21 29	21 38		21 42	
St Pancras International 15 ⊖ d																								
Farringdon 3 ⊖ d																								
City Thameslink 3 d																								
London Blackfriars 3 ⊖ d																								
London Bridge 4 ⊖ d	20 42				20 36			20 50					21 08	21 12		21 06			21 20					21 42
New Cross Gate d					20 41											21 11								
Norwood Junction 2 a					20 59			21 02					21 19			21 29			21 32					
East Croydon a	20 53		20 57	20 59	21 03	21 12	21 03	21 06	21 09	21 18	21 22		21 22	21 24	21 27	21 33	21 42	21 33	21 36	21 39	21 48		21 52	21 54
South Croydon 4 a					21 06	21 15										21 36	21 45							
Purley Oaks a					21 09	21 18										21 39	21 48							
Purley 4 a			21 03		21 12	21 21		21 15							21 33	21 42	21 51		21 45					

Table 175

Saturdays
until 3 September

London - East Croydon and Purley

COMPLETE SERVICE

	SN 1	SN	SN ◇1	SN	SN	SN 1	SN ◇1		SN ◇1	SN 1	FC 1	SN 1	SN	SN ◇1	SN	SN	SN 1		SN 1	SN ◇1	FC 1	SN 1	SN	SN
London Victoria 15 ⊖ d	21 40	21 43	21 47			21 53	22 02		22 06			22 10	22 13	22 17			22 23		22 32	22 36		22 40		22 43
Clapham Junction 10 d	21 46	21 51	21 53			21 59	22 08		22 12			22 16	22 21	22 23			22 29		22 38	22 42		22 46		22 51
St Pancras International 15 ⊖ d																								
Farringdon 3 ⊖ d																								
City Thameslink 3 d																								
London Blackfriars 3 ⊖ d																								
London Bridge 4 ⊖ d				21 36	21 50					22 08	22 12				22 06	22 20					22 42		22 36	
New Cross Gate d				21 41											22 11								22 41	
Norwood Junction 2 a				21 59	22 02					22 19					22 29	22 32							22 59	
East Croydon a	21 57	22 12	22 03	22 04	22 07	22 09	22 18		22 22	22 22	22 24	22 27	22 42	22 33	22 35	22 37	22 39		22 48	22 52	22 54	22 57	23 03	23 13
South Croydon 4 a		22 15		22 07									22 46		22 38								23 06	23 16
Purley Oaks a		22 18		22 10									22 49		22 41								23 09	23 19
Purley 4 a	22 03	22 21		22 13	22 16							22 33	22 52		22 44	22 47						23 03	23 12	23 22

	SN ◇1	SN	SN 1		SN ◇1	SN 1	SN ◇1	FC 1	SN 1	SN	SN	SN ◇1	SN 1		SN 1	FC 1	SN	SN	SN 1	SN 1				
London Victoria 15 ⊖ d	22 47		22 53		23 02		23 06		23 10		23 15	23 17	23 24		23 32			23 45	23 47	23 49				
Clapham Junction 10 d	22 53		22 59		23 08		23 12		23 16		23 23	23 23	23 30		23 38			23 53	23 53	23 56				
St Pancras International 15 ⊖ d																								
Farringdon 3 ⊖ d																								
City Thameslink 3 d																								
London Blackfriars 3 ⊖ d																								
London Bridge 4 ⊖ d		22 50				23 04		23 12		23 06						23 42	23 36							
New Cross Gate d										23 11							23 41							
Norwood Junction 2 a		23 02				23 15				23 29							23 59							
East Croydon a	23 03	23 06	23 09		23 18	23 19	23 22	23 24	23 27	23 33	23 44	23 33	23 40		23 52	23 56	00 03	00 14	00 05	00 09				
South Croydon 4 a										23 36	23 47						00 06	00 17						
Purley Oaks a										23 39	23 50						00 09	00 20						
Purley 4 a		23 15							23 33	23 42	23 53						00 13	00 23	00 11					

Saturdays
from 10 September

	SN 1	SN	SN	SN 1	SN 1	SN ◇1	FC	SN 1	SN		SN	FC	SN	SN	SN ◇1	FC 1	FC 1	SN 1	FC 1		SN 1	FC 1	FC 1	SN ◇1
London Victoria 15 ⊖ d			23p45	23p47	23p49	00 05		00 14			00 16			00 42	01 00			02 00			03 00			04 00
Clapham Junction 10 d	23p40		23p53	23p53	23p56	00 11		00 20			00 24			00 50	01 08			02 08			03 08			04 08
St Pancras International 15 ⊖ d																								
Farringdon 3 ⊖ d																								
City Thameslink 3 d																								
London Blackfriars 3 ⊖ d																								
London Bridge 4 ⊖ d		23p36					00 12		00 06			00 42	00 36			01 05	01 35		02 05			03 05	03 35	
New Cross Gate d		23p41							00 11				00 41											
Norwood Junction 2 a		23p59							00 29				00 59											
East Croydon a	00 01	00 03	00 14	00 05	00 09	00 24	00 26	00 31	00 33		00 44	00 56	01 03	01 10	01 21	01 32	02 02	02 21	02 30		03 21	03 30	04 00	04 21
South Croydon 4 a		00 06	00 17						00 36		00 50													
Purley Oaks a		00 09	00 20						00 39		00 53													
Purley 4 a		00 12	00 23	00 11				00 37	00 42		00 56				01 27			02 27			03 27			04 27

	FC 1	FC 1	SN ◇1	FC 1	SN 1		SN ◇1	FC 1	SN 1	SN 1	SN 1	FC 1	SN 1	FC 1	SN 1		SN	SN	FC 1	SN	SN 1	SN 1	SN ◇1	SN 1
London Victoria 15 ⊖ d			05 02		05 23		05 32		06 02		06 23		06 32							06 43	06 53		07 06	
Clapham Junction 10 d			05 08		05 31		05 38		06 08		06 29		06 38		06 34					06 51	06 59		07 12	
St Pancras International 15 ⊖ d																								
Farringdon 3 ⊖ d																								
City Thameslink 3 d																								
London Blackfriars 3 ⊖ d																								
London Bridge 4 ⊖ d	04 05	04 35		05 05				05 52		06 08		06 27		06 42			06 36	06 50	06 57			07 03		07 08
New Cross Gate d																	06 41					07 08		
Norwood Junction 2 a					05 47												06 59	07 02				07 16		
East Croydon a	04 30	05 00	05 21	05 31	05 51		05 48	06 04	06 18	06 22	06 39	06 39	06 48	06 54	06 57		07 03	07 06	07 09	07 12	07 09	07 20	07 22	07 22
South Croydon 4 a					05 54										07 01		07 06			07 15				
Purley Oaks a																	07 09			07 18				
Purley 4 a			05 26				05 53		06 23				06 53				07 12	07 15		07 21		07 26		

	FC 1		SN	SN	SN	SN ◇1	SN 1	FC 1	SN ◇1	SN 1	SN ◇1		FC 1	SN 1	SN 1	SN	SN	SN ◇1	SN	SN ◇1	SN 1		FC 1	SN ◇1
London Victoria 15 ⊖ d					07 13	07 21	07 23		07 32		07 36						07 43	07 47		07 51	07 53			08 02
Clapham Junction 10 d					07 21		07 29		07 38		07 42			07 34			07 51	07 53			07 59			08 08
St Pancras International 15 ⊖ d																								
Farringdon 3 ⊖ d																								
City Thameslink 3 d																								
London Blackfriars 3 ⊖ d																								
London Bridge 4 ⊖ d	07 12		07 06	07 20				07 27		07 33			07 42		07 45	07 36			07 50				07 57	
New Cross Gate d			07 11							07 38						07 41								
Norwood Junction 2 a			07 29	07 32						07 46					07 56	07 59			08 02					
East Croydon a	07 24		07 33	07 36	07 42	07 37	07 39	07 39	07 48	07 50	07 52		07 54	07 57	08 00	08 03	08 12	08 03	08 06	08 07	08 09		08 09	08 18
South Croydon 4 a			07 36		07 45									08 01		08 06	08 15							
Purley Oaks a			07 39		07 48											08 09	08 18							
Purley 4 a			07 42	07 45	07 51					07 56					08 05	08 12	08 21		08 15					

Table 175

Saturdays

from 10 September

London - East Croydon and Purley

COMPLETE SERVICE

	SN 1	SN ◇1	SN 1	FC 1	SN 1	SN	SN		SN ◇1	SN	and at the same minutes past each hour until	SN	SN ◇1	SN 1	FC 1	SN ◇1		SN 1	SN ◇1 ⌶	FC 1	SN 1	SN 1	SN
London Victoria 15 ⊖ d		08 06					08 13		08 17				17 21	17 23		17 32			17 36				
Clapham Junction 10 d		08 12					08 21		08 23					17 29		17 38			17 42		17 34		
St Pancras International 15 ⊖ d																							
Farringdon 3 ⊖ d																							
City Thameslink 3 d																							
London Blackfriars 3 ⊖ d																							
London Bridge 4 ⊖ d	08 03		08 08	08 12	08 15	08 06				08 20		17 20			17 27			17 33		17 42		17 45	17 36
New Cross Gate d	08 08					08 11												17 38					17 41
Norwood Junction 2 a	08 16				08 26	08 29				08 32		17 32						17 46				17 57	17 59
East Croydon a	08 20	08 22	08 22	08 24	08 30	08 33	08 42		08 33	08 36		17 36	17 37	17 39	17 39	17 48		17 50	17 52	17 54	17 57	18 00	18 03
South Croydon 4 a						08 36	08 45														18 01		18 06
Purley Oaks a						08 39	08 48																18 09
Purley 4 a	08 26				08 35	08 42	08 51			08 45		17 45						17 56				18 06	18 12

	SN	SN ◇1	SN		SN ◇1	SN 1	FC 1	SN ◇1 ⌶	SN 1	SN ◇1 ⌶	SN 1	FC 1	SN 1		SN	SN	SN ◇1	SN	SN ◇1	SN 1	FC 1	SN ◇1	SN 1	
London Victoria 15 ⊖ d	17 43	17 47			17 51	17 53		18 02		18 06						18 13	18 17		18 21	18 23		18 32		
Clapham Junction 10 d	17 51	17 53				17 59		18 08		18 12						18 21	18 23			18 29		18 38		
St Pancras International 15 ⊖ d																								
Farringdon 3 ⊖ d																								
City Thameslink 3 d																								
London Blackfriars 3 ⊖ d																								
London Bridge 4 ⊖ d			17 50				17 57		18 03		18 08	18 12	18 15		18 06			18 20			18 27		18 33	
New Cross Gate d									18 08						18 11								18 38	
Norwood Junction 2 a			18 02						18 16				18 26		18 29			18 32					18 46	
East Croydon a	18 12	18 03	18 06		18 07	18 09	18 09	18 18	18 20	18 22	18 22	18 24	18 30		18 33	18 42	18 33	18 36	18 37	18 39	18 39	18 48	18 50	
South Croydon 4 a	18 15														18 36	18 45								
Purley Oaks a	18 18														18 39	18 48								
Purley 4 a	18 21		18 15						18 26				18 35		18 42	18 51		18 45					18 56	

	SN ◇1 ⌶	FC 1	SN 1	SN 1	SN	SN	SN ◇1	SN	SN ◇1		SN 1	FC 1	SN ◇1 ⌶	SN 1	SN ◇1 ⌶	SN 1	FC 1	SN	SN		SN ◇1	SN	SN ◇1	SN 1
London Victoria 15 ⊖ d	18 36					18 43	18 47		18 51		18 53		19 02		19 06				19 13		19 17		19 21	19 23
Clapham Junction 10 d	18 42		18 34			18 51	18 53				18 59		19 08		19 12				19 21		19 23			19 29
St Pancras International 15 ⊖ d																								
Farringdon 3 ⊖ d																								
City Thameslink 3 d																								
London Blackfriars 3 ⊖ d																								
London Bridge 4 ⊖ d		18 42		18 45	18 36			18 50				18 57		19 03		19 08	19 12	19 06				19 20		
New Cross Gate d					18 41									19 08				19 11						
Norwood Junction 2 a				18 56	18 59			19 02						19 16				19 29				19 32		
East Croydon a	18 52	18 54	18 57	19 00	19 03	19 12	19 03	19 06	19 07		19 09	19 09	19 18	19 20	19 22	19 22	19 24	19 33	19 42		19 33	19 36	19 37	19 39
South Croydon 4 a			19 01		19 06	19 15												19 36	19 45					
Purley Oaks a					19 09	19 18												19 39	19 48					
Purley 4 a				19 05	19 12	19 21		19 15						19 26				19 42	19 51			19 45		

	FC 1	SN ◇1	SN 1	SN ◇1	FC 1		SN 1	SN	SN	SN ◇1	SN	SN ◇1	SN 1	FC 1	SN ◇1		SN ◇1	SN 1	FC 1	SN 1	SN	SN	SN ◇1	SN
London Victoria 15 ⊖ d		19 32		19 36					19 43	19 47		19 51	19 53		20 02		20 06			20 10		20 13	20 17	
Clapham Junction 10 d		19 38		19 42			19 34		19 51	19 53			19 59		20 08		20 12			20 16		20 21	20 23	
St Pancras International 15 ⊖ d																								
Farringdon 3 ⊖ d																								
City Thameslink 3 d																								
London Blackfriars 3 ⊖ d																								
London Bridge 4 ⊖ d	19 27		19 33		19 42			19 36			19 50			19 57				20 08	20 12		20 06			20 20
New Cross Gate d			19 38					19 41													20 11			
Norwood Junction 2 a			19 46					19 59			20 02							20 19			20 29			20 32
East Croydon a	19 39	19 48	19 50	19 52	19 54		19 57	20 03	20 12	20 03	20 06	20 07	20 09	20 09	20 19		20 22	20 22	20 24	20 27	20 33	20 42	20 33	20 36
South Croydon 4 a								20 06	20 15												20 36	20 45		
Purley Oaks a								20 09	20 18												20 39	20 48		
Purley 4 a			19 56					20 12	20 21		20 15									20 33	20 42	20 51		20 45

	SN ◇1		SN 1	SN ◇1	SN ◇1	FC 1	SN 1	SN 1	SN	SN	SN ◇1		SN	SN 1	SN ◇1	SN ◇1	SN 1	FC 1	SN 1	SN	SN		SN ◇1	SN
London Victoria 15 ⊖ d	20 21		20 23	20 32	20 36		20 40			20 43	20 47			20 53	21 02	21 06			21 10		21 13		21 17	
Clapham Junction 10 d			20 29	20 38	20 42		20 46	20 34		20 51	20 53			20 59	21 08	21 12			21 16		21 21		21 23	
St Pancras International 15 ⊖ d																								
Farringdon 3 ⊖ d																								
City Thameslink 3 d																								
London Blackfriars 3 ⊖ d																								
London Bridge 4 ⊖ d						20 42			20 36				20 50				21 08	21 12		21 06				21 20
New Cross Gate d									20 41											21 11				
Norwood Junction 2 a									20 59				21 02				21 19			21 29				21 32
East Croydon a	20 37		20 39	20 48	20 52	20 53	20 57	20 59	21 03	21 12	21 03		21 06	21 09	21 18	21 22	21 22	21 24	21 27	21 33	21 42		21 33	21 36
South Croydon 4 a									21 06	21 15										21 36	21 45			
Purley Oaks a									21 09	21 18										21 39	21 48			
Purley 4 a							21 03		21 12	21 21			21 15						21 33	21 42	21 51			21 45

Table 175

London - East Croydon and Purley

COMPLETE SERVICE

Saturdays

from 10 September

		SN	SN	SN	FC	SN	SN	SN		SN	SN	SN	SN	SN	SN	FC	SN	SN		SN	SN	SN	SN	SN	SN
		1	1	◇1	1	1		◇1				1	◇1	◇1	1	1	1			◇1			1	1	◇1
London Victoria 15 ⊖	d	21 23	21 32	21 36		21 40	21 43	21 47				21 53	22 02	22 06			22 10	22 13		22 17			22 23	22 32	22 36
Clapham Junction 10	d	21 29	21 38	21 42		21 46	21 51	21 53				21 59	22 08	22 12			22 16	22 21		22 23			22 29	22 38	22 42
St Pancras International 15 ⊖	d																								
Farringdon 3 ⊖	d																								
City Thameslink 3	d																								
London Blackfriars 3 ⊖	d																								
London Bridge 4 ⊖	d				21 42					21 36	21 50				22 08	22 12					22 06	22 20			
New Cross Gate	d									21 41											22 11				
Norwood Junction 2	a									21 59	22 02				22 19						22 29	22 32			
East Croydon	a	21 39	21 48	21 52	21 54	21 57	22 12	22 03		22 04	22 07	22 09	22 18	22 22	22 22	22 24	22 27	22 42		22 33	22 35	22 37	22 39	22 48	22 52
South Croydon 4	a						22 15			22 07								22 46			22 38				
Purley Oaks	a						22 18			22 10								22 49			22 41				
Purley 4	a					22 03	22 21			22 13	22 16						22 33	22 52			22 44	22 47			

		FC	SN	SN		SN	SN	SN	SN	SN	SN	SN	FC	SN		SN	SN	SN	SN	SN	FC	SN	SN	SN	
		1	1				◇1		1	◇1	1	◇1	1	1				◇1	1	1	1			1	
London Victoria 15 ⊖	d		22 40			22 43	22 47		22 53	23 02		23 06		23 10			23 15	23 17	23 24	23 32			23 45	23 47	
Clapham Junction 10	d		22 46			22 51	22 53		22 59	23 08		23 12		23 16			23 23	23 23	23 30	23 38			23 53	23 53	
St Pancras International 15 ⊖	d																								
Farringdon 3 ⊖	d																								
City Thameslink 3	d																								
London Blackfriars 3 ⊖	d																								
London Bridge 4 ⊖	d	22 42		22 36				22 50			23 04		23 12			23 06					23 42	23 36			
New Cross Gate	d			22 41												23 11						23 41			
Norwood Junction 2	a			22 59				23 02			23 15					23 29						23 59			
East Croydon	a	22 54	22 57	23 03		23 13	23 03	23 06	23 09	23 18	23 19	23 22	23 24	23 27		23 33	23 44	23 33	23 40	23 52	23 56	00 03	00 14	00 05	
South Croydon 4	a			23 06		23 16										23 36	23 47					00 06	00 17		
Purley Oaks	a			23 09		23 19										23 39	23 50					00 09	00 20		
Purley 4	a		23 03	23 12		23 22		23 15						23 33		23 42	23 53					00 13	00 23	00 11	

		SN
		1
London Victoria 15 ⊖	d	23 49
Clapham Junction 10	d	23 56
St Pancras International 15 ⊖	d	
Farringdon 3 ⊖	d	
City Thameslink 3	d	
London Blackfriars 3 ⊖	d	
London Bridge 4 ⊖	d	
New Cross Gate	d	
Norwood Junction 2	a	
East Croydon	a	00 09
South Croydon 4	a	
Purley Oaks	a	
Purley 4	a	

Sundays

until 4 September

		SN	SN	SN	SN	SN	FC	SN	SN	SN		FC	SN	SN	SN	FC	SN	SN	SN	SN		SN	SN	SN	SN
				1	1	◇1	1	1				1			1	1	1	1	1	1		◇1	◇1		◇1
		A	A	A	A																				
London Victoria 15 ⊖	d		23p45	23p47	23p49	00 05		00 14		00 16				00 42	01 00		02 00	03 00	04 00	05 02		05 47	06 32	06 36	07 02
Clapham Junction 10	d		23p53	23p53	23p56	00 11		00 20		00 24				00 50	01 08		02 08	03 08	04 08	05 08		05 53	06 38	06 42	07 08
St Pancras International 15 ⊖	d																								
Farringdon 3 ⊖	d																								
City Thameslink 3	d																								
London Blackfriars 3 ⊖	d																								
London Bridge 4 ⊖	d	23p36					00 12		00 06			00 42	00 36			01 05									
New Cross Gate	d	23p41							00 11				00 41												
Norwood Junction 2	a	23p59							00 29				00 59												
East Croydon	a	00 03	00 14	00 05	00 09	00 24	00 27	00 31	00 33	00 44		00 56	01 03	01 10	01 21	01 32	02 21	03 21	04 21	05 22		06 05	06 51	07 03	07 19
South Croydon 4	a	00 06	00 17						00 36	00 50															
Purley Oaks	a	00 09	00 20						00 39	00 53															
Purley 4	a	00 13	00 23	00 11				00 37	00 42	00 56					01 27		02 27	03 27	04 27	05 28			06 56	07 10	07 25

		SN	FC	SN	SN	SN		FC	SN	SN	SN	SN	SN	SN	FC	SN		SN	SN	SN	SN	SN	FC	SN	SN
		1	1		◇1	1		1		1			◇1	1	1				◇1		◇1	1	1		1
London Victoria 15 ⊖	d			07 06	07 27				07 36	07 40			08 02					08 06	08 17		08 27			08 36	08 40
Clapham Junction 10	d			07 12	07 33				07 42	07 45			08 08					08 12	08 23		08 33			08 42	08 45
St Pancras International 15 ⊖	d																								
Farringdon 3 ⊖	d																								
City Thameslink 3	d																								
London Blackfriars 3 ⊖	d																								
London Bridge 4 ⊖	d	07 05	07 12			07 37		07 42			07 21	07 39		08 05	08 12	07 51				08 09		08 37	08 42		
New Cross Gate	d											07 44								08 14					
Norwood Junction 2	a	07 17				07 48						08 02		08 16						08 32		08 48			
East Croydon	a	07 21	07 24	07 33	07 42	07 54		07 54	08 03	07 57	08 01	08 07	08 17	08 20	08 24	08 30		08 33	08 32	08 37	08 42	08 54	08 54	09 03	08 57
South Croydon 4	a											08 10								08 40					
Purley Oaks	a											08 13								08 43					
Purley 4	a	07 28		07 40		08 00			08 10			08 16	08 23	08 26				08 40		08 46		09 00		09 10	

A not 22 May

Table 175

Sundays
until 4 September

London - East Croydon and Purley

COMPLETE SERVICE

	SN		SN	SN	SN	SN	SN	FC	SN	SN	SN		SN	SN	SN		SN	SN	FC	SN		SN	SN
			◇1		◇1	1	◇1	1			◇1			◇1	◇1		◇1	1	1			1	
London Victoria 15 ⊖ d			08 47		09 02		09 06			09 06	09 17			09 27	09 36	and at the same minutes past each hour until	20 36			20 36		20 40	
Clapham Junction 10 d			08 53		09 08		09 12			09 12	09 23			09 33	09 42		20 42			20 42		20 45	
St Pancras International 15 ⊖ d																							
Farringdon 3 ⊖ d																							
City Thameslink 3 d																							
London Blackfriars 3 ⊖ d																							
London Bridge 4 ⊖ d	08 21			08 39		09 05		09 12	08 51				09 09					20 37	20 42				20 21
New Cross Gate d				08 44									09 14										
Norwood Junction 2 a				09 02		09 16							09 32					20 48					
East Croydon a	09 01		09 02	09 07	09 17	09 20	09 22	09 24	09 30	09 33	09 32		09 37	09 42	09 52		20 52	20 54	20 54	21 03		20 57	21 01
South Croydon 4 a				09 10									09 40										
Purley Oaks a				09 13									09 43										
Purley 4 a				09 16	09 23	09 26				09 40			09 46					21 00		21 10			

	SN	SN	SN	SN	SN	FC	SN		SN	SN	SN	SN	SN	FC	SN	SN	SN		SN	SN	SN	SN	FC	SN
	◇1		◇1	1	◇1	1				◇1		◇1	1	1		1			◇1		◇1	1	1	
London Victoria 15 ⊖ d	20 47		21 02		21 06				21 06	21 17		21 27			21 36	21 40			21 47		22 02			
Clapham Junction 10 d	20 53		21 08		21 12				21 12	21 23		21 33			21 42	21 45			21 53		22 08			
St Pancras International 15 ⊖ d																								
Farringdon 3 ⊖ d																								
City Thameslink 3 d																								
London Blackfriars 3 ⊖ d																								
London Bridge 4 ⊖ d		20 39		21 05		21 12	20 51				21 09		21 37	21 42			21 21			21 39		22 05	22 12	21 51
New Cross Gate d		20 44									21 14									21 44				
Norwood Junction 2 a		21 02		21 16							21 32		21 48							22 02		22 16		
East Croydon a	21 02	21 07	21 17	21 20	21 22	21 24	21 30		21 33	21 32	21 37	21 42	21 54	21 54	22 03	21 57	22 01		22 02	22 07	22 17	22 20	22 24	22 30
South Croydon 4 a		21 10									21 40									22 10				
Purley Oaks a		21 13									21 43									22 13				
Purley 4 a		21 16	21 23	21 26					21 40		21 46		22 00		22 10					22 16	22 23	22 26		

	SN	SN	SN		SN	SN	FC	SN	SN	SN	SN	SN	SN		FC	SN	SN	SN	SN	SN	FC	SN	SN	
		◇1			◇1	1	1		1		◇1		1		1			◇1		◇1	1			
London Victoria 15 ⊖ d	22 06	22 17			22 27			22 36	22 40		22 47		23 04				23 06	23 17		23 32			23 47	
Clapham Junction 10 d	22 12	22 23			22 33			22 42	22 45		22 53		23 10				23 12	23 23		23 38			23 53	
St Pancras International 15 ⊖ d																								
Farringdon 3 ⊖ d																								
City Thameslink 3 d																								
London Blackfriars 3 ⊖ d																								
London Bridge 4 ⊖ d			22 09			22 37	22 42			22 21		22 39			23 12	22 51			23 09		23 42	23 21		
New Cross Gate d			22 14									22 44							23 14					
Norwood Junction 2 a			22 32			22 48						23 02							23 32					
East Croydon a	22 33	22 32	22 37		22 42	22 54	22 54	23 03	22 57	23 00	23 03	23 07	23 22		23 24	23 30	23 34	23 37	23 38	23 52	23 56	00 01	00 06	
South Croydon 4 a			22 40									23 10					23 37							
Purley Oaks a			22 43									23 13					23 40							
Purley 4 a	22 40		22 46			23 00		23 10				23 16	23 28				23 43							

	SN	SN
London Victoria 15 ⊖ d		23 50
Clapham Junction 10 d		23 56
St Pancras International 15 ⊖ d		
Farringdon 3 ⊖ d		
City Thameslink 3 d		
London Blackfriars 3 ⊖ d		
London Bridge 4 ⊖ d	23 39	
New Cross Gate d	23 44	
Norwood Junction 2 a	00 02	
East Croydon a	00 06	00 17
South Croydon 4 a	00 09	00 20
Purley Oaks a	00 12	00 23
Purley 4 a	00 15	00 26

Sundays
from 11 September

	SN	SN	SN	SN	SN	FC	SN	SN	SN		FC	SN	SN	SN	FC	SN	SN	SN	SN		SN	SN	SN	SN
			1	1	◇1	1	1				1			1	1	1	1	1	1		◇1	◇1		◇1
London Victoria 15 ⊖ d		23p45	23p47	23p49	00 05		00 14		00 16				00 42	01 00		02 00	03 00	04 00	05 02		05 47	06 32	06 36	07 02
Clapham Junction 10 d		23p53	23p53	23p56	00 11		00 20		00 24				00 50	01 08		02 08	03 08	04 08	05 08		05 53	06 38	06 42	07 08
St Pancras International 15 ⊖ d																								
Farringdon 3 ⊖ d																								
City Thameslink 3 d																								
London Blackfriars 3 ⊖ d																								
London Bridge 4 ⊖ d	23p36					00 12		00 06			00 42	00 36			01 05									
New Cross Gate d	23p41							00 11				00 41												
Norwood Junction 2 a	23p59							00 29				00 59												
East Croydon a	00 03	00 14	00 05	00 09	00 24	00 27	00 31	00 33	00 44		00 56	01 03	01 10	01 21	01 32	02 21	03 21	04 21	05 22		06 05	06 51	07 03	07 23
South Croydon 4 a	00 06	00 17						00 36	00 50															
Purley Oaks a	00 09	00 20						00 39	00 53															
Purley 4 a	00 13	00 23	00 11				00 37	00 42	00 56					01 27		02 27	03 27	04 27	05 28			06 56	07 10	07 29

Table 175

London - East Croydon and Purley

COMPLETE SERVICE

Sundays

from 11 September

	FC	SN	SN	SN	FC		SN	SN	SN	SN	SN	FC	SN	SN	SN		SN	SN	SN	FC	SN	SN	SN	SN
	1		◇1	1	1		1				◇1	1			◇1			◇1	1	1	1			◇1
London Victoria [15] ⊖ d		07 06	07 32				07 34		07 36		08 04			08 06	08 17			08 32			08 34		08 36	08 47
Clapham Junction [10] d		07 12	07 38				07 40		07 42		08 10			08 12	08 23			08 38			08 40		08 42	08 53
St Pancras International [15] ⊖ d																								
Farringdon [3] ⊖ d																								
City Thameslink [3] d																								
London Blackfriars [3] ⊖ d																								
London Bridge [4] ⊖ d	07 12			07 37	07 42			07 21		07 39		08 12	07 51				08 09		08 37	08 42		08 21		
New Cross Gate d										07 44							08 14							
Norwood Junction [2] a				07 48						08 02							08 32		08 48					
East Croydon a	07 26	07 33	07 50	07 54	07 56		07 57	08 01	08 03	08 07	08 24	08 27	08 30	08 33	08 36		08 37	08 50	08 54	08 56	08 57	09 01	09 03	09 06
South Croydon [4] a										08 10							08 40							
Purley Oaks a										08 13							08 43							
Purley [4] a		07 40		08 00					08 10	08 16	08 30			08 40			08 46		09 00				09 10	

	SN		SN		SN	SN	FC	SN	SN	SN		SN	SN	SN	FC	SN	SN	SN	SN	SN		SN	FC
			◇1		◇1	◇1	1			◇1			◇1	1	1	1			◇1			◇1	1
London Victoria [15] ⊖ d			09 02	and at	21 02	21 04			21 06	21 17			21 32			21 34		21 36	21 47			22 04	
Clapham Junction [10] d			09 08	the same	21 08	21 10			21 12	21 23			21 38			21 40		21 42	21 53			22 10	
St Pancras International [15] ⊖ d				minutes																			
Farringdon [3] ⊖ d				past																			
City Thameslink [3] d				each																			
London Blackfriars [3] ⊖ d				hour until																			
London Bridge [4] ⊖ d	08 39						21 12	20 51				21 09		21 37	21 42		21 21			21 39			22 12
New Cross Gate d	08 44											21 14								21 44			
Norwood Junction [2] a	09 02											21 32		21 48						22 02			
East Croydon a	09 07		09 21		21 21	21 24	21 27	21 30	21 33	21 36		21 37	21 50	21 54	21 56	21 57	22 01	22 03	22 06	22 07		22 24	22 27
South Croydon [4] a	09 10											21 40								22 10			
Purley Oaks a	09 13											21 43								22 13			
Purley [4] a	09 16					21 30			21 40			21 46		22 00				22 10		22 16		22 30	

	SN	SN	SN	SN	SN	SN	FC		SN	SN	SN	SN	SN	SN	FC	SN	SN		SN	SN	SN	FC	SN	SN
			◇1		◇1	1	1		1			◇1		1	1				◇1		◇1	1		
London Victoria [15] ⊖ d		22 06	22 17		22 32				22 34		22 36	22 47		23 04			23 06		23 17		23 32			23 47
Clapham Junction [10] d		22 12	22 23		22 38				22 40		22 42	22 53		23 10			23 12		23 23		23 38			23 53
St Pancras International [15] ⊖ d																								
Farringdon [3] ⊖ d																								
City Thameslink [3] d																								
London Blackfriars [3] ⊖ d																								
London Bridge [4] ⊖ d	21 51			22 09		22 37	22 42			22 21			22 39		23 12	22 51				23 09		23 42	23 21	
New Cross Gate d				22 14									22 44							23 14				
Norwood Junction [2] a				22 32		22 48							23 02							23 32				
East Croydon a	22 30	22 33	22 36	22 37	22 50	22 54	22 56		22 57	23 00	23 03	23 06	23 07	23 22	23 27	23 30	23 34		23 37	23 38	23 52	23 56	00 01	00 06
South Croydon [4] a				22 40									23 10				23 37							
Purley Oaks a				22 43									23 13				23 40							
Purley [4] a		22 40		22 46		23 00					23 10		23 16	23 28			23 43							

	SN	SN
London Victoria [15] ⊖ d		23 50
Clapham Junction [10] d		23 56
St Pancras International [15] ⊖ d		
Farringdon [3] ⊖ d		
City Thameslink [3] d		
London Blackfriars [3] ⊖ d		
London Bridge [4] ⊖ d	23 39	
New Cross Gate d	23 44	
Norwood Junction [2] a	00 02	
East Croydon a	00 06	00 17
South Croydon [4] a	00 09	00 20
Purley Oaks a	00 12	00 23
Purley [4] a	00 15	00 26

Table 175

Mondays to Fridays

until 2 September

Purley and East Croydon - London

COMPLETE SERVICE

		SN MO 1	SN MO 1	SN MX 1	FC 1	SN ◇1	FC MX 1	FC MO 1	SN	SN 1		FC 1	SN 1	FC 1	SN 1	FC 1	SN 1	FC	SN	FC 1		SN 1	SN	FC 1	SN
Purley 4	d		23p50	23p49		00 11				01 22			02 22		03 22		04 22		05 07			05 23			05 39
Purley Oaks	d																								05 42
South Croydon 4	d																								05 45
East Croydon	d	23p50	23p56	23p58	00 04	00 17	00 36	00 36	00 49	01 28		01 50	02 28	02 47	03 28	03 47	04 28	04 47	05 13	05 17		05 29	05 33	05 47	05 48
Norwood Junction 2	d																		05 17				05 37		
New Cross Gate	d				00a19		00a52	00a53				02a14		03a12		04a12			05 34						
London Bridge 4 ⊖	a																			05 34				06 02	
London Blackfriars 3 ⊖	a																	05 13		05 41				06 10	
City Thameslink 3	a																	05 16		05 44				06 14	
Farringdon 3 ⊖	a																	05 20		05 47				06 18	
St Pancras International 15 ⊖	a																	05 23		05 51				06 21	
Clapham Junction 10	a	00 02	00 11	00 11		00 29			01 01	01 40			02 40		03 40		04 47					05 48	05 57		06 09
London Victoria 15 ⊖	a	00 08	00 21	00 18		00 37			01 09	01 49			02 49		03 49		04 54					05 58	06 06		06 18

		SN	FC 1	SN 1	SN 1	SN		SN ◇1	SN	SN 1	SN 1	SN	SN 1	FC 1	SN	SN 1		SN 1	FC 1	SN	SN 1	SN	SN 1	SN 1	SN 1
Purley 4	d			06 00		06 04						06 22	06 26		06 27							06 47		06 54	06 59
Purley Oaks	d					06 07						06 25			06 30							06 50			
South Croydon 4	d					06 10						06 28			06 33					06 42	06 51	06 53			
East Croydon	d	05 51	06 02	06 07	06 11	06 13		06 15	06 17	06 23	06 27	06 31	06 31	06 32	06 36	06 39		06 42	06 44	06 45	06 54	06 57	06 57	07 00	07 05
Norwood Junction 2	d	05 55				06 18						06 37			06 40										
New Cross Gate	d	06a24				06 35				06a39		06a49			06a52	06a55					07a11		07a13	07a16	
London Bridge 4 ⊖	a		06 15											06 46					06 58						
London Blackfriars 3 ⊖	a		06 23											06 52					07 04						
City Thameslink 3	a		06 26											06 54					07 08						
Farringdon 3 ⊖	a		06 30											06 58					07 12						
St Pancras International 15 ⊖	a		06 33											07 01					07 15						
Clapham Junction 10	a			06 18	06 21			06 25	06 37		06 38		06 41					06 51		07 05		07 06			07 16
London Victoria 15 ⊖	a			06 25	06 28			06 32	06 45		06 45		06 48					07 00		07 16		07 15			07 23

		FC 1		SN	SN ◇1	SN 1	SN	FC 1	SN	SN 1	SN 1	SN ◇1 🚲		SN 1	SN 1	SN ◇1 🚲	SN	SN 1	SN 1	SN 1	SN	SN		FC 1	SN
Purley 4	d			07 01					07 17						07 29		07 31	07 37			07 39				07 47
Purley Oaks	d			07 04					07 20								07 34				07 42				07 50
South Croydon 4	d			07 07					07 23		07 25						07 37				07 45				07 53
East Croydon	d	07 09		07 10	07 15	07 15	07 18	07 24	07 26	07 27	07 28	07 31		07 32	07 35	07 39	07 40	07 42	07 45	07 46	07 48	07 50		07 54	07 56
Norwood Junction 2	d			07 14													07 44								
New Cross Gate	d			07a28						07a43	07a47			07a49	07a49		07a58			08a01					
London Bridge 4 ⊖	a	07 23																							
London Blackfriars 3 ⊖	a	07 30						07 51																08 20	
City Thameslink 3	a	07 32						07 56																08 23	
Farringdon 3 ⊖	a	07 36						08 00																08 27	
St Pancras International 15 ⊖	a	07 39						08 03																08 31	
Clapham Junction 10	a				07 24	07 27	07 38		07 36			07 40				07 48		07 51	07 55		08 08	08 13			08 06
London Victoria 15 ⊖	a				07 33	07 36	07 48		07 46			07 49				07 57		08 00	08 04		08 19				08 15

		SN 1	SN 1	SN ◇1 🚲	SN 1	SN 1	SN 1	SN 1		SN ◇1	SN	SN 1	SN ◇1 🚲	SN 1	SN	SN 1	FC 1	SN 1		SN	SN 1	SN 1	SN ◇1	SN 1	SN 1
Purley 4	d				07 55						08 01					08 15				08 17					
Purley Oaks	d										08 04									08 20					
South Croydon 4	d		07 54								08 07									08 23		08 26			
East Croydon	d	07 57	07 59	08 01	08 02	08 03	08 05	08 07		08 08	08 10	08 11	08 14	08 15	08 18	08 21	08 21	08 25		08 26	08 27	08 29	08 30	08 32	08 33
Norwood Junction 2	d										08 14														
New Cross Gate	d	08a13	08a16		08a17	08a19	08a23				08a28					08a37		08a41			08a45	08a47		08a54	08a52
London Bridge 4 ⊖	a																								
London Blackfriars 3 ⊖	a																08 53								
City Thameslink 3	a																08 56								
Farringdon 3 ⊖	a																09 00								
St Pancras International 15 ⊖	a																09 03								
Clapham Junction 10	a			08 10				08 36		08 17		08 20	08 23	08 26	08 38					08 36			08 39		
London Victoria 15 ⊖	a			08 19						08 26		08 29	08 32	08 35	08 48					08 45			08 48		

		SN 1	SN	FC 1		SN	SN ◇1 🚲	SN 1	SN	SN ◇1 🚲	SN 1	SN	FC 1	SN 1		SN ◇1	SN 1	SN 1	SN	SN 1	FC 1	SN 1	SN ◇1 🚲	SN 1	
Purley 4	d	08 31				08 33						08 45					08 52		08 56			09 05			
Purley Oaks	d					08 36						08 48							08 59						
South Croydon 4	d		08 35			08 39		08 42				08 51		08 52					09 02						
East Croydon	d	08 37	08 39	08 39		08 42	08 43	08 45	08 48	08 50	08 51	08 54	08 54	08 56		08 58	08 59	09 02	09 05	09 08	09 09	09 11	09 14	09 14	
Norwood Junction 2	d					08 47													09 09						
New Cross Gate	d					09a01					09a06			09a13			09a16	09a20	09a23						
London Bridge 4 ⊖	a												09 08												
London Blackfriars 3 ⊖	a			09 09									09 21								09 37				
City Thameslink 3	a			09 12									09 25								09 40				
Farringdon 3 ⊖	a			09 16									09 28								09 44				
St Pancras International 15 ⊖	a			09 19									09 32								09 47				
Clapham Junction 10	a	08 47	09 04				08 52	08 55	09 08	09 00		09 04				09 07				09 34		09 20	09 23	09 26	
London Victoria 15 ⊖	a	08 56					09 01	09 04	09 18	09 09		09 13				09 16						09 27	09 32	09 35	

Table 175

Mondays to Fridays

until 2 September

Purley and East Croydon - London

COMPLETE SERVICE

		SN	SN	SN ◇1 trolley	SN 1 trolley	SN	SN 1	FC 1	SN 1	SN 1		SN ◇1 trolley	SN ◇1	SN 1	SN	FC 1	SN	SN ◇1 trolley	SN 1	SN		SN ◇1 trolley	FC 1	SN 1	SN 1
Purley 4	d	09 08	09 14			09 21				09 32					09 38		09 45		09 49	09 51				10 02	
Purley Oaks	d	09 11				09 24									09 41					09 54					
South Croydon 4	d	09 14				09 27									09 44					09 57					
East Croydon	d	09 17	09 20	09 22	09 27	09 30	09 30	09 32	09 33	09 37		09 39	09 43	09 44	09 47	09 47	09 51	09 53	09 55	10 00		10 00	10 02	10 07	10 08
Norwood Junction 2	d		09 25			09 35				09 42							09 55		09 59	10 05				10 13	
New Cross Gate	d		09 33			09 52			09a51	09a54							10a09		10 07	10 22				10a25	
London Bridge 4 ⊖	a							09 46								10 00							10 15		
London Blackfriars 3 ⊖	a							09 53								10 08							10 23		
City Thameslink 3	a							09 56								10 10							10 26		
Farringdon 3 ⊖	a							10 00								10 14							10 30		
St Pancras International 15 ⊖	a							10 03								10 17							10 33		
Clapham Junction 10	a	09 38		09 32	09 36		09 39					09 48	09 52	09 55	10 07			10 02				10 09			10 17
London Victoria 15 ⊖	a	09 48		09 42	09 45		09 50					09 58	10 00	10 05	10 16			10 10				10 16			10 24

		SN 1	SN ◇1 trolley	SN 1	SN	FC 1		SN	SN 1	SN ◇1 trolley	SN ◇1	SN	FC 1	SN 1	SN 1	SN ◇1 trolley		SN 1	SN	FC 1	SN	SN ◇1 trolley	SN 1	SN	SN ◇1
Purley 4	d				10 08			10 15	10 19			10 21			10 33				10 38		10 45		10 49	10 51	
Purley Oaks	d				10 11							10 24							10 41					10 54	
South Croydon 4	d	10 07			10 14							10 27							10 44					10 57	
East Croydon	d	10 10	10 12	10 14	10 17	10 17		10 21	10 25	10 25	10 28	10 30	10 32	10 33	10 38	10 42		10 44	10 47	10 47	10 51	10 53	10 55	11 00	11 00
Norwood Junction 2	d							10 25	10 29			10 35			10 43						10 55		10 59	11 05	
New Cross Gate	d							10a39	10 37			10 52		10a49	10a55						11a09		11 07	11 22	
London Bridge 4 ⊖	a					10 30							10 45							11 00					
London Blackfriars 3 ⊖	a					10 37							10 52							11 07					
City Thameslink 3	a					10 40							10 56							11 10					
Farringdon 3 ⊖	a					10 44							11 00							11 14					
St Pancras International 15 ⊖	a					10 47							11 03							11 17					
Clapham Junction 10	a	10 35	10 21	10 25	10 37					10 34	10 37					10 51		10 55	11 07			11 02			11 09
London Victoria 15 ⊖	a		10 28	10 35	10 46					10 41	10 45					10 58		11 05	11 16			11 10			11 16

		FC 1		SN 1	SN 1	SN 1	SN ◇1	SN 1	SN	FC 1	SN	SN ◇1 trolley		SN 1	SN ◇1	SN	FC 1	SN 1	SN 1	SN ◇1	SN 1	SN		FC 1	SN
Purley 4	d			11 01					11 08		11 15			11 19		11 21			11 32			11 38			11 45
Purley Oaks	d								11 11							11 24						11 41			
South Croydon 4	d					11 07			11 14							11 27						11 44			
East Croydon	d	11 02		11 07	11 08	11 11	11 12	11 14	11 17	11 17	11 21	11 23		11 25	11 28	11 30	11 32	11 33	11 37	11 42	11 44	11 47		11 47	11 51
Norwood Junction 2	d			11 13							11 25			11 29		11 35			11 43						11 55
New Cross Gate	d			11a25							11a39			11 37		11 52		11a49	11a55						12a09
London Bridge 4 ⊖	a	11 15								11 30							11 45							12 00	
London Blackfriars 3 ⊖	a	11 22								11 37							11 52							12 07	
City Thameslink 3	a	11 26								11 40							11 56							12 10	
Farringdon 3 ⊖	a	11 30								11 44							12 00							12 14	
St Pancras International 15 ⊖	a	11 33								11 47							12 03							12 17	
Clapham Junction 10	a				11 17	11 33	11 21	11 25	11 37			11 32			11 37					11 51	11 55	12 07			
London Victoria 15 ⊖	a				11 24		11 28	11 32				11 41			11 45					11 58	12 02				

		SN ◇1 trolley	SN 1	SN	SN ◇1	FC 1	SN 1	SN 1		SN 1	SN ◇1	SN 1	SN	FC 1	SN	SN ◇1 trolley	SN 1	SN ◇1		SN	FC 1	SN 1	SN 1	SN ◇1	SN 1
Purley 4	d		11 49	11 51			12 02						12 08		12 15		12 19			12 21			12 32		
Purley Oaks	d			11 54									12 11							12 24					
South Croydon 4	d			11 57						12 07			12 14							12 27					
East Croydon	d	11 53	11 55	12 00	12 00	12 02	12 07	12 08		12 10	12 12	12 14	12 17	12 17	12 21	12 23	12 25	12 28		12 30	12 32	12 33	12 37	12 42	12 44
Norwood Junction 2	d		11 59	12 05			12 13								12 25		12 29			12 35			12 43		
New Cross Gate	d		12 07	12 22			12a25								12a39		12 37			12 52		12a49	12a55		
London Bridge 4 ⊖	a					12 15								12 30							12 45				
London Blackfriars 3 ⊖	a					12 22								12 37							12 52				
City Thameslink 3	a					12 26								12 40							12 56				
Farringdon 3 ⊖	a					12 30								12 44							13 00				
St Pancras International 15 ⊖	a					12 33								12 47							13 03				
Clapham Junction 10	a	12 02			12 09			12 17		12 34	12 21	12 25	12 37			12 32		12 37						12 51	12 55
London Victoria 15 ⊖	a	12 11			12 18			12 24			12 28	12 32				12 40		12 44						12 58	13 02

		SN	FC 1	SN		SN ◇1 trolley	SN 1	SN	SN ◇1	FC 1	SN 1	SN 1	SN 1	SN ◇1		SN 1	SN	FC 1	SN	SN ◇1 trolley	SN 1	SN ◇1	SN	FC 1	
Purley 4	d	12 38		12 45			12 49	12 51			13 02						13 08		13 15		13 19		13 21		
Purley Oaks	d	12 41						12 54									13 11						13 24		
South Croydon 4	d	12 44						12 57					13 07				13 14						13 27		
East Croydon	d	12 47	12 47	12 51		12 53	12 55	13 00	13 00	13 02	13 07	13 08	13 10	13 12		13 14	13 17	13 17	13 21	13 23	13 25	13 28	13 30	13 32	
Norwood Junction 2	d			12 55			12 59	13 05			13 13								13 25		13 29		13 35		
New Cross Gate	d			13a09			13 07	13 22			13a25								13a39		13 37		13 52		
London Bridge 4 ⊖	a		13 00							13 15								13 30						13 45	
London Blackfriars 3 ⊖	a		13 07							13 22								13 37						13 52	
City Thameslink 3	a		13 10							13 26								13 40						13 56	
Farringdon 3 ⊖	a		13 14							13 30								13 44						14 00	
St Pancras International 15 ⊖	a		13 17							13 33								13 47						14 03	
Clapham Junction 10	a	13 07				13 02			13 09			13 17	13 34	13 21		13 25	13 37			13 32		13 37			
London Victoria 15 ⊖	a	13 16				13 10			13 16			13 24		13 28		13 32				13 40		13 44			

Table 175

Mondays to Fridays

until 2 September

Purley and East Croydon - London

COMPLETE SERVICE

		SN	SN	SN	SN	SN	FC	SN	SN	SN		SN	SN	FC	SN	SN	SN	SN	SN	SN		FC	SN	SN	SN
		1	1	◇1	1		1		◇1 ⚲	1			◇1	1	1	1	1	◇1	1			1		◇1 ⚲	1
Purley 4	d		13 32			13 38		13 45		13 49		13 51			14 02					14 08			14 15		14 19
Purley Oaks	d					13 41						13 54								14 11					
South Croydon 4	d					13 44						13 57					14 07			14 14					
East Croydon	d	13 33	13 37	13 42	13 44	13 47	13 47	13 51	13 53	13 55		14 00	14 00	14 02	14 08	14 08	14 10	14 12	14 14	14 17		14 17	14 21	14 23	14 25
Norwood Junction 2	d		13 43					13 55		13 59		14 05			14 13								14 25		14 29
New Cross Gate	d	13a49	13a55					14a09		14 07		14 22			14a25								14a39		14 37
London Bridge 4 ⊖	a						14 00							14 15								14 30			
London Blackfriars 3 ⊖	a						14 07							14 22								14 37			
City Thameslink 3	a						14 10							14 26								14 40			
Farringdon 3 ⊖	a						14 14							14 30								14 44			
St Pancras International 15 ⊖	a						14 17							14 33								14 47			
Clapham Junction 10	a			13 51	13 55	14 07			14 02				14 09			14 17	14 34	14 21	14 25	14 37				14 32	
London Victoria 15 ⊖	a			13 58	14 03				14 10				14 16			14 24		14 28	14 32					14 40	

		SN	SN	FC	SN	SN		SN	SN	SN	FC	SN	SN	SN	SN	SN		FC	SN	SN	SN	SN	SN	SN	FC
		◇1		1	1	1		◇1	1		1		◇1 ⚲	1		◇1		1	1	1	1	◇1	1		1
Purley 4	d		14 21			14 32				14 38		14 45		14 49	14 51				15 02					15 08	
Purley Oaks	d		14 24							14 41					14 54									15 11	
South Croydon 4	d		14 27							14 44					14 57						15 07			15 14	
East Croydon	d	14 28	14 30	14 32	14 33	14 37		14 42	14 44	14 47	14 47	14 51	14 53	14 55	15 00	15 00		15 02	15 07	15 08	15 10	15 12	15 14	15 17	15 17
Norwood Junction 2	d		14 35			14 43						14 55		14 59	15 05				15 13						
New Cross Gate	d		14 52		14a49	14a55						15a09		15 07	15 22				15a25						
London Bridge 4 ⊖	a			14 45							15 00							15 15							15 30
London Blackfriars 3 ⊖	a			14 52							15 07							15 22							15 37
City Thameslink 3	a			14 56							15 10							15 26							15 40
Farringdon 3 ⊖	a			15 00							15 14							15 30							15 44
St Pancras International 15 ⊖	a			15 03							15 17							15 33							15 47
Clapham Junction 10	a	14 37						14 51	14 55	15 07			15 02			15 09				15 17	15 35	15 21	15 25	15 37	
London Victoria 15 ⊖	a	14 44						14 58	15 02	15 16			15 10			15 20				15 24		15 28	15 35	15 46	

		SN		SN	SN	SN	SN	FC	SN	SN	SN	SN		SN	FC	SN	SN	SN	SN	SN	FC	SN		SN	SN
				◇1 ⚲	1	◇1		1	1	1	◇1 ⚲	1			1		◇1 ⚲	1		◇1 ⚲	1	1		1	1
Purley 4	d	15 15			15 19		15 21			15 32				15 38		15 45		15 49	15 51			16 02			
Purley Oaks	d						15 24							15 41					15 54						
South Croydon 4	d						15 27							15 44					15 57						16 07
East Croydon	d	15 21		15 23	15 25	15 28	15 30	15 32	15 33	15 37	15 42	15 44		15 47	15 47	15 51	15 53	15 55	16 00	16 00	16 02	16 07		16 08	16 10
Norwood Junction 2	d	15 25			15 29		15 35			15 43						15 55		15 59	16 05			16 13			
New Cross Gate	d	15a39			15 37		15 52		15a49	15a55						16a09		16 07	16 22			16a25			
London Bridge 4 ⊖	a							15 45							16 00						16 15				
London Blackfriars 3 ⊖	a							15 52							16 07						16 25				
City Thameslink 3	a							15 56							16 10						16 28				
Farringdon 3 ⊖	a							16 00							16 13						16 31				
St Pancras International 15 ⊖	a							16 03							16 17						16 35				
Clapham Junction 10	a			15 32		15 37					15 51	15 55		16 07			16 02			16 09				16 17	16 34
London Victoria 15 ⊖	a			15 40		15 46					15 58	16 05		16 16			16 10			16 16				16 24	

		SN	SN	SN	FC	SN	SN	SN		FC	SN	SN	SN	SN	SN	SN	SN	SN		FC	SN	SN	SN	FC	SN
		◇1 ⚲	1		1		1	◇1 ⚲		1		◇1 ⚲	1	◇1	1	◇1 ⚲	1			1		1 ⚲	1	1	
Purley 4	d			16 08		16 15	16 18				16 21				16 34			16 38			16 45		16 49		16 51
Purley Oaks	d			16 11							16 24							16 41							16 54
South Croydon 4	d			16 14							16 27							16 44							16 57
East Croydon	d	16 12	16 14	16 17	16 17	16 21	16 24	16 25		16 28	16 30	16 30	16 33	16 38	16 40	16 42	16 44	16 47		16 47	16 51	16 54	16 55	16 58	17 00
Norwood Junction 2	d					16 25	16 28				16 35				16 45						16 55		16 59		17 05
New Cross Gate	d					16a39	16 36				16 52		16a47		17a00						17a08		17 06		17 22
London Bridge 4 ⊖	a																								
London Blackfriars 3 ⊖	a				16 47					16 55										17 19				17 25	
City Thameslink 3	a				16 54					16 58										17 24				17 28	
Farringdon 3 ⊖	a				16 57					17 01										17 27				17 31	
St Pancras International 15 ⊖	a				17 01					17 05										17 31				17 35	
Clapham Junction 10	a	16 21	16 25	16 37				16 34				16 39		16 47		16 51	16 55	17 07				17 03			
London Victoria 15 ⊖	a	16 28	16 35	16 46				16 42				16 46		16 54		16 58	17 05	17 16				17 10			

		SN	SN	FC		SN	SN	SN	SN	SN	FC	SN	SN	SN		SN	SN	SN	SN	SN	SN	SN	FC	SN	
		◇1	1	1		1	◇1 ⚲	1			1	1	1 ⚲			◇1 ⚲	1	1	◇1 ⚲	1	1		1		
Purley 4	d		17 02						17 08	17 15		17 19		17 21								17 38		17 45	
Purley Oaks	d								17 11					17 24								17 41			
South Croydon 4	d					17 07			17 14					17 27								17 44			
East Croydon	d	17 01	17 07	17 09		17 10	17 13	17 14	17 17	17 21	17 23	17 25	17 26	17 30		17 30	17 36	17 38	17 41	17 41	17 44	17 47	17 47	17 51	
Norwood Junction 2	d		17 12							17 25		17 31		17 35						17 45				17 55	
New Cross Gate	d		17a26							17a37		17 38		17 52			17a52			17a58				18a09	
London Bridge 4 ⊖	a			17 27																			18 13		
London Blackfriars 3 ⊖	a			17 35							17 49												18 21		
City Thameslink 3	a			17 38							17 54												18 24		
Farringdon 3 ⊖	a			17 41							17 57												18 27		
St Pancras International 15 ⊖	a			17 45							18 01												18 31		
Clapham Junction 10	a	17 10				17 34	17 22	17 25	17 37				17 35			17 39		17 47	17 50		17 55	18 07			
London Victoria 15 ⊖	a	17 17					17 29	17 35	17 48				17 42			17 46		17 54	17 58		18 05	18 16			

Table 175

Mondays to Fridays

until 2 September

Purley and East Croydon - London

COMPLETE SERVICE

		SN	SN	SN	FC	SN	SN	SN	SN	SN		SN	SN	FC	SN	SN	SN	SN	SN	FC		SN	SN	SN	SN
		1	1	1	1	◇1		1	1	◇1		1		1		1	1		◇1	1		1	1	◇1	1
				🚲		🚲				🚲						🚲			🚲					🚲	
Purley [4]	d		17 49				17 59						18 08		18 15		18 19	18 21							
Purley Oaks	d						18 02						18 11					18 24							
South Croydon [4]	d						18 05						18 14					18 27							
East Croydon 🚊	d	17 53	17 55	17 57	17 58	18 02	18 08	18 08	18 10	18 12		18 14	18 17	18 17	18 21	18 25	18 26	18 30	18 30	18 33		18 36	18 40	18 43	18 44
Norwood Junction [2]	d		17 59				18 12								18 29			18 35							
New Cross Gate	d		18 07				18a26								18a41			18 52				18a50			
London Bridge [4] ⊖	a																			18 46					
London Blackfriars [3] ⊖	a				18 25									18 51						18 55					
City Thameslink [3]	a				18 28									18 54						18 58					
Farringdon [3] ⊖	a				18 31									18 57						19 01					
St Pancras International [15] ⊖	a				18 35									19 01						19 05					
Clapham Junction [10]	a	18 02		18 06		18 13		18 18	18 34	18 21		18 25	18 39			18 34	18 37		18 40				18 49	18 52	18 55
London Victoria [15] ⊖	a	18 09		18 14		18 20		18 26		18 29		18 35	18 46			18 41	18 44		18 47				18 56	18 59	19 05

		SN	FC	SN	SN	SN		SN	SN	SN	FC	SN	SN	SN	SN	SN		FC	SN	SN	SN	SN	FC	SN	SN
			1	1	1	1		1		◇1	1	1	1	◇1	1			1	◇1	1	◇1		1	1	1
														🚲											
Purley [4]	d	18 37			18 49				18 51							19 08				19 19		19 21			
Purley Oaks	d	18 40							18 54							19 11						19 24			
South Croydon [4]	d	18 44							18 57							19 14						19 27			
East Croydon 🚊	d	18 47	18 47	18 53	18 55	18 57		18 57	19 00	19 00	19 02	19 09	19 10	19 12	19 14	19 17		19 17	19 24	19 25	19 29	19 30	19 32	19 33	19 40
Norwood Junction [2]	d					19 02			19 05			19 13										19 35			
New Cross Gate	d					19a15			19 22			19a25										19 52		19a49	
London Bridge [4] ⊖	a		19 00								19 15							19 30					19 45		
London Blackfriars [3] ⊖	a		19 09								19 22							19 37					19 52		
City Thameslink [3]	a		19 12								19 26							19 40					19 56		
Farringdon [3] ⊖	a		19 15								19 30							19 44					20 00		
St Pancras International [15] ⊖	a		19 19								19 33							19 47					20 03		
Clapham Junction [10]	a	19 08		19 02	19 05			19 08		19 11			19 34	19 21	19 25	19 37			19 33	19 37	19 40				19 49
London Victoria [15] ⊖	a	19 15		19 09	19 13			19 15		19 18				19 29	19 32	19 48			19 41	19 44	19 47				19 56

		SN		SN	SN	FC	SN	SN	SN	SN	FC	SN		SN	SN	SN	FC	SN	SN	SN	SN	FC		SN	SN
		◇1		1		1	◇1	1		1	1	1		◇1	1		1	◇1	1	◇1		1		1	◇1
Purley [4]	d				19 38			19 53	19 51							20 08			20 18		20 22				
Purley Oaks	d				19 41				19 54							20 11					20 25				
South Croydon [4]	d				19 44				19 57							20 14					20 28				
East Croydon 🚊	d	19 43		19 44	19 47	19 47	19 53	19 59	20 00	20 01	20 02	20 07		20 11	20 14	20 17	20 17	20 23	20 26	20 30	20 31	20 32		20 34	20 41
Norwood Junction [2]	d								20 05												20 35				
New Cross Gate	d								20 22			20a21									20 52			20a49	
London Bridge [4] ⊖	a					20 00					20 15						20 30					20 45			
London Blackfriars [3] ⊖	a					20 07					20 22						20 37					20 52			
City Thameslink [3]	a					20 10					20 26						20 40					20 56			
Farringdon [3] ⊖	a					20 14					20 30						20 44					21 00			
St Pancras International [15] ⊖	a					20 17					20 33						20 47					21 03			
Clapham Junction [10]	a	19 52		19 55	20 07		20 02	20 08		20 11				20 20	20 25	20 37		20 32	20 37	20 40					20 50
London Victoria [15] ⊖	a	19 59		20 02			20 10	20 15		20 20				20 28	20 32	20 46		20 40	20 44	20 50					20 58

		SN	SN	FC	SN	SN	SN	SN		SN	FC	SN	SN	SN	FC	SN	SN	SN		SN	FC	SN	SN	SN	SN
		1		1	◇1	1	1			◇1	1	◇1	1		1	◇1	1			◇1	1	1	◇1	1	
Purley [4]	d		20 38				20 49	20 51						21 08			21 19	21 21							21 38
Purley Oaks	d		20 41					20 54						21 11				21 24							21 41
South Croydon [4]	d		20 44					20 57						21 14				21 27							21 44
East Croydon 🚊	d	20 44	20 47	20 47	20 53	20 54	20 57	21 00		21 00	21 02	21 09	21 14	21 17	21 17	21 23	21 26	21 30		21 30	21 32	21 33	21 42	21 44	21 47
Norwood Junction [2]	d							21 05										21 35							
New Cross Gate	d					21a09		21 22										21 52				21a49			
London Bridge [4] ⊖	a			21 00							21 15				21 30						21 45				
London Blackfriars [3] ⊖	a			21 07							21 22				21 37						21 52				
City Thameslink [3]	a			21 10							21 26				21 40						21 56				
Farringdon [3] ⊖	a			21 14							21 30				21 44						22 00				
St Pancras International [15] ⊖	a			21 17							21 33				21 47						22 03				
Clapham Junction [10]	a	20 55	21 07		21 02		21 07			21 11		21 18	21 25	21 37		21 32	21 37			21 40			21 51	21 55	22 07
London Victoria [15] ⊖	a	21 05	21 18		21 10		21 15			21 18		21 26	21 35	21 48		21 40	21 45			21 50			21 58	22 05	22 18

		SN	SN	SN		SN	FC	SN	SN	SN	SN	SN	SN	SN		SN	FC	SN	SN	SN	SN	SN	SN	SN	
		◇1	1			◇1	1	◇1	1		1	◇1	1			◇1	1	1	◇1	1		◇1	1	◇1	
																			🚲						
Purley [4]	d		21 49	21 51						22 08			22 19	22 21							22 38		22 50		
Purley Oaks	d			21 54						22 11				22 24							22 41				
South Croydon [4]	d			21 57						22 14				22 27							22 44				
East Croydon 🚊	d	21 53	21 57	22 00		22 00	22 02	22 09	22 14	22 17	22 17	22 23	22 25	22 30		22 30	22 32	22 34	22 41	22 44	22 47	22 53	22 56	23 00	
Norwood Junction [2]	d			22 05										22 35											
New Cross Gate	d			22 22			22a17				22a33			22 52			22a47	22a49							
London Bridge [4] ⊖	a																								
London Blackfriars [3] ⊖	a																								
City Thameslink [3]	a																								
Farringdon [3] ⊖	a																								
St Pancras International [15] ⊖	a																								
Clapham Junction [10]	a	22 02	22 07			22 10		22 18	22 25	22 37		22 32	22 37			22 40			22 50	22 55	23 07	23 02	23 06	23 10	
London Victoria [15] ⊖	a	22 10	22 14			22 20		22 26	22 35	22 48		22 40	22 44			22 50			22 57	23 05	23 18	23 13	23 15	23 20	

Table 175

Purley and East Croydon - London

COMPLETE SERVICE

Mondays to Fridays

until 2 September

		SN	FC 1	SN 1	SN	SN 1	SN ◇1	FC 1	SN	SN 1
Purley 4	d	22 52			23 08				23 34	23 49
Purley Oaks	d	22 55			23 11				23 37	
South Croydon 4	d	22 58			23 14				23 40	
East Croydon	d	23 01	23 02	23 14	23 17	23 20	23 30	23 32	23 43	23 58
Norwood Junction 2	d	23 06							23a47	
New Cross Gate	d	23 23	23a17					23a47		
London Bridge 4 ⊖	a									
London Blackfriars 3 ⊖	a									
City Thameslink 3	a									
Farringdon 3 ⊖	a									
St Pancras International 15 ⊖	a									
Clapham Junction 10	a			23 25	23 37	23 32	23 42			00 11
London Victoria 15 ⊖	a			23 35	23 46	23 40	23 52			00 18

Mondays to Fridays

from 5 September

		SN MO 1	SN MO 1	SN MX 1	FC 1	SN ◇1	FC MX 1	FC MO 1	SN	SN 1		FC 1	SN 1	FC 1	SN 1	FC 1	SN 1	FC	SN	FC 1		SN 1	SN	FC 1	SN
Purley 4	d		23p50	23p49		00 11				01 22			02 22		03 22		04 22		05 07			05 23			05 39
Purley Oaks	d																								05 42
South Croydon 4	d																								05 45
East Croydon	d	23p50	23p56	23p58	00 04	00 17	00 36	00 36	00 49	01 28		01 50	02 28	02 47	03 28	03 47	04 28	04 47	05 13	05 17		05 29	05 33	05 47	05 48
Norwood Junction 2	d																		05 17				05 37		
New Cross Gate	d				00a19		00a52	00a53				02a14		03a12		04a12			05 34						
London Bridge 4 ⊖	a																			05 34				06 02	
London Blackfriars 3 ⊖	a																	05 13		05 41				06 10	
City Thameslink 3	a																	05 16		05 44				06 14	
Farringdon 3 ⊖	a																	05 20		05 47				06 18	
St Pancras International 15 ⊖	a																	05 23		05 51				06 21	
Clapham Junction 10	a	00 02	00 11	00 11		00 29			01 01	01 40			02 40		03 40		04 47					05 48	05 57		06 09
London Victoria 15 ⊖	a	00 08	00 21	00 18		00 37			01 09	01 49			02 49		03 49		04 54					05 58	06 06		06 18

		SN	FC 1	SN 1	SN 1	SN		SN ◇1	SN	SN 1	SN 1	SN	SN 1	FC 1	SN	SN 1		SN 1	FC 1	SN	SN 1	SN	SN 1	SN 1	SN 1
Purley 4	d			06 00		06 04						06 22	06 26		06 27							06 47		06 54	06 59
Purley Oaks	d					06 07						06 25			06 30							06 50			
South Croydon 4	d					06 10						06 28			06 33					06 42	06 51	06 53			
East Croydon	d	05 51	06 02	06 07	06 11	06 13		06 15	06 17	06 23	06 27	06 31	06 31	06 32	06 36	06 39		06 42	06 44	06 45	06 54	06 57	06 57	07 00	07 05
Norwood Junction 2	d	05 55				06 18						06 37			06 40										
New Cross Gate	d	06a24				06 35				06a39		06a49			06a52	06a55					07a11		07a13	07a16	
London Bridge 4 ⊖	a		06 15											06 46					06 58						
London Blackfriars 3 ⊖	a		06 23											06 52					07 04						
City Thameslink 3	a		06 26											06 54					07 08						
Farringdon 3 ⊖	a		06 30											06 58					07 12						
St Pancras International 15 ⊖	a		06 33											07 01					07 15						
Clapham Junction 10	a			06 18	06 21			06 25	06 37		06 38		06 41					06 51		07 05		07 06			07 16
London Victoria 15 ⊖	a			06 25	06 28			06 32	06 45		06 45		06 48					07 00		07 16		07 15			07 23

		FC 1		SN	SN ◇1	SN 1	SN	FC 1	SN	SN 1	SN 1	SN ◇1 trolley		SN 1	SN 1	SN ◇1 trolley	SN	SN 1	SN 1	SN 1	SN	SN		FC 1	SN
Purley 4	d			07 01					07 17						07 29		07 31	07 37			07 39				07 47
Purley Oaks	d			07 04					07 20								07 34				07 42				07 50
South Croydon 4	d			07 07					07 23		07 25						07 37				07 45				07 53
East Croydon	d	07 09		07 10	07 15	07 15	07 18	07 24	07 26	07 27	07 28	07 31		07 32	07 35	07 39	07 40	07 42	07 45	07 46	07 48	07 50		07 54	07 56
Norwood Junction 2	d			07 14													07 44								
New Cross Gate	d			07a28						07a43	07a47			07a49	07a49		07a58			08a01					
London Bridge 4 ⊖	a	07 23																							
London Blackfriars 3 ⊖	a	07 30						07 51																08 20	
City Thameslink 3	a	07 32						07 56																08 23	
Farringdon 3 ⊖	a	07 36						08 00																08 27	
St Pancras International 15 ⊖	a	07 39						08 03																08 31	
Clapham Junction 10	a				07 24	07 27	07 38		07 36			07 40				07 48		07 51	07 55		08 08	08 13			08 06
London Victoria 15 ⊖	a				07 33	07 36	07 48		07 46			07 49				07 57		08 00	08 04		08 19				08 15

		SN 1	SN 1	SN ◇1 trolley	SN 1	SN 1	SN 1	SN 1		SN ◇1	SN	SN 1	SN ◇1 trolley	SN 1	SN	SN 1	FC 1	SN 1		SN	SN 1	SN 1	SN ◇1	SN 1	SN 1
Purley 4	d				07 55						08 01					08 15				08 17					
Purley Oaks	d										08 04									08 20					
South Croydon 4	d		07 54								08 07									08 23		08 26			
East Croydon	d	07 57	07 59	08 01	08 02	08 03	08 05	08 07		08 08	08 10	08 11	08 14	08 15	08 18	08 21	08 21	08 25		08 26	08 27	08 29	08 30	08 32	08 33
Norwood Junction 2	d										08 14														
New Cross Gate	d	08a13	08a16		08a17	08a19	08a23				08a28					08a37		08a41			08a45	08a47		08a54	08a52
London Bridge 4 ⊖	a																								
London Blackfriars 3 ⊖	a																08 53								
City Thameslink 3	a																08 56								
Farringdon 3 ⊖	a																09 00								
St Pancras International 15 ⊖	a																09 03								
Clapham Junction 10	a			08 10				08 36		08 17		08 20	08 23	08 26	08 38					08 36			08 39		
London Victoria 15 ⊖	a			08 19						08 26		08 29	08 32	08 35	08 48					08 45			08 48		

Table 175

Mondays to Fridays

from 5 September

Purley and East Croydon - London

COMPLETE SERVICE

		SN 1	SN	FC 1	SN	SN ◇1 🚲	SN 1	SN	SN ◇1 🚲	SN 1	SN	FC 1	SN 1	SN ◇1	SN 1	SN 1	SN	SN 1	FC 1	SN 1	SN ◇1 🚲	SN 1
Purley 4	d	08 31			08 33						08 45				08 52		08 56			09 05		
Purley Oaks	d				08 36						08 48						08 59					
South Croydon 4	d		08 35		08 39		08 42				08 51		08 52				09 02					
East Croydon 🚊	d	08 37	08 39	08 39	08 42	08 43	08 45	08 48	08 50	08 51	08 54	08 54	08 56	08 58	08 59	09 02	09 05	09 08	09 09	09 11	09 14	09 14
Norwood Junction 2	d				08 47												09 09					
New Cross Gate	d				09a01					09a06			09a13		09a16	09a20	09a23					
London Bridge 4 ⊖	a											09 08										
London Blackfriars 3 ⊖	a			09 09								09 21							09 37			
City Thameslink 3	a			09 12								09 25							09 40			
Farringdon 3 ⊖	a			09 16								09 28							09 44			
St Pancras International 15 ⊖	a			09 19								09 32							09 47			
Clapham Junction 10	a	08 47	09 04			08 52	08 55	09 08	09 00		09 04			09 07				09 34		09 20	09 23	09 26
London Victoria 15 ⊖	a	08 56				09 01	09 04	09 18	09 09		09 13			09 16						09 27	09 32	09 35

		SN	SN	SN ◇1 🚲	SN 1 🚲	SN	SN 1	FC 1	SN 1	SN 1	SN ◇1 🚲	SN ◇1	SN 1	SN	FC 1	SN	SN ◇1 🚲	SN 1	SN	SN ◇1 🚲	FC 1	SN 1	SN 1
Purley 4	d	09 08	09 14			09 21				09 32				09 38		09 45		09 49	09 51			10 02	
Purley Oaks	d	09 11				09 24								09 41					09 54				
South Croydon 4	d	09 14				09 27								09 44					09 57				
East Croydon 🚊	d	09 17	09 20	09 22	09 27	09 30	09 30	09 32	09 33	09 37	09 39	09 43	09 44	09 47	09 47	09 51	09 53	09 55	10 00	10 00	10 02	10 07	10 08
Norwood Junction 2	d		09 25			09 35				09 42						09 55		09 59	10 05			10 13	
New Cross Gate	d		09 33			09 52			09a51	09a54						10a09		10 07	10 22			10a25	
London Bridge 4 ⊖	a							09 46							10 00						10 15		
London Blackfriars 3 ⊖	a							09 53							10 08						10 23		
City Thameslink 3	a							09 56							10 10						10 26		
Farringdon 3 ⊖	a							10 00							10 14						10 30		
St Pancras International 15 ⊖	a							10 03							10 17						10 33		
Clapham Junction 10	a	09 38		09 32	09 36		09 39				09 48	09 52	09 55	10 07			10 02			10 09			10 17
London Victoria 15 ⊖	a	09 48		09 42	09 45		09 50				09 58	10 00	10 05	10 16			10 10			10 16			10 24

		SN 1	SN ◇1 🚲	SN 1	SN	FC 1	SN	SN 1	SN ◇1 🚲	SN ◇1	SN	FC 1	SN 1	SN 1	SN ◇1 🚲	SN 1	SN	FC 1	SN	SN ◇1 🚲	SN 1	SN	SN ◇1
Purley 4	d				10 08		10 15	10 19			10 21			10 33			10 38		10 45		10 49	10 51	
Purley Oaks	d				10 11						10 24						10 41					10 54	
South Croydon 4	d	10 07			10 14						10 27						10 44					10 57	
East Croydon 🚊	d	10 10	10 12	10 14	10 17	10 17	10 21	10 25	10 25	10 28	10 30	10 32	10 33	10 38	10 42	10 44	10 47	10 47	10 51	10 53	10 55	11 00	11 00
Norwood Junction 2	d						10 25	10 29			10 35			10 43					10 55		10 59	11 05	
New Cross Gate	d						10a39	10 37			10 52		10a49	10a55					11a09		11 07	11 22	
London Bridge 4 ⊖	a					10 30						10 45						11 00					
London Blackfriars 3 ⊖	a					10 37						10 52						11 07					
City Thameslink 3	a					10 40						10 56						11 10					
Farringdon 3 ⊖	a					10 44						11 00						11 14					
St Pancras International 15 ⊖	a					10 47						11 03						11 17					
Clapham Junction 10	a	10 35	10 21	10 25	10 37				10 34	10 37					10 51	10 55	11 07			11 02			11 09
London Victoria 15 ⊖	a		10 28	10 35	10 46				10 41	10 45					10 58	11 05	11 16			11 10			11 16

		FC 1	SN 1	SN 1	SN 1	SN ◇1	SN 1	SN	FC 1	SN	SN ◇1 🚲	SN 1	SN ◇1	SN	FC 1	SN 1	SN 1	SN ◇1	SN 1	SN	FC 1	SN
Purley 4	d		11 01					11 08		11 15		11 19		11 21			11 32			11 38		11 45
Purley Oaks	d							11 11						11 24						11 41		
South Croydon 4	d				11 07			11 14						11 27						11 44		
East Croydon 🚊	d	11 02	11 07	11 08	11 11	11 12	11 14	11 17	11 17	11 21	11 23	11 25	11 28	11 30	11 32	11 33	11 37	11 42	11 44	11 47	11 47	11 51
Norwood Junction 2	d		11 13							11 25		11 29		11 35			11 43					11 55
New Cross Gate	d		11a25							11a39		11 37		11 52		11a49	11a55					12a09
London Bridge 4 ⊖	a	11 15							11 30						11 45						12 00	
London Blackfriars 3 ⊖	a	11 22							11 37						11 52						12 07	
City Thameslink 3	a	11 26							11 40						11 56						12 10	
Farringdon 3 ⊖	a	11 30							11 44						12 00						12 14	
St Pancras International 15 ⊖	a	11 33							11 47						12 03						12 17	
Clapham Junction 10	a			11 17	11 33	11 21	11 25	11 37			11 32		11 37					11 51	11 55	12 07		
London Victoria 15 ⊖	a			11 24		11 28	11 32				11 41		11 45					11 58	12 02			

		SN ◇1 🚲	SN 1	SN	SN ◇1	FC 1	SN 1	SN 1	SN 1	SN ◇1	SN 1	SN	FC 1	SN	SN ◇1 🚲	SN 1	SN ◇1	SN	FC 1	SN 1	SN 1	SN ◇1	SN 1
Purley 4	d		11 49	11 51			12 02					12 08		12 15		12 19		12 21			12 32		
Purley Oaks	d			11 54								12 11						12 24					
South Croydon 4	d			11 57					12 07			12 14						12 27					
East Croydon 🚊	d	11 53	11 55	12 00	12 00	12 02	12 07	12 08	12 10	12 12	12 14	12 17	12 17	12 21	12 23	12 25	12 28	12 30	12 32	12 33	12 37	12 42	12 44
Norwood Junction 2	d		11 59	12 05			12 13							12 25		12 29		12 35			12 43		
New Cross Gate	d		12 07	12 22			12a25							12a39		12 37		12 52		12a49	12a55		
London Bridge 4 ⊖	a					12 15							12 30						12 45				
London Blackfriars 3 ⊖	a					12 22							12 37						12 52				
City Thameslink 3	a					12 26							12 40						12 56				
Farringdon 3 ⊖	a					12 30							12 44						13 00				
St Pancras International 15 ⊖	a					12 33							12 47						13 03				
Clapham Junction 10	a	12 02			12 09			12 17	12 34	12 21	12 25	12 37			12 32		12 37					12 51	12 55
London Victoria 15 ⊖	a	12 11			12 18			12 24		12 28	12 32				12 40		12 44					12 58	13 02

Table 175

Mondays to Fridays

from 5 September

Purley and East Croydon - London

COMPLETE SERVICE

		SN	FC 1	SN		SN ◇1 (trolley)	SN 1	SN	SN ◇1	FC 1	SN 1	SN 1	SN 1	SN ◇1		SN 1	SN	FC 1	SN	SN ◇1 (trolley)	SN 1	SN ◇1	SN	FC 1	
Purley 4	d	12 38		12 45			12 49	12 51			13 02						13 08		13 15		13 19		13 21		
Purley Oaks	d	12 41						12 54									13 11						13 24		
South Croydon 4	d	12 44						12 57					13 07				13 14						13 27		
East Croydon	d	12 47	12 47	12 51		12 53	12 55	13 00	13 00	13 02	13 07	13 08	13 10	13 12		13 14	13 17	13 17	13 21	13 23	13 25	13 28	13 30	13 32	
Norwood Junction 2	d			12 55			12 59	13 05			13 13								13 25		13 29		13 35		
New Cross Gate	d			13a09			13 07	13 22			13a25								13a39		13 37		13 52		
London Bridge 4 ⊖	a		13 00							13 15								13 30						13 45	
London Blackfriars 3 ⊖	a		13 07							13 22								13 37						13 52	
City Thameslink 3	a		13 10							13 26								13 40						13 56	
Farringdon 3 ⊖	a		13 14							13 30								13 44						14 00	
St Pancras International 15 ⊖	a		13 17							13 33								13 47						14 03	
Clapham Junction 10	a	13 07				13 02			13 09			13 17	13 34	13 21		13 25	13 37			13 32		13 37			
London Victoria 15 ⊖	a	13 16				13 10			13 16			13 24		13 28		13 32				13 40		13 44			

		SN 1	SN 1	SN ◇1	SN 1	SN	FC 1	SN	SN ◇1 (trolley)	SN 1		SN	SN ◇1	FC 1	SN 1	SN 1	SN 1	SN ◇1	SN 1	SN		FC 1	SN	SN ◇1 (trolley)	SN 1
Purley 4	d		13 32			13 38		13 45		13 49		13 51			14 02					14 08			14 15		14 19
Purley Oaks	d					13 41						13 54								14 11					
South Croydon 4	d					13 44						13 57					14 07			14 14					
East Croydon	d	13 33	13 37	13 42	13 44	13 47	13 47	13 51	13 53	13 55		14 00	14 00	14 02	14 08	14 08	14 10	14 12	14 14	14 17		14 17	14 21	14 23	14 25
Norwood Junction 2	d		13 43					13 55		13 59		14 05			14 13								14 25		14 29
New Cross Gate	d	13a49	13a55					14a09		14 07		14 22			14a25								14a39		14 37
London Bridge 4 ⊖	a						14 00							14 15								14 30			
London Blackfriars 3 ⊖	a						14 07							14 22								14 37			
City Thameslink 3	a						14 10							14 26								14 40			
Farringdon 3 ⊖	a						14 14							14 30								14 44			
St Pancras International 15 ⊖	a						14 17							14 33								14 47			
Clapham Junction 10	a			13 51	13 55	14 07			14 02				14 09			14 17	14 34	14 21	14 25	14 37				14 32	
London Victoria 15 ⊖	a			13 58	14 03				14 10				14 16			14 24		14 28	14 32					14 40	

		SN ◇1	SN	FC 1	SN 1	SN 1		SN ◇1	SN 1	SN	FC 1	SN	SN ◇1 (trolley)	SN 1	SN	SN ◇1		FC 1	SN 1	SN 1	SN 1	SN ◇1	SN 1	SN	FC 1
Purley 4	d		14 21			14 32				14 38		14 45		14 49	14 51				15 02					15 08	
Purley Oaks	d		14 24							14 41					14 54									15 11	
South Croydon 4	d		14 27							14 44					14 57						15 07			15 14	
East Croydon	d	14 28	14 30	14 32	14 33	14 37		14 42	14 44	14 47	14 47	14 51	14 53	14 55	15 00	15 00		15 02	15 07	15 08	15 10	15 12	15 14	15 17	15 17
Norwood Junction 2	d		14 35			14 43						14 55		14 59	15 05				15 13						
New Cross Gate	d		14 52		14a49	14a55						15a09		15 07	15 22				15a25						
London Bridge 4 ⊖	a			14 45							15 00							15 15							15 30
London Blackfriars 3 ⊖	a			14 52							15 07							15 22							15 37
City Thameslink 3	a			14 56							15 10							15 26							15 40
Farringdon 3 ⊖	a			15 00							15 14							15 30							15 44
St Pancras International 15 ⊖	a			15 03							15 17							15 33							15 47
Clapham Junction 10	a	14 37						14 51	14 55	15 07			15 02			15 09				15 17	15 35	15 21	15 25	15 37	
London Victoria 15 ⊖	a	14 44						14 58	15 02	15 16			15 10			15 20				15 24		15 28	15 35	15 46	

		SN		SN ◇1 (trolley)	SN 1	SN ◇1	SN	FC 1	SN 1	SN 1	SN ◇1 (trolley)	SN 1		SN	FC 1	SN	SN ◇1 (trolley)	SN 1	SN	SN ◇1 (trolley)	FC 1	SN 1		SN 1	SN 1
Purley 4	d	15 15			15 19		15 21			15 32				15 38		15 45		15 49	15 51			16 02			
Purley Oaks	d						15 24							15 41					15 54						
South Croydon 4	d						15 27							15 44					15 57						16 07
East Croydon	d	15 21		15 23	15 25	15 28	15 30	15 32	15 33	15 37	15 42	15 44		15 47	15 47	15 51	15 53	15 55	16 00	16 00	16 02	16 07		16 08	16 10
Norwood Junction 2	d	15 25			15 29		15 35			15 43						15 55		15 59	16 05			16 13			
New Cross Gate	d	15a39			15 37		15 52		15a49	15a55						16a09		16 07	16 22			16a25			
London Bridge 4 ⊖	a							15 45							16 00						16 15				
London Blackfriars 3 ⊖	a							15 52							16 07						16 25				
City Thameslink 3	a							15 56							16 10						16 28				
Farringdon 3 ⊖	a							16 00							16 13						16 31				
St Pancras International 15 ⊖	a							16 03							16 17						16 35				
Clapham Junction 10	a			15 32		15 37					15 51	15 55		16 07			16 02			16 09				16 17	16 34
London Victoria 15 ⊖	a			15 40		15 46					15 58	16 05		16 16			16 10			16 16				16 24	

		SN ◇1 (trolley)	SN 1	SN	FC 1	SN	SN 1	SN ◇1 (trolley)		FC 1	SN	SN ◇1 (trolley)	SN 1	SN ◇1	SN 1	SN ◇1 (trolley)	SN 1	SN		FC 1	SN	SN 1 (trolley)	SN 1	FC 1	SN
Purley 4	d			16 08		16 15	16 18				16 21				16 34			16 38			16 45		16 49		16 51
Purley Oaks	d			16 11							16 24							16 41							16 54
South Croydon 4	d			16 14							16 27							16 44							16 57
East Croydon	d	16 12	16 14	16 17	16 17	16 21	16 24	16 25		16 28	16 30	16 30	16 33	16 38	16 40	16 42	16 44	16 47		16 47	16 51	16 54	16 55	16 58	17 00
Norwood Junction 2	d					16 25	16 28				16 35				16 45						16 55		16 59		17 05
New Cross Gate	d					16a39	16 36				16 52		16a47		17a00						17a08		17 06		17 22
London Bridge 4 ⊖	a																								
London Blackfriars 3 ⊖	a				16 47					16 55										17 19				17 25	
City Thameslink 3	a				16 54					16 58										17 24				17 28	
Farringdon 3 ⊖	a				16 57					17 01										17 27				17 31	
St Pancras International 15 ⊖	a				17 01					17 05										17 31				17 35	
Clapham Junction 10	a	16 21	16 25	16 37				16 34				16 39		16 47		16 51	16 55	17 07				17 03			
London Victoria 15 ⊖	a	16 28	16 35	16 46				16 42				16 46		16 54		16 58	17 05	17 16				17 10			

Table 175

Mondays to Fridays

from 5 September

Purley and East Croydon - London

COMPLETE SERVICE

		SN ◇1	SN 1	FC 1		SN 1	SN ◇1 🛒	SN 1	SN	SN	FC 1	SN 1	SN 1 🛒	SN		SN ◇1 🛒	SN 1	SN 1	SN ◇1 🛒	SN 1	SN 1	SN	FC 1	SN	
Purley 4	d		17 02						17 08	17 15		17 19		17 21								17 38		17 45	
Purley Oaks	d								17 11					17 24								17 41			
South Croydon 4	d					17 07			17 14					17 27								17 44			
East Croydon 🚊	d	17 01	17 07	17 09		17 10	17 13	17 14	17 17	17 21	17 23	17 25	17 26	17 30		17 30	17 36	17 38	17 41	17 41	17 44	17 47	17 47	17 51	
Norwood Junction 2	d		17 12							17 25		17 31		17 35						17 45				17 55	
New Cross Gate	d		17a26							17a37		17 38		17 52			17a52			17a58				18a09	
London Bridge 4 ⊖	a			17 27																			18 13		
London Blackfriars 3 ⊖	a			17 35							17 49												18 21		
City Thameslink 3	a			17 38							17 54												18 24		
Farringdon 3 ⊖	a			17 41							17 57												18 27		
St Pancras International 15 ⊖	a			17 45							18 01												18 31		
Clapham Junction 10	a	17 10				17 34	17 22	17 25	17 37				17 35			17 39		17 47	17 50		17 55	18 07			
London Victoria 15 ⊖	a	17 17					17 29	17 35	17 48				17 42			17 46		17 54	17 58		18 05	18 16			

		SN 1	SN 1	SN 1 🛒	FC 1	SN ◇1 🛒	SN	SN 1	SN 1	SN ◇1 🛒		SN 1	SN	FC 1	SN	SN 1 🛒	SN 1	SN	SN ◇1 🛒	FC 1		SN 1	SN 1	SN ◇1 🛒	SN 1
Purley 4	d		17 49				17 59						18 08		18 15		18 19	18 21							
Purley Oaks	d						18 02						18 11					18 24							
South Croydon 4	d						18 05						18 14					18 27							
East Croydon 🚊	d	17 53	17 55	17 57	17 58	18 02	18 08	18 08	18 10	18 12		18 14	18 17	18 17	18 21	18 25	18 26	18 30	18 30	18 33		18 36	18 40	18 43	18 44
Norwood Junction 2	d		17 59				18 12								18 29			18 35							
New Cross Gate	d		18 07				18a26								18a41			18 52				18a50			
London Bridge 4 ⊖	a																			18 46					
London Blackfriars 3 ⊖	a				18 25									18 51						18 55					
City Thameslink 3	a				18 28									18 54						18 58					
Farringdon 3 ⊖	a				18 31									18 57						19 01					
St Pancras International 15 ⊖	a				18 35									19 01						19 05					
Clapham Junction 10	a	18 02		18 06		18 13		18 18	18 34	18 21		18 25	18 39			18 34	18 37		18 40				18 49	18 52	18 55
London Victoria 15 ⊖	a	18 09		18 14		18 20		18 26		18 29		18 35	18 46			18 41	18 44		18 47				18 56	18 59	19 05

		SN	FC 1	SN 1	SN 1	SN 1		SN 1	SN	SN ◇1	FC 1	SN 1	SN 1	SN ◇1 🛒	SN 1	SN		FC 1	SN ◇1	SN 1	SN ◇1	SN	FC 1	SN 1	SN 1
Purley 4	d	18 37			18 49				18 51							19 08				19 19		19 21			
Purley Oaks	d	18 40							18 54							19 11						19 24			
South Croydon 4	d	18 44							18 57							19 14						19 27			
East Croydon 🚊	d	18 47	18 47	18 53	18 55	18 57		18 57	19 00	19 00	19 02	19 09	19 10	19 12	19 14	19 17		19 17	19 24	19 25	19 29	19 30	19 32	19 33	19 40
Norwood Junction 2	d					19 02			19 05			19 13										19 35			
New Cross Gate	d					19a15			19 22			19a25										19 52		19a49	
London Bridge 4 ⊖	a		19 00								19 15							19 30					19 45		
London Blackfriars 3 ⊖	a		19 09								19 22							19 37					19 52		
City Thameslink 3	a		19 12								19 26							19 40					19 56		
Farringdon 3 ⊖	a		19 15								19 30							19 44					20 00		
St Pancras International 15 ⊖	a		19 19								19 33							19 47					20 03		
Clapham Junction 10	a	19 08		19 02	19 05			19 08		19 11			19 34	19 21	19 25	19 37			19 33	19 37	19 40				19 49
London Victoria 15 ⊖	a	19 15		19 09	19 13			19 15		19 18				19 29	19 32	19 48			19 41	19 44	19 47				19 56

		SN ◇1		SN 1	SN	FC 1	SN ◇1	SN 1	SN	SN 1	FC 1	SN 1		SN ◇1	SN 1	SN	FC 1	SN ◇1	SN 1	SN ◇1	SN	FC 1		SN 1	SN ◇1
Purley 4	d				19 38			19 53	19 51							20 08			20 18		20 22				
Purley Oaks	d				19 41				19 54							20 11					20 25				
South Croydon 4	d				19 44				19 57							20 14					20 28				
East Croydon 🚊	d	19 43		19 44	19 47	19 47	19 53	19 59	20 00	20 01	20 02	20 07		20 11	20 14	20 17	20 17	20 23	20 26	20 30	20 31	20 32		20 34	20 41
Norwood Junction 2	d								20 05												20 35				
New Cross Gate	d								20 22			20a21									20 52			20a49	
London Bridge 4 ⊖	a					20 00					20 15						20 30					20 45			
London Blackfriars 3 ⊖	a					20 07					20 22						20 37					20 52			
City Thameslink 3	a					20 10					20 26						20 40					20 56			
Farringdon 3 ⊖	a					20 14					20 30						20 44					21 00			
St Pancras International 15 ⊖	a					20 17					20 33						20 47					21 03			
Clapham Junction 10	a	19 52		19 55	20 07		20 02	20 08		20 11				20 20	20 25	20 37		20 32	20 37	20 40					20 50
London Victoria 15 ⊖	a	19 59		20 02			20 10	20 15		20 20				20 28	20 32	20 46		20 40	20 44	20 50					20 58

		SN 1	SN	FC 1	SN ◇1	SN 1	SN 1	SN		SN ◇1	FC 1	SN ◇1	SN 1	SN	FC 1	SN ◇1	SN 1	SN		SN ◇1	FC 1	SN 1	SN ◇1	SN 1	SN
Purley 4	d		20 38				20 49	20 51						21 08			21 19	21 21							21 38
Purley Oaks	d		20 41					20 54						21 11				21 24							21 41
South Croydon 4	d		20 44					20 57						21 14				21 27							21 44
East Croydon 🚊	d	20 44	20 47	20 47	20 53	20 54	20 57	21 00		21 00	21 02	21 09	21 14	21 17	21 17	21 23	21 26	21 30		21 30	21 32	21 33	21 42	21 44	21 47
Norwood Junction 2	d							21 05										21 35							
New Cross Gate	d					21a09		21 22										21 52				21a49			
London Bridge 4 ⊖	a			21 00							21 15				21 30						21 45				
London Blackfriars 3 ⊖	a			21 07							21 22				21 37						21 52				
City Thameslink 3	a			21 10							21 26				21 40						21 56				
Farringdon 3 ⊖	a			21 14							21 30				21 44						22 00				
St Pancras International 15 ⊖	a			21 17							21 33				21 47						22 03				
Clapham Junction 10	a	20 55	21 07		21 02		21 07			21 11		21 18	21 25	21 37		21 32	21 37			21 40			21 51	21 55	22 07
London Victoria 15 ⊖	a	21 05	21 18		21 10		21 15			21 18		21 26	21 35	21 48		21 40	21 45			21 50			21 58	22 05	22 18

Table 175

Mondays to Fridays

from 5 September

Purley and East Croydon - London

COMPLETE SERVICE

		SN	SN	SN	SN	FC	SN	SN	SN	SN	SN	SN	SN	SN	FC	SN	SN	SN	SN	SN	SN	SN
		◇1	1		◇1	1	◇1	1		1	◇1	1		◇1	1	1	◇1 ⚲	1		◇1	1	◇1
Purley 4	d		21 49	21 51					22 08			22 19	22 21						22 38		22 50	
Purley Oaks	d			21 54					22 11				22 24						22 41			
South Croydon 4	d			21 57					22 14				22 27						22 44			
East Croydon	d	21 53	21 57	22 00	22 00	22 02	22 09	22 14	22 17	22 17	22 23	22 25	22 30	22 30	22 32	22 34	22 41	22 44	22 47	22 53	22 56	23 00
Norwood Junction 2	d			22 05									22 35									
New Cross Gate	d			22 22		22a17				22a33			22 52		22a47	22a49						
London Bridge 4 ⊖	a																					
London Blackfriars 3 ⊖	a																					
City Thameslink 3	a																					
Farringdon 3 ⊖	a																					
St Pancras International 15 ⊖	a																					
Clapham Junction 10	a	22 02	22 07		22 10		22 18	22 25	22 37		22 32	22 37		22 40			22 50	22 55	23 07	23 02	23 06	23 10
London Victoria 15 ⊖	a	22 10	22 14		22 20		22 26	22 35	22 48		22 40	22 44		22 50			22 57	23 05	23 18	23 13	23 15	23 20

		SN	FC	SN	SN	SN	SN	FC	SN	SN
			1	1		1	◇1	1		1
Purley 4	d	22 52			23 08				23 34	23 49
Purley Oaks	d	22 55			23 11				23 37	
South Croydon 4	d	22 58			23 14				23 40	
East Croydon	d	23 01	23 02	23 14	23 17	23 20	23 30	23 32	23 43	23 58
Norwood Junction 2	d	23 06							23a47	
New Cross Gate	d	23 23	23a17					23a47		
London Bridge 4 ⊖	a									
London Blackfriars 3 ⊖	a									
City Thameslink 3	a									
Farringdon 3 ⊖	a									
St Pancras International 15 ⊖	a									
Clapham Junction 10	a			23 25	23 37	23 32	23 42			00 11
London Victoria 15 ⊖	a			23 35	23 46	23 40	23 52			00 18

Saturdays

until 3 September

		SN	FC	SN	FC	SN	SN	FC	SN	FC	SN	FC	SN	FC	FC	SN	FC	SN	SN	SN	FC	SN	SN
		1	1	◇1	1		1	1	1	1	1	1	1	1	1	1	1	◇1	1	◇1	1	1	
Purley 4	d	23p49		00 11			01 22		02 22		03 22		04 22			05 24		05 58				06 19	06 21
Purley Oaks	d																						06 24
South Croydon 4	d																						06 27
East Croydon	d	23p58	00 04	00 17	00 36	00 49	01 28	01 50	02 28	02 47	03 28	03 47	04 28	04 47	05 17	05 29	05 42	06 07	06 10	06 11	06 17	06 25	06 30
Norwood Junction 2	d																					06 29	06 35
New Cross Gate	d		00a19		00a52			02a14		03a12		04a12		05a12	05a42		05a57				06a32	06 37	06 52
London Bridge 4 ⊖	a																						
London Blackfriars 3 ⊖	a																						
City Thameslink 3	a																						
Farringdon 3 ⊖	a																						
St Pancras International 15 ⊖	a																						
Clapham Junction 10	a	00 11		00 29		01 01	01 40		02 40		03 40		04 41			05 49		06 18	06 34	06 21			
London Victoria 15 ⊖	a	00 18		00 37		01 09	01 49		02 49		03 49		04 50			05 58		06 26		06 30			

		SN	SN	SN	FC	SN	SN	SN	SN	SN	SN	SN	SN	FC	SN	SN	SN	SN	FC	SN	SN	SN	SN
		◇1			1	◇1	1		1	1	◇1	1		1	◇1	1		◇1	1	1	1	◇1	1
Purley 4	d			06 38			06 49	06 51	07 02				07 08			07 19	07 21				07 34		
Purley Oaks	d			06 41				06 54					07 11				07 24						
South Croydon 4	d			06 44				06 57		07 07			07 14				07 27						
East Croydon	d	06 41	06 43	06 47	06 47	06 53	06 55	07 00	07 07	07 10	07 11	07 14	07 17	07 17	07 23	07 25	07 30	07 30	07 32	07 33	07 39	07 42	07 44
Norwood Junction 2	d		06 50				06 59	07 05	07 13							07 29	07 35				07 45		
New Cross Gate	d		07 04		07a02		07 07	07 22	07a25					07a32		07 37	07 52		07a47	07a49	07a57		
London Bridge 4 ⊖	a																						
London Blackfriars 3 ⊖	a																						
City Thameslink 3	a																						
Farringdon 3 ⊖	a																						
St Pancras International 15 ⊖	a																						
Clapham Junction 10	a	06 50		07 07		07 02				07 34	07 20	07 25	07 37		07 32			07 39				07 51	07 55
London Victoria 15 ⊖	a	06 57		07 16		07 09					07 27	07 32	07 46		07 40			07 46				07 58	08 02

		SN	FC	SN	SN	SN	SN	SN	FC	SN	SN	SN	SN	SN	SN	FC	SN	SN	SN	SN	SN	FC
			1		◇1	1		◇1	1	1	1	1	◇1	1		1		◇1 ⚲	1	◇1		1
Purley 4	d	07 38		07 45		07 49	07 51			08 02					08 08		08 15		08 19		08 21	
Purley Oaks	d	07 41					07 54								08 11						08 24	
South Croydon 4	d	07 44					07 57					08 07			08 14						08 27	
East Croydon	d	07 47	07 47	07 51	07 53	07 55	08 00	08 00	08 02	08 07	08 08	08 10	08 12	08 14	08 17	08 17	08 21	08 23	08 25	08 28	08 30	08 32
Norwood Junction 2	d			07 55		07 59	08 05			08 13							08 25		08 29		08 35	
New Cross Gate	d		08a02	08a09		08 07	08 22		08a17	08a25						08a32	08a39		08 37		08 52	08a47
London Bridge 4 ⊖	a																					
London Blackfriars 3 ⊖	a																					
City Thameslink 3	a																					
Farringdon 3 ⊖	a																					
St Pancras International 15 ⊖	a																					
Clapham Junction 10	a	08 07			08 02			08 09			08 17	08 34	08 21	08 25	08 37			08 32		08 37		
London Victoria 15 ⊖	a	08 16			08 10			08 16			08 24		08 28	08 32	08 46			08 40		08 44		

Table 175

Purley and East Croydon - London

COMPLETE SERVICE

Saturdays

until 3 September

		SN 1	SN 1		SN 1	SN ◇1	SN 1		SN	FC 1	SN	SN ◇1 🛒	SN 1	SN	SN ◇1	FC 1	SN 1		SN 1	SN 1	SN ◇1	SN 1	SN	FC 1
Purley 4	d		08 32		11 32				11 38		11 45		11 49	11 51			12 02						12 08	
Purley Oaks	d			and at the same minutes past each hour until					11 41					11 54									12 11	
South Croydon 4	d								11 44					11 57						12 07			12 14	
East Croydon	d	08 33	08 37		11 37	11 42	11 44		11 47	11 47	11 51	11 53	11 55	12 00	12 00	12 02	12 07		12 08	12 10	12 12	12 14	12 17	12 17
Norwood Junction 2	d		08 43		11 43						11 55		11 59	12 05			12 13							
New Cross Gate	d	08a49	08a55		11a55					12a02	12a09		12 07	12 22		12a17	12a25							12a32
London Bridge 4 ⊖	a																							
London Blackfriars 3 ⊖	a																							
City Thameslink 3	a																							
Farringdon 3 ⊖	a																							
St Pancras International 15 ⊖	a																							
Clapham Junction 10	a					11 51	11 55		12 07			12 02			12 09				12 17	12 34	12 21	12 25	12 37	
London Victoria 15 ⊖	a					11 58	12 02		12 16			12 10			12 16				12 24		12 28	12 32	12 46	

		SN	SN ◇1 🛒	SN 1		SN ◇1 🛒	SN	FC 1	SN 1	SN 1	SN ◇1	SN 1	SN	FC 1		SN	SN ◇1 🛒	SN 1	SN	SN ◇1	FC 1	SN 1	SN 1	SN 1	
Purley 4	d	12 15		12 19			12 21			12 32			12 38			12 45		12 49	12 51			13 02			
Purley Oaks	d						12 24						12 41						12 54						
South Croydon 4	d						12 27						12 44						12 57					13 07	
East Croydon	d	12 21	12 23	12 25		12 28	12 30	12 32	12 33	12 38	12 42	12 44	12 47	12 47		12 51	12 53	12 55	13 00	13 00	13 02	13 07	13 08	13 10	
Norwood Junction 2	d	12 25		12 29			12 35			12 43						12 55		12 59	13 05			13 13			
New Cross Gate	d	12a39		12 37			12 52	12a47	12a49	12a55				13a02		13a09		13 07	13 22		13a17	13a25			
London Bridge 4 ⊖	a																								
London Blackfriars 3 ⊖	a																								
City Thameslink 3	a																								
Farringdon 3 ⊖	a																								
St Pancras International 15 ⊖	a																								
Clapham Junction 10	a		12 32			12 37					12 51	12 55	13 07				13 02			13 09			13 17	13 34	
London Victoria 15 ⊖	a		12 40			12 44					12 58	13 02	13 16				13 10			13 16			13 24		

		SN ◇1	SN 1	SN	FC 1	SN	SN ◇1 🛒	SN 1	SN ◇1 🛒	SN		FC 1	SN 1	SN 1	SN ◇1	SN 1	SN	FC 1	SN	SN ◇1 🛒		SN 1	SN	SN ◇1	FC 1
Purley 4	d			13 08		13 15		13 19		13 21				13 32			13 38		13 45			13 49	13 51		
Purley Oaks	d			13 11						13 24							13 41						13 54		
South Croydon 4	d			13 14						13 27							13 44						13 57		
East Croydon	d	13 12	13 14	13 17	13 17	13 21	13 23	13 25	13 28	13 30		13 32	13 33	13 37	13 42	13 44	13 47	13 47	13 51	13 53		13 55	14 00	14 00	14 02
Norwood Junction 2	d					13 25		13 29		13 35				13 43					13 55			13 59	14 05		
New Cross Gate	d				13a32	13a39		13 37		13 52		13a47	13a49	13a55				14a02	14a09			14 07	14 22		14a17
London Bridge 4 ⊖	a																								
London Blackfriars 3 ⊖	a																								
City Thameslink 3	a																								
Farringdon 3 ⊖	a																								
St Pancras International 15 ⊖	a																								
Clapham Junction 10	a	13 21	13 25	13 37			13 32		13 37						13 51	13 55	14 07			14 02				14 09	
London Victoria 15 ⊖	a	13 28	13 32	13 46			13 40		13 44						13 58	14 02	14 16			14 10				14 16	

		SN 1	SN 1	SN 1	SN ◇1	SN 1		SN	FC 1	SN	SN ◇1 🛒	SN 1	SN ◇1 🛒	SN	FC 1	SN 1		SN 1	SN ◇1	SN 1	SN	FC 1	SN	SN ◇1 🛒	SN 1
Purley 4	d	14 02						14 08		14 15		14 19		14 21				14 32			14 38		14 45		14 49
Purley Oaks	d							14 11						14 24							14 41				
South Croydon 4	d			14 07				14 14						14 27							14 44				
East Croydon	d	14 07	14 08	14 10	14 12	14 14		14 17	14 17	14 21	14 23	14 25	14 28	14 30	14 32	14 33		14 37	14 42	14 44	14 47	14 47	14 51	14 53	14 55
Norwood Junction 2	d	14 13								14 25		14 29		14 35				14 43					14 55		14 59
New Cross Gate	d	14a25							14a32	14a39		14 37		14 52	14a47	14a49		14a55				15a02	15a09		15 07
London Bridge 4 ⊖	a																								
London Blackfriars 3 ⊖	a																								
City Thameslink 3	a																								
Farringdon 3 ⊖	a																								
St Pancras International 15 ⊖	a																								
Clapham Junction 10	a		14 17	14 34	14 21	14 25		14 37			14 32		14 37						14 51	14 55	15 07			15 02	
London Victoria 15 ⊖	a		14 24		14 28	14 32		14 46			14 40		14 44						14 58	15 02	15 16			15 10	

		SN		SN ◇1	FC 1	SN 1	SN 1	SN 1	SN ◇1	SN 1	SN	FC 1		SN	SN ◇1 🛒	SN 1	SN ◇1 🛒	SN	FC 1	SN 1	SN 1	SN ◇1		SN 1	SN
Purley 4	d	14 51				15 02					15 08			15 15		15 19		15 21			15 32				15 38
Purley Oaks	d	14 54									15 11							15 24							15 41
South Croydon 4	d	14 57						15 07			15 14							15 27							15 44
East Croydon	d	15 00		15 00	15 02	15 07	15 08	15 10	15 12	15 14	15 17	15 17		15 21	15 23	15 25	15 28	15 30	15 32	15 33	15 37	15 42		15 44	15 47
Norwood Junction 2	d	15 05				15 13								15 25		15 29		15 35			15 43				
New Cross Gate	d	15 22			15a17	15a25						15a32		15a39		15 37		15 52	15a47	15a49	15a55				
London Bridge 4 ⊖	a																								
London Blackfriars 3 ⊖	a																								
City Thameslink 3	a																								
Farringdon 3 ⊖	a																								
St Pancras International 15 ⊖	a																								
Clapham Junction 10	a			15 09			15 17	15 35	15 21	15 25	15 37				15 32		15 37					15 51		15 55	16 07
London Victoria 15 ⊖	a			15 16			15 24		15 28	15 32	15 46				15 40		15 44					15 58		16 02	16 16

Table 175

Saturdays
until 3 September

Purley and East Croydon - London

COMPLETE SERVICE

	FC 1	SN	SN ◇1 🚲	SN 1	SN	SN ◇1	FC 1		SN 1	SN 1	SN 1	SN ◇1	SN 1	SN	FC 1	SN	SN ◇1 🚲		SN 1	SN ◇1 🚲	SN	FC 1	SN 1	SN 1
Purley 4 d		15 45		15 49	15 51				16 02					16 08		16 15			16 19		16 21			16 32
Purley Oaks d					15 54									16 11							16 24			
South Croydon 4 d					15 57						16 07			16 14							16 27			
East Croydon d	15 47	15 51	15 53	15 55	16 00	16 00	16 02		16 07	16 08	16 10	16 12	16 14	16 17	16 17	16 21	16 23		16 25	16 28	16 30	16 32	16 33	16 37
Norwood Junction 2 d		15 55		15 59	16 05				16 13							16 25			16 29		16 35			16 43
New Cross Gate d	16a02	16a09		16 07	16 22		16a17		16a25						16a32	16a39			16 37		16 52	16a47	16a49	16a55
London Bridge 4 ⊖ a																								
London Blackfriars 3 ⊖ a																								
City Thameslink 3 a																								
Farringdon 3 ⊖ a																								
St Pancras International 15 ⊖ a																								
Clapham Junction 10 a			16 02			16 09				16 17	16 34	16 21	16 25	16 37			16 32			16 37				
London Victoria 15 ⊖ a			16 10			16 16				16 24		16 28	16 32	16 46			16 40			16 44				

	SN ◇1	SN 1	SN		FC 1	SN	SN ◇1 🚲	SN 1	SN	SN ◇1	FC 1	SN 1	SN 1		SN 1	SN ◇1	SN 1	SN	FC 1	SN	SN ◇1 🚲	SN 1	SN ◇1 🚲	
Purley 4 d			16 38			16 45		16 49	16 51			17 02						17 08		17 15		17 19		
Purley Oaks d			16 41						16 54									17 11						
South Croydon 4 d			16 44						16 57						17 07			17 14						
East Croydon d	16 42	16 44	16 47		16 47	16 51	16 53	16 55	17 00	17 00	17 02	17 07	17 08		17 10	17 12	17 14	17 17	17 17	17 21	17 23	17 25	17 28	
Norwood Junction 2 d						16 55		16 59	17 05			17 13								17 25		17 29		
New Cross Gate d					17a02	17a09		17 07	17 22		17a17	17a25							17a32	17a39		17 37		
London Bridge 4 ⊖ a																								
London Blackfriars 3 ⊖ a																								
City Thameslink 3 a																								
Farringdon 3 ⊖ a																								
St Pancras International 15 ⊖ a																								
Clapham Junction 10 a	16 51	16 55	17 07				17 02			17 09			17 17		17 34	17 21	17 25	17 38			17 32		17 37	
London Victoria 15 ⊖ a	16 58	17 02	17 16				17 10			17 16			17 24			17 28	17 32	17 47			17 40		17 44	

	SN	FC 1	SN 1	SN 1	SN ◇1	SN 1	SN	FC 1	SN		SN ◇1 🚲	SN 1	SN	SN ◇1	FC 1	SN 1	SN 1	SN 1	SN ◇1		SN 1	SN	FC 1	SN
Purley 4 d	17 21			17 32			17 38		17 45			17 49	17 51			18 02						18 08		18 15
Purley Oaks d	17 24						17 41						17 54									18 11		
South Croydon 4 d	17 27						17 44						17 57					18 07				18 14		
East Croydon d	17 30	17 32	17 33	17 37	17 42	17 44	17 47	17 47	17 51		17 53	17 55	18 00	18 00	18 02	18 07	18 08	18 10	18 12		18 14	18 17	18 17	18 21
Norwood Junction 2 d	17 35			17 43					17 55			17 59	18 05			18 13								18 25
New Cross Gate d	17 52	17a47	17a49	17a55				18a02	18a09			18 07	18 22		18a17	18a25							18a32	18a39
London Bridge 4 ⊖ a																								
London Blackfriars 3 ⊖ a																								
City Thameslink 3 a																								
Farringdon 3 ⊖ a																								
St Pancras International 15 ⊖ a																								
Clapham Junction 10 a					17 51	17 55	18 07				18 02			18 09			18 17	18 34	18 21		18 25	18 37		
London Victoria 15 ⊖ a					17 58	18 02	18 16				18 10			18 16			18 24		18 28		18 32	18 46		

	SN ◇1 🚲	SN 1	SN ◇1 🚲	SN	FC 1		SN 1	SN 1	SN ◇1	SN 1	SN	FC 1	SN	SN ◇1	SN 1		SN	SN ◇1	FC 1	SN 1	SN 1	SN 1	SN ◇1	SN 1
Purley 4 d		18 19		18 21				18 32			18 38		18 45		18 49		18 51			19 02				
Purley Oaks d				18 24							18 41						18 54							
South Croydon 4 d				18 27							18 44						18 57					19 07		
East Croydon d	18 23	18 25	18 28	18 30	18 32		18 33	18 37	18 42	18 44	18 47	18 47	18 51	18 53	18 55		19 00	19 00	19 02	19 07	19 08	19 10	19 12	19 14
Norwood Junction 2 d		18 29		18 35				18 43					18 55		18 59		19 05			19 13				
New Cross Gate d		18 37		18 52	18a47		18a49	18a55				19a02	19a09		19 07		19 22		19a17	19a25				
London Bridge 4 ⊖ a																								
London Blackfriars 3 ⊖ a																								
City Thameslink 3 a																								
Farringdon 3 ⊖ a																								
St Pancras International 15 ⊖ a																								
Clapham Junction 10 a	18 32		18 37						18 51	18 55	19 07			19 02				19 09			19 17	19 34	19 21	19 25
London Victoria 15 ⊖ a	18 40		18 44						18 58	19 02	19 16			19 10				19 16			19 24		19 28	19 32

	SN		FC 1	SN	SN ◇1	SN 1	SN ◇1	SN	FC 1	SN 1	SN ◇1		SN ◇1	SN 1	SN	FC 1	SN	SN ◇1	SN 1	SN	SN 1		FC 1	SN ◇1
Purley 4 d	19 08			19 15		19 19		19 21							19 38		19 45		19 49	19 51				
Purley Oaks d	19 11							19 24							19 41					19 54				
South Croydon 4 d	19 14							19 27							19 44					19 57				
East Croydon d	19 17		19 17	19 21	19 23	19 25	19 29	19 30	19 32	19 33	19 38		19 42	19 44	19 47	19 47	19 51	19 53	19 57	20 00	20 00		20 02	20 12
Norwood Junction 2 d				19 25				19 35									19 55			20 05				
New Cross Gate d			19a32	19a39				19 52	19a47	19a49						20a02	20a09			20 22			20a17	
London Bridge 4 ⊖ a																								
London Blackfriars 3 ⊖ a																								
City Thameslink 3 a																								
Farringdon 3 ⊖ a																								
St Pancras International 15 ⊖ a																								
Clapham Junction 10 a	19 37				19 32	19 37	19 40				19 47		19 51	19 55	20 07			20 02	20 08		20 11			20 21
London Victoria 15 ⊖ a	19 46				19 40	19 44	19 50				19 54		19 58	20 05	20 16			20 10	20 15		20 20			20 28

Table 175

Saturdays
until 3 September

Purley and East Croydon - London

COMPLETE SERVICE

		SN 1	SN	FC 1	SN	SN ◇1	SN 1	SN		SN ◇1	FC 1	SN 1	SN ◇1	SN 1	SN	FC 1	SN	SN ◇1		SN 1	SN	SN ◇1	FC 1	SN ◇1	SN 1
Purley 4	d		20 08		20 15		20 19	20 21							20 38		20 45			20 49	20 51				
Purley Oaks	d		20 11					20 24							20 41						20 54				
South Croydon 4	d		20 14					20 27							20 44						20 57				
East Croydon	d	20 14	20 17	20 17	20 21	20 23	20 26	20 30		20 30	20 32	20 33	20 42	20 44	20 47	20 47	20 51	20 53		20 56	21 00	21 00	21 02	21 09	21 14
Norwood Junction 2	d				20 25			20 35									20 55				21 05				
New Cross Gate	d			20a32	20a39			20 52			20a47	20a49				21a02	21a09				21 22		21a17		
London Bridge 4 ⊖	a																								
London Blackfriars 3 ⊖	a																								
City Thameslink 3	a																								
Farringdon 3 ⊖	a																								
St Pancras International 15 ⊖	a																								
Clapham Junction 10	a	20 25	20 37			20 32	20 37			20 40			20 51	20 55	21 07			21 02		21 07		21 10		21 18	21 25
London Victoria 15 ⊖	a	20 32	20 46			20 40	20 44			20 50			20 58	21 02	21 16			21 10		21 14		21 17		21 26	21 32

		SN	FC 1	SN		SN ◇1	SN 1	SN	SN ◇1	FC 1	SN 1	SN ◇1	SN 1	SN		SN	SN ◇1	SN 1	SN	SN ◇1	FC 1	SN ◇1	SN 1	SN	
Purley 4	d	21 08		21 15			21 19	21 21						21 38		21 45		21 49	21 51					22 08	
Purley Oaks	d	21 11						21 24						21 41					21 54					22 11	
South Croydon 4	d	21 14						21 27						21 44					21 57					22 14	
East Croydon	d	21 17	21 17	21 21		21 23	21 26	21 30	21 30	21 32	21 33	21 42	21 44	21 47		21 51	21 53	21 56	22 00	22 00	22 02	22 09	22 14	22 17	
Norwood Junction 2	d			21 25				21 35								21 55			22 05						
New Cross Gate	d		21a32	21a39				21 52		21a47	21a49					22a09			22 22		22a17				
London Bridge 4 ⊖	a																								
London Blackfriars 3 ⊖	a																								
City Thameslink 3	a																								
Farringdon 3 ⊖	a																								
St Pancras International 15 ⊖	a																								
Clapham Junction 10	a	21 37				21 32	21 37		21 40			21 51	21 55	22 07			22 02	22 07		22 10		22 18	22 25	22 37	
London Victoria 15 ⊖	a	21 46				21 40	21 44		21 50			21 58	22 02	22 16			22 13	22 15		22 20		22 26	22 35	22 46	

		SN	SN ◇1	SN 1	SN	SN ◇1	FC 1	SN 1	SN ◇1 ⚲	SN 1		SN	SN	SN 1	SN ◇1	SN	FC 1	SN 1	SN	SN		SN ◇1	FC 1	SN	SN 1
Purley 4	d	22 15		22 19	22 21							22 38	22 45	22 50		22 52			23 08	23 15				23 34	23 49
Purley Oaks	d				22 24							22 41				22 55			23 11					23 37	
South Croydon 4	d				22 27							22 44				22 58			23 14					23 40	
East Croydon	d	22 21	22 23	22 26	22 30	22 30	22 32	22 33	22 40	22 44		22 47	22 51	22 56	23 00	23 01	23 02	23 14	23 17	23 21		23 30	23 32	23 43	23 56
Norwood Junction 2	d	22 25			22 35								22 55			23 06				23 25				23a47	
New Cross Gate	d	22a39			22 52		22a47	22a49					23a09			23 23	23a17			23a39			23a47		
London Bridge 4 ⊖	a																								
London Blackfriars 3 ⊖	a																								
City Thameslink 3	a																								
Farringdon 3 ⊖	a																								
St Pancras International 15 ⊖	a																								
Clapham Junction 10	a		22 32	22 37		22 40			22 49	22 55		23 07		23 06	23 10			23 25	23 37			23 42			00 11
London Victoria 15 ⊖	a		22 40	22 44		22 50			22 57	23 05		23 16		23 14	23 20			23 35	23 48			23 52			00 18

Saturdays
from 10 September

		SN 1	FC 1	SN ◇1	FC 1	SN	SN 1	FC 1	SN 1	FC 1		SN 1	FC 1	SN 1	FC 1	FC 1	SN 1	FC 1	SN ◇1	SN 1		SN ◇1	FC 1	SN 1	SN
Purley 4	d	23p49		00 11			01 22		02 22			03 22		04 22			05 24		05 58					06 19	06 21
Purley Oaks	d																								06 24
South Croydon 4	d																								06 27
East Croydon	d	23p58	00 04	00 17	00 36	00 49	01 28	01 50	02 28	02 47		03 28	03 47	04 28	04 47	05 17	05 29	05 42	06 07	06 10		06 11	06 17	06 25	06 30
Norwood Junction 2	d																							06 29	06 35
New Cross Gate	d		00a19		00a52			02a14		03a12			04a12		05a12	05a42		05a57					06a32	06 37	06 52
London Bridge 4 ⊖	a																								
London Blackfriars 3 ⊖	a																								
City Thameslink 3	a																								
Farringdon 3 ⊖	a																								
St Pancras International 15 ⊖	a																								
Clapham Junction 10	a	00 11		00 29		01 01	01 40		02 40			03 40		04 41			05 49		06 18	06 34		06 21			
London Victoria 15 ⊖	a	00 18		00 37		01 09	01 49		02 49			03 49		04 50			05 58		06 26			06 30			

		SN ◇1	SN	SN	FC 1	SN ◇1		SN 1	SN	SN 1	SN 1	SN ◇1	SN 1	SN	FC 1	SN ◇1		SN 1	SN	SN ◇1	FC 1	SN 1	SN ◇1	SN 1	SN ◇1
Purley 4	d			06 38				06 49	06 51	07 02				07 08				07 19	07 21					07 34	
Purley Oaks	d			06 41					06 54					07 11					07 24						
South Croydon 4	d			06 44					06 57		07 07			07 14					07 27						
East Croydon	d	06 41	06 43	06 47	06 47	06 53		06 55	07 00	07 07	07 10	07 11	07 14	07 17	07 17	07 23		07 25	07 30	07 30	07 32	07 33	07 38	07 39	07 42
Norwood Junction 2	d		06 50					06 59	07 05	07 13								07 29	07 35					07 45	
New Cross Gate	d		07 04		07a02			07 07	07 22	07a25					07a32			07 37	07 52		07a47	07a49		07a57	
London Bridge 4 ⊖	a																								
London Blackfriars 3 ⊖	a																								
City Thameslink 3	a																								
Farringdon 3 ⊖	a																								
St Pancras International 15 ⊖	a																								
Clapham Junction 10	a	06 50		07 07		07 02					07 34	07 20	07 25	07 37		07 32				07 39			07 47		07 51
London Victoria 15 ⊖	a	06 57		07 16		07 09						07 27	07 32	07 46		07 40				07 46			07 54		07 58

Table 175

Saturdays
from 10 September

Purley and East Croydon - London

COMPLETE SERVICE

		SN 1		SN	FC 1	SN	SN ◇1	SN 1	SN	SN ◇1	FC 1	SN 1		SN 1	SN 1	SN ◇1	SN 1	SN	FC 1	SN	SN ◇1 🚲	SN 1		SN ◇1	SN
Purley 4	d			07 38		07 45		07 49	07 51			08 02						08 08		08 15		08 19			08 21
Purley Oaks	d			07 41					07 54									08 11							08 24
South Croydon 4	d			07 44					07 57						08 07			08 14							08 27
East Croydon	d	07 44		07 47	07 47	07 51	07 53	07 55	08 00	08 00	08 02	08 07		08 08	08 10	08 12	08 14	08 17	08 17	08 21	08 23	08 25		08 28	08 30
Norwood Junction 2	d					07 55		07 59	08 05			08 13								08 25		08 29			08 35
New Cross Gate	d				08a02	08a09		08 07	08 22		08a17	08a25							08a32	08a39		08 37			08 52
London Bridge 4 ⊖	a																								
London Blackfriars 3 ⊖	a																								
City Thameslink 3	a																								
Farringdon 3 ⊖	a																								
St Pancras International 15 ⊖	a																								
Clapham Junction 10	a	07 55		08 07			08 02			08 09				08 17	08 34	08 21	08 25	08 37			08 32			08 37	
London Victoria 15 ⊖	a	08 02		08 16			08 10			08 16				08 24		08 28	08 32	08 46			08 40			08 44	

		FC 1	SN 1	SN 1	SN ◇1		SN ◇1		SN ◇1	SN 1	SN	FC 1	SN	SN ◇1 🚲	SN 1	SN	SN ◇1		FC 1	SN 1	SN 1	SN 1	SN ◇1	SN 1
Purley 4	d			08 32		and at the same minutes past each hour until					11 38		11 45		11 49	11 51				12 02				
Purley Oaks	d										11 41					11 54								
South Croydon 4	d										11 44					11 57						12 07		
East Croydon	d	08 32	08 33	08 37	08 38		11 38		11 42	11 44	11 47	11 47	11 51	11 53	11 55	12 00	12 00		12 02	12 07	12 08	12 10	12 12	12 14
Norwood Junction 2	d			08 43									11 55		11 59	12 05				12 13				
New Cross Gate	d	08a47	08a49	08a55								12a02	12a09		12 07	12 22			12a17	12a25				
London Bridge 4 ⊖	a																							
London Blackfriars 3 ⊖	a																							
City Thameslink 3	a																							
Farringdon 3 ⊖	a																							
St Pancras International 15 ⊖	a																							
Clapham Junction 10	a				08 47		11 47		11 51	11 55	12 07			12 02			12 09				12 17	12 34	12 21	12 25
London Victoria 15 ⊖	a				08 54		11 54		11 58	12 02	12 16			12 10			12 16				12 24		12 28	12 32

		SN	FC 1	SN		SN ◇1 🚲	SN 1	SN ◇1 🚲	SN	FC 1	SN 1	SN 1	SN ◇1	SN ◇1		SN 1	SN	FC 1	SN	SN ◇1 🚲	SN 1	SN	SN ◇1	FC 1
Purley 4	d	12 08		12 15			12 19		12 21			12 32					12 38		12 45		12 49	12 51		
Purley Oaks	d	12 11							12 24								12 41					12 54		
South Croydon 4	d	12 14							12 27								12 44					12 57		
East Croydon	d	12 17	12 17	12 21		12 23	12 25	12 28	12 30	12 32	12 33	12 38	12 38	12 42		12 44	12 47	12 47	12 51	12 53	12 55	13 00	13 00	13 02
Norwood Junction 2	d			12 25			12 29		12 35			12 43							12 55		12 59	13 05		
New Cross Gate	d		12a32	12a39			12 37		12 52	12a47	12a49	12a55						13a02	13a09		13 07	13 22		13a17
London Bridge 4 ⊖	a																							
London Blackfriars 3 ⊖	a																							
City Thameslink 3	a																							
Farringdon 3 ⊖	a																							
St Pancras International 15 ⊖	a																							
Clapham Junction 10	a	12 37				12 32		12 37					12 47	12 51		12 55	13 07			13 02			13 09	
London Victoria 15 ⊖	a	12 46				12 40		12 44					12 54	12 58		13 02	13 16			13 10			13 16	

		SN 1	SN 1	SN 1	SN ◇1	SN 1	SN	FC 1	SN	SN ◇1 🚲		SN 1	SN ◇1 🚲	SN	FC 1	SN 1	SN 1	SN ◇1	SN ◇1	SN 1		SN	FC 1	SN	SN ◇1 🚲
Purley 4	d	13 02					13 08		13 15			13 19		13 21			13 32					13 38		13 45	
Purley Oaks	d						13 11							13 24								13 41			
South Croydon 4	d			13 07			13 14							13 27								13 44			
East Croydon	d	13 07	13 08	13 10	13 12	13 14	13 17	13 17	13 21	13 23		13 25	13 28	13 30	13 32	13 33	13 37	13 38	13 42	13 44		13 47	13 47	13 51	13 53
Norwood Junction 2	d	13 13							13 25			13 29		13 35			13 43							13 55	
New Cross Gate	d	13a25						13a32	13a39			13 37		13 52	13a47	13a49	13a55						14a02	14a09	
London Bridge 4 ⊖	a																								
London Blackfriars 3 ⊖	a																								
City Thameslink 3	a																								
Farringdon 3 ⊖	a																								
St Pancras International 15 ⊖	a																								
Clapham Junction 10	a		13 17	13 34	13 21	13 25	13 37			13 32			13 37					13 47	13 51	13 55		14 07			14 02
London Victoria 15 ⊖	a		13 24		13 28	13 32	13 46			13 40			13 44					13 54	13 58	14 02		14 16			14 10

		SN 1	SN	SN ◇1	FC 1	SN 1		SN 1	SN 1	SN ◇1	SN 1	SN	FC 1	SN	SN ◇1 🚲	SN 1		SN ◇1 🚲	SN	FC 1	SN 1	SN 1	SN ◇1	SN ◇1	SN 1
Purley 4	d	13 49	13 51			14 02						14 08		14 15		14 19			14 21			14 32			
Purley Oaks	d		13 54									14 11							14 24						
South Croydon 4	d		13 57						14 07			14 14							14 27						
East Croydon	d	13 55	14 00	14 00	14 02	14 07		14 08	14 10	14 12	14 14	14 17	14 17	14 21	14 23	14 25		14 28	14 30	14 32	14 33	14 37	14 38	14 42	14 44
Norwood Junction 2	d	13 59	14 05			14 13								14 25		14 29			14 35			14 43			
New Cross Gate	d	14 07	14 22		14a17	14a25							14a32	14a39		14 37			14 52	14a47	14a49	14a55			
London Bridge 4 ⊖	a																								
London Blackfriars 3 ⊖	a																								
City Thameslink 3	a																								
Farringdon 3 ⊖	a																								
St Pancras International 15 ⊖	a																								
Clapham Junction 10	a			14 09				14 17	14 34	14 21	14 25	14 37			14 32			14 37					14 47	14 51	14 55
London Victoria 15 ⊖	a			14 16				14 24		14 28	14 32	14 46			14 40			14 44					14 54	14 58	15 02

Table 175

Saturdays

from 10 September

Purley and East Croydon - London

COMPLETE SERVICE

		SN		FC	SN	SN	SN	SN	SN	FC	SN	SN		SN	SN	SN	SN	FC	SN	SN	SN	SN		SN	FC
		1		1		◇1 ⊤	1		◇1	1	1	1		1	◇1	1		1		◇1 ⊤	1	◇1 ⊤			1
Purley 4	d	14 38			14 45		14 49	14 51			15 02						15 08		15 15		15 19			15 21	
Purley Oaks	d	14 41						14 54									15 11							15 24	
South Croydon 4	d	14 44						14 57						15 07			15 14							15 27	
East Croydon	d	14 47		14 47	14 51	14 53	14 55	15 00	15 00	15 02	15 07	15 08		15 10	15 12	15 14	15 17	15 17	15 21	15 23	15 25	15 28		15 30	15 32
Norwood Junction 2	d				14 55		14 59	15 05			15 13								15 25		15 29			15 35	
New Cross Gate	d			15a02	15a09		15 07	15 22		15a17	15a25							15a32	15a39		15 37			15 52	15a47
London Bridge 4 ⊖	a																								
London Blackfriars 3 ⊖	a																								
City Thameslink 3	a																								
Farringdon 3 ⊖	a																								
St Pancras International 15 ⊖	a																								
Clapham Junction 10	a	15 07				15 02			15 09			15 17		15 35	15 21	15 25	15 37			15 32		15 37			
London Victoria 15 ⊖	a	15 16				15 10			15 16			15 24			15 28	15 32	15 46			15 40		15 44			

		SN	SN	SN	SN	SN	SN	FC		SN	SN	SN	SN	SN	FC	SN	SN	SN		SN	SN	SN	FC	SN	SN
		1	1	◇1	◇1	1		1			◇1 ⊤	1		◇1	1	1	1	1		◇1	1		1		◇1 ⊤
Purley 4	d		15 32				15 38			15 45		15 49	15 51			16 02						16 08		16 15	
Purley Oaks	d						15 41						15 54									16 11			
South Croydon 4	d						15 44						15 57					16 07				16 14			
East Croydon	d	15 33	15 37	15 38	15 42	15 44	15 47	15 47		15 51	15 53	15 55	16 00	16 00	16 02	16 07	16 08	16 10		16 12	16 14	16 17	16 17	16 21	16 23
Norwood Junction 2	d		15 43							15 55		15 59	16 05			16 13								16 25	
New Cross Gate	d	15a49	15a55					16a02		16a09		16 07	16 22		16a17	16a25							16a32	16a39	
London Bridge 4 ⊖	a																								
London Blackfriars 3 ⊖	a																								
City Thameslink 3	a																								
Farringdon 3 ⊖	a																								
St Pancras International 15 ⊖	a																								
Clapham Junction 10	a			15 47	15 51	15 55	16 07				16 02			16 09			16 17	16 34		16 21	16 25	16 37			16 32
London Victoria 15 ⊖	a			15 54	15 58	16 02	16 16				16 10			16 16			16 24			16 28	16 32	16 46			16 40

		SN	SN	SN		FC	SN	SN	SN	SN	SN	SN	FC	SN		SN	SN	SN	SN	FC	SN	SN	SN	SN	
		1	◇1 ⊤			1	1	1	◇1	◇1	1		1			◇1 ⊤	1		◇1	1	1	1	1	◇1	
Purley 4	d	16 19		16 21				16 32				16 38		16 45			16 49	16 51			17 02				
Purley Oaks	d			16 24								16 41						16 54							
South Croydon 4	d			16 27								16 44						16 57					17 07		
East Croydon	d	16 25	16 28	16 30		16 32	16 33	16 37	16 38	16 42	16 44	16 47	16 47	16 51		16 53	16 55	17 00	17 00	17 02	17 07	17 08	17 10	17 12	
Norwood Junction 2	d	16 29		16 35				16 43						16 55			16 59	17 05			17 13				
New Cross Gate	d	16 37		16 52		16a47	16a49	16a55					17a02	17a09			17 07	17 22		17a17	17a25				
London Bridge 4 ⊖	a																								
London Blackfriars 3 ⊖	a																								
City Thameslink 3	a																								
Farringdon 3 ⊖	a																								
St Pancras International 15 ⊖	a																								
Clapham Junction 10	a		16 37						16 47	16 51	16 55	17 07				17 02			17 09			17 17	17 34	17 21	
London Victoria 15 ⊖	a		16 44						16 54	16 58	17 02	17 16				17 10			17 16			17 24		17 28	

		SN	SN	FC	SN	SN	SN	SN	SN	FC		SN	SN	SN	SN	SN	SN	FC	SN	SN		SN	SN	SN	FC
		1		1		◇1 ⊤	1	◇1 ⊤		1		1	1	◇1	◇1	1		1		◇1 ⊤		1		◇1	1
Purley 4	d		17 08		17 15		17 19		17 21				17 32				17 38		17 45			17 49	17 51		
Purley Oaks	d		17 11						17 24								17 41						17 54		
South Croydon 4	d		17 14						17 27								17 44						17 57		
East Croydon	d	17 14	17 17	17 17	17 21	17 23	17 25	17 28	17 30	17 32		17 33	17 37	17 38	17 42	17 44	17 47	17 47	17 51	17 53		17 55	18 00	18 00	18 02
Norwood Junction 2	d				17 25		17 29		17 35				17 43						17 55			17 59	18 05		
New Cross Gate	d			17a32	17a39		17 37		17 52	17a47		17a49	17a55					18a02	18a09			18 07	18 22		18a17
London Bridge 4 ⊖	a																								
London Blackfriars 3 ⊖	a																								
City Thameslink 3	a																								
Farringdon 3 ⊖	a																								
St Pancras International 15 ⊖	a																								
Clapham Junction 10	a	17 25	17 38			17 32		17 37						17 47	17 51	17 55	18 07			18 02				18 09	
London Victoria 15 ⊖	a	17 32	17 47			17 40		17 44						17 54	17 58	18 02	18 16			18 10				18 16	

		SN	SN	SN	SN	SN		SN	FC	SN	SN	SN	SN	SN	FC	SN		SN	SN	SN	SN	SN	FC	SN	SN
		1	1	1	◇1	1			1		◇1 ⊤	1	◇1 ⊤		1	1		1	◇1	◇1	1		1		◇1
Purley 4	d	18 02						18 08		18 15		18 19		18 21				18 32				18 38		18 45	
Purley Oaks	d							18 11						18 24								18 41			
South Croydon 4	d			18 07				18 14						18 27								18 44			
East Croydon	d	18 07	18 08	18 10	18 12	18 14		18 17	18 17	18 21	18 23	18 25	18 28	18 30	18 32	18 33		18 37	18 38	18 42	18 44	18 47	18 47	18 51	18 53
Norwood Junction 2	d	18 13								18 25		18 29		18 35				18 43						18 55	
New Cross Gate	d	18a25							18a32	18a39		18 37		18 52	18a47	18a49		18a55					19a02	19a09	
London Bridge 4 ⊖	a																								
London Blackfriars 3 ⊖	a																								
City Thameslink 3	a																								
Farringdon 3 ⊖	a																								
St Pancras International 15 ⊖	a																								
Clapham Junction 10	a		18 17	18 34	18 21	18 25		18 37			18 32		18 37						18 47	18 51	18 55	19 07			19 02
London Victoria 15 ⊖	a		18 24		18 28	18 32		18 46			18 40		18 44						18 54	18 58	19 02	19 16			19 10

Table 175

Saturdays

from 10 September

Purley and East Croydon - London

COMPLETE SERVICE

		SN 1		SN	SN ◇1	FC 1	SN 1	SN 1	SN 1	SN ◇1	SN 1	SN		FC 1	SN	SN ◇1	SN 1	SN ◇1	SN	FC 1	SN 1	SN ◇1		SN ◇1	SN 1
Purley 4	d	18 49		18 51			19 02					19 08			19 15		19 19		19 21						
Purley Oaks	d			18 54								19 11							19 24						
South Croydon 4	d			18 57					19 07			19 14							19 27						
East Croydon	d	18 55		19 00	19 00	19 02	19 07	19 08	19 10	19 12	19 14	19 17		19 17	19 21	19 23	19 25	19 29	19 30	19 32	19 33	19 38		19 42	19 44
Norwood Junction 2	d	18 59		19 05			19 13								19 25				19 35						
New Cross Gate	d	19 07		19 22		19a17	19a25							19a32	19a39				19 52	19a47	19a49				
London Bridge 4	a																								
London Blackfriars 3	a																								
City Thameslink 3	a																								
Farringdon 3	a																								
St Pancras International 15	a																								
Clapham Junction 10	a				19 09			19 17	19 34	19 21	19 25	19 37				19 32	19 37	19 40				19 47		19 51	19 55
London Victoria 15	a				19 16			19 24		19 28	19 32	19 46				19 40	19 44	19 50				19 54		19 58	20 05

		SN	FC 1	SN	SN ◇1	SN 1	SN	SN 1		FC 1	SN ◇1	SN 1	SN	FC 1	SN	SN ◇1	SN 1	SN		SN ◇1	FC 1	SN 1	SN ◇1	SN 1	SN
Purley 4	d	19 38		19 45		19 49	19 51						20 08		20 15		20 19	20 21							20 38
Purley Oaks	d	19 41					19 54						20 11					20 24							20 41
South Croydon 4	d	19 44					19 57						20 14					20 27							20 44
East Croydon	d	19 47	19 47	19 51	19 53	19 57	20 00	20 00		20 02	20 12	20 14	20 17	20 17	20 21	20 23	20 26	20 30		20 30	20 32	20 33	20 42	20 44	20 47
Norwood Junction 2	d			19 55			20 05								20 25			20 35							
New Cross Gate	d		20a02	20a09			20 22			20a17				20a32	20a39			20 52			20a47	20a49			
London Bridge 4	a																								
London Blackfriars 3	a																								
City Thameslink 3	a																								
Farringdon 3	a																								
St Pancras International 15	a																								
Clapham Junction 10	a	20 07			20 02	20 08		20 11			20 21	20 25	20 37			20 32	20 37			20 40			20 51	20 55	21 07
London Victoria 15	a	20 16			20 10	20 15		20 20			20 28	20 32	20 46			20 40	20 44			20 50			20 58	21 02	21 16

		FC 1	SN	SN ◇1		SN 1	SN	SN ◇1	FC 1	SN ◇1	SN 1	SN	FC 1	SN		SN ◇1	SN 1	SN	SN ◇1	FC 1	SN 1	SN ◇1	SN 1	SN	
Purley 4	d		20 45			20 49	20 51					21 08		21 15			21 19	21 21						21 38	
Purley Oaks	d						20 54					21 11						21 24						21 41	
South Croydon 4	d						20 57					21 14						21 27						21 44	
East Croydon	d	20 47	20 51	20 53		20 56	21 00	21 00	21 02	21 09	21 14	21 17	21 17	21 21		21 23	21 26	21 30	21 30	21 32	21 33	21 42	21 44	21 47	
Norwood Junction 2	d		20 55				21 05							21 25				21 35							
New Cross Gate	d	21a02	21a09				21 22		21a17				21a32	21a39				21 52		21a47	21a49				
London Bridge 4	a																								
London Blackfriars 3	a																								
City Thameslink 3	a																								
Farringdon 3	a																								
St Pancras International 15	a																								
Clapham Junction 10	a			21 02		21 07		21 10		21 18	21 25	21 37				21 32	21 37		21 40			21 51	21 55	22 07	
London Victoria 15	a			21 10		21 14		21 17		21 26	21 32	21 46				21 40	21 44		21 50			21 58	22 02	22 16	

		SN	SN ◇1	SN 1	SN	SN ◇1	FC 1	SN ◇1	SN 1	SN		SN	SN ◇1	SN 1	SN	SN ◇1	FC 1	SN 1	SN ◇1 ⚲	SN 1		SN	SN	SN 1	SN ◇1
Purley 4	d	21 45		21 49	21 51					22 08		22 15		22 19	22 21							22 38	22 45	22 50	
Purley Oaks	d				21 54					22 11					22 24							22 41			
South Croydon 4	d				21 57					22 14					22 27							22 44			
East Croydon	d	21 51	21 53	21 56	22 00	22 00	22 02	22 09	22 14	22 17		22 21	22 23	22 26	22 30	22 30	22 32	22 33	22 40	22 44		22 47	22 51	22 56	23 00
Norwood Junction 2	d	21 55			22 05							22 25			22 35								22 55		
New Cross Gate	d	22a09			22 22		22a17					22a39			22 52		22a47	22a49					23a09		
London Bridge 4	a																								
London Blackfriars 3	a																								
City Thameslink 3	a																								
Farringdon 3	a																								
St Pancras International 15	a																								
Clapham Junction 10	a		22 02	22 07		22 10		22 18	22 25	22 37			22 32	22 37		22 40			22 49	22 55		23 07		23 06	23 10
London Victoria 15	a		22 13	22 15		22 20		22 26	22 35	22 46			22 40	22 44		22 50			22 57	23 05		23 16		23 14	23 20

		SN	FC 1	SN 1	SN	SN		SN ◇1	FC 1	SN	SN 1
Purley 4	d	22 52			23 08	23 15				23 34	23 49
Purley Oaks	d	22 55			23 11					23 37	
South Croydon 4	d	22 58			23 14					23 40	
East Croydon	d	23 01	23 02	23 14	23 17	23 21		23 30	23 32	23 43	23 56
Norwood Junction 2	d	23 06				23 25				23a47	
New Cross Gate	d	23 23	23a17			23a39			23a47		
London Bridge 4	a										
London Blackfriars 3	a										
City Thameslink 3	a										
Farringdon 3	a										
St Pancras International 15	a										
Clapham Junction 10	a			23 25	23 37			23 42			00 11
London Victoria 15	a			23 35	23 48			23 52			00 18

Table 175

Sundays
until 4 September

Purley and East Croydon - London

COMPLETE SERVICE

	SN	FC	SN	FC	SN	SN	SN	SN	SN		SN	FC	SN	FC	SN	SN	FC	SN	SN		SN	SN	FC	SN
	[1]	[1]	◇[1]	[1]		[1]	[1]	[1]	[1]		◇[1]	[1]	[1]	[1]			[1]	◇[1]				[1]	[1]	
	A	A	A	A																				
Purley [4] d	23p49		00 11			01 37	02 33	03 33	04 33		05 22		05 56			06 38					07 08	07 20		
Purley Oaks d																06 41					07 11			
South Croydon [4] d																06 44					07 14	07 24		
East Croydon d	23p56	00 04	00 17	00 36	00 49	01 43	02 40	03 40	04 40		05 28	05 32	06 02	06 32	06 40	06 47	07 02	07 10	07 12		07 17	07 27	07 32	07 42
Norwood Junction [2] d												05 36		06 36		06 52					07 22			
New Cross Gate d		00a19		00a52								05a59		06a59		07 09	07a15		07a50		07 39		07a45	08a19
London Bridge [4] ⊖ a																								
London Blackfriars [3] ⊖ a																								
City Thameslink [3] a																								
Farringdon [3] ⊖ a																								
St Pancras International [15] ⊖ a																								
Clapham Junction [10] a	00 11		00 28		01 03	01 53	02 52	03 52	04 52		05 47		06 14		07 00			07 24				07 40		
London Victoria [15] ⊖ a	00 18		00 36		01 10	02 05	03 05	04 05	05 05		05 58		06 22		07 09			07 31				07 48		

	SN	SN	SN	SN	FC		SN	SN	SN	SN	SN	FC	SN	SN	SN		SN	SN	SN	SN	SN	SN	FC	SN
			[1]	◇[1]	[1]		◇[1] 🛒			◇[1]		[1]	[1]	◇[1]			◇[1] 🛒		[1]		[1]	◇[1]	[1]	◇[1] 🛒
Purley [4] d	07 38	07 47	07 50						08 08	08 14	08 17		08 27					08 38		08 47	08 50			
Purley Oaks d	07 41								08 11									08 41						
South Croydon [4] d	07 44								08 14									08 44						
East Croydon d	07 47	07 53	07 56	08 00	08 02		08 09	08 12	08 17	08 20	08 23	08 32	08 34	08 39	08 42		08 46	08 47	08 50	08 53	08 56	09 00	09 02	09 09
Norwood Junction [2] d	07 52		08 01						08 22				08 38					08 52			09 01			
New Cross Gate d	08 09		08a13		08a15			08a49	08 39			08a45	08a51		09a19			09 09			09a13		09a15	
London Bridge [4] ⊖ a																								
London Blackfriars [3] ⊖ a																								
City Thameslink [3] a																								
Farringdon [3] ⊖ a																								
St Pancras International [15] ⊖ a																								
Clapham Junction [10] a		08 12		08 09			08 18			08 31	08 42			08 48			08 55		09 02	09 12		09 09		09 18
London Victoria [15] ⊖ a		08 20		08 16			08 25			08 39	08 50			08 55			09 03		09 09	09 20		09 16		09 25

	SN		SN	SN		SN	SN	SN	FC	SN		SN	SN	SN	SN	SN	SN	SN	SN	FC		SN	SN
				◇[1] 🛒		◇[1] 🛒	◇[1] 🛒		[1]	[1]		◇[1]		◇[1] 🛒		[1]		[1]	◇[1]	[1]		◇[1] 🛒	
Purley [4] d			09 08				17 14	17 17		17 27					17 38		17 47	17 50					
Purley Oaks d			09 11												17 41								
South Croydon [4] d			09 14												17 44								
East Croydon d	09 12		09 17	09 17	and at the same minutes past each hour until	17 17	17 20	17 23	17 32	17 34		17 39	17 42	17 46	17 47	17 50	17 53	17 56	18 00	18 02		18 09	18 12
Norwood Junction [2] d			09 22							17 38					17 52			18 01					
New Cross Gate d	09a49		09 39						17a45	17a51			18a19		18 09			18a13		18a15			18a49
London Bridge [4] ⊖ a																							
London Blackfriars [3] ⊖ a																							
City Thameslink [3] a																							
Farringdon [3] ⊖ a																							
St Pancras International [15] ⊖ a																							
Clapham Junction [10] a				09 26		17 26	17 31	17 42				17 48		17 55		18 02	18 12		18 09			18 18	
London Victoria [15] ⊖ a				09 33		17 33	17 39	17 50				17 55		18 03		18 09	18 20		18 16			18 25	

	SN	SN	SN	SN	FC	SN	SN		SN	SN	SN	SN	SN	SN	SN	FC	SN		SN	SN	SN	SN	SN	FC
		◇[1] 🛒	◇[1] 🛒		[1]	[1]	◇[1]			◇[1]		[1]		[1]	◇[1]	[1]	◇[1] 🛒				◇[1]	◇[1]		[1]
Purley [4] d	18 08		18 14	18 17		18 27					18 38		18 47	18 50						19 08		19 14	19 17	
Purley Oaks d	18 11										18 41									19 11				
South Croydon [4] d	18 14										18 44									19 14				
East Croydon d	18 17	18 17	18 20	18 23	18 32	18 34	18 39		18 42	18 46	18 47	18 50	18 53	18 56	19 00	19 02	19 09		19 12	19 17	19 17	19 20	19 23	19 32
Norwood Junction [2] d	18 22					18 38					18 52			19 01						19 22				
New Cross Gate d	18 40				18a45	18a51			19a19		19 09			19a13		19a15			19a49	19 39				19a45
London Bridge [4] ⊖ a																								
London Blackfriars [3] ⊖ a																								
City Thameslink [3] a																								
Farringdon [3] ⊖ a																								
St Pancras International [15] ⊖ a																								
Clapham Junction [10] a		18 26	18 31	18 42			18 48			18 55		19 02	19 12		19 09		19 18				19 26	19 31	19 42	
London Victoria [15] ⊖ a		18 33	18 39	18 50			18 55			19 03		19 09	19 20		19 16		19 25				19 33	19 39	19 50	

	SN	SN	SN		SN	SN	SN	SN	SN	SN	FC	SN	SN		SN	SN	SN	SN	FC	SN	SN	SN	SN	
	[1]	◇[1]			◇[1]		[1]		[1]	◇[1]	[1]	◇[1]				◇[1]	◇[1]		[1]	[1]	◇[1]		◇[1]	
Purley [4] d	19 27					19 38		19 47	19 50						20 08		20 14	20 17		20 27				
Purley Oaks d						19 41									20 11									
South Croydon [4] d						19 44									20 14									
East Croydon d	19 34	19 39	19 42		19 46	19 47	19 50	19 53	19 56	20 00	20 02	20 09	20 12		20 17	20 17	20 20	20 23	20 32	20 34	20 39	20 42	20 46	
Norwood Junction [2] d	19 38					19 52			20 01						20 22					20 38				
New Cross Gate d	19a51		20a19			20 09			20a13		20a15		20a49		20 39				20a45	20a51		21a19		
London Bridge [4] ⊖ a																								
London Blackfriars [3] ⊖ a																								
City Thameslink [3] a																								
Farringdon [3] ⊖ a																								
St Pancras International [15] ⊖ a																								
Clapham Junction [10] a		19 48			19 55		20 02	20 12		20 09		20 18				20 26	20 31	20 42			20 48		20 55	
London Victoria [15] ⊖ a		19 55			20 03		20 09	20 20		20 16		20 25				20 33	20 39	20 50			20 55		21 03	

A not 22 May

Table 175

Sundays until 4 September

Purley and East Croydon - London

COMPLETE SERVICE

		SN	SN 1	SN	SN 1	SN ◇1	FC 1	SN ◇1	SN	SN	SN ◇1	SN ◇1	SN	FC 1	SN 1	SN ◇1	SN	SN	SN 1	SN	SN 1	SN ◇1	FC 1
Purley 4	d	20 38		20 47	20 50					21 08		21 14	21 17		21 27			21 38		21 47	21 50		
Purley Oaks	d	20 41								21 11								21 41					
South Croydon 4	d	20 44								21 14								21 44					
East Croydon	d	20 47	20 50	20 53	20 56	21 00	21 02	21 09	21 12	21 17	21 17	21 20	21 23	21 32	21 34	21 39	21 42	21 47	21 50	21 53	21 56	22 00	22 02
Norwood Junction 2	d	20 52			21 01					21 22					21 38			21 52			22 01		
New Cross Gate	d	21 09			21a13		21a15		21a49	21 39				21a45	21a51		22a19	22 09			22a13		22a15
London Bridge 4 ⊖	a																						
London Blackfriars 3 ⊖	a																						
City Thameslink 3	a																						
Farringdon 3 ⊖	a																						
St Pancras International 15 ⊖	a																						
Clapham Junction 10	a		21 02	21 12		21 09		21 18			21 26	21 31	21 42			21 48			22 02	22 12		22 09	
London Victoria 15 ⊖	a		21 09	21 20		21 16		21 25			21 33	21 39	21 50			21 55			22 09	22 20		22 16	

		SN ◇1	SN	SN	SN ◇1	SN	FC 1	SN 1	SN	SN	SN 1	SN	SN 1	SN ◇1	FC 1	SN	SN ◇1	SN	FC 1	SN 1	SN 1
Purley 4	d			22 08	22 14	22 17		22 27		22 38		22 47	22 50			23 08	23 14	23 17			23 50
Purley Oaks	d			22 11						22 41						23 11		23 20			
South Croydon 4	d			22 14						22 44						23 14		23 23			
East Croydon	d	22 09	22 12	22 17	22 20	22 23	22 32	22 34	22 42	22 47	22 50	22 53	22 56	23 00	23 02	23 17	23 21	23a25	23 32	23 50	23 56
Norwood Junction 2	d			22 22				22 38		22 52						23a21					
New Cross Gate	d		22a49	22 39			22a45	22a51	23a19	23 09					23a15				23a45		
London Bridge 4 ⊖	a																				
London Blackfriars 3 ⊖	a																				
City Thameslink 3	a																				
Farringdon 3 ⊖	a																				
St Pancras International 15 ⊖	a																				
Clapham Junction 10	a	22 18			22 31	22 42					23 02	23 12	23 07	23 10			23 31			00 02	00 11
London Victoria 15 ⊖	a	22 25			22 39	22 50					23 09	23 23	23 14	23 17			23 38			00 08	00 21

Sundays from 11 September

		SN 1	FC 1	SN ◇1	FC 1	SN	SN 1	SN 1	SN 1	SN 1	SN ◇1	FC 1	SN 1	FC 1	SN	SN	FC 1	SN ◇1	SN	SN	SN 1	FC 1	SN
Purley 4	d	23p49		00 11			01 37	02 33	03 33	04 33	05 22		05 56			06 38				07 08	07 20		
Purley Oaks	d															06 41				07 11			
South Croydon 4	d															06 44				07 14	07 24		
East Croydon	d	23p56	00 04	00 17	00 36	00 49	01 43	02 40	03 40	04 40	05 28	05 32	06 02	06 32	06 40	06 47	07 02	07 10	07 12	07 17	07 27	07 32	07 42
Norwood Junction 2	d											05 36		06 36		06 52				07 22			
New Cross Gate	d		00a19		00a52							05a59		06a59		07 09	07a15		07a50	07 39		07a45	08a19
London Bridge 4 ⊖	a																						
London Blackfriars 3 ⊖	a																						
City Thameslink 3	a																						
Farringdon 3 ⊖	a																						
St Pancras International 15 ⊖	a																						
Clapham Junction 10	a	00 11		00 28		01 03	01 53	02 52	03 52	04 52	05 47		06 14		07 00			07 24			07 40		
London Victoria 15 ⊖	a	00 18		00 36		01 10	02 05	03 05	04 05	05 05	05 56		06 22		07 09			07 31			07 48		

		SN	SN	SN 1	SN ◇1	FC 1	SN ◇1 🛒	SN	SN	SN	SN ◇1	FC 1	SN ◇1	SN	SN	SN 1	SN	SN 1	SN ◇1	FC 1	SN ◇1 🛒	SN
Purley 4	d	07 38	07 47	07 50					08 08	08 17	08 20				08 38		08 47	08 50				
Purley Oaks	d	07 41							08 11						08 41							
South Croydon 4	d	07 44							08 14						08 44							
East Croydon	d	07 47	07 53	07 56	08 00	08 02	08 10	08 12	08 17	08 23	08 26	08 32	08 40	08 42	08 47	08 50	08 53	08 56	09 00	09 02	09 10	09 12
Norwood Junction 2	d	07 52		08 01					08 22						08 52			09 01				
New Cross Gate	d	08 09		08a13		08a15		08a49	08 39			08a45		09a19	09 09			09a13		09a15		09a49
London Bridge 4 ⊖	a																					
London Blackfriars 3 ⊖	a																					
City Thameslink 3	a																					
Farringdon 3 ⊖	a																					
St Pancras International 15 ⊖	a																					
Clapham Junction 10	a		08 12		08 11		08 24			08 42	08 37		08 54			09 01	09 12		09 11		09 24	
London Victoria 15 ⊖	a		08 20		08 18		08 31			08 50	08 46		09 01			09 08	09 20		09 18		09 31	

		SN ◇1 🛒		SN ◇1 🛒	SN	SN	SN ◇1 🛒	FC 1	SN ◇1	SN	SN	SN 1	SN	SN 1	SN ◇1	FC 1	SN ◇1 🛒	SN	SN ◇1 🛒	SN	SN
Purley 4	d		and at the same minutes past each hour until		13 08	13 17	13 19				13 38		13 47	13 50						14 08	14 17
Purley Oaks	d				13 11						13 41									14 11	
South Croydon 4	d				13 14						13 44									14 14	
East Croydon	d	09 13		13 13	13 17	13 23	13 26	13 32	13 40	13 42	13 47	13 50	13 53	13 56	14 00	14 02	14 10	14 12	14 13	14 17	14 23
Norwood Junction 2	d				13 22						13 52			14 01						14 22	
New Cross Gate	d				13 39			13a45		14a19	14 09			14a13		14a15		14a49		14 39	
London Bridge 4 ⊖	a																				
London Blackfriars 3 ⊖	a																				
City Thameslink 3	a																				
Farringdon 3 ⊖	a																				
St Pancras International 15 ⊖	a																				
Clapham Junction 10	a	09 27		13 27		13 42	13 37		13 54			14 01	14 12		14 11		14 24		14 27		14 42
London Victoria 15 ⊖	a	09 35		13 35		13 50	13 46		14 01			14 08	14 20		14 18		14 31		14 35		14 50

Table 175

Sundays
from 11 September

Purley and East Croydon - London

COMPLETE SERVICE

		SN		SN		FC	SN	SN	SN	SN	SN	SN	SN	FC		SN	SN	SN	SN	SN	SN	FC	SN	SN
		◇1		◇1		1	◇1			1		1	◇1	1		◇1		◇1			◇1	1	◇1	
		🛒		🛒												🛒		🛒			🛒			
Purley 4	d	14 20		17 20					17 38		17 47	17 50							18 08	18 17	18 20			
Purley Oaks	d		and at the same minutes past each hour until						17 41										18 11					
South Croydon 4	d								17 44										18 14					
East Croydon	d	14 26		17 26		17 32	17 40	17 42	17 47	17 50	17 53	17 56	18 00	18 02		18 10	18 12	18 13	18 17	18 23	18 26	18 32	18 40	18 42
Norwood Junction 2	d								17 52			18 01							18 22					
New Cross Gate	d					17a45		18a19	18 09			18a13		18a15			18a49		18 40			18a45		19a19
London Bridge 4 ⊖	a																							
London Blackfriars 3 ⊖	a																							
City Thameslink 3	a																							
Farringdon 3 ⊖	a																							
St Pancras International 15 ⊖	a																							
Clapham Junction 10	a	14 37		17 37			17 54			18 01	18 12		18 11			18 24		18 27		18 42	18 37		18 54	
London Victoria 15 ⊖	a	14 46		17 46			18 01			18 08	18 20		18 18			18 31		18 35		18 50	18 46		19 01	

			SN	SN	SN	SN	SN	FC	SN	SN	SN		SN	SN	SN	FC	SN	SN	SN	SN	SN		SN	SN	FC
				1		1	◇1	1	◇1		◇1				◇1	1	◇1			1			1	◇1	1
									🛒																
Purley 4	d		18 38		18 47	18 50							19 08	19 17	19 20				19 38		19 47		19 50		
Purley Oaks	d		18 41										19 11						19 41						
South Croydon 4	d		18 44										19 14						19 44						
East Croydon	d		18 47	18 50	18 53	18 56	19 00	19 02	19 10	19 12	19 13		19 17	19 23	19 26	19 32	19 40	19 42	19 47	19 50	19 53		19 56	20 00	20 02
Norwood Junction 2	d		18 52			19 01							19 22						19 52				20 01		
New Cross Gate	d		19 09			19a13		19a15		19a49			19 39			19a45		20a19	20 09				20a13		20a15
London Bridge 4 ⊖	a																								
London Blackfriars 3 ⊖	a																								
City Thameslink 3	a																								
Farringdon 3 ⊖	a																								
St Pancras International 15 ⊖	a																								
Clapham Junction 10	a			19 01	19 12		19 11		19 24		19 27			19 42	19 37		19 54			20 01	20 12			20 11	
London Victoria 15 ⊖	a			19 08	19 20		19 18		19 31		19 35			19 50	19 46		20 01			20 08	20 20			20 18	

		SN	SN	SN	SN	SN	SN		FC	SN	SN	SN	SN	SN	SN	SN	FC		SN	SN	SN	SN	SN	SN	FC
		◇1		◇1			◇1		1	◇1			1		1	◇1	1		◇1		◇1			◇1	1
Purley 4	d				20 08	20 17	20 20					20 38		20 47	20 50							21 08	21 17	21 20	
Purley Oaks	d				20 11							20 41										21 11			
South Croydon 4	d				20 14							20 44										21 14			
East Croydon	d	20 10	20 12	20 13	20 17	20 23	20 26		20 32	20 40	20 42	20 47	20 50	20 53	20 56	21 00	21 02		21 10	21 12	21 13	21 17	21 23	21 26	21 32
Norwood Junction 2	d				20 22							20 52			21 01							21 22			
New Cross Gate	d		20a49		20 39				20a45		21a19	21 09			21a13		21a15			21a49		21 39			21a45
London Bridge 4 ⊖	a																								
London Blackfriars 3 ⊖	a																								
City Thameslink 3	a																								
Farringdon 3 ⊖	a																								
St Pancras International 15 ⊖	a																								
Clapham Junction 10	a	20 24		20 27		20 42	20 37			20 54			21 01	21 12		21 11			21 24		21 27		21 42	21 37	
London Victoria 15 ⊖	a	20 31		20 35		20 50	20 46			21 01			21 08	21 20		21 18			21 31		21 35		21 50	21 46	

		SN	SN		SN	SN	SN	SN	SN	FC	SN	SN	SN		SN	SN	FC	SN	SN	SN	SN	SN	SN		FC
		◇1				1		1	◇1	1	◇1					◇1	1			1		1	◇1		1
Purley 4	d				21 38		21 47	21 50					22 08		22 17	22 20			22 38		22 47	22 50			
Purley Oaks	d				21 41								22 11						22 41						
South Croydon 4	d				21 44								22 14						22 44						
East Croydon	d	21 40	21 42		21 47	21 50	21 53	21 56	22 00	22 02	22 10	22 12	22 17		22 23	22 26	22 32	22 42	22 47	22 50	22 53	22 56	23 00		23 02
Norwood Junction 2	d				21 52			22 01					22 22						22 52						
New Cross Gate	d		22a19		22 09			22a13		22a15		22a49	22 39				22a45	23a19	23 09						23a15
London Bridge 4 ⊖	a																								
London Blackfriars 3 ⊖	a																								
City Thameslink 3	a																								
Farringdon 3 ⊖	a																								
St Pancras International 15 ⊖	a																								
Clapham Junction 10	a	21 54				22 01	22 12		22 11		22 24				22 42	22 37				23 01	23 12	23 07	23 12		
London Victoria 15 ⊖	a	22 01				22 08	22 20		22 18		22 31				22 50	22 46				23 08	23 23	23 14	23 20		

		SN	SN	SN	FC	SN	SN
				◇1	1	1	1
Purley 4	d	23 08	23 17	23 20			23 50
Purley Oaks	d	23 11	23 20				
South Croydon 4	d	23 14	23 23				
East Croydon	d	23 17	23a25	23 27	23 32	23 50	23 56
Norwood Junction 2	d	23a21					
New Cross Gate	d				23a45		
London Bridge 4 ⊖	a						
London Blackfriars 3 ⊖	a						
City Thameslink 3	a						
Farringdon 3 ⊖	a						
St Pancras International 15 ⊖	a						
Clapham Junction 10	a			23 38		00 02	00 11
London Victoria 15 ⊖	a			23 46		00 08	00 21

Network Diagram for Table 176

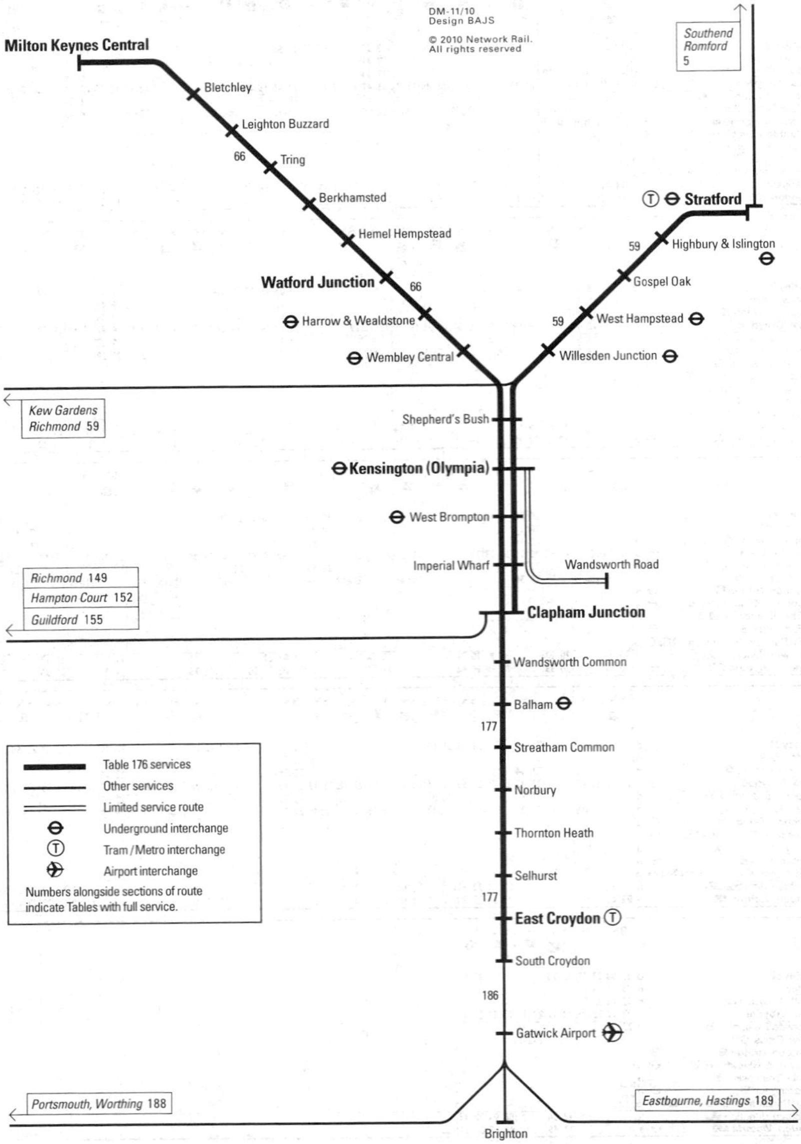

Table 176

Mondays to Fridays

East Croydon, Clapham Junction, Kensington (Olympia) - Watford Junction and Milton Keynes Central

Miles	Miles			SN [1]	SN [1]	LO	SN [1]	LO	LO	SN [1]	LO		LO	LO	LO	SN [1]	LO	LO	LO	SN	LO		SN [1]	LO
—	—	**South Croydon**	d																					
0	—	**East Croydon**	d																	07 50			08 07	
1	—	Selhurst [4]	d																	07 54			08 13	
1¾	—	Thornton Heath	d																	07 56			08 16	
3	—	Norbury	d																	07 59			08 20	
4	—	Streatham Common [4]	d																	08 02			08 23	
5¾	—	Balham [4]	d		05 25															08 06			08 28	
6½	—	Wandsworth Common	d																	08 08			08 31	
—	—	Wandsworth Road	d																					
7¾	—	**Clapham Junction [10]**	a		05 29															08 13			08 36	
—	—		d	05 03	05 30	05 47	05 55	06 14	06 29	06 38	06 44		06 59	07 14	07 29	07 39	07 44	07 59	08 09	08 14	08 29		08 39	08 44
8¾	—	Imperial Wharf	d	05 07	05 39	05 51	06 00	06 18	06 33	06 42	06 48		07 03	07 18	07 33	07 44	07 48	08 03	08 13	08 18	08 33		08 44	08 48
9½	—	West Brompton ⊖	d	05 10	05 41	05 54	06 03	06 21	06 36	06 45	06 51		07 06	07 21	07 36	07 47	07 51	08 06	08 16	08 21	08 36		08 47	08 51
11½	—	**Kensington (Olympia)** ⊖	d	05 14	05 44	05 57	06 07	06 24	06 39	06 49	06 54		07 09	07 24	07 39	07 50	07 54	08 09	08 19	08 25	08 39		08 50	08 54
12¾	0	Shepherd's Bush ⊖	d	05 17	05 47	05 59	06 10	06 26	06 41	06 52	06 56		07 11	07 26	07 41	07 53	07 56	08 11	08 21	08a27	08 41		08 53	08 56
—	1½	Willesden Jn. High Level ⊖	a			06 09		06 34	06 50		07 04		07 19	07 35	07 49		08 05	08 19	08 36		08 49			09 05
—	4	West Hampstead ⊖	a					06 43	06 58		07 13		07 28	07 43	07 58		08 14	08 28			08 58			09 14
—	6	Gospel Oak	a					06 49	07 04		07 19		07 34	07 49	08 04		08 20	08 34			09 04			09 20
—	8¾	Highbury & Islington ⊖	a					07 00	07 15		07 30		07 45	08 00	08 15		08 31	08 45			09 15			09 31
—	13½	Stratford	a					07 18	07 33		07 48		08 03	08 18	08 33		08 49	09 03			09 33			09 51
17	—	Wembley Central ⊖	a		06s00		06 23			07s07						08s08							09s08	
20½	—	Harrow & Wealdstone ⊖	a	05 33	06 07		06 28			07 12						08 13							09 13	
25	—	**Watford Junction**	a	05 40	06 14		06 35			07 19						08 20							09 20	
32	—	Hemel Hempstead	a		06 22					07 27						08 28							09 28	
35½	—	Berkhamsted	a		06 26					07 31						08 32							09 32	
39¼	—	Tring	a		06 33					07 39						08 37							09 39	
47¾	—	Leighton Buzzard	a		06 41					07 50						08 47							09 47	
54¼	—	Bletchley	a		06 48					07 57						08 55							09 55	
57¼	—	**Milton Keynes Central [10]**	a		06 55					08 03						09 01							10 01	

		SN	LO	SN	LO	SN	LO	SN [1]		LO	LO	LO	LO	SN [1]	LO	LO	LO	LO		SN [1]	LO	LO	LO	LO	SN [1]
South Croydon	d			08 35										10 07						11 07					12 07
East Croydon	d			08 39				09 08						10 10						11 11					12 10
Selhurst [4]	d			08 43				09 13						10 14						11 16					12 14
Thornton Heath	d			08 46				09 16						10 16						11 18					12 16
Norbury	d			08 49				09 19						10 19						11 21					12 19
Streatham Common [4]	d			08 52				09 21						10 22						11 24					12 22
Balham [4]	d			08 58				09 28						10 29						11 28					12 28
Wandsworth Common	d			09 00				09 30						10 31						11 30					12 30
Wandsworth Road	d																								
Clapham Junction [10]	a			09 04				09 34						10 35						11 33					12 34
	d	08 48	08 59	09 05	09 15	09 24	09 30	09 39		09 45	10 00	10 15	10 30	10 39	10 45	11 00	11 15	11 30		11 39	11 45	12 00	12 15	12 30	12 39
Imperial Wharf	d	08 52	09 03	09 09	09 19	09 28	09 34	09 44		09 49	10 04	10 19	10 34	10 44	10 49	11 04	11 19	11 34		11 44	11 49	12 04	12 19	12 34	12 44
West Brompton ⊖	d	08 55	09 06	09 12	09 22	09 31	09 37	09 47		09 52	10 07	10 22	10 37	10 47	10 52	11 07	11 22	11 37		11 47	11 52	12 07	12 22	12 37	12 47
Kensington (Olympia) ⊖	d	08 59	09 09	09 15	09 25	09 35	09 40	09 50		09 55	10 10	10 25	10 40	10 50	10 55	11 10	11 25	11 40		11 50	11 55	12 10	12 25	12 40	12 50
Shepherd's Bush ⊖	d	09a01	09 11	09a18	09 27	09a37	09 42	09 53		09 57	10 12	10 27	10 42	10 53	10 57	11 12	11 27	11 42		11 53	11 57	12 12	12 27	12 42	12 53
Willesden Jn. High Level ⊖	a		09 19		09 35		09 52			10 05	10 22	10 35	10 52		11 05	11 22	11 35	11 52			12 05	12 22	12 35	12 52	
West Hampstead ⊖	a		09 28		09 44					10 14		10 44			11 14		11 44				12 14		12 44		
Gospel Oak	a		09 34		09 50					10 20		10 50			11 20		11 50				12 20		12 50		
Highbury & Islington ⊖	a		09 45		10 01					10 31		11 01			11 31		12 01				12 31		13 01		
Stratford	a		10 03		10 20					10 50		11 20			11 49		12 20				12 50		13 20		
Wembley Central ⊖	a							10s08						11s08						12s08					13s08
Harrow & Wealdstone ⊖	a							10 13						11 13						12 13					13 13
Watford Junction	a							10 20						11 20						12 20					13 20
Hemel Hempstead	a							10 28						11 28						12 28					13 28
Berkhamsted	a							10 32						11 32						12 32					13 32
Tring	a							10 39						11 39						12 39					13 39
Leighton Buzzard	a							10 47						11 48						12 48					13 48
Bletchley	a							10 57						11 55						12 55					13 55
Milton Keynes Central [10]	a							11 02						12 01						13 01					14 01

East Croydon, Clapham Junction, Kensington (Olympia) - Watford Junction and Milton Keynes Central

		LO	LO	LO		LO	SN [1]	LO	LO	LO	LO	SN [1]	LO	LO		LO	LO	SN [1]	LO	LO	SN	LO	LO	SN [1]	LO
South Croydon	d						13 07					14 07						15 07						16 07	
East Croydon	d						13 10					14 10						15 10						16 10	
Selhurst [4]	d						13 13					14 13						15 13						16 13	
Thornton Heath	d						13 16					14 16						15 16						16 16	
Norbury	d						13 19					14 19						15 19						16 19	
Streatham Common [4]	d						13 21					14 21						15 21						16 21	
Balham [4]	d						13 28					14 28						15 29						16 28	
Wandsworth Common	d						13 30					14 30						15 31						16 30	
Wandsworth Road	d																				16 12				
Clapham Junction [10]	a						13 34					14 34						15 35						16 34	
	d	12 45	13 00	13 15		13 30	13 39	13 45	14 00	14 15	14 30	14 39	14 45	15 00		15 15	15 30	15 39	15 44	15 59		16 14	16 29	16 39	16 44
Imperial Wharf	d	12 49	13 04	13 19		13 34	13 44	13 49	14 04	14 19	14 34	14 44	14 49	15 04		15 19	15 34	15 44	15 48	16 03		16 18	16 33	16 44	16 48
West Brompton ⊖	d	12 52	13 07	13 22		13 37	13 47	13 52	14 07	14 22	14 37	14 47	14 52	15 07		15 22	15 37	15 47	15 51	16 06		16 21	16 36	16 47	16 51
Kensington (Olympia) ⊖	d	12 55	13 10	13 25		13 40	13 50	13 55	14 10	14 25	14 40	14 50	14 55	15 10		15 25	15 40	15 50	15 54	16 09	16a29	16 24	16 39	16 50	16 54
Shepherd's Bush ⊖	d	12 57	13 12	13 27		13 42	13 53	13 57	14 12	14 27	14 42	14 53	14 57	15 12		15 27	15 42	15 53	15 56	16 11		16 26	16 41	16 53	16 56
Willesden Jn. High Level ⊖	a	13 05	13 22	13 35		13 52		14 05	14 22	14 35	14 52		15 05	15 22		15 35	15 52		16 04	16 19		16 34	16 49		17 04
West Hampstead ⊖	a	13 14		13 44				14 14		14 44			15 14			15 44			16 13	16 28		16 43	16 58		17 13
Gospel Oak	a	13 20		13 50				14 20		14 50			15 20			15 50			16 19	16 34		16 49	17 04		17 19
Highbury & Islington ⊖	a	13 31		14 01				14 31		15 01			15 32			16 01			16 30	16 45		17 00	17 15		17 30
Stratford	a	13 50		14 20				14 50		15 20			15 51			16 20			16 49	17 05		17 20	17 35		17 50
Wembley Central ⊖	a						14s08					15s08						16s08						17s08	
Harrow & Wealdstone ⊖	a						14 13					15 13						16 13						17 13	
Watford Junction	a						14 20					15 20						16 20						17 20	
Hemel Hempstead	a						14 28					15 28						16 28						17 28	
Berkhamsted	a						14 32					15 32						16 32						17 33	
Tring	a						14 39					15 39						16 39						17 38	
Leighton Buzzard	a						14 48					15 48						16 47						17 47	
Bletchley	a						14 55					15 55						16 55						17 54	
Milton Keynes Central [10]	a						15 01					16 01						17 00						17 59	

		SN	LO	LO	SN	LO	SN [1]	LO	LO	LO		LO	SN [1]	LO	LO	LO	LO	SN [1]	LO	LO		LO	LO	SN [1]	LO
South Croydon	d						17 07																		
East Croydon	d						17 10						18 10					19 10							
Selhurst [4]	d						17 13						18 13					19 13							
Thornton Heath	d						17 16						18 16					19 16							
Norbury	d						17 19						18 19					19 19							
Streatham Common [4]	d						17 21						18 21					19 21							
Balham [4]	d						17 28						18 26					19 28							
Wandsworth Common	d						17 30						18 28					19 30							
Wandsworth Road	d																								
Clapham Junction [10]	a						17 34						18 34					19 34							
	d	16 48	16 59	17 14	17 20	17 29	17 39	17 44	17 59	18 14		18 29	18 39	18 44	18 59	19 15	19 30	19 39	19 45	20 00		20 15	20 30	20 39	20 45
Imperial Wharf	d		17 03	17 18	17 24	17 33	17 44	17 48	18 03	18 18		18 33	18 44	18 48	19 03	19 19	19 34	19 44	19 49	20 04		20 19	20 34	20 44	20 49
West Brompton ⊖	d		17 06	17 21	17 27	17 36	17 47	17 51	18 06	18 21		18 36	18 47	18 51	19 06	19 22	19 37	19 47	19 52	20 07		20 22	20 37	20 47	20 52
Kensington (Olympia) ⊖	d	16a57	17 09	17 24	17 30	17 39	17 50	17 54	18 09	18 24		18 39	18 50	18 54	19 09	19 25	19 40	19 50	19 55	20 10		20 25	20 40	20 50	20 55
Shepherd's Bush ⊖	d		17 11	17 26	17a32	17 41	17 53	17 56	18 11	18 26		18 41	18 53	18 56	19 11	19 27	19 42	19 53	19 57	20 12		20 27	20 42	20 53	20 57
Willesden Jn. High Level ⊖	a		17 19	17 34		17 49		18 04	18 19	18 34		18 49		19 04	19 19	19 35	19 52		20 05	20 22		20 35	20 52		21 05
West Hampstead ⊖	a		17 28	17 43		17 58		18 13	18 28	18 43		18 58		19 13	19 28	19 44			20 14			20 44			21 14
Gospel Oak	a		17 34	17 49		18 04		18 19	18 34	18 49		19 04		19 19	19 34	19 50			20 20			20 50			21 20
Highbury & Islington ⊖	a		17 45	18 00		18 15		18 30	18 45	19 00		19 15		19 30	19 45	20 01			20 31			21 01			21 31
Stratford	a		18 05	18 20		18 35		18 50	19 05	19 21		19 35		19 50	20 04	20 20			20 50			21 20			21 50
Wembley Central ⊖	a						18s08						19s08					20s08						21s08	
Harrow & Wealdstone ⊖	a						18 13						19 13					20 13						21 13	
Watford Junction	a						18 20						19 20					20 20						21 20	
Hemel Hempstead	a						18 28						19 28					20 28						21 28	
Berkhamsted	a						18 32						19 33					20 32						21 32	
Tring	a						18 38						19 40					20 39						21 39	
Leighton Buzzard	a						18 46						19 51					20 48						21 50	
Bletchley	a						18 53						20 00					20 55						21 58	
Milton Keynes Central [10]	a						19 00						20 06					21 01						22 03	

Table 176

Mondays to Fridays

East Croydon, Clapham Junction, Kensington (Olympia) - Watford Junction and Milton Keynes Central

		LO	LO	LO	SN 1	LO		LO	LO	SN 1	LO	LO
South Croydon	d											
East Croydon ⇌	d											
Selhurst 4	d											
Thornton Heath	d											
Norbury	d											
Streatham Common 4	d											
Balham 4	d											
Wandsworth Common	d											
Wandsworth Road	d											
Clapham Junction 10	a											
	d	21 00	21 15	21 30	21 39	21 45		22 00	22 30	22 39	23 00	23 30
Imperial Wharf	d	21 04	21 19	21 34	21 44	21 49		22 04	22 34	22 44	23 04	23 34
West Brompton ⊖	d	21 07	21 22	21 37	21 47	21 52		22 07	22 37	22 47	23 07	23 37
Kensington (Olympia) ⊖	d	21 10	21 25	21 40	21 50	21 55		22 10	22 40	22 50	23 10	23 40
Shepherd's Bush ⊖	d	21 12	21 27	21 42	21 53	21 57		22 12	22 42	22 53	23 12	23 42
Willesden Jn. High Level ⊖	a	21 22	21 35	21 52		22 05		22 22	22 52		23 24	23 52
West Hampstead ⊖	a		21 44			22 14						
Gospel Oak	a		21 50			22 20						
Highbury & Islington ⊖	a		22 01			22 31						
Stratford	a		22 20			22 50						
Wembley Central ⊖	a											
Harrow & Wealdstone ⊖	a				22 16					23 16		
Watford Junction	a				22 23					23 23		
Hemel Hempstead	a											
Berkhamsted	a											
Tring	a											
Leighton Buzzard	a											
Bletchley	a											
Milton Keynes Central 10	a											

Saturdays

		SN 1	SN 1	LO	SN 1	LO	LO	SN 1	LO	LO		LO	LO	SN 1	LO	LO	LO	LO	SN 1	LO		LO	LO	LO	SN 1
South Croydon	d													07 07					08 07						09 07
East Croydon ⇌	d							06 10						07 10					08 10						09 10
Selhurst 4	d							06 13						07 13					08 13						09 13
Thornton Heath	d							06 16						07 16					08 16						09 16
Norbury	d							06 19						07 19					08 19						09 19
Streatham Common 4	d							06 21						07 21					08 21						09 21
Balham 4	d		05 33					06 28						07 28					08 28						09 28
Wandsworth Common	d							06 30						07 30					08 30						09 30
Wandsworth Road	d																								
Clapham Junction 10	a		05 37					06 34						07 34					08 34						09 34
	d	05 08	05 38	05 47	06 09	06 15	06 30	06 39	06 45	07 00		07 15	07 30	07 39	07 45	08 00	08 15	08 30	08 39	08 45		09 00	09 15	09 30	09 39
Imperial Wharf	d	05 12	05 42	05 51	06 13	06 19	06 34	06 44	06 49	07 04		07 19	07 34	07 44	07 49	08 04	08 19	08 34	08 44	08 49		09 04	09 19	09 34	09 44
West Brompton ⊖	d	05 15	05 45	05 54	06 16	06 22	06 37	06 47	06 52	07 07		07 22	07 37	07 47	07 52	08 07	08 22	08 37	08 47	08 52		09 07	09 22	09 37	09 47
Kensington (Olympia) ⊖	d	05 19	05 49	05 57	06 20	06 25	06 40	06 50	06 55	07 10		07 25	07 40	07 50	07 55	08 10	08 25	08 40	08 50	08 55		09 10	09 25	09 40	09 50
Shepherd's Bush ⊖	d	05 22	05 52	05 59	06 23	06 27	06 42	06 53	06 57	07 12		07 27	07 42	07 53	07 57	08 12	08 27	08 42	08 53	08 57		09 12	09 27	09 42	09 53
Willesden Jn. High Level ⊖	a			06 09		06 35	06 52		07 05	07 22		07 35	07 52		08 05	08 22	08 35	08 52		09 05		09 22	09 35	09 52	
West Hampstead ⊖	a					06 44			07 14			07 44			08 14		08 44			09 14			09 44		
Gospel Oak	a					06 50			07 20			07 50			08 20		08 50			09 20			09 50		
Highbury & Islington ⊖	a					07 01			07 31			08 01			08 31		09 01			09 31			10 01		
Stratford	a					07 20			07 50			08 20			08 50		09 20			09 50			10 20		
Wembley Central ⊖	a		06s07		06 38			07s07						08s07					09s07						10s07
Harrow & Wealdstone ⊖	a	05 40	06 12		06 43			07 12						08 12					09 12						10 12
Watford Junction	a	05 47	06 19		06 50			07 19						08 19					09 19						10 19
Hemel Hempstead	a		06 27					07 27						08 27					09 27						10 27
Berkhamsted	a		06 31					07 32						08 31					09 33						10 31
Tring	a		06 37					07 39						08 37					09 38						10 37
Leighton Buzzard	a		06 46					07 47						08 46					09 47						10 47
Bletchley	a		06 54					07 54						08 54					09 54						10 54
Milton Keynes Central 10	a		07 00					08 00						09 00					10 00						11 00

Table 176

Saturdays

East Croydon, Clapham Junction, Kensington (Olympia) - Watford Junction and Milton Keynes Central

Station		LO	LO	LO	LO	SN 1		LO	LO	LO	LO	SN 1	LO	LO	LO	LO		SN 1	LO	LO	LO	LO	SN 1	LO	LO
South Croydon	d					10 07						11 07						12 07					13 07		
East Croydon	d					10 10						11 10						12 10					13 10		
Selhurst 4	d					10 13						11 13						12 13					13 13		
Thornton Heath	d					10 16						11 16						12 16					13 16		
Norbury	d					10 19						11 19						12 19					13 19		
Streatham Common 4	d					10 21						11 21						12 21					13 21		
Balham 4	d					10 28						11 28						12 28					13 28		
Wandsworth Common	d					10 30						11 30						12 30					13 30		
Wandsworth Road	d																								
Clapham Junction 10	a					10 34						11 34						12 34					13 34		
	d	09 45	10 00	10 15	10 30	10 39		10 45	11 00	11 15	11 30	11 39	11 45	12 00	12 15	12 30		12 39	12 45	13 00	13 15	13 30	13 39	13 45	14 00
Imperial Wharf	d	09 49	10 04	10 19	10 34	10 44		10 49	11 04	11 19	11 34	11 44	11 49	12 04	12 19	12 34		12 44	12 49	13 04	13 19	13 34	13 44	13 49	14 04
West Brompton ⊖	d	09 52	10 07	10 22	10 37	10 47		10 52	11 07	11 22	11 37	11 47	11 52	12 07	12 22	12 37		12 47	12 52	13 07	13 22	13 37	13 47	13 52	14 07
Kensington (Olympia) ⊖	d	09 55	10 10	10 25	10 40	10 50		10 55	11 10	11 25	11 40	11 50	11 55	12 10	12 25	12 40		12 50	12 55	13 10	13 25	13 40	13 50	13 55	14 10
Shepherd's Bush ⊖	d	09 57	10 12	10 27	10 42	10 53		10 57	11 12	11 27	11 42	11 53	11 57	12 12	12 27	12 42		12 53	12 57	13 12	13 27	13 42	13 53	13 57	14 12
Willesden Jn. High Level ⊖	a	10 05	10 22	10 35	10 52			11 05	11 22	11 35	11 52		12 05	12 22	12 35	12 52			13 05	13 22	13 35	13 52		14 05	14 22
West Hampstead ⊖	a	10 14		10 44				11 14		11 44			12 14		12 44				13 14		13 44			14 14	
Gospel Oak	a	10 20		10 50				11 20		11 50			12 20		12 50				13 20		13 50			14 20	
Highbury & Islington ⊖	a	10 31		11 01				11 31		12 01			12 31		13 01				13 31		14 01			14 31	
Stratford	a	10 50		11 20				11 50		12 20			12 50		13 20				13 50		14 20			14 50	
Wembley Central ⊖	a					11s08						12s07						13s07					14s08		
Harrow & Wealdstone ⊖	a					11 13						12 12						13 12					14 13		
Watford Junction	a					11 20						12 19						13 19					14 20		
Hemel Hempstead	a					11 28						12 28						13 27					14 28		
Berkhamsted	a					11 33						12 32						13 32					14 32		
Tring	a					11 38						12 37						13 37					14 37		
Leighton Buzzard	a					11 47						12 47						13 47					14 47		
Bletchley	a					11 54						12 54						13 54					14 54		
Milton Keynes Central 10	a					12 00						13 00						14 00					15 00		

Station		LO		LO	SN 1	LO	LO	LO	LO	SN 1	LO	LO		LO	LO	SN 1	LO	LO	LO	LO	SN 1	LO		LO	LO
South Croydon	d				14 07					15 07						16 07					17 07				
East Croydon	d				14 10					15 10						16 10					17 10				
Selhurst 4	d				14 13					15 13						16 13					17 13				
Thornton Heath	d				14 16					15 16						16 16					17 16				
Norbury	d				14 19					15 19						16 19					17 19				
Streatham Common 4	d				14 21					15 21						16 21					17 21				
Balham 4	d				14 28					15 29						16 28					17 28				
Wandsworth Common	d				14 30					15 31						16 30					17 30				
Wandsworth Road	d																								
Clapham Junction 10	a				14 34					15 35						16 34					17 34				
	d	14 15		14 30	14 39	14 45	15 00	15 15	15 30	15 39	15 45	16 00		16 15	16 30	16 39	16 45	17 00	17 15	17 30	17 39	17 45		18 00	18 15
Imperial Wharf	d	14 19		14 34	14 44	14 49	15 04	15 19	15 34	15 44	15 49	16 04		16 19	16 34	16 44	16 49	17 04	17 19	17 34	17 44	17 49		18 04	18 19
West Brompton ⊖	d	14 22		14 37	14 47	14 52	15 07	15 22	15 37	15 47	15 52	16 07		16 22	16 37	16 47	16 52	17 07	17 22	17 37	17 47	17 52		18 07	18 22
Kensington (Olympia) ⊖	d	14 25		14 40	14 50	14 55	15 10	15 25	15 40	15 50	15 55	16 10		16 25	16 40	16 50	16 55	17 10	17 25	17 40	17 50	17 55		18 10	18 25
Shepherd's Bush ⊖	d	14 27		14 42	14 53	14 57	15 12	15 27	15 42	15 53	15 57	16 12		16 27	16 42	16 53	16 57	17 12	17 27	17 42	17 53	17 57		18 12	18 27
Willesden Jn. High Level ⊖	a	14 35		14 52		15 05	15 22	15 35	15 52		16 05	16 22		16 35	16 52		17 05	17 22	17 35	17 52		18 05		18 22	18 35
West Hampstead ⊖	a	14 44				15 14		15 44			16 14			16 44			17 14		17 44			18 14			18 44
Gospel Oak	a	14 50				15 20		15 50			16 20			16 50			17 20		17 50			18 20			18 50
Highbury & Islington ⊖	a	15 01				15 31		16 01			16 31			17 01			17 31		18 01			18 31			19 01
Stratford	a	15 20				15 50		16 20			16 50			17 20			17 50		18 20			18 50			19 20
Wembley Central ⊖	a				15s07					16s07						17s07					18s07				
Harrow & Wealdstone ⊖	a				15 12					16 12						17 12					18 12				
Watford Junction	a				15 19					16 19						17 19					18 19				
Hemel Hempstead	a				15 27					16 27						17 27					18 27				
Berkhamsted	a				15 32					16 32						17 32					18 32				
Tring	a				15 37					16 37						17 37					18 37				
Leighton Buzzard	a				15 47					16 47						17 46					18 46				
Bletchley	a				15 54					16 54						17 54					18 54				
Milton Keynes Central 10	a				16 00					17 00						18 00					19 00				

East Croydon, Clapham Junction, Kensington (Olympia) - Watford Junction and Milton Keynes Central

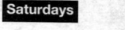

		LO	SN 1	LO	LO	LO	LO	SN 1		LO	LO	LO	SN 1	LO	LO	LO	LO	LO		SN 1	LO	LO	LO	SN 1	LO
South Croydon	d		18 07					19 07																	
East Croydon	🚋 d		18 10					19 10																	
Selhurst 4	d		18 13					19 13																	
Thornton Heath	d		18 16					19 16																	
Norbury	d		18 19					19 19																	
Streatham Common 4	d		18 21					19 21																	
Balham 4	d		18 28					19 28																	
Wandsworth Common	d		18 30					19 30																	
Wandsworth Road	d																								
Clapham Junction 10	a		18 34					19 34																	
	d	18 30	18 39	18 45	19 00	19 15	19 30	19 38		19 45	20 00	20 15	20 25	20 30	20 45	21 00	21 15	21 30		21 39	21 45	22 00	22 30	22 39	23 00
Imperial Wharf	d	18 34	18 44	18 49	19 04	19 19	19 34	19 42		19 49	20 04	20 19	20 29	20 34	20 49	21 04	21 19	21 34		21 44	21 49	22 04	22 34	22 44	23 04
West Brompton	⊖ d	18 37	18 47	18 52	19 07	19 22	19 37	19 45		19 52	20 07	20 22	20 32	20 37	20 52	21 07	21 22	21 37		21 47	21 52	22 07	22 37	22 47	23 07
Kensington (Olympia)	⊖ d	18 40	18 50	18 55	19 10	19 25	19 40	19 48		19 55	20 10	20 25	20 36	20 40	20 55	21 10	21 25	21 40		21 50	21 55	22 10	22 40	22 50	23 10
Shepherd's Bush	⊖ d	18 42	18 53	18 57	19 12	19 27	19 42	19 50		19 57	20 12	20 27	20 39	20 42	20 57	21 12	21 27	21 42		21 53	21 57	22 12	22 42	22 53	23 12
Willesden Jn. High Level	⊖ a	18 52		19 05	19 22	19 35	19 52			20 05	20 22	20 35		20 52	21 05	21 22	21 35	21 53			22 05	22 22	22 53		23 22
West Hampstead	⊖ a			19 14		19 44				20 14		20 44			21 14		21 44				22 14				
Gospel Oak	a			19 20		19 50				20 20		20 50			21 20		21 50				22 20				
Highbury & Islington	⊖ a			19 31		20 01				20 31		21 01			21 31		22 01				22 31				
Stratford	a			19 50		20 20				20 50		21 20			21 50		22 20				22 50				
Wembley Central	⊖ a		19 08																						
Harrow & Wealdstone	⊖ a		19 13					20 08					21 02							22 13				23 12	
Watford Junction	a		19 21					20 15					21 09							22 20				23 19	
Hemel Hempstead	a																								
Berkhamsted	a																								
Tring	a																								
Leighton Buzzard	a																								
Bletchley	a																								
Milton Keynes Central 10	a																								

		LO
South Croydon	d	
East Croydon	🚋 d	
Selhurst 4	d	
Thornton Heath	d	
Norbury	d	
Streatham Common 4	d	
Balham 4	d	
Wandsworth Common	d	
Wandsworth Road	d	
Clapham Junction 10	a	
	d	23 30
Imperial Wharf	d	23 34
West Brompton	⊖ d	23 37
Kensington (Olympia)	⊖ d	23 40
Shepherd's Bush	⊖ d	23 42
Willesden Jn. High Level	⊖ a	23 52
West Hampstead	⊖ a	
Gospel Oak	a	
Highbury & Islington	⊖ a	
Stratford	a	
Wembley Central	⊖ a	
Harrow & Wealdstone	⊖ a	
Watford Junction	a	
Hemel Hempstead	a	
Berkhamsted	a	
Tring	a	
Leighton Buzzard	a	
Bletchley	a	
Milton Keynes Central 10	a	

Table 176

Sundays

East Croydon, Clapham Junction, Kensington (Olympia) - Watford Junction and Milton Keynes Central

		SN [1]	SN [1]	LO	LO	SN [1]	LO	LO	SN [1]	LO		LO	LO	LO	SN [1]	LO	LO	LO	LO	SN [1]		LO	LO	LO	LO
South Croydon	d																								
East Croydon	d																								
Selhurst [4]	d																								
Thornton Heath	d																								
Norbury	d																								
Streatham Common [4]	d																								
Balham [4]	d																								
Wandsworth Common	d																								
Wandsworth Road	d																								
Clapham Junction [10]	a																								
	d	07 24	08 15	08 30	09 00	09 15	09 30	10 00	10 15	10 20		10 30	10 45	11 00	11 15	11 20	11 30	11 45	12 00	12 05		12 15	12 30	12 45	13 00
Imperial Wharf	d	07 28	08 19	08 34	09 04	09 19	09 34	10 04	10 19	10 24		10 34	10 49	11 04	11 19	11 24	11 34	11 49	12 04	12 09		12 19	12 34	12 49	13 04
West Brompton	⊖ d	07 31	08 22	08 37	09 07	09 22	09 37	10 07	10 22	10 27		10 37	10 52	11 07	11 22	11 27	11 37	11 52	12 07	12 12		12 22	12 37	12 52	13 07
Kensington (Olympia)	⊖ d	07 34	08 26	08 40	09 10	09 26	09 40	10 10	10 26	10 30		10 40	10 55	11 10	11 26	11 30	11 40	11 55	12 10	12 16		12 25	12 40	12 55	13 10
Shepherd's Bush	⊖ d	07a36	08 29	08 42	09 12	09 29	09 42	10 12	10 29	10 32		10 42	10 57	11 12	11 29	11 32	11 42	11 57	12 12	12 19		12 27	12 42	12 57	13 12
Willesden Jn. High Level	⊖ a			08 52	09 22		09 52	10 22		10 40		10 52	11 05	11 22		11 40	11 54	12 05	12 22			12 35	12 52	13 05	13 22
West Hampstead	⊖ a									10 49			11 14			11 49		12 14				12 44		13 14	
Gospel Oak	a									10 55			11 20			11 55		12 20				12 50		13 20	
Highbury & Islington	⊖ a									11 06			11 31			12 06		12 31				13 01		13 31	
Stratford	a									11 25			11 50			12 25		12 50				13 20		13 50	
Wembley Central	⊖ a																								
Harrow & Wealdstone	⊖ a		08 48			09 48			10 48						11 48					12 36					
Watford Junction	a		08 56			09 58			10 56						11 56					12 44					
Hemel Hempstead	a																								
Berkhamsted	a																								
Tring	a																								
Leighton Buzzard	a																								
Bletchley	a																								
Milton Keynes Central [10]	a																								

		SN [1]	LO	LO	LO	LO		SN [1]	LO	LO	LO	LO	SN [1]	LO	LO	LO		LO	SN [1]	LO	LO	LO	LO	SN [1]	LO
South Croydon	d																								
East Croydon	d																								
Selhurst [4]	d																								
Thornton Heath	d																								
Norbury	d																								
Streatham Common [4]	d																								
Balham [4]	d																								
Wandsworth Common	d																								
Wandsworth Road	d																								
Clapham Junction [10]	a																								
	d	13 05	13 15	13 30	13 45	14 00		14 05	14 15	14 30	14 45	15 00	15 05	15 15	15 30	15 45		16 00	16 05	16 15	16 30	16 45	17 00	17 05	17 15
Imperial Wharf	d	13 09	13 19	13 34	13 49	14 04		14 09	14 19	14 34	14 49	15 04	15 09	15 19	15 34	15 49		16 04	16 09	16 19	16 34	16 49	17 04	17 09	17 19
West Brompton	⊖ d	13 12	13 22	13 37	13 52	14 07		14 12	14 22	14 37	14 52	15 07	15 12	15 22	15 37	15 52		16 07	16 12	16 22	16 37	16 52	17 07	17 12	17 22
Kensington (Olympia)	⊖ d	13 16	13 25	13 40	13 55	14 10		14 16	14 25	14 40	14 55	15 10	15 16	15 25	15 40	15 55		16 10	16 16	16 25	16 40	16 55	17 10	17 16	17 25
Shepherd's Bush	⊖ d	13 19	13 27	13 42	13 57	14 12		14 19	14 27	14 42	14 57	15 12	15 19	15 27	15 42	15 57		16 12	16 19	16 27	16 42	16 57	17 12	17 19	17 27
Willesden Jn. High Level	⊖ a		13 35	13 52	14 05	14 22			14 35	14 52	15 05	15 22		15 35	15 52	16 05		16 22		16 35	16 52	17 05	17 22		17 35
West Hampstead	⊖ a		13 44		14 14				14 44		15 14			15 44		16 14				16 44		17 14			17 44
Gospel Oak	a		13 50		14 20				14 50		15 20			15 50		16 20				16 50		17 20			17 50
Highbury & Islington	⊖ a		14 01		14 31				15 01		15 31			16 01		16 31				17 01		17 31			18 01
Stratford	a		14 20		14 50				15 20		15 50			16 20		16 50				17 20		17 50			18 20
Wembley Central	⊖ a																								
Harrow & Wealdstone	⊖ a	13 36						14 36					15 36						16 36					17 36	
Watford Junction	a	13 44						14 44					15 44						16 44					17 44	
Hemel Hempstead	a																								
Berkhamsted	a																								
Tring	a																								
Leighton Buzzard	a																								
Bletchley	a																								
Milton Keynes Central [10]	a																								

Table 176

Sundays

East Croydon, Clapham Junction, Kensington (Olympia) - Watford Junction and Milton Keynes Central

		LO		LO	LO	SN 1	LO	LO	LO	LO	SN 1	LO
South Croydon	d											
East Croydon ⛴	d											
Selhurst 4	d											
Thornton Heath	d											
Norbury	d											
Streatham Common 4	d											
Balham 4	d											
Wandsworth Common	d											
Wandsworth Road	d											
Clapham Junction 10	a											
	d	17 30		17 45	18 00	18 05	18 15	18 30	18 45	19 00	19 05	19 15
Imperial Wharf	d	17 34		17 49	18 04	18 09	18 19	18 34	18 49	19 04	19 09	19 19
West Brompton ⊖	d	17 37		17 52	18 07	18 12	18 22	18 37	18 52	19 07	19 12	19 22
Kensington (Olympia) ⊖	d	17 40		17 55	18 10	18 16	18 25	18 40	18 55	19 10	19 16	19 25
Shepherd's Bush ⊖	d	17 42		17 57	18 12	18 19	18 27	18 42	18 57	19 12	19 19	19 27
Willesden Jn. High Level ⊖	a	17 52		18 05	18 22		18 35	18 52	19 05	19 22		19 35
West Hampstead ⊖	a			18 14			18 44		19 14			19 44
Gospel Oak	a			18 20			18 50		19 20			19 50
Highbury & Islington ⊖	a			18 31			19 01		19 31			20 01
Stratford	a			18 50			19 20		19 50			20 20
Wembley Central ⊖	a											
Harrow & Wealdstone ⊖	a					18 36					19 36	
Watford Junction	a					18 44					19 43	
Hemel Hempstead	a											
Berkhamsted	a											
Tring	a											
Leighton Buzzard	a											
Bletchley	a											
Milton Keynes Central 10	a											

			LO	LO	LO	SN 1	LO	LO	LO	LO	SN 1		LO	LO
South Croydon	d													
East Croydon ⛴	d													
Selhurst 4	d													
Thornton Heath	d													
Norbury	d													
Streatham Common 4	d													
Balham 4	d													
Wandsworth Common	d													
Wandsworth Road	d													
Clapham Junction 10	a													
	d		19 30	19 45	20 00	20 05	20 15	20 30	20 45	21 00	21 15		21 20	21 30
Imperial Wharf	d		19 34	19 49	20 04	20 09	20 19	20 34	20 49	21 04	21 19		21 27	21 34
West Brompton ⊖	d		19 37	19 52	20 07	20 12	20 22	20 37	20 52	21 07	21 22		21 30	21 37
Kensington (Olympia) ⊖	d		19 40	19 55	20 10	20 16	20 25	20 40	20 55	21 10	21 26		21 33	21 40
Shepherd's Bush ⊖	d		19 42	19 57	20 12	20 19	20 27	20 42	20 57	21 12	21 29		21 35	21 42
Willesden Jn. High Level ⊖	a		19 52	20 07	20 22		20 37	20 53	21 10	21 22			21 45	21 52
West Hampstead ⊖	a													
Gospel Oak	a													
Highbury & Islington ⊖	a													
Stratford	a													
Wembley Central ⊖	a													
Harrow & Wealdstone ⊖	a					20 36					21 47			
Watford Junction	a					20 44					21 54			
Hemel Hempstead	a													
Berkhamsted	a													
Tring	a													
Leighton Buzzard	a													
Bletchley	a													
Milton Keynes Central 10	a													

		LO	LO	LO	SN 1	LO	LO
South Croydon	d						
East Croydon ⛴	d						
Selhurst 4	d						
Thornton Heath	d						
Norbury	d						
Streatham Common 4	d						
Balham 4	d						
Wandsworth Common	d						
Wandsworth Road	d						
Clapham Junction 10	a						
	d	21 45	22 00	22 15	22 15	22 44	23 15
Imperial Wharf	d	21 49	22 04	22 19	22 19	22 48	23 19
West Brompton ⊖	d	21 52	22 07	22 22	22 22	22 51	23 22
Kensington (Olympia) ⊖	d	21 55	22 10	22 25	22 26	22 54	23 25
Shepherd's Bush ⊖	d	21 57	22 12	22 27	22 29	22 56	23 27
Willesden Jn. High Level ⊖	a	22 10	22 22	22 37		23 10	23 37
West Hampstead ⊖	a						
Gospel Oak	a						
Highbury & Islington ⊖	a						
Stratford	a						
Wembley Central ⊖	a						
Harrow & Wealdstone ⊖	a				22 48		
Watford Junction	a				22 56		
Hemel Hempstead	a						
Berkhamsted	a						
Tring	a						
Leighton Buzzard	a						
Bletchley	a						
Milton Keynes Central 10	a						

Milton Keynes Central, Watford Junction, Kensington (Olympia) - Clapham Junction and East Croydon

Miles	Miles			SN	SN	LO	SN	LO	SN	LO	LO	LO		SN	LO	LO	LO	SN	LO	LO	SN	LO		LO	SN
				MX	MO	MX	MX																		
				[1]	[1]		[1]		[1]					[1]				[1]							
0	—	**Milton Keynes Central** [10]	d	22p11														07 01							
3	—	Bletchley	d	22p15														07 05							
9½	—	Leighton Buzzard	d	22p22														07 13							
18	—	Tring	d	22p34														07 22							
21¾	—	Berkhamsted	d	22p39														07 27							
25¼	—	Hemel Hempstead	d	22p43														07 31							
32¼	—	**Watford Junction**	d	22p54	23p17		23p29		05 54					06 53				07 39							
36¾	—	Harrow & Wealdstone ⊖	d	23p01	23p23		23p35		06 00					06 59				07 45							
40¼	—	Wembley Central ⊖	d						06 05					07 04				07u50							
—	0	Stratford [7] ⊖	d								06 05	06 20			06 35	06 50	07 00		07 20	07 35		07 50		08 05	
—	4¾	Highbury & Islington ⊖	d								06 20	06 35			06 50	07 05	07 15		07 35	07 50		08 05		08 20	
—	7½	Gospel Oak	d								06 30	06 45			07 00	07 15	07 25		07 45	08 00		08 15		08 30	
—	9½	West Hampstead ⊖	d								06 36	06 51			07 06	07 21	07 31		07 51	08 06		08 21		08 36	
—	12	Willesden Jn. High Level ⊖	d			23p40		06 01		06 33	06 46	07 01			07 16	07 31	07 41		08 01	08 16		08 31		08 46	
44½	13½	Shepherd's Bush ⊖	d	23p21	23p45	23p48	23p54	06 08	06 19	06 40	06 54	07 09		07 19	07 24	07 39	07 49	08 05	08 09	08 24	08 31	08 39		08 54	09 06
45¾	—	**Kensington (Olympia)** ⊖	d	23p23	23p48	23p50	23p56	06 10	06 22	06 42	06 56	07 11		07 22	07 26	07 41	07 51	08 07	08 11	08 26	08 33	08 41		08 56	09 09
47¾	—	West Brompton ⊖	d	23p26	23p50	23p52	23p59	06 13	06 25	06 45	06 58	07 13		07 25	07 28	07 43	07 53	08 10	08 13	08 28	08 36	08 43		08 58	09 12
48½	—	Imperial Wharf	d	23p28	23p53	23p55	00 02	06 16	06 27	06 48	07 01	07 16		07 27	07 31	07 46	07 56	08 13	08 16	08 31	08 38	08 46		09 01	09 15
49½	—	**Clapham Junction** [10]	a	23p33	23p58	00 04	00 07	06 23	06 32	06 54	07 11	07 27		07 32	07 42	07 56	08 06	08 18	08 27	08 42	08 43	08 57		09 12	09 19
—	—		d	23p40	00 05													08 36							
—	—	Wandsworth Road	a																						
50¾	—	Wandsworth Common	a															08 39							
51½	—	Balham [4]	a	23p44														08 42							
53¼	—	Streatham Common [4]	a	23p48														08 46							
54¼	—	Norbury	a	23p51														08 49							
55½	—	Thornton Heath	a	23p54														08 52							
56¼	—	Selhurst [4]	a	23p56	00 18													08 54							
57¼	—	**East Croydon**	a	00 01	00 22													09 05							
—	—	**South Croydon**	a																						

		LO	SN	LO	LO	SN	LO	SN		LO	SN	LO	LO	LO	LO	SN	LO	LO		LO	LO	SN	LO	LO	LO
			[1]								[1]					[1]						[1]			
Milton Keynes Central [10]	d		08 13								09 13					10 13						11 13			
Bletchley	d		08 17								09 17					10 17						11 17			
Leighton Buzzard	d		08 24								09 24					10 24						11 24			
Tring	d		08 34								09 34					10 34						11 34			
Berkhamsted	d		08 39								09 39					10 39						11 39			
Hemel Hempstead	d		08 43								09 43					10 43						11 43			
Watford Junction	d		08 51								09 51					10 51						11 51			
Harrow & Wealdstone ⊖	d		08 58								09 58					10 59						11 59			
Wembley Central ⊖	d		09u05								10u05					11u04						12u04			
Stratford [7] ⊖	d	08 20		08 35	08 50		09 05					09 35		10 05			10 35			11 05			11 35		12 05
Highbury & Islington ⊖	d	08 35		08 50	09 05		09 20					09 50		10 20			10 50			11 20			11 50		12 20
Gospel Oak	d	08 45		09 00	09 15		09 30					10 00		10 30			11 00			11 31			12 00		12 30
West Hampstead ⊖	d	08 51		09 06	09 21		09 36					10 06		10 36			11 06			11 37			12 06		12 36
Willesden Jn. High Level ⊖	d	09 01		09 16	09 31		09 46			10 01		10 16	10 31	10 46	11 01		11 16	11 31		11 46	12 01		12 16	12 31	12 46
Shepherd's Bush ⊖	d	09 09	09 18	09 24	09 39	09 42	09 54			10 09	10 21	10 26	10 39	10 54	11 09	11 19	11 24	11 39		11 54	12 09	12 19	12 24	12 39	12 54
Kensington (Olympia) ⊖	d	09 11	09 21	09 26	09 41	09 45	09 56	10 04		10 11	10 24	10 28	10 41	10 56	11 11	11 21	11 26	11 41		11 56	12 11	12 22	12 26	12 41	12 56
West Brompton ⊖	d	09 13	09 23	09 28	09 43	09 48	09 58			10 13	10 27	10 30	10 43	10 58	11 13	11 23	11 28	11 43		11 58	12 13	12 25	12 28	12 43	12 58
Imperial Wharf	d	09 16	09 26	09 31	09 46	09 50	10 01			10 16	10 29	10 33	10 46	11 01	11 16	11 26	11 31	11 46		12 01	12 16	12 27	12 31	12 46	13 01
Clapham Junction [10]	a	09 27	09 31	09 42	09 56	09 55	10 08			10 25	10 34	10 40	10 55	11 08	11 25	11 30	11 38	11 55		12 08	12 25	12 32	12 38	12 55	13 08
	d		09 34								10 34					11 34						12 34			
Wandsworth Road	a							10 20																	
Wandsworth Common	a		09 37								10 37					11 37						12 37			
Balham [4]	a		09 41								10 40					11 40						12 40			
Streatham Common [4]	a		09 45								10 45					11 45						12 45			
Norbury	a		09 48								10 48					11 48						12 48			
Thornton Heath	a		09 51								10 51					11 51						12 51			
Selhurst [4]	a		09 53								10 53					11 53						12 53			
East Croydon	a		09 57								10 57					11 57						12 57			
South Croydon	a		10 01								11 01					12 01						13 01			

Table 176

Mondays to Fridays

Milton Keynes Central, Watford Junction, Kensington (Olympia) - Clapham Junction and East Croydon

		LO	SN [1]	LO		LO	LO	LO	SN [1]	LO	LO	LO	LO	SN [1]		LO	LO	LO	LO	SN [1]	LO	SN	LO	LO	
Milton Keynes Central [10]	d		12 13						13 13					14 13						15 13					
Bletchley	d		12 17						13 17					14 17						15 17					
Leighton Buzzard	d		12 24						13 24					14 24						15 24					
Tring	d		12 34						13 34					14 34						15 34					
Berkhamsted	d		12 39						13 39					14 39						15 39					
Hemel Hempstead	d		12 43						13 43					14 43						15 43					
Watford Junction	d		12 51						13 51					14 51						15 51					
Harrow & Wealdstone ⊖	d		12 59						13 59					14 59						15 59					
Wembley Central ⊖	d		13u04						14u04					15u04						16u05					
Stratford [7] ⊖	d			12 35			13 05			13 35		14 05				14 35		15 05			15 35		15 50		
Highbury & Islington ⊖	d			12 50			13 20			13 50		14 20				14 50		15 20			15 50		16 05		
Gospel Oak	d			13 00			13 30			14 00		14 30				15 00		15 30			16 02		16 15		
West Hampstead ⊖	d			13 06			13 36			14 06		14 36				15 06		15 36			16 08		16 21		
Willesden Jn. High Level ⊖	d	13 01		13 16		13 31	13 46	14 01		14 16	14 31	14 46	15 01			15 16	15 31	15 46	16 01		16 17		16 31	16 46	
Shepherd's Bush ⊖	d	13 09	13 19	13 24		13 39	13 54	14 09	14 19	14 24	14 39	14 54	15 09	15 22		15 26	15 39	15 54	16 09	16 19	16 25		16 39	16 53	
Kensington (Olympia) ⊖	d	13 11	13 22	13 26		13 41	13 56	14 11	14 22	14 26	14 41	14 56	15 11	15 24		15 28	15 41	15 56	16 11	16 22	16 27	16 34	16 41	16 55	
West Brompton ⊖	d	13 13	13 25	13 28		13 43	13 58	14 13	14 25	14 28	14 43	14 58	15 13	15 26		15 30	15 43	15 58	16 13	16 25	16 29	16 36	16 43	16 58	
Imperial Wharf	d	13 16	13 28	13 31		13 46	14 01	14 16	14 28	14 31	14 46	15 01	15 16	15 29		15 33	15 46	16 01	16 16	16 27	16 32	16 39	16 46	17 01	
Clapham Junction [10]	a	13 25	13 32	13 38		13 55	14 08	14 25	14 32	14 38	14 55	15 08	15 25	15 33		15 40	15 55	16 08	16 25	16 32	16 39	16 43	16 55	17 10	
	d		13 34						14 34					15 34						16 34					
Wandsworth Road	a																								
Wandsworth Common	a		13 37						14 37					15 37						16 37					
Balham [4]	a		13 40						14 40					15 40						16 40					
Streatham Common [4]	a		13 45						14 45					15 45						16 45					
Norbury	a		13 48						14 48					15 48						16 48					
Thornton Heath	a		13 51						14 51					15 51						16 51					
Selhurst [4]	a		13 53						14 53					15 53						16 54					
East Croydon 🚋	a		13 57						14 57					15 57						16 58					
South Croydon	a		14 01						15 01					16 01						17 02					

		SN	LO	SN [1]	LO	LO	SN	LO	LO	SN [1]		LO	LO	LO	LO	SN [1]	LO	LO	LO	LO		SN [1]	LO	LO	LO
Milton Keynes Central [10]	d			16 13						17 13						18 13						19 15			
Bletchley	d			16 17						17 17						18 17						19 19			
Leighton Buzzard	d			16 24						17 24						18 24						19 26			
Tring	d			16 34						17 34						18 34						19 36			
Berkhamsted	d			16 39						17 39						18 39						19 41			
Hemel Hempstead	d			16 43						17 43						18 43						19 45			
Watford Junction	d			16 51						17 51						18 51						19 54			
Harrow & Wealdstone ⊖	d			16 59						17 59						18 59						20 02			
Wembley Central ⊖	d			17u05						18u05						19u05						20u06			
Stratford [7] ⊖	d		16 20		16 35	16 50		17 05	17 21			17 36	17 50	18 05	18 20		18 35	18 50	19 05				19 37		20 05
Highbury & Islington ⊖	d		16 35		16 50	17 05		17 20	17 35			17 50	18 05	18 20	18 35		18 50	19 05	19 20				19 52		20 20
Gospel Oak	d		16 45		17 00	17 15		17 30	17 45			18 00	18 15	18 30	18 45		19 00	19 15	19 30				20 01		20 30
West Hampstead ⊖	d		16 51		17 06	17 21		17 36	17 51			18 06	18 21	18 36	18 51		19 06	19 21	19 36				20 07		20 36
Willesden Jn. High Level ⊖	d		17 01		17 16	17 31		17 46	18 01			18 16	18 31	18 46	19 01		19 16	19 31	19 46	20 05			20 17	20 31	20 46
Shepherd's Bush ⊖	d		17 09	17 19	17 24	17 39	17 45	17 54	18 09	18 19		18 24	18 39	18 54	19 09	19 18	19 24	19 39	19 54	20 13		20 21	20 26	20 39	20 54
Kensington (Olympia) ⊖	d	17 00	17 11	17 22	17 26	17 41	17 47	17 56	18 11	18 22		18 26	18 41	18 56	19 11	19 20	19 26	19 41	19 56	20 15		20 23	20 28	20 41	20 56
West Brompton ⊖	d	17 02	17 13	17 25	17 28	17 43	17 50	17 58	18 13	18 25		18 28	18 43	18 58	19 13	19 23	19 28	19 43	19 58	20 17		20 25	20 30	20 43	20 58
Imperial Wharf	d	17 05	17 16	17 28	17 31	17 46	17 53	18 01	18 16	18 27		18 31	18 46	19 01	19 16	19 25	19 31	19 46	20 01	20 20		20 28	20 33	20 46	21 01
Clapham Junction [10]	a	17 09	17 27	17 32	17 38	17 57	17 57	18 10	18 25	18 32		18 40	18 53	19 12	19 26	19 30	19 38	19 53	20 08	20 29		20 33	20 40	20 55	21 08
	d			17 33			18 02			18 34						19 34									
Wandsworth Road	a																								
Wandsworth Common	a			17 36			18 05			18 37						19 37									
Balham [4]	a			17 39			18 08			18 40						19 40									
Streatham Common [4]	a			17 46			18 15			18 46						19 45									
Norbury	a			17 48			18 18			18 49						19 48									
Thornton Heath	a			17 51			18 21			18 52						19 51									
Selhurst [4]	a			17 54			18 24			18 54						19 53									
East Croydon 🚋	a			17 59			18 32			19 02															
South Croydon	a						18 35																		

Milton Keynes Central, Watford Junction, Kensington (Olympia) - Clapham Junction and East Croydon

		LO	SN 1	LO	LO	LO	LO	SN 1	LO	LO	SN 1	LO	SN 1	LO	SN 1
Milton Keynes Central 10	d		20 13					21 13					22 11		
Bletchley	d		20 17					21 17					22 15		
Leighton Buzzard	d		20 24					21 24					22 22		
Tring	d		20 34					21 34					22 34		
Berkhamsted	d		20 39					21 39					22 39		
Hemel Hempstead	d		20 43					21 43					22 43		
Watford Junction	d		20 51					21 51			22 27		22 54		23 29
Harrow & Wealdstone ⊖	d		20 59					21 59			22 33		23 01		23 35
Wembley Central ⊖	d		21u04												
Stratford 7 ⊖	d			20 35		21 05			21 35						
Highbury & Islington ⊖	d			20 50		21 20			21 50						
Gospel Oak	d			21 00		21 30			22 00						
West Hampstead ⊖	d			21 06		21 36			22 06						
Willesden Jn. High Level ⊖	d	21 01		21 16	21 31	21 46	22 01		22 16	22 31		23 01		23 40	
Shepherd's Bush ⊖	d	21 09	21 22	21 26	21 39	21 54	22 09	22 23	22 26	22 39	22 49	23 09	23 21	23 48	23 54
Kensington (Olympia) ⊖	d	21 11	21 24	21 28	21 41	21 56	22 11	22 25	22 28	22 41	22 51	23 11	23 23	23 50	23 56
West Brompton ⊖	d	21 13	21 27	21 30	21 43	21 58	22 13	22 27	22 30	22 43	22 54	23 13	23 26	23 52	23 59
Imperial Wharf	d	21 16	21 29	21 33	21 46	22 01	22 16	22 30	22 33	22 46	22 56	23 16	23 28	23 55	00 02
Clapham Junction 10	a	21 25	21 34	21 40	21 55	22 08	22 25	22 34	22 40	22 55	23 01	23 25	23 33	00 04	00 07
	d												23 40		
Wandsworth Road	a														
Wandsworth Common	a														
Balham 4	a												23 44		
Streatham Common 4	a												23 48		
Norbury	a												23 51		
Thornton Heath	a												23 54		
Selhurst 4	a												23 56		
East Croydon	a												00 01		
South Croydon	a														

Saturdays

		SN 1	LO	SN 1	LO	SN 1	LO	LO	LO	SN 1	LO	LO	LO	LO	SN 1	LO	LO	LO	LO	SN 1	LO	LO	LO
Milton Keynes Central 10	d	22p11													07 13					08 13			
Bletchley	d	22p15													07 17					08 17			
Leighton Buzzard	d	22p22													07 24					08 24			
Tring	d	22p34													07 34					08 34			
Berkhamsted	d	22p39													07 39					08 39			
Hemel Hempstead	d	22p43													07 43					08 43			
Watford Junction	d	22p54		23p29		05 52				06 55					07 52					08 52			
Harrow & Wealdstone ⊖	d	23p01		23p35		05 58				07 01					07 59					08 59			
Wembley Central ⊖	d									07 06					08u04					09u04			
Stratford 7 ⊖	d							06 05			06 35		07 05			07 35		08 05			08 35		09 05
Highbury & Islington ⊖	d							06 20			06 50		07 20			07 50		08 20			08 50		09 20
Gospel Oak	d							06 30			07 00		07 30			08 00		08 30			09 00		09 30
West Hampstead ⊖	d							06 36			07 06		07 36			08 06		08 36			09 06		09 36
Willesden Jn. High Level ⊖	d		23p40		06 02		06 31	06 46	07 01		07 16	07 31	07 46	08 01		08 16	08 31	08 46	09 01		09 16	09 31	09 46
Shepherd's Bush ⊖	d	23p21	23p48	23p54	06 10	06 20	06 39	06 54	07 09	07 19	07 24	07 39	07 54	08 09	08 19	08 24	08 39	08 54	09 09	09 19	09 24	09 39	09 54
Kensington (Olympia) ⊖	d	23p23	23p50	23p56	06 12	06 23	06 41	06 56	07 11	07 22	07 26	07 41	07 56	08 11	08 22	08 26	08 41	08 56	09 11	09 22	09 26	09 41	09 56
West Brompton ⊖	d	23p26	23p52	23p59	06 14	06 26	06 43	06 58	07 13	07 25	07 28	07 43	07 58	08 13	08 25	08 28	08 43	08 58	09 13	09 25	09 28	09 43	09 58
Imperial Wharf	d	23p28	23p55	00 02	06 17	06 28	06 46	07 01	07 16	07 27	07 31	07 46	08 01	08 16	08 27	08 31	08 46	09 01	09 16	09 27	09 31	09 46	10 01
Clapham Junction 10	a	23p33	00 04	00 07	06 26	06 33	06 55	07 08	07 25	07 33	07 38	07 55	08 08	08 25	08 33	08 38	08 55	09 08	09 25	09 33	09 38	09 55	10 08
	d	23p40				06 34				07 34					08 34					09 34			
Wandsworth Road	a																						
Wandsworth Common	a					06 37				07 37					08 37					09 37			
Balham 4	a	23p44				06 40				07 40					08 40					09 40			
Streatham Common 4	a	23p48				06 45				07 45					08 45					09 45			
Norbury	a	23p51				06 48				07 48					08 48					09 48			
Thornton Heath	a	23p54				06 51				07 51					08 51					09 51			
Selhurst 4	a	23p56				06 53				07 53					08 53					09 53			
East Croydon	a	00 01				06 57				07 57					08 57					09 57			
South Croydon	a					07 01				08 01					09 01					10 01			

Table 176

Saturdays

Milton Keynes Central, Watford Junction, Kensington (Olympia) - Clapham Junction and East Croydon

		LO	SN 1	LO	LO	LO		LO	SN 1	LO	LO	LO	LO	SN 1	LO	LO		LO	LO	SN 1	LO	LO	LO	LO	SN 1
Milton Keynes Central 10	d		09 13						10 13					11 13						12 13					13 13
Bletchley	d		09 17						10 17					11 17						12 17					13 17
Leighton Buzzard	d		09 24						10 24					11 24						12 24					13 24
Tring	d		09 34						10 34					11 34						12 34					13 34
Berkhamsted	d		09 39						10 39					11 39						12 39					13 39
Hemel Hempstead	d		09 43						10 43					11 43						12 43					13 43
Watford Junction	d		09 52						10 52					11 52						12 52					13 52
Harrow & Wealdstone ⊖	d		09 59						10 59					11 59						12 59					13 59
Wembley Central ⊖	d		10u04						11u04					12u04						13u04					14u04
Stratford 7 ⊖	d			09 35		10 05				10 35		11 05			11 35			12 05			12 35		13 05		
Highbury & Islington ⊖	d			09 50		10 20				10 50		11 20			11 50			12 20			12 50		13 20		
Gospel Oak	d			10 00		10 30				11 00		11 30			12 00			12 30			13 00		13 30		
West Hampstead ⊖	d			10 06		10 36				11 06		11 36			12 06			12 36			13 06		13 36		
Willesden Jn. High Level ⊖	d	10 01		10 16	10 31	10 46		11 01		11 16	11 31	11 46	12 01		12 16	12 31		12 46	13 01		13 16	13 31	13 46	14 01	
Shepherd's Bush ⊖	d	10 09	10 19	10 24	10 39	10 54		11 09	11 19	11 24	11 39	11 54	12 09	12 19	12 24	12 39		12 54	13 09	13 19	13 24	13 39	13 54	14 09	14 19
Kensington (Olympia) ⊖	d	10 11	10 22	10 26	10 41	10 56		11 11	11 22	11 26	11 41	11 56	12 11	12 22	12 26	12 41		12 56	13 11	13 22	13 26	13 41	13 56	14 11	14 22
West Brompton ⊖	d	10 13	10 25	10 28	10 43	10 58		11 13	11 25	11 28	11 43	11 58	12 13	12 25	12 28	12 43		12 58	13 13	13 25	13 28	13 43	13 58	14 13	14 25
Imperial Wharf	d	10 16	10 27	10 31	10 46	11 01		11 16	11 27	11 31	11 46	12 01	12 16	12 27	12 31	12 46		13 01	13 16	13 27	13 31	13 46	14 01	14 16	14 27
Clapham Junction 10	a	10 25	10 33	10 38	10 55	11 08		11 25	11 33	11 38	11 55	12 08	12 25	12 33	12 38	12 55		13 08	13 25	13 33	13 38	13 55	14 08	14 25	14 33
	d		10 34						11 34					12 34						13 34					14 34
Wandsworth Road	a																								
Wandsworth Common	a		10 37						11 37					12 37						13 37					14 37
Balham 4	a		10 40						11 40					12 40						13 40					14 40
Streatham Common 4	a		10 45						11 45					12 45						13 45					14 45
Norbury	a		10 48						11 48					12 48						13 48					14 48
Thornton Heath	a		10 51						11 51					12 51						13 51					14 51
Selhurst 4	a		10 53						11 53					12 53						13 53					14 53
East Croydon	a		10 57						11 57					12 57						13 57					14 57
South Croydon	a		11 01						12 01					13 01						14 01					15 01

		LO		LO	LO	LO	SN 1	LO	LO	LO	LO	SN 1		LO	LO	LO	LO	SN 1	LO	LO	LO	LO		SN 1	LO
Milton Keynes Central 10	d						14 13					15 13						16 13						17 13	
Bletchley	d						14 17					15 17						16 17						17 17	
Leighton Buzzard	d						14 24					15 24						16 24						17 24	
Tring	d						14 34					15 34						16 34						17 34	
Berkhamsted	d						14 39					15 39						16 39						17 39	
Hemel Hempstead	d						14 43					15 43						16 43						17 43	
Watford Junction	d						14 52					15 52						16 52						17 52	
Harrow & Wealdstone ⊖	d						14 59					15 59						16 59						17 59	
Wembley Central ⊖	d						15u04					16u04						17u04						18u04	
Stratford 7 ⊖	d	13 35			14 05			14 35		15 05				15 35		16 05			16 35		17 05				17 35
Highbury & Islington ⊖	d	13 50			14 20			14 50		15 20				15 50		16 20			16 50		17 20				17 50
Gospel Oak	d	14 00			14 30			15 00		15 30				16 00		16 30			17 00		17 30				18 00
West Hampstead ⊖	d	14 06			14 36			15 06		15 36				16 06		16 36			17 06		17 36				18 06
Willesden Jn. High Level ⊖	d	14 16		14 31	14 46	15 01		15 16	15 31	15 46	16 01			16 16	16 31	16 46	17 01		17 16	17 31	17 46	18 01			18 16
Shepherd's Bush ⊖	d	14 24		14 39	14 54	15 09	15 19	15 24	15 39	15 54	16 09	16 19		16 24	16 39	16 54	17 09	17 19	17 24	17 39	17 54	18 09		18 19	18 24
Kensington (Olympia) ⊖	d	14 26		14 41	14 56	15 11	15 22	15 26	15 41	15 56	16 11	16 22		16 26	16 41	16 56	17 11	17 22	17 26	17 41	17 56	18 11		18 22	18 26
West Brompton ⊖	d	14 28		14 43	14 58	15 13	15 25	15 28	15 43	15 58	16 13	16 25		16 28	16 43	16 58	17 13	17 25	17 28	17 43	17 58	18 13		18 25	18 28
Imperial Wharf	d	14 31		14 46	15 01	15 16	15 27	15 31	15 46	16 01	16 16	16 27		16 31	16 46	17 01	17 16	17 27	17 31	17 46	18 01	18 16		18 27	18 31
Clapham Junction 10	a	14 38		14 55	15 08	15 25	15 33	15 38	15 55	16 08	16 25	16 33		16 38	16 55	17 08	17 25	17 32	17 38	17 55	18 08	18 25		18 32	18 38
	d						15 34					16 34						17 34						18 34	
Wandsworth Road	a																								
Wandsworth Common	a						15 37					16 37						17 37						18 37	
Balham 4	a						15 40					16 40						17 40						18 40	
Streatham Common 4	a						15 45					16 45						17 45						18 45	
Norbury	a						15 48					16 48						17 48						18 48	
Thornton Heath	a						15 51					16 51						17 51						18 51	
Selhurst 4	a						15 53					16 53						17 53						18 53	
East Croydon	a						15 57					16 57						17 57						18 57	
South Croydon	a						16 01					17 01						18 01						19 01	

Table 176

Saturdays

Milton Keynes Central, Watford Junction, Kensington (Olympia) - Clapham Junction and East Croydon

		LO	LO	LO	SN 1	LO	LO	LO		SN 1	LO	SN 1	LO	LO	LO	SN 1	LO	LO		LO	LO	SN 1	LO	LO	LO
Milton Keynes Central 10	d				18 13							19 13													
Bletchley	d				18 17							19 17													
Leighton Buzzard	d				18 24							19 24													
Tring	d				18 34							19 34													
Berkhamsted	d				18 39							19 39													
Hemel Hempstead	d				18 43							19 43													
Watford Junction	d				18 52					19 31		19 51				20 43						21 43			
Harrow & Wealdstone ⊖	d				18 59					19 38		19 58				20 50						21 50			
Wembley Central ⊖	d				19u04					19 43															
Stratford 7 ⊖	d		18 05			18 35		19 05					19 35		20 05			20 35			21 05			21 35	
Highbury & Islington ⊖	d		18 20			18 50		19 20					19 50		20 20			20 50			21 20			21 50	
Gospel Oak	d		18 30			19 00		19 30					20 00		20 30			21 00			21 30			22 00	
West Hampstead ⊖	d		18 36			19 06		19 36					20 06		20 36			21 06			21 36			22 06	
Willesden Jn. High Level ⊖	d	18 31	18 46	19 01		19 16	19 31	19 46			20 01		20 16	20 31	20 46		21 01	21 16		21 31	21 46		22 01	22 16	22 31
Shepherd's Bush ⊖	d	18 39	18 54	19 09	19 19	19 24	19 39	19 54		19 57	20 09	20 19	20 24	20 39	20 54	21 07	21 10	21 24		21 39	21 54	22 07	22 10	22 24	22 39
Kensington (Olympia) ⊖	d	18 41	18 56	19 11	19 22	19 26	19 41	19 56		20 00	20 11	20 22	20 26	20 41	20 56	21 10	21 12	21 26		21 41	21 56	22 10	22 12	22 26	22 41
West Brompton ⊖	d	18 43	18 58	19 13	19 25	19 28	19 43	19 58		20 03	20 13	20 25	20 28	20 43	20 58	21 13	21 14	21 28		21 43	21 58	22 13	22 14	22 28	22 43
Imperial Wharf	d	18 46	19 01	19 16	19 27	19 31	19 46	20 01		20 05	20 16	20 27	20 31	20 46	21 01	21 15	21 17	21 31		21 46	22 01	22 15	22 17	22 31	22 46
Clapham Junction 10	a	18 55	19 08	19 25	19 32	19 38	19 55	20 08		20 10	20 25	20 32	20 38	20 55	21 08	21 20	21 27	21 38		21 55	22 08	22 20	22 27	22 38	22 55
	d				19 34							20 34													
Wandsworth Road	a																								
Wandsworth Common	a				19 37							20 37													
Balham 4	a				19 40							20 40													
Streatham Common 4	a				19 45							20 45													
Norbury	a				19 48							20 48													
Thornton Heath	a				19 51							20 51													
Selhurst 4	a				19 53							20 53													
East Croydon	a				19 57							20 59													
South Croydon	a																								

		LO	SN 1	LO		SN 1
Milton Keynes Central 10	d					
Bletchley	d					
Leighton Buzzard	d					
Tring	d					
Berkhamsted	d					
Hemel Hempstead	d					
Watford Junction	d		22 48			23 25
Harrow & Wealdstone ⊖	d		22 55			23 31
Wembley Central ⊖	d					
Stratford 7 ⊖	d					
Highbury & Islington ⊖	d					
Gospel Oak	d					
West Hampstead ⊖	d					
Willesden Jn. High Level ⊖	d	23 01		23 31		
Shepherd's Bush ⊖	d	23 09	23 14	23 39		23 49
Kensington (Olympia) ⊖	d	23 11	23 16	23 41		23 51
West Brompton ⊖	d	23 13	23 19	23 43		23 54
Imperial Wharf	d	23 16	23 21	23 46		23 57
Clapham Junction 10	a	23 25	23 26	23 55		00 02
	d					
Wandsworth Road	a					
Wandsworth Common	a					
Balham 4	a					
Streatham Common 4	a					
Norbury	a					
Thornton Heath	a					
Selhurst 4	a					
East Croydon	a					
South Croydon	a					

Table 176

Sundays

Milton Keynes Central, Watford Junction, Kensington (Olympia) - Clapham Junction and East Croydon

		SN 1 A	SN 1	SN 1	LO	LO	SN 1	LO	LO	LO	LO	SN 1	LO	LO	LO	LO	SN 1	LO	LO	LO	LO	SN 1	LO
Milton Keynes Central 10	d																						
Bletchley	d																						
Leighton Buzzard	d																						
Tring	d																						
Berkhamsted	d																						
Hemel Hempstead	d																						
Watford Junction	d	23p25					09 17					10 17					11 22					12 22	
Harrow & Wealdstone ⊖	d	23p31					09 23					10 23					11 28					12 29	
Wembley Central ⊖	d																						
Stratford 7 ⊖	d														10 35			11 05		11 35			12 05
Highbury & Islington ⊖	d														10 50			11 20		11 50			12 20
Gospel Oak	d														11 00			11 30		12 00			12 30
West Hampstead ⊖	d														11 06			11 36		12 06			12 36
Willesden Jn. High Level ⊖	d				09 02	09 32		09 48	10 02	10 16	10 32		10 46	11 02	11 16	11 32		11 46	12 02	12 16	12 32		12 46
Shepherd's Bush ⊖	d	23p49	07 47	08 50	09 10	09 40	09 45	09 54	10 10	10 24	10 40	10 45	10 55	11 10	11 24	11 40	11 45	11 54	12 10	12 24	12 40	12 45	12 54
Kensington (Olympia) ⊖	d	23p51	07 49	08 53	09 12	09 42	09 48	09 56	10 12	10 26	10 42	10 48	10 56	11 12	11 26	11 42	11 48	11 56	12 12	12 26	12 42	12 48	12 56
West Brompton ⊖	d	23p54	07 51	08 56	09 14	09 44	09 50	09 58	10 14	10 28	10 44	10 50	10 58	11 14	11 28	11 44	11 50	11 58	12 14	12 28	12 44	12 50	12 58
Imperial Wharf	d	23p57	07 54	08 58	09 17	09 47	09 53	10 01	10 17	10 31	10 47	10 53	11 01	11 17	11 31	11 47	11 53	12 01	12 17	12 31	12 47	12 53	13 01
Clapham Junction 10	a	00 02	07 58	09 03	09 25	09 55	09 58	10 09	10 25	10 38	10 55	10 58	11 08	11 30	11 39	11 55	11 58	12 08	12 25	12 38	12 55	12 58	13 08
	d																						
Wandsworth Road	a																						
Wandsworth Common	a																						
Balham 4	a																						
Streatham Common 4	a																						
Norbury	a																						
Thornton Heath	a																						
Selhurst 4	a																						
East Croydon	a																						
South Croydon	a																						

		LO	LO	LO	SN 1	LO	LO	LO	LO	SN 1	LO	LO	LO	LO	SN 1	LO	LO	LO	LO	SN 1	LO	LO	LO
Milton Keynes Central 10	d																						
Bletchley	d																						
Leighton Buzzard	d																						
Tring	d																						
Berkhamsted	d																						
Hemel Hempstead	d																						
Watford Junction	d				13 22					14 22					15 22					16 22			
Harrow & Wealdstone ⊖	d				13 28					14 28					15 28					16 28			
Wembley Central ⊖	d																						
Stratford 7 ⊖	d		12 35			13 05		13 35			14 05		14 35			15 05		15 35			16 05		16 35
Highbury & Islington ⊖	d		12 50			13 20		13 50			14 20		14 50			15 20		15 50			16 20		16 50
Gospel Oak	d		13 00			13 30		14 00			14 30		15 00			15 30		16 00			16 30		17 00
West Hampstead ⊖	d		13 06			13 36		14 06			14 36		15 06			15 36		16 06			16 36		17 06
Willesden Jn. High Level ⊖	d	13 02	13 16	13 32		13 46	14 02	14 16	14 32		14 46	15 02	15 16	15 32		15 46	16 02	16 16	16 32		16 46	17 02	17 16
Shepherd's Bush ⊖	d	13 10	13 24	13 40	13 45	13 54	14 10	14 24	14 40	14 45	14 54	15 10	15 24	15 40	15 45	15 54	16 10	16 24	16 40	16 45	16 54	17 10	17 24
Kensington (Olympia) ⊖	d	13 12	13 26	13 42	13 48	13 56	14 12	14 26	14 42	14 48	14 56	15 12	15 26	15 42	15 48	15 56	16 12	16 26	16 42	16 48	16 56	17 12	17 26
West Brompton ⊖	d	13 14	13 28	13 44	13 50	13 58	14 14	14 28	14 44	14 50	14 58	15 14	15 28	15 44	15 50	15 58	16 14	16 28	16 44	16 50	16 58	17 14	17 28
Imperial Wharf	d	13 17	13 31	13 47	13 53	14 01	14 17	14 31	14 47	14 53	15 01	15 17	15 31	15 47	15 53	16 01	16 17	16 31	16 47	16 53	17 01	17 17	17 31
Clapham Junction 10	a	13 25	13 38	13 55	13 58	14 08	14 25	14 38	14 56	14 58	15 08	15 25	15 38	15 55	15 58	16 08	16 25	16 38	16 56	16 58	17 08	17 26	17 38
	d																						
Wandsworth Road	a																						
Wandsworth Common	a																						
Balham 4	a																						
Streatham Common 4	a																						
Norbury	a																						
Thornton Heath	a																						
Selhurst 4	a																						
East Croydon	a																						
South Croydon	a																						

A not 22 May

Table 176

Sundays

Milton Keynes Central, Watford Junction, Kensington (Olympia) - Clapham Junction and East Croydon

		LO		SN 1	LO	LO	LO	LO	SN 1	LO	LO	LO		LO	SN 1	LO	LO	LO	LO	SN 1	LO	LO		LO	LO
Milton Keynes Central 10	d																								
Bletchley	d																								
Leighton Buzzard	d																								
Tring	d																								
Berkhamsted	d																								
Hemel Hempstead	d																								
Watford Junction	d			17 22					18 22						19 22					20 22					
Harrow & Wealdstone ⊖	d			17 28					18 28						19 28					20 28					
Wembley Central ⊖	d																								
Stratford 7 ⊖	d				17 05		17 35			18 05		18 35				19 05		19 35			20 05			20 35	
Highbury & Islington ⊖	d				17 20		17 50			18 20		18 50				19 20		19 50			20 20			20 50	
Gospel Oak	d				17 30		18 00			18 30		19 00				19 30		20 00			20 30			21 00	
West Hampstead ⊖	d				17 36		18 06			18 36		19 06				19 36		20 06			20 36			21 06	
Willesden Jn. High Level ⊖	d	17 32			17 46	18 02	18 16	18 32		18 46	19 02	19 16		19 32		19 46	20 02	20 16	20 32		20 46	21 02		21 16	21 32
Shepherd's Bush ⊖	d	17 40		17 45	17 54	18 10	18 24	18 40	18 45	18 54	19 10	19 24		19 40	19 45	19 54	20 10	20 24	20 40	20 45	20 54	21 10		21 24	21 40
Kensington (Olympia) ⊖	d	17 42		17 48	17 56	18 12	18 26	18 42	18 48	18 56	19 12	19 26		19 42	19 48	19 56	20 12	20 26	20 42	20 48	20 56	21 12		21 26	21 42
West Brompton ⊖	d	17 44		17 50	17 58	18 14	18 28	18 44	18 50	18 58	19 14	19 28		19 44	19 50	19 58	20 14	20 28	20 44	20 50	20 58	21 14		21 28	21 44
Imperial Wharf	d	17 47		17 53	18 01	18 17	18 31	18 47	18 53	19 01	19 17	19 31		19 47	19 53	20 01	20 17	20 31	20 47	20 53	21 01	21 17		21 31	21 47
Clapham Junction 10	a	17 56		17 58	18 08	18 26	18 38	18 56	18 58	19 08	19 26	19 38		19 56	19 58	20 08	20 26	20 38	20 56	20 58	21 08	21 26		21 38	21 56
	d																								
Wandsworth Road	a																								
Wandsworth Common	a																								
Balham 4	a																								
Streatham Common 4	a																								
Norbury	a																								
Thornton Heath	a																								
Selhurst 4	a																								
East Croydon	a																								
South Croydon	a																								

		SN 1	LO	LO	LO	SN 1	LO	LO		SN 1
Milton Keynes Central 10	d									
Bletchley	d									
Leighton Buzzard	d									
Tring	d									
Berkhamsted	d									
Hemel Hempstead	d									
Watford Junction	d	21 17				22 17				23 17
Harrow & Wealdstone ⊖	d	21 23				22 23				23 23
Wembley Central ⊖	d									
Stratford 7 ⊖	d									
Highbury & Islington ⊖	d									
Gospel Oak	d									
West Hampstead ⊖	d									
Willesden Jn. High Level ⊖	d		21 46	22 02	22 32		22 46	23 16		
Shepherd's Bush ⊖	d	21 45	21 54	22 10	22 40	22 45	22 54	23 24		23 45
Kensington (Olympia) ⊖	d	21 48	21 56	22 12	22 42	22 48	22 56	23 26		23 48
West Brompton ⊖	d	21 50	21 58	22 14	22 44	22 50	22 58	23 28		23 50
Imperial Wharf	d	21 53	22 01	22 17	22 47	22 53	23 01	23 31		23 53
Clapham Junction 10	a	21 58	22 11	22 26	22 56	22 58	23 13	23 43		23 58
	d									00 05
Wandsworth Road	a									
Wandsworth Common	a									
Balham 4	a									
Streatham Common 4	a									
Norbury	a									
Thornton Heath	a									
Selhurst 4	a									00 18
East Croydon	a									00 22
South Croydon	a									

Network Diagram for Tables 177, 178, 179, 181, 182 | also 175★

DM-17/10
Design BAJS

© Network Rail OPSU 2010
All rights reserved

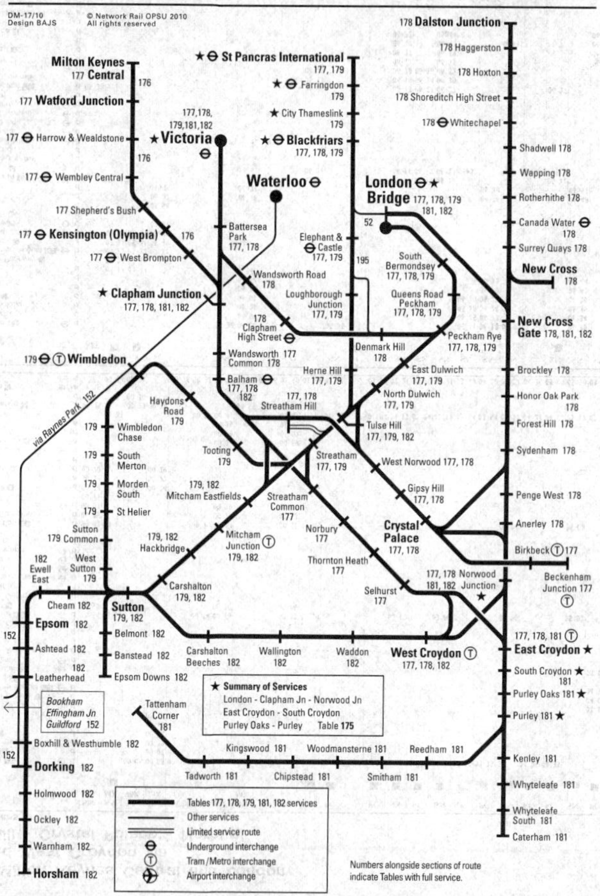

Luton, Milton Keynes Central and London East and West Croydon via Tulse Hill - Crystal Palace - Norbury

Local Services

Miles	Miles	Miles	Miles	Miles			SN MX 1	SN MO	SN MX	SN MX	SN MO	SN MX	SN MX	SN MX 1	SN MO	SN MX 1	SN MO	LO MO	SN MX	SN MO 1	SN MX		SN MX	FC MX	LO MX
—	0	—	—	0	London Bridge 4 ⊖	d		23p21		23p36	23p39	23p33									23p48			23p58	
—	1¾	—	—	1¾	South Bermondsey	d		23p25				23p37									23p52				
—	2¾	—	—	2¾	Queens Rd Peckham	d		23p27				23p39									23p54				
—	3½	—	—	3½	Peckham Rye 4	d		23p30				23p42									23p57				
—	4¼	—	—	4¼	East Dulwich	d		23p33				23p45									00 01				
—	4¾	—	—	4¾	North Dulwich	d		23p35				23p47									00 03				
—	—	—	—	—	Luton 10	d																			
—	—	—	—	—	Luton Airport Parkway 7	d																			
—	—	—	—	—	St Pancras International 15 ⊖	d																			
—	—	—	—	—	City Thameslink 3	d																			
—	—	—	—	—	London Blackfriars 3 ⊖	d																			
—	—	—	—	—	Elephant & Castle ⊖	d																			
—	—	—	—	—	Loughborough Jn	d																			
—	—	—	—	—	Herne Hill 4	d																			
—	6	—	—	6	Tulse Hill 3	d		23p39				23p51									00 06			00 10	
—	7½	—	—	—	Streatham 4	d		23p42													00 10			00a14	
0	—	0	0	—	London Victoria 15 ⊖	d			23p34				23p38	23p47	23p47	23p49	23p50		23p51				23p54		
1¼	—	1¼	1¼	—	Battersea Park 4	d			23p38				23p42						23p55				23p58		
—	—	—	—	—	Milton Keynes Central	d	22p11																		
—	—	—	—	—	Watford Junction	d	22p54													23p17					
—	—	—	—	—	Harrow & Wealdstone ⊖	d	23p01													23p23					
—	—	—	—	—	Wembley Central ⊖	d																			
—	—	—	—	—	Shepherd's Bush ⊖	d	23p21													23p45					
—	—	—	—	—	Kensington (Olympia) ⊖	d	23p23													23p48					
—	—	—	—	—	West Brompton ⊖	d	23p26													23p50					
—	—	—	—	—	Imperial Wharf	d	23p28													23p53					
2¾	—	2¾	2¾	—	Clapham Junction 10	d	23b40		23p42				23p46	23p53	23p53	23p56	23p56		23p59	00 05			00 02		
4	—	4	4	—	Wandsworth Common	d			23p45				23p49				23p59		00 02				00 05		
4¾	—	4¾	4¾	—	Balham 4 ⊖	d	23p44		23p47				23p51				00 02		00 04				00 07		
5¾	—	5¾	—	—	Streatham Hill	d							23p54										00 10		
7	—	7	—	6½	West Norwood 4	d						23p54	23p58										00 14		
8	—	8	—	7½	Gipsy Hill	d						23p57	00 01										00 17		
8¾	—	8¾	—	8¼	Crystal Palace 4	d						23p59	00 03										00a19		
—	—	10¼	—	—	Birkbeck 🚊	d																			
—	—	11¾	—	—	Beckenham Junction 4 🚊	a																			
—	8	—	6½	—	Streatham Common 4	d	23p48	23p48	23p51								00 06		00 08		00 13				
—	9	—	7½	—	Norbury	d	23p51	23p51	23p54								00 08		00 11		00 15				
—	10¼	—	8¾	—	Thornton Heath	d	23p54	23p54	23p57								00 11		00 14		00 18				
—	11	—	9½	—	Selhurst 4	d	23p57	23p57	23p59								00 14		00 17	00 19	00 21				
10¼	—	—	—	9¾	Norwood Junction 2	a				23p59	00 02	00 04	00 08												
—	—	—	—	—		d				23p59	00 03		00 09					00 08							00 20
—	12	—	—	—	West Croydon 4 🚊	a			00 03				00 14					00 15	00 21		00 27				00 27
11½	—	—	10½	11	East Croydon 🚊	a	00 01	00 01		00 03	00 06			00 05	00 06	00 09	00 17			00 22					

b Previous night, arr. 2333

Luton, Milton Keynes Central and London East and West Croydon via Tulse Hill - Crystal Palace - Norbury

Local Services

		SN MO	SN MX ◇1	SN MX	SN MX	FC	SN 1	SN	SN MX	FC	SN	SN ◇1	FC 1		FC 1	SN 1	FC 1	SN 1	FC	FC 1	SN ◇1	FC 1	FC 1	SN ◇1	FC 1
London Bridge	d			00 06	00 03	00 12			00 36	00 42			01 05		01 35		02 05		03 05	03 35		04 05	04 35		
South Bermondsey	d				00 07																				
Queens Rd Peckham	d				00 09																				
Peckham Rye	d				00 12																				
East Dulwich	d				00 15																				
North Dulwich	d				00 17																				
Luton	d																								04 06
Luton Airport Parkway	d																								04 08
St Pancras International	d																								04 54
City Thameslink	d																								
London Blackfriars	d																								05 04
Elephant & Castle	d																								
Loughborough Jn.	d																								
Herne Hill	d																								
Tulse Hill	d				00 21																				
Streatham	d																								
London Victoria	d	23p54	00 05				00 14	00 16			00 42	01 00				02 00		03 00			04 00			05 02	
Battersea Park	d	23p58						00 20			00 46														
Milton Keynes Central	d																								
Watford Junction	d																								
Harrow & Wealdstone	d																								
Wembley Central	d																								
Shepherd's Bush	d																								
Kensington (Olympia)	d																								
West Brompton	d																								
Imperial Wharf	d																								
Clapham Junction	d	00 02	00 11				00 20	00 24			00 50	01 08				02 08		03 08			04 08			05 08	
Wandsworth Common	d	00 05						00 27			00 53														
Balham	d	00 07						00 29			00 55														
Streatham Hill	d	00 11																							
West Norwood	d	00 14			00 24																				
Gipsy Hill	d	00 17			00 27																				
Crystal Palace	d	00 20			00 29																				
Birkbeck	d																								
Beckenham Junction	a																								
Streatham Common	d							00 33			00 59														
Norbury	d							00 36			01 02														
Thornton Heath	d							00 39			01 05														
Selhurst	d		00 21				00 28	00 41			01 07	01 17	01 26		01 54	02 17	02 24	03 17	03 24	03 54	04 17	04 24	04 54	05 17	05 27
Norwood Junction	a	00 25		00 29	00 34				00 59																
	d			00 30					01 00																
West Croydon	a																								
East Croydon	a		00 24	00 33		00 26	00 31	00 44	01 03	00 56	01 10	01 21	01 32		02 02	02 21	02 30	03 21	03 30	04 00	04 21	04 30	05 00	05 20	05 30

		SN ◇1	FC 1	FC 1	FC		SN	SN	SN	LO	LO	SN	SN	FC 1	LO	SN	SN	SN	SN	SN	SN		SN ◇1	SN	SN
London Bridge	d							05 36	06 00				06 06						06 11	06 18	06 19			06 30	
South Bermondsey	d								06 04										06 15	06 22				06 34	
Queens Rd Peckham	d								06 06										06 18	06 24				06 36	
Peckham Rye	d								06 09										06 20	06 27				06 39	
East Dulwich	d								06 12											06 30				06 42	
North Dulwich	d								06 14											06 32				06 44	
Luton	d		04 34	04 44										05 24											
Luton Airport Parkway	d		04 36	04 46										05 26											
St Pancras International	d		05 12	05 32	05 38									06 02											
City Thameslink	d		05 21	05 41	05 45									06 11											
London Blackfriars	d		05 24	05 44	05 48									06 14											
Elephant & Castle	d				05 51																				
Loughborough Jn.	d																								
Herne Hill	d				05 58																				
Tulse Hill	d				06 02				06 18											06 36				06 48	
Streatham	d				06a05				06a21											06 39				06a51	
London Victoria	d	05 32										06 00				06 07	06 13	06 19					06 21		
Battersea Park	d											06 04				06 11	06 17	06 23	06a32						
Milton Keynes Central	d																								
Watford Junction	d																								
Harrow & Wealdstone	d																								
Wembley Central	d																								
Shepherd's Bush	d																								
Kensington (Olympia)	d																								
West Brompton	d																								
Imperial Wharf	d																								
Clapham Junction	d	05 38										06 08				06 15	06 21	06 27					06 27		
Wandsworth Common	d											06 11				06 18	06 24	06 30							
Balham	d											06 13				06 20	06 26	06 32							
Streatham Hill	d															06 23		06 35							06 42
West Norwood	d															06 27		06 39							06 45
Gipsy Hill	d															06 30		06 42			06a41				06 48
Crystal Palace	d															06 32		06a44							06a51
Birkbeck	d																								
Beckenham Junction	a																								
Streatham Common	d											06 17					06 30			06 42					
Norbury	d											06 20					06 33			06 45					
Thornton Heath	d											06 23					06 36			06 48					
Selhurst	d											06 26					06 39			06 51					
Norwood Junction	a							06 00					06 29			06 37									
	d						05 53	06 00		06 05	06 20		06 30		06 35	06 39									
West Croydon	a						05 57	06 05		06 13	06 30	06 31			06 41	06 44				06 55					

Luton, Milton Keynes Central and London East and West Croydon via Tulse Hill - Crystal Palace - Norbury

Local Services

		SN	LO	SN	SN ◇1	FC 1	FC	SN	LO	SN	SN	SN ◇1	SN		SN	SN	SN	SN 1	FC 1	SN	SN	SN	SN	LO	SN
London Bridge	d	06 33						06 36							06 41	06 48	06 51			06 54	06 58		07 03		
South Bermondsey	d	06 37													06 45	06 52					07 02		07 07		
Queens Rd Peckham	d	06 39													06 48	06 54					07 04		07 09		
Peckham Rye	d	06 42													06 50	06 57					07 07		07 12		
East Dulwich	d	06 45														07 00					07 10		07 15		
North Dulwich	d	06 47														07 02					07 12		07 17		
Luton	d					05 44	05 48												06 04						
Luton Airport Parkway	d					05 46	05 50												06 06						
St Pancras International	d					06 22	06 34												06 38						
City Thameslink	d					06 31	06 43												06 47						
London Blackfriars	d					06 34	06 46												06 50						
Elephant & Castle	d						06 49																		
Loughborough Jn.	d						06 53																		
Herne Hill	d						06 57																		
Tulse Hill	d	06 50					07 02									07 07					07 16		07 20		
Streatham	d						07a05									07 10					07a19				
London Victoria	d			06 30	06 32					06 36	06 44	06 47	06 49					06 51							07 00
Battersea Park	d			06 34						06 40			06 53		07a02										07 04
Milton Keynes Central	d																								
Watford Junction	d																								
Harrow & Wealdstone	d																								
Wembley Central	d																								
Shepherd's Bush	d																								
Kensington (Olympia)	d																								
West Brompton	d																								
Imperial Wharf	d																								
Clapham Junction	d			06 38	06 38					06 44	06 50	06 53	06 57					06 57							07 08
Wandsworth Common	d			06 41						06 47	06 53		07 00												07 11
Balham	d			06 44						06 49	06 56		07 02												07 13
Streatham Hill	d									06 53			07 05									07 12			
West Norwood	d	06 53								06 56			07 09									07 15	07 23		
Gipsy Hill	d	06 56								06 59			07 12				07a15					07 18	07 26		
Crystal Palace	d	06 59								07 02			07a14									07a21	07 29		
Birkbeck	d	07 03																					07 33		
Beckenham Junction	a	07 06																					07 36		
Streatham Common	d			06 48							07 00					07 13									07 18
Norbury	d			06 50							07 02					07 16									07 21
Thornton Heath	d			06 53							07 05					07 19									07 24
Selhurst	d			06 56							07 09					07 21									07 27
Norwood Junction	a							06 59		07 07										07 17					
	d		06 50					07 00	07 05	07 09										07 18				07 20	
West Croydon	a		07 00	07 02					07 11	07 13						07 25								07 30	07 32
East Croydon	a				06 48	06 55		07 03			07 12	07 03						07 06	07 14	07 21					

		SN 1	FC 1	SN	LO		SN	SN ◇1	SN	SN	SN	SN	FC 1	SN	SN 1	SN	SN	SN 1	SN	SN 1	LO		SN	SN 1	FC 1
London Bridge	d			07 06							07 11	07 16		07 21	07 27		07 29	07 30	07 33	07 33					
South Bermondsey	d										07 15	07 20					07 33		07 37						
Queens Rd Peckham	d										07 17	07 22					07 35		07 39						
Peckham Rye	d										07 20	07 25					07 38		07 42						
East Dulwich	d											07 28					07 41		07 45						
North Dulwich	d											07 30					07 43		07 47						
Luton	d		06 22										06 34												06 46
Luton Airport Parkway	d		06 24																						06 48
St Pancras International	d		06 58										07 06												07 20
City Thameslink	d		07 05										07 15												07 29
London Blackfriars	d		07 08										07 18												07 32
Elephant & Castle	d												07 21												
Loughborough Jn.	d												07 25												
Herne Hill	d												07 31												
Tulse Hill	d											07 34	07 37				07 47		07 50						
Streatham	d											07 37	07a40				07a51								
London Victoria	d	07 02					07 06	07 17	07 17	07 20						07 23							07 30	07 36	
Battersea Park	d						07 10		07 21	07 24	07a32												07 34		
Milton Keynes Central	d																								
Watford Junction	d																								
Harrow & Wealdstone	d																								
Wembley Central	d																								
Shepherd's Bush	d																								
Kensington (Olympia)	d																								
West Brompton	d																								
Imperial Wharf	d																								
Clapham Junction	d	07 08					07 14	07 23	07 25	07 28						07 30							07 38	07 42	
Wandsworth Common	d						07 17			07 31													07 41		
Balham	d						07 20		07 29	07 33													07 44		
Streatham Hill	d						07 23		07 32																
West Norwood	d						07 27		07 38										07 53						
Gipsy Hill	d						07 30		07 41					07a45					07 56						
Crystal Palace	d						07 32		07a43										07 59						
Birkbeck	d																		08 03						
Beckenham Junction	a																		08 06						
Streatham Common	d									07 37		07 40											07 48		
Norbury	d									07 40		07 43											07 50		
Thornton Heath	d									07 43		07 46											07 53		
Selhurst	d									07 46		07 51											07 56		
Norwood Junction	a			07 29			07 38								07 38			07 41							
	d			07 31	07 35		07 39								07 38			07 42			07 50				
West Croydon	a				07 42		07 44					07 55									08 00		08 02		
East Croydon	a	07 17	07 30	07 37				07 33		07 49					07 42	07 44		07 45		07 48				07 52	07 55

Luton, Milton Keynes Central and London East and West Croydon via Tulse Hill - Crystal Palace - Norbury

Local Services

	FC	FC ■1	SN	SN	SN	LO	SN ■1	SN	SN	SN	FC	SN ◇■1		SN	SN	SN ■1	SN ◇■1	SN ■1	SN	LO	SN	SN ◇■1	FC ■1	SN
London Bridge ■4 ⊖ d			07 36	07 41	07 46		07 56			07 47					07 51	07 53		08 02						08 03
South Bermondsey d				07 45																				08 07
Queens Rd Peckham d				07 47																				08 09
Peckham Rye ■4 d				07 50						07 53														08 12
East Dulwich d										07 56														08 15
North Dulwich d										07 58														08 17
Luton ■10 d	06 36	06 56									06 50												07 16	
Luton Airport Parkway ■7 d	06 38										06 52													
St Pancras International ■15 ⊖ d	07 24	07 28									07 32												07 48	
City Thameslink ■3 d	07 33	07 37									07 41												07 57	
London Blackfriars ■3 ⊖ d	07 36	07 40									07 44												08 00	
Elephant & Castle ⊖ d	07 40	07a43									07 47													
Loughborough Jn. d											07 51													
Herne Hill ■4 d	07a46										07 56													
Tulse Hill ■3 d										08 02	08 05												08 13	08 21
Streatham ■4 d										08 05	08a09													
London Victoria ■15 ⊖ d								07 36	07 45			07 47		07 52			07 52				08 03	08 07		
Battersea Park ■4 d				08a02				07 40													08 07			
Milton Keynes Central d																								
Watford Junction d																								
Harrow & Wealdstone ⊖ d																								
Wembley Central ⊖ d																								
Shepherd's Bush ⊖ d																								
Kensington (Olympia) ⊖ d																								
West Brompton ⊖ d																								
Imperial Wharf d																								
Clapham Junction ■10 d								07 44	07 51			07 53		07 58			07 58				08 11	08 13		
Wandsworth Common d								07 47	07 54												08 14			
Balham ■4 ⊖ d								07 50	07 57					08 03							08 16			
Streatham Hill d								07 53						08 06					08 15					
West Norwood ■4 d								07 58						08 09					08 19					08 24
Gipsy Hill d								08 01						08 12	08a15				08 22					08 27
Crystal Palace ■4 d								08 04						08a15					08a24					08 29
Birkbeck 🚊 d																								08 33
Beckenham Junction ■4 🚊 a																								08 37
Streatham Common ■4 d									08 01	08 08											08 20			
Norbury d									08 03	08 11											08 23			
Thornton Heath d									08 06	08 14											08 26			
Selhurst ■4 d									08 09	08 17											08 32			
Norwood Junction ■2 a			07 59				08 07	08 08										08 15						
d			08 00			08 05	08 07	08 09										08 15		08 20				
West Croydon ■4 🚊 a						08 12		08 14		08 22										08 30	08 36			
East Croydon 🚊 a			08 03		08 00		08 10		08 12			08 03				08 06	08 09	08 19				08 22	08 25	

	SN	SN	SN	SN ■1		LO	SN	SN	SN ◇■1	FC ■1	SN ◇■1	SN	SN	SN	SN	FC	SN	SN ■1	SN	SN		SN	SN ■1	SN ■1
London Bridge ■4 ⊖ d	08 06	08 14	08 06	08 08										08 10	08 17		08 20	08 23	08 24			08 27	08 32	
South Bermondsey d	08 11													08 14					08 28					
Queens Rd Peckham d	08 13													08 16					08 30					
Peckham Rye ■4 d	08 16													08 19	08 23				08 33					
East Dulwich d	08 19														08 26				08 36					
North Dulwich d	08 21														08 28				08 38					
Luton ■10 d										07 24						07 30								
Luton Airport Parkway ■7 d										07 26						07 32								
St Pancras International ■15 ⊖ d										08 00						08 12								
City Thameslink ■3 d										08 07						08 21								
London Blackfriars ■3 ⊖ d										08 10						08 24								
Elephant & Castle ⊖ d																08 27								
Loughborough Jn. d																08 31								
Herne Hill ■4 d																08 36								
Tulse Hill ■3 d	08 25														08 32	08 40			08 47					
Streatham ■4 d	08a28														08 36	08a44			08a50					
London Victoria ■15 ⊖ d							08 07	08 15	08 17		08 21		08 22							08 26				
Battersea Park ■4 d							08 11	08 19					08 26	08a32										
Milton Keynes Central d																								07 01
Watford Junction d																								07 39
Harrow & Wealdstone ⊖ d																								07 45
Wembley Central ⊖ d																								07u50
Shepherd's Bush ⊖ d																								08 05
Kensington (Olympia) ⊖ d																								08 07
West Brompton ⊖ d																								08 10
Imperial Wharf d																								08 13
Clapham Junction ■10 d							08 16	08 23	08 23		08 27		08 30							08 33				08 36
Wandsworth Common d							08 19	08 26					08 33							08 36				08 39
Balham ■4 ⊖ d							08 21	08 28					08 35							08 38				08 42
Streatham Hill d							08 24					08 35	08 38											
West Norwood ■4 d							08 28					08 38	08 42											
Gipsy Hill d							08 31					08 41	08 45				08a43							
Crystal Palace ■4 d							08 33					08a44	08a47											
Birkbeck 🚊 d																								
Beckenham Junction ■4 🚊 a																								
Streatham Common ■4 d								08 32							08 39					08 42				08 46
Norbury d								08 35							08 41					08 45				08 49
Thornton Heath d								08 38							08 44					08 48				08 52
Selhurst ■4 d								08 41							08 47					08 51				08 55
Norwood Junction ■2 a		08 27	08 29				08 38																08 45	
d		08 27	08 30			08 35	08 39																08 45	
West Croydon ■4 🚊 a						08 43	08 44								08 52					08 55				
East Croydon 🚊 a		08 30	08 33	08 22				08 44	08 33	08 36	08 39							08 37				08 42	08 49	09 05

Luton, Milton Keynes Central and London East and West Croydon via Tulse Hill - Crystal Palace - Norbury

Local Services

	SN	LO	SN	SN ◇■1 工	SN ◇■1 工	FC ■1	FC ■1	SN ■1	SN	LO	SN	SN		SN ◇■1 工	SN	SN ◇■1	SN	SN	SN	SN	SN	SN	SN ■1	LO
London Bridge ■4 ⊖ d	08 33							08 45	08 36									08 41	08 47	08 48	08 51	09 03	09 03	
South Bermondsey d	08 37																	08 45		08 52		09 07		
Queens Rd Peckham d	08 39																	08 48		08 54		09 09		
Peckham Rye ■4 d	08 42																	08 50		08 57		09 12		
East Dulwich d	08 45																			09 00		09 15		
North Dulwich d	08 47																			09 02		09 17		
Luton ■10 d						07 48	07 56																	
Luton Airport Parkway ■7 d							07 58																	
St Pancras International ■15 ⊖ d						08 20	08 32																	
City Thameslink ■3 d						08 29	08 41																	
London Blackfriars ■3 ⊖ d						08 32	08 44																	
Elephant & Castle ⊖ d							08 47																	
Loughborough Jn. d							08 51																	
Herne Hill ■4 d							08 57																	
Tulse Hill ■3 d	08 50						09 01													09 05		09 20		
Streatham ■4 d							09a05													09 09				
London Victoria ■15 ⊖ d			08 31	08 32	08 36						08 36	08 43		08 47	08 49	08 51	08 52							
Battersea Park ■4 d			08 36								08 40	08 47			08 53		08 56	09a02						
Milton Keynes Central d																								
Watford Junction d																								
Harrow & Wealdstone ⊖ d																								
Wembley Central ⊖ d																								
Shepherd's Bush ⊖ d																								
Kensington (Olympia) ⊖ d																								
West Brompton ⊖ d																								
Imperial Wharf d																								
Clapham Junction ■10 d			08 40	08 38	08 43						08 44	08 51		08 53	08 57		09 00							
Wandsworth Common d			08 43								08 47	08 54			09 00		09 03							
Balham ■4 ⊖ d			08 46								08 50	08 56			09 02		09 05							
Streatham Hill d											08 53				09 05									
West Norwood ■4 d	08 53										08 57				09 09							09 23		
Gipsy Hill d	08 56										09 00				09 12						09a14	09 26		
Crystal Palace ■4 d	08 59										09 02				09a14							09 29		
Birkbeck 🚊 d	09 03																					09 33		
Beckenham Junction ■4 🚊 a	09 06																					09 36		
Streatham Common ■4 d			08 51									09 00					09 09			09 13				
Norbury d			08 54									09 03					09 12			09 15				
Thornton Heath d			08 57									09 06					09 15			09 18				
Selhurst ■4 d			09 00									09 09					09 18			09 21				
Norwood Junction ■2 a								08 56	08 59		09 07												09 16	
d		08 50						08 56	09 00	09 05	09 09												09 16	09 20
West Croydon ■4 🚊 a		09 00	09 05							09 12	09 13						09 22			09 25				09 30
East Croydon 🚊 a				08 48	08 52	08 56		08 59	09 06			09 12		09 03		09 07			09 02				09 20	

	SN	SN ■1	SN	SN		SN	LO	SN	SN ◇■1 工	FC ■1	FC	SN	SN ◇■1 工	SN	SN ◇■1 A	FC ■1	SN	SN	SN ■1	SN		SN ◇■1 工	SN ■1	SN
London Bridge ■4 ⊖ d		09 15	09 06	09 11		09 20												09 18		09 22			09 32	09 33
South Bermondsey d				09 15														09 22						09 37
Queens Rd Peckham d				09 18														09 24						09 39
Peckham Rye ■4 d				09 20														09 27						09 42
East Dulwich d																		09 30						09 45
North Dulwich d																		09 32						09 47
Luton ■10 d										08 12						08 28								
Luton Airport Parkway ■7 d										08 14						08 30								
St Pancras International ■15 ⊖ d										08 48	08 56					09 04								
City Thameslink ■3 d										08 57	09 05					09 13								
London Blackfriars ■3 ⊖ d										09 00	09 08					09 16								
Elephant & Castle ⊖ d											09 12													
Loughborough Jn. d											09 16													
Herne Hill ■4 d											09 25													
Tulse Hill ■3 d											09 31							09 35						09 50
Streatham ■4 d											09a35							09 39						
London Victoria ■15 ⊖ d	09 03							09 05	09 06			09 13	09 17	09 19	09 21		09 22					09 32		
Battersea Park ■4 d	09 07			09a32				09 10				09 17		09 23										
Milton Keynes Central d																			08 13					
Watford Junction d																			08 51					
Harrow & Wealdstone ⊖ d																			08 58					
Wembley Central ⊖ d																			09u05					
Shepherd's Bush ⊖ d																			09 18					
Kensington (Olympia) ⊖ d																			09 21					
West Brompton ⊖ d																			09 23					
Imperial Wharf d																			09 26					
Clapham Junction ■10 d	09 11							09 14	09 12			09 21	09 23	09 27			09 30		09 34			09 38		
Wandsworth Common d	09 14							09 17				09 24		09 30			09 33		09 37					
Balham ■4 ⊖ d	09 16							09 20				09 26		09 32			09 35		09 41					
Streatham Hill d								09 23						09 35										
West Norwood ■4 d								09 27						09 40										09 53
Gipsy Hill d								09 30						09 43						09a46				09 56
Crystal Palace ■4 d								09 32						09a46										09 59
Birkbeck 🚊 d																								10 03
Beckenham Junction ■4 🚊 a																								10 06
Streatham Common ■4 d	09 20											09 30					09 39	09 42	09 45					
Norbury d	09 23											09 33					09 42	09 45	09 48					
Thornton Heath d	09 26											09 36					09 45	09 48	09 51					
Selhurst ■4 d	09 29											09 39					09 48	09 51	09 54					
Norwood Junction ■2 a		09 26	09 30			09 32		09 37															09 45	
d		09 26	09 30			09 33	09 35	09 39															09 45	
West Croydon ■4 🚊 a	09 33						09 42	09 43									09 52	09 55						
East Croydon 🚊 a		09 30	09 33			09 36			09 22	09 24		09 42	09 33		09 37	09 39			09 57			09 48	09 49	

A from 5 September

Table 177

Luton, Milton Keynes Central and London East and West Croydon via Tulse Hill - Crystal Palace - Norbury

Local Services

Station		LO	SN	SN	SN	SN	SN	LO	SN	SN	FC	FC	SN		SN	SN	SN	FC	SN	SN	SN	SN	SN	LO	SN
				■						◇■	■				◇■ H		◇■	■					■		
London Bridge	d			09 45	09 36	09 41	09 50													09 48	09 52	10 03	10 03		
South Bermondsey	d					09 45														09 52		10 07			
Queens Rd Peckham	d					09 48														09 54		10 09			
Peckham Rye	d					09 50														09 57		10 12			
East Dulwich	d																			10 00		10 15			
North Dulwich	d																			10 02		10 17			
Luton	d										08 48	08 54						09 04							
Luton Airport Parkway	d										08 50	08 56						09 06							
St Pancras International	d										09 24	09 34						09 40							
City Thameslink	d										09 32	09 43						09 47							
London Blackfriars	d										09 34	09 46						09 50							
Elephant & Castle	d											09 49													
Loughborough Jn.	d											09 53													
Herne Hill	d											09 57													
Tulse Hill	d											10 01								10 05		10 20			
Streatham	d											10a05								10 09					
London Victoria	d		09 33						09 35	09 36			09 43		09 47	09 49	09 51		09 53						10 03
Battersea Park	d		09 37			10a02			09 40				09 47			09 53									10 07
Milton Keynes Central	d																								
Watford Junction	d																								
Harrow & Wealdstone	d																								
Wembley Central	d																								
Shepherd's Bush	d																								
Kensington (Olympia)	d																								
West Brompton	d																								
Imperial Wharf	d																								
Clapham Junction	d		09 41						09 44	09 42			09 51		09 53	09 57			10 00						10 11
Wandsworth Common	d		09 44						09 47				09 54			10 00			10 03						10 14
Balham	d		09 46						09 50				09 56			10 02			10 05						10 16
Streatham Hill	d								09 53							10 05									
West Norwood	d								09 57							10 10						10 23			
Gipsy Hill	d								10 00							10 13					10a15	10 26			
Crystal Palace	d								10 02							10a16						10 29			
Birkbeck	d																					10 33			
Beckenham Junction	a																					10 36			
Streatham Common	d		09 50										10 00						10 09	10 12					10 20
Norbury	d		09 53										10 03						10 12	10 15					10 23
Thornton Heath	d		09 56										10 06						10 15	10 18					10 26
Selhurst	d		09 59										10 09						10 18	10 21					10 29
Norwood Junction	a			09 56	09 59		10 02		10 07														10 16		
Norwood Junction	d	09 50		09 56	10 00		10 03	10 05	10 09														10 16	10 20	
West Croydon	a	10 00	10 03					10 12	10 13										10 22	10 25				10 30	10 33
East Croydon	a			10 00	10 03		10 06			09 52	09 54		10 12		10 03		10 07	10 09					10 20		

Station		SN	FC	FC	SN		SN	SN	SN	LO	SN	SN	SN	SN	SN	FC	SN	SN	SN	SN	SN		SN	SN	LO
		◇■ H	■		■								◇■ H		◇■ A	■			■		◇■ H			■	
London Bridge	d				10 15		10 06	10 11	10 20									10 18		10 22			10 33	10 33	
South Bermondsey	d							10 15										10 22					10 37		
Queens Rd Peckham	d							10 18										10 24					10 39		
Peckham Rye	d							10 20										10 27					10 42		
East Dulwich	d																	10 30					10 45		
North Dulwich	d																	10 32					10 47		
Luton	d		09 18	09 14												09 34									
Luton Airport Parkway	d		09 20	09 16												09 36									
St Pancras International	d		09 54	10 04												10 10									
City Thameslink	d		10 02	10 13												10 17									
London Blackfriars	d		10 05	10 16												10 20									
Elephant & Castle	d			10 19																					
Loughborough Jn.	d			10 23																					
Herne Hill	d			10 27																					
Tulse Hill	d			10 31														10 35					10 50		
Streatham	d			10a35														10 39							
London Victoria	d	10 06									10 06	10 13	10 17	10 19	10 21		10 23				10 32				
Battersea Park	d							10a32			10 10	10 17		10 23											
Milton Keynes Central	d																		09 13						
Watford Junction	d																		09 51						
Harrow & Wealdstone	d																		09 58						
Wembley Central	d																		10u05						
Shepherd's Bush	d																		10 21						
Kensington (Olympia)	d																		10 24						
West Brompton	d																		10 27						
Imperial Wharf	d																		10 29						
Clapham Junction	d	10 12									10 14	10 21	10 23	10 27			10 30		10 34		10 38				
Wandsworth Common	d										10 17	10 24		10 30			10 33		10 37						
Balham	d										10 20	10 26		10 32			10 35		10 40						
Streatham Hill	d										10 23			10 35											
West Norwood	d										10 27			10 40									10 53		
Gipsy Hill	d										10 30			10 43						10a45			10 56		
Crystal Palace	d										10 32			10a46									10 59		
Birkbeck	d																						11 03		
Beckenham Junction	a																						11 06		
Streatham Common	d											10 30					10 39	10 42	10 45						
Norbury	d											10 33					10 42	10 45	10 48						
Thornton Heath	d											10 36					10 45	10 48	10 51						
Selhurst	d											10 39					10 48	10 51	10 54						
Norwood Junction	a				10 26		10 29		10 32		10 37													10 46	
Norwood Junction	d				10 26		10 30		10 33	10 35	10 39													10 46	10 50
West Croydon	a									10 42	10 43						10 52	10 55							11 00
East Croydon	a	10 22	10 24		10 30		10 33		10 36			10 42	10 33		10 37	10 39			10 57		10 48			10 50	

Table 177

Luton, Milton Keynes Central and London East and West Croydon via Tulse Hill - Crystal Palace - Norbury

Local Services

Station		SN	SN	FC	FC	SN	SN	SN	SN	LO	SN	SN	SN		SN	SN	FC	SN	SN	SN	SN	SN	LO	SN	SN
			◇■	■		■							◇■ H			◇■	■					■			◇■
London Bridge	d					10 45	10 36	10 41	10 50										10 48	10 52	11 03	11 03			
South Bermondsey	d							10 45											10 52		11 07				
Queens Rd Peckham	d							10 48											10 54		11 09				
Peckham Rye	d							10 50											10 57		11 12				
East Dulwich	d																		11 00		11 15				
North Dulwich	d																		11 02		11 17				
Luton	d			09 48	09 44												10 04								
Luton Airport Parkway	d			09 50	09 46												10 06								
St Pancras International	d			10 24	10 34												10 40								
City Thameslink	d			10 32	10 43												10 47								
London Blackfriars	d			10 35	10 46												10 50								
Elephant & Castle	d				10 49																				
Loughborough Jn.	d				10 53																				
Herne Hill	d				10 57																				
Tulse Hill	d				11 01														11 05		11 20				
Streatham	d				11a05														11 09						
London Victoria	d	10 33	10 36								10 36	10 43	10 47		10 49	10 51		10 53						11 03	11 06
Battersea Park	d	10 37						11a02			10 40	10 47			10 53									11 07	
Milton Keynes Central	d																								
Watford Junction	d																								
Harrow & Wealdstone	d																								
Wembley Central	d																								
Shepherd's Bush	d																								
Kensington (Olympia)	d																								
West Brompton	d																								
Imperial Wharf	d																								
Clapham Junction	d	10 41	10 42								10 44	10 51	10 53		10 57			11 00						11 11	11 12
Wandsworth Common	d	10 44									10 47	10 54			11 00			11 03						11 14	
Balham	d	10 46									10 50	10 56			11 02			11 05						11 16	
Streatham Hill	d										10 53				11 05										
West Norwood	d										10 57				11 10						11 23				
Gipsy Hill	d										11 00				11 13					11a15	11 26				
Crystal Palace	d										11 02				11a16						11 29				
Birkbeck	d																				11 33				
Beckenham Junction	a																				11 36				
Streatham Common	d	10 50										11 00						11 09	11 12					11 20	
Norbury	d	10 53										11 03						11 12	11 15					11 23	
Thornton Heath	d	10 56										11 06						11 15	11 18					11 26	
Selhurst	d	10 59										11 09						11 18	11 21					11 29	
Norwood Junction	a					10 56	10 59		11 02		11 07											11 16			
Norwood Junction	d					10 56	11 00		11 03	11 05	11 09											11 16	11 20		
West Croydon	a	11 03								11 12	11 13							11 22	11 25				11 30	11 33	
East Croydon	a		10 52	10 54		11 00	11 03		11 06			11 12	11 03			11 07	11 09					11 20			11 22

Station		FC	FC	SN	SN		SN	SN	LO	SN	SN	SN	SN	SN	FC	SN	SN	SN	SN	SN	SN		SN	LO	SN
		■		■								◇■		◇■ A	■			■		◇■			■		
London Bridge	d			11 15	11 06		11 11	11 20									11 18		11 22		11 33		11 33		
South Bermondsey	d						11 15										11 22				11 37				
Queens Rd Peckham	d						11 18										11 24				11 39				
Peckham Rye	d						11 20										11 27				11 42				
East Dulwich	d																11 30				11 45				
North Dulwich	d																11 32				11 47				
Luton	d	10 18	10 14												10 34										
Luton Airport Parkway	d	10 20	10 16												10 36										
St Pancras International	d	10 54	11 04												11 10										
City Thameslink	d	11 02	11 13												11 17										
London Blackfriars	d	11 05	11 16												11 20										
Elephant & Castle	d		11 19																						
Loughborough Jn.	d		11 23																						
Herne Hill	d		11 27																						
Tulse Hill	d		11 31														11 35				11 50				
Streatham	d		11a35														11 39								
London Victoria	d									11 06	11 13	11 17	11 19	11 21		11 23				11 32					11 33
Battersea Park	d						11a32			11 10	11 17		11 23												11 37
Milton Keynes Central	d																	10 13							
Watford Junction	d																	10 51							
Harrow & Wealdstone	d																	10 59							
Wembley Central	d																	11u04							
Shepherd's Bush	d																	11 19							
Kensington (Olympia)	d																	11 21							
West Brompton	d																	11 23							
Imperial Wharf	d																	11 26							
Clapham Junction	d									11 14	11 21	11 23	11 27			11 30		11 34		11 38					11 41
Wandsworth Common	d									11 17	11 24		11 30			11 33		11 37							11 44
Balham	d									11 20	11 26		11 32			11 35		11 40							11 46
Streatham Hill	d									11 23			11 35												
West Norwood	d									11 27			11 40								11 53				
Gipsy Hill	d									11 30			11 43						11a45		11 56				
Crystal Palace	d									11 32			11a46								11 59				
Birkbeck	d																				12 03				
Beckenham Junction	a																				12 06				
Streatham Common	d										11 30					11 39	11 42	11 45							11 50
Norbury	d										11 33					11 42	11 45	11 48							11 53
Thornton Heath	d										11 36					11 45	11 48	11 51							11 56
Selhurst	d										11 39					11 48	11 51	11 54							11 59
Norwood Junction	a			11 26	11 29			11 32		11 37													11 46		
Norwood Junction	d			11 26	11 30			11 33	11 35	11 39													11 46	11 50	
West Croydon	a								11 42	11 43						11 52	11 55							12 00	12 03
East Croydon	a	11 24		11 30	11 33			11 36			11 42	11 33		11 37	11 39			11 57		11 48			11 50		

A from 5 September

Luton, Milton Keynes Central and London East and West Croydon via Tulse Hill - Crystal Palace - Norbury

Local Services

		SN ◇1	FC 1	FC	SN 1	SN	SN	SN	LO	SN	SN	SN ◇1	SN	SN ◇1	FC 1	SN	SN	SN	SN	SN 1	LO	SN	SN ◇1	FC 1
London Bridge 4 ⊖	d				11 45	11 36	11 41	11 50									11 48	11 52	12 03	12 03				
South Bermondsey	d						11 45										11 52		12 07					
Queens Rd Peckham	d						11 48										11 54		12 09					
Peckham Rye 4	d						11 50										11 57		12 12					
East Dulwich	d																12 00		12 15					
North Dulwich	d																12 02		12 17					
Luton 10	d		10 48	10 44											11 04									11 18
Luton Airport Parkway 7	d		10 50	10 46											11 06									11 20
St Pancras International 15 ⊖	d		11 24	11 34											11 40									11 54
City Thameslink 3	d		11 32	11 43											11 47									12 02
London Blackfriars 3 ⊖	d		11 35	11 46											11 50									12 05
Elephant & Castle ⊖	d			11 49																				
Loughborough Jn.	d			11 53																				
Herne Hill 4	d			11 57																				
Tulse Hill 3	d			12 01													12 05		12 20					
Streatham 4	d			12a05													12 09							
London Victoria 15 ⊖	d	11 36								11 36	11 43	11 47	11 49	11 51								12 03	12 06	
Battersea Park 4	d						12a02			11 40	11 47		11 53									12 07		
Milton Keynes Central	d																							
Watford Junction	d																							
Harrow & Wealdstone ⊖	d																							
Wembley Central ⊖	d																							
Shepherd's Bush ⊖	d																							
Kensington (Olympia) ⊖	d																							
West Brompton ⊖	d																							
Imperial Wharf	d																							
Clapham Junction 10	d	11 42								11 44	11 51	11 53	11 57			12 00						12 11	12 12	
Wandsworth Common	d									11 47	11 54		12 00			12 03						12 14		
Balham 4 ⊖	d									11 50	11 56		12 02			12 05						12 16		
Streatham Hill	d									11 53			12 05											
West Norwood 4	d									11 57			12 10						12 23					
Gipsy Hill	d									12 00			12 13					12a15	12 26					
Crystal Palace 4	d									12 02			12a16						12 29					
Birkbeck	d																		12 33					
Beckenham Junction 4	a																		12 36					
Streatham Common 4	d										12 00					12 09	12 12					12 20		
Norbury	d										12 03					12 12	12 15					12 23		
Thornton Heath	d										12 06					12 15	12 18					12 26		
Selhurst 4	d										12 09					12 18	12 21					12 29		
Norwood Junction 2	a				11 56	11 59		12 02		12 07										12 16				
	d				11 56	12 00		12 03	12 05	12 09										12 16	12 20			
West Croydon 4	a								12 12	12 13						12 22	12 25				12 30	12 33		
East Croydon	a	11 52	11 54		12 00	12 03		12 06			12 12	12 03		12 07	12 09					12 20			12 22	12 24

Luton, Milton Keynes Central and London East and West Croydon via Tulse Hill - Crystal Palace - Norbury

Local Services

		FC	SN 1	SN	SN	SN	LO	SN	SN	SN ◇1	SN	SN ◇1 A	FC 1	SN	SN	SN 1	SN	SN ◇1	SN	SN 1	LO	SN	SN ◇1
London Bridge 4 ⊖	d		12 15	12 06	12 11	12 20									12 18		12 22		12 33	12 33			
South Bermondsey	d				12 15										12 22				12 37				
Queens Rd Peckham	d				12 18										12 24				12 39				
Peckham Rye 4	d				12 20										12 27				12 42				
East Dulwich	d														12 30				12 45				
North Dulwich	d														12 32				12 47				
Luton 10	d	11 14											11 34										
Luton Airport Parkway 7	d	11 16											11 36										
St Pancras International 15 ⊖	d	12 04											12 10										
City Thameslink 3	d	12 13											12 17										
London Blackfriars 3 ⊖	d	12 16											12 20										
Elephant & Castle ⊖	d	12 19																					
Loughborough Jn.	d	12 23																					
Herne Hill 4	d	12 27																					
Tulse Hill 3	d	12 31													12 35				12 50				
Streatham 4	d	12a35													12 39								
London Victoria 15 ⊖	d							12 06	12 13	12 17	12 19	12 21						12 32				12 33	12 36
Battersea Park 4	d				12a32			12 10	12 17		12 23											12 37	
Milton Keynes Central	d															11 13							
Watford Junction	d															11 51							
Harrow & Wealdstone ⊖	d															11 59							
Wembley Central ⊖	d															12u04							
Shepherd's Bush ⊖	d															12 19							
Kensington (Olympia) ⊖	d															12 22							
West Brompton ⊖	d															12 25							
Imperial Wharf	d															12 27							
Clapham Junction 10	d							12 14	12 21	12 23	12 27			12 30		12 34		12 38				12 41	12 42
Wandsworth Common	d							12 17	12 24		12 30			12 33		12 37						12 44	
Balham 4 ⊖	d							12 20	12 26		12 32			12 35		12 40						12 46	
Streatham Hill	d							12 23			12 35												
West Norwood 4	d							12 27			12 40								12 53				
Gipsy Hill	d							12 30			12 43						12a45		12 56				
Crystal Palace 4	d							12 32			12a46								12 59				
Birkbeck	d																		13 03				
Beckenham Junction 4	a																		13 06				
Streatham Common 4	d								12 30					12 39	12 42	12 45						12 50	
Norbury	d								12 33					12 42	12 45	12 48						12 53	
Thornton Heath	d								12 36					12 45	12 48	12 51						12 56	
Selhurst 4	d								12 39					12 48	12 51	12 54						12 59	
Norwood Junction 2	a		12 26	12 29		12 32		12 37												12 46			
	d		12 26	12 30		12 33	12 35	12 39												12 46	12 50		
West Croydon 4	a						12 42	12 43						12 52	12 55						13 00	13 03	
East Croydon	a		12 30	12 33		12 36			12 42	12 33		12 37	12 39			12 57		12 48		12 50			12 52

A from 5 September

Luton, Milton Keynes Central and London East and West Croydon via Tulse Hill - Crystal Palace - Norbury

Local Services

		FC ■	FC	SN ■	SN	SN	SN	LO	SN	SN	SN ◇■	SN	SN ◇■		FC ■	SN	SN	SN	SN	SN ■	LO	SN	SN ◇■ H	FC ■	FC
London Bridge ■ ⊖	d			12 45	12 36	12 41	12 50										12 48	12 52	13 03	13 03					
South Bermondsey	d					12 45											12 52		13 07						
Queens Rd Peckham	d					12 48											12 54		13 09						
Peckham Rye ■	d					12 50											12 57		13 12						
East Dulwich	d																13 00		13 15						
North Dulwich	d																13 02		13 17						
Luton ■	d	11 48	11 44												12 04									12 18	12 14
Luton Airport Parkway ■	d	11 50	11 46												12 06									12 20	12 16
St Pancras International ■ ⊖	d	12 24	12 34												12 40									12 54	13 04
City Thameslink ■	d	12 32	12 43												12 47									13 02	13 13
London Blackfriars ■ ⊖	d	12 35	12 46												12 50									13 05	13 16
Elephant & Castle ⊖	d		12 49																						13 19
Loughborough Jn.	d		12 53																						13 23
Herne Hill ■	d		12 57																						13 27
Tulse Hill ■	d		13 01														13 05		13 20						13 31
Streatham ■	d		13a05														13 09								13a35
London Victoria ■ ⊖	d								12 36	12 43	12 47	12 49	12 51									13 03	13 06		
Battersea Park ■	d					13a02			12 40	12 47		12 53										13 07			
Milton Keynes Central	d																								
Watford Junction	d																								
Harrow & Wealdstone ⊖	d																								
Wembley Central ⊖	d																								
Shepherd's Bush ⊖	d																								
Kensington (Olympia) ⊖	d																								
West Brompton ⊖	d																								
Imperial Wharf	d																								
Clapham Junction ■	d								12 44	12 51	12 53	12 57				13 00						13 11	13 12		
Wandsworth Common	d								12 47	12 54		13 00				13 03						13 14			
Balham ■ ⊖	d								12 50	12 56		13 02				13 05						13 16			
Streatham Hill	d								12 53			13 05													
West Norwood ■	d								12 57			13 10							13 23						
Gipsy Hill	d								13 00			13 13						13a15	13 26						
Crystal Palace ■	d								13 02			13a16							13 29						
Birkbeck 🚊	d																		13 33						
Beckenham Junction ■ 🚊	a																		13 36						
Streatham Common ■	d									13 00						13 09	13 12					13 20			
Norbury	d									13 03						13 12	13 15					13 23			
Thornton Heath	d									13 06						13 15	13 18					13 26			
Selhurst ■	d									13 09						13 18	13 21					13 29			
Norwood Junction ■	a			12 56	12 59		13 02		13 07											13 16					
	d			12 56	13 00		13 03	13 05	13 09											13 16	13 20				
West Croydon ■ 🚊	a							13 12	13 13							13 22	13 25				13 30	13 33			
East Croydon 🚊	a	12 54		13 00	13 03		13 06			13 12	13 03		13 07		13 09					13 20			13 22	13 24	

Luton, Milton Keynes Central and London East and West Croydon via Tulse Hill - Crystal Palace - Norbury

Local Services

		SN ■	SN	SN	SN		LO	SN	SN	SN ◇■	SN	SN ◇■ A	FC ■	SN	SN	SN ■	SN	SN ◇■ H	SN	SN ■	LO		SN	SN ◇■ H	FC ■
London Bridge ■ ⊖	d	13 15	13 06	13 11	13 20										13 18		13 22		13 33	13 33					
South Bermondsey	d			13 15											13 22				13 37						
Queens Rd Peckham	d			13 18											13 24				13 39						
Peckham Rye ■	d			13 20											13 27				13 42						
East Dulwich	d														13 30				13 45						
North Dulwich	d														13 32				13 47						
Luton ■	d												12 34												12 48
Luton Airport Parkway ■	d												12 36												12 50
St Pancras International ■ ⊖	d												13 10												13 24
City Thameslink ■	d												13 17												13 32
London Blackfriars ■ ⊖	d												13 20												13 35
Elephant & Castle ⊖	d																								
Loughborough Jn.	d																								
Herne Hill ■	d																								
Tulse Hill ■	d														13 35				13 50						
Streatham ■	d														13 39										
London Victoria ■ ⊖	d							13 06	13 13	13 17	13 19	13 21		13 23				13 32					13 33	13 36	
Battersea Park ■	d			13a32				13 10	13 17		13 23												13 37		
Milton Keynes Central	d															12 13									
Watford Junction	d															12 51									
Harrow & Wealdstone ⊖	d															12 59									
Wembley Central ⊖	d															13u04									
Shepherd's Bush ⊖	d															13 19									
Kensington (Olympia) ⊖	d															13 22									
West Brompton ⊖	d															13 25									
Imperial Wharf	d															13 28									
Clapham Junction ■	d							13 14	13 21	13 23	13 27			13 30		13 34		13 38					13 41	13 42	
Wandsworth Common	d							13 17	13 24		13 30			13 33		13 37							13 44		
Balham ■ ⊖	d							13 20	13 26		13 32			13 35		13 40							13 46		
Streatham Hill	d							13 23			13 35														
West Norwood ■	d							13 27			13 40								13 53						
Gipsy Hill	d							13 30			13 43						13a45		13 56						
Crystal Palace ■	d							13 32			13a46								13 59						
Birkbeck 🚊	d																		14 03						
Beckenham Junction ■ 🚊	a																		14 06						
Streatham Common ■	d								13 30					13 39	13 42	13 45							13 50		
Norbury	d								13 33					13 42	13 45	13 48							13 53		
Thornton Heath	d								13 36					13 45	13 48	13 51							13 56		
Selhurst ■	d								13 39					13 48	13 51	13 54							13 59		
Norwood Junction ■	a	13 26	13 29		13 32			13 37												13 46					
	d	13 26	13 30		13 33		13 35	13 39												13 46	13 50				
West Croydon ■ 🚊	a						13 42	13 43						13 52	13 55						14 00		14 03		
East Croydon 🚊	a	13 30	13 33		13 36				13 42	13 33		13 37	13 39			13 57		13 48		13 50				13 52	13 54

A from 5 September

Luton, Milton Keynes Central and London East and West Croydon via Tulse Hill - Crystal Palace - Norbury

Local Services

		FC	SN 1	SN	SN	SN	LO	SN	SN	SN ◇1	SN	SN ◇1	FC 1	SN	SN	SN	SN	SN 1	LO	SN	SN ◇1	FC 1	FC	SN 1
London Bridge 4 ⊖	d		13 45	13 36	13 41	13 50									13 48	13 52	14 03	14 03						14 15
South Bermondsey	d				13 45										13 52		14 07							
Queens Rd Peckham	d				13 48										13 54		14 09							
Peckham Rye 4	d				13 50										13 57		14 12							
East Dulwich	d														14 00		14 15							
North Dulwich	d														14 02		14 17							
Luton 10	d	12 44											13 04									13 18	13 14	
Luton Airport Parkway 7	d	12 46											13 06									13 20	13 16	
St Pancras International 15 ⊖	d	13 34											13 40									13 54	14 04	
City Thameslink 3	d	13 43											13 47									14 02	14 13	
London Blackfriars 3 ⊖	d	13 46											13 50									14 05	14 16	
Elephant & Castle ⊖	d	13 49																					14 19	
Loughborough Jn.	d	13 53																					14 23	
Herne Hill 4	d	13 57																					14 27	
Tulse Hill 3	d	14 01													14 05		14 20						14 31	
Streatham 4	d	14a05													14 09								14a35	
London Victoria 15 ⊖	d							13 36	13 43	13 47	13 49	13 51								14 03	14 06			
Battersea Park 4	d				14a02			13 40	13 47		13 53									14 07				
Milton Keynes Central	d																							
Watford Junction	d																							
Harrow & Wealdstone ⊖	d																							
Wembley Central ⊖	d																							
Shepherd's Bush ⊖	d																							
Kensington (Olympia) ⊖	d																							
West Brompton ⊖	d																							
Imperial Wharf	d																							
Clapham Junction 10	d							13 44	13 51	13 53	13 57			14 00						14 11	14 12			
Wandsworth Common	d							13 47	13 54		14 00			14 03						14 14				
Balham 4 ⊖	d							13 50	13 56		14 02			14 05						14 16				
Streatham Hill	d							13 53			14 05													
West Norwood 4	d							13 57			14 10						14 23							
Gipsy Hill	d							14 00			14 13					14a15	14 26							
Crystal Palace 4	d							14 02			14a16						14 29							
Birkbeck	d																14 33							
Beckenham Junction 4	a																14 36							
Streatham Common 4	d								14 00					14 09	14 12					14 20				
Norbury	d								14 03					14 12	14 15					14 23				
Thornton Heath	d								14 06					14 15	14 18					14 26				
Selhurst 4	d								14 09					14 18	14 21					14 29				
Norwood Junction 2	a		13 56	13 59		14 02		14 07										14 16						14 26
	d		13 56	14 00		14 03	14 05	14 09										14 16	14 20					14 26
West Croydon 4	a						14 12	14 13						14 22	14 25				14 30	14 33				
East Croydon	a		14 00	14 03		14 06			14 12	14 03		14 07	14 09					14 20			14 22	14 24		14 30

Luton, Milton Keynes Central and London East and West Croydon via Tulse Hill - Crystal Palace - Norbury

Local Services

		SN	SN	SN	LO	SN	SN	SN ◇1	SN	SN ◇1 A	FC 1	SN	SN	SN 1	SN	SN ◇1	SN	SN 1	LO	SN	SN ◇1	FC 1	FC
London Bridge 4 ⊖	d	14 06	14 11	14 20									14 18		14 22		14 33	14 33					
South Bermondsey	d		14 15										14 22				14 37						
Queens Rd Peckham	d		14 18										14 24				14 39						
Peckham Rye 4	d		14 20										14 27				14 42						
East Dulwich	d												14 30				14 45						
North Dulwich	d												14 32				14 47						
Luton 10	d										13 34											13 48	13 44
Luton Airport Parkway 7	d										13 36											13 50	13 46
St Pancras International 15 ⊖	d										14 10											14 24	14 34
City Thameslink 3	d										14 17											14 32	14 43
London Blackfriars 3 ⊖	d										14 20											14 35	14 46
Elephant & Castle ⊖	d																						14 49
Loughborough Jn.	d																						14 53
Herne Hill 4	d																						14 57
Tulse Hill 3	d												14 35				14 50						15 01
Streatham 4	d												14 39										15a05
London Victoria 15 ⊖	d					14 06	14 13	14 17	14 19	14 21						14 32				14 33	14 36		
Battersea Park 4	d		14a32			14 10	14 17		14 23											14 37			
Milton Keynes Central	d													13 13									
Watford Junction	d													13 51									
Harrow & Wealdstone ⊖	d													13 59									
Wembley Central ⊖	d													14u04									
Shepherd's Bush ⊖	d													14 19									
Kensington (Olympia) ⊖	d													14 22									
West Brompton ⊖	d													14 25									
Imperial Wharf	d													14 28									
Clapham Junction 10	d					14 14	14 21	14 23	14 27			14 30		14 34		14 38				14 41	14 42		
Wandsworth Common	d					14 17	14 24		14 30			14 33		14 37						14 44			
Balham 4 ⊖	d					14 20	14 26		14 32			14 35		14 40						14 46			
Streatham Hill	d					14 23			14 35														
West Norwood 4	d					14 27			14 40								14 53						
Gipsy Hill	d					14 30			14 43								14 56						
Crystal Palace 4	d					14 32			14a46						14a45		14 59						
Birkbeck	d																15 03						
Beckenham Junction 4	a																15 06						
Streatham Common 4	d						14 30					14 39	14 42	14 45						14 50			
Norbury	d						14 33					14 42	14 45	14 48						14 53			
Thornton Heath	d						14 36					14 45	14 48	14 51						14 56			
Selhurst 4	d						14 39					14 48	14 51	14 54						14 59			
Norwood Junction 2	a	14 29		14 32		14 37												14 46					
	d	14 30		14 33	14 35	14 39												14 46	14 50				
West Croydon 4	a				14 42	14 43						14 52	14 55						15 00	15 03			
East Croydon	a	14 33		14 36			14 43	14 33		14 37	14 39			14 57		14 48		14 50			14 52	14 54	

A from 5 September

Table 177

Luton, Milton Keynes Central and London East and West Croydon via Tulse Hill - Crystal Palace - Norbury

Local Services

		SN 1	SN	SN	SN	LO	SN	SN	SN ◇1	SN	SN ◇1	FC 1	SN		SN	SN	SN	SN 1	LO	SN	SN ◇1	FC 1	FC	SN 1	SN
London Bridge 4 ⊖	d	14 45	14 36	14 41	14 50										14 48	14 52	15 03	15 03						15 15	15 06
South Bermondsey	d			14 45											14 52		15 07								
Queens Rd Peckham	d			14 48											14 54		15 09								
Peckham Rye 4	d			14 50											14 57		15 12								
East Dulwich	d														15 00		15 15								
North Dulwich	d														15 02		15 17								
Luton 10	d											14 04										14 18	14 14		
Luton Airport Parkway 7	d											14 06										14 20	14 16		
St Pancras International 15 ⊖	d											14 40										14 54	15 04		
City Thameslink 3	d											14 47										15 02	15 13		
London Blackfriars 3 ⊖	d											14 50										15 05	15 16		
Elephant & Castle ⊖	d																						15 19		
Loughborough Jn.	d																						15 23		
Herne Hill 4	d																						15 27		
Tulse Hill 3	d														15 05		15 20						15 31		
Streatham 4	d														15 09								15a35		
London Victoria 15 ⊖	d						14 36	14 43	14 47	14 49	14 51									15 03	15 06				
Battersea Park 4	d			15a02			14 40	14 47		14 53										15 07					
Milton Keynes Central	d																								
Watford Junction	d																								
Harrow & Wealdstone ⊖	d																								
Wembley Central ⊖	d																								
Shepherd's Bush ⊖	d																								
Kensington (Olympia) ⊖	d																								
West Brompton ⊖	d																								
Imperial Wharf	d																								
Clapham Junction 10	d						14 44	14 51	14 53	14 57			15 00							15 11	15 12				
Wandsworth Common	d						14 47	14 54		15 00			15 03							15 14					
Balham 4 ⊖	d						14 50	14 56		15 02			15 05							15 16					
Streatham Hill	d						14 53			15 05															
West Norwood 4	d						14 57			15 10							15 23								
Gipsy Hill	d						15 00			15 13						15a15	15 26								
Crystal Palace 4	d						15 02			15a16							15 29								
Birkbeck 🚋	d																15 33								
Beckenham Junction 4 🚋	a																15 36								
Streatham Common 4	d							15 00					15 09		15 12					15 20					
Norbury	d							15 03					15 12		15 15					15 23					
Thornton Heath	d							15 06					15 15		15 18					15 26					
Selhurst 4	d							15 09					15 18		15 21					15 29					
Norwood Junction 2	a	14 56	14 59		15 02		15 07											15 16						15 26	15 29
	d	14 56	15 00		15 03	15 05	15 09											15 16	15 20					15 26	15 30
West Croydon 4 🚋	a					15 12	15 13						15 22		15 25				15 30	15 33					
East Croydon 🚋	a	15 00	15 03		15 06			15 12	15 03		15 07	15 09						15 20			15 22	15 24		15 30	15 33

Table 177

Luton, Milton Keynes Central and London East and West Croydon via Tulse Hill - Crystal Palace - Norbury

Local Services

		SN	SN	LO	SN		SN	SN ◇1	SN	SN ◇1 A	FC 1	SN	SN	SN 1	SN	SN ◇1	SN	SN 1	LO	SN	SN ◇1		FC 1	FC	SN 1
London Bridge 4 ⊖	d	15 11	15 20										15 18		15 22		15 33	15 33							15 45
South Bermondsey	d	15 15											15 22				15 37								
Queens Rd Peckham	d	15 18											15 24				15 39								
Peckham Rye 4	d	15 20											15 27				15 42								
East Dulwich	d												15 30				15 45								
North Dulwich	d												15 32				15 47								
Luton 10	d										14 34												14 48	14 44	
Luton Airport Parkway 7	d										14 36												14 50	14 46	
St Pancras International 15 ⊖	d										15 10												15 24	15 34	
City Thameslink 3	d										15 17												15 32	15 43	
London Blackfriars 3 ⊖	d										15 20												15 35	15 46	
Elephant & Castle ⊖	d																							15 49	
Loughborough Jn.	d																							15 53	
Herne Hill 4	d																							15 57	
Tulse Hill 3	d												15 35				15 50							16 01	
Streatham 4	d												15 39											16a05	
London Victoria 15 ⊖	d				15 06		15 13	15 17	15 19	15 21		15 23				15 32				15 33	15 36				
Battersea Park 4	d	15a32			15 10		15 17		15 23											15 37					
Milton Keynes Central	d													14 13											
Watford Junction	d													14 51											
Harrow & Wealdstone ⊖	d													14 59											
Wembley Central ⊖	d													15u04											
Shepherd's Bush ⊖	d													15 22											
Kensington (Olympia) ⊖	d													15 24											
West Brompton ⊖	d													15 26											
Imperial Wharf	d													15 29											
Clapham Junction 10	d				15 14		15 21	15 23	15 27			15 30		15 34		15 38				15 41	15 42				
Wandsworth Common	d				15 17		15 24		15 30			15 33		15 37						15 44					
Balham 4 ⊖	d				15 20		15 26		15 32			15 35		15 40						15 46					
Streatham Hill	d				15 23				15 35																
West Norwood 4	d				15 27				15 40								15 53								
Gipsy Hill	d				15 30				15 43						15a45		15 56								
Crystal Palace 4	d				15 32				15a46								15 59								
Birkbeck 🚋	d																16 03								
Beckenham Junction 4 🚋	a																16 06								
Streatham Common 4	d						15 30					15 39	15 42	15 45						15 50					
Norbury	d						15 33					15 42	15 45	15 48						15 53					
Thornton Heath	d						15 36					15 45	15 48	15 51						15 56					
Selhurst 4	d						15 39					15 48	15 51	15 54						15 59					
Norwood Junction 2	a		15 32		15 37													15 46							15 56
	d		15 33	15 35	15 39													15 46	15 50						15 56
West Croydon 4 🚋	a			15 42	15 43							15 52	15 55						16 00	16 03					
East Croydon 🚋	a		15 36				15 43	15 33		15 37	15 39			15 57		15 48		15 50			15 52		15 54		16 00

A from 5 September

Luton, Milton Keynes Central and London East and West Croydon via Tulse Hill - Crystal Palace - Norbury

Local Services

		SN	SN	SN	LO	SN	SN	SN ◇1	SN	SN ◇1	FC 1	SN	SN		SN	SN	SN 1	LO	SN	SN 1	FC 1	FC	SN 1	SN	SN
London Bridge	d	15 36	15 41	15 50									15 48		15 52	16 03	16 03						16 15	16 06	16 11
South Bermondsey	d		15 45										15 52			16 07									16 15
Queens Rd Peckham	d		15 48										15 54			16 09									16 18
Peckham Rye	d		15 50										15 57			16 12									16 20
East Dulwich	d												16 00			16 15									
North Dulwich	d												16 02			16 17									
Luton	d										15 04										15 18	15 14			
Luton Airport Parkway	d										15 06										15 20	15 16			
St Pancras International	d										15 40										15 54	16 04			
City Thameslink	d										15 47										16 02	16 13			
London Blackfriars	d										15 50										16 05	16 16			
Elephant & Castle	d																					16 19			
Loughborough Jn.	d																					16 23			
Herne Hill	d																					16 27			
Tulse Hill	d												16 05			16 20							16 32			
Streatham	d												16 09										16a35			
London Victoria	d					15 36	15 43	15 47	15 49	15 51		15 53							16 03	16 06					
Battersea Park	d		16a02			15 40	15 47		15 53										16 07						16a32
Milton Keynes Central	d																								
Watford Junction	d																								
Harrow & Wealdstone	d																								
Wembley Central	d																								
Shepherd's Bush	d																								
Kensington (Olympia)	d																								
West Brompton	d																								
Imperial Wharf	d																								
Clapham Junction	d					15 44	15 51	15 53	15 57			16 00							16 11	16 12					
Wandsworth Common	d					15 47	15 54		16 00			16 03							16 14						
Balham	d					15 50	15 56		16 02			16 05							16 16						
Streatham Hill	d					15 53			16 05																
West Norwood	d					15 57			16 10							16 23									
Gipsy Hill	d					16 00			16 13						16a15	16 26									
Crystal Palace	d					16 02			16a16							16 29									
Birkbeck	d															16 33									
Beckenham Junction	a															16 38									
Streatham Common	d						16 00					16 09	16 12						16 20						
Norbury	d						16 03					16 12	16 15						16 23						
Thornton Heath	d						16 06					16 15	16 18						16 26						
Selhurst	d						16 09					16 18	16 21						16 29						
Norwood Junction	a	15 59		16 02		16 07											16 16						16 26	16 29	
	d	16 00		16 03	16 05	16 09											16 16	16 20					16 26	16 30	
West Croydon	a				16 12	16 13						16 22	16 25					16 30	16 33						
East Croydon	a	16 03		16 06			16 12	16 03		16 07	16 09						16 20			16 22	16 24		16 30	16 33	

		SN	LO	SN	SN		SN ◇1	SN	SN 1	FC 1	SN	SN 1	SN	SN ◇1	SN	SN 1	LO	SN	SN	SN 1	SN		SN	LO	SN
London Bridge	d	16 20						16 18					16 22		16 33	16 33			16 36		16 41		16 48		
South Bermondsey	d							16 22							16 37						16 45				
Queens Rd Peckham	d							16 24							16 39						16 48				
Peckham Rye	d							16 27							16 42						16 50				
East Dulwich	d							16 30							16 45										
North Dulwich	d							16 32							16 47										
Luton	d									15 34															
Luton Airport Parkway	d									15 36															
St Pancras International	d									16 10															
City Thameslink	d									16 17															
London Blackfriars	d									16 20															
Elephant & Castle	d																								
Loughborough Jn.	d																								
Herne Hill	d																								
Tulse Hill	d							16 35							16 50										
Streatham	d							16 39																	
London Victoria	d			16 07	16 13		16 17		16 19		16 19			16 32				16 33		16 36					16 37
Battersea Park	d			16 11	16 17						16 23							16 37			17a02				16 41
Milton Keynes Central	d											15 13													
Watford Junction	d											15 51													
Harrow & Wealdstone	d											15 59													
Wembley Central	d											16u05													
Shepherd's Bush	d											16 19													
Kensington (Olympia)	d											16 22													
West Brompton	d											16 25													
Imperial Wharf	d											16 27													
Clapham Junction	d			16 15	16 21		16 23		16 26		16 27	16 34		16 38				16 41		16 42					16 45
Wandsworth Common	d			16 18	16 24						16 30	16 37						16 44							16 48
Balham	d			16 20	16 26						16 32	16 40						16 46							16 50
Streatham Hill	d			16 23							16 35														16 53
West Norwood	d			16 27							16 39				16 53										16 57
Gipsy Hill	d			16 30							16 44		16a45		16 56										17 00
Crystal Palace	d			16 32							16a46				16 59										17 02
Birkbeck	d														17 03										
Beckenham Junction	a														17 08										
Streatham Common	d				16 30			16 42				16 45						16 50							
Norbury	d				16 33			16 45				16 48						16 53							
Thornton Heath	d				16 36			16 48				16 51						16 56							
Selhurst	d				16 39			16 51				16 55						16 59							
Norwood Junction	a	16 32		16 37													16 44			16 59				17 01		17 07
	d	16 33	16 35	16 39													16 45	16 50		17 00				17 02	17 05	17 09
West Croydon	a		16 42	16 43				16 57										17 00	17 03	17 07					17 12	17 13
East Croydon	a	16 36			16 42		16 33		16 36	16 39		16 58		16 47		16 48				16 52			17 05		

		SN	FC 1	FC	FC 1	SN	SN ◇1	SN	SN 1	SN	SN	SN 1	SN		SN 1	SN	LO	SN	SN	SN 1	FC 1	FC	SN	SN	LO
London Bridge	d							16 48		16 52		16 57	16 58		16 59	17 03			17 05				17 11	17 17	
South Bermondsey	d							16 52					17 02										17 15		
Queens Rd Peckham	d							16 54					17 04										17 18		
Peckham Rye	d							16 57					17 07										17 20		
East Dulwich	d							17 00					17 10												
North Dulwich	d							17 02					17 12												
Luton	d		15 48	15 44	16 04																16 14	16 16			
Luton Airport Parkway	d		15 50	15 46	16 06																16 17	16 18			
St Pancras International	d		16 24	16 34	16 40																16 46	17 02			
City Thameslink	d		16 33	16 43	16 49																16 55	17 11			
London Blackfriars	d		16 36	16 46	16 52																17 00	17 14			
Elephant & Castle	d			16 49	16 56																17 04	17 18			
Loughborough Jn.	d			16 53	17 00																	17 22			
Herne Hill	d			16 57	17a04																	17 26			
Tulse Hill	d			17 02					17 05					17 17									17 31			
Streatham	d			17a05					17 09														17a35			
London Victoria	d	16 39				16 43	16 47		16 49		16 52							17 01		17 06					
Battersea Park	d					16 47					16 56							17 05					17a32		
Milton Keynes Central	d																								
Watford Junction	d																								
Harrow & Wealdstone	d																								
Wembley Central	d																								
Shepherd's Bush	d																								
Kensington (Olympia)	d																								
West Brompton	d																								
Imperial Wharf	d																								
Clapham Junction	d	16 45				16 51	16 53		16 56		17 00							17 09		17 12					
Wandsworth Common	d					16 54					17 03							17 12							
Balham	d					16 56					17 06							17 14							
Streatham Hill	d										17 09														
West Norwood	d										17 12		17 20												
Gipsy Hill	d									17a15	17 15		17 23												
Crystal Palace	d										17a18		17 26												
Birkbeck	d												17 30												
Beckenham Junction	a												17 35												
Streatham Common	d					17 00		17 12										17 18							
Norbury	d					17 03		17 15										17 21							
Thornton Heath	d					17 06		17 18										17 24							
Selhurst	d					17 09		17 21										17 27							
Norwood Junction	a														17 10	17 16			17 29					17 30	
	d														17 11	17 16	17 20		17 30					17 31	17 35
West Croydon	a							17 27								17 21	17 30	17 32	17 37						17 42
East Croydon	a	16 55	16 59			17 12	17 03		17 06			17 09			17 14					17 22	17 25			17 34	

		SN	SN	SN	SN ◇1		SN	SN 1	SN	SN	SN 1	FC 1	SN	SN	SN 1	SN 1	SN ◇1	LO	SN	SN ◇1	SN		SN	SN 1	FC 1
London Bridge	d						17 18			17 21	17 23		17 28	17 29	17 32						17 36		17 41	17 42	
South Bermondsey	d						17 22						17 32										17 45		
Queens Rd Peckham	d						17 24						17 35										17 47		
Peckham Rye	d						17 27						17 37										17 50		
East Dulwich	d						17 30						17 40												
North Dulwich	d						17 32						17 42												
Luton	d											16 34													16 50
Luton Airport Parkway	d											16 36													16 52
St Pancras International	d											17 10													17 28
City Thameslink	d											17 19													17 37
London Blackfriars	d											17 22													17 40
Elephant & Castle	d																								
Loughborough Jn.	d																								
Herne Hill	d																								
Tulse Hill	d						17 36						17 46												
Streatham	d						17 39																		
London Victoria	d	17 06	17 09	17 13	17 17			17 21	17 22								17 32		17 33	17 35					
Battersea Park	d	17 10		17 17					17 26										17 37				18a02		
Milton Keynes Central	d															16 13									
Watford Junction	d															16 51									
Harrow & Wealdstone	d															16 59									
Wembley Central	d															17u05									
Shepherd's Bush	d															17 19									
Kensington (Olympia)	d															17 22									
West Brompton	d															17 25									
Imperial Wharf	d															17 28									
Clapham Junction	d	17 14	17 15	17 21	17 23			17 27	17 30							17 33	17 38		17 41	17 42					
Wandsworth Common	d	17 17		17 24					17 33							17 36			17 44						
Balham	d	17 19		17 26					17 35							17 39			17 46						
Streatham Hill	d	17 22							17 38																
West Norwood	d	17 27							17 42				17 49												
Gipsy Hill	d	17 30							17 45	17a46			17 52												
Crystal Palace	d	17 32							17a47				17 54												
Birkbeck	d												17 58												
Beckenham Junction	a												18 04												
Streatham Common	d			17 30			17 42									17 46			17 50						
Norbury	d			17 33			17 45									17 48			17 53						
Thornton Heath	d			17 36			17 48									17 51			17 56						
Selhurst	d			17a40			17 50									17 55			17 59						
Norwood Junction	a	17 37												17 41	17 43						17 59				
	d	17 38												17 43	17 44			17 50			18 00				
West Croydon	a	17 43					17 57							17 47				18 01	18 03		18 08				
East Croydon	a		17 27		17 32			17 36			17 35	17 46			17 48	17 59	17 48			17 51				17 54	18 08

Table 177

Mondays to Fridays

Luton, Milton Keynes Central and London East and West Croydon via Tulse Hill - Crystal Palace - Norbury

Local Services

		FC	SN	SN	LO	SN	SN	SN	SN ◇1	SN 1	SN	SN	SN 1		SN	SN 1	SN	SN	LO	SN	SN	SN ◇1 H	FC 1	FC	FC
London Bridge	d		17 48	17 49							17 53		17 57		17 58	17 59		18 02			18 06				
South Bermondsey	d		17 52												18 02										
Queens Rd Peckham	d		17 54												18 04										
Peckham Rye	d		17 57												18 07										
East Dulwich	d		18 00												18 10										
North Dulwich	d		18 02												18 12										
Luton	d	16 46																						17 10	17 18
Luton Airport Parkway	d	16 48																						17 12	17 20
St Pancras International	d	17 32																					17 40	17 44	18 04
City Thameslink	d	17 41																					17 49	17 53	18 13
London Blackfriars	d	17 44																					17 52	17 56	18 16
Elephant & Castle	d	17 48																					17 56	18 00	18 20
Loughborough Jn.	d	17 52																							18 24
Herne Hill	d	17 57																						18a06	18 28
Tulse Hill	d	18 02	18 05												18 17										18 32
Streatham	d	18a05	18 09																						18a35
London Victoria	d					17 37	17 39	17 45	17 47	17 49		17 52								18 03		18 06			
Battersea Park	d					17 41		17 49				17 56								18 07					
Milton Keynes Central	d																								
Watford Junction	d																								
Harrow & Wealdstone	d																								
Wembley Central	d																								
Shepherd's Bush	d																17 45								
Kensington (Olympia)	d																17 47								
West Brompton	d																17 50								
Imperial Wharf	d																17 53								
Clapham Junction	d					17 45	17 45	17 53	17 53	17 56		18 00					18 02			18 11		18 12			
Wandsworth Common	d					17 48		17 56				18 03					18 05			18 14					
Balham	d					17 50		17 58				18 05					18 08			18 16					
Streatham Hill	d					17 53						18 08													
West Norwood	d					17 57						18 14			18 20										
Gipsy Hill	d					18 00					18a16	18 17			18 23										
Crystal Palace	d					18 02						18a19			18 26										
Birkbeck	d														18 30										
Beckenham Junction	a														18 35										
Streatham Common	d		18 12					18 02									18 15			18 20					
Norbury	d		18 14					18 05									18 18			18 23					
Thornton Heath	d		18 17					18 08									18 21			18 26					
Selhurst	d		18 21					18a12									18 26			18 29					
Norwood Junction	a			18 01		18 08										18 11		18 15			18 29				
	d			18 02	18 05	18 09										18 11		18 16	18 20		18 32				
West Croydon	a		18 27		18 12	18 14												18 20	18 30	18 34	18 39				
East Croydon	a			18 05			17 55		18 02	18 05			18 11			18 15	18 32					18 22	18 24		

		SN	SN 1	SN	LO		SN	SN	SN	SN ◇1	SN	SN	SN 1	SN 1	FC 1	SN	SN	SN 1	SN 1	SN	SN ◇1		LO	SN	SN
London Bridge	d	18 11	18 12	18 18							18 18	18 21	18 23				18 28	18 30		18 32					18 36
South Bermondsey	d	18 15									18 22						18 32								
Queens Rd Peckham	d	18 18									18 24						18 34								
Peckham Rye	d	18 20									18 27						18 37								
East Dulwich	d										18 30						18 40								
North Dulwich	d										18 32						18 42								
Luton	d														17 32										
Luton Airport Parkway	d														17 34										
St Pancras International	d														18 08										
City Thameslink	d														18 17										
London Blackfriars	d														18 20										
Elephant & Castle	d																								
Loughborough Jn.	d																								
Herne Hill	d																								
Tulse Hill	d										18 35						18 47								
Streatham	d										18 39														
London Victoria	d						18 07	18 09	18 13	18 17				18 19		18 22					18 32			18 32	
Battersea Park	d	18a32					18 11		18 17							18 26								18 36	
Milton Keynes Central	d																		17 13						
Watford Junction	d																		17 51						
Harrow & Wealdstone	d																		17 59						
Wembley Central	d																		18u05						
Shepherd's Bush	d																		18 19						
Kensington (Olympia)	d																		18 22						
West Brompton	d																		18 25						
Imperial Wharf	d																		18 27						
Clapham Junction	d						18 15	18 15	18 21	18 23				18 26		18 30			18 34		18 38			18 40	
Wandsworth Common	d						18 18		18 24							18 33			18 37					18 43	
Balham	d						18 20		18 26							18 35			18 40					18 45	
Streatham Hill	d						18 23									18 38									
West Norwood	d						18 27									18 42	18 50								
Gipsy Hill	d						18 30					18a45				18 45	18 53								
Crystal Palace	d						18 32									18a47	18 56								
Birkbeck	d																19 00								
Beckenham Junction	a																19 05								
Streatham Common	d								18 30		18 42								18 46					18 50	
Norbury	d								18 33		18 44								18 49					18 52	
Thornton Heath	d								18 36		18 47								18 52					18 55	
Selhurst	d								18a40		18 51								18 56					19 00	
Norwood Junction	a			18 30			18 37											18 41		18 45					18 59
	d			18 31	18 35		18 39											18 42		18 46			18 50		19 02
West Croydon	a				[illegible]		18 44				18 57									18 50			19 01	19 04	19 09

Table 177

Mondays to Fridays

Luton, Milton Keynes Central and London East and West Croydon via Tulse Hill - Crystal Palace - Norbury

Local Services

		SN 1	FC 1	SN	SN	LO	SN	SN	SN	SN ◇1 H	SN	SN	SN 1		FC 1	FC	SN	SN 1	LO	SN	SN 1 H	FC 1	SN	SN	LO
London Bridge	d			18 41	18 49						18 48	18 51						19 03					19 06	18 58	
South Bermondsey	d			18 45							18 52													19 02	
Queens Rd Peckham	d			18 48							18 54													19 04	
Peckham Rye	d			18 50							18 57													19 07	
East Dulwich	d										19 00													19 10	
North Dulwich	d										19 02													19 12	
Luton	d		17 46												18 00							18 18			
Luton Airport Parkway	d		17 48												18 02							18 20			
St Pancras International	d		18 20												18 34	18 38						18 54			
City Thameslink	d		18 29												18 43	18 47						19 03			
London Blackfriars	d		18 32												18 46	18 50						19 05			
Elephant & Castle	d		18 36													18 54									
Loughborough Jn.	d															18 58									
Herne Hill	d															19 02									
Tulse Hill	d										19 05					19 07								19 17	
Streatham	d										19 09					19a11									
London Victoria	d	18 36					18 36	18 39	18 45	18 47			18 51				18 52			18 59	19 06				
Battersea Park	d			19a02			18 40		18 49								18 56			19 04					
Milton Keynes Central	d																								
Watford Junction	d																								
Harrow & Wealdstone	d																								
Wembley Central	d																								
Shepherd's Bush	d																								
Kensington (Olympia)	d																								
West Brompton	d																								
Imperial Wharf	d																								
Clapham Junction	d	18 42					18 44	18 45	18 53	18 53			18 57				19 00			19 08	19 12				
Wandsworth Common	d						18 47		18 56								19 03			19 11					
Balham	d						18 49		18 58								19 05			19 14					
Streatham Hill	d						18 52										19 08								
West Norwood	d						18 56										19 12							19 20	
Gipsy Hill	d						18 59					19a15					19 15							19 23	
Crystal Palace	d						19 01										19a19							19 26	
Birkbeck	d																								
Beckenham Junction	a																								
Streatham Common	d								19 02		19 12									19 18					
Norbury	d								19 05		19 15									19 20					
Thornton Heath	d								19 08		19 18									19 23					
Selhurst	d								19 10		19 21									19 27					
Norwood Junction	a				19 01		19 06											19 14					19 29	19 32	
	d				19 02	19 05	19 09											19 15	19 20				19 30	19 33	19 35
West Croydon	a					19 12	19 14				19 27								19 30	19 32				19 40	19 42
East Croydon	a	18 52	18 55		19 05			18 57	19 13	19 02			19 07		19 10			19 18			19 22	19 24	19 33		

		SN	SN	FC	SN 1		SN	SN ◇1 H	FC 1	SN	SN	SN	SN	SN	LO	SN	SN	SN ◇1 H	SN 1	FC 1	SN		SN 1	LO	SN
London Bridge	d		19 08								19 11	19 18	19 22	19 31			19 28				19 36		19 52		
South Bermondsey	d		19 12								19 15	19 22					19 32								
Queens Rd Peckham	d		19 14								19 18	19 24					19 34								
Peckham Rye	d		19 17								19 20	19 27					19 37								
East Dulwich	d		19 20									19 30					19 40								
North Dulwich	d		19 22									19 32					19 42								
Luton	d			18 22					18 34											18 48					
Luton Airport Parkway	d			18 25					18 36											18 50					
St Pancras International	d			19 04					19 10											19 24					
City Thameslink	d			19 13					19 17											19 32					
London Blackfriars	d			19 16					19 20											19 35					
Elephant & Castle	d			19 19																					
Loughborough Jn.	d			19 23																					
Herne Hill	d			19 27																					
Tulse Hill	d		19 27	19 31								19 35					19 46								
Streatham	d			19a35								19 39													
London Victoria	d	19 06			19 10		19 15	19 17		19 22						19 30		19 32	19 36						19 36
Battersea Park	d	19 10					19 19			19 26	19a32					19 34									19 40
Milton Keynes Central	d																								
Watford Junction	d																								
Harrow & Wealdstone	d																								
Wembley Central	d																								
Shepherd's Bush	d																								
Kensington (Olympia)	d																								
West Brompton	d																								
Imperial Wharf	d																								
Clapham Junction	d	19 14			19 16		19 23	19 23		19 30						19 38		19 38	19 42						19 44
Wandsworth Common	d	19 17					19 26			19 33						19 41									19 47
Balham	d	19 20					19 28			19 35						19 44									19 50
Streatham Hill	d	19 23								19 38															19 53
West Norwood	d	19 27	19 30							19 42							19 49								19 57
Gipsy Hill	d	19 30	19 33							19 45			19a45				19 52								20 00
Crystal Palace	d	19 32	19 35							19a47							19 54								20 02
Birkbeck	d		19 39																						
Beckenham Junction	a		19 43																						
Streatham Common	d						19 32					19 42				19 48									
Norbury	d						19 35					19 45				19 51									
Thornton Heath	d						19 38					19 48				19 54									
Selhurst	d						19 41					19 51				19 57									
Norwood Junction	a	19 37												19 44			19 59				19 59		20 03		20 07
	d	19 39												19 44	19 50		20 02				20 00		20 03	20 05	20 09
West Croydon	a	[illegible]										19 55		19 49	20 00	20 02	20 06							20 12	20 13

Luton, Milton Keynes Central and London East and West Croydon via Tulse Hill - Crystal Palace - Norbury

Local Services

Station		SN	FC	SN ■	SN	SN ◇■	FC ■	SN	SN	SN	SN	SN	LO		SN	SN ◇■	FC ■	FC	SN	LO	SN	SN ■	SN	SN ◇■	SN
London Bridge ⊖	d	19 38							19 41	19 48	19 54	20 03							20 06						
South Bermondsey	d	19 42							19 45	19 52		20 07													
Queens Rd Peckham	d	19 44							19 48	19 54		20 09													
Peckham Rye	d	19 47							19 50	19 57		20 12													
East Dulwich	d	19 50								20 00		20 15													
North Dulwich	d	19 52								20 02		20 17													
Luton	d		18 54				19 04										19 18	19 24							
Luton Airport Parkway	d		18 57				19 06										19 20	19 27							
St Pancras International ⊖	d		19 34				19 40										19 54	20 04							
City Thameslink	d		19 43				19 47										20 02	20 13							
London Blackfriars ⊖	d		19 46				19 50										20 05	20 16							
Elephant & Castle ⊖	d		19 49															20 19							
Loughborough Jn.	d		19 53															20 23							
Herne Hill	d		19 57															20 27							
Tulse Hill	d	19 57	20 01							20 05		20 21						20 31							
Streatham	d		20a05							20 09								20a35							
London Victoria ⊖	d			19 40	19 45	19 47		19 52							20 00	20 06					20 06	20 10	20 15	20 17	20 22
Battersea Park	d				19 49			19 56	20a02						20 04						20 10		20 19		20 26
Milton Keynes Central	d																								
Watford Junction	d																								
Harrow & Wealdstone ⊖	d																								
Wembley Central ⊖	d																								
Shepherd's Bush ⊖	d																								
Kensington (Olympia) ⊖	d																								
West Brompton ⊖	d																								
Imperial Wharf	d																								
Clapham Junction	d			19 46	19 53	19 53		20 00							20 08	20 12					20 14	20 16	20 23	20 23	20 30
Wandsworth Common	d				19 56			20 03							20 11						20 17		20 26		20 33
Balham ⊖	d				19 59			20 05							20 14						20 20		20 28		20 35
Streatham Hill	d							20 08													20 23				20 38
West Norwood	d	20 00						20 12				20 24									20 27				20 42
Gipsy Hill	d	20 03						20 15			20a16	20 27									20 30				20 45
Crystal Palace	d	20 05						20a17				20 29									20 33				20a47
Birkbeck	d	20 09										20 33													
Beckenham Junction	a	20 13										20 37													
Streatham Common	d				20 03					20 12					20 18								20 32		
Norbury	d				20 05					20 15					20 20								20 35		
Thornton Heath	d				20 08					20 18					20 23								20 38		
Selhurst	d				20 11					20 21					20 27								20 41		
Norwood Junction	a																		20 29		20 37				
	d												20 20						20 30	20 35	20 39				
West Croydon	a									20 25			20 29		20 32					20 42	20 43				
East Croydon	a			19 57	20 14	20 03	20 09									20 22	20 24		20 33			20 27	20 44	20 33	

Station		SN	SN	SN	SN ■		SN	SN ■	LO	SN	SN ◇■	SN ◇■	FC ■	FC	SN	LO	SN	SN ■	SN	SN ◇■	SN		SN	SN	SN
London Bridge ⊖	d	20 11	20 18	20 22	20 28		20 33	20 34							20 36								20 41	20 48	20 52
South Bermondsey	d	20 15	20 22				20 37																20 45	20 52	
Queens Rd Peckham	d	20 18	20 24				20 39																20 48	20 54	
Peckham Rye	d	20 20	20 27				20 42																20 50	20 57	
East Dulwich	d		20 30				20 45																	21 00	
North Dulwich	d		20 32				20 47																	21 02	
Luton	d												19 46	19 50											
Luton Airport Parkway	d												19 48	19 52											
St Pancras International ⊖	d												20 24	20 36											
City Thameslink	d												20 32	20 43											
London Blackfriars ⊖	d												20 35	20 46											
Elephant & Castle ⊖	d													20 49											
Loughborough Jn.	d													20 53											
Herne Hill	d													20 57											
Tulse Hill	d		20 35				20 51							21 01										21 05	
Streatham	d		20 39											21a05										21 09	
London Victoria ⊖	d									20 30	20 32	20 36					20 36	20 40	20 45	20 47	20 52				
Battersea Park	d	20a32								20 34							20 40		20 49		20 56		21a02		
Milton Keynes Central	d																								
Watford Junction	d																								
Harrow & Wealdstone ⊖	d																								
Wembley Central ⊖	d																								
Shepherd's Bush ⊖	d																								
Kensington (Olympia) ⊖	d																								
West Brompton ⊖	d																								
Imperial Wharf	d																								
Clapham Junction	d									20 38	20 38	20 42					20 44	20 46	20 53	20 53	21 00				
Wandsworth Common	d									20 41							20 47		20 56		21 03				
Balham ⊖	d									20 44							20 50		20 58		21 05				
Streatham Hill	d																20 53				21 08				
West Norwood	d						20 54										20 57				21 12				
Gipsy Hill	d			20a45			20 57										21 00				21 15				21a15
Crystal Palace	d						20 59										21 03				21a17				
Birkbeck	d						21 03																		
Beckenham Junction	a						21 07																		
Streatham Common	d		20 42							20 48									21 02					21 12	
Norbury	d		20 45							20 50									21 05					21 15	
Thornton Heath	d		20 48							20 53									21 08					21 18	
Selhurst	d		20 51							20 57									21 11					21 21	
Norwood Junction	a							20 45							20 59		21 07								
	d							20 45	20 50						21 00	21 05	21 09								
West Croydon	a		20 55						21 00	21 02						21 12	21 13							21 25	
East Croydon	a				20 40			20 49			20 48	20 52	20 54		21 03			20 57	21 14	21 03					

Luton, Milton Keynes Central and London East and West Croydon via Tulse Hill - Crystal Palace - Norbury

Local Services

Station		SN ■	SN	LO	SN	SN ■	SN ◇■	FC ■	FC	SN	LO	SN	SN ■		SN	SN ◇■	SN	SN	SN	SN	SN ■	SN	LO	SN	SN ◇■
London Bridge ⊖	d	20 58	21 03							21 06								21 11	21 18	21 22	21 26	21 33			
South Bermondsey	d		21 07															21 15	21 22			21 37			
Queens Rd Peckham	d		21 09															21 18	21 24			21 39			
Peckham Rye	d		21 12															21 20	21 27			21 42			
East Dulwich	d		21 15																21 30			21 45			
North Dulwich	d		21 17																21 32			21 47			
Luton	d							20 16	20 20																
Luton Airport Parkway	d							20 18	20 22																
St Pancras International ⊖	d							20 54	21 06																
City Thameslink	d							21 02	21 13																
London Blackfriars ⊖	d							21 05	21 16																
Elephant & Castle ⊖	d								21 19																
Loughborough Jn.	d								21 23																
Herne Hill	d								21 27																
Tulse Hill	d		21 21						21 31										21 35			21 51			
Streatham	d								21a35										21 39						
London Victoria ⊖	d				21 00	21 02	21 06					21 06	21 10		21 15	21 17	21 23							21 30	21 36
Battersea Park	d				21 04							21 10			21 19		21 27	21a32						21 34	
Milton Keynes Central	d																								
Watford Junction	d																								
Harrow & Wealdstone ⊖	d																								
Wembley Central ⊖	d																								
Shepherd's Bush ⊖	d																								
Kensington (Olympia) ⊖	d																								
West Brompton ⊖	d																								
Imperial Wharf	d																								
Clapham Junction	d				21 08	21 08	21 12					21 14	21 16		21 23	21 23	21 31							21 38	21 42
Wandsworth Common	d				21 11							21 17			21 26		21 34							21 41	
Balham ⊖	d				21 14							21 20			21 29		21 36							21 44	
Streatham Hill	d											21 23					21 39								
West Norwood	d		21 24									21 27					21 43					21 54			
Gipsy Hill	d		21 27									21 30					21 46			21a45		21 57			
Crystal Palace	d		21 29									21 33					21a48					21 59			
Birkbeck	d		21 33																			22 03			
Beckenham Junction	a		21 37																			22 07			
Streatham Common	d				21 18										21 33				21 42					21 48	
Norbury	d				21 20										21 35				21 45					21 50	
Thornton Heath	d				21 23										21 38				21 48					21 53	
Selhurst	d				21 27										21 41				21 51					21 57	
Norwood Junction	a									21 29		21 37									21 37				
	d			21 20						21 30	21 35	21 39									21 38		21 50		
West Croydon	a			21 30	21 32						21 42	21 43							21 55				22 00	22 02	
East Croydon	a	21 10				21 18	21 22	21 24		21 33			21 27		21 44	21 33					21 41				21 52

Station		FC ■	FC	SN	LO		SN	SN ■	SN	SN ◇■	SN	SN	SN	SN	SN	LO	SN	SN ◇■	SN ◇■	FC ■	FC		SN	LO	SN
London Bridge ⊖	d			21 36								21 41	21 48	21 52	22 03								22 08		
South Bermondsey	d											21 45	21 52		22 07										
Queens Rd Peckham	d											21 48	21 54		22 09										
Peckham Rye	d											21 50	21 57		22 12										
East Dulwich	d												22 00		22 15										
North Dulwich	d												22 02		22 17										
Luton	d	20 46	20 50																	21 16	21 20				
Luton Airport Parkway	d	20 48	20 52																	21 18	21 22				
St Pancras International ⊖	d	21 24	21 36																	21 54	22 06				
City Thameslink	d	21 32	21 43																	22 02	22 13				
London Blackfriars ⊖	d	21 35	21 46																	22 05	22 16				
Elephant & Castle ⊖	d		21 49																		22 19				
Loughborough Jn.	d		21 53																		22 23				
Herne Hill	d		21 57																		22 27				
Tulse Hill	d		22 01										22 05		22 21						22 31				
Streatham	d		22a05										22 09								22a35				
London Victoria ⊖	d						21 36	21 40	21 45	21 47	21 52						22 00	22 02	22 06						22 06
Battersea Park	d						21 40		21 49		21 56	22a02					22 04								22 10
Milton Keynes Central	d																								
Watford Junction	d																								
Harrow & Wealdstone ⊖	d																								
Wembley Central ⊖	d																								
Shepherd's Bush ⊖	d																								
Kensington (Olympia) ⊖	d																								
West Brompton ⊖	d																								
Imperial Wharf	d																								
Clapham Junction	d						21 44	21 46	21 53	21 53	22 00						22 08	22 08	22 12						22 14
Wandsworth Common	d						21 47		21 56		22 03						22 11								22 17
Balham ⊖	d						21 50		21 58		22 05						22 14								22 20
Streatham Hill	d						21 53				22 08														22 23
West Norwood	d						21 57				22 12				22 24										22 27
Gipsy Hill	d						22 00				22 15			22a15	22 27										22 30
Crystal Palace	d						22 03				22a17				22 29										22 33
Birkbeck	d														22 35										
Beckenham Junction	a														22 38										
Streatham Common	d								22 02				22 12				22 18								
Norbury	d								22 05				22 15				22 20								
Thornton Heath	d								22 08				22 18				22 23								
Selhurst	d								22 11				22 21				22 27								
Norwood Junction	a			21 59			22 07																22 31		22 37
	d			22 00	22 05		22 09									22 20							22 32	22 35	22 39
West Croydon	a				22 12		22 13						22 25			22 30	22 32							22 42	22 43
East Croydon	a	21 54		22 03				21 57	22 14	22 03								22 18	22 22	22 24			22 35		

Luton, Milton Keynes Central and London East and West Croydon via Tulse Hill - Crystal Palace - Norbury

Local Services

Station		SN 1	SN	SN	SN	SN	SN	SN	SN	LO	SN	SN 1	SN 1
London Bridge	d				22 11	22 18	22 23	22 26	22 33				
South Bermondsey	d				22 15	22 22			22 37				
Queens Rd Peckham	d				22 18	22 24			22 39				
Peckham Rye	d				22 20	22 27			22 42				
East Dulwich	d					22 30			22 45				
North Dulwich	d					22 32			22 47				
Luton	d												
Luton Airport Parkway	d												
St Pancras International	d												
City Thameslink	d												
London Blackfriars	d												
Elephant & Castle	d												
Loughborough Jn.	d												
Herne Hill	d												
Tulse Hill	d					22 35			22 51				
Streatham	d					22 39							
London Victoria	d	22 10	22 15	22 22							22 30	22 32	22 36
Battersea Park	d		22 19	22 26	22a32						22 34		
Milton Keynes Central	d												
Watford Junction	d												
Harrow & Wealdstone	d												
Wembley Central	d												
Shepherd's Bush	d												
Kensington (Olympia)	d												
West Brompton	d												
Imperial Wharf	d												
Clapham Junction	d	22 16	22 23	22 30							22 38	22 38	22 42
Wandsworth Common	d		22 26	22 33							22 41		
Balham	d		22 28	22 35							22 44		
Streatham Hill	d			22 38									
West Norwood	d			22 42					22 54				
Gipsy Hill	d			22 45			22a45		22 57				
Crystal Palace	d			22a47					22 59				
Birkbeck	d								23 03				
Beckenham Junction	a								23 07				
Streatham Common	d		22 32			22 42					22 48		
Norbury	d		22 35			22 45					22 50		
Thornton Heath	d		22 38			22 48					22 53		
Selhurst	d		22 41			22 51					22 57		
Norwood Junction	a							22 38					
	d							22 38		22 50			
West Croydon	a					22 55				23 00	23 02		
East Croydon	a	22 26	22 44					22 42				22 48	22 52

Station			SN	SN	FC 1	SN	SN	SN 1	SN	SN ◇1	SN	SN	SN
London Bridge	d		22 38	22 41	22 42	22 56					22 48	22 52	
South Bermondsey	d			22 45							22 52		
Queens Rd Peckham	d			22 48							22 54		
Peckham Rye	d			22 50							22 57		
East Dulwich	d										23 00		
North Dulwich	d										23 02		
Luton	d												
Luton Airport Parkway	d												
St Pancras International	d												
City Thameslink	d												
London Blackfriars	d												
Elephant & Castle	d												
Loughborough Jn.	d												
Herne Hill	d												
Tulse Hill	d										23 05		
Streatham	d										23 09		
London Victoria	d						22 36	22 40	22 45	22 47			22 52
Battersea Park	d			23a02			22 40		22 49				22 56
Milton Keynes Central	d												
Watford Junction	d												
Harrow & Wealdstone	d												
Wembley Central	d												
Shepherd's Bush	d												
Kensington (Olympia)	d												
West Brompton	d												
Imperial Wharf	d												
Clapham Junction	d						22 44	22 46	22 53	22 53			23 00
Wandsworth Common	d						22 47		22 56				23 03
Balham	d						22 50		22 58				23 05
Streatham Hill	d						22 53						23 08
West Norwood	d						22 57						23 12
Gipsy Hill	d						23 00					23a15	23 15
Crystal Palace	d						23 03						23a17
Birkbeck	d												
Beckenham Junction	a												
Streatham Common	d								23 02		23 12		
Norbury	d								23 05		23 15		
Thornton Heath	d								23 08		23 18		
Selhurst	d								23 11		23 21		
Norwood Junction	a		23 01			23 07	23 08						
	d		23 02			23 07	23 09						
West Croydon	a						23 13				23 25		
East Croydon	a		23 06		22 54	23 11		22 57	23 14	23 03			

Station		FC	LO	SN	SN ◇1		SN ◇1	SN	SN	SN	SN 1	SN	SN ◇1
London Bridge	d	23 01						23 06	23 05				
South Bermondsey	d								23 09				
Queens Rd Peckham	d								23 11				
Peckham Rye	d								23 14				
East Dulwich	d								23 17				
North Dulwich	d								23 19				
Luton	d												
Luton Airport Parkway	d												
St Pancras International	d												
City Thameslink	d												
London Blackfriars	d												
Elephant & Castle	d												
Loughborough Jn.	d												
Herne Hill	d												
Tulse Hill	d	23 11							23 23				
Streatham	d	23a15											
London Victoria	d			23 00	23 02		23 06			23 06	23 10	23 15	23 17
Battersea Park	d			23 04						23 10		23 19	
Milton Keynes Central	d												
Watford Junction	d												
Harrow & Wealdstone	d												
Wembley Central	d												
Shepherd's Bush	d												
Kensington (Olympia)	d												
West Brompton	d												
Imperial Wharf	d												
Clapham Junction	d			23 08	23 08		23 12			23 14	23 16	23 23	23 23
Wandsworth Common	d			23 11						23 17		23 26	
Balham	d			23 14						23 20		23 28	
Streatham Hill	d									23 23			
West Norwood	d								23 26	23 29			
Gipsy Hill	d								23 29	23 32			
Crystal Palace	d								23 31	23 35			
Birkbeck	d												
Beckenham Junction	a												
Streatham Common	d			23 18								23 32	
Norbury	d			23 20								23 35	
Thornton Heath	d			23 23								23 38	
Selhurst	d			23 27								23 41	
Norwood Junction	a							23 29	23 36	23 39			
	d		23 20					23 30		23 40			
West Croydon	a		23 30	23 32						23 44			

Station		SN	SN	FC 1	SN	SN	FC	SN ◇1	LO		SN	SN	FC 1
London Bridge	d		23 11	23 12	23 18	23 22	23 28				23 36	23 33	23 42
South Bermondsey	d		23 15		23 22							23 37	
Queens Rd Peckham	d		23 18		23 24							23 39	
Peckham Rye	d		23 20		23 27							23 42	
East Dulwich	d				23 30							23 45	
North Dulwich	d				23 32							23 47	
Luton	d												
Luton Airport Parkway	d												
St Pancras International	d												
City Thameslink	d												
London Blackfriars	d												
Elephant & Castle	d												
Loughborough Jn.	d												
Herne Hill	d												
Tulse Hill	d				23 35		23 40					23 51	
Streatham	d				23 39		23a44						
London Victoria	d	23 22						23 32					
Battersea Park	d	23 26	23a32										
Milton Keynes Central	d												
Watford Junction	d												
Harrow & Wealdstone	d												
Wembley Central	d												
Shepherd's Bush	d												
Kensington (Olympia)	d												
West Brompton	d												
Imperial Wharf	d												
Clapham Junction	d	23 30						23 38					
Wandsworth Common	d	23 33											
Balham	d	23 35											
Streatham Hill	d	23 38											
West Norwood	d	23 42										23 54	
Gipsy Hill	d	23 45				23a45						23 57	
Crystal Palace	d	23a47										23 59	
Birkbeck	d												
Beckenham Junction	a												
Streatham Common	d				23 42								
Norbury	d				23 45								
Thornton Heath	d				23 48								
Selhurst	d				23 51								
Norwood Junction	a										23 59	00 04	
	d								23 50		23 59		
West Croydon	a				23 55				23 59				

Luton, Milton Keynes Central and London East and West Croydon via Tulse Hill - Crystal Palace - Norbury

Local Services

Station		SN 1	SN	SN	SN FO	SN 1	SN 1	SN FX	SN	SN	SN	FC	SN FO
London Bridge	d								23 48	23 52		23 58	
South Bermondsey	d								23 52				
Queens Rd Peckham	d								23 54				
Peckham Rye	d								23 57				
East Dulwich	d								00 01				
North Dulwich	d								00 03				
Luton	d												
Luton Airport Parkway	d												
St Pancras International	d												
City Thameslink	d												
London Blackfriars	d												
Elephant & Castle	d												
Loughborough Jn.	d												
Herne Hill	d												
Tulse Hill	d								00 06			00 10	
Streatham	d								00 10			00a14	
London Victoria	d		23 34	23 38	23 45	23 47	23 49	23 51			23 54		23 59
Battersea Park	d		23 38	23 42	23 49			23 55			23 58		00 03
Milton Keynes Central	d	22 11											
Watford Junction	d	22 54											
Harrow & Wealdstone	d	23 01											
Wembley Central	d												
Shepherd's Bush	d	23 21											
Kensington (Olympia)	d	23 23											
West Brompton	d	23 26											
Imperial Wharf	d	23 28											
Clapham Junction	d	23 40	23 42	23 46	23 53	23 53	23 56	23 59			00 02		00 07
Wandsworth Common	d		23 45	23 49	23 56			00 02			00 05		00 10
Balham	d	23 44	23 47	23 51	23 58			00 04			00 07		00 12
Streatham Hill	d			23 54							00 10		
West Norwood	d			23 58							00 14		
Gipsy Hill	d			00 01						00a15	00 17		
Crystal Palace	d			00 03							00a19		
Birkbeck	d												
Beckenham Junction	a												
Streatham Common	d	23 48	23 51		00 02			00 08	00 13				00 16
Norbury	d	23 51	23 54		00 05			00 11	00 15				00 19
Thornton Heath	d	23 54	23 57		00 08			00 14	00 18				00 22
Selhurst	d	23 57	23 59		00 11			00 17	00 21				00 25
Norwood Junction	a			00 08									
	d			00 09									
West Croydon	a		00 03	00 14				00 21	00 27				00 30
East Croydon	a	00 01			00 14	00 05	00 09						

Luton, Milton Keynes Central and London East and West Croydon via Tulse Hill - Crystal Palace - Norbury

Local Services

		SN 1	SN	SN	SN	SN	SN	SN 1	SN	SN 1	SN	FC	LO	SN	SN ◇1	SN	SN	SN	FC	SN 1	SN	SN	SN	SN
London Bridge 4 ⊖	d			23p36	23p33				23p48			23p58				00 06	00 03		00 12			00 18		
South Bermondsey	d				23p37				23p52								00 07					00 22		
Queens Rd Peckham	d				23p39				23p54								00 09					00 24		
Peckham Rye 4	d				23p42				23p57								00 12					00 27		
East Dulwich	d				23p45				00 01								00 15					00 30		
North Dulwich	d				23p47				00 03								00 17					00 32		
Luton 10	d																							
Luton Airport Parkway 7	d																							
St Pancras International 15 ⊖	d																							
City Thameslink 3	d																							
London Blackfriars 3 ⊖	d																							
Elephant & Castle ⊖	d																							
Loughborough Jn	d																							
Herne Hill 4	d																							
Tulse Hill 3	d				23p51				00 06			00 10					00 21					00 35		
Streatham 4	d								00 10			00a14										00 39		
London Victoria 15 ⊖	d		23p34			23p38	23p45	23p47		23p49	23p54			23p59	00 05			00 07		00 14	00 16		00 22	00 34
Battersea Park 4	d		23p38			23p42	23p49				23p58			00 03				00 11			00 20		00 26	00 38
Milton Keynes Central	d	22p11																						
Watford Junction	d	22p54																						
Harrow & Wealdstone ⊖	d	23p01																						
Wembley Central ⊖	d																							
Shepherd's Bush ⊖	d	23p21																						
Kensington (Olympia) ⊖	d	23p23																						
West Brompton ⊖	d	23p26																						
Imperial Wharf	d	23p28																						
Clapham Junction 10	d	23b40	23p42			23p46	23p53	23p53		23p56	00 02			00 07	00 11			00 15		00 20	00 24		00 30	00 42
Wandsworth Common	d		23p45			23p49	23p56				00 05			00 10				00 18			00 27		00 33	00 45
Balham 4 ⊖	d	23p44	23p47			23p51	23p58				00 07			00 12				00 20			00 29		00 35	00 47
Streatham Hill	d					23p54					00 10							00 23					00 38	
West Norwood 4	d				23p54	23p58					00 14						00 24	00 28					00 42	
Gipsy Hill	d				23p57	00 01					00 17						00 27	00 31					00 45	
Crystal Palace 4	d				23p59	00 03					00a19						00 29	00 33					00 47	
Birkbeck	d																							
Beckenham Junction 4	a																							
Streatham Common 4	d	23p48	23p51				00 02		00 13					00 16							00 33	00 42		00 51
Norbury	d	23p51	23p54				00 05		00 15					00 19							00 36	00 45		00 54
Thornton Heath	d	23p54	23p57				00 08		00 18					00 22							00 39	00 48		00 57
Selhurst 4	d	23p57	23p59				00 11		00 21					00 25	00 21					00 28	00 41	00 51		01 00
Norwood Junction 2	a			23p59	00 04	00 08										00 29	00 34	00 38					00 52	
	d			23p59		00 09							00 20			00 30		00 38					00 52	
West Croydon 4	a		00 03			00 14			00 27				00 27	00 30				00 43				00 55	00 58	01 04
East Croydon	a	00 01		00 03			00 14	00 05		00 09					00 24	00 33			00 26	00 31	00 44			

		SN	SN	SN	FC	SN	SN ◇1	FC 1	FC 1	SN 1	FC 1	SN 1	FC 1	FC 1	SN ◇1	FC 1	FC 1	SN ◇1	FC 1	SN ◇1	FC 1	SN 1	LO
London Bridge 4 ⊖	d	00 36	00 33		00 42			01 05	01 35		02 05		03 05	03 35		04 05	04 35		05 05		05 52		
South Bermondsey	d		00 37																				
Queens Rd Peckham	d		00 39																				
Peckham Rye 4	d		00 42																				
East Dulwich	d		00 45																				
North Dulwich	d		00 47																				
Luton 10	d																						
Luton Airport Parkway 7	d																						
St Pancras International 15 ⊖	d																						
City Thameslink 3	d																						
London Blackfriars 3 ⊖	d																						
Elephant & Castle ⊖	d																						
Loughborough Jn	d																						
Herne Hill 4	d																						
Tulse Hill 3	d		00 51																				
Streatham 4	d																						
London Victoria 15 ⊖	d			00 37		00 42	01 00			02 00		03 00			04 00			05 02		05 32		06 02	
Battersea Park 4	d			00 41		00 46																	
Milton Keynes Central	d																						
Watford Junction	d																						
Harrow & Wealdstone ⊖	d																						
Wembley Central ⊖	d																						
Shepherd's Bush ⊖	d																						
Kensington (Olympia) ⊖	d																						
West Brompton ⊖	d																						
Imperial Wharf	d																						
Clapham Junction 10	d			00 45		00 50	01 08			02 08		03 08			04 08			05 08		05 38		06 08	
Wandsworth Common	d			00 48		00 53																	
Balham 4 ⊖	d			00 50		00 55																	
Streatham Hill	d			00 53																			
West Norwood 4	d		00 54	00 58																			
Gipsy Hill	d		00 57	01 01																			
Crystal Palace 4	d		00 59	01 03																			
Birkbeck	d																						
Beckenham Junction 4	a																						
Streatham Common 4	d					00 59																	
Norbury	d					01 02																	
Thornton Heath	d					01 05																	
Selhurst 4	d					01 07	01 16	01 29	01 54	02 16	02 24	03 16	03 24	03 54	04 16	04 24	04 54	05 16	05 27				
Norwood Junction 2	a	00 59	01 04	01 08																			
	d	01 00		01 08																			06 05
West Croydon 4	a			01 13																			06 12
East Croydon	a	01 03			00 56	01 10	01 21	01 32	02 02	02 21	02 30	03 21	03 30	04 00	04 21	04 30	05 00	05 21	05 31	05 48	06 04	06 18	

b Previous night, arr. 2333

Luton, Milton Keynes Central and London East and West Croydon via Tulse Hill - Crystal Palace - Norbury

Local Services

		SN	LO	FC	SN	FC 1	LO	SN	SN 1	SN 1	LO	SN	SN	SN	FC 1	FC	SN	SN	SN	FC 1	LO	SN	SN 1	SN ◇1
London Bridge 4 ⊖	d	06 11		06 21		06 27						06 36		06 41	06 42	06 45		06 48	06 50	06 57			07 03	
South Bermondsey	d	06 15												06 45				06 52						
Queens Rd Peckham	d	06 18												06 48				06 54						
Peckham Rye 4	d	06 20												06 50				06 57						
East Dulwich	d																	07 00						
North Dulwich	d																	07 02						
Luton 10	d																							
Luton Airport Parkway 7	d																							
St Pancras International 15 ⊖	d																							
City Thameslink 3	d																							
London Blackfriars 3 ⊖	d																							
Elephant & Castle ⊖	d																							
Loughborough Jn	d																							
Herne Hill 4	d																							
Tulse Hill 3	d			06 31												07 01		07 05						
Streatham 4	d			06a35												07a05		07 09						
London Victoria 15 ⊖	d							06 23		06 32			06 43				06 53							07 06
Battersea Park 4	d	06a32											06 47	07a02										
Milton Keynes Central	d																							
Watford Junction	d								05 52															
Harrow & Wealdstone ⊖	d								05 58															
Wembley Central ⊖	d																							
Shepherd's Bush ⊖	d								06 20															
Kensington (Olympia) ⊖	d								06 23															
West Brompton ⊖	d								06 26															
Imperial Wharf	d								06 28															
Clapham Junction 10	d							06 30	06 34	06 38			06 51				07 00							07 12
Wandsworth Common	d							06 33	06 37				06 54				07 03							
Balham 4 ⊖	d							06 35	06 40				06 56				07 05							
Streatham Hill	d																					06 53		
West Norwood 4	d																					06 57		
Gipsy Hill	d																					07 00		
Crystal Palace 4	d																					07 02		
Birkbeck	d																							
Beckenham Junction 4	a																							
Streatham Common 4	d							06 39	06 45				07 00				07 09	07 12						
Norbury	d							06 42	06 48				07 03				07 12	07 15						
Thornton Heath	d							06 45	06 51				07 06				07 15	07 18						
Selhurst 4	d							06 48	06 54				07 09				07 18	07 21						
Norwood Junction 2	a											06 59							07 02			07 07	07 16	
	d		06 18		06 33		06 35				06 50	07 00							07 03		07 05	07 09	07 16	
West Croydon 4	a		06 30				06 41	06 52			07 00						07 22	07 25			07 11	07 14		
East Croydon	a				06 36	06 39			06 57	06 48		07 03	07 12		06 54				07 06	07 09			07 20	07 22

Table 177

Luton, Milton Keynes Central and London East and West Croydon via Tulse Hill - Crystal Palace - Norbury

Local Services

		LO	SN	SN	FC 1	FC	SN	LO		SN	SN	SN ◇1 A	SN	SN	FC 1	SN 1	SN ◇1	SN	SN 1	LO	SN	SN ◇1	SN 1	SN
London Bridge 4 ⊖	d		07 06	07 11	07 12	07 15	07 20							07 18	07 27			07 33	07 33				07 45	07 36
South Bermondsey	d			07 15										07 22				07 37						
Queens Rd Peckham	d			07 18										07 24				07 39						
Peckham Rye 4	d			07 20										07 27				07 42						
East Dulwich	d													07 30				07 45						
North Dulwich	d													07 32				07 47						
Luton 10	d																							
Luton Airport Parkway 7	d																							
St Pancras International 15 ⊖	d																							
City Thameslink 3	d																							
London Blackfriars 3 ⊖	d																							
Elephant & Castle ⊖	d																							
Loughborough Jn	d																							
Herne Hill 4	d																							
Tulse Hill 3	d					07 31								07 35				07 50						
Streatham 4	d					07a35								07 39										
London Victoria 15 ⊖	d									07 06	07 13	07 21	07 23				07 32				07 33	07 36		
Battersea Park 4	d			07a32						07 10	07 17										07 37			
Milton Keynes Central	d																							
Watford Junction	d															06 55								
Harrow & Wealdstone ⊖	d															07 01								
Wembley Central ⊖	d															07 06								
Shepherd's Bush ⊖	d															07 19								
Kensington (Olympia) ⊖	d															07 22								
West Brompton ⊖	d															07 25								
Imperial Wharf	d															07 27								
Clapham Junction 10	d									07 14	07 21		07 30			07 34	07 38				07 41	07 42		
Wandsworth Common	d									07 17	07 24		07 33			07 37					07 44			
Balham 4 ⊖	d									07 20	07 26		07 35			07 40					07 46			
Streatham Hill	d									07 23														
West Norwood 4	d									07 27								07 53						
Gipsy Hill	d									07 30								07 56						
Crystal Palace 4	d									07 32								07 59						
Birkbeck	d																	08 03						
Beckenham Junction 4	a																	08 06						
Streatham Common 4	d										07 30		07 39	07 42		07 45					07 50			
Norbury	d										07 33		07 42	07 45		07 48					07 53			
Thornton Heath	d										07 36		07 45	07 48		07 51					07 56			
Selhurst 4	d										07 39		07 48	07 51		07 54					07 59			
Norwood Junction 2	a		07 29				07 32			07 37									07 46				07 56	07 59
	d	07 20	07 30				07 33	07 35		07 39									07 46	07 50			07 56	08 00
West Croydon 4	a	07 30						07 41		07 43			07 52	07 55						08 00	08 03			
East Croydon	a		07 33		07 24		07 36				07 42	07 37			07 39	07 57	07 48		07 50			07 52	08 00	08 03

A from 10 September

Table 177

Luton, Milton Keynes Central and London East and West Croydon via Tulse Hill - Crystal Palace - Norbury

Local Services

		SN	FC 1	FC	SN	LO	SN	SN	SN ◇1	SN	SN ◇1	SN	SN	FC 1	SN	SN 1		LO	SN	SN ◇1	SN 1	SN	SN	FC 1	FC
London Bridge 4 ⊖	d	07 41	07 42	07 45	07 50								07 48	07 57	08 03	08 03					08 15	08 06	08 11	08 12	08 15
South Bermondsey	d	07 45											07 52		08 07								08 15		
Queens Rd Peckham	d	07 48											07 54		08 09								08 18		
Peckham Rye 4	d	07 50											07 57		08 12								08 20		
East Dulwich	d												08 00		08 15										
North Dulwich	d												08 02		08 17										
Luton 10	d																								
Luton Airport Parkway 7	d																								
St Pancras International 15 ⊖	d																								
City Thameslink 3	d																								
London Blackfriars 3 ⊖	d																								
Elephant & Castle ⊖	d																								
Loughborough Jn	d																								
Herne Hill 4	d																								
Tulse Hill 3	d			08 01									08 05		08 20										08 31
Streatham 4	d			08a05									08 09												08a35
London Victoria 15 ⊖	d						07 36	07 43	07 47	07 49	07 51	07 53							08 03	08 06					
Battersea Park 4	d	08a02					07 40	07 47		07 53									08 07				08a32		
Milton Keynes Central	d																								
Watford Junction	d																								
Harrow & Wealdstone ⊖	d																								
Wembley Central ⊖	d																								
Shepherd's Bush ⊖	d																								
Kensington (Olympia) ⊖	d																								
West Brompton ⊖	d																								
Imperial Wharf	d																								
Clapham Junction 10	d						07 44	07 51	07 53	07 57		08 00							08 11	08 12					
Wandsworth Common	d						07 47	07 54		08 00		08 03							08 14						
Balham 4 ⊖	d						07 50	07 56		08 02		08 05							08 16						
Streatham Hill	d						07 53			08 05															
West Norwood 4	d						07 57			08 10					08 23										
Gipsy Hill	d						08 00			08 13					08 26										
Crystal Palace 4	d						08 02			08a16					08 29										
Birkbeck	d														08 33										
Beckenham Junction 4	a														08 36										
Streatham Common 4	d							08 00				08 09	08 12						08 20						
Norbury	d							08 03				08 12	08 15						08 23						
Thornton Heath	d							08 06				08 15	08 18						08 26						
Selhurst 4	d							08 09				08 18	08 21						08 29						
Norwood Junction 2	a				08 02		08 07									08 16					08 26	08 29			
	d				08 03	08 05	08 09									08 16		08 20			08 26	08 30			
West Croydon 4	a					08 11	08 13					08 22	08 25					08 30	08 33						
East Croydon	a		07 54		08 06			08 12	08 03		08 07			08 09		08 20				08 22	08 30	08 33		08 24	

Luton, Milton Keynes Central and London East and West Croydon via Tulse Hill - Crystal Palace - Norbury

Local Services

		SN	LO	SN	SN	SN ◇1	SN	SN ◇1 A		SN	SN	SN	FC 1	SN 1	SN ◇1	SN	SN 1	LO	SN	SN ◇1	SN 1	SN	SN	FC 1
London Bridge 4 ⊖	d	08 20									08 18	08 22	08 27			08 33	08 33				08 45	08 36	08 41	08 42
South Bermondsey	d										08 22					08 37							08 45	
Queens Rd Peckham	d										08 24					08 39							08 48	
Peckham Rye 4	d										08 27					08 42							08 50	
East Dulwich	d										08 30					08 45								
North Dulwich	d										08 32					08 47								
Luton 10	d																							
Luton Airport Parkway 7	d																							
St Pancras International 15 ⊖	d																							
City Thameslink 3	d																							
London Blackfriars 3 ⊖	d																							
Elephant & Castle ⊖	d																							
Loughborough Jn.	d																							
Herne Hill 4	d																							
Tulse Hill 3	d										08 35					08 50								
Streatham 4	d										08 39													
London Victoria 15 ⊖	d			08 06	08 13	08 17	08 19	08 21		08 23					08 32				08 33	08 36				
Battersea Park 4	d			08 10	08 17		08 23												08 37				09a02	
Milton Keynes Central	d													07 13										
Watford Junction	d													07 52										
Harrow & Wealdstone ⊖	d													07 59										
Wembley Central ⊖	d													08u04										
Shepherd's Bush ⊖	d													08 19										
Kensington (Olympia) ⊖	d													08 22										
West Brompton ⊖	d													08 25										
Imperial Wharf	d													08 27										
Clapham Junction 10	d			08 14	08 21	08 23	08 27			08 30				08 34	08 38				08 41	08 42				
Wandsworth Common	d			08 17	08 24		08 30			08 33				08 37					08 44					
Balham 4 ⊖	d			08 20	08 26		08 32			08 35				08 40					08 46					
Streatham Hill	d			08 23			08 35																	
West Norwood 4	d			08 27			08 40									08 53								
Gipsy Hill	d			08 30			08 43					08a45				08 56								
Crystal Palace 4	d			08 32			08a46									08 59								
Birkbeck	d															09 03								
Beckenham Junction 4	a															09 06								
Streatham Common 4	d				08 30					08 39	08 42			08 45					08 50					
Norbury	d				08 33					08 42	08 45			08 48					08 53					
Thornton Heath	d				08 36					08 45	08 48			08 51					08 56					
Selhurst 4	d				08 39					08 48	08 51			08 54					08 59					
Norwood Junction 2	a	08 32		08 37													08 46				08 56	08 59		
	d	08 33	08 35	08 39													08 46	08 50			08 56	09 00		
West Croydon 4	a		08 41	08 43						08 52	08 55							09 00	09 03					
East Croydon	a	08 36			08 42	08 33		08 37					08 39	08 57	08 48		08 50			08 52	09 00	09 03		08 54

A from 10 September

Luton, Milton Keynes Central and London East and West Croydon via Tulse Hill - Crystal Palace - Norbury

Local Services

		FC	SN	LO	SN	SN	SN ◇1	SN	SN ◇1	SN	SN	SN	FC 1	SN	SN 1	LO		SN	SN ◇1 H	SN 1	SN	SN	FC 1	FC	SN
London Bridge 4 ⊖	d	08 45	08 50								08 48	08 52	08 57	09 03	09 03					09 15	09 06	09 11	09 12	09 15	09 20
South Bermondsey	d										08 52			09 07								09 15			
Queens Rd Peckham	d										08 54			09 09								09 18			
Peckham Rye 4	d										08 57			09 12								09 20			
East Dulwich	d										09 00			09 15											
North Dulwich	d										09 02			09 17											
Luton 10	d																								
Luton Airport Parkway 7	d																								
St Pancras International 15 ⊖	d																								
City Thameslink 3	d																								
London Blackfriars 3 ⊖	d																								
Elephant & Castle ⊖	d																								
Loughborough Jn.	d																								
Herne Hill 4	d																								
Tulse Hill 3	d	09 01									09 05			09 20										09 31	
Streatham 4	d	09a05									09 09													09a35	
London Victoria 15 ⊖	d				08 36	08 43	08 47	08 49	08 51	08 53								09 03	09 06						
Battersea Park 4	d				08 40	08 47		08 53										09 07				09a32			
Milton Keynes Central	d																								
Watford Junction	d																								
Harrow & Wealdstone ⊖	d																								
Wembley Central ⊖	d																								
Shepherd's Bush ⊖	d																								
Kensington (Olympia) ⊖	d																								
West Brompton ⊖	d																								
Imperial Wharf	d																								
Clapham Junction 10	d				08 44	08 51	08 53	08 57		09 00								09 11	09 12						
Wandsworth Common	d				08 47	08 54		09 00		09 03								09 14							
Balham 4 ⊖	d				08 50	08 56		09 02		09 05								09 16							
Streatham Hill	d				08 53			09 05																	
West Norwood 4	d				08 57			09 10						09 23											
Gipsy Hill	d				09 00			09 13				09a15		09 26											
Crystal Palace 4	d				09 02			09a16						09 29											
Birkbeck	d													09 33											
Beckenham Junction 4	a													09 36											
Streatham Common 4	d					09 00				09 09	09 12							09 20							
Norbury	d					09 03				09 12	09 15							09 23							
Thornton Heath	d					09 06				09 15	09 18							09 26							
Selhurst 4	d					09 09				09 18	09 21							09 29							
Norwood Junction 2	a		09 02		09 07										09 16					09 26	09 29				09 32
	d		09 03	09 05	09 09										09 16	09 20				09 26	09 30				09 33
West Croydon 4	a			09 12	09 13					09 22	09 25					09 30		09 33							
East Croydon	a		09 06			09 12	09 03		09 07				09 09		09 20				09 22	09 30	09 33		09 24		09 36

Table 177

Saturdays

Luton, Milton Keynes Central and London East and West Croydon via Tulse Hill - Crystal Palace - Norbury

Local Services

		LO	SN	SN	SN	SN	SN	SN	SN	SN	FC	SN	SN	SN	SN	LO	SN	SN	SN	SN	SN	FC	FC
					◇1		◇1				1	1	◇1		1			◇1	1			1	
							A											H					
London Bridge 4 ⊖	d								09 18	09 22	09 27			09 33	09 33				09 45	09 36	09 41	09 42	09 45
South Bermondsey	d								09 22					09 37							09 45		
Queens Rd Peckham	d								09 24					09 39							09 48		
Peckham Rye 4	d								09 27					09 42							09 50		
East Dulwich	d								09 30					09 45									
North Dulwich	d								09 32					09 47									
Luton 10	d																						
Luton Airport Parkway 7	d																						
St Pancras International 15 ⊖	d																						
City Thameslink 3	d																						
London Blackfriars 3 ⊖	d																						
Elephant & Castle ⊖	d																						
Loughborough Jn	d																						
Herne Hill 4	d																						
Tulse Hill 3	d								09 35					09 50									10 01
Streatham 4	d								09 39														10a05
London Victoria 15 ⊖	d		09 06	09 13	09 17	09 19	09 21	09 23					09 32				09 33	09 36					
Battersea Park 4	d		09 10	09 17		09 23											09 37				10a02		
Milton Keynes Central	d											08 13											
Watford Junction	d											08 52											
Harrow & Wealdstone ⊖	d											08 59											
Wembley Central ⊖	d											09u04											
Shepherd's Bush ⊖	d											09 19											
Kensington (Olympia) ⊖	d											09 22											
West Brompton ⊖	d											09 25											
Imperial Wharf	d											09 27											
Clapham Junction 10	d		09 14	09 21	09 23	09 27		09 30				09 34	09 38				09 41	09 42					
Wandsworth Common	d		09 17	09 24		09 30		09 33				09 37					09 44						
Balham 4 ⊖	d		09 20	09 26		09 32		09 35				09 40					09 46						
Streatham Hill	d		09 23			09 35																	
West Norwood 4	d		09 27			09 40								09 53									
Gipsy Hill	d		09 30			09 43				09a45				09 56									
Crystal Palace 4	d		09 32			09a46								09 59									
Birkbeck	d													10 03									
Beckenham Junction 4	a													10 06									
Streatham Common 4	d			09 30				09 39	09 42			09 45					09 50						
Norbury	d			09 33				09 42	09 45			09 48					09 53						
Thornton Heath	d			09 36				09 45	09 48			09 51					09 56						
Selhurst 4	d			09 39				09 48	09 51			09 54					09 59						
Norwood Junction 2	a		09 37												09 46				09 56	09 59			
	d	09 35	09 39												09 46	09 50			09 56	10 00			
West Croydon 4	a	09 42	09 43					09 52	09 55							10 00	10 03						
East Croydon	a			09 42	09 33		09 37				09 39	09 57	09 48		09 50			09 52	10 00	10 03		09 54	

A from 10 September

Table 177

Saturdays

Luton, Milton Keynes Central and London East and West Croydon via Tulse Hill - Crystal Palace - Norbury

Local Services

		SN	LO	SN	SN	SN	SN	SN	SN	SN	SN	FC	SN	SN	LO	SN	SN	SN	SN	SN	FC	FC	SN	LO
						◇1		◇1				1		1			◇1	1			1			
																	H							
London Bridge 4 ⊖	d	09 50								09 48	09 52	09 57	10 03	10 03				10 15	10 06	10 11	10 12	10 15	10 20	
South Bermondsey	d									09 52			10 07							10 15				
Queens Rd Peckham	d									09 54			10 09							10 18				
Peckham Rye 4	d									09 57			10 12							10 20				
East Dulwich	d									10 00			10 15											
North Dulwich	d									10 02			10 17											
Luton 10	d																							
Luton Airport Parkway 7	d																							
St Pancras International 15 ⊖	d																							
City Thameslink 3	d																							
London Blackfriars 3 ⊖	d																							
Elephant & Castle ⊖	d																							
Loughborough Jn	d																							
Herne Hill 4	d																							
Tulse Hill 3	d									10 05			10 20									10 31		
Streatham 4	d									10 09												10a35		
London Victoria 15 ⊖	d			09 36	09 43	09 47	09 49	09 51	09 53							10 03	10 06							
Battersea Park 4	d			09 40	09 47		09 53									10 07				10a32				
Milton Keynes Central	d																							
Watford Junction	d																							
Harrow & Wealdstone ⊖	d																							
Wembley Central ⊖	d																							
Shepherd's Bush ⊖	d																							
Kensington (Olympia) ⊖	d																							
West Brompton ⊖	d																							
Imperial Wharf	d																							
Clapham Junction 10	d			09 44	09 51	09 53	09 57		10 00							10 11	10 12							
Wandsworth Common	d			09 47	09 54		10 00		10 03							10 14								
Balham 4 ⊖	d			09 50	09 56		10 02		10 05							10 16								
Streatham Hill	d			09 53			10 05																	
West Norwood 4	d			09 57			10 10						10 23											
Gipsy Hill	d			10 00			10 13				10a15		10 26											
Crystal Palace 4	d			10 02			10a16						10 29											
Birkbeck	d												10 33											
Beckenham Junction 4	a												10 36											
Streatham Common 4	d				10 00				10 09	10 12						10 20								
Norbury	d				10 03				10 12	10 15						10 23								
Thornton Heath	d				10 06				10 15	10 18						10 26								
Selhurst 4	d				10 09				10 18	10 21						10 29								
Norwood Junction 2	a	10 02		10 07										10 16				10 26	10 29				10 32	
	d	10 03	10 05	10 09										10 16	10 20			10 26	10 30				10 33	10 35
West Croydon 4	a		10 12	10 13					10 22	10 25					10 30	10 33								10 42
East Croydon	a	10 06			10 12	10 03		10 07				10 09		10 20			10 22	10 30	10 33		10 24		10 36	

Luton, Milton Keynes Central and London East and West Croydon via Tulse Hill - Crystal Palace - Norbury

Local Services

Station		SN	SN	SN ◇1	SN	SN ◇1 A	SN	SN		SN	FC 1	SN 1	SN ◇1	SN	SN 1	LO	SN	SN ◇1	SN 1	SN	SN	FC 1	FC	SN
London Bridge 4 ⊖	d							10 18		10 22	10 27			10 33	10 33				10 45	10 36	10 41	10 42	10 45	10 50
South Bermondsey	d							10 22						10 37							10 45			
Queens Rd Peckham	d							10 24						10 39							10 48			
Peckham Rye 4	d							10 27						10 42							10 50			
East Dulwich	d							10 30						10 45										
North Dulwich	d							10 32						10 47										
Luton 10	d																							
Luton Airport Parkway 7	d																							
St Pancras International 15 ⊖	d																							
City Thameslink 3	d																							
London Blackfriars 3 ⊖	d																							
Elephant & Castle ⊖	d																							
Loughborough Jn.	d																							
Herne Hill 4	d																							
Tulse Hill 3	d							10 35						10 50									11 01	
Streatham 4	d							10 39															11a05	
London Victoria 15 ⊖	d	10 06	10 13	10 17	10 19	10 21	10 23						10 32				10 33	10 36						
Battersea Park 4	d	10 10	10 17		10 23												10 37				11a02			
Milton Keynes Central	d											09 13												
Watford Junction	d											09 52												
Harrow & Wealdstone ⊖	d											09 59												
Wembley Central ⊖	d											10u04												
Shepherd's Bush ⊖	d											10 19												
Kensington (Olympia) ⊖	d											10 22												
West Brompton ⊖	d											10 25												
Imperial Wharf	d											10 27												
Clapham Junction 10	d	10 14	10 21	10 23	10 27		10 30					10 34	10 38				10 41	10 42						
Wandsworth Common	d	10 17	10 24		10 30		10 33					10 37					10 44							
Balham 4 ⊖	d	10 20	10 26		10 32		10 35					10 40					10 46							
Streatham Hill	d	10 23			10 35																			
West Norwood 4	d	10 27			10 40									10 53										
Gipsy Hill	d	10 30			10 43					10a45				10 56										
Crystal Palace 4	d	10 32			10a46									10 59										
Birkbeck	d													11 03										
Beckenham Junction 4	a													11 06										
Streatham Common 4	d		10 30				10 39	10 42				10 45					10 50							
Norbury	d		10 33				10 42	10 45				10 48					10 53							
Thornton Heath	d		10 36				10 45	10 48				10 51					10 56							
Selhurst 4	d		10 39				10 48	10 51				10 54					10 59							
Norwood Junction 2	a	10 37													10 46				10 56	10 59				11 02
	d	10 39													10 46	10 50			10 56	11 00				11 03
West Croydon 4	a	10 43					10 52	10 55								11 00	11 03							
East Croydon	a		10 42	10 33		10 37					10 39	10 57	10 48		10 50			10 52	11 00	11 03		10 54		11 06

A from 10 September

Luton, Milton Keynes Central and London East and West Croydon via Tulse Hill - Crystal Palace - Norbury

Local Services

Station		LO	SN	SN	SN ◇1	SN	SN ◇1	SN	SN	SN	FC 1	SN	SN 1	LO	SN	SN ◇1		SN 1	SN	SN	FC 1	FC	SN	LO	SN
London Bridge 4 ⊖	d								10 48	10 52	10 57	11 03	11 03					11 15	11 06	11 11	11 12	11 15	11 20		
South Bermondsey	d								10 52			11 07								11 15					
Queens Rd Peckham	d								10 54			11 09								11 18					
Peckham Rye 4	d								10 57			11 12								11 20					
East Dulwich	d								11 00			11 15													
North Dulwich	d								11 02			11 17													
Luton 10	d																								
Luton Airport Parkway 7	d																								
St Pancras International 15 ⊖	d																								
City Thameslink 3	d																								
London Blackfriars 3 ⊖	d																								
Elephant & Castle ⊖	d																								
Loughborough Jn.	d																								
Herne Hill 4	d																								
Tulse Hill 3	d								11 05			11 20										11 31			
Streatham 4	d								11 09													11a35			
London Victoria 15 ⊖	d		10 36	10 43	10 47	10 49	10 51	10 53							11 03	11 06									11 06
Battersea Park 4	d		10 40	10 47		10 53									11 07					11a32					11 10
Milton Keynes Central	d																								
Watford Junction	d																								
Harrow & Wealdstone ⊖	d																								
Wembley Central ⊖	d																								
Shepherd's Bush ⊖	d																								
Kensington (Olympia) ⊖	d																								
West Brompton ⊖	d																								
Imperial Wharf	d																								
Clapham Junction 10	d		10 44	10 51	10 53	10 57		11 00							11 11	11 12									11 14
Wandsworth Common	d		10 47	10 54		11 00		11 03							11 14										11 17
Balham 4 ⊖	d		10 50	10 56		11 02		11 05							11 16										11 20
Streatham Hill	d		10 53			11 05																			11 23
West Norwood 4	d		10 57			11 10						11 23													11 27
Gipsy Hill	d		11 00			11 13				11a15		11 26													11 30
Crystal Palace 4	d		11 02			11a16						11 29													11 32
Birkbeck	d											11 33													
Beckenham Junction 4	a											11 36													
Streatham Common 4	d			11 00				11 09	11 12						11 20										
Norbury	d			11 03				11 12	11 15						11 23										
Thornton Heath	d			11 06				11 15	11 18						11 26										
Selhurst 4	d			11 09				11 18	11 21						11 29										
Norwood Junction 2	a		11 07										11 16					11 26	11 29				11 32		11 37
	d	11 05	11 09										11 16	11 20				11 26	11 30				11 33	11 35	11 39
West Croydon 4	a	11 12	11 13					11 22	11 25					11 30	11 33									11 42	11 43
East Croydon	a			11 12	11 03		11 07				11 09		11 20			11 22		11 30	11 33		11 24		11 36		

Table 177

Saturdays

Luton, Milton Keynes Central and London East and West Croydon via Tulse Hill - Crystal Palace - Norbury

Local Services

		SN	SN ◇1	SN	SN ◇1 A	SN	SN	SN		FC 1	SN 1	SN ◇1	SN	SN 1	LO	SN	SN ◇1	SN 1	SN	SN	FC 1	FC	SN	LO
London Bridge 4 ⊖	d						11 18	11 22		11 27			11 33	11 33				11 45	11 36	11 41	11 42	11 45	11 50	
South Bermondsey	d						11 22						11 37							11 45				
Queens Rd Peckham	d						11 24						11 39							11 48				
Peckham Rye 4	d						11 27						11 42							11 50				
East Dulwich	d						11 30						11 45											
North Dulwich	d						11 32						11 47											
Luton 10	d																							
Luton Airport Parkway 7	d																							
St Pancras International 15 ⊖	d																							
City Thameslink 3	d																							
London Blackfriars 3 ⊖	d																							
Elephant & Castle ⊖	d																							
Loughborough Jn	d																							
Herne Hill 4	d																							
Tulse Hill 3	d						11 35						11 50									12 01		
Streatham 4	d						11 39															12a05		
London Victoria 15 ⊖	d	11 13	11 17	11 19	11 21	11 23						11 32				11 33	11 36							
Battersea Park 4	d	11 17		11 23												11 37				12a02				
Milton Keynes Central	d										10 13													
Watford Junction	d										10 52													
Harrow & Wealdstone ⊖	d										10 59													
Wembley Central ⊖	d										11u04													
Shepherd's Bush ⊖	d										11 19													
Kensington (Olympia) ⊖	d										11 22													
West Brompton ⊖	d										11 25													
Imperial Wharf	d										11 27													
Clapham Junction 10	d	11 21	11 23	11 27		11 30					11 34	11 38				11 41	11 42							
Wandsworth Common	d	11 24		11 30		11 33					11 37					11 44								
Balham 4 ⊖	d	11 26		11 32		11 35					11 40					11 46								
Streatham Hill	d			11 35																				
West Norwood 4	d			11 40									11 53											
Gipsy Hill	d			11 43				11a45					11 56											
Crystal Palace 4	d			11a46									11 59											
Birkbeck 🚊	d												12 03											
Beckenham Junction 4 🚊	a												12 06											
Streatham Common 4	d	11 30				11 39	11 42				11 45					11 50								
Norbury	d	11 33				11 42	11 45				11 48					11 53								
Thornton Heath	d	11 36				11 45	11 48				11 51					11 56								
Selhurst 4	d	11 39				11 48	11 51				11 54					11 59								
Norwood Junction 2	a													11 46				11 56	11 59				12 02	
	d													11 46	11 50			11 56	12 00				12 03	12 05
West Croydon 4 🚊	a					11 52	11 55								12 00	12 03								12 12
East Croydon 🚊	a	11 42	11 33		11 37					11 39	11 57	11 48		11 50			11 52	12 00	12 03		11 54		12 06	

A from 10 September

Table 177

Saturdays

Luton, Milton Keynes Central and London East and West Croydon via Tulse Hill - Crystal Palace - Norbury

Local Services

		SN	SN	SN ◇1	SN	SN ◇1	SN	SN	SN	FC 1	SN	SN 1	LO	SN	SN ◇1	SN 1		SN	SN	FC 1	FC	SN	LO	SN	SN
London Bridge 4 ⊖	d							11 48	11 52	11 57	12 03	12 03				12 15		12 06	12 11	12 12	12 15	12 20			
South Bermondsey	d							11 52			12 07								12 15						
Queens Rd Peckham	d							11 54			12 09								12 18						
Peckham Rye 4	d							11 57			12 12								12 20						
East Dulwich	d							12 00			12 15														
North Dulwich	d							12 02			12 17														
Luton 10	d																								
Luton Airport Parkway 7	d																								
St Pancras International 15 ⊖	d																								
City Thameslink 3	d																								
London Blackfriars 3 ⊖	d																								
Elephant & Castle ⊖	d																								
Loughborough Jn	d																								
Herne Hill 4	d																								
Tulse Hill 3	d							12 05			12 20										12 31				
Streatham 4	d							12 09													12a35				
London Victoria 15 ⊖	d	11 36	11 43	11 47	11 49	11 51	11 53							12 03	12 06									12 06	12 13
Battersea Park 4	d	11 40	11 47		11 53									12 07					12a32					12 10	12 17
Milton Keynes Central	d																								
Watford Junction	d																								
Harrow & Wealdstone ⊖	d																								
Wembley Central ⊖	d																								
Shepherd's Bush ⊖	d																								
Kensington (Olympia) ⊖	d																								
West Brompton ⊖	d																								
Imperial Wharf	d																								
Clapham Junction 10	d	11 44	11 51	11 53	11 57		12 00							12 11	12 12									12 14	12 21
Wandsworth Common	d	11 47	11 54		12 00		12 03							12 14										12 17	12 24
Balham 4 ⊖	d	11 50	11 56		12 02		12 05							12 16										12 20	12 26
Streatham Hill	d	11 53			12 05																			12 23	
West Norwood 4	d	11 57			12 10						12 23													12 27	
Gipsy Hill	d	12 00			12 13				12a15		12 26													12 30	
Crystal Palace 4	d	12 02			12a16						12 29													12 32	
Birkbeck 🚊	d										12 33														
Beckenham Junction 4 🚊	a										12 36														
Streatham Common 4	d		12 00				12 09	12 12						12 20											12 30
Norbury	d		12 03				12 12	12 15						12 23											12 33
Thornton Heath	d		12 06				12 15	12 18						12 26											12 36
Selhurst 4	d		12 09				12 18	12 21						12 29											12 39
Norwood Junction 2	a	12 07										12 16				12 26		12 29				12 32		12 37	
	d	12 09										12 16	12 20			12 26		12 30				12 33	12 35	12 39	
West Croydon 4 🚊	a	12 13					12 22	12 25					12 30	12 33									12 42	12 43	
East Croydon 🚊	a		12 12	12 03		12 07				12 09		12 20			12 22	12 30		12 33		12 24		12 36			12 42

Luton, Milton Keynes Central and London East and West Croydon via Tulse Hill - Crystal Palace - Norbury

Local Services

		SN ◇1	SN	SN ◇1 A	SN	SN	SN	FC 1	SN 1	SN ◇1	SN	SN 1	LO	SN	SN ◇1 🚲	SN 1	SN	SN	FC 1	FC	SN	LO	SN
London Bridge 4 ⊖	d					12 18	12 22	12 27			12 33	12 33				12 45	12 36	12 41	12 42	12 45	12 50		
South Bermondsey	d					12 22					12 37							12 45					
Queens Rd Peckham	d					12 24					12 39							12 48					
Peckham Rye 4	d					12 27					12 42							12 50					
East Dulwich	d					12 30					12 45												
North Dulwich	d					12 32					12 47												
Luton 10	d																						
Luton Airport Parkway 7	d																						
St Pancras International 15 ⊖	d																						
City Thameslink 3	d																						
London Blackfriars 3 ⊖	d																						
Elephant & Castle ⊖	d																						
Loughborough Jn.	d																						
Herne Hill 4	d																						
Tulse Hill 3	d					12 35					12 50									13 01			
Streatham 4	d					12 39														13a05			
London Victoria 15 ⊖	d	12 17	12 19	12 21	12 23					12 32				12 33	12 36								12 36
Battersea Park 4	d		12 23											12 37				13a02					12 40
Milton Keynes Central	d								11 13														
Watford Junction	d								11 52														
Harrow & Wealdstone ⊖	d								11 59														
Wembley Central ⊖	d								12u04														
Shepherd's Bush ⊖	d								12 19														
Kensington (Olympia) ⊖	d								12 22														
West Brompton ⊖	d								12 25														
Imperial Wharf	d								12 27														
Clapham Junction 10	d	12 23	12 27		12 30				12 34	12 38				12 41	12 42								12 44
Wandsworth Common	d		12 30		12 33				12 37					12 44									12 47
Balham 4 ⊖	d		12 32		12 35				12 40					12 46									12 50
Streatham Hill	d		12 35																				12 53
West Norwood 4	d		12 40								12 53												12 57
Gipsy Hill	d		12 43				12a45				12 56												13 00
Crystal Palace 4	d		12a46								12 59												13 02
Birkbeck 🚊	d										13 03												
Beckenham Junction 4 🚊	a										13 06												
Streatham Common 4	d				12 39	12 42			12 45					12 50									
Norbury	d				12 42	12 45			12 48					12 53									
Thornton Heath	d				12 45	12 48			12 51					12 56									
Selhurst 4	d				12 48	12 51			12 54					12 59									
Norwood Junction 2	a											12 46				12 56	12 59				13 02		13 07
	d											12 46	12 50			12 56	13 00				13 03	13 05	13 09
West Croydon 4 🚊	a				12 52	12 55							13 00	13 03								13 12	13 13
East Croydon 🚊	a	12 33		12 37				12 39	12 57	12 48		12 50			12 52	13 00	13 03		12 54		13 06		

A from 10 September

Luton, Milton Keynes Central and London East and West Croydon via Tulse Hill - Crystal Palace - Norbury

Local Services

		SN	SN ◇1	SN	SN ◇1	SN	SN	SN	FC 1	SN	SN 1	LO	SN	SN ◇1 🚲	SN 1	SN	SN	FC 1	FC	SN	LO	SN	SN	SN ◇1
London Bridge 4 ⊖	d						12 48	12 52	12 57	13 03	13 03				13 15	13 06	13 11	13 12	13 15	13 20				
South Bermondsey	d						12 52			13 07							13 15							
Queens Rd Peckham	d						12 54			13 09							13 18							
Peckham Rye 4	d						12 57			13 12							13 20							
East Dulwich	d						13 00			13 15														
North Dulwich	d						13 02			13 17														
Luton 10	d																							
Luton Airport Parkway 7	d																							
St Pancras International 15 ⊖	d																							
City Thameslink 3	d																							
London Blackfriars 3 ⊖	d																							
Elephant & Castle ⊖	d																							
Loughborough Jn.	d																							
Herne Hill 4	d																							
Tulse Hill 3	d						13 05			13 20									13 31					
Streatham 4	d						13 09												13a35					
London Victoria 15 ⊖	d	12 43	12 47	12 49	12 51	12 53							13 03	13 06								13 06	13 13	13 17
Battersea Park 4	d	12 47		12 53									13 07				13a32					13 10	13 17	
Milton Keynes Central	d																							
Watford Junction	d																							
Harrow & Wealdstone ⊖	d																							
Wembley Central ⊖	d																							
Shepherd's Bush ⊖	d																							
Kensington (Olympia) ⊖	d																							
West Brompton ⊖	d																							
Imperial Wharf	d																							
Clapham Junction 10	d	12 51	12 53	12 57		13 00							13 11	13 12								13 14	13 21	13 23
Wandsworth Common	d	12 54		13 00		13 03							13 14									13 17	13 24	
Balham 4 ⊖	d	12 56		13 02		13 05							13 16									13 20	13 26	
Streatham Hill	d			13 05																		13 23		
West Norwood 4	d			13 10						13 23												13 27		
Gipsy Hill	d			13 13				13a15		13 26												13 30		
Crystal Palace 4	d			13a16						13 29												13 32		
Birkbeck 🚊	d									13 33														
Beckenham Junction 4 🚊	a									13 36														
Streatham Common 4	d	13 00				13 09	13 12						13 20										13 30	
Norbury	d	13 03				13 12	13 15						13 23										13 33	
Thornton Heath	d	13 06				13 15	13 18						13 26										13 36	
Selhurst 4	d	13 09				13 18	13 21						13 29										13 39	
Norwood Junction 2	a										13 16				13 26	13 29				13 32		13 37		
	d										13 16	13 20			13 26	13 30				13 33	13 35	13 39		
West Croydon 4 🚊	a					13 22	13 25					13 30	13 33								13 42	13 43		
East Croydon 🚊	a	13 12	13 03		13 07				13 09		13 20			13 22	13 30	13 33		13 24		13 36			13 42	13 33

Table 177

Luton, Milton Keynes Central and London East and West Croydon via Tulse Hill - Crystal Palace - Norbury

Local Services

	SN	SN ◇[1] A	SN	SN	SN	FC [1]	SN [1]		SN ◇[1]	SN	SN [1]	LO	SN	SN ◇[1] 🚌	SN [1]	SN	SN	FC [1]	FC	SN	LO	SN	SN
London Bridge [4] ⊖ d				13 18	13 22	13 27				13 33	13 33				13 45	13 36	13 41	13 42	13 45	13 50			
South Bermondsey d				13 22						13 37							13 45						
Queens Rd Peckham d				13 24						13 39							13 48						
Peckham Rye [4] d				13 27						13 42							13 50						
East Dulwich d				13 30						13 45													
North Dulwich d				13 32						13 47													
Luton [10] d																							
Luton Airport Parkway [7] d																							
St Pancras International [15] ⊖ d																							
City Thameslink [3] d																							
London Blackfriars [3] ⊖ d																							
Elephant & Castle ⊖ d																							
Loughborough Jn d																							
Herne Hill [4] d																							
Tulse Hill [3] d				13 35						13 50									14 01				
Streatham [4] d				13 39															14a05				
London Victoria [15] ⊖ d	13 19	13 21	13 23						13 32				13 33	13 36								13 36	13 43
Battersea Park [4] d	13 23												13 37				14a02					13 40	13 47
Milton Keynes Central d							12 13																
Watford Junction d							12 52																
Harrow & Wealdstone ⊖ d							12 59																
Wembley Central ⊖ d							13u04																
Shepherd's Bush ⊖ d							13 19																
Kensington (Olympia) ⊖ d							13 22																
West Brompton ⊖ d							13 25																
Imperial Wharf d							13 27																
Clapham Junction [10] d	13 27		13 30				13 34		13 38				13 41	13 42								13 44	13 51
Wandsworth Common d	13 30		13 33				13 37						13 44									13 47	13 54
Balham [4] ⊖ d	13 32		13 35				13 40						13 46									13 50	13 56
Streatham Hill d	13 35																					13 53	
West Norwood [4] d	13 40									13 53												13 57	
Gipsy Hill d	13 43				13a45					13 56												14 00	
Crystal Palace [4] d	13a46									13 59												14 02	
Birkbeck 🚋 d										14 03													
Beckenham Junction [4] 🚋 a										14 06													
Streatham Common [4] d			13 39	13 42			13 45						13 50										14 00
Norbury d			13 42	13 45			13 48						13 53										14 03
Thornton Heath d			13 45	13 48			13 51						13 56										14 06
Selhurst [4] d			13 48	13 51			13 54						13 59										14 09
Norwood Junction [2] a											13 46				13 56	13 59				14 02		14 07	
d											13 46	13 50			13 56	14 00				14 03	14 05	14 09	
West Croydon [4] 🚋 a			13 52	13 55								14 00	14 03								14 12	14 13	
East Croydon 🚋 a		13 37				13 39	13 57		13 48		13 50			13 52	14 00	14 03		13 54		14 06			14 12

A from 10 September

Table 177

Saturdays

Luton, Milton Keynes Central and London East and West Croydon via Tulse Hill - Crystal Palace - Norbury

Local Services

	SN ◇[1]	SN	SN ◇[1]	SN	SN	SN	FC [1]	SN	SN [1]	LO	SN	SN ◇[1] 🚌	SN [1]	SN	SN		FC [1]	FC	SN	LO	SN	SN	SN ◇[1]	SN
London Bridge [4] ⊖ d					13 48	13 52	13 57	14 03	14 03				14 15	14 06	14 11		14 12	14 15	14 20					
South Bermondsey d					13 52			14 07							14 15									
Queens Rd Peckham d					13 54			14 09							14 18									
Peckham Rye [4] d					13 57			14 12							14 20									
East Dulwich d					14 00			14 15																
North Dulwich d					14 02			14 17																
Luton [10] d																								
Luton Airport Parkway [7] d																								
St Pancras International [15] ⊖ d																								
City Thameslink [3] d																								
London Blackfriars [3] ⊖ d																								
Elephant & Castle ⊖ d																								
Loughborough Jn d																								
Herne Hill [4] d																								
Tulse Hill [3] d					14 05			14 20										14 31						
Streatham [4] d					14 09													14a35						
London Victoria [15] ⊖ d	13 47	13 49	13 51	13 53							14 03	14 06									14 06	14 13	14 17	14 19
Battersea Park [4] d		13 53									14 07				14a32						14 10	14 17		14 23
Milton Keynes Central d																								
Watford Junction d																								
Harrow & Wealdstone ⊖ d																								
Wembley Central ⊖ d																								
Shepherd's Bush ⊖ d																								
Kensington (Olympia) ⊖ d																								
West Brompton ⊖ d																								
Imperial Wharf d																								
Clapham Junction [10] d	13 53	13 57		14 00							14 11	14 12									14 14	14 21	14 23	14 27
Wandsworth Common d		14 00		14 03							14 14										14 17	14 24		14 30
Balham [4] ⊖ d		14 02		14 05							14 16										14 20	14 26		14 32
Streatham Hill d		14 05																			14 23			14 35
West Norwood [4] d		14 10						14 23													14 27			14 40
Gipsy Hill d		14 13				14a15		14 26													14 30			14 43
Crystal Palace [4] d		14a16						14 29													14 32			14a46
Birkbeck 🚋 d								14 33																
Beckenham Junction [4] 🚋 a								14 36																
Streatham Common [4] d				14 09	14 12						14 20											14 30		
Norbury d				14 12	14 15						14 23											14 33		
Thornton Heath d				14 15	14 18						14 26											14 36		
Selhurst [4] d				14 18	14 21						14 29											14 39		
Norwood Junction [2] a									14 16				14 26	14 29					14 32		14 37			
d									14 16	14 20			14 26	14 30					14 33	14 35	14 39			
West Croydon [4] 🚋 a				14 22	14 25					14 30	14 33									14 42	14 43			
East Croydon 🚋 a	14 03		14 07				14 09		14 20			14 22	14 30	14 33			14 24		14 36			14 42	14 33	

Luton, Milton Keynes Central and London East and West Croydon via Tulse Hill - Crystal Palace - Norbury

Local Services

		SN ◇[1] A	SN	SN	SN	FC [1]	SN [1]	SN ◇[1]		SN	SN [1]	LO	SN	SN ◇[1] H	SN [1]	SN	SN	FC [1]	FC	SN	LO	SN	SN	SN ◇[1]
London Bridge [4] ⊖	d			14 18	14 22	14 27				14 33	14 33				14 45	14 36	14 41	14 42	14 45	14 50				
South Bermondsey	d			14 22						14 37							14 45							
Queens Rd Peckham	d			14 24						14 39							14 48							
Peckham Rye [4]	d			14 27						14 42							14 50							
East Dulwich	d			14 30						14 45														
North Dulwich	d			14 32						14 47														
Luton [10]	d																							
Luton Airport Parkway [7]	d																							
St Pancras International [15] ⊖	d																							
City Thameslink [3]	d																							
London Blackfriars [3] ⊖	d																							
Elephant & Castle ⊖	d																							
Loughborough Jn.	d																							
Herne Hill [4]	d																							
Tulse Hill [3]	d			14 35						14 50									15 01					
Streatham [4]	d			14 39															15a05					
London Victoria [15] ⊖	d	14 21	14 23					14 32					14 33	14 36								14 36	14 43	14 47
Battersea Park [4]	d												14 37				15a02					14 40	14 47	
Milton Keynes Central	d						13 13																	
Watford Junction	d						13 52																	
Harrow & Wealdstone ⊖	d						13 59																	
Wembley Central ⊖	d						14u04																	
Shepherd's Bush ⊖	d						14 19																	
Kensington (Olympia) ⊖	d						14 22																	
West Brompton ⊖	d						14 25																	
Imperial Wharf	d						14 27																	
Clapham Junction [10]	d		14 30				14 34	14 38					14 41	14 42								14 44	14 51	14 53
Wandsworth Common	d		14 33				14 37						14 44									14 47	14 54	
Balham [4] ⊖	d		14 35				14 40						14 46									14 50	14 56	
Streatham Hill	d																					14 53		
West Norwood [4]	d									14 53												14 57		
Gipsy Hill	d				14a45					14 56												15 00		
Crystal Palace [4]	d									14 59												15 02		
Birkbeck 🚋	d									15 03														
Beckenham Junction [4] 🚋	a									15 06														
Streatham Common [4]	d		14 39	14 42			14 45						14 50										15 00	
Norbury	d		14 42	14 45			14 48						14 53										15 03	
Thornton Heath	d		14 45	14 48			14 51						14 56										15 06	
Selhurst [4]	d		14 48	14 51			14 54						14 59										15 09	
Norwood Junction [2]	a										14 46				14 56	14 59				15 02		15 07		
	d										14 46	14 50			14 56	15 00				15 03	15 05	15 09		
West Croydon [4] 🚋	a		14 52	14 55								15 00	15 03								15 12	15 13		
East Croydon 🚋	a	14 37				14 39	14 57	14 48			14 50			14 52	15 00	15 03		14 54		15 06			15 12	15 03

A from 10 September

Luton, Milton Keynes Central and London East and West Croydon via Tulse Hill - Crystal Palace - Norbury

Local Services

		SN	SN ◇[1]	SN	SN	SN	FC [1]	SN	SN [1]	LO	SN	SN ◇[1] H	SN [1]	SN	SN	FC [1]		FC	SN	LO	SN	SN	SN ◇[1]	SN	SN ◇[1] A
London Bridge [4] ⊖	d				14 48	14 52	14 57	15 03	15 03				15 15	15 06	15 11	15 12		15 15	15 20						
South Bermondsey	d				14 52			15 07							15 15										
Queens Rd Peckham	d				14 54			15 09							15 18										
Peckham Rye [4]	d				14 57			15 12							15 20										
East Dulwich	d				15 00			15 15																	
North Dulwich	d				15 02			15 17																	
Luton [10]	d																								
Luton Airport Parkway [7]	d																								
St Pancras International [15] ⊖	d																								
City Thameslink [3]	d																								
London Blackfriars [3] ⊖	d																								
Elephant & Castle ⊖	d																								
Loughborough Jn.	d																								
Herne Hill [4]	d																								
Tulse Hill [3]	d				15 05			15 20										15 31							
Streatham [4]	d				15 09													15a35							
London Victoria [15] ⊖	d	14 49	14 51	14 53							15 03	15 06									15 06	15 13	15 17	15 19	15 21
Battersea Park [4]	d	14 53									15 07				15a32						15 10	15 17		15 23	
Milton Keynes Central	d																								
Watford Junction	d																								
Harrow & Wealdstone ⊖	d																								
Wembley Central ⊖	d																								
Shepherd's Bush ⊖	d																								
Kensington (Olympia) ⊖	d																								
West Brompton ⊖	d																								
Imperial Wharf	d																								
Clapham Junction [10]	d	14 57		15 00							15 11	15 12									15 14	15 21	15 23	15 27	
Wandsworth Common	d	15 00		15 03							15 14										15 17	15 24		15 30	
Balham [4] ⊖	d	15 02		15 05							15 16										15 20	15 26		15 32	
Streatham Hill	d	15 05																			15 23			15 35	
West Norwood [4]	d	15 10						15 23													15 27			15 40	
Gipsy Hill	d	15 13				15a15		15 26													15 30			15 43	
Crystal Palace [4]	d	15a16						15 29													15 32			15a46	
Birkbeck 🚋	d							15 33																	
Beckenham Junction [4] 🚋	a							15 36																	
Streatham Common [4]	d			15 09	15 12						15 20											15 30			
Norbury	d			15 12	15 15						15 23											15 33			
Thornton Heath	d			15 15	15 18						15 26											15 36			
Selhurst [4]	d			15 18	15 21						15 29											15 39			
Norwood Junction [2]	a								15 16				15 26	15 29					15 32		15 37				
	d								15 16	15 20			15 26	15 30					15 33	15 35	15 39				
West Croydon [4] 🚋	a			15 22	15 25					15 30	15 33									15 42	15 43				
East Croydon 🚋	a		15 07				15 09		15 20			15 22	15 30	15 33		15 24			15 36			15 42	15 33		15 37

A from 10 September

Table 177

Luton, Milton Keynes Central and London East and West Croydon via Tulse Hill - Crystal Palace - Norbury

Local Services

		SN	SN	SN	FC 1	SN 1	SN ◇1	SN	SN 1	LO	SN	SN ◇1	SN 1	SN	SN	FC 1	FC	SN	LO	SN	SN	SN ◇1	SN
London Bridge ⊖	d		15 18	15 22	15 27			15 33	15 33				15 45	15 36	15 41	15 42	15 45	15 50					
South Bermondsey	d		15 22					15 37							15 45								
Queens Rd Peckham	d		15 24					15 39							15 48								
Peckham Rye	d		15 27					15 42							15 50								
East Dulwich	d		15 30					15 45															
North Dulwich	d		15 32					15 47															
Luton	d																						
Luton Airport Parkway	d																						
St Pancras International ⊖	d																						
City Thameslink	d																						
London Blackfriars ⊖	d																						
Elephant & Castle ⊖	d																						
Loughborough Jn	d																						
Herne Hill	d																						
Tulse Hill	d		15 35					15 50									16 01						
Streatham	d		15 39														16a05						
London Victoria ⊖	d	15 23					15 32				15 33	15 36								15 36	15 43	15 47	15 49
Battersea Park	d										15 37				16a02					15 40	15 47		15 53
Milton Keynes Central	d					14 13																	
Watford Junction	d					14 52																	
Harrow & Wealdstone ⊖	d					14 59																	
Wembley Central ⊖	d					15u04																	
Shepherd's Bush ⊖	d					15 19																	
Kensington (Olympia) ⊖	d					15 22																	
West Brompton ⊖	d					15 25																	
Imperial Wharf	d					15 27																	
Clapham Junction	d	15 30				15 34	15 38				15 41	15 42								15 44	15 51	15 53	15 57
Wandsworth Common	d	15 33				15 37					15 44									15 47	15 54		16 00
Balham ⊖	d	15 35				15 40					15 46									15 50	15 56		16 02
Streatham Hill	d																			15 53			16 05
West Norwood	d							15 53												15 57			16 10
Gipsy Hill	d			15a45				15 56												16 00			16 13
Crystal Palace	d							15 59												16 02			16a16
Birkbeck	d							16 03															
Beckenham Junction	a							16 06															
Streatham Common	d	15 39	15 42			15 45					15 50										16 00		
Norbury	d	15 42	15 45			15 48					15 53										16 03		
Thornton Heath	d	15 45	15 48			15 51					15 56										16 06		
Selhurst	d	15 48	15 51			15 54					15 59										16 09		
Norwood Junction	a								15 46				15 56	15 59				16 02		16 07			
	d								15 46	15 50			15 56	16 00				16 03	16 05	16 09			
West Croydon	a	15 52	15 55							16 00	16 03								16 12	16 13			
East Croydon	a				15 39	15 57	15 48		15 50			15 52	16 00	16 03		15 54		16 06			16 12	16 03	

Table 177

Luton, Milton Keynes Central and London East and West Croydon via Tulse Hill - Crystal Palace - Norbury

Local Services

		SN ◇1	SN	SN	SN	FC 1	SN	SN 1	LO	SN	SN ◇1	SN 1	SN	SN	FC 1	FC	SN	LO	SN	SN	SN ◇1	SN	SN ◇1 A	SN
London Bridge ⊖	d			15 48	15 52	15 57	16 03	16 03				16 15	16 06	16 11	16 12	16 15	16 20							
South Bermondsey	d			15 52			16 07							16 15										
Queens Rd Peckham	d			15 54			16 09							16 18										
Peckham Rye	d			15 57			16 12							16 20										
East Dulwich	d			16 00			16 15																	
North Dulwich	d			16 02			16 17																	
Luton	d																							
Luton Airport Parkway	d																							
St Pancras International ⊖	d																							
City Thameslink	d																							
London Blackfriars ⊖	d																							
Elephant & Castle ⊖	d																							
Loughborough Jn	d																							
Herne Hill	d																							
Tulse Hill	d			16 05			16 20									16 31								
Streatham	d			16 09												16a35								
London Victoria ⊖	d	15 51	15 53							16 03	16 06								16 06	16 13	16 17	16 19	16 21	16 23
Battersea Park	d									16 07				16a32					16 10	16 17		16 23		
Milton Keynes Central	d																							
Watford Junction	d																							
Harrow & Wealdstone ⊖	d																							
Wembley Central ⊖	d																							
Shepherd's Bush ⊖	d																							
Kensington (Olympia) ⊖	d																							
West Brompton ⊖	d																							
Imperial Wharf	d																							
Clapham Junction	d		16 00							16 11	16 12								16 14	16 21	16 23	16 27		16 30
Wandsworth Common	d		16 03							16 14									16 17	16 24		16 30		16 33
Balham ⊖	d		16 05							16 16									16 20	16 26		16 32		16 35
Streatham Hill	d																		16 23			16 35		
West Norwood	d						16 23												16 27			16 40		
Gipsy Hill	d				16a15		16 26												16 30			16 43		
Crystal Palace	d						16 29												16 32			16a46		
Birkbeck	d						16 33																	
Beckenham Junction	a						16 36																	
Streatham Common	d		16 09	16 12						16 20										16 30				16 39
Norbury	d		16 12	16 15						16 23										16 33				16 42
Thornton Heath	d		16 15	16 18						16 26										16 36				16 45
Selhurst	d		16 18	16 21						16 29										16 39				16 48
Norwood Junction	a							16 16				16 26	16 29				16 32		16 37					
	d							16 16	16 20			16 26	16 30				16 33	16 35	16 39					
West Croydon	a		16 22	16 25					16 30	16 33								16 42	16 43					16 52
East Croydon	a	16 07				16 09		16 20			16 22	16 30	16 33		16 24		16 36			16 42	16 33		16 37	

A from 10 September

Luton, Milton Keynes Central and London East and West Croydon via Tulse Hill - Crystal Palace - Norbury

Local Services

Station		SN	SN	FC 1	SN 1	SN ◇1	SN	SN 1		LO	SN	SN ◇1 🚲	SN 1	SN	SN	FC 1	FC	SN	LO	SN	SN	SN ◇1	SN	SN ◇1	
London Bridge 4 ⊖	d	16 18	16 22	16 27			16 33	16 33					16 45	16 36	16 41	16 42	16 45	16 50							
South Bermondsey	d	16 22					16 37								16 45										
Queens Rd Peckham	d	16 24					16 39								16 48										
Peckham Rye 4	d	16 27					16 42								16 50										
East Dulwich	d	16 30					16 45																		
North Dulwich	d	16 32					16 47																		
Luton 10	d																								
Luton Airport Parkway 7	d																								
St Pancras International 15 ⊖	d																								
City Thameslink 3	d																								
London Blackfriars 3 ⊖	d																								
Elephant & Castle ⊖	d																								
Loughborough Jn.	d																								
Herne Hill 4	d																								
Tulse Hill 3	d	16 35					16 50										17 01								
Streatham 4	d	16 39															17a05								
London Victoria 15 ⊖	d					16 32					16 33	16 36								16 36	16 43	16 47	16 49	16 51	
Battersea Park 4	d										16 37				17a02					16 40	16 47		16 53		
Milton Keynes Central	d				15 13																				
Watford Junction	d				15 52																				
Harrow & Wealdstone ⊖	d				15 59																				
Wembley Central ⊖	d				16u04																				
Shepherd's Bush ⊖	d				16 19																				
Kensington (Olympia) ⊖	d				16 22																				
West Brompton ⊖	d				16 25																				
Imperial Wharf	d				16 27																				
Clapham Junction 10	d				16 34	16 38					16 41	16 42								16 44	16 51	16 53	16 57		
Wandsworth Common	d				16 37						16 44									16 47	16 54		17 00		
Balham 4 ⊖	d				16 40						16 46									16 50	16 56		17 02		
Streatham Hill	d																			16 53			17 05		
West Norwood 4	d						16 53													16 57			17 10		
Gipsy Hill	d		16a45				16 56													17 00			17 13		
Crystal Palace 4	d						16 59													17 02			17a16		
Birkbeck	d						17 03																		
Beckenham Junction 4	a						17 06																		
Streatham Common 4	d	16 42			16 45						16 50										17 00				
Norbury	d	16 45			16 48						16 53										17 03				
Thornton Heath	d	16 48			16 51						16 56										17 06				
Selhurst 4	d	16 51			16 54						16 59										17 09				
Norwood Junction 2	a							16 46					16 56	16 59				17 02		17 07					
	d							16 46		16 50			16 56	17 00				17 03	17 05	17 09					
West Croydon 4	a	16 55								17 00	17 03								17 12	17 13					
East Croydon	a			16 39	16 57	16 48		16 50				16 52	17 00	17 03		16 54		17 06			17 12	17 03		17 07	

Luton, Milton Keynes Central and London East and West Croydon via Tulse Hill - Crystal Palace - Norbury

Local Services

Station		SN	SN	SN	FC 1	SN	SN 1	LO	SN	SN ◇1 🚲	SN 1	SN	SN	FC 1	FC	SN		LO	SN	SN	SN ◇1	SN	SN ◇1 A	SN	SN
London Bridge 4 ⊖	d		16 48	16 52	16 57	17 03	17 03				17 15	17 06	17 11	17 12	17 15	17 20									17 18
South Bermondsey	d		16 52			17 07							17 15												17 22
Queens Rd Peckham	d		16 54			17 09							17 18												17 24
Peckham Rye 4	d		16 57			17 12							17 20												17 27
East Dulwich	d		17 00			17 15																			17 30
North Dulwich	d		17 02			17 17																			17 32
Luton 10	d																								
Luton Airport Parkway 7	d																								
St Pancras International 15 ⊖	d																								
City Thameslink 3	d																								
London Blackfriars 3 ⊖	d																								
Elephant & Castle ⊖	d																								
Loughborough Jn.	d																								
Herne Hill 4	d																								
Tulse Hill 3	d		17 05			17 20									17 31										17 35
Streatham 4	d		17 09												17a35										17 39
London Victoria 15 ⊖	d	16 53							17 03	17 06									17 06	17 13	17 17	17 19	17 21	17 23	
Battersea Park 4	d								17 07				17a32						17 10	17 17		17 23			
Milton Keynes Central	d																								
Watford Junction	d																								
Harrow & Wealdstone ⊖	d																								
Wembley Central ⊖	d																								
Shepherd's Bush ⊖	d																								
Kensington (Olympia) ⊖	d																								
West Brompton ⊖	d																								
Imperial Wharf	d																								
Clapham Junction 10	d	17 00							17 11	17 12									17 14	17 21	17 23	17 27		17 30	
Wandsworth Common	d	17 03							17 14										17 17	17 24		17 30		17 33	
Balham 4 ⊖	d	17 05							17 16										17 20	17 26		17 32		17 35	
Streatham Hill	d																		17 23			17 35			
West Norwood 4	d					17 23													17 27			17 40			
Gipsy Hill	d			17a15		17 26													17 30			17 43			
Crystal Palace 4	d					17 29													17 32			17a46			
Birkbeck	d					17 33																			
Beckenham Junction 4	a					17 36																			
Streatham Common 4	d	17 09	17 12						17 20											17 30				17 39	17 42
Norbury	d	17 12	17 15						17 23											17 33				17 42	17 45
Thornton Heath	d	17 15	17 18						17 26											17 36				17 45	17 48
Selhurst 4	d	17 18	17 21						17 29											17 39				17 48	17 51
Norwood Junction 2	a						17 16				17 26	17 29				17 32			17 37						
	d						17 16	17 20			17 26	17 30				17 33		17 35	17 39						
West Croydon 4	a	17 22	17 25					17 30	17 33									17 42	17 43					17 52	17 55
East Croydon	a				17 09		17 20			17 22	17 30	17 33		17 24		17 36				17 42	17 33		17 37		

A from 10 September

Table 177

Saturdays

Luton, Milton Keynes Central and London East and West Croydon via Tulse Hill - Crystal Palace - Norbury

Local Services

			SN	FC ■	SN ■	SN ◇■	SN	SN ■	LO		SN	SN ◇■	SN ■	SN	SN	FC ■	FC	SN	LO	SN	SN	SN ◇■	SN	SN ◇■	SN
London Bridge 4	⊖	d	17 22	17 27			17 33	17 33					17 45	17 36	17 41	17 42	17 45	17 50							
South Bermondsey		d					17 37								17 45										
Queens Rd Peckham		d					17 39								17 48										
Peckham Rye 4		d					17 42								17 50										
East Dulwich		d					17 45																		
North Dulwich		d					17 47																		
Luton 10		d																							
Luton Airport Parkway 7		d																							
St Pancras International 15	⊖	d																							
City Thameslink 3		d																							
London Blackfriars 3	⊖	d																							
Elephant & Castle	⊖	d																							
Loughborough Jn		d																							
Herne Hill 4		d																							
Tulse Hill 3		d					17 50										18 01								
Streatham 4		d															18a05								
London Victoria 15	⊖	d				17 32					17 33	17 36								17 36	17 43	17 47	17 49	17 51	17 53
Battersea Park 4		d									17 37				18a02					17 40	17 47		17 53		
Milton Keynes Central		d			16 13																				
Watford Junction		d			16 52																				
Harrow & Wealdstone	⊖	d			16 59																				
Wembley Central	⊖	d			17u04																				
Shepherd's Bush	⊖	d			17 19																				
Kensington (Olympia)	⊖	d			17 22																				
West Brompton	⊖	d			17 25																				
Imperial Wharf		d			17 27																				
Clapham Junction 10		d			17 34	17 38					17 41	17 42								17 44	17 51	17 53	17 57		18 00
Wandsworth Common		d			17 37						17 44									17 47	17 54		18 00		18 03
Balham 4	⊖	d			17 40						17 46									17 50	17 56		18 02		18 05
Streatham Hill		d																		17 53			18 05		
West Norwood 4		d					17 53													17 57			18 10		
Gipsy Hill		d	17a45				17 56													18 00			18 13		
Crystal Palace 4		d					17 59													18 02			18a16		
Birkbeck	🚋	d					18 03																		
Beckenham Junction 4	🚋	a					18 06																		
Streatham Common 4		d			17 45						17 50										18 00				18 09
Norbury		d			17 48						17 53										18 03				18 12
Thornton Heath		d			17 51						17 56										18 06				18 15
Selhurst 4		d			17 54						17 59										18 09				18 18
Norwood Junction 2		a						17 46					17 57	17 59				18 02		18 07					
		d						17 46	17 50				17 57	18 00				18 03	18 05	18 09					
West Croydon 4	🚋	a							18 00		18 03								18 11	18 13					18 22
East Croydon	🚋	a		17 39	17 57	17 48		17 50				17 52	18 00	18 03		17 54		18 06			18 12	18 03		18 07	

Table 177

Saturdays

Luton, Milton Keynes Central and London East and West Croydon via Tulse Hill - Crystal Palace - Norbury

Local Services

			SN	SN	FC ■	SN	SN ■	LO	SN	SN ◇■	SN ■	SN	SN	FC ■	FC	SN	LO		SN	SN	SN ◇■	SN	SN ◇■ A	SN	SN	SN
London Bridge 4	⊖	d	17 48	17 52	17 57	18 03	18 03				18 15	18 06	18 11	18 12	18 15	18 20									18 18	18 22
South Bermondsey		d	17 52			18 07							18 15												18 22	
Queens Rd Peckham		d	17 54			18 09							18 18												18 24	
Peckham Rye 4		d	17 57			18 12							18 20												18 27	
East Dulwich		d	18 00			18 15																			18 30	
North Dulwich		d	18 02			18 17																			18 32	
Luton 10		d																								
Luton Airport Parkway 7		d																								
St Pancras International 15	⊖	d																								
City Thameslink 3		d																								
London Blackfriars 3	⊖	d																								
Elephant & Castle	⊖	d																								
Loughborough Jn		d																								
Herne Hill 4		d																								
Tulse Hill 3		d	18 05			18 20									18 31										18 35	
Streatham 4		d	18 09												18a35										18 39	
London Victoria 15	⊖	d							18 03	18 06									18 06	18 13	18 17	18 19	18 21	18 23		
Battersea Park 4		d							18 07				18a32						18 10	18 17		18 23				
Milton Keynes Central		d																								
Watford Junction		d																								
Harrow & Wealdstone	⊖	d																								
Wembley Central	⊖	d																								
Shepherd's Bush	⊖	d																								
Kensington (Olympia)	⊖	d																								
West Brompton	⊖	d																								
Imperial Wharf		d																								
Clapham Junction 10		d							18 11	18 12									18 14	18 21	18 23	18 27		18 30		
Wandsworth Common		d							18 14										18 17	18 24		18 30		18 33		
Balham 4	⊖	d							18 16										18 20	18 26		18 32		18 35		
Streatham Hill		d																	18 23			18 35				
West Norwood 4		d				18 23													18 27			18 40				
Gipsy Hill		d		18a15		18 26													18 30			18 43				18a45
Crystal Palace 4		d				18 29													18 32			18a46				
Birkbeck	🚋	d				18 33																				
Beckenham Junction 4	🚋	a				18 36																				
Streatham Common 4		d	18 12						18 20											18 30				18 39	18 42	
Norbury		d	18 15						18 23											18 33				18 42	18 45	
Thornton Heath		d	18 18						18 26											18 36				18 45	18 48	
Selhurst 4		d	18 21						18 29											18 39				18 48	18 51	
Norwood Junction 2		a					18 16				18 26	18 29				18 32			18 37							
		d					18 16	18 20			18 26	18 30				18 33	18 35		18 39							
West Croydon 4	🚋	a	18 25					18 30	18 33								18 41		18 43					18 52	18 55	
East Croydon	🚋	a			18 09		18 20			18 22	18 30	18 33		18 24		18 36				18 42	18 33		18 37			

A from 10 September

Luton, Milton Keynes Central and London East and West Croydon via Tulse Hill - Crystal Palace - Norbury

Local Services

		FC	SN	SN	SN	SN	LO	SN		SN	SN	SN	SN	FC	FC	SN	LO	SN	SN	SN	SN	SN	SN	SN
		1	1	◇1		1				◇1	1			1						◇1		◇1		
London Bridge 4 ⊖	d	18 27			18 33	18 33					18 45	18 36	18 41	18 42	18 45	18 50								18 48
South Bermondsey	d				18 37								18 45											18 52
Queens Rd Peckham	d				18 39								18 48											18 54
Peckham Rye 4	d				18 42								18 50											18 57
East Dulwich	d				18 45																			19 00
North Dulwich	d				18 47																			19 02
Luton 10	d																							
Luton Airport Parkway 7	d																							
St Pancras International 15 ⊖	d																							
City Thameslink 3	d																							
London Blackfriars 3 ⊖	d																							
Elephant & Castle ⊖	d																							
Loughborough Jn.	d																							
Herne Hill 4	d																							
Tulse Hill 3	d				18 50										19 01									19 05
Streatham 4	d														19a05									19 09
London Victoria 15 ⊖	d			18 32				18 33		18 36								18 36	18 43	18 47	18 49	18 51	18 53	
Battersea Park 4	d							18 37					19a02					18 40	18 47		18 53			
Milton Keynes Central	d		17 13																					
Watford Junction	d		17 52																					
Harrow & Wealdstone ⊖	d		17 59																					
Wembley Central ⊖	d		18u04																					
Shepherd's Bush ⊖	d		18 19																					
Kensington (Olympia) ⊖	d		18 22																					
West Brompton ⊖	d		18 25																					
Imperial Wharf	d		18 27																					
Clapham Junction 10	d		18 34	18 38				18 41		18 42								18 44	18 51	18 53	18 57		19 00	
Wandsworth Common	d		18 37					18 44										18 47	18 54		19 00		19 03	
Balham 4 ⊖	d		18 40					18 46										18 50	18 56		19 02		19 05	
Streatham Hill	d																	18 53			19 05			
West Norwood 4	d				18 53													18 57			19 10			
Gipsy Hill	d				18 56													19 00			19 13			
Crystal Palace 4	d				18 59													19 02			19a16			
Birkbeck	d				19 03																			
Beckenham Junction 4	a				19 06																			
Streatham Common 4	d		18 45					18 50											19 00				19 09	19 12
Norbury	d		18 48					18 53											19 03				19 12	19 15
Thornton Heath	d		18 51					18 56											19 06				19 15	19 18
Selhurst 4	d		18 54					18 59											19 09				19 18	19 21
Norwood Junction 2	a					18 46					18 56	18 59				19 02		19 07						
	d					18 46	18 50				18 56	19 00				19 03	19 05	19 09						
West Croydon 4	a						19 00	19 03									19 11	19 13					19 22	19 25
East Croydon	a	18 39	18 57	18 48		18 50				18 52	19 00	19 03		18 54		19 06			19 12	19 03		19 07		

Luton, Milton Keynes Central and London East and West Croydon via Tulse Hill - Crystal Palace - Norbury

Local Services

		SN	FC	SN	SN	LO	SN	SN	SN	SN	FC	FC	SN	LO	SN	SN		SN	SN	SN	SN	SN	SN	FC	SN
			1		1			◇1			1							◇1		◇1 A				1	1
London Bridge 4 ⊖	d	18 52	18 57	19 03	19 03				19 06	19 11	19 12	19 15	19 20									19 18	19 22	19 27	
South Bermondsey	d			19 07						19 15												19 22			
Queens Rd Peckham	d			19 09						19 18												19 24			
Peckham Rye 4	d			19 12						19 20												19 27			
East Dulwich	d			19 15																		19 30			
North Dulwich	d			19 17																		19 32			
Luton 10	d																								
Luton Airport Parkway 7	d																								
St Pancras International 15 ⊖	d																								
City Thameslink 3	d																								
London Blackfriars 3 ⊖	d																								
Elephant & Castle ⊖	d																								
Loughborough Jn.	d																								
Herne Hill 4	d																								
Tulse Hill 3	d			19 20								19 31										19 35			
Streatham 4	d											19a35										19 39			
London Victoria 15 ⊖	d						19 03	19 06							19 06	19 13		19 17	19 19	19 21	19 23				
Battersea Park 4	d						19 07			19a32					19 10	19 17			19 23						
Milton Keynes Central	d																								18 13
Watford Junction	d																								18 52
Harrow & Wealdstone ⊖	d																								18 59
Wembley Central ⊖	d																								19u04
Shepherd's Bush ⊖	d																								19 19
Kensington (Olympia) ⊖	d																								19 22
West Brompton ⊖	d																								19 25
Imperial Wharf	d																								19 27
Clapham Junction 10	d						19 11	19 12							19 14	19 21		19 23	19 27		19 30				19 34
Wandsworth Common	d						19 14								19 17	19 24			19 30		19 33				19 37
Balham 4 ⊖	d						19 16								19 20	19 26			19 32		19 35				19 40
Streatham Hill	d														19 23				19 35						
West Norwood 4	d			19 23											19 27				19 40						
Gipsy Hill	d	19a15		19 26											19 30				19 43				19a45		
Crystal Palace 4	d			19 29											19 32				19a46						
Birkbeck	d			19 33																					
Beckenham Junction 4	a			19 36																					
Streatham Common 4	d						19 20									19 30					19 39	19 42			19 45
Norbury	d						19 23									19 33					19 42	19 45			19 48
Thornton Heath	d						19 26									19 36					19 45	19 48			19 51
Selhurst 4	d						19 29									19 39					19 48	19 51			19 54
Norwood Junction 2	a				19 16				19 29				19 32		19 37										
	d				19 16	19 20			19 30				19 33	19 35	19 39										
West Croydon 4	a					19 30	19 33							19 41	19 43						19 52	19 55			
East Croydon	a		19 09		19 20			19 22	19 33		19 24		19 36			19 42		19 33		19 37				19 39	19 57

A from 10 September

Luton, Milton Keynes Central and London East and West Croydon via Tulse Hill - Crystal Palace - Norbury

Local Services

		SN	SN	SN	LO	SN	SN	SN		SN	FC	FC	SN	LO	SN	SN	SN	SN	SN	SN	SN	SN	FC	SN
		◇1		1			◇1				1						◇1		◇1				1	
London Bridge	d		19 33	19 33				19 36		19 41	19 42	19 45	19 50								19 48	19 52	19 57	20 03
South Bermondsey	d		19 37							19 45											19 52			20 07
Queens Rd Peckham	d		19 39							19 48											19 54			20 09
Peckham Rye	d		19 42							19 50											19 57			20 12
East Dulwich	d		19 45																		20 00			20 15
North Dulwich	d		19 47																		20 02			20 17
Luton	d																							
Luton Airport Parkway	d																							
St Pancras International	d																							
City Thameslink	d																							
London Blackfriars	d																							
Elephant & Castle	d																							
Loughborough Jn	d																							
Herne Hill	d																							
Tulse Hill	d		19 50									20 01									20 05			20 20
Streatham	d											20a05									20 09			
London Victoria	d	19 32				19 33	19 36								19 36	19 43	19 47	19 49	19 51	19 53				
Battersea Park	d					19 37				20a02					19 40	19 47		19 53						
Milton Keynes Central	d																							
Watford Junction	d																							
Harrow & Wealdstone	d																							
Wembley Central	d																							
Shepherd's Bush	d																							
Kensington (Olympia)	d																							
West Brompton	d																							
Imperial Wharf	d																							
Clapham Junction	d	19 38				19 41	19 42								19 44	19 51	19 53	19 57		20 00				
Wandsworth Common	d					19 44									19 47	19 54		20 00		20 03				
Balham	d					19 46									19 50	19 56		20 02		20 05				
Streatham Hill	d														19 53			20 05						
West Norwood	d		19 53												19 57			20 10						20 23
Gipsy Hill	d		19 56												20 00			20 13				20a15		20 26
Crystal Palace	d		19 59												20 02			20a16						20 29
Birkbeck	d		20 03																					20 33
Beckenham Junction	a		20 06																					20 36
Streatham Common	d					19 50										20 00				20 09	20 12			
Norbury	d					19 53										20 03				20 12	20 15			
Thornton Heath	d					19 56										20 06				20 15	20 18			
Selhurst	d					19 59										20 09				20 18	20 21			
Norwood Junction	a			19 46				19 59					20 02		20 07									
	d			19 46	19 50			20 00					20 03	20 05	20 09									
West Croydon	a				20 00	20 03								20 15	20 14					20 24	20 26			
East Croydon	a	19 48		19 50			19 52	20 03			19 54		20 06			20 12	20 03		20 07				20 09	

		LO	SN	SN	SN	SN	FC	FC	SN	LO	SN	SN	SN	SN	SN	SN		SN	SN	SN	SN	SN	SN	LO	SN
				◇1			1					1		◇1		◇1				1		◇1			
London Bridge	d				20 06	20 11	20 12	20 15	20 20										20 18		20 22		20 33		
South Bermondsey	d					20 15													20 22				20 37		
Queens Rd Peckham	d					20 18													20 24				20 39		
Peckham Rye	d					20 20													20 27				20 42		
East Dulwich	d																		20 30				20 45		
North Dulwich	d																		20 32				20 47		
Luton	d																								
Luton Airport Parkway	d																								
St Pancras International	d																								
City Thameslink	d																								
London Blackfriars	d																								
Elephant & Castle	d																								
Loughborough Jn	d																								
Herne Hill	d																								
Tulse Hill	d							20 31											20 35				20 50		
Streatham	d							20a35											20 39						
London Victoria	d		20 03	20 06							20 06	20 10	20 13	20 17	20 19	20 21		20 23				20 32			20 33
Battersea Park	d		20 07			20a32					20 10		20 17		20 23										20 37
Milton Keynes Central	d																			19 13					
Watford Junction	d																			19 51					
Harrow & Wealdstone	d																			19 58					
Wembley Central	d																								
Shepherd's Bush	d																			20 19					
Kensington (Olympia)	d																			20 22					
West Brompton	d																			20 25					
Imperial Wharf	d																			20 27					
Clapham Junction	d		20 11	20 12							20 14	20 16	20 21	20 23	20 27			20 30		20 34		20 38			20 41
Wandsworth Common	d		20 14								20 17		20 24		20 30			20 33		20 37					20 44
Balham	d		20 16								20 20		20 26		20 32			20 35		20 40					20 46
Streatham Hill	d										20 23				20 35										
West Norwood	d										20 27				20 40								20 53		
Gipsy Hill	d										20 30				20 43						20a45		20 56		
Crystal Palace	d										20 32				20a46								20 59		
Birkbeck	d																						21 03		
Beckenham Junction	a																						21 06		
Streatham Common	d		20 20										20 30					20 39	20 42	20 45					20 50
Norbury	d		20 23										20 33					20 42	20 45	20 48					20 53
Thornton Heath	d		20 26										20 36					20 45	20 48	20 51					20 56
Selhurst	d		20 29										20 39					20 48	20 51	20 55					20 59
Norwood Junction	a				20 29				20 32		20 37														
	d	20 20			20 30				20 33	20 35	20 39													20 50	
West Croydon	a	20 30	20 33							20 45	20 44							20 54	20 56					21 00	21 03
East Croydon	a			20 22	20 33		20 24		20 36			20 27	20 42	20 33		20 37				20 59		20 48			

Luton, Milton Keynes Central and London East and West Croydon via Tulse Hill - Crystal Palace - Norbury

Local Services

		SN	SN	SN	FC	FC	SN	LO		SN	SN	SN	SN	SN	SN	SN	SN	SN	SN	LO	SN	SN	SN	SN
		◇1			1						1		◇1					◇1				◇1		
London Bridge	d		20 36	20 41	20 42	20 45	20 50									20 48	20 52		21 03				21 06	21 11
South Bermondsey	d			20 45												20 52			21 07					21 15
Queens Rd Peckham	d			20 48												20 54			21 09					21 18
Peckham Rye	d			20 50												20 57			21 12					21 20
East Dulwich	d															21 00			21 15					
North Dulwich	d															21 02			21 17					
Luton	d																							
Luton Airport Parkway	d																							
St Pancras International	d																							
City Thameslink	d																							
London Blackfriars	d																							
Elephant & Castle	d																							
Loughborough Jn	d																							
Herne Hill	d																							
Tulse Hill	d					21 01										21 05			21 20					
Streatham	d					21a05										21 09								
London Victoria	d	20 36								20 36	20 40	20 43	20 47	20 49	20 53			21 02			21 03	21 06		
Battersea Park	d			21a02						20 40		20 47		20 53							21 07			21a32
Milton Keynes Central	d																							
Watford Junction	d																							
Harrow & Wealdstone	d																							
Wembley Central	d																							
Shepherd's Bush	d																							
Kensington (Olympia)	d																							
West Brompton	d																							
Imperial Wharf	d																							
Clapham Junction	d	20 42								20 44	20 46	20 51	20 53	20 57	21 00			21 08			21 11	21 12		
Wandsworth Common	d									20 47		20 54		21 00	21 03						21 14			
Balham	d									20 50		20 56		21 02	21 05						21 16			
Streatham Hill	d									20 53				21 05										
West Norwood	d									20 57				21 10					21 23					
Gipsy Hill	d									21 00				21 13			21a15		21 26					
Crystal Palace	d									21 02				21a16					21 29					
Birkbeck	d																		21 33					
Beckenham Junction	a																		21 36					
Streatham Common	d											21 00			21 09	21 12					21 20			
Norbury	d											21 03			21 12	21 15					21 23			
Thornton Heath	d											21 06			21 15	21 18					21 26			
Selhurst	d											21 09			21 18	21 21					21 29			
Norwood Junction	a		20 59				21 02			21 07													21 29	
	d		21 00				21 03	21 05		21 09										21 20			21 30	
West Croydon	a							21 15		21 14					21 24	21 26				21 30	21 33			
East Croydon	a	20 52	21 03		20 53		21 06				20 57	21 12	21 03					21 18				21 22	21 33	

		FC	FC	SN	LO	SN	SN	SN	SN	SN	SN	SN	SN	SN	LO	SN		SN	SN	SN	FC	FC	SN	LO	SN
		1					1		◇1									◇1			1				
London Bridge	d	21 12	21 15	21 20								21 18	21 22	21 33					21 36	21 41	21 42	21 45	21 50		
South Bermondsey	d											21 22		21 37						21 45					
Queens Rd Peckham	d											21 24		21 39						21 48					
Peckham Rye	d											21 27		21 42						21 50					
East Dulwich	d											21 30		21 45											
North Dulwich	d											21 32		21 47											
Luton	d																								
Luton Airport Parkway	d																								
St Pancras International	d																								
City Thameslink	d																								
London Blackfriars	d																								
Elephant & Castle	d																								
Loughborough Jn	d																								
Herne Hill	d																								
Tulse Hill	d		21 31									21 35		21 50								22 01			
Streatham	d		21a35									21 39										22a05			
London Victoria	d					21 06	21 10	21 13	21 17	21 19	21 23					21 33		21 36							21 36
Battersea Park	d					21 10		21 17		21 23						21 37				22a02					21 40
Milton Keynes Central	d																								
Watford Junction	d																								
Harrow & Wealdstone	d																								
Wembley Central	d																								
Shepherd's Bush	d																								
Kensington (Olympia)	d																								
West Brompton	d																								
Imperial Wharf	d																								
Clapham Junction	d					21 14	21 16	21 21	21 23	21 27	21 30					21 41		21 42							21 44
Wandsworth Common	d					21 17		21 24		21 30	21 33					21 44									21 47
Balham	d					21 20		21 26		21 32	21 35					21 46									21 50
Streatham Hill	d					21 23				21 35															21 53
West Norwood	d					21 27				21 40				21 53											21 57
Gipsy Hill	d					21 30				21 43			21a45	21 56											22 00
Crystal Palace	d					21 32				21a46				21 59											22 02
Birkbeck	d													22 03											
Beckenham Junction	a													22 06											
Streatham Common	d							21 30			21 39	21 42				21 50									
Norbury	d							21 33			21 42	21 45				21 53									
Thornton Heath	d							21 36			21 45	21 48				21 56									
Selhurst	d							21 39			21 48	21 51				21 59									
Norwood Junction	a			21 32		21 37													21 59				22 02		22 07
	d			21 33	21 35	21 39									21 50				22 00				22 03	22 05	22 09
West Croydon	a				21 45	21 44					21 54	21 56			22 00	22 03								22 12	22 13
East Croydon	a	21 24		21 36			21 27	21 42	21 33									21 52	22 04		21 54		22 07		

Luton, Milton Keynes Central and London East and West Croydon via Tulse Hill - Crystal Palace - Norbury

Local Services

Station		SN 1	SN	SN ◇1	SN	SN	SN	SN		SN ◇1	SN	LO	SN	SN ◇1	SN	SN	FC 1	FC	SN	LO	SN	SN 1	SN	SN
London Bridge ⊖	d						21 48	21 52			22 03				22 06	22 11	22 12	22 15	22 20					
South Bermondsey	d						21 52				22 07					22 15								
Queens Rd Peckham	d						21 54				22 09					22 18								
Peckham Rye	d						21 57				22 12					22 20								
East Dulwich	d						22 00				22 15													
North Dulwich	d						22 02				22 17													
Luton	d																							
Luton Airport Parkway	d																							
St Pancras International ⊖	d																							
City Thameslink	d																							
London Blackfriars ⊖	d																							
Elephant & Castle ⊖	d																							
Loughborough Jn.	d																							
Herne Hill	d																							
Tulse Hill	d						22 05				22 20							22 31						
Streatham	d						22 09											22a35						
London Victoria ⊖	d	21 40	21 43	21 47	21 49	21 53				22 02			22 03	22 06							22 06	22 10	22 13	22 19
Battersea Park	d		21 47		21 53								22 07			22a32					22 10		22 17	22 23
Milton Keynes Central	d																							
Watford Junction	d																							
Harrow & Wealdstone ⊖	d																							
Wembley Central ⊖	d																							
Shepherd's Bush ⊖	d																							
Kensington (Olympia) ⊖	d																							
West Brompton ⊖	d																							
Imperial Wharf	d																							
Clapham Junction	d	21 46	21 51	21 53	21 57	22 00				22 08			22 11	22 12							22 14	22 16	22 21	22 27
Wandsworth Common	d		21 54		22 00	22 03							22 14								22 17		22 24	22 30
Balham ⊖	d		21 56		22 02	22 05							22 16								22 20		22 26	22 32
Streatham Hill	d				22 05																22 23			22 35
West Norwood	d				22 10						22 23										22 27			22 40
Gipsy Hill	d				22 13			22a15			22 26										22 30			22 43
Crystal Palace	d				22a16						22 29										22 32			22a46
Birkbeck	d										22 33													
Beckenham Junction	a										22 36													
Streatham Common	d		22 00			22 09	22 12						22 20										22 30	
Norbury	d		22 03			22 12	22 15						22 23										22 33	
Thornton Heath	d		22 06			22 15	22 18						22 26										22 36	
Selhurst	d		22 09			22 18	22 21						22 29										22 39	
Norwood Junction	a														22 29				22 32		22 37			
	d											22 20			22 30				22 33	22 35	22 39			
West Croydon	a					22 22	22 26					22 30	22 33							22 42	22 43			
East Croydon	a	21 57	22 12	22 03						22 18				22 22	22 35		22 24		22 37			22 27	22 42	

Station		SN	SN	SN	SN 1	SN	LO	SN	SN ◇1	SN	SN	FC 1	FC	SN	SN	SN 1		SN	SN ◇1	SN	SN	SN	SN	SN ◇1	LO
London Bridge ⊖	d		22 18	22 22		22 33				22 36	22 41	22 42	22 45	22 50								22 48	22 52		
South Bermondsey	d		22 22			22 37					22 45											22 52			
Queens Rd Peckham	d		22 24			22 39					22 48											22 54			
Peckham Rye	d		22 27			22 42					22 50											22 57			
East Dulwich	d		22 30			22 45																23 00			
North Dulwich	d		22 32			22 47																23 02			
Luton	d																								
Luton Airport Parkway	d																								
St Pancras International ⊖	d																								
City Thameslink	d																								
London Blackfriars ⊖	d																								
Elephant & Castle ⊖	d																								
Loughborough Jn.	d																								
Herne Hill	d																								
Tulse Hill	d		22 35			22 50							23 01									23 05			
Streatham	d		22 39										23a05									23 09			
London Victoria ⊖	d	22 23			22 32			22 33	22 36						22 36	22 40		22 43	22 47	22 49	22 53			23 02	
Battersea Park	d							22 37			23a02				22 40			22 47		22 53					
Milton Keynes Central	d																								
Watford Junction	d																								
Harrow & Wealdstone ⊖	d																								
Wembley Central ⊖	d																								
Shepherd's Bush ⊖	d																								
Kensington (Olympia) ⊖	d																								
West Brompton ⊖	d																								
Imperial Wharf	d																								
Clapham Junction	d	22 30			22 38			22 41	22 42						22 44	22 46		22 51	22 53	22 57	23 00			23 08	
Wandsworth Common	d	22 33						22 44							22 47			22 54		23 00	23 03				
Balham ⊖	d	22 35						22 46							22 50			22 56		23 02	23 05				
Streatham Hill	d														22 53					23 05					
West Norwood	d					22 53									22 57					23 10					
Gipsy Hill	d			22a45		22 56									23 00					23 13			23a15		
Crystal Palace	d					22 59									23 03					23a16					
Birkbeck	d					23 03																			
Beckenham Junction	a					23 06																			
Streatham Common	d	22 39	22 42					22 50										23 00			23 09	23 12			
Norbury	d	22 42	22 45					22 53										23 03			23 12	23 15			
Thornton Heath	d	22 45	22 48					22 56										23 06			23 15	23 18			
Selhurst	d	22 48	22 51					22 59										23 09			23 18	23 21			
Norwood Junction	a									22 59				23 02	23 07										
	d						22 50			23 00				23 03	23 09										23 20
West Croydon	a	22 52	22 55				23 00	23 03							23 13						23 22	23 25			23 30
East Croydon	a				22 48				22 52	23 03		22 54		23 06		22 57		23 13	23 03					23 18	

Luton, Milton Keynes Central and London East and West Croydon via Tulse Hill - Crystal Palace - Norbury

Local Services

Station		SN	SN ◇1	SN	SN	SN	SN 1	SN		SN ◇1	SN	SN	FC 1	FC	SN	SN	SN 1	LO	SN	SN	SN	SN	FC 1	FC
London Bridge ⊖	d			23 06	23 03							23 11	23 12	23 15	23 18	23 22				23 36	23 33		23 42	23 45
South Bermondsey	d				23 07							23 15			23 22						23 37			
Queens Rd Peckham	d				23 09							23 18			23 24						23 39			
Peckham Rye	d				23 12							23 20			23 27						23 42			
East Dulwich	d				23 15										23 30						23 45			
North Dulwich	d				23 17										23 32						23 47			
Luton	d																							
Luton Airport Parkway	d																							
St Pancras International ⊖	d																							
City Thameslink	d																							
London Blackfriars ⊖	d																							
Elephant & Castle ⊖	d																							
Loughborough Jn.	d																							
Herne Hill	d																							
Tulse Hill	d				23 21									23 31	23 35						23 51			00 01
Streatham	d													23a35	23 39									00a05
London Victoria ⊖	d	23 03	23 06			23 06	23 10	23 15		23 17	23 19						23 32		23 34			23 38		
Battersea Park	d	23 07				23 10		23 19			23 23	23a32							23 38			23 42		
Milton Keynes Central	d																							
Watford Junction	d																							
Harrow & Wealdstone ⊖	d																							
Wembley Central ⊖	d																							
Shepherd's Bush ⊖	d																							
Kensington (Olympia) ⊖	d																							
West Brompton ⊖	d																							
Imperial Wharf	d																							
Clapham Junction	d	23 11	23 12			23 14	23 16	23 23		23 23	23 27						23 38		23 42			23 46		
Wandsworth Common	d	23 14				23 17		23 26			23 30								23 45			23 49		
Balham ⊖	d	23 16				23 20		23 28			23 32								23 47			23 51		
Streatham Hill	d					23 23					23 35											23 54		
West Norwood	d				23 24	23 27					23 40										23 54	23 58		
Gipsy Hill	d				23 27	23 30					23 43					23a45					23 57	00 01		
Crystal Palace	d				23 29	23 32					23a46										23 59	00 03		
Birkbeck	d																							
Beckenham Junction	a																							
Streatham Common	d	23 20						23 32							23 42				23 51					
Norbury	d	23 23						23 35							23 45				23 54					
Thornton Heath	d	23 26						23 38							23 48				23 57					
Selhurst	d	23 29						23 41							23 51				23 59					
Norwood Junction	a			23 29	23 34	23 37														23 59	00 04	00 08		
	d			23 30		23 39												23 50		23 59		00 09		
West Croydon	a	23 33				23 43									23 55			23 59	00 03			00 14		
East Croydon	a		23 22	23 33			23 27	23 44		23 33			23 24				23 52			00 03			23 56	

Station		SN	SN 1	SN	SN 1	SN	SN	SN
London Bridge ⊖	d			23 48		23 52		
South Bermondsey	d			23 52				
Queens Rd Peckham	d			23 54				
Peckham Rye	d			23 57				
East Dulwich	d			00 01				
North Dulwich	d			00 03				
Luton	d							
Luton Airport Parkway	d							
St Pancras International ⊖	d							
City Thameslink	d							
London Blackfriars ⊖	d							
Elephant & Castle ⊖	d							
Loughborough Jn.	d							
Herne Hill	d							
Tulse Hill	d			00 06				
Streatham	d			00 10				
London Victoria ⊖	d	23 45	23 47		23 49		23 54	23 59
Battersea Park	d	23 49					23 58	00 03
Milton Keynes Central	d							
Watford Junction	d							
Harrow & Wealdstone ⊖	d							
Wembley Central ⊖	d							
Shepherd's Bush ⊖	d							
Kensington (Olympia) ⊖	d							
West Brompton ⊖	d							
Imperial Wharf	d							
Clapham Junction	d	23 53	23 53		23 56		00 02	00 07
Wandsworth Common	d	23 56					00 05	00 10
Balham ⊖	d	23 58					00 07	00 12
Streatham Hill	d						00 10	
West Norwood	d						00 14	
Gipsy Hill	d					00a15	00 17	
Crystal Palace	d						00a19	
Birkbeck	d							
Beckenham Junction	a							
Streatham Common	d	00 02		00 13				00 16
Norbury	d	00 05		00 15				00 19
Thornton Heath	d	00 08		00 18				00 22
Selhurst	d	00 11	00 01	00 21				00 25
Norwood Junction	a							
	d							
West Croydon	a			00 27				00 30
East Croydon	a	00 14	00 05		00 09			

Table 177

Sundays
until 4 September

Luton, Milton Keynes Central and London East and West Croydon via Tulse Hill - Crystal Palace - Norbury

Local Services

Station		SN	SN	SN	SN	FC	SN	SN 1	SN	SN 1	SN	LO	SN	SN ◇1	SN	SN	SN	FC 1	SN 1	SN	SN	SN	SN	SN
		A	A	A	A	A	A	A	A	A	A	A	A											
London Bridge	d		23p36	23p33		23p45			23p48						00 06	00 03		00 12			00 18			00 36
South Bermondsey	d			23p37					23p52							00 07					00 22			
Queens Rd Peckham	d			23p39					23p54							00 09					00 24			
Peckham Rye	d			23p42					23p57							00 12					00 27			
East Dulwich	d			23p45					00 01							00 15					00 30			
North Dulwich	d			23p47					00 03							00 17					00 32			
Luton	d																							
Luton Airport Parkway	d																							
St Pancras International	d																							
City Thameslink	d																							
London Blackfriars	d																							
Elephant & Castle	d																							
Loughborough Jn	d																							
Herne Hill	d																							
Tulse Hill	d			23p51		00 01			00 06							00 21					00 35			
Streatham	d					00a05			00 10												00 39			
London Victoria	d	23p34			23p38		23p45	23p47		23p49	23p54		23p59	00 05			00 07		00 14	00 16		00 22	00 34	
Battersea Park	d	23p38			23p42		23p49				23p58		00 03				00 11			00 20		00 26	00 38	
Milton Keynes Central	d																							
Watford Junction	d																							
Harrow & Wealdstone	d																							
Wembley Central	d																							
Shepherd's Bush	d																							
Kensington (Olympia)	d																							
West Brompton	d																							
Imperial Wharf	d																							
Clapham Junction	d	23p42			23p46		23p53	23p53		23p56	00 02		00 07	00 11			00 15		00 20	00 24		00 30	00 42	
Wandsworth Common	d	23p45			23p49		23p56				00 05		00 10				00 18			00 27		00 33	00 45	
Balham	d	23p47			23p51		23p58				00 07		00 12				00 20			00 29		00 35	00 47	
Streatham Hill	d				23p54						00 10						00 23					00 38		
West Norwood	d			23p54	23p58						00 14					00 24	00 28					00 42		
Gipsy Hill	d			23p57	00 01						00 17					00 27	00 31					00 45		
Crystal Palace	d			23p59	00 03						00a19					00 29	00 33					00 47		
Birkbeck	d																							
Beckenham Junction	a																							
Streatham Common	d	23p51					00 02		00 13				00 16							00 33	00 42		00 51	
Norbury	d	23p54					00 05		00 15				00 19							00 36	00 45		00 54	
Thornton Heath	d	23p57					00 08		00 18				00 22							00 39	00 48		00 57	
Selhurst	d	23p59					00 11	00 01	00 21				00 25	00 21					00 28	00 41	00 51		01 00	
Norwood Junction	a		23p59	00 04	00 08										00 29	00 34	00 38					00 52		00 59
	d		23p59		00 09							00 20			00 30		00 38					00 52		01 00
West Croydon	a	00 03			00 14				00 27			00 27	00 30				00 43				00 55	00 58	01 04	
East Croydon	a		00 03				00 14	00 05		00 09				00 24	00 33			00 27	00 31	00 44				01 03

A not 22 May

Table 177

Sundays
until 4 September

Luton, Milton Keynes Central and London East and West Croydon via Tulse Hill - Crystal Palace - Norbury

Local Services

Station		SN	SN	FC 1	SN	SN 1	FC 1	SN 1	SN 1	SN 1	SN 1	SN ◇1	SN ◇1	SN	SN	SN 1	SN	FC 1	SN	LO	SN	SN	SN
London Bridge	d	00 33		00 42			01 05									07 05	07 11	07 12				07 21	07 24
South Bermondsey	d	00 37															07 15					07 25	
Queens Rd Peckham	d	00 39															07 18					07 27	
Peckham Rye	d	00 42															07 20					07 30	
East Dulwich	d	00 45																				07 33	
North Dulwich	d	00 47																				07 35	
Luton	d																						
Luton Airport Parkway	d																						
St Pancras International	d																						
City Thameslink	d																						
London Blackfriars	d																						
Elephant & Castle	d																						
Loughborough Jn	d																						
Herne Hill	d																						
Tulse Hill	d	00 51																				07 39	
Streatham	d																					07 42	
London Victoria	d		00 37		00 42	01 00		02 00	03 00	04 00	05 02	05 47	06 32	06 36	06 49				07 06		07 19		
Battersea Park	d		00 41		00 46										06 53		07a32						
Milton Keynes Central	d																						
Watford Junction	d																						
Harrow & Wealdstone	d																						
Wembley Central	d																						
Shepherd's Bush	d																						
Kensington (Olympia)	d																						
West Brompton	d																						
Imperial Wharf	d																						
Clapham Junction	d		00 45		00 50	01 08		02 08	03 08	04 08	05 08	05 53	06 38	06 42	06 57				07 12		07 26		
Wandsworth Common	d		00 48		00 53										07 00								
Balham	d		00 50		00 55									06 47	07 02				07 17		07 30		
Streatham Hill	d		00 53																				
West Norwood	d	00 54	00 58																				
Gipsy Hill	d	00 57	01 01																				
Crystal Palace	d	00 59	01 03																				
Birkbeck	d																						
Beckenham Junction	a																						
Streatham Common	d				00 59									06 51	07 06				07 21		07 34	07 48	
Norbury	d				01 02									06 54	07 09				07 24		07 37	07 51	
Thornton Heath	d				01 05									06 57	07 12				07 27		07 40	07 54	
Selhurst	d				01 07	01 16	01 26	02 16	03 16	04 16	05 18	06 02		07 00	07 16				07 30		07 44	07 57	
Norwood Junction	a	01 04	01 08													07 17							07 44
	d		01 08													07 17				07 22			07 48
West Croydon	a		01 13												07 20					07 29	07 48		07 55
East Croydon	a			00 56	01 10	01 21	01 32	02 21	03 21	04 21	05 22	06 05	06 51	07 03		07 21		07 24	07 33			08 01	

Station		SN 1	LO	SN	SN ◇1	SN	SN	SN	FC 1	SN	SN	SN	SN	SN 1	LO	SN	SN	SN	SN	FC 1	SN	SN ◇1	SN	SN
London Bridge	d	07 37				07 36	07 39	07 41	07 42			07 51	07 54	08 05			08 06	08 09	08 11	08 12				08 21
South Bermondsey	d					07 40		07 45				07 55					08 10		08 15					08 25
Queens Rd Peckham	d					07 42		07 48				07 57					08 12		08 18					08 27
Peckham Rye	d					07 45		07 50				08 00					08 15		08 20					08 30
East Dulwich	d					07 48						08 03					08 18							08 33
North Dulwich	d					07 50						08 05					08 20							08 35
Luton	d																							
Luton Airport Parkway	d																							
St Pancras International	d																							
City Thameslink	d																							
London Blackfriars	d																							
Elephant & Castle	d																							
Loughborough Jn	d																							
Herne Hill	d																							
Tulse Hill	d					07 54						08 09					08 24							08 39
Streatham	d											08 12												08 42
London Victoria	d			07 24	07 27					07 36	07 49					07 54					08 06	08 17	08 19	
Battersea Park	d			07 28				08a02								07 58			08a32					
Milton Keynes Central	d																							
Watford Junction	d																							
Harrow & Wealdstone	d																							
Wembley Central	d																							
Shepherd's Bush	d																							
Kensington (Olympia)	d																							
West Brompton	d																							
Imperial Wharf	d																							
Clapham Junction	d			07 32	07 33					07 42	07 56					08 02					08 12	08 23	08 26	
Wandsworth Common	d			07 35												08 05								
Balham	d			07 37						07 47	08 00					08 07					08 17		08 30	
Streatham Hill	d			07 41												08 11								
West Norwood	d			07 46		07 57										08 16	08 27							
Gipsy Hill	d			07 49		08 00										08 19	08 30							
Crystal Palace	d			07 51		08a02										08 21	08a32							
Birkbeck	d																							
Beckenham Junction	a																							
Streatham Common	d									07 51	08 04	08 18									08 21		08 34	08 48
Norbury	d									07 54	08 07	08 21									08 24		08 37	08 51
Thornton Heath	d									07 57	08 10	08 24									08 27		08 40	08 54
Selhurst	d									08 00	08 13	08 27									08 30		08 43	08 57
Norwood Junction	a	07 48		07 56			08 02						08 14	08 16		08 26		08 32						
	d	07 48	07 52	07 57			08 03						08 16	08 16	08 22	08 27		08 33						
West Croydon	a		07 59	08 01							08 18		08 24		08 28	08 31							08 48	
East Croydon	a	07 54			07 42		08 07		07 54	08 03		08 30		08 20				08 37		08 24	08 33	08 32		09 01

Luton, Milton Keynes Central and London East and West Croydon via Tulse Hill - Crystal Palace - Norbury

Local Services

	SN	SN 1	LO	SN	SN ◇1	SN	SN	SN	FC 1	SN	SN ◇1 H	SN	SN	SN	SN 1	LO	SN	SN	SN ◇1	SN	SN	FC 1
London Bridge 4 ⊖ d	08 24	08 37				08 36	08 39	08 41	08 42				08 51	08 54	09 05			09 06		09 09	09 11	09 12
South Bermondsey d						08 40		08 45					08 55					09 10			09 15	
Queens Rd Peckham d						08 42		08 48					08 57					09 12			09 18	
Peckham Rye 4 d						08 45		08 50					09 00					09 15			09 20	
East Dulwich d						08 48							09 03					09 18				
North Dulwich d						08 50							09 05					09 20				
Luton 10 d																						
Luton Airport Parkway 7 d																						
St Pancras International 15 ⊖ d																						
City Thameslink 3 d																						
London Blackfriars 3 ⊖ d																						
Elephant & Castle ⊖ d																						
Loughborough Jn d																						
Herne Hill 4 d																						
Tulse Hill 3 d						08 54							09 09					09 24				
Streatham 4 d													09 12									
London Victoria 15 ⊖ d				08 24	08 27					08 36	08 47	08 49					08 54		09 06			
Battersea Park 4 d				08 28				09a02									08 58				09a32	
Milton Keynes Central d																						
Watford Junction d																						
Harrow & Wealdstone ⊖ d																						
Wembley Central ⊖ d																						
Shepherd's Bush ⊖ d																						
Kensington (Olympia) ⊖ d																						
West Brompton ⊖ d																						
Imperial Wharf d																						
Clapham Junction 10 d				08 32	08 33					08 42	08 53	08 56					09 02		09 12			
Wandsworth Common d				08 35													09 05					
Balham 4 ⊖ d				08 37						08 47		09 00					09 07					
Streatham Hill d				08 41													09 11					
West Norwood 4 d				08 46		08 57											09 16	09 27				
Gipsy Hill d				08 49		09 00											09 19	09 30				
Crystal Palace 4 d				08 51		09a02											09 21	09a32				
Birkbeck ⇌ d																						
Beckenham Junction 4 ⇌ a																						
Streatham Common 4 d										08 51		09 04	09 18									
Norbury d										08 54		09 07	09 21									
Thornton Heath d										08 57		09 10	09 24									
Selhurst 4 d										09 00		09 13	09 27									
Norwood Junction 2 a	08 44	08 48		08 56			09 02							09 14	09 16		09 26			09 32		
d	08 46	08 48	08 52	08 57			09 03							09 16	09 16	09 22	09 27			09 33		
West Croydon 4 ⇌ a	08 54		08 58	09 01								09 18		09 24		09 28	09 31					
East Croydon ⇌ a		08 54			08 42		09 07		08 54	09 03	09 02		09 30		09 20				09 22	09 37		09 24

	SN	SN ◇1	SN	SN	SN	FC	SN 1	LO	SN	SN ◇1	SN	SN ◇1	SN	SN	FC 1	SN	SN ◇1 H	SN	SN	SN	FC	SN 1	LO
London Bridge 4 ⊖ d				09 21	09 24	09 32	09 37				09 36		09 39	09 41	09 42				09 51	09 54	10 02	10 05	
South Bermondsey d				09 25							09 40			09 45					09 55				
Queens Rd Peckham d				09 27							09 42			09 48					09 57				
Peckham Rye 4 d				09 30							09 45			09 50					10 00				
East Dulwich d				09 33							09 48								10 03				
North Dulwich d				09 35							09 50								10 05				
Luton 10 d																							
Luton Airport Parkway 7 d																							
St Pancras International 15 ⊖ d																							
City Thameslink 3 d																							
London Blackfriars 3 ⊖ d																							
Elephant & Castle ⊖ d																							
Loughborough Jn d																							
Herne Hill 4 d																							
Tulse Hill 3 d				09 39		09 43					09 54								10 09		10 13		
Streatham 4 d				09 42		09a46													10 12		10a16		
London Victoria 15 ⊖ d	09 06	09 17	09 19						09 24	09 27		09 36				09 36	09 47	09 49					
Battersea Park 4 d									09 28					10a02									
Milton Keynes Central d																							
Watford Junction d																							
Harrow & Wealdstone ⊖ d																							
Wembley Central ⊖ d																							
Shepherd's Bush ⊖ d																							
Kensington (Olympia) ⊖ d																							
West Brompton ⊖ d																							
Imperial Wharf d																							
Clapham Junction 10 d	09 12	09 23	09 26						09 32	09 33		09 42				09 42	09 53	09 56					
Wandsworth Common d									09 35														
Balham 4 ⊖ d	09 17		09 30						09 37							09 47		10 00					
Streatham Hill d									09 41														
West Norwood 4 d									09 46		09 57												
Gipsy Hill d									09 49		10 00												
Crystal Palace 4 d									09 51		10a02												
Birkbeck ⇌ d																							
Beckenham Junction 4 ⇌ a																							
Streatham Common 4 d	09 21		09 34	09 48												09 51		10 04	10 18				
Norbury d	09 24		09 37	09 51												09 54		10 07	10 21				
Thornton Heath d	09 27		09 40	09 54												09 57		10 10	10 24				
Selhurst 4 d	09 30		09 43	09 57												10 00		10 13	10 27				
Norwood Junction 2 a					09 44		09 48		09 56				10 02							10 14		10 16	
d					09 46		09 48	09 52	09 57				10 03							10 16		10 16	10 22
West Croydon 4 ⇌ a			09 48		09 54			09 58	10 01									10 18		10 24			10 28
East Croydon ⇌ a	09 33	09 32		10 01			09 54			09 42		09 52	10 07		09 54	10 03	10 02		10 30			10 20	

Luton, Milton Keynes Central and London East and West Croydon via Tulse Hill - Crystal Palace - Norbury

Local Services

	SN	SN	SN ◇1 H	SN	SN	FC 1	SN	SN ◇1	SN	SN	SN	FC	SN 1	LO	SN	SN ◇1	SN	SN ◇1 H	SN	SN	FC 1	SN
London Bridge 4 ⊖ d		10 06		10 09	10 11	10 12				10 21	10 24	10 32	10 37				10 36		10 39	10 41	10 42	
South Bermondsey d		10 10			10 15					10 25							10 40			10 45		
Queens Rd Peckham d		10 12			10 18					10 27							10 42			10 48		
Peckham Rye 4 d		10 15			10 20					10 30							10 45			10 50		
East Dulwich d		10 18								10 33							10 48					
North Dulwich d		10 20								10 35							10 50					
Luton 10 d																						
Luton Airport Parkway 7 d																						
St Pancras International 15 ⊖ d																						
City Thameslink 3 d																						
London Blackfriars 3 ⊖ d																						
Elephant & Castle ⊖ d																						
Loughborough Jn d																						
Herne Hill 4 d																						
Tulse Hill 3 d		10 24								10 39		10 43					10 54					
Streatham 4 d										10 42		10a46										
London Victoria 15 ⊖ d	09 54		10 06				10 06	10 17	10 19						10 24	10 27		10 36				10 36
Battersea Park 4 d	09 58				10a32										10 28					11a02		
Milton Keynes Central d																						
Watford Junction d																						
Harrow & Wealdstone ⊖ d																						
Wembley Central ⊖ d																						
Shepherd's Bush ⊖ d																						
Kensington (Olympia) ⊖ d																						
West Brompton ⊖ d																						
Imperial Wharf d																						
Clapham Junction 10 d	10 02		10 12				10 12	10 23	10 26						10 32	10 33		10 42				10 42
Wandsworth Common d	10 05														10 35							
Balham 4 ⊖ d	10 07						10 17		10 30						10 37							10 47
Streatham Hill d	10 11														10 41							
West Norwood 4 d	10 16	10 27													10 46		10 57					
Gipsy Hill d	10 19	10 30													10 49		11 00					
Crystal Palace 4 d	10 21	10a32													10 51		11a02					
Birkbeck ⇌ d																						
Beckenham Junction 4 ⇌ a																						
Streatham Common 4 d							10 21		10 34	10 48												10 51
Norbury d							10 24		10 37	10 51												10 54
Thornton Heath d							10 27		10 40	10 54												10 57
Selhurst 4 d							10 30		10 43	10 57												11 00
Norwood Junction 2 a	10 26			10 32							10 44		10 48		10 56				11 02			
d	10 27			10 33							10 46		10 48	10 52	10 57				11 03			
West Croydon 4 ⇌ a	10 31								10 48		10 54			10 58	11 01							
East Croydon ⇌ a			10 22	10 37		10 24	10 33	10 32		11 01			10 54			10 42		10 52	11 07		10 54	11 03

	SN ◇1 H	SN	SN	SN	FC	SN 1	LO	SN	SN	SN ◇1 H	SN	SN	FC 1	SN	SN ◇1	SN	SN	SN	FC	SN 1	LO	SN	SN ◇1
London Bridge 4 ⊖ d			10 51	10 54	11 02	11 05			11 06		11 09	11 11	11 12				11 21	11 24	11 32	11 37			
South Bermondsey d			10 55						11 10			11 15					11 25						
Queens Rd Peckham d			10 57						11 12			11 18					11 27						
Peckham Rye 4 d			11 00						11 15			11 20					11 30						
East Dulwich d			11 03						11 18								11 33						
North Dulwich d			11 05						11 20								11 35						
Luton 10 d																							
Luton Airport Parkway 7 d																							
St Pancras International 15 ⊖ d																							
City Thameslink 3 d																							
London Blackfriars 3 ⊖ d																							
Elephant & Castle ⊖ d																							
Loughborough Jn d																							
Herne Hill 4 d																							
Tulse Hill 3 d			11 09		11 13				11 24								11 39		11 43				
Streatham 4 d			11 12		11a16												11 42		11a46				
London Victoria 15 ⊖ d	10 47	10 49						10 54		11 06				11 06	11 17	11 19						11 24	11 27
Battersea Park 4 d								10 58				11a32										11 28	
Milton Keynes Central d																							
Watford Junction d																							
Harrow & Wealdstone ⊖ d																							
Wembley Central ⊖ d																							
Shepherd's Bush ⊖ d																							
Kensington (Olympia) ⊖ d																							
West Brompton ⊖ d																							
Imperial Wharf d																							
Clapham Junction 10 d	10 53	10 56						11 02		11 12				11 12	11 23	11 26						11 32	11 33
Wandsworth Common d								11 05														11 35	
Balham 4 ⊖ d		11 00						11 07						11 17		11 30						11 37	
Streatham Hill d								11 11														11 41	
West Norwood 4 d								11 16	11 27													11 46	
Gipsy Hill d								11 19	11 30													11 49	
Crystal Palace 4 d								11 21	11a32													11 51	
Birkbeck ⇌ d																							
Beckenham Junction 4 ⇌ a																							
Streatham Common 4 d		11 04	11 18											11 21		11 34	11 48						
Norbury d		11 07	11 21											11 24		11 37	11 51						
Thornton Heath d		11 10	11 24											11 27		11 40	11 54						
Selhurst 4 d		11 13	11 27											11 30		11 43	11 57						
Norwood Junction 2 a				11 14		11 16		11 26			11 32							11 44		11 48		11 56	
d				11 16		11 16	11 22	11 27			11 33							11 46		11 48	11 52	11 57	
West Croydon 4 ⇌ a		11 18		11 24			11 28	11 31								11 48		11 54			11 58	12 01	
East Croydon ⇌ a	11 02		11 30			11 20				11 22	11 37		11 24	11 33	11 32		12 01			11 54			11 42

Table 177

Sundays
until 4 September

Luton, Milton Keynes Central and London East and West Croydon via Tulse Hill - Crystal Palace - Norbury

Local Services

	SN	SN ◇■ 🛒	SN	SN	FC ■	SN	SN ◇■ 🛒		SN	SN	SN	FC	SN ■	LO	SN	SN	SN ◇■ 🛒	SN	SN	FC ■	SN	SN ◇■	LO
London Bridge ⊖ d	11 36		11 39	11 41	11 42					11 51	11 54	12 02	12 05			12 06		12 09	12 11	12 12			
South Bermondsey d	11 40			11 45						11 55						12 10			12 15				
Queens Rd Peckham d	11 42			11 48						11 57						12 12			12 18				
Peckham Rye d	11 45			11 50						12 00						12 15			12 20				
East Dulwich d	11 48									12 03						12 18							
North Dulwich d	11 50									12 05						12 20							
Luton d																							
Luton Airport Parkway d																							
St Pancras International ⊖ d																							
City Thameslink d																							
London Blackfriars ⊖ d																							
Elephant & Castle ⊖ d																							
Loughborough Jn d																							
Herne Hill d																							
Tulse Hill d	11 54									12 09		12 13				12 24							
Streatham d										12 12		12a16											
London Victoria ⊖ d		11 36				11 36	11 47		11 49						11 54		12 06				12 06	12 17	
Battersea Park d				12a02											11 58				12a32				
Milton Keynes Central d																							
Watford Junction d																							
Harrow & Wealdstone ⊖ d																							
Wembley Central ⊖ d																							
Shepherd's Bush ⊖ d																							
Kensington (Olympia) ⊖ d																							
West Brompton ⊖ d																							
Imperial Wharf d																							
Clapham Junction d		11 42				11 42	11 53		11 56						12 02		12 12				12 12	12 23	
Wandsworth Common d															12 05								
Balham ⊖ d						11 47			12 00						12 07						12 17		
Streatham Hill d															12 11								
West Norwood d	11 57														12 16	12 27							
Gipsy Hill d	12 00														12 19	12 30							
Crystal Palace d	12a02														12 21	12a32							
Birkbeck d																							
Beckenham Junction a																							
Streatham Common d						11 51			12 04	12 18											12 21		
Norbury d						11 54			12 07	12 21											12 24		
Thornton Heath d						11 57			12 10	12 24											12 27		
Selhurst d						12 00			12 13	12 27											12 30		
Norwood Junction a			12 02								12 14		12 16		12 26			12 32					
Norwood Junction d			12 03								12 16		12 16	12 22	12 27			12 33					12 38
West Croydon a									12 18		12 24			12 28	12 31								12 45
East Croydon a		11 52	12 07		11 54	12 03	12 02			12 30			12 20				12 22	12 37		12 24	12 33	12 32	

	SN	SN	SN	FC	SN ■	LO	SN	SN ◇■	SN	SN ◇■ 🛒	SN	SN	FC ■	SN	SN ◇■ 🛒		LO	SN	SN	SN	FC	SN ■	LO	SN
London Bridge ⊖ d		12 21	12 24	12 32	12 37				12 36		12 39	12 41	12 42						12 51	12 54	13 02	13 05		
South Bermondsey d		12 25							12 40			12 45							12 55					
Queens Rd Peckham d		12 27							12 42			12 48							12 57					
Peckham Rye d		12 30							12 45			12 50							13 00					
East Dulwich d		12 33							12 48										13 03					
North Dulwich d		12 35							12 50										13 05					
Luton d																								
Luton Airport Parkway d																								
St Pancras International ⊖ d																								
City Thameslink d																								
London Blackfriars ⊖ d																								
Elephant & Castle ⊖ d																								
Loughborough Jn d																								
Herne Hill d																								
Tulse Hill d		12 39		12 43					12 54										13 09		13 13			
Streatham d		12 42		12a46															13 12		13a16			
London Victoria ⊖ d	12 19						12 24	12 27		12 36				12 36	12 47			12 49						12 54
Battersea Park d							12 28					13a02												12 58
Milton Keynes Central d																								
Watford Junction d																								
Harrow & Wealdstone ⊖ d																								
Wembley Central ⊖ d																								
Shepherd's Bush ⊖ d																								
Kensington (Olympia) ⊖ d																								
West Brompton ⊖ d																								
Imperial Wharf d																								
Clapham Junction d	12 26						12 32	12 33		12 42				12 42	12 53			12 56						13 02
Wandsworth Common d							12 35																	13 05
Balham ⊖ d	12 30						12 37							12 47				13 00						13 07
Streatham Hill d							12 41																	13 11
West Norwood d							12 46		12 57															13 16
Gipsy Hill d							12 49		13 00															13 19
Crystal Palace d							12 51		13a02															13 21
Birkbeck d																								
Beckenham Junction a																								
Streatham Common d	12 34	12 48												12 51				13 04	13 18					
Norbury d	12 37	12 51												12 54				13 07	13 21					
Thornton Heath d	12 40	12 54												12 57				13 10	13 24					
Selhurst d	12 43	12 57												13 00				13 13	13 27					
Norwood Junction a			12 44		12 48		12 56				13 02									13 14		13 16		13 26
Norwood Junction d			12 46		12 48	12 53	12 57				13 03						13 08			13 16		13 16	13 23	13 27
West Croydon a	[illegible]		[illegible]			[illegible]	[illegible]										13 15	13 18		13 24			13 29	13 31

Table 177

Sundays
until 4 September

Luton, Milton Keynes Central and London East and West Croydon via Tulse Hill - Crystal Palace - Norbury

Local Services

	SN	SN ◇■ 🛒	SN	SN	FC ■	SN	SN ◇■		LO	SN	SN	SN	FC	SN ■	LO	SN	SN ◇■	SN	SN ◇■ 🛒	SN	SN	FC ■	SN
London Bridge ⊖ d	13 06		13 09	13 11	13 12						13 21	13 24	13 32	13 37				13 36		13 39	13 41	13 42	
South Bermondsey d	13 10			13 15							13 25							13 40			13 45		
Queens Rd Peckham d	13 12			13 18							13 27							13 42			13 48		
Peckham Rye d	13 15			13 20							13 30							13 45			13 50		
East Dulwich d	13 18										13 33							13 48					
North Dulwich d	13 20										13 35							13 50					
Luton d																							
Luton Airport Parkway d																							
St Pancras International ⊖ d																							
City Thameslink d																							
London Blackfriars ⊖ d																							
Elephant & Castle ⊖ d																							
Loughborough Jn d																							
Herne Hill d																							
Tulse Hill d	13 24										13 39		13 43					13 54					
Streatham d											13 42		13a46										
London Victoria ⊖ d		13 06				13 06	13 17			13 19						13 24	13 27		13 36				13 36
Battersea Park d				13a32												13 28					14a02		
Milton Keynes Central d																							
Watford Junction d																							
Harrow & Wealdstone ⊖ d																							
Wembley Central ⊖ d																							
Shepherd's Bush ⊖ d																							
Kensington (Olympia) ⊖ d																							
West Brompton ⊖ d																							
Imperial Wharf d																							
Clapham Junction d		13 12				13 12	13 23			13 26						13 32	13 33		13 42				13 42
Wandsworth Common d																13 35							
Balham ⊖ d						13 17				13 30						13 37							13 47
Streatham Hill d																13 41							
West Norwood d	13 27															13 46		13 57					
Gipsy Hill d	13 30															13 49		14 00					
Crystal Palace d	13a32															13 51		14a02					
Birkbeck d																							
Beckenham Junction a																							
Streatham Common d						13 21				13 34	13 48												13 51
Norbury d						13 24				13 37	13 51												13 54
Thornton Heath d						13 27				13 40	13 54												13 57
Selhurst d						13 30				13 43	13 57												14 00
Norwood Junction a			13 32									13 44		13 48		13 56				14 02			
Norwood Junction d			13 33						13 38			13 46		13 48	13 53	13 57				14 03			
West Croydon a									13 45	13 48		13 54			13 59	14 01							
East Croydon a		13 22	13 37		13 24	13 33	13 32				14 01			13 54			13 42		13 52	14 07		13 54	14 03

	SN ◇■ 🛒	LO	SN	SN	SN	FC	SN ■	LO	SN	SN	SN ◇■ 🛒	SN	SN	FC ■	SN		SN ◇■	LO	SN	SN	SN	FC	SN ■	LO
London Bridge ⊖ d				13 51	13 54	14 02	14 05			14 06		14 09	14 11	14 12						14 21	14 24	14 32	14 37	
South Bermondsey d				13 55						14 10			14 15							14 25				
Queens Rd Peckham d				13 57						14 12			14 18							14 27				
Peckham Rye d				14 00						14 15			14 20							14 30				
East Dulwich d				14 03						14 18										14 33				
North Dulwich d				14 05						14 20										14 35				
Luton d																								
Luton Airport Parkway d																								
St Pancras International ⊖ d																								
City Thameslink d																								
London Blackfriars ⊖ d																								
Elephant & Castle ⊖ d																								
Loughborough Jn d																								
Herne Hill d																								
Tulse Hill d				14 09		14 13				14 24										14 39		14 43		
Streatham d				14 12		14a16														14 42		14a46		
London Victoria ⊖ d	13 47		13 49						13 54		14 06				14 06		14 17		14 19					
Battersea Park d									13 58				14a32											
Milton Keynes Central d																								
Watford Junction d																								
Harrow & Wealdstone ⊖ d																								
Wembley Central ⊖ d																								
Shepherd's Bush ⊖ d																								
Kensington (Olympia) ⊖ d																								
West Brompton ⊖ d																								
Imperial Wharf d																								
Clapham Junction d	13 53		13 56						14 02		14 12				14 12		14 23		14 26					
Wandsworth Common d									14 05															
Balham ⊖ d			14 00						14 07						14 17				14 30					
Streatham Hill d									14 11															
West Norwood d									14 16	14 27														
Gipsy Hill d									14 19	14 30														
Crystal Palace d									14 21	14a32														
Birkbeck d																								
Beckenham Junction a																								
Streatham Common d			14 04	14 18											14 21				14 34	14 48				
Norbury d			14 07	14 21											14 24				14 37	14 51				
Thornton Heath d			14 10	14 24											14 27				14 40	14 54				
Selhurst d			14 13	14 27											14 30				14 43	14 57				
Norwood Junction a					14 14		14 16		14 26			14 32									14 44		14 48	
Norwood Junction d		14 08			14 16		14 16	14 23	14 27			14 33						14 38			14 46		14 48	14 53
West Croydon a		14 15	14 18		14 24			14 29	14 31									14 45	14 48		14 54			14 59

Luton, Milton Keynes Central and London East and West Croydon via Tulse Hill - Crystal Palace - Norbury

Local Services

		SN	SN	SN	SN	SN	SN	FC		SN	SN	LO	SN	SN	SN	FC	SN	LO	SN	SN	SN	SN	SN	FC
			◇1		◇1 🍴			1			◇1 🍴						1				◇1 🍴			1
London Bridge 4 ⊖	d			14 36		14 39	14 41	14 42						14 51	14 54	15 02	15 05			15 06		15 09	15 11	15 12
South Bermondsey	d			14 40			14 45							14 55						15 10			15 15	
Queens Rd Peckham	d			14 42			14 48							14 57						15 12			15 18	
Peckham Rye 4	d			14 45			14 50							15 00						15 15			15 20	
East Dulwich	d			14 48										15 03						15 18				
North Dulwich	d			14 50										15 05						15 20				
Luton 10	d																							
Luton Airport Parkway 7	d																							
St Pancras International 15 ⊖	d																							
City Thameslink 3	d																							
London Blackfriars 3 ⊖	d																							
Elephant & Castle ⊖	d																							
Loughborough Jn	d																							
Herne Hill 4	d																							
Tulse Hill 3	d			14 54										15 09		15 13				15 24				
Streatham 4	d													15 12		15a16								
London Victoria 15 ⊖	d	14 24	14 27		14 36					14 36	14 47		14 49						14 54		15 06			
Battersea Park 4	d	14 28					15a02												14 58				15a32	
Milton Keynes Central	d																							
Watford Junction	d																							
Harrow & Wealdstone ⊖	d																							
Wembley Central ⊖	d																							
Shepherd's Bush ⊖	d																							
Kensington (Olympia) ⊖	d																							
West Brompton ⊖	d																							
Imperial Wharf	d																							
Clapham Junction 10	d	14 32	14 33		14 42					14 42	14 53		14 56						15 02		15 12			
Wandsworth Common	d	14 35																	15 05					
Balham 4 ⊖	d	14 37								14 47			15 00						15 07					
Streatham Hill	d	14 41																	15 11					
West Norwood 4	d	14 46		14 57															15 16	15 27				
Gipsy Hill	d	14 49		15 00															15 19	15 30				
Crystal Palace 4	d	14 51		15a02															15 21	15a32				
Birkbeck 🚊	d																							
Beckenham Junction 4 🚊	a																							
Streatham Common 4	d									14 51			15 04	15 18										
Norbury	d									14 54			15 07	15 21										
Thornton Heath	d									14 57			15 10	15 24										
Selhurst 4	d									15 00			15 13	15 27										
Norwood Junction 2	a	14 56				15 02									15 14		15 16		15 26			15 32		
	d	14 57				15 03						15 08			15 16		15 16	15 23	15 27			15 33		
West Croydon 4 🚊	a	15 01										15 15	15 18		15 24			15 29	15 31					
East Croydon 🚊	a		14 42		14 52	15 07		14 54		15 03	15 02			15 30			15 20				15 22	15 37		15 24

		SN	SN	LO	SN	SN	SN	FC	SN	LO	SN	SN	SN	SN	SN	SN		FC	SN	SN	LO	SN	SN	SN	FC
			◇1						1			◇1		◇1 🍴				1		◇1 🍴					
London Bridge 4 ⊖	d					15 21	15 24	15 32	15 37				15 36		15 39	15 41		15 42					15 51	15 54	16 02
South Bermondsey	d					15 25							15 40			15 45							15 55		
Queens Rd Peckham	d					15 27							15 42			15 48							15 57		
Peckham Rye 4	d					15 30							15 45			15 50							16 00		
East Dulwich	d					15 33							15 48										16 03		
North Dulwich	d					15 35							15 50										16 05		
Luton 10	d																								
Luton Airport Parkway 7	d																								
St Pancras International 15 ⊖	d																								
City Thameslink 3	d																								
London Blackfriars 3 ⊖	d																								
Elephant & Castle ⊖	d																								
Loughborough Jn	d																								
Herne Hill 4	d																								
Tulse Hill 3	d					15 39		15 43					15 54										16 09		16 13
Streatham 4	d					15 42		15a46															16 12		16a16
London Victoria 15 ⊖	d	15 06	15 17		15 19						15 24	15 27		15 36					15 36	15 47		15 49			
Battersea Park 4	d										15 28					16a02									
Milton Keynes Central	d																								
Watford Junction	d																								
Harrow & Wealdstone ⊖	d																								
Wembley Central ⊖	d																								
Shepherd's Bush ⊖	d																								
Kensington (Olympia) ⊖	d																								
West Brompton ⊖	d																								
Imperial Wharf	d																								
Clapham Junction 10	d	15 12	15 23		15 26						15 32	15 33		15 42					15 42	15 53		15 56			
Wandsworth Common	d										15 35														
Balham 4 ⊖	d	15 17			15 30						15 37								15 47			16 00			
Streatham Hill	d										15 41														
West Norwood 4	d										15 46		15 57												
Gipsy Hill	d										15 49		16 00												
Crystal Palace 4	d										15 51		16a02												
Birkbeck 🚊	d																								
Beckenham Junction 4 🚊	a																								
Streatham Common 4	d	15 21			15 34	15 48													15 51			16 04	16 18		
Norbury	d	15 24			15 37	15 51													15 54			16 07	16 21		
Thornton Heath	d	15 27			15 40	15 54													15 57			16 10	16 24		
Selhurst 4	d	15 30			15 43	15 57													16 00			16 13	16 27		
Norwood Junction 2	a						15 44		15 48		15 56				16 02									16 14	
	d			15 38			15 46		15 48	15 53	15 57				16 03						16 08			16 16	
West Croydon 4 🚊	a			15 45	15 48		15 54			15 59	16 01										16 15	16 18		16 24	
East Croydon 🚊	a	15 33	15 32			16 01			15 54			15 42		15 52	16 07			15 54	16 03	16 02			16 30		

Luton, Milton Keynes Central and London East and West Croydon via Tulse Hill - Crystal Palace - Norbury

Local Services

		SN	LO	SN	SN	SN	SN	SN		FC	SN	SN	LO	SN	SN	SN	FC	SN	LO	SN	SN	SN	SN	SN
		1				◇1 🍴				1		◇1						1			◇1		◇1 🍴	
London Bridge 4 ⊖	d	16 05			16 06		16 09	16 11		16 12					16 21	16 24	16 32	16 37				16 36		16 39
South Bermondsey	d				16 10			16 15							16 25							16 40		
Queens Rd Peckham	d				16 12			16 18							16 27							16 42		
Peckham Rye 4	d				16 15			16 20							16 30							16 45		
East Dulwich	d				16 18										16 33							16 48		
North Dulwich	d				16 20										16 35							16 50		
Luton 10	d																							
Luton Airport Parkway 7	d																							
St Pancras International 15 ⊖	d																							
City Thameslink 3	d																							
London Blackfriars 3 ⊖	d																							
Elephant & Castle ⊖	d																							
Loughborough Jn	d																							
Herne Hill 4	d																							
Tulse Hill 3	d				16 24										16 39		16 43					16 54		
Streatham 4	d														16 42		16a46							
London Victoria 15 ⊖	d			15 54		16 06					16 06	16 17		16 19						16 24	16 27		16 36	
Battersea Park 4	d			15 58				16a32												16 28				
Milton Keynes Central	d																							
Watford Junction	d																							
Harrow & Wealdstone ⊖	d																							
Wembley Central ⊖	d																							
Shepherd's Bush ⊖	d																							
Kensington (Olympia) ⊖	d																							
West Brompton ⊖	d																							
Imperial Wharf	d																							
Clapham Junction 10	d			16 02		16 12					16 12	16 23		16 26						16 32	16 33		16 42	
Wandsworth Common	d			16 05																16 35				
Balham 4 ⊖	d			16 07							16 17			16 30						16 37				
Streatham Hill	d			16 11																16 41				
West Norwood 4	d			16 16	16 27															16 46		16 57		
Gipsy Hill	d			16 19	16 30															16 49		17 00		
Crystal Palace 4	d			16 21	16a32															16 51		17a02		
Birkbeck 🚊	d																							
Beckenham Junction 4 🚊	a																							
Streatham Common 4	d										16 21			16 34	16 48									
Norbury	d										16 24			16 37	16 51									
Thornton Heath	d										16 27			16 40	16 54									
Selhurst 4	d										16 30			16 43	16 57									
Norwood Junction 2	a	16 16		16 26			16 32									16 44		16 48		16 56				17 02
	d	16 16	16 23	16 27			16 33						16 38			16 46		16 48	16 53	16 57				17 03
West Croydon 4 🚊	a		16 29	16 31									16 45	16 48		16 54			16 59	17 01				
East Croydon 🚊	a	16 20				16 22	16 37			16 24	16 33	16 32			17 01			16 54			16 42		16 52	17 07

		SN	FC	SN	SN	LO	SN	SN	SN	FC	SN	LO	SN	SN	SN	SN		SN	FC	SN	SN	LO	SN	SN	SN
			1		◇1 🍴						1				◇1 🍴				1		◇1				
London Bridge 4 ⊖	d	16 41	16 42					16 51	16 54	17 02	17 05			17 06		17 09		17 11	17 12					17 21	17 24
South Bermondsey	d	16 45						16 55						17 10				17 15						17 25	
Queens Rd Peckham	d	16 48						16 57						17 12				17 18						17 27	
Peckham Rye 4	d	16 50						17 00						17 15				17 20						17 30	
East Dulwich	d							17 03						17 18										17 33	
North Dulwich	d							17 05						17 20										17 35	
Luton 10	d																								
Luton Airport Parkway 7	d																								
St Pancras International 15 ⊖	d																								
City Thameslink 3	d																								
London Blackfriars 3 ⊖	d																								
Elephant & Castle ⊖	d																								
Loughborough Jn	d																								
Herne Hill 4	d																								
Tulse Hill 3	d							17 09		17 13				17 24										17 39	
Streatham 4	d							17 12		17a16														17 42	
London Victoria 15 ⊖	d			16 36	16 47		16 49						16 54		17 06					17 06	17 17		17 19		
Battersea Park 4	d	17a02											16 58					17a32							
Milton Keynes Central	d																								
Watford Junction	d																								
Harrow & Wealdstone ⊖	d																								
Wembley Central ⊖	d																								
Shepherd's Bush ⊖	d																								
Kensington (Olympia) ⊖	d																								
West Brompton ⊖	d																								
Imperial Wharf	d																								
Clapham Junction 10	d			16 42	16 53		16 56						17 02		17 12					17 12	17 23		17 26		
Wandsworth Common	d												17 05												
Balham 4 ⊖	d			16 47			17 00						17 07							17 17			17 30		
Streatham Hill	d												17 11												
West Norwood 4	d												17 16	17 27											
Gipsy Hill	d												17 19	17 30											
Crystal Palace 4	d												17 21	17a32											
Birkbeck 🚊	d																								
Beckenham Junction 4 🚊	a																								
Streatham Common 4	d			16 51			17 04	17 18												17 21			17 34	17 48	
Norbury	d			16 54			17 07	17 21												17 24			17 37	17 51	
Thornton Heath	d			16 57			17 10	17 24												17 27			17 40	17 54	
Selhurst 4	d			17 00			17 13	17 27												17 30			17 43	17 57	
Norwood Junction 2	a								17 14		17 16		17 26			17 32									17 44
	d					17 08			17 16		17 16	17 23	17 27			17 33						17 38			17 46
West Croydon 4 🚊	a					17 15	17 18		17 24			17 29	17 31									17 45	17 48		17 54
East Croydon 🚊	a		16 54	17 03	17 02			17 30			17 20				17 22	17 37			17 24	17 33	17 32			18 01	

Table 177

Sundays
until 4 September

Luton, Milton Keynes Central and London East and West Croydon via Tulse Hill - Crystal Palace - Norbury

Local Services

Station		FC	SN 1	LO	SN	SN ◇1	SN	SN ◇1 H	SN	SN	FC 1	SN	SN ◇1 H	LO	SN	SN	SN	FC	SN 1	LO	SN	SN	SN ◇1 H
London Bridge ⊖	d	17 32	17 37				17 36		17 39	17 41	17 42					17 51	17 54	18 02	18 05			18 06	
South Bermondsey	d						17 40			17 45						17 55						18 10	
Queens Rd Peckham	d						17 42			17 48						17 57						18 12	
Peckham Rye	d						17 45			17 50						18 00						18 15	
East Dulwich	d						17 48									18 03						18 18	
North Dulwich	d						17 50									18 05						18 20	
Luton	d																						
Luton Airport Parkway	d																						
St Pancras International ⊖	d																						
City Thameslink	d																						
London Blackfriars ⊖	d																						
Elephant & Castle ⊖	d																						
Loughborough Jn.	d																						
Herne Hill	d																						
Tulse Hill	d	17 43					17 54									18 09		18 13				18 24	
Streatham	d	17a46														18 12		18a16					
London Victoria ⊖	d				17 24	17 27		17 36				17 36	17 47		17 49						17 54		18 06
Battersea Park	d				17 28					18a02											17 58		
Milton Keynes Central	d																						
Watford Junction	d																						
Harrow & Wealdstone ⊖	d																						
Wembley Central ⊖	d																						
Shepherd's Bush ⊖	d																						
Kensington (Olympia) ⊖	d																						
West Brompton ⊖	d																						
Imperial Wharf	d																						
Clapham Junction	d				17 32	17 33		17 42				17 42	17 53		17 56						18 02		18 12
Wandsworth Common	d				17 35																18 05		
Balham ⊖	d				17 37							17 47			18 00						18 07		
Streatham Hill	d				17 41																18 11		
West Norwood	d				17 46		17 57														18 16	18 27	
Gipsy Hill	d				17 49		18 00														18 19	18 30	
Crystal Palace	d				17 51		18a02														18 21	18a32	
Birkbeck	d																						
Beckenham Junction	a																						
Streatham Common	d											17 51			18 04	18 18							
Norbury	d											17 54			18 07	18 21							
Thornton Heath	d											17 57			18 10	18 24							
Selhurst	d											18 00			18 13	18 27							
Norwood Junction	a		17 48		17 56				18 02								18 14		18 16		18 26		
	d		17 48	17 53	17 57				18 03					18 08			18 16		18 16	18 23	18 27		
West Croydon	a			17 59	18 01									18 14	18 18		18 24			18 29	18 31		
East Croydon	a		17 54			17 42		17 52	18 07		17 54	18 03	18 02			18 30			18 20				18 22

Station		SN	SN	FC 1	SN	SN ◇1	LO	SN	SN	SN	FC	SN 1	LO	SN	SN ◇1	SN	SN ◇1 H	SN	SN	FC 1	SN	SN ◇1 H	LO	SN
London Bridge ⊖	d	18 09	18 11	18 12					18 21	18 24	18 32	18 37				18 36		18 39	18 41	18 42				
South Bermondsey	d		18 15						18 25							18 40			18 45					
Queens Rd Peckham	d		18 18						18 27							18 42			18 48					
Peckham Rye	d		18 20						18 30							18 45			18 50					
East Dulwich	d								18 33							18 48								
North Dulwich	d								18 35							18 50								
Luton	d																							
Luton Airport Parkway	d																							
St Pancras International ⊖	d																							
City Thameslink	d																							
London Blackfriars ⊖	d																							
Elephant & Castle ⊖	d																							
Loughborough Jn.	d																							
Herne Hill	d																							
Tulse Hill	d								18 39		18 43					18 54								
Streatham	d								18 42		18a46													
London Victoria ⊖	d				18 06	18 17		18 19						18 24	18 27		18 36				18 36	18 47		18 49
Battersea Park	d		18a32											18 28					19a02					
Milton Keynes Central	d																							
Watford Junction	d																							
Harrow & Wealdstone ⊖	d																							
Wembley Central ⊖	d																							
Shepherd's Bush ⊖	d																							
Kensington (Olympia) ⊖	d																							
West Brompton ⊖	d																							
Imperial Wharf	d																							
Clapham Junction	d				18 12	18 23		18 26						18 32	18 33		18 42				18 42	18 53		18 56
Wandsworth Common	d													18 35										
Balham ⊖	d				18 17			18 30						18 37							18 47			19 00
Streatham Hill	d													18 41										
West Norwood	d													18 46		18 57								
Gipsy Hill	d													18 49		19 00								
Crystal Palace	d													18 51		19a02								
Birkbeck	d																							
Beckenham Junction	a																							
Streatham Common	d				18 21			18 34	18 48												18 51			19 04
Norbury	d				18 24			18 37	18 51												18 54			19 07
Thornton Heath	d				18 27			18 40	18 54												18 57			19 10
Selhurst	d				18 30			18 43	18 57												19 00			19 13
Norwood Junction	a	18 32								18 44		18 48		18 56				19 02						
	d	18 33					18 38			18 46		18 48	18 53	18 57				19 03					19 08	
West Croydon	a						18 44	18 48		18 54			18 59	19 01									19 14	19 18

Table 177

Sundays
until 4 September

Luton, Milton Keynes Central and London East and West Croydon via Tulse Hill - Crystal Palace - Norbury

Local Services

Station		SN	SN	FC	SN 1	LO	SN	SN	SN ◇1 H	SN	SN	FC 1	SN	SN ◇1	LO	SN	SN	SN	FC	SN 1	LO	SN	SN ◇1
London Bridge ⊖	d	18 51	18 54	19 02	19 05			19 06		19 09	19 11	19 12					19 21	19 24	19 32	19 37			
South Bermondsey	d	18 55						19 10			19 15						19 25						
Queens Rd Peckham	d	18 57						19 12			19 18						19 27						
Peckham Rye	d	19 00						19 15			19 20						19 30						
East Dulwich	d	19 03						19 18									19 33						
North Dulwich	d	19 05						19 20									19 35						
Luton	d																						
Luton Airport Parkway	d																						
St Pancras International ⊖	d																						
City Thameslink	d																						
London Blackfriars ⊖	d																						
Elephant & Castle ⊖	d																						
Loughborough Jn.	d																						
Herne Hill	d																						
Tulse Hill	d	19 09		19 13				19 24									19 39		19 43				
Streatham	d	19 12		19a16													19 42		19a46				
London Victoria ⊖	d						18 54		19 06				19 06	19 17		19 19						19 24	19 27
Battersea Park	d						18 58				19a32											19 28	
Milton Keynes Central	d																						
Watford Junction	d																						
Harrow & Wealdstone ⊖	d																						
Wembley Central ⊖	d																						
Shepherd's Bush ⊖	d																						
Kensington (Olympia) ⊖	d																						
West Brompton ⊖	d																						
Imperial Wharf	d																						
Clapham Junction	d						19 02		19 12				19 12	19 23		19 26						19 32	19 33
Wandsworth Common	d						19 05															19 35	
Balham ⊖	d						19 07						19 17			19 30						19 37	
Streatham Hill	d						19 11															19 41	
West Norwood	d						19 16	19 27														19 46	
Gipsy Hill	d						19 19	19 30														19 49	
Crystal Palace	d						19 21	19a32														19 51	
Birkbeck	d																						
Beckenham Junction	a																						
Streatham Common	d	19 18											19 21			19 34	19 48						
Norbury	d	19 21											19 24			19 37	19 51						
Thornton Heath	d	19 24											19 27			19 40	19 54						
Selhurst	d	19 27											19 30			19 43	19 57						
Norwood Junction	a		19 14		19 16		19 26			19 32								19 44		19 48		19 56	
	d		19 16		19 16	19 23	19 27			19 33					19 38			19 46		19 48	19 53	19 57	
West Croydon	a		19 24			19 29	19 31								19 44	19 48		19 54			19 59	20 01	
East Croydon	a	19 30			19 20				19 22	19 37		19 24	19 33	19 32			20 01			19 54			19 42

Luton, Milton Keynes Central and London East and West Croydon via Tulse Hill - Crystal Palace - Norbury

Local Services

		SN	SN ◇1	SN	SN	FC 1	SN	SN ◇1	LO	SN	SN	SN	FC	SN 1	LO	SN		SN	SN ◇1	SN	SN	FC 1	SN	SN ◇1	LO
London Bridge	d	19 36		19 39	19 41	19 42					19 51	19 54	20 02	20 05				20 06		20 09	20 11	20 12			
South Bermondsey	d	19 40			19 45						19 55							20 10			20 15				
Queens Rd Peckham	d	19 42			19 48						19 57							20 12			20 18				
Peckham Rye	d	19 45			19 50						20 00							20 15			20 20				
East Dulwich	d	19 48									20 03							20 18							
North Dulwich	d	19 50									20 05							20 20							
Luton	d																								
Luton Airport Parkway	d																								
St Pancras International	d																								
City Thameslink	d																								
London Blackfriars	d																								
Elephant & Castle	d																								
Loughborough Jn.	d																								
Herne Hill	d																								
Tulse Hill	d	19 54									20 09		20 13					20 24							
Streatham	d										20 12		20a16												
London Victoria	d		19 36				19 36	19 47		19 49						19 54			20 06				20 06	20 17	
Battersea Park	d				20a02											19 58					20a32				
Milton Keynes Central	d																								
Watford Junction	d																								
Harrow & Wealdstone	d																								
Wembley Central	d																								
Shepherd's Bush	d																								
Kensington (Olympia)	d																								
West Brompton	d																								
Imperial Wharf	d																								
Clapham Junction	d		19 42				19 42	19 53		19 56						20 02			20 12				20 12	20 23	
Wandsworth Common	d															20 05									
Balham	d						19 47			20 00						20 07							20 17		
Streatham Hill	d															20 11									
West Norwood	d	19 57														20 16		20 27							
Gipsy Hill	d	20 00														20 19		20 30							
Crystal Palace	d	20a02														20 21		20a32							
Birkbeck	d																								
Beckenham Junction	a																								
Streatham Common	d						19 51			20 04	20 18												20 21		
Norbury	d						19 54			20 07	20 21												20 24		
Thornton Heath	d						19 57			20 10	20 24												20 27		
Selhurst	d						20 00			20 13	20 27												20 30		
Norwood Junction	a			20 02								20 14		20 16		20 26				20 32					
	d			20 03					20 08			20 16		20 16	20 23	20 27				20 33					20 38
West Croydon	a								20 15	20 18		20 24			20 29	20 31									20 45
East Croydon	a		19 52	20 07		19 54	20 03	20 02			20 30			20 20					20 22	20 37		20 24	20 33	20 32	

		SN	SN	SN	FC	SN 1	LO	SN		SN ◇1	SN	SN ◇1	SN	SN	FC 1	SN	SN ◇1	LO	SN	SN	SN	FC	SN 1	LO
London Bridge	d		20 21	20 24	20 32	20 37					20 36		20 39	20 41	20 42					20 51	20 54	21 02	21 05	
South Bermondsey	d		20 25								20 40			20 45						20 55				
Queens Rd Peckham	d		20 27								20 42			20 48						20 57				
Peckham Rye	d		20 30								20 45			20 50						21 00				
East Dulwich	d		20 33								20 48									21 03				
North Dulwich	d		20 35								20 50									21 05				
Luton	d																							
Luton Airport Parkway	d																							
St Pancras International	d																							
City Thameslink	d																							
London Blackfriars	d																							
Elephant & Castle	d																							
Loughborough Jn.	d																							
Herne Hill	d																							
Tulse Hill	d		20 39		20 43						20 54									21 09		21 13		
Streatham	d		20 42		20a46															21 12		21a16		
London Victoria	d	20 19						20 24		20 27		20 36				20 36	20 47		20 49					
Battersea Park	d							20 28						21a02										
Milton Keynes Central	d																							
Watford Junction	d																							
Harrow & Wealdstone	d																							
Wembley Central	d																							
Shepherd's Bush	d																							
Kensington (Olympia)	d																							
West Brompton	d																							
Imperial Wharf	d																							
Clapham Junction	d	20 26						20 32		20 33		20 42				20 42	20 53		20 56					
Wandsworth Common	d							20 35																
Balham	d	20 30						20 37								20 47			21 00					
Streatham Hill	d							20 41																
West Norwood	d							20 46			20 57													
Gipsy Hill	d							20 49			21 00													
Crystal Palace	d							20 51			21a02													
Birkbeck	d																							
Beckenham Junction	a																							
Streatham Common	d	20 34	20 48													20 51			21 04	21 18				
Norbury	d	20 37	20 51													20 54			21 07	21 21				
Thornton Heath	d	20 40	20 54													20 57			21 10	21 24				
Selhurst	d	20 43	20 57													21 00			21 13	21 27				
Norwood Junction	a			20 44		20 48		20 56					21 02								21 14		21 16	
	d			20 46		20 48	20 53	20 57					21 03					21 08			21 16		21 16	21 23
West Croydon	a	20 48		20 54			20 59	21 01										21 15	21 18		21 24			21 29
East Croydon	a		21 01			20 54				20 42		20 52	21 07		20 54	21 03	21 02			21 30			21 20	

Luton, Milton Keynes Central and London East and West Croydon via Tulse Hill - Crystal Palace - Norbury

Local Services

		SN	SN	SN ◇1	SN	SN	FC 1	SN	SN ◇1	LO	SN	SN	SN	SN 1	LO	SN		SN ◇1	SN	SN	SN	FC 1	SN	SN ◇1	LO
London Bridge	d		21 06		21 09	21 11	21 12					21 21	21 24	21 37					21 36	21 39	21 41	21 42			
South Bermondsey	d		21 10			21 15						21 25							21 40		21 45				
Queens Rd Peckham	d		21 12			21 18						21 27							21 42		21 48				
Peckham Rye	d		21 15			21 20						21 30							21 45		21 50				
East Dulwich	d		21 18									21 33							21 48						
North Dulwich	d		21 20									21 35							21 50						
Luton	d																								
Luton Airport Parkway	d																								
St Pancras International	d																								
City Thameslink	d																								
London Blackfriars	d																								
Elephant & Castle	d																								
Loughborough Jn.	d																								
Herne Hill	d																								
Tulse Hill	d		21 24									21 39							21 54						
Streatham	d											21 42													
London Victoria	d	20 54		21 06				21 06	21 17		21 19					21 24		21 27					21 36	21 47	
Battersea Park	d	20 58				21a32										21 28					22a02				
Milton Keynes Central	d																								
Watford Junction	d																								
Harrow & Wealdstone	d																								
Wembley Central	d																								
Shepherd's Bush	d																								
Kensington (Olympia)	d																								
West Brompton	d																								
Imperial Wharf	d																								
Clapham Junction	d	21 02		21 12				21 12	21 23		21 26					21 32		21 33					21 42	21 53	
Wandsworth Common	d	21 05														21 35									
Balham	d	21 07						21 17			21 30					21 38							21 47		
Streatham Hill	d	21 11														21 41									
West Norwood	d	21 16	21 27													21 46			21 57						
Gipsy Hill	d	21 19	21 30													21 49			22 00						
Crystal Palace	d	21 21	21a32													21 51			22a02						
Birkbeck	d																								
Beckenham Junction	a																								
Streatham Common	d							21 21			21 34	21 48											21 51		
Norbury	d							21 24			21 37	21 51											21 54		
Thornton Heath	d							21 27			21 40	21 54											21 57		
Selhurst	d							21 30			21 43	21 57											22 00		
Norwood Junction	a	21 26			21 32								21 44	21 48		21 56				22 02					
	d	21 27			21 33					21 38			21 46	21 48	21 53	21 57				22 03					22 08
West Croydon	a	21 31								21 45	21 48		21 54		21 59	22 01									22 15
East Croydon	a			21 22	21 37		21 24	21 33	21 32			22 01		21 54				21 42		22 07		21 54	22 03	22 02	

		SN	SN	SN	SN 1	LO	SN	SN		SN	SN	FC 1	SN	SN ◇1	LO	SN	SN	SN 1	SN	SN ◇1	SN	SN	SN ◇1	SN
London Bridge	d		21 51	21 54	22 05			22 06		22 09	22 11	22 12					22 21	22 37			22 36			22 39
South Bermondsey	d		21 55					22 10			22 15						22 25				22 40			
Queens Rd Peckham	d		21 57					22 12			22 18						22 27				22 42			
Peckham Rye	d		22 00					22 15			22 20						22 30				22 45			
East Dulwich	d		22 03					22 18									22 33				22 48			
North Dulwich	d		22 05					22 20									22 35				22 50			
Luton	d																							
Luton Airport Parkway	d																							
St Pancras International	d																							
City Thameslink	d																							
London Blackfriars	d																							
Elephant & Castle	d																							
Loughborough Jn.	d																							
Herne Hill	d																							
Tulse Hill	d		22 09					22 24									22 39				22 54			
Streatham	d		22 12														22 42							
London Victoria	d	21 49					21 54						22 06	22 17		22 19			22 24	22 27		22 36	22 47	
Battersea Park	d						21 58				22a32								22 28					
Milton Keynes Central	d																							
Watford Junction	d																							
Harrow & Wealdstone	d																							
Wembley Central	d																							
Shepherd's Bush	d																							
Kensington (Olympia)	d																							
West Brompton	d																							
Imperial Wharf	d																							
Clapham Junction	d	21 56					22 02						22 12	22 23		22 26			22 32	22 33		22 42	22 53	
Wandsworth Common	d						22 05												22 35					
Balham	d	22 00					22 07						22 17			22 30			22 38			22 47		
Streatham Hill	d						22 11												22 41					
West Norwood	d						22 16	22 27											22 46		22 57			
Gipsy Hill	d						22 19	22 30											22 49		23 00			
Crystal Palace	d						22 21	22a32											22 51		23a02			
Birkbeck	d																							
Beckenham Junction	a																							
Streatham Common	d	22 04	22 18										22 21			22 34	22 48					22 51		
Norbury	d	22 07	22 21										22 24			22 37	22 51					22 54		
Thornton Heath	d	22 10	22 24										22 27			22 40	22 54					22 57		
Selhurst	d	22 13	22 27										22 30			22 43	22 57					23 00		
Norwood Junction	a			22 14	22 16		22 26			22 32								22 48	22 56					23 02
	d			22 16	22 16	22 23	22 27			22 33					22 38			22 48	22 57					23 03
West Croydon	a	22 18		22 24		22 29	22 31								22 45	22 48			23 01					
East Croydon	a		22 30		22 20					22 37		22 24	22 33	22 32			23 00	22 54		22 42		23 03	23 03	23 07

Table 177

Sundays until 4 September

Luton, Milton Keynes Central and London East and West Croydon via Tulse Hill - Crystal Palace - Norbury

Local Services

		LO	SN	SN	SN	FC ■	SN ■	SN	SN	SN	SN ◇■	SN	LO	SN	SN	SN		FC ■	SN ◇■	SN	SN	SN	FC ■	SN	SN
London Bridge ⊖	d				22 41	22 42		22 51	23 06			23 09				23 11		23 12		23 21		23 39	23 42		
South Bermondsey	d				22 45			22 55	23 10							23 15				23 25					
Queens Rd Peckham	d				22 48			22 57	23 12							23 18				23 27					
Peckham Rye	d				22 50			23 00	23 15							23 20				23 30					
East Dulwich	d							23 03	23 18											23 33					
North Dulwich	d							23 05	23 20											23 35					
Luton	d																								
Luton Airport Parkway	d																								
St Pancras International ⊖	d																								
City Thameslink	d																								
London Blackfriars ⊖	d																								
Elephant & Castle ⊖	d																								
Loughborough Jn.	d																								
Herne Hill	d																								
Tulse Hill	d							23 09	23 24											23 39					
Streatham	d							23 12												23 42					
London Victoria ⊖	d		22 49	22 54			23 04			23 06	23 17			23 19	23 24				23 32		23 36			23 47	23 50
Battersea Park	d			22 58	23a02									23 23	23 28	23a32					23 40				
Milton Keynes Central	d																								
Watford Junction	d																								
Harrow & Wealdstone ⊖	d																								
Wembley Central ⊖	d																								
Shepherd's Bush ⊖	d																								
Kensington (Olympia) ⊖	d																								
West Brompton ⊖	d																								
Imperial Wharf	d																								
Clapham Junction	d		22 56	23 02			23 10			23 12	23 23			23 27	23 32				23 38		23 44			23 53	23 56
Wandsworth Common	d			23 05										23 30	23 35						23 47				23 59
Balham ⊖	d		23 00	23 07						23 17				23 32	23 37						23 49				00 02
Streatham Hill	d			23 11											23 41										
West Norwood	d			23 16					23 27						23 44										
Gipsy Hill	d			23 19					23 30						23 47										
Crystal Palace	d			23 21					23a32						23 50										
Birkbeck	d																								
Beckenham Junction	a																								
Streatham Common	d		23 04					23 18		23 21				23 36						23 48	23 53				00 06
Norbury	d		23 07					23 21		23 24				23 39						23 51	23 56				00 08
Thornton Heath	d		23 10					23 24		23 27				23 42						23 54	23 59				00 11
Selhurst	d		23 13					23 27		23 30				23 45					23 48	23 57	00a01				00 14
Norwood Junction	a			23 26								23 32			23 54							00 02			
	d	23 08		23 27								23 33	23 38		23 55							00 03			
West Croydon	a	23 14	23 18	23 31									23 44	23 49	23 59										
East Croydon	a					22 54	23 22	23 30		23 34	23 37	23 38						23 24	23 52	00 01		00 06	23 56	00 06	00 17

		SN ■	SN
London Bridge ⊖	d		
South Bermondsey	d		
Queens Rd Peckham	d		
Peckham Rye	d		
East Dulwich	d		
North Dulwich	d		
Luton	d		
Luton Airport Parkway	d		
St Pancras International ⊖	d		
City Thameslink	d		
London Blackfriars ⊖	d		
Elephant & Castle ⊖	d		
Loughborough Jn.	d		
Herne Hill	d		
Tulse Hill	d		
Streatham	d		
London Victoria ⊖	d		23 54
Battersea Park	d		23 58
Milton Keynes Central	d		
Watford Junction	d	23 17	
Harrow & Wealdstone ⊖	d	23 23	
Wembley Central ⊖	d		
Shepherd's Bush ⊖	d	23 45	
Kensington (Olympia) ⊖	d	23 48	
West Brompton ⊖	d	23 50	
Imperial Wharf	d	23 53	
Clapham Junction	d	00 05	00 02
Wandsworth Common	d		00 05
Balham ⊖	d		00 07
Streatham Hill	d		00 11
West Norwood	d		00 14
Gipsy Hill	d		00 17
Crystal Palace	d		00 20
Birkbeck	d		
Beckenham Junction	a		
Streatham Common	d		
Norbury	d		
Thornton Heath	d		
Selhurst	d	00 19	
Norwood Junction	a		00 25
	d		
West Croydon	a		
East Croydon	a	00 22	

Table 177

Sundays from 11 September

Luton, Milton Keynes Central and London East and West Croydon via Tulse Hill - Crystal Palace - Norbury

Local Services

		SN	SN	SN	SN	FC	SN	SN ■	SN	SN ■	SN	LO	SN	SN ◇■	SN	SN		SN	FC ■	SN ■	SN	SN	SN	SN	SN
London Bridge ⊖	d		23p36	23p33		23p45			23p48						00 06	00 03			00 12			00 18			00 36
South Bermondsey	d			23p37					23p52							00 07						00 22			
Queens Rd Peckham	d			23p39					23p54							00 09						00 24			
Peckham Rye	d			23p42					23p57							00 12						00 27			
East Dulwich	d			23p45					00 01							00 15						00 30			
North Dulwich	d			23p47					00 03							00 17						00 32			
Luton	d																								
Luton Airport Parkway	d																								
St Pancras International ⊖	d																								
City Thameslink	d																								
London Blackfriars ⊖	d																								
Elephant & Castle ⊖	d																								
Loughborough Jn.	d																								
Herne Hill	d																								
Tulse Hill	d			23p51		00 01			00 06							00 21						00 35			
Streatham	d					00a05			00 10													00 39			
London Victoria ⊖	d	23p34			23p38		23p45	23p47		23p49	23p54		23p59	00 05				00 07		00 14	00 16		00 22	00 34	
Battersea Park	d	23p38			23p42		23p49				23p58		00 03					00 11			00 20		00 26	00 38	
Milton Keynes Central	d																								
Watford Junction	d																								
Harrow & Wealdstone ⊖	d																								
Wembley Central ⊖	d																								
Shepherd's Bush ⊖	d																								
Kensington (Olympia) ⊖	d																								
West Brompton ⊖	d																								
Imperial Wharf	d																								
Clapham Junction	d	23p42			23p46		23p53	23p53		23p56	00 02		00 07	00 11				00 15		00 20	00 24		00 30	00 42	
Wandsworth Common	d	23p45			23p49		23p56				00 05		00 10					00 18			00 27		00 33	00 45	
Balham ⊖	d	23p47			23p51		23p58				00 07		00 12					00 20			00 29		00 35	00 47	
Streatham Hill	d				23p54						00 10							00 23					00 38		
West Norwood	d			23p54	23p58						00 14					00 24		00 28					00 42		
Gipsy Hill	d			23p57	00 01						00 17					00 27		00 31					00 45		
Crystal Palace	d			23p59	00 03						00a19					00 29		00 33					00 47		
Birkbeck	d																								
Beckenham Junction	a																								
Streatham Common	d	23p51					00 02		00 13				00 16								00 33	00 42		00 51	
Norbury	d	23p54					00 05		00 15				00 19								00 36	00 45		00 54	
Thornton Heath	d	23p57					00 08		00 18				00 22								00 39	00 48		00 57	
Selhurst	d	23p59					00 11	00 01	00 21				00 25	00 21						00 28	00 41	00 51		01 00	
Norwood Junction	a		23p59	00 04	00 08										00 29	00 34		00 38					00 52		00 59
	d		23p59		00 09							00 20			00 30			00 38					00 52		01 00
West Croydon	a	00 03			00 14				00 27			00 27	00 30					00 43				00 55	00 58	01 04	
East Croydon	a		00 03				00 14	00 05		00 09				00 24	00 33				00 27	00 31	00 44				01 03

		SN	SN	FC ■	SN	SN ■	FC ■	SN ■		SN ■	SN ■	SN ■	SN ◇■	SN ◇■	SN	SN	SN	FC ■	SN	LO	SN	SN	SN	SN ■
London Bridge ⊖	d	00 33		00 42			01 05										07 11	07 12				07 21	07 24	07 37
South Bermondsey	d	00 37															07 15					07 25		
Queens Rd Peckham	d	00 39															07 18					07 27		
Peckham Rye	d	00 42															07 20					07 30		
East Dulwich	d	00 45																				07 33		
North Dulwich	d	00 47																				07 35		
Luton	d																							
Luton Airport Parkway	d																							
St Pancras International ⊖	d																							
City Thameslink	d																							
London Blackfriars ⊖	d																							
Elephant & Castle ⊖	d																							
Loughborough Jn.	d																							
Herne Hill	d																							
Tulse Hill	d	00 51																				07 39		
Streatham	d																					07 42		
London Victoria ⊖	d		00 37		00 42	01 00		02 00		03 00	04 00	05 02	05 47	06 32	06 36	06 49			07 06		07 19			
Battersea Park	d		00 41		00 46											06 53	07a32							
Milton Keynes Central	d																							
Watford Junction	d																							
Harrow & Wealdstone ⊖	d																							
Wembley Central ⊖	d																							
Shepherd's Bush ⊖	d																							
Kensington (Olympia) ⊖	d																							
West Brompton ⊖	d																							
Imperial Wharf	d																							
Clapham Junction	d		00 45		00 50	01 08		02 08		03 08	04 08	05 08	05 53	06 38	06 42	06 57			07 12		07 26			
Wandsworth Common	d		00 48		00 53											07 00								
Balham ⊖	d		00 50		00 55										06 47	07 02			07 17		07 30			
Streatham Hill	d		00 53																					
West Norwood	d	00 54	00 58																					
Gipsy Hill	d	00 57	01 01																					
Crystal Palace	d	00 59	01 03																					
Birkbeck	d																							
Beckenham Junction	a																							
Streatham Common	d				00 59										06 51	07 06			07 21		07 34	07 48		
Norbury	d				01 02										06 54	07 09			07 24		07 37	07 51		
Thornton Heath	d				01 05										06 57	07 12			07 27		07 40	07 54		
Selhurst	d				01 07	01 16	01 26	02 16		03 16	04 16	05 18	06 02		07 00	07 16			07 30		07 44	07 57		
Norwood Junction	a	01 04	01 08																				07 44	07 48
	d		01 08																	07 22			07 48	07 48
West Croydon	a		01 13													07 20				07 29	07 48		07 55	
East Croydon	a			00 56	01 10	01 21	01 32	02 21		03 21	04 21	05 22	06 05	06 51	07 03			07 26	07 33			08 01		07 54

Luton, Milton Keynes Central and London East and West Croydon via Tulse Hill - Crystal Palace - Norbury

Local Services

		LO	SN	SN ◇1	SN	SN	SN	FC 1	SN	SN	SN	SN	LO	SN	SN	SN		SN	FC 1	SN	SN ◇1	SN	SN	SN	SN 1
London Bridge	d				07 36	07 39	07 41	07 42			07 51	07 54			08 06	08 09		08 11	08 12				08 21	08 24	08 37
South Bermondsey	d				07 40		07 45				07 55				08 10			08 15					08 25		
Queens Rd Peckham	d				07 42		07 48				07 57				08 12			08 18					08 27		
Peckham Rye	d				07 45		07 50				08 00				08 15			08 20					08 30		
East Dulwich	d				07 48						08 03				08 18								08 33		
North Dulwich	d				07 50						08 05				08 20								08 35		
Luton	d																								
Luton Airport Parkway	d																								
St Pancras International	d																								
City Thameslink	d																								
London Blackfriars	d																								
Elephant & Castle	d																								
Loughborough Jn.	d																								
Herne Hill	d																								
Tulse Hill	d				07 54						08 09				08 24								08 39		
Streatham	d										08 12												08 42		
London Victoria	d		07 24	07 32					07 36	07 49				07 54						08 06	08 17	08 19			
Battersea Park	d		07 28				08a02							07 58				08a32							
Milton Keynes Central	d																								
Watford Junction	d																								
Harrow & Wealdstone	d																								
Wembley Central	d																								
Shepherd's Bush	d																								
Kensington (Olympia)	d																								
West Brompton	d																								
Imperial Wharf	d																								
Clapham Junction	d		07 32	07 38					07 42	07 56				08 02						08 12	08 23	08 26			
Wandsworth Common	d		07 35											08 05											
Balham	d		07 37						07 47	08 00				08 07						08 17		08 30			
Streatham Hill	d		07 41											08 11											
West Norwood	d		07 46		07 57									08 16	08 27										
Gipsy Hill	d		07 49		08 00									08 19	08 30										
Crystal Palace	d		07 51		08a02									08 21	08a32										
Birkbeck	d																								
Beckenham Junction	a																								
Streatham Common	d								07 51	08 04	08 18									08 21		08 34	08 48		
Norbury	d								07 54	08 07	08 21									08 24		08 37	08 51		
Thornton Heath	d								07 57	08 10	08 24									08 27		08 40	08 54		
Selhurst	d								08 00	08 13	08 27									08 30		08 43	08 57		
Norwood Junction	a		07 56			08 02						08 14		08 26		08 32								08 44	08 48
	d	07 52	07 57			08 03						08 16	08 22	08 27		08 33								08 46	08 48
West Croydon	a	07 59	08 01							08 18		08 24	08 28	08 31								08 48		08 54	
East Croydon	a			07 50		08 07		07 56	08 03		08 30					08 37			08 27	08 33	08 36		09 01		08 54

		LO	SN	SN ◇1	SN	SN	SN	FC 1		SN	SN ◇1 ⚒	SN	SN	SN	LO	SN	SN ◇1	SN	SN	SN	FC 1	SN	SN ◇1	SN	
London Bridge	d				08 36	08 39	08 41	08 42					08 51	08 54				09 06	09 09	09 11	09 12				
South Bermondsey	d				08 40		08 45						08 55					09 10		09 15					
Queens Rd Peckham	d				08 42		08 48						08 57					09 12		09 18					
Peckham Rye	d				08 45		08 50						09 00					09 15		09 20					
East Dulwich	d				08 48								09 03					09 18							
North Dulwich	d				08 50								09 05					09 20							
Luton	d																								
Luton Airport Parkway	d																								
St Pancras International	d																								
City Thameslink	d																								
London Blackfriars	d																								
Elephant & Castle	d																								
Loughborough Jn.	d																								
Herne Hill	d																								
Tulse Hill	d				08 54								09 09					09 24							
Streatham	d												09 12												
London Victoria	d		08 24	08 32						08 36	08 47	08 49				08 54	09 02					09 06	09 17	09 19	
Battersea Park	d		08 28				09a02									08 58				09a32					
Milton Keynes Central	d																								
Watford Junction	d																								
Harrow & Wealdstone	d																								
Wembley Central	d																								
Shepherd's Bush	d																								
Kensington (Olympia)	d																								
West Brompton	d																								
Imperial Wharf	d																								
Clapham Junction	d		08 32	08 38						08 42	08 53	08 56				09 02	09 08					09 12	09 23	09 26	
Wandsworth Common	d		08 35													09 05									
Balham	d		08 37							08 47		09 00				09 07						09 17		09 30	
Streatham Hill	d		08 41													09 11									
West Norwood	d		08 46		08 57											09 16		09 27							
Gipsy Hill	d		08 49		09 00											09 19		09 30							
Crystal Palace	d		08 51		09a02											09 21		09a32							
Birkbeck	d																								
Beckenham Junction	a																								
Streatham Common	d									08 51		09 04	09 18									09 21		09 34	
Norbury	d									08 54		09 07	09 21									09 24		09 37	
Thornton Heath	d									08 57		09 10	09 24									09 27		09 40	
Selhurst	d									09 00		09 13	09 27									09 30		09 43	
Norwood Junction	a		08 56			09 02								09 14		09 26			09 32						
	d	08 52	08 57			09 03								09 16	09 22	09 27			09 33						
West Croydon	a	08 58	09 01									09 18		09 24	09 28	09 31							09 48		
East Croydon	a			08 50		09 07		08 56		09 03	09 06		09 30				09 21		09 37		09 27	09 33	09 36		

Luton, Milton Keynes Central and London East and West Croydon via Tulse Hill - Crystal Palace - Norbury

Local Services

		SN	SN	FC	SN 1	LO	SN	SN ◇1	SN	SN	SN	FC 1	SN	SN ◇1 ⚒	SN	SN		SN	FC	LO	SN	SN ◇1 ⚒	SN	SN	SN
London Bridge	d	09 21	09 24	09 32	09 37				09 36	09 39	09 41	09 42				09 51		09 54	10 02				10 06	10 09	10 11
South Bermondsey	d	09 25							09 40		09 45					09 55							10 10		10 15
Queens Rd Peckham	d	09 27							09 42		09 48					09 57							10 12		10 18
Peckham Rye	d	09 30							09 45		09 50					10 00							10 15		10 20
East Dulwich	d	09 33							09 48							10 03							10 18		
North Dulwich	d	09 35							09 50							10 05							10 20		
Luton	d																								
Luton Airport Parkway	d																								
St Pancras International	d																								
City Thameslink	d																								
London Blackfriars	d																								
Elephant & Castle	d																								
Loughborough Jn.	d																								
Herne Hill	d																								
Tulse Hill	d	09 39		09 43					09 54							10 09			10 13				10 24		
Streatham	d	09 42		09a46												10 12			10a16						
London Victoria	d						09 24	09 32					09 36	09 47	09 49						09 54	10 02			
Battersea Park	d						09 28				10a02										09 58				10a32
Milton Keynes Central	d																								
Watford Junction	d																								
Harrow & Wealdstone	d																								
Wembley Central	d																								
Shepherd's Bush	d																								
Kensington (Olympia)	d																								
West Brompton	d																								
Imperial Wharf	d																								
Clapham Junction	d						09 32	09 38					09 42	09 53	09 56						10 02	10 08			
Wandsworth Common	d						09 35														10 05				
Balham	d						09 37						09 47		10 00						10 07				
Streatham Hill	d						09 41														10 11				
West Norwood	d						09 46		09 57												10 16		10 27		
Gipsy Hill	d						09 49		10 00												10 19		10 30		
Crystal Palace	d						09 51		10a02												10 21		10a32		
Birkbeck	d																								
Beckenham Junction	a																								
Streatham Common	d	09 48											09 51		10 04	10 18									
Norbury	d	09 51											09 54		10 07	10 21									
Thornton Heath	d	09 54											09 57		10 10	10 24									
Selhurst	d	09 57											10 00		10 13	10 27									
Norwood Junction	a		09 44		09 48		09 56			10 02								10 14			10 26			10 32	
	d		09 46		09 48	09 52	09 57			10 03								10 16		10 22	10 27			10 33	
West Croydon	a		09 54			09 58	10 01								10 18			10 24		10 28	10 31				
East Croydon	a	10 01			09 54			09 50		10 07		09 56	10 03	10 06		10 30						10 21		10 37	

		FC 1	SN	SN ◇1	SN	SN	SN	FC		SN 1	LO	SN	SN ◇1	SN	SN	SN	FC 1	SN	SN ◇1 ⚒	SN	SN	SN	FC	LO	
London Bridge	d	10 12				10 21	10 24	10 32		10 37				10 36	10 39	10 41	10 42				10 51	10 54	11 02		
South Bermondsey	d					10 25								10 40		10 45					10 55				
Queens Rd Peckham	d					10 27								10 42		10 48					10 57				
Peckham Rye	d					10 30								10 45		10 50					11 00				
East Dulwich	d					10 33								10 48							11 03				
North Dulwich	d					10 35								10 50							11 05				
Luton	d																								
Luton Airport Parkway	d																								
St Pancras International	d																								
City Thameslink	d																								
London Blackfriars	d																								
Elephant & Castle	d																								
Loughborough Jn.	d																								
Herne Hill	d																								
Tulse Hill	d					10 39		10 43						10 54							11 09		11 13		
Streatham	d					10 42		10a46													11 12		11a16		
London Victoria	d		10 06	10 17	10 19							10 24	10 32					10 36	10 47	10 49					
Battersea Park	d											10 28				11a02									
Milton Keynes Central	d																								
Watford Junction	d																								
Harrow & Wealdstone	d																								
Wembley Central	d																								
Shepherd's Bush	d																								
Kensington (Olympia)	d																								
West Brompton	d																								
Imperial Wharf	d																								
Clapham Junction	d		10 12	10 23	10 26							10 32	10 38					10 42	10 53	10 56					
Wandsworth Common	d											10 35													
Balham	d		10 17		10 30							10 37						10 47		11 00					
Streatham Hill	d											10 41													
West Norwood	d											10 46		10 57											
Gipsy Hill	d											10 49		11 00											
Crystal Palace	d											10 51		11a02											
Birkbeck	d																								
Beckenham Junction	a																								
Streatham Common	d		10 21		10 34	10 48												10 51		11 04	11 18				
Norbury	d		10 24		10 37	10 51												10 54		11 07	11 21				
Thornton Heath	d		10 27		10 40	10 54												10 57		11 10	11 24				
Selhurst	d		10 30		10 43	10 57												11 00		11 13	11 27				
Norwood Junction	a						10 44			10 48		10 56			11 02							11 14			
	d						10 46			10 48	10 52	10 57			11 03							11 16		11 22	
West Croydon	a				10 48		10 54				10 58	11 01								11 18		11 24		11 28	
East Croydon	a	10 27	10 33	10 36		11 01				10 54			10 50		11 07		10 56	11 03	11 06		11 30				

Table 177

Sundays from 11 September

Luton, Milton Keynes Central and London East and West Croydon via Tulse Hill - Crystal Palace - Norbury

Local Services

		SN	SN ◇1 H	SN	SN	SN	FC 1	SN	SN ◇1	SN	SN	SN	FC	SN 1	LO	SN		SN ◇1	SN	SN	SN	FC 1	SN	SN ◇1 H	SN
London Bridge ⊖	d			11 06	11 09	11 11	11 12				11 21	11 24	11 32	11 37					11 36	11 39	11 41	11 42			
South Bermondsey	d			11 10		11 15					11 25								11 40		11 45				
Queens Rd Peckham	d			11 12		11 18					11 27								11 42		11 48				
Peckham Rye	d			11 15		11 20					11 30								11 45		11 50				
East Dulwich	d			11 18							11 33								11 48						
North Dulwich	d			11 20							11 35								11 50						
Luton	d																								
Luton Airport Parkway	d																								
St Pancras International ⊖	d																								
City Thameslink	d																								
London Blackfriars ⊖	d																								
Elephant & Castle ⊖	d																								
Loughborough Jn	d																								
Herne Hill	d																								
Tulse Hill	d			11 24							11 39		11 43						11 54						
Streatham	d										11 42		11a46												
London Victoria ⊖	d	10 54	11 02					11 06	11 17	11 19						11 24		11 32					11 36	11 47	11 49
Battersea Park	d	10 58				11a32										11 28					12a02				
Milton Keynes Central	d																								
Watford Junction	d																								
Harrow & Wealdstone ⊖	d																								
Wembley Central ⊖	d																								
Shepherd's Bush ⊖	d																								
Kensington (Olympia) ⊖	d																								
West Brompton ⊖	d																								
Imperial Wharf	d																								
Clapham Junction	d	11 02	11 08					11 12	11 23	11 26						11 32		11 38					11 42	11 53	11 56
Wandsworth Common	d	11 05														11 35									
Balham ⊖	d	11 07						11 17		11 30						11 37							11 47		12 00
Streatham Hill	d	11 11														11 41									
West Norwood	d	11 16		11 27												11 46			11 57						
Gipsy Hill	d	11 19		11 30												11 49			12 00						
Crystal Palace	d	11 21		11a32												11 51			12a02						
Birkbeck	d																								
Beckenham Junction	a																								
Streatham Common	d							11 21		11 34	11 48												11 51		12 04
Norbury	d							11 24		11 37	11 51												11 54		12 07
Thornton Heath	d							11 27		11 40	11 54												11 57		12 10
Selhurst	d							11 30		11 43	11 57												12 00		12 13
Norwood Junction	a	11 26			11 32								11 44	11 48		11 56				12 02					
	d	11 27			11 33								11 46	11 48	11 52	11 57				12 03					
West Croydon	a	11 31								11 48			11 54		11 58	12 01									12 18
East Croydon	a		11 21		11 37		11 27	11 33	11 36		12 01			11 54				11 50		12 07		11 56	12 03	12 06	

		SN	SN	FC	LO	SN	SN ◇1 H	SN		SN	SN	FC 1	SN	SN ◇1	LO	SN	SN	SN	FC	SN 1	LO	SN	SN ◇1	SN	
London Bridge ⊖	d	11 51	11 54	12 02				12 06		12 09	12 11	12 12					12 21	12 24	12 32	12 37				12 36	
South Bermondsey	d	11 55						12 10			12 15						12 25							12 40	
Queens Rd Peckham	d	11 57						12 12			12 18						12 27							12 42	
Peckham Rye	d	12 00						12 15			12 20						12 30							12 45	
East Dulwich	d	12 03						12 18									12 33							12 48	
North Dulwich	d	12 05						12 20									12 35							12 50	
Luton	d																								
Luton Airport Parkway	d																								
St Pancras International ⊖	d																								
City Thameslink	d																								
London Blackfriars ⊖	d																								
Elephant & Castle ⊖	d																								
Loughborough Jn	d																								
Herne Hill	d																								
Tulse Hill	d	12 09		12 13				12 24									12 39		12 43					12 54	
Streatham	d	12 12		12a16													12 42		12a46						
London Victoria ⊖	d					11 54	12 02						12 06	12 17		12 19						12 24	12 32		
Battersea Park	d					11 58					12a32											12 28			
Milton Keynes Central	d																								
Watford Junction	d																								
Harrow & Wealdstone ⊖	d																								
Wembley Central ⊖	d																								
Shepherd's Bush ⊖	d																								
Kensington (Olympia) ⊖	d																								
West Brompton ⊖	d																								
Imperial Wharf	d																								
Clapham Junction	d					12 02	12 08						12 12	12 23		12 26						12 32	12 38		
Wandsworth Common	d					12 05																12 35			
Balham ⊖	d					12 07							12 17			12 30						12 37			
Streatham Hill	d					12 11																12 41			
West Norwood	d					12 16		12 27														12 46		12 57	
Gipsy Hill	d					12 19		12 30														12 49		13 00	
Crystal Palace	d					12 21		12a32														12 51		13a02	
Birkbeck	d																								
Beckenham Junction	a																								
Streatham Common	d	12 18											12 21			12 34	12 48								
Norbury	d	12 21											12 24			12 37	12 51								
Thornton Heath	d	12 24											12 27			12 40	12 54								
Selhurst	d	12 27											12 30			12 43	12 57								
Norwood Junction	a		12 14			12 26				12 32								12 44		12 48		12 56			
	d		12 16		12 22	12 27				12 33					12 38			12 46		12 48	12 53	12 57			
West Croydon	a		12 24		12 28	12 31									12 45	12 48		12 54			12 59	13 01			

Table 177

Sundays from 11 September

Luton, Milton Keynes Central and London East and West Croydon via Tulse Hill - Crystal Palace - Norbury

Local Services

		SN	SN	FC 1	SN	SN ◇1 H	LO	SN	SN	SN	FC	LO	SN	SN ◇1 H	SN	SN		SN	FC 1	SN	SN ◇1	LO	SN	SN	SN
London Bridge ⊖	d	12 39	12 41	12 42					12 51	12 54	13 02				13 06	13 09		13 11	13 12					13 21	13 24
South Bermondsey	d		12 45						12 55						13 10			13 15						13 25	
Queens Rd Peckham	d		12 48						12 57						13 12			13 18						13 27	
Peckham Rye	d		12 50						13 00						13 15			13 20						13 30	
East Dulwich	d								13 03						13 18									13 33	
North Dulwich	d								13 05						13 20									13 35	
Luton	d																								
Luton Airport Parkway	d																								
St Pancras International ⊖	d																								
City Thameslink	d																								
London Blackfriars ⊖	d																								
Elephant & Castle ⊖	d																								
Loughborough Jn	d																								
Herne Hill	d																								
Tulse Hill	d								13 09		13 13				13 24									13 39	
Streatham	d								13 12		13a16													13 42	
London Victoria ⊖	d				12 36	12 47		12 49					12 54	13 02						13 06	13 17		13 19		
Battersea Park	d		13a02										12 58					13a32							
Milton Keynes Central	d																								
Watford Junction	d																								
Harrow & Wealdstone ⊖	d																								
Wembley Central ⊖	d																								
Shepherd's Bush ⊖	d																								
Kensington (Olympia) ⊖	d																								
West Brompton ⊖	d																								
Imperial Wharf	d																								
Clapham Junction	d				12 42	12 53		12 56					13 02	13 08						13 12	13 23		13 26		
Wandsworth Common	d												13 05												
Balham ⊖	d				12 47			13 00					13 07							13 17			13 30		
Streatham Hill	d												13 11												
West Norwood	d												13 16		13 27										
Gipsy Hill	d												13 19		13 30										
Crystal Palace	d												13 21		13a32										
Birkbeck	d																								
Beckenham Junction	a																								
Streatham Common	d				12 51			13 04	13 18											13 21			13 34	13 48	
Norbury	d				12 54			13 07	13 21											13 24			13 37	13 51	
Thornton Heath	d				12 57			13 10	13 24											13 27			13 40	13 54	
Selhurst	d				13 00			13 13	13 27											13 30			13 43	13 57	
Norwood Junction	a	13 02								13 14			13 26			13 32									13 44
	d	13 03					13 08			13 16		13 23	13 27			13 33						13 38			13 46
West Croydon	a						13 15	13 18		13 24		13 29	13 31									13 45	13 48		13 54
East Croydon	a	13 07		12 56	13 03	13 06			13 30					13 21		13 37			13 27	13 33	13 36			14 01	

		FC	SN 1	LO	SN	SN ◇1	SN	SN		SN	FC 1	SN	SN ◇1 H	LO	SN	SN	SN	FC	LO	SN	SN ◇1 H	SN	SN	SN	
London Bridge ⊖	d	13 32	13 37				13 36	13 39		13 41	13 42					13 51	13 54	14 02				14 06	14 09	14 11	
South Bermondsey	d						13 40			13 45						13 55						14 10		14 15	
Queens Rd Peckham	d						13 42			13 48						13 57						14 12		14 18	
Peckham Rye	d						13 45			13 50						14 00						14 15		14 20	
East Dulwich	d						13 48									14 03						14 18			
North Dulwich	d						13 50									14 05						14 20			
Luton	d																								
Luton Airport Parkway	d																								
St Pancras International ⊖	d																								
City Thameslink	d																								
London Blackfriars ⊖	d																								
Elephant & Castle ⊖	d																								
Loughborough Jn	d																								
Herne Hill	d																								
Tulse Hill	d	13 43					13 54									14 09		14 13				14 24			
Streatham	d	13a46														14 12		14a16							
London Victoria ⊖	d				13 24	13 32						13 36	13 47		13 49					13 54	14 02				
Battersea Park	d				13 28					14a02										13 58				14a32	
Milton Keynes Central	d																								
Watford Junction	d																								
Harrow & Wealdstone ⊖	d																								
Wembley Central ⊖	d																								
Shepherd's Bush ⊖	d																								
Kensington (Olympia) ⊖	d																								
West Brompton ⊖	d																								
Imperial Wharf	d																								
Clapham Junction	d				13 32	13 38						13 42	13 53		13 56					14 02	14 08				
Wandsworth Common	d				13 35															14 05					
Balham ⊖	d				13 37							13 47			14 00					14 07					
Streatham Hill	d				13 41															14 11					
West Norwood	d				13 46		13 57													14 16		14 27			
Gipsy Hill	d				13 49		14 00													14 19		14 30			
Crystal Palace	d				13 51		14a02													14 21		14a32			
Birkbeck	d																								
Beckenham Junction	a																								
Streatham Common	d											13 51			14 04	14 18									
Norbury	d											13 54			14 07	14 21									
Thornton Heath	d											13 57			14 10	14 24									
Selhurst	d											14 00			14 13	14 27									
Norwood Junction	a		13 48		13 56			14 02									14 14			14 26			14 32		
	d		13 48	13 53	13 57			14 03						14 08			14 16		14 23	14 27			14 33		
West Croydon	a			13 59	14 01									14 15	14 18		14 24		14 29	14 31					
East Croydon	a		13 54			13 50		14 07			13 56	14 03	14 06			14 30					14 21		14 37		

Luton, Milton Keynes Central and London East and West Croydon via Tulse Hill - Crystal Palace - Norbury

Local Services

	FC 1	SN	SN ◇1	LO	SN	SN	SN	FC	SN 1	LO	SN	SN ◇1	SN	SN	SN		FC 1	SN	SN ◇1	LO	SN	SN	SN	FC
London Bridge 4 ⊖ d	14 12					14 21	14 24	14 32	14 37				14 36	14 39	14 41		14 42					14 51	14 54	15 02
South Bermondsey d						14 25							14 40		14 45							14 55		
Queens Rd Peckham d						14 27							14 42		14 48							14 57		
Peckham Rye 4 d						14 30							14 45		14 50							15 00		
East Dulwich d						14 33							14 48									15 03		
North Dulwich d						14 35							14 50									15 05		
Luton 10 d																								
Luton Airport Parkway 7 d																								
St Pancras International 15 ⊖ d																								
City Thameslink 3 d																								
London Blackfriars 3 ⊖ d																								
Elephant & Castle ⊖ d																								
Loughborough Jn. d																								
Herne Hill 4 d																								
Tulse Hill 3 d						14 39		14 43					14 54									15 09		15 13
Streatham 4 d						14 42		14a46														15 12		15a16
London Victoria 15 ⊖ d		14 06	14 17		14 19						14 24	14 32						14 36	14 47		14 49			
Battersea Park 4 d											14 28				15a02									
Milton Keynes Central d																								
Watford Junction d																								
Harrow & Wealdstone ⊖ d																								
Wembley Central ⊖ d																								
Shepherd's Bush ⊖ d																								
Kensington (Olympia) ⊖ d																								
West Brompton ⊖ d																								
Imperial Wharf d																								
Clapham Junction 10 d		14 12	14 23		14 26						14 32	14 38						14 42	14 53		14 56			
Wandsworth Common d											14 35													
Balham 4 ⊖ d		14 17			14 30						14 37							14 47			15 00			
Streatham Hill d											14 41													
West Norwood 4 d											14 46		14 57											
Gipsy Hill d											14 49		15 00											
Crystal Palace 4 d											14 51		15a02											
Birkbeck d																								
Beckenham Junction 4 a																								
Streatham Common 4 d		14 21			14 34	14 48												14 51			15 04	15 18		
Norbury d		14 24			14 37	14 51												14 54			15 07	15 21		
Thornton Heath d		14 27			14 40	14 54												14 57			15 10	15 24		
Selhurst 4 d		14 30			14 43	14 57												15 00			15 13	15 27		
Norwood Junction 2 a							14 44		14 48		14 56			15 02									15 14	
d				14 38			14 46		14 48	14 53	14 57			15 03						15 08			15 16	
West Croydon 4 a				14 45	14 48		14 54			14 59	15 01									15 15	15 18		15 24	
East Croydon a	14 27	14 33	14 36			15 01			14 54			14 50		15 07			14 56	15 03	15 06			15 30		

	LO	SN	SN ◇1	SN	SN	SN	FC 1		SN	SN ◇1	LO	SN	SN	SN	FC	SN 1	LO	SN	SN ◇1	SN	SN	SN	FC 1	
London Bridge 4 ⊖ d				15 06	15 09	15 11	15 12						15 21	15 24	15 32	15 37				15 36	15 39	15 41	15 42	
South Bermondsey d				15 10		15 15							15 25							15 40		15 45		
Queens Rd Peckham d				15 12		15 18							15 27							15 42		15 48		
Peckham Rye 4 d				15 15		15 20							15 30							15 45		15 50		
East Dulwich d				15 18									15 33							15 48				
North Dulwich d				15 20									15 35							15 50				
Luton 10 d																								
Luton Airport Parkway 7 d																								
St Pancras International 15 ⊖ d																								
City Thameslink 3 d																								
London Blackfriars 3 ⊖ d																								
Elephant & Castle ⊖ d																								
Loughborough Jn. d																								
Herne Hill 4 d																								
Tulse Hill 3 d				15 24									15 39		15 43					15 54				
Streatham 4 d													15 42		15a46									
London Victoria 15 ⊖ d		14 54	15 02						15 06	15 17		15 19						15 24	15 32					
Battersea Park 4 d		14 58				15a32												15 28				16a02		
Milton Keynes Central d																								
Watford Junction d																								
Harrow & Wealdstone ⊖ d																								
Wembley Central ⊖ d																								
Shepherd's Bush ⊖ d																								
Kensington (Olympia) ⊖ d																								
West Brompton ⊖ d																								
Imperial Wharf d																								
Clapham Junction 10 d		15 02	15 08						15 12	15 23		15 26						15 32	15 38					
Wandsworth Common d		15 05																15 35						
Balham 4 ⊖ d		15 07							15 17			15 30						15 37						
Streatham Hill d		15 11																15 41						
West Norwood 4 d		15 16		15 27														15 46		15 57				
Gipsy Hill d		15 19		15 30														15 49		16 00				
Crystal Palace 4 d		15 21		15a32														15 51		16a02				
Birkbeck d																								
Beckenham Junction 4 a																								
Streatham Common 4 d									15 21			15 34	15 48											
Norbury d									15 24			15 37	15 51											
Thornton Heath d									15 27			15 40	15 54											
Selhurst 4 d									15 30			15 43	15 57											
Norwood Junction 2 a		15 26			15 32									15 44		15 48		15 56			16 02			
d	15 23	15 27			15 33						15 38			15 46		15 48	15 53	15 57			16 03			
West Croydon 4 a	15 29	15 31									15 45	15 48		15 54			15 59	16 01						
East Croydon a			15 21		15 37		15 27		15 33	15 36			16 01			15 54			15 50		16 07		15 56	

Luton, Milton Keynes Central and London East and West Croydon via Tulse Hill - Crystal Palace - Norbury

Local Services

	SN	SN ◇1	LO	SN	SN	SN	FC	LO	SN	SN ◇1	SN	SN	SN	FC 1	SN		SN ◇1	LO	SN	SN	SN	FC	SN 1	LO
London Bridge 4 ⊖ d					15 51	15 54	16 02				16 06	16 09	16 11	16 12						16 21	16 24	16 32	16 37	
South Bermondsey d					15 55						16 10		16 15							16 25				
Queens Rd Peckham d					15 57						16 12		16 18							16 27				
Peckham Rye 4 d					16 00						16 15		16 20							16 30				
East Dulwich d					16 03						16 18									16 33				
North Dulwich d					16 05						16 20									16 35				
Luton 10 d																								
Luton Airport Parkway 7 d																								
St Pancras International 15 ⊖ d																								
City Thameslink 3 d																								
London Blackfriars 3 ⊖ d																								
Elephant & Castle ⊖ d																								
Loughborough Jn. d																								
Herne Hill 4 d																								
Tulse Hill 3 d					16 09		16 13				16 24									16 39		16 43		
Streatham 4 d					16 12		16a16													16 42		16a46		
London Victoria 15 ⊖ d	15 36	15 47		15 49					15 54	16 02					16 06		16 17		16 19					
Battersea Park 4 d									15 58				16a32											
Milton Keynes Central d																								
Watford Junction d																								
Harrow & Wealdstone ⊖ d																								
Wembley Central ⊖ d																								
Shepherd's Bush ⊖ d																								
Kensington (Olympia) ⊖ d																								
West Brompton ⊖ d																								
Imperial Wharf d																								
Clapham Junction 10 d	15 42	15 53		15 56					16 02	16 08					16 12		16 23		16 26					
Wandsworth Common d									16 05															
Balham 4 ⊖ d	15 47			16 00					16 07						16 17				16 30					
Streatham Hill d									16 11															
West Norwood 4 d									16 16		16 27													
Gipsy Hill d									16 19		16 30													
Crystal Palace 4 d									16 21		16a32													
Birkbeck d																								
Beckenham Junction 4 a																								
Streatham Common 4 d	15 51			16 04	16 18										16 21				16 34	16 48				
Norbury d	15 54			16 07	16 21										16 24				16 37	16 51				
Thornton Heath d	15 57			16 10	16 24										16 27				16 40	16 54				
Selhurst 4 d	16 00			16 13	16 27										16 30				16 43	16 57				
Norwood Junction 2 a						16 14			16 26			16 32									16 44		16 48	
d			16 08			16 16		16 23	16 27			16 33						16 38			16 46		16 48	16 53
West Croydon 4 a			16 15	16 18		16 24		16 29	16 31									16 45	16 48		16 54			16 59
East Croydon a	16 03	16 06			16 30					16 21		16 37		16 27	16 33		16 36			17 01			16 54	

	SN	SN ◇1	SN	SN	SN	FC 1	SN		SN ◇1	LO	SN	SN	SN	FC	LO	SN	SN ◇1	SN	SN	SN	FC 1	SN	SN ◇1	
London Bridge 4 ⊖ d			16 36	16 39	16 41	16 42						16 51	16 54	17 02				17 06	17 09	17 11	17 12			
South Bermondsey d			16 40		16 45							16 55						17 10		17 15				
Queens Rd Peckham d			16 42		16 48							16 57						17 12		17 18				
Peckham Rye 4 d			16 45		16 50							17 00						17 15		17 20				
East Dulwich d			16 48									17 03						17 18						
North Dulwich d			16 50									17 05						17 20						
Luton 10 d																								
Luton Airport Parkway 7 d																								
St Pancras International 15 ⊖ d																								
City Thameslink 3 d																								
London Blackfriars 3 ⊖ d																								
Elephant & Castle ⊖ d																								
Loughborough Jn. d																								
Herne Hill 4 d																								
Tulse Hill 3 d			16 54									17 09		17 13				17 24						
Streatham 4 d												17 12		17a16										
London Victoria 15 ⊖ d	16 24	16 32					16 36		16 47		16 49					16 54	17 02					17 06	17 17	
Battersea Park 4 d	16 28				17a02											16 58				17a32				
Milton Keynes Central d																								
Watford Junction d																								
Harrow & Wealdstone ⊖ d																								
Wembley Central ⊖ d																								
Shepherd's Bush ⊖ d																								
Kensington (Olympia) ⊖ d																								
West Brompton ⊖ d																								
Imperial Wharf d																								
Clapham Junction 10 d	16 32	16 38					16 42		16 53		16 56					17 02	17 08					17 12	17 23	
Wandsworth Common d	16 35															17 05								
Balham 4 ⊖ d	16 37						16 47				17 00					17 07						17 17		
Streatham Hill d	16 41															17 11								
West Norwood 4 d	16 46		16 57													17 16		17 27						
Gipsy Hill d	16 49		17 00													17 19		17 30						
Crystal Palace 4 d	16 51		17a02													17 21		17a32						
Birkbeck d																								
Beckenham Junction 4 a																								
Streatham Common 4 d							16 51				17 04	17 18										17 21		
Norbury d							16 54				17 07	17 21										17 24		
Thornton Heath d							16 57				17 10	17 24										17 27		
Selhurst 4 d							17 00				17 13	17 27										17 30		
Norwood Junction 2 a	16 56			17 02									17 14			17 26			17 32					
d	16 57			17 03						17 08			17 16		17 23	17 27			17 33					
West Croydon 4 a	17 01									17 15	17 18		17 24		17 29	17 31								
East Croydon a		16 50		17 07		16 56	17 03		17 06			17 30					17 21		17 37		17 27	17 33	17 36	

Table 177

Luton, Milton Keynes Central and London East and West Croydon via Tulse Hill - Crystal Palace - Norbury

Local Services

		LO	SN	SN	SN	FC	SN ■	LO	SN	SN ◇■	SN	SN	SN	FC ■	SN	SN ◇■		LO	SN	SN	SN	FC	LO	SN	SN ◇■
London Bridge ■ ⊖	d			17 21	17 24	17 32	17 37				17 36	17 39	17 41	17 42						17 51	17 54	18 02			
South Bermondsey	d			17 25							17 40		17 45							17 55					
Queens Rd Peckham	d			17 27							17 42		17 48							17 57					
Peckham Rye ■	d			17 30							17 45		17 50							18 00					
East Dulwich	d			17 33							17 48									18 03					
North Dulwich	d			17 35							17 50									18 05					
Luton ■	d																								
Luton Airport Parkway ■	d																								
St Pancras International ■ ⊖	d																								
City Thameslink ■	d																								
London Blackfriars ■ ⊖	d																								
Elephant & Castle ⊖	d																								
Loughborough Jn.	d																								
Herne Hill ■	d																								
Tulse Hill ■	d			17 39		17 43					17 54									18 09		18 13			
Streatham ■	d			17 42		17a46														18 12		18a16			
London Victoria ■ ⊖	d		17 19						17 24	17 32					17 36	17 47			17 49					17 54	18 02
Battersea Park ■	d								17 28				18a02											17 58	
Milton Keynes Central	d																								
Watford Junction	d																								
Harrow & Wealdstone ⊖	d																								
Wembley Central ⊖	d																								
Shepherd's Bush ⊖	d																								
Kensington (Olympia) ⊖	d																								
West Brompton ⊖	d																								
Imperial Wharf	d																								
Clapham Junction ■	d		17 26						17 32	17 38					17 42	17 53			17 56					18 02	18 08
Wandsworth Common	d								17 35															18 05	
Balham ■ ⊖	d		17 30						17 37						17 47				18 00					18 07	
Streatham Hill	d								17 41															18 11	
West Norwood ■	d								17 46		17 57													18 16	
Gipsy Hill	d								17 49		18 00													18 19	
Crystal Palace ■	d								17 51		18a02													18 21	
Birkbeck	d																								
Beckenham Junction ■	a																								
Streatham Common ■	d		17 34	17 48											17 51				18 04	18 18					
Norbury	d		17 37	17 51											17 54				18 07	18 21					
Thornton Heath	d		17 40	17 54											17 57				18 10	18 24					
Selhurst ■	d		17 43	17 57											18 00				18 13	18 27					
Norwood Junction ■	a				17 44		17 48		17 56			18 02									18 14			18 26	
	d	17 38			17 46		17 48	17 53	17 57			18 03						18 08			18 16		18 23	18 27	
West Croydon ■	a	17 45	17 48		17 54			17 59	18 01									18 14	18 18		18 24		18 29	18 31	
East Croydon	a			18 01			17 54			17 50		18 07		17 56	18 03	18 06				18 30					18 21

		SN	SN	SN	FC ■	SN	SN ◇■	LO		SN	SN	SN	FC	SN ■	LO	SN	SN ◇■	SN	SN	SN	FC ■	SN	SN ◇■	LO
London Bridge ■ ⊖	d	18 06	18 09	18 11	18 12						18 21	18 24	18 32	18 37				18 36	18 39	18 41	18 42			
South Bermondsey	d	18 10		18 15							18 25							18 40		18 45				
Queens Rd Peckham	d	18 12		18 18							18 27							18 42		18 48				
Peckham Rye ■	d	18 15		18 20							18 30							18 45		18 50				
East Dulwich	d	18 18									18 33							18 48						
North Dulwich	d	18 20									18 35							18 50						
Luton ■	d																							
Luton Airport Parkway ■	d																							
St Pancras International ■ ⊖	d																							
City Thameslink ■	d																							
London Blackfriars ■ ⊖	d																							
Elephant & Castle ⊖	d																							
Loughborough Jn.	d																							
Herne Hill ■	d																							
Tulse Hill ■	d	18 24									18 39		18 43					18 54						
Streatham ■	d										18 42		18a46											
London Victoria ■ ⊖	d					18 06	18 17			18 19						18 24	18 32					18 36	18 47	
Battersea Park ■	d			18a32												18 28				19a02				
Milton Keynes Central	d																							
Watford Junction	d																							
Harrow & Wealdstone ⊖	d																							
Wembley Central ⊖	d																							
Shepherd's Bush ⊖	d																							
Kensington (Olympia) ⊖	d																							
West Brompton ⊖	d																							
Imperial Wharf	d																							
Clapham Junction ■	d					18 12	18 23			18 26						18 32	18 38					18 42	18 53	
Wandsworth Common	d															18 35								
Balham ■ ⊖	d					18 17				18 30						18 37						18 47		
Streatham Hill	d															18 41								
West Norwood ■	d	18 27														18 46		18 57						
Gipsy Hill	d	18 30														18 49		19 00						
Crystal Palace ■	d	18a32														18 51		19a02						
Birkbeck	d																							
Beckenham Junction ■	a																							
Streatham Common ■	d					18 21				18 34	18 48											18 51		
Norbury	d					18 24				18 37	18 51											18 54		
Thornton Heath	d					18 27				18 40	18 54											18 57		
Selhurst ■	d					18 30				18 43	18 57											19 00		
Norwood Junction ■	a		18 32									18 44		18 48		18 56			19 02					
	d		18 33					18 38				18 46		18 48	18 53	18 57			19 03					19 08
West Croydon ■	a							18 44		18 48		18 54			18 59	19 01								19 14

Table 177

Sundays
from 11 September

Luton, Milton Keynes Central and London East and West Croydon via Tulse Hill - Crystal Palace - Norbury

Local Services

		SN	SN	SN	FC	LO	SN	SN ◇■	SN	SN	SN	FC ■	SN	SN ◇■	LO	SN		SN	SN	FC	SN ■	LO	SN	SN ◇■	SN
London Bridge ■ ⊖	d		18 51	18 54	19 02				19 06	19 09	19 11	19 12						19 21	19 24	19 32	19 37				19 36
South Bermondsey	d		18 55						19 10		19 15							19 25							19 40
Queens Rd Peckham	d		18 57						19 12		19 18							19 27							19 42
Peckham Rye ■	d		19 00						19 15		19 20							19 30							19 45
East Dulwich	d		19 03						19 18									19 33							19 48
North Dulwich	d		19 05						19 20									19 35							19 50
Luton ■	d																								
Luton Airport Parkway ■	d																								
St Pancras International ■ ⊖	d																								
City Thameslink ■	d																								
London Blackfriars ■ ⊖	d																								
Elephant & Castle ⊖	d																								
Loughborough Jn.	d																								
Herne Hill ■	d																								
Tulse Hill ■	d		19 09		19 13				19 24									19 39		19 43					19 54
Streatham ■	d		19 12		19a16													19 42		19a46					
London Victoria ■ ⊖	d	18 49					18 54	19 02					19 06	19 17		19 19							19 24	19 32	
Battersea Park ■	d						18 58				19a32												19 28		
Milton Keynes Central	d																								
Watford Junction	d																								
Harrow & Wealdstone ⊖	d																								
Wembley Central ⊖	d																								
Shepherd's Bush ⊖	d																								
Kensington (Olympia) ⊖	d																								
West Brompton ⊖	d																								
Imperial Wharf	d																								
Clapham Junction ■	d	18 56					19 02	19 08					19 12	19 23		19 26							19 32	19 38	
Wandsworth Common	d						19 05																19 35		
Balham ■ ⊖	d	19 00					19 07						19 17			19 30							19 37		
Streatham Hill	d						19 11																19 41		
West Norwood ■	d						19 16		19 27														19 46		19 57
Gipsy Hill	d						19 19		19 30														19 49		20 00
Crystal Palace ■	d						19 21		19a32														19 51		20a02
Birkbeck	d																								
Beckenham Junction ■	a																								
Streatham Common ■	d	19 04	19 18										19 21			19 34		19 48							
Norbury	d	19 07	19 21										19 24			19 37		19 51							
Thornton Heath	d	19 10	19 24										19 27			19 40		19 54							
Selhurst ■	d	19 13	19 27										19 30			19 43		19 57							
Norwood Junction ■	a			19 14			19 26			19 32									19 44		19 48		19 56		
	d			19 16		19 23	19 27			19 33					19 38				19 46		19 48	19 53	19 57		
West Croydon ■	a	19 18		19 24		19 29	19 31								19 44	19 48			19 54			19 59	20 01		
East Croydon	a		19 30					19 21		19 37		19 27	19 33	19 36				20 01			19 54			19 50	

Luton, Milton Keynes Central and London East and West Croydon via Tulse Hill - Crystal Palace - Norbury

Local Services

	SN	SN	FC 1	SN	SN ◇1	LO	SN	SN	SN	FC 1	LO	SN	SN ◇1	SN	SN	SN	FC 1	SN	SN ◇1	LO	SN	SN
London Bridge ⊖ d	19 39	19 41	19 42					19 51	19 54	20 02				20 06	20 09	20 11	20 12					20 21
South Bermondsey d		19 45						19 55						20 10		20 15						20 25
Queens Rd Peckham d		19 48						19 57						20 12		20 18						20 27
Peckham Rye d		19 50						20 00						20 15		20 20						20 30
East Dulwich d								20 03						20 18								20 33
North Dulwich d								20 05						20 20								20 35
Luton d																						
Luton Airport Parkway d																						
St Pancras International ⊖ d																						
City Thameslink d																						
London Blackfriars ⊖ d																						
Elephant & Castle ⊖ d																						
Loughborough Jn d																						
Herne Hill d																						
Tulse Hill d								20 09		20 13				20 24								20 39
Streatham d								20 12		20a16												20 42
London Victoria ⊖ d				19 36	19 47		19 49					19 54	20 02					20 06	20 17		20 19	
Battersea Park d		20a02										19 58				20a32						
Milton Keynes Central d																						
Watford Junction d																						
Harrow & Wealdstone ⊖ d																						
Wembley Central ⊖ d																						
Shepherd's Bush ⊖ d																						
Kensington (Olympia) ⊖ d																						
West Brompton ⊖ d																						
Imperial Wharf d																						
Clapham Junction d				19 42	19 53		19 56					20 02	20 08					20 12	20 23		20 26	
Wandsworth Common d												20 05										
Balham ⊖ d				19 47			20 00					20 07						20 17			20 30	
Streatham Hill d												20 11										
West Norwood d												20 16		20 27								
Gipsy Hill d												20 19		20 30								
Crystal Palace d												20 21		20a32								
Birkbeck 🚊 d																						
Beckenham Junction 🚊 a																						
Streatham Common d				19 51			20 04	20 18										20 21			20 34	20 48
Norbury d				19 54			20 07	20 21										20 24			20 37	20 51
Thornton Heath d				19 57			20 10	20 24										20 27			20 40	20 54
Selhurst d				20 00			20 13	20 27										20 30			20 43	20 57
Norwood Junction a	20 02								20 14			20 26			20 32							
Norwood Junction d	20 03					20 08			20 16		20 23	20 27			20 33					20 38		
West Croydon 🚊 a						20 15	20 18		20 24		20 29	20 31								20 45	20 48	
East Croydon 🚊 a	20 07		19 56	20 03	20 06			20 30					20 21		20 37		20 27	20 33	20 36			21 01

	SN	FC	SN 1	LO	SN	SN ◇1	SN	SN	SN	FC 1	SN	SN ◇1	LO	SN	SN	SN	FC	LO	SN	SN ◇1	SN	SN	SN
London Bridge ⊖ d	20 24	20 32	20 37				20 36	20 39	20 41	20 42					20 51	20 54	21 02				21 06	21 09	21 11
South Bermondsey d							20 40		20 45						20 55						21 10		21 15
Queens Rd Peckham d							20 42		20 48						20 57						21 12		21 18
Peckham Rye d							20 45		20 50						21 00						21 15		21 20
East Dulwich d							20 48								21 03						21 18		
North Dulwich d							20 50								21 05						21 20		
Luton d																							
Luton Airport Parkway d																							
St Pancras International ⊖ d																							
City Thameslink d																							
London Blackfriars ⊖ d																							
Elephant & Castle ⊖ d																							
Loughborough Jn d																							
Herne Hill d																							
Tulse Hill d		20 43					20 54								21 09		21 13				21 24		
Streatham d		20a46													21 12		21a16						
London Victoria ⊖ d					20 24	20 32					20 36	20 47		20 49					20 54	21 02			
Battersea Park d					20 28				21a02										20 58				21a32
Milton Keynes Central d																							
Watford Junction d																							
Harrow & Wealdstone ⊖ d																							
Wembley Central ⊖ d																							
Shepherd's Bush ⊖ d																							
Kensington (Olympia) ⊖ d																							
West Brompton ⊖ d																							
Imperial Wharf d																							
Clapham Junction d					20 32	20 38					20 42	20 53		20 56					21 02	21 08			
Wandsworth Common d					20 35														21 05				
Balham ⊖ d					20 37						20 47			21 00					21 07				
Streatham Hill d					20 41														21 11				
West Norwood d					20 46		20 57												21 16		21 27		
Gipsy Hill d					20 49		21 00												21 19		21 30		
Crystal Palace d					20 51		21a02												21 21		21a32		
Birkbeck 🚊 d																							
Beckenham Junction 🚊 a																							
Streatham Common d											20 51			21 04	21 18								
Norbury d											20 54			21 07	21 21								
Thornton Heath d											20 57			21 10	21 24								
Selhurst d											21 00			21 13	21 27								
Norwood Junction a	20 44		20 48		20 56			21 02								21 14			21 26			21 32	
Norwood Junction d	20 46		20 48	20 53	20 57			21 03					21 08			21 16		21 23	21 27			21 33	
West Croydon 🚊 a	20 54			20 59	21 01								21 15	21 18		21 24		21 29	21 31				
East Croydon 🚊 a			20 54			20 50		21 07		20 56	21 03	21 06			21 30					21 21		21 37	

Luton, Milton Keynes Central and London East and West Croydon via Tulse Hill - Crystal Palace - Norbury

Local Services

	FC 1	SN	SN ◇1	LO	SN	SN	SN	SN 1	LO	SN	SN ◇1	SN	SN	SN	FC 1	SN	SN ◇1	LO	SN	SN	SN	LO
London Bridge ⊖ d	21 12					21 21	21 24	21 37				21 36	21 39	21 41	21 42					21 51	21 54	
South Bermondsey d						21 25						21 40		21 45						21 55		
Queens Rd Peckham d						21 27						21 42		21 48						21 57		
Peckham Rye d						21 30						21 45		21 50						22 00		
East Dulwich d						21 33						21 48								22 03		
North Dulwich d						21 35						21 50								22 05		
Luton d																						
Luton Airport Parkway d																						
St Pancras International ⊖ d																						
City Thameslink d																						
London Blackfriars ⊖ d																						
Elephant & Castle ⊖ d																						
Loughborough Jn d																						
Herne Hill d																						
Tulse Hill d						21 39						21 54								22 09		
Streatham d						21 42														22 12		
London Victoria ⊖ d		21 06	21 17		21 19					21 24	21 32					21 36	21 47		21 49			
Battersea Park d										21 28				22a02								
Milton Keynes Central d																						
Watford Junction d																						
Harrow & Wealdstone ⊖ d																						
Wembley Central ⊖ d																						
Shepherd's Bush ⊖ d																						
Kensington (Olympia) ⊖ d																						
West Brompton ⊖ d																						
Imperial Wharf d																						
Clapham Junction d		21 12	21 23		21 26					21 32	21 38					21 42	21 53		21 56			
Wandsworth Common d										21 35												
Balham ⊖ d		21 17			21 30					21 38						21 47			22 00			
Streatham Hill d										21 41												
West Norwood d										21 46		21 57										
Gipsy Hill d										21 49		22 00										
Crystal Palace d										21 51		22a02										
Birkbeck 🚊 d																						
Beckenham Junction 🚊 a																						
Streatham Common d		21 21			21 34	21 48										21 51			22 04	22 18		
Norbury d		21 24			21 37	21 51										21 54			22 07	22 21		
Thornton Heath d		21 27			21 40	21 54										21 57			22 10	22 24		
Selhurst d		21 30			21 43	21 57										22 00			22 13	22 27		
Norwood Junction a							21 44	21 48		21 56			22 02								22 14	
Norwood Junction d				21 38			21 46	21 48	21 53	21 57			22 03					22 08			22 16	22 23
West Croydon 🚊 a				21 45	21 48		21 54		21 59	22 01								22 15	22 18		22 24	22 29
East Croydon 🚊 a	21 27	21 33	21 36			22 01		21 54			21 50		22 07		21 56	22 03	22 06			22 30		

	SN	SN	SN	SN	FC 1	SN	SN ◇1	LO	SN	SN	SN 1	SN	SN ◇1	SN	SN	SN ◇1	SN	LO	SN	SN	SN	FC 1	SN 1
London Bridge ⊖ d		22 06	22 09	22 11	22 12					22 21	22 37			22 36			22 39				22 41	22 42	
South Bermondsey d		22 10		22 15						22 25				22 40							22 45		
Queens Rd Peckham d		22 12		22 18						22 27				22 42							22 48		
Peckham Rye d		22 15		22 20						22 30				22 45							22 50		
East Dulwich d		22 18								22 33				22 48									
North Dulwich d		22 20								22 35				22 50									
Luton d																							
Luton Airport Parkway d																							
St Pancras International ⊖ d																							
City Thameslink d																							
London Blackfriars ⊖ d																							
Elephant & Castle ⊖ d																							
Loughborough Jn d																							
Herne Hill d																							
Tulse Hill d		22 24								22 39				22 54									
Streatham d										22 42													
London Victoria ⊖ d	21 54					22 06	22 17		22 19			22 24	22 32		22 36	22 47			22 49	22 54			23 04
Battersea Park d	21 58			22a32								22 28								22 58	23a02		
Milton Keynes Central d																							
Watford Junction d																							
Harrow & Wealdstone ⊖ d																							
Wembley Central ⊖ d																							
Shepherd's Bush ⊖ d																							
Kensington (Olympia) ⊖ d																							
West Brompton ⊖ d																							
Imperial Wharf d																							
Clapham Junction d	22 02					22 12	22 23		22 26			22 32	22 38		22 42	22 53			22 56	23 02			23 10
Wandsworth Common d	22 05											22 35								23 05			
Balham ⊖ d	22 07					22 17			22 30			22 38			22 47				23 00	23 07			
Streatham Hill d	22 11											22 41								23 11			
West Norwood d	22 16	22 27										22 46		22 57						23 16			
Gipsy Hill d	22 19	22 30										22 49		23 00						23 19			
Crystal Palace d	22 21	22a32										22 51		23a02						23 21			
Birkbeck 🚊 d																							
Beckenham Junction 🚊 a																							
Streatham Common d						22 21			22 34	22 48					22 51				23 04				
Norbury d						22 24			22 37	22 51					22 54				23 07				
Thornton Heath d						22 27			22 40	22 54					22 57				23 10				
Selhurst d						22 30			22 43	22 57					23 00				23 13				
Norwood Junction a	22 26		22 32								22 48	22 56					23 02			23 26			
Norwood Junction d	22 27		22 33					22 38			22 48	22 57					23 03	23 08		23 27			
West Croydon 🚊 a	22 31							22 45	22 48			23 01						23 14	23 18	23 31			
East Croydon 🚊 a			22 37		22 27	22 33	22 36			23 00	22 54		22 50		23 03	23 06	23 07					22 56	23 22

Table 177

Sundays from 11 September

Luton, Milton Keynes Central and London East and West Croydon via Tulse Hill - Crystal Palace - Norbury

Local Services

Station		SN	SN	SN	SN ◇1	SN	LO	SN		SN	SN	FC 1	SN ◇1	SN	SN	SN	FC 1	SN	SN	SN 1	SN
London Bridge ⊖	d	22 51	23 06			23 09					23 11	23 12		23 21		23 39	23 42				
South Bermondsey	d	22 55	23 10								23 15			23 25							
Queens Rd Peckham	d	22 57	23 12								23 18			23 27							
Peckham Rye	d	23 00	23 15								23 20			23 30							
East Dulwich	d	23 03	23 18											23 33							
North Dulwich	d	23 05	23 20											23 35							
Luton	d																				
Luton Airport Parkway	d																				
St Pancras International ⊖	d																				
City Thameslink	d																				
London Blackfriars ⊖	d																				
Elephant & Castle ⊖	d																				
Loughborough Jn	d																				
Herne Hill	d																				
Tulse Hill	d	23 09	23 24											23 39							
Streatham	d	23 12												23 42							
London Victoria ⊖	d			23 06	23 17			23 19		23 24			23 32		23 36			23 47	23 50		23 54
Battersea Park	d							23 23		23 28	23a32				23 40						23 58
Milton Keynes Central	d																				
Watford Junction	d																			23 17	
Harrow & Wealdstone ⊖	d																			23 23	
Wembley Central ⊖	d																				
Shepherd's Bush ⊖	d																			23 45	
Kensington (Olympia) ⊖	d																			23 48	
West Brompton ⊖	d																			23 50	
Imperial Wharf	d																			23 53	
Clapham Junction	d			23 12	23 23			23 27		23 32			23 38		23 44			23 53	23 56	00 05	00 02
Wandsworth Common	d							23 30		23 35					23 47				23 59		00 05
Balham ⊖	d			23 17				23 32		23 37					23 49				00 02		00 07
Streatham Hill	d									23 41											00 11
West Norwood	d		23 27							23 44											00 14
Gipsy Hill	d		23 30							23 47											00 17
Crystal Palace	d		23a32							23 50											00 20
Birkbeck	d																				
Beckenham Junction	a																				
Streatham Common	d	23 18		23 21				23 36						23 48	23 53				00 06		
Norbury	d	23 21		23 24				23 39						23 51	23 56				00 08		
Thornton Heath	d	23 24		23 27				23 42						23 54	23 59				00 11		
Selhurst	d	23 27		23 30				23 45					23 48	23 57	00a01				00 14	00 19	
Norwood Junction	a					23 32				23 54						00 02					00 25
	d					23 33	23 38			23 55						00 03					
West Croydon	a						23 44	23 49		23 59											
East Croydon	a	23 30		23 34	23 37	23 38						23 27	23 52	00 01		00 06	23 56	00 06	00 17	00 22	

Table 177

Mondays to Fridays

East and West Croydon, London Milton Keynes Central and Luton via Norbury Crystal Palace - Tulse Hill

Local Services

Miles	Miles	Miles	Miles	Miles	Station		SN MO	SN MO	SN MX	SN MX	SN MO	SN MO 1	SN MX 1	SN MX	SN MX	SN	SN 1	FC 1	SN 1	FC 1	SN 1		FC 1	SN 1	FC
0	—	—	0	0	**East Croydon**	d						23p56	23p58			00 49	01 28	01 50	02 28	02 47	03 28		03 47	04 28	04 47
—	0	—	—	—	**West Croydon**	d	23p37				23p52														
1¼	—	—	—	1¼	Norwood Junction	a																			
—	—	—	—	—		d																			
—	1	—	1	—	Selhurst	d	23p41				23p56	00 01	00 02				01 30	01 53	02 30	02 50	03 30		03 50	04 31	04 50
—	1¾	—	1¾	—	Thornton Heath	d	23p43				23p58													04 33	
—	3	—	3	—	Norbury	d	23p46				00 01													04 36	
—	4	—	4	—	Streatham Common	d	23p49				00 04													04 39	
—	—	0	—	—	Beckenham Junction	d																			
—	—	1½	—	—	Birkbeck	d																			
2¾	—	3	—	2¾	**Crystal Palace**	d		23p37	23p43	23p51				00 13	00 21										
3½	—	3¾	—	3½	Gipsy Hill	d		23p39	23p45					00 15											
4½	—	4¾	—	4½	West Norwood	d		23p42	23p48					00 18											
5¾	—	6	—	—	Streatham Hill	d			23p52					00 22											
6¾	—	7	5¾	—	Balham ⊖	d	23p53		23p55		00 08			00 25										04 43	
7½	—	7¾	6½	—	Wandsworth Common	d			23p58					00 27											
8¾	—	9	7¼	—	Clapham Junction	d	23p58		00 02		00 12	00 11	00 11	00 31		01 01	01 41		02 41		03 41			04 47	
—	—	—	—	—	Imperial Wharf	d																			
—	—	—	—	—	West Brompton ⊖	d																			
—	—	—	—	—	Kensington (Olympia) ⊖	d																			
—	—	—	—	—	Shepherd's Bush ⊖	d																			
—	—	—	—	—	Wembley Central ⊖	d																			
—	—	—	—	—	Harrow & Wealdstone ⊖	d																			
—	—	—	—	—	Watford Junction	d																			
—	—	—	—	—	Milton Keynes Central	a																			
10¼	—	10½	9¼	—	Battersea Park	d			00 05					00 35											
11½	—	11¼	10¼	—	**London Victoria** ⊖	a	00 04		00 10		00 19	00 21	00 18	00 42		01 09	01 49		02 49		03 49			04 54	
—	4¼	—	—	—	Streatham	d																			
—	6	—	—	5	Tulse Hill	d		23p46																	
—	—	—	—	—	Herne Hill	a																			
—	—	—	—	—	Loughborough Jn	a																			
—	—	—	—	—	Elephant & Castle ⊖	a																			
—	—	—	—	—	London Blackfriars ⊖	a																			05 13
—	—	—	—	—	City Thameslink	a																			05 16
—	—	—	—	—	St Pancras International ⊖	a																			05 23
—	—	—	—	—	Luton Airport Parkway	a																			06 09
—	—	—	—	—	**Luton**	a																			06 12
—	7¼	—	—	6¼	North Dulwich	d		23p49																	
—	7¾	—	—	6¾	East Dulwich	d		23p51																	
—	8½	—	—	7½	Peckham Rye	d		23p53																	
—	9¼	—	—	8¼	Queens Rd Peckham	d		23p56																	
—	10¼	—	—	9¼	South Bermondsey	d		23p58																	
—	12	—	—	11	**London Bridge** ⊖	a		00 03		00 11					00 41			02 14		03 12			04 12		

Station		SN	SN	FC 1	SN	FC	LO	SN	FC 1	SN	SN	LO	FC		SN	SN 1	LO	SN	SN ◇1	SN	SN	SN 1	SN 1	FC	SN
East Croydon	d		05 13	05 17	05 33				05 47	05 48	05 51					06 07		06 13	06 15		06 17	06 23	06 31		
West Croydon	d						05 39	05 45				05 52			06 01		06 09			06 15					
Norwood Junction	a		05 17		05 37		05 43	05 50			05 54	05 58					06 13	06 17		06 19					
	d		05 17		05 37			05 50			05 55							06 18		06 20					
Selhurst	d					05 36				05 52			05 56		06 06	06 10					06 20				
Thornton Heath	d					05 38				05 54			05 58		06 08						06 22				
Norbury	d					05 40				05 57			06 00		06 11						06 25				
Streatham Common	d					05 43				05 59			06 03		06 13						06 27				
Beckenham Junction	d																								
Birkbeck	d																								
Crystal Palace	d				05 41						05 59														
Gipsy Hill	d				05 43						06 01														
West Norwood	d				05 46						06 04														
Streatham Hill	d				05 50																				
Balham ⊖	d	04 58			05 53					06 03					06 17						06 31				
Wandsworth Common	d									06 05					06 19						06 33				
Clapham Junction	d	05 02			05 57					06 09					06 23	06 18			06 25		06 37		06 41		
Imperial Wharf	d																								
West Brompton ⊖	d																								
Kensington (Olympia) ⊖	d																								
Shepherd's Bush ⊖	d																								
Wembley Central ⊖	d																								
Harrow & Wealdstone ⊖	d																								
Watford Junction	d																								
Milton Keynes Central	a																								
Battersea Park	d	05 05			06 01					06 13					06 27						06 41				06 45
London Victoria ⊖	a	05 10			06 06					06 18					06 31	06 25			06 32		06 45		06 48		
Streatham	d					05 46							06 06											06 38	
Tulse Hill	d					05 50					06 07		06 10											06 42	
Herne Hill	a					05 54							06 14											06 46	
Loughborough Jn	a												06 19											06 49	
Elephant & Castle ⊖	a					06 00							06 23											06 53	
London Blackfriars ⊖	a			05 41		06 03			06 10				06 27											06 57	
City Thameslink	a			05 44		06 06			06 14				06 32											07 02	
St Pancras International ⊖	a			05 51		06 13			06 21				06 39											07 09	
Luton Airport Parkway	a			06 35					06 54				07 23											07 49	
Luton	a			06 38					06 58				07 26											07 54	
North Dulwich	d										06 10														
East Dulwich	d										06 12														
Peckham Rye	d										06 15														06 56
Queens Rd Peckham	d										06 17														06 59
South Bermondsey	d										06 20														07 01
London Bridge ⊖	a		05 41					06 14			06 24							06 42		06 33		06 39			07 08

Table 177

Mondays to Fridays

East and West Croydon, London Milton Keynes Central and Luton via Norbury Crystal Palace - Tulse Hill

Local Services

		SN	SN	LO	SN 1		SN	SN	SN 1	SN	FC	SN	SN ◇1	SN	LO	SN	SN 1	SN	SN	SN ◇1	SN		SN	SN	LO
East Croydon ⇌	d		10 51		10 55			11 00	11 07				11 12				11 11	11 17		11 28				11 21	
West Croydon 4 ⇌	d	10 45		10 52			10 58					11 01		11 04	11 09								11 15		11 22
Norwood Junction 2	a	10 49	10 55	10 58	10 59			11 04	11 12						11 13								11 19	11 25	11 28
	d	10 52	10 55		10 59			11 05	11 13														11 22	11 25	
Selhurst 4	d						11 02					11 05		11 09			11 16	11 20							
Thornton Heath	d						11 04					11 07		11 11			11 18	11 22							
Norbury	d						11 07					11 10		11 14			11 21	11 25							
Streatham Common 4	d						11 10					11 13		11 17			11 24	11 28							
Beckenham Junction 4 ⇌	d									10 53															
Birkbeck ⇌	d									10 56															
Crystal Palace 4	d	10 56								11 00						11 13			11 21				11 26		
Gipsy Hill	d	10 59								11 02						11 15							11 29		
West Norwood 4	d	11 02								11 05						11 18							11 32		
Streatham Hill	d	11 05														11 22							11 35		
Balham 4 ⊖	d	11 09					11 14							11 21		11 25	11 28	11 32					11 40		
Wandsworth Common	d	11 11					11 16							11 23		11 27	11 30	11 34					11 42		
Clapham Junction 10	d	11 15					11 20						11 21	11 27		11 31	11 39	11 38		11 37			11 46		
Imperial Wharf	d																11 44								
West Brompton ⊖	d																11 47								
Kensington (Olympia) ⊖	d																11 50								
Shepherd's Bush ⊖	d																11 53								
Wembley Central ⊖	d																12s08								
Harrow & Wealdstone ⊖	d																12 13								
Watford Junction	d																12 20								
Milton Keynes Central 10	a																13 01								
Battersea Park 4	d	11 18					11 23									11 35		11a41			11 45		11 49		
London Victoria 15 ⊖	a	11 23					11 28						11 28	11 34		11 39				11 45			11 54		
Streatham 4	d										11 08	11 16													
Tulse Hill 3	d									11 09	11 12	11 24													
Herne Hill 4	a										11 16														
Loughborough Jn	a										11 19														
Elephant & Castle ⊖	a										11 23														
London Blackfriars 3 ⊖	a										11 27														
City Thameslink 3	a										11 32														
St Pancras International 15 ⊖	a										11 39														
Luton Airport Parkway 7	a										12 25														
Luton 10	a										12 30														
North Dulwich	d									11 12		11 27													
East Dulwich	d									11 14		11 29													
Peckham Rye 4	d									11 16		11 31									11 56				
Queens Rd Peckham	d									11 19		11 34									11 59				
South Bermondsey	d									11 21		11 36									12 01				
London Bridge 4 ⊖	a		11 09		11 13			11 29	11 25	11 26		11 41							11 41		12 06			11 39	

		SN 1	SN	SN	SN 1	SN	FC	SN	SN ◇1	SN	LO	SN	SN		SN	SN ◇1	SN	SN	SN	LO	SN 1	SN	SN	SN 1	SN
East Croydon ⇌	d	11 25		11 30	11 37				11 42				11 47			12 00			11 51		11 55		12 00	12 07	
West Croydon 4 ⇌	d		11 28					11 31		11 34	11 39							11 45		11 52		11 58			
Norwood Junction 2	a	11 29		11 34	11 42						11 43							11 49	11 55	11 58	11 59		12 04	12 12	
	d	11 29		11 35	11 43													11 52	11 55		11 59		12 05	12 13	
Selhurst 4	d		11 32					11 35		11 39			11 50									12 02			
Thornton Heath	d		11 34					11 37		11 41			11 52									12 04			
Norbury	d		11 37					11 40		11 44			11 55									12 07			
Streatham Common 4	d		11 40					11 43		11 47			11 58									12 10			
Beckenham Junction 4 ⇌	d					11 23																			11 53
Birkbeck ⇌	d					11 26																			11 56
Crystal Palace 4	d					11 30						11 43			11 51			11 56							12 00
Gipsy Hill	d					11 32						11 45						11 59							12 02
West Norwood 4	d					11 35						11 48						12 02							12 05
Streatham Hill	d											11 52						12 05							
Balham 4 ⊖	d		11 44							11 51		11 55	12 02					12 09				12 14			
Wandsworth Common	d		11 46							11 53		11 57	12 04					12 11				12 16			
Clapham Junction 10	d		11 50						11 51	11 57		12 01	12 08			12 12		12 15				12 20			
Imperial Wharf	d																								
West Brompton ⊖	d																								
Kensington (Olympia) ⊖	d																								
Shepherd's Bush ⊖	d																								
Wembley Central ⊖	d																								
Harrow & Wealdstone ⊖	d																								
Watford Junction	d																								
Milton Keynes Central 10	a																								
Battersea Park 4	d		11 53									12 05	12a11				12 15	12 18				12 23			
London Victoria 15 ⊖	a		11 58						11 58	12 04		12 09				12 18		12 23				12 28			
Streatham 4	d						11 38	11 46																	
Tulse Hill 3	d					11 39	11 42	11 54																	12 09
Herne Hill 4	a						11 46																		
Loughborough Jn	a						11 49																		
Elephant & Castle ⊖	a						11 53																		
London Blackfriars 3 ⊖	a						11 57																		
City Thameslink 3	a						12 02																		
St Pancras International 15 ⊖	a						12 09																		
Luton Airport Parkway 7	a						12 55																		
Luton 10	a						13 00																		
North Dulwich	d					11 42		11 57																	12 12
East Dulwich	d					11 44		11 59																	12 14
Peckham Rye 4	d					11 46		12 01									12 26								12 16
Queens Rd Peckham	d					11 49		12 04									12 29								12 19
South Bermondsey	d					11 51		12 06									12 31								12 21
London Bridge 4 ⊖	a	11 43		11 59	11 55	11 56		12 11							12 11		12 36		12 09		12 13		12 29	12 25	12 26

Table 177

East and West Croydon, London Milton Keynes Central and Luton via Norbury Crystal Palace - Tulse Hill

Local Services

		FC	SN	SN ◇1	SN		LO	SN	SN 1	SN	SN	SN ◇1	SN	SN	SN	LO	SN 1	SN	SN	SN 1	SN		FC	SN	SN ◇1
East Croydon ⇌	d			12 12					12 10	12 17		12 28			12 21		12 25		12 30	12 37					12 42
West Croydon 4 ⇌	d		12 01		12 04		12 09							12 15		12 22		12 28						12 31	
Norwood Junction 2	a						12 13							12 19	12 25	12 28	12 29		12 34	12 42					
	d													12 22	12 25		12 29		12 35	12 43					
Selhurst 4	d		12 05		12 09				12 14	12 20								12 32						12 35	
Thornton Heath	d		12 07		12 11				12 16	12 22								12 34						12 37	
Norbury	d		12 10		12 14				12 19	12 25								12 37						12 40	
Streatham Common 4	d		12 13		12 17				12 22	12 28								12 40						12 43	
Beckenham Junction 4 ⇌	d																				12 23				
Birkbeck ⇌	d																				12 26				
Crystal Palace 4	d							12 13			12 21			12 26							12 30				
Gipsy Hill	d							12 15						12 29							12 32				
West Norwood 4	d							12 18						12 32							12 35				
Streatham Hill	d							12 22						12 35											
Balham 4 ⊖	d				12 21			12 25	12 28	12 32				12 39				12 44							
Wandsworth Common	d				12 23			12 27	12 30	12 34				12 41				12 46							
Clapham Junction 10	d			12 22	12 27			12 31	12 39	12 38		12 37		12 45				12 50							12 51
Imperial Wharf	d								12 44																
West Brompton ⊖	d								12 47																
Kensington (Olympia) ⊖	d								12 50																
Shepherd's Bush ⊖	d								12 53																
Wembley Central ⊖	d								13s08																
Harrow & Wealdstone ⊖	d								13 13																
Watford Junction	d								13 20																
Milton Keynes Central 10	a								14 01																
Battersea Park 4	d							12 35		12a41			12 45	12 48				12 53							
London Victoria 15 ⊖	a			12 28	12 34			12 39				12 44		12 53				12 58							12 58
Streatham 4	d	12 08	12 16																				12 38	12 46	
Tulse Hill 3	d	12 12	12 24																		12 39		12 42	12 54	
Herne Hill 4	a	12 16																					12 46		
Loughborough Jn	a	12 19																					12 49		
Elephant & Castle ⊖	a	12 23																					12 53		
London Blackfriars 3 ⊖	a	12 27																					12 57		
City Thameslink 3	a	12 32																					13 02		
St Pancras International 15 ⊖	a	12 39																					13 09		
Luton Airport Parkway 7	a	13 25																					13 56		
Luton 10	a	13 30																					14 00		
North Dulwich	d		12 27																		12 42			12 57	
East Dulwich	d		12 29																		12 44			12 59	
Peckham Rye 4	d		12 31										12 56								12 46			13 01	
Queens Rd Peckham	d		12 34										12 59								12 49			13 04	
South Bermondsey	d		12 36										13 01								12 51			13 06	
London Bridge 4 ⊖	a		12 41								12 41		13 06		12 39		12 43		12 59	12 55	12 56			13 11	

		SN	LO	SN	SN	SN	SN ◇1	SN	SN	SN	LO	SN 1	SN		SN	SN 1	SN	FC	SN	SN ◇1	SN	LO	SN	SN 1	SN
East Croydon ⇌	d				12 47		13 00			12 51		12 55			13 00	13 07				13 12				13 10	13 17
West Croydon 4 ⇌	d	12 34	12 39						12 45		12 52		12 58						13 01		13 04	13 09			
Norwood Junction 2	a		12 43						12 49	12 55	12 58	12 59			13 04	13 12						13 13			
	d								12 52	12 55		12 59			13 05	13 13									
Selhurst 4	d	12 39			12 50								13 02						13 05		13 09			13 13	13 20
Thornton Heath	d	12 41			12 52								13 04						13 07		13 11			13 16	13 22
Norbury	d	12 44			12 55								13 07						13 10		13 14			13 19	13 25
Streatham Common 4	d	12 47			12 58								13 10						13 13		13 17			13 21	13 28
Beckenham Junction 4 ⇌	d																12 53								
Birkbeck ⇌	d																12 56								
Crystal Palace 4	d			12 43		12 51			12 56								13 00						13 13		
Gipsy Hill	d			12 45					12 59								13 02						13 15		
West Norwood 4	d			12 48					13 02								13 05						13 18		
Streatham Hill	d			12 52					13 05														13 22		
Balham 4 ⊖	d	12 51		12 55	13 02				13 09				13 14								13 21		13 25	13 28	13 32
Wandsworth Common	d	12 53		12 57	13 04				13 11				13 16								13 23		13 27	13 30	13 34
Clapham Junction 10	d	12 57		13 01	13 08		13 10		13 15				13 20							13 21	13 27		13 31	13 39	13 38
Imperial Wharf	d																							13 44	
West Brompton ⊖	d																							13 47	
Kensington (Olympia) ⊖	d																							13 50	
Shepherd's Bush ⊖	d																							13 53	
Wembley Central ⊖	d																							14s08	
Harrow & Wealdstone ⊖	d																							14 13	
Watford Junction	d																							14 20	
Milton Keynes Central 10	a																							15 01	
Battersea Park 4	d			13 05	13 11			13 15	13 18				13 23										13 35		13a41
London Victoria 15 ⊖	a	13 04		13 09	13 16		13 16		13 23				13 28							13 28	13 34		13 39		
Streatham 4	d																	13 08	13 16						
Tulse Hill 3	d																13 09	13 12	13 24						
Herne Hill 4	a																	13 16							
Loughborough Jn	a																	13 19							
Elephant & Castle ⊖	a																	13 23							
London Blackfriars 3 ⊖	a																	13 27							
City Thameslink 3	a																	13 32							
St Pancras International 15 ⊖	a																	13 39							
Luton Airport Parkway 7	a																	14 25							
Luton 10	a																	14 30							
North Dulwich	d																13 12		13 27						
East Dulwich	d																13 14		13 29						
Peckham Rye 4	d							13 26									13 16		13 31						
Queens Rd Peckham	d							13 29									13 19		13 34						
South Bermondsey	d							13 31									13 21		13 36						
London Bridge 4 ⊖	a					13 11		13 36		13 09		13 13			13 29	13 25	13 26		13 41						

East and West Croydon, London
Milton Keynes Central and Luton via Norbury
Crystal Palace - Tulse Hill

Local Services

		SN	SN ◇1	SN	SN		SN	LO	SN 1	SN	SN	SN 1	SN	FC	SN	SN ◇1	SN	LO	SN	SN	SN		SN ◇1	SN	SN
East Croydon	d		13 28				13 21		13 25		13 30	13 37				13 42				13 47			14 00		
West Croydon 4	d				13 15			13 22		13 28					13 31		13 34	13 39							13 45
Norwood Junction 2	a				13 19		13 25	13 28	13 29		13 34	13 42						13 43							13 49
	d				13 22		13 25		13 29		13 35	13 43													13 52
Selhurst 4	d									13 32					13 35		13 39			13 50					
Thornton Heath	d									13 34					13 37		13 41			13 52					
Norbury	d									13 37					13 40		13 44			13 55					
Streatham Common 4	d									13 40					13 43		13 47			13 58					
Beckenham Junction 4	d												13 23												
Birkbeck	d												13 26												
Crystal Palace 4	d	13 21			13 26								13 30						13 43		13 51				13 56
Gipsy Hill	d				13 29								13 32						13 45						13 59
West Norwood 4	d				13 32								13 35						13 48						14 02
Streatham Hill	d				13 35														13 52						14 05
Balham 4	⊖ d				13 39					13 44							13 51		13 55	14 02					14 09
Wandsworth Common	d				13 41					13 46							13 53		13 57	14 04					14 11
Clapham Junction 10	d		13 37		13 45					13 50						13 51	13 57		14 01	14 08			14 10		14 15
Imperial Wharf	d																								
West Brompton	⊖ d																								
Kensington (Olympia)	⊖ d																								
Shepherd's Bush	⊖ d																								
Wembley Central	⊖ d																								
Harrow & Wealdstone	⊖ d																								
Watford Junction	d																								
Milton Keynes Central 10	a																								
Battersea Park 4	d			13 45	13 48					13 53									14 05	14a11				14 15	14 18
London Victoria 15	⊖ a		13 44		13 53					13 58						13 58	14 04		14 09				14 16		14 23
Streatham 4	d													13 38	13 46										
Tulse Hill 3	d												13 39	13 42	13 54										
Herne Hill 4	a													13 46											
Loughborough Jn	a													13 49											
Elephant & Castle	⊖ a													13 53											
London Blackfriars 3	⊖ a													13 57											
City Thameslink 3	a													14 02											
St Pancras International 15	⊖ a													14 09											
Luton Airport Parkway 7	a													14 55											
Luton 10	a													15 00											
North Dulwich	d												13 42		13 57										
East Dulwich	d												13 44		13 59										
Peckham Rye 4	d			13 56									13 46		14 01									14 26	
Queens Rd Peckham	d			13 59									13 49		14 04									14 29	
South Bermondsey	d			14 01									13 51		14 06									14 31	
London Bridge 4	⊖ a	13 41		14 06			13 39		13 43		13 59	13 55	13 56		14 11						14 11			14 36	

		SN	LO	SN 1	SN	SN	SN 1	SN	FC	SN	SN ◇1	SN	LO		SN	SN 1	SN	SN	SN ◇1	SN	SN	SN	LO	SN 1	SN
East Croydon	d	13 51		13 55		14 00	14 08				14 12					14 10	14 17		14 28			14 21		14 25	
West Croydon 4	d		13 52		13 58					14 01		14 04	14 09								14 15		14 22		14 28
Norwood Junction 2	a	13 55	13 58	13 59		14 04	14 12						14 13								14 19	14 25	14 28	14 29	
	d	13 55		13 59		14 05	14 13														14 22	14 25		14 29	
Selhurst 4	d				14 02					14 05		14 09				14 13	14 20								14 32
Thornton Heath	d				14 04					14 07		14 11				14 16	14 22								14 34
Norbury	d				14 07					14 10		14 14				14 19	14 25								14 37
Streatham Common 4	d				14 10					14 13		14 17				14 21	14 28								14 40
Beckenham Junction 4	d							13 53																	
Birkbeck	d							13 56																	
Crystal Palace 4	d							14 00							14 13			14 21			14 26				
Gipsy Hill	d							14 02							14 15						14 29				
West Norwood 4	d							14 05							14 18						14 32				
Streatham Hill	d														14 22						14 35				
Balham 4	⊖ d				14 14							14 21			14 25	14 28	14 32				14 39				14 44
Wandsworth Common	d				14 16							14 23			14 27	14 30	14 34				14 41				14 46
Clapham Junction 10	d				14 20						14 21	14 27			14 31	14 39	14 38		14 37		14 45				14 50
Imperial Wharf	d															14 44									
West Brompton	⊖ d															14 47									
Kensington (Olympia)	⊖ d															14 50									
Shepherd's Bush	⊖ d															14 53									
Wembley Central	⊖ d															15s08									
Harrow & Wealdstone	⊖ d															15 13									
Watford Junction	d															15 20									
Milton Keynes Central 10	a															16 01									
Battersea Park 4	d				14 23										14 35		14a41			14 45	14 48				14 53
London Victoria 15	⊖ a				14 28						14 28	14 34			14 39				14 44		14 53				14 58
Streatham 4	d								14 08	14 16															
Tulse Hill 3	d							14 09	14 12	14 24															
Herne Hill 4	a								14 16																
Loughborough Jn	a								14 19																
Elephant & Castle	⊖ a								14 23																
London Blackfriars 3	⊖ a								14 27																
City Thameslink 3	a								14 32																
St Pancras International 15	⊖ a								14 39																
Luton Airport Parkway 7	a								15 25																
Luton 10	a								15 30																
North Dulwich	d							14 12		14 27															
East Dulwich	d							14 14		14 29															
Peckham Rye 4	d							14 16		14 31										14 56					
Queens Rd Peckham	d							14 19		14 34										14 59					
South Bermondsey	d							14 21		14 36										15 01					
London Bridge 4	⊖ a	14 09		14 13		14 29	14 25	14 26		14 41								14 41		15 06		14 39		14 43	

Table 177 Mondays to Fridays

East and West Croydon, London
Milton Keynes Central and Luton via Norbury
Crystal Palace - Tulse Hill

Local Services

		SN	SN 1	SN	FC		SN	SN ◇1	SN	LO	SN	SN	SN	SN ◇1	SN	SN	SN	LO	SN 1	SN	SN		SN 1	SN	FC
East Croydon	d	14 30	14 37					14 42				14 47		15 00			14 51		14 55		15 00		15 07		
West Croydon 4	d						14 31		14 34	14 39						14 45		14 52		14 58					
Norwood Junction 2	a	14 34	14 42							14 43						14 49	14 55	14 58	14 59		15 04		15 12		
	d	14 35	14 43													14 52	14 55		14 59		15 05		15 13		
Selhurst 4	d						14 35		14 39			14 50								15 02					
Thornton Heath	d						14 37		14 41			14 52								15 04					
Norbury	d						14 40		14 44			14 55								15 07					
Streatham Common 4	d						14 43		14 47			14 58								15 10					
Beckenham Junction 4	d			14 23																				14 53	
Birkbeck	d			14 26																				14 56	
Crystal Palace 4	d			14 30							14 43		14 51			14 56								15 01	
Gipsy Hill	d			14 32							14 45					14 59								15 03	
West Norwood 4	d			14 35							14 48					15 02								15 06	
Streatham Hill	d										14 52					15 05									
Balham 4	⊖ d								14 51		14 55	15 02				15 09				15 14					
Wandsworth Common	d								14 53		14 57	15 04				15 11				15 16					
Clapham Junction 10	d							14 51	14 57		15 01	15 08		15 10		15 15				15 20					
Imperial Wharf	d																								
West Brompton	⊖ d																								
Kensington (Olympia)	⊖ d																								
Shepherd's Bush	⊖ d																								
Wembley Central	⊖ d																								
Harrow & Wealdstone	⊖ d																								
Watford Junction	d																								
Milton Keynes Central 10	a																								
Battersea Park 4	d										15 05	15 11			15 15	15 18				15 23					
London Victoria 15	⊖ a							14 58	15 04		15 09	15 16		15 20		15 24				15 28					
Streatham 4	d				14 38		14 46																		15 08
Tulse Hill 3	d			14 39	14 42		14 54																	15 10	15 12
Herne Hill 4	a				14 46																				15 16
Loughborough Jn	a				14 49																				15 19
Elephant & Castle	⊖ a				14 53																				15 23
London Blackfriars 3	⊖ a				14 57																				15 27
City Thameslink 3	a				15 02																				15 32
St Pancras International 15	⊖ a				15 09																				15 39
Luton Airport Parkway 7	a				15 55																				16 25
Luton 10	a				16 00																				16 30
North Dulwich	d			14 42			14 57																	15 13	
East Dulwich	d			14 44			14 59																	15 15	
Peckham Rye 4	d			14 46			15 01								15 26									15 17	
Queens Rd Peckham	d			14 49			15 04								15 29									15 20	
South Bermondsey	d			14 51			15 06								15 31									15 22	
London Bridge 4	⊖ a	14 59	14 55	14 56			15 11						15 11		15 36		15 09		15 13		15 29		15 25	15 27	

		SN	SN ◇1	SN	LO	SN	SN 1	SN	SN	SN ◇1	SN	SN	SN		LO	SN 1	SN	SN	SN 1	SN	FC	SN	SN ◇1	SN	LO
East Croydon	d		15 12				15 10	15 17		15 28			15 21			15 25		15 30	15 37				15 42		
West Croydon 4	d	15 01		15 04	15 09							15 15			15 22		15 28					15 31		15 34	15 39
Norwood Junction 2	a				15 13							15 19	15 25		15 28	15 29		15 34	15 42						15 43
	d											15 22	15 25			15 29		15 35	15 43						
Selhurst 4	d	15 05		15 09			15 13	15 20									15 32					15 35		15 39	
Thornton Heath	d	15 07		15 11			15 16	15 22									15 34					15 37		15 41	
Norbury	d	15 10		15 14			15 19	15 25									15 37					15 40		15 44	
Streatham Common 4	d	15 13		15 17			15 21	15 28									15 40					15 43		15 47	
Beckenham Junction 4	d																			15 23					
Birkbeck	d																			15 26					
Crystal Palace 4	d					15 13			15 21			15 26								15 30					
Gipsy Hill	d					15 15						15 29								15 32					
West Norwood 4	d					15 18						15 32								15 35					
Streatham Hill	d					15 22						15 35													
Balham 4	⊖ d			15 21		15 25	15 29	15 32				15 39					15 44							15 51	
Wandsworth Common	d			15 23		15 27	15 31	15 34				15 41					15 46							15 53	
Clapham Junction 10	d		15 21	15 27		15 31	15 39	15 38		15 38		15 45					15 50						15 51	15 57	
Imperial Wharf	d						15 44																		
West Brompton	⊖ d						15 47																		
Kensington (Olympia)	⊖ d						15 50																		
Shepherd's Bush	⊖ d						15 53																		
Wembley Central	⊖ d						16s08																		
Harrow & Wealdstone	⊖ d						16 13																		
Watford Junction	d						16 20																		
Milton Keynes Central 10	a						17 00																		
Battersea Park 4	d					15 35		15 41			15 45	15 49					15 53								
London Victoria 15	⊖ a		15 28	15 34		15 39		15 46		15 46		15 54					15 58						15 58	16 04	
Streatham 4	d	15 16																			15 38	15 46			
Tulse Hill 3	d	15 24																		15 39	15 42	15 54			
Herne Hill 4	a																				15 46				
Loughborough Jn	a																				15 49				
Elephant & Castle	⊖ a																				15 53				
London Blackfriars 3	⊖ a																				15 57				
City Thameslink 3	a																				16 02				
St Pancras International 15	⊖ a																				16 09				
Luton Airport Parkway 7	a																				16 59				
Luton 10	a																				17 04				
North Dulwich	d	15 27																		15 42		15 57			
East Dulwich	d	15 29																		15 44		15 59			
Peckham Rye 4	d	15 31									15 56									15 46		16 01			
Queens Rd Peckham	d	15 34									15 59									15 49		16 04			
South Bermondsey	d	15 36									16 01									15 51		16 06			
London Bridge 4	⊖ a	15 41							15 41		16 06		15 39			15 43		15 59	[illegible]	[illegible]		[illegible]			

Table 177

East and West Croydon, London Milton Keynes Central and Luton via Norbury Crystal Palace - Tulse Hill

Local Services

		SN	SN	SN	SN		SN ◇1 ⌶	SN	SN	SN	LO	SN 1	SN	SN	SN 1	SN	FC	SN	SN ◇1 ⌶	SN	LO		SN	SN 1	SN
East Croydon ⇌	d		15 47				16 00			15 51		15 55		16 00	16 07				16 12					16 10	16 17
West Croydon 4 ⇌	d								15 45		15 52		15 58					16 01		16 04	16 09				
Norwood Junction 2	a								15 49	15 55	15 58	15 59		16 04	16 12						16 13				
	d								15 52	15 55		15 59		16 05	16 13										
Selhurst 4	d		15 50										16 02					16 05		16 09				16 13	16 20
Thornton Heath	d		15 52										16 04					16 07		16 11				16 16	16 22
Norbury	d		15 55										16 07					16 10		16 14				16 19	16 25
Streatham Common 4	d		15 58										16 10					16 13		16 17				16 21	16 28
Beckenham Junction 4 ⇌	d															15 53									
Birkbeck ⇌	d															15 56									
Crystal Palace 4	d	15 43		15 51					15 56							16 00							16 13		
Gipsy Hill	d	15 45							15 59							16 02							16 15		
West Norwood 4	d	15 48							16 02							16 05							16 18		
Streatham Hill	d	15 52			15 56				16 05														16 22		
Balham 4 ⊖	d	15 55	16 02						16 09				16 14							16 21			16 25	16 28	16 32
Wandsworth Common	d	15 57	16 04						16 11				16 16							16 23			16 27	16 30	16 34
Clapham Junction 10	d	16 01	16 08				16 09		16 15				16 20						16 21	16 27			16 31	16 39	16 38
Imperial Wharf	d																							16 44	
West Brompton ⊖	d																							16 47	
Kensington (Olympia) ⊖	d																							16 50	
Shepherd's Bush ⊖	d																							16 53	
Wembley Central ⊖	d																							17s08	
Harrow & Wealdstone ⊖	d																							17 13	
Watford Junction	d																							17 21	
Milton Keynes Central 10	a																							17 59	
Battersea Park 4	d	16 05	16 11					16 15	16 18				16 23										16 35		16 41
London Victoria 15 ⊖	a	16 10	16 16				16 16		16 23				16 28						16 28	16 34			16 40		16 46
Streatham 4	d																16 08	16 16							
Tulse Hill 3	d				16 00											16 09	16 12	16 24							
Herne Hill 4	a																16 16								
Loughborough Jn.	a																16 19								
Elephant & Castle ⊖	a																16 23								
London Blackfriars 3 ⊖	a																16 29								
City Thameslink 3	a																16 32								
St Pancras International 15 ⊖	a																16 39								
Luton Airport Parkway 7	a																17 25								
Luton 10	a																17 30								
North Dulwich	d				16 03											16 12		16 27							
East Dulwich	d				16 05											16 14		16 29							
Peckham Rye 4	d				16 07			16 26								16 16		16 31							
Queens Rd Peckham	d				16 10			16 29								16 19		16 34							
South Bermondsey	d				16 12			16 31								16 21		16 36							
London Bridge 4 ⊖	a			16 11	16 17			16 38		16 09		16 13		16 29	16 25	16 26		16 41							

		SN	SN ◇1 ⌶	SN	SN	SN	LO	SN 1	SN	SN	SN	FC	SN		LO	SN 1	SN ◇1 ⌶	SN	SN	SN	SN	SN ◇1	SN	SN	SN
East Croydon ⇌	d		16 30			16 21		16 24			16 30					16 40	16 42			16 47		17 01			16 51
West Croydon 4 ⇌	d				16 15		16 22			16 28			16 31		16 39			16 34						16 45	
Norwood Junction 2	a				16 20	16 25	16 28	16 28			16 34				16 43	16 44								16 50	16 55
	d				16 22	16 25		16 28			16 35					16 45								16 52	16 55
Selhurst 4	d									16 32			16 35					16 39		16 50					
Thornton Heath	d									16 34			16 37					16 41		16 52					
Norbury	d									16 37			16 40					16 44		16 55					
Streatham Common 4	d									16 40			16 43					16 47		16 58					
Beckenham Junction 4 ⇌	d								16 23																
Birkbeck ⇌	d								16 26																
Crystal Palace 4	d	16 21			16 26				16 30										16 43		16 50			16 56	
Gipsy Hill	d				16 29				16 32										16 45					16 59	
West Norwood 4	d				16 32				16 35										16 48					17 02	
Streatham Hill	d				16 35														16 52					17 05	
Balham 4 ⊖	d				16 39					16 44								16 51	16 55	17 02				17 09	
Wandsworth Common	d				16 41					16 46								16 53	16 57	17 04				17 11	
Clapham Junction 10	d		16 40		16 45					16 50							16 51	16 57	17 01	17 08		17 11		17 15	
Imperial Wharf	d																								
West Brompton ⊖	d																								
Kensington (Olympia) ⊖	d																								
Shepherd's Bush ⊖	d																								
Wembley Central ⊖	d																								
Harrow & Wealdstone ⊖	d																								
Watford Junction	d																								
Milton Keynes Central 10	a																								
Battersea Park 4	d			16 45	16 49					16 53									17 05	17 11			17 15	17 18	
London Victoria 15 ⊖	a		16 46		16 55					16 58							16 58	17 04	17 10	17 16		17 17		17 23	
Streatham 4	d											16 40	16 46												
Tulse Hill 3	d								16 39			16 46	16 53												
Herne Hill 4	a											16 50													
Loughborough Jn.	a											16 53													
Elephant & Castle ⊖	a											16 59													
London Blackfriars 3 ⊖	a											17 03													
City Thameslink 3	a											17 06													
St Pancras International 15 ⊖	a											17 13													
Luton Airport Parkway 7	a																								
Luton 10	a																								
North Dulwich	d								16 42				16 56												
East Dulwich	d								16 44				16 58												
Peckham Rye 4	d			16 56					16 46				17 00										17 26		
Queens Rd Peckham	d			16 59					16 49				17 03										17 29		
South Bermondsey	d			17 01					16 51				17 05										17 31		
London Bridge 4 ⊖	a	16 41		17 08		16 39		16 43	16 56		17 02		17 10			17 00					17 12		17 38		17 08

Table 177

East and West Croydon, London Milton Keynes Central and Luton via Norbury Crystal Palace - Tulse Hill

Local Services

		LO	SN 1	SN	SN		SN 1	SN	FC	SN	SN ◇1 ⌶	SN	LO	SN	SN	SN 1	SN	SN	SN ◇1 ⌶	SN	SN 1		FC	SN	SN
East Croydon ⇌	d		16 55		17 00		17 07				17 13					17 10			17 30	17 17	17 38				
West Croydon 4 ⇌	d	16 52		16 58						17 01		17 04	17 09	17 12											17 18
Norwood Junction 2	a	16 58	16 59		17 04		17 11						17 13												17 22
	d		16 59		17 05		17 12																		17 23
Selhurst 4	d			17 02						17 05		17 09				17 13				17 20					
Thornton Heath	d			17 04						17 07		17 11				17 16				17 22					
Norbury	d			17 07						17 10		17 14				17 19				17 25					
Streatham Common 4	d			17 10						17 13		17 17				17 21				17 28					
Beckenham Junction 4 ⇌	d							16 53									17 11								
Birkbeck ⇌	d							16 56									17 14								
Crystal Palace 4	d							17 00							17 13		17 18	17 21							17 27
Gipsy Hill	d							17 02							17 15		17 20								17 29
West Norwood 4	d							17 05							17 18		17 23								17 32
Streatham Hill	d														17 22										17 36
Balham 4 ⊖	d			17 14								17 21			17 25	17 28				17 32					17 39
Wandsworth Common	d			17 16								17 23			17 27	17 30				17 34					17 41
Clapham Junction 10	d			17 20							17 23	17 27			17 31	17 39			17 40	17 38	17 47				17 45
Imperial Wharf	d															17 44									
West Brompton ⊖	d															17 47									
Kensington (Olympia) ⊖	d															17 50									
Shepherd's Bush ⊖	d															17 53									
Wembley Central ⊖	d															18s08									
Harrow & Wealdstone ⊖	d															18 13									
Watford Junction	d															18 20									
Milton Keynes Central 10	a															19 00									
Battersea Park 4	d			17 23											17 35					17 41				17 45	17 48
London Victoria 15 ⊖	a			17 28							17 29	17 34			17 42				17 46	17 48	17 54				17 55
Streatham 4	d								17 10	17 16													17 40		
Tulse Hill 3	d							17 09	17 16	17 22							17 27						17 44		
Herne Hill 4	a								17 20														17 47		
Loughborough Jn.	a								17 23														17 51		
Elephant & Castle ⊖	a								17 28														17 55		
London Blackfriars 3 ⊖	a								17 31														17 59		
City Thameslink 3	a								17 34														18 02		
St Pancras International 15 ⊖	a								17 41														18 09		
Luton Airport Parkway 7	a								18 27														18 57		
Luton 10	a								18 32														19 02		
North Dulwich	d							17 12		17 25							17 30								
East Dulwich	d							17 14		17 27							17 32								
Peckham Rye 4	d							17 16		17 29							17 34							17 57	
Queens Rd Peckham	d							17 19		17 32							17 37							17 59	
South Bermondsey	d							17 21		17 34							17 39							18 02	
London Bridge 4 ⊖	a		17 14		17 31		17 26	17 27		17 40				17 28			17 44	17 43						18 08	

		SN	LO	SN 1	SN	SN	SN	SN	LO	SN ◇1 ⌶	SN 1	SN	SN		SN	SN	SN	SN	SN ◇1 ⌶	FC	SN	SN	LO	SN 1	SN 1
East Croydon ⇌	d	17 21		17 25			17 30			17 41	17 41				17 47	17 51			18 02					17 55	18 08
West Croydon 4 ⇌	d		17 22		17 28			17 31	17 39			17 42										17 48	17 52		
Norwood Junction 2	a	17 25	17 28	17 30			17 34		17 43		17 45					17 55						17 54	17 58	17 59	
	d	17 25		17 31		17 32	17 35				17 45					17 55						17 55		17 59	
Selhurst 4	d				17 32			17 35							17 50										
Thornton Heath	d				17 34			17 37							17 52										
Norbury	d				17 37			17 40							17 55										
Streatham Common 4	d				17 40			17 43							17 58										
Beckenham Junction 4 ⇌	d																	17 48							
Birkbeck ⇌	d																	17 51							
Crystal Palace 4	d					17 36							17 44				17 48	17 55				17 59			
Gipsy Hill	d					17 38							17 46					17 57				18 01			
West Norwood 4	d					17 42							17 49					18 00				18 04			
Streatham Hill	d												17 53									18 08			
Balham 4 ⊖	d				17 44								17 56		18 02							18 11			
Wandsworth Common	d				17 46								17 58		18 04							18 13			
Clapham Junction 10	d				17 50					17 51			18 02		18 08				18 13			18 17			18 19
Imperial Wharf	d																								
West Brompton ⊖	d																								
Kensington (Olympia) ⊖	d																								
Shepherd's Bush ⊖	d																								
Wembley Central ⊖	d																								
Harrow & Wealdstone ⊖	d																								
Watford Junction	d																								
Milton Keynes Central 10	a																								
Battersea Park 4	d				17 53								18 06		18 11						18 15	18 20			
London Victoria 15 ⊖	a				17 58					17 58			18 12		18 16				18 20			18 25			18 26
Streatham 4	d							17 46												18 10					
Tulse Hill 3	d					17 45		17 54										18 05		18 16					
Herne Hill 4	a																			18 20					
Loughborough Jn.	a																			18 23					
Elephant & Castle ⊖	a																			18 27					
London Blackfriars 3 ⊖	a																			18 31					
City Thameslink 3	a																			18 34					
St Pancras International 15 ⊖	a																			18 41					
Luton Airport Parkway 7	a																			19 29					
Luton 10	a																			19 34					
North Dulwich	d					17 48		17 57										18 08							
East Dulwich	d					17 50		17 59										18 10							
Peckham Rye 4	d					17 53		18 01										18 12			18 26				
Queens Rd Peckham	d					17 55		18 04										18 15			18 29				
South Bermondsey	d					17 58		18 06										18 17			18 31				
London Bridge 4 ⊖	a	17 37		17 45		18 02	17 59	18 11			17 58	18 00				18 09	18 13	18 22			18 38			18 16	

Table 177 — Mondays to Fridays

East and West Croydon, London Milton Keynes Central and Luton via Norbury Crystal Palace - Tulse Hill

Local Services

Station		SN	SN	SN	LO		SN 1	SN ◇1 H	SN	SN	SN 1	SN	SN	SN	SN	SN ◇1 H	FC	SN	SN	SN	LO		SN	SN 1	SN
East Croydon	d		18 08				18 10	18 12			18 26			18 17		18 30				18 21			18 30	18 40	
West Croydon	d	17 58		18 01	18 09				18 13										18 18		18 22				18 28
Norwood Junction	a		18 12		18 13														18 23	18 28	18 28		18 34		
	d		18 12																18 24	18 29			18 35		
Selhurst	d	18 02		18 05			18 13							18 20											18 32
Thornton Heath	d	18 04		18 07			18 16							18 22											18 34
Norbury	d	18 07		18 10			18 19							18 25											18 37
Streatham Common	d	18 10		18 13			18 21							18 28											18 40
Beckenham Junction	d												18 11												
Birkbeck	d												18 14												
Crystal Palace	d											18 13	18 18		18 20				18 28						
Gipsy Hill	d											18 16	18 20						18 30						
West Norwood	d											18 19	18 23						18 33						
Streatham Hill	d											18 22							18 37						
Balham ⊖	d	18 14					18 26					18 29		18 33					18 40						18 44
Wandsworth Common	d	18 16					18 28					18 31		18 35					18 42						18 46
Clapham Junction	d	18 20					18 39	18 22			18 37	18 36		18 39		18 40			18 46					18 49	18 50
Imperial Wharf	d						18 44																		
West Brompton ⊖	d						18 47																		
Kensington (Olympia) ⊖	d						18 50																		
Shepherd's Bush ⊖	d						18 53																		
Wembley Central ⊖	d						19s08																		
Harrow & Wealdstone ⊖	d						19 13																		
Watford Junction	d						19 21																		
Milton Keynes Central	a						20 06																		
Battersea Park	d	18 23										18 40						18 45	18 49						
London Victoria ⊖	a	18 28						18 29			18 44	18 46		18 46		18 47			18 54					18 56	18 57
Streatham	d			18 16						18 20							18 40								
Tulse Hill	d			18 20						18 24			18 28				18 44								
Herne Hill	a																18 47								
Loughborough Jn	a																18 51								
Elephant & Castle ⊖	a																18 55								
London Blackfriars ⊖	a																18 59								
City Thameslink	a																19 02								
St Pancras International ⊖	a																19 09								
Luton Airport Parkway	a																19 53								
Luton	a																19 58								
North Dulwich	d			18 23						18 27			18 31												
East Dulwich	d			18 25						18 29			18 33												
Peckham Rye	d			18 29						18 32			18 36					18 57							
Queens Rd Peckham	d			18 32						18 35			18 38					19 00							
South Bermondsey	d			18 34						18 37			18 41					19 02							
London Bridge ⊖	a		18 26	18 39					18 29	18 42			18 45		18 45			19 09		18 41			18 59		

Station		SN	LO	SN ◇1 H	SN	SN	SN 1	SN	SN	SN	SN ◇1	FC	SN		SN	LO	SN	SN	SN 1	SN	LO	SN 1	SN ◇1 H	SN	SN
East Croydon	d			18 43			18 55	18 47			19 00							19 00	19 09			19 10	19 12		
West Croydon	d	18 31	18 39												18 47	18 52	18 58			19 01	19 09				
Norwood Junction	a		18 43												18 51	18 58		19 04	19 12		19 13				
	d														18 52			19 05	19 13						
Selhurst	d	18 35						18 51									19 02			19 05		19 13			
Thornton Heath	d	18 37						18 53									19 04			19 07		19 16			
Norbury	d	18 40						18 56									19 07			19 10		19 19			
Streatham Common	d	18 43						18 58									19 10			19 13		19 21			
Beckenham Junction	d									18 44															
Birkbeck	d									18 47															
Crystal Palace	d				18 43	18 51				18 51					18 56									19 13	19 21
Gipsy Hill	d				18 45					18 53					18 59									19 15	
West Norwood	d				18 48					18 56					19 02									19 18	
Streatham Hill	d				18 52										19 05									19 22	
Balham ⊖	d				18 55			19 02							19 09		19 14					19 28		19 25	
Wandsworth Common	d				18 57			19 04							19 11		19 16					19 30		19 27	
Clapham Junction	d			18 52	19 01		19 06	19 08			19 12				19 15		19 20					19 39	19 22	19 31	
Imperial Wharf	d																					19 44			
West Brompton ⊖	d																					19 47			
Kensington (Olympia) ⊖	d																					19 50			
Shepherd's Bush ⊖	d																					19 53			
Wembley Central ⊖	d																					20s08			
Harrow & Wealdstone ⊖	d																					20 13			
Watford Junction	d																					20 20			
Milton Keynes Central	a																					21 01			
Battersea Park	d				19 05								19 15		19 18		19 23							19 35	
London Victoria ⊖	a			18 59	19 12		19 13	19 15			19 18				19 25		19 28						19 29	19 41	
Streatham	d	18 46							18 56			19 10								19 16					
Tulse Hill	d	18 54							19 00	19 10		19 14								19 22					
Herne Hill	a											19 17													
Loughborough Jn	a											19 20													
Elephant & Castle ⊖	a											19 24													
London Blackfriars ⊖	a											19 28													
City Thameslink	a											19 32													
St Pancras International ⊖	a											19 39													
Luton Airport Parkway	a											20 25													
Luton	a											20 30													
North Dulwich	d	18 57							19 03	19 13										19 25					
East Dulwich	d	18 59							19 05	19 15										19 27					
Peckham Rye	d	19 01							19 07	19 17			19 26							19 29					
Queens Rd Peckham	d	19 04							19 10	19 20			19 29							19 32					
South Bermondsey	d	19 06							19 12	19 22			19 31							19 34					
London Bridge ⊖	a	19 11				19 13			19 17	19 27			19 36					19 29	19 25	19 41					19 41

Table 177 — Mondays to Fridays

East and West Croydon, London Milton Keynes Central and Luton via Norbury Crystal Palace - Tulse Hill

Local Services

Station		SN 1	SN	SN ◇1	SN		SN	SN	LO	SN	SN	SN 1	SN	FC	SN ◇1	SN	FC 1	SN	SN	LO	SN		SN 1	SN 1	SN
East Croydon	d	19 25		19 29	19 17						19 30	19 40			19 43		19 47				19 47		19 59	20 01	
West Croydon	d							19 17	19 22				19 28						19 31	19 39					
Norwood Junction	a							19 21	19 28		19 34									19 43					
	d							19 22			19 35														
Selhurst	d				19 20								19 32						19 35		19 50				
Thornton Heath	d				19 22								19 34						19 37		19 52				
Norbury	d				19 25								19 37						19 40		19 55				
Streatham Common	d				19 28								19 40						19 43		19 58				
Beckenham Junction	d									19 25															
Birkbeck	d									19 28															
Crystal Palace	d							19 26		19 32						19 43		19 51							
Gipsy Hill	d							19 29		19 34						19 45									
West Norwood	d							19 32		19 37						19 48									
Streatham Hill	d							19 35								19 52									
Balham ⊖	d				19 32			19 39					19 45			19 55					20 02				
Wandsworth Common	d				19 34			19 41					19 47			19 57					20 04				
Clapham Junction	d	19 38		19 41	19 38			19 45				19 49	19 51		19 52	20 01					20 08		20 08	20 11	
Imperial Wharf	d																								
West Brompton ⊖	d																								
Kensington (Olympia) ⊖	d																								
Shepherd's Bush ⊖	d																								
Wembley Central ⊖	d																								
Harrow & Wealdstone ⊖	d																								
Watford Junction	d																								
Milton Keynes Central	a																								
Battersea Park	d				19 41		19 45	19 48					19 54			20 05					20a11				20 15
London Victoria ⊖	a	19 44		19 47	19 48			19 53				19 56	19 59		19 59	20 09							20 15	20 20	
Streatham	d		19 26											19 40					19 46						
Tulse Hill	d		19 31							19 41				19 44					19 54						
Herne Hill	a													19 47											
Loughborough Jn	a													19 50											
Elephant & Castle ⊖	a													19 54											
London Blackfriars ⊖	a													19 58			20 07								
City Thameslink	a													20 02			20 10								
St Pancras International ⊖	a													20 09			20 17								
Luton Airport Parkway	a													20 55			20 51								
Luton	a													21 00			20 54								
North Dulwich	d		19 34							19 44									19 57						
East Dulwich	d		19 36							19 46									19 59						
Peckham Rye	d		19 38				19 56			19 48									20 01						20 26
Queens Rd Peckham	d		19 41				19 59			19 51									20 04						20 29
South Bermondsey	d		19 43				20 01			19 53									20 06						20 31
London Bridge ⊖	a		19 51				20 06			19 58	19 59							20 11	20 14						20 36

Station		SN	LO	SN	SN	SN	FC	SN	LO	SN ◇1	SN	SN	SN 1		SN	SN ◇1	SN FO	SN FX	SN	LO	SN	SN	FC	SN	SN ◇1
East Croydon	d					20 00				20 11			20 26		20 17	20 30						20 31			20 41
West Croydon	d	19 47	19 52		19 58			20 01	20 09										20 18	20 22				20 31	
Norwood Junction	a	19 51	19 58			20 04			20 13										20 22	20 28		20 35			
	d	19 52				20 05													20 23			20 35			
Selhurst	d				20 02			20 05							20 20									20 35	
Thornton Heath	d				20 04			20 07							20 22									20 37	
Norbury	d				20 07			20 10							20 25									20 40	
Streatham Common	d				20 10			20 13							20 28									20 43	
Beckenham Junction	d			19 54																	20 24				
Birkbeck	d			19 57																	20 27				
Crystal Palace	d	19 56		20 01							20 13	20 21							20 27		20 31				
Gipsy Hill	d	19 58		20 03							20 16								20 29		20 33				
West Norwood	d	20 01		20 06							20 19								20 32		20 36				
Streatham Hill	d	20 05									20 22								20 36						
Balham ⊖	d	20 08			20 14						20 25				20 32				20 39						
Wandsworth Common	d	20 10			20 16						20 27				20 34				20 41						
Clapham Junction	d	20 14			20 20					20 21	20 31		20 37		20 38	20 41			20 45						20 51
Imperial Wharf	d																								
West Brompton ⊖	d																								
Kensington (Olympia) ⊖	d																								
Shepherd's Bush ⊖	d																								
Wembley Central ⊖	d																								
Harrow & Wealdstone ⊖	d																								
Watford Junction	d																								
Milton Keynes Central	a																								
Battersea Park	d	20 18			20 23						20 35				20 41		20 45	20 45	20 48						
London Victoria ⊖	a	20 22			20 28					20 28	20 39		20 44		20 46	20 50			20 53						20 58
Streatham	d						20 06	20 17															20 36	20 46	
Tulse Hill	d			20 11			20 12	20 24													20 40		20 42	20 54	
Herne Hill	a						20 16																20 46		
Loughborough Jn	a						20 19																20 49		
Elephant & Castle ⊖	a						20 23																20 53		
London Blackfriars ⊖	a						20 27																20 57		
City Thameslink	a						20 32																21 02		
St Pancras International ⊖	a						20 39																21 09		
Luton Airport Parkway	a						21 25																21 55		
Luton	a						21 30																22 00		
North Dulwich	d			20 14				20 27													20 43			20 57	
East Dulwich	d			20 16				20 29													20 45			20 59	
Peckham Rye	d			20 18				20 31									20 56	20 56			20 47			21 01	
Queens Rd Peckham	d			20 21				20 34									20 59	20 59			20 50			21 04	
South Bermondsey	d			20 23				20 36									21 01	21 01			20 52			21 06	
London Bridge ⊖	a			20 28		20 29		20 41				20 41					21 06	21 07			20 57	[illegible]		[illegible]	

East and West Croydon, London Milton Keynes Central and Luton via Norbury Crystal Palace - Tulse Hill

Local Services

		SN	LO	SN	SN	SN	SN ■	SN	SN	SN	LO	SN	SN	SN	SN	SN ■	SN	SN ■	SN ■	SN	SN	LO	SN
East Croydon	d				06 31	06 36	06 42							06 57	06 45	06 57		07 00	07 05				
West Croydon	d		06 22	06 26						06 31	06 39		06 45									06 52	06 58
Norwood Junction	a		06 28		06 35	06 40					06 43		06 49									06 58	
	d	06 23			06 37	06 40						06 47	06 50								06 53		
Selhurst	d			06 31						06 35					06 48								07 02
Thornton Heath	d			06 33						06 37					06 50								07 04
Norbury	d			06 36						06 40					06 53								07 07
Streatham Common	d			06 38						06 43					06 56								07 10
Beckenham Junction	d																						
Birkbeck	d																						
Crystal Palace	d	06 27						06 39	06 44			06 51					06 51				06 57		
Gipsy Hill	d	06 29						06 41				06 53									06 59		
West Norwood	d	06 32						06 44				06 56									07 02		
Streatham Hill	d	06 36						06 48													07 06		
Balham	d	06 39		06 42				06 51							07 00						07 09		07 14
Wandsworth Common	d	06 41		06 44											07 02						07 11		07 16
Clapham Junction	d	06 45		06 48			06 51	06 56						07 07	07 06				07 17		07 15		07 20
Imperial Wharf	d																						
West Brompton	d																						
Kensington (Olympia)	d																						
Shepherd's Bush	d																						
Wembley Central	d																						
Harrow & Wealdstone	d																						
Watford Junction	d																						
Milton Keynes Central	a																						
Battersea Park	d	06 48		06 52											07 09					07 15	07 18		07 23
London Victoria	a	06 53		06 56			07 00	07 05						07 15	07 16				07 23		07 25		07 30
Streatham	d									06 46													
Tulse Hill	d									06 50		07 00											
Herne Hill	a																						
Loughborough Jn.	a																						
Elephant & Castle	a																						
London Blackfriars	a																						
City Thameslink	a																						
St Pancras International	a																						
Luton Airport Parkway	a																						
Luton	a																						
North Dulwich	d									06 53		07 03											
East Dulwich	d									06 55		07 05											
Peckham Rye	d									06 59		07 07								07 26			
Queens Rd Peckham	d									07 02		07 10								07 29			
South Bermondsey	d									07 04		07 12								07 31			
London Bridge	a				06 49	06 52			07 06	07 11		07 19	07 04			07 13	07 16	07 16		07 38			

		FC	SN	LO	SN	SN	SN ◇■	SN	SN	SN	SN	SN ■	SN	SN	SN ◇■	SN ■	FC	SN	SN	LO	SN ◇■	SN	SN	LO
East Croydon	d				07 10		07 15			07 26	07 18	07 27			07 31	07 35					07 39			
West Croydon	d		07 01	07 09		07 13													07 17	07 22		07 28	07 31	07 39
Norwood Junction	a			07 13	07 14	07 17													07 21	07 28				07 43
	d				07 14	07 18													07 22					
Selhurst	d		07 05								07 21											07 32	07 35	
Thornton Heath	d		07 07								07 23											07 34	07 37	
Norbury	d		07 10								07 26											07 37	07 40	
Streatham Common	d		07 13								07 28											07 40	07 43	
Beckenham Junction	d												07 13											
Birkbeck	d												07 16											
Crystal Palace	d							07 13	07 14				07 20	07 21					07 26					
Gipsy Hill	d							07 15					07 22						07 28					
West Norwood	d							07 18					07 25						07 31					
Streatham Hill	d							07 22											07 35					
Balham	d							07 25			07 32								07 39			07 44		
Wandsworth Common	d							07 27			07 34								07 41			07 46		
Clapham Junction	d						07 24	07 31		07 37	07 38				07 41				07 45		07 48	07 50		
Imperial Wharf	d																							
West Brompton	d																							
Kensington (Olympia)	d																							
Shepherd's Bush	d																							
Wembley Central	d																							
Harrow & Wealdstone	d																							
Watford Junction	d																							
Milton Keynes Central	a																							
Battersea Park	d							07 35			07 42							07 45	07 48			07 53		
London Victoria	a						07 33	07 41		07 46	07 48				07 49				07 57		07 57	08 00		
Streatham	d	07 16	07 19														07 38						07 46	
Tulse Hill	d	07 20	07 24										07 29				07 42						07 52	
Herne Hill	a	07 23															07 46							
Loughborough Jn.	a	07 27															07 49							
Elephant & Castle	a	07 31															07 53							
London Blackfriars	a	07 35															07 57							
City Thameslink	a	07 38															08 00							
St Pancras International	a	07 45															08 07							
Luton Airport Parkway	a	08 21																						
Luton	a	08 24																						
North Dulwich	d		07 27										07 32										07 55	
East Dulwich	d		07 29										07 34										07 57	
Peckham Rye	d		07 31										07 36					07 56					07 59	
Queens Rd Peckham	d		07 34										07 39					07 59					08 02	
South Bermondsey	d		07 36										07 41					08 01					08 04	
London Bridge	a		07 43		07 28	07 32			07 36			07 43	07 48	07 45		07 49		08 08					08 11	

East and West Croydon, London Milton Keynes Central and Luton via Norbury Crystal Palace - Tulse Hill

Local Services

		SN	SN ■	SN	SN	SN ■	SN	SN	SN	SN	SN	SN ■	SN	SN	SN ◇■	SN ■	SN ■	FC	SN	SN	LO	SN ◇■	SN ■
East Croydon	d	07 40	07 42			07 46			07 56	07 48	07 50	07 57			08 01	08 02	08 03					08 08	08 11
West Croydon	d			07 34			07 44													07 47	07 52		
Norwood Junction	a	07 44					07 48													07 51	07 58		
	d	07 44					07 49													07 52			
Selhurst	d			07 38						07 51	07 54												
Thornton Heath	d			07 40						07 53	07 56												
Norbury	d			07 43						07 56	07 59												
Streatham Common	d			07 46						07 59	08 02												
Beckenham Junction	d												07 42										
Birkbeck	d												07 45										
Crystal Palace	d				07 43			07 44					07 49	07 52						07 56			
Gipsy Hill	d				07 45								07 51							07 58			
West Norwood	d				07 48								07 54							08 01			
Streatham Hill	d				07 52															08 05			
Balham	d			07 50	07 55					08 03	08 06									08 09			
Wandsworth Common	d			07 52	07 57					08 05	08 08									08 11			
Clapham Junction	d		07 51	07 56	08 01				08 07	08 09	08 14				08 11					08 16		08 18	08 21
Imperial Wharf	d										08 18												
West Brompton	d										08 21												
Kensington (Olympia)	d										08 25												
Shepherd's Bush	d										08a27												
Wembley Central	d																						
Harrow & Wealdstone	d																						
Watford Junction	d																						
Milton Keynes Central	a																						
Battersea Park	d			07 59	08 05					08 12									08 15	08 19			
London Victoria	a		08 00	08 06	08 11				08 15	08 19					08 19					08 26		08 26	08 27
Streatham	d																	08 09					
Tulse Hill	d												07 59					08 13					
Herne Hill	a																	08 17					
Loughborough Jn.	a																	08 23					
Elephant & Castle	a																	08 27					
London Blackfriars	a																	08 32					
City Thameslink	a																	08 35					
St Pancras International	a																	08 43					
Luton Airport Parkway	a																	09 27					
Luton	a																	09 32					
North Dulwich	d												08 02										
East Dulwich	d												08 04										
Peckham Rye	d												08 06						08 26				
Queens Rd Peckham	d												08 09						08 29				
South Bermondsey	d												08 11						08 31				
London Bridge	a	07 58				08 01	08 05	08 07				08 13	08 18	08 15		08 17	08 19		08 38				

		SN	SN	SN ◇■	SN	LO	SN	SN ■	SN	SN	SN	SN	SN	SN ■	SN ■	SN	SN	SN ◇■	SN ■	SN ■	FC	SN	SN	LO
East Croydon	d			08 14				08 07	08 10			08 26	08 18	08 21	08 27			08 30	08 33	08 37				
West Croydon	d	07 58	08 01		08 05	08 09				08 16													08 19	08 22
Norwood Junction	a					08 13			08 14	08 20													08 24	08 28
	d								08 14	08 21													08 25	
Selhurst	d	08 02	08 05		08 09			08 13					08 21											
Thornton Heath	d	08 04	08 07		08 11			08 16					08 23											
Norbury	d	08 07	08 10		08 14			08 20					08 26											
Streatham Common	d	08 10	08 13		08 17			08 23					08 28											
Beckenham Junction	d															08 12								
Birkbeck	d															08 15								
Crystal Palace	d						08 13				08 15					08 19	08 24						08 29	
Gipsy Hill	d						08 15									08 21							08 31	
West Norwood	d						08 18									08 24							08 34	
Streatham Hill	d						08 22																08 38	
Balham	d	08 14			08 21		08 25	08 28					08 32										08 41	
Wandsworth Common	d	08 16					08 27	08 31					08 34										08 43	
Clapham Junction	d	08 20		08 24	08 26		08 31	08 39				08 37	08 38					08 40		08 48			08 47	
Imperial Wharf	d							08 44																
West Brompton	d							08 47																
Kensington (Olympia)	d							08 50																
Shepherd's Bush	d							08 53																
Wembley Central	d							09s08																
Harrow & Wealdstone	d							09 13																
Watford Junction	d							09 20																
Milton Keynes Central	a							10 01																
Battersea Park	d	08 23					08 35						08 42									08 45	08 50	
London Victoria	a	08 30		08 32	08 36		08 41					08 45	08 48					08 48		08 56			08 57	
Streatham	d		08 16																		08 39			
Tulse Hill	d		08 22													08 28					08 43			
Herne Hill	a																				08 46			
Loughborough Jn.	a																				08 50			
Elephant & Castle	a																				08 57			
London Blackfriars	a																				09 01			
City Thameslink	a																				09 04			
St Pancras International	a																				09 11			
Luton Airport Parkway	a																				09 59			
Luton	a																				10 04			
North Dulwich	d		08 25													08 31								
East Dulwich	d		08 27													08 33								
Peckham Rye	d		08 29													08 35						08 56		
Queens Rd Peckham	d		08 32													08 38						08 59		
South Bermondsey	d		08 34													08 40						09 01		
London Bridge	a		08 41						08 28	08 35	08 37			08 37	08 45	08 49	08 47		08 52			09 08		

East and West Croydon, London
Milton Keynes Central and Luton via Norbury
Crystal Palace - Tulse Hill

Local Services

Station		SN	SN	SN	LO	SN	SN ◇1 H	SN	SN ◇1 H	SN	SN	SN	SN ◇1	SN	SN 1	SN 1	SN	SN	FC	SN	SN	LO	SN
East Croydon	d			08 39		08 42	08 43		08 50			08 54	08 58	08 48	08 51	08 57							09 05
West Croydon 4	d	08 26	08 31		08 39			08 44													08 49	08 53	
Norwood Junction 2	a				08 43	08 46		08 49													08 53	08 58	09 09
	d					08 47		08 49													08 54		09 09
Selhurst 4	d	08 31	08 35	08 43										08 51									
Thornton Heath	d	08 33	08 37	08 46										08 53									
Norbury	d	08 36	08 40	08 49										08 56									
Streatham Common 4	d	08 38	08 43	08 52										08 58									
Beckenham Junction 4	d																08 43						
Birkbeck	d																08 46						
Crystal Palace 4	d									08 40	08 44						08 50	08 51			08 58		
Gipsy Hill	d									08 43							08 52				09 00		
West Norwood 4	d									08 46							08 55				09 03		
Streatham Hill	d									08 49											09 07		
Balham 4	d	08 43		08 58						08 55				09 02							09 10		
Wandsworth Common	d	08 45		09 00						08 57				09 04							09 12		
Clapham Junction 10	d	08 50		09 05			08 53		09 01	09 01		09 04	09 08	09 08							09 16		
Imperial Wharf	d			09 09																			
West Brompton	d			09 12																			
Kensington (Olympia)	d			09 15																			
Shepherd's Bush	d			09a18																			
Wembley Central	d																						
Harrow & Wealdstone	d																						
Watford Junction	d																						
Milton Keynes Central 10	a																						
Battersea Park 4	d	08 53								09 05				09 12						09 15	09 19		
London Victoria 15	a	09 00					09 01		09 09	09 11		09 13	09 16	09 18							09 27		
Streatham 4	d		08 50																09 08				
Tulse Hill 3	d		08 54														08 59		09 16				
Herne Hill 4	a																		09 19				
Loughborough Jn	a																		09 23				
Elephant & Castle	a																		09 29				
London Blackfriars 3	a																		09 33				
City Thameslink 3	a																		09 36				
St Pancras International 15	a																		09 43				
Luton Airport Parkway 7	a																		10 29				
Luton 10	a																		10 34				
North Dulwich	d		08 57														09 02						
East Dulwich	d		08 59														09 04						
Peckham Rye 4	d		09 01														09 06			09 26			
Queens Rd Peckham	d		09 04														09 09			09 29			
South Bermondsey	d		09 06														09 11			09 31			
London Bridge 4	a		09 14			09 01		09 04			09 06				09 06	09 13	09 19	09 14		09 38			09 23

Station		SN 1	SN	SN	SN 1	LO	SN ◇1 H	SN	SN	SN	SN ◇1 H	SN	SN 1	SN	SN	SN	LO	SN	SN 1	SN	FC	SN ◇1 H	SN	SN
East Croydon	d	09 11			09 08		09 14				09 22	09 17	09 30			09 20		09 30	09 37			09 39		
West Croydon 4	d		08 57	09 01		09 09									09 15		09 22						09 28	09 31
Norwood Junction 2	a					09 13									09 19	09 24	09 28	09 34	09 41					
	d														09 22	09 25		09 35	09 42					
Selhurst 4	d		09 01	09 05	09 13							09 21											09 32	09 35
Thornton Heath	d		09 03	09 07	09 16							09 23											09 34	09 37
Norbury	d		09 06	09 10	09 19							09 26											09 37	09 40
Streatham Common 4	d		09 09	09 13	09 21							09 28											09 40	09 43
Beckenham Junction 4	d																			09 23				
Birkbeck	d																			09 26				
Crystal Palace 4	d							09 11	09 14	09 21					09 26					09 30				
Gipsy Hill	d							09 14							09 28					09 32				
West Norwood 4	d							09 17							09 31					09 35				
Streatham Hill	d							09 21							09 35									
Balham 4	d		09 13		09 28			09 25				09 32			09 41								09 44	
Wandsworth Common	d		09 15		09 30			09 27				09 34			09 43								09 46	
Clapham Junction 10	d	09 21	09 19		09 39		09 24	09 31			09 33	09 38	09 40		09 47							09 48	09 50	
Imperial Wharf	d				09 44																			
West Brompton	d				09 47																			
Kensington (Olympia)	d				09 50																			
Shepherd's Bush	d				09 53																			
Wembley Central	d				10s08																			
Harrow & Wealdstone	d				10 13																			
Watford Junction	d				10 20																			
Milton Keynes Central 10	a				11 02																			
Battersea Park 4	d		09 22					09 35				09 42		09 45	09 50								09 53	
London Victoria 15	a	09 27	09 31				09 32	09 42			09 42	09 48	09 50		09 58							09 58	10 00	
Streatham 4	d			09 20																	09 38			09 46
Tulse Hill 3	d			09 25																09 39	09 42			09 54
Herne Hill 4	a																				09 46			
Loughborough Jn	a																				09 50			
Elephant & Castle	a																				09 54			
London Blackfriars 3	a																				09 59			
City Thameslink 3	a																				10 02			
St Pancras International 15	a																				10 09			
Luton Airport Parkway 7	a																				10 57			
Luton 10	a																				11 02			
North Dulwich	d			09 28																09 42				09 57
East Dulwich	d			09 30																09 44				09 59
Peckham Rye 4	d			09 32										09 56						09 46				10 01
Queens Rd Peckham	d			09 35										09 59						09 49				10 04
South Bermondsey	d			09 37										10 01						09 51				10 06
London Bridge 4	a			09 44					09 37	09 44				10 06		09 42		09 59	09 54	09 58				10 11

Table 177 Mondays to Fridays

East and West Croydon, London
Milton Keynes Central and Luton via Norbury
Crystal Palace - Tulse Hill

Local Services

Station		SN ◇1	SN	LO	SN	SN	SN	SN ◇1 H	SN	SN	SN	LO	SN 1	SN	SN	SN 1	SN	FC	SN	SN ◇1 H	SN	LO	SN
East Croydon	d	09 43				09 47		10 00			09 51		09 55		10 00	10 07				10 12			
West Croydon 4	d		09 35	09 39						09 45		09 52		09 58					10 01		10 04	10 09	
Norwood Junction 2	a			09 43						09 50	09 55	09 58	09 59		10 04	10 12						10 13	
	d									09 52	09 55		09 59		10 05	10 13							
Selhurst 4	d		09 39			09 50								10 02					10 05		10 09		
Thornton Heath	d		09 41			09 52								10 04					10 07		10 11		
Norbury	d		09 44			09 55								10 07					10 10		10 14		
Streatham Common 4	d		09 47			09 58								10 10					10 13		10 17		
Beckenham Junction 4	d																09 53						
Birkbeck	d																09 56						
Crystal Palace 4	d				09 43		09 51			09 56							10 00						10 13
Gipsy Hill	d				09 46					09 58							10 02						10 15
West Norwood 4	d				09 49					10 01							10 05						10 18
Streatham Hill	d				09 52					10 05													10 22
Balham 4	d		09 52		09 56	10 02				10 09				10 14							10 21		10 25
Wandsworth Common	d		09 54		09 58	10 04				10 11				10 16							10 23		10 27
Clapham Junction 10	d	09 53	09 58		10 02	10 08		10 09		10 15				10 20						10 21	10 27		10 31
Imperial Wharf	d																						
West Brompton	d																						
Kensington (Olympia)	d																						
Shepherd's Bush	d																						
Wembley Central	d																						
Harrow & Wealdstone	d																						
Watford Junction	d																						
Milton Keynes Central 10	a																						
Battersea Park 4	d				10 05	10 11			10 15	10 19				10 23									10 35
London Victoria 15	a	10 00	10 05		10 11	10 16		10 16		10 24				10 28						10 28	10 34		10 39
Streatham 4	d																	10 08	10 16				
Tulse Hill 3	d																10 09	10 12	10 24				
Herne Hill 4	a																	10 16					
Loughborough Jn	a																	10 19					
Elephant & Castle	a																	10 23					
London Blackfriars 3	a																	10 27					
City Thameslink 3	a																	10 32					
St Pancras International 15	a																	10 39					
Luton Airport Parkway 7	a																	11 27					
Luton 10	a																	11 32					
North Dulwich	d																10 12		10 27				
East Dulwich	d																10 14		10 29				
Peckham Rye 4	d								10 26								10 16		10 31				
Queens Rd Peckham	d								10 29								10 19		10 34				
South Bermondsey	d								10 31								10 21		10 36				
London Bridge 4	a						10 11		10 36		10 09		10 13		10 29	10 25	10 26		10 41				

Station		SN 1	SN	SN ◇1	SN	SN	SN	SN	LO	SN 1	SN	SN	SN 1	SN	FC	SN	SN ◇1 H	SN	LO	SN	SN	SN	SN ◇1	SN
East Croydon	d	10 10		10 28	10 17			10 21		10 25		10 30	10 38				10 42				10 47		11 00	
West Croydon 4	d						10 15		10 22		10 28					10 31		10 34	10 39					
Norwood Junction 2	a						10 19	10 25	10 28	10 29		10 34	10 42						10 43					
	d						10 22	10 25		10 29		10 35	10 43											
Selhurst 4	d	10 14			10 20						10 32					10 35		10 39			10 50			
Thornton Heath	d	10 16			10 22						10 34					10 37		10 41			10 52			
Norbury	d	10 19			10 25						10 37					10 40		10 44			10 55			
Streatham Common 4	d	10 22			10 28						10 40					10 43		10 47			10 58			
Beckenham Junction 4	d													10 23										
Birkbeck	d													10 26										
Crystal Palace 4	d		10 21				10 26							10 30						10 43		10 51		
Gipsy Hill	d						10 29							10 32						10 45				
West Norwood 4	d						10 32							10 35						10 48				
Streatham Hill	d						10 35													10 52				
Balham 4	d	10 29			10 32		10 39				10 44							10 51		10 55	11 02			
Wandsworth Common	d	10 31			10 34		10 41				10 46							10 53		10 57	11 04			
Clapham Junction 10	d	10 39		10 38	10 38		10 45				10 50						10 51	10 57		11 01	11 08		11 10	
Imperial Wharf	d	10 44																						
West Brompton	d	10 47																						
Kensington (Olympia)	d	10 50																						
Shepherd's Bush	d	10 53																						
Wembley Central	d	11s08																						
Harrow & Wealdstone	d	11 13																						
Watford Junction	d	11 20																						
Milton Keynes Central 10	a	12 01																						
Battersea Park 4	d				10 41	10 45	10 49				10 53									11 05	11 11			11 15
London Victoria 15	a			10 44	10 46		10 53				10 58						10 58	11 04		11 09	11 16		11 16	
Streatham 4	d														10 38	10 46								
Tulse Hill 3	d													10 39	10 42	10 54								
Herne Hill 4	a														10 46									
Loughborough Jn	a														10 49									
Elephant & Castle	a														10 53									
London Blackfriars 3	a														10 57									
City Thameslink 3	a														11 02									
St Pancras International 15	a														11 09									
Luton Airport Parkway 7	a														11 55									
Luton 10	a														12 00									
North Dulwich	d													10 42		10 57								
East Dulwich	d													10 44		10 59								
Peckham Rye 4	d					10 56								10 46		11 01								11 26
Queens Rd Peckham	d					10 59								10 49		11 04								11 29
South Bermondsey	d					11 01								10 51		11 06								11 31
London Bridge 4	a		10 41			11 06		10 39		10 43		10 59	10 55	10 56		11 11						11 11		[illegible]

Table 177

Mondays to Fridays

East and West Croydon, London Milton Keynes Central and Luton via Norbury Crystal Palace - Tulse Hill

Local Services

		SN	LO	SN	SN	SN 1	SN	SN	SN	LO	SN	SN	FC	SN	SN ◇1	SN	LO	SN	SN	SN 1	SN	SN ◇1	SN
East Croydon	d					20 57	20 47					21 00			21 09					21 26	21 17	21 30	
West Croydon [4]	d	20 35	20 39						20 45	20 52				21 01		21 04	21 09						
Norwood Junction [2]	a		20 43						20 49	20 58		21 04					21 13						
	d								20 52			21 05											
Selhurst [4]	d	20 39					20 50							21 05		21 09					21 20		
Thornton Heath	d	20 41					20 52							21 07		21 11					21 22		
Norbury	d	20 44					20 55							21 10		21 14					21 25		
Streatham Common [4]	d	20 47					20 58							21 13		21 17					21 28		
Beckenham Junction [4]	d										20 53												
Birkbeck	d										20 56												
Crystal Palace [4]	d			20 43	20 51				20 56		21 00							21 13	21 21				
Gipsy Hill	d			20 45					20 59		21 02							21 15					
West Norwood [4]	d			20 48					21 02		21 05							21 18					
Streatham Hill	d			20 52					21 05									21 22					
Balham [4] ⊖	d	20 51		20 56			21 02		21 08							21 21		21 26			21 32		
Wandsworth Common	d	20 53		20 58			21 04		21 10							21 23		21 28			21 34		
Clapham Junction [10]	d	20 57		21 03		21 08	21 08		21 14						21 18	21 27		21 33		21 38	21 38	21 41	
Imperial Wharf	d																						
West Brompton ⊖	d																						
Kensington (Olympia) ⊖	d																						
Shepherd's Bush ⊖	d																						
Wembley Central ⊖	d																						
Harrow & Wealdstone ⊖	d																						
Watford Junction	d																						
Milton Keynes Central [10]	a																						
Battersea Park [4]	d			21 06			21 11	21 15	21 18									21 36			21 41		21 45
London Victoria [15] ⊖	a	21 04		21 11		21 15	21 18		21 22						21 26	21 34		21 41		21 45	21 48	21 50	
Streatham [4]	d												21 06	21 16									
Tulse Hill [3]	d										21 09		21 12	21 24									
Herne Hill [4]	a												21 16										
Loughborough Jn	a												21 19										
Elephant & Castle ⊖	a												21 23										
London Blackfriars [3] ⊖	a												21 27										
City Thameslink [3]	a												21 32										
St Pancras International [15] ⊖	a												21 39										
Luton Airport Parkway [7]	a												22 25										
Luton [10]	a												22 30										
North Dulwich	d										21 12			21 27									
East Dulwich	d										21 14			21 29									
Peckham Rye [4]	d							21 26			21 16			21 31									21 56
Queens Rd Peckham	d							21 29			21 19			21 34									21 59
South Bermondsey	d							21 31			21 21			21 36									22 01
London Bridge [4] ⊖	a				21 13			21 36			21 26	21 29		21 41					21 43				22 06

		SN	LO	SN	SN	SN ◇1	FC	SN	SN	LO	SN	SN	SN 1	SN	SN	SN	LO	SN	SN	SN	SN ◇1	SN	LO	SN
East Croydon	d				21 30	21 42							21 57	21 47					22 00		22 09			
West Croydon [4]	d	21 18	21 22					21 31	21 34	21 39						21 48	21 52			22 01		22 04	22 09	
Norwood Junction [2]	a	21 22	21 28		21 34					21 43						21 52	21 58		22 04				22 13	
	d	21 23			21 35											21 53			22 05					
Selhurst [4]	d							21 35	21 39					21 50						22 05		22 09		
Thornton Heath	d							21 37	21 41					21 52						22 07		22 11		
Norbury	d							21 40	21 44					21 55						22 10		22 14		
Streatham Common [4]	d							21 43	21 47					21 58						22 13		22 17		
Beckenham Junction [4]	d			21 23														21 53						
Birkbeck	d			21 26														21 56						
Crystal Palace [4]	d	21 27		21 30							21 43	21 51				21 57		22 00						22 13
Gipsy Hill	d	21 29		21 32							21 45					21 59		22 02						22 15
West Norwood [4]	d	21 32		21 35							21 48					22 02		22 05						22 18
Streatham Hill	d	21 36									21 52					22 06								22 22
Balham [4] ⊖	d	21 39							21 51		21 56			22 02		22 09						22 21		22 26
Wandsworth Common	d	21 41							21 53		21 58			22 04		22 11						22 23		22 28
Clapham Junction [10]	d	21 45				21 51			21 57		22 03		22 08	22 08		22 15					22 18	22 27		22 33
Imperial Wharf	d																							
West Brompton ⊖	d																							
Kensington (Olympia) ⊖	d																							
Shepherd's Bush ⊖	d																							
Wembley Central ⊖	d																							
Harrow & Wealdstone ⊖	d																							
Watford Junction	d																							
Milton Keynes Central [10]	a																							
Battersea Park [4]	d	21 48									22 06			22 11	22 15	22 18								22 36
London Victoria [15] ⊖	a	21 53				21 58			22 04		22 11		22 14	22 18		22 23					22 26	22 34		22 41
Streatham [4]	d						21 46	21 50												22 16				
Tulse Hill [3]	d			21 39			21 50	21 54										22 09		22 24				
Herne Hill [4]	a						21 54																	
Loughborough Jn	a						21 57																	
Elephant & Castle ⊖	a						22 01																	
London Blackfriars [3] ⊖	a						22 05																	
City Thameslink [3]	a						22 10																	
St Pancras International [15] ⊖	a						22 17																	
Luton Airport Parkway [7]	a						23 01																	
Luton [10]	a						23 04																	
North Dulwich	d			21 42				21 57										22 12		22 27				
East Dulwich	d			21 44				21 59										22 14		22 29				
Peckham Rye [4]	d			21 46				22 01							22 26			22 16		22 31				
Queens Rd Peckham	d			21 49				22 04							22 29			22 19		22 34				
South Bermondsey	d			21 51				22 06							22 31			22 21		22 36				
London Bridge [4] ⊖	a			21 56	21 59			22 11				22 13			22 36			22 26	22 29	22 41				

East and West Croydon, London Milton Keynes Central and Luton via Norbury Crystal Palace - Tulse Hill

Local Services

		SN	SN	SN 1	SN	SN ◇1	FC	SN	SN	LO	SN	SN	SN ◇1	SN	LO	SN	SN	SN 1	SN	SN	SN	LO	SN
East Croydon	d			22 25	22 17	22 30					22 30		22 41					22 56	22 47				
West Croydon [4]	d								22 18	22 22		22 31		22 34	22 39						22 48	22 52	
Norwood Junction [2]	a								22 22	22 28	22 34				22 43						22 52	22 58	
	d								22 23		22 35										22 53		
Selhurst [4]	d				22 20							22 35		22 39					22 50				
Thornton Heath	d				22 22							22 37		22 41					22 52				
Norbury	d				22 25							22 40		22 44					22 55				
Streatham Common [4]	d				22 28							22 43		22 47					22 58				
Beckenham Junction [4]	d		22 15																				22 53
Birkbeck	d		22 18																				22 56
Crystal Palace [4]	d	22 21	22 22						22 27							22 43	22 51				22 57		23 00
Gipsy Hill	d		22 24						22 29							22 45					22 59		23 02
West Norwood [4]	d		22 27						22 32							22 48					23 02		23 05
Streatham Hill	d								22 36							22 52					23 06		
Balham [4] ⊖	d				22 32				22 39					22 51		22 56			23 02		23 09		
Wandsworth Common	d				22 34				22 41					22 53		22 58			23 04		23 11		
Clapham Junction [10]	d			22 38	22 38	22 41			22 45				22 51	22 57		23 03		23 07	23 08		23 15		
Imperial Wharf	d																						
West Brompton ⊖	d																						
Kensington (Olympia) ⊖	d																						
Shepherd's Bush ⊖	d																						
Wembley Central ⊖	d																						
Harrow & Wealdstone ⊖	d																						
Watford Junction	d																						
Milton Keynes Central [10]	a																						
Battersea Park [4]	d				22 41			22 45	22 48							23 07			23 11	23 15	23 19		
London Victoria [15] ⊖	a			22 44	22 48	22 50			22 53				22 57	23 04		23 14		23 15	23 18		23 25		
Streatham [4]	d						22 40					22 46											
Tulse Hill [3]	d		22 35				22 43					22 54											23 09
Herne Hill [4]	a																						
Loughborough Jn	a																						
Elephant & Castle ⊖	a																						
London Blackfriars [3] ⊖	a																						
City Thameslink [3]	a																						
St Pancras International [15] ⊖	a																						
Luton Airport Parkway [7]	a																						
Luton [10]	a																						
North Dulwich	d		22 38									22 57											23 12
East Dulwich	d		22 40									22 59											23 14
Peckham Rye [4]	d		22 42					22 56				23 01								23 26			23 16
Queens Rd Peckham	d		22 45					22 59				23 04								23 29			23 19
South Bermondsey	d		22 47					23 01				23 06								23 31			23 21
London Bridge [4] ⊖	a	22 45	22 52				22 55	23 06			22 59	23 11					23 14			23 36			23 26

		SN	SN	SN	SN	SN	SN	SN ◇1	SN	LO	SN	SN	SN	SN	SN 1
East Croydon	d	23 01				23 17		23 30				23 43			23 58
West Croydon [4]	d		23 01	23 04					23 18	23 22					
Norwood Junction [2]	a	23 05							23 22	23 28		23 47			
	d	23 06							23 23						
Selhurst [4]	d		23 05	23 09		23 20									00 02
Thornton Heath	d		23 07	23 11		23 22									
Norbury	d		23 10	23 14		23 25									
Streatham Common [4]	d		23 13	23 17		23 28									
Beckenham Junction [4]	d										23 23				
Birkbeck	d										23 26				
Crystal Palace [4]	d				23 13		23 21		23 27		23 30		23 43	23 51	
Gipsy Hill	d				23 15				23 29		23 32		23 45		
West Norwood [4]	d				23 18				23 32		23 35		23 48		
Streatham Hill	d				23 22				23 36				23 52		
Balham [4] ⊖	d			23 21	23 26	23 32			23 40				23 55		
Wandsworth Common	d			23 23	23 28	23 34			23 42				23 58		
Clapham Junction [10]	d			23 27	23 33	23 38		23 42	23 46				00 02		00 11
Imperial Wharf	d														
West Brompton ⊖	d														
Kensington (Olympia) ⊖	d														
Shepherd's Bush ⊖	d														
Wembley Central ⊖	d														
Harrow & Wealdstone ⊖	d														
Watford Junction	d														
Milton Keynes Central [10]	a														
Battersea Park [4]	d				23 37	23 41			23 49				00 05		
London Victoria [15] ⊖	a			23 34	23 41	23 46		23 52	23 54				00 10		00 18
Streatham [4]	d		23 16												
Tulse Hill [3]	d		23 24								23 39				
Herne Hill [4]	a														
Loughborough Jn	a														
Elephant & Castle ⊖	a														
London Blackfriars [3] ⊖	a														
City Thameslink [3]	a														
St Pancras International [15] ⊖	a														
Luton Airport Parkway [7]	a														
Luton [10]	a														
North Dulwich	d		23 27								23 42				
East Dulwich	d		23 29								23 44				
Peckham Rye [4]	d		23 31								23 46				
Queens Rd Peckham	d		23 34								23 49				
South Bermondsey	d		23 36								23 51				
London Bridge [4] ⊖	a	23 30	23 41				23 45				23 56			00 11	

Table 177 — **Saturdays**

East and West Croydon, London Milton Keynes Central and Luton via Norbury Crystal Palace - Tulse Hill

Local Services

		SN	SN	SN ■	SN	SN	SN	SN ■	FC ■	SN ■	FC ■	SN ■	FC ■	SN ■	FC ■	SN		FC ■	LO	FC ■	FC	SN	LO	SN	FC
East Croydon	d			23p58			00 49	01 28	01 50	02 28	02 47	03 28	03 47	04 28	04 47			05 17		05 42					
West Croydon	d																		05 39				05 52		
Norwood Junction	a																		05 43				05 58		
	d																					05 52			
Selhurst	d			00 02				01 30	01 53	02 30	02 50	03 30	03 50	04 31	04 50			05 20			05 39			06 01	06 09
Thornton Heath	d																				05 41			06 03	06 11
Norbury	d																				05 43			06 06	06 13
Streatham Common	d																				05 46			06 08	06 16
Beckenham Junction	d																								
Birkbeck	d																								
Crystal Palace	d	23p43	23p51		00 13	00 21																05 56			
Gipsy Hill	d	23p45			00 15																	05 59			
West Norwood	d	23p48			00 18																	06 02			
Streatham Hill	d	23p52			00 22																	06 05			
Balham	d	23p55			00 25																	06 09		06 12	
Wandsworth Common	d	23p58			00 27																	06 11		06 14	
Clapham Junction	d	00 02		00 11	00 31		01 01	01 41		02 41		03 41		04 41		05 00						06 15		06 18	
Imperial Wharf	d																								
West Brompton	d																								
Kensington (Olympia)	d																								
Shepherd's Bush	d																								
Wembley Central	d																								
Harrow & Wealdstone	d																								
Watford Junction	d																								
Milton Keynes Central	a																								
Battersea Park	d	00 05			00 35											05 03						06 18		06 22	
London Victoria	a	00 10		00 18	00 42		01 09	01 49		02 49		03 49		04 50		05 08						06 23		06 26	
Streatham	d																				05 49				06 19
Tulse Hill	d																				05 55				06 23
Herne Hill	a																								
Loughborough Jn	a																								
Elephant & Castle	a																								
London Blackfriars	a																								
City Thameslink	a																								
St Pancras International	a																								
Luton Airport Parkway	a																								
Luton	a																								
North Dulwich	d																								
East Dulwich	d																								
Peckham Rye	d																								
Queens Rd Peckham	d																								
South Bermondsey	d																								
London Bridge	a		00 11			00 41			02 14		03 12		04 12		05 12			05 42		05 57	06 09				06 35

		SN ◇■	LO	SN ■	SN	SN	LO	SN ■		SN	SN ◇■	SN	FC	LO	SN	SN	SN	SN	LO	SN ■	SN	SN ■	FC	SN ◇■	
East Croydon	d	06 07		06 10				06 25		06 30	06 41				06 43	06 47				06 55	07 00	07 07		07 11	
West Croydon	d		06 09			06 18	06 22							06 39				06 45	06 52						
Norwood Junction	a		06 13			06 22	06 28	06 29		06 34				06 43	06 49			06 52	06 58	06 59	07 04	07 12			
	d					06 23		06 29		06 35		06 41			06 50			06 53		06 59	07 05	07 13			
Selhurst	d	06 10		06 13									06 39			06 50									
Thornton Heath	d			06 16									06 41			06 52									
Norbury	d			06 19									06 43			06 55									
Streatham Common	d			06 21									06 46			06 58									
Beckenham Junction	d																								
Birkbeck	d																								
Crystal Palace	d					06 27						06 45						06 57							
Gipsy Hill	d					06 29						06 47						06 59							
West Norwood	d					06 32						06 50						07 02							
Streatham Hill	d					06 36												07 06							
Balham	d			06 28		06 39										07 02		07 09							
Wandsworth Common	d			06 30		06 41										07 04		07 11							
Clapham Junction	d	06 18		06 39		06 45					06 50					07 08		07 15						07 20	
Imperial Wharf	d			06 44																					
West Brompton	d			06 47																					
Kensington (Olympia)	d			06 50																					
Shepherd's Bush	d			06 53																					
Wembley Central	d			07s07																					
Harrow & Wealdstone	d			07 12																					
Watford Junction	d			07 19																					
Milton Keynes Central	a			08 00																					
Battersea Park	d				06 45	06 48										07 11	07 15	07 19							
London Victoria	a	06 26				06 53					06 57					07 16		07 24						07 27	
Streatham	d												06 49										07 10		
Tulse Hill	d											06 54	06 57										07 17		
Herne Hill	a												07 01												
Loughborough Jn	a																								
Elephant & Castle	a																								
London Blackfriars	a																								
City Thameslink	a																								
St Pancras International	a																								
Luton Airport Parkway	a																								
Luton	a																								
North Dulwich	d											06 57													
East Dulwich	d											06 59													
Peckham Rye	d				06 56							07 01					07 26								
Queens Rd Peckham	d				06 59							07 04					07 29								
South Bermondsey	d				07 01							07 06					07 31								
London Bridge	a				07 06			06 43		06 59		07 14			07 11		07 36			07 13	07 29	07 25	07 30		

Table 177 — **Saturdays**

East and West Croydon, London Milton Keynes Central and Luton via Norbury Crystal Palace - Tulse Hill

Local Services

		SN	SN	LO	SN ■	SN	SN	SN ◇■	SN	SN	LO	SN ■	SN	SN	FC	SN		LO	SN ■	SN ◇■	SN	SN	SN	SN ◇■	SN
East Croydon	d				07 10		07 17	07 30				07 25		07 30					07 39	07 42			07 47	08 00	
West Croydon	d	06 58	07 01	07 09		07 15					07 22		07 28			07 31		07 39				07 45			
Norwood Junction	a			07 13		07 19					07 28	07 29		07 34				07 43	07 44			07 49			
	d					07 20				07 23		07 29		07 35					07 45			07 50			
Selhurst	d	07 02	07 05		07 13		07 20						07 32			07 35							07 50		
Thornton Heath	d	07 04	07 07		07 16		07 22						07 34			07 37							07 52		
Norbury	d	07 07	07 10		07 19		07 25						07 37			07 40							07 55		
Streatham Common	d	07 10	07 13		07 21		07 28						07 40			07 43							07 58		
Beckenham Junction	d																								
Birkbeck	d																								
Crystal Palace	d									07 27											07 43				
Gipsy Hill	d									07 29											07 45				
West Norwood	d									07 32											07 48				
Streatham Hill	d									07 36											07 52				
Balham	d	07 14			07 28		07 32			07 39			07 44								07 55		08 02		
Wandsworth Common	d	07 16			07 30		07 34			07 41			07 46								07 57		08 04		
Clapham Junction	d	07 20			07 39		07 38	07 39		07 45			07 50							07 51	08 01		08 08	08 10	
Imperial Wharf	d				07 44																				
West Brompton	d				07 47																				
Kensington (Olympia)	d				07 50																				
Shepherd's Bush	d				07 53																				
Wembley Central	d				08s07																				
Harrow & Wealdstone	d				08 12																				
Watford Junction	d				08 19																				
Milton Keynes Central	a				09 00																				
Battersea Park	d	07 23					07 41		07 45	07 48			07 53								08 05		08 11		08 15
London Victoria	a	07 28					07 46	07 46		07 53			07 58							07 58	08 09		08 16	08 16	
Streatham	d		07 16												07 40	07 46									
Tulse Hill	d		07 24												07 47	07 54									
Herne Hill	a																								
Loughborough Jn	a																								
Elephant & Castle	a																								
London Blackfriars	a																								
City Thameslink	a																								
St Pancras International	a																								
Luton Airport Parkway	a																								
Luton	a																								
North Dulwich	d		07 27													07 57									
East Dulwich	d		07 29													07 59									
Peckham Rye	d		07 31						07 56							08 01									08 26
Queens Rd Peckham	d		07 34						07 59							08 04									08 29
South Bermondsey	d		07 36						08 01							08 06									08 31
London Bridge	a		07 41			07 41			08 06			07 43		07 59	08 00	08 11			07 57			08 11			08 36

		SN	SN	LO	SN ■	SN	SN	SN ■		FC	SN	LO	SN ■	SN ◇■	SN	SN	SN ◇■	SN	SN	SN	SN	LO	SN ■	SN	
East Croydon	d		07 51		07 55		08 00	08 07					08 10	08 12			08 28	08 17			08 21		08 25		
West Croydon	d			07 52		07 58					08 01	08 09								08 15		08 22		08 28	
Norwood Junction	a		07 55	07 58	07 59		08 04	08 12				08 13								08 19	08 25	08 28	08 29		
	d	07 53	07 55		07 59		08 05	08 13												08 22	08 25		08 29		
Selhurst	d					08 02					08 05		08 13					08 20						08 32	
Thornton Heath	d					08 04					08 07		08 16					08 22						08 34	
Norbury	d					08 07					08 10		08 19					08 25						08 37	
Streatham Common	d					08 10					08 13		08 21					08 28						08 40	
Beckenham Junction	d																								
Birkbeck	d																								
Crystal Palace	d	07 57													08 13	08 21				08 26					
Gipsy Hill	d	07 59													08 15					08 29					
West Norwood	d	08 02													08 18					08 32					
Streatham Hill	d	08 06													08 22					08 35					
Balham	d	08 09				08 14							08 28		08 25			08 32		08 39				08 44	
Wandsworth Common	d	08 11				08 16							08 30		08 27			08 34		08 41				08 46	
Clapham Junction	d	08 15				08 20							08 39	08 21	08 31		08 37	08 38		08 45				08 50	
Imperial Wharf	d												08 44												
West Brompton	d												08 47												
Kensington (Olympia)	d												08 50												
Shepherd's Bush	d												08 53												
Wembley Central	d												09s07												
Harrow & Wealdstone	d												09 12												
Watford Junction	d												09 19												
Milton Keynes Central	a												10 00												
Battersea Park	d	08 18				08 23									08 35			08 41	08 45	08 48				08 53	
London Victoria	a	08 23				08 28								08 28	08 39		08 44	08 46		08 53				08 58	
Streatham	d									08 10	08 16														
Tulse Hill	d									08 17	08 24														
Herne Hill	a																								
Loughborough Jn	a																								
Elephant & Castle	a																								
London Blackfriars	a																								
City Thameslink	a																								
St Pancras International	a																								
Luton Airport Parkway	a																								
Luton	a																								
North Dulwich	d										08 27														
East Dulwich	d										08 29														
Peckham Rye	d										08 31								08 56						
Queens Rd Peckham	d										08 34								08 59						
South Bermondsey	d										08 36								09 01						
London Bridge	a		08 09		08 13		08 29	08 25		08 30	08 41	[illegible]	[illegible]	[illegible]	[illegible]	[illegible]	[illegible]	[illegible]	[illegible]	[illegible]	[illegible]	[illegible]	[illegible]	[illegible]	[illegible]

East and West Croydon, London Milton Keynes Central and Luton via Norbury Crystal Palace - Tulse Hill

Local Services

		SN	SN ■	SN	FC	SN	SN ◇■	SN	LO	SN	SN	SN	SN ◇■	SN	SN	SN	LO	SN ■	SN	SN	SN ■	SN	FC	SN
East Croydon	d	08 30	08 37				08 42				08 47		09 00			08 51		08 55		09 00	09 07			
West Croydon	d					08 31		08 34	08 39						08 45		08 52		08 58					09 01
Norwood Junction	a	08 34	08 42						08 43						08 49	08 55	08 58	08 59		09 04	09 12			
	d	08 35	08 43												08 52	08 55		08 59		09 05	09 13			
Selhurst	d					08 35		08 39			08 50								09 02					09 05
Thornton Heath	d					08 37		08 41			08 52								09 04					09 07
Norbury	d					08 40		08 44			08 55								09 07					09 10
Streatham Common	d					08 43		08 47			08 58								09 10					09 13
Beckenham Junction	d			08 23																		08 53		
Birkbeck	d			08 26																		08 56		
Crystal Palace	d			08 30						08 43		08 51			08 56							09 00		
Gipsy Hill	d			08 32						08 45					08 58							09 02		
West Norwood	d			08 35						08 48					09 01							09 05		
Streatham Hill	d									08 52					09 06									
Balham	d							08 51		08 55	09 02				09 09				09 14					
Wandsworth Common	d							08 53		08 57	09 04				09 11				09 16					
Clapham Junction	d						08 51	08 57		09 01	09 08		09 10		09 15				09 20					
Imperial Wharf	d																							
West Brompton	d																							
Kensington (Olympia)	d																							
Shepherd's Bush	d																							
Wembley Central	d																							
Harrow & Wealdstone	d																							
Watford Junction	d																							
Milton Keynes Central	a																							
Battersea Park	d									09 05	09 11			09 15	09 18				09 23					
London Victoria	a						08 58	09 04		09 09	09 16		09 16		09 23				09 28					
Streatham	d				08 40	08 46																	09 10	09 16
Tulse Hill	d			08 39	08 47	08 54																09 09	09 17	09 24
Herne Hill	a																							
Loughborough Jn.	a																							
Elephant & Castle	a																							
London Blackfriars	a																							
City Thameslink	a																							
St Pancras International	a																							
Luton Airport Parkway	a																							
Luton	a																							
North Dulwich	d			08 42		08 57																09 12		09 27
East Dulwich	d			08 44		08 59																09 14		09 29
Peckham Rye	d			08 46		09 01								09 26								09 16		09 31
Queens Rd Peckham	d			08 49		09 04								09 29								09 19		09 34
South Bermondsey	d			08 51		09 06								09 31								09 21		09 36
London Bridge	a	08 59	08 55	08 56	09 00	09 11						09 11		09 36		09 09		09 13		09 29	09 25	09 26	09 30	09 41

		SN ◇■	SN	LO	SN	SN ■	SN	SN ◇■	SN	SN	SN	SN	LO	SN ■	SN	SN	SN ■	SN	FC	SN	SN ◇■	SN	LO
East Croydon	d	09 12				09 10		09 28	09 17			09 21		09 25		09 30	09 37				09 42		
West Croydon	d		09 04	09 09							09 15		09 22		09 28					09 31		09 34	09 39
Norwood Junction	a			09 13							09 19	09 25	09 28	09 29		09 34	09 42						09 43
	d										09 22	09 25		09 29		09 35	09 43						
Selhurst	d		09 09			09 13			09 20						09 32					09 35		09 39	
Thornton Heath	d		09 11			09 16			09 22						09 34					09 37		09 41	
Norbury	d		09 14			09 19			09 25						09 37					09 40		09 44	
Streatham Common	d		09 17			09 21			09 28						09 40					09 43		09 47	
Beckenham Junction	d																	09 23					
Birkbeck	d																	09 26					
Crystal Palace	d				09 13		09 21				09 26							09 30					
Gipsy Hill	d				09 15						09 29							09 32					
West Norwood	d				09 18						09 32							09 35					
Streatham Hill	d				09 22						09 35												
Balham	d		09 21		09 25	09 28			09 32		09 39				09 44							09 51	
Wandsworth Common	d		09 23		09 27	09 30			09 34		09 41				09 46							09 53	
Clapham Junction	d	09 21	09 27		09 31	09 39		09 37	09 38		09 45				09 50						09 51	09 57	
Imperial Wharf	d					09 44																	
West Brompton	d					09 47																	
Kensington (Olympia)	d					09 50																	
Shepherd's Bush	d					09 53																	
Wembley Central	d					10s07																	
Harrow & Wealdstone	d					10 12																	
Watford Junction	d					10 19																	
Milton Keynes Central	a					11 00																	
Battersea Park	d				09 35				09 41	09 45	09 48				09 53								
London Victoria	a	09 28	09 34		09 39			09 44	09 46		09 54				09 58						09 58	10 04	
Streatham	d																		09 40	09 46			
Tulse Hill	d																	09 39	09 47	09 54			
Herne Hill	a																						
Loughborough Jn.	a																						
Elephant & Castle	a																						
London Blackfriars	a																						
City Thameslink	a																						
St Pancras International	a																						
Luton Airport Parkway	a																						
Luton	a																						
North Dulwich	d																	09 42		09 57			
East Dulwich	d																	09 44		09 59			
Peckham Rye	d									09 56								09 46		10 01			
Queens Rd Peckham	d									09 59								09 49		10 04			
South Bermondsey	d									10 01								09 51		10 06			
London Bridge	a						09 41			10 06		09 39		09 43		09 59	09 55	09 56	10 00	10 11			

East and West Croydon, London Milton Keynes Central and Luton via Norbury Crystal Palace - Tulse Hill

Local Services

		SN	SN	SN	SN ◇■	SN	SN	SN	LO	SN ■	SN	SN	SN ■	SN	FC	SN	SN ◇■	SN	LO	SN	SN ■	SN	SN ◇■	SN
East Croydon	d		09 47		10 00			09 51		09 55		10 00	10 07				10 12				10 10		10 28	10 17
West Croydon	d						09 45		09 52		09 58					10 01		10 04	10 09					
Norwood Junction	a						09 49	09 55	09 58	09 59		10 04	10 12						10 13					
	d						09 52	09 55		09 59		10 05	10 13											
Selhurst	d		09 50								10 02					10 05		10 09			10 13			10 20
Thornton Heath	d		09 52								10 04					10 07		10 11			10 16			10 22
Norbury	d		09 55								10 07					10 10		10 14			10 19			10 25
Streatham Common	d		09 58								10 10					10 13		10 17			10 21			10 28
Beckenham Junction	d													09 53										
Birkbeck	d													09 56										
Crystal Palace	d	09 43		09 51			09 56							10 00						10 13		10 21		
Gipsy Hill	d	09 45					09 59							10 02						10 15				
West Norwood	d	09 48					10 02							10 05						10 18				
Streatham Hill	d	09 52					10 05													10 22				
Balham	d	09 55	10 02				10 09				10 14							10 21		10 25	10 28			10 32
Wandsworth Common	d	09 57	10 04				10 11				10 16							10 23		10 27	10 30			10 34
Clapham Junction	d	10 01	10 08		10 10		10 15				10 20						10 21	10 27		10 31	10 39		10 37	10 38
Imperial Wharf	d																				10 44			
West Brompton	d																				10 47			
Kensington (Olympia)	d																				10 50			
Shepherd's Bush	d																				10 53			
Wembley Central	d																				11s08			
Harrow & Wealdstone	d																				11 13			
Watford Junction	d																				11 20			
Milton Keynes Central	a																				12 00			
Battersea Park	d	10 05	10 11			10 15	10 18				10 23									10 35				10 41
London Victoria	a	10 09	10 16		10 16		10 23				10 28						10 28	10 34		10 39			10 44	10 46
Streatham	d														10 10	10 16								
Tulse Hill	d													10 09	10 17	10 24								
Herne Hill	a																							
Loughborough Jn.	a																							
Elephant & Castle	a																							
London Blackfriars	a																							
City Thameslink	a																							
St Pancras International	a																							
Luton Airport Parkway	a																							
Luton	a																							
North Dulwich	d													10 12		10 27								
East Dulwich	d													10 14		10 29								
Peckham Rye	d					10 26								10 16		10 31								
Queens Rd Peckham	d					10 29								10 19		10 34								
South Bermondsey	d					10 31								10 21		10 36								
London Bridge	a			10 11		10 36		10 09		10 13		10 29	10 25	10 26	10 30	10 41						10 41		

		SN	SN	SN	LO	SN ■	SN	SN	SN ■	SN	FC	SN	SN ◇■	SN	LO	SN	SN	SN	SN ◇■	SN	SN	SN	LO
East Croydon	d			10 21		10 25		10 30	10 37				10 42				10 47		11 00			10 51	
West Croydon	d		10 15		10 22		10 28					10 31		10 34	10 39						10 45		10 52
Norwood Junction	a		10 19	10 25	10 28	10 29		10 34	10 42						10 43						10 49	10 55	10 58
	d		10 22	10 25		10 29		10 35	10 43												10 52	10 55	
Selhurst	d						10 32					10 35		10 39			10 50						
Thornton Heath	d						10 34					10 37		10 41			10 52						
Norbury	d						10 37					10 40		10 44			10 55						
Streatham Common	d						10 40					10 43		10 47			10 58						
Beckenham Junction	d									10 23													
Birkbeck	d									10 26													
Crystal Palace	d		10 26							10 30						10 43		10 51			10 56		
Gipsy Hill	d		10 29							10 32						10 45					10 59		
West Norwood	d		10 32							10 35						10 48					11 02		
Streatham Hill	d		10 35													10 52					11 05		
Balham	d		10 39				10 44							10 51		10 55	11 02				11 09		
Wandsworth Common	d		10 41				10 46							10 53		10 57	11 04				11 11		
Clapham Junction	d		10 45				10 50						10 51	10 57		11 01	11 08		11 10		11 15		
Imperial Wharf	d																						
West Brompton	d																						
Kensington (Olympia)	d																						
Shepherd's Bush	d																						
Wembley Central	d																						
Harrow & Wealdstone	d																						
Watford Junction	d																						
Milton Keynes Central	a																						
Battersea Park	d	10 45	10 48				10 53									11 05	11 11			11 15	11 18		
London Victoria	a		10 53				10 58						10 58	11 04		11 09	11 16		11 16		11 23		
Streatham	d										10 40	10 46											
Tulse Hill	d									10 39	10 47	10 54											
Herne Hill	a																						
Loughborough Jn.	a																						
Elephant & Castle	a																						
London Blackfriars	a																						
City Thameslink	a																						
St Pancras International	a																						
Luton Airport Parkway	a																						
Luton	a																						
North Dulwich	d									10 42		10 57											
East Dulwich	d									10 44		10 59											
Peckham Rye	d	10 56								10 46		11 01								11 26			
Queens Rd Peckham	d	10 59								10 49		11 04								11 29			
South Bermondsey	d	11 01								10 51		11 06								11 31			
London Bridge	a	11 06		10 39		10 43		10 59	10 55	10 56	11 00	11 11						11 11		11 36		11 09	

East and West Croydon, London Milton Keynes Central and Luton via Norbury Crystal Palace - Tulse Hill

Local Services

		SN 1	SN	SN	SN 1	SN	FC	SN	SN ◇1	SN	LO	SN	SN 1	SN	SN ◇1 H	SN		SN	SN	SN	LO	SN 1	SN	SN	SN 1
East Croydon	d	10 55		11 00	11 07				11 12				11 10		11 28	11 17				11 21		11 25		11 30	11 37
West Croydon 4	d		10 58					11 01		11 04	11 09								11 15		11 22		11 28		
Norwood Junction 2	a	10 59		11 04	11 12						11 13								11 19	11 25	11 28	11 29		11 34	11 42
	d	10 59		11 05	11 13														11 22	11 25		11 29		11 35	11 43
Selhurst 4	d		11 02					11 05		11 09			11 13			11 20							11 32		
Thornton Heath	d		11 04					11 07		11 11			11 16			11 22							11 34		
Norbury	d		11 07					11 10		11 14			11 19			11 25							11 37		
Streatham Common 4	d		11 10					11 13		11 17			11 21			11 28							11 40		
Beckenham Junction 4	d					10 53																			
Birkbeck	d					10 56																			
Crystal Palace 4	d					11 00						11 13		11 21					11 26						
Gipsy Hill	d					11 02						11 15							11 29						
West Norwood 4	d					11 05						11 18							11 32						
Streatham Hill	d											11 22							11 35						
Balham 4 ⊖	d		11 14							11 21		11 25	11 28			11 32			11 39				11 44		
Wandsworth Common	d		11 16							11 23		11 27	11 30			11 34			11 41				11 46		
Clapham Junction 10	d		11 20						11 21	11 27		11 31	11 39		11 37	11 38			11 45				11 50		
Imperial Wharf	d												11 44												
West Brompton ⊖	d												11 47												
Kensington (Olympia) ⊖	d												11 50												
Shepherd's Bush ⊖	d												11 53												
Wembley Central ⊖	d												12s07												
Harrow & Wealdstone ⊖	d												12 12												
Watford Junction	d												12 19												
Milton Keynes Central 10	a												13 00												
Battersea Park 4	d		11 23									11 35				11 41		11 45	11 48				11 53		
London Victoria 15 ⊖	a		11 28						11 28	11 34		11 39			11 44	11 46			11 53				11 58		
Streatham 4	d						11 10	11 16																	
Tulse Hill 3	d					11 09	11 17	11 24																	
Herne Hill 4	a																								
Loughborough Jn	a																								
Elephant & Castle ⊖	a																								
London Blackfriars 3 ⊖	a																								
City Thameslink 3	a																								
St Pancras International 15 ⊖	a																								
Luton Airport Parkway 7	a																								
Luton 10	a																								
North Dulwich	d					11 12		11 27																	
East Dulwich	d					11 14		11 29																	
Peckham Rye 4	d					11 16		11 31										11 56							
Queens Rd Peckham	d					11 19		11 34										11 59							
South Bermondsey	d					11 21		11 36										12 01							
London Bridge 4 ⊖	a	11 13		11 29	11 25	11 26	11 30	11 41						11 41				12 06		11 39		11 43		11 59	11 55

		SN	FC	SN	SN ◇1	SN	LO	SN		SN	SN	SN ◇1	SN	SN	SN	LO	SN 1	SN	SN	SN 1	SN	FC	SN	SN ◇1
East Croydon	d				11 42					11 47		12 00			11 51		11 55		12 00	12 07				12 12
West Croydon 4	d			11 31		11 34	11 39							11 45		11 52		11 58					12 01	
Norwood Junction 2	a						11 43							11 49	11 55	11 58	11 59		12 04	12 12				
	d													11 52	11 55		11 59		12 05	12 13				
Selhurst 4	d			11 35		11 39				11 50								12 02					12 05	
Thornton Heath	d			11 37		11 41				11 52								12 04					12 07	
Norbury	d			11 40		11 44				11 55								12 07					12 10	
Streatham Common 4	d			11 43		11 47				11 58								12 10					12 13	
Beckenham Junction 4	d	11 23																			11 53			
Birkbeck	d	11 26																			11 56			
Crystal Palace 4	d	11 30						11 43			11 51			11 56							12 00			
Gipsy Hill	d	11 32						11 45						11 59							12 02			
West Norwood 4	d	11 35						11 48						12 02							12 05			
Streatham Hill	d							11 52						12 05										
Balham 4 ⊖	d					11 51		11 55		12 02				12 09				12 14						
Wandsworth Common	d					11 53		11 57		12 04				12 11				12 16						
Clapham Junction 10	d				11 51	11 57		12 01		12 08		12 10		12 15				12 20						12 21
Imperial Wharf	d																							
West Brompton ⊖	d																							
Kensington (Olympia) ⊖	d																							
Shepherd's Bush ⊖	d																							
Wembley Central ⊖	d																							
Harrow & Wealdstone ⊖	d																							
Watford Junction	d																							
Milton Keynes Central 10	a																							
Battersea Park 4	d							12 05		12 11			12 15	12 18				12 23						
London Victoria 15 ⊖	a				11 58	12 04		12 09		12 16		12 16		12 23				12 28						12 28
Streatham 4	d		11 40	11 46																		12 10	12 16	
Tulse Hill 3	d	11 39	11 47	11 54																	12 09	12 17	12 24	
Herne Hill 4	a																							
Loughborough Jn	a																							
Elephant & Castle ⊖	a																							
London Blackfriars 3 ⊖	a																							
City Thameslink 3	a																							
St Pancras International 15 ⊖	a																							
Luton Airport Parkway 7	a																							
Luton 10	a																							
North Dulwich	d	11 42		11 57																	12 12		12 27	
East Dulwich	d	11 44		11 59																	12 14		12 29	
Peckham Rye 4	d	11 46		12 01									12 26								12 16		12 31	
Queens Rd Peckham	d	11 49		12 04									12 29								12 19		12 34	
South Bermondsey	d	11 51		12 06									12 31								12 21		12 36	
London Bridge 4 ⊖	a	11 56	12 00	12 11							12 11		12 36		12 09		12 13		12 29	12 25	12 26	12 30	12 41	

East and West Croydon, London Milton Keynes Central and Luton via Norbury Crystal Palace - Tulse Hill

Local Services

		SN	LO	SN	SN 1	SN	SN ◇1 H	SN	SN	SN	SN	LO	SN 1	SN	SN	SN 1		SN	FC	SN	SN ◇1	SN	LO	SN	SN
East Croydon	d				12 10		12 28	12 17			12 21		12 25		12 30	12 38					12 42				12 47
West Croydon 4	d	12 04	12 09							12 15		12 22		12 28						12 31		12 34	12 39		
Norwood Junction 2	a		12 13							12 19	12 25	12 28	12 29		12 34	12 42							12 43		
	d									12 22	12 25		12 29		12 35	12 43									
Selhurst 4	d	12 09			12 13			12 20						12 32						12 35		12 39			12 50
Thornton Heath	d	12 11			12 16			12 22						12 34						12 37		12 41			12 52
Norbury	d	12 14			12 19			12 25						12 37						12 40		12 44			12 55
Streatham Common 4	d	12 17			12 21			12 28						12 40						12 43		12 47			12 57
Beckenham Junction 4	d																	12 23							
Birkbeck	d																	12 26							
Crystal Palace 4	d			12 13		12 21				12 26								12 30						12 43	
Gipsy Hill	d			12 15						12 29								12 32						12 45	
West Norwood 4	d			12 18						12 32								12 35						12 48	
Streatham Hill	d			12 22						12 35														12 52	
Balham 4 ⊖	d	12 21		12 25	12 28			12 32		12 39				12 44								12 51		12 55	13 01
Wandsworth Common	d	12 23		12 27	12 30			12 34		12 41				12 46								12 53		12 57	13 03
Clapham Junction 10	d	12 27		12 31	12 39		12 37	12 38		12 45				12 50							12 51	12 57		13 01	13 07
Imperial Wharf	d				12 44																				
West Brompton ⊖	d				12 47																				
Kensington (Olympia) ⊖	d				12 50																				
Shepherd's Bush ⊖	d				12 53																				
Wembley Central ⊖	d				13s07																				
Harrow & Wealdstone ⊖	d				13 12																				
Watford Junction	d				13 19																				
Milton Keynes Central 10	a				14 00																				
Battersea Park 4	d			12 35				12 41	12 45	12 48				12 53										13 05	13 11
London Victoria 15 ⊖	a	12 34		12 39			12 44	12 46		12 53				12 58							12 58	13 04		13 09	13 16
Streatham 4	d																		12 40	12 46					
Tulse Hill 3	d																	12 39	12 47	12 54					
Herne Hill 4	a																								
Loughborough Jn	a																								
Elephant & Castle ⊖	a																								
London Blackfriars 3 ⊖	a																								
City Thameslink 3	a																								
St Pancras International 15 ⊖	a																								
Luton Airport Parkway 7	a																								
Luton 10	a																								
North Dulwich	d																	12 42		12 57					
East Dulwich	d																	12 44		12 59					
Peckham Rye 4	d								12 56									12 46		13 01					
Queens Rd Peckham	d								12 59									12 49		13 04					
South Bermondsey	d								13 01									12 51		13 06					
London Bridge 4 ⊖	a					12 44			13 06		12 39		12 43		12 59	12 55		12 56	13 00	13 11					

East and West Croydon, London Milton Keynes Central and Luton via Norbury Crystal Palace - Tulse Hill

Local Services

Station		SN	SN ◇■	SN	SN	SN	LO	SN ■	SN	SN	SN ■	SN	FC	SN	SN ◇■	SN	LO	SN	SN ■	SN	SN ◇■	SN	SN
East Croydon	d		13 00			12 51		12 55		13 00	13 07				13 12				13 10		13 28	13 17	
West Croydon	d				12 45		12 52		12 58					13 01		13 04	13 09						
Norwood Junction	a				12 49	12 55	12 58	12 59		13 04	13 12						13 13						
	d				12 52	12 55		12 59		13 05	13 13												
Selhurst	d								13 02					13 05		13 09			13 13			13 20	
Thornton Heath	d								13 04					13 07		13 11			13 16			13 22	
Norbury	d								13 07					13 10		13 14			13 19			13 25	
Streatham Common	d								13 10					13 13		13 17			13 21			13 28	
Beckenham Junction	d											12 53											
Birkbeck	d											12 56											
Crystal Palace	d	12 51			12 56							13 00						13 13		13 21			
Gipsy Hill	d				12 59							13 02						13 15					
West Norwood	d				13 02							13 05						13 18					
Streatham Hill	d				13 05													13 22					
Balham	d				13 09				13 14							13 21		13 25	13 28			13 32	
Wandsworth Common	d				13 11				13 16							13 23		13 27	13 30			13 34	
Clapham Junction	d		13 10		13 15				13 20						13 21	13 27		13 31	13 39		13 37	13 38	
Imperial Wharf	d																		13 44				
West Brompton	d																		13 47				
Kensington (Olympia)	d																		13 50				
Shepherd's Bush	d																		13 53				
Wembley Central	d																		14s08				
Harrow & Wealdstone	d																		14 13				
Watford Junction	d																		14 20				
Milton Keynes Central	a																		15 00				
Battersea Park	d			13 15	13 18				13 23									13 35				13 41	13 45
London Victoria	a		13 16		13 23				13 28						13 28	13 34		13 39			13 44	13 46	
Streatham	d												13 10	13 16									
Tulse Hill	d											13 09	13 17	13 24									
Herne Hill	a																						
Loughborough Jn.	a																						
Elephant & Castle	a																						
London Blackfriars	a																						
City Thameslink	a																						
St Pancras International	a																						
Luton Airport Parkway	a																						
Luton	a																						
North Dulwich	d											13 12		13 27									
East Dulwich	d											13 14		13 29									
Peckham Rye	d			13 26								13 16		13 31									13 56
Queens Rd Peckham	d			13 29								13 19		13 34									13 59
South Bermondsey	d			13 31								13 21		13 36									14 01
London Bridge	a	13 11		13 36		13 09		13 13		13 29	13 25	13 26	13 30	13 41						13 44			14 06

Station		SN	SN	LO	SN ■	SN	SN	SN ■	SN	FC	SN	SN ◇■	SN	LO	SN	SN	SN	SN ◇■	SN	SN	SN	LO	SN ■	SN
East Croydon	d		13 21		13 25		13 30	13 37				13 42				13 47		14 00			13 51		13 55	
West Croydon	d	13 15		13 22		13 28					13 31		13 34	13 39						13 45		13 52		13 58
Norwood Junction	a	13 19	13 25	13 28	13 29		13 34	13 42						13 43						13 49	13 55	13 58	13 59	
	d	13 22	13 25		13 29		13 35	13 43												13 52	13 55		13 59	
Selhurst	d					13 32					13 35		13 39			13 50								14 02
Thornton Heath	d					13 34					13 37		13 41			13 52								14 04
Norbury	d					13 37					13 40		13 44			13 55								14 07
Streatham Common	d					13 40					13 43		13 47			13 58								14 10
Beckenham Junction	d								13 23															
Birkbeck	d								13 26															
Crystal Palace	d	13 26							13 30						13 43		13 51			13 56				
Gipsy Hill	d	13 29							13 32						13 45					13 59				
West Norwood	d	13 32							13 35						13 48					14 02				
Streatham Hill	d	13 35													13 52					14 05				
Balham	d	13 39				13 44							13 51		13 55	14 02				14 09				14 14
Wandsworth Common	d	13 41				13 46							13 53		13 57	14 04				14 11				14 16
Clapham Junction	d	13 45				13 50						13 51	13 57		14 01	14 08		14 10		14 15				14 20
Imperial Wharf	d																							
West Brompton	d																							
Kensington (Olympia)	d																							
Shepherd's Bush	d																							
Wembley Central	d																							
Harrow & Wealdstone	d																							
Watford Junction	d																							
Milton Keynes Central	a																							
Battersea Park	d	13 48				13 53									14 05	14 11			14 15	14 18				14 23
London Victoria	a	13 53				13 58						13 58	14 04		14 09	14 16		14 16		14 23				14 28
Streatham	d									13 40	13 46													
Tulse Hill	d								13 39	13 47	13 54													
Herne Hill	a																							
Loughborough Jn.	a																							
Elephant & Castle	a																							
London Blackfriars	a																							
City Thameslink	a																							
St Pancras International	a																							
Luton Airport Parkway	a																							
Luton	a																							
North Dulwich	d								13 42		13 57													
East Dulwich	d								13 44		13 59													
Peckham Rye	d								13 46		14 01								14 26					
Queens Rd Peckham	d								13 49		14 04								14 29					
South Bermondsey	d								13 51		14 06								14 31					
London Bridge	a		13 39		13 43		13 59	13 55	13 56	14 00	14 11						14 11		14 36		14 09		14 13	

East and West Croydon, London Milton Keynes Central and Luton via Norbury Crystal Palace - Tulse Hill

Local Services

Station		SN	SN ■	SN	FC	SN	SN ◇■	SN	LO	SN	SN ■	SN	SN ◇■	SN	SN	SN	SN	LO	SN ■	SN	SN	SN ■	SN
East Croydon	d	14 00	14 07				14 12				14 10		14 28	14 17			14 21		14 25		14 30	14 37	
West Croydon	d					14 01		14 04	14 09							14 15		14 22		14 28			
Norwood Junction	a	14 04	14 12						14 13							14 19	14 25	14 28	14 29		14 34	14 42	
	d	14 05	14 13													14 22	14 25		14 29		14 35	14 43	
Selhurst	d					14 05		14 09			14 13			14 20						14 32			
Thornton Heath	d					14 07		14 11			14 16			14 22						14 34			
Norbury	d					14 10		14 14			14 19			14 25						14 37			
Streatham Common	d					14 13		14 17			14 21			14 28						14 40			
Beckenham Junction	d			13 53																			14 23
Birkbeck	d			13 56																			14 26
Crystal Palace	d			14 00						14 13		14 21				14 26							14 30
Gipsy Hill	d			14 02						14 15						14 29							14 32
West Norwood	d			14 05						14 18						14 32							14 35
Streatham Hill	d									14 22						14 35							
Balham	d							14 21		14 25	14 28			14 32		14 39				14 44			
Wandsworth Common	d							14 23		14 27	14 30			14 34		14 41				14 46			
Clapham Junction	d						14 21	14 27		14 31	14 39		14 37	14 38		14 45				14 50			
Imperial Wharf	d										14 44												
West Brompton	d										14 47												
Kensington (Olympia)	d										14 50												
Shepherd's Bush	d										14 53												
Wembley Central	d										15s07												
Harrow & Wealdstone	d										15 12												
Watford Junction	d										15 19												
Milton Keynes Central	a										16 00												
Battersea Park	d									14 35				14 41	14 45	14 48				14 53			
London Victoria	a						14 28	14 34		14 39			14 44	14 46		14 53				14 58			
Streatham	d				14 10	14 16																	
Tulse Hill	d			14 09	14 17	14 24																	14 39
Herne Hill	a																						
Loughborough Jn.	a																						
Elephant & Castle	a																						
London Blackfriars	a																						
City Thameslink	a																						
St Pancras International	a																						
Luton Airport Parkway	a																						
Luton	a																						
North Dulwich	d			14 12		14 27																	14 42
East Dulwich	d			14 14		14 29																	14 44
Peckham Rye	d			14 16		14 31									14 56								14 46
Queens Rd Peckham	d			14 19		14 34									14 59								14 49
South Bermondsey	d			14 21		14 36									15 01								14 51
London Bridge	a	14 29	14 25	14 26	14 30	14 41						14 44			15 06		14 39		14 43		14 59	14 55	14 56

Station		FC	SN	SN ◇■	SN	LO	SN	SN	SN	SN ◇■	SN	SN	SN	LO	SN ■	SN	SN	SN ■	SN	FC	SN	SN ◇■	SN	LO
East Croydon	d			14 42				14 47		15 00			14 51		14 55		15 00	15 07				15 12		
West Croydon	d		14 31		14 34	14 39						14 45		14 52		14 58					15 01		15 04	15 09
Norwood Junction	a					14 43						14 49	14 55	14 58	14 59		15 04	15 12						15 13
	d											14 52	14 55		14 59		15 05	15 13						
Selhurst	d		14 35		14 39			14 50								15 02					15 05		15 09	
Thornton Heath	d		14 37		14 41			14 52								15 04					15 07		15 11	
Norbury	d		14 40		14 44			14 55								15 07					15 10		15 14	
Streatham Common	d		14 43		14 47			14 58								15 10					15 13		15 17	
Beckenham Junction	d																		14 53					
Birkbeck	d																		14 56					
Crystal Palace	d						14 43		14 51			14 56							15 00					
Gipsy Hill	d						14 45					14 59							15 02					
West Norwood	d						14 48					15 02							15 05					
Streatham Hill	d						14 52					15 05												
Balham	d				14 51		14 55	15 02				15 09				15 14							15 21	
Wandsworth Common	d				14 53		14 57	15 04				15 11				15 16							15 23	
Clapham Junction	d			14 51	14 57		15 01	15 08		15 10		15 15				15 20						15 21	15 27	
Imperial Wharf	d																							
West Brompton	d																							
Kensington (Olympia)	d																							
Shepherd's Bush	d																							
Wembley Central	d																							
Harrow & Wealdstone	d																							
Watford Junction	d																							
Milton Keynes Central	a																							
Battersea Park	d						15 05	15 11			15 15	15 18				15 23								
London Victoria	a			14 58	15 04		15 09	15 16		15 16		15 23				15 28						15 28	15 34	
Streatham	d	14 40	14 46																	15 10	15 16			
Tulse Hill	d	14 47	14 54																15 09	15 17	15 24			
Herne Hill	a																							
Loughborough Jn.	a																							
Elephant & Castle	a																							
London Blackfriars	a																							
City Thameslink	a																							
St Pancras International	a																							
Luton Airport Parkway	a																							
Luton	a																							
North Dulwich	d		14 57																15 12		15 27			
East Dulwich	d		14 59																15 14		15 29			
Peckham Rye	d		15 01								15 26								15 16		15 31			
Queens Rd Peckham	d		15 04								15 29								15 19		15 34			
South Bermondsey	d		15 06								15 31								15 21		15 36			
London Bridge	a	15 00	15 11						15 11		15 36		15 09		15 13		15 29	15 25	15 26	15 30	15 41			

Table 177

East and West Croydon, London Milton Keynes Central and Luton via Norbury Crystal Palace - Tulse Hill

Local Services

		SN	SN ■1	SN	SN ◇1	SN	SN	SN		SN	LO	SN ■1	SN	SN	SN ■1	SN	FC	SN	SN ◇1	SN	LO	SN	SN	SN
East Croydon	d		15 10		15 28	15 17				15 21		15 25		15 30	15 37				15 42				15 47	
West Croydon ■4	d							15 15			15 22		15 28					15 31		15 34	15 39			
Norwood Junction ■2	a							15 19		15 25	15 28	15 29		15 34	15 42						15 43			
	d							15 22		15 25		15 29		15 35	15 43									
Selhurst ■4	d		15 13			15 20							15 32					15 35		15 39			15 50	
Thornton Heath	d		15 16			15 22							15 34					15 37		15 41			15 52	
Norbury	d		15 19			15 25							15 37					15 40		15 44			15 55	
Streatham Common ■4	d		15 21			15 28							15 40					15 43		15 47			15 58	
Beckenham Junction ■4	d															15 23								
Birkbeck	d															15 26								
Crystal Palace ■4	d	15 13		15 21				15 26								15 30						15 43		15 51
Gipsy Hill	d	15 15						15 29								15 32						15 45		
West Norwood ■4	d	15 18						15 32								15 35						15 48		
Streatham Hill	d	15 22						15 35														15 52		
Balham ■4 ⊖	d	15 25	15 29			15 32		15 39					15 44							15 51		15 55	16 02	
Wandsworth Common	d	15 27	15 31			15 34		15 41					15 46							15 53		15 57	16 04	
Clapham Junction ■10	d	15 31	15 39		15 37	15 38		15 45					15 50						15 51	15 57		16 01	16 08	
Imperial Wharf	d		15 44																					
West Brompton ⊖	d		15 47																					
Kensington (Olympia) ⊖	d		15 50																					
Shepherd's Bush ⊖	d		15 53																					
Wembley Central ⊖	d		16s07																					
Harrow & Wealdstone ⊖	d		16 12																					
Watford Junction	d		16 19																					
Milton Keynes Central ■10	a		17 00																					
Battersea Park ■4	d	15 35				15 41	15 45	15 48					15 53									16 05	16 11	
London Victoria ■15 ⊖	a	15 39			15 44	15 46		15 53					15 58						15 58	16 04		16 09	16 16	
Streatham ■4	d																15 40	15 46						
Tulse Hill ■3	d															15 39	15 47	15 54						
Herne Hill ■4	a																							
Loughborough Jn	a																							
Elephant & Castle ⊖	a																							
London Blackfriars ■3 ⊖	a																							
City Thameslink ■3	a																							
St Pancras International ■15 ⊖	a																							
Luton Airport Parkway ■7	a																							
Luton ■10	a																							
North Dulwich	d															15 42		15 57						
East Dulwich	d															15 44		15 59						
Peckham Rye ■4	d						15 56									15 46		16 01						
Queens Rd Peckham	d						15 59									15 49		16 04						
South Bermondsey	d						16 01									15 51		16 06						
London Bridge ■4 ⊖	a			15 44			16 06			15 39		15 43		15 59	15 55	15 56	16 00	16 11						16 11

Table 177

East and West Croydon, London Milton Keynes Central and Luton via Norbury Crystal Palace - Tulse Hill

Local Services

		SN ◇1	SN	SN	SN	LO	SN ■1	SN	SN	SN ■1	SN	FC	SN	SN ◇1	SN	LO		SN	SN ■1	SN	SN ◇1	SN	SN	SN	SN
East Croydon	d	16 00			15 51		15 55		16 00	16 07				16 12					16 10		16 28	16 17			16 21
West Croydon ■4	d			15 45		15 52		15 58					16 01		16 04	16 09								16 15	
Norwood Junction ■2	a			15 49	15 55	15 58	15 59		16 04	16 12						16 13								16 19	16 25
	d			15 52	15 55		15 59		16 05	16 13														16 22	16 25
Selhurst ■4	d							16 02					16 05		16 09				16 13			16 20			
Thornton Heath	d							16 04					16 07		16 11				16 16			16 22			
Norbury	d							16 07					16 10		16 14				16 19			16 25			
Streatham Common ■4	d							16 10					16 13		16 17				16 21			16 28			
Beckenham Junction ■4	d										15 53														
Birkbeck	d										15 56														
Crystal Palace ■4	d			15 56							16 00							16 13		16 21				16 26	
Gipsy Hill	d			15 59							16 02							16 15						16 29	
West Norwood ■4	d			16 02							16 05							16 18						16 32	
Streatham Hill	d			16 05														16 22						16 35	
Balham ■4 ⊖	d			16 09				16 14							16 21			16 25	16 28			16 32		16 39	
Wandsworth Common	d			16 11				16 16							16 23			16 27	16 30			16 34		16 41	
Clapham Junction ■10	d	16 10		16 15				16 20						16 21	16 27			16 31	16 39		16 37	16 38		16 45	
Imperial Wharf	d																		16 44						
West Brompton ⊖	d																		16 47						
Kensington (Olympia) ⊖	d																		16 50						
Shepherd's Bush ⊖	d																		16 53						
Wembley Central ⊖	d																		17s07						
Harrow & Wealdstone ⊖	d																		17 12						
Watford Junction	d																		17 19						
Milton Keynes Central ■10	a																		18 00						
Battersea Park ■4	d		16 15	16 18				16 23										16 35				16 41	16 45	16 48	
London Victoria ■15 ⊖	a	16 16		16 23				16 28						16 28	16 34			16 39			16 44	16 46		16 53	
Streatham ■4	d											16 10	16 16												
Tulse Hill ■3	d										16 09	16 17	16 24												
Herne Hill ■4	a																								
Loughborough Jn	a																								
Elephant & Castle ⊖	a																								
London Blackfriars ■3 ⊖	a																								
City Thameslink ■3	a																								
St Pancras International ■15 ⊖	a																								
Luton Airport Parkway ■7	a																								
Luton ■10	a																								
North Dulwich	d										16 12		16 27												
East Dulwich	d										16 14		16 29												
Peckham Rye ■4	d		16 26								16 16		16 31										16 56		
Queens Rd Peckham	d		16 29								16 19		16 34										16 59		
South Bermondsey	d		16 31								16 21		16 36										17 01		
London Bridge ■4 ⊖	a		16 36		16 09		16 13		16 29	16 25	16 26	16 30	16 41							16 41			17 06		16 39

		LO	SN ■1	SN	SN	SN ■1	SN	FC		SN	SN ◇1	SN	LO	SN	SN	SN	SN ◇1	SN	SN	SN	LO	SN ■1	SN	SN
East Croydon	d		16 25		16 30	16 37					16 42				16 47		17 00			16 51		16 55		17 00
West Croydon ■4	d	16 22		16 28						16 31		16 34	16 39						16 45		16 52		16 58	
Norwood Junction ■2	a	16 28	16 29		16 34	16 42							16 43						16 49	16 55	16 58	16 59		17 04
	d		16 29		16 35	16 43													16 52	16 55		16 59		17 05
Selhurst ■4	d			16 32						16 35		16 39			16 50								17 02	
Thornton Heath	d			16 34						16 37		16 41			16 52								17 04	
Norbury	d			16 37						16 40		16 44			16 55								17 07	
Streatham Common ■4	d			16 40						16 43		16 47			16 58								17 10	
Beckenham Junction ■4	d						16 23																	
Birkbeck	d						16 26																	
Crystal Palace ■4	d						16 30							16 43		16 51			16 56					
Gipsy Hill	d						16 32							16 45					16 59					
West Norwood ■4	d						16 35							16 48					17 02					
Streatham Hill	d													16 52					17 05					
Balham ■4 ⊖	d			16 44								16 51		16 55	17 02				17 09				17 14	
Wandsworth Common	d			16 46								16 53		16 57	17 04				17 11				17 16	
Clapham Junction ■10	d			16 50							16 51	16 57		17 01	17 08		17 10		17 15				17 20	
Imperial Wharf	d																							
West Brompton ⊖	d																							
Kensington (Olympia) ⊖	d																							
Shepherd's Bush ⊖	d																							
Wembley Central ⊖	d																							
Harrow & Wealdstone ⊖	d																							
Watford Junction	d																							
Milton Keynes Central ■10	a																							
Battersea Park ■4	d			16 53										17 05	17 11			17 15	17 18				17 23	
London Victoria ■15 ⊖	a			16 58							16 58	17 04		17 09	17 16		17 16		17 23				17 28	
Streatham ■4	d							16 40		16 46														
Tulse Hill ■3	d						16 39	16 47		16 54														
Herne Hill ■4	a																							
Loughborough Jn	a																							
Elephant & Castle ⊖	a																							
London Blackfriars ■3 ⊖	a																							
City Thameslink ■3	a																							
St Pancras International ■15 ⊖	a																							
Luton Airport Parkway ■7	a																							
Luton ■10	a																							
North Dulwich	d						16 42			16 57														
East Dulwich	d						16 44			16 59														
Peckham Rye ■4	d						16 46			17 01								17 26						
Queens Rd Peckham	d						16 49			17 04								17 29						
South Bermondsey	d						16 51			17 06								17 31						
London Bridge ■4 ⊖	a		16 43		16 59	16 55	16 56	17 00		17 11						[illegible]								

East and West Croydon, London Milton Keynes Central and Luton via Norbury Crystal Palace - Tulse Hill

Local Services

		SN 1	SN	FC	SN	SN ◇1	SN	LO	SN	SN 1	SN	SN ◇1	SN	SN	SN	SN		LO	SN 1	SN	SN	SN 1	SN	FC	SN
East Croydon	d	17 07				17 12				17 10		17 28	17 17			17 21			17 25		17 30	17 37			
West Croydon	d				17 01		17 04	17 09							17 15			17 22		17 28					17 31
Norwood Junction	a	17 12						17 13							17 19	17 25		17 28	17 29		17 34	17 42			
	d	17 13													17 22	17 25			17 29		17 35	17 43			
Selhurst	d				17 05		17 09			17 13			17 20							17 32					17 35
Thornton Heath	d				17 07		17 11			17 16			17 22							17 34					17 37
Norbury	d				17 10		17 14			17 19			17 25							17 37					17 40
Streatham Common	d				17 13		17 17			17 21			17 28							17 40					17 43
Beckenham Junction	d		16 53																				17 23		
Birkbeck	d		16 56																				17 26		
Crystal Palace	d		17 00						17 13		17 21				17 26								17 30		
Gipsy Hill	d		17 02						17 15						17 29								17 32		
West Norwood	d		17 05						17 18						17 32								17 35		
Streatham Hill	d								17 22						17 35										
Balham	d						17 21		17 25	17 28			17 33		17 39					17 44					
Wandsworth Common	d						17 23		17 27	17 30			17 35		17 41					17 46					
Clapham Junction	d					17 21	17 27		17 32	17 39		17 37	17 39		17 45					17 50					
Imperial Wharf	d									17 44															
West Brompton	d									17 47															
Kensington (Olympia)	d									17 50															
Shepherd's Bush	d									17 53															
Wembley Central	d									18s07															
Harrow & Wealdstone	d									18 12															
Watford Junction	d									18 19															
Milton Keynes Central	a									19 00															
Battersea Park	d								17 36				17 42	17 45	17 48					17 53					
London Victoria	a					17 28	17 34		17 40			17 44	17 47		17 53					17 58					
Streatham	d			17 10	17 16																			17 40	17 46
Tulse Hill	d		17 09	17 17	17 24																		17 39	17 47	17 54
Herne Hill	a																								
Loughborough Jn.	a																								
Elephant & Castle	a																								
London Blackfriars	a																								
City Thameslink	a																								
St Pancras International	a																								
Luton Airport Parkway	a																								
Luton	a																								
North Dulwich	d		17 12		17 27																		17 42		17 57
East Dulwich	d		17 14		17 29																		17 44		17 59
Peckham Rye	d		17 16		17 31									17 56									17 46		18 01
Queens Rd Peckham	d		17 19		17 34									17 59									17 49		18 04
South Bermondsey	d		17 21		17 36									18 01									17 51		18 06
London Bridge	a	17 25	17 26	17 30	17 41						17 41			18 06		17 39			17 43		17 59	17 55	17 56	18 00	18 11

		SN ◇1	SN	LO	SN	SN	SN	SN ◇1		SN	SN	SN	LO	SN 1	SN	SN	SN 1	SN	FC	SN	SN ◇1	SN	LO	SN
East Croydon	d	17 42				17 47		18 00				17 51		17 55		18 00	18 07				18 12			
West Croydon	d		17 34	17 39							17 45		17 52		17 58					18 01		18 04	18 09	
Norwood Junction	a			17 43							17 49	17 55	17 58	17 59		18 04	18 12						18 13	
	d										17 52	17 55		17 59		18 05	18 13							
Selhurst	d		17 39			17 50									18 02					18 05		18 09		
Thornton Heath	d		17 41			17 52									18 04					18 07		18 11		
Norbury	d		17 44			17 55									18 07					18 10		18 14		
Streatham Common	d		17 47			17 58									18 10					18 13		18 17		
Beckenham Junction	d																	17 53						
Birkbeck	d																	17 56						
Crystal Palace	d				17 43		17 51				17 56							18 00						18 13
Gipsy Hill	d				17 45						17 59							18 02						18 15
West Norwood	d				17 48						18 02							18 05						18 18
Streatham Hill	d				17 52						18 05													18 22
Balham	d		17 51		17 55	18 02					18 09				18 14							18 21		18 25
Wandsworth Common	d		17 53		17 57	18 04					18 11				18 16							18 23		18 27
Clapham Junction	d	17 51	17 57		18 01	18 08		18 10			18 15				18 20						18 21	18 27		18 31
Imperial Wharf	d																							
West Brompton	d																							
Kensington (Olympia)	d																							
Shepherd's Bush	d																							
Wembley Central	d																							
Harrow & Wealdstone	d																							
Watford Junction	d																							
Milton Keynes Central	a																							
Battersea Park	d				18 05	18 11				18 15	18 18				18 23									18 35
London Victoria	a	17 58	18 04		18 09	18 16		18 16			18 23				18 28						18 28	18 34		18 39
Streatham	d																		18 10	18 16				
Tulse Hill	d																	18 09	18 17	18 24				
Herne Hill	a																							
Loughborough Jn.	a																							
Elephant & Castle	a																							
London Blackfriars	a																							
City Thameslink	a																							
St Pancras International	a																							
Luton Airport Parkway	a																							
Luton	a																							
North Dulwich	d																	18 12		18 27				
East Dulwich	d																	18 14		18 29				
Peckham Rye	d									18 26								18 16		18 31				
Queens Rd Peckham	d									18 29								18 19		18 34				
South Bermondsey	d									18 31								18 21		18 36				
London Bridge	a						18 11			18 36		18 09		18 13		18 29	18 25	18 26	18 30	18 41				

East and West Croydon, London Milton Keynes Central and Luton via Norbury Crystal Palace - Tulse Hill

Local Services

		SN 1	SN	SN ◇1	SN	SN	SN	SN	LO	SN 1	SN	SN	SN 1	SN	FC	SN		SN ◇1	SN	LO	SN	SN	SN	SN ◇1	SN
East Croydon	d	18 10		18 28	18 17			18 21		18 25		18 30	18 37					18 42				18 47		19 00	
West Croydon	d						18 15		18 22		18 28					18 31			18 34	18 39					
Norwood Junction	a						18 19	18 25	18 28	18 29		18 34	18 42							18 43					
	d						18 22	18 25		18 29		18 35	18 43												
Selhurst	d	18 13			18 20						18 32					18 35			18 39			18 50			
Thornton Heath	d	18 16			18 22						18 34					18 37			18 41			18 52			
Norbury	d	18 19			18 25						18 37					18 40			18 44			18 55			
Streatham Common	d	18 21			18 28						18 40					18 43			18 47			18 58			
Beckenham Junction	d													18 23											
Birkbeck	d													18 26											
Crystal Palace	d		18 21				18 26							18 30							18 43		18 51		
Gipsy Hill	d						18 29							18 32							18 45				
West Norwood	d						18 32							18 35							18 48				
Streatham Hill	d						18 35														18 52				
Balham	d	18 28			18 32		18 39				18 44								18 51		18 55	19 02			
Wandsworth Common	d	18 30			18 34		18 41				18 46								18 53		18 57	19 04			
Clapham Junction	d	18 39		18 37	18 38		18 45				18 50							18 51	18 57		19 01	19 08		19 10	
Imperial Wharf	d	18 44																							
West Brompton	d	18 47																							
Kensington (Olympia)	d	18 50																							
Shepherd's Bush	d	18 53																							
Wembley Central	d	19 08																							
Harrow & Wealdstone	d	19 13																							
Watford Junction	d	19a21																							
Milton Keynes Central	a																								
Battersea Park	d				18 41	18 45	18 48				18 53										19 05	19 11			19 15
London Victoria	a			18 44	18 46		18 53				18 58							18 58	19 04		19 09	19 16		19 16	
Streatham	d														18 40	18 46									
Tulse Hill	d													18 39	18 47	18 54									
Herne Hill	a																								
Loughborough Jn.	a																								
Elephant & Castle	a																								
London Blackfriars	a																								
City Thameslink	a																								
St Pancras International	a																								
Luton Airport Parkway	a																								
Luton	a																								
North Dulwich	d													18 42		18 57									
East Dulwich	d													18 44		18 59									
Peckham Rye	d					18 56								18 46		19 01									19 26
Queens Rd Peckham	d					18 59								18 49		19 04									19 29
South Bermondsey	d					19 01								18 51		19 06									19 31
London Bridge	a		18 41			19 06		18 39		18 43		18 59	18 55	18 56	19 00	19 11							19 11		19 36

		SN	SN	LO	SN 1	SN	SN	SN 1		SN	FC	SN	SN ◇1	SN	LO	SN	SN 1	SN	SN 1	SN	SN ◇1	SN	SN	SN
East Croydon	d		18 51		18 55		19 00	19 07					19 12				19 10		19 25	19 17	19 29			19 21
West Croydon	d	18 45		18 52		18 58						19 01		19 04	19 09								19 15	
Norwood Junction	a	18 49	18 55	18 58	18 59		19 04	19 12							19 13								19 19	19 25
	d	18 52	18 55		18 59		19 05	19 13															19 22	19 25
Selhurst	d					19 02						19 05		19 09			19 13			19 20				
Thornton Heath	d					19 04						19 07		19 11			19 16			19 22				
Norbury	d					19 07						19 10		19 14			19 19			19 25				
Streatham Common	d					19 10						19 13		19 17			19 21			19 28				
Beckenham Junction	d									18 53														
Birkbeck	d									18 56														
Crystal Palace	d	18 56								19 00						19 13		19 21					19 26	
Gipsy Hill	d	18 59								19 02						19 15							19 29	
West Norwood	d	19 02								19 05						19 18							19 32	
Streatham Hill	d	19 05														19 22							19 35	
Balham	d	19 09				19 14								19 21		19 25	19 28			19 32			19 39	
Wandsworth Common	d	19 11				19 16								19 23		19 27	19 30			19 34			19 41	
Clapham Junction	d	19 15				19 20							19 21	19 27		19 31	19 38		19 37	19 38	19 40		19 45	
Imperial Wharf	d																19 42							
West Brompton	d																19 45							
Kensington (Olympia)	d																19 48							
Shepherd's Bush	d																19 50							
Wembley Central	d																							
Harrow & Wealdstone	d																20 08							
Watford Junction	d																20a15							
Milton Keynes Central	a																							
Battersea Park	d	19 18				19 23										19 35				19 41		19 45	19 48	
London Victoria	a	19 23				19 28							19 28	19 34		19 39			19 44	19 46	19 50		19 53	
Streatham	d										19 10	19 16												
Tulse Hill	d									19 09	19 17	19 24												
Herne Hill	a																							
Loughborough Jn.	a																							
Elephant & Castle	a																							
London Blackfriars	a																							
City Thameslink	a																							
St Pancras International	a																							
Luton Airport Parkway	a																							
Luton	a																							
North Dulwich	d									19 12		19 27												
East Dulwich	d									19 14		19 29												
Peckham Rye	d									19 16		19 31										19 56		
Queens Rd Peckham	d									19 19		19 34										19 59		
South Bermondsey	d									19 21		19 36										20 01		
London Bridge	a		19 09		19 13		19 29	19 25		19 26	19 30	19 41						19 41				20 06		19 39

Table 177

Saturdays

East and West Croydon, London Milton Keynes Central and Luton via Norbury Crystal Palace - Tulse Hill

Local Services

		LO	SN	SN	SN	FC	SN	SN ◇1	SN	LO	SN	SN	SN 1	SN	SN 1	SN		SN	SN	LO	SN	SN	SN	FC	SN
East Croydon	d				19 30			19 42					19 57	19 47	20 00				19 51				20 00		
West Croydon	d	19 22		19 28			19 31		19 34	19 39								19 45		19 52		19 58			20 01
Norwood Junction	a	19 28			19 34					19 43								19 49	19 55	19 58			20 04		
	d				19 35													19 52	19 55				20 05		
Selhurst	d			19 32			19 35		19 39					19 50								20 02			20 05
Thornton Heath	d			19 34			19 37		19 41					19 52								20 04			20 07
Norbury	d			19 37			19 40		19 44					19 55								20 07			20 10
Streatham Common	d			19 40			19 43		19 47					19 58								20 10			20 13
Beckenham Junction	d		19 23																		19 53				
Birkbeck	d		19 26																		19 56				
Crystal Palace	d		19 30								19 43	19 51						19 56			20 00				
Gipsy Hill	d		19 32								19 45							19 59			20 03				
West Norwood	d		19 35								19 48							20 02			20 06				
Streatham Hill	d										19 52							20 05							
Balham	d			19 44					19 51		19 55			20 02				20 09				20 14			
Wandsworth Common	d			19 46					19 53		19 57			20 04				20 11				20 16			
Clapham Junction	d			19 50				19 51	19 57		20 01		20 09	20 08	20 12			20 15				20 20			
Imperial Wharf	d																								
West Brompton	d																								
Kensington (Olympia)	d																								
Shepherd's Bush	d																								
Wembley Central	d																								
Harrow & Wealdstone	d																								
Watford Junction	d																								
Milton Keynes Central	a																								
Battersea Park	d			19 53							20 05			20 11		20 15		20 18				20 23			
London Victoria	a			19 58				19 58	20 04		20 09		20 15	20 16	20 20			20 23				20 28			
Streatham	d					19 40	19 46																	20 10	20 16
Tulse Hill	d		19 39			19 47	19 54														20 09			20 17	20 24
Herne Hill	a																								
Loughborough Jn	a																								
Elephant & Castle	a																								
London Blackfriars	a																								
City Thameslink	a																								
St Pancras International	a																								
Luton Airport Parkway	a																								
Luton	a																								
North Dulwich	d		19 42				19 57														20 12				20 27
East Dulwich	d		19 44				19 59														20 14				20 29
Peckham Rye	d		19 46				20 01									20 26					20 16				20 31
Queens Rd Peckham	d		19 49				20 04									20 29					20 19				20 34
South Bermondsey	d		19 51				20 06									20 31					20 21				20 36
London Bridge	a		19 56		19 59	20 00	20 11					20 11				20 36			20 09		20 26		20 29	20 30	20 41

		SN ◇1	SN	LO	SN	SN	SN 1	SN		SN ◇1	SN	SN	SN	LO	SN	SN	SN	FC	SN	SN ◇1	SN	LO	SN	SN	
East Croydon	d	20 12					20 26	20 17		20 30			20 21				20 30			20 42					
West Croydon	d		20 04	20 09								20 15		20 22		20 28			20 31		20 34	20 39			
Norwood Junction	a			20 13								20 19	20 25	20 28			20 34					20 43			
	d											20 22	20 25				20 35								
Selhurst	d		20 09					20 20								20 32			20 35		20 39				
Thornton Heath	d		20 11					20 22								20 34			20 37		20 41				
Norbury	d		20 14					20 25								20 37			20 40		20 44				
Streatham Common	d		20 17					20 28								20 40			20 43		20 47				
Beckenham Junction	d														20 23										
Birkbeck	d														20 26										
Crystal Palace	d				20 13	20 21						20 26			20 30								20 43	20 51	
Gipsy Hill	d				20 15							20 29			20 33								20 45		
West Norwood	d				20 18							20 32			20 36								20 48		
Streatham Hill	d				20 22							20 35											20 52		
Balham	d		20 21		20 25			20 32				20 39				20 44					20 51		20 55		
Wandsworth Common	d		20 23		20 27			20 34				20 41				20 46					20 53		20 57		
Clapham Junction	d	20 21	20 27		20 31		20 37	20 38		20 41		20 45				20 50				20 51	20 57		21 01		
Imperial Wharf	d																								
West Brompton	d																								
Kensington (Olympia)	d																								
Shepherd's Bush	d																								
Wembley Central	d																								
Harrow & Wealdstone	d																								
Watford Junction	d																								
Milton Keynes Central	a																								
Battersea Park	d				20 35			20 41			20 45	20 48				20 53							21 05		
London Victoria	a	20 28	20 34		20 39		20 44	20 46		20 50		20 53				20 58				20 58	21 04		21 09		
Streatham	d																	20 40	20 46						
Tulse Hill	d														20 39			20 47	20 54						
Herne Hill	a																								
Loughborough Jn	a																								
Elephant & Castle	a																								
London Blackfriars	a																								
City Thameslink	a																								
St Pancras International	a																								
Luton Airport Parkway	a																								
Luton	a																								
North Dulwich	d														20 42				20 57						
East Dulwich	d														20 44				20 59						
Peckham Rye	d										20 56				20 46				21 01						
Queens Rd Peckham	d										20 59				20 49				21 04						
South Bermondsey	d										21 01				20 51				21 06						
London Bridge	a					20 41					21 06		20 39		20 56		20 59	21 00	21 11					21 13	

Table 177

Saturdays

East and West Croydon, London Milton Keynes Central and Luton via Norbury Crystal Palace - Tulse Hill

Local Services

		SN 1	SN	SN	SN	SN	LO	SN	SN	SN ◇1	SN	FC	SN	SN	LO	SN		SN	SN 1	SN	SN ◇1	SN	SN	SN	LO
East Croydon	d	20 56	20 47			20 51			21 00	21 09									21 26	21 17	21 30			21 21	
West Croydon	d				20 45		20 52				20 58		21 02	21 04	21 09								21 15		21 22
Norwood Junction	a				20 49	20 55	20 58		21 04						21 13								21 19	21 25	21 28
	d				20 52	20 55			21 05														21 22	21 25	
Selhurst	d		20 50								21 02		21 06	21 09						21 20					
Thornton Heath	d		20 52								21 04		21 08	21 11						21 22					
Norbury	d		20 55								21 07		21 11	21 14						21 25					
Streatham Common	d		20 58								21 10		21 14	21 17						21 28					
Beckenham Junction	d							20 53																	
Birkbeck	d							20 56																	
Crystal Palace	d				20 56			21 00								21 13		21 21					21 26		
Gipsy Hill	d				20 59			21 02								21 15							21 29		
West Norwood	d				21 02			21 05								21 18							21 32		
Streatham Hill	d				21 05											21 22							21 35		
Balham	d		21 02		21 09						21 14			21 21		21 25				21 32			21 39		
Wandsworth Common	d		21 04		21 11						21 16			21 23		21 27				21 34			21 41		
Clapham Junction	d	21 07	21 08		21 15					21 18	21 20			21 27		21 31			21 37	21 38	21 41		21 45		
Imperial Wharf	d																								
West Brompton	d																								
Kensington (Olympia)	d																								
Shepherd's Bush	d																								
Wembley Central	d																								
Harrow & Wealdstone	d																								
Watford Junction	d																								
Milton Keynes Central	a																								
Battersea Park	d		21 11	21 15	21 18						21 23					21 35				21 41		21 45	21 48		
London Victoria	a	21 14	21 16		21 23					21 26	21 28			21 34		21 39			21 44	21 46	21 50		21 53		
Streatham	d											21 10	21 17												
Tulse Hill	d							21 09				21 17	21 24												
Herne Hill	a																								
Loughborough Jn	a																								
Elephant & Castle	a																								
London Blackfriars	a																								
City Thameslink	a																								
St Pancras International	a																								
Luton Airport Parkway	a																								
Luton	a																								
North Dulwich	d							21 12					21 27												
East Dulwich	d							21 14					21 29												
Peckham Rye	d			21 26				21 16					21 31									21 56			
Queens Rd Peckham	d			21 29				21 19					21 34									21 59			
South Bermondsey	d			21 31				21 21					21 36									22 01			
London Bridge	a			21 36		21 09		21 26	21 29			21 30	21 41					21 43				22 06		21 39	

		SN	SN	SN	FC	SN	SN ◇1	SN		LO	SN	SN	SN 1	SN	SN	SN	SN	LO	SN	SN	SN ◇1	SN	FC	SN	
East Croydon	d			21 30			21 42						21 56	21 47			21 51			22 00	22 09				
West Croydon	d		21 28			21 31		21 34		21 39						21 45		21 52				21 58		22 01	
Norwood Junction	a			21 34						21 43						21 49	21 55	21 58		22 04					
	d			21 35												21 52	21 55			22 05					
Selhurst	d		21 32			21 35		21 39						21 50								22 02		22 05	
Thornton Heath	d		21 34			21 37		21 41						21 52								22 04		22 07	
Norbury	d		21 37			21 40		21 44						21 55								22 07		22 10	
Streatham Common	d		21 40			21 43		21 47						21 58								22 10		22 13	
Beckenham Junction	d	21 23																	21 53						
Birkbeck	d	21 26																	21 56						
Crystal Palace	d	21 30									21 43	21 51				21 56			22 00						
Gipsy Hill	d	21 32									21 45					21 59			22 02						
West Norwood	d	21 35									21 48					22 02			22 05						
Streatham Hill	d										21 52					22 05									
Balham	d		21 44					21 51			21 55			22 02		22 09						22 14			
Wandsworth Common	d		21 46					21 53			21 57			22 04		22 11						22 16			
Clapham Junction	d		21 50				21 52	21 57			22 01		22 07	22 08		22 15					22 18	22 20			
Imperial Wharf	d																								
West Brompton	d																								
Kensington (Olympia)	d																								
Shepherd's Bush	d																								
Wembley Central	d																								
Harrow & Wealdstone	d																								
Watford Junction	d																								
Milton Keynes Central	a																								
Battersea Park	d		21 53								22 05			22 11	22 15	22 18						22 23			
London Victoria	a		21 58				21 58	22 04			22 09		22 15	22 16		22 23					22 26	22 28			
Streatham	d				21 40	21 46																	22 10	22 16	
Tulse Hill	d	21 39			21 47	21 54													22 09				22 17	22 24	
Herne Hill	a																								
Loughborough Jn	a																								
Elephant & Castle	a																								
London Blackfriars	a																								
City Thameslink	a																								
St Pancras International	a																								
Luton Airport Parkway	a																								
Luton	a																								
North Dulwich	d	21 42				21 57													22 12					22 27	
East Dulwich	d	21 44				21 59													22 14					22 29	
Peckham Rye	d	21 46				22 01									22 26				22 16					22 31	
Queens Rd Peckham	d	21 49				22 04									22 29				22 19					22 34	
South Bermondsey	d	21 51				22 06									22 31				22 21					[illegible]	
London Bridge	a	21 56		21 59	22 00	22 11						22 13			[illegible]		[illegible]								

East and West Croydon, London
Milton Keynes Central and Luton via Norbury
Crystal Palace - Tulse Hill

Local Services

		SN	LO	SN	SN	SN ■1	SN	SN ◇■1	SN	SN	SN	LO	SN	SN	SN ◇■1	SN		FC	SN	SN	LO	SN	SN	SN ■1	SN
East Croydon 🚊	d					22 26	22 17	22 30			22 21			22 30	22 40									22 56	22 47
West Croydon [4] 🚊	d	22 04	22 09							22 15		22 22				22 28			22 31	22 34	22 39				
Norwood Junction [2]	a		22 13							22 19	22 25	22 28		22 34							22 43				
	d									22 22	22 25			22 35											
Selhurst [4]	d	22 10					22 20									22 32			22 35	22 39					22 50
Thornton Heath	d	22 12					22 22									22 34			22 37	22 41					22 52
Norbury	d	22 15					22 25									22 37			22 40	22 44					22 55
Streatham Common [4]	d	22 17					22 28									22 40			22 43	22 47					22 58
Beckenham Junction [4] 🚊	d												22 23												
Birkbeck 🚊	d												22 26												
Crystal Palace [4]	d			22 13	22 21					22 26			22 30									22 43	22 51		
Gipsy Hill	d			22 15						22 29			22 32									22 45			
West Norwood [4]	d			22 18						22 32			22 35									22 48			
Streatham Hill	d			22 22						22 35												22 52			
Balham [4] ⊖	d	22 22		22 25			22 32			22 39						22 44				22 51		22 55			23 02
Wandsworth Common	d	22 24		22 27			22 34			22 41						22 46				22 53		22 57			23 04
Clapham Junction [10]	d	22 27		22 31		22 37	22 38	22 41		22 45					22 50	22 50				22 57		23 01		23 07	23 08
Imperial Wharf	d																								
West Brompton ⊖	d																								
Kensington (Olympia) ⊖	d																								
Shepherd's Bush ⊖	d																								
Wembley Central ⊖	d																								
Harrow & Wealdstone ⊖	d																								
Watford Junction	d																								
Milton Keynes Central [10]	a																								
Battersea Park [4]	d			22 35			22 41		22 45	22 48						22 53						23 05			23 11
London Victoria [15] ⊖	a	22 34		22 39		22 44	22 46	22 50		22 53					22 57	22 58				23 04		23 09		23 14	23 16
Streatham [4]	d																	22 40	22 46						
Tulse Hill [3]	d												22 39					22 47	22 54						
Herne Hill [4]	a																								
Loughborough Jn.	a																								
Elephant & Castle ⊖	a																								
London Blackfriars [3] ⊖	a																								
City Thameslink [3]	a																								
St Pancras International [15] ⊖	a																								
Luton Airport Parkway [7]	a																								
Luton [10]	a																								
North Dulwich	d												22 42						22 57						
East Dulwich	d												22 44						22 59						
Peckham Rye [4]	d								22 56				22 46						23 01						
Queens Rd Peckham	d								22 59				22 49						23 04						
South Bermondsey	d								23 01				22 51						23 06						
London Bridge [4] ⊖	a				22 43				23 06		22 39		22 56	22 59				23 00	23 11				23 13		

		SN	SN	SN	LO	SN	SN	SN		SN	SN	SN	SN	SN	SN ◇■1	SN	SN	LO	SN	SN	SN	SN	SN	SN	
East Croydon 🚊	d			22 51				23 01					23 17		23 30		23 21					23 43			
West Croydon [4] 🚊	d		22 45		22 52		22 58			23 01	23 04					23 15		23 22		23 28	23 34				
Norwood Junction [2]	a		22 49	22 55	22 58			23 05								23 19	23 25	23 28				23 47			
	d		22 52	22 55				23 06								23 22	23 25								
Selhurst [4]	d						23 02			23 05	23 09		23 20							23 32	23 39				
Thornton Heath	d						23 04			23 07	23 11		23 22							23 34	23 41				
Norbury	d						23 07			23 10	23 14		23 25							23 37	23 44				
Streatham Common [4]	d						23 10			23 13	23 17		23 28							23 40	23 46				
Beckenham Junction [4] 🚊	d					22 53													23 23						
Birkbeck 🚊	d					22 56													23 26						
Crystal Palace [4]	d		22 56			23 00						23 13		23 21		23 26			23 30				23 43	23 51	
Gipsy Hill	d		22 59			23 02						23 15				23 29			23 32				23 45		
West Norwood [4]	d		23 02			23 05						23 18				23 32			23 35				23 48		
Streatham Hill	d		23 05									23 22				23 35							23 52		
Balham [4] ⊖	d		23 09				23 14				23 21	23 25	23 32			23 39				23 44	23 50		23 55		
Wandsworth Common	d		23 11				23 16				23 23	23 27	23 34			23 41				23 46	23 52		23 57		
Clapham Junction [10]	d		23 15				23 20				23 27	23 31	23 38		23 42	23 45				23 50	23 56		00 02		
Imperial Wharf	d																								
West Brompton ⊖	d																								
Kensington (Olympia) ⊖	d																								
Shepherd's Bush ⊖	d																								
Wembley Central ⊖	d																								
Harrow & Wealdstone ⊖	d																								
Watford Junction	d																								
Milton Keynes Central [10]	a																								
Battersea Park [4]	d	23 15	23 18				23 23					23 35	23 41			23 49				23 53			00 05		
London Victoria [15] ⊖	a		23 24				23 29				23 34	23 41	23 48		23 52	23 53				23 58	00 04		00 10		
Streatham [4]	d									23 19															
Tulse Hill [3]	d					23 09				23 24									23 39						
Herne Hill [4]	a																								
Loughborough Jn.	a																								
Elephant & Castle ⊖	a																								
London Blackfriars [3] ⊖	a																								
City Thameslink [3]	a																								
St Pancras International [15] ⊖	a																								
Luton Airport Parkway [7]	a																								
Luton [10]	a																								
North Dulwich	d					23 12				23 27									23 42						
East Dulwich	d					23 14				23 29									23 44						
Peckham Rye [4]	d	23 26				23 16				23 31									23 46						
Queens Rd Peckham	d	23 29				23 19				23 34									23 49						
South Bermondsey	d	23 31				23 21				23 36									23 51						
London Bridge [4] ⊖	a	23 36		23 09		23 26		23 30		23 41				23 43			23 39		23 56					00 11	

East and West Croydon, London
Milton Keynes Central and Luton via Norbury
Crystal Palace - Tulse Hill

Local Services

		SN ■1
East Croydon 🚊	d	23 56
West Croydon [4] 🚊	d	
Norwood Junction [2]	a	
	d	
Selhurst [4]	d	00 02
Thornton Heath	d	
Norbury	d	
Streatham Common [4]	d	
Beckenham Junction [4] 🚊	d	
Birkbeck 🚊	d	
Crystal Palace [4]	d	
Gipsy Hill	d	
West Norwood [4]	d	
Streatham Hill	d	
Balham [4] ⊖	d	
Wandsworth Common	d	
Clapham Junction [10]	d	00 11
Imperial Wharf	d	
West Brompton ⊖	d	
Kensington (Olympia) ⊖	d	
Shepherd's Bush ⊖	d	
Wembley Central ⊖	d	
Harrow & Wealdstone ⊖	d	
Watford Junction	d	
Milton Keynes Central [10]	a	
Battersea Park [4]	d	
London Victoria [15] ⊖	a	00 18
Streatham [4]	d	
Tulse Hill [3]	d	
Herne Hill [4]	a	
Loughborough Jn.	a	
Elephant & Castle ⊖	a	
London Blackfriars [3] ⊖	a	
City Thameslink [3]	a	
St Pancras International [15] ⊖	a	
Luton Airport Parkway [7]	a	
Luton [10]	a	
North Dulwich	d	
East Dulwich	d	
Peckham Rye [4]	d	
Queens Rd Peckham	d	
South Bermondsey	d	
London Bridge [4] ⊖	a	

Table 177

Sundays until 4 September

East and West Croydon, London Milton Keynes Central and Luton via Norbury Crystal Palace - Tulse Hill

Local Services

		SN	SN	SN	SN	SN	SN	SN	SN	SN	SN	SN	FC	SN	SN	LO	SN	SN	SN	SN	SN	SN	LO	SN
					1				1	1	1	1	1	1										
		A	A	A	A	A	A																	
East Croydon ⇌	d				23p56			00 49	01 43	02 40	03 40	04 40	05 32	06 02	06 40		06 47					07 12		07 17
West Croydon 4 ⇌	d	23p34														06 42				07 07			07 12	
Norwood Junction 2	a												05 36			06 47	06 51						07 17	07 21
	d												05 36				06 52		06 57					07 22
Selhurst 4	d	23p39			00 02			00 53	01 45	02 42	03 42	04 42		06 05	06 43			06 47		07 11		07 15		
Thornton Heath	d	23p41													06 45			06 49		07 13		07 17		
Norbury	d	23p44													06 48			06 52		07 16		07 20		
Streatham Common 4	d	23p46													06 51			06 55		07 19		07 23		
Beckenham Junction 4 ⇌	d																							
Birkbeck ⇌	d																							
Crystal Palace 4	d		23p43	23p51		00 13	00 21												07 01		07 07			
Gipsy Hill	d		23p45			00 15													07 03		07 09			
West Norwood 4	d		23p48			00 18													07 06		07 12			
Streatham Hill	d		23p52			00 22													07 10					
Balham 4 ⊖	d	23p50	23p55			00 26									06 55				07 13	07 23				
Wandsworth Common	d	23p52	23p57			00 28									06 57				07 15					
Clapham Junction 10	d	23p56	00 02		00 11	00 32		01 03	01 54	02 53	03 53	04 53		06 14	07 00				07 19	07 27				
Imperial Wharf	d																							
West Brompton ⊖	d																							
Kensington (Olympia) ⊖	d																							
Shepherd's Bush ⊖	d																							
Wembley Central ⊖	d																							
Harrow & Wealdstone ⊖	d																							
Watford Junction	d																							
Milton Keynes Central 10	a																							
Battersea Park 4	d		00 05			00 35									07 04				07 23					
London Victoria 15 ⊖	a	00 04	00 10		00 18	00 42		01 10	02 05	03 05	04 05	05 05		06 22	07 09				07 27	07 34				
Streatham 4	d																	06 58				07 28		
Tulse Hill 3	d																	07 02			07 16	07 32		
Herne Hill 4	a																							
Loughborough Jn.	a																							
Elephant & Castle ⊖	a																							
London Blackfriars 3 ⊖	a																							
City Thameslink 3	a																							
St Pancras International 15 ⊖	a																							
Luton Airport Parkway 7	a																							
Luton 10	a																							
North Dulwich	d																	07 05			07 19	07 35		
East Dulwich	d																	07 07			07 21	07 37		
Peckham Rye 4	d																	07 09			07 23	07 39		
Queens Rd Peckham	d																	07 12			07 26	07 42		
South Bermondsey	d																	07 14			07 28	07 44		
London Bridge 4 ⊖	a			00 11			00 41						05 59				07 17	07 19			07 33	07 49		07 48

A not 22 May

Table 177

Sundays until 4 September

East and West Croydon, London Milton Keynes Central and Luton via Norbury Crystal Palace - Tulse Hill

Local Services

		SN	SN	SN	SN	SN	SN	SN	LO	SN	SN	SN	SN	SN	SN	SN	SN	SN	SN	LO	SN	SN	SN
		1										◇1 ⚲			1							◇1	
East Croydon ⇌	d	07 27						07 42		07 47	07 53	08 09			07 56				08 12		08 17	08 20	08 23
West Croydon 4 ⇌	d			07 22	07 34	07 37			07 42					07 52		08 04	08 07			08 12			
Norwood Junction 2	a			07 26	07 39				07 47	07 51				07 56	08 00	08 09				08 17	08 21		
	d			07 27	07 40					07 52				07 57	08 01	08 10					08 22		
Selhurst 4	d	07 31				07 41		07 46			07 57						08 11		08 16				08 26
Thornton Heath	d					07 43		07 48			07 59						08 13		08 18				08 28
Norbury	d					07 46		07 51			08 02						08 16		08 21				08 31
Streatham Common 4	d					07 49		07 53			08 04						08 19		08 23				08 34
Beckenham Junction 4 ⇌	d																						
Birkbeck ⇌	d																						
Crystal Palace 4	d			07 31			07 37							08 01				08 07					
Gipsy Hill	d			07 33			07 39							08 03				08 09					
West Norwood 4	d			07 36			07 42							08 06				08 12					
Streatham Hill	d			07 40										08 10									
Balham 4 ⊖	d			07 43		07 53					08 08			08 13			08 23						08 38
Wandsworth Common	d			07 45										08 15									
Clapham Junction 10	d	07 41		07 49		07 57					08 13	08 19		08 19			08 27					08 32	08 42
Imperial Wharf	d																						
West Brompton ⊖	d																						
Kensington (Olympia) ⊖	d																						
Shepherd's Bush ⊖	d																						
Wembley Central ⊖	d																						
Harrow & Wealdstone ⊖	d																						
Watford Junction	d																						
Milton Keynes Central 10	a																						
Battersea Park 4	d		07 45	07 53									08 15	08 23									
London Victoria 15 ⊖	a	07 48		07 57		08 04					08 20	08 25		08 27			08 34					08 39	08 50
Streatham 4	d							07 58											08 28				
Tulse Hill 3	d						07 46	08 02										08 16	08 32				
Herne Hill 4	a																						
Loughborough Jn.	a																						
Elephant & Castle ⊖	a																						
London Blackfriars 3 ⊖	a																						
City Thameslink 3	a																						
St Pancras International 15 ⊖	a																						
Luton Airport Parkway 7	a																						
Luton 10	a																						
North Dulwich	d						07 49	08 05										08 19	08 35				
East Dulwich	d						07 51	08 07										08 21	08 37				
Peckham Rye 4	d		07 56				07 53	08 10					08 26					08 23	08 40				
Queens Rd Peckham	d		07 59				07 56	08 12					08 29					08 26	08 42				
South Bermondsey	d		08 01				07 58	08 15					08 31					08 28	08 45				
London Bridge 4 ⊖	a		08 06		08 01		08 03	08 19		08 17			08 36		08 13	08 31		08 33	08 49		08 48		

		SN	SN	SN	SN	SN	SN	SN	SN	LO	SN	SN	SN	SN	SN	SN	SN	SN	SN	SN	LO	SN	SN	SN
		◇1			1								◇1 ⚲			1							◇1	
East Croydon ⇌	d	08 39			08 34				08 42		08 47	08 53	09 09			08 56				09 12		09 17	09 20	09 23
West Croydon 4 ⇌	d			08 22		08 34	08 37			08 42					08 52		09 04	09 07			09 12			
Norwood Junction 2	a			08 26	08 38	08 39				08 47	08 51				08 56	09 00	09 09				09 17	09 21		
	d			08 27	08 38	08 40					08 52				08 57	09 01	09 10					09 22		
Selhurst 4	d						08 41		08 46			08 57						09 11		09 16				09 26
Thornton Heath	d						08 43		08 48			08 59						09 13		09 18				09 28
Norbury	d						08 46		08 51			09 02						09 16		09 21				09 31
Streatham Common 4	d						08 49		08 53			09 04						09 19		09 23				09 34
Beckenham Junction 4 ⇌	d																							
Birkbeck ⇌	d																							
Crystal Palace 4	d			08 31				08 37							09 01				09 07					
Gipsy Hill	d			08 33				08 39							09 03				09 09					
West Norwood 4	d			08 36				08 42							09 06				09 12					
Streatham Hill	d			08 40											09 10									
Balham 4 ⊖	d			08 43			08 53					09 08			09 13			09 23						09 38
Wandsworth Common	d			08 45											09 15									
Clapham Junction 10	d	08 49		08 49			08 57					09 13	09 19		09 19			09 27					09 32	09 42
Imperial Wharf	d																							
West Brompton ⊖	d																							
Kensington (Olympia) ⊖	d																							
Shepherd's Bush ⊖	d																							
Wembley Central ⊖	d																							
Harrow & Wealdstone ⊖	d																							
Watford Junction	d																							
Milton Keynes Central 10	a																							
Battersea Park 4	d		08 45	08 52										09 15	09 23									
London Victoria 15 ⊖	a	08 55		08 57			09 04					09 20	09 25		09 27			09 34					09 39	09 50
Streatham 4	d								08 58											09 28				
Tulse Hill 3	d							08 46	09 02										09 16	09 32				
Herne Hill 4	a																							
Loughborough Jn.	a																							
Elephant & Castle ⊖	a																							
London Blackfriars 3 ⊖	a																							
City Thameslink 3	a																							
St Pancras International 15 ⊖	a																							
Luton Airport Parkway 7	a																							
Luton 10	a																							
North Dulwich	d							08 49	09 05										09 19	09 35				
East Dulwich	d							08 51	09 07										09 21	09 37				
Peckham Rye 4	d		08 56					08 53	09 10					09 26					09 23	09 40				
Queens Rd Peckham	d		08 59					08 56	09 12					09 29					09 26	09 42				
South Bermondsey	d		09 01					08 58	09 15					09 31					09 28	09 45				
London Bridge 4 ⊖	a		09 06		08 51	09 01		09 03	09 19		09 18			[illegible]		[illegible]	[illegible]							

Table 177

Sundays until 4 September

East and West Croydon, London Milton Keynes Central and Luton via Norbury Crystal Palace - Tulse Hill

Local Services

		SN	SN	SN	SN	SN	SN	SN		SN	LO	SN	SN	SN	SN	SN	SN	SN	SN	SN	SN	LO	SN	SN
		◇1			1									◇1 H			1							◇1
East Croydon	d	09 39			09 34					09 42		09 47	09 53	10 09			09 56				10 12		10 17	10 20
West Croydon 4	d			09 22		09 34	09 37				09 42					09 52		10 04	10 07			10 12		
Norwood Junction 2	a			09 26	09 38	09 39					09 47	09 51				09 56	10 00	10 09				10 17	10 21	
	d			09 27	09 38	09 40						09 52				09 57	10 01	10 10					10 22	
Selhurst 4	d						09 41			09 46			09 57						10 11		10 16			
Thornton Heath	d						09 43			09 48			09 59						10 13		10 18			
Norbury	d						09 46			09 51			10 02						10 16		10 21			
Streatham Common 4	d						09 49			09 53			10 04						10 19		10 23			
Beckenham Junction 4	d																							
Birkbeck	d																							
Crystal Palace 4	d			09 31				09 37								10 01				10 07				
Gipsy Hill	d			09 33				09 39								10 03				10 09				
West Norwood 4	d			09 36				09 42								10 06				10 12				
Streatham Hill	d			09 40												10 10								
Balham 4 ⊖	d			09 43			09 53						10 08			10 13			10 23					
Wandsworth Common	d			09 45												10 15								
Clapham Junction 10	d	09 49		09 49			09 57						10 13	10 19		10 19			10 27					10 32
Imperial Wharf	d																							
West Brompton ⊖	d																							
Kensington (Olympia) ⊖	d																							
Shepherd's Bush ⊖	d																							
Wembley Central ⊖	d																							
Harrow & Wealdstone ⊖	d																							
Watford Junction	d																							
Milton Keynes Central 10	a																							
Battersea Park 4	d		09 45	09 53											10 15	10 22								
London Victoria 15 ⊖	a	09 55		09 57			10 04						10 20	10 25		10 27			10 34					10 39
Streatham 4	d									09 58											10 28			
Tulse Hill 3	d							09 46		10 02										10 16	10 32			
Herne Hill 4	a																							
Loughborough Jn	a																							
Elephant & Castle ⊖	a																							
London Blackfriars 3 ⊖	a																							
City Thameslink 3	a																							
St Pancras International 15 ⊖	a																							
Luton Airport Parkway 7	a																							
Luton 10	a																							
North Dulwich	d							09 49		10 05										10 19	10 35			
East Dulwich	d							09 51		10 07										10 21	10 37			
Peckham Rye 4	d		09 56					09 53		10 10					10 26					10 23	10 40			
Queens Rd Peckham	d		09 59					09 56		10 12					10 29					10 26	10 42			
South Bermondsey	d		10 01					09 58		10 15					10 31					10 28	10 45			
London Bridge 4 ⊖	a		10 06		09 51	10 01		10 03		10 19		10 18			10 36		10 13	10 31		10 33	10 49		10 48	

		SN	SN	SN	SN	SN	SN	SN	SN	LO	FC	SN	SN	SN	SN	SN		SN	SN	SN	SN	SN	LO	FC	SN
			◇1			1									◇1 H				1						
East Croydon	d	10 23	10 39			10 34						10 42	10 47	10 53	11 09				10 56						11 12
West Croydon 4	d				10 22		10 34	10 37		10 42								10 52		11 04	11 07		11 12		
Norwood Junction 2	a				10 26	10 38	10 39			10 47			10 51					10 56	11 00	11 09			11 17		
	d				10 27	10 38	10 40						10 52					10 57	11 01	11 10					
Selhurst 4	d	10 26						10 41				10 46		10 57							11 11				11 16
Thornton Heath	d	10 28						10 43				10 48		10 59							11 13				11 18
Norbury	d	10 31						10 46				10 51		11 02							11 16				11 21
Streatham Common 4	d	10 34						10 49				10 53		11 04							11 19				11 23
Beckenham Junction 4	d																								
Birkbeck	d																								
Crystal Palace 4	d				10 31				10 37									11 01				11 07			
Gipsy Hill	d				10 33				10 39									11 03				11 09			
West Norwood 4	d				10 36				10 42									11 06				11 12			
Streatham Hill	d				10 40													11 10							
Balham 4 ⊖	d	10 38			10 43			10 53						11 08				11 13			11 23				
Wandsworth Common	d				10 45													11 15							
Clapham Junction 10	d	10 42	10 49		10 49			10 57						11 13	11 19			11 19			11 27				
Imperial Wharf	d																								
West Brompton ⊖	d																								
Kensington (Olympia) ⊖	d																								
Shepherd's Bush ⊖	d																								
Wembley Central ⊖	d																								
Harrow & Wealdstone ⊖	d																								
Watford Junction	d																								
Milton Keynes Central 10	a																								
Battersea Park 4	d			10 45	10 52											11 15		11 22							
London Victoria 15 ⊖	a	10 50	10 55		10 57			11 04						11 20	11 25			11 27			11 34				
Streatham 4	d										10 55	10 58												11 25	11 28
Tulse Hill 3	d								10 46		10 59	11 02										11 16		11 29	11 32
Herne Hill 4	a																								
Loughborough Jn	a																								
Elephant & Castle ⊖	a																								
London Blackfriars 3 ⊖	a																								
City Thameslink 3	a																								
St Pancras International 15 ⊖	a																								
Luton Airport Parkway 7	a																								
Luton 10	a																								
North Dulwich	d								10 49			11 05										11 19			11 35
East Dulwich	d								10 51			11 07										11 21			11 37
Peckham Rye 4	d			10 56					10 53			11 10				11 26						11 23			11 40
Queens Rd Peckham	d			10 59					10 56			11 12				11 29						11 26			11 42
South Bermondsey	d			11 01					10 58			11 15				11 31						11 28			11 45
London Bridge 4 ⊖	a			11 06		10 51	11 01		11 03		11 10	11 19	11 18			11 36			11 13	11 31		11 33		11 40	11 49

Table 177

until 4 September

East and West Croydon, London Milton Keynes Central and Luton via Norbury Crystal Palace - Tulse Hill

Local Services

		SN	SN	SN	SN	SN	SN	SN		SN	SN	SN	LO	FC	SN	SN	SN	SN	SN	SN	SN	SN	SN	SN
			◇1 H		◇1			1										◇1 H			1			
East Croydon	d	11 17	11 20	11 23	11 39			11 34							11 42	11 47	11 53	12 09			11 56			
West Croydon 4	d						11 22			11 34	11 37		11 42							11 52		12 04	12 07	
Norwood Junction 2	a	11 21					11 26	11 38		11 39			11 47			11 51				11 56	12 00	12 09		
	d	11 22					11 27	11 38		11 40						11 52				11 57	12 01	12 10		
Selhurst 4	d			11 26							11 41				11 46		11 57						12 11	
Thornton Heath	d			11 28							11 43				11 48		11 59						12 13	
Norbury	d			11 31							11 46				11 51		12 02						12 16	
Streatham Common 4	d			11 34							11 49				11 53		12 04						12 19	
Beckenham Junction 4	d																							
Birkbeck	d																							
Crystal Palace 4	d						11 31					11 37								12 01				12 07
Gipsy Hill	d						11 33					11 39								12 03				12 09
West Norwood 4	d						11 36					11 42								12 06				12 12
Streatham Hill	d						11 40													12 10				
Balham 4 ⊖	d			11 38			11 43				11 53						12 08			12 13			12 23	
Wandsworth Common	d						11 45													12 15				
Clapham Junction 10	d		11 32	11 42	11 49		11 49				11 57						12 13	12 19		12 19			12 27	
Imperial Wharf	d																							
West Brompton ⊖	d																							
Kensington (Olympia) ⊖	d																							
Shepherd's Bush ⊖	d																							
Wembley Central ⊖	d																							
Harrow & Wealdstone ⊖	d																							
Watford Junction	d																							
Milton Keynes Central 10	a																							
Battersea Park 4	d					11 45	11 52												12 15	12 22				
London Victoria 15 ⊖	a		11 39	11 50	11 55		11 57				12 04						12 20	12 25		12 27			12 34	
Streatham 4	d													11 55	11 58									
Tulse Hill 3	d											11 46		11 59	12 02									12 16
Herne Hill 4	a																							
Loughborough Jn	a																							
Elephant & Castle ⊖	a																							
London Blackfriars 3 ⊖	a																							
City Thameslink 3	a																							
St Pancras International 15 ⊖	a																							
Luton Airport Parkway 7	a																							
Luton 10	a																							
North Dulwich	d											11 49			12 05									12 19
East Dulwich	d											11 51			12 07									12 21
Peckham Rye 4	d					11 56						11 53			12 10				12 26					12 23
Queens Rd Peckham	d					11 59						11 56			12 12				12 29					12 26
South Bermondsey	d					12 01						11 58			12 15				12 31					12 28
London Bridge 4 ⊖	a	11 48				12 06		11 51		12 01		12 03		12 10	12 19	12 18			12 36		12 13	12 31		12 33

		LO	FC	SN	SN	SN	SN	SN	SN	SN	SN	SN	SN	SN	LO	FC		SN	SN	SN	SN	SN	SN	SN	LO
						◇1 H		◇1			1										◇1 H			1	
East Croydon	d			12 12	12 17	12 20	12 23	12 39			12 34							12 42	12 47	12 53	13 09			12 56	
West Croydon 4	d	12 12								12 22		12 34	12 37		12 42								12 52		12 57
Norwood Junction 2	a	12 16			12 21					12 26	12 38	12 39			12 46				12 51				12 56	13 00	13 01
	d				12 22					12 27	12 38	12 40							12 52				12 57	13 01	
Selhurst 4	d			12 16			12 26						12 41					12 46		12 57					
Thornton Heath	d			12 18			12 28						12 43					12 48		12 59					
Norbury	d			12 21			12 31						12 46					12 51		13 02					
Streatham Common 4	d			12 23			12 34						12 49					12 53		13 04					
Beckenham Junction 4	d																								
Birkbeck	d																								
Crystal Palace 4	d									12 31				12 37									13 01		
Gipsy Hill	d									12 33				12 39									13 03		
West Norwood 4	d									12 36				12 42									13 06		
Streatham Hill	d									12 40													13 10		
Balham 4 ⊖	d						12 38			12 43			12 53							13 08			13 13		
Wandsworth Common	d									12 45													13 15		
Clapham Junction 10	d					12 32	12 42	12 49		12 49			12 57							13 13	13 19		13 19		
Imperial Wharf	d																								
West Brompton ⊖	d																								
Kensington (Olympia) ⊖	d																								
Shepherd's Bush ⊖	d																								
Wembley Central ⊖	d																								
Harrow & Wealdstone ⊖	d																								
Watford Junction	d																								
Milton Keynes Central 10	a																								
Battersea Park 4	d								12 45	12 52												13 15	13 23		
London Victoria 15 ⊖	a					12 39	12 50	12 55		12 57			13 04							13 20	13 25		13 27		
Streatham 4	d		12 25	12 28												12 55		12 58							
Tulse Hill 3	d		12 29	12 32										12 46		12 59		13 02							
Herne Hill 4	a																								
Loughborough Jn	a																								
Elephant & Castle ⊖	a																								
London Blackfriars 3 ⊖	a																								
City Thameslink 3	a																								
St Pancras International 15 ⊖	a																								
Luton Airport Parkway 7	a																								
Luton 10	a																								
North Dulwich	d			12 35										12 49				13 05							
East Dulwich	d			12 37										12 51				13 07							
Peckham Rye 4	d			12 40					12 56					12 53				13 10				13 26			
Queens Rd Peckham	d			12 42					12 59					12 56				13 12				13 29			
South Bermondsey	d			12 45					13 01					12 58				13 15				13 31			
London Bridge 4 ⊖	a		12 40	12 49	12 48				13 06		12 51	13 01		13 03		13 10		13 19	13 18			13 36		13 13	

East and West Croydon, London Milton Keynes Central and Luton via Norbury Crystal Palace - Tulse Hill

Local Services

		SN	SN	SN	LO	FC	SN	SN	SN ◇1 H	SN	SN ◇1	SN	SN	LO	SN 1	SN	SN	SN	LO	FC	SN	SN	SN
East Croydon	d						13 12	13 17	13 20	13 23	13 39				13 34						13 42	13 47	13 53
West Croydon 4	d	13 04	13 07		13 12								13 22	13 27		13 34	13 37		13 42				
Norwood Junction 2	a	13 09			13 16			13 21					13 26	13 31	13 38	13 39			13 46			13 51	
	d	13 10						13 22					13 27		13 38	13 40						13 52	
Selhurst 4	d		13 11				13 16			13 26							13 41				13 46		13 57
Thornton Heath	d		13 13				13 18			13 28							13 43				13 48		13 59
Norbury	d		13 16				13 21			13 31							13 46				13 51		14 02
Streatham Common 4	d		13 19				13 23			13 34							13 49				13 53		14 04
Beckenham Junction 4	d																						
Birkbeck	d																						
Crystal Palace 4	d			13 07									13 31					13 37					
Gipsy Hill	d			13 09									13 33					13 39					
West Norwood 4	d			13 12									13 36					13 42					
Streatham Hill	d												13 40										
Balham 4 ⊖	d		13 23							13 38			13 43				13 53						14 08
Wandsworth Common	d												13 45										
Clapham Junction 10	d		13 27						13 32	13 42	13 49		13 49				13 57						14 13
Imperial Wharf	d																						
West Brompton ⊖	d																						
Kensington (Olympia) ⊖	d																						
Shepherd's Bush ⊖	d																						
Wembley Central ⊖	d																						
Harrow & Wealdstone ⊖	d																						
Watford Junction	d																						
Milton Keynes Central 10	a																						
Battersea Park 4	d											13 45	13 52										
London Victoria 15 ⊖	a		13 34						13 39	13 50	13 55		13 57				14 04						14 20
Streatham 4	d					13 25	13 28													13 55	13 58		
Tulse Hill 3	d			13 16		13 29	13 32											13 46		13 59	14 02		
Herne Hill 4	a																						
Loughborough Jn	a																						
Elephant & Castle ⊖	a																						
London Blackfriars 3 ⊖	a																						
City Thameslink 3	a																						
St Pancras International 15 ⊖	a																						
Luton Airport Parkway 7	a																						
Luton 10	a																						
North Dulwich	d			13 19			13 35											13 49			14 05		
East Dulwich	d			13 21			13 37											13 51			14 07		
Peckham Rye 4	d			13 23			13 40					13 56						13 53			14 10		
Queens Rd Peckham	d			13 26			13 42					13 59						13 56			14 12		
South Bermondsey	d			13 28			13 45					14 01						13 58			14 15		
London Bridge 4 ⊖	a	13 31		13 33		13 40	13 49	13 48				14 06			13 51	14 01		14 03		14 10	14 19	14 18	

		SN ◇1 H	SN	SN	SN 1	LO	SN	SN	SN	LO	FC	SN	SN	SN ◇1 H	SN	SN ◇1	SN	SN	LO	SN 1	SN	SN	SN	LO
East Croydon	d	14 09			13 56							14 12	14 17	14 20	14 23	14 39				14 34				
West Croydon 4	d			13 52		13 57	14 04	14 07		14 12								14 22	14 27		14 34	14 37		14 42
Norwood Junction 2	a			13 56	14 00	14 01	14 09			14 16			14 21					14 26	14 31	14 38	14 39			14 46
	d			13 57	14 01		14 10						14 22					14 27		14 38	14 40			
Selhurst 4	d							14 11				14 16			14 26							14 41		
Thornton Heath	d							14 13				14 18			14 28							14 43		
Norbury	d							14 16				14 21			14 31							14 46		
Streatham Common 4	d							14 19				14 23			14 34							14 49		
Beckenham Junction 4	d																							
Birkbeck	d																							
Crystal Palace 4	d			14 01					14 07									14 31					14 37	
Gipsy Hill	d			14 03					14 09									14 33					14 39	
West Norwood 4	d			14 06					14 12									14 36					14 42	
Streatham Hill	d			14 10														14 40						
Balham 4 ⊖	d			14 13				14 23							14 38			14 43				14 53		
Wandsworth Common	d			14 15														14 45						
Clapham Junction 10	d	14 19		14 19				14 27						14 32	14 42	14 49		14 49				14 57		
Imperial Wharf	d																							
West Brompton ⊖	d																							
Kensington (Olympia) ⊖	d																							
Shepherd's Bush ⊖	d																							
Wembley Central ⊖	d																							
Harrow & Wealdstone ⊖	d																							
Watford Junction	d																							
Milton Keynes Central 10	a																							
Battersea Park 4	d		14 15	14 23													14 45	14 52						
London Victoria 15 ⊖	a	14 25		14 27				14 34						14 39	14 50	14 55		14 57				15 04		
Streatham 4	d										14 25	14 28												
Tulse Hill 3	d								14 16		14 29	14 32											14 46	
Herne Hill 4	a																							
Loughborough Jn	a																							
Elephant & Castle ⊖	a																							
London Blackfriars 3 ⊖	a																							
City Thameslink 3	a																							
St Pancras International 15 ⊖	a																							
Luton Airport Parkway 7	a																							
Luton 10	a																							
North Dulwich	d								14 19			14 35											14 49	
East Dulwich	d								14 21			14 37											14 51	
Peckham Rye 4	d		14 26						14 23			14 40					14 56						14 53	
Queens Rd Peckham	d		14 29						14 26			14 42					14 59						14 56	
South Bermondsey	d		14 31						14 28			14 45					15 01						14 58	
London Bridge 4 ⊖	a		14 36		14 13		14 31		14 33		14 40	14 49	14 48				15 06			14 51	15 01		15 03	

East and West Croydon, London Milton Keynes Central and Luton via Norbury Crystal Palace - Tulse Hill

Local Services

		FC	SN	SN	SN	SN ◇1 H	SN	SN	SN 1	LO	SN	SN	SN	LO	FC	SN	SN	SN ◇1 H	SN	SN ◇1	SN	SN	LO
East Croydon	d		14 42	14 47	14 53	15 09			14 56							15 12	15 17	15 20	15 23	15 39			
West Croydon 4	d							14 52		14 57	15 04	15 07		15 12								15 22	15 27
Norwood Junction 2	a			14 51				14 56	15 00	15 01	15 09			15 16			15 21					15 26	15 31
	d			14 52				14 57	15 01		15 10						15 22					15 27	
Selhurst 4	d		14 46		14 57							15 11				15 16			15 26				
Thornton Heath	d		14 48		14 59							15 13				15 18			15 28				
Norbury	d		14 51		15 02							15 16				15 21			15 31				
Streatham Common 4	d		14 53		15 04							15 19				15 23			15 34				
Beckenham Junction 4	d																						
Birkbeck	d																						
Crystal Palace 4	d							15 01					15 07									15 31	
Gipsy Hill	d							15 03					15 09									15 33	
West Norwood 4	d							15 06					15 12									15 36	
Streatham Hill	d							15 10														15 40	
Balham 4 ⊖	d				15 08			15 13				15 23							15 38			15 43	
Wandsworth Common	d							15 15														15 45	
Clapham Junction 10	d				15 13	15 19		15 19				15 27						15 32	15 42	15 49		15 49	
Imperial Wharf	d																						
West Brompton ⊖	d																						
Kensington (Olympia) ⊖	d																						
Shepherd's Bush ⊖	d																						
Wembley Central ⊖	d																						
Harrow & Wealdstone ⊖	d																						
Watford Junction	d																						
Milton Keynes Central 10	a																						
Battersea Park 4	d						15 15	15 23													15 45	15 52	
London Victoria 15 ⊖	a				15 20	15 25		15 27				15 34						15 39	15 50	15 55		15 57	
Streatham 4	d	14 55	14 58												15 25	15 28							
Tulse Hill 3	d	14 59	15 02										15 16		15 29	15 32							
Herne Hill 4	a																						
Loughborough Jn	a																						
Elephant & Castle ⊖	a																						
London Blackfriars 3 ⊖	a																						
City Thameslink 3	a																						
St Pancras International 15 ⊖	a																						
Luton Airport Parkway 7	a																						
Luton 10	a																						
North Dulwich	d		15 05										15 19			15 35							
East Dulwich	d		15 07										15 21			15 37							
Peckham Rye 4	d		15 10				15 26						15 23			15 40					15 56		
Queens Rd Peckham	d		15 12				15 29						15 26			15 42					15 59		
South Bermondsey	d		15 15				15 31						15 28			15 45					16 01		
London Bridge 4 ⊖	a	15 10	15 19	15 18			15 36		15 13		15 31		15 33		15 40	15 49	15 48				16 06		

		SN 1	SN	SN	SN	LO	FC	SN	SN	SN	SN ◇1 H	SN	SN	SN 1	LO	SN	SN	SN	LO	FC	SN	SN	SN ◇1 H	SN
East Croydon	d	15 34						15 42	15 47	15 53	16 09			15 56							16 12	16 17	16 20	16 23
West Croydon 4	d		15 34	15 37		15 42							15 52		15 57	16 04	16 07		16 12					
Norwood Junction 2	a	15 38	15 39			15 46			15 51				15 56	16 00	16 01	16 09			16 16			16 21		
	d	15 38	15 40						15 52				15 57	16 01		16 10						16 22		
Selhurst 4	d			15 41				15 46		15 57							16 11				16 16			16 26
Thornton Heath	d			15 43				15 48		15 59							16 13				16 18			16 28
Norbury	d			15 46				15 51		16 02							16 16				16 21			16 31
Streatham Common 4	d			15 49				15 53		16 04							16 19				16 23			16 34
Beckenham Junction 4	d																							
Birkbeck	d																							
Crystal Palace 4	d				15 37								16 01					16 07						
Gipsy Hill	d				15 39								16 03					16 09						
West Norwood 4	d				15 42								16 06					16 12						
Streatham Hill	d												16 10											
Balham 4 ⊖	d			15 53						16 08			16 13				16 23							16 38
Wandsworth Common	d												16 15											
Clapham Junction 10	d			15 57						16 13	16 19		16 19				16 27						16 32	16 42
Imperial Wharf	d																							
West Brompton ⊖	d																							
Kensington (Olympia) ⊖	d																							
Shepherd's Bush ⊖	d																							
Wembley Central ⊖	d																							
Harrow & Wealdstone ⊖	d																							
Watford Junction	d																							
Milton Keynes Central 10	a																							
Battersea Park 4	d											16 15	16 23											
London Victoria 15 ⊖	a			16 04						16 20	16 25		16 27				16 34						16 39	16 50
Streatham 4	d						15 55	15 58												16 25	16 28			
Tulse Hill 3	d				15 46		15 59	16 02										16 16		16 29	16 32			
Herne Hill 4	a																							
Loughborough Jn	a																							
Elephant & Castle ⊖	a																							
London Blackfriars 3 ⊖	a																							
City Thameslink 3	a																							
St Pancras International 15 ⊖	a																							
Luton Airport Parkway 7	a																							
Luton 10	a																							
North Dulwich	d				15 49			16 05										16 19			16 35			
East Dulwich	d				15 51			16 07										16 21			16 37			
Peckham Rye 4	d				15 53			16 10				16 26						16 23			16 40			
Queens Rd Peckham	d				15 56			16 12				16 29						16 26			16 42			
South Bermondsey	d				15 58			16 15				16 31						16 28			16 45			
London Bridge 4 ⊖	a	15 51	16 01		16 03		16 10	16 19	16 18			16 36		16 13		16 31		[illegible]			[illegible]			

Table 177

Sundays until 4 September

East and West Croydon, London Milton Keynes Central and Luton via Norbury Crystal Palace - Tulse Hill

Local Services

		SN ◇1	SN	SN	LO	SN 1	SN	SN		SN	LO	FC	SN	SN	SN	SN ◇1	SN	SN	SN 1	LO	SN	SN	SN	LO	
East Croydon	d	16 39				16 34							16 42	16 47	16 53	17 09			16 56						
West Croydon 4	d			16 22	16 27		16 34	16 37			16 42							16 52		16 57	17 04	17 07		17 12	
Norwood Junction 2	a			16 26	16 31	16 38	16 39				16 46			16 51				16 56	17 00	17 01	17 09			17 16	
	d			16 27		16 38	16 40							16 52				16 57	17 01		17 10				
Selhurst 4	d							16 41					16 46		16 57							17 11			
Thornton Heath	d							16 43					16 48		16 59							17 13			
Norbury	d							16 46					16 51		17 02							17 16			
Streatham Common 4	d							16 49					16 53		17 04							17 19			
Beckenham Junction 4	d																								
Birkbeck	d																								
Crystal Palace 4	d			16 31						16 37								17 01					17 07		
Gipsy Hill	d			16 33						16 39								17 03					17 09		
West Norwood 4	d			16 36						16 42								17 06					17 12		
Streatham Hill	d			16 40														17 10							
Balham 4 ⊖	d			16 43				16 53							17 08			17 13				17 23			
Wandsworth Common	d			16 45														17 15							
Clapham Junction 10	d	16 49		16 49				16 57							17 13	17 19		17 19				17 27			
Imperial Wharf	d																								
West Brompton ⊖	d																								
Kensington (Olympia) ⊖	d																								
Shepherd's Bush ⊖	d																								
Wembley Central ⊖	d																								
Harrow & Wealdstone ⊖	d																								
Watford Junction	d																								
Milton Keynes Central 10	a																								
Battersea Park 4	d		16 45	16 52													17 15	17 23							
London Victoria 15 ⊖	a	16 55		16 57				17 04							17 20	17 25		17 27				17 34			
Streatham 4	d											16 55	16 58												
Tulse Hill 3	d									16 46		16 59	17 02										17 16		
Herne Hill 4	a																								
Loughborough Jn	a																								
Elephant & Castle ⊖	a																								
London Blackfriars 3 ⊖	a																								
City Thameslink 3	a																								
St Pancras International 15 ⊖	a																								
Luton Airport Parkway 7	a																								
Luton 10	a																								
North Dulwich	d									16 49			17 05										17 19		
East Dulwich	d									16 51			17 07										17 21		
Peckham Rye 4	d		16 56							16 53			17 10				17 26						17 23		
Queens Rd Peckham	d		16 59							16 56			17 12				17 29						17 26		
South Bermondsey	d		17 01							16 58			17 15				17 31						17 28		
London Bridge 4 ⊖	a		17 06			16 51	17 01			17 03		17 10	17 19	17 18			17 36		17 13		17 31		17 33		

		FC	SN	SN	SN ◇1	SN	SN ◇1	SN	SN	LO	SN 1	SN	SN	SN	LO	FC		SN	SN	SN	SN ◇1	SN	SN	SN 1	LO
East Croydon	d		17 12	17 17	17 20	17 23	17 39				17 34							17 42	17 47	17 53	18 09			17 56	
West Croydon 4	d								17 22	17 27		17 34	17 37		17 42								17 52		17 57
Norwood Junction 2	a			17 21					17 26	17 31	17 38	17 39			17 46				17 51				17 56	18 00	18 01
	d			17 22					17 27		17 38	17 40							17 52				17 57	18 01	
Selhurst 4	d		17 16			17 26							17 41					17 46		17 57					
Thornton Heath	d		17 18			17 28							17 43					17 48		17 59					
Norbury	d		17 21			17 31							17 46					17 51		18 02					
Streatham Common 4	d		17 23			17 34							17 49					17 53		18 04					
Beckenham Junction 4	d																								
Birkbeck	d																								
Crystal Palace 4	d								17 31					17 37									18 01		
Gipsy Hill	d								17 33					17 39									18 03		
West Norwood 4	d								17 36					17 42									18 06		
Streatham Hill	d								17 40														18 10		
Balham 4 ⊖	d					17 38			17 43				17 53							18 08			18 13		
Wandsworth Common	d								17 45														18 15		
Clapham Junction 10	d				17 32	17 42	17 49		17 49				17 57							18 13	18 19		18 19		
Imperial Wharf	d																								
West Brompton ⊖	d																								
Kensington (Olympia) ⊖	d																								
Shepherd's Bush ⊖	d																								
Wembley Central ⊖	d																								
Harrow & Wealdstone ⊖	d																								
Watford Junction	d																								
Milton Keynes Central 10	a																								
Battersea Park 4	d							17 45	17 52													18 15	18 23		
London Victoria 15 ⊖	a				17 39	17 50	17 55		17 57				18 04							18 20	18 25		18 27		
Streatham 4	d	17 25	17 28													17 55		17 58							
Tulse Hill 3	d	17 29	17 32											17 46		17 59		18 02							
Herne Hill 4	a																								
Loughborough Jn	a																								
Elephant & Castle ⊖	a																								
London Blackfriars 3 ⊖	a																								
City Thameslink 3	a																								
St Pancras International 15 ⊖	a																								
Luton Airport Parkway 7	a																								
Luton 10	a																								
North Dulwich	d		17 35											17 49				18 05							
East Dulwich	d		17 37											17 51				18 07							
Peckham Rye 4	d		17 40					17 56						17 53				18 10				18 26			
Queens Rd Peckham	d		17 42					17 59						17 56				18 12				18 29			
South Bermondsey	d		17 45					18 01						17 58				18 15				18 31			
London Bridge 4 ⊖	a	17 40	17 49	17 48				18 06			17 51	18 01		18 03		18 10		18 19	18 18			18 36		18 13	

until 4 September

East and West Croydon, London Milton Keynes Central and Luton via Norbury Crystal Palace - Tulse Hill

Local Services

		SN	SN	SN	LO	FC	SN	SN		SN ◇1	SN	SN ◇1	SN	SN	LO	SN 1	SN	SN	SN	LO	FC	SN	SN	SN	
East Croydon	d						18 12	18 17		18 20	18 23	18 39				18 34						18 42	18 47	18 53	
West Croydon 4	d	18 04	18 07		18 12									18 22	18 27		18 34	18 37		18 42					
Norwood Junction 2	a	18 09			18 16			18 21						18 26	18 31	18 38	18 39			18 46			18 51		
	d	18 10						18 22						18 27		18 38	18 40						18 52		
Selhurst 4	d		18 11				18 16				18 26							18 41				18 46		18 57	
Thornton Heath	d		18 13				18 18				18 28							18 43				18 48		18 59	
Norbury	d		18 16				18 21				18 31							18 46				18 51		19 02	
Streatham Common 4	d		18 19				18 23				18 34							18 49				18 53		19 04	
Beckenham Junction 4	d																								
Birkbeck	d																								
Crystal Palace 4	d			18 07										18 31					18 37						
Gipsy Hill	d			18 09										18 33					18 39						
West Norwood 4	d			18 12										18 36					18 42						
Streatham Hill	d													18 40											
Balham 4 ⊖	d		18 23								18 38			18 43				18 53						19 08	
Wandsworth Common	d													18 45											
Clapham Junction 10	d		18 27							18 32	18 42	18 49		18 49				18 57						19 13	
Imperial Wharf	d																								
West Brompton ⊖	d																								
Kensington (Olympia) ⊖	d																								
Shepherd's Bush ⊖	d																								
Wembley Central ⊖	d																								
Harrow & Wealdstone ⊖	d																								
Watford Junction	d																								
Milton Keynes Central 10	a																								
Battersea Park 4	d												18 45	18 52											
London Victoria 15 ⊖	a		18 34							18 39	18 50	18 55		18 57				19 04						19 20	
Streatham 4	d					18 25	18 28														18 55	18 58			
Tulse Hill 3	d			18 16		18 29	18 32												18 46		18 59	19 02			
Herne Hill 4	a																								
Loughborough Jn	a																								
Elephant & Castle ⊖	a																								
London Blackfriars 3 ⊖	a																								
City Thameslink 3	a																								
St Pancras International 15 ⊖	a																								
Luton Airport Parkway 7	a																								
Luton 10	a																								
North Dulwich	d			18 19			18 35												18 49			19 05			
East Dulwich	d			18 21			18 37												18 51			19 07			
Peckham Rye 4	d			18 23			18 40						18 56						18 53			19 10			
Queens Rd Peckham	d			18 26			18 42						18 59						18 56			19 12			
South Bermondsey	d			18 28			18 45						19 01						18 58			19 15			
London Bridge 4 ⊖	a	18 31		18 33		18 40	18 49	18 48					19 06			18 51	19 01		19 03		19 10	19 19	19 18		

Table 177

Sundays
until 4 September

East and West Croydon, London Milton Keynes Central and Luton via Norbury Crystal Palace - Tulse Hill

Local Services

		SN ◇1	SN	SN	SN 1	LO	SN	SN	SN	LO	FC	SN	SN	SN ◇1	SN	SN ◇1		SN	SN	LO	SN 1	SN	SN	SN	LO
East Croydon	d	19 09			18 56							19 12	19 17	19 20	19 23	19 39					19 34				
West Croydon 4	d			18 52		18 57	19 04	19 07		19 12									19 22	19 27		19 34	19 37		19 42
Norwood Junction 2	a			18 56	19 00	19 01	19 09			19 16			19 21						19 26	19 31	19 38	19 39			19 46
	d			18 57	19 01		19 10						19 22						19 27		19 38	19 40			
Selhurst 4	d							19 11				19 16			19 26								19 41		
Thornton Heath	d							19 13				19 18			19 28								19 43		
Norbury	d							19 16				19 21			19 31								19 46		
Streatham Common 4	d							19 19				19 23			19 34								19 49		
Beckenham Junction 4	d																								
Birkbeck	d																								
Crystal Palace 4	d			19 01					19 07										19 31					19 37	
Gipsy Hill	d			19 03					19 09										19 33					19 39	
West Norwood 4	d			19 06					19 12										19 36					19 42	
Streatham Hill	d			19 10															19 40						
Balham 4 ⊖	d			19 13				19 23							19 38				19 43				19 53		
Wandsworth Common	d			19 15															19 45						
Clapham Junction 10	d	19 19		19 19				19 27						19 32	19 42	19 49			19 49				19 57		
Imperial Wharf	d																								
West Brompton ⊖	d																								
Kensington (Olympia) ⊖	d																								
Shepherd's Bush ⊖	d																								
Wembley Central ⊖	d																								
Harrow & Wealdstone ⊖	d																								
Watford Junction	d																								
Milton Keynes Central 10	a																								
Battersea Park 4	d		19 15	19 23														19 45	19 52						
London Victoria 15 ⊖	a	19 25		19 27				19 34						19 39	19 50	19 55			19 57				20 04		
Streatham 4	d										19 25	19 28													
Tulse Hill 3	d								19 16		19 29	19 32												19 46	
Herne Hill 4	a																								
Loughborough Jn	a																								
Elephant & Castle ⊖	a																								
London Blackfriars 3 ⊖	a																								
City Thameslink 3	a																								
St Pancras International 15 ⊖	a																								
Luton Airport Parkway 7	a																								
Luton 10	a																								
North Dulwich	d								19 19			19 35												19 49	
East Dulwich	d								19 21			19 37												19 51	
Peckham Rye 4	d		19 26						19 23			19 40						19 56						19 53	
Queens Rd Peckham	d		19 29						19 26			19 42						19 59						19 56	
South Bermondsey	d		19 31						19 28			19 45						20 01						19 58	
London Bridge 4 ⊖	a		19 36		19 13		19 31		19 33		19 40	19 49	19 48					20 06			19 51	20 01		20 03	

		FC	SN	SN	SN	SN ◇1	SN	SN		SN 1	LO	SN	SN	SN	LO	FC	SN	SN	SN ◇1	SN	SN ◇1	SN	SN	LO
East Croydon	d		19 42	19 47	19 53	20 09				19 56							20 12	20 17	20 20	20 23	20 39			
West Croydon 4	d							19 52			19 57	20 04	20 07		20 12								20 22	20 27
Norwood Junction 2	a			19 51				19 56		20 00	20 01	20 09			20 16			20 21					20 26	20 31
	d			19 52				19 57		20 01		20 10						20 22					20 27	
Selhurst 4	d		19 46		19 57								20 11				20 16			20 26				
Thornton Heath	d		19 48		19 59								20 13				20 18			20 28				
Norbury	d		19 51		20 02								20 16				20 21			20 31				
Streatham Common 4	d		19 53		20 04								20 19				20 23			20 34				
Beckenham Junction 4	d																							
Birkbeck	d																							
Crystal Palace 4	d							20 01						20 07									20 31	
Gipsy Hill	d							20 03						20 09									20 33	
West Norwood 4	d							20 06						20 12									20 36	
Streatham Hill	d							20 10															20 40	
Balham 4 ⊖	d				20 08			20 13					20 23							20 38			20 43	
Wandsworth Common	d							20 15															20 45	
Clapham Junction 10	d				20 13	20 19		20 19					20 27						20 32	20 42	20 49		20 49	
Imperial Wharf	d																							
West Brompton ⊖	d																							
Kensington (Olympia) ⊖	d																							
Shepherd's Bush ⊖	d																							
Wembley Central ⊖	d																							
Harrow & Wealdstone ⊖	d																							
Watford Junction	d																							
Milton Keynes Central 10	a																							
Battersea Park 4	d						20 15	20 22														20 45	20 52	
London Victoria 15 ⊖	a				20 20	20 25		20 27					20 34						20 39	20 50	20 55		20 57	
Streatham 4	d	19 55	19 58													20 25	20 28							
Tulse Hill 3	d	19 59	20 02											20 16		20 29	20 32							
Herne Hill 4	a																							
Loughborough Jn	a																							
Elephant & Castle ⊖	a																							
London Blackfriars 3 ⊖	a																							
City Thameslink 3	a																							
St Pancras International 15 ⊖	a																							
Luton Airport Parkway 7	a																							
Luton 10	a																							
North Dulwich	d		20 05											20 19			20 35							
East Dulwich	d		20 07											20 21			20 37							
Peckham Rye 4	d		20 10				20 26							20 23			20 40					20 56		
Queens Rd Peckham	d		20 12				20 29							20 26			20 42					20 59		
South Bermondsey	d		20 15				20 31							20 28			20 45					21 01		
London Bridge 4 ⊖	a	20 10	20 19	20 18			20 36			20 13		20 31		20 33		20 40	20 49	20 48				21 06		

Table 177

Sundays
until 4 September

East and West Croydon, London Milton Keynes Central and Luton via Norbury Crystal Palace - Tulse Hill

Local Services

		SN 1	SN	SN	SN	LO	FC	SN	SN	SN	SN ◇1	SN	SN	SN 1	LO	SN		SN	SN	LO	FC	SN	SN	SN	SN ◇1
East Croydon	d	20 34						20 42	20 47	20 53	21 09			20 56								21 12	21 17	21 23	21 39
West Croydon 4	d		20 34	20 37		20 42							20 52		20 57	21 04		21 07		21 12					
Norwood Junction 2	a	20 38	20 39			20 46			20 51				20 56	21 00	21 01	21 09				21 16			21 21		
	d	20 38	20 40						20 52				20 57	21 01		21 10							21 22		
Selhurst 4	d			20 41				20 46		20 57								21 11				21 16		21 26	
Thornton Heath	d			20 43				20 48		20 59								21 13				21 18		21 28	
Norbury	d			20 46				20 51		21 02								21 16				21 21		21 31	
Streatham Common 4	d			20 49				20 53		21 04								21 19				21 23		21 34	
Beckenham Junction 4	d																								
Birkbeck	d																								
Crystal Palace 4	d				20 37								21 01						21 07						
Gipsy Hill	d				20 39								21 03						21 09						
West Norwood 4	d				20 42								21 06						21 12						
Streatham Hill	d												21 10												
Balham 4 ⊖	d			20 53						21 08			21 13					21 23						21 38	
Wandsworth Common	d												21 15												
Clapham Junction 10	d			20 57						21 13	21 19		21 19					21 27						21 42	21 49
Imperial Wharf	d																								
West Brompton ⊖	d																								
Kensington (Olympia) ⊖	d																								
Shepherd's Bush ⊖	d																								
Wembley Central ⊖	d																								
Harrow & Wealdstone ⊖	d																								
Watford Junction	d																								
Milton Keynes Central 10	a																								
Battersea Park 4	d											21 15	21 23												
London Victoria 15 ⊖	a			21 04						21 20	21 25		21 27					21 34						21 50	21 55
Streatham 4	d						20 55	20 58													21 25	21 28			
Tulse Hill 3	d				20 46		20 59	21 02											21 16		21 29	21 32			
Herne Hill 4	a																								
Loughborough Jn	a																								
Elephant & Castle ⊖	a																								
London Blackfriars 3 ⊖	a																								
City Thameslink 3	a																								
St Pancras International 15 ⊖	a																								
Luton Airport Parkway 7	a																								
Luton 10	a																								
North Dulwich	d				20 49			21 05											21 19			21 35			
East Dulwich	d				20 51			21 07											21 21			21 37			
Peckham Rye 4	d				20 53			21 10				21 26							21 23			21 40			
Queens Rd Peckham	d				20 56			21 12				21 29							21 26			21 42			
South Bermondsey	d				20 58			21 15				21 31							21 28			21 45			
London Bridge 4 ⊖	a	20 51	21 01		21 03		21 10	21 19	21 18			21 36		21 13		21 31			21 33		21 40	21 49	21 48		

		SN	SN	LO	SN 1	SN	SN	SN		LO	FC	SN	SN	SN	SN ◇1	SN	SN	SN 1	LO	SN	SN	SN	SN	LO
East Croydon	d				21 34							21 42	21 47	21 53	22 09			21 56					22 12	
West Croydon 4	d		21 22	21 27		21 34	21 37			21 42							21 52		21 57	22 04	22 07			22 12
Norwood Junction 2	a		21 26	21 31	21 38	21 39				21 46			21 51				21 56	22 00	22 01	22 09				22 16
	d		21 27		21 38	21 40							21 52				21 57	22 01		22 10				
Selhurst 4	d						21 41					21 46		21 56							22 11		22 16	
Thornton Heath	d						21 43					21 48		21 58							22 13		22 18	
Norbury	d						21 46					21 51		22 01							22 16		22 21	
Streatham Common 4	d						21 49					21 53		22 04							22 19		22 23	
Beckenham Junction 4	d																							
Birkbeck	d																							
Crystal Palace 4	d		21 31					21 37									22 01					22 07		
Gipsy Hill	d		21 33					21 39									22 03					22 09		
West Norwood 4	d		21 36					21 42									22 06					22 12		
Streatham Hill	d		21 40														22 10							
Balham 4 ⊖	d		21 43				21 53							22 08			22 13				22 23			
Wandsworth Common	d		21 45														22 15							
Clapham Junction 10	d		21 49				21 57							22 12	22 19		22 19				22 27			
Imperial Wharf	d																							
West Brompton ⊖	d																							
Kensington (Olympia) ⊖	d																							
Shepherd's Bush ⊖	d																							
Wembley Central ⊖	d																							
Harrow & Wealdstone ⊖	d																							
Watford Junction	d																							
Milton Keynes Central 10	a																							
Battersea Park 4	d	21 45	21 53													22 15	22 23							
London Victoria 15 ⊖	a		21 57				22 04							22 20	22 25		22 27				22 34			
Streatham 4	d										21 55	21 58											22 28	
Tulse Hill 3	d							21 46			21 59	22 02										22 16	22 32	
Herne Hill 4	a																							
Loughborough Jn	a																							
Elephant & Castle ⊖	a																							
London Blackfriars 3 ⊖	a																							
City Thameslink 3	a																							
St Pancras International 15 ⊖	a																							
Luton Airport Parkway 7	a																							
Luton 10	a																							
North Dulwich	d							21 49				22 05										22 19	22 35	
East Dulwich	d							21 51				22 07										22 21	22 37	
Peckham Rye 4	d	21 56						21 53				22 10				22 26						22 23	22 40	
Queens Rd Peckham	d	21 59						21 56				22 12				22 29						22 26	22 42	
South Bermondsey	d	22 01						21 58				22 15				22 31						22 28	22 45	
London Bridge 4 ⊖	a	22 06			21 51	22 01		22 03			22 10	22 19	22 18			22 36		22 13		22 31		22 33	22 49	

Sundays
until 4 September

East and West Croydon, London Milton Keynes Central and Luton via Norbury Crystal Palace - Tulse Hill

Local Services

		SN	SN ◇1	SN	SN	SN	LO	SN 1	SN	SN	SN	SN	LO	SN	SN	SN 1	SN	SN	LO	SN	SN	SN	SN ◇1	SN
East Croydon	d	22 17	22 20	22 23				22 34				22 42		22 47	22 53	22 56						23 17	23 21	
West Croydon 4	d					22 22	22 27		22 34	22 37			22 42					22 52	22 57	23 07				23 22
Norwood Junction 2	a	22 21				22 26	22 31	22 38	22 39				22 46	22 51				22 56	23 01			23 21		23 26
	d	22 22				22 27		22 38	22 40					22 52				22 57						23 27
Selhurst 4	d			22 26						22 41		22 46			22 57	22 59				23 11				
Thornton Heath	d			22 28						22 43		22 48			22 59					23 13				
Norbury	d			22 31						22 46		22 51			23 02					23 16				
Streatham Common 4	d			22 34						22 49		22 53			23 04					23 19				
Beckenham Junction 4	d																							
Birkbeck	d																							
Crystal Palace 4	d					22 31					22 37							23 01			23 07			23 31
Gipsy Hill	d					22 33					22 39							23 03			23 09			23 33
West Norwood 4	d					22 36					22 42							23 06			23 12			23 36
Streatham Hill	d					22 40												23 10						23 40
Balham 4 ⊖	d			22 38		22 43				22 53					23 08			23 13		23 23				23 43
Wandsworth Common	d					22 45												23 15						23 45
Clapham Junction 10	d		22 32	22 42		22 49				22 57					23 13	23 08		23 19		23 27			23 32	23 49
Imperial Wharf	d																							
West Brompton ⊖	d																							
Kensington (Olympia) ⊖	d																							
Shepherd's Bush ⊖	d																							
Wembley Central ⊖	d																							
Harrow & Wealdstone ⊖	d																							
Watford Junction	d																							
Milton Keynes Central 10	a																							
Battersea Park 4	d				22 45	22 53											23 15	23 23						23 53
London Victoria 15 ⊖	a		22 39	22 50		22 57				23 04					23 20	23 14		23 27		23 34			23 38	23 57
Streatham 4	d											22 58												
Tulse Hill 3	d										22 46	23 02									23 16			
Herne Hill 4	a																							
Loughborough Jn.	a																							
Elephant & Castle ⊖	a																							
London Blackfriars 3 ⊖	a																							
City Thameslink 3	a																							
St Pancras International 15 ⊖	a																							
Luton Airport Parkway 7	a																							
Luton 10	a																							
North Dulwich	d										22 49	23 05									23 19			
East Dulwich	d										22 51	23 07									23 21			
Peckham Rye 4	d				22 56						22 53	23 10					23 26				23 23			
Queens Rd Peckham	d				22 59						22 56	23 12					23 29				23 26			
South Bermondsey	d				23 01						22 58	23 15					23 31				23 28			
London Bridge 4 ⊖	a	22 48			23 06			22 51	23 01		23 03	23 19		23 17			23 36				23 33			

		SN	SN	SN	SN	SN 1
East Croydon	d	23 26				23 56
West Croydon 4	d		23 37		23 52	
Norwood Junction 2	a					
	d					
Selhurst 4	d	23a29	23 41		23 56	00 01
Thornton Heath	d		23 43		23 58	
Norbury	d		23 46		00 01	
Streatham Common 4	d		23 49		00 04	
Beckenham Junction 4	d					
Birkbeck	d					
Crystal Palace 4	d			23 37		
Gipsy Hill	d			23 39		
West Norwood 4	d			23 42		
Streatham Hill	d					
Balham 4 ⊖	d		23 53		00 08	
Wandsworth Common	d					
Clapham Junction 10	d		23 58		00 12	00 11
Imperial Wharf	d					
West Brompton ⊖	d					
Kensington (Olympia) ⊖	d					
Shepherd's Bush ⊖	d					
Wembley Central ⊖	d					
Harrow & Wealdstone ⊖	d					
Watford Junction	d					
Milton Keynes Central 10	a					
Battersea Park 4	d					
London Victoria 15 ⊖	a		00 04		00 19	00 21
Streatham 4	d					
Tulse Hill 3	d			23 46		
Herne Hill 4	a					
Loughborough Jn.	a					
Elephant & Castle ⊖	a					
London Blackfriars 3 ⊖	a					
City Thameslink 3	a					
St Pancras International 15 ⊖	a					
Luton Airport Parkway 7	a					
Luton 10	a					
North Dulwich	d			23 49		
East Dulwich	d			23 51		
Peckham Rye 4	d			23 53		
Queens Rd Peckham	d			23 56		
South Bermondsey	d			23 58		
London Bridge 4 ⊖	a			00 03		

from 11 September

East and West Croydon, London Milton Keynes Central and Luton via Norbury Crystal Palace - Tulse Hill

Local Services

		SN	SN	SN	SN 1	SN	SN	SN	SN 1	SN 1	SN 1	SN 1	FC 1	SN 1	SN	LO	SN	SN	SN	SN	SN	SN	LO	SN
East Croydon	d				23p56			00 49	01 43	02 40	03 40	04 40	05 32	06 02	06 40		06 47					07 12		07 17
West Croydon 4	d	23p34														06 42				07 07			07 12	
Norwood Junction 2	a												05 36			06 47	06 51						07 17	07 21
	d												05 36				06 52		06 57					07 22
Selhurst 4	d	23p39			00 02			00 53	01 45	02 42	03 42	04 42		06 05	06 43			06 47		07 11		07 15		
Thornton Heath	d	23p41													06 45			06 49		07 13		07 17		
Norbury	d	23p44													06 48			06 52		07 16		07 20		
Streatham Common 4	d	23p46													06 51			06 55		07 19		07 23		
Beckenham Junction 4	d																							
Birkbeck	d																							
Crystal Palace 4	d		23p43	23p51		00 13	00 21												07 01		07 07			
Gipsy Hill	d		23p45			00 15													07 03		07 09			
West Norwood 4	d		23p48			00 18													07 06		07 12			
Streatham Hill	d		23p52			00 22													07 10					
Balham 4 ⊖	d	23p50	23p55			00 26									06 55				07 13	07 23				
Wandsworth Common	d	23p52	23p57			00 28									06 57				07 15					
Clapham Junction 10	d	23p56	00 02		00 11	00 32		01 03	01 54	02 53	03 53	04 53		06 14	07 00				07 19	07 27				
Imperial Wharf	d																							
West Brompton ⊖	d																							
Kensington (Olympia) ⊖	d																							
Shepherd's Bush ⊖	d																							
Wembley Central ⊖	d																							
Harrow & Wealdstone ⊖	d																							
Watford Junction	d																							
Milton Keynes Central 10	a																							
Battersea Park 4	d		00 05			00 35									07 04				07 23					
London Victoria 15 ⊖	a	00 04	00 10		00 18	00 42		01 10	02 05	03 05	04 05	05 05		06 22	07 09				07 27	07 34				
Streatham 4	d																	06 58				07 28		
Tulse Hill 3	d																	07 02			07 16	07 32		
Herne Hill 4	a																							
Loughborough Jn.	a																							
Elephant & Castle ⊖	a																							
London Blackfriars 3 ⊖	a																							
City Thameslink 3	a																							
St Pancras International 15 ⊖	a																							
Luton Airport Parkway 7	a																							
Luton 10	a																							
North Dulwich	d																	07 05			07 19	07 35		
East Dulwich	d																	07 07			07 21	07 37		
Peckham Rye 4	d																	07 09			07 23	07 39		
Queens Rd Peckham	d																	07 12			07 26	07 42		
South Bermondsey	d																	07 14			07 28	07 44		
London Bridge 4 ⊖	a			00 11			00 41						05 59				07 17	07 19			07 33	07 49		07 48

		SN 1	SN	SN	SN	SN	SN	SN	LO	SN	SN	SN	SN	SN 1	SN	SN	SN ◇1	SN	SN	LO	SN	SN ◇1	SN
East Croydon	d	07 27						07 42		07 47	07 53			07 56			08 10		08 12		08 17	08 26	08 23
West Croydon 4	d			07 22	07 34	07 37			07 42				07 52		08 04			08 07		08 12			
Norwood Junction 2	a			07 26	07 39				07 47	07 51			07 56	08 00	08 09					08 17	08 21		
	d			07 27	07 40					07 52			07 57	08 01	08 10						08 22		
Selhurst 4	d	07 31				07 41		07 46			07 57							08 11	08 16				08 26
Thornton Heath	d					07 43		07 48			07 59							08 13	08 18				08 28
Norbury	d					07 46		07 51			08 02							08 16	08 21				08 31
Streatham Common 4	d					07 49		07 53			08 04							08 19	08 23				08 34
Beckenham Junction 4	d																						
Birkbeck	d																						
Crystal Palace 4	d			07 31			07 37						08 01			08 07							
Gipsy Hill	d			07 33			07 39						08 03			08 09							
West Norwood 4	d			07 36			07 42						08 06			08 12							
Streatham Hill	d			07 40									08 10										
Balham 4 ⊖	d			07 43		07 53					08 08		08 13					08 23					08 38
Wandsworth Common	d			07 45									08 15										
Clapham Junction 10	d	07 41		07 49		07 57					08 13		08 19				08 25	08 27				08 38	08 42
Imperial Wharf	d																						
West Brompton ⊖	d																						
Kensington (Olympia) ⊖	d																						
Shepherd's Bush ⊖	d																						
Wembley Central ⊖	d																						
Harrow & Wealdstone ⊖	d																						
Watford Junction	d																						
Milton Keynes Central 10	a																						
Battersea Park 4	d		07 45	07 53								08 15	08 23										
London Victoria 15 ⊖	a	07 48		07 57		08 04					08 20		08 27				08 31	08 34				08 46	08 50
Streatham 4	d							07 58											08 28				
Tulse Hill 3	d						07 46	08 02								08 16			08 32				
Herne Hill 4	a																						
Loughborough Jn.	a																						
Elephant & Castle ⊖	a																						
London Blackfriars 3 ⊖	a																						
City Thameslink 3	a																						
St Pancras International 15 ⊖	a																						
Luton Airport Parkway 7	a																						
Luton 10	a																						
North Dulwich	d						07 49	08 05								08 19			08 35				
East Dulwich	d						07 51	08 07								08 21			08 37				
Peckham Rye 4	d		07 56				07 53	08 10				08 26				08 23			08 40				
Queens Rd Peckham	d		07 59				07 56	08 12				08 29				08 26			08 42				
South Bermondsey	d		08 01				07 58	08 15				08 31				08 28			08 45				
London Bridge 4 ⊖	a		08 06		08 01		08 03	08 19		08 17		08 36		08 13	08 31	08 33			08 49		08 48		

Table 177

Sundays from 11 September

East and West Croydon, London
Milton Keynes Central and Luton via Norbury
Crystal Palace - Tulse Hill

Local Services

Station		SN	SN	SN	SN	SN	SN	SN	LO	SN	SN	SN	SN	SN	SN	SN		SN	SN	SN	LO	SN	SN	SN	SN
						◇1								1				◇1 H					◇1 H		
East Croydon	d					08 40		08 42		08 47	08 53			08 56				09 10		09 12		09 17	09 26	09 23	
West Croydon	d		08 22	08 34			08 37		08 42				08 52		09 04				09 07		09 12				
Norwood Junction	a		08 26	08 39					08 47	08 51			08 56	09 00	09 09						09 17	09 21			
	d		08 27	08 40						08 52			08 57	09 01	09 10							09 22			
Selhurst	d						08 41	08 46			08 57								09 11	09 16				09 26	
Thornton Heath	d						08 43	08 48			08 59								09 13	09 18				09 28	
Norbury	d						08 46	08 51			09 02								09 16	09 21				09 31	
Streatham Common	d						08 49	08 53			09 04								09 19	09 23				09 34	
Beckenham Junction	d																								
Birkbeck	d																								
Crystal Palace	d		08 31		08 37								09 01			09 07									
Gipsy Hill	d		08 33		08 39								09 03			09 09									
West Norwood	d		08 36		08 42								09 06			09 12									
Streatham Hill	d		08 40										09 10												
Balham	d		08 43				08 53				09 08		09 13						09 23					09 38	
Wandsworth Common	d		08 45										09 15												
Clapham Junction	d		08 49			08 55	08 57				09 13		09 19					09 25	09 27				09 38	09 42	
Imperial Wharf	d																								
West Brompton	d																								
Kensington (Olympia)	d																								
Shepherd's Bush	d																								
Wembley Central	d																								
Harrow & Wealdstone	d																								
Watford Junction	d																								
Milton Keynes Central	a																								
Battersea Park	d	08 45	08 52									09 15	09 23												09 45
London Victoria	a		08 57			09 01	09 04				09 20		09 27					09 31	09 34				09 46	09 50	
Streatham	d							08 58												09 28					
Tulse Hill	d				08 46			09 02								09 16				09 32					
Herne Hill	a																								
Loughborough Jn	a																								
Elephant & Castle	a																								
London Blackfriars	a																								
City Thameslink	a																								
St Pancras International	a																								
Luton Airport Parkway	a																								
Luton	a																								
North Dulwich	d				08 49			09 05								09 19				09 35					
East Dulwich	d				08 51			09 07								09 21				09 37					
Peckham Rye	d	08 56			08 53			09 10				09 26				09 23				09 40					09 56
Queens Rd Peckham	d	08 59			08 56			09 12				09 29				09 26				09 42					09 59
South Bermondsey	d	09 01			08 58			09 15				09 31				09 28				09 45					10 01
London Bridge	a	09 06		09 01	09 03			09 19		09 18		09 36		09 13	09 31	09 33				09 49		09 48			10 06

Station		SN	SN	SN	SN	SN	SN	LO		SN	SN	SN	SN	SN	SN	SN	SN	SN	SN	LO	SN	SN	SN	SN
					◇1									1			◇1 H					◇1 H		
East Croydon	d				09 40		09 42			09 47	09 53			09 56			10 10		10 12		10 17	10 26	10 23	
West Croydon	d	09 22	09 34			09 37		09 42					09 52		10 04			10 07		10 12				
Norwood Junction	a	09 26	09 39					09 47		09 51			09 56	10 00	10 09					10 17	10 21			
	d	09 27	09 40							09 52			09 57	10 01	10 10						10 22			
Selhurst	d					09 41	09 46				09 57							10 11	10 16				10 26	
Thornton Heath	d					09 43	09 48				09 59							10 13	10 18				10 28	
Norbury	d					09 46	09 51				10 02							10 16	10 21				10 31	
Streatham Common	d					09 49	09 53				10 04							10 19	10 23				10 34	
Beckenham Junction	d																							
Birkbeck	d																							
Crystal Palace	d	09 31		09 37									10 01			10 07								
Gipsy Hill	d	09 33		09 39									10 03			10 09								
West Norwood	d	09 36		09 42									10 06			10 12								
Streatham Hill	d	09 40											10 10											
Balham	d	09 43				09 53					10 08		10 13					10 23					10 38	
Wandsworth Common	d	09 45											10 15											
Clapham Junction	d	09 49			09 55	09 57					10 13		10 19				10 25	10 27				10 38	10 42	
Imperial Wharf	d																							
West Brompton	d																							
Kensington (Olympia)	d																							
Shepherd's Bush	d																							
Wembley Central	d																							
Harrow & Wealdstone	d																							
Watford Junction	d																							
Milton Keynes Central	a																							
Battersea Park	d	09 53										10 15	10 22											10 45
London Victoria	a	09 57			10 01	10 04					10 20		10 27				10 31	10 34				10 46	10 50	
Streatham	d						09 58												10 28					
Tulse Hill	d			09 46			10 02									10 16			10 32					
Herne Hill	a																							
Loughborough Jn	a																							
Elephant & Castle	a																							
London Blackfriars	a																							
City Thameslink	a																							
St Pancras International	a																							
Luton Airport Parkway	a																							
Luton	a																							
North Dulwich	d			09 49			10 05									10 19			10 35					
East Dulwich	d			09 51			10 07									10 21			10 37					
Peckham Rye	d			09 53			10 10					10 26				10 23			10 40					10 56
Queens Rd Peckham	d			09 56			10 12					10 29				10 26			10 42					10 59
South Bermondsey	d			09 58			10 15					10 31				10 28			10 45					11 01
London Bridge	a		10 01	10 03			10 19			10 18		10 36		10 13	10 31	10 33			10 49		10 48			11 06

Table 177

Sundays from 11 September

East and West Croydon, London
Milton Keynes Central and Luton via Norbury
Crystal Palace - Tulse Hill

Local Services

Station		SN	SN	SN	SN	SN	LO	FC	SN	SN	SN	SN	SN	SN	SN	SN		SN	SN	LO	FC	SN	SN	SN	SN
					◇1									1				◇1 H						◇1 H	
East Croydon	d				10 40				10 42	10 47	10 53			10 56				11 10				11 12	11 17	11 26	11 23
West Croydon	d	10 22	10 34			10 37	10 42						10 52		11 04				11 07	11 12					
Norwood Junction	a	10 26	10 39				10 47			10 51			10 56	11 00	11 09					11 17			11 21		
	d	10 27	10 40							10 52			10 57	11 01	11 10								11 22		
Selhurst	d					10 41			10 46		10 57								11 11			11 16			11 26
Thornton Heath	d					10 43			10 48		10 59								11 13			11 18			11 28
Norbury	d					10 46			10 51		11 02								11 16			11 21			11 31
Streatham Common	d					10 49			10 53		11 04								11 19			11 23			11 34
Beckenham Junction	d																								
Birkbeck	d																								
Crystal Palace	d	10 31		10 37									11 01			11 07									
Gipsy Hill	d	10 33		10 39									11 03			11 09									
West Norwood	d	10 36		10 42									11 06			11 12									
Streatham Hill	d	10 40											11 10												
Balham	d	10 43				10 53					11 08		11 13						11 23						11 38
Wandsworth Common	d	10 45											11 15												
Clapham Junction	d	10 49			10 55	10 57					11 13		11 19					11 25	11 27					11 38	11 42
Imperial Wharf	d																								
West Brompton	d																								
Kensington (Olympia)	d																								
Shepherd's Bush	d																								
Wembley Central	d																								
Harrow & Wealdstone	d																								
Watford Junction	d																								
Milton Keynes Central	a																								
Battersea Park	d	10 52										11 15	11 22												
London Victoria	a	10 57			11 01	11 04					11 20		11 27					11 31	11 34					11 46	11 50
Streatham	d							10 55	10 58												11 25	11 28			
Tulse Hill	d			10 46				10 59	11 02							11 16					11 29	11 32			
Herne Hill	a																								
Loughborough Jn	a																								
Elephant & Castle	a																								
London Blackfriars	a																								
City Thameslink	a																								
St Pancras International	a																								
Luton Airport Parkway	a																								
Luton	a																								
North Dulwich	d			10 49					11 05							11 19						11 35			
East Dulwich	d			10 51					11 07							11 21						11 37			
Peckham Rye	d			10 53					11 10			11 26				11 23						11 40			
Queens Rd Peckham	d			10 56					11 12			11 29				11 26						11 42			
South Bermondsey	d			10 58					11 15			11 31				11 28						11 45			
London Bridge	a		11 01	11 03				11 10	11 19	11 18		11 36		11 13	11 31	11 33					11 40	11 49	11 48		

Station		SN	SN	SN	SN	SN	SN	LO		FC	SN	SN	SN	SN	SN	SN	SN	SN	SN	SN	LO	FC	SN	SN
						◇1										1			◇1 H					
East Croydon	d					11 40					11 42	11 47	11 53			11 56			12 10				12 12	12 17
West Croydon	d		11 22	11 34			11 37	11 42							11 52		12 04			12 07	12 12			
Norwood Junction	a		11 26	11 39				11 47				11 51			11 56	12 00	12 09				12 16			12 21
	d		11 27	11 40								11 52			11 57	12 01	12 10							12 22
Selhurst	d						11 41				11 46		11 57							12 11			12 16	
Thornton Heath	d						11 43				11 48		11 59							12 13			12 18	
Norbury	d						11 46				11 51		12 02							12 16			12 21	
Streatham Common	d						11 49				11 53		12 04							12 19			12 23	
Beckenham Junction	d																							
Birkbeck	d																							
Crystal Palace	d		11 31		11 37										12 01			12 07						
Gipsy Hill	d		11 33		11 39										12 03			12 09						
West Norwood	d		11 36		11 42										12 06			12 12						
Streatham Hill	d		11 40												12 10									
Balham	d		11 43				11 53						12 08		12 13					12 23				
Wandsworth Common	d		11 45												12 15									
Clapham Junction	d		11 49			11 55	11 57						12 13		12 19				12 25	12 27				
Imperial Wharf	d																							
West Brompton	d																							
Kensington (Olympia)	d																							
Shepherd's Bush	d																							
Wembley Central	d																							
Harrow & Wealdstone	d																							
Watford Junction	d																							
Milton Keynes Central	a																							
Battersea Park	d	11 45	11 52											12 15	12 22									
London Victoria	a		11 57			12 01	12 04						12 20		12 27				12 31	12 34				
Streatham	d									11 55	11 58											12 25	12 28	
Tulse Hill	d				11 46					11 59	12 02							12 16				12 29	12 32	
Herne Hill	a																							
Loughborough Jn	a																							
Elephant & Castle	a																							
London Blackfriars	a																							
City Thameslink	a																							
St Pancras International	a																							
Luton Airport Parkway	a																							
Luton	a																							
North Dulwich	d				11 49						12 05							12 19					12 35	
East Dulwich	d				11 51						12 07							12 21					12 37	
Peckham Rye	d	11 56			11 53						12 10			12 26				12 23					12 40	
Queens Rd Peckham	d	11 59			11 56						12 12			12 29				12 26					12 42	
South Bermondsey	d	12 01			11 58						12 15			12 31				12 28					12 45	
London Bridge	a	12 06		12 01	12 03					12 10	12 19	12 18		12 36		12 13	12 31	12 33				[illegible]	[illegible]	[illegible]

East and West Croydon, London Milton Keynes Central and Luton via Norbury Crystal Palace - Tulse Hill

Local Services

		SN ◇1	SN	SN	SN	SN	SN	SN ◇1	SN	LO	FC	SN	SN	SN	SN	SN		SN 1	LO	SN	SN	SN ◇1	SN	LO	FC
East Croydon	d	12 26	12 23					12 40				12 42	12 47	12 53				12 56				13 10			
West Croydon	d				12 22	12 34			12 37	12 42						12 52			12 57	13 04			13 07	13 12	
Norwood Junction	a				12 26	12 39				12 46			12 51			12 56		13 00	13 01	13 09				13 16	
	d				12 27	12 40							12 52			12 57		13 01		13 10					
Selhurst	d		12 26						12 41			12 46		12 57									13 11		
Thornton Heath	d		12 28						12 43			12 48		12 59									13 13		
Norbury	d		12 31						12 46			12 51		13 02									13 16		
Streatham Common	d		12 34						12 49			12 53		13 04									13 19		
Beckenham Junction	d																								
Birkbeck	d																								
Crystal Palace	d				12 31		12 37									13 01					13 07				
Gipsy Hill	d				12 33		12 39									13 03					13 09				
West Norwood	d				12 36		12 42									13 06					13 12				
Streatham Hill	d				12 40											13 10									
Balham	d		12 38		12 43				12 53					13 08		13 13							13 23		
Wandsworth Common	d				12 45											13 15									
Clapham Junction	d	12 38	12 42		12 49			12 55	12 57					13 13		13 19						13 25	13 27		
Imperial Wharf	d																								
West Brompton	d																								
Kensington (Olympia)	d																								
Shepherd's Bush	d																								
Wembley Central	d																								
Harrow & Wealdstone	d																								
Watford Junction	d																								
Milton Keynes Central	a																								
Battersea Park	d			12 45	12 52										13 15	13 23									
London Victoria	a	12 46	12 50		12 57			13 01	13 04					13 20		13 27						13 31	13 34		
Streatham	d										12 55	12 58													13 25
Tulse Hill	d						12 46				12 59	13 02									13 16				13 29
Herne Hill	a																								
Loughborough Jn	a																								
Elephant & Castle	a																								
London Blackfriars	a																								
City Thameslink	a																								
St Pancras International	a																								
Luton Airport Parkway	a																								
Luton	a																								
North Dulwich	d						12 49					13 05									13 19				
East Dulwich	d						12 51					13 07									13 21				
Peckham Rye	d			12 56			12 53					13 10			13 26						13 23				
Queens Rd Peckham	d			12 59			12 56					13 12			13 29						13 26				
South Bermondsey	d			13 01			12 58					13 15			13 31						13 28				
London Bridge	a			13 06		13 01	13 03				13 10	13 19	13 18		13 36			13 13		13 31	13 33				13 40

		SN	SN	SN ◇1	SN	SN	SN	LO		SN	SN	SN ◇1	SN	LO	FC	SN	SN	SN	SN	SN	SN 1	LO	SN	SN	
East Croydon	d	13 12	13 17	13 26	13 23							13 40				13 42	13 47	13 53			13 56				
West Croydon	d						13 22	13 27		13 34			13 37	13 42						13 52		13 57	14 04		
Norwood Junction	a		13 21				13 26	13 31		13 39				13 46			13 51			13 56	14 00	14 01	14 09		
	d		13 22				13 27			13 40							13 52			13 57	14 01		14 10		
Selhurst	d	13 16			13 26								13 41			13 46		13 57							
Thornton Heath	d	13 18			13 28								13 43			13 48		13 59							
Norbury	d	13 21			13 31								13 46			13 51		14 02							
Streatham Common	d	13 23			13 34								13 49			13 53		14 04							
Beckenham Junction	d																								
Birkbeck	d																								
Crystal Palace	d						13 31				13 37									14 01				14 07	
Gipsy Hill	d						13 33				13 39									14 03				14 09	
West Norwood	d						13 36				13 42									14 06				14 12	
Streatham Hill	d						13 40													14 10					
Balham	d				13 38		13 43						13 53					14 08		14 13					
Wandsworth Common	d						13 45													14 15					
Clapham Junction	d			13 38	13 42		13 49					13 55	13 57					14 13		14 19					
Imperial Wharf	d																								
West Brompton	d																								
Kensington (Olympia)	d																								
Shepherd's Bush	d																								
Wembley Central	d																								
Harrow & Wealdstone	d																								
Watford Junction	d																								
Milton Keynes Central	a																								
Battersea Park	d					13 45	13 52												14 15	14 23					
London Victoria	a			13 46	13 50		13 57					14 01	14 04					14 20		14 27					
Streatham	d	13 28													13 55	13 58									
Tulse Hill	d	13 32									13 46				13 59	14 02								14 16	
Herne Hill	a																								
Loughborough Jn	a																								
Elephant & Castle	a																								
London Blackfriars	a																								
City Thameslink	a																								
St Pancras International	a																								
Luton Airport Parkway	a																								
Luton	a																								
North Dulwich	d	13 35									13 49					14 05								14 19	
East Dulwich	d	13 37									13 51					14 07								14 21	
Peckham Rye	d	13 40				13 56					13 53					14 10			14 26					14 23	
Queens Rd Peckham	d	13 42				13 59					13 56					14 12			14 29					14 26	
South Bermondsey	d	13 45				14 01					13 58					14 15			14 31					14 28	
London Bridge	a	13 49	13 48			14 06				14 01	14 03				14 10	14 19	14 18		14 36		14 13		14 31	14 33	

East and West Croydon, London Milton Keynes Central and Luton via Norbury Crystal Palace - Tulse Hill

Local Services

		SN ◇1	SN	LO	FC	SN	SN	SN ◇1	SN	SN	SN	LO	SN	SN	SN ◇1	SN		LO	FC	SN	SN	SN	SN	SN	SN 1
East Croydon	d	14 10				14 12	14 17	14 26	14 23						14 40					14 42	14 47	14 53			14 56
West Croydon	d		14 07	14 12							14 22	14 27	14 34			14 37		14 42						14 52	
Norwood Junction	a			14 16			14 21				14 26	14 31	14 39					14 46			14 51			14 56	15 00
	d						14 22				14 27		14 40								14 52			14 57	15 01
Selhurst	d		14 11			14 16			14 26							14 41				14 46		14 57			
Thornton Heath	d		14 13			14 18			14 28							14 43				14 48		14 59			
Norbury	d		14 16			14 21			14 31							14 46				14 51		15 02			
Streatham Common	d		14 19			14 23			14 34							14 49				14 53		15 04			
Beckenham Junction	d																								
Birkbeck	d																								
Crystal Palace	d										14 31			14 37										15 01	
Gipsy Hill	d										14 33			14 39										15 03	
West Norwood	d										14 36			14 42										15 06	
Streatham Hill	d										14 40													15 10	
Balham	d		14 23						14 38		14 43					14 53						15 08		15 13	
Wandsworth Common	d										14 45													15 15	
Clapham Junction	d	14 25	14 27					14 38	14 42		14 49				14 55	14 57						15 13		15 19	
Imperial Wharf	d																								
West Brompton	d																								
Kensington (Olympia)	d																								
Shepherd's Bush	d																								
Wembley Central	d																								
Harrow & Wealdstone	d																								
Watford Junction	d																								
Milton Keynes Central	a																								
Battersea Park	d									14 45	14 52												15 15	15 23	
London Victoria	a	14 31	14 34					14 46	14 50		14 57				15 01	15 04						15 20		15 27	
Streatham	d				14 25	14 28													14 55	14 58					
Tulse Hill	d				14 29	14 32								14 46					14 59	15 02					
Herne Hill	a																								
Loughborough Jn	a																								
Elephant & Castle	a																								
London Blackfriars	a																								
City Thameslink	a																								
St Pancras International	a																								
Luton Airport Parkway	a																								
Luton	a																								
North Dulwich	d					14 35								14 49						15 05					
East Dulwich	d					14 37								14 51						15 07					
Peckham Rye	d					14 40				14 56				14 53						15 10			15 26		
Queens Rd Peckham	d					14 42				14 59				14 56						15 12			15 29		
South Bermondsey	d					14 45				15 01				14 58						15 15			15 31		
London Bridge	a				14 40	14 49	14 48			15 06			15 01	15 03					15 10	15 19	15 18		15 36		15 13

		LO	SN	SN	SN ◇1	SN	LO	FC		SN	SN	SN ◇1	SN	SN	SN	LO	SN	SN	SN ◇1	SN	LO	FC	SN	SN	
East Croydon	d				15 10					15 12	15 17	15 26	15 23						15 40				15 42	15 47	
West Croydon	d	14 57	15 04			15 07	15 12								15 22	15 27	15 34			15 37	15 42				
Norwood Junction	a	15 01	15 09				15 16				15 21				15 26	15 31	15 39				15 46			15 51	
	d		15 10								15 22				15 27		15 40							15 52	
Selhurst	d					15 11				15 16			15 26							15 41			15 46		
Thornton Heath	d					15 13				15 18			15 28							15 43			15 48		
Norbury	d					15 16				15 21			15 31							15 46			15 51		
Streatham Common	d					15 19				15 23			15 34							15 49			15 53		
Beckenham Junction	d																								
Birkbeck	d																								
Crystal Palace	d			15 07											15 31			15 37							
Gipsy Hill	d			15 09											15 33			15 39							
West Norwood	d			15 12											15 36			15 42							
Streatham Hill	d														15 40										
Balham	d					15 23							15 38		15 43					15 53					
Wandsworth Common	d														15 45										
Clapham Junction	d				15 25	15 27						15 38	15 42		15 49				15 55	15 57					
Imperial Wharf	d																								
West Brompton	d																								
Kensington (Olympia)	d																								
Shepherd's Bush	d																								
Wembley Central	d																								
Harrow & Wealdstone	d																								
Watford Junction	d																								
Milton Keynes Central	a																								
Battersea Park	d													15 45	15 52										
London Victoria	a				15 31	15 34						15 46	15 50		15 57				16 01	16 04					
Streatham	d							15 25		15 28												15 55	15 58		
Tulse Hill	d			15 16				15 29		15 32								15 46				15 59	16 02		
Herne Hill	a																								
Loughborough Jn	a																								
Elephant & Castle	a																								
London Blackfriars	a																								
City Thameslink	a																								
St Pancras International	a																								
Luton Airport Parkway	a																								
Luton	a																								
North Dulwich	d			15 19						15 35								15 49					16 05		
East Dulwich	d			15 21						15 37								15 51					16 07		
Peckham Rye	d			15 23						15 40				15 56				15 53					16 10		
Queens Rd Peckham	d			15 26						15 42				15 59				15 56					16 12		
South Bermondsey	d			15 28						15 45				16 01				15 58					16 15		
London Bridge	a		15 31	15 33				15 40		15 49	15 48			16 06			16 01	16 03				16 10	16 19	16 18	

Table 177

Sundays from 11 September

East and West Croydon, London Milton Keynes Central and Luton via Norbury Crystal Palace - Tulse Hill

Local Services

		SN	SN	SN	SN	LO	SN	SN	SN	SN	LO	FC	SN	SN	SN	SN		SN	SN	LO	SN	SN	SN	SN	LO
					1				◇1						◇1								◇1		
East Croydon	d	15 53			15 56				16 10				16 12	16 17	16 26	16 23							16 40		
West Croydon	d			15 52		15 57	16 04			16 07	16 12								16 22	16 27	16 34			16 37	16 42
Norwood Junction	a			15 56	16 00	16 01	16 09				16 16			16 21					16 26	16 31	16 39				16 46
	d			15 57	16 01		16 10							16 22					16 27		16 40				
Selhurst	d	15 57								16 11			16 16			16 26								16 41	
Thornton Heath	d	15 59								16 13			16 18			16 28								16 43	
Norbury	d	16 02								16 16			16 21			16 31								16 46	
Streatham Common	d	16 04								16 19			16 23			16 34								16 49	
Beckenham Junction	d																								
Birkbeck	d																								
Crystal Palace	d			16 01				16 07											16 31			16 37			
Gipsy Hill	d			16 03				16 09											16 33			16 39			
West Norwood	d			16 06				16 12											16 36			16 42			
Streatham Hill	d			16 10															16 40						
Balham	d	16 08		16 13						16 23						16 38			16 43					16 53	
Wandsworth Common	d			16 15															16 45						
Clapham Junction	d	16 13		16 19					16 25	16 27					16 38	16 42			16 49				16 55	16 57	
Imperial Wharf	d																								
West Brompton	d																								
Kensington (Olympia)	d																								
Shepherd's Bush	d																								
Wembley Central	d																								
Harrow & Wealdstone	d																								
Watford Junction	d																								
Milton Keynes Central	a																								
Battersea Park	d		16 15	16 23														16 45	16 52						
London Victoria	a	16 20		16 27					16 31	16 34					16 46	16 50			16 57				17 01	17 04	
Streatham	d											16 25	16 28												
Tulse Hill	d							16 16				16 29	16 32									16 46			
Herne Hill	a																								
Loughborough Jn	a																								
Elephant & Castle	a																								
London Blackfriars	a																								
City Thameslink	a																								
St Pancras International	a																								
Luton Airport Parkway	a																								
Luton	a																								
North Dulwich	d							16 19					16 35									16 49			
East Dulwich	d							16 21					16 37									16 51			
Peckham Rye	d		16 26					16 23					16 40					16 56				16 53			
Queens Rd Peckham	d		16 29					16 26					16 42					16 59				16 56			
South Bermondsey	d		16 31					16 28					16 45					17 01				16 58			
London Bridge	a		16 36		16 13		16 31	16 33				16 40	16 49	16 48				17 06			17 01	17 03			

		FC	SN	SN	SN	SN	SN	SN		LO	SN	SN	SN	SN	LO	FC	SN	SN	SN	SN	SN	SN	LO	SN
								1					◇1						◇1					
East Croydon	d		16 42	16 47	16 53			16 56					17 10				17 12	17 17	17 26	17 23				
West Croydon	d						16 52			16 57	17 04			17 07	17 12							17 22	17 27	17 34
Norwood Junction	a			16 51			16 56	17 00		17 01	17 09				17 16			17 21				17 26	17 31	17 39
	d			16 52			16 57	17 01			17 10							17 22				17 27		17 40
Selhurst	d		16 46		16 57									17 11			17 16			17 26				
Thornton Heath	d		16 48		16 59									17 13			17 18			17 28				
Norbury	d		16 51		17 02									17 16			17 21			17 31				
Streatham Common	d		16 53		17 04									17 19			17 23			17 34				
Beckenham Junction	d																							
Birkbeck	d																							
Crystal Palace	d						17 01					17 07										17 31		
Gipsy Hill	d						17 03					17 09										17 33		
West Norwood	d						17 06					17 12										17 36		
Streatham Hill	d						17 10															17 40		
Balham	d				17 08		17 13							17 23						17 38		17 43		
Wandsworth Common	d						17 15															17 45		
Clapham Junction	d				17 13		17 19						17 25	17 27					17 38	17 42		17 49		
Imperial Wharf	d																							
West Brompton	d																							
Kensington (Olympia)	d																							
Shepherd's Bush	d																							
Wembley Central	d																							
Harrow & Wealdstone	d																							
Watford Junction	d																							
Milton Keynes Central	a																							
Battersea Park	d					17 15	17 23														17 45	17 52		
London Victoria	a				17 20		17 27						17 31	17 34					17 46	17 50		17 57		
Streatham	d	16 55	16 58													17 25	17 28							
Tulse Hill	d	16 59	17 02									17 16				17 29	17 32							
Herne Hill	a																							
Loughborough Jn	a																							
Elephant & Castle	a																							
London Blackfriars	a																							
City Thameslink	a																							
St Pancras International	a																							
Luton Airport Parkway	a																							
Luton	a																							
North Dulwich	d		17 05									17 19					17 35							
East Dulwich	d		17 07									17 21					17 37							
Peckham Rye	d		17 10			17 26						17 23					17 40				17 56			
Queens Rd Peckham	d		17 12			17 29						17 26					17 42				17 59			
South Bermondsey	d		17 15			17 31						17 28					17 45				18 01			
London Bridge	a	17 10	17 19	17 18		17 36		17 13			17 31	17 33				17 40	17 49	17 48			18 06			18 01

Table 177

Sundays from 11 September

East and West Croydon, London Milton Keynes Central and Luton via Norbury Crystal Palace - Tulse Hill

Local Services

		SN	SN	SN	LO	FC	SN	SN	SN	SN	SN	SN	LO	SN	SN	SN		SN	LO	FC	SN	SN	SN	SN	SN
			◇1									1				◇1							◇1		
East Croydon	d		17 40				17 42	17 47	17 53			17 56				18 10					18 12	18 17	18 26	18 23	
West Croydon	d			17 37	17 42						17 52		17 57	18 04				18 07	18 12						
Norwood Junction	a				17 46			17 51			17 56	18 00	18 01	18 09					18 16			18 21			
	d							17 52			17 57	18 01		18 10								18 22			
Selhurst	d			17 41			17 46		17 57									18 11			18 16			18 26	
Thornton Heath	d			17 43			17 48		17 59									18 13			18 18			18 28	
Norbury	d			17 46			17 51		18 02									18 16			18 21			18 31	
Streatham Common	d			17 49			17 53		18 04									18 19			18 23			18 34	
Beckenham Junction	d																								
Birkbeck	d																								
Crystal Palace	d	17 37									18 01				18 07										
Gipsy Hill	d	17 39									18 03				18 09										
West Norwood	d	17 42									18 06				18 12										
Streatham Hill	d										18 10														
Balham	d			17 53					18 08		18 13							18 23						18 38	
Wandsworth Common	d										18 15														
Clapham Junction	d		17 55	17 57					18 13		18 19					18 25		18 27					18 38	18 42	
Imperial Wharf	d																								
West Brompton	d																								
Kensington (Olympia)	d																								
Shepherd's Bush	d																								
Wembley Central	d																								
Harrow & Wealdstone	d																								
Watford Junction	d																								
Milton Keynes Central	a																								
Battersea Park	d									18 15	18 23														18 45
London Victoria	a		18 01	18 04					18 20		18 27					18 31		18 34					18 46	18 50	
Streatham	d					17 55	17 58													18 25	18 28				
Tulse Hill	d	17 46				17 59	18 02								18 16					18 29	18 32				
Herne Hill	a																								
Loughborough Jn	a																								
Elephant & Castle	a																								
London Blackfriars	a																								
City Thameslink	a																								
St Pancras International	a																								
Luton Airport Parkway	a																								
Luton	a																								
North Dulwich	d	17 49					18 05								18 19						18 35				
East Dulwich	d	17 51					18 07								18 21						18 37				
Peckham Rye	d	17 53					18 10			18 26					18 23						18 40				18 56
Queens Rd Peckham	d	17 56					18 12			18 29					18 26						18 42				18 59
South Bermondsey	d	17 58					18 15			18 31					18 28						18 45				19 01
London Bridge	a	18 03				18 10	18 19	18 18		18 36		18 13		18 31	18 33					18 40	18 49	18 48			19 06

Table 177

Sundays
from 11 September

East and West Croydon, London Milton Keynes Central and Luton via Norbury Crystal Palace - Tulse Hill

Local Services

		SN	LO	SN	SN	SN	SN	LO	FC	SN	SN	SN	SN	SN	SN	LO	SN	SN	SN	SN	LO	FC	SN
						◇1									1				◇1				
East Croydon	d					18 40				18 42	18 47	18 53			18 56				19 10				19 12
West Croydon 4	d	18 22	18 27	18 34			18 37	18 42						18 52		18 57	19 04			19 07	19 12		
Norwood Junction 2	a	18 26	18 31	18 39				18 46			18 51			18 56	19 00	19 01	19 09				19 16		
	d	18 27		18 40							18 52			18 57	19 01		19 10						
Selhurst 4	d						18 41			18 46		18 57								19 11			19 16
Thornton Heath	d						18 43			18 48		18 59								19 13			19 18
Norbury	d						18 46			18 51		19 02								19 16			19 21
Streatham Common 4	d						18 49			18 53		19 04								19 19			19 23
Beckenham Junction 4	d																						
Birkbeck	d																						
Crystal Palace 4	d	18 31			18 37									19 01				19 07					
Gipsy Hill	d	18 33			18 39									19 03				19 09					
West Norwood 4	d	18 36			18 42									19 06				19 12					
Streatham Hill	d	18 40												19 10									
Balham 4 ⊖	d	18 43					18 53					19 08		19 13						19 23			
Wandsworth Common	d	18 45												19 15									
Clapham Junction 10	d	18 49				18 55	18 57					19 13		19 19					19 25	19 27			
Imperial Wharf	d																						
West Brompton ⊖	d																						
Kensington (Olympia) ⊖	d																						
Shepherd's Bush ⊖	d																						
Wembley Central ⊖	d																						
Harrow & Wealdstone ⊖	d																						
Watford Junction	d																						
Milton Keynes Central 10	a																						
Battersea Park 4	d	18 52											19 15	19 23									
London Victoria 15 ⊖	a	18 57				19 01	19 04					19 20		19 27					19 31	19 34			
Streatham 4	d								18 55	18 58												19 25	19 28
Tulse Hill 3	d				18 46				18 59	19 02								19 16				19 29	19 32
Herne Hill 4	a																						
Loughborough Jn	a																						
Elephant & Castle ⊖	a																						
London Blackfriars 3 ⊖	a																						
City Thameslink 3	a																						
St Pancras International 15 ⊖	a																						
Luton Airport Parkway 7	a																						
Luton 10	a																						
North Dulwich	d				18 49					19 05								19 19					19 35
East Dulwich	d				18 51					19 07								19 21					19 37
Peckham Rye 4	d				18 53					19 10			19 26					19 23					19 40
Queens Rd Peckham	d				18 56					19 12			19 29					19 26					19 42
South Bermondsey	d				18 58					19 15			19 31					19 28					19 45
London Bridge 4 ⊖	a			19 01	19 03				19 10	19 19	19 18		19 36		19 13		19 31	19 33				19 40	19 49

		SN	SN	SN	SN	SN	LO	SN	SN	SN	SN	LO	FC	SN	SN	SN	SN	SN	SN	LO	SN	SN	SN	SN
			◇1							◇1									1				◇1	
East Croydon	d	19 17	19 26	19 23						19 40				19 42	19 47	19 53			19 56				20 10	
West Croydon 4	d					19 22	19 27	19 34			19 37	19 42						19 52		19 57	20 04			20 07
Norwood Junction 2	a	19 21				19 26	19 31	19 39				19 46			19 51			19 56	20 00	20 01	20 09			
	d	19 22				19 27		19 40							19 52			19 57	20 01		20 10			
Selhurst 4	d			19 26							19 41			19 46		19 57								20 11
Thornton Heath	d			19 28							19 43			19 48		19 59								20 13
Norbury	d			19 31							19 46			19 51		20 02								20 16
Streatham Common 4	d			19 34							19 49			19 53		20 04								20 19
Beckenham Junction 4	d																							
Birkbeck	d																							
Crystal Palace 4	d					19 31			19 37									20 01				20 07		
Gipsy Hill	d					19 33			19 39									20 03				20 09		
West Norwood 4	d					19 36			19 42									20 06				20 12		
Streatham Hill	d					19 40												20 10						
Balham 4 ⊖	d			19 38		19 43					19 53					20 08		20 13						20 23
Wandsworth Common	d					19 45												20 15						
Clapham Junction 10	d		19 38	19 42		19 49				19 55	19 57					20 13		20 19					20 25	20 27
Imperial Wharf	d																							
West Brompton ⊖	d																							
Kensington (Olympia) ⊖	d																							
Shepherd's Bush ⊖	d																							
Wembley Central ⊖	d																							
Harrow & Wealdstone ⊖	d																							
Watford Junction	d																							
Milton Keynes Central 10	a																							
Battersea Park 4	d				19 45	19 52											20 15	20 22						
London Victoria 15 ⊖	a		19 46	19 50		19 57				20 01	20 04					20 20		20 27					20 31	20 34
Streatham 4	d												19 55	19 58										
Tulse Hill 3	d								19 46				19 59	20 02								20 16		
Herne Hill 4	a																							
Loughborough Jn	a																							
Elephant & Castle ⊖	a																							
London Blackfriars 3 ⊖	a																							
City Thameslink 3	a																							
St Pancras International 15 ⊖	a																							
Luton Airport Parkway 7	a																							
Luton 10	a																							
North Dulwich	d								19 49					20 05								20 19		
East Dulwich	d								19 51					20 07								20 21		
Peckham Rye 4	d				19 56				19 53					20 10			20 26					20 23		
Queens Rd Peckham	d				19 59				19 56					20 12			20 29					20 26		
South Bermondsey	d				20 01				19 58					20 15			20 31					20 28		
London Bridge 4 ⊖	a	19 48			20 06			20 01	20 03				20 10	20 19	20 18		20 36		20 13		20 31	20 33		

East and West Croydon, London Milton Keynes Central and Luton via Norbury Crystal Palace - Tulse Hill

Local Services

		LO	FC	SN	SN	SN	SN	SN	SN	LO	SN	SN	SN	SN	LO	FC	SN	SN	SN	SN	SN	SN	LO
						◇1							◇1									1	
East Croydon	d			20 12	20 17	20 26	20 23						20 40				20 42	20 47	20 53			20 56	
West Croydon 4	d	20 12							20 22	20 27	20 34			20 37	20 42						20 52		20 57
Norwood Junction 2	a	20 16			20 21				20 26	20 31	20 39				20 46			20 51			20 56	21 00	21 01
	d				20 22				20 27		20 40							20 52			20 57	21 01	
Selhurst 4	d			20 16			20 26							20 41			20 46		20 57				
Thornton Heath	d			20 18			20 28							20 43			20 48		20 59				
Norbury	d			20 21			20 31							20 46			20 51		21 02				
Streatham Common 4	d			20 23			20 34							20 49			20 53		21 04				
Beckenham Junction 4	d																						
Birkbeck	d																						
Crystal Palace 4	d								20 31			20 37									21 01		
Gipsy Hill	d								20 33			20 39									21 03		
West Norwood 4	d								20 36			20 42									21 06		
Streatham Hill	d								20 40												21 10		
Balham 4 ⊖	d						20 38		20 43					20 53					21 08		21 13		
Wandsworth Common	d								20 45												21 15		
Clapham Junction 10	d					20 38	20 42		20 49				20 55	20 57					21 13		21 19		
Imperial Wharf	d																						
West Brompton ⊖	d																						
Kensington (Olympia) ⊖	d																						
Shepherd's Bush ⊖	d																						
Wembley Central ⊖	d																						
Harrow & Wealdstone ⊖	d																						
Watford Junction	d																						
Milton Keynes Central 10	a																						
Battersea Park 4	d							20 45	20 52											21 15	21 23		
London Victoria 15 ⊖	a					20 46	20 50		20 57				21 01	21 04					21 20		21 27		
Streatham 4	d		20 25	20 28												20 55	20 58						
Tulse Hill 3	d		20 29	20 32								20 46				20 59	21 02						
Herne Hill 4	a																						
Loughborough Jn	a																						
Elephant & Castle ⊖	a																						
London Blackfriars 3 ⊖	a																						
City Thameslink 3	a																						
St Pancras International 15 ⊖	a																						
Luton Airport Parkway 7	a																						
Luton 10	a																						
North Dulwich	d			20 35								20 49					21 05						
East Dulwich	d			20 37								20 51					21 07						
Peckham Rye 4	d			20 40				20 56				20 53					21 10			21 26			
Queens Rd Peckham	d			20 42				20 59				20 56					21 12			21 29			
South Bermondsey	d			20 45				21 01				20 58					21 15			21 31			
London Bridge 4 ⊖	a		20 40	20 49	20 48			21 06			21 01	21 03				21 10	21 19	21 18		21 36		21 13	

		SN	SN	SN	SN	LO	FC	SN	SN	SN	SN	SN	SN	LO	SN	SN	SN	SN	LO	FC	SN	SN	SN	SN
				◇1						◇1							◇1							
East Croydon	d			21 10				21 12	21 17	21 26	21 23						21 40				21 42	21 47	21 53	
West Croydon 4	d	21 04			21 07	21 12							21 22	21 27	21 34			21 37	21 42					
Norwood Junction 2	a	21 09				21 16			21 21				21 26	21 31	21 39				21 46			21 51		
	d	21 10							21 22				21 27		21 40							21 52		
Selhurst 4	d				21 11			21 16			21 26							21 41			21 46		21 56	
Thornton Heath	d				21 13			21 18			21 28							21 43			21 48		21 58	
Norbury	d				21 16			21 21			21 31							21 46			21 51		22 01	
Streatham Common 4	d				21 19			21 23			21 34							21 49			21 53		22 04	
Beckenham Junction 4	d																							
Birkbeck	d																							
Crystal Palace 4	d		21 07										21 31			21 37								
Gipsy Hill	d		21 09										21 33			21 39								
West Norwood 4	d		21 12										21 36			21 42								
Streatham Hill	d												21 40											
Balham 4 ⊖	d				21 23						21 38		21 43					21 53					22 08	
Wandsworth Common	d												21 45											
Clapham Junction 10	d			21 25	21 27					21 38	21 42		21 49				21 55	21 57					22 12	
Imperial Wharf	d																							
West Brompton ⊖	d																							
Kensington (Olympia) ⊖	d																							
Shepherd's Bush ⊖	d																							
Wembley Central ⊖	d																							
Harrow & Wealdstone ⊖	d																							
Watford Junction	d																							
Milton Keynes Central 10	a																							
Battersea Park 4	d											21 45	21 53											22 15
London Victoria 15 ⊖	a			21 31	21 34					21 46	21 50		21 57				22 01	22 04					22 20	
Streatham 4	d						21 25	21 28												21 55	21 58			
Tulse Hill 3	d		21 16				21 29	21 32								21 46				21 59	22 02			
Herne Hill 4	a																							
Loughborough Jn	a																							
Elephant & Castle ⊖	a																							
London Blackfriars 3 ⊖	a																							
City Thameslink 3	a																							
St Pancras International 15 ⊖	a																							
Luton Airport Parkway 7	a																							
Luton 10	a																							
North Dulwich	d		21 19					21 35								21 49					22 05			
East Dulwich	d		21 21					21 37								21 51					22 07			
Peckham Rye 4	d		21 23					21 40				21 56				21 53					22 10			22 26
Queens Rd Peckham	d		21 26					21 42				21 59				21 56					22 12			22 29
South Bermondsey	d		21 28					21 45				22 01				21 58					22 15			22 31
London Bridge 4 ⊖	a	21 31	21 33				21 40	21 49	21 48			22 06			22 01	22 03				22 10	22 19	22 18		22 36

East and West Croydon, London Milton Keynes Central and Luton via Norbury Crystal Palace - Tulse Hill

Local Services

Station		SN	SN [1]	LO	SN	SN	SN ◇[1]	SN		SN	LO	SN	SN ◇[1]	SN	SN	SN	LO	SN	SN	SN	SN	LO	SN	SN
East Croydon	d		21 56				22 10			22 12		22 17	22 26	22 23							22 42		22 47	22 53
West Croydon [4]	d	21 52		21 57	22 04			22 07			22 12					22 22	22 27	22 34	22 37			22 42		
Norwood Junction [2]	a	21 56	22 00	22 01	22 09						22 16	22 21				22 26	22 31	22 39				22 46	22 51	
	d	21 57	22 01		22 10							22 22				22 27		22 40					22 52	
Selhurst [4]	d							22 11		22 16				22 26					22 41		22 46			22 57
Thornton Heath	d							22 13		22 18				22 28					22 43		22 48			22 59
Norbury	d							22 16		22 21				22 31					22 46		22 51			23 02
Streatham Common [4]	d							22 19		22 23				22 34					22 49		22 53			23 04
Beckenham Junction [4]	d																							
Birkbeck	d																							
Crystal Palace [4]	d	22 01				22 07										22 31				22 37				
Gipsy Hill	d	22 03				22 09										22 33				22 39				
West Norwood [4]	d	22 06				22 12										22 36				22 42				
Streatham Hill	d	22 10														22 40								
Balham [4] ⊖	d	22 13						22 23						22 38		22 43			22 53					23 08
Wandsworth Common	d	22 15														22 45								
Clapham Junction [10]	d	22 19					22 25	22 27					22 38	22 42		22 49			22 57					23 13
Imperial Wharf	d																							
West Brompton ⊖	d																							
Kensington (Olympia) ⊖	d																							
Shepherd's Bush ⊖	d																							
Wembley Central ⊖	d																							
Harrow & Wealdstone ⊖	d																							
Watford Junction	d																							
Milton Keynes Central [10]	a																							
Battersea Park [4]	d	22 23													22 45	22 53								
London Victoria [15] ⊖	a	22 27					22 31	22 34					22 46	22 50		22 57			23 04					23 20
Streatham [4]	d									22 28											22 58			
Tulse Hill [3]	d					22 16				22 32										22 46	23 02			
Herne Hill [4]	a																							
Loughborough Jn	a																							
Elephant & Castle ⊖	a																							
London Blackfriars [3] ⊖	a																							
City Thameslink [3]	a																							
St Pancras International [15] ⊖	a																							
Luton Airport Parkway [7]	a																							
Luton [10]	a																							
North Dulwich	d					22 19				22 35										22 49	23 05			
East Dulwich	d					22 21				22 37										22 51	23 07			
Peckham Rye [4]	d					22 23				22 40					22 56					22 53	23 10			
Queens Rd Peckham	d					22 26				22 42					22 59					22 56	23 12			
South Bermondsey	d					22 28				22 45					23 01					22 58	23 15			
London Bridge [4] ⊖	a		22 13		22 31	22 33				22 49		22 48			23 06			23 01		23 03	23 19		23 17	

Station		SN [1]	SN	SN	LO	SN	SN	SN	SN	SN ◇[1]	SN	SN	SN	SN	SN [1]
East Croydon	d	22 56						23 17	23 26	23 27					23 56
West Croydon [4]	d			22 52	22 57	23 07					23 22	23 37		23 52	
Norwood Junction [2]	a			22 56	23 01			23 21			23 26				
	d			22 57							23 27				
Selhurst [4]	d	22 59				23 11			23a29			23 41		23 56	00 01
Thornton Heath	d					23 13						23 43		23 58	
Norbury	d					23 16						23 46		00 01	
Streatham Common [4]	d					23 19						23 49		00 04	
Beckenham Junction [4]	d														
Birkbeck	d														
Crystal Palace [4]	d			23 01			23 07				23 31		23 37		
Gipsy Hill	d			23 03			23 09				23 33		23 39		
West Norwood [4]	d			23 06			23 12				23 36		23 42		
Streatham Hill	d			23 10							23 40				
Balham [4] ⊖	d			23 13		23 23					23 43	23 53		00 08	
Wandsworth Common	d			23 15							23 45				
Clapham Junction [10]	d	23 08		23 19		23 27				23 39	23 49	23 58		00 12	00 11
Imperial Wharf	d														
West Brompton ⊖	d														
Kensington (Olympia) ⊖	d														
Shepherd's Bush ⊖	d														
Wembley Central ⊖	d														
Harrow & Wealdstone ⊖	d														
Watford Junction	d														
Milton Keynes Central [10]	a														
Battersea Park [4]	d		23 15	23 23							23 53				
London Victoria [15] ⊖	a	23 14		23 27		23 34				23 46	23 57	00 04		00 19	00 21
Streatham [4]	d														
Tulse Hill [3]	d						23 16						23 46		
Herne Hill [4]	a														
Loughborough Jn	a														
Elephant & Castle ⊖	a														
London Blackfriars [3] ⊖	a														
City Thameslink [3]	a														
St Pancras International [15] ⊖	a														
Luton Airport Parkway [7]	a														
Luton [10]	a														
North Dulwich	d						23 19						23 49		
East Dulwich	d						23 21						23 51		
Peckham Rye [4]	d		23 26				23 23						23 53		
Queens Rd Peckham	d		23 29				23 26						23 56		
South Bermondsey	d		23 31				23 28						23 58		
London Bridge [4] ⊖	a		23 36				23 33						00 03		

London Bridge to London Victoria - Croydon and East London Line

Miles	Miles	Miles	Miles	Miles	Station		SN MX	SN MX	SN MO	SN MX	LO MO	LO MX	SN MX	LO MX	LO MX		SN MX	SN MX	LO MX	LO MX	SN MX	SE	SE	SN	LO
0	0	0	—	—	**London Bridge** [4] ⊖	d	23p22	23p36	23p39				23p52				00 03	00 06			00 36			06 00	
—	—	—	—	—	Highbury & Islington	d					23p23	23p25		23p35	23p42				23p56	00 10					
—	—	—	—	—	Canonbury	d					23p25	23p27		23p37	23p44				23p58	00 12					
—	—	—	0	—	**Dalston Junction Stn ELL**	d					23p28	23p30		23p40	23p47				00 02	00 15					
—	—	—	0½	—	Haggerston	d					23p29	23p31		23p41	23p48				00 03	00 16					
—	—	—	1	—	Hoxton	d					23p31	23p33		23p43	23p50				00 05	00 18					
—	—	—	1¾	—	Shoreditch High Street	d					23p34	23p36		23p46	23p53				00 08	00 21					
—	—	—	2½	—	Whitechapel	d					23p36	23p38		23p48	23p55				00 10	00 23					
—	—	—	3¼	—	Shadwell	d					23p38	23p40		23p50	23p57				00 12	00 25					
—	—	—	3¾	—	Wapping	d					23p40	23p42		23p52	23p59				00 14	00 27					
—	—	—	4	—	Rotherhithe	d					23p42	23p44		23p54	00 01				00 16	00 29					
—	—	—	4¼	—	Canada Water	d					23p44	23p46		23p56	00 03				00 18	00 31					
—	—	—	4½	—	Surrey Quays	d					23p45	23p47		23p57	00 05				00 19	00 32					
—	—	—	5¼	—	**New Cross ELL**	a																			
—	2¾	2¾	5¼	—	**New Cross Gate** [4]	a	23p27	23p41	23p44		23p49	23p51	23p57	00 01	00 08			00 11	00 23	00 36	00 41				
—	—	—	—	—		d	23p27	23p41	23p44		23p50	23p52	23p57	00 02				00 11			00 41				05 47
—	3¾	3¾	—	—	Brockley	d	23p30	23p44	23p47		23p52	23p54	00 01	00 04				00 14			00 44				05 49
—	4¾	4¾	—	—	Honor Oak Park	d	23p33	23p47	23p50		23p55	23p57	00 04	00 07				00 17			00 47				05 52
—	5¾	5¾	—	—	Forest Hill [4]	d	23p35	23p49	23p52		23p58	23p59	00 06	00 10				00 19			00 49				05 55
—	6½	6½	—	—	Sydenham	d	23p38	23p52	23p55		00 01	00 02	00 09	00 12				00 22			00 52				05 57
—	7¼	—	—	—	**Crystal Palace** [4]	d	23p43			00 03		00a07	00 13												
—	8½	—	—	—	Gipsy Hill	d	23p45						00 15												
—	9½	—	—	—	West Norwood [4]	d	23p48						00 18												
—	10¾	—	—	—	Streatham Hill	d	23p52						00 22												
—	11¾	—	—	—	Balham [4] ⊖	d	23p55						00 25												
—	12½	—	—	—	Wandsworth Common	d	23p58						00 27												
—	13¾	—	—	—	Clapham Junction [10]	d	00 02						00 31												
1¼	—	—	—	—	South Bermondsey	d											00 07							06 04	
2¼	—	—	—	—	Queens Rd Peckham	d											00 09							06 06	
3½	—	—	0	0	Peckham Rye [4]	d											00 12					05 04	06 04	06a09	
4¼	—	—	0¾	0¾	Denmark Hill [4]	d																05 07	06 07		
—	—	—	—	4½	**London Blackfriars** [3] ⊖	a																05 17	06 17		
6¼	—	—	—	—	Clapham High Street ⊖	d																			
6¾	—	—	—	—	Wandsworth Road	d																			
7½	15¼	—	—	—	Battersea Park [4]	d	00 05						00 35												
8¼	16½	—	5	—	**London Victoria** [15] ⊖	a	00 10						00 42												
—	—	7¼	—	—	Penge West	d		23p54	23p57		00 03			00 15				00 24			00 54				06 00
—	—	7½	—	—	Anerley	d		23p56	23p59		00 05			00 17				00 26			00 56				06 02
—	—	8¾	—	0	Norwood Junction [2]	d		23p59	00 03	00 09	00 08			00 20			00a34	00 30			01 00				06 05
—	—	—	—	1¾	**West Croydon** [4]	a				00 14	00 15			00 27											06 13
—	—	10	—	—	**East Croydon**	a		00 03	00 06									00 33			01 03				

Station		LO	LO	LO	LO	SN	SN	SE	LO	LO		SN	LO	LO	SN	SN	SE	SN	LO	SN		SN	SE	LO
London Bridge [4] ⊖	d					06 06	06 11					06 19			06 30	06 33				06 36		06 41		
Highbury & Islington	d		05 35							05 55			06 05											
Canonbury	d		05 37							05 57			06 07											
Dalston Junction Stn ELL	d		05 40	05 50						06 00			06 10	06 20										
Haggerston	d		05 41	05 51						06 01			06 11	06 21										
Hoxton	d		05 43	05 53						06 03			06 13	06 23										
Shoreditch High Street	d		05 46	05 56						06 06			06 16	06 26										
Whitechapel	d		05 48	05 58						06 08			06 18	06 28										
Shadwell	d		05 50	06 00						06 10			06 20	06 30										
Wapping	d		05 52	06 02						06 12			06 22	06 32										
Rotherhithe	d		05 54	06 04						06 14			06 24	06 34										
Canada Water	d		05 56	06 06						06 16			06 26	06 36										
Surrey Quays	d		05 57	06 07						06 17			06 27	06 37										
New Cross ELL	a			06 13										06 43										
New Cross Gate [4]	a		06 01			06 11				06 21		06 25	06 31							06 41				
	d	05 52	06 02		06 07	06 11			06 17	06 22		06 25	06 32						06 37	06 41				06 47
Brockley	d	05 54	06 04		06 09	06 14			06 19	06 24		06 27	06 34						06 39	06 44				06 49
Honor Oak Park	d	05 57	06 07		06 12	06 17			06 22	06 27		06 30	06 37						06 42	06 47				06 52
Forest Hill [4]	d	06 00	06 10		06 15	06 19			06 25	06 30		06 33	06 40						06 45	06 49				06 55
Sydenham	d	06 02	06 12		06 17	06 22			06 27	06 32		06 35	06 42						06 47	06 52				06 57
Crystal Palace [4]	d	06a07			06a22					06a37		06 39						06 51	06a52					
Gipsy Hill	d											06 41						06 53						
West Norwood [4]	d											06 44						06 56						
Streatham Hill	d											06 48												
Balham [4] ⊖	d											06 51												
Wandsworth Common	d																							
Clapham Junction [10]	d											06 56												
South Bermondsey	d						06 15								06 34	06 37						06 45		
Queens Rd Peckham	d						06 18								06 36	06 39						06 48		
Peckham Rye [4]	d						06 20	06 30							06a39	06a42	06 47	07a07				06 50	07 02	
Denmark Hill [4]	d						06 23	06 33									06 50					06 53	07 05	
London Blackfriars [3] ⊖	a							06 45															07 16	
Clapham High Street ⊖	d						06 28															06 58		
Wandsworth Road	d						06 29															06 59		
Battersea Park [4]	d						06 32															07 02		
London Victoria [15] ⊖	a						06 36					07 05					07 04					07 08		
Penge West	d		06 15			06 24			06 30				06 45							06 54				07 00
Anerley	d		06 17			06 26			06 32				06 47							06 56				07 02
Norwood Junction [2]	d		06 20			06 30			06 35				06 50							07 00				07 05
West Croydon [4]	a		06 30						06 41				07 00											07 11
East Croydon	a					06 33														07 03				

London Bridge to London Victoria - Croydon and East London Line

		LO	LO	SN	SN	LO	SN		SN	SN	LO	LO	SN	LO	LO	LO	SN		SE	SN	LO	SE	SN	SN	SN
London Bridge 4 ⊖	d			06 51	06 54		06 58		07 03				07 06				07 11			07 21			07 29	07 33	
Highbury & Islington	d	06 25				06 33					06 40			06 48	06 55						07 03				
Canonbury	d	06 27				06 35					06 42			06 50	06 57						07 05				
Dalston Junction Stn ELL	d	06 30	06 35			06 40					06 45	06 50		06 55	07 00	07 05					07 10				
Haggerston	d	06 31	06 36			06 41					06 46	06 51		06 56	07 01	07 06					07 11				
Hoxton	d	06 33	06 38			06 43					06 48	06 53		06 58	07 03	07 08					07 13				
Shoreditch High Street	d	06 36	06 41			06 46					06 51	06 56		07 01	07 06	07 11					07 16				
Whitechapel	d	06 38	06 43			06 48					06 53	06 58		07 03	07 08	07 13					07 18				
Shadwell	d	06 40	06 45			06 50					06 55	07 00		07 05	07 10	07 15					07 20				
Wapping	d	06 42	06 47			06 52					06 57	07 02		07 07	07 12	07 17					07 22				
Rotherhithe	d	06 44	06 49			06 54					06 59	07 04		07 09	07 14	07 19					07 24				
Canada Water	d	06 46	06 51			06 56					07 01	07 06		07 11	07 16	07 21					07 26				
Surrey Quays	d	06 47	06 52			06 57					07 02	07 07		07 12	07 17	07 22					07 27				
New Cross ELL	a		06 58									07 13				07 28									
New Cross Gate 4	a	06 51		06 56	06 59	07 00					07 06		07 11	07 15	07 21					07 26	07 31				
	d	06 52		06 56	06 59	07 02					07 07		07 11	07 17	07 22					07 26	07 32				
Brockley	d	06 54		06 59	07 02	07 04					07 09		07 14	07 19	07 24					07 29	07 34				
Honor Oak Park	d	06 57		07 02	07 05	07 07					07 12		07 17	07 22	07 27					07 32	07 37				
Forest Hill 4	d	07 00		07 04	07 07	07 10					07 15		07 19	07 25	07 30					07 34	07 40				
Sydenham	d	07 02		07 07	07 10	07 12					07 17		07 22	07 27	07 32					07 37	07 42				
Crystal Palace 4	d	07a07		07 13						07 20	07a22				07a37					07 43					07 49
Gipsy Hill	d			07 15						07 22										07 45					07 51
West Norwood 4	d			07 18						07 25										07 48					07 54
Streatham Hill	d			07 22																07 52					
Balham 4 ⊖	d			07 25																07 55					
Wandsworth Common	d			07 27																07 57					
Clapham Junction 10	d			07 31																08 01					
South Bermondsey	d						07 02		07 07								07 15						07 33	07 37	
Queens Rd Peckham	d						07 04		07 09								07 17						07 35	07 39	
Peckham Rye 4	d						07a07		07a12	07a36							07 20		07 23			07 34	07a38	07a42	08a06
Denmark Hill 4	d																07 23		07 29			07 37			
London Blackfriars 3 ⊖	a																					07 48			
Clapham High Street ⊖	d																07 28								
Wandsworth Road	d																07 29								
Battersea Park 4	d			07 35													07 32			08 05					
London Victoria 15 ⊖	a			07 41													07 38		07 42	08 11					
Penge West	d				07 12	07 15							07 24	07 30							07 45				
Anerley	d				07 14	07 17							07 26	07 32							07 47				
Norwood Junction 2	d				07 18	07 20							07 31	07 35							07 50				
West Croydon 4 ⇌	a					07 30								07 42							08 00				
East Croydon ⇌	a				07 21								07 37												

		LO	LO		SN	LO	LO	LO	SN	SE	SN	LO	SE		SN	SE	SN	SE	SN	LO	LO	SN	LO		LO
London Bridge 4 ⊖	d				07 36				07 41		07 51				08 03		08 06					08 06			
Highbury & Islington	d	07 10				07 18	07 25					07 33								07 40			07 48		07 55
Canonbury	d	07 12				07 20	07 27					07 35								07 42			07 50		07 57
Dalston Junction Stn ELL	d	07 15	07 20			07 25	07 30	07 35				07 40								07 45	07 50		07 55		08 00
Haggerston	d	07 16	07 21			07 26	07 31	07 36				07 41								07 46	07 51		07 56		08 01
Hoxton	d	07 18	07 23			07 28	07 33	07 38				07 43								07 48	07 53		07 58		08 03
Shoreditch High Street	d	07 21	07 26			07 31	07 36	07 41				07 46								07 51	07 56		08 01		08 06
Whitechapel	d	07 23	07 28			07 33	07 38	07 43				07 48								07 53	07 58		08 03		08 08
Shadwell	d	07 25	07 30			07 35	07 40	07 45				07 50								07 55	08 00		08 05		08 10
Wapping	d	07 27	07 32			07 37	07 42	07 47				07 52								07 57	08 02		08 07		08 12
Rotherhithe	d	07 29	07 34			07 39	07 44	07 49				07 54								07 59	08 04		08 09		08 14
Canada Water	d	07 31	07 36			07 41	07 46	07 51				07 56								08 01	08 06		08 11		08 16
Surrey Quays	d	07 32	07 37			07 42	07 47	07 52				07 57								08 02	08 07		08 12		08 17
New Cross ELL	a		07 43					07 58													08 13				
New Cross Gate 4	a	07 36			07 41	07 45	07 51				07 56	08 01								08 06		08 11	08 16		08 21
	d	07 37			07 41	07 47	07 52				07 56	08 02								08 07		08 11	08 17		08 22
Brockley	d	07 39			07 44	07 49	07 54				07 59	08 04								08 09		08 14	08 19		08 24
Honor Oak Park	d	07 42			07 47	07 52	07 57				08 02	08 07								08 12		08 17	08 22		08 27
Forest Hill 4	d	07 45			07 49	07 55	08 00				08 04	08 10								08 15		08 19	08 25		08 30
Sydenham	d	07 47			07 52	07 57	08 02				08 07	08 12								08 17		08 22	08 27		08 32
Crystal Palace 4	d	07a52					08a07				08 13								08 19	08a22					08a37
Gipsy Hill	d										08 15								08 21						
West Norwood 4	d										08 18								08 24						
Streatham Hill	d										08 22														
Balham 4 ⊖	d										08 25														
Wandsworth Common	d										08 27														
Clapham Junction 10	d										08 31														
South Bermondsey	d								07 45						08 07		08 11								
Queens Rd Peckham	d								07 47						08 09		08 13								
Peckham Rye 4	d								07 50	07 54			08 01		08a12	08 13	08a16	08 16	08a35						
Denmark Hill 4	d								07 53	07 59			08 04			08 17		08 19							
London Blackfriars 3 ⊖	a												08 17					08 29							
Clapham High Street ⊖	d								07 58																
Wandsworth Road	d								07 59																
Battersea Park 4	d								08 02		08 35														
London Victoria 15 ⊖	a								08 08	08 11	08 41					08 29									
Penge West	d				07 54	08 00						08 15										08 24	08 30		
Anerley	d				07 56	08 02						08 17										08 26	08 32		
Norwood Junction 2	d				08 00	08 05						08 20										08 30	08 35		
West Croydon 4 ⇌	a					08 12						08 30											08 43		
East Croydon ⇌	a				08 03																	08 33			

London Bridge to London Victoria - Croydon and East London Line

		LO	SN	SE	SE [1]	SE	SN	LO	SE [1]		SN	SE	SN	LO	LO	SN	LO	LO	LO		SN	SE	SN	LO	LO
London Bridge 4 ⊖	d		08 10				08 20				08 33					08 36					08 41		08 51		
Highbury & Islington	d							08 03						08 10			08 18	08 25						08 33	08 40
Canonbury	d							08 05						08 12			08 20	08 27						08 35	08 42
Dalston Junction Stn ELL	d	08 05						08 10						08 15	08 20		08 25	08 30	08 35					08 40	08 45
Haggerston	d	08 06						08 11						08 16	08 21		08 26	08 31	08 36					08 41	08 46
Hoxton	d	08 08						08 13						08 18	08 23		08 28	08 33	08 38					08 43	08 48
Shoreditch High Street	d	08 11						08 16						08 21	08 26		08 31	08 36	08 41					08 46	08 51
Whitechapel	d	08 13						08 18						08 23	08 28		08 33	08 38	08 43					08 48	08 53
Shadwell	d	08 15						08 20						08 25	08 30		08 35	08 40	08 45					08 50	08 55
Wapping	d	08 17						08 22						08 27	08 32		08 37	08 42	08 47					08 52	08 57
Rotherhithe	d	08 19						08 24						08 29	08 34		08 39	08 44	08 49					08 54	08 59
Canada Water	d	08 21						08 26						08 31	08 36		08 41	08 46	08 51					08 56	09 01
Surrey Quays	d	08 22						08 27						08 32	08 37		08 42	08 47	08 52					08 57	09 02
New Cross ELL	a	08 28													08 43				08 58						
New Cross Gate 4	a						08 26	08 31						08 36		08 41	08 46	08 51					08 57	09 01	09 06
	d						08 26	08 32						08 37		08 41	08 47	08 52					08 57	09 02	09 07
Brockley	d						08 29	08 34						08 39		08 44	08 49	08 54					09 00	09 04	09 09
Honor Oak Park	d						08 32	08 37						08 42		08 47	08 52	08 57					09 03	09 07	09 12
Forest Hill 4	d						08 34	08 40						08 45		08 49	08 55	09 00					09 05	09 10	09 15
Sydenham	d						08 37	08 42						08 47		08 52	08 57	09 02					09 08	09 12	09 17
Crystal Palace 4	d						08 40						08 50	08a52				09a07					09 11		09a22
Gipsy Hill	d						08 43						08 52										09 14		
West Norwood 4	d						08 46						08 55										09 17		
Streatham Hill	d						08 49																09 21		
Balham 4 ⊖	d						08 55																09 25		
Wandsworth Common	d						08 57																09 27		
Clapham Junction 10	d						09 01																09 31		
South Bermondsey	d		08 14								08 37										08 45				
Queens Rd Peckham	d		08 16								08 39										08 48				
Peckham Rye 4	d		08 19			08 33			08 36		08a42	08 44	09a06								08 50	08 55			
Denmark Hill 4	d		08 22	08 26	08 30	08 36			08 39			08 47									08 53	09 02			
London Blackfriars 3 ⊖	a			08 41					08 50			08 58													
Clapham High Street ⊖	d		08 27																		08 58				
Wandsworth Road	d		08 29																		08 59				
Battersea Park 4	d		08 32				09 05														09 02		09 35		
London Victoria 15 ⊖	a		08 39		08 42	08 49	09 11														09 08	09 11	09 42		
Penge West	d							08 45								08 54	09 00							09 15	
Anerley	d							08 47								08 56	09 02							09 17	
Norwood Junction 2	d							08 50								09 00	09 05							09 20	
West Croydon 4 ⇌	a							09 00									09 12							09 30	
East Croydon ⇌	a															09 06									

		LO	SE	SE [1]	SN		SN	LO	SE	SE	SN	SE	SN	LO	LO		SN	LO	LO	LO	SN	SN	LO	SE	SN
London Bridge 4 ⊖	d				09 03		09 06				09 11						09 22				09 33	09 36			09 41
Highbury & Islington	d							08 48						08 55				09 03	09 10				09 18		
Canonbury	d							08 50						08 57				09 05	09 12				09 20		
Dalston Junction Stn ELL	d	08 50						08 55						09 00	09 05			09 10	09 15	09 20			09 25		
Haggerston	d	08 51						08 56						09 01	09 06			09 11	09 16	09 21			09 26		
Hoxton	d	08 53						08 58						09 03	09 08			09 13	09 18	09 23			09 28		
Shoreditch High Street	d	08 56						09 01						09 06	09 11			09 16	09 21	09 26			09 31		
Whitechapel	d	08 58						09 03						09 08	09 13			09 18	09 23	09 28			09 33		
Shadwell	d	09 00						09 05						09 10	09 15			09 20	09 25	09 30			09 35		
Wapping	d	09 02						09 07						09 12	09 17			09 22	09 27	09 32			09 37		
Rotherhithe	d	09 04						09 09						09 14	09 19			09 24	09 29	09 34			09 39		
Canada Water	d	09 06						09 11						09 16	09 21			09 26	09 31	09 36			09 41		
Surrey Quays	d	09 07						09 12						09 17	09 22			09 27	09 32	09 37			09 42		
New Cross ELL	a	09 13													09 28					09 43					
New Cross Gate 4	a						09 12	09 16						09 21			09 28	09 30	09 36			09 41	09 46		
	d						09 12	09 17						09 22			09 28	09 32	09 37			09 41	09 47		
Brockley	d						09 14	09 19						09 24			09 30	09 34	09 39			09 44	09 49		
Honor Oak Park	d						09 17	09 22						09 27			09 33	09 37	09 42			09 47	09 52		
Forest Hill 4	d						09 20	09 25						09 30			09 36	09 40	09 45			09 49	09 55		
Sydenham	d						09 22	09 27						09 32			09 38	09 42	09 47			09 52	09 57		
Crystal Palace 4	d												09 30	09a37			09 43		09a52						
Gipsy Hill	d												09 32				09 46								
West Norwood 4	d												09 35				09 49								
Streatham Hill	d																09 52								
Balham 4 ⊖	d																09 56								
Wandsworth Common	d																09 58								
Clapham Junction 10	d																10 02								
South Bermondsey	d				09 07						09 15										09 37				09 45
Queens Rd Peckham	d				09 09						09 18										09 39				09 48
Peckham Rye 4	d		09 04	09 09	09a12				09 14	09 17	09 20	09 31	09a46								09a42			09 45	09 50
Denmark Hill 4	d		09 07	09 12					09 17	09 19	09 23	09 34												09 49	09 53
London Blackfriars 3 ⊖	a		09 18	09 26						09 30		09 46													
Clapham High Street ⊖	d										09 28														09 58
Wandsworth Road	d										09 29														09 59
Battersea Park 4	d										09 32						10 05								10 03
London Victoria 15 ⊖	a								09 29		09 38						10 11							10 00	10 07
Penge West	d						09 25	09 30										09 45				09 54	10 00		
Anerley	d						09 27	09 32										09 47				09 56	10 02		
Norwood Junction 2	d						09 30	09 35										09 50				10 00	10 05		
West Croydon 4 ⇌	a							09 42										10 00					10 12		
East Croydon ⇌	a						09 33															10 03			

London Bridge to London Victoria - Croydon and East London Line

			SE	SN	LO	LO	SN	LO	LO	LO	SN		SN	LO	SE	SN	SE	SN	LO	LO	SN		LO	LO	LO
London Bridge 4 ⊖	d						09 52				10 03		10 06			10 11					10 22				
Highbury & Islington	d				09 25			09 33	09 40					09 48					09 55				10 03	10 10	
Canonbury	d				09 27			09 35	09 42					09 50					09 57				10 05	10 12	
Dalston Junction Stn ELL	d				09 30	09 35		09 40	09 45	09 50				09 55					10 00	10 05			10 10	10 15	10 20
Haggerston	d				09 31	09 36		09 41	09 46	09 51				09 56					10 01	10 06			10 11	10 16	10 21
Hoxton	d				09 33	09 38		09 43	09 48	09 53				09 58					10 03	10 08			10 13	10 18	10 23
Shoreditch High Street	d				09 36	09 41		09 46	09 51	09 56				10 01					10 06	10 11			10 16	10 21	10 26
Whitechapel	d				09 38	09 43		09 48	09 53	09 58				10 03					10 08	10 13			10 18	10 23	10 28
Shadwell	d				09 40	09 45		09 50	09 55	10 00				10 05					10 10	10 15			10 20	10 25	10 30
Wapping	d				09 42	09 47		09 52	09 57	10 02				10 07					10 12	10 17			10 22	10 27	10 32
Rotherhithe	d				09 44	09 49		09 54	09 59	10 04				10 09					10 14	10 19			10 24	10 29	10 34
Canada Water	d				09 46	09 51		09 56	10 01	10 06				10 11					10 16	10 21			10 26	10 31	10 36
Surrey Quays	d				09 47	09 52		09 57	10 02	10 07				10 12					10 17	10 22			10 27	10 32	10 37
New Cross ELL	a					09 58				10 13										10 28					10 43
New Cross Gate 4	a				09 51		09 57	10 01	10 06				10 11	10 16					10 21		10 27		10 31	10 36	
	d				09 52		09 57	10 02	10 07				10 11	10 17					10 22		10 27		10 32	10 37	
Brockley	d				09 54		10 00	10 04	10 09				10 14	10 19					10 24		10 30		10 34	10 39	
Honor Oak Park	d				09 57		10 03	10 07	10 12				10 17	10 22					10 27		10 33		10 37	10 42	
Forest Hill 4	d				10 00		10 05	10 10	10 15				10 19	10 25					10 30		10 35		10 40	10 45	
Sydenham	d				10 02		10 08	10 12	10 17				10 22	10 27					10 32		10 38		10 42	10 47	
Crystal Palace 4	d			10 00	10a07		10 13		10a22									10 30	10a37		10 43			10a52	
Gipsy Hill	d			10 02			10 15											10 32			10 45				
West Norwood 4	d			10 05			10 18											10 35			10 48				
Streatham Hill	d						10 22														10 52				
Balham 4 ⊖	d						10 25														10 55				
Wandsworth Common	d						10 27														10 57				
Clapham Junction 10	d						10 31														11 01				
South Bermondsey	d										10 07					10 15									
Queens Rd Peckham	d										10 09					10 18									
Peckham Rye 4	d		10 04	10a16							10a12				10 15	10 20	10 34	10a46							
Denmark Hill 4	d		10 07												10 19	10 23	10 37								
London Blackfriars 3 ⊖	a		10 18														10 48								
Clapham High Street ⊖	d															10 28									
Wandsworth Road	d															10 29									
Battersea Park 4	d						10 35									10 32					11 05				
London Victoria 15 ⊖	a						10 39								10 28	10 36					11 09				
Penge West	d							10 15					10 24	10 30									10 45		
Anerley	d							10 17					10 26	10 32									10 47		
Norwood Junction 2	d							10 20					10 30	10 35									10 50		
West Croydon 4	a							10 30						10 42									11 00		
East Croydon	a												10 33												

		SN	SN	LO	SE	SN	SE		SN	LO	LO	SN	LO	LO	LO	SN	SN		LO	SE	SN	SE	SN	LO	LO
London Bridge 4 ⊖	d	10 33	10 36			10 41						10 52				11 03	11 06				11 11				
Highbury & Islington	d			10 18						10 25			10 33	10 40					10 48					10 55	
Canonbury	d			10 20						10 27			10 35	10 42					10 50					10 57	
Dalston Junction Stn ELL	d			10 25						10 30	10 35		10 40	10 45	10 50				10 55					11 00	11 05
Haggerston	d			10 26						10 31	10 36		10 41	10 46	10 51				10 56					11 01	11 06
Hoxton	d			10 28						10 33	10 38		10 43	10 48	10 53				10 58					11 03	11 08
Shoreditch High Street	d			10 31						10 36	10 41		10 46	10 51	10 56				11 01					11 06	11 11
Whitechapel	d			10 33						10 38	10 43		10 48	10 53	10 58				11 03					11 08	11 13
Shadwell	d			10 35						10 40	10 45		10 50	10 55	11 00				11 05					11 10	11 15
Wapping	d			10 37						10 42	10 47		10 52	10 57	11 02				11 07					11 12	11 17
Rotherhithe	d			10 39						10 44	10 49		10 54	10 59	11 04				11 09					11 14	11 19
Canada Water	d			10 41						10 46	10 51		10 56	11 01	11 06				11 11					11 16	11 21
Surrey Quays	d			10 42						10 47	10 52		10 57	11 02	11 07				11 12					11 17	11 22
New Cross ELL	a										10 58				11 13										11 28
New Cross Gate 4	a		10 41	10 46						10 51		10 57	11 01	11 06			11 11		11 16					11 21	
	d		10 41	10 47						10 52		10 57	11 02	11 07			11 11		11 17					11 22	
Brockley	d		10 44	10 49						10 54		11 00	11 04	11 09			11 14		11 19					11 24	
Honor Oak Park	d		10 47	10 52						10 57		11 03	11 07	11 12			11 17		11 22					11 27	
Forest Hill 4	d		10 49	10 55						11 00		11 05	11 10	11 15			11 19		11 25					11 30	
Sydenham	d		10 52	10 57						11 02		11 08	11 12	11 17			11 22		11 27					11 32	
Crystal Palace 4	d								11 00	11a07		11 13		11a22									11 30	11a37	
Gipsy Hill	d								11 02			11 15											11 32		
West Norwood 4	d								11 05			11 18											11 35		
Streatham Hill	d											11 22													
Balham 4 ⊖	d											11 25													
Wandsworth Common	d											11 27													
Clapham Junction 10	d											11 31													
South Bermondsey	d	10 37				10 45										11 07					11 15				
Queens Rd Peckham	d	10 39				10 48										11 09					11 18				
Peckham Rye 4	d	10a42			10 45	10 50	10 50		11a16							11a12				11 15	11 20	11 20	11a46		
Denmark Hill 4	d				10 49	10 53	10 54													11 19	11 23	11 24			
London Blackfriars 3 ⊖	a						11 04															11 34			
Clapham High Street ⊖	d					10 58															11 28				
Wandsworth Road	d					10 59															11 29				
Battersea Park 4	d					11 02						11 35									11 32				
London Victoria 15 ⊖	a				10 58	11 06						11 39								11 28	11 36				
Penge West	d		10 54	11 00									11 15				11 24		11 30						
Anerley	d		10 56	11 02									11 17				11 26		11 32						
Norwood Junction 2	d		11 00	11 05									11 20				11 30		11 35						
West Croydon 4	a			11 12									11 30						11 42						
East Croydon	a		11 03														11 33								

London Bridge to London Victoria - Croydon and East London Line

		SN	LO		LO	LO	SN	SN	LO	SE	SN	SE	SN		LO	LO	SN	LO	LO	LO	SN	SN	LO		SE
London Bridge 4 ⊖	d	11 22					11 33	11 36			11 41						11 52				12 03	12 06			
Highbury & Islington	d		11 03		11 10				11 18						11 25			11 33	11 40				11 48		
Canonbury	d		11 05		11 12				11 20						11 27			11 35	11 42				11 50		
Dalston Junction Stn ELL	d		11 10		11 15	11 20			11 25						11 30	11 35		11 40	11 45	11 50			11 55		
Haggerston	d		11 11		11 16	11 21			11 26						11 31	11 36		11 41	11 46	11 51			11 56		
Hoxton	d		11 13		11 18	11 23			11 28						11 33	11 38		11 43	11 48	11 53			11 58		
Shoreditch High Street	d		11 16		11 21	11 26			11 31						11 36	11 41		11 46	11 51	11 56			12 01		
Whitechapel	d		11 18		11 23	11 28			11 33						11 38	11 43		11 48	11 53	11 58			12 03		
Shadwell	d		11 20		11 25	11 30			11 35						11 40	11 45		11 50	11 55	12 00			12 05		
Wapping	d		11 22		11 27	11 32			11 37						11 42	11 47		11 52	11 57	12 02			12 07		
Rotherhithe	d		11 24		11 29	11 34			11 39						11 44	11 49		11 54	11 59	12 04			12 09		
Canada Water	d		11 26		11 31	11 36			11 41						11 46	11 51		11 56	12 01	12 06			12 11		
Surrey Quays	d		11 27		11 32	11 37			11 42						11 47	11 52		11 57	12 02	12 07			12 12		
New Cross ELL	a					11 43										11 58				12 13					
New Cross Gate 4	a	11 27	11 31		11 36			11 41	11 46						11 51		11 57	12 01	12 06			12 11	12 16		
	d	11 27	11 32		11 37			11 41	11 47						11 52		11 57	12 02	12 07			12 11	12 17		
Brockley	d	11 30	11 34		11 39			11 44	11 49						11 54		12 00	12 04	12 09			12 14	12 19		
Honor Oak Park	d	11 33	11 37		11 42			11 47	11 52						11 57		12 03	12 07	12 12			12 17	12 22		
Forest Hill 4	d	11 35	11 40		11 45			11 49	11 55						12 00		12 05	12 10	12 15			12 19	12 25		
Sydenham	d	11 38	11 42		11 47			11 52	11 57						12 02		12 08	12 12	12 17			12 22	12 27		
Crystal Palace 4	d	11 43			11a52								12 00		12a07		12 13		12a22						
Gipsy Hill	d	11 45											12 02				12 15								
West Norwood 4	d	11 48											12 05				12 18								
Streatham Hill	d	11 52															12 22								
Balham 4 ⊖	d	11 55															12 25								
Wandsworth Common	d	11 57															12 27								
Clapham Junction 10	d	12 01															12 31								
South Bermondsey	d						11 37				11 45										12 07				
Queens Rd Peckham	d						11 39				11 48										12 09				
Peckham Rye 4	d						11a42			11 45	11 50	11 50	12a16								12a12				12 15
Denmark Hill 4	d									11 49	11 54	11 54													12 19
London Blackfriars 3 ⊖	a											12 04													
Clapham High Street ⊖	d										11 58														
Wandsworth Road	d										12 00														
Battersea Park 4	d	12 05									12 02						12 35								
London Victoria 15 ⊖	a	12 09								11 58	12 07						12 39								12 28
Penge West	d		11 45					11 54	12 00									12 15				12 24	12 30		
Anerley	d		11 47					11 56	12 02									12 17				12 26	12 32		
Norwood Junction 2	d		11 50					12 00	12 05									12 20				12 30	12 35		
West Croydon 4	a		12 00						12 12									12 30					12 42		
East Croydon	a							12 03														12 33			

		SN	SE	SN	LO	LO	SN	LO	LO		LO	SN	SN	LO	SE	SN	SE	SN	LO		LO	SN	LO	LO	LO
London Bridge 4 ⊖	d	12 11					12 22					12 33	12 36			12 41						12 52			
Highbury & Islington	d				11 55			12 03	12 10					12 18					12 25				12 33	12 40	
Canonbury	d				11 57			12 05	12 12					12 20					12 27				12 35	12 42	
Dalston Junction Stn ELL	d				12 00	12 05		12 10	12 15		12 20			12 25					12 30		12 35		12 40	12 45	12 50
Haggerston	d				12 01	12 06		12 11	12 16		12 21			12 26					12 31		12 36		12 41	12 46	12 51
Hoxton	d				12 03	12 08		12 13	12 18		12 23			12 28					12 33		12 38		12 43	12 48	12 53
Shoreditch High Street	d				12 06	12 11		12 16	12 21		12 26			12 31					12 36		12 41		12 46	12 51	12 56
Whitechapel	d				12 08	12 13		12 18	12 23		12 28			12 33					12 38		12 43		12 48	12 53	12 58
Shadwell	d				12 10	12 15		12 20	12 25		12 30			12 35					12 40		12 45		12 50	12 55	13 00
Wapping	d				12 12	12 17		12 22	12 27		12 32			12 37					12 42		12 47		12 52	12 57	13 02
Rotherhithe	d				12 14	12 19		12 24	12 29		12 34			12 39					12 44		12 49		12 54	12 59	13 04
Canada Water	d				12 16	12 21		12 26	12 31		12 36			12 41					12 46		12 51		12 56	13 01	13 06
Surrey Quays	d				12 17	12 22		12 27	12 32		12 37			12 42					12 47		12 52		12 57	13 02	13 07
New Cross ELL	a					12 28					12 43										12 58				13 13
New Cross Gate 4	a				12 21		12 27	12 31	12 36				12 41	12 46					12 51			12 57	13 01	13 06	
	d				12 22		12 27	12 32	12 37				12 41	12 47					12 52			12 57	13 02	13 07	
Brockley	d				12 24		12 30	12 34	12 39				12 44	12 49					12 54			13 00	13 04	13 09	
Honor Oak Park	d				12 27		12 33	12 37	12 42				12 47	12 52					12 57			13 03	13 07	13 12	
Forest Hill 4	d				12 30		12 35	12 40	12 45				12 49	12 55					13 00			13 05	13 10	13 15	
Sydenham	d				12 32		12 38	12 42	12 47				12 52	12 57					13 02			13 08	13 12	13 17	
Crystal Palace 4	d			12 30	12a37		12 43		12a52									13 00	13a07			13 13		13a22	
Gipsy Hill	d			12 32			12 45											13 02				13 15			
West Norwood 4	d			12 35			12 48											13 05				13 18			
Streatham Hill	d						12 52															13 22			
Balham 4 ⊖	d						12 55															13 25			
Wandsworth Common	d						12 57															13 27			
Clapham Junction 10	d						13 01															13 31			
South Bermondsey	d	12 15										12 37				12 45									
Queens Rd Peckham	d	12 18										12 39				12 48									
Peckham Rye 4	d	12 20	12 20	12a46								12a42			12 45	12 50	12 50	13a16							
Denmark Hill 4	d	12 23	12 24												12 49	12 53	12 54								
London Blackfriars 3 ⊖	a		12 34														13 04								
Clapham High Street ⊖	d	12 28														12 58									
Wandsworth Road	d	12 29														12 59									
Battersea Park 4	d	12 32					13 05									13 02						13 35			
London Victoria 15 ⊖	a	12 36					13 09								12 58	13 06						13 39			
Penge West	d							12 45					12 54	13 00									13 15		
Anerley	d							12 47					12 56	13 02									13 17		
Norwood Junction 2	d							12 50					13 00	13 05									13 20		
West Croydon 4	a							13 00						13 12									13 30		
East Croydon	a												13 03												

London Bridge to London Victoria - Croydon and East London Line

Station		SN	SN	LO	SE	SN	SE	SN	LO	LO	SN	LO	LO	LO	SN	SN	LO	SE	SN	SE	SN	LO	LO
London Bridge 4 ⊖	d	13 03	13 06			13 11					13 22				13 33	13 36			13 41				
Highbury & Islington	d			12 48					12 55			13 03	13 10				13 18					13 25	
Canonbury	d			12 50					12 57			13 05	13 12				13 20					13 27	
Dalston Junction Stn ELL	d			12 55					13 00	13 05		13 10	13 15	13 20			13 25					13 30	13 35
Haggerston	d			12 56					13 01	13 06		13 11	13 16	13 21			13 26					13 31	13 36
Hoxton	d			12 58					13 03	13 08		13 13	13 18	13 23			13 28					13 33	13 38
Shoreditch High Street	d			13 01					13 06	13 11		13 16	13 21	13 26			13 31					13 36	13 41
Whitechapel	d			13 03					13 08	13 13		13 18	13 23	13 28			13 33					13 38	13 43
Shadwell	d			13 05					13 10	13 15		13 20	13 25	13 30			13 35					13 40	13 45
Wapping	d			13 07					13 12	13 17		13 22	13 27	13 32			13 37					13 42	13 47
Rotherhithe	d			13 09					13 14	13 19		13 24	13 29	13 34			13 39					13 44	13 49
Canada Water	d			13 11					13 16	13 21		13 26	13 31	13 36			13 41					13 46	13 51
Surrey Quays	d			13 12					13 17	13 22		13 27	13 32	13 37			13 42					13 47	13 52
New Cross ELL	a									13 28				13 43									13 58
New Cross Gate 4	a		13 11	13 16					13 21		13 27	13 31	13 36			13 41	13 46					13 51	
	d		13 11	13 17					13 22		13 27	13 32	13 37			13 41	13 47					13 52	
Brockley	d		13 14	13 19					13 24		13 30	13 34	13 39			13 44	13 49					13 54	
Honor Oak Park	d		13 17	13 22					13 27		13 33	13 37	13 42			13 47	13 52					13 57	
Forest Hill 4	d		13 19	13 25					13 30		13 35	13 40	13 45			13 49	13 55					14 00	
Sydenham	d		13 22	13 27					13 32		13 38	13 42	13 47			13 52	13 57					14 02	
Crystal Palace 4	d							13 30	13a37		13 43		13a52								14 00	14a07	
Gipsy Hill	d							13 32			13 45										14 02		
West Norwood 4	d							13 35			13 48										14 05		
Streatham Hill	d										13 52												
Balham 4 ⊖	d										13 55												
Wandsworth Common	d										13 57												
Clapham Junction 10	d										14 01												
South Bermondsey	d	13 07				13 15									13 37				13 45				
Queens Rd Peckham	d	13 09				13 18									13 39				13 48				
Peckham Rye 4	d	13a12			13 15	13 20	13 20	13a46							13a42			13 45	13 50	13 50	14a16		
Denmark Hill 4	d				13 19	13 23	13 24											13 49	13 53	13 54			
London Blackfriars 3 ⊖	a						13 34													14 04			
Clapham High Street ⊖	d					13 28													13 58				
Wandsworth Road	d					13 29													13 59				
Battersea Park 4	d					13 32					14 05								14 02				
London Victoria 15 ⊖	a				13 28	13 36					14 09							13 58	14 06				
Penge West	d		13 24	13 30								13 45				13 54	14 00						
Anerley	d		13 26	13 32								13 47				13 56	14 02						
Norwood Junction 2	d		13 30	13 35								13 50				14 00	14 05						
West Croydon 4	a			13 42								14 00					14 12						
East Croydon	a		13 33													14 03							

Station		SN	LO	LO	LO	SN	SN	LO	SE	SN	SE	SN	LO	LO	SN	LO	LO	LO	SN	SN	LO	SE
London Bridge 4 ⊖	d	13 52				14 03	14 06			14 11					14 22				14 33	14 36		
Highbury & Islington	d		13 33	13 40				13 48					13 55			14 03	14 10				14 18	
Canonbury	d		13 35	13 42				13 50					13 57			14 05	14 12				14 20	
Dalston Junction Stn ELL	d		13 40	13 45	13 50			13 55					14 00	14 05		14 10	14 15	14 20			14 25	
Haggerston	d		13 41	13 46	13 51			13 56					14 01	14 06		14 11	14 16	14 21			14 26	
Hoxton	d		13 43	13 48	13 53			13 58					14 03	14 08		14 13	14 18	14 23			14 28	
Shoreditch High Street	d		13 46	13 51	13 56			14 01					14 06	14 11		14 16	14 21	14 26			14 31	
Whitechapel	d		13 48	13 53	13 58			14 03					14 08	14 13		14 18	14 23	14 28			14 33	
Shadwell	d		13 50	13 55	14 00			14 05					14 10	14 15		14 20	14 25	14 30			14 35	
Wapping	d		13 52	13 57	14 02			14 07					14 12	14 17		14 22	14 27	14 32			14 37	
Rotherhithe	d		13 54	13 59	14 04			14 09					14 14	14 19		14 24	14 29	14 34			14 39	
Canada Water	d		13 56	14 01	14 06			14 11					14 16	14 21		14 26	14 31	14 36			14 41	
Surrey Quays	d		13 57	14 02	14 07			14 12					14 17	14 22		14 27	14 32	14 37			14 42	
New Cross ELL	a				14 13									14 28				14 43				
New Cross Gate 4	a	13 57	14 01	14 06			14 11	14 16					14 21		14 27	14 31	14 36			14 41	14 46	
	d	13 57	14 02	14 07			14 11	14 17					14 22		14 27	14 32	14 37			14 41	14 47	
Brockley	d	14 00	14 04	14 09			14 14	14 19					14 24		14 30	14 34	14 39			14 44	14 49	
Honor Oak Park	d	14 03	14 07	14 12			14 17	14 22					14 27		14 33	14 37	14 42			14 47	14 52	
Forest Hill 4	d	14 05	14 10	14 15			14 19	14 25					14 30		14 35	14 40	14 45			14 49	14 55	
Sydenham	d	14 08	14 12	14 17			14 22	14 27					14 32		14 38	14 42	14 47			14 52	14 57	
Crystal Palace 4	d	14 13		14a22								14 30	14a37		14 43		14a52					
Gipsy Hill	d	14 15										14 32			14 45							
West Norwood 4	d	14 18										14 35			14 48							
Streatham Hill	d	14 22													14 52							
Balham 4 ⊖	d	14 25													14 55							
Wandsworth Common	d	14 27													14 57							
Clapham Junction 10	d	14 31													15 01							
South Bermondsey	d					14 07				14 15									14 37			
Queens Rd Peckham	d					14 09				14 18									14 39			
Peckham Rye 4	d					14a12			14 15	14 20	14 20	14a46							14a42			14 45
Denmark Hill 4	d								14 19	14 23	14 24											14 49
London Blackfriars 3 ⊖	a										14 34											
Clapham High Street ⊖	d									14 28												
Wandsworth Road	d									14 29												
Battersea Park 4	d	14 35								14 32					15 05							
London Victoria 15 ⊖	a	14 39							14 28	14 36					15 09							14 58
Penge West	d		14 15				14 24	14 30								14 45				14 54	15 00	
Anerley	d		14 17				14 26	14 32								14 47				14 56	15 02	
Norwood Junction 2	d		14 20				14 30	14 35								14 50				15 00	15 05	
West Croydon 4	a		14 30					14 42								15 00					15 12	
East Croydon	a						14 33													15 03		

London Bridge to London Victoria - Croydon and East London Line

Station		SN	SE	SN	LO	LO	SN	LO	LO	LO	SN	SN	LO	SE	SN	SE	SN	LO	LO	SN	LO	LO	LO
London Bridge 4 ⊖	d	14 41					14 52				15 03	15 06			15 11					15 22			
Highbury & Islington	d				14 25			14 33	14 40				14 48					14 55			15 03	15 10	
Canonbury	d				14 27			14 35	14 42				14 50					14 57			15 05	15 12	
Dalston Junction Stn ELL	d				14 30	14 35		14 40	14 45	14 50			14 55					15 00	15 05		15 10	15 15	15 20
Haggerston	d				14 31	14 36		14 41	14 46	14 51			14 56					15 01	15 06		15 11	15 16	15 21
Hoxton	d				14 33	14 38		14 43	14 48	14 53			14 58					15 03	15 08		15 13	15 18	15 23
Shoreditch High Street	d				14 36	14 41		14 46	14 51	14 56			15 01					15 06	15 11		15 16	15 21	15 26
Whitechapel	d				14 38	14 43		14 48	14 53	14 58			15 03					15 08	15 13		15 18	15 23	15 28
Shadwell	d				14 40	14 45		14 50	14 55	15 00			15 05					15 10	15 15		15 20	15 25	15 30
Wapping	d				14 42	14 47		14 52	14 57	15 02			15 07					15 12	15 17		15 22	15 27	15 32
Rotherhithe	d				14 44	14 49		14 54	14 59	15 04			15 09					15 14	15 19		15 24	15 29	15 34
Canada Water	d				14 46	14 51		14 56	15 01	15 06			15 11					15 16	15 21		15 26	15 31	15 36
Surrey Quays	d				14 47	14 52		14 57	15 02	15 07			15 12					15 17	15 22		15 27	15 32	15 37
New Cross ELL	a					14 58				15 13									15 28				15 43
New Cross Gate 4	a				14 51		14 57	15 01	15 06			15 11	15 16					15 21		15 27	15 31	15 36	
	d				14 52		14 57	15 02	15 07			15 11	15 17					15 22		15 27	15 32	15 37	
Brockley	d				14 54		15 00	15 04	15 09			15 14	15 19					15 24		15 30	15 34	15 39	
Honor Oak Park	d				14 57		15 03	15 07	15 12			15 17	15 22					15 27		15 33	15 37	15 42	
Forest Hill 4	d				15 00		15 05	15 10	15 15			15 19	15 25					15 30		15 35	15 40	15 45	
Sydenham	d				15 02		15 08	15 12	15 17			15 22	15 27					15 32		15 38	15 42	15 47	
Crystal Palace 4	d			15 01	15a07		15 13		15a22								15 30	15a37		15 43		15a52	
Gipsy Hill	d			15 03			15 15										15 32			15 45			
West Norwood 4	d			15 06			15 18										15 35			15 48			
Streatham Hill	d						15 22													15 52			
Balham 4 ⊖	d						15 25													15 55			
Wandsworth Common	d						15 27													15 57			
Clapham Junction 10	d						15 31													16 01			
South Bermondsey	d	14 45									15 07				15 15								
Queens Rd Peckham	d	14 48									15 09				15 18								
Peckham Rye 4	d	14 50	14 50	15a17							15a12			15 15	15 20	15 20	15a46						
Denmark Hill 4	d	14 53	14 54											15 19	15 23	15 24							
London Blackfriars 3 ⊖	a		15 04													15 34							
Clapham High Street ⊖	d	14 58													15 28								
Wandsworth Road	d	14 59													15 29								
Battersea Park 4	d	15 02					15 35								15 32					16 05			
London Victoria 15 ⊖	a	15 06					15 39							15 28	15 36					16 10			
Penge West	d							15 15				15 24	15 30								15 45		
Anerley	d							15 17				15 26	15 32								15 47		
Norwood Junction 2	d							15 20				15 30	15 35								15 50		
West Croydon 4	a							15 30					15 42								16 00		
East Croydon	a											15 33											

Station		SN	SN	LO	SE	SN	SE	SN	SN	LO	LO	SN	LO	LO	LO	SN	SN	LO	SE	SN	SE 1	SN
London Bridge 4 ⊖	d	15 33	15 36			15 41						15 52				16 03	16 06			16 11		
Highbury & Islington	d			15 18						15 25			15 33	15 40				15 48				
Canonbury	d			15 20						15 27			15 35	15 42				15 50				
Dalston Junction Stn ELL	d			15 25						15 30	15 35		15 40	15 45	15 50			15 55				
Haggerston	d			15 26						15 31	15 36		15 41	15 46	15 51			15 56				
Hoxton	d			15 28						15 33	15 38		15 43	15 48	15 53			15 58				
Shoreditch High Street	d			15 31						15 36	15 41		15 46	15 51	15 56			16 01				
Whitechapel	d			15 33						15 38	15 43		15 48	15 53	15 58			16 03				
Shadwell	d			15 35						15 40	15 45		15 50	15 55	16 00			16 05				
Wapping	d			15 37						15 42	15 47		15 52	15 57	16 02			16 07				
Rotherhithe	d			15 39						15 44	15 49		15 54	15 59	16 04			16 09				
Canada Water	d			15 41						15 46	15 51		15 56	16 01	16 06			16 11				
Surrey Quays	d			15 42						15 47	15 52		15 57	16 02	16 07			16 12				
New Cross ELL	a										15 58				16 13							
New Cross Gate 4	a		15 41	15 46						15 51		15 57	16 01	16 06			16 11	16 16				
	d		15 41	15 47						15 52		15 57	16 02	16 07			16 11	16 17				
Brockley	d		15 44	15 49						15 54		16 00	16 04	16 09			16 14	16 19				
Honor Oak Park	d		15 47	15 52						15 57		16 03	16 07	16 12			16 17	16 22				
Forest Hill 4	d		15 49	15 55						16 00		16 05	16 10	16 15			16 19	16 25				
Sydenham	d		15 52	15 57						16 02		16 08	16 12	16 17			16 22	16 27				
Crystal Palace 4	d								16 00	16a07		16 13		16a22								16 30
Gipsy Hill	d								16 02			16 15										16 32
West Norwood 4	d								16 05			16 18										16 35
Streatham Hill	d							15 56				16 22										
Balham 4 ⊖	d											16 25										
Wandsworth Common	d											16 27										
Clapham Junction 10	d											16 31										
South Bermondsey	d	15 37				15 45										16 07				16 15		
Queens Rd Peckham	d	15 39				15 48										16 09				16 18		
Peckham Rye 4	d	15a42			15 45	15 50	15 50	16a07	16a16							16a12			16 15	16 20	16 20	16a46
Denmark Hill 4	d				15 49	15 53	15 54												16 19	16 23	16 24	
London Blackfriars 3 ⊖	a						16 04														16 34	
Clapham High Street ⊖	d					15 58														16 28		
Wandsworth Road	d					15 59														16 29		
Battersea Park 4	d					16 02						16 35								16 32		
London Victoria 15 ⊖	a				15 58	16 06						16 40							16 28	16 38		
Penge West	d		15 54	16 00									16 15				16 24	16 30				
Anerley	d		15 56	16 02									16 17				16 26	16 32				
Norwood Junction 2	d		16 00	16 05									16 20				16 30	16 35				
West Croydon 4	a			16 12									16 30					16 42				
East Croydon	a		16 03														16 33					

London Bridge to London Victoria - Croydon and East London Line

	LO	LO	SN	LO	LO	LO	SN	SN	LO	SE	SN	SE 1	SE	SN	LO	LO	SN	LO	SN	SE	SE	SN
London Bridge ⊖ d			16 22				16 33	16 36			16 41						16 52		16 58			
Highbury & Islington d	15 55			16 03	16 10				16 18						16 25			16 33				
Canonbury d	15 57			16 05	16 12				16 20						16 27			16 35				
Dalston Junction Stn ELL d	16 00	16 05		16 10	16 15	16 20			16 25						16 30	16 35		16 40				
Haggerston d	16 01	16 06		16 11	16 16	16 21			16 26						16 31	16 36		16 41				
Hoxton d	16 03	16 08		16 13	16 18	16 23			16 28						16 33	16 38		16 43				
Shoreditch High Street d	16 06	16 11		16 16	16 21	16 26			16 31						16 36	16 41		16 46				
Whitechapel d	16 08	16 13		16 18	16 23	16 28			16 33						16 38	16 43		16 48				
Shadwell d	16 10	16 15		16 20	16 25	16 30			16 35						16 40	16 45		16 50				
Wapping d	16 12	16 17		16 22	16 27	16 32			16 37						16 42	16 47		16 52				
Rotherhithe d	16 14	16 19		16 24	16 29	16 34			16 39						16 44	16 49		16 54				
Canada Water d	16 16	16 21		16 26	16 31	16 36			16 41						16 46	16 51		16 56				
Surrey Quays d	16 17	16 22		16 27	16 32	16 37			16 42						16 47	16 52		16 57				
New Cross ELL a		16 28				16 43										16 58						
New Cross Gate a	16 21		16 27	16 31	16 36			16 41	16 46						16 51		16 57	17 01				
d	16 22		16 27	16 32	16 37			16 41	16 47						16 52		16 57	17 02				
Brockley d	16 24		16 30	16 34	16 39			16 44	16 49						16 54		17 00	17 04				
Honor Oak Park d	16 27		16 33	16 37	16 42			16 47	16 52						16 57		17 03	17 07				
Forest Hill d	16 30		16 35	16 40	16 45			16 49	16 55						17 00		17 05	17 10				
Sydenham d	16 32		16 38	16 42	16 47			16 52	16 57						17 02		17 08	17 12				
Crystal Palace d	16a37		16 43		16a52									17 00	17a07		17 13					17 18
Gipsy Hill d			16 45											17 02			17 15					17 20
West Norwood d			16 48											17 05			17 18					17 23
Streatham Hill d			16 52														17 22					
Balham ⊖ d			16 55														17 25					
Wandsworth Common d			16 57														17 27					
Clapham Junction d			17 01														17 31					
South Bermondsey d							16 37				16 45								17 02			
Queens Rd Peckham d							16 39				16 48								17 04			
Peckham Rye d							16a42			16 45	16 50	16 50	17 02	17a16					17a07	17 15	17 20	17a34
Denmark Hill d										16 49	16 53	16 54	17 05							17 19	17 24	
London Blackfriars ⊖ a												17 08	17 16								17 40	
Clapham High Street ⊖ d											16 58											
Wandsworth Road d											16 59											
Battersea Park d			17 05								17 02						17 35					
London Victoria ⊖ a			17 10							17 01	17 08						17 42			17 28		
Penge West d				16 45				16 54	17 00									17 15				
Anerley d				16 47				16 56	17 02									17 17				
Norwood Junction d				16 50				17 00	17 05									17 20				
West Croydon a				17 00				17 07	17 12									17 30				
East Croydon a																						

	LO	LO	SN	LO	SN	SN	LO	LO	SN	SN	LO	LO	LO	SN	SN	LO	SE	SN	SE 1	SN	LO	LO
London Bridge ⊖ d			17 05		17 11				17 21	17 25				17 28	17 36			17 41				
Highbury & Islington d	16 40			16 48			16 55				17 03	17 10				17 18					17 25	
Canonbury d	16 42			16 50			16 57				17 05	17 12				17 20					17 27	
Dalston Junction Stn ELL d	16 45	16 50		16 55			17 00	17 05			17 10	17 15	17 20			17 25					17 30	17 35
Haggerston d	16 46	16 51		16 56			17 01	17 06			17 11	17 16	17 21			17 26					17 31	17 36
Hoxton d	16 48	16 53		16 58			17 03	17 08			17 13	17 18	17 23			17 28					17 33	17 38
Shoreditch High Street d	16 51	16 56		17 01			17 06	17 11			17 16	17 21	17 26			17 31					17 36	17 41
Whitechapel d	16 53	16 58		17 03			17 08	17 13			17 18	17 23	17 28			17 33					17 38	17 43
Shadwell d	16 55	17 00		17 05			17 10	17 15			17 20	17 25	17 30			17 35					17 40	17 45
Wapping d	16 57	17 02		17 07			17 12	17 17			17 22	17 27	17 32			17 37					17 42	17 47
Rotherhithe d	16 59	17 04		17 09			17 14	17 19			17 24	17 29	17 34			17 39					17 44	17 49
Canada Water d	17 01	17 06		17 11			17 16	17 21			17 26	17 31	17 36			17 41					17 46	17 51
Surrey Quays d	17 02	17 07		17 12			17 17	17 22			17 27	17 32	17 37			17 42					17 47	17 52
New Cross ELL a		17 13						17 28					17 43									17 58
New Cross Gate a	17 06		17 11	17 16			17 21		17 26	17 30	17 30	17 36			17 41	17 46					17 51	
d	17 07		17 11	17 17			17 22		17 26	17 30	17 32	17 37			17 41	17 47					17 52	
Brockley d	17 09		17 14	17 19			17 24		17 29	17 33	17 34	17 39			17 44	17 49					17 54	
Honor Oak Park d	17 12		17 17	17 22			17 27		17 32	17 36	17 37	17 42			17 47	17 52					17 57	
Forest Hill d	17 15		17 19	17 25			17 30		17 34	17 38	17 40	17 45			17 49	17 55					18 00	
Sydenham d	17 17		17 22	17 27			17 32		17 37	17 41	17 42	17 47			17 52	17 57					18 02	
Crystal Palace d	17a22					17 36	17a37		17 44	17a47		17a52								17 55	18a07	
Gipsy Hill d						17 38			17 46											17 57		
West Norwood d						17 42			17 49											18 00		
Streatham Hill d									17 53													
Balham ⊖ d									17 56													
Wandsworth Common d									17 58													
Clapham Junction d									18 02													
South Bermondsey d					17 15									17 32				17 45				
Queens Rd Peckham d					17 18									17 35				17 47				
Peckham Rye d					17 20	17a53								17a37			17 45	17 50	17 50	18a12		
Denmark Hill d					17 23												17 49	17 53	17 54			
London Blackfriars ⊖ a																			18 05			
Clapham High Street ⊖ d					17 28													17 58				
Wandsworth Road d					17 29													17 59				
Battersea Park d					17 32				18 06									18 02				
London Victoria ⊖ a					17 38				18 12								17 59	18 08				
Penge West d			17 24	17 30							17 45				17 54	18 00						
Anerley d			17 26	17 32							17 47				17 56	18 02						
Norwood Junction d			17 30	17 35							17 50				18 00	18 05						
West Croydon a			17 37	17 42							18 01				18 08	18 12						
East Croydon a																						

London Bridge to London Victoria - Croydon and East London Line

	SN	LO	SN	SE	SE 1	SN	LO	LO	SN	LO	LO	LO	SN	SN	SN	LO	SN	SE	SE	SN	LO
London Bridge ⊖ d	17 53		17 58						18 06				18 11	18 21	18 24		18 28				
Highbury & Islington d		17 33					17 40			17 48	17 55					18 03					18 10
Canonbury d		17 35					17 42			17 50	17 57					18 05					18 12
Dalston Junction Stn ELL d		17 40					17 45	17 50		17 55	18 00	18 05				18 10					18 15
Haggerston d		17 41					17 46	17 51		17 56	18 01	18 06				18 11					18 16
Hoxton d		17 43					17 48	17 53		17 58	18 03	18 08				18 13					18 18
Shoreditch High Street d		17 46					17 51	17 56		18 01	18 06	18 11				18 16					18 21
Whitechapel d		17 48					17 53	17 58		18 03	18 08	18 13				18 18					18 23
Shadwell d		17 50					17 55	18 00		18 05	18 10	18 15				18 20					18 25
Wapping d		17 52					17 57	18 02		18 07	18 12	18 17				18 22					18 27
Rotherhithe d		17 54					17 59	18 04		18 09	18 14	18 19				18 24					18 29
Canada Water d		17 56					18 01	18 06		18 11	18 16	18 21				18 26					18 31
Surrey Quays d		17 57					18 02	18 07		18 12	18 17	18 22				18 27					18 32
New Cross ELL a								18 13				18 28									
New Cross Gate a	17 58	18 01					18 06		18 11	18 16	18 21			18 26	18 30	18 30					18 36
d	17 58	18 02					18 07		18 11	18 17	18 22			18 26	18 30	18 32					18 37
Brockley d	18 01	18 04					18 09		18 14	18 19	18 24			18 29	18 33	18 34					18 39
Honor Oak Park d	18 04	18 07					18 12		18 17	18 22	18 27			18 32	18 36	18 37					18 42
Forest Hill d	18 06	18 10					18 15		18 19	18 25	18 30			18 34	18 38	18 40					18 45
Sydenham d	18 09	18 12					18 17		18 22	18 27	18 32			18 37	18 41	18 42					18 47
Crystal Palace d	18 13					18 18	18a22				18a37			18 43	18a46					18 51	18a52
Gipsy Hill d	18 16					18 20								18 45						18 53	
West Norwood d	18 19					18 23								18 48						18 56	
Streatham Hill d	18 22													18 52							
Balham ⊖ d	18 29													18 55							
Wandsworth Common d	18 31													18 57							
Clapham Junction d	18 36													19 01							
South Bermondsey d			18 02										18 15				18 32				
Queens Rd Peckham d			18 04										18 18				18 34				
Peckham Rye d			18a07	18 15	18 20	18a36							18 20				18a37	18 45	18 50	19a17	
Denmark Hill d				18 19	18 23								18 23					18 49	18 54		
London Blackfriars ⊖ a					18 36														19 04		
Clapham High Street ⊖ d													18 28								
Wandsworth Road d													18 29								
Battersea Park d	18 40												18 32	19 05							
London Victoria ⊖ a	18 46			18 29									18 39	19 12				18 58			
Penge West d		18 15							18 24	18 30						18 45					
Anerley d		18 17							18 26	18 32						18 47					
Norwood Junction d		18 20							18 32	18 35						18 50					
West Croydon a		18 30							18 39	18 42						19 01					
East Croydon a																					

	LO	SN	LO	LO	LO	SN	SE	SN	LO	LO	LO	SN	SN	LO	SE	SN	SN	SE	SE	SN	LO	LO
London Bridge ⊖ d		18 36				18 41		18 51				18 58	19 06			19 08	19 11					
Highbury & Islington d			18 18	18 25					18 33	18 40				18 48							18 55	
Canonbury d			18 20	18 27					18 35	18 42				18 50							18 57	
Dalston Junction Stn ELL d	18 20		18 25	18 30	18 35				18 40	18 45	18 50			18 55							19 00	19 05
Haggerston d	18 21		18 26	18 31	18 36				18 41	18 46	18 51			18 56							19 01	19 06
Hoxton d	18 23		18 28	18 33	18 38				18 43	18 48	18 53			18 58							19 03	19 08
Shoreditch High Street d	18 26		18 31	18 36	18 41				18 46	18 51	18 56			19 01							19 06	19 11
Whitechapel d	18 28		18 33	18 38	18 43				18 48	18 53	18 58			19 03							19 08	19 13
Shadwell d	18 30		18 35	18 40	18 45				18 50	18 55	19 00			19 05							19 10	19 15
Wapping d	18 32		18 37	18 42	18 47				18 52	18 57	19 02			19 07							19 12	19 17
Rotherhithe d	18 34		18 39	18 44	18 49				18 54	18 59	19 04			19 09							19 14	19 19
Canada Water d	18 36		18 41	18 46	18 51				18 56	19 01	19 06			19 11							19 16	19 21
Surrey Quays d	18 37		18 42	18 47	18 52				18 57	19 02	19 07			19 12							19 17	19 22
New Cross ELL a	18 43				18 58						19 13											19 28
New Cross Gate a		18 41	18 46	18 51				18 56	19 01	19 06			19 11	19 16							19 21	
d		18 41	18 47	18 52				18 56	19 02	19 07			19 11	19 17							19 22	
Brockley d		18 44	18 49	18 54				18 59	19 04	19 09			19 14	19 19							19 24	
Honor Oak Park d		18 47	18 52	18 57				19 02	19 07	19 12			19 17	19 22							19 27	
Forest Hill d		18 49	18 55	19 00				19 04	19 10	19 15			19 19	19 25							19 30	
Sydenham d		18 52	18 57	19 02				19 07	19 12	19 17			19 22	19 27							19 32	
Crystal Palace d				19a07				19 13		19a22										19 32	19a37	
Gipsy Hill d								19 15												19 34		
West Norwood d								19 18												19 37		
Streatham Hill d								19 22														
Balham ⊖ d								19 25														
Wandsworth Common d								19 27														
Clapham Junction d								19 31														
South Bermondsey d						18 45						19 02				19 12	19 15					
Queens Rd Peckham d						18 48						19 04				19 14	19 18					
Peckham Rye d						18 50						19 07			19 15	19a17	19 20	19 20		19a48		
Denmark Hill d						18 53	18 59								19 19		19 23	19 24	19 28			
London Blackfriars ⊖ a																		19 34				
Clapham High Street ⊖ d						18 58											19 28					
Wandsworth Road d						18 59											19 29					
Battersea Park d						19 02		19 35									19 32					
London Victoria ⊖ a						19 08	19 13	19 41							19 28		19 36		19 43			
Penge West d		18 54	19 00						19 15				19 24	19 30								
Anerley d		18 56	19 02						19 17				19 26	19 32								
Norwood Junction d		19 02	19 05						19 20			19 33	19 30	19 35								
West Croydon a		19 09	19 12						19 30			19 40		19 42								
East Croydon a													19 33									

London Bridge to London Victoria - Croydon and East London Line

Station		SN	LO		LO	LO	SN	SN	LO	SN	SN	SE	SN		LO	LO	SN	LO	LO	LO	SN	SN	LO		SN
London Bridge 4 ⊖	d	19 22					19 28	19 36		19 38	19 41						19 54				20 03	20 06			20 11
Highbury & Islington	d		19 03		19 10				19 18						19 25			19 33	19 40				19 48		
Canonbury	d		19 05		19 12				19 20						19 27			19 35	19 42				19 50		
Dalston Junction Stn ELL	d		19 10		19 15	19 20			19 25						19 30	19 35		19 40	19 45	19 50			19 55		
Haggerston	d		19 11		19 16	19 21			19 26						19 31	19 36		19 41	19 46	19 51			19 56		
Hoxton	d		19 13		19 18	19 23			19 28						19 33	19 38		19 43	19 48	19 53			19 58		
Shoreditch High Street	d		19 16		19 21	19 26			19 31						19 36	19 41		19 46	19 51	19 56			20 01		
Whitechapel	d		19 18		19 23	19 28			19 33						19 38	19 43		19 48	19 53	19 58			20 03		
Shadwell	d		19 20		19 25	19 30			19 35						19 40	19 45		19 50	19 55	20 00			20 05		
Wapping	d		19 22		19 27	19 32			19 37						19 42	19 47		19 52	19 57	20 02			20 07		
Rotherhithe	d		19 24		19 29	19 34			19 39						19 44	19 49		19 54	19 59	20 04			20 09		
Canada Water	d		19 26		19 31	19 36			19 41						19 46	19 51		19 56	20 01	20 06			20 11		
Surrey Quays	d		19 27		19 32	19 37			19 42						19 47	19 52		19 57	20 02	20 07			20 12		
New Cross ELL	a					19 43										19 58				20 13					
New Cross Gate 4	a	19 27	19 31		19 36			19 41	19 46						19 51		19 59	20 00	20 06			20 11	20 16		
	d	19 27	19 32		19 37			19 41	19 47						19 52		19 59	20 02	20 07			20 11	20 17		
Brockley	d	19 30	19 34		19 39			19 44	19 49						19 54		20 02	20 04	20 09			20 14	20 19		
Honor Oak Park	d	19 33	19 37		19 42			19 47	19 52						19 57		20 05	20 07	20 12			20 17	20 22		
Forest Hill 4	d	19 35	19 40		19 45			19 49	19 55						20 00		20 07	20 10	20 15			20 19	20 25		
Sydenham	d	19 38	19 42		19 47			19 52	19 57						20 02		20 10	20 12	20 17			20 22	20 27		
Crystal Palace 4	d	19 43			19a52								20 01		20a07		20 13		20a22						
Gipsy Hill	d	19 45											20 03				20 16								
West Norwood 4	d	19 48											20 06				20 19								
Streatham Hill	d	19 52															20 22								
Balham 4 ⊖	d	19 55															20 25								
Wandsworth Common	d	19 57															20 27								
Clapham Junction 10	d	20 01															20 31								
South Bermondsey	d						19 32			19 42	19 45										20 07				20 15
Queens Rd Peckham	d						19 34			19 44	19 48										20 09				20 18
Peckham Rye 4	d						19 37			19a47	19 50	19 50	20a18								20a12				20 20
Denmark Hill 4	d										19 53	19 54													20 23
London Blackfriars 3 ⊖	a											20 04													
Clapham High Street ⊖	d										19 58														20 28
Wandsworth Road	d										19 59														20 29
Battersea Park 4	d	20 05									20 02						20 35								20 32
London Victoria 15 ⊖	a	20 09									20 06						20 39								20 36
Penge West	d		19 45					19 54	20 00									20 15				20 24	20 30		
Anerley	d		19 47					19 56	20 02									20 17				20 26	20 32		
Norwood Junction 2	d		19 50				20 02	20 00	20 05									20 20				20 30	20 35		
West Croydon 4	a		20 00				20 06		20 12									20 29					20 42		
East Croydon	a							20 03														20 33			

Station		SE	SN	LO	LO	SN	LO	LO	LO		SN	SN	LO	SN	SE	SN	LO	LO	SN		LO	LO	LO	SN	SN
London Bridge 4 ⊖	d					20 22					20 33	20 36		20 41					20 52					21 03	21 06
Highbury & Islington	d			19 55			20 03	20 10					20 18				20 25				20 33	20 40			
Canonbury	d			19 57			20 05	20 12					20 20				20 27				20 35	20 42			
Dalston Junction Stn ELL	d			20 00	20 05		20 10	20 15	20 20				20 25				20 30	20 35			20 40	20 45	20 50		
Haggerston	d			20 01	20 06		20 11	20 16	20 21				20 26				20 31	20 36			20 41	20 46	20 51		
Hoxton	d			20 03	20 08		20 13	20 18	20 23				20 28				20 33	20 38			20 43	20 48	20 53		
Shoreditch High Street	d			20 06	20 11		20 16	20 21	20 26				20 31				20 36	20 41			20 46	20 51	20 56		
Whitechapel	d			20 08	20 13		20 18	20 23	20 28				20 33				20 38	20 43			20 48	20 53	20 58		
Shadwell	d			20 10	20 15		20 20	20 25	20 30				20 35				20 40	20 45			20 50	20 55	21 00		
Wapping	d			20 12	20 17		20 22	20 27	20 32				20 37				20 42	20 47			20 52	20 57	21 02		
Rotherhithe	d			20 14	20 19		20 24	20 29	20 34				20 39				20 44	20 49			20 54	20 59	21 04		
Canada Water	d			20 16	20 21		20 26	20 31	20 36				20 41				20 46	20 51			20 56	21 01	21 06		
Surrey Quays	d			20 17	20 22		20 27	20 32	20 37				20 42				20 47	20 52			20 57	21 02	21 07		
New Cross ELL	a				20 28				20 43									20 58					21 13		
New Cross Gate 4	a			20 21		20 27	20 31	20 36				20 41	20 46				20 51		20 57		21 01	21 06			21 11
	d			20 22		20 27	20 32	20 37				20 41	20 47				20 52		20 57		21 02	21 07			21 11
Brockley	d			20 24		20 30	20 34	20 39				20 44	20 49				20 54		21 00		21 04	21 09			21 14
Honor Oak Park	d			20 27		20 33	20 37	20 42				20 47	20 52				20 57		21 03		21 07	21 12			21 17
Forest Hill 4	d			20 30		20 35	20 40	20 45				20 49	20 55				21 00		21 05		21 10	21 15			21 19
Sydenham	d			20 32		20 38	20 42	20 47				20 52	20 57				21 02		21 08		21 12	21 17			21 22
Crystal Palace 4	d		20 31	20a37		20 43		20a52								21 00	21a07		21 13			21a22			
Gipsy Hill	d		20 33			20 45										21 02			21 15						
West Norwood 4	d		20 36			20 48										21 05			21 18						
Streatham Hill	d					20 52													21 22						
Balham 4 ⊖	d					20 56													21 26						
Wandsworth Common	d					20 58													21 28						
Clapham Junction 10	d					21 03													21 33						
South Bermondsey	d										20 37			20 45										21 07	
Queens Rd Peckham	d										20 39			20 48										21 09	
Peckham Rye 4	d	20 20	20a47								20a42			20 50	20 50	21a16								21a12	
Denmark Hill 4	d	20 24												20 53	20 54										
London Blackfriars 3 ⊖	a	20 34													21 04										
Clapham High Street ⊖	d													20 58											
Wandsworth Road	d													20 59											
Battersea Park 4	d					21 06								21 02					21 36						
London Victoria 15 ⊖	a					21 11								21 06					21 41						
Penge West	d						20 45					20 54	21 00								21 15				21 24
Anerley	d						20 47					20 56	21 02								21 17				21 26
Norwood Junction 2	d						20 50					21 00	21 05								21 20				21 30
West Croydon 4	a						21 00						21 12								21 30				
East Croydon	a											21 03													21 33

London Bridge to London Victoria - Croydon and East London Line

Station		LO	SE	SN	SN		LO	LO	SN	LO	LO	LO	SN	SN	LO		SE	SN	SN	LO	LO	SN	LO	LO	LO
London Bridge 4 ⊖	d			21 11					21 22				21 33	21 36				21 41				21 52			
Highbury & Islington	d	20 48					20 55			21 03	21 10				21 18					21 25			21 33	21 40	
Canonbury	d	20 50					20 57			21 05	21 12				21 20					21 27			21 35	21 42	
Dalston Junction Stn ELL	d	20 55					21 00	21 05		21 10	21 15	21 20			21 25					21 30	21 35		21 40	21 45	21 50
Haggerston	d	20 56					21 01	21 06		21 11	21 16	21 21			21 26					21 31	21 36		21 41	21 46	21 51
Hoxton	d	20 58					21 03	21 08		21 13	21 18	21 23			21 28					21 33	21 38		21 43	21 48	21 53
Shoreditch High Street	d	21 01					21 06	21 11		21 16	21 21	21 26			21 31					21 36	21 41		21 46	21 51	21 56
Whitechapel	d	21 03					21 08	21 13		21 18	21 23	21 28			21 33					21 38	21 43		21 48	21 53	21 58
Shadwell	d	21 05					21 10	21 15		21 20	21 25	21 30			21 35					21 40	21 45		21 50	21 55	22 00
Wapping	d	21 07					21 12	21 17		21 22	21 27	21 32			21 37					21 42	21 47		21 52	21 57	22 02
Rotherhithe	d	21 09					21 14	21 19		21 24	21 29	21 34			21 39					21 44	21 49		21 54	21 59	22 04
Canada Water	d	21 11					21 16	21 21		21 26	21 31	21 36			21 41					21 46	21 51		21 56	22 01	22 06
Surrey Quays	d	21 12					21 17	21 22		21 27	21 32	21 37			21 42					21 47	21 52		21 57	22 02	22 07
New Cross ELL	a							21 28				21 43									21 58				22 13
New Cross Gate 4	a	21 16					21 21		21 27	21 31	21 36			21 41	21 46					21 51		21 57	22 01	22 06	
	d	21 17					21 22		21 27	21 32	21 37			21 41	21 47					21 52		21 57	22 02	22 07	
Brockley	d	21 19					21 24		21 30	21 34	21 39			21 44	21 49					21 54		22 00	22 04	22 09	
Honor Oak Park	d	21 22					21 27		21 33	21 37	21 42			21 47	21 52					21 57		22 03	22 07	22 12	
Forest Hill 4	d	21 25					21 30		21 35	21 40	21 45			21 49	21 55					22 00		22 05	22 10	22 15	
Sydenham	d	21 27					21 32		21 38	21 42	21 47			21 52	21 57					22 02		22 08	22 12	22 17	
Crystal Palace 4	d				21 30		21a37		21 43		21a52								22 00	22a07		22 13		22a22	
Gipsy Hill	d				21 32				21 45										22 02			22 15			
West Norwood 4	d				21 35				21 48										22 05			22 18			
Streatham Hill	d								21 52													22 22			
Balham 4 ⊖	d								21 56													22 26			
Wandsworth Common	d								21 58													22 28			
Clapham Junction 10	d								22 03													22 33			
South Bermondsey	d			21 15									21 37					21 45							
Queens Rd Peckham	d			21 18									21 39					21 48							
Peckham Rye 4	d		21 20	21 20	21a46								21a42				21 50	21 50	22a16						
Denmark Hill 4	d		21 23	21 23													21 53	21 53							
London Blackfriars 3 ⊖	a																								
Clapham High Street ⊖	d			21 28														21 58							
Wandsworth Road	d			21 29														21 59							
Battersea Park 4	d			21 32					22 06									22 02				22 36			
London Victoria 15 ⊖	a		21 33	21 36					22 11								22 03	22 06				22 41			
Penge West	d	21 30								21 45				21 54	22 00								22 15		
Anerley	d	21 32								21 47				21 56	22 02								22 17		
Norwood Junction 2	d	21 35								21 50				22 00	22 05								22 20		
West Croydon 4	a	21 42								22 00					22 12								22 30		
East Croydon	a													22 03											

Station			SN	SN	LO	SE	SN	SN	LO	SN	LO		LO	SN	SN	SE	SN	SN	LO	SN	LO		LO	SN	SN
London Bridge 4 ⊖	d		22 03	22 08			22 11			22 23				22 33	22 38		22 41			22 52				23 05	23 06
Highbury & Islington	d				21 48				21 55		22 05								22 25		22 35				
Canonbury	d				21 50				21 57		22 07								22 27		22 37				
Dalston Junction Stn ELL	d				21 55				22 00		22 10		22 20						22 30		22 40		22 50		
Haggerston	d				21 56				22 01		22 11		22 21						22 31		22 41		22 51		
Hoxton	d				21 58				22 03		22 13		22 23						22 33		22 43		22 53		
Shoreditch High Street	d				22 01				22 06		22 16		22 26						22 36		22 46		22 56		
Whitechapel	d				22 03				22 08		22 18		22 28						22 38		22 48		22 58		
Shadwell	d				22 05				22 10		22 20		22 30						22 40		22 50		23 00		
Wapping	d				22 07				22 12		22 22		22 32						22 42		22 52		23 02		
Rotherhithe	d				22 09				22 14		22 24		22 34						22 44		22 54		23 04		
Canada Water	d				22 11				22 16		22 26		22 36						22 46		22 56		23 06		
Surrey Quays	d				22 12				22 17		22 27		22 37						22 47		22 57		23 07		
New Cross ELL	a												22 43										23 13		
New Cross Gate 4	a			22 13	22 16				22 21	22 28	22 31				22 43				22 51	22 57	23 01				23 11
	d			22 13	22 17				22 22	22 28	22 32				22 43				22 52	22 57	23 02				23 11
Brockley	d			22 16	22 19				22 24	22 31	22 34				22 46				22 54	23 00	23 04				23 14
Honor Oak Park	d			22 19	22 22				22 27	22 34	22 37				22 49				22 57	23 03	23 07				23 17
Forest Hill 4	d			22 21	22 25				22 30	22 36	22 40				22 51				23 00	23 05	23 10				23 19
Sydenham	d			22 24	22 27				22 32	22 39	22 42				22 54				23 02	23 08	23 12				23 22
Crystal Palace 4	d							22 22	22a37	22 43								23 00	23a07	23 13					
Gipsy Hill	d							22 24		22 45								23 02		23 15					
West Norwood 4	d							22 27		22 48								23 05		23 18					
Streatham Hill	d									22 52										23 22					
Balham 4 ⊖	d									22 56										23 26					
Wandsworth Common	d									22 58										23 28					
Clapham Junction 10	d									23 03										23 33					
South Bermondsey	d		22 07				22 15							22 37			22 45							23 09	
Queens Rd Peckham	d		22 09				22 18							22 39			22 48							23 11	
Peckham Rye 4	d		22a12			22 20	22 20	22a42						22a42		22 50	22 50	23a16						23 14	
Denmark Hill 4	d					22 23	22 23									22 53	22 53								
London Blackfriars 3 ⊖	a																								
Clapham High Street ⊖	d						22 28										22 58								
Wandsworth Road	d						22 29										22 59								
Battersea Park 4	d						22 32			23 07							23 02			23 37					
London Victoria 15 ⊖	a					22 33	22 36			23 14						23 03	23 06			23 41					
Penge West	d			22 26	22 30						22 45				22 56						23 15				23 24
Anerley	d			22 28	22 32						22 47				22 58						23 17				23 26
Norwood Junction 2	d			22 32	22 35						22 50				23 02						23 20			23a36	23 30
West Croydon 4	a				22 42						23 00										23 30				
East Croydon	a			22 35											23 06										23 33

Table 178

Mondays to Fridays

London Bridge to London Victoria - Croydon and East London Line

Station		SE	SN	SN	LO	SN	LO	LO	SN	SN	LO	SN	LO	LO	LO
London Bridge 4 ⊖	d		23 11			23 22			23 33	23 36		23 52			
Highbury & Islington	d				22 55		23 05				23 25		23 35	23 42	23 56
Canonbury	d				22 57		23 07				23 27		23 37	23 44	23 58
Dalston Junction Stn ELL	d				23 00		23 10	23 20			23 30		23 40	23 47	00 02
Haggerston	d				23 01		23 11	23 21			23 31		23 41	23 48	00 03
Hoxton	d				23 03		23 13	23 23			23 33		23 43	23 50	00 05
Shoreditch High Street	d				23 06		23 16	23 26			23 36		23 46	23 53	00 08
Whitechapel	d				23 08		23 18	23 28			23 38		23 48	23 55	00 10
Shadwell	d				23 10		23 20	23 30			23 40		23 50	23 57	00 12
Wapping	d				23 12		23 22	23 32			23 42		23 52	23 59	00 14
Rotherhithe	d				23 14		23 24	23 34			23 44		23 54	00 01	00 16
Canada Water	d				23 16		23 26	23 36			23 46		23 56	00 03	00 18
Surrey Quays	d				23 17		23 27	23 37			23 47		23 57	00 05	00 19
New Cross ELL	a							23 43							
New Cross Gate 4	a				23 21	23 27	23 31			23 41	23 51	23 57	00 01	00 08	00 23
	d				23 22	23 27	23 32			23 41	23 52	23 57	00 02		
Brockley	d				23 24	23 30	23 34			23 44	23 54	00 01	00 04		
Honor Oak Park	d				23 27	23 33	23 37			23 47	23 57	00 04	00 07		
Forest Hill 4	d				23 30	23 35	23 40			23 49	23 59	00 06	00 10		
Sydenham	d				23 32	23 38	23 42			23 52	00 02	00 09	00 12		
Crystal Palace 4	d			23 30	23a37	23 43					00a07	00 13			
Gipsy Hill	d			23 32		23 45						00 15			
West Norwood 4	d			23 35		23 48						00 18			
Streatham Hill	d					23 52						00 22			
Balham 4 ⊖	d					23 55						00 25			
Wandsworth Common	d					23 58						00 27			
Clapham Junction 10	d					00 02						00 31			
South Bermondsey	d		23 15						23 37						
Queens Rd Peckham	d		23 18						23 39						
Peckham Rye 4	d	23 20	23 20	23a46					23 42						
Denmark Hill 4	d	23 23	23 23												
London Blackfriars 3 ⊖	a														
Clapham High Street ⊖	d		23 28												
Wandsworth Road	d		23 29												
Battersea Park 4	d		23 32			00 05						00 35			
London Victoria 15 ⊖	a	23 33	23 37			00 10						00 42			
Penge West	d						23 45			23 54			00 15		
Anerley	d						23 47			23 56			00 17		
Norwood Junction 2	d						23 50		00a04	23 59			00 20		
West Croydon 4	a						23 59						00 27		
East Croydon	a									00 03					

Saturdays

Station		SN	SN	SN	LO	SN	LO	LO	SN	SN	LO	LO
London Bridge 4 ⊖	d	23p22	23p36			23p52			00 03	00 06		
Highbury & Islington	d				23p25		23p35	23p42			23p56	00 10
Canonbury	d				23p27		23p37	23p44			23p58	00 12
Dalston Junction Stn ELL	d				23p30		23p40	23p47			00 02	00 15
Haggerston	d				23p31		23p41	23p48			00 03	00 16
Hoxton	d				23p33		23p43	23p50			00 05	00 18
Shoreditch High Street	d				23p36		23p46	23p53			00 08	00 21
Whitechapel	d				23p38		23p48	23p55			00 10	00 23
Shadwell	d				23p40		23p50	23p57			00 12	00 25
Wapping	d				23p42		23p52	23p59			00 14	00 27
Rotherhithe	d				23p44		23p54	00 01			00 16	00 29
Canada Water	d				23p46		23p56	00 03			00 18	00 31
Surrey Quays	d				23p47		23p57	00 05			00 19	00 32
New Cross ELL	a											
New Cross Gate 4	a	23p27	23p41		23p51	23p57	00 01	00 08		00 11	00 23	00 36
	d	23p27	23p41		23p52	23p57	00 02			00 11		
Brockley	d	23p30	23p44		23p54	00 01	00 04			00 14		
Honor Oak Park	d	23p33	23p47		23p57	00 04	00 07			00 17		
Forest Hill 4	d	23p35	23p49		23p59	00 06	00 10			00 19		
Sydenham	d	23p38	23p52		00 02	00 09	00 12			00 22		
Crystal Palace 4	d	23p43		00 03	00a07	00 13						
Gipsy Hill	d	23p45				00 15						
West Norwood 4	d	23p48				00 18						
Streatham Hill	d	23p52				00 22						
Balham 4 ⊖	d	23p55				00 25						
Wandsworth Common	d	23p58				00 27						
Clapham Junction 10	d	00 02				00 31						
South Bermondsey	d								00 07			
Queens Rd Peckham	d								00 09			
Peckham Rye 4	d								00 12			
Denmark Hill 4	d											
London Blackfriars 3 ⊖	a											
Clapham High Street ⊖	d											
Wandsworth Road	d											
Battersea Park 4	d	00 05				00 35						
London Victoria 15 ⊖	a	00 10				00 42						
Penge West	d		23p54				00 15			00 24		
Anerley	d		23p56				00 17			00 26		
Norwood Junction 2	d		23p59	00 09			00 20		00a34	00 30		
West Croydon 4	a			00 14			00 27					
East Croydon	a		00 03							00 33		

Station		SN	SN	SN	SN	SN	SE	SN	LO	LO	LO	LO
London Bridge 4 ⊖	d			00 33	00 36			06 11				
Highbury & Islington	d										05 35	
Canonbury	d										05 37	
Dalston Junction Stn ELL	d										05 40	05 50
Haggerston	d										05 41	05 51
Hoxton	d										05 43	05 53
Shoreditch High Street	d										05 46	05 56
Whitechapel	d										05 48	05 58
Shadwell	d										05 50	06 00
Wapping	d										05 52	06 02
Rotherhithe	d										05 54	06 04
Canada Water	d										05 56	06 06
Surrey Quays	d										05 57	06 07
New Cross ELL	a											06 13
New Cross Gate 4	a				00 41						06 01	
	d				00 41				05 47	05 52	06 02	
Brockley	d				00 44				05 49	05 54	06 04	
Honor Oak Park	d				00 47				05 52	05 57	06 07	
Forest Hill 4	d				00 49				05 55	06 00	06 10	
Sydenham	d				00 52				05 57	06 02	06 12	
Crystal Palace 4	d	00 33	00 47			01 03				06a07		
Gipsy Hill	d											
West Norwood 4	d											
Streatham Hill	d											
Balham 4 ⊖	d											
Wandsworth Common	d											
Clapham Junction 10	d											
South Bermondsey	d			00 37				06 15				
Queens Rd Peckham	d			00 39				06 18				
Peckham Rye 4	d			00 42			06 13	06 20				
Denmark Hill 4	d						06 17	06 23				
London Blackfriars 3 ⊖	a											
Clapham High Street ⊖	d							06 28				
Wandsworth Road	d							06 29				
Battersea Park 4	d							06 32				
London Victoria 15 ⊖	a						06 26	06 36				
Penge West	d				00 54				06 00		06 15	
Anerley	d				00 56				06 02		06 17	
Norwood Junction 2	d	00 38	00 52	01a04	01 00	01 08			06 05		06 18	
West Croydon 4	a	00 43	00 58			01 13			06 12		06 30	
East Croydon	a				01 03							

Table 178

Saturdays

London Bridge to London Victoria - Croydon and East London Line

Station		SE	LO	LO	LO	LO	LO	SN	LO	SN	SN	SE	SE
London Bridge 4 ⊖	d									06 36	06 41		
Highbury & Islington	d				05 55	06 05							
Canonbury	d				05 57	06 07							
Dalston Junction Stn ELL	d				06 00	06 10	06 20						
Haggerston	d				06 01	06 11	06 21						
Hoxton	d				06 03	06 13	06 23						
Shoreditch High Street	d				06 06	06 16	06 26						
Whitechapel	d				06 08	06 18	06 28						
Shadwell	d				06 10	06 20	06 30						
Wapping	d				06 12	06 22	06 32						
Rotherhithe	d				06 14	06 24	06 34						
Canada Water	d				06 16	06 26	06 36						
Surrey Quays	d				06 17	06 27	06 37						
New Cross ELL	a						06 43						
New Cross Gate 4	a				06 21	06 31				06 41			
	d		06 07	06 17	06 22	06 32			06 37	06 41			
Brockley	d		06 09	06 19	06 24	06 34			06 39	06 44			
Honor Oak Park	d		06 12	06 22	06 27	06 37			06 42	06 47			
Forest Hill 4	d		06 15	06 25	06 30	06 40			06 45	06 49			
Sydenham	d		06 17	06 27	06 32	06 42			06 47	06 52			
Crystal Palace 4	d		06a22		06a37			06 45	06a52				
Gipsy Hill	d							06 47					
West Norwood 4	d							06 50					
Streatham Hill	d												
Balham 4 ⊖	d												
Wandsworth Common	d												
Clapham Junction 10	d												
South Bermondsey	d										06 45		
Queens Rd Peckham	d										06 48		
Peckham Rye 4	d	06 43						07a01			06 50	07 13	07 17
Denmark Hill 4	d	06 47									06 53	07 17	07 21
London Blackfriars 3 ⊖	a												
Clapham High Street ⊖	d										06 58		
Wandsworth Road	d										06 59		
Battersea Park 4	d										07 02		
London Victoria 15 ⊖	a	06 56									07 06	07 26	07 30
Penge West	d			06 30		06 45				06 54			
Anerley	d			06 32		06 47				06 56			
Norwood Junction 2	d			06 35		06 50				07 00			
West Croydon 4	a			06 41		07 00							
East Croydon	a									07 03			

Station		LO	LO	LO	LO	LO	LO	SN	LO	LO	LO
London Bridge 4 ⊖	d							07 06			
Highbury & Islington	d		06 25		06 33	06 40			06 48	06 55	
Canonbury	d		06 27		06 35	06 42			06 50	06 57	
Dalston Junction Stn ELL	d		06 30	06 35	06 40	06 45	06 50		06 55	07 00	07 05
Haggerston	d		06 31	06 36	06 41	06 46	06 51		06 56	07 01	07 06
Hoxton	d		06 33	06 38	06 43	06 48	06 53		06 58	07 03	07 08
Shoreditch High Street	d		06 36	06 41	06 46	06 51	06 56		07 01	07 06	07 11
Whitechapel	d		06 38	06 43	06 48	06 53	06 58		07 03	07 08	07 13
Shadwell	d		06 40	06 45	06 50	06 55	07 00		07 05	07 10	07 15
Wapping	d		06 42	06 47	06 52	06 57	07 02		07 07	07 12	07 17
Rotherhithe	d		06 44	06 49	06 54	06 59	07 04		07 09	07 14	07 19
Canada Water	d		06 46	06 51	06 56	07 01	07 06		07 11	07 16	07 21
Surrey Quays	d		06 47	06 52	06 57	07 02	07 07		07 12	07 17	07 22
New Cross ELL	a			06 58			07 13				07 28
New Cross Gate 4	a		06 51		07 01	07 06		07 11	07 16	07 21	
	d	06 47	06 52		07 02	07 07		07 11	07 17	07 22	
Brockley	d	06 49	06 54		07 04	07 09		07 14	07 19	07 24	
Honor Oak Park	d	06 52	06 57		07 07	07 12		07 17	07 22	07 27	
Forest Hill 4	d	06 55	07 00		07 10	07 15		07 19	07 25	07 30	
Sydenham	d	06 57	07 02		07 12	07 17		07 22	07 27	07 32	
Crystal Palace 4	d		07a07			07a22				07a37	
Gipsy Hill	d										
West Norwood 4	d										
Streatham Hill	d										
Balham 4 ⊖	d										
Wandsworth Common	d										
Clapham Junction 10	d										
South Bermondsey	d										
Queens Rd Peckham	d										
Peckham Rye 4	d										
Denmark Hill 4	d										
London Blackfriars 3 ⊖	a										
Clapham High Street ⊖	d										
Wandsworth Road	d										
Battersea Park 4	d										
London Victoria 15 ⊖	a										
Penge West	d	07 00			07 15			07 24	07 30		
Anerley	d	07 02			07 17			07 26	07 32		
Norwood Junction 2	d	07 05			07 20			07 30	07 35		
West Croydon 4	a	07 11			07 30				07 41		
East Croydon	a							07 33			

Station		LO	LO	SN	LO	SN	SN	LO	LO	LO	LO
London Bridge 4 ⊖	d			07 11		07 33	07 36				
Highbury & Islington	d	07 03	07 10					07 18	07 25		07 33
Canonbury	d	07 05	07 12					07 20	07 27		07 35
Dalston Junction Stn ELL	d	07 10	07 15		07 20			07 25	07 30	07 35	07 40
Haggerston	d	07 11	07 16		07 21			07 26	07 31	07 36	07 41
Hoxton	d	07 13	07 18		07 23			07 28	07 33	07 38	07 43
Shoreditch High Street	d	07 16	07 21		07 26			07 31	07 36	07 41	07 46
Whitechapel	d	07 18	07 23		07 28			07 33	07 38	07 43	07 48
Shadwell	d	07 20	07 25		07 30			07 35	07 40	07 45	07 50
Wapping	d	07 22	07 27		07 32			07 37	07 42	07 47	07 52
Rotherhithe	d	07 24	07 29		07 34			07 39	07 44	07 49	07 54
Canada Water	d	07 26	07 31		07 36			07 41	07 46	07 51	07 56
Surrey Quays	d	07 27	07 32		07 37			07 42	07 47	07 52	07 57
New Cross ELL	a				07 43					07 58	
New Cross Gate 4	a	07 31	07 36				07 41	07 46	07 51		08 01
	d	07 32	07 37				07 41	07 47	07 52		08 02
Brockley	d	07 34	07 39				07 44	07 49	07 54		08 04
Honor Oak Park	d	07 37	07 42				07 47	07 52	07 57		08 07
Forest Hill 4	d	07 40	07 45				07 49	07 55	08 00		08 10
Sydenham	d	07 42	07 47				07 52	07 57	08 02		08 12
Crystal Palace 4	d		07a52						08a07		
Gipsy Hill	d										
West Norwood 4	d										
Streatham Hill	d										
Balham 4 ⊖	d										
Wandsworth Common	d										
Clapham Junction 10	d										
South Bermondsey	d			07 15		07 37					
Queens Rd Peckham	d			07 18		07 39					
Peckham Rye 4	d			07 20		07a42					
Denmark Hill 4	d			07 23							
London Blackfriars 3 ⊖	a										
Clapham High Street ⊖	d			07 28							
Wandsworth Road	d			07 29							
Battersea Park 4	d			07 32							
London Victoria 15 ⊖	a			07 36							
Penge West	d	07 45					07 54	08 00			08 15
Anerley	d	07 47					07 56	08 02			08 17
Norwood Junction 2	d	07 50					08 00	08 05			08 20
West Croydon 4	a	08 00						08 11			08 30
East Croydon	a						08 03				

Station		LO	LO	SE	SE	SN	SN	SN	LO	SE	SE	SN
London Bridge 4 ⊖	d					07 41	08 03	08 06				08 11
Highbury & Islington	d	07 40							07 48			
Canonbury	d	07 42							07 50			
Dalston Junction Stn ELL	d	07 45	07 50						07 55			
Haggerston	d	07 46	07 51						07 56			
Hoxton	d	07 48	07 53						07 58			
Shoreditch High Street	d	07 51	07 56						08 01			
Whitechapel	d	07 53	07 58						08 03			
Shadwell	d	07 55	08 00						08 05			
Wapping	d	07 57	08 02						08 07			
Rotherhithe	d	07 59	08 04						08 09			
Canada Water	d	08 01	08 06						08 11			
Surrey Quays	d	08 02	08 07						08 12			
New Cross ELL	a		08 13									
New Cross Gate 4	a	08 06						08 11	08 16			
	d	08 07						08 11	08 17			
Brockley	d	08 09						08 14	08 19			
Honor Oak Park	d	08 12						08 17	08 22			
Forest Hill 4	d	08 15						08 19	08 25			
Sydenham	d	08 17						08 22	08 27			
Crystal Palace 4	d	08a22										
Gipsy Hill	d											
West Norwood 4	d											
Streatham Hill	d											
Balham 4 ⊖	d											
Wandsworth Common	d											
Clapham Junction 10	d											
South Bermondsey	d					07 45	08 07					08 15
Queens Rd Peckham	d					07 48	08 09					08 18
Peckham Rye 4	d			07 43	07 47	07 50	08a12			08 13	08 17	08 20
Denmark Hill 4	d			07 47	07 51	07 53				08 17	08 21	08 23
London Blackfriars 3 ⊖	a											
Clapham High Street ⊖	d					07 58						08 28
Wandsworth Road	d					07 59						08 29
Battersea Park 4	d					08 02						08 32
London Victoria 15 ⊖	a			07 56	08 00	08 06				08 26	08 30	08 36
Penge West	d							08 24	08 30			
Anerley	d							08 26	08 32			
Norwood Junction 2	d							08 30	08 35			
West Croydon 4	a								08 41			
East Croydon	a							08 33				

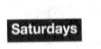

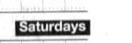

London Bridge to London Victoria - Croydon and East London Line

Station		SN	LO	LO	SN	LO	LO	LO	SN	SN	LO	SE	SE	SN	SN	LO	LO	SN	LO	LO	LO	SN	SN
London Bridge 4	d				08 22				08 33	08 36				08 41				08 52				09 03	09 06
Highbury & Islington	d		07 55			08 03	08 10				08 18					08 25			08 33	08 40			
Canonbury	d		07 57			08 05	08 12				08 20					08 27			08 35	08 42			
Dalston Junction Stn ELL	d		08 00	08 05		08 10	08 15	08 20			08 25					08 30	08 35		08 40	08 45	08 50		
Haggerston	d		08 01	08 06		08 11	08 16	08 21			08 26					08 31	08 36		08 41	08 46	08 51		
Hoxton	d		08 03	08 08		08 13	08 18	08 23			08 28					08 33	08 38		08 43	08 48	08 53		
Shoreditch High Street	d		08 06	08 11		08 16	08 21	08 26			08 31					08 36	08 41		08 46	08 51	08 56		
Whitechapel	d		08 08	08 13		08 18	08 23	08 28			08 33					08 38	08 43		08 48	08 53	08 58		
Shadwell	d		08 10	08 15		08 20	08 25	08 30			08 35					08 40	08 45		08 50	08 55	09 00		
Wapping	d		08 12	08 17		08 22	08 27	08 32			08 37					08 42	08 47		08 52	08 57	09 02		
Rotherhithe	d		08 14	08 19		08 24	08 29	08 34			08 39					08 44	08 49		08 54	08 59	09 04		
Canada Water	d		08 16	08 21		08 26	08 31	08 36			08 41					08 46	08 51		08 56	09 01	09 06		
Surrey Quays	d		08 17	08 22		08 27	08 32	08 37			08 42					08 47	08 52		08 57	09 02	09 07		
New Cross ELL	a			08 28				08 43									08 58				09 13		
New Cross Gate 4	a		08 21		08 27	08 31	08 36			08 41	08 46					08 51		08 57	09 01	09 06			09 11
	d		08 22		08 27	08 32	08 37			08 41	08 47					08 52		08 57	09 02	09 07			09 11
Brockley	d		08 24		08 30	08 34	08 39			08 44	08 49					08 54		09 00	09 04	09 09			09 14
Honor Oak Park	d		08 27		08 33	08 37	08 42			08 47	08 52					08 57		09 03	09 07	09 12			09 17
Forest Hill 4	d		08 30		08 35	08 40	08 45			08 49	08 55					09 00		09 05	09 10	09 15			09 19
Sydenham	d		08 32		08 38	08 42	08 47			08 52	08 57					09 02		09 08	09 12	09 17			09 22
Crystal Palace 4	d	08 30	08a37		08 43		08a52								09 00	09a07		09 13		09a22			
Gipsy Hill	d	08 32			08 45										09 02			09 15					
West Norwood 4	d	08 35			08 48										09 05			09 18					
Streatham Hill	d				08 52													09 22					
Balham 4	d				08 55													09 25					
Wandsworth Common	d				08 57													09 27					
Clapham Junction 10	d				09 01													09 31					
South Bermondsey	d								08 37					08 45								09 07	
Queens Rd Peckham	d								08 39					08 48								09 09	
Peckham Rye 4	d	08a46							08a42			08 43	08 47	08 50	09a16							09a12	
Denmark Hill 4	d											08 47	08 51	08 53									
London Blackfriars 3	a																						
Clapham High Street	d													08 58									
Wandsworth Road	d													08 59									
Battersea Park 4	d				09 05									09 02				09 35					
London Victoria 15	a				09 09							08 56	09 00	09 06				09 39					
Penge West	d					08 45				08 54	09 00								09 15				09 24
Anerley	d					08 47				08 56	09 02								09 17				09 26
Norwood Junction 2	d					08 50				09 00	09 05								09 20				09 30
West Croydon 4	a					09 00					09 12								09 30				
East Croydon	a									09 03													09 33

Station		LO	SE	SE	SN	SN	LO	LO	SN	LO	LO	LO	SN	SN	LO	SE	SE	SN	SN	LO	LO	SN
London Bridge 4	d				09 11				09 22				09 33	09 36				09 41				09 52
Highbury & Islington	d	08 48					08 55			09 03	09 10				09 18					09 25		
Canonbury	d	08 50					08 57			09 05	09 12				09 20					09 27		
Dalston Junction Stn ELL	d	08 55					09 00	09 05		09 10	09 15	09 20			09 25					09 30	09 35	
Haggerston	d	08 56					09 01	09 06		09 11	09 16	09 21			09 26					09 31	09 36	
Hoxton	d	08 58					09 03	09 08		09 13	09 18	09 23			09 28					09 33	09 38	
Shoreditch High Street	d	09 01					09 06	09 11		09 16	09 21	09 26			09 31					09 36	09 41	
Whitechapel	d	09 03					09 08	09 13		09 18	09 23	09 28			09 33					09 38	09 43	
Shadwell	d	09 05					09 10	09 15		09 20	09 25	09 30			09 35					09 40	09 45	
Wapping	d	09 07					09 12	09 17		09 22	09 27	09 32			09 37					09 42	09 47	
Rotherhithe	d	09 09					09 14	09 19		09 24	09 29	09 34			09 39					09 44	09 49	
Canada Water	d	09 11					09 16	09 21		09 26	09 31	09 36			09 41					09 46	09 51	
Surrey Quays	d	09 12					09 17	09 22		09 27	09 32	09 37			09 42					09 47	09 52	
New Cross ELL	a							09 28				09 43									09 58	
New Cross Gate 4	a	09 16					09 21		09 27	09 31	09 36			09 41	09 46					09 51		09 57
	d	09 17					09 22		09 27	09 32	09 37			09 41	09 47					09 52		09 57
Brockley	d	09 19					09 24		09 30	09 34	09 39			09 44	09 49					09 54		10 00
Honor Oak Park	d	09 22					09 27		09 33	09 37	09 42			09 47	09 52					09 57		10 03
Forest Hill 4	d	09 25					09 30		09 35	09 40	09 45			09 49	09 55					10 00		10 05
Sydenham	d	09 27					09 32		09 38	09 42	09 47			09 52	09 57					10 02		10 08
Crystal Palace 4	d					09 30	09a37		09 43		09a52								10 00	10a07		10 13
Gipsy Hill	d					09 32			09 45										10 02			10 15
West Norwood 4	d					09 35			09 48										10 05			10 18
Streatham Hill	d								09 52													10 22
Balham 4	d								09 55													10 25
Wandsworth Common	d								09 57													10 27
Clapham Junction 10	d								10 01													10 31
South Bermondsey	d				09 15								09 37					09 45				
Queens Rd Peckham	d				09 18								09 39					09 48				
Peckham Rye 4	d		09 13	09 17	09 20	09a46							09a42			09 43	09 47	09 50	10a16			
Denmark Hill 4	d		09 17	09 21	09 23											09 47	09 51	09 53				
London Blackfriars 3	a																					
Clapham High Street	d				09 28													09 58				
Wandsworth Road	d				09 29													09 59				
Battersea Park 4	d				09 32				10 05									10 02				10 35
London Victoria 15	a		09 26	09 30	09 36				10 09							09 56	10 00	10 06				10 39
Penge West	d	09 30								09 45				09 54	10 00							
Anerley	d	09 32								09 47				09 56	10 02							
Norwood Junction 2	d	09 35								09 50				10 00	10 05							
West Croydon 4	a	09 42								10 00					10 12							
East Croydon	a													10 03								

London Bridge to London Victoria - Croydon and East London Line

Station		LO	LO	LO	SN	SN	LO	SE	SE	SN	SN	LO	LO	SN	LO	LO	LO	SN	SN	LO	SE	SE	SN
London Bridge 4	d				10 03	10 06				10 11				10 22				10 33	10 36				10 41
Highbury & Islington	d	09 33	09 40				09 48					09 55			10 03	10 10				10 18			
Canonbury	d	09 35	09 42				09 50					09 57			10 05	10 12				10 20			
Dalston Junction Stn ELL	d	09 40	09 45	09 50			09 55					10 00	10 05		10 10	10 15	10 20			10 25			
Haggerston	d	09 41	09 46	09 51			09 56					10 01	10 06		10 11	10 16	10 21			10 26			
Hoxton	d	09 43	09 48	09 53			09 58					10 03	10 08		10 13	10 18	10 23			10 28			
Shoreditch High Street	d	09 46	09 51	09 56			10 01					10 06	10 11		10 16	10 21	10 26			10 31			
Whitechapel	d	09 48	09 53	09 58			10 03					10 08	10 13		10 18	10 23	10 28			10 33			
Shadwell	d	09 50	09 55	10 00			10 05					10 10	10 15		10 20	10 25	10 30			10 35			
Wapping	d	09 52	09 57	10 02			10 07					10 12	10 17		10 22	10 27	10 32			10 37			
Rotherhithe	d	09 54	09 59	10 04			10 09					10 14	10 19		10 24	10 29	10 34			10 39			
Canada Water	d	09 56	10 01	10 06			10 11					10 16	10 21		10 26	10 31	10 36			10 41			
Surrey Quays	d	09 57	10 02	10 07			10 12					10 17	10 22		10 27	10 32	10 37			10 42			
New Cross ELL	a			10 13									10 28				10 43						
New Cross Gate 4	a	10 01	10 06			10 11	10 16					10 21		10 27	10 31	10 36			10 41	10 46			
	d	10 02	10 07			10 11	10 17					10 22		10 27	10 32	10 37			10 41	10 47			
Brockley	d	10 04	10 09			10 14	10 19					10 24		10 30	10 34	10 39			10 44	10 49			
Honor Oak Park	d	10 07	10 12			10 17	10 22					10 27		10 33	10 37	10 42			10 47	10 52			
Forest Hill 4	d	10 10	10 15			10 19	10 25					10 30		10 35	10 40	10 45			10 49	10 55			
Sydenham	d	10 12	10 17			10 22	10 27					10 32		10 38	10 42	10 47			10 52	10 57			
Crystal Palace 4	d		10a22								10 30	10a37		10 43		10a52							
Gipsy Hill	d										10 32			10 45									
West Norwood 4	d										10 35			10 48									
Streatham Hill	d													10 52									
Balham 4	d													10 55									
Wandsworth Common	d													10 57									
Clapham Junction 10	d													11 01									
South Bermondsey	d				10 07					10 15								10 37					10 45
Queens Rd Peckham	d				10 09					10 18								10 39					10 48
Peckham Rye 4	d				10a12			10 13	10 17	10 20	10a46							10a42			10 43	10 47	10 50
Denmark Hill 4	d							10 17	10 21	10 23											10 47	10 51	10 53
London Blackfriars 3	a																						
Clapham High Street	d									10 28													10 58
Wandsworth Road	d									10 29													10 59
Battersea Park 4	d									10 32				11 05									11 02
London Victoria 15	a							10 26	10 30	10 36				11 09							10 56	11 00	11 06
Penge West	d	10 15				10 24	10 30								10 45				10 54	11 00			
Anerley	d	10 17				10 26	10 32								10 47				10 56	11 02			
Norwood Junction 2	d	10 20				10 30	10 35								10 50				11 00	11 05			
West Croydon 4	a	10 30					10 42								11 00					11 12			
East Croydon	a					10 33													11 03				

Station		SN	LO	LO	SN	LO	LO	LO	SN	SN	LO	SE	SE	SN	SN	LO	LO	SN	LO	LO	LO	SN	SN
London Bridge 4	d				10 52				11 03	11 06				11 11				11 22				11 33	11 36
Highbury & Islington	d		10 25			10 33	10 40				10 48					10 55			11 03	11 10			
Canonbury	d		10 27			10 35	10 42				10 50					10 57			11 05	11 12			
Dalston Junction Stn ELL	d		10 30	10 35		10 40	10 45	10 50			10 55					11 00	11 05		11 10	11 15	11 20		
Haggerston	d		10 31	10 36		10 41	10 46	10 51			10 56					11 01	11 06		11 11	11 16	11 21		
Hoxton	d		10 33	10 38		10 43	10 48	10 53			10 58					11 03	11 08		11 13	11 18	11 23		
Shoreditch High Street	d		10 36	10 41		10 46	10 51	10 56			11 01					11 06	11 11		11 16	11 21	11 26		
Whitechapel	d		10 38	10 43		10 48	10 53	10 58			11 03					11 08	11 13		11 18	11 23	11 28		
Shadwell	d		10 40	10 45		10 50	10 55	11 00			11 05					11 10	11 15		11 20	11 25	11 30		
Wapping	d		10 42	10 47		10 52	10 57	11 02			11 07					11 12	11 17		11 22	11 27	11 32		
Rotherhithe	d		10 44	10 49		10 54	10 59	11 04			11 09					11 14	11 19		11 24	11 29	11 34		
Canada Water	d		10 46	10 51		10 56	11 01	11 06			11 11					11 16	11 21		11 26	11 31	11 36		
Surrey Quays	d		10 47	10 52		10 57	11 02	11 07			11 12					11 17	11 22		11 27	11 32	11 37		
New Cross ELL	a			10 58				11 13									11 28				11 43		
New Cross Gate 4	a		10 51		10 57	11 01	11 06			11 11	11 16					11 21		11 27	11 31	11 36			11 41
	d		10 52		10 57	11 02	11 07			11 11	11 17					11 22		11 27	11 32	11 37			11 41
Brockley	d		10 54		11 00	11 04	11 09			11 14	11 19					11 24		11 30	11 34	11 39			11 44
Honor Oak Park	d		10 57		11 03	11 07	11 12			11 17	11 22					11 27		11 33	11 37	11 42			11 47
Forest Hill 4	d		11 00		11 05	11 10	11 15			11 19	11 25					11 30		11 35	11 40	11 45			11 49
Sydenham	d		11 02		11 08	11 12	11 17			11 22	11 27					11 32		11 38	11 42	11 47			11 52
Crystal Palace 4	d	11 00	11a07		11 13		11a22								11 30	11a37		11 43		11a52			
Gipsy Hill	d	11 02			11 15										11 32			11 45					
West Norwood 4	d	11 05			11 18										11 35			11 48					
Streatham Hill	d				11 22													11 52					
Balham 4	d				11 25													11 55					
Wandsworth Common	d				11 27													11 57					
Clapham Junction 10	d				11 31													12 01					
South Bermondsey	d								11 07					11 15								11 37	
Queens Rd Peckham	d								11 09					11 18								11 39	
Peckham Rye 4	d	11a16							11a12			11 13	11 17	11 20	11a46							11a42	
Denmark Hill 4	d											11 17	11 21	11 23									
London Blackfriars 3	a																						
Clapham High Street	d													11 28									
Wandsworth Road	d													11 29									
Battersea Park 4	d				11 35									11 32				12 05					
London Victoria 15	a				11 39							11 26	11 30	11 36				12 09					
Penge West	d					11 15				11 24	11 30								11 45				11 54
Anerley	d					11 17				11 26	11 32								11 47				11 56
Norwood Junction 2	d					11 20				11 30	11 35								11 50				12 00
West Croydon 4	a					11 30					11 42								12 00				
East Croydon	a									11 33													12 03

London Bridge to London Victoria - Croydon and East London Line

		LO		SE	SE	SN	SN	LO	LO	SN	LO	LO		LO	SN	SN	LO	SE	SE	SN	SN	LO		LO	SN
London Bridge ⊖	d					11 41				11 52					12 03	12 06				12 11					12 22
Highbury & Islington	d	11 18						11 25			11 33	11 40					11 48					11 55			
Canonbury	d	11 20						11 27			11 35	11 42					11 50					11 57			
Dalston Junction Stn ELL	d	11 25						11 30	11 35		11 40	11 45		11 50			11 55					12 00		12 05	
Haggerston	d	11 26						11 31	11 36		11 41	11 46		11 51			11 56					12 01		12 06	
Hoxton	d	11 28						11 33	11 38		11 43	11 48		11 53			11 58					12 03		12 08	
Shoreditch High Street	d	11 31						11 36	11 41		11 46	11 51		11 56			12 01					12 06		12 11	
Whitechapel	d	11 33						11 38	11 43		11 48	11 53		11 58			12 03					12 08		12 13	
Shadwell	d	11 35						11 40	11 45		11 50	11 55		12 00			12 05					12 10		12 15	
Wapping	d	11 37						11 42	11 47		11 52	11 57		12 02			12 07					12 12		12 17	
Rotherhithe	d	11 39						11 44	11 49		11 54	11 59		12 04			12 09					12 14		12 19	
Canada Water	d	11 41						11 46	11 51		11 56	12 01		12 06			12 11					12 16		12 21	
Surrey Quays	d	11 42						11 47	11 52		11 57	12 02		12 07			12 12					12 17		12 22	
New Cross ELL	a								11 58					12 13										12 28	
New Cross Gate	a	11 46						11 51		11 57	12 01	12 06				12 11	12 16					12 21			12 27
	d	11 47						11 52		11 57	12 02	12 07				12 11	12 17					12 22			12 27
Brockley	d	11 49						11 54		12 00	12 04	12 09				12 14	12 19					12 24			12 30
Honor Oak Park	d	11 52						11 57		12 03	12 07	12 12				12 17	12 22					12 27			12 33
Forest Hill	d	11 55						12 00		12 05	12 10	12 15				12 19	12 25					12 30			12 35
Sydenham	d	11 57						12 02		12 08	12 12	12 17				12 22	12 27					12 32			12 38
Crystal Palace	d						12 00	12a07		12 13		12a22									12 30	12a37			12 43
Gipsy Hill	d						12 02			12 15											12 32				12 45
West Norwood	d						12 05			12 18											12 35				12 48
Streatham Hill	d									12 22															12 52
Balham ⊖	d									12 25															12 55
Wandsworth Common	d									12 27															12 57
Clapham Junction	d									12 31															13 01
South Bermondsey	d					11 45									12 07					12 15					
Queens Rd Peckham	d					11 48									12 09					12 18					
Peckham Rye	d			11 43	11 47	11 50	12a16								12a12			12 13	12 17	12 20	12a46				
Denmark Hill	d			11 47	11 51	11 53												12 17	12 21	12 23					
London Blackfriars ⊖	a																								
Clapham High Street ⊖	d					11 58														12 28					
Wandsworth Road	d					11 59														12 29					
Battersea Park	d					12 02				12 35										12 32					13 05
London Victoria ⊖	a			11 56	12 00	12 06				12 39								12 26	12 30	12 36					13 09
Penge West	d	12 00									12 15					12 24	12 30								
Anerley	d	12 02									12 17					12 26	12 32								
Norwood Junction	d	12 05									12 20					12 30	12 35								
West Croydon	a	12 12									12 30						12 42								
East Croydon	a															12 33									

		LO	LO	LO	SN	SN	LO	SE		SE	SN	SN	LO	LO	SN	LO	LO	LO		SN	SN	LO	SE	SE	SN
London Bridge ⊖	d				12 33	12 36					12 41				12 52					13 03	13 06				13 11
Highbury & Islington	d	12 03	12 10				12 18						12 25			12 33	12 40					12 48			
Canonbury	d	12 05	12 12				12 20						12 27			12 35	12 42					12 50			
Dalston Junction Stn ELL	d	12 10	12 15	12 20			12 25						12 30	12 35		12 40	12 45	12 50				12 55			
Haggerston	d	12 11	12 16	12 21			12 26						12 31	12 36		12 41	12 46	12 51				12 56			
Hoxton	d	12 13	12 18	12 23			12 28						12 33	12 38		12 43	12 48	12 53				12 58			
Shoreditch High Street	d	12 16	12 21	12 26			12 31						12 36	12 41		12 46	12 51	12 56				13 01			
Whitechapel	d	12 18	12 23	12 28			12 33						12 38	12 43		12 48	12 53	12 58				13 03			
Shadwell	d	12 20	12 25	12 30			12 35						12 40	12 45		12 50	12 55	13 00				13 05			
Wapping	d	12 22	12 27	12 32			12 37						12 42	12 47		12 52	12 57	13 02				13 07			
Rotherhithe	d	12 24	12 29	12 34			12 39						12 44	12 49		12 54	12 59	13 04				13 09			
Canada Water	d	12 26	12 31	12 36			12 41						12 46	12 51		12 56	13 01	13 06				13 11			
Surrey Quays	d	12 27	12 32	12 37			12 42						12 47	12 52		12 57	13 02	13 07				13 12			
New Cross ELL	a			12 43										12 58				13 13							
New Cross Gate	a	12 31	12 36			12 41	12 46						12 51		12 57	13 01	13 06				13 11	13 16			
	d	12 32	12 37			12 41	12 47						12 52		12 57	13 02	13 07				13 11	13 17			
Brockley	d	12 34	12 39			12 44	12 49						12 54		13 00	13 04	13 09				13 14	13 19			
Honor Oak Park	d	12 37	12 42			12 47	12 52						12 57		13 03	13 07	13 12				13 17	13 22			
Forest Hill	d	12 40	12 45			12 49	12 55						13 00		13 05	13 10	13 15				13 19	13 25			
Sydenham	d	12 42	12 47			12 52	12 57						13 02		13 08	13 12	13 17				13 22	13 27			
Crystal Palace	d		12a52									13 00	13a07		13 13		13a22								
Gipsy Hill	d											13 02			13 15										
West Norwood	d											13 05			13 18										
Streatham Hill	d														13 22										
Balham ⊖	d														13 25										
Wandsworth Common	d														13 27										
Clapham Junction	d														13 31										
South Bermondsey	d				12 37						12 45									13 07					13 15
Queens Rd Peckham	d				12 39						12 48									13 09					13 18
Peckham Rye	d				12a42			12 43		12 47	12 50	13a16								13a12			13 13	13 17	13 20
Denmark Hill	d							12 47		12 51	12 53												13 17	13 21	13 23
London Blackfriars ⊖	a																								
Clapham High Street ⊖	d										12 58														13 28
Wandsworth Road	d										12 59														13 29
Battersea Park	d										13 02				13 35										13 32
London Victoria ⊖	a							12 56		13 00	13 06				13 39								13 26	13 30	13 36
Penge West	d	12 45				12 54	13 00									13 15					13 24	13 30			
Anerley	d	12 47				12 56	13 02									13 17					13 26	13 32			
Norwood Junction	d	12 50				13 00	13 05									13 20					13 30	13 35			
West Croydon	a	13 00					13 12									13 30						13 42			
East Croydon	a					13 03															13 33				

London Bridge to London Victoria - Croydon and East London Line

		SN	LO	LO		SN	LO	LO	LO	SN	SN	LO	SE	SE		SN	SN	LO	LO	SN	LO	LO	LO	SN
London Bridge ⊖	d					13 22				13 33	13 36					13 41				13 52				14 03
Highbury & Islington	d		12 55				13 03	13 10				13 18						13 25			13 33	13 40		
Canonbury	d		12 57				13 05	13 12				13 20						13 27			13 35	13 42		
Dalston Junction Stn ELL	d		13 00	13 05			13 10	13 15	13 20			13 25						13 30	13 35		13 40	13 45	13 50	
Haggerston	d		13 01	13 06			13 11	13 16	13 21			13 26						13 31	13 36		13 41	13 46	13 51	
Hoxton	d		13 03	13 08			13 13	13 18	13 23			13 28						13 33	13 38		13 43	13 48	13 53	
Shoreditch High Street	d		13 06	13 11			13 16	13 21	13 26			13 31						13 36	13 41		13 46	13 51	13 56	
Whitechapel	d		13 08	13 13			13 18	13 23	13 28			13 33						13 38	13 43		13 48	13 53	13 58	
Shadwell	d		13 10	13 15			13 20	13 25	13 30			13 35						13 40	13 45		13 50	13 55	14 00	
Wapping	d		13 12	13 17			13 22	13 27	13 32			13 37						13 42	13 47		13 52	13 57	14 02	
Rotherhithe	d		13 14	13 19			13 24	13 29	13 34			13 39						13 44	13 49		13 54	13 59	14 04	
Canada Water	d		13 16	13 21			13 26	13 31	13 36			13 41						13 46	13 51		13 56	14 01	14 06	
Surrey Quays	d		13 17	13 22			13 27	13 32	13 37			13 42						13 47	13 52		13 57	14 02	14 07	
New Cross ELL	a			13 28					13 43										13 58				14 13	
New Cross Gate	a		13 21			13 27	13 31	13 36			13 41	13 46						13 51		13 57	14 01	14 06		
	d		13 22			13 27	13 32	13 37			13 41	13 47						13 52		13 57	14 02	14 07		
Brockley	d		13 24			13 30	13 34	13 39			13 44	13 49						13 54		14 00	14 04	14 09		
Honor Oak Park	d		13 27			13 33	13 37	13 42			13 47	13 52						13 57		14 03	14 07	14 12		
Forest Hill	d		13 30			13 35	13 40	13 45			13 49	13 55						14 00		14 05	14 10	14 15		
Sydenham	d		13 32			13 38	13 42	13 47			13 52	13 57						14 02		14 08	14 12	14 17		
Crystal Palace	d	13 30	13a37			13 43		13a52									14 00	14a07		14 13		14a22		
Gipsy Hill	d	13 32				13 45											14 02			14 15				
West Norwood	d	13 35				13 48											14 05			14 18				
Streatham Hill	d					13 52														14 22				
Balham ⊖	d					13 55														14 25				
Wandsworth Common	d					13 57														14 27				
Clapham Junction	d					14 01														14 31				
South Bermondsey	d									13 37						13 45								14 07
Queens Rd Peckham	d									13 39						13 48								14 09
Peckham Rye	d	13a46								13a42			13 43	13 47		13 50	14a16							14a12
Denmark Hill	d												13 47	13 51		13 53								
London Blackfriars ⊖	a																							
Clapham High Street ⊖	d															13 58								
Wandsworth Road	d															13 59								
Battersea Park	d					14 05										14 02				14 35				
London Victoria ⊖	a					14 09							13 56	14 00		14 06				14 39				
Penge West	d						13 45				13 54	14 00									14 15			
Anerley	d						13 47				13 56	14 02									14 17			
Norwood Junction	d						13 50				14 00	14 05									14 20			
West Croydon	a						14 00					14 12									14 30			
East Croydon	a										14 03													

		SN	LO	SE	SE	SN	SN	LO	LO	SN		LO	LO	LO	SN	SN	LO	SE	SE	SN		SN	LO	LO	SN
London Bridge ⊖	d	14 06				14 11				14 22					14 33	14 36				14 41					14 52
Highbury & Islington	d		13 48					13 55				14 03	14 10				14 18						14 25		
Canonbury	d		13 50					13 57				14 05	14 12				14 20						14 27		
Dalston Junction Stn ELL	d		13 55					14 00	14 05			14 10	14 15	14 20			14 25						14 30	14 35	
Haggerston	d		13 56					14 01	14 06			14 11	14 16	14 21			14 26						14 31	14 36	
Hoxton	d		13 58					14 03	14 08			14 13	14 18	14 23			14 28						14 33	14 38	
Shoreditch High Street	d		14 01					14 06	14 11			14 16	14 21	14 26			14 31						14 36	14 41	
Whitechapel	d		14 03					14 08	14 13			14 18	14 23	14 28			14 33						14 38	14 43	
Shadwell	d		14 05					14 10	14 15			14 20	14 25	14 30			14 35						14 40	14 45	
Wapping	d		14 07					14 12	14 17			14 22	14 27	14 32			14 37						14 42	14 47	
Rotherhithe	d		14 09					14 14	14 19			14 24	14 29	14 34			14 39						14 44	14 49	
Canada Water	d		14 11					14 16	14 21			14 26	14 31	14 36			14 41						14 46	14 51	
Surrey Quays	d		14 12					14 17	14 22			14 27	14 32	14 37			14 42						14 47	14 52	
New Cross ELL	a								14 28					14 43										14 58	
New Cross Gate	a	14 11	14 16					14 21		14 27		14 31	14 36			14 41	14 46						14 51		14 57
	d	14 11	14 17					14 22		14 27		14 32	14 37			14 41	14 47						14 52		14 57
Brockley	d	14 14	14 19					14 24		14 30		14 34	14 39			14 44	14 49						14 54		15 00
Honor Oak Park	d	14 17	14 22					14 27		14 33		14 37	14 42			14 47	14 52						14 57		15 03
Forest Hill	d	14 19	14 25					14 30		14 35		14 40	14 45			14 49	14 55						15 00		15 05
Sydenham	d	14 22	14 27					14 32		14 38		14 42	14 47			14 52	14 57						15 02		15 08
Crystal Palace	d						14 30	14a37		14 43			14a52									15 00	15a07		15 13
Gipsy Hill	d						14 32			14 45												15 02			15 15
West Norwood	d						14 35			14 48												15 05			15 18
Streatham Hill	d									14 52															15 22
Balham ⊖	d									14 55															15 25
Wandsworth Common	d									14 57															15 27
Clapham Junction	d									15 01															15 31
South Bermondsey	d					14 15									14 37					14 45					
Queens Rd Peckham	d					14 18									14 39					14 48					
Peckham Rye	d			14 13	14 17	14 20	14a46								14a42			14 43	14 47	14 50		15a16			
Denmark Hill	d			14 17	14 21	14 23												14 47	14 51	14 53					
London Blackfriars ⊖	a																								
Clapham High Street ⊖	d					14 28														14 58					
Wandsworth Road	d					14 29														14 59					
Battersea Park	d					14 32				15 05										15 02					15 35
London Victoria ⊖	a			14 26	14 30	14 36				15 09								14 56	15 00	15 06					15 39
Penge West	d	14 24	14 30									14 45				14 54	15 00								
Anerley	d	14 26	14 32									14 47				14 56	15 02								
Norwood Junction	d	14 30	14 35									14 50				15 00	15 05								
West Croydon	a		14 42									15 00					15 12								
East Croydon	a	14 33														15 03									

Table 178

London Bridge to London Victoria - Croydon and East London Line

		LO	LO	LO	SN	SN		LO	SE	SE	SN	SN	LO	LO	SN	LO		LO	LO	SN	SN	LO	SE	SE	SN
London Bridge 4 ⊖	d				15 03	15 06					15 11				15 22					15 33	15 36				15 41
Highbury & Islington	d	14 33	14 40					14 48					14 55			15 03		15 10				15 18			
Canonbury	d	14 35	14 42					14 50					14 57			15 05		15 12				15 20			
Dalston Junction Stn ELL	d	14 40	14 45	14 50				14 55					15 00	15 05		15 10		15 15	15 20			15 25			
Haggerston	d	14 41	14 46	14 51				14 56					15 01	15 06		15 11		15 16	15 21			15 26			
Hoxton	d	14 43	14 48	14 53				14 58					15 03	15 08		15 13		15 18	15 23			15 28			
Shoreditch High Street	d	14 46	14 51	14 56				15 01					15 06	15 11		15 16		15 21	15 26			15 31			
Whitechapel	d	14 48	14 53	14 58				15 03					15 08	15 13		15 18		15 23	15 28			15 33			
Shadwell	d	14 50	14 55	15 00				15 05					15 10	15 15		15 20		15 25	15 30			15 35			
Wapping	d	14 52	14 57	15 02				15 07					15 12	15 17		15 22		15 27	15 32			15 37			
Rotherhithe	d	14 54	14 59	15 04				15 09					15 14	15 19		15 24		15 29	15 34			15 39			
Canada Water	d	14 56	15 01	15 06				15 11					15 16	15 21		15 26		15 31	15 36			15 41			
Surrey Quays	d	14 57	15 02	15 07				15 12					15 17	15 22		15 27		15 32	15 37			15 42			
New Cross ELL	a			15 13										15 28					15 43						
New Cross Gate 4	a	15 01	15 06			15 11		15 16					15 21		15 27	15 31		15 36			15 41	15 46			
	d	15 02	15 07			15 11		15 17					15 22		15 27	15 32		15 37			15 41	15 47			
Brockley	d	15 04	15 09			15 14		15 19					15 24		15 30	15 34		15 39			15 44	15 49			
Honor Oak Park	d	15 07	15 12			15 17		15 22					15 27		15 33	15 37		15 42			15 47	15 52			
Forest Hill 4	d	15 10	15 15			15 19		15 25					15 30		15 35	15 40		15 45			15 49	15 55			
Sydenham	d	15 12	15 17			15 22		15 27					15 32		15 38	15 42		15 47			15 52	15 57			
Crystal Palace 4	d		15a22									15 30	15a37		15 43			15a52							
Gipsy Hill	d											15 32			15 45										
West Norwood 4	d											15 35			15 48										
Streatham Hill	d														15 52										
Balham 4 ⊖	d														15 55										
Wandsworth Common	d														15 57										
Clapham Junction 10	d														16 01										
South Bermondsey	d				15 07						15 15									15 37					15 45
Queens Rd Peckham	d				15 09						15 18									15 39					15 48
Peckham Rye 4	d				15a12				15 13	15 17	15 20	15a46								15a42			15 43	15 47	15 50
Denmark Hill 4	d								15 17	15 21	15 23												15 47	15 51	15 53
London Blackfriars 3 ⊖	a																								
Clapham High Street ⊖	d										15 28														15 58
Wandsworth Road	d										15 29														15 59
Battersea Park 4	d										15 32				16 05										16 02
London Victoria 15 ⊖	a								15 26	15 30	15 36				16 09								15 56	16 00	16 06
Penge West	d	15 15				15 24		15 30								15 45					15 54	16 00			
Anerley	d	15 17				15 26		15 32								15 47					15 56	16 02			
Norwood Junction 2	d	15 20				15 30		15 35								15 50					16 00	16 05			
West Croydon 4	a	15 30						15 42								16 00						16 12			
East Croydon	a					15 33															16 03				

		SN		LO	LO	SN	LO	LO	LO	SN	SN	LO		SE	SE	SN	SN	LO	LO	SN	LO	LO		LO	SN
London Bridge 4 ⊖	d					15 52				16 03	16 06					16 11				16 22					16 33
Highbury & Islington	d			15 25			15 33	15 40				15 48						15 55			16 03	16 10			
Canonbury	d			15 27			15 35	15 42				15 50						15 57			16 05	16 12			
Dalston Junction Stn ELL	d			15 30	15 35		15 40	15 45	15 50			15 55						16 00	16 05		16 10	16 15		16 20	
Haggerston	d			15 31	15 36		15 41	15 46	15 51			15 56						16 01	16 06		16 11	16 16		16 21	
Hoxton	d			15 33	15 38		15 43	15 48	15 53			15 58						16 03	16 08		16 13	16 18		16 23	
Shoreditch High Street	d			15 36	15 41		15 46	15 51	15 56			16 01						16 06	16 11		16 16	16 21		16 26	
Whitechapel	d			15 38	15 43		15 48	15 53	15 58			16 03						16 08	16 13		16 18	16 23		16 28	
Shadwell	d			15 40	15 45		15 50	15 55	16 00			16 05						16 10	16 15		16 20	16 25		16 30	
Wapping	d			15 42	15 47		15 52	15 57	16 02			16 07						16 12	16 17		16 22	16 27		16 32	
Rotherhithe	d			15 44	15 49		15 54	15 59	16 04			16 09						16 14	16 19		16 24	16 29		16 34	
Canada Water	d			15 46	15 51		15 56	16 01	16 06			16 11						16 16	16 21		16 26	16 31		16 36	
Surrey Quays	d			15 47	15 52		15 57	16 02	16 07			16 12						16 17	16 22		16 27	16 32		16 37	
New Cross ELL	a				15 58				16 13										16 28					16 43	
New Cross Gate 4	a			15 51		15 57	16 01	16 06			16 11	16 16						16 21		16 27	16 31	16 36			
	d			15 52		15 57	16 02	16 07			16 11	16 17						16 22		16 27	16 32	16 37			
Brockley	d			15 54		16 00	16 04	16 09			16 14	16 19						16 24		16 30	16 34	16 39			
Honor Oak Park	d			15 57		16 03	16 07	16 12			16 17	16 22						16 27		16 33	16 37	16 42			
Forest Hill 4	d			16 00		16 05	16 10	16 15			16 19	16 25						16 30		16 35	16 40	16 45			
Sydenham	d			16 02		16 08	16 12	16 17			16 22	16 27						16 32		16 38	16 42	16 47			
Crystal Palace 4	d	16 00		16a07		16 13		16a22									16 30	16a37		16 43		16a52			
Gipsy Hill	d	16 02				16 15											16 32			16 45					
West Norwood 4	d	16 05				16 18											16 35			16 48					
Streatham Hill	d					16 22														16 52					
Balham 4 ⊖	d					16 25														16 55					
Wandsworth Common	d					16 27														16 57					
Clapham Junction 10	d					16 31														17 01					
South Bermondsey	d									16 07						16 15									16 37
Queens Rd Peckham	d									16 09						16 18									16 39
Peckham Rye 4	d	16a16								16a12				16 13	16 17	16 20	16a46								16a42
Denmark Hill 4	d													16 17	16 21	16 23									
London Blackfriars 3 ⊖	a																								
Clapham High Street ⊖	d															16 28									
Wandsworth Road	d															16 29									
Battersea Park 4	d					16 35										16 32				17 05					
London Victoria 15 ⊖	a					16 39								16 26	16 30	16 36				17 09					
Penge West	d						16 15				16 24	16 30									16 45				
Anerley	d						16 17				16 26	16 32									16 47				
Norwood Junction 2	d						16 20				16 30	16 35									16 50				
West Croydon 4	a						16 30					16 42									17 00				
East Croydon	a										16 33														

London Bridge to London Victoria - Croydon and East London Line

		SN	LO	SE	SE	SN	SN	LO		LO	SN	LO	LO	LO	SN	SN	LO	SE		SE	SN	SN	LO	LO	SN
London Bridge 4 ⊖	d	16 36				16 41					16 52				17 03	17 06					17 11				17 22
Highbury & Islington	d		16 18					16 25				16 33	16 40				16 48						16 55		
Canonbury	d		16 20					16 27				16 35	16 42				16 50						16 57		
Dalston Junction Stn ELL	d		16 25					16 30		16 35		16 40	16 45	16 50			16 55						17 00	17 05	
Haggerston	d		16 26					16 31		16 36		16 41	16 46	16 51			16 56						17 01	17 06	
Hoxton	d		16 28					16 33		16 38		16 43	16 48	16 53			16 58						17 03	17 08	
Shoreditch High Street	d		16 31					16 36		16 41		16 46	16 51	16 56			17 01						17 06	17 11	
Whitechapel	d		16 33					16 38		16 43		16 48	16 53	16 58			17 03						17 08	17 13	
Shadwell	d		16 35					16 40		16 45		16 50	16 55	17 00			17 05						17 10	17 15	
Wapping	d		16 37					16 42		16 47		16 52	16 57	17 02			17 07						17 12	17 17	
Rotherhithe	d		16 39					16 44		16 49		16 54	16 59	17 04			17 09						17 14	17 19	
Canada Water	d		16 41					16 46		16 51		16 56	17 01	17 06			17 11						17 16	17 21	
Surrey Quays	d		16 42					16 47		16 52		16 57	17 02	17 07			17 12						17 17	17 22	
New Cross ELL	a									16 58				17 13										17 28	
New Cross Gate 4	a	16 41	16 46					16 51			16 57	17 01	17 06			17 11	17 16						17 21		17 27
	d	16 41	16 47					16 52			16 57	17 02	17 07			17 11	17 17						17 22		17 27
Brockley	d	16 44	16 49					16 54			17 00	17 04	17 09			17 14	17 19						17 24		17 30
Honor Oak Park	d	16 47	16 52					16 57			17 03	17 07	17 12			17 17	17 22						17 27		17 33
Forest Hill 4	d	16 49	16 55					17 00			17 05	17 10	17 15			17 19	17 25						17 30		17 35
Sydenham	d	16 52	16 57					17 02			17 08	17 12	17 17			17 22	17 27						17 32		17 38
Crystal Palace 4	d						17 00	17a07			17 13		17a22									17 30	17a37		17 43
Gipsy Hill	d						17 02				17 15											17 32			17 45
West Norwood 4	d						17 05				17 18											17 35			17 48
Streatham Hill	d										17 22														17 52
Balham 4 ⊖	d										17 25														17 55
Wandsworth Common	d										17 27														17 57
Clapham Junction 10	d										17 32														18 01
South Bermondsey	d					16 45									17 07						17 15				
Queens Rd Peckham	d					16 48									17 09						17 18				
Peckham Rye 4	d			16 43	16 47	16 50	17a16								17a12			17 13		17 17	17 20	17a46			
Denmark Hill 4	d			16 47	16 51	16 53												17 17		17 21	17 23				
London Blackfriars 3 ⊖	a																								
Clapham High Street ⊖	d					16 58															17 28				
Wandsworth Road	d					16 59															17 29				
Battersea Park 4	d					17 02					17 36										17 32				18 05
London Victoria 15 ⊖	a			16 56	17 00	17 06					17 40							17 26		17 30	17 36				18 09
Penge West	d	16 54	17 00									17 15				17 24	17 30								
Anerley	d	16 56	17 02									17 17				17 26	17 32								
Norwood Junction 2	d	17 00	17 05									17 20				17 30	17 35								
West Croydon 4	a		17 12									17 30					17 42								
East Croydon	a	17 03														17 33									

		LO	LO	LO		SN	SN	LO	SE	SE	SN	SN	LO	LO		SN	LO	LO	LO	SN	SN	LO	SE	SE	
London Bridge 4 ⊖	d					17 33	17 36				17 41					17 52				18 03	18 06				
Highbury & Islington	d	17 03	17 10					17 18					17 25				17 33	17 40				17 48			
Canonbury	d	17 05	17 12					17 20					17 27				17 35	17 42				17 50			
Dalston Junction Stn ELL	d	17 10	17 15	17 20				17 25					17 30	17 35			17 40	17 45	17 50			17 55			
Haggerston	d	17 11	17 16	17 21				17 26					17 31	17 36			17 41	17 46	17 51			17 56			
Hoxton	d	17 13	17 18	17 23				17 28					17 33	17 38			17 43	17 48	17 53			17 58			
Shoreditch High Street	d	17 16	17 21	17 26				17 31					17 36	17 41			17 46	17 51	17 56			18 01			
Whitechapel	d	17 18	17 23	17 28				17 33					17 38	17 43			17 48	17 53	17 58			18 03			
Shadwell	d	17 20	17 25	17 30				17 35					17 40	17 45			17 50	17 55	18 00			18 05			
Wapping	d	17 22	17 27	17 32				17 37					17 42	17 47			17 52	17 57	18 02			18 07			
Rotherhithe	d	17 24	17 29	17 34				17 39					17 44	17 49			17 54	17 59	18 04			18 09			
Canada Water	d	17 26	17 31	17 36				17 41					17 46	17 51			17 56	18 01	18 06			18 11			
Surrey Quays	d	17 27	17 32	17 37				17 42					17 47	17 52			17 57	18 02	18 07			18 12			
New Cross ELL	a			17 43										17 58					18 13						
New Cross Gate 4	a	17 31	17 36				17 41	17 46					17 51			17 57	18 01	18 06			18 11	18 16			
	d	17 32	17 37				17 41	17 47					17 52			17 57	18 02	18 07			18 11	18 17			
Brockley	d	17 34	17 39				17 44	17 49					17 54			18 00	18 04	18 09			18 14	18 19			
Honor Oak Park	d	17 37	17 42				17 47	17 52					17 57			18 03	18 07	18 12			18 17	18 22			
Forest Hill 4	d	17 40	17 45				17 49	17 55					18 00			18 05	18 10	18 15			18 19	18 25			
Sydenham	d	17 42	17 47				17 52	17 57					18 02			18 08	18 12	18 17			18 22	18 27			
Crystal Palace 4	d		17a52									18 00	18a07			18 13		18a22							
Gipsy Hill	d											18 02				18 15									
West Norwood 4	d											18 05				18 18									
Streatham Hill	d															18 22									
Balham 4 ⊖	d															18 25									
Wandsworth Common	d															18 27									
Clapham Junction 10	d															18 31									
South Bermondsey	d					17 37					17 45									18 07					
Queens Rd Peckham	d					17 39					17 48									18 09					
Peckham Rye 4	d					17a42			17 43	17 47	17 50	18a16								18a12			18 13	18 17	
Denmark Hill 4	d								17 47	17 51	17 53												18 17	18 21	
London Blackfriars 3 ⊖	a																								
Clapham High Street ⊖	d										17 58														
Wandsworth Road	d										17 59														
Battersea Park 4	d										18 02					18 35									
London Victoria 15 ⊖	a								17 56	18 00	18 06					18 39							18 26	18 30	
Penge West	d	17 45					17 54	18 00									18 15				18 24	18 30			
Anerley	d	17 47					17 56	18 02									18 17				18 26	18 32			
Norwood Junction 2	d	17 50					18 00	18 05									18 20				18 30	18 35			
West Croydon 4	a	18 00						18 11									18 30					18 41			
East Croydon	a						18 03														18 33				

London Bridge to London Victoria - Croydon and East London Line

		SN	SN	LO	LO	SN	LO	LO	LO	SN	SN	LO	SE	SE	SN	SN	LO	LO	SN	LO	LO	LO	SN
London Bridge 4 ⊖	d	18 11				18 22				18 33	18 36				18 41				18 52				19 03
Highbury & Islington	d			17 55			18 03	18 10				18 18					18 25			18 33	18 40		
Canonbury	d			17 57			18 05	18 12				18 20					18 27			18 35	18 42		
Dalston Junction Stn ELL	d			18 00	18 05		18 10	18 15	18 20			18 25					18 30	18 35		18 40	18 45	18 50	
Haggerston	d			18 01	18 06		18 11	18 16	18 21			18 26					18 31	18 36		18 41	18 46	18 51	
Hoxton	d			18 03	18 08		18 13	18 18	18 23			18 28					18 33	18 38		18 43	18 48	18 53	
Shoreditch High Street	d			18 06	18 11		18 16	18 21	18 26			18 31					18 36	18 41		18 46	18 51	18 56	
Whitechapel	d			18 08	18 13		18 18	18 23	18 28			18 33					18 38	18 43		18 48	18 53	18 58	
Shadwell	d			18 10	18 15		18 20	18 25	18 30			18 35					18 40	18 45		18 50	18 55	19 00	
Wapping	d			18 12	18 17		18 22	18 27	18 32			18 37					18 42	18 47		18 52	18 57	19 02	
Rotherhithe	d			18 14	18 19		18 24	18 29	18 34			18 39					18 44	18 49		18 54	18 59	19 04	
Canada Water	d			18 16	18 21		18 26	18 31	18 36			18 41					18 46	18 51		18 56	19 01	19 06	
Surrey Quays	d			18 17	18 22		18 27	18 32	18 37			18 42					18 47	18 52		18 57	19 02	19 07	
New Cross ELL	a				18 28				18 43									18 58				19 13	
New Cross Gate 4	a			18 21		18 27	18 31	18 36			18 41	18 46					18 51		18 57	19 01	19 06		
	d			18 22		18 27	18 32	18 37			18 41	18 47					18 52		18 57	19 02	19 07		
Brockley	d			18 24		18 30	18 34	18 39			18 44	18 49					18 54		19 00	19 04	19 09		
Honor Oak Park	d			18 27		18 33	18 37	18 42			18 47	18 52					18 57		19 03	19 07	19 12		
Forest Hill 4	d			18 30		18 35	18 40	18 45			18 49	18 55					19 00		19 05	19 10	19 15		
Sydenham	d			18 32		18 38	18 42	18 47			18 52	18 57					19 02		19 08	19 12	19 17		
Crystal Palace 4	d		18 30	18a37		18 43		18a52								19 00	19a07		19 13		19a22		
Gipsy Hill	d		18 32			18 45										19 02			19 15				
West Norwood 4	d		18 35			18 48										19 05			19 18				
Streatham Hill	d					18 52													19 22				
Balham 4 ⊖	d					18 55													19 25				
Wandsworth Common	d					18 57													19 27				
Clapham Junction 10	d					19 01													19 31				
South Bermondsey	d	18 15								18 37					18 45								19 07
Queens Rd Peckham	d	18 18								18 39					18 48								19 09
Peckham Rye 4	d	18 20	18a46							18a42			18 43	18 47	18 50	19a16							19a12
Denmark Hill 4	d	18 23											18 47	18 51	18 53								
London Blackfriars 3 ⊖	a																						
Clapham High Street ⊖	d	18 28													18 58								
Wandsworth Road	d	18 29													18 59								
Battersea Park 4	d	18 32				19 05									19 02				19 35				
London Victoria 15 ⊖	a	18 36				19 09							18 56	19 00	19 06				19 39				
Penge West	d						18 45				18 54	19 00								19 15			
Anerley	d						18 47				18 56	19 02								19 17			
Norwood Junction 2	d						18 50				19 00	19 05								19 20			
West Croydon 4	a						19 00					19 11								19 30			
East Croydon	a										19 03												

		SN	LO	SE	SE	SN	SN	LO	LO	SN	LO	LO	LO	SN	SN	LO	SE	SN	SN	LO	LO	SN	LO
London Bridge 4 ⊖	d	19 06				19 11				19 22				19 33	19 36			19 41				19 52	
Highbury & Islington	d		18 48					18 55			19 03	19 10				19 18				19 25			19 33
Canonbury	d		18 50					18 57			19 05	19 12				19 20				19 27			19 35
Dalston Junction Stn ELL	d		18 55					19 00	19 05		19 10	19 15	19 20			19 25				19 30	19 35		19 40
Haggerston	d		18 56					19 01	19 06		19 11	19 16	19 21			19 26				19 31	19 36		19 41
Hoxton	d		18 58					19 03	19 08		19 13	19 18	19 23			19 28				19 33	19 38		19 43
Shoreditch High Street	d		19 01					19 06	19 11		19 16	19 21	19 26			19 31				19 36	19 41		19 46
Whitechapel	d		19 03					19 08	19 13		19 18	19 23	19 28			19 33				19 38	19 43		19 48
Shadwell	d		19 05					19 10	19 15		19 20	19 25	19 30			19 35				19 40	19 45		19 50
Wapping	d		19 07					19 12	19 17		19 22	19 27	19 32			19 37				19 42	19 47		19 52
Rotherhithe	d		19 09					19 14	19 19		19 24	19 29	19 34			19 39				19 44	19 49		19 54
Canada Water	d		19 11					19 16	19 21		19 26	19 31	19 36			19 41				19 46	19 51		19 56
Surrey Quays	d		19 12					19 17	19 22		19 27	19 32	19 37			19 42				19 47	19 52		19 57
New Cross ELL	a								19 28				19 43								19 58		
New Cross Gate 4	a	19 11	19 16					19 21		19 27	19 31	19 36			19 41	19 46				19 51		19 57	20 01
	d	19 11	19 17					19 22		19 27	19 32	19 37			19 41	19 47				19 52		19 57	20 02
Brockley	d	19 14	19 19					19 24		19 30	19 34	19 39			19 44	19 49				19 54		20 00	20 04
Honor Oak Park	d	19 17	19 22					19 27		19 33	19 37	19 42			19 47	19 52				19 57		20 03	20 07
Forest Hill 4	d	19 19	19 25					19 30		19 35	19 40	19 45			19 49	19 55				20 00		20 05	20 10
Sydenham	d	19 22	19 27					19 32		19 38	19 42	19 47			19 52	19 57				20 02		20 08	20 12
Crystal Palace 4	d						19 30	19a37		19 43		19a52							20 00	20a07		20 13	
Gipsy Hill	d						19 32			19 45									20 03			20 15	
West Norwood 4	d						19 35			19 48									20 06			20 18	
Streatham Hill	d									19 52												20 22	
Balham 4 ⊖	d									19 55												20 25	
Wandsworth Common	d									19 57												20 27	
Clapham Junction 10	d									20 01												20 31	
South Bermondsey	d					19 15								19 37				19 45					
Queens Rd Peckham	d					19 18								19 39				19 48					
Peckham Rye 4	d			19 13	19 17	19 20	19a46							19a42			19 43	19 50	20a16				
Denmark Hill 4	d			19 17	19 21	19 23											19 47	19 53					
London Blackfriars 3 ⊖	a																						
Clapham High Street ⊖	d					19 28												19 58					
Wandsworth Road	d					19 29												19 59					
Battersea Park 4	d					19 32				20 05								20 02				20 35	
London Victoria 15 ⊖	a			19 26	19 30	19 36				20 09							19 56	20 06				20 39	
Penge West	d	19 24	19 30								19 45				19 54	20 00							20 15
Anerley	d	19 26	19 32								19 47				19 56	20 02							20 17
Norwood Junction 2	d	19 30	19 35								19 50				20 00	20 05							20 20
West Croydon 4	a		19 41								20 00					20 15							20 30
East Croydon	a	19 33													20 03								

London Bridge to London Victoria - Croydon and East London Line

		LO	LO	SN	SN	LO	SE	SN	SN	LO	LO	SN	LO	LO	LO	SN	SN	LO	SE	SN	SN	LO
London Bridge 4 ⊖	d			20 03	20 06			20 11				20 22				20 33	20 36			20 41		
Highbury & Islington	d	19 40				19 48				19 55			20 03	20 10				20 18				20 25
Canonbury	d	19 42				19 50				19 57			20 05	20 12				20 20				20 27
Dalston Junction Stn ELL	d	19 45	19 50			19 55				20 00	20 05		20 10	20 15	20 20			20 25				20 30
Haggerston	d	19 46	19 51			19 56				20 01	20 06		20 11	20 16	20 21			20 26				20 31
Hoxton	d	19 48	19 53			19 58				20 03	20 08		20 13	20 18	20 23			20 28				20 33
Shoreditch High Street	d	19 51	19 56			20 01				20 06	20 11		20 16	20 21	20 26			20 31				20 36
Whitechapel	d	19 53	19 58			20 03				20 08	20 13		20 18	20 23	20 28			20 33				20 38
Shadwell	d	19 55	20 00			20 05				20 10	20 15		20 20	20 25	20 30			20 35				20 40
Wapping	d	19 57	20 02			20 07				20 12	20 17		20 22	20 27	20 32			20 37				20 42
Rotherhithe	d	19 59	20 04			20 09				20 14	20 19		20 24	20 29	20 34			20 39				20 44
Canada Water	d	20 01	20 06			20 11				20 16	20 21		20 26	20 31	20 36			20 41				20 46
Surrey Quays	d	20 02	20 07			20 12				20 17	20 22		20 27	20 32	20 37			20 42				20 47
New Cross ELL	a		20 13								20 28				20 43							
New Cross Gate 4	a	20 06			20 11	20 16				20 21		20 27	20 31	20 36			20 41	20 46				20 51
	d	20 07			20 11	20 17				20 22		20 27	20 32	20 37			20 41	20 47				20 52
Brockley	d	20 09			20 14	20 19				20 24		20 30	20 34	20 39			20 44	20 49				20 54
Honor Oak Park	d	20 12			20 17	20 22				20 27		20 33	20 37	20 42			20 47	20 52				20 57
Forest Hill 4	d	20 15			20 19	20 25				20 30		20 35	20 40	20 45			20 49	20 55				21 00
Sydenham	d	20 17			20 22	20 27				20 32		20 38	20 42	20 47			20 52	20 57				21 02
Crystal Palace 4	d	20a22							20 30	20a37		20 43		20a52							21 00	21a07
Gipsy Hill	d								20 33			20 45									21 02	
West Norwood 4	d								20 36			20 48									21 05	
Streatham Hill	d											20 52										
Balham 4 ⊖	d											20 55										
Wandsworth Common	d											20 57										
Clapham Junction 10	d											21 01										
South Bermondsey	d			20 07				20 15								20 37				20 45		
Queens Rd Peckham	d			20 09				20 18								20 39				20 48		
Peckham Rye 4	d			20a12			20 13	20 20	20a46							20a42			20 43	20 50	21a16	
Denmark Hill 4	d						20 17	20 23											20 47	20 53		
London Blackfriars 3 ⊖	a																					
Clapham High Street ⊖	d							20 28												20 58		
Wandsworth Road	d							20 29												20 59		
Battersea Park 4	d							20 32				21 05								21 02		
London Victoria 15 ⊖	a						20 26	20 36				21 09							20 56	21 06		
Penge West	d				20 24	20 30							20 45				20 54	21 00				
Anerley	d				20 26	20 32							20 47				20 56	21 02				
Norwood Junction 2	d				20 30	20 35							20 50				21 00	21 05				
West Croydon 4	a					20 45							21 00					21 15				
East Croydon	a				20 33												21 03					

		LO	SN	LO	LO	LO	SN	SN	LO	SE	SN	SN	LO	LO	SN	LO	LO	LO	SN	SN	LO	SE	SN
London Bridge 4 ⊖	d		20 52				21 03	21 06			21 11				21 22				21 33	21 36			21 41
Highbury & Islington	d			20 33	20 40				20 48				20 55			21 03	21 10				21 18		
Canonbury	d			20 35	20 42				20 50				20 57			21 05	21 12				21 20		
Dalston Junction Stn ELL	d	20 35		20 40	20 45	20 50			20 55				21 00	21 05		21 10	21 15	21 20			21 25		
Haggerston	d	20 36		20 41	20 46	20 51			20 56				21 01	21 06		21 11	21 16	21 21			21 26		
Hoxton	d	20 38		20 43	20 48	20 53			20 58				21 03	21 08		21 13	21 18	21 23			21 28		
Shoreditch High Street	d	20 41		20 46	20 51	20 56			21 01				21 06	21 11		21 16	21 21	21 26			21 31		
Whitechapel	d	20 43		20 48	20 53	20 58			21 03				21 08	21 13		21 18	21 23	21 28			21 33		
Shadwell	d	20 45		20 50	20 55	21 00			21 05				21 10	21 15		21 20	21 25	21 30			21 35		
Wapping	d	20 47		20 52	20 57	21 02			21 07				21 12	21 17		21 22	21 27	21 32			21 37		
Rotherhithe	d	20 49		20 54	20 59	21 04			21 09				21 14	21 19		21 24	21 29	21 34			21 39		
Canada Water	d	20 51		20 56	21 01	21 06			21 11				21 16	21 21		21 26	21 31	21 36			21 41		
Surrey Quays	d	20 52		20 57	21 02	21 07			21 12				21 17	21 22		21 27	21 32	21 37			21 42		
New Cross ELL	a	20 58				21 13								21 28				21 43					
New Cross Gate 4	a		20 57	21 01	21 06			21 11	21 16				21 21		21 27	21 31	21 36			21 41	21 46		
	d		20 57	21 02	21 07			21 11	21 17				21 22		21 27	21 32	21 37			21 41	21 47		
Brockley	d		21 00	21 04	21 09			21 14	21 19				21 24		21 30	21 34	21 39			21 44	21 49		
Honor Oak Park	d		21 03	21 07	21 12			21 17	21 22				21 27		21 33	21 37	21 42			21 47	21 52		
Forest Hill 4	d		21 05	21 10	21 15			21 19	21 25				21 30		21 35	21 40	21 45			21 49	21 55		
Sydenham	d		21 08	21 12	21 17			21 22	21 27				21 32		21 38	21 42	21 47			21 52	21 57		
Crystal Palace 4	d		21 13		21a22							21 30	21a37		21 43		21a52						
Gipsy Hill	d		21 15									21 32			21 45								
West Norwood 4	d		21 18									21 35			21 48								
Streatham Hill	d		21 22												21 52								
Balham 4 ⊖	d		21 25												21 55								
Wandsworth Common	d		21 27												21 57								
Clapham Junction 10	d		21 31												22 01								
South Bermondsey	d						21 07				21 15								21 37				21 45
Queens Rd Peckham	d						21 09				21 18								21 39				21 48
Peckham Rye 4	d						21a12			21 13	21 20	21a46							21a42			21 43	21 50
Denmark Hill 4	d									21 17	21 23											21 47	21 53
London Blackfriars 3 ⊖	a																						
Clapham High Street ⊖	d										21 28												21 58
Wandsworth Road	d										21 29												21 59
Battersea Park 4	d		21 35								21 32				22 05								22 02
London Victoria 15 ⊖	a		21 39							21 26	21 36				22 09							21 56	22 06
Penge West	d			21 15				21 24	21 30							21 45				21 54	22 00		
Anerley	d			21 17				21 26	21 32							21 47				21 56	22 02		
Norwood Junction 2	d			21 20				21 30	21 35							21 50				22 00	22 05		
West Croydon 4	a			21 30					21 45							22 00					22 12		
East Croydon	a							21 33												22 04			

London Bridge to London Victoria - Croydon and East London Line

		SN	LO	LO	SN	LO	LO	LO	SN	SN	LO	SE	SN	SN	LO	SN	LO	LO	SN	SN	SE	SN
London Bridge	d				21 52				22 03	22 06			22 11			22 22			22 33	22 36		22 41
Highbury & Islington	d		21 25			21 33	21 40				21 48				21 55		22 05					
Canonbury	d		21 27			21 35	21 42				21 50				21 57		22 07					
Dalston Junction Stn ELL	d		21 30	21 35		21 40	21 45	21 50			21 55				22 00		22 10	22 20				
Haggerston	d		21 31	21 36		21 41	21 46	21 51			21 56				22 01		22 11	22 21				
Hoxton	d		21 33	21 38		21 43	21 48	21 53			21 58				22 03		22 13	22 23				
Shoreditch High Street	d		21 36	21 41		21 46	21 51	21 56			22 01				22 06		22 16	22 26				
Whitechapel	d		21 38	21 43		21 48	21 53	21 58			22 03				22 08		22 18	22 28				
Shadwell	d		21 40	21 45		21 50	21 55	22 00			22 05				22 10		22 20	22 30				
Wapping	d		21 42	21 47		21 52	21 57	22 02			22 07				22 12		22 22	22 32				
Rotherhithe	d		21 44	21 49		21 54	21 59	22 04			22 09				22 14		22 24	22 34				
Canada Water	d		21 46	21 51		21 56	22 01	22 06			22 11				22 16		22 26	22 36				
Surrey Quays	d		21 47	21 52		21 57	22 02	22 07			22 12				22 17		22 27	22 37				
New Cross ELL	a			21 58				22 13										22 43				
New Cross Gate	a		21 51		21 57	22 01	22 06			22 11	22 16				22 21	22 27	22 31			22 41		
	d		21 52		21 57	22 02	22 07			22 11	22 17				22 22	22 27	22 32			22 41		
Brockley	d		21 54		22 00	22 04	22 09			22 14	22 19				22 24	22 30	22 34			22 44		
Honor Oak Park	d		21 57		22 03	22 07	22 12			22 17	22 22				22 27	22 33	22 37			22 47		
Forest Hill	d		22 00		22 05	22 10	22 15			22 19	22 25				22 30	22 35	22 40			22 49		
Sydenham	d		22 02		22 08	22 12	22 17			22 22	22 27				22 32	22 38	22 42			22 52		
Crystal Palace	d	22 00	22a07		22 13		22a22							22 30	22a37	22 43						
Gipsy Hill	d	22 02			22 15									22 32		22 45						
West Norwood	d	22 05			22 18									22 35		22 48						
Streatham Hill	d				22 22											22 52						
Balham	d				22 25											22 55						
Wandsworth Common	d				22 27											22 57						
Clapham Junction	d				22 31											23 01						
South Bermondsey	d								22 07				22 15						22 37			22 45
Queens Rd Peckham	d								22 09				22 18						22 39			22 48
Peckham Rye	d	22a16							22a12			22 13	22 20	22a46					22a42		22 43	22 50
Denmark Hill	d											22 17	22 23								22 47	22 53
London Blackfriars	a																					
Clapham High Street	d												22 28									22 58
Wandsworth Road	d												22 29									22 59
Battersea Park	d				22 35								22 32			23 05						23 02
London Victoria	a				22 39							22 26	22 36			23 09					22 56	23 06
Penge West	d					22 15				22 24	22 30						22 45			22 54		
Anerley	d					22 17				22 26	22 32						22 47			22 56		
Norwood Junction	d					22 20				22 30	22 35						22 50			23 00		
West Croydon	a					22 30					22 42						23 00					
East Croydon	a									22 35										23 03		

		SN	LO	SN	LO	LO	SN	SN	SE	SN	SN	LO	SN	LO	LO	SN	SN	LO	SN	LO	LO	LO
London Bridge	d			22 52			23 03	23 06		23 11			23 22			23 33	23 36		23 52			
Highbury & Islington	d		22 25		22 35							22 55		23 05				23 25		23 35	23 42	23 56
Canonbury	d		22 27		22 37							22 57		23 07				23 27		23 37	23 44	23 58
Dalston Junction Stn ELL	d		22 30		22 40	22 50						23 00		23 10	23 20			23 30		23 40	23 47	00 02
Haggerston	d		22 31		22 41	22 51						23 01		23 11	23 21			23 31		23 41	23 48	00 03
Hoxton	d		22 33		22 43	22 53						23 03		23 13	23 23			23 33		23 43	23 50	00 05
Shoreditch High Street	d		22 36		22 46	22 56						23 06		23 16	23 26			23 36		23 46	23 53	00 08
Whitechapel	d		22 38		22 48	22 58						23 08		23 18	23 28			23 38		23 48	23 55	00 10
Shadwell	d		22 40		22 50	23 00						23 10		23 20	23 30			23 40		23 50	23 57	00 12
Wapping	d		22 42		22 52	23 02						23 12		23 22	23 32			23 42		23 52	23 59	00 14
Rotherhithe	d		22 44		22 54	23 04						23 14		23 24	23 34			23 44		23 54	00 01	00 16
Canada Water	d		22 46		22 56	23 06						23 16		23 26	23 36			23 46		23 56	00 03	00 18
Surrey Quays	d		22 47		22 57	23 07						23 17		23 27	23 37			23 47		23 57	00 05	00 19
New Cross ELL	a					23 13									23 43							
New Cross Gate	a		22 51	22 57	23 01			23 11				23 21	23 27	23 31			23 41	23 51	23 57	00 02	00 08	00 23
	d		22 52	22 57	23 02			23 11				23 22	23 27	23 32			23 41	23 52	23 57	00 02		
Brockley	d		22 54	23 00	23 04			23 14				23 24	23 30	23 34			23 44	23 54	00 01	00 04		
Honor Oak Park	d		22 57	23 03	23 07			23 17				23 27	23 33	23 37			23 47	23 57	00 04	00 07		
Forest Hill	d		23 00	23 05	23 10			23 19				23 30	23 35	23 40			23 49	23 59	00 06	00 10		
Sydenham	d		23 02	23 08	23 12			23 22				23 32	23 38	23 42			23 52	00 02	00 09	00 12		
Crystal Palace	d	23 00	23a07	23 13							23 30	23a37	23 43					00a07	00 13			
Gipsy Hill	d	23 02		23 15							23 32		23 45						00 15			
West Norwood	d	23 05		23 18							23 35		23 48						00 18			
Streatham Hill	d			23 22									23 52						00 22			
Balham	d			23 25									23 55						00 26			
Wandsworth Common	d			23 27									23 57						00 28			
Clapham Junction	d			23 31									00 02						00 32			
South Bermondsey	d						23 07			23 15						23 37						
Queens Rd Peckham	d						23 09			23 18						23 39						
Peckham Rye	d	23a16					23 12		23 13	23 20	23a46					23 42						
Denmark Hill	d								23 17	23 23												
London Blackfriars	a																					
Clapham High Street	d									23 28												
Wandsworth Road	d									23 29												
Battersea Park	d			23 35						23 32			00 05						00 35			
London Victoria	a			23 41					23 26	23 37			00 10						00 42			
Penge West	d				23 15			23 24						23 45			23 54			00 15		
Anerley	d				23 17			23 26						23 47			23 56			00 17		
Norwood Junction	d				23 20		23a34	23 30						23 50		00a04	23 59			00 20		
West Croydon	a				23 30									23 59						00 27		
East Croydon	a							23 33									00 03					

London Bridge to London Victoria - Croydon and East London Line

		SN A	SN A	SN A	LO A	SN A	LO A	LO A	SN	SN	LO A	LO	SN	SN	SN	SN	SN	SE	SN	SN	LO	LO	SN
London Bridge	d	23p22	23p36			23p52			00 03	00 06					00 33	00 36			07 11				07 24
Highbury & Islington	d				23p25		23p35	23p42			23p56	00 10										06 51	
Canonbury	d				23p27		23p37	23p44			23p58	00 12										06 53	
Dalston Junction Stn ELL	d				23p30		23p40	23p47			00 02	00 15										06 56	
Haggerston	d				23p31		23p41	23p48			00 03	00 16										06 57	
Hoxton	d				23p33		23p43	23p50			00 05	00 18										06 59	
Shoreditch High Street	d				23p36		23p46	23p53			00 08	00 21										07 02	
Whitechapel	d				23p38		23p48	23p55			00 10	00 23										07 04	
Shadwell	d				23p40		23p50	23p57			00 12	00 25										07 06	
Wapping	d				23p42		23p52	23p59			00 14	00 27										07 08	
Rotherhithe	d				23p44		23p54	00 01			00 16	00 29										07 10	
Canada Water	d				23p46		23p56	00 03			00 18	00 31										07 12	
Surrey Quays	d				23p47		23p57	00 05			00 19	00 32										07 13	
New Cross ELL	a																						
New Cross Gate	a	23p27	23p41		23p51	23p57	00 02	00 08		00 11	00 23	00 36				00 41						07 17	07 29
	d	23p27	23p41		23p52	23p57	00 02			00 11						00 41					07 04	07 18	07 29
Brockley	d	23p30	23p44		23p54	00 01	00 04			00 14						00 44					07 06	07 20	07 32
Honor Oak Park	d	23p33	23p47		23p57	00 04	00 07			00 17						00 47					07 09	07 23	07 35
Forest Hill	d	23p35	23p49		23p59	00 06	00 10			00 19						00 49					07 12	07 26	07 37
Sydenham	d	23p38	23p52		00 02	00 09	00 12			00 22						00 52					07 14	07 28	07 40
Crystal Palace	d	23p43		00 03	00a07	00 13							00 33	00 47			01 03			07 07		07a33	
Gipsy Hill	d	23p45				00 15														07 09			
West Norwood	d	23p48				00 18														07 12			
Streatham Hill	d	23p52				00 22																	
Balham	d	23p55				00 26																	
Wandsworth Common	d	23p57				00 28																	
Clapham Junction	d	00 02				00 32																	
South Bermondsey	d								00 07						00 37				07 15				
Queens Rd Peckham	d								00 09						00 39				07 18				
Peckham Rye	d								00 12						00 42			07 12	07 20	07a23			
Denmark Hill	d																	07 16	07 23				
London Blackfriars	a																						
Clapham High Street	d																		07 28				
Wandsworth Road	d																		07 29				
Battersea Park	d	00 05				00 35													07 32				
London Victoria	a	00 10				00 42												07 25	07 36				
Penge West	d		23p54				00 15			00 24						00 54					07 17		
Anerley	d		23p56				00 17			00 26						00 56					07 19		
Norwood Junction	d		23p59	00 09			00 20		00a34	00 30			00 38	00 52	01a04	01 00	01 08				07 22		07 48
West Croydon	a			00 14			00 27						00 43	00 58			01 13				07 29		07 55
East Croydon	a		00 03							00 33						01 03							

		LO	SE	SN	SN	SN	SN	LO	SN	LO	SE	SN	SN	SN	SN	LO	SN	LO	LO	SE	SN	SN	SN
London Bridge	d			07 36	07 39	07 41			07 54			08 06	08 09	08 11			08 24				08 36	08 39	08 41
Highbury & Islington	d	07 05						07 21		07 35						07 51		08 05					
Canonbury	d	07 07						07 23		07 37						07 53		08 07					
Dalston Junction Stn ELL	d	07 12						07 26		07 42						07 56		08 12	08 22				
Haggerston	d	07 13						07 27		07 43						07 57		08 13	08 23				
Hoxton	d	07 15						07 29		07 45						07 59		08 15	08 25				
Shoreditch High Street	d	07 18						07 32		07 48						08 02		08 18	08 28				
Whitechapel	d	07 20						07 34		07 50						08 04		08 20	08 30				
Shadwell	d	07 22						07 36		07 52						08 06		08 22	08 32				
Wapping	d	07 24						07 38		07 54						08 08		08 24	08 34				
Rotherhithe	d	07 26						07 40		07 56						08 10		08 26	08 36				
Canada Water	d	07 28						07 42		07 58						08 12		08 28	08 38				
Surrey Quays	d	07 29						07 43		07 59						08 13		08 29	08 39				
New Cross ELL	a																		08 45				
New Cross Gate	a	07 33			07 44			07 47	07 59	08 03			08 14			08 17	08 29	08 33				08 44	
	d	07 34			07 44			07 48	07 59	08 03			08 14			08 18	08 29	08 34				08 44	
Brockley	d	07 36			07 47			07 50	08 02	08 06			08 17			08 20	08 32	08 36				08 47	
Honor Oak Park	d	07 39			07 50			07 53	08 05	08 09			08 20			08 23	08 35	08 39				08 50	
Forest Hill	d	07 42			07 52			07 56	08 07	08 12			08 22			08 26	08 37	08 42				08 52	
Sydenham	d	07 44			07 55			07 58	08 10	08 14			08 25			08 28	08 40	08 44				08 55	
Crystal Palace	d						07 37	08a03							08 07	08a33							
Gipsy Hill	d						07 39								08 09								
West Norwood	d						07 42								08 12								
Streatham Hill	d																						
Balham	d																						
Wandsworth Common	d																						
Clapham Junction	d																						
South Bermondsey	d			07 40		07 45						08 10		08 15							08 40		08 45
Queens Rd Peckham	d			07 42		07 48						08 12		08 18							08 42		08 48
Peckham Rye	d		07 42	07a45		07 50	07a53				08 12	08a15		08 20	08a23					08 42	08a45		08 50
Denmark Hill	d		07 46			07 53					08 16			08 23						08 46			08 53
London Blackfriars	a																						
Clapham High Street	d					07 58								08 28									08 58
Wandsworth Road	d					07 59								08 29									08 59
Battersea Park	d					08 02								08 32									09 02
London Victoria	a		07 55			08 06					08 25			08 36						08 55			09 06
Penge West	d	07 47			07 57					08 17			08 27					08 47				08 57	
Anerley	d	07 49			07 59					08 19			08 29					08 49				08 59	
Norwood Junction	d	07 52			08 03				08 16	08 22			08 33				08 46	08 52				09 03	
West Croydon	a	07 59							08 24	08 28							08 54	08 58					
East Croydon	a				08 07								08 37									09 07	

A not 22 May

Table 178

Sundays

London Bridge to London Victoria - Croydon and East London Line

		SN	LO	LO	SN	LO	LO	SE	SN	SN	SN	SN	LO	LO	SN	LO	LO	SE	SN	SN	SN	SN
London Bridge	d				08 54				09 06	09 09	09 11				09 24				09 36	09 39	09 41	
Highbury & Islington	d		08 21			08 35							08 51			09 05						
Canonbury	d		08 23			08 37							08 53			09 07						
Dalston Junction Stn ELL	d		08 26	08 37		08 42	08 52						08 56	09 07		09 12	09 22					
Haggerston	d		08 27	08 38		08 43	08 53						08 57	09 08		09 13	09 23					
Hoxton	d		08 29	08 40		08 45	08 55						08 59	09 10		09 15	09 25					
Shoreditch High Street	d		08 32	08 43		08 48	08 58						09 02	09 13		09 18	09 28					
Whitechapel	d		08 34	08 45		08 50	09 00						09 04	09 15		09 20	09 30					
Shadwell	d		08 36	08 47		08 52	09 02						09 06	09 17		09 22	09 32					
Wapping	d		08 38	08 49		08 54	09 04						09 08	09 19		09 24	09 34					
Rotherhithe	d		08 40	08 51		08 56	09 06						09 10	09 21		09 26	09 36					
Canada Water	d		08 42	08 53		08 58	09 08						09 12	09 23		09 28	09 38					
Surrey Quays	d		08 43	08 54		08 59	09 09						09 13	09 24		09 29	09 39					
New Cross ELL	a			09 00			09 15							09 30			09 45					
New Cross Gate	a		08 47		08 59	09 03				09 14			09 17		09 29	09 33				09 44		
	d		08 48		08 59	09 04				09 14			09 18		09 29	09 34				09 44		
Brockley	d		08 50		09 02	09 06				09 17			09 20		09 32	09 36				09 47		
Honor Oak Park	d		08 53		09 05	09 09				09 20			09 23		09 35	09 39				09 50		
Forest Hill	d		08 56		09 07	09 12				09 22			09 26		09 37	09 42				09 52		
Sydenham	d		08 58		09 10	09 14				09 25			09 28		09 40	09 44				09 55		
Crystal Palace	d	08 37	09a03									09 07	09a33									09 37
Gipsy Hill	d	08 39										09 09										09 39
West Norwood	d	08 42										09 12										09 42
Streatham Hill	d																					
Balham	d																					
Wandsworth Common	d																					
Clapham Junction	d																					
South Bermondsey	d								09 10		09 15								09 40		09 45	
Queens Rd Peckham	d								09 12		09 18								09 42		09 48	
Peckham Rye	d	08a53						09 12	09a15		09 20	09a23						09 42	09a45		09 50	09a53
Denmark Hill	d							09 16			09 23							09 46			09 53	
London Blackfriars	a																					
Clapham High Street	d										09 28										09 58	
Wandsworth Road	d										09 29										09 59	
Battersea Park	d										09 32										10 02	
London Victoria	a							09 25			09 36							09 55			10 06	
Penge West	d					09 17				09 27						09 47				09 57		
Anerley	d					09 19				09 29						09 49				09 59		
Norwood Junction	d				09 16	09 22				09 33					09 46	09 52				10 03		
West Croydon	a				09 24	09 28									09 54	09 58						
East Croydon	a									09 37										10 07		

		LO	LO	SN	LO	LO	SE	SN	SN	SN	SN	LO	LO	SN	LO	LO	SE	SN	SN	SN	SN	LO	LO
London Bridge	d			09 54				10 06	10 09	10 11				10 24				10 36	10 39	10 41			
Highbury & Islington	d	09 21			09 35							09 51			10 05							10 21	
Canonbury	d	09 23			09 37							09 53			10 07							10 23	
Dalston Junction Stn ELL	d	09 26	09 37		09 42	09 52						09 56	10 07		10 12	10 22						10 26	10 37
Haggerston	d	09 27	09 38		09 43	09 53						09 57	10 08		10 13	10 23						10 27	10 38
Hoxton	d	09 29	09 40		09 45	09 55						09 59	10 10		10 15	10 25						10 29	10 40
Shoreditch High Street	d	09 32	09 43		09 48	09 58						10 02	10 13		10 18	10 28						10 32	10 43
Whitechapel	d	09 34	09 45		09 50	10 00						10 04	10 15		10 20	10 30						10 34	10 45
Shadwell	d	09 36	09 47		09 52	10 02						10 06	10 17		10 22	10 32						10 36	10 47
Wapping	d	09 38	09 49		09 54	10 04						10 08	10 19		10 24	10 34						10 38	10 49
Rotherhithe	d	09 40	09 51		09 56	10 06						10 10	10 21		10 26	10 36						10 40	10 51
Canada Water	d	09 42	09 53		09 58	10 08						10 12	10 23		10 28	10 38						10 42	10 53
Surrey Quays	d	09 43	09 54		09 59	10 09						10 13	10 24		10 29	10 39						10 43	10 54
New Cross ELL	a		10 00			10 15							10 30			10 45							11 00
New Cross Gate	a	09 47		09 59	10 03				10 14			10 17		10 29	10 33				10 44			10 47	
	d	09 48		09 59	10 04				10 14			10 18		10 29	10 34				10 44			10 48	
Brockley	d	09 50		10 02	10 06				10 17			10 20		10 32	10 36				10 47			10 50	
Honor Oak Park	d	09 53		10 05	10 09				10 20			10 23		10 35	10 39				10 50			10 53	
Forest Hill	d	09 56		10 07	10 12				10 22			10 26		10 37	10 42				10 52			10 56	
Sydenham	d	09 58		10 10	10 14				10 25			10 28		10 40	10 44				10 55			10 58	
Crystal Palace	d	10a03									10 07	10a33									10 37	11a03	
Gipsy Hill	d										10 09										10 39		
West Norwood	d										10 12										10 42		
Streatham Hill	d																						
Balham	d																						
Wandsworth Common	d																						
Clapham Junction	d																						
South Bermondsey	d							10 10		10 15								10 40		10 45			
Queens Rd Peckham	d							10 12		10 18								10 42		10 48			
Peckham Rye	d						10 12	10a15		10 20	10a23						10 42	10a45		10 50	10a53		
Denmark Hill	d						10 16			10 23							10 46			10 53			
London Blackfriars	a																						
Clapham High Street	d									10 28										10 58			
Wandsworth Road	d									10 29										10 59			
Battersea Park	d									10 32										11 02			
London Victoria	a						10 25			10 36							10 55			11 06			
Penge West	d				10 17				10 27						10 47				10 57				
Anerley	d				10 19				10 29						10 49				10 59				
Norwood Junction	d			10 16	10 22				10 33					10 46	10 52				11 03				
West Croydon	a			10 24	10 28									10 54	10 58								
East Croydon	a								10 37										11 07				

Table 178

Sundays

London Bridge to London Victoria - Croydon and East London Line

		SN	LO	LO	SE	SN	SN	SN	SN	LO	LO	SN	LO	LO	SE	SN	SN	SN	SN	LO	LO	SN
London Bridge	d	10 54				11 06	11 09	11 11				11 24				11 36	11 39	11 41				11 54
Highbury & Islington	d		10 35							10 51			11 05							11 21		
Canonbury	d		10 37							10 53			11 07							11 23		
Dalston Junction Stn ELL	d		10 42	10 52						10 56	11 07		11 12	11 22						11 26	11 37	
Haggerston	d		10 43	10 53						10 57	11 08		11 13	11 23						11 27	11 38	
Hoxton	d		10 45	10 55						10 59	11 10		11 15	11 25						11 29	11 40	
Shoreditch High Street	d		10 48	10 58						11 02	11 13		11 18	11 28						11 32	11 43	
Whitechapel	d		10 50	11 00						11 04	11 15		11 20	11 30						11 34	11 45	
Shadwell	d		10 52	11 02						11 06	11 17		11 22	11 32						11 36	11 47	
Wapping	d		10 54	11 04						11 08	11 19		11 24	11 34						11 38	11 49	
Rotherhithe	d		10 56	11 06						11 10	11 21		11 26	11 36						11 40	11 51	
Canada Water	d		10 58	11 08						11 12	11 23		11 28	11 38						11 42	11 53	
Surrey Quays	d		10 59	11 09						11 13	11 24		11 29	11 39						11 43	11 54	
New Cross ELL	a			11 15							11 30			11 45							12 00	
New Cross Gate	a	10 59	11 03				11 14			11 17		11 29	11 33				11 44			11 47		11 59
	d	10 59	11 04				11 14			11 18		11 29	11 34				11 44			11 48		11 59
Brockley	d	11 02	11 06				11 17			11 20		11 32	11 36				11 47			11 50		12 02
Honor Oak Park	d	11 05	11 09				11 20			11 23		11 35	11 39				11 50			11 53		12 05
Forest Hill	d	11 07	11 12				11 22			11 26		11 37	11 42				11 52			11 56		12 07
Sydenham	d	11 10	11 14				11 25			11 28		11 40	11 44				11 55			11 58		12 10
Crystal Palace	d								11 07	11a33									11 37	12a03		
Gipsy Hill	d								11 09										11 39			
West Norwood	d								11 12										11 42			
Streatham Hill	d																					
Balham	d																					
Wandsworth Common	d																					
Clapham Junction	d																					
South Bermondsey	d					11 10		11 15								11 40		11 45				
Queens Rd Peckham	d					11 12		11 18								11 42		11 48				
Peckham Rye	d				11 12	11a15		11 20	11a23						11 42	11a45		11 50	11a53			
Denmark Hill	d				11 16			11 23							11 46			11 53				
London Blackfriars	a																					
Clapham High Street	d							11 28										11 58				
Wandsworth Road	d							11 29										11 59				
Battersea Park	d							11 32										12 02				
London Victoria	a				11 25			11 36							11 55			12 06				
Penge West	d		11 17				11 27						11 47				11 57					
Anerley	d		11 19				11 29						11 49				11 59					
Norwood Junction	d	11 16	11 22				11 33					11 46	11 52				12 03					12 16
West Croydon	a	11 24	11 28									11 54	11 58									12 24
East Croydon	a						11 37										12 07					

		LO	SE	SN	SN	LO	LO	SN	LO	SN	SE	SN	LO	LO	SN	LO	LO	LO	SN	SN	LO	SN	SE
London Bridge	d			12 06				12 09		12 11					12 24				12 36	12 39		12 41	
Highbury & Islington	d	11 35				11 43			11 51				11 58			12 06	12 13				12 21		
Canonbury	d	11 37				11 45			11 53				12 00			12 08	12 15				12 23		
Dalston Junction Stn ELL	d	11 42				11 48	11 52		11 58				12 03	12 08		12 13	12 18	12 23			12 28		
Haggerston	d	11 43				11 49	11 53		11 59				12 04	12 09		12 14	12 19	12 24			12 29		
Hoxton	d	11 45				11 51	11 55		12 01				12 06	12 11		12 16	12 21	12 26			12 31		
Shoreditch High Street	d	11 48				11 54	11 58		12 04				12 09	12 14		12 19	12 24	12 29			12 34		
Whitechapel	d	11 50				11 56	12 00		12 06				12 11	12 16		12 21	12 26	12 31			12 36		
Shadwell	d	11 52				11 58	12 02		12 08				12 13	12 18		12 23	12 28	12 33			12 38		
Wapping	d	11 54				12 00	12 04		12 10				12 15	12 20		12 25	12 30	12 35			12 40		
Rotherhithe	d	11 56				12 02	12 06		12 12				12 17	12 22		12 27	12 32	12 37			12 42		
Canada Water	d	11 58				12 04	12 08		12 14				12 19	12 24		12 29	12 34	12 39			12 44		
Surrey Quays	d	11 59				12 05	12 09		12 15				12 20	12 25		12 30	12 35	12 40			12 45		
New Cross ELL	a						12 15							12 31				12 46					
New Cross Gate	a	12 03				12 09		12 14	12 19				12 24		12 29	12 34	12 39			12 44	12 49		
	d	12 04				12 10		12 14	12 20				12 25		12 29	12 35	12 40			12 44	12 50		
Brockley	d	12 06				12 12		12 17	12 22				12 27		12 32	12 37	12 42			12 47	12 52		
Honor Oak Park	d	12 09				12 15		12 20	12 25				12 30		12 35	12 40	12 45			12 50	12 55		
Forest Hill	d	12 12				12 18		12 22	12 28				12 33		12 37	12 43	12 48			12 52	12 58		
Sydenham	d	12 14				12 20		12 25	12 30				12 35		12 40	12 45	12 50			12 55	13 00		
Crystal Palace	d				12 07	12a25						12 37	12a40				12a55						
Gipsy Hill	d				12 09							12 39											
West Norwood	d				12 12							12 42											
Streatham Hill	d																						
Balham	d																						
Wandsworth Common	d																						
Clapham Junction	d																						
South Bermondsey	d			12 10						12 15									12 40			12 45	
Queens Rd Peckham	d			12 12						12 18									12 42			12 48	
Peckham Rye	d		12 12	12a15	12a23					12 20	12 42	12a53							12a45			12 50	13 12
Denmark Hill	d		12 16							12 23	12 46											12 53	13 16
London Blackfriars	a																						
Clapham High Street	d									12 28												12 58	
Wandsworth Road	d									12 29												12 59	
Battersea Park	d									12 32												13 02	
London Victoria	a		12 25							12 36	12 55											13 06	13 25
Penge West	d	12 17						12 27	12 33							12 48				12 57	13 03		
Anerley	d	12 19						12 29	12 35							12 50				12 59	13 05		
Norwood Junction	d	12 22						12 33	12 38						12 46	12 53				13 03	13 08		
West Croydon	a	12 28							12 45						12 54	12 59					13 15		
East Croydon	a							12 37												13 07			

London Bridge to London Victoria - Croydon and East London Line

		SN	LO	LO	SN	LO	LO	LO	SN	SN	LO	SN	SE	SN	LO	LO	SN	LO	LO	LO	SN	SN	LO
London Bridge 4 ⊖	d				12 54				13 06	13 09		13 11					13 24				13 36	13 39	
Highbury & Islington	d		12 28			12 36	12 43				12 51				12 58			13 06	13 13				13 21
Canonbury	d		12 30			12 38	12 45				12 53				13 00			13 08	13 15				13 23
Dalston Junction Stn ELL	d		12 33	12 38		12 43	12 48	12 53			12 58				13 03	13 08		13 13	13 18	13 23			13 28
Haggerston	d		12 34	12 39		12 44	12 49	12 54			12 59				13 04	13 09		13 14	13 19	13 24			13 29
Hoxton	d		12 36	12 41		12 46	12 51	12 56			13 01				13 06	13 11		13 16	13 21	13 26			13 31
Shoreditch High Street	d		12 39	12 44		12 49	12 54	12 59			13 04				13 09	13 14		13 19	13 24	13 29			13 34
Whitechapel	d		12 41	12 46		12 51	12 56	13 01			13 06				13 11	13 16		13 21	13 26	13 31			13 36
Shadwell	d		12 43	12 48		12 53	12 58	13 03			13 08				13 13	13 18		13 23	13 28	13 33			13 38
Wapping	d		12 45	12 50		12 55	13 00	13 05			13 10				13 15	13 20		13 25	13 30	13 35			13 40
Rotherhithe	d		12 47	12 52		12 57	13 02	13 07			13 12				13 17	13 22		13 27	13 32	13 37			13 42
Canada Water	d		12 49	12 54		12 59	13 04	13 09			13 14				13 19	13 24		13 29	13 34	13 39			13 44
Surrey Quays	d		12 50	12 55		13 00	13 05	13 10			13 15				13 20	13 25		13 30	13 35	13 40			13 45
New Cross ELL	a			13 01				13 16								13 31				13 46			
New Cross Gate 4	a		12 54		12 59	13 04	13 09			13 14	13 19				13 24		13 29	13 34	13 39			13 44	13 49
	d		12 55		12 59	13 05	13 10			13 14	13 20				13 25		13 29	13 35	13 40			13 44	13 50
Brockley	d		12 57		13 02	13 07	13 12			13 17	13 22				13 27		13 32	13 37	13 42			13 47	13 52
Honor Oak Park	d		13 00		13 05	13 10	13 15			13 20	13 25				13 30		13 35	13 40	13 45			13 50	13 55
Forest Hill 4	d		13 03		13 07	13 13	13 18			13 22	13 28				13 33		13 37	13 43	13 48			13 52	13 58
Sydenham	d		13 05		13 10	13 15	13 20			13 25	13 30				13 35		13 40	13 45	13 50			13 55	14 00
Crystal Palace 4	d	13 07	13a10				13a25							13 37	13a40				13a55				
Gipsy Hill	d	13 09												13 39									
West Norwood 4	d	13 12												13 42									
Streatham Hill	d																						
Balham 4 ⊖	d																						
Wandsworth Common	d																						
Clapham Junction 10	d																						
South Bermondsey	d								13 10			13 15									13 40		
Queens Rd Peckham	d								13 12			13 18									13 42		
Peckham Rye 4	d	13a23							13a15			13 20	13 42	13a53							13a45		
Denmark Hill 4	d											13 23	13 46										
London Blackfriars 3 ⊖	a																						
Clapham High Street ⊖	d											13 28											
Wandsworth Road	d											13 29											
Battersea Park 4	d											13 32											
London Victoria 15 ⊖	a											13 36	13 55										
Penge West	d					13 18				13 27	13 33							13 48				13 57	14 03
Anerley	d					13 20				13 29	13 35							13 50				13 59	14 05
Norwood Junction 2	d				13 16	13 23				13 33	13 38						13 46	13 53				14 03	14 08
West Croydon 4	a				13 24	13 29					13 45						13 54	13 59					14 15
East Croydon	a									13 37												14 07	

		SN	SE	SN	LO	LO	SN	LO	LO	LO	SN	SN	LO	SN	SE	SN	LO	LO	SN	LO	LO	LO
London Bridge 4 ⊖	d	13 41					13 54				14 06	14 09		14 11					14 24			
Highbury & Islington	d				13 28			13 36	13 43				13 51				13 58			14 06	14 13	
Canonbury	d				13 30			13 38	13 45				13 53				14 00			14 08	14 15	
Dalston Junction Stn ELL	d				13 33	13 38		13 43	13 48	13 53			13 58				14 03	14 08		14 13	14 18	14 23
Haggerston	d				13 34	13 39		13 44	13 49	13 54			13 59				14 04	14 09		14 14	14 19	14 24
Hoxton	d				13 36	13 41		13 46	13 51	13 56			14 01				14 06	14 11		14 16	14 21	14 26
Shoreditch High Street	d				13 39	13 44		13 49	13 54	13 59			14 04				14 09	14 14		14 19	14 24	14 29
Whitechapel	d				13 41	13 46		13 51	13 56	14 01			14 06				14 11	14 16		14 21	14 26	14 31
Shadwell	d				13 43	13 48		13 53	13 58	14 03			14 08				14 13	14 18		14 23	14 28	14 33
Wapping	d				13 45	13 50		13 55	14 00	14 05			14 10				14 15	14 20		14 25	14 30	14 35
Rotherhithe	d				13 47	13 52		13 57	14 02	14 07			14 12				14 17	14 22		14 27	14 32	14 37
Canada Water	d				13 49	13 54		13 59	14 04	14 09			14 14				14 19	14 24		14 29	14 34	14 39
Surrey Quays	d				13 50	13 55		14 00	14 05	14 10			14 15				14 20	14 25		14 30	14 35	14 40
New Cross ELL	a					14 01				14 16								14 31				14 46
New Cross Gate 4	a				13 54		13 59	14 04	14 09			14 14	14 19				14 24		14 29	14 34	14 39	
	d				13 55		13 59	14 05	14 10			14 14	14 20				14 25		14 29	14 35	14 40	
Brockley	d				13 57		14 02	14 07	14 12			14 17	14 22				14 27		14 32	14 37	14 42	
Honor Oak Park	d				14 00		14 05	14 10	14 15			14 20	14 25				14 30		14 35	14 40	14 45	
Forest Hill 4	d				14 03		14 07	14 13	14 18			14 22	14 28				14 33		14 37	14 43	14 48	
Sydenham	d				14 05		14 10	14 15	14 20			14 25	14 30				14 35		14 40	14 45	14 50	
Crystal Palace 4	d			14 07	14a10				14a25							14 37	14a40				14a55	
Gipsy Hill	d			14 09												14 39						
West Norwood 4	d			14 12												14 42						
Streatham Hill	d																					
Balham 4 ⊖	d																					
Wandsworth Common	d																					
Clapham Junction 10	d																					
South Bermondsey	d	13 45									14 10			14 15								
Queens Rd Peckham	d	13 48									14 12			14 18								
Peckham Rye 4	d	13 50	14 12	14a23							14a15			14 20	14 42	14a53						
Denmark Hill 4	d	13 53	14 16											14 23	14 46							
London Blackfriars 3 ⊖	a																					
Clapham High Street ⊖	d	13 58												14 28								
Wandsworth Road	d	13 59												14 29								
Battersea Park 4	d	14 02												14 32								
London Victoria 15 ⊖	a	14 06	14 25											14 36	14 55							
Penge West	d							14 18				14 27	14 33							14 48		
Anerley	d							14 20				14 29	14 35							14 50		
Norwood Junction 2	d						14 16	14 23				14 33	14 38						14 46	14 53		
West Croydon 4	a						14 24	14 29					14 45						14 54	14 59		
East Croydon	a											14 37										

London Bridge to London Victoria - Croydon and East London Line

		SN	SN	LO	SN	SE	SN	LO	LO	SN	LO	LO	LO	SN	SN	LO	SN	SE	SN	LO	LO	SN	LO
London Bridge 4 ⊖	d	14 36	14 39		14 41					14 54				15 06	15 09		15 11					15 24	
Highbury & Islington	d			14 21				14 28			14 36	14 43				14 51				14 58			15 06
Canonbury	d			14 23				14 30			14 38	14 45				14 53				15 00			15 08
Dalston Junction Stn ELL	d			14 28				14 33	14 38		14 43	14 48	14 53			14 58				15 03	15 08		15 13
Haggerston	d			14 29				14 34	14 39		14 44	14 49	14 54			14 59				15 04	15 09		15 14
Hoxton	d			14 31				14 36	14 41		14 46	14 51	14 56			15 01				15 06	15 11		15 16
Shoreditch High Street	d			14 34				14 39	14 44		14 49	14 54	14 59			15 04				15 09	15 14		15 19
Whitechapel	d			14 36				14 41	14 46		14 51	14 56	15 01			15 06				15 11	15 16		15 21
Shadwell	d			14 38				14 43	14 48		14 53	14 58	15 03			15 08				15 13	15 18		15 23
Wapping	d			14 40				14 45	14 50		14 55	15 00	15 05			15 10				15 15	15 20		15 25
Rotherhithe	d			14 42				14 47	14 52		14 57	15 02	15 07			15 12				15 17	15 22		15 27
Canada Water	d			14 44				14 49	14 54		14 59	15 04	15 09			15 14				15 19	15 24		15 29
Surrey Quays	d			14 45				14 50	14 55		15 00	15 05	15 10			15 15				15 20	15 25		15 30
New Cross ELL	a								15 01				15 16								15 31		
New Cross Gate 4	a		14 44	14 49				14 54		14 59	15 04	15 09			15 14	15 19				15 24		15 29	15 34
	d		14 44	14 50				14 55		14 59	15 05	15 10			15 14	15 20				15 25		15 29	15 35
Brockley	d		14 47	14 52				14 57		15 02	15 07	15 12			15 17	15 22				15 27		15 32	15 37
Honor Oak Park	d		14 50	14 55				15 00		15 05	15 10	15 15			15 20	15 25				15 30		15 35	15 40
Forest Hill 4	d		14 52	14 58				15 03		15 07	15 13	15 18			15 22	15 28				15 33		15 37	15 43
Sydenham	d		14 55	15 00				15 05		15 10	15 15	15 20			15 25	15 30				15 35		15 40	15 45
Crystal Palace 4	d						15 07	15a10				15a25							15 37	15a40			
Gipsy Hill	d						15 09												15 39				
West Norwood 4	d						15 12												15 42				
Streatham Hill	d																						
Balham 4 ⊖	d																						
Wandsworth Common	d																						
Clapham Junction 10	d																						
South Bermondsey	d	14 40			14 45									15 10			15 15						
Queens Rd Peckham	d	14 42			14 48									15 12			15 18						
Peckham Rye 4	d	14a45			14 50	15 12	15a23							15a15			15 20	15 42	15a53				
Denmark Hill 4	d				14 53	15 16											15 23	15 46					
London Blackfriars 3 ⊖	a																						
Clapham High Street ⊖	d				14 58												15 28						
Wandsworth Road	d				14 59												15 29						
Battersea Park 4	d				15 02												15 32						
London Victoria 15 ⊖	a				15 06	15 25											15 36	15 55					
Penge West	d		14 57	15 03							15 18				15 27	15 33							15 48
Anerley	d		14 59	15 05							15 20				15 29	15 35							15 50
Norwood Junction 2	d		15 03	15 08						15 16	15 23				15 33	15 38						15 46	15 53
West Croydon 4	a			15 15						15 24	15 29					15 45						15 54	15 59
East Croydon	a		15 07												15 37								

		LO	LO	SN	SN	LO	SN	SE	SN	LO	LO	SN	LO	LO	LO	SN	SN	LO	SN	SE	SN	LO
London Bridge 4 ⊖	d			15 36	15 39		15 41					15 54				16 06	16 09		16 11			
Highbury & Islington	d	15 13				15 21				15 28			15 36	15 43				15 51				15 58
Canonbury	d	15 15				15 23				15 30			15 38	15 45				15 53				16 00
Dalston Junction Stn ELL	d	15 18	15 23			15 28				15 33	15 38		15 43	15 48	15 53			15 58				16 03
Haggerston	d	15 19	15 24			15 29				15 34	15 39		15 44	15 49	15 54			15 59				16 04
Hoxton	d	15 21	15 26			15 31				15 36	15 41		15 46	15 51	15 56			16 01				16 06
Shoreditch High Street	d	15 24	15 29			15 34				15 39	15 44		15 49	15 54	15 59			16 04				16 09
Whitechapel	d	15 26	15 31			15 36				15 41	15 46		15 51	15 56	16 01			16 06				16 11
Shadwell	d	15 28	15 33			15 38				15 43	15 48		15 53	15 58	16 03			16 08				16 13
Wapping	d	15 30	15 35			15 40				15 45	15 50		15 55	16 00	16 05			16 10				16 15
Rotherhithe	d	15 32	15 37			15 42				15 47	15 52		15 57	16 02	16 07			16 12				16 17
Canada Water	d	15 34	15 39			15 44				15 49	15 54		15 59	16 04	16 09			16 14				16 19
Surrey Quays	d	15 35	15 40			15 45				15 50	15 55		16 00	16 05	16 10			16 15				16 20
New Cross ELL	a		15 46								16 01				16 16							
New Cross Gate 4	a	15 39			15 44	15 49				15 54		15 59	16 04	16 09			16 14	16 19				16 24
	d	15 40			15 44	15 50				15 55		15 59	16 05	16 10			16 14	16 20				16 25
Brockley	d	15 42			15 47	15 52				15 57		16 02	16 07	16 12			16 17	16 22				16 27
Honor Oak Park	d	15 45			15 50	15 55				16 00		16 05	16 10	16 15			16 20	16 25				16 30
Forest Hill 4	d	15 48			15 52	15 58				16 03		16 07	16 13	16 18			16 22	16 28				16 33
Sydenham	d	15 50			15 55	16 00				16 05		16 10	16 15	16 20			16 25	16 30				16 35
Crystal Palace 4	d	15a55							16 07	16a10				16a25							16 37	16a40
Gipsy Hill	d								16 09												16 39	
West Norwood 4	d								16 12												16 42	
Streatham Hill	d																					
Balham 4 ⊖	d																					
Wandsworth Common	d																					
Clapham Junction 10	d																					
South Bermondsey	d			15 40			15 45									16 10			16 15			
Queens Rd Peckham	d			15 42			15 48									16 12			16 18			
Peckham Rye 4	d			15a45			15 50	16 12	16a23							16a15			16 20	16 42	16a53	
Denmark Hill 4	d						15 53	16 16											16 23	16 46		
London Blackfriars 3 ⊖	a																					
Clapham High Street ⊖	d						15 58												16 28			
Wandsworth Road	d						15 59												16 29			
Battersea Park 4	d						16 02												16 32			
London Victoria 15 ⊖	a						16 06	16 25											16 36	16 55		
Penge West	d				15 57	16 03							16 18				16 27	16 33				
Anerley	d				15 59	16 05							16 20				16 29	16 35				
Norwood Junction 2	d				16 03	16 08						16 16	16 23				16 33	16 38				
West Croydon 4	a					16 15						16 24	16 29					16 45				
East Croydon	a				16 07												16 37					

Table 178

Sundays

London Bridge to London Victoria - Croydon and East London Line

		LO	SN	LO	LO	LO	SN	SN	LO	SN		SE	SN	LO	LO	SN	LO	LO	LO	SN		SN	LO	SN	SE
London Bridge 4 ⊖	d		16 24				16 36	16 39		16 41						16 54				17 06		17 09		17 11	
Highbury & Islington	d			16 06	16 13				16 21					16 28			16 36	16 43					16 51		
Canonbury	d			16 08	16 15				16 23					16 30			16 38	16 45					16 53		
Dalston Junction Stn ELL	d	16 08		16 13	16 18	16 23			16 28					16 33	16 38		16 43	16 48	16 53				16 58		
Haggerston	d	16 09		16 14	16 19	16 24			16 29					16 34	16 39		16 44	16 49	16 54				16 59		
Hoxton	d	16 11		16 16	16 21	16 26			16 31					16 36	16 41		16 46	16 51	16 56				17 01		
Shoreditch High Street	d	16 14		16 19	16 24	16 29			16 34					16 39	16 44		16 49	16 54	16 59				17 04		
Whitechapel	d	16 16		16 21	16 26	16 31			16 36					16 41	16 46		16 51	16 56	17 01				17 06		
Shadwell	d	16 18		16 23	16 28	16 33			16 38					16 43	16 48		16 53	16 58	17 03				17 08		
Wapping	d	16 20		16 25	16 30	16 35			16 40					16 45	16 50		16 55	17 00	17 05				17 10		
Rotherhithe	d	16 22		16 27	16 32	16 37			16 42					16 47	16 52		16 57	17 02	17 07				17 12		
Canada Water	d	16 24		16 29	16 34	16 39			16 44					16 49	16 54		16 59	17 04	17 09				17 14		
Surrey Quays	d	16 25		16 30	16 35	16 40			16 45					16 50	16 55		17 00	17 05	17 10				17 15		
New Cross ELL	a	16 31				16 46									17 01				17 16						
New Cross Gate 4	a		16 29	16 34	16 39			16 44	16 49					16 54		16 59	17 04	17 09				17 14	17 19		
	d		16 29	16 35	16 40			16 44	16 50					16 55		16 59	17 05	17 10				17 14	17 20		
Brockley	d		16 32	16 37	16 42			16 47	16 52					16 57		17 02	17 07	17 12				17 17	17 22		
Honor Oak Park	d		16 35	16 40	16 45			16 50	16 55					17 00		17 05	17 10	17 15				17 20	17 25		
Forest Hill 4	d		16 37	16 43	16 48			16 52	16 58					17 03		17 07	17 13	17 18				17 22	17 28		
Sydenham	d		16 40	16 45	16 50			16 55	17 00					17 05		17 10	17 15	17 20				17 25	17 30		
Crystal Palace 4	d				16a55								17 07	17a10				17a25							
Gipsy Hill	d												17 09												
West Norwood 4	d												17 12												
Streatham Hill	d																								
Balham 4 ⊖	d																								
Wandsworth Common	d																								
Clapham Junction 10	d																								
South Bermondsey	d						16 40			16 45										17 10				17 15	
Queens Rd Peckham	d						16 42			16 48										17 12				17 18	
Peckham Rye 4	d						16a45			16 50		17 12	17a23							17a15				17 20	17 42
Denmark Hill 4	d									16 53		17 16												17 23	17 46
London Blackfriars 3 ⊖	a																								
Clapham High Street ⊖	d									16 58														17 28	
Wandsworth Road	d									16 59														17 29	
Battersea Park 4	d									17 02														17 32	
London Victoria 15 ⊖	a									17 06		17 25												17 36	17 55
Penge West	d			16 48				16 57	17 03								17 18					17 27	17 33		
Anerley	d			16 50				16 59	17 05								17 20					17 29	17 35		
Norwood Junction 2	d		16 46	16 53				17 03	17 08							17 16	17 23					17 33	17 38		
West Croydon 4	a		16 54	16 59					17 15							17 24	17 29						17 45		
East Croydon	a							17 07														17 37			

		SN	LO	LO	SN	LO		LO	LO	SN	SN	LO	SN	SE	SN	LO		LO	SN	LO	LO	LO	SN	SN	LO
London Bridge 4 ⊖	d				17 24					17 36	17 39		17 41						17 54				18 06	18 09	
Highbury & Islington	d		16 58			17 06		17 13				17 21				17 28				17 36	17 43				17 51
Canonbury	d		17 00			17 08		17 15				17 23				17 30				17 38	17 45				17 53
Dalston Junction Stn ELL	d		17 03	17 08		17 13		17 18	17 23			17 28				17 33		17 38		17 43	17 48	17 53			17 58
Haggerston	d		17 04	17 09		17 14		17 19	17 24			17 29				17 34		17 39		17 44	17 49	17 54			17 59
Hoxton	d		17 06	17 11		17 16		17 21	17 26			17 31				17 36		17 41		17 46	17 51	17 56			18 01
Shoreditch High Street	d		17 09	17 14		17 19		17 24	17 29			17 34				17 39		17 44		17 49	17 54	17 59			18 04
Whitechapel	d		17 11	17 16		17 21		17 26	17 31			17 36				17 41		17 46		17 51	17 56	18 01			18 06
Shadwell	d		17 13	17 18		17 23		17 28	17 33			17 38				17 43		17 48		17 53	17 58	18 03			18 08
Wapping	d		17 15	17 20		17 25		17 30	17 35			17 40				17 45		17 50		17 55	18 00	18 05			18 10
Rotherhithe	d		17 17	17 22		17 27		17 32	17 37			17 42				17 47		17 52		17 57	18 02	18 07			18 12
Canada Water	d		17 19	17 24		17 29		17 34	17 39			17 44				17 49		17 54		17 59	18 04	18 09			18 14
Surrey Quays	d		17 20	17 25		17 30		17 35	17 40			17 45				17 50		17 55		18 00	18 05	18 10			18 15
New Cross ELL	a			17 31					17 46									18 01				18 16			
New Cross Gate 4	a		17 24		17 29	17 34		17 39			17 44	17 49				17 54			17 59	18 04	18 09			18 14	18 19
	d		17 25		17 29	17 35		17 40			17 44	17 50				17 55			17 59	18 05	18 10			18 14	18 20
Brockley	d		17 27		17 32	17 37		17 42			17 47	17 52				17 57			18 02	18 07	18 12			18 17	18 22
Honor Oak Park	d		17 30		17 35	17 40		17 45			17 50	17 55				18 00			18 05	18 10	18 15			18 20	18 25
Forest Hill 4	d		17 33		17 37	17 43		17 48			17 52	17 58				18 03			18 07	18 13	18 18			18 22	18 28
Sydenham	d		17 35		17 40	17 45		17 50			17 55	18 00				18 05			18 10	18 15	18 20			18 25	18 30
Crystal Palace 4	d	17 37	17a40					17a55							18 07	18a10					18a25				
Gipsy Hill	d	17 39													18 09										
West Norwood 4	d	17 42													18 12										
Streatham Hill	d																								
Balham 4 ⊖	d																								
Wandsworth Common	d																								
Clapham Junction 10	d																								
South Bermondsey	d									17 40			17 45										18 10		
Queens Rd Peckham	d									17 42			17 48										18 12		
Peckham Rye 4	d	17a53								17a45			17 50	18 12	18a23								18a15		
Denmark Hill 4	d												17 53	18 16											
London Blackfriars 3 ⊖	a																								
Clapham High Street ⊖	d												17 58												
Wandsworth Road	d												17 59												
Battersea Park 4	d												18 02												
London Victoria 15 ⊖	a												18 06	18 25											
Penge West	d					17 48					17 57	18 03								18 18				18 27	18 33
Anerley	d					17 50					17 59	18 05								18 20				18 29	18 35
Norwood Junction 2	d				17 46	17 53					18 03	18 08							18 16	18 23				18 33	18 38
West Croydon 4	a				17 54	17 59						18 14							18 24	18 29					18 44
East Croydon	a										18 07													18 37	

Table 178

Sundays

London Bridge to London Victoria - Croydon and East London Line

		SN		SE	SN	LO	LO	SN	LO	LO	LO	SN		SN	LO	SN	SE	SN	LO	LO	SN	LO		LO	LO
London Bridge 4 ⊖	d	18 11						18 24				18 36		18 39		18 41					18 54				
Highbury & Islington	d					17 58			18 06	18 13					18 21				18 28			18 36		18 43	
Canonbury	d					18 00			18 08	18 15					18 23				18 30			18 38		18 45	
Dalston Junction Stn ELL	d					18 03	18 08		18 13	18 18	18 23				18 28				18 33	18 38		18 43		18 48	18 53
Haggerston	d					18 04	18 09		18 14	18 19	18 24				18 29				18 34	18 39		18 44		18 49	18 54
Hoxton	d					18 06	18 11		18 16	18 21	18 26				18 31				18 36	18 41		18 46		18 51	18 56
Shoreditch High Street	d					18 09	18 14		18 19	18 24	18 29				18 34				18 39	18 44		18 49		18 54	18 59
Whitechapel	d					18 11	18 16		18 21	18 26	18 31				18 36				18 41	18 46		18 51		18 56	19 01
Shadwell	d					18 13	18 18		18 23	18 28	18 33				18 38				18 43	18 48		18 53		18 58	19 03
Wapping	d					18 15	18 20		18 25	18 30	18 35				18 40				18 45	18 50		18 55		19 00	19 05
Rotherhithe	d					18 17	18 22		18 27	18 32	18 37				18 42				18 47	18 52		18 57		19 02	19 07
Canada Water	d					18 19	18 24		18 29	18 34	18 39				18 44				18 49	18 54		18 59		19 04	19 09
Surrey Quays	d					18 20	18 25		18 30	18 35	18 40				18 45				18 50	18 55		19 00		19 05	19 10
New Cross ELL	a						18 31				18 46									19 01					19 16
New Cross Gate 4	a					18 24		18 29	18 34	18 39				18 44	18 49				18 54		18 59	19 04		19 09	
	d					18 25		18 29	18 35	18 40				18 44	18 50				18 55		18 59	19 05		19 10	
Brockley	d					18 27		18 32	18 37	18 42				18 47	18 52				18 57		19 02	19 07		19 12	
Honor Oak Park	d					18 30		18 35	18 40	18 45				18 50	18 55				19 00		19 05	19 10		19 15	
Forest Hill 4	d					18 33		18 37	18 43	18 48				18 52	18 58				19 03		19 07	19 13		19 18	
Sydenham	d					18 35		18 40	18 45	18 50				18 55	19 00				19 05		19 10	19 15		19 20	
Crystal Palace 4	d				18 37	18a40				18a55								19 07	19a10					19a25	
Gipsy Hill	d				18 39													19 09							
West Norwood 4	d				18 42													19 12							
Streatham Hill	d																								
Balham 4 ⊖	d																								
Wandsworth Common	d																								
Clapham Junction 10	d																								
South Bermondsey	d	18 15										18 40				18 45									
Queens Rd Peckham	d	18 18										18 42				18 48									
Peckham Rye 4	d	18 20		18 42	18a53							18a45				18 50	19 12	19a23							
Denmark Hill 4	d	18 23		18 46												18 53	19 16								
London Blackfriars 3 ⊖	a																								
Clapham High Street ⊖	d	18 28														18 58									
Wandsworth Road	d	18 29														18 59									
Battersea Park 4	d	18 32														19 02									
London Victoria 15 ⊖	a	18 36		18 55												19 06	19 25								
Penge West	d								18 48					18 57	19 03							19 18			
Anerley	d								18 50					18 59	19 05							19 20			
Norwood Junction 2	d							18 46	18 53					19 03	19 08						19 16	19 23			
West Croydon 4	a							18 54	18 59						19 14						19 24	19 29			
East Croydon	a													19 07											

		SN	SN	LO	SN	SE	SN	LO		LO	SN	LO	LO	LO	SN	SN	LO	SN		SE	SN	LO	LO	SN	LO
London Bridge 4 ⊖	d	19 06	19 09		19 11						19 24				19 36	19 39		19 41						19 54	
Highbury & Islington	d			18 51				18 58				19 06	19 13				19 21					19 28			19 36
Canonbury	d			18 53				19 00				19 08	19 15				19 23					19 30			19 38
Dalston Junction Stn ELL	d			18 58				19 03		19 08		19 13	19 18	19 23			19 28					19 33	19 38		19 43
Haggerston	d			18 59				19 04		19 09		19 14	19 19	19 24			19 29					19 34	19 39		19 44
Hoxton	d			19 01				19 06		19 11		19 16	19 21	19 26			19 31					19 36	19 41		19 46
Shoreditch High Street	d			19 04				19 09		19 14		19 19	19 24	19 29			19 34					19 39	19 44		19 49
Whitechapel	d			19 06				19 11		19 16		19 21	19 26	19 31			19 36					19 41	19 46		19 51
Shadwell	d			19 08				19 13		19 18		19 23	19 28	19 33			19 38					19 43	19 48		19 53
Wapping	d			19 10				19 15		19 20		19 25	19 30	19 35			19 40					19 45	19 50		19 55
Rotherhithe	d			19 12				19 17		19 22		19 27	19 32	19 37			19 42					19 47	19 52		19 57
Canada Water	d			19 14				19 19		19 24		19 29	19 34	19 39			19 44					19 49	19 54		19 59
Surrey Quays	d			19 15				19 20		19 25		19 30	19 35	19 40			19 45					19 50	19 55		20 00
New Cross ELL	a									19 31				19 46									20 01		
New Cross Gate 4	a		19 14	19 19				19 24			19 29	19 34	19 39			19 44	19 49					19 54		19 59	20 04
	d		19 14	19 20				19 25			19 29	19 35	19 40			19 44	19 50					19 55		19 59	20 05
Brockley	d		19 17	19 22				19 27			19 32	19 37	19 42			19 47	19 52					19 57		20 02	20 07
Honor Oak Park	d		19 20	19 25				19 30			19 35	19 40	19 45			19 50	19 55					20 00		20 05	20 10
Forest Hill 4	d		19 22	19 28				19 33			19 37	19 43	19 48			19 52	19 58					20 03		20 07	20 13
Sydenham	d		19 25	19 30				19 35			19 40	19 45	19 50			19 55	20 00					20 05		20 10	20 15
Crystal Palace 4	d						19 37	19a40					19a55								20 07	20a10			
Gipsy Hill	d						19 39														20 09				
West Norwood 4	d						19 42														20 12				
Streatham Hill	d																								
Balham 4 ⊖	d																								
Wandsworth Common	d																								
Clapham Junction 10	d																								
South Bermondsey	d	19 10			19 15										19 40			19 45							
Queens Rd Peckham	d	19 12			19 18										19 42			19 48							
Peckham Rye 4	d	19a15			19 20	19 42	19a53								19a45			19 50		20 12	20a23				
Denmark Hill 4	d				19 23	19 46												19 53		20 16					
London Blackfriars 3 ⊖	a																								
Clapham High Street ⊖	d				19 28													19 58							
Wandsworth Road	d				19 29													19 59							
Battersea Park 4	d				19 32													20 02							
London Victoria 15 ⊖	a				19 36	19 55												20 06		20 25					
Penge West	d		19 27	19 33								19 48				19 57	20 03								20 18
Anerley	d		19 29	19 35								19 50				19 59	20 05								20 20
Norwood Junction 2	d		19 33	19 38							19 46	19 53				20 03	20 08							20 16	20 23
West Croydon 4	a			19 44							19 54	19 59					20 15							20 24	20 29
East Croydon	a		19 37													20 07									

London Bridge to London Victoria - Croydon and East London Line

		LO	LO	SN	SN	LO	SN	SE	SN	LO	LO	SN	LO	LO	LO	SN	SN	LO	SN	SE	SN	LO
London Bridge [4] ⊖	d			20 06	20 09		20 11					20 24				20 36	20 39		20 41			
Highbury & Islington	d	19 43				19 51				19 58			20 06	20 13				20 21				20 28
Canonbury	d	19 45				19 53				20 00			20 08	20 15				20 23				20 30
Dalston Junction Stn ELL	d	19 48	19 53			19 58				20 03	20 08		20 13	20 18	20 23			20 28				20 33
Haggerston	d	19 49	19 54			19 59				20 04	20 09		20 14	20 19	20 24			20 29				20 34
Hoxton	d	19 51	19 56			20 01				20 06	20 11		20 16	20 21	20 26			20 31				20 36
Shoreditch High Street	d	19 54	19 59			20 04				20 09	20 14		20 19	20 24	20 29			20 34				20 39
Whitechapel	d	19 56	20 01			20 06				20 11	20 16		20 21	20 26	20 31			20 36				20 41
Shadwell	d	19 58	20 03			20 08				20 13	20 18		20 23	20 28	20 33			20 38				20 43
Wapping	d	20 00	20 05			20 10				20 15	20 20		20 25	20 30	20 35			20 40				20 45
Rotherhithe	d	20 02	20 07			20 12				20 17	20 22		20 27	20 32	20 37			20 42				20 47
Canada Water	d	20 04	20 09			20 14				20 19	20 24		20 29	20 34	20 39			20 44				20 49
Surrey Quays	d	20 05	20 10			20 15				20 20	20 25		20 30	20 35	20 40			20 45				20 50
New Cross ELL	a		20 16								20 31				20 46							
New Cross Gate [4]	a	20 09			20 14	20 19				20 24		20 29	20 34	20 39			20 44	20 49				20 54
	d	20 10			20 14	20 20				20 25		20 29	20 35	20 40			20 44	20 50				20 55
Brockley	d	20 12			20 17	20 22				20 27		20 32	20 37	20 42			20 47	20 52				20 57
Honor Oak Park	d	20 15			20 20	20 25				20 30		20 35	20 40	20 45			20 50	20 55				21 00
Forest Hill [4]	d	20 18			20 22	20 28				20 33		20 37	20 43	20 48			20 52	20 58				21 03
Sydenham	d	20 20			20 25	20 30				20 35		20 40	20 45	20 50			20 55	21 00				21 05
Crystal Palace [4]	d	20a25							20 37	20a40				20a55							21 07	21a10
Gipsy Hill	d								20 39												21 09	
West Norwood [4]	d								20 42												21 12	
Streatham Hill	d																					
Balham [4] ⊖	d																					
Wandsworth Common	d																					
Clapham Junction [10]	d																					
South Bermondsey	d			20 10			20 15									20 40			20 45			
Queens Rd Peckham	d			20 12			20 18									20 42			20 48			
Peckham Rye [4]	d			20a15			20 20	20 42	20a53							20a45			20 50	21 12	21a23	
Denmark Hill [4]	d						20 23	20 46											20 53	21 16		
London Blackfriars [3] ⊖	a																					
Clapham High Street ⊖	d						20 28												20 58			
Wandsworth Road	d						20 29												20 59			
Battersea Park [4]	d						20 32												21 02			
London Victoria [15] ⊖	a						20 36	20 55											21 06	21 25		
Penge West	d				20 27	20 33							20 48				20 57	21 03				
Anerley	d				20 29	20 35							20 50				20 59	21 05				
Norwood Junction [2]	d				20 33	20 38						20 46	20 53				21 03	21 08				
West Croydon [4]	a					20 45						20 54	20 59					21 15				
East Croydon	a				20 37												21 07					

		LO	SN	LO	LO	LO	SN	SN	LO	SN	SE	SN	LO	LO	SN	LO	LO	LO	SN	SN	LO	SN	SE
London Bridge [4] ⊖	d		20 54				21 06	21 09		21 11					21 24				21 36	21 39		21 41	
Highbury & Islington	d			20 36	20 43				20 51				20 58			21 06	21 13				21 21		
Canonbury	d			20 38	20 45				20 53				21 00			21 08	21 15				21 23		
Dalston Junction Stn ELL	d	20 38		20 43	20 48	20 53			20 58				21 03	21 08		21 13	21 18	21 23			21 28		
Haggerston	d	20 39		20 44	20 49	20 54			20 59				21 04	21 09		21 14	21 19	21 24			21 29		
Hoxton	d	20 41		20 46	20 51	20 56			21 01				21 06	21 11		21 16	21 21	21 26			21 31		
Shoreditch High Street	d	20 44		20 49	20 54	20 59			21 04				21 09	21 14		21 19	21 24	21 29			21 34		
Whitechapel	d	20 46		20 51	20 56	21 01			21 06				21 11	21 16		21 21	21 26	21 31			21 36		
Shadwell	d	20 48		20 53	20 58	21 03			21 08				21 13	21 18		21 23	21 28	21 33			21 38		
Wapping	d	20 50		20 55	21 00	21 05			21 10				21 15	21 20		21 25	21 30	21 35			21 40		
Rotherhithe	d	20 52		20 57	21 02	21 07			21 12				21 17	21 22		21 27	21 32	21 37			21 42		
Canada Water	d	20 54		20 59	21 04	21 09			21 14				21 19	21 24		21 29	21 34	21 39			21 44		
Surrey Quays	d	20 55		21 00	21 05	21 10			21 15				21 20	21 25		21 30	21 35	21 40			21 45		
New Cross ELL	a	21 01				21 16								21 31				21 46					
New Cross Gate [4]	a		20 59	21 04	21 09			21 14	21 19				21 24		21 29	21 34	21 39			21 44	21 49		
	d		20 59	21 05	21 10			21 14	21 20				21 25		21 29	21 35	21 40			21 44	21 50		
Brockley	d		21 02	21 07	21 12			21 17	21 22				21 27		21 32	21 37	21 42			21 47	21 52		
Honor Oak Park	d		21 05	21 10	21 15			21 20	21 25				21 30		21 35	21 40	21 45			21 50	21 55		
Forest Hill [4]	d		21 07	21 13	21 18			21 22	21 28				21 33		21 37	21 43	21 48			21 52	21 58		
Sydenham	d		21 10	21 15	21 20			21 25	21 30				21 35		21 40	21 45	21 50			21 55	22 00		
Crystal Palace [4]	d				21a25							21 37	21a40				21a55						
Gipsy Hill	d											21 39											
West Norwood [4]	d											21 42											
Streatham Hill	d																						
Balham [4] ⊖	d																						
Wandsworth Common	d																						
Clapham Junction [10]	d																						
South Bermondsey	d						21 10			21 15									21 40			21 45	
Queens Rd Peckham	d						21 12			21 18									21 42			21 48	
Peckham Rye [4]	d						21a15			21 20	21 42	21a53							21a45			21 50	22 12
Denmark Hill [4]	d									21 23	21 46											21 53	22 16
London Blackfriars [3] ⊖	a																						
Clapham High Street ⊖	d									21 28												21 58	
Wandsworth Road	d									21 29												21 59	
Battersea Park [4]	d									21 32												22 02	
London Victoria [15] ⊖	a									21 36	21 55											22 06	22 25
Penge West	d			21 18				21 27	21 33							21 48				21 57	22 03		
Anerley	d			21 20				21 29	21 35							21 50				21 59	22 05		
Norwood Junction [2]	d		21 16	21 23				21 33	21 38						21 46	21 53				22 03	22 08		
West Croydon [4]	a		21 24	21 29					21 45						21 54	21 59					22 15		
East Croydon	a							21 37												22 07			

London Bridge to London Victoria - Croydon and East London Line

		SN	LO	LO	SN	LO	LO	LO	SN	SN	LO	LO	SN	SE	SN	SN	LO	SN	LO	LO	SN	SE	SN
London Bridge [4] ⊖	d				21 54				22 06	22 09			22 11		22 36			22 39			22 41		23 06
Highbury & Islington	d		21 28			21 36	21 43				21 51						22 13		22 23				
Canonbury	d		21 30			21 38	21 45				21 53						22 15		22 25				
Dalston Junction Stn ELL	d		21 33	21 38		21 43	21 48	21 53			21 58	22 08					22 18		22 28	22 38			
Haggerston	d		21 34	21 39		21 44	21 49	21 54			21 59	22 09					22 19		22 29	22 39			
Hoxton	d		21 36	21 41		21 46	21 51	21 56			22 01	22 11					22 21		22 31	22 41			
Shoreditch High Street	d		21 39	21 44		21 49	21 54	21 59			22 04	22 14					22 24		22 34	22 44			
Whitechapel	d		21 41	21 46		21 51	21 56	22 01			22 06	22 16					22 26		22 36	22 46			
Shadwell	d		21 43	21 48		21 53	21 58	22 03			22 08	22 18					22 28		22 38	22 48			
Wapping	d		21 45	21 50		21 55	22 00	22 05			22 10	22 20					22 30		22 40	22 50			
Rotherhithe	d		21 47	21 52		21 57	22 02	22 07			22 12	22 22					22 32		22 42	22 52			
Canada Water	d		21 49	21 54		21 59	22 04	22 09			22 14	22 24					22 34		22 44	22 54			
Surrey Quays	d		21 50	21 55		22 00	22 05	22 10			22 15	22 25					22 35		22 45	22 55			
New Cross ELL	a			22 01				22 17				22 31								23 01			
New Cross Gate [4]	a		21 54		21 59	22 04	22 09			22 14	22 19						22 39	22 44	22 49				
	d		21 55		21 59	22 05	22 10			22 14	22 20						22 40	22 44	22 50				
Brockley	d		21 57		22 02	22 07	22 12			22 17	22 22						22 42	22 47	22 52				
Honor Oak Park	d		22 00		22 05	22 10	22 15			22 20	22 25						22 45	22 50	22 55				
Forest Hill [4]	d		22 03		22 07	22 13	22 18			22 22	22 28						22 48	22 52	22 58				
Sydenham	d		22 05		22 10	22 15	22 20			22 25	22 30						22 50	22 55	23 00				
Crystal Palace [4]	d	22 07	22a10				22a25									22 37	22a55						
Gipsy Hill	d	22 09														22 39							
West Norwood [4]	d	22 12														22 42							
Streatham Hill	d																						
Balham [4] ⊖	d																						
Wandsworth Common	d																						
Clapham Junction [10]	d																						
South Bermondsey	d								22 10				22 15		22 40						22 45		23 10
Queens Rd Peckham	d								22 12				22 18		22 42						22 48		23 12
Peckham Rye [4]	d	22a23							22a15				22 20	22 42	22a45	22a53					22 50	23 12	23a15
Denmark Hill [4]	d												22 23	22 46							22 53	23 16	
London Blackfriars [3] ⊖	a																						
Clapham High Street ⊖	d												22 28								22 58		
Wandsworth Road	d												22 29								22 59		
Battersea Park [4]	d												22 32								23 02		
London Victoria [15] ⊖	a												22 36	22 55							23 06	23 25	
Penge West	d					22 18				22 27	22 33							22 57	23 03				
Anerley	d					22 20				22 29	22 35							22 59	23 05				
Norwood Junction [2]	d				22 16	22 23				22 33	22 38							23 03	23 08				
West Croydon [4]	a				22 24	22 29					22 45								23 14				
East Croydon	a									22 37								23 07					

		SN	LO	SN	LO	LO	SN	SE	SN	SN	LO	SN	LO
London Bridge [4] ⊖	d			23 09			23 11					23 39	
Highbury & Islington	d		22 43		22 53						23 13		23 23
Canonbury	d		22 45		22 55						23 15		23 25
Dalston Junction Stn ELL	d		22 48		22 58	23 08					23 18		23 28
Haggerston	d		22 49		22 59	23 09					23 19		23 29
Hoxton	d		22 51		23 01	23 11					23 21		23 31
Shoreditch High Street	d		22 54		23 04	23 14					23 24		23 34
Whitechapel	d		22 56		23 06	23 16					23 26		23 36
Shadwell	d		22 58		23 08	23 18					23 28		23 38
Wapping	d		23 00		23 10	23 20					23 30		23 40
Rotherhithe	d		23 02		23 12	23 22					23 32		23 42
Canada Water	d		23 04		23 14	23 24					23 34		23 44
Surrey Quays	d		23 05		23 15	23 25					23 35		23 45
New Cross ELL	a					23 31							
New Cross Gate [4]	a		23 09	23 14	23 19						23 39	23 44	23 49
	d		23 10	23 14	23 20						23 40	23 44	23 50
Brockley	d		23 12	23 17	23 22						23 42	23 47	23 52
Honor Oak Park	d		23 15	23 20	23 25						23 45	23 50	23 55
Forest Hill [4]	d		23 18	23 22	23 28						23 48	23 52	23 58
Sydenham	d		23 20	23 25	23 30						23 50	23 55	00 01
Crystal Palace [4]	d	23 07	23a25						23 37	23 50	23a55		
Gipsy Hill	d	23 09							23 39				
West Norwood [4]	d	23 12							23 42				
Streatham Hill	d												
Balham [4] ⊖	d												
Wandsworth Common	d												
Clapham Junction [10]	d												
South Bermondsey	d						23 15						
Queens Rd Peckham	d						23 18						
Peckham Rye [4]	d	23a23					23 20	23 42	23a53				
Denmark Hill [4]	d						23 23	23 46					
London Blackfriars [3] ⊖	a												
Clapham High Street ⊖	d						23 28						
Wandsworth Road	d						23 29						
Battersea Park [4]	d						23 32						
London Victoria [15] ⊖	a						23 37	23 55					
Penge West	d			23 27	23 33							23 57	00 03
Anerley	d			23 29	23 35							23 59	00 05
Norwood Junction [2]	d			23 33	23 38					23 55		00 03	00 08
West Croydon [4]	a				23 44					23 59			00 15
East Croydon	a			23 38								00 06	

East London Line and Croydon - London Victoria to London Bridge

Miles	Miles	Miles	Miles	Miles		LO MX	LO MX	SN MO	SN MX	SN MX	SN MX	SN	SE	LO	SN	LO	LO	LO	SE	LO	LO	LO	SN
—	—	0	—	—	East Croydon d							05 13			05 51								06 13
—	—	—	—	0	West Croydon d	23p22								05 39				05 52				06 09	
—	—	1¼	—	1¼	Norwood Junction d	23p28						05 17		05 43	05 55			05 58				06 13	06 18
—	—	2½	—	—	Anerley d	23p31						05 20		05 46				06 01				06 16	06 21
—	—	2¾	—	—	Penge West d	23p33						05 22		05 48				06 03				06 18	06 23
0	0	—	0	—	London Victoria d				23p22	23p54													
1¼	1¼	—	—	—	Battersea Park d				23p26	23p58													
2	—	—	—	—	Wandsworth Road d																		
2½	—	—	—	—	Clapham High Street d																		
—	—	—	—	0	London Blackfriars d								05 28						06 10				
4½	—	—	4¼	3¾	Denmark Hill d								05 39						06 22				
5¼	—	—	5	4¼	Peckham Rye d			23p53			00 12		05a41		06 15				06a25				
6	—	—	—	—	Queens Rd Peckham d			23p56							06 17								
7	—	—	—	—	South Bermondsey d			23p58							06 20								
—	2¾	—	—	—	Clapham Junction d				23p30	00 02													
—	4	—	—	—	Wandsworth Common d				23p33	00 05													
—	4¾	—	—	—	Balham d				23p35	00 07													
—	5¾	—	—	—	Streatham Hill d				23p38	00 10													
—	7	—	—	—	West Norwood d				23p42	00 14	00 24												
—	8	—	—	—	Gipsy Hill d				23p45	00 17	00 27												
—	8¾	—	—	—	Crystal Palace d		23p43		23p51	00 21	00a29						05 58				06 13		
—	10	3½	—	—	Sydenham d	23p36	23p46		23p54	00 24		05 24		05 51			06 01	06 06			06 16	06 21	06 25
—	10¾	4¼	—	—	Forest Hill d	23p38	23p49		23p57	00 27		05 27		05 53			06 04	06 08			06 19	06 23	06 28
—	11¾	5¼	—	—	Honor Oak Park d	23p41	23p51		23p59	00 29		05 29		05 56			06 06	06 11			06 21	06 26	06 30
—	12¾	6¼	—	—	Brockley d	23p43	23p54		00 02	00 32		05 32		05 58			06 09	06 13			06 24	06 28	06 33
—	13¾	7¼	—	—	New Cross Gate a	23p46	23p56		00 04	00 34		05 34		06 01			06 11	06 16			06 26	06 31	06 35
—	—	—	—	—	d	23p46	23p56		00 04	00 34		05 34		06 01			06 11	06 16			06 26	06 31	06 35
—	—	—	0	—	New Cross ELL d											06 06				06 21			
—	—	—	1¼	—	Surrey Quays d	23p49	23p59							06 05		06 10	06 15	06 19		06 25	06 30	06 35	
—	—	—	1½	—	Canada Water d	23p51	00 02							06 07		06 12	06 17	06 21		06 27	06 32	06 37	
—	—	—	1¾	—	Rotherhithe d	23p53	00 03							06 08		06 13	06 18	06 23		06 28	06 33	06 38	
—	—	—	2	—	Wapping d	23p54	00 05							06 10		06 15	06 20	06 24		06 30	06 35	06 40	
—	—	—	2½	—	Shadwell d	23p56	00 07							06 12		06 17	06 22	06 26		06 32	06 37	06 42	
—	—	—	3¼	—	Whitechapel d	23p59	00 09							06 14		06 19	06 24	06 29		06 34	06 39	06 44	
—	—	—	4	—	Shoreditch High Street d	00 01	00 11							06 16		06 21	06 26	06 31		06 36	06 41	06 46	
—	—	—	4¾	—	Hoxton d	00 03	00 13							06 18		06 23	06 28	06 33		06 38	06 43	06 48	
—	—	—	5¼	—	Haggerston d	00 05	00 15							06 20		06 25	06 30	06 35		06 40	06 45	06 50	
—	—	—	5¾	—	Dalston Junction Stn ELL a	00 07	00 17							06 22		06 29	06 32	06 37		06 44	06 47	06 52	
—	—	—	—	—	Canonbury d	00 12	00 20							06 27			06 35	06 42			06 50	06 57	
—	—	—	—	—	Highbury & Islington d	00a14	00a23							06a30			06a38	06a44			06a54	07a00	
8¾	16½	10	—	—	London Bridge a			00 03	00 11	00 41		05 41			06 24								06 42

	LO	LO	LO	SN	LO	LO	SN	SN	LO	SN	SE	SN	SN	LO	SN	FC 1	LO	LO	SN	LO	LO
East Croydon d																					
West Croydon d			06 22										06 31	06 39				06 52			
Norwood Junction d			06 28	06 32										06 43	06 47			06 58	07 02		
Anerley d			06 31	06 35										06 46				07 01	07 05		
Penge West d			06 33	06 37										06 48				07 03	07 07		
London Victoria d							06 19					06 41									
Battersea Park d							06 23					06 45									
Wandsworth Road d												06 47									
Clapham High Street d												06 49									
London Blackfriars d											06 42					06 58					
Denmark Hill d											06 52	06 54				07 09					
Peckham Rye d										06 42	06a55	06 56	06 59		07 07	07a12					
Queens Rd Peckham d												06 59	07 02		07 10						
South Bermondsey d												07 01	07 04		07 12						
Clapham Junction d							06 27														
Wandsworth Common d							06 30														
Balham d							06 32														
Streatham Hill d							06 35	06 42													
West Norwood d							06 39	06 45		06 53											
Gipsy Hill d							06 42	06 48		06 56											
Crystal Palace d		06 28				06 41	06 44	06 51	06 58	06a59											07 11
Sydenham d		06 31	06 36	06 39		06 44	06 48	06 54	07 01					06 51				07 06	07 09		07 14
Forest Hill d		06 34	06 38	06 42		06 47	06 50	06 57	07 04					06 53				07 08	07 12		07 17
Honor Oak Park d		06 36	06 41	06 44		06 49	06 53	06 59	07 06					06 56				07 11	07 14		07 19
Brockley d		06 39	06 43	06 47		06 52	06 55	07 02	07 09					06 58				07 13	07 17		07 22
New Cross Gate a		06 41	06 46	06 49		06 54	06 58	07 04	07 11					07 01				07 16	07 19		07 24
d		06 41	06 46	06 49		06 54	06 58	07 04	07 11					07 01				07 16	07 19		07 24
New Cross ELL d	06 36				06 51												07 06			07 21	
Surrey Quays d	06 40	06 45	06 49		06 55	07 00			07 15					07 05			07 10	07 19		07 25	07 30
Canada Water d	06 42	06 47	06 51		06 57	07 02			07 17					07 07			07 12	07 21		07 27	07 32
Rotherhithe d	06 43	06 48	06 53		06 58	07 03			07 18					07 08			07 13	07 23		07 28	07 33
Wapping d	06 45	06 50	06 54		07 00	07 05			07 20					07 10			07 15	07 24		07 30	07 35
Shadwell d	06 47	06 52	06 56		07 02	07 07			07 22					07 12			07 17	07 26		07 32	07 37
Whitechapel d	06 49	06 54	06 59		07 04	07 09			07 24					07 14			07 19	07 29		07 34	07 39
Shoreditch High Street d	06 51	06 56	07 01		07 06	07 11			07 26					07 16			07 21	07 31		07 36	07 41
Hoxton d	06 53	06 58	07 03		07 08	07 13			07 28					07 18			07 23	07 33		07 38	07 43
Haggerston d	06 55	07 00	07 05		07 10	07 15			07 30					07 20			07 25	07 35		07 40	07 45
Dalston Junction Stn ELL a	06 59	07 02	07 07		07 14	07 17			07 32					07 23			07 29	07 37		07 44	07 47
Canonbury d		07 05	07 12			07 20			07 35					07 27				07 42			07 50
Highbury & Islington d		07a08	07a14			07a23			07a38					07a30				07a44			07a53
London Bridge a				06 59			07 06	07 16				07 08	07 11		07 19				07 30		

Table 178

Mondays to Fridays

East London Line and Croydon - London Victoria to London Bridge

	SN	SN	SN	SN	SN	LO	SN	FC	SN	LO	LO	LO	SN	LO	LO	SN	SN	SN	FC 1	SN	SE	SN
East Croydon d																						
West Croydon d					07 01	07 09	07 17					07 22										07 31
Norwood Junction d						07 13	07 22					07 28	07 32									
Anerley d						07 16						07 31	07 35									
Penge West d						07 18						07 33	07 37									
London Victoria d	06 49			07 11												07 17				07 41	07 43	
Battersea Park d	06 53			07 15												07 21				07 45		
Wandsworth Road d				07 17																07 47		
Clapham High Street d				07 19																07 49		
London Blackfriars d								07 24											07 40			
Denmark Hill d				07 24				07 34											07 50	07 54	07 53	
Peckham Rye d			07 12	07 26	07 31			07a36	07 36									07 42	07a53	07 56	07a56	07 59
Queens Rd Peckham d				07 29	07 34				07 39											07 59		08 02
South Bermondsey d				07 31	07 36				07 41											08 01		08 04
Clapham Junction d	06 57															07 25						
Wandsworth Common d	07 00																					
Balham d	07 02															07 29						
Streatham Hill d	07 05	07 12														07 32						
West Norwood d	07 09	07 15	07 23													07 38		07 53				
Gipsy Hill d	07 12	07 18	07 26													07 41		07 56				
Crystal Palace d	07 14	07 21	07a29				07a26				07 28				07 41	07 44	07 52	07a59				
Sydenham d	07 18	07 24				07 21					07 31	07 36	07 39		07 44	07 48	07 56					
Forest Hill d	07 20	07 27				07 23					07 34	07 38	07 42		07 47	07 50	07 58					
Honor Oak Park d	07 23	07 29				07 26					07 36	07 41	07 44		07 49	07 53	08 01					
Brockley d	07 25	07 32				07 28					07 39	07 43	07 47		07 52	07 55	08 03					
New Cross Gate a	07 28	07 34				07 31					07 41	07 46	07 49		07 54	07 58	08 06					
d	07 28	07 34				07 31					07 41	07 46	07 49		07 54	07 58	08 06					
New Cross ELL d										07 36				07 51								
Surrey Quays d						07 35				07 40	07 45	07 49		07 55	08 00							
Canada Water d						07 37				07 42	07 47	07 51		07 57	08 02							
Rotherhithe d						07 38				07 43	07 48	07 53		07 58	08 03							
Wapping d						07 40				07 45	07 50	07 54		08 00	08 05							
Shadwell d						07 42				07 47	07 52	07 56		08 02	08 07							
Whitechapel d						07 44				07 49	07 54	07 59		08 04	08 09							
Shoreditch High Street d						07 46				07 51	07 56	08 01		08 06	08 11							
Hoxton d						07 48				07 53	07 58	08 03		08 08	08 13							
Haggerston d						07 50				07 55	08 00	08 05		08 10	08 15							
Dalston Junction Stn ELL a						07 53				07 59	08 02	08 07		08 14	08 17							
Canonbury d						07 57					08 05	08 12			08 20							
Highbury & Islington d						08a00					08a08	08a14			08a23							
London Bridge a	07 36	07 45		07 38	07 43				07 48				07 58			08 07	08 15			08 08		08 11

	LO	SN	FC	SN	FC	LO	LO	LO	SN	LO	LO	SN	SN	LO	SN	SE	SN	SN	LO	SN	SN
East Croydon d																					
West Croydon d	07 39	07 47						07 52										08 01	08 09	08 19	
Norwood Junction d	07 43	07 52						07 58	08 02										08 13	08 25	
Anerley d	07 46							08 01	08 05										08 16		
Penge West d	07 48							08 03	08 07										08 18		
London Victoria d												07 52				08 09	08 11				
Battersea Park d																	08 15				
Wandsworth Road d																	08 17				
Clapham High Street d																	08 19				
London Blackfriars d			07 50		07 56																
Denmark Hill d			08 00		08 09											08 18	08 24				
Peckham Rye d			08a03	08 06	08a12										08 12	08a21	08 26	08 29			08 35
Queens Rd Peckham d				08 09													08 29	08 32			08 38
South Bermondsey d				08 11													08 31	08 34			08 40
Clapham Junction d												07 58									
Wandsworth Common d																					
Balham d												08 03									
Streatham Hill d												08 06	08 15								
West Norwood d												08 09	08 19		08 24						
Gipsy Hill d												08 12	08 22		08 27						
Crystal Palace d		07a56					07 58				08 11	08 15	08 24	08 28	08a29					08a29	
Sydenham d	07 51						08 01	08 06	08 09		08 14	08 18	08 28	08 31					08 21		
Forest Hill d	07 53						08 04	08 08	08 12		08 17	08 21	08 30	08 34					08 23		
Honor Oak Park d	07 56						08 06	08 11	08 14		08 19	08 23	08 33	08 36					08 26		
Brockley d	07 58						08 09	08 13	08 17		08 22	08 26	08 35	08 39					08 28		
New Cross Gate a	08 01						08 11	08 16	08 19		08 24	08 28	08 38	08 41					08 31		
d	08 01						08 11	08 16	08 19		08 24	08 28	08 38	08 41					08 31		
New Cross ELL d						08 06				08 21											
Surrey Quays d	08 05					08 10	08 15	08 19		08 25	08 30			08 45					08 35		
Canada Water d	08 07					08 12	08 17	08 21		08 27	08 32			08 47					08 37		
Rotherhithe d	08 08					08 13	08 18	08 23		08 28	08 33			08 48					08 38		
Wapping d	08 10					08 15	08 20	08 24		08 30	08 35			08 50					08 40		
Shadwell d	08 12					08 17	08 22	08 26		08 32	08 37			08 52					08 42		
Whitechapel d	08 14					08 19	08 24	08 29		08 34	08 39			08 54					08 44		
Shoreditch High Street d	08 16					08 21	08 26	08 31		08 36	08 41			08 56					08 46		
Hoxton d	08 18					08 23	08 28	08 33		08 38	08 43			08 58					08 48		
Haggerston d	08 20					08 25	08 30	08 35		08 40	08 45			09 00					08 50		
Dalston Junction Stn ELL a	08 23					08 29	08 32	08 37		08 44	08 47			09 02					08 53		
Canonbury d	08 27						08 35	08 42			08 50			09 05					08 57		
Highbury & Islington d	08a30						08a38	08a44			08a53			09a08					09a00		
London Bridge a				08 18					08 31			08 37	08 47				08 38	08 41			08 49

East London Line and Croydon - London Victoria to London Bridge

		FC 1	LO	LO	SN	LO	LO	SN	SN		LO	SN	SE	FC	SN	SN	LO	SN	FC		SN	LO	LO	SN	LO
East Croydon	d																								
West Croydon 4	d			08 22												08 31	08 39	08 49					08 53		
Norwood Junction 2	d			08 28	08 32												08 43	08 54					08 58	09 02	
Anerley	d			08 31	08 35												08 46						09 01	09 05	
Penge West	d			08 33	08 37												08 48						09 03	09 07	
London Victoria 15 ⊖	d								08 22				08 39		08 41										
Battersea Park 4	d								08 26						08 45										
Wandsworth Road	d														08 47										
Clapham High Street ⊖	d														08 49										
London Blackfriars 3 ⊖	d	08 28												08 40					08 52						
Denmark Hill 4	d	08 38											08 48	08 52	08 54				09a02						
Peckham Rye 4	d	08a41										08 42	08a51	08a55	08 56	09 01					09 06				
Queens Rd Peckham	d														08 59	09 04					09 09				
South Bermondsey	d														09 01	09 06					09 11				
Clapham Junction 10	d								08 30																
Wandsworth Common	d								08 33																
Balham 4 ⊖	d								08 35																
Streatham Hill	d							08 35	08 38																
West Norwood 4	d							08 38	08 42			08 53													
Gipsy Hill	d							08 41	08 45			08 56													
Crystal Palace 4	d						08 41	08 44	08 51		08 58	08a59						08a58							
Sydenham	d			08 36	08 39		08 44	08 47	08 54		09 01						08 51						09 06	09 09	
Forest Hill 4	d			08 38	08 42		08 47	08 50	08 57		09 04						08 53						09 08	09 12	
Honor Oak Park	d			08 41	08 44		08 49	08 52	08 59		09 06						08 56						09 11	09 14	
Brockley	d			08 43	08 47		08 52	08 55	09 02		09 09						08 58						09 13	09 17	
New Cross Gate 4	a			08 46	08 49		08 54	08 57	09 04		09 11						09 01						09 16	09 19	
	d			08 46	08 49		08 54	08 57	09 04		09 11						09 01						09 16	09 19	
New Cross ELL	d		08 36			08 51																09 06			09 21
Surrey Quays	d		08 40	08 49		08 55	09 00				09 15						09 05					09 10	09 19		09 25
Canada Water	d		08 42	08 51		08 57	09 02				09 17						09 07					09 12	09 21		09 27
Rotherhithe	d		08 43	08 53		08 58	09 03				09 18						09 08					09 13	09 23		09 28
Wapping	d		08 45	08 54		09 00	09 05				09 20						09 10					09 15	09 24		09 30
Shadwell	d		08 47	08 56		09 02	09 07				09 22						09 12					09 17	09 26		09 32
Whitechapel	d		08 49	08 59		09 04	09 09				09 24						09 14					09 19	09 29		09 34
Shoreditch High Street	d		08 51	09 01		09 06	09 11				09 26						09 16					09 21	09 31		09 36
Hoxton	d		08 53	09 03		09 08	09 13				09 28						09 18					09 23	09 33		09 38
Haggerston	d		08 55	09 05		09 10	09 15				09 30						09 20					09 25	09 35		09 40
Dalston Junction Stn ELL	a		08 59	09 07		09 14	09 17				09 32						09 23					09 29	09 37		09 44
Canonbury	d			09 12			09 20				09 35						09 27						09 42		
Highbury & Islington	d			09a14			09a23				09a38						09a30						09a44		
London Bridge 4 ⊖	a				08 58			09 06	09 14						09 08	09 14					09 19			09 29	

		LO	SN	SN	LO		SN	SE	FC	SN	SN	LO	SN	LO	LO		SN	LO	LO	SN	LO	SN	SN	SE	FC
East Croydon	d												09 20				09 30								
West Croydon 4	d										09 01	09 09			09 22										
Norwood Junction 2	d											09 13	09 25		09 28		09 35								
Anerley	d											09 16			09 31		09 38								
Penge West	d											09 18			09 33		09 40								
London Victoria 15 ⊖	d		08 49					09 09		09 11										09 19				09 39	
Battersea Park 4	d		08 53							09 15										09 23					
Wandsworth Road	d									09 17															
Clapham High Street ⊖	d									09 19															
London Blackfriars 3 ⊖	d								09 12																09 42
Denmark Hill 4	d							09 18	09 22	09 24														09 48	09 52
Peckham Rye 4	d						09 12	09a21	09a25	09 26	09 32											09 42	09 46	09a51	09a55
Queens Rd Peckham	d									09 29	09 35												09 49		
South Bermondsey	d									09 31	09 37												09 51		
Clapham Junction 10	d		08 57																	09 27					
Wandsworth Common	d		09 00																	09 30					
Balham 4 ⊖	d		09 02																	09 32					
Streatham Hill	d		09 05																	09 35					
West Norwood 4	d		09 09				09 23													09 40		09 53			
Gipsy Hill	d		09 12				09 26													09 43		09 56			
Crystal Palace 4	d	09 11	09 14	09 21	09 28		09a29												09 43	09 51	09 58	09a59			
Sydenham	d	09 14	09 18	09 24	09 31							09 21			09 36		09 42		09 46	09 54	10 01				
Forest Hill 4	d	09 17	09 20	09 27	09 34							09 23			09 38		09 45		09 49	09 57	10 04				
Honor Oak Park	d	09 19	09 23	09 29	09 36							09 26			09 41		09 47		09 51	09 59	10 06				
Brockley	d	09 22	09 25	09 32	09 39							09 28			09 43		09 50		09 54	10 02	10 09				
New Cross Gate 4	a	09 24	09 28	09 34	09 41							09 31	09 32		09 46		09 52		09 56	10 04	10 11				
	d	09 24	09 28	09 34	09 41							09 31	09 33		09 46		09 52		09 56	10 04	10 11				
New Cross ELL	d													09 36				09 51							
Surrey Quays	d	09 30			09 45							09 35		09 40	09 49			09 55	10 00		10 15				
Canada Water	d	09 32			09 47							09 37		09 42	09 51			09 57	10 02		10 17				
Rotherhithe	d	09 33			09 48							09 38		09 43	09 53			09 58	10 03		10 18				
Wapping	d	09 35			09 50							09 40		09 45	09 54			10 00	10 05		10 20				
Shadwell	d	09 37			09 52							09 42		09 47	09 56			10 02	10 07		10 22				
Whitechapel	d	09 39			09 54							09 44		09 49	09 59			10 04	10 09		10 24				
Shoreditch High Street	d	09 41			09 56							09 46		09 51	10 01			10 06	10 11		10 26				
Hoxton	d	09 43			09 58							09 48		09 53	10 03			10 08	10 13		10 28				
Haggerston	d	09 45			10 00							09 50		09 55	10 05			10 10	10 15		10 30				
Dalston Junction Stn ELL	a	09 47			10 02							09 53		09 59	10 07			10 14	10 17		10 32				
Canonbury	d	09 50			10 05							09 57			10 12				10 20		10 35				
Highbury & Islington	d	09a53			10a08							10a00			10a14				10a23		10a38				
London Bridge 4 ⊖	a		09 37	09 44						09 38	09 44		09 42				09 59			10 11			09 58		

East London Line and Croydon - London Victoria to London Bridge

			SN	SN	LO	LO	LO	SN	LO	LO	SN		LO	SN	SN	SE	FC	SN	SN	LO	LO		LO	SN	LO
East Croydon	d							10 00																10 30	
West Croydon 4	d			09 31	09 39		09 52												10 01	10 09			10 22		
Norwood Junction 2	d				09 43		09 58	10 05												10 13			10 28	10 35	
Anerley	d				09 46		10 01	10 08												10 16			10 31	10 38	
Penge West	d				09 48		10 03	10 10												10 18			10 33	10 40	
London Victoria 15 ⊖	d		09 41								09 49					10 09		10 11							
Battersea Park 4	d		09 45								09 53							10 15							
Wandsworth Road	d		09 47															10 17							
Clapham High Street ⊖	d		09 49															10 19							
London Blackfriars 3 ⊖	d																10 12								
Denmark Hill 4	d		09 54													10 18	10 22	10 24							
Peckham Rye 4	d		09 56	10 01										10 12	10 16	10a21	10a25	10 26	10 31						
Queens Rd Peckham	d		09 59	10 04											10 19			10 29	10 34						
South Bermondsey	d		10 01	10 06											10 21			10 31	10 36						
Clapham Junction 10	d										09 57														
Wandsworth Common	d										10 00														
Balham 4 ⊖	d										10 02														
Streatham Hill	d										10 05														
West Norwood 4	d										10 10			10 23											
Gipsy Hill	d										10 13			10 26											
Crystal Palace 4	d									10 13	10 21		10 28	10a29											
Sydenham	d				09 51		10 06	10 12		10 16	10 24		10 31							10 21			10 36	10 42	
Forest Hill 4	d				09 53		10 08	10 15		10 19	10 27		10 34							10 23			10 38	10 45	
Honor Oak Park	d				09 56		10 11	10 17		10 21	10 29		10 36							10 26			10 41	10 47	
Brockley	d				09 58		10 13	10 20		10 24	10 32		10 39							10 28			10 43	10 50	
New Cross Gate 4	a				10 01		10 16	10 22		10 26	10 34		10 41							10 31			10 46	10 52	
	d				10 01		10 16	10 22		10 26	10 34		10 41							10 31			10 46	10 52	
New Cross ELL	d					10 06			10 21												10 36				10 51
Surrey Quays	d				10 05	10 10	10 19		10 25	10 30			10 45							10 35	10 40		10 49		10 55
Canada Water	d				10 07	10 12	10 21		10 27	10 32			10 47							10 37	10 42		10 51		10 57
Rotherhithe	d				10 08	10 13	10 23		10 28	10 33			10 48							10 38	10 43		10 53		10 58
Wapping	d				10 10	10 15	10 24		10 30	10 35			10 50							10 40	10 45		10 54		11 00
Shadwell	d				10 12	10 17	10 26		10 32	10 37			10 52							10 42	10 47		10 56		11 02
Whitechapel	d				10 14	10 19	10 29		10 34	10 39			10 54							10 44	10 49		10 59		11 04
Shoreditch High Street	d				10 16	10 21	10 31		10 36	10 41			10 56							10 46	10 51		11 01		11 06
Hoxton	d				10 18	10 23	10 33		10 38	10 43			10 58							10 48	10 53		11 03		11 08
Haggerston	d				10 20	10 25	10 35		10 40	10 45			11 00							10 50	10 55		11 05		11 10
Dalston Junction Stn ELL	a				10 22	10 29	10 37		10 44	10 47			11 02							10 52	10 59		11 07		11 14
Canonbury	d				10 27		10 42			10 50			11 05							10 57			11 12		
Highbury & Islington	d				10a30		10a44			10a53			11a08							11a00			11a14		
London Bridge 4 ⊖	a		10 06	10 11				10 29			10 41				10 26			10 36	10 41					10 59	

		LO	SN	LO	SN	SN	SE		FC	SN	SN	LO	LO	LO	SN	LO	LO		SN	LO	SN	SN	SE	FC	SN
East Croydon	d														11 00										
West Croydon 4	d										10 31	10 39		10 52											
Norwood Junction 2	d											10 43		10 58	11 05										
Anerley	d											10 46		11 01	11 08										
Penge West	d											10 48		11 03	11 10										
London Victoria 15 ⊖	d		10 19				10 39			10 41									10 49				11 09		11 11
Battersea Park 4	d		10 23							10 45									10 53						11 15
Wandsworth Road	d									10 47															11 17
Clapham High Street ⊖	d									10 49															11 19
London Blackfriars 3 ⊖	d								10 42															11 12	
Denmark Hill 4	d						10 48		10 52	10 54													11 18	11 22	11 24
Peckham Rye 4	d				10 42	10 46	10a51		10a55	10 56	11 01										11 12	11 16	11a21	11a25	11 26
Queens Rd Peckham	d					10 49				10 59	11 04											11 19			11 29
South Bermondsey	d					10 51				11 01	11 06											11 21			11 31
Clapham Junction 10	d		10 27																10 57						
Wandsworth Common	d		10 30																11 00						
Balham 4 ⊖	d		10 32																11 02						
Streatham Hill	d		10 35																11 05						
West Norwood 4	d		10 40		10 53														11 10		11 23				
Gipsy Hill	d		10 43		10 56														11 13		11 26				
Crystal Palace 4	d	10 43	10 51	10 58	10a59												11 13		11 21	11 28	11a29				
Sydenham	d	10 46	10 54	11 01								10 51		11 06	11 12		11 16		11 24	11 31					
Forest Hill 4	d	10 49	10 57	11 04								10 53		11 08	11 15		11 19		11 27	11 34					
Honor Oak Park	d	10 51	10 59	11 06								10 56		11 11	11 17		11 21		11 29	11 36					
Brockley	d	10 54	11 02	11 09								10 58		11 13	11 20		11 24		11 32	11 39					
New Cross Gate 4	a	10 56	11 04	11 11								11 01		11 16	11 22		11 26		11 34	11 41					
	d	10 56	11 04	11 11								11 01		11 16	11 22		11 26		11 34	11 41					
New Cross ELL	d												11 06			11 21									
Surrey Quays	d	11 00		11 15								11 05	11 10	11 19		11 25	11 30			11 45					
Canada Water	d	11 02		11 17								11 07	11 12	11 21		11 27	11 32			11 47					
Rotherhithe	d	11 03		11 18								11 08	11 13	11 23		11 28	11 33			11 48					
Wapping	d	11 05		11 20								11 10	11 15	11 24		11 30	11 35			11 50					
Shadwell	d	11 07		11 22								11 12	11 17	11 26		11 32	11 37			11 52					
Whitechapel	d	11 09		11 24								11 14	11 19	11 29		11 34	11 39			11 54					
Shoreditch High Street	d	11 11		11 26								11 16	11 21	11 31		11 36	11 41			11 56					
Hoxton	d	11 13		11 28								11 18	11 23	11 33		11 38	11 43			11 58					
Haggerston	d	11 15		11 30								11 20	11 25	11 35		11 40	11 45			12 00					
Dalston Junction Stn ELL	a	11 17		11 32								11 22	11 29	11 37		11 44	11 47			12 02					
Canonbury	d	11 20		11 35								11 27		11 42			11 50			12 05					
Highbury & Islington	d	11a23		11a38								11a30		11a44			11a53			12a08					
London Bridge 4 ⊖	a		11 11			10 56				11 06	11 11				11 29				11 41			11 26			11 36

East London Line and Croydon - London Victoria to London Bridge

		SN	LO		LO	LO	SN	LO	LO	SN	LO	SN	SN		SE	FC	SN	SN	LO	LO	LO	SN	LO		LO
East Croydon	d						11 30															12 00			
West Croydon	d	11 01	11 09			11 22												11 31	11 39		11 52				
Norwood Junction	d		11 13			11 28	11 35												11 43		11 58	12 05			
Anerley	d		11 16			11 31	11 38												11 46		12 01	12 08			
Penge West	d		11 18			11 33	11 40												11 48		12 03	12 10			
London Victoria ⊖	d									11 19					11 39		11 41								
Battersea Park	d									11 23							11 45								
Wandsworth Road	d																11 47								
Clapham High Street ⊖	d																11 49								
London Blackfriars ⊖	d															11 42									
Denmark Hill	d														11 48	11 52	11 54								
Peckham Rye	d	11 31										11 42	11 46		11a51	11a55	11 56	12 01							
Queens Rd Peckham	d	11 34											11 49				11 59	12 04							
South Bermondsey	d	11 36											11 51				12 01	12 06							
Clapham Junction	d									11 27															
Wandsworth Common	d									11 30															
Balham ⊖	d									11 32															
Streatham Hill	d									11 35															
West Norwood	d									11 40		11 53													
Gipsy Hill	d									11 43		11 56													
Crystal Palace	d								11 43	11 51	11 58	11a59													12 13
Sydenham	d		11 21			11 36	11 42		11 46	11 54	12 01								11 51		12 06	12 12			12 16
Forest Hill	d		11 23			11 38	11 45		11 49	11 57	12 04								11 53		12 08	12 15			12 19
Honor Oak Park	d		11 26			11 41	11 47		11 51	11 59	12 06								11 56		12 11	12 17			12 21
Brockley	d		11 28			11 43	11 50		11 54	12 02	12 09								11 58		12 13	12 20			12 24
New Cross Gate	a		11 31			11 46	11 52		11 56	12 04	12 11								12 01		12 16	12 22			12 26
	d		11 31			11 46	11 52		11 56	12 04	12 11								12 01		12 16	12 22			12 26
New Cross ELL	d				11 36			11 51												12 06			12 21		
Surrey Quays	d		11 35		11 40	11 49		11 55	12 00		12 15								12 05	12 10	12 19		12 25		12 30
Canada Water	d		11 37		11 42	11 51		11 57	12 02		12 17								12 07	12 12	12 21		12 27		12 32
Rotherhithe	d		11 38		11 43	11 53		11 58	12 03		12 18								12 08	12 13	12 23		12 28		12 33
Wapping	d		11 40		11 45	11 54		12 00	12 05		12 20								12 10	12 15	12 24		12 30		12 35
Shadwell	d		11 42		11 47	11 56		12 02	12 07		12 22								12 12	12 17	12 26		12 32		12 37
Whitechapel	d		11 44		11 49	11 59		12 04	12 09		12 24								12 14	12 19	12 29		12 34		12 39
Shoreditch High Street	d		11 46		11 51	12 01		12 06	12 11		12 26								12 16	12 21	12 31		12 36		12 41
Hoxton	d		11 48		11 53	12 03		12 08	12 13		12 28								12 18	12 23	12 33		12 38		12 43
Haggerston	d		11 50		11 55	12 05		12 10	12 15		12 30								12 20	12 25	12 35		12 40		12 45
Dalston Junction Stn ELL	a		11 52		11 59	12 07		12 14	12 17		12 32								12 22	12 29	12 37		12 44		12 47
Canonbury	d		11 57			12 12			12 20		12 35								12 27		12 42				12 50
Highbury & Islington	d		12a00			12a14			12a23		12a38								12a30		12a44				12a53
London Bridge ⊖	a	11 41					11 59			12 11			11 56				12 06	12 11				12 29			

		SN	LO	SN	SN	SE	FC	SN	SN		LO	LO	LO	SN	LO	LO	SN	LO	SN		SN	SE	FC	SN	SN
East Croydon	d													12 30											
West Croydon	d								12 01		12 09		12 22												12 31
Norwood Junction	d										12 13		12 28	12 35											
Anerley	d										12 16		12 31	12 38											
Penge West	d										12 18		12 33	12 40											
London Victoria ⊖	d	11 49				12 09		12 11									12 19					12 39		12 41	
Battersea Park	d	11 53						12 15									12 23							12 45	
Wandsworth Road	d							12 17																12 47	
Clapham High Street ⊖	d							12 19																12 49	
London Blackfriars ⊖	d						12 12																12 42		
Denmark Hill	d					12 18	12 22	12 24														12 48	12 52	12 54	
Peckham Rye	d			12 12	12 16	12a21	12a25	12 26	12 31										12 42		12 46	12a51	12a55	12 56	13 01
Queens Rd Peckham	d				12 19			12 29	12 34												12 49			12 59	13 04
South Bermondsey	d				12 21			12 31	12 36												12 51			13 01	13 06
Clapham Junction	d	11 57															12 27								
Wandsworth Common	d	12 00															12 30								
Balham ⊖	d	12 02															12 32								
Streatham Hill	d	12 05															12 35								
West Norwood	d	12 10		12 23													12 40		12 53						
Gipsy Hill	d	12 13		12 26													12 43		12 56						
Crystal Palace	d	12 21	12 28	12a29												12 43	12 51	12 58	12a59						
Sydenham	d	12 24	12 31								12 21		12 36	12 42		12 46	12 54	13 01							
Forest Hill	d	12 27	12 34								12 23		12 38	12 45		12 49	12 57	13 04							
Honor Oak Park	d	12 29	12 36								12 26		12 41	12 47		12 51	12 59	13 06							
Brockley	d	12 32	12 39								12 28		12 43	12 50		12 54	13 02	13 09							
New Cross Gate	a	12 34	12 41								12 31		12 46	12 52		12 56	13 04	13 11							
	d	12 34	12 41								12 31		12 46	12 52		12 56	13 04	13 11							
New Cross ELL	d											12 36			12 51										
Surrey Quays	d		12 45								12 35	12 40	12 49		12 55	13 00		13 15							
Canada Water	d		12 47								12 37	12 42	12 51		12 57	13 02		13 17							
Rotherhithe	d		12 48								12 38	12 43	12 53		12 58	13 03		13 18							
Wapping	d		12 50								12 40	12 45	12 54		13 00	13 05		13 20							
Shadwell	d		12 52								12 42	12 47	12 56		13 02	13 07		13 22							
Whitechapel	d		12 54								12 44	12 49	12 59		13 04	13 09		13 24							
Shoreditch High Street	d		12 56								12 46	12 51	13 01		13 06	13 11		13 26							
Hoxton	d		12 58								12 48	12 53	13 03		13 08	13 13		13 28							
Haggerston	d		13 00								12 50	12 55	13 05		13 10	13 15		13 30							
Dalston Junction Stn ELL	a		13 02								12 52	12 59	13 07		13 14	13 17		13 32							
Canonbury	d		13 05								12 57		13 12			13 20		13 35							
Highbury & Islington	d		13a08								13a00		13a14			13a23		13a38							
London Bridge ⊖	a	12 41			12 26			12 36	12 41					12 59			13 11				12 56			13 06	13 11

East London Line and Croydon - London Victoria to London Bridge

		LO	LO	LO	SN		LO	LO	SN	LO	SN	SN	SE	FC	SN		SN	LO	LO	LO	SN	LO	LO	SN	LO
East Croydon	d				13 00																13 30				
West Croydon	d	12 39		12 52													13 01	13 09		13 22					
Norwood Junction	d	12 43		12 58	13 05													13 13		13 28	13 35				
Anerley	d	12 46		13 01	13 08													13 16		13 31	13 38				
Penge West	d	12 48		13 03	13 10													13 18		13 33	13 40				
London Victoria ⊖	d								12 49				13 09		13 11									13 19	
Battersea Park	d								12 53						13 15									13 23	
Wandsworth Road	d														13 17										
Clapham High Street ⊖	d														13 19										
London Blackfriars ⊖	d													13 12											
Denmark Hill	d												13 18	13 22	13 24										
Peckham Rye	d										13 12	13 16	13a21	13a25	13 26		13 31								
Queens Rd Peckham	d											13 19			13 29		13 34								
South Bermondsey	d											13 21			13 31		13 36								
Clapham Junction	d								12 57															13 27	
Wandsworth Common	d								13 00															13 30	
Balham ⊖	d								13 02															13 32	
Streatham Hill	d								13 05															13 35	
West Norwood	d								13 10		13 23													13 40	
Gipsy Hill	d								13 13		13 26													13 43	
Crystal Palace	d							13 13	13 21	13 28	13a29												13 43	13 51	13 58
Sydenham	d	12 51		13 06	13 12			13 16	13 24	13 31								13 21		13 36	13 42		13 46	13 54	14 01
Forest Hill	d	12 53		13 08	13 15			13 19	13 27	13 34								13 23		13 38	13 45		13 49	13 57	14 04
Honor Oak Park	d	12 56		13 11	13 17			13 21	13 29	13 36								13 26		13 41	13 47		13 51	13 59	14 06
Brockley	d	12 58		13 13	13 20			13 24	13 32	13 39								13 28		13 43	13 50		13 54	14 02	14 09
New Cross Gate	a	13 01		13 16	13 22			13 26	13 34	13 41								13 31		13 46	13 52		13 56	14 04	14 11
	d	13 01		13 16	13 22			13 26	13 34	13 41								13 31		13 46	13 52		13 56	14 04	14 11
New Cross ELL	d		13 06				13 21												13 36			13 51			
Surrey Quays	d	13 05	13 10	13 19			13 25	13 30		13 45								13 35	13 40	13 49		13 55	14 00		14 15
Canada Water	d	13 07	13 12	13 21			13 27	13 32		13 47								13 37	13 42	13 51		13 57	14 02		14 17
Rotherhithe	d	13 08	13 13	13 23			13 28	13 33		13 48								13 38	13 43	13 53		13 58	14 03		14 18
Wapping	d	13 10	13 15	13 24			13 30	13 35		13 50								13 40	13 45	13 54		14 00	14 05		14 20
Shadwell	d	13 12	13 17	13 26			13 32	13 37		13 52								13 42	13 47	13 56		14 02	14 07		14 22
Whitechapel	d	13 14	13 19	13 29			13 34	13 39		13 54								13 44	13 49	13 59		14 04	14 09		14 24
Shoreditch High Street	d	13 16	13 21	13 31			13 36	13 41		13 56								13 46	13 51	14 01		14 06	14 11		14 26
Hoxton	d	13 18	13 23	13 33			13 38	13 43		13 58								13 48	13 53	14 03		14 08	14 13		14 28
Haggerston	d	13 20	13 25	13 35			13 40	13 45		14 00								13 50	13 55	14 05		14 10	14 15		14 30
Dalston Junction Stn ELL	a	13 22	13 29	13 37			13 44	13 47		14 02								13 52	13 59	14 07		14 14	14 17		14 32
Canonbury	d	13 27		13 42				13 50		14 05								13 57		14 12			14 20		14 35
Highbury & Islington	d	13a30		13a44				13a53		14a08								14a00		14a14			14a23		14a38
London Bridge ⊖	a				13 29				13 41			13 26			13 36		13 41				13 59			14 11	

			SN	SN	SE	FC	SN	SN	LO	LO	LO		SN	LO	LO	SN	LO	SN	SN	SE	FC		SN	SN	LO
East Croydon	d												14 00												
West Croydon	d							13 31	13 39		13 52													14 01	14 09
Norwood Junction	d								13 43		13 58		14 05												14 13
Anerley	d								13 46		14 01		14 08												14 16
Penge West	d								13 48		14 03		14 10												14 18
London Victoria ⊖	d				13 39		13 41									13 49				14 09			14 11		
Battersea Park	d						13 45									13 53							14 15		
Wandsworth Road	d						13 47																14 17		
Clapham High Street ⊖	d						13 49																14 19		
London Blackfriars ⊖	d					13 42															14 12				
Denmark Hill	d				13 48	13 52	13 54													14 18	14 22		14 24		
Peckham Rye	d		13 42	13 46	13a51	13a55	13 56	14 01										14 12	14 16	14a21	14a25		14 26	14 31	
Queens Rd Peckham	d			13 49			13 59	14 04											14 19				14 29	14 34	
South Bermondsey	d			13 51			14 01	14 06											14 21				14 31	14 36	
Clapham Junction	d															13 57									
Wandsworth Common	d															14 00									
Balham ⊖	d															14 02									
Streatham Hill	d															14 05									
West Norwood	d		13 53													14 10		14 23							
Gipsy Hill	d		13 56													14 13		14 26							
Crystal Palace	d		13a59												14 13	14 21	14 28	14a29							
Sydenham	d								13 51		14 06		14 12		14 16	14 24	14 31								14 21
Forest Hill	d								13 53		14 08		14 15		14 19	14 27	14 34								14 23
Honor Oak Park	d								13 56		14 11		14 17		14 21	14 29	14 36								14 26
Brockley	d								13 58		14 13		14 20		14 24	14 32	14 39								14 28
New Cross Gate	a								14 01		14 16		14 22		14 26	14 34	14 41								14 31
	d								14 01		14 16		14 22		14 26	14 34	14 41								14 31
New Cross ELL	d									14 06				14 21											
Surrey Quays	d								14 05	14 10	14 19			14 25	14 30		14 45								14 35
Canada Water	d								14 07	14 12	14 21			14 27	14 32		14 47								14 37
Rotherhithe	d								14 08	14 13	14 23			14 28	14 33		14 48								14 38
Wapping	d								14 10	14 15	14 24			14 30	14 35		14 50								14 40
Shadwell	d								14 12	14 17	14 26			14 32	14 37		14 52								14 42
Whitechapel	d								14 14	14 19	14 29			14 34	14 39		14 54								14 44
Shoreditch High Street	d								14 16	14 21	14 31			14 36	14 41		14 56								14 46
Hoxton	d								14 18	14 23	14 33			14 38	14 43		14 58								14 48
Haggerston	d								14 20	14 25	14 35			14 40	14 45		15 00								14 50
Dalston Junction Stn ELL	a								14 22	14 29	14 37			14 44	14 47		15 02								14 52
Canonbury	d								14 27		14 42				14 50		15 05								14 57
Highbury & Islington	d								14a30		14a44				14a53		15a08								15a00
London Bridge ⊖	a			13 56			14 06	14 11					14 29			14 41			14 26				14 36	14 41	

East London Line and Croydon - London Victoria to London Bridge

Station		LO	LO	SN	LO	LO	SN		LO	SN	SN	SE	FC	SN	SN	LO	LO		LO	SN	LO	LO	SN	LO	SN
East Croydon	d			14 30																15 00					
West Croydon 4	d		14 22												14 31	14 39			14 52						
Norwood Junction 2	d		14 28	14 35												14 43			14 58	15 05					
Anerley	d		14 31	14 38												14 46			15 01	15 08					
Penge West	d		14 33	14 40												14 48			15 03	15 10					
London Victoria 15	d					14 19					14 39		14 41									14 49		
Battersea Park 4	d					14 23							14 45									14 53		
Wandsworth Road	d												14 47											
Clapham High Street	d												14 49											
London Blackfriars 3	d											14 42												
Denmark Hill 4	d										14 48	14 52	14 54											
Peckham Rye 4	d								14 42	14 46	14a51	14a55	14 56	15 01										15 12
Queens Rd Peckham	d									14 49			14 59	15 04										
South Bermondsey	d									14 51			15 01	15 06										
Clapham Junction 10	d					14 27																14 57		
Wandsworth Common	d					14 30																15 00		
Balham 4	d					14 32																15 02		
Streatham Hill	d					14 35																15 05		
West Norwood 4	d					14 40			14 53													15 10		15 23
Gipsy Hill	d					14 43			14 56													15 13		15 26
Crystal Palace 4	d				14 43	14 51		14 58	14a59												15 13	15 21	15 28	15a29
Sydenham	d		14 36	14 42		14 46	14 54		15 01							14 51			15 06	15 12		15 16	15 24	15 31	
Forest Hill 4	d		14 38	14 45		14 49	14 57		15 04							14 53			15 08	15 15		15 19	15 27	15 34	
Honor Oak Park	d		14 41	14 47		14 51	14 59		15 06							14 56			15 11	15 17		15 21	15 29	15 36	
Brockley	d		14 43	14 50		14 54	15 02		15 09							14 58			15 13	15 20		15 24	15 32	15 39	
New Cross Gate 4	a		14 46	14 52		14 56	15 04		15 11							15 01			15 16	15 22		15 26	15 34	15 41	
	d		14 46	14 52		14 56	15 04		15 11							15 01			15 16	15 22		15 26	15 34	15 41	
New Cross ELL	d	14 36			14 51												15 06				15 21				
Surrey Quays	d	14 40	14 49		14 55	15 00			15 15							15 05	15 10		15 19		15 25	15 30		15 45	
Canada Water	d	14 42	14 51		14 57	15 02			15 17							15 07	15 12		15 21		15 27	15 32		15 47	
Rotherhithe	d	14 43	14 53		14 58	15 03			15 18							15 08	15 13		15 23		15 28	15 33		15 48	
Wapping	d	14 45	14 54		15 00	15 05			15 20							15 10	15 15		15 24		15 30	15 35		15 50	
Shadwell	d	14 47	14 56		15 02	15 07			15 22							15 12	15 17		15 26		15 32	15 37		15 52	
Whitechapel	d	14 49	14 59		15 04	15 09			15 24							15 14	15 19		15 29		15 34	15 39		15 54	
Shoreditch High Street	d	14 51	15 01		15 06	15 11			15 26							15 16	15 21		15 31		15 36	15 41		15 56	
Hoxton	d	14 53	15 03		15 08	15 13			15 28							15 18	15 23		15 33		15 38	15 43		15 58	
Haggerston	d	14 55	15 05		15 10	15 15			15 30							15 20	15 25		15 35		15 40	15 45		16 00	
Dalston Junction Stn ELL	a	14 59	15 07		15 14	15 17			15 32							15 22	15 29		15 37		15 44	15 47		16 02	
Canonbury	d		15 12			15 20			15 35							15 27			15 42			15 50		16 05	
Highbury & Islington	d		15a14			15a23			15a38							15a30			15a44			15a53		16a08	
London Bridge 4	a			14 59			15 11				14 56			15 06	15 11					15 29			15 41		

Station		SN	SE		FC	SN	SN	LO	LO	LO	SN	LO	LO		SN	LO	SN	SN	SE	FC	SN	SN	LO		LO
East Croydon	d									15 30														
West Croydon 4	d					15 01	15 09		15 22												15 31	15 39		
Norwood Junction 2	d						15 13		15 28	15 35												15 43		
Anerley	d						15 16		15 31	15 38												15 46		
Penge West	d						15 18		15 33	15 40												15 48		
London Victoria 15	d		15 09			15 11									15 19				15 39		15 41				
Battersea Park 4	d				15 15									15 23						15 45				
Wandsworth Road	d				15 17															15 47				
Clapham High Street	d				15 19															15 49				
London Blackfriars 3	d			15 12															15 42					
Denmark Hill 4	d		15 18		15 22	15 24													15 48	15 52	15 54				
Peckham Rye 4	d	15 17	15a21		15a25	15 26	15 31										15 42	15 46	15a51	15a55	15 56	16 01			
Queens Rd Peckham	d	15 20				15 29	15 34											15 49			15 59	16 04			
South Bermondsey	d	15 22				15 31	15 36											15 51			16 01	16 06			
Clapham Junction 10	d													15 27										
Wandsworth Common	d													15 30										
Balham 4	d													15 32										
Streatham Hill	d													15 35										
West Norwood 4	d													15 40		15 53								
Gipsy Hill	d													15 43		15 56								
Crystal Palace 4	d											15 43		15 51	15 58	15a59								
Sydenham	d						15 21		15 36	15 42		15 46		15 54	16 01							15 51		
Forest Hill 4	d						15 23		15 38	15 45		15 49		15 57	16 04							15 53		
Honor Oak Park	d						15 26		15 41	15 47		15 51		15 59	16 06							15 56		
Brockley	d						15 28		15 43	15 50		15 54		16 02	16 09							15 58		
New Cross Gate 4	a						15 31		15 46	15 52		15 56		16 04	16 11							16 01		
	d						15 31		15 46	15 52		15 56		16 04	16 11							16 01		
New Cross ELL	d							15 36			15 51													16 06
Surrey Quays	d						15 35	15 40	15 49		15 55	16 00			16 15							16 05		16 10
Canada Water	d						15 37	15 42	15 51		15 57	16 02			16 17							16 07		16 12
Rotherhithe	d						15 38	15 43	15 53		15 58	16 03			16 18							16 08		16 13
Wapping	d						15 40	15 45	15 54		16 00	16 05			16 20							16 10		16 15
Shadwell	d						15 42	15 47	15 56		16 02	16 07			16 22							16 12		16 17
Whitechapel	d						15 44	15 49	15 59		16 04	16 09			16 24							16 14		16 19
Shoreditch High Street	d						15 46	15 51	16 01		16 06	16 11			16 26							16 16		16 21
Hoxton	d						15 48	15 53	16 03		16 08	16 13			16 28							16 18		16 23
Haggerston	d						15 50	15 55	16 05		16 10	16 15			16 30							16 20		16 25
Dalston Junction Stn ELL	a						15 52	15 59	16 07		16 14	16 17			16 32							16 22		16 29
Canonbury	d						15 57		16 12			16 20			16 35							16 27		
Highbury & Islington	d						16a00		16a14			16a23			16a38							16a30		
London Bridge 4	a	15 27				15 36	15 41				15 59				16 11			15 56			16 06	16 11			

East London Line and Croydon - London Victoria to London Bridge

Station		LO	SN	SN	LO	LO	SN	LO	SN		SN	SE	FC	SN	SN	LO	FC	LO	LO		SN	LO	LO	SN	LO
East Croydon	d			16 00																	16 30				
West Croydon 4	d	15 52													16 01	16 09			16 22						
Norwood Junction 2	d	15 58		16 05												16 13			16 28		16 35				
Anerley	d	16 01		16 08												16 16			16 31		16 38				
Penge West	d	16 03		16 10												16 18			16 33		16 40				
London Victoria 15	d					15 49					16 09		16 11										16 19	
Battersea Park 4	d					15 53							16 15										16 23	
Wandsworth Road	d												16 17											
Clapham High Street	d												16 19											
London Blackfriars 3	d											16 12				16 26								
Denmark Hill 4	d										16 18	16 22	16 24			16 39								
Peckham Rye 4	d		16 07						16 12		16 16	16a21	16a25	16 26	16 31		16a42								
Queens Rd Peckham	d		16 10								16 19			16 29	16 34										
South Bermondsey	d		16 12								16 21			16 31	16 36										
Clapham Junction 10	d					15 57																	16 27	
Wandsworth Common	d					16 00																	16 30	
Balham 4	d					16 02																	16 32	
Streatham Hill	d					16 05																	16 35	
West Norwood 4	d					16 10		16 23															16 39	
Gipsy Hill	d					16 13		16 26															16 44	
Crystal Palace 4	d				16 13	16 21	16 28	16a29														16 43	16 50	16 58
Sydenham	d	16 06		16 12		16 16	16 24	16 31								16 21			16 36		16 42		16 46	16 54	17 01
Forest Hill 4	d	16 08		16 15		16 19	16 27	16 34								16 23			16 38		16 45		16 49	16 56	17 04
Honor Oak Park	d	16 11		16 17		16 21	16 29	16 36								16 26			16 41		16 47		16 51	16 59	17 06
Brockley	d	16 13		16 20		16 24	16 32	16 39								16 28			16 43		16 50		16 54	17 01	17 09
New Cross Gate 4	a	16 16		16 22		16 26	16 34	16 41								16 31			16 46		16 52		16 56	17 04	17 11
	d	16 16		16 22		16 26	16 34	16 41								16 31			16 46		16 52		16 56	17 04	17 11
New Cross ELL	d			16 21													16 36				16 51			
Surrey Quays	d	16 19			16 25	16 30		16 45								16 35		16 40	16 49			16 55	17 00		17 15
Canada Water	d	16 21			16 27	16 32		16 47								16 37		16 42	16 51			16 57	17 02		17 17
Rotherhithe	d	16 23			16 28	16 33		16 48								16 38		16 43	16 53			16 58	17 03		17 18
Wapping	d	16 24			16 30	16 35		16 50								16 40		16 45	16 54			17 00	17 05		17 20
Shadwell	d	16 26			16 32	16 37		16 52								16 42		16 47	16 56			17 02	17 07		17 22
Whitechapel	d	16 29			16 34	16 39		16 54								16 44		16 49	16 59			17 04	17 09		17 24
Shoreditch High Street	d	16 31			16 36	16 41		16 56								16 46		16 51	17 01			17 06	17 11		17 26
Hoxton	d	16 33			16 38	16 43		16 58								16 48		16 53	17 03			17 08	17 13		17 28
Haggerston	d	16 35			16 40	16 45		17 00								16 50		16 55	17 05			17 10	17 15		17 30
Dalston Junction Stn ELL	a	16 37			16 44	16 47		17 02								16 52		16 59	17 07			17 14	17 17		17 32
Canonbury	d	16 42				16 50		17 05								16 57			17 12				17 20		17 35
Highbury & Islington	d	16a44				16a53		17a08								17a00			17a14				17a23		17a38
London Bridge 4	a		16 17	16 29			16 41				16 26			16 38	16 41						17 02			17 12	

Station		SN	SN	SE	FC		SN	SN	LO	LO	LO	SN	LO	LO	SN		SN	SN	SE	FC	SN	SN	LO	SN	SN
East Croydon	d										17 00													
West Croydon 4	d						16 31	16 39		16 52											17 01	17 09	17 12	
Norwood Junction 2	d							16 43		16 58	17 05											17 13		
Anerley	d							16 46		17 01	17 08											17 16		
Penge West	d							16 48		17 03	17 10											17 18		
London Victoria 15	d			16 39			16 41								16 52				17 04		17 11				
Battersea Park 4	d					16 45								16 56						17 15				
Wandsworth Road	d					16 47														17 17				
Clapham High Street	d					16 49														17 19				
London Blackfriars 3	d			16 42															17 10					
Denmark Hill 4	d			16 48	16 52		16 54												17 13	17 20	17 24				
Peckham Rye 4	d	16 42	16 46	16a51	16a55		16 56	17 00									17 07	17 16	17a16	17a23	17 26	17 29			17 34
Queens Rd Peckham	d		16 49				16 59	17 03										17 19			17 29	17 32			17 37
South Bermondsey	d		16 51				17 01	17 05										17 21			17 31	17 34			17 39
Clapham Junction 10	d													17 00										
Wandsworth Common	d													17 03										
Balham 4	d													17 06										
Streatham Hill	d													17 09										
West Norwood 4	d	16 53													17 12		17 20								
Gipsy Hill	d	16 56													17 15		17 23								
Crystal Palace 4	d	16a59												17 13	17 21		17a26								
Sydenham	d							16 51		17 06	17 12		17 16	17 24								17 21		
Forest Hill 4	d							16 53		17 08	17 15		17 19	17 27								17 23		
Honor Oak Park	d							16 56		17 11	17 17		17 21	17 29								17 26		
Brockley	d							16 58		17 13	17 20		17 24	17 32								17 28		
New Cross Gate 4	a							17 01		17 16	17 22		17 26	17 34								17 31		
	d							17 01		17 16	17 22		17 26	17 34								17 31		
New Cross ELL	d								17 06			17 21												
Surrey Quays	d							17 05	17 10	17 19		17 25	17 30									17 35		
Canada Water	d							17 07	17 12	17 21		17 27	17 32									17 37		
Rotherhithe	d							17 08	17 13	17 23		17 28	17 33									17 38		
Wapping	d							17 10	17 15	17 24		17 30	17 35									17 40		
Shadwell	d							17 12	17 17	17 26		17 32	17 37									17 42		
Whitechapel	d							17 14	17 19	17 29		17 34	17 39									17 44		
Shoreditch High Street	d							17 16	17 21	17 31		17 36	17 41									17 46		
Hoxton	d							17 18	17 23	17 33		17 38	17 43									17 48		
Haggerston	d							17 20	17 25	17 35		17 40	17 45									17 50		
Dalston Junction Stn ELL	a							17 22	17 29	17 37		17 44	17 47									17 52		
Canonbury	d							17 27		17 42			17 50									17 57		
Highbury & Islington	d							17a30		17a44			17a53									18a00		
London Bridge 4	a		16 56				17 08	17 10				17 31			17 43			17 27			17 38	17 40		17 28	17 44

East London Line and Croydon - London Victoria to London Bridge

		LO	LO	LO	LO	LO	SN	SN	SE	FC	SN	SN	SN	SN	LO	SN	LO	LO	LO	SN	LO	LO
East Croydon	d											17 30										
West Croydon 4	d			17 22										17 31	17 39	17 42			17 52			
Norwood Junction 2	d			17 28							17 32	17 35			17 43				17 58	18 04		
Anerley	d			17 31								17 38			17 46				18 01	18 07		
Penge West	d			17 33								17 40			17 48				18 03	18 09		
London Victoria 15 ⊖	d						17 22		17 34				17 41									
Battersea Park 4	d						17 26						17 45									
Wandsworth Road	d												17 47									
Clapham High Street ⊖	d												17 49									
London Blackfriars 3 ⊖	d									17 36												
Denmark Hill 4	d								17 43	17 47			17 54									
Peckham Rye 4	d							17 37	17a46	17a49	17 53		17 57	18 01								
Queens Rd Peckham	d										17 55		17 59	18 04								
South Bermondsey	d										17 58		18 02	18 06								
Clapham Junction 10	d						17 30															
Wandsworth Common	d						17 33															
Balham 4 ⊖	d						17 35															
Streatham Hill	d						17 38															
West Norwood 4	d						17 42	17 49														
Gipsy Hill	d						17 45	17 52														
Crystal Palace 4	d		17 28			17 43	17 48	17a54										17 58				18 13
Sydenham	d		17 31	17 36		17 46	17 54					17 42			17 51			18 01	18 06	18 11		18 16
Forest Hill 4	d		17 34	17 38		17 49	17 57					17 45			17 53			18 04	18 08	18 14		18 19
Honor Oak Park	d		17 36	17 41		17 51	17 59					17 47			17 56			18 06	18 11	18 16		18 21
Brockley	d		17 39	17 43		17 54	18 02					17 50			17 58			18 09	18 13	18 19		18 24
New Cross Gate 4	a		17 41	17 46		17 56	18 04					17 52			18 01			18 11	18 16	18 21		18 26
	d		17 41	17 46		17 56	18 04					17 52			18 01			18 11	18 16	18 21		18 26
New Cross ELL	d	17 36			17 51												18 06				18 21	
Surrey Quays	d	17 40	17 45	17 49	17 55	18 00									18 05		18 10	18 15	18 19		18 25	18 30
Canada Water	d	17 42	17 47	17 51	17 57	18 02									18 07		18 12	18 17	18 21		18 27	18 32
Rotherhithe	d	17 43	17 48	17 53	17 58	18 03									18 08		18 13	18 18	18 23		18 28	18 33
Wapping	d	17 45	17 50	17 54	18 00	18 05									18 10		18 15	18 20	18 24		18 30	18 35
Shadwell	d	17 47	17 52	17 56	18 02	18 07									18 12		18 17	18 22	18 26		18 32	18 37
Whitechapel	d	17 49	17 54	17 59	18 04	18 09									18 14		18 19	18 24	18 29		18 34	18 39
Shoreditch High Street	d	17 51	17 56	18 01	18 06	18 11									18 16		18 21	18 26	18 31		18 36	18 41
Hoxton	d	17 53	17 58	18 03	18 08	18 13									18 18		18 23	18 28	18 33		18 38	18 43
Haggerston	d	17 55	18 00	18 05	18 10	18 15									18 20		18 25	18 30	18 35		18 40	18 45
Dalston Junction Stn ELL	a	17 59	18 02	18 07	18 14	18 17									18 23		18 29	18 32	18 37		18 44	18 47
Canonbury	d		18 05	18 12		18 20									18 27			18 35	18 42			18 50
Highbury & Islington	d		18a08	18a14		18a23									18a30			18a38	18a44			18a53
London Bridge 4 ⊖	a						18 13				18 02	17 59	18 08	18 11		18 00				18 31		

		SN	SN	SE	SN	FC	SN	SN	LO	SN	LO	LO	LO	LO	SE	SN	SN	FC	SN	LO	SN	SN	SE
East Croydon	d																		18 30				
West Croydon 4	d							18 01	18 09	18 13			18 22										
Norwood Junction 2	d								18 13				18 28						18 35				
Anerley	d								18 16				18 31						18 38				
Penge West	d								18 18				18 33						18 40				
London Victoria 15 ⊖	d	17 52		17 56			18 11								18 18						18 22		18 39
Battersea Park 4	d	17 56					18 15														18 26		
Wandsworth Road	d						18 17																
Clapham High Street ⊖	d						18 19																
London Blackfriars 3 ⊖	d					18 00												18 24					
Denmark Hill 4	d			18 06		18 15	18 24								18 28			18 34					18 48
Peckham Rye 4	d		18 07	18a08	18 12	18a17	18 26	18 29							18a31	18 32	18 36	18a37				18 37	18a51
Queens Rd Peckham	d				18 15		18 29	18 32								18 35	18 38						
South Bermondsey	d				18 17		18 31	18 34								18 37	18 41						
Clapham Junction 10	d	18 00																			18 30		
Wandsworth Common	d	18 03																			18 33		
Balham 4 ⊖	d	18 05																			18 35		
Streatham Hill	d	18 08																			18 38		
West Norwood 4	d	18 14	18 20																		18 42	18 50	
Gipsy Hill	d	18 17	18 23																		18 45	18 53	
Crystal Palace 4	d	18 20	18a26									18 28								18 43	18 51	18a56	
Sydenham	d	18 24							18 21			18 31	18 36						18 42	18 46	18 54		
Forest Hill 4	d	18 27							18 23			18 34	18 38						18 45	18 49	18 57		
Honor Oak Park	d	18 29							18 26			18 36	18 41						18 47	18 51	18 59		
Brockley	d	18 32							18 28			18 39	18 43						18 50	18 54	19 02		
New Cross Gate 4	a	18 34							18 31			18 41	18 46						18 52	18 56	19 04		
	d	18 34							18 31			18 41	18 46						18 52	18 56	19 04		
New Cross ELL	d										18 36			18 51									
Surrey Quays	d								18 35		18 40	18 45	18 49	18 55						19 00			
Canada Water	d								18 37		18 42	18 47	18 51	18 57						19 02			
Rotherhithe	d								18 38		18 43	18 48	18 53	18 58						19 03			
Wapping	d								18 40		18 45	18 50	18 54	19 00						19 05			
Shadwell	d								18 42		18 47	18 52	18 56	19 02						19 07			
Whitechapel	d								18 44		18 49	18 54	18 59	19 04						19 09			
Shoreditch High Street	d								18 46		18 51	18 56	19 01	19 06						19 11			
Hoxton	d								18 48		18 53	18 58	19 03	19 08						19 13			
Haggerston	d								18 50		18 55	19 00	19 05	19 10						19 15			
Dalston Junction Stn ELL	a								18 52		18 59	19 02	19 07	19 14						19 17			
Canonbury	d								18 57			19 05	19 12							19 20			
Highbury & Islington	d								19a00			19a08	19a14							19a23			
London Bridge 4 ⊖	a	18 45			18 22		18 38	18 39		18 29						18 42	18 45		18 59		19 13		

East London Line and Croydon - London Victoria to London Bridge

		FC 1	SN	SN	LO	LO	LO	LO	SN	SN	SN	LO	LO	SN	LO	SN	SE	FC	SN	SN	LO	LO
East Croydon	d										19 00											
West Croydon 4	d			18 31	18 39			18 52												19 01	19 09	
Norwood Junction 2	d				18 43			18 58			19 05										19 13	
Anerley	d				18 46			19 01			19 08										19 16	
Penge West	d				18 48			19 03			19 10										19 18	
London Victoria 15 ⊖	d		18 41											18 52			19 09		19 11			
Battersea Park 4	d		18 45											18 56					19 15			
Wandsworth Road	d		18 47																19 17			
Clapham High Street ⊖	d		18 49																19 19			
London Blackfriars 3 ⊖	d	18 42																19 12				
Denmark Hill 4	d	18 52	18 54														19 18	19 22	19 24			
Peckham Rye 4	d	18a55	18 57	19 01					19 07	19 17						19 17	19a21	19a25	19 26	19 29		
Queens Rd Peckham	d		19 00	19 04					19 10	19 20									19 29	19 32		
South Bermondsey	d		19 02	19 06					19 12	19 22									19 31	19 34		
Clapham Junction 10	d													19 00								
Wandsworth Common	d													19 03								
Balham 4 ⊖	d													19 05								
Streatham Hill	d													19 08								
West Norwood 4	d													19 12		19 30						
Gipsy Hill	d													19 15		19 33						
Crystal Palace 4	d						18 58						19 13	19 21	19 28	19a35						
Sydenham	d				18 51		19 01	19 06			19 12		19 16	19 24	19 31						19 21	
Forest Hill 4	d				18 53		19 04	19 08			19 15		19 19	19 27	19 34						19 23	
Honor Oak Park	d				18 56		19 06	19 11			19 17		19 21	19 29	19 36						19 26	
Brockley	d				18 58		19 09	19 13			19 20		19 24	19 32	19 39						19 28	
New Cross Gate 4	a				19 01		19 11	19 16			19 22		19 26	19 34	19 41						19 31	
	d				19 01		19 11	19 16			19 22		19 26	19 34	19 41						19 31	
New Cross ELL	d					19 06						19 21										19 36
Surrey Quays	d				19 05	19 10	19 15	19 19				19 25	19 30		19 45						19 35	19 40
Canada Water	d				19 07	19 12	19 17	19 21				19 27	19 32		19 47						19 37	19 42
Rotherhithe	d				19 08	19 13	19 18	19 23				19 28	19 33		19 48						19 38	19 43
Wapping	d				19 10	19 15	19 20	19 24				19 30	19 35		19 50						19 40	19 45
Shadwell	d				19 12	19 17	19 22	19 26				19 32	19 37		19 52						19 42	19 47
Whitechapel	d				19 14	19 19	19 24	19 29				19 34	19 39		19 54						19 44	19 49
Shoreditch High Street	d				19 16	19 21	19 26	19 31				19 36	19 41		19 56						19 46	19 51
Hoxton	d				19 18	19 23	19 28	19 33				19 38	19 43		19 58						19 48	19 53
Haggerston	d				19 20	19 25	19 30	19 35				19 40	19 45		20 00						19 50	19 55
Dalston Junction Stn ELL	a				19 22	19 29	19 32	19 37				19 44	19 47		20 02						19 52	19 59
Canonbury	d				19 27		19 35	19 42					19 50		20 05						19 57	
Highbury & Islington	d				19a30		19a38	19a44					19a53		20a08						20a00	
London Bridge 4 ⊖	a		19 09	19 11					19 17	19 27	19 29			19 41					19 36	19 41		

		LO	SN	SN	LO	LO	SN	LO	SN	SN	SE	FC	SN	SN	LO	LO	LO	SN	LO	LO	SN	LO	SN
East Croydon	d			19 30														20 00					
West Croydon 4	d	19 22												19 31	19 39		19 52						
Norwood Junction 2	d	19 28		19 35											19 43		19 58	20 05					
Anerley	d	19 31		19 38											19 46		20 01	20 08					
Penge West	d	19 33		19 40											19 48		20 03	20 10					
London Victoria 15 ⊖	d						19 22				19 39		19 41								19 52		
Battersea Park 4	d						19 26						19 45								19 56		
Wandsworth Road	d												19 47										
Clapham High Street ⊖	d												19 49										
London Blackfriars 3 ⊖	d											19 42											
Denmark Hill 4	d										19 48	19 52	19 54										
Peckham Rye 4	d		19 38						19 47	19 48	19a51	19a55	19 56	20 01									20 12
Queens Rd Peckham	d		19 41							19 51			19 59	20 04									
South Bermondsey	d		19 43							19 53			20 01	20 06									
Clapham Junction 10	d						19 30														20 00		
Wandsworth Common	d						19 33														20 03		
Balham 4 ⊖	d						19 35														20 05		
Streatham Hill	d						19 38														20 08		
West Norwood 4	d						19 42		20 00												20 12		20 24
Gipsy Hill	d						19 45		20 03												20 15		20 27
Crystal Palace 4	d					19 43	19 51	19 58	20a05											20 13	20 21	20 28	20a29
Sydenham	d	19 36		19 42		19 46	19 54	20 01							19 51		20 06	20 12		20 16	20 24	20 31	
Forest Hill 4	d	19 38		19 45		19 49	19 57	20 04							19 53		20 08	20 15		20 19	20 27	20 34	
Honor Oak Park	d	19 41		19 47		19 51	19 59	20 06							19 56		20 11	20 17		20 21	20 29	20 36	
Brockley	d	19 43		19 50		19 54	20 02	20 09							19 58		20 13	20 20		20 24	20 32	20 39	
New Cross Gate 4	a	19 46		19 52		19 56	20 04	20 11							20 01		20 16	20 22		20 26	20 34	20 41	
	d	19 46		19 52		19 56	20 04	20 11							20 01		20 16	20 22		20 26	20 34	20 41	
New Cross ELL	d				19 51											20 06			20 21				
Surrey Quays	d	19 49			19 55	20 00		20 15							20 05	20 10	20 19		20 25	20 30		20 45	
Canada Water	d	19 51			19 57	20 02		20 17							20 07	20 12	20 21		20 27	20 32		20 47	
Rotherhithe	d	19 53			19 58	20 03		20 18							20 08	20 13	20 23		20 28	20 33		20 48	
Wapping	d	19 54			20 00	20 05		20 20							20 10	20 15	20 24		20 30	20 35		20 50	
Shadwell	d	19 56			20 02	20 07		20 22							20 12	20 17	20 26		20 32	20 37		20 52	
Whitechapel	d	19 59			20 04	20 09		20 24							20 14	20 19	20 29		20 34	20 39		20 54	
Shoreditch High Street	d	20 01			20 06	20 11		20 26							20 16	20 21	20 31		20 36	20 41		20 56	
Hoxton	d	20 03			20 08	20 13		20 28							20 18	20 23	20 33		20 38	20 43		20 58	
Haggerston	d	20 05			20 10	20 15		20 30							20 20	20 25	20 35		20 40	20 45		21 00	
Dalston Junction Stn ELL	a	20 07			20 14	20 17		20 32							20 22	20 29	20 37		20 44	20 47		21 02	
Canonbury	d	20 12				20 20		20 35							20 27		20 42			20 50		21 05	
Highbury & Islington	d	20a14				20a23		20a38							20a30		20a44			20a53		21a08	
London Bridge 4 ⊖	a		19 51	19 59			20 11			19 58			20 06	20 14				20 29			20 41		

East London Line and Croydon - London Victoria to London Bridge

Station		SN	FC	SN	SN	LO	LO	LO	SN	LO	LO	SN	LO	SN	SN	FC	SN FO	SN FX	SN	LO	LO	LO	SN
East Croydon	d								20 31														21 00
West Croydon 4	d				20 01	20 09		20 22											20 31	20 39		20 52	
Norwood Junction 2	d					20 13		20 28	20 35											20 43		20 58	21 05
Anerley	d					20 16		20 31	20 38											20 46		21 01	21 08
Penge West	d					20 18		20 33	20 40											20 48		21 03	21 10
London Victoria 15	d			20 11								20 22					20 41	20 41					
Battersea Park 4	d			20 15								20 26					20 45	20 45					
Wandsworth Road	d			20 17													20 47	20 47					
Clapham High Street	d			20 19													20 49	20 49					
London Blackfriars 3	d		20 12													20 42							
Denmark Hill 4	d		20 22	20 24												20 52	20 54	20 54					
Peckham Rye 4	d	20 18	20a25	20 26	20 31									20 42	20 47	20a55	20 56	20 56	21 01				
Queens Rd Peckham	d	20 21		20 29	20 34										20 50		20 59	20 59	21 04				
South Bermondsey	d	20 23		20 31	20 36										20 52		21 01	21 01	21 06				
Clapham Junction 10	d											20 30											
Wandsworth Common	d											20 33											
Balham 4	d											20 35											
Streatham Hill	d											20 38											
West Norwood 4	d											20 42		20 54									
Gipsy Hill	d											20 45		20 57									
Crystal Palace 4	d										20 43	20 51	20 58	20a59									
Sydenham	d					20 21		20 36	20 42		20 46	20 54	21 01							20 51		21 06	21 12
Forest Hill 4	d					20 23		20 38	20 45		20 49	20 57	21 04							20 53		21 08	21 15
Honor Oak Park	d					20 26		20 41	20 47		20 51	20 59	21 06							20 56		21 11	21 17
Brockley	d					20 28		20 43	20 50		20 54	21 02	21 09							20 58		21 13	21 20
New Cross Gate 4	a					20 31		20 46	20 52		20 56	21 04	21 11							21 01		21 16	21 22
	d					20 31		20 46	20 52		20 56	21 04	21 11							21 01		21 16	21 22
New Cross ELL	d						20 36			20 51											21 06		
Surrey Quays	d					20 35	20 40	20 49		20 55	21 00		21 15							21 05	21 10	21 19	
Canada Water	d					20 37	20 42	20 51		20 57	21 02		21 17							21 07	21 12	21 21	
Rotherhithe	d					20 38	20 43	20 53		20 58	21 03		21 18							21 08	21 13	21 23	
Wapping	d					20 40	20 45	20 54		21 00	21 05		21 20							21 10	21 15	21 24	
Shadwell	d					20 42	20 47	20 56		21 02	21 07		21 22							21 12	21 17	21 26	
Whitechapel	d					20 44	20 49	20 59		21 04	21 09		21 24							21 14	21 19	21 29	
Shoreditch High Street	d					20 46	20 51	21 01		21 06	21 11		21 26							21 16	21 21	21 31	
Hoxton	d					20 48	20 53	21 03		21 08	21 13		21 28							21 18	21 23	21 33	
Haggerston	d					20 50	20 55	21 05		21 10	21 15		21 30							21 20	21 25	21 35	
Dalston Junction Stn ELL	a					20 52	20 59	21 07		21 14	21 17		21 32							21 22	21 29	21 37	
Canonbury	d					20 57		21 12			21 20		21 35							21 27		21 42	
Highbury & Islington	d					21a00		21a14			21a23		21a38							21a30		21a44	
London Bridge 4	a	20 28		20 36	20 41				20 59			21 13			20 57		21 06	21 07	21 11				21 29

Station		LO	LO	SN	LO	SN	SN	FC	SN	SN	LO	LO	LO	SN	LO	LO	SN	LO	SN	SN	SN	SE
East Croydon	d													21 30								
West Croydon 4	d									21 01	21 09		21 22									
Norwood Junction 2	d										21 13		21 28	21 35								
Anerley	d										21 16		21 31	21 38								
Penge West	d										21 18		21 33	21 40								
London Victoria 15	d			20 52					21 11								21 23				21 41	21 43
Battersea Park 4	d			20 56					21 15								21 27				21 45	
Wandsworth Road	d								21 17												21 47	
Clapham High Street	d								21 19												21 49	
London Blackfriars 3	d							21 12														
Denmark Hill 4	d							21 22	21 24												21 54	21 52
Peckham Rye 4	d					21 12	21 16	21a25	21 26	21 31									21 42	21 46	21 56	21a55
Queens Rd Peckham	d						21 19		21 29	21 34										21 49	21 59	
South Bermondsey	d						21 21		21 31	21 36										21 51	22 01	
Clapham Junction 10	d			21 00													21 31					
Wandsworth Common	d			21 03													21 34					
Balham 4	d			21 05													21 36					
Streatham Hill	d			21 08													21 39					
West Norwood 4	d			21 12		21 24											21 43		21 54			
Gipsy Hill	d			21 15		21 27											21 46		21 57			
Crystal Palace 4	d		21 13	21 21	21 28	21a29										21 43	21 51	21 58	21a59			
Sydenham	d		21 16	21 27	21 31						21 21		21 36	21 42		21 46	21 54	22 01				
Forest Hill 4	d		21 19	21 29	21 34						21 23		21 38	21 45		21 49	21 57	22 04				
Honor Oak Park	d		21 21	21 32	21 36						21 26		21 41	21 47		21 51	21 59	22 06				
Brockley	d		21 24	21 34	21 39						21 28		21 43	21 50		21 54	22 02	22 09				
New Cross Gate 4	a		21 26	21 37	21 41						21 31		21 46	21 52		21 56	22 04	22 11				
	d		21 26	21 37	21 41						21 31		21 46	21 52		21 56	22 04	22 11				
New Cross ELL	d	21 21										21 36			21 51							
Surrey Quays	d	21 25	21 30		21 45						21 35	21 40	21 49		21 55	22 00		22 15				
Canada Water	d	21 27	21 32		21 47						21 37	21 42	21 51		21 57	22 02		22 17				
Rotherhithe	d	21 28	21 33		21 48						21 38	21 43	21 53		21 58	22 03		22 18				
Wapping	d	21 30	21 35		21 50						21 40	21 45	21 54		22 00	22 05		22 20				
Shadwell	d	21 32	21 37		21 52						21 42	21 47	21 56		22 02	22 07		22 22				
Whitechapel	d	21 34	21 39		21 54						21 44	21 49	21 59		22 04	22 09		22 24				
Shoreditch High Street	d	21 36	21 41		21 56						21 46	21 51	22 01		22 06	22 11		22 26				
Hoxton	d	21 38	21 43		21 58						21 48	21 53	22 03		22 08	22 13		22 28				
Haggerston	d	21 40	21 45		22 00						21 50	21 55	22 05		22 10	22 15		22 30				
Dalston Junction Stn ELL	a	21 44	21 47		22 02						21 52	21 59	22 07		22 14	22 17		22 32				
Canonbury	d		21 50		22 05						21 57		22 12			22 20		22 35				
Highbury & Islington	d		21a53		22a08						22a00		22a14			22a23		22a38				
London Bridge 4	a			21 43			21 26		21 36	21 41				21 59			22 13			21 56	22 06	

East London Line and Croydon - London Victoria to London Bridge

Station		SN	LO	LO	LO	SN	LO	SN	LO	SN	SN	SN	SE	SN	LO	LO	LO	SN	SN	LO	SN	SN	SN
East Croydon	d					22 00													22 30				
West Croydon 4	d	21 31	21 39		21 52									22 01	22 09		22 22						
Norwood Junction 2	d		21 43		21 58	22 05									22 13		22 28		22 35				
Anerley	d		21 46		22 01	22 08									22 16		22 31		22 38				
Penge West	d		21 48		22 03	22 10									22 18		22 33		22 40				
London Victoria 15	d							21 52				22 11	22 13								22 22		22 41
Battersea Park 4	d							21 56				22 15									22 26		22 45
Wandsworth Road	d											22 17											22 47
Clapham High Street	d											22 19											22 49
London Blackfriars 3	d																						
Denmark Hill 4	d											22 24	22 22										22 54
Peckham Rye 4	d	22 01								22 12	22 16	22 26	22a25	22 31				22 42				22 42	22 56
Queens Rd Peckham	d	22 04									22 19	22 29		22 34				22 45					22 59
South Bermondsey	d	22 06									22 21	22 31		22 36				22 47					23 01
Clapham Junction 10	d							22 00													22 30		
Wandsworth Common	d							22 03													22 33		
Balham 4	d							22 05													22 35		
Streatham Hill	d							22 08													22 38		
West Norwood 4	d							22 12		22 24											22 42	22 54	
Gipsy Hill	d							22 15		22 27											22 45	22 57	
Crystal Palace 4	d						22 13	22 21	22 28	22a29										22 43	22 51	22a59	
Sydenham	d		21 51		22 06	22 12	22 16	22 24	22 31						22 21		22 36		22 42	22 46	22 54		
Forest Hill 4	d		21 53		22 08	22 15	22 19	22 27	22 34						22 23		22 38		22 45	22 49	22 57		
Honor Oak Park	d		21 56		22 11	22 17	22 21	22 29	22 36						22 26		22 41		22 47	22 51	22 59		
Brockley	d		21 58		22 13	22 20	22 24	22 32	22 39						22 28		22 43		22 50	22 54	23 02		
New Cross Gate 4	a		22 01		22 16	22 22	22 26	22 34	22 41						22 31		22 46		22 52	22 56	23 04		
	d		22 01		22 16	22 22	22 26	22 34	22 41						22 31		22 46		22 52	22 56	23 04		
New Cross ELL	d			22 06												22 36							
Surrey Quays	d		22 05	22 10	22 19		22 30		22 45						22 35	22 40	22 49			23 00			
Canada Water	d		22 07	22 12	22 21		22 32		22 47						22 37	22 42	22 51			23 02			
Rotherhithe	d		22 08	22 13	22 23		22 33		22 48						22 38	22 43	22 53			23 03			
Wapping	d		22 10	22 15	22 24		22 35		22 50						22 40	22 45	22 54			23 05			
Shadwell	d		22 12	22 17	22 26		22 37		22 52						22 42	22 47	22 56			23 07			
Whitechapel	d		22 14	22 19	22 29		22 39		22 54						22 44	22 49	22 59			23 09			
Shoreditch High Street	d		22 16	22 21	22 31		22 41		22 56						22 46	22 51	23 01			23 11			
Hoxton	d		22 18	22 23	22 33		22 43		22 58						22 48	22 53	23 03			23 13			
Haggerston	d		22 20	22 25	22 35		22 45		23 00						22 50	22 55	23 05			23 15			
Dalston Junction Stn ELL	a		22 22	22 29	22 37		22 47		23 02						22 52	22 59	23 07			23 17			
Canonbury	d		22 27		22 42		22 50		23 05						22 57		23 12			23 20			
Highbury & Islington	d		22a30		22a44		22a53		23a08						23a00		23a14			23a23			
London Bridge 4	a	22 11				22 29		22 45			22 26	22 36		22 41				22 52	22 59		23 14		23 06

Station		SE	SN	LO	LO	LO	SN	LO	SN	SN	SN	SN	LO	SE	SN	LO	LO	SN	SN	SN	SE	SN
East Croydon	d						23 01															
West Croydon 4	d		22 31	22 39		22 52									23 01	23 22						
Norwood Junction 2	d			22 43		22 58	23 06									23 28						
Anerley	d			22 46		23 01	23 09									23 31						
Penge West	d			22 48		23 03	23 11									23 33						
London Victoria 15	d	22 43							22 52			23 11		23 13				23 22			23 43	23 54
Battersea Park 4	d								22 56			23 15						23 26				23 58
Wandsworth Road	d											23 17										
Clapham High Street	d											23 19										
London Blackfriars 3	d																					
Denmark Hill 4	d	22 52										23 24		23 22							23 52	
Peckham Rye 4	d	22a55	23 01							23 14	23 16	23 26		23a25	23 31				23 42	23 46	23a55	
Queens Rd Peckham	d		23 04								23 19	23 29			23 34					23 49		
South Bermondsey	d		23 06								23 21	23 31			23 36					23 51		
Clapham Junction 10	d								23 00									23 30				00 02
Wandsworth Common	d								23 03									23 33				00 05
Balham 4	d								23 05									23 35				00 07
Streatham Hill	d								23 08									23 38				00 10
West Norwood 4	d								23 12	23 26								23 42	23 54			00 14
Gipsy Hill	d								23 15	23 29								23 45	23 57			00 17
Crystal Palace 4	d							23 13	23 21	23a31							23 43	23 51	23a59			00 21
Sydenham	d			22 51		23 06	23 13	23 16	23 24							23 36	23 46	23 54				00 24
Forest Hill 4	d			22 53		23 08	23 16	23 19	23 27							23 38	23 49	23 57				00 27
Honor Oak Park	d			22 56		23 11	23 18	23 21	23 29							23 41	23 51	23 59				00 29
Brockley	d			22 58		23 13	23 21	23 24	23 32							23 43	23 54	00 02				00 32
New Cross Gate 4	a			23 01		23 16	23 23	23 26	23 34							23 46	23 56	00 04				00 34
	d			23 01		23 16	23 23	23 26	23 34							23 46	23 56	00 04				00 34
New Cross ELL	d				23 06								23 36									
Surrey Quays	d			23 05	23 10	23 19		23 30					23 40			23 49	23 59					
Canada Water	d			23 07	23 12	23 21		23 32					23 42			23 51	00 02					
Rotherhithe	d			23 08	23 13	23 23		23 33					23 43			23 53	00 03					
Wapping	d			23 10	23 15	23 24		23 35					23 45			23 54	00 05					
Shadwell	d			23 12	23 17	23 26		23 37					23 47			23 56	00 07					
Whitechapel	d			23 14	23 19	23 29		23 39					23 49			23 59	00 09					
Shoreditch High Street	d			23 16	23 21	23 31		23 41					23 51			00 01	00 11					
Hoxton	d			23 18	23 23	23 33		23 43					23 53			00 03	00 13					
Haggerston	d			23 20	23 25	23 35		23 45					23 55			00 05	00 15					
Dalston Junction Stn ELL	a			23 22	23 29	23 37		23 47					23 59			00 07	00 17					
Canonbury	d			23 27		23 42		23 50								00 12	00 20					
Highbury & Islington	d			23a30		23a44		23a53								00a14	00a23					
London Bridge 4	a		23 11				23 30		23 45		23 26	23 36			23 41			00 11		23 56		00 41

East London Line and Croydon - London Victoria to London Bridge

		LO	LO	SN	SN	SN	SN	LO	LO	LO	LO	LO	LO	LO	SN	LO	LO	LO	SN	LO	LO	SE	SN
East Croydon	d																		06 30				
West Croydon	d	23p22						05 39			05 52			06 09	06 18			06 22					
Norwood Junction	d	23p28						05 43			05 58			06 13	06 23			06 28	06 35				
Anerley	d	23p31						05 46			06 01			06 16				06 31	06 38				
Penge West	d	23p33						05 48			06 03			06 18				06 33	06 40				
London Victoria	d			23p22	23p54																	06 13	06 41
Battersea Park	d			23p26	23p58																		06 45
Wandsworth Road	d																						06 47
Clapham High Street	d																						06 49
London Blackfriars	d																						
Denmark Hill	d																					06 22	06 54
Peckham Rye	d					00 12	00 42															06a25	06 56
Queens Rd Peckham	d																						06 59
South Bermondsey	d																						07 01
Clapham Junction	d			23p30	00 02																		
Wandsworth Common	d			23p33	00 05																		
Balham	d			23p35	00 07																		
Streatham Hill	d			23p38	00 10																		
West Norwood	d			23p42	00 14	00 24	00 54																
Gipsy Hill	d			23p45	00 17	00 27	00 57																
Crystal Palace	d		23p43	23p51	00 21	00a29	00a59			05 58			06 13		06a27		06 28				06 43		
Sydenham	d	23p36	23p46	23p54	00 24			05 51		06 01	06 06		06 16	06 21			06 31	06 36	06 42		06 46		
Forest Hill	d	23p38	23p49	23p57	00 27			05 53		06 04	06 08		06 19	06 23			06 34	06 38	06 45		06 49		
Honor Oak Park	d	23p41	23p51	23p59	00 29			05 56		06 06	06 11		06 21	06 26			06 36	06 41	06 47		06 51		
Brockley	d	23p43	23p54	00 02	00 32			05 58		06 09	06 13		06 24	06 28			06 39	06 43	06 50		06 54		
New Cross Gate	a	23p46	23p56	00 04	00 34			06 01		06 11	06 16		06 26	06 31			06 41	06 46	06 52		06 56		
	d	23p46	23p56	00 04	00 34			06 01		06 11	06 16		06 26	06 31			06 41	06 46	06 52		06 56		
New Cross ELL	d								06 06			06 21				06 36				06 51			
Surrey Quays	d	23p49	23p59					06 05	06 10	06 15	06 19	06 25	06 30	06 35		06 40	06 45	06 49		06 55	07 00		
Canada Water	d	23p51	00 02					06 07	06 12	06 17	06 21	06 27	06 32	06 37		06 42	06 47	06 51		06 57	07 02		
Rotherhithe	d	23p53	00 03					06 08	06 13	06 18	06 23	06 28	06 33	06 38		06 43	06 48	06 53		06 58	07 03		
Wapping	d	23p54	00 05					06 10	06 15	06 20	06 24	06 30	06 35	06 40		06 45	06 50	06 54		07 00	07 05		
Shadwell	d	23p56	00 07					06 12	06 17	06 22	06 26	06 32	06 37	06 42		06 47	06 52	06 56		07 02	07 07		
Whitechapel	d	23p59	00 09					06 14	06 19	06 24	06 29	06 34	06 39	06 44		06 49	06 54	06 59		07 04	07 09		
Shoreditch High Street	d	00 01	00 11					06 16	06 21	06 26	06 31	06 36	06 41	06 46		06 51	06 56	07 01		07 06	07 11		
Hoxton	d	00 03	00 13					06 18	06 23	06 28	06 33	06 38	06 43	06 48		06 53	06 58	07 03		07 08	07 13		
Haggerston	d	00 05	00 15					06 20	06 25	06 30	06 35	06 40	06 45	06 50		06 55	07 00	07 05		07 10	07 15		
Dalston Junction Stn ELL	a	00 07	00 17					06 22	06 29	06 32	06 37	06 44	06 47	06 52		06 59	07 02	07 07		07 14	07 17		
Canonbury	d	00 12	00 20					06 27		06 35	06 42		06 50	06 57			07 05	07 12			07 20		
Highbury & Islington	d	00a14	00a23					06a30		06a38	06a44		06a54	07a00			07a08	07a14			07a23		
London Bridge	a			00 11	00 41														06 59				07 06

		SE	SN	LO	SN	SN	LO	LO	LO	SN	SN	LO	LO	SE	SN	LO	LO	LO	LO	SN	LO	LO	LO
East Croydon	d				06 43					07 00										07 30			
West Croydon	d			06 39		06 45			06 52						07 01	07 09			07 22				
Norwood Junction	d		06 41	06 43	06 50	06 53			06 58	07 05						07 13			07 28	07 35			
Anerley	d			06 46					07 01	07 08						07 16			07 31	07 38			
Penge West	d			06 48					07 03	07 10						07 18			07 33	07 40			
London Victoria	d	06 43									07 11			07 13									
Battersea Park	d										07 15												
Wandsworth Road	d										07 17												
Clapham High Street	d										07 19												
London Blackfriars	d																						
Denmark Hill	d	06 52									07 24			07 22									
Peckham Rye	d	06a55	07 01								07 26			07a25	07 31								
Queens Rd Peckham	d		07 04								07 29				07 34								
South Bermondsey	d		07 06								07 31				07 36								
Clapham Junction	d																						
Wandsworth Common	d																						
Balham	d																						
Streatham Hill	d																						
West Norwood	d																						
Gipsy Hill	d																						
Crystal Palace	d					06a57		06 58					07 13					07 28				07 43	07 58
Sydenham	d			06 51	06 54			07 01	07 06	07 12			07 16			07 21		07 31	07 36	07 42		07 46	08 01
Forest Hill	d			06 53	06 57			07 04	07 08	07 15			07 19			07 23		07 34	07 38	07 45		07 49	08 04
Honor Oak Park	d			06 56	06 59			07 06	07 11	07 17			07 21			07 26		07 36	07 41	07 47		07 51	08 06
Brockley	d			06 58	07 02			07 09	07 13	07 20			07 24			07 28		07 39	07 43	07 50		07 54	08 09
New Cross Gate	a			07 01	07 04			07 11	07 16	07 22			07 26			07 31		07 41	07 46	07 52		07 56	08 11
	d			07 01	07 04			07 11	07 16	07 22			07 26			07 31		07 41	07 46	07 52		07 56	08 11
New Cross ELL	d						07 06					07 21					07 36				07 51		
Surrey Quays	d			07 05			07 10	07 15	07 19			07 25	07 30			07 35	07 40	07 45	07 49		07 55	08 00	08 15
Canada Water	d			07 07			07 12	07 17	07 21			07 27	07 32			07 37	07 42	07 47	07 51		07 57	08 02	08 17
Rotherhithe	d			07 08			07 13	07 18	07 23			07 28	07 33			07 38	07 43	07 48	07 53		07 58	08 03	08 18
Wapping	d			07 10			07 15	07 20	07 24			07 30	07 35			07 40	07 45	07 50	07 54		08 00	08 05	08 20
Shadwell	d			07 12			07 17	07 22	07 26			07 32	07 37			07 42	07 47	07 52	07 56		08 02	08 07	08 22
Whitechapel	d			07 14			07 19	07 24	07 29			07 34	07 39			07 44	07 49	07 54	07 59		08 04	08 09	08 24
Shoreditch High Street	d			07 16			07 21	07 26	07 31			07 36	07 41			07 46	07 51	07 56	08 01		08 06	08 11	08 26
Hoxton	d			07 18			07 23	07 28	07 33			07 38	07 43			07 48	07 53	07 58	08 03		08 08	08 13	08 28
Haggerston	d			07 20			07 25	07 30	07 35			07 40	07 45			07 50	07 55	08 00	08 05		08 10	08 15	08 30
Dalston Junction Stn ELL	a			07 22			07 29	07 32	07 37			07 44	07 47			07 52	07 59	08 02	08 07		08 14	08 17	08 32
Canonbury	d			07 27				07 35	07 42				07 50			07 57		08 05	08 12			08 20	08 35
Highbury & Islington	d			07a30				07a38	07a44				07a53			08a00		08a08	08a14			08a23	08a38
London Bridge	a		07 14		07 11					07 29	07 36				07 41					07 59			

East London Line and Croydon - London Victoria to London Bridge

		SN	SE	SN	SE	SN	LO	LO	LO	SN	LO	LO	SN	LO	SN	SE	SN	SE	SN	LO	LO	LO
East Croydon	d									08 00												
West Croydon	d					07 31	07 39		07 52										08 01	08 09		08 22
Norwood Junction	d						07 43		07 58	08 05										08 13		08 28
Anerley	d						07 46		08 01	08 08										08 16		08 31
Penge West	d						07 48		08 03	08 10										08 18		08 33
London Victoria	d		07 39	07 41	07 43								07 49			08 09	08 11	08 13				
Battersea Park	d			07 45									07 53				08 15					
Wandsworth Road	d			07 47													08 17					
Clapham High Street	d			07 49													08 19					
London Blackfriars	d																					
Denmark Hill	d		07 48	07 54	07 52											08 18	08 24	08 22				
Peckham Rye	d	07 42	07a51	07 56	07a55	08 01									08 12	08a21	08 26	08a25	08 31			
Queens Rd Peckham	d			07 59		08 04											08 29		08 34			
South Bermondsey	d			08 01		08 06											08 31		08 36			
Clapham Junction	d												07 57									
Wandsworth Common	d												08 00									
Balham	d												08 02									
Streatham Hill	d												08 05									
West Norwood	d	07 53											08 10		08 23							
Gipsy Hill	d	07 56											08 13		08 26							
Crystal Palace	d	07a59										08 13	08 21	08 28	08a29							
Sydenham	d						07 51		08 06	08 12		08 16	08 24	08 31						08 21		08 36
Forest Hill	d						07 53		08 08	08 15		08 19	08 27	08 34						08 23		08 38
Honor Oak Park	d						07 56		08 11	08 17		08 21	08 29	08 36						08 26		08 41
Brockley	d						07 58		08 13	08 20		08 24	08 32	08 39						08 28		08 43
New Cross Gate	a						08 01		08 16	08 22		08 26	08 34	08 41						08 31		08 46
	d						08 01		08 16	08 22		08 26	08 34	08 41						08 31		08 46
New Cross ELL	d							08 06			08 21										08 36	
Surrey Quays	d						08 05	08 10	08 19		08 25	08 30		08 45						08 35	08 40	08 49
Canada Water	d						08 07	08 12	08 21		08 27	08 32		08 47						08 37	08 42	08 51
Rotherhithe	d						08 08	08 13	08 23		08 28	08 33		08 48						08 38	08 43	08 53
Wapping	d						08 10	08 15	08 24		08 30	08 35		08 50						08 40	08 45	08 54
Shadwell	d						08 12	08 17	08 26		08 32	08 37		08 52						08 42	08 47	08 56
Whitechapel	d						08 14	08 19	08 29		08 34	08 39		08 54						08 44	08 49	08 59
Shoreditch High Street	d						08 16	08 21	08 31		08 36	08 41		08 56						08 46	08 51	09 01
Hoxton	d						08 18	08 23	08 33		08 38	08 43		08 58						08 48	08 53	09 03
Haggerston	d						08 20	08 25	08 35		08 40	08 45		09 00						08 50	08 55	09 05
Dalston Junction Stn ELL	a						08 22	08 29	08 37		08 44	08 47		09 02						08 52	08 59	09 07
Canonbury	d						08 27		08 42			08 50		09 05						08 57		09 12
Highbury & Islington	d						08a30		08a44			08a53		09a08						09a00		09a14
London Bridge	a			08 06		08 11				08 29			08 41				08 36		08 41			

		SN	LO	LO	SN	LO	SN	SN	SE	SN	SE	SN	LO	LO	LO	SN	LO	LO	SN	LO	SN	SN	SE
East Croydon	d	08 30														09 00							
West Croydon	d											08 31	08 39		08 52								
Norwood Junction	d	08 35											08 43		08 58	09 05							
Anerley	d	08 38											08 46		09 01	09 08							
Penge West	d	08 40											08 48		09 03	09 10							
London Victoria	d				08 19				08 39	08 41	08 43								08 49				09 09
Battersea Park	d				08 23					08 45									08 53				
Wandsworth Road	d									08 47													
Clapham High Street	d									08 49													
London Blackfriars	d																						
Denmark Hill	d								08 48	08 54	08 52												09 18
Peckham Rye	d						08 42	08 46	08a51	08 56	08a55	09 01									09 12	09 16	09a21
Queens Rd Peckham	d							08 49		08 59		09 04										09 19	
South Bermondsey	d							08 51		09 01		09 06										09 21	
Clapham Junction	d				08 27														08 57				
Wandsworth Common	d				08 30														09 00				
Balham	d				08 32														09 02				
Streatham Hill	d				08 35														09 05				
West Norwood	d				08 40		08 53												09 10		09 23		
Gipsy Hill	d				08 43		08 56												09 13		09 26		
Crystal Palace	d			08 43	08 51	08 58	08a59											09 13	09 21	09 28	09a29		
Sydenham	d	08 42		08 46	08 54	09 01							08 51		09 06	09 12		09 16	09 24	09 31			
Forest Hill	d	08 45		08 49	08 57	09 04							08 53		09 08	09 15		09 19	09 27	09 34			
Honor Oak Park	d	08 47		08 51	08 59	09 06							08 56		09 11	09 17		09 21	09 29	09 36			
Brockley	d	08 50		08 54	09 02	09 09							08 58		09 13	09 20		09 24	09 32	09 39			
New Cross Gate	a	08 52		08 56	09 04	09 11							09 01		09 16	09 22		09 26	09 34	09 41			
	d	08 52		08 56	09 04	09 11							09 01		09 16	09 22		09 26	09 34	09 41			
New Cross ELL	d		08 51											09 06			09 21						
Surrey Quays	d		08 55	09 00		09 15							09 05	09 10	09 19		09 25	09 30		09 45			
Canada Water	d		08 57	09 02		09 17							09 07	09 12	09 21		09 27	09 32		09 47			
Rotherhithe	d		08 58	09 03		09 18							09 08	09 13	09 23		09 28	09 33		09 48			
Wapping	d		09 00	09 05		09 20							09 10	09 15	09 24		09 30	09 35		09 50			
Shadwell	d		09 02	09 07		09 22							09 12	09 17	09 26		09 32	09 37		09 52			
Whitechapel	d		09 04	09 09		09 24							09 14	09 19	09 29		09 34	09 39		09 54			
Shoreditch High Street	d		09 06	09 11		09 26							09 16	09 21	09 31		09 36	09 41		09 56			
Hoxton	d		09 08	09 13		09 28							09 18	09 23	09 33		09 38	09 43		09 58			
Haggerston	d		09 10	09 15		09 30							09 20	09 25	09 35		09 40	09 45		10 00			
Dalston Junction Stn ELL	a		09 14	09 17		09 32							09 22	09 29	09 37		09 44	09 47		10 02			
Canonbury	d			09 20		09 35							09 27		09 42			09 50		10 05			
Highbury & Islington	d			09a23		09a38							09a30		09a44			09a53		10a08			
London Bridge	a	08 59			09 11			08 56		09 06		09 11				09 29			09 41			09 26	

East London Line and Croydon - London Victoria to London Bridge

		SN	SE	SN	LO	LO	LO	SN	LO	LO	SN	LO	SN	SN	SE	SN	SE	SN	LO	LO	LO	SN
East Croydon	d							09 30														10 00
West Croydon	d			09 01	09 09		09 22											09 31	09 39		09 52	
Norwood Junction	d				09 13		09 28	09 35											09 43		09 58	10 05
Anerley	d				09 16		09 31	09 38											09 46		10 01	10 08
Penge West	d				09 18		09 33	09 40											09 48		10 03	10 10
London Victoria	d	09 11	09 13								09 19				09 39	09 41	09 43					
Battersea Park	d	09 15									09 23					09 45						
Wandsworth Road	d	09 17														09 47						
Clapham High Street	d	09 19														09 49						
London Blackfriars	d																					
Denmark Hill	d	09 24	09 22												09 48	09 54	09 52					
Peckham Rye	d	09 26	09a25	09 31									09 42	09 46	09a51	09 56	09a55	10 01				
Queens Rd Peckham	d	09 29		09 34										09 49		09 59		10 04				
South Bermondsey	d	09 31		09 36										09 51		10 01		10 06				
Clapham Junction	d										09 27											
Wandsworth Common	d										09 30											
Balham	d										09 32											
Streatham Hill	d										09 35											
West Norwood	d										09 40		09 53									
Gipsy Hill	d										09 43		09 56									
Crystal Palace	d									09 43	09 51	09 58	09a59									
Sydenham	d				09 21		09 36	09 42		09 46	09 54	10 01							09 51		10 06	10 12
Forest Hill	d				09 23		09 38	09 45		09 49	09 57	10 04							09 53		10 08	10 15
Honor Oak Park	d				09 26		09 41	09 47		09 51	09 59	10 06							09 56		10 11	10 17
Brockley	d				09 28		09 43	09 50		09 54	10 02	10 09							09 58		10 13	10 20
New Cross Gate	a				09 31		09 46	09 52		09 56	10 04	10 11							10 01		10 16	10 22
	d				09 31		09 46	09 52		09 56	10 04	10 11							10 01		10 16	10 22
New Cross ELL	d					09 36			09 51											10 06		
Surrey Quays	d				09 35	09 40	09 49		09 55	10 00		10 15							10 05	10 10	10 19	
Canada Water	d				09 37	09 42	09 51		09 57	10 02		10 17							10 07	10 12	10 21	
Rotherhithe	d				09 38	09 43	09 53		09 58	10 03		10 18							10 08	10 13	10 23	
Wapping	d				09 40	09 45	09 54		10 00	10 05		10 20							10 10	10 15	10 24	
Shadwell	d				09 42	09 47	09 56		10 02	10 07		10 22							10 12	10 17	10 26	
Whitechapel	d				09 44	09 49	09 59		10 04	10 09		10 24							10 14	10 19	10 29	
Shoreditch High Street	d				09 46	09 51	10 01		10 06	10 11		10 26							10 16	10 21	10 31	
Hoxton	d				09 48	09 53	10 03		10 08	10 13		10 28							10 18	10 23	10 33	
Haggerston	d				09 50	09 55	10 05		10 10	10 15		10 30							10 20	10 25	10 35	
Dalston Junction Stn ELL	a				09 52	09 59	10 07		10 14	10 17		10 32							10 22	10 29	10 37	
Canonbury	d				09 57		10 12			10 20		10 35							10 27		10 42	
Highbury & Islington	d				10a00		10a14			10a23		10a38							10a30		10a44	
London Bridge	a	09 36		09 41				09 59			10 11			09 56		10 06		10 11				10 29

		LO	LO	SN	LO	SN	SN	SE	SN	SE	SN	LO	LO	LO	SN	LO	LO	SN	LO	SN	SN	SE	SN
East Croydon	d														10 30								
West Croydon	d										10 01	10 09		10 22									
Norwood Junction	d											10 13		10 28	10 35								
Anerley	d											10 16		10 31	10 38								
Penge West	d											10 18		10 33	10 40								
London Victoria	d			09 49				10 09	10 11	10 13								10 19				10 39	10 41
Battersea Park	d			09 53					10 15									10 23					10 45
Wandsworth Road	d								10 17														10 47
Clapham High Street	d								10 19														10 49
London Blackfriars	d																						
Denmark Hill	d							10 18	10 24	10 22												10 48	10 54
Peckham Rye	d					10 12	10 16	10a21	10 26	10a25	10 31									10 42	10 46	10a51	10 56
Queens Rd Peckham	d						10 19		10 29		10 34										10 49		10 59
South Bermondsey	d						10 21		10 31		10 36										10 51		11 01
Clapham Junction	d			09 57														10 27					
Wandsworth Common	d			10 00														10 30					
Balham	d			10 02														10 32					
Streatham Hill	d			10 05														10 35					
West Norwood	d			10 10		10 23												10 40		10 53			
Gipsy Hill	d			10 13		10 26												10 43		10 56			
Crystal Palace	d		10 13	10 21	10 28	10a29											10 43	10 51	10 58	10a59			
Sydenham	d		10 16	10 24	10 31							10 21		10 36	10 42		10 46	10 54	11 01				
Forest Hill	d		10 19	10 27	10 34							10 23		10 38	10 45		10 49	10 57	11 04				
Honor Oak Park	d		10 21	10 29	10 36							10 26		10 41	10 47		10 51	10 59	11 06				
Brockley	d		10 24	10 32	10 39							10 28		10 43	10 50		10 54	11 02	11 09				
New Cross Gate	a		10 26	10 34	10 41							10 31		10 46	10 52		10 56	11 04	11 11				
	d		10 26	10 34	10 41							10 31		10 46	10 52		10 56	11 04	11 11				
New Cross ELL	d	10 21											10 36			10 51							
Surrey Quays	d	10 25	10 30		10 45							10 35	10 40	10 49		10 55	11 00		11 15				
Canada Water	d	10 27	10 32		10 47							10 37	10 42	10 51		10 57	11 02		11 17				
Rotherhithe	d	10 28	10 33		10 48							10 38	10 43	10 53		10 58	11 03		11 18				
Wapping	d	10 30	10 35		10 50							10 40	10 45	10 54		11 00	11 05		11 20				
Shadwell	d	10 32	10 37		10 52							10 42	10 47	10 56		11 02	11 07		11 22				
Whitechapel	d	10 34	10 39		10 54							10 44	10 49	10 59		11 04	11 09		11 24				
Shoreditch High Street	d	10 36	10 41		10 56							10 46	10 51	11 01		11 06	11 11		11 26				
Hoxton	d	10 38	10 43		10 58							10 48	10 53	11 03		11 08	11 13		11 28				
Haggerston	d	10 40	10 45		11 00							10 50	10 55	11 05		11 10	11 15		11 30				
Dalston Junction Stn ELL	a	10 44	10 47		11 02							10 52	10 59	11 07		11 14	11 17		11 32				
Canonbury	d		10 50		11 05							10 57		11 12			11 20		11 35				
Highbury & Islington	d		10a53		11a08							11a00		11a14			11a23		11a38				
London Bridge	a			10 41			10 26		10 36		10 41				10 59			11 11			10 56		11 06

East London Line and Croydon - London Victoria to London Bridge

		SE	SN	LO	LO	LO	SN	LO	LO	SN	LO	SN	SN	SE	SN	SE	SN	LO	LO	LO	SN	LO	LO
East Croydon	d						11 00														11 30		
West Croydon	d		10 31	10 39		10 52											11 01	11 09		11 22			
Norwood Junction	d			10 43		10 58	11 05											11 13		11 28	11 35		
Anerley	d			10 46		11 01	11 08											11 16		11 31	11 38		
Penge West	d			10 48		11 03	11 10											11 18		11 33	11 40		
London Victoria	d	10 43								10 49				11 09	11 11	11 13							
Battersea Park	d									10 53					11 15								
Wandsworth Road	d														11 17								
Clapham High Street	d														11 19								
London Blackfriars	d																						
Denmark Hill	d	10 52												11 18	11 24	11 22							
Peckham Rye	d	10a55	11 01									11 12	11 16	11a21	11 26	11a25	11 31						
Queens Rd Peckham	d		11 04										11 19		11 29		11 34						
South Bermondsey	d		11 06										11 21		11 31		11 36						
Clapham Junction	d									10 57													
Wandsworth Common	d									11 00													
Balham	d									11 02													
Streatham Hill	d									11 05													
West Norwood	d									11 10		11 23											
Gipsy Hill	d									11 13		11 26											
Crystal Palace	d								11 13	11 21	11 28	11a29											11 43
Sydenham	d			10 51		11 06	11 12		11 16	11 24	11 31							11 21		11 36	11 42		11 46
Forest Hill	d			10 53		11 08	11 15		11 19	11 27	11 34							11 23		11 38	11 45		11 49
Honor Oak Park	d			10 56		11 11	11 17		11 21	11 29	11 36							11 26		11 41	11 47		11 51
Brockley	d			10 58		11 13	11 20		11 24	11 32	11 39							11 28		11 43	11 50		11 54
New Cross Gate	a			11 01		11 16	11 22		11 26	11 34	11 41							11 31		11 46	11 52		11 56
	d			11 01		11 16	11 22		11 26	11 34	11 41							11 31		11 46	11 52		11 56
New Cross ELL	d				11 06			11 21											11 36			11 51	
Surrey Quays	d			11 05	11 10	11 19		11 25	11 30		11 45							11 35	11 40	11 49		11 55	12 00
Canada Water	d			11 07	11 12	11 21		11 27	11 32		11 47							11 37	11 42	11 51		11 57	12 02
Rotherhithe	d			11 08	11 13	11 23		11 28	11 33		11 48							11 38	11 43	11 53		11 58	12 03
Wapping	d			11 10	11 15	11 24		11 30	11 35		11 50							11 40	11 45	11 54		12 00	12 05
Shadwell	d			11 12	11 17	11 26		11 32	11 37		11 52							11 42	11 47	11 56		12 02	12 07
Whitechapel	d			11 14	11 19	11 29		11 34	11 39		11 54							11 44	11 49	11 59		12 04	12 09
Shoreditch High Street	d			11 16	11 21	11 31		11 36	11 41		11 56							11 46	11 51	12 01		12 06	12 11
Hoxton	d			11 18	11 23	11 33		11 38	11 43		11 58							11 48	11 53	12 03		12 08	12 13
Haggerston	d			11 20	11 25	11 35		11 40	11 45		12 00							11 50	11 55	12 05		12 10	12 15
Dalston Junction Stn ELL	a			11 22	11 29	11 37		11 44	11 47		12 02							11 52	11 59	12 07		12 14	12 17
Canonbury	d			11 27		11 42			11 50		12 05							11 57		12 12			12 20
Highbury & Islington	d			11a30		11a44			11a53		12a08							12a00		12a14			12a23
London Bridge	a		11 11				11 29			11 41			11 26		11 36		11 41				11 59		

		SN	LO	SN	SN	SE	SN	SE	SN	LO	LO	LO	SN	LO	LO	SN	LO	SN	SN	SE	SN	SE
East Croydon	d												12 00									
West Croydon	d								11 31	11 39		11 52										
Norwood Junction	d									11 43		11 58	12 05									
Anerley	d									11 46		12 01	12 08									
Penge West	d									11 48		12 03	12 10									
London Victoria	d	11 19				11 39	11 41	11 43								11 49				12 09	12 11	12 13
Battersea Park	d	11 23					11 45									11 53					12 15	
Wandsworth Road	d						11 47														12 17	
Clapham High Street	d						11 49														12 19	
London Blackfriars	d																					
Denmark Hill	d					11 48	11 54	11 52												12 18	12 24	12 22
Peckham Rye	d			11 42	11 46	11a51	11 56	11a55	12 01									12 12	12 16	12a21	12 26	12a25
Queens Rd Peckham	d				11 49		11 59		12 04										12 19		12 29	
South Bermondsey	d				11 51		12 01		12 06										12 21		12 31	
Clapham Junction	d	11 27														11 57						
Wandsworth Common	d	11 30														12 00						
Balham	d	11 32														12 02						
Streatham Hill	d	11 35														12 05						
West Norwood	d	11 40		11 53												12 10		12 23				
Gipsy Hill	d	11 43		11 56												12 13		12 26				
Crystal Palace	d	11 51	11 58	11a59											12 13	12 21	12 28	12a29				
Sydenham	d	11 54	12 01							11 51		12 06	12 12		12 16	12 24	12 31					
Forest Hill	d	11 57	12 04							11 53		12 08	12 15		12 19	12 27	12 34					
Honor Oak Park	d	11 59	12 06							11 56		12 11	12 17		12 21	12 29	12 36					
Brockley	d	12 02	12 09							11 58		12 13	12 20		12 24	12 32	12 39					
New Cross Gate	a	12 04	12 11							12 01		12 16	12 22		12 26	12 34	12 41					
	d	12 04	12 11							12 01		12 16	12 22		12 26	12 34	12 41					
New Cross ELL	d										12 06			12 21								
Surrey Quays	d		12 15							12 05	12 10	12 19		12 25	12 30		12 45					
Canada Water	d		12 17							12 07	12 12	12 21		12 27	12 32		12 47					
Rotherhithe	d		12 18							12 08	12 13	12 23		12 28	12 33		12 48					
Wapping	d		12 20							12 10	12 15	12 24		12 30	12 35		12 50					
Shadwell	d		12 22							12 12	12 17	12 26		12 32	12 37		12 52					
Whitechapel	d		12 24							12 14	12 19	12 29		12 34	12 39		12 54					
Shoreditch High Street	d		12 26							12 16	12 21	12 31		12 36	12 41		12 56					
Hoxton	d		12 28							12 18	12 23	12 33		12 38	12 43		12 58					
Haggerston	d		12 30							12 20	12 25	12 35		12 40	12 45		13 00					
Dalston Junction Stn ELL	a		12 32							12 22	12 29	12 37		12 44	12 47		13 02					
Canonbury	d		12 35							12 27		12 42			12 50		13 05					
Highbury & Islington	d		12a38							12a30		12a44			12a53		13a08					
London Bridge	a	12 11			11 56		12 06		12 11				12 29			12 44			12 26		12 36	

East London Line and Croydon - London Victoria to London Bridge

		SN	LO	LO	LO	SN	LO	LO	SN	LO	SN	SN	SE	SN	SE	SN	LO	LO	LO	SN	LO	LO	SN
East Croydon	d					12 30														13 00			
West Croydon	d	12 01	12 09		12 22											12 31	12 39		12 52				
Norwood Junction	d		12 13		12 28	12 35											12 43		12 58	13 05			
Anerley	d		12 16		12 31	12 38											12 46		13 01	13 08			
Penge West	d		12 18		12 33	12 40											12 48		13 03	13 10			
London Victoria	d								12 19				12 39	12 41	12 43								12 49
Battersea Park	d								12 23					12 45									12 53
Wandsworth Road	d													12 47									
Clapham High Street	d													12 49									
London Blackfriars	d																						
Denmark Hill	d												12 48	12 54	12 52								
Peckham Rye	d	12 31									12 42	12 46	12a51	12 56	12a55	13 01							
Queens Rd Peckham	d	12 34										12 49		12 59		13 04							
South Bermondsey	d	12 36										12 51		13 01		13 06							
Clapham Junction	d								12 27														12 57
Wandsworth Common	d								12 30														13 00
Balham	d								12 32														13 02
Streatham Hill	d								12 35														13 05
West Norwood	d								12 40		12 53												13 10
Gipsy Hill	d								12 43		12 56												13 13
Crystal Palace	d							12 43	12 51	12 58	12a59											13 13	13 21
Sydenham	d		12 21		12 36	12 42		12 46	12 54	13 01							12 51		13 06	13 12		13 16	13 24
Forest Hill	d		12 23		12 38	12 45		12 49	12 57	13 04							12 53		13 08	13 15		13 19	13 27
Honor Oak Park	d		12 26		12 41	12 47		12 51	12 59	13 06							12 56		13 11	13 17		13 21	13 29
Brockley	d		12 28		12 43	12 50		12 54	13 02	13 09							12 58		13 13	13 20		13 24	13 32
New Cross Gate	a		12 31		12 46	12 52		12 56	13 04	13 11							13 01		13 16	13 22		13 26	13 34
	d		12 31		12 46	12 52		12 56	13 04	13 11							13 01		13 16	13 22		13 26	13 34
New Cross ELL	d			12 36			12 51											13 06			13 21		
Surrey Quays	d		12 35	12 40	12 49		12 55	13 00		13 15							13 05	13 10	13 19		13 25	13 30	
Canada Water	d		12 37	12 42	12 51		12 57	13 02		13 17							13 07	13 12	13 21		13 27	13 32	
Rotherhithe	d		12 38	12 43	12 53		12 58	13 03		13 18							13 08	13 13	13 23		13 28	13 33	
Wapping	d		12 40	12 45	12 54		13 00	13 05		13 20							13 10	13 15	13 24		13 30	13 35	
Shadwell	d		12 42	12 47	12 56		13 02	13 07		13 22							13 12	13 17	13 26		13 32	13 37	
Whitechapel	d		12 44	12 49	12 59		13 04	13 09		13 24							13 14	13 19	13 29		13 34	13 39	
Shoreditch High Street	d		12 46	12 51	13 01		13 06	13 11		13 26							13 16	13 21	13 31		13 36	13 41	
Hoxton	d		12 48	12 53	13 03		13 08	13 13		13 28							13 18	13 23	13 33		13 38	13 43	
Haggerston	d		12 50	12 55	13 05		13 10	13 15		13 30							13 20	13 25	13 35		13 40	13 45	
Dalston Junction Stn ELL	a		12 52	12 59	13 07		13 14	13 17		13 32							13 22	13 29	13 37		13 44	13 47	
Canonbury	d		12 57		13 12			13 20		13 35							13 27		13 42			13 50	
Highbury & Islington	d		13a00		13a14			13a23		13a38							13a30		13a44			13a53	
London Bridge	a	12 41				12 59			13 11			12 56		13 06		13 11				13 29			13 44

		LO	SN	SN	SE	SN	SE	SN	LO	LO	LO	SN	LO	LO	SN	LO	SN	SN	SE	SN	SE	SN
East Croydon	d											13 30										
West Croydon	d							13 01	13 09		13 22											13 31
Norwood Junction	d								13 13		13 28	13 35										
Anerley	d								13 16		13 31	13 38										
Penge West	d								13 18		13 33	13 40										
London Victoria	d				13 09	13 11	13 13								13 19				13 39	13 41	13 43	
Battersea Park	d					13 15									13 23					13 45		
Wandsworth Road	d					13 17														13 47		
Clapham High Street	d					13 19														13 49		
London Blackfriars	d																					
Denmark Hill	d				13 18	13 24	13 22												13 48	13 54	13 52	
Peckham Rye	d		13 12	13 16	13a21	13 26	13a25	13 31									13 42	13 46	13a51	13 56	13a55	14 01
Queens Rd Peckham	d			13 19		13 29		13 34										13 49		13 59		14 04
South Bermondsey	d			13 21		13 31		13 36										13 51		14 01		14 06
Clapham Junction	d														13 27							
Wandsworth Common	d														13 30							
Balham	d														13 32							
Streatham Hill	d														13 35							
West Norwood	d		13 23												13 40		13 53					
Gipsy Hill	d		13 26												13 43		13 56					
Crystal Palace	d	13 28	13a29											13 43	13 51	13 58	13a59					
Sydenham	d	13 31							13 21		13 36	13 42		13 46	13 54	14 01						
Forest Hill	d	13 34							13 23		13 38	13 45		13 49	13 57	14 04						
Honor Oak Park	d	13 36							13 26		13 41	13 47		13 51	13 59	14 06						
Brockley	d	13 39							13 28		13 43	13 50		13 54	14 02	14 09						
New Cross Gate	a	13 41							13 31		13 46	13 52		13 56	14 04	14 11						
	d	13 41							13 31		13 46	13 52		13 56	14 04	14 11						
New Cross ELL	d									13 36			13 51									
Surrey Quays	d	13 45							13 35	13 40	13 49		13 55	14 00		14 15						
Canada Water	d	13 47							13 37	13 42	13 51		13 57	14 02		14 17						
Rotherhithe	d	13 48							13 38	13 43	13 53		13 58	14 03		14 18						
Wapping	d	13 50							13 40	13 45	13 54		14 00	14 05		14 20						
Shadwell	d	13 52							13 42	13 47	13 56		14 02	14 07		14 22						
Whitechapel	d	13 54							13 44	13 49	13 59		14 04	14 09		14 24						
Shoreditch High Street	d	13 56							13 46	13 51	14 01		14 06	14 11		14 26						
Hoxton	d	13 58							13 48	13 53	14 03		14 08	14 13		14 28						
Haggerston	d	14 00							13 50	13 55	14 05		14 10	14 15		14 30						
Dalston Junction Stn ELL	a	14 02							13 52	13 59	14 07		14 14	14 17		14 32						
Canonbury	d	14 05							13 57		14 12			14 20		14 35						
Highbury & Islington	d	14a08							14a00		14a14			14a23		14a38						
London Bridge	a			13 26		13 36		13 41				13 59			14 11			13 56		14 06		14 11

Table 178 Saturdays

East London Line and Croydon - London Victoria to London Bridge

		LO	LO	LO	SN	LO	LO	SN	LO	SN	SN	SE	SN	SE	SN	LO	LO	LO	SN	LO	LO	SN	LO
East Croydon	d				14 00														14 30				
West Croydon	d	13 39		13 52											14 01	14 09		14 22					
Norwood Junction	d	13 43		13 58	14 05											14 13		14 28	14 35				
Anerley	d	13 46		14 01	14 08											14 16		14 31	14 38				
Penge West	d	13 48		14 03	14 10											14 18		14 33	14 40				
London Victoria	d							13 49				14 09	14 11	14 13								14 19	
Battersea Park	d							13 53					14 15									14 23	
Wandsworth Road	d												14 17										
Clapham High Street	d												14 19										
London Blackfriars	d																						
Denmark Hill	d											14 18	14 24	14 22									
Peckham Rye	d									14 12	14 16	14a21	14 26	14a25	14 31								
Queens Rd Peckham	d										14 19		14 29		14 34								
South Bermondsey	d										14 21		14 31		14 36								
Clapham Junction	d							13 57														14 27	
Wandsworth Common	d							14 00														14 30	
Balham	d							14 02														14 32	
Streatham Hill	d							14 05														14 35	
West Norwood	d							14 10		14 23												14 40	
Gipsy Hill	d							14 13		14 26												14 43	
Crystal Palace	d						14 13	14 21	14 28	14a29											14 43	14 51	14 58
Sydenham	d	13 51		14 06	14 12		14 16	14 24	14 31							14 21		14 36	14 42		14 46	14 54	15 01
Forest Hill	d	13 53		14 08	14 15		14 19	14 27	14 34							14 23		14 38	14 45		14 49	14 57	15 04
Honor Oak Park	d	13 56		14 11	14 17		14 21	14 29	14 36							14 26		14 41	14 47		14 51	14 59	15 06
Brockley	d	13 58		14 13	14 20		14 24	14 32	14 39							14 28		14 43	14 50		14 54	15 02	15 09
New Cross Gate	a	14 01		14 16	14 22		14 26	14 34	14 41							14 31		14 46	14 52		14 56	15 04	15 11
	d	14 01		14 16	14 22		14 26	14 34	14 41							14 31		14 46	14 52		14 56	15 04	15 11
New Cross ELL	d		14 06			14 21											14 36			14 51			
Surrey Quays	d	14 05	14 10	14 19		14 25	14 30		14 45							14 35	14 40	14 49		14 55	15 00		15 15
Canada Water	d	14 07	14 12	14 21		14 27	14 32		14 47							14 37	14 42	14 51		14 57	15 02		15 17
Rotherhithe	d	14 08	14 13	14 23		14 28	14 33		14 48							14 38	14 43	14 53		14 58	15 03		15 18
Wapping	d	14 10	14 15	14 24		14 30	14 35		14 50							14 40	14 45	14 54		15 00	15 05		15 20
Shadwell	d	14 12	14 17	14 26		14 32	14 37		14 52							14 42	14 47	14 56		15 02	15 07		15 22
Whitechapel	d	14 14	14 19	14 29		14 34	14 39		14 54							14 44	14 49	14 59		15 04	15 09		15 24
Shoreditch High Street	d	14 16	14 21	14 31		14 36	14 41		14 56							14 46	14 51	15 01		15 06	15 11		15 26
Hoxton	d	14 18	14 23	14 33		14 38	14 43		14 58							14 48	14 53	15 03		15 08	15 13		15 28
Haggerston	d	14 20	14 25	14 35		14 40	14 45		15 00							14 50	14 55	15 05		15 10	15 15		15 30
Dalston Junction Stn ELL	a	14 22	14 29	14 37		14 44	14 47		15 02							14 52	14 59	15 07		15 14	15 17		15 32
Canonbury	d	14 27		14 42			14 50		15 05							14 57		15 12			15 20		15 35
Highbury & Islington	d	14a30		14a44			14a53		15a08							15a00		15a14			15a23		15a38
London Bridge	a				14 29			14 44			14 26		14 36		14 41				14 59			15 11	

		SN	SN	SE	SN	SE	SN	LO	LO	LO	SN	LO	LO	SN	LO	SN	SN	SE	SN	SE	SN	LO	LO
East Croydon	d										15 00												
West Croydon	d						14 31	14 39		14 52											15 01	15 09	
Norwood Junction	d							14 43		14 58	15 05											15 13	
Anerley	d							14 46		15 01	15 08											15 16	
Penge West	d							14 48		15 03	15 10											15 18	
London Victoria	d			14 39	14 41	14 43								14 49				15 09	15 11	15 13			
Battersea Park	d				14 45									14 53					15 15				
Wandsworth Road	d				14 47														15 17				
Clapham High Street	d				14 49														15 19				
London Blackfriars	d																						
Denmark Hill	d			14 48	14 54	14 52												15 18	15 24	15 22			
Peckham Rye	d	14 42	14 46	14a51	14 56	14a55	15 01									15 12	15 16	15a21	15 26	15a25	15 31		
Queens Rd Peckham	d		14 49		14 59		15 04										15 19		15 29		15 34		
South Bermondsey	d		14 51		15 01		15 06										15 21		15 31		15 36		
Clapham Junction	d													14 57									
Wandsworth Common	d													15 00									
Balham	d													15 02									
Streatham Hill	d													15 05									
West Norwood	d	14 53												15 10		15 23							
Gipsy Hill	d	14 56												15 13		15 26							
Crystal Palace	d	14a59											15 13	15 21	15 28	15a29							
Sydenham	d							14 51		15 06	15 12		15 16	15 24	15 31							15 21	
Forest Hill	d							14 53		15 08	15 15		15 19	15 27	15 34							15 23	
Honor Oak Park	d							14 56		15 11	15 17		15 21	15 29	15 36							15 26	
Brockley	d							14 58		15 13	15 20		15 24	15 32	15 39							15 28	
New Cross Gate	a							15 01		15 16	15 22		15 26	15 34	15 41							15 31	
	d							15 01		15 16	15 22		15 26	15 34	15 41							15 31	
New Cross ELL	d								15 06			15 21											15 36
Surrey Quays	d							15 05	15 10	15 19		15 25	15 30		15 45							15 35	15 40
Canada Water	d							15 07	15 12	15 21		15 27	15 32		15 47							15 37	15 42
Rotherhithe	d							15 08	15 13	15 23		15 28	15 33		15 48							15 38	15 43
Wapping	d							15 10	15 15	15 24		15 30	15 35		15 50							15 40	15 45
Shadwell	d							15 12	15 17	15 26		15 32	15 37		15 52							15 42	15 47
Whitechapel	d							15 14	15 19	15 29		15 34	15 39		15 54							15 44	15 49
Shoreditch High Street	d							15 16	15 21	15 31		15 36	15 41		15 56							15 46	15 51
Hoxton	d							15 18	15 23	15 33		15 38	15 43		15 58							15 48	15 53
Haggerston	d							15 20	15 25	15 35		15 40	15 45		16 00							15 50	15 55
Dalston Junction Stn ELL	a							15 22	15 29	15 37		15 44	15 47		16 02							15 52	15 59
Canonbury	d							15 27		15 42			15 50		16 05							15 57	
Highbury & Islington	d							15a30		15a44			15a53		16a08							16a00	
London Bridge	a		14 56		15 06		15 11				15 29			15 44			15 26		15 36		15 41		

East London Line and Croydon - London Victoria to London Bridge

		LO	SN	LO	LO	SN	LO	SN	SN	SE	SN	SE	SN	LO	LO	LO	SN	LO	LO	SN	LO	SN
East Croydon	d		15 30														16 00					
West Croydon	d	15 22											15 31	15 39		15 52						
Norwood Junction	d	15 28	15 35											15 43		15 58	16 05					
Anerley	d	15 31	15 38											15 46		16 01	16 08					
Penge West	d	15 33	15 40											15 48		16 03	16 10					
London Victoria ⊖	d					15 19				15 39	15 41	15 43								15 49		
Battersea Park	d					15 23					15 45									15 53		
Wandsworth Road	d										15 47											
Clapham High Street ⊖	d										15 49											
London Blackfriars ⊖	d																					
Denmark Hill	d									15 48	15 54	15 52										
Peckham Rye	d							15 42	15 46	15a51	15 56	15a55	16 01									16 12
Queens Rd Peckham	d								15 49		15 59		16 04									
South Bermondsey	d								15 51		16 01		16 06									
Clapham Junction	d					15 27														15 57		
Wandsworth Common	d					15 30														16 00		
Balham ⊖	d					15 32														16 02		
Streatham Hill	d					15 35														16 05		
West Norwood	d					15 40		15 53												16 10		16 23
Gipsy Hill	d					15 43		15 56												16 13		16 26
Crystal Palace	d				15 43	15 51	15 58	15a59											16 13	16 21	16 28	16a29
Sydenham	d	15 36	15 42		15 46	15 54	16 01							15 51		16 06	16 12		16 16	16 24	16 31	
Forest Hill	d	15 38	15 45		15 49	15 57	16 04							15 53		16 08	16 15		16 19	16 27	16 34	
Honor Oak Park	d	15 41	15 47		15 51	15 59	16 06							15 56		16 11	16 17		16 21	16 29	16 36	
Brockley	d	15 43	15 50		15 54	16 02	16 09							15 58		16 13	16 20		16 24	16 32	16 39	
New Cross Gate	a	15 46	15 52		15 56	16 04	16 11							16 01		16 16	16 22		16 26	16 34	16 41	
	d	15 46	15 52		15 56	16 04	16 11							16 01		16 16	16 22		16 26	16 34	16 41	
New Cross ELL	d			15 51											16 06			16 21				
Surrey Quays	d	15 49		15 55	16 00		16 15							16 05	16 10	16 19		16 25	16 30		16 45	
Canada Water	d	15 51		15 57	16 02		16 17							16 07	16 12	16 21		16 27	16 32		16 47	
Rotherhithe	d	15 53		15 58	16 03		16 18							16 08	16 13	16 23		16 28	16 33		16 48	
Wapping	d	15 54		16 00	16 05		16 20							16 10	16 15	16 24		16 30	16 35		16 50	
Shadwell	d	15 56		16 02	16 07		16 22							16 12	16 17	16 26		16 32	16 37		16 52	
Whitechapel	d	15 59		16 04	16 09		16 24							16 14	16 19	16 29		16 34	16 39		16 54	
Shoreditch High Street	d	16 01		16 06	16 11		16 26							16 16	16 21	16 31		16 36	16 41		16 56	
Hoxton	d	16 03		16 08	16 13		16 28							16 18	16 23	16 33		16 38	16 43		16 58	
Haggerston	d	16 05		16 10	16 15		16 30							16 20	16 25	16 35		16 40	16 45		17 00	
Dalston Junction Stn ELL	a	16 07		16 14	16 17		16 32							16 22	16 29	16 37		16 44	16 47		17 02	
Canonbury	d	16 12			16 20		16 35							16 27		16 42			16 50		17 05	
Highbury & Islington	d	16a14			16a23		16a38							16a30		16a44			16a53		17a08	
London Bridge ⊖	a		15 59			16 11			15 56		16 06		16 11				16 29			16 41		

		SN	SE	SN	SE	SN	LO	LO	LO	SN	LO	LO	SN	LO	SN	SN	SE	SN	SE	SN	LO	LO	LO
East Croydon	d									16 30													
West Croydon	d					16 01	16 09		16 22											16 31	16 39		16 52
Norwood Junction	d						16 13		16 28	16 35											16 43		16 58
Anerley	d						16 16		16 31	16 38											16 46		17 01
Penge West	d						16 18		16 33	16 40											16 48		17 03
London Victoria ⊖	d		16 09	16 11	16 13								16 19				16 39	16 41	16 43				
Battersea Park	d			16 15									16 23					16 45					
Wandsworth Road	d			16 17														16 47					
Clapham High Street ⊖	d			16 19														16 49					
London Blackfriars ⊖	d																						
Denmark Hill	d		16 18	16 24	16 22												16 48	16 54	16 52				
Peckham Rye	d	16 16	16a21	16 26	16a25	16 31									16 42	16 46	16a51	16 56	16a55	17 01			
Queens Rd Peckham	d	16 19		16 29		16 34										16 49		16 59		17 04			
South Bermondsey	d	16 21		16 31		16 36										16 51		17 01		17 06			
Clapham Junction	d												16 27										
Wandsworth Common	d												16 30										
Balham ⊖	d												16 32										
Streatham Hill	d												16 35										
West Norwood	d												16 40		16 53								
Gipsy Hill	d												16 43		16 56								
Crystal Palace	d											16 43	16 51	16 58	16a59								
Sydenham	d						16 21		16 36	16 42		16 46	16 54	17 01							16 51		17 06
Forest Hill	d						16 23		16 38	16 45		16 49	16 57	17 04							16 53		17 08
Honor Oak Park	d						16 26		16 41	16 47		16 51	16 59	17 06							16 56		17 11
Brockley	d						16 28		16 43	16 50		16 54	17 02	17 09							16 58		17 13
New Cross Gate	a						16 31		16 46	16 52		16 56	17 04	17 11							17 01		17 16
	d						16 31		16 46	16 52		16 56	17 04	17 11							17 01		17 16
New Cross ELL	d							16 36			16 51											17 06	
Surrey Quays	d						16 35	16 40	16 49		16 55	17 00		17 15							17 05	17 10	17 19
Canada Water	d						16 37	16 42	16 51		16 57	17 02		17 17							17 07	17 12	17 21
Rotherhithe	d						16 38	16 43	16 53		16 58	17 03		17 18							17 08	17 13	17 23
Wapping	d						16 40	16 45	16 54		17 00	17 05		17 20							17 10	17 15	17 24
Shadwell	d						16 42	16 47	16 56		17 02	17 07		17 22							17 12	17 17	17 26
Whitechapel	d						16 44	16 49	16 59		17 04	17 09		17 24							17 14	17 19	17 29
Shoreditch High Street	d						16 46	16 51	17 01		17 06	17 11		17 26							17 16	17 21	17 31
Hoxton	d						16 48	16 53	17 03		17 08	17 13		17 28							17 18	17 23	17 33
Haggerston	d						16 50	16 55	17 05		17 10	17 15		17 30							17 20	17 25	17 35
Dalston Junction Stn ELL	a						16 52	16 59	17 07		17 14	17 17		17 32							17 22	17 29	17 37
Canonbury	d						16 57		17 12			17 20		17 35							17 27		17 42
Highbury & Islington	d						17a00		17a14			17a23		17a38							17a30		17a44
London Bridge ⊖	a	16 26		16 36		16 41				16 59			17 11			16 56		17 06		17 11			

East London Line and Croydon - London Victoria to London Bridge

		SN	LO	LO	SN	LO	SN	SN	SE	SN	SE	SN	LO	LO	LO	SN	LO	LO	SN	LO	SN	SN
East Croydon	d	17 00														17 30						
West Croydon	d											17 01	17 09		17 22							
Norwood Junction	d	17 05											17 13		17 28	17 35						
Anerley	d	17 08											17 16		17 31	17 38						
Penge West	d	17 10											17 18		17 33	17 40						
London Victoria ⊖	d				16 49				17 09	17 11	17 13								17 19			
Battersea Park	d				16 53					17 15									17 23			
Wandsworth Road	d									17 17												
Clapham High Street ⊖	d									17 19												
London Blackfriars ⊖	d																					
Denmark Hill	d								17 18	17 24	17 22											
Peckham Rye	d						17 12	17 16	17a21	17 26	17a25	17 31									17 42	17 46
Queens Rd Peckham	d							17 19		17 29		17 34										17 49
South Bermondsey	d							17 21		17 31		17 36										17 51
Clapham Junction	d				16 57														17 27			
Wandsworth Common	d				17 00														17 30			
Balham ⊖	d				17 02														17 32			
Streatham Hill	d				17 05														17 35			
West Norwood	d				17 10		17 23												17 40		17 53	
Gipsy Hill	d				17 13		17 26												17 43		17 56	
Crystal Palace	d			17 13	17 21	17 28	17a29											17 43	17 51	17 58	17a59	
Sydenham	d	17 12		17 16	17 24	17 31							17 21		17 36	17 42		17 46	17 54	18 01		
Forest Hill	d	17 15		17 19	17 27	17 34							17 23		17 38	17 45		17 49	17 57	18 04		
Honor Oak Park	d	17 17		17 21	17 29	17 36							17 26		17 41	17 47		17 51	17 59	18 06		
Brockley	d	17 20		17 24	17 32	17 39							17 28		17 43	17 50		17 54	18 02	18 09		
New Cross Gate	a	17 22		17 26	17 34	17 41							17 31		17 46	17 52		17 56	18 04	18 11		
	d	17 22		17 26	17 34	17 41							17 31		17 46	17 52		17 56	18 04	18 11		
New Cross ELL	d		17 21											17 36			17 51					
Surrey Quays	d		17 25	17 30		17 45							17 35	17 40	17 49		17 55	18 00		18 15		
Canada Water	d		17 27	17 32		17 47							17 37	17 42	17 51		17 57	18 02		18 17		
Rotherhithe	d		17 28	17 33		17 48							17 38	17 43	17 53		17 58	18 03		18 18		
Wapping	d		17 30	17 35		17 50							17 40	17 45	17 54		18 00	18 05		18 20		
Shadwell	d		17 32	17 37		17 52							17 42	17 47	17 56		18 02	18 07		18 22		
Whitechapel	d		17 34	17 39		17 54							17 44	17 49	17 59		18 04	18 09		18 24		
Shoreditch High Street	d		17 36	17 41		17 56							17 46	17 51	18 01		18 06	18 11		18 26		
Hoxton	d		17 38	17 43		17 58							17 48	17 53	18 03		18 08	18 13		18 28		
Haggerston	d		17 40	17 45		18 00							17 50	17 55	18 05		18 10	18 15		18 30		
Dalston Junction Stn ELL	a		17 44	17 47		18 02							17 52	17 59	18 07		18 14	18 17		18 32		
Canonbury	d			17 50		18 05							17 57		18 12			18 20		18 35		
Highbury & Islington	d			17a53		18a08							18a00		18a14			18a23		18a38		
London Bridge ⊖	a	17 30			17 41			17 26		17 36		17 41				17 59			18 11			17 56

		SE	SN	SE	SN	LO	LO	LO	SN	LO	LO	SN	LO	SN	SN	SE	SN	SE	SN	LO	LO	LO	SN
East Croydon	d								18 00														18 30
West Croydon	d				17 31	17 39		17 52											18 01	18 09		18 22	
Norwood Junction	d					17 43		17 58	18 05											18 13		18 28	18 35
Anerley	d					17 46		18 01	18 08											18 16		18 31	18 38
Penge West	d					17 48		18 03	18 10											18 18		18 33	18 40
London Victoria ⊖	d	17 39	17 41	17 43								17 49				18 09	18 11	18 13					
Battersea Park	d		17 45									17 53					18 15						
Wandsworth Road	d		17 47														18 17						
Clapham High Street ⊖	d		17 49														18 19						
London Blackfriars ⊖	d																						
Denmark Hill	d	17 48	17 54	17 52												18 18	18 24	18 22					
Peckham Rye	d	17a51	17 56	17a55	18 01									18 12	18 16	18a21	18 26	18a25	18 31				
Queens Rd Peckham	d		17 59		18 04										18 19		18 29		18 34				
South Bermondsey	d		18 01		18 06										18 21		18 31		18 36				
Clapham Junction	d											17 57											
Wandsworth Common	d											18 00											
Balham ⊖	d											18 02											
Streatham Hill	d											18 05											
West Norwood	d											18 10		18 23									
Gipsy Hill	d											18 13		18 26									
Crystal Palace	d										18 13	18 21	18 28	18a29									
Sydenham	d					17 51		18 06	18 12		18 16	18 24	18 31							18 21		18 36	18 42
Forest Hill	d					17 53		18 08	18 15		18 19	18 27	18 34							18 23		18 38	18 45
Honor Oak Park	d					17 56		18 11	18 17		18 21	18 29	18 36							18 26		18 41	18 47
Brockley	d					17 58		18 13	18 20		18 24	18 32	18 39							18 28		18 43	18 50
New Cross Gate	a					18 01		18 16	18 22		18 26	18 34	18 41							18 31		18 46	18 52
	d					18 01		18 16	18 22		18 26	18 34	18 41							18 31		18 46	18 52
New Cross ELL	d						18 06			18 21											18 36		
Surrey Quays	d					18 05	18 10	18 19		18 25	18 30		18 45							18 35	18 40	18 49	
Canada Water	d					18 07	18 12	18 21		18 27	18 32		18 47							18 37	18 42	18 51	
Rotherhithe	d					18 08	18 13	18 23		18 28	18 33		18 48							18 38	18 43	18 53	
Wapping	d					18 10	18 15	18 24		18 30	18 35		18 50							18 40	18 45	18 54	
Shadwell	d					18 12	18 17	18 26		18 32	18 37		18 52							18 42	18 47	18 56	
Whitechapel	d					18 14	18 19	18 29		18 34	18 39		18 54							18 44	18 49	18 59	
Shoreditch High Street	d					18 16	18 21	18 31		18 36	18 41		18 56							18 46	18 51	19 01	
Hoxton	d					18 18	18 23	18 33		18 38	18 43		18 58							18 48	18 53	19 03	
Haggerston	d					18 20	18 25	18 35		18 40	18 45		19 00							18 50	18 55	19 05	
Dalston Junction Stn ELL	a					18 22	18 29	18 37		18 44	18 47		19 02							18 52	18 59	19 07	
Canonbury	d					18 27		18 42			18 50		19 05							18 57		19 12	
Highbury & Islington	d					18a30		18a44			18a53		19a08							19a00		19a14	
London Bridge ⊖	a		18 06		18 11				18 29			18 41			18 26		18 36		18 41				18 59

Table 178

Saturdays

East London Line and Croydon - London Victoria to London Bridge

Station		LO	LO	SN	LO	SN	SN	SE	SN	SE	SN	LO	LO	LO	SN	LO	LO	SN	LO	SN	SN	SE	SN
East Croydon 🚊	d														19 00								
West Croydon 4 🚊	d										18 31	18 39		18 52									
Norwood Junction 2	d											18 43		18 58	19 05								
Anerley	d											18 46		19 01	19 08								
Penge West	d											18 48		19 03	19 10								
London Victoria 15 ⊖	d			18 19				18 39	18 41	18 43								18 49				19 09	19 11
Battersea Park 4	d			18 23					18 45									18 53					19 15
Wandsworth Road	d								18 47														19 17
Clapham High Street ⊖	d								18 49														19 19
London Blackfriars 3 ⊖	d																						
Denmark Hill 4	d							18 48	18 54	18 52												19 18	19 24
Peckham Rye 4	d					18 42	18 46	18a51	18 56	18a55	19 01									19 12	19 16	19a21	19 26
Queens Rd Peckham	d						18 49		18 59		19 04										19 19		19 29
South Bermondsey	d						18 51		19 01		19 06										19 21		19 31
Clapham Junction 10	d			18 27														18 57					
Wandsworth Common	d			18 30														19 00					
Balham 4 ⊖	d			18 32														19 02					
Streatham Hill	d			18 35														19 05					
West Norwood 4	d			18 40		18 53												19 10		19 23			
Gipsy Hill	d			18 43		18 56												19 13		19 26			
Crystal Palace 4	d		18 43	18 51	18 58	18a59											19 13	19 21	19 28	19a29			
Sydenham	d		18 46	18 54	19 01							18 51		19 06	19 12		19 16	19 24	19 31				
Forest Hill 4	d		18 49	18 57	19 04							18 53		19 08	19 15		19 19	19 27	19 34				
Honor Oak Park	d		18 51	18 59	19 06							18 56		19 11	19 17		19 21	19 29	19 36				
Brockley	d		18 54	19 02	19 09							18 58		19 13	19 20		19 24	19 32	19 39				
New Cross Gate 4	a		18 56	19 04	19 11							19 01		19 16	19 22		19 26	19 34	19 41				
	d		18 56	19 04	19 11							19 01		19 16	19 22		19 26	19 34	19 41				
New Cross ELL	d	18 51											19 06			19 21							
Surrey Quays	d	18 55	19 00		19 15							19 05	19 10	19 19		19 25	19 30		19 45				
Canada Water	d	18 57	19 02		19 17							19 07	19 12	19 21		19 27	19 32		19 47				
Rotherhithe	d	18 58	19 03		19 18							19 08	19 13	19 23		19 28	19 33		19 48				
Wapping	d	19 00	19 05		19 20							19 10	19 15	19 24		19 30	19 35		19 50				
Shadwell	d	19 02	19 07		19 22							19 12	19 17	19 26		19 32	19 37		19 52				
Whitechapel	d	19 04	19 09		19 24							19 14	19 19	19 29		19 34	19 39		19 54				
Shoreditch High Street	d	19 06	19 11		19 26							19 16	19 21	19 31		19 36	19 41		19 56				
Hoxton	d	19 08	19 13		19 28							19 18	19 23	19 33		19 38	19 43		19 58				
Haggerston	d	19 10	19 15		19 30							19 20	19 25	19 35		19 40	19 45		20 00				
Dalston Junction Stn ELL	a	19 14	19 17		19 32							19 22	19 29	19 37		19 44	19 47		20 02				
Canonbury	d		19 20		19 35							19 27		19 42			19 50		20 05				
Highbury & Islington	d		19a23		19a38							19a30		19a44			19a53		20a08				
London Bridge 4 ⊖	a			19 11			18 56		19 06		19 11				19 29			19 41			19 26		19 36

Station		SE	SN	LO	LO	LO	SN	LO	LO	SN	LO	SN	SN	SE	SN	SE	SN	LO	LO	LO	SN	LO
East Croydon 🚊	d						19 30														20 00	
West Croydon 4 🚊	d		19 01	19 09		19 22											19 31	19 39		19 52		
Norwood Junction 2	d			19 13		19 28	19 35											19 43		19 58	20 05	
Anerley	d			19 16		19 31	19 38											19 46		20 01	20 08	
Penge West	d			19 18		19 33	19 40											19 48		20 03	20 10	
London Victoria 15 ⊖	d	19 13								19 19				19 39	19 41	19 43						
Battersea Park 4	d									19 23					19 45							
Wandsworth Road	d														19 47							
Clapham High Street ⊖	d														19 49							
London Blackfriars 3 ⊖	d																					
Denmark Hill 4	d	19 22												19 48	19 54	19 52						
Peckham Rye 4	d	19a25	19 31									19 42	19 46	19a51	19 56	19a55	20 01					
Queens Rd Peckham	d		19 34										19 49		19 59		20 04					
South Bermondsey	d		19 36										19 51		20 01		20 06					
Clapham Junction 10	d									19 27												
Wandsworth Common	d									19 30												
Balham 4 ⊖	d									19 32												
Streatham Hill	d									19 35												
West Norwood 4	d									19 40		19 53										
Gipsy Hill	d									19 43		19 56										
Crystal Palace 4	d								19 43	19 51	19 58	19a59										
Sydenham	d			19 21		19 36	19 42		19 46	19 54	20 01							19 51		20 06	20 12	
Forest Hill 4	d			19 23		19 38	19 45		19 49	19 57	20 04							19 53		20 08	20 15	
Honor Oak Park	d			19 26		19 41	19 47		19 51	19 59	20 06							19 56		20 11	20 17	
Brockley	d			19 28		19 43	19 50		19 54	20 02	20 09							19 58		20 13	20 20	
New Cross Gate 4	a			19 31		19 46	19 52		19 56	20 04	20 11							20 01		20 16	20 22	
	d			19 31		19 46	19 52		19 56	20 04	20 11							20 01		20 16	20 22	
New Cross ELL	d				19 36			19 51											20 06			20 21
Surrey Quays	d			19 35	19 40	19 49		19 55	20 00		20 15							20 05	20 10	20 19		20 25
Canada Water	d			19 37	19 42	19 51		19 57	20 02		20 17							20 07	20 12	20 21		20 27
Rotherhithe	d			19 38	19 43	19 53		19 58	20 03		20 18							20 08	20 13	20 23		20 28
Wapping	d			19 40	19 45	19 54		20 00	20 05		20 20							20 10	20 15	20 24		20 30
Shadwell	d			19 42	19 47	19 56		20 02	20 07		20 22							20 12	20 17	20 26		20 32
Whitechapel	d			19 44	19 49	19 59		20 04	20 09		20 24							20 14	20 19	20 29		20 34
Shoreditch High Street	d			19 46	19 51	20 01		20 06	20 11		20 26							20 16	20 21	20 31		20 36
Hoxton	d			19 48	19 53	20 03		20 08	20 13		20 28							20 18	20 23	20 33		20 38
Haggerston	d			19 50	19 55	20 05		20 10	20 15		20 30							20 20	20 25	20 35		20 40
Dalston Junction Stn ELL	a			19 52	19 59	20 07		20 14	20 17		20 32							20 22	20 29	20 37		20 44
Canonbury	d			19 57		20 12			20 20		20 35							20 27		20 42		
Highbury & Islington	d			20a00		20a14			20a23		20a38							20a30		20a44		
London Bridge 4 ⊖	a		19 41				19 59			20 11			19 56		20 06		20 11				20 29	

Table 178

Saturdays

East London Line and Croydon - London Victoria to London Bridge

Station		LO	SN	LO	SN	SN	SN	SE	SN	LO	LO	LO	SN	LO	LO	SN	LO	SN	SN	SN	SE	SN	LO
East Croydon 🚊	d												20 30										
West Croydon 4 🚊	d								20 01	20 09		20 22										20 31	20 39
Norwood Junction 2	d									20 13		20 28	20 35										20 43
Anerley	d									20 16		20 31	20 38										20 46
Penge West	d									20 18		20 33	20 40										20 48
London Victoria 15 ⊖	d		19 49				20 11	20 13								20 19				20 41	20 43		
Battersea Park 4	d		19 53				20 15									20 23				20 45			
Wandsworth Road	d						20 17													20 47			
Clapham High Street ⊖	d						20 19													20 49			
London Blackfriars 3 ⊖	d																						
Denmark Hill 4	d						20 24	20 22												20 54	20 52		
Peckham Rye 4	d				20 12	20 16	20 26	20a25	20 31									20 42	20 46	20 56	20a55	21 01	
Queens Rd Peckham	d					20 19	20 29		20 34										20 49	20 59		21 04	
South Bermondsey	d					20 21	20 31		20 36										20 51	21 01		21 06	
Clapham Junction 10	d		19 57													20 27							
Wandsworth Common	d		20 00													20 30							
Balham 4 ⊖	d		20 02													20 32							
Streatham Hill	d		20 05													20 35							
West Norwood 4	d		20 10		20 23											20 40		20 53					
Gipsy Hill	d		20 13		20 26											20 43		20 56					
Crystal Palace 4	d	20 13	20 21	20 28	20a29										20 43	20 51	20 58	20a59					
Sydenham	d	20 16	20 24	20 31						20 21		20 36	20 42		20 46	20 54	21 01						20 51
Forest Hill 4	d	20 19	20 27	20 34						20 23		20 38	20 45		20 49	20 57	21 04						20 53
Honor Oak Park	d	20 21	20 29	20 36						20 26		20 41	20 47		20 51	20 59	21 06						20 56
Brockley	d	20 24	20 32	20 39						20 28		20 43	20 50		20 54	21 02	21 09						20 58
New Cross Gate 4	a	20 26	20 34	20 41						20 31		20 46	20 52		20 56	21 04	21 11						21 01
	d	20 26	20 34	20 41						20 31		20 46	20 52		20 56	21 04	21 11						21 01
New Cross ELL	d										20 36			20 51									
Surrey Quays	d	20 30		20 45						20 35	20 40	20 49		20 55	21 00		21 15						21 05
Canada Water	d	20 32		20 47						20 37	20 42	20 51		20 57	21 02		21 17						21 07
Rotherhithe	d	20 33		20 48						20 38	20 43	20 53		20 58	21 03		21 18						21 08
Wapping	d	20 35		20 50						20 40	20 45	20 54		21 00	21 05		21 20						21 10
Shadwell	d	20 37		20 52						20 42	20 47	20 56		21 02	21 07		21 22						21 12
Whitechapel	d	20 39		20 54						20 44	20 49	20 59		21 04	21 09		21 24						21 14
Shoreditch High Street	d	20 41		20 56						20 46	20 51	21 01		21 06	21 11		21 26						21 16
Hoxton	d	20 43		20 58						20 48	20 53	21 03		21 08	21 13		21 28						21 18
Haggerston	d	20 45		21 00						20 50	20 55	21 05		21 10	21 15		21 30						21 20
Dalston Junction Stn ELL	a	20 47		21 02						20 52	20 59	21 07		21 14	21 17		21 32						21 22
Canonbury	d	20 50		21 05						20 57		21 12			21 20		21 35						21 27
Highbury & Islington	d	20a53		21a08						21a00		21a14			21a23		21a38						21a30
London Bridge 4 ⊖	a		20 41			20 26	20 36		20 41				20 59			21 13			20 56	21 06		21 11	

Station		LO	LO	SN	LO	LO	SN	LO	SN	SN	SN	SE	SN	LO	LO	LO	SN	LO	LO	SN	LO	SN
East Croydon 🚊	d			21 00													21 30					
West Croydon 4 🚊	d		20 52										21 02	21 09		21 22						
Norwood Junction 2	d		20 58	21 05										21 13		21 28	21 35					
Anerley	d		21 01	21 08										21 16		21 31	21 38					
Penge West	d		21 03	21 10										21 18		21 33	21 40					
London Victoria 15 ⊖	d						20 49				21 11	21 13								21 19		
Battersea Park 4	d						20 53				21 15									21 23		
Wandsworth Road	d										21 17											
Clapham High Street ⊖	d										21 19											
London Blackfriars 3 ⊖	d																					
Denmark Hill 4	d										21 24	21 22										
Peckham Rye 4	d								21 12	21 16	21 26	21a25	21 31									21 42
Queens Rd Peckham	d									21 19	21 29		21 34									
South Bermondsey	d									21 21	21 31		21 36									
Clapham Junction 10	d						20 57													21 27		
Wandsworth Common	d						21 00													21 30		
Balham 4 ⊖	d						21 02													21 32		
Streatham Hill	d						21 05													21 35		
West Norwood 4	d						21 10		21 23											21 40		21 53
Gipsy Hill	d						21 13		21 26											21 43		21 56
Crystal Palace 4	d					21 13	21 21	21 28	21a29										21 43	21 51	21 58	21a59
Sydenham	d		21 06	21 12		21 16	21 24	21 31						21 21		21 36	21 42		21 46	21 54	22 01	
Forest Hill 4	d		21 08	21 15		21 19	21 27	21 34						21 23		21 38	21 45		21 49	21 57	22 04	
Honor Oak Park	d		21 11	21 17		21 21	21 29	21 36						21 26		21 41	21 47		21 51	21 59	22 06	
Brockley	d		21 13	21 20		21 24	21 32	21 39						21 28		21 43	21 50		21 54	22 02	22 09	
New Cross Gate 4	a		21 16	21 22		21 26	21 34	21 41						21 31		21 46	21 52		21 56	22 04	22 11	
	d		21 16	21 22		21 26	21 34	21 41						21 31		21 46	21 52		21 56	22 04	22 11	
New Cross ELL	d	21 06			21 21										21 36			21 51				
Surrey Quays	d	21 10	21 19		21 25	21 30		21 45						21 35	21 40	21 49		21 55	22 00		22 15	
Canada Water	d	21 12	21 21		21 27	21 32		21 47						21 37	21 42	21 51		21 57	22 02		22 17	
Rotherhithe	d	21 13	21 23		21 28	21 33		21 48						21 38	21 43	21 53		21 58	22 03		22 18	
Wapping	d	21 15	21 24		21 30	21 35		21 50						21 40	21 45	21 54		22 00	22 05		22 20	
Shadwell	d	21 17	21 26		21 32	21 37		21 52						21 42	21 47	21 56		22 02	22 07		22 22	
Whitechapel	d	21 19	21 29		21 34	21 39		21 54						21 44	21 49	21 59		22 04	22 09		22 24	
Shoreditch High Street	d	21 21	21 31		21 36	21 41		21 56						21 46	21 51	22 01		22 06	22 11		22 26	
Hoxton	d	21 23	21 33		21 38	21 43		21 58						21 48	21 53	22 03		22 08	22 13		22 28	
Haggerston	d	21 25	21 35		21 40	21 45		22 00						21 50	21 55	22 05		22 10	22 15		22 30	
Dalston Junction Stn ELL	a	21 29	21 37		21 44	21 47		22 02						21 52	21 59	22 07		22 14	22 17		22 32	
Canonbury	d		21 42			21 50		22 05						21 57		22 12			22 20		22 35	
Highbury & Islington	d		21a44			21a53		22a08						22a00		22a14			22a23		22a38	
London Bridge 4 ⊖	a			21 29			21 43			21 26	21 36		21 41				21 59			22 13		

East London Line and Croydon - London Victoria to London Bridge

Station		SN	SN	SE	SN	LO	LO	LO	SN	LO		SN	LO	SN	SN	SN	SE	SN	LO	LO		LO	SN	LO	SN
East Croydon	d								22 00														22 30		
West Croydon 4	d				21 31	21 39		21 52										22 01	22 09			22 22			
Norwood Junction 2	d					21 43		21 58	22 05										22 13			22 28	22 35		
Anerley	d					21 46		22 01	22 08										22 16			22 31	22 38		
Penge West	d					21 48		22 03	22 10										22 18			22 33	22 40		
London Victoria 15 ⊖	d		21 41	21 43								21 49				22 11	22 13								22 19
Battersea Park 4	d		21 45									21 53				22 15									22 23
Wandsworth Road	d		21 47													22 17									
Clapham High Street ⊖	d		21 49													22 19									
London Blackfriars 3 ⊖	d																								
Denmark Hill 4	d		21 54	21 52												22 24	22 22								
Peckham Rye 4	d	21 46	21 56	21a55	22 01									22 12	22 16	22 26	22a25	22 31							
Queens Rd Peckham	d	21 49	21 59		22 04										22 19	22 29		22 34							
South Bermondsey	d	21 51	22 01		22 06										22 21	22 31		22 36							
Clapham Junction 10	d											21 57													22 27
Wandsworth Common	d											22 00													22 30
Balham 4 ⊖	d											22 02													22 32
Streatham Hill	d											22 05													22 35
West Norwood 4	d											22 10		22 23											22 40
Gipsy Hill	d											22 13		22 26											22 43
Crystal Palace 4	d									22 13		22 21	22 28	22a29										22 43	22 51
Sydenham	d					21 51		22 06	22 12	22 16		22 24	22 31						22 21			22 36	22 42	22 46	22 54
Forest Hill 4	d					21 53		22 08	22 15	22 19		22 27	22 34						22 23			22 38	22 45	22 49	22 57
Honor Oak Park	d					21 56		22 11	22 17	22 21		22 29	22 36						22 26			22 41	22 47	22 51	22 59
Brockley	d					21 58		22 13	22 20	22 24		22 32	22 39						22 28			22 43	22 50	22 54	23 02
New Cross Gate 4	a					22 01		22 16	22 22	22 26		22 34	22 41						22 31			22 46	22 52	22 56	23 04
	d					22 01		22 16	22 22	22 26		22 34	22 41						22 31			22 46	22 52	22 56	23 04
New Cross ELL	d						22 06													22 36					
Surrey Quays	d					22 05	22 10	22 19		22 30			22 45						22 35	22 40		22 49		23 00	
Canada Water	d					22 07	22 12	22 21		22 32			22 47						22 37	22 42		22 51		23 02	
Rotherhithe	d					22 08	22 13	22 23		22 33			22 48						22 38	22 43		22 53		23 03	
Wapping	d					22 10	22 15	22 24		22 35			22 50						22 40	22 45		22 54		23 05	
Shadwell	d					22 12	22 17	22 26		22 37			22 52						22 42	22 47		22 56		23 07	
Whitechapel	d					22 14	22 19	22 29		22 39			22 54						22 44	22 49		22 59		23 09	
Shoreditch High Street	d					22 16	22 21	22 31		22 41			22 56						22 46	22 51		23 01		23 11	
Hoxton	d					22 18	22 23	22 33		22 43			22 58						22 48	22 53		23 03		23 13	
Haggerston	d					22 20	22 25	22 35		22 45			23 00						22 50	22 55		23 05		23 15	
Dalston Junction Stn ELL	a					22 22	22 29	22 37		22 47			23 02						22 52	22 59		23 07		23 17	
Canonbury	d					22 27		22 42		22 50			23 05						22 57			23 12		23 20	
Highbury & Islington	d					22a30		22a44		22a53			23a08						23a00			23a14		23a23	
London Bridge 4 ⊖	a	21 56	22 06		22 11				22 29			22 43			22 26	22 36		22 41					22 59		23 13

Station		SN	SN	SN	SE	SN		LO	LO	LO	SN	LO	SN	SN	SN	SN		LO	SE	SN	LO	LO	SN	SN	SN
East Croydon	d										23 01														
West Croydon 4	d					22 31		22 39		22 52										23 01	23 22				
Norwood Junction 2	d							22 43		22 58	23 06										23 28				
Anerley	d							22 46		23 01	23 09										23 31				
Penge West	d							22 48		23 03	23 11										23 33				
London Victoria 15 ⊖	d			22 41	22 43								22 49			23 11			23 13				23 19		
Battersea Park 4	d			22 45									22 53			23 15							23 23		
Wandsworth Road	d			22 47												23 17									
Clapham High Street ⊖	d			22 49												23 19									
London Blackfriars 3 ⊖	d																								
Denmark Hill 4	d			22 54	22 52											23 24			23 22						
Peckham Rye 4	d	22 42	22 46	22 56	22a55	23 01								23 12	23 16	23 26			23a25	23 31				23 42	23 46
Queens Rd Peckham	d		22 49	22 59		23 04									23 19	23 29				23 34					23 49
South Bermondsey	d		22 51	23 01		23 06									23 21	23 31				23 36					23 51
Clapham Junction 10	d												22 57										23 27		
Wandsworth Common	d												23 00										23 30		
Balham 4 ⊖	d												23 02										23 32		
Streatham Hill	d												23 05										23 35		
West Norwood 4	d	22 53											23 10	23 24									23 40	23 54	
Gipsy Hill	d	22 56											23 13	23 27									23 43	23 57	
Crystal Palace 4	d	22a59										23 13	23 21	23a29								23 43	23 51	23a59	
Sydenham	d							22 51		23 06	23 13	23 16	23 24								23 36	23 46	23 54		
Forest Hill 4	d							22 53		23 08	23 16	23 19	23 27								23 38	23 49	23 57		
Honor Oak Park	d							22 56		23 11	23 18	23 21	23 29								23 41	23 51	23 59		
Brockley	d							22 58		23 13	23 21	23 24	23 32								23 43	23 54	00 02		
New Cross Gate 4	a							23 01		23 16	23 23	23 26	23 34								23 46	23 56	00 04		
	d							23 01		23 16	23 23	23 26	23 34								23 46	23 56	00 04		
New Cross ELL	d								23 06									23 36							
Surrey Quays	d							23 05	23 10	23 19		23 30						23 40			23 49	23 59			
Canada Water	d							23 07	23 12	23 21		23 32						23 42			23 51	00 02			
Rotherhithe	d							23 08	23 13	23 23		23 33						23 43			23 53	00 03			
Wapping	d							23 10	23 15	23 24		23 35						23 45			23 54	00 05			
Shadwell	d							23 12	23 17	23 26		23 37						23 47			23 56	00 07			
Whitechapel	d							23 14	23 19	23 29		23 39						23 49			23 59	00 09			
Shoreditch High Street	d							23 16	23 21	23 31		23 41						23 51			00 01	00 11			
Hoxton	d							23 18	23 23	23 33		23 43						23 53			00 03	00 13			
Haggerston	d							23 20	23 25	23 35		23 45						23 55			00 05	00 15			
Dalston Junction Stn ELL	a							23 22	23 29	23 37		23 47						23 59			00 07	00 17			
Canonbury	d							23 27		23 42		23 50									00 12	00 20			
Highbury & Islington	d							23a30		23a44		23a53									00a14	00a23			
London Bridge 4 ⊖	a		22 56	23 06		23 11					23 30		23 43		23 26	23 36				23 41			00 11		23 56

East London Line and Croydon - London Victoria to London Bridge

Station		SE	SN
East Croydon	d		
West Croydon 4	d		
Norwood Junction 2	d		
Anerley	d		
Penge West	d		
London Victoria 15 ⊖	d	23 43	23 54
Battersea Park 4	d		23 58
Wandsworth Road	d		
Clapham High Street ⊖	d		
London Blackfriars 3 ⊖	d		
Denmark Hill 4	d	23 52	
Peckham Rye 4	d	23a55	
Queens Rd Peckham	d		
South Bermondsey	d		
Clapham Junction 10	d		00 02
Wandsworth Common	d		00 05
Balham 4 ⊖	d		00 07
Streatham Hill	d		00 10
West Norwood 4	d		00 14
Gipsy Hill	d		00 17
Crystal Palace 4	d		00 21
Sydenham	d		00 24
Forest Hill 4	d		00 27
Honor Oak Park	d		00 29
Brockley	d		00 32
New Cross Gate 4	a		00 35
	d		00 35
New Cross ELL	d		
Surrey Quays	d		
Canada Water	d		
Rotherhithe	d		
Wapping	d		
Shadwell	d		
Whitechapel	d		
Shoreditch High Street	d		
Hoxton	d		
Haggerston	d		
Dalston Junction Stn ELL	a		
Canonbury	d		
Highbury & Islington	d		
London Bridge 4 ⊖	a		00 41

Sundays

Station		LO A	LO A	SN A	SN A	SN	SN	LO	SN	LO		SN	LO	SN	SN	SN	SN	LO	SN	LO		SN	SE	SN	SN
East Croydon	d								06 47						07 12	07 17									
West Croydon 4	d	23p22						06 42					07 12				07 22		07 34	07 42					
Norwood Junction 2	d	23p28						06 47	06 52				07 17			07 22	07 27		07 40	07 47					
Anerley	d	23p31						06 50	06 55				07 20			07 25				07 50					
Penge West	d	23p33						06 52	06 57				07 22			07 27				07 52					
London Victoria 15 ⊖	d			23p19	23p54																		07 39		07 41
Battersea Park 4	d			23p23	23p58																				07 45
Wandsworth Road	d																								07 47
Clapham High Street ⊖	d																								07 49
London Blackfriars 3 ⊖	d																								
Denmark Hill 4	d																						07 48		07 54
Peckham Rye 4	d					00 12	00 42					07 09		07 23	07 39							07 45	07a51	07 53	07 56
Queens Rd Peckham	d											07 12		07 26	07 42									07 56	07 59
South Bermondsey	d											07 14		07 28	07 44									07 58	08 01
Clapham Junction 10	d			23p27	00 02																				
Wandsworth Common	d			23p30	00 05																				
Balham 4 ⊖	d			23p32	00 07																				
Streatham Hill	d			23p35	00 10																				
West Norwood 4	d			23p40	00 14	00 24	00 54															07 57			
Gipsy Hill	d			23p43	00 17	00 27	00 57															08 00			
Crystal Palace 4	d		23p43	23p51	00 21	00a29	00a59			07 07							07a31	07 37				08a02			
Sydenham	d	23p36	23p46	23p54	00 24			06 55	06 59	07 10			07 25			07 29		07 40	07 44	07 55					
Forest Hill 4	d	23p38	23p49	23p57	00 27			06 57	07 02	07 13			07 27			07 32		07 43	07 47	07 57					
Honor Oak Park	d	23p41	23p51	23p59	00 29			07 00	07 04	07 15			07 30			07 34		07 45	07 49	08 00					
Brockley	d	23p43	23p54	00 02	00 32			07 02	07 07	07 18			07 32			07 37		07 48	07 52	08 02					
New Cross Gate 4	a	23p46	23p56	00 04	00 35			07 05	07 09	07 20			07 35			07 39		07 50	07 54	08 05					
	d	23p46	23p56	00 04	00 35			07 05	07 09	07 20			07 35			07 39		07 50	07 54	08 05					
New Cross ELL	d																								
Surrey Quays	d	23p49	23p59					07 09		07 24			07 39					07 54		08 09					
Canada Water	d	23p51	00 02					07 11		07 26			07 41					07 56		08 11					
Rotherhithe	d	23p53	00 03					07 12		07 27			07 42					07 57		08 12					
Wapping	d	23p54	00 05					07 14		07 29			07 44					07 59		08 14					
Shadwell	d	23p56	00 07					07 16		07 31			07 46					08 01		08 16					
Whitechapel	d	23p59	00 09					07 18		07 33			07 48					08 03		08 18					
Shoreditch High Street	d	00 01	00 11					07 20		07 35			07 50					08 05		08 20					
Hoxton	d	00 03	00 13					07 22		07 37			07 52					08 07		08 22					
Haggerston	d	00 05	00 15					07 24		07 39			07 54					08 09		08 24					
Dalston Junction Stn ELL	a	00 07	00 17					07 26		07 41			07 56					08 11		08 26					
Canonbury	d	00 12	00 20					07 31		07 44			08 01					08 14		08 31					
Highbury & Islington	d	00a14	00a23					07a34		07a47			08a04					08a17		08a34					
London Bridge 4 ⊖	a			00 11	00 41				07 17			07 19		07 33	07 49	07 48			08 01					08 03	08 06

A not 22 May

East London Line and Croydon - London Victoria to London Bridge

Station		SN	SN	SN	LO	SN		LO	SN	SE	SN	SN	SN	SN	LO	SN		SN	LO	LO	LO	SE	SN	SN	SN
East Croydon ⇌	d	07 42	07 47										08 12	08 17											08 42
West Croydon 4 ⇌	d			07 52		08 04		08 12								08 34				08 42					
Norwood Junction 2	d		07 52	07 57		08 10		08 17						08 22		08 40				08 47					
Anerley	d		07 55					08 20						08 25						08 50					
Penge West	d		07 57					08 22						08 27						08 52					
London Victoria 15 ⊖	d									08 09		08 11										08 39		08 41	
Battersea Park 4	d											08 15												08 45	
Wandsworth Road	d											08 17												08 47	
Clapham High Street ⊖	d											08 19												08 49	
London Blackfriars 3 ⊖	d																								
Denmark Hill 4	d									08 18		08 24										08 48		08 54	
Peckham Rye 4	d	08 10							08 15	08a21	08 23	08 26	08 40					08 45				08a51	08 53	08 56	09 10
Queens Rd Peckham	d	08 12									08 26	08 29	08 42										08 56	08 59	09 12
South Bermondsey	d	08 15									08 28	08 31	08 45										08 58	09 01	09 15
Clapham Junction 10	d																								
Wandsworth Common	d																								
Balham 4 ⊖	d																								
Streatham Hill	d																								
West Norwood 4	d								08 27									08 57							
Gipsy Hill	d								08 30									09 00							
Crystal Palace 4	d			08a01	08 07				08a32						08 37			09a02							
Sydenham	d		07 59		08 10	08 14		08 25						08 29	08 40	08 44				08 55					
Forest Hill 4	d		08 02		08 13	08 17		08 27						08 32	08 43	08 47				08 57					
Honor Oak Park	d		08 04		08 15	08 19		08 30						08 34	08 45	08 49				09 00					
Brockley	d		08 07		08 18	08 22		08 32						08 37	08 48	08 52				09 02					
New Cross Gate 4	a		08 09		08 20	08 24		08 35						08 39	08 50	08 54				09 05					
	d		08 09		08 20	08 24		08 35						08 39	08 50	08 54				09 05					
New Cross ELL	d																		08 54		09 09				
Surrey Quays	d				08 24			08 39							08 54				08 58	09 09	09 13				
Canada Water	d				08 26			08 41							08 56				09 00	09 11	09 15				
Rotherhithe	d				08 27			08 42							08 57				09 01	09 12	09 16				
Wapping	d				08 29			08 44							08 59				09 03	09 14	09 18				
Shadwell	d				08 31			08 46							09 01				09 05	09 16	09 20				
Whitechapel	d				08 33			08 48							09 03				09 07	09 18	09 22				
Shoreditch High Street	d				08 35			08 50							09 05				09 09	09 20	09 24				
Hoxton	d				08 37			08 52							09 07				09 11	09 22	09 26				
Haggerston	d				08 39			08 54							09 09				09 13	09 24	09 28				
Dalston Junction Stn ELL	a				08 41			08 56							09 11				09 17	09 26	09 32				
Canonbury	d				08 44			09 01							09 14					09 31					
Highbury & Islington	d				08a47			09a04							09a17					09a34					
London Bridge 4 ⊖	a	08 19	08 17			08 31					08 33	08 36	08 49	08 48		09 01							09 03	09 06	09 19

Station		SN		LO	SN	SN	LO	LO	LO	SE	SN	SN		SN	SN	LO	SN	SN	LO	LO	LO	SE		SN	SN
East Croydon ⇌	d	08 47												09 12	09 17										
West Croydon 4 ⇌	d				09 04			09 12									09 34			09 42					
Norwood Junction 2	d	08 52			09 10			09 17							09 22		09 40			09 47					
Anerley	d	08 55						09 20							09 25					09 50					
Penge West	d	08 57						09 22							09 27					09 52					
London Victoria 15 ⊖	d									09 09		09 11										09 39			09 41
Battersea Park 4	d											09 15													09 45
Wandsworth Road	d											09 17													09 47
Clapham High Street ⊖	d											09 19													09 49
London Blackfriars 3 ⊖	d																								
Denmark Hill 4	d									09 18		09 24										09 48			09 54
Peckham Rye 4	d					09 15				09a21	09 23	09 26		09 40				09 45				09a51		09 53	09 56
Queens Rd Peckham	d										09 26	09 29		09 42										09 56	09 59
South Bermondsey	d										09 28	09 31		09 45										09 58	10 01
Clapham Junction 10	d																								
Wandsworth Common	d																								
Balham 4 ⊖	d																								
Streatham Hill	d																								
West Norwood 4	d					09 27												09 57							
Gipsy Hill	d					09 30												10 00							
Crystal Palace 4	d			09 07		09a32										09 37		10a02							
Sydenham	d	08 59		09 10	09 14			09 25							09 29	09 40	09 44			09 55					
Forest Hill 4	d	09 02		09 13	09 17			09 27							09 32	09 43	09 47			09 57					
Honor Oak Park	d	09 04		09 15	09 19			09 30							09 34	09 45	09 49			10 00					
Brockley	d	09 07		09 18	09 22			09 32							09 37	09 48	09 52			10 02					
New Cross Gate 4	a	09 09		09 20	09 24			09 35							09 39	09 50	09 54			10 05					
	d	09 09		09 20	09 24			09 35							09 39	09 50	09 54			10 05					
New Cross ELL	d						09 24		09 39										09 54		10 09				
Surrey Quays	d			09 24			09 28	09 39	09 43							09 54			09 58	10 09	10 13				
Canada Water	d			09 26			09 30	09 41	09 45							09 56			10 00	10 11	10 15				
Rotherhithe	d			09 27			09 31	09 42	09 46							09 57			10 01	10 12	10 16				
Wapping	d			09 29			09 33	09 44	09 48							09 59			10 03	10 14	10 18				
Shadwell	d			09 31			09 35	09 46	09 50							10 01			10 05	10 16	10 20				
Whitechapel	d			09 33			09 37	09 48	09 52							10 03			10 07	10 18	10 22				
Shoreditch High Street	d			09 35			09 39	09 50	09 54							10 05			10 09	10 20	10 24				
Hoxton	d			09 37			09 41	09 52	09 56							10 07			10 11	10 22	10 26				
Haggerston	d			09 39			09 43	09 54	09 58							10 09			10 13	10 24	10 28				
Dalston Junction Stn ELL	a			09 41			09 47	09 56	10 02							10 11			10 17	10 26	10 32				
Canonbury	d			09 44				10 01								10 14				10 31					
Highbury & Islington	d			09a47				10a04								10a17				10a34					
London Bridge 4 ⊖	a	09 18			09 31						09 33	09 36		09 49	09 48		10 01							10 03	10 06

East London Line and Croydon - London Victoria to London Bridge

Station		SN	SN	LO	SN	SN	LO	LO		LO	SE	SN	SN	SN	SN	LO	SN	SN		LO	LO	LO	SE	SN	SN
East Croydon ⇌	d	09 42	09 47											10 12	10 17										
West Croydon 4 ⇌	d				10 04			10 12									10 34				10 42				
Norwood Junction 2	d		09 52		10 10			10 17							10 22		10 40				10 47				
Anerley	d		09 55					10 20							10 25						10 50				
Penge West	d		09 57					10 22							10 27						10 52				
London Victoria 15 ⊖	d										10 09		10 11										10 39		10 41
Battersea Park 4	d												10 15												10 45
Wandsworth Road	d												10 17												10 47
Clapham High Street ⊖	d												10 19												10 49
London Blackfriars 3 ⊖	d																								
Denmark Hill 4	d										10 18		10 24										10 48		10 54
Peckham Rye 4	d	10 10				10 15					10a21	10 23	10 26	10 40				10 45					10a51	10 53	10 56
Queens Rd Peckham	d	10 12										10 26	10 29	10 42										10 56	10 59
South Bermondsey	d	10 15										10 28	10 31	10 45										10 58	11 01
Clapham Junction 10	d																								
Wandsworth Common	d																								
Balham 4 ⊖	d																								
Streatham Hill	d																								
West Norwood 4	d					10 27												10 57							
Gipsy Hill	d					10 30												11 00							
Crystal Palace 4	d			10 07		10a32										10 37		11a02							
Sydenham	d		09 59	10 10	10 14			10 25							10 29	10 40	10 44				10 55				
Forest Hill 4	d		10 02	10 13	10 17			10 27							10 32	10 43	10 47				10 57				
Honor Oak Park	d		10 04	10 15	10 19			10 30							10 34	10 45	10 49				11 00				
Brockley	d		10 07	10 18	10 22			10 32							10 37	10 48	10 52				11 02				
New Cross Gate 4	a		10 09	10 20	10 24			10 35							10 39	10 50	10 54				11 05				
	d		10 09	10 20	10 24			10 35							10 39	10 50	10 54				11 05				
New Cross ELL	d						10 24			10 39										10 54		11 09			
Surrey Quays	d			10 24			10 28	10 39		10 43						10 54				10 58	11 09	11 13			
Canada Water	d			10 26			10 30	10 41		10 45						10 56				11 00	11 11	11 15			
Rotherhithe	d			10 27			10 31	10 42		10 46						10 57				11 01	11 12	11 16			
Wapping	d			10 29			10 33	10 44		10 48						10 59				11 03	11 14	11 18			
Shadwell	d			10 31			10 35	10 46		10 50						11 01				11 05	11 16	11 20			
Whitechapel	d			10 33			10 37	10 48		10 52						11 03				11 07	11 18	11 22			
Shoreditch High Street	d			10 35			10 39	10 50		10 54						11 05				11 09	11 20	11 24			
Hoxton	d			10 37			10 41	10 52		10 56						11 07				11 11	11 22	11 26			
Haggerston	d			10 39			10 43	10 54		10 58						11 09				11 13	11 24	11 28			
Dalston Junction Stn ELL	a			10 41			10 47	10 56		11 02						11 11				11 17	11 26	11 32			
Canonbury	d			10 44				11 01								11 14					11 31				
Highbury & Islington	d			10a47				11a04								11a17					11a34				
London Bridge 4 ⊖	a	10 19	10 18		10 31							10 33	10 36	10 49	10 48		11 01							11 03	11 06

Station		SN	SN	LO		SN	SN	LO	LO	LO	SE	SN	SN	SN		SN	LO	SN	SN	LO	LO	LO	SE	SN	
East Croydon ⇌	d	10 42	10 47											11 12		11 17									
West Croydon 4 ⇌	d					11 04			11 12									11 34			11 42				
Norwood Junction 2	d		10 52			11 10			11 17							11 22		11 40			11 47				
Anerley	d		10 55						11 20							11 25					11 50				
Penge West	d		10 57						11 22							11 27					11 52				
London Victoria 15 ⊖	d										11 09		11 11										11 39		
Battersea Park 4	d												11 15												
Wandsworth Road	d												11 17												
Clapham High Street ⊖	d												11 19												
London Blackfriars 3 ⊖	d																								
Denmark Hill 4	d										11 18		11 24										11 48		
Peckham Rye 4	d	11 10					11 15				11a21	11 23	11 26	11 40					11 45				11a51	11 53	
Queens Rd Peckham	d	11 12										11 26	11 29	11 42										11 56	
South Bermondsey	d	11 15										11 28	11 31	11 45										11 58	
Clapham Junction 10	d																								
Wandsworth Common	d																								
Balham 4 ⊖	d																								
Streatham Hill	d																								
West Norwood 4	d						11 27												11 57						
Gipsy Hill	d						11 30												12 00						
Crystal Palace 4	d			11 07			11a32										11 37		12a02						
Sydenham	d		10 59	11 10		11 14			11 25							11 29	11 40	11 44			11 55				
Forest Hill 4	d		11 02	11 13		11 17			11 27							11 32	11 43	11 47			11 57				
Honor Oak Park	d		11 04	11 15		11 19			11 30							11 34	11 45	11 49			12 00				
Brockley	d		11 07	11 18		11 22			11 32							11 37	11 48	11 52			12 02				
New Cross Gate 4	a		11 09	11 20		11 24			11 35							11 39	11 50	11 54			12 05				
	d		11 09	11 20		11 24			11 35							11 39	11 50	11 54			12 05				
New Cross ELL	d							11 24		11 39										11 54		12 09			
Surrey Quays	d			11 24				11 28	11 39	11 43							11 54			11 58	12 09	12 13			
Canada Water	d			11 26				11 30	11 41	11 45							11 56			12 00	12 11	12 15			
Rotherhithe	d			11 27				11 31	11 42	11 46							11 57			12 01	12 12	12 16			
Wapping	d			11 29				11 33	11 44	11 48							11 59			12 03	12 14	12 18			
Shadwell	d			11 31				11 35	11 46	11 50							12 01			12 05	12 16	12 20			
Whitechapel	d			11 33				11 37	11 48	11 52							12 03			12 07	12 18	12 22			
Shoreditch High Street	d			11 35				11 39	11 50	11 54							12 05			12 09	12 20	12 24			
Hoxton	d			11 37				11 41	11 52	11 56							12 07			12 11	12 22	12 26			
Haggerston	d			11 39				11 43	11 54	11 58							12 09			12 13	12 24	12 28			
Dalston Junction Stn ELL	a			11 41				11 47	11 56	12 02							12 11			12 17	12 26	12 32			
Canonbury	d			11 44					12 01								12 14				12 31				
Highbury & Islington	d			11a47					12a04								12a17				12a34				
London Bridge 4 ⊖	a	11 19	11 18			11 31						11 33	11 36	11 49		11 48		12 01						12 03	

East London Line and Croydon - London Victoria to London Bridge

		SN	SN	SN	LO	SN	LO	LO	LO	LO	SN	LO	LO	SE	SN	SN	SN	SN	SN	LO	LO	LO	LO
East Croydon	d		11 42	11 47													12 12	12 17					
West Croydon 4	d					12 04		12 12											12 34		12 42		
Norwood Junction 2	d			11 52		12 10		12 16										12 22	12 40		12 46		
Anerley	d			11 55				12 19										12 25			12 49		
Penge West	d			11 57				12 21										12 27			12 51		
London Victoria 15 ⊖	d	11 41												12 09		12 11							
Battersea Park 4	d	11 45														12 15							
Wandsworth Road	d	11 47														12 17							
Clapham High Street ⊖	d	11 49														12 19							
London Blackfriars 3 ⊖	d																						
Denmark Hill 4	d	11 54												12 18		12 24							
Peckham Rye 4	d	11 56	12 10								12 15			12a21	12 23	12 26	12 40						
Queens Rd Peckham	d	11 59	12 12												12 26	12 29	12 42						
South Bermondsey	d	12 01	12 15												12 28	12 31	12 45						
Clapham Junction 10	d																						
Wandsworth Common	d																						
Balham 4 ⊖	d																						
Streatham Hill	d																						
West Norwood 4	d										12 27												
Gipsy Hill	d										12 30												
Crystal Palace 4	d				12 07					12 31	12a32									12 46			13 01
Sydenham	d			11 59	12 10	12 14		12 24		12 34								12 29	12 44	12 49	12 54		13 04
Forest Hill 4	d			12 02	12 13	12 17		12 26		12 37								12 32	12 47	12 52	12 56		13 07
Honor Oak Park	d			12 04	12 15	12 19		12 29		12 39								12 34	12 49	12 54	12 59		13 09
Brockley	d			12 07	12 18	12 22		12 31		12 42								12 37	12 52	12 57	13 01		13 12
New Cross Gate 4	a			12 09	12 20	12 24		12 34		12 44								12 39	12 54	12 59	13 04		13 14
	d			12 09	12 20	12 24		12 34		12 44								12 39	12 54	12 59	13 04		13 14
New Cross ELL	d						12 24		12 39				12 54									13 09	
Surrey Quays	d				12 24		12 28	12 38	12 43	12 48		12 53	12 58							13 03	13 08	13 13	13 18
Canada Water	d				12 26		12 30	12 40	12 45	12 50		12 55	13 00							13 05	13 10	13 15	13 20
Rotherhithe	d				12 27		12 31	12 41	12 46	12 51		12 56	13 01							13 06	13 11	13 16	13 21
Wapping	d				12 29		12 33	12 43	12 48	12 53		12 58	13 03							13 08	13 13	13 18	13 23
Shadwell	d				12 31		12 35	12 45	12 50	12 55		13 00	13 05							13 10	13 15	13 20	13 25
Whitechapel	d				12 33		12 37	12 47	12 52	12 57		13 02	13 07							13 12	13 17	13 22	13 27
Shoreditch High Street	d				12 35		12 39	12 49	12 54	12 59		13 04	13 09							13 14	13 19	13 24	13 29
Hoxton	d				12 37		12 41	12 51	12 56	13 01		13 06	13 11							13 16	13 21	13 26	13 31
Haggerston	d				12 39		12 43	12 53	12 58	13 03		13 08	13 13							13 18	13 23	13 28	13 33
Dalston Junction Stn ELL	a				12 41		12 47	12 55	13 02	13 05		13 10	13 17							13 20	13 25	13 32	13 35
Canonbury	d				12 44			13 00		13 08		13 15								13 23	13 30		13 38
Highbury & Islington	d				12a47			13a03		13a11		13a18								13a26	13a33		13a41
London Bridge 4 ⊖	a	12 06	12 19	12 18		12 31									12 33	12 36	12 49	12 48	13 01				

		SN	SE	SN	SN	SN	SN	LO	SN	LO	LO	LO	LO	LO	SN	SE	SN	SN	SN	SN	LO	SN	LO
East Croydon	d					12 42	12 47												13 12	13 17			
West Croydon 4	d							12 57	13 04			13 12									13 27	13 34	
Norwood Junction 2	d						12 52	13 01	13 10			13 16								13 22	13 31	13 40	
Anerley	d						12 55	13 04				13 19								13 25	13 34		
Penge West	d						12 57	13 06				13 21								13 27	13 36		
London Victoria 15 ⊖	d		12 39		12 41											13 09		13 11					
Battersea Park 4	d				12 45													13 15					
Wandsworth Road	d				12 47													13 17					
Clapham High Street ⊖	d				12 49													13 19					
London Blackfriars 3 ⊖	d																						
Denmark Hill 4	d		12 48		12 54											13 18		13 24					
Peckham Rye 4	d	12 45	12a51	12 53	12 56	13 10									13 15	13a21	13 23	13 26	13 40				
Queens Rd Peckham	d			12 56	12 59	13 12											13 26	13 29	13 42				
South Bermondsey	d			12 58	13 01	13 15											13 28	13 31	13 45				
Clapham Junction 10	d																						
Wandsworth Common	d																						
Balham 4 ⊖	d																						
Streatham Hill	d																						
West Norwood 4	d	12 57													13 27								
Gipsy Hill	d	13 00													13 30								
Crystal Palace 4	d	13a02									13 16			13 31	13a32								
Sydenham	d						12 59	13 09	13 14		13 19	13 24		13 34						13 29	13 39	13 44	
Forest Hill 4	d						13 02	13 11	13 17		13 22	13 26		13 37						13 32	13 41	13 47	
Honor Oak Park	d						13 04	13 14	13 19		13 24	13 29		13 39						13 34	13 44	13 49	
Brockley	d						13 07	13 16	13 22		13 27	13 31		13 42						13 37	13 46	13 52	
New Cross Gate 4	a						13 09	13 19	13 24		13 29	13 34		13 44						13 39	13 49	13 54	
	d						13 09	13 19	13 24		13 29	13 34		13 44						13 39	13 49	13 54	
New Cross ELL	d									13 24			13 39										13 54
Surrey Quays	d							13 23		13 28	13 33	13 38	13 43	13 48							13 53		13 58
Canada Water	d							13 25		13 30	13 35	13 40	13 45	13 50							13 55		14 00
Rotherhithe	d							13 26		13 31	13 36	13 41	13 46	13 51							13 56		14 01
Wapping	d							13 28		13 33	13 38	13 43	13 48	13 53							13 58		14 03
Shadwell	d							13 30		13 35	13 40	13 45	13 50	13 55							14 00		14 05
Whitechapel	d							13 32		13 37	13 42	13 47	13 52	13 57							14 02		14 07
Shoreditch High Street	d							13 34		13 39	13 44	13 49	13 54	13 59							14 04		14 09
Hoxton	d							13 36		13 41	13 46	13 51	13 56	14 01							14 06		14 11
Haggerston	d							13 38		13 43	13 48	13 53	13 58	14 03							14 08		14 13
Dalston Junction Stn ELL	a							13 40		13 47	13 50	13 55	14 02	14 05							14 10		14 17
Canonbury	d							13 45			13 53	14 00		14 08							14 15		
Highbury & Islington	d							13a48			13a56	14a03		14a11							14a18		
London Bridge 4 ⊖	a			13 03	13 06	13 19	13 18		13 31								13 33	13 36	13 49	13 48		14 01	

East London Line and Croydon - London Victoria to London Bridge

		LO	LO	LO	LO	SN	SE	SN	SN	SN	SN	LO	SN	LO	LO	LO	LO	LO	SN	SE	SN	SN
East Croydon	d									13 42	13 47											
West Croydon 4	d		13 42									13 57	14 04			14 12						
Norwood Junction 2	d		13 46								13 52	14 01	14 10			14 16						
Anerley	d		13 49								13 55	14 04				14 19						
Penge West	d		13 51								13 57	14 06				14 21						
London Victoria 15 ⊖	d						13 39		13 41											14 09		14 11
Battersea Park 4	d								13 45													14 15
Wandsworth Road	d								13 47													14 17
Clapham High Street ⊖	d								13 49													14 19
London Blackfriars 3 ⊖	d																					
Denmark Hill 4	d						13 48		13 54											14 18		14 24
Peckham Rye 4	d					13 45	13a51	13 53	13 56	14 10									14 15	14a21	14 23	14 26
Queens Rd Peckham	d							13 56	13 59	14 12											14 26	14 29
South Bermondsey	d							13 58	14 01	14 15											14 28	14 31
Clapham Junction 10	d																					
Wandsworth Common	d																					
Balham 4 ⊖	d																					
Streatham Hill	d																					
West Norwood 4	d					13 57													14 27			
Gipsy Hill	d					14 00													14 30			
Crystal Palace 4	d	13 46			14 01	14a02									14 16			14 31	14a32			
Sydenham	d	13 49	13 54		14 04						13 59	14 09	14 14		14 19	14 24		14 34				
Forest Hill 4	d	13 52	13 56		14 07						14 02	14 11	14 17		14 22	14 26		14 37				
Honor Oak Park	d	13 54	13 59		14 09						14 04	14 14	14 19		14 24	14 29		14 39				
Brockley	d	13 57	14 01		14 12						14 07	14 16	14 22		14 27	14 31		14 42				
New Cross Gate 4	a	13 59	14 04		14 14						14 09	14 19	14 24		14 29	14 34		14 44				
	d	13 59	14 04		14 14						14 09	14 19	14 24		14 29	14 34		14 44				
New Cross ELL	d			14 09										14 24			14 39					
Surrey Quays	d	14 03	14 08	14 13	14 18							14 23		14 28	14 33	14 38	14 43	14 48				
Canada Water	d	14 05	14 10	14 15	14 20							14 25		14 30	14 35	14 40	14 45	14 50				
Rotherhithe	d	14 06	14 11	14 16	14 21							14 26		14 31	14 36	14 41	14 46	14 51				
Wapping	d	14 08	14 13	14 18	14 23							14 28		14 33	14 38	14 43	14 48	14 53				
Shadwell	d	14 10	14 15	14 20	14 25							14 30		14 35	14 40	14 45	14 50	14 55				
Whitechapel	d	14 12	14 17	14 22	14 27							14 32		14 37	14 42	14 47	14 52	14 57				
Shoreditch High Street	d	14 14	14 19	14 24	14 29							14 34		14 39	14 44	14 49	14 54	14 59				
Hoxton	d	14 16	14 21	14 26	14 31							14 36		14 41	14 46	14 51	14 56	15 01				
Haggerston	d	14 18	14 23	14 28	14 33							14 38		14 43	14 48	14 53	14 58	15 03				
Dalston Junction Stn ELL	a	14 20	14 25	14 32	14 35							14 40		14 47	14 50	14 55	15 02	15 05				
Canonbury	d	14 23	14 30		14 38							14 45			14 53	15 00		15 08				
Highbury & Islington	d	14a26	14a33		14a41							14a48			14a56	15a03		15a11				
London Bridge 4 ⊖	a							14 03	14 06	14 19	14 18		14 31								14 33	14 36

		SN	SN	LO	SN	LO	LO	LO	LO	LO	SN	SE	SN	SN	SN	SN	LO	SN	LO	LO	LO	LO	LO
East Croydon	d	14 12	14 17												14 42	14 47							
West Croydon 4	d			14 27	14 34			14 42									14 57	15 04			15 12		
Norwood Junction 2	d		14 22	14 31	14 40			14 46								14 52	15 01	15 10			15 16		
Anerley	d		14 25	14 34				14 49								14 55	15 04				15 19		
Penge West	d		14 27	14 36				14 51								14 57	15 06				15 21		
London Victoria 15 ⊖	d											14 39		14 41									
Battersea Park 4	d													14 45									
Wandsworth Road	d													14 47									
Clapham High Street ⊖	d													14 49									
London Blackfriars 3 ⊖	d																						
Denmark Hill 4	d											14 48		14 54									
Peckham Rye 4	d	14 40									14 45	14a51	14 53	14 56	15 10								
Queens Rd Peckham	d	14 42											14 56	14 59	15 12								
South Bermondsey	d	14 45											14 58	15 01	15 15								
Clapham Junction 10	d																						
Wandsworth Common	d																						
Balham 4 ⊖	d																						
Streatham Hill	d																						
West Norwood 4	d										14 57												
Gipsy Hill	d										15 00												
Crystal Palace 4	d						14 46			15 01	15a02									15 16			15 31
Sydenham	d		14 29	14 39	14 44		14 49	14 54		15 04						14 59	15 09	15 14		15 19	15 24		15 34
Forest Hill 4	d		14 32	14 41	14 47		14 52	14 56		15 07						15 02	15 11	15 17		15 22	15 26		15 37
Honor Oak Park	d		14 34	14 44	14 49		14 54	14 59		15 09						15 04	15 14	15 19		15 24	15 29		15 39
Brockley	d		14 37	14 46	14 52		14 57	15 01		15 12						15 07	15 16	15 22		15 27	15 31		15 42
New Cross Gate 4	a		14 39	14 49	14 54		14 59	15 04		15 14						15 09	15 19	15 24		15 29	15 34		15 44
	d		14 39	14 49	14 54		14 59	15 04		15 14						15 09	15 19	15 24		15 29	15 34		15 44
New Cross ELL	d					14 54			15 09										15 24			15 39	
Surrey Quays	d			14 53		14 58	15 03	15 08	15 13	15 18							15 23		15 28	15 33	15 38	15 43	15 48
Canada Water	d			14 55		15 00	15 05	15 10	15 15	15 20							15 25		15 30	15 35	15 40	15 45	15 50
Rotherhithe	d			14 56		15 01	15 06	15 11	15 16	15 21							15 26		15 31	15 36	15 41	15 46	15 51
Wapping	d			14 58		15 03	15 08	15 13	15 18	15 23							15 28		15 33	15 38	15 43	15 48	15 53
Shadwell	d			15 00		15 05	15 10	15 15	15 20	15 25							15 30		15 35	15 40	15 45	15 50	15 55
Whitechapel	d			15 02		15 07	15 12	15 17	15 22	15 27							15 32		15 37	15 42	15 47	15 52	15 57
Shoreditch High Street	d			15 04		15 09	15 14	15 19	15 24	15 29							15 34		15 39	15 44	15 49	15 54	15 59
Hoxton	d			15 06		15 11	15 16	15 21	15 26	15 31							15 36		15 41	15 46	15 51	15 56	16 01
Haggerston	d			15 08		15 13	15 18	15 23	15 28	15 33							15 38		15 43	15 48	15 53	15 58	16 03
Dalston Junction Stn ELL	a			15 10		15 17	15 20	15 25	15 32	15 35							15 40		15 47	15 50	15 55	16 02	16 05
Canonbury	d			15 15			15 23	15 30		15 38							15 45			15 53	16 00		16 08
Highbury & Islington	d			15a18			15a26	15a33		15a41							15a48			15a56	16a03		16a11
London Bridge 4 ⊖	a	14 49	14 48		15 01								15 03	15 06	15 19	15 18		15 31					

East London Line and Croydon - London Victoria to London Bridge

		SN	SE	SN	SN	SN	SN	LO	SN	LO	LO	LO	LO	LO	SN	SE	SN	SN	SN	SN	LO	SN
East Croydon	d					15 12	15 17												15 42	15 47		
West Croydon	d							15 27	15 34			15 42									15 57	16 04
Norwood Junction	d						15 22	15 31	15 40			15 46								15 52	16 01	16 10
Anerley	d						15 25	15 34				15 49								15 55	16 04	
Penge West	d						15 27	15 36				15 51								15 57	16 06	
London Victoria	d		15 09		15 11											15 39		15 41				
Battersea Park	d				15 15													15 45				
Wandsworth Road	d				15 17													15 47				
Clapham High Street	d				15 19													15 49				
London Blackfriars	d																					
Denmark Hill	d		15 18		15 24											15 48		15 54				
Peckham Rye	d	15 15	15a21	15 23	15 26	15 40									15 45	15a51	15 53	15 56	16 10			
Queens Rd Peckham	d			15 26	15 29	15 42											15 56	15 59	16 12			
South Bermondsey	d			15 28	15 31	15 45											15 58	16 01	16 15			
Clapham Junction	d																					
Wandsworth Common	d																					
Balham	d																					
Streatham Hill	d																					
West Norwood	d	15 27													15 57							
Gipsy Hill	d	15 30													16 00							
Crystal Palace	d	15a32									15 46			16 01	16a02							
Sydenham	d						15 29	15 39	15 44		15 49	15 54		16 04						15 59	16 09	16 14
Forest Hill	d						15 32	15 41	15 47		15 52	15 56		16 07						16 02	16 11	16 17
Honor Oak Park	d						15 34	15 44	15 49		15 54	15 59		16 09						16 04	16 14	16 19
Brockley	d						15 37	15 46	15 52		15 57	16 01		16 12						16 07	16 16	16 22
New Cross Gate	a						15 39	15 49	15 54		15 59	16 04		16 14						16 09	16 19	16 24
	d						15 39	15 49	15 54		15 59	16 04		16 14						16 09	16 19	16 24
New Cross ELL	d									15 54			16 09									
Surrey Quays	d							15 53		15 58	16 03	16 08	16 13	16 18							16 23	
Canada Water	d							15 55		16 00	16 05	16 10	16 15	16 20							16 25	
Rotherhithe	d							15 56		16 01	16 06	16 11	16 16	16 21							16 26	
Wapping	d							15 58		16 03	16 08	16 13	16 18	16 23							16 28	
Shadwell	d							16 00		16 05	16 10	16 15	16 20	16 25							16 30	
Whitechapel	d							16 02		16 07	16 12	16 17	16 22	16 27							16 32	
Shoreditch High Street	d							16 04		16 09	16 14	16 19	16 24	16 29							16 34	
Hoxton	d							16 06		16 11	16 16	16 21	16 26	16 31							16 36	
Haggerston	d							16 08		16 13	16 18	16 23	16 28	16 33							16 38	
Dalston Junction Stn ELL	a							16 10		16 17	16 20	16 25	16 32	16 35							16 40	
Canonbury	d							16 15			16 23	16 30		16 38							16 45	
Highbury & Islington	d							16a18			16a26	16a33		16a41							16a48	
London Bridge	a			15 33	15 36	15 49	15 48		16 01								16 03	16 06	16 19	16 18		16 31

		LO	LO	LO	LO	LO	SN	SE	SN	SN	SN	SN	LO	SN	LO	LO	LO	LO	LO	SN	SE	SN	SN
East Croydon	d										16 12	16 17											
West Croydon	d			16 12									16 27	16 34			16 42						
Norwood Junction	d			16 16								16 22	16 31	16 40			16 46						
Anerley	d			16 19								16 25	16 34				16 49						
Penge West	d			16 21								16 27	16 36				16 51						
London Victoria	d							16 09		16 11											16 39		16 41
Battersea Park	d									16 15													16 45
Wandsworth Road	d									16 17													16 47
Clapham High Street	d									16 19													16 49
London Blackfriars	d																						
Denmark Hill	d							16 18		16 24											16 48		16 54
Peckham Rye	d						16 15	16a21	16 23	16 26	16 40									16 45	16a51	16 53	16 56
Queens Rd Peckham	d								16 26	16 29	16 42											16 56	16 59
South Bermondsey	d								16 28	16 31	16 45											16 58	17 01
Clapham Junction	d																						
Wandsworth Common	d																						
Balham	d																						
Streatham Hill	d																						
West Norwood	d						16 27													16 57			
Gipsy Hill	d						16 30													17 00			
Crystal Palace	d		16 16			16 31	16a32									16 46			17 01	17a02			
Sydenham	d		16 19	16 24		16 34						16 29	16 39	16 44		16 49	16 54		17 04				
Forest Hill	d		16 22	16 26		16 37						16 32	16 41	16 47		16 52	16 56		17 07				
Honor Oak Park	d		16 24	16 29		16 39						16 34	16 44	16 49		16 54	16 59		17 09				
Brockley	d		16 27	16 31		16 42						16 37	16 46	16 52		16 57	17 01		17 12				
New Cross Gate	a		16 29	16 34		16 44						16 39	16 49	16 54		16 59	17 04		17 14				
	d		16 29	16 34		16 44						16 39	16 49	16 54		16 59	17 04		17 14				
New Cross ELL	d	16 24			16 39										16 54			17 09					
Surrey Quays	d	16 28	16 33	16 38	16 43	16 48							16 53		16 58	17 03	17 08	17 13	17 18				
Canada Water	d	16 30	16 35	16 40	16 45	16 50							16 55		17 00	17 05	17 10	17 15	17 20				
Rotherhithe	d	16 31	16 36	16 41	16 46	16 51							16 56		17 01	17 06	17 11	17 16	17 21				
Wapping	d	16 33	16 38	16 43	16 48	16 53							16 58		17 03	17 08	17 13	17 18	17 23				
Shadwell	d	16 35	16 40	16 45	16 50	16 55							17 00		17 05	17 10	17 15	17 20	17 25				
Whitechapel	d	16 37	16 42	16 47	16 52	16 57							17 02		17 07	17 12	17 17	17 22	17 27				
Shoreditch High Street	d	16 39	16 44	16 49	16 54	16 59							17 04		17 09	17 14	17 19	17 24	17 29				
Hoxton	d	16 41	16 46	16 51	16 56	17 01							17 06		17 11	17 16	17 21	17 26	17 31				
Haggerston	d	16 43	16 48	16 53	16 58	17 03							17 08		17 13	17 18	17 23	17 28	17 33				
Dalston Junction Stn ELL	a	16 47	16 50	16 55	17 02	17 05							17 10		17 17	17 20	17 25	17 32	17 35				
Canonbury	d		16 53	17 00		17 08							17 15			17 23	17 30		17 38				
Highbury & Islington	d		16a56	17a03		17a11							17a18			17a26	17a33		17a41				
London Bridge	a								16 33	16 36	16 49	16 48		17 01								17 03	17 06

Table 178

Sundays

East London Line and Croydon - London Victoria to London Bridge

		SN	SN	LO	SN	LO	LO	LO	LO	LO	SN	SE	SN	SN	SN	SN	LO	SN	LO	LO	LO	LO	LO
East Croydon	d	16 42	16 47												17 12	17 17							
West Croydon	d			16 57	17 04			17 12									17 27	17 34			17 42		
Norwood Junction	d		16 52	17 01	17 10			17 16								17 22	17 31	17 40			17 46		
Anerley	d		16 55	17 04				17 19								17 25	17 34				17 49		
Penge West	d		16 57	17 06				17 21								17 27	17 36				17 51		
London Victoria	d											17 09		17 11									
Battersea Park	d													17 15									
Wandsworth Road	d													17 17									
Clapham High Street	d													17 19									
London Blackfriars	d																						
Denmark Hill	d											17 18		17 24									
Peckham Rye	d	17 10									17 15	17a21	17 23	17 26	17 40								
Queens Rd Peckham	d	17 12											17 26	17 29	17 42								
South Bermondsey	d	17 15											17 28	17 31	17 45								
Clapham Junction	d																						
Wandsworth Common	d																						
Balham	d																						
Streatham Hill	d																						
West Norwood	d										17 27												
Gipsy Hill	d										17 30												
Crystal Palace	d						17 16			17 31	17a32									17 46			18 01
Sydenham	d		16 59	17 09	17 14		17 19	17 24		17 34						17 29	17 39	17 44		17 49	17 54		18 04
Forest Hill	d		17 02	17 11	17 17		17 22	17 26		17 37						17 32	17 41	17 47		17 52	17 56		18 07
Honor Oak Park	d		17 04	17 14	17 19		17 24	17 29		17 39						17 34	17 44	17 49		17 54	17 59		18 09
Brockley	d		17 07	17 16	17 22		17 27	17 31		17 42						17 37	17 46	17 52		17 57	18 01		18 12
New Cross Gate	a		17 09	17 19	17 24		17 29	17 34		17 44						17 39	17 49	17 54		17 59	18 04		18 14
	d		17 09	17 19	17 24		17 29	17 34		17 44						17 39	17 49	17 54		17 59	18 04		18 14
New Cross ELL	d					17 24			17 39										17 54			18 09	
Surrey Quays	d			17 23		17 28	17 33	17 38	17 43	17 48							17 53		17 58	18 03	18 08	18 13	18 18
Canada Water	d			17 25		17 30	17 35	17 40	17 45	17 50							17 55		18 00	18 05	18 10	18 15	18 20
Rotherhithe	d			17 26		17 31	17 36	17 41	17 46	17 51							17 56		18 01	18 06	18 11	18 16	18 21
Wapping	d			17 28		17 33	17 38	17 43	17 48	17 53							17 58		18 03	18 08	18 13	18 18	18 23
Shadwell	d			17 30		17 35	17 40	17 45	17 50	17 55							18 00		18 05	18 10	18 15	18 20	18 25
Whitechapel	d			17 32		17 37	17 42	17 47	17 52	17 57							18 02		18 07	18 12	18 17	18 22	18 27
Shoreditch High Street	d			17 34		17 39	17 44	17 49	17 54	17 59							18 04		18 09	18 14	18 19	18 24	18 29
Hoxton	d			17 36		17 41	17 46	17 51	17 56	18 01							18 06		18 11	18 16	18 21	18 26	18 31
Haggerston	d			17 38		17 43	17 48	17 53	17 58	18 03							18 08		18 13	18 18	18 23	18 28	18 33
Dalston Junction Stn ELL	a			17 40		17 47	17 50	17 55	18 02	18 05							18 10		18 17	18 20	18 25	18 32	18 35
Canonbury	d			17 45			17 53	18 00		18 08							18 15			18 23	18 30		18 38
Highbury & Islington	d			17a48			17a56	18a03		18a11							18a18			18a26	18a33		18a41
London Bridge	a	17 19	17 18		17 31								17 33	17 36	17 49	17 48		18 01					

		SN	SE	SN	SN	SN	SN	LO	SN	LO	LO	LO	LO	LO	SN	SE	SN	SN	SN	SN	LO	SN
East Croydon	d					17 42	17 47												18 12	18 17		
West Croydon	d							17 57	18 04			18 12									18 27	18 34
Norwood Junction	d						17 52	18 01	18 10			18 16								18 22	18 31	18 40
Anerley	d						17 55	18 04				18 19								18 25	18 34	
Penge West	d						17 57	18 06				18 21								18 27	18 36	
London Victoria	d		17 39		17 41											18 09		18 11				
Battersea Park	d				17 45													18 15				
Wandsworth Road	d				17 47													18 17				
Clapham High Street	d				17 49													18 19				
London Blackfriars	d																					
Denmark Hill	d		17 48		17 54											18 18		18 24				
Peckham Rye	d	17 45	17a51	17 53	17 56	18 10									18 15	18a21	18 23	18 26	18 40			
Queens Rd Peckham	d			17 56	17 59	18 12											18 26	18 29	18 42			
South Bermondsey	d			17 58	18 01	18 15											18 28	18 31	18 45			
Clapham Junction	d																					
Wandsworth Common	d																					
Balham	d																					
Streatham Hill	d																					
West Norwood	d	17 57													18 27							
Gipsy Hill	d	18 00													18 30							
Crystal Palace	d	18a02									18 16			18 31	18a32							
Sydenham	d						17 59	18 09	18 14		18 19	18 24		18 34						18 29	18 39	18 44
Forest Hill	d						18 02	18 11	18 17		18 22	18 26		18 37						18 32	18 41	18 47
Honor Oak Park	d						18 04	18 14	18 19		18 24	18 29		18 39						18 34	18 44	18 49
Brockley	d						18 07	18 16	18 22		18 27	18 31		18 42						18 37	18 46	18 52
New Cross Gate	a						18 09	18 19	18 24		18 29	18 34		18 44						18 39	18 49	18 54
	d						18 09	18 19	18 24		18 29	18 34		18 44						18 40	18 49	18 54
New Cross ELL	d									18 24			18 39									
Surrey Quays	d							18 23		18 28	18 33	18 38	18 43	18 48							18 53	
Canada Water	d							18 25		18 30	18 35	18 40	18 45	18 50							18 55	
Rotherhithe	d							18 26		18 31	18 36	18 41	18 46	18 51							18 56	
Wapping	d							18 28		18 33	18 38	18 43	18 48	18 53							18 58	
Shadwell	d							18 30		18 35	18 40	18 45	18 50	18 55							19 00	
Whitechapel	d							18 32		18 37	18 42	18 47	18 52	18 57							19 02	
Shoreditch High Street	d							18 34		18 39	18 44	18 49	18 54	18 59							19 04	
Hoxton	d							18 36		18 41	18 46	18 51	18 56	19 01							19 06	
Haggerston	d							18 38		18 43	18 48	18 53	18 58	19 03							19 08	
Dalston Junction Stn ELL	a							18 40		18 47	18 50	18 55	19 02	19 05							19 10	
Canonbury	d							18 45			18 53	19 00		19 08							19 15	
Highbury & Islington	d							18a48			18a56	19a03		19a11							19a18	
London Bridge	a			18 03	18 06	18 19	18 18		18 31								18 33	18 36	18 49	18 48		19 01

East London Line and Croydon - London Victoria to London Bridge

Station		LO	LO	LO	LO	LO	SN	SE		SN	SN	SN	SN	LO	SN	LO	LO	LO		LO	LO	SN	SE	SN	SN
East Croydon	d											18 42	18 47												
West Croydon 4	d			18 42										18 57	19 04			19 12							
Norwood Junction 2	d			18 46									18 52	19 01	19 10			19 16							
Anerley	d			18 49									18 55	19 04				19 19							
Penge West	d			18 51									18 57	19 06				19 21							
London Victoria 15 ⊖	d							18 39			18 41												19 09		19 11
Battersea Park 4	d										18 45														19 15
Wandsworth Road	d										18 47														19 17
Clapham High Street ⊖	d										18 49														19 19
London Blackfriars 3 ⊖	d																								
Denmark Hill 4	d							18 48			18 54												19 18		19 24
Peckham Rye 4	d						18 45	18a51		18 53	18 56	19 10										19 15	19a21	19 23	19 26
Queens Rd Peckham	d									18 56	18 59	19 12												19 26	19 29
South Bermondsey	d									18 58	19 01	19 15												19 28	19 31
Clapham Junction 10	d																								
Wandsworth Common	d																								
Balham 4 ⊖	d																								
Streatham Hill	d																								
West Norwood 4	d						18 57															19 27			
Gipsy Hill	d						19 00															19 30			
Crystal Palace 4	d		18 46			19 01	19a02										19 16				19 31	19a32			
Sydenham	d		18 49	18 54		19 04							18 59	19 09	19 14		19 19	19 24			19 34				
Forest Hill 4	d		18 52	18 56		19 07							19 02	19 11	19 17		19 22	19 26			19 37				
Honor Oak Park	d		18 54	18 59		19 09							19 04	19 14	19 19		19 24	19 29			19 39				
Brockley	d		18 57	19 01		19 12							19 07	19 16	19 22		19 27	19 31			19 42				
New Cross Gate 4	a		18 59	19 04		19 14							19 09	19 19	19 24		19 29	19 34			19 44				
	d		18 59	19 04		19 14							19 09	19 19	19 24		19 29	19 34			19 44				
New Cross ELL	d	18 54			19 09											19 24				19 39					
Surrey Quays	d	18 58	19 03	19 08	19 13	19 18								19 23		19 28	19 33	19 38		19 43	19 48				
Canada Water	d	19 00	19 05	19 10	19 15	19 20								19 25		19 30	19 35	19 40		19 45	19 50				
Rotherhithe	d	19 01	19 06	19 11	19 16	19 21								19 26		19 31	19 36	19 41		19 46	19 51				
Wapping	d	19 03	19 08	19 13	19 18	19 23								19 28		19 33	19 38	19 43		19 48	19 53				
Shadwell	d	19 05	19 10	19 15	19 20	19 25								19 30		19 35	19 40	19 45		19 50	19 55				
Whitechapel	d	19 07	19 12	19 17	19 22	19 27								19 32		19 37	19 42	19 47		19 52	19 57				
Shoreditch High Street	d	19 09	19 14	19 19	19 24	19 29								19 34		19 39	19 44	19 49		19 54	19 59				
Hoxton	d	19 11	19 16	19 21	19 26	19 31								19 36		19 41	19 46	19 51		19 56	20 01				
Haggerston	d	19 13	19 18	19 23	19 28	19 33								19 38		19 43	19 48	19 53		19 58	20 03				
Dalston Junction Stn ELL	a	19 17	19 20	19 25	19 32	19 35								19 40		19 47	19 50	19 55		20 02	20 05				
Canonbury	d		19 23	19 30		19 38								19 45			19 53	20 00			20 08				
Highbury & Islington	d		19a26	19a33		19a41								19a48			19a56	20a03			20a11				
London Bridge 4 ⊖	a									19 03	19 06	19 19	19 18		19 31									19 33	19 36

Station		SN	SN	LO		SN	LO	LO	LO	LO	LO	SN	SE	SN		SN	SN	SN	LO	SN	LO	LO	LO	LO	
East Croydon	d	19 12	19 17														19 42	19 47							
West Croydon 4	d			19 27		19 34			19 42										19 57	20 04			20 12		
Norwood Junction 2	d		19 22	19 31		19 40			19 46									19 52	20 01	20 10			20 16		
Anerley	d		19 25	19 34					19 49									19 55	20 04				20 19		
Penge West	d		19 27	19 36					19 51									19 57	20 06				20 21		
London Victoria 15 ⊖	d												19 39			19 41									
Battersea Park 4	d															19 45									
Wandsworth Road	d															19 47									
Clapham High Street ⊖	d															19 49									
London Blackfriars 3 ⊖	d																								
Denmark Hill 4	d												19 48			19 54									
Peckham Rye 4	d	19 40										19 45	19a51	19 53		19 56	20 10								
Queens Rd Peckham	d	19 42												19 56		19 59	20 12								
South Bermondsey	d	19 45												19 58		20 01	20 15								
Clapham Junction 10	d																								
Wandsworth Common	d																								
Balham 4 ⊖	d																								
Streatham Hill	d																								
West Norwood 4	d											19 57													
Gipsy Hill	d											20 00													
Crystal Palace 4	d							19 46			20 01	20a02										20 16			
Sydenham	d		19 29	19 39		19 44		19 49	19 54		20 04							19 59	20 09	20 14		20 19	20 24		
Forest Hill 4	d		19 32	19 41		19 47		19 52	19 56		20 07							20 02	20 11	20 17		20 22	20 26		
Honor Oak Park	d		19 34	19 44		19 49		19 54	19 59		20 09							20 04	20 14	20 19		20 24	20 29		
Brockley	d		19 37	19 46		19 52		19 57	20 01		20 12							20 07	20 16	20 22		20 27	20 31		
New Cross Gate 4	a		19 39	19 49		19 54		19 59	20 04		20 14							20 09	20 19	20 24		20 29	20 34		
	d		19 39	19 49		19 54		19 59	20 04		20 14							20 09	20 19	20 24		20 29	20 34		
New Cross ELL	d						19 54			20 09											20 24			20 39	
Surrey Quays	d			19 53			19 58	20 03	20 08	20 13	20 18								20 23		20 28	20 33	20 38	20 43	
Canada Water	d			19 55			20 00	20 05	20 10	20 15	20 20								20 25		20 30	20 35	20 40	20 45	
Rotherhithe	d			19 56			20 01	20 06	20 11	20 16	20 21								20 26		20 31	20 36	20 41	20 46	
Wapping	d			19 58			20 03	20 08	20 13	20 18	20 23								20 28		20 33	20 38	20 43	20 48	
Shadwell	d			20 00			20 05	20 10	20 15	20 20	20 25								20 30		20 35	20 40	20 45	20 50	
Whitechapel	d			20 02			20 07	20 12	20 17	20 22	20 27								20 32		20 37	20 42	20 47	20 52	
Shoreditch High Street	d			20 04			20 09	20 14	20 19	20 24	20 29								20 34		20 39	20 44	20 49	20 54	
Hoxton	d			20 06			20 11	20 16	20 21	20 26	20 31								20 36		20 41	20 46	20 51	20 56	
Haggerston	d			20 08			20 13	20 18	20 23	20 28	20 33								20 38		20 43	20 48	20 53	20 58	
Dalston Junction Stn ELL	a			20 10			20 17	20 20	20 25	20 32	20 35								20 40		20 47	20 50	20 55	21 02	
Canonbury	d			20 15				20 23	20 30		20 38								20 45			20 53	21 00		
Highbury & Islington	d			20a18				20a26	20a33		20a41								20a48			20a56	21a03		
London Bridge 4 ⊖	a	19 49	19 48			20 01								20 03		20 06	20 19	20 18		20 31					

East London Line and Croydon - London Victoria to London Bridge

Station		LO	SN	SE	SN	SN	SN	SN	LO	SN		LO	LO	LO	LO	LO	SN	SE	SN	SN		SN	SN	LO	SN
East Croydon	d						20 12	20 17														20 42	20 47		
West Croydon 4	d								20 27	20 34				20 42										20 57	21 04
Norwood Junction 2	d							20 22	20 31	20 40				20 46									20 52	21 01	21 10
Anerley	d							20 25	20 34					20 49									20 55	21 04	
Penge West	d							20 27	20 36					20 51									20 57	21 06	
London Victoria 15 ⊖	d			20 09		20 11												20 39		20 41					
Battersea Park 4	d					20 15														20 45					
Wandsworth Road	d					20 17														20 47					
Clapham High Street ⊖	d					20 19														20 49					
London Blackfriars 3 ⊖	d																								
Denmark Hill 4	d			20 18		20 24												20 48		20 54					
Peckham Rye 4	d		20 15	20a21	20 23	20 26	20 40										20 45	20a51	20 53	20 56		21 10			
Queens Rd Peckham	d				20 26	20 29	20 42												20 56	20 59		21 12			
South Bermondsey	d				20 28	20 31	20 45												20 58	21 01		21 15			
Clapham Junction 10	d																								
Wandsworth Common	d																								
Balham 4 ⊖	d																								
Streatham Hill	d																								
West Norwood 4	d		20 27														20 57								
Gipsy Hill	d		20 30														21 00								
Crystal Palace 4	d	20 31	20a32										20 46			21 01	21a02								
Sydenham	d	20 34						20 29	20 39	20 44			20 49	20 54		21 04							20 59	21 09	21 14
Forest Hill 4	d	20 37						20 32	20 41	20 47			20 52	20 56		21 07							21 02	21 11	21 17
Honor Oak Park	d	20 39						20 34	20 44	20 49			20 54	20 59		21 09							21 04	21 14	21 19
Brockley	d	20 42						20 37	20 46	20 52			20 57	21 01		21 12							21 07	21 16	21 22
New Cross Gate 4	a	20 44						20 39	20 49	20 54			20 59	21 04		21 14							21 09	21 19	21 24
	d	20 44						20 39	20 49	20 54			20 59	21 04		21 14							21 09	21 19	21 24
New Cross ELL	d											20 54			21 09										
Surrey Quays	d	20 48							20 53			20 58	21 03	21 08	21 13	21 18								21 23	
Canada Water	d	20 50							20 55			21 00	21 05	21 10	21 15	21 20								21 25	
Rotherhithe	d	20 51							20 56			21 01	21 06	21 11	21 16	21 21								21 26	
Wapping	d	20 53							20 58			21 03	21 08	21 13	21 18	21 23								21 28	
Shadwell	d	20 55							21 00			21 05	21 10	21 15	21 20	21 25								21 30	
Whitechapel	d	20 57							21 02			21 07	21 12	21 17	21 22	21 27								21 32	
Shoreditch High Street	d	20 59							21 04			21 09	21 14	21 19	21 24	21 29								21 34	
Hoxton	d	21 01							21 06			21 11	21 16	21 21	21 26	21 31								21 36	
Haggerston	d	21 03							21 08			21 13	21 18	21 23	21 28	21 33								21 38	
Dalston Junction Stn ELL	a	21 05							21 10			21 17	21 20	21 25	21 32	21 35								21 40	
Canonbury	d	21 08							21 15				21 23	21 30		21 38								21 45	
Highbury & Islington	d	21a11							21a18				21a26	21a33		21a41								21a48	
London Bridge 4 ⊖	a				20 33	20 36	20 49	20 48		21 01									21 03	21 06		21 19	21 18		21 31

Station		LO	LO	LO	LO	LO		SN	SE	SN	SN	SN	SN	LO	SN	LO		LO	LO	LO	LO	SN	SE	SN	SN
East Croydon	d											21 12	21 17												
West Croydon 4	d			21 12										21 27	21 34				21 42						
Norwood Junction 2	d			21 16									21 22	21 31	21 40				21 46						
Anerley	d			21 19									21 25	21 34					21 49						
Penge West	d			21 21									21 27	21 36					21 51						
London Victoria 15 ⊖	d								21 09		21 11												21 39		21 41
Battersea Park 4	d										21 15														21 45
Wandsworth Road	d										21 17														21 47
Clapham High Street ⊖	d										21 19														21 49
London Blackfriars 3 ⊖	d																								
Denmark Hill 4	d								21 18		21 24												21 48		21 54
Peckham Rye 4	d							21 15	21a21	21 23	21 26	21 40										21 45	21a51	21 53	21 56
Queens Rd Peckham	d									21 26	21 29	21 42												21 56	21 59
South Bermondsey	d									21 28	21 31	21 45												21 58	22 01
Clapham Junction 10	d																								
Wandsworth Common	d																								
Balham 4 ⊖	d																								
Streatham Hill	d																								
West Norwood 4	d							21 27														21 57			
Gipsy Hill	d							21 30														22 00			
Crystal Palace 4	d		21 16			21 31		21a32										21 46			22 01	22a02			
Sydenham	d		21 19	21 24		21 34							21 29	21 39	21 44			21 49	21 54		22 04				
Forest Hill 4	d		21 22	21 26		21 37							21 32	21 41	21 47			21 52	21 56		22 07				
Honor Oak Park	d		21 24	21 29		21 39							21 34	21 44	21 49			21 54	21 59		22 09				
Brockley	d		21 27	21 31		21 42							21 37	21 46	21 52			21 57	22 01		22 12				
New Cross Gate 4	a		21 29	21 34		21 44							21 39	21 49	21 54			21 59	22 04		22 14				
	d		21 29	21 34		21 44							21 39	21 49	21 54			21 59	22 04		22 14				
New Cross ELL	d	21 24			21 39											21 54				22 09					
Surrey Quays	d	21 28	21 33	21 38	21 43	21 48								21 53		21 58		22 03	22 08	22 13	22 18				
Canada Water	d	21 30	21 35	21 40	21 45	21 50								21 55		22 00		22 05	22 10	22 15	22 20				
Rotherhithe	d	21 31	21 36	21 41	21 46	21 51								21 56		22 01		22 06	22 11	22 16	22 21				
Wapping	d	21 33	21 38	21 43	21 48	21 53								21 58		22 03		22 08	22 13	22 18	22 23				
Shadwell	d	21 35	21 40	21 45	21 50	21 55								22 00		22 05		22 10	22 15	22 20	22 25				
Whitechapel	d	21 37	21 42	21 47	21 52	21 57								22 02		22 07		22 12	22 17	22 22	22 27				
Shoreditch High Street	d	21 39	21 44	21 49	21 54	21 59								22 04		22 09		22 14	22 19	22 24	22 29				
Hoxton	d	21 41	21 46	21 51	21 56	22 01								22 06		22 11		22 16	22 21	22 26	22 31				
Haggerston	d	21 43	21 48	21 53	21 58	22 03								22 08		22 13		22 18	22 23	22 28	22 33				
Dalston Junction Stn ELL	a	21 47	21 50	21 55	22 02	22 05								22 10		22 17		22 20	22 25	22 32	22 35				
Canonbury	d		21 53	22 00		22 08								22 15				22 23	22 30		22 38				
Highbury & Islington	d		21a56	22a03		22a11								22a18				22a26	22a33		22a41				
London Bridge 4 ⊖	a									21 33	21 36	21 49	21 48		22 01									22 03	22 06

Table 178

Sundays

East London Line and Croydon - London Victoria to London Bridge

		SN		SN	LO	SN	LO	SN	LO	SE	SN	SN		SN	SN	LO	SN	LO	LO	SN	LO	SE		SN	SN
East Croydon	d	21 42		21 47										22 12	22 17										
West Croydon 4	d				21 57	22 04	22 12									22 27	22 34		22 42						
Norwood Junction 2	d			21 52	22 01	22 10	22 16								22 22	22 31	22 40		22 46						
Anerley	d			21 55	22 04		22 19								22 25	22 34			22 49						
Penge West	d			21 57	22 06		22 21								22 27	22 36			22 51						
London Victoria 15 ⊖	d									22 09		22 11										22 39			22 41
Battersea Park 4	d											22 15													22 45
Wandsworth Road	d											22 17													22 47
Clapham High Street ⊖	d											22 19													22 49
London Blackfriars 3 ⊖	d																								
Denmark Hill 4	d									22 18		22 24										22 48			22 54
Peckham Rye 4	d	22 10						22 15		22a21	22 23	22 26		22 40						22 45		22a51		22 53	22 56
Queens Rd Peckham	d	22 12									22 26	22 29		22 42										22 56	22 59
South Bermondsey	d	22 15									22 28	22 31		22 45										22 58	23 01
Clapham Junction 10	d																								
Wandsworth Common	d																								
Balham 4 ⊖	d																								
Streatham Hill	d																								
West Norwood 4	d							22 27												22 57					
Gipsy Hill	d							22 30												23 00					
Crystal Palace 4	d							22a32										22 46		23a02					
Sydenham	d			21 59	22 09	22 14	22 24								22 29	22 39	22 44	22 49	22 54						
Forest Hill 4	d			22 02	22 11	22 17	22 26								22 32	22 41	22 47	22 52	22 56						
Honor Oak Park	d			22 04	22 14	22 19	22 29								22 34	22 44	22 49	22 54	22 59						
Brockley	d			22 07	22 16	22 22	22 31								22 37	22 46	22 52	22 57	23 01						
New Cross Gate 4	a			22 09	22 19	22 24	22 34								22 39	22 49	22 54	22 59	23 04						
	d			22 09	22 19	22 24	22 34								22 39	22 49	22 54	22 59	23 04						
New Cross ELL	d								22 39												23 09				
Surrey Quays	d				22 23		22 38		22 43							22 53		23 03	23 08		23 13				
Canada Water	d				22 25		22 40		22 45							22 55		23 05	23 10		23 15				
Rotherhithe	d				22 26		22 41		22 46							22 56		23 06	23 11		23 16				
Wapping	d				22 28		22 43		22 48							22 58		23 08	23 13		23 18				
Shadwell	d				22 30		22 45		22 50							23 00		23 10	23 15		23 20				
Whitechapel	d				22 32		22 47		22 52							23 02		23 12	23 17		23 22				
Shoreditch High Street	d				22 34		22 49		22 54							23 04		23 14	23 19		23 24				
Hoxton	d				22 36		22 51		22 56							23 06		23 16	23 21		23 26				
Haggerston	d				22 38		22 53		22 58							23 08		23 18	23 23		23 28				
Dalston Junction Stn ELL	a				22 40		22 55		23 02							23 10		23 20	23 25		23 32				
Canonbury	d				22 45		23 00									23 15		23 23	23 30						
Highbury & Islington	d				22a48		23a03									23a18		23a26	23a33						
London Bridge 4 ⊖	a	22 19		22 18		22 31					22 33	22 36		22 49	22 48		23 01							23 03	23 06

		SN	SN	LO	LO	SN	SE	SN		SN	SN
East Croydon	d	22 42	22 47								
West Croydon 4	d			22 57							
Norwood Junction 2	d		22 52	23 01							
Anerley	d		22 55	23 04							
Penge West	d		22 57	23 06							
London Victoria 15 ⊖	d						23 09			23 11	
Battersea Park 4	d									23 15	
Wandsworth Road	d									23 17	
Clapham High Street ⊖	d									23 19	
London Blackfriars 3 ⊖	d										
Denmark Hill 4	d						23 18			23 24	
Peckham Rye 4	d	23 10				23 15	23a21	23 23		23 26	23 53
Queens Rd Peckham	d	23 12						23 26		23 29	23 56
South Bermondsey	d	23 15						23 28		23 31	23 58
Clapham Junction 10	d										
Wandsworth Common	d										
Balham 4 ⊖	d										
Streatham Hill	d										
West Norwood 4	d					23 27					
Gipsy Hill	d					23 30					
Crystal Palace 4	d				23 16	23a32					
Sydenham	d		22 59	23 09	23 19						
Forest Hill 4	d		23 02	23 11	23 22						
Honor Oak Park	d		23 04	23 14	23 24						
Brockley	d		23 07	23 16	23 27						
New Cross Gate 4	a		23 09	23 19	23 29						
	d		23 09	23 19	23 29						
New Cross ELL	d										
Surrey Quays	d			23 23	23 33						
Canada Water	d			23 25	23 35						
Rotherhithe	d			23 26	23 36						
Wapping	d			23 28	23 38						
Shadwell	d			23 30	23 40						
Whitechapel	d			23 32	23 42						
Shoreditch High Street	d			23 34	23 44						
Hoxton	d			23 36	23 46						
Haggerston	d			23 38	23 48						
Dalston Junction Stn ELL	a			23 40	23 50						
Canonbury	d			23 45	23 53						
Highbury & Islington	d			23a48	23a56						
London Bridge 4 ⊖	a	23 19	23 17					23 33		23 36	00 03

Luton and London - Wimbledon and Sutton via Streatham

Miles	Miles	Station		FC MX	FC MX	FC	SN	FC	FC	SN	FC	SN		FC	FC 1	FC	FC 1	SN	FC	FC	SN	FC		SN	FC 1
—	—	**Luton** 10	d					05 08			05 48			06 06	06 34	06 36	06 40		06 50	07 10		07 30			
—	—	Luton Airport Parkway 7	d					05 10			05 50			06 08		06 38	06 42		06 52	07 12		07 32			
—	—	St Pancras International 15 ⊖	d			05 38		05 54	06 12		06 34			06 52	07 06	07 24	07 16		07 32	07 52		08 12			08 24
—	—	Farringdon 3 ⊖	d			05 42		05 58	06 17		06 39			06 57	07 11	07 29	07 21		07 37	07 57		08 17			08 29
—	0	City Thameslink 3	d			05 45		06 01	06 21		06 43			07 01	07 15	07 33	07 25		07 41	08 01		08 21			08 33
—	0½	**London Blackfriars** 3 ⊖	d			05 48		06 06	06 24		06 46			07 04	07 18	07 36	07 28		07 44	08 04		08 24			08 36
—	1½	Elephant & Castle ⊖	d			05 51		06 09	06 27		06 49			07 07	07 21	07 40	07 33		07 47	08 07		08 27			
—	3½	Loughborough Jn	d					06 13	06 31		06 53			07 11	07 25		07 37		07 51	08 11		08 31			
—	4½	Herne Hill 4	d			05 58		06 16	06 34		06 57			07 16	07 31	07a46	07 41		07 56	08 15		08 36			08 46
0	—	**London Bridge** 4 ⊖	d	23p28	23p58		06 00			06 30		06 58						07 29			08 06			08 24	
1¾	—	South Bermondsey	d				06 04			06 34		07 02						07 33			08 11			08 28	
2¾	—	Queens Rd Peckham	d				06 06			06 36		07 04						07 35			08 13			08 30	
3½	—	Peckham Rye 4	d				06 09			06 39		07 07						07 38			08 16			08 33	
4½	—	East Dulwich	d				06 12			06 42		07 10						07 41			08 19			08 36	
4¾	—	North Dulwich	d				06 14			06 44		07 12						07 43			08 21			08 38	
6	5½	Tulse Hill 3	d	23p40	00 10	06 02	06 18	06 22	06 42	06 48	07 02	07 16		07 20	07 37		07 45	07 47	08 05	08 20	08 25	08 40		08 47	08 50
7½	7	Streatham 4	d	23p44	00 14	06 05	06 21	06 25	06 46	06 51	07 05	07 19		07 23	07 40		07 48	07 51	08 09	08 24	08 28	08 44		08 50	08 54
—	8	Mitcham Eastfields	d					06 29	06 50					07 27			07 52			08 28					08 58
—	9	Mitcham Junction	d					06 32	06 53					07 30			07 55			08 31					09 01
—	11	Hackbridge	d					06 35	06 56					07 33			07 58			08 34					09 04
—	11¾	Carshalton	d					06 38	06 59					07 36			08 01			08 37					09 07
9	—	Tooting	d	23p48	00 18	06 09	06 25			06 55	07 10	07 23			07 44			07 55	08 12		08 33	08 48			
10¼	—	Haydons Road	d	23p51	00 21	06 12	06 28			06 58	07 13	07 26			07 47			07 58	08 15		08 36	08 51			
11½	—	**Wimbledon** 6 ⊖	a	23p54	00 24	06 15	06 31			07 01	07 16	07 30			07 50			08 01	08 18		08 38	08 54			
—	—		d	23p55	00 25	06 15					07 17				07 51				08 19			08 55			
12½	—	Wimbledon Chase	d	23p58	00 28	06 18					07 20				07 54				08 22			08 58			
13	—	South Merton	d	00 01	00 30	06 20					07 22				07 56				08 24			09 00			
13½	—	Morden South	d	00 03	00 32	06 22					07 24				07 58				08 26			09 02			
14	—	St Helier	d	00 05	00 34	06 24					07 26				08 00				08 28			09 04			
15	—	Sutton Common	d	00 08	00 36	06 27					07 28				08 02				08 30			09 06			
16	—	West Sutton	d	00 11	00 39	06 29					07 31				08 05				08 33			09 09			
17	13	**Sutton (Surrey)** 4	a	00 14	00 43	06 33		06 43	07 04		07 35			07 39	08 08		08 04		08 37	08 40		09 12		09 02	09 10

Station		FC 1	FC	FC	FC	FC	FC	FC		FC	FC		FC	FC	FC	FC	FC		FC 1	FC	SN	FC	FC 1	FC
Luton 10	d	07 56	08 02			08 54		09 14			09 44		14 44		15 14		15 44		16 04			16 16	16 42	
Luton Airport Parkway 7	d	07 58	08 04			08 56		09 16			09 46		14 46		15 16		15 46		16 06			16 18	16 45	
St Pancras International 15 ⊖	d	08 32	08 44	08 56	09 16	09 34	09 48	10 04		10 18	10 34		15 34	15 48	16 04	16 18	16 34		16 40	16 52		17 02	17 14	17 18
Farringdon 3 ⊖	d	08 37	08 49	09 01	09 21	09 39	09 53	10 09		10 23	10 39		15 39	15 53	16 09	16 23	16 39		16 45	16 57		17 07	17 19	17 23
City Thameslink 3	d	08 41	08 53	09 05	09 25	09 43	09 57	10 13		10 27	10 43		15 43	15 57	16 13	16 27	16 43		16 49	17 01		17 11	17 23	17 27
London Blackfriars 3 ⊖	d	08 44	08 56	09 08	09 28	09 46	10 00	10 16		10 30	10 46		15 46	16 00	16 16	16 30	16 46		16 52	17 04		17 14	17 26	17 30
Elephant & Castle ⊖	d	08 47	09 00	09 12	09 31	09 49	10 03	10 19		10 33	10 49		15 49	16 03	16 19	16 33	16 49		16 56	17 08		17 18	17 30	17 34
Loughborough Jn	d	08 51	09 04	09 16	09 35	09 53	10 07	10 23		10 37	10 53		15 53	16 07	16 23	16 37	16 53		17 00	17 12		17 22		17 38
Herne Hill 4	d	08 57	09 11	09 25	09 41	09 57	10 11	10 27		10 41	10 57		15 57	16 11	16 27	16 41	16 57		17a04	17 16		17 26	17a36	17 44
London Bridge 4 ⊖	d																				17 06			
South Bermondsey	d																				17 10			
Queens Rd Peckham	d											and at									17 12			
Peckham Rye 4	d											the same									17 15			
East Dulwich	d											minutes									17 18			
North Dulwich	d											past									17 20			
Tulse Hill 3	d	09 01	09 16	09 31	09 46	10 01	10 16	10 31		10 46	11 01	each	16 01	16 16	16 32	16 46	17 02			17 20	17 24	17 31		17 48
Streatham 4	d	09 05	09 20	09 35	09 50	10 05	10 20	10 35		10 50	11 05	hour until	16 05	16 20	16 36	16 50	17 06			17 24	17 28	17 36		17 52
Mitcham Eastfields	d		09 24		09 54		10 24			10 54				16 24		16 56				17 28	17 32			17 56
Mitcham Junction	d		09 27		09 57		10 27			10 57				16 27		16 59				17 31	17 35			17 59
Hackbridge	d		09 30		10 00		10 30			11 00				16 30		17 02				17 34	17 38			18 02
Carshalton	d		09 33		10 03		10 33			11 03				16 33		17 05				17 37	17 41			18 05
Tooting	d	09 10		09 40		10 10		10 40			11 10		16 10		16 40		17 10					17 40		
Haydons Road	d	09 13		09 43		10 13		10 43			11 13		16 13		16 43		17 13					17 43		
Wimbledon 6 ⊖	a	09 16		09 46		10 16		10 46			11 16		16 16		16 46		17 16					17 46		
	d	09 17		09 47		10 17		10 47			11 17		16 17		16 47		17 19					17 49		
Wimbledon Chase	d	09 20		09 50		10 20		10 50			11 20		16 20		16 50		17 22					17 52		
South Merton	d	09 22		09 52		10 22		10 52			11 22		16 22		16 52		17 24					17 54		
Morden South	d	09 24		09 54		10 24		10 54			11 24		16 24		16 54		17 26					17 56		
St Helier	d	09 26		09 56		10 26		10 56			11 26		16 26		16 56		17 28					17 58		
Sutton Common	d	09 28		09 58		10 28		10 58			11 28		16 28		16 58		17 30					18 00		
West Sutton	d	09 31		10 01		10 31		11 01			11 31		16 31		17 01		17 33					18 03		
Sutton (Surrey) 4	a	09 37	09 36	10 05	10 06	10 35	10 36	11 05		11 06	11 35		16 35	16 36	17 05	17 08	17 39			17 40	17 44	18 07		18 08

Luton and London - Wimbledon and Sutton via Streatham

		SN	FC	FC	FC	SN	FC	FC 1	FC	SN	FC	FC	FC	FC	FC	FC	FC	FC	FC		FC
Luton 10	d		16 46	17 10			17 18	17 22	17 38			18 06	18 22		18 54		19 24		19 50		21 20
Luton Airport Parkway 7	d		16 48	17 12			17 20	17 24	17 40			18 08	18 25		18 57		19 27		19 52		21 22
St Pancras International 15 ⊖	d		17 32	17 44	17 52		18 04	17 58	18 24		18 38	18 48	19 04	19 18	19 34	19 48	20 04	20 18	20 36		22 06
Farringdon 3 ⊖	d		17 37	17 49	17 57		18 09	18 03	18 29		18 43	18 53	19 09	19 23	19 39	19 53	20 09	20 23	20 40		22 10
City Thameslink 3	d		17 41	17 53	18 01		18 13	18 07	18 33		18 47	18 57	19 13	19 27	19 43	19 57	20 13	20 27	20 43		22 13
London Blackfriars 3 ⊖	d		17 44	17 56	18 04		18 16	18 10	18 36		18 50	19 00	19 16	19 30	19 46	20 00	20 16	20 30	20 46		22 16
Elephant & Castle ⊖	d		17 48	18 00	18 08		18 20	18 14	18 40		18 54	19 04	19 19	19 33	19 49	20 03	20 19	20 33	20 49		22 19
Loughborough Jn	d		17 52		18 12		18 24		18 44		18 58	19 08	19 23	19 37	19 53	20 07	20 23	20 37	20 53		22 23
Herne Hill 4	d		17 57	18a06	18 18		18 28	18a21	18 48		19 02	19 12	19 27	19 41	19 57	20 11	20 27	20 41	20 57		22 27
London Bridge 4 ⊖	d	17 37				18 08				18 38											
South Bermondsey	d	17 41				18 12				18 42											
Queens Rd Peckham	d	17 43				18 14				18 44											
Peckham Rye 4	d	17 46				18 17				18 47										and every 30 minutes until	
East Dulwich	d	17 49				18 20				18 50											
North Dulwich	d	17 51				18 22				18 52											
Tulse Hill 3	d	17 55	18 02		18 22	18 27	18 32		18 52	18 56	19 07	19 16	19 31	19 46	20 01	20 16	20 31	20 46	21 01		22 31
Streatham 4	d	17 58	18 06		18 26	18 30	18 36		18 56	18 59	19 11	19 20	19 35	19 50	20 05	20 20	20 35	20 50	21 05		22 35
Mitcham Eastfields	d	18 02			18 30	18 34			19 00	19 03		19 24		19 54		20 24		20 54			
Mitcham Junction	d	18 05			18 33	18 37			19 03	19 06		19 27		19 57		20 27		20 57			
Hackbridge	d	18 09			18 36	18 41			19 06	19 10		19 30		20 00		20 30		21 00			
Carshalton	d	18 11			18 39	18 43			19 09	19 12		19 33		20 03		20 33		21 03			
Tooting	d		18 10				18 40				19 16		19 40		20 10		20 40		21 10		22 40
Haydons Road	d		18 13				18 43				19 19		19 43		20 13		20 43		21 13		22 43
Wimbledon 6 ⊖	a		18 16				18 46				19 22		19 46		20 16		20 46		21 16		22 46
	d		18 19				18 47				19 23		19 49		20 19		20 49		21 19		22 49
Wimbledon Chase	d		18 22				18 50				19 26		19 52		20 22		20 52		21 22		22 52
South Merton	d		18 24				18 52				19 28		19 54		20 24		20 54		21 24		22 54
Morden South	d		18 26				18 54				19 30		19 56		20 26		20 56		21 26		22 56
St Helier	d		18 28				18 56				19 32		19 58		20 28		20 58		21 28		22 58
Sutton Common	d		18 30				18 58				19 34		20 00		20 30		21 00		21 30		23 00
West Sutton	d		18 33				19 01				19 37		20 03		20 33		21 03		21 33		23 03
Sutton (Surrey) 4	a	18 15	18 37		18 42	18 47	19 07		19 12	19 16	19 40	19 36	20 07	20 06	20 39	20 36	21 09	21 06	21 39		23 09

		FC	FC	FC
Luton 10	d			
Luton Airport Parkway 7	d			
St Pancras International 15 ⊖	d			
Farringdon 3 ⊖	d			
City Thameslink 3	d			
London Blackfriars 3 ⊖	d			
Elephant & Castle ⊖	d			
Loughborough Jn	d			
Herne Hill 4	d			
London Bridge 4 ⊖	d	23 01	23 28	23 58
South Bermondsey	d			
Queens Rd Peckham	d			
Peckham Rye 4	d			
East Dulwich	d			
North Dulwich	d			
Tulse Hill 3	d	23 11	23 40	00 10
Streatham 4	d	23 15	23 44	00 14
Mitcham Eastfields	d			
Mitcham Junction	d			
Hackbridge	d			
Carshalton	d			
Tooting	d	23 20	23 48	00 18
Haydons Road	d	23 23	23 51	00 21
Wimbledon 6 ⊖	a	23 26	23 54	00 24
	d	23 26	23 55	00 25
Wimbledon Chase	d	23 29	23 58	00 28
South Merton	d	23 31	00 01	00 30
Morden South	d	23 33	00 03	00 32
St Helier	d	23 35	00 05	00 34
Sutton Common	d	23 38	00 08	00 36
West Sutton	d	23 40	00 11	00 39
Sutton (Surrey) 4	a	23 45	00 14	00 43

Table 179

Saturdays

Luton and London - Wimbledon and Sutton via Streatham

Station		FC	FC	FC	FC	FC	FC	FC	
Luton 10	d								
Luton Airport Parkway 7	d								
St Pancras International 15 ⊖	d								
Farringdon 3 ⊖	d								
City Thameslink 3	d								
London Blackfriars 3 ⊖	d								
Elephant & Castle ⊖	d								
Loughborough Jn	d								
Herne Hill 4	d				06 42		07 12		
London Bridge 4 ⊖	d	23p28	23p58	06 21		06 45		07 15	
South Bermondsey	d								
Queens Rd Peckham	d								
Peckham Rye 4	d								and at the same minutes past each hour until
East Dulwich	d								
North Dulwich	d								
Tulse Hill 3	d	23p40	00 10	06 31	06 46	07 01	07 16	07 31	
Streatham 4	d	23p44	00 14	06 35	06 50	07 05	07 20	07 35	
Mitcham Eastfields	d				06 54		07 24		
Mitcham Junction 🚊	d				06 57		07 27		
Hackbridge	d				07 00		07 30		
Carshalton	d				07 03		07 33		
Tooting	d	23p48	00 18	06 40		07 10		07 40	
Haydons Road	d	23p51	00 21	06 43		07 13		07 43	
Wimbledon 6 ⊖ 🚊	a	23p54	00 24	06 46		07 16		07 46	
	d	23p55	00 25	06 47		07 17		07 47	
Wimbledon Chase	d	23p58	00 28	06 50		07 20		07 50	
South Merton	d	00 01	00 30	06 52		07 22		07 52	
Morden South	d	00 03	00 32	06 54		07 24		07 54	
St Helier	d	00 05	00 34	06 56		07 26		07 56	
Sutton Common	d	00 08	00 36	06 58		07 28		07 58	
West Sutton	d	00 11	00 39	07 01		07 31		08 01	
Sutton (Surrey) 4	a	00 14	00 43	07 05	07 06	07 35	07 36	08 05	

Station		FC		FC	FC	FC	FC	FC	FC	FC	FC	FC		FC	FC	FC
Luton 10	d															
Luton Airport Parkway 7	d															
St Pancras International 15 ⊖	d															
Farringdon 3 ⊖	d															
City Thameslink 3	d															
London Blackfriars 3 ⊖	d															
Elephant & Castle ⊖	d															
Loughborough Jn	d															
Herne Hill 4	d			18 42		19 12		19 42								
London Bridge 4 ⊖	d	18 15			18 45		19 15		19 45	20 15	20 45	21 15		21 45	22 15	22 45
South Bermondsey	d															
Queens Rd Peckham	d															
Peckham Rye 4	d															
East Dulwich	d															
North Dulwich	d															
Tulse Hill 3	d	18 31		18 46	19 01	19 16	19 31	19 46	20 01	20 31	21 01	21 31		22 01	22 31	23 01
Streatham 4	d	18 35		18 50	19 05	19 20	19 35	19 51	20 05	20 35	21 05	21 35		22 05	22 35	23 05
Mitcham Eastfields	d			18 54		19 24		19 55								
Mitcham Junction 🚊	d			18 57		19 27		19 58								
Hackbridge	d			19 00		19 30		20 01								
Carshalton	d			19 03		19 33		20 04								
Tooting	d	18 40			19 10		19 40		20 10	20 40	21 10	21 40		22 10	22 40	23 10
Haydons Road	d	18 43			19 13		19 43		20 13	20 43	21 13	21 43		22 13	22 43	23 13
Wimbledon 6 ⊖ 🚊	a	18 46			19 16		19 46		20 16	20 46	21 16	21 46		22 16	22 46	23 16
	d	18 47			19 17		19 47		20 17	20 47	21 17	21 47		22 17	22 47	23 17
Wimbledon Chase	d	18 50			19 20		19 50		20 20	20 50	21 20	21 50		22 20	22 50	23 20
South Merton	d	18 52			19 22		19 52		20 22	20 52	21 22	21 52		22 22	22 52	23 22
Morden South	d	18 54			19 24		19 54		20 24	20 54	21 24	21 54		22 24	22 54	23 24
St Helier	d	18 56			19 26		19 56		20 26	20 56	21 26	21 56		22 26	22 56	23 26
Sutton Common	d	18 58			19 28		19 58		20 28	20 58	21 28	21 58		22 28	22 58	23 28
West Sutton	d	19 01			19 31		20 01		20 31	21 01	21 31	22 01		22 31	23 01	23 31
Sutton (Surrey) 4	a	19 05		19 06	19 39	19 36	20 05	20 07	20 37	21 05	21 37	22 05		22 39	23 05	23 35

Station		FC	FC
Luton 10	d		
Luton Airport Parkway 7	d		
St Pancras International 15 ⊖	d		
Farringdon 3 ⊖	d		
City Thameslink 3	d		
London Blackfriars 3 ⊖	d		
Elephant & Castle ⊖	d		
Loughborough Jn	d		
Herne Hill 4	d		
London Bridge 4 ⊖	d	23 15	23 45
South Bermondsey	d		
Queens Rd Peckham	d		
Peckham Rye 4	d		
East Dulwich	d		
North Dulwich	d		
Tulse Hill 3	d	23 31	00 01
Streatham 4	d	23 35	00 05
Mitcham Eastfields	d		
Mitcham Junction 🚊	d		
Hackbridge	d		
Carshalton	d		
Tooting	d	23 40	00 10
Haydons Road	d	23 43	00 13
Wimbledon 6 ⊖ 🚊	a	23 46	00 16
	d	23 47	00 17
Wimbledon Chase	d	23 50	00 20
South Merton	d	23 52	00 22
Morden South	d	23 54	00 24
St Helier	d	23 56	00 26
Sutton Common	d	23 58	00 28
West Sutton	d	00 01	00 31
Sutton (Surrey) 4	a	00 05	00 35

Table 179

Sundays

Luton and London - Wimbledon and Sutton via Streatham

		FC A	FC A	FC		FC
Luton 10	d					
Luton Airport Parkway 7	d					
St Pancras International 15 ⊖	d					
Farringdon 3 ⊖	d					
City Thameslink 3	d					
London Blackfriars 3 ⊖	d					
Elephant & Castle ⊖	d					
Loughborough Jn	d					
Herne Hill 4	d					
London Bridge 4 ⊖	d	23p15	23p45	09 32	and every 30 minutes until	21 02
South Bermondsey	d					
Queens Rd Peckham	d					
Peckham Rye 4	d					
East Dulwich	d					
North Dulwich	d					
Tulse Hill 3	d	23p31	00 01	09 43		21 13
Streatham 4	d	23p35	00 05	09 46		21 16
Mitcham Eastfields	d					
Mitcham Junction	d					
Hackbridge	d					
Carshalton	d					
Tooting	d	23p40	00 10	09 50		21 20
Haydons Road	d	23p43	00 13	09 53		21 23
Wimbledon 6 ⊖	a	23p46	00 16	09 57		21 27
	d	23p47	00 17	09 58		21 28
Wimbledon Chase	d	23p50	00 20	10 01		21 31
South Merton	d	23p52	00 22	10 03		21 33
Morden South	d	23p54	00 24	10 05		21 35
St Helier	d	23p56	00 26	10 07		21 37
Sutton Common	d	23p58	00 28	10 09		21 39
West Sutton	d	00 01	00 31	10 12		21 42
Sutton (Surrey) 4	a	00 05	00 35	10 16		21 46

A not 22 May

Sutton and Wimbledon - London and Luton via Streatham

Miles	Miles			SE	SN	SN	FC	FC	SN	FC	SN	SE		FC	SE	FC	SN	SE 1	FC	FC	SN	FC		SE 1	FC
0	0	**Sutton (Surrey)** 4	d		05 37	06 14	06 05	06 34	06 50	06 46	07 20			07 06		07 37	07 49		07 40	08 09	08 20	08 08			08 39
1	—	West Sutton	d				06 09			06 49				07 09					07 43			08 11			
2	—	Sutton Common	d				06 11			06 51				07 11					07 45			08 13			
3	—	St Helier	d				06 14			06 54				07 14					07 48			08 16			
3½	—	Morden South	d				06 16			06 56				07 16					07 50			08 18			
4	—	South Merton	d				06 18			06 58				07 18					07 52			08 20			
4½	—	Wimbledon Chase	d				06 20			07 00				07 20					07 54			08 22			
5½	—	Wimbledon 6 ⊖	a				06 23			07 05				07 23					07 57			08 25			
—	—		d				06 28			07 06				07 26					07 58			08 28			
6¾	—	Haydons Road	d				06 30			07 08				07 28					08 00			08 30			
8	—	Tooting	d				06 33			07 11				07 31					08 03			08 33			
—	1¼	Carshalton	d		05 40	06 17		06 37	06 53		07 23					07 40	07 52			08 12	08 23				08 42
—	2	Hackbridge	d		05 42	06 19		06 39	06 55		07 25					07 42	07 54			08 14	08 25				08 44
—	4	Mitcham Junction	d		05 46	06 23		06 42	06 59		07 29					07 45	07 58			08 17	08 29				08 47
—	5	Mitcham Eastfields	d		05 49	06 26		06 45	07 02		07 32					07 48	08 01			08 20	08 32				08 50
9½	6	Streatham 4	d		05 53	06 30	06 38	06 49	07 05	07 16	07 35			07 38		07 52	08 05		08 09	08 24	08 36	08 39			08 54
11	7½	Tulse Hill 3	d		05 57	06 34	06 42	06 53	07 10	07 20	07 41			07 42		07 57	08 09		08 13	08 28	08 40	08 43			08 58
12¼	—	North Dulwich	d			06 37			07 13		07 44						08 12				08 43				
12½	—	East Dulwich	d			06 39			07 15		07 46						08 14				08 45				
13½	—	Peckham Rye 4	d		06 02	06 42			07 17		07 48						08 16				08 48				
14¼	—	Queens Rd Peckham	d			06 44			07 20		07 51						08 19				08 50				
15¼	—	South Bermondsey	d			06 47			07 22		07 53						08 21				08 53				
17	—	**London Bridge** 4 ⊖	a		06 08	06 51			07 28		07 59						08 28				08 57				
—	8½	Herne Hill 4	d	05 23			06 46	06 57		07 24		07 31		07 46	07 57	08 01		08 12	08 20	08 31		08 47		08 52	09 02
—	9½	Loughborough Jn	d				06 49	07 00		07 27		07 34		07 49	08 00	08 04		08 16	08 23	08 35		08 50		08 55	09 05
—	11½	Elephant & Castle ⊖	d	05 29			06 54	07 06		07 32		07 38		07 54	08 05	08 09		08 21	08 28	08 40		08 58		09 02	09 10
—	12½	**London Blackfriars** 3 ⊖	a	05 33			06 57	07 09		07 35		07 42		07 57	08 08	08 12		08 25	08 32	08 45		09 01		09 06	09 13
—	13	City Thameslink 3	a	05 35			07 02	07 14		07 38		07 44		08 00	08 11	08 15		08 27	08 35	08 48		09 04		09 08	09 16
—	—	Farringdon 3 ⊖	a				07 06	07 18		07 42		07 48		08 03	08 15	08 19		08 30	08 39	08 52		09 08		09 12	09 20
—	—	St Pancras International 15 ⊖	a				07 09	07 21		07 45		07 51		08 07	08 19	08 23		08 35	08 43	08 55		09 11		09 15	09 23
—	—	Luton Airport Parkway 7	a				07 49			08 21					09 01			09 09	09 27			09 59		09 43	10 03
—	—	**Luton** 10	a				07 54			08 24					09 04			09 12	09 32			10 04		09 46	10 06

		FC	SN	FC	FC	FC	FC	FC		FC	FC	FC	FC	FC	FC	FC	FC	FC		FC	FC	FC	FC	FC	FC
Sutton (Surrey) 4	d	08 41	08 57	09 13	09 11	09 38	09 37	10 08		10 07	10 38	10 37	11 08	11 07	11 38	11 37	12 08	12 07		12 38	12 37	13 08	13 07	13 38	13 37
West Sutton	d	08 44			09 14		09 40			10 10		10 40		11 10		11 40		12 10			12 40		13 10		13 40
Sutton Common	d	08 46			09 16		09 42			10 12		10 42		11 12		11 42		12 12			12 42		13 12		13 42
St Helier	d	08 49			09 19		09 45			10 15		10 45		11 15		11 45		12 15			12 45		13 15		13 45
Morden South	d	08 51			09 21		09 47			10 17		10 47		11 17		11 47		12 17			12 47		13 17		13 47
South Merton	d	08 53			09 23		09 49			10 19		10 49		11 19		11 49		12 19			12 49		13 19		13 49
Wimbledon Chase	d	08 55			09 25		09 51			10 21		10 51		11 21		11 51		12 21			12 51		13 21		13 51
Wimbledon 6 ⊖	a	08 58			09 28		09 54			10 24		10 54		11 24		11 54		12 24			12 54		13 24		13 54
	d	08 58			09 28		09 58			10 28		10 58		11 28		11 58		12 28			12 58		13 28		13 58
Haydons Road	d	09 00			09 30		10 00			10 30		11 00		11 30		12 00		12 30			13 00		13 30		14 00
Tooting	d	09 03			09 33		10 03			10 33		11 03		11 33		12 03		12 33			13 03		13 33		14 03
Carshalton	d		09 00	09 16		09 41		10 11			10 41		11 11		11 41		12 11			12 41		13 11		13 41	
Hackbridge	d		09 02	09 18		09 43		10 13			10 43		11 13		11 43		12 13			12 43		13 13		13 43	
Mitcham Junction	d		09 06	09 21		09 46		10 16			10 46		11 16		11 46		12 16			12 46		13 16		13 46	
Mitcham Eastfields	d		09 09	09 24		09 49		10 19			10 49		11 19		11 49		12 19			12 49		13 19		13 49	
Streatham 4	d	09 08	09 12	09 28	09 38	09 53	10 08	10 23		10 38	10 53	11 08	11 23	11 38	11 53	12 08	12 23	12 38		12 53	13 08	13 23	13 38	13 53	14 08
Tulse Hill 3	d	09 16	09 16	09 32	09 42	09 57	10 12	10 27		10 42	10 57	11 12	11 27	11 42	11 57	12 12	12 27	12 42		12 57	13 12	13 27	13 42	13 57	14 12
North Dulwich	d		09 19																						
East Dulwich	d		09 21																						
Peckham Rye 4	d		09 23																						
Queens Rd Peckham	d		09 26																						
South Bermondsey	d		09 28																						
London Bridge 4 ⊖	a		09 35																						
Herne Hill 4	d	09 20		09 35	09 47	10 01	10 16	10 31		10 46	11 01	11 16	11 31	11 46	12 01	12 16	12 31	12 46		13 01	13 16	13 31	13 46	14 01	14 16
Loughborough Jn	d	09 23		09 39	09 50	10 04	10 19	10 34		10 49	11 04	11 19	11 34	11 49	12 04	12 19	12 34	12 49		13 04	13 19	13 34	13 49	14 04	14 19
Elephant & Castle ⊖	d	09 30		09 46	09 55	10 09	10 24	10 39		10 54	11 09	11 24	11 39	11 54	12 09	12 24	12 39	12 54		13 09	13 24	13 39	13 54	14 09	14 24
London Blackfriars 3 ⊖	a	09 33		09 49	09 59	10 12	10 27	10 42		10 57	11 12	11 27	11 42	11 57	12 12	12 27	12 42	12 57		13 12	13 27	13 42	13 57	14 12	14 27
City Thameslink 3	a	09 36		09 52	10 02	10 15	10 32	10 45		11 02	11 15	11 32	11 45	12 02	12 15	12 32	12 45	13 02		13 15	13 32	13 45	14 02	14 15	14 32
Farringdon 3 ⊖	a	09 40		09 56	10 06	10 19	10 35	10 49		11 06	11 19	11 36	11 49	12 06	12 19	12 36	12 49	13 06		13 19	13 36	13 49	14 06	14 19	14 36
St Pancras International 15 ⊖	a	09 43		09 59	10 09	10 22	10 39	10 52		11 09	11 22	11 39	11 52	12 09	12 22	12 39	12 52	13 09		13 22	13 39	13 52	14 09	14 22	14 39
Luton Airport Parkway 7	a	10 29			10 57		11 27			11 55		12 25		12 55		13 25		13 56			14 25		14 55		15 25
Luton 10	a	10 34			11 02		11 32			12 00		12 30		13 00		13 30		14 00			14 30		15 00		15 30

Sutton and Wimbledon - London and Luton via Streatham

		FC	FC	FC	FC	FC	FC	FC	FC	FC	FC	FC 1	FC	FC	SE 1	FC	FC	FC	SN	FC	FC	FC
Sutton (Surrey) 4	d	14 08	14 07	14 38	14 37	15 08	15 07	15 38	15 37	16 08	16 07	16 38	16 37	17 08		17 11	17 42	17 41		18 08	18 09	18 38
West Sutton	d		14 10		14 40		15 10		15 40		16 10		16 40			17 14		17 44			18 12	
Sutton Common	d		14 12		14 42		15 12		15 42		16 12		16 42			17 16		17 46			18 14	
St Helier	d		14 15		14 45		15 15		15 45		16 15		16 45			17 19		17 49			18 17	
Morden South	d		14 17		14 47		15 17		15 47		16 17		16 47			17 21		17 51			18 19	
South Merton	d		14 19		14 49		15 19		15 49		16 19		16 49			17 23		17 53			18 21	
Wimbledon Chase	d		14 21		14 51		15 21		15 51		16 21		16 51			17 25		17 55			18 23	
Wimbledon 6 ⊖	a		14 24		14 54		15 24		15 54		16 24		16 54			17 28		17 58			18 26	
	d		14 28		14 58		15 28		15 58		16 30		17 00			17 30		18 00	18 10		18 28	
Haydons Road	d		14 30		15 00		15 30		16 00		16 32		17 02			17 32		18 02	18 12		18 30	
Tooting	d		14 33		15 03		15 33		16 03		16 35		17 05			17 35		18 05	18 15		18 33	
Carshalton	d	14 11		14 41		15 11		15 41		16 11		16 41		17 11			17 45			18 11		18 41
Hackbridge	d	14 13		14 43		15 13		15 43		16 13		16 43		17 13			17 47			18 13		18 43
Mitcham Junction	d	14 16		14 46		15 16		15 46		16 16		16 46		17 16			17 50			18 16		18 46
Mitcham Eastfields	d	14 19		14 49		15 19		15 49		16 19		16 49		17 19			17 53			18 19		18 49
Streatham 4	d	14 23	14 38	14 53	15 08	15 23	15 38	15 53	16 08	16 23	16 40	16 53	17 10	17 23		17 40	17 57	18 10	18 20	18 23	18 40	18 53
Tulse Hill 3	d	14 27	14 42	14 57	15 12	15 27	15 42	15 57	16 12	16 27	16 46	16 57	17 16	17 27		17 44	18 01	18 16	18 24	18 27	18 44	18 57
North Dulwich	d																		18 27			
East Dulwich	d																		18 29			
Peckham Rye 4	d																		18 32			
Queens Rd Peckham	d																		18 35			
South Bermondsey	d																		18 37			
London Bridge 4 ⊖	a																		18 42			
Herne Hill 4	d	14 31	14 46	15 01	15 16	15 31	15 46	16 01	16 16	16 31	16 50	17 01	17 20	17 31	17 43	17 48	18 06	18 20		18 31	18 48	19 01
Loughborough Jn	d	14 34	14 49	15 04	15 19	15 34	15 49	16 04	16 19	16 34	16 53		17 23	17 34	17 46	17 51	18 09	18 23		18 34	18 51	19 04
Elephant & Castle ⊖	d	14 39	14 54	15 09	15 24	15 39	15 54	16 09	16 24	16 39	17 00	17 08	17 28	17 39	17 52	17 56	18 14	18 28		18 40	18 56	19 09
London Blackfriars 3 ⊖	a	14 42	14 57	15 12	15 27	15 42	15 57	16 13	16 29	16 43	17 03	17 11	17 31	17 43	17 55	17 59	18 17	18 31		18 43	18 59	19 14
City Thameslink 3	a	14 45	15 02	15 15	15 32	15 45	16 02	16 16	16 32	16 46	17 06	17 14	17 34	17 48	17 58	18 02	18 20	18 34		18 46	19 02	19 20
Farringdon 3 ⊖	a	14 49	15 06	15 19	15 36	15 49	16 06	16 19	16 35	16 49	17 09	17 17	17 37	17 51	18 01	18 05	18 23	18 37		18 49	19 05	19 23
St Pancras International 15 ⊖	a	14 52	15 09	15 22	15 39	15 52	16 09	16 23	16 39	16 53	17 13	17 21	17 41	17 55	18 05	18 09	18 27	18 41		18 53	19 09	19 27
Luton Airport Parkway 7	a		15 55		16 25		16 59		17 25			17 55	18 27		18 39	18 57		19 29		19 35	19 53	
Luton 10	a		16 00		16 30		17 04		17 30			17 58	18 32		18 42	19 02		19 34		19 38	19 58	

		SN	FC	FC	SN	FC	FC	FC	FC	FC	FC	FC	FC	FC	FC
Sutton (Surrey) 4	d		18 43	19 08		19 13	19 42	19 38	20 10	20 07	20 40	20 37	21 10	21 10	22 12
West Sutton	d		18 46			19 16		19 41		20 10		20 40		21 13	22 15
Sutton Common	d		18 48			19 18		19 43		20 12		20 42		21 15	22 17
St Helier	d		18 51			19 21		19 46		20 15		20 45		21 18	22 20
Morden South	d		18 53			19 23		19 48		20 17		20 47		21 20	22 22
South Merton	d		18 55			19 25		19 50		20 19		20 49		21 22	22 24
Wimbledon Chase	d		18 57			19 27		19 52		20 21		20 51		21 24	22 26
Wimbledon 6 ⊖	a		19 00			19 30		19 55		20 24		20 54		21 27	22 29
	d	18 43	19 00		19 17	19 30		19 56		20 26		20 56		21 36	22 30
Haydons Road	d	18 45	19 02		19 19	19 32		19 58		20 28		20 58		21 38	22 32
Tooting	d	18 48	19 05		19 22	19 35		20 01		20 31		21 01		21 41	22 35
Carshalton	d			19 11			19 45		20 13		20 43		21 13		
Hackbridge	d			19 13			19 47		20 15		20 45		21 15		
Mitcham Junction	d			19 16			19 50		20 18		20 48		21 18		
Mitcham Eastfields	d			19 19			19 53		20 21		20 51		21 21		
Streatham 4	d	18 56	19 10	19 23	19 26	19 40	19 57	20 06	20 25	20 36	20 55	21 06	21 25	21 46	22 40
Tulse Hill 3	d	19 00	19 14	19 27	19 31	19 44	20 01	20 12	20 29	20 42	20 59	21 12	21 29	21 50	22 43
North Dulwich	d	19 03			19 34										
East Dulwich	d	19 05			19 36										
Peckham Rye 4	d	19 07			19 38										
Queens Rd Peckham	d	19 10			19 41										
South Bermondsey	d	19 12			19 43										
London Bridge 4 ⊖	a	19 17			19 51										22 55
Herne Hill 4	d		19 17	19 31		19 47	20 05	20 16	20 35	20 46	21 05	21 16	21 35	21 54	
Loughborough Jn	d		19 20	19 34		19 50	20 08	20 19	20 38	20 49	21 08	21 19	21 38	21 57	
Elephant & Castle ⊖	d		19 25	19 39		19 55	20 13	20 24	20 43	20 54	21 13	21 24	21 43	22 02	
London Blackfriars 3 ⊖	a		19 28	19 43		19 58	20 16	20 27	20 46	20 57	21 16	21 27	21 46	22 05	
City Thameslink 3	a		19 32	19 48		20 02	20 20	20 32	20 50	21 02	21 20	21 32	21 50	22 10	
Farringdon 3 ⊖	a		19 36	19 52		20 06	20 24	20 36	20 54	21 06	21 24	21 36	21 54	22 14	
St Pancras International 15 ⊖	a		19 39	19 55		20 09	20 27	20 39	20 57	21 09	21 27	21 39	21 57	22 17	
Luton Airport Parkway 7	a		20 25			20 55		21 25		21 55		22 25		23 01	
Luton 10	a		20 30			21 00		21 30		22 00		22 30		23 04	

Table 179

Saturdays

Sutton and Wimbledon - London and Luton via Streatham

		FC	FC	FC	FC	FC		FC	FC		FC	FC	FC	FC		FC
Sutton (Surrey) 4	d		07 08	07 07	07 38	07 37		18 37	19 08		19 07	19 37	20 08	20 37		22 07
West Sutton	d			07 10		07 40		18 40			19 10	19 40	20 11	20 40		22 10
Sutton Common	d			07 12		07 42		18 42			19 12	19 42	20 13	20 42		22 12
St Helier	d			07 15		07 45		18 45			19 15	19 45	20 16	20 45		22 15
Morden South	d			07 17		07 47		18 47			19 17	19 47	20 18	20 47		22 17
South Merton	d			07 19		07 49		18 49			19 19	19 49	20 20	20 49		22 19
Wimbledon Chase	d			07 21		07 51		18 51			19 21	19 51	20 22	20 51		22 21
Wimbledon 6 ⊖	a			07 25		07 55		18 55			19 25	19 55	20 25	20 55		22 25
	d	07 00		07 30		08 00		19 00			19 30	20 00	20 30	21 00		22 30
Haydons Road	d	07 02		07 32		08 02		19 02			19 32	20 02	20 32	21 02		22 32
Tooting	d	07 05		07 35		08 05		19 05			19 35	20 05	20 35	21 05		22 35
Carshalton	d		07 11		07 41				19 11							
Hackbridge	d		07 13		07 43		and at the same minutes past each hour until		19 13							
Mitcham Junction	d		07 16		07 46				19 16						and every 30 minutes until	
Mitcham Eastfields	d		07 19		07 49				19 19							
Streatham 4	d	07 10	07 23	07 40	07 53	08 10		19 10	19 23		19 40	20 10	20 40	21 10		22 40
Tulse Hill 3	d	07 17	07 27	07 47	07 57	08 17		19 17	19 27		19 47	20 17	20 47	21 17		22 47
North Dulwich	d															
East Dulwich	d															
Peckham Rye 4	d															
Queens Rd Peckham	d															
South Bermondsey	d															
London Bridge 4 ⊖	a	07 30		08 00		08 30		19 30			20 00	20 30	21 00	21 30		23 00
Herne Hill 4	d		07a31		08a01				19a31							
Loughborough Jn	d															
Elephant & Castle ⊖	d															
London Blackfriars 3 ⊖	a															
City Thameslink 3	a															
Farringdon 3 ⊖	a															
St Pancras International 15 ⊖	a															
Luton Airport Parkway 7	a															
Luton 10	a															

Sundays

		FC		FC
Sutton (Surrey) 4	d	10 28		21 28
West Sutton	d	10 31		21 31
Sutton Common	d	10 33		21 33
St Helier	d	10 36		21 36
Morden South	d	10 38		21 38
South Merton	d	10 40		21 40
Wimbledon Chase	d	10 42		21 42
Wimbledon 6 ⊖	a	10 45		21 45
	d	10 45		21 45
Haydons Road	d	10 48		21 48
Tooting	d	10 51		21 51
Carshalton	d			
Hackbridge	d			
Mitcham Junction	d		and every 30 minutes until	
Mitcham Eastfields	d			
Streatham 4	d	10 55		21 55
Tulse Hill 3	d	10 59		21 59
North Dulwich	d			
East Dulwich	d			
Peckham Rye 4	d			
Queens Rd Peckham	d			
South Bermondsey	d			
London Bridge 4 ⊖	a	11 10		22 10
Herne Hill 4	d			
Loughborough Jn	d			
Elephant & Castle ⊖	d			
London Blackfriars 3 ⊖	a			
City Thameslink 3	a			
Farringdon 3 ⊖	a			
St Pancras International 15 ⊖	a			
Luton Airport Parkway 7	a			
Luton 10	a			

London and Croydon - Caterham and Tattenham Corner

Miles	Miles			SN MX	SN MX	SN MO	SN MO	SN MX	SN	SN	SN	SN	
0	—	**London Victoria** 15 ⊖	d	23p15			23p50			06 13			
2¾	—	Clapham Junction 10	d	23p23			23p56			06 21			
—	0	**London Bridge** 4 ⊖	d		23p36	23p39		00 06	06 06		06 36	06 54	
—	2¾	New Cross Gate 4 ⊖	d		23p41	23p44		00 11	06 11		06 41	06 59	
—	8¾	Norwood Junction 2	d		23p59	00 03		00 30	06 30		07 00	07 18	
10½	10	**East Croydon**	d	23p45	00 04	00 07	00 18	00 35	06 34	06 44	07 04	07 22	
11½	11	South Croydon 4	d	23p47	00 06	00 09	00 20	00 37	06 36		07 06	07 25	
12½	12	Purley Oaks	d	23p50	00 09	00 12	00 23	00 40	06 39		07 09	07 28	
13½	13	Purley 4	a	23p54	00 12	00 15	00 26	00 43	06 42	06 51	07 12	07 31	
—	—		d	23p55	00 15	00 16	00 27	00 46	06 45	06 54	07 13	07 34	07 36
—	14¼	Kenley	d		00 18	00 19	00 30	00 49	06 48		07 16	07 37	
—	15½	Whyteleafe	d		00 21	00 22	00 33	00 52	06 51		07 19	07 40	
—	16	Whyteleafe South	d		00 23	00 24	00 35	00 54	06 53		07 21	07 42	
—	17¾	**Caterham**	a		00 28	00 29	00 40	00 59	06 58		07 26	07 48	
14¼	—	Reedham	d	23p57						06 56			07 38
15	—	Coulsdon Town	d										
15¾	—	Woodmansterne	d	00 03						07 02			07 44
16¾	—	Chipstead	d	00 06						07 05			07 47
19¼	—	Kingswood	d	00 11						07 10			07 52
20½	—	Tadworth	d	00 15						07 14			07 56
21¾	—	**Tattenham Corner**	a	00 18						07 18			07 59

			SN	SN	SN	SN		SN	SN	SN	SN		SN
London Victoria 15 ⊖	d			07 23	07 20			07 45			08 15		
Clapham Junction 10	d			07 30	07 28			07 51			08 23		
London Bridge 4 ⊖	d		07 06			07 36			08 14	08 06			08 47
New Cross Gate 4 ⊖	d		07 11			07 41				08 11			
Norwood Junction 2	d		07 31			08 00			08 27	08 30			
East Croydon	d		07 38	07 45	07 49	08 04		08 13	08 31	08 34	08 45		09 03
South Croydon 4	d		07 40		07 52	08 06		08 15		08 36	08 47		
Purley Oaks	d		07 43		07 55	08 09		08 18		08 39	08 50		
Purley 4	a		07 46	07 52	07 58	08 12		08 21	08 38	08 42	08 53		09 09
	d		07 49	07 53	07 58	08 16	08 18	08 24	08 39	08 43	08 54		09 11
Kenley	d		07 52	08 00		08 19		08 27		08 46	08 57		
Whyteleafe	d		07 55	08 04		08 22		08 30		08 49	09 00		
Whyteleafe South	d		07 57	08 06		08 24		08 32		08 51	09 02		
Caterham	a		08 02	08 10		08 29		08 37		08 56	09 07		
Reedham	d				08 00		08 20		08 42				09 14
Coulsdon Town	d												
Woodmansterne	d				08 06		08 26		08 47				09 19
Chipstead	d				08 09		08 29		08 50				09 22
Kingswood	d				08 14		08 34		08 56				09 28
Tadworth	d				08 18		08 38		08 59				09 31
Tattenham Corner	a				08 21		08 41		09 03				09 36

		SN	SN	SN	SN	SN	SN	SN	SN		SN	SN	
London Victoria 15 ⊖	d		08 43			09 13					09 43		and at the same minutes past each hour until
Clapham Junction 10	d		08 51			09 21					09 51		
London Bridge 4 ⊖	d	08 36		09 06	09 20			09 36	09 50			10 06	
New Cross Gate 4 ⊖	d	08 41		09 12				09 41				10 11	
Norwood Junction 2	d	09 00		09 30	09 33			10 00	10 03			10 30	
East Croydon	d	09 07	09 13	09 34	09 37	09 43		10 04	10 07		10 13	10 34	
South Croydon 4	d	09 09	09 15	09 36		09 45		10 06			10 15	10 36	
Purley Oaks	d	09 12	09 18	09 39		09 48		10 09			10 18	10 39	
Purley 4	a	09 15	09 21	09 42	09 45	09 51		10 12	10 15		10 21	10 42	
	d	09 18	09 26	09 43	09 46	09 52	10 02	10 13	10 16		10 22	10 43	
Kenley	d	09 21	09 29	09 46		09 55		10 16			10 25	10 46	
Whyteleafe	d	09 24	09 32	09 49		09 58		10 19			10 28	10 49	
Whyteleafe South	d	09 26	09 34	09 51		10 00		10 21			10 30	10 51	
Caterham	a	09 31	09 40	09 56		10 05		10 26			10 35	10 56	
Reedham	d				09 48		10 04		10 18				
Coulsdon Town	d												
Woodmansterne	d				09 54		10 10		10 24				
Chipstead	d				09 57		10 13		10 27				
Kingswood	d				10 02		10 18		10 32				
Tadworth	d				10 06		10 22		10 36				
Tattenham Corner	a				10 09		10 25		10 39				

		SN	SN	SN	SN	SN		SN	SN	SN	SN	SN
London Victoria 15 ⊖	d			14 13					14 43			15 13
Clapham Junction 10	d			14 21					14 51			15 21
London Bridge 4 ⊖	d	14 06	14 20			14 36		14 50		15 06	15 20	
New Cross Gate 4 ⊖	d	14 11				14 41				15 11		
Norwood Junction 2	d	14 30	14 33			15 00		15 03		15 30	15 33	
East Croydon	d	14 34	14 37	14 43		15 04		15 07	15 13	15 34	15 37	15 43
South Croydon 4	d	14 36		14 46		15 06			15 15	15 36		15 46
Purley Oaks	d	14 39		14 49		15 09			15 18	15 39		15 49
Purley 4	a	14 42	14 45	14 52		15 12		15 15	15 21	15 42	15 45	15 52
	d	14 43	14 46	14 54	15 02	15 13		15 16	15 22	15 43	15 46	15 52
Kenley	d	14 46		14 57		15 16			15 25	15 46		15 55
Whyteleafe	d	14 49		15 01		15 19			15 28	15 49		15 59
Whyteleafe South	d	14 51		15 03		15 21			15 30	15 51		16 01
Caterham	a	14 56		15 07		15 26			15 35	15 56		16 05
Reedham	d		14 48		15 04			15 18			15 48	
Coulsdon Town	d											
Woodmansterne	d		14 54		15 10			15 24			15 54	
Chipstead	d		14 57		15 13			15 27			15 57	
Kingswood	d		15 02		15 18			15 32			16 02	
Tadworth	d		15 06		15 22			15 36			16 06	
Tattenham Corner	a		15 09		15 25			15 39			16 09	

		SN	SN	SN	SN		SN	SN	SN	SN	SN		SN
London Victoria 15 ⊖	d				15 43				16 13	16 39			16 43
Clapham Junction 10	d				15 51				16 21	16 45			16 51
London Bridge 4 ⊖	d		15 36	15 50			16 06	16 20			16 48		
New Cross Gate 4 ⊖	d		15 41				16 11						
Norwood Junction 2	d		16 00	16 03			16 30	16 33			17 02		
East Croydon	d		16 04	16 07	16 13		16 34	16 37	16 43	16 56	17 06		17 17
South Croydon 4	d		16 06		16 15		16 36		16 45	16 58	17 08		17 19
Purley Oaks	d		16 09		16 18		16 39		16 48	17 01	17 11		17 22
Purley 4	a		16 12	16 15	16 21		16 42	16 45	16 51	17 04	17 14		17 25
	d	16 02	16 13	16 16	16 24		16 43	16 48	16 52	17 05	17 18	17 22	17 28
Kenley	d		16 16		16 27		16 46		16 55	17 08	17 21		17 31
Whyteleafe	d		16 19		16 30		16 49		16 58	17 11	17 24		17 34
Whyteleafe South	d		16 21		16 32		16 51		17 00	17 13	17 26		17 36
Caterham	a		16 26		16 37		16 58		17 07	17 20	17 33		17 43
Reedham	d	16 04		16 18				16 50				17 24	
Coulsdon Town	d												
Woodmansterne	d	16 10		16 24				16 56				17 30	
Chipstead	d	16 13		16 27				16 59				17 33	
Kingswood	d	16 18		16 32				17 04				17 38	
Tadworth	d	16 22		16 36				17 08				17 42	
Tattenham Corner	a	16 25		16 39				17 11				17 47	

		SN			SN		SN		SN		SN		
London Victoria 15 ⊖	d	17 09					17 39				18 09		
Clapham Junction 10	d	17 15					17 45				18 15		
London Bridge 4 ⊖	d				17 17				17 49				
New Cross Gate 4 ⊖	d												
Norwood Junction 2	d				17 31				18 02				
East Croydon	d	17 27			17 35		17 56		18 06		18 28		
South Croydon 4	d	17 30			17 37		17 58		18 08		18 30		
Purley Oaks	d	17 33			17 40		18 01		18 11		18 33		
Purley 4	a	17 36			17 44		18 04		18 14		18 36		
	d	17 40	17 42		17 48	17 50	18 08	18 10	18 18	18 21	18 40	18 42	
Kenley	d	17 43			17 51		18 11		18 21		18 43		
Whyteleafe	d	17 46			17 54		18 14		18 24		18 46		
Whyteleafe South	d	17 48			17 56		18 16		18 26		18 48		
Caterham	a	17 55			18 03		18 23		18 33		18 55		
Reedham	d		17 44			17 52		18 12		18 23		18 44	
Coulsdon Town	d												
Woodmansterne	d		17 50			17 58		18 18		18 29		18 50	
Chipstead	d		17 53			18 01		18 21		18 32		18 53	
Kingswood	d		17 58			18 06		18 26		18 37		18 58	
Tadworth	d		18 02			18 10		18 30		18 41		19 02	
Tattenham Corner	a		18 05			18 15		18 33		18 45		19 05	

		SN			SN	SN	SN		SN		SN	SN	SN	
London Victoria 15 ⊖	d				18 39				18 45			19 15		
Clapham Junction 10	d				18 45				18 53			19 23		
London Bridge 4 ⊖	d	18 18					18 49				19 06		19 36	
New Cross Gate 4 ⊖	d										19 11		19 41	
Norwood Junction 2	d	18 31					19 02				19 30		20 00	
East Croydon	d	18 37			18 57		19 06		19 14		19 34	19 44	20 04	
South Croydon 4	d	18 42			19 00		19 08		19 16		19 36	19 47	20 06	
Purley Oaks	d	18 45			19 03		19 11		19 19		19 39	19 50	20 09	
Purley 4	a	18 48			19 06		19 14		19 22		19 42	19 53	20 12	
	d	18 51	18 54		19 10	19 12	19 18	19 21	19 26	19 28	19 45	19 53	20 15	
Kenley	d	18 54			19 13		19 21		19 29		19 48		20 18	
Whyteleafe	d	18 57			19 16		19 24		19 32		19 51		20 21	
Whyteleafe South	d	18 59			19 18		19 26		19 34		19 53		20 23	
Caterham	a	19 06			19 25		19 33		19 41		19 58		20 28	
Reedham	d		18 56			19 14		19 23		19 31		19 56		
Coulsdon Town	d													
Woodmansterne	d		19 02			19 20		19 29		19 37		20 01		
Chipstead	d		19 05			19 23		19 32		19 40		20 04		
Kingswood	d		19 10			19 28		19 37		19 45		20 10		
Tadworth	d		19 14			19 32		19 41		19 49		20 13		
Tattenham Corner	a		19 17			19 35		19 45		19 52		20 17		

		SN	SN	SN	SN	SN	SN	SN	SN	SN		SN
London Victoria 15 ⊖	d	19 45		20 15		20 45		21 15		21 45		
Clapham Junction 10	d	19 53		20 23		20 53		21 23		21 53		
London Bridge 4 ⊖	d		20 06		20 36		21 06		21 36			22 08
New Cross Gate 4 ⊖	d		20 11		20 41		21 11		21 41			22 13
Norwood Junction 2	d		20 30		21 00		21 30		22 00			22 32
East Croydon	d	20 15	20 34	20 44	21 04	21 14	21 34	21 45	22 04	22 14		22 36
South Croydon 4	d	20 17	20 36	20 47	21 06	21 17	21 36	21 47	22 06	22 17		22 38
Purley Oaks	d	20 21	20 39	20 50	21 09	21 20	21 39	21 50	22 09	22 20		22 41
Purley 4	a	20 24	20 42	20 53	21 12	21 23	21 42	21 53	22 12	22 23		22 44
	d	20 24	20 45	20 53	21 15	21 23	21 45	21 54	22 15	22 23		22 47
Kenley	d		20 48		21 18		21 48		22 18			22 50
Whyteleafe	d		20 51		21 21		21 51		22 21			22 53
Whyteleafe South	d		20 53		21 23		21 53		22 23			22 55
Caterham	a		20 58		21 28		21 58		22 28			23 00
Reedham	d	20 27		20 56		21 26		21 56		22 26		
Coulsdon Town	d											
Woodmansterne	d	20 32		21 01		21 31		22 02		22 31		
Chipstead	d	20 35		21 04		21 34		22 05		22 34		
Kingswood	d	20 41		21 10		21 40		22 10		22 40		
Tadworth	d	20 44		21 13		21 43		22 14		22 43		
Tattenham Corner	a	20 48		21 17		21 47		22 17		22 47		

Table 181

Mondays to Fridays

London and Croydon - Caterham and Tattenham Corner

		SN	SN	SN	SN	SN	SN	SN FO
London Victoria 15 ⊖	d	22 15		22 45		23 15		23 45
Clapham Junction 10	d	22 23		22 53		23 23		23 53
London Bridge 4 ⊖	d		22 38		23 06		23 36	
New Cross Gate 4 ⊖	d		22 43		23 11		23 41	
Norwood Junction 2	d		23 02		23 30		23 59	
East Croydon	d	22 45	23 07	23 14	23 34	23 45	00 04	00 14
South Croydon 4	d	22 47	23 09	23 17	23 36	23 47	00 06	00 17
Purley Oaks	d	22 50	23 12	23 20	23 39	23 50	00 09	00 20
Purley 4	a	22 53	23 15	23 23	23 42	23 54	00 12	00 23
	d	22 54	23 15	23 24	23 45	23 55	00 15	00 23
Kenley	d		23 18		23 48		00 18	
Whyteleafe	d		23 22		23 51		00 21	
Whyteleafe South	d		23 24		23 53		00 23	
Caterham	a		23 28		23 58		00 28	
Reedham	d	22 56		23 26		23 57		00 26
Coulsdon Town	d							
Woodmansterne	d	23 02		23 32		00 03		00 31
Chipstead	d	23 05		23 35		00 06		00 34
Kingswood	d	23 10		23 40		00 11		00 40
Tadworth	d	23 14		23 44		00 15		00 43
Tattenham Corner	a	23 17		23 47		00 18		00 47

Saturdays

		SN	SN	SN	SN	SN	SN	SN	SN	SN		SN	SN	SN	SN		SN	SN	SN		SN	SN	SN	SN
London Victoria 15 ⊖	d	23p15		23p45		00 16				06 43				07 13		and at the same minutes past each hour until					19 43			20 13
Clapham Junction 10	d	23p23		23p53		00 24				06 51				07 21							19 51			20 21
London Bridge 4 ⊖	d		23p36		00 06			06 36	06 50			07 06	07 20					19 36	19 50			20 06	20 20	
New Cross Gate 4 ⊖	d		23p41		00 11			06 41				07 11						19 41				20 11		
Norwood Junction 2	d		23p59		00 30		06 33	07 00	07 03			07 30	07 33					20 00	20 03			20 30	20 33	
East Croydon	d	23p45	00 04	00 14	00 34	00 48	06 37	07 04	07 07	07 13		07 34	07 37	07 43				20 04	20 07		20 13	20 34	20 37	20 43
South Croydon 4	d	23p47	00 06	00 17	00 36	00 50		07 06		07 15		07 36		07 45				20 06			20 15	20 36		20 45
Purley Oaks	d	23p50	00 09	00 20	00 39	00 53		07 09		07 18		07 39		07 48				20 09			20 18	20 39		20 48
Purley 4	a	23p54	00 12	00 23	00 42	00 56	06 45	07 12	07 15	07 21		07 42	07 45	07 51				20 12	20 15		20 21	20 42	20 45	20 51
	d	23p55	00 15	00 23	00 45	00 57	06 46	07 13	07 16	07 22		07 43	07 46	07 52	08 02		20 02	20 13	20 16		20 22	20 43	20 46	20 52
Kenley	d		00 18		00 48			07 16		07 25		07 46		07 55				20 16			20 25	20 46		20 55
Whyteleafe	d		00 21		00 51			07 19		07 28		07 49		07 58				20 19			20 28	20 49		20 58
Whyteleafe South	d		00 23		00 53			07 21		07 30		07 51		08 00				20 21			20 30	20 51		21 00
Caterham	a		00 28		00 58			07 26		07 35		07 56		08 05				20 26			20 35	20 56		21 05
Reedham	d	23p57		00 26		00 59	06 48		07 18				07 48		08 04		20 04		20 18				20 48	
Coulsdon Town	d																							
Woodmansterne	d	00 03		00 31		01 05	06 54		07 24				07 54		08 10		20 10		20 24				20 54	
Chipstead	d	00 06		00 34		01 08	06 57		07 27				07 57		08 13		20 13		20 27				20 57	
Kingswood	d	00 11		00 40		01 13	07 02		07 32				08 02		08 18		20 18		20 32				21 02	
Tadworth	d	00 15		00 43		01 17	07 06		07 36				08 06		08 22		20 22		20 36				21 06	
Tattenham Corner	a	00 18		00 47		01 20	07 09		07 39				08 09		08 25		20 25		20 39				21 09	

		SN	SN	SN	SN	SN		SN	SN	SN	SN	SN	SN	SN	SN	SN		SN	SN	SN	SN	SN	SN	SN
London Victoria 15 ⊖	d				20 43				21 13				21 43			22 13				22 43		23 15		23 45
Clapham Junction 10	d				20 51				21 21				21 51			22 21				22 51		23 23		23 53
London Bridge 4 ⊖	d		20 36	20 50		21 06		21 20			21 36	21 50		22 06	22 20			22 36	22 50		23 06		23 36	
New Cross Gate 4 ⊖	d		20 41			21 11					21 41			22 11				22 41			23 11		23 41	
Norwood Junction 2	d		21 00	21 03		21 30		21 33			22 00	22 03		22 30	22 33			23 00	23 03		23 30		23 59	
East Croydon	d		21 04	21 07	21 13	21 34		21 37	21 43		22 05	22 07	22 13	22 36	22 38	22 43		23 04	23 07	23 14	23 34	23 44	00 04	00 14
South Croydon 4	d		21 06		21 15	21 36			21 45		22 07		22 15	22 38		22 46		23 06		23 16	23 36	23 47	00 06	00 17
Purley Oaks	d		21 09		21 18	21 39			21 48		22 10		22 18	22 41		22 49		23 09		23 19	23 39	23 50	00 09	00 20
Purley 4	a		21 12	21 15	21 21	21 42		21 45	21 51		22 13	22 16	22 21	22 44	22 47	22 52		23 12	23 15	23 22	23 42	23 53	00 13	00 23
	d	21 04	21 13	21 16	21 22	21 43		21 46	21 52	22 04	22 14	22 17	22 22	22 45	22 48	22 52		23 13	23 16	23 23	23 43	23 53	00 16	00 23
Kenley	d		21 16		21 25	21 46			21 55		22 17		22 25	22 48		22 55		23 16		23 26	23 46		00 19	
Whyteleafe	d		21 19		21 28	21 49			21 58		22 20		22 28	22 51		22 59		23 19		23 29	23 49		00 22	
Whyteleafe South	d		21 21		21 30	21 51			22 00		22 22		22 30	22 53		23 01		23 21		23 31	23 51		00 24	
Caterham	a		21 26		21 35	21 56			22 05		22 27		22 36	22 58		23 06		23 26		23 36	23 56		00 29	
Reedham	d	21 06		21 18				21 48		22 06		22 19			22 50				23 18			23 56		00 26
Coulsdon Town	d																							
Woodmansterne	d	21 12		21 24				21 54		22 12		22 25			22 56				23 24			00 01		00 31
Chipstead	d	21 15		21 27				21 57		22 15		22 28			22 59				23 27			00 04		00 34
Kingswood	d	21 20		21 32				22 02		22 20		22 33			23 04				23 32			00 10		00 40
Tadworth	d	21 24		21 36				22 06		22 24		22 37			23 08				23 36			00 13		00 43
Tattenham Corner	a	21 27		21 39				22 09		22 27		22 40			23 11				23 39			00 17		00 47

Table 181

Sundays

London and Croydon - Caterham and Tattenham Corner

		SN A	SN A	SN A	SN	SN	SN	SN	SN	SN		SN	SN		SN	SN	SN	SN	SN		SN
London Victoria 15 ⊖	d	23p15		23p45		00 16	06 36	07 06	07 36			08 06				22 36		23 06			23 50
Clapham Junction 10	d	23p23		23p53		00 24	06 42	07 12	07 42			08 12				22 42		23 12			23 56
London Bridge 4 ⊖	d		23p36		00 06					07 39			08 09		22 09		22 39		23 39		
New Cross Gate 4 ⊖	d		23p41		00 11					07 44			08 14		22 14		22 44		23 44		
Norwood Junction 2	d		23p59		00 30					08 03			08 33		22 33		23 03		00 03		
East Croydon	d	23p44	00 04	00 14	00 34	00 48	07 04	07 34	08 04	08 08		08 34	08 38		22 38	23 04	23 08	23 35	00 07		00 18
South Croydon 4	d	23p47	00 06	00 17	00 36	00 50				08 10			08 40	and at the same minutes past each hour until	22 40		23 10	23 37	00 09		00 20
Purley Oaks	d	23p50	00 09	00 20	00 39	00 53				08 13			08 43		22 43		23 13	23 40	00 12		00 23
Purley 4	a	23p53	00 13	00 23	00 42	00 56	07 10	07 40	08 10	08 16		08 40	08 46		22 46	23 10	23 16	23 43	00 15		00 26
	d	23p53	00 16	00 23	00 45	00 57	07 10	07 40	08 10	08 17		08 40	08 47		22 47	23 10	23 32	23 44	00 16		00 27
Kenley	d		00 19		00 48		07 13	07 43	08 13			08 43				23 13		23 47	00 19		00 30
Whyteleafe	d		00 22		00 51		07 17	07 47	08 17			08 47				23 17		23 50	00 22		00 33
Whyteleafe South	d		00 24		00 53		07 19	07 49	08 19			08 49				23 19		23 52	00 24		00 35
Caterham	a		00 29		00 58		07 23	07 53	08 23			08 53				23 23		23 57	00 29		00 40
Reedham	d	23p56		00 26		00 59				08 19			08 49		22 49		23 34				
Coulsdon Town	d																				
Woodmansterne	d	00 01		00 31		01 05				08 25			08 55		22 55		23 40				
Chipstead	d	00 04		00 34		01 08				08 28			08 58		22 58		23 43				
Kingswood	d	00 10		00 40		01 13				08 33			09 03		23 03		23 48				
Tadworth	d	00 13		00 43		01 17				08 37			09 07		23 07		23 52				
Tattenham Corner	a	00 17		00 47		01 20				08 40			09 10		23 10		23 55				

A not 22 May

Table 181

Tattenham Corner and Caterham - Croydon and London

Miles	Miles	Station		SN	SN	SN	SN	SN	SN	SN	SN	SN		SN	SN	SN	SN	SN	SN	SN	SN	SN		SN	SN
0	—	**Tattenham Corner**	d		05 56			06 32		06 48		07 02			07 18		07 32		07 48		08 04			08 16	
1¼	—	Tadworth	d		05 59			06 35		06 51		07 05			07 21		07 35		07 51		08 07			08 19	
2½	—	Kingswood	d		06 02			06 38		06 54		07 08			07 24		07 38		07 54		08 10			08 22	
5	—	Chipstead	d		06 08			06 44		07 00		07 14			07 30		07 44		08 00		08 16			08 28	
6	—	Woodmansterne	d		06 11			06 47		07 03		07 17			07 33		07 47		08 03		08 19			08 31	
6¾	—	Coulsdon Town	d																						
7½	—	Reedham	d		06 16			06 52		07 08		07 22			07 38		07 52		08 08		08 24			08 36	
—	0	**Caterham**	d	05 52		06 15	06 35		06 45		07 01			07 15		07 31		07 45		08 01		08 17			08 29
—	1¾	Whyteleafe South	d	05 55		06 18	06 38		06 48		07 04			07 18		07 34		07 48		08 04		08 20			08 32
—	2¼	Whyteleafe	d	05 57		06 20	06 40		06 50		07 06			07 20		07 36		07 50		08 06		08 22			08 34
—	3½	Kenley	d	06 00		06 23	06 43		06 53		07 09			07 23		07 39		07 53		08 09		08 25			08 37
8¼	4¾	Purley 4	a	06 03	06 19	06 26	06 46	06 55	06 57	07 11	07 13	07 25		07 27	07 41	07 43	07 55	07 57	08 11	08 13	08 27	08 29		08 39	08 41
—	—																								
—	—		d	06 04	06 22	06 27	06 47	07 01		07 17		07 31			07 47		08 01		08 17		08 33			08 45	
9¼	5¾	Purley Oaks	d	06 07	06 25	06 30	06 50	07 04		07 20		07 34			07 50		08 04		08 20		08 36			08 48	
10¼	6¾	South Croydon 4	d	06 10	06 28	06 33	06 53	07 07		07 23		07 37			07 53		08 07		08 23		08 39			08 51	
11¼	7¾	**East Croydon**	d	06 13	06 31	06 36	06 57	07 10		07 26		07 40			07 56		08 10		08 26		08 42			08 54	
—	9	Norwood Junction 2	d	06 18	06 37	06 40		07 14				07 44					08 14				08 47				
—	15	New Cross Gate 4 ⊖	a	06 35																					
—	17¾	**London Bridge 4** ⊖	a	06 42	06 49	06 52		07 28				07 58					08 28				09 01				
19	—	Clapham Junction 10	a				07 06			07 36					08 06				08 36					09 04	
21¾	—	**London Victoria 15** ⊖	a				07 15			07 46					08 15				08 45					09 13	

Station		SN	SN	SN	SN	SN	SN	SN		SN	SN	SN	SN	SN	SN	SN	SN	SN		SN	SN	SN	SN	SN	SN
Tattenham Corner	d	08 27			08 51			09 21			09 33		09 49			10 21		10 33			10 51			11 21	
Tadworth	d	08 30			08 54			09 24			09 36		09 52			10 24		10 36			10 54			11 24	
Kingswood	d	08 33			08 57			09 27			09 39		09 55			10 27		10 39			10 57			11 27	
Chipstead	d	08 39			09 03			09 33			09 45		10 01			10 33		10 45			11 03			11 33	
Woodmansterne	d	08 42			09 06			09 36			09 48		10 04			10 36		10 48			11 06			11 36	
Coulsdon Town	d																								
Reedham	d	08 47			09 11			09 41			09 53		10 09			10 41		10 53			11 11			11 41	
Caterham	d		08 40	08 56		09 09	09 26			09 37		09 56		10 09	10 26		10 39			10 56		11 09	11 26		11 39
Whyteleafe South	d		08 43	08 59		09 12	09 29			09 40		09 59		10 12	10 29		10 42			10 59		11 12	11 29		11 42
Whyteleafe	d		08 45	09 01		09 14	09 31			09 42		10 01		10 14	10 31		10 44			11 01		11 14	11 31		11 44
Kenley	d		08 48	09 04		09 17	09 34			09 45		10 04		10 17	10 34		10 47			11 04		11 17	11 34		11 47
Purley 4	a	08 50	08 52	09 07	09 14	09 20	09 37	09 44		09 48	09 56	10 07	10 12	10 20	10 37	10 44	10 50	10 56		11 07	11 14	11 20	11 37	11 44	11 50
	d	08 56		09 08	09 14	09 21	09 38	09 45		09 51		10 08	10 15	10 21	10 38	10 45	10 51			11 08	11 15	11 21	11 38	11 45	11 51
Purley Oaks	d	08 59		09 11		09 24	09 41			09 54		10 11		10 24	10 41		10 54			11 11		11 24	11 41		11 54
South Croydon 4	d	09 02		09 14		09 27	09 44			09 57		10 14		10 27	10 44		10 57			11 14		11 27	11 44		11 57
East Croydon	d	09 05		09 17	09 20	09 30	09 47	09 51		10 00		10 17	10 21	10 30	10 47	10 51	11 00			11 17	11 21	11 30	11 47	11 51	12 00
Norwood Junction 2	d	09 09			09 25	09 35		09 55		10 05			10 25	10 35		10 55	11 05				11 25	11 35		11 55	12 05
New Cross Gate 4 ⊖	a				09 32	09 52				10 22				10 52			11 22					11 52			12 22
London Bridge 4 ⊖	a	09 23			09 42	09 59		10 09		10 29			10 39	10 59		11 09	11 29				11 39	11 59		12 09	12 29
Clapham Junction 10	a			09 38			10 07					10 37			11 07					11 37			12 07		
London Victoria 15 ⊖	a			09 48			10 16					10 46			11 16					11 46			12 16		

Station		SN	SN	SN		SN	SN	SN	SN	SN	SN	SN	SN	SN		SN	SN	SN	SN	SN	SN	SN	SN	SN	
Tattenham Corner	d	11 33		11 51				12 21		12 33		12 51				13 21		13 33		13 51			14 21		
Tadworth	d	11 36		11 54				12 24		12 36		12 54				13 24		13 36		13 54			14 24		
Kingswood	d	11 39		11 57				12 27		12 39		12 57				13 27		13 39		13 57			14 27		
Chipstead	d	11 45		12 03				12 33		12 45		13 03				13 33		13 45		14 03			14 33		
Woodmansterne	d	11 48		12 06				12 36		12 48		13 06				13 36		13 48		14 06			14 36		
Coulsdon Town	d																								
Reedham	d	11 53		12 11				12 41		12 53		13 11				13 41		13 53		14 11			14 41		
Caterham	d		11 56			12 09	12 26		12 39		12 56		13 09	13 26			13 39		13 56		14 09	14 26		14 39	
Whyteleafe South	d		11 59			12 12	12 29		12 42		12 59		13 12	13 29			13 42		13 59		14 12	14 29		14 42	
Whyteleafe	d		12 01			12 14	12 31		12 44		13 01		13 14	13 31			13 44		14 01		14 14	14 31		14 44	
Kenley	d		12 04			12 17	12 34		12 47		13 04		13 17	13 34			13 47		14 04		14 17	14 34		14 47	
Purley 4	a	11 56	12 07	12 14		12 20	12 37	12 44	12 50	12 56	13 07	13 14	13 20	13 37		13 44	13 50	13 56	14 07	14 14	14 20	14 37	14 44	14 50	
	d		12 08	12 15		12 21	12 38	12 45	12 51		13 08	13 15	13 21	13 38		13 45	13 51		14 08	14 15	14 21	14 38	14 45	14 51	
Purley Oaks	d		12 11			12 24	12 41		12 54		13 11		13 24	13 41			13 54		14 11		14 24	14 41		14 54	
South Croydon 4	d		12 14			12 27	12 44		12 57		13 14		13 27	13 44			13 57		14 14		14 27	14 44		14 57	
East Croydon	d		12 17	12 21		12 30	12 47	12 51	13 00		13 17	13 21	13 30	13 47		13 51	14 00		14 17	14 21	14 30	14 47	14 51	15 00	
Norwood Junction 2	d			12 25		12 35		12 55	13 05			13 25	13 35			13 55	14 05			14 25	14 35		14 55	15 05	
New Cross Gate 4 ⊖	a					12 52			13 22				13 52				14 22				14 52			15 22	
London Bridge 4 ⊖	a			12 39		12 59		13 09	13 29			13 39	13 59			14 09	14 29			14 39	14 59		15 09	15 29	
Clapham Junction 10	a		12 37				13 07				13 37			14 07					14 37			15 07			
London Victoria 15 ⊖	a		12 46				13 16				13 46			14 16					14 46			15 16			

Station		SN	SN	SN	SN	SN	SN	SN	SN	SN		SN	SN	SN	SN	SN	SN	SN	SN	SN		SN	SN	SN	SN
Tattenham Corner	d	14 33		14 51			15 21		15 33			15 51			16 21		16 33		16 51				17 19		
Tadworth	d	14 36		14 54			15 24		15 36			15 54			16 24		16 36		16 54				17 22		
Kingswood	d	14 39		14 57			15 27		15 39			15 57			16 27		16 39		16 57				17 25		
Chipstead	d	14 45		15 03			15 33		15 45			16 03			16 33		16 45		17 03				17 31		
Woodmansterne	d	14 48		15 06			15 36		15 48			16 06			16 36		16 48		17 06				17 34		
Coulsdon Town	d																								
Reedham	d	14 53		15 11			15 41		15 53			16 11			16 41		16 53		17 11				17 39		
Caterham	d		14 56		15 09	15 26		15 39		15 56			16 09	16 26		16 39		16 52		17 09		17 26		17 45	17 56
Whyteleafe South	d		14 59		15 12	15 29		15 42		15 59			16 12	16 29		16 42		16 55		17 12		17 29		17 48	17 59
Whyteleafe	d		15 01		15 14	15 31		15 44		16 01			16 14	16 31		16 44		16 57		17 14		17 31		17 50	18 01
Kenley	d		15 04		15 17	15 34		15 47		16 04			16 17	16 34		16 47		17 00		17 17		17 34		17 53	18 04
Purley 4	a	14 56	15 07	15 14	15 20	15 37	15 44	15 50	15 56	16 07		16 14	16 20	16 37	16 44	16 50	16 56	17 04	17 14	17 20		17 37	17 42	17 56	18 07
	d		15 08	15 15	15 21	15 38	15 45	15 51		16 08		16 15	16 21	16 38	16 45	16 51	17 08		17 15	17 21		17 38	17 45	17 59	18 08
Purley Oaks	d		15 11		15 24	15 41		15 54		16 11			16 24	16 41		16 54	17 11			17 24		17 41		18 02	18 11
South Croydon 4	d		15 14		15 27	15 44		15 57		16 14			16 27	16 44		16 57	17 14			17 27		17 44		18 05	18 14
East Croydon	d		15 17	15 21	15 30	15 47	15 51	16 00		16 17		16 21	16 30	16 47	16 51	17 00	17 17		17 21	17 30		17 47	17 51	18 08	18 17
Norwood Junction 2	d			15 25	15 35		15 55	16 05				16 25	16 35		16 55	17 05			17 25	17 35			17 55	18 12	
New Cross Gate 4 ⊖	a				15 52			16 22					16 52			17 22				17 52					
London Bridge 4 ⊖	a			15 39	15 59		16 09	16 29				16 39	17 02		17 08	17 31			17 37	17 59			18 09	18 26	
Clapham Junction 10	a		15 37			16 07				16 37				17 07			17 37					18 07			18 39
London Victoria 15 ⊖	a		15 46			16 16				16 46				17 16			17 48					18 16			18 46

Tattenham Corner and Caterham - Croydon and London

		SN	SN	SN	SN	SN		SN	SN	SN	SN	SN	SN	SN	SN	SN		SN	SN	SN	SN	SN	SN	SN	SN
Tattenham Corner	d	17 51		18 12		18 42			19 14		19 42	19 53		20 12		20 42			21 12		21 42		22 12		22 42
Tadworth	d	17 54		18 15		18 45			19 17		19 45	19 56		20 15		20 45			21 15		21 45		22 15		22 45
Kingswood	d	17 57		18 18		18 48			19 20		19 48	19 59		20 18		20 48			21 18		21 48		22 18		22 48
Chipstead	d	18 03		18 24		18 54			19 26		19 54	20 05		20 24		20 54			21 24		21 54		22 24		22 54
Woodmansterne	d	18 06		18 27		18 57			19 29		19 57	20 08		20 27		20 57			21 27		21 57		22 27		22 57
Coulsdon Town	d																								
Reedham	d	18 11		18 32		19 02			19 34		20 02	20 13		20 32		21 02			21 32		22 02		22 32		23 02
Caterham	d		18 09		18 39			19 09		19 39			20 08		20 37			21 07		21 39		22 09		22 38	
Whyteleafe South	d		18 12		18 42			19 12		19 42			20 11		20 40			21 10		21 42		22 12		22 41	
Whyteleafe	d		18 14		18 44			19 14		19 44			20 13		20 42			21 12		21 44		22 14		22 43	
Kenley	d		18 17		18 47			19 17		19 47			20 16		20 45			21 15		21 47		22 17		22 46	
Purley 4	a	18 14	18 20	18 35	18 50	19 05		19 20	19 37	19 50	20 05	20 16	20 19	20 35	20 48	21 05		21 18	21 35	21 50	22 05	22 20	22 35	22 49	23 05
	d	18 15	18 21	18 37	18 51	19 08		19 21	19 38	19 51	20 08		20 22	20 38	20 51	21 08		21 21	21 38	21 51	22 08	22 21	22 38	22 52	23 08
Purley Oaks	d		18 24	18 40	18 54	19 11		19 24	19 41	19 54	20 11		20 25	20 41	20 54	21 11		21 24	21 41	21 54	22 11	22 24	22 41	22 55	23 11
South Croydon 4	d		18 27	18 44	18 57	19 14		19 27	19 44	19 57	20 14		20 28	20 44	20 57	21 14		21 27	21 44	21 57	22 14	22 27	22 44	22 58	23 14
East Croydon	d	18 21	18 30	18 47	19 00	19 17		19 30	19 47	20 00	20 17		20 31	20 47	21 00	21 17		21 30	21 47	22 00	22 17	22 30	22 47	23 01	23 17
Norwood Junction 2	d	18 29	18 35		19 05			19 35		20 05			20 35		21 05			21 35		22 05		22 35		23 06	
New Cross Gate 4 ⊖	a		18 52		19 22			19 52		20 22			20 52		21 22			21 52		22 22		22 52		23 23	
London Bridge 4 ⊖	a	18 41	18 59		19 29			19 59		20 29			20 59		21 29			21 59		22 29		22 59		23 30	
Clapham Junction 10	a			19 08		19 37			20 07		20 37			21 07		21 37			22 07		22 37		23 07		23 37
London Victoria 15 ⊖	a			19 15		19 48			20 18		20 46			21 18		21 48			22 18		22 48		23 18		23 46

		SN
Tattenham Corner	d	
Tadworth	d	
Kingswood	d	
Chipstead	d	
Woodmansterne	d	
Coulsdon Town	d	
Reedham	d	
Caterham	d	23 20
Whyteleafe South	d	23 23
Whyteleafe	d	23 25
Kenley	d	23 28
Purley 4	a	23 31
	d	23 34
Purley Oaks	d	23 37
South Croydon 4	d	23 40
East Croydon	d	23 43
Norwood Junction 2	d	23a47
New Cross Gate 4 ⊖	a	
London Bridge 4 ⊖	a	
Clapham Junction 10	a	
London Victoria 15 ⊖	a	

Saturdays

		SN	SN	SN	SN	SN	SN	SN	SN	SN		SN	SN	SN	SN	SN	SN	SN	SN	SN		SN	SN	SN	
Tattenham Corner	d		06 12		06 42			07 21				07 51			08 21		08 35		08 51				09 21		
Tadworth	d		06 15		06 45			07 24				07 54			08 24		08 38		08 54				09 24		
Kingswood	d		06 18		06 48			07 27				07 57			08 27		08 41		08 57				09 27		
Chipstead	d		06 24		06 54			07 33				08 03			08 33		08 47		09 03				09 33		
Woodmansterne	d		06 27		06 57			07 36				08 06			08 36		08 50		09 06				09 36		
Coulsdon Town	d																								
Reedham	d		06 32		07 02			07 41				08 11			08 41		08 55		09 11				09 41		
Caterham	d	06 07		06 39		07 09	07 26		07 39	07 56			08 09	08 26		08 39		08 56		09 09		09 26		09 39	
Whyteleafe South	d	06 10		06 42		07 12	07 29		07 42	07 59			08 12	08 29		08 42		08 59		09 12		09 29		09 42	
Whyteleafe	d	06 12		06 44		07 14	07 31		07 44	08 01			08 14	08 31		08 44		09 01		09 14		09 31		09 44	
Kenley	d	06 15		06 47		07 17	07 34		07 47	08 04			08 17	08 34		08 47		09 04		09 17		09 34		09 47	
Purley 4	a	06 18	06 35	06 50	07 05	07 20	07 37	07 44	07 50	08 07		08 14	08 20	08 37	08 44	08 50	08 58	09 07	09 14	09 20		09 37	09 44	09 50	
	d	06 21	06 38	06 51	07 08	07 21	07 38	07 45	07 51	08 08		08 15	08 21	08 38	08 45	08 51		09 08	09 15	09 21		09 38	09 45	09 51	
Purley Oaks	d	06 24	06 41	06 54	07 11	07 24	07 41		07 54	08 11			08 24	08 41		08 54		09 11		09 24		09 41		09 54	
South Croydon 4	d	06 27	06 44	06 57	07 14	07 27	07 44		07 57	08 14			08 27	08 44		08 57		09 14		09 27		09 44		09 57	
East Croydon	d	06 30	06 47	07 00	07 17	07 30	07 47	07 51	08 00	08 17		08 21	08 30	08 47	08 51	09 00		09 17	09 21	09 30		09 47	09 51	10 00	
Norwood Junction 2	d	06 35		07 05		07 35		07 55	08 05			08 25	08 35		08 55	09 05			09 25	09 35			09 55	10 05	
New Cross Gate 4 ⊖	a	06 52		07 22		07 52			08 22				08 52			09 22				09 52				10 22	
London Bridge 4 ⊖	a	06 59		07 29		07 59		08 09	08 29			08 39	08 59		09 09	09 29			09 39	09 59			10 09	10 29	
Clapham Junction 10	a		07 07		07 37		08 07			08 37				09 07				09 37				10 07			
London Victoria 15 ⊖	a		07 16		07 46		08 16			08 46				09 16				09 46				10 16			

		SN		SN	SN	SN		SN	SN	SN	SN	SN	SN	SN	SN	SN		SN	SN	SN	SN		SN
Tattenham Corner	d	09 33		15 33		15 51				16 21		16 33		16 51				17 21		17 33			
Tadworth	d	09 36		15 36		15 54				16 24		16 36		16 54				17 24		17 36			
Kingswood	d	09 39		15 39		15 57				16 27		16 39		16 57				17 27		17 39			
Chipstead	d	09 45		15 45		16 03				16 33		16 45		17 03				17 33		17 45			
Woodmansterne	d	09 48		15 48		16 06				16 36		16 48		17 06				17 36		17 48			
Coulsdon Town	d																						
Reedham	d	09 53	and at	15 53		16 11				16 41		16 53		17 11				17 41		17 53		and at	
Caterham	d		the same		15 56			16 09	16 26		16 39		16 56		17 09	17 26			17 39		17 56	the same	21 56
Whyteleafe South	d		minutes		15 59			16 12	16 29		16 42		16 59		17 12	17 29			17 42		17 59	minutes	21 59
Whyteleafe	d		past		16 01			16 14	16 31		16 44		17 01		17 14	17 31			17 44		18 01	past	22 01
Kenley	d		each		16 04			16 17	16 34		16 47		17 04		17 17	17 34			17 47		18 04	each	22 04
Purley 4	a	09 56	hour until	15 56	16 07	16 14		16 20	16 37	16 44	16 50	16 56	17 07	17 14	17 20	17 37		17 44	17 50	17 56	18 07	hour until	22 07
	d				16 08	16 15		16 21	16 38	16 45	16 51		17 08	17 15	17 21	17 38		17 45	17 51		18 08		22 08
Purley Oaks	d				16 11			16 24	16 41		16 54		17 11		17 24	17 41			17 54		18 11		22 11
South Croydon 4	d				16 14			16 27	16 44		16 57		17 14		17 27	17 44			17 57		18 14		22 14
East Croydon	d				16 17	16 21		16 30	16 47	16 51	17 00		17 17	17 21	17 30	17 47		17 51	18 00		18 17		22 17
Norwood Junction 2	d					16 25		16 35		16 55	17 05			17 25	17 35			17 55	18 05				
New Cross Gate 4 ⊖	a							16 52			17 22				17 52				18 22				
London Bridge 4 ⊖	a					16 39		16 59		17 09	17 30			17 39	17 59			18 09	18 29				
Clapham Junction 10	a				16 37				17 07				17 38			18 07					18 37		22 37
London Victoria 15 ⊖	a				16 46				17 16				17 47			18 16					18 46		22 46

Table 181

Saturdays

Tattenham Corner and Caterham - Croydon and London

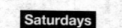

		SN	SN		SN	SN	SN	SN	SN	SN	SN
Tattenham Corner	d	21 51				22 21		22 33		22 51	
Tadworth	d	21 54				22 24		22 36		22 54	
Kingswood	d	21 57				22 27		22 39		22 57	
Chipstead	d	22 03				22 33		22 45		23 03	
Woodmansterne	d	22 06				22 36		22 48		23 06	
Coulsdon Town	d										
Reedham	d	22 11				22 41		22 53		23 11	
Caterham	d		22 09		22 26		22 39		22 56		23 20
Whyteleafe South	d		22 12		22 29		22 42		22 59		23 23
Whyteleafe	d		22 14		22 31		22 44		23 01		23 25
Kenley	d		22 17		22 34		22 47		23 04		23 28
Purley 4	a	22 14	22 20		22 37	22 44	22 50	22 56	23 07	23 14	23 31
	d	22 15	22 21		22 38	22 45	22 52		23 08	23 15	23 34
Purley Oaks	d		22 24		22 41		22 55		23 11		23 37
South Croydon 4	d		22 27		22 44		22 58		23 14		23 40
East Croydon	d	22 21	22 30		22 47	22 51	23 01		23 17	23 21	23 43
Norwood Junction 2	d	22 25	22 35			22 55	23 06			23 25	23a47
New Cross Gate 4 ⊖	a		22 52				23 23				
London Bridge 4 ⊖	a	22 39	22 59			23 09	23 30			23 39	
Clapham Junction 10	a				23 07				23 37		
London Victoria 15 ⊖	a				23 16				23 48		

Sundays

		SN	SN	SN	SN	SN		SN	SN		SN	SN	SN	SN	SN	SN
Tattenham Corner	d			07 45		08 15		21 15			21 45		22 15		22 45	
Tadworth	d			07 48		08 18		21 18			21 48		22 18		22 48	
Kingswood	d			07 51		08 21		21 21			21 51		22 21		22 51	
Chipstead	d			07 57		08 27		21 27			21 57		22 27		22 57	
Woodmansterne	d			08 00		08 30		21 30			22 00		22 30		23 00	
Coulsdon Town	d															
Reedham	d			08 05		08 35	and at	21 35			22 05		22 35		23 05	
Caterham	d	07 24	07 35		08 05		the same		21 35			22 05		22 35		23 05
Whyteleafe South	d	07 27	07 38		08 08		minutes		21 38			22 08		22 38		23 08
Whyteleafe	d	07 29	07 40		08 10		past		21 40			22 10		22 40		23 10
Kenley	d	07 32	07 43		08 13		each		21 43			22 13		22 43		23 13
Purley 4	a	07 35	07 46	08 08	08 16	08 38	hour until	21 38	21 46		22 08	22 16	22 38	22 46	23 08	23 16
	d	07 38	07 47	08 08	08 17	08 38		21 38	21 47		22 08	22 17	22 38	22 47	23 08	23 17
Purley Oaks	d	07 41		08 11		08 41		21 41			22 11		22 41		23 11	23 20
South Croydon 4	d	07 44		08 14		08 44		21 44			22 14		22 44		23 14	23 23
East Croydon	d	07 47	07 53	08 17	08 23	08 47		21 47	21 53		22 17	22 23	22 47	22 53	23 17	23a25
Norwood Junction 2	d	07 52		08 22		08 52		21 52			22 22		22 52		23a21	
New Cross Gate 4 ⊖	a	08 09		08 39		09 09		22 09			22 39		23 09			
London Bridge 4 ⊖	a	08 17		08 48		09 18		22 18			22 48		23 17			
Clapham Junction 10	a		08 12		08 42				22 12			22 42		23 12		
London Victoria 15 ⊖	a		08 20		08 50				22 20			22 50		23 20		

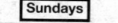

Table 182

Mondays to Fridays
until 30 September

London - Sutton, Epsom, Guildford, Dorking and Horsham

Miles	Miles	Miles			SN MO	SW MO	SN MO	SN MX	SN MX	SW MX	SN MX	SW MX	SN	SW	SN	SN	SN	FC MX	FC MX	FC	FC	SN	SN
—	0	—	**London Victoria** 15 ⊖	d	23p08		23p19	23p26	23p34		23p51					05 52							06 00
—	—	—	**London Waterloo** 15 ⊖	d		23p32				23p42		00 15		05 47									
—	2¾	—	Clapham Junction 10	d	23p16	23p41	23p27	23p34	23p42	23p51	23p59	00 25		05 56		05 58							06 08
—	4¾	—	Balham 4 ⊖	d	23p21		23p32	23p40	23p47		00 04					06 03							06 13
—	—	—	**London Bridge** 4 ⊖	d														23p28	23p58			05 36	
—	—	6	Tulse Hill 3	d														23p40	00 10	06 02	06 22		
—	—	6	New Cross Gate 4 ⊖	d																		05 42	
8¾	—	—	Norwood Junction 2	d											05 53							06 00	
10½	—	12	**West Croydon** 4	d			23p50		00 04		00 21		05 45		05 58							06 05	06 32
11½	—	—	Waddon	d			23p52		00 06		00 24		05 47		06 00							06 08	06 34
13	—	—	Wallington	d			23p56		00 10		00 27		05 51		06 04							06 11	06 38
13¾	—	—	Carshalton Beeches	d			23p58		00 12		00 30		05 53		06 06							06 14	06 40
—	8	—	Mitcham Eastfields	d	23p28			23p46								06 12					06 29		
—	9	—	Mitcham Junction	d	23p31			23p49								06 15					06 32		
—	9¾	—	Hackbridge	d	23p34			23p53								06 19					06 35		
—	10¾	—	Carshalton	d	23p37			23p55								06 21					06 38		
14¾	12	0	**Sutton (Surrey)** 4	a	23p40		00 02	23p59	00 16		00 33		05 57		06 10	06 25		00 14	00 43	06 33	06 43	06 17	06 44
—	—	—		d	23p41		00 04	00 01							06 11	06 25	06 39						06 48
—	13	—	Belmont	d											06 14								06 51
—	14½	—	Banstead	d											06 18								06 55
—	16	—	**Epsom Downs**	a											06 21								06 58
15¾	—	—	Cheam	d	23p43		00 06	00 03								06 28	06 41						
17¼	—	—	Ewell East	d	23p47		00 10	00 07								06 31	06 45						
18¾	—	—	**Epsom** 3	a	23p51	00 06	00 14	00 11		00 15		00 50		06 20		06 35	06 49						
—	—	—		d	23p51			00 11		00 19				06 21		06 36	06 50						
20½	—	—	Ashtead	d	23p55			00 15		00 23				06 25		06 40							
22½	—	0	Leatherhead	d	23p58			00 18		00 26				06 28		06 43	06 56						
25	—	—	Bookham	d						00 31				06 33			07 01						
26¾	—	—	Effingham Junction 6	d						00 36				06 37			07 05						
35	—	—	**Guildford**	a						00 53				06 50			07 17						
—	—	3¼	Boxhill & Westhumble	d	00 03			00 23								06 48							
—	—	4	**Dorking** 4	a	00 06			00 26								06 50							
—	—	—		d				00 26								06 51							
—	—	9	Holmwood	d				00s33								06 58							
—	—	11¼	Ockley	d				00s37								07 02							
—	—	15¾	Warnham	d				00s43								07 08							
—	—	17¾	**Horsham** 4	a				00 47								07 12							

		SW	SN	SN	SN	SW	FC	SW	SN	SN	FC	SW	SN	FC	SN	SW	SN	FC 1	SW	FC 1	SW	SN	SN
London Victoria 15 ⊖	d		06 07	06 17	06 30				06 36	07 00			07 06		07 15		07 30					07 36	07 47
London Waterloo 15 ⊖	d	06 24				06 39		06 54				07 09				07 24			07 39		07 54		
Clapham Junction 10	d	06 33	06 15	06 24	06 38	06 48		07 03	06 44	07 08		07 18	07 14		07 21	07 33	07 38		07 48		08 03	07 44	07 55
Balham 4 ⊖	d		06 20	06 30	06 44				06 49	07 13			07 20		07 26		07 44					07 50	08 00
London Bridge 4 ⊖	d																						
Tulse Hill 3	d						06 42				07 02			07 20				07 37		07 45			
New Cross Gate 4 ⊖	d																						
Norwood Junction 2	d		06 39						07 09				07 39									08 09	
West Croydon 4	d		06 46		07 03				07 14	07 32			07 46				08 04					08 15	
Waddon	d		06 48		07 05				07 16	07 35			07 48				08 06					08 17	
Wallington	d		06 52		07 09				07 20	07 38			07 52				08 10					08 21	
Carshalton Beeches	d		06 54		07 11				07 22	07 41			07 54				08 12					08 23	
Mitcham Eastfields	d			06 38			06 50							07 27						07 52			08 07
Mitcham Junction	d			06 41			06 53							07 30	07 34					07 55			08 10
Hackbridge	d			06 45			06 56							07 33	07 37					07 58			08 13
Carshalton	d			06 47			06 59							07 36	07 40					08 01			08 16
Sutton (Surrey) 4	a		06 58	06 51	07 15		07 04		07 26	07 44	07 35		07 58	07 39	07 43		08 16	08 08		08 04		08 27	08 19
	d		07 00	06 52	07 18				07 26	07 45			07 59		07 44		08 16					08 27	
Belmont	d				07 21					07 48							08 20						
Banstead	d				07 25					07 52							08 23						
Epsom Downs	a				07 28					07 55							08 27						
Cheam	d		07 02	06 54					07 29				08 01		07 46							08 30	
Ewell East	d		07 06	06 58					07 32				08 05		07 50							08 33	
Epsom 3	a	06 57	07 10	07 02		07 11		07 27	07 36			07 42	08 09		07 54	07 58			08 13		08 27	08 37	
	d	06 58		07 02		07 12		07 28	07 37						07 54	07 58			08 17		08 28	08 38	
Ashtead	d	07 02		07 06		07 16		07 32	07 41						07 58	08 02			08 21		08 32	08 42	
Leatherhead	d	07 05		07 09		07 19		07 35	07 44						08 01	08 05			08 24		08 35	08 45	
Bookham	d					07 24			07 49										08 29				
Effingham Junction 6	d					07a28			07 53										08 33				
Guildford	a								08 06										08 50				
Boxhill & Westhumble	d														08 06							08 50	
Dorking 4	a	07 11		07 15				07 41							08 09	08 12					08 41	08 52	
	d			07 16											08 09								
Holmwood	d			07 23											08 17								
Ockley	d			07 27											08 21								
Warnham	d			07 33											08 26								
Horsham 4	a			07 37											08 30								

Table 182

Mondays to Fridays
until 30 September

London - Sutton, Epsom, Guildford, Dorking and Horsham

		SN	SN	FC	SN	SW	FC	SW	SN	SN	FC	SN	SN	SN	SW	FC 1	SW	SN	SN	FC 1	SN	SN	SN
London Victoria 15 ⊖	d	07 55	08 03		08 07				08 19	08 26			08 31	08 36				08 47	08 52		09 01	09 03	09 05
London Waterloo 15 ⊖	d					08 09		08 24							08 39		08 54						
Clapham Junction 10	d	08 02	08 11		08 16	08 18		08 33	08 26	08 33			08 40	08 44	08 48		09 03	08 54	09 00		09 08	09 11	09 14
Balham 4 ⊖	d		08 16		08 21				08 30	08 38			08 46	08 50				09 00	09 05			09 16	09 20
London Bridge 4 ⊖	d											08 24											
Tulse Hill 3	d			08 05			08 20				08 40	08 47				08 50				09 01			
New Cross Gate 4 ⊖	d																						
Norwood Junction 2	d				08 39									09 09									09 39
West Croydon 4	d		08 36		08 45					08 56			09 06	09 14					09 24			09 34	09 44
Waddon	d		08 39		08 47					08 58			09 08	09 16					09 26			09 36	09 46
Wallington	d		08 42		08 51					09 02			09 12	09 20					09 30			09 40	09 50
Carshalton Beeches	d		08 45		08 53					09 04			09 14	09 22					09 32			09 42	09 52
Mitcham Eastfields	d						08 28		08 37							08 58		09 06					
Mitcham Junction	d						08 31		08 40							09 01		09 09					
Hackbridge	d						08 34		08 44							09 04		09 13					
Carshalton	d						08 37		08 46							09 07		09 15					
Sutton (Surrey) 4	a	08 22	08 48	08 37	08 57		08 40		08 50	09 08	09 12	09 02	09 18	09 26		09 10		09 19	09 39	09 37	09 28	09 46	09 56
	d	08 23	08 53						08 50			09 02	09 19					09 19	09 40		09 29		
Belmont	d		08 56										09 22										
Banstead	d		09 00										09 26										
Epsom Downs	a		09 03										09 29										
Cheam	d	08 25							08 53			09 05						09 22	09 42		09 31		
Ewell East	d	08 29							08 56			09 08						09 25	09 46				
Epsom 3	a	08 33				08 42		08 57	09 00			09 12			09 16		09 27	09 29	09 50		09 37		
	d	08 33				08 47		08 58	09 01						09 17		09 28				09 37		
Ashtead	d	08 37				08 51		09 02	09 05						09 21		09 32				09 41		
Leatherhead	d	08 40				08 54		09 05	09 08						09 24		09 35				09 44		
Bookham	d					08 59									09 29								
Effingham Junction 6	d					09 03									09 33								
Guildford	a					09 20									09 50								
Boxhill & Westhumble	d								09 13												09 49		
Dorking 4	a	08 46						09 11	09 15								09 41				09 52		
	d	08 47							09 16														
Holmwood	d								09 23														
Ockley	d								09 27														
Warnham	d								09 33														
Horsham 4	a	09 03							09 37														

		SW	FC	SW	SN	SN	FC	SN	SN	SN	SW	FC	SW	SN	SN	FC	SN	SN	SN	SW	FC	SW
London Victoria 15 ⊖	d				09 17	09 22		09 31	09 33	09 35				09 47	09 53		10 01	10 03	10 06			
London Waterloo 15 ⊖	d	09 09		09 24							09 39		09 54							10 09		10 24
Clapham Junction 10	d	09 18		09 33	09 24	09 30		09 38	09 41	09 44	09 48		10 03	09 54	10 00		10 08	10 11	10 14	10 18		10 33
Balham 4 ⊖	d				09 30	09 35			09 46	09 50				10 00	10 05			10 16	10 20			
London Bridge 4 ⊖	d																					
Tulse Hill 3	d		09 16				09 31					09 46				10 01					10 16	
New Cross Gate 4 ⊖	d																					
Norwood Junction 2	d									10 09									10 39			
West Croydon 4	d					09 54			10 04	10 14					10 24			10 34	10 44			
Waddon	d					09 56			10 06	10 16					10 26			10 36	10 46			
Wallington	d					10 00			10 10	10 20					10 30			10 40	10 50			
Carshalton Beeches	d					10 02			10 12	10 22					10 32			10 42	10 52			
Mitcham Eastfields	d		09 24		09 36							09 54		10 06							10 24	
Mitcham Junction	d		09 27		09 39							09 57		10 09							10 27	
Hackbridge	d		09 30		09 43							10 00		10 13							10 30	
Carshalton	d		09 33		09 45							10 03		10 15							10 33	
Sutton (Surrey) 4	a		09 36		09 49	10 06	10 05	09 58	10 16	10 26		10 06		10 19	10 39	10 35	10 28	10 46	10 56		10 36	
	d				09 49	10 07		09 59						10 19	10 40		10 29					
Belmont	d					10 10																
Banstead	d					10 14																
Epsom Downs	a					10 17																
Cheam	d				09 52			10 01						10 22	10 42		10 31					
Ewell East	d				09 55			10 05						10 25	10 46							
Epsom 3	a	09 42		09 57	09 59			10 09			10 16		10 27	10 29	10 52		10 37			10 46		10 57
	d	09 47		09 58				10 09			10 17		10 28				10 37			10 47		10 58
Ashtead	d	09 51		10 02				10 13			10 21		10 32				10 41			10 51		11 02
Leatherhead	d	09 54		10 05				10 16			10 24		10 35				10 44			10 54		11 05
Bookham	d	09 59									10 29									10 59		
Effingham Junction 6	d	10 03									10 33									11 03		
Guildford	a	10 20									10 50									11 20		
Boxhill & Westhumble	d							10 21														
Dorking 4	a			10 11				10 24					10 41				10 50					11 11
	d							10 24														
Holmwood	d							10 32														
Ockley	d							10 36														
Warnham	d							10 41														
Horsham 4	a							10 45														

London - Sutton, Epsom, Guildford, Dorking and Horsham

until 30 September

Station		SN	SN	FC	SN	SN	SN	SW	FC	SW	SN	SN	FC	SN	SN	SN	SW	FC	SW	SN	SN	FC	SN
London Victoria ⊖	d	10 17	10 23		10 31	10 33	10 36				10 47	10 53		11 01	11 03	11 06				11 17	11 23		11 31
London Waterloo ⊖	d							10 39		10 54							11 09		11 24				
Clapham Junction	d	10 24	10 30		10 38	10 41	10 44	10 48		11 03	10 54	11 00		11 08	11 11	11 14	11 18		11 33	11 24	11 30		11 38
Balham ⊖	d	10 30	10 35			10 46	10 50				11 00	11 05			11 16	11 20				11 30	11 35		
London Bridge ⊖	d																						
Tulse Hill	d			10 31					10 46				11 01					11 16				11 31	
New Cross Gate ⊖	d																						
Norwood Junction	d						11 09									11 39							
West Croydon	d		10 54			11 04	11 14					11 24			11 34	11 44					11 54		
Waddon	d		10 56			11 06	11 16					11 26			11 36	11 46					11 56		
Wallington	d		11 00			11 10	11 20					11 30			11 40	11 50					12 00		
Carshalton Beeches	d		11 02			11 12	11 22					11 32			11 42	11 52					12 02		
Mitcham Eastfields	d	10 36							10 54		11 06							11 24		11 36			
Mitcham Junction	d	10 39							10 57		11 09							11 27		11 39			
Hackbridge	d	10 43							11 00		11 13							11 30		11 43			
Carshalton	d	10 45							11 03		11 15							11 33		11 45			
Sutton (Surrey)	a	10 49	11 06	11 05	10 58	11 16	11 26		11 06		11 19	11 39	11 35	11 28	11 46	11 56		11 36		11 49	12 06	12 05	11 58
	d	10 49	11 07		10 59						11 19	11 40		11 29						11 49	12 07		11 59
Belmont	d		11 10																		12 10		
Banstead	d		11 14																		12 14		
Epsom Downs	a		11 17																		12 17		
Cheam	d	10 52			11 01						11 22	11 42		11 31						11 52			12 01
Ewell East	d	10 55			11 05						11 25	11 46								11 55			12 05
Epsom	a	10 59			11 09			11 16		11 27	11 29	11 52		11 37			11 46		11 57	11 59			12 09
	d				11 09			11 17		11 28				11 37			11 47		11 58				12 09
Ashtead	d				11 13			11 21		11 32				11 41			11 51		12 02				12 13
Leatherhead	d				11 16			11 24		11 35				11 44			11 54		12 05				12 16
Bookham	d							11 29									11 59						
Effingham Junction	d							11 33									12 03						
Guildford	a							11 50									12 20						
Boxhill & Westhumble	d				11 21																		12 21
Dorking	a				11 24					11 41				11 50					12 11				12 24
	d				11 24																		12 24
Holmwood	d				11 32																		12 32
Ockley	d				11 36																		12 36
Warnham	d				11 41																		12 41
Horsham	a				11 45																		12 45

Station		SN	SN	SW	FC	SW	SN	FC	SN	SW	SN	SN	SN	FC	SW	SN	FC	SN	SN	SN	SN	SW
London Victoria ⊖	d	11 33	11 36				11 47		12 01		11 53	12 03	12 06			12 17		12 31	12 23	12 33	12 36	
London Waterloo ⊖	d			11 39		11 54				12 09					12 24							12 39
Clapham Junction	d	11 41	11 44	11 48		12 03	11 54		12 08	12 18	12 00	12 11	12 14		12 33	12 24		12 38	12 30	12 41	12 44	12 48
Balham ⊖	d	11 46	11 50				12 00				12 05	12 16	12 20			12 30			12 35	12 46	12 50	
London Bridge ⊖	d																					
Tulse Hill	d				11 46			12 01						12 16			12 31					
New Cross Gate ⊖	d																					
Norwood Junction	d		12 09										12 39								13 09	
West Croydon	d	12 04	12 14								12 24	12 34	12 44						12 54	13 04	13 14	
Waddon	d	12 06	12 16								12 26	12 36	12 46						12 56	13 06	13 16	
Wallington	d	12 10	12 20								12 30	12 40	12 50						13 00	13 10	13 20	
Carshalton Beeches	d	12 12	12 22								12 32	12 42	12 52						13 02	13 12	13 22	
Mitcham Eastfields	d				11 54		12 06							12 24		12 36						
Mitcham Junction	d				11 57		12 09							12 27		12 39						
Hackbridge	d				12 00		12 13							12 30		12 43						
Carshalton	d				12 03		12 15							12 33		12 45						
Sutton (Surrey)	a	12 16	12 26		12 06		12 19	12 35	12 28		12 39	12 46	12 56	12 36		12 49	13 05	12 58	13 06	13 16	13 26	
	d						12 19		12 29		12 40					12 49		12 59	13 07			
Belmont	d																		13 10			
Banstead	d																		13 14			
Epsom Downs	a																		13 17			
Cheam	d						12 22		12 31		12 42					12 52		13 01				
Ewell East	d						12 25				12 46					12 55		13 05				
Epsom	a			12 16		12 27	12 29		12 37	12 46	12 52				12 57	12 59		13 09				13 16
	d			12 17		12 28			12 37	12 47					12 58			13 09				13 17
Ashtead	d			12 21		12 32			12 41	12 51					13 02			13 13				13 21
Leatherhead	d			12 24		12 35			12 44	12 54					13 05			13 16				13 24
Bookham	d			12 29						12 59												13 29
Effingham Junction	d			12 33						13 03												13 33
Guildford	a			12 50						13 20												13 50
Boxhill & Westhumble	d																	13 21				
Dorking	a					12 41			12 50						13 11			13 24				
	d																	13 24				
Holmwood	d																	13 32				
Ockley	d																	13 36				
Warnham	d																	13 41				
Horsham	a																	13 45				

London - Sutton, Epsom, Guildford, Dorking and Horsham

until 30 September

Station		FC	SW	SN	FC	SN	SW	SN	SN	SN	FC	SW	SN	SN	FC	SN	SN	SN	SW	FC	SW	SN	FC
London Victoria ⊖	d			12 47		13 01		12 53	13 03	13 06			13 17	13 23		13 31	13 33	13 36				13 47	
London Waterloo ⊖	d		12 54				13 09					13 24							13 39		13 54		
Clapham Junction	d		13 03	12 54		13 08	13 18	13 00	13 11	13 14		13 33	13 24	13 30		13 38	13 41	13 44	13 48		14 03	13 54	
Balham ⊖	d			13 00				13 05	13 16	13 20			13 30	13 35			13 46	13 50				14 00	
London Bridge ⊖	d																						
Tulse Hill	d	12 46			13 01						13 16				13 31					13 46			14 01
New Cross Gate ⊖	d																						
Norwood Junction	d									13 39								14 09					
West Croydon	d							13 24	13 34	13 44				13 54			14 04	14 14					
Waddon	d							13 26	13 36	13 46				13 56			14 06	14 16					
Wallington	d							13 30	13 40	13 50				14 00			14 10	14 20					
Carshalton Beeches	d							13 32	13 42	13 52				14 02			14 12	14 22					
Mitcham Eastfields	d	12 54		13 06							13 24		13 36							13 54		14 06	
Mitcham Junction	d	12 57		13 09							13 27		13 39							13 57		14 09	
Hackbridge	d	13 00		13 13							13 30		13 43							14 00		14 13	
Carshalton	d	13 03		13 15							13 33		13 45							14 03		14 15	
Sutton (Surrey)	a	13 06		13 19	13 35	13 28		13 39	13 46	13 56	13 36		13 49	14 06	14 05	13 58	14 16	14 26		14 06		14 19	14 35
	d			13 19		13 29		13 40					13 49	14 07		13 59						14 19	
Belmont	d													14 10									
Banstead	d													14 14									
Epsom Downs	a													14 17									
Cheam	d			13 22		13 31		13 42					13 52			14 01						14 22	
Ewell East	d			13 25				13 46					13 55			14 05						14 25	
Epsom	a		13 27	13 29		13 37	13 46	13 52				13 57	13 59			14 09			14 16		14 27	14 29	
	d		13 28			13 37	13 47					13 58				14 09			14 17		14 28		
Ashtead	d		13 32			13 41	13 51					14 02				14 13			14 21		14 32		
Leatherhead	d		13 35			13 44	13 54					14 05				14 16			14 24		14 35		
Bookham	d						13 59												14 29				
Effingham Junction	d						14 03												14 33				
Guildford	a						14 20												14 50				
Boxhill & Westhumble	d															14 21							
Dorking	a		13 41			13 50						14 11				14 24					14 41		
	d															14 24							
Holmwood	d															14 32							
Ockley	d															14 36							
Warnham	d															14 41							
Horsham	a															14 45							

Station		SN	SW	SN	SN	SN	FC	SW	SN	FC	SN	SN	SN	SN	SW	FC	SW	SN	FC	SN	SW	SN	SN
London Victoria ⊖	d	14 01		13 53	14 03	14 06			14 17		14 31	14 23	14 33	14 36				14 47		15 01		14 53	15 03
London Waterloo ⊖	d		14 09					14 24							14 39		14 54				15 09		
Clapham Junction	d	14 08	14 18	14 00	14 11	14 14		14 33	14 24		14 38	14 30	14 41	14 44	14 48		15 03	14 54		15 08	15 18	15 00	15 11
Balham ⊖	d			14 05	14 16	14 20			14 30			14 35	14 46	14 50				15 00				15 05	15 16
London Bridge ⊖	d																						
Tulse Hill	d						14 16			14 31						14 46			15 01				
New Cross Gate ⊖	d																						
Norwood Junction	d					14 39								15 09									
West Croydon	d			14 24	14 34	14 44						14 54	15 04	15 14								15 24	15 34
Waddon	d			14 26	14 36	14 46						14 56	15 06	15 16								15 26	15 36
Wallington	d			14 30	14 40	14 50						15 00	15 10	15 20								15 30	15 40
Carshalton Beeches	d			14 32	14 42	14 52						15 02	15 12	15 22								15 32	15 42
Mitcham Eastfields	d						14 24		14 36							14 54		15 06					
Mitcham Junction	d						14 27		14 39							14 57		15 09					
Hackbridge	d						14 30		14 43							15 00		15 13					
Carshalton	d						14 33		14 45							15 03		15 15					
Sutton (Surrey)	a	14 28		14 39	14 46	14 56	14 36		14 50	15 05	14 58	15 06	15 16	15 26		15 06		15 19	15 35	15 28		15 39	15 47
	d	14 29		14 40					14 50		14 59	15 07						15 19		15 29		15 40	
Belmont	d											15 10											
Banstead	d											15 14											
Epsom Downs	a											15 17											
Cheam	d	14 31		14 42					14 53		15 01							15 22		15 31		15 42	
Ewell East	d			14 46					14 56		15 05							15 25				15 46	
Epsom	a	14 37	14 46	14 52				14 57	15 00		15 09				15 16		15 27	15 29		15 37	15 46	15 52	
	d	14 37	14 47					14 58			15 09				15 17		15 28			15 37	15 47		
Ashtead	d	14 41	14 51					15 02			15 13				15 21		15 32			15 41	15 51		
Leatherhead	d	14 44	14 54					15 05			15 16				15 24		15 35			15 44	15 54		
Bookham	d		14 59												15 29						15 59		
Effingham Junction	d		15 03												15 33						16 03		
Guildford	a		15 20												15 50						16 20		
Boxhill & Westhumble	d										15 21												
Dorking	a	14 50						15 11			15 24						15 41			15 50			
	d										15 24												
Holmwood	d										15 32												
Ockley	d										15 36												
Warnham	d										15 41												
Horsham	a										15 45												

Table 182

Mondays to Fridays

until 30 September

London - Sutton, Epsom, Guildford, Dorking and Horsham

		SN	FC	SW	SN	SN	FC	SN	SN	SN	SW	FC	SW	SN	SN	FC	SN	SN	SN	SW	FC	SW
London Victoria ⊖	d	15 06			15 17	15 23		15 31	15 33	15 36				15 47	15 53		16 01	16 03	16 07			
London Waterloo ⊖	d			15 24							15 39		15 54							16 09		16 24
Clapham Junction	d	15 14		15 33	15 24	15 30		15 38	15 41	15 44	15 48		16 03	15 54	16 00		16 08	16 11	16 15	16 18		16 33
Balham ⊖	d	15 20			15 30	15 35			15 46	15 50				16 00	16 05			16 16	16 20			
London Bridge ⊖	d																					
Tulse Hill	d		15 16				15 31					15 46				16 01					16 16	
New Cross Gate ⊖	d																					
Norwood Junction	d	15 39								16 09									16 39			
West Croydon	d	15 44				15 54			16 04	16 14					16 24			16 34	16 44			
Waddon	d	15 46				15 56			16 06	16 16					16 26			16 36	16 46			
Wallington	d	15 50				16 00			16 10	16 20					16 30			16 40	16 50			
Carshalton Beeches	d	15 52				16 02			16 12	16 22					16 32			16 42	16 52			
Mitcham Eastfields	d		15 24		15 36							15 54		16 06							16 24	
Mitcham Junction	d		15 27		15 39							15 57		16 09			16 22				16 27	
Hackbridge	d		15 30		15 43							16 00		16 13							16 30	
Carshalton	d		15 33		15 45							16 03		16 15							16 33	
Sutton (Surrey)	a	15 56	15 36		15 49	16 06	16 05	15 58	16 16	16 26		16 06		16 19	16 36	16 35	16 29	16 48	16 58		16 36	
	d				15 49	16 07		15 59						16 19	16 37		16 30					
Belmont	d					16 10									16 40							
Banstead	d					16 14									16 44							
Epsom Downs	a					16 17									16 47							
Cheam	d				15 52			16 01						16 22			16 32					
Ewell East	d				15 55			16 05						16 25			16 36					
Epsom	a			15 57	15 59			16 09			16 15		16 27	16 29			16 40			16 46		16 57
	d			15 58				16 09			16 17		16 28				16 40			16 47		16 58
Ashtead	d			16 02				16 13			16 21		16 32				16 44			16 51		17 02
Leatherhead	d			16 05				16 16			16 24		16 35				16 47			16 54		17 05
Bookham	d										16 29									16 59		
Effingham Junction	d										16 33									17 03		
Guildford	a										16 50									17 22		
Boxhill & Westhumble	d							16 21									16 52					17 10
Dorking	a			16 11				16 24					16 41				16 57					17 14
	d							16 24														
Holmwood	d							16 32														
Ockley	d							16 36														
Warnham	d							16 41														
Horsham	a							16 45														

		SN	SN	FC	SN	SW	FC	SW	SN	SN	FC	FC	SN	SN	SN	SW	SW	SN	SN	SW	FC	SN	SN
London Victoria ⊖	d	16 17	16 31		16 33				16 37	16 50				17 01	17 06				17 20				17 31
London Waterloo ⊖	d					16 39		16 54								17 09	17 24			17 30			
Clapham Junction	d	16 24	16 38		16 41	16 48		17 03	16 45	16 56				17 09	17 14	17 18	17 33		17 26	17 39			17 37
Balham ⊖	d	16 30			16 46				16 50	17 01				17 14	17 19				17 32				17 42
London Bridge ⊖	d												17 03					17 06				17 29	
Tulse Hill	d			16 32			16 46				17 02	17 20						17 24			17 31		
New Cross Gate ⊖	d																						
Norwood Junction	d								17 09				17 16		17 38							17 43	
West Croydon	d				17 04				17 14				17 22	17 33	17 44							17 48	
Waddon	d				17 06				17 16				17 24	17 35	17 46							17 51	
Wallington	d				17 10				17 20				17 28	17 39	17 50							17 54	
Carshalton Beeches	d				17 12				17 22				17 30	17 41	17 52							17 57	
Mitcham Eastfields	d	16 36	16 51				16 56			17 08		17 28						17 32	17 38				17 48
Mitcham Junction	d	16 39	16 54				16 59			17 11		17 31						17 35	17 41				17 51
Hackbridge	d	16 43	16 57				17 02			17 15		17 34						17 38	17 45				17 55
Carshalton	d	16 45	17 00				17 05			17 17		17 37						17 41	17 47				17 57
Sutton (Surrey)	a	16 49	17 03	17 05	17 16		17 08		17 26	17 21	17 39	17 40	17 34	17 45	17 58			17 44	17 51		18 07	18 00	18 03
	d	16 49	17 04		17 16				17 27	17 21			17 34	17 45					17 51			18 01	18 05
Belmont	d				17 20									17 49									
Banstead	d				17 23									17 52									
Epsom Downs	a				17 28									17 58									
Cheam	d	16 52	17 06						17 29	17 24			17 37						17 54			18 03	18 07
Ewell East	d	16 55	17 10						17 33	17 27			17 40						17 57			18 07	18 11
Epsom	a	17 01	17 16			17 12		17 27	17 37	17 31			17 46			17 42	17 54		18 01	18 07		18 11	18 17
	d	17 02				17 17		17 28	17 37	17 32						17 47	17 54		18 02			18 12	
Ashtead	d	17 06				17 21		17 32	17 41	17 36						17 51	17 58		18 06			18 16	
Leatherhead	d	17 09				17 24		17 35	17 44	17 39						17 54	18 01		18 09			18 19	
Bookham	d					17 29			17 50							17 59						18 24	
Effingham Junction	d					17 33			17 53							18a05						18 28	
Guildford	a					17 52			18 13													18 46	
Boxhill & Westhumble	d	17 14						17 40		17 44							18 06		18 14				
Dorking	a	17 16						17 44		17 46							18 11		18 16				
	d	17 17								17 47									18 19				
Holmwood	d	17 24								17 54									18 26				
Ockley	d	17 28								17 58									18 30				
Warnham	d	17 34								18 04									18 36				
Horsham	a	17 40								18 10									18 42				

Table 182

Mondays to Fridays

until 30 September

London - Sutton, Epsom, Guildford, Dorking and Horsham

		SN	SN	SW	FC	SW	SN	SN	SW	FC	SN	SW	SN	SN	SN	FC	SW	SN	SN	SW	FC	FC
London Victoria ⊖	d	17 33	17 37					17 50					18 01	18 03	18 07				18 20			
London Waterloo ⊖	d			17 39		17 54			18 00			18 09					18 24			18 30		
Clapham Junction	d	17 41	17 45	17 48		18 03		17 56	18 09			18 13	18 08	18 11	18 15		18 33		18 26	18 39		
Balham ⊖	d	17 46	17 50					18 02					18 12	18 16	18 20				18 32			
London Bridge ⊖	d						17 37				18 02							18 08				
Tulse Hill	d				17 48		17 55			18 02						18 22		18 27			18 32	18 52
New Cross Gate ⊖	d																					
Norwood Junction	d		18 09								18 16				18 39							
West Croydon	d	18 04	18 15								18 21			18 35	18 45							
Waddon	d	18 06	18 17								18 23			18 37	18 47							
Wallington	d	18 10	18 21								18 27			18 41	18 51							
Carshalton Beeches	d	18 12	18 23								18 29			18 43	18 53							
Mitcham Eastfields	d				17 56		18 02	18 08					18 19			18 30		18 34	18 38			19 00
Mitcham Junction	d				17 59		18 05	18 11					18 22			18 33		18 37	18 41			19 03
Hackbridge	d				18 02		18 09	18 15					18 25			18 36		18 41	18 45			19 06
Carshalton	d				18 05		18 11	18 17					18 28			18 39		18 43	18 47			19 09
Sutton (Surrey)	a	18 18	18 29		18 08		18 15	18 21		18 37	18 33		18 36	18 47	18 58	18 42		18 47	18 51		19 07	19 12
	d	18 19						18 21			18 33		18 36	18 48					18 51			
Belmont	d	18 22												18 51								
Banstead	d	18 26												18 55								
Epsom Downs	a	18 31												19 00								
Cheam	d							18 24			18 36		18 39						18 54			
Ewell East	d							18 27			18 39		18 42						18 57			
Epsom	a			18 15		18 24		18 31	18 35		18 43	18 46	18 48				18 54		19 01	19 07		
	d			18 17		18 24		18 34			18 44	18 47					18 54		19 02			
Ashtead	d			18 21		18 28		18 38			18 48	18 51					18 58		19 06			
Leatherhead	d			18 24		18 31		18 41			18 51	18 54					19 01		19 09			
Bookham	d			18 29								18 59										
Effingham Junction	d			18a42								19 03										
Guildford	a											19 22										
Boxhill & Westhumble	d					18 36		18 46			18 56						19 06		19 14			
Dorking	a					18 41		18 48			19 00						19 11		19 16			
	d							18 49											19 19			
Holmwood	d							18 56											19 26			
Ockley	d							19 00											19 30			
Warnham	d							19 06											19 36			
Horsham	a							19 12											19 42			

		SN	SW	SW	SN	SN	SN	SN	SW	FC	SW	SN	SN	FC	SW	SN	FC	FC	FC	SN	SN	SW	SN
London Victoria ⊖	d					18 32	18 36	18 50				18 59	19 06			19 20					19 30		19 34
London Waterloo ⊖	d		18 39	18 54					19 00		19 09				19 24							19 39	
Clapham Junction	d		18 48	19 03		18 40	18 44	18 56	19 09		19 18	19 08	19 14		19 33	19 26					19 38	19 48	19 41
Balham ⊖	d					18 45	18 49	19 02				19 14	19 20			19 32					19 44		19 46
London Bridge ⊖	d	18 32			18 38															19 31			
Tulse Hill	d				18 56					19 07				19 16			19 31	19 46	20 01				
New Cross Gate ⊖	d																						
Norwood Junction	d	18 46					19 09						19 39							19 44			
West Croydon	d	18 51				19 04	19 15					19 32	19 45							19 49	20 02		
Waddon	d	18 53				19 07	19 17					19 35	19 47							19 52	20 05		
Wallington	d	18 57				19 10	19 21					19 38	19 51							19 55	20 08		
Carshalton Beeches	d	18 59				19 13	19 23					19 41	19 53							19 58	20 11		
Mitcham Eastfields	d				19 03			19 08						19 24		19 38		19 54					19 57
Mitcham Junction	d				19 06			19 11						19 27		19 41		19 57					20 00
Hackbridge	d				19 10			19 15						19 30		19 45		20 00					20 03
Carshalton	d				19 12			19 17						19 33		19 47		20 03					20 06
Sutton (Surrey)	a	19 03			19 16	19 16	19 28	19 21		19 40		19 44	19 57	19 36		19 51	20 07	20 06	20 39	20 01	20 14		20 09
	d	19 03			19 16	19 17		19 21				19 45	19 58			19 51				20 02			20 10
Belmont	d					19 20							20 01										
Banstead	d					19 24							20 05										
Epsom Downs	a					19 29							20 08										
Cheam	d	19 06			19 19			19 24				19 47				19 54				20 04			20 12
Ewell East	d	19 09			19 22			19 27				19 51				19 57				20 08			20 16
Epsom	a	19 13	19 16	19 24	19 26			19 31	19 35		19 44	19 55			19 57	20 01				20 12		20 16	20 20
	d	19 14	19 17	19 24				19 34			19 47				19 58	20 02				20 12		20 17	
Ashtead	d	19 18	19 21	19 28				19 38			19 51				20 02	20 06				20 16		20 21	
Leatherhead	d	19 21	19 24	19 31				19 41			19 54				20 05	20 09				20 19		20 24	
Bookham	d		19 29								19 59											20 29	
Effingham Junction	d		19 33								20 03											20 33	
Guildford	a		19 52								20 20											20 50	
Boxhill & Westhumble	d	19 26		19 36				19 46							20 10	20 14							
Dorking	a	19 30		19 41				19 50							20 12	20 16				20 25			
	d															20 17							
Holmwood	d															20 24							
Ockley	d															20 28							
Warnham	d															20 34							
Horsham	a															20 38							

London - Sutton, Epsom, Guildford, Dorking and Horsham

		SN	SW	SN	SN		SW	FC	SN	SW	SN	SN	SN	FC	SW		FC	SN	SN	SW	SN	SN	FC	SW	SN
London Victoria 15 ⊖	d	19 36		19 50	20 00				20 03		20 06	20 20	20 30					20 33	20 36		20 50	21 00			21 03
London Waterloo 15 ⊖	d		19 54				20 09			20 24					20 39					20 54				21 09	
Clapham Junction 10	d	19 44	20 03	19 56	20 08		20 18		20 11	20 33	20 14	20 26	20 38		20 48			20 41	20 44	21 03	20 56	21 08		21 18	21 11
Balham 4 ⊖	d	19 50		20 02	20 14				20 16		20 20	20 31	20 44					20 46	20 50		21 02	21 14			21 16
London Bridge 4 ⊖	d																								
Tulse Hill 3	d							20 16						20 31			20 46						21 01		
New Cross Gate 4 ⊖	d																								
Norwood Junction 2	d	20 09									20 39								21 09						
West Croydon 4	d	20 14			20 32						20 44		21 02						21 14			21 32			
Waddon	d	20 16			20 35						20 46		21 05						21 16			21 35			
Wallington	d	20 20			20 38						20 50		21 08						21 20			21 38			
Carshalton Beeches	d	20 22			20 41						20 52		21 11						21 22			21 41			
Mitcham Eastfields	d			20 08				20 24	20 27			20 38					20 54	20 58			21 08				21 23
Mitcham Junction	d			20 11				20 27	20 30			20 41					20 57	21 01			21 11				21 26
Hackbridge	d			20 15				20 30	20 34			20 45					21 00	21 04			21 15				21 30
Carshalton	d			20 17				20 33	20 36			20 47					21 03	21 07			21 17				21 32
Sutton (Surrey) 4	a	20 26		20 21	20 44			20 36	20 40		20 56	20 51	21 14	21 09			21 06	21 12	21 26		21 21	21 44	21 39		21 36
	d	20 27		20 21					20 40		20 57	20 51						21 13	21 27		21 21				21 36
Belmont	d	20 30																	21 30						
Banstead	d	20 34																	21 34						
Epsom Downs	a	20 37																	21 37						
Cheam	d			20 24					20 43		20 59	20 54						21 15			21 24				21 39
Ewell East	d			20 27					20 46		21 03	20 57						21 19			21 27				21 42
Epsom 3	a		20 27	20 31			20 42		20 50	20 57	21 07	21 01			21 12			21 23		21 27	21 31			21 42	21 46
	d			20 32			20 43					21 02			21 13						21 32			21 43	
Ashtead	d			20 36			20 47					21 06			21 17						21 36			21 47	
Leatherhead	d			20 39			20 50					21 09			21 20						21 39			21 50	
Bookham	d														21 25										
Effingham Junction 6	d														21 29										
Guildford	a														21 46										
Boxhill & Westhumble	d			20 44			20 55					21 14									21 44			21 55	
Dorking 4	a			20 46			20 57					21 16									21 46			21 57	
	d																								
Holmwood	d																								
Ockley	d																								
Warnham	d																								
Horsham 4	a																								

			SW	SN	SN	SN	FC	SW	SN	SN	SW		SN	SN	FC	SW	SN	SN	SN	SN	FC		SW	SN	SN
London Victoria 15 ⊖	d			21 06	21 20	21 30			21 33	21 36			21 50	22 00			22 03	22 06	22 20	22 30				22 33	22 36
London Waterloo 15 ⊖	d		21 24					21 39			21 54					22 09							22 39		
Clapham Junction 10	d		21 33	21 14	21 26	21 38		21 48	21 41	21 44	22 03		21 56	22 08		22 18	22 11	22 14	22 26	22 38			22 48	22 41	22 44
Balham 4 ⊖	d			21 20	21 31	21 44			21 46	21 50			22 02	22 14			22 16	22 20	22 32	22 44				22 46	22 50
London Bridge 4 ⊖	d																								
Tulse Hill 3	d						21 31								22 01						22 31				
New Cross Gate 4 ⊖	d																								
Norwood Junction 2	d			21 39						22 09								22 39							23 09
West Croydon 4	d			21 44		22 02				22 14				22 32				22 44		23 02					23 14
Waddon	d			21 46		22 05				22 16				22 35				22 46		23 05					23 16
Wallington	d			21 50		22 08				22 20				22 38				22 50		23 08					23 20
Carshalton Beeches	d			21 52		22 11				22 22				22 41				22 52		23 11					23 22
Mitcham Eastfields	d				21 38				21 53				22 08				22 23		22 38					22 53	
Mitcham Junction	d				21 41				21 56				22 11				22 26		22 41					22 56	
Hackbridge	d				21 45				21 59				22 15				22 29		22 45					22 59	
Carshalton	d				21 47				22 02				22 17				22 32		22 47					23 02	
Sutton (Surrey) 4	a			21 56	21 51	22 14	22 09		22 05	22 26			22 21	22 44	22 39		22 35	22 56	22 51	23 14	23 09			23 05	23 26
	d			21 57	21 51				22 06	22 27			22 21				22 36	22 57	22 51					23 06	23 27
Belmont	d									22 30															23 30
Banstead	d									22 34															23 34
Epsom Downs	a									22 37															23 37
Cheam	d			21 59	21 54				22 08				22 24				22 38	22 59	22 54					23 08	
Ewell East	d			22 03	21 57				22 12				22 27				22 42	23 03	22 57					23 12	
Epsom 3	a		21 57	22 07	22 01			22 12	22 16		22 27		22 31			22 42	22 46	23 07	23 01				23 12	23 16	
	d				22 02			22 13					22 32			22 43			23 02				23 13		
Ashtead	d				22 06			22 17					22 36			22 47			23 06				23 17		
Leatherhead	d				22 09			22 20					22 39			22 50			23 09				23 20		
Bookham	d							22 25															23 25		
Effingham Junction 6	d							22 29															23 29		
Guildford	a							22 46															23 46		
Boxhill & Westhumble	d												22 44			22 55									
Dorking 4	a				22 15								22 46			22 57			23 15						
	d																								
Holmwood	d																								
Ockley	d																								
Warnham	d																								
Horsham 4	a																								

London - Sutton, Epsom, Guildford, Dorking and Horsham

		SN	SW	SN	SN	SN	SN		SN	SW	SN FX	SN FO	FC	FC	FC
London Victoria 15 ⊖	d	22 50		23 00	23 03	23 06	23 26		23 34		23 51	23 59			
London Waterloo 15 ⊖	d		23 09							23 42					
Clapham Junction 10	d	22 56	23 18	23 08	23 11	23 14	23 34		23 42	23 51	23 59	00 07			
Balham 4 ⊖	d	23 01		23 14	23 16	23 20	23 40		23 47		00 04	00 12			
London Bridge 4 ⊖	d												23 01	23 28	23 58
Tulse Hill 3	d												23 11	23 40	00 10
New Cross Gate 4 ⊖	d														
Norwood Junction 2	d					23 40									
West Croydon 4	d			23 32		23 45			00 04		00 21	00 31			
Waddon	d			23 35		23 47			00 06		00 24	00 33			
Wallington	d			23 38		23 51			00 10		00 27	00 37			
Carshalton Beeches	d			23 41		23 53			00 12		00 30	00 39			
Mitcham Eastfields	d	23 07			23 23		23 46								
Mitcham Junction	d	23 10			23 26		23 49								
Hackbridge	d	23 14			23 29		23 53								
Carshalton	d	23 16			23 32		23 55								
Sutton (Surrey) 4	a	23 20		23 44	23 35	23 57	23 59		00 16		00 33	00 43	23 45	00 14	00 43
	d	23 20		23 45	23 36		00 01								
Belmont	d														
Banstead	d														
Epsom Downs	a														
Cheam	d	23 23		23 47	23 38		00 03								
Ewell East	d	23 26		23 51	23 42		00 07								
Epsom 3	a	23 30	23 42	23 55	23 46		00 11			00 15					
	d	23 31	23 43				00 11			00 19					
Ashtead	d	23 35	23 47				00 15			00 23					
Leatherhead	d	23 38	23 50				00 18			00 26					
Bookham	d									00 31					
Effingham Junction 6	d									00 36					
Guildford	a									00 53					
Boxhill & Westhumble	d	23 43	23 55				00 23								
Dorking 4	a	23 45	23 57				00 26								
	d						00 26								
Holmwood	d						00s33								
Ockley	d						00s37								
Warnham	d						00s43								
Horsham 4	a						00 47								

Mondays to Fridays

from 3 October

		SN MO	SW MO	SN MO	SN MX	SN MX	SW MX	SN MX	SW MX	SN		SW	SN	SN	SN	FC MX	FC MX	FC	FC	SN		SN	SW	SN	SN
London Victoria 15 ⊖	d	23p08		23p19	23p26	23p34		23p51						05 52								06 00		06 07	06 17
London Waterloo 15 ⊖	d		23p32				23p42		00 15			05 47											06 24		
Clapham Junction 10	d	23p16	23p41	23p27	23p34	23p42	23p51	23p59	00 25			05 56		05 58								06 08	06 33	06 15	06 24
Balham 4 ⊖	d	23p21		23p32	23p40	23p47		00 04						06 03								06 13		06 20	06 30
London Bridge 4 ⊖	d															23p28	23p58			05 36					
Tulse Hill 3	d															23p40	00 10	06 02	06 22						
New Cross Gate 4 ⊖	d																			05 42					
Norwood Junction 2	d												05 53							06 00				06 39	
West Croydon 4	d			23p50		00 04		00 21		05 45			05 58							06 05		06 32		06 46	
Waddon	d			23p52		00 06		00 24		05 47			06 00							06 08		06 34		06 48	
Wallington	d			23p56		00 10		00 27		05 51			06 04							06 11		06 38		06 52	
Carshalton Beeches	d			23p58		00 12		00 30		05 53			06 06							06 14		06 40		06 54	
Mitcham Eastfields	d	23p28			23p46									06 12					06 29						06 38
Mitcham Junction	d	23p31			23p49									06 15					06 32						06 41
Hackbridge	d	23p34			23p53									06 19					06 35						06 45
Carshalton	d	23p37			23p55									06 21					06 38						06 47
Sutton (Surrey) 4	a	23p40		00 02	23p59	00 16		00 33		05 57			06 10	06 25		00 14	00 43	06 33	06 43	06 17		06 44		06 58	06 51
	d	23p41		00 04	00 01								06 11	06 25	06 39							06 48		07 00	06 52
Belmont	d												06 14									06 51			
Banstead	d												06 18									06 55			
Epsom Downs	a												06 21									06 58			
Cheam	d	23p43		00 06	00 03									06 28	06 41									07 02	06 54
Ewell East	d	23p47		00 10	00 07									06 31	06 45									07 06	06 58
Epsom 3	a	23p51	00 06	00 14	00 11		00 15		00 50			06 20		06 35	06 49								06 57	07 10	07 02
	d	23p51			00 11		00 19					06 21		06 36	06 50								06 58		07 02
Ashtead	d	23p55			00 15		00 23					06 25		06 40									07 02		07 06
Leatherhead	d	23p58			00 18		00 26					06 28		06 43	06 56								07 05		07 09
Bookham	d						00 31					06 33			07 01										
Effingham Junction 6	d						00 36					06 37			07 05										
Guildford	a						00 56					06 53			07 17										
Boxhill & Westhumble	d	00 03			00 23									06 48											
Dorking 4	a	00 06			00 26									06 50									07 13		07 15
	d				00 26									06 51											07 16
Holmwood	d				00s33									06 58											07 23
Ockley	d				00s37									07 02											07 27
Warnham	d				00s43									07 08											07 33
Horsham 4	a				00 47									07 12											07 37

Table 182

Mondays to Fridays

from 3 October

London - Sutton, Epsom, Guildford, Dorking and Horsham

Station		SN	SW	FC	SW	SN	SN	FC	SW	SN	FC	SN	SW	SN	FC 1	SW	FC 1	SW	SN	SN	SN	SN	FC
London Victoria 15 ⊖	d	06 30				06 36	07 00			07 06		07 15		07 30					07 36	07 47	07 55	08 03	
London Waterloo 15 ⊖	d		06 39		06 54				07 09				07 24			07 39		07 54					
Clapham Junction 10	d	06 38	06 48		07 03	06 44	07 08		07 18	07 14		07 21	07 33	07 38		07 48		08 03	07 44	07 55	08 02	08 11	
Balham 4 ⊖	d	06 44				06 49	07 13			07 20		07 26		07 44					07 50	08 00		08 16	
London Bridge 4 ⊖	d																						
Tulse Hill 3	d			06 42				07 02			07 20				07 37		07 45						08 05
New Cross Gate 4 ⊖	d																						
Norwood Junction 2	d					07 09				07 39									08 09				
West Croydon 4	d	07 03				07 14	07 32			07 46				08 04					08 15			08 36	
Waddon	d	07 05				07 16	07 35			07 48				08 06					08 17			08 39	
Wallington	d	07 09				07 20	07 38			07 52				08 10					08 21			08 42	
Carshalton Beeches	d	07 11				07 22	07 41			07 54				08 12					08 23			08 45	
Mitcham Eastfields	d			06 50							07 27						07 52			08 07			
Mitcham Junction	d			06 53							07 30	07 34					07 55			08 10			
Hackbridge	d			06 56							07 33	07 37					07 58			08 13			
Carshalton	d			06 59							07 36	07 40					08 01			08 16			
Sutton (Surrey) 4	a	07 15		07 04		07 26	07 44	07 35		07 58	07 39	07 43		08 16	08 08		08 04		08 27	08 19	08 22	08 48	08 37
	d	07 18				07 26	07 45			07 59		07 44		08 16					08 27		08 23	08 53	
Belmont	d	07 21					07 48							08 20								08 56	
Banstead	d	07 25					07 52							08 23								09 00	
Epsom Downs	a	07 28					07 55							08 27								09 03	
Cheam	d					07 29				08 01		07 46							08 30		08 25		
Ewell East	d					07 32				08 05		07 50							08 33		08 29		
Epsom 3	a		07 11		07 27	07 36			07 42	08 09		07 54	07 58			08 13		08 27	08 37		08 33		
	d		07 12		07 28	07 37						07 54	07 58			08 17		08 28	08 38		08 33		
Ashtead	d		07 16		07 32	07 41						07 58	08 02			08 21		08 32	08 42		08 37		
Leatherhead	d		07 19		07 35	07 44						08 01	08 05			08 24		08 35	08 45		08 40		
Bookham	d		07 24			07 49										08 29							
Effingham Junction 6	d		07a28			07 53										08 33							
Guildford	a					08 06										08 53							
Boxhill & Westhumble	d											08 06							08 50				
Dorking 4	a				07 43							08 09	08 14					08 43	08 52		08 46		
	d											08 09									08 47		
Holmwood	d											08 17											
Ockley	d											08 21											
Warnham	d											08 26											
Horsham 4	a											08 30									09 03		

Station		SN	SW	FC	SW	SN	SN	FC	SN	SN	SN	SW	FC 1	SW	SN	SN	FC 1	SN	SN	SN	SW	FC
London Victoria 15 ⊖	d	08 07				08 19	08 26			08 31	08 36				08 47	08 52		09 01	09 03	09 05		
London Waterloo 15 ⊖	d		08 09		08 24							08 39		08 54							09 09	
Clapham Junction 10	d	08 16	08 18		08 33	08 26	08 33			08 40	08 44	08 48		09 03	08 54	09 00		09 08	09 11	09 14	09 18	
Balham 4 ⊖	d	08 21				08 30	08 38			08 46	08 50				09 00	09 05			09 16	09 20		
London Bridge 4 ⊖	d								08 24													
Tulse Hill 3	d			08 20				08 40	08 47				08 50				09 01					09 16
New Cross Gate 4 ⊖	d																					
Norwood Junction 2	d	08 39									09 09									09 39		
West Croydon 4	d	08 45					08 56			09 06	09 14					09 24			09 34	09 44		
Waddon	d	08 47					08 58			09 08	09 16					09 26			09 36	09 46		
Wallington	d	08 51					09 02			09 12	09 20					09 30			09 40	09 50		
Carshalton Beeches	d	08 53					09 04			09 14	09 22					09 32			09 42	09 52		
Mitcham Eastfields	d			08 28		08 37							08 58		09 06							09 24
Mitcham Junction	d			08 31		08 40							09 01		09 09							09 27
Hackbridge	d			08 34		08 44							09 04		09 13							09 30
Carshalton	d			08 37		08 46							09 07		09 15							09 33
Sutton (Surrey) 4	a	08 57		08 40		08 50	09 08	09 12	09 02	09 18	09 26		09 10		09 19	09 39	09 37	09 28	09 46	09 56		09 36
	d					08 50			09 02	09 19					09 19	09 40		09 29				
Belmont	d									09 22												
Banstead	d									09 26												
Epsom Downs	a									09 29												
Cheam	d					08 53			09 05						09 22	09 42		09 31				
Ewell East	d					08 56			09 08						09 25	09 46						
Epsom 3	a		08 42		08 57	09 00			09 12			09 16		09 27	09 29	09 50		09 37			09 42	
	d		08 47		08 58	09 01						09 17		09 28				09 37			09 47	
Ashtead	d		08 51		09 02	09 05						09 21		09 32				09 41			09 51	
Leatherhead	d		08 54		09 05	09 08						09 24		09 35				09 44			09 54	
Bookham	d		08 59									09 29									09 59	
Effingham Junction 6	d		09 03									09 33									10 03	
Guildford	a		09 23									09 53									10 23	
Boxhill & Westhumble	d					09 13												09 49				
Dorking 4	a				09 13	09 15								09 43				09 52				
	d					09 16																
Holmwood	d					09 23																
Ockley	d					09 27																
Warnham	d					09 33																
Horsham 4	a					09 37																

Table 182

Mondays to Fridays

from 3 October

London - Sutton, Epsom, Guildford, Dorking and Horsham

Station		SW	SN	SN	FC	SN	SN	SN	SW	FC	SW	SN	SN	FC	SN	SN	SN	SW	FC	SW	SN	SN	FC
London Victoria 15 ⊖	d		09 17	09 22		09 31	09 33	09 35				09 47	09 53		10 01	10 03	10 06				10 17	10 23	
London Waterloo 15 ⊖	d	09 24							09 39		09 54							10 09		10 24			
Clapham Junction 10	d	09 33	09 24	09 30		09 38	09 41	09 44	09 48		10 03	09 54	10 00		10 08	10 11	10 14	10 18		10 33	10 24	10 30	
Balham 4 ⊖	d		09 30	09 35			09 46	09 50				10 00	10 05			10 16	10 20				10 30	10 35	
London Bridge 4 ⊖	d																						
Tulse Hill 3	d				09 31					09 46				10 01					10 16				10 31
New Cross Gate 4 ⊖	d																						
Norwood Junction 2	d							10 09									10 39						
West Croydon 4	d			09 54			10 04	10 14					10 24			10 34	10 44					10 54	
Waddon	d			09 56			10 06	10 16					10 26			10 36	10 46					10 56	
Wallington	d			10 00			10 10	10 20					10 30			10 40	10 50					11 00	
Carshalton Beeches	d			10 02			10 12	10 22					10 32			10 42	10 52					11 02	
Mitcham Eastfields	d		09 36							09 54		10 06							10 24		10 36		
Mitcham Junction	d		09 39							09 57		10 09							10 27		10 39		
Hackbridge	d		09 43							10 00		10 13							10 30		10 43		
Carshalton	d		09 45							10 03		10 15							10 33		10 45		
Sutton (Surrey) 4	a		09 49	10 06	10 05	09 58	10 16	10 26		10 06		10 19	10 39	10 35	10 28	10 46	10 56		10 36		10 49	11 06	11 05
	d		09 49	10 07		09 59						10 19	10 40		10 29						10 49	11 07	
Belmont	d			10 10																		11 10	
Banstead	d			10 14																		11 14	
Epsom Downs	a			10 17																		11 17	
Cheam	d		09 52			10 01						10 22	10 42		10 31						10 52		
Ewell East	d		09 55			10 05						10 25	10 46								10 55		
Epsom 3	a	09 57	09 59			10 09			10 16		10 27	10 29	10 52		10 37			10 46		10 57	10 59		
	d	09 58				10 09			10 17		10 28				10 37			10 47		10 58			
Ashtead	d	10 02				10 13			10 21		10 32				10 41			10 51		11 02			
Leatherhead	d	10 05				10 16			10 24		10 35				10 44			10 54		11 05			
Bookham	d								10 29									10 59					
Effingham Junction 6	d								10 33									11 03					
Guildford	a								10 53									11 23					
Boxhill & Westhumble	d					10 21																	
Dorking 4	a	10 13				10 24					10 43				10 50					11 13			
	d					10 24																	
Holmwood	d					10 32																	
Ockley	d					10 36																	
Warnham	d					10 41																	
Horsham 4	a					10 45																	

Station		SN	SN	SN	SW	FC	SW	SN	SN	FC	SN	SN	SN	SW	FC	SW	SN	SN	FC	SN	SN	SN
London Victoria 15 ⊖	d	10 31	10 33	10 36				10 47	10 53		11 01	11 03	11 06				11 17	11 23		11 31	11 33	11 36
London Waterloo 15 ⊖	d				10 39		10 54							11 09		11 24						
Clapham Junction 10	d	10 38	10 41	10 44	10 48		11 03	10 54	11 00		11 08	11 11	11 14	11 18		11 33	11 24	11 30		11 38	11 41	11 44
Balham 4 ⊖	d		10 46	10 50				11 00	11 05			11 16	11 20				11 30	11 35			11 46	11 50
London Bridge 4 ⊖	d																					
Tulse Hill 3	d					10 46				11 01					11 16				11 31			
New Cross Gate 4 ⊖	d																					
Norwood Junction 2	d			11 09									11 39									12 09
West Croydon 4	d		11 04	11 14					11 24			11 34	11 44					11 54			12 04	12 14
Waddon	d		11 06	11 16					11 26			11 36	11 46					11 56			12 06	12 16
Wallington	d		11 10	11 20					11 30			11 40	11 50					12 00			12 10	12 20
Carshalton Beeches	d		11 12	11 22					11 32			11 42	11 52					12 02			12 12	12 22
Mitcham Eastfields	d					10 54		11 06							11 24		11 36					
Mitcham Junction	d					10 57		11 09							11 27		11 39					
Hackbridge	d					11 00		11 13							11 30		11 43					
Carshalton	d					11 03		11 15							11 33		11 45					
Sutton (Surrey) 4	a	10 58	11 16	11 26		11 06		11 19	11 39	11 35	11 28	11 46	11 56		11 36		11 49	12 06	12 05	11 58	12 16	12 26
	d	10 59						11 19	11 40		11 29						11 49	12 07		11 59		
Belmont	d																	12 10				
Banstead	d																	12 14				
Epsom Downs	a																	12 17				
Cheam	d	11 01						11 22	11 42		11 31						11 52			12 01		
Ewell East	d	11 05						11 25	11 46								11 55			12 05		
Epsom 3	a	11 09			11 16		11 27	11 29	11 52		11 37			11 46		11 57	11 59			12 09		
	d	11 09			11 17		11 28				11 37			11 47		11 58				12 09		
Ashtead	d	11 13			11 21		11 32				11 41			11 51		12 02				12 13		
Leatherhead	d	11 16			11 24		11 35				11 44			11 54		12 05				12 16		
Bookham	d				11 29									11 59								
Effingham Junction 6	d				11 33									12 03								
Guildford	a				11 53									12 23								
Boxhill & Westhumble	d	11 21																		12 21		
Dorking 4	a	11 24					11 43				11 50					12 13				12 24		
	d	11 24																		12 24		
Holmwood	d	11 32																		12 32		
Ockley	d	11 36																		12 36		
Warnham	d	11 41																		12 41		
Horsham 4	a	11 45																		12 45		

London - Sutton, Epsom, Guildford, Dorking and Horsham

from 3 October

		SW	FC	SW	SN	FC	SN	SW	SN	SN	SN	FC	SW	SN	FC	SN	SN	SN	SN	SW	FC	SW	SN
London Victoria	⊖ d				11 47		12 01		11 53	12 03	12 06			12 17		12 31	12 23	12 33	12 36				12 47
London Waterloo	⊖ d	11 39		11 54				12 09					12 24							12 39		12 54	
Clapham Junction	d	11 48		12 03	11 54		12 08	12 18	12 00	12 11	12 14		12 33	12 24		12 38	12 30	12 41	12 44	12 48		13 03	12 54
Balham	⊖ d				12 00				12 05	12 16	12 20			12 30			12 35	12 46	12 50				13 00
London Bridge	⊖ d																						
Tulse Hill	d		11 46			12 01						12 16			12 31						12 46		
New Cross Gate	⊖ d																						
Norwood Junction	d										12 39								13 09				
West Croydon	d								12 24	12 34	12 44						12 54	13 04	13 14				
Waddon	d								12 26	12 36	12 46						12 56	13 06	13 16				
Wallington	d								12 30	12 40	12 50						13 00	13 10	13 20				
Carshalton Beeches	d								12 32	12 42	12 52						13 02	13 12	13 22				
Mitcham Eastfields	d		11 54		12 06							12 24		12 36							12 54		13 06
Mitcham Junction	d		11 57		12 09							12 27		12 39							12 57		13 09
Hackbridge	d		12 00		12 13							12 30		12 43							13 00		13 13
Carshalton	d		12 03		12 15							12 33		12 45							13 03		13 15
Sutton (Surrey)	a		12 06		12 19	12 35	12 28		12 39	12 46	12 56	12 36		12 49	13 05	12 58	13 06	13 16	13 26		13 06		13 19
	d				12 19		12 29		12 40					12 49		12 59	13 07						13 19
Belmont	d																13 10						
Banstead	d																13 14						
Epsom Downs	a																13 17						
Cheam	d				12 22		12 31		12 42					12 52		13 01							13 22
Ewell East	d				12 25				12 46					12 55		13 05							13 25
Epsom	a	12 16		12 27	12 29		12 37	12 46	12 52				12 57	12 59		13 09				13 16		13 27	13 29
	d	12 17		12 28			12 37	12 47					12 58			13 09				13 17		13 28	
Ashtead	d	12 21		12 32			12 41	12 51					13 02			13 13				13 21		13 32	
Leatherhead	d	12 24		12 35			12 44	12 54					13 05			13 16				13 24		13 35	
Bookham	d	12 29						12 59												13 29			
Effingham Junction	d	12 33						13 03												13 33			
Guildford	a	12 53						13 23												13 53			
Boxhill & Westhumble	d															13 21							
Dorking	a			12 43			12 50						13 13			13 24						13 43	
	d															13 24							
Holmwood	d															13 32							
Ockley	d															13 36							
Warnham	d															13 41							
Horsham	a															13 45							

		FC	SN	SW	SN	SN	SN	FC	SW	SN	SN	FC	SN	SN	SN	SW	FC	SW	SN	FC	SN	SW	SN
London Victoria	⊖ d		13 01		12 53	13 03	13 06			13 17	13 23		13 31	13 33	13 36				13 47		14 01		13 53
London Waterloo	⊖ d			13 09					13 24							13 39		13 54				14 09	
Clapham Junction	d		13 08	13 18	13 00	13 11	13 14		13 33	13 24	13 30		13 38	13 41	13 44	13 48		14 03	13 54		14 08	14 18	14 00
Balham	⊖ d				13 05	13 16	13 20			13 30	13 35			13 46	13 50				14 00				14 05
London Bridge	⊖ d																						
Tulse Hill	d	13 01						13 16				13 31					13 46			14 01			
New Cross Gate	⊖ d																						
Norwood Junction	d						13 39								14 09								
West Croydon	d				13 24	13 34	13 44				13 54			14 04	14 14								14 24
Waddon	d				13 26	13 36	13 46				13 56			14 06	14 16								14 26
Wallington	d				13 30	13 40	13 50				14 00			14 10	14 20								14 30
Carshalton Beeches	d				13 32	13 42	13 52				14 02			14 12	14 22								14 32
Mitcham Eastfields	d							13 24		13 36							13 54		14 06				
Mitcham Junction	d							13 27		13 39							13 57		14 09				
Hackbridge	d							13 30		13 43							14 00		14 13				
Carshalton	d							13 33		13 45							14 03		14 15				
Sutton (Surrey)	a	13 35	13 28		13 39	13 46	13 56	13 36		13 49	14 06	14 05	13 58	14 16	14 26		14 06		14 19	14 35	14 28		14 39
	d		13 29		13 40					13 49	14 07		13 59						14 19		14 29		14 40
Belmont	d										14 10												
Banstead	d										14 14												
Epsom Downs	a										14 17												
Cheam	d		13 31		13 42					13 52			14 01						14 22		14 31		14 42
Ewell East	d				13 46					13 55			14 05						14 25				14 46
Epsom	a		13 37	13 46	13 52				13 57	13 59			14 09			14 16		14 27	14 29		14 37	14 46	14 52
	d		13 37	13 47					13 58				14 09			14 17		14 28			14 37	14 47	
Ashtead	d		13 41	13 51					14 02				14 13			14 21		14 32			14 41	14 51	
Leatherhead	d		13 44	13 54					14 05				14 16			14 24		14 35			14 44	14 54	
Bookham	d			13 59												14 29						14 59	
Effingham Junction	d			14 03												14 33						15 03	
Guildford	a			14 23												14 53						15 23	
Boxhill & Westhumble	d												14 21										
Dorking	a		13 50						14 13				14 24					14 43			14 50		
	d												14 24										
Holmwood	d												14 32										
Ockley	d												14 36										
Warnham	d												14 41										
Horsham	a												14 45										

London - Sutton, Epsom, Guildford, Dorking and Horsham

from 3 October

		SN	SN	FC	SW	SN	FC	SN	SN	SN	SN	SW	FC	SW	SN	FC	SN	SW	SN	SN	SN	FC
London Victoria	⊖ d	14 03	14 06			14 17		14 31	14 23	14 33	14 36				14 47		15 01		14 53	15 03	15 06	
London Waterloo	⊖ d				14 24							14 39		14 54				15 09				
Clapham Junction	d	14 11	14 14		14 33	14 24		14 38	14 30	14 41	14 44	14 48		15 03	14 54		15 08	15 18	15 00	15 11	15 14	
Balham	⊖ d	14 16	14 20			14 30			14 35	14 46	14 50				15 00				15 05	15 16	15 20	
London Bridge	⊖ d																					
Tulse Hill	d			14 16			14 31						14 46			15 01						15 16
New Cross Gate	⊖ d																					
Norwood Junction	d		14 39								15 09										15 39	
West Croydon	d	14 34	14 44						14 54	15 04	15 14								15 24	15 34	15 44	
Waddon	d	14 36	14 46						14 56	15 06	15 16								15 26	15 36	15 46	
Wallington	d	14 40	14 50						15 00	15 10	15 20								15 30	15 40	15 50	
Carshalton Beeches	d	14 42	14 52						15 02	15 12	15 22								15 32	15 42	15 52	
Mitcham Eastfields	d			14 24		14 36							14 54		15 06							15 24
Mitcham Junction	d			14 27		14 39							14 57		15 09							15 27
Hackbridge	d			14 30		14 43							15 00		15 13							15 30
Carshalton	d			14 33		14 45							15 03		15 15							15 33
Sutton (Surrey)	a	14 46	14 56	14 36		14 50	15 05	14 58	15 06	15 16	15 26		15 06		15 19	15 35	15 28		15 39	15 47	15 56	15 36
	d					14 50		14 59	15 07						15 19		15 29		15 40			
Belmont	d								15 10													
Banstead	d								15 14													
Epsom Downs	a								15 17													
Cheam	d					14 53		15 01							15 22		15 31		15 42			
Ewell East	d					14 56		15 05							15 25				15 46			
Epsom	a				14 57	15 00		15 09				15 16		15 27	15 29		15 37	15 46	15 52			
	d				14 58			15 09				15 17		15 28			15 37	15 47				
Ashtead	d				15 02			15 13				15 21		15 32			15 41	15 51				
Leatherhead	d				15 05			15 16				15 24		15 35			15 44	15 54				
Bookham	d											15 29						15 59				
Effingham Junction	d											15 33						16 03				
Guildford	a											15 53						16 23				
Boxhill & Westhumble	d							15 21														
Dorking	a				15 13			15 24						15 43			15 50					
	d							15 24														
Holmwood	d							15 32														
Ockley	d							15 36														
Warnham	d							15 41														
Horsham	a							15 45														

		SW	SN	SN	FC	SN	SN	SN	SW	FC	SW	SN	SN	FC	SN	SN	SN	SW	FC	SW	SN	SN	FC
London Victoria	⊖ d		15 17	15 23		15 31	15 33	15 36				15 47	15 53		16 01	16 03	16 07				16 17	16 31	
London Waterloo	⊖ d	15 24							15 39		15 54							16 09		16 24			
Clapham Junction	d	15 33	15 24	15 30		15 38	15 41	15 44	15 48		16 03	15 54	16 00		16 08	16 11	16 15	16 18		16 33	16 24	16 38	
Balham	⊖ d		15 30	15 35			15 46	15 50				16 00	16 05			16 16	16 20				16 30		
London Bridge	⊖ d																						
Tulse Hill	d				15 31					15 46				16 01					16 16				16 32
New Cross Gate	⊖ d																						
Norwood Junction	d							16 09									16 39						
West Croydon	d			15 54			16 04	16 14					16 24			16 34	16 44						
Waddon	d			15 56			16 06	16 16					16 26			16 36	16 46						
Wallington	d			16 00			16 10	16 20					16 30			16 40	16 50						
Carshalton Beeches	d			16 02			16 12	16 22					16 32			16 42	16 52						
Mitcham Eastfields	d		15 36							15 54		16 06							16 24		16 36	16 51	
Mitcham Junction	d		15 39							15 57		16 09			16 22				16 27		16 39	16 54	
Hackbridge	d		15 43							16 00		16 13							16 30		16 43	16 57	
Carshalton	d		15 45							16 03		16 15							16 33		16 45	17 00	
Sutton (Surrey)	a		15 49	16 06	16 05	15 58	16 16	16 26		16 06		16 19	16 36	16 35	16 29	16 48	16 58		16 36		16 49	17 03	17 05
	d		15 49	16 07		15 59						16 19	16 37		16 30						16 49	17 04	
Belmont	d			16 10									16 40										
Banstead	d			16 14									16 44										
Epsom Downs	a			16 17									16 47										
Cheam	d		15 52			16 01						16 22			16 32						16 52	17 06	
Ewell East	d		15 55			16 05						16 25			16 36						16 55	17 10	
Epsom	a	15 57	15 59			16 09			16 15		16 27	16 29			16 40			16 46		16 57	17 01	17 16	
	d	15 58				16 09			16 17		16 28				16 40			16 47		16 58	17 02		
Ashtead	d	16 02				16 13			16 21		16 32				16 44			16 51		17 02	17 06		
Leatherhead	d	16 05				16 16			16 24		16 35				16 47			16 54		17 05	17 09		
Bookham	d								16 29									16 59					
Effingham Junction	d								16 33									17 03					
Guildford	a								16 53									17 25					
Boxhill & Westhumble	d					16 21									16 52					17 10	17 14		
Dorking	a	16 13				16 24					16 43				16 57					17 16	17 16		
	d					16 24															17 17		
Holmwood	d					16 32															17 24		
Ockley	d					16 36															17 28		
Warnham	d					16 41															17 34		
Horsham	a					16 45															17 40		

Table 182

Mondays to Fridays
from 3 October

London - Sutton, Epsom, Guildford, Dorking and Horsham

Station		SN	SW	FC		SW	SN	SN	FC	FC	SN	SN	SN	SW		SW	SN	SN	SW	FC	SN	SN	SN	SN	
London Victoria 15 ⊖	d	16 33					16 37	16 50				17 01	17 06					17 20				17 31	17 33	17 37	
London Waterloo 15 ⊖	d		16 39			16 54								17 09		17 24			17 30						
Clapham Junction 10	d	16 41	16 48			17 03	16 45	16 56				17 09	17 14	17 18		17 33		17 26	17 39			17 37	17 41	17 45	
Balham 4 ⊖	d	16 46					16 50	17 01				17 14	17 19					17 32				17 42	17 46	17 50	
London Bridge 4 ⊖	d										17 03						17 06				17 29				
Tulse Hill 3	d			16 46					17 02	17 20							17 24			17 31					
New Cross Gate 4 ⊖	d																								
Norwood Junction 2	d						17 09				17 16		17 38								17 43			18 09	
West Croydon 4	d	17 04					17 14				17 22	17 33	17 44								17 48		18 04	18 15	
Waddon	d	17 06					17 16				17 24	17 35	17 46								17 51		18 06	18 17	
Wallington	d	17 10					17 20				17 28	17 39	17 50								17 54		18 10	18 21	
Carshalton Beeches	d	17 12					17 22				17 30	17 41	17 52								17 57		18 12	18 23	
Mitcham Eastfields	d			16 56				17 08		17 28							17 32	17 38				17 48			
Mitcham Junction	d			16 59				17 11		17 31							17 35	17 41				17 51			
Hackbridge	d			17 02				17 15		17 34							17 38	17 45				17 55			
Carshalton	d			17 05				17 17		17 37							17 41	17 47				17 57			
Sutton (Surrey) 4	a	17 16		17 08			17 26	17 21	17 39	17 40	17 34	17 45	17 58				17 44	17 51		18 07	18 00	18 03	18 18	18 29	
	d	17 16					17 27	17 21			17 34	17 45						17 51			18 01	18 05	18 19		
Belmont	d	17 20										17 49											18 22		
Banstead	d	17 23										17 52											18 26		
Epsom Downs	a	17 28										17 58											18 31		
Cheam	d						17 29	17 24			17 37							17 54			18 03	18 07			
Ewell East	d						17 33	17 27			17 40							17 57			18 07	18 11			
Epsom 3	a		17 12			17 27	17 37	17 31			17 46			17 42		17 54		18 01	18 07		18 11	18 17			
	d		17 17			17 28	17 37	17 32						17 47		17 54		18 02			18 12				
Ashtead	d		17 21			17 32	17 41	17 36						17 51		17 58		18 06			18 16				
Leatherhead	d		17 24			17 35	17 44	17 39						17 54		18 01		18 09			18 19				
Bookham	d		17 29				17 50							17 59							18 24				
Effingham Junction 6	d		17 33				17 53							18a05							18 28				
Guildford	a		17 55				18 13														18 46				
Boxhill & Westhumble	d					17 40		17 44								18 06		18 14							
Dorking 4	a					17 46		17 46								18 13		18 16							
	d							17 47										18 19							
Holmwood	d							17 54										18 26							
Ockley	d							17 58										18 30							
Warnham	d							18 04										18 36							
Horsham 4	a							18 10										18 42							

Station		SW	FC	SW	SN	SN	SW	FC	SN	SW		SN	SN	SN	FC	SW	SN	SN	SW	FC		FC	SN	SW	SW
London Victoria 15 ⊖	d					17 50						18 01	18 03	18 07				18 20							
London Waterloo 16 ⊖	d	17 39		17 54			18 00			18 09						18 24			18 30					18 39	18 54
Clapham Junction 10	d	17 48		18 03		17 56	18 09			18 18		18 08	18 11	18 15		18 33		18 26	18 39					18 48	19 03
Balham 4 ⊖	d					18 02						18 12	18 16	18 20				18 32							
London Bridge 4 ⊖	d				17 37				18 02								18 08						18 32		
Tulse Hill 3	d		17 48		17 55			18 02							18 22		18 27			18 32		18 52			
New Cross Gate 4 ⊖	d																								
Norwood Junction 2	d								18 16					18 39									18 46		
West Croydon 4	d								18 21				18 35	18 45									18 51		
Waddon	d								18 23				18 37	18 47									18 53		
Wallington	d								18 27				18 41	18 51									18 57		
Carshalton Beeches	d								18 29				18 43	18 53									18 59		
Mitcham Eastfields	d		17 56		18 02	18 08						18 19			18 30		18 34	18 38				19 00			
Mitcham Junction	d		17 59		18 05	18 11						18 22			18 33		18 37	18 41				19 03			
Hackbridge	d		18 02		18 09	18 15						18 25			18 36		18 41	18 45				19 06			
Carshalton	d		18 05		18 11	18 17						18 28			18 39		18 43	18 47				19 09			
Sutton (Surrey) 4	a		18 08		18 15	18 21		18 37	18 33			18 36	18 47	18 58	18 42		18 47	18 51		19 07		19 12	19 03		
	d					18 21			18 33			18 36	18 48					18 51					19 03		
Belmont	d												18 51												
Banstead	d												18 55												
Epsom Downs	a												19 00												
Cheam	d					18 24			18 36			18 39						18 54					19 06		
Ewell East	d					18 27			18 39			18 42						18 57					19 09		
Epsom 3	a	18 15		18 24		18 31	18 35		18 43	18 46		18 48				18 54		19 01	19 07				19 13	19 16	19 24
	d	18 17		18 24		18 34			18 44	18 47						18 54		19 02					19 14	19 17	19 24
Ashtead	d	18 21		18 28		18 38			18 48	18 51						18 58		19 06					19 18	19 21	19 28
Leatherhead	d	18 24		18 31		18 41			18 51	18 54						19 01		19 09					19 21	19 24	19 31
Bookham	d	18 29								18 59														19 29	
Effingham Junction 6	d	18a42								19 03														19 33	
Guildford	a									19 25														19 55	
Boxhill & Westhumble	d			18 36		18 46			18 56							19 06		19 14					19 26		19 36
Dorking 4	a			18 43		18 48			19 00							19 13		19 16					19 30		19 43
	d					18 49												19 19							
Holmwood	d					18 56												19 26							
Ockley	d					19 00												19 30							
Warnham	d					19 06												19 36							
Horsham 4	a					19 12												19 42							

Table 182

Mondays to Fridays
from 3 October

London - Sutton, Epsom, Guildford, Dorking and Horsham

Station		SN	SN	SN	SN	SW		FC	SW	SN	SN	FC	SW	SN	FC	FC		FC	SN	SN	SW	SN	SN	SW	SN
London Victoria 15 ⊖	d		18 32	18 36	18 50					18 59	19 06			19 20						19 30		19 34	19 36		19 50
London Waterloo 15 ⊖	d					19 00			19 09				19 24								19 39			19 54	
Clapham Junction 10	d		18 40	18 44	18 56	19 09			19 18	19 08	19 14		19 33	19 26						19 38	19 48	19 41	19 44	20 03	19 56
Balham 4 ⊖	d		18 45	18 49	19 02					19 14	19 20			19 32						19 44		19 46	19 50		20 02
London Bridge 4 ⊖	d	18 38																	19 31						
Tulse Hill 3	d	18 56						19 07				19 16			19 31	19 46		20 01							
New Cross Gate 4 ⊖	d																								
Norwood Junction 2	d			19 09							19 39								19 44				20 09		
West Croydon 4	d		19 04	19 15						19 32	19 45								19 49	20 02			20 14		
Waddon	d		19 07	19 17						19 35	19 47								19 52	20 05			20 16		
Wallington	d		19 10	19 21						19 38	19 51								19 55	20 08			20 20		
Carshalton Beeches	d		19 13	19 23						19 41	19 53								19 58	20 11			20 22		
Mitcham Eastfields	d	19 03			19 08							19 24		19 38		19 54						19 57			20 08
Mitcham Junction	d	19 06			19 11							19 27		19 41		19 57						20 00			20 11
Hackbridge	d	19 10			19 15							19 30		19 45		20 00						20 03			20 15
Carshalton	d	19 12			19 17							19 33		19 47		20 03						20 06			20 17
Sutton (Surrey) 4	a	19 16	19 16	19 28	19 21			19 40		19 44	19 57	19 36		19 51	20 07	20 06		20 39	20 01	20 14		20 09	20 26		20 21
	d	19 16	19 17		19 21					19 45	19 58			19 51					20 02			20 10	20 27		20 21
Belmont	d		19 20								20 01												20 30		
Banstead	d		19 24								20 05												20 34		
Epsom Downs	a		19 29								20 08												20 37		
Cheam	d	19 19			19 24					19 47				19 54					20 04			20 12			20 24
Ewell East	d	19 22			19 27					19 51				19 57					20 08			20 16			20 27
Epsom 3	a	19 26			19 31	19 35			19 44	19 55			19 57	20 01					20 12		20 16	20 20		20 27	20 31
	d				19 34				19 47				19 58	20 02					20 12		20 17				20 32
Ashtead	d				19 38				19 51				20 02	20 06					20 16		20 21				20 36
Leatherhead	d				19 41				19 54				20 05	20 09					20 19		20 24				20 39
Bookham	d								19 59												20 29				
Effingham Junction 6	d								20 03												20 33				
Guildford	a								20 23												20 53				
Boxhill & Westhumble	d				19 46								20 10	20 14											20 44
Dorking 4	a				19 50								20 14	20 16					20 25						20 46
	d													20 17											
Holmwood	d													20 24											
Ockley	d													20 28											
Warnham	d													20 34											
Horsham 4	a													20 38											

Station		SN		SW	FC	SN	SW	SN	SN	SN	FC	SW		FC	SN	SN	SW	SN	SN	FC	SW	SN		SW	SN
London Victoria 15 ⊖	d	20 00				20 03		20 06	20 20	20 30					20 33	20 36		20 50	21 00			21 03			21 06
London Waterloo 15 ⊖	d			20 09			20 24					20 39					20 54				21 09			21 24	
Clapham Junction 10	d	20 08		20 18		20 11	20 33	20 14	20 26	20 38		20 48			20 41	20 44	21 03	20 56	21 08		21 18	21 11		21 33	21 14
Balham 4 ⊖	d	20 14				20 16		20 20	20 31	20 44					20 46	20 50		21 02	21 14			21 16			21 20
London Bridge 4 ⊖	d																								
Tulse Hill 3	d				20 16						20 31			20 46						21 01					
New Cross Gate 4 ⊖	d																								
Norwood Junction 2	d							20 39								21 09									21 39
West Croydon 4	d	20 32						20 44		21 02						21 14			21 32						21 44
Waddon	d	20 35						20 46		21 05						21 16			21 35						21 46
Wallington	d	20 38						20 50		21 08						21 20			21 38						21 50
Carshalton Beeches	d	20 41						20 52		21 11						21 22			21 41						21 52
Mitcham Eastfields	d				20 24	20 27			20 38					20 54	20 58			21 08				21 23			
Mitcham Junction	d				20 27	20 30			20 41					20 57	21 01			21 11				21 26			
Hackbridge	d				20 30	20 34			20 45					21 00	21 04			21 15				21 30			
Carshalton	d				20 33	20 36			20 47					21 03	21 07			21 17				21 32			
Sutton (Surrey) 4	a	20 44			20 36	20 40		20 56	20 51	21 14	21 09			21 06	21 12	21 26		21 21	21 44	21 39		21 36			21 56
	d					20 40		20 57	20 51						21 13	21 27		21 21				21 36			21 57
Belmont	d															21 30									
Banstead	d															21 34									
Epsom Downs	a															21 37									
Cheam	d					20 43		20 59	20 54						21 15			21 24				21 39			21 59
Ewell East	d					20 46		21 03	20 57						21 19			21 27				21 42			22 03
Epsom 3	a			20 42		20 50	20 57	21 07	21 01			21 12			21 23		21 27	21 31			21 42	21 46		21 57	22 07
	d			20 43					21 02			21 13						21 32			21 43				
Ashtead	d			20 47					21 06			21 17						21 36			21 47				
Leatherhead	d			20 50					21 09			21 20						21 39			21 50				
Bookham	d											21 25													
Effingham Junction 6	d											21 29													
Guildford	a											21 49													
Boxhill & Westhumble	d			20 55					21 14									21 44			21 55				
Dorking 4	a			20 59					21 16									21 46			21 59				
	d																								
Holmwood	d																								
Ockley	d																								
Warnham	d																								
Horsham 4	a																								

London - Sutton, Epsom, Guildford, Dorking and Horsham

from 3 October

		SN	SN	FC	SW	SN	SN	SW	SN	SN	FC	SW	SN	SN	SN	SN	FC	SW	SN	SN	SN	SW	SN
London Victoria ⊖	d	21 20	21 30			21 33	21 36		21 50	22 00			22 03	22 06	22 20	22 30			22 33	22 36	22 50		23 00
London Waterloo ⊖	d				21 39			21 54				22 09						22 39				23 09	
Clapham Junction	d	21 26	21 38		21 48	21 41	21 44	22 03	21 56	22 08		22 18	22 11	22 14	22 26	22 38		22 48	22 41	22 44	22 56	23 18	23 08
Balham ⊖	d	21 31	21 44			21 46	21 50		22 02	22 14			22 16	22 20	22 32	22 44			22 46	22 50	23 01		23 14
London Bridge ⊖	d																						
Tulse Hill	d			21 31							22 01						22 31						
New Cross Gate ⊖	d																						
Norwood Junction	d						22 09							22 39						23 09			
West Croydon	d		22 02				22 14			22 32				22 44		23 02				23 14			23 32
Waddon	d		22 05				22 16			22 35				22 46		23 05				23 16			23 35
Wallington	d		22 08				22 20			22 38				22 50		23 08				23 20			23 38
Carshalton Beeches	d		22 11				22 22			22 41				22 52		23 11				23 22			23 41
Mitcham Eastfields	d	21 38				21 53			22 08				22 23		22 38				22 53		23 07		
Mitcham Junction	d	21 41				21 56			22 11				22 26		22 41				22 56		23 10		
Hackbridge	d	21 45				21 59			22 15				22 29		22 45				22 59		23 14		
Carshalton	d	21 47				22 02			22 17				22 32		22 47				23 02		23 16		
Sutton (Surrey)	a	21 51	22 14	22 09		22 05	22 26		22 21	22 44	22 39		22 35	22 56	22 51	23 14	23 09		23 05	23 26	23 20		23 44
	d	21 51				22 06	22 27		22 21				22 36	22 57	22 51				23 06	23 27	23 20		23 45
Belmont	d						22 30													23 30			
Banstead	d						22 34													23 34			
Epsom Downs	a						22 37													23 37			
Cheam	d	21 54				22 08			22 24				22 38	22 59	22 54				23 08		23 23		23 47
Ewell East	d	21 57				22 12			22 27				22 42	23 03	22 57				23 12		23 26		23 51
Epsom	a	22 01			22 12	22 16		22 27	22 31			22 42	22 46	23 07	23 01			23 12	23 16		23 30	23 42	23 55
	d	22 02			22 13				22 32			22 43			23 02			23 13			23 31	23 43	
Ashtead	d	22 06			22 17				22 36			22 47			23 06			23 17			23 35	23 47	
Leatherhead	d	22 09			22 20				22 39			22 50			23 09			23 20			23 38	23 50	
Bookham	d				22 25													23 25					
Effingham Junction	d				22 29													23 29					
Guildford	a				22 49													23 49					
Boxhill & Westhumble	d								22 44			22 55									23 43	23 55	
Dorking	a	22 15							22 46			22 59			23 15						23 45	23 59	
	d																						
Holmwood	d																						
Ockley	d																						
Warnham	d																						
Horsham	a																						

		SN	SN	SN	SN	SW	SN FX	SN FO	FC	FC	FC
London Victoria ⊖	d	23 03	23 06	23 26	23 34		23 51	23 59			
London Waterloo ⊖	d					23 42					
Clapham Junction	d	23 11	23 14	23 34	23 42	23 51	23 59	00 07			
Balham ⊖	d	23 16	23 20	23 40	23 47		00 04	00 12			
London Bridge ⊖	d								23 01	23 28	23 58
Tulse Hill	d								23 11	23 40	00 10
New Cross Gate ⊖	d										
Norwood Junction	d		23 40								
West Croydon	d		23 45		00 04		00 21	00 31			
Waddon	d		23 47		00 06		00 24	00 33			
Wallington	d		23 51		00 10		00 27	00 37			
Carshalton Beeches	d		23 53		00 12		00 30	00 39			
Mitcham Eastfields	d	23 23		23 46							
Mitcham Junction	d	23 26		23 49							
Hackbridge	d	23 29		23 53							
Carshalton	d	23 32		23 55							
Sutton (Surrey)	a	23 35	23 57	23 59	00 16		00 33	00 43	23 45	00 14	00 43
	d	23 36		00 01							
Belmont	d										
Banstead	d										
Epsom Downs	a										
Cheam	d	23 38		00 03							
Ewell East	d	23 42		00 07							
Epsom	a	23 46		00 11		00 15					
	d			00 11		00 19					
Ashtead	d			00 15		00 23					
Leatherhead	d			00 18		00 26					
Bookham	d					00 31					
Effingham Junction	d					00 36					
Guildford	a					00 56					
Boxhill & Westhumble	d			00 23							
Dorking	a			00 26							
	d			00 26							
Holmwood	d			00s33							
Ockley	d			00s37							
Warnham	d			00s43							
Horsham	a			00 47							

London - Sutton, Epsom, Guildford, Dorking and Horsham

		SN	SN	SW	SN	SW	SN	SN	SN	SN	SW	SN	FC	FC	FC	FC	SN	SW	SN	SN	SW	FC	FC
London Victoria ⊖	d	23p26	23p34		23p59		00 20	00 34		06 23							06 47		06 53	07 06			
London Waterloo ⊖	d			23p42		00 15					06 39							07 09			07 24		
Clapham Junction	d	23p34	23p42	23p51	00 07	00 25	00 27	00 42		06 30	06 48						06 54	07 18	07 00	07 14	07 33		
Balham ⊖	d	23p40	23p47		00 12		00 32	00 47		06 35							07 00		07 05	07 20			
London Bridge ⊖	d												23p28	23p58	06 21							06 45	
Tulse Hill	d												23p40	00 10	06 31	06 46						07 01	07 16
New Cross Gate ⊖	d																						
Norwood Junction	d											07 09								07 39			
West Croydon	d		00 04		00 31			01 04	06 45	06 54		07 15							07 24	07 44			
Waddon	d		00 06		00 33			01 07	06 47	06 56		07 17							07 26	07 46			
Wallington	d		00 10		00 37			01 10	06 51	07 00		07 21							07 30	07 50			
Carshalton Beeches	d		00 12		00 39			01 13	06 53	07 02		07 23							07 32	07 52			
Mitcham Eastfields	d	23p46					00 38									06 54	07 06						07 24
Mitcham Junction	d	23p49					00 41									06 57	07 09						07 27
Hackbridge	d	23p53					00 45									07 00	07 13						07 30
Carshalton	d	23p55					00 47									07 03	07 15						07 33
Sutton (Surrey)	a	23p59	00 16		00 43		00 51	01 16	06 57	07 06		07 27	00 14	00 43	07 05	07 06	07 19		07 39	07 56		07 35	07 36
	d	00 01							06 57	07 07							07 19		07 40				
Belmont	d									07 10													
Banstead	d									07 14													
Epsom Downs	a									07 17													
Cheam	d	00 03							07 00								07 22		07 42				
Ewell East	d	00 07							07 03								07 25		07 46				
Epsom	a	00 11		00 15		00 50			07 07		07 16						07 29	07 46	07 52		07 57		
	d	00 11		00 19					07 08		07 17						07 30	07 47			07 58		
Ashtead	d	00 15		00 23					07 12		07 21						07 34	07 51			08 02		
Leatherhead	d	00 18		00 26					07 15		07 24						07 37	07 54			08 05		
Bookham	d			00 31							07 29							07 59					
Effingham Junction	d			00 36							07 33							08 03					
Guildford	a			00 53							07 50							08 20					
Boxhill & Westhumble	d	00 23															07 42						
Dorking	a	00 26							07 21								07 44				08 11		
	d	00 26																					
Holmwood	d	00s33																					
Ockley	d	00s37																					
Warnham	d	00s43																					
Horsham	a	00 47																					

		SN	SN	SN	SN	SN	SW	SW	FC	FC	SN	SN	SN	SN	SN	SW	SW	FC	FC	SN	SN	SN	SN
London Victoria ⊖	d	07 17	07 23	07 31	07 33	07 36					07 47	07 53	08 01	08 03	08 06					08 17	08 23	08 31	08 33
London Waterloo ⊖	d						07 39	07 54								08 09	08 24						
Clapham Junction	d	07 24	07 30	07 38	07 41	07 44	07 48	08 03			07 54	08 00	08 08	08 11	08 14	08 18	08 33			08 24	08 30	08 38	08 41
Balham ⊖	d	07 30	07 35		07 46	07 50					08 00	08 05		08 16	08 20					08 30	08 35		08 46
London Bridge ⊖	d								07 15									07 45					
Tulse Hill	d								07 31	07 46								08 01	08 16				
New Cross Gate ⊖	d																						
Norwood Junction	d					08 09									08 39								
West Croydon	d		07 54		08 04	08 14						08 24		08 34	08 44						08 54		09 04
Waddon	d		07 56		08 06	08 16						08 26		08 36	08 46						08 56		09 06
Wallington	d		08 00		08 10	08 20						08 30		08 40	08 50						09 00		09 10
Carshalton Beeches	d		08 02		08 12	08 22						08 32		08 42	08 52						09 02		09 12
Mitcham Eastfields	d	07 36								07 54	08 06								08 24	08 36			
Mitcham Junction	d	07 39								07 57	08 09								08 27	08 39			
Hackbridge	d	07 43								08 00	08 13								08 30	08 43			
Carshalton	d	07 45								08 03	08 15								08 33	08 45			
Sutton (Surrey)	a	07 49	08 06	07 58	08 16	08 26			08 05	08 06	08 19	08 39	08 28	08 46	08 56			08 35	08 36	08 49	09 06	08 58	09 16
	d	07 49	08 07	07 59							08 19	08 40	08 29							08 49	09 07	08 59	
Belmont	d		08 10																		09 10		
Banstead	d		08 14																		09 14		
Epsom Downs	a		08 17																		09 17		
Cheam	d	07 52		08 01							08 22	08 42	08 31							08 52		09 01	
Ewell East	d	07 55		08 05							08 25	08 46								08 55		09 05	
Epsom	a	07 59		08 09			08 16	08 27			08 29	08 52	08 37			08 46	08 57			08 59		09 09	
	d			08 09			08 17	08 28					08 37			08 47	08 58					09 09	
Ashtead	d			08 13			08 21	08 32					08 41			08 51	09 02					09 13	
Leatherhead	d			08 16			08 24	08 35					08 44			08 54	09 05					09 16	
Bookham	d						08 29									08 59							
Effingham Junction	d						08 33									09 03							
Guildford	a						08 50									09 20							
Boxhill & Westhumble	d			08 21																		09 21	
Dorking	a			08 24				08 41					08 50				09 11					09 24	
	d			08 24																		09 24	
Holmwood	d			08 32																		09 32	
Ockley	d			08 36																		09 36	
Warnham	d			08 41																		09 41	
Horsham	a			08 45																		09 45	

Table 182

London - Sutton, Epsom, Guildford, Dorking and Horsham

		SN	SW	SW	FC	FC	SN	SN	SN	SN	SN	SW	SW	FC	FC	SN	SN	SN	SN	SN	SW	SW
London Victoria 15 ⊖	d	08 36					08 47	08 53	09 01	09 03	09 06					09 17	09 23	09 31	09 33	09 36		
London Waterloo 15 ⊖	d		08 39	08 54								09 09	09 24								09 39	09 54
Clapham Junction 10	d	08 44	08 48	09 03			08 54	09 00	09 08	09 11	09 14	09 18	09 33			09 24	09 30	09 38	09 41	09 44	09 48	10 03
Balham 4 ⊖	d	08 50					09 00	09 05		09 16	09 20					09 30	09 35		09 46	09 50		
London Bridge 4 ⊖	d				08 15									08 45								
Tulse Hill 3	d				08 31	08 46								09 01	09 16							
New Cross Gate 4 ⊖	d																					
Norwood Junction 2	d	09 09									09 39									10 09		
West Croydon 4	d	09 14						09 24		09 34	09 44						09 54		10 04	10 14		
Waddon	d	09 16						09 26		09 36	09 46						09 56		10 06	10 16		
Wallington	d	09 20						09 30		09 40	09 50						10 00		10 10	10 20		
Carshalton Beeches	d	09 22						09 32		09 42	09 52						10 02		10 12	10 22		
Mitcham Eastfields	d					08 54	09 06								09 24	09 36						
Mitcham Junction	d					08 57	09 09								09 27	09 39						
Hackbridge	d					09 00	09 13								09 30	09 43						
Carshalton	d					09 03	09 15								09 33	09 45						
Sutton (Surrey) 4	a	09 26			09 05	09 06	09 19	09 39	09 28	09 46	09 56			09 35	09 36	09 49	10 06	09 58	10 16	10 26		
	d						09 19	09 40	09 29							09 49	10 07	09 59				
Belmont	d																10 10					
Banstead	d																10 14					
Epsom Downs	a																10 17					
Cheam	d						09 22	09 42	09 31							09 52		10 01				
Ewell East	d						09 25	09 46								09 55		10 05				
Epsom 3	a		09 16	09 27			09 29	09 52	09 37			09 46	09 57			09 59		10 09			10 16	10 27
	d		09 17	09 28					09 37			09 47	09 58					10 09			10 17	10 28
Ashtead	d		09 21	09 32					09 41			09 51	10 02					10 13			10 21	10 32
Leatherhead	d		09 24	09 35					09 44			09 54	10 05					10 16			10 24	10 35
Bookham	d		09 29									09 59									10 29	
Effingham Junction 6	d		09 33									10 03									10 33	
Guildford	a		09 50									10 20									10 50	
Boxhill & Westhumble	d																	10 21				
Dorking 4	a			09 41					09 50				10 11					10 24				10 41
	d																	10 24				
Holmwood	d																	10 32				
Ockley	d																	10 36				
Warnham	d																	10 41				
Horsham 4	a																	10 45				

		FC	FC	SN	SN	SN	SN	SN	SW	SW	FC	FC	SN	SN	SN	SN	SN	SW	SW	FC	FC	SN	SN
London Victoria 15 ⊖	d			09 47	09 53	10 01	10 03	10 06					10 17	10 23	10 31	10 33	10 36					10 47	10 53
London Waterloo 15 ⊖	d								10 09	10 24								10 39	10 54				
Clapham Junction 10	d			09 54	10 00	10 08	10 11	10 14	10 18	10 33			10 24	10 30	10 38	10 41	10 44	10 48	11 03			10 54	11 00
Balham 4 ⊖	d			10 00	10 05		10 16	10 20					10 30	10 35		10 46	10 50					11 00	11 05
London Bridge 4 ⊖	d	09 15									09 45									10 15			
Tulse Hill 3	d	09 31	09 46								10 01	10 16								10 31	10 46		
New Cross Gate 4 ⊖	d																						
Norwood Junction 2	d							10 39									11 09						
West Croydon 4	d				10 24		10 34	10 44						10 54		11 04	11 14						11 24
Waddon	d				10 26		10 36	10 46						10 56		11 06	11 16						11 26
Wallington	d				10 30		10 40	10 50						11 00		11 10	11 20						11 30
Carshalton Beeches	d				10 32		10 42	10 52						11 02		11 12	11 22						11 32
Mitcham Eastfields	d		09 54	10 06								10 24	10 36								10 54	11 08	
Mitcham Junction	d		09 57	10 09								10 27	10 39								10 57	11 11	
Hackbridge	d		10 00	10 13								10 30	10 43								11 00	11 15	
Carshalton	d		10 03	10 15								10 33	10 45								11 03	11 17	
Sutton (Surrey) 4	a	10 05	10 06	10 19	10 39	10 28	10 46	10 56			10 35	10 36	10 49	11 06	10 58	11 16	11 26			11 05	11 06	11 21	11 39
	d			10 19	10 40	10 29							10 49	11 07	10 59							11 21	11 40
Belmont	d													11 10									
Banstead	d													11 14									
Epsom Downs	a													11 17									
Cheam	d			10 22	10 42	10 31							10 52		11 01							11 24	11 42
Ewell East	d			10 25	10 46								10 55		11 05							11 27	11 46
Epsom 3	a			10 29	10 52	10 37			10 46	10 57			10 59		11 09			11 16	11 27			11 31	11 52
	d					10 37			10 47	10 58					11 09			11 17	11 28				
Ashtead	d					10 41			10 51	11 02					11 13			11 21	11 32				
Leatherhead	d					10 44			10 54	11 05					11 16			11 24	11 35				
Bookham	d								10 59									11 29					
Effingham Junction 6	d								11 03									11 33					
Guildford	a								11 20									11 50					
Boxhill & Westhumble	d														11 21								
Dorking 4	a					10 50				11 11					11 24				11 41				
	d														11 24								
Holmwood	d														11 32								
Ockley	d														11 36								
Warnham	d														11 41								
Horsham 4	a														11 45								

Table 182

London - Sutton, Epsom, Guildford, Dorking and Horsham

		SN	SN	SN	SW	SW	FC	FC	SN	SN	SN	SN	SN	SW	SW	FC	FC	SN	SN	SN	SN	SN
London Victoria 15 ⊖	d	11 01	11 03	11 06					11 17	11 23	11 31	11 33	11 36					11 47	11 53	12 01	12 03	12 06
London Waterloo 15 ⊖	d				11 09	11 24								11 39	11 54							
Clapham Junction 10	d	11 08	11 11	11 14	11 18	11 33			11 24	11 30	11 38	11 41	11 44	11 48	12 03			11 54	12 00	12 08	12 11	12 14
Balham 4 ⊖	d		11 16	11 20					11 30	11 35		11 46	11 50					12 00	12 05		12 16	12 20
London Bridge 4 ⊖	d						10 45									11 15						
Tulse Hill 3	d						11 01	11 16								11 31	11 46					
New Cross Gate 4 ⊖	d																					
Norwood Junction 2	d			11 39									12 09									12 39
West Croydon 4	d		11 34	11 44						11 54		12 04	12 14						12 24		12 34	12 44
Waddon	d		11 36	11 46						11 56		12 06	12 16						12 26		12 36	12 46
Wallington	d		11 40	11 50						12 00		12 10	12 20						12 30		12 40	12 50
Carshalton Beeches	d		11 42	11 52						12 02		12 12	12 22						12 32		12 42	12 52
Mitcham Eastfields	d							11 24	11 36								11 54	12 06				
Mitcham Junction	d							11 27	11 39								11 57	12 09				
Hackbridge	d							11 30	11 43								12 00	12 13				
Carshalton	d							11 33	11 45								12 03	12 15				
Sutton (Surrey) 4	a	11 28	11 46	11 56			11 35	11 36	11 49	12 06	11 58	12 16	12 26			12 05	12 06	12 19	12 39	12 28	12 46	12 56
	d	11 29							11 49	12 07	11 59							12 19	12 40	12 29		
Belmont	d									12 10												
Banstead	d									12 14												
Epsom Downs	a									12 17												
Cheam	d	11 31							11 52		12 01							12 22	12 42	12 31		
Ewell East	d								11 55		12 05							12 25	12 46			
Epsom 3	a	11 37			11 46	11 57			11 59		12 09			12 16	12 27			12 29	12 52	12 37		
	d	11 37			11 47	11 58					12 09			12 17	12 28					12 37		
Ashtead	d	11 41			11 51	12 02					12 13			12 21	12 32					12 41		
Leatherhead	d	11 44			11 54	12 05					12 16			12 24	12 35					12 44		
Bookham	d				11 59									12 29								
Effingham Junction 6	d				12 03									12 33								
Guildford	a				12 20									12 50								
Boxhill & Westhumble	d										12 21											
Dorking 4	a	11 50				12 11					12 24				12 41					12 50		
	d										12 24											
Holmwood	d										12 32											
Ockley	d										12 36											
Warnham	d										12 41											
Horsham 4	a										12 45											

		SW	SW	FC	FC	SN	SN	SN	SN	SN	SW	SW	FC	FC	SN	SN	SN	SN	SN	SW	SW	FC	FC
London Victoria 15 ⊖	d					12 17	12 23	12 31	12 33	12 36					12 47	12 53	13 01	13 03	13 06				
London Waterloo 15 ⊖	d	12 09	12 24								12 39	12 54								13 09	13 24		
Clapham Junction 10	d	12 18	12 33			12 24	12 30	12 38	12 41	12 44	12 48	13 03			12 54	13 00	13 08	13 11	13 14	13 18	13 33		
Balham 4 ⊖	d					12 30	12 35		12 46	12 50					13 00	13 05		13 16	13 20				
London Bridge 4 ⊖	d			11 45									12 15									12 45	
Tulse Hill 3	d			12 01	12 16								12 31	12 46								13 01	13 16
New Cross Gate 4 ⊖	d																						
Norwood Junction 2	d									13 09									13 39				
West Croydon 4	d						12 54		13 04	13 14						13 24		13 34	13 44				
Waddon	d						12 56		13 06	13 16						13 26		13 36	13 46				
Wallington	d						13 00		13 10	13 20						13 30		13 40	13 50				
Carshalton Beeches	d						13 02		13 12	13 22						13 32		13 42	13 52				
Mitcham Eastfields	d				12 24	12 36								12 54	13 06								13 24
Mitcham Junction	d				12 27	12 39								12 57	13 09								13 27
Hackbridge	d				12 30	12 43								13 00	13 13								13 30
Carshalton	d				12 33	12 45								13 03	13 15								13 33
Sutton (Surrey) 4	a			12 35	12 36	12 49	13 06	12 58	13 16	13 26			13 05	13 06	13 19	13 39	13 28	13 46	13 56			13 35	13 36
	d					12 49	13 07	12 59							13 19	13 40	13 29						
Belmont	d						13 10																
Banstead	d						13 14																
Epsom Downs	a						13 17																
Cheam	d					12 52		13 01							13 22	13 42	13 31						
Ewell East	d					12 55		13 05							13 25	13 46							
Epsom 3	a	12 46	12 57			12 59		13 09			13 16	13 27			13 29	13 52	13 37			13 46	13 57		
	d	12 47	12 58					13 09			13 17	13 28					13 37			13 47	13 58		
Ashtead	d	12 51	13 02					13 13			13 21	13 32					13 41			13 51	14 02		
Leatherhead	d	12 54	13 05					13 16			13 24	13 35					13 44			13 54	14 05		
Bookham	d	12 59									13 29									13 59			
Effingham Junction 6	d	13 03									13 33									14 03			
Guildford	a	13 20									13 50									14 20			
Boxhill & Westhumble	d							13 21															
Dorking 4	a		13 11					13 24				13 41					13 50				14 11		
	d							13 24															
Holmwood	d							13 32															
Ockley	d							13 36															
Warnham	d							13 41															
Horsham 4	a							13 45															

London - Sutton, Epsom, Guildford, Dorking and Horsham

		SN	SN	SN	SN	SN	SW	SW	FC	FC	SN	SN	SN	SN	SN	SW	SW	FC	FC	SN	SN	SN	SN
London Victoria 15 ⊖	d	13 17	13 23	13 31	13 33	13 36					13 47	13 53	14 01	14 03	14 06					14 17	14 23	14 31	14 33
London Waterloo 15 ⊖	d						13 39	13 54								14 09	14 24						
Clapham Junction 10	d	13 24	13 30	13 38	13 41	13 44	13 48	14 03			13 54	14 00	14 08	14 11	14 14	14 18	14 33			14 24	14 30	14 38	14 41
Balham 4 ⊖	d	13 30	13 35		13 46	13 50					14 00	14 05		14 16	14 20					14 30	14 35		14 46
London Bridge 4 ⊖	d								13 15									13 45					
Tulse Hill 3	d								13 31	13 46								14 01	14 16				
New Cross Gate 4 ⊖	d																						
Norwood Junction 2	d					14 09									14 39								
West Croydon 4	d		13 54		14 04	14 14						14 24		14 34	14 44						14 54		15 04
Waddon	d		13 56		14 06	14 16						14 26		14 36	14 46						14 56		15 06
Wallington	d		14 00		14 10	14 20						14 30		14 40	14 50						15 00		15 10
Carshalton Beeches	d		14 02		14 12	14 22						14 32		14 42	14 52						15 02		15 12
Mitcham Eastfields	d	13 36								13 54	14 06								14 24	14 36			
Mitcham Junction	d	13 39								13 57	14 09								14 27	14 39			
Hackbridge	d	13 43								14 00	14 13								14 30	14 43			
Carshalton	d	13 45								14 03	14 15								14 33	14 45			
Sutton (Surrey) 4	a	13 49	14 06	13 58	14 16	14 26			14 05	14 06	14 19	14 39	14 28	14 46	14 56			14 35	14 36	14 49	15 06	14 58	15 16
	d	13 49	14 07	13 59							14 19	14 40	14 29							14 49	15 07	14 59	
Belmont	d		14 10																		15 10		
Banstead	d		14 14																		15 14		
Epsom Downs	a		14 17																		15 17		
Cheam	d	13 52		14 01							14 22	14 42	14 31							14 52		15 01	
Ewell East	d	13 55		14 05							14 25	14 46								14 55		15 05	
Epsom 3	a	13 59		14 09			14 16	14 27			14 29	14 52	14 37			14 46	14 57			14 59		15 09	
	d			14 09			14 17	14 28					14 37			14 47	14 58					15 09	
Ashtead	d			14 13			14 21	14 32					14 41			14 51	15 02					15 13	
Leatherhead	d			14 16			14 24	14 35					14 44			14 54	15 05					15 16	
Bookham	d						14 29									14 59							
Effingham Junction 6	d						14 33									15 03							
Guildford	a						14 50									15 20							
Boxhill & Westhumble	d			14 21																		15 21	
Dorking 4	a			14 24				14 41					14 50				15 11					15 24	
	d			14 24																		15 24	
Holmwood	d			14 32																		15 32	
Ockley	d			14 36																		15 36	
Warnham	d			14 41																		15 41	
Horsham 4	a			14 45																		15 45	

		SN	SW	SW	FC	FC	SN	SN	SN	SN	SN	SW	SW	FC	FC	SN	SN	SN	SN	SN	SW	SW
London Victoria 15 ⊖	d	14 36					14 47	14 53	15 01	15 03	15 06					15 17	15 23	15 31	15 33	15 36		
London Waterloo 15 ⊖	d		14 39	14 54								15 09	15 24								15 39	15 54
Clapham Junction 10	d	14 44	14 48	15 03			14 54	15 00	15 08	15 11	15 14	15 18	15 33			15 24	15 30	15 38	15 41	15 44	15 48	16 03
Balham 4 ⊖	d	14 50					15 00	15 05		15 16	15 20					15 30	15 35		15 46	15 50		
London Bridge 4 ⊖	d				14 15									14 45								
Tulse Hill 3	d				14 31	14 46								15 01	15 16							
New Cross Gate 4 ⊖	d																					
Norwood Junction 2	d	15 09									15 39									16 09		
West Croydon 4	d	15 14						15 24		15 34	15 44						15 54		16 04	16 14		
Waddon	d	15 16						15 26		15 36	15 46						15 56		16 06	16 16		
Wallington	d	15 20						15 30		15 40	15 50						16 00		16 10	16 20		
Carshalton Beeches	d	15 22						15 32		15 42	15 52						16 02		16 12	16 22		
Mitcham Eastfields	d					14 54	15 06								15 24	15 36						
Mitcham Junction	d					14 57	15 09								15 27	15 39						
Hackbridge	d					15 00	15 13								15 30	15 43						
Carshalton	d					15 03	15 15								15 33	15 45						
Sutton (Surrey) 4	a	15 26			15 05	15 06	15 19	15 39	15 28	15 46	15 56			15 35	15 36	15 49	16 06	15 58	16 16	16 26		
	d						15 19	15 40	15 29							15 49	16 07	15 59				
Belmont	d																16 10					
Banstead	d																16 14					
Epsom Downs	a																16 17					
Cheam	d						15 22	15 42	15 31							15 52		16 01				
Ewell East	d						15 25	15 46								15 55		16 05				
Epsom 3	a		15 16	15 27			15 29	15 52	15 37			15 46	15 57			15 59		16 09			16 16	16 27
	d		15 17	15 28					15 37			15 47	15 58					16 09			16 17	16 28
Ashtead	d		15 21	15 32					15 41			15 51	16 02					16 13			16 21	16 32
Leatherhead	d		15 24	15 35					15 44			15 54	16 05					16 16			16 24	16 35
Bookham	d		15 29									15 59									16 29	
Effingham Junction 6	d		15 33									16 03									16 33	
Guildford	a		15 50									16 20									16 50	
Boxhill & Westhumble	d																	16 21				
Dorking 4	a			15 41					15 50				16 11					16 24				16 41
	d																	16 24				
Holmwood	d																	16 32				
Ockley	d																	16 36				
Warnham	d																	16 41				
Horsham 4	a																	16 45				

London - Sutton, Epsom, Guildford, Dorking and Horsham

		FC	FC	SN	SN	SN	SN	SN	SW	SW	FC	FC	SN	SN	SN	SN	SN	SW	SW	FC	FC	SN	SN
London Victoria 15 ⊖	d			15 47	15 53	16 01	16 03	16 06					16 17	16 23	16 31	16 33	16 36					16 47	16 53
London Waterloo 15 ⊖	d								16 09	16 24								16 39	16 54				
Clapham Junction 10	d			15 54	16 00	16 08	16 11	16 14	16 18	16 33			16 24	16 30	16 38	16 41	16 44	16 48	17 03			16 54	17 00
Balham 4 ⊖	d			16 00	16 05		16 16	16 20					16 30	16 35		16 46	16 50					17 00	17 05
London Bridge 4 ⊖	d	15 15									15 45									16 15			
Tulse Hill 3	d	15 31	15 46								16 01	16 16								16 31	16 46		
New Cross Gate 4 ⊖	d																						
Norwood Junction 2	d							16 39									17 09						
West Croydon 4	d				16 24		16 34	16 44						16 54		17 04	17 14						17 24
Waddon	d				16 26		16 36	16 46						16 56		17 06	17 16						17 26
Wallington	d				16 30		16 40	16 50						17 00		17 10	17 20						17 30
Carshalton Beeches	d				16 32		16 42	16 52						17 02		17 12	17 22						17 32
Mitcham Eastfields	d		15 54	16 06								16 24	16 36								16 54	17 06	
Mitcham Junction	d		15 57	16 09								16 27	16 39								16 57	17 09	
Hackbridge	d		16 00	16 13								16 30	16 43								17 00	17 13	
Carshalton	d		16 03	16 15								16 33	16 45								17 03	17 15	
Sutton (Surrey) 4	a	16 05	16 06	16 19	16 39	16 28	16 46	16 56			16 35	16 36	16 49	17 06	16 58	17 16	17 26			17 05	17 06	17 19	17 39
	d			16 19	16 40	16 29							16 49	17 07	16 59							17 19	17 40
Belmont	d													17 10									
Banstead	d													17 14									
Epsom Downs	a													17 17									
Cheam	d			16 22	16 42	16 31							16 52		17 01							17 22	17 42
Ewell East	d			16 25	16 46								16 55		17 05							17 25	17 46
Epsom 3	a			16 29	16 52	16 37			16 46	16 57			16 59		17 09			17 16	17 27			17 29	17 52
	d					16 37			16 47	16 58					17 09			17 17	17 28				
Ashtead	d					16 41			16 51	17 02					17 13			17 21	17 32				
Leatherhead	d					16 44			16 54	17 05					17 16			17 24	17 35				
Bookham	d								16 59									17 29					
Effingham Junction 6	d								17 03									17 33					
Guildford	a								17 20									17 50					
Boxhill & Westhumble	d														17 21								
Dorking 4	a					16 50				17 11					17 24				17 41				
	d														17 24								
Holmwood	d														17 32								
Ockley	d														17 36								
Warnham	d														17 41								
Horsham 4	a														17 45								

		SN	SN	SN	SW	SW	FC	FC	SN	SN	SN	SN	SN	SW	SW	FC	FC	SN	SN	SN	SN	SN
London Victoria 15 ⊖	d	17 01	17 03	17 06					17 17	17 23	17 31	17 33	17 36					17 47	17 53	18 01	18 03	18 06
London Waterloo 15 ⊖	d				17 09	17 24								17 39	17 54							
Clapham Junction 10	d	17 08	17 11	17 14	17 18	17 33			17 24	17 30	17 38	17 41	17 44	17 48	18 03			17 54	18 00	18 08	18 11	18 14
Balham 4 ⊖	d		17 16	17 20					17 30	17 35		17 46	17 50					18 00	18 05		18 16	18 20
London Bridge 4 ⊖	d						16 45									17 15						
Tulse Hill 3	d						17 01	17 16								17 31	17 46					
New Cross Gate 4 ⊖	d																					
Norwood Junction 2	d			17 39									18 09									18 39
West Croydon 4	d		17 34	17 44						17 54		18 04	18 14						18 24		18 34	18 44
Waddon	d		17 36	17 46						17 56		18 06	18 16						18 26		18 36	18 46
Wallington	d		17 40	17 50						18 00		18 10	18 20						18 30		18 40	18 50
Carshalton Beeches	d		17 42	17 52						18 02		18 12	18 22						18 32		18 42	18 52
Mitcham Eastfields	d							17 24	17 36								17 54	18 06				
Mitcham Junction	d							17 27	17 39								17 57	18 09				
Hackbridge	d							17 30	17 43								18 00	18 13				
Carshalton	d							17 33	17 45								18 03	18 15				
Sutton (Surrey) 4	a	17 28	17 46	17 56			17 35	17 36	17 49	18 06	17 58	18 16	18 26			18 05	18 06	18 19	18 39	18 28	18 46	18 56
	d	17 29							17 49	18 07	17 59							18 19	18 40	18 29		
Belmont	d									18 10												
Banstead	d									18 14												
Epsom Downs	a									18 17												
Cheam	d	17 31							17 52		18 01							18 22	18 42	18 31		
Ewell East	d								17 55		18 05							18 25	18 46			
Epsom 3	a	17 37			17 46	17 57			17 59		18 09			18 16	18 27			18 29	18 52	18 37		
	d	17 37			17 47	17 58					18 09			18 17	18 28					18 37		
Ashtead	d	17 41			17 51	18 02					18 13			18 21	18 32					18 41		
Leatherhead	d	17 44			17 54	18 05					18 16			18 24	18 35					18 44		
Bookham	d				17 59									18 29								
Effingham Junction 6	d				18 03									18 33								
Guildford	a				18 20									18 50								
Boxhill & Westhumble	d										18 21									18 49		
Dorking 4	a	17 50				18 11					18 24				18 41					18 52		
	d										18 24											
Holmwood	d										18 32											
Ockley	d										18 36											
Warnham	d										18 41											
Horsham 4	a										18 45											

London - Sutton, Epsom, Guildford, Dorking and Horsham

		SW	SW	FC	FC	SN	SN	SN	SN	SN	SW	SW	FC	FC	SN	SN	SN	SN	SN	SW	SW	FC	FC
London Victoria ⊖	d					18 17	18 23	18 31	18 33	18 36					18 47	18 53	19 01	19 03	19 06				
London Waterloo ⊖	d	18 09	18 24								18 39	18 54								19 09	19 24		
Clapham Junction	d	18 18	18 33			18 24	18 30	18 38	18 41	18 44	18 48	19 03			18 54	19 00	19 08	19 11	19 14	19 18	19 33		
Balham ⊖	d					18 30	18 35		18 46	18 50					19 00	19 05		19 16	19 20				
London Bridge ⊖	d			17 45									18 15									18 45	
Tulse Hill	d			18 01	18 16								18 31	18 46								19 01	19 16
New Cross Gate ⊖	d																						
Norwood Junction	d									19 09									19 39				
West Croydon	d						18 54		19 04	19 14						19 24		19 34	19 44				
Waddon	d						18 56		19 06	19 16						19 26		19 36	19 46				
Wallington	d						19 00		19 10	19 20						19 30		19 40	19 50				
Carshalton Beeches	d						19 02		19 12	19 22						19 32		19 42	19 52				
Mitcham Eastfields	d				18 24	18 36								18 54	19 06								19 24
Mitcham Junction	d				18 27	18 39								18 57	19 09								19 27
Hackbridge	d				18 30	18 43								19 00	19 13								19 30
Carshalton	d				18 33	18 45								19 03	19 15								19 33
Sutton (Surrey)	a			18 35	18 36	18 49	19 06	18 58	19 16	19 26			19 05	19 06	19 19	19 39	19 28	19 46	19 56			19 39	19 36
	d					18 49	19 07	18 59							19 19	19 40	19 29						
Belmont	d						19 10																
Banstead	d						19 14																
Epsom Downs	a						19 17																
Cheam	d					18 52		19 01							19 22	19 42	19 31						
Ewell East	d					18 55		19 05							19 25	19 46							
Epsom	a	18 46	18 57			18 59		19 09			19 16	19 27			19 29	19 52	19 37			19 46	19 57		
	d	18 47	18 58					19 09			19 17	19 28					19 37			19 47	19 58		
Ashtead	d	18 51	19 02					19 13			19 21	19 32					19 41			19 51	20 02		
Leatherhead	d	18 54	19 05					19 16			19 24	19 35					19 44			19 54	20 05		
Bookham	d	18 59									19 29									19 59			
Effingham Junction	d	19 03									19 33									20 03			
Guildford	a	19 20									19 50									20 20			
Boxhill & Westhumble	d																19 49						
Dorking	a		19 11					19 22				19 41					19 52				20 11		
	d																						
Holmwood	d																						
Ockley	d																						
Warnham	d																						
Horsham	a																						

		SN	SN	SN	SN	SN	SW	SW	FC	FC	SN	SN	SN	SN	SN	SW	SW	SN	SN	SN	SN	SN	SW
London Victoria ⊖	d	19 17	19 23	19 31	19 33	19 36					19 47	19 53	20 01	20 03	20 06			20 17	20 23	20 31	20 33	20 36	
London Waterloo ⊖	d						19 39	19 54								20 09	20 24						20 39
Clapham Junction	d	19 24	19 30	19 38	19 41	19 44	19 48	20 03			19 54	20 00	20 08	20 11	20 14	20 18	20 33	20 24	20 30	20 38	20 41	20 44	20 48
Balham ⊖	d	19 30	19 35		19 46	19 50					20 00	20 05		20 16	20 20			20 30	20 35		20 46	20 50	
London Bridge ⊖	d								19 15														
Tulse Hill	d								19 31	19 46													
New Cross Gate ⊖	d																						
Norwood Junction	d					20 09									20 39							21 09	
West Croydon	d		19 54		20 04	20 15						20 25		20 34	20 45				20 55		21 04	21 15	
Waddon	d		19 56		20 06	20 17						20 27		20 36	20 47				20 57		21 06	21 17	
Wallington	d		20 00		20 10	20 21						20 31		20 40	20 51				21 01		21 10	21 21	
Carshalton Beeches	d		20 02		20 12	20 23						20 33		20 42	20 53				21 03		21 12	21 23	
Mitcham Eastfields	d	19 36								19 55	20 06							20 36					
Mitcham Junction	d	19 39								19 58	20 09							20 39					
Hackbridge	d	19 43								20 01	20 13							20 43					
Carshalton	d	19 45								20 04	20 15							20 45					
Sutton (Surrey)	a	19 49	20 06	19 58	20 16	20 27			20 05	20 07	20 19	20 39	20 28	20 46	20 57			20 49	21 07	20 58	21 16	21 27	
	d	19 49	20 07	19 59							20 19	20 40	20 29					20 49	21 08	20 59			
Belmont	d		20 10																21 11				
Banstead	d		20 14																21 15				
Epsom Downs	a		20 17																21 18				
Cheam	d	19 52		20 01							20 22	20 42	20 31					20 52		21 01			
Ewell East	d	19 55		20 05							20 25	20 46						20 55		21 05			
Epsom	a	19 59		20 09			20 16	20 27			20 29	20 52	20 37			20 46	20 57	20 59		21 09			21 16
	d			20 09			20 17						20 37			20 47				21 09			21 17
Ashtead	d			20 13			20 21						20 41			20 51				21 13			21 21
Leatherhead	d			20 16			20 24						20 44			20 54				21 16			21 24
Bookham	d						20 29																21 29
Effingham Junction	d						20 33																21 33
Guildford	a						20 50																21 50
Boxhill & Westhumble	d												20 49										
Dorking	a			20 22									20 52			21 00				21 22			
	d																						
Holmwood	d																						
Ockley	d																						
Warnham	d																						
Horsham	a																						

London - Sutton, Epsom, Guildford, Dorking and Horsham

		SW	SN	SN	SN	SN	SN	SW	SW	SN	SN	SN	SN	SN	SW	SW	SN	SN	SN	SN	SN	SW
London Victoria ⊖	d		20 47	20 53	21 01	21 03	21 06			21 17	21 23	21 31	21 33	21 36			21 47	21 53	22 01	22 03	22 06	
London Waterloo ⊖	d	20 54						21 09	21 24						21 39	21 54						22 09
Clapham Junction	d	21 03	20 54	21 00	21 08	21 11	21 14	21 18	21 33	21 24	21 30	21 38	21 41	21 44	21 48	22 03	21 54	22 00	22 08	22 11	22 14	22 18
Balham ⊖	d		21 00	21 05		21 16	21 20			21 30	21 35		21 46	21 50			22 00	22 05		22 16	22 20	
London Bridge ⊖	d																					
Tulse Hill	d																					
New Cross Gate ⊖	d																					
Norwood Junction	d						21 39							22 09							22 39	
West Croydon	d			21 25		21 34	21 45				21 55		22 04	22 14				22 24		22 34	22 44	
Waddon	d			21 27		21 36	21 47				21 57		22 06	22 16				22 26		22 36	22 46	
Wallington	d			21 31		21 40	21 51				22 01		22 10	22 20				22 30		22 40	22 50	
Carshalton Beeches	d			21 33		21 42	21 53				22 03		22 12	22 22				22 32		22 42	22 52	
Mitcham Eastfields	d		21 06							21 36							22 06					
Mitcham Junction	d		21 09							21 39							22 09					
Hackbridge	d		21 13							21 43							22 13					
Carshalton	d		21 15							21 45							22 15					
Sutton (Surrey)	a		21 19	21 39	21 28	21 46	21 57			21 49	22 07	21 58	22 16	22 26			22 19	22 39	22 28	22 46	22 56	
	d		21 19	21 40	21 29					21 49	22 08	21 59					22 19	22 40	22 29			
Belmont	d										22 11											
Banstead	d										22 15											
Epsom Downs	a										22 18											
Cheam	d		21 22	21 42	21 31					21 52		22 01					22 22	22 42	22 31			
Ewell East	d		21 25	21 46						21 55		22 05					22 25	22 46				
Epsom	a	21 27	21 29	21 52	21 37			21 46	21 57	21 59		22 09			22 16	22 27	22 29	22 52	22 37			22 46
	d				21 37			21 47				22 09			22 17				22 37			22 47
Ashtead	d				21 41			21 51				22 13			22 21				22 41			22 51
Leatherhead	d				21 44			21 54				22 16			22 24				22 44			22 54
Bookham	d														22 29							
Effingham Junction	d														22 33							
Guildford	a														22 50							
Boxhill & Westhumble	d				21 49														22 49			
Dorking	a				21 52			22 00				22 22							22 52			23 00
	d																					
Holmwood	d																					
Ockley	d																					
Warnham	d																					
Horsham	a																					

		SN	SN	SN	SN	SN	SW	SN	SN	SN	SN	SN	SW	SN	SN	SW	SN	FC	FC	FC	FC	FC
London Victoria ⊖	d	22 17	22 23	22 31	22 33	22 36		22 47	22 53	23 01	23 03	23 06		23 26	23 34		23 59					
London Waterloo ⊖	d						22 39						23 09			23 42						
Clapham Junction	d	22 24	22 30	22 38	22 41	22 44	22 48	22 54	23 00	23 08	23 11	23 14	23 18	23 32	23 42	23 51	00 07					
Balham ⊖	d	22 30	22 35		22 46	22 50		23 00	23 05		23 16	23 20		23 37	23 47		00 12					
London Bridge ⊖	d																	19 45	20 15	20 45	21 15	21 45
Tulse Hill	d																	20 01	20 31	21 01	21 31	22 01
New Cross Gate ⊖	d																					
Norwood Junction	d					23 09						23 39										
West Croydon	d		22 54		23 04	23 14			23 24		23 34	23 44			00 04		00 31					
Waddon	d		22 56		23 06	23 16			23 26		23 36	23 46			00 06		00 33					
Wallington	d		23 00		23 10	23 20			23 30		23 40	23 50			00 10		00 37					
Carshalton Beeches	d		23 02		23 12	23 22			23 32		23 42	23 52			00 12		00 39					
Mitcham Eastfields	d	22 36						23 06						23 43								
Mitcham Junction	d	22 39						23 09						23 46								
Hackbridge	d	22 43						23 13						23 50								
Carshalton	d	22 45						23 15						23 52								
Sutton (Surrey)	a	22 49	23 06	22 58	23 16	23 26		23 19	23 39	23 28	23 46	23 56		23 59	00 16		00 43	20 37	21 05	21 37	22 05	22 39
	d	22 49	23 07	22 59		23 33		23 19	23 40	23 29				00 01								
Belmont	d		23 10			23 36																
Banstead	d		23 14			23 40																
Epsom Downs	a		23 17			23 43																
Cheam	d	22 52		23 01				23 22	23 42	23 31				00 03								
Ewell East	d	22 55		23 05				23 25	23 46					00 07								
Epsom	a	22 59		23 09			23 12	23 29	23 52	23 37			23 42	00 11		00 15						
	d			23 09			23 17			23 37			23 47	00 11		00 19						
Ashtead	d			23 13			23 21			23 41			23 51	00 15		00 23						
Leatherhead	d			23 16			23 24			23 44			23 54	00 18		00 26						
Bookham	d						23 29									00 31						
Effingham Junction	d						23 33									00 36						
Guildford	a						23 50									00 53						
Boxhill & Westhumble	d			23 21										00 23								
Dorking	a			23 24						23 50			00 01	00 26								
	d																					
Holmwood	d																					
Ockley	d																					
Warnham	d																					
Horsham	a																					

London - Sutton, Epsom, Guildford, Dorking and Horsham

until 1 October

Station		FC		FC
London Victoria ⊖	d			
London Waterloo ⊖	d			
Clapham Junction	d			
Balham ⊖	d			
London Bridge ⊖	d	22 15		23 45
Tulse Hill	d	22 31		00 01
New Cross Gate ⊖	d			
Norwood Junction	d			
West Croydon	d			
Waddon	d			
Wallington	d			
Carshalton Beeches	d			
Mitcham Eastfields	d			
Mitcham Junction	d			
Hackbridge	d			
Carshalton	d			
Sutton (Surrey)	a	23 05	and every 30 minutes until	00 35
	d			
Belmont	d			
Banstead	d			
Epsom Downs	a			
Cheam	d			
Ewell East	d			
Epsom	a			
	d			
Ashtead	d			
Leatherhead	d			
Bookham	d			
Effingham Junction	d			
Guildford	a			
Boxhill & Westhumble	d			
Dorking	a			
	d			
Holmwood	d			
Ockley	d			
Warnham	d			
Horsham	a			

Saturdays

from 8 October

Station		SN	SN	SW	SN	SW	SN	SN	SN	SN	SW	SN	FC	FC	FC	FC	SN	SW	SN	SN	SW	FC	FC
London Victoria ⊖	d	23p26	23p34		23p59		00 20	00 34		06 23							06 47		06 53	07 06			
London Waterloo ⊖	d			23p42		00 15					06 39							07 09			07 24		
Clapham Junction	d	23p34	23p42	23p51	00 07	00 25	00 27	00 42		06 30	06 48						06 54	07 18	07 00	07 14	07 33		
Balham ⊖	d	23p40	23p47		00 12		00 32	00 47		06 35							07 00		07 05	07 20			
London Bridge ⊖	d												23p28	23p58	06 21							06 45	
Tulse Hill	d												23p40	00 10	06 31	06 46						07 01	07 16
New Cross Gate ⊖	d																						
Norwood Junction	d											07 09								07 39			
West Croydon	d		00 04		00 31			01 04	06 45	06 54		07 15							07 24	07 44			
Waddon	d		00 06		00 33			01 07	06 47	06 56		07 17							07 26	07 46			
Wallington	d		00 10		00 37			01 10	06 51	07 00		07 21							07 30	07 50			
Carshalton Beeches	d		00 12		00 39			01 13	06 53	07 02		07 23							07 32	07 52			
Mitcham Eastfields	d	23p46					00 38									06 54	07 06						07 24
Mitcham Junction	d	23p49					00 41									06 57	07 09						07 27
Hackbridge	d	23p53					00 45									07 00	07 13						07 30
Carshalton	d	23p55					00 47									07 03	07 15						07 33
Sutton (Surrey)	a	23p59	00 16		00 43		00 51	01 16	06 57	07 06		07 27	00 14	00 43	07 05	07 06	07 19		07 39	07 56		07 35	07 36
	d	00 01							06 57	07 07							07 19		07 40				
Belmont	d									07 10													
Banstead	d									07 14													
Epsom Downs	a									07 17													
Cheam	d	00 03							07 00								07 22		07 42				
Ewell East	d	00 07							07 03								07 25		07 46				
Epsom	a	00 11		00 15		00 50			07 07		07 16						07 29	07 46	07 52		07 57		
	d	00 11		00 19					07 08		07 17						07 30	07 47			07 58		
Ashtead	d	00 15		00 23					07 12		07 21						07 34	07 51			08 02		
Leatherhead	d	00 18		00 26					07 15		07 24						07 37	07 54			08 05		
Bookham	d			00 31							07 29							07 59					
Effingham Junction	d			00 36							07 33							08 03					
Guildford	a			00 56							07 53							08 23					
Boxhill & Westhumble	d	00 23															07 42						
Dorking	a	00 26							07 21								07 44				08 13		
	d	00 26																					
Holmwood	d	00s33																					
Ockley	d	00s37																					
Warnham	d	00s43																					
Horsham	a	00 47																					

London - Sutton, Epsom, Guildford, Dorking and Horsham

from 8 October

Station		SN	SN	SN	SN	SN	SW	SW	FC	FC	SN	SN	SN	SN	SN	SW	SW	FC	FC	SN	SN	SN	SN
London Victoria ⊖	d	07 17	07 23	07 31	07 33	07 36					07 47	07 53	08 01	08 03	08 06					08 17	08 23	08 31	08 33
London Waterloo ⊖	d						07 39	07 54								08 09	08 24						
Clapham Junction	d	07 24	07 30	07 38	07 41	07 44	07 48	08 03			07 54	08 00	08 08	08 11	08 14	08 18	08 33			08 24	08 30	08 38	08 41
Balham ⊖	d	07 30	07 35		07 46	07 50					08 00	08 05		08 16	08 20					08 30	08 35		08 46
London Bridge ⊖	d								07 15									07 45					
Tulse Hill	d								07 31	07 46								08 01	08 16				
New Cross Gate ⊖	d																						
Norwood Junction	d					08 09									08 39								
West Croydon	d		07 54		08 04	08 14						08 24		08 34	08 44						08 54		09 04
Waddon	d		07 56		08 06	08 16						08 26		08 36	08 46						08 56		09 06
Wallington	d		08 00		08 10	08 20						08 30		08 40	08 50						09 00		09 10
Carshalton Beeches	d		08 02		08 12	08 22						08 32		08 42	08 52						09 02		09 12
Mitcham Eastfields	d	07 36								07 54	08 06								08 24	08 36			
Mitcham Junction	d	07 39								07 57	08 09								08 27	08 39			
Hackbridge	d	07 43								08 00	08 13								08 30	08 43			
Carshalton	d	07 45								08 03	08 15								08 33	08 45			
Sutton (Surrey)	a	07 49	08 06	07 58	08 16	08 26			08 05	08 06	08 19	08 39	08 28	08 46	08 56			08 35	08 36	08 49	09 06	08 58	09 16
	d	07 49	08 07	07 59							08 19	08 40	08 29							08 49	09 07	08 59	
Belmont	d		08 10																		09 10		
Banstead	d		08 14																		09 14		
Epsom Downs	a		08 17																		09 17		
Cheam	d	07 52		08 01							08 22	08 42	08 31							08 52		09 01	
Ewell East	d	07 55		08 05							08 25	08 46								08 55		09 05	
Epsom	a	07 59		08 09			08 16	08 27			08 29	08 52	08 37			08 46	08 57			08 59		09 09	
	d			08 09			08 17	08 28					08 37			08 47	08 58					09 09	
Ashtead	d			08 13			08 21	08 32					08 41			08 51	09 02					09 13	
Leatherhead	d			08 16			08 24	08 35					08 44			08 54	09 05					09 16	
Bookham	d						08 29									08 59							
Effingham Junction	d						08 33									09 03							
Guildford	a						08 53									09 23							
Boxhill & Westhumble	d			08 21																		09 21	
Dorking	a			08 24				08 43					08 50				09 13					09 24	
	d			08 24																		09 24	
Holmwood	d			08 32																		09 32	
Ockley	d			08 36																		09 36	
Warnham	d			08 41																		09 41	
Horsham	a			08 45																		09 45	

Station		SN	SW	SW	FC	FC	SN	SN	SN	SN	SN	SW	SW	FC	FC	SN	SN	SN	SN	SN	SW	SW
London Victoria ⊖	d	08 36					08 47	08 53	09 01	09 03	09 06					09 17	09 23	09 31	09 33	09 36		
London Waterloo ⊖	d		08 39	08 54								09 09	09 24								09 39	09 54
Clapham Junction	d	08 44	08 48	09 03			08 54	09 00	09 08	09 11	09 14	09 18	09 33			09 24	09 30	09 38	09 41	09 44	09 48	10 03
Balham ⊖	d	08 50					09 00	09 05		09 16	09 20					09 30	09 35		09 46	09 50		
London Bridge ⊖	d				08 15									08 45								
Tulse Hill	d				08 31	08 46								09 01	09 16							
New Cross Gate ⊖	d																					
Norwood Junction	d	09 09									09 39									10 09		
West Croydon	d	09 14						09 24		09 34	09 44						09 54		10 04	10 14		
Waddon	d	09 16						09 26		09 36	09 46						09 56		10 06	10 16		
Wallington	d	09 20						09 30		09 40	09 50						10 00		10 10	10 20		
Carshalton Beeches	d	09 22						09 32		09 42	09 52						10 02		10 12	10 22		
Mitcham Eastfields	d					08 54	09 06								09 24	09 36						
Mitcham Junction	d					08 57	09 09								09 27	09 39						
Hackbridge	d					09 00	09 13								09 30	09 43						
Carshalton	d					09 03	09 15								09 33	09 45						
Sutton (Surrey)	a	09 26			09 05	09 06	09 19	09 39	09 28	09 46	09 56			09 35	09 36	09 49	10 06	09 58	10 16	10 26		
	d						09 19	09 40	09 29							09 49	10 07	09 59				
Belmont	d																10 10					
Banstead	d																10 14					
Epsom Downs	a																10 17					
Cheam	d						09 22	09 42	09 31							09 52		10 01				
Ewell East	d						09 25	09 46								09 55		10 05				
Epsom	a		09 16	09 27			09 29	09 52	09 37			09 46	09 57			09 59		10 09			10 16	10 27
	d		09 17	09 28					09 37			09 47	09 58					10 09			10 17	10 28
Ashtead	d		09 21	09 32					09 41			09 51	10 02					10 13			10 21	10 32
Leatherhead	d		09 24	09 35					09 44			09 54	10 05					10 16			10 24	10 35
Bookham	d		09 29									09 59									10 29	
Effingham Junction	d		09 33									10 03									10 33	
Guildford	a		09 53									10 23									10 53	
Boxhill & Westhumble	d																	10 21				
Dorking	a			09 43					09 50				10 13					10 24				10 43
	d																	10 24				
Holmwood	d																	10 32				
Ockley	d																	10 36				
Warnham	d																	10 41				
Horsham	a																	10 45				

Table 182

Saturdays from 8 October

London - Sutton, Epsom, Guildford, Dorking and Horsham

		FC	FC	SN	SN	SN	SN	SN		SW	SW	FC	FC	SN	SN	SN	SN	SN		SW	SW	FC	FC	SN	SN
London Victoria 15 ⊖	d			09 47	09 53	10 01	10 03	10 06						10 17	10 23	10 31	10 33	10 36						10 47	10 53
London Waterloo 15 ⊖	d									10 09	10 24									10 39	10 54				
Clapham Junction 10	d			09 54	10 00	10 08	10 11	10 14		10 18	10 33			10 24	10 30	10 38	10 41	10 44		10 48	11 03			10 54	11 00
Balham 4 ⊖	d			10 00	10 05		10 16	10 20						10 30	10 35		10 46	10 50						11 00	11 05
London Bridge 4 ⊖	d	09 15										09 45										10 15			
Tulse Hill 3	d	09 31	09 46									10 01	10 16									10 31	10 46		
New Cross Gate 4 ⊖	d																								
Norwood Junction 2	d							10 39										11 09							
West Croydon 4	d				10 24		10 34	10 44							10 54		11 04	11 14							11 24
Waddon	d				10 26		10 36	10 46							10 56		11 06	11 16							11 26
Wallington	d				10 30		10 40	10 50							11 00		11 10	11 20							11 30
Carshalton Beeches	d				10 32		10 42	10 52							11 02		11 12	11 22							11 32
Mitcham Eastfields	d		09 54	10 06									10 24	10 36									10 54	11 08	
Mitcham Junction	d		09 57	10 09									10 27	10 39									10 57	11 11	
Hackbridge	d		10 00	10 13									10 30	10 43									11 00	11 15	
Carshalton	d		10 03	10 15									10 33	10 45									11 03	11 17	
Sutton (Surrey) 4	a	10 05	10 06	10 19	10 39	10 28	10 46	10 56				10 35	10 36	10 49	11 06	10 58	11 16	11 26				11 05	11 06	11 21	11 39
	d			10 19	10 40	10 29								10 49	11 07	10 59								11 21	11 40
Belmont	d														11 10										
Banstead	d														11 14										
Epsom Downs	a														11 17										
Cheam	d			10 22	10 42	10 31								10 52		11 01								11 24	11 42
Ewell East	d			10 25	10 46									10 55		11 05								11 27	11 46
Epsom 3	a			10 29	10 52	10 37				10 46	10 57			10 59		11 09				11 16	11 27			11 31	11 52
	d					10 37				10 47	10 58					11 09				11 17	11 28				
Ashtead	d					10 41				10 51	11 02					11 13				11 21	11 32				
Leatherhead	d					10 44				10 54	11 05					11 16				11 24	11 35				
Bookham	d									10 59										11 29					
Effingham Junction 6	d									11 03										11 33					
Guildford	a									11 23										11 53					
Boxhill & Westhumble	d															11 21									
Dorking 4	a					10 50					11 13					11 24					11 43				
	d															11 24									
Holmwood	d															11 32									
Ockley	d															11 36									
Warnham	d															11 41									
Horsham 4	a															11 45									

		SN	SN	SN		SW	SW	FC	FC	SN	SN	SN	SN	SN		SW	SW	FC	FC	SN	SN	SN	SN	SN
London Victoria 15 ⊖	d	11 01	11 03	11 06						11 17	11 23	11 31	11 33	11 36						11 47	11 53	12 01	12 03	12 06
London Waterloo 15 ⊖	d					11 09	11 24									11 39	11 54							
Clapham Junction 10	d	11 08	11 11	11 14		11 18	11 33			11 24	11 30	11 38	11 41	11 44		11 48	12 03			11 54	12 00	12 08	12 11	12 14
Balham 4 ⊖	d		11 16	11 20						11 30	11 35		11 46	11 50						12 00	12 05		12 16	12 20
London Bridge 4 ⊖	d							10 45										11 15						
Tulse Hill 3	d							11 01	11 16									11 31	11 46					
New Cross Gate 4 ⊖	d																							
Norwood Junction 2	d			11 39										12 09										12 39
West Croydon 4	d		11 34	11 44							11 54		12 04	12 14							12 24		12 34	12 44
Waddon	d		11 36	11 46							11 56		12 06	12 16							12 26		12 36	12 46
Wallington	d		11 40	11 50							12 00		12 10	12 20							12 30		12 40	12 50
Carshalton Beeches	d		11 42	11 52							12 02		12 12	12 22							12 32		12 42	12 52
Mitcham Eastfields	d								11 24	11 36									11 54	12 06				
Mitcham Junction	d								11 27	11 39									11 57	12 09				
Hackbridge	d								11 30	11 43									12 00	12 13				
Carshalton	d								11 33	11 45									12 03	12 15				
Sutton (Surrey) 4	a	11 28	11 46	11 56				11 35	11 36	11 49	12 06	11 58	12 16	12 26				12 05	12 06	12 19	12 39	12 28	12 46	12 56
	d	11 29								11 49	12 07	11 59								12 19	12 40	12 29		
Belmont	d										12 10													
Banstead	d										12 14													
Epsom Downs	a										12 17													
Cheam	d	11 31								11 52		12 01								12 22	12 42	12 31		
Ewell East	d									11 55		12 05								12 25	12 46			
Epsom 3	a	11 37				11 46	11 57			11 59		12 09				12 16	12 27			12 29	12 52	12 37		
	d	11 37				11 47	11 58					12 09				12 17	12 28					12 37		
Ashtead	d	11 41				11 51	12 02					12 13				12 21	12 32					12 41		
Leatherhead	d	11 44				11 54	12 05					12 16				12 24	12 35					12 44		
Bookham	d					11 59										12 29								
Effingham Junction 6	d					12 03										12 33								
Guildford	a					12 23										12 53								
Boxhill & Westhumble	d											12 21												
Dorking 4	a	11 50					12 13					12 24					12 43					12 50		
	d											12 24												
Holmwood	d											12 32												
Ockley	d											12 36												
Warnham	d											12 41												
Horsham 4	a											12 45												

Table 182

Saturdays from 8 October

London - Sutton, Epsom, Guildford, Dorking and Horsham

		SW	SW	FC	FC	SN	SN	SN	SN	SN		SW	SW	FC	FC	SN	SN	SN	SN	SN		SW	SW	FC	FC
London Victoria 15 ⊖	d					12 17	12 23	12 31	12 33	12 36						12 47	12 53	13 01	13 03	13 06					
London Waterloo 15 ⊖	d	12 09	12 24									12 39	12 54									13 09	13 24		
Clapham Junction 10	d	12 18	12 33			12 24	12 30	12 38	12 41	12 44		12 48	13 03			12 54	13 00	13 08	13 11	13 14		13 18	13 33		
Balham 4 ⊖	d					12 30	12 35		12 46	12 50						13 00	13 05		13 16	13 20					
London Bridge 4 ⊖	d			11 45										12 15										12 45	
Tulse Hill 3	d			12 01	12 16									12 31	12 46									13 01	13 16
New Cross Gate 4 ⊖	d																								
Norwood Junction 2	d									13 09										13 39					
West Croydon 4	d						12 54		13 04	13 14							13 24		13 34	13 44					
Waddon	d						12 56		13 06	13 16							13 26		13 36	13 46					
Wallington	d						13 00		13 10	13 20							13 30		13 40	13 50					
Carshalton Beeches	d						13 02		13 12	13 22							13 32		13 42	13 52					
Mitcham Eastfields	d				12 24	12 36									12 54	13 06									13 24
Mitcham Junction	d				12 27	12 39									12 57	13 09									13 27
Hackbridge	d				12 30	12 43									13 00	13 13									13 30
Carshalton	d				12 33	12 45									13 03	13 15									13 33
Sutton (Surrey) 4	a			12 35	12 36	12 49	13 06	12 58	13 16	13 26				13 05	13 06	13 19	13 39	13 28	13 46	13 56				13 35	13 36
	d					12 49	13 07	12 59								13 19	13 40	13 29							
Belmont	d						13 10																		
Banstead	d						13 14																		
Epsom Downs	a						13 17																		
Cheam	d					12 52		13 01								13 22	13 42	13 31							
Ewell East	d					12 55		13 05								13 25	13 46								
Epsom 3	a	12 46	12 57			12 59		13 09				13 16	13 27			13 29	13 52	13 37				13 46	13 57		
	d	12 47	12 58					13 09				13 17	13 28					13 37				13 47	13 58		
Ashtead	d	12 51	13 02					13 13				13 21	13 32					13 41				13 51	14 02		
Leatherhead	d	12 54	13 05					13 16				13 24	13 35					13 44				13 54	14 05		
Bookham	d	12 59										13 29										13 59			
Effingham Junction 6	d	13 03										13 33										14 03			
Guildford	a	13 23										13 53										14 23			
Boxhill & Westhumble	d							13 21																	
Dorking 4	a		13 13					13 24					13 43					13 50					14 13		
	d							13 24																	
Holmwood	d							13 32																	
Ockley	d							13 36																	
Warnham	d							13 41																	
Horsham 4	a							13 45																	

		SN	SN	SN	SN	SN		SW	SW	FC	FC	SN	SN	SN	SN	SN		SW	SW	FC	FC	SN	SN	SN	SN
London Victoria 15 ⊖	d	13 17	13 23	13 31	13 33	13 36						13 47	13 53	14 01	14 03	14 06						14 17	14 23	14 31	14 33
London Waterloo 15 ⊖	d							13 39	13 54									14 09	14 24						
Clapham Junction 10	d	13 24	13 30	13 38	13 41	13 44		13 48	14 03			13 54	14 00	14 08	14 11	14 14		14 18	14 33			14 24	14 30	14 38	14 41
Balham 4 ⊖	d	13 30	13 35		13 46	13 50						14 00	14 05		14 16	14 20						14 30	14 35		14 46
London Bridge 4 ⊖	d									13 15										13 45					
Tulse Hill 3	d									13 31	13 46									14 01	14 16				
New Cross Gate 4 ⊖	d																								
Norwood Junction 2	d					14 09										14 39									
West Croydon 4	d		13 54		14 04	14 14							14 24		14 34	14 44							14 54		15 04
Waddon	d		13 56		14 06	14 16							14 26		14 36	14 46							14 56		15 06
Wallington	d		14 00		14 10	14 20							14 30		14 40	14 50							15 00		15 10
Carshalton Beeches	d		14 02		14 12	14 22							14 32		14 42	14 52							15 02		15 12
Mitcham Eastfields	d	13 36									13 54	14 06									14 24	14 36			
Mitcham Junction	d	13 39									13 57	14 09									14 27	14 39			
Hackbridge	d	13 43									14 00	14 13									14 30	14 43			
Carshalton	d	13 45									14 03	14 15									14 33	14 45			
Sutton (Surrey) 4	a	13 49	14 06	13 58	14 16	14 26				14 05	14 06	14 19	14 39	14 28	14 46	14 56				14 35	14 36	14 49	15 06	14 58	15 16
	d	13 49	14 07	13 59								14 19	14 40	14 29								14 49	15 07	14 59	
Belmont	d		14 10																				15 10		
Banstead	d		14 14																				15 14		
Epsom Downs	a		14 17																				15 17		
Cheam	d	13 52		14 01								14 22	14 42	14 31								14 52		15 01	
Ewell East	d	13 55		14 05								14 25	14 46									14 55		15 05	
Epsom 3	a	13 59		14 09				14 16	14 27			14 29	14 52	14 37				14 46	14 57			14 59		15 09	
	d			14 09				14 17	14 28					14 37				14 47	14 58					15 09	
Ashtead	d			14 13				14 21	14 32					14 41				14 51	15 02					15 13	
Leatherhead	d			14 16				14 24	14 35					14 44				14 54	15 05					15 16	
Bookham	d							14 29										14 59							
Effingham Junction 6	d							14 33										15 03							
Guildford	a							14 53										15 23							
Boxhill & Westhumble	d			14 21																				15 21	
Dorking 4	a			14 24					14 43					14 50					15 13					15 24	
	d			14 24																				15 24	
Holmwood	d			14 32																				15 32	
Ockley	d			14 36																				15 36	
Warnham	d			14 41																				15 41	
Horsham 4	a			14 45																				15 45	

London - Sutton, Epsom, Guildford, Dorking and Horsham

from 8 October

		SN		SW	SW	FC	FC	SN	SN	SN	SN	SN		SW	SW	FC	FC	SN	SN	SN	SN	SN		SW	SW
London Victoria 15 ⊖	d	14 36						14 47	14 53	15 01	15 03	15 06						15 17	15 23	15 31	15 33	15 36			
London Waterloo 15 ⊖	d			14 39	14 54									15 09	15 24									15 39	15 54
Clapham Junction 10	d	14 44		14 48	15 03			14 54	15 00	15 08	15 11	15 14		15 18	15 33			15 24	15 30	15 38	15 41	15 44		15 48	16 03
Balham 4 ⊖	d	14 50						15 00	15 05		15 16	15 20						15 30	15 35		15 46	15 50			
London Bridge 4 ⊖	d					14 15										14 45									
Tulse Hill 3	d					14 31	14 46									15 01	15 16								
New Cross Gate 4 ⊖	d																								
Norwood Junction 2	d	15 09										15 39										16 09			
West Croydon 4	d	15 14							15 24		15 34	15 44							15 54		16 04	16 14			
Waddon	d	15 16							15 26		15 36	15 46							15 56		16 06	16 16			
Wallington	d	15 20							15 30		15 40	15 50							16 00		16 10	16 20			
Carshalton Beeches	d	15 22							15 32		15 42	15 52							16 02		16 12	16 22			
Mitcham Eastfields	d						14 54	15 06									15 24	15 36							
Mitcham Junction	d						14 57	15 09									15 27	15 39							
Hackbridge	d						15 00	15 13									15 30	15 43							
Carshalton	d						15 03	15 15									15 33	15 45							
Sutton (Surrey) 4	a	15 26				15 05	15 06	15 19	15 39	15 28	15 46	15 56				15 35	15 36	15 49	16 06	15 58	16 16	16 26			
	d							15 19	15 40	15 29								15 49	16 07	15 59					
Belmont	d																		16 10						
Banstead	d																		16 14						
Epsom Downs	a																		16 17						
Cheam	d							15 22	15 42	15 31								15 52		16 01					
Ewell East	d							15 25	15 46									15 55		16 05					
Epsom 3	a			15 16	15 27			15 29	15 52	15 37				15 46	15 57			15 59		16 09				16 16	16 27
	d			15 17	15 28					15 37				15 47	15 58					16 09				16 17	16 28
Ashtead	d			15 21	15 32					15 41				15 51	16 02					16 13				16 21	16 32
Leatherhead	d			15 24	15 35					15 44				15 54	16 05					16 16				16 24	16 35
Bookham	d			15 29										15 59										16 29	
Effingham Junction 6	d			15 33										16 03										16 33	
Guildford	a			15 53										16 23										16 53	
Boxhill & Westhumble	d																			16 21					
Dorking 4	a				15 43					15 50					16 13					16 24					16 43
	d																			16 24					
Holmwood	d																			16 32					
Ockley	d																			16 36					
Warnham	d																			16 41					
Horsham 4	a																			16 45					

		FC	FC	SN	SN	SN	SN	SN		SW	SW	FC	FC	SN	SN	SN	SN	SN		SW	SW	FC	FC	SN	SN
London Victoria 15 ⊖	d			15 47	15 53	16 01	16 03	16 06						16 17	16 23	16 31	16 33	16 36						16 47	16 53
London Waterloo 15 ⊖	d									16 09	16 24									16 39	16 54				
Clapham Junction 10	d			15 54	16 00	16 08	16 11	16 14		16 18	16 33			16 24	16 30	16 38	16 41	16 44		16 48	17 03			16 54	17 00
Balham 4 ⊖	d			16 00	16 05		16 16	16 20						16 30	16 35		16 46	16 50						17 00	17 05
London Bridge 4 ⊖	d	15 15										15 45										16 15			
Tulse Hill 3	d	15 31	15 46									16 01	16 16									16 31	16 46		
New Cross Gate 4 ⊖	d																								
Norwood Junction 2	d							16 39										17 09							
West Croydon 4	d				16 24		16 34	16 44							16 54		17 04	17 14							17 24
Waddon	d				16 26		16 36	16 46							16 56		17 06	17 16							17 26
Wallington	d				16 30		16 40	16 50							17 00		17 10	17 20							17 30
Carshalton Beeches	d				16 32		16 42	16 52							17 02		17 12	17 22							17 32
Mitcham Eastfields	d		15 54	16 06									16 24	16 36									16 54	17 06	
Mitcham Junction	d		15 57	16 09									16 27	16 39									16 57	17 09	
Hackbridge	d		16 00	16 13									16 30	16 43									17 00	17 13	
Carshalton	d		16 03	16 15									16 33	16 45									17 03	17 15	
Sutton (Surrey) 4	a	16 05	16 06	16 19	16 39	16 28	16 46	16 56				16 35	16 36	16 49	17 06	16 58	17 16	17 26				17 05	17 06	17 19	17 39
	d			16 19	16 40	16 29								16 49	17 07	16 59								17 19	17 40
Belmont	d														17 10										
Banstead	d														17 14										
Epsom Downs	a														17 17										
Cheam	d			16 22	16 42	16 31								16 52		17 01								17 22	17 42
Ewell East	d			16 25	16 46									16 55		17 05								17 25	17 46
Epsom 3	a			16 29	16 52	16 37				16 46	16 57			16 59		17 09				17 16	17 27			17 29	17 52
	d					16 37				16 47	16 58					17 09				17 17	17 28				
Ashtead	d					16 41				16 51	17 02					17 13				17 21	17 32				
Leatherhead	d					16 44				16 54	17 05					17 16				17 24	17 35				
Bookham	d									16 59										17 29					
Effingham Junction 6	d									17 03										17 33					
Guildford	a									17 23										17 53					
Boxhill & Westhumble	d															17 21									
Dorking 4	a					16 50					17 13					17 24					17 43				
	d															17 24									
Holmwood	d															17 32									
Ockley	d															17 36									
Warnham	d															17 41									
Horsham 4	a															17 45									

London - Sutton, Epsom, Guildford, Dorking and Horsham

		SN	SN	SN		SW	SW	FC	FC	SN	SN	SN	SN	SN		SW	SW	FC	FC	SN	SN	SN	SN	SN	
London Victoria 15 ⊖	d	17 01	17 03	17 06						17 17	17 23	17 31	17 33	17 36						17 47	17 53	18 01	18 03	18 06	
London Waterloo 15 ⊖	d					17 09	17 24									17 39	17 54								
Clapham Junction 10	d	17 08	17 11	17 14		17 18	17 33			17 24	17 30	17 38	17 41	17 44		17 48	18 03			17 54	18 00	18 08	18 11	18 14	
Balham 4 ⊖	d		17 16	17 20						17 30	17 35		17 46	17 50						18 00	18 05		18 16	18 20	
London Bridge 4 ⊖	d							16 45										17 15							
Tulse Hill 3	d							17 01	17 16									17 31	17 46						
New Cross Gate 4 ⊖	d																								
Norwood Junction 2	d			17 39										18 09										18 39	
West Croydon 4	d		17 34	17 44							17 54		18 04	18 14							18 24		18 34	18 44	
Waddon	d		17 36	17 46							17 56		18 06	18 16							18 26		18 36	18 46	
Wallington	d		17 40	17 50							18 00		18 10	18 20							18 30		18 40	18 50	
Carshalton Beeches	d		17 42	17 52							18 02		18 12	18 22							18 32		18 42	18 52	
Mitcham Eastfields	d								17 24	17 36									17 54	18 06					
Mitcham Junction	d								17 27	17 39									17 57	18 09					
Hackbridge	d								17 30	17 43									18 00	18 13					
Carshalton	d								17 33	17 45									18 03	18 15					
Sutton (Surrey) 4	a	17 28	17 46	17 56				17 35	17 36	17 49	18 06	17 58	18 16	18 26				18 05	18 06	18 19	18 39	18 28	18 46	18 56	
	d	17 29								17 49	18 07	17 59								18 19	18 40	18 29			
Belmont	d										18 10														
Banstead	d										18 14														
Epsom Downs	a										18 17														
Cheam	d	17 31								17 52		18 01								18 22	18 42	18 31			
Ewell East	d									17 55		18 05								18 25	18 46				
Epsom 3	a	17 37				17 46	17 57			17 59		18 09				18 16	18 27			18 29	18 52	18 37			
	d	17 37				17 47	17 58					18 09				18 17	18 28					18 37			
Ashtead	d	17 41				17 51	18 02					18 13				18 21	18 32					18 41			
Leatherhead	d	17 44				17 54	18 05					18 16				18 24	18 35					18 44			
Bookham	d					17 59										18 29									
Effingham Junction 6	d					18 03										18 33									
Guildford	a					18 23										18 53									
Boxhill & Westhumble	d											18 21										18 49			
Dorking 4	a	17 50					18 13					18 24					18 43					18 52			
	d											18 24													
Holmwood	d											18 32													
Ockley	d											18 36													
Warnham	d											18 41													
Horsham 4	a											18 45													

		SW	SW	FC	FC	SN	SN	SN	SN	SN		SW	SW	FC	FC	SN	SN	SN	SN	SN		SW	SW	FC	FC
London Victoria 15 ⊖	d					18 17	18 23	18 31	18 33	18 36						18 47	18 53	19 01	19 03	19 06					
London Waterloo 15 ⊖	d	18 09	18 24									18 39	18 54									19 09	19 24		
Clapham Junction 10	d	18 18	18 33			18 24	18 30	18 38	18 41	18 44		18 48	19 03			18 54	19 00	19 08	19 11	19 14		19 18	19 33		
Balham 4 ⊖	d					18 30	18 35		18 46	18 50						19 00	19 05		19 16	19 20					
London Bridge 4 ⊖	d			17 45										18 15										18 45	
Tulse Hill 3	d			18 01	18 16									18 31	18 46									19 01	19 16
New Cross Gate 4 ⊖	d																								
Norwood Junction 2	d									19 09										19 39					
West Croydon 4	d						18 54		19 04	19 14							19 24		19 34	19 44					
Waddon	d						18 56		19 06	19 16							19 26		19 36	19 46					
Wallington	d						19 00		19 10	19 20							19 30		19 40	19 50					
Carshalton Beeches	d						19 02		19 12	19 22							19 32		19 42	19 52					
Mitcham Eastfields	d				18 24	18 36									18 54	19 06									19 24
Mitcham Junction	d				18 27	18 39									18 57	19 09									19 27
Hackbridge	d				18 30	18 43									19 00	19 13									19 30
Carshalton	d				18 33	18 45									19 03	19 15									19 33
Sutton (Surrey) 4	a			18 35	18 36	18 49	19 06	18 58	19 16	19 26				19 05	19 06	19 19	19 39	19 28	19 46	19 56				19 39	19 36
	d					18 49	19 07	18 59								19 19	19 40	19 29							
Belmont	d						19 10																		
Banstead	d						19 14																		
Epsom Downs	a						19 17																		
Cheam	d					18 52		19 01								19 22	19 42	19 31							
Ewell East	d					18 55		19 05								19 25	19 46								
Epsom 3	a	18 46	18 57			18 59		19 09				19 16	19 27			19 29	19 52	19 37				19 46	19 57		
	d	18 47	18 58					19 09				19 17	19 28					19 37				19 47	19 58		
Ashtead	d	18 51	19 02					19 13				19 21	19 32					19 41				19 51	20 02		
Leatherhead	d	18 54	19 05					19 16				19 24	19 35					19 44				19 54	20 05		
Bookham	d	18 59										19 29										19 59			
Effingham Junction 6	d	19 03										19 33										20 03			
Guildford	a	19 23										19 53										20 23			
Boxhill & Westhumble	d																	19 49							
Dorking 4	a		19 13					19 22					19 43					19 52					20 13		
	d																								
Holmwood	d																								
Ockley	d																								
Warnham	d																								
Horsham 4	a																								

London - Sutton, Epsom, Guildford, Dorking and Horsham

		SN	SN	SN	SN	SN	SW	SW	FC	FC	SN	SN	SN	SN	SN	SW	SW	SN	SN	SN	SN	SN	SW
London Victoria 15	⊖ d	19 17	19 23	19 31	19 33	19 36					19 47	19 53	20 01	20 03	20 06			20 17	20 23	20 31	20 33	20 36	
London Waterloo 15	⊖ d						19 39	19 54								20 09	20 24						20 39
Clapham Junction 10	d	19 24	19 30	19 38	19 41	19 44	19 48	20 03			19 54	20 00	20 08	20 11	20 14	20 18	20 33	20 24	20 30	20 38	20 41	20 44	20 48
Balham 4	⊖ d	19 30	19 35		19 46	19 50					20 00	20 05		20 16	20 20			20 30	20 35		20 46	20 50	
London Bridge 4	⊖ d								19 15														
Tulse Hill 3	d								19 31	19 46													
New Cross Gate 4	⊖ d																						
Norwood Junction 2	d					20 09									20 39							21 09	
West Croydon 4	d		19 54		20 04	20 15						20 25		20 34	20 45				20 55		21 04	21 15	
Waddon	d		19 56		20 06	20 17						20 27		20 36	20 47				20 57		21 06	21 17	
Wallington	d		20 00		20 10	20 21						20 31		20 40	20 51				21 01		21 10	21 21	
Carshalton Beeches	d		20 02		20 12	20 23						20 33		20 42	20 53				21 03		21 12	21 23	
Mitcham Eastfields	d	19 36								19 55	20 06							20 36					
Mitcham Junction	d	19 39								19 58	20 09							20 39					
Hackbridge	d	19 43								20 01	20 13							20 43					
Carshalton	d	19 45								20 04	20 15							20 45					
Sutton (Surrey) 4	a	19 49	20 06	19 58	20 16	20 27			20 05	20 07	20 19	20 39	20 28	20 46	20 57			20 49	21 07	20 58	21 16	21 27	
	d	19 49	20 07	19 59							20 19	20 40	20 29					20 49	21 08	20 59			
Belmont	d		20 10																21 11				
Banstead	d		20 14																21 15				
Epsom Downs	a		20 17																21 18				
Cheam	d	19 52		20 01							20 22	20 42	20 31					20 52		21 01			
Ewell East	d	19 55		20 05							20 25	20 46						20 55		21 05			
Epsom 8	a	19 59		20 09			20 16	20 27			20 29	20 52	20 37			20 46	20 57	20 59		21 09			21 16
	d			20 09			20 17						20 37			20 47				21 09			21 17
Ashtead	d			20 13			20 21						20 41			20 51				21 13			21 21
Leatherhead	d			20 16			20 24						20 44			20 54				21 16			21 24
Bookham	d						20 29																21 29
Effingham Junction 6	d						20 33																21 33
Guildford	a						20 53																21 53
Boxhill & Westhumble	d												20 49										
Dorking 4	a			20 22									20 52			21 02				21 22			
	d																						
Holmwood	d																						
Ockley	d																						
Warnham	d																						
Horsham 4	a																						

		SW	SN	SN	SN	SN	SN	SW	SW	SN	SN	SN	SN	SN	SW	SW	SN	SN	SN	SN	SN	SW
London Victoria 15	⊖ d		20 47	20 53	21 01	21 03	21 06			21 17	21 23	21 31	21 33	21 36			21 47	21 53	22 01	22 03	22 06	
London Waterloo 15	⊖ d	20 54						21 09	21 24						21 39	21 54						22 09
Clapham Junction 10	d	21 03	20 54	21 00	21 08	21 11	21 14	21 18	21 33	21 24	21 30	21 38	21 41	21 44	21 48	22 03	21 54	22 00	22 08	22 11	22 14	22 18
Balham 4	⊖ d		21 00	21 05		21 16	21 20			21 30	21 35		21 46	21 50			22 00	22 05		22 16	22 20	
London Bridge 4	⊖ d																					
Tulse Hill 3	d																					
New Cross Gate 4	⊖ d																					
Norwood Junction 2	d						21 39							22 09							22 39	
West Croydon 4	d			21 25		21 34	21 45				21 55		22 04	22 14				22 24		22 34	22 44	
Waddon	d			21 27		21 36	21 47				21 57		22 06	22 16				22 26		22 36	22 46	
Wallington	d			21 31		21 40	21 51				22 01		22 10	22 20				22 30		22 40	22 50	
Carshalton Beeches	d			21 33		21 42	21 53				22 03		22 12	22 22				22 32		22 42	22 52	
Mitcham Eastfields	d		21 06							21 36							22 06					
Mitcham Junction	d		21 09							21 39							22 09					
Hackbridge	d		21 13							21 43							22 13					
Carshalton	d		21 15							21 45							22 15					
Sutton (Surrey) 4	a		21 19	21 39	21 28	21 46	21 57			21 49	22 07	21 58	22 16	22 26			22 19	22 39	22 28	22 46	22 56	
	d		21 19	21 40	21 29					21 49	22 08	21 59					22 19	22 40	22 29			
Belmont	d										22 11											
Banstead	d										22 15											
Epsom Downs	a										22 18											
Cheam	d		21 22	21 42	21 31					21 52		22 01					22 22	22 42	22 31			
Ewell East	d		21 25	21 46						21 55		22 05					22 25	22 46				
Epsom 8	a	21 27	21 29	21 52	21 37			21 46	21 57	21 59		22 09			22 16	22 27	22 29	22 52	22 37			22 46
	d				21 37			21 47				22 09			22 17				22 37			22 47
Ashtead	d				21 41			21 51				22 13			22 21				22 41			22 51
Leatherhead	d				21 44			21 54				22 16			22 24				22 44			22 54
Bookham	d														22 29							
Effingham Junction 6	d														22 33							
Guildford	a														22 53							
Boxhill & Westhumble	d				21 49														22 49			
Dorking 4	a				21 52			22 02				22 22							22 52			23 02
	d																					
Holmwood	d																					
Ockley	d																					
Warnham	d																					
Horsham 4	a																					

London - Sutton, Epsom, Guildford, Dorking and Horsham

		SN	SN	SN	SN	SN	SW	SN	SN	SN	SN	SN	SW	SN	SN	SW	SN	FC	FC	FC	FC	FC
London Victoria 15	⊖ d	22 17	22 23	22 31	22 33	22 36		22 47	22 53	23 01	23 03	23 06		23 26	23 34		23 59					
London Waterloo 15	⊖ d						22 39						23 09			23 42						
Clapham Junction 10	d	22 24	22 30	22 38	22 41	22 44	22 48	22 54	23 00	23 08	23 11	23 14	23 18	23 32	23 42	23 51	00 07					
Balham 4	⊖ d	22 30	22 35		22 46	22 50		23 00	23 05		23 16	23 20		23 37	23 47		00 12					
London Bridge 4	⊖ d																	19 45	20 15	20 45	21 15	21 45
Tulse Hill 3	d																	20 01	20 31	21 01	21 31	22 01
New Cross Gate 4	⊖ d																					
Norwood Junction 2	d					23 09						23 39										
West Croydon 4	d		22 54		23 04	23 14			23 24		23 34	23 44			00 04		00 31					
Waddon	d		22 56		23 06	23 16			23 26		23 36	23 46			00 06		00 33					
Wallington	d		23 00		23 10	23 20			23 30		23 40	23 50			00 10		00 37					
Carshalton Beeches	d		23 02		23 12	23 22			23 32		23 42	23 52			00 12		00 39					
Mitcham Eastfields	d	22 36						23 06						23 43								
Mitcham Junction	d	22 39						23 09						23 46								
Hackbridge	d	22 43						23 13						23 50								
Carshalton	d	22 45						23 15						23 52								
Sutton (Surrey) 4	a	22 49	23 06	22 58	23 16	23 26		23 19	23 39	23 28	23 46	23 56		23 59	00 16		00 43	20 37	21 05	21 37	22 05	22 39
	d	22 49	23 07	22 59		23 33		23 19	23 40	23 29				00 01								
Belmont	d		23 10			23 36																
Banstead	d		23 14			23 40																
Epsom Downs	a		23 17			23 43																
Cheam	d	22 52		23 01				23 22	23 42	23 31				00 03								
Ewell East	d	22 55		23 05				23 25	23 46					00 07								
Epsom 8	a	22 59		23 09			23 12	23 29	23 52	23 37			23 42	00 11		00 15						
	d			23 09			23 17			23 37			23 47	00 11		00 19						
Ashtead	d			23 13			23 21			23 41			23 51	00 15		00 23						
Leatherhead	d			23 16			23 24			23 44			23 54	00 18		00 26						
Bookham	d						23 29									00 31						
Effingham Junction 6	d						23 33									00 36						
Guildford	a						23 53									00 56						
Boxhill & Westhumble	d			23 21										00 23								
Dorking 4	a			23 24						23 50			00 03	00 26								
	d																					
Holmwood	d																					
Ockley	d																					
Warnham	d																					
Horsham 4	a																					

		FC		FC
London Victoria 15	⊖ d			
London Waterloo 15	⊖ d			
Clapham Junction 10	d			
Balham 4	⊖ d			
London Bridge 4	⊖ d	22 15		23 45
Tulse Hill 3	d	22 31		00 01
New Cross Gate 4	⊖ d			
Norwood Junction 2	d			
West Croydon 4	d			
Waddon	d			
Wallington	d			
Carshalton Beeches	d			
Mitcham Eastfields	d			
Mitcham Junction	d			
Hackbridge	d			
Carshalton	d			
Sutton (Surrey) 4	a	23 05	and every 30 minutes until	00 35
	d			
Belmont	d			
Banstead	d			
Epsom Downs	a			
Cheam	d			
Ewell East	d			
Epsom 8	a			
	d			
Ashtead	d			
Leatherhead	d			
Bookham	d			
Effingham Junction 6	d			
Guildford	a			
Boxhill & Westhumble	d			
Dorking 4	a			
	d			
Holmwood	d			
Ockley	d			
Warnham	d			
Horsham 4	a			

London - Sutton, Epsom, Guildford, Dorking and Horsham

until 25 September

		SW A	SN A	SN A	SW A	SN A	SW	SN	SN	SN	SN	SN	SN	SW	SN	SN	SW	SN	SN	SN	SN	SW	SN
London Victoria 15 ⊖	d		23p26	23p34		23p59		00 34	06 49	07 19	07 22	07 24	07 49		07 52	07 54		08 08	08 19	08 22	08 24		08 38
London Waterloo 15 ⊖	d	23p09			23p42		00 15										08 02					08 32	
Clapham Junction 10	d	23p18	23p32	23p42	23p51	00 07	00 25	00 42	06 57	07 26	07 29	07 32	07 56		07 59	08 02	08 11	08 16	08 26	08 29	08 32	08 41	08 46
Balham 4 ⊖	d		23p37	23p47		00 12		00 47	07 02	07 30	07 33	07 37	08 00		08 03	08 07		08 22	08 30	08 33	08 37		08 51
London Bridge 4 ⊖	d																						
Tulse Hill 3	d																						
New Cross Gate 4 ⊖	d																						
Norwood Junction 2	d											07 57				08 27					08 57		
West Croydon 4	d			00 04		00 31		01 04	07 21	07 49		08 04	08 19			08 34			08 49		09 04		
Waddon	d			00 06		00 33		01 07	07 23	07 51		08 06	08 21			08 36			08 51		09 06		
Wallington	d			00 10		00 37		01 10	07 27	07 55		08 10	08 25			08 40			08 55		09 10		
Carshalton Beeches	d			00 12		00 39		01 13	07 29	07 57		08 12	08 27			08 42			08 57		09 12		
Mitcham Eastfields	d		23p43								07 40				08 10			08 28		08 40			08 58
Mitcham Junction	d		23p46								07 43				08 13			08 31		08 43			09 01
Hackbridge	d		23p50								07 46				08 16			08 35		08 46			09 04
Carshalton	d		23p52								07 49				08 19			08 37		08 49			09 07
Sutton (Surrey) 4	a		23p59	00 16		00 43		01 16	07 33	08 01	07 52	08 16	08 31		08 22	08 46		08 41	09 01	08 52	09 16		09 10
	d		00 01						07 41	08 11	07 53				08 23			08 41		08 53			09 11
Belmont	d																						
Banstead	d																						
Epsom Downs	a																						
Cheam	d		00 03						07 43	08 13	07 55				08 25			08 44		08 55			09 13
Ewell East	d		00 07						07 47	08 17	07 59				08 29			08 47		08 59			09 17
Epsom 3	a	23p42	00 11		00 15		00 50		07 52	08 22	08 03				08 33		08 36	08 51		09 03		09 06	09 21
	d	23p47	00 11		00 19				07 53	08 23				08 08			08 38	08 52				09 08	09 21
Ashtead	d	23p51	00 15		00 23				07 57	08 27				08 12			08 42	08 56				09 12	09 25
Leatherhead	d	23p54	00 18		00 26				08 00	08 30				08 15			08 45	08 59				09 15	09 28
Bookham	d				00 31									08 21								09 21	
Effingham Junction 6	d				00 36									08 25								09 25	
Guildford	a				00 53									08 41								09 41	
Boxhill & Westhumble	d		00 23						08 05	08 35								09 04					09 33
Dorking 4	a	00 01	00 26						08 07	08 37							08 51	09 06					09 36
	d																						
Holmwood	d																						
Ockley	d																						
Warnham	d																						
Horsham 4	a																						

		SN	SN	SN	SW	SN		SN	SN	SN	SN	SW	SN	SN	SN	SN	SW	SN	SN	SN	
London Victoria 15 ⊖	d	08 49	08 52	08 54		09 08		12 08	12 19	12 22	12 24		12 38	12 49	12 52	12 54		13 08	13 19	13 22	
London Waterloo 15 ⊖	d				09 02							12 32					13 02				
Clapham Junction 10	d	08 56	08 59	09 02	09 11	09 16		12 16	12 26	12 29	12 32	12 41	12 46	12 56	12 59	13 02	13 11	13 16	13 26	13 29	
Balham 4 ⊖	d	09 00	09 03	09 07		09 21		12 21	12 30	12 33	12 37		12 51	13 00	13 03	13 07		13 21	13 30	13 33	
London Bridge 4 ⊖	d																				
Tulse Hill 3	d																				
New Cross Gate 4 ⊖	d																				
Norwood Junction 2	d			09 27							12 57					13 27					
West Croydon 4	d	09 19		09 34					12 49		13 04			13 19		13 34			13 49		
Waddon	d	09 21		09 36					12 51		13 06			13 21		13 36			13 51		
Wallington	d	09 25		09 40					12 55		13 10			13 25		13 40			13 55		
Carshalton Beeches	d	09 27		09 42					12 57		13 12			13 27		13 42			13 57		
Mitcham Eastfields	d		09 10			09 28		12 28		12 40			12 58		13 10			13 28		13 40	
Mitcham Junction	d		09 13			09 31		12 31		12 43			13 01		13 13			13 31		13 43	
Hackbridge	d		09 16			09 34	and at the same minutes past each hour until	12 34		12 46			13 04		13 16			13 34		13 46	and at the same minutes past each hour until
Carshalton	d		09 19			09 37		12 37		12 49			13 07		13 19			13 37		13 49	
Sutton (Surrey) 4	a	09 31	09 22	09 46		09 40		12 40	13 01	12 52	13 16		13 10	13 31	13 22	13 46		13 40	14 01	13 52	
	d		09 23			09 41		12 41		12 53			13 11		13 23			13 41		13 53	
Belmont	d																				
Banstead	d																				
Epsom Downs	a																				
Cheam	d		09 25			09 43		12 43		12 55			13 13		13 25			13 43		13 55	
Ewell East	d		09 29			09 47		12 47		12 59			13 17		13 29			13 47		13 59	
Epsom 3	a		09 33		09 36	09 51		12 51		13 05		13 06	13 21		13 33		13 36	13 51		14 03	
	d				09 38	09 51		12 51				13 08	13 21				13 38	13 51			
Ashtead	d				09 42	09 55		12 55				13 12	13 25				13 42	13 55			
Leatherhead	d				09 45	09 58		12 58				13 15	13 28				13 45	13 58			
Bookham	d											13 21									
Effingham Junction 6	d											13 25									
Guildford	a											13 41									
Boxhill & Westhumble	d					10 03		13 03					13 33					14 03			
Dorking 4	a				09 51	10 06		13 06					13 36				13 51	14 06			
	d																				
Holmwood	d																				
Ockley	d																				
Warnham	d																				
Horsham 4	a																				

A not 22 May

London - Sutton, Epsom, Guildford, Dorking and Horsham

until 25 September

		SN	SN	SW	SN	SN	SN	SN	SW	SN	SN	SN	SW	SN	SN	SN	SW	SN	SN	SN	SW	SN	SN
London Victoria 15 ⊖	d	17 22	17 24		17 38	17 49	17 52	17 54		18 08	18 19	18 24		18 38	18 49	18 54		19 08	19 19	19 24		19 38	19 49
London Waterloo 15 ⊖	d			17 32					18 02				18 32				19 02				19 32		
Clapham Junction 10	d	17 29	17 32	17 41	17 46	17 56	17 59	18 02	18 11	18 16	18 26	18 32	18 41	18 46	18 56	19 02	19 11	19 16	19 26	19 32	19 41	19 46	19 56
Balham 4 ⊖	d	17 33	17 37		17 51	18 00	18 03	18 07		18 21	18 30	18 37		18 51	19 00	19 07		19 21	19 30	19 37		19 51	20 00
London Bridge 4 ⊖	d																						
Tulse Hill 3	d																						
New Cross Gate 4 ⊖	d																						
Norwood Junction 2	d		17 57					18 27				18 57				19 27				19 57			
West Croydon 4	d		18 04			18 19		18 34			18 49	19 04			19 19	19 34			19 49	20 04			20 19
Waddon	d		18 06			18 21		18 36			18 51	19 06			19 21	19 36			19 51	20 06			20 21
Wallington	d		18 10			18 25		18 40			18 55	19 10			19 25	19 40			19 55	20 10			20 25
Carshalton Beeches	d		18 12			18 27		18 42			18 57	19 12			19 27	19 42			19 57	20 12			20 27
Mitcham Eastfields	d	17 40			17 58		18 10			18 28				18 58				19 28				19 58	
Mitcham Junction	d	17 43			18 01		18 13			18 31				19 01				19 31				20 01	
Hackbridge	d	17 46			18 04		18 16			18 34				19 04				19 34				20 04	
Carshalton	d	17 49			18 07		18 19			18 37				19 07				19 37				20 07	
Sutton (Surrey) 4	a	17 52	18 16		18 10	18 31	18 22	18 46		18 40	19 01	19 16		19 10	19 31	19 46		19 40	20 01	20 16		20 10	20 31
	d	17 53			18 11		18 23			18 41				19 11				19 41				20 11	
Belmont	d																						
Banstead	d																						
Epsom Downs	a																						
Cheam	d	17 55			18 13		18 25			18 43				19 13				19 43				20 13	
Ewell East	d	17 59			18 17		18 29			18 47				19 17				19 47				20 17	
Epsom 3	a	18 03		18 06	18 21		18 33		18 36	18 51			19 06	19 21			19 36	19 51			20 06	20 21	
	d			18 08	18 21				18 38	18 51			19 08	19 21			19 38	19 51			20 08	20 21	
Ashtead	d			18 12	18 25				18 42	18 55			19 12	19 25			19 42	19 55			20 12	20 25	
Leatherhead	d			18 15	18 28				18 45	18 58			19 15	19 28			19 45	19 58			20 15	20 28	
Bookham	d			18 21									19 21								20 21		
Effingham Junction 6	d			18 25									19 25								20 25		
Guildford	a			18 41									19 41								20 41		
Boxhill & Westhumble	d				18 33					19 03				19 33				20 03				20 33	
Dorking 4	a				18 36				18 51	19 06				19 36			19 51	20 06				20 36	
	d																						
Holmwood	d																						
Ockley	d																						
Warnham	d																						
Horsham 4	a																						

		SN	SW	SN	SN	SN	SW	SN	SN	SN	SW	SN	SN	SN	SW	SN	SN	SN	SW	SN	SN	SN
London Victoria 15 ⊖	d	19 54		20 08	20 19	20 24		20 38	20 49	20 54		21 08	21 19	21 24		21 38	21 49	21 54		22 08	22 19	22 24
London Waterloo 15 ⊖	d		20 02				20 32				21 02				21 32				22 02			
Clapham Junction 10	d	20 02	20 11	20 16	20 26	20 32	20 41	20 46	20 56	21 02	21 11	21 16	21 26	21 32	21 41	21 46	21 56	22 02	22 11	22 16	22 26	22 32
Balham 4 ⊖	d	20 07		20 21	20 30	20 37		20 51	21 00	21 07		21 21	21 30	21 38		21 51	22 00	22 07		22 21	22 30	22 38
London Bridge 4 ⊖	d																					
Tulse Hill 3	d																					
New Cross Gate 4 ⊖	d																					
Norwood Junction 2	d	20 27				20 57				21 27				21 57				22 27				22 57
West Croydon 4	d	20 34			20 49	21 04			21 19	21 34			21 49	22 04			22 19	22 34			22 49	23 04
Waddon	d	20 36			20 51	21 06			21 21	21 36			21 51	22 06			22 21	22 36			22 51	23 06
Wallington	d	20 40			20 55	21 10			21 25	21 40			21 55	22 10			22 25	22 40			22 55	23 10
Carshalton Beeches	d	20 42			20 57	21 12			21 27	21 42			21 57	22 12			22 27	22 42			22 57	23 12
Mitcham Eastfields	d			20 28				20 58				21 28				21 58				22 28		
Mitcham Junction	d			20 31				21 01				21 31				22 01				22 31		
Hackbridge	d			20 34				21 04				21 34				22 04				22 34		
Carshalton	d			20 37				21 07				21 37				22 07				22 37		
Sutton (Surrey) 4	a	20 46		20 40	21 01	21 16		21 10	21 31	21 46		21 40	22 01	22 16		22 10	22 31	22 46		22 40	23 01	23 16
	d			20 41				21 11				21 41				22 11				22 41		
Belmont	d																					
Banstead	d																					
Epsom Downs	a																					
Cheam	d			20 43				21 13				21 43				22 13				22 43		
Ewell East	d			20 47				21 17				21 47				22 17				22 47		
Epsom 3	a		20 36	20 51			21 06	21 21			21 36	21 51			22 06	22 21			22 36	22 51		
	d		20 38	20 51			21 08	21 21			21 38	21 51			22 08	22 21			22 38	22 51		
Ashtead	d		20 42	20 55			21 12	21 25			21 42	21 55			22 12	22 25			22 42	22 55		
Leatherhead	d		20 45	20 58			21 15	21 28			21 45	21 58			22 15	22 28			22 45	22 58		
Bookham	d						21 21								22 21							
Effingham Junction 6	d						21 25								22 25							
Guildford	a						21 41								22 41							
Boxhill & Westhumble	d			21 03				21 33				22 03				22 33				23 03		
Dorking 4	a		20 51	21 06				21 36			21 51	22 06				22 36			22 51	23 06		
	d																					
Holmwood	d																					
Ockley	d																					
Warnham	d																					
Horsham 4	a																					

Table 182

Sundays until 25 September

London - Sutton, Epsom, Guildford, Dorking and Horsham

		SW	SN	SN	SN	SW	SN	SW	SN	FC A	FC A	FC		FC
London Victoria ⊖	d		22 38	22 49	22 54		23 08		23 19					
London Waterloo ⊖	d	22 32				23 02		23 32						
Clapham Junction	d	22 41	22 46	22 56	23 02	23 11	23 16	23 41	23 27					
Balham ⊖	d		22 51	23 00	23 07		23 21		23 32					
London Bridge ⊖	d									23p15	23p45	09 32		21 02
Tulse Hill	d									23p31	00 01	09 43		21 13
New Cross Gate ⊖	d													
Norwood Junction	d				23 27									
West Croydon	d			23 19	23 34				23 50					
Waddon	d			23 21	23 36				23 52					
Wallington	d			23 25	23 40				23 56					
Carshalton Beeches	d			23 27	23 42				23 58					
Mitcham Eastfields	d		22 58				23 28							
Mitcham Junction	d		23 01				23 31							
Hackbridge	d		23 04				23 34							
Carshalton	d		23 07				23 37							
Sutton (Surrey)	a		23 10	23 31	23 46		23 40		00 02	00 05	00 35	10 16	and every 30 minutes until	21 46
	d		23 11				23 41		00 04					
Belmont	d													
Banstead	d													
Epsom Downs	a													
Cheam	d		23 13				23 43		00 06					
Ewell East	d		23 17				23 47		00 10					
Epsom	a	23 06	23 21			23 36	23 51	00 06	00 14					
	d	23 08	23 21				23 51							
Ashtead	d	23 12	23 25				23 55							
Leatherhead	d	23 15	23 28				23 58							
Bookham	d	23 21												
Effingham Junction	d	23 25												
Guildford	a	23 41												
Boxhill & Westhumble	d		23 33				00 03							
Dorking	a		23 36				00 06							
	d													
Holmwood	d													
Ockley	d													
Warnham	d													
Horsham	a													

Sundays from 2 October

		SW B	SW C	SN	SN	SW B	SW C	SN	SW	SN	SN	SN	SN	SN	SN	SW	SN	SN	SW	SN	SN	SN	SN
London Victoria ⊖	d			23p26	23p34			23p59		00 34	06 49	07 19	07 22	07 24	07 49		07 52	07 54		08 08	08 19	08 22	08 24
London Waterloo ⊖	d	23p09	23p09			23p42	23p42		00 15										08 02				
Clapham Junction	d	23p18	23p18	23p32	23p42	23p51	23p51	00 07	00 25	00 42	06 57	07 26	07 29	07 32	07 56		07 59	08 02	08 11	08 16	08 26	08 29	08 32
Balham ⊖	d			23p37	23p47			00 12		00 47	07 02	07 30	07 33	07 37	08 00		08 03	08 07		08 22	08 30	08 33	08 37
London Bridge ⊖	d																						
Tulse Hill	d																						
New Cross Gate ⊖	d																						
Norwood Junction	d													07 57				08 27					08 57
West Croydon	d				00 04			00 31		01 04	07 21	07 49		08 04	08 19			08 34			08 49		09 04
Waddon	d				00 06			00 33		01 07	07 23	07 51		08 06	08 21			08 36			08 51		09 06
Wallington	d				00 10			00 37		01 10	07 27	07 55		08 10	08 25			08 40			08 55		09 10
Carshalton Beeches	d				00 12			00 39		01 13	07 29	07 57		08 12	08 27			08 42			08 57		09 12
Mitcham Eastfields	d			23p43									07 40				08 10			08 28		08 40	
Mitcham Junction	d			23p46									07 43				08 13			08 31		08 43	
Hackbridge	d			23p50									07 46				08 16			08 35		08 46	
Carshalton	d			23p52									07 49				08 19			08 37		08 49	
Sutton (Surrey)	a			23p59	00 16			00 43		01 16	07 33	08 01	07 52	08 16	08 31		08 22	08 46		08 41	09 01	08 52	09 16
	d			00 01							07 41	08 11	07 53				08 23			08 41		08 53	
Belmont	d																						
Banstead	d																						
Epsom Downs	a																						
Cheam	d			00 03							07 43	08 13	07 55				08 25			08 44		08 55	
Ewell East	d			00 07							07 47	08 17	07 59				08 29			08 47		08 59	
Epsom	a	23p42	23p42	00 11		00 15	00 15		00 50		07 52	08 22	08 03				08 33		08 36	08 51		09 03	
	d	23p47	23p47	00 11		00 19	00 19				07 53	08 23				08 08			08 38	08 52			
Ashtead	d	23p51	23p51	00 15		00 23	00 23				07 57	08 27				08 12			08 42	08 56			
Leatherhead	d	23p54	23p54	00 18		00 26	00 26				08 00	08 30				08 15			08 45	08 59			
Bookham	d					00 31	00 31									08 21							
Effingham Junction	d					00 36	00 36									08 25							
Guildford	a					00 53	00 56									08 44							
Boxhill & Westhumble	d			00 23							08 05	08 35								09 04			
Dorking	a	00 01	00 03	00 26							08 07	08 37							08 53	09 06			
	d																						
Holmwood	d																						
Ockley	d																						
Warnham	d																						
Horsham	a																						

A not 22 May

B 2 October

C not 2 October

Table 182

Sundays from 2 October

London - Sutton, Epsom, Guildford, Dorking and Horsham

		SW	SN	SN	SN	SN	SW	SN		SN	SN	SN	SN	SW	SN	SN	SN	SN	SW	SN	SN
London Victoria ⊖	d		08 38	08 49	08 52	08 54		09 08		12 08	12 19	12 22	12 24		12 38	12 49	12 52	12 54		13 08	13 19
London Waterloo ⊖	d	08 32					09 02							12 32					13 02		
Clapham Junction	d	08 41	08 46	08 56	08 59	09 02	09 11	09 16		12 16	12 26	12 29	12 32	12 41	12 46	12 56	12 59	13 02	13 11	13 16	13 26
Balham ⊖	d		08 51	09 00	09 03	09 07		09 21		12 21	12 30	12 33	12 37		12 51	13 00	13 03	13 07		13 21	13 30
London Bridge ⊖	d																				
Tulse Hill	d																				
New Cross Gate ⊖	d																				
Norwood Junction	d					09 27							12 57					13 27			
West Croydon	d			09 19		09 34					12 49		13 04			13 19		13 34			13 49
Waddon	d			09 21		09 36					12 51		13 06			13 21		13 36			13 51
Wallington	d			09 25		09 40					12 55		13 10			13 25		13 40			13 55
Carshalton Beeches	d			09 27		09 42					12 57		13 12			13 27		13 42			13 57
Mitcham Eastfields	d		08 58		09 10			09 28		12 28		12 40			12 58		13 10			13 28	
Mitcham Junction	d		09 01		09 13			09 31		12 31		12 43			13 01		13 13			13 31	
Hackbridge	d		09 04		09 16			09 34	and at the same	12 34		12 46			13 04		13 16			13 34	
Carshalton	d		09 07		09 19			09 37	minutes	12 37		12 49			13 07		13 19			13 37	
Sutton (Surrey)	a		09 10	09 31	09 22	09 46		09 40	past each	12 40	13 01	12 52	13 16		13 10	13 31	13 22	13 46		13 40	14 01
	d		09 11		09 23			09 41	hour until	12 41		12 53			13 11		13 23			13 41	
Belmont	d																				
Banstead	d																				
Epsom Downs	a																				
Cheam	d		09 13		09 25			09 43		12 43		12 55			13 13		13 25			13 43	
Ewell East	d		09 17		09 29			09 47		12 47		12 59			13 17		13 29			13 47	
Epsom	a	09 06	09 21		09 33		09 36	09 51		12 51		13 05		13 06	13 21		13 33		13 36	13 51	
	d	09 08	09 21				09 38	09 51		12 51				13 08	13 21				13 38	13 51	
Ashtead	d	09 12	09 25				09 42	09 55		12 55				13 12	13 25				13 42	13 55	
Leatherhead	d	09 15	09 28				09 45	09 58		12 58				13 15	13 28				13 45	13 58	
Bookham	d	09 21												13 21							
Effingham Junction	d	09 25												13 25							
Guildford	a	09 44												13 44							
Boxhill & Westhumble	d		09 33					10 03		13 03					13 33					14 03	
Dorking	a		09 36				09 53	10 06		13 06					13 36				13 53	14 06	
	d																				
Holmwood	d																				
Ockley	d																				
Warnham	d																				
Horsham	a																				

		SN		SN	SN	SW	SN	SN	SN	SN	SW	SN	SN	SN	SW	SN	SN	SN	SW	SN	SN	SN
London Victoria ⊖	d	13 22		17 22	17 24		17 38	17 49	17 52	17 54		18 08	18 19	18 24		18 38	18 49	18 54		19 08	19 19	19 24
London Waterloo ⊖	d					17 32					18 02				18 32				19 02			
Clapham Junction	d	13 29		17 29	17 32	17 41	17 46	17 56	17 59	18 02	18 11	18 16	18 26	18 32	18 41	18 46	18 56	19 02	19 11	19 16	19 26	19 32
Balham ⊖	d	13 33		17 33	17 37		17 51	18 00	18 03	18 07		18 21	18 30	18 37		18 51	19 00	19 07		19 21	19 30	19 37
London Bridge ⊖	d																					
Tulse Hill	d																					
New Cross Gate ⊖	d																					
Norwood Junction	d				17 57					18 27				18 57				19 27				19 57
West Croydon	d				18 04			18 19		18 34			18 49	19 04			19 19	19 34			19 49	20 04
Waddon	d				18 06			18 21		18 36			18 51	19 06			19 21	19 36			19 51	20 06
Wallington	d				18 10			18 25		18 40			18 55	19 10			19 25	19 40			19 55	20 10
Carshalton Beeches	d				18 12			18 27		18 42			18 57	19 12			19 27	19 42			19 57	20 12
Mitcham Eastfields	d	13 40		17 40			17 58		18 10			18 28				18 58				19 28		
Mitcham Junction	d	13 43		17 43			18 01		18 13			18 31				19 01				19 31		
Hackbridge	d	13 46	and at the same	17 46			18 04		18 16			18 34				19 04				19 34		
Carshalton	d	13 49	minutes	17 49			18 07		18 19			18 37				19 07				19 37		
Sutton (Surrey)	a	13 52	past each	17 52	18 16		18 10	18 31	18 22	18 46		18 40	19 01	19 16		19 10	19 31	19 46		19 40	20 01	20 16
	d	13 53	hour until	17 53			18 11		18 23			18 41				19 11				19 41		
Belmont	d																					
Banstead	d																					
Epsom Downs	a																					
Cheam	d	13 55		17 55			18 13		18 25			18 43				19 13				19 43		
Ewell East	d	13 59		17 59			18 17		18 29			18 47				19 17				19 47		
Epsom	a	14 03		18 03		18 06	18 21		18 33		18 36	18 51			19 06	19 21			19 36	19 51		
	d					18 08	18 21				18 38	18 51			19 08	19 21			19 38	19 51		
Ashtead	d					18 12	18 25				18 42	18 55			19 12	19 25			19 42	19 55		
Leatherhead	d					18 15	18 28				18 45	18 58			19 15	19 28			19 45	19 58		
Bookham	d					18 21									19 21							
Effingham Junction	d					18 25									19 25							
Guildford	a					18 44									19 44							
Boxhill & Westhumble	d						18 33					19 03				19 33				20 03		
Dorking	a						18 36				18 53	19 06				19 36			19 53	20 06		
	d																					
Holmwood	d																					
Ockley	d																					
Warnham	d																					
Horsham	a																					

from 2 October

London - Sutton, Epsom, Guildford, Dorking and Horsham

		SW	SN	SN	SN	SW	SN	SN	SN	SW	SN	SN	SN	SW	SN	SN	SN	SW	SN	SN	SN	SW
London Victoria ⊖	d		19 38	19 49	19 54		20 08	20 19	20 24		20 38	20 49	20 54		21 08	21 19	21 24		21 38	21 49	21 54	
London Waterloo ⊖	d	19 32				20 02				20 32				21 02				21 32				22 02
Clapham Junction	d	19 41	19 46	19 56	20 02	20 11	20 16	20 26	20 32	20 41	20 46	20 56	21 02	21 11	21 16	21 26	21 32	21 41	21 46	21 56	22 02	22 11
Balham ⊖	d		19 51	20 00	20 07		20 21	20 30	20 37		20 51	21 00	21 07		21 21	21 30	21 38		21 51	22 00	22 07	
London Bridge ⊖	d																					
Tulse Hill	d																					
New Cross Gate ⊖	d																					
Norwood Junction	d				20 27				20 57				21 27				21 57				22 27	
West Croydon	d			20 19	20 34			20 49	21 04			21 19	21 34			21 49	22 04			22 19	22 34	
Waddon	d			20 21	20 36			20 51	21 06			21 21	21 36			21 51	22 06			22 21	22 36	
Wallington	d			20 25	20 40			20 55	21 10			21 25	21 40			21 55	22 10			22 25	22 40	
Carshalton Beeches	d			20 27	20 42			20 57	21 12			21 27	21 42			21 57	22 12			22 27	22 42	
Mitcham Eastfields	d		19 58				20 28				20 58				21 28				21 58			
Mitcham Junction	d		20 01				20 31				21 01				21 31				22 01			
Hackbridge	d		20 04				20 34				21 04				21 34				22 04			
Carshalton	d		20 07				20 37				21 07				21 37				22 07			
Sutton (Surrey)	a		20 10	20 31	20 46		20 40	21 01	21 16		21 10	21 31	21 46		21 40	22 01	22 16		22 10	22 31	22 46	
	d		20 11				20 41				21 11				21 41				22 11			
Belmont	d																					
Banstead	d																					
Epsom Downs	a																					
Cheam	d		20 13				20 43				21 13				21 43				22 13			
Ewell East	d		20 17				20 47				21 17				21 47				22 17			
Epsom	a	20 06	20 21			20 36	20 51			21 06	21 21			21 36	21 51			22 06	22 21			22 36
	d	20 08	20 21			20 38	20 51			21 08	21 21			21 38	21 51			22 08	22 21			22 38
Ashtead	d	20 12	20 25			20 42	20 55			21 12	21 25			21 42	21 55			22 12	22 25			22 42
Leatherhead	d	20 15	20 28			20 45	20 58			21 15	21 28			21 45	21 58			22 15	22 28			22 45
Bookham	d	20 21								21 21								22 21				
Effingham Junction	d	20 25								21 25								22 25				
Guildford	a	20 44								21 44								22 44				
Boxhill & Westhumble	d		20 33				21 03				21 33				22 03				22 33			
Dorking	a		20 36			20 53	21 06				21 36			21 53	22 06				22 36			22 53
	d																					
Holmwood	d																					
Ockley	d																					
Warnham	d																					
Horsham	a																					

		SN	SN	SN	SW	SN	SN	SN	SW	SN	SW	SN	FC	FC	FC		FC
London Victoria ⊖	d	22 08	22 19	22 24		22 38	22 49	22 54		23 08		23 19					
London Waterloo ⊖	d				22 32				23 02		23 32						
Clapham Junction	d	22 16	22 26	22 32	22 41	22 46	22 56	23 02	23 11	23 16	23 41	23 27					
Balham ⊖	d	22 21	22 30	22 38		22 51	23 00	23 07		23 21		23 32					
London Bridge ⊖	d												23p15	23p45	09 32		21 02
Tulse Hill	d												23p31	00 01	09 43		21 13
New Cross Gate ⊖	d																
Norwood Junction	d			22 57				23 27									
West Croydon	d		22 49	23 04			23 19	23 34				23 50					
Waddon	d		22 51	23 06			23 21	23 36				23 52					
Wallington	d		22 55	23 10			23 25	23 40				23 56					
Carshalton Beeches	d		22 57	23 12			23 27	23 42				23 58					
Mitcham Eastfields	d	22 28				22 58				23 28							
Mitcham Junction	d	22 31				23 01				23 31							
Hackbridge	d	22 34				23 04				23 34							
Carshalton	d	22 37				23 07				23 37							
Sutton (Surrey)	a	22 40	23 01	23 16		23 10	23 31	23 46		23 40		00 02	00 05	00 35	10 16	and every 30 minutes until	21 46
	d	22 41				23 11				23 41		00 04					
Belmont	d																
Banstead	d																
Epsom Downs	a																
Cheam	d	22 43				23 13				23 43		00 06					
Ewell East	d	22 47				23 17				23 47		00 10					
Epsom	a	22 51			23 06	23 21			23 36	23 51	00 06	00 14					
	d	22 51			23 08	23 21				23 51							
Ashtead	d	22 55			23 12	23 25				23 55							
Leatherhead	d	22 58			23 15	23 28				23 58							
Bookham	d				23 21												
Effingham Junction	d				23 25												
Guildford	a				23 44												
Boxhill & Westhumble	d	23 03				23 33				00 03							
Dorking	a	23 06				23 36				00 06							
	d																
Holmwood	d																
Ockley	d																
Warnham	d																
Horsham	a																

until 30 September

Horsham, Dorking, Guildford, Epsom and Sutton - London

Miles	Miles	Miles			SN MO	SN MO	SN MO	SN MX	SN	SW	SN	SN	SN	FC	SN	SW	SN	SW	SN	SN	FC	SN	SW
—	—	0	Horsham	d																		05 49	
—	—	2	Warnham	d																		05 53	
—	—	6½	Ockley	d																		06 00	
—	—	8¾	Holmwood	d																		06 04	
—	—	13¾	Dorking	a																		06 10	
—	—	—		d			23p16									05 48						06 11	
—	—	14½	Boxhill & Westhumble	d			23p18									05 50						06 13	
0	—	—	Guildford	d						04 58													05 58
8¼	—	—	Effingham Junction	d						05 16													06 16
10	—	—	Bookham	d						05 19													06 19
12½	—	17¾	Leatherhead	d			23p23			05 24						05 56						06 18	06 24
14½	—	—	Ashtead	d			23p27			05 28						05 59						06 22	06 28
16¼	—	—	Epsom	a			23p31			05 32						06 04						06 26	06 32
—	—	—		d			23p32		05 23	05 34		05 39			05 57	06 04		06 18				06 27	06 34
17¾	—	—	Ewell East	d			23p36		05 27			05 43			06 01							06 31	
19¼	—	—	Cheam	d			23p39		05 30			05 46			06 04							06 34	
—	0	—	Epsom Downs	d				23p43															
—	1½	—	Banstead	d				23p46															
—	3	—	Belmont	d				23p49															
20¼	4	5½	Sutton (Surrey)	a			23p42	23p52	05 33			05 49			06 07							06 37	
—	—	—		d	23p25	23p40	23p43	23p53	05 33		05 37	05 49	06 03	06 05	06 08		06 14		06 14	06 33	06 34	06 37	
—	5¼	—	Carshalton	d			23p46				05 40				06 11		06 17				06 37	06 40	
—	6¼	—	Hackbridge	d			23p48				05 42				06 13		06 19				06 39	06 43	
—	7	—	Mitcham Junction	d			23p52				05 46				06 17		06 23				06 42	06 46	
—	8	—	Mitcham Eastfields	d			23p55				05 49				06 20		06 26				06 45	06 49	
21¼	—	—	Carshalton Beeches	d	23p28	23p43		23p56	05 36			05 52	06 06						06 17	06 36			
22	—	—	Wallington	d	23p30	23p45		23p58	05 39			05 55	06 08						06 20	06 38			
23½	—	—	Waddon	d	23p33	23p48		00 01	05 42			05 58	06 11						06 23	06 41			
24½	—	0	West Croydon	d	23p37	23p52		00a04	05 45			06 01	06 15						06 26	06 45			
26¼	—	—	Norwood Junction	d					05 50				06 20							06 50			
32¼	—	—	New Cross Gate ⊖	d					06 08														
—	—	6	Tulse Hill	a							05 57			06 42			06 34				06 53		
—	—	—		d							05 57						06 34						
35	—	12	London Bridge ⊖	a					06 14		06 08		06 33				06 51			07 04			
—	11¼	—	Balham ⊖	d	23p53	00 08	00 01					06 17			06 27				06 42			06 57	
—	13¼	—	Clapham Junction	a	23p57	00 12	00 06			06 00		06 23			06 31	06 30		06 45	06 48			07 01	07 00
—	—	—	London Waterloo ⊖	a						06 11						06 40		06 55					07 12
—	16	—	London Victoria ⊖	a	00 04	00 19	00 15					06 31			06 38				06 56			07 08	

		SW	SN	FC	SN	SN	FC	SN	SW	SN	SN	SN	SN	SW	SN	SW	FC	SN	SW	SW	FC	SN	SN
Horsham	d							06 20										06 55					
Warnham	d							06 24										06 59					
Ockley	d							06 31										07 06					
Holmwood	d							06 35										07 10					
Dorking	a							06 41										07 16					
	d	06 32						06 44					06 59	07 02				07 17		07 32			
Boxhill & Westhumble	d	06 34						06 46					07 01	07 04						07 34			
Guildford	d								06 28										06 58				
Effingham Junction	d								06 48										07 16				
Bookham	d								06 51										07 19				
Leatherhead	d	06 39						06 51	06 56				07 06	07 09				07 23	07 26	07 39			
Ashtead	d	06 43						06 55	06 59				07 10	07 13				07 26	07 29	07 43			
Epsom	a	06 47						06 59	07 04				07 14	07 17				07 31	07 34	07 47			
	d	06 48				06 49		07 00	07 04				07 15	07 18	07 21	07 22		07 31	07 34	07 48			
Ewell East	d					06 53		07 04					07 19		07 25								
Cheam	d					06 56		07 07					07 22		07 28			07 37					
Epsom Downs	d		06 34							07 05												07 34	
Banstead	d		06 37							07 08												07 37	
Belmont	d		06 40							07 11												07 40	
Sutton (Surrey)	a		06 43			06 59		07 10		07 14			07 25		07 31			07 40				07 43	
	d		06 44	06 46	06 50	07 00	07 06	07 10		07 15	07 20	07 22	07 26		07 32		07 37	07 42			07 40	07 45	07 49
Carshalton	d				06 53			07 13			07 23		07 29				07 40	07 45					07 52
Hackbridge	d				06 55			07 16			07 25		07 31				07 42						07 54
Mitcham Junction	d				06 59			07 19			07 29		07 35				07 45	07 49					07 58
Mitcham Eastfields	d				07 02			07 22			07 32		07 38				07 48	07 52					08 01
Carshalton Beeches	d		06 47			07 03				07 18		07 25			07 35							07 48	
Wallington	d		06 50			07 05				07 20		07 27			07 37							07 50	
Waddon	d		06 53			07 08				07 23		07 30			07 40							07 53	
West Croydon	d		06 58			07 13				07 28		07 34			07 44							07 58	
Norwood Junction	d					07 18									07 49								
New Cross Gate ⊖	d																						
Tulse Hill	a			07 20	07 09		07 42				07 39						07 56				08 13		08 08
	d				07 10						07 41												08 09
London Bridge ⊖	a				07 28	07 32					07 59				08 05								08 28
Balham ⊖	d		07 14					07 29		07 44		07 50	07 47					07 59				08 14	
Clapham Junction	a	07 15	07 19					07 34	07 30	07 49		07 55	07 51	07 42		07 48		08 04	08 01	08 12		08 19	
London Waterloo ⊖	a	07 27							07 42					07 54		08 00			08 13	08 24			
London Victoria ⊖	a		07 30					07 41		08 00		08 06	08 00					08 11				08 30	

Table 182

Mondays to Fridays

until 30 September

Horsham, Dorking, Guildford, Epsom and Sutton - London

		SN	SN	SW	SN	FC	FC	SN	SW	SW	SW	SN	SN	SN	SN	SW	FC	FC	SN	SN	SW	SN	SN
Horsham [4]	d							07 21												07 56			
Warnham	d							07 25												08 00			
Ockley	d							07 32												08 07			
Holmwood	d							07 36												08 11			
Dorking [4]	a							07 42												08 17			
	d							07 46		08 02										08 22	08 31		
Boxhill & Westhumble	d									08 04										08 24	08 33		
Guildford	d				07 26											07 58							08 16
Effingham Junction [6]	d				07 38				07 46							08 16							08 32
Bookham	d				07 41				07 49							08 19							08 35
Leatherhead	d				07 46			07 52	07 56	08 09						08 25				08 29	08 38		08 41
Ashtead	d				07 50			07 55	07 59	08 13						08 28				08 33	08 42		08 45
Epsom [3]	a				07 54			08 00	08 04	08 17						08 33				08 37	08 46		08 49
	d		07 49	07 52	07 55			08 02	08 04	08 18	08 22				08 22	08 34				08 38	08 48		08 50
Ewell East	d		07 53		07 59			08 06							08 26					08 42			08 54
Cheam	d		07 56		08 02			08 09							08 29					08 45			08 57
Epsom Downs	d											08 04							08 34				
Banstead	d											08 07							08 37				
Belmont	d											08 10							08 40				
Sutton (Surrey) [4]	a		07 59		08 05			08 12				08 13			08 32				08 43	08 48			09 00
	d	07 53	08 00		08 05	08 08	08 09	08 12				08 14	08 20	08 29	08 32		08 39	08 41	08 45	08 48		08 57	09 00
Carshalton	d		08 03				08 12	08 15					08 23	08 32			08 42			08 51		09 00	09 03
Hackbridge	d		08 05				08 14	08 18					08 25	08 34			08 44			08 54		09 02	09 06
Mitcham Junction	d		08 09				08 17	08 21					08 29	08 38			08 47			08 57		09 06	09 09
Mitcham Eastfields	d		08 12				08 20	08 24					08 32	08 41			08 50			09 00		09 09	09 12
Carshalton Beeches	d	07 56			08 08							08 17			08 35				08 48				
Wallington	d	07 58			08 11							08 19			08 38				08 50				
Waddon	d	08 01										08 22			08 41				08 53				
West Croydon [4]	d	08 05			08 16							08 26			08 44				08 57				
Norwood Junction [2]	d				08 21										08 49								
New Cross Gate [4] ⊖	d																						
Tulse Hill [3]	a					08 43	08 28						08 40				08 58	09 13				09 16	
	d												08 40									09 16	
London Bridge [4] ⊖	a				08 35								08 57		09 04							09 35	
Balham [4] ⊖	d	08 21	08 18									08 43		08 47					09 13	09 07			09 18
Clapham Junction [10]	a	08 25	08 22	08 18				08 32	08 31	08 42	08 48	08 49		08 52		09 00			09 18	09 11	09 15		09 22
London Waterloo [15] ⊖	a			08 30					08 43	08 54	09 00					09 12					09 27		
London Victoria [15] ⊖	a	08 36	08 30					08 39				09 00		09 00					09 31	09 20			09 33

		SW	SN	FC	FC	SN	SN	SW	SN	SN	SW	SN	FC	FC	SN	SN	SN	SN	SW	SW	SN	FC
Horsham [4]	d																	09 09				
Warnham	d																	09 13				
Ockley	d																	09 20				
Holmwood	d																	09 24				
Dorking [4]	a																	09 30				
	d						08 57	09 02										09 31	09 35			
Boxhill & Westhumble	d						08 59	09 04										09 33				
Guildford	d										08 58									09 28		
Effingham Junction [6]	d	08 48									09 16									09 46		
Bookham	d	08 51									09 19									09 49		
Leatherhead	d	08 56					09 04	09 09			09 24							09 38	09 41	09 54		
Ashtead	d	08 59					09 08	09 13			09 28							09 42	09 45	09 58		
Epsom [3]	a	09 04					09 12	09 17			09 32							09 46	09 49	10 02		
	d	09 04					09 13	09 18		09 19	09 35					09 42		09 49	09 50	10 05		
Ewell East	d						09 17			09 23						09 46		09 53				
Cheam	d						09 20			09 26						09 49		09 56				
Epsom Downs	d								09 09						09 35							
Banstead	d								09 12						09 38							
Belmont	d								09 15						09 41							
Sutton (Surrey) [4]	a						09 23		09 18	09 29					09 44	09 52		09 59				
	d		09 03	09 11	09 13	09 15	09 23		09 23	09 30		09 33	09 37	09 38	09 45	09 53	09 52	10 00			10 03	10 07
Carshalton	d				09 16					09 33				09 41				10 03				
Hackbridge	d				09 18					09 35				09 43				10 05				
Mitcham Junction	d				09 21					09 39				09 46				10 09				
Mitcham Eastfields	d				09 24		09 32			09 42				09 49				10 12				
Carshalton Beeches	d		09 06			09 18			09 26			09 36			09 48		09 55				10 06	
Wallington	d		09 08			09 20			09 28			09 38			09 50		09 57				10 08	
Waddon	d		09 11			09 23			09 31			09 41			09 53		10 00				10 11	
West Croydon [4]	d		09 15			09 28			09 35			09 45			09 58		10 04				10 15	
Norwood Junction [2]	d		09 22									09 52									10 22	
New Cross Gate [4] ⊖	d																					
Tulse Hill [3]	a			09 42	09 32								10 12	09 57								10 42
	d																					
London Bridge [4] ⊖	a																					
Balham [4] ⊖	d		09 41			09 44			09 52	09 49		10 09			10 14		10 21	10 18			10 39	
Clapham Junction [10]	a	09 30	09 46			09 49	09 42	09 45	09 57	09 53	10 00	10 15			10 19	10 11	10 26	10 22	10 15	10 30	10 45	
London Waterloo [15] ⊖	a	09 42						09 57			10 10								10 25	10 40		
London Victoria [15] ⊖	a		09 58			10 00	09 52		10 05	10 00		10 24			10 28	10 20	10 34	10 31			10 53	

Table 182

Mondays to Fridays

until 30 September

Horsham, Dorking, Guildford, Epsom and Sutton - London

		FC	SN	SN	SN	SW	SN	SW	SN	FC	FC	SN	SN	SW	SN	SN	SW	SN	FC	FC	SN	SN	SW
Horsham [4]	d												10 04										
Warnham	d												10 08										
Ockley	d												10 15										
Holmwood	d												10 19										
Dorking [4]	a												10 25										
	d				09 57	10 05							10 26	10 35								10 58	11 05
Boxhill & Westhumble	d				09 59								10 28										
Guildford	d							09 58									10 28						
Effingham Junction [6]	d							10 16									10 46						
Bookham	d							10 19									10 49						
Leatherhead	d				10 04	10 11		10 24					10 33	10 41			10 54					11 04	11 11
Ashtead	d				10 08	10 14		10 28					10 37	10 44			10 58					11 07	11 14
Epsom [3]	a				10 12	10 19		10 32					10 41	10 49			11 02					11 12	11 19
	d		10 04		10 13	10 20	10 19	10 35					10 42	10 50		10 49	11 05				11 04	11 13	11 20
Ewell East	d		10 08		10 17		10 23						10 46			10 53					11 08		
Cheam	d		10 11		10 20		10 26						10 49			10 56					11 11	11 18	
Epsom Downs	d											10 35											
Banstead	d											10 38											
Belmont	d											10 41											
Sutton (Surrey) [4]	a		10 14		10 23		10 29					10 44	10 52			10 59					11 14	11 21	
	d	10 08	10 15	10 22	10 23		10 30		10 33	10 37	10 38	10 45	10 53		10 52	11 00		11 03	11 07	11 08	11 15	11 23	
Carshalton	d	10 11					10 33				10 41					11 03				11 11			
Hackbridge	d	10 13					10 35				10 43					11 05				11 13			
Mitcham Junction	d	10 16					10 39				10 46					11 09				11 16			
Mitcham Eastfields	d	10 19					10 42				10 49					11 12				11 19			
Carshalton Beeches	d		10 18	10 25					10 36			10 48			10 55			11 06			11 18		
Wallington	d		10 20	10 27					10 38			10 50			10 57			11 08			11 20		
Waddon	d		10 23	10 30					10 41			10 53			11 00			11 11			11 23		
West Croydon [4]	d		10 28	10 34					10 45			10 58			11 04			11 15			11 28		
Norwood Junction [2]	d								10 52									11 22					
New Cross Gate [4] ⊖	d																						
Tulse Hill [3]	a	10 27								11 12	10 57								11 42	11 27			
	d																						
London Bridge [4] ⊖	a																						
Balham [4] ⊖	d		10 44	10 51			10 48		11 09			11 14			11 21	11 18		11 40			11 44		
Clapham Junction [10]	a		10 49	10 56	10 40	10 45	10 52	11 00	11 14			11 19	11 10	11 15	11 26	11 22	11 30	11 45			11 49	11 40	11 45
London Waterloo [15] ⊖	a					10 55		11 10						11 25			11 40						11 55
London Victoria [15] ⊖	a		10 58	11 04	10 48		11 00		11 23			11 28	11 20		11 34	11 30		11 54			11 58	11 50	

		SN	SN	SW	SN	FC	FC	SN	SN	SW	SN	SN	SW	SN	FC	FC	SN	SN	SW	SN	SN	SW
Horsham [4]	d								11 04													
Warnham	d								11 08													
Ockley	d								11 15													
Holmwood	d								11 19													
Dorking [4]	a								11 25													
	d								11 26	11 35								11 58	12 05			
Boxhill & Westhumble	d								11 28													
Guildford	d			10 58									11 28									11 58
Effingham Junction [6]	d			11 16									11 46									12 16
Bookham	d			11 19									11 49									12 19
Leatherhead	d			11 24					11 33	11 41			11 54					12 04	12 11			12 24
Ashtead	d			11 28					11 37	11 44			11 58					12 07	12 14			12 28
Epsom [3]	a			11 32					11 41	11 49			12 02					12 12	12 19			12 32
	d		11 19	11 35					11 42	11 50		11 49	12 05				12 04	12 13	12 20		12 19	12 35
Ewell East	d		11 23						11 46			11 53					12 08				12 23	
Cheam	d		11 26						11 49			11 56					12 11	12 18			12 26	
Epsom Downs	d							11 35														
Banstead	d							11 38														
Belmont	d							11 41														
Sutton (Surrey) [4]	a		11 29					11 44	11 52			11 59					12 14	12 21			12 29	
	d	11 22	11 30		11 33	11 37	11 38	11 45	11 53		11 52	12 00		12 03	12 07	12 08	12 15	12 23		12 22	12 30	
Carshalton	d		11 33				11 41					12 03				12 11					12 33	
Hackbridge	d		11 35				11 43					12 05				12 13					12 35	
Mitcham Junction	d		11 39				11 46					12 09				12 16					12 39	
Mitcham Eastfields	d		11 42				11 49					12 12				12 19					12 42	
Carshalton Beeches	d	11 25			11 36			11 48			11 55			12 06			12 18			12 25		
Wallington	d	11 27			11 38			11 50			11 57			12 08			12 20			12 27		
Waddon	d	11 30			11 41			11 53			12 00			12 11			12 23			12 30		
West Croydon [4]	d	11 34			11 45			11 58			12 04			12 15			12 28			12 34		
Norwood Junction [2]	d				11 52									12 22								
New Cross Gate [4] ⊖	d																					
Tulse Hill [3]	a					12 12	11 57								12 42	12 27						
	d																					
London Bridge [4] ⊖	a																					
Balham [4] ⊖	d	11 51	11 48		12 09			12 14			12 21	12 18		12 39			12 44			12 51	12 48	
Clapham Junction [10]	a	11 56	11 52	12 00	12 14			12 19	12 10	12 15	12 26	12 22	12 30	12 44			12 49	12 40	12 45	12 56	12 52	13 00
London Waterloo [15] ⊖	a			12 10						12 25			12 40						12 55			13 10
London Victoria [15] ⊖	a	12 04	12 00		12 23			12 28	12 18		12 34	12 30		12 53			12 58	12 48		13 04	13 00	

Horsham, Dorking, Guildford, Epsom and Sutton - London

until 30 September

		SN	FC	FC	SN	SN	SW	SN	SN		SW	SN	FC	FC	SN	SN	SW	SN	SN		SW	SN	FC	FC	SN
Horsham 4	d					12 04																			
Warnham	d					12 08																			
Ockley	d					12 15																			
Holmwood	d					12 19																			
Dorking 4	a					12 25																			
	d					12 26	12 35									12 58	13 05								
Boxhill & Westhumble	d					12 28																			
Guildford	d										12 28										12 58				
Effingham Junction 6	d										12 46										13 16				
Bookham	d										12 49										13 19				
Leatherhead	d					12 33	12 41				12 54					13 04	13 11				13 24				
Ashtead	d					12 37	12 44				12 58					13 07	13 14				13 28				
Epsom 3	a					12 41	12 49				13 02					13 12	13 19				13 32				
	d					12 42	12 50		12 49		13 05				13 04	13 13	13 20		13 19		13 35				
Ewell East	d					12 46			12 53						13 08				13 23						
Cheam	d					12 49			12 56						13 11	13 18			13 26						
Epsom Downs	d				12 35																				13 35
Banstead	d				12 38																				13 38
Belmont	d				12 41																				13 41
Sutton (Surrey) 4	a				12 44	12 52			12 59						13 14	13 21			13 29						13 44
	d	12 33	12 37	12 38	12 45	12 53		12 52	13 00			13 03	13 07	13 08	13 15	13 23		13 22	13 30			13 33	13 37	13 38	13 45
Carshalton	d			12 41					13 03					13 11					13 33					13 41	
Hackbridge	d			12 43					13 05					13 13					13 35					13 43	
Mitcham Junction	d			12 46					13 09					13 16					13 39					13 46	
Mitcham Eastfields	d			12 49					13 12					13 19					13 42					13 49	
Carshalton Beeches	d	12 36			12 48			12 55				13 06			13 18			13 25				13 36			13 48
Wallington	d	12 38			12 50			12 57				13 08			13 20			13 27				13 38			13 50
Waddon	d	12 41			12 53			13 00				13 11			13 23			13 30				13 41			13 53
West Croydon 4	d	12 45			12 58			13 04				13 15			13 28			13 34				13 45			13 58
Norwood Junction 2	d	12 52										13 22										13 52			
New Cross Gate 4 ⊖	d																								
Tulse Hill 3	a		13 12	12 57									13 42	13 27									14 12	13 57	
	d																								
London Bridge 4 ⊖	a																								
Balham 4 ⊖	d	13 09			13 14			13 21	13 18			13 39			13 44			13 51	13 48			14 09			14 14
Clapham Junction 10	a	13 14			13 19	13 10	13 15	13 26	13 22		13 30	13 44			13 49	13 40	13 45	13 56	13 52		14 00	14 14			14 19
London Waterloo 15 ⊖	a						13 25				13 40						13 55				14 10				
London Victoria 15 ⊖	a	13 23			13 28	13 18		13 34	13 30			13 53			13 58	13 48		14 04	14 00			14 23			14 28

		SN	SW	SN	SN		SW	SN	FC	FC	SN	SN	SW	SN	SN		SW	SN	FC	FC	SN	SN	SW	SN	SN
Horsham 4	d	13 04																				14 04			
Warnham	d	13 08																				14 08			
Ockley	d	13 15																				14 15			
Holmwood	d	13 19																				14 19			
Dorking 4	a	13 25																				14 25			
	d	13 26	13 35									13 58	14 05									14 26	14 35		
Boxhill & Westhumble	d	13 28																				14 28			
Guildford	d						13 28										13 58								
Effingham Junction 6	d						13 46										14 16								
Bookham	d						13 49										14 19								
Leatherhead	d	13 33	13 41				13 54					14 04	14 11				14 24					14 33	14 41		
Ashtead	d	13 37	13 44				13 58					14 07	14 14				14 28					14 37	14 44		
Epsom 3	a	13 41	13 49				14 02					14 12	14 19				14 32					14 41	14 49		
	d	13 42	13 50		13 49		14 05				14 04	14 13	14 20		14 19		14 35					14 42	14 50		14 49
Ewell East	d	13 46			13 53						14 08				14 23							14 46			14 53
Cheam	d	13 49			13 56						14 11	14 18			14 26							14 49			14 56
Epsom Downs	d																				14 35				
Banstead	d																				14 38				
Belmont	d																				14 41				
Sutton (Surrey) 4	a	13 52			13 59						14 14	14 21			14 29						14 44	14 52			14 59
	d	13 53		13 52	14 00			14 03	14 07	14 08	14 15	14 23		14 22	14 30			14 33	14 37	14 38	14 45	14 53		14 52	15 00
Carshalton	d				14 03					14 11					14 33					14 41					15 03
Hackbridge	d				14 05					14 13					14 35					14 43					15 05
Mitcham Junction	d				14 09					14 16					14 39					14 46					15 09
Mitcham Eastfields	d				14 12					14 19					14 42					14 49					15 12
Carshalton Beeches	d			13 55				14 06			14 18			14 25				14 36			14 48			14 55	
Wallington	d			13 57				14 08			14 20			14 27				14 38			14 50			14 57	
Waddon	d			14 00				14 11			14 23			14 30				14 41			14 53			15 00	
West Croydon 4	d			14 04				14 15			14 28			14 34				14 45			14 58			15 04	
Norwood Junction 2	d							14 22										14 52							
New Cross Gate 4 ⊖	d																								
Tulse Hill 3	a								14 42	14 27									15 12	14 57					
	d																								
London Bridge 4 ⊖	a																								
Balham 4 ⊖	d			14 21	14 18			14 39			14 44			14 51	14 48			15 09			15 14			15 21	15 18
Clapham Junction 10	a	14 10	14 15	14 26	14 22		14 30	14 44			14 49	14 40	14 45	14 56	14 52		15 00	15 14			15 19	15 10	15 15	15 26	15 22
London Waterloo 15 ⊖	a		14 25				14 40						14 55				15 10						15 25		
London Victoria 15 ⊖	a	14 18		14 34	14 30			14 53			14 58	14 48		15 04	15 00			15 24			15 28	15 22		15 34	15 30

Horsham, Dorking, Guildford, Epsom and Sutton - London

until 30 September

			SW	SN	FC	FC	SN	SN	SW	SN	SN		SW	SN	FC	FC	SN	SN	SW	SN	SN		SW	SN	FC
Horsham 4	d																	15 04							
Warnham	d																	15 08							
Ockley	d																	15 15							
Holmwood	d																	15 19							
Dorking 4	a																	15 25							
	d							14 58	15 05									15 26	15 35						
Boxhill & Westhumble	d																	15 28							
Guildford	d		14 28										14 58										15 28		
Effingham Junction 6	d		14 46										15 16										15 46		
Bookham	d		14 49										15 19										15 49		
Leatherhead	d		14 54					15 04	15 11				15 24					15 33	15 41				15 54		
Ashtead	d		14 58					15 07	15 14				15 28					15 37	15 44				15 58		
Epsom 3	a		15 02					15 12	15 19				15 32					15 41	15 49				16 02		
	d		15 05				15 04	15 13	15 20		15 19		15 35					15 42	15 50		15 49		16 05		
Ewell East	d						15 08				15 23							15 46			15 53				
Cheam	d						15 11	15 18			15 26							15 49			15 56				
Epsom Downs	d																15 35								
Banstead	d																15 38								
Belmont	d																15 41								
Sutton (Surrey) 4	a						15 14	15 21			15 29						15 44	15 52			15 59				
	d			15 03	15 07	15 08	15 15	15 23		15 22	15 30			15 33	15 37	15 38	15 45	15 53		15 52	16 00			16 03	16 07
Carshalton	d					15 11					15 33					15 41					16 03				
Hackbridge	d					15 13					15 35					15 43					16 05				
Mitcham Junction	d					15 16					15 39					15 46					16 09				
Mitcham Eastfields	d					15 19					15 42					15 49					16 12				
Carshalton Beeches	d			15 06			15 18			15 25				15 36			15 48			15 55				16 06	
Wallington	d			15 08			15 20			15 27				15 38			15 50			15 57				16 08	
Waddon	d			15 11			15 23			15 30				15 41			15 53			16 00				16 11	
West Croydon 4	d			15 15			15 28			15 34				15 45			15 58			16 04				16 15	
Norwood Junction 2	d			15 22										15 52										16 22	
New Cross Gate 4 ⊖	d																								
Tulse Hill 3	a				15 42	15 27									16 12	15 57									16 44
	d																								
London Bridge 4 ⊖	a																								
Balham 4 ⊖	d			15 39			15 44			15 51	15 48			16 09			16 14			16 21	16 18			16 39	
Clapham Junction 10	a		15 30	15 44			15 49	15 40	15 45	15 56	15 52		16 00	16 14			16 19	16 10	16 15	16 26	16 23		16 30	16 45	
London Waterloo 15 ⊖	a		15 40						15 55				16 10						16 25				16 40		
London Victoria 15 ⊖	a			15 54			15 58	15 52		16 04	16 00			16 23			16 28	16 18		16 34	16 30			16 55	

		FC	SN	SN	SW	SN	SN		SW	SN	SN	FC	FC 1	SN	SW	SN	SN		SW	SN	FC	SN	FC	SN	SW
Horsham 4	d													16 04											
Warnham	d													16 08											
Ockley	d													16 15											
Holmwood	d													16 19											
Dorking 4	a													16 25											
	d			15 56	16 05									16 26	16 35									17 00	17 05
Boxhill & Westhumble	d			15 58										16 28										17 02	
Guildford	d								15 58										16 28						
Effingham Junction 6	d								16 16										16 46						
Bookham	d								16 19										16 49						
Leatherhead	d			16 03	16 11				16 24					16 33	16 41				16 54					17 07	17 11
Ashtead	d			16 07	16 14				16 28					16 37	16 44				16 58					17 11	17 14
Epsom 3	a			16 11	16 19				16 32					16 41	16 49				17 02					17 15	17 19
	d		16 04	16 12	16 20		16 19		16 35					16 42	16 50		16 49		17 05					17 19	17 20
Ewell East	d		16 08	16 16			16 23							16 46			16 53							17 23	
Cheam	d		16 11	16 19			16 26							16 49			16 56							17 26	
Epsom Downs	d										16 26											17 02			
Banstead	d										16 29											17 05			
Belmont	d										16 32											17 08			
Sutton (Surrey) 4	a		16 14	16 22			16 29				16 35			16 52			16 59					17 11		17 29	
	d	16 08	16 15	16 23		16 22	16 30			16 33	16 45	16 37	16 38	16 53		16 52	17 00			17 03	17 08	17 15	17 11	17 30	
Carshalton	d	16 11					16 33						16 41				17 03				17 11			17 33	
Hackbridge	d	16 13					16 35						16 43				17 05				17 13			17 35	
Mitcham Junction	d	16 16					16 39						16 46				17 09				17 16			17 39	
Mitcham Eastfields	d	16 19					16 42						16 49				17 12				17 19			17 42	
Carshalton Beeches	d		16 18			16 25				16 36	16 48					16 55				17 06		17 18			
Wallington	d		16 20			16 27				16 38	16 50					16 57				17 08		17 20			
Waddon	d		16 23			16 30				16 41	16 53					17 00				17 11		17 23			
West Croydon 4	d		16 28			16 34				16 45	16 58					17 04				17 18		17 28			
Norwood Junction 2	d									16 52										17 23					
New Cross Gate 4 ⊖	d																								
Tulse Hill 3	a	16 27										17 14	16 57								17 27		17 44		
	d																								
London Bridge 4 ⊖	a																								
Balham 4 ⊖	d		16 44			16 51	16 48			17 09	17 14					17 21	17 18			17 39		17 44		17 48	
Clapham Junction 10	a		16 49	16 40	16 45	16 56	16 53		17 00	17 14	17 19			17 10	17 15	17 26	17 23		17 30	17 44		17 49		17 52	17 45
London Waterloo 15 ⊖	a				16 55				17 10						17 25				17 40						17 55
London Victoria 15 ⊖	a		16 58	16 48		17 04	17 00			17 23	17 28			17 18		17 34	17 30			17 55		17 58		18 00	

Table 182

Mondays to Fridays

until 30 September

Horsham, Dorking, Guildford, Epsom and Sutton - London

		SN	SW		FC	FC	SN	SN	SW	SN	SW	FC	FC		SN	SN	SW	SN	SW	FC	FC	SN	SN		SW
Horsham	d							17 07								17 34							18 04		
Warnham	d							17 11								17 38							18 08		
Ockley	d							17 18								17 45							18 15		
Holmwood	d							17 22								17 49							18 19		
Dorking	a							17 28								17 55							18 25		
	d							17 31	17 35							17 56	18 05						18 26		18 35
Boxhill & Westhumble	d							17 33								17 58							18 28		
Guildford	d		16 58								17 28								17 58						
Effingham Junction	d		17 16								17 46								18 16						
Bookham	d		17 19								17 49								18 19						
Leatherhead	d		17 24					17 38	17 41		17 54					18 03	18 11		18 24				18 33		18 41
Ashtead	d		17 28					17 42	17 45		17 58					18 07	18 14		18 28				18 37		18 45
Epsom	a		17 32					17 46	17 49		18 02					18 14	18 19		18 32				18 43		18 49
	d	17 23	17 35					17 49	17 50	17 52	18 05					18 17	18 20	18 22	18 35				18 49		18 50
Ewell East	d	17 27						17 53		17 56						18 23		18 26					18 53		
Cheam	d	17 30						17 56		17 59						18 26		18 29					18 56		
Epsom Downs	d						17 35								18 02							18 35			
Banstead	d						17 38								18 05							18 38			
Belmont	d						17 41								18 08							18 41			
Sutton (Surrey)	a	17 33					17 44	17 59		18 02					18 11	18 29		18 32				18 44	18 59		
	d	17 33			17 41	17 42	17 45	18 00		18 04		18 08	18 09		18 12	18 30		18 33		18 38	18 43	18 45	19 00		
Carshalton	d					17 45		18 03				18 11				18 33				18 41			19 03		
Hackbridge	d					17 47		18 05				18 13				18 35				18 43			19 05		
Mitcham Junction	d					17 50		18 09				18 16				18 39				18 46			19 09		
Mitcham Eastfields	d					17 53		18 12				18 19				18 42				18 49			19 12		
Carshalton Beeches	d	17 36					17 48			18 07					18 15			18 36				18 48			
Wallington	d	17 39					17 50			18 09					18 17			18 38				18 50			
Waddon	d	17 42					17 53			18 12					18 20			18 41				18 53			
West Croydon	d	17 48					17 58			18 18					18 28			18 47				18 58			
Norwood Junction	d	17 55								18 24								18 52							
New Cross Gate ⊖	d																								
Tulse Hill	a				18 14	18 01						18 27	18 44							18 57	19 14				
	d																								
London Bridge ⊖	a																								
Balham ⊖	d	18 11					18 14	18 18		18 40					18 44	18 48		19 09				19 14	19 18		
Clapham Junction	a	18 16	18 00				18 19	18 22	18 15	18 45	18 30				18 49	18 52	18 45	19 14	19 00			19 19	19 22		19 16
London Waterloo ⊖	a		18 10						18 25		18 40						18 55		19 10						19 27
London Victoria ⊖	a	18 25					18 28	18 33		18 54					18 57	19 01		19 25				19 28	19 30		

		SN	SW	FC	FC	SN	SN	SW	SN		SW	FC	FC	SN	SN	SN	SW	SN	SW		FC	FC	SN	SN	SW
Horsham	d						18 34									19 04									
Warnham	d						18 38									19 08									
Ockley	d						18 45									19 15									
Holmwood	d						18 49									19 19									
Dorking	a						18 55									19 25									
	d		18 50				18 56		19 05							19 28	19 33	19 37						19 57	20 05
Boxhill & Westhumble	d						18 58									19 30								19 59	
Guildford	d	18 22													19 04				19 28						
Effingham Junction	d	18 39						18 59							19 20				19 46						
Bookham	d	18 42						19 02							19 23				19 49						
Leatherhead	d	18 47	18 56				19 03	19 08	19 11						19 28	19 35	19 39	19 43	19 54					20 04	20 11
Ashtead	d	18 51	18 59				19 07	19 12	19 15						19 32	19 39	19 42	19 46	19 58					20 08	20 14
Epsom	a	18 57	19 04				19 11	19 16	19 19						19 36	19 43	19 47	19 51	20 02					20 12	20 19
	d	18 57	19 05				19 12	19 20	19 20		19 35				19 37	19 46	19 50	19 52	20 05					20 13	20 20
Ewell East	d						19 16		19 24						19 41	19 50		19 56						20 17	
Cheam	d						19 19		19 27						19 44	19 53		19 59						20 20	
Epsom Downs	d					19 06								19 36									20 13		
Banstead	d					19 09								19 39									20 16		
Belmont	d					19 12								19 42									20 19		
Sutton (Surrey)	a	19 04				19 15	19 22		19 30					19 45	19 47	19 56		20 02					20 22	20 23	
	d	19 05		19 08	19 13	19 16	19 22		19 33			19 38	19 42	19 46		19 56		20 03			20 07	20 10	20 23	20 25	
Carshalton	d			19 11			19 25						19 45			19 59						20 13		20 28	
Hackbridge	d			19 13			19 28						19 47			20 02						20 15		20 31	
Mitcham Junction	d			19 16			19 31						19 50			20 05						20 18		20 34	
Mitcham Eastfields	d			19 19			19 34						19 53			20 08						20 21		20 37	
Carshalton Beeches	d	19 08				19 19			19 36					19 49				20 06					20 26		
Wallington	d	19 10				19 21			19 38					19 51				20 08					20 28		
Waddon	d	19 13				19 24			19 41					19 54				20 11					20 31		
West Croydon	d	19 17				19 28			19 47					19 58				20 18					20 35		
Norwood Junction	d	19 22							19 52									20 23							
New Cross Gate ⊖	d																								
Tulse Hill	a			19 27	19 44							20 10	20 01								20 40	20 29			
	d																								
London Bridge ⊖	a																								
Balham ⊖	d	19 39				19 45	19 42		20 08					20 14		20 17		20 39					20 51	20 44	
Clapham Junction	a	19 44	19 30			19 50	19 47	19 45	20 14		20 00			20 19		20 22	20 15	20 44	20 30				20 56	20 48	20 45
London Waterloo ⊖	a		19 41					19 55			20 10						20 25		20 41						20 55
London Victoria ⊖	a	19 53				19 59	19 55		20 22					20 28		20 30		20 53					21 04	20 56	

Table 182

Mondays to Fridays

until 30 September

Horsham, Dorking, Guildford, Epsom and Sutton - London

		SN	SN	SW	FC		FC	SN	SN	SW	SN	SW	SN	FC	FC		SN	SN	SW	SN	SN	SW	SN	SN	SW
Horsham	d								20 06																
Warnham	d								20 10																
Ockley	d								20 17																
Holmwood	d								20 21																
Dorking	a								20 27																
	d								20 30	20 35								20 59						21 30	21 35
Boxhill & Westhumble	d																	21 01							
Guildford	d			19 58															20 46						
Effingham Junction	d			20 16															21 03						
Bookham	d			20 19															21 06						
Leatherhead	d			20 24					20 36	20 41								21 06	21 11					21 36	21 41
Ashtead	d			20 28					20 39	20 44								21 10	21 14					21 40	21 44
Epsom	a			20 32					20 44	20 49								21 14	21 19					21 44	21 49
	d	20 22	20 25	20 35					20 45	20 50	20 55	21 05						21 15	21 20	21 21	21 28	21 35		21 45	21 50
Ewell East	d	20 26	20 29						20 49		20 59							21 19		21 25				21 49	
Cheam	d	20 29	20 32						20 52		21 02							21 22		21 28				21 52	
Epsom Downs	d												20 54												
Banstead	d												20 57												
Belmont	d												21 00												
Sutton (Surrey)	a	20 32	20 35						20 55		21 05		21 03					21 25		21 31	21 35			21 55	
	d	20 33	20 36		20 37		20 40	20 52	20 55		21 06		21 06	21 10	21 10		21 22	21 25		21 32	21 35		21 52	21 55	
Carshalton	d		20 39				20 43		20 58		21 09			21 13				21 28			21 38			21 58	
Hackbridge	d		20 41				20 45		21 01		21 11			21 15				21 31			21 41			22 01	
Mitcham Junction	d		20 45				20 48		21 04		21 15			21 18				21 34			21 44			22 04	
Mitcham Eastfields	d		20 48				20 51		21 07		21 18			21 21				21 37			21 47			22 07	
Carshalton Beeches	d	20 36						20 55					21 09				21 25			21 35			21 55		
Wallington	d	20 38						20 57					21 11				21 27			21 37			21 57		
Waddon	d	20 41						21 00					21 14				21 30			21 40			22 00		
West Croydon	d	20 45						21 04					21 18				21 34			21 48			22 04		
Norwood Junction	d	20 52											21 23							21 53					
New Cross Gate ⊖	d																								
Tulse Hill	a				21 10		20 59							21 29	21 50										
	d																								
London Bridge ⊖	a																								
Balham ⊖	d	21 08	20 54					21 21	21 14		21 24		21 39				21 51	21 44		22 09	21 54		22 21	22 14	
Clapham Junction	a	21 14	20 59	21 00				21 26	21 18	21 15	21 29	21 30	21 44				21 56	21 49	21 45	22 14	21 59	22 00	22 26	22 19	22 15
London Waterloo ⊖	a			21 10						21 25		21 40							21 55			22 10			22 25
London Victoria ⊖	a	21 22	21 09					21 34	21 26		21 39		21 53				22 04	21 57		22 23	22 09		22 34	22 27	

			SN	SN	FC	SN	SN	SW	SN	SN	SN		SN	SW	SN	SN	SN	SN	SW	SN	SN		SN		
Horsham	d																								
Warnham	d																								
Ockley	d																								
Holmwood	d																								
Dorking	a																								
	d						21 59						22 30	22 35				23 00			23 30				
Boxhill & Westhumble	d						22 01											23 02							
Guildford	d							21 46											22 46						
Effingham Junction	d							22 03											23 03						
Bookham	d							22 06											23 06						
Leatherhead	d						22 06	22 11					22 36	22 41				23 07	23 11		23 36				
Ashtead	d						22 10	22 14					22 40	22 44				23 11	23 14		23 39				
Epsom	a						22 14	22 19					22 44	22 49				23 15	23 19		23 45				
	d		21 55				22 15	22 20	22 21	22 25			22 45	22 50	22 55			23 16	23 20	23 25					
Ewell East	d		21 59				22 19		22 25	22 29			22 49		22 59			23 20		23 29					
Cheam	d		22 02				22 22		22 28	22 32			22 52		23 02			23 23		23 32					
Epsom Downs	d			21 54												22 54							23 43		
Banstead	d			21 57												22 57							23 46		
Belmont	d			22 00												23 00							23 49		
Sutton (Surrey)	a		22 05	22 03			22 25		22 31	22 35			22 55		23 05	23 03		23 26		23 35			23 52		
	d		22 06	22 06	22 12	22 22	22 25		22 32	22 36	22 52		22 55		23 06	23 06	23 20	23 30		23 40			23 53		
Carshalton	d		22 09				22 28			22 39			22 58		23 09										
Hackbridge	d		22 11				22 31			22 41			23 01		23 11										
Mitcham Junction	d		22 15				22 34			22 45			23 04		23 15										
Mitcham Eastfields	d		22 18				22 37			22 48			23 07		23 18										
Carshalton Beeches	d			22 09		22 25			22 35		22 55					23 09	23 23	23 33		23 43			23 56		
Wallington	d			22 11		22 27			22 37		22 57					23 11	23 25	23 35		23 45			23 58		
Waddon	d			22 14		22 30			22 40		23 00					23 14	23 28	23 38		23 48			00 01		
West Croydon	d			22 18		22 34			22 48		23 04					23 18	23a31	23a41		23a57			00a04		
Norwood Junction	d			22 23					22 53							23 23									
New Cross Gate ⊖	d																								
Tulse Hill	a				22 43																				
	d				22 43																				
London Bridge ⊖	a				22 55																				
Balham ⊖	d		22 24	22 39		22 51	22 44		23 09	22 54	23 21		23 14		23 24	23 40									
Clapham Junction	a		22 29	22 44		22 56	22 48	22 45	23 15	22 59	23 26		23 18	23 15	23 29	23 45			23 48						
London Waterloo ⊖	a							22 55						23 27					23 58						
London Victoria ⊖	a		22 39	22 53		23 04	22 56		23 25	23 09	23 34		23 27		23 39	23 54									

Horsham, Dorking, Guildford, Epsom and Sutton - London

from 3 October

		SN MO	SN MO	SN MO	SN MX	SN	SW	SN	SN	SN	FC	SN	SW	SN	SW	SN	SN	FC	SN	SW	SW	SN	FC
Horsham	d																		05 49				
Warnham	d																		05 53				
Ockley	d																		06 00				
Holmwood	d																		06 04				
Dorking	a																		06 10				
	d			23p16									05 48						06 11		06 32		
Boxhill & Westhumble	d			23p18									05 50						06 13		06 34		
Guildford	d						04 58													05 58			
Effingham Junction	d						05 16													06 16			
Bookham	d						05 19													06 19			
Leatherhead	d			23p23			05 24						05 56						06 18	06 24	06 39		
Ashtead	d			23p27			05 28						05 59						06 22	06 28	06 43		
Epsom	a			23p31			05 32						06 04						06 26	06 32	06 47		
	d			23p32		05 23	05 34		05 39			05 57	06 04		06 18				06 27	06 34	06 48		
Ewell East	d			23p36		05 27			05 43			06 01							06 31				
Cheam	d			23p39		05 30			05 46			06 04							06 34				
Epsom Downs	d				23p43																	06 34	
Banstead	d				23p46																	06 37	
Belmont	d				23p49																	06 40	
Sutton (Surrey)	a			23p42	23p52	05 33			05 49			06 07							06 37			06 43	
	d	23p25	23p40	23p43	23p53	05 33		05 37	05 49	06 03	06 05	06 08		06 14		06 14	06 33	06 34	06 37			06 44	06 46
Carshalton	d			23p46				05 40				06 11		06 17				06 37	06 40				
Hackbridge	d			23p48				05 42				06 13		06 19				06 39	06 43				
Mitcham Junction	d			23p52				05 46				06 17		06 23				06 42	06 46				
Mitcham Eastfields	d			23p55				05 49				06 20		06 26				06 45	06 49				
Carshalton Beeches	d	23p28	23p43		23p56	05 36			05 52	06 06						06 17	06 36					06 47	
Wallington	d	23p30	23p45		23p58	05 39			05 55	06 08						06 20	06 38					06 50	
Waddon	d	23p33	23p48		00 01	05 42			05 58	06 11						06 23	06 41					06 53	
West Croydon	d	23p37	23p52		00a04	05 45			06 01	06 15						06 26	06 45					06 58	
Norwood Junction	d					05 50				06 20							06 50						
New Cross Gate ⊖	d					06 08																	
Tulse Hill	a							05 57			06 42			06 34				06 53					07 20
	d							05 57						06 34									
London Bridge ⊖	a					06 14		06 08		06 33				06 51			07 04						
Balham ⊖	d	23p53	00 08	00 01					06 17			06 27				06 42			06 57			07 14	
Clapham Junction	a	23p57	00 12	00 06			06 00		06 23			06 31	06 30		06 45	06 48			07 01	07 00	07 15	07 19	
London Waterloo ⊖	a						06 11						06 40		06 55					07 12	07 27		
London Victoria ⊖	a	00 04	00 19	00 15					06 31			06 38				06 56			07 08			07 30	

		SN	SN	FC	SN	SW	SN	SN	SN	SN	SW	SN	SW	FC	SN	SW	SW	FC	SN	SN	SN	SN	SW
Horsham	d				06 20										06 55								
Warnham	d				06 24										06 59								
Ockley	d				06 31										07 06								
Holmwood	d				06 35										07 10								
Dorking	a				06 41										07 16								
	d				06 44					06 59	07 02				07 17		07 32						
Boxhill & Westhumble	d				06 46					07 01	07 04						07 34						
Guildford	d					06 28										06 58							
Effingham Junction	d					06 48										07 16							
Bookham	d					06 51										07 19							
Leatherhead	d				06 51	06 56				07 06	07 09				07 23	07 26	07 39						
Ashtead	d				06 55	06 59				07 10	07 13				07 26	07 29	07 43						
Epsom	a				06 59	07 04				07 14	07 17				07 31	07 34	07 47						
	d		06 49		07 00	07 04				07 15	07 18	07 21	07 22		07 31	07 34	07 48					07 49	07 52
Ewell East	d		06 53		07 04					07 19		07 25										07 53	
Cheam	d		06 56		07 07					07 22		07 28			07 37							07 56	
Epsom Downs	d						07 05												07 34				
Banstead	d						07 08												07 37				
Belmont	d						07 11												07 40				
Sutton (Surrey)	a		06 59		07 10		07 14			07 25		07 31			07 40				07 43			07 59	
	d	06 50	07 00	07 06	07 10		07 15	07 20	07 22	07 26		07 32		07 37	07 42			07 40	07 45	07 49	07 53	08 00	
Carshalton	d	06 53			07 13			07 23		07 29				07 40	07 45					07 52		08 03	
Hackbridge	d	06 55			07 16			07 25		07 31				07 42						07 54		08 05	
Mitcham Junction	d	06 59			07 19			07 29		07 35				07 45	07 49					07 58		08 09	
Mitcham Eastfields	d	07 02			07 22			07 32		07 38				07 48	07 52					08 01		08 12	
Carshalton Beeches	d		07 03				07 18		07 25			07 35							07 48		07 56		
Wallington	d		07 05				07 20		07 27			07 37							07 50		07 58		
Waddon	d		07 08				07 23		07 30			07 40							07 53		08 01		
West Croydon	d		07 13				07 28		07 34			07 44							07 58		08 05		
Norwood Junction	d		07 18									07 49											
New Cross Gate ⊖	d																						
Tulse Hill	a	07 09		07 42				07 39						07 56				08 13		08 08			
	d	07 10						07 41												08 09			
London Bridge ⊖	a	07 28	07 32					07 59				08 05								08 28			
Balham ⊖	d				07 29		07 44		07 50	07 47					07 59				08 14		08 21	08 18	
Clapham Junction	a				07 34	07 30	07 49		07 55	07 51	07 42		07 48		08 04	08 01	08 12		08 19		08 25	08 22	08 18
London Waterloo ⊖	a					07 42					07 54		08 00			08 13	08 24						08 30
London Victoria ⊖	a				07 41		08 00		08 06	08 00					08 11				08 30		08 36	08 30	

Horsham, Dorking, Guildford, Epsom and Sutton - London

from 3 October

		SN	FC	FC	SN	SW	SW	SW	SN	SN	SN	SN	SW	FC	FC	SN	SN	SW	SN	SN	SW	SN
Horsham	d				07 21												07 56					
Warnham	d				07 25												08 00					
Ockley	d				07 32												08 07					
Holmwood	d				07 36												08 11					
Dorking	a				07 42												08 17					
	d				07 46		08 02										08 22	08 31				
Boxhill & Westhumble	d						08 04										08 24	08 33				
Guildford	d	07 26											07 58							08 16		
Effingham Junction	d	07 38				07 46							08 16							08 32	08 48	
Bookham	d	07 41				07 49							08 19							08 35	08 51	
Leatherhead	d	07 46			07 52	07 56	08 09						08 25				08 29	08 38		08 41	08 56	
Ashtead	d	07 50			07 55	07 59	08 13						08 28				08 33	08 42		08 45	08 59	
Epsom	a	07 54			08 00	08 04	08 17						08 33				08 37	08 46		08 49	09 04	
	d	07 55			08 02	08 04	08 18	08 22				08 22	08 34				08 38	08 48		08 50	09 04	
Ewell East	d	07 59			08 06							08 26					08 42			08 54		
Cheam	d	08 02			08 09							08 29					08 45			08 57		
Epsom Downs	d								08 04							08 34						
Banstead	d								08 07							08 37						
Belmont	d								08 10							08 40						
Sutton (Surrey)	a	08 05			08 12				08 13			08 32				08 43	08 48			09 00		
	d	08 05	08 08	08 09	08 12				08 14	08 20	08 29	08 32		08 39	08 41	08 45	08 48		08 57	09 00		09 03
Carshalton	d			08 12	08 15					08 23	08 32			08 42			08 51		09 00	09 03		
Hackbridge	d			08 14	08 18					08 25	08 34			08 44			08 54		09 02	09 06		
Mitcham Junction	d			08 17	08 21					08 29	08 38			08 47			08 57		09 06	09 09		
Mitcham Eastfields	d			08 20	08 24					08 32	08 41			08 50			09 00		09 09	09 12		
Carshalton Beeches	d	08 08							08 17			08 35				08 48						09 06
Wallington	d	08 11							08 19			08 38				08 50						09 08
Waddon	d								08 22			08 41				08 53						09 11
West Croydon	d	08 16							08 26			08 44				08 57						09 15
Norwood Junction	d	08 21										08 49										09 22
New Cross Gate ⊖	d																					
Tulse Hill	a		08 43	08 28						08 40				08 58	09 13				09 16			
	d									08 40									09 16			
London Bridge ⊖	a	08 35								08 57		09 04							09 35			
Balham ⊖	d								08 43		08 47					09 13	09 07			09 18		09 41
Clapham Junction	a				08 32	08 31	08 42	08 48	08 49		08 52		09 00			09 18	09 11	09 15		09 22	09 30	09 46
London Waterloo ⊖	a					08 43	08 54	09 00					09 12					09 27			09 42	
London Victoria ⊖	a				08 39				09 00		09 00					09 31	09 20			09 33		09 58

		FC	FC	SN	SN	SW	SN	SN	SW	SN	FC	FC	SN	SN	SN	SN	SW	SW	SN	FC	FC	SN	SN
Horsham	d															09 09							
Warnham	d															09 13							
Ockley	d															09 20							
Holmwood	d															09 24							
Dorking	a															09 30							
	d				08 57	09 02										09 31	09 35						
Boxhill & Westhumble	d				08 59	09 04										09 33							
Guildford	d								08 58									09 28					
Effingham Junction	d								09 16									09 46					
Bookham	d								09 19									09 49					
Leatherhead	d				09 04	09 09			09 24							09 38	09 41	09 54					
Ashtead	d				09 08	09 13			09 28							09 42	09 45	09 58					
Epsom	a				09 12	09 17			09 32							09 46	09 49	10 02					
	d				09 13	09 18		09 19	09 35					09 42		09 49	09 50	10 05				10 04	
Ewell East	d				09 17			09 23						09 46		09 53						10 08	
Cheam	d				09 20			09 26						09 49		09 56						10 11	
Epsom Downs	d						09 09						09 35										
Banstead	d						09 12						09 38										
Belmont	d						09 15						09 41										
Sutton (Surrey)	a				09 23		09 18	09 29					09 44	09 52		09 59						10 14	
	d	09 11	09 13	09 15	09 23		09 23	09 30		09 33	09 37	09 38	09 45	09 53	09 52	10 00			10 03	10 07	10 08	10 15	10 22
Carshalton	d		09 16					09 33				09 41				10 03					10 11		
Hackbridge	d		09 18					09 35				09 43				10 05					10 13		
Mitcham Junction	d		09 21					09 39				09 46				10 09					10 16		
Mitcham Eastfields	d		09 24		09 32			09 42				09 49				10 12					10 19		
Carshalton Beeches	d			09 18			09 26			09 36			09 48		09 55				10 06			10 18	10 25
Wallington	d			09 20			09 28			09 38			09 50		09 57				10 08			10 20	10 27
Waddon	d			09 23			09 31			09 41			09 53		10 00				10 11			10 23	10 30
West Croydon	d			09 28			09 35			09 45			09 58		10 04				10 15			10 28	10 34
Norwood Junction	d									09 52									10 22				
New Cross Gate ⊖	d																						
Tulse Hill	a	09 42	09 32								10 12	09 57								10 42	10 27		
	d																						
London Bridge ⊖	a																						
Balham ⊖	d			09 44			09 52	09 49		10 09			10 14		10 21	10 18			10 39			10 44	10 51
Clapham Junction	a			09 49	09 42	09 45	09 57	09 53	10 00	10 15			10 19	10 11	10 26	10 22	10 15	10 30	10 45			10 49	10 56
London Waterloo ⊖	a					09 57			10 10								10 25	10 40					
London Victoria ⊖	a			10 00	09 52		10 05	10 00		10 24			10 28	10 20	10 34	10 31			10 53			10 58	11 04

Table 182

Mondays to Fridays

from 3 October

Horsham, Dorking, Guildford, Epsom and Sutton - London

		SN	SW	SN		SW	SN	FC	FC	SN	SN	SW	SN	SN		SW	SN	FC	FC	SN	SN	SW	SN	SN	
Horsham	d										10 04														
Warnham	d										10 08														
Ockley	d										10 15														
Holmwood	d										10 19														
Dorking	a										10 25														
	d	09 57	10 05								10 26	10 35									10 58	11 05			
Boxhill & Westhumble	d	09 59									10 28														
Guildford	d					09 58										10 28									
Effingham Junction	d					10 16										10 46									
Bookham	d					10 19										10 49									
Leatherhead	d	10 04	10 11			10 24					10 33	10 41				10 54					11 04	11 11			
Ashtead	d	10 08	10 14			10 28					10 37	10 44				10 58					11 07	11 14			
Epsom	a	10 12	10 19			10 32					10 41	10 49				11 02					11 12	11 19			
	d	10 13	10 20	10 19		10 35					10 42	10 50		10 49		11 05				11 04	11 13	11 20		11 19	
Ewell East	d	10 17		10 23							10 46			10 53						11 08				11 23	
Cheam	d	10 20		10 26							10 49			10 56						11 11	11 18			11 26	
Epsom Downs	d									10 35															
Banstead	d									10 38															
Belmont	d									10 41															
Sutton (Surrey)	a	10 23		10 29						10 44	10 52			10 59						11 14	11 21			11 29	
	d	10 23		10 30			10 33	10 37	10 38	10 45	10 53		10 52	11 00			11 03	11 07	11 08	11 15	11 23		11 22	11 30	
Carshalton	d			10 33					10 41					11 03					11 11					11 33	
Hackbridge	d			10 35					10 43					11 05					11 13					11 35	
Mitcham Junction	d			10 39					10 46					11 09					11 16					11 39	
Mitcham Eastfields	d			10 42					10 49					11 12					11 19					11 42	
Carshalton Beeches	d						10 36			10 48			10 55				11 06			11 18			11 25		
Wallington	d						10 38			10 50			10 57				11 08			11 20			11 27		
Waddon	d						10 41			10 53			11 00				11 11			11 23			11 30		
West Croydon	d						10 45			10 58			11 04				11 15			11 28			11 34		
Norwood Junction	d						10 52										11 22								
New Cross Gate	⊖ d																								
Tulse Hill	a							11 12	10 57									11 42	11 27						
	d																								
London Bridge	⊖ a																								
Balham	⊖ d			10 48			11 09			11 14			11 21	11 18			11 40			11 44			11 51	11 48	
Clapham Junction	a	10 40	10 45	10 52		11 00	11 14			11 19	11 10	11 15	11 26	11 22		11 30	11 45			11 49	11 40	11 45	11 56	11 52	
London Waterloo	⊖ a		10 55			11 10						11 25				11 40						11 55			
London Victoria	⊖ a	10 48		11 00			11 23			11 28	11 20		11 34	11 30			11 54			11 58	11 50		12 04	12 00	

		SW	SN	FC	FC	SN	SN	SW	SN	SN		SW	SN	FC	FC	SN	SN	SW	SN	SN		SW	SN	FC	FC
Horsham	d						11 04																		
Warnham	d						11 08																		
Ockley	d						11 15																		
Holmwood	d						11 19																		
Dorking	a						11 25																		
	d						11 26	11 35									11 58	12 05							
Boxhill & Westhumble	d						11 28																		
Guildford	d	10 58										11 28										11 58			
Effingham Junction	d	11 16										11 46										12 16			
Bookham	d	11 19										11 49										12 19			
Leatherhead	d	11 24					11 33	11 41				11 54					12 04	12 11				12 24			
Ashtead	d	11 28					11 37	11 44				11 58					12 07	12 14				12 28			
Epsom	a	11 32					11 41	11 49				12 02					12 12	12 19				12 32			
	d	11 35					11 42	11 50		11 49		12 05				12 04	12 13	12 20		12 19		12 35			
Ewell East	d						11 46			11 53						12 08				12 23					
Cheam	d						11 49			11 56						12 11	12 18			12 26					
Epsom Downs	d					11 35																			
Banstead	d					11 38																			
Belmont	d					11 41																			
Sutton (Surrey)	a					11 44	11 52			11 59						12 14	12 21			12 29					
	d		11 33	11 37	11 38	11 45	11 53		11 52	12 00			12 03	12 07	12 08	12 15	12 23		12 22	12 30			12 33	12 37	12 38
Carshalton	d				11 41					12 03					12 11					12 33					12 41
Hackbridge	d				11 43					12 05					12 13					12 35					12 43
Mitcham Junction	d				11 46					12 09					12 16					12 39					12 46
Mitcham Eastfields	d				11 49					12 12					12 19					12 42					12 49
Carshalton Beeches	d		11 36			11 48			11 55				12 06			12 18			12 25				12 36		
Wallington	d		11 38			11 50			11 57				12 08			12 20			12 27				12 38		
Waddon	d		11 41			11 53			12 00				12 11			12 23			12 30				12 41		
West Croydon	d		11 45			11 58			12 04				12 15			12 28			12 34				12 45		
Norwood Junction	d		11 52										12 22										12 52		
New Cross Gate	⊖ d																								
Tulse Hill	a			12 12	11 57									12 42	12 27									13 12	12 57
	d																								
London Bridge	⊖ a																								
Balham	⊖ d		12 09			12 14			12 21	12 18			12 39			12 44			12 51	12 48			13 09		
Clapham Junction	a	12 00	12 14			12 19	12 10	12 15	12 26	12 22		12 30	12 44			12 49	12 40	12 45	12 56	12 52		13 00	13 14		
London Waterloo	⊖ a	12 10						12 25				12 40						12 55				13 10			
London Victoria	⊖ a		12 23			12 28	12 18		12 34	12 30			12 53			12 58	12 48		13 04	13 00			13 23		

Table 182

Mondays to Fridays

from 3 October

Horsham, Dorking, Guildford, Epsom and Sutton - London

		SN	SN	SW	SN	SN		SW	SN	FC	FC	SN	SN	SW	SN	SN		SW	SN	FC	FC	SN	SN	SW	SN
Horsham	d		12 04																				13 04		
Warnham	d		12 08																				13 08		
Ockley	d		12 15																				13 15		
Holmwood	d		12 19																				13 19		
Dorking	a		12 25																				13 25		
	d		12 26	12 35									12 58	13 05									13 26	13 35	
Boxhill & Westhumble	d		12 28																				13 28		
Guildford	d							12 28										12 58							
Effingham Junction	d							12 46										13 16							
Bookham	d							12 49										13 19							
Leatherhead	d		12 33	12 41				12 54					13 04	13 11				13 24					13 33	13 41	
Ashtead	d		12 37	12 44				12 58					13 07	13 14				13 28					13 37	13 44	
Epsom	a		12 41	12 49				13 02					13 12	13 19				13 32					13 41	13 49	
	d		12 42	12 50		12 49		13 05				13 04	13 13	13 20		13 19		13 35					13 42	13 50	
Ewell East	d		12 46			12 53						13 08				13 23							13 46		
Cheam	d		12 49			12 56						13 11	13 18			13 26							13 49		
Epsom Downs	d	12 35																				13 35			
Banstead	d	12 38																				13 38			
Belmont	d	12 41																				13 41			
Sutton (Surrey)	a	12 44	12 52			12 59						13 14	13 21			13 29						13 44	13 52		
	d	12 45	12 53		12 52	13 00			13 03	13 07	13 08	13 15	13 23		13 22	13 30			13 33	13 37	13 38	13 45	13 53		13 52
Carshalton	d					13 03					13 11					13 33					13 41				
Hackbridge	d					13 05					13 13					13 35					13 43				
Mitcham Junction	d					13 09					13 16					13 39					13 46				
Mitcham Eastfields	d					13 12					13 19					13 42					13 49				
Carshalton Beeches	d	12 48			12 55				13 06			13 18			13 25				13 36			13 48			13 55
Wallington	d	12 50			12 57				13 08			13 20			13 27				13 38			13 50			13 57
Waddon	d	12 53			13 00				13 11			13 23			13 30				13 41			13 53			14 00
West Croydon	d	12 58			13 04				13 15			13 28			13 34				13 45			13 58			14 04
Norwood Junction	d								13 22										13 52						
New Cross Gate	⊖ d																								
Tulse Hill	a									13 42	13 27									14 12	13 57				
	d																								
London Bridge	⊖ a																								
Balham	⊖ d	13 14			13 21	13 18			13 39			13 44			13 51	13 48			14 09			14 14			14 21
Clapham Junction	a	13 19	13 10	13 15	13 26	13 22		13 30	13 44			13 49	13 40	13 45	13 56	13 52		14 00	14 14			14 19	14 10	14 15	14 26
London Waterloo	⊖ a			13 25				13 40						13 55				14 10						14 25	
London Victoria	⊖ a	13 28	13 18		13 34	13 30			13 53			13 58	13 48		14 04	14 00			14 23			14 28	14 18		14 34

		SN		SW	SN	FC	FC	SN	SN	SW	SN	SN		SW	SN	FC	FC	SN	SN	SW	SN	SN		SW	SN
Horsham	d																		14 04						
Warnham	d																		14 08						
Ockley	d																		14 15						
Holmwood	d																		14 19						
Dorking	a																		14 25						
	d								13 58	14 05									14 26	14 35					
Boxhill & Westhumble	d																		14 28						
Guildford	d			13 28										13 58										14 28	
Effingham Junction	d			13 46										14 16										14 46	
Bookham	d			13 49										14 19										14 49	
Leatherhead	d			13 54					14 04	14 11				14 24					14 33	14 41				14 54	
Ashtead	d			13 58					14 07	14 14				14 28					14 37	14 44				14 58	
Epsom	a			14 02					14 12	14 19				14 32					14 41	14 49				15 02	
	d	13 49		14 05				14 04	14 13	14 20		14 19		14 35					14 42	14 50		14 49		15 05	
Ewell East	d	13 53						14 08				14 23							14 46			14 53			
Cheam	d	13 56						14 11	14 18			14 26							14 49			14 56			
Epsom Downs	d																	14 35							
Banstead	d																	14 38							
Belmont	d																	14 41							
Sutton (Surrey)	a	13 59						14 14	14 21			14 29						14 44	14 52			14 59			
	d	14 00			14 03	14 07	14 08	14 15	14 23		14 22	14 30			14 33	14 37	14 38	14 45	14 53		14 52	15 00			15 03
Carshalton	d	14 03					14 11					14 33					14 41					15 03			
Hackbridge	d	14 05					14 13					14 35					14 43					15 05			
Mitcham Junction	d	14 09					14 16					14 39					14 46					15 09			
Mitcham Eastfields	d	14 12					14 19					14 42					14 49					15 12			
Carshalton Beeches	d				14 06			14 18			14 25				14 36			14 48			14 55				15 06
Wallington	d				14 08			14 20			14 27				14 38			14 50			14 57				15 08
Waddon	d				14 11			14 23			14 30				14 41			14 53			15 00				15 11
West Croydon	d				14 15			14 28			14 34				14 45			14 58			15 04				15 15
Norwood Junction	d				14 22										14 52										15 22
New Cross Gate	⊖ d																								
Tulse Hill	a					14 42	14 27									15 12	14 57								
	d																								
London Bridge	⊖ a																								
Balham	⊖ d	14 18			14 39			14 44			14 51	14 48			15 09			15 14			15 21	15 18			15 39
Clapham Junction	a	14 22		14 30	14 44			14 49	14 40	14 45	14 56	14 52		15 00	15 14			15 19	15 10	15 15	15 26	15 22		15 30	15 44
London Waterloo	⊖ a			14 40						14 55				15 10						15 25				15 40	
London Victoria	⊖ a	14 30			14 53			14 58	14 48		15 04	15 00			15 24			15 28	15 22		15 34	15 30			15 54

Horsham, Dorking, Guildford, Epsom and Sutton - London

		FC	FC	SN	SN	SW	SN	SN		SW	SN	FC	FC	SN	SN	SW	SN	SN		SW	SN	FC	FC	SN	SN
Horsham 4	d														15 04										
Warnham	d														15 08										
Ockley	d														15 15										
Holmwood	d														15 19										
Dorking 4	a														15 25										
	d				14 58	15 05									15 26	15 35									15 56
Boxhill & Westhumble	d														15 28										15 58
Guildford	d									14 58										15 28					
Effingham Junction 6	d									15 16										15 46					
Bookham	d									15 19										15 49					
Leatherhead	d				15 04	15 11				15 24					15 33	15 41				15 54					16 03
Ashtead	d				15 07	15 14				15 28					15 37	15 44				15 58					16 07
Epsom 3	a				15 12	15 19				15 32					15 41	15 49				16 02					16 11
	d			15 04	15 13	15 20		15 19		15 35					15 42	15 50		15 49		16 05				16 04	16 12
Ewell East	d			15 08				15 23							15 46			15 53						16 08	16 16
Cheam	d			15 11	15 18			15 26							15 49			15 56						16 11	16 19
Epsom Downs	d													15 35											
Banstead	d													15 38											
Belmont	d													15 41											
Sutton (Surrey) 4	a			15 14	15 21			15 29						15 44	15 52			15 59						16 14	16 22
	d	15 07	15 08	15 15	15 23		15 22	15 30			15 33	15 37	15 38	15 45	15 53		15 52	16 00			16 03	16 07	16 08	16 15	16 23
Carshalton	d		15 11					15 33					15 41					16 03					16 11		
Hackbridge	d		15 13					15 35					15 43					16 05					16 13		
Mitcham Junction	d		15 16					15 39					15 46					16 09					16 16		
Mitcham Eastfields	d		15 19					15 42					15 49					16 12					16 19		
Carshalton Beeches	d			15 18			15 25				15 36			15 48			15 55				16 06			16 18	
Wallington	d			15 20			15 27				15 38			15 50			15 57				16 08			16 20	
Waddon	d			15 23			15 30				15 41			15 53			16 00				16 11			16 23	
West Croydon 4	d			15 28			15 34				15 45			15 58			16 04				16 15			16 28	
Norwood Junction 2	d										15 52										16 22				
New Cross Gate 4 ⊖	d																								
Tulse Hill 3	a	15 42	15 27									16 12	15 57									16 44	16 27		
	d																								
London Bridge 4 ⊖	a																								
Balham 4 ⊖	d			15 44			15 51	15 48			16 09			16 14			16 21	16 18			16 39			16 44	
Clapham Junction 10	a			15 49	15 40	15 45	15 56	15 52		16 00	16 14			16 19	16 10	16 15	16 26	16 23		16 30	16 45			16 49	16 40
London Waterloo 15 ⊖	a					15 55				16 10						16 25				16 40					
London Victoria 15 ⊖	a			15 58	15 52		16 04	16 00			16 23			16 28	16 18		16 34	16 30			16 55			16 58	16 48

		SW	SN	SN		SW	SN	SN	FC	FC 1	SN	SW	SN	SN		SW	SN	FC	SN	FC	SN	SW	SN	SW	
Horsham 4	d										16 04														
Warnham	d										16 08														
Ockley	d										16 15														
Holmwood	d										16 19														
Dorking 4	a										16 25														
	d	16 05									16 26	16 35									17 00	17 05			
Boxhill & Westhumble	d										16 28										17 02				
Guildford	d					15 58										16 28								16 58	
Effingham Junction 6	d					16 16										16 46								17 16	
Bookham	d					16 19										16 49								17 19	
Leatherhead	d	16 11				16 24					16 33	16 41				16 54					17 07	17 11		17 24	
Ashtead	d	16 14				16 28					16 37	16 44				16 58					17 11	17 14		17 28	
Epsom 3	a	16 19				16 32					16 41	16 49				17 02					17 15	17 19		17 32	
	d	16 20		16 19		16 35					16 42	16 50		16 49		17 05					17 19	17 20	17 23	17 35	
Ewell East	d			16 23							16 46			16 53							17 23		17 27		
Cheam	d			16 26							16 49			16 56							17 26		17 30		
Epsom Downs	d							16 26											17 02						
Banstead	d							16 29											17 05						
Belmont	d							16 32											17 08						
Sutton (Surrey) 4	a			16 29				16 35			16 52			16 59					17 11		17 29		17 33		
	d		16 22	16 30			16 33	16 45	16 37	16 38	16 53		16 52	17 00			17 03	17 08	17 15	17 11	17 30		17 33		
Carshalton	d			16 33						16 41				17 03				17 11			17 33				
Hackbridge	d			16 35						16 43				17 05				17 13			17 35				
Mitcham Junction	d			16 39						16 46				17 09				17 16			17 39				
Mitcham Eastfields	d			16 42						16 49				17 12				17 19			17 42				
Carshalton Beeches	d		16 25				16 36	16 48					16 55				17 06		17 18				17 36		
Wallington	d		16 27				16 38	16 50					16 57				17 08		17 20				17 39		
Waddon	d		16 30				16 41	16 53					17 00				17 11		17 23				17 42		
West Croydon 4	d		16 34				16 45	16 58					17 04				17 18		17 28				17 48		
Norwood Junction 2	d						16 52										17 23						17 55		
New Cross Gate 4 ⊖	d																								
Tulse Hill 3	a								17 14	16 57								17 27		17 44					
	d																								
London Bridge 4 ⊖	a																								
Balham 4 ⊖	d		16 51	16 48			17 09	17 14					17 21	17 18			17 39		17 44		17 48		18 11		
Clapham Junction 10	a	16 45	16 56	16 53		17 00	17 14	17 19			17 10	17 15	17 26	17 23		17 30	17 44		17 49		17 52	17 45	18 16	18 00	
London Waterloo 15 ⊖	a	16 55				17 10						17 25				17 40						17 55		18 10	
London Victoria 15 ⊖	a		17 04	17 00			17 23	17 28			17 18		17 34	17 30			17 55		17 58		18 00		18 25		

Horsham, Dorking, Guildford, Epsom and Sutton - London

		FC	FC	SN	SN	SW	SN	SW	FC	FC		SN	SN	SW	SN	SW	FC	FC	SN	SN		SW	SN	SW	FC
Horsham 4	d				17 07								17 34							18 04					
Warnham	d				17 11								17 38							18 08					
Ockley	d				17 18								17 45							18 15					
Holmwood	d				17 22								17 49							18 19					
Dorking 4	a				17 28								17 55							18 25					
	d				17 31	17 35							17 56	18 05						18 26		18 35		18 50	
Boxhill & Westhumble	d				17 33								17 58							18 28					
Guildford	d							17 28								17 58							18 22		
Effingham Junction 6	d							17 46								18 16							18 39		
Bookham	d							17 49								18 19							18 42		
Leatherhead	d				17 38	17 41		17 54					18 03	18 11		18 24				18 33		18 41	18 47	18 56	
Ashtead	d				17 42	17 45		17 58					18 07	18 14		18 28				18 37		18 45	18 51	18 59	
Epsom 3	a				17 46	17 49		18 02					18 14	18 19		18 32				18 43		18 49	18 57	19 04	
	d				17 49	17 50	17 52	18 05					18 17	18 20	18 22	18 35				18 49		18 50	18 57	19 05	
Ewell East	d				17 53		17 56						18 23		18 26					18 53					
Cheam	d				17 56		17 59						18 26		18 29					18 56					
Epsom Downs	d			17 35								18 02							18 35						
Banstead	d			17 38								18 05							18 38						
Belmont	d			17 41								18 08							18 41						
Sutton (Surrey) 4	a			17 44	17 59		18 02					18 11	18 29		18 32				18 44	18 59			19 04		
	d	17 41	17 42	17 45	18 00		18 04		18 08	18 09		18 12	18 30		18 33		18 38	18 43	18 45	19 00			19 05		19 08
Carshalton	d		17 45		18 03				18 11				18 33				18 41			19 03					19 11
Hackbridge	d		17 47		18 05				18 13				18 35				18 43			19 05					19 13
Mitcham Junction	d		17 50		18 09				18 16				18 39				18 46			19 09					19 16
Mitcham Eastfields	d		17 53		18 12				18 19				18 42				18 49			19 12					19 19
Carshalton Beeches	d			17 48			18 07					18 15			18 36				18 48				19 08		
Wallington	d			17 50			18 09					18 17			18 38				18 50				19 10		
Waddon	d			17 53			18 12					18 20			18 41				18 53				19 13		
West Croydon 4	d			17 58			18 18					18 28			18 47				18 58				19 17		
Norwood Junction 2	d						18 24								18 52								19 22		
New Cross Gate 4 ⊖	d																								
Tulse Hill 3	a	18 14	18 01						18 27	18 44							18 57	19 14							19 27
	d																								
London Bridge 4 ⊖	a																								
Balham 4 ⊖	d			18 14	18 18		18 40					18 44	18 48		19 09				19 14	19 18			19 39		
Clapham Junction 10	a			18 19	18 22	18 15	18 45	18 30				18 49	18 52	18 45	19 14	19 00			19 19	19 22		19 16	19 44	19 30	
London Waterloo 15 ⊖	a					18 25		18 40						18 55		19 10						19 27		19 41	
London Victoria 15 ⊖	a			18 28	18 33		18 54					18 57	19 01		19 25				19 28	19 30			19 53		

		FC	SN	SN	SW	SN		SW	FC	FC	SN	SN	SN	SW	SN	SW		FC	FC	SN	SN	SW	SN	SN	SW
Horsham 4	d			18 34									19 04												
Warnham	d			18 38									19 08												
Ockley	d			18 45									19 15												
Holmwood	d			18 49									19 19												
Dorking 4	a			18 55									19 25												
	d			18 56		19 05							19 28	19 33	19 37						19 57	20 05			
Boxhill & Westhumble	d			18 58									19 30								19 59				
Guildford	d											19 04				19 28									19 58
Effingham Junction 6	d				18 59							19 20				19 46									20 16
Bookham	d				19 02							19 23				19 49									20 19
Leatherhead	d			19 03	19 08	19 11						19 28	19 35	19 39	19 43	19 54					20 04	20 11			20 24
Ashtead	d			19 07	19 12	19 15						19 32	19 39	19 42	19 46	19 58					20 08	20 14			20 28
Epsom 3	a			19 11	19 16	19 19						19 36	19 43	19 47	19 51	20 02					20 12	20 19			20 32
	d			19 12	19 20	19 20		19 35				19 37	19 46	19 50	19 52	20 05					20 13	20 20	20 22	20 25	20 35
Ewell East	d			19 16		19 24						19 41	19 50		19 56						20 17		20 26	20 29	
Cheam	d			19 19		19 27						19 44	19 53		19 59						20 20		20 29	20 32	
Epsom Downs	d		19 06								19 36									20 13					
Banstead	d		19 09								19 39									20 16					
Belmont	d		19 12								19 42									20 19					
Sutton (Surrey) 4	a		19 15	19 22		19 30					19 45	19 47	19 56		20 02					20 22	20 23		20 32	20 35	
	d	19 13	19 16	19 22		19 33			19 38	19 42	19 46		19 56		20 03			20 07	20 10	20 23	20 25		20 33	20 36	
Carshalton	d			19 25						19 45			19 59						20 13		20 28			20 39	
Hackbridge	d			19 28						19 47			20 02						20 15		20 31			20 41	
Mitcham Junction	d			19 31						19 50			20 05						20 18		20 34			20 45	
Mitcham Eastfields	d			19 34						19 53			20 08						20 21		20 37			20 48	
Carshalton Beeches	d		19 19			19 36					19 49				20 06					20 26			20 36		
Wallington	d		19 21			19 38					19 51				20 08					20 28			20 38		
Waddon	d		19 24			19 41					19 54				20 11					20 31			20 41		
West Croydon 4	d		19 28			19 47					19 58				20 18					20 35			20 45		
Norwood Junction 2	d					19 52									20 23								20 52		
New Cross Gate 4 ⊖	d																								
Tulse Hill 3	a	19 44							20 10	20 01								20 40	20 29						
	d																								
London Bridge 4 ⊖	a																								
Balham 4 ⊖	d		19 45	19 42		20 08					20 14		20 17		20 39					20 51	20 44		21 08	20 54	
Clapham Junction 10	a		19 50	19 47	19 45	20 14		20 00			20 19		20 22	20 15	20 44	20 30				20 56	20 48	20 45	21 14	20 59	21 00
London Waterloo 15 ⊖	a				19 55			20 10						20 25		20 41						20 55			21 10
London Victoria 15 ⊖	a		19 59	19 55		20 22					20 28		20 30		20 53					21 04	20 56		21 22	21 09	

Table 182

Horsham, Dorking, Guildford, Epsom and Sutton - London

Mondays to Fridays from 3 October

		FC		FC	SN	SN	SW	SN	SW	SN	FC	FC		SN	SN	SW	SN	SN	SW	SN	SN	SW		SN	SN
Horsham	d					20 06																			
Warnham	d					20 10																			
Ockley	d					20 17																			
Holmwood	d					20 21																			
Dorking	a					20 27																			
	d					20 30	20 35								20 59						21 30	21 35			
Boxhill & Westhumble	d														21 01										
Guildford	d															20 46									
Effingham Junction	d															21 03									
Bookham	d															21 06									
Leatherhead	d					20 36	20 41								21 06	21 11					21 36	21 41			
Ashtead	d					20 39	20 44								21 10	21 14					21 40	21 44			
Epsom	a					20 44	20 49								21 14	21 19					21 44	21 49			
	d					20 45	20 50	20 55	21 05						21 15	21 20	21 21	21 28	21 35		21 45	21 50		21 55	
Ewell East	d					20 49		20 59							21 19		21 25				21 49			21 59	
Cheam	d					20 52		21 02							21 22		21 28				21 52			22 02	
Epsom Downs	d									20 54															21 54
Banstead	d									20 57															21 57
Belmont	d									21 00															22 00
Sutton (Surrey)	a					20 55		21 05		21 03					21 25		21 31	21 35			21 55			22 05	22 03
	d	20 37		20 40	20 52	20 55		21 06		21 06	21 10	21 10		21 22	21 25		21 32	21 35		21 52	21 55			22 06	22 06
Carshalton	d			20 43		20 58		21 09			21 13				21 28			21 38			21 58			22 09	
Hackbridge	d			20 45		21 01		21 11			21 15				21 31			21 41			22 01			22 11	
Mitcham Junction	d			20 48		21 04		21 15			21 18				21 34			21 44			22 04			22 15	
Mitcham Eastfields	d			20 51		21 07		21 18			21 21				21 37			21 47			22 07			22 18	
Carshalton Beeches	d				20 55					21 09				21 25			21 35			21 55					22 09
Wallington	d				20 57					21 11				21 27			21 37			21 57					22 11
Waddon	d				21 00					21 14				21 30			21 40			22 00					22 14
West Croydon	d				21 04					21 18				21 34			21 48			22 04					22 18
Norwood Junction	d									21 23							21 53								22 23
New Cross Gate ⊖	d																								
Tulse Hill	a	21 10		20 59							21 29	21 50													
	d																								
London Bridge ⊖	a																								
Balham ⊖	d				21 21	21 14		21 24		21 39				21 51	21 44		22 09	21 54		22 21	22 14			22 24	22 39
Clapham Junction	a				21 26	21 18	21 15	21 29	21 30	21 44				21 56	21 49	21 45	22 14	21 59	22 00	22 26	22 19	22 15		22 29	22 44
London Waterloo ⊖	a						21 25		21 40							21 55			22 10			22 25			
London Victoria ⊖	a				21 34	21 26		21 39		21 53				22 04	21 57		22 23	22 09		22 34	22 27			22 39	22 53

		FC	SN	SN	SW	SN	SN	SN		SN	SW	SN	SN	SN	SN	SW	SN	SN		SN					
Horsham	d																								
Warnham	d																								
Ockley	d																								
Holmwood	d																								
Dorking	a																								
	d			21 59						22 30	22 35				23 00			23 30							
Boxhill & Westhumble	d			22 01											23 02										
Guildford	d				21 46											22 46									
Effingham Junction	d				22 03											23 03									
Bookham	d				22 06											23 06									
Leatherhead	d			22 06	22 11					22 36	22 41				23 07	23 11		23 36							
Ashtead	d			22 10	22 14					22 40	22 44				23 11	23 14		23 39							
Epsom	a			22 14	22 19					22 44	22 49				23 15	23 19		23 45							
	d			22 15	22 20	22 21	22 25			22 45	22 50	22 55			23 16	23 20	23 25								
Ewell East	d			22 19		22 25	22 29			22 49		22 59			23 20		23 29								
Cheam	d			22 22		22 28	22 32			22 52		23 02			23 23		23 32								
Epsom Downs	d												22 54							23 43					
Banstead	d												22 57							23 46					
Belmont	d												23 00							23 49					
Sutton (Surrey)	a			22 25		22 31	22 35			22 55		23 05	23 03		23 26		23 35			23 52					
	d	22 12	22 22	22 25		22 32	22 36	22 52		22 55		23 06	23 06	23 20	23 30		23 40			23 53					
Carshalton	d			22 28			22 39			22 58		23 09													
Hackbridge	d			22 31			22 41			23 01		23 11													
Mitcham Junction	d			22 34			22 45			23 04		23 15													
Mitcham Eastfields	d			22 37			22 48			23 07		23 18													
Carshalton Beeches	d		22 25			22 35		22 55					23 09	23 23	23 33		23 43			23 56					
Wallington	d		22 27			22 37		22 57					23 11	23 25	23 35		23 45			23 58					
Waddon	d		22 30			22 40		23 00					23 14	23 28	23 38		23 48			00 01					
West Croydon	d		22 34			22 48		23 04					23 18	23a31	23a41		23a57			00a04					
Norwood Junction	d					22 53							23 23												
New Cross Gate ⊖	d																								
Tulse Hill	a	22 43																							
	d	22 43																							
London Bridge ⊖	a	22 55																							
Balham ⊖	d		22 51	22 44		23 09	22 54	23 21		23 14		23 24	23 40												
Clapham Junction	a		22 56	22 48	22 45	23 15	22 59	23 26		23 18	23 15	23 29	23 45			23 48									
London Waterloo ⊖	a				22 55						23 27					23 58									
London Victoria ⊖	a		23 04	22 56		23 25	23 09	23 34		23 27		23 39	23 54												

Table 182

Horsham, Dorking, Guildford, Epsom and Sutton - London

Saturdays until 1 October

		SN	SW	SW	SW	SN	SN	SN	SW	SN		FC	FC	SN	SN	SN	SW	SN	FC	FC		SN	SN	SN	SW
Horsham	d																								
Warnham	d																								
Ockley	d																								
Holmwood	d																								
Dorking	a																								
	d						06 28								06 57								07 26		
Boxhill & Westhumble	d														06 59								07 28		
Guildford	d								06 28								06 58								07 28
Effingham Junction	d								06 46								07 16								07 46
Bookham	d								06 49								07 19								07 49
Leatherhead	d						06 34		06 54						07 04		07 24						07 33		07 54
Ashtead	d						06 37		06 58						07 08		07 28						07 37		07 58
Epsom	a						06 42		07 02						07 12		07 32						07 41		08 02
	d		05 35	06 05	06 35		06 42	06 49	07 05					07 04	07 13	07 19	07 35						07 42	07 49	08 05
Ewell East	d						06 46	06 53						07 08		07 23							07 46	07 53	
Cheam	d						06 49	06 56						07 11	07 18	07 26							07 49	07 56	
Epsom Downs	d	23p43																				07 35			
Banstead	d	23p46																				07 38			
Belmont	d	23p49																				07 41			
Sutton (Surrey)	a	23p52					06 52	06 59						07 14	07 22	07 29						07 44	07 52	07 59	
	d	23p53				06 45	06 53	07 00		07 03		07 07	07 08	07 15	07 23	07 30		07 33	07 37	07 38		07 45	07 53	08 00	
Carshalton	d							07 03					07 11			07 33				07 41				08 03	
Hackbridge	d							07 05					07 13			07 35				07 43				08 05	
Mitcham Junction	d							07 09					07 16			07 39				07 46				08 09	
Mitcham Eastfields	d							07 12					07 19			07 42				07 49				08 12	
Carshalton Beeches	d	23p56				06 48				07 06				07 18				07 36				07 48			
Wallington	d	23p58				06 50				07 08				07 20				07 38				07 50			
Waddon	d	00 01				06 53				07 11				07 23				07 41				07 53			
West Croydon	d	00a04				06 58				07 15				07 28				07 45				07 58			
Norwood Junction	d									07 20								07 50							
New Cross Gate ⊖	d									07 34								08 04							
Tulse Hill	a											07 44	07 27						08 14	07 57					
	d											07 47							08 17						
London Bridge ⊖	a									07 41		08 00						08 11	08 30						
Balham ⊖	d					07 14		07 18						07 44		07 48						08 14		08 18	
Clapham Junction	a		06 01	06 30	07 00	07 19	07 10	07 22	07 30					07 49	07 40	07 52	08 00					08 19	08 10	08 22	08 30
London Waterloo ⊖	a		06 11	06 40	07 10				07 40								08 10								08 40
London Victoria ⊖	a					07 28	07 18	07 30						07 58	07 48	08 00						08 28	08 18	08 30	

		SN	FC	FC	SN	SN		SW	SN	SN	SW	SN	FC	FC	SN	SN		SW	SN	SN	SW	SN	FC	FC	SN
Horsham	d															08 04									
Warnham	d															08 08									
Ockley	d															08 15									
Holmwood	d															08 19									
Dorking	a															08 25									
	d					07 58		08 05								08 26		08 35							
Boxhill & Westhumble	d															08 28									
Guildford	d										07 58										08 28				
Effingham Junction	d										08 16										08 46				
Bookham	d										08 19										08 49				
Leatherhead	d					08 04		08 11			08 24					08 33		08 41			08 54				
Ashtead	d					08 07		08 14			08 28					08 37		08 44			08 58				
Epsom	a					08 12		08 19			08 32					08 41		08 49			09 02				
	d				08 04	08 13		08 20		08 19	08 35					08 42		08 50		08 49	09 05				09 04
Ewell East	d				08 08					08 23						08 46				08 53					09 08
Cheam	d				08 11	08 18				08 26						08 49				08 56					09 11
Epsom Downs	d														08 35										
Banstead	d														08 38										
Belmont	d														08 41										
Sutton (Surrey)	a				08 14	08 21				08 29					08 44	08 52				08 59					09 14
	d	08 03	08 07	08 08	08 15	08 23			08 22	08 30		08 33	08 37	08 38	08 45	08 53			08 52	09 00		09 03	09 07	09 08	09 15
Carshalton	d			08 11						08 33				08 41						09 03				09 11	
Hackbridge	d			08 13						08 35				08 43						09 05				09 13	
Mitcham Junction	d			08 16						08 39				08 46						09 09				09 16	
Mitcham Eastfields	d			08 19						08 42				08 49						09 12				09 19	
Carshalton Beeches	d	08 06			08 18				08 25			08 36			08 48				08 55			09 06			09 18
Wallington	d	08 08			08 20				08 27			08 38			08 50				08 57			09 08			09 20
Waddon	d	08 11			08 23				08 30			08 41			08 53				09 00			09 11			09 23
West Croydon	d	08 15			08 28				08 34			08 45			08 58				09 04			09 16			09 28
Norwood Junction	d	08 22										08 52										09 22			
New Cross Gate ⊖	d																								
Tulse Hill	a		08 44	08 27									09 14	08 57									09 44	09 27	
	d		08 47										09 17										09 47		
London Bridge ⊖	a		09 00										09 30										10 00		
Balham ⊖	d	08 39			08 44				08 51	08 48		09 09			09 14				09 21	09 18		09 39			09 44
Clapham Junction	a	08 44			08 49	08 40		08 45	08 56	08 52	09 00	09 14			09 19	09 10		09 15	09 26	09 22	09 30	09 44			09 49
London Waterloo ⊖	a							08 55			09 10							09 25			09 40				
London Victoria ⊖	a	08 53			08 58	08 48			09 04	09 00		09 23			09 28	09 18			09 34	09 30		09 54			09 58

until 1 October

Horsham, Dorking, Guildford, Epsom and Sutton - London

		SN		SW	SN	SN	SW	SN	FC	FC	SN	SN		SW	SN	SN	SW	SN	FC	FC	SN	SN		SW	SN
Horsham 4	d											09 04													
Warnham	d											09 08													
Ockley	d											09 15													
Holmwood	d											09 19													
Dorking 4	a											09 25													
	d	08 58		09 05								09 26		09 35								09 58		10 05	
Boxhill & Westhumble	d											09 28													
Guildford	d						08 58										09 28								
Effingham Junction 6	d						09 16										09 46								
Bookham	d						09 19										09 49								
Leatherhead	d	09 04		09 11			09 24					09 33		09 41			09 54					10 04		10 11	
Ashtead	d	09 07		09 14			09 28					09 37		09 44			09 58					10 07		10 14	
Epsom 3	a	09 12		09 19			09 32					09 41		09 49			10 02					10 12		10 19	
	d	09 13		09 20		09 19	09 35					09 42		09 50		09 49	10 05				10 04	10 12		10 20	
Ewell East	d					09 23						09 46				09 53					10 08				
Cheam	d	09 18				09 26						09 49				09 56					10 11	10 18			
Epsom Downs	d										09 35														
Banstead	d										09 38														
Belmont	d										09 41														
Sutton (Surrey) 4	a	09 21				09 29					09 44	09 52				09 59					10 14	10 22			
	d	09 23			09 22	09 30		09 33	09 37	09 38	09 45	09 53			09 52	10 00		10 03	10 07	10 08	10 15	10 23			10 22
Carshalton	d					09 33				09 41						10 03				10 11					
Hackbridge	d					09 35				09 43						10 05				10 13					
Mitcham Junction	d					09 39				09 46						10 09				10 16					
Mitcham Eastfields	d					09 42				09 49						10 12				10 19					
Carshalton Beeches	d				09 25			09 36			09 48				09 55			10 06			10 18				10 25
Wallington	d				09 27			09 38			09 50				09 57			10 08			10 20				10 27
Waddon	d				09 30			09 41			09 53				10 00			10 11			10 23				10 30
West Croydon 4	d				09 34			09 45			09 58				10 04			10 15			10 28				10 34
Norwood Junction 2	d							09 52										10 22							
New Cross Gate 4	⊖ d																								
Tulse Hill 3	a								10 14	09 57									10 44	10 27					
	d								10 17										10 47						
London Bridge 4	⊖ a								10 30										11 00						
Balham 4	⊖ d				09 51	09 48		10 09			10 14				10 21	10 18		10 39			10 44				10 51
Clapham Junction 10	a	09 40		09 45	09 56	09 52	10 00	10 14			10 19	10 10		10 15	10 26	10 22	10 30	10 44			10 49	10 40		10 45	10 56
London Waterloo 15	⊖ a			09 55			10 10							10 25			10 40							10 55	
London Victoria 15	⊖ a	09 48			10 04	10 00		10 23			10 28	10 18			10 34	10 30		10 53			10 58	10 48			11 04

		SN	SW	SN	FC	FC	SN	SN		SW	SN	SN	SW	SN	FC	FC	SN	SN		SW	SN	SN	SW	SN	FC
Horsham 4	d							10 04																	
Warnham	d							10 08																	
Ockley	d							10 15																	
Holmwood	d							10 19																	
Dorking 4	a							10 25																	
	d							10 26		10 35								10 58		11 05					
Boxhill & Westhumble	d							10 28																	
Guildford	d		09 58										10 28										10 58		
Effingham Junction 6	d		10 16										10 46										11 16		
Bookham	d		10 19										10 49										11 19		
Leatherhead	d		10 24					10 33		10 41			10 54					11 04		11 11			11 24		
Ashtead	d		10 28					10 37		10 44			10 58					11 07		11 14			11 28		
Epsom 3	a		10 32					10 41		10 49			11 02					11 12		11 19			11 32		
	d	10 19	10 35					10 42		10 50		10 49	11 05				11 04	11 13		11 20		11 19	11 35		
Ewell East	d	10 23						10 46				10 53					11 08					11 23			
Cheam	d	10 26						10 49				10 56					11 11	11 18				11 26			
Epsom Downs	d						10 35																		
Banstead	d						10 38																		
Belmont	d						10 41																		
Sutton (Surrey) 4	a	10 29					10 44	10 52				10 59					11 14	11 21				11 29			
	d	10 30		10 33	10 37	10 38	10 45	10 53			10 52	11 00		11 03	11 07	11 08	11 15	11 23			11 22	11 30		11 33	11 37
Carshalton	d	10 33				10 41						11 03				11 11						11 33			
Hackbridge	d	10 35				10 43						11 05				11 13						11 35			
Mitcham Junction	d	10 39				10 46						11 09				11 16						11 39			
Mitcham Eastfields	d	10 42				10 49						11 12				11 19						11 42			
Carshalton Beeches	d			10 36			10 48				10 55			11 06			11 18				11 25			11 36	
Wallington	d			10 38			10 50				10 57			11 08			11 20				11 27			11 38	
Waddon	d			10 41			10 53				11 00			11 11			11 23				11 30			11 41	
West Croydon 4	d			10 45			10 58				11 04			11 15			11 28				11 34			11 45	
Norwood Junction 2	d			10 52										11 22										11 52	
New Cross Gate 4	⊖ d																								
Tulse Hill 3	a				11 14	10 57									11 44	11 27									12 14
	d				11 17										11 47										12 17
London Bridge 4	⊖ a				11 30										12 00										12 30
Balham 4	⊖ d	10 48		11 09			11 14				11 21	11 18		11 39			11 44				11 51	11 48		12 09	
Clapham Junction 10	a	10 52	11 00	11 14			11 19	11 10		11 15	11 26	11 22	11 30	11 44			11 49	11 40		11 45	11 56	11 52	12 00	12 14	
London Waterloo 15	⊖ a		11 10							11 25			11 40							11 55			12 10		
London Victoria 15	⊖ a	11 00		11 23			11 28	11 18			11 34	11 30		11 53			11 58	11 48			12 04	12 00		12 23	

Horsham, Dorking, Guildford, Epsom and Sutton - London

until 1 October

		FC	SN	SN		SW	SN	SN	SW	SN	FC	FC	SN	SN		SW	SN	SN	SW	SN	FC	FC	SN	SN	
Horsham 4	d			11 04																				12 04	
Warnham	d			11 08																				12 08	
Ockley	d			11 15																				12 15	
Holmwood	d			11 19																				12 19	
Dorking 4	a			11 25																				12 25	
	d			11 26		11 35								11 58		12 05								12 26	
Boxhill & Westhumble	d			11 28																				12 28	
Guildford	d								11 28										11 58						
Effingham Junction 6	d								11 46										12 16						
Bookham	d								11 49										12 19						
Leatherhead	d			11 33		11 41			11 54					12 04		12 11			12 24					12 33	
Ashtead	d			11 37		11 44			11 58					12 07		12 14			12 28					12 37	
Epsom 3	a			11 41		11 49			12 02					12 12		12 19			12 32					12 41	
	d			11 42		11 50		11 49	12 05				12 04	12 13		12 20		12 19	12 35					12 42	
Ewell East	d			11 46				11 53					12 08					12 23						12 46	
Cheam	d			11 49				11 56					12 11	12 18				12 26						12 49	
Epsom Downs	d		11 35																				12 35		
Banstead	d		11 38																				12 38		
Belmont	d		11 41																				12 41		
Sutton (Surrey) 4	a		11 44	11 52				11 59					12 14	12 21				12 29					12 44	12 52	
	d	11 38	11 45	11 53			11 52	12 00		12 03	12 07	12 08	12 15	12 23			12 22	12 30		12 33	12 37	12 38	12 45	12 53	
Carshalton	d	11 41						12 03				12 11						12 33				12 41			
Hackbridge	d	11 43						12 05				12 13						12 35				12 43			
Mitcham Junction	d	11 46						12 09				12 16						12 39				12 46			
Mitcham Eastfields	d	11 49						12 12				12 19						12 42				12 49			
Carshalton Beeches	d		11 48				11 55			12 06			12 18				12 25			12 36			12 48		
Wallington	d		11 50				11 57			12 08			12 20				12 27			12 38			12 50		
Waddon	d		11 53				12 00			12 11			12 23				12 30			12 41			12 53		
West Croydon 4	d		11 58				12 04			12 15			12 28				12 34			12 45			12 58		
Norwood Junction 2	d									12 22										12 52					
New Cross Gate 4	⊖ d																								
Tulse Hill 3	a	11 57									12 44	12 27									13 14	12 57			
	d										12 47										13 17				
London Bridge 4	⊖ a										13 00										13 30				
Balham 4	⊖ d		12 14				12 21	12 18		12 39			12 44				12 51	12 48		13 09			13 14		
Clapham Junction 10	a		12 19	12 10		12 15	12 26	12 22	12 30	12 44			12 49	12 40		12 45	12 56	12 52	13 00	13 14			13 19	13 10	
London Waterloo 15	⊖ a					12 25			12 40							12 55			13 10						
London Victoria 15	⊖ a		12 28	12 18			12 34	12 30		12 53			12 58	12 48			13 04	13 00		13 23			13 28	13 18	

		SW	SN	SN	SW	SN	FC	FC	SN	SN		SW	SN	SN	SW	SN	FC	FC	SN	SN		SW	SN	SN	SW
Horsham 4	d																			13 04					
Warnham	d																			13 08					
Ockley	d																			13 15					
Holmwood	d																			13 19					
Dorking 4	a																			13 25					
	d	12 35								12 58		13 05								13 26		13 35			
Boxhill & Westhumble	d																			13 28					
Guildford	d				12 28										12 58										13 28
Effingham Junction 6	d				12 46										13 16										13 46
Bookham	d				12 49										13 19										13 49
Leatherhead	d	12 41			12 54					13 04		13 11			13 24					13 33		13 41			13 54
Ashtead	d	12 44			12 58					13 07		13 14			13 28					13 37		13 44			13 58
Epsom 3	a	12 49			13 02					13 12		13 19			13 32					13 41		13 49			14 02
	d	12 50		12 49	13 05				13 04	13 13		13 20		13 19	13 35					13 42		13 50		13 49	14 05
Ewell East	d			12 53					13 08					13 23						13 46				13 53	
Cheam	d			12 56					13 11	13 18				13 26						13 49				13 56	
Epsom Downs	d																		13 35						
Banstead	d																		13 38						
Belmont	d																		13 41						
Sutton (Surrey) 4	a			12 59					13 14	13 21				13 29					13 44	13 52				13 59	
	d		12 52	13 00		13 03	13 07	13 08	13 15	13 23			13 22	13 30		13 33	13 37	13 38	13 45	13 53			13 52	14 00	
Carshalton	d			13 03				13 11						13 33				13 41						14 03	
Hackbridge	d			13 05				13 13						13 35				13 43						14 05	
Mitcham Junction	d			13 09				13 16						13 39				13 46						14 09	
Mitcham Eastfields	d			13 12				13 19						13 42				13 49						14 12	
Carshalton Beeches	d		12 55			13 06			13 18				13 25			13 36			13 48				13 55		
Wallington	d		12 57			13 08			13 20				13 27			13 38			13 50				13 57		
Waddon	d		13 00			13 11			13 23				13 30			13 41			13 53				14 00		
West Croydon 4	d		13 04			13 15			13 28				13 34			13 45			13 58				14 04		
Norwood Junction 2	d					13 22										13 52									
New Cross Gate 4	⊖ d																								
Tulse Hill 3	a						13 44	13 27									14 14	13 57							
	d						13 47										14 17								
London Bridge 4	⊖ a						14 00										14 30								
Balham 4	⊖ d		13 21	13 18		13 39			13 44				13 51	13 48		14 09			14 14				14 21	14 18	
Clapham Junction 10	a	13 15	13 26	13 22	13 30	13 44			13 49	13 40		13 45	13 56	13 52	14 00	14 14			14 19	14 10		14 15	14 26	14 22	14 30
London Waterloo 15	⊖ a	13 25			13 40							13 55			14 10							14 25			14 40
London Victoria 15	⊖ a		13 34	13 30		13 53			13 58	13 48			14 04	14 00		14 23			14 28	14 18			14 34	14 30	

Table 182

Saturdays until 1 October

Horsham, Dorking, Guildford, Epsom and Sutton - London

		SN	FC	FC	SN	SN		SW	SN	SN	SW	SN	FC	FC	SN	SN		SW	SN	SN	SW	SN	FC	FC	SN
Horsham	d															14 04									
Warnham	d															14 08									
Ockley	d															14 15									
Holmwood	d															14 19									
Dorking	a															14 25									
	d					13 58		14 05								14 26		14 35							
Boxhill & Westhumble	d															14 28									
Guildford	d										13 58										14 28				
Effingham Junction	d										14 16										14 46				
Bookham	d										14 19										14 49				
Leatherhead	d					14 04		14 11			14 24					14 33		14 41			14 54				
Ashtead	d					14 07		14 14			14 28					14 37		14 44			14 58				
Epsom	a					14 12		14 19			14 32					14 41		14 49			15 02				
	d				14 04	14 13		14 20		14 19	14 35					14 42		14 50		14 49	15 05				15 04
Ewell East	d				14 08					14 23						14 46				14 53					15 08
Cheam	d				14 11	14 18				14 26						14 49				14 56					15 11
Epsom Downs	d														14 35										
Banstead	d														14 38										
Belmont	d														14 41										
Sutton (Surrey)	a				14 14	14 21				14 29					14 44	14 52				14 59					15 14
	d	14 03	14 07	14 08	14 15	14 23			14 22	14 30		14 33	14 37	14 38	14 45	14 53			14 52	15 00		15 03	15 07	15 08	15 15
Carshalton	d			14 11						14 33				14 41						15 03				15 11	
Hackbridge	d			14 13						14 35				14 43						15 05				15 13	
Mitcham Junction	d			14 16						14 39				14 46						15 09				15 16	
Mitcham Eastfields	d			14 19						14 42				14 49						15 12				15 19	
Carshalton Beeches	d	14 06			14 18				14 25			14 36			14 48				14 55			15 06			15 18
Wallington	d	14 08			14 20				14 27			14 38			14 50				14 57			15 08			15 20
Waddon	d	14 11			14 23				14 30			14 41			14 53				15 00			15 11			15 23
West Croydon	d	14 15			14 28				14 34			14 45			14 58				15 04			15 15			15 28
Norwood Junction	d	14 22										14 52										15 22			
New Cross Gate ⊖	d																								
Tulse Hill	a		14 44	14 27									15 14	14 57									15 44	15 27	
	d		14 47										15 17										15 47		
London Bridge ⊖	a		15 00										15 30										16 00		
Balham ⊖	d	14 39			14 44				14 51	14 48		15 09			15 14				15 21	15 18		15 39			15 44
Clapham Junction	a	14 44			14 49	14 40		14 45	14 56	14 52	15 00	15 14			15 19	15 10		15 15	15 26	15 22	15 30	15 44			15 49
London Waterloo ⊖	a							14 55			15 10							15 25			15 40				
London Victoria ⊖	a	14 53			14 58	14 48			15 04	15 00		15 23			15 28	15 18			15 34	15 30		15 53			15 58

		SN		SW	SN	SN	SW	SN	FC	FC	SN	SN		SW	SN	SN	SW	SN	FC	FC	SN	SN		SW	SN
Horsham	d											15 04													
Warnham	d											15 08													
Ockley	d											15 15													
Holmwood	d											15 19													
Dorking	a											15 25													
	d	14 58		15 05								15 26		15 35								15 58		16 05	
Boxhill & Westhumble	d											15 28													
Guildford	d						14 58										15 28								
Effingham Junction	d						15 16										15 46								
Bookham	d						15 19										15 49								
Leatherhead	d	15 04		15 11			15 24					15 33		15 41			15 54					16 04		16 11	
Ashtead	d	15 07		15 14			15 28					15 37		15 44			15 58					16 07		16 14	
Epsom	a	15 12		15 19			15 32					15 41		15 49			16 02					16 12		16 19	
	d	15 13		15 20		15 19	15 35					15 42		15 50		15 49	16 05				16 04	16 13		16 20	
Ewell East	d					15 23						15 46				15 53					16 08				
Cheam	d	15 18				15 26						15 49				15 56					16 11	16 18			
Epsom Downs	d										15 35														
Banstead	d										15 38														
Belmont	d										15 41														
Sutton (Surrey)	a	15 21				15 29					15 44	15 52				15 59					16 14	16 21			
	d	15 23			15 22	15 30		15 33	15 37	15 38	15 45	15 53			15 52	16 00		16 03	16 07	16 08	16 15	16 23			16 22
Carshalton	d					15 33				15 41						16 03				16 11					
Hackbridge	d					15 35				15 43						16 05				16 13					
Mitcham Junction	d					15 39				15 46						16 09				16 16					
Mitcham Eastfields	d					15 42				15 49						16 12				16 19					
Carshalton Beeches	d				15 25			15 36			15 48				15 55			16 06			16 18				16 25
Wallington	d				15 27			15 38			15 50				15 57			16 08			16 20				16 27
Waddon	d				15 30			15 41			15 53				16 00			16 11			16 23				16 30
West Croydon	d				15 34			15 45			15 58				16 04			16 15			16 28				16 34
Norwood Junction	d							15 52										16 22							
New Cross Gate ⊖	d																								
Tulse Hill	a								16 14	15 57									16 44	16 27					
	d								16 17										16 47						
London Bridge ⊖	a								16 30										17 00						
Balham ⊖	d				15 51	15 48		16 09			16 14				16 21	16 18		16 39			16 44				16 51
Clapham Junction	a	15 40		15 45	15 56	15 52	16 00	16 14			16 19	16 10		16 15	16 26	16 22	16 30	16 44			16 49	16 40		16 45	16 56
London Waterloo ⊖	a			15 55			16 10							16 25			16 40							16 55	
London Victoria ⊖	a	15 48			16 04	16 00		16 23			16 28	16 18			16 34	16 30		16 53			16 58	16 48			17 04

Table 182

Saturdays until 1 October

Horsham, Dorking, Guildford, Epsom and Sutton - London

		SN	SW	SN	FC	FC	SN	SN		SW	SN	SN	SW	SN	FC	FC	SN	SN		SW	SN	SN	SW	SN	FC
Horsham	d							16 04																	
Warnham	d							16 08																	
Ockley	d							16 15																	
Holmwood	d							16 19																	
Dorking	a							16 25																	
	d							16 26		16 35								16 58		17 05					
Boxhill & Westhumble	d							16 28																	
Guildford	d		15 58										16 28										16 58		
Effingham Junction	d		16 16										16 46										17 16		
Bookham	d		16 19										16 49										17 19		
Leatherhead	d		16 24					16 33		16 41			16 54					17 04		17 11			17 24		
Ashtead	d		16 28					16 37		16 44			16 58					17 07		17 14			17 28		
Epsom	a		16 32					16 41		16 49			17 02					17 12		17 19			17 32		
	d	16 19	16 35					16 42		16 50		16 49	17 05				17 04	17 13		17 20		17 19	17 35		
Ewell East	d	16 23						16 46				16 53					17 08					17 23			
Cheam	d	16 26						16 49				16 56					17 11	17 18				17 26			
Epsom Downs	d						16 35																		
Banstead	d						16 38																		
Belmont	d						16 41																		
Sutton (Surrey)	a	16 29					16 44	16 52				16 59					17 14	17 21				17 29			
	d	16 30		16 33	16 37	16 38	16 45	16 53			16 52	17 00		17 03	17 07	17 08	17 15	17 23			17 22	17 30		17 33	17 37
Carshalton	d	16 33				16 41						17 03				17 11						17 33			
Hackbridge	d	16 35				16 43						17 05				17 13						17 35			
Mitcham Junction	d	16 39				16 46						17 09				17 16						17 39			
Mitcham Eastfields	d	16 42				16 49						17 12				17 19						17 42			
Carshalton Beeches	d			16 36			16 48				16 55			17 06			17 18				17 25			17 36	
Wallington	d			16 38			16 50				16 57			17 08			17 20				17 27			17 38	
Waddon	d			16 41			16 53				17 00			17 11			17 23				17 30			17 41	
West Croydon	d			16 45			16 58				17 04			17 15			17 28				17 34			17 45	
Norwood Junction	d			16 52										17 22										17 52	
New Cross Gate ⊖	d																								
Tulse Hill	a				17 14	16 57									17 44	17 27									18 14
	d				17 17										17 47										18 17
London Bridge ⊖	a				17 30										18 00										18 30
Balham ⊖	d	16 48		17 09			17 14				17 21	17 18		17 39			17 44				17 51	17 48		18 09	
Clapham Junction	a	16 52	17 00	17 14			17 19	17 10		17 15	17 26	17 22	17 30	17 44			17 49	17 41		17 45	17 56	17 52	18 00	18 14	
London Waterloo ⊖	a		17 10							17 25			17 40							17 55			18 10		
London Victoria ⊖	a	17 00		17 23			17 28	17 18			17 34	17 30		17 53			17 58	17 49			18 04	18 00		18 23	

		FC	SN	SN		SW	SN	SN	SW	SN	FC	FC	SN	SN		SW	SN	SN	SW	SN	FC	FC	SN	SN	
Horsham	d			17 04																				18 04	
Warnham	d			17 08																				18 08	
Ockley	d			17 15																				18 15	
Holmwood	d			17 19																				18 19	
Dorking	a			17 25																				18 25	
	d			17 26		17 35								17 58		18 05								18 26	
Boxhill & Westhumble	d			17 28																				18 28	
Guildford	d								17 28										17 58						
Effingham Junction	d								17 46										18 16						
Bookham	d								17 49										18 19						
Leatherhead	d			17 33		17 41			17 54					18 04		18 11			18 24					18 33	
Ashtead	d			17 37		17 44			17 58					18 07		18 14			18 28					18 37	
Epsom	a			17 41		17 49			18 02					18 12		18 19			18 32					18 41	
	d			17 42		17 50		17 49	18 05				18 04	18 13		18 20		18 19	18 35					18 42	
Ewell East	d			17 46				17 53					18 08					18 23						18 46	
Cheam	d			17 49				17 56					18 11	18 18				18 26						18 49	
Epsom Downs	d		17 35																				18 35		
Banstead	d		17 38																				18 38		
Belmont	d		17 41																				18 41		
Sutton (Surrey)	a		17 44	17 52				17 59					18 14	18 21				18 29					18 44	18 52	
	d	17 38	17 45	17 53			17 52	18 00		18 03	18 07	18 08	18 15	18 23			18 22	18 30		18 33	18 37	18 38	18 45	18 53	
Carshalton	d	17 41						18 03				18 11						18 33				18 41			
Hackbridge	d	17 43						18 05				18 13						18 35				18 43			
Mitcham Junction	d	17 46						18 09				18 16						18 39				18 46			
Mitcham Eastfields	d	17 49						18 12				18 19						18 42				18 49			
Carshalton Beeches	d		17 48				17 55			18 06			18 18				18 25			18 36			18 48		
Wallington	d		17 50				17 57			18 08			18 20				18 27			18 38			18 50		
Waddon	d		17 53				18 00			18 11			18 23				18 30			18 41			18 53		
West Croydon	d		17 58				18 04			18 15			18 28				18 34			18 45			18 58		
Norwood Junction	d									18 22										18 52					
New Cross Gate ⊖	d																								
Tulse Hill	a	17 57									18 44	18 27									19 14	18 57			
	d										18 47										19 17				
London Bridge ⊖	a										19 00										19 30				
Balham ⊖	d		18 14				18 21	18 18		18 39			18 44				18 51	18 48		19 09			19 14		
Clapham Junction	a		18 19	18 10		18 15	18 26	18 22	18 30	18 44			18 49	18 40		18 45	18 56	18 52	19 00	19 14			19 19	19 10	
London Waterloo ⊖	a					18 25			18 40							18 55			19 10						
London Victoria ⊖	a		18 28	18 18			18 34	18 30		18 53			18 58	18 48			19 04	19 00		19 23			19 28	19 18	

Saturdays until 1 October

Horsham, Dorking, Guildford, Epsom and Sutton - London

		SW	SN	SN	SW	SN	FC	FC	SN	SN	SW	SN	SN	SW	SN	FC	SN	SN	SW	SN	SN	SW	SN
Horsham	d																						
Warnham	d																						
Ockley	d																						
Holmwood	d																						
Dorking	a																						
	d	18 35								18 58	19 05							19 28	19 35				
Boxhill & Westhumble	d									19 00													
Guildford	d				18 28									18 58								19 28	
Effingham Junction	d				18 46									19 16								19 46	
Bookham	d				18 49									19 19								19 49	
Leatherhead	d	18 41			18 54					19 05	19 11			19 24				19 34	19 41			19 54	
Ashtead	d	18 44			18 58					19 09	19 14			19 28				19 37	19 44			19 58	
Epsom	a	18 49			19 02					19 13	19 19			19 32				19 42	19 49			20 02	
	d	18 50		18 49	19 05				19 04	19 14	19 20		19 19	19 35				19 42	19 50		19 49	20 05	
Ewell East	d			18 53					19 08				19 23					19 46			19 53		
Cheam	d			18 56					19 11	19 19			19 26					19 49			19 56		
Epsom Downs	d																19 35						
Banstead	d																19 38						
Belmont	d																19 41						
Sutton (Surrey)	a			18 59					19 14	19 22			19 29				19 44	19 52			19 59		
	d		18 52	19 00		19 03	19 07	19 08	19 15	19 23		19 22	19 30		19 33	19 37	19 45	19 53		19 52	20 00		20 03
Carshalton	d			19 03				19 11					19 33								20 03		
Hackbridge	d			19 05				19 13					19 35								20 05		
Mitcham Junction	d			19 09				19 16					19 39								20 09		
Mitcham Eastfields	d			19 12				19 19					19 42								20 12		
Carshalton Beeches	d		18 55			19 06			19 18			19 25			19 36		19 48			19 55			20 06
Wallington	d		18 57			19 08			19 20			19 27			19 38		19 50			19 57			20 08
Waddon	d		19 00			19 11			19 23			19 30			19 41		19 53			20 00			20 11
West Croydon	d		19 04			19 15			19 28			19 34			19 45		19 58			20 04			20 15
Norwood Junction	d					19 22									19 52								20 22
New Cross Gate	d																						
Tulse Hill	a						19 44	19 27								20 14							
	d						19 47									20 17							
London Bridge	a						20 00									20 30							
Balham	d		19 21	19 18		19 39			19 44			19 51	19 48		20 09		20 14			20 21	20 18		20 39
Clapham Junction	a	19 15	19 26	19 22	19 30	19 44			19 49	19 40	19 45	19 56	19 52	20 00	20 14		20 19	20 10	20 15	20 26	20 22	20 30	20 44
London Waterloo	a	19 25			19 40						19 55			20 10					20 25			20 40	
London Victoria	a		19 34	19 30		19 53			19 58	19 48		20 04	20 00		20 23		20 28	20 18		20 34	20 30		20 53

		FC	SN	SN	SW	SN	SN	SW	SN	FC	SN	SN	SW	SN	SN	SN	FC	SN	SW	SN	SW	SN	SN
Horsham	d																						
Warnham	d																						
Ockley	d																						
Holmwood	d																						
Dorking	a																						
	d			19 58	20 05							20 28	20 35							20 58			
Boxhill & Westhumble	d			20 00																21 00			
Guildford	d							19 58													20 46		
Effingham Junction	d							20 16													21 03		
Bookham	d							20 19													21 06		
Leatherhead	d			20 05	20 11			20 24				20 34	20 41							21 05	21 11		
Ashtead	d			20 09	20 14			20 28				20 37	20 44							21 09	21 14		
Epsom	a			20 13	20 19			20 32				20 42	20 49							21 13	21 19		
	d		20 04	20 14	20 20		20 19	20 35				20 42	20 50		20 49			21 03	21 05	21 14	21 20		21 19
Ewell East	d		20 08				20 23					20 46			20 53			21 08					21 23
Cheam	d		20 11	20 19			20 26					20 49			20 56			21 11		21 19			21 26
Epsom Downs	d										20 35												
Banstead	d										20 38												
Belmont	d										20 41												
Sutton (Surrey)	a		20 14	20 22			20 29				20 44	20 52			20 59			21 14		21 22			21 29
	d	20 08	20 15	20 23		20 22	20 30		20 33	20 37	20 45	20 53		20 52	21 00	21 03	21 07	21 15		21 23		21 22	21 30
Carshalton	d						20 33								21 03								21 33
Hackbridge	d						20 35								21 05								21 35
Mitcham Junction	d						20 39								21 09								21 39
Mitcham Eastfields	d						20 42								21 12								21 42
Carshalton Beeches	d		20 18			20 25			20 36		20 48			20 55		21 06		21 18				21 25	
Wallington	d		20 20			20 27			20 38		20 50			20 57		21 08		21 20				21 27	
Waddon	d		20 23			20 30			20 41		20 53			21 00		21 11		21 23				21 30	
West Croydon	d		20 28			20 34			20 45		20 58			21 04		21 15		21 28				21 34	
Norwood Junction	d								20 52							21 22							
New Cross Gate	d																						
Tulse Hill	a	20 44								21 14							21 44						
	d	20 47								21 17							21 47						
London Bridge	a	21 00								21 30							22 00						
Balham	d		20 44			20 51	20 48		21 09		21 14			21 21	21 18	21 39		21 44				21 51	21 48
Clapham Junction	a		20 49	20 40	20 45	20 56	20 52	21 00	21 14		21 19	21 10	21 15	21 26	21 22	21 44		21 49	21 30	21 40	21 45	21 56	21 52
London Waterloo	a				20 55			21 10					21 25						21 40		21 55		
London Victoria	a		20 58	20 48		21 04	21 00		21 23		21 28	21 18		21 34	21 30	21 53		21 58		21 48		22 04	22 00

Horsham, Dorking, Guildford, Epsom and Sutton - London

until 1 October

		SW	SN	FC	SN	SN	SW	SN	SN	SN	FC	SN	SN	SW	SN	SN	SN	SN	SN	SW	SN	SN
Horsham	d																					
Warnham	d																					
Ockley	d																					
Holmwood	d																					
Dorking	a																					
	d					21 28	21 35						21 58						22 28	22 35		
Boxhill & Westhumble	d												22 00									
Guildford	d													21 46								
Effingham Junction	d													22 03								
Bookham	d													22 06								
Leatherhead	d					21 34	21 41						22 05	22 11					22 34	22 41		
Ashtead	d					21 37	21 44						22 09	22 14					22 37	22 44		
Epsom	a					21 42	21 49						22 13	22 19					22 42	22 49		
	d	21 35				21 42	21 50		21 49			22 04	22 14	22 20		22 19			22 42	22 50		22 49
Ewell East	d					21 46			21 53			22 08				22 23			22 46			22 53
Cheam	d					21 49			21 56			22 11	22 19			22 26			22 49			22 56
Epsom Downs	d				21 35													22 35				
Banstead	d				21 38													22 38				
Belmont	d				21 41													22 41				
Sutton (Surrey)	a				21 44	21 52			21 59			22 14	22 22			22 29		22 44	22 52			22 59
	d		21 33	21 37	21 45	21 53		21 52	22 00	22 03	22 07	22 15	22 23		22 22	22 30	22 33	22 45	22 53		22 52	23 00
Carshalton	d								22 03							22 33						23 03
Hackbridge	d								22 05							22 35						23 05
Mitcham Junction	d								22 09							22 39						23 09
Mitcham Eastfields	d								22 12							22 42						23 12
Carshalton Beeches	d		21 36		21 48			21 55		22 06		22 18			22 25		22 36	22 48			22 55	
Wallington	d		21 38		21 50			21 57		22 08		22 20			22 27		22 38	22 51			22 57	
Waddon	d		21 41		21 53			22 00		22 11		22 23			22 30		22 41	22 54			23 00	
West Croydon	d		21 45		21 58			22 04		22 15		22 28			22 34		22 45	22 58			23 04	
Norwood Junction	d		21 52							22 22							22 52					
New Cross Gate	d																					
Tulse Hill	a			22 14							22 44											
	d			22 17							22 47											
London Bridge	a			22 30							23 00											
Balham	d		22 09		22 14			22 22	22 18	22 39		22 44			22 51	22 48	23 09	23 14			23 21	23 18
Clapham Junction	a	22 00	22 14		22 19	22 10	22 15	22 27	22 22	22 44		22 49	22 40	22 45	22 56	22 52	23 14	23 19	23 10	23 15	23 26	23 22
London Waterloo	a	22 10					22 25							22 55						23 25		
London Victoria	a		22 23		22 28	22 18		22 34	22 30	22 53		22 58	22 48		23 04	23 00	23 24	23 29	23 22		23 34	23 31

		SN	SN	SN	SN	SW	SN	SN	SN	SN
Horsham	d									
Warnham	d									
Ockley	d									
Holmwood	d									
Dorking	a									
	d				23 00				23 30	
Boxhill & Westhumble	d				23 02					
Guildford	d					22 46				
Effingham Junction	d					23 03				
Bookham	d					23 06				
Leatherhead	d				23 07	23 11			23 36	
Ashtead	d				23 11	23 14			23 39	
Epsom	a				23 15	23 19			23 45	
	d		23 04		23 16	23 20		23 35		
Ewell East	d		23 08		23 20			23 39		
Cheam	d		23 11		23 23			23 42		
Epsom Downs	d						23 23			23 50
Banstead	d						23 26			23 53
Belmont	d						23 29			23 56
Sutton (Surrey)	a		23 14		23 26		23 32	23 45		23 59
	d	23 03	23 15	23 22	23 30		23 34	23 46		00 01
Carshalton	d									
Hackbridge	d									
Mitcham Junction	d									
Mitcham Eastfields	d									
Carshalton Beeches	d	23 06	23 18	23 25	23 33		23 37	23 49		00 04
Wallington	d	23 08	23 20	23 27	23 35		23 39	23 51		00 06
Waddon	d	23 11	23 23	23 30	23 38		23 44	23 54		00 09
West Croydon	d	23 15	23 28	23 34	23a41		23a47	23a57		00a12
Norwood Junction	d	23 22								
New Cross Gate	d									
Tulse Hill	a									
	d									
London Bridge	a									
Balham	d	23 39	23 44	23 50						
Clapham Junction	a	23 45	23 49	23 56		23 48				
London Waterloo	a					23 58				
London Victoria	a	23 53	23 58	00 04						

Table 182

Saturdays
from 8 October

Horsham, Dorking, Guildford, Epsom and Sutton - London

		SN	SW	SW	SW	SN	SN	SN	SW	SN		FC	FC	SN	SN	SN	SW	SN	FC	FC		SN	SN	SN	SW
Horsham [4]	d																								
Warnham	d																								
Ockley	d																								
Holmwood	d																								
Dorking [4]	a																								
	d						06 28								06 57								07 26		
Boxhill & Westhumble	d														06 59								07 28		
Guildford	d								06 28								06 58								07 28
Effingham Junction [6]	d								06 46								07 16								07 46
Bookham	d								06 49								07 19								07 49
Leatherhead	d						06 34		06 54						07 04		07 24						07 33		07 54
Ashtead	d						06 37		06 58						07 08		07 28						07 37		07 58
Epsom [3]	a						06 42		07 02						07 12		07 32						07 41		08 02
	d		05 35	06 05	06 35		06 42	06 49	07 05					07 04	07 13	07 19	07 35						07 42	07 49	08 05
Ewell East	d						06 46	06 53						07 08		07 23							07 46	07 53	
Cheam	d						06 49	06 56						07 11	07 18	07 26							07 49	07 56	
Epsom Downs	d	23p43																				07 35			
Banstead	d	23p46																				07 38			
Belmont	d	23p49																				07 41			
Sutton (Surrey) [4]	a	23p52					06 52	06 59						07 14	07 22	07 29						07 44	07 52	07 59	
	d	23p53				06 45	06 53	07 00		07 03		07 07	07 08	07 15	07 23	07 30		07 33	07 37	07 38		07 45	07 53	08 00	
Carshalton	d							07 03					07 11			07 33				07 41				08 03	
Hackbridge	d							07 05					07 13			07 35				07 43				08 05	
Mitcham Junction	d							07 09					07 16			07 39				07 46				08 09	
Mitcham Eastfields	d							07 12					07 19			07 42				07 49				08 12	
Carshalton Beeches	d	23p56				06 48				07 06				07 18				07 36				07 48			
Wallington	d	23p58				06 50				07 08				07 20				07 38				07 50			
Waddon	d	00 01				06 53				07 11				07 23				07 41				07 53			
West Croydon [4]	d	00a04				06 58				07 15				07 28				07 45				07 58			
Norwood Junction [2]	d									07 20								07 50							
New Cross Gate [4] ⊖	d									07 34								08 04							
Tulse Hill [3]	a											07 44	07 27						08 14	07 57					
	d											07 47							08 17						
London Bridge [4] ⊖	a									07 41		08 00						08 11	08 30						
Balham [4] ⊖	d					07 14		07 18						07 44		07 48						08 14		08 18	
Clapham Junction [10]	a		06 01	06 30	07 00	07 19	07 10	07 22	07 30					07 49	07 40	07 52	08 00					08 19	08 10	08 22	08 30
London Waterloo [15] ⊖	a		06 11	06 40	07 10				07 40								08 10								08 40
London Victoria [15] ⊖	a					07 28	07 18	07 30						07 58	07 48	08 00						08 28	08 18	08 30	

		SN	FC	FC	SN	SN		SW	SN	SN	SW	SN	FC	FC	SN	SN		SW	SN	SN	SW	SN	FC	FC	SN
Horsham [4]	d															08 04									
Warnham	d															08 08									
Ockley	d															08 15									
Holmwood	d															08 19									
Dorking [4]	a															08 25									
	d					07 58		08 05								08 26		08 35							
Boxhill & Westhumble	d															08 28									
Guildford	d										07 58										08 28				
Effingham Junction [6]	d										08 16										08 46				
Bookham	d										08 19										08 49				
Leatherhead	d					08 04		08 11			08 24					08 33		08 41			08 54				
Ashtead	d					08 07		08 14			08 28					08 37		08 44			08 58				
Epsom [3]	a					08 12		08 19			08 32					08 41		08 49			09 02				
	d				08 04	08 13		08 20		08 19	08 35					08 42		08 50		08 49	09 05				09 04
Ewell East	d				08 08					08 23						08 46				08 53					09 08
Cheam	d				08 11	08 18				08 26						08 49				08 56					09 11
Epsom Downs	d														08 35										
Banstead	d														08 38										
Belmont	d														08 41										
Sutton (Surrey) [4]	a				08 14	08 21				08 29					08 44	08 52				08 59					09 14
	d	08 03	08 07	08 08	08 15	08 23			08 22	08 30		08 33	08 37	08 38	08 45	08 53			08 52	09 00		09 03	09 07	09 08	09 15
Carshalton	d			08 11						08 33				08 41						09 03				09 11	
Hackbridge	d			08 13						08 35				08 43						09 05				09 13	
Mitcham Junction	d			08 16						08 39				08 46						09 09				09 16	
Mitcham Eastfields	d			08 19						08 42				08 49						09 12				09 19	
Carshalton Beeches	d	08 06			08 18				08 25			08 36			08 48				08 55			09 06			09 18
Wallington	d	08 08			08 20				08 27			08 38			08 50				08 57			09 08			09 20
Waddon	d	08 11			08 23				08 30			08 41			08 53				09 00			09 11			09 23
West Croydon [4]	d	08 15			08 28				08 34			08 45			08 58				09 04			09 16			09 28
Norwood Junction [2]	d	08 22										08 52										09 22			
New Cross Gate [4] ⊖	d																								
Tulse Hill [3]	a		08 44	08 27									09 14	08 57									09 44	09 27	
	d		08 47										09 17										09 47		
London Bridge [4] ⊖	a		09 00										09 30										10 00		
Balham [4] ⊖	d	08 39			08 44				08 51	08 48		09 09			09 14				09 21	09 18		09 39			09 44
Clapham Junction [10]	a	08 44			08 49	08 40		08 45	08 56	08 52	09 00	09 14			09 19	09 10		09 15	09 26	09 22	09 30	09 44			09 49
London Waterloo [15] ⊖	a							08 55			09 10							09 25			09 40				
London Victoria [15] ⊖	a	08 53			08 58	08 48			09 04	09 00		09 23			09 28	09 18			09 34	09 30		09 54			09 58

Table 182

Saturdays
from 8 October

Horsham, Dorking, Guildford, Epsom and Sutton - London

		SN		SW	SN	SN	SW	SN	FC	FC	SN	SN		SW	SN	SN	SW	SN	FC	FC	SN	SN		SW	SN
Horsham [4]	d											09 04													
Warnham	d											09 08													
Ockley	d											09 15													
Holmwood	d											09 19													
Dorking [4]	a											09 25													
	d	08 58		09 05								09 26		09 35								09 58		10 05	
Boxhill & Westhumble	d											09 28													
Guildford	d						08 58										09 28								
Effingham Junction [6]	d						09 16										09 46								
Bookham	d						09 19										09 49								
Leatherhead	d	09 04		09 11			09 24					09 33		09 41			09 54					10 04		10 11	
Ashtead	d	09 07		09 14			09 28					09 37		09 44			09 58					10 07		10 14	
Epsom [3]	a	09 12		09 19			09 32					09 41		09 49			10 02					10 12		10 19	
	d	09 13		09 20		09 19	09 35					09 42		09 50		09 49	10 05				10 04	10 12		10 20	
Ewell East	d					09 23						09 46				09 53					10 08				
Cheam	d	09 18				09 26						09 49				09 56					10 11	10 18			
Epsom Downs	d										09 35														
Banstead	d										09 38														
Belmont	d										09 41														
Sutton (Surrey) [4]	a	09 21				09 29					09 44	09 52				09 59					10 14	10 22			
	d	09 23			09 22	09 30		09 33	09 37	09 38	09 45	09 53			09 52	10 00		10 03	10 07	10 08	10 15	10 23			10 22
Carshalton	d					09 33				09 41						10 03				10 11					
Hackbridge	d					09 35				09 43						10 05				10 13					
Mitcham Junction	d					09 39				09 46						10 09				10 16					
Mitcham Eastfields	d					09 42				09 49						10 12				10 19					
Carshalton Beeches	d				09 25			09 36			09 48				09 55			10 06			10 18				10 25
Wallington	d				09 27			09 38			09 50				09 57			10 08			10 20				10 27
Waddon	d				09 30			09 41			09 53				10 00			10 11			10 23				10 30
West Croydon [4]	d				09 34			09 45			09 58				10 04			10 15			10 28				10 34
Norwood Junction [2]	d							09 52										10 22							
New Cross Gate [4] ⊖	d																								
Tulse Hill [3]	a								10 14	09 57									10 44	10 27					
	d								10 17										10 47						
London Bridge [4] ⊖	a								10 30										11 00						
Balham [4] ⊖	d				09 51	09 48		10 09			10 14				10 21	10 18		10 39			10 44				10 51
Clapham Junction [10]	a	09 40		09 45	09 56	09 52	10 00	10 14			10 19	10 10		10 15	10 26	10 22	10 30	10 44			10 49	10 40		10 45	10 56
London Waterloo [15] ⊖	a			09 55			10 10							10 25			10 40							10 55	
London Victoria [15] ⊖	a	09 48			10 04	10 00		10 23			10 28	10 18			10 34	10 30		10 53			10 58	10 48			11 04

		SN	SW	SN	FC	FC	SN	SN		SW	SN	SN	SW	SN	FC	FC	SN	SN		SW	SN	SN	SW	SN	FC
Horsham [4]	d							10 04																	
Warnham	d							10 08																	
Ockley	d							10 15																	
Holmwood	d							10 19																	
Dorking [4]	a							10 25																	
	d							10 26		10 35								10 58		11 05					
Boxhill & Westhumble	d							10 28																	
Guildford	d		09 58										10 28										10 58		
Effingham Junction [6]	d		10 16										10 46										11 16		
Bookham	d		10 19										10 49										11 19		
Leatherhead	d		10 24					10 33		10 41			10 54					11 04		11 11			11 24		
Ashtead	d		10 28					10 37		10 44			10 58					11 07		11 14			11 28		
Epsom [3]	a		10 32					10 41		10 49			11 02					11 12		11 19			11 32		
	d	10 19	10 35					10 42		10 50		10 49	11 05				11 04	11 13		11 20		11 19	11 35		
Ewell East	d	10 23						10 46				10 53					11 08					11 23			
Cheam	d	10 26						10 49				10 56					11 11	11 18				11 26			
Epsom Downs	d						10 35																		
Banstead	d						10 38																		
Belmont	d						10 41																		
Sutton (Surrey) [4]	a	10 29					10 44	10 52				10 59					11 14	11 21				11 29			
	d	10 30		10 33	10 37	10 38	10 45	10 53			10 52	11 00		11 03	11 07	11 08	11 15	11 23			11 22	11 30		11 33	11 37
Carshalton	d	10 33				10 41						11 03				11 11						11 33			
Hackbridge	d	10 35				10 43						11 05				11 13						11 35			
Mitcham Junction	d	10 39				10 46						11 09				11 16						11 39			
Mitcham Eastfields	d	10 42				10 49						11 12				11 19						11 42			
Carshalton Beeches	d			10 36			10 48				10 55			11 06			11 18				11 25			11 36	
Wallington	d			10 38			10 50				10 57			11 08			11 20				11 27			11 38	
Waddon	d			10 41			10 53				11 00			11 11			11 23				11 30			11 41	
West Croydon [4]	d			10 45			10 58				11 04			11 15			11 28				11 34			11 45	
Norwood Junction [2]	d			10 52										11 22										11 52	
New Cross Gate [4] ⊖	d																								
Tulse Hill [3]	a				11 14	10 57									11 44	11 27									12 14
	d				11 17										11 47										12 17
London Bridge [4] ⊖	a				11 30										12 00										12 30
Balham [4] ⊖	d	10 48		11 09			11 14				11 21	11 18		11 39			11 44				11 51	11 48		12 09	
Clapham Junction [10]	a	10 52	11 00	11 14			11 19	11 10		11 15	11 26	11 22	11 30	11 44			11 49	11 40		11 45	11 56	11 52	12 00	12 14	
London Waterloo [15] ⊖	a		11 10							11 25			11 40							11 55			12 10		
London Victoria [15] ⊖	a	11 00		11 23			11 28	11 18			11 34	11 30		11 53			11 58	11 48			12 04	12 00		12 23	

Horsham, Dorking, Guildford, Epsom and Sutton - London

		FC	SN	SN	SW	SN	SN	SW	SN	FC	FC	SN	SN	SW	SN	SN	SW	SN	FC	FC	SN	SN
Horsham 4	d			11 04																		12 04
Warnham	d			11 08																		12 08
Ockley	d			11 15																		12 15
Holmwood	d			11 19																		12 19
Dorking 4	a			11 25																		12 25
	d			11 26	11 35								11 58	12 05								12 26
Boxhill & Westhumble	d			11 28																		12 28
Guildford	d							11 28									11 58					
Effingham Junction 6	d							11 46									12 16					
Bookham	d							11 49									12 19					
Leatherhead	d			11 33	11 41			11 54					12 04	12 11			12 24					12 33
Ashtead	d			11 37	11 44			11 58					12 07	12 14			12 28					12 37
Epsom 3	a			11 41	11 49			12 02					12 12	12 19			12 32					12 41
	d			11 42	11 50		11 49	12 05				12 04	12 13	12 20		12 19	12 35					12 42
Ewell East	d			11 46			11 53					12 08				12 23						12 46
Cheam	d			11 49			11 56					12 11	12 18			12 26						12 49
Epsom Downs	d		11 35																		12 35	
Banstead	d		11 38																		12 38	
Belmont	d		11 41																		12 41	
Sutton (Surrey) 4	a		11 44	11 52			11 59					12 14	12 21			12 29					12 44	12 52
	d	11 38	11 45	11 53		11 52	12 00		12 03	12 07	12 08	12 15	12 23		12 22	12 30		12 33	12 37	12 38	12 45	12 53
Carshalton	d	11 41					12 03				12 11					12 33				12 41		
Hackbridge	d	11 43					12 05				12 13					12 35				12 43		
Mitcham Junction	d	11 46					12 09				12 16					12 39				12 46		
Mitcham Eastfields	d	11 49					12 12				12 19					12 42				12 49		
Carshalton Beeches	d		11 48			11 55			12 06			12 18			12 25			12 36			12 48	
Wallington	d		11 50			11 57			12 08			12 20			12 27			12 38			12 50	
Waddon	d		11 53			12 00			12 11			12 23			12 30			12 41			12 53	
West Croydon 4	d		11 58			12 04			12 15			12 28			12 34			12 45			12 58	
Norwood Junction 2	d								12 22									12 52				
New Cross Gate 4 ⊖	d																					
Tulse Hill 3	a	11 57								12 44	12 27								13 14	12 57		
	d									12 47									13 17			
London Bridge 4 ⊖	a									13 00									13 30			
Balham 4 ⊖	d		12 14			12 21	12 18		12 39			12 44			12 51	12 48		13 09			13 14	
Clapham Junction 10	a		12 19	12 10	12 15	12 26	12 22	12 30	12 44			12 49	12 40	12 45	12 56	12 52	13 00	13 14			13 19	13 10
London Waterloo 15 ⊖	a				12 25			12 40						12 55			13 10					
London Victoria 15 ⊖	a		12 28	12 18		12 34	12 30		12 53			12 58	12 48		13 04	13 00		13 23			13 28	13 18

		SW	SN	SN	SW	SN	FC	FC	SN	SN	SW	SN	SN	SW	SN	FC	FC	SN	SN	SW	SN	SN	SW
Horsham 4	d																		13 04				
Warnham	d																		13 08				
Ockley	d																		13 15				
Holmwood	d																		13 19				
Dorking 4	a																		13 25				
	d	12 35								12 58	13 05								13 26	13 35			
Boxhill & Westhumble	d																		13 28				
Guildford	d				12 28									12 58									13 28
Effingham Junction 6	d				12 46									13 16									13 46
Bookham	d				12 49									13 19									13 49
Leatherhead	d	12 41			12 54					13 04	13 11			13 24					13 33	13 41			13 54
Ashtead	d	12 44			12 58					13 07	13 14			13 28					13 37	13 44			13 58
Epsom 3	a	12 49			13 02					13 12	13 19			13 32					13 41	13 49			14 02
	d	12 50		12 49	13 05				13 04	13 13	13 20		13 19	13 35					13 42	13 50		13 49	14 05
Ewell East	d			12 53					13 08				13 23						13 46			13 53	
Cheam	d			12 56					13 11	13 18			13 26						13 49			13 56	
Epsom Downs	d																	13 35					
Banstead	d																	13 38					
Belmont	d																	13 41					
Sutton (Surrey) 4	a			12 59					13 14	13 21			13 29					13 44	13 52			13 59	
	d		12 52	13 00		13 03	13 07	13 08	13 15	13 23		13 22	13 30		13 33	13 37	13 38	13 45	13 53		13 52	14 00	
Carshalton	d			13 03				13 11					13 33				13 41					14 03	
Hackbridge	d			13 05				13 13					13 35				13 43					14 05	
Mitcham Junction	d			13 09				13 16					13 39				13 46					14 09	
Mitcham Eastfields	d			13 12				13 19					13 42				13 49					14 12	
Carshalton Beeches	d		12 55			13 06			13 18			13 25			13 36			13 48			13 55		
Wallington	d		12 57			13 08			13 20			13 27			13 38			13 50			13 57		
Waddon	d		13 00			13 11			13 23			13 30			13 41			13 53			14 00		
West Croydon 4	d		13 04			13 15			13 28			13 34			13 45			13 58			14 04		
Norwood Junction 2	d					13 22									13 52								
New Cross Gate 4 ⊖	d																						
Tulse Hill 3	a						13 44	13 27								14 14	13 57						
	d						13 47									14 17							
London Bridge 4 ⊖	a						14 00									14 30							
Balham 4 ⊖	d		13 21	13 18		13 39			13 44			13 51	13 48		14 09			14 14			14 21	14 18	
Clapham Junction 10	a	13 15	13 26	13 22	13 30	13 44			13 49	13 40	13 45	13 56	13 52	14 00	14 14			14 19	14 10	14 15	14 26	14 22	14 30
London Waterloo 15 ⊖	a	13 25			13 40						13 55			14 10						14 25			14 40
London Victoria 15 ⊖	a		13 34	13 30		13 53			13 58	13 48		14 04	14 00		14 23			14 28	14 18		14 34	14 30	

Horsham, Dorking, Guildford, Epsom and Sutton - London

		SN	FC	FC	SN	SN	SW	SN	SN	SW	SN	FC	FC	SN	SN	SW	SN	SN	SW	SN	FC	FC	SN
Horsham 4	d														14 04								
Warnham	d														14 08								
Ockley	d														14 15								
Holmwood	d														14 19								
Dorking 4	a														14 25								
	d					13 58	14 05								14 26	14 35							
Boxhill & Westhumble	d														14 28								
Guildford	d									13 58									14 28				
Effingham Junction 6	d									14 16									14 46				
Bookham	d									14 19									14 49				
Leatherhead	d					14 04	14 11			14 24					14 33	14 41			14 54				
Ashtead	d					14 07	14 14			14 28					14 37	14 44			14 58				
Epsom 3	a					14 12	14 19			14 32					14 41	14 49			15 02				
	d				14 04	14 13	14 20		14 19	14 35					14 42	14 50		14 49	15 05				15 04
Ewell East	d				14 08				14 23						14 46			14 53					15 08
Cheam	d				14 11	14 18			14 26						14 49			14 56					15 11
Epsom Downs	d													14 35									
Banstead	d													14 38									
Belmont	d													14 41									
Sutton (Surrey) 4	a				14 14	14 21			14 29					14 44	14 52			14 59					15 14
	d	14 03	14 07	14 08	14 15	14 23		14 22	14 30		14 33	14 37	14 38	14 45	14 53		14 52	15 00		15 03	15 07	15 08	15 15
Carshalton	d			14 11					14 33				14 41					15 03				15 11	
Hackbridge	d			14 13					14 35				14 43					15 05				15 13	
Mitcham Junction	d			14 16					14 39				14 46					15 09				15 16	
Mitcham Eastfields	d			14 19					14 42				14 49					15 12				15 19	
Carshalton Beeches	d	14 06			14 18			14 25			14 36			14 48			14 55			15 06			15 18
Wallington	d	14 08			14 20			14 27			14 38			14 50			14 57			15 08			15 20
Waddon	d	14 11			14 23			14 30			14 41			14 53			15 00			15 11			15 23
West Croydon 4	d	14 15			14 28			14 34			14 45			14 58			15 04			15 15			15 28
Norwood Junction 2	d	14 22									14 52									15 22			
New Cross Gate 4 ⊖	d																						
Tulse Hill 3	a		14 44	14 27								15 14	14 57								15 44	15 27	
	d		14 47									15 17									15 47		
London Bridge 4 ⊖	a		15 00									15 30									16 00		
Balham 4 ⊖	d	14 39			14 44			14 51	14 48		15 09			15 14			15 21	15 18		15 39			15 44
Clapham Junction 10	a	14 44			14 49	14 40	14 45	14 56	14 52	15 00	15 14			15 19	15 10	15 15	15 26	15 22	15 30	15 44			15 49
London Waterloo 15 ⊖	a						14 55			15 10						15 25			15 40				
London Victoria 15 ⊖	a	14 53			14 58	14 48		15 04	15 00		15 23			15 28	15 18		15 34	15 30		15 53			15 58

		SN	SW	SN	SN	SW	SN	FC	FC	SN	SN	SW	SN	SN	SW	SN	FC	FC	SN	SN	SW	SN
Horsham 4	d										15 04											
Warnham	d										15 08											
Ockley	d										15 15											
Holmwood	d										15 19											
Dorking 4	a										15 25											
	d	14 58	15 05								15 26	15 35								15 58	16 05	
Boxhill & Westhumble	d										15 28											
Guildford	d					14 58									15 28							
Effingham Junction 6	d					15 16									15 46							
Bookham	d					15 19									15 49							
Leatherhead	d	15 04	15 11			15 24					15 33	15 41			15 54					16 04	16 11	
Ashtead	d	15 07	15 14			15 28					15 37	15 44			15 58					16 07	16 14	
Epsom 3	a	15 12	15 19			15 32					15 41	15 49			16 02					16 12	16 19	
	d	15 13	15 20		15 19	15 35					15 42	15 50		15 49	16 05				16 04	16 13	16 20	
Ewell East	d				15 23						15 46			15 53					16 08			
Cheam	d	15 18			15 26						15 49			15 56					16 11	16 18		
Epsom Downs	d									15 35												
Banstead	d									15 38												
Belmont	d									15 41												
Sutton (Surrey) 4	a	15 21			15 29					15 44	15 52			15 59					16 14	16 21		
	d	15 23		15 22	15 30		15 33	15 37	15 38	15 45	15 53		15 52	16 00		16 03	16 07	16 08	16 15	16 23		16 22
Carshalton	d				15 33				15 41					16 03				16 11				
Hackbridge	d				15 35				15 43					16 05				16 13				
Mitcham Junction	d				15 39				15 46					16 09				16 16				
Mitcham Eastfields	d				15 42				15 49					16 12				16 19				
Carshalton Beeches	d			15 25			15 36			15 48			15 55			16 06			16 18			16 25
Wallington	d			15 27			15 38			15 50			15 57			16 08			16 20			16 27
Waddon	d			15 30			15 41			15 53			16 00			16 11			16 23			16 30
West Croydon 4	d			15 34			15 45			15 58			16 04			16 15			16 28			16 34
Norwood Junction 2	d						15 52									16 22						
New Cross Gate 4 ⊖	d																					
Tulse Hill 3	a							16 14	15 57								16 44	16 27				
	d							16 17									16 47					
London Bridge 4 ⊖	a							16 30									17 00					
Balham 4 ⊖	d			15 51	15 48		16 09			16 14			16 21	16 18		16 39			16 44			16 51
Clapham Junction 10	a	15 40	15 45	15 56	15 52	16 00	16 14			16 19	16 10	16 15	16 26	16 22	16 30	16 44			16 49	16 40	16 45	16 56
London Waterloo 15 ⊖	a		15 55			16 10						16 25			16 40						16 55	
London Victoria 15 ⊖	a	15 48		16 04	16 00		16 23			16 28	16 18		16 34	16 30		16 53			16 58	16 48		17 04

Table 182

Saturdays from 8 October

Horsham, Dorking, Guildford, Epsom and Sutton - London

		SN	SW	SN	FC	FC	SN	SN	SW	SN	SN	SW	SN	FC	FC	SN	SN	SW	SN	SN	SW	SN	FC
Horsham	d							16 04															
Warnham	d							16 08															
Ockley	d							16 15															
Holmwood	d							16 19															
Dorking	a							16 25															
	d							16 26	16 35								16 58	17 05					
Boxhill & Westhumble	d							16 28															
Guildford	d		15 58									16 28									16 58		
Effingham Junction	d		16 16									16 46									17 16		
Bookham	d		16 19									16 49									17 19		
Leatherhead	d		16 24					16 33	16 41			16 54					17 04	17 11			17 24		
Ashtead	d		16 28					16 37	16 44			16 58					17 07	17 14			17 28		
Epsom	a		16 32					16 41	16 49			17 02					17 12	17 19			17 32		
	d	16 19	16 35					16 42	16 50		16 49	17 05				17 04	17 13	17 20		17 19	17 35		
Ewell East	d	16 23						16 46			16 53					17 08				17 23			
Cheam	d	16 26						16 49			16 56					17 11	17 18			17 26			
Epsom Downs	d						16 35																
Banstead	d						16 38																
Belmont	d						16 41																
Sutton (Surrey)	a	16 29					16 44	16 52			16 59					17 14	17 21			17 29			
	d	16 30		16 33	16 37	16 38	16 45	16 53		16 52	17 00		17 03	17 07	17 08	17 15	17 23		17 22	17 30		17 33	17 37
Carshalton	d	16 33				16 41					17 03				17 11					17 33			
Hackbridge	d	16 35				16 43					17 05				17 13					17 35			
Mitcham Junction	d	16 39				16 46					17 09				17 16					17 39			
Mitcham Eastfields	d	16 42				16 49					17 12				17 19					17 42			
Carshalton Beeches	d			16 36			16 48			16 55			17 06			17 18			17 25			17 36	
Wallington	d			16 38			16 50			16 57			17 08			17 20			17 27			17 38	
Waddon	d			16 41			16 53			17 00			17 11			17 23			17 30			17 41	
West Croydon	d			16 45			16 58			17 04			17 15			17 28			17 34			17 45	
Norwood Junction	d			16 52									17 22									17 52	
New Cross Gate ⊖	d																						
Tulse Hill	a				17 14	16 57								17 44	17 27								18 14
	d				17 17									17 47									18 17
London Bridge ⊖	a				17 30									18 00									18 30
Balham ⊖	d	16 48		17 09			17 14			17 21	17 18		17 39			17 44			17 51	17 48		18 09	
Clapham Junction	a	16 52	17 00	17 14			17 19	17 10	17 15	17 26	17 22	17 30	17 44			17 49	17 41	17 45	17 56	17 52	18 00	18 14	
London Waterloo ⊖	a		17 10						17 25			17 40						17 55			18 10		
London Victoria ⊖	a	17 00		17 23			17 28	17 18		17 34	17 30		17 53			17 58	17 49		18 04	18 00		18 23	

		FC	SN	SN	SW	SN	SN	SW	SN	FC	FC	SN	SN	SW	SN	SN	SW	SN	FC	FC	SN	SN
Horsham	d			17 04																		18 04
Warnham	d			17 08																		18 08
Ockley	d			17 15																		18 15
Holmwood	d			17 19																		18 19
Dorking	a			17 25																		18 25
	d			17 26	17 35								17 58	18 05								18 26
Boxhill & Westhumble	d			17 28																		18 28
Guildford	d							17 28									17 58					
Effingham Junction	d							17 46									18 16					
Bookham	d							17 49									18 19					
Leatherhead	d			17 33	17 41			17 54					18 04	18 11			18 24					18 33
Ashtead	d			17 37	17 44			17 58					18 07	18 14			18 28					18 37
Epsom	a			17 41	17 49			18 02					18 12	18 19			18 32					18 41
	d			17 42	17 50		17 49	18 05				18 04	18 13	18 20		18 19	18 35					18 42
Ewell East	d			17 46			17 53					18 08				18 23						18 46
Cheam	d			17 49			17 56					18 11	18 18			18 26						18 49
Epsom Downs	d		17 35																		18 35	
Banstead	d		17 38																		18 38	
Belmont	d		17 41																		18 41	
Sutton (Surrey)	a		17 44	17 52			17 59					18 14	18 21			18 29					18 44	18 52
	d	17 38	17 45	17 53		17 52	18 00		18 03	18 07	18 08	18 15	18 23		18 22	18 30		18 33	18 37	18 38	18 45	18 53
Carshalton	d	17 41					18 03				18 11					18 33				18 41		
Hackbridge	d	17 43					18 05				18 13					18 35				18 43		
Mitcham Junction	d	17 46					18 09				18 16					18 39				18 46		
Mitcham Eastfields	d	17 49					18 12				18 19					18 42				18 49		
Carshalton Beeches	d		17 48			17 55			18 06			18 18			18 25			18 36			18 48	
Wallington	d		17 50			17 57			18 08			18 20			18 27			18 38			18 50	
Waddon	d		17 53			18 00			18 11			18 23			18 30			18 41			18 53	
West Croydon	d		17 58			18 04			18 15			18 28			18 34			18 45			18 58	
Norwood Junction	d								18 22									18 52				
New Cross Gate ⊖	d																					
Tulse Hill	a	17 57								18 44	18 27								19 14	18 57		
	d									18 47									19 17			
London Bridge ⊖	a									19 00									19 30			
Balham ⊖	d		18 14			18 21	18 18		18 39			18 44			18 51	18 48		19 09			19 14	
Clapham Junction	a		18 19	18 10	18 15	18 26	18 22	18 30	18 44			18 49	18 40	18 45	18 56	18 52	19 00	19 14			19 19	19 10
London Waterloo ⊖	a				18 25			18 40						18 55			19 10					
London Victoria ⊖	a		18 28	18 18		18 34	18 30		18 53			18 58	18 48		19 04	19 00		19 23			19 28	19 18

Table 182

Saturdays from 8 October

Horsham, Dorking, Guildford, Epsom and Sutton - London

		SW	SN	SN	SW	SN	FC	FC	SN	SN	SW	SN	SN	SW	SN	FC	SN	SN	SW	SN	SN	SW	SN
Horsham	d																						
Warnham	d																						
Ockley	d																						
Holmwood	d																						
Dorking	a																						
	d	18 35								18 58	19 05							19 28	19 35				
Boxhill & Westhumble	d									19 00													
Guildford	d				18 28									18 58								19 28	
Effingham Junction	d				18 46									19 16								19 46	
Bookham	d				18 49									19 19								19 49	
Leatherhead	d	18 41			18 54					19 05	19 11			19 24				19 34	19 41			19 54	
Ashtead	d	18 44			18 58					19 09	19 14			19 28				19 37	19 44			19 58	
Epsom	a	18 49			19 02					19 13	19 19			19 32				19 42	19 49			20 02	
	d	18 50		18 49	19 05				19 04	19 14	19 20		19 19	19 35				19 42	19 50		19 49	20 05	
Ewell East	d			18 53					19 08				19 23					19 46			19 53		
Cheam	d			18 56					19 11	19 19			19 26					19 49			19 56		
Epsom Downs	d																19 35						
Banstead	d																19 38						
Belmont	d																19 41						
Sutton (Surrey)	a			18 59					19 14	19 22			19 29				19 44	19 52			19 59		
	d		18 52	19 00		19 03	19 07	19 08	19 15	19 23		19 22	19 30		19 33	19 37	19 45	19 53		19 52	20 00		20 03
Carshalton	d			19 03				19 11					19 33								20 03		
Hackbridge	d			19 05				19 13					19 35								20 05		
Mitcham Junction	d			19 09				19 16					19 39								20 09		
Mitcham Eastfields	d			19 12				19 19					19 42								20 12		
Carshalton Beeches	d		18 55			19 06			19 18			19 25			19 36		19 48			19 55			20 06
Wallington	d		18 57			19 08			19 20			19 27			19 38		19 50			19 57			20 08
Waddon	d		19 00			19 11			19 23			19 30			19 41		19 53			20 00			20 11
West Croydon	d		19 04			19 15			19 28			19 34			19 45		19 58			20 04			20 15
Norwood Junction	d					19 22									19 52								20 22
New Cross Gate ⊖	d																						
Tulse Hill	a						19 44	19 27								20 14							
	d						19 47									20 17							
London Bridge ⊖	a						20 00									20 30							
Balham ⊖	d		19 21	19 18		19 39			19 44			19 51	19 48		20 09		20 14			20 21	20 18		20 39
Clapham Junction	a	19 15	19 26	19 22	19 30	19 44			19 49	19 40	19 45	19 56	19 52	20 00	20 14		20 19	20 10	20 15	20 26	20 22	20 30	20 44
London Waterloo ⊖	a	19 25			19 40						19 55			20 10					20 25			20 40	
London Victoria ⊖	a		19 34	19 30		19 53			19 58	19 48		20 04	20 00		20 23		20 28	20 18		20 34	20 30		20 53

		FC	SN	SN	SW	SN	SN	SW	SN	FC	SN	SN	SW	SN	SN	SN	FC	SN	SW	SN	SW	SN	SN
Horsham	d																						
Warnham	d																						
Ockley	d																						
Holmwood	d																						
Dorking	a																						
	d			19 58	20 05							20 28	20 35							20 58			
Boxhill & Westhumble	d			20 00																21 00			
Guildford	d							19 58													20 46		
Effingham Junction	d							20 16													21 03		
Bookham	d							20 19													21 06		
Leatherhead	d			20 05	20 11			20 24				20 34	20 41							21 05	21 11		
Ashtead	d			20 09	20 14			20 28				20 37	20 44							21 09	21 14		
Epsom	a			20 13	20 19			20 32				20 42	20 49							21 13	21 19		
	d		20 04	20 14	20 20		20 19	20 35				20 42	20 50		20 49			21 03	21 05	21 14	21 20		21 19
Ewell East	d		20 08				20 23					20 46			20 53			21 08					21 23
Cheam	d		20 11	20 19			20 26					20 49			20 56			21 11		21 19			21 26
Epsom Downs	d										20 35												
Banstead	d										20 38												
Belmont	d										20 41												
Sutton (Surrey)	a		20 14	20 22			20 29				20 44	20 52			20 59			21 14		21 22			21 29
	d	20 08	20 15	20 23		20 22	20 30		20 33	20 37	20 45	20 53		20 52	21 00	21 03	21 07	21 15		21 23		21 22	21 30
Carshalton	d						20 33								21 03								21 33
Hackbridge	d						20 35								21 05								21 35
Mitcham Junction	d						20 39								21 09								21 39
Mitcham Eastfields	d						20 42								21 12								21 42
Carshalton Beeches	d		20 18			20 25			20 36		20 48			20 55		21 06		21 18				21 25	
Wallington	d		20 20			20 27			20 38		20 50			20 57		21 08		21 20				21 27	
Waddon	d		20 23			20 30			20 41		20 53			21 00		21 11		21 23				21 30	
West Croydon	d		20 28			20 34			20 45		20 58			21 04		21 15		21 28				21 34	
Norwood Junction	d								20 52							21 22							
New Cross Gate ⊖	d																						
Tulse Hill	a	20 44								21 14							21 44						
	d	20 47								21 17							21 47						
London Bridge ⊖	a	21 00								21 30							22 00						
Balham ⊖	d		20 44			20 51	20 48		21 09		21 14			21 21	21 18	21 39		21 44				21 51	21 48
Clapham Junction	a		20 49	20 40	20 45	20 56	20 52	21 00	21 14		21 19	21 10	21 15	21 26	21 22	21 44		21 49	21 30	21 40	21 45	21 56	21 52
London Waterloo ⊖	a				20 55			21 10					21 25						21 40		21 55		
London Victoria ⊖	a		20 58	20 48		21 04	21 00		21 23		21 28	21 18		21 34	21 30	21 53		21 58		21 48		22 04	22 00

Horsham, Dorking, Guildford, Epsom and Sutton - London

from 8 October

		SW		SN	FC	SN	SN	SW	SN	SN	SN	FC		SN	SN	SW	SN	SN	SN	SN	SN	SW		SN	SN
Horsham 4	d																								
Warnham	d																								
Ockley	d																								
Holmwood	d																								
Dorking 4	a																								
	d						21 28	21 35							21 58						22 28	22 35			
Boxhill & Westhumble	d														22 00										
Guildford	d															21 46									
Effingham Junction 6	d															22 03									
Bookham	d															22 06									
Leatherhead	d						21 34	21 41							22 05	22 11					22 34	22 41			
Ashtead	d						21 37	21 44							22 09	22 14					22 37	22 44			
Epsom 3	a						21 42	21 49							22 13	22 19					22 42	22 49			
	d	21 35					21 42	21 50		21 49				22 04	22 14	22 20		22 19			22 42	22 50			22 49
Ewell East	d						21 46			21 53				22 08				22 23			22 46				22 53
Cheam	d						21 49			21 56				22 11	22 19			22 26			22 49				22 56
Epsom Downs	d					21 35														22 35					
Banstead	d					21 38														22 38					
Belmont	d					21 41														22 41					
Sutton (Surrey) 4	a					21 44	21 52			21 59				22 14	22 22			22 29		22 44	22 52				22 59
	d			21 33	21 37	21 45	21 53		21 52	22 00	22 03	22 07		22 15	22 23		22 22	22 30	22 33	22 45	22 53			22 52	23 00
Carshalton	d									22 03								22 33							23 03
Hackbridge	d									22 05								22 35							23 05
Mitcham Junction	d									22 09								22 39							23 09
Mitcham Eastfields	d									22 12								22 42							23 12
Carshalton Beeches	d			21 36		21 48			21 55		22 06			22 18			22 25		22 36	22 48				22 55	
Wallington	d			21 38		21 50			21 57		22 08			22 20			22 27		22 38	22 51				22 57	
Waddon	d			21 41		21 53			22 00		22 11			22 23			22 30		22 41	22 54				23 00	
West Croydon 4	d			21 45		21 58			22 04		22 15			22 28			22 34		22 45	22 58				23 04	
Norwood Junction 2	d			21 52							22 22								22 52						
New Cross Gate 4 ⊖	d																								
Tulse Hill 3	a				22 14							22 44													
	d				22 17							22 47													
London Bridge 4 ⊖	a				22 30							23 00													
Balham 4 ⊖	d			22 09		22 14			22 22	22 18	22 39			22 44			22 51	22 48	23 09	23 14				23 21	23 18
Clapham Junction 10	a	22 00		22 14		22 19	22 10	22 15	22 27	22 22	22 44			22 49	22 40	22 45	22 56	22 52	23 14	23 19	23 10	23 15		23 26	23 22
London Waterloo 15 ⊖	a	22 10						22 25								22 55						23 25			
London Victoria 15 ⊖	a			22 23		22 28	22 18		22 34	22 30	22 53			22 58	22 48		23 04	23 00	23 24	23 29	23 22			23 34	23 31

		SN	SN	SN	SN	SW	SN	SN		SN	SN
Horsham 4	d										
Warnham	d										
Ockley	d										
Holmwood	d										
Dorking 4	a										
	d				23 00					23 30	
Boxhill & Westhumble	d				23 02						
Guildford	d					22 46					
Effingham Junction 6	d					23 03					
Bookham	d					23 06					
Leatherhead	d				23 07	23 11				23 36	
Ashtead	d				23 11	23 14				23 39	
Epsom 3	a				23 15	23 19				23 45	
	d		23 04		23 16	23 20		23 35			
Ewell East	d		23 08		23 20			23 39			
Cheam	d		23 11		23 23			23 42			
Epsom Downs	d						23 23				23 50
Banstead	d						23 26				23 53
Belmont	d						23 29				23 56
Sutton (Surrey) 4	a		23 14		23 26		23 32	23 45			23 59
	d	23 03	23 15	23 22	23 30		23 34	23 46			00 01
Carshalton	d										
Hackbridge	d										
Mitcham Junction	d										
Mitcham Eastfields	d										
Carshalton Beeches	d	23 06	23 18	23 25	23 33		23 37	23 49			00 04
Wallington	d	23 08	23 20	23 27	23 35		23 39	23 51			00 06
Waddon	d	23 11	23 23	23 30	23 38		23 44	23 54			00 09
West Croydon 4	d	23 15	23 28	23 34	23a41		23a47	23a57			00a12
Norwood Junction 2	d	23 22									
New Cross Gate 4 ⊖	d										
Tulse Hill 3	a										
	d										
London Bridge 4 ⊖	a										
Balham 4 ⊖	d	23 39	23 44	23 50							
Clapham Junction 10	a	23 45	23 49	23 56		23 48					
London Waterloo 15 ⊖	a					23 58					
London Victoria 15 ⊖	a	23 53	23 58	00 04							

Horsham, Dorking, Guildford, Epsom and Sutton - London

until 25 September

		SN A	SN A	SN	SN	SN	SW	SN	SN	SN		SW	SN	SN	SN	SN	SW	SN	SN	SN		SN	SW	SN	SN
Horsham 4	d																								
Warnham	d																								
Ockley	d																								
Holmwood	d																								
Dorking 4	a																								
	d							07 16						07 46					08 16						08 46
Boxhill & Westhumble	d							07 18						07 48					08 18						08 48
Guildford	d																						08 20		
Effingham Junction 6	d																						08 36		
Bookham	d																						08 39		
Leatherhead	d							07 23						07 53					08 23				08 45		08 53
Ashtead	d							07 27						07 57					08 27				08 48		08 57
Epsom 3	a							07 31						08 01					08 31				08 53		09 01
	d			06 44		07 17	07 24	07 32		07 47		07 54		08 02		08 17	08 24		08 32			08 47	08 54		09 02
Ewell East	d			06 48		07 21		07 36		07 51				08 06		08 21			08 36			08 51			09 06
Cheam	d			06 51		07 24		07 39		07 54				08 09		08 24			08 39			08 54			09 09
Epsom Downs	d		23p50																						
Banstead	d		23p53																						
Belmont	d		23p56																						
Sutton (Surrey) 4	a		23p59	06 54		07 27		07 42		07 57				08 12		08 27			08 42			08 57			09 12
	d	23p22	00 01	06 55	07 25	07 28		07 43	07 55	07 58			08 10	08 13	08 25	08 28		08 40	08 43	08 55		08 58		09 10	09 13
Carshalton	d					07 31		07 46		08 01				08 16		08 31			08 46			09 01			09 16
Hackbridge	d					07 33		07 48		08 03				08 18		08 33			08 48			09 03			09 18
Mitcham Junction	d					07 37		07 52		08 07				08 22		08 37			08 52			09 07			09 22
Mitcham Eastfields	d					07 40		07 55		08 10				08 25		08 40			08 55			09 10			09 25
Carshalton Beeches	d	23p25	00 04	06 58	07 28				07 58				08 13		08 28			08 43		08 58				09 13	
Wallington	d	23p27	00 06	07 00	07 30				08 00				08 15		08 30			08 45		09 00				09 15	
Waddon	d	23p30	00 09	07 03	07 33				08 03				08 18		08 33			08 48		09 03				09 18	
West Croydon 4	d	23p34	00a12	07 07	07 37				08 07				08 22		08 37			08 52		09 07				09 22	
Norwood Junction 2	d												08 27					08 57						09 27	
New Cross Gate 4 ⊖	d																								
Tulse Hill 3	a																								
	d																								
London Bridge 4 ⊖	a																								
Balham 4 ⊖	d	23p50		07 23	07 53	07 48		08 01	08 23	08 18			08 43	08 31	08 53	08 48		09 13	09 01	09 23		09 18		09 43	09 31
Clapham Junction 10	a	23p56		07 27	07 57	07 52	07 49	08 06	08 27	08 22		08 19	08 48	08 36	08 57	08 52	08 49	09 19	09 06	09 27		09 22	09 19	09 49	09 36
London Waterloo 15 ⊖	a						08 04					08 34					09 04						09 34		
London Victoria 15 ⊖	a	00 04		07 34	08 04	07 59		08 15	08 34	08 29			08 57	08 45	09 04	08 59		09 27	09 15	09 34		09 29		09 57	09 45

		SN	SN	SW	SN	SN		SN	SN	SW	SN	SN	SN	SN	SW	FC		SN	SN	SN	SN	SW	FC	SN	SN
Horsham 4	d																								
Warnham	d																								
Ockley	d																								
Holmwood	d																								
Dorking 4	a																								
	d			09 08		09 16						09 46			10 08				10 16						10 46
Boxhill & Westhumble	d					09 18						09 48							10 18						10 48
Guildford	d									09 20												10 20			
Effingham Junction 6	d									09 36												10 36			
Bookham	d									09 39												10 39			
Leatherhead	d			09 15		09 23				09 45		09 53			10 15				10 23			10 45			10 53
Ashtead	d			09 18		09 27				09 48		09 57			10 18				10 27			10 48			10 57
Epsom 3	a			09 23		09 31				09 53		10 01			10 23				10 31			10 53			11 01
	d		09 17	09 24		09 32			09 47	09 54		10 02		10 17	10 24				10 32		10 47	10 54			11 02
Ewell East	d		09 21			09 36			09 51			10 06		10 21					10 36		10 51				11 06
Cheam	d		09 24			09 39			09 54			10 09		10 24					10 39		10 54				11 09
Epsom Downs	d																								
Banstead	d																								
Belmont	d																								
Sutton (Surrey) 4	a		09 27			09 42			09 57			10 12		10 27					10 42		10 57				11 12
	d	09 25	09 28		09 40	09 43		09 55	09 58		10 10	10 13	10 25	10 28		10 28		10 40	10 43	10 55	10 58		10 58	11 10	11 13
Carshalton	d		09 31			09 46			10 01			10 16		10 31					10 46		11 01				11 16
Hackbridge	d		09 33			09 48			10 03			10 18		10 33					10 48		11 03				11 18
Mitcham Junction	d		09 37			09 52			10 07			10 22		10 37					10 52		11 07				11 22
Mitcham Eastfields	d		09 40			09 55			10 10			10 25		10 40					10 55		11 10				11 25
Carshalton Beeches	d	09 28			09 43			09 58			10 13		10 28					10 43		10 58				11 13	
Wallington	d	09 30			09 45			10 00			10 15		10 30					10 45		11 00				11 15	
Waddon	d	09 33			09 48			10 03			10 18		10 33					10 48		11 03				11 18	
West Croydon 4	d	09 37			09 52			10 07			10 22		10 37					10 52		11 07				11 22	
Norwood Junction 2	d				09 57						10 27							10 57						11 27	
New Cross Gate 4 ⊖	d																								
Tulse Hill 3	a															10 59							11 29		
	d															10 59							11 29		
London Bridge 4 ⊖	a															11 10							11 40		
Balham 4 ⊖	d	09 53	09 48		10 13	10 01		10 23	10 18		10 43	10 31	10 53	10 48				11 13	11 01	11 23	11 18			11 43	11 31
Clapham Junction 10	a	09 57	09 52	09 49	10 18	10 06		10 27	10 22	10 19	10 48	10 36	10 57	10 52	10 49			11 18	11 06	11 27	11 22	11 19		11 48	11 36
London Waterloo 15 ⊖	a			10 04						10 34					11 04							11 34			
London Victoria 15 ⊖	a	10 04	09 59		10 27	10 15		10 34	10 29		10 57	10 45	11 04	10 59				11 27	11 15	11 34	11 29			11 57	11 45

A not 22 May

Table 182

Sundays until 25 September

Horsham, Dorking, Guildford, Epsom and Sutton - London

		SN		SN	SW	FC	SN	SN	SN	SN	SW	FC		SN	SN	SN	SN	SW	FC	SN	SN	SN		SN	SW
Horsham	d																								
Warnham	d																								
Ockley	d																								
Holmwood	d																								
Dorking	a																								
	d				11 08			11 16							11 46			12 08			12 16				
Boxhill & Westhumble	d							11 18							11 48						12 18				
Guildford	d										11 20														12 20
Effingham Junction	d										11 36														12 36
Bookham	d										11 39														12 39
Leatherhead	d				11 15			11 23			11 45				11 53			12 15			12 23				12 45
Ashtead	d				11 18			11 27			11 48				11 57			12 18			12 27				12 48
Epsom	a				11 23			11 31			11 53				12 01			12 23			12 31				12 53
	d			11 17	11 24			11 32		11 47	11 54				12 02		12 17	12 24			12 32			12 47	12 54
Ewell East	d			11 21				11 36		11 51					12 06		12 21				12 36			12 51	
Cheam	d			11 24				11 39		11 54					12 09		12 24				12 39			12 54	
Epsom Downs	d																								
Banstead	d																								
Belmont	d																								
Sutton (Surrey)	a			11 27				11 42		11 57					12 12		12 27				12 42			12 57	
	d	11 25		11 28		11 28	11 40	11 43	11 55	11 58		11 58		12 10	12 13	12 25	12 28		12 28	12 40	12 43	12 55		12 58	
Carshalton	d			11 31				11 46		12 01					12 16		12 31				12 46			13 01	
Hackbridge	d			11 33				11 48		12 03					12 18		12 33				12 48			13 03	
Mitcham Junction	d			11 37				11 52		12 07					12 22		12 37				12 52			13 07	
Mitcham Eastfields	d			11 40				11 55		12 10					12 25		12 40				12 55			13 10	
Carshalton Beeches	d	11 28					11 43		11 58					12 13		12 28				12 43		12 58			
Wallington	d	11 30					11 45		12 00					12 15		12 30				12 45		13 00			
Waddon	d	11 33					11 48		12 03					12 18		12 33				12 48		13 03			
West Croydon	d	11 37					11 52		12 07					12 22		12 37				12 52		13 07			
Norwood Junction	d						11 57							12 27						12 57					
New Cross Gate ⊖	d																								
Tulse Hill	a					11 59						12 29							12 59						
	d					11 59						12 29							12 59						
London Bridge ⊖	a					12 10						12 40							13 10						
Balham ⊖	d	11 53		11 48			12 13	12 01	12 23	12 18				12 43	12 31	12 53	12 48			13 13	13 01	13 23		13 18	
Clapham Junction	a	11 57		11 52	11 49		12 18	12 06	12 27	12 22	12 19			12 48	12 36	12 57	12 52	12 49		13 19	13 06	13 27		13 22	13 19
London Waterloo ⊖	a				12 04						12 34							13 04							13 34
London Victoria ⊖	a	12 04		11 59			12 27	12 15	12 34	12 29				12 57	12 45	13 04	12 59			13 27	13 15	13 34		13 29	

		FC	SN	SN	SN	SN	SW	FC		SN	SN	SN	SN	SW	FC	SN	SN	SN		SN	SW	FC	SN	SN	SN
Horsham	d																								
Warnham	d																								
Ockley	d																								
Holmwood	d																								
Dorking	a																								
	d			12 46			13 08				13 16						13 46				14 08			14 16	
Boxhill & Westhumble	d			12 48							13 18						13 48							14 18	
Guildford	d													13 20											
Effingham Junction	d													13 36											
Bookham	d													13 39											
Leatherhead	d			12 53			13 15				13 23			13 45			13 53				14 15			14 23	
Ashtead	d			12 57			13 18				13 27			13 48			13 57				14 18			14 27	
Epsom	a			13 01			13 23				13 31			13 53			14 01				14 23			14 31	
	d			13 02		13 17	13 24				13 32		13 47	13 54			14 02			14 17	14 24			14 32	
Ewell East	d			13 06		13 21					13 36		13 51				14 06			14 21				14 36	
Cheam	d			13 09		13 24					13 39		13 54				14 09			14 24				14 39	
Epsom Downs	d																								
Banstead	d																								
Belmont	d																								
Sutton (Surrey)	a			13 12		13 27					13 42		13 57				14 12			14 27				14 42	
	d	12 58	13 10	13 13	13 25	13 28		13 28		13 40	13 43	13 55	13 58		13 58	14 10	14 13	14 25		14 28		14 28	14 40	14 43	14 55
Carshalton	d			13 16		13 31					13 46		14 01				14 16			14 31				14 46	
Hackbridge	d			13 18		13 33					13 48		14 03				14 18			14 33				14 48	
Mitcham Junction	d			13 22		13 37					13 52		14 07				14 22			14 37				14 52	
Mitcham Eastfields	d			13 25		13 40					13 55		14 10				14 25			14 40				14 55	
Carshalton Beeches	d		13 13		13 28					13 43		13 58				14 13		14 28					14 43		14 58
Wallington	d		13 15		13 30					13 45		14 00				14 15		14 30					14 45		15 00
Waddon	d		13 18		13 33					13 48		14 03				14 18		14 33					14 48		15 03
West Croydon	d		13 22		13 37					13 52		14 07				14 22		14 37					14 52		15 07
Norwood Junction	d		13 27							13 57						14 27							14 57		
New Cross Gate ⊖	d																								
Tulse Hill	a	13 29						13 59							14 29							14 59			
	d	13 29						13 59							14 29							14 59			
London Bridge ⊖	a	13 40						14 10							14 40							15 10			
Balham ⊖	d		13 43	13 31	13 53	13 48				14 13	14 01	14 23	14 18			14 43	14 31	14 53		14 48			15 13	15 01	15 23
Clapham Junction	a		13 48	13 36	13 57	13 52	13 49			14 19	14 06	14 27	14 22	14 19		14 48	14 36	14 57		14 52	14 49		15 19	15 06	15 27
London Waterloo ⊖	a						14 04							14 34							14 59				
London Victoria ⊖	a		13 57	13 45	14 04	13 59				14 27	14 15	14 34	14 29			14 57	14 45	15 04		14 59			15 27	15 15	15 34

Table 182

Sundays until 25 September

Horsham, Dorking, Guildford, Epsom and Sutton - London

		SN	SW	FC		SN	SN	SN	SN	SW	FC	SN	SN	SN		SN	SW	FC	SN	SN	SN	SN	SW	FC	
Horsham	d																								
Warnham	d																								
Ockley	d																								
Holmwood	d																								
Dorking	a																								
	d						14 46			15 08			15 16							15 46			16 08		
Boxhill & Westhumble	d						14 48						15 18							15 48					
Guildford	d		14 20														15 20								
Effingham Junction	d		14 36														15 36								
Bookham	d		14 39														15 39								
Leatherhead	d		14 45				14 53			15 15			15 23				15 45			15 53			16 15		
Ashtead	d		14 48				14 57			15 18			15 27				15 48			15 57			16 18		
Epsom	a		14 53				15 01			15 23			15 31				15 53			16 01			16 23		
	d	14 47	14 54				15 02		15 17	15 24			15 32			15 47	15 54			16 02		16 17	16 24		
Ewell East	d	14 51					15 06		15 21				15 36			15 51				16 06		16 21			
Cheam	d	14 54					15 09		15 24				15 39			15 54				16 09		16 24			
Epsom Downs	d																								
Banstead	d																								
Belmont	d																								
Sutton (Surrey)	a	14 57					15 12		15 27				15 42			15 57				16 12		16 27			
	d	14 58		14 58		15 10	15 13	15 25	15 28		15 28	15 40	15 43	15 55		15 58		15 58	16 10	16 13	16 25	16 28		16 28	
Carshalton	d	15 01					15 16		15 31				15 46			16 01				16 16		16 31			
Hackbridge	d	15 03					15 18		15 33				15 48			16 03				16 18		16 33			
Mitcham Junction	d	15 07					15 22		15 37				15 52			16 07				16 22		16 37			
Mitcham Eastfields	d	15 10					15 25		15 40				15 55			16 10				16 25		16 40			
Carshalton Beeches	d					15 13		15 28				15 43		15 58					16 13		16 28				
Wallington	d					15 15		15 30				15 45		16 00					16 15		16 30				
Waddon	d					15 18		15 33				15 48		16 03					16 18		16 33				
West Croydon	d					15 22		15 37				15 52		16 07					16 22		16 37				
Norwood Junction	d					15 27						15 57							16 27						
New Cross Gate ⊖	d																								
Tulse Hill	a			15 29							15 59							16 29						16 59	
	d			15 29							15 59							16 29						16 59	
London Bridge ⊖	a			15 40							16 10							16 40						17 10	
Balham ⊖	d	15 18				15 43	15 31	15 53	15 48			16 13	16 01	16 23		16 18			16 43	16 31	16 53	16 48			
Clapham Junction	a	15 22	15 19			15 48	15 36	15 57	15 52	15 49		16 19	16 06	16 27		16 22	16 19		16 48	16 36	16 57	16 52	16 49		
London Waterloo ⊖	a		15 29							15 59							16 29						16 59		
London Victoria ⊖	a	15 29				15 57	15 45	16 04	15 59			16 27	16 15	16 34		16 29			16 57	16 45	17 04	16 59			

		SN	SN	SN	SN	SW	FC	SN	SN	SN		SN	SW	FC	SN	SN	SN	SN	SW	FC		SN	SN	SN	SN
Horsham	d																								
Warnham	d																								
Ockley	d																								
Holmwood	d																								
Dorking	a																								
	d		16 16						16 46				17 08			17 16							17 46		
Boxhill & Westhumble	d		16 18						16 48							17 18							17 48		
Guildford	d					16 20													17 20						
Effingham Junction	d					16 36													17 36						
Bookham	d					16 39													17 39						
Leatherhead	d		16 23			16 45			16 53				17 15			17 23			17 45				17 53		
Ashtead	d		16 27			16 48			16 57				17 18			17 27			17 48				17 57		
Epsom	a		16 31			16 53			17 01				17 23			17 31			17 53				18 01		
	d		16 32		16 47	16 54			17 02			17 17	17 24			17 32		17 47	17 54				18 02		18 17
Ewell East	d		16 36		16 51				17 06			17 21				17 36		17 51					18 06		18 21
Cheam	d		16 39		16 54				17 09			17 24				17 39		17 54					18 09		18 24
Epsom Downs	d																								
Banstead	d																								
Belmont	d																								
Sutton (Surrey)	a		16 42		16 57				17 12			17 27				17 42		17 57					18 12		18 27
	d	16 40	16 43	16 55	16 58		16 58	17 10	17 13	17 25		17 28		17 28	17 40	17 43	17 55	17 58		17 58		18 10	18 13	18 25	18 28
Carshalton	d		16 46		17 01				17 16			17 31				17 46		18 01					18 16		18 31
Hackbridge	d		16 48		17 03				17 18			17 33				17 48		18 03					18 18		18 33
Mitcham Junction	d		16 52		17 07				17 22			17 37				17 52		18 07					18 22		18 37
Mitcham Eastfields	d		16 55		17 10				17 25			17 40				17 55		18 10					18 25		18 40
Carshalton Beeches	d	16 43		16 58				17 13		17 28					17 43		17 58					18 13		18 28	
Wallington	d	16 45		17 00				17 15		17 30					17 45		18 00					18 15		18 30	
Waddon	d	16 48		17 03				17 18		17 33					17 48		18 03					18 18		18 33	
West Croydon	d	16 52		17 07				17 22		17 37					17 52		18 07					18 22		18 37	
Norwood Junction	d	16 57						17 27							17 57							18 27			
New Cross Gate ⊖	d																								
Tulse Hill	a						17 29							17 59						18 29					
	d						17 29							17 59						18 29					
London Bridge ⊖	a						17 40							18 10						18 40					
Balham ⊖	d	17 13	17 01	17 23	17 18			17 43	17 31	17 53		17 48			18 13	18 01	18 23	18 18				18 43	18 31	18 53	18 48
Clapham Junction	a	17 19	17 06	17 27	17 22	17 19		17 48	17 36	17 57		17 52	17 49		18 19	18 06	18 27	18 22	18 19			18 48	18 36	18 57	18 52
London Waterloo ⊖	a					17 29							17 59						18 29						
London Victoria ⊖	a	17 27	17 15	17 34	17 29			17 57	17 45	18 04		17 59			18 27	18 15	18 34	18 29				18 57	18 45	19 04	18 59

Horsham, Dorking, Guildford, Epsom and Sutton - London

until 25 September

		SW	FC	SN	SN	SN	SN	SW	FC	SN	SN	SW	SN	FC	SN	SN	SW	SN	FC	SN	SN	SW	SN
Horsham	d																						
Warnham	d																						
Ockley	d																						
Holmwood	d																						
Dorking	a																						
	d	18 08			18 16						18 46	19 08				19 16					19 46	20 08	
Boxhill & Westhumble	d				18 18						18 48					19 18					19 48		
Guildford	d							18 20									19 20						
Effingham Junction	d							18 36									19 36						
Bookham	d							18 39									19 39						
Leatherhead	d	18 15			18 23			18 45			18 53	19 15				19 23	19 45				19 53	20 15	
Ashtead	d	18 18			18 27			18 48			18 57	19 18				19 27	19 48				19 57	20 18	
Epsom	a	18 23			18 31			18 53			19 01	19 23				19 31	19 53				20 01	20 23	
	d	18 24			18 32		18 47	18 54			19 02	19 24				19 32	19 54				20 02	20 24	
Ewell East	d				18 36		18 51				19 06					19 36					20 06		
Cheam	d				18 39		18 54				19 09					19 39					20 09		
Epsom Downs	d																						
Banstead	d																						
Belmont	d																						
Sutton (Surrey)	a				18 42		18 57				19 12					19 42					20 12		
	d		18 28	18 40	18 43	18 55	18 58		18 58	19 10	19 13		19 25	19 28	19 40	19 43		19 55	19 58	20 10	20 13		20 25
Carshalton	d				18 46		19 01				19 16					19 46					20 16		
Hackbridge	d				18 48		19 03				19 18					19 48					20 18		
Mitcham Junction	d				18 52		19 07				19 22					19 52					20 22		
Mitcham Eastfields	d				18 55		19 10				19 25					19 55					20 25		
Carshalton Beeches	d			18 43		18 58				19 13			19 28		19 43			19 58		20 13			20 28
Wallington	d			18 45		19 00				19 15			19 30		19 45			20 00		20 15			20 30
Waddon	d			18 48		19 03				19 18			19 33		19 48			20 03		20 18			20 33
West Croydon	d			18 52		19 07				19 22			19 37		19 52			20 07		20 22			20 37
Norwood Junction	d			18 57						19 27					19 57					20 27			
New Cross Gate ⊖	d																						
Tulse Hill	a		18 59						19 29					19 59					20 29				
	d		18 59						19 29					19 59					20 29				
London Bridge ⊖	a		19 10						19 40					20 10					20 40				
Balham ⊖	d			19 13	19 01	19 23	19 18			19 43	19 31		19 53		20 13	20 01		20 23		20 43	20 31		20 53
Clapham Junction	a	18 49		19 19	19 06	19 27	19 22	19 19		19 48	19 36	19 49	19 57		20 18	20 06	20 19	20 27		20 48	20 36	20 49	20 57
London Waterloo ⊖	a	18 59						19 29				19 59					20 29					21 00	
London Victoria ⊖	a			19 27	19 15	19 34	19 29			19 57	19 45		20 04		20 27	20 15		20 34		20 57	20 45		21 04

		FC	SN	SN	SW	SN	FC	SN	SN	SW	SN	FC	SN	SN	SW	SN	SN	SN	SW	SN	SN	SN
Horsham	d																					
Warnham	d																					
Ockley	d																					
Holmwood	d																					
Dorking	a																					
	d			20 16					20 46	21 08				21 16				21 46	22 08			22 16
Boxhill & Westhumble	d			20 18					20 48					21 18				21 48				22 18
Guildford	d				20 20										21 20							
Effingham Junction	d				20 36										21 36							
Bookham	d				20 39										21 39							
Leatherhead	d			20 23	20 45				20 53	21 15				21 23	21 45			21 53	22 15			22 23
Ashtead	d			20 27	20 48				20 57	21 18				21 27	21 48			21 57	22 18			22 27
Epsom	a			20 31	20 53				21 01	21 23				21 31	21 53			22 01	22 23			22 31
	d			20 32	20 54				21 02	21 24				21 32	21 54			22 02	22 24			22 32
Ewell East	d			20 36					21 06					21 36				22 06				22 36
Cheam	d			20 39					21 09					21 39				22 09				22 39
Epsom Downs	d																					
Banstead	d																					
Belmont	d																					
Sutton (Surrey)	a			20 42					21 12					21 42				22 12				22 42
	d	20 28	20 40	20 43		20 55	20 58	21 10	21 13		21 25	21 28	21 40	21 43		21 55	22 10	22 13		22 25	22 40	22 43
Carshalton	d			20 46					21 16					21 46				22 16				22 46
Hackbridge	d			20 48					21 18					21 48				22 18				22 48
Mitcham Junction	d			20 52					21 22					21 52				22 22				22 52
Mitcham Eastfields	d			20 55					21 25					21 55				22 25				22 55
Carshalton Beeches	d		20 43			20 58		21 13			21 28		21 43			21 58	22 13			22 28	22 43	
Wallington	d		20 45			21 00		21 15			21 30		21 45			22 00	22 15			22 30	22 45	
Waddon	d		20 48			21 03		21 18			21 33		21 48			22 03	22 18			22 33	22 48	
West Croydon	d		20 52			21 07		21 22			21 37		21 52			22 07	22 22			22 37	22 52	
Norwood Junction	d		20 57					21 27					21 57				22 27				22 57	
New Cross Gate ⊖	d																					
Tulse Hill	a	20 59					21 29					21 59										
	d	20 59					21 29					21 59										
London Bridge ⊖	a	21 10					21 40					22 10										
Balham ⊖	d		21 13	21 01		21 23		21 43	21 31		21 53		22 13	22 01		22 23	22 43	22 31		22 53	23 13	23 01
Clapham Junction	a		21 19	21 06	21 19	21 27		21 49	21 36	21 49	21 57		22 19	22 06	22 19	22 27	22 49	22 36	22 49	22 57	23 19	23 06
London Waterloo ⊖	a				21 29					22 00					22 29				23 00			
London Victoria ⊖	a		21 27	21 15		21 34		21 57	21 45		22 04		22 27	22 15		22 34	22 57	22 45		23 04	23 27	23 15

Horsham, Dorking, Guildford, Epsom and Sutton - London

until 25 September

		SW	SN	SN	SN	SW	SN	SN	SN
Horsham	d								
Warnham	d								
Ockley	d								
Holmwood	d								
Dorking	a								
	d				22 46	23 08			23 16
Boxhill & Westhumble	d				22 48				23 18
Guildford	d	22 20							
Effingham Junction	d	22 36							
Bookham	d	22 39							
Leatherhead	d	22 45			22 53	23 15			23 23
Ashtead	d	22 48			22 57	23 18			23 27
Epsom	a	22 53			23 01	23 23			23 31
	d	22 54			23 02	23 24			23 32
Ewell East	d				23 06				23 36
Cheam	d				23 09				23 39
Epsom Downs	d								
Banstead	d								
Belmont	d								
Sutton (Surrey)	a				23 12				23 42
	d		22 55	23 10	23 13		23 25	23 40	23 43
Carshalton	d				23 16				23 46
Hackbridge	d				23 18				23 48
Mitcham Junction	d				23 22				23 52
Mitcham Eastfields	d				23 25				23 55
Carshalton Beeches	d		22 58	23 13			23 28	23 43	
Wallington	d		23 00	23 15			23 30	23 45	
Waddon	d		23 03	23 18			23 33	23 48	
West Croydon	d		23 07	23 22			23 37	23 52	
Norwood Junction	d			23 27					
New Cross Gate ⊖	d								
Tulse Hill	a								
	d								
London Bridge ⊖	a								
Balham ⊖	d		23 23	23 43	23 31		23 53	00 08	00 01
Clapham Junction	a	23 19	23 27	23 49	23 36	23 49	23 57	00 12	00 06
London Waterloo ⊖	a	23 29				23 59			
London Victoria ⊖	a		23 34	23 57	23 45		00 04	00 19	00 15

Sundays

from 2 October

		SN	SN	SN	SN	SN	SW	SN	SN	SN	SW	SN	SN	SN	SN	SW	SN	SN	SN	SN	SW	SN	SN
Horsham	d																						
Warnham	d																						
Ockley	d																						
Holmwood	d																						
Dorking	a																						
	d							07 16					07 46					08 16					08 46
Boxhill & Westhumble	d							07 18					07 48					08 18					08 48
Guildford	d																				08 18		
Effingham Junction	d																				08 34		
Bookham	d																				08 37		
Leatherhead	d							07 23					07 53					08 23			08 45		08 53
Ashtead	d							07 27					07 57					08 27			08 48		08 57
Epsom	a							07 31					08 01					08 31			08 53		09 01
	d			06 44		07 17	07 24	07 32		07 47	07 54		08 02		08 17	08 24		08 32		08 47	08 54		09 02
Ewell East	d			06 48		07 21		07 36		07 51			08 06		08 21			08 36		08 51			09 06
Cheam	d			06 51		07 24		07 39		07 54			08 09		08 24			08 39		08 54			09 09
Epsom Downs	d		23p50																				
Banstead	d		23p53																				
Belmont	d		23p56																				
Sutton (Surrey)	a		23p59	06 54		07 27		07 42		07 57			08 12		08 27			08 42		08 57			09 12
	d	23p22	00 01	06 55	07 25	07 28		07 43	07 55	07 58		08 10	08 13	08 25	08 28		08 40	08 43	08 55	08 58		09 10	09 13
Carshalton	d					07 31		07 46		08 01			08 16		08 31			08 46		09 01			09 16
Hackbridge	d					07 33		07 48		08 03			08 18		08 33			08 48		09 03			09 18
Mitcham Junction	d					07 37		07 52		08 07			08 22		08 37			08 52		09 07			09 22
Mitcham Eastfields	d					07 40		07 55		08 10			08 25		08 40			08 55		09 10			09 25
Carshalton Beeches	d	23p25	00 04	06 58	07 28				07 58			08 13		08 28			08 43		08 58			09 13	
Wallington	d	23p27	00 06	07 00	07 30				08 00			08 15		08 30			08 45		09 00			09 15	
Waddon	d	23p30	00 09	07 03	07 33				08 03			08 18		08 33			08 48		09 03			09 18	
West Croydon	d	23p34	00a12	07 07	07 37				08 07			08 22		08 37			08 52		09 07			09 22	
Norwood Junction	d											08 27					08 57					09 27	
New Cross Gate ⊖	d																						
Tulse Hill	a																						
	d																						
London Bridge ⊖	a																						
Balham ⊖	d	23p50		07 23	07 53	07 48		08 01	08 23	08 18		08 43	08 31	08 53	08 48		09 13	09 01	09 23	09 18		09 43	09 31
Clapham Junction	a	23p56		07 27	07 57	07 52	07 49	08 06	08 27	08 22	08 19	08 48	08 36	08 57	08 52	08 49	09 19	09 06	09 27	09 22	09 19	09 49	09 36
London Waterloo ⊖	a						08 04				08 34					09 04					09 34		
London Victoria ⊖	a	00 04		07 34	08 04	07 59		08 15	08 34	08 29		08 57	08 45	09 04	08 59		09 27	09 15	09 34	09 29		09 57	09 45

Table 182

Sundays from 2 October

Horsham, Dorking, Guildford, Epsom and Sutton - London

		SN	SN	SW	SN	SN	SN	SN	SW	SN	SN	SN	SN	SW	FC	SN	SN	SN	SN	SW	FC	SN	SN
Horsham 4	d																						
Warnham	d																						
Ockley	d																						
Holmwood	d																						
Dorking 4	a																						
	d			09 08		09 16					09 46			10 08			10 16						10 46
Boxhill & Westhumble	d					09 18					09 48						10 18						10 48
Guildford	d								09 18											10 18			
Effingham Junction 6	d								09 34											10 34			
Bookham	d								09 37											10 37			
Leatherhead	d			09 15		09 23			09 45		09 53			10 15			10 23			10 45			10 53
Ashtead	d			09 18		09 27			09 48		09 57			10 18			10 27			10 48			10 57
Epsom 3	a			09 23		09 31			09 53		10 01			10 23			10 31			10 53			11 01
	d		09 17	09 24		09 32		09 47	09 54		10 02		10 17	10 24			10 32		10 47	10 54			11 02
Ewell East	d		09 21			09 36		09 51			10 06		10 21				10 36		10 51				11 06
Cheam	d		09 24			09 39		09 54			10 09		10 24				10 39		10 54				11 09
Epsom Downs	d																						
Banstead	d																						
Belmont	d																						
Sutton (Surrey) 4	a		09 27			09 42		09 57			10 12		10 27				10 42		10 57				11 12
	d	09 25	09 28		09 40	09 43	09 55	09 58		10 10	10 13	10 25	10 28		10 28	10 40	10 43	10 55	10 58		10 58	11 10	11 13
Carshalton	d		09 31			09 46		10 01			10 16		10 31				10 46		11 01				11 16
Hackbridge	d		09 33			09 48		10 03			10 18		10 33				10 48		11 03				11 18
Mitcham Junction	d		09 37			09 52		10 07			10 22		10 37				10 52		11 07				11 22
Mitcham Eastfields	d		09 40			09 55		10 10			10 25		10 40				10 55		11 10				11 25
Carshalton Beeches	d	09 28			09 43		09 58			10 13		10 28				10 43		10 58				11 13	
Wallington	d	09 30			09 45		10 00			10 15		10 30				10 45		11 00				11 15	
Waddon	d	09 33			09 48		10 03			10 18		10 33				10 48		11 03				11 18	
West Croydon 4	d	09 37			09 52		10 07			10 22		10 37				10 52		11 07				11 22	
Norwood Junction 2	d				09 57					10 27						10 57						11 27	
New Cross Gate 4	⊖ d																						
Tulse Hill 3	a														10 59						11 29		
	d														10 59						11 29		
London Bridge 4	⊖ a														11 10						11 40		
Balham 4	⊖ d	09 53	09 48		10 13	10 01	10 23	10 18		10 43	10 31	10 53	10 48			11 13	11 01	11 23	11 18			11 43	11 31
Clapham Junction 10	a	09 57	09 52	09 49	10 18	10 06	10 27	10 22	10 19	10 48	10 36	10 57	10 52	10 49		11 18	11 06	11 27	11 22	11 19		11 48	11 36
London Waterloo 15	⊖ a			10 04					10 34					11 04						11 34			
London Victoria 15	⊖ a	10 04	09 59		10 27	10 15	10 34	10 29		10 57	10 45	11 04	10 59			11 27	11 15	11 34	11 29			11 57	11 45

		SN	SN	SW	FC	SN	SN	SN	SN	SW	FC	SN	SN	SN	SN	SW	FC	SN	SN	SN	SN	SW
Horsham 4	d																					
Warnham	d																					
Ockley	d																					
Holmwood	d																					
Dorking 4	a																					
	d			11 08			11 16						11 46			12 08			12 16			
Boxhill & Westhumble	d						11 18						11 48						12 18			
Guildford	d									11 18												12 18
Effingham Junction 6	d									11 34												12 34
Bookham	d									11 37												12 37
Leatherhead	d			11 15			11 23			11 45			11 53			12 15			12 23			12 45
Ashtead	d			11 18			11 27			11 48			11 57			12 18			12 27			12 48
Epsom 3	a			11 23			11 31			11 53			12 01			12 23			12 31			12 53
	d		11 17	11 24			11 32		11 47	11 54			12 02		12 17	12 24			12 32		12 47	12 54
Ewell East	d		11 21				11 36		11 51				12 06		12 21				12 36		12 51	
Cheam	d		11 24				11 39		11 54				12 09		12 24				12 39		12 54	
Epsom Downs	d																					
Banstead	d																					
Belmont	d																					
Sutton (Surrey) 4	a		11 27				11 42		11 57				12 12		12 27				12 42		12 57	
	d	11 25	11 28		11 28	11 40	11 43	11 55	11 58		11 58	12 10	12 13	12 25	12 28		12 28	12 40	12 43	12 55	12 58	
Carshalton	d		11 31				11 46		12 01				12 16		12 31				12 46		13 01	
Hackbridge	d		11 33				11 48		12 03				12 18		12 33				12 48		13 03	
Mitcham Junction	d		11 37				11 52		12 07				12 22		12 37				12 52		13 07	
Mitcham Eastfields	d		11 40				11 55		12 10				12 25		12 40				12 55		13 10	
Carshalton Beeches	d	11 28				11 43		11 58				12 13		12 28				12 43		12 58		
Wallington	d	11 30				11 45		12 00				12 15		12 30				12 45		13 00		
Waddon	d	11 33				11 48		12 03				12 18		12 33				12 48		13 03		
West Croydon 4	d	11 37				11 52		12 07				12 22		12 37				12 52		13 07		
Norwood Junction 2	d					11 57						12 27						12 57				
New Cross Gate 4	⊖ d																					
Tulse Hill 3	a				11 59						12 29						12 59					
	d				11 59						12 29						12 59					
London Bridge 4	⊖ a				12 10						12 40						13 10					
Balham 4	⊖ d	11 53	11 48			12 13	12 01	12 23	12 18			12 43	12 31	12 53	12 48			13 13	13 01	13 23	13 18	
Clapham Junction 10	a	11 57	11 52	11 49		12 18	12 06	12 27	12 22	12 19		12 48	12 36	12 57	12 52	12 49		13 19	13 06	13 27	13 22	13 19
London Waterloo 15	⊖ a			12 04						12 34						13 04						13 34
London Victoria 15	⊖ a	12 04	11 59			12 27	12 15	12 34	12 29			12 57	12 45	13 04	12 59			13 27	13 15	13 34	13 29	

Table 182

Sundays from 2 October

Horsham, Dorking, Guildford, Epsom and Sutton - London

		FC	SN	SN	SN	SN	SW	FC	SN	SN	SN	SN	SW	FC	SN	SN	SN	SN	SW	FC	SN	SN	SN
Horsham 4	d																						
Warnham	d																						
Ockley	d																						
Holmwood	d																						
Dorking 4	a																						
	d			12 46			13 08			13 16						13 46			14 08			14 16	
Boxhill & Westhumble	d			12 48						13 18						13 48						14 18	
Guildford	d												13 18										
Effingham Junction 6	d												13 34										
Bookham	d												13 37										
Leatherhead	d			12 53			13 15			13 23			13 45			13 53			14 15			14 23	
Ashtead	d			12 57			13 18			13 27			13 48			13 57			14 18			14 27	
Epsom 3	a			13 01			13 23			13 31			13 53			14 01			14 23			14 31	
	d			13 02		13 17	13 24			13 32		13 47	13 54			14 02		14 17	14 24			14 32	
Ewell East	d			13 06		13 21				13 36		13 51				14 06		14 21				14 36	
Cheam	d			13 09		13 24				13 39		13 54				14 09		14 24				14 39	
Epsom Downs	d																						
Banstead	d																						
Belmont	d																						
Sutton (Surrey) 4	a			13 12		13 27				13 42		13 57				14 12		14 27				14 42	
	d	12 58	13 10	13 13	13 25	13 28		13 28	13 40	13 43	13 55	13 58		13 58	14 10	14 13	14 25	14 28		14 28	14 40	14 43	14 55
Carshalton	d			13 16		13 31				13 46		14 01				14 16		14 31				14 46	
Hackbridge	d			13 18		13 33				13 48		14 03				14 18		14 33				14 48	
Mitcham Junction	d			13 22		13 37				13 52		14 07				14 22		14 37				14 52	
Mitcham Eastfields	d			13 25		13 40				13 55		14 10				14 25		14 40				14 55	
Carshalton Beeches	d		13 13		13 28				13 43		13 58				14 13		14 28				14 43		14 58
Wallington	d		13 15		13 30				13 45		14 00				14 15		14 30				14 45		15 00
Waddon	d		13 18		13 33				13 48		14 03				14 18		14 33				14 48		15 03
West Croydon 4	d		13 22		13 37				13 52		14 07				14 22		14 37				14 52		15 07
Norwood Junction 2	d		13 27						13 57						14 27						14 57		
New Cross Gate 4	⊖ d																						
Tulse Hill 3	a	13 29						13 59						14 29						14 59			
	d	13 29						13 59						14 29						14 59			
London Bridge 4	⊖ a	13 40						14 10						14 40						15 10			
Balham 4	⊖ d		13 43	13 31	13 53	13 48			14 13	14 01	14 23	14 18			14 43	14 31	14 53	14 48			15 13	15 01	15 23
Clapham Junction 10	a		13 48	13 36	13 57	13 52	13 49		14 19	14 06	14 27	14 22	14 19		14 48	14 36	14 57	14 52	14 49		15 19	15 06	15 27
London Waterloo 15	⊖ a						14 04						14 34						14 59				
London Victoria 15	⊖ a		13 57	13 45	14 04	13 59			14 27	14 15	14 34	14 29			14 57	14 45	15 04	14 59			15 27	15 15	15 34

		SN	SW	FC	SN	SN	SN	SN	SW	FC	SN	SN	SN	SN	SW	FC	SN	SN	SN	SN	SW	FC
Horsham 4	d																					
Warnham	d																					
Ockley	d																					
Holmwood	d																					
Dorking 4	a																					
	d					14 46			15 08			15 16						15 46			16 08	
Boxhill & Westhumble	d					14 48						15 18						15 48				
Guildford	d		14 18												15 18							
Effingham Junction 6	d		14 34												15 34							
Bookham	d		14 37												15 37							
Leatherhead	d		14 45			14 53			15 15			15 23			15 45			15 53			16 15	
Ashtead	d		14 48			14 57			15 18			15 27			15 48			15 57			16 18	
Epsom 3	a		14 53			15 01			15 23			15 31			15 53			16 01			16 23	
	d	14 47	14 54			15 02		15 17	15 24			15 32		15 47	15 54			16 02		16 17	16 24	
Ewell East	d	14 51				15 06		15 21				15 36		15 51				16 06		16 21		
Cheam	d	14 54				15 09		15 24				15 39		15 54				16 09		16 24		
Epsom Downs	d																					
Banstead	d																					
Belmont	d																					
Sutton (Surrey) 4	a	14 57				15 12		15 27				15 42		15 57				16 12		16 27		
	d	14 58		14 58	15 10	15 13	15 25	15 28		15 28	15 40	15 43	15 55	15 58		15 58	16 10	16 13	16 25	16 28		16 28
Carshalton	d	15 01				15 16		15 31				15 46		16 01				16 16		16 31		
Hackbridge	d	15 03				15 18		15 33				15 48		16 03				16 18		16 33		
Mitcham Junction	d	15 07				15 22		15 37				15 52		16 07				16 22		16 37		
Mitcham Eastfields	d	15 10				15 25		15 40				15 55		16 10				16 25		16 40		
Carshalton Beeches	d				15 13		15 28				15 43		15 58				16 13		16 28			
Wallington	d				15 15		15 30				15 45		16 00				16 15		16 30			
Waddon	d				15 18		15 33				15 48		16 03				16 18		16 33			
West Croydon 4	d				15 22		15 37				15 52		16 07				16 22		16 37			
Norwood Junction 2	d				15 27						15 57						16 27					
New Cross Gate 4	⊖ d																					
Tulse Hill 3	a			15 29						15 59						16 29						16 59
	d			15 29						15 59						16 29						16 59
London Bridge 4	⊖ a			15 40						16 10						16 40						17 10
Balham 4	⊖ d	15 18			15 43	15 31	15 53	15 48			16 13	16 01	16 23	16 18			16 43	16 31	16 53	16 48		
Clapham Junction 10	a	15 22	15 19		15 48	15 36	15 57	15 52	15 49		16 19	16 06	16 27	16 22	16 19		16 48	16 36	16 57	16 52	16 49	
London Waterloo 15	⊖ a		15 29						15 59						16 29						16 59	
London Victoria 15	⊖ a	15 29			15 57	15 45	16 04	15 59			16 27	16 15	16 34	16 29			16 57	16 45	17 04	16 59		

Horsham, Dorking, Guildford, Epsom and Sutton - London

from 2 October

		SN	SN	SN	SN	SW	FC	SN	SN	SN		SN	SW	FC	SN	SN	SN	SN	SW	FC		SN	SN	SN	SN
Horsham [4]	d																								
Warnham	d																								
Ockley	d																								
Holmwood	d																								
Dorking [4]	a																								
	d		16 16						16 46				17 08			17 16							17 46		
Boxhill & Westhumble	d		16 18						16 48							17 18							17 48		
Guildford	d					16 18													17 18						
Effingham Junction [6]	d					16 34													17 34						
Bookham	d					16 37													17 37						
Leatherhead	d		16 23			16 45			16 53				17 15			17 23			17 45				17 53		
Ashtead	d		16 27			16 48			16 57				17 18			17 27			17 48				17 57		
Epsom [3]	a		16 31			16 53			17 01				17 23			17 31			17 53				18 01		
	d		16 32		16 47	16 54			17 02			17 17	17 24			17 32		17 47	17 54				18 02		18 17
Ewell East	d		16 36		16 51				17 06			17 21				17 36		17 51					18 06		18 21
Cheam	d		16 39		16 54				17 09			17 24				17 39		17 54					18 09		18 24
Epsom Downs	d																								
Banstead	d																								
Belmont	d																								
Sutton (Surrey) [4]	a		16 42		16 57				17 12			17 27				17 42		17 57					18 12		18 27
	d	16 40	16 43	16 55	16 58		16 58	17 10	17 13	17 25		17 28		17 28	17 40	17 43	17 55	17 58		17 58		18 10	18 13	18 25	18 28
Carshalton	d		16 46		17 01				17 16			17 31				17 46		18 01					18 16		18 31
Hackbridge	d		16 48		17 03				17 18			17 33				17 48		18 03					18 18		18 33
Mitcham Junction	d		16 52		17 07				17 22			17 37				17 52		18 07					18 22		18 37
Mitcham Eastfields	d		16 55		17 10				17 25			17 40				17 55		18 10					18 25		18 40
Carshalton Beeches	d	16 43		16 58				17 13		17 28					17 43		17 58					18 13		18 28	
Wallington	d	16 45		17 00				17 15		17 30					17 45		18 00					18 15		18 30	
Waddon	d	16 48		17 03				17 18		17 33					17 48		18 03					18 18		18 33	
West Croydon [4]	d	16 52		17 07				17 22		17 37					17 52		18 07					18 22		18 37	
Norwood Junction [2]	d	16 57						17 27							17 57							18 27			
New Cross Gate [4]	⊖ d																								
Tulse Hill [3]	a						17 29							17 59						18 29					
	d						17 29							17 59						18 29					
London Bridge [4]	⊖ a						17 40							18 10						18 40					
Balham [4]	⊖ d	17 13	17 01	17 23	17 18			17 43	17 31	17 53		17 48			18 13	18 01	18 23	18 18				18 43	18 31	18 53	18 48
Clapham Junction [10]	a	17 19	17 06	17 27	17 22	17 19		17 48	17 36	17 57		17 52	17 49		18 19	18 06	18 27	18 22	18 19			18 48	18 36	18 57	18 52
London Waterloo [15]	⊖ a					17 29							17 59						18 29						
London Victoria [15]	⊖ a	17 27	17 15	17 34	17 29			17 57	17 45	18 04		17 59			18 27	18 15	18 34	18 29				18 57	18 45	19 04	18 59

		SW	FC	SN	SN	SN		SN	SW	FC	SN	SN	SW	SN	FC	SN		SN	SW	SN	FC	SN	SN	SW	SN
Horsham [4]	d																								
Warnham	d																								
Ockley	d																								
Holmwood	d																								
Dorking [4]	a																								
	d	18 08			18 16							18 46	19 08					19 16					19 46	20 08	
Boxhill & Westhumble	d				18 18							18 48						19 18					19 48		
Guildford	d								18 18										19 18						
Effingham Junction [6]	d								18 34										19 34						
Bookham	d								18 37										19 37						
Leatherhead	d	18 15			18 23				18 45			18 53	19 15					19 23	19 45				19 53	20 15	
Ashtead	d	18 18			18 27				18 48			18 57	19 18					19 27	19 48				19 57	20 18	
Epsom [3]	a	18 23			18 31				18 53			19 01	19 23					19 31	19 53				20 01	20 23	
	d	18 24			18 32			18 47	18 54			19 02	19 24					19 32	19 54				20 02	20 24	
Ewell East	d				18 36			18 51				19 06						19 36					20 06		
Cheam	d				18 39			18 54				19 09						19 39					20 09		
Epsom Downs	d																								
Banstead	d																								
Belmont	d																								
Sutton (Surrey) [4]	a				18 42			18 57				19 12						19 42					20 12		
	d		18 28	18 40	18 43	18 55		18 58		18 58	19 10	19 13		19 25	19 28	19 40		19 43		19 55	19 58	20 10	20 13		20 25
Carshalton	d				18 46			19 01				19 16						19 46					20 16		
Hackbridge	d				18 48			19 03				19 18						19 48					20 18		
Mitcham Junction	d				18 52			19 07				19 22						19 52					20 22		
Mitcham Eastfields	d				18 55			19 10				19 25						19 55					20 25		
Carshalton Beeches	d			18 43		18 58					19 13			19 28		19 43				19 58		20 13			20 28
Wallington	d			18 45		19 00					19 15			19 30		19 45				20 00		20 15			20 30
Waddon	d			18 48		19 03					19 18			19 33		19 48				20 03		20 18			20 33
West Croydon [4]	d			18 52		19 07					19 22			19 37		19 52				20 07		20 22			20 37
Norwood Junction [2]	d			18 57							19 27					19 57						20 27			
New Cross Gate [4]	⊖ d																								
Tulse Hill [3]	a		18 59							19 29					19 59						20 29				
	d		18 59							19 29					19 59						20 29				
London Bridge [4]	⊖ a		19 10							19 40					20 10						20 40				
Balham [4]	⊖ d			19 13	19 01	19 23		19 18			19 43	19 31		19 53		20 13		20 01		20 23		20 43	20 31		20 53
Clapham Junction [10]	a	18 49		19 19	19 06	19 27		19 22	19 19		19 48	19 36	19 49	19 57		20 18		20 06	20 19	20 27		20 48	20 36	20 49	20 57
London Waterloo [15]	⊖ a	18 59							19 29				19 59						20 29					21 00	
London Victoria [15]	⊖ a			19 27	19 15	19 34		19 29			19 57	19 45		20 04		20 27		20 15		20 34		20 57	20 45		21 04

Horsham, Dorking, Guildford, Epsom and Sutton - London

from 2 October

		FC		SN	SN	SW	SN	FC	SN	SN	SW	SN		FC	SN	SN	SW	SN	SN	SN	SW	SN		SN	SN
Horsham [4]	d																								
Warnham	d																								
Ockley	d																								
Holmwood	d																								
Dorking [4]	a																								
	d				20 16					20 46	21 08					21 16				21 46	22 08				22 16
Boxhill & Westhumble	d				20 18					20 48						21 18				21 48					22 18
Guildford	d					20 18											21 18								
Effingham Junction [6]	d					20 34											21 34								
Bookham	d					20 37											21 37								
Leatherhead	d				20 23	20 45				20 53	21 15					21 23	21 45			21 53	22 15				22 23
Ashtead	d				20 27	20 48				20 57	21 18					21 27	21 48			21 57	22 18				22 27
Epsom [3]	a				20 31	20 53				21 01	21 23					21 31	21 53			22 01	22 23				22 31
	d				20 32	20 54				21 02	21 24					21 32	21 54			22 02	22 24				22 32
Ewell East	d				20 36					21 06						21 36				22 06					22 36
Cheam	d				20 39					21 09						21 39				22 09					22 39
Epsom Downs	d																								
Banstead	d																								
Belmont	d																								
Sutton (Surrey) [4]	a				20 42					21 12						21 42				22 12					22 42
	d	20 28		20 40	20 43		20 55	20 58	21 10	21 13		21 25		21 28	21 40	21 43		21 55	22 10	22 13		22 25		22 40	22 43
Carshalton	d				20 46					21 16						21 46				22 16					22 46
Hackbridge	d				20 48					21 18						21 48				22 18					22 48
Mitcham Junction	d				20 52					21 22						21 52				22 22					22 52
Mitcham Eastfields	d				20 55					21 25						21 55				22 25					22 55
Carshalton Beeches	d			20 43			20 58		21 13			21 28			21 43			21 58	22 13			22 28		22 43	
Wallington	d			20 45			21 00		21 15			21 30			21 45			22 00	22 15			22 30		22 45	
Waddon	d			20 48			21 03		21 18			21 33			21 48			22 03	22 18			22 33		22 48	
West Croydon [4]	d			20 52			21 07		21 22			21 37			21 52			22 07	22 22			22 37		22 52	
Norwood Junction [2]	d			20 57					21 27						21 57				22 27					22 57	
New Cross Gate [4]	⊖ d																								
Tulse Hill [3]	a	20 59						21 29						21 59											
	d	20 59						21 29						21 59											
London Bridge [4]	⊖ a	21 10						21 40						22 10											
Balham [4]	⊖ d			21 13	21 01		21 23		21 43	21 31		21 53			22 13	22 01		22 23	22 43	22 31		22 53		23 13	23 01
Clapham Junction [10]	a			21 19	21 06	21 19	21 27		21 49	21 36	21 49	21 57			22 19	22 06	22 19	22 27	22 49	22 36	22 49	22 57		23 19	23 06
London Waterloo [15]	⊖ a					21 29					22 00						22 29				23 00				
London Victoria [15]	⊖ a			21 27	21 15		21 34		21 57	21 45		22 04			22 27	22 15		22 34	22 57	22 45		23 04		23 27	23 15

		SW	SN	SN	SN	SW	SN	SN		SN
Horsham [4]	d									
Warnham	d									
Ockley	d									
Holmwood	d									
Dorking [4]	a									
	d				22 46	23 08				23 16
Boxhill & Westhumble	d				22 48					23 18
Guildford	d	22 20								
Effingham Junction [6]	d	22 36								
Bookham	d	22 39								
Leatherhead	d	22 45			22 53	23 15				23 23
Ashtead	d	22 48			22 57	23 18				23 27
Epsom [3]	a	22 53			23 01	23 23				23 31
	d	22 54			23 02	23 24				23 32
Ewell East	d				23 06					23 36
Cheam	d				23 09					23 39
Epsom Downs	d									
Banstead	d									
Belmont	d									
Sutton (Surrey) [4]	a				23 12					23 42
	d		22 55	23 10	23 13		23 25	23 40		23 43
Carshalton	d				23 16					23 46
Hackbridge	d				23 18					23 48
Mitcham Junction	d				23 22					23 52
Mitcham Eastfields	d				23 25					23 55
Carshalton Beeches	d		22 58	23 13			23 28	23 43		
Wallington	d		23 00	23 15			23 30	23 45		
Waddon	d		23 03	23 18			23 33	23 48		
West Croydon [4]	d		23 07	23 22			23 37	23 52		
Norwood Junction [2]	d			23 27						
New Cross Gate [4]	⊖ d									
Tulse Hill [3]	a									
	d									
London Bridge [4]	⊖ a									
Balham [4]	⊖ d		23 23	23 43	23 31		23 53	00 08		00 01
Clapham Junction [10]	a	23 19	23 27	23 49	23 36	23 49	23 57	00 12		00 06
London Waterloo [15]	⊖ a	23 29				23 59				
London Victoria [15]	⊖ a		23 34	23 57	23 45		00 04	00 19		00 15

Network Diagram for Tables 184, 189

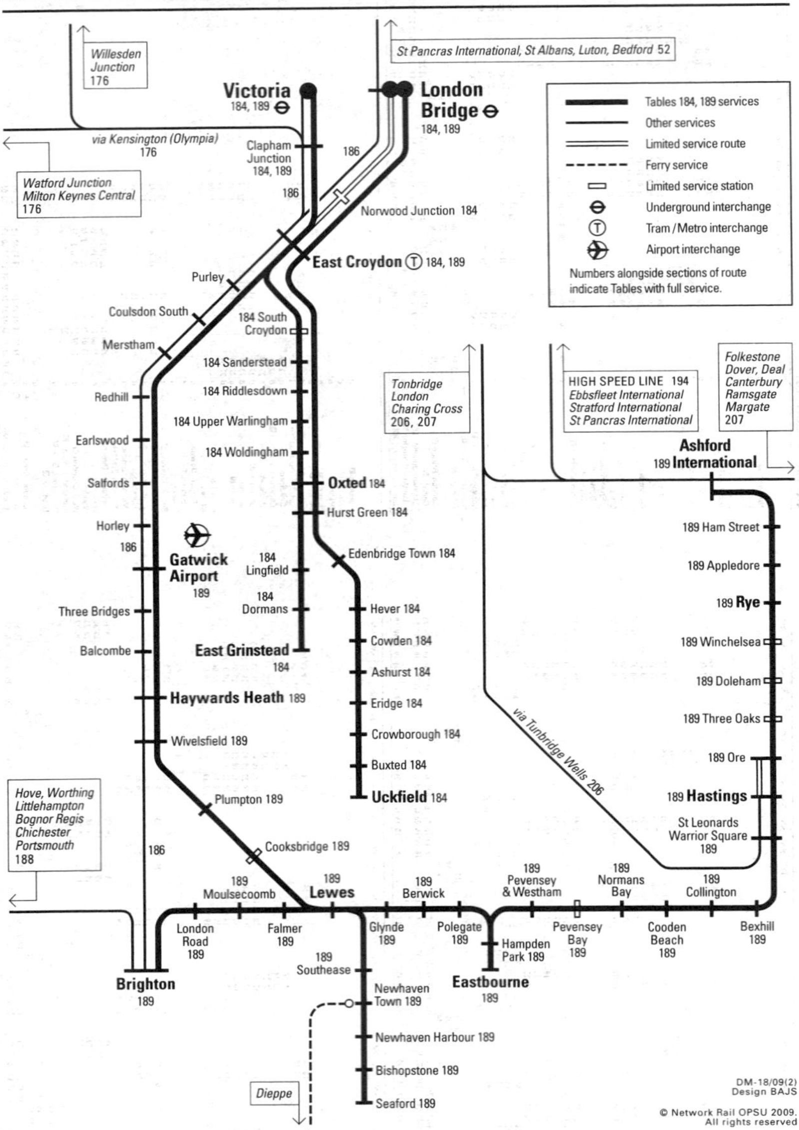

© Network Rail OPSU 2009. All rights reserved

Table 184

Mondays to Fridays

London - Oxted, East Grinstead and Uckfield

Miles	Miles			SN MX 1	SN MX 1	SN MX 1	SN 1	SN 1	SN 1	SN 1	SN 1	SN 1	SN 1	SN 1	SN 1	SN 1	SN 1	SN 1	SN 1	SN 1	SN 1	SN 1	SN 1
0	—	**London Victoria** 15 ⊖175,177	d		23p24	23p49		05 23	05 53		06 24		06 54		07 10		07 32		08 10		08 53		09 23
2¾	—	Clapham Junction 10 175,177	d		23p30	23p56		05 33	05 59		06 30		07 00		07 16		07 38		08 16		08 59		09 29
—	0	**London Bridge** 4 ⊖175,177	d	23p04						06 08		06 32		07 03		07 19		08 00		08 25		09 08	
—	8¾	Norwood Junction 2 175,177	d	23p15				05 50								07 30				08 36			
10½	10¼	**East Croydon** 175,177	d	23p19	23p41	00 10	05 26	05 54	06 10	06 22	06 41	06 55	07 11	07 17	07 27	07 35	07 52	08 16	08 27	08 41	09 10	09 23	09 40
11½	—	South Croydon 4 175	d					05 56															
12½	—	Sanderstead	d	23p24	23p46	00s14			06 14		06 45		07 15	07 21	07 31	07 39	07 57	08 20	08 31	08 45	09 14		09 44
13¾	—	Riddlesdown	d		23p49	00s17			06 17		06 48			07 24		07 42	08 00	08 23		08 48	09 17		09 47
15½	—	Upper Warlingham	d	23p29	23p53	00s21			06 21		06 52			07 28		07 46	08 04	08 27		08 52	09 21		09 51
17¼	—	Woldingham	d		23p57	00s25			06 25		06 56			07 32		07 50	08 08	08 31		08 56	09 25		09 55
20½	—	**Oxted** 3	a	23p36	00 02	00 30	05 41	06 08	06 30	06 36	07 01	07 07	07 26	07 37	07 43	07 55	08 13	08 36	08 42	09 01	09 30	09 36	10 00
—	—		d	23p37	00 02		05 41	06 08	06 31	06 36	07 02	07 08	07 26	07 38	07 43	07 56	08 13	08 37	08 42	09 02	09 31	09 37	10 00
21½	0	Hurst Green	d	23p39	00 05		05 44	06 10	06 33	06 39	07 04	07 11	07 29	07 40	07 46	07 58	08 16	08 39	08 46	09 04	09 33	09 39	10 03
26¼	—	Lingfield	d		00 11			06 16	06 39		07 10		07 35		07 52	08 04	08 22		08 52	09 10	09 39		10 09
28	—	Dormans	d		00 14			06 20	06 43		07 14		07 38		07 55	08 08	08 25		08 55	09 14	09 43		10 12
30¼	—	**East Grinstead**	a		00 19			06 24	06 47		07 18		07 43		08 00	08 12	08 30		09 00	09 18	09 47		10 17
—	4¼	Edenbridge Town	d	23b45			05 50			06 45		07 17		07 46				08 45				09 45	
—	6	Hever	d							06 48		07 20		07 50				08 49				09 49	
—	8	Cowden	d							06 52		07 24		07 54				08 53				09 53	
—	10¾	Ashurst	d							06 57		07 29		07 58				08 57				09 57	
—	14½	Eridge	d	23b58			06 11			07 02		07 34		08 04				09 03				10 03	
—	17¾	Crowborough	d	00s04			06 17			07 13		07 40		08 10				09 09				10 09	
—	22½	Buxted	d	00s10			06 23			07 19		07 46		08 16				09 15				10 15	
—	25	**Uckfield**	a	00 16			06 29			07 25		07 52		08 22				09 21				10 21	

		SN 1	SN 1	SN 1	SN 1	SN 1	SN 1	SN 1	SN 1	SN 1	SN 1	SN 1	SN 1	SN 1	SN 1	SN 1	SN 1	SN 1	SN 1	SN 1	SN 1	SN 1	SN 1
London Victoria 15 ⊖175,177	d	09 53		10 23	10 53		11 23	11 53		12 23	12 53		13 23	13 53		14 23	14 53		15 23		15 53		16 23
Clapham Junction 10 175,177	d	09 59		10 29	10 59		11 29	11 59		12 29	12 59		13 29	13 59		14 29	14 59		15 29		15 59		16 29
London Bridge 4 ⊖175,177	d		10 08			11 08			12 08			13 08			14 08			15 08		15 38		16 08	
Norwood Junction 2 175,177	d											13 19			14 19			15 19				16 19	
East Croydon 175,177	d	10 10	10 23	10 40	11 10	11 24	11 40	12 10	12 23	12 40	13 10	13 24	13 40	14 10	14 23	14 40	15 10	15 23	15 40	15 53	16 10	16 23	16 40
South Croydon 4 175	d																		15 43		16 12		16 42
Sanderstead	d	10 14		10 44	11 14		11 44	12 14		12 44	13 14		13 44	14 14		14 45	15 14		15 46		16 15		16 45
Riddlesdown	d	10 17		10 47	11 17		11 47	12 17		12 47	13 17		13 47	14 17		14 48	15 17		15 49		16 18		16 48
Upper Warlingham	d	10 21		10 51	11 21		11 51	12 21		12 51	13 21		13 51	14 21		14 52	15 21		15 53		16 22		16 52
Woldingham	d	10 25		10 55	11 25		11 55	12 25		12 55	13 25		13 55	14 25		14 56	15 25		15 57		16 26		16 56
Oxted 3	a	10 30	10 36	11 00	11 30	11 36	12 00	12 30	12 36	13 00	13 30	13 36	14 00	14 30	14 36	15 01	15 30	15 36	16 02	16 06	16 31	16 36	17 01
	d	10 30	10 37	11 00	11 30	11 37	12 00	12 30	12 37	13 00	13 30	13 37	14 00	14 30	14 37	15 01	15 30	15 37	16 02	16 07	16 31	16 37	17 02
Hurst Green	d	10 33	10 39	11 03	11 33	11 39	12 03	12 33	12 39	13 03	13 33	13 39	14 03	14 33	14 39	15 03	15 33	15 39	16 04	16 09	16 34	16 39	17 04
Lingfield	d	10 39		11 09	11 39		12 09	12 39		13 09	13 39		14 09	14 39		15 09	15 39		16 10		16 40		17 10
Dormans	d	10 42		11 12	11 42		12 12	12 42		13 12	13 42		14 12	14 42		15 13	15 42		16 14		16 43		17 14
East Grinstead	a	10 47		11 17	11 47		12 17	12 47		13 17	13 47		14 17	14 47		15 17	15 47		16 18		16 48		17 20
Edenbridge Town	d		10 45			11 45			12 45			13 45			14 45			15 45		16 15		16 45	
Hever	d		10 49			11 49			12 49			13 49			14 49			15 49		16 19		16 49	
Cowden	d		10 53			11 53			12 53			13 53			14 53			15 53		16 23		16 53	
Ashurst	d		10 57			11 57			12 57			13 57			14 57			15 57		16 27		16 57	
Eridge	d		11 03			12 03			13 03			14 03			15 03			16 03		16 33		17 03	
Crowborough	d		11 09			12 09			13 09			14 09			15 09			16 09		16 39		17 09	
Buxted	d		11 15			12 15			13 15			14 15			15 15			16 15		16 45		17 15	
Uckfield	a		11 21			12 21			13 21			14 21			15 21			16 21		16 51		17 21	

		SN 1	SN 1	SN 1	SN 1	SN 1	SN 1	SN 1	SN 1	SN 1	SN 1	SN 1	SN 1	SN 1	SN 1	SN 1	SN 1	SN 1	SN 1	SN 1	SN 1	SN 1
London Victoria 15 ⊖175,177	d		16 53			17 23		17 53			18 23		18 53		19 23	19 53		20 23	20 53		21 23	21 53
Clapham Junction 10 175,177	d		16 59			17 30		18 00			18 30		19 00		19 29	19 59		20 29	20 59		21 29	21 59
London Bridge 4 ⊖175,177	d	16 38		17 09	17 15		17 44		18 08	18 16		18 47		19 08			20 04			21 04		
Norwood Junction 2 175,177	d																20 16			21 15		
East Croydon 175,177	d	16 53	17 10	17 23	17 30	17 41	17 58	18 11	18 22	18 31	18 42	19 00	19 11	19 23	19 40	20 10	20 20	20 40	21 10	21 19	21 40	22 10
South Croydon 4 175	d		17 12		17 32		18 01			18 33		19 03										
Sanderstead	d		17 15		17 35	17 45	18 04	18 15		18 36	18 47	19 06	19 15		19 44	20 14	20 24	20 44	21 14	21 24	21 44	22 14
Riddlesdown	d		17 18		17 38	17 48	18 07	18 18		18 39	18 50	19 09	19 18		19 47	20 17		20 47	21 17		21 47	22 17
Upper Warlingham	d		17 22		17 42	17 52	18 11	18 22		18 43	18 54	19 13	19 22		19 51	20 21	20 30	20 51	21 21	21 29	21 51	22 21
Woldingham	d		17 26		17 46	17 56	18 15	18 26		18 47	18 58	19 17	19 26		19 55	20 25		20 55	21 25		21 55	22 25
Oxted 3	a	17 06	17 31	17 36	17 51	18 01	18 20	18 31	18 36	18 52	19 03	19 22	19 31	19 36	20 00	20 30	20 37	21 00	21 30	21 36	22 00	22 30
	d	17 07	17 32	17 37	17 52	18 02	18 20	18 32	18 37	18 53	19 03	19 22	19 32	19 37	20 00	20 30	20 37	21 00	21 30	21 37	22 00	22 30
Hurst Green	d	17 09	17 34	17 40	17 54	18 04	18 23	18 34	18 39	18 55	19 06	19 25	19 34	19 39	20 03	20 33	20 40	21 03	21 33	21 39	22 03	22 33
Lingfield	d		17 40		18 00	18 10	18 29	18 40		19 01	19 12	19 31	19 40		20 09	20 39		21 09	21 39		22 09	22 39
Dormans	d		17 44		18 04	18 14	18 32	18 44		19 05	19 15	19 34	19 44		20 12	20 42		21 12	21 42		22 12	22 42
East Grinstead	a		17 50		18 12	18 22	18 40	18 52		19 12	19 22	19 42	19 52		20 17	20 47		21 17	21 47		22 17	22 47
Edenbridge Town	d	17 15		17 46					18 45					19 45			20 46			21 45		
Hever	d	17 19												19 49			20 49			21 49		
Cowden	d	17 23												19 53			20 53			21 53		
Ashurst	d	17 27												19 57			20 58			21 57		
Eridge	d	17 33		17 58					18 57					20 03			21 03			22 03		
Crowborough	d	17 39		18 04					19 03					20 09			21 09			22 09		
Buxted	d	17 45		18 10					19 09					20 15			21 15			22 15		
Uckfield	a	17 51		18 18					19 17					20 21			21 21			22 21		

b Previous night, stops to set down only

London - Oxted, East Grinstead and Uckfield

Mondays to Fridays

		SN [1]	SN [1]	SN [1]	SN [1]	SN [1]	SN [1]
London Victoria [15] ⊖175,177	d		22 23	22 53		23 24	23 49
Clapham Junction [10] 175,177	d		22 29	22 59		23 30	23 56
London Bridge [4] ⊖175,177	d	22 04			23 04		
Norwood Junction [2] 175,177	d	22 15			23 15		
East Croydon 175,177	d	22 19	22 40	23 10	23 19	23 41	00 10
South Croydon [4] 175	d						
Sanderstead	d	22 24	22 44	23 14	23 24	23 46	00s14
Riddlesdown	d		22 47	23 17		23 49	00s17
Upper Warlingham	d	22 29	22 51	23 21	23 29	23 53	00s21
Woldingham	d		22 55	23 25		23 57	00s25
Oxted [3]	a	22 36	23 00	23 30	23 36	00 02	00 30
	d	22 37	23 00	23 30	23 37	00 02	
Hurst Green	d	22 39	23 03	23 33	23 39	00 05	
Lingfield	d		23 09	23 39		00 11	
Dormans	d		23 12	23 42		00 14	
East Grinstead	a		23 17	23 47		00 19	
Edenbridge Town	d	22 45			23s45		
Hever	d	22s49					
Cowden	d	22s53					
Ashurst	d	22s57					
Eridge	d	23 03			23s58		
Crowborough	d	23 09			00s04		
Buxted	d	23 15			00s10		
Uckfield	a	23 21			00 16		

Saturdays

		SN [1]	SN [1]	SN [1]	SN [1]	SN [1]	SN [1]	SN [1]		SN [1]
London Victoria [15] ⊖175,177	d		23p24	23p49	05 23		06 23	06 53		19 53
Clapham Junction [10] 175,177	d		23p30	23p56	05 31		06 29	06 59		19 59
London Bridge [4] ⊖175,177	d	23p04				06 08				
Norwood Junction [2] 175,177	d	23p15			05 48					
East Croydon 175,177	d	23p19	23p41	00 10	05 52	06 23	06 40	07 10		20 10
South Croydon [4] 175	d				05 54					
Sanderstead	d	23p24	23p46	00s14			06 44	07 14		20 14
Riddlesdown	d		23p49	00s17			06 47	07 17	and at	20 17
Upper Warlingham	d	23p29	23p53	00s21			06 51	07 21	the same	20 21
Woldingham	d		23p57	00s25			06 55	07 25	minutes	20 25
Oxted [3]	a	23p36	00 02	00 30	06 06	06 36	07 00	07 30	past	20 30
	d	23p37	00 02		06 06	06 37	07 00	07 30	each	20 30
Hurst Green	d	23p39	00 05		06 09	06 39	07 03	07 33	hour until	20 33
Lingfield	d		00 11		06 15		07 09	07 39		20 39
Dormans	d		00 14		06 18		07 12	07 42		20 42
East Grinstead	a		00 19		06 23		07 17	07 47		20 47
Edenbridge Town	d	23b45				06 45				
Hever	d					06 49				
Cowden	d					06 53				
Ashurst	d					06 57				
Eridge	d	23b58				07 03				
Crowborough	d	00s04				07 09				
Buxted	d	00s10				07 15				
Uckfield	a	00 16				07 21				

		SN [1]	SN [1]	SN [1]	SN [1]	SN [1]	SN [1]	SN [1]	SN [1]	SN [1]	SN [1]	SN [1]	SN [1]
London Victoria [15] ⊖175,177	d		20 23	20 53		21 23	21 53		22 23	22 53		23 24	23 49
Clapham Junction [10] 175,177	d		20 29	20 59		21 29	21 59		22 29	22 59		23 30	23 56
London Bridge [4] ⊖175,177	d	20 08			21 08			22 08			23 04		
Norwood Junction [2] 175,177	d	20 19			21 19			22 19			23 15		
East Croydon 175,177	d	20 23	20 40	21 10	21 23	21 40	22 10	22 23	22 40	23 10	23 19	23 41	00 10
South Croydon [4] 175	d												
Sanderstead	d		20 44	21 14		21 44	22 14		22 44	23 14	23 24	23 46	00s14
Riddlesdown	d		20 47	21 17		21 47	22 17		22 47	23 17		23 49	00s17
Upper Warlingham	d		20 51	21 21		21 51	22 21		22 51	23 21	23 29	23 53	00s21
Woldingham	d		20 55	21 25		21 55	22 25		22 55	23 25		23 57	00s25
Oxted [3]	a	20 36	21 00	21 30	21 36	22 00	22 30	22 36	23 00	23 30	23 36	00 02	00 30
	d	20 37	21 00	21 30	21 37	22 00	22 30	22 37	23 00	23 30	23 37	00 02	
Hurst Green	d	20 39	21 03	21 33	21 39	22 03	22 33	22 39	23 03	23 33	23 39	00 05	
Lingfield	d		21 09	21 39		22 09	22 39		23 09	23 39		00 11	
Dormans	d		21 12	21 42		22 12	22 42		23 12	23 42		00 14	
East Grinstead	a		21 17	21 47		22 17	22 47		23 17	23 47		00 19	
Edenbridge Town	d	20 45			21 45			22 45			23s45		
Hever	d	20 49			21 49			22s49					
Cowden	d	20 53			21 53			22s53					
Ashurst	d	20 57			21 57			22s57					
Eridge	d	21 03			22 03			23 03			23s58		
Crowborough	d	21 09			22 09			23 09			00s04		
Buxted	d	21 15			22 15			23 15			00s10		
Uckfield	a	21 21			22 21			23 21			00 16		

Sundays
until 4 September

		SN [1] A	SN [1] A	SN [1] A	SN [1]	SN [1]	SN [1]	SN [1]	SN [1]	SN [1]		SN [1]
London Victoria [15] ⊖175,177	d		23p24	23p49	07 40	08 40		09 40		10 40		22 40
Clapham Junction [10] 175,177	d		23p30	23p56	07 45	08 45		09 45		10 45		22 45
London Bridge [4] ⊖175,177	d	23p04										
Norwood Junction [2] 175,177	d	23p15										
East Croydon 175,177	d	23p19	23p41	00 10	07 58	08 58	09 15	09 58	10 15	10 58		22 58
South Croydon [4] 175	d											
Sanderstead	d	23p24	23p46	00s14	08 02	09 02		10 02		11 02		23 02
Riddlesdown	d		23p49	00s17	08 05	09 05		10 05		11 05		23 05
Upper Warlingham	d	23p29	23p53	00s21	08 09	09 09		10 09		11 09	and	23 09
Woldingham	d		23p57	00s25	08 13	09 13		10 13		11 13	hourly	23 13
Oxted [3]	a	23p36	00 02	00 30	08 18	09 18	09 27	10 18	10 27	11 18	until	23 18
	d	23p37	00 02		08 18	09 18	09 33	10 18	10 33	11 18		23 18
Hurst Green	d	23p39	00 05		08 21	09 21	09 36	10 21	10 36	11 21		23 21
Lingfield	d		00 11		08 27	09 27		10 27		11 27		23 27
Dormans	d		00 14		08 30	09 30		10 30		11 30		23 30
East Grinstead	a		00 19		08 35	09 35		10 35		11 35		23 35
Edenbridge Town	d	23b45					09 42		10 42			
Hever	d						09 46		10 46			
Cowden	d						09 50		10 50			
Ashurst	d						09 54		10 54			
Eridge	d	23b58					10 00		11 00			
Crowborough	d	00s04					10 06		11 06			
Buxted	d	00s10					10 12		11 12			
Uckfield	a	00 16					10 18		11 18			

A not 22 May

b Previous night, stops to set down only

Table 184

Sundays
from 11 September

London - Oxted, East Grinstead and Uckfield

		SN 1	SN 1	SN 1	SN 1	SN 1	SN 1	SN 1	SN 1	SN 1		SN 1
London Victoria 15 ⊖175,177	d		23p24	23p49	07 34	08 34		09 34		10 34		22 34
Clapham Junction 10 175,177	d		23p30	23p56	07 40	08 40		09 40		10 40		22 40
London Bridge 4 ⊖175,177	d	23p04										
Norwood Junction 2 175,177	d	23p15										
East Croydon 175,177 ⇌	d	23p19	23p41	00 10	07 58	08 58	09 15	09 58	10 15	10 58		22 58
South Croydon 4 175	d											
Sanderstead	d	23p24	23p46	00s14	08 02	09 02		10 02		11 02		23 02
Riddlesdown	d		23p49	00s17	08 05	09 05		10 05		11 05		23 05
Upper Warlingham	d	23p29	23p53	00s21	08 09	09 09		10 09		11 09		23 09
Woldingham	d		23p57	00s25	08 13	09 13		10 13		11 13	and	23 13
Oxted 3	a	23p36	00 02	00 30	08 18	09 18	09 27	10 18	10 27	11 18	hourly	23 18
	d	23p37	00 02		08 18	09 18	09 33	10 18	10 33	11 18	until	23 18
Hurst Green	d	23p39	00 05		08 21	09 21	09 36	10 21	10 36	11 21		23 21
Lingfield	d		00 11		08 27	09 27		10 27		11 27		23 27
Dormans	d		00 14		08 30	09 30		10 30		11 30		23 30
East Grinstead	a		00 19		08 35	09 35		10 35		11 35		23 35
Edenbridge Town	d	23b45					09 42		10 42			
Hever	d						09 46		10 46			
Cowden	d						09 50		10 50			
Ashurst	d						09 54		10 54			
Eridge	d	23b58					10 00		11 00			
Crowborough	d	00s04					10 06		11 06			
Buxted	d	00s10					10 12		11 12			
Uckfield	a	00 16					10 18		11 18			

b Previous night, stops to set down only

Uckfield, East Grinstead and Oxted - London

Miles	Miles			SN MO 1	SN 1	SN 1	SN 1	SN 1	SN 1	SN 1	SN 1	SN 1	SN 1	SN 1	SN 1	SN 1	SN 1	SN 1	SN 1	SN 1	SN 1	SN 1	SN 1
—	0	**Uckfield**	d				05 45				06 34			07 08			07 34			08 04		08 34	
—	2½	Buxted	d				05 50				06 39			07 14			07 39			08 09		08 39	
—	7¼	Crowborough	d				05 57				06 46			07 21			07 46			08 16		08 46	
—	10½	Eridge	d				06 02				06 51			07 27			07 51			08 21		08 51	
—	14¼	Ashurst	d								06 56						07 56			08 26		08 56	
—	17	Cowden	d				06 10				07 01						08 01			08 31		09 01	
—	19	Hever	d								07 05						08 05			08 35		09 05	
—	20¾	Edenbridge Town	d				06 15				07 09			07 39			08 09			08 39		09 08	
0	—	**East Grinstead**	d	23p12		05 58		06 16	06 37	06 49		07 07	07 19		07 37	07 49		08 07	08 19		08 37		09 07
2¼	—	Dormans	d	23p16		06 02		06 20	06 41	06 53		07 11	07 23		07 41	07 53		08 11	08 23		08 41		09 11
4	—	Lingfield	d	23p19		06 05		06 23	06 44	06 56		07 14	07 26		07 44	07 56		08 14	08 26		08 44		09 14
8¾	—	Hurst Green	d	23p26	06 00	06 12	06 22	06 30	06 51	07 03	07 17	07 21	07 33	07 47	07 51	08 03	08 16	08 21	08 33	08 46	08 51	09 15	09 21
9¾	25	**Oxted 3**	a	23p28	06 02	06 14	06 24	06 32	06 53	07 05	07 19	07 23	07 35	07 49	07 53	08 05	08 19	08 23	08 35	08 48	08 53	09 18	09 23
—	—		d	23p28	06 03	06 15	06 25	06 32	06 54	07 06	07 20	07 24	07 36	07 50	07 54	08 06	08 20	08 24	08 36	08 50	08 53	09 19	09 23
13	—	Woldingham	d	23p34	06 08			06 38	06 59	07 11		07 29	07 41		07 59	08 11		08 29	08 41		08 59		09 29
14¾	—	Upper Warlingham	d	23p37	06 12			06 41	07 03	07 15		07 33	07 45		08 03	08 15		08 33	08 45		09 02		09 32
16½	—	Riddlesdown	d	23p41	06 15			06 45	07 06	07 18		07 36	07 48		08 06	08 18		08 36	08 48		09 06		09 36
17¾	—	Sanderstead	d	23p44	06 18			06 48	07 10	07 22		07 40	07 51		08 10	08 22		08 39	08 51		09 09		09 39
18¾	—	South Croydon 4 175	d					06 51		07 25			07 54			08 26		08 42	08 54				
19¾	0	**East Croydon** 175,177	a	23p49	06 23	06 27	06 38	06 53	07 15	07 27	07 31	07 44	07 58	08 04	08 14	08 29	08 32	08 45	08 57	09 01	09 13	09 32	09 43
—	1½	Norwood Junction 2 175,177	a																				
—	10¼	**London Bridge 4** ⊖175,177	a		06 39		06 55	07 11		07 47	07 49		08 16	08 23		08 47	08 54		09 16	09 20		09 51	
27½	—	Clapham Junction 10 175,177	a	00 02		06 38			07 27			07 55			08 26			08 55			09 26		09 55
30¼	—	**London Victoria 15** ⊖175,177	a	00 08		06 45			07 36			08 04			08 35			09 04			09 35		10 05

		SN 1	SN 1	SN 1	SN 1	SN 1	SN 1	SN 1	SN 1	SN 1	SN 1	SN 1	SN 1	SN 1	SN 1	SN 1	SN 1	SN 1	SN 1	SN 1	SN 1	SN 1	SN 1
Uckfield	d		09 34			10 34			11 34			12 34			13 34			14 34			15 34		
Buxted	d		09 39			10 39			11 39			12 39			13 39			14 39			15 39		
Crowborough	d		09 46			10 46			11 46			12 46			13 46			14 46			15 46		
Eridge	d		09 51			10 51			11 51			12 51			13 51			14 51			15 51		
Ashurst	d		09 56			10 56			11 56			12 56			13 56			14 56			15 56		
Cowden	d		10 01			11 01			12 01			13 01			14 01			15 01			16 01		
Hever	d		10 05			11 05			12 05			13 05			14 05			15 05			16 05		
Edenbridge Town	d		10 08			11 08			12 08			13 08			14 08			15 08			16 08		
East Grinstead	d	09 37		10 07	10 37		11 07	11 37		12 07	12 37		13 07	13 37		14 07	14 37		15 07	15 37		16 07	16 37
Dormans	d	09 41		10 11	10 41		11 11	11 41		12 11	12 41		13 11	13 41		14 11	14 41		15 11	15 41		16 11	16 41
Lingfield	d	09 44		10 14	10 44		11 14	11 44		12 14	12 44		13 14	13 44		14 14	14 44		15 14	15 44		16 14	16 44
Hurst Green	d	09 51	10 15	10 21	10 51	11 15	11 21	11 51	12 15	12 21	12 51	13 15	13 21	13 51	14 15	14 21	14 51	15 15	15 21	15 51	16 15	16 21	16 51
Oxted 3	a	09 53	10 17	10 23	10 53	11 17	11 23	11 53	12 17	12 23	12 53	13 17	13 23	13 53	14 17	14 23	14 53	15 17	15 23	15 53	16 17	16 23	16 53
	d	09 53	10 18	10 23	10 53	11 18	11 23	11 53	12 18	12 23	12 53	13 18	13 23	13 53	14 18	14 23	14 53	15 18	15 23	15 53	16 18	16 23	16 53
Woldingham	d	09 59		10 29	10 59		11 29	11 59		12 29	12 59		13 29	13 59		14 29	14 59		15 29	15 59		16 29	16 59
Upper Warlingham	d	10 02		10 32	11 02		11 32	12 02		12 32	13 02		13 32	14 02		14 32	15 02		15 32	16 02		16 32	17 02
Riddlesdown	d	10 06		10 36	11 06		11 36	12 06		12 36	13 06		13 36	14 06		14 36	15 06		15 36	16 06		16 36	17 06
Sanderstead	d	10 09		10 39	11 09		11 39	12 09		12 39	13 09		13 39	14 09		14 39	15 09		15 39	16 09		16 39	17 09
South Croydon 4 175	d																						
East Croydon 175,177	a	10 13	10 32	10 43	11 13	11 32	11 43	12 13	12 32	12 43	13 13	13 32	13 43	14 13	14 32	14 43	15 13	15 32	15 43	16 13	16 32	16 43	17 13
Norwood Junction 2 175,177	a																						
London Bridge 4 ⊖175,177	a		10 49			11 49			12 49			13 49			14 49			15 49			16 47		
Clapham Junction 10 175,177	a	10 25		10 55	11 25		11 55	12 25		12 55	13 25		13 55	14 25		14 55	15 25		15 55	16 25		16 55	17 25
London Victoria 15 ⊖175,177	a	10 35		11 05	11 32		12 05	12 35		13 02	13 32		14 03	14 32		15 02	15 35		16 05	16 35		17 05	17 35

		SN 1	SN 1	SN 1	SN 1	SN 1	SN 1	SN 1	SN 1	SN 1	SN 1	SN 1	SN 1	SN 1	SN 1	SN 1	SN 1	SN 1	SN 1	SN 1	SN 1	SN 1
Uckfield	d	16 33		17 03		17 32			17 58			18 30			18 57			19 33		20 04		20 34
Buxted	d	16 38		17 08		17 37			18 03			18 35			19 02			19 38		20 09		20 39
Crowborough	d	16 46		17 16		17 44			18 16			18 43			19 16			19 46		20 16		20 46
Eridge	d	16 51		17 21		17 49			18 21			18 48			19 21			19 51		20 21		20 51
Ashurst	d	16 56				17 54						18 53			19 26			19 56				20 56
Cowden	d	17 01				17 59						18 57			19 31			20 01				21 01
Hever	d	17 05				18 03						19 01			19 35			20 05				21 05
Edenbridge Town	d	17 08		17 34		18 06			18 34			19 05			19 38			20 08		20 33		21 08
East Grinstead	d		17 07		17 37		18 07	18 17		18 37	18 47		19 07	19 17		19 37	19 47		20 07		20 37	
Dormans	d		17 11		17 41		18 11	18 21		18 41	18 51		19 11	19 21		19 41	19 51		20 11		20 41	
Lingfield	d		17 14		17 44		18 14	18 24		18 44	18 54		19 14	19 24		19 44	19 54		20 14		20 44	
Hurst Green	d	17 15	17 21	17 40	17 51	18 13	18 21	18 31	18 40	18 51	19 01	19 11	19 21	19 31	19 45	19 51	20 01	20 15	20 21	20 39	20 51	21 15
Oxted 3	a	17 17	17 23	17 43	17 53	18 15	18 23	18 33	18 43	18 53	19 03	19 14	19 23	19 33	19 47	19 53	20 03	20 17	20 23	20 42	20 53	21 17
	d	17 18	17 23		17 53	18 20	18 23	18 34		18 53	19 04	19 18	19 23	19 34	19 48	19 53	20 04	20 18	20 23	20 42	20 53	21 18
Woldingham	d		17 29		17 59		18 29	18 39		18 59	19 09		19 29	19 39		19 59	20 09		20 29		20 59	
Upper Warlingham	d		17 32		18 02		18 32	18 43		19 02	19 13		19 32	19 43		20 02	20 13		20 32		21 02	
Riddlesdown	d		17 36		18 06		18 36	18 46		19 06	19 16		19 36	19 46		20 06	20 16		20 36		21 06	
Sanderstead	d		17 39		18 09		18 39	18 49		19 09	19 19		19 39	19 49		20 09	20 19		20 39		21 09	
South Croydon 4 175	d																					
East Croydon 175,177	a	17 35	17 43		18 13	18 35	18 43	18 56		19 13	19 25	19 31	19 43	19 55	20 06	20 13	20 25	20 30	20 43	20 54	21 13	21 30
Norwood Junction 2 175,177	a							19 01														
London Bridge 4 ⊖175,177	a	17 52				18 50		19 15				19 49			20 21			20 48		21 09		21 49
Clapham Junction 10 175,177	a		17 55		18 25		18 55			19 25			19 55			20 25			20 55		21 25	
London Victoria 15 ⊖175,177	a		18 05		18 35		19 05			19 32			20 02			20 32			21 05		21 35	

Table 184

Mondays to Fridays

Uckfield, East Grinstead and Oxted - London

		SN 1	SN 1	SN 1	SN 1	SN 1	SN 1	SN 1
Uckfield	d			21 34				22 34
Buxted	d			21 39				22 39
Crowborough	d			21 46				22 46
Eridge	d			21 51				22 51
Ashurst	d			21 56				
Cowden	d			22 01				
Hever	d			22 05				
Edenbridge Town	d			22 08				23 04
East Grinstead	d	21 07	21 37		22 07	22 37	22 54	
Dormans	d	21 11	21 41		22 11	22 41		
Lingfield	d	21 14	21 44		22 14	22 44		
Hurst Green	d	21 21	21 51	22 15	22 21	22 51		23 10
Oxted 3	a	21 23	21 53	22 17	22 23	22 53	23 06	23 13
	d	21 23	21 53	22 18	22 23	22 53	23 07	23 13
Woldingham	d	21 29	21 59		22 29	22 59		
Upper Warlingham	d	21 32	22 02		22 32	23 02		
Riddlesdown	d	21 36	22 06		22 36	23 06		
Sanderstead	d	21 39	22 09		22 39	23 09		
South Croydon 4 175	d							
East Croydon 175,177	a	21 43	22 13	22 33	22 43	23 13	23 19	23 28
Norwood Junction 2 175,177	a							
London Bridge 4 ⊖175,177	a			22 49				
Clapham Junction 10 175,177	a	21 55	22 25		22 55	23 25	23 32	
London Victoria 15 ⊖175,177	a	22 05	22 35		23 05	23 35	23 40	

Saturdays

		SN 1	SN 1	SN 1	SN 1	SN 1	SN 1	SN 1	SN 1		SN 1	SN 1	SN 1	SN 1	SN 1	SN 1	SN 1	SN 1	SN 1	SN 1	SN 1	SN 1
Uckfield	d		06 34			07 34			08 34		18 34			19 34			20 34			21 34		
Buxted	d		06 39			07 39			08 39		18 39			19 39			20 39			21 39		
Crowborough	d		06 46			07 46			08 46		18 46			19 46			20 46			21 46		
Eridge	d		06 51			07 51			08 51		18 51			19 51			20 51			21 51		
Ashurst	d		06 56			07 56			08 56		18 56			19 56			20 56			21 56		
Cowden	d		07 01			08 01			09 01		19 01			20 01			21 01			22 01		
Hever	d		07 05			08 05			09 05		19 05			20 05			21 05			22 05		
Edenbridge Town	d		07 08			08 08			09 08	and at	19 08			20 08			21 08			22 08		
East Grinstead	d	06 37		07 07	07 37		08 07	08 37		the same		19 07	19 37		20 07	20 37		21 07	21 37		22 07	22 37
Dormans	d	06 41		07 11	07 41		08 11	08 41		minutes		19 11	19 41		20 11	20 41		21 11	21 41		22 11	22 41
Lingfield	d	06 44		07 14	07 44		08 14	08 44		past		19 14	19 44		20 14	20 44		21 14	21 44		22 14	22 44
Hurst Green	d	06 51	07 15	07 21	07 51	08 15	08 21	08 51	09 15	each	19 15	19 21	19 51	20 15	20 21	20 51	21 15	21 21	21 51	22 15	22 21	22 51
Oxted 3	a	06 53	07 18	07 23	07 53	08 18	08 23	08 53	09 17	hour until	19 17	19 23	19 53	20 17	20 23	20 53	21 17	21 23	21 53	22 17	22 23	22 53
	d	06 53	07 19	07 23	07 53	08 19	08 23	08 53	09 18		19 18	19 23	19 53	20 18	20 23	20 53	21 18	21 23	21 53	22 18	22 23	22 53
Woldingham	d	06 59		07 29	07 59		08 29	08 59				19 29	19 59		20 29	20 59		21 29	21 59		22 29	22 59
Upper Warlingham	d	07 02		07 32	08 02		08 32	09 02				19 32	20 02		20 32	21 02		21 32	22 02		22 32	23 02
Riddlesdown	d	07 06		07 36	08 06		08 36	09 06				19 36	20 06		20 36	21 06		21 36	22 06		22 36	23 06
Sanderstead	d	07 09		07 39	08 09		08 39	09 09				19 39	20 09		20 39	21 09		21 39	22 09		22 39	23 09
South Croydon 4 175	d																					
East Croydon 175,177	a	07 13	07 33	07 43	08 13	08 32	08 43	09 13	09 32		19 32	19 43	20 13	20 32	20 43	21 13	21 32	21 43	22 13	22 32	22 43	23 13
Norwood Junction 2 175,177	a																					
London Bridge 4 ⊖175,177	a		07 49			08 49			09 49		19 49			20 49			21 49			22 49		
Clapham Junction 10 175,177	a	07 25		07 55	08 25		08 55	09 25				19 55	20 25		20 55	21 25		21 55	22 25		22 55	23 25
London Victoria 15 ⊖175,177	a	07 32		08 02	08 32		09 02	09 32				20 05	20 32		21 02	21 32		22 02	22 35		23 05	23 35

		SN 1
Uckfield	d	22 34
Buxted	d	22 39
Crowborough	d	22 46
Eridge	d	22 51
Ashurst	d	
Cowden	d	
Hever	d	
Edenbridge Town	d	23 04
East Grinstead	d	
Dormans	d	
Lingfield	d	
Hurst Green	d	23 10
Oxted 3	a	23 13
	d	23 13
Woldingham	d	
Upper Warlingham	d	
Riddlesdown	d	
Sanderstead	d	
South Croydon 4 175	d	
East Croydon 175,177	a	23 26
Norwood Junction 2 175,177	a	
London Bridge 4 ⊖175,177	a	
Clapham Junction 10 175,177	a	
London Victoria 15 ⊖175,177	a	

Table 184

Sundays
until 4 September

Uckfield, East Grinstead and Oxted - London

		SN 1	SN 1	SN 1	SN 1		SN 1	SN 1	SN 1	SN 1
Uckfield	d				10 32		21 32		22 32	
Buxted	d				10 37		21 37		22 37	
Crowborough	d				10 44		21 44		22 44	
Eridge	d				10 49		21 49		22 49	
Ashurst	d				10 54		21 54		22 54	
Cowden	d				10 59		21 59		22 59	
Hever	d				11 03		22 03		23 03	
Edenbridge Town	d				11 06	and at	22 06		23 06	
East Grinstead	d	08 12	09 12	10 12		the same		22 12		23 12
Dormans	d	08 16	09 16	10 16		minutes		22 16		23 16
Lingfield	d	08 19	09 19	10 19		past		22 19		23 19
Hurst Green	d	08 26	09 26	10 26	11 13	each	22 13	22 26	23 13	23 26
Oxted 3	a	08 28	09 28	10 28	11 16	hour until	22 16	22 28	23 16	23 28
	d	08 28	09 28	10 28				22 28	23 17	23 28
Woldingham	d	08 34	09 34	10 34				22 34		23 34
Upper Warlingham	d	08 37	09 37	10 37				22 37		23 37
Riddlesdown	d	08 41	09 41	10 41				22 41		23 41
Sanderstead	d	08 44	09 44	10 44				22 44		23 44
South Croydon 4 175	d									
East Croydon 175,177 ⇌	a	08 49	09 49	10 49				22 49	23 29	23 49
Norwood Junction 2 175,177	a									
London Bridge 4 ⊖175,177	a									
Clapham Junction 10 175,177	a	09 02	10 02	11 02				23 02		00 02
London Victoria 15 ⊖175,177	a	09 09	10 09	11 09				23 09		00 08

Sundays
from 11 September

		SN 1	SN 1	SN 1	SN 1		SN 1	SN 1	SN 1	SN 1
Uckfield	d				10 32		21 32		22 32	
Buxted	d				10 37		21 37		22 37	
Crowborough	d				10 44		21 44		22 44	
Eridge	d				10 49		21 49		22 49	
Ashurst	d				10 54		21 54		22 54	
Cowden	d				10 59		21 59		22 59	
Hever	d				11 03		22 03		23 03	
Edenbridge Town	d				11 06	and at	22 06		23 06	
East Grinstead	d	08 12	09 12	10 12		the same		22 12		23 12
Dormans	d	08 16	09 16	10 16		minutes		22 16		23 16
Lingfield	d	08 19	09 19	10 19		past		22 19		23 19
Hurst Green	d	08 26	09 26	10 26	11 13	each	22 13	22 26	23 13	23 26
Oxted 3	a	08 28	09 28	10 28	11 16	hour until	22 16	22 28	23 16	23 28
	d	08 28	09 28	10 28				22 28	23 17	23 28
Woldingham	d	08 34	09 34	10 34				22 34		23 34
Upper Warlingham	d	08 37	09 37	10 37				22 37		23 37
Riddlesdown	d	08 41	09 41	10 41				22 41		23 41
Sanderstead	d	08 44	09 44	10 44				22 44		23 44
South Croydon 4 175	d									
East Croydon 175,177 ⇌	a	08 49	09 49	10 49				22 49	23 29	23 49
Norwood Junction 2 175,177	a									
London Bridge 4 ⊖175,177	a									
Clapham Junction 10 175,177	a	09 01	10 01	11 01				23 01		00 02
London Victoria 15 ⊖175,177	a	09 08	10 08	11 08				23 08		00 08

Network Diagram for Tables 186, 188

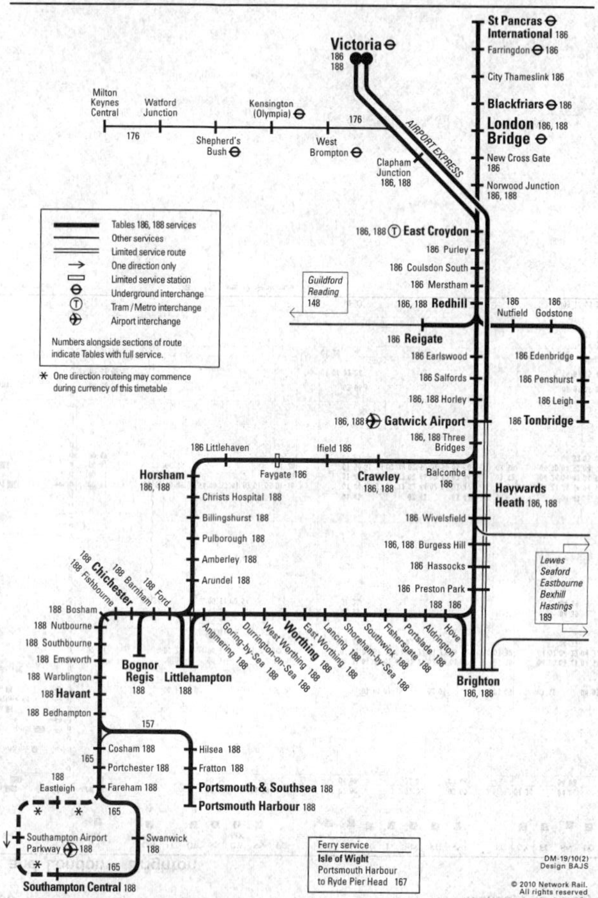

Bedford and London - Brighton

Miles	Miles	Miles			SN MX ◇1	SN MO 1	SN MX ◇1	FC 1 A	FC MX 1	FC 1 B	SN MX 1	SN MX ◇1	SN MO 1	SN MX 1	SN MO ◇1	GX 1	SN MX 1	SN MX ◇1	SN MO ◇1	FC 1	GX 1	SN MX 1	SN 1
0	—	—	**London Victoria** 15 ⊖	d	23p02	23p04	23p06				23p10	23p17			23p17	23p30		23p32	23p32		23p45	23p47	00 02
2¾	50¾	6¼	Clapham Junction 10	d	23p08	23p10	23p12				23p16	23p23			23p23			23p38	23p38			23p53	
—	—	—	**Bedford**	d																			
—	—	—	Luton 10	d																			
—	—	—	Luton Airport Parkway 7 ✈	d																			
—	—	—	St Albans City	d																			
—	—	—	St Pancras International 15 ⊖	d																			
—	—	—	Farringdon 3 ⊖	d																			
—	—	—	City Thameslink 3	d																			
—	—	—	**London Blackfriars** 3 ⊖	d																			
—	0	—	**London Bridge** 4 ⊖	d				23p12	23p12	23p12										23p42			
—	—	—	New Cross Gate	d																			
—	9	—	Norwood Junction 2	d																			
10½	10¼	—	**East Croydon**	a	23p19	23p22	23p22	23p24	23p24	23p27	23p27	23p33			23p37			23p51	23p52	23p56		00 05	
—	—	—		d	23p20	23p22	23p23	23p24	23p25	23p27	23p28	23p33			23p38			23p52	23p53	23p57		00 06	
13½	—	—	Purley 4	d		23p29					23p33											00 12	
15½	—	—	Coulsdon South	d		23p33					23p37											00 15	
19	—	—	Merstham	d		23p38					23p42											00 21	
21	0	0	**Redhill**	a	23p31	23p42					23p46							00 03	00 05			00 24	
—	—	—		d	23p31	23p42					23p46						23p55	00 05	00 05			00 25	
—	1¾	—	**Reigate**	a																			
—	—	2	Nutfield	d																			
—	—	5¾	Godstone	d																			
—	—	10½	Edenbridge	d													00 06						
—	—	15½	Penshurst	d																			
—	—	17¼	Leigh (Kent)	d																			
—	—	19¾	**Tonbridge** 4	a													00 15						
21¾	—	—	Earlswood (Surrey)	d							23p49												
23¾	—	—	Salfords	d							23p52												
26	—	—	Horley 4	d		23p50					23p56		←	←								00 31	
26¾	—	—	**Gatwick Airport** 10 ✈	a	23p38	23p54		23p41	23p40	23p48	23p58	23p50	23p54	23p58	23p59	00 05		00 14	00 14	00 18	00 20	00 33	00 37
—	—	—		d	23p39	23p55		23p41	23p41	23p50	23p59	23p51	23p55	23p59	00 01			00 15	00 15	00 19		00 34	
29½	0	—	Three Bridges 15	a	23p44	→		23p47	23p47	23p54	→	23p55	00 01	00 04	00 05			00 20	00 19	00 24		00 39	
—	—	—		d	23p44			23p47	23p47	23p54		23p56	00 01	00 04	00 06			00 20	00 20			00 39	
—	1½	—	Crawley	d									00 05	00 07								00 43	
—	2¾	—	Ifield	d									00 07	00 10								00 46	
—	5¼	—	Faygate	d																			
—	7½	—	Littlehaven	d									00 14	00 16								00 52	
—	8½	—	**Horsham** 4	a									00 17	00 19								00 55	
34	—	—	Balcombe	d					23p53									00 26	00 26				
38	—	—	**Haywards Heath**	a	23p52		23p46	23p56	23p58	00 03		00 04			00 14			00 31	00 31				
—	—	—		d	23p53		23p46	23p56	23p59	00 03		00 05			00 15			00 31	00 31				
41	0	—	Wivelsfield	d	23p57				00 03									00 35	00 35				
—	9¼	—	Lewes 4	a																			
41¾	—	—	Burgess Hill 4	d	23p59			00 02	00 05	00 08		00 10			00 20			00 37	00 37				
43¾	—	—	Hassocks 4	d	00 02			00 06	00 08	00 12								00 41	00 41				
49½	0	—	Preston Park	d	00 09				00 15									00 48	00 48				
—	1½	—	Hove 2	a								00 21			00 31								
51	—	—	Brighton 10	a	00 15		00 01	00 15	00 20	00 22								00 52	00 52				

A MO until 5 September

B MO from 12 September

Bedford and London - Brighton

Station		SN MX ◇1		GW 1 A	FC	GW 1 B	SN 1	GW MX 1	SN 1	FC		SN MX ◇1	SN ◇1	FC 1	FC 1	SN 1	FC 1	SN 1		FC	GX 1	FC 1	SN ◇1	FC 1
London Victoria 15 ⊖	d	00 05					00 14		00 30				01 00			02 00		03 00			03 30		04 00	
Clapham Junction 10	d	00 11					00 20						01 08			02 08		03 08					04 08	
Bedford	d																							
Luton 10	d																							
Luton Airport Parkway 7 ✈	d																							
St Albans City	d																							
St Pancras International 15 ⊖	d																							
Farringdon 3 ⊖	d																							
City Thameslink 3	d																							
London Blackfriars 3 ⊖	d																							
London Bridge 4 ⊖	d				00 12					00 42				01 05	01 35		02 05			03 05		03 35		04 05
New Cross Gate	d																							
Norwood Junction 2	d																							
East Croydon	a	00 24			00 26		00 31			00 56			01 21	01 32	02 02	02 21	02 30	03 21		03 30		04 00	04 21	04 30
	d	00 24			00 27		00 32			00 57			01 22	01 32	02 02	02 22	02 32	03 22		03 32		04 02	04 22	04 32
Purley 4	d						00 37						01 27			02 27		03 27					04 27	
Coulsdon South	d						00 41																	
Merstham	d						00 47																	
Redhill	a						00 50						01 35										04 35	
	d			00 34		00 46	00 51	00 54					01 36										04 35	
Reigate	a																							
Nutfield	d																							
Godstone	d																							
Edenbridge	d																							
Penshurst	d																							
Leigh (Kent)	d																							
Tonbridge 4	a																							
Earlswood (Surrey)	d																							
Salfords	d																							
Horley 4	d						00 57						01 42			02 42		03 42					04 43	
Gatwick Airport 10 ✈	a	00 41		00 41	00 49	00 54	00 59	01 03	01 05	01 18			01 44	01 51	02 21	02 44	02 51	03 44		03 51	04 05	04 24	04 46	04 51
	d	00 42			00 50					01 22			01 46	01 52	02 22	02 46	02 52	03 46		03 52		04 24	04 47	04 52
Three Bridges 15	a	00 47			00 55					01 28			01 50	01 58	02 28	02 50	02 58	03 50		03 58		04 30	04 52	04 58
	d	00 47											01 52										04 52	05 00
Crawley	d																							
Ifield	d																							
Faygate	d																							
Littlehaven	d																							
Horsham 4	a																							
Balcombe	d																							
Haywards Heath	a	00 58											02 06										05 01	05 09
	d	01 02	01 06									01 06	02 06										05 01	05 10
Wivelsfield	d																							
Lewes 4	a		01 20									01 20												
Burgess Hill 4	d																							05 15
Hassocks 4	d																							05 18
Preston Park	d																							
Hove 2	a																							
Brighton 10	a	01s16											02 23										05 16	05 29

A MO from 19 September

B MO until 12 September

Bedford and London - Brighton

Station		SN 1	FC 1		GX 1	SN 1	SN ◇1	SN	GW 1	SN 1	SN		FC 1	SN 1	GX 1	SN ◇1	FC 1	GX	SN ◇1		FC 1	GX 1	GW 1	GW 1	SN 1
London Victoria 15 ⊖	d	04 30			05 00		05 02	05 15							05 30	05 32		05 45				06 00			
Clapham Junction 10	d						05 08									05 38									
Bedford	d												03 42				04 10				04 20				
Luton 10	d												04 06				04 34				04 44				
Luton Airport Parkway 7 ✈	d												04 08				04 36				04 46				
St Albans City	d												04 20				04 48				04 58				
St Pancras International 15 ⊖	d												04 54				05 12				05 32				
Farringdon 3 ⊖	d												04 59				05 17				05 37				
City Thameslink 3	d																05 21				05 41				
London Blackfriars 3 ⊖	d												05 04				05 24				05 44				
London Bridge 4 ⊖	d		04 35														05 30				05 50				
New Cross Gate	d																								
Norwood Junction 2	d																								
East Croydon	a		05 00				05 20						05 30			05 48	05 51				06 04				
	d		05 02				05 20						05 32			05 49	05 52				06 06				
Purley 4	d						05 25									05 54									
Coulsdon South	d						05 28									05 58									
Merstham	d						05 34									06 03									
Redhill	a						05 37									06 07									
	d					05 35	05 38		05 44	05 56						06 07							06 24	06 36	06 39
Reigate	a																						06 28		06 43
Nutfield	d					05 39				06 00															
Godstone	d					05 45				06 06															
Edenbridge	d					05 50				06 11															
Penshurst	d					05 57				06 18															
Leigh (Kent)	d					06 00				06 21															
Tonbridge 4	a					06 05				06 26															
Earlswood (Surrey)	d															06 10									
Salfords	d															06 13									
Horley 4	d						05 44									06 17			←						
Gatwick Airport 10 ✈	a	05 05	05 21		05 35		05 46	05 50	05 54				05 53		06 00	06 19	06 09	06 15	06 19		06 21	06 30		06 46	
	d		05 22				05 47						05 54	05 56		06 20	06 10		06 20		06 22				
Three Bridges 15	a		05 26				05 52						05 59	06 00		→	06 14		06 25		06 27				
	d		05 27				05 52						06 00	06 01			06 14		06 25		06 27				
Crawley	d													06 05											
Ifield	d													06 07											
Faygate	d																								
Littlehaven	d													06 14											
Horsham 4	a													06 17											
Balcombe	d						05 58										06 20				06 34				
Haywards Heath	a		05 35				06 03						06 09				06 25		06 33		06 39				
	d		05 36				06 04				06 07		06 10				06 26		06 34		06 40				
Wivelsfield	d		05 40				06 08				06 11		06 14				06 30		06 38		06 44				
Lewes 4	a										06 22								06 49						
Burgess Hill 4	d		05 42				06 10						06 16				06 32				06 46				
Hassocks 4	d		05 45				06 13						06 19				06 35				06 49				
Preston Park	d		05 52				06 20						06 26				06 42				06 56				
Hove 2	a																								
Brighton 10	a		05 57				06 26						06 33				06 47				07 00				

Bedford and London - Brighton

		SN ◇1		GX 1	FC 1	SN ◇1	SN 1	SN 1	SN ◇1		GX 1	SN ◇1	SN ◇1	FC 1	GX 1	SN ◇1	SN ◇1	SN ◇1	SN 1	GW 1
London Victoria 15 ⊖	d	06 02		06 15					06 21		06 30		06 32		06 45	06 47		06 32		
Clapham Junction 10	d	06 08							06 27				06 38			06 53		06 38		
Bedford	d				05 00									05 20						
Luton 10	d				05 24									05 44						
Luton Airport Parkway 7 ✈	d				05 26									05 46						
St Albans City	d				05 38									05 58						
St Pancras International 15 ⊖	d				06 02									06 22						
Farringdon 3 ⊖	d				06 07									06 27						
City Thameslink 3	d				06 11									06 31						
London Blackfriars 3 ⊖	d				06 14									06 34						
London Bridge 4 ⊖	d				06 20									06 42						
New Cross Gate	d																			
Norwood Junction 2	d																			
East Croydon	a	06 17			06 35				06 38				06 48	06 55		07 03		06 48		
	d	06 18			06 36				06 39				06 49	06 56		07 03		06 49		
Purley 4	d	06 23							06 44				06 54					06 54		
Coulsdon South	d	06 26											06 57					06 57		
Merstham	d	06 32											07 03					07 03		
Redhill	a	06 35							06 52				07 06					07 06		
	d	06 39	06 41					07 00	06 56	07 03			07 07					07 07		07 28
Reigate	a							07 04												07 32
Nutfield	d		06 45							07 07										
Godstone	d		06 51							07 13										
Edenbridge	d		06 56							07 18										
Penshurst	d		07 03							07 25										
Leigh (Kent)	d		07 06							07 28										
Tonbridge 4	a		07 11							07 33										
Earlswood (Surrey)	d	06 41											07 09					07 09		
Salfords	d	06 45											07 13					07 13		
Horley 4	d	06 48				←			07 02			←	07 16				←	07 16	←	
Gatwick Airport 10 ✈	a	06 54		06 43	06 51	06 54			07 04		06 59	07 04	07 19	07 11	07 16	07 18	07 19	07 19	07 16	
	d	06 55		06 48	06 52	06 55			07 05		07 04	07 05	07 20	07 12	07 25	07 19	07 20	07 20	07 25	
Three Bridges 15	a	→			06 57	06 59			→			07 10	→	07 17	→	07 24	07 24	→		
	d				06 57	07 00						07 11		07 17		07 24	07 28			
Crawley	d					07 03														
Ifield	d																			
Faygate	d																			
Littlehaven	d																			
Horsham 4	a					07 11														
Balcombe	d											07 17					07 35			
Haywards Heath	a			06 58	07 05						07 14	07 22		07 26		07 32	07 40			
	d			07 00	07 06		07 10				07 16	07 22		07 26		07 33	07 40			
Wivelsfield	d				07 10		07 14					07 26		07 30		07 37	07 44			
Lewes 4	a						07 29									07 52				
Burgess Hill 4	d				07 12							07 28		07 32			07 46			
Hassocks 4	d				07 15							07 32		07 36			07 50			
Preston Park	d				07 22							07 39		07 43			07 57			
Hove 2	a																			
Brighton 10	a			07 13	07 27						07 33	07 43		07 47			08 01		07 53	

Bedford and London - Brighton

		SN 1		GX 1	FC 1	SN 1	SN 1	GX 1	FC 1	GW 1	SN ◇1	GX 1	SN 1	SN 1	SN 1	SN 1	FC 1	GX 1	SN ◇1	SN 1	SN 1
London Victoria 15 ⊖	d	06 51		07 00			07 02	07 15			07 17	07 30				07 36		07 45	07 47		
Clapham Junction 10	d	06 57					07 08				07 23					07 42			07 53		
Bedford	d				05 40				05 58								06 22				
Luton 10	d				06 04				06 22								06 46				
Luton Airport Parkway 7 ✈	d				06 06				06 24								06 48				
St Albans City	d				06 18				06 36								07 00				
St Pancras International 15 ⊖	d				06 38				06 58								07 20				
Farringdon 3 ⊖	d				06 43				07 03								07 25				
City Thameslink 3	d				06 47				07 05								07 29				
London Blackfriars 3 ⊖	d				06 50				07 08								07 32				
London Bridge 4 ⊖	d				07 00				07 16					07 30	07 33		07 42				
New Cross Gate	d														07 38						
Norwood Junction 2	d													07 42							
East Croydon	a	07 06			07 14		07 17		07 30		07 33			07 45	07 48	07 52	07 55		08 03		
	d	07 07			07 15		07 18		07 31		07 34			07 46	07 49	07 52	07 56		08 03		
Purley 4	d						07 23									07 57					
Coulsdon South	d	07 13					07 26							07 52		08 01					
Merstham	d	07 19					07 32							07 58		08 07					
Redhill	a	07 22					07 35				07 46			08 01		08 10					
	d	07 27	07 29				07 40			07 41	07 47		08 00	08 02		08 11					08 17
Reigate	a						07 44						08 04								08 21
Nutfield	d		07 33											08 06							
Godstone	d		07 39											08 12							
Edenbridge	d		07 44											08 17							
Penshurst	d		07 51											08 24							
Leigh (Kent)	d		07 54											08 27							
Tonbridge 4	a		08 02											08 32							
Earlswood (Surrey)	d	07 29									07 49					08 13					
Salfords	d	07 33									07 53					08 17					
Horley 4	d	07 36				←					07 56					08 21				←	
Gatwick Airport 10 ✈	a	07 39		07 30	07 31	07 39		07 45	07 46	07 50	07 59	08 02			08 04	08 23	08 10	08 15	08 18	08 23	
	d	07 40			07 32	07 40			07 47		08 00				08 05	08 24	08 11		08 19	08 24	
Three Bridges 15	a	→			07 36	07 44			07 52		08 04				08 09	→	08 15			08 29	
	d				07 37	07 45			07 52		08 05				08 10		08 15			08 30	
Crawley	d					07 49					08 09									08 34	
Ifield	d					07 52					08 11									08 36	
Faygate	d										08 15									08 40	
Littlehaven	d					07 58					08 19									08 44	
Horsham 4	a					08 01					08 22									08 48	
Balcombe	d								07 58								08 21				
Haywards Heath	a				07 45				08 03						08 19		08 27		08 30		
	d				07 46				08 04						08 19		08 27		08 31		
Wivelsfield	d				07 50				08 08								08 31		08 35		
Lewes 4	a																		08 50		
Burgess Hill 4	d				07 52				08 10						08 25		08 33				
Hassocks 4	d				07 55				08 13								08 36				
Preston Park	d								08 20								08 43				
Hove 2	a																				
Brighton 10	a				08 05				08 25						08 36		08 48				

Bedford and London - Brighton

		SN		SN	SN	SN	SN	GW	SN	SN	FC	GX	SN		FC	SN	GW	SN		SN	SN	SN
		1		◇1	1	1	◇1	1	1	◇1	1	1	◇1		1	1	1	1		◇1	1	◇1
																						A
						⌶						⌶									⌶	⌶
London Victoria 15 ⊖	d			07 52		08 00	08 02			08 07		08 15	08 17							08 21	08 30	08 32
Clapham Junction 10	d			07 58			08 08			08 13			08 23							08 27		08 38
Bedford	d										06 56				07 00							
Luton 10	d										07 16				07 24							
Luton Airport Parkway 7 ✈	d														07 26							
St Albans City	d										07 28				07 38							
St Pancras International 15 ⊖	d										07 48				08 00							
Farringdon 3 ⊖	d										07 53				08 05							
City Thameslink 3	d										07 57				08 07							
London Blackfriars 3 ⊖	d										08 00				08 10							
London Bridge 4 ⊖	d	07 53							08 02						08 18			08 23				
New Cross Gate	d								08 07													
Norwood Junction 2	d								08 15													
East Croydon	a	08 06		08 09			08 18		08 19	08 22	08 25		08 33		08 36			08 37		08 39		08 48
	d	08 06		08 09			08 18		08 19	08 23	08 26		08 33		08 37			08 38		08 40		08 48
Purley 4	d								08 25													
Coulsdon South	d								08 28									08 47				
Merstham	d								08 34													
Redhill	a	08 17					08 30		08 37									08 54				09 02
	d	08 21	08 23				08 30	08 33	08 41								08 50	08 58	09 00			09 03
Reigate	a							08 37											09 04			
Nutfield	d		08 27															09 02				
Godstone	d		08 33															09 08				
Edenbridge	d		08 38															09 13				
Penshurst	d		08 45															09 20				
Leigh (Kent)	d		08 48															09 23				
Tonbridge 4	a		08 53															09 28				
Earlswood (Surrey)	d								08 43													
Salfords	d								08 47													
Horley 4	d				←				08 50							←						
Gatwick Airport 10 ✈	a	08 28		08 24	08 28	08 30	08 37		08 53		08 40	08 45	08 48		08 51	08 53	08 59			08 55	09 00	09 10
	d	08 29		08 25	08 29		08 40		08 54		08 41		08 49		08 52	08 54				08 56		09 11
Three Bridges 15	a	→			08 33		08 44		→	08 41	08 45				08 57	08 59				09 00		09 16
	d				08 34		08 45			08 42	08 45				08 57	08 59				09 01		09 16
Crawley	d						08 48									09 03						09 19
Ifield	d															09 06						
Faygate	d															09 10						
Littlehaven	d															09 14						
Horsham 4	a						08 56									09 17						09 27
Balcombe	d										08 51											
Haywards Heath	a			08 36	08 42					08 50	08 57		09 00		09 07					09 12		
	d			08 37	08 43					08 51	08 57		09 04	09 10	09 08					09 21		
Wivelsfield	d				08 47						09 01			09 14						09 25		
Lewes 4	a													09 25								
Burgess Hill 4	d				08 49						09 03		09 09		09 13					09 27		
Hassocks 4	d				08 52						09 06									09 30		
Preston Park	d				08 59						09 13		09 18							09 37		
Hove 2	a			08 53									09 21									
Brighton 10	a				09 03					09 06	09 18				09 25					09 41		

A ⌶ to Crawley

Table 186 Mondays to Fridays

Bedford and London - Brighton

		SN	SN	FC	GX	SN	SN		SN	SN	SN	SN	GW	SN	SN	FC	GX	GW	SN	SN		SN
		1	◇1	1	1	1	◇1		◇1	1	1	◇1	1	1	◇1	1	1	1	1	◇1		1
							A					B								C		
			⌶		⌶		⌶				⌶	⌶			⌶		⌶			⌶		
London Victoria 15 ⊖	d		08 36		08 45		08 47		08 51		09 00	09 02			09 06		09 15			09 17		
Clapham Junction 10	d		08 43				08 53					09 08			09 12					09 23		
Bedford	d			07 28												07 48						
Luton 10	d			07 48												08 12						
Luton Airport Parkway 7 ✈	d															08 14						
St Albans City	d			08 00												08 26						
St Pancras International 15 ⊖	d			08 20												08 48						
Farringdon 3 ⊖	d			08 25												08 53						
City Thameslink 3	d			08 29												08 57						
London Blackfriars 3 ⊖	d			08 32												09 00						
London Bridge 4 ⊖	d	08 32				08 45								09 03		09 12			09 15			
New Cross Gate	d	08 37												09 08								
Norwood Junction 2	d	08 45				08 56								09 16					09 26			
East Croydon	a	08 49	08 52	08 56		08 59	09 03		09 07			09 18		09 20	09 22	09 24			09 30	09 33		
	d	08 51	08 53	08 56		09 00	09 03		09 08			09 19		09 21	09 23	09 25			09 30	09 33		
Purley 4	d	08 59				09 06								09 27					09 36			
Coulsdon South	d	09 02				09 09								09 30					09 39			
Merstham	d	09 08												09 36					09 45			
Redhill	a	09 12				09 16						09 30		09 39					09 48			
	d	09 12				09 17						09 30	09 34	09 40				09 51	09 53			
Reigate	a												09 38						09 57			
Nutfield	d					09 21																
Godstone	d					09 27																
Edenbridge	d					09 32																
Penshurst	d					09 39																
Leigh (Kent)	d					09 42																
Tonbridge 4	a					09 47																
Earlswood (Surrey)	d	09 15												09 42								
Salfords	d	09 18												09 46								
Horley 4	d	09 22								←		09 36		09 50								←
Gatwick Airport 10 ✈	a	09 24		09 11	09 15		09 18		09 22	09 24	09 30	09 39		09 53		09 40	09 45	09 59		09 48		09 53
	d	09 25		09 13			09 19		09 23	09 25		09 40		09 54		09 41				09 49		09 54
Three Bridges 15	a	→		09 17						09 30		09 44		→		09 45						09 59
	d			09 17						09 30		09 45				09 45						10 00
Crawley	d									09 34		09 48										10 03
Ifield	d									09 36												10 06
Faygate	d																					
Littlehaven	d									09 43												10 12
Horsham 4	a									09 46		09 56										10 15
Balcombe	d															09 51						
Haywards Heath	a			09 26			09 30									09 56				10 00		
	d			09 26			09 35	09 37								09 57				10 05	10 07	
Wivelsfield	d			09 30												10 01					10 11	
Lewes 4	a						09 53														10 22	
Burgess Hill 4	d			09 33					09 38							10 03				10 10		
Hassocks 4	d			09 36					09 41							10 06						
Preston Park	d			09 43												10 13				10 19		
Hove 2	a							09 53												10 22		
Brighton 10	a		09 28	09 48					09 52						09 58	10 18						

A ⌶ to Haywards Heath B ⌶ to Crawley C ⌶ to Gatwick Airport

Bedford and London - Brighton

		FC 1	GX 1 ⌶	SN ◇1 A ⌶	SN 1	SN ◇1	FC 1	SN 1 ⌶	SN 1	SN ◇1 B ⌶		SN ◇1	SN 1	FC 1	SN 1 ⌶	SN ◇1 A ⌶	GW 1	GW 1	SN 1	SN ◇1 ⌶	FC 1	GX 1 ⌶
London Victoria 15 ⊖	d		09 30	09 32		09 36		09 45		09 47		09 51			10 00	10 02				10 06		10 15
Clapham Junction 10	d			09 38		09 42				09 53						10 08				10 12		
Bedford	d	08 04					08 24							08 40							08 54	
Luton 10	d	08 28					08 48							09 04							09 18	
Luton Airport Parkway 7 ✈	d	08 30					08 50							09 06							09 20	
St Albans City	d	08 44					09 04							09 18							09 32	
St Pancras International 15 ⊖	d	09 04					09 24							09 40							09 54	
Farringdon 3 ⊖	d	09 09					09 29							09 44							09 59	
City Thameslink 3	d	09 13					09 32							09 47							10 02	
London Blackfriars 3 ⊖	d	09 16					09 34							09 50							10 05	
London Bridge 4 ⊖	d	09 27			09 32		09 42		09 45					09 57					10 03		10 12	
New Cross Gate	d				09 37														10 08			
Norwood Junction 2	d				09 45				09 56										10 16			
East Croydon	a	09 39		09 48	09 49	09 52	09 54		10 00	10 03		10 07		10 09		10 18			10 20	10 22	10 24	
	d	09 41		09 48	09 51	09 53	09 55		10 00	10 03		10 08		10 11		10 18			10 21	10 23	10 25	
Purley 4	d				09 57				10 06										10 27			
Coulsdon South	d				10 00				10 09										10 30			
Merstham	d				10 06														10 36			
Redhill	a			10 00	10 09				10 16							10 30			10 39			
	d			10 00	10 10				10 17							10 30	10 34	10 41	10 45			
Reigate	a																10 38					
Nutfield	d								10 21													
Godstone	d								10 27													
Edenbridge	d								10 32													
Penshurst	d								10 39													
Leigh (Kent)	d								10 42													
Tonbridge 4	a								10 47													
Earlswood (Surrey)	d				10 12																	
Salfords	d				10 16																	
Horley 4	d				10 19								←			10 36			10 53			
Gatwick Airport 10 ✈	a	09 56	10 00	10 08	10 23		10 10	10 15		10 18		10 22	10 23	10 26	10 30	10 39		10 50	10 55		10 40	10 45
	d	09 57		10 09	10 24		10 11			10 19		10 23	10 24	10 27		10 40			10 56		10 41	
Three Bridges 15	a	10 01		10 14	→		10 15						10 29	10 31		10 44			→		10 45	
	d	10 02		10 14			10 15						10 30	10 32		10 45					10 45	
Crawley	d			10 18									10 33			10 48						
Ifield	d												10 36									
Faygate	d																					
Littlehaven	d												10 42									
Horsham 4	a			10 26									10 47			10 56						
Balcombe	d						10 21															
Haywards Heath	a	10 10					10 26			10 30				10 40							10 54	
	d	10 11					10 27			10 35	10 37			10 41							10 55	
Wivelsfield	d						10 31														10 59	
Lewes 4	a									10 52												
Burgess Hill 4	d						10 33					10 38									11 01	
Hassocks 4	d						10 36					10 41									11 04	
Preston Park	d						10 43														11 11	
Hove 2	a										10 53											
Brighton 10	a	10 25				10 28	10 48					10 52		10 55						10 58	11 16	

A ⌶ to Crawley

B ⌶ to Haywards Heath

Bedford and London - Brighton

		SN 1	SN ◇1 A ⌶		SN 1	FC 1	SN 1 ⌶	SN ◇1 B ⌶	SN 1	SN ◇1	FC 1	GX 1 ⌶	SN 1	SN ◇1 C ⌶		SN ◇1	SN 1	FC 1	GX 1 ⌶	SN ◇1	GW 1	GW 1
London Victoria 15 ⊖	d		10 17				10 30	10 32		10 36		10 45		10 47		10 51			11 00	11 02		
Clapham Junction 10	d		10 23					10 38		10 42				10 53						11 08		
Bedford	d					09 10					09 24							09 40				
Luton 10	d					09 34					09 48							10 04				
Luton Airport Parkway 7 ✈	d					09 36					09 50							10 06				
St Albans City	d					09 48					10 02							10 18				
St Pancras International 15 ⊖	d					10 10					10 24							10 40				
Farringdon 3 ⊖	d					10 14					10 29							10 44				
City Thameslink 3	d					10 17					10 32							10 47				
London Blackfriars 3 ⊖	d					10 20					10 35							10 50				
London Bridge 4 ⊖	d	10 15				10 27			10 33		10 42		10 45					10 57				
New Cross Gate	d								10 38													
Norwood Junction 2	d	10 26							10 46				10 56									
East Croydon	a	10 30	10 33			10 39		10 48	10 50	10 52	10 54		11 00	11 03		11 07		11 09		11 18		
	d	10 30	10 33			10 41		10 48	10 51	10 53	10 55		11 00	11 03		11 08		11 11		11 18		
Purley 4	d	10 36							10 57				11 06									
Coulsdon South	d	10 39							11 00				11 09									
Merstham	d	10 45							11 06													
Redhill	a	10 48						11 00	11 10				11 16							11 30		
	d	10 52						11 00	11 11				11 17							11 30	11 34	11 41
Reigate	a	10 56																			11 38	
Nutfield	d												11 21									
Godstone	d												11 27									
Edenbridge	d												11 32									
Penshurst	d												11 39									
Leigh (Kent)	d												11 42									
Tonbridge 4	a												11 47									
Earlswood (Surrey)	d								11 13													
Salfords	d								11 17													
Horley 4	d				←				11 20								←			11 36		
Gatwick Airport 10 ✈	a		10 48		10 55	10 56	11 00	11 08	11 23		11 10	11 15		11 18		11 22	11 23	11 26	11 30	11 39		11 50
	d		10 49		10 56	10 57		11 09	11 24		11 11			11 19		11 23	11 24	11 27		11 40		
Three Bridges 15	a				11 01	11 01		11 14	→		11 15						11 29	11 31		11 44		
	d				11 01	11 02		11 14			11 15						11 30	11 32		11 45		
Crawley	d				11 05			11 18									11 33			11 48		
Ifield	d				11 07												11 36					
Faygate	d																					
Littlehaven	d				11 14												11 42					
Horsham 4	a				11 17			11 26									11 45			11 56		
Balcombe	d										11 21											
Haywards Heath	a		11 00			11 10					11 26			11 30				11 40				
	d		11 05	11 07		11 11					11 27			11 35	11 37			11 41				
Wivelsfield	d			11 11							11 31											
Lewes 4	a			11 22										11 52								
Burgess Hill 4	d		11 10								11 33					11 38						
Hassocks 4	d										11 36					11 41						
Preston Park	d		11 18								11 43											
Hove 2	a		11 22												11 53							
Brighton 10	a					11 25				11 28	11 48					11 52		11 55				

A ⌶ to Gatwick Airport

B ⌶ to Crawley

C ⌶ to Haywards Heath

Bedford and London - Brighton

		SN 1	SN ◇1	FC 1	GX 1 🛒		SN 1	SN ◇1		SN 1	FC 1	SN 1 🛒	SN ◇1		SN 1	SN ◇1 🛒	FC 1	GX 1 🛒	SN 1	SN ◇1			SN ◇1	SN 1	FC 1
London Victoria 15 ⊖	d		11 06		11 15			11 17				11 30	11 32			11 36		11 45		11 47			11 51		
Clapham Junction 10	d		11 12					11 23					11 38			11 42				11 53					
Bedford	d			09 54							10 10						10 24								10 40
Luton 10	d			10 18							10 34						10 48								11 04
Luton Airport Parkway 7 ✈	d			10 20							10 36						10 50								11 06
St Albans City	d			10 32							10 48						11 02								11 18
St Pancras International 15 ⊖	d			10 54							11 10						11 24								11 40
Farringdon 3 ⊖	d			10 59							11 14						11 29								11 44
City Thameslink 3	d			11 02							11 17						11 32								11 47
London Blackfriars 3 ⊖	d			11 05							11 20						11 35								11 50
London Bridge 4 ⊖	d	11 03		11 12			11 15				11 27				11 33		11 42		11 45						11 57
New Cross Gate	d	11 08													11 38										
Norwood Junction 2	d	11 16					11 26								11 46				11 56						
East Croydon 🚊	a	11 20	11 22	11 24			11 30	11 33			11 39		11 48		11 50	11 52	11 54		12 00	12 03			12 07		12 09
	d	11 21	11 23	11 25			11 30	11 33			11 41		11 48		11 51	11 53	11 55		12 00	12 03			12 08		12 11
Purley 4	d	11 27					11 36								11 57				12 06						
Coulsdon South	d	11 30					11 39								12 00				12 09						
Merstham	d	11 36					11 45								12 06										
Redhill	a	11 39					11 48						12 00		12 09				12 16						
	d	11 45					11 52						12 00		12 10				12 17						
Reigate	a						11 56																		
Nutfield	d																		12 21						
Godstone	d																		12 27						
Edenbridge	d																		12 32						
Penshurst	d																		12 39						
Leigh (Kent)	d																		12 42						
Tonbridge 4	a																		12 47						
Earlswood (Surrey)	d														12 12										
Salfords	d														12 16										
Horley 4	d	11 53								←					12 19									←	
Gatwick Airport 10 ✈	a	11 55		11 40	11 45			11 48		11 55	11 56	12 00	12 08		12 23		12 10	12 15		12 18			12 22	12 23	12 26
	d	11 56		11 41				11 49		11 56	11 57		12 09		12 24		12 11			12 19			12 23	12 24	12 27
Three Bridges 15	a	→		11 45						12 01	12 01		12 14		→		12 15							12 29	12 31
	d			11 45						12 01	12 02		12 14				12 15							12 30	12 32
Crawley	d									12 05			12 18											12 33	
Ifield	d									12 07														12 36	
Faygate	d									12 11															
Littlehaven	d									12 15														12 42	
Horsham 4	a									12 18			12 26											12 45	
Balcombe	d																12 21								
Haywards Heath	a			11 54				12 00			12 10						12 26			12 30					12 40
	d			11 55				12 05	12 07		12 11						12 27			12 35	12 37				12 41
Wivelsfield	d			11 59					12 11								12 31								
Lewes 4	a								12 22											12 52					
Burgess Hill 4	d			12 01				12 10									12 33						12 38		
Hassocks 4	d			12 04													12 36						12 41		
Preston Park	d			12 11				12 18									12 43								
Hove 2	a							12 22													12 53				
Brighton 10	a		11 58	12 16							12 25					12 28	12 48						12 52		12 55

Bedford and London - Brighton

		SN 1 🛒	SN ◇1	GW 1	GW 1		SN 1	SN ◇1 🛒	FC 1	GX 1 🛒	SN 1	SN ◇1			SN 1	FC 1	GX 1 🛒	SN ◇1	SN 1	SN ◇1 🛒	FC 1		GX 1 🛒	SN 1
London Victoria 15 ⊖	d	12 00	12 02					12 06		12 15		12 17					12 30	12 32		12 36			12 45	
Clapham Junction 10	d		12 08					12 12				12 23						12 38		12 42				
Bedford	d								10 54							11 10					11 24			
Luton 10	d								11 18							11 34					11 48			
Luton Airport Parkway 7 ✈	d								11 20							11 36					11 50			
St Albans City	d								11 32							11 48					12 02			
St Pancras International 15 ⊖	d								11 54							12 10					12 24			
Farringdon 3 ⊖	d								11 59							12 14					12 29			
City Thameslink 3	d								12 02							12 17					12 32			
London Blackfriars 3 ⊖	d								12 05							12 20					12 35			
London Bridge 4 ⊖	d						12 03		12 12		12 15					12 27			12 33		12 42			12 45
New Cross Gate	d						12 08												12 38					
Norwood Junction 2	d						12 16				12 26								12 46					12 56
East Croydon 🚊	a		12 18				12 20	12 22	12 24		12 30	12 33				12 39		12 48	12 50	12 52	12 54			13 00
	d		12 18				12 21	12 23	12 25		12 30	12 33				12 41		12 48	12 51	12 53	12 55			13 00
Purley 4	d						12 27				12 36								12 57					13 06
Coulsdon South	d						12 30				12 39								13 00					13 09
Merstham	d						12 36				12 45								13 06					
Redhill	a		12 30				12 39				12 48							13 00	13 09					13 16
	d		12 30	12 34	12 41		12 45				12 52							13 00	13 10					13 17
Reigate	a			12 38							12 56													
Nutfield	d																							13 21
Godstone	d																							13 27
Edenbridge	d																							13 32
Penshurst	d																							13 39
Leigh (Kent)	d																							13 42
Tonbridge 4	a																							13 47
Earlswood (Surrey)	d																		13 12					
Salfords	d																		13 16					
Horley 4	d		12 36				12 53								←				13 19					
Gatwick Airport 10 ✈	a	12 30	12 39		12 50		12 55		12 40	12 45		12 48			12 55	12 56	13 00	13 08	13 23		13 10		13 15	
	d		12 40				12 56		12 41			12 49			12 56	12 57		13 09	13 24		13 11			
Three Bridges 15	a		12 44				→		12 45						13 01	13 01		13 14	→		13 15			
	d		12 45						12 45						13 01	13 02		13 14			13 15			
Crawley	d		12 48												13 05			13 18						
Ifield	d														13 07									
Faygate	d																							
Littlehaven	d														13 14									
Horsham 4	a		12 56												13 17			13 26						
Balcombe	d																				13 21			
Haywards Heath	a								12 54			13 00				13 10					13 26			
	d								12 55			13 05	13 07			13 11					13 27			
Wivelsfield	d								12 59				13 11								13 31			
Lewes 4	a												13 22											
Burgess Hill 4	d								13 01			13 10									13 33			
Hassocks 4	d								13 04												13 36			
Preston Park	d								13 11			13 18									13 43			
Hove 2	a											13 22												
Brighton 10	a							12 58	13 16							13 25				13 28	13 48			

Bedford and London - Brighton

		SN ◇1		SN ◇1	SN 1	FC 1	GX 1 ᅲ	SN ◇1	GW 1	GW 1	SN 1	SN ◇1 ᅲ	FC 1	GX 1 ᅲ	SN 1	SN ◇1		SN 1	FC 1	GX 1 ᅲ	SN ◇1 A ᅲ	SN 1
London Victoria 15 ⊖	d	12 47		12 51			13 00	13 02				13 06		13 15		13 17				13 30	13 32	
Clapham Junction 10	d	12 53						13 08				13 12				13 23					13 38	
Bedford	d					11 40							11 54						12 10			
Luton 10	d					12 04							12 18						12 34			
Luton Airport Parkway 7 ✈	d					12 06							12 20						12 36			
St Albans City	d					12 18							12 32						12 48			
St Pancras International 15 ⊖	d					12 40							12 54						13 10			
Farringdon 3 ⊖	d					12 44							12 59						13 14			
City Thameslink 3	d					12 47							13 02						13 17			
London Blackfriars 3 ⊖	d					12 50							13 05						13 20			
London Bridge 4 ⊖	d					12 57					13 03		13 12		13 15				13 27			13 33
New Cross Gate	d										13 08											13 38
Norwood Junction 2	d										13 16				13 26							13 46
East Croydon ⇌	a	13 03		13 07		13 09		13 18			13 20	13 22	13 24		13 30	13 33			13 39		13 48	13 50
	d	13 03		13 08		13 11		13 18			13 21	13 23	13 25		13 30	13 33			13 41		13 48	13 51
Purley 4	d										13 27				13 36							13 57
Coulsdon South	d										13 30				13 39							14 00
Merstham	d										13 36				13 45							14 06
Redhill	a							13 30			13 39				13 48						14 00	14 09
	d							13 30	13 34	13 41	13 45				13 52						14 00	14 10
Reigate	a								13 38						13 56							
Nutfield	d																					
Godstone	d																					
Edenbridge	d																					
Penshurst	d																					
Leigh (Kent)	d																					
Tonbridge 4	a																					
Earlswood (Surrey)	d																					14 12
Salfords	d																					14 16
Horley 4	d				←			13 36			13 53							←				14 19
Gatwick Airport 10 ✈	a	13 18		13 22	13 23	13 26	13 30	13 39		13 50	13 55		13 40	13 45		13 48		13 55	13 56	14 00	14 08	14 23
	d	13 19		13 23	13 24	13 27		13 40			13 56		13 41			13 49		13 56	13 57		14 09	14 24
Three Bridges 15	a				13 29	13 31		13 44			→		13 45					14 01	14 01		14 14	→
	d				13 30	13 32		13 45					13 45					14 01	14 02		14 14	
Crawley	d				13 33			13 48										14 05			14 18	
Ifield	d				13 36													14 07				
Faygate	d																					
Littlehaven	d				13 42													14 14				
Horsham 4	a				13 45			13 56										14 17			14 26	
Balcombe	d																					
Haywards Heath	a	13 30				13 40							13 54			14 00			14 10			
	d	13 35	13 37			13 41							13 55			14 05	14 07		14 11			
Wivelsfield	d												13 59				14 11					
Lewes 4	a	13 52															14 22					
Burgess Hill 4	d			13 38									14 01			14 10						
Hassocks 4	d			13 41									14 04									
Preston Park	d												14 11			14 18						
Hove 2	a		13 53													14 22						
Brighton 10	a			13 52		13 55						13 58	14 16						14 25			

A ᅲ to Crawley

Bedford and London - Brighton

		SN ◇1 ᅲ	FC 1	GX 1 ᅲ	SN 1	SN ◇1		SN ◇1	SN 1	FC 1	GX 1 ᅲ	SN ◇1	GW 1	GW 1	SN 1	SN ◇1 ᅲ	FC 1	GX 1 ᅲ	SN 1	SN ◇1		SN 1
London Victoria 15 ⊖	d	13 36		13 45		13 47		13 51			14 00	14 02				14 06		14 15		14 17		
Clapham Junction 10	d	13 42				13 53						14 08				14 12				14 23		
Bedford	d		12 24							12 40							12 54					
Luton 10	d		12 48							13 04							13 18					
Luton Airport Parkway 7 ✈	d		12 50							13 06							13 20					
St Albans City	d		13 02							13 18							13 32					
St Pancras International 15 ⊖	d		13 24							13 40							13 54					
Farringdon 3 ⊖	d		13 29							13 44							13 59					
City Thameslink 3	d		13 32							13 47							14 02					
London Blackfriars 3 ⊖	d		13 35							13 50							14 05					
London Bridge 4 ⊖	d		13 42		13 45					13 57					14 03		14 12		14 15			
New Cross Gate	d														14 08							
Norwood Junction 2	d				13 56										14 16				14 26			
East Croydon ⇌	a	13 52	13 54		14 00	14 03		14 07		14 09		14 18			14 20	14 22	14 24		14 30	14 33		
	d	13 53	13 55		14 00	14 03		14 08		14 11		14 18			14 21	14 23	14 25		14 30	14 33		
Purley 4	d				14 06										14 27				14 36			
Coulsdon South	d				14 09										14 30				14 39			
Merstham	d														14 36				14 45			
Redhill	a				14 16							14 30			14 39				14 48			
	d				14 17							14 30	14 34	14 41	14 45				14 52			
Reigate	a												14 38						14 56			
Nutfield	d				14 21																	
Godstone	d				14 27																	
Edenbridge	d				14 32																	
Penshurst	d				14 39																	
Leigh (Kent)	d				14 42																	
Tonbridge 4	a				14 47																	
Earlswood (Surrey)	d																					
Salfords	d																					
Horley 4	d								←			14 36			14 53							←
Gatwick Airport 10 ✈	a		14 10	14 15		14 18		14 22	14 23	14 26	14 30	14 39		14 50	14 55		14 40	14 45		14 48		14 55
	d		14 11			14 19		14 23	14 24	14 27		14 40			14 56		14 41			14 49		14 56
Three Bridges 15	a		14 15						14 29	14 31		14 44			→		14 45					15 01
	d		14 15						14 30	14 32		14 45					14 45					15 01
Crawley	d								14 33			14 48										15 05
Ifield	d								14 36													15 07
Faygate	d																					
Littlehaven	d								14 42													15 14
Horsham 4	a								14 45			14 56										15 17
Balcombe	d		14 21																			
Haywards Heath	a		14 26			14 30				14 40							14 54			15 00		
	d		14 27			14 35	14 37			14 41							14 55			15 05	15 07	
Wivelsfield	d		14 31														14 59				15 11	
Lewes 4	a					14 52															15 22	
Burgess Hill 4	d		14 33					14 38									15 01			15 10		
Hassocks 4	d		14 36					14 41									15 04					
Preston Park	d		14 43														15 11			15 18		
Hove 2	a						14 53													15 22		
Brighton 10	a	14 28	14 48					14 52		14 55						14 58	15 16					

Bedford and London - Brighton

		FC ■	GX ■ ⌶	SN ◇■ A ⌶	SN ■	SN ◇■ ⌶	FC ■	GX ■ ⌶	SN ■	SN ◇■		SN ◇■	SN ■	FC ■	GX ■ ⌶	GW ■	SN ◇■	GW ■	SN ■	SN ◇■ ⌶	FC ■	GX ■ ⌶
London Victoria [15] ⊖	d		14 30	14 32		14 36		14 45		14 47		14 51			15 00		15 02			15 06		15 15
Clapham Junction [10]	d			14 38		14 42				14 53							15 08			15 12		
Bedford	d	13 10					13 24							13 40							13 54	
Luton [10]	d	13 34					13 48							14 04							14 18	
Luton Airport Parkway [7] ✈	d	13 36					13 50							14 06							14 20	
St Albans City	d	13 48					14 02							14 18							14 32	
St Pancras International [15] ⊖	d	14 10					14 24							14 40							14 54	
Farringdon [3] ⊖	d	14 14					14 29							14 44							14 59	
City Thameslink [3]	d	14 17					14 32							14 47							15 02	
London Blackfriars [3] ⊖	d	14 20					14 35							14 50							15 05	
London Bridge [4] ⊖	d	14 27			14 33		14 42		14 45					14 57					15 03		15 12	
New Cross Gate	d				14 38														15 08			
Norwood Junction [2]	d				14 46				14 56										15 16			
East Croydon	a	14 39		14 48	14 50	14 52	14 54		15 00	15 03		15 07		15 09			15 18		15 20	15 22	15 24	
	d	14 41		14 48	14 51	14 53	14 55		15 00	15 03		15 08		15 11			15 18		15 21	15 23	15 25	
Purley [4]	d				14 57				15 06										15 27			
Coulsdon South	d				15 00				15 09										15 30			
Merstham	d				15 06														15 36			
Redhill	a			15 00	15 09				15 16								15 30		15 39			
	d			15 00	15 10				15 17							15 29	15 30	15 41	15 45			
Reigate	a															15 33						
Nutfield	d								15 21													
Godstone	d								15 27													
Edenbridge	d								15 32													
Penshurst	d								15 39													
Leigh (Kent)	d								15 42													
Tonbridge [4]	a								15 47													
Earlswood (Surrey)	d				15 12														15 48			
Salfords	d				15 16														15 51			
Horley [4]	d				15 19								←				15 36		15 55			
Gatwick Airport [10] ✈	a	14 56	15 00	15 08	15 23		15 10	15 15		15 18		15 22	15 23	15 26	15 30		15 39	15 50	15 57		15 40	15 45
	d	14 57		15 09	15 24		15 11			15 19		15 23	15 24	15 27			15 40		15 58		15 41	
Three Bridges [15]	a	15 01		15 14	→		15 15						15 29	15 31			15 44		→		15 45	
	d	15 02		15 14			15 15						15 30	15 32			15 45				15 45	
Crawley	d			15 18									15 33				15 48					
Ifield	d												15 36									
Faygate	d																					
Littlehaven	d												15 42									
Horsham [4]	a			15 26									15 48				15 56					
Balcombe	d						15 21															
Haywards Heath	a	15 10					15 26			15 30				15 40							15 54	
	d	15 11					15 27			15 35	15 37			15 41							15 55	
Wivelsfield	d						15 31			15 39											15 59	
Lewes [4]	a									15 52												
Burgess Hill [4]	d						15 33					15 38									16 01	
Hassocks [4]	d						15 36					15 41									16 04	
Preston Park	d						15 43														16 11	
Hove [2]	a										15 53											
Brighton [10]	a	15 25				15 28	15 48					15 52		15 55						15 58	16 16	

A ⌶ to Crawley

Bedford and London - Brighton

		SN ■	SN ◇■		FC ■	SN ■	GX ■ ⌶	SN ◇■	SN ■	SN ◇■ ⌶	FC ■	GX ■ ⌶	SN ■	SN ◇■		SN ◇■	SN ■	FC ■	SN ■ ⌶	SN ◇■	GW ■	SN ■	
London Victoria [15] ⊖	d		15 17				15 30	15 32		15 36		15 45		15 47		15 51			16 00	16 02			
Clapham Junction [10]	d		15 23					15 38		15 42				15 53						16 08			
Bedford	d				14 10						14 24							14 40					
Luton [10]	d				14 34						14 48							15 04					
Luton Airport Parkway [7] ✈	d				14 36						14 50							15 06					
St Albans City	d				14 48						15 02							15 18					
St Pancras International [15] ⊖	d				15 10						15 24							15 40					
Farringdon [3] ⊖	d				15 14						15 29							15 44					
City Thameslink [3]	d				15 17						15 32							15 47					
London Blackfriars [3] ⊖	d				15 20						15 35							15 50					
London Bridge [4] ⊖	d	15 15			15 27				15 33		15 42		15 45					15 57				16 03	
New Cross Gate	d								15 38													16 08	
Norwood Junction [2]	d	15 26							15 46				15 56									16 16	
East Croydon	a	15 30	15 33		15 39			15 48	15 50	15 52	15 54		16 00	16 03		16 07		16 09		16 18		16 20	
	d	15 30	15 33		15 41			15 48	15 51	15 53	15 55		16 00	16 03		16 08		16 11		16 18		16 21	
Purley [4]	d	15 36							15 57				16 06									16 27	
Coulsdon South	d	15 39							16 00				16 09									16 30	
Merstham	d	15 45							16 06				16 15									16 36	
Redhill	a	15 48						16 00	16 09				16 18							16 30		16 39	
	d	15 52						16 00	16 10				16 20							16 30	16 32	16 43	16 45
Reigate	a	15 56																			16 36		
Nutfield	d												16 24										16 49
Godstone	d												16 30										16 55
Edenbridge	d												16 35										17 00
Penshurst	d												16 42										17 07
Leigh (Kent)	d												16 45										17 10
Tonbridge [4]	a												16 52										17 15
Earlswood (Surrey)	d								16 12													16 45	
Salfords	d								16 16													16 49	
Horley [4]	d					←			16 19								←			16 36		16 52	
Gatwick Airport [10] ✈	a		15 48		15 56	15 57	16 00	16 08	16 23		16 10	16 15		16 18		16 22	16 23	16 26	16 30	16 39		16 55	
	d		15 49		15 57	15 58		16 09	16 24		16 11			16 19		16 23	16 24	16 27		16 40		16 56	
Three Bridges [15]	a				16 01	16 03		16 14	→		16 15						16 29	16 31		16 44		→	
	d				16 02	16 03		16 14			16 15						16 30	16 32		16 45			
Crawley	d					16 07		16 18									16 34			16 48			
Ifield	d					16 10											16 36						
Faygate	d					16 14											16 40						
Littlehaven	d					16 18											16 44						
Horsham [4]	a					16 21		16 26									16 47			16 56			
Balcombe	d										16 21												
Haywards Heath	a		16 00		16 10						16 26			16 30				16 40					
	d		16 05	16 07	16 11						16 27			16 35	16 37			16 41					
Wivelsfield	d			16 11							16 31			16 39									
Lewes [4]	a			16 22										16 54									
Burgess Hill [4]	d		16 10								16 33					16 38							
Hassocks [4]	d										16 36					16 41							
Preston Park	d		16 18								16 43												
Hove [2]	a		16 22												16 53								
Brighton [10]	a				16 25					16 28	16 48					16 52		16 55					

Bedford and London - Brighton

		SN 1 🛒	FC 1	GX 1	GW 1	SN 1	SN ◇1 A 🛒		SN 1	SN 1	FC 1	GX 1 🛒	SN ◇1 A 🛒		SN 1	SN 1 🛒		FC 1	GX 1 🛒	SN ◇1 B 🛒	SN 1	SN 1
London Victoria 15 ⊖	d	16 06		16 15			16 17		16 19			16 30	16 32			16 36			16 45	16 47		
Clapham Junction 10	d	16 12					16 23		16 26				16 38			16 42				16 53		
Bedford	d		14 54								15 10							15 24				
Luton 10	d		15 18								15 34							15 48				
Luton Airport Parkway 7 ✈	d		15 20								15 36							15 50				
St Albans City	d		15 32								15 48							16 02				
St Pancras International 15 ⊖	d		15 54								16 10							16 24				
Farringdon 3 ⊖	d		15 59								16 14							16 29				
City Thameslink 3	d		16 02								16 17							16 33				
London Blackfriars 3 ⊖	d		16 05								16 20							16 36				
London Bridge 4 ⊖	d		16 12			16 15					16 27				16 33			16 43				
New Cross Gate	d																					
Norwood Junction 2	d					16 26									16 45							
East Croydon 🚋	a	16 22	16 24			16 30	16 33		16 36		16 39		16 47		16 48	16 52		16 59		17 03		
	d	16 23	16 25			16 30	16 33		16 36		16 41		16 48		16 49	16 52		17 00		17 03		
Purley 4	d					16 36									16 55							
Coulsdon South	d					16 39									16 59							
Merstham	d					16 45									17 04							
Redhill	a					16 48							16 59		17 08							
	d				16 51	16 53							17 00		17 08							17 12
Reigate	a					16 59																
Nutfield	d																					17 16
Godstone	d																					17 22
Edenbridge	d																					17 27
Penshurst	d																					17 34
Leigh (Kent)	d																					17 37
Tonbridge 4	a																					17 42
Earlswood (Surrey)	d														17 11							
Salfords	d														17 14							
Horley 4	d									←			17 06		17 18						←	
Gatwick Airport 10 ✈	a		16 40	16 45	16 59		16 48		16 52	16 55	16 56	17 00	17 08		17 20			17 15	17 15	17 19	17 20	
	d		16 41				16 49		16 53	16 56	16 57		17 09		17 21			17 16		17 20	17 21	
Three Bridges 15	a		16 45						16 57	17 00	17 01		17 14		→	17 10		17 21		17 25	17 26	
	d		16 46						16 58	17 02	17 02		17 18	17 20		17 10		17 21		17 25	17 26	
Crawley	d								17 02	17 06			17 22	17 26							17 30	
Ifield	d									17 08				17 28							17 33	
Faygate	d									17 12											17 37	
Littlehaven	d									17 16				17 35							17 41	
Horsham 4	a								17 12	17 19			17 30	17 38							17 44	
Balcombe	d																	17 27				
Haywards Heath	a		16 54				17 00				17 10					17 19		17 32		17 35		
	d		16 55				17 04	17 06			17 11					17 23	17 26	17 33		17 36		
Wivelsfield	d		16 59					17 10									17 30	17 37		17 41		
Lewes 4	a							17 21												17 56		
Burgess Hill 4	d		17 01				17 09				17 16						17 32	17 40				
Hassocks 4	d		17 04														17 35	17 44				
Preston Park	d		17 11														17 42	17 51				
Hove 2	a						17 20															
Brighton 10	a	17 00	17 16								17 27					17 39	17 47	17 55				

A 🛒 to Gatwick Airport

B 🛒 to Wivelsfield

Bedford and London - Brighton

		SN 1		SN 1	GX 1 🛒	SN 1		SN 1	FC 1	SN 1 🛒	SN ◇1	SN 1	SN 1	GW 1	GW 1	SN 1		GX 1 🛒	FC 1	SN 1		SN ◇1 A 🛒
London Victoria 15 ⊖	d	16 49			17 00			17 06		17 15	17 17					17 21		17 30				17 35
Clapham Junction 10	d	16 56						17 12			17 23					17 27						17 42
Bedford	d								15 52										16 10			
Luton 10	d								16 14										16 34			
Luton Airport Parkway 7 ✈	d								16 17										16 36			
St Albans City	d								16 25										16 48			
St Pancras International 15 ⊖	d								16 46										17 10			
Farringdon 3 ⊖	d								16 51										17 15			
City Thameslink 3	d								16 55										17 19			
London Blackfriars 3 ⊖	d								17 00										17 22			
London Bridge 4 ⊖	d			16 57		16 59							17 23							17 32		
New Cross Gate	d																					
Norwood Junction 2	d					17 11														17 44		
East Croydon 🚋	a	17 06		17 09		17 14		17 22	17 25		17 32		17 35			17 36			17 46	17 48		17 51
	d	17 07		17 10		17 15		17 23	17 26		17 33		17 36			17 38			17 47	17 49		17 52
Purley 4	d					17 21														17 54		
Coulsdon South	d	17 13				17 24										17 44				17 57		
Merstham	d	17 19				17 30										17 50				18 03		
Redhill	a	17 22				17 33										17 53			18 02	18 06		
	d	17 27	17 29			17 37	17 39							17 41	17 43	17 57	17 59		18 03	18 10	18 12	
Reigate	a		17 35												17 48		18 05					
Nutfield	d						17 43														18 16	
Godstone	d						17 49														18 22	
Edenbridge	d						17 54														18 27	
Penshurst	d						18 01														18 34	
Leigh (Kent)	d						18 04														18 37	
Tonbridge 4	a						18 09														18 44	
Earlswood (Surrey)	d	17 29				17 39										17 59				18 12		
Salfords	d	17 33				17 43										18 03				18 16		
Horley 4	d	17 36				17 46						←	17 50			18 06				18 19		
Gatwick Airport 10 ✈	a	17 39			17 30	17 49			17 40	17 45	17 47	17 49		17 54		18 09		17 57	18 13	18 22		18 06
	d	17 40				17 50			17 41		17 48	17 50				18 10		18 00	18 14	18 23		18 07
Three Bridges 15	a	17 44		17 29		→			17 46			17 54	17 55			→			→	→		
	d			17 29					17 46			17 55	17 56									
Crawley	d											17 59										
Ifield	d											18 01										
Faygate	d																					
Littlehaven	d											18 08										
Horsham 4	a											18 11										
Balcombe	d								17 52													
Haywards Heath	a			17 38				17 46	17 57		18 00		18 04					18 11				18 18
	d			17 39				17 47	17 58		18 01		18 05					18 12				18 18
Wivelsfield	d							17 52					18 09									18 23
Lewes 4	a												18 20									18 38
Burgess Hill 4	d			17 46				17 55	18 03		18 07							18 18				
Hassocks 4	d			17 49				17 59	18 07		18 11							18 22				
Preston Park	d			17 56				18 06	18 15													
Hove 2	a			18 00							18 21											
Brighton 10	a							18 12	18 20									18 34				

A 🛒 to Wivelsfield

Table 186

Bedford and London - Brighton

		SN 1	SN 1	FC 1	SN 1 🛒	SN ◇1	SN 1	SN 1		FC 1	SN 1	SN 1 🛒	SN 1	SN 1	SN 1	SN ◇1 A 🛒	SN 1	SN 1 🛒	SN 1	FC 1	SN ◇1	SN 1
London Victoria 15 ⊖	d				17 45	17 47		17 49				18 00				18 06		18 15			18 17	
Clapham Junction 10	d					17 53		17 56								18 12					18 23	
Bedford	d									16 26												
Luton 10	d									16 50												
Luton Airport Parkway 7 ✈	d									16 52												
St Albans City	d									17 04												
St Pancras International 15 ⊖	d									17 28										17 40		
Farringdon 3 ⊖	d									17 33										17 45		
City Thameslink 3	d									17 37										17 49		
London Blackfriars 3 ⊖	d									17 40										17 52		
London Bridge 4 ⊖	d		17 42								17 57				17 59		18 12					18 23
New Cross Gate	d																					
Norwood Junction 2	d														18 11							
East Croydon 🚊	a		17 54			18 02		18 05		18 08	18 11				18 15	18 22	18 24			18 24	18 33	18 36
	d		17 55			18 03		18 06		18 09	18 15				18 15	18 22	18 25			18 26	18 33	18 37
Purley 4	d														18 21							
Coulsdon South	d							18 12							18 24							
Merstham	d							18 18							18 30							
Redhill	a							18 21							18 33					18 37		
	d							18 25	18 27					18 32	18 34					18 39		
Reigate	a								18 33													
Nutfield	d													18 36								
Godstone	d													18 42								
Edenbridge	d													18 47								
Penshurst	d													18 54								
Leigh (Kent)	d													18 57								
Tonbridge 4	a													19 02								
Earlswood (Surrey)	d							18 27							18 36							
Salfords	d							18 31							18 40							
Horley 4	d	←		←		18 18	←	18 34					←		18 43				←		18 48	
Gatwick Airport 10 ✈	a	18 09		18 13	18 12	18 20	18 22	18 37		18 24		18 28	18 37		18 46	18 37		18 44	18 46	18 49		
	d	18 10		18 14	18 15	18 21	18 23	18 38		18 25		18 35	18 38		18 47	18 38		18 46	18 47	18 50		
Three Bridges 15	a	18 16		18 18			18 27	→		18 30	18 34		18 42		→		18 44		18 51	18 56		18 55
	d			18 19			18 28			18 30	18 34						18 45		18 52			18 56
Crawley	d						18 32												18 56			
Ifield	d						18 34												18 58			
Faygate	d						18 38															
Littlehaven	d						18 42												19 05			
Horsham 4	a						18 47												19 08			
Balcombe	d			18 25																	18 57	
Haywards Heath	a		18 21	18 30	18 25	18 33				18 39	18 43	18 46				18 49	18 54	18 57			19 02	19 05
	d		18 22	18 31	18 26	18 33				18 39	18 44	18 47				18 50	18 54	18 58			19 03	19 06
Wivelsfield	d									18 43						18 54						19 11
Lewes 4	a															19 09						19 27
Burgess Hill 4	d		18 27	18 36		18 41				18 46	18 49	18 53					19 00				19 09	
Hassocks 4	d		18 31	18 40		18 45				18 50	18 53	18 57					19 04				19 13	
Preston Park	d		18 39	18 48	18 43	18 53				18 57	19 01						19 11	19 15				
Hove 2	a		18 43			18 57											19 17				19 22	
Brighton 10	a			18 53	18 49					19 03	19 07	19 10						19 22				

A 🛒 to Wivelsfield

Table 186

Bedford and London - Brighton

		GW 1	GW 1	SN 1	SN 1		FC 1	SN 1 🛒	SN 1		SN 1	FC 1	SN 1	SN 1 🛒	SN 1	SN ◇1 A 🛒		SN 1	FC 1	SN 1 🛒	SN 1	SN ◇1 B 🛒
London Victoria 15 ⊖	d				18 19			18 30			18 36			18 45		18 47		18 51		19 00		19 02
Clapham Junction 10	d				18 26						18 42					18 53		18 57				19 08
Bedford	d						17 08					17 22							17 36			
Luton 10	d						17 32					17 46							18 00			
Luton Airport Parkway 7 ✈	d						17 34					17 48							18 02			
St Albans City	d						17 46					18 00							18 14			
St Pancras International 15 ⊖	d						18 08					18 20							18 34			
Farringdon 3 ⊖	d						18 13					18 25							18 39			
City Thameslink 3	d						18 17					18 29							18 43			
London Blackfriars 3 ⊖	d						18 20					18 32							18 46			
London Bridge 4 ⊖	d						18 27		18 30										18 57			
New Cross Gate	d																					
Norwood Junction 2	d								18 42													
East Croydon 🚊	a				18 37		18 41		18 45		18 52	18 55				19 02		19 07	19 10			19 18
	d				18 38		18 41		18 46		18 52	18 56				19 03		19 08	19 11			19 18
Purley 4	d				18 43				18 51													
Coulsdon South	d				18 46				18 54									19 14				
Merstham	d				18 52				19 00									19 20				
Redhill	a				18 55				19 03									19 23				19 30
	d	18 43	18 51	18 54	18 59	19 01			19 07	19 09								19 24				19 31
Reigate	a	18 47		18 58						19 15												
Nutfield	d					19 05																
Godstone	d					19 11																
Edenbridge	d					19 16																
Penshurst	d					19 23																
Leigh (Kent)	d					19 26																
Tonbridge 4	a					19 34																
Earlswood (Surrey)	d				19 01				19 09									19 26				
Salfords	d				19 05				19 13									19 30				
Horley 4	d				19 08				19 16				←		←			19 33			←	
Gatwick Airport 10 ✈	a		19 00		19 13		18 56	19 00	19 19			19 10	19 13	19 14	19 19	19 19		19 36	19 25	19 30	19 36	19 39
	d				19 14		18 57	19 05	19 20			19 11	19 14	19 16	19 20	19 20		19 37	19 27		19 37	19 40
Three Bridges 15	a				→		19 02		→				19 19		19 24			→	19 31		19 41	19 45
	d						19 02						19 19		19 25				19 32			19 45
Crawley	d												19 23		19 29							19 49
Ifield	d												19 26		19 31							
Faygate	d														19 35							
Littlehaven	d												19 32		19 39							
Horsham 4	a												19 35		19 43							19 57
Balcombe	d						19 08					19 19										
Haywards Heath	a						19 13	19 16			19 18	19 24		19 27		19 31			19 40			
	d						19 14	19 17			19 20	19 31		19 28		19 34	19 37		19 41			
Wivelsfield	d										19 24					19 38						
Lewes 4	a															19 53						
Burgess Hill 4	d						19 19	19 23				19 36					19 42		19 46			
Hassocks 4	d						19 23	19 27				19 40					19 46		19 49			
Preston Park	d											19 48		19 40								
Hove 2	a																19 56					
Brighton 10	a						19 33	19 39			19 42	19 53		19 47					19 59			

A 🛒 to Wivelsfield

B 🛒 to Crawley

Bedford and London - Brighton

		SN 1	SN 1	SN 1 ⚭	FC 1	GW 1	SN 1	SN 1 ⚭	SN ◇1 A ⚭		SN 1	FC 1	SN 1	GX 1 ⚭	SN 1	SN ◇1 B ⚭	SN 1	FC 1	SN 1	SN 1	GX 1 ⚭
London Victoria 15 ⊖	d			19 06			19 10	19 15	19 17					19 30		19 32	19 36			19 40	19 45
Clapham Junction 10	d			19 12			19 16		19 23							19 38	19 42			19 46	
Bedford	d				17 54							18 10						18 24			
Luton 10	d				18 18							18 34						18 48			
Luton Airport Parkway 7 ✈	d				18 20							18 36						18 50			
St Albans City	d				18 32							18 48						19 02			
St Pancras International 15 ⊖	d				18 54							19 10						19 24			
Farringdon 3 ⊖	d				18 59							19 14						19 29			
City Thameslink 3	d				19 03							19 17						19 32			
London Blackfriars 3 ⊖	d				19 05							19 20						19 35			
London Bridge 4 ⊖	d		19 03		19 12							19 27						19 42			
New Cross Gate	d																				
Norwood Junction 2	d		19 15																		
East Croydon 🚊	a		19 18	19 22	19 24		19 27		19 33			19 39				19 48	19 52	19 54		19 57	
	d		19 19	19 23	19 25		19 28		19 33			19 41				19 48	19 53	19 55		19 58	
Purley 4	d		19 24				19 33													20 03	
Coulsdon South	d		19 28				19 36													20 06	
Merstham	d		19 33				19 42													20 12	
Redhill	a		19 37				19 45									20 00				20 15	
	d	19 36	19 37			19 43	19 46								19 51	20 00			20 05	20 16	
Reigate	a	19 40																	20 10		
Nutfield	d														19 55						
Godstone	d														20 01						
Edenbridge	d														20 06						
Penshurst	d														20 13						
Leigh (Kent)	d														20 16						
Tonbridge 4	a														20 21						
Earlswood (Surrey)	d		19 40				19 48													20 18	
Salfords	d		19 43				19 52													20 22	
Horley 4	d		19 47				19 55				←		←							20 25	
Gatwick Airport 10 ✈	a		19 49		19 40	19 55	19 58	19 45	19 48		19 49	19 55	19 58	20 00		20 08		20 10		20 28	20 15
	d		19 50		19 41		19 59		19 49		19 50	19 57	19 59			20 09		20 11		20 29	
Three Bridges 15	a		→		19 45		→				19 55	20 01	20 03			20 14		20 15		→	
	d				19 45						19 55	20 02	20 04			20 14		20 15			
Crawley	d										19 59		20 08			20 18					
Ifield	d										20 02		20 10								
Faygate	d												20 14								
Littlehaven	d										20 08		20 18								
Horsham 4	a										20 11		20 21			20 26					
Balcombe	d				19 51																
Haywards Heath	a			19 46	19 56				20 00			20 10					20 16	20 24			
	d			19 47	19 57				20 04	20 07		20 11					20 17	20 25			
Wivelsfield	d				20 01					20 11								20 29			
Lewes 4	a									20 22											
Burgess Hill 4	d				20 03				20 09			20 16						20 31			
Hassocks 4	d				20 06							20 19						20 34			
Preston Park	d				20 13													20 41			
Hove 2	a								20 21												
Brighton 10	a			20 02	20 18							20 29					20 33	20 46			

A ⚭ to Gatwick Airport

B ⚭ to Crawley

Bedford and London - Brighton

		SN ◇1 A ⚭		SN 1	FC 1	SN 1	GX 1 ⚭	SN ◇1 ⚭	SN ◇1	FC 1	GW 1	GW 1	SN 1	SN 1	SN ◇1		SN 1	SN 1	GX 1	SN 1	SN ◇1	SN ◇1
London Victoria 15 ⊖	d	19 47					20 00	20 02	20 06				20 10	20 15	20 17				20 30		20 32	20 36
Clapham Junction 10	d	19 53						20 08	20 12				20 16		20 23						20 38	20 42
Bedford	d				18 40					18 54												
Luton 10	d				19 04					19 18												
Luton Airport Parkway 7 ✈	d				19 06					19 20												
St Albans City	d				19 18					19 32												
St Pancras International 15 ⊖	d				19 40					19 54												
Farringdon 3 ⊖	d				19 44					19 59												
City Thameslink 3	d				19 47					20 02												
London Blackfriars 3 ⊖	d				19 50					20 05												
London Bridge 4 ⊖	d			19 52	19 57					20 12							20 28					
New Cross Gate	d																					
Norwood Junction 2	d			20 03																		
East Croydon 🚊	a	20 03		20 06	20 09			20 19	20 22	20 24			20 27		20 33		20 40				20 48	20 52
	d	20 03		20 07	20 11			20 19	20 23	20 25			20 28		20 33		20 41				20 48	20 53
Purley 4	d			20 12									20 33									
Coulsdon South	d			20 15									20 36									
Merstham	d			20 21									20 42									
Redhill	a			20 24				20 30					20 45								21 00	
	d			20 25				20 31			20 34	20 41	20 46							20 51	21 00	
Reigate	a			20 30							20 38											
Nutfield	d																			20 55		
Godstone	d																			21 01		
Edenbridge	d																			21 06		
Penshurst	d																			21 13		
Leigh (Kent)	d																			21 16		
Tonbridge 4	a																			21 21		
Earlswood (Surrey)	d												20 48									
Salfords	d																					
Horley 4	d					←							20 54					←				
Gatwick Airport 10 ✈	a	20 18			20 25	20 28	20 30	20 38		20 40		20 50	20 56	20 45	20 48		20 55	20 56	21 00		21 08	
	d	20 19			20 27	20 29		20 39		20 41			20 57		20 49		20 56	20 57			21 09	
Three Bridges 15	a				20 31	20 33		20 44		20 45			→				21 01	21 02			21 14	
	d				20 32	20 34		20 44		20 45							21 01	21 03			21 14	
Crawley	d					20 37		20 48										21 06			21 18	
Ifield	d					20 40												21 09				
Faygate	d																					
Littlehaven	d					20 46												21 15				
Horsham 4	a					20 49		20 56										21 18			21 26	
Balcombe	d									20 51												
Haywards Heath	a	20 30			20 40				20 47	20 56					21 00		21 10					21 16
	d	20 34	20 36		20 41				20 47	20 57					21 04	21 07	21 11					21 16
Wivelsfield	d		20 40							21 01						21 11						
Lewes 4	a		20 55													21 22						
Burgess Hill 4	d	20 39			20 46					21 03					21 09							
Hassocks 4	d	20 42								21 06												
Preston Park	d	20 49								21 13												
Hove 2	a	20 53													21 21							
Brighton 10	a				20 57				21 01	21 18							21 26					21 30

A ⚭ to Gatwick Airport

Bedford and London - Brighton

Station		FC 1	SN 1	SN 1	GX 1	SN ◇1		SN 1	SN 1	GX 1	SN 1	SN 1	SN ◇1	FC 1	GW 1	SN 1	GX 1	SN ◇1		SN 1	GX 1	GW 1
London Victoria 15 ⊖	d			20 40	20 45	20 47				21 00		21 02	21 06			21 10	21 15	21 17			21 30	
Clapham Junction 10	d			20 46		20 53						21 08	21 12			21 16		21 23				
Bedford	d	19 22												19 52								
Luton 10	d	19 46												20 16								
Luton Airport Parkway 7 ✈	d	19 48												20 18								
St Albans City	d	20 00												20 30								
St Pancras International 15 ⊖	d	20 24												20 54								
Farringdon 3 ⊖	d	20 29												20 59								
City Thameslink 3	d	20 32												21 02								
London Blackfriars 3 ⊖	d	20 35												21 05								
London Bridge 4 ⊖	d	20 42						20 58						21 12								
New Cross Gate	d																					
Norwood Junction 2	d																					
East Croydon	a	20 54		20 57		21 03		21 10				21 18	21 22	21 24		21 27		21 33				
	d	20 55		20 58		21 04		21 11				21 18	21 23	21 25		21 28		21 33				
Purley 4	d			21 03												21 33						
Coulsdon South	d			21 06												21 36						
Merstham	d			21 12												21 42						
Redhill	a			21 15								21 30				21 45						
	d		21 05	21 16							21 22	21 31			21 35	21 46						21 53
Reigate	a		21 09								21 26				21 39							
Nutfield	d																					
Godstone	d																					
Edenbridge	d																					
Penshurst	d																					
Leigh (Kent)	d																					
Tonbridge 4	a																					
Earlswood (Surrey)	d			21 18												21 48						
Salfords	d			21 22																		
Horley 4	d			21 25					←							21 54				←		
Gatwick Airport 10 ✈	a	21 10		21 28	21 15	21 18		21 26	21 28	21 30		21 38		21 40		21 56	21 45	21 48		21 56	22 00	22 06
	d	21 11		21 29		21 19		21 27	21 29			21 39		21 41		21 57		21 49		21 57		
Three Bridges 15	a	21 15		→				21 31	21 33			21 44		21 45		→		21 53		22 02		
	d	21 15						21 32	21 34			21 44		21 45				21 53		22 03		
Crawley	d								21 37											22 06		
Ifield	d								21 40											22 09		
Faygate	d																					
Littlehaven	d								21 46											22 15		
Horsham 4	a								21 49											22 18		
Balcombe	d													21 53								
Haywards Heath	a	21 24				21 30		21 40				21 52	21 46	21 58				22 02				
	d	21 25				21 34	21 37	21 41				21 53	21 46	21 59				22 06	22 08			
Wivelsfield	d	21 29					21 41					21 57		22 03					22 12			
Lewes 4	a						21 54												22 23			
Burgess Hill 4	d	21 31				21 39						21 59		22 05				22 11				
Hassocks 4	d	21 34				21 42						22 02		22 08								
Preston Park	d	21 41				21 49						22 09		22 15								
Hove 2	a					21 53												22 22				
Brighton 10	a	21 46						21 56				22 15	22 00	22 20								

Table 186 Mondays to Fridays

Bedford and London - Brighton

Station		SN 1	SN 1	SN ◇1	FC 1	SN 1	SN 1	GX 1	SN ◇1		SN 1	SN 1	SN 1	SN ◇1	SN ◇1	FC 1	SN 1	GX 1	SN ◇1	SN 1	GX 1	GW 1
London Victoria 15 ⊖	d		21 32	21 36			21 40	21 45	21 47			22 00		22 02	22 06		22 10	22 15	22 17		22 30	
Clapham Junction 10	d		21 38	21 42			21 46		21 53					22 08	22 12		22 16		22 23			
Bedford	d				20 22											20 52						
Luton 10	d				20 46											21 16						
Luton Airport Parkway 7 ✈	d				20 48											21 18						
St Albans City	d				21 00											21 30						
St Pancras International 15 ⊖	d				21 24											21 54						
Farringdon 3 ⊖	d				21 29											21 59						
City Thameslink 3	d				21 32											22 02						
London Blackfriars 3 ⊖	d				21 35											22 05						
London Bridge 4 ⊖	d				21 42											22 12						
New Cross Gate	d																					
Norwood Junction 2	d																					
East Croydon	a		21 48	21 52	21 54		21 57		22 03					22 18	22 22	22 24	22 26		22 33			
	d		21 48	21 53	21 55		21 58		22 03					22 18	22 23	22 25	22 28		22 34			
Purley 4	d						22 03										22 33					
Coulsdon South	d						22 06										22 36					
Merstham	d						22 12										22 42					
Redhill	a		21 59				22 15							22 30			22 45					
	d	21 55	22 00			22 05	22 16						22 22	22 31			22 46					22 52
Reigate	a					22 09							22 26									
Nutfield	d	21 59																				
Godstone	d	22 05																				
Edenbridge	d	22 10																				
Penshurst	d	22 17																				
Leigh (Kent)	d	22 20																				
Tonbridge 4	a	22 28																				
Earlswood (Surrey)	d						22 18										22 48					
Salfords	d						22 22															
Horley 4	d						22 25				←						22 54			←		
Gatwick Airport 10 ✈	a		22 08		22 10		22 28	22 15	22 18		22 28	22 30		22 38		22 40	22 56	22 45	22 48	22 56	23 00	23 06
	d		22 09		22 11		22 29		22 19		22 29			22 39		22 41	22 57		22 49	22 57		
Three Bridges 15	a		22 14		22 15		→				22 33			22 44		22 45	→		22 54	23 02		
	d		22 14		22 15						22 36			22 44		22 45			22 54	23 03		
Crawley	d		22 18								22 39									23 06		
Ifield	d										22 42									23 09		
Faygate	d																					
Littlehaven	d										22 48									23 15		
Horsham 4	a		22 26								22 51									23 18		
Balcombe	d															22 53						
Haywards Heath	a			22 16	22 24				22 30					22 52	22 46	22 58			23 02			
	d			22 16	22 25				22 34	22 37				22 53	22 46	22 59			23 03			
Wivelsfield	d				22 29				22 38					22 57		23 03						
Lewes 4	a								22 51													
Burgess Hill 4	d				22 31									22 59		23 05			23 08			
Hassocks 4	d				22 34									23 02		23 08						
Preston Park	d				22 41									23 09		23 15						
Hove 2	a									22 51									23 21			
Brighton 10	a			22 30	22 46									23 15	23 00	23 20						

Bedford and London - Brighton

		SN 1	SN 1	SN 1	FC 1	SN 1	SN 1	SN 1	SN ◇1	SN 1	GX 1	SN ◇1	SN ◇1	FC 1	SN 1	SN 1	SN ◇1	SN 1	GX 1	SN 1	SN ◇1
London Victoria 15 ⊖	d		22 32	22 36			22 40	22 45	22 47		23 00	23 02	23 06		23 10	23 15	23 17		23 30		23 32
Clapham Junction 10	d		22 38	22 42			22 46		22 53			23 08	23 12		23 16		23 23				23 38
Bedford	d																				
Luton 10	d																				
Luton Airport Parkway 7 ✈	d																				
St Albans City	d																				
St Pancras International 15 ⊖	d																				
Farringdon 3 ⊖	d																				
City Thameslink 3	d																				
London Blackfriars 3 ⊖	d																				
London Bridge 4 ⊖	d				22 42									23 12							
New Cross Gate	d																				
Norwood Junction 2	d																				
East Croydon ⛴	a		22 48	22 52	22 54		22 57		23 03			23 19	23 22	23 24	23 27		23 33				23 51
	d		22 48	22 53	22 55		22 58		23 03			23 20	23 23	23 25	23 28		23 33				23 52
Purley 4	d						23 03								23 33						
Coulsdon South	d						23 06								23 37						
Merstham	d						23 12								23 42						
Redhill	a		23 00				23 15					23 31			23 46						00 03
	d	22 55	23 01			23 05	23 16					23 31			23 46					23 55	00 05
Reigate	a					23 09															
Nutfield	d	22 59																			
Godstone	d	23 05																			
Edenbridge	d	23 10																			
Penshurst	d	23 17																		00 06	
Leigh (Kent)	d	23 20																			
Tonbridge 4	a	23 25																		00 15	
Earlswood (Surrey)	d						23 18								23 49						
Salfords	d						23 22								23 52						
Horley 4	d						23 25			←					23 56			←			
Gatwick Airport 10 ✈	a		23 08		23 10		23 28	23 15	23 18	23 28	23 30	23 38		23 40	23 58	23 45	23 50	23 58	00 05		00 14
	d		23 09		23 11		23 29		23 19	23 29		23 39		23 41	23 59		23 51	23 59			00 15
Three Bridges 15	a		23 15		23 15		→			23 33		23 44		23 47	→		23 55	00 04			00 20
	d		23 16		23 15					23 38		23 44		23 47			23 56	00 04			00 20
Crawley	d		23 19							23 41								00 07			
Ifield	d									23 44								00 10			
Faygate	d																				
Littlehaven	d									23 50								00 16			
Horsham 4	a		23 27							23 53								00 19			
Balcombe	d													23 53							00 26
Haywards Heath	a			23 16	23 24				23 30			23 52	23 46	23 58			00 04				00 31
	d			23 16	23 25				23 34 / 23 37			23 53	23 46	23 59			00 05				00 31
Wivelsfield	d				23 29				23 38			23 57		00 03							00 35
Lewes 4	a								23 51												
Burgess Hill 4	d				23 31							23 59		00 05			00 10				00 37
Hassocks 4	d				23 34							00 02		00 08							00 41
Preston Park	d				23 41							00 09		00 15							00 48
Hove 2	a								23 51								00 21				
Brighton 10	a			23 30	23 46							00 15	00 01	00 20							00 52

Bedford and London - Brighton

		FC 1	GX 1	SN 1
London Victoria 15 ⊖	d		23 45	23 47
Clapham Junction 10	d			23 53
Bedford	d			
Luton 10	d			
Luton Airport Parkway 7 ✈	d			
St Albans City	d			
St Pancras International 15 ⊖	d			
Farringdon 3 ⊖	d			
City Thameslink 3	d			
London Blackfriars 3 ⊖	d			
London Bridge 4 ⊖	d	23 42		
New Cross Gate	d			
Norwood Junction 2	d			
East Croydon ⛴	a	23 56		00 05
	d	23 57		00 06
Purley 4	d			00 12
Coulsdon South	d			00 15
Merstham	d			00 21
Redhill	a			00 24
	d			00 25
Reigate	a			
Nutfield	d			
Godstone	d			
Edenbridge	d			
Penshurst	d			
Leigh (Kent)	d			
Tonbridge 4	a			
Earlswood (Surrey)	d			
Salfords	d			
Horley 4	d			00 31
Gatwick Airport 10 ✈	a	00 18	00 20	00 33
	d	00 19		00 34
Three Bridges 15	a	00 24		00 39
	d			00 39
Crawley	d			00 43
Ifield	d			00 46
Faygate	d			
Littlehaven	d			00 52
Horsham 4	a			00 55
Balcombe	d			
Haywards Heath	a			
	d			
Wivelsfield	d			
Lewes 4	a			
Burgess Hill 4	d			
Hassocks 4	d			
Preston Park	d			
Hove 2	a			
Brighton 10	a			

Bedford and London - Brighton

		SN ◇1	SN ◇1	FC 1	SN 1	SN ◇1	SN 1	GX 1	SN 1	SN ◇1	FC 1	SN 1	SN 1	GX 1	SN ◇1		FC	SN 1	GW 1	GX 1	FC	SN ◇1	FC 1
London Victoria ⊖	d	23p02	23p06		23p10	23p17		23p30		23p32		23p45	23p47	00 02	00 05			00 14		00 30		01 00	
Clapham Junction	d	23p08	23p12		23p16	23p23				23p38			23p53		00 11			00 20				01 08	
Bedford	d																						
Luton	d																						
Luton Airport Parkway ✈	d																						
St Albans City	d																						
St Pancras International ⊖	d																						
Farringdon ⊖	d																						
City Thameslink	d																						
London Blackfriars ⊖	d																						
London Bridge ⊖	d			23p12							23p42						00 12				00 42		01 05
New Cross Gate	d																						
Norwood Junction	d																						
East Croydon	a	23p19	23p22	23p24	23p27	23p33				23p51	23p56		00 05		00 24		00 26	00 31			00 56	01 21	01 32
	d	23p20	23p23	23p25	23p28	23p33				23p52	23p57		00 06		00 25		00 27	00 32			00 57	01 22	01 32
Purley	d				23p33								00 12					00 37				01 27	
Coulsdon South	d				23p37								00 15					00 41					
Merstham	d				23p42								00 21					00 47					
Redhill	a	23p31			23p46					00 03			00 24					00 50				01 36	
	d	23p31			23p46				23p55	00 05			00 25					00 51	00 54			01 36	
Reigate	a																						
Nutfield	d																						
Godstone	d																						
Edenbridge	d								00 06														
Penshurst	d																						
Leigh (Kent)	d																						
Tonbridge	a								00 15														
Earlswood (Surrey)	d				23p49																		
Salfords	d				23p52																		
Horley	d				23p56		←						00 31					00 57				01 43	
Gatwick Airport ✈	a	23p38		23p40	23p58	23p50	23p58	00 05		00 14	00 18	00 20	00 33	00 37	00 42		00 48	00 59	01 03	01 20	01 18	01 45	01 51
	d	23p39		23p41	23p59	23p51	23p59			00 15	00 19		00 34		00 43		00 49				01 22	01 47	01 52
Three Bridges	a	23p44		23p47	→	23p55	00 04			00 20	00 24		00 39		00 47		00 54				01 28	01 51	01 58
	d	23p44		23p47		23p56	00 04			00 20			00 39		00 47							01 52	
Crawley	d						00 07						00 43										
Ifield	d						00 10						00 46										
Faygate	d																						
Littlehaven	d						00 16						00 52										
Horsham	a						00 19						00 55										
Balcombe	d			23p53						00 26													
Haywards Heath	a	23p52	23p46	23p58		00 04				00 31					00 58							02 06	
	d	23p53	23p46	23p59		00 05				00 31					01 02	01 06						02 06	
Wivelsfield	d	23p57		00 03						00 35													
Lewes	a															01 20							
Burgess Hill	d	23p59		00 05		00 10				00 37													
Hassocks	d	00 02		00 08						00 41													
Preston Park	d	00 09		00 15						00 48													
Hove	a					00 21																	
Brighton	a	00 15	00 01	00 20						00 52					01s16							02 23	

Table 186

Saturdays

Bedford and London - Brighton

		FC 1	SN 1	FC 1	SN 1	FC 1	GX 1	FC 1	SN ◇1	FC 1	GX 1	FC 1	SN 1	SN ◇1	GX 1	FC 1	GW 1	SN 1	GX 1	SN 1	SN ◇1	GX 1
London Victoria ⊖	d		02 00		03 00		03 30		04 00		04 30		05 00	05 02	05 15				05 30		05 32	05 45
Clapham Junction	d		02 08		03 08				04 08					05 08							05 38	
Bedford	d																					
Luton	d																					
Luton Airport Parkway ✈	d																					
St Albans City	d																					
St Pancras International ⊖	d																					
Farringdon ⊖	d																					
City Thameslink	d																					
London Blackfriars ⊖	d																					
London Bridge ⊖	d	01 35		02 05		03 05		03 35		04 05		04 35				05 05						
New Cross Gate	d																					
Norwood Junction	d																					
East Croydon	a	02 02	02 21	02 30	03 21	03 30		04 00	04 21	04 30		05 00		05 21		05 31					05 48	
	d	02 02	02 22	02 32	03 22	03 32		04 02	04 22	04 32		05 02		05 22		05 32					05 48	
Purley	d		02 27		03 27				04 27					05 26							05 53	
Coulsdon South	d													05 30							05 57	
Merstham	d													05 35							06 03	
Redhill	a								04 36					05 39							06 06	
	d								04 36					05 39			05 49				06 07	
Reigate	a																					
Nutfield	d																					
Godstone	d																					
Edenbridge	d																					
Penshurst	d																					
Leigh (Kent)	d																					
Tonbridge	a																					
Earlswood (Surrey)	d																				06 11	
Salfords	d																				06 15	
Horley	d		02 42		03 42				04 43					05 45							06 18	
Gatwick Airport ✈	a	02 21	02 44	02 51	03 44	03 51	04 05	04 24	04 45	04 51	05 05	05 21	05 35	05 48	05 50	05 55	05 58		06 00		06 21	06 15
	d	02 22	02 46	02 52	03 46	03 52		04 24	04 47	04 52		05 22		05 49		05 56		05 58		06 11	06 22	
Three Bridges	a	02 28	02 50	02 58	03 50	03 58		04 30	04 51	04 58		05 27		05 53		06 00		06 02		06 15	→	
	d								04 52			05 28		05 54		06 01		06 03		06 16		
Crawley	d																	06 06				
Ifield	d																	06 09				
Faygate	d																					
Littlehaven	d																	06 15				
Horsham	a																	06 18				
Balcombe	d											05 34				06 07						
Haywards Heath	a								05 00			05 39		06 02		06 12				06 25		
	d								05 01			05 40		06 03		06 12				06 25		
Wivelsfield	d											05 44		06 07		06 16				06 29		
Lewes	a																			06 40		
Burgess Hill	d											05 46		06 09		06 18						
Hassocks	d											05 50		06 12		06 22						
Preston Park	d											05 57		06 19		06 29						
Hove	a																					
Brighton	a								05 16			06 02		06 24		06 34						

Bedford and London - Brighton

Station		FC	SN	SN	GX	SN	GW	GW	SN		GX	FC	SN	GX	SN		FC	GX	SN	SN	GW
		1	◇1	◇1	1	1	1	1	1		1	1	1	1	1		1	1	1	1	1
London Victoria 15 ⊖	d			05 32	06 00				06 02		06 15			06 30	06 32			06 45			
Clapham Junction 10	d			05 38					06 08						06 38						
Bedford	d																				
Luton 10	d																				
Luton Airport Parkway 7 ✈	d																				
St Albans City	d																				
St Pancras International 15 ⊖	d																				
Farringdon 3 ⊖	d																				
City Thameslink 3	d																				
London Blackfriars 3 ⊖	d																				
London Bridge 4 ⊖	d	05 52										06 27					06 42				
New Cross Gate	d																				
Norwood Junction 2	d																				
East Croydon	a	06 04		05 48					06 18			06 39			06 48		06 54				
	d	06 05		05 48					06 18			06 41			06 48		06 55				
Purley 4	d			05 53					06 23						06 53						
Coulsdon South	d			05 57					06 27						06 57						
Merstham	d			06 03					06 32						07 02						
Redhill	a			06 06					06 36						07 06						
	d			06 07		06 22	06 34	06 41	06 46	06 52					07 10	07 22					07 34
Reigate	a						06 38			06 56											07 38
Nutfield	d					06 26										07 26					
Godstone	d					06 32										07 32					
Edenbridge	d					06 37										07 37					
Penshurst	d					06 44										07 44					
Leigh (Kent)	d					06 47										07 47					
Tonbridge 4	a					06 52										07 52					
Earlswood (Surrey)	d			06 11					06 48						07 12						
Salfords	d			06 15					06 52						07 16						
Horley 4	d		←	06 18					06 55				←		07 19				←		
Gatwick Airport 10 ✈	a	06 19	06 21	06 21	06 30			06 50	06 58		06 45	06 56	06 58	07 00	07 23		07 10	07 15	07 23		
	d	06 20	06 22	06 22					06 59			06 57	06 59		07 24		07 11		07 24		
Three Bridges 15	a	06 25	06 26	→					→			07 01	07 03		→		07 15		07 29		
	d	06 25	06 30									07 02	07 04				07 15		07 30		
Crawley	d												07 07						07 33		
Ifield	d												07 10						07 36		
Faygate	d																				
Littlehaven	d												07 16						07 42		
Horsham 4	a												07 19						07 45		
Balcombe	d		06 36														07 21				
Haywards Heath	a	06 34	06 41									07 10					07 26				
	d	06 34	06 41									07 11					07 27			07 33	
Wivelsfield	d		06 45														07 31			07 37	
Lewes 4	a																			07 48	
Burgess Hill 4	d	06 40	06 47														07 33				
Hassocks 4	d		06 51														07 36				
Preston Park	d		06 58														07 43				
Hove 2	a																				
Brighton 10	a	06 52	07 03									07 24					07 48				

Bedford and London - Brighton

Station		SN	FC	GX	GW	SN		SN	FC	SN	SN	FC	SN	SN	SN	SN	FC	SN	SN	SN	
		◇1	1	1	1	1		◇1	1	1	1	1	1	◇1	1	◇1	1	1	1	◇1	
London Victoria 15 ⊖	d			07 00				07 06		07 15			07 30	07 32		07 36		07 45		07 47	
Clapham Junction 10	d							07 12						07 38		07 42				07 53	
Bedford	d																				
Luton 10	d																				
Luton Airport Parkway 7 ✈	d																				
St Albans City	d																				
St Pancras International 15 ⊖	d																				
Farringdon 3 ⊖	d																				
City Thameslink 3	d																				
London Blackfriars 3 ⊖	d																				
London Bridge 4 ⊖	d		06 57			07 03			07 12			07 27			07 33		07 42		07 45		
New Cross Gate	d					07 08									07 38						
Norwood Junction 2	d					07 16									07 46				07 56		
East Croydon	a		07 09			07 20		07 22	07 24			07 39		07 48	07 50	07 52	07 54		08 00	08 03	
	d		07 11			07 21		07 23	07 25			07 41		07 48	07 51	07 53	07 55		08 00	08 03	
Purley 4	d					07 27									07 57				08 06		
Coulsdon South	d					07 30									08 00				08 09		
Merstham	d					07 36									08 06						
Redhill	a					07 39								08 00	08 09				08 16		
	d				07 41	07 44	07 52							08 00	08 10				08 17		
Reigate	a						07 56														
Nutfield	d																		08 21		
Godstone	d																		08 27		
Edenbridge	d																		08 32		
Penshurst	d																		08 39		
Leigh (Kent)	d																		08 42		
Tonbridge 4	a																		08 47		
Earlswood (Surrey)	d														08 12						
Salfords	d														08 16						
Horley 4	d					07 51					←				08 19						
Gatwick Airport 10 ✈	a		07 26	07 30	07 50	07 55			07 40	07 45	07 55	07 56	08 00	08 08	08 23		08 10	08 15		08 18	
	d		07 27			07 56			07 41		07 56	07 57		08 09	08 24		08 11			08 19	
Three Bridges 15	a		07 31			→			07 45		08 01	08 01		08 14	→		08 15				
	d		07 32						07 45		08 01	08 02		08 14			08 15				
Crawley	d										08 05			08 18							
Ifield	d										08 07										
Faygate	d																				
Littlehaven	d										08 14										
Horsham 4	a										08 17			08 26							
Balcombe	d																08 21				
Haywards Heath	a		07 40						07 54			08 10					08 26			08 30	
	d	07 37	07 41						07 55			08 11					08 27			08 35	08 37
Wivelsfield	d								07 59								08 31				
Lewes 4	a																			08 49	
Burgess Hill 4	d								08 01								08 33				
Hassocks 4	d								08 04								08 36				
Preston Park	d								08 11								08 43				
Hove 2	a	07 51																			08 53
Brighton 10	a		07 54					07 57	08 16			08 24				08 27	08 48				

Table 186

Saturdays

Bedford and London - Brighton

		SN	SN	FC	SN	SN	GW	GW	SN	SN	FC	SN	SN	SN	SN	FC	SN	SN	SN	SN
		◇1	1	1	1	◇1	1	1	1	◇1	1	1	1	◇1	1	1	1	◇1	1	◇1
					H							H					H			
London Victoria 15 ⊖	d	07 51			08 00	08 02				08 06		08 15		08 17			08 30	08 32		08 36
Clapham Junction 10	d					08 08				08 12				08 23				08 38		08 42
Bedford	d																			
Luton 10	d																			
Luton Airport Parkway 7 ✈	d																			
St Albans City	d																			
St Pancras International 15 ⊖	d																			
Farringdon 3 ⊖	d																			
City Thameslink 3	d																			
London Blackfriars 3 ⊖	d																			
London Bridge 4 ⊖	d			07 57					08 03		08 12		08 15			08 27			08 33	
New Cross Gate	d								08 08										08 38	
Norwood Junction 2	d								08 16				08 26						08 46	
East Croydon	a	08 07		08 09		08 18			08 20	08 22	08 24		08 30	08 33		08 39		08 48	08 50	08 52
	d	08 08		08 11		08 18			08 21	08 23	08 25		08 30	08 33		08 40		08 48	08 51	08 53
Purley 4	d								08 27				08 36						08 57	
Coulsdon South	d								08 30				08 39						09 00	
Merstham	d								08 36				08 45						09 06	
Redhill	a					08 30			08 39				08 48					09 00	09 09	
	d					08 30	08 34	08 41	08 44				08 52					09 00	09 10	
Reigate	a						08 38						08 56							
Nutfield	d																			
Godstone	d																			
Edenbridge	d																			
Penshurst	d																			
Leigh (Kent)	d																			
Tonbridge 4	a																			
Earlswood (Surrey)	d																		09 12	
Salfords	d																		09 16	
Horley 4	d		←			08 36			08 51						←				09 19	
Gatwick Airport 10 ✈	a	08 22	08 23	08 26	08 30	08 39		08 50	08 55		08 40	08 45		08 48	08 55	08 56	09 00	09 08	09 23	
	d	08 23	08 24	08 27		08 40			08 56		08 41			08 49	08 56	08 57		09 09	09 24	
Three Bridges 15	a		08 29	08 31		08 44			→		08 45				09 01	09 01		09 14	→	
	d		08 30	08 32		08 45					08 45				09 01	09 02		09 14		
Crawley	d		08 33			08 48									09 05			09 18		
Ifield	d		08 36												09 07					
Faygate	d																			
Littlehaven	d		08 42												09 14					
Horsham 4	a		08 45			08 56									09 17			09 26		
Balcombe	d																			
Haywards Heath	a			08 40							08 54			09 00		09 10				
	d			08 41							08 55			09 05 09 07		09 11				
Wivelsfield	d										08 59			09 11						
Lewes 4	a													09 22						
Burgess Hill 4	d	08 38									09 01			09 10						
Hassocks 4	d	08 41									09 04									
Preston Park	d										09 11			09 18						
Hove 2	a													09 22						
Brighton 10	a	08 52		08 55						08 57	09 16					09 25				09 27

Table 186

Saturdays

Bedford and London - Brighton

		FC	SN	SN	SN	SN	SN	FC	SN	SN	GW	GW	SN	SN	FC	SN	SN	SN	SN
		1	1	1	◇1	◇1	1	1	1	◇1	1	1	1	◇1	1	1	1	◇1	1
			H						H					H		H			
London Victoria 15 ⊖	d		08 45		08 47	08 51			09 00	09 02				09 06		09 15		09 17	
Clapham Junction 10	d				08 53					09 08				09 12				09 23	
Bedford	d																		
Luton 10	d																		
Luton Airport Parkway 7 ✈	d																		
St Albans City	d																		
St Pancras International 15 ⊖	d																		
Farringdon 3 ⊖	d																		
City Thameslink 3	d																		
London Blackfriars 3 ⊖	d																		
London Bridge 4 ⊖	d	08 42		08 45				08 57					09 03		09 12		09 15		
New Cross Gate	d												09 08						
Norwood Junction 2	d			08 56									09 16				09 26		
East Croydon	a	08 54		09 00	09 03	09 07		09 09		09 18			09 20	09 22	09 24		09 30	09 33	
	d	08 55		09 00	09 03	09 08		09 11		09 18			09 21	09 23	09 25		09 30	09 33	
Purley 4	d			09 06									09 27				09 36		
Coulsdon South	d			09 09									09 30				09 39		
Merstham	d												09 36				09 45		
Redhill	a			09 16						09 30			09 39				09 48		
	d			09 17						09 30	09 34	09 41	09 44				09 52		
Reigate	a										09 38						09 56		
Nutfield	d			09 21															
Godstone	d			09 27															
Edenbridge	d			09 32															
Penshurst	d			09 39															
Leigh (Kent)	d			09 42															
Tonbridge 4	a			09 47															
Earlswood (Surrey)	d																		
Salfords	d																		
Horley 4	d						←			09 36			09 51						←
Gatwick Airport 10 ✈	a	09 10	09 15		09 18	09 22	09 23	09 26	09 30	09 39		09 50	09 55		09 40	09 45		09 48	09 55
	d	09 11			09 19	09 23	09 24	09 27		09 40			09 56		09 41			09 49	09 56
Three Bridges 15	a	09 15					09 29	09 31		09 44			→		09 45				10 01
	d	09 15					09 30	09 32		09 45					09 45				10 01
Crawley	d						09 33			09 48									10 05
Ifield	d						09 36												10 07
Faygate	d																		
Littlehaven	d						09 42												10 14
Horsham 4	a						09 45			09 56									10 17
Balcombe	d	09 21																	
Haywards Heath	a	09 26			09 30			09 40							09 54			10 00	
	d	09 27			09 35 09 37			09 41							09 55			10 05 10 07	
Wivelsfield	d	09 31													09 59			10 11	
Lewes 4	a				09 52													10 22	
Burgess Hill 4	d	09 33				09 38									10 01			10 10	
Hassocks 4	d	09 36				09 41									10 04				
Preston Park	d	09 43													10 11			10 18	
Hove 2	a				09 53													10 22	
Brighton 10	a	09 48				09 52		09 55						09 57	10 16				

Bedford and London - Brighton

Station		FC	SN	SN	SN	SN	FC	SN	SN	SN		SN	SN	FC	SN	SN	GW	GW	SN	SN	FC	SN
		1	1	◇1	1	◇1	1	1	1	◇1		◇1	1	1	1	◇1	1	1	1	◇1	1	1
			⌶			⌶		⌶							⌶	A ⌶				⌶		⌶
London Victoria 15 ⊖	d		09 30	09 32		09 36		09 45		09 47		09 51			10 00	10 02				10 06		10 15
Clapham Junction 10	d			09 38		09 42				09 53						10 08				10 12		
Bedford	d																					
Luton 10	d																					
Luton Airport Parkway 7 ✈	d																					
St Albans City	d																					
St Pancras International 15 ⊖	d																					
Farringdon 3 ⊖	d																					
City Thameslink 3	d																					
London Blackfriars 3 ⊖	d																					
London Bridge 4 ⊖	d	09 27			09 33		09 42		09 45					09 57					10 03		10 12	
New Cross Gate	d				09 38														10 08			
Norwood Junction 2	d				09 46				09 56										10 16			
East Croydon	a	09 39		09 48	09 50	09 52	09 54		10 00	10 03		10 07		10 09		10 18			10 20	10 22	10 24	
	d	09 41		09 48	09 51	09 53	09 55		10 00	10 03		10 08		10 11		10 18			10 21	10 23	10 25	
Purley 4	d				09 57				10 06										10 27			
Coulsdon South	d				10 00				10 09										10 30			
Merstham	d				10 06														10 36			
Redhill	a			10 00	10 09				10 16							10 30			10 39			
	d			10 00	10 10				10 17							10 30	10 34	10 41	10 44			
Reigate	a																10 38					
Nutfield	d								10 21													
Godstone	d								10 27													
Edenbridge	d								10 32													
Penshurst	d								10 39													
Leigh (Kent)	d								10 42													
Tonbridge 4	a								10 47													
Earlswood (Surrey)	d				10 12																	
Salfords	d				10 16																	
Horley 4	d				10 19								←			10 36			10 51			
Gatwick Airport 10 ✈	a	09 56	10 00	10 08	10 23		10 10	10 15		10 18		10 22	10 23	10 26	10 30	10 39		10 50	10 55		10 40	10 45
	d	09 57		10 09	10 24		10 11			10 19		10 23	10 24	10 27		10 40			10 56		10 41	
Three Bridges 15	a	10 01		10 14	→		10 15						10 29	10 31		10 44			→		10 45	
	d	10 02		10 14			10 15						10 30	10 32		10 45					10 45	
Crawley	d			10 18									10 33			10 48						
Ifield	d												10 36									
Faygate	d																					
Littlehaven	d												10 42									
Horsham 4	a			10 26									10 45			10 56						
Balcombe	d						10 21															
Haywards Heath	a	10 10					10 26			10 30				10 40							10 54	
	d	10 11					10 27			10 35	10 37			10 41							10 55	
Wivelsfield	d						10 31														10 59	
Lewes 4	a									10 52												
Burgess Hill 4	d						10 33					10 38									11 01	
Hassocks 4	d						10 36					10 41									11 04	
Preston Park	d						10 43														11 11	
Hove 2	a										10 53											
Brighton 10	a	10 25				10 27	10 48					10 52		10 55						10 57	11 16	

A ⌶ to Crawley

Bedford and London - Brighton

Station		SN	SN		SN	FC	SN	SN	SN	SN	FC	SN	SN	SN		SN	SN	FC	SN	SN	GW
		1	◇1		1	1	1	◇1	1	◇1	1	1	1	◇1		◇1	1	1	1	◇1	1
							⌶			⌶		⌶							⌶	B ⌶	
London Victoria 15 ⊖	d		10 17				10 30	10 32		10 36		10 45		10 47		10 51			11 00	11 02	
Clapham Junction 10	d		10 23					10 38		10 42				10 53						11 08	
Bedford	d																				
Luton 10	d																				
Luton Airport Parkway 7 ✈	d																				
St Albans City	d																				
St Pancras International 15 ⊖	d																				
Farringdon 3 ⊖	d																				
City Thameslink 3	d																				
London Blackfriars 3 ⊖	d																				
London Bridge 4 ⊖	d	10 15				10 27			10 33		10 42		10 45					10 57			
New Cross Gate	d								10 38												
Norwood Junction 2	d	10 26							10 46				10 56								
East Croydon	a	10 30	10 33			10 39		10 48	10 50	10 52	10 54		11 00	11 03		11 07		11 09		11 18	
	d	10 30	10 33			10 41		10 48	10 51	10 53	10 55		11 00	11 03		11 08		11 11		11 18	
Purley 4	d	10 36							10 57				11 06								
Coulsdon South	d	10 39							11 00				11 09								
Merstham	d	10 45							11 06												
Redhill	a	10 48						11 00	11 09				11 16							11 30	
	d	10 52						11 00	11 10				11 17							11 30	11 34
Reigate	a	10 56																			11 38
Nutfield	d												11 21								
Godstone	d												11 27								
Edenbridge	d												11 32								
Penshurst	d												11 39								
Leigh (Kent)	d												11 42								
Tonbridge 4	a												11 47								
Earlswood (Surrey)	d								11 12												
Salfords	d								11 16												
Horley 4	d				←				11 19								←			11 36	
Gatwick Airport 10 ✈	a		10 48		10 55	10 56	11 00	11 08	11 23		11 10	11 15		11 18		11 22	11 23	11 26	11 30	11 39	
	d		10 49		10 56	10 57		11 09	11 24		11 11			11 19		11 23	11 24	11 27		11 40	
Three Bridges 15	a				11 01	11 01		11 14	→		11 15						11 29	11 31		11 44	
	d				11 01	11 02		11 14			11 15						11 30	11 32		11 45	
Crawley	d				11 05			11 18									11 33			11 48	
Ifield	d				11 07												11 36				
Faygate	d																				
Littlehaven	d				11 14												11 42				
Horsham 4	a				11 17			11 26									11 45			11 56	
Balcombe	d										11 21										
Haywards Heath	a		11 00			11 10					11 26			11 30				11 40			
	d		11 05	11 07		11 11					11 27			11 35	11 37			11 41			
Wivelsfield	d			11 11							11 31										
Lewes 4	a			11 22										11 52							
Burgess Hill 4	d		11 10								11 33					11 38					
Hassocks 4	d										11 36					11 41					
Preston Park	d		11 18								11 43										
Hove 2	a		11 22												11 53						
Brighton 10	a					11 25				11 27	11 48					11 52		11 55			

B ⌶ to Crawley

Table 186

Bedford and London - Brighton

		GW 1	SN 1	SN ◇1 ✕	FC 1	SN 1 ✕	SN 1	SN ◇1		SN 1	FC 1	SN 1 ✕	SN ◇1	SN 1	SN ◇1 ✕	FC 1	SN 1 ✕	SN 1	SN ◇1		SN ◇1
London Victoria 15 ⊖	d			11 06		11 15		11 17				11 30	11 32		11 36		11 45		11 47		11 51
Clapham Junction 10	d			11 12				11 23					11 38		11 42				11 53		
Bedford	d																				
Luton 10	d																				
Luton Airport Parkway 7 ✈	d																				
St Albans City	d																				
St Pancras International 15 ⊖	d																				
Farringdon 3 ⊖	d																				
City Thameslink 3	d																				
London Blackfriars 3 ⊖	d																				
London Bridge 4 ⊖	d		11 03		11 12		11 15				11 27			11 33		11 42		11 45			
New Cross Gate	d		11 08											11 38							
Norwood Junction 2	d		11 16				11 26							11 46				11 56			
East Croydon	a		11 20	11 22	11 24		11 30	11 33			11 39		11 48	11 50	11 52	11 54		12 00	12 03		12 07
	d		11 21	11 23	11 25		11 30	11 33			11 41		11 48	11 51	11 53	11 55		12 00	12 03		12 08
Purley 4	d		11 27				11 36							11 57				12 06			
Coulsdon South	d		11 30				11 39							12 00				12 09			
Merstham	d		11 36				11 45							12 06							
Redhill	a		11 39				11 48						12 00	12 09				12 16			
	d	11 41	11 44				11 52						12 00	12 10				12 17			
Reigate	a						11 56														
Nutfield	d																	12 21			
Godstone	d																	12 27			
Edenbridge	d																	12 32			
Penshurst	d																	12 39			
Leigh (Kent)	d																	12 42			
Tonbridge 4	a																	12 47			
Earlswood (Surrey)	d													12 12							
Salfords	d													12 16							
Horley 4	d		11 51							←				12 19							
Gatwick Airport 10 ✈	a	11 50	11 55		11 40	11 45		11 48		11 55	11 56	12 00	12 08	12 23		12 10	12 15		12 18		12 22
	d		11 56		11 41			11 49		11 56	11 57		12 09	12 24		12 11			12 19		12 23
Three Bridges 10	a		→		11 45					12 01	12 01		12 14	→		12 15					
	d				11 45					12 01	12 02		12 14			12 15					
Crawley	d									12 05			12 18								
Ifield	d									12 07											
Faygate	d																				
Littlehaven	d									12 14											
Horsham 4	a									12 17			12 26								
Balcombe	d															12 21					
Haywards Heath	a				11 54			12 00			12 10					12 26			12 30		
	d				11 55			12 05	12 07		12 11					12 27			12 35	12 37	
Wivelsfield	d				11 59				12 11							12 31					
Lewes 4	a								12 22										12 52		
Burgess Hill 4	d				12 01			12 10								12 33					12 38
Hassocks 4	d				12 04											12 36					12 41
Preston Park	d				12 11			12 18								12 43					
Hove 2	a							12 22												12 53	
Brighton 10	a			11 57	12 16						12 25				12 27	12 48					12 52

Table 186

Bedford and London - Brighton

		SN 1	FC 1	SN 1 ✕	SN ◇1 A ✕	GW 1	GW 1	SN 1	SN ◇1 ✕	FC 1	SN 1 ✕	SN 1	SN ◇1		SN 1	FC 1	SN 1 ✕	SN ◇1	SN 1	SN ◇1 ✕	FC 1
London Victoria 15 ⊖	d			12 00	12 02				12 06		12 15		12 17				12 30	12 32		12 36	
Clapham Junction 10	d				12 08				12 12				12 23					12 38		12 42	
Bedford	d																				
Luton 10	d																				
Luton Airport Parkway 7 ✈	d																				
St Albans City	d																				
St Pancras International 15 ⊖	d																				
Farringdon 3 ⊖	d																				
City Thameslink 3	d																				
London Blackfriars 3 ⊖	d																				
London Bridge 4 ⊖	d		11 57					12 03		12 12		12 15				12 27			12 33		12 42
New Cross Gate	d							12 08											12 38		
Norwood Junction 2	d							12 16				12 26							12 46		
East Croydon	a		12 09		12 18			12 20	12 22	12 24		12 30	12 33			12 39		12 48	12 50	12 52	12 54
	d		12 11		12 18			12 21	12 23	12 25		12 30	12 33			12 41		12 48	12 51	12 53	12 55
Purley 4	d							12 27				12 36							12 57		
Coulsdon South	d							12 30				12 39							13 00		
Merstham	d							12 36				12 45							13 06		
Redhill	a				12 30			12 39				12 48						13 00	13 09		
	d				12 30	12 34	12 41	12 44				12 52						13 00	13 10		
Reigate	a					12 38						12 56									
Nutfield	d																				
Godstone	d																				
Edenbridge	d																				
Penshurst	d																				
Leigh (Kent)	d																				
Tonbridge 4	a																				
Earlswood (Surrey)	d																		13 12		
Salfords	d																		13 16		
Horley 4	d	←			12 36			12 51							←				13 19		
Gatwick Airport 10 ✈	a	12 23	12 26	12 30	12 39		12 50	12 55		12 40	12 45		12 48		12 55	12 56	13 00	13 08	13 23		13 10
	d	12 24	12 27		12 40			12 56		12 41			12 49		12 56	12 57		13 09	13 24		13 11
Three Bridges 10	a	12 29	12 31		12 44			→		12 45					13 01	13 01		13 14	→		13 15
	d	12 30	12 32		12 45					12 45					13 01	13 02		13 14			13 15
Crawley	d	12 33			12 48										13 05			13 18			
Ifield	d	12 36													13 07						
Faygate	d																				
Littlehaven	d	12 42													13 14						
Horsham 4	a	12 45			12 56										13 17			13 26			
Balcombe	d																				13 21
Haywards Heath	a		12 40							12 54			13 00			13 10					13 26
	d		12 41							12 55			13 05	13 07		13 11					13 27
Wivelsfield	d									12 59				13 11							13 31
Lewes 4	a													13 22							
Burgess Hill 4	d									13 01			13 10								13 33
Hassocks 4	d									13 04											13 36
Preston Park	d									13 11			13 18								13 43
Hove 2	a												13 22								
Brighton 10	a		12 55						12 57	13 16						13 25				13 27	13 48

A ✕ to Crawley

B from 10 September

Bedford and London - Brighton

Station		SN	SN	SN		SN	SN	FC	SN	SN	GW	GW	SN	SN	FC	SN	SN	SN		SN	FC
		■	■	◇■		◇■	■	■	■	◇■	■	■	■	◇■	■	■	■	◇■		■	■
		🍴							🍴	A 🍴				🍴		🍴					
London Victoria 15 ⊖	d	12 45		12 47		12 51			13 00	13 02				13 06		13 15		13 17			
Clapham Junction 10	d			12 53						13 08				13 12				13 23			
Bedford	d																				
Luton 10	d																				
Luton Airport Parkway 7 ✈	d																				
St Albans City	d																				
St Pancras International 15 ⊖	d																				
Farringdon 3 ⊖	d																				
City Thameslink 3	d																				
London Blackfriars 3 ⊖	d																				
London Bridge 4 ⊖	d		12 45					12 57					13 03		13 12		13 15				13 27
New Cross Gate	d												13 08								
Norwood Junction 2	d		12 56										13 16				13 26				
East Croydon 🚊	a		13 00	13 03		13 07		13 09		13 18			13 20	13 22	13 24		13 30	13 33			13 39
	d		13 00	13 03		13 08		13 11		13 18			13 21	13 23	13 25		13 30	13 33			13 41
Purley 4	d		13 06										13 27				13 36				
Coulsdon South	d		13 09										13 30				13 39				
Merstham	d												13 36				13 45				
Redhill	a		13 16							13 30			13 39				13 48				
	d		13 17							13 30	13 34	13 41	13 44				13 52				
Reigate	a										13 38						13 56				
Nutfield	d		13 21																		
Godstone	d		13 27																		
Edenbridge	d		13 32																		
Penshurst	d		13 39																		
Leigh (Kent)	d		13 42																		
Tonbridge 4	a		13 47																		
Earlswood (Surrey)	d																				
Salfords	d																				
Horley 4	d						←			13 36			13 51							←	
Gatwick Airport 10 ✈	a	13 15		13 18		13 22	13 23	13 26	13 30	13 39		13 50	13 55		13 40	13 45		13 48		13 55	13 56
	d			13 19		13 23	13 24	13 27		13 40			13 56		13 41			13 49		13 56	13 57
Three Bridges 15	a						13 29	13 31		13 44			→		13 45					14 01	14 01
	d						13 30	13 32		13 45					13 45					14 01	14 02
Crawley	d						13 33			13 48										14 05	
Ifield	d						13 36													14 07	
Faygate	d																				
Littlehaven	d						13 42													14 14	
Horsham 4	a						13 45			13 56										14 17	
Balcombe	d																				
Haywards Heath	a			13 30				13 40							13 54			14 00			14 10
	d			13 35	13 37			13 41							13 55			14 05	14 07		14 11
Wivelsfield	d														13 59				14 11		
Lewes 4	a			13 52															14 22		
Burgess Hill 4	d					13 38									14 01			14 10			
Hassocks 4	d					13 41									14 04						
Preston Park	d														14 11			14 18			
Hove 2	a				13 53													14 22			
Brighton 10	a					13 52		13 55						13 57	14 16						14 25

A 🍴 to Crawley

Bedford and London - Brighton

Station		SN	SN	SN	SN	FC	SN	SN	SN		SN	SN	FC	SN	SN	GW	GW	SN	SN	FC	SN	SN
		■	◇■	■	◇■	■	■	■	◇■		◇■	■	■	■	◇■	■	■	■	◇■	■	■	■
		🍴			🍴		🍴							🍴	A 🍴				🍴		🍴	
London Victoria 15 ⊖	d	13 30	13 32		13 36		13 45		13 47		13 51			14 00	14 02				14 06		14 15	
Clapham Junction 10	d		13 38		13 42				13 53						14 08				14 12			
Bedford	d																					
Luton 10	d																					
Luton Airport Parkway 7 ✈	d																					
St Albans City	d																					
St Pancras International 15 ⊖	d																					
Farringdon 3 ⊖	d																					
City Thameslink 3	d																					
London Blackfriars 3 ⊖	d																					
London Bridge 4 ⊖	d			13 33		13 42		13 45					13 57					14 03		14 12		14 15
New Cross Gate	d			13 38														14 08				
Norwood Junction 2	d			13 46				13 56										14 16				14 26
East Croydon 🚊	a		13 48	13 50	13 52	13 54		14 00	14 03		14 07		14 09		14 18			14 20	14 22	14 24		14 30
	d		13 48	13 51	13 53	13 55		14 00	14 03		14 08		14 11		14 18			14 21	14 23	14 25		14 30
Purley 4	d			13 57				14 06										14 27				14 36
Coulsdon South	d			14 00				14 09										14 30				14 39
Merstham	d			14 06														14 36				14 45
Redhill	a		14 00	14 09				14 16							14 30			14 39				14 48
	d		14 00	14 10				14 17							14 30	14 34	14 41	14 44				14 52
Reigate	a															14 38						14 56
Nutfield	d							14 21														
Godstone	d							14 27														
Edenbridge	d							14 32														
Penshurst	d							14 39														
Leigh (Kent)	d							14 42														
Tonbridge 4	a							14 47														
Earlswood (Surrey)	d			14 12																		
Salfords	d			14 16																		
Horley 4	d			14 19								←			14 36			14 51				
Gatwick Airport 10 ✈	a	14 00	14 08	14 23		14 10	14 15		14 18		14 22	14 23	14 26	14 30	14 39		14 50	14 55		14 40	14 45	
	d		14 09	14 24		14 11			14 19		14 23	14 24	14 27		14 40			14 56		14 41		
Three Bridges 15	a		14 14	→		14 15						14 29	14 31		14 44			→		14 45		
	d		14 14			14 15						14 30	14 32		14 45					14 45		
Crawley	d		14 18									14 33			14 48							
Ifield	d											14 36										
Faygate	d																					
Littlehaven	d											14 42										
Horsham 4	a		14 26									14 45			14 56							
Balcombe	d					14 21																
Haywards Heath	a					14 26			14 30				14 40							14 54		
	d					14 27			14 35	14 37			14 41							14 55		
Wivelsfield	d					14 31														14 59		
Lewes 4	a								14 52													
Burgess Hill 4	d					14 33					14 38									15 01		
Hassocks 4	d					14 36					14 41									15 04		
Preston Park	d					14 43														15 11		
Hove 2	a									14 53												
Brighton 10	a				14 27	14 48					14 52		14 55						14 57	15 16		

A 🍴 to Crawley

Bedford and London - Brighton

		SN ◇1		SN 1	FC 1	SN 1 ⌶	SN ◇1	SN 1	SN ◇1 ⌶	FC 1	SN 1 ⌶	SN 1	SN ◇1		SN ◇1	SN 1	FC 1	SN 1 ⌶	SN ◇1 B ⌶	GW 1	GW 1
London Victoria 15 ⊖	d	14 17				14 30	14 32		14 36		14 45		14 47		14 51			15 00	15 02		
Clapham Junction 10	d	14 23					14 38		14 42				14 53						15 08		
Bedford	d																				
Luton 10	d																				
Luton Airport Parkway 7 ✈	d																				
St Albans City	d																				
St Pancras International 15 ⊖	d																				
Farringdon 3 ⊖	d																				
City Thameslink 3	d																				
London Blackfriars 3 ⊖	d																				
London Bridge 4 ⊖	d				14 27			14 33		14 42		14 45					14 57				
New Cross Gate	d							14 38													
Norwood Junction 2	d							14 46				14 56									
East Croydon	a	14 33			14 39		14 48	14 50	14 52	14 54		15 00	15 03		15 07		15 09		15 18		
	d	14 33			14 41		14 48	14 51	14 53	14 55		15 00	15 03		15 08		15 11		15 18		
Purley 4	d							14 57				15 06									
Coulsdon South	d							15 00				15 09									
Merstham	d							15 06													
Redhill	a						15 00	15 09				15 16							15 30		
	d						15 00	15 10				15 17							15 30	15 34	15 41
Reigate	a																			15 38	
Nutfield	d											15 21									
Godstone	d											15 27									
Edenbridge	d											15 32									
Penshurst	d											15 39									
Leigh (Kent)	d											15 42									
Tonbridge 4	a											15 47									
Earlswood (Surrey)	d							15 12													
Salfords	d							15 16													
Horley 4	d			←				15 19								←			15 36		
Gatwick Airport 10 ✈	a	14 48		14 55	14 56	15 00	15 08	15 23		15 10	15 15		15 18		15 22	15 23	15 26	15 30	15 39		15 50
	d	14 49		14 56	14 57		15 09	15 24		15 11			15 19		15 23	15 24	15 27		15 40		
Three Bridges 15	a			15 01	15 01		15 14	→		15 15						15 29	15 31		15 44		
	d			15 01	15 02		15 14			15 15						15 30	15 32		15 45		
Crawley	d			15 05			15 18									15 33			15 48		
Ifield	d			15 07												15 36					
Faygate	d																				
Littlehaven	d			15 14												15 42					
Horsham 4	a			15 17			15 26									15 45			15 56		
Balcombe	d									15 21											
Haywards Heath	a	15 00			15 10					15 26			15 30				15 40				
	d	15 05	15 07		15 11					15 27			15 35	15 37			15 41				
Wivelsfield	d		15 11							15 31											
Lewes 4	a		15 22										15 52								
Burgess Hill 4	d	15 10								15 33					15 38						
Hassocks 4	d									15 36					15 41						
Preston Park	d	15 18								15 43											
Hove 2	a	15 22												15 53							
Brighton 10	a				15 25				15 27	15 48					15 52		15 55				

B ⌶ to Crawley

Bedford and London - Brighton

		SN 1	SN ◇1 ⌶	FC 1	SN 1 ⌶	SN 1	SN ◇1		SN 1	FC 1	SN 1 ⌶	SN ◇1	SN 1	SN ◇1 ⌶	FC 1	SN 1 ⌶	SN 1	SN ◇1		SN ◇1	SN 1
London Victoria 15 ⊖	d		15 06		15 15		15 17				15 30	15 32		15 36		15 45		15 47		15 51	
Clapham Junction 10	d		15 12				15 23					15 38		15 42				15 53			
Bedford	d																				
Luton 10	d																				
Luton Airport Parkway 7 ✈	d																				
St Albans City	d																				
St Pancras International 15 ⊖	d																				
Farringdon 3 ⊖	d																				
City Thameslink 3	d																				
London Blackfriars 3 ⊖	d																				
London Bridge 4 ⊖	d	15 03		15 12		15 15				15 27			15 33		15 42		15 45				
New Cross Gate	d	15 08											15 38								
Norwood Junction 2	d	15 16				15 26							15 46				15 56				
East Croydon	a	15 20	15 22	15 24		15 30	15 33			15 39		15 48	15 50	15 52	15 54		16 00	16 03		16 07	
	d	15 21	15 23	15 25		15 30	15 33			15 41		15 48	15 51	15 53	15 55		16 00	16 03		16 08	
Purley 4	d	15 27				15 36							15 57				16 06				
Coulsdon South	d	15 30				15 39							16 00				16 09				
Merstham	d	15 36				15 45							16 06								
Redhill	a	15 39				15 48						16 00	16 09				16 16				
	d	15 44				15 52						16 00	16 10				16 17				
Reigate	a					15 56															
Nutfield	d																16 21				
Godstone	d																16 27				
Edenbridge	d																16 32				
Penshurst	d																16 39				
Leigh (Kent)	d																16 42				
Tonbridge 4	a																16 47				
Earlswood (Surrey)	d												16 12								
Salfords	d												16 16								
Horley 4	d	15 51							←				16 19								←
Gatwick Airport 10 ✈	a	15 55		15 40	15 45		15 48		15 55	15 56	16 00	16 08	16 23		16 10	16 15		16 18		16 22	16 23
	d	15 56		15 41			15 49		15 56	15 57		16 09	16 24		16 11			16 19		16 23	16 24
Three Bridges 15	a	→		15 45					16 01	16 01		16 14	→		16 15						16 29
	d			15 45					16 01	16 02		16 14			16 15						16 30
Crawley	d								16 05			16 18									16 33
Ifield	d								16 07												16 36
Faygate	d																				
Littlehaven	d								16 14												16 42
Horsham 4	a								16 17			16 26									16 45
Balcombe	d														16 21						
Haywards Heath	a			15 54			16 00			16 10					16 26			16 30			
	d			15 55			16 05	16 07		16 11					16 27			16 35	16 37		
Wivelsfield	d			15 59				16 11							16 31						
Lewes 4	a							16 22										16 52			
Burgess Hill 4	d			16 01			16 10								16 33					16 38	
Hassocks 4	d			16 04											16 36					16 41	
Preston Park	d			16 11			16 18								16 43						
Hove 2	a						16 22												16 53		
Brighton 10	a		15 57	16 16						16 25				16 27	16 48					16 52	

Bedford and London - Brighton

		FC 1	SN 1 🚲	SN ◇1 A 🚲	GW 1	GW 1	SN 1	SN ◇1 🚲	FC 1	SN 1 🚲	SN 1	SN ◇1		SN 1	FC 1	SN 1 🚲	SN ◇1	SN 1	SN ◇1 🚲	FC 1	SN 1 🚲
London Victoria 15 ⊖	d		16 00	16 02				16 06		16 15		16 17				16 30	16 32		16 36		16 45
Clapham Junction 10	d			16 08				16 12				16 23					16 38		16 42		
Bedford	d																				
Luton 10	d																				
Luton Airport Parkway 7 ✈	d																				
St Albans City	d																				
St Pancras International 15 ⊖	d																				
Farringdon 3 ⊖	d																				
City Thameslink 3	d																				
London Blackfriars 3 ⊖	d																				
London Bridge 4 ⊖	d	15 57					16 03		16 12		16 15				16 27			16 33		16 42	
New Cross Gate	d						16 08											16 38			
Norwood Junction 2	d						16 16				16 26							16 46			
East Croydon	a	16 09		16 18			16 20	16 22	16 24		16 30	16 33			16 39		16 48	16 50	16 52	16 54	
	d	16 11		16 18			16 21	16 23	16 25		16 30	16 33			16 41		16 48	16 51	16 53	16 55	
Purley 4	d						16 27				16 36							16 57			
Coulsdon South	d						16 30				16 39							17 00			
Merstham	d						16 36				16 45							17 06			
Redhill	a			16 30			16 39				16 48						17 00	17 09			
	d			16 30	16 34	16 41	16 44				16 52						17 00	17 10			
Reigate	a				16 38						16 56										
Nutfield	d																				
Godstone	d																				
Edenbridge	d																				
Penshurst	d																				
Leigh (Kent)	d																				
Tonbridge 4	a																				
Earlswood (Surrey)	d																	17 12			
Salfords	d																	17 16			
Horley 4	d			16 36			16 51							←				17 19			
Gatwick Airport 10 ✈	a	16 26	16 30	16 39		16 50	16 55		16 40	16 45		16 48		16 55	16 56	17 00	17 08	17 23		17 10	17 15
	d	16 27		16 40			16 56		16 41			16 49		16 56	16 57		17 09	17 24		17 11	
Three Bridges 15	a	16 31		16 44			→		16 45					17 01	17 01		17 14	→		17 15	
	d	16 32		16 45					16 45					17 01	17 02		17 14			17 15	
Crawley	d			16 48										17 05			17 18				
Ifield	d													17 07							
Faygate	d																				
Littlehaven	d													17 14							
Horsham 4	a			16 56										17 17			17 26				
Balcombe	d																			17 21	
Haywards Heath	a	16 40							16 54			17 00			17 10					17 26	
	d	16 41							16 55			17 05	17 07		17 11					17 27	
Wivelsfield	d								16 59				17 11							17 31	
Lewes 4	a												17 22								
Burgess Hill 4	d								17 01			17 10								17 33	
Hassocks 4	d								17 04											17 36	
Preston Park	d								17 11			17 18								17 43	
Hove 2	a											17 22									
Brighton 10	a	16 55						16 57	17 16						17 25				17 27	17 48	

A 🚲 to Crawley

Bedford and London - Brighton

		SN 1	SN ◇1		SN ◇1	SN 1	FC 1	SN 1 🚲	SN ◇1 A 🚲	GW 1	GW 1	SN 1	SN ◇1 🚲	FC 1	SN 1 🚲	SN 1	SN ◇1		SN 1	FC 1	SN 1 🚲
London Victoria 15 ⊖	d		16 47		16 51			17 00	17 02				17 06		17 15		17 17				17 30
Clapham Junction 10	d		16 53						17 08				17 12				17 23				
Bedford	d																				
Luton 10	d																				
Luton Airport Parkway 7 ✈	d																				
St Albans City	d																				
St Pancras International 15 ⊖	d																				
Farringdon 3 ⊖	d																				
City Thameslink 3	d																				
London Blackfriars 3 ⊖	d																				
London Bridge 4 ⊖	d	16 45					16 57					17 03		17 12		17 15				17 27	
New Cross Gate	d											17 08									
Norwood Junction 2	d	16 56										17 16				17 26					
East Croydon	a	17 00	17 03		17 07		17 09		17 18			17 20	17 22	17 24		17 30	17 33			17 39	
	d	17 00	17 03		17 08		17 11		17 18			17 21	17 23	17 25		17 30	17 33			17 41	
Purley 4	d	17 06										17 27				17 36					
Coulsdon South	d	17 09										17 30				17 39					
Merstham	d											17 36				17 45					
Redhill	a	17 16							17 30			17 39				17 48					
	d	17 17							17 30	17 34	17 41	17 44				17 52					
Reigate	a									17 38						17 56					
Nutfield	d	17 21																			
Godstone	d	17 27																			
Edenbridge	d	17 32																			
Penshurst	d	17 39																			
Leigh (Kent)	d	17 42																			
Tonbridge 4	a	17 47																			
Earlswood (Surrey)	d																				
Salfords	d																				
Horley 4	d					←			17 36			17 51							←		
Gatwick Airport 10 ✈	a		17 18		17 22	17 23	17 26	17 30	17 39		17 50	17 55		17 40	17 45		17 48		17 55	17 56	18 00
	d		17 19		17 23	17 24	17 27		17 40			17 56		17 41			17 49		17 56	17 57	
Three Bridges 15	a					17 29	17 31		17 44			→		17 45					18 01	18 01	
	d					17 30	17 32		17 45					17 45					18 01	18 02	
Crawley	d					17 33			17 48										18 05		
Ifield	d					17 36													18 07		
Faygate	d																				
Littlehaven	d					17 42													18 14		
Horsham 4	a					17 45			17 56										18 17		
Balcombe	d																				
Haywards Heath	a		17 30				17 40							17 54			18 00			18 10	
	d		17 35	17 37			17 41							17 55			18 05	18 07		18 11	
Wivelsfield	d													17 59				18 11			
Lewes 4	a		17 52															18 22			
Burgess Hill 4	d				17 38									18 01			18 10				
Hassocks 4	d				17 41									18 04							
Preston Park	d													18 11			18 18				
Hove 2	a			17 53													18 22				
Brighton 10	a				17 52		17 55						17 57	18 16						18 25	

A 🚲 to Crawley

Table 186

Saturdays

Bedford and London - Brighton

		SN ◇1	SN 1	SN ◇1 ⊼	FC 1	SN 1 ⊼	SN 1	SN ◇1	SN ◇1	SN 1	SN 1	FC 1	SN 1 ⊼	SN ◇1 A ⊼	GW 1	GW 1	SN 1	SN ◇1 ⊼	FC 1	SN 1 ⊼	SN 1
London Victoria [15] ⊖	d	17 32		17 36		17 45		17 47	17 51				18 00	18 02				18 06		18 15	
Clapham Junction [10]	d	17 38		17 42				17 53						18 08				18 12			
Bedford	d																				
Luton [10]	d																				
Luton Airport Parkway [7] ✈	d																				
St Albans City	d																				
St Pancras International [15] ⊖	d																				
Farringdon [3] ⊖	d																				
City Thameslink [3]	d																				
London Blackfriars [3] ⊖	d																				
London Bridge [4] ⊖	d		17 33		17 42		17 45					17 57					18 03		18 12		18 15
New Cross Gate	d		17 38														18 08				
Norwood Junction [2]	d		17 46				17 57										18 16				18 26
East Croydon ⇌	a	17 48	17 50	17 52	17 54		18 00	18 03	18 07			18 09		18 18			18 20	18 22	18 24		18 30
	d	17 48	17 51	17 53	17 55		18 00	18 03	18 08			18 11		18 18			18 21	18 23	18 25		18 30
Purley [4]	d		17 57				18 06										18 27				18 36
Coulsdon South	d		18 00				18 09										18 30				18 39
Merstham	d		18 06														18 36				18 45
Redhill	a	18 00	18 09				18 16							18 30			18 39				18 48
	d	18 00	18 10				18 17							18 30	18 34	18 41	18 44				18 52
Reigate	a														18 38						18 56
Nutfield	d						18 21														
Godstone	d						18 27														
Edenbridge	d						18 32														
Penshurst	d						18 39														
Leigh (Kent)	d						18 42														
Tonbridge [4]	a						18 47														
Earlswood (Surrey)	d		18 12																		
Salfords	d		18 16																		
Horley [4]	d		18 19							←				18 36			18 51				
Gatwick Airport [10] ✈	a	18 08	18 23		18 10	18 15		18 18	18 22	18 23		18 26	18 30	18 39		18 50	18 55		18 40	18 45	
	d	18 09	18 24		18 11			18 19	18 23	18 24		18 27		18 40			18 56		18 41		
Three Bridges [10]	a	18 14	→		18 15					18 29		18 31		18 44			→		18 45		
	d	18 14			18 15					18 30		18 32		18 45					18 45		
Crawley	d	18 18								18 33				18 48							
Ifield	d									18 36											
Faygate	d																				
Littlehaven	d									18 42											
Horsham [4]	a	18 26								18 47				18 56							
Balcombe	d				18 21																
Haywards Heath	a				18 26			18 30				18 40							18 54		
	d				18 27			18 35 18 37			18 37	18 41							18 55		
Wivelsfield	d				18 31														18 59		
Lewes [4]	a							18 52													
Burgess Hill [4]	d				18 33				18 38										19 01		
Hassocks [4]	d				18 36				18 41										19 04		
Preston Park	d				18 43														19 11		
Hove [2]	a							18 53			18 53										
Brighton [10]	a			18 27	18 48				18 52			18 55						18 57	19 16		

A ⊼ to Crawley

Table 186

Saturdays

Bedford and London - Brighton

		SN ◇1	SN 1	FC 1	SN 1 ⊼	SN ◇1	SN 1	SN ◇1 ⊼	FC 1	SN 1 ⊼	SN 1	SN ◇1	SN ◇1	SN 1	FC 1	SN 1 ⊼	SN ◇1 B ⊼	GW 1	GW 1
London Victoria [15] ⊖	d	18 17			18 30	18 32		18 36		18 45		18 47	18 51			19 00	19 02		
Clapham Junction [10]	d	18 23				18 38		18 42				18 53					19 08		
Bedford	d																		
Luton [10]	d																		
Luton Airport Parkway [7] ✈	d																		
St Albans City	d																		
St Pancras International [15] ⊖	d																		
Farringdon [3] ⊖	d																		
City Thameslink [3]	d																		
London Blackfriars [3] ⊖	d																		
London Bridge [4] ⊖	d			18 27			18 33		18 42		18 45				18 57				
New Cross Gate	d						18 38												
Norwood Junction [2]	d						18 46				18 56								
East Croydon ⇌	a	18 33		18 39		18 48	18 50	18 52	18 54		19 00	19 03	19 07		19 09		19 18		
	d	18 33		18 41		18 48	18 51	18 53	18 55		19 00	19 03	19 08		19 11		19 18		
Purley [4]	d						18 57				19 06								
Coulsdon South	d						19 00				19 09								
Merstham	d						19 06												
Redhill	a					19 00	19 09				19 16						19 30		
	d					19 00	19 10				19 17						19 30	19 34	19 41
Reigate	a																	19 38	
Nutfield	d										19 21								
Godstone	d										19 27								
Edenbridge	d										19 32								
Penshurst	d										19 39								
Leigh (Kent)	d										19 42								
Tonbridge [4]	a										19 47								
Earlswood (Surrey)	d						19 12												
Salfords	d						19 16												
Horley [4]	d		←				19 19							←			19 36		
Gatwick Airport [10] ✈	a	18 48	18 55	18 56	19 00	19 08	19 23		19 10	19 15		19 18	19 22	19 23	19 26	19 30	19 39		19 50
	d	18 49	18 56	18 57		19 09	19 24		19 11			19 19	19 23	19 24	19 27		19 40		
Three Bridges [10]	a		19 01	19 01		19 14	→		19 15					19 28	19 31		19 44		
	d		19 01	19 02		19 14			19 15					19 30	19 32		19 45		
Crawley	d		19 05			19 18								19 33			19 48		
Ifield	d		19 07											19 36					
Faygate	d																		
Littlehaven	d		19 14											19 42					
Horsham [4]	a		19 17			19 26								19 45			19 56		
Balcombe	d								19 21										
Haywards Heath	a	19 00		19 10					19 26			19 30			19 40				
	d	19 05 19 07		19 11					19 27			19 35 19 37			19 41				
Wivelsfield	d	19 11							19 31										
Lewes [4]	a	19 22										19 52							
Burgess Hill [4]	d	19 10							19 33				19 37						
Hassocks [4]	d								19 36				19 41						
Preston Park	d	19 18							19 43										
Hove [2]	a	19 22										19 52							
Brighton [10]	a			19 25				19 27	19 48				19 52		19 54				

B ⊼ to Crawley

Bedford and London - Brighton

Station		SN 1	SN ◇1	FC 1	SN 1	SN ◇1		SN 1	FC 1	SN 1	SN 1	SN ◇1	SN 1	SN ◇1	FC 1	SN 1	SN ◇1		SN ◇1	SN 1	FC 1
London Victoria	d		19 06		19 15	19 17				19 30		19 32		19 36		19 45	19 47		19 51		
Clapham Junction	d		19 12			19 23						19 38		19 42			19 53				
Bedford	d																				
Luton	d																				
Luton Airport Parkway	d																				
St Albans City	d																				
St Pancras International	d																				
Farringdon	d																				
City Thameslink	d																				
London Blackfriars	d																				
London Bridge	d	19 03		19 12					19 27				19 33		19 42						19 57
New Cross Gate	d	19 08											19 38								
Norwood Junction	d	19 16											19 46								
East Croydon	a	19 20	19 22	19 24		19 33			19 39			19 48	19 50	19 52	19 54		20 03		20 07		20 09
	d	19 21	19 23	19 25		19 33			19 41			19 48	19 51	19 53	19 55		20 03		20 08		20 11
Purley	d	19 27											19 57								
Coulsdon South	d	19 30											20 00								
Merstham	d	19 36											20 06								
Redhill	a	19 39										20 00	20 09								
	d	19 46									19 51	20 00	20 10								
Reigate	a																				
Nutfield	d										19 55										
Godstone	d										20 01										
Edenbridge	d										20 06										
Penshurst	d										20 13										
Leigh (Kent)	d										20 16										
Tonbridge	a										20 21										
Earlswood (Surrey)	d												20 12								
Salfords	d												20 16								
Horley	d	19 52						←					20 19							←	
Gatwick Airport	a	19 55		19 40	19 45	19 48		19 55	19 56	20 00		20 08	20 23		20 10	20 15	20 18		20 22	20 23	20 26
	d	19 56		19 41		19 49		19 56	19 57			20 09	20 24		20 11		20 19		20 23	20 24	20 27
Three Bridges	a	→		19 45				20 01	20 01			20 14	→		20 15					20 29	20 31
	d			19 45				20 01	20 02			20 14			20 15					20 33	20 32
Crawley	d							20 05				20 18								20 36	
Ifield	d							20 07												20 39	
Faygate	d																				
Littlehaven	d							20 14												20 45	
Horsham	a							20 17				20 26								20 48	
Balcombe	d														20 21						
Haywards Heath	a			19 54		20 00			20 10						20 26		20 30				20 40
	d			19 55		20 05	20 07		20 11						20 27		20 35	20 37			20 41
Wivelsfield	d			19 59			20 11								20 31		20 39				
Lewes	a						20 22										20 52				
Burgess Hill	d			20 01		20 10									20 33				20 38		
Hassocks	d			20 04											20 36				20 41		
Preston Park	d			20 11		20 18									20 43						
Hove	a					20 22												20 53			
Brighton	a		19 58	20 16					20 25					20 27	20 48				20 52		20 55

Bedford and London - Brighton

Station		SN 1	SN ◇1	SN ◇1	FC 1	GW 1 A	GW 1	SN 1	SN 1	SN ◇1		SN ◇1	SN 1	SN 1	SN 1	SN ◇1	SN ◇1	FC 1	SN 1	SN 1	SN ◇1	
London Victoria	d	20 00	20 02	20 06				20 10	20 15	20 17		20 21		20 30		20 32	20 36		20 40	20 45	20 47	
Clapham Junction	d		20 08	20 12				20 16		20 23						20 38	20 42		20 46		20 53	
Bedford	d																					
Luton	d																					
Luton Airport Parkway	d																					
St Albans City	d																					
St Pancras International	d																					
Farringdon	d																					
City Thameslink	d																					
London Blackfriars	d																					
London Bridge	d				20 12													20 42				
New Cross Gate	d																					
Norwood Junction	d																					
East Croydon	a		20 19	20 22	20 24			20 27		20 33		20 37				20 48	20 52	20 53	20 57		21 03	
	d		20 19	20 23	20 25			20 28		20 33		20 38				20 48	20 53	20 54	20 58		21 03	
Purley	d							20 33											21 03			
Coulsdon South	d							20 37											21 06			
Merstham	d							20 42											21 12			
Redhill	a		20 30					20 46								21 00			21 15			
	d		20 31			20 34	20 41	20 46							20 51	21 00			21 16			
Reigate	a					20 38																
Nutfield	d														20 55							
Godstone	d														21 01							
Edenbridge	d														21 06							
Penshurst	d														21 13							
Leigh (Kent)	d														21 16							
Tonbridge	a														21 21							
Earlswood (Surrey)	d																		21 18			
Salfords	d																		21 22			
Horley	d							20 52					←						21 25			
Gatwick Airport	a	20 30	20 38		20 40		20 50	20 56	20 45	20 48		20 52	20 56	21 00		21 08		21 10	21 28	21 15	21 18	
	d		20 39		20 41			20 57		20 49		20 53	20 57			21 09		21 11	21 29		21 19	
Three Bridges	a		20 44		20 45			→					21 02			21 14		21 15	→			
	d		20 44		20 45								21 02			21 14		21 15				
Crawley	d		20 48										21 06			21 18						
Ifield	d												21 08									
Faygate	d																					
Littlehaven	d												21 15									
Horsham	a		20 56										21 18			21 26						
Balcombe	d				20 51																	
Haywards Heath	a				20 56					21 00								21 24			21 30	
	d				20 57					21 05	21 07							21 25			21 34	21 37
Wivelsfield	d				21 01						21 11							21 29			21 38	
Lewes	a										21 22										21 51	
Burgess Hill	d				21 03					21 10								21 31				
Hassocks	d				21 06							21 10						21 34				
Preston Park	d				21 13					21 19								21 41				
Hove	a									21 22												21 51
Brighton	a			20 57	21 18							21 22					21 27	21 46				

A from 17 September

Table 186

Saturdays

Bedford and London - Brighton

		SN 1	SN 1	SN ◇1	SN ◇1	FC 1	GW 1	SN 1	SN 1	SN ◇1		SN 1	GW 1	SN 1	SN 1	SN 1	SN ◇1	FC 1	SN 1	SN 1	SN ◇1	
London Victoria 15 ⊖	d		21 00	21 02	21 06			21 10	21 15	21 17				21 30		21 32	21 36		21 40	21 45	21 47	
Clapham Junction 10	d			21 08	21 12			21 16		21 23						21 38	21 42		21 46		21 53	
Bedford	d																					
Luton 10	d																					
Luton Airport Parkway 7 ✈	d																					
St Albans City	d																					
St Pancras International 15 ⊖	d																					
Farringdon 3 ⊖	d																					
City Thameslink 3	d																					
London Blackfriars 3 ⊖	d																					
London Bridge 4 ⊖	d					21 12												21 42				
New Cross Gate	d																					
Norwood Junction 2	d																					
East Croydon	a			21 18	21 22	21 24		21 27		21 33						21 48	21 52	21 54	21 57		22 03	
	d			21 18	21 23	21 25		21 28		21 33						21 48	21 53	21 55	21 58		22 03	
Purley 4	d							21 33											22 03			
Coulsdon South	d							21 37											22 06			
Merstham	d							21 42											22 12			
Redhill	a			21 30				21 46								21 59			22 15			
	d			21 31			21 36	21 46					21 49		21 51	22 00			22 16			
Reigate	a						21 40															
Nutfield	d														21 55							
Godstone	d														22 01							
Edenbridge	d														22 06							
Penshurst	d														22 13							
Leigh (Kent)	d														22 16							
Tonbridge 4	a														22 21							
Earlswood (Surrey)	d																		22 18			
Salfords	d																		22 22			
Horley 4	d	←						21 52				←							22 25			
Gatwick Airport 10 ✈	a	21 28	21 30	21 38		21 40		21 55	21 45	21 48		21 55	21 59	22 00		22 08		22 10	22 28	22 15	22 18	
	d	21 29		21 39		21 41		21 56		21 49		21 56				22 09		22 11	22 29		22 19	
Three Bridges 15	a	21 33		21 44		21 45		→		21 53		22 00				22 14		22 15	→			
	d	21 36		21 44		21 45				21 53		22 01				22 14		22 15				
Crawley	d	21 39										22 04				22 18						
Ifield	d	21 42										22 07										
Faygate	d																					
Littlehaven	d	21 48										22 13										
Horsham 4	a	21 52										22 16				22 26						
Balcombe	d					21 53																
Haywards Heath	a			21 52	21 46	21 58				22 02							22 16	22 24			22 30	
	d			21 53	21 46	21 59				22 06	22 08						22 16	22 25			22 34	22 37
Wivelsfield	d			21 57		22 03					22 12							22 29			22 38	
Lewes 4	a										22 23										22 51	
Burgess Hill 4	d			21 59		22 05				22 11								22 31				
Hassocks 4	d			22 02		22 08												22 34				
Preston Park	d			22 09		22 15												22 41				
Hove 2	a									22 22												22 51
Brighton 10	a			22 15	22 00	22 20											22 30	22 46				

Table 186

Saturdays

Bedford and London - Brighton

		SN 1	SN 5	SN ◇1	SN ◇1	FC 1	SN 1	SN 1	SN ◇1	SN 1	SN 1	SN 1	GW 1	SN 1	SN ◇1	FC 1	SN 1	SN 1	SN ◇1		SN 1	SN 1
London Victoria 15 ⊖	d		22 00	22 02	22 06		22 10	22 15	22 17		22 30			22 32	22 36		22 40	22 45	22 47			23 00
Clapham Junction 10	d			22 08	22 12		22 16		22 23					22 38	22 42		22 46		22 53			
Bedford	d																					
Luton 10	d																					
Luton Airport Parkway 7 ✈	d																					
St Albans City	d																					
St Pancras International 15 ⊖	d																					
Farringdon 3 ⊖	d																					
City Thameslink 3	d																					
London Blackfriars 3 ⊖	d																					
London Bridge 4 ⊖	d					22 12										22 42						
New Cross Gate	d																					
Norwood Junction 2	d																					
East Croydon	a			22 18	22 22	22 24	22 27		22 33					22 48	22 52	22 54	22 57		23 03			
	d			22 18	22 23	22 25	22 28		22 33					22 48	22 53	22 55	22 58		23 03			
Purley 4	d						22 33										23 03					
Coulsdon South	d						22 37										23 07					
Merstham	d						22 42										23 12					
Redhill	a			22 30			22 46							23 00			23 16					
	d			22 31			22 46					22 55	22 56	23 01			23 16					
Reigate	a																					
Nutfield	d											22 59										
Godstone	d											23 05										
Edenbridge	d											23 10										
Penshurst	d											23 17										
Leigh (Kent)	d											23 20										
Tonbridge 4	a											23 25										
Earlswood (Surrey)	d																23 19					
Salfords	d																23 22					
Horley 4	d	←					22 52			←							23 26				←	
Gatwick Airport 10 ✈	a	22 28	22 30	22 38		22 40	22 55	22 45	22 48	22 55	23 00		23 05	23 08		23 10	23 28	23 15	23 18		23 28	23 30
	d	22 29		22 39		22 41	22 56		22 49	22 56				23 09		23 11	23 29		23 19		23 29	
Three Bridges 15	a	22 33		22 44		22 45	→		22 54	23 00				23 14		23 15	→				23 34	
	d	22 36		22 44		22 45			22 54	23 01				23 15		23 15					23 38	
Crawley	d	22 39								23 04				23 18							23 41	
Ifield	d	22 42								23 07											23 44	
Faygate	d																					
Littlehaven	d	22 48								23 13											23 50	
Horsham 4	a	22 52								23 16				23 26							23 53	
Balcombe	d					22 53																
Haywards Heath	a			22 52	22 46	22 58			23 02						23 16	23 24			23 30			
	d			22 53	22 46	22 59			23 03						23 16	23 25			23 34	23 37		
Wivelsfield	d			22 57		23 03										23 29			23 38			
Lewes 4	a																		23 51			
Burgess Hill 4	d			22 59		23 05			23 08							23 31						
Hassocks 4	d			23 02		23 08										23 34						
Preston Park	d			23 09		23 15										23 41						
Hove 2	a								23 21											23 51		
Brighton 10	a			23 15	23 00	23 20									23 30	23 46						

Bedford and London - Brighton

		SN ◇1	SN ◇1	FC 1	SN 1	SN 1	SN ◇1	SN 1	SN 1	SN 1	SN 1	FC 1	SN	SN 1
London Victoria 15 ⊖	d	23 02	23 06		23 10	23 15	23 17		23 30		23 32		23 45	23 47
Clapham Junction 10	d	23 08	23 12		23 16		23 23				23 38			23 53
Bedford	d													
Luton 10	d													
Luton Airport Parkway 7 ✈	d													
St Albans City	d													
St Pancras International 15 ⊖	d													
Farringdon 3 ⊖	d													
City Thameslink 3	d													
London Blackfriars 3 ⊖	d													
London Bridge 4 ⊖	d			23 12								23 42		
New Cross Gate	d													
Norwood Junction 2	d													
East Croydon	a	23 18	23 22	23 24	23 27		23 33				23 52	23 56		00 05
	d	23 18	23 23	23 25	23 28		23 33				23 52	23 57		00 06
Purley 4	d				23 33									00 12
Coulsdon South	d				23 37									00 15
Merstham	d				23 42									00 21
Redhill	a	23 30			23 46						00 03			00 24
	d	23 31			23 46					23 55	00 05			00 25
Reigate	a													
Nutfield	d													
Godstone	d													
Edenbridge	d									00 06				
Penshurst	d													
Leigh (Kent)	d													
Tonbridge 4	a									00 15				
Earlswood (Surrey)	d				23 49									
Salfords	d				23 52									
Horley 4	d				23 56			←						00 31
Gatwick Airport 10 ✈	a	23 38		23 40	23 58	23 45	23 50	23 58	00 05		00 14	00 18	00 20	00 33
	d	23 39		23 41	23 59		23 51	23 59			00 15	00 19		00 34
Three Bridges 15	a	23 44		23 47	→		23 55	00 04			00 20	00 24		00 39
	d	23 44		23 47			23 56	00 04			00 20			00 39
Crawley	d							00 07						00 43
Ifield	d							00 10						00 46
Faygate	d													
Littlehaven	d							00 16						00 52
Horsham 4	a							00 19						00 55
Balcombe	d			23 53							00 27			
Haywards Heath	a	23 52	23 46	23 58			00 04				00 34			
	d	23 53	23 46	23 59			00 05				00 34			
Wivelsfield	d	23 57		00 03							00 38			
Lewes 4	a													
Burgess Hill 4	d	23 59		00 05			00 10				00 40			
Hassocks 4	d	00 02		00 08							00 44			
Preston Park	d	00 09		00 15							00 51			
Hove 2	a						00 21							
Brighton 10	a	00 15	00 01	00 20							00 55			

Bedford and London - Brighton

until 11 September

		SN ◇1 A	SN ◇1 A	FC 1 A	SN 1 A	SN ◇1 A	SN 1 A	SN 1 A	SN 1 A	GW 1 A	SN 1 A	FC 1 A	SN A	SN 1 A	SN 1	SN ◇1	FC 1	SN 1	SN 1	FC 1	GW 1
London Victoria 15 ⊖	d	23p02	23p06		23p10	23p17		23p30			23p32		23p45	23p47	00 02	00 05		00 14	00 30		
Clapham Junction 10	d	23p08	23p12		23p16	23p23					23p38			23p53		00 11		00 20			
Bedford	d																				
Luton 10	d																				
Luton Airport Parkway 7 ✈	d																				
St Albans City	d																				
St Pancras International 15 ⊖	d																				
Farringdon 3 ⊖	d																				
City Thameslink 3	d																				
London Blackfriars 3 ⊖	d																				
London Bridge 4 ⊖	d			23p12								23p42					00 12			00 42	
New Cross Gate	d																				
Norwood Junction 2	d																				
East Croydon	a	23p18	23p22	23p24	23p27	23p33					23p52	23p56		00 05		00 24	00 27	00 31		00 56	
	d	23p18	23p23	23p25	23p28	23p33					23p52	23p57		00 06		00 25	00 27	00 32		00 57	
Purley 4	d				23p33									00 12				00 37			
Coulsdon South	d				23p37									00 15				00 41			
Merstham	d				23p42									00 21				00 47			
Redhill	a	23p30			23p46						00 03			00 24				00 50			
	d	23p31			23p46				23p55	00 03	00 05			00 25				00 51			01 18
Reigate	a																				
Nutfield	d																				
Godstone	d																				
Edenbridge	d								00 06												
Penshurst	d																				
Leigh (Kent)	d																				
Tonbridge 4	a								00 15												
Earlswood (Surrey)	d				23p49																
Salfords	d				23p52																
Horley 4	d				23p56		←							00 31				00 57			
Gatwick Airport 10 ✈	a	23p38		23p40	23p58	23p50	23p58	00 05		00 10	00 14	00 18	00 20	00 33	00 38	00 43	00 48	00 59	01 05	01 19	01 26
	d	23p39		23p41	23p59	23p51	23p59				00 15	00 19		00 34		00 44	00 49	01 00		01 20	
Three Bridges 15	a	23p44		23p47	→	23p55	00 04				00 20	00 24		00 39		00 48	00 54	01 05		01 24	
	d	23p44		23p47		23p56	00 04				00 20			00 39		00 48					
Crawley	d						00 07							00 43							
Ifield	d						00 10							00 46							
Faygate	d																				
Littlehaven	d						00 16							00 52							
Horsham 4	a						00 19							00 55							
Balcombe	d			23p53							00 27										
Haywards Heath	a	23p52	23p46	23p58		00 04					00 34					00 58					
	d	23p53	23p46	23p59		00 05					00 34					01 02 / 01 06					
Wivelsfield	d	23p57		00 03							00 38										
Lewes 4	a															01 20					
Burgess Hill 4	d	23p59		00 05		00 10					00 40										
Hassocks 4	d	00 02		00 08							00 44										
Preston Park	d	00 09		00 15							00 51										
Hove 2	a					00 21															
Brighton 10	a	00 15	00 01	00 20							00 55					01s16					

A not 22 May

Table 186

Sundays

until 11 September

Bedford and London - Brighton

		SN	FC	SN	SN	SN	SN	SN	SN	SN	SN	SN	SN	SN	SN	SN	SN	SN	SN	SN	SN	SN
		■	■	■	■	■	■	■	■	■	■	■	■	■	◇■	■	■	■	◇■	■	■	■
																				A	B	A
																🚌	🚌	🚌		🚌	🚌	🚌
London Victoria 15 ⊖	d	01 00		02 00	03 00	03 30	04 00	04 30	05 00	05 02	05 15	05 30	05 45		05 47	06 00	06 15	06 30	06 32	06 45	06 45	07 00
Clapham Junction 10	d	01 08		02 08	03 08		04 08			05 08					05 53				06 38			
Bedford	d																					
Luton 10	d																					
Luton Airport Parkway 7 ✈	d																					
St Albans City	d																					
St Pancras International 15 ⊖	d																					
Farringdon 3 ⊖	d																					
City Thameslink 3	d																					
London Blackfriars 3 ⊖	d																					
London Bridge 4 ⊖	d		01 05																			
New Cross Gate	d																					
Norwood Junction 2	d																					
East Croydon	a	01 21	01 32	02 21	03 21		04 21			05 22					06 05				06 51			
	d	01 22	01 32	02 22	03 22		04 22			05 23					06 06				06 52			
Purley 4	d	01 27		02 27	03 27		04 27			05 29									06 56			
Coulsdon South	d																		07 00			
Merstham	d																		07 05			
Redhill	a	01 36					04 36			05 37					06 18				07 09			
	d	01 36					04 36			05 38					06 19				07 09			
Reigate	a																					
Nutfield	d																					
Godstone	d																					
Edenbridge	d																					
Penshurst	d																					
Leigh (Kent)	d																					
Tonbridge 4	a																					
Earlswood (Surrey)	d																					
Salfords	d																					
Horley 4	d	01 43		02 42	03 42		04 43								06 25				07 15			
Gatwick Airport 10 ✈	a	01 45	01 51	02 44	03 44	04 05	04 45	05 05	05 35	05 45	05 50	06 05	06 20		06 31	06 35	06 47	07 05	07 18	07 15	07 20	07 30
	d	01 47	01 52	02 46	03 46		04 47			05 46				06 29	06 32				07 19			
Three Bridges 15	a	01 51	01 58	03 00	04 00		04 54			05 50				06 33	06 36				07 23			
	d	01 52					04 55			05 51				06 40	06 36				07 24			
Crawley	d													06 43								
Ifield	d													06 46								
Faygate	d																					
Littlehaven	d													06 52								
Horsham 4	a													06 56								
Balcombe	d																		07 30			
Haywards Heath	a	02 06					05 07			05 59					06 46				07 35			
	d	02 06					05 07			06 00					06 47				07 36			
Wivelsfield	d														06 51				07 40			
Lewes 4	a																					
Burgess Hill 4	d														06 53				07 42			
Hassocks 4	d														06 56				07 45			
Preston Park	d														07 03				07 52			
Hove 2	a																					
Brighton 10	a	02 23					05 21			06 18					07 08				07 58			

A not 11 September

B 11 September

Table 186

Sundays

until 11 September

Bedford and London - Brighton

		SN	SN	SN	SN	FC	SN	SN	SN	FC	SN	GW	SN	SN	SN	SN	SN	SN	SN	FC	SN	FC
		■	◇■	■	◇■	■	◇■	■	◇■	■	■	■	◇■	■	■	◇■	■	■	■	■	■	■
		A	B	B	A	B	B	B	A	A	A		B	B	A	A	A	A	B	B	B	A
		🚌						🚌			🚌			🚌	🚌						🚌	
London Victoria 15 ⊖	d	07 00	07 02		07 02			07 15			07 15		07 27	07 30	07 30	07 32					07 45	
Clapham Junction 10	d		07 08		07 08								07 33			07 38						
Bedford	d																					
Luton 10	d																					
Luton Airport Parkway 7 ✈	d																					
St Albans City	d																					
St Pancras International 15 ⊖	d																					
Farringdon 3 ⊖	d																					
City Thameslink 3	d																					
London Blackfriars 3 ⊖	d																					
London Bridge 4 ⊖	d			07 05		07 12				07 12								07 37	07 37	07 42		07 42
New Cross Gate	d																					
Norwood Junction 2	d			07 17														07 48	07 48			
East Croydon	a		07 19	07 21	07 23	07 24				07 26			07 42			07 50		07 54	07 54	07 54		07 56
	d		07 20	07 22	07 23	07 24				07 27			07 43			07 51		07 55	07 55	07 54		07 57
Purley 4	d		07 25	07 28	07 29													08 00	08 00			
Coulsdon South	d			07 31														08 04	08 04			
Merstham	d			07 37														08 09	08 09			
Redhill	a		07 33	07 40	07 37								07 57			08 03		08 13	08 13			
	d		07 34	07 41	07 37							07 45	07 57			08 04	08 10	08 13	08 13			
Reigate	a																					
Nutfield	d			07 45													08 14					
Godstone	d			07 51													08 20					
Edenbridge	d			07 56													08 25					
Penshurst	d			08 03													08 32					
Leigh (Kent)	d			08 06													08 35					
Tonbridge 4	a			08 11													08 40					
Earlswood (Surrey)	d																		08 18			
Salfords	d																		08 22			
Horley 4	d		07 40		07 43		←		←									08 22	08 25			
Gatwick Airport 10 ✈	a	07 35	07 42		07 46	07 41	07 42	07 45	07 46	07 48	07 50	07 55	08 04	08 00	08 05	08 11		08 24	08 28	08 11	08 15	08 18
	d		07 43		07 47	07 41	07 43		07 47	07 50			08 05			08 12		08 25	08 29	08 11		08 20
Three Bridges 15	a		→		→	07 47	07 48		07 51	07 54			08 10			08 16		→	→	08 17		08 24
	d					07 47	07 48		07 52	07 54			08 10			08 17				08 17		08 24
Crawley	d						07 52		07 55													
Ifield	d						07 54		07 58													
Faygate	d																					
Littlehaven	d						08 01		08 04													
Horsham 4	a						08 04		08 07													
Balcombe	d												08 16			08 23						
Haywards Heath	a					07 56				08 03			08 21			08 28				08 26		08 33
	d					07 56				08 03			08 22			08 28				08 26		08 33
Wivelsfield	d												08 26			08 32						
Lewes 4	a																					
Burgess Hill 4	d					08 01				08 08			08 28			08 34				08 31		08 38
Hassocks 4	d					08 05				08 12			08 31			08 38				08 35		08 42
Preston Park	d												08 38			08 45						
Hove 2	a																					
Brighton 10	a					08 14				08 22			08 43			08 50				08 45		08 52

A 11 September

B not 11 September

Bedford and London - Brighton

		SN 1 A ⌶	SN 1 A	SN 1 B	SN 1 B ⌶	SN 1 A ⌶	SN ◇1 B	SN 1 B	FC 1 B	SN ◇1 A	SN 1 B ⌶	FC 1 A	SN 1 A ⌶	SN ◇1 B	SN ◇1 A	GW 1	SN ◇1 B	SN 1 B ⌶	SN 1 A ⌶	SN ◇1 A	SN 1 A	SN 1 B
London Victoria 15 ⊖	d	07 45			08 00	08 00	08 02			08 04	08 15		08 15	08 17	08 17		08 27	08 30	08 30	08 32		
Clapham Junction 10	d						08 08			08 10				08 23	08 23		08 33			08 38		
Bedford	d																					
Luton 10	d																					
Luton Airport Parkway 7 ✈	d																					
St Albans City	d																					
St Pancras International 15 ⊖	d																					
Farringdon 3 ⊖	d																					
City Thameslink 3	d																					
London Blackfriars 3 ⊖	d																					
London Bridge 4 ⊖	d							08 05	08 12			08 12										08 37
New Cross Gate	d																					
Norwood Junction 2	d							08 16														08 48
East Croydon	a						08 17	08 20	08 24	08 24		08 27		08 32	08 36		08 42			08 50		08 54
	d						08 18	08 21	08 24	08 24		08 27		08 33	08 37		08 43			08 51		08 55
Purley 4	d						08 23	08 27		08 30												09 00
Coulsdon South	d							08 30														09 04
Merstham	d							08 36														09 09
Redhill	a						08 31	08 39		08 38							08 57			09 03		09 13
	d						08 32	08 40		08 39						08 49	08 57			09 04	09 10	09 13
Reigate	a																					
Nutfield	d							08 44													09 14	
Godstone	d							08 50													09 20	
Edenbridge	d							08 55													09 25	
Penshurst	d							09 02													09 32	
Leigh (Kent)	d							09 05													09 35	
Tonbridge 4	a							09 10													09 40	
Earlswood (Surrey)	d																					09 18
Salfords	d																					09 22
Horley 4	d		←	←			08 38			08 45												09 25
Gatwick Airport 10 ✈	a	08 20	08 24	08 28	08 30	08 35	08 40		08 41	08 47	08 45	08 48	08 50	08 48	08 54	08 57	09 04	09 00	09 05	09 11		09 28
	d		08 25	08 29			08 41		08 41	08 48		08 50		08 49	08 56		09 05			09 12		09 29
Three Bridges 15	a		08 30	08 33			08 46		08 47	08 53		08 54					09 10			09 16		→
	d		08 33	08 34			08 46		08 47	08 53		08 54					09 10			09 17		
Crawley	d		08 36	08 37			08 50			08 56												
Ifield	d		08 39	08 40																		
Faygate	d																					
Littlehaven	d		08 45	08 46																		
Horsham 4	a		08 49	08 49			08 58			09 04												
Balcombe	d																09 16			09 23		
Haywards Heath	a								08 56			09 03		09 00	09 06		09 21			09 28		
	d								08 56			09 03		09 00	09 07		09 22			09 28		
Wivelsfield	d																09 26			09 32		
Lewes 4	a																					
Burgess Hill 4	d								09 01			09 08		09 06	09 12		09 28			09 34		
Hassocks 4	d								09 05			09 12					09 31			09 38		
Preston Park	d																09 38			09 45		
Hove 2	a													09 18	09 24							
Brighton 10	a								09 14			09 22					09 43			09 50		

A 11 September

B not 11 September

Bedford and London - Brighton

		SN 1 A	FC 1 B	SN 1 B ⌶	FC 1 A	SN 1 A ⌶	SN ◇1 C ⌶	SN 1 A	SN 1 B	SN ◇1 D ⌶	SN 1 B ⌶	SN 1 A ⌶	SN ◇1 B	SN 1 B	SN ◇1 A	SN ◇1 A	SN ◇1 B	SN ◇1 A	SN ◇1 B	FC 1 B	SN 1 B ⌶	SN ◇1 A
London Victoria 15 ⊖	d			08 45		08 45	08 47			08 47	09 00	09 00	09 02		09 02	09 04	09 06				09 15	
Clapham Junction 10	d						08 53			08 53			09 08		09 08	09 10	09 12					
Bedford	d																					
Luton 10	d																					
Luton Airport Parkway 7 ✈	d																					
St Albans City	d																					
St Pancras International 15 ⊖	d																					
Farringdon 3 ⊖	d																					
City Thameslink 3	d																					
London Blackfriars 3 ⊖	d																					
London Bridge 4 ⊖	d	08 37	08 42		08 42									09 05						09 12		
New Cross Gate	d																					
Norwood Junction 2	d	08 48												09 16								
East Croydon	a	08 54	08 54		08 56		09 02			09 06			09 17	09 20	09 21	09 24	09 22			09 24		
	d	08 55	08 54		08 57		09 03			09 07			09 18	09 21	09 22	09 24	09 23			09 24		
Purley 4	d	09 00											09 23	09 27		09 30						
Coulsdon South	d	09 04												09 30								
Merstham	d	09 09												09 36								
Redhill	a	09 13											09 31	09 39		09 38						
	d	09 16											09 32	09 40		09 39						
Reigate	a																					
Nutfield	d													09 44								
Godstone	d													09 50								
Edenbridge	d													09 55								
Penshurst	d													10 02								
Leigh (Kent)	d													10 05								
Tonbridge 4	a													10 10								
Earlswood (Surrey)	d																					
Salfords	d																					
Horley 4	d	09 22						←	←				09 38			09 45		←	←			←
Gatwick Airport 10 ✈	a	09 24	09 11	09 15	09 18	09 20	09 18	09 24	09 28	09 27	09 30	09 35	09 40		09 39	09 47	09 37	09 39	09 40	09 41	09 45	09 47
	d	09 25	09 11		09 20		09 19	09 25	09 29	09 29			09 41		09 40	09 48	09 39	09 40	09 41	09 41		09 48
Three Bridges 15	a	→	09 17		09 24			09 30	09 33				→		→	→			09 46	09 47		09 53
	d		09 17		09 24			09 33	09 34										09 46	09 47		09 53
Crawley	d							09 37	09 37										09 50			09 56
Ifield	d							09 39	09 40													
Faygate	d																					
Littlehaven	d							09 46	09 46													
Horsham 4	a							09 49	09 49										09 58			10 04
Balcombe	d																					
Haywards Heath	a		09 26		09 33		09 30			09 40										09 56		
	d		09 26		09 33		09 30			09 41										09 56		
Wivelsfield	d						09 34			09 45												
Lewes 4	a						09 48			09 58												
Burgess Hill 4	d		09 31		09 38															10 01		
Hassocks 4	d		09 35		09 42															10 05		
Preston Park	d																					
Hove 2	a																					
Brighton 10	a		09 46		09 52												10 03	10 03		10 14		

A 11 September

B not 11 September

C not 11 September. ⌶ to Wivelsfield

D 11 September. ⌶ to Wivelsfield

Table 186

Sundays until 11 September

Bedford and London - Brighton

		FC	SN	SN	SN	GW	SN	SN	SN	SN	SN	SN	SN	SN	FC	SN	FC	SN	SN	SN	SN	SN
		1	1	◇1	◇1	1	◇1	1	1	◇1	◇1	1	1	1	1	1	1	1	◇1	1	1	◇1
		A	A ⌶	B	A		B	B ⌶	A ⌶	A	B	A	B	A	B	B ⌶	A	A ⌶	C ⌶	A	B	D ⌶
London Victoria 15 ⊖	d		09 15	09 17	09 17		09 27	09 30	09 30	09 32	09 36					09 45		09 45	09 47			09 47
Clapham Junction 10	d			09 23	09 23		09 33			09 38	09 42								09 53			09 53
Bedford	d																					
Luton 10	d																					
Luton Airport Parkway 7 ✈	d																					
St Albans City	d																					
St Pancras International 15 ⊖	d																					
Farringdon 3 ⊖	d																					
City Thameslink 3	d																					
London Blackfriars 3 ⊖	d																					
London Bridge 4 ⊖	d	09 12											09 37	09 37	09 42		09 42					
New Cross Gate	d																					
Norwood Junction 2	d												09 48	09 48								
East Croydon	a	09 27		09 32	09 36		09 42			09 50	09 52		09 54	09 54	09 54		09 56		10 02			10 06
	d	09 27		09 33	09 37		09 43			09 51	09 53		09 55	09 55	09 54		09 57		10 03			10 07
Purley 4	d												10 00	10 00								
Coulsdon South	d												10 04	10 04								
Merstham	d												10 09	10 09								
Redhill	a						09 57			10 03			10 13	10 13								
	d					09 47	09 57			10 04		10 10	10 13	10 16								
Reigate	a																					
Nutfield	d											10 14										
Godstone	d											10 20										
Edenbridge	d											10 25										
Penshurst	d											10 32										
Leigh (Kent)	d											10 35										
Tonbridge 4	a											10 40										
Earlswood (Surrey)	d												10 18									
Salfords	d												10 22									
Horley 4	d												10 25	10 22						←	←	
Gatwick Airport 10 ✈	a	09 48	09 50	09 48	09 54	09 56	10 04	10 00	10 05	10 11			10 28	10 24	10 11	10 15	10 18	10 20	10 18	10 24	10 28	10 27
	d	09 50		09 49	09 56		10 05			10 12			10 29	10 25	10 11		10 20		10 19	10 25	10 29	10 29
Three Bridges 15	a	09 54					10 10			10 16			→	→	10 17		10 24			10 30	10 33	
	d	09 54					10 10			10 17					10 17		10 24			10 33	10 34	
Crawley	d																			10 37	10 37	
Ifield	d																			10 39	10 40	
Faygate	d																					
Littlehaven	d																			10 46	10 46	
Horsham 4	a																			10 49	10 49	
Balcombe	d						10 16			10 23												
Haywards Heath	a	10 03		10 00	10 06		10 21			10 28					10 26		10 33		10 30			10 40
	d	10 03		10 00	10 07		10 22			10 28					10 26		10 33		10 30			10 41
Wivelsfield	d						10 26			10 32									10 34			10 45
Lewes 4	a																		10 48			10 58
Burgess Hill 4	d	10 08		10 06	10 12		10 28			10 34					10 31		10 38					
Hassocks 4	d	10 12					10 31			10 38					10 35		10 42					
Preston Park	d						10 38			10 45												
Hove 2	a			10 18	10 24																	
Brighton 10	a	10 22					10 43			10 50	10 27				10 46		10 52					

A 11 September
B not 11 September
C not 11 September. ⌶ to Wivelsfield
D 11 September. ⌶ to Wivelsfield

Table 186

Sundays until 11 September

Bedford and London - Brighton

		SN	SN	SN	SN	SN	SN	SN	SN	SN	FC	SN	SN	FC	SN	SN	SN	GW	SN	SN	SN	SN
		1	1	◇1	1	◇1	◇1	◇1	◇1	◇1	1	1	◇1	1	1	◇1	◇1	1	◇1	1	1	◇1
		A ⌶	B ⌶	A	A	B ⌶	B ⌶	A ⌶	B ⌶	A	A	A ⌶	B ⌶	B	B ⌶	A	B		A	A ⌶	B ⌶	B
London Victoria 15 ⊖	d	10 00	10 00	10 02		10 02	10 04	10 06				10 15			10 15	10 17	10 17		10 27	10 30	10 30	10 32
Clapham Junction 10	d			10 08		10 08	10 10	10 12								10 23	10 23		10 33			10 38
Bedford	d																					
Luton 10	d																					
Luton Airport Parkway 7 ✈	d																					
St Albans City	d																					
St Pancras International 15 ⊖	d																					
Farringdon 3 ⊖	d																					
City Thameslink 3	d																					
London Blackfriars 3 ⊖	d																					
London Bridge 4 ⊖	d				10 05						10 12			10 12								
New Cross Gate	d																					
Norwood Junction 2	d				10 16																	
East Croydon	a			10 17	10 20	10 21	10 24	10 22			10 24			10 27		10 32	10 36		10 42			10 50
	d			10 18	10 21	10 22	10 24	10 23			10 24			10 27		10 33	10 37		10 43			10 51
Purley 4	d			10 23	10 27		10 30															
Coulsdon South	d				10 30																	
Merstham	d				10 36																	
Redhill	a			10 31	10 39		10 38												10 57			11 03
	d			10 32	10 40		10 39											10 49	10 57			11 04
Reigate	a																					
Nutfield	d				10 44																	
Godstone	d				10 50																	
Edenbridge	d				10 55																	
Penshurst	d				11 02																	
Leigh (Kent)	d				11 05																	
Tonbridge 4	a				11 10																	
Earlswood (Surrey)	d																					
Salfords	d																					
Horley 4	d			10 38			10 45		←	←			←									
Gatwick Airport 10 ✈	a	10 30	10 35	10 40		10 39	10 47	10 37	10 39	10 40	10 41	10 45	10 47	10 48	10 50	10 48	10 54	10 57	11 04	11 00	11 05	11 11
	d			10 41		10 40	10 48	10 39	10 40	10 41	10 41		10 48	10 50		10 49	10 56		11 05			11 12
Three Bridges 15	a			→		→	→			10 46	10 47		10 53	10 54					11 10			11 16
	d									10 46	10 47		10 53	10 54					11 10			11 17
Crawley	d									10 50			10 56									
Ifield	d																					
Faygate	d																					
Littlehaven	d																					
Horsham 4	a									10 58			11 04									
Balcombe	d																		11 16			11 23
Haywards Heath	a										10 56			11 03		11 00	11 06		11 21			11 28
	d										10 56			11 03		11 00	11 07		11 22			11 28
Wivelsfield	d																		11 26			11 32
Lewes 4	a																					
Burgess Hill 4	d										11 01			11 08		11 06	11 12		11 28			11 34
Hassocks 4	d										11 05			11 12					11 31			11 38
Preston Park	d																		11 38			11 45
Hove 2	a															11 18	11 24					
Brighton 10	a							11 03	11 03		11 14			11 22					11 43			11 50

A not 11 September
B 11 September

Table 186

Bedford and London - Brighton

Sundays

until 11 September

		SN	SN	SN	SN	FC	SN	FC	SN	SN	SN	SN	SN	SN	SN	SN	SN	SN	SN	SN	SN	SN
		◇1	1	1	1	1	1	1	1	◇1	1	1	◇1	1	1	◇1	1	◇1	◇1	◇1	◇1	◇1
		A	B	A	B	A	A	B	B	C	B	A	D	A	B	A	A	B	B	A	B	A
		⊥					⊥		⊥	⊥			⊥	⊥	⊥	⊥		⊥	⊥	⊥	⊥	⊥
London Victoria 15 ⊖	d	10 36					10 45		10 45	10 47			10 47	11 00	11 00	11 02		11 02	11 04	11 06		
Clapham Junction 10	d	10 42								10 53			10 53			11 08		11 08	11 10	11 12		
Bedford	d																					
Luton 10	d																					
Luton Airport Parkway 7 ✈	d																					
St Albans City	d																					
St Pancras International 15 ⊖	d																					
Farringdon 3 ⊖	d																					
City Thameslink 3	d																					
London Blackfriars 3 ⊖	d																					
London Bridge 4 ⊖	d			10 37	10 37	10 42		10 42									11 05					
New Cross Gate	d																					
Norwood Junction 2	d			10 48	10 48												11 16					
East Croydon	a	10 52		10 54	10 54	10 54		10 56		11 02			11 06			11 17	11 20	11 21	11 24	11 22		
	d	10 53		10 55	10 55	10 54		10 57		11 03			11 07			11 18	11 21	11 22	11 24	11 23		
Purley 4	d			11 00	11 00											11 23	11 27		11 30			
Coulsdon South	d			11 04	11 04												11 30					
Merstham	d			11 09	11 09												11 36					
Redhill	a			11 13	11 13											11 31	11 39		11 38			
	d		11 10	11 13	11 16											11 32	11 40		11 39			
Reigate	a																					
Nutfield	d		11 14														11 44					
Godstone	d		11 20														11 50					
Edenbridge	d		11 25														11 55					
Penshurst	d		11 32														12 02					
Leigh (Kent)	d		11 35														12 05					
Tonbridge 4	a		11 40														12 10					
Earlswood (Surrey)	d			11 18																		
Salfords	d			11 22																		
Horley 4	d			11 25	11 22						←	←				11 38			11 45		←	←
Gatwick Airport 10 ✈	a			11 28	11 24	11 11	11 15	11 18	11 20	11 18	11 24	11 28	11 27	11 30	11 35	11 40		11 39	11 47	11 37	11 39	11 40
	d			11 29	11 25	11 11		11 20		11 19	11 25	11 29	11 29			11 41		11 40	11 48	11 39	11 40	11 41
Three Bridges 15	a			→	→	11 17		11 24			11 30	11 33				→		→	→			11 46
	d					11 17		11 24			11 33	11 34										11 46
Crawley	d										11 37	11 37										11 50
Ifield	d										11 39	11 40										
Faygate	d																					
Littlehaven	d										11 46	11 46										
Horsham 4	a										11 49	11 49										11 58
Balcombe	d																					
Haywards Heath	a					11 26		11 33		11 30			11 40									
	d					11 26		11 33		11 30			11 41									
Wivelsfield	d									11 34			11 45									
Lewes 4	a									11 48			11 58									
Burgess Hill 4	d					11 31		11 38														
Hassocks 4	d					11 35		11 42														
Preston Park	d																					
Hove 2	a																					
Brighton 10	a	11 27				11 46		11 52												12 03	12 03	

A not 11 September
B 11 September
C not 11 September. ⊥ to Wivelsfield
D 11 September. ⊥ to Wivelsfield

Bedford and London - Brighton

until 11 September

		FC	SN	SN	FC	SN	SN	SN	GW	SN	SN	SN	SN	SN	SN	SN	SN	FC	SN	FC	SN	SN
		1	1	◇1	1	1	◇1	◇1	1	◇1	1	1	◇1	◇1	1	1	1	1	1	1	1	◇1
		A	A	B	B	B	A	B		A	A	B	B	A	B	A	B	A	A	B	B	C
			⊥	⊥		⊥					⊥	⊥		⊥					⊥		⊥	⊥
London Victoria 15 ⊖	d		11 15			11 15	11 17	11 17		11 27	11 30	11 30	11 32	11 36					11 45		11 45	11 47
Clapham Junction 10	d						11 23	11 23		11 33			11 38	11 42								11 53
Bedford	d																					
Luton 10	d																					
Luton Airport Parkway 7 ✈	d																					
St Albans City	d																					
St Pancras International 15 ⊖	d																					
Farringdon 3 ⊖	d																					
City Thameslink 3	d																					
London Blackfriars 3 ⊖	d																					
London Bridge 4 ⊖	d	11 12			11 12											11 37	11 37	11 42		11 42		
New Cross Gate	d																					
Norwood Junction 2	d															11 48	11 48					
East Croydon	a	11 24			11 27		11 32	11 36		11 42			11 50	11 52		11 54	11 54	11 54		11 56		12 02
	d	11 24			11 27		11 33	11 37		11 43			11 51	11 53		11 55	11 55	11 54		11 57		12 03
Purley 4	d															12 00	12 00					
Coulsdon South	d															12 04	12 04					
Merstham	d															12 09	12 09					
Redhill	a									11 57			12 03			12 13	12 13					
	d								11 46	11 57			12 04		12 10	12 13	12 16					
Reigate	a																					
Nutfield	d														12 14							
Godstone	d														12 20							
Edenbridge	d														12 25							
Penshurst	d														12 32							
Leigh (Kent)	d														12 35							
Tonbridge 4	a														12 40							
Earlswood (Surrey)	d															12 18						
Salfords	d															12 22						
Horley 4	d			←												12 25	12 22					
Gatwick Airport 10 ✈	a	11 41	11 45	11 47	11 48	11 50	11 48	11 54	11 54	12 04	12 00	12 05	12 11			12 28	12 24	12 11	12 15	12 18	12 20	12 18
	d	11 41		11 48	11 50		11 49	11 56		12 05			12 12			12 29	12 25	12 11		12 20		12 19
Three Bridges 15	a	11 47		11 53	11 54					12 10			12 16			→	→	12 17		12 24		
	d	11 47		11 53	11 54					12 10			12 17					12 17		12 24		
Crawley	d			11 56																		
Ifield	d																					
Faygate	d																					
Littlehaven	d																					
Horsham 4	a			12 04																		
Balcombe	d									12 16			12 23									
Haywards Heath	a	11 56			12 03		12 00	12 06		12 21			12 28					12 26		12 33		12 30
	d	11 56			12 03		12 00	12 07		12 22			12 28					12 26		12 33		12 30
Wivelsfield	d									12 26			12 32									12 34
Lewes 4	a																					12 48
Burgess Hill 4	d	12 01			12 08		12 06	12 12		12 28			12 34					12 31		12 38		
Hassocks 4	d	12 05			12 12					12 31			12 38					12 35		12 42		
Preston Park	d									12 38			12 45									
Hove 2	a						12 18	12 24														
Brighton 10	a	12 14			12 22					12 43			12 49	12 27				12 46		12 52		

A not 11 September
B 11 September
C not 11 September. ⊥ to Wivelsfield

Bedford and London - Brighton

Sundays
until 11 September

		SN	SN	SN	SN	SN	SN	SN	SN	SN	SN	SN	SN	FC	SN	SN	FC	SN	SN	SN	GW	SN
		1	1	◇1	1	1	◇1	1	◇1	◇1	◇1	◇1	◇1	1	1	◇1	1	1	◇1	◇1	1	◇1
		A	B	C	B	A	B	B	A	A	B	A	B	B	B	A	A	A	B	A		B
				✠	✠	✠			✠	✠	✠	✠			✠	✠		✠				
London Victoria 15 ⊖	d			11 47	12 00	12 00	12 02		12 02	12 04	12 06				12 15			12 15	12 17	12 17		12 27
Clapham Junction 10	d			11 53			12 08		12 08	12 10	12 12								12 23	12 23		12 33
Bedford	d																					
Luton 10	d																					
Luton Airport Parkway 7 ✈	d																					
St Albans City	d																					
St Pancras International 15 ⊖	d																					
Farringdon 3 ⊖	d																					
City Thameslink 3	d																					
London Blackfriars 3 ⊖	d																					
London Bridge 4 ⊖	d							12 05						12 12			12 12					
New Cross Gate	d																					
Norwood Junction 2	d							12 16														
East Croydon	a			12 06			12 17	12 20	12 21	12 24	12 22			12 24			12 27		12 32	12 36		12 42
	d			12 07			12 18	12 21	12 22	12 24	12 23			12 24			12 27		12 33	12 37		12 43
Purley 4	d						12 23	12 27		12 30												
Coulsdon South	d							12 30														
Merstham	d							12 36														
Redhill	a						12 31	12 39		12 38												12 57
	d						12 32	12 40		12 39											12 46	12 57
Reigate	a																					
Nutfield	d							12 44														
Godstone	d							12 50														
Edenbridge	d							12 55														
Penshurst	d							13 02														
Leigh (Kent)	d							13 05														
Tonbridge 4	a							13 10														
Earlswood (Surrey)	d																					
Salfords	d																					
Horley 4	d	←	←				12 38			12 45		←	←			←						
Gatwick Airport 10 ✈	a	12 24	12 28	12 27	12 30	12 35	12 40		12 39	12 47	12 37	12 39	12 40	12 41	12 45	12 47	12 48	12 50	12 48	12 54	12 54	13 04
	d	12 25	12 29	12 29			12 41		12 40	12 48	12 39	12 40	12 41	12 41		12 48	12 50		12 49	12 56		13 05
Three Bridges 15	a	12 30	12 33				→		→	→			12 46	12 47		12 53	12 54					13 10
	d	12 33	12 34										12 46	12 47		12 53	12 54					13 10
Crawley	d	12 37	12 37										12 50			12 56						
Ifield	d	12 39	12 40																			
Faygate	d																					
Littlehaven	d	12 46	12 46																			
Horsham 4	a	12 49	12 49										12 58			13 04						
Balcombe	d																					13 16
Haywards Heath	a			12 40										12 56			13 03		13 00	13 06		13 21
	d			12 41										12 56			13 03		13 00	13 07		13 22
Wivelsfield	d			12 45																		13 26
Lewes 4	a			12 58																		
Burgess Hill 4	d													13 01			13 08		13 06	13 12		13 28
Hassocks 4	d													13 05			13 12					13 31
Preston Park	d																					13 38
Hove 2	a																		13 18	13 24		
Brighton 10	a										13 03	13 03		13 14			13 22					13 43

A 11 September
B not 11 September
C 11 September. ✠ to Wivelsfield

Bedford and London - Brighton

Sundays
until 11 September

		SN	SN	SN	SN	SN	SN	SN	FC	SN	FC	SN	SN	SN	SN	SN	SN	SN	SN	SN	SN	SN
		1	1	◇1	◇1	1	1	1	1	1	1	1	◇1	1	1	◇1	1	1	◇1	1	◇1	◇1
		A	B	B	A	B	A	B	A	A	B	B	C	B	A	D	A	B	A	A	B	B
		✠	✠		✠					✠		✠	✠			✠	✠	✠			✠	✠
London Victoria 15 ⊖	d	12 30	12 30	12 32	12 36					12 45		12 45	12 47			12 47	13 00	13 00	13 02		13 02	13 04
Clapham Junction 10	d			12 38	12 42								12 53			12 53			13 08		13 08	13 10
Bedford	d																					
Luton 10	d																					
Luton Airport Parkway 7 ✈	d																					
St Albans City	d																					
St Pancras International 15 ⊖	d																					
Farringdon 3 ⊖	d																					
City Thameslink 3	d																					
London Blackfriars 3 ⊖	d																					
London Bridge 4 ⊖	d						12 37	12 37	12 42		12 42									13 05		
New Cross Gate	d																					
Norwood Junction 2	d						12 48	12 48												13 16		
East Croydon	a			12 50	12 52		12 54	12 54	12 54		12 56		13 02			13 06			13 17	13 20	13 21	13 24
	d			12 51	12 53		12 55	12 55	12 54		12 57		13 03			13 07			13 18	13 21	13 22	13 24
Purley 4	d						13 00	13 00											13 23	13 27		13 30
Coulsdon South	d						13 04	13 04												13 30		
Merstham	d						13 09	13 09												13 36		
Redhill	a			13 03			13 13	13 13											13 31	13 39		13 38
	d			13 04		13 10	13 13	13 16											13 32	13 40		13 39
Reigate	a																					
Nutfield	d					13 14														13 44		
Godstone	d					13 20														13 50		
Edenbridge	d					13 25														13 55		
Penshurst	d					13 32														14 02		
Leigh (Kent)	d					13 35														14 05		
Tonbridge 4	a					13 40														14 10		
Earlswood (Surrey)	d						13 18															
Salfords	d						13 22															
Horley 4	d						13 25	13 22						←	←				13 38			13 45
Gatwick Airport 10 ✈	a	13 00	13 05	13 11			13 28	13 24	13 11	13 15	13 18	13 20	13 18	13 24	13 28	13 27	13 30	13 35	13 40		13 39	13 47
	d			13 12			13 29	13 25	13 11		13 20		13 19	13 25	13 29	13 29			13 41		13 40	13 48
Three Bridges 15	a			13 16			→	→	13 17		13 24			13 30	13 33				→		→	→
	d			13 17					13 17		13 24			13 33	13 34							
Crawley	d													13 37	13 37							
Ifield	d													13 39	13 40							
Faygate	d																					
Littlehaven	d													13 46	13 46							
Horsham 4	a													13 49	13 49							
Balcombe	d			13 23																		
Haywards Heath	a			13 28					13 26		13 33		13 30			13 40						
	d			13 28					13 26		13 33		13 30			13 41						
Wivelsfield	d			13 32									13 34			13 45						
Lewes 4	a												13 48			13 56						
Burgess Hill 4	d			13 34					13 31		13 38											
Hassocks 4	d			13 38					13 35		13 42											
Preston Park	d			13 45																		
Hove 2	a																					
Brighton 10	a			13 50	13 27				13 46		13 52											

A not 11 September
B 11 September
C not 11 September. ✠ to Wivelsfield
D 11 September. ✠ to Wivelsfield

until 11 September

Bedford and London - Brighton

		SN	SN	SN	FC	SN	SN	FC	SN	SN	SN	GW	SN	SN	SN	SN	SN	SN	SN	SN	FC	SN
		◇1	◇1	◇1	1	1	◇1	1	1	◇1	◇1	1	◇1	1	1	◇1	◇1	1	1	1	1	1
		A 🍴	B 🍴	A	A	A 🍴	B 🍴	B	B 🍴	A	B		A	A 🍴	B 🍴	B	A 🍴	B	A	B	A	A 🍴
London Victoria 15 ⊖	d	13 06				13 15			13 15	13 17	13 17		13 27	13 30	13 30	13 32	13 36					13 45
Clapham Junction 10	d	13 12								13 23	13 23		13 33			13 38	13 42					
Bedford	d																					
Luton 10	d																					
Luton Airport Parkway 7 ✈	d																					
St Albans City	d																					
St Pancras International 15 ⊖	d																					
Farringdon 3 ⊖	d																					
City Thameslink 3	d																					
London Blackfriars 3 ⊖	d																					
London Bridge 4 ⊖	d				13 12			13 12											13 37	13 37	13 42	
New Cross Gate	d																					
Norwood Junction 2	d																		13 48	13 48		
East Croydon	a	13 22			13 24			13 27		13 32	13 36		13 42			13 50	13 52		13 54	13 54	13 54	
	d	13 23			13 24			13 27		13 33	13 37		13 43			13 51	13 53		13 55	13 55	13 54	
Purley 4	d																		14 00	14 00		
Coulsdon South	d																		14 04	14 04		
Merstham	d																		14 09	14 09		
Redhill	a												13 57			14 03			14 13	14 13		
	d											13 46	13 57			14 04		14 10	14 13	14 16		
Reigate	a																					
Nutfield	d																	14 14				
Godstone	d																	14 20				
Edenbridge	d																	14 25				
Penshurst	d																	14 32				
Leigh (Kent)	d																	14 35				
Tonbridge 4	a																	14 40				
Earlswood (Surrey)	d																		14 18			
Salfords	d																		14 22			
Horley 4	d		←	←			←												14 25	14 22		
Gatwick Airport 10 ✈	a	13 37	13 39	13 40	13 41	13 45	13 47	13 48	13 50	13 48	13 54	13 54	14 04	14 00	14 05	14 11			14 28	14 24	14 11	14 15
	d	13 39	13 40	13 41	13 41		13 48	13 50		13 49	13 56		14 05			14 12			14 29	14 25	14 11	
Three Bridges 15	a			13 46	13 47		13 53	13 54					14 10			14 16			→	→	14 17	
	d			13 46	13 47		13 53	13 54					14 10			14 17					14 17	
Crawley	d			13 50			13 56															
Ifield	d																					
Faygate	d																					
Littlehaven	d																					
Horsham 4	a			13 58			14 04															
Balcombe	d												14 16			14 23						
Haywards Heath	a				13 56			14 03		14 00	14 06		14 21			14 28					14 26	
	d				13 56			14 03		14 00	14 07		14 22			14 28					14 26	
Wivelsfield	d												14 26			14 32						
Lewes 4	a																					
Burgess Hill 4	d				14 01			14 08		14 06	14 12		14 28			14 34					14 31	
Hassocks 4	d				14 05			14 12					14 31			14 38					14 35	
Preston Park	d												14 38			14 45						
Hove 2	a									14 18	14 24											
Brighton 10	a	14 03	14 03		14 14			14 22					14 43			14 50	14 27				14 46	

A not 11 September

B 11 September

until 11 September

Bedford and London - Brighton

		FC	SN	SN	SN	SN	SN	SN	SN	SN	SN	SN	SN	SN	SN	SN	FC	SN	SN	FC	SN	SN
		1	1	◇1	1	1	◇1	1	1	◇1	1	◇1	◇1	◇1	◇1	◇1	1	1	◇1	1	1	◇1
		A	A 🍴	B 🍴	A	C	D 🍴	C 🍴	A 🍴	C	C	A 🍴	A 🍴	C 🍴	A 🍴	C	C	C 🍴	A 🍴	A	A 🍴	C
London Victoria 15 ⊖	d		13 45	13 47			13 47	14 00	14 00	14 02		14 02	14 04	14 06				14 15			14 15	14 17
Clapham Junction 10	d			13 53			13 53			14 08		14 08	14 10	14 12								14 23
Bedford	d																					
Luton 10	d																					
Luton Airport Parkway 7 ✈	d																					
St Albans City	d																					
St Pancras International 15 ⊖	d																					
Farringdon 3 ⊖	d																					
City Thameslink 3	d																					
London Blackfriars 3 ⊖	d																					
London Bridge 4 ⊖	d	13 42									14 05						14 12			14 12		
New Cross Gate	d																					
Norwood Junction 2	d										14 16											
East Croydon	a	13 56		14 02			14 06			14 17	14 20	14 21	14 24	14 22			14 24			14 27		14 32
	d	13 57		14 03			14 07			14 18	14 21	14 22	14 24	14 23			14 24			14 27		14 33
Purley 4	d									14 23	14 27		14 30									
Coulsdon South	d										14 30											
Merstham	d										14 36											
Redhill	a									14 31	14 39		14 38									
	d									14 32	14 40		14 39									
Reigate	a																					
Nutfield	d										14 44											
Godstone	d										14 50											
Edenbridge	d										14 55											
Penshurst	d										15 02											
Leigh (Kent)	d										15 05											
Tonbridge 4	a										15 10											
Earlswood (Surrey)	d																					
Salfords	d																					
Horley 4	d				←	←				14 38			14 45		←	←			←			
Gatwick Airport 10 ✈	a	14 18	14 20	14 18	14 24	14 28	14 27	14 30	14 35	14 40		14 39	14 47	14 37	14 39	14 40	14 41	14 45	14 47	14 48	14 50	14 48
	d	14 20		14 19	14 25	14 29	14 29			14 41		14 40	14 48	14 39	14 40	14 41	14 41		14 48	14 50		14 49
Three Bridges 15	a	14 24			14 30	14 33				→		→	→			14 46	14 47		14 53	14 54		
	d	14 24			14 33	14 34										14 46	14 47		14 53	14 54		
Crawley	d				14 37	14 37										14 50			14 56			
Ifield	d				14 39	14 40																
Faygate	d																					
Littlehaven	d				14 46	14 46																
Horsham 4	a				14 49	14 49										14 58			15 04			
Balcombe	d																					
Haywards Heath	a	14 33		14 30			14 40										14 56			15 03		15 00
	d	14 33		14 30			14 41										14 56			15 03		15 00
Wivelsfield	d			14 34			14 45															
Lewes 4	a			14 48			14 56															
Burgess Hill 4	d	14 38															15 01			15 08		15 06
Hassocks 4	d	14 42															15 05			15 12		
Preston Park	d																					
Hove 2	a																					15 18
Brighton 10	a	14 52												15 03	15 03		15 14			15 22		

A 11 September

B not 11 September. 🍴 to Wivelsfield

C not 11 September

D 11 September. 🍴 to Wivelsfield

Table 186

Sundays until 11 September

Bedford and London - Brighton

		SN ◇1 A	GW 1	SN ◇1 B	SN 1 B 🚌	SN 1 A 🚌	SN ◇1 A	SN ◇1 B 🚌	SN 1 A	SN 1 B	SN 1 A	FC 1 B	SN 1 B 🚌	FC 1 A	SN 1 A 🚌	SN ◇1 C 🚌	SN 1 A	SN 1 B	SN ◇1 D 🚌	SN 1 B 🚌	SN 1 A 🚌	SN ◇1 B
London Victoria 15 ⊖	d	14 17		14 27	14 30	14 30	14 32	14 36					14 45		14 45	14 47			14 47	15 00	15 00	15 02
Clapham Junction 10	d	14 23		14 33			14 38	14 42								14 53			14 53			15 08
Bedford	d																					
Luton 10	d																					
Luton Airport Parkway 7 ✈	d																					
St Albans City	d																					
St Pancras International 15 ⊖	d																					
Farringdon 3 ⊖	d																					
City Thameslink 3	d																					
London Blackfriars 3 ⊖	d																					
London Bridge 4 ⊖	d									14 37	14 37	14 42		14 42								
New Cross Gate	d																					
Norwood Junction 2	d									14 48	14 48											
East Croydon	a	14 36		14 42			14 50	14 52		14 54	14 54	14 54		14 56		15 02			15 06			15 17
	d	14 37		14 43			14 51	14 53		14 55	14 55	14 54		14 57		15 03			15 07			15 18
Purley 4	d									15 00	15 00											15 23
Coulsdon South	d									15 04	15 04											
Merstham	d									15 09	15 09											
Redhill	a			14 57			15 03			15 13	15 13											15 31
	d		14 46	14 57			15 04		15 10	15 13	15 16											15 32
Reigate	a																					
Nutfield	d								15 14													
Godstone	d								15 20													
Edenbridge	d								15 25													
Penshurst	d								15 32													
Leigh (Kent)	d								15 35													
Tonbridge 4	a								15 40													
Earlswood (Surrey)	d									15 18												
Salfords	d									15 22												
Horley 4	d									15 25	15 22						←	←				15 38
Gatwick Airport 10 ✈	a	14 54	14 54	15 04	15 00	15 05	15 11			15 28	15 24	15 11	15 15	15 18	15 20	15 18	15 24	15 28	15 27	15 30	15 35	15 40
	d	14 56		15 05			15 12			15 29	15 25	15 11		15 20		15 19	15 25	15 29	15 29			15 41
Three Bridges 10	a			15 10			15 16			→	→	15 17		15 24			15 30	15 33				→
	d			15 10			15 17					15 17		15 24			15 33	15 34				
Crawley	d																15 37	15 37				
Ifield	d																15 39	15 40				
Faygate	d																					
Littlehaven	d																15 46	15 46				
Horsham 4	a																15 49	15 49				
Balcombe	d			15 16			15 23															
Haywards Heath	a	15 06		15 21			15 28					15 26		15 33		15 30			15 40			
	d	15 07		15 22			15 28					15 26		15 33		15 30			15 41			
Wivelsfield	d			15 26			15 32									15 34			15 45			
Lewes 4	a															15 48			15 56			
Burgess Hill 4	d	15 12		15 28			15 34					15 31		15 38								
Hassocks 4	d			15 31			15 38					15 35		15 42								
Preston Park	d			15 38			15 45															
Hove 2	a	15 24																				
Brighton 10	a			15 43			15 50	15 27				15 46		15 52								

A 11 September
B not 11 September
C not 11 September. 🚌 to Wivelsfield
D 11 September. 🚌 to Wivelsfield

Table 186

Sundays until 11 September

Bedford and London - Brighton

		SN 1 A	SN ◇1 B 🚌	SN ◇1 B 🚌	SN ◇1 A 🚌	SN ◇1 B 🚌	SN ◇1 A	FC 1 A	SN 1 A 🚌	SN ◇1 B 🚌	FC 1 B	SN 1 B 🚌	SN ◇1 A	SN ◇1 B	GW 1	SN ◇1 A	SN 1 A 🚌	SN 1 B 🚌	SN ◇1 B	SN ◇1 A 🚌	SN 1 B	SN 1 A
London Victoria 15 ⊖	d		15 02	15 04	15 06				15 15			15 15	15 17	15 17		15 27	15 30	15 30	15 32	15 36		
Clapham Junction 10	d		15 08	15 10	15 12								15 23	15 23		15 33			15 38	15 42		
Bedford	d																					
Luton 10	d																					
Luton Airport Parkway 7 ✈	d																					
St Albans City	d																					
St Pancras International 15 ⊖	d																					
Farringdon 3 ⊖	d																					
City Thameslink 3	d																					
London Blackfriars 3 ⊖	d																					
London Bridge 4 ⊖	d	15 05						15 12			15 12											15 37
New Cross Gate	d																					
Norwood Junction 2	d	15 16																				15 48
East Croydon	a	15 20	15 21	15 24	15 22			15 24			15 27		15 32	15 36		15 42			15 50	15 52		15 54
	d	15 21	15 22	15 24	15 23			15 24			15 27		15 33	15 37		15 43			15 51	15 53		15 55
Purley 4	d	15 27		15 30																		16 00
Coulsdon South	d	15 30																				16 04
Merstham	d	15 36																				16 09
Redhill	a	15 39		15 38												15 57			16 03			16 13
	d	15 40		15 39											15 46	15 57			16 04		16 10	16 13
Reigate	a																					
Nutfield	d	15 44																			16 14	
Godstone	d	15 50																			16 20	
Edenbridge	d	15 55																			16 25	
Penshurst	d	16 02																			16 32	
Leigh (Kent)	d	16 05																			16 35	
Tonbridge 4	a	16 10																			16 40	
Earlswood (Surrey)	d																					16 18
Salfords	d																					16 22
Horley 4	d			15 45		←	←			←												16 25
Gatwick Airport 10 ✈	a		15 39	15 47	15 37	15 39	15 40	15 41	15 45	15 47	15 48	15 50	15 48	15 54	15 54	16 04	16 00	16 05	16 11			16 28
	d		15 40	15 48	15 39	15 40	15 41	15 41		15 48	15 50		15 49	15 56		16 05			16 12			16 29
Three Bridges 10	a		→	→			15 46	15 47		15 53	15 54					16 10			16 16			→
	d						15 46	15 47		15 53	15 54					16 10			16 17			
Crawley	d						15 50			15 56												
Ifield	d																					
Faygate	d																					
Littlehaven	d																					
Horsham 4	a						15 58			16 04												
Balcombe	d															16 16			16 23			
Haywards Heath	a							15 56			16 03		16 00	16 06		16 21			16 28			
	d							15 56			16 03		16 00	16 07		16 22			16 28			
Wivelsfield	d															16 26			16 32			
Lewes 4	a																					
Burgess Hill 4	d							16 01			16 08		16 06	16 12		16 28			16 34			
Hassocks 4	d							16 05			16 12					16 31			16 38			
Preston Park	d															16 38			16 45			
Hove 2	a												16 18	16 24								
Brighton 10	a				16 03	16 03		16 14			16 22					16 43			16 50	16 27		

A not 11 September
B 11 September

until 11 September

Bedford and London - Brighton

Station		SN	FC	SN	FC	SN	SN	SN	SN	SN	SN	SN	SN	SN	SN	SN	SN	SN	SN	FC	SN	SN
		1	1	1	1	1	◇1	1	1	◇1	1	1	◇1	1	◇1	◇1	◇1	◇1	◇1	1	1	◇1
		A	B	B	A	A	C	A	B	D	B	A	B	B	A	A	B	A	B	B	B	A
				(trolley)		(trolley)	(trolley)			(trolley)	(trolley)	(trolley)			(trolley)	(trolley)	(trolley)	(trolley)			(trolley)	(trolley)
London Victoria [15] ⊖	d			15 45		15 45	15 47			15 47	16 00	16 00	16 02		16 02	16 04	16 06				16 15	
Clapham Junction [10]	d						15 53			15 53			16 08		16 08	16 10	16 12					
Bedford	d																					
Luton [10]	d																					
Luton Airport Parkway [7] ✈	d																					
St Albans City	d																					
St Pancras International [15] ⊖	d																					
Farringdon [3] ⊖	d																					
City Thameslink [3]	d																					
London Blackfriars [3] ⊖	d																					
London Bridge [4] ⊖	d	15 37	15 42		15 42									16 05						16 12		
New Cross Gate	d																					
Norwood Junction [2]	d	15 48												16 16								
East Croydon	a	15 54	15 54		15 56		16 02			16 06			16 17	16 20	16 21	16 24	16 22			16 24		
	d	15 55	15 54		15 57		16 03			16 07			16 18	16 21	16 22	16 24	16 23			16 24		
Purley [4]	d	16 00											16 23	16 27		16 30						
Coulsdon South	d	16 04												16 30								
Merstham	d	16 09												16 36								
Redhill	a	16 13											16 31	16 39		16 38						
	d	16 16											16 32	16 40		16 39						
Reigate	a																					
Nutfield	d													16 44								
Godstone	d													16 50								
Edenbridge	d													16 55								
Penshurst	d													17 02								
Leigh (Kent)	d													17 05								
Tonbridge [4]	a													17 10								
Earlswood (Surrey)	d																					
Salfords	d																					
Horley [4]	d	16 22						←	←				16 38			16 45		←	←			←
Gatwick Airport [10] ✈	a	16 24	16 11	16 15	16 18	16 20	16 18	16 24	16 28	16 27	16 30	16 35	16 40		16 39	16 47	16 37	16 39	16 40	16 41	16 45	16 47
	d	16 25	16 11		16 20		16 19	16 25	16 29	16 29			16 41		16 40	16 48	16 39	16 40	16 41	16 41		16 48
Three Bridges [15]	a	→	16 17		16 24			16 30	16 33				→		→	→			16 46	16 47		16 53
	d		16 17		16 24			16 33	16 34										16 46	16 47		16 53
Crawley	d							16 37	16 37										16 50			16 56
Ifield	d							16 39	16 40													
Faygate	d																					
Littlehaven	d							16 46	16 46													
Horsham [4]	a							16 49	16 49										16 58			17 04
Balcombe	d																					
Haywards Heath	a		16 26		16 33		16 30			16 40										16 56		
	d		16 26		16 33		16 30			16 41										16 56		
Wivelsfield	d						16 34			16 45												
Lewes [4]	a						16 48			16 58												
Burgess Hill [4]	d		16 31		16 38															17 01		
Hassocks [4]	d		16 35		16 42															17 05		
Preston Park	d																					
Hove [2]	a																					
Brighton [10]	a		16 46		16 52												17 03	17 03		17 14		

A 11 September
B not 11 September
C not 11 September. (trolley) to Wivelsfield
D 11 September. (trolley) to Wivelsfield

Bedford and London - Brighton

until 11 September

Station		FC	SN	SN	SN	GW	SN	SN	SN	SN	SN	SN	SN	SN	FC	SN	FC	SN	SN	SN	SN	SN
		1	1	◇1	◇1	1	◇1	1	1	◇1	◇1	1	1	1	1	1	1	1	◇1	1	1	◇1
		A	A	B	A		B	B	A	A	B	A	B	A	B	B	A	A	C	A	B	D
			(trolley)					(trolley)	(trolley)		(trolley)					(trolley)		(trolley)	(trolley)			(trolley)
London Victoria [15] ⊖	d		16 15	16 17	16 17		16 27	16 30	16 30	16 32	16 36					16 45		16 45	16 47			16 47
Clapham Junction [10]	d			16 23	16 23		16 33			16 38	16 42								16 53			16 53
Bedford	d																					
Luton [10]	d																					
Luton Airport Parkway [7] ✈	d																					
St Albans City	d																					
St Pancras International [15] ⊖	d																					
Farringdon [3] ⊖	d																					
City Thameslink [3]	d																					
London Blackfriars [3] ⊖	d																					
London Bridge [4] ⊖	d	16 12											16 37	16 37	16 42		16 42					
New Cross Gate	d																					
Norwood Junction [2]	d												16 48	16 48								
East Croydon	a	16 27		16 32	16 36		16 42			16 50	16 52		16 54	16 54	16 54		16 56		17 02			17 06
	d	16 27		16 33	16 37		16 43			16 51	16 53		16 55	16 55	16 54		16 57		17 03			17 07
Purley [4]	d												17 00	17 00								
Coulsdon South	d												17 04	17 04								
Merstham	d												17 09	17 09								
Redhill	a						16 57			17 03			17 13	17 13								
	d					16 46	16 57			17 04		17 10	17 13	17 16								
Reigate	a																					
Nutfield	d											17 14										
Godstone	d											17 20										
Edenbridge	d											17 25										
Penshurst	d											17 32										
Leigh (Kent)	d											17 35										
Tonbridge [4]	a											17 40										
Earlswood (Surrey)	d												17 18									
Salfords	d												17 22									
Horley [4]	d												17 25	17 22						←	←	
Gatwick Airport [10] ✈	a	16 48	16 50	16 48	16 54	16 54	17 04	17 00	17 05	17 11			17 28	17 24	17 11	17 15	17 18	17 20	17 18	17 24	17 28	17 27
	d	16 50		16 49	16 56		17 05			17 12			17 29	17 25	17 11		17 20		17 19	17 25	17 29	17 29
Three Bridges [15]	a	16 54					17 10			17 16			→	→	17 17		17 24			17 30	17 33	
	d	16 54					17 10			17 17					17 17		17 24			17 33	17 34	
Crawley	d																			17 37	17 37	
Ifield	d																			17 39	17 40	
Faygate	d																					
Littlehaven	d																			17 46	17 46	
Horsham [4]	a																			17 49	17 49	
Balcombe	d						17 16			17 23												
Haywards Heath	a	17 03		17 00	17 06		17 21			17 28					17 26		17 33		17 30			17 40
	d	17 03		17 00	17 07		17 22			17 28					17 26		17 33		17 30			17 41
Wivelsfield	d						17 26			17 32									17 34			17 45
Lewes [4]	a																		17 48			17 58
Burgess Hill [4]	d	17 08		17 06	17 12		17 28			17 34					17 31		17 38					
Hassocks [4]	d	17 12					17 31			17 38					17 35		17 42					
Preston Park	d						17 38			17 45												
Hove [2]	a			17 18	17 24																	
Brighton [10]	a	17 22					17 43			17 50	17 27				17 46		17 52					

A 11 September
B not 11 September
C not 11 September. (trolley) to Wivelsfield
D 11 September. (trolley) to Wivelsfield

Table 186

Bedford and London - Brighton

Sundays
until 11 September

		SN	SN	SN	SN	SN	SN	SN	SN	SN	FC	SN	SN	FC	SN	SN	SN	GW	SN	SN	SN	SN
		1	1	◇1	1	◇1	◇1	◇1	◇1	◇1	1	1	◇1	1	1	◇1	◇1	1	◇1	1	1	◇1
		A	B	A	A	B	B	A	B	A	A	A	B	B	B	A	B		A	A	B	B
		bus	bus			bus	bus	bus	bus			bus	bus		bus					bus	bus	
London Victoria 15 ⊖	d	17 00	17 00	17 02		17 02	17 04	17 06				17 15			17 15	17 17	17 17		17 27	17 30	17 30	17 32
Clapham Junction 10	d			17 08		17 08	17 10	17 12								17 23	17 23		17 33			17 38
Bedford	d																					
Luton 10	d																					
Luton Airport Parkway 7 ✈	d																					
St Albans City	d																					
St Pancras International 15 ⊖	d																					
Farringdon 3 ⊖	d																					
City Thameslink 3	d																					
London Blackfriars 3 ⊖	d																					
London Bridge 4 ⊖	d				17 05						17 12			17 12								
New Cross Gate	d																					
Norwood Junction 2	d				17 16																	
East Croydon	a			17 17	17 20	17 21	17 24	17 22			17 24			17 27		17 32	17 36		17 42			17 50
	d			17 18	17 21	17 22	17 24	17 23			17 24			17 27		17 33	17 37		17 43			17 51
Purley 4	d			17 23	17 27		17 30															
Coulsdon South	d				17 30																	
Merstham	d				17 36																	
Redhill	a			17 31	17 39		17 38												17 57			18 03
	d			17 32	17 40		17 39											17 46	17 57			18 04
Reigate	a																					
Nutfield	d				17 44																	
Godstone	d				17 50																	
Edenbridge	d				17 55																	
Penshurst	d				18 02																	
Leigh (Kent)	d				18 05																	
Tonbridge 4	a				18 10																	
Earlswood (Surrey)	d																					
Salfords	d																					
Horley 4	d			17 38			17 45		←	←			←									
Gatwick Airport 10 ✈	a	17 30	17 35	17 40		17 39	17 47	17 37	17 39	17 40	17 41	17 45	17 47	17 48	17 50	17 48	17 54	17 54	18 04	18 00	18 05	18 11
	d			17 41		17 40	17 48	17 39	17 40	17 41	17 41		17 48	17 50		17 49	17 56		18 05			18 12
Three Bridges 15	a			→		→	→			17 46	17 47		17 53	17 54					18 10			18 16
	d									17 46	17 47		17 53	17 54					18 10			18 17
Crawley	d									17 50			17 56									
Ifield	d																					
Faygate	d																					
Littlehaven	d																					
Horsham 4	a									17 58			18 04									
Balcombe	d																		18 16			18 23
Haywards Heath	a										17 56			18 03		18 00	18 06		18 21			18 28
	d										17 56			18 03		18 00	18 07		18 22			18 28
Wivelsfield	d																		18 26			18 32
Lewes 4	a																					
Burgess Hill 4	d										18 01			18 08		18 06	18 12		18 28			18 34
Hassocks 4	d										18 05			18 12					18 31			18 38
Preston Park	d																		18 38			18 45
Hove 2	a															18 18	18 24					
Brighton 10	a							18 03	18 03		18 14			18 22					18 43			18 50

A not 11 September

B 11 September

Table 186

Bedford and London - Brighton

Sundays
until 11 September

		SN	SN	SN	SN	FC	SN	FC	SN	SN	SN	SN	SN	SN	SN	SN	SN	SN	SN	SN	SN	SN
		◇1	1	1	1	1	1	1	1	◇1	1	1	◇1	1	1	◇1	1	◇1	◇1	◇1	◇1	◇1
		A	B	A	B	A	A	B	B	C	B	A	D	A	B	A	A	B	B	A	B	A
		bus					bus		bus	bus			bus	bus	bus			bus	bus	bus	bus	
London Victoria 15 ⊖	d	17 36					17 45		17 45	17 47			17 47	18 00	18 00	18 02		18 02	18 04	18 06		
Clapham Junction 10	d	17 42								17 53			17 53			18 08		18 08	18 10	18 12		
Bedford	d																					
Luton 10	d																					
Luton Airport Parkway 7 ✈	d																					
St Albans City	d																					
St Pancras International 15 ⊖	d																					
Farringdon 3 ⊖	d																					
City Thameslink 3	d																					
London Blackfriars 3 ⊖	d																					
London Bridge 4 ⊖	d			17 37	17 37	17 42		17 42									18 05					
New Cross Gate	d																					
Norwood Junction 2	d			17 48	17 48												18 16					
East Croydon	a	17 52		17 54	17 54	17 54		17 56		18 02			18 06			18 17	18 20	18 21	18 24	18 22		
	d	17 53		17 55	17 55	17 54		17 57		18 03			18 07			18 18	18 21	18 22	18 24	18 23		
Purley 4	d			18 00	18 00											18 23	18 27		18 30			
Coulsdon South	d			18 04	18 04												18 30					
Merstham	d			18 09	18 09												18 36					
Redhill	a			18 13	18 13											18 31	18 39		18 38			
	d		18 10	18 13	18 16											18 32	18 40		18 39			
Reigate	a																					
Nutfield	d		18 14														18 44					
Godstone	d		18 20														18 50					
Edenbridge	d		18 25														18 55					
Penshurst	d		18 32														19 02					
Leigh (Kent)	d		18 35														19 05					
Tonbridge 4	a		18 40														19 10					
Earlswood (Surrey)	d			18 18																		
Salfords	d			18 22																		
Horley 4	d			18 25	18 22						←	←				18 38			18 45		←	←
Gatwick Airport 10 ✈	a			18 28	18 24	18 11	18 15	18 18	18 20	18 18	18 24	18 28	18 27	18 30	18 35	18 40		18 39	18 47	18 37	18 39	18 40
	d			18 29	18 25	18 11		18 20		18 19	18 25	18 29	18 29			18 41		18 40	18 48	18 39	18 40	18 41
Three Bridges 15	a			→	→	18 17		18 24			18 30	18 33				→		→	→			18 46
	d					18 17		18 24			18 33	18 34										18 46
Crawley	d										18 37	18 37										18 50
Ifield	d										18 39	18 40										
Faygate	d																					
Littlehaven	d										18 46	18 46										
Horsham 4	a										18 49	18 49										18 58
Balcombe	d																					
Haywards Heath	a					18 26		18 33		18 30			18 40									
	d					18 26		18 33		18 30			18 41									
Wivelsfield	d									18 34			18 45									
Lewes 4	a									18 48			18 58									
Burgess Hill 4	d					18 31		18 38														
Hassocks 4	d					18 35		18 42														
Preston Park	d																					
Hove 2	a																					
Brighton 10	a	18 27				18 46		18 52												19 03	19 03	

A not 11 September

B 11 September

C not 11 September. bus to Wivelsfield

D 11 September. bus to Wivelsfield

Table 186

Bedford and London - Brighton

Sundays until 11 September

Station		FC	SN	SN	FC	SN	SN	SN	GW	SN	SN	SN	SN	SN	SN	SN	SN	FC	SN	FC	SN	SN
		1	1	◇1	1	1	◇1	◇1	1	◇1	1	1	◇1	◇1	1	1	1	1	1	1	1	◇1
		A	A	B	B	B	A	B		A	A	B	B	A	B	A	B	A	A	B	B	C
			⌶	⌶		⌶					⌶	⌶		⌶					⌶		⌶	⌶
London Victoria 15 ⊖	d		18 15			18 15	18 17	18 17		18 27	18 30	18 30	18 32	18 36					18 45		18 45	18 47
Clapham Junction 10	d						18 23	18 23		18 33			18 38	18 42								18 53
Bedford	d																					
Luton 10	d																					
Luton Airport Parkway 7 ✈	d																					
St Albans City	d																					
St Pancras International 15 ⊖	d																					
Farringdon 3 ⊖	d																					
City Thameslink 3	d																					
London Blackfriars 3 ⊖	d																					
London Bridge 4 ⊖	d	18 12			18 12											18 37	18 37	18 42		18 42		
New Cross Gate	d																					
Norwood Junction 2	d															18 48	18 48					
East Croydon	a	18 24			18 27		18 32	18 36		18 42			18 50	18 52		18 54	18 54	18 54		18 56		19 02
	d	18 24			18 27		18 33	18 37		18 43			18 51	18 53		18 55	18 55	18 54		18 57		19 03
Purley 4	d															19 00	19 00					
Coulsdon South	d															19 04	19 04					
Merstham	d															19 09	19 09					
Redhill	a									18 57			19 03			19 13	19 13					
	d								18 46	18 57			19 04		19 10	19 13	19 16					
Reigate	a																					
Nutfield	d														19 14							
Godstone	d														19 20							
Edenbridge	d														19 25							
Penshurst	d														19 32							
Leigh (Kent)	d														19 35							
Tonbridge 4	a														19 40							
Earlswood (Surrey)	d															19 18						
Salfords	d															19 22						
Horley 4	d			←												19 25	19 22					
Gatwick Airport 10 ✈	a	18 41	18 45	18 47	18 48	18 50	18 48	18 54	18 55	19 04	19 00	19 05	19 11			19 28	19 24	19 11	19 15	19 18	19 20	19 18
	d	18 41		18 48	18 50		18 49	18 56		19 05			19 12			19 29	19 25	19 11		19 20		19 19
Three Bridges 15	a	18 47		18 53	18 54					19 10			19 16			→	→	19 17		19 24		
	d	18 47		18 53	18 54					19 10			19 17					19 17		19 24		
Crawley	d			18 56																		
Ifield	d																					
Faygate	d																					
Littlehaven	d																					
Horsham 4	a			19 04																		
Balcombe	d									19 16			19 23									
Haywards Heath	a	18 56			19 03		19 00	19 06		19 21			19 28					19 26		19 33		19 30
	d	18 56			19 03		19 00	19 07		19 22			19 28					19 26		19 33		19 30
Wivelsfield	d									19 26			19 32									19 34
Lewes 4	a																					19 48
Burgess Hill 4	d	19 01			19 08		19 06	19 12		19 28			19 34					19 31		19 38		
Hassocks 4	d	19 05			19 12					19 31			19 38					19 35		19 42		
Preston Park	d									19 38			19 45									
Hove 2	a						19 18	19 24														
Brighton 10	a	19 14			19 22					19 43			19 50	19 27				19 46		19 52		

A not 11 September
B 11 September
C not 11 September. ⌶ to Wivelsfield

Bedford and London - Brighton

until 11 September

Station		SN	SN	SN	SN	SN	SN	SN	SN	SN	SN	SN	SN	FC	SN	SN	FC	SN	SN	SN	GW	SN
		1	1	◇1	1	1	◇1	1	◇1	◇1	◇1	◇1	◇1	1	1	◇1	1	1	◇1	◇1	1	◇1
		A	B	C	B	A	B	B	A	A	B	A	B	B	B	A	A	A	B	A		B
				⌶	⌶	⌶			⌶	⌶	⌶	⌶				⌶						
London Victoria 15 ⊖	d			18 47	19 00	19 00	19 02		19 02	19 04	19 06				19 15			19 15	19 17	19 17		19 27
Clapham Junction 10	d			18 53			19 08		19 08	19 10	19 12								19 23	19 23		19 33
Bedford	d																					
Luton 10	d																					
Luton Airport Parkway 7 ✈	d																					
St Albans City	d																					
St Pancras International 15 ⊖	d																					
Farringdon 3 ⊖	d																					
City Thameslink 3	d																					
London Blackfriars 3 ⊖	d																					
London Bridge 4 ⊖	d							19 05						19 12			19 12					
New Cross Gate	d																					
Norwood Junction 2	d							19 16														
East Croydon	a			19 06			19 17	19 20	19 21	19 24	19 22			19 24			19 27		19 32	19 36		19 42
	d			19 07			19 18	19 21	19 22	19 24	19 23			19 24			19 27		19 33	19 37		19 43
Purley 4	d						19 23	19 27		19 30												
Coulsdon South	d							19 30														
Merstham	d							19 36														
Redhill	a						19 31	19 39		19 38												19 57
	d						19 32	19 40		19 39											19 46	19 57
Reigate	a																					
Nutfield	d							19 44														
Godstone	d							19 50														
Edenbridge	d							19 55														
Penshurst	d							20 02														
Leigh (Kent)	d							20 05														
Tonbridge 4	a							20 10														
Earlswood (Surrey)	d																					
Salfords	d																					
Horley 4	d	←	←				19 38			19 45		←	←			←						
Gatwick Airport 10 ✈	a	19 24	19 28	19 27	19 30	19 35	19 40		19 39	19 47	19 37	19 39	19 40	19 41	19 45	19 47	19 48	19 50	19 48	19 54	19 55	20 04
	d	19 25	19 29	19 29			19 41		19 40	19 48	19 39	19 40	19 41	19 41		19 48	19 50		19 49	19 56		20 05
Three Bridges 15	a	19 30	19 33				→		→	→			19 46	19 47		19 53	19 54					20 10
	d	19 33	19 34										19 46	19 47		19 53	19 54					20 10
Crawley	d	19 37	19 37										19 50			19 56						
Ifield	d	19 39	19 40																			
Faygate	d																					
Littlehaven	d	19 46	19 46																			
Horsham 4	a	19 49	19 49										19 58			20 04						
Balcombe	d																					20 16
Haywards Heath	a			19 40										19 56			20 03		20 00	20 06		20 21
	d			19 41										19 56			20 03		20 00	20 07		20 22
Wivelsfield	d			19 45																		20 26
Lewes 4	a			19 58																		
Burgess Hill 4	d													20 01			20 08		20 06	20 12		20 28
Hassocks 4	d													20 05			20 12					20 31
Preston Park	d																					20 38
Hove 2	a																		20 18	20 24		
Brighton 10	a										20 03	20 03		20 14			20 22					20 43

A 11 September
B not 11 September
C 11 September. ⌶ to Wivelsfield

Table 186

Sundays until 11 September

Bedford and London - Brighton

		SN	SN	SN	SN	SN	SN	SN	FC	SN	FC	SN	SN	SN	SN	SN	SN	SN	SN	SN	SN	SN
		1	1	◇1	◇1	1	1	1	1	1	1	1	◇1	1	1	◇1	1	1	◇1	1	◇1	◇1
		A	B	B	A	B	A	B	A	A	B	B	C	B	A	D	A	B	A	A	B	B
London Victoria 15 ⊖	d	19 30	19 30	19 32	19 36					19 45		19 45	19 47			19 47	20 00	20 00	20 02		20 02	20 04
Clapham Junction 10	d			19 38	19 42								19 53			19 53			20 08		20 08	20 10
Bedford	d																					
Luton 10	d																					
Luton Airport Parkway 7 ✈	d																					
St Albans City	d																					
St Pancras International 15 ⊖	d																					
Farringdon 3 ⊖	d																					
City Thameslink 3	d																					
London Blackfriars 3 ⊖	d																					
London Bridge 4 ⊖	d						19 37	19 37	19 42		19 42									20 05		
New Cross Gate	d																					
Norwood Junction 2	d						19 48	19 48												20 16		
East Croydon ⇌	a			19 50	19 52		19 54	19 54	19 54		19 56		20 02			20 06			20 17	20 20	20 21	20 24
	d			19 51	19 53		19 55	19 55	19 54		19 57		20 03			20 07			20 18	20 21	20 22	20 24
Purley 4	d						20 00	20 00											20 23	20 27		20 30
Coulsdon South	d						20 04	20 04												20 30		
Merstham	d						20 09	20 09												20 36		
Redhill	a			20 03			20 13	20 13											20 31	20 39		20 38
	d			20 04		20 10	20 13	20 16											20 32	20 40		20 39
Reigate	a																					
Nutfield	d					20 14														20 44		
Godstone	d					20 20														20 50		
Edenbridge	d					20 25														20 55		
Penshurst	d					20 32														21 02		
Leigh (Kent)	d					20 35														21 05		
Tonbridge 4	a					20 40														21 10		
Earlswood (Surrey)	d						20 18															
Salfords	d						20 22															
Horley 4	d						20 25	20 22						←	←				20 38			20 45
Gatwick Airport 10 ✈	a	20 00	20 05	20 11			20 28	20 24	20 11	20 15	20 18	20 20	20 18	20 24	20 28	20 27	20 30	20 35	20 40		20 39	20 47
	d			20 12			20 29	20 25	20 11		20 20		20 19	20 25	20 29	20 29			20 41		20 40	20 48
Three Bridges 15	a			20 16			→	→	20 17		20 24			20 30	20 33				→		→	→
	d			20 17					20 17		20 24			20 33	20 34							
Crawley	d													20 37	20 37							
Ifield	d													20 39	20 40							
Faygate	d																					
Littlehaven	d													20 46	20 46							
Horsham 4	a													20 49	20 49							
Balcombe	d			20 23																		
Haywards Heath	a			20 28					20 26		20 33		20 30			20 40						
	d			20 28					20 26		20 33		20 30			20 41						
Wivelsfield	d			20 32									20 34			20 45						
Lewes 4	a												20 48			20 58						
Burgess Hill 4	d			20 34					20 31		20 38											
Hassocks 4	d			20 38					20 35		20 42											
Preston Park	d			20 45																		
Hove 2	a																					
Brighton 10	a			20 50	20 27				20 46		20 52											

A not 11 September
B 11 September
C not 11 September. 🚌 to Wivelsfield
D 11 September. 🚌 to Wivelsfield

Table 186

Sundays until 11 September

Bedford and London - Brighton

		SN	SN	SN	FC	SN	SN	FC	SN	SN	SN	GW	SN	SN	SN	SN	SN	SN	SN	SN	FC	SN
		◇1	◇1	◇1	1	1	◇1	1	1	◇1	◇1	1	◇1	1	1	◇1	◇1	1	1	1	1	1
		A	B	A	A	A	B	B	B	A	B		A	A	B	B	A	B	A	B	A	A
London Victoria 15 ⊖	d	20 06				20 15			20 15	20 17	20 17		20 27	20 30	20 30	20 32	20 36					20 45
Clapham Junction 10	d	20 12								20 23	20 23		20 33			20 38	20 42					
Bedford	d																					
Luton 10	d																					
Luton Airport Parkway 7 ✈	d																					
St Albans City	d																					
St Pancras International 15 ⊖	d																					
Farringdon 3 ⊖	d																					
City Thameslink 3	d																					
London Blackfriars 3 ⊖	d																					
London Bridge 4 ⊖	d				20 12			20 12											20 37	20 37	20 42	
New Cross Gate	d																					
Norwood Junction 2	d																		20 48	20 48		
East Croydon ⇌	a	20 22			20 24			20 27		20 32	20 36		20 42			20 50	20 52		20 54	20 54	20 54	
	d	20 23			20 24			20 27		20 33	20 37		20 43			20 51	20 53		20 55	20 55	20 54	
Purley 4	d																		21 00	21 00		
Coulsdon South	d																		21 04	21 04		
Merstham	d																		21 09	21 09		
Redhill	a												20 57			21 03			21 13	21 13		
	d											20 46	20 57			21 04		21 10	21 13	21 16		
Reigate	a																					
Nutfield	d																	21 14				
Godstone	d																	21 20				
Edenbridge	d																	21 25				
Penshurst	d																	21 32				
Leigh (Kent)	d																	21 35				
Tonbridge 4	a																	21 40				
Earlswood (Surrey)	d																		21 18			
Salfords	d																		21 22			
Horley 4	d		←	←			←												21 25	21 22		
Gatwick Airport 10 ✈	a	20 37	20 39	20 40	20 41	20 45	20 47	20 48	20 50	20 48	20 54	20 55	21 04	21 00	21 05	21 11			21 28	21 24	21 11	21 15
	d	20 39	20 40	20 41	20 41		20 48	20 50		20 49	20 56		21 05			21 12			21 29	21 25	21 11	
Three Bridges 15	a			20 46	20 47		20 53	20 54					21 10			21 16			→	→	21 17	
	d			20 46	20 47		20 53	20 54					21 10			21 17					21 17	
Crawley	d			20 50			20 56															
Ifield	d																					
Faygate	d																					
Littlehaven	d																					
Horsham 4	a			20 58			21 04															
Balcombe	d												21 16			21 23						
Haywards Heath	a				20 56			21 03		21 00	21 06		21 21			21 28					21 26	
	d				20 56			21 03		21 00	21 07		21 22			21 28					21 26	
Wivelsfield	d												21 26			21 32						
Lewes 4	a																					
Burgess Hill 4	d				21 01			21 08		21 06	21 12		21 28			21 34					21 31	
Hassocks 4	d				21 05			21 12					21 31			21 38					21 35	
Preston Park	d												21 38			21 45						
Hove 2	a									21 18	21 24											
Brighton 10	a	21 03	21 03		21 14			21 22					21 43			21 50	21 27				21 46	

A not 11 September
B 11 September

Bedford and London - Brighton

until 11 September

Station		FC	SN	SN	SN	SN	SN	SN	SN	SN	SN	SN	SN	SN	SN	SN	FC	SN	SN	FC	SN	SN
		1	1	◇1	1	1	◇1	1	1	◇1	1	◇1	◇1	◇1	◇1	◇1	1	1	◇1	1	1	◇1
		A	A	B	A	B	A	B	A	B	B	A	A	B	A	B	B	B	A	A	A	B
London Victoria 15 ⊖	d		20 45	20 47			20 47	21 00	21 00	21 02		21 02	21 04	21 06				21 15			21 15	21 17
Clapham Junction 10	d			20 53			20 53			21 08		21 08	21 10	21 12								21 23
Bedford	d																					
Luton 10	d																					
Luton Airport Parkway 7 ✈	d																					
St Albans City	d																					
St Pancras International 15 ⊖	d																					
Farringdon 3 ⊖	d																					
City Thameslink 3	d																					
London Blackfriars 3 ⊖	d																					
London Bridge 4 ⊖	d	20 42									21 05						21 12			21 12		
New Cross Gate	d																					
Norwood Junction 2	d										21 16											
East Croydon	a	20 56		21 02			21 06			21 17	21 20	21 21	21 24	21 22			21 24			21 27		21 32
	d	20 57		21 03			21 07			21 18	21 21	21 22	21 24	21 23			21 24			21 27		21 33
Purley 4	d									21 23	21 27		21 30									
Coulsdon South	d										21 30											
Merstham	d										21 36											
Redhill	a									21 31	21 39		21 38									
	d									21 32	21 40		21 39									
Reigate	a																					
Nutfield	d										21 44											
Godstone	d										21 50											
Edenbridge	d										21 55											
Penshurst	d										22 02											
Leigh (Kent)	d										22 05											
Tonbridge 4	a										22 10											
Earlswood (Surrey)	d																					
Salfords	d																					
Horley 4	d				←	←				21 38			21 45		←	←			←			
Gatwick Airport 10 ✈	a	21 18	21 20	21 18	21 24	21 28	21 27	21 30	21 35	21 40		21 39	21 47	21 37	21 39	21 40	21 41	21 45	21 47	21 48	21 50	21 48
	d	21 20		21 19	21 25	21 29	21 29			21 41		21 40	21 48	21 39	21 40	21 41	21 41		21 48	21 50		21 49
Three Bridges 15	a	21 24			21 30	21 33				→		→	→			21 46	21 47		21 53	21 54		
	d	21 24			21 33	21 34										21 46	21 47		21 53	21 54		
Crawley	d				21 37	21 37										21 50			21 56			
Ifield	d				21 39	21 40																
Faygate	d																					
Littlehaven	d				21 46	21 46																
Horsham 4	a				21 49	21 49										21 58			22 04			
Balcombe	d																					
Haywards Heath	a	21 33		21 30			21 40										21 56			22 03		22 00
	d	21 33		21 30			21 41										21 56			22 03		22 00
Wivelsfield	d			21 34			21 45															
Lewes 4	a			21 48			21 58															
Burgess Hill 4	d	21 38															22 01			22 08		22 06
Hassocks 4	d	21 42															22 05			22 12		
Preston Park	d																					
Hove 2	a																					22 18
Brighton 10	a	21 52												22 03	22 03		22 14			22 22		

A 11 September B not 11 September

Bedford and London - Brighton

until 11 September

Station		SN	GW	SN	SN	SN	SN	SN	SN	SN	FC	SN	SN	FC	SN	SN	SN	SN	SN	SN	SN	SN
		◇1	1	◇1	1	1	◇1	1	1	1	1	◇1	1	1	1	◇1	1	1	◇1	1	1	◇1
		A		B	B	A	A	A	B	A	B	A	B	A	A	B	A	B	A	B	A	B
London Victoria 15 ⊖	d	21 17		21 27	21 30	21 30	21 32						21 45		21 45	21 47			21 47	22 00	22 00	22 02
Clapham Junction 10	d	21 23		21 33			21 38									21 53			21 53			22 08
Bedford	d																					
Luton 10	d																					
Luton Airport Parkway 7 ✈	d																					
St Albans City	d																					
St Pancras International 15 ⊖	d																					
Farringdon 3 ⊖	d																					
City Thameslink 3	d																					
London Blackfriars 3 ⊖	d																					
London Bridge 4 ⊖	d								21 37	21 37	21 42			21 42								
New Cross Gate	d																					
Norwood Junction 2	d								21 48	21 48												
East Croydon	a	21 36		21 42			21 50		21 54	21 54	21 54			21 56		22 02			22 06			22 17
	d	21 37		21 43			21 51		21 55	21 55	21 54			21 57		22 03			22 07			22 18
Purley 4	d								22 00	22 00												22 23
Coulsdon South	d								22 04	22 04												
Merstham	d								22 09	22 09												
Redhill	a			21 57			22 03		22 13	22 13												22 31
	d		21 46	21 57			22 04	22 10	22 13	22 16												22 32
Reigate	a																					
Nutfield	d							22 14														
Godstone	d							22 20														
Edenbridge	d							22 25														
Penshurst	d							22 32														
Leigh (Kent)	d							22 35														
Tonbridge 4	a							22 40														
Earlswood (Surrey)	d								22 18													
Salfords	d								22 22													
Horley 4	d								22 25	22 22		←					←	←				22 38
Gatwick Airport 10 ✈	a	21 55	21 55	22 04	22 00	22 05	22 12		22 28	22 24	22 11	22 12	22 15	22 18	22 20	22 18	22 24	22 28	22 27	22 30	22 35	22 40
	d	21 56		22 05			22 13		22 29	22 25	22 11	22 13		22 20		22 19	22 25	22 29	22 29			22 41
Three Bridges 15	a			22 10			→		→	→	22 17	22 18		22 24			22 30	22 33				22 46
	d			22 10							22 17	22 18		22 24			22 33	22 34				22 46
Crawley	d																22 37	22 37				22 50
Ifield	d																22 39	22 40				
Faygate	d																					
Littlehaven	d																22 46	22 46				
Horsham 4	a																22 49	22 49				22 58
Balcombe	d			22 16								22 24										
Haywards Heath	a	22 06		22 21							22 26	22 29		22 33		22 30			22 40			
	d	22 07		22 22							22 26	22 30		22 33		22 30			22 41			
Wivelsfield	d			22 26								22 34				22 34			22 45			
Lewes 4	a															22 48			22 58			
Burgess Hill 4	d	22 12		22 28							22 31	22 36		22 38								
Hassocks 4	d			22 31							22 35	22 39		22 42								
Preston Park	d			22 38								22 46										
Hove 2	a	22 24																				
Brighton 10	a			22 43							22 46	22 50		22 52								

A 11 September B not 11 September

Table 186

Sundays
until 11 September

Bedford and London - Brighton

		SN 1 A	FC 1 A	SN ◇1 B	SN 1 A	FC 1 B	SN 1 B	SN ◇1 A	SN ◇1 B	GW 1	SN ◇1 A	SN 1 A	SN 1 B	SN ◇1 B	SN 1	SN 1 A	SN 1 B	FC 1 A	SN 1 A	FC 1 B	SN 1 B	SN ◇1 A
London Victoria 15 ⊖	d			22 04	22 15		22 15	22 17	22 17		22 27	22 30	22 30	22 32					22 45		22 45	22 47
Clapham Junction 10	d			22 10				22 23	22 23		22 33			22 38								22 53
Bedford	d																					
Luton 10	d																					
Luton Airport Parkway 7 ✈	d																					
St Albans City	d																					
St Pancras International 15 ⊖	d																					
Farringdon 3 ⊖	d																					
City Thameslink 3	d																					
London Blackfriars 3 ⊖	d																					
London Bridge 4 ⊖	d	22 05	22 12			22 12										22 37	22 37	22 42		22 42		
New Cross Gate	d																					
Norwood Junction 2	d	22 16														22 48	22 48					
East Croydon ⇌	a	22 20	22 24	22 24		22 27		22 32	22 36		22 42			22 50		22 54	22 54	22 54		22 56		23 03
	d	22 21	22 24	22 24		22 27		22 33	22 37		22 43			22 51		22 55	22 55	22 54		22 57		23 03
Purley 4	d	22 27		22 30												23 00	23 00					
Coulsdon South	d	22 30														23 04	23 04					
Merstham	d	22 36														23 09	23 09					
Redhill	a	22 39		22 38							22 57			23 03		23 13	23 13					
	d	22 40		22 39						22 46	22 57			23 04	23 10	23 13	23 16					
Reigate	a																					
Nutfield	d	22 44													23 14							
Godstone	d	22 50													23 20							
Edenbridge	d	22 55													23 25							
Penshurst	d	23 02													23 32							
Leigh (Kent)	d	23 05													23 35							
Tonbridge 4	a	23 10													23 40							
Earlswood (Surrey)	d															23 18						
Salfords	d															23 22						
Horley 4	d			22 45												23 25	23 22					
Gatwick Airport 10 ✈	a		22 41	22 47	22 45	22 48	22 50	22 48	22 54	22 54	23 04	23 00	23 05	23 11		23 28	23 24	23 11	23 15	23 18	23 20	23 18
	d		22 41	22 48		22 50		22 49	22 56		23 05			23 12		23 29	23 25	23 11		23 20		23 19
Three Bridges 15	a		22 47	22 53		22 54					23 10			23 16		→	→	23 17		23 24		
	d		22 47	22 53		22 54					23 10			23 17				23 17		23 24		
Crawley	d			22 56																		
Ifield	d																					
Faygate	d																					
Littlehaven	d																					
Horsham 4	a			23 04																		
Balcombe	d										23 16			23 23								
Haywards Heath	a		22 56			23 03		23 00	23 06		23 21			23 28				23 26		23 33		23 30
	d		22 56			23 03		23 00	23 07		23 22			23 28				23 26		23 33		23 30
Wivelsfield	d										23 26			23 32								23 34
Lewes 4	a																					23 48
Burgess Hill 4	d		23 01			23 08		23 06	23 12		23 28			23 34				23 31		23 38		
Hassocks 4	d		23 05			23 12					23 31			23 38				23 35		23 42		
Preston Park	d										23 38			23 45								
Hove 2	a							23 19	23 24													
Brighton 10	a		23 14			23 22					23 42			23 50				23 46		23 52		

A not 11 September

B 11 September

Table 186

Sundays
until 11 September

Bedford and London - Brighton

		SN 1 A	SN 1 B	SN ◇1 A	SN 1 B	SN 1 A	SN 1	FC 1 B	FC 1 A	SN 1	SN 1	GW 1	SN ◇1	SN 1	SN ◇1	FC 1	SN 1
London Victoria 15 ⊖	d			22 47	23 00	23 00	23 04			23 15			23 17	23 30	23 32		23 45
Clapham Junction 10	d			22 53			23 10						23 23		23 38		
Bedford	d																
Luton 10	d																
Luton Airport Parkway 7 ✈	d																
St Albans City	d																
St Pancras International 15 ⊖	d																
Farringdon 3 ⊖	d																
City Thameslink 3	d																
London Blackfriars 3 ⊖	d																
London Bridge 4 ⊖	d							23 12	23 12							23 42	
New Cross Gate	d																
Norwood Junction 2	d																
East Croydon ⇌	a			23 06			23 22	23 24	23 27				23 37		23 52	23 56	
	d			23 07			23 22	23 24	23 27				23 38		23 53	23 57	
Purley 4	d						23 29										
Coulsdon South	d						23 33										
Merstham	d						23 38										
Redhill	a						23 42								00 05		
	d						23 42					23 48			00 05		
Reigate	a																
Nutfield	d																
Godstone	d																
Edenbridge	d																
Penshurst	d																
Leigh (Kent)	d																
Tonbridge 4	a																
Earlswood (Surrey)	d																
Salfords	d																
Horley 4	d	←	←				23 50				←						
Gatwick Airport 10 ✈	a	23 24	23 28	23 27	23 30	23 35	23 54	23 41	23 48	23 50	23 54	23 56	23 59	00 05	00 14	00 18	00 20
	d	23 25	23 29	23 29			23 55	23 41	23 50		23 55		00 01		00 15	00 19	
Three Bridges 15	a	23 30	23 33				→	23 47	23 54		00 01		00 05		00 19	00 24	
	d	23 33	23 34					23 47	23 54		00 01		00 06		00 20		
Crawley	d	23 37	23 37								00 05						
Ifield	d	23 39	23 40								00 07						
Faygate	d																
Littlehaven	d	23 46	23 46								00 14						
Horsham 4	a	23 49	23 49								00 17						
Balcombe	d														00 26		
Haywards Heath	a			23 40				23 56	00 03				00 14		00 31		
	d			23 41				23 56	00 03				00 15		00 31		
Wivelsfield	d			23 45											00 35		
Lewes 4	a			23 58													
Burgess Hill 4	d							00 02	00 08				00 20		00 37		
Hassocks 4	d							00 06	00 12						00 41		
Preston Park	d														00 48		
Hove 2	a												00 31				
Brighton 10	a							00 15	00 22						00 52		

A 11 September

B not 11 September

Bedford and London - Brighton

from 18 September

Station		SN ◇1	SN ◇1	FC 1	SN 1	SN ◇1	SN 1	SN 1	SN 1	GW 1	SN 1	FC 1	SN	SN 1	SN 1	SN ◇1	FC 1	SN 1	GW 1	SN 1	FC 1
London Victoria 15 ⊖	d	23p02	23p06		23p10	23p17		23p30			23p32		23p45	23p47	00 02	00 05		00 14		00 30	
Clapham Junction 10	d	23p08	23p12		23p16	23p23					23p38			23p53		00 11		00 20			
Bedford	d																				
Luton 10	d																				
Luton Airport Parkway 7 ✈	d																				
St Albans City	d																				
St Pancras International 15 ⊖	d																				
Farringdon 3 ⊖	d																				
City Thameslink 3	d																				
London Blackfriars 3 ⊖	d																				
London Bridge 4 ⊖	d			23p12								23p42					00 12				00 42
New Cross Gate	d																				
Norwood Junction 2	d																				
East Croydon	a	23p18	23p22	23p24	23p27	23p33					23p52	23p56		00 05		00 24	00 27	00 31			00 56
	d	23p18	23p23	23p25	23p28	23p33					23p52	23p57		00 06		00 25	00 27	00 32			00 57
Purley 4	d				23p33									00 12				00 37			
Coulsdon South	d				23p37									00 15				00 41			
Merstham	d				23p42									00 21				00 47			
Redhill	a	23p30			23p46						00 03			00 24				00 50			
	d	23p31			23p46				23p55	00 03	00 05			00 25				00 51	00 54		
Reigate	a																				
Nutfield	d																				
Godstone	d																				
Edenbridge	d								00 06												
Penshurst	d																				
Leigh (Kent)	d																				
Tonbridge 4	a								00 15												
Earlswood (Surrey)	d				23p49																
Salfords	d				23p52																
Horley 4	d				23p56		←							00 31				00 57			
Gatwick Airport 10 ✈	a	23p38		23p40	23p58	23p50	23p58	00 05		00 10	00 14	00 18	00 20	00 33	00 38	00 43	00 48	00 59	01 02	01 05	01 19
	d	23p39		23p41	23p59	23p51	23p59				00 15	00 19		00 34		00 44	00 49	01 00			01 20
Three Bridges 15	a	23p44		23p47	→	23p55	00 04				00 20	00 24		00 39		00 48	00 54	01 05			01 24
	d	23p44		23p47		23p56	00 04				00 20			00 39		00 48					
Crawley	d						00 07							00 43							
Ifield	d						00 10							00 46							
Faygate	d																				
Littlehaven	d						00 16							00 52							
Horsham 4	a						00 19							00 55							
Balcombe	d			23p53							00 27										
Haywards Heath	a	23p52	23p46	23p58		00 04					00 34					00 58					
	d	23p53	23p46	23p59		00 05					00 34					01 02 01 06					
Wivelsfield	d	23p57		00 03							00 38										
Lewes 4	a															01 20					
Burgess Hill 4	d	23p59		00 05		00 10					00 40										
Hassocks 4	d	00 02		00 08							00 44										
Preston Park	d	00 09		00 15							00 51										
Hove 2	a					00 21															
Brighton 10	a	00 15	00 01	00 20							00 55					01s16					

Bedford and London - Brighton

from 18 September

Station		SN 1	FC 1	SN 1	SN 1	SN 1	SN 1	SN 1	SN 1	SN 1	SN 1	SN 1	SN 1	SN 1	SN ◇1	SN 1 ⌶	SN 1 ⌶	SN 1 ⌶	SN ◇1	SN 1 ⌶	GW 1	SN 1 ⌶
London Victoria 15 ⊖	d	01 00		02 00	03 00	03 30	04 00	04 30	05 00	05 02	05 15	05 30	05 45		05 47	06 00	06 15	06 30	06 32	06 45		07 00
Clapham Junction 10	d	01 08		02 08	03 08		04 08			05 08					05 53				06 38			
Bedford	d																					
Luton 10	d																					
Luton Airport Parkway 7 ✈	d																					
St Albans City	d																					
St Pancras International 15 ⊖	d																					
Farringdon 3 ⊖	d																					
City Thameslink 3	d																					
London Blackfriars 3 ⊖	d																					
London Bridge 4 ⊖	d		01 05																			
New Cross Gate	d																					
Norwood Junction 2	d																					
East Croydon	a	01 21	01 32	02 21	03 21		04 21			05 22					06 05				06 51			
	d	01 22	01 32	02 22	03 22		04 22			05 23					06 06				06 52			
Purley 4	d	01 27		02 27	03 27		04 27			05 29									06 56			
Coulsdon South	d																		07 00			
Merstham	d																		07 05			
Redhill	a	01 36					04 36			05 37					06 18				07 09			
	d	01 36					04 36			05 38					06 19				07 09		07 15	
Reigate	a																					
Nutfield	d																					
Godstone	d																					
Edenbridge	d																					
Penshurst	d																					
Leigh (Kent)	d																					
Tonbridge 4	a																					
Earlswood (Surrey)	d																					
Salfords	d																					
Horley 4	d	01 43		02 42	03 42		04 43								06 25				07 15			
Gatwick Airport 10 ✈	a	01 45	01 51	02 44	03 44	04 05	04 45	05 05	05 35	05 45	05 50	06 05	06 20		06 31	06 35	06 47	07 05	07 18	07 20	07 27	07 35
	d	01 47	01 52	02 46	03 46		04 47			05 46				06 29	06 32				07 19			
Three Bridges 15	a	01 51	01 58	03 00	04 00		04 54			05 50				06 33	06 36				07 23			
	d	01 52					04 55			05 51				06 40	06 36				07 24			
Crawley	d													06 43								
Ifield	d													06 46								
Faygate	d																					
Littlehaven	d													06 52								
Horsham 4	a													06 56								
Balcombe	d																		07 30			
Haywards Heath	a	02 06					05 07			05 59					06 46				07 35			
	d	02 06					05 07			06 00					06 47				07 36			
Wivelsfield	d														06 51				07 40			
Lewes 4	a																					
Burgess Hill 4	d														06 53				07 42			
Hassocks 4	d														06 56				07 45			
Preston Park	d														07 03				07 52			
Hove 2	a																					
Brighton 10	a	02 23					05 21			06 18					07 08				07 58			

Table 186

Sundays
from 18 September

Bedford and London - Brighton

		SN	FC	SN	SN	SN	SN	SN	SN	FC	SN	GW	SN	SN	FC	SN	SN	SN	SN	SN	SN	SN
		◇1	1	1	1	◇1	1	1	1	1	1	1	1	◇1	1	1	◇1	1	◇1	1	1	1
				⌶	⌶		⌶						⌶			⌶		⌶		⌶		
London Victoria 15 ⊖	d	07 02		07 15	07 30	07 32	07 45						08 00	08 04		08 15	08 17	08 30	08 32	08 45		
Clapham Junction 10	d	07 08				07 38								08 10			08 23		08 38			
Bedford	d																					
Luton 10	d																					
Luton Airport Parkway 7 ✈	d																					
St Albans City	d																					
St Pancras International 15 ⊖	d																					
Farringdon 3 ⊖	d																					
City Thameslink 3	d																					
London Blackfriars 3 ⊖	d																					
London Bridge 4 ⊖	d		07 12						07 37	07 42					08 12							08 37
New Cross Gate	d																					
Norwood Junction 2	d								07 48													08 48
East Croydon	a	07 23	07 26			07 50			07 54	07 56				08 24	08 27		08 36		08 50			08 54
	d	07 23	07 27			07 51			07 55	07 57				08 24	08 27		08 37		08 51			08 55
Purley 4	d	07 29							08 00					08 30								09 00
Coulsdon South	d								08 04													09 04
Merstham	d								08 09													09 09
Redhill	a	07 37				08 03			08 13					08 38					09 03			09 13
	d	07 37				08 04		08 10	08 13			08 21		08 39					09 04		09 10	09 16
Reigate	a																					
Nutfield	d							08 14													09 14	
Godstone	d							08 20													09 20	
Edenbridge	d							08 25													09 25	
Penshurst	d							08 32													09 32	
Leigh (Kent)	d							08 35													09 35	
Tonbridge 4	a							08 40													09 40	
Earlswood (Surrey)	d																					
Salfords	d																					
Horley 4	d	07 43							08 22		←			08 45								09 22
Gatwick Airport 10 ✈	a	07 46	07 48	07 50	08 05	08 11	08 20		08 24	08 18	08 24	08 31	08 35	08 47	08 48	08 50	08 54	09 05	09 11	09 20		09 24
	d	07 47	07 50			08 12			08 25	08 20	08 25			08 48	08 50		08 56		09 12			09 25
Three Bridges 15	a	07 51	07 54			08 16			→	08 24	08 30			08 53	08 54				09 16			→
	d	07 52	07 54			08 17				08 24	08 33			08 53	08 54				09 17			
Crawley	d	07 55									08 36			08 56								
Ifield	d	07 58									08 39											
Faygate	d																					
Littlehaven	d	08 04									08 45											
Horsham 4	a	08 07									08 49			09 04								
Balcombe	d					08 23													09 23			
Haywards Heath	a		08 03			08 28				08 33					09 03		09 06		09 28			
	d		08 03			08 28				08 33					09 03		09 07		09 28			
Wivelsfield	d					08 32													09 32			
Lewes 4	a																					
Burgess Hill 4	d		08 08			08 34				08 38					09 08		09 12		09 34			
Hassocks 4	d		08 12			08 38				08 42					09 12				09 38			
Preston Park	d					08 45													09 45			
Hove 2	a																09 24					
Brighton 10	a		08 22			08 50				08 52					09 22				09 50			

Table 186

Sundays
from 18 September

Bedford and London - Brighton

		FC	SN	SN	GW	SN	SN	SN	FC	SN	SN	SN	SN	SN	SN	SN	FC	SN	SN	GW	SN	SN
		1	1	◇1	1	1	◇1	◇1	1	1	◇1	1	◇1	1	1	1	1	1	◇1	1	1	◇1
				A ⌶		⌶				⌶		⌶		⌶					A ⌶		⌶	⌶
London Victoria 15 ⊖	d			08 47		09 00	09 02	09 04		09 15	09 17	09 30	09 32	09 45					09 47		10 00	10 02
Clapham Junction 10	d			08 53			09 08	09 10			09 23		09 38						09 53			10 08
Bedford	d																					
Luton 10	d																					
Luton Airport Parkway 7 ✈	d																					
St Albans City	d																					
St Pancras International 15 ⊖	d																					
Farringdon 3 ⊖	d																					
City Thameslink 3	d																					
London Blackfriars 3 ⊖	d																					
London Bridge 4 ⊖	d	08 42							09 12							09 37	09 42					
New Cross Gate	d																					
Norwood Junction 2	d															09 48						
East Croydon	a	08 56		09 06			09 21	09 24	09 27		09 36		09 50			09 54	09 56		10 06			10 21
	d	08 57		09 07			09 22	09 24	09 27		09 37		09 51			09 55	09 57		10 07			10 22
Purley 4	d							09 30								10 00						
Coulsdon South	d															10 04						
Merstham	d															10 09						
Redhill	a							09 38					10 03			10 13						
	d				09 21			09 39					10 04		10 10	10 16				10 21		
Reigate	a																					
Nutfield	d														10 14							
Godstone	d														10 20							
Edenbridge	d														10 25							
Penshurst	d														10 32							
Leigh (Kent)	d														10 35							
Tonbridge 4	a														10 40							
Earlswood (Surrey)	d																					
Salfords	d																					
Horley 4	d		←					09 45								10 22		←				
Gatwick Airport 10 ✈	a	09 18	09 24	09 27	09 30	09 35	09 39	09 47	09 48	09 50	09 54	10 05	10 11	10 20		10 24	10 18	10 24	10 27	10 30	10 35	10 39
	d	09 20	09 25	09 29			09 40	09 48	09 50		09 56		10 12			10 25	10 20	10 25	10 29			10 40
Three Bridges 15	a	09 24	09 30					09 53	09 54				10 16			→	10 24	10 30				
	d	09 24	09 33					09 53	09 54				10 17				10 24	10 33				
Crawley	d		09 37					09 56										10 37				
Ifield	d		09 39															10 39				
Faygate	d																					
Littlehaven	d		09 46															10 46				
Horsham 4	a		09 49					10 04										10 49				
Balcombe	d												10 23									
Haywards Heath	a	09 33		09 40					10 03		10 06		10 28				10 33		10 40			
	d	09 33		09 41					10 03		10 07		10 28				10 33		10 41			
Wivelsfield	d			09 45									10 32						10 45			
Lewes 4	a			09 58															10 58			
Burgess Hill 4	d	09 38							10 08		10 12		10 34				10 38					
Hassocks 4	d	09 42							10 12				10 38				10 42					
Preston Park	d												10 45									
Hove 2	a										10 24											
Brighton 10	a	09 52					10 03		10 22				10 50				10 52					11 03

A ⌶ to Wivelsfield

Bedford and London - Brighton

from 18 September

Station		SN ◇1 ⊤	FC 1	SN 1 ⊤	SN ◇1	SN 1 ⊤	SN ◇1	SN 1 ⊤
London Victoria 15 ⊖	d	10 04		10 15	10 17	10 30	10 32	10 45
Clapham Junction 10	d	10 10			10 23		10 38	
Bedford	d							
Luton 10	d							
Luton Airport Parkway 7 ✈	d							
St Albans City	d							
St Pancras International 15 ⊖	d							
Farringdon 3 ⊖	d							
City Thameslink 3	d							
London Blackfriars 3 ⊖	d							
London Bridge 4 ⊖	d		10 12					
New Cross Gate	d							
Norwood Junction 2	d							
East Croydon	a	10 24	10 27		10 36		10 50	
	d	10 24	10 27		10 37		10 51	
Purley 4	d	10 30						
Coulsdon South	d							
Merstham	d							
Redhill	a	10 38					11 03	
	d	10 39					11 04	
Reigate	a							
Nutfield	d							
Godstone	d							
Edenbridge	d							
Penshurst	d							
Leigh (Kent)	d							
Tonbridge 4	a							
Earlswood (Surrey)	d							
Salfords	d							
Horley 4	d	10 45						
Gatwick Airport 10 ✈	a	10 47	10 48	10 50	10 54	11 05	11 11	11 20
	d	10 48	10 50		10 56		11 12	
Three Bridges 15	a	10 53	10 54				11 16	
	d	10 53	10 54				11 17	
Crawley	d	10 56						
Ifield	d							
Faygate	d							
Littlehaven	d							
Horsham 4	a	11 04						
Balcombe	d						11 23	
Haywards Heath	a		11 03		11 06		11 28	
	d		11 03		11 07		11 28	
Wivelsfield	d						11 32	
Lewes 4	a							
Burgess Hill 4	d		11 08		11 12		11 34	
Hassocks 4	d		11 12				11 38	
Preston Park	d						11 45	
Hove 2	a				11 24			
Brighton 10	a		11 22				11 50	

Station		SN 1	SN 1	FC 1	SN 1	SN ◇1 A ⊤	GW 1	SN 1 ⊤
London Victoria 15 ⊖	d					10 47		11 00
Clapham Junction 10	d					10 53		
Bedford	d							
Luton 10	d							
Luton Airport Parkway 7 ✈	d							
St Albans City	d							
St Pancras International 15 ⊖	d							
Farringdon 3 ⊖	d							
City Thameslink 3	d							
London Blackfriars 3 ⊖	d							
London Bridge 4 ⊖	d		10 37	10 42				
New Cross Gate	d							
Norwood Junction 2	d		10 48					
East Croydon	a		10 54	10 56		11 06		
	d		10 55	10 57		11 07		
Purley 4	d		11 00					
Coulsdon South	d		11 04					
Merstham	d		11 09					
Redhill	a		11 13					
	d	11 10	11 16				11 21	
Reigate	a							
Nutfield	d	11 14						
Godstone	d	11 20						
Edenbridge	d	11 25						
Penshurst	d	11 32						
Leigh (Kent)	d	11 35						
Tonbridge 4	a	11 40						
Earlswood (Surrey)	d							
Salfords	d							
Horley 4	d		11 22		←			
Gatwick Airport 10 ✈	a		11 24	11 18	11 24	11 27	11 30	11 35
	d		11 25	11 20	11 25	11 29		
Three Bridges 15	a		→	11 24	11 30			
	d			11 24	11 33			
Crawley	d				11 37			
Ifield	d				11 39			
Faygate	d							
Littlehaven	d				11 46			
Horsham 4	a				11 49			
Balcombe	d							
Haywards Heath	a			11 33		11 40		
	d			11 33		11 41		
Wivelsfield	d					11 45		
Lewes 4	a					11 58		
Burgess Hill 4	d			11 38				
Hassocks 4	d			11 42				
Preston Park	d							
Hove 2	a							
Brighton 10	a			11 52				

Station		SN ◇1 ⊤	SN ◇1 ⊤	FC 1	SN 1 ⊤	SN ◇1	SN 1 ⊤	SN ◇1
London Victoria 15 ⊖	d	11 02	11 04		11 15	11 17	11 30	11 32
Clapham Junction 10	d	11 08	11 10			11 23		11 38
Bedford	d							
Luton 10	d							
Luton Airport Parkway 7 ✈	d							
St Albans City	d							
St Pancras International 15 ⊖	d							
Farringdon 3 ⊖	d							
City Thameslink 3	d							
London Blackfriars 3 ⊖	d							
London Bridge 4 ⊖	d			11 12				
New Cross Gate	d							
Norwood Junction 2	d							
East Croydon	a	11 21	11 24	11 27		11 36		11 50
	d	11 22	11 24	11 27		11 37		11 51
Purley 4	d		11 30					
Coulsdon South	d							
Merstham	d							
Redhill	a		11 38					12 03
	d		11 39					12 04
Reigate	a							
Nutfield	d							
Godstone	d							
Edenbridge	d							
Penshurst	d							
Leigh (Kent)	d							
Tonbridge 4	a							
Earlswood (Surrey)	d							
Salfords	d							
Horley 4	d		11 45					
Gatwick Airport 10 ✈	a	11 39	11 47	11 48	11 50	11 54	12 05	12 11
	d	11 40	11 48	11 50		11 56		12 12
Three Bridges 15	a		11 53	11 54				12 16
	d		11 53	11 54				12 17
Crawley	d		11 56					
Ifield	d							
Faygate	d							
Littlehaven	d							
Horsham 4	a		12 04					
Balcombe	d							12 23
Haywards Heath	a			12 03		12 06		12 28
	d			12 03		12 07		12 28
Wivelsfield	d							12 32
Lewes 4	a							
Burgess Hill 4	d			12 08		12 12		12 34
Hassocks 4	d			12 12				12 38
Preston Park	d							12 45
Hove 2	a					12 24		
Brighton 10	a	12 03		12 22				12 49

A ⊤ to Wivelsfield

Bedford and London - Brighton

from 18 September

Station		SN 1 ⊤	SN 1	SN 1	FC 1	SN 1	SN ◇1 A ⊤	GW 1
London Victoria 15 ⊖	d	11 45					11 47	
Clapham Junction 10	d						11 53	
Bedford	d							
Luton 10	d							
Luton Airport Parkway 7 ✈	d							
St Albans City	d							
St Pancras International 15 ⊖	d							
Farringdon 3 ⊖	d							
City Thameslink 3	d							
London Blackfriars 3 ⊖	d							
London Bridge 4 ⊖	d			11 37	11 42			
New Cross Gate	d							
Norwood Junction 2	d			11 48				
East Croydon	a			11 54	11 56		12 06	
	d			11 55	11 57		12 07	
Purley 4	d			12 00				
Coulsdon South	d			12 04				
Merstham	d			12 09				
Redhill	a			12 13				
	d		12 10	12 16				12 21
Reigate	a							
Nutfield	d		12 14					
Godstone	d		12 20					
Edenbridge	d		12 25					
Penshurst	d		12 32					
Leigh (Kent)	d		12 35					
Tonbridge 4	a		12 40					
Earlswood (Surrey)	d							
Salfords	d							
Horley 4	d			12 22		←		
Gatwick Airport 10 ✈	a	12 20		12 24	12 18	12 24	12 27	12 30
	d			12 25	12 20	12 25	12 29	
Three Bridges 15	a			→	12 24	12 30		
	d				12 24	12 33		
Crawley	d					12 37		
Ifield	d					12 39		
Faygate	d							
Littlehaven	d					12 46		
Horsham 4	a					12 49		
Balcombe	d							
Haywards Heath	a				12 33		12 40	
	d				12 33		12 41	
Wivelsfield	d						12 45	
Lewes 4	a						12 58	
Burgess Hill 4	d				12 38			
Hassocks 4	d				12 42			
Preston Park	d							
Hove 2	a							
Brighton 10	a				12 52			

Station		SN 1 ⊤	SN ◇1 ⊤	SN ◇1 ⊤	FC 1	SN 1 ⊤	SN ◇1	SN 1 ⊤
London Victoria 15 ⊖	d	12 00	12 02	12 04		12 15	12 17	12 30
Clapham Junction 10	d		12 08	12 10			12 23	
Bedford	d							
Luton 10	d							
Luton Airport Parkway 7 ✈	d							
St Albans City	d							
St Pancras International 15 ⊖	d							
Farringdon 3 ⊖	d							
City Thameslink 3	d							
London Blackfriars 3 ⊖	d							
London Bridge 4 ⊖	d				12 12			
New Cross Gate	d							
Norwood Junction 2	d							
East Croydon	a		12 21	12 24	12 27		12 36	
	d		12 22	12 24	12 27		12 37	
Purley 4	d			12 30				
Coulsdon South	d							
Merstham	d							
Redhill	a			12 38				
	d			12 39				
Reigate	a							
Nutfield	d							
Godstone	d							
Edenbridge	d							
Penshurst	d							
Leigh (Kent)	d							
Tonbridge 4	a							
Earlswood (Surrey)	d							
Salfords	d							
Horley 4	d			12 45				
Gatwick Airport 10 ✈	a	12 35	12 39	12 47	12 48	12 50	12 54	13 05
	d		12 40	12 48	12 50		12 56	
Three Bridges 15	a			12 53	12 54			
	d			12 53	12 54			
Crawley	d			12 56				
Ifield	d							
Faygate	d							
Littlehaven	d							
Horsham 4	a			13 04				
Balcombe	d							
Haywards Heath	a				13 03		13 06	
	d				13 03		13 07	
Wivelsfield	d							
Lewes 4	a							
Burgess Hill 4	d				13 08		13 12	
Hassocks 4	d				13 12			
Preston Park	d							
Hove 2	a						13 24	
Brighton 10	a		13 03		13 22			

Station		SN ◇1	SN 1 ⊤	SN 1	SN 1	FC 1	SN 1	SN ◇1 A ⊤
London Victoria 15 ⊖	d	12 32	12 45					12 47
Clapham Junction 10	d	12 38						12 53
Bedford	d							
Luton 10	d							
Luton Airport Parkway 7 ✈	d							
St Albans City	d							
St Pancras International 15 ⊖	d							
Farringdon 3 ⊖	d							
City Thameslink 3	d							
London Blackfriars 3 ⊖	d							
London Bridge 4 ⊖	d				12 37	12 42		
New Cross Gate	d							
Norwood Junction 2	d				12 48			
East Croydon	a	12 50			12 54	12 56		13 06
	d	12 51			12 55	12 57		13 07
Purley 4	d				13 00			
Coulsdon South	d				13 04			
Merstham	d				13 09			
Redhill	a	13 03			13 13			
	d	13 04		13 10	13 16			
Reigate	a							
Nutfield	d			13 14				
Godstone	d			13 20				
Edenbridge	d			13 25				
Penshurst	d			13 32				
Leigh (Kent)	d			13 35				
Tonbridge 4	a			13 40				
Earlswood (Surrey)	d							
Salfords	d							
Horley 4	d				13 22		←	
Gatwick Airport 10 ✈	a	13 11	13 20		13 24	13 18	13 24	13 27
	d	13 12			13 25	13 20	13 25	13 29
Three Bridges 15	a	13 16			→	13 24	13 30	
	d	13 17				13 24	13 33	
Crawley	d						13 37	
Ifield	d						13 39	
Faygate	d							
Littlehaven	d						13 46	
Horsham 4	a						13 49	
Balcombe	d	13 23						
Haywards Heath	a	13 28				13 33		13 40
	d	13 28				13 33		13 41
Wivelsfield	d	13 32						13 45
Lewes 4	a							13 56
Burgess Hill 4	d	13 34				13 38		
Hassocks 4	d	13 38				13 42		
Preston Park	d	13 45						
Hove 2	a							
Brighton 10	a	13 50				13 52		

A ⊤ to Wivelsfield

Table 186

Sundays from 18 September

Bedford and London - Brighton

		GW 1	SN 1 🚌	SN ◇1 🚌	SN ◇1 🚌	FC 1	SN 1 🚌	SN ◇1	SN 1 🚌	SN ◇1	SN 1 🚌	SN 1	SN 1	FC 1	SN 1	SN ◇1 A 🚌	GW 1	SN 1 🚌	SN ◇1 🚌	SN ◇1 🚌	FC 1	SN 1 🚌
London Victoria 15 ⊖	d		13 00	13 02	13 04		13 15	13 17	13 30	13 32	13 45					13 47		14 00	14 02	14 04		14 15
Clapham Junction 10	d			13 08	13 10			13 23		13 38						13 53			14 08	14 10		
Bedford	d																					
Luton 10	d																					
Luton Airport Parkway 7 ✈	d																					
St Albans City	d																					
St Pancras International 15 ⊖	d																					
Farringdon 3 ⊖	d																					
City Thameslink 3	d																					
London Blackfriars 3 ⊖	d																					
London Bridge 4 ⊖	d					13 12							13 37	13 42							14 12	
New Cross Gate	d																					
Norwood Junction 2	d												13 48									
East Croydon	a			13 21	13 24	13 27		13 36		13 50			13 54	13 56		14 06			14 21	14 24	14 27	
	d			13 22	13 24	13 27		13 37		13 51			13 55	13 57		14 07			14 22	14 24	14 27	
Purley 4	d				13 30								14 00							14 30		
Coulsdon South	d												14 04									
Merstham	d												14 09									
Redhill	a				13 38					14 03			14 13							14 38		
	d	13 21			13 39					14 04		14 10	14 16				14 21			14 39		
Reigate	a																					
Nutfield	d											14 14										
Godstone	d											14 20										
Edenbridge	d											14 25										
Penshurst	d											14 32										
Leigh (Kent)	d											14 35										
Tonbridge 4	a											14 40										
Earlswood (Surrey)	d																					
Salfords	d																					
Horley 4	d				13 45								14 22		←					14 45		
Gatwick Airport 10 ✈	a	13 30	13 35	13 39	13 47	13 48	13 50	13 54	14 05	14 11	14 20		14 24	14 18	14 24	14 27	14 30	14 35	14 39	14 47	14 48	14 50
	d			13 40	13 48	13 50		13 56		14 12			14 25	14 20	14 25	14 29			14 40	14 48	14 50	
Three Bridges 15	a				13 53	13 54				14 16			→	14 24	14 30					14 53	14 54	
	d				13 53	13 54				14 17				14 24	14 33					14 53	14 54	
Crawley	d				13 56										14 37					14 56		
Ifield	d														14 39							
Faygate	d																					
Littlehaven	d														14 46							
Horsham 4	a				14 04										14 49					15 04		
Balcombe	d									14 23												
Haywards Heath	a					14 03		14 06		14 28				14 33		14 40					15 03	
	d					14 03		14 07		14 28				14 33		14 41					15 03	
Wivelsfield	d									14 32						14 45						
Lewes 4	a															14 56						
Burgess Hill 4	d					14 08		14 12		14 34				14 38							15 08	
Hassocks 4	d					14 12				14 38				14 42							15 12	
Preston Park	d									14 45												
Hove 2	a							14 24														
Brighton 10	a			14 03		14 22				14 50				14 52					15 03		15 22	

A 🚌 to Wivelsfield

Table 186

Sundays from 18 September

Bedford and London - Brighton

		SN ◇1	SN 1 🚌	SN ◇1	SN 1 🚌	SN 1	SN 1	FC 1	SN 1	SN ◇1 A 🚌	GW 1	SN 1 🚌	SN ◇1 🚌	SN ◇1 🚌	FC 1	SN 1 🚌	SN ◇1	SN 1 🚌	SN ◇1	SN 1 🚌	SN 1	SN 1
London Victoria 15 ⊖	d	14 17	14 30	14 32	14 45					14 47		15 00	15 02	15 04		15 15	15 17	15 30	15 32	15 45		
Clapham Junction 10	d	14 23		14 38						14 53			15 08	15 10			15 23		15 38			
Bedford	d																					
Luton 10	d																					
Luton Airport Parkway 7 ✈	d																					
St Albans City	d																					
St Pancras International 15 ⊖	d																					
Farringdon 3 ⊖	d																					
City Thameslink 3	d																					
London Blackfriars 3 ⊖	d																					
London Bridge 4 ⊖	d						14 37	14 42							15 12							15 37
New Cross Gate	d																					
Norwood Junction 2	d						14 48															15 48
East Croydon	a	14 36		14 50			14 54	14 56		15 06			15 21	15 24	15 27		15 36		15 50			15 54
	d	14 37		14 51			14 55	14 57		15 07			15 22	15 24	15 27		15 37		15 51			15 55
Purley 4	d						15 00							15 30								16 00
Coulsdon South	d						15 04															16 04
Merstham	d						15 09															16 09
Redhill	a			15 03			15 13							15 38					16 03			16 13
	d			15 04		15 10	15 16				15 21			15 39					16 04		16 10	16 16
Reigate	a																					
Nutfield	d					15 14															16 14	
Godstone	d					15 20															16 20	
Edenbridge	d					15 25															16 25	
Penshurst	d					15 32															16 32	
Leigh (Kent)	d					15 35															16 35	
Tonbridge 4	a					15 40															16 40	
Earlswood (Surrey)	d																					
Salfords	d																					
Horley 4	d						15 22		←					15 45								16 22
Gatwick Airport 10 ✈	a	14 54	15 05	15 11	15 20		15 24	15 18	15 24	15 27	15 30	15 35	15 39	15 47	15 48	15 50	15 54	16 05	16 11	16 20		16 24
	d	14 56		15 12			15 25	15 20	15 25	15 29			15 40	15 48	15 50		15 56		16 12			16 25
Three Bridges 15	a			15 16			→	15 24	15 30					15 53	15 54				16 16			→
	d			15 17				15 24	15 33					15 53	15 54				16 17			
Crawley	d								15 37					15 56								
Ifield	d								15 39													
Faygate	d																					
Littlehaven	d								15 46													
Horsham 4	a								15 49					16 04								
Balcombe	d			15 23															16 23			
Haywards Heath	a	15 06		15 28				15 33		15 40					16 03		16 06		16 28			
	d	15 07		15 28				15 33		15 41					16 03		16 07		16 28			
Wivelsfield	d			15 32						15 45									16 32			
Lewes 4	a									15 56												
Burgess Hill 4	d	15 12		15 34				15 38							16 08		16 12		16 34			
Hassocks 4	d			15 38				15 42							16 12				16 38			
Preston Park	d			15 45															16 45			
Hove 2	a	15 24															16 24					
Brighton 10	a			15 50				15 52					16 03		16 22				16 50			

A 🚌 to Wivelsfield

Bedford and London - Brighton

from 18 September

		FC	SN	SN	GW	SN	SN	SN	FC	SN	SN	SN	SN	SN	SN	SN	FC	SN	SN	GW	SN	SN
		1	1	◇1	1	1	◇1	◇1	1	1	◇1	1	◇1	1	1	1	1	1	◇1	1	1	◇1
				A															A			
				⊼		⊼	⊼	⊼		⊼		⊼		⊼					⊼		⊼	⊼
London Victoria 15 ⊖	d			15 47		16 00	16 02	16 04		16 15	16 17	16 30	16 32	16 45					16 47		17 00	17 02
Clapham Junction 10	d			15 53			16 08	16 10			16 23		16 38						16 53			17 08
Bedford	d																					
Luton 10	d																					
Luton Airport Parkway 7 ✈	d																					
St Albans City	d																					
St Pancras International 15 ⊖	d																					
Farringdon 3 ⊖	d																					
City Thameslink 3	d																					
London Blackfriars 3 ⊖	d																					
London Bridge 4 ⊖	d	15 42							16 12							16 37	16 42					
New Cross Gate	d																					
Norwood Junction 2	d															16 48						
East Croydon	a	15 56		16 06			16 21	16 24	16 27		16 36		16 50			16 54	16 56		17 06			17 21
	d	15 57		16 07			16 22	16 24	16 27		16 37		16 51			16 55	16 57		17 07			17 22
Purley 4	d							16 30								17 00						
Coulsdon South	d															17 04						
Merstham	d															17 09						
Redhill	a							16 38					17 03			17 13						
	d				16 21			16 39					17 04		17 10	17 16				17 21		
Reigate	a																					
Nutfield	d														17 14							
Godstone	d														17 20							
Edenbridge	d														17 25							
Penshurst	d														17 32							
Leigh (Kent)	d														17 35							
Tonbridge 4	a														17 40							
Earlswood (Surrey)	d																					
Salfords	d																					
Horley 4	d		←					16 45								17 22		←				
Gatwick Airport 10 ✈	a	16 18	16 24	16 27	16 30	16 35	16 39	16 47	16 48	16 50	16 54	17 05	17 11	17 20		17 24	17 18	17 24	17 27	17 30	17 35	17 39
	d	16 20	16 25	16 29			16 40	16 48	16 50		16 56		17 12			17 25	17 20	17 25	17 29			17 40
Three Bridges 15	a	16 24	16 30					16 53	16 54				17 16			→	17 24	17 30				
	d	16 24	16 33					16 53	16 54				17 17				17 24	17 33				
Crawley	d		16 37					16 56										17 37				
Ifield	d		16 39															17 39				
Faygate	d																					
Littlehaven	d		16 46															17 46				
Horsham 4	a		16 49					17 04										17 49				
Balcombe	d												17 23									
Haywards Heath	a	16 33		16 40					17 03		17 06		17 28				17 33		17 40			
	d	16 33		16 41					17 03		17 07		17 28				17 33		17 41			
Wivelsfield	d			16 45									17 32						17 45			
Lewes 4	a			16 58															17 58			
Burgess Hill 4	d	16 38							17 08		17 12		17 34				17 38					
Hassocks 4	d	16 42							17 12				17 38				17 42					
Preston Park	d												17 45									
Hove 2	a										17 24											
Brighton 10	a	16 52					17 03		17 22				17 50				17 52					18 03

A ⊼ to Wivelsfield

Bedford and London - Brighton

from 18 September

		SN	FC	SN	SN	SN	SN	SN	SN	SN	FC	SN	SN	GW	SN	SN	SN	FC	SN	SN	SN	SN
		◇1	1	1	◇1	1	◇1	1	1	1	1	1	◇1	1	1	◇1	◇1	1	1	◇1	1	◇1
													A									
		⊼		⊼		⊼		⊼					⊼		⊼	⊼	⊼		⊼		⊼	
London Victoria 15 ⊖	d	17 04		17 15	17 17	17 30	17 32	17 45					17 47		18 00	18 02	18 04		18 15	18 17	18 30	18 32
Clapham Junction 10	d	17 10			17 23		17 38						17 53			18 08	18 10			18 23		18 38
Bedford	d																					
Luton 10	d																					
Luton Airport Parkway 7 ✈	d																					
St Albans City	d																					
St Pancras International 15 ⊖	d																					
Farringdon 3 ⊖	d																					
City Thameslink 3	d																					
London Blackfriars 3 ⊖	d																					
London Bridge 4 ⊖	d		17 12							17 37	17 42							18 12				
New Cross Gate	d																					
Norwood Junction 2	d									17 48												
East Croydon	a	17 24	17 27		17 36		17 50			17 54	17 56		18 06			18 21	18 24	18 27		18 36		18 50
	d	17 24	17 27		17 37		17 51			17 55	17 57		18 07			18 22	18 24	18 27		18 37		18 51
Purley 4	d	17 30								18 00							18 30					
Coulsdon South	d									18 04												
Merstham	d									18 09												
Redhill	a	17 38					18 03			18 13							18 38					19 03
	d	17 39					18 04		18 10	18 16				18 21			18 39					19 04
Reigate	a																					
Nutfield	d								18 14													
Godstone	d								18 20													
Edenbridge	d								18 25													
Penshurst	d								18 32													
Leigh (Kent)	d								18 35													
Tonbridge 4	a								18 40													
Earlswood (Surrey)	d																					
Salfords	d																					
Horley 4	d	17 45								18 22		←					18 45					
Gatwick Airport 10 ✈	a	17 47	17 48	17 50	17 54	18 05	18 11	18 20		18 24	18 18	18 24	18 27	18 30	18 35	18 39	18 47	18 48	18 50	18 54	19 05	19 11
	d	17 48	17 50		17 56		18 12			18 25	18 20	18 25	18 29			18 40	18 48	18 50		18 56		19 12
Three Bridges 15	a	17 53	17 54				18 16			→	18 24	18 30					18 53	18 54				19 16
	d	17 53	17 54				18 17				18 24	18 33					18 53	18 54				19 17
Crawley	d	17 56										18 37					18 56					
Ifield	d											18 39										
Faygate	d																					
Littlehaven	d											18 46										
Horsham 4	a	18 04										18 49					19 04					
Balcombe	d						18 23															19 23
Haywards Heath	a		18 03		18 06		18 28				18 33		18 40					19 03		19 06		19 28
	d		18 03		18 07		18 28				18 33		18 41					19 03		19 07		19 28
Wivelsfield	d						18 32						18 45									19 32
Lewes 4	a												18 58									
Burgess Hill 4	d		18 08		18 12		18 34				18 38							19 08		19 12		19 34
Hassocks 4	d		18 12				18 38				18 42							19 12				19 38
Preston Park	d						18 45															19 45
Hove 2	a				18 24															19 24		
Brighton 10	a		18 22				18 50				18 52					19 03		19 22				19 50

A ⊼ to Wivelsfield

Table 186

Sundays from 18 September

Bedford and London - Brighton

		SN 1 ⌶	SN 1	SN 1	FC 1	SN 1	SN ◇1 A ⌶	GW 1	SN 1 ⌶	SN ◇1 ⌶	SN ◇1 ⌶	FC 1	SN 1	SN ◇1	SN 1	SN ◇1	SN 1	SN 1	SN 1	FC 1	SN 1	SN ◇1 A ⌶
London Victoria 15 ⊖	d	18 45					18 47		19 00	19 02	19 04		19 15	19 17	19 30	19 32	19 45					19 47
Clapham Junction 10	d						18 53			19 08	19 10			19 23		19 38						19 53
Bedford	d																					
Luton 10	d																					
Luton Airport Parkway 7 ✈	d																					
St Albans City	d																					
St Pancras International 15 ⊖	d																					
Farringdon 3 ⊖	d																					
City Thameslink 3	d																					
London Blackfriars 3 ⊖	d																					
London Bridge 4 ⊖	d			18 37	18 42							19 12							19 37	19 42		
New Cross Gate	d																					
Norwood Junction 2	d			18 48															19 48			
East Croydon	a			18 54	18 56		19 06			19 21	19 24	19 27		19 36		19 50			19 54	19 56		20 06
	d			18 55	18 57		19 07			19 22	19 24	19 27		19 37		19 51			19 55	19 57		20 07
Purley 4	d			19 00							19 30								20 00			
Coulsdon South	d			19 04															20 04			
Merstham	d			19 09															20 09			
Redhill	a			19 13							19 38					20 03			20 13			
	d		19 10	19 16				19 21			19 39					20 04		20 10	20 16			
Reigate	a																					
Nutfield	d		19 14															20 14				
Godstone	d		19 20															20 20				
Edenbridge	d		19 25															20 25				
Penshurst	d		19 32															20 32				
Leigh (Kent)	d		19 35															20 35				
Tonbridge 4	a		19 40															20 40				
Earlswood (Surrey)	d																					
Salfords	d																					
Horley 4	d			19 22		←					19 45								20 22		←	
Gatwick Airport 10 ✈	a	19 20		19 24	19 18	19 24	19 27	19 30	19 35	19 39	19 47	19 48	19 50	19 54	20 05	20 11	20 20		20 24	20 18	20 24	20 27
	d			19 25	19 20	19 25	19 29			19 40	19 48	19 50		19 56		20 12			20 25	20 20	20 25	20 29
Three Bridges 15	a			→	19 24	19 30					19 53	19 54				20 16			→	20 24	20 30	
	d				19 24	19 33					19 53	19 54				20 17				20 24	20 33	
Crawley	d					19 37					19 56										20 37	
Ifield	d					19 39															20 39	
Faygate	d																					
Littlehaven	d					19 46															20 46	
Horsham 4	a					19 49					20 04										20 49	
Balcombe	d															20 23						
Haywards Heath	a				19 33		19 40					20 03		20 06		20 28				20 33		20 40
	d				19 33		19 41					20 03		20 07		20 28				20 33		20 41
Wivelsfield	d						19 45									20 32						20 45
Lewes 4	a						19 58															20 58
Burgess Hill 4	d				19 38							20 08		20 12		20 34				20 38		
Hassocks 4	d				19 42							20 12				20 38				20 42		
Preston Park	d															20 45						
Hove 2	a													20 24								
Brighton 10	a				19 52					20 03		20 22				20 50				20 52		

A ⌶ to Wivelsfield

Table 186

Sundays from 18 September

Bedford and London - Brighton

		GW 1	SN 1	SN ◇1	SN ◇1	FC 1	SN 1	SN ◇1	SN 1	SN ◇1	SN 1	SN 1	SN 1	FC 1	SN 1	SN ◇1	GW 1	SN 1	SN ◇1	SN ◇1	FC 1	SN 1
London Victoria 15 ⊖	d		20 00	20 02	20 04		20 15	20 17	20 30	20 32	20 45					20 47		21 00	21 02	21 04		21 15
Clapham Junction 10	d			20 08	20 10			20 23		20 38						20 53			21 08	21 10		
Bedford	d																					
Luton 10	d																					
Luton Airport Parkway 7 ✈	d																					
St Albans City	d																					
St Pancras International 15 ⊖	d																					
Farringdon 3 ⊖	d																					
City Thameslink 3	d																					
London Blackfriars 3 ⊖	d																					
London Bridge 4 ⊖	d					20 12							20 37	20 42							21 12	
New Cross Gate	d																					
Norwood Junction 2	d												20 48									
East Croydon	a			20 21	20 24	20 27		20 36		20 50			20 54	20 56		21 06			21 21	21 24	21 27	
	d			20 22	20 24	20 27		20 37		20 51			20 55	20 57		21 07			21 22	21 24	21 27	
Purley 4	d				20 30								21 00							21 30		
Coulsdon South	d												21 04									
Merstham	d												21 09									
Redhill	a				20 38					21 03			21 13							21 38		
	d	20 21			20 39					21 04		21 10	21 16				21 21			21 39		
Reigate	a																					
Nutfield	d											21 14										
Godstone	d											21 20										
Edenbridge	d											21 25										
Penshurst	d											21 32										
Leigh (Kent)	d											21 35										
Tonbridge 4	a											21 40										
Earlswood (Surrey)	d																					
Salfords	d																					
Horley 4	d				20 45								21 22		←					21 45		
Gatwick Airport 10 ✈	a	20 30	20 35	20 39	20 47	20 48	20 50	20 54	21 05	21 11	21 20		21 24	21 18	21 24	21 27	21 30	21 35	21 39	21 47	21 48	21 50
	d			20 40	20 48	20 50		20 56		21 12			21 25	21 20	21 25	21 29			21 40	21 48	21 50	
Three Bridges 15	a				20 53	20 54				21 16			→	21 24	21 30					21 53	21 54	
	d				20 53	20 54				21 17				21 24	21 33					21 53	21 54	
Crawley	d				20 56										21 37					21 56		
Ifield	d														21 39							
Faygate	d																					
Littlehaven	d														21 46							
Horsham 4	a				21 04										21 49					22 04		
Balcombe	d									21 23												
Haywards Heath	a					21 03		21 06		21 28				21 33		21 40					22 03	
	d					21 03		21 07		21 28				21 33		21 41					22 03	
Wivelsfield	d									21 32						21 45						
Lewes 4	a															21 58						
Burgess Hill 4	d					21 08		21 12		21 34				21 38							22 08	
Hassocks 4	d					21 12				21 38				21 42							22 12	
Preston Park	d									21 45												
Hove 2	a							21 24														
Brighton 10	a			21 03		21 22				21 50				21 52					22 03		22 22	

Bedford and London - Brighton

		SN ◇1	SN 1	SN ◇1	SN 1	SN 1	SN 1	FC 1	SN 1	SN ◇1	GW 1	SN 1	SN ◇1	FC 1	SN 1	SN ◇1	SN 1	SN ◇1	SN 1	SN 1	SN 1	FC 1
London Victoria 15 ⊖	d	21 17	21 30	21 32	21 45					21 47		22 00	22 04		22 15	22 17	22 30	22 32	22 45			
Clapham Junction 10	d	21 23		21 38						21 53			22 10			22 23		22 38				
Bedford	d																					
Luton 10	d																					
Luton Airport Parkway 7 ✈	d																					
St Albans City	d																					
St Pancras International 15 ⊖	d																					
Farringdon 3 ⊖	d																					
City Thameslink 3	d																					
London Blackfriars 3 ⊖	d																					
London Bridge 4 ⊖	d						21 37	21 42						22 12							22 37	22 42
New Cross Gate	d																					
Norwood Junction 2	d						21 48														22 48	
East Croydon	a	21 36		21 50			21 54	21 56		22 06			22 24	22 27		22 36		22 50			22 54	22 56
	d	21 37		21 51			21 55	21 57		22 07			22 24	22 27		22 37		22 51			22 55	22 57
Purley 4	d						22 00						22 30								23 00	
Coulsdon South	d						22 04														23 04	
Merstham	d						22 09														23 09	
Redhill	a			22 03			22 13						22 38					23 03			23 13	
	d			22 04		22 10	22 16				22 21		22 39					23 04		23 10	23 16	
Reigate	a																					
Nutfield	d					22 14														23 14		
Godstone	d					22 20														23 20		
Edenbridge	d					22 25														23 25		
Penshurst	d					22 32														23 32		
Leigh (Kent)	d					22 35														23 35		
Tonbridge 4	a					22 40														23 40		
Earlswood (Surrey)	d																					
Salfords	d																					
Horley 4	d						22 22		←				22 45								23 22	
Gatwick Airport 10 ✈	a	21 55	22 05	22 12	22 20		22 24	22 18	22 24	22 27	22 30	22 35	22 47	22 48	22 50	22 54	23 05	23 11	23 20		23 24	23 18
	d	21 56		22 13			22 25	22 20	22 25	22 29			22 48	22 50		22 56		23 12			23 25	23 20
Three Bridges 15	a			22 18			→	22 24	22 30				22 53	22 54				23 16			→	23 24
	d			22 18				22 24	22 33				22 53	22 54				23 17				23 24
Crawley	d								22 37				22 56									
Ifield	d								22 39													
Faygate	d																					
Littlehaven	d								22 46													
Horsham 4	a								22 49				23 04									
Balcombe	d			22 24														23 23				
Haywards Heath	a	22 06		22 29				22 33		22 40				23 03		23 06		23 28				23 33
	d	22 07		22 30				22 33		22 41				23 03		23 07		23 28				23 33
Wivelsfield	d			22 34						22 45								23 32				
Lewes 4	a									22 58												
Burgess Hill 4	d	22 12		22 36				22 38						23 08		23 12		23 34				23 38
Hassocks 4	d			22 39				22 42						23 12				23 38				23 42
Preston Park	d			22 46														23 45				
Hove 2	a	22 24														23 24						
Brighton 10	a			22 50				22 52						23 22				23 50				23 52

Bedford and London - Brighton

		SN 1	SN ◇1	GW 1	SN 1	SN 1	FC 1	SN 1	SN 1	SN ◇1	SN 1	SN ◇1	FC 1	SN 1
London Victoria 15 ⊖	d		22 47		23 00	23 04		23 15		23 17	23 30	23 32		23 45
Clapham Junction 10	d		22 53			23 10				23 23		23 38		
Bedford	d													
Luton 10	d													
Luton Airport Parkway 7 ✈	d													
St Albans City	d													
St Pancras International 15 ⊖	d													
Farringdon 3 ⊖	d													
City Thameslink 3	d													
London Blackfriars 3 ⊖	d													
London Bridge 4 ⊖	d						23 12						23 42	
New Cross Gate	d													
Norwood Junction 2	d													
East Croydon	a		23 06			23 22	23 27			23 37		23 52	23 56	
	d		23 07			23 22	23 27			23 38		23 53	23 57	
Purley 4	d					23 29								
Coulsdon South	d					23 33								
Merstham	d					23 38								
Redhill	a					23 42						00 05		
	d			23 21		23 42						00 05		
Reigate	a													
Nutfield	d													
Godstone	d													
Edenbridge	d													
Penshurst	d													
Leigh (Kent)	d													
Tonbridge 4	a													
Earlswood (Surrey)	d													
Salfords	d													
Horley 4	d	←				23 50			←					
Gatwick Airport 10 ✈	a	23 24	23 27	23 30	23 35	23 54	23 48	23 50	23 54	23 59	00 05	00 14	00 18	00 20
	d	23 25	23 29			23 55	23 50		23 55	00 01		00 15	00 19	
Three Bridges 15	a	23 30				→	23 54		00 01	00 05		00 19	00 24	
	d	23 33					23 54		00 01	00 06		00 20		
Crawley	d	23 37							00 05					
Ifield	d	23 39							00 07					
Faygate	d													
Littlehaven	d	23 46							00 14					
Horsham 4	a	23 49							00 17					
Balcombe	d											00 26		
Haywards Heath	a		23 40				00 03			00 14		00 31		
	d		23 41				00 03			00 15		00 31		
Wivelsfield	d		23 45									00 35		
Lewes 4	a		23 58											
Burgess Hill 4	d						00 08			00 20		00 37		
Hassocks 4	d						00 12					00 41		
Preston Park	d											00 48		
Hove 2	a									00 31				
Brighton 10	a						00 22					00 52		

Brighton - London and Bedford

Miles	Miles	Miles	Station		SN MO 1	SN MX 1	SN MO 1	SN 1	SN MX 1	SN MX ◇1	SN MO ◇1	FC MX 1	FC 1 A	FC 1 B	SN 1	SN MX ◇1	SN MO ◇1	SN 1	FC MX 1	FC MO 1	SN 1	SN	SN 1
0	—	—	**Brighton** 10	d						23p02	23p02	23p11	23p14	23p15					23p37	23p45			
—	0	—	Hove 2	d																			
1½	1½	—	Preston Park	d						23p06	23p06								23p41				
7¼	—	—	Hassocks 4	d						23p12	23p12	23p19	23p22	23p23					23p47	23p53			
9¼	—	—	Burgess Hill 4	d						23p16	23p16	23p23	23p26	23p27					23p51	23p57			
—	—	—	Lewes 4	d																			
10	9¼	—	Wivelsfield 4	d						23p19	23p19								23p53				
13	—	—	**Haywards Heath** 3	a						23p23	23p23	23p27	23p30	23p31					23p58	00 01			
—	—	—		d						23p24	23p24	23p28	23p31	23p32					23p59	00 01			
17	—	—	Balcombe	d							23p29								00 04				
—	0	—	**Horsham** 4	d		23p02	23p03																
—	1	—	Littlehaven	d		23p05	23p06																
—	3¼	—	Faygate	d																			
—	5¾	—	Ifield	d		23p11	23p12																
—	7	—	Crawley	d		23p14	23p16																
21½	8½	—	Three Bridges 4	a		23p18	23p20			23p33	23p36	23p38	23p40	23p41					00 10	00 10			
—	—	—		d		23p18	23p20			23p47	23p42	23p38	23p40	23p41					00 10	00 10			
24¼	—	—	**Gatwick Airport** 10 ✈	a		23p22	23p24			23p52	23p46	23p42	23p44	23p45					00 14	00 14			
—	—	—		d		23p23	23p25	23p35		23p53	23p47	23p43	23p45	23p46	23p50			00 05	00 15	00 15	00 20		00 35
25	—	—	Horley 4	d		23p26	23p28			23p56	23p49												
27¼	—	—	Salfords	d		23p30																	
29¼	—	—	Earlswood (Surrey)	d		23p33																	
—	—	0	**Tonbridge** 4	d																			
—	—	2½	Leigh (Kent)	d																			
—	—	4¼	Penshurst	d																			
—	—	9¼	Edenbridge	d																			
—	—	14	Godstone	d																			
—	—	17¾	Nutfield	d																			
—	0	—	**Reigate**	d																			
30	1¾	19¾	**Redhill** 5	a		23p36	23p34			00 03	23p57								00 22	00 22			
—	—	—		d		23p37	23p35			00 03	00 02								00 22	00 23			
32	—	—	Merstham	d		23p41	23p39																
35½	—	—	Coulsdon South	d		23p46	23p44																
37½	—	—	Purley 4	d		23p49	23p50		←	00 11	00 11					←	←						
40½	0	—	**East Croydon**	a		23p54	23p55		23p54	00 16	00 16	00 02	00 02	00 02		00 16	00 16		00 35	00 36			
—	—	—		d	23p50	23p58	23p56		23p58	00 17	00 17	00 04	00 04	00 04		00 17	00 17		00 36	00 36		00 49	
—	1¼	—	Norwood Junction 2	a		→				→	→												
—	—	—	New Cross Gate	d																			
—	10¼	—	**London Bridge** 4 ⊖	a								00 19	00 19	00 19					00 52	00 53			
—	—	—	**London Blackfriars** 3 ⊖	a																			
—	—	—	City Thameslink 3	a																			
—	—	—	Farringdon 3 ⊖	a																			
—	—	—	St Pancras International 15 ⊖	a																			
—	—	—	St Albans City	a																			
—	—	—	Luton Airport Parkway 4 ✈	a																			
—	—	—	Luton 7	a																			
—	—	—	**Bedford** 10	a																			
48¼	0	0	Clapham Junction 10	d	00 02		00 11		00 11							00 30	00 30					01 01	
51	—	—	**London Victoria** 15 ⊖	a	00 08		00 21	00 10	00 18						00 25	00 37	00 37	00 40			00 55	01 09	01 11

A MO from 12 September

B MO until 5 September

Brighton - London and Bedford

Station		SN 1	SN 1	FC 1	SN 1	SN 1	FC 1	SN 1	FC 1	FC	SN 1	FC 1	SN 1	SN 1	FC 1	GW 1	SN 1	FC 1	SN 1	SN 1	SN 1	SN 1	GW 1
Brighton 10	d																	05 09				05 23	
Hove 2	d																						
Preston Park	d																	05 13					
Hassocks 4	d																	05 19					
Burgess Hill 4	d																	05 23				05 33	
Lewes 4	d																						
Wivelsfield 4	d																	05 25					
Haywards Heath 3	a																	05 30				05 38	
	d																	05 30				05 38	
Balcombe	d																	05 36				05 44	
Horsham 4	d																05 17						
Littlehaven	d																05 20						
Faygate	d																						
Ifield	d																05 26						
Crawley	d																05 29						
Three Bridges 4	a																05 33	05 41				05 49	
	d			01 25		01 59	02 25	02 55	03 25	04 25		04 55					05 33	05 41				05 50	
Gatwick Airport 10 ✈	a			01 29		02 03	02 29	02 59	03 29	04 29		04 59					05 37	05 45				05 54	
	d	00 50	01 05	01 30	01 35	02 05	02 30	03 05	03 30	04 30	04 35	05 00		05 20	05 27	05 31	05 38	05 46		05 50		05 55	05 56
Horley 4	d		01 07			02 07		03 07									05 40						
Salfords	d																						
Earlswood (Surrey)	d																						
Tonbridge 4	d												04 59						05 20				
Leigh (Kent)	d												05 03						05 24				
Penshurst	d												05 07						05 28				
Edenbridge	d												05 13						05 34				
Godstone	d												05 20						05 41				
Nutfield	d												05 25						05 46				
Reigate	d																						
Redhill 5	a												05 30		05 34	05 41	05 47		05 51				06 07
	d														05 35		05 48						
Merstham	d																05 52						
Coulsdon South	d																05 57						
Purley 4	d		01 22			02 22		03 22									06 00				←		
East Croydon	a		01 27	01 50		02 27	02 47	03 27	03 47	04 47		05 17			05 46		06 06	06 01			06 06	06 10	
	d		01 28	01 50		02 28	02 47	03 28	03 47	04 47		05 17			05 47		06 07	06 02			06 07	06 11	
Norwood Junction 2	a																→						
New Cross Gate	d																						
London Bridge 4 ⊖	a			02 14			03 12		04 12			05 34			06 02			06 15					
London Blackfriars 3 ⊖	a									05 13		05 41			06 10			06 23					
City Thameslink 3	a									05 16		05 44			06 14			06 26					
Farringdon 3 ⊖	a									05 20		05 47			06 18			06 30					
St Pancras International 15 ⊖	a									05 23		05 51			06 21			06 33					
St Albans City	a									05 57		06 23			06 41			06 56					
Luton Airport Parkway 4 ✈	a									06 09		06 35			06 54			07 08					
Luton 7	a									06 12		06 38			06 58			07 11					
Bedford 10	a									06 40		07 04			07 24			07 36					
Clapham Junction 10	d		01 41			02 41		03 41													06 18	06 21	
London Victoria 15 ⊖	a	01 25	01 49		02 10	02 49		03 49			05 12			05 55						06 20	06 25	06 28	

Brighton - London and Bedford

Station		SN ◇1	SN 1	SN 1	SN 1 ⊼	FC 1	SN 1 ⊼	FC 1	SN 1	FC 1	SN 1	SN 1	SN 1 ⊼	SN 1	SN 1	SN 1	SN 1	SN 1	FC 1	SN 1 ⊼	SN ◇1	SN ◇1	SN ◇1 A
Brighton 10	d					05 39		05 49						06 01					06 07				06 17
Hove 2	d								05 57														
Preston Park	d					05 43		05 53											06 11				
Hassocks 4	d					05 49		05 59						06 09					06 18				06 26
Burgess Hill 4	d					05 53		06 03						06 12					06 22				06 30
Lewes 4	d	05 29													06 05								
Wivelsfield 4	d					05 55		06 05						06 15					06 25				
Haywards Heath 3	a	05 46				06 00		06 10	06 12					06 19	06 23				06 29				06 35
	d	05 47				06 00		06 10	06 12					06 27					06 30				06 35
Balcombe	d					06 06													06 35				
Horsham 4	d			05 38								06 10										06 24	
Littlehaven	d			05 41								06 13										06 27	
Faygate	d																						
Ifield	d			05 47								06 19										06 33	
Crawley	d			05 50								06 23										06 37	
Three Bridges 4	a			05 54		06 11		06 19	06 21			06 26		06 36					06 41			06 40	06 45
	d			05 54		06 11		06 20	06 21			06 27		06 36					06 41				06 48
Gatwick Airport 10 ✈	a	05 58		05 58		06 15		06 24	06 25			06 31		06 40					06 45				06 52
	d	06 00		06 00	06 05	06 16	06 20	06 25	06 26			06 32	06 35	06 41					06 46	06 50			06 53
Horley 4	d			06 02								06 35											06 56
Salfords	d			06 06								06 39											
Earlswood (Surrey)	d			06 10								06 42											
Tonbridge 4	d										06 10												
Leigh (Kent)	d										06 14												
Penshurst	d										06 18												
Edenbridge	d										06 24												
Godstone	d										06 31												
Nutfield	d										06 36												
Reigate	d																	06 49					
Redhill 5	a			06 13				06 32			06 42	06 46						06 53	06 54				07 02
	d			06 13				06 33			06 43	06 46							06 56				07 03
Merstham	d			06 17								06 50											
Coulsdon South	d			06 22							06 50	06 55											
Purley 4	d			06 26						←	06 54	06 59				←	←				←		
East Croydon	a	06 15		06 30		06 32		06 43	06 41	06 43	06 59	07 04		06 56		06 59	07 04		07 08		07 14		07 14
	d	06 15	06 27	06 31		06 32		06 44	06 42	06 44	07 00	07 05		06 57		07 00	07 05		07 09		07 15		07 15
Norwood Junction 2	a							→			→	→											→
New Cross Gate	d																						
London Bridge 4 ⊖	a					06 46				06 58				07 13		07 16			07 23				
London Blackfriars 3 ⊖	a					06 52				07 04									07 30				
City Thameslink 3	a					06 54				07 08									07 32				
Farringdon 3 ⊖	a					06 58				07 12									07 36				
St Pancras International 15 ⊖	a					07 01				07 15									07 39				
St Albans City	a					07 25				07 41													
Luton Airport Parkway 4 ✈	a					07 37				07 53									08 10				
Luton 7	a					07 40				07 58									08 12				
Bedford 10	a					08 06				08 24													
Clapham Junction 10	d	06 25	06 38	06 41					06 51								07 17				07 24		
London Victoria 15 ⊖	a	06 32	06 45	06 48	06 35		06 50		07 00				07 05				07 23			07 20	07 33		

A ◇ from Three Bridges

Brighton - London and Bedford

Station		GW 1	SN 1	FC 1	SN 1	SN 1 ⊼	SN 1	SN 1	SN 1	SN 1	SN ◇1 ⊼	SN 1	SN 1 ⊼	SN ◇1 ⊼	SN ◇1 A ⊼	SN 1	GW 1	SN 1	SN 1	SN 1	SN 1
Brighton 10	d			06 24		06 30				06 37			06 40	06 51							
Hove 2	d								06 31												
Preston Park	d			06 28					06 36				06 44								
Hassocks 4	d			06 35					06 43				06 52								
Burgess Hill 4	d			06 39		06 43			06 47				06 56	07 01							
Lewes 4	d																				06 51
Wivelsfield 4	d					06 46			06 50												07 08
Haywards Heath 3	a			06 43		06 50			06 54	06 58			07 01	07 05							07 12
	d			06 44		06 51			07 00				07 03	07 06							07 13
Balcombe	d			06 50																	07 19
Horsham 4	d				06 38						06 50				07 04						
Littlehaven	d				06 41						06 53										
Faygate	d				06 45																
Ifield	d				06 49						07 00										
Crawley	d				06 52						07 04				07 13						
Three Bridges 4	a			06 55	06 56						07 07			07 16	07 18						07 24
	d			06 56	06 56			07 04			07 08				07 22					07 14	07 25
Gatwick Airport 10 ✈	a			07 00	07 01	07 03		07 08	07 11		07 12		07 15							07 21	07 29
	d	07 00		07 01	07 02	07 05		07 09	07 12		07 14		07 20							07 22	07 30
Horley 4	d				07 04			07 12			07 16									07 25	
Salfords	d				07 08			07 16												07 29	
Earlswood (Surrey)	d				07 12			07 19												07 32	
Tonbridge 4	d						06 47														
Leigh (Kent)	d						06 51														
Penshurst	d						06 55														
Edenbridge	d						07 01														
Godstone	d						07 08														
Nutfield	d						07 13														
Reigate	d																07 18		07 27		
Redhill 5	a	07 07		07 10	07 15		07 18	07 22									07 24		07 31	07 36	
	d			07 11	07 15			07 23												07 40	
Merstham	d				07 19			07 27												07 44	
Coulsdon South	d				07 25			07 33												07 50	
Purley 4	d				07 29			07 37				←				←				07 55	
East Croydon	a			07 23	07 34			07 41	07 27		07 31	07 34			07 38	07 41				08 01	07 45
	d		07 15	07 24	07 35			07 42	07 27		07 31	07 35			07 39	07 42		07 45		08 02	07 46
Norwood Junction 2	a				→			→												→	
New Cross Gate	d																				
London Bridge 4 ⊖	a								07 43			07 49									08 01
London Blackfriars 3 ⊖	a			07 51																	
City Thameslink 3	a			07 56																	
Farringdon 3 ⊖	a			08 00																	
St Pancras International 15 ⊖	a			08 03																	
St Albans City	a			08 24																	
Luton Airport Parkway 4 ✈	a			08 37																	
Luton 7	a			08 40																	
Bedford 10	a			09 06																	
Clapham Junction 10	d		07 27								07 41				07 48	07 51		07 56			
London Victoria 15 ⊖	a		07 36			07 36					07 49		07 50		07 57	08 00		08 04			

A ⊼ from Three Bridges

Brighton - London and Bedford

		SN 1	SN 1	SN 1 H	FC 1	SN 1	SN 1	SN ◇1 H	SN 1		SN 1	SN 1	SN 1	SN 1	SN 1	SN 1	SN 1 H	SN ◇1	SN 1		SN ◇1 H	SN ◇1 H	GW 1	SN 1	SN 1
Brighton 10	d			06 56	07 00												07 15								
Hove 2	d					07 11												07 20							
Preston Park	d			07 00	07 04												07 19								
Hassocks 4	d				07 10	07 21												07 30							
Burgess Hill 4	d			07 10	07 14												07 29								
Lewes 4	d																				07 22	07 22			
Wivelsfield 4	d			07 14	07 18	07 26												07 35			07 39	07 39			
Haywards Heath 3	a			07 18	07 23	07 30											07 34	07 40			07 43	07 43			
	d			07 20	07 23	07 31											07 35	07 40			07 44	07 44			
Balcombe	d																								
Horsham 4	d		07 09				07 17	07 25																	
Littlehaven	d		07 12				07 20	07 29																	
Faygate	d		07 16																						
Ifield	d		07 20				07 27																		
Crawley	d		07 23				07 31	07 37																	
Three Bridges 4	a		07 27		07 32		07 34	07 40																	
	d		07 28		07 32		07 35	07 41																	
Gatwick Airport 10	a		07 32	07 32	07 37		07 39										07 47								
	d		07 33	07 35	07 38		07 40									07 44	07 50						07 58		
Horley 4	d		07 36				07 43									07 47					07 58	07 58			
Salfords	d		07 40				07 47									07 51									
Earlswood (Surrey)	d		07 43				07 50									07 54									
Tonbridge 4	d														07 25										
Leigh (Kent)	d														07 29										
Penshurst	d														07 33										
Edenbridge	d														07 39										
Godstone	d														07 46										
Nutfield	d														07 51										
Reigate	d	07 40												07 52											
Redhill 5	a	07 45	07 47				07 53							07 56	07 56	07 58							08 05		
	d		07 51				07 54									08 02									
Merstham	d						07 59									08 06									
Coulsdon South	d						08 04									08 11									
Purley 4	d								←		←	←	←			08 15			←						←
East Croydon	a		08 02		07 53	07 57	08 11	08 00	08 01		08 01	08 02	08 02			08 20		08 08	08 11		08 14	08 14			08 20
	d		08 03		07 54	07 57	08 11	08 01	08 02		08 02	08 03	08 03			08 21		08 08	08 11		08 14	08 14		08 15	08 21
Norwood Junction 2	a		→				→									→									
New Cross Gate	d																								
London Bridge 4	a					08 13			08 17		08 17	08 19	08 19												08 37
London Blackfriars 3	a				08 20																				
City Thameslink 3	a				08 23																				
Farringdon 3	a				08 27																				
St Pancras International 15	a				08 31																				
St Albans City	a				08 51																				
Luton Airport Parkway 4	a				09 00																				
Luton 7	a				09 04																				
Bedford 10	a				09 26																				
Clapham Junction 10	d							08 11										08 18	08 21		08 24	08 24		08 27	
London Victoria 15	a			08 06				08 19									08 20	08 26	08 29		08 32	08 32		08 35	

Brighton - London and Bedford

		SN 1	FC 1	SN 1 H	SN 1		SN 1	SN 1	SN ◇1	SN 1	SN 1	SN 1 H	SN 1 H	SN 1	FC 1		SN ◇1 H	GW 1	SN 1 H	SN ◇1 H	SN 1	SN 1	SN 1	SN 1	SN 1
Brighton 10	d		07 24	07 30				07 33					07 44		07 50										
Hove 2	d								07 41																
Preston Park	d		07 28					07 37					07 48		07 54										
Hassocks 4	d		07 35	07 39									07 56		08 00										
Burgess Hill 4	d		07 39					07 46	07 52				08 00												
Lewes 4	d									07 42										07 55					
Wivelsfield 4	d			07 45				07 49												08 11					
Haywards Heath 3	a		07 45	07 49				07 53	07 57	08 02			08 05		08 09					08 16					
	d		07 46	07 51				07 54	07 59	08 03			08 06		08 09					08 16					
Balcombe	d							07 59							08 15					08 22					
Horsham 4	d						07 40				07 51						08 09								08 12
Littlehaven	d						07 43				07 54														08 15
Faygate	d										07 58														08 19
Ifield	d						07 50				08 02														08 23
Crawley	d						07 53				08 06						08 18								08 26
Three Bridges 4	a		07 55				07 57	08 05			08 09						08 22			08 28					08 29
	d		07 56				07 58	08 05			08 10						08 22			08 28					08 30
Gatwick Airport 10	a		08 00	08 02			08 04		08 12		08 14		08 17		08 22										08 34
	d		08 01	08 05			08 05		08 13		08 15	08 17	08 20		08 23				08 35						08 35
Horley 4	d						08 07				08 17						08 28								08 38
Salfords	d						08 11				08 21														08 42
Earlswood (Surrey)	d						08 15				08 25														08 45
Tonbridge 4	d																						07 59	08 16	
Leigh (Kent)	d																						08 03	08 20	
Penshurst	d																						08 07	08 24	
Edenbridge	d																						08 13	08 30	
Godstone	d																						08 20	08 37	
Nutfield	d																						08 25	08 42	
Reigate	d				08 09													08 24				08 27			
Redhill 5	a		08 08		08 13		08 18				08 28							08 30				08 32	08 34	08 47	08 49
	d		08 09				08 18				08 28												08 38		08 53
Merstham	d						08 22																08 43		08 57
Coulsdon South	d						08 27				08 36												08 48		09 02
Purley 4	d	←					08 31							←							←		08 52		09 05
East Croydon	a	08 20	08 20				08 36	08 24	08 29	08 31	08 50			08 36	08 38		08 43			08 46	08 50		08 58		09 10
	d	08 21	08 21				08 37	08 25	08 30	08 33	08 51			08 37	08 39		08 43			08 50	08 51		08 59		09 11
Norwood Junction 2	a						→				→												→		→
New Cross Gate	d																								
London Bridge 4	a	08 37						08 41		08 52											09 06				
London Blackfriars 3	a		08 53												09 09										
City Thameslink 3	a		08 56												09 12										
Farringdon 3	a		09 00												09 16										
St Pancras International 15	a		09 03												09 19										
St Albans City	a		09 25												09 39										
Luton Airport Parkway 4	a		09 37												09 52										
Luton 7	a		09 40												09 56										
Bedford 10	a		10 08												10 22										
Clapham Junction 10	d								08 40					08 48			08 53			09 01					
London Victoria 15	a			08 35					08 48			08 50	08 52	08 56			09 01		09 05	09 09					

Brighton - London and Bedford

		FC	SN	SN	SN	SN	FC	SN	SN	SN	SN	SN	SN	GW	SN	SN	FC	SN	SN	SN	FC	SN
		1	◇1	1	1	◇1	1	1	1	1	1	◇1	1	1	1	◇1	1	1	1	1	1	1
						H						H	H			H		H				
Brighton 10	d	08 02				08 13	08 16										08 36	08 45				
Hove 2	d		08 08																			
Preston Park	d	08 06	08 12				08 20										08 40					
Hassocks 4	d	08 12	08 19				08 26										08 46					
Burgess Hill 4	d	08 16	08 23				08 30										08 50					
Lewes 4	d											08 23										
Wivelsfield 4	d	08 18					08 34					08 39										
Haywards Heath 3	a	08 23	08 28				08 38					08 44					08 55	08 57				
	d	08 23	08 28				08 39					08 44					09 00	08 58				
Balcombe	d																09 06					
Horsham 4	d										08 35					08 49						
Littlehaven	d										08 38											
Faygate	d																					
Ifield	d										08 44											
Crawley	d										08 47					08 58						
Three Bridges 4	a	08 33	08 38				08 48				08 51					09 01	09 11					
	d	08 34	08 39				08 48				08 51					09 02	09 12					
Gatwick Airport 10 ✈	a	08 38				08 46	08 52				08 55	08 56				09 06	09 16	09 09				
	d	08 38				08 50	08 53				08 56	08 57	09 05	09 07		09 07	09 16	09 10				
Horley 4	d										08 59	08 59										
Salfords	d										09 03											
Earlswood (Surrey)	d										09 06											
Tonbridge 4	d									08 37												
Leigh (Kent)	d									08 41												
Penshurst	d									08 45												
Edenbridge	d									08 51												
Godstone	d									08 58												
Nutfield	d									09 03												
Reigate	d																					09 14
Redhill 5	a									09 08	09 10			09 15								09 18
	d									09 14												09 19
Merstham	d									09 18												09 23
Coulsdon South	d									09 23												09 28
Purley 4	d			←	←			←	←										←	←	←	09 32
East Croydon	a	08 54	08 57	08 58	08 58		09 08	09 10	09 10	09 29		09 14				09 22	09 32	09 25	09 29	09 29	09 32	09 37
	d	08 54	08 58	08 59	08 59		09 09	09 11	09 11	09 30		09 14			09 14	09 22	09 32	09 27	09 30	09 30	09 32	09 37
Norwood Junction 2	a									→							→					09 41
New Cross Gate	d																					
London Bridge 4 ⊖	a	09 08		09 16	09 16																09 46	09 54
London Blackfriars 3 ⊖	a	09 21					09 37														09 53	
City Thameslink 3	a	09 25					09 40														09 56	
Farringdon 3 ⊖	a	09 28					09 44														10 00	
St Pancras International 15 ⊖	a	09 32					09 47														10 03	
St Albans City	a	09 52					10 10														10 24	
Luton Airport Parkway 4 ✈	a	10 01					10 21														10 37	
Luton 7	a	10 04					10 24														10 40	
Bedford 10	a	10 28					10 50														11 06	
Clapham Junction 10	d		09 08					09 21	09 21			09 24			09 27	09 33		09 37	09 40	09 40		
London Victoria 15 ⊖	a		09 16			09 20		09 27	09 27			09 32	09 35		09 35	09 42		09 45	09 50	09 50		

Brighton - London and Bedford

		SN	GW	SN	SN	SN	SN	SN	SN	FC	SN	SN	FC	SN	SN	SN	FC	SN	SN	SN	SN	SN
		1	1		1	◇1	◇1	◇1	1	1	1	◇1	1	◇1	1	◇1	1	1	1		1	1
		H				H	H				H	H		H		H			H			
Brighton 10	d									09 00			09 07	09 19							09 25	
Hove 2	d							08 52														
Preston Park	d							08 57					09 11									
Hassocks 4	d							09 04		09 08			09 17								09 34	
Burgess Hill 4	d							09 08		09 12			09 21								09 38	
Lewes 4	d					08 48	08 48															
Wivelsfield 4	d					09 01	09 01						09 23									
Haywards Heath 3	a					09 05	09 05	09 12		09 16			09 28									
	d					09 08	09 08	09 14		09 17			09 32									
Balcombe	d												09 37									
Horsham 4	d				09 00							09 20										09 30
Littlehaven	d				09 03																	09 33
Faygate	d																					09 37
Ifield	d				09 09																	09 41
Crawley	d				09 13							09 29										09 44
Three Bridges 4	a				09 16	09 17	09 17			09 26		09 32	09 42									09 48
	d				09 18	09 18	09 18			09 26		09 33	09 42									09 48
Gatwick Airport 10 ✈	a				09 22	09 22	09 22	09 26		09 30		09 37	09 46								09 51	09 53
	d	09 20			09 23	09 23	09 23	09 27		09 31	09 35	09 38	09 46						09 50		09 53	09 54
Horley 4	d				09 26							09 41										09 56
Salfords	d				09 30																	
Earlswood (Surrey)	d				09 33																	
Tonbridge 4	d																	09 19				
Leigh (Kent)	d																	09 23				
Penshurst	d																	09 27				
Edenbridge	d																	09 33				
Godstone	d																	09 40				
Nutfield	d																	09 45				
Reigate	d		09 24																			
Redhill 5	a		09 30		09 36							09 47						09 50				10 03
	d				09 37							09 48						09 51				10 07
Merstham	d				09 41																	10 11
Coulsdon South	d				09 46													09 58				10 16
Purley 4	d				09 49										←	←	←	10 02				10 19
East Croydon	a				09 54	09 38	09 38	09 42		09 46		09 59	10 02	09 52	09 54	09 59	10 02	10 07			10 08	10 24
	d				09 55	09 39	09 39	09 43	09 44	09 47		10 00	10 02	09 53	09 55	10 00	10 02	10 07			10 08	10 25
Norwood Junction 2	a				→							→	→		09 59			10 12				→
New Cross Gate	d														10 07							
London Bridge 4 ⊖	a									10 00					10 13		10 15	10 25				
London Blackfriars 3 ⊖	a									10 08							10 23					
City Thameslink 3	a									10 10							10 26					
Farringdon 3 ⊖	a									10 14							10 30					
St Pancras International 15 ⊖	a									10 17							10 33					
St Albans City	a									10 39							10 54					
Luton Airport Parkway 4 ✈	a									10 51							11 06					
Luton 7	a									10 54							11 09					
Bedford 10	a									11 20							11 36					
Clapham Junction 10	d			09 42		09 48	09 48	09 53	09 56					10 03		10 09				10 11	10 18	
London Victoria 15 ⊖	a	09 50		09 52		09 58	09 58	10 00	10 05		10 05			10 10		10 16			10 20	10 20	10 24	

Brighton - London and Bedford

		SN	SN	SN	FC	SN	GW	SN	SN	FC	SN	SN	FC	SN	GW	SN	SN	SN	SN	SN	SN	FC	SN
		◇1	◇1	1	1	1	1	1	◇1	1	◇1	◇1	1	1	1		1	1	◇1	◇1	1	1	1
		⊼	A ⊼					⊼			⊼						⊼		⊼	A ⊼			⊼
Brighton 10	d				09 34					09 37	09 49											10 04	
Hove 2	d		09 22																	09 51			
Preston Park	d									09 41										09 55			
Hassocks 4	d		09 31							09 47													
Burgess Hill 4	d									09 51										10 04			
Lewes 4	d	09 18																	09 49				
Wivelsfield 4	d	09 34								09 53													
Haywards Heath 3	a	09 38	09 40		09 46					09 58									10 07	10 10		10 16	
	d	09 44			09 47					09 58									10 14			10 17	
Balcombe	d																						
Horsham 4	d								09 51									10 00					
Littlehaven	d																	10 03					
Faygate	d																						
Ifield	d																	10 09					
Crawley	d								10 00									10 13					
Three Bridges 4	a				09 56				10 03	10 07								10 16				10 26	
	d				09 56				10 04	10 10								10 18				10 26	
Gatwick Airport 10 ✈	a	09 55			10 00				10 08	10 15								10 22	10 25			10 30	
	d	09 56			10 01		10 03	10 05	10 09	10 16							10 20	10 23	10 26			10 31	10 35
Horley 4	d																	10 26					
Salfords	d																	10 30					
Earlswood (Surrey)	d																	10 33					
Tonbridge 4	d																						
Leigh (Kent)	d																						
Penshurst	d																						
Edenbridge	d																						
Godstone	d																						
Nutfield	d																						
Reigate	d													10 14	10 19								
Redhill 5	a						10 10		10 16					10 18	10 25			10 36					
	d								10 17					10 20				10 37					
Merstham	d													10 24				10 41					
Coulsdon South	d													10 29				10 46					
Purley 4	d					←						←	←	10 33				10 49					
East Croydon	a	10 11			10 16	10 24			10 28	10 32	10 24	10 28	10 32	10 38				10 54	10 41			10 46	
	d	10 12		10 14	10 17	10 25			10 28	10 32	10 25	10 28	10 32	10 38				10 55	10 42		10 44	10 47	
Norwood Junction 2	a					10 29			→	→				10 42				→					
New Cross Gate	d					10 37																	
London Bridge 4 ⊖	a				10 30	10 43							10 45	10 55								11 00	
London Blackfriars 3 ⊖	a				10 37								10 52									11 07	
City Thameslink 3	a				10 40								10 56									11 10	
Farringdon 3 ⊖	a				10 44								11 00									11 14	
St Pancras International 15 ⊖	a				10 47								11 03									11 17	
St Albans City	a				11 10								11 24									11 39	
Luton Airport Parkway 4 ✈	a				11 21								11 37									11 51	
Luton 7	a				11 24								11 40									11 54	
Bedford 10	a				11 50								12 06									12 20	
Clapham Junction 10	d	10 21		10 26							10 35	10 38				10 41			10 51		10 56		
London Victoria 15 ⊖	a	10 28		10 35				10 35			10 41	10 45				10 48	10 50		10 58		11 05		11 05

A ⊼ from Haywards Heath

Brighton - London and Bedford

		SN	FC	SN	SN	SN	FC	SN	SN	SN	SN	SN	SN	SN	FC	GW	SN	SN	FC	SN	SN	SN
		◇1	1	◇1	1	◇1	1	1	1	1	1	◇1	◇1	1	1	1	1	◇1	1	◇1	1	◇1
				⊼					⊼								⊼			⊼		
Brighton 10	d		10 07	10 19						10 25					10 34				10 37	10 49		
Hove 2	d											10 21										
Preston Park	d		10 11																10 41			
Hassocks 4	d		10 17							10 34									10 47			
Burgess Hill 4	d		10 21							10 38									10 51			
Lewes 4	d												10 19									
Wivelsfield 4	d		10 23										10 35						10 53			
Haywards Heath 3	a		10 28									10 35	10 40		10 46				10 58			
	d		10 32									10 44			10 47				11 02			
Balcombe	d		10 37																			
Horsham 4	d	10 20									10 30							10 50				
Littlehaven	d										10 33											
Faygate	d																					
Ifield	d										10 39											
Crawley	d	10 29									10 43							10 59				
Three Bridges 4	a	10 32	10 42								10 46				10 56			11 02	11 11			
	d	10 33	10 42								10 48				10 56			11 03	11 12			
Gatwick Airport 10 ✈	a	10 37	10 46							10 51	10 52	10 55			11 00			11 07	11 16			
	d	10 38	10 46						10 50	10 53	10 53	10 56			11 01	11 03	11 05	11 08	11 16			
Horley 4	d	10 41									10 56											
Salfords	d																					
Earlswood (Surrey)	d																					
Tonbridge 4	d							10 19														
Leigh (Kent)	d							10 23														
Penshurst	d							10 27														
Edenbridge	d							10 33														
Godstone	d							10 40														
Nutfield	d							10 45														
Reigate	d																					
Redhill 5	a	10 47						10 50			11 02					11 10		11 15				
	d	10 48						10 51			11 07							11 16				
Merstham	d										11 11											
Coulsdon South	d							10 58			11 16											
Purley 4	d				←	←	←	11 01			11 19										←	←
East Croydon	a	10 59	11 02	10 52	10 54	10 59	11 02	11 06		11 08	11 24	11 11			11 16			11 27	11 32	11 22	11 24	11 27
	d	11 00	11 02	10 53	10 55	11 00	11 02	11 07		11 08	11 25	11 12		11 14	11 17			11 28	11 32	11 23	11 25	11 28
Norwood Junction 2	a	→	→		10 59			11 12			→							→	→		11 29	
New Cross Gate	d				11 07																11 37	
London Bridge 4 ⊖	a				11 13		11 15	11 25							11 30						11 43	
London Blackfriars 3 ⊖	a						11 22								11 37							
City Thameslink 3	a						11 26								11 40							
Farringdon 3 ⊖	a						11 30								11 44							
St Pancras International 15 ⊖	a						11 33								11 47							
St Albans City	a						11 54								12 09							
Luton Airport Parkway 4 ✈	a						12 07								12 21							
Luton 7	a						12 10								12 24							
Bedford 10	a						12 36								12 50							
Clapham Junction 10	d			11 03		11 10				11 18		11 21		11 26						11 33		11 37
London Victoria 15 ⊖	a			11 10		11 16			11 20	11 24		11 28		11 32			11 35			11 41		11 45

Brighton - London and Bedford

Station		FC 1	SN 1	GW 1	SN 1 🚲	SN	SN 1	SN ◇1	SN ◇1	SN 1	FC 1	SN 1 🚲	SN ◇1	FC 1	SN ◇1 🚲	SN 1	SN ◇1	FC 1	SN 1	SN 1 🚲	SN 1	SN 1
Brighton 10	d										11 04			11 07	11 19						11 25	
Hove 2	d								10 51													
Preston Park	d								10 55					11 11								
Hassocks 4	d													11 17							11 34	
Burgess Hill 4	d								11 04					11 21							11 38	
Lewes 4	d							10 50														
Wivelsfield 4	d													11 23								
Haywards Heath 3	a							11 05	11 09		11 16			11 28								
	d							11 14			11 17			11 32								
Balcombe	d													11 37								
Horsham 4	d						11 00						11 20									11 30
Littlehaven	d						11 03															11 33
Faygate	d																					
Ifield	d						11 09															11 39
Crawley	d						11 13						11 29									11 43
Three Bridges 4	a						11 16				11 26		11 32	11 42								11 46
	d						11 18				11 26		11 33	11 42								11 48
Gatwick Airport 10 ✈	a						11 22	11 25			11 30		11 37	11 46							11 51	11 52
	d				11 20		11 23	11 26			11 31	11 35	11 38	11 46						11 50	11 53	11 53
Horley 4	d						11 26						11 41									11 56
Salfords	d						11 30															
Earlswood (Surrey)	d						11 33															
Tonbridge 4	d																		11 19			
Leigh (Kent)	d																		11 23			
Penshurst	d																		11 27			
Edenbridge	d																		11 33			
Godstone	d																		11 40			
Nutfield	d																		11 45			
Reigate	d		11 14	11 19																		
Redhill 5	a		11 18	11 25			11 36						11 47						11 50			12 02
	d		11 19				11 37						11 48						11 51			12 07
Merstham	d		11 23				11 41															12 11
Coulsdon South	d		11 28				11 46												11 58			12 16
Purley 4	d	←	11 32				11 49									←	←	←	12 02			12 19
East Croydon 🚋	a	11 32	11 37				11 54	11 41			11 46		11 59	12 02	11 52	11 54	11 59	12 02	12 07		12 08	12 24
	d	11 32	11 37				11 55	11 42		11 44	11 47		12 00	12 02	11 53	11 55	12 00	12 02	12 07		12 08	12 25
Norwood Junction 2	a		11 42				→						→	→		11 59			12 12			→
New Cross Gate	d															12 07						
London Bridge 4 ⊖	a	11 45	11 55								12 00					12 13		12 15	12 25			
London Blackfriars 3 ⊖	a	11 52									12 07							12 22				
City Thameslink 3	a	11 56									12 10							12 26				
Farringdon 3 ⊖	a	12 00									12 14							12 30				
St Pancras International 15 ⊖	a	12 03									12 17							12 33				
St Albans City	a	12 24									12 39							12 54				
Luton Airport Parkway 4 ✈	a	12 37									12 51							13 07				
Luton 7	a	12 40									12 54							13 10				
Bedford 10	a	13 06									13 20							13 36				
Clapham Junction 10	d					11 41		11 51		11 56					12 03		12 12				12 18	
London Victoria 15 ⊖	a				11 50	11 50		11 58		12 02		12 05			12 11		12 18			12 20	12 24	

Brighton - London and Bedford

Station		SN ◇1	SN ◇1	SN 1	FC 1	GW 1	SN 1 🚲	SN ◇1	FC 1	SN ◇1 🚲	SN 1	SN ◇1	FC 1	SN 1	GW 1	SN	SN 1 🚲	SN 1	SN ◇1	SN ◇1	SN 1	FC 1
Brighton 10	d				11 34				11 37	11 49												12 04
Hove 2	d	11 21																		11 51		
Preston Park	d								11 41											11 55		
Hassocks 4	d								11 47													
Burgess Hill 4	d								11 51											12 04		
Lewes 4	d		11 20																11 50			
Wivelsfield 4	d		11 35						11 53													
Haywards Heath 3	a	11 35	11 40		11 46				11 58										12 05	12 09		12 16
	d	11 44			11 47				12 02										12 14			12 17
Balcombe	d																					
Horsham 4	d							11 50										12 00				
Littlehaven	d																	12 03				
Faygate	d																					
Ifield	d																	12 09				
Crawley	d							11 59										12 13				
Three Bridges 4	a				11 56			12 02	12 11									12 16				12 26
	d				11 56			12 03	12 12									12 18				12 26
Gatwick Airport 10 ✈	a	11 55			12 00			12 07	12 16									12 22	12 25			12 30
	d	11 56			12 01	12 03	12 05	12 08	12 16								12 20	12 23	12 26			12 31
Horley 4	d																	12 26				
Salfords	d																	12 30				
Earlswood (Surrey)	d																	12 33				
Tonbridge 4	d																					
Leigh (Kent)	d																					
Penshurst	d																					
Edenbridge	d																					
Godstone	d																					
Nutfield	d																					
Reigate	d													12 14	12 19							
Redhill 5	a					12 10		12 15						12 18	12 25			12 36				
	d							12 16						12 19				12 37				
Merstham	d													12 23				12 41				
Coulsdon South	d													12 28				12 46				
Purley 4	d										←	←	←	12 32				12 49				
East Croydon 🚋	a	12 11			12 16			12 27	12 32	12 22	12 24	12 27	12 32	12 37				12 54	12 41			12 46
	d	12 12		12 14	12 17			12 28	12 32	12 23	12 25	12 28	12 32	12 37				12 55	12 42		12 44	12 47
Norwood Junction 2	a							→	→		12 29			12 42				→				
New Cross Gate	d										12 37											
London Bridge 4 ⊖	a				12 30						12 43		12 45	12 55								13 00
London Blackfriars 3 ⊖	a				12 37								12 52									13 07
City Thameslink 3	a				12 40								12 56									13 10
Farringdon 3 ⊖	a				12 44								13 00									13 14
St Pancras International 15 ⊖	a				12 47								13 03									13 17
St Albans City	a				13 09								13 24									13 40
Luton Airport Parkway 4 ✈	a				13 21								13 37									13 52
Luton 7	a				13 24								13 40									13 55
Bedford 10	a				13 50								14 06									14 20
Clapham Junction 10	d	12 22		12 26						12 33		12 37				12 41			12 51		12 56	
London Victoria 15 ⊖	a	12 28		12 32			12 35			12 40		12 44				12 48	12 50		12 58		13 02	

Table 186

Mondays to Fridays

Brighton - London and Bedford

		SN 1 🛒	SN ◇1	FC 1	SN ◇1 🛒	SN 1	SN ◇1	FC 1	SN 1	SN 1 🛒	SN 1	SN 1	SN ◇1	SN ◇1	SN 1	FC 1	GW 1	SN 1 🛒	SN ◇1	FC 1	SN ◇1 🛒	SN 1	SN ◇1
Brighton 10	d			12 07	12 19						12 25					12 34				12 37	12 49		
Hove 2	d												12 21										
Preston Park	d			12 11																12 41			
Hassocks 4	d			12 17							12 34									12 47			
Burgess Hill 4	d			12 21							12 38									12 51			
Lewes 4	d													12 20									
Wivelsfield 4	d			12 23										12 35						12 53			
Haywards Heath 3	a			12 28									12 35	12 40		12 46				12 58			
	d			12 32									12 44			12 47				13 02			
Balcombe	d			12 37																			
Horsham 4	d		12 20									12 30							12 50				
Littlehaven	d											12 33											
Faygate	d											12 37											
Ifield	d											12 41											
Crawley	d		12 29									12 44							12 59				
Three Bridges 4	a		12 32	12 42								12 47				12 56			13 02	13 11			
	d		12 33	12 42								12 48				12 56			13 03	13 12			
Gatwick Airport 10 ✈	a		12 37	12 46							12 51	12 52	12 55			13 00			13 07	13 16			
	d	12 35	12 38	12 46						12 50	12 53	12 53	12 56			13 01	13 03	13 05	13 08	13 16			
Horley 4	d		12 41									12 56											
Salfords	d																						
Earlswood (Surrey)	d																						
Tonbridge 4	d								12 19														
Leigh (Kent)	d								12 23														
Penshurst	d								12 27														
Edenbridge	d								12 33														
Godstone	d								12 40														
Nutfield	d								12 45														
Reigate	d																						
Redhill 5	a		12 47						12 50			13 02					13 10		13 15				
	d		12 48						12 51			13 07							13 16				
Merstham	d											13 11											
Coulsdon South	d								12 58			13 16											
Purley 4	d					←	←	←	13 02			13 19										←	←
East Croydon	a		12 59	13 02	12 52	12 54	12 59	13 02	13 07		13 08	13 24	13 11			13 16			13 27	13 32	13 22	13 24	13 27
	d		13 00	13 02	12 53	12 55	13 00	13 02	13 07		13 08	13 25	13 12		13 14	13 17			13 28	13 32	13 23	13 25	13 28
Norwood Junction 2	a		→	→		12 59			13 12			→							→	→		13 29	
New Cross Gate	d					13 07																13 37	
London Bridge 4 ⊖	a					13 13		13 15	13 25							13 30						13 43	
London Blackfriars 3 ⊖	a							13 22								13 37							
City Thameslink 3	a							13 26								13 40							
Farringdon 3 ⊖	a							13 30								13 44							
St Pancras International 15 ⊖	a							13 33								13 47							
St Albans City	a							13 54								14 09							
Luton Airport Parkway 4 ✈	a							14 07								14 21							
Luton 7	a							14 10								14 24							
Bedford 10	a							14 36								14 50							
Clapham Junction 10	d				13 03		13 10				13 18		13 21		13 26						13 33		13 37
London Victoria 15 ⊖	a	13 05			13 10		13 16			13 20	13 24		13 28		13 32			13 35			13 40		13 44

Table 186

Mondays to Fridays

Brighton - London and Bedford

		FC 1	SN 1	GW 1	SN	SN 1 🛒	SN 1	SN ◇1	SN ◇1	SN 1	FC 1	SN 1 🛒	SN ◇1	FC 1	SN ◇1 🛒	SN 1	SN ◇1	FC 1	SN 1	SN 1 🛒	SN 1	SN 1
Brighton 10	d										13 04			13 07	13 19						13 25	
Hove 2	d								12 51													
Preston Park	d								12 55					13 11								
Hassocks 4	d													13 17							13 34	
Burgess Hill 4	d								13 04					13 21							13 38	
Lewes 4	d							12 50														
Wivelsfield 4	d													13 23								
Haywards Heath 3	a							13 05	13 09		13 16			13 28								
	d							13 14			13 17			13 32								
Balcombe	d													13 37								
Horsham 4	d						13 00						13 20									13 30
Littlehaven	d						13 03															13 33
Faygate	d																					
Ifield	d						13 09															13 39
Crawley	d						13 13						13 29									13 43
Three Bridges 4	a						13 16				13 26		13 32	13 42								13 46
	d						13 18				13 26		13 33	13 42								13 48
Gatwick Airport 10 ✈	a						13 22	13 25			13 30		13 37	13 46							13 51	13 52
	d					13 20	13 23	13 26			13 31	13 35	13 38	13 46						13 50	13 53	13 53
Horley 4	d						13 26						13 41									13 56
Salfords	d						13 30															
Earlswood (Surrey)	d						13 33															
Tonbridge 4	d																		13 19			
Leigh (Kent)	d																		13 23			
Penshurst	d																		13 27			
Edenbridge	d																		13 33			
Godstone	d																		13 40			
Nutfield	d																		13 45			
Reigate	d		13 14	13 19																		
Redhill 5	a		13 18	13 25			13 36						13 47						13 50			14 02
	d		13 19				13 37						13 48						13 51			14 07
Merstham	d		13 23				13 41															14 11
Coulsdon South	d		13 28				13 46												13 58			14 16
Purley 4	d	←	13 32				13 49									←	←	←	14 02			14 19
East Croydon	a	13 32	13 37				13 54	13 41			13 46		13 59	14 02	13 52	13 54	13 59	14 02	14 07		14 08	14 24
	d	13 32	13 37				13 55	13 42		13 44	13 47		14 00	14 02	13 53	13 55	14 00	14 02	14 08		14 08	14 25
Norwood Junction 2	a		13 42				→						→	→		13 59			14 12			→
New Cross Gate	d															14 07						
London Bridge 4 ⊖	a	13 45	13 55								14 00					14 13		14 15	14 25			
London Blackfriars 3 ⊖	a	13 52									14 07							14 22				
City Thameslink 3	a	13 56									14 10							14 26				
Farringdon 3 ⊖	a	14 00									14 14							14 30				
St Pancras International 15 ⊖	a	14 03									14 17							14 33				
St Albans City	a	14 24									14 39							14 54				
Luton Airport Parkway 4 ✈	a	14 37									14 51							15 07				
Luton 7	a	14 40									14 54							15 10				
Bedford 10	a	15 06									15 20							15 36				
Clapham Junction 10	d				13 41			13 51		13 56					14 03		14 10				14 18	
London Victoria 15 ⊖	a				13 48	13 50		13 58		14 03		14 05			14 10		14 16			14 20	14 24	

Brighton - London and Bedford

		SN ◇1	SN ◇1		SN 1	FC 1	GW 1	SN 1 ⌶	SN ◇1	FC 1	SN ◇1 ⌶	SN 1	SN ◇1		FC 1	SN 1	GW 1	SN	SN 1 ⌶	SN 1	SN ◇1	SN ◇1	SN 1		FC 1
Brighton 10	d					13 34				13 37	13 49														14 04
Hove 2	d	13 21																				13 51			
Preston Park	d									13 41												13 55			
Hassocks 4	d									13 47															
Burgess Hill 4	d									13 51												14 04			
Lewes 4	d		13 20																		13 50				
Wivelsfield 4	d		13 35							13 53															
Haywards Heath 3	a	13 35	13 40			13 46				13 58											14 05	14 09			14 16
	d	13 44				13 47				14 02											14 14				14 17
Balcombe	d																								
Horsham 4	d								13 50											14 00					
Littlehaven	d																			14 03					
Faygate	d																								
Ifield	d																			14 09					
Crawley	d								13 59											14 13					
Three Bridges 4	a					13 56			14 02	14 11										14 16					14 26
	d					13 56			14 03	14 12										14 18					14 26
Gatwick Airport 10 ✈	a	13 55				14 00			14 07	14 16										14 22	14 25				14 30
	d	13 56				14 01	14 03	14 05	14 08	14 16									14 20	14 23	14 26				14 31
Horley 4	d																			14 26					
Salfords	d																			14 30					
Earlswood (Surrey)	d																			14 33					
Tonbridge 4	d																								
Leigh (Kent)	d																								
Penshurst	d																								
Edenbridge	d																								
Godstone	d																								
Nutfield	d																								
Reigate	d															14 14	14 19								
Redhill 5	a						14 10		14 15							14 18	14 25			14 36					
	d								14 16							14 19				14 37					
Merstham	d															14 23				14 41					
Coulsdon South	d															14 28				14 46					
Purley 4	d											←	←		←	14 32				14 49					
East Croydon 🚌	a	14 11				14 16			14 27	14 32	14 22	14 24	14 27		14 32	14 37				14 54	14 41				14 46
	d	14 12			14 14	14 17			14 28	14 32	14 23	14 25	14 28		14 32	14 37				14 55	14 42		14 44		14 47
Norwood Junction 2	a								→	→		14 29				14 42				→					
New Cross Gate	d											14 37													
London Bridge 4 ⊖	a					14 30						14 43			14 45	14 55									15 00
London Blackfriars 3 ⊖	a					14 37									14 52										15 07
City Thameslink 3	a					14 40									14 56										15 10
Farringdon 3 ⊖	a					14 44									15 00										15 14
St Pancras International 15 ⊖	a					14 47									15 03										15 17
St Albans City	a					15 09									15 24										15 39
Luton Airport Parkway 4 ✈	a					15 21									15 37										15 51
Luton 7	a					15 24									15 40										15 54
Bedford 10	a					15 50									16 06										16 20
Clapham Junction 10	d	14 21			14 26						14 33		14 37					14 41			14 51		14 56		
London Victoria 15 ⊖	a	14 28			14 32			14 35			14 40		14 44					14 48	14 50		14 58		15 02		

Brighton - London and Bedford

		SN 1 ⌶	SN ◇1	FC 1	SN ◇1 ⌶	SN 1	SN ◇1	FC 1	SN 1		SN 1 ⌶	SN 1	SN 1	SN ◇1	SN ◇1	SN 1	FC 1	GW 1	SN 1 ⌶		SN ◇1	FC 1	SN ◇1 ⌶	SN 1	SN ◇1
Brighton 10	d			14 07	14 19							14 25					14 34					14 37	14 49		
Hove 2	d													14 21											
Preston Park	d			14 11																		14 41			
Hassocks 4	d			14 17								14 34										14 47			
Burgess Hill 4	d			14 21								14 38										14 51			
Lewes 4	d														14 20										
Wivelsfield 4	d			14 23											14 35							14 53			
Haywards Heath 3	a			14 28										14 35	14 40		14 46					14 58			
	d			14 32										14 44			14 47					15 02			
Balcombe	d			14 37																					
Horsham 4	d		14 20										14 30								14 50				
Littlehaven	d												14 33												
Faygate	d																								
Ifield	d												14 39												
Crawley	d		14 29										14 43								14 59				
Three Bridges 4	a		14 32	14 42									14 46				14 56				15 02	15 11			
	d		14 33	14 42									14 48				14 56				15 03	15 12			
Gatwick Airport 10 ✈	a		14 37	14 46								14 51	14 52	14 55			15 00				15 07	15 16			
	d	14 35	14 38	14 46							14 50	14 53	14 53	14 56			15 01	15 03	15 05		15 08	15 16			
Horley 4	d		14 41										14 56												
Salfords	d																								
Earlswood (Surrey)	d																								
Tonbridge 4	d								14 19																
Leigh (Kent)	d								14 23																
Penshurst	d								14 27																
Edenbridge	d								14 33																
Godstone	d								14 40																
Nutfield	d								14 45																
Reigate	d																								
Redhill 5	a		14 47						14 50				15 02					15 10			15 16				
	d		14 48						14 51				15 07								15 17				
Merstham	d												15 11												
Coulsdon South	d								14 58				15 16												
Purley 4	d					←	←	←	15 02				15 19											←	←
East Croydon 🚌	a		14 59	15 02	14 52	14 54	14 59	15 02	15 07			15 08	15 24	15 11			15 16				15 28	15 32	15 22	15 24	15 28
	d		15 00	15 02	14 53	14 55	15 00	15 02	15 07			15 08	15 25	15 12		15 14	15 17				15 28	15 32	15 23	15 25	15 28
Norwood Junction 2	a		→	→		14 59			15 12				→								→	→		15 29	
New Cross Gate	d					15 07																		15 37	
London Bridge 4 ⊖	a					15 13		15 15	15 25								15 30							15 43	
London Blackfriars 3 ⊖	a							15 22									15 37								
City Thameslink 3	a							15 26									15 40								
Farringdon 3 ⊖	a							15 30									15 44								
St Pancras International 15 ⊖	a							15 33									15 47								
St Albans City	a							15 54									16 09								
Luton Airport Parkway 4 ✈	a							16 06									16 21								
Luton 7	a							16 09									16 24								
Bedford 10	a							16 36									16 50								
Clapham Junction 10	d				15 03		15 10					15 18		15 21		15 26							15 33		15 38
London Victoria 15 ⊖	a	15 05			15 10		15 20				15 20	15 24		15 28		15 35			15 35				15 40		15 46

Table 186

Mondays to Fridays

Brighton - London and Bedford

		FC	SN	GW	SN	SN	SN	SN	SN	SN	FC	SN	SN	FC	SN	SN	SN	FC	SN	SN	SN	SN
		1	1	1	1		1	◇1	◇1	1	1	1	◇1	1	◇1	1	◇1	1	1	1	1	1
									A													
					⊼			⊼	⊼			⊼	⊼		⊼		⊼			⊼		
Brighton 10	d										15 04			15 07	15 19						15 25	
Hove 2	d								14 51													
Preston Park	d								14 55					15 11								
Hassocks 4	d													15 17							15 34	
Burgess Hill 4	d								15 04					15 21							15 38	
Lewes 4	d							14 50														
Wivelsfield 4	d													15 23								
Haywards Heath 3	a							15 05	15 09		15 16			15 28								
	d							15 14			15 17			15 32								
Balcombe	d													15 37								
Horsham 4	d						15 00						15 20									15 30
Littlehaven	d						15 03															15 33
Faygate	d																					
Ifield	d						15 09															15 39
Crawley	d						15 13						15 29									15 43
Three Bridges 4	a						15 16				15 26		15 32	15 42								15 46
	d						15 18				15 26		15 33	15 42								15 48
Gatwick Airport 10 ✈	a						15 22	15 25			15 30		15 37	15 46							15 51	15 52
	d				15 20		15 23	15 26			15 31	15 35	15 38	15 46						15 50	15 53	15 53
Horley 4	d						15 26						15 41									15 56
Salfords	d						15 30															
Earlswood (Surrey)	d						15 33															
Tonbridge 4	d																		15 19			
Leigh (Kent)	d																		15 23			
Penshurst	d																		15 27			
Edenbridge	d																		15 33			
Godstone	d																		15 40			
Nutfield	d																		15 45			
Reigate	d		15 14	15 19																		
Redhill 5	a		15 18	15 25			15 36						15 47						15 50			16 02
	d		15 19				15 37						15 48						15 51			16 06
Merstham	d		15 23				15 41															16 10
Coulsdon South	d		15 28				15 46												15 58			16 15
Purley 4	d	←	15 32				15 49									←	←	←	16 02			16 18
East Croydon	a	15 32	15 37				15 54	15 41			15 46		15 59	16 02	15 52	15 54	15 59	16 02	16 07		16 08	16 23
	d	15 32	15 37				15 55	15 42		15 44	15 47		16 00	16 02	15 53	15 55	16 00	16 02	16 07		16 08	16 24
Norwood Junction 2	a		15 42				→						→	→		15 59			16 12			→
New Cross Gate	d															16 07						
London Bridge 4 ⊖	a	15 45	15 55								16 00					16 13		16 15	16 25			
London Blackfriars 3 ⊖	a	15 52									16 07							16 25				
City Thameslink 3	a	15 56									16 10							16 28				
Farringdon 3 ⊖	a	16 00									16 13							16 31				
St Pancras International 15 ⊖	a	16 03									16 17							16 35				
St Albans City	a	16 24									16 39							16 56				
Luton Airport Parkway 4 ✈	a	16 37									16 51							17 09				
Luton 7	a	16 40									16 54							17 12				
Bedford 10	a	17 06									17 20							17 38				
Clapham Junction 10	d					15 41		15 51		15 56					16 03		16 09				16 18	
London Victoria 15 ⊖	a				15 50	15 52		15 58		16 05		16 05			16 10		16 16			16 22	16 24	

A ⊼ from Haywards Heath

Table 186

Mondays to Fridays

Brighton - London and Bedford

		SN	SN	SN	FC	SN	GW	SN	SN	FC	SN	FC	SN	SN	SN	SN	SN	GW	SN	SN	SN	SN
		◇1	◇1	1	1	1	1	1	◇1	1	◇1	1	◇1		1	◇1	1	1	1	◇1	◇1	1
		A																			A	
		⊼	⊼					⊼	⊼		⊼		⊼		⊼					⊼	⊼	
Brighton 10	d				15 34					15 37	15 49					15 55						
Hove 2	d	15 21																			15 52	
Preston Park	d									15 41											15 56	
Hassocks 4	d									15 47						16 06						
Burgess Hill 4	d									15 51											16 05	
Lewes 4	d		15 19																	15 50		
Wivelsfield 4	d		15 35							15 53												
Haywards Heath 3	a	15 35	15 40		15 46					15 58										16 05	16 10	
	d	15 44			15 47					15 58										16 14		
Balcombe	d																					
Horsham 4	d								15 50										16 00			
Littlehaven	d																		16 03			
Faygate	d																					
Ifield	d																		16 09			
Crawley	d								15 59										16 13			
Three Bridges 4	a				15 56				16 02	16 07									16 16			
	d				15 56				16 03	16 07									16 18			
Gatwick Airport 10 ✈	a	15 55			16 00				16 07	16 11						16 21			16 22	16 25		
	d	15 56			16 01		16 03	16 05	16 08	16 11					16 20	16 23			16 23	16 26		
Horley 4	d																		16 26			
Salfords	d																		16 30			
Earlswood (Surrey)	d																		16 33			
Tonbridge 4	d																					
Leigh (Kent)	d																					
Penshurst	d																					
Edenbridge	d																					
Godstone	d																					
Nutfield	d																					
Reigate	d																16 14	16 21				
Redhill 5	a						16 10		16 17								16 18	16 27	16 36			
	d								16 18								16 21		16 37			
Merstham	d																16 25		16 41			
Coulsdon South	d																16 30		16 46			
Purley 4	d					←						←	←				16 34		16 49			
East Croydon	a	16 11			16 16	16 23			16 30	16 28	16 24	16 28	16 30			16 38	16 39		16 54	16 41		
	d	16 12		16 14	16 17	16 24			16 30	16 28	16 25	16 28	16 30			16 38	16 40		16 55	16 42		16 44
Norwood Junction 2	a					16 28			→	→							16 44		→			
New Cross Gate	d					16 36																
London Bridge 4 ⊖	a					16 43											17 00					
London Blackfriars 3 ⊖	a				16 47							16 55										
City Thameslink 3	a				16 54							16 58										
Farringdon 3 ⊖	a				16 57							17 01										
St Pancras International 15 ⊖	a				17 01							17 05										
St Albans City	a				17 21							17 26										
Luton Airport Parkway 4 ✈	a											17 39										
Luton 7	a				17 34							17 42										
Bedford 10	a				17 58							18 08										
Clapham Junction 10	d	16 21		16 26							16 35		16 40	16 41		16 48				16 51		16 56
London Victoria 15 ⊖	a	16 28		16 35				16 35			16 42		16 46	16 48	16 52	16 54				16 58		17 05

A ⊼ from Haywards Heath

Brighton - London and Bedford

		FC 1	SN 1 🛒	SN ◇1	FC 1	SN 1 🛒	SN 1	FC 1	SN ◇1	SN 1	SN 1 🛒	SN 1	SN 1	FC 1	SN ◇1 🛒	SN ◇1 A 🛒	SN ◇1 🛒	GW 1	SN 1	SN 1 🛒	FC 1	SN 1	SN 1 🛒
Brighton 10	d	16 04			16 07	16 19								16 24							16 30		16 49
Hove 2	d															16 21							
Preston Park	d				16 11																16 34		
Hassocks 4	d				16 17																16 40		
Burgess Hill 4	d				16 21																16 44		
Lewes 4	d																16 20						
Wivelsfield 4	d																16 38				16 46		
Haywards Heath 3	a	16 16			16 25									16 37		16 34	16 42				16 50		
	d	16 17			16 26									16 38		16 46					16 50		
Balcombe	d				16 31																16 57		
Horsham 4	d			16 20								16 30											
Littlehaven	d											16 33											
Faygate	d											16 37											
Ifield	d											16 41											
Crawley	d			16 29								16 44											
Three Bridges 4	a	16 26		16 32	16 37							16 47		16 47							17 02		
	d	16 26		16 33	16 37							16 48		16 47							17 03		
Gatwick Airport 10 ✈	a	16 30		16 37	16 41							16 52		16 52		16 57					17 07		
	d	16 31	16 35	16 38	16 42						16 50	16 53		16 53		16 58		17 03		17 05	17 08		
Horley 4	d											16 56											
Salfords	d											17 00											
Earlswood (Surrey)	d											17 03											
Tonbridge 4	d									16 19													
Leigh (Kent)	d									16 23													
Penshurst	d									16 27													
Edenbridge	d									16 33													
Godstone	d									16 40													
Nutfield	d									16 45													
Reigate	d												17 03										
Redhill 5	a			16 46						16 50		17 06	17 07					17 10					
	d			16 47						16 51		17 07											
Merstham	d											17 11											
Coulsdon South	d									16 58		17 16											
Purley 4	d						←	←	←	17 02		17 19			←							←	
East Croydon	a	16 46		17 01	16 58	16 53	16 54	16 58	17 01	17 07		17 24		17 08	17 13	17 13					17 23	17 24	17 26
	d	16 47		17 01	16 58	16 54	16 55	16 58	17 01	17 07		17 25		17 09	17 13	17 13			17 14		17 23	17 25	17 26
Norwood Junction 2	a			→	→		16 59			17 11		→				→						17 30	
New Cross Gate	d						17 06															17 38	
London Bridge 4 ⊖	a						17 14			17 26				17 27								17 45	
London Blackfriars 3 ⊖	a	17 19						17 25						17 35							17 49		
City Thameslink 3	a	17 24						17 28						17 38							17 54		
Farringdon 3 ⊖	a	17 27						17 31						17 41							17 57		
St Pancras International 15 ⊖	a	17 31						17 35						17 45							18 01		
St Albans City	a	17 51						17 56						18 06							18 21		
Luton Airport Parkway 4 ✈	a							18 09						18 20									
Luton 7	a	18 04						18 12						18 23							18 34		
Bedford 10	a	18 28						18 38						18 48							18 58		
Clapham Junction 10	d					17 03			17 11						17 23				17 25				17 36
London Victoria 15 ⊖	a		17 05			17 10			17 17		17 20				17 29				17 35	17 38			17 42

A 🛒 from Haywards Heath

Brighton - London and Bedford

		SN ◇1 🛒	SN 1 🛒	SN 1	SN 1	GW 1	SN 1	SN ◇1 🛒	SN ◇1 A 🛒	SN 1	SN 1	FC 1	SN 1 🛒	SN 1	SN 1	FC 1	SN 1 🛒	FC 1	SN ◇1 🛒	SN 1 🛒	SN 1	SN 1	SN 1
Brighton 10	d										16 55	17 03				17 07	17 19						
Hove 2	d								16 51														
Preston Park	d										16 58					17 11							
Hassocks 4	d										17 05					17 17							
Burgess Hill 4	d								17 02		17 08	17 13				17 21							
Lewes 4	d							16 50															
Wivelsfield 4	d										17 11												
Haywards Heath 3	a							17 05	17 09		17 15	17 17				17 25							
	d							17 13			17 21	17 18				17 26							
Balcombe	d										17 26												
Horsham 4	d	16 52					17 00												17 22				
Littlehaven	d						17 03																
Faygate	d						17 07																
Ifield	d						17 11																
Crawley	d	17 01					17 14												17 31				
Three Bridges 4	a	17 04					17 17				17 32	17 27							17 34				
	d	17 05					17 18				17 32	17 27							17 36				
Gatwick Airport 10 ✈	a	17 09					17 22	17 24			17 36	17 31				17 38			17 41				
	d	17 10	17 20				17 23	17 25			17 38	17 31	17 35			17 39			17 42	17 50			
Horley 4	d						17 26																
Salfords	d						17 30																
Earlswood (Surrey)	d						17 33																
Tonbridge 4	d			16 49	17 03																		17 21
Leigh (Kent)	d			16 53																			17 25
Penshurst	d			16 57																			17 29
Edenbridge	d			17 03	17 13																		17 35
Godstone	d			17 10																			17 42
Nutfield	d			17 15																			17 47
Reigate	d					17 26																17 44	
Redhill 5	a	17 17		17 20	17 25	17 32	17 36												17 49			17 48	17 53
	d	17 18		17 21	17 28		17 37												17 49			17 57	
Merstham	d			17 25			17 41																
Coulsdon South	d			17 30			17 46																
Purley 4	d						17 49							←	←			←			←		
East Croydon	a	17 30		17 37	17 40		17 54	17 40			17 53	17 46		17 53	17 54	17 57	17 56	17 57	18 01		18 08	18 08	
	d	17 30		17 38	17 41		17 55	17 41		17 44	17 53	17 47		17 53	17 55	17 58	17 57	17 58	18 02		18 08	18 08	
Norwood Junction 2	a				17 45		→				→				17 59	→						→	
New Cross Gate	d														18 07								
London Bridge 4 ⊖	a				17 58							18 13			18 16								
London Blackfriars 3 ⊖	a											18 21						18 25					
City Thameslink 3	a											18 24						18 28					
Farringdon 3 ⊖	a											18 27						18 31					
St Pancras International 15 ⊖	a											18 31						18 35					
St Albans City	a											18 51						18 56					
Luton Airport Parkway 4 ✈	a																	19 09					
Luton 7	a											19 04						19 12					
Bedford 10	a											19 26						19 38					
Clapham Junction 10	d	17 40		17 47				17 51		17 56				18 03			18 07		18 13		18 19		
London Victoria 15 ⊖	a	17 46	17 52	17 54				17 58		18 05			18 05	18 09			18 14		18 20	18 22	18 26		

A 🛒 from Haywards Heath

Brighton - London and Bedford

Station		SN 1	SN ◇1 A ✠	SN ◇1 ✠	SN 1	FC 1	GW 1	SN 1 ✠	SN ◇1 ✠	FC 1	SN 1 ✠	SN 1	SN ◇1 ✠	FC 1	SN 1 ✠	SN 1	SN 1	GW 1	SN 1	SN ◇1 ✠	SN ◇1 A ✠	SN 1
Brighton 10	d					17 24				17 37	17 49											
Hove 2	d		17 21																		17 51	
Preston Park	d					17 28				17 41												
Hassocks 4	d					17 34				17 47												
Burgess Hill 4	d					17 38				17 51											18 04	
Lewes 4	d			17 19																17 50		
Wivelsfield 4	d			17 35		17 40				17 53												
Haywards Heath 3	a		17 35	17 39		17 45				17 58										18 06	18 10	
	d		17 43			17 46				18 02										18 13		
Balcombe	d									18 07												
Horsham 4	d	17 30							17 52										18 00			
Littlehaven	d	17 33																	18 03			
Faygate	d	17 37																	18 07			
Ifield	d	17 41																	18 11			
Crawley	d	17 44							18 01										18 14			
Three Bridges 4	a	17 47				17 55			18 04	18 13									18 17			
	d	17 48				17 55			18 05	18 13									18 18			
Gatwick Airport 10 ✈	a	17 52		17 54		17 59			18 09	18 17									18 22	18 26		
	d	17 53		17 55		18 00	18 03	18 05	18 10	18 17					18 20				18 23	18 27		
Horley 4	d	17 56																	18 26			
Salfords	d	18 00																	18 30			
Earlswood (Surrey)	d	18 03																	18 33			
Tonbridge 4	d																17 49					
Leigh (Kent)	d																17 53					
Penshurst	d																17 57					
Edenbridge	d																18 03					
Godstone	d																18 10					
Nutfield	d																18 15					
Reigate	d															18 14		18 26				18 38
Redhill 5	a	18 06					18 10		18 17							18 19	18 21	18 32	18 36			18 42
	d	18 07							18 18							18 24			18 37			
Merstham	d	18 11														18 28			18 41			
Coulsdon South	d	18 16														18 33			18 46			
Purley 4	d	18 19										←	←	←					18 49			
East Croydon	a	18 24		18 11		18 15			18 29	18 32	18 24	18 24	18 29	18 32		18 39			18 54	18 42		
	d	18 26		18 12	18 14	18 17			18 30	18 33	18 25	18 26	18 30	18 33		18 40			18 55	18 43		
Norwood Junction 2	a	→							→	→									→			
New Cross Gate	d																					
London Bridge 4 ⊖	a													18 46								
London Blackfriars 3 ⊖	a					18 51								18 55								
City Thameslink 3	a					18 54								18 58								
Farringdon 3 ⊖	a					18 57								19 01								
St Pancras International 15 ⊖	a					19 01								19 05								
St Albans City	a					19 21								19 26								
Luton Airport Parkway 4 ✈	a													19 39								
Luton 7	a					19 34								19 43								
Bedford 10	a					19 58								20 08								
Clapham Junction 10	d			18 22	18 26						18 34	18 37	18 40			18 49				18 52		
London Victoria 15 ⊖	a			18 29	18 35			18 35			18 41	18 44	18 47		18 50	18 56				18 59		

A ✠ from Haywards Heath

Brighton - London and Bedford

Station		SN 1	SN 1	FC 1	SN 1 ✠	SN 1	SN 1	SN ◇1	FC 1	SN 1	SN ◇1	FC 1	SN 1	SN 1 ✠	SN 1	SN 1	SN ◇1 ✠	SN ◇1 A ✠	SN 1	FC 1	SN 1 ✠	SN ◇1	FC 1
Brighton 10	d		17 55	18 04					18 07	18 19										18 34			18 37
Hove 2	d																	18 21					
Preston Park	d		17 59						18 11														18 41
Hassocks 4	d		18 05						18 17														18 47
Burgess Hill 4	d		18 09	18 14					18 21									18 34					18 51
Lewes 4	d																18 18						
Wivelsfield 4	d		18 11						18 23								18 34						18 53
Haywards Heath 3	a		18 16	18 18					18 28								18 38	18 41		18 46			18 58
	d		18 22	18 18					18 32								18 45			18 47			19 02
Balcombe	d								18 37														
Horsham 4	d							18 22								18 30						18 52	
Littlehaven	d															18 33							
Faygate	d															18 37							
Ifield	d															18 41							
Crawley	d							18 31								18 44						19 01	
Three Bridges 4	a		18 31					18 34	18 42							18 47				18 56		19 04	19 12
	d		18 31					18 35	18 42							18 48				18 56		19 05	19 12
Gatwick Airport 10 ✈	a		18 36	18 30				18 39	18 46							18 52	18 56			19 00		19 09	19 16
	d		18 38	18 31	18 35			18 40	18 46					18 50		18 53	18 57			19 01	19 05	19 10	19 16
Horley 4	d															18 56							
Salfords	d															19 00							
Earlswood (Surrey)	d															19 03							
Tonbridge 4	d												18 23										
Leigh (Kent)	d												18 27										
Penshurst	d												18 31										
Edenbridge	d												18 37										
Godstone	d												18 44										
Nutfield	d												18 49										
Reigate	d														19 02								
Redhill 5	a							18 47					18 54		19 06	19 06						19 17	
	d							18 48					18 57			19 07						19 18	
Merstham	d															19 11							
Coulsdon South	d															19 16							
Purley 4	d					←	←				←	←				19 19							
East Croydon	a		18 53	18 46		18 53	18 54	18 59	19 02	18 56	18 59	19 02	19 09			19 24	19 12			19 16		19 28	19 32
	d	18 44	18 53	18 47		18 53	18 55	19 00	19 02	18 57	19 00	19 02	19 09			19 25	19 12		19 14	19 17		19 29	19 32
Norwood Junction 2	a		→					→	→				19 12			→						→	→
New Cross Gate	d																						
London Bridge 4 ⊖	a			19 00								19 15	19 25							19 30			
London Blackfriars 3 ⊖	a			19 09								19 22								19 37			
City Thameslink 3	a			19 12								19 26								19 40			
Farringdon 3 ⊖	a			19 15								19 30								19 44			
St Pancras International 15 ⊖	a			19 19								19 33								19 47			
St Albans City	a			19 45								19 55								20 09			
Luton Airport Parkway 4 ✈	a			19 57								20 07								20 21			
Luton 7	a			20 00								20 10								20 24			
Bedford 10	a			20 26								20 36								20 50			
Clapham Junction 10	d	18 56				19 03	19 06			19 09	19 12						19 22		19 26				
London Victoria 15 ⊖	a	19 05			19 05	19 09	19 13			19 15	19 18			19 20			19 29		19 32		19 35		

A ✠ from Haywards Heath

Brighton - London and Bedford

		SN	SN	SN	FC	SN	GW	SN	SN	GW	SN	SN	SN	SN	SN	FC	SN	SN	SN	SN	FC	SN
		◇1	1	◇1	1	1	1	1	1	1	1	◇1	◇1	1	1	1	1	1	◇1	1	1	◇1
								bus									bus		A			
Brighton 10	d	18 49																	18 59		19 07	19 19
Hove 2	d											18 52										
Preston Park	d																		19 03		19 11	
Hassocks 4	d																		19 09		19 17	
Burgess Hill 4	d																		19 13		19 21	
Lewes 4	d												18 50									
Wivelsfield 4	d												19 06						19 15		19 23	
Haywards Heath 3	a											19 06	19 10						19 20		19 28	
	d											19 14							19 21		19 32	
Balcombe	d																				19 37	
Horsham 4	d										19 02							19 17				
Littlehaven	d										19 05											
Faygate	d																					
Ifield	d										19 11											
Crawley	d										19 14							19 26				
Three Bridges 4	a										19 18							19 29	19 31		19 42	
	d										19 18					19 27		19 35			19 42	
Gatwick Airport 10 ✈	a										19 22	19 25				19 31		19 39			19 46	
	d						19 16	19 20			19 23	19 26				19 31	19 35	19 40			19 46	
Horley 4	d										19 26											
Salfords	d										19 30											
Earlswood (Surrey)	d										19 33											
Tonbridge 4	d					18 50								19 10								
Leigh (Kent)	d					18 54								19 14								
Penshurst	d					18 58								19 18								
Edenbridge	d					19 04								19 24								
Godstone	d					19 11								19 31								
Nutfield	d					19 16								19 36								
Reigate	d								19 21	19 30										19 51		
Redhill 5	a					19 21	19 23		19 25	19 35	19 38			19 41				19 47		19 55		
	d					19 23					19 39							19 48				
Merstham	d					19 27					19 43											
Coulsdon South	d					19 32					19 48											
Purley 4	d		←	←	←						19 53											
East Croydon ⇌	a	19 23	19 24	19 28	19 32	19 39					19 58	19 42				19 47		20 00			20 02	19 52
	d	19 24	19 25	19 29	19 32	19 40					19 59	19 43			19 44	19 47		20 01			20 02	19 53
Norwood Junction 2	a										→							→			→	
New Cross Gate	d																					
London Bridge 4 ⊖	a				19 45											20 00						
London Blackfriars 3 ⊖	a				19 52											20 07						
City Thameslink 3	a				19 56											20 10						
Farringdon 3 ⊖	a				20 00											20 14						
St Pancras International 15 ⊖	a				20 03											20 17						
St Albans City	a				20 25											20 39						
Luton Airport Parkway 4 ✈	a				20 37											20 51						
Luton 7	a				20 40											20 54						
Bedford 10	a				21 06											21 20						
Clapham Junction 10	d	19 34	19 38	19 41		19 49						19 52			19 56							20 03
London Victoria 15 ⊖	a	19 41	19 44	19 47		19 56		19 50				19 59			20 02		20 05					20 10

A ◇ to Three Bridges

Brighton - London and Bedford

		SN	SN	SN	FC	SN	SN	SN	SN	SN	FC	GW	SN	SN	SN	FC	SN	SN	SN	FC	SN	SN
		1	1	1	1	1	◇1	◇1	1	1	1	1	1	1	◇1	1	◇1	1	◇1	1	1	1
						bus																
Brighton 10	d										19 34					19 37	19 49					
Hove 2	d						19 22															
Preston Park	d															19 41						
Hassocks 4	d															19 47						
Burgess Hill 4	d						19 32									19 51						
Lewes 4	d							19 21														
Wivelsfield 4	d															19 53						
Haywards Heath 3	a						19 36	19 40			19 46					19 58						
	d						19 44				19 47					20 02						
Balcombe	d																					
Horsham 4	d									19 32					19 52							20 02
Littlehaven	d									19 35												20 05
Faygate	d																					
Ifield	d									19 41												20 11
Crawley	d									19 45					20 01							20 14
Three Bridges 4	a									19 49	19 56				20 04	20 11						20 18
	d									19 51	19 56				20 05	20 12						20 18
Gatwick Airport 10 ✈	a						19 55			19 55	20 00				20 10	20 16						20 22
	d					19 50	19 56			19 56	20 01	20 03	20 05		20 11	20 16					20 20	20 23
Horley 4	d									19 59												20 26
Salfords	d																					20 30
Earlswood (Surrey)	d																					20 33
Tonbridge 4	d																					
Leigh (Kent)	d																					
Penshurst	d																					
Edenbridge	d																					
Godstone	d																					
Nutfield	d																					
Reigate	d													20 14								
Redhill 5	a									20 05		20 11		20 18	20 18							20 36
	d									20 06					20 18							20 37
Merstham	d									20 10												20 41
Coulsdon South	d									20 15												20 46
Purley 4	d	←	←	←	←					20 18								←	←	←		20 49
East Croydon ⇌	a	19 58	20 00	20 00	20 02		20 11			20 23	20 16				20 30	20 32	20 22	20 23	20 30	20 32		20 57
	d	19 59	20 01	20 01	20 02		20 11		20 14	20 26	20 17				20 30	20 32	20 23	20 26	20 30	20 32		20 57
Norwood Junction 2	a									→					→	→						→
New Cross Gate	d																					
London Bridge 4 ⊖	a				20 15						20 30									20 45		
London Blackfriars 3 ⊖	a				20 22						20 37									20 52		
City Thameslink 3	a				20 26						20 40									20 56		
Farringdon 3 ⊖	a				20 30						20 44									21 00		
St Pancras International 15 ⊖	a				20 33						20 47									21 03		
St Albans City	a				20 55						21 09									21 25		
Luton Airport Parkway 4 ✈	a				21 07						21 21									21 37		
Luton 7	a				21 10						21 24									21 40		
Bedford 10	a				21 36						21 50									22 06		
Clapham Junction 10	d	20 08	20 11	20 11			20 21		20 26								20 33	20 37	20 41			
London Victoria 15 ⊖	a	20 15	20 20	20 20		20 20	20 28		20 32				20 35				20 40	20 44	20 50		20 50	

Brighton - London and Bedford

		SN	SN	SN	SN	SN	FC	SN	SN	FC	SN	SN	SN	FC	SN	SN	SN	SN	FC	GW	SN	SN	SN
		◇1	◇1	1	1	◇1	1	1	1	1	◇1	1	◇1	1	1	◇1	1	1	1	1	1	1	◇1
Brighton 10	d					19 55	20 04			20 07	20 19								20 34				
Hove 2	d	19 52														20 22							
Preston Park	d					19 58				20 11													
Hassocks 4	d					20 05				20 17													
Burgess Hill 4	d					20 08				20 21						20 33							
Lewes 4	d		19 50																				
Wivelsfield 4	d		20 05			20 11				20 23													
Haywards Heath 3	a	20 04	20 10			20 15	20 17			20 28						20 37			20 46				
	d	20 14				20 22	20 17			20 32						20 38			20 47				
Balcombe	d									20 37													
Horsham 4	d																	20 32					20 52
Littlehaven	d																	20 35					
Faygate	d																						
Ifield	d																	20 41					
Crawley	d																	20 45					21 01
Three Bridges 4	a					20 32	20 26			20 42						20 47		20 48	20 56				21 05
	d					20 32	20 26			20 42						20 47		20 51	20 56				21 05
Gatwick Airport 10 ✈	a	20 25				20 37	20 31			20 46						20 51		20 56	21 00				21 10
	d	20 26				20 38	20 31	20 35		20 46					20 50	20 53		20 57	21 01	21 03	21 05		21 11
Horley 4	d																	20 59					
Salfords	d																						
Earlswood (Surrey)	d																						
Tonbridge 4	d			20 10																			
Leigh (Kent)	d			20 14																			
Penshurst	d			20 18																			
Edenbridge	d			20 24																			
Godstone	d			20 31																			
Nutfield	d			20 36																			
Reigate	d								20 50													21 13	
Redhill 5	a			20 45		20 47			20 54									21 06		21 10		21 17	21 18
	d					20 48												21 07					21 18
Merstham	d																	21 11					
Coulsdon South	d																	21 16					
Purley 4	d											←	←	←				21 19					
East Croydon ⛴	a	20 41				20 59	20 47			21 02	20 52	20 57	20 59	21 02		21 08		21 25	21 16				21 30
	d	20 41			20 44	21 00	20 47			21 02	20 53	20 57	21 00	21 02		21 09	21 14	21 26	21 17				21 30
Norwood Junction 2	a					→				→								→					→
New Cross Gate	d																						
London Bridge 4 ⊖	a						21 00							21 15					21 30				
London Blackfriars 3 ⊖	a						21 07							21 22					21 37				
City Thameslink 3	a						21 10							21 26					21 40				
Farringdon 3 ⊖	a						21 14							21 30					21 44				
St Pancras International 15 ⊖	a						21 17							21 33					21 47				
St Albans City	a						21 39							21 55					22 09				
Luton Airport Parkway 4 ✈	a						21 51							22 07					22 21				
Luton 7	a						21 54							22 10					22 24				
Bedford 10	a						22 22							22 36					22 50				
Clapham Junction 10	d	20 51			20 57						21 03	21 08	21 11			21 18	21 26						
London Victoria 15 ⊖	a	20 58			21 05			21 05			21 10	21 15	21 18		21 20	21 26	21 35				21 35		

Brighton - London and Bedford

		GW	FC	SN	SN	SN	FC	SN	SN	SN	SN	SN	SN	SN	SN	SN	FC	SN	SN	SN	FC	SN
		1	1	◇1	1	◇1	1	1	1	◇1	◇1	1	1	1	◇1	1	1	◇1	1	◇1	1	1
Brighton 10	d		20 37	20 49											21 02		21 11	21 19				
Hove 2	d									20 52												
Preston Park	d		20 41												21 06							
Hassocks 4	d		20 47												21 12		21 19					
Burgess Hill 4	d		20 51												21 16		21 23					
Lewes 4	d										20 50											
Wivelsfield 4	d		20 53								21 05				21 18							
Haywards Heath 3	a		20 58							21 05	21 09				21 23		21 27					
	d		21 02							21 13					21 23		21 32					
Balcombe	d																21 37					
Horsham 4	d								21 02													
Littlehaven	d								21 05													
Faygate	d																					
Ifield	d								21 11													
Crawley	d								21 14													
Three Bridges 4	a		21 11						21 18						21 32		21 42					
	d		21 12						21 18						21 33		21 42					
Gatwick Airport 10 ✈	a		21 16						21 22	21 25					21 37		21 46					
	d		21 16					21 20	21 23	21 26			21 35		21 38		21 46					21 50
Horley 4	d								21 26													
Salfords	d								21 30													
Earlswood (Surrey)	d								21 33													
Tonbridge 4	d											21 10										
Leigh (Kent)	d											21 14										
Penshurst	d											21 18										
Edenbridge	d											21 24										
Godstone	d											21 31										
Nutfield	d											21 36										
Reigate	d	21 24														21 52						
Redhill 5	a	21 30							21 36			21 42			21 45	21 57						
	d								21 37						21 46							
Merstham	d								21 41													
Coulsdon South	d								21 46													
Purley 4	d				←	←	←		21 49										←	←	←	
East Croydon ⛴	a		21 32	21 22	21 25	21 30	21 32		21 54	21 41					21 59		22 02	21 52	21 54	21 59	22 02	
	d		21 32	21 23	21 26	21 30	21 32		21 57	21 42				21 44	22 00		22 02	21 53	21 57	22 00	22 02	
Norwood Junction 2	a		→						→						→		→					
New Cross Gate	d																					
London Bridge 4 ⊖	a						21 45														22 17	
London Blackfriars 3 ⊖	a						21 52															
City Thameslink 3	a						21 56															
Farringdon 3 ⊖	a						22 00															
St Pancras International 15 ⊖	a						22 03															
St Albans City	a						22 25															
Luton Airport Parkway 4 ✈	a						22 37															
Luton 7	a						22 40															
Bedford 10	a						23 06															
Clapham Junction 10	d			21 33	21 38	21 41				21 51				21 56				22 03	22 08	22 11		
London Victoria 15 ⊖	a			21 40	21 45	21 50		21 50		21 58			22 05	22 05				22 10	22 14	22 20		22 20

Brighton - London and Bedford

Station		SN ◇1	SN 1	SN 1	SN 1	SN 1	SN 1	SN ◇1	FC 1	SN ◇1	SN 1	SN ◇1	FC 1	SN 1	GW 1	SN 1	SN 1	SN ◇1 ⌶	SN ◇1 A ⌶	SN 1	SN 1	SN 1	SN ◇1
Brighton	d				21 34				21 37	21 49													22 00
Hove	d	21 22																	21 52				
Preston Park	d								21 41														22 04
Hassocks	d								21 47														22 10
Burgess Hill	d	21 33							21 51										22 04				22 14
Lewes	d																	21 50					
Wivelsfield	d								21 53									22 02					22 16
Haywards Heath	a	21 37			21 46				21 58									22 06	22 10				22 21
	d	21 38			21 47				22 02									22 14					22 22
Balcombe	d																						
Horsham	d			21 32				21 52									22 02						
Littlehaven	d			21 35													22 05						
Faygate	d																						
Ifield	d			21 41													22 11						
Crawley	d			21 45				22 01									22 14						
Three Bridges	a	21 47		21 48	21 56			22 05	22 11								22 18						22 32
	d	21 47		21 51	21 56			22 05	22 12								22 19						22 32
Gatwick Airport	a	21 51		21 55	22 00			22 10	22 16								22 23	22 25					22 37
	d	21 53		21 56	22 02	22 05		22 11	22 16					22 20	22 22		22 24	22 26			22 35		22 38
Horley	d			21 59													22 27						
Salfords	d																22 31						
Earlswood (Surrey)	d																22 34						
Tonbridge	d																			22 10			
Leigh (Kent)	d																			22 14			
Penshurst	d																			22 18			
Edenbridge	d																			22 24			
Godstone	d																			22 31			
Nutfield	d																			22 36			
Reigate	d						22 13									22 33							
Redhill	a			22 05			22 17	22 18							22 30	22 37	22 37			22 42			22 45
	d			22 06				22 18									22 38						22 46
Merstham	d			22 10													22 42						
Coulsdon South	d			22 15													22 47						
Purley	d			22 19							←	←	←				22 50						
East Croydon	a	22 08		22 24	22 17			22 30	22 32	22 22	22 24	22 30	22 32				22 55	22 41					22 59
	d	22 09	22 14	22 25	22 17			22 30	22 32	22 23	22 25	22 30	22 32				22 56	22 41				22 44	23 00
Norwood Junction	a			→				→	→								→						→
New Cross Gate	d																						
London Bridge	a				22 33								22 47										
London Blackfriars	a																						
City Thameslink	a																						
Farringdon	a																						
St Pancras International	a																						
St Albans City	a																						
Luton Airport Parkway	a																						
Luton	a																						
Bedford	a																						
Clapham Junction	d	22 18	22 26							22 33	22 38	22 41						22 51				22 56	
London Victoria	a	22 26	22 35			22 35				22 40	22 44	22 50		22 50				22 57			23 05	23 05	

A ⌶ from Haywards Heath

Brighton - London and Bedford

Station		FC 1	SN ◇1	SN 1	SN ◇1	FC 1	SN 1	SN 1	SN 1	SN 1	FC 1	SN ◇1	FC 1	GW 1	SN 1	SN 1	SN 1	SN 1	SN ◇1	FC 1	SN 1	SN ◇1	FC 1
Brighton	d	22 07	22 19								22 33								23 02	23 11			23 37
Hove	d																						
Preston Park	d	22 11									22 37								23 06				23 41
Hassocks	d	22 17									22 43								23 12	23 19			23 47
Burgess Hill	d	22 21									22 47								23 16	23 23			23 51
Lewes	d											22 40											
Wivelsfield	d	22 23									22 49	22 54							23 19				23 53
Haywards Heath	a	22 28									22 54	22 58							23 23	23 27			23 58
	d	22 32									22 54	22 59							23 24	23 28			23 59
Balcombe	d	22 37									23 00												00 04
Horsham	d															23 02							
Littlehaven	d															23 05							
Faygate	d																						
Ifield	d															23 11							
Crawley	d															23 14							
Three Bridges	a	22 42									23 05	23 08				23 18			23 33	23 38			00 10
	d	22 42									23 12	23 08				23 18			23 47	23 38			00 10
Gatwick Airport	a	22 46									23 16	23 12				23 22			23 52	23 42			00 14
	d	22 46					22 50	23 05			23 16	23 13		23 18	23 20	23 23		23 35	23 53	23 43	23 50		00 15
Horley	d															23 26			23 56				
Salfords	d															23 30							
Earlswood (Surrey)	d															23 33							
Tonbridge	d																23 17						
Leigh (Kent)	d																23 21						
Penshurst	d																23 25						
Edenbridge	d																23 31						
Godstone	d																23 38						
Nutfield	d																23 43						
Reigate	d																						
Redhill	a													23 25		23 36	23 49		00 03				00 22
	d															23 37			00 03				00 22
Merstham	d															23 41							
Coulsdon South	d															23 46							
Purley	d			←	←	←							←			23 49			00 11			←	
East Croydon	a	23 02	22 52	22 55	22 59	23 02					23 32	23 30	23 32			23 54			00 16	00 02		00 16	00 35
	d	23 02	22 53	22 56	23 00	23 02			23 14	23 20	23 32	23 30	23 32			23 58			00 17	00 04		00 17	00 36
Norwood Junction	a	→									→								→				
New Cross Gate	d																						
London Bridge	a					23 17							23 47							00 19			00 52
London Blackfriars	a																						
City Thameslink	a																						
Farringdon	a																						
St Pancras International	a																						
St Albans City	a																						
Luton Airport Parkway	a																						
Luton	a																						
Bedford	a																						
Clapham Junction	d		23 03	23 07	23 11				23 26	23 33		23 42				00 11						00 30	
London Victoria	a		23 13	23 15	23 20		23 20	23 35	23 35	23 40		23 52			23 55	00 18		00 10			00 25	00 37	

Table 186

Saturdays

Brighton - London and Bedford

Station		SN	SN	SN	FC	SN	SN	SN	FC	SN	SN	SN	SN	SN	FC	SN	SN	FC	SN	FC	SN	FC	SN
		1	1	◇1	1	1	◇1	1	1	1		1	1	1	1	1	1	1	1	1	1	1	1
Brighton 10	d			23p02	23p11				23p37														
Hove 2	d																						
Preston Park	d			23p06					23p41														
Hassocks 4	d			23p12	23p19				23p47														
Burgess Hill 4	d			23p16	23p23				23p51														
Lewes 4	d																						
Wivelsfield 4	d			23p19					23p53														
Haywards Heath 3	a			23p23	23p27				23p58														
	d			23p24	23p28				23p59														
Balcombe	d								00 04														
Horsham 4	d	23p02																					
Littlehaven	d	23p05																					
Faygate	d																						
Ifield	d	23p11																					
Crawley	d	23p14																					
Three Bridges 4	a	23p18		23p33	23p38				00 10														
	d	23p18		23p47	23p38				00 10						01 25		01 59	02 25	02 55	03 25	03 55	04 25	
Gatwick Airport 10 ✈	a	23p22		23p52	23p42				00 14						01 29		02 03	02 29	02 59	03 29	03 59	04 29	
	d	23p23	23p35	23p53	23p43	23p50		00 05	00 15	00 20		00 35	00 50	01 05	01 30	01 35	02 05	02 30	03 05	03 30	04 05	04 30	04 35
Horley 4	d	23p26		23p56										01 07			02 07		03 07		04 07		
Salfords	d	23p30																					
Earlswood (Surrey)	d	23p33																					
Tonbridge 4	d																						
Leigh (Kent)	d																						
Penshurst	d																						
Edenbridge	d																						
Godstone	d																						
Nutfield	d																						
Reigate	d																						
Redhill 5	a	23p36		00 03					00 22												04 14		
	d	23p37		00 03					00 22												04 14		
Merstham	d	23p41																					
Coulsdon South	d	23p46																					
Purley 4	d	23p49		00 11			←							01 22			02 22		03 22		04 22		
East Croydon	a	23p54		00 16	00 02		00 16		00 35					01 27	01 50		02 27	02 47	03 27	03 47	04 27	04 47	
	d	23p58		00 17	00 04		00 17		00 36		00 49			01 28	01 50		02 28	02 47	03 28	03 47	04 28	04 47	
Norwood Junction 2	a			→																			
New Cross Gate	d																						
London Bridge 4 ⊖	a				00 19				00 52						02 14			03 12		04 12		05 12	
London Blackfriars 3 ⊖	a																						
City Thameslink 3	a																						
Farringdon 3 ⊖	a																						
St Pancras International 15 ⊖	a																						
St Albans City	a																						
Luton Airport Parkway 4 ✈	a																						
Luton 7	a																						
Bedford 10	a																						
Clapham Junction 10	d	00 11					00 30				01 01			01 41			02 41		03 41		04 41		
London Victoria 15 ⊖	a	00 18	00 10			00 25	00 37	00 40		00 55	01 09	01 11	01 25	01 49		02 10	02 49		03 49		04 50		05 10

Table 186

Saturdays

Brighton - London and Bedford

Station		FC	SN	FC	GW	SN	SN	SN	SN	SN	SN	FC	SN	GW	SN	SN	SN	SN	SN	SN	FC	SN	SN
		1	1	1	1	◇1	1	1	◇1	1	1	1	1	1	1 🚲	1 🚲	1	◇1	◇1	◇1	1	1 🚲	◇1
Brighton 10	d								05 21			05 24						05 50		05 56	06 04		
Hove 2	d																		05 54				
Preston Park	d											05 28								06 00			
Hassocks 4	d											05 34								06 06			
Burgess Hill 4	d								05 31			05 38									06 14		
Lewes 4	d										05 26												
Wivelsfield 4	d											05 40								06 11			
Haywards Heath 3	a								05 36		05 40	05 45						06 02	06 07	06 15	06 18		
	d								05 37		05 49	05 45						06 11		06 16	06 18		
Balcombe	d											05 51											
Horsham 4	d									05 30							06 00						
Littlehaven	d									05 33							06 03						
Faygate	d																						
Ifield	d									05 39							06 09						
Crawley	d									05 43							06 13						
Three Bridges 4	a								05 46	05 46	05 59	05 56					06 16	06 20		06 25			
	d	04 55		05 20		05 33			05 46	05 48	05 59	05 56					06 18	06 20		06 31			
Gatwick Airport 10 ✈	a	04 59		05 24		05 37			05 50	05 52	06 03	06 00					06 22	06 24		06 35	06 30		
	d	05 00	05 20	05 26	05 31	05 38		05 50	05 53	05 53		06 01		06 03	06 05	06 20	06 23	06 25		06 38	06 31	06 35	
Horley 4	d					05 40				05 56							06 26						
Salfords	d									06 00							06 30						
Earlswood (Surrey)	d									06 03							06 33						
Tonbridge 4	d						05 24																
Leigh (Kent)	d						05 28																
Penshurst	d						05 32																
Edenbridge	d						05 38																
Godstone	d						05 45																
Nutfield	d						05 50																
Reigate	d																						
Redhill 5	a				05 38	05 47	05 55			06 06				06 12			06 36						
	d					05 48				06 07							06 37						
Merstham	d									06 11							06 41						
Coulsdon South	d									06 16							06 46						
Purley 4	d					05 58				06 19			←				06 49						←
East Croydon	a	05 17		05 42		06 02			06 10	06 24		06 16	06 24				06 54	06 40		06 53	06 46		06 53
	d	05 17		05 42		06 07			06 11	06 25		06 17	06 25				06 55	06 41		06 53	06 47		06 53
Norwood Junction 2	a									→			06 29				→			→			
New Cross Gate	d												06 37										
London Bridge 4 ⊖	a	05 42		05 57								06 32	06 43								07 02		
London Blackfriars 3 ⊖	a																						
City Thameslink 3	a																						
Farringdon 3 ⊖	a																						
St Pancras International 15 ⊖	a																						
St Albans City	a																						
Luton Airport Parkway 4 ✈	a																						
Luton 7	a																						
Bedford 10	a																						
Clapham Junction 10	d					06 18			06 22									06 50					07 03
London Victoria 15 ⊖	a		05 55			06 26		06 20	06 30						06 35	06 50		06 57				07 05	07 09

Brighton - London and Bedford

		SN ■		SN ■	SN	SN ■	SN ■	SN ◇■	SN ◇■	SN ■	FC ■	GW ■		SN ■	SN ◇■	FC ■	SN ◇■	SN ■	SN ◇■	FC ■	SN	SN ■			SN ■
						🛒			A					🛒								🛒			
Brighton 10	d							06 10			06 24					06 37	06 49								
Hove 2	d								06 21																
Preston Park	d							06 14			06 28					06 41									
Hassocks 4	d							06 20			06 34					06 47									
Burgess Hill 4	d							06 24			06 38					06 51									
Lewes 4	d																								
Wivelsfield 4	d							06 26			06 40					06 53									
Haywards Heath 3	a							06 31	06 35		06 45					06 58									
	d							06 40			06 45					07 02									
Balcombe	d										06 51														
Horsham 4	d						06 30								06 52										
Littlehaven	d						06 33																		
Faygate	d																								
Ifield	d						06 39																		
Crawley	d						06 43								07 01										
Three Bridges 4	a						06 46	06 49			06 56				07 04	07 11									
	d						06 48	06 49			06 56				07 05	07 12									
Gatwick Airport 10 ✈	a						06 52	06 53			07 00				07 09	07 16									
	d					06 50	06 53	06 55			07 01	07 03		07 05	07 10	07 16						07 20			
Horley 4	d						06 56																		
Salfords	d																								
Earlswood (Surrey)	d																								
Tonbridge 4	d			06 19																					
Leigh (Kent)	d			06 23																					
Penshurst	d			06 27																					
Edenbridge	d			06 33																					
Godstone	d			06 40																					
Nutfield	d			06 45																					
Reigate	d																								07 14
Redhill 5	a			06 50			07 02					07 10			07 17										07 18
	d			06 51			07 07								07 18										07 21
Merstham	d						07 11																		07 25
Coulsdon South	d			06 58			07 16																		07 30
Purley 4	d	←		07 02			07 19											←	←	←					07 34
East Croydon	a	06 54		07 07			07 24	07 10			07 16				07 29	07 32	07 22	07 24	07 29	07 32					07 39
	d	06 55		07 07			07 25	07 11		07 14	07 17				07 30	07 32	07 23	07 25	07 30	07 32					07 39
Norwood Junction 2	a	06 59		07 12			→								→	→		07 29							07 44
New Cross Gate	d	07 07																07 37							
London Bridge 4 ⊖	a	07 13		07 25							07 32							07 43		07 47					07 57
London Blackfriars 3 ⊖	a																								
City Thameslink 3	a																								
Farringdon 3 ⊖	a																								
St Pancras International 15 ⊖	a																								
St Albans City	a																								
Luton Airport Parkway 4 ✈	a																								
Luton 7	a																								
Bedford 10	a																								
Clapham Junction 10	d				07 11			07 20		07 26							07 33		07 39		07 41				
London Victoria 15 ⊖	a				07 18	07 20		07 27		07 32				07 35			07 40		07 46		07 48	07 50			

A ◇ from Haywards Heath

Brighton - London and Bedford

		GW ■	SN ■	SN ◇■	SN ◇■	SN ■	FC ■	SN ■		SN ◇■	FC ■	SN ◇■	SN ■	SN ◇■	FC ■	SN ■	SN	SN ■		SN ■	SN ■	SN ◇■	SN ◇■	SN ■	FC ■
								🛒										🛒					A		
Brighton 10	d						07 04				07 07	07 19								07 24					07 34
Hove 2	d				06 51																	07 22			
Preston Park	d				06 55						07 11														
Hassocks 4	d										07 17									07 34					
Burgess Hill 4	d				07 04						07 21									07 38					
Lewes 4	d			06 50																			07 20		
Wivelsfield 4	d										07 23												07 35		
Haywards Heath 3	a			07 05	07 09		07 16				07 28											07 35	07 40		07 46
	d			07 14			07 17				07 32											07 44			07 47
Balcombe	d										07 37														
Horsham 4	d		07 00							07 20											07 30				
Littlehaven	d		07 03																		07 33				
Faygate	d																								
Ifield	d		07 09																		07 39				
Crawley	d		07 13							07 29											07 43				
Three Bridges 4	a		07 16				07 26			07 32	07 42										07 46				07 56
	d		07 18				07 26			07 33	07 42										07 48				07 56
Gatwick Airport 10 ✈	a		07 22	07 25			07 30			07 37	07 46									07 51	07 52	07 55			08 00
	d		07 23	07 26			07 31	07 35		07 38	07 46							07 50		07 53	07 53	07 56			08 01
Horley 4	d		07 26							07 41											07 56				
Salfords	d		07 30																						
Earlswood (Surrey)	d		07 33																						
Tonbridge 4	d															07 19									
Leigh (Kent)	d															07 23									
Penshurst	d															07 27									
Edenbridge	d															07 33									
Godstone	d															07 40									
Nutfield	d															07 45									
Reigate	d	07 18																							
Redhill 5	a	07 25	07 36							07 47						07 50					08 02				
	d		07 37							07 48						07 51					08 07				
Merstham	d		07 41																		08 11				
Coulsdon South	d		07 46													07 58					08 16				
Purley 4	d		07 49										←	←	←	08 02					08 19				
East Croydon	a		07 54	07 41			07 46			07 59	08 02	07 52	07 54	07 59	08 02	08 07				08 08	08 24	08 11			08 16
	d		07 55	07 42		07 44	07 47			08 00	08 02	07 53	07 55	08 00	08 02	08 07				08 08	08 25	08 12		08 14	08 17
Norwood Junction 2	a		→							→	→		07 59			08 12					→				
New Cross Gate	d												08 07												
London Bridge 4 ⊖	a						08 02						08 13		08 17	08 25									08 32
London Blackfriars 3 ⊖	a																								
City Thameslink 3	a																								
Farringdon 3 ⊖	a																								
St Pancras International 15 ⊖	a																								
St Albans City	a																								
Luton Airport Parkway 4 ✈	a																								
Luton 7	a																								
Bedford 10	a																								
Clapham Junction 10	d			07 51		07 56						08 03		08 10			08 11			08 18		08 21		08 26	
London Victoria 15 ⊖	a			07 58		08 02		08 05				08 10		08 16			08 18	08 20		08 24		08 28		08 32	

A ◇ from Haywards Heath

Brighton - London and Bedford

Station		GW 1	SN 1 H	SN ◇1	FC 1	SN ◇1 H	SN 1	SN ◇1	FC 1	SN 1	GW 1	SN	SN 1 H	SN 1	SN ◇1	SN ◇1 B	SN 1	FC 1	SN 1 H	SN ◇1	FC 1
Brighton 10	d				07 37	07 49												08 04			08 07
Hove 2	d															07 51					
Preston Park	d				07 41											07 55					08 11
Hassocks 4	d				07 47																08 17
Burgess Hill 4	d				07 51											08 04					08 21
Lewes 4	d														07 50						
Wivelsfield 4	d				07 53																08 23
Haywards Heath 3	a				07 58										08 05	08 09		08 16			08 28
	d				08 02										08 14			08 17			08 32
Balcombe	d																				08 37
Horsham 4	d			07 50										08 00						08 20	
Littlehaven	d													08 03							
Faygate	d																				
Ifield	d													08 09							
Crawley	d			07 59										08 13						08 29	
Three Bridges 4	a			08 02	08 11									08 16				08 26		08 32	08 42
	d			08 03	08 12									08 18				08 26		08 33	08 42
Gatwick Airport 10 ✈	a			08 07	08 16									08 22	08 25			08 30		08 37	08 46
	d	08 03	08 05	08 08	08 16								08 20	08 23	08 26			08 31	08 35	08 38	08 46
Horley 4	d													08 26						08 41	
Salfords	d													08 30							
Earlswood (Surrey)	d													08 33							
Tonbridge 4	d																				
Leigh (Kent)	d																				
Penshurst	d																				
Edenbridge	d																				
Godstone	d																				
Nutfield	d																				
Reigate	d									08 14	08 19										
Redhill 5	a	08 10		08 15						08 18	08 25			08 36						08 47	
	d			08 16						08 19				08 37						08 48	
Merstham	d									08 23				08 41							
Coulsdon South	d									08 28				08 46							
Purley 4	d						←	←	←	08 32				08 49							
East Croydon	a			08 27	08 32	08 22	08 24	08 27	08 32	08 37				08 54	08 41			08 46		08 59	09 02
	d			08 28	08 32	08 23	08 25	08 28	08 32	08 37				08 55	08 42		08 44	08 47		09 00	09 02
Norwood Junction 2	a			→	→		08 29			08 42				→						→	→
New Cross Gate	d						08 37														
London Bridge 4 ⊖	a						08 43		08 47	08 55								09 02			
London Blackfriars 3 ⊖	a																				
City Thameslink 3	a																				
Farringdon 3 ⊖	a																				
St Pancras International 15 ⊖	a																				
St Albans City	a																				
Luton Airport Parkway 4 ✈	a																				
Luton 7	a																				
Bedford 10	a																				
Clapham Junction 10	d					08 33		08 37				08 41			08 51		08 56				
London Victoria 15 ⊖	a		08 35			08 40		08 44				08 48	08 50		08 58		09 02		09 05		

B ◇ from Haywards Heath

Brighton - London and Bedford

Station		SN ◇1 H	SN 1	SN ◇1	FC 1	SN 1	SN 1 H	SN 1	SN 1	SN ◇1	SN ◇1 A	SN 1	FC 1	GW 1	SN 1 H	SN ◇1 H	FC 1	SN ◇1 H	SN 1	SN ◇1 H	FC 1	SN 1	GW 1
Brighton 10	d	08 19						08 24					08 34				08 37	08 49					
Hove 2	d									08 21													
Preston Park	d																08 41						
Hassocks 4	d							08 34									08 47						
Burgess Hill 4	d							08 38									08 51						
Lewes 4	d										08 20												
Wivelsfield 4	d										08 35						08 53						
Haywards Heath 3	a									08 35	08 40		08 46				08 58						
	d									08 44			08 47				09 02						
Balcombe	d																						
Horsham 4	d								08 30							08 50							
Littlehaven	d								08 33														
Faygate	d																						
Ifield	d								08 39														
Crawley	d								08 43							08 59							
Three Bridges 4	a								08 46				08 56			09 02	09 11						
	d								08 48				08 56			09 03	09 12						
Gatwick Airport 10 ✈	a							08 51	08 52	08 55			09 00			09 07	09 16						
	d						08 50	08 53	08 53	08 56			09 01	09 03	09 05	09 08	09 16						
Horley 4	d								08 56														
Salfords	d																						
Earlswood (Surrey)	d																						
Tonbridge 4	d					08 19																	
Leigh (Kent)	d					08 23																	
Penshurst	d					08 27																	
Edenbridge	d					08 33																	
Godstone	d					08 40																	
Nutfield	d					08 45																	
Reigate	d																					09 14	09 18
Redhill 5	a					08 50			09 02					09 10		09 15						09 18	09 25
	d					08 51			09 07							09 16						09 19	
Merstham	d								09 11													09 23	
Coulsdon South	d					08 58			09 16													09 28	
Purley 4	d		←	←	←	09 02			09 19										←	←	←	09 32	
East Croydon	a	08 52	08 54	08 59	09 02	09 07		09 08	09 24	09 11			09 16			09 27	09 32	09 22	09 24	09 27	09 32	09 37	
	d	08 53	08 55	09 00	09 02	09 07		09 08	09 25	09 12		09 14	09 17			09 28	09 32	09 23	09 25	09 28	09 32	09 37	
Norwood Junction 2	a		08 59			09 12			→							→	→		09 29			09 42	
New Cross Gate	d		09 07																09 37				
London Bridge 4 ⊖	a		09 13		09 17	09 25							09 32						09 43		09 47	09 55	
London Blackfriars 3 ⊖	a																						
City Thameslink 3	a																						
Farringdon 3 ⊖	a																						
St Pancras International 15 ⊖	a																						
St Albans City	a																						
Luton Airport Parkway 6 ✈	a																						
Luton 7	a																						
Bedford 10	a																						
Clapham Junction 10	d	09 03		09 10				09 18		09 21		09 26						09 33		09 37			
London Victoria 15 ⊖	a	09 10		09 16			09 20	09 24		09 28		09 32			09 35			09 40		09 44			

A ◇ from Haywards Heath

Brighton - London and Bedford

		SN	SN	SN	SN	SN	SN	FC	SN	SN	FC	SN	SN	SN	FC	SN	SN	SN	SN	SN	SN	SN
			1	1	◇1	◇1	1	1	1	◇1	1	◇1	1	◇1	1	1	1	1	1	◇1	◇1	1
						B																
			⊼						⊼			⊼					⊼					
Brighton 10	d							09 04			09 07	09 19						09 24				
Hove 2	d					08 51														09 21		
Preston Park	d					08 55					09 11											
Hassocks 4	d										09 17							09 34				
Burgess Hill 4	d					09 04					09 21							09 38				
Lewes 4	d				08 50																09 20	
Wivelsfield 4	d										09 23										09 35	
Haywards Heath 3	a				09 05	09 09		09 16			09 28									09 35	09 40	
	d				09 14			09 17			09 32									09 44		
Balcombe	d										09 37											
Horsham 4	d			09 00						09 20									09 30			
Littlehaven	d			09 03															09 33			
Faygate	d																					
Ifield	d			09 09															09 39			
Crawley	d			09 13						09 29									09 43			
Three Bridges 4	a			09 16				09 26		09 32	09 42								09 46			
	d			09 18				09 26		09 33	09 42								09 48			
Gatwick Airport 10 ✈	a			09 22	09 25			09 30		09 37	09 46							09 51	09 52	09 55		
	d		09 20	09 23	09 26			09 31	09 35	09 38	09 46						09 50	09 53	09 53	09 56		
Horley 4	d			09 26						09 41									09 56			
Salfords	d			09 30																		
Earlswood (Surrey)	d			09 33																		
Tonbridge 4	d															09 19						
Leigh (Kent)	d															09 23						
Penshurst	d															09 27						
Edenbridge	d															09 33						
Godstone	d															09 40						
Nutfield	d															09 45						
Reigate	d																					
Redhill 5	a			09 36						09 47						09 50			10 02			
	d			09 37						09 48						09 51			10 07			
Merstham	d			09 41															10 11			
Coulsdon South	d			09 46												09 58			10 16			
Purley 4	d			09 49									←	←	←	10 02			10 19			
East Croydon	a			09 54	09 41			09 46		09 59	10 02	09 52	09 54	09 59	10 02	10 07		10 08	10 24	10 11		
	d			09 55	09 42		09 44	09 47		10 00	10 02	09 53	09 55	10 00	10 02	10 07		10 08	10 25	10 12		10 14
Norwood Junction 2	a			→						→	→		09 59			10 12			→			
New Cross Gate	d												10 07									
London Bridge 4 ⊖	a							10 02					10 13		10 17	10 25						
London Blackfriars 3 ⊖	a																					
City Thameslink 3	a																					
Farringdon 3 ⊖	a																					
St Pancras International 15 ⊖	a																					
St Albans City	a																					
Luton Airport Parkway 4 ✈	a																					
Luton 7	a																					
Bedford 10	a																					
Clapham Junction 10	d	09 41			09 51		09 56					10 03		10 10				10 18		10 21		10 26
London Victoria 15 ⊖	a	09 48	09 50		09 58		10 02		10 05			10 10		10 16			10 20	10 24		10 28		10 32

B ◇ from Haywards Heath

Brighton - London and Bedford

		FC	GW	SN	SN	FC	SN	SN	SN	FC	SN	GW	SN	SN	SN	SN	SN	SN	FC	SN	SN
		1	1	1	◇1	1	◇1	1	◇1	1	1	1		1	1	◇1	◇1	1	1	1	◇1
				⊼	⊼		⊼		⊼					⊼						⊼	
Brighton 10	d	09 34				09 37	09 49												10 04		
Hove 2	d																09 51				
Preston Park	d					09 41											09 55				
Hassocks 4	d					09 47															
Burgess Hill 4	d					09 51											10 04				
Lewes 4	d															09 50					
Wivelsfield 4	d					09 53															
Haywards Heath 3	a	09 46				09 58										10 05	10 09		10 16		
	d	09 47				10 02										10 14			10 17		
Balcombe	d																				
Horsham 4	d				09 50										10 00						10 20
Littlehaven	d														10 03						
Faygate	d																				
Ifield	d														10 09						
Crawley	d				09 59										10 13						10 29
Three Bridges 4	a	09 56			10 02	10 11									10 16				10 26		10 32
	d	09 56			10 03	10 12									10 18				10 26		10 33
Gatwick Airport 10 ✈	a	10 00			10 07	10 16									10 22	10 25			10 30		10 37
	d	10 01	10 03	10 05	10 08	10 16								10 20	10 23	10 26			10 31	10 35	10 38
Horley 4	d														10 26						10 41
Salfords	d														10 30						
Earlswood (Surrey)	d														10 33						
Tonbridge 4	d																				
Leigh (Kent)	d																				
Penshurst	d																				
Edenbridge	d																				
Godstone	d																				
Nutfield	d																				
Reigate	d										10 14	10 19									
Redhill 5	a		10 10		10 15						10 18	10 25			10 36						10 47
	d				10 16						10 19				10 37						10 48
Merstham	d										10 23				10 41						
Coulsdon South	d										10 28				10 46						
Purley 4	d							←	←	←	10 32				10 49						
East Croydon	a	10 16			10 27	10 32	10 22	10 24	10 27	10 32	10 37				10 54	10 41			10 46		10 59
	d	10 17			10 28	10 32	10 23	10 25	10 28	10 32	10 37				10 55	10 42		10 44	10 47		11 00
Norwood Junction 2	a				→	→		10 29			10 42				→						→
New Cross Gate	d							10 37													
London Bridge 4 ⊖	a	10 32						10 43		10 47	10 55								11 02		
London Blackfriars 3 ⊖	a																				
City Thameslink 3	a																				
Farringdon 3 ⊖	a																				
St Pancras International 15 ⊖	a																				
St Albans City	a																				
Luton Airport Parkway 4 ✈	a																				
Luton 7	a																				
Bedford 10	a																				
Clapham Junction 10	d						10 33		10 37				10 41			10 51		10 56			
London Victoria 15 ⊖	a			10 35			10 40		10 44				10 48	10 50		10 58		11 02		11 05	

Table 186

Saturdays

Brighton - London and Bedford

		FC	SN	SN	SN	FC	SN	SN	SN	SN	SN	SN	SN	FC	GW	SN	SN	FC	SN	SN	SN	FC	SN
		1	◇1	1	◇1	1	1	1	1	1	◇1	◇1	1	1	1	1	◇1	1	◇1	1	◇1	1	1
			H					H								H	H		H		H		
Brighton 10	d	10 07	10 19						10 24					10 34				10 37	10 49				
Hove 2	d										10 21												
Preston Park	d	10 11																10 41					
Hassocks 4	d	10 17							10 34									10 47					
Burgess Hill 4	d	10 21							10 38									10 51					
Lewes 4	d											10 20											
Wivelsfield 4	d	10 23										10 35						10 53					
Haywards Heath 3	a	10 28									10 35	10 40		10 46				10 58					
	d	10 32										10 44		10 47				11 02					
Balcombe	d	10 37																					
Horsham 4	d									10 30							10 50						
Littlehaven	d									10 33													
Faygate	d																						
Ifield	d									10 39													
Crawley	d									10 43							10 59						
Three Bridges 4	a	10 42								10 46				10 56			11 02	11 11					
	d	10 42								10 48				10 56			11 03	11 12					
Gatwick Airport 10 ✈	a	10 46							10 51	10 52		10 55		11 00			11 07	11 16					
	d	10 46						10 50	10 53	10 53		10 56		11 01	11 03	11 05	11 08	11 16					
Horley 4	d									10 56													
Salfords	d																						
Earlswood (Surrey)	d																						
Tonbridge 4	d						10 19																
Leigh (Kent)	d						10 23																
Penshurst	d						10 27																
Edenbridge	d						10 33																
Godstone	d						10 40																
Nutfield	d						10 45																
Reigate	d																						11 14
Redhill 5	a						10 50			11 02					11 10		11 15						11 18
	d						10 51			11 07							11 16						11 19
Merstham	d									11 11													11 23
Coulsdon South	d						10 58			11 16													11 28
Purley 4	d			←	←	←	11 02			11 19										←	←	←	11 32
East Croydon	a	11 02	10 52	10 54	10 59	11 02	11 07		11 08	11 24		11 11		11 16			11 27	11 32	11 22	11 24	11 27	11 32	11 37
	d	11 02	10 53	10 55	11 00	11 02	11 07		11 08	11 25		11 12	11 14	11 17			11 28	11 32	11 23	11 25	11 28	11 32	11 37
Norwood Junction 2	a	→		10 59			11 12			→							→	→		11 29			11 42
New Cross Gate	d			11 07																11 37			
London Bridge 4 ⊖	a			11 13		11 17	11 25							11 32						11 43		11 47	11 55
London Blackfriars 3 ⊖	a																						
City Thameslink 3	a																						
Farringdon 3 ⊖	a																						
St Pancras International 15 ⊖	a																						
St Albans City	a																						
Luton Airport Parkway 4 ✈	a																						
Luton 7	a																						
Bedford 10	a																						
Clapham Junction 10	d		11 03		11 10				11 18			11 21	11 26						11 33		11 37		
London Victoria 15 ⊖	a		11 10		11 16			11 20	11 24			11 28	11 32			11 35			11 40		11 44		

Table 186

Saturdays

Brighton - London and Bedford

		GW	SN	SN	SN	SN	SN	SN	FC	SN	SN	FC	SN	SN	SN	FC	SN	SN	SN	SN	SN	SN
		1		1	1	◇1	◇1	1	1	1	◇1	1	◇1	1	◇1	1	1	1	1	1	◇1	◇1
							B															
				H						H			H					H				
Brighton 10	d								11 04			11 07	11 19						11 24			
Hove 2	d						10 51														11 21	
Preston Park	d						10 55					11 11										
Hassocks 4	d											11 17							11 34			
Burgess Hill 4	d						11 04					11 21							11 38			
Lewes 4	d					10 50																11 20
Wivelsfield 4	d											11 23										11 35
Haywards Heath 3	a					11 05	11 09		11 16			11 28									11 35	11 40
	d						11 14		11 17			11 32										11 44
Balcombe	d											11 37										
Horsham 4	d				11 00						11 20									11 30		
Littlehaven	d				11 03															11 33		
Faygate	d																					
Ifield	d				11 09															11 39		
Crawley	d				11 13						11 29									11 43		
Three Bridges 4	a				11 16				11 26		11 32	11 42								11 46		
	d				11 18				11 26		11 33	11 42								11 48		
Gatwick Airport 10 ✈	a				11 22		11 25		11 30		11 37	11 46							11 51	11 52		11 55
	d			11 20	11 23		11 26		11 31	11 35	11 38	11 46						11 50	11 53	11 53		11 56
Horley 4	d				11 26						11 41									11 56		
Salfords	d				11 30																	
Earlswood (Surrey)	d				11 33																	
Tonbridge 4	d																11 19					
Leigh (Kent)	d																11 23					
Penshurst	d																11 27					
Edenbridge	d																11 33					
Godstone	d																11 40					
Nutfield	d																11 45					
Reigate	d	11 18																				
Redhill 5	a	11 25			11 36						11 47						11 50			12 02		
	d				11 37						11 48						11 51			12 07		
Merstham	d				11 41															12 11		
Coulsdon South	d				11 46												11 58			12 16		
Purley 4	d				11 49									←	←	←	12 02			12 19		
East Croydon	a				11 54	11 41			11 46		11 59	12 02	11 52	11 54	11 59	12 02	12 07		12 08	12 24		12 11
	d				11 55	11 42		11 44	11 47		12 00	12 02	11 53	11 55	12 00	12 02	12 07		12 08	12 25		12 12
Norwood Junction 2	a				→						→	→		11 59			12 12			→		
New Cross Gate	d													12 07								
London Bridge 4 ⊖	a								12 02					12 13		12 17	12 25					
London Blackfriars 3 ⊖	a																					
City Thameslink 3	a																					
Farringdon 3 ⊖	a																					
St Pancras International 15 ⊖	a																					
St Albans City	a																					
Luton Airport Parkway 4 ✈	a																					
Luton 7	a																					
Bedford 10	a																					
Clapham Junction 10	d		11 41			11 51		11 56					12 03		12 10				12 18			12 21
London Victoria 15 ⊖	a		11 48	11 50		11 58		12 02		12 05			12 10		12 16			12 20	12 24			12 28

B ◇ from Haywards Heath

Brighton - London and Bedford

		SN [1]	FC [1]	GW [1]	SN [1] 🛒	SN ◇[1] 🛒	FC [1]	SN ◇[1] 🛒	SN [1]	SN ◇[1] 🛒	FC [1]	SN [1]	GW [1]	SN	SN [1] 🛒	SN [1]	SN ◇[1]	SN ◇[1] B	SN [1]	FC [1]	SN [1] 🛒
Brighton [10]	d		11 34				11 37	11 49												12 04	
Hove [2]	d																	11 51			
Preston Park	d						11 41											11 55			
Hassocks [4]	d						11 47														
Burgess Hill [4]	d						11 51											12 04			
Lewes [4]	d																11 50				
Wivelsfield [4]	d						11 53														
Haywards Heath [3]	a		11 46				11 58										12 05	12 09		12 16	
	d		11 47				12 02										12 14			12 17	
Balcombe	d																				
Horsham [4]	d					11 50										12 00					
Littlehaven	d															12 03					
Faygate	d																				
Ifield	d															12 09					
Crawley	d					11 59										12 13					
Three Bridges [4]	a		11 56			12 02	12 11									12 16				12 26	
	d		11 56			12 03	12 12									12 18				12 26	
Gatwick Airport [10] ✈	a		12 00			12 07	12 16									12 22	12 25			12 30	
	d		12 01	12 03	12 05	12 08	12 16								12 20	12 23	12 26			12 31	12 35
Horley [4]	d															12 26					
Salfords	d															12 30					
Earlswood (Surrey)	d															12 33					
Tonbridge [4]	d																				
Leigh (Kent)	d																				
Penshurst	d																				
Edenbridge	d																				
Godstone	d																				
Nutfield	d																				
Reigate	d											12 14	12 19								
Redhill [5]	a			12 10		12 15						12 18	12 25			12 36					
	d					12 16						12 19				12 37					
Merstham	d											12 23				12 41					
Coulsdon South	d											12 28				12 46					
Purley [4]	d								←	←	←	12 32				12 49					
East Croydon ⇌	a		12 16			12 27	12 32	12 22	12 24	12 27	12 32	12 37				12 54	12 41			12 46	
	d	12 14	12 17			12 28	12 32	12 23	12 25	12 28	12 32	12 38				12 55	12 42		12 44	12 47	
Norwood Junction [2]	a					→	→		12 29			12 42				→					
New Cross Gate	d								12 37												
London Bridge [4] ⊖	a		12 32						12 43		12 47	12 55								13 02	
London Blackfriars [3] ⊖	a																				
City Thameslink [3]	a																				
Farringdon [3] ⊖	a																				
St Pancras International [15] ⊖	a																				
St Albans City	a																				
Luton Airport Parkway [4] ✈	a																				
Luton [7]	a																				
Bedford [10]	a																				
Clapham Junction [10]	d	12 26						12 33		12 37				12 41			12 51		12 56		
London Victoria [15] ⊖	a	12 32			12 35			12 40		12 44				12 48	12 50		12 58		13 02		13 05

B ◇ from Haywards Heath

Brighton - London and Bedford

		SN ◇[1]	FC [1]	SN ◇[1] 🛒	SN [1]	SN ◇[1]	FC [1]	SN [1]	SN [1] 🛒	SN [1]	SN [1]	SN ◇[1]	SN ◇[1]	SN [1]	FC [1]	GW [1]	SN [1] 🛒	SN ◇[1] 🛒	FC [1]	SN ◇[1] 🛒	SN [1]	SN ◇[1] 🛒	FC [1]
Brighton [10]	d		12 07	12 19						12 24					12 34				12 37	12 49			
Hove [2]	d											12 21											
Preston Park	d		12 11																12 41				
Hassocks [4]	d		12 17							12 34									12 47				
Burgess Hill [4]	d		12 21							12 38									12 51				
Lewes [4]	d												12 20										
Wivelsfield [4]	d		12 23										12 35						12 53				
Haywards Heath [3]	a		12 28									12 35	12 40		12 46				12 58				
	d		12 32									12 44			12 47				13 02				
Balcombe	d		12 37																				
Horsham [4]	d	12 20									12 30							12 50					
Littlehaven	d										12 33												
Faygate	d																						
Ifield	d										12 39												
Crawley	d	12 29									12 43							12 59					
Three Bridges [4]	a	12 32	12 42								12 46				12 56			13 02	13 11				
	d	12 33	12 42								12 48				12 56			13 03	13 12				
Gatwick Airport [10] ✈	a	12 37	12 46							12 51	12 52	12 55			13 00			13 07	13 16				
	d	12 38	12 46						12 50	12 53	12 53	12 56			13 01	13 03	13 05	13 08	13 16				
Horley [4]	d	12 41									12 56												
Salfords	d																						
Earlswood (Surrey)	d																						
Tonbridge [4]	d							12 19															
Leigh (Kent)	d							12 23															
Penshurst	d							12 27															
Edenbridge	d							12 33															
Godstone	d							12 40															
Nutfield	d							12 45															
Reigate	d																						
Redhill [5]	a	12 47						12 50			13 02					13 10		13 15					
	d	12 48						12 51			13 07							13 16					
Merstham	d										13 11												
Coulsdon South	d							12 58			13 16												
Purley [4]	d				←	←	←	13 02			13 19										←	←	←
East Croydon ⇌	a	12 59	13 02	12 52	12 54	12 59	13 02	13 07		13 08	13 24	13 11			13 16			13 27	13 32	13 22	13 24	13 27	13 32
	d	13 00	13 02	12 53	12 55	13 00	13 02	13 07		13 08	13 25	13 12		13 14	13 17			13 28	13 32	13 23	13 25	13 28	13 32
Norwood Junction [2]	a	→	→		12 59			13 12			→							→	→		13 29		
New Cross Gate	d				13 07																13 37		
London Bridge [4] ⊖	a				13 13		13 17	13 25							13 32						13 43		13 47
London Blackfriars [3] ⊖	a																						
City Thameslink [3]	a																						
Farringdon [3] ⊖	a																						
St Pancras International [15] ⊖	a																						
St Albans City	a																						
Luton Airport Parkway [4] ✈	a																						
Luton [7]	a																						
Bedford [10]	a																						
Clapham Junction [10]	d			13 03		13 10				13 18		13 21		13 26						13 33		13 37	
London Victoria [15] ⊖	a			13 10		13 16			13 20	13 24		13 28		13 32			13 35			13 40		13 44	

Table 186

Saturdays

Brighton - London and Bedford

		SN	GW	SN	SN	SN	SN	SN	SN	FC	SN	SN	FC	SN	SN	SN	FC	SN	SN	SN	SN
		1	1		1	1	◇1	◇1	1	1	1	◇1	1	◇1	1	◇1	1	1	1	1	1
								B													
					🛒						🛒			🛒					🛒		
Brighton 10	d									13 04			13 07	13 19						13 24	
Hove 2	d							12 51													
Preston Park	d							12 55					13 11								
Hassocks 4	d												13 17							13 34	
Burgess Hill 4	d							13 04					13 21							13 38	
Lewes 4	d						12 50														
Wivelsfield 4	d												13 23								
Haywards Heath 3	a						13 05	13 09		13 16			13 28								
	d							13 14		13 17			13 32								
Balcombe	d												13 37								
Horsham 4	d					13 00						13 20									13 30
Littlehaven	d					13 03															13 33
Faygate	d																				
Ifield	d					13 09															13 39
Crawley	d					13 13						13 29									13 43
Three Bridges 4	a					13 16				13 26		13 32	13 42								13 46
	d					13 18				13 26		13 33	13 42								13 48
Gatwick Airport 10 ✈	a					13 22		13 25		13 30		13 37	13 46							13 51	13 52
	d				13 20	13 23		13 26		13 31	13 35	13 38	13 46						13 50	13 53	13 53
Horley 4	d					13 26						13 41									13 56
Salfords	d					13 30															
Earlswood (Surrey)	d					13 33															
Tonbridge 4	d																	13 19			
Leigh (Kent)	d																	13 23			
Penshurst	d																	13 27			
Edenbridge	d																	13 33			
Godstone	d																	13 40			
Nutfield	d																	13 45			
Reigate	d	13 14	13 18																		
Redhill 5	a	13 18	13 25			13 36						13 47						13 50			14 02
	d	13 19				13 37						13 48						13 51			14 07
Merstham	d	13 23				13 41															14 11
Coulsdon South	d	13 28				13 46												13 58			14 16
Purley 4	d	13 32				13 49									←	←	←	14 02			14 19
East Croydon	a	13 37				13 54		13 41		13 46		13 59	14 02	13 52	13 54	13 59	14 02	14 07		14 08	14 24
	d	13 37				13 55		13 42	13 44	13 47		14 00	14 02	13 53	13 55	14 00	14 02	14 07		14 08	14 25
Norwood Junction 2	a	13 42				→						→	→		13 59			14 12			→
New Cross Gate	d														14 07						
London Bridge 4 ⊖	a	13 55								14 02					14 13		14 17	14 25			
London Blackfriars 3 ⊖	a																				
City Thameslink 3	a																				
Farringdon 3 ⊖	a																				
St Pancras International 15 ⊖	a																				
St Albans City	a																				
Luton Airport Parkway 4 ✈	a																				
Luton 7	a																				
Bedford 10	a																				
Clapham Junction 10	d			13 41				13 51	13 56					14 03		14 10				14 18	
London Victoria 15 ⊖	a			13 48	13 50			13 58	14 02		14 05			14 10		14 16			14 20	14 24	

B ◇ from Haywards Heath

Table 186

Saturdays

Brighton - London and Bedford

		SN	SN	SN	FC	GW	SN	SN	FC	SN	SN	SN	FC	SN	GW	SN	SN	SN	SN	SN	SN	FC
		◇1	◇1	1	1	1	1	◇1	1	◇1	1	◇1	1	1	1		1	1	◇1	◇1	1	1
																				B		
							🛒	🛒		🛒		🛒					🛒					
Brighton 10	d				13 34				13 37	13 49												14 04
Hove 2	d	13 21																		13 51		
Preston Park	d								13 41											13 55		
Hassocks 4	d								13 47													
Burgess Hill 4	d								13 51											14 04		
Lewes 4	d		13 20																13 50			
Wivelsfield 4	d		13 35						13 53													
Haywards Heath 3	a	13 35	13 40		13 46				13 58										14 05	14 09		14 16
	d		13 44		13 47				14 02											14 14		14 17
Balcombe	d																					
Horsham 4	d							13 50										14 00				
Littlehaven	d																	14 03				
Faygate	d																					
Ifield	d																	14 09				
Crawley	d							13 59										14 13				
Three Bridges 4	a				13 56			14 02	14 11									14 16				14 26
	d				13 56			14 03	14 12									14 18				14 26
Gatwick Airport 10 ✈	a		13 55		14 00			14 07	14 16									14 22		14 25		14 30
	d		13 56		14 01	14 03	14 05	14 08	14 16								14 20	14 23		14 26		14 31
Horley 4	d																	14 26				
Salfords	d																	14 30				
Earlswood (Surrey)	d																	14 33				
Tonbridge 4	d																					
Leigh (Kent)	d																					
Penshurst	d																					
Edenbridge	d																					
Godstone	d																					
Nutfield	d																					
Reigate	d													14 14	14 19							
Redhill 5	a					14 10		14 15						14 18	14 25			14 36				
	d							14 16						14 19				14 37				
Merstham	d													14 23				14 41				
Coulsdon South	d													14 28				14 46				
Purley 4	d										←	←	←	14 32				14 49				
East Croydon	a		14 11		14 16			14 27	14 32	14 22	14 24	14 27	14 32	14 37				14 54		14 41		14 46
	d		14 12	14 14	14 17			14 28	14 32	14 23	14 25	14 28	14 32	14 37				14 55		14 42	14 44	14 47
Norwood Junction 2	a							→	→		14 29			14 42				→				
New Cross Gate	d										14 37											
London Bridge 4 ⊖	a				14 32						14 43		14 47	14 55								15 02
London Blackfriars 3 ⊖	a																					
City Thameslink 3	a																					
Farringdon 3 ⊖	a																					
St Pancras International 15 ⊖	a																					
St Albans City	a																					
Luton Airport Parkway 4 ✈	a																					
Luton 7	a																					
Bedford 10	a																					
Clapham Junction 10	d		14 21	14 26						14 33		14 37				14 41				14 51	14 56	
London Victoria 15 ⊖	a		14 28	14 32			14 35			14 40		14 44				14 48	14 50			14 58	15 02	

B ◇ from Haywards Heath

Brighton - London and Bedford

		SN	SN	FC	SN	SN	SN	FC	SN	SN	SN	SN	SN	SN	SN	FC	GW	SN	SN	FC	SN	SN	SN
		1	◇1	1	◇1	1	◇1	1	1	1	1	1	◇1	◇1	1	1	1	1	◇1	1	◇1	1	◇1
		⊼			⊼					⊼								⊼	⊼		⊼		⊼
Brighton 10	d			14 07	14 19						14 24					14 34				14 37	14 49		
Hove 2	d												14 21										
Preston Park	d			14 11																14 41			
Hassocks 4	d			14 17							14 34									14 47			
Burgess Hill 4	d			14 21							14 38									14 51			
Lewes 4	d													14 20									
Wivelsfield 4	d			14 23										14 35						14 53			
Haywards Heath 3	a			14 28									14 35	14 40		14 46				14 58			
	d			14 32									14 44			14 47				15 02			
Balcombe	d			14 37																			
Horsham 4	d		14 20									14 30							14 50				
Littlehaven	d											14 33											
Faygate	d																						
Ifield	d											14 39											
Crawley	d		14 29									14 43							14 59				
Three Bridges 4	a		14 32	14 42								14 46				14 56			15 02	15 11			
	d		14 33	14 42								14 48				14 56			15 03	15 12			
Gatwick Airport 10 ✈	a		14 37	14 46							14 51	14 52	14 55			15 00			15 07	15 16			
	d	14 35	14 38	14 46						14 50	14 53	14 53	14 56			15 01	15 03	15 05	15 08	15 16			
Horley 4	d		14 41									14 56											
Salfords	d																						
Earlswood (Surrey)	d																						
Tonbridge 4	d								14 19														
Leigh (Kent)	d								14 23														
Penshurst	d								14 27														
Edenbridge	d								14 33														
Godstone	d								14 40														
Nutfield	d								14 45														
Reigate	d																						
Redhill 5	a		14 47						14 50			15 02					15 10		15 15				
	d		14 48						14 51			15 07							15 16				
Merstham	d											15 11											
Coulsdon South	d								14 58			15 16											
Purley 4	d					←	←	←	15 02			15 19										←	←
East Croydon	a		14 59	15 02	14 52	14 54	14 59	15 02	15 07		15 08	15 24	15 11			15 16			15 27	15 32	15 22	15 24	15 27
	d		15 00	15 02	14 53	14 55	15 00	15 02	15 07		15 08	15 25	15 12		15 14	15 17			15 28	15 32	15 23	15 25	15 28
Norwood Junction 2	a		→	→		14 59			15 12			→							→	→		15 29	
New Cross Gate	d					15 07																15 37	
London Bridge 4 ⊖	a					15 13		15 17	15 25							15 32						15 43	
London Blackfriars 3 ⊖	a																						
City Thameslink 3	a																						
Farringdon 3 ⊖	a																						
St Pancras International 15 ⊖	a																						
St Albans City	a																						
Luton Airport Parkway 4 ✈	a																						
Luton 7	a																						
Bedford 10	a																						
Clapham Junction 10	d				15 03		15 10				15 18		15 21		15 26						15 33		15 37
London Victoria 15 ⊖	a	15 05			15 10		15 16			15 20	15 24		15 28		15 32			15 35			15 40		15 44

Brighton - London and Bedford

		FC	SN	GW	SN	SN	SN	SN	SN	SN	FC	SN	SN	FC	SN	SN	SN	FC	SN	SN	SN
		1	1	1		1	1	◇1	◇1	1	1	1	◇1	1	◇1	1	◇1	1	1	1	1
									B												
						⊼						⊼			⊼					⊼	
Brighton 10	d										15 04			15 07	15 19						15 24
Hove 2	d								14 51												
Preston Park	d								14 55					15 11							
Hassocks 4	d													15 17							15 34
Burgess Hill 4	d								15 04					15 21							15 38
Lewes 4	d							14 50													
Wivelsfield 4	d													15 23							
Haywards Heath 3	a							15 05	15 09		15 16			15 28							
	d							15 14			15 17			15 32							
Balcombe	d													15 37							
Horsham 4	d						15 00						15 20								
Littlehaven	d						15 03														
Faygate	d																				
Ifield	d						15 09														
Crawley	d						15 13						15 29								
Three Bridges 4	a						15 16				15 26		15 32	15 42							
	d						15 18				15 26		15 33	15 42							
Gatwick Airport 10 ✈	a						15 22	15 25			15 30		15 37	15 46							15 51
	d					15 20	15 23	15 26			15 31	15 35	15 38	15 46						15 50	15 53
Horley 4	d						15 26						15 41								
Salfords	d						15 30														
Earlswood (Surrey)	d						15 33														
Tonbridge 4	d																		15 19		
Leigh (Kent)	d																		15 23		
Penshurst	d																		15 27		
Edenbridge	d																		15 33		
Godstone	d																		15 40		
Nutfield	d																		15 45		
Reigate	d		15 14	15 18																	
Redhill 5	a		15 18	15 25			15 36						15 47						15 50		
	d		15 19				15 37						15 48						15 51		
Merstham	d		15 23				15 41														
Coulsdon South	d		15 28				15 46												15 58		
Purley 4	d	←	15 32				15 49									←	←	←	16 02		
East Croydon	a	15 32	15 37				15 54	15 41			15 46		15 59	16 02	15 52	15 54	15 59	16 02	16 07		16 08
	d	15 32	15 37				15 55	15 42		15 44	15 47		16 00	16 02	15 53	15 55	16 00	16 02	16 07		16 08
Norwood Junction 2	a		15 42				→						→	→		15 59			16 12		
New Cross Gate	d															16 07					
London Bridge 4 ⊖	a	15 47	15 55								16 02					16 13		16 17	16 25		
London Blackfriars 3 ⊖	a																				
City Thameslink 3	a																				
Farringdon 3 ⊖	a																				
St Pancras International 15 ⊖	a																				
St Albans City	a																				
Luton Airport Parkway 4 ✈	a																				
Luton 7	a																				
Bedford 10	a																				
Clapham Junction 10	d				15 41			15 51		15 56					16 03		16 10				16 18
London Victoria 15 ⊖	a				15 48	15 50		15 58		16 02		16 05			16 10		16 16			16 20	16 24

B ◇ from Haywards Heath

Brighton - London and Bedford

		SN 1	SN ◇1	SN ◇1	SN 1	FC 1	GW 1	SN 1 H	SN ◇1 H	FC 1	SN ◇1 H	SN 1	SN ◇1 H	FC 1	SN 1	GW 1	SN	SN 1 H	SN 1	SN ◇1	SN ◇1 B	SN 1
Brighton 10	d					15 34				15 37	15 49											
Hove 2	d		15 21																		15 51	
Preston Park	d									15 41											15 55	
Hassocks 4	d									15 47												
Burgess Hill 4	d									15 51											16 04	
Lewes 4	d			15 20																15 50		
Wivelsfield 4	d			15 35						15 53												
Haywards Heath 3	a		15 35	15 40		15 46				15 58										16 05	16 09	
	d		15 44			15 47				16 02										16 14		
Balcombe	d																					
Horsham 4	d	15 30							15 50										16 00			
Littlehaven	d	15 33																	16 03			
Faygate	d																					
Ifield	d	15 39																	16 09			
Crawley	d	15 43							15 59										16 13			
Three Bridges 4	a	15 46				15 56			16 02	16 11									16 16			
	d	15 48				15 56			16 03	16 12									16 18			
Gatwick Airport 10 ✈	a	15 52	15 55			16 00			16 07	16 16									16 22	16 25		
	d	15 53	15 56			16 01	16 03	16 05	16 08	16 16								16 20	16 23	16 26		
Horley 4	d	15 56																	16 26			
Salfords	d																		16 30			
Earlswood (Surrey)	d																		16 33			
Tonbridge 4	d																					
Leigh (Kent)	d																					
Penshurst	d																					
Edenbridge	d																					
Godstone	d																					
Nutfield	d																					
Reigate	d														16 14	16 19						
Redhill 5	a	16 02					16 10		16 15						16 18	16 25			16 36			
	d	16 07							16 16						16 19				16 37			
Merstham	d	16 11													16 23				16 41			
Coulsdon South	d	16 16													16 28				16 46			
Purley 4	d	16 19										←	←	←	16 32				16 49			
East Croydon	a	16 24	16 11			16 16			16 27	16 32	16 22	16 24	16 27	16 32	16 37				16 54	16 41		
	d	16 25	16 12		16 14	16 17			16 28	16 32	16 23	16 25	16 28	16 32	16 37				16 55	16 42		16 44
Norwood Junction 2	a	→							→	→		16 29			16 42				→			
New Cross Gate	d											16 37										
London Bridge 4 ⊖	a					16 32						16 43		16 47	16 55							
London Blackfriars 3 ⊖	a																					
City Thameslink 3	a																					
Farringdon 3 ⊖	a																					
St Pancras International 15 ⊖	a																					
St Albans City	a																					
Luton Airport Parkway 4 ✈	a																					
Luton 7	a																					
Bedford 10	a																					
Clapham Junction 10	d		16 21		16 26						16 33		16 37				16 41			16 51		16 56
London Victoria 15 ⊖	a		16 28		16 32			16 35			16 40		16 44				16 48	16 50		16 58		17 02

B ◇ from Haywards Heath

Brighton - London and Bedford

		FC 1	SN 1 H	SN ◇1	FC 1	SN ◇1 H	SN 1	SN ◇1	FC 1	SN 1	SN 1 H	SN 1	SN 1	SN ◇1	SN ◇1	SN 1	FC 1	GW 1	SN 1 H	SN ◇1 H	FC 1	SN ◇1 H
Brighton 10	d	16 04			16 07	16 19						16 24					16 34				16 37	16 49
Hove 2	d													16 21								
Preston Park	d				16 11																16 41	
Hassocks 4	d				16 17							16 34									16 47	
Burgess Hill 4	d				16 21							16 38									16 51	
Lewes 4	d														16 20							
Wivelsfield 4	d				16 23										16 35						16 53	
Haywards Heath 3	a	16 16			16 28									16 35	16 40		16 46				16 58	
	d	16 17			16 32									16 44			16 47				17 02	
Balcombe	d				16 37																	
Horsham 4	d			16 20									16 30							16 50		
Littlehaven	d												16 33									
Faygate	d																					
Ifield	d												16 39									
Crawley	d			16 29									16 43							16 59		
Three Bridges 4	a	16 26		16 32	16 42								16 46				16 56			17 02	17 11	
	d	16 26		16 33	16 42								16 48				16 56			17 03	17 12	
Gatwick Airport 10 ✈	a	16 30		16 37	16 46							16 51	16 52	16 55			17 00			17 07	17 16	
	d	16 31	16 35	16 38	16 46						16 50	16 53	16 53	16 56			17 01	17 03	17 05	17 08	17 16	
Horley 4	d			16 41									16 56									
Salfords	d																					
Earlswood (Surrey)	d																					
Tonbridge 4	d									16 19												
Leigh (Kent)	d									16 23												
Penshurst	d									16 27												
Edenbridge	d									16 33												
Godstone	d									16 40												
Nutfield	d									16 45												
Reigate	d																					
Redhill 5	a			16 47						16 50			17 02					17 10		17 15		
	d			16 48						16 51			17 07							17 16		
Merstham	d												17 11									
Coulsdon South	d									16 58			17 16									
Purley 4	d						←	←	←	17 02			17 19									
East Croydon	a	16 46		16 59	17 02	16 52	16 54	16 59	17 02	17 07		17 08	17 24	17 11			17 16			17 27	17 32	17 22
	d	16 47		17 00	17 02	16 53	16 55	17 00	17 02	17 07		17 08	17 25	17 12		17 14	17 17			17 28	17 32	17 23
Norwood Junction 2	a			→	→		16 59			17 12			→							→	→	
New Cross Gate	d						17 07															
London Bridge 4 ⊖	a	17 02					17 13		17 17	17 25							17 32					
London Blackfriars 3 ⊖	a																					
City Thameslink 3	a																					
Farringdon 3 ⊖	a																					
St Pancras International 15 ⊖	a																					
St Albans City	a																					
Luton Airport Parkway 4 ✈	a																					
Luton 7	a																					
Bedford 10	a																					
Clapham Junction 10	d					17 03		17 10				17 18		17 21		17 26						17 33
London Victoria 15 ⊖	a		17 05			17 10		17 16			17 20	17 24		17 28		17 32			17 35			17 40

Brighton - London and Bedford

		SN	SN	FC	SN	GW	SN	SN	SN	SN	SN	SN	FC	SN	SN	FC	SN	SN	SN	FC	SN	SN
		1	◇1	1	1	1		1	1	◇1	◇1	1	1	1	◇1	1	◇1	1	◇1	1	1	1
											B											
			✠					✠						✠			✠					✠
Brighton 10	d												17 04			17 07	17 19					
Hove 2	d										16 51											
Preston Park	d										16 55					17 11						
Hassocks 4	d															17 17						
Burgess Hill 4	d										17 04					17 21						
Lewes 4	d									16 50												
Wivelsfield 4	d															17 23						
Haywards Heath 3	a									17 05	17 09		17 16			17 28						
	d									17 14			17 17			17 32						
Balcombe	d															17 37						
Horsham 4	d								17 00						17 20							
Littlehaven	d								17 03													
Faygate	d																					
Ifield	d								17 09													
Crawley	d								17 13						17 29							
Three Bridges 4	a								17 16				17 26		17 32	17 42						
	d								17 18				17 26		17 33	17 42						
Gatwick Airport 10 ✈	a								17 22	17 25			17 30		17 37	17 46						
	d							17 20	17 23	17 26			17 31	17 35	17 38	17 46						17 50
Horley 4	d								17 26						17 41							
Salfords	d								17 30													
Earlswood (Surrey)	d								17 33													
Tonbridge 4	d																				17 19	
Leigh (Kent)	d																				17 23	
Penshurst	d																				17 27	
Edenbridge	d																				17 33	
Godstone	d																				17 40	
Nutfield	d																				17 45	
Reigate	d				17 14	17 18																
Redhill 5	a				17 18	17 25			17 36						17 47						17 50	
	d				17 19				17 37						17 48						17 51	
Merstham	d				17 23				17 41													
Coulsdon South	d				17 28				17 46												17 58	
Purley 4	d	←	←	←	17 32				17 49									←	←	←	18 02	
East Croydon	a	17 24	17 27	17 32	17 37				17 54	17 41			17 46		17 59	18 02	17 52	17 54	17 59	18 02	18 07	
	d	17 25	17 28	17 32	17 37				17 55	17 42		17 44	17 47		18 00	18 02	17 53	17 55	18 00	18 02	18 07	
Norwood Junction 2	a	17 29			17 42				→						→	→		17 59			18 12	
New Cross Gate	d	17 37																18 07				
London Bridge 4 ⊖	a	17 45		17 47	17 55								18 02					18 13		18 17	18 25	
London Blackfriars 3 ⊖	a																					
City Thameslink 3	a																					
Farringdon 3 ⊖	a																					
St Pancras International 15 ⊖	a																					
St Albans City	a																					
Luton Airport Parkway 4 ✈	a																					
Luton 7	a																					
Bedford 10	a																					
Clapham Junction 10	d		17 37				17 42			17 51		17 56					18 03		18 10			
London Victoria 15 ⊖	a		17 44				17 49	17 50		17 58		18 02		18 05			18 10		18 16			18 20

B ◇ from Haywards Heath

Brighton - London and Bedford

		SN	SN	SN	SN	SN	FC	GW	SN	SN	FC	SN	SN	SN	FC	SN	GW	SN	SN	SN	SN	SN
		1	1	◇1	◇1	1	1	1	1	◇1	1	◇1	1	◇1	1	1	1		1	1	◇1	◇1
																						B
									✠	✠		✠		✠					✠			
Brighton 10	d	17 24					17 34				17 37	17 49										
Hove 2	d			17 21																		17 51
Preston Park	d										17 41											17 55
Hassocks 4	d	17 34									17 47											
Burgess Hill 4	d	17 38									17 51											18 04
Lewes 4	d				17 20																17 50	
Wivelsfield 4	d				17 35						17 53											
Haywards Heath 3	a			17 35	17 40		17 46				17 58										18 05	18 09
	d			17 44			17 47				18 02										18 14	
Balcombe	d																					
Horsham 4	d		17 30							17 50										18 00		
Littlehaven	d		17 33																	18 03		
Faygate	d																					
Ifield	d		17 39																	18 09		
Crawley	d		17 43							17 59										18 13		
Three Bridges 4	a		17 46				17 56			18 02	18 11									18 16		
	d		17 48				17 56			18 03	18 12									18 18		
Gatwick Airport 10 ✈	a	17 51	17 52	17 55			18 00			18 07	18 16									18 22	18 25	
	d	17 53	17 53	17 56			18 01	18 03	18 05	18 08	18 16								18 20	18 23	18 26	
Horley 4	d		17 56																	18 26		
Salfords	d																			18 30		
Earlswood (Surrey)	d																			18 33		
Tonbridge 4	d																					
Leigh (Kent)	d																					
Penshurst	d																					
Edenbridge	d																					
Godstone	d																					
Nutfield	d																					
Reigate	d															18 14	18 19					
Redhill 5	a		18 02					18 10		18 15						18 18	18 25			18 36		
	d		18 07							18 16						18 19				18 37		
Merstham	d		18 11													18 23				18 41		
Coulsdon South	d		18 16													18 28				18 46		
Purley 4	d		18 19										←	←	←	18 32				18 49		
East Croydon	a	18 08	18 24	18 11			18 16			18 27	18 32	18 22	18 24	18 27	18 32	18 37				18 54	18 41	
	d	18 08	18 25	18 12		18 14	18 17			18 28	18 32	18 23	18 25	18 28	18 32	18 37				18 55	18 42	
Norwood Junction 2	a		→							→	→		18 29			18 42				→		
New Cross Gate	d												18 37									
London Bridge 4 ⊖	a						18 32						18 43		18 47	18 55						
London Blackfriars 3 ⊖	a																					
City Thameslink 3	a																					
Farringdon 3 ⊖	a																					
St Pancras International 15 ⊖	a																					
St Albans City	a																					
Luton Airport Parkway 4 ✈	a																					
Luton 7	a																					
Bedford 10	a																					
Clapham Junction 10	d	18 18		18 21		18 26						18 33		18 37				18 41			18 51	
London Victoria 15 ⊖	a	18 24		18 28		18 32			18 35			18 40		18 44				18 48	18 50		18 58	

B ◇ from Haywards Heath

Table 186

Saturdays

Brighton - London and Bedford

Station		SN	FC	SN	SN ◇	FC	SN ◇	SN	SN ◇	FC	SN	SN	SN	SN	SN ◇	SN ◇	SN	FC	GW	SN	SN ◇	SN
Brighton	d		18 04			18 07	18 19						18 24					18 34				
Hove	d														18 21							
Preston Park	d					18 11																
Hassocks	d					18 17							18 34									
Burgess Hill	d					18 21							18 38									
Lewes	d															18 20						
Wivelsfield	d					18 23										18 35						
Haywards Heath	a		18 16			18 28									18 35	18 40		18 46				
	d		18 17			18 32									18 44			18 47				
Balcombe	d					18 37																
Horsham	d				18 20									18 32							18 50	
Littlehaven	d													18 35								
Faygate	d																					
Ifield	d													18 41								
Crawley	d				18 29									18 45							18 59	
Three Bridges	a		18 26		18 32	18 42								18 48				18 56			19 02	
	d		18 26		18 33	18 42								18 50				18 56			19 03	
Gatwick Airport	a		18 30		18 37	18 46							18 51	18 54	18 55			19 00			19 07	
	d		18 31	18 35	18 38	18 46						18 50	18 53	18 55	18 56			19 01	19 03	19 05	19 08	
Horley	d				18 41									18 58							19 11	
Salfords	d																					
Earlswood (Surrey)	d																					
Tonbridge	d										18 19											
Leigh (Kent)	d										18 23											
Penshurst	d										18 27											
Edenbridge	d										18 33											
Godstone	d										18 40											
Nutfield	d										18 45											
Reigate	d																					19 14
Redhill	a				18 47						18 50			19 04					19 10		19 17	19 18
	d				18 48						18 51			19 07							19 18	
Merstham	d													19 11								
Coulsdon South	d										18 58			19 16								
Purley	d							←	←	←	19 02			19 19								
East Croydon	a		18 46		18 59	19 02	18 52	18 54	18 59	19 02	19 07		19 08	19 24	19 11			19 16			19 28	
	d	18 44	18 47		19 00	19 02	18 53	18 55	19 00	19 02	19 07		19 08	19 25	19 12		19 14	19 17			19 29	
Norwood Junction	a				→	→		18 59			19 12			→							→	
New Cross Gate	d							19 07														
London Bridge	a		19 02					19 13		19 17	19 25							19 32				
London Blackfriars	a																					
City Thameslink	a																					
Farringdon	a																					
St Pancras International	a																					
St Albans City	a																					
Luton Airport Parkway	a																					
Luton	a																					
Bedford	a																					
Clapham Junction	d	18 56					19 03		19 10				19 18		19 21		19 26					
London Victoria	a	19 02		19 05			19 10		19 16			19 20	19 24		19 28		19 32			19 35		

Table 186

Saturdays

Brighton - London and Bedford

Station		GW	FC	SN ◇	SN	SN	SN ◇	FC	SN	SN ◇	SN	SN ◇	SN ◇ A	SN	SN	FC	SN	SN	FC	SN ◇	SN	SN	SN
Brighton	d		18 37	18 49						18 54						19 04			19 07	19 19			
Hove	d												18 51										
Preston Park	d		18 41										18 55						19 11				
Hassocks	d		18 47							19 06									19 17				
Burgess Hill	d		18 51										19 04						19 21				
Lewes	d											18 50											
Wivelsfield	d		18 53																19 23				
Haywards Heath	a		18 58									19 05	19 09			19 16			19 28				
	d		19 02									19 14				19 17			19 32				
Balcombe	d																		19 37				
Horsham	d										19 02							19 21					
Littlehaven	d										19 05												
Faygate	d																						
Ifield	d										19 11												
Crawley	d										19 14							19 30					
Three Bridges	a		19 11								19 18					19 26		19 33	19 42				
	d		19 12								19 18					19 26		19 34	19 42				
Gatwick Airport	a		19 16							19 21	19 22	19 25				19 30		19 38	19 46				
	d		19 16						19 20	19 23	19 23	19 26				19 31	19 35	19 39	19 46				
Horley	d										19 26												
Salfords	d										19 30												
Earlswood (Surrey)	d										19 33												
Tonbridge	d													19 10									
Leigh (Kent)	d													19 14									
Penshurst	d													19 18									
Edenbridge	d													19 24									
Godstone	d													19 31									
Nutfield	d													19 36									
Reigate	d	19 18																					
Redhill	a	19 25									19 36			19 45				19 47					
	d										19 37							19 48					
Merstham	d										19 41												
Coulsdon South	d										19 46												
Purley	d				←		←	←			19 49										←		←
East Croydon	a		19 32	19 22	19 24		19 28	19 32		19 38	19 54	19 41				19 46		19 59	20 02	19 52	19 54		19 59
	d		19 32	19 23	19 25		19 29	19 32		19 38	19 57	19 42			19 44	19 47		20 00	20 02	19 53	19 57		20 00
Norwood Junction	a		→								→							→	→				
New Cross Gate	d																						
London Bridge	a							19 47								20 02							
London Blackfriars	a																						
City Thameslink	a																						
Farringdon	a																						
St Pancras International	a																						
St Albans City	a																						
Luton Airport Parkway	a																						
Luton	a																						
Bedford	a																						
Clapham Junction	d			19 33	19 37	19 41	19 40			19 48		19 51			19 56					20 03	20 09	20 11	20 12
London Victoria	a			19 40	19 44	19 48	19 50		19 50	19 54		19 58			20 05		20 05			20 10	20 15	20 18	20 20

A ◇ from Haywards Heath

Brighton - London and Bedford

		FC 1	SN 1		SN 1	SN ◇1	SN ◇1 A	SN 1	FC 1	GW 1	SN 1	SN ◇1	GW 1		FC 1	SN ◇1	SN 1	SN	SN ◇1	FC 1	SN 1	SN 1	SN ◇1	SN ◇1 A
Brighton 10	d								19 34						19 37	19 49								
Hove 2	d					19 21																		19 52
Preston Park	d														19 41									
Hassocks 4	d														19 47									
Burgess Hill 4	d														19 51									20 02
Lewes 4	d						19 20																19 50	
Wivelsfield 4	d						19 35								19 53								20 02	
Haywards Heath 3	a					19 35	19 40		19 46						19 58								20 07	20 10
	d					19 44			19 47						20 02								20 14	
Balcombe	d																							
Horsham 4	d				19 32							19 52										20 02		
Littlehaven	d				19 35																	20 05		
Faygate	d																							
Ifield	d				19 41																	20 11		
Crawley	d				19 45							20 01										20 14		
Three Bridges 4	a				19 48				19 56			20 05			20 11							20 18		
	d				19 50				19 56			20 05			20 12							20 18		
Gatwick Airport 10 ✈	a				19 54	19 55			20 00			20 10			20 16							20 22	20 25	
	d		19 50		19 55	19 56			20 01	20 03	20 05	20 11			20 16						20 20	20 23	20 26	
Horley 4	d				19 58																	20 26		
Salfords	d																					20 30		
Earlswood (Surrey)	d																					20 33		
Tonbridge 4	d																							
Leigh (Kent)	d																							
Penshurst	d																							
Edenbridge	d																							
Godstone	d																							
Nutfield	d																							
Reigate	d												20 19											
Redhill 5	a				20 04					20 10		20 18	20 25									20 36		
	d				20 07							20 18										20 37		
Merstham	d				20 11																	20 41		
Coulsdon South	d				20 16																	20 46		
Purley 4	d	←			20 19												←		←	←		20 49		
East Croydon	a	20 02			20 24	20 11			20 16			20 30			20 32	20 22	20 24		20 30	20 32		20 54	20 41	
	d	20 02			20 26	20 12		20 14	20 17			20 30			20 32	20 23	20 26		20 30	20 32		20 56	20 42	
Norwood Junction 2	a				→							→			→							→		
New Cross Gate	d																							
London Bridge 4 ⊖	a	20 17							20 32											20 47				
London Blackfriars 3 ⊖	a																							
City Thameslink 3	a																							
Farringdon 3 ⊖	a																							
St Pancras International 15 ⊖	a																							
St Albans City	a																							
Luton Airport Parkway 4 ✈	a																							
Luton 7	a																							
Bedford 10	a																							
Clapham Junction 10	d					20 21		20 26								20 33	20 37	20 41	20 41				20 51	
London Victoria 15 ⊖	a		20 20			20 28		20 32			20 35					20 40	20 44	20 48	20 50		20 50		20 58	

A ◇ from Haywards Heath

Brighton - London and Bedford

		SN 1	SN 1	SN ◇1	FC 1	SN 1	FC 1	SN ◇1	SN 1	SN ◇1		FC 1	SN	SN 1	SN ◇1	SN 1	SN 1	FC 1	GW 1	SN 1		SN ◇1	GW 1	FC 1	SN ◇1
Brighton 10	d			19 54	20 04		20 07	20 19										20 34						20 37	20 49
Hove 2	d														20 22										
Preston Park	d			19 57			20 11																	20 41	
Hassocks 4	d			20 04			20 17																	20 47	
Burgess Hill 4	d			20 07			20 21																	20 51	
Lewes 4	d																								
Wivelsfield 4	d			20 10			20 23																	20 53	
Haywards Heath 3	a			20 14	20 17		20 28								20 35			20 46						20 58	
	d			20 22	20 18		20 32								20 38			20 47						21 02	
Balcombe	d						20 37																		
Horsham 4	d																20 32					20 52			
Littlehaven	d																20 35								
Faygate	d																								
Ifield	d																20 41								
Crawley	d																20 45					21 01			
Three Bridges 4	a			20 32	20 26		20 42								20 47		20 48	20 56				21 05		21 11	
	d			20 32	20 26		20 42								20 47		20 51	20 56				21 05		21 12	
Gatwick Airport 10 ✈	a			20 37	20 31		20 46								20 51		20 56	21 00				21 10		21 16	
	d			20 38	20 31	20 35	20 46							20 50	20 53		20 57	21 01	21 03	21 05		21 11		21 16	
Horley 4	d																20 59								
Salfords	d																								
Earlswood (Surrey)	d																								
Tonbridge 4	d	20 10																							
Leigh (Kent)	d	20 14																							
Penshurst	d	20 18																							
Edenbridge	d	20 24																							
Godstone	d	20 31																							
Nutfield	d	20 36																							
Reigate	d																						21 18		
Redhill 5	a	20 45		20 47													21 06		21 10			21 18	21 25		
	d			20 48													21 07					21 18			
Merstham	d																21 11								
Coulsdon South	d																21 16								
Purley 4	d								←	←		←					21 19								
East Croydon	a			20 59	20 47		21 02	20 52	20 54	20 59		21 02			21 08		21 24	21 16				21 30		21 32	21 22
	d		20 44	21 00	20 47		21 02	20 53	20 56	21 00		21 02			21 09	21 14	21 26	21 17				21 30		21 32	21 23
Norwood Junction 2	a			→			→										→					→		→	
New Cross Gate	d																								
London Bridge 4 ⊖	a				21 02							21 17						21 32							
London Blackfriars 3 ⊖	a																								
City Thameslink 3	a																								
Farringdon 3 ⊖	a																								
St Pancras International 15 ⊖	a																								
St Albans City	a																								
Luton Airport Parkway 4 ✈	a																								
Luton 7	a																								
Bedford 10	a																								
Clapham Junction 10	d		20 56					21 03	21 07	21 11			21 11		21 18	21 26									21 33
London Victoria 15 ⊖	a		21 02			21 05		21 10	21 14	21 17			21 18	21 20	21 26	21 32				21 35					21 40

Brighton - London and Bedford

Station		SN 1	SN	SN ◇1	FC 1	SN 1	SN 1	SN ◇1	SN ◇1 A	SN 1	SN 1	SN 1	SN ◇1	FC 1	SN ◇1	SN 1	SN	SN ◇1	FC 1	SN 1	SN ◇1	SN 1	SN 1
Brighton 10	d												21 00	21 07	21 19								
Hove 2	d								20 52												21 22		
Preston Park	d												21 04	21 11									
Hassocks 4	d												21 10	21 17									
Burgess Hill 4	d								21 04				21 14	21 21									
Lewes 4	d							20 50															
Wivelsfield 4	d							21 04					21 16	21 23									
Haywards Heath 3	a							21 09	21 11				21 21	21 28							21 35		
	d							21 15					21 22	21 32							21 38		
Balcombe	d													21 37									
Horsham 4	d						21 02																21 32
Littlehaven	d						21 05																21 35
Faygate	d																						
Ifield	d						21 11																21 41
Crawley	d						21 14																21 45
Three Bridges 4	a						21 18						21 32	21 42							21 47		21 48
	d						21 18						21 32	21 42							21 47		21 52
Gatwick Airport 10 ✈	a						21 22	21 26					21 37	21 46							21 51		21 56
	d					21 20	21 23	21 27				21 35	21 38	21 46						21 50	21 53		21 57
Horley 4	d						21 26																22 00
Salfords	d						21 30																
Earlswood (Surrey)	d						21 33																
Tonbridge 4	d									21 10													
Leigh (Kent)	d									21 14													
Penshurst	d									21 18													
Edenbridge	d									21 24													
Godstone	d									21 31													
Nutfield	d									21 36													
Reigate	d																						
Redhill 5	a						21 36			21 41			21 47										22 06
	d						21 37						21 48										22 07
Merstham	d						21 41																22 11
Coulsdon South	d						21 46																22 16
Purley 4	d	←		←	←		21 49									←		←	←				22 19
East Croydon	a	21 24		21 30	21 32		21 54	21 42					21 59	22 02	21 52	21 54		21 59	22 02		22 08		22 24
	d	21 26		21 30	21 32		21 56	21 42			21 44		22 00	22 02	21 53	21 56		22 00	22 02		22 09	22 14	22 26
Norwood Junction 2	a						→						→	→									→
New Cross Gate	d																						
London Bridge 4 ⊖	a				21 47														22 17				
London Blackfriars 3 ⊖	a																						
City Thameslink 3	a																						
Farringdon 3 ⊖	a																						
St Pancras International 15 ⊖	a																						
St Albans City	a																						
Luton Airport Parkway 4 ✈	a																						
Luton 7	a																						
Bedford 10	a																						
Clapham Junction 10	d	21 37	21 41	21 41				21 52			21 56				22 03	22 07	22 11	22 11			22 18	22 26	
London Victoria 15 ⊖	a	21 44	21 48	21 50		21 50		21 58			22 02	22 05			22 13	22 15	22 18	22 20		22 20	22 26	22 35	

A ◇ from Haywards Heath

Brighton - London and Bedford

Station		SN 1	SN ◇1	FC 1	SN ◇1	SN 1	SN	SN ◇1	FC 1	SN 1	GW 1	SN 1	SN ◇1 ⌶	SN ◇1 A ⌶	SN 1	SN 1	SN 1	SN 1	SN ◇1	FC 1	SN 1	SN
Brighton 10	d			21 37	21 49														22 00	22 07		
Hove 2	d													21 52								
Preston Park	d			21 41															22 04	22 11		
Hassocks 4	d			21 47															22 10	22 17		
Burgess Hill 4	d			21 51										22 04					22 14	22 21		
Lewes 4	d												21 50									
Wivelsfield 4	d			21 53									22 02						22 16	22 23		
Haywards Heath 3	a			21 58									22 06	22 09					22 21	22 28		
	d			22 02									22 13						22 22	22 32		
Balcombe	d																			22 37		
Horsham 4	d		21 52									22 02										
Littlehaven	d											22 05										
Faygate	d																					
Ifield	d											22 11										
Crawley	d		22 01									22 14										
Three Bridges 4	a		22 05	22 11								22 18							22 32	22 42		
	d		22 05	22 12								22 19							22 32	22 42		
Gatwick Airport 10 ✈	a		22 10	22 16								22 23	22 24						22 37	22 46		
	d	22 05	22 11	22 16						22 20	22 22	22 24	22 25			22 35			22 38	22 46	22 50	
Horley 4	d											22 27										
Salfords	d											22 31										
Earlswood (Surrey)	d											22 34										
Tonbridge 4	d														22 10							
Leigh (Kent)	d														22 14							
Penshurst	d														22 18							
Edenbridge	d														22 24							
Godstone	d														22 31							
Nutfield	d														22 36							
Reigate	d																					
Redhill 5	a		22 18								22 30	22 37			22 42				22 46			
	d		22 18									22 38							22 47			
Merstham	d											22 42										
Coulsdon South	d											22 47										
Purley 4	d					←		←	←			22 50						←				
East Croydon	a		22 30	22 32	22 22	22 24		22 30	22 32			22 55	22 40					22 55	22 59	23 02		
	d		22 30	22 32	22 23	22 26		22 30	22 32			22 56	22 40				22 44	22 56	23 00	23 02		
Norwood Junction 2	a		→	→								→										
New Cross Gate	d																					
London Bridge 4 ⊖	a								22 47											23 17		
London Blackfriars 3 ⊖	a																					
City Thameslink 3	a																					
Farringdon 3 ⊖	a																					
St Pancras International 15 ⊖	a																					
St Albans City	a																					
Luton Airport Parkway 4 ✈	a																					
Luton 7	a																					
Bedford 10	a																					
Clapham Junction 10	d				22 33	22 37	22 41	22 41					22 50				22 56	23 07	23 11			23 11
London Victoria 15 ⊖	a	22 35			22 40	22 44	22 48	22 50		22 50			22 57			23 05	23 05	23 14	23 20		23 20	23 22

A ⌶ from Haywards Heath ◇ from Haywards Heath

Brighton - London and Bedford

		SN	SN	FC	SN	FC	GW	SN		SN	SN	SN	SN	FC	SN	SN	FC
		1	1	1	◇1	1	1	1		1	1	1	◇1	1	1	◇1	1
Brighton 10	d			22 33									23 02	23 11			23 37
Hove 2	d																
Preston Park	d			22 37									23 06				23 41
Hassocks 4	d			22 43									23 12	23 19			23 47
Burgess Hill 4	d			22 47									23 16	23 23			23 51
Lewes 4	d				22 40												
Wivelsfield 4	d			22 49	22 54								23 19				23 53
Haywards Heath 3	a			22 54	22 58								23 23	23 27			23 58
	d			22 54	22 59								23 24	23 28			23 59
Balcombe	d			23 00													00 04
Horsham 4	d									23 02							
Littlehaven	d									23 05							
Faygate	d																
Ifield	d									23 11							
Crawley	d									23 14							
Three Bridges 4	a			23 05	23 08					23 18			23 33	23 38			00 10
	d			23 12	23 08					23 18			23 47	23 38			00 10
Gatwick Airport 10 ✈	a			23 16	23 12					23 22			23 52	23 42			00 14
	d	23 05		23 16	23 13		23 18	23 20		23 23		23 35	23 53	23 43	23 50		00 15
Horley 4	d									23 26			23 56				
Salfords	d									23 30							
Earlswood (Surrey)	d									23 33							
Tonbridge 4	d										23 17						
Leigh (Kent)	d										23 21						
Penshurst	d										23 25						
Edenbridge	d										23 31						
Godstone	d										23 38						
Nutfield	d										23 43						
Reigate	d																
Redhill 5	a						23 25			23 36	23 49		00 03				00 22
	d									23 37			00 03				00 22
Merstham	d									23 41							
Coulsdon South	d									23 46							
Purley 4	d					←				23 49			00 11			←	
East Croydon	a			23 32	23 30	23 32				23 55			00 16	00 02		00 16	00 35
	d		23 14	23 32	23 30	23 32				23 56			00 17	00 04		00 17	00 36
Norwood Junction 2	a			→									→				
New Cross Gate	d																
London Bridge 4 ⊖	a					23 47								00 19			00 52
London Blackfriars 3 ⊖	a																
City Thameslink 3	a																
Farringdon 3 ⊖	a																
St Pancras International 15 ⊖	a																
St Albans City	a																
Luton Airport Parkway 4 ✈	a																
Luton 7	a																
Bedford 10	a																
Clapham Junction 10	d		23 26		23 42					00 11						00 29	
London Victoria 15 ⊖	a	23 35	23 35		23 52			23 55		00 18		00 10			00 25	00 36	

Brighton - London and Bedford

until 4 September

		SN	SN	SN	FC	SN	SN	SN	FC	SN		SN	SN	SN	SN	SN	SN	SN	SN	SN		FC	SN	SN	SN
		1	1	◇1	1	1	◇1	1	1	1			1	1	1	1	1	1	1	1		1	1	1	1
		A	A	A	A	A	A		A																
Brighton 10	d			23p02	23p11				23p37																
Hove 2	d																								
Preston Park	d			23p06					23p41																
Hassocks 4	d			23p12	23p19				23p47																
Burgess Hill 4	d			23p16	23p23				23p51																
Lewes 4	d																								
Wivelsfield 4	d			23p19					23p53																
Haywards Heath 3	a			23p23	23p27				23p58																
	d			23p24	23p28				23p59																
Balcombe	d								00 04																
Horsham 4	d	23p02																							
Littlehaven	d	23p05																							
Faygate	d																								
Ifield	d	23p11																							
Crawley	d	23p14																							
Three Bridges 4	a	23p18		23p33	23p38				00 10																
	d	23p18		23p47	23p38				00 10						01 10		02 10	03 10	04 10			05 10		05 30	
Gatwick Airport 10 ✈	a	23p22		23p52	23p42				00 14						01 19		02 14	03 14	04 14			05 14		05 34	
	d	23p23	23p35	23p53	23p43	23p50		00 05	00 15	00 20			00 35	00 50	01 20	01 35	02 15	03 15	04 15	04 35		05 15	05 20	05 36	05 50
Horley 4	d	23p26		23p56											01 22		02 18	03 18	04 18					05 38	
Salfords	d	23p30																							
Earlswood (Surrey)	d	23p33																							
Tonbridge 4	d																								
Leigh (Kent)	d																								
Penshurst	d																								
Edenbridge	d																								
Godstone	d																								
Nutfield	d																								
Reigate	d																								
Redhill 5	a	23p36		00 03					00 22															05 46	
	d	23p37		00 03					00 22															05 46	
Merstham	d	23p41																							
Coulsdon South	d	23p46																							
Purley 4	d	23p49		00 11			←								01 37		02 33	03 33	04 33					05 56	
East Croydon	a	23p55		00 16	00 02		00 16		00 35						01 42		02 39	03 39	04 39			05 31		06 01	
	d	23p56		00 17	00 04		00 17		00 36			00 49			01 43		02 40	03 40	04 40			05 32		06 02	
Norwood Junction 2	a			→																		05 36			
New Cross Gate	d																								
London Bridge 4 ⊖	a				00 19				00 52													05 59			
London Blackfriars 3 ⊖	a																								
City Thameslink 3	a																								
Farringdon 3 ⊖	a																								
St Pancras International 15 ⊖	a																								
St Albans City	a																								
Luton Airport Parkway 4 ✈	a																								
Luton 7	a																								
Bedford 10	a																								
Clapham Junction 10	d	00 11					00 29					01 03			01 54		02 53	03 53	04 53					06 14	
London Victoria 15 ⊖	a	00 18	00 10			00 25	00 36	00 42		00 55		01 10	01 11	01 25	02 05	02 10	03 05	04 05	05 05	05 10			05 55	06 22	06 25

A not 22 May

Table 186

Brighton - London and Bedford

		SN	GW	FC	SN	SN		SN	FC	SN	SN	SN	GW	FC	SN	SN		SN	SN	FC	SN	SN	SN	SN	SN
		1	1	1	1	1		1	1	1	◇1	1	1	1	1	1		1	◇1	1	1	◇1	◇1	1	1
		🚲				🚲		🚲		🚲		🚲			🚲			🚲			🚲	🚲			🚲
Brighton 10	d			05 45					06 11		06 16			06 45					07 04	07 15					
Hove 2	d																								
Preston Park	d										06 19								07 07						
Hassocks 4	d			05 53					06 19		06 26			06 53					07 14	07 23					
Burgess Hill 4	d			05 56					06 26		06 29			06 57					07 17	07 27					
Lewes 4	d																					07 22			
Wivelsfield 4	d										06 32								07 20			07 36			
Haywards Heath 3	a			06 01					06 30		06 36			07 01					07 24	07 31		07 40			
	d			06 01					06 31		06 40			07 02					07 25	07 32		07 41			
Balcombe	d																		07 30						
Horsham 4	d				06 04											07 00							07 37		
Littlehaven	d				06 07											07 03									
Faygate	d																								
Ifield	d				06 13											07 09									
Crawley	d				06 17											07 13							07 46		
Three Bridges 4	a			06 10	06 20				06 40		06 49			07 11		07 16			07 36	07 41			07 50		
	d			06 10	06 21				06 40		06 49			07 11		07 18			07 36	07 41			07 50		
Gatwick Airport 10 ✈	a			06 14	06 25				06 44		06 53			07 15		07 22			07 41	07 45		07 52	07 55		
	d	06 05	06 08	06 15		06 20		06 35	06 45	06 50	06 54	07 05	07 08	07 16	07 20	07 23		07 35	07 42	07 46	07 50	07 53	07 56		08 05
Horley 4	d															07 26							07 58		
Salfords	d															07 30									
Earlswood (Surrey)	d															07 33									
Tonbridge 4	d																							07 41	
Leigh (Kent)	d																							07 45	
Penshurst	d																							07 49	
Edenbridge	d																							07 55	
Godstone	d																							08 02	
Nutfield	d																							08 07	
Reigate	d																								
Redhill 5	a		06 16										07 16			07 36			07 49				08 05	08 12	
	d															07 37			07 49				08 05	08 13	
Merstham	d															07 41								08 17	
Coulsdon South	d															07 46								08 22	
Purley 4	d															07 50							08 14	08 27	
East Croydon	a			06 31					07 01		07 10			07 32		07 56			08 00	08 02		08 09	08 19	08 32	
	d			06 32					07 02		07 10			07 32		07 56			08 00	08 02		08 09	08 20	08 34	
Norwood Junction 2	a			06 36												08 00								08 38	
New Cross Gate	d																								
London Bridge 4 ⊖	a			06 59					07 15					07 45		08 13				08 15				08 51	
London Blackfriars 3 ⊖	a																								
City Thameslink 3	a																								
Farringdon 3 ⊖	a																								
St Pancras International 15 ⊖	a																								
St Albans City	a																								
Luton Airport Parkway 4 ✈	a																								
Luton 7	a																								
Bedford 10	a																								
Clapham Junction 10	d										07 24								08 10			08 19	08 32		
London Victoria 15 ⊖	a	06 40				06 55		07 10		07 20	07 31	07 35			07 50			08 05	08 16		08 20	08 25	08 39		08 35

Table 186

Brighton - London and Bedford

		GW		FC	SN	SN	SN	SN	SN	SN	SN	SN		SN	FC	SN	SN	SN	SN	SN	SN	SN		GW	FC
		1		1	1	◇1	1	1	◇1	◇1	1	1		◇1	1	1	◇1	◇1	◇1	1	◇1	1		1	1
					🚲			🚲		🚲						🚲	🚲		🚲	🚲					
Brighton 10	d			07 45					08 00	08 10					08 15				08 40						08 45
Hove 2	d					07 54																			
Preston Park	d								08 03																
Hassocks 4	d			07 53					08 10						08 23										08 53
Burgess Hill 4	d			07 57		08 04			08 13						08 27										08 57
Lewes 4	d																08 22								
Wivelsfield 4	d								08 16								08 36								
Haywards Heath 3	a			08 01		08 09			08 20						08 31		08 40								09 01
	d			08 02		08 11			08 25						08 32		08 41								09 02
Balcombe	d								08 30																
Horsham 4	d						08 00											08 37							
Littlehaven	d						08 03																		
Faygate	d																								
Ifield	d						08 09																		
Crawley	d						08 13											08 46							
Three Bridges 4	a			08 11			08 16		08 36						08 41			08 50							09 11
	d			08 11			08 18		08 36						08 41			08 50							09 11
Gatwick Airport 10 ✈	a			08 15		08 22	08 22		08 41						08 45		08 52	08 55	09 01						09 15
	d	08 08		08 16	08 20	08 23	08 23	08 35	08 42						08 46	08 50	08 53	08 56	09 02	09 05				09 08	09 16
Horley 4	d						08 26											08 58							
Salfords	d						08 30																		
Earlswood (Surrey)	d						08 33																		
Tonbridge 4	d																					08 41			
Leigh (Kent)	d																					08 45			
Penshurst	d																					08 49			
Edenbridge	d																					08 55			
Godstone	d																					09 02			
Nutfield	d																					09 07			
Reigate	d																								
Redhill 5	a	08 16					08 36		08 49									09 05				09 12		09 16	
	d						08 37		08 49									09 05				09 13			
Merstham	d						08 41															09 17			
Coulsdon South	d						08 46															09 22			
Purley 4	d						08 50					←		←				09 14			←	09 27			
East Croydon	a			08 32		08 39	08 56		09 00	08 45		08 56		09 00	09 02		09 09	09 19	09 17		09 19	09 32			09 32
	d			08 32		08 39	08 56		09 00	08 46	08 50	08 56		09 00	09 02		09 09	09 20	09 17		09 20	09 34			09 32
Norwood Junction 2	a						→		→			09 00						→				09 38			
New Cross Gate	d																								
London Bridge 4 ⊖	a			08 45								09 13			09 15							09 51			09 45
London Blackfriars 3 ⊖	a																								
City Thameslink 3	a																								
Farringdon 3 ⊖	a																								
St Pancras International 15 ⊖	a																								
St Albans City	a																								
Luton Airport Parkway 4 ✈	a																								
Luton 7	a																								
Bedford 10	a																								
Clapham Junction 10	d					08 49				08 56	09 03			09 10			09 19		09 27		09 32				
London Victoria 15 ⊖	a				08 50	08 55		09 05		09 03	09 09			09 16		09 20	09 25		09 33	09 35	09 39				

Sundays
until 4 September

Brighton - London and Bedford

Station		SN ■ ✠	SN ◇■	SN ■	SN ■ ✠	SN ◇■	SN ◇■ ✠	SN ■	SN ■	SN ◇■	FC ■	SN ■ ✠	SN ◇■ ✠	SN ◇■	SN ◇■ ✠	SN ■ ✠	SN ◇■	SN ■	GW ■	FC ■	SN ■ ✠	SN ◇■	SN ■
Brighton 10	d					09 00	09 10				09 15				09 40					09 45			
Hove 2	d		08 54																			09 54	
Preston Park	d					09 03																	
Hassocks 4	d					09 10					09 23									09 53			
Burgess Hill 4	d		09 04			09 13					09 27									09 57		10 04	
Lewes 4	d												09 22										
Wivelsfield 4	d					09 16							09 36										
Haywards Heath 3	a		09 09			09 20					09 31		09 40							10 01		10 09	
	d		09 11			09 25					09 32		09 41							10 02		10 11	
Balcombe	d					09 30																	
Horsham 4	d			09 00										09 37									10 00
Littlehaven	d			09 03																			10 03
Faygate	d																						
Ifield	d			09 09																			10 09
Crawley	d			09 13										09 46									10 13
Three Bridges 4	a			09 16		09 36					09 41			09 50						10 11			10 16
	d			09 18		09 36					09 41			09 50						10 11			10 18
Gatwick Airport 10 ✈	a		09 22	09 22		09 41					09 45		09 52	09 55	10 01					10 15		10 22	10 22
	d	09 20	09 23	09 23	09 35	09 42					09 46	09 50	09 53	09 56	10 02	10 05			10 08	10 16	10 20	10 23	10 23
Horley 4	d			09 26										09 58									10 26
Salfords	d			09 30																			10 30
Earlswood (Surrey)	d			09 33																			10 33
Tonbridge 4	d																	09 41					
Leigh (Kent)	d																	09 45					
Penshurst	d																	09 49					
Edenbridge	d																	09 55					
Godstone	d																	10 02					
Nutfield	d																	10 07					
Reigate	d																						
Redhill 5	a			09 36		09 49								10 05				10 12	10 16				10 36
	d			09 37		09 49								10 05				10 13					10 37
Merstham	d			09 41														10 17					10 41
Coulsdon South	d			09 46														10 22					10 46
Purley 4	d			09 50					←	←				10 14			←	10 27					10 50
East Croydon	a		09 39	09 56		10 00	09 45		09 56	10 00	10 02		10 09	10 19	10 17		10 19	10 32		10 32		10 39	10 56
	d		09 39	09 56		10 00	09 46	09 50	09 56	10 00	10 02		10 09	10 20	10 17		10 20	10 34		10 32		10 39	10 56
Norwood Junction 2	a			→		→			10 00					→				10 38					→
New Cross Gate	d																						
London Bridge 4 ⊖	a								10 13		10 15							10 51		10 45			
London Blackfriars 3 ⊖	a																						
City Thameslink 3	a																						
Farringdon 3 ⊖	a																						
St Pancras International 15 ⊖	a																						
St Albans City	a																						
Luton Airport Parkway 4 ✈	a																						
Luton 7	a																						
Bedford 10	a																						
Clapham Junction 10	d		09 49				09 56	10 03		10 10			10 19		10 27		10 32					10 49	
London Victoria 15 ⊖	a	09 50	09 55		10 05		10 03	10 09		10 16		10 20	10 25		10 33	10 35	10 39				10 50	10 55	

until 4 September

Brighton - London and Bedford

Station		SN ■ ✠	SN ◇■	SN ◇■ ✠	SN ■	SN ■	SN ◇■	FC ■	SN ■ ✠	SN ◇■ ✠	SN ◇■ ✠	SN ◇■ ✠	SN ■ ✠	SN ◇■ ✠	SN ■	GW ■	FC ■	SN ■ ✠	SN ◇■	SN ■	SN ■ ✠	SN ◇■
Brighton 10	d		10 00	10 10				10 15				10 40					10 45					11 00
Hove 2	d																		10 54			
Preston Park	d		10 03																			11 03
Hassocks 4	d		10 10					10 23									10 53					11 10
Burgess Hill 4	d		10 13					10 27									10 57		11 04			11 13
Lewes 4	d									10 22												
Wivelsfield 4	d		10 16							10 36												11 16
Haywards Heath 3	a		10 20					10 31		10 40							11 01		11 09			11 20
	d		10 25					10 32		10 41							11 02		11 11			11 25
Balcombe	d		10 30																			11 30
Horsham 4	d										10 37									11 00		
Littlehaven	d																			11 03		
Faygate	d																					
Ifield	d																			11 09		
Crawley	d										10 46									11 13		
Three Bridges 4	a		10 36					10 41			10 50						11 11			11 16		11 36
	d		10 36					10 41			10 50						11 11			11 18		11 36
Gatwick Airport 10 ✈	a		10 41					10 45		10 52	10 55	11 01					11 15		11 22	11 22		11 41
	d	10 35	10 42					10 46	10 50	10 53	10 56	11 02	11 05			11 08	11 16	11 20	11 23	11 23	11 35	11 42
Horley 4	d										10 58									11 26		
Salfords	d																			11 30		
Earlswood (Surrey)	d																			11 33		
Tonbridge 4	d														10 41							
Leigh (Kent)	d														10 45							
Penshurst	d														10 49							
Edenbridge	d														10 55							
Godstone	d														11 02							
Nutfield	d														11 07							
Reigate	d																					
Redhill 5	a		10 49								11 05				11 12	11 16				11 36		11 49
	d		10 49								11 05				11 13					11 37		11 49
Merstham	d														11 17					11 41		
Coulsdon South	d														11 22					11 46		
Purley 4	d					←	←				11 14			←	11 27					11 50		
East Croydon	a		11 00	10 45		10 56	11 00	11 02		11 09	11 19	11 17		11 19	11 32		11 32		11 39	11 56		12 00
	d		11 00	10 46	10 50	10 56	11 00	11 02		11 09	11 20	11 17		11 20	11 34		11 32		11 39	11 56		12 00
Norwood Junction 2	a		→			11 00					→				11 38					→		→
New Cross Gate	d																					
London Bridge 4 ⊖	a					11 13		11 15							11 51		11 45					
London Blackfriars 3 ⊖	a																					
City Thameslink 3	a																					
Farringdon 3 ⊖	a																					
St Pancras International 15 ⊖	a																					
St Albans City	a																					
Luton Airport Parkway 4 ✈	a																					
Luton 7	a																					
Bedford 10	a																					
Clapham Junction 10	d			10 56	11 03		11 10			11 19		11 27		11 32					11 49			
London Victoria 15 ⊖	a	11 05		11 03	11 09		11 16		11 20	11 25		11 33	11 35	11 39				11 50	11 55		12 05	

Table 186

Sundays
until 4 September

Brighton - London and Bedford

		SN	SN	SN	SN	FC	SN	SN	SN	SN	SN	SN	SN	GW	FC	SN	SN	SN	SN	SN	SN	SN	SN
		◇1 🛒	1	1	◇1	1	1 🛒	◇1 🛒	◇1 🛒	◇1 🛒	1 🛒	◇1 🛒	1	1	1	1 🛒	◇1	1	1 🛒	◇1	◇1 🛒	1	1
Brighton 10	d	11 10				11 15				11 40					11 45					12 00	12 10		
Hove 2	d																11 54						
Preston Park	d																			12 03			
Hassocks 4	d					11 23									11 53					12 10			
Burgess Hill 4	d					11 27									11 57		12 04			12 13			
Lewes 4	d							11 22															
Wivelsfield 4	d							11 36												12 16			
Haywards Heath 3	a					11 31		11 40							12 01		12 09			12 20			
	d					11 32		11 41							12 02		12 11			12 25			
Balcombe	d																			12 30			
Horsham 4	d								11 37									12 00					
Littlehaven	d																	12 03					
Faygate	d																						
Ifield	d																	12 09					
Crawley	d								11 46									12 13					
Three Bridges 4	a					11 41			11 50						12 11			12 16		12 36			
	d					11 41			11 50						12 11			12 18		12 36			
Gatwick Airport 10	✈ a					11 45		11 52	11 55	12 01					12 15		12 22	12 22		12 41			
	d					11 46	11 50	11 53	11 56	12 02	12 05			12 08	12 16	12 20	12 23	12 23	12 35	12 42			
Horley 4	d								11 58									12 26					
Salfords	d																	12 30					
Earlswood (Surrey)	d																	12 33					
Tonbridge 4	d												11 41										
Leigh (Kent)	d												11 45										
Penshurst	d												11 49										
Edenbridge	d												11 55										
Godstone	d												12 02										
Nutfield	d												12 07										
Reigate	d																						
Redhill 5	a								12 05				12 12	12 16				12 36		12 49			
	d								12 05				12 13					12 37		12 49			
Merstham	d												12 17					12 41					
Coulsdon South	d												12 22					12 46					
Purley 4	d			←	←				12 14			←	12 27					12 50					←
East Croydon	🚉 a	11 45		11 56	12 00	12 02		12 09	12 19	12 17		12 19	12 32		12 32		12 39	12 56		13 00	12 45		12 56
	d	11 46	11 50	11 56	12 00	12 02		12 09	12 20	12 17		12 20	12 34		12 32		12 39	12 56		13 00	12 46	12 50	12 56
Norwood Junction 2	a			12 00					→				12 38					→		→			13 00
New Cross Gate	d																						
London Bridge 4	⊖ a			12 13		12 15							12 51		12 45								13 13
London Blackfriars 3	⊖ a																						
City Thameslink 3	a																						
Farringdon 3	⊖ a																						
St Pancras International 15	⊖ a																						
St Albans City	a																						
Luton Airport Parkway 4	✈ a																						
Luton 7	a																						
Bedford 10	a																						
Clapham Junction 10	d	11 56	12 03		12 10			12 19		12 27		12 32					12 49				12 56	13 03	
London Victoria 15	⊖ a	12 03	12 09		12 16		12 20	12 25		12 33	12 35	12 39				12 50	12 55		13 05		13 03	13 09	

Table 186

Sundays
until 4 September

Brighton - London and Bedford

		SN	FC	SN	SN	SN	SN	SN	SN	SN	GW	FC	SN	SN	SN	SN	SN	SN	SN	SN	SN	FC	SN
		◇1	1	1 🛒	◇1 🛒	◇1 🛒	◇1 🛒	1 🛒	◇1 🛒	1	1	1	1 🛒	◇1	1	1 🛒	◇1	◇1 🛒	1	1	◇1	1	1 🛒
Brighton 10	d		12 15				12 40					12 45					13 00	13 10				13 15	
Hove 2	d													12 54									
Preston Park	d																13 03						
Hassocks 4	d		12 23									12 53					13 10					13 23	
Burgess Hill 4	d		12 27									12 57		13 04			13 13					13 27	
Lewes 4	d				12 22																		
Wivelsfield 4	d				12 36												13 16						
Haywards Heath 3	a		12 31		12 40							13 01		13 09			13 20					13 31	
	d		12 32		12 41							13 02		13 11			13 25					13 32	
Balcombe	d																13 30						
Horsham 4	d					12 37									13 00								
Littlehaven	d														13 03								
Faygate	d																						
Ifield	d														13 09								
Crawley	d					12 46									13 13								
Three Bridges 4	a		12 41			12 50						13 11			13 16		13 36					13 41	
	d		12 41			12 50						13 11			13 18		13 36					13 41	
Gatwick Airport 10	✈ a		12 45		12 52	12 55	13 01					13 15		13 22	13 22		13 41					13 45	
	d		12 46	12 50	12 53	12 56	13 02	13 05			13 08	13 16	13 20	13 23	13 23	13 35	13 42					13 46	13 50
Horley 4	d					12 58									13 26								
Salfords	d														13 30								
Earlswood (Surrey)	d														13 33								
Tonbridge 4	d									12 41													
Leigh (Kent)	d									12 45													
Penshurst	d									12 49													
Edenbridge	d									12 55													
Godstone	d									13 02													
Nutfield	d									13 07													
Reigate	d																						
Redhill 5	a					13 05				13 12	13 16				13 36		13 49						
	d					13 05				13 13					13 37		13 49						
Merstham	d									13 17					13 41								
Coulsdon South	d									13 22					13 46								
Purley 4	d	←				13 14			←	13 27					13 50					←	←		
East Croydon	🚉 a	13 00	13 02		13 09	13 19	13 17		13 19	13 32		13 32		13 39	13 56		14 00	13 45		13 56	14 00	14 02	
	d	13 00	13 02		13 09	13 20	13 17		13 20	13 34		13 32		13 39	13 56		14 00	13 46	13 50	13 56	14 00	14 02	
Norwood Junction 2	a					→				13 38					→		→			14 00			
New Cross Gate	d																						
London Bridge 4	⊖ a		13 15							13 51		13 45								14 13		14 15	
London Blackfriars 3	⊖ a																						
City Thameslink 3	a																						
Farringdon 3	⊖ a																						
St Pancras International 15	⊖ a																						
St Albans City	a																						
Luton Airport Parkway 4	✈ a																						
Luton 7	a																						
Bedford 10	a																						
Clapham Junction 10	d	13 10			13 19		13 27		13 32					13 49				13 56	14 03		14 10		
London Victoria 15	⊖ a	13 16		13 20	13 25		13 33	13 35	13 39				13 50	13 55		14 05		14 03	14 09		14 16		14 20

Brighton - London and Bedford

		SN ◇1 🚲	SN ◇1 🚲	SN ◇1 🚲	SN 1 🚲	SN ◇1 🚲	SN 1	GW 1	FC 1	SN 1 🚲	SN ◇1	SN 1	SN 1 🚲	SN ◇1	SN ◇1 🚲	SN 1	SN 1	SN ◇1	FC 1	SN 1 🚲	SN ◇1 🚲	SN ◇1 🚲
Brighton 10	d			13 40					13 45					14 00	14 10				14 15			
Hove 2	d										13 54											
Preston Park	d													14 03								
Hassocks 4	d								13 53					14 10					14 23			
Burgess Hill 4	d								13 57		14 04			14 13					14 27			
Lewes 4	d	13 22																			14 22	
Wivelsfield 4	d	13 36												14 16							14 36	
Haywards Heath 3	a	13 40							14 01		14 09			14 20					14 31		14 40	
	d	13 41							14 02		14 11			14 25					14 32		14 41	
Balcombe	d													14 30								
Horsham 4	d		13 37									14 00										14 37
Littlehaven	d											14 03										
Faygate	d																					
Ifield	d											14 09										
Crawley	d		13 46									14 13										14 46
Three Bridges 4	a		13 50						14 11			14 16		14 36					14 41			14 50
	d		13 50						14 11			14 18		14 36					14 41			14 50
Gatwick Airport 10 ✈	a	13 52	13 55	14 01					14 15		14 22	14 22		14 41					14 45		14 52	14 55
	d	13 53	13 56	14 02	14 05			14 08	14 16	14 20	14 23	14 23	14 35	14 42					14 46	14 50	14 53	14 56
Horley 4	d		13 58									14 26										14 58
Salfords	d											14 30										
Earlswood (Surrey)	d											14 33										
Tonbridge 4	d						13 41															
Leigh (Kent)	d						13 45															
Penshurst	d						13 49															
Edenbridge	d						13 55															
Godstone	d						14 02															
Nutfield	d						14 07															
Reigate	d																					
Redhill 5	a		14 05				14 12	14 16				14 36		14 49								15 05
	d		14 05				14 13					14 37		14 49								15 05
Merstham	d						14 17					14 41										
Coulsdon South	d						14 22					14 46										
Purley 4	d		14 14			←	14 27					14 50					←	←				15 14
East Croydon	a	14 09	14 19	14 17		14 19	14 32		14 32		14 39	14 56		15 00	14 45		14 56	15 00	15 02		15 09	15 19
	d	14 09	14 20	14 17		14 20	14 34		14 32		14 39	14 56		15 00	14 46	14 50	14 56	15 00	15 02		15 09	15 20
Norwood Junction 2	a		→				14 38					→		→			15 00					→
New Cross Gate	d																					
London Bridge 4 ⊖	a						14 51		14 45								15 13		15 15			
London Blackfriars 3 ⊖	a																					
City Thameslink 3	a																					
Farringdon 3 ⊖	a																					
St Pancras International 15 ⊖	a																					
St Albans City	a																					
Luton Airport Parkway 4 ✈	a																					
Luton 7	a																					
Bedford 10	a																					
Clapham Junction 10	d	14 19		14 27		14 32					14 49				14 56	15 03		15 10			15 19	
London Victoria 15 ⊖	a	14 25		14 33	14 35	14 39				14 50	14 55		15 05		15 03	15 09		15 16		15 20	15 25	

Brighton - London and Bedford

		SN ◇1 🚲	SN 1 🚲	SN ◇1 🚲	SN 1	GW 1	FC 1	SN 1 🚲	SN ◇1	SN 1	SN 1 🚲	SN ◇1	SN ◇1 🚲	SN 1	SN 1	SN ◇1	FC 1	SN 1 🚲	SN ◇1 🚲	SN ◇1 🚲	SN ◇1 🚲	SN 1 🚲	SN ◇1 🚲
Brighton 10	d	14 40					14 45					15 00	15 10				15 15				15 40		
Hove 2	d								14 54														
Preston Park	d											15 03											
Hassocks 4	d						14 53					15 10					15 23						
Burgess Hill 4	d						14 57		15 04			15 13					15 27						
Lewes 4	d																		15 22				
Wivelsfield 4	d											15 16							15 36				
Haywards Heath 3	a						15 01		15 09			15 20					15 31		15 40				
	d						15 02		15 11			15 25					15 32		15 41				
Balcombe	d											15 30											
Horsham 4	d									15 00										15 37			
Littlehaven	d									15 03													
Faygate	d																						
Ifield	d									15 09													
Crawley	d									15 13										15 46			
Three Bridges 4	a						15 11			15 16		15 36					15 41			15 50			
	d						15 11			15 18		15 36					15 41			15 50			
Gatwick Airport 10 ✈	a	15 01					15 15		15 22	15 22		15 41					15 45		15 52	15 55	16 01		
	d	15 02	15 05			15 08	15 16	15 20	15 23	15 23	15 35	15 42					15 46	15 50	15 53	15 56	16 02	16 05	
Horley 4	d									15 26										15 58			
Salfords	d									15 30													
Earlswood (Surrey)	d									15 33													
Tonbridge 4	d				14 41																		
Leigh (Kent)	d				14 45																		
Penshurst	d				14 49																		
Edenbridge	d				14 55																		
Godstone	d				15 02																		
Nutfield	d				15 07																		
Reigate	d																						
Redhill 5	a				15 12	15 16				15 36		15 49								16 05			
	d				15 13					15 37		15 49								16 05			
Merstham	d				15 17					15 41													
Coulsdon South	d				15 22					15 46													
Purley 4	d			←	15 27					15 50					←	←				16 14			←
East Croydon	a	15 17		15 19	15 32		15 32		15 39	15 56		16 00	15 45		15 56	16 00	16 02		16 09	16 19	16 17		16 19
	d	15 17		15 20	15 34		15 32		15 39	15 56		16 00	15 46	15 50	15 56	16 00	16 02		16 09	16 20	16 17		16 20
Norwood Junction 2	a				15 38					→		→			16 00					→			
New Cross Gate	d																						
London Bridge 4 ⊖	a				15 51		15 45								16 13		16 15						
London Blackfriars 3 ⊖	a																						
City Thameslink 3	a																						
Farringdon 3 ⊖	a																						
St Pancras International 15 ⊖	a																						
St Albans City	a																						
Luton Airport Parkway 4 ✈	a																						
Luton 7	a																						
Bedford 10	a																						
Clapham Junction 10	d	15 27		15 32					15 49				15 56	16 03		16 10			16 19		16 27		16 32
London Victoria 15 ⊖	a	15 33	15 35	15 39				15 50	15 55		16 05		16 03	16 09		16 16		16 20	16 25		16 33	16 35	16 39

Table 186

Sundays
until 4 September

Brighton - London and Bedford

		SN 1	GW 1	FC 1	SN 1 ⊼	SN ◇1	SN 1	SN 1 ⊼	SN ◇1	SN ◇1 ⊼	SN 1	SN 1	SN ◇1	FC 1	SN 1 ⊼	SN ◇1 ⊼	SN ◇1 ⊼	SN ◇1 ⊼	SN 1 ⊼	SN ◇1 ⊼	SN 1	GW 1
Brighton 10	d			15 45					16 00	16 10				16 15				16 40				
Hove 2	d					15 54																
Preston Park	d								16 03													
Hassocks 4	d			15 53					16 10					16 23								
Burgess Hill 4	d			15 57		16 04			16 13					16 27								
Lewes 4	d															16 22						
Wivelsfield 4	d								16 16							16 36						
Haywards Heath 3	a			16 01		16 09			16 20					16 31		16 40						
	d			16 02		16 11			16 25					16 32		16 41						
Balcombe	d								16 30													
Horsham 4	d						16 00										16 37					
Littlehaven	d						16 03															
Faygate	d																					
Ifield	d						16 09															
Crawley	d						16 13										16 46					
Three Bridges 4	a			16 11			16 16		16 36					16 41			16 50					
	d			16 11			16 18		16 36					16 41			16 50					
Gatwick Airport 10 ✈	a			16 15		16 22	16 22		16 41					16 45		16 52	16 55	17 01				
	d		16 08	16 16	16 20	16 23	16 23	16 35	16 42					16 46	16 50	16 53	16 56	17 02	17 05			17 08
Horley 4	d						16 26										16 58					
Salfords	d						16 30															
Earlswood (Surrey)	d						16 33															
Tonbridge 4	d	15 41																			16 41	
Leigh (Kent)	d	15 45																			16 45	
Penshurst	d	15 49																			16 49	
Edenbridge	d	15 55																			16 55	
Godstone	d	16 02																			17 02	
Nutfield	d	16 07																			17 07	
Reigate	d																					
Redhill 5	a	16 12	16 16				16 36		16 49								17 05				17 12	17 16
	d	16 13					16 37		16 49								17 05				17 13	
Merstham	d	16 17					16 41														17 17	
Coulsdon South	d	16 22					16 46														17 22	
Purley 4	d	16 27					16 50					←	←				17 14			←	17 27	
East Croydon ⇌	a	16 32		16 32		16 39	16 56		17 00	16 45		16 56	17 00	17 02		17 09	17 19	17 17		17 19	17 32	
	d	16 34		16 32		16 39	16 56		17 00	16 46	16 50	16 56	17 00	17 02		17 09	17 20	17 17		17 20	17 34	
Norwood Junction 2	a	16 38					→		→			17 00					→				17 38	
New Cross Gate	d																					
London Bridge 4 ⊖	a	16 51		16 45								17 13		17 15							17 51	
London Blackfriars 3 ⊖	a																					
City Thameslink 3	a																					
Farringdon 3 ⊖	a																					
St Pancras International 15 ⊖	a																					
St Albans City	a																					
Luton Airport Parkway 4 ✈	a																					
Luton 7	a																					
Bedford 10	a																					
Clapham Junction 10	d					16 49				16 56	17 03		17 10			17 19		17 27		17 32		
London Victoria 15 ⊖	a				16 50	16 55		17 05		17 03	17 09		17 16		17 20	17 25		17 33	17 35	17 39		

Table 186

Sundays
until 4 September

Brighton - London and Bedford

		FC 1	SN 1 ⊼	SN ◇1	SN 1	SN 1 ⊼	SN ◇1	SN ◇1 ⊼	SN 1	SN 1	SN ◇1	FC 1	SN 1 ⊼	SN ◇1 ⊼	SN ◇1 ⊼	SN ◇1 ⊼	SN 1 ⊼	SN ◇1 ⊼	SN 1	GW 1	FC 1	SN 1 ⊼	SN ◇1
Brighton 10	d	16 45					17 00	17 10				17 15				17 40					17 45		
Hove 2	d			16 54																			17 54
Preston Park	d						17 03																
Hassocks 4	d	16 53					17 10					17 23									17 53		
Burgess Hill 4	d	16 57		17 04			17 13					17 27									17 57		18 04
Lewes 4	d													17 22									
Wivelsfield 4	d						17 16							17 36									
Haywards Heath 3	a	17 01		17 09			17 20					17 31		17 40							18 01		18 09
	d	17 02		17 11			17 25					17 32		17 41							18 02		18 11
Balcombe	d						17 30																
Horsham 4	d				17 00										17 37								
Littlehaven	d				17 03																		
Faygate	d																						
Ifield	d				17 09																		
Crawley	d				17 13										17 46								
Three Bridges 4	a	17 11			17 16		17 36					17 41			17 50						18 11		
	d	17 11			17 18		17 36					17 41			17 50						18 11		
Gatwick Airport 10 ✈	a	17 15		17 22	17 22		17 41					17 45		17 52	17 55	18 01					18 15		18 22
	d	17 16	17 20	17 23	17 23	17 35	17 42					17 46	17 50	17 53	17 56	18 02	18 05			18 08	18 16	18 20	18 23
Horley 4	d				17 26										17 58								
Salfords	d				17 30																		
Earlswood (Surrey)	d				17 33																		
Tonbridge 4	d																		17 41				
Leigh (Kent)	d																		17 45				
Penshurst	d																		17 49				
Edenbridge	d																		17 55				
Godstone	d																		18 02				
Nutfield	d																		18 07				
Reigate	d																						
Redhill 5	a				17 36		17 49								18 05				18 12	18 16			
	d				17 37		17 49								18 05				18 13				
Merstham	d				17 41														18 17				
Coulsdon South	d				17 46														18 22				
Purley 4	d				17 50					←	←				18 14			←	18 27				
East Croydon ⇌	a	17 32		17 39	17 56		18 00	17 45		17 56	18 00	18 02		18 09	18 19	18 17		18 19	18 32		18 32		18 39
	d	17 32		17 39	17 56		18 00	17 46	17 50	17 56	18 00	18 02		18 09	18 20	18 17		18 20	18 34		18 32		18 39
Norwood Junction 2	a				→		→			18 00					→				18 38				
New Cross Gate	d																						
London Bridge 4 ⊖	a	17 45								18 13		18 15							18 51		18 45		
London Blackfriars 3 ⊖	a																						
City Thameslink 3	a																						
Farringdon 3 ⊖	a																						
St Pancras International 15 ⊖	a																						
St Albans City	a																						
Luton Airport Parkway 4 ✈	a																						
Luton 7	a																						
Bedford 10	a																						
Clapham Junction 10	d			17 49				17 56	18 03		18 10			18 19		18 27		18 32					18 49
London Victoria 15 ⊖	a		17 50	17 55		18 05		18 03	18 09		18 16		18 20	18 25		18 33	18 35	18 39				18 50	18 55

Brighton - London and Bedford

until 4 September

		SN 1	SN 1 🛒	SN ◇1	SN ◇1	SN 1	SN 1	SN ◇1	FC 1	SN 1 🛒	SN ◇1 🛒	SN ◇1	SN ◇1	SN 1	SN ◇1	SN 1	GW 1	FC 1	SN 1	SN ◇1	SN 1	SN 1	SN ◇1
Brighton 10	d			18 00	18 10				18 15				18 40					18 45					19 00
Hove 2	d																			18 54			
Preston Park	d			18 03																			19 03
Hassocks 4	d			18 10					18 23									18 53					19 10
Burgess Hill 4	d			18 13					18 27									18 57		19 04			19 13
Lewes 4	d										18 22												
Wivelsfield 4	d			18 16							18 36												19 16
Haywards Heath 3	a			18 20					18 31		18 40							19 01		19 09			19 20
	d			18 25					18 32		18 41							19 02		19 11			19 25
Balcombe	d			18 30																			19 30
Horsham 4	d	18 00										18 37									19 00		
Littlehaven	d	18 03																			19 03		
Faygate	d																						
Ifield	d	18 09																			19 09		
Crawley	d	18 13										18 46									19 13		
Three Bridges 4	a	18 16		18 36					18 41			18 50						19 11			19 16		19 36
	d	18 18		18 36					18 41			18 50						19 11			19 18		19 36
Gatwick Airport 10 ✈	a	18 22		18 41					18 45		18 52	18 55	19 01					19 15		19 22	19 22		19 41
	d	18 23	18 35	18 42					18 46	18 50	18 53	18 56	19 02	19 05			19 08	19 16	19 20	19 23	19 23	19 35	19 42
Horley 4	d	18 26										18 58									19 26		
Salfords	d	18 30																			19 30		
Earlswood (Surrey)	d	18 33																			19 33		
Tonbridge 4	d															18 41							
Leigh (Kent)	d															18 45							
Penshurst	d															18 49							
Edenbridge	d															18 55							
Godstone	d															19 02							
Nutfield	d															19 07							
Reigate	d																						
Redhill 5	a	18 36		18 49								19 05				19 12	19 16				19 36		19 49
	d	18 37		18 49								19 05				19 13					19 37		19 49
Merstham	d	18 41														19 17					19 41		
Coulsdon South	d	18 46														19 22					19 46		
Purley 4	d	18 50					←	←				19 14			←	19 27					19 50		
East Croydon ⇌	a	18 56		19 00	18 45		18 56	19 00	19 02		19 09	19 19	19 17		19 19	19 32		19 32		19 39	19 56		20 00
	d	18 56		19 00	18 46	18 50	18 56	19 00	19 02		19 09	19 20	19 17		19 20	19 34		19 32		19 39	19 56		20 00
Norwood Junction 2	a	→		→			19 00					→				19 38					→		→
New Cross Gate	d																						
London Bridge 4 ⊖	a						19 13		19 15							19 51		19 45					
London Blackfriars 3 ⊖	a																						
City Thameslink 3	a																						
Farringdon 3 ⊖	a																						
St Pancras International 15 ⊖	a																						
St Albans City	a																						
Luton Airport Parkway 4 ✈	a																						
Luton 7	a																						
Bedford 10	a																						
Clapham Junction 10	d				18 56	19 03		19 10			19 19		19 27		19 32					19 49			
London Victoria 15 ⊖	a		19 05		19 03	19 09		19 16		19 20	19 25		19 33	19 35	19 39				19 50	19 55		20 05	

Brighton - London and Bedford

until 4 September

		SN ◇1	SN 1	SN 1	SN ◇1	FC 1	SN 1	SN ◇1	SN ◇1	SN ◇1	SN 1	SN ◇1	SN 1	GW 1	FC 1	SN 1	SN ◇1	SN 1	SN 1	SN ◇1	SN ◇1	SN 1
Brighton 10	d	19 10				19 15				19 40					19 45					20 00	20 10	
Hove 2	d																19 54					
Preston Park	d																			20 03		
Hassocks 4	d					19 23									19 53					20 10		
Burgess Hill 4	d					19 27									19 57		20 04			20 13		
Lewes 4	d							19 22														
Wivelsfield 4	d							19 36												20 16		
Haywards Heath 3	a					19 31		19 40							20 01		20 09			20 20		
	d					19 32		19 41							20 02		20 11			20 25		
Balcombe	d																			20 30		
Horsham 4	d								19 37									20 00				
Littlehaven	d																	20 03				
Faygate	d																					
Ifield	d																	20 09				
Crawley	d								19 46									20 13				
Three Bridges 4	a					19 41			19 50						20 11			20 16		20 36		
	d					19 41			19 50						20 11			20 18		20 36		
Gatwick Airport 10 ✈	a					19 45		19 52	19 55	20 01					20 15		20 22	20 22		20 41		
	d					19 46	19 50	19 53	19 56	20 02	20 05			20 08	20 16	20 20	20 23	20 23	20 35	20 42		
Horley 4	d								19 58									20 26				
Salfords	d																	20 30				
Earlswood (Surrey)	d																	20 33				
Tonbridge 4	d												19 41									
Leigh (Kent)	d												19 45									
Penshurst	d												19 49									
Edenbridge	d												19 55									
Godstone	d												20 02									
Nutfield	d												20 07									
Reigate	d																					
Redhill 5	a								20 05				20 12	20 16				20 36		20 49		
	d								20 05				20 13					20 37		20 49		
Merstham	d												20 17					20 41				
Coulsdon South	d												20 22					20 46				
Purley 4	d			←	←				20 14			←	20 27					20 50				
East Croydon ⇌	a	19 45		19 56	20 00	20 02		20 09	20 19	20 17		20 19	20 32		20 32		20 39	20 56		21 00	20 45	
	d	19 46	19 50	19 56	20 00	20 02		20 09	20 20	20 17		20 20	20 34		20 32		20 39	20 56		21 00	20 46	20 50
Norwood Junction 2	a			20 00					→				20 38					→		→		
New Cross Gate	d																					
London Bridge 4 ⊖	a			20 13		20 15							20 51		20 45							
London Blackfriars 3 ⊖	a																					
City Thameslink 3	a																					
Farringdon 3 ⊖	a																					
St Pancras International 15 ⊖	a																					
St Albans City	a																					
Luton Airport Parkway 4 ✈	a																					
Luton 7	a																					
Bedford 10	a																					
Clapham Junction 10	d	19 56	20 03		20 10			20 19		20 27		20 32					20 49				20 56	21 03
London Victoria 15 ⊖	a	20 03	20 09		20 16		20 20	20 25		20 33	20 35	20 39				20 50	20 55		21 05		21 03	21 09

Table 186

Sundays until 4 September

Brighton - London and Bedford

		SN	SN	FC	SN	SN	SN	SN	SN	SN	SN	GW	FC	SN	SN	SN	SN	SN	SN	FC	SN	SN	SN
		■	◇■	■	■	◇■	◇■	◇■	■	◇■	■	■	■	■	◇■	■	■	■	◇■	■	■	◇■	◇■
Brighton ■	d			20 15				20 40					20 45						21 04	21 15			
Hove ■	d														20 54								
Preston Park	d																		21 07				
Hassocks ■	d			20 23									20 53						21 14	21 23			
Burgess Hill ■	d			20 27									20 57		21 04				21 17	21 27			
Lewes ■	d					20 22																21 22	
Wivelsfield ■	d					20 36													21 20			21 36	
Haywards Heath ■	a			20 31		20 40							21 01		21 09				21 24	21 31		21 40	
	d			20 32		20 41							21 02		21 11				21 25	21 32		21 41	
Balcombe	d																		21 30				
Horsham ■	d						20 37										21 00						21 37
Littlehaven	d																21 03						
Faygate	d																						
Ifield	d																21 09						
Crawley	d						20 46										21 13						21 46
Three Bridges ■	a			20 41			20 50						21 11				21 16		21 36	21 41			21 50
	d			20 41			20 50						21 11				21 18		21 36	21 41			21 50
Gatwick Airport ■ ✈	a			20 45		20 52	20 55	21 01					21 15		21 22		21 22		21 41	21 45		21 52	21 55
	d			20 46	20 50	20 53	20 56	21 02	21 05			21 08	21 16	21 20	21 23		21 23	21 35	21 42	21 46	21 50	21 53	21 56
Horley ■	d						20 58										21 26						21 58
Salfords	d																21 30						
Earlswood (Surrey)	d																21 33						
Tonbridge ■	d										20 41												
Leigh (Kent)	d										20 45												
Penshurst	d										20 49												
Edenbridge	d										20 55												
Godstone	d										21 02												
Nutfield	d										21 07												
Reigate	d																						
Redhill ■	a						21 05				21 12	21 16					21 36		21 49				22 05
	d						21 05				21 13						21 37		21 49				22 05
Merstham	d										21 17						21 41						
Coulsdon South	d										21 22						21 46						
Purley ■	d	←	←				21 14			←	21 27						21 50						22 14
East Croydon	a	20 56	21 00	21 02		21 09	21 19	21 17		21 19	21 32		21 32		21 39		21 56		22 00	22 02		22 09	22 19
	d	20 56	21 00	21 02		21 09	21 20	21 17		21 20	21 34		21 32		21 39	21 50	21 56		22 00	22 02		22 09	22 20
Norwood Junction ■	a	21 00					→				21 38						22 00						
New Cross Gate	d																						
London Bridge ■ ⊖	a	21 13		21 15							21 51		21 45				22 13			22 15			
London Blackfriars ■ ⊖	a																						
City Thameslink ■	a																						
Farringdon ■ ⊖	a																						
St Pancras International ■ ⊖	a																						
St Albans City	a																						
Luton Airport Parkway ■ ✈	a																						
Luton ■	a																						
Bedford ■	a																						
Clapham Junction ■	d		21 10			21 19		21 27		21 32					21 49	22 03			22 10			22 19	22 32
London Victoria ■ ⊖	a		21 16		21 20	21 25		21 33	21 35	21 39				21 50	21 55	22 09		22 05	22 16		22 20	22 25	22 39

Table 186

Sundays until 4 September

Brighton - London and Bedford

		SN	SN	GW	FC	SN	SN	SN	SN	SN	FC	SN	SN	SN	SN	GW	FC	SN	SN	SN	SN	SN
		■	■	■	■	■	■	■	■	◇■	■	■	■	◇■	■	■	■	■	■	■	■	◇■
Brighton ■	d				21 45					22 04	22 15						22 45					23 02
Hove ■	d																					
Preston Park	d									22 07												23 06
Hassocks ■	d				21 53					22 14	22 23						22 53					23 12
Burgess Hill ■	d				21 57					22 17	22 27						22 57					23 16
Lewes ■	d																					
Wivelsfield ■	d									22 20												23 19
Haywards Heath ■	a				22 01					22 24	22 31						23 01					23 23
	d				22 02					22 25	22 32						23 02					23 24
Balcombe	d									22 30												23 29
Horsham ■	d							22 00						22 37						23 03		
Littlehaven	d							22 03												23 06		
Faygate	d																					
Ifield	d							22 09												23 12		
Crawley	d							22 13						22 46						23 16		
Three Bridges ■	a				22 11			22 16		22 36	22 41			22 50			23 11			23 20		23 36
	d				22 11			22 18		22 36	22 41			22 50			23 11			23 20		23 42
Gatwick Airport ■ ✈	a				22 15			22 22		22 41	22 45			22 55			23 15			23 24		23 46
	d		22 05	22 08	22 16	22 20		22 23	22 35	22 42	22 46		22 50	22 56	23 05	23 09	23 16	23 20		23 25	23 35	23 47
Horley ■	d							22 26						22 58						23 28		23 49
Salfords	d							22 30														
Earlswood (Surrey)	d							22 33														
Tonbridge ■	d	21 41										22 29										
Leigh (Kent)	d	21 45										22 33										
Penshurst	d	21 49										22 37										
Edenbridge	d	21 55										22 43										
Godstone	d	22 02										22 50										
Nutfield	d	22 07										22 55										
Reigate	d																					
Redhill ■	a	22 12		22 16				22 36		22 49		23 00		23 05		23 16				23 34		23 57
	d	22 13						22 37		22 49				23 05						23 35		00 02
Merstham	d	22 17						22 41												23 39		
Coulsdon South	d	22 22						22 46												23 44		
Purley ■	d	22 27						22 50						23 14						23 50		00 11
East Croydon	a	22 32			22 32			22 56		23 00	23 02			23 20			23 32			23 55		00 16
	d	22 34			22 32		22 50	22 56		23 00	23 02			23 21			23 32		23 50	23 56		00 17
Norwood Junction ■	a	22 38																				→
New Cross Gate	d																					
London Bridge ■ ⊖	a	22 51			22 45						23 15						23 45					
London Blackfriars ■ ⊖	a																					
City Thameslink ■	a																					
Farringdon ■ ⊖	a																					
St Pancras International ■ ⊖	a																					
St Albans City	a																					
Luton Airport Parkway ■ ✈	a																					
Luton ■	a																					
Bedford ■	a																					
Clapham Junction ■	d						23 03	23 08		23 11				23 32					00 02	00 11		
London Victoria ■ ⊖	a		22 35			22 50	23 09	23 14	23 07	23 17			23 20	23 38	23 35			23 55	00 08	00 21	00 10	

Sundays
until 4 September

Brighton - London and Bedford

		FC	SN	SN ◇	FC
Brighton	d	23 15			23 45
Hove	d				
Preston Park	d				
Hassocks	d	23 23			23 53
Burgess Hill	d	23 27			23 57
Lewes	d				
Wivelsfield	d				
Haywards Heath	a	23 31			00 01
	d	23 32			00 01
Balcombe	d				
Horsham	d				
Littlehaven	d				
Faygate	d				
Ifield	d				
Crawley	d				
Three Bridges	a	23 41			00 10
	d	23 41			00 10
Gatwick Airport ✈	a	23 45			00 14
	d	23 46	23 50		00 15
Horley	d				
Salfords	d				
Earlswood (Surrey)	d				
Tonbridge	d				
Leigh (Kent)	d				
Penshurst	d				
Edenbridge	d				
Godstone	d				
Nutfield	d				
Reigate	d				
Redhill	a				00 22
	d				00 23
Merstham	d				
Coulsdon South	d				
Purley	d			←	
East Croydon	a	00 02		00 16	00 36
	d	00 04		00 17	00 36
Norwood Junction	a				
New Cross Gate	d				
London Bridge ⊖	a	00 19			00 53
London Blackfriars ⊖	a				
City Thameslink	a				
Farringdon ⊖	a				
St Pancras International ⊖	a				
St Albans City	a				
Luton Airport Parkway ✈	a				
Luton	a				
Bedford	a				
Clapham Junction	d			00 30	
London Victoria ⊖	a		00 25	00 37	

from 11 September

Brighton - London and Bedford

		SN	SN	SN ◇	FC	SN	SN ◇	SN	FC	SN	SN	SN	SN	SN	SN	SN	SN	SN	SN	FC	SN	SN	SN
Brighton	d			23p02	23p11				23p37														
Hove	d																						
Preston Park	d			23p06					23p41														
Hassocks	d			23p12	23p19				23p47														
Burgess Hill	d			23p16	23p23				23p51														
Lewes	d																						
Wivelsfield	d			23p19					23p53														
Haywards Heath	a			23p23	23p27				23p58														
	d			23p24	23p28				23p59														
Balcombe	d								00 04														
Horsham	d	23p02																					
Littlehaven	d	23p05																					
Faygate	d																						
Ifield	d	23p11																					
Crawley	d	23p14																					
Three Bridges	a	23p18		23p33	23p38				00 10														
	d	23p18		23p47	23p38				00 10					01 10		02 10	03 10	04 10		05 10		05 30	
Gatwick Airport ✈	a	23p22		23p52	23p42				00 14					01 19		02 14	03 14	04 14		05 14		05 34	
	d	23p23	23p35	23p53	23p43	23p50		00 05	00 15	00 20		00 35	00 50	01 20	01 35	02 15	03 15	04 15	04 35	05 15	05 20	05 36	05 50
Horley	d	23p26		23p56										01 22		02 18	03 18	04 18				05 38	
Salfords	d	23p30																					
Earlswood (Surrey)	d	23p33																					
Tonbridge	d																						
Leigh (Kent)	d																						
Penshurst	d																						
Edenbridge	d																						
Godstone	d																						
Nutfield	d																						
Reigate	d																						
Redhill	a	23p36		00 03					00 22													05 46	
	d	23p37		00 03					00 22													05 46	
Merstham	d	23p41																					
Coulsdon South	d	23p46																					
Purley	d	23p49		00 11			←							01 37		02 33	03 33	04 33				05 56	
East Croydon	a	23p55		00 16	00 02		00 16		00 35					01 42		02 39	03 39	04 39		05 31		06 01	
	d	23p56		00 17	00 04		00 17		00 36		00 49			01 43		02 40	03 40	04 40		05 32		06 02	
Norwood Junction	a			→																05 36			
New Cross Gate	d																						
London Bridge ⊖	a				00 19				00 52											05 59			
London Blackfriars ⊖	a																						
City Thameslink	a																						
Farringdon ⊖	a																						
St Pancras International ⊖	a																						
St Albans City	a																						
Luton Airport Parkway ✈	a																						
Luton	a																						
Bedford	a																						
Clapham Junction	d	00 11					00 29				01 03			01 54		02 53	03 53	04 53				06 14	
London Victoria ⊖	a	00 18	00 10			00 25	00 36	00 42		00 55	01 10	01 11	01 25	02 05	02 10	03 05	04 05	05 05	05 10		05 58	06 22	06 25

Table 186

Sundays from 11 September

Brighton - London and Bedford

		SN 1 ⊼	GW 1	FC 1	SN 1	SN 1 ⊼	SN 1 ⊼	FC 1	SN 1 ⊼	SN ◇1	SN 1 ⊼	GW 1	FC 1	SN 1 ⊼	SN 1	SN 1 ⊼	SN ◇1	FC 1	SN 1	SN 1 ⊼	SN ◇1 ⊼	SN ◇1	SN 1 ⊼
Brighton 10	d			05 45				06 11		06 16			06 44				07 00	07 14					
Hove 2	d																						
Preston Park	d									06 19							07 03						
Hassocks 4	d			05 53				06 19		06 26			06 52				07 10	07 22					
Burgess Hill 4	d			05 56				06 26		06 29			06 56				07 13	07 26					
Lewes 4	d																				07 20		
Wivelsfield 4	d									06 32							07 16				07 32		
Haywards Heath 3	a			06 01				06 30		06 36			07 00				07 20	07 30			07 36		
	d			06 01				06 31		06 40			07 01				07 21	07 31			07 39		
Balcombe	d																07 26						
Horsham 4	d				06 04										07 03							07 42	
Littlehaven	d				06 07										07 06								
Faygate	d																						
Ifield	d				06 13										07 12								
Crawley	d				06 17										07 16							07 51	
Three Bridges 4	a			06 10	06 20			06 40		06 49			07 10		07 19		07 32	07 40				07 54	
	d			06 10	06 21			06 40		06 49			07 10		07 20		07 32	07 40				07 55	
Gatwick Airport 10 ✈	a			06 14	06 25			06 44		06 53			07 14		07 24		07 37	07 44			07 51	07 59	
	d	06 05	06 08	06 15		06 20	06 35	06 45	06 50	06 54	07 05	07 08	07 15	07 20	07 25	07 35	07 38	07 45		07 50	07 53	08 00	08 05
Horley 4	d														07 28							08 02	
Salfords	d																						
Earlswood (Surrey)	d																						
Tonbridge 4	d																		07 29				
Leigh (Kent)	d																		07 33				
Penshurst	d																		07 37				
Edenbridge	d																		07 43				
Godstone	d																		07 50				
Nutfield	d																		07 55				
Reigate	d																						
Redhill 5	a		06 16									07 16			07 34		07 45		08 00			08 09	
	d														07 35		07 46					08 09	
Merstham	d														07 39								
Coulsdon South	d														07 44								
Purley 4	d														07 50							08 20	
East Croydon	a			06 31				07 01		07 10			07 31		07 56		07 58	08 01			08 09	08 26	
	d			06 32				07 02		07 10			07 32		07 56		08 00	08 02			08 10	08 26	
Norwood Junction 2	a			06 36											08 00								
New Cross Gate	d																						
London Bridge 4 ⊖	a			06 59				07 15					07 45		08 13			08 15					
London Blackfriars 3 ⊖	a																						
City Thameslink 3	a																						
Farringdon 3 ⊖	a																						
St Pancras International 15 ⊖	a																						
St Albans City	a																						
Luton Airport Parkway 4 ✈	a																						
Luton 7	a																						
Bedford 10	a																						
Clapham Junction 10	d									07 24							08 12				08 25	08 38	
London Victoria 15 ⊖	a	06 40				06 55	07 10		07 25	07 31	07 40			07 55		08 10	08 18			08 25	08 31	08 46	08 40

Table 186

Sundays from 11 September

Brighton - London and Bedford

		GW 1	FC 1	SN 1 ⊼	SN ◇1	SN 1	SN 1	SN 1 ⊼	SN ◇1	FC 1	SN 1	SN 1 ⊼	SN ◇1 ⊼	SN ◇1 ⊼	SN ◇1 ⊼	SN 1 ⊼	GW 1	FC 1	SN 1 ⊼	SN ◇1	SN 1	SN 1
Brighton 10	d		07 44						08 00	08 14				08 34				08 44				
Hove 2	d				07 54															08 54		
Preston Park	d								08 03													
Hassocks 4	d		07 52						08 10	08 22								08 52				
Burgess Hill 4	d		07 56		08 04				08 13	08 26								08 56		09 04		
Lewes 4	d												08 16									
Wivelsfield 4	d								08 16				08 31									
Haywards Heath 3	a		08 00		08 09				08 20	08 30			08 36					09 00		09 09		
	d		08 01		08 10				08 21	08 31			08 39					09 01		09 10		
Balcombe	d								08 26													
Horsham 4	d						08 03								08 42							09 03
Littlehaven	d						08 06															09 06
Faygate	d																					
Ifield	d						08 12															09 12
Crawley	d						08 16								08 51							09 16
Three Bridges 4	a		08 10				08 19		08 32	08 40					08 54			09 10				09 19
	d		08 10				08 20		08 32	08 40					08 55			09 10				09 20
Gatwick Airport 10 ✈	a		08 14		08 22		08 24		08 37	08 44			08 51	08 55	08 59			09 14		09 21		09 24
	d	08 08	08 15	08 20	08 23		08 25	08 35	08 38	08 45		08 50	08 53	08 56	09 00	09 05	09 08	09 15	09 20	09 23		09 25
Horley 4	d						08 28								09 02							09 28
Salfords	d																					
Earlswood (Surrey)	d																					
Tonbridge 4	d										08 29											
Leigh (Kent)	d										08 33											
Penshurst	d										08 37											
Edenbridge	d										08 43											
Godstone	d										08 50											
Nutfield	d										08 55											
Reigate	d																					
Redhill 5	a	08 16					08 34		08 45		09 00				09 09		09 16					09 34
	d						08 35		08 46						09 10							09 35
Merstham	d						08 39															09 39
Coulsdon South	d						08 44															09 44
Purley 4	d						08 50								09 20							09 50
East Croydon	a		08 31		08 39		08 56		08 58	09 01			09 09	09 12	09 26			09 31		09 39		09 56
	d		08 32		08 40	08 50	08 56		09 00	09 02			09 10	09 13	09 26			09 32		09 40	09 50	09 56
Norwood Junction 2	a						09 00															10 00
New Cross Gate	d																					
London Bridge 4 ⊖	a		08 45				09 13			09 15								09 45				10 13
London Blackfriars 3 ⊖	a																					
City Thameslink 3	a																					
Farringdon 3 ⊖	a																					
St Pancras International 15 ⊖	a																					
St Albans City	a																					
Luton Airport Parkway 4 ✈	a																					
Luton 7	a																					
Bedford 10	a																					
Clapham Junction 10	d				08 55	09 01			09 12				09 25	09 28	09 38					09 55	10 01	
London Victoria 15 ⊖	a			08 55	09 01	09 08		09 10	09 18			09 25	09 31	09 35	09 46	09 40			09 55	10 01	10 08	

Sundays

from 11 September

Brighton - London and Bedford

		SN	SN	FC	SN	SN	SN	SN	SN	SN	GW	FC	SN	SN	SN	SN	SN	SN	FC	SN	SN	SN	SN
		1	◇1	1	1	1	◇1	◇1	◇1	1	1	1	1	◇1	1	1	1	◇1	1	1	1	◇1	◇1
		🛒				🛒	🛒	🛒	🛒	🛒			🛒				🛒				🛒	🛒	🛒
Brighton 10	d		09 00	09 14				09 34				09 44						10 00	10 14				10 34
Hove 2	d													09 54									
Preston Park	d		09 03															10 03					
Hassocks 4	d		09 10	09 22								09 52						10 10	10 22				
Burgess Hill 4	d		09 13	09 26								09 56		10 04				10 13	10 26				
Lewes 4	d						09 16															10 16	
Wivelsfield 4	d		09 16				09 31											10 16				10 31	
Haywards Heath 3	a		09 20	09 30			09 35					10 00		10 09				10 20	10 30			10 35	
	d		09 21	09 31			09 39					10 01		10 10				10 21	10 31			10 39	
Balcombe	d		09 26															10 26					
Horsham 4	d								09 42							10 03							
Littlehaven	d															10 06							
Faygate	d																						
Ifield	d															10 12							
Crawley	d								09 51							10 16							
Three Bridges 4	a		09 32	09 40					09 54			10 10				10 19		10 32	10 40				
	d		09 32	09 40					09 55			10 10				10 20		10 32	10 40				
Gatwick Airport 10 ✈	a		09 37	09 44			09 51	09 55	09 59			10 14		10 21		10 24		10 37	10 44			10 51	10 55
	d	09 35	09 38	09 45		09 50	09 53	09 56	10 00	10 05	10 08	10 15	10 20	10 23		10 25	10 35	10 38	10 45		10 50	10 53	10 56
Horley 4	d								10 02							10 28							
Salfords	d																						
Earlswood (Surrey)	d																						
Tonbridge 4	d				09 29															10 29			
Leigh (Kent)	d				09 33															10 33			
Penshurst	d				09 37															10 37			
Edenbridge	d				09 43															10 43			
Godstone	d				09 50															10 50			
Nutfield	d				09 55															10 55			
Reigate	d																						
Redhill 5	a		09 45		10 00				10 09		10 16					10 34		10 45		11 00			
	d		09 46						10 10							10 35		10 46					
Merstham	d															10 39							
Coulsdon South	d															10 44							
Purley 4	d								10 20							10 50							
East Croydon 🚊	a		09 58	10 01			10 09	10 12	10 26			10 31		10 39		10 56		10 58	11 01			11 09	11 12
	d		10 00	10 02			10 10	10 13	10 26			10 32		10 40	10 50	10 56		11 00	11 02			11 10	11 13
Norwood Junction 2	a															11 00							
New Cross Gate	d																						
London Bridge 4 ⊖	a			10 15								10 45				11 13			11 15				
London Blackfriars 3 ⊖	a																						
City Thameslink 3	a																						
Farringdon 3 ⊖	a																						
St Pancras International 15 ⊖	a																						
St Albans City	a																						
Luton Airport Parkway 4 ✈	a																						
Luton 7	a																						
Bedford 10	a																						
Clapham Junction 10	d		10 12				10 25	10 28	10 38					10 55	11 01			11 12				11 25	11 28
London Victoria 15 ⊖	a	10 10	10 18			10 25	10 31	10 35	10 46	10 40			10 55	11 01	11 08		11 10	11 18			11 25	11 31	11 35

from 11 September

Brighton - London and Bedford

		SN	SN	GW	FC	SN	SN	SN	SN	SN	SN	FC	SN	SN	SN	SN	SN	SN	GW	FC	SN	SN
		◇1	1	1	1	1	◇1	1	1	1	◇1	1	1	1	◇1	◇1	◇1	1	1	1	1	◇1
		🛒	🛒			🛒				🛒				🛒	🛒	🛒	🛒	🛒			🛒	
Brighton 10	d				10 44						11 00	11 14				11 34				11 44		
Hove 2	d						10 54															11 54
Preston Park	d										11 03											
Hassocks 4	d				10 52						11 10	11 22								11 52		
Burgess Hill 4	d				10 56		11 04				11 13	11 26								11 56		12 04
Lewes 4	d														11 16							
Wivelsfield 4	d										11 16				11 31							
Haywards Heath 3	a				11 00		11 09				11 20	11 30			11 35					12 00		12 09
	d				11 01		11 10				11 21	11 31			11 39					12 01		12 10
Balcombe	d										11 26											
Horsham 4	d	10 42							11 03								11 42					
Littlehaven	d								11 06													
Faygate	d																					
Ifield	d								11 12													
Crawley	d	10 51							11 16								11 51					
Three Bridges 4	a	10 54			11 10				11 19		11 32	11 40					11 54			12 10		
	d	10 55			11 10				11 20		11 32	11 40					11 55			12 10		
Gatwick Airport 10 ✈	a	10 59			11 14		11 21		11 24		11 37	11 44			11 51	11 55	11 59			12 14		12 22
	d	11 00	11 05	11 08	11 15	11 20	11 23		11 25	11 35	11 38	11 45		11 50	11 53	11 56	12 00	12 05	12 08	12 15	12 20	12 23
Horley 4	d	11 02							11 28								12 02					
Salfords	d																					
Earlswood (Surrey)	d																					
Tonbridge 4	d												11 29									
Leigh (Kent)	d												11 33									
Penshurst	d												11 37									
Edenbridge	d												11 43									
Godstone	d												11 50									
Nutfield	d												11 55									
Reigate	d																					
Redhill 5	a	11 09		11 16					11 34		11 45		12 00				12 09		12 16			
	d	11 10							11 35		11 46						12 10					
Merstham	d								11 39													
Coulsdon South	d								11 44													
Purley 4	d	11 20							11 50								12 20					
East Croydon 🚊	a	11 26			11 31		11 39		11 56		11 58	12 01			12 09	12 12	12 26			12 31		12 39
	d	11 26			11 32		11 40	11 50	11 56		12 00	12 02			12 10	12 13	12 26			12 32		12 40
Norwood Junction 2	a								12 00													
New Cross Gate	d																					
London Bridge 4 ⊖	a				11 45				12 13			12 15								12 45		
London Blackfriars 3 ⊖	a																					
City Thameslink 3	a																					
Farringdon 3 ⊖	a																					
St Pancras International 15 ⊖	a																					
St Albans City	a																					
Luton Airport Parkway 4 ✈	a																					
Luton 7	a																					
Bedford 10	a																					
Clapham Junction 10	d	11 38					11 55	12 01			12 12				12 25	12 28	12 38					12 55
London Victoria 15 ⊖	a	11 46	11 40			11 55	12 01	12 08		12 10	12 18			12 25	12 31	12 35	12 46	12 40			12 55	13 01

Table 186

Sundays from 11 September

Brighton - London and Bedford

		SN ■	SN ■	SN ■ 🚲	SN ◇■	FC ■	SN ■	SN ■ 🚲	SN ◇■ 🚲	SN ◇■ 🚲	SN ◇■ 🚲	SN ■ 🚲	GW ■	FC ■	SN ■ 🚲	SN ◇■	SN ■	SN ■	SN ■ 🚲	SN ◇■	FC ■	SN ■	SN ■ 🚲
Brighton 10	d				12 00	12 14				12 34				12 44						13 00	13 14		
Hove 2	d															12 54							
Preston Park	d				12 03															13 03			
Hassocks 4	d				12 10	12 22								12 52						13 10	13 22		
Burgess Hill 4	d				12 13	12 26								12 56		13 04				13 13	13 26		
Lewes 4	d								12 16														
Wivelsfield 4	d				12 16				12 31											13 16			
Haywards Heath 3	a				12 20	12 30			12 35					13 00		13 09				13 20	13 30		
	d				12 21	12 31			12 39					13 01		13 10				13 21	13 31		
Balcombe	d				12 26															13 26			
Horsham 4	d		12 03								12 42							13 03					
Littlehaven	d		12 06															13 06					
Faygate	d																						
Ifield	d		12 12															13 12					
Crawley	d		12 16								12 51							13 16					
Three Bridges 4	a		12 19		12 32	12 40					12 54			13 10				13 19		13 32	13 40		
	d		12 20		12 32	12 40					12 55			13 10				13 20		13 32	13 40		
Gatwick Airport 10 ✈	a		12 24		12 37	12 44			12 52	12 55	12 59			13 14		13 22		13 24		13 37	13 44		
	d		12 25	12 35	12 38	12 45		12 50	12 53	12 56	13 00	13 05	13 08	13 15	13 20	13 23		13 25	13 35	13 38	13 45		13 50
Horley 4	d		12 28								13 02							13 28					
Salfords	d																						
Earlswood (Surrey)	d																						
Tonbridge 4	d						12 29															13 29	
Leigh (Kent)	d						12 33															13 33	
Penshurst	d						12 37															13 37	
Edenbridge	d						12 43															13 43	
Godstone	d						12 50															13 50	
Nutfield	d						12 55															13 55	
Reigate	d																						
Redhill 5	a		12 34		12 45		13 00				13 09		13 16					13 34		13 45		14 00	
	d		12 35		12 46						13 10							13 35		13 46			
Merstham	d		12 39															13 39					
Coulsdon South	d		12 44															13 44					
Purley 4	d		12 50								13 19							13 50					
East Croydon	a		12 56		12 58	13 01			13 09	13 12	13 26			13 31		13 39		13 56		13 58	14 01		
	d	12 50	12 56		13 00	13 02			13 10	13 13	13 26			13 32		13 40	13 50	13 56		14 00	14 02		
Norwood Junction 2	a		13 00															14 00					
New Cross Gate	d																						
London Bridge 4 ⊖	a		13 13			13 15								13 45				14 13			14 15		
London Blackfriars 5 ⊖	a																						
City Thameslink 3	a																						
Farringdon 3 ⊖	a																						
St Pancras International 15 ⊖	a																						
St Albans City	a																						
Luton Airport Parkway 4 ✈	a																						
Luton 7	a																						
Bedford 10	a																						
Clapham Junction 10	d	13 01			13 12				13 25	13 28	13 38					13 55	14 01			14 12			
London Victoria 15 ⊖	a	13 08		13 10	13 18			13 25	13 31	13 35	13 46	13 40			13 55	14 01	14 08		14 10	14 18			14 25

Table 186

Sundays from 11 September

Brighton - London and Bedford

		SN ◇■ 🚲	SN ◇■ 🚲	SN ◇■ 🚲	SN ■ 🚲	GW ■	FC ■	SN ■ 🚲	SN ◇■	SN ■	SN ■	SN ■ 🚲	SN ◇■	FC ■	SN ■	SN ■ 🚲	SN ◇■ 🚲	SN ◇■ 🚲	SN ◇■ 🚲	SN ■ 🚲	GW ■	FC ■	SN ■ 🚲
Brighton 10	d		13 34				13 44						14 00	14 14				14 34				14 44	
Hove 2	d								13 54														
Preston Park	d												14 03										
Hassocks 4	d						13 52						14 10	14 22								14 52	
Burgess Hill 4	d						13 56		14 04				14 13	14 26								14 56	
Lewes 4	d	13 16															14 16						
Wivelsfield 4	d	13 31											14 16				14 31						
Haywards Heath 3	a	13 35					14 00		14 09				14 20	14 30			14 35					15 00	
	d	13 39					14 01		14 10				14 21	14 31			14 39					15 01	
Balcombe	d												14 26										
Horsham 4	d			13 42							14 03								14 42				
Littlehaven	d										14 06												
Faygate	d																						
Ifield	d										14 12												
Crawley	d			13 51							14 16								14 51				
Three Bridges 4	a			13 54			14 10				14 19		14 32	14 40					14 54			15 10	
	d			13 55			14 10				14 20		14 32	14 40					14 55			15 10	
Gatwick Airport 10 ✈	a	13 52	13 55	13 59			14 14		14 22		14 24		14 37	14 44			14 52	14 55	14 59			15 14	
	d	13 53	13 56	14 00	14 05	14 08	14 15	14 20	14 23		14 25	14 35	14 38	14 45		14 50	14 53	14 56	15 00	15 05	15 08	15 15	15 20
Horley 4	d			14 02							14 28								15 02				
Salfords	d																						
Earlswood (Surrey)	d																						
Tonbridge 4	d														14 29								
Leigh (Kent)	d														14 33								
Penshurst	d														14 37								
Edenbridge	d														14 43								
Godstone	d														14 50								
Nutfield	d														14 55								
Reigate	d																						
Redhill 5	a			14 09		14 16					14 34		14 45		15 00				15 09		15 16		
	d			14 10							14 35		14 46						15 10				
Merstham	d										14 39												
Coulsdon South	d										14 44												
Purley 4	d			14 20							14 50								15 20				
East Croydon	a	14 09	14 12	14 26			14 31		14 39		14 56		14 58	15 01			15 09	15 12	15 26			15 31	
	d	14 10	14 13	14 26			14 32		14 40	14 50	14 56		15 00	15 02			15 10	15 13	15 26			15 32	
Norwood Junction 2	a										15 00												
New Cross Gate	d																						
London Bridge 4 ⊖	a						14 45				15 13			15 15								15 45	
London Blackfriars 5 ⊖	a																						
City Thameslink 3	a																						
Farringdon 3 ⊖	a																						
St Pancras International 15 ⊖	a																						
St Albans City	a																						
Luton Airport Parkway 4 ✈	a																						
Luton 7	a																						
Bedford 10	a																						
Clapham Junction 10	d	14 25	14 28	14 38					14 55	15 01			15 12				15 25	15 28	15 38				
London Victoria 15 ⊖	a	14 31	14 35	14 46	14 40			14 55	15 01	15 08		15 10	15 18			15 25	15 31	15 35	15 46	15 40			15 55

Brighton - London and Bedford

		SN ◇1	SN 1	SN 1	SN 1 ✠	SN ◇1	FC 1	SN 1	SN 1 ✠	SN ◇1 ✠	SN ◇1 ✠	SN ◇1 ✠	SN 1 ✠	GW 1	FC 1	SN 1 ✠	SN ◇1	SN 1	SN 1	SN 1 ✠	SN ◇1	FC 1
Brighton 10	d					15 00	15 14				15 34				15 44						16 00	16 14
Hove 2	d	14 54															15 54					
Preston Park	d					15 03															16 03	
Hassocks 4	d					15 10	15 22								15 52						16 10	16 22
Burgess Hill 4	d	15 04				15 13	15 26								15 56		16 04				16 13	16 26
Lewes 4	d									15 16												
Wivelsfield 4	d					15 16				15 31											16 16	
Haywards Heath 3	a	15 09				15 20	15 30			15 35					16 00		16 09				16 20	16 30
	d	15 10				15 21	15 31			15 39					16 01		16 10				16 21	16 31
Balcombe	d					15 26															16 26	
Horsham 4	d			15 03								15 42							16 03			
Littlehaven	d			15 06															16 06			
Faygate	d																					
Ifield	d			15 12															16 12			
Crawley	d			15 16								15 51							16 16			
Three Bridges 4	a			15 19		15 32	15 40					15 54			16 10				16 19		16 32	16 40
	d			15 20		15 32	15 40					15 55			16 10				16 20		16 32	16 40
Gatwick Airport 10 ✈	a	15 22		15 24		15 37	15 44			15 52	15 55	15 59			16 14		16 22		16 24		16 37	16 44
	d	15 23		15 25	15 35	15 38	15 45		15 50	15 53	15 56	16 00	16 05	16 08	16 15	16 20	16 23		16 25	16 35	16 38	16 45
Horley 4	d			15 28								16 02							16 28			
Salfords	d																					
Earlswood (Surrey)	d																					
Tonbridge 4	d							15 29														
Leigh (Kent)	d							15 33														
Penshurst	d							15 37														
Edenbridge	d							15 43														
Godstone	d							15 50														
Nutfield	d							15 55														
Reigate	d																					
Redhill 5	a			15 34		15 45		16 00				16 09		16 16					16 34		16 45	
	d			15 35		15 46						16 10							16 35		16 46	
Merstham	d			15 39															16 39			
Coulsdon South	d			15 44															16 44			
Purley 4	d			15 50								16 20							16 50			
East Croydon	a	15 39		15 56		15 58	16 01			16 09	16 12	16 26			16 31		16 39		16 56		16 58	17 01
	d	15 40	15 50	15 56		16 00	16 02			16 10	16 13	16 26			16 32		16 40	16 50	16 56		17 00	17 02
Norwood Junction 2	a			16 00															17 00			
New Cross Gate	d																					
London Bridge 4 ⊖	a			16 13			16 15								16 45				17 13			17 15
London Blackfriars 3 ⊖	a																					
City Thameslink 3	a																					
Farringdon 3 ⊖	a																					
St Pancras International 15 ⊖	a																					
St Albans City	a																					
Luton Airport Parkway 4 ✈	a																					
Luton 7	a																					
Bedford 10	a																					
Clapham Junction 10	d	15 55	16 01			16 12				16 25	16 28	16 38					16 55	17 01			17 12	
London Victoria 15 ⊖	a	16 01	16 08		16 10	16 18			16 25	16 31	16 35	16 46	16 40			16 55	17 01	17 08		17 10	17 18	

Brighton - London and Bedford

		SN 1	SN 1 ✠	SN ◇1 ✠	SN ◇1 ✠	SN ◇1 ✠	SN 1 ✠	GW 1	FC 1	SN 1 ✠	SN ◇1	SN 1	SN 1	SN 1 ✠	SN ◇1	FC 1	SN 1	SN 1 ✠	SN ◇1 ✠	SN ◇1 ✠	SN ◇1 ✠	SN 1 ✠	GW 1
Brighton 10	d				16 34				16 44						17 00	17 14				17 34			
Hove 2	d										16 54												
Preston Park	d														17 03								
Hassocks 4	d								16 52						17 10	17 22							
Burgess Hill 4	d								16 56		17 04				17 13	17 26							
Lewes 4	d			16 16															17 16				
Wivelsfield 4	d			16 31											17 16				17 31				
Haywards Heath 3	a			16 35					17 00		17 09				17 20	17 30			17 35				
	d			16 39					17 01		17 10				17 21	17 31			17 39				
Balcombe	d														17 26								
Horsham 4	d					16 42							17 03								17 42		
Littlehaven	d												17 06										
Faygate	d																						
Ifield	d												17 12										
Crawley	d					16 51							17 16								17 51		
Three Bridges 4	a					16 54			17 10				17 19		17 32	17 40					17 54		
	d					16 55			17 10				17 20		17 32	17 40					17 55		
Gatwick Airport 10 ✈	a			16 52	16 55	16 59			17 14		17 22		17 24		17 37	17 44			17 52	17 55	17 59		
	d		16 50	16 53	16 56	17 00	17 05	17 08	17 15	17 20	17 23		17 25	17 35	17 38	17 45		17 50	17 53	17 56	18 00	18 05	18 08
Horley 4	d					17 02							17 28								18 02		
Salfords	d																						
Earlswood (Surrey)	d																						
Tonbridge 4	d	16 29															17 29						
Leigh (Kent)	d	16 33															17 33						
Penshurst	d	16 37															17 37						
Edenbridge	d	16 43															17 43						
Godstone	d	16 50															17 50						
Nutfield	d	16 55															17 55						
Reigate	d																						
Redhill 5	a	17 00				17 09		17 16					17 34		17 45		18 00				18 09		18 16
	d					17 10							17 35		17 46						18 10		
Merstham	d												17 39										
Coulsdon South	d												17 44										
Purley 4	d					17 20							17 50								18 20		
East Croydon	a			17 09	17 12	17 26			17 31		17 39		17 56		17 58	18 01			18 09	18 12	18 26		
	d			17 10	17 13	17 26			17 32		17 40	17 50	17 56		18 00	18 02			18 10	18 13	18 26		
Norwood Junction 2	a												18 00										
New Cross Gate	d																						
London Bridge 4 ⊖	a								17 45				18 13			18 15							
London Blackfriars 3 ⊖	a																						
City Thameslink 3	a																						
Farringdon 3 ⊖	a																						
St Pancras International 15 ⊖	a																						
St Albans City	a																						
Luton Airport Parkway 4 ✈	a																						
Luton 7	a																						
Bedford 10	a																						
Clapham Junction 10	d			17 25	17 28	17 38					17 55	18 01			18 12				18 25	18 28	18 38		
London Victoria 15 ⊖	a		17 25	17 31	17 35	17 46	17 40			17 55	18 01	18 08		18 10	18 18			18 25	18 31	18 35	18 46	18 40	

Table 186

Sundays from 11 September

Brighton - London and Bedford

		FC ■	SN ■ 🛒	SN ◇■	SN ■	SN ■	SN ■ 🛒	SN ◇■	FC ■	SN ■	SN ■ 🛒	SN ◇■ 🛒	SN ◇■	SN ◇■	SN ■	GW ■	FC ■	SN ■	SN ◇■	SN ■	SN ■	SN ■
Brighton [10]	d	17 44						18 00	18 14				18 34				18 44					
Hove [2]	d			17 54															18 54			
Preston Park	d							18 03														
Hassocks [4]	d	17 52						18 10	18 22								18 52					
Burgess Hill [4]	d	17 56		18 04				18 13	18 26								18 56		19 04			
Lewes [4]	d											18 16										
Wivelsfield [4]	d							18 16				18 31										
Haywards Heath [3]	a	18 00		18 09				18 20	18 30			18 35					19 00		19 09			
	d	18 01		18 10				18 21	18 31			18 39					19 01		19 10			
Balcombe	d							18 26														
Horsham [4]	d					18 03								18 42							19 03	
Littlehaven	d					18 06															19 06	
Faygate	d																					
Ifield	d					18 12															19 12	
Crawley	d					18 16								18 51							19 16	
Three Bridges [4]	a	18 10				18 19		18 32	18 40					18 54			19 10				19 19	
	d	18 10				18 20		18 32	18 40					18 55			19 10				19 20	
Gatwick Airport [10] ✈	a	18 14		18 22		18 24		18 37	18 44			18 52	18 55	18 59			19 14		19 22		19 24	
	d	18 15	18 20	18 23		18 25	18 35	18 38	18 45		18 50	18 53	18 56	19 00	19 05	19 08	19 15	19 20	19 23		19 25	19 35
Horley [4]	d					18 28								19 02							19 28	
Salfords	d																					
Earlswood (Surrey)	d																					
Tonbridge [4]	d									18 29												
Leigh (Kent)	d									18 33												
Penshurst	d									18 37												
Edenbridge	d									18 43												
Godstone	d									18 50												
Nutfield	d									18 55												
Reigate	d																					
Redhill [5]	a					18 34		18 45		19 00				19 09		19 16					19 34	
	d					18 35		18 46						19 10							19 35	
Merstham	d					18 39															19 39	
Coulsdon South	d					18 44															19 44	
Purley [4]	d					18 50								19 20							19 50	
East Croydon	a	18 31		18 39		18 56		18 58	19 01			19 09	19 12	19 26			19 31		19 39		19 56	
	d	18 32		18 40	18 50	18 56		19 00	19 02			19 10	19 13	19 26			19 32		19 40	19 50	19 56	
Norwood Junction [2]	a					19 00															20 00	
New Cross Gate	d																					
London Bridge [4] ⊖	a	18 45				19 13			19 15								19 45				20 13	
London Blackfriars [3] ⊖	a																					
City Thameslink [3]	a																					
Farringdon [3] ⊖	a																					
St Pancras International [15] ⊖	a																					
St Albans City	a																					
Luton Airport Parkway [4] ✈	a																					
Luton [7]	a																					
Bedford [10]	a																					
Clapham Junction [10]	d			18 55	19 01			19 12				19 25	19 28	19 38					19 55	20 01		
London Victoria [15] ⊖	a		18 55	19 01	19 08		19 10	19 18			19 25	19 31	19 35	19 46	19 40			19 55	20 01	20 08		20 10

Table 186

Sundays from 11 September

Brighton - London and Bedford

		SN ◇■	FC ■	SN ■	SN ■	SN ◇■	SN ◇■	SN ◇■	SN ■	GW ■	FC ■	SN ■	SN ◇■	SN ■	SN ■	SN ■	SN ◇■	FC ■	SN ■	SN ■	SN ◇■	SN ◇■	SN ◇■
Brighton [10]	d	19 00	19 14				19 34				19 44						20 00	20 14				20 34	
Hove [2]	d												19 54										
Preston Park	d	19 03															20 03						
Hassocks [4]	d	19 10	19 22								19 52						20 10	20 22					
Burgess Hill [4]	d	19 13	19 26								19 56		20 04				20 13	20 26					
Lewes [4]	d					19 16															20 16		
Wivelsfield [4]	d	19 16				19 31											20 16				20 31		
Haywards Heath [3]	a	19 20	19 30			19 35					20 00		20 09				20 20	20 30			20 35		
	d	19 21	19 31			19 39					20 01		20 10				20 21	20 31			20 39		
Balcombe	d	19 26															20 26						
Horsham [4]	d							19 42							20 03								20 42
Littlehaven	d														20 06								
Faygate	d																						
Ifield	d														20 12								
Crawley	d							19 51							20 16								20 51
Three Bridges [4]	a	19 32	19 40					19 54			20 10				20 19		20 32	20 40					20 54
	d	19 32	19 40					19 55			20 10				20 20		20 32	20 40					20 55
Gatwick Airport [10] ✈	a	19 37	19 44			19 52	19 55	19 59			20 14		20 22		20 24		20 37	20 44			20 52	20 55	20 59
	d	19 38	19 45		19 50	19 53	19 56	20 00	20 05	20 08	20 15	20 20	20 23		20 25	20 35	20 38	20 45		20 50	20 53	20 56	21 00
Horley [4]	d							20 02							20 28								21 02
Salfords	d																						
Earlswood (Surrey)	d																						
Tonbridge [4]	d			19 29															20 29				
Leigh (Kent)	d			19 33															20 33				
Penshurst	d			19 37															20 37				
Edenbridge	d			19 43															20 43				
Godstone	d			19 50															20 50				
Nutfield	d			19 55															20 55				
Reigate	d																						
Redhill [5]	a	19 45		20 00				20 09		20 16					20 34		20 45		21 00				21 09
	d	19 46						20 10							20 35		20 46						21 10
Merstham	d														20 39								
Coulsdon South	d														20 44								
Purley [4]	d							20 20							20 50								21 20
East Croydon	a	19 58	20 01			20 09	20 12	20 26			20 31		20 39		20 56		20 58	21 01			21 09	21 12	21 26
	d	20 00	20 02			20 10	20 13	20 26			20 32		20 40	20 50	20 56		21 00	21 02			21 10	21 13	21 26
Norwood Junction [2]	a														21 00								
New Cross Gate	d																						
London Bridge [4] ⊖	a		20 15								20 45				21 13			21 15					
London Blackfriars [3] ⊖	a																						
City Thameslink [3]	a																						
Farringdon [3] ⊖	a																						
St Pancras International [15] ⊖	a																						
St Albans City	a																						
Luton Airport Parkway [4] ✈	a																						
Luton [7]	a																						
Bedford [10]	a																						
Clapham Junction [10]	d	20 12				20 25	20 28	20 38					20 55	21 01			21 12				21 25	21 28	21 38
London Victoria [15] ⊖	a	20 18			20 25	20 31	20 35	20 46	20 41			20 55	21 01	21 08		21 10	21 18			21 25	21 31	21 35	21 46

Brighton - London and Bedford

from 11 September

		SN 1	GW 1	FC 1	SN 1	SN ◇1	SN 1	SN 1	SN 1	SN ◇1	FC 1	SN 1	SN 1	SN ◇1	SN ◇1	SN 1	GW 1	FC 1	SN 1	SN 1	SN 1	SN 1	SN ◇1
Brighton 10	d			20 44						21 00	21 14							21 44					22 00
Hove 2	d					20 54																	
Preston Park	d									21 03													22 03
Hassocks 4	d			20 52						21 10	21 22							21 52					22 10
Burgess Hill 4	d			20 56		21 04				21 13	21 26							21 56					22 13
Lewes 4	d													21 16									
Wivelsfield 4	d									21 16				21 31									22 16
Haywards Heath 3	a			21 00		21 09				21 20	21 30			21 35				22 00					22 20
	d			21 01		21 10				21 21	21 31			21 39				22 01					22 21
Balcombe	d									21 26													22 26
Horsham 4	d							21 03							21 42						22 03		
Littlehaven	d							21 06													22 06		
Faygate	d																						
Ifield	d							21 12													22 12		
Crawley	d							21 16							21 51						22 16		
Three Bridges 4	a			21 10				21 19		21 32	21 40				21 54			22 10			22 19		22 32
	d			21 10				21 20		21 32	21 40				21 55			22 10			22 20		22 32
Gatwick Airport 10 ✈	a			21 14		21 22		21 24		21 37	21 44			21 52	21 59			22 14			22 24		22 37
	d	21 05	21 08	21 15	21 20	21 23		21 25	21 35	21 38	21 45		21 50	21 53	22 00	22 05	22 08	22 15	22 20		22 25	22 35	22 38
Horley 4	d							21 28							22 02						22 28		
Salfords	d																						
Earlswood (Surrey)	d																						
Tonbridge 4	d											21 29											
Leigh (Kent)	d											21 33											
Penshurst	d											21 37											
Edenbridge	d											21 43											
Godstone	d											21 50											
Nutfield	d											21 55											
Reigate	d																						
Redhill 5	a		21 16					21 34		21 45		22 00			22 09		22 16				22 34		22 45
	d							21 35		21 46					22 10						22 35		22 46
Merstham	d							21 39													22 39		
Coulsdon South	d							21 44													22 44		
Purley 4	d							21 50							22 20						22 50		
East Croydon	a			21 31		21 39		21 56		21 58	22 01			22 09	22 26			22 31			22 56		22 58
	d			21 32		21 40	21 50	21 56		22 00	22 02			22 10	22 26			22 32		22 50	22 56		23 00
Norwood Junction 2	a							22 00															
New Cross Gate	d																						
London Bridge 4 ⊖	a			21 45				22 13			22 15							22 45					
London Blackfriars 3 ⊖	a																						
City Thameslink 3	a																						
Farringdon 3 ⊖	a																						
St Pancras International 15 ⊖	a																						
St Albans City	a																						
Luton Airport Parkway 4 ✈	a																						
Luton 7	a																						
Bedford 10	a																						
Clapham Junction 10	d					21 55	22 01			22 12				22 25	22 38					23 01	23 08		23 13
London Victoria 15 ⊖	a	21 40			21 55	22 01	22 08		22 10	22 18			22 25	22 31	22 46	22 40			22 55	23 08	23 14	23 10	23 20

Brighton - London and Bedford

from 11 September

		FC 1	SN 1	SN 1	SN ◇1	SN 1	GW 1 A	GW 1 B	FC 1	SN 1	SN 1	SN 1	SN 1	SN ◇1	FC 1	SN 1	SN ◇1	FC 1
Brighton 10	d	22 14							22 44					23 02	23 14			23 45
Hove 2	d																	
Preston Park	d													23 06				
Hassocks 4	d	22 22							22 52					23 12	23 22			23 53
Burgess Hill 4	d	22 26							22 56					23 16	23 26			23 57
Lewes 4	d																	
Wivelsfield 4	d													23 19				
Haywards Heath 3	a	22 30							23 00					23 23	23 30			00 01
	d	22 31							23 01					23 24	23 31			00 01
Balcombe	d													23 29				
Horsham 4	d				22 42							23 03						
Littlehaven	d											23 06						
Faygate	d																	
Ifield	d											23 12						
Crawley	d				22 51							23 16						
Three Bridges 4	a	22 40			22 54				23 10			23 20		23 36	23 40			00 10
	d	22 40			22 55				23 10			23 20		23 42	23 40			00 10
Gatwick Airport 10 ✈	a	22 44			22 59				23 14			23 24		23 46	23 44			00 14
	d	22 45		22 50	23 00	23 05	23 08	23 09	23 15	23 20		23 25	23 35	23 47	23 45	23 50		00 15
Horley 4	d				23 02							23 28		23 49				
Salfords	d																	
Earlswood (Surrey)	d																	
Tonbridge 4	d		22 29															
Leigh (Kent)	d		22 33															
Penshurst	d		22 37															
Edenbridge	d		22 43															
Godstone	d		22 50															
Nutfield	d		22 55															
Reigate	d																	
Redhill 5	a		23 00		23 09		23 16	23 16				23 34		23 57				00 22
	d				23 10							23 35		00 02				00 23
Merstham	d											23 39						
Coulsdon South	d											23 44						
Purley 4	d				23 20							23 50		00 11			←	
East Croydon	a	23 01			23 26				23 31			23 55		00 16	00 02		00 16	00 36
	d	23 02			23 27				23 32		23 50	23 56		00 17	00 04		00 17	00 36
Norwood Junction 2	a													→				
New Cross Gate	d																	
London Bridge 4 ⊖	a	23 15							23 45						00 19			00 53
London Blackfriars 3 ⊖	a																	
City Thameslink 3	a																	
Farringdon 3 ⊖	a																	
St Pancras International 15 ⊖	a																	
St Albans City	a																	
Luton Airport Parkway 4 ✈	a																	
Luton 7	a																	
Bedford 10	a																	
Clapham Junction 10	d				23 39						00 02	00 11					00 30	
London Victoria 15 ⊖	a			23 25	23 46	23 40				23 55	00 08	00 21	00 10			00 25	00 37	

A not 11 September

B 11 September

London, Gatwick Airport, Brighton - Sussex Coast, Portsmouth and Southampton

Miles	Miles	Miles	Station		SN MX ◇1	SN MX 1	SN MX ◇1	SN MX ◇1	SN MX ◇	SN ◇	SN MX ◇1	SN MO 1	SN MX 1	SN MO ◇1	SN MX 1	SN MX ◇1	SN ◇1	SN ◇	SN ◇	SN ◇	SN ◇1	SN ◇1	SN ◇
0	—	0	London Victoria 15 ⊖	d	22p17	22p32		22p47			23p17	23p04	23p10	23p17	23p47	00 05							
2¾	—	—	Clapham Junction 10	d	22p23	22p38		22p53			23p23	23p10	23p16	23p23	23p53	00 11							
—	0	—	London Bridge 4 ⊖	d																			
10½	10¼	—	East Croydon	d	22p34	22p48		23p03			23p33	23p22	23p28	23p38	00 06	00 24							
21	—	—	Redhill 5	d		23p01						23p42	23p46		00 25								
26	—	—	Horley	d								23p50	23p56		00 31								
26¾	—	—	Gatwick Airport 10 ✈	d	22p49	23p09		23p19			23p51	23p55	23p59	00 01	00 34	00 42							
29½	—	29½	Three Bridges 4	a	22p54	23p15					23p55	00 01	00 04	00 05	00 39	00 47							
—	—	—		d	22p54	23p16					23p56	00 01	00 04	00 06	00 39	00 47							
—	—	31	Crawley	d		23p19						00 05	00 07		00 43								
—	—	38	Horsham 4	a		23p27						00 17	00 19		00 55								
—	—	—		d		23p28																	
—	—	40½	Christs Hospital	d		23p31																	
—	—	45¼	Billingshurst	d		23p37																	
—	—	50¼	Pulborough	d		23p44																	
—	—	55	Amberley	d		23p50																	
—	—	58¾	Arundel	d		23p55																	
38	—	—	Haywards Heath 3	d	23p03			23b37			00 05			00 15		01 02							
41¾	—	—	Burgess Hill	d	23p08						00 10			00 20									
—	—	—	Preston Park	d																			
—	0	—	Brighton 10	d					00 03	00 10						01s16						05 14	
51	1½	—	Hove 2	d	23p22			23p52	00 07	00a13	00 22			00 31		01s24						05 18	
—	2	—	Aldrington	d					00 09													05 20	
—	3	—	Portslade	d	23p25			23p55	00 11		00s25			00s34		01s27						05 22	
—	3½	—	Fishersgate	d					00 13													05 24	
—	4½	—	Southwick	d	23p28			23p58	00 15		00s28			00s37		01s30						05 26	
—	5½	—	Shoreham-by-Sea	d	23p31			00 01	00 19		00s31			00s40		01s33						05 29	
—	8¼	—	Lancing	d	23p35			00 05	00 23		00s35			00s44		01s37						05 33	
—	9¾	—	East Worthing	d					00 26													05 36	
—	10½	—	Worthing 4	a	23p39			00 09	00 28		00 39			00 48		01 41						05 39	
—	—	—		d	23p39				00 29													05 39	
—	11½	—	West Worthing	d	23p41				00a31													05 41	
—	12¼	—	Durrington-on-Sea	d	23p44																	05 44	
—	13	—	Goring-by-Sea	d	23p46																	05 46	
0	15½	—	Angmering 3	d	23p50																	05 50	
6	—	—	Littlehampton 4	a																			
—	—	—		d																	05 35		06 04
8	19¾	61	Ford 4	d	23p56	00 01															05 39	05 56	06 08
—	—	—	Bognor Regis 4	d			←																
0	22½	—	Barnham	a	00 01	00 06	00 01														05 43	06 01	06 12
—	—	—		d	00 09	00 06	00 09										04 58	05 02	05 21	05 36	05 44	06 01	06 13
3½	—	—	Bognor Regis	a	→		00 15													05 42			06 19
—	28¾	—	Chichester 4	a		00 14											05 05	05 09	05 28		05 51	06 09	
—	—	—		d													05 06	05 10	05 29		05 52	06 09	
—	30¼	—	Fishbourne (Sussex)	d																	05 55		
—	31¼	—	Bosham	d																	05 58		
—	33¼	—	Nutbourne	d																	06 01		
—	34¼	—	Southbourne	d																	06 04		
—	35¾	—	Emsworth	d																	06 07		
—	37	—	Warblington	d																	06 10		
0	37½	—	Havant	d													05 17	05 21	05 40		06 13	06 20	
—	38¼	—	Bedhampton	a																	06 15		
—	41¼	—	Hilsea	a																	06 20		
—	44	—	Fratton	a														05 29	05 48		06 24		
—	44¾	—	Portsmouth & Southsea	a														05 33	05 52		06 28		
—	45½	—	Portsmouth Harbour ⛴	a														05 37	05 56		06 32		
4	—	—	Cosham	a													05 23					06 27	
6½	—	—	Portchester	a													05 28						
9¾	—	—	Fareham	a													05 33					06 36	
13½	—	—	Swanwick	a													05 40					06 43	
24¼	—	—	Southampton Central ⛴	a													05 59					07 02	

b Previous night, arr. 2330

London, Gatwick Airport, Brighton - Sussex Coast, Portsmouth and Southampton

Station		SN ◇1	SN ◇	SN ◇	SN ◇1	SN ◇	SN ◇	SN ◇	SN ◇	SN ◇1	SN ◇1	SN 1		SN ◇1	SN ◇	SN ◇	SN ◇	SN ◇	SN ◇1	SN ◇1	SN 1	SN ◇	SN ◇
London Victoria 15 ⊖	d																			06 02			
Clapham Junction 10	d																			06 08			
London Bridge 4 ⊖	d																						
East Croydon	d																			06 18			
Redhill 5	d																			06 39			
Horley	d																			06 48			
Gatwick Airport 10 ✈	d											05 56								06 55			
Three Bridges 4	a											06 00								06 59			
	d											06 01								07 00	07 05		
Crawley	d											06 05								07 03	07 08		
Horsham 4	a											06 17								07 11	07 22		
	d											06 17								07 12			
Christs Hospital	d											06 21								07 15			
Billingshurst	d											06 27								07 21			
Pulborough	d											06 34								07 28			
Amberley	d											06 40								07 34			
Arundel	d											06 46								07 39			
Haywards Heath 3	d																						
Burgess Hill	d																						
Preston Park	d																						
Brighton 10	d	05 30	05 44		05 53			05 57	06 15	06 27				06 35				06 53	07 06			07 15	
Hove 2	d	05 34	05a47		05 57			06 01	06 19	06 31				06 39				06 57	07 10			07 19	
Aldrington	d	05 36						06 03	06 21									06 59					
Portslade	d	05 38						06 05	06 23					06 42				07 01				07 22	
Fishersgate	d	05 40						06 07	06 25									07 03					
Southwick	d	05 42						06 09	06 27					06 45				07 05				07 25	
Shoreham-by-Sea	d	05 45			06 03			06 12	06 30	06 37				06 48				07 09	07 16			07 28	
Lancing	d	05 49						06 16	06 34					06 52				07 13				07 32	
East Worthing	d	05 52						06 19	06 37									07 16					
Worthing 4	a	05 55			06 09			06 22	06 40	06 43				06 56				07 18	07 22			07 36	
	d	05 55			06 09			06 22	06 40	06 43				06 56				07 19	07 23			07 36	
West Worthing	d	05 57						06 24	06a42	06 45				06 58				07 21	07 25				
Durrington-on-Sea	d	06 00						06 27		06 48				07 01				07 23	07 27				
Goring-by-Sea	d	06 02						06 29		06 50				07 03				07 26	07 30				
Angmering 3	d	06 06						06 33		06 54				07 07				07 30	07 34				
Littlehampton 4	a							06 42										07 38					
	d						06 35				06 58				07 18			07 48					
Ford 4	d	06 13					06 39				07 04	06 51		07 13	07 22			07 52		07 44		07 48	
Bognor Regis 4	d			06 13												07 27							←
Barnham	a	06 17		06 19	06 24		06 43			07 04	07 08	06 55		07 18	07 26	07 33		07 56	07 43	07 49		07 53	07 56
	d	06 18			06 24	06 27	06 48			07 05	07 09	07 00	07 13	07 18	07 27		07 39	07 57	07 44	07 50		07 53	07 57
Bognor Regis	a					06 33	06 54						07 20				07 45	→		07 58			
Chichester 4	a	06 25			06 32					07 12	07 16	07 07		07 26	07 34				07 51			08 01	08 05
	d	06 26			06 32					07 13	07 17	07 08		07 28	07 35				07 52			08 01	
Fishbourne (Sussex)	d				06 35						07 20				07 38							08 04	
Bosham	d				06 38					07 17					07 41							08 07	
Nutbourne	d				06 42						07 25				07 44							08 11	
Southbourne	d	06 33			06 44					07 22	07 27				07 47							08 13	
Emsworth	d	06 36			06 47					07 25	07 30				07 50							08 16	
Warblington	d				06 50					07 28					07 53							08 19	
Havant	d	06 40			06 53					07 31	07 35	07 19		07 41	07 58				08 03			08 22	
Bedhampton	a				06 56						07 37				08 00							08 25	
Hilsea	a				07 01						07 42				08 05							08 30	
Fratton	a				07 05						07 46			07 49	08 09							08 34	
Portsmouth & Southsea	a				07 08						07 50			07 53	08 15							08 37	
Portsmouth Harbour ⛴	a				07 12									07 58	08 20							08 41	
Cosham	a	06 49								07 38		07 25							08 09				
Portchester	a	06 54										07 30							08 13				
Fareham	a	06 59								07 46		07 35							08 18				
Swanwick	a	07 06								07 53		07 42							08 26				
Southampton Central ⛴	a	07 25								08 13		08 01							08 52				

London, Gatwick Airport, Brighton - Sussex Coast, Portsmouth and Southampton

		SN	SN	SN	SN	SN	SN	SN	SN	SN	SN	SN	SN	SN	SN	SN	SN	SN	SN	SN	SN	SN	SN
		◇	◇	1	◇1	◇	◇1	1	◇	◇	◇1	◇	◇	◇	◇	◇	◇1	1	◇	◇	1	◇	◇1
							A																
London Victoria 15 ⊖	d						06 32	06 51									07 17	07 36					07 52
Clapham Junction 10	d						06 38	06 57									07 23	07 42					07 58
London Bridge 4 ⊖	d																						
East Croydon	d						06 49	07 07									07 34	07 52					08 09
Redhill 5	d						07 07	07 27									07 47	08 11					
Horley	d						07 16	07 36									07 56	08 21					
Gatwick Airport 10 ✈	d						07 20	07 40									08 00	08 24					08 25
Three Bridges 4	a						07 24	07 44									08 04	08 29					
	d						07 30	07 45									08 05	08 30					
Crawley	d						07 34	07 49									08 09	08 34					
Horsham 4	a						07 46	08 01									08 22	08 48					
	d						07 46										08 23						
Christs Hospital	d						07 50										08 26						
Billingshurst	d						07 56										08 32						
Pulborough	d						08 03										08 39						
Amberley	d						08 09										08 45						
Arundel	d						08 14										08 50						
Haywards Heath 3	d																						08 37
Burgess Hill	d																						
Preston Park	d																						
Brighton 10	d		07 20	07 30	07 37	07 47			07 50		08 03		08 07	08 14	08 23						08 33	08 44	
Hove 2	d		07 24	07 34	07 41	07 51			07 54		08 07		08 11	08a17	08 27						08 37	08a47	08 54
Aldrington	d		07 26						07 56						08 29								
Portslade	d		07 28	07 37	07 44	07 54			07 58				08 14		08 31						08 40		
Fishersgate	d		07 30						08 00						08 33								
Southwick	d		07 32	07 40	07 47	07 57			08 02				08 17		08 35						08 43		
Shoreham-by-Sea	d		07 35	07 43	07 50	08 00			08 06		08 13		08 20		08 39						08 46		09 00
Lancing	d		07 39	07 47	07 54	08 04			08 10				08 24		08 43						08 50		09 04
East Worthing	d		07 42						08 13						08 46								
Worthing 4	a		07 45	07 51	07 58	08 08			08 15		08 19		08 28		08 48						08 54		09 08
	d		07 45	07 52	07 59	08 08			08 16		08 20		08 28		08 49						08 55		09 08
West Worthing	d		07 47	07 54	08 01				08 18		08 22		08 30		08a51						08 57		09 10
Durrington-on-Sea	d		07 50	07 56	08 03	08 12			08 20		08 24		08 33								08 59		09 13
Goring-by-Sea	d		07 52	07 59	08 06				08 23		08 27		08 35								09 02		09 15
Angmering 3	d		07 56	08 03	08 10	08 17			08 27		08 31		08 39								09 06		09 19
Littlehampton 4	a		08 05				08 21		08 35														09 28
	d	07 58					08 26												08 54				
Ford 4	d	08 02		08 09	08 17		08 30				08 37		08 45				08 55		08 59				
Bognor Regis 4	d									08 32						08 48							
Barnham	a	08 06		08 13	08 21	08 27	08 34			08 38	08 41		08 50			08 55	08 59		09 03		09 15		
	d	08 07		08 14	08 22	08 28	08 35				08 42	08 45	08 52				09 00		09 04	09 12	09 16		
Bognor Regis	a	08 13				08 36						08 51	08 58							09 18			
Chichester 4	a			08 21	08 29		08 42				08 49						09 07		09 11		09 23		
	d			08 22	08 30						08 50						09 08		09 12		09 24		
Fishbourne (Sussex)	d																		09 15				
Bosham	d																		09 18				
Nutbourne	d																		09 21				
Southbourne	d			08 29	08 37												09 15		09 24		09 31		
Emsworth	d			08 32	08 40												09 18		09 27		09 34		
Warblington	d																		09 30				
Havant	d			08 37	08 44						09 01						09 23		09 33		09 38		
Bedhampton	a																		09 36				
Hilsea	a																		09 42				
Fratton	a				08 53						09 11								09 46				
Portsmouth & Southsea	a				08 56						09 17								09 50				
Portsmouth Harbour ⛴	a				09 02						09 21												
Cosham	a			08 45													09 29				09 45		
Portchester	a			08 49																			
Fareham	a			08 54													09 37				09 53		
Swanwick	a			09 01													09 44				10 00		
Southampton Central ⛴	a			09 19													10 01				10 20		

A ◇ to Three Bridges

London, Gatwick Airport, Brighton - Sussex Coast, Portsmouth and Southampton

		SN	SN	GW	SN		SN	SN	SN	SN	SN	SN	SN	SN	SN		SN	SN	SN	SN	SN
		◇	◇	◇	◇1		◇1	◇	◇1	1	◇	◇	◇	◇1	◇1		1	◇	◇	◇1	1
				A ✠											B ✠					C ✠	
London Victoria 15 ⊖	d				08 02				08 17						08 32					08 47	
Clapham Junction 10	d				08 08				08 23						08 38					08 53	
London Bridge 4 ⊖	d									08 02											08 32
East Croydon	d				08 18				08 33	08 19					08 48					09 03	08 49
Redhill 5	d				08 32					08 41					09 03						09 12
Horley	d									08 50											09 21
Gatwick Airport 10 ✈	d				08 40				08 49	08 54					09 11					09 19	09 25
Three Bridges 4	a				08 44					08 59					09 16						09 29
	d				08 45					08 59					09 16						09 30
Crawley	d				08 48					09 03					09 19						09 34
Horsham 4	a				08 56					09 17					09 27						09 46
	d				09 00	09 05									09 31	09 36					
Christs Hospital	d					09 08										09 39					
Billingshurst	d					09 14										09 45					
Pulborough	d					09 21										09 52					
Amberley	d					09 27										09 58					
Arundel	d					09 32										10 03					
Haywards Heath 3	d								09 04											09 37	
Burgess Hill	d								09 09												
Preston Park	d								09 18												
Brighton 10	d	08 53		09 00			09 03	09 14			09 23						09 33	09 44			
Hove 2	d	08 57		09 04			09 07	09a18	09 22		09 27						09 37	09a47		09 53	
Aldrington	d	08 59									09 29										
Portslade	d	09 01					09 10		09 25		09 31						09 40				
Fishersgate	d	09 03									09 33										
Southwick	d	09 05					09 13				09 35						09 43				
Shoreham-by-Sea	d	09 08		09 13			09 17		09 30		09 39						09 46			10 00	
Lancing	d	09 12					09 21				09 43						09 50			10 04	
East Worthing	d	09 15									09 46										
Worthing 4	a	09 18		09 21			09 25		09 36		09 48						09 54			10 08	
	d	09 18		09 22			09 25		09 37		09 49						09 55			10 08	
West Worthing	d	09a20							09 39		09a51						09 57			10 10	
Durrington-on-Sea	d								09 41								09 59			10 13	
Goring-by-Sea	d								09 44								10 02			10 15	
Angmering 3	d						09 34		09 48								10 06			10 19	
Littlehampton 4	a								09 58											10 28	
	d													09 54					10 11		
Ford 4	d					09 37								09 58		10 08	10 12		10 16		
Bognor Regis 4	d											09 39									
Barnham	a			09 37	09 26	09 41	09 44					09 45		10 02	09 57	10 12	10 16		10 20		
	d		09 19	09 38	09 27	09 42	09 45						09 52	10 03	09 58	10 13	10 17		10 22		
Bognor Regis	a		09 25			09 48							09 58			10 19			10 28		
Chichester 4	a			09 45	09 34		09 52							10 10	10 05		10 24				
	d			09 47	09 35		09 53							10 11	10 06		10 25				
Fishbourne (Sussex)	d													10 14							
Bosham	d													10 17							
Nutbourne	d													10 20							
Southbourne	d						10 00							10 23	10 13						
Emsworth	d						10 03							10 26	10 16		10 33				
Warblington	d													10 29							
Havant	d			09 59	09 46		10 07							10 32	10 20		10 37				
Bedhampton	a													10 34							
Hilsea	a													10 42							
Fratton	a				09 54		10 16							10 46							
Portsmouth & Southsea	a				09 58		10 19							10 50							
Portsmouth Harbour ⛴	a				10 02		10 23														
Cosham	a			10 05											10 28		10 45				
Portchester	a														10 32						
Fareham	a			10 14											10 37		10 53				
Swanwick	a														10 44		11 00				
Southampton Central ⛴	a			10 41											11 01		11 19				

A ✠ to Fareham B ✠ to Crawley C ✠ to Haywards Heath

Table 188

London, Gatwick Airport, Brighton - Sussex Coast, Portsmouth and Southampton

		SN ◇■ A ⊼		SN ◇	SN ◇	SN ◇	SN ◇■ B ⊼	SN ■	SN ◇	SN ◇	SN ◇	SN ◇	SN ◇■ A ⊼		SN ■	SN ◇	SN ◇	SN ◇■ C ⊼	SN ■	SN ◇■ A ⊼		SN ◇	SN ◇
London Victoria 15 ⊖	d	09 02					09 17						09 32					09 47		10 02			
Clapham Junction 10	d	09 08					09 23						09 38					09 53		10 08			
London Bridge 4 ⊖	d							09 03											09 32				
East Croydon ⇌	d	09 19					09 33	09 21					09 48					10 03	09 51	10 18			
Redhill 5	d	09 30						09 40					10 00						10 10	10 30			
Horley	d	09 36						09 50											10 19	10 36			
Gatwick Airport 10 ✈	d	09 40					09 49	09 54					10 09					10 19	10 24	10 40			
Three Bridges 4	a	09 44						09 59					10 14						10 29	10 44			
	d	09 45						10 00					10 14						10 30	10 45			
Crawley	d	09 48						10 03					10 18						10 33	10 48			
Horsham 4	a	09 56						10 15					10 26						10 47	10 56			
	d	10 00	10 05										10 30	10 35						11 00	11 05		
Christs Hospital	d													10 38									
Billingshurst	d		10 14											10 44							11 14		
Pulborough	d		10 20											10 51							11 20		
Amberley	d													10 57									
Arundel	d		10 29											11 02							11 29		
Haywards Heath 3	d						10 05											10 37					
Burgess Hill	d						10 10																
Preston Park	d						10 19																
Brighton 10	d			09 53	10 03	10 14			10 23						10 33	10 44						10 53	11 03
Hove 2	d			09 57	10 07	10a17	10 23		10 27						10 37	10a47		10 53				10 57	11 07
Aldrington	d			09 59					10 29													10 59	
Portslade	d			10 01	10 10		10 26		10 31						10 40							11 01	11 10
Fishersgate	d			10 03					10 33													11 03	
Southwick	d			10 05	10 13				10 35						10 43							11 05	11 13
Shoreham-by-Sea	d			10 09	10 16		10 31		10 39						10 46			11 00				11 09	11 16
Lancing	d			10 13	10 20				10 43						10 50			11 04				11 13	11 20
East Worthing	d			10 16					10 46													11 16	
Worthing 4	a			10 18	10 24		10 37		10 48						10 54			11 08				11 18	11 24
	d			10 19	10 25		10 37		10 49						10 55			11 08				11 19	11 25
West Worthing	d			10a21			10 39		10a51						10 57			11 10				11a21	
Durrington-on-Sea	d						10 42								10 59			11 13					
Goring-by-Sea	d						10 44								11 02			11 15					
Angmering 3	d				10 31		10 48								11 06			11 19					11 31
Littlehampton 4	a						10 57											11 28					
	d											10 54					11 11						
Ford 4	d		10 34									10 58		11 07	11 12		11 16				11 34		
Bognor Regis 4	d									10 39													
Barnham	a	10 26	10 39		10 42					10 45		11 02	10 56	11 11	11 16		11 20			11 26	11 39		11 42
	d	10 27	10 39		10 42						10 52	11 03	10 57	11 12	11 17		11 22			11 27	11 39		11 42
Bognor Regis	a		10 46								10 58			11 18			11 28				11 46		
Chichester 4	a	10 34			10 50							11 10	11 04		11 24					11 34			11 50
	d	10 35			10 50							11 11	11 05		11 25					11 35			11 50
Fishbourne (Sussex)	d											11 14											
Bosham	d											11 17											
Nutbourne	d											11 20											
Southbourne	d				10 57							11 23	11 12										11 57
Emsworth	d				11 00							11 26	11 15		11 33								12 00
Warblington	d											11 29											
Havant	d	10 46			11 05							11 32	11 19		11 37					11 46			12 05
Bedhampton	a											11 34											
Hilsea	a											11 42											
Fratton	a	10 54			11 13							11 46								11 54			12 13
Portsmouth & Southsea	a	10 58			11 17							11 50								11 58			12 17
Portsmouth Harbour ⛴	a	11 02			11 21															12 02			12 21
Cosham	a												11 26		11 45								
Portchester	a												11 30										
Fareham	a												11 35		11 53								
Swanwick	a												11 42		12 00								
Southampton Central ⛴	a												12 01		12 19								

A ⊼ to Crawley B ⊼ to Gatwick Airport C ⊼ to Haywards Heath

Table 188

Mondays to Fridays

London, Gatwick Airport, Brighton - Sussex Coast, Portsmouth and Southampton

		SN ◇	SN ◇■ A ⊼	SN ■	SN ◇	SN ◇	SN ◇	SN ◇	SN ◇■ B ⊼		SN ■	SN ■	SN ◇	SN ◇	SN ◇■		SN ◇■	SN ◇	SN ◇■	SN ◇	SN ◇■	SN ■
London Victoria 15 ⊖	d		10 17						10 32						11 02						11 17	
Clapham Junction 10	d		10 23						10 38						11 08						11 23	
London Bridge 4 ⊖	d			10 03							10 33											11 03
East Croydon ⇌	d		10 33	10 21					10 48		10 51				11 18						11 33	11 21
Redhill 5	d			10 45					11 00		11 11				11 30							11 45
Horley	d			10 53							11 20				11 36							11 53
Gatwick Airport 10 ✈	d		10 49	10 56					11 09		11 24				11 40						11 49	11 56
Three Bridges 4	a			11 01					11 14		11 29				11 44							12 01
	d			11 01					11 14		11 30				11 45							12 01
Crawley	d			11 05					11 18		11 33				11 48							12 05
Horsham 4	a			11 17					11 26		11 45				11 56							12 18
	d								11 30	11 35					12 00	12 05						
Christs Hospital	d									11 38												
Billingshurst	d									11 44						12 14						
Pulborough	d									11 51						12 20						
Amberley	d									11 57												
Arundel	d									12 02						12 29						
Haywards Heath 3	d		11 05														11 37				12 05	
Burgess Hill	d		11 10																		12 10	
Preston Park	d		11 18																		12 18	
Brighton 10	d	11 14			11 23							11 33	11 44					11 53	12 03	12 14		
Hove 2	d	11a17	11 22		11 27							11 37	11a47				11 53	11 57	12 07	12a17	12 22	
Aldrington	d				11 29													11 59				
Portslade	d		11 25		11 31							11 40						12 01	12 10		12 25	
Fishersgate	d				11 33													12 03				
Southwick	d				11 35							11 43						12 05	12 13			
Shoreham-by-Sea	d		11 30		11 39							11 46					12 00	12 09	12 16		12 30	
Lancing	d				11 43							11 50					12 04	12 13	12 20			
East Worthing	d				11 46													12 16				
Worthing 4	a		11 36		11 48							11 54					12 08	12 18	12 24		12 36	
	d		11 37		11 49							11 55					12 08	12 19	12 25		12 37	
West Worthing	d		11 39		11a51							11 57					12 10	12a21			12 39	
Durrington-on-Sea	d		11 41									11 59					12 13				12 41	
Goring-by-Sea	d		11 44									12 02					12 15				12 44	
Angmering 3	d		11 48									12 06					12 19		12 31		12 48	
Littlehampton 4	a		11 57														12 28				12 57	
	d							11 54						12 11								
Ford 4	d							11 58		12 07		12 12		12 16		12 34						
Bognor Regis 4	d					11 39																
Barnham	a					11 45		12 02	11 56	12 11		12 16		12 20	12 26	12 39			12 42			
	d						11 52	12 03	11 57	12 12		12 17		12 22	12 27	12 39			12 42			
Bognor Regis	a						11 58			12 18				12 28		12 46						
Chichester 4	a							12 10	12 04			12 24			12 34				12 50			
	d							12 11	12 05			12 25			12 35				12 50			
Fishbourne (Sussex)	d							12 14														
Bosham	d							12 17														
Nutbourne	d							12 20														
Southbourne	d							12 23	12 12										12 57			
Emsworth	d							12 26	12 15			12 33							13 00			
Warblington	d							12 29														
Havant	d							12 32	12 19			12 37			12 46				13 05			
Bedhampton	a							12 34														
Hilsea	a							12 42														
Fratton	a							12 46							12 54				13 13			
Portsmouth & Southsea	a							12 50							12 58				13 17			
Portsmouth Harbour ⛴	a														13 02				13 21			
Cosham	a								12 26			12 45										
Portchester	a								12 30													
Fareham	a								12 35			12 53										
Swanwick	a								12 42			13 00										
Southampton Central ⛴	a								12 59			13 19										

A ⊼ to Gatwick Airport
B ⊼ to Crawley

London, Gatwick Airport, Brighton - Sussex Coast, Portsmouth and Southampton

		SN ◇	SN ◇	SN ◇	SN ◇	SN ◇1		SN ◇1	SN ◇	SN ◇	SN ◇1	SN 1	SN ◇1		SN ◇	SN ◇	SN ◇	SN ◇1	SN 1	SN ◇	SN ◇	SN ◇	SN ◇1
London Victoria 15 ⊖	d					11 32					11 47		12 02					12 17					
Clapham Junction 10	d					11 38					11 53		12 08					12 23					
London Bridge 4 ⊖	d											11 33							12 03				
East Croydon	d					11 48					12 03	11 51	12 18					12 33	12 21				
Redhill 5	d					12 00						12 10	12 30						12 45				
Horley	d											12 19	12 36						12 53				
Gatwick Airport 10 ✈	d					12 09					12 19	12 24	12 40					12 49	12 56				
Three Bridges 4	a					12 14						12 29	12 44						13 01				
	d					12 14						12 30	12 45						13 01				
Crawley	d					12 18						12 33	12 48						13 05				
Horsham 4	a					12 26						12 45	12 56						13 17				
	d					12 30	12 35						13 00	13 05									
Christs Hospital	d						12 38																
Billingshurst	d						12 44							13 14									
Pulborough	d						12 51							13 20									
Amberley	d						12 57																
Arundel	d						13 02							13 29									
Haywards Heath 3	d										12 37							13 05					
Burgess Hill	d																	13 10					
Preston Park	d																	13 18					
Brighton 10	d	12 23						12 33	12 44						12 53	13 03	13 14			13 23			
Hove 2	d	12 27						12 37	12a47		12 53				12 57	13 07	13a19	13 22		13 27			
Aldrington	d	12 29													12 59					13 29			
Portslade	d	12 31						12 40							13 01	13 10		13 25		13 31			
Fishersgate	d	12 33													13 03					13 33			
Southwick	d	12 35						12 43							13 05	13 13				13 35			
Shoreham-by-Sea	d	12 39						12 46			13 00				13 09	13 16		13 30		13 39			
Lancing	d	12 43						12 50			13 04				13 13	13 20				13 43			
East Worthing	d	12 46													13 16					13 46			
Worthing 4	a	12 48						12 54			13 08				13 18	13 24		13 36		13 48			
	d	12 49						12 55			13 08				13 19	13 25		13 37		13 49			
West Worthing	d	12a51						12 57			13 10				13a21			13 39		13a51			
Durrington-on-Sea	d							12 59			13 13							13 41					
Goring-by-Sea	d							13 02			13 15							13 44					
Angmering 3	d							13 06			13 19					13 31		13 48					
Littlehampton 4	a										13 28							13 57					
	d				12 54					13 11													13 54
Ford 4	d				12 58		13 07	13 12		13 16				13 34									13 58
Bognor Regis 4	d		12 39																		13 39		
Barnham	a		12 45		13 02	12 56	13 11	13 16		13 20			13 26	13 39		13 42					13 45		14 02
	d			12 52	13 03	12 57	13 12	13 17		13 22			13 27	13 39		13 42						13 52	14 03
Bognor Regis	a			12 58			13 18			13 28				13 46								13 58	
Chichester 4	a				13 10	13 04		13 24					13 34			13 50							14 10
	d				13 11	13 05		13 25					13 35			13 50							14 11
Fishbourne (Sussex)	d				13 14																		14 14
Bosham	d				13 17																		14 17
Nutbourne	d				13 20																		14 20
Southbourne	d				13 23	13 12										13 57							14 23
Emsworth	d				13 26	13 15		13 33								14 00							14 26
Warblington	d				13 29																		14 29
Havant	d				13 32	13 19		13 37					13 46			14 05							14 32
Bedhampton	a				13 34																		14 34
Hilsea	a				13 42																		14 42
Fratton	a				13 46								13 54			14 13							14 46
Portsmouth & Southsea	a				13 50								13 58			14 17							14 50
Portsmouth Harbour ⛴	a												14 02			14 21							
Cosham	a					13 26		13 45															
Portchester	a					13 30																	
Fareham	a					13 35		13 53															
Swanwick	a					13 42		14 02															
Southampton Central ⛴	a					13 59		14 19															

London, Gatwick Airport, Brighton - Sussex Coast, Portsmouth and Southampton

		SN ◇1		SN 1	SN ◇	SN ◇	SN ◇1	SN 1	SN ◇1		SN ◇	SN ◇	SN ◇	SN ◇1	SN 1	SN ◇	SN ◇	SN ◇	SN ◇1	SN ◇1 A 🚌		SN 1	SN ◇
London Victoria 15 ⊖	d	12 32					12 47		13 02					13 17						13 32			
Clapham Junction 10	d	12 38					12 53		13 08					13 23						13 38			
London Bridge 4 ⊖	d							12 33							13 03								
East Croydon	d	12 48					13 03	12 51	13 18					13 33	13 21					13 48			
Redhill 5	d	13 00						13 10	13 30						13 45					14 00			
Horley	d							13 19	13 36						13 53								
Gatwick Airport 10 ✈	d	13 09					13 19	13 24	13 40					13 49	13 56					14 09			
Three Bridges 4	a	13 14						13 29	13 44						14 01					14 14			
	d	13 14						13 30	13 45						14 01					14 14			
Crawley	d	13 18						13 33	13 48						14 05					14 18			
Horsham 4	a	13 26						13 45	13 56						14 17					14 26			
	d	13 30	13 35						14 00	14 05										14 30	14 35		
Christs Hospital	d		13 38																		14 38		
Billingshurst	d		13 44							14 14											14 44		
Pulborough	d		13 51							14 20											14 51		
Amberley	d		13 57																		14 57		
Arundel	d		14 02							14 29											15 02		
Haywards Heath 3	d						13 37							14 05									
Burgess Hill	d													14 10									
Preston Park	d													14 18									
Brighton 10	d			13 33	13 44						13 53	14 03	14 14			14 23						14 33	14 44
Hove 2	d			13 37	13a47		13 53				13 57	14 07	14a17	14 22		14 27						14 37	14a47
Aldrington	d										13 59					14 29							
Portslade	d			13 40							14 01	14 10		14 25		14 31						14 40	
Fishersgate	d										14 03					14 33							
Southwick	d			13 43							14 05	14 13				14 35						14 43	
Shoreham-by-Sea	d			13 46			14 00				14 09	14 16		14 30		14 39						14 46	
Lancing	d			13 50			14 04				14 13	14 20				14 43						14 50	
East Worthing	d										14 16					14 46							
Worthing 4	a			13 54			14 08				14 18	14 24		14 36		14 48						14 54	
	d			13 55			14 08				14 19	14 25		14 37		14 49						14 55	
West Worthing	d			13 57			14 10				14a21			14 39		14a51						14 57	
Durrington-on-Sea	d			13 59			14 13							14 41								14 59	
Goring-by-Sea	d			14 02			14 15							14 44								15 02	
Angmering 3	d			14 06			14 19					14 31		14 48								15 06	
Littlehampton 4	a						14 28							14 57									
	d					14 11													14 54				
Ford 4	d		14 07	14 12		14 16				14 34									14 58		15 07	15 12	
Bognor Regis 4	d																14 40						
Barnham	a	13 56	14 11	14 16		14 20			14 27	14 39		14 42					14 46		15 02	14 56	15 11	15 16	
	d	13 57	14 12	14 17		14 22			14 28	14 39		14 42						14 52	15 03	14 57	15 12	15 17	
Bognor Regis	a		14 18			14 28				14 46								14 58			15 18		
Chichester 4	a	14 04		14 24					14 35			14 50							15 10	15 04		15 24	
	d	14 05		14 25					14 36			14 50							15 11	15 05		15 25	
Fishbourne (Sussex)	d																		15 14				
Bosham	d																		15 17				
Nutbourne	d																		15 20				
Southbourne	d	14 12										14 57							15 23	15 12			
Emsworth	d	14 15		14 33								15 00							15 26	15 15		15 33	
Warblington	d																		15 29				
Havant	d	14 19		14 37					14 47			15 05							15 32	15 19		15 37	
Bedhampton	a																		15 34				
Hilsea	a																		15 42				
Fratton	a								14 55			15 13							15 46				
Portsmouth & Southsea	a								14 59			15 17							15 50				
Portsmouth Harbour ⛴	a								15 03			15 21											
Cosham	a	14 26		14 45																15 26		15 45	
Portchester	a	14 30																		15 30			
Fareham	a	14 35		14 53																15 35		15 53	
Swanwick	a	14 42		15 00																15 42		16 00	
Southampton Central ⛴	a	14 59		15 19																15 59		16 20	

A 🚌 to Crawley

London, Gatwick Airport, Brighton - Sussex Coast, Portsmouth and Southampton

		SN	SN	SN	SN	SN	SN		SN	SN	SN	SN	SN	SN	SN	SN		SN	SN	SN	SN	SN
		◇	◇1	1	◇	◇	◇1		◇	◇1	◇	◇1	1	◇	◇	◇1 A ⌶		◇1	◇	◇1	◇	◇1
London Victoria 15 ⊖	d		13 47				14 02					14 17				14 32						14 47
Clapham Junction 10	d		13 53				14 08					14 23				14 38						14 53
London Bridge 4 ⊖	d			13 33									14 03									
East Croydon	d		14 03	13 51			14 18					14 33	14 21			14 48						15 03
Redhill 5	d			14 10			14 30						14 45			15 00						
Horley	d			14 19			14 36						14 53									
Gatwick Airport 10 ✈	d		14 19	14 24			14 40					14 49	14 56			15 09						15 19
Three Bridges 4	a			14 29			14 44						15 01			15 14						
	d			14 30			14 45						15 01			15 14						
Crawley	d			14 33			14 48						15 05			15 18						
Horsham 4	a			14 45			14 56						15 17			15 26						
	d						15 00	15 05								15 30	15 35					
Christs Hospital	d							15 08									15 38					
Billingshurst	d							15 14									15 44					
Pulborough	d							15 21									15 51					
Amberley	d																15 57					
Arundel	d							15 30									16 02					
Haywards Heath 3	d		14 37									15 05										15 37
Burgess Hill	d											15 10										
Preston Park	d											15 18										
Brighton 10	d				14 53					15 03	15 14							15 23		15 33	15 44	
Hove 2	d		14 53		14 57					15 07	15a17	15 22						15 27		15 37	15a47	15 53
Aldrington	d				14 59													15 29				
Portslade	d				15 01					15 10		15 25						15 31		15 40		
Fishersgate	d				15 03													15 33				
Southwick	d				15 05					15 13								15 35		15 43		
Shoreham-by-Sea	d		15 00		15 09					15 16		15 30						15 39		15 46		16 00
Lancing	d		15 04		15 13					15 20								15 43		15 50		16 04
East Worthing	d				15 16							15 35						15 46				
Worthing 4	a		15 08		15 18					15 24		15 38						15 48		15 54		16 08
	d		15 08		15 19					15 25		15 38						15 49		15 55		16 08
West Worthing	d		15 10		15a21					15 27		15 40						15 51		15 57		16 10
Durrington-on-Sea	d		15 13							15 29		15 43						15 53		15 59		16 13
Goring-by-Sea	d		15 15							15 32		15 45						15 56		16 02		16 15
Angmering 3	d		15 19							15 36		15 49						16 00		16 06		16 19
Littlehampton 4	a		15 28									15 58						16 11				16 28
	d	15 11				15 23									15 54							
Ford 4	d	15 16				15 27		15 35		15 42					15 58		16 07			16 12		
Bognor Regis 4	d								15 39										16 09			
Barnham	a	15 20				15 31	15 26	15 39	15 45	15 46					16 02	15 56	16 11		16 15	16 16		
	d	15 22				15 33	15 27	15 40		15 47				15 53	16 03	15 57	16 12			16 17		
Bognor Regis	a	15 28						15 46						15 59			16 18					
Chichester 4	a					15 40	15 34			15 54					16 10	16 04				16 24		
	d					15 41	15 35			15 55					16 11	16 05				16 25		
Fishbourne (Sussex)	d					15 44									16 14							
Bosham	d					15 47									16 17							
Nutbourne	d					15 50									16 20							
Southbourne	d					15 53				16 02					16 23	16 12						
Emsworth	d					15 56				16 05					16 26	16 15				16 33		
Warblington	d					15 59									16 29							
Havant	d					16 02	15 46			16 09					16 32	16 19				16 37		
Bedhampton	a					16 04									16 34							
Hilsea	a														16 42							
Fratton	a					16 12	15 54			16 18					16 46							
Portsmouth & Southsea	a					16 15	15 58			16 21					16 50							
Portsmouth Harbour ⛴	a					16 21	16 02			16 26												
Cosham	a															16 26				16 45		
Portchester	a															16 30						
Fareham	a															16 35				16 53		
Swanwick	a															16 42						
Southampton Central ⛴	a															17 01				17 28		

A ⌶ to Crawley

London, Gatwick Airport, Brighton - Sussex Coast, Portsmouth and Southampton

		SN	SN	SN	SN	SN		SN	SN	SN	SN	SN	SN	SN	SN	SN		SN	SN	SN	SN	SN	SN
		1	◇	◇	◇	◇1		◇	◇	◇	◇1	1	◇	◇	◇1	◇1		1	◇	◇	◇1	1	◇1
London Victoria 15 ⊖	d					15 02					15 17					15 32					15 47		
Clapham Junction 10	d					15 08					15 23					15 38					15 53		
London Bridge 4 ⊖	d	14 33										15 03										15 33	
East Croydon	d	14 51				15 18					15 33	15 21				15 48					16 03	15 51	
Redhill 5	d	15 10				15 30						15 45				16 00						16 10	
Horley	d	15 19				15 36						15 55										16 19	
Gatwick Airport 10 ✈	d	15 24				15 40					15 49	15 58				16 09					16 19	16 24	
Three Bridges 4	a	15 29				15 44						16 03				16 14						16 29	
	d	15 30				15 45						16 03				16 14						16 30	
Crawley	d	15 33				15 48						16 07				16 18						16 34	
Horsham 4	a	15 48				15 56						16 21				16 26						16 47	
	d					16 00	16 05									16 30	16 35						
Christs Hospital	d						16 08										16 38						
Billingshurst	d						16 14										16 44						
Pulborough	d						16 21										16 51						
Amberley	d																16 57						
Arundel	d						16 30										17 02						
Haywards Heath 3	d										16 05										16 37		
Burgess Hill	d										16 10												
Preston Park	d										16 18												
Brighton 10	d		15 53						16 03	16 14			16 24					16 33	16 44				16 53
Hove 2	d		15 57						16 07	16a17	16 22		16 28					16 37	16a47		16 53		16 57
Aldrington	d		15 59										16 30										16 59
Portslade	d		16 01						16 10		16 25		16 32					16 40			16 56		17 01
Fishersgate	d		16 03										16 34										17 03
Southwick	d		16 05						16 13				16 36					16 43					17 05
Shoreham-by-Sea	d		16 09						16 16		16 30		16 40					16 46			17 01		17 08
Lancing	d		16 13						16 20				16 44					16 50			17 05		17 12
East Worthing	d		16 16										16 47										17 15
Worthing 4	a		16 18						16 24		16 36		16 49					16 54			17 09		17 18
	d		16 19						16 25		16 37		16 50					16 55			17 10		17 18
West Worthing	d		16a21						16 27		16 39		16a52					16 57			17 12		17 20
Durrington-on-Sea	d								16 29		16 41							16 59			17 14		
Goring-by-Sea	d								16 32		16 44							17 02			17 17		
Angmering 3	d								16 36		16 48							17 06			17 21		
Littlehampton 4	a										16 57										17 29		17 33
	d				16 22										16 54					17 11			17 41
Ford 4	d				16 26		16 35		16 42						16 58		17 07	17 12		17 16			17 46
Bognor Regis 4	d							16 39															
Barnham	a				16 30	16 26	16 39	16 45	16 46						17 02	16 56	17 11	17 16		17 20			17 50
	d			16 24	16 31	16 27	16 40		16 47					16 54	17 03	16 57	17 12	17 17		17 24			17 54
Bognor Regis	a			16 30			16 46							17 00			17 18			17 30			→
Chichester 4	a				16 38	16 34			16 54						17 10	17 04		17 24					
	d				16 39	16 35			16 55						17 11	17 05		17 25					
Fishbourne (Sussex)	d				16 42										17 14								
Bosham	d				16 45										17 17								
Nutbourne	d				16 48										17 20								
Southbourne	d				16 51				17 02						17 23	17 12							
Emsworth	d				16 54				17 05						17 26	17 15		17 33					
Warblington	d				16 57										17 29								
Havant	d				17 00	16 46			17 09						17 32	17 19		17 37					
Bedhampton	a				17 02										17 34								
Hilsea	a				17 07										17 42								
Fratton	a				17 11	16 54			17 18						17 46								
Portsmouth & Southsea	a				17 16	16 58			17 22						17 50								
Portsmouth Harbour ⛴	a				17 20	17 02																	
Cosham	a															17 26		17 45					
Portchester	a															17 31							
Fareham	a															17 36		17 53					
Swanwick	a															17 43		18 00					
Southampton Central ⛴	a															18 03		18 20					

London, Gatwick Airport, Brighton - Sussex Coast, Portsmouth and Southampton

Station		GW ◇ ⌶	SN ◇1		SN ◇	SN ◇1	SN ◇	SN ◇1 A ⌶	SN 1	SN 1	SN ◇	SN ◇	SN ◇	SN ◇	SN ◇1 A ⌶		SN 1	SN 1	SN ◇	SN ◇	SN 1	SN ◇
London Victoria 15 ⊖	d		16 02					16 17	16 19						16 32							
Clapham Junction 10	d		16 08					16 23	16 26						16 38							
London Bridge 4 ⊖	d									16 03							16 33				16 57	
East Croydon 🚊	d		16 18					16 33	16 36	16 21					16 48		16 49				17 10	
Redhill 5	d		16 30							16 43					17 00		17 08					
Horley	d		16 36							16 52					17 06		17 18					
Gatwick Airport 10 ✈	d		16 40					16 49	16 53	16 56					17 09		17 21					
Three Bridges 4	a		16 44						16 57	17 00					17 14		17 26				17 29	
	d		16 45						16 58	17 02					17 18	17 20	17 26				17 29	
Crawley	d		16 48						17 02	17 06					17 22	17 26	17 30					
Horsham 4	a		16 56						17 12	17 19					17 30	17 38	17 44					
	d		17 00	17 05											17 30	17 38						
Christs Hospital	d			17 08												17 42						
Billingshurst	d			17 15												17 48						
Pulborough	d			17 21												17 54						
Amberley	d			17 27																		
Arundel	d			17 32												18 03						
Haywards Heath 3	d							17 04													17 39	
Burgess Hill	d							17 09													17 46	
Preston Park	d																				17 56	
Brighton 10	d	17 00			17 03		17 14						17 23					17 33	17 45	17 53		
Hove 2	d	17 04			17 07		17a17	17 21					17 27					17 37	17 49	17a56	18 01	
Aldrington	d												17 29						17 51			
Portslade	d				17 10			17 24					17 31					17 40	17 53		18 04	
Fishersgate	d												17 33						17 55			
Southwick	d				17 13								17 35					17 43	17 57			
Shoreham-by-Sea	d	17 13			17 16			17 29					17 39					17 46	18 01		18 09	
Lancing	d				17 20			17 33					17 43					17 50	18 05		18 13	
East Worthing	d												17 46						18 08			
Worthing 4	a	17 21			17 24			17 37					17 48					17 54	18 10		18 17	
	d	17 22			17 25			17 38					17 49					17 55	18 11		18 17	
West Worthing	d				17 27			17 40					17 51					17 57	18 13		18 19	
Durrington-on-Sea	d				17 29			17 42					17 53					17 59	18 15		18 22	
Goring-by-Sea	d				17 32			17 45					17 56					18 02	18 18		18 24	
Angmering 3	d				17 36			17 49					18 00					18 06	18 22		18 28	
Littlehampton 4	a							18 00					18 08						18 30		18 39	
	d											17 54										
Ford 4	d			17 37	17 42							17 58				18 08		18 12				
Bognor Regis 4	d					←					17 51											18 19
Barnham	a	17 38	17 26	17 42	17 46	17 50					17 57	18 02			17 57	18 13		18 16				18 25
	d	17 39	17 27	17 42	17 47	17 54						18 04		18 08	17 57	18 14		18 17				
Bognor Regis	a			17 49		18 00								18 14		18 22						
Chichester 4	a	17 46	17 34		17 54							18 11			18 05			18 24				
	d	17 47	17 35		17 55							18 12			18 05			18 25				
Fishbourne (Sussex)	d		17 38									18 15										
Bosham	d		17 41									18 18			18 10							
Nutbourne	d											18 21										
Southbourne	d		17 45		18 04							18 24			18 14							
Emsworth	d		17 48		18 07							18 27			18 17			18 33				
Warblington	d				18 10							18 30										
Havant	d	17 58	17 54		18 13							18 34			18 23			18 37				
Bedhampton	a		17 56									18 36										
Hilsea	a		18 01									18 42										
Fratton	a		18 05		18 22							18 46										
Portsmouth & Southsea	a		18 09		18 25							18 49										
Portsmouth Harbour ⛴	a		18 15		18 31																	
Cosham	a	18 04													18 29			18 44				
Portchester	a														18 34							
Fareham	a	18 12													18 39			18 52				
Swanwick	a														18 46			18 59				
Southampton Central ⛴	a	18 41													19 05			19 20				

A ⌶ to Gatwick Airport

London, Gatwick Airport, Brighton - Sussex Coast, Portsmouth and Southampton

Station		SN ◇	SN ◇1 A ⌶		SN ◇	SN ◇	SN ◇1	SN 1	SN ◇	SN ◇	SN ◇1		SN 1	SN 1	SN 1	SN ◇	SN ◇1	SN 1	SN ◇	SN ◇1		SN 1	SN ◇
London Victoria 15 ⊖	d		17 02				17 17				17 32						17 47			18 02			
Clapham Junction 10	d		17 08				17 23				17 38						17 53			18 08			
London Bridge 4 ⊖	d							16 59						17 42	17 47			17 32				17 59	
East Croydon 🚊	d		17 18				17 33	17 15			17 49			17 55	18 00		18 03	17 49		18 18		18 15	
Redhill 5	d							17 37										18 10				18 34	
Horley	d							17 46									18 18	18 19				18 43	
Gatwick Airport 10 ✈	d						17 48	17 50									18 21	18 23				18 47	
Three Bridges 4	a		17 36					17 54			18 06				18 21			18 27		18 36		18 51	
	d		17 37					17 55			18 07				18 22			18 28		18 37		18 52	
Crawley	d		17 41					17 59			18 11				18 26			18 32		18 41		18 56	
Horsham 4	a		17 49					18 11			18 22				18 38			18 47		18 49		19 08	
	d		17 53	17 58							18 26	18 31			18 39					18 53	18 58		
Christs Hospital	d			18 01								18 35			18 42						19 01		
Billingshurst	d			18 07								18 41			18 49						19 07		
Pulborough	d			18 14								18 48			18 56						19 14		
Amberley	d			18 20											19 02								
Arundel	d			18 25								18 57			19 07						19 23		
Haywards Heath 3	d						18 01							18 22			18 33						
Burgess Hill	d						18 07							18 27			18 41						
Preston Park	d													18 39			18 53						
Brighton 10	d				18 00	18 14							18 28			18 48							19 00
Hove 2	d				18 04	18a17	18 21						18 32	18 44		18a53	18 58						19 04
Aldrington	d				18 06								18 34										19 06
Portslade	d				18 08		18 24						18 36	18 47			19 01						19 08
Fishersgate	d				18 10								18 38										19 10
Southwick	d				18 12								18 40										19 12
Shoreham-by-Sea	d				18 16		18 29						18 44	18 52			19 06						19 16
Lancing	d				18 20		18 33						18 48	18 56			19 10						19 20
East Worthing	d				18 23								18 51										19 23
Worthing 4	a				18 25		18 37						18 53	19 00			19 14						19 25
	d				18 27		18 38						18 54	19 00			19 14						19 26
West Worthing	d				18 29		18 40							19 02			19 16						19 28
Durrington-on-Sea	d				18 31		18 42							19 05			19 19						19 30
Goring-by-Sea	d				18 34		18 45							19 07			19 21						19 33
Angmering 3	d				18 38		18 49						19 00	19 11			19 25						19 37
Littlehampton 4	a						19 00							19 24			19 36						
	d	18 18								18 48									19 11				
Ford 4	d	18 22		18 30	18 44					18 53		19 02	19 07						19 19		19 28		19 43
Bognor Regis 4	d																						
Barnham	a	18 26	18 20	18 34	18 48					18 57	18 53	19 06	19 11		19 15				19 23	19 20	19 32		19 47
	d	18 27	18 21	18 35	18 49				18 55	19 00	18 54	19 07	19 12		19 16				19 24	19 21	19 33		19 48
Bognor Regis	a	18 33		18 41					19 01			19 13			19 24				19 30		19 39		
Chichester 4	a		18 28		18 56					19 07	19 01		19 19							19 28			19 55
	d		18 29		18 57					19 11	19 02		19 20							19 29			19 56
Fishbourne (Sussex)	d		18 32							19 14	19 05												
Bosham	d		18 35							19 17	19 08												
Nutbourne	d		18 38							19 20													
Southbourne	d		18 41							19 23	19 12									19 36			
Emsworth	d		18 44							19 26	19 15		19 30							19 39			
Warblington	d		18 47							19 29													
Havant	d		18 54		19 08					19 33	19 20		19 37							19 46			20 07
Bedhampton	a		18 57							19 35													
Hilsea	a		19 02							19 43													
Fratton	a		19 06		19 17					19 47										19 56			20 15
Portsmouth & Southsea	a		19 09		19 21					19 50										20 01			20 19
Portsmouth Harbour ⛴	a				19 26															20 07			
Cosham	a										19 29		19 46										
Portchester	a										19 33												
Fareham	a										19 38		19 54										
Swanwick	a										19 45		20 01										
Southampton Central ⛴	a										20 03		20 18										

A ⌶ to Crawley

London, Gatwick Airport, Brighton - Sussex Coast, Portsmouth and Southampton

		SN 1	SN ◇	SN ◇1	SN ◇	SN ◇1		SN 1	SN 1	SN 1	SN ◇	SN ◇	SN ◇1 A ⊼	SN ◇1 B ⊼		SN ◇1	SN ◇	SN ◇	SN ◇1 C ⊼	SN 1	SN 1	SN ◇1 B ⊼	
London Victoria 15 ⊖	d			18 17		18 32		18 19					18 47	19 02					19 17		19 10	19 32	
Clapham Junction 10	d			18 23		18 38		18 26					18 53	19 08					19 23		19 16	19 38	
London Bridge 4 ⊖	d	18 12							18 30											19 03			
East Croydon	d	18 25		18 33		18 48		18 38	18 46				19 03	19 18					19 33	19 19	19 28	19 48	
Redhill 5	d							18 59	19 07					19 31						19 37	19 46	20 00	
Horley	d			18 48				19 08	19 16											19 47	19 55		
Gatwick Airport 10 ✈	d							19 14	19 20				19 20	19 40					19 49	19 50	19 59	20 09	
Three Bridges 4	a	18 44				19 06		19 19	19 24					19 45						19 55	20 03	20 14	
	d	18 45				19 07		19 19	19 25					19 45						19 55	20 04	20 14	
Crawley	d					19 11		19 23	19 29					19 49						19 59	20 08	20 18	
Horsham 4	a					19 22		19 35	19 43					19 57						20 11	20 21	20 26	
	d					19 26	19 31							20 01	20 06							20 30	20 35
Christs Hospital	d						19 34								20 09								20 38
Billingshurst	d						19 41								20 15								20 44
Pulborough	d						19 48								20 22								20 51
Amberley	d						19 54								20 28								20 57
Arundel	d						19 59								20 33								21 02
Haywards Heath 3	d	18 54		19 03									19 37						20 04				
Burgess Hill	d	19 00		19 09									19 42						20 09				
Preston Park	d	19 11																					
Brighton 10	d		19 15							19 30	19 44					20 03	20 14						
Hove 2	d	19 18	19a19	19 23						19 34	19a48		19 57			20 07	20a17		20 22				
Aldrington	d									19 36						20 09							
Portslade	d	19 21		19 26						19 38			20 00			20 11			20 25				
Fishersgate	d									19 40						20 13							
Southwick	d									19 42						20 15							
Shoreham-by-Sea	d	19 26		19 31						19 46			20 04			20 19			20 30				
Lancing	d	19 30		19 36						19 50			20 08			20 23			20 34				
East Worthing	d									19 53						20 26							
Worthing 4	a	19 34		19 40						19 55			20 12			20 28			20 38				
	d	19 35		19 40						19 56			20 13			20 29			20 38				
West Worthing	d	19 37		19 42						19 58			20 15			20 31			20 40				
Durrington-on-Sea	d	19 39		19 45						20 00			20 17			20 33			20 43				
Goring-by-Sea	d	19 42		19 47						20 03			20 20			20 36			20 45				
Angmering 3	d	19 46		19 51						20 07			20 24			20 40			20 49				
Littlehampton 4	a	19 57		20 03									20 35						20 58				
	d				19 35							20 06						20 37					
Ford 4	d				19 39					20 13		20 10			20 38	20 46		20 42					21 07
Bognor Regis 4	d																						
Barnham	a				19 43	19 52	20 07			20 18		20 14		20 27	20 42	20 50		20 46				20 56	21 11
	d				19 55	19 53	20 08			20 18		20 22		20 28	20 43	20 51		20 52				20 57	21 12
Bognor Regis	a				20 01		20 14					20 28			20 49			20 58					21 18
Chichester 4	a					20 00				20 26				20 35		20 58						21 04	
	d					20 01				20 26				20 36		20 59						21 05	
Fishbourne (Sussex)	d					20 04																21 08	
Bosham	d					20 07																21 11	
Nutbourne	d					20 10																21 14	
Southbourne	d					20 13								20 43								21 17	
Emsworth	d					20 16								20 46								21 20	
Warblington	d					20 19																21 23	
Havant	d					20 22				20 37				20 52		21 10						21 26	
Bedhampton	a																						
Hilsea	a																						
Fratton	a													21 01		21 18							
Portsmouth & Southsea	a													21 06		21 23							
Portsmouth Harbour ⛴	a															21 27							
Cosham	a					20 28				20 44												21 33	
Portchester	a									20 48												21 38	
Fareham	a					20 36				20 53												21 43	
Swanwick	a					20 43				21 00												21 49	
Southampton Central ⛴	a					21 01				21 19												22 07	

A ⊼ to Haywards Heath B ⊼ to Crawley C ⊼ to Gatwick Airport

London, Gatwick Airport, Brighton - Sussex Coast, Portsmouth and Southampton

		SN ◇1	SN ◇	SN ◇	SN ◇1 A ⊼	SN 1	SN ◇1 ⊼		SN ◇	SN ◇1	SN ◇	SN ◇1	SN 1	SN ◇	SN ◇	SN ◇1		SN ◇1	SN ◇1	SN ◇	SN ◇1	SN 1
London Victoria 15 ⊖	d				19 47	19 40	20 02					20 17	20 10			20 32					20 47	20 40
Clapham Junction 10	d				19 53	19 46	20 08					20 23	20 16			20 38					20 53	20 46
London Bridge 4 ⊖	d																					
East Croydon	d				20 03	19 58	20 19					20 33	20 28			20 48					21 04	20 58
Redhill 5	d					20 16	20 31						20 46			21 00						21 16
Horley	d					20 25							20 54									21 25
Gatwick Airport 10 ✈	d				20 19	20 29	20 39					20 49	20 57			21 09					21 19	21 29
Three Bridges 4	a					20 33	20 44						21 02			21 14						21 33
	d					20 34	20 44						21 03			21 14						21 34
Crawley	d					20 37	20 48						21 06			21 18						21 37
Horsham 4	a					20 49	20 56						21 18			21 26						21 49
	d						21 00	21 05								21 30	21 35					
Christs Hospital	d							21 08									21 38					
Billingshurst	d							21 14									21 44					
Pulborough	d							21 21									21 51					
Amberley	d							21 27									21 57					
Arundel	d							21 32									22 02					
Haywards Heath 3	d				20 34							21 04									21 34	
Burgess Hill	d				20 39							21 09									21 39	
Preston Park	d				20 49																21 49	
Brighton 10	d	20 30	20 47							21 03	21 14								21 33	21 44		
Hove 2	d	20 34	20a50		20 54					21 07	21a17	21 22							21 37	21a48	21 54	
Aldrington	d	20 36								21 09									21 39			
Portslade	d	20 38			20 57					21 11		21 25							21 41		21 57	
Fishersgate	d	20 40								21 13									21 43			
Southwick	d	20 42								21 15									21 45			
Shoreham-by-Sea	d	20 46			21 01					21 19		21 30							21 49		22 01	
Lancing	d	20 50			21 05					21 23		21 34							21 53		22 05	
East Worthing	d	20 53								21 26									21 56			
Worthing 4	a	20 55			21 09					21 28		21 38							21 58		22 09	
	d	20 56			21 10					21 29		21 38							21 59		22 10	
West Worthing	d	20 58			21 12					21 31		21 40							22 01		22 12	
Durrington-on-Sea	d	21 00			21 14					21 33		21 43							22 03		22 14	
Goring-by-Sea	d	21 03			21 17					21 36		21 45							22 06		22 17	
Angmering 3	d	21 07			21 21					21 40		21 49							22 10		22 21	
Littlehampton 4	a				21 29							21 58									22 30	
	d			21 06														22 08				
Ford 4	d	21 13		21 10				21 37		21 46							22 07	22 12	22 16			
Bognor Regis 4	d								21 39						22 00							
Barnham	a	21 17		21 14			21 26	21 41	21 45	21 50					22 06	21 56	22 11	22 16	22 20			
	d	21 18		21 22			21 27	21 42		21 51				21 52		21 57	22 12	22 17	22 21			
Bognor Regis	a			21 28				21 48						21 58			22 18					
Chichester 4	a	21 25					21 34			21 58						22 04		22 24	22 28			
	d	21 26					21 35			21 59						22 05			22 29			
Fishbourne (Sussex)	d															22 08						
Bosham	d															22 11						
Nutbourne	d															22 14						
Southbourne	d						21 42									22 17			22 36			
Emsworth	d						21 45									22 20			22 39			
Warblington	d															22 23						
Havant	d	21 37					21 49			22 10						22 26			22 43			
Bedhampton	a																					
Hilsea	a																					
Fratton	a						21 58			22 18									22 52			
Portsmouth & Southsea	a						22 01			22 22									22 55			
Portsmouth Harbour ⛴	a						22 05			22 26									22 59			
Cosham	a	21 43														22 33						
Portchester	a																					
Fareham	a	21 51														22 42						
Swanwick	a	21 58														22 49						
Southampton Central ⛴	a	22 16														23 07						

A ⊼ to Gatwick Airport

London, Gatwick Airport, Brighton - Sussex Coast, Portsmouth and Southampton

		SN ◇	SN ◇	SN ◇	SN ◇	SN ◇1	SN 1	SN 1	SN ◇1	SN ◇	SN ◇1	SN ◇
London Victoria 15 ⊖	d					21 17	21 10	21 32				
Clapham Junction 10	d					21 23	21 16	21 38				
London Bridge 4 ⊖	d											
East Croydon	d					21 33	21 28	21 48				
Redhill 5	d						21 46	22 00				
Horley	d						21 54					
Gatwick Airport 10 ✈	d					21 49	21 57	22 09				
Three Bridges 4	a					21 53	22 02	22 14				
	d					21 53	22 03	22 14				
Crawley	d						22 06	22 18				
Horsham 4	a						22 18	22 26				
	d							22 27				
Christs Hospital	d							22 30				
Billingshurst	d							22 36				
Pulborough	d							22 43				
Amberley	d							22 49				
Arundel	d							22 54				
Haywards Heath 3	d					22 06						
Burgess Hill	d					22 11						
Preston Park	d											
Brighton 10	d		22 03	22 14							22 33	22 44
Hove 2	d		22 07	22a17		22 23					22 37	22a47
Aldrington	d		22 09								22 39	
Portslade	d		22 11			22 26					22 41	
Fishersgate	d		22 13								22 43	
Southwick	d		22 15								22 45	
Shoreham-by-Sea	d		22 19			22 31					22 49	
Lancing	d		22 23			22 35					22 53	
East Worthing	d		22 26								22 56	
Worthing 4	a		22 28			22 39					22 58	
	d		22 29			22 39					22 59	
West Worthing	d		22 31			22 41					23 01	
Durrington-on-Sea	d		22 33			22 44					23 03	
Goring-by-Sea	d		22 36			22 46					23 06	
Angmering 3	d		22 40			22 50					23 10	
Littlehampton 4	a										23 18	
	d				22 38						23 23	
Ford 4	d		22 46		22 42	22 56		23 00			23 27	
Bognor Regis 4	d								←	23 15		
Barnham	a		22 50		22 46	23 01		23 04	23 01	23 21	23 31	
	d	22 22	22 51		22 52	23 06		23 05	23 06		23 32	
Bognor Regis	a	22 28			22 58	→			23 12			
Chichester 4	a		22 58					23 12			23 39	
	d		22 59					23 13				
Fishbourne (Sussex)	d							23 16				
Bosham	d							23 19				
Nutbourne	d							23 22				
Southbourne	d							23 25				
Emsworth	d							23 28				
Warblington	d							23 31				
Havant	d		23 11					23 34				
Bedhampton	a											
Hilsea	a											
Fratton	a		23 20					23 47				
Portsmouth & Southsea	a		23 23					23 54				
Portsmouth Harbour ⛴	a		23 27									
Cosham	a											
Portchester	a											
Fareham	a											
Swanwick	a											
Southampton Central ⛴	a											

		SN ◇1	SN 1	SN ◇	SN ◇	SN ◇	SN ◇1	SN 1	SN 1	SN ◇1	SN ◇	SN ◇1
London Victoria 15 ⊖	d	21 47	21 40				22 17	22 10	22 32			22 47
Clapham Junction 10	d	21 53	21 46				22 23	22 16	22 38			22 53
London Bridge 4 ⊖	d											
East Croydon	d	22 03	21 58				22 34	22 28	22 48			23 03
Redhill 5	d		22 16					22 46	23 01			
Horley	d		22 25					22 54				
Gatwick Airport 10 ✈	d	22 19	22 29				22 49	22 57	23 09			23 19
Three Bridges 4	a		22 33				22 54	23 02	23 15			
	d		22 36				22 54	23 03	23 16			
Crawley	d		22 39					23 06	23 19			
Horsham 4	a		22 51					23 18	23 27			
	d								23 28			
Christs Hospital	d								23 31			
Billingshurst	d								23 37			
Pulborough	d								23 44			
Amberley	d								23 50			
Arundel	d								23 55			
Haywards Heath 3	d	22 37					23 03					23c37
Burgess Hill	d						23 08					
Preston Park	d											
Brighton 10	d			23 03	23 14						23 44	
Hove 2	d	22 52		23 07	23a17		23 22				23a47	23 52
Aldrington	d			23 09								
Portslade	d	22 55		23 11			23 25					23 55
Fishersgate	d			23 13								
Southwick	d			23 15			23 28					23 58
Shoreham-by-Sea	d	23 00		23 19			23 31					00 01
Lancing	d	23 04		23 23			23 35					00 05
East Worthing	d			23 26								
Worthing 4	a	23 08		23 28			23 39					00 09
	d	23 08		23 29			23 39					
West Worthing	d	23 10		23a31			23 41					
Durrington-on-Sea	d	23 13					23 44					
Goring-by-Sea	d	23 15					23 46					
Angmering 3	d	23 19					23 50					
Littlehampton 4	a	23 28										
	d											
Ford 4	d						23 56		00 01			
Bognor Regis 4	d									←		
Barnham	a						00 01		00 06	00 01		
	d					23 36	00 09		00 06	00 09		
Bognor Regis	a					23 42	→			00 15		
Chichester 4	a								00 14			
	d											
Fishbourne (Sussex)	d											
Bosham	d											
Nutbourne	d											
Southbourne	d											
Emsworth	d											
Warblington	d											
Havant	d											
Bedhampton	a											
Hilsea	a											
Fratton	a											
Portsmouth & Southsea	a											
Portsmouth Harbour ⛴	a											
Cosham	a											
Portchester	a											
Fareham	a											
Swanwick	a											
Southampton Central ⛴	a											

London, Gatwick Airport, Brighton - Sussex Coast, Portsmouth and Southampton

		SN 1	SN ◇1	SN 1	SN 1
London Victoria 15 ⊖	d	22 40	23 17	23 10	23 47
Clapham Junction 10	d	22 46	23 23	23 16	23 53
London Bridge 4 ⊖	d				
East Croydon	d	22 58	23 33	23 28	00 06
Redhill 5	d	23 16		23 46	00 25
Horley	d	23 25		23 56	00 31
Gatwick Airport 10 ✈	d	23 29	23 51	23 59	00 34
Three Bridges 4	a	23 33	23 55	00 04	00 39
	d	23 38	23 56	00 04	00 39
Crawley	d	23 41		00 07	00 43
Horsham 4	a	23 53		00 19	00 55
	d				
Christs Hospital	d				
Billingshurst	d				
Pulborough	d				
Amberley	d				
Arundel	d				
Haywards Heath 3	d		00 05		
Burgess Hill	d		00 10		
Preston Park	d				
Brighton 10	d				
Hove 2	d		00 22		
Aldrington	d				
Portslade	d		00s25		
Fishersgate	d				
Southwick	d		00s28		
Shoreham-by-Sea	d		00s31		
Lancing	d		00s35		
East Worthing	d				
Worthing 4	a		00 39		
	d				
West Worthing	d				
Durrington-on-Sea	d				
Goring-by-Sea	d				
Angmering 3	d				
Littlehampton 4	a				
	d				
Ford 4	d				
Bognor Regis 4	d				
Barnham	a				
	d				
Bognor Regis	a				
Chichester 4	a				
	d				
Fishbourne (Sussex)	d				
Bosham	d				
Nutbourne	d				
Southbourne	d				
Emsworth	d				
Warblington	d				
Havant	d				
Bedhampton	a				
Hilsea	a				
Fratton	a				
Portsmouth & Southsea	a				
Portsmouth Harbour ⛴	a				
Cosham	a				
Portchester	a				
Fareham	a				
Swanwick	a				
Southampton Central ⛴	a				

London, Gatwick Airport, Brighton - Sussex Coast, Portsmouth and Southampton

		SN	SN	SN	SN	SN	SN	SN	SN	SN	SN	SN	SN	SN	SN	SN	SN	SN	SN	SN	SN	SN	SN
		◇■	■	◇■	◇■	◇	◇	◇■	■	■	◇■	◇■	◇■	◇■	◇■	◇■	◇■	◇	◇	◇■	◇	◇	◇
London Victoria [15] ⊖	d	22p17	22p32		22p47			23p17	23p10	23p47	00 05												
Clapham Junction [10]	d	22p23	22p38		22p53			23p23	23p16	23p53	00 11												
London Bridge [4] ⊖	d																						
East Croydon	d	22p34	22p48		23p03			23p33	23p28	00 06	00 25												
Redhill [5]	d		23p01						23p46	00 25													
Horley	d								23p56	00 31													
Gatwick Airport [10] ✈	d	22p49	23p09		23p19			23p51	23p59	00 34	00 43												
Three Bridges [4]	a	22p54	23p15					23p55	00 04	00 39	00 47												
	d	22p54	23p16					23p56	00 04	00 39	00 47												
Crawley	d		23p19						00 07	00 43													
Horsham [4]	a		23p27						00 19	00 55													
	d		23p28																				
Christs Hospital	d		23p31																				
Billingshurst	d		23p37																				
Pulborough	d		23p44																				
Amberley	d		23p50																				
Arundel	d		23p55																				
Haywards Heath [3]	d	23p03			23b37			00 05			01 02												
Burgess Hill	d	23p08						00 10															
Preston Park	d																						
Brighton [10]	d					00 03	00 10				01s16						05 15			05 27	05 44	05 53	
Hove [2]	d	23p22			23p52	00 07	00a13	00 22			01s24						05 20			05 31	05a47	05 57	
Aldrington	d					00 09														05 33		05 59	
Portslade	d	23p25			23p55	00 11		00s25			01s27						05 23			05 35		06 01	
Fishersgate	d					00 13														05 37		06 03	
Southwick	d	23p28			23p58	00 15		00s28			01s30									05 39		06 05	
Shoreham-by-Sea	d	23p31			00 01	00 19		00s31			01s33						05 27			05 43		06 09	
Lancing	d	23p35			00 05	00 23		00s35			01s37						05 31			05 47		06 13	
East Worthing	d					00 26														05 50		06 16	
Worthing [4]	a	23p39			00 09	00 28		00 39			01 41						05 35			05 52		06 18	
	d	23p39				00 29											05 36			05 53		06 19	
West Worthing	d	23p41				00a31											05 38			05 55		06a21	
Durrington-on-Sea	d	23p44															05 40			05 57			
Goring-by-Sea	d	23p46															05 43			06 00			
Angmering [3]	d	23p50															05 47			06 04			
Littlehampton [4]	a																						
	d																	05 54					
Ford [4]	d	23p56	00 01														05 53	05 58		06 10			
Bognor Regis [4]	d			←															06 04				
Barnham	a	00 01	00 06	00 01													05 57	06 02	06 10	06 14			
	d	00 09	00 06	00 09								04 57	05 15	05 20	05 30	05 38	05 58	06 03		06 15			06 22
Bognor Regis	a	→		00 15																			06 28
Chichester [4]	a		00 14									05 04	05 22	05 27	05 37	05 45	06 05	06 10		06 22			
	d											05 05	05 23	05 28	05 38	05 46	06 06	06 11		06 23			
Fishbourne (Sussex)	d																	06 14					
Bosham	d																06 10	06 17					
Nutbourne	d																	06 20					
Southbourne	d																06 15	06 23		06 30			
Emsworth	d																06 18	06 26		06 33			
Warblington	d																06 21	06 29					
Havant	d											05 16	05 34	05 39	05 49	05 57	06 24	06 32		06 37			
Bedhampton	a																	06 34					
Hilsea	a																	06 42					
Fratton	a												05 42		05 57	06 05		06 46					
Portsmouth & Southsea	a												05 46		06 01	06 09		06 50					
Portsmouth Harbour ⛴	a														06 05	06 16							
Cosham	a											05 22		05 49			06 30			06 45			
Portchester	a											05 27					06 34						
Fareham	a											05 32		05 57			06 39			06 53			
Swanwick	a											05 39		06 04			06 46						
Southampton Central ⛴	a											05 58		06 24			07 05			07 28			

b Previous night, arr. 2330

London, Gatwick Airport, Brighton - Sussex Coast, Portsmouth and Southampton

		SN	SN	SN	SN	SN	SN	SN	SN	SN	SN	SN	SN	SN	SN	SN	SN	SN	SN	SN	SN	SN
		◇■	◇■	◇	◇	◇	◇	◇	■	◇■	◇	◇	◇■ A	◇	◇	◇■	◇	◇	◇	◇	■	◇
London Victoria [15] ⊖	d												05 32								06 02	
Clapham Junction [10]	d												05 38								06 08	
London Bridge [4] ⊖	d																					
East Croydon	d												05 48								06 18	
Redhill [5]	d												06 07								06 46	
Horley	d												06 18								06 55	
Gatwick Airport [10] ✈	d								05 58				06 22								06 59	
Three Bridges [4]	a								06 02				06 26								07 03	
	d								06 03				06 34								07 04	
Crawley	d								06 06				06 37								07 07	
Horsham [4]	a								06 18				06 49								07 19	
	d								06 19				06 50								07 20	
Christs Hospital	d								06 22				06 53								07 23	
Billingshurst	d								06 28				06 59								07 29	
Pulborough	d								06 35				07 06								07 36	
Amberley	d								06 41				07 12								07 42	
Arundel	d								06 46				07 17								07 47	
Haywards Heath [3]	d																					
Burgess Hill	d																					
Preston Park	d																					
Brighton [10]	d		06 01	06 14	06 23					06 33	06 44			06 48	06 53	07 03	07 14	07 23				
Hove [2]	d		06 05	06a17	06 27					06 37	06a47			06 52	06 57	07 07	07a17	07 27				
Aldrington	d				06 29										06 59			07 29				
Portslade	d		06 08		06 31					06 40				06 55	07 01	07 10		07 31				
Fishersgate	d				06 33										07 03			07 33				
Southwick	d		06 11		06 35					06 43					07 05	07 13		07 35				
Shoreham-by-Sea	d		06 14		06 39					06 46				06 59	07 09	07 16		07 39				
Lancing	d		06 18		06 43					06 50				07 03	07 13	07 20		07 43				
East Worthing	d				06 46										07 16			07 46				
Worthing [4]	a		06 22		06 48					06 54				07 07	07 18	07 24		07 48				
	d		06 23		06 49					06 55				07 08	07 19	07 25		07 49				
West Worthing	d		06 25		06a51					06 57				07 10	07a21			07a51				
Durrington-on-Sea	d		06 27							06 59				07 12								
Goring-by-Sea	d		06 30							07 02				07 15								
Angmering [3]	d		06 34							07 06				07 19		07 31						
Littlehampton [4]	a													07 27								
	d	06 19						06 54														07 54
Ford [4]	d		06 40					06 58	06 51	07 12		07 16	07 22								07 52	07 58
Bognor Regis [4]	d					06 39													07 39			
Barnham	a	06 26	06 44			06 45		07 02	06 55	07 16		07 20	07 27			07 41			07 45		07 57	08 02
	d	06 27	06 45				06 52	07 03	06 59 / 07 05	07 17		07 22	07 27			07 41				07 52	07 57	08 03
Bognor Regis	a						06 58		07 11			07 28								07 58		
Chichester [4]	a	06 34	06 52					07 10	07 06	07 24			07 35			07 49					08 05	08 10
	d	06 35	06 53					07 11	07 07	07 25			07 35			07 49					08 05	08 11
Fishbourne (Sussex)	d							07 14														08 14
Bosham	d							07 17														08 17
Nutbourne	d							07 20														08 20
Southbourne	d							07 23	07 14							07 56					08 12	08 23
Emsworth	d							07 26	07 17	07 33						07 59					08 15	08 26
Warblington	d							07 29														08 29
Havant	d	06 46	07 04					07 32	07 23	07 37			07 46			08 04					08 20	08 32
Bedhampton	a							07 34														08 34
Hilsea	a							07 42														08 42
Fratton	a	06 54	07 12					07 46					07 55			08 12						08 46
Portsmouth & Southsea	a	06 58	07 16					07 50					07 58			08 16						08 50
Portsmouth Harbour ⛴	a	07 02	07 20										08 02			08 20						
Cosham	a								07 29	07 45											08 28	
Portchester	a								07 34												08 32	
Fareham	a								07 39	07 53											08 37	
Swanwick	a								07 45												08 44	
Southampton Central ⛴	a								08 03	08 28											09 01	

A ◇ to Three Bridges

London, Gatwick Airport, Brighton - Sussex Coast, Portsmouth and Southampton

		SN 1	SN ◇	SN ◇	SN 1	SN 1	SN ◇1	SN ◇	SN ◇1	SN ◇	SN ◇	SN ◇	SN ◇	SN ◇		SN ◇1	SN ◇1	SN ◇	SN ◇	SN ◇1	SN 1
London Victoria 15 ⊖	d				06 32											07 32				07 47	
Clapham Junction 10	d				06 38											07 38				07 53	
London Bridge 4 ⊖	d					07 03															07 33
East Croydon	d				06 48	07 21										07 48				08 03	07 51
Redhill 5	d				07 10	07 44										08 00					08 10
Horley	d				07 19	07 51															08 19
Gatwick Airport 10 ✈	d				07 24	07 56										08 09				08 19	08 24
Three Bridges 4	a				07 29	08 01										08 14					08 29
	d				07 30	08 01										08 14					08 30
Crawley	d				07 33	08 05										08 18					08 33
Horsham 4	a				07 45	08 17										08 26					08 45
	d				07 50										08 30	08 35					
Christs Hospital	d				07 53											08 38					
Billingshurst	d				07 59											08 44					
Pulborough	d				08 06											08 51					
Amberley	d				08 12											08 57					
Arundel	d				08 17											09 02					
Haywards Heath 3	d						07 37													08 37	
Burgess Hill	d																				
Preston Park	d																				
Brighton 10	d	07 33	07 44					07 53	08 03	08 14	08 23						08 33	08 44			
Hove 2	d	07 37	07a47				07 52	07 57	08 07	08a17	08 27						08 37	08a47		08 53	
Aldrington	d							07 59			08 29										
Portslade	d	07 40						08 01	08 10		08 31						08 40				
Fishersgate	d							08 03			08 33										
Southwick	d	07 43						08 05	08 13		08 35						08 43				
Shoreham-by-Sea	d	07 46					07 58	08 09	08 16		08 39						08 46			09 00	
Lancing	d	07 50					08 02	08 13	08 20		08 43						08 50			09 04	
East Worthing	d							08 16			08 46										
Worthing 4	a	07 54					08 06	08 18	08 24		08 48						08 54			09 08	
	d	07 55					08 07	08 19	08 25		08 49						08 55			09 08	
West Worthing	d	07 57					08 09	08a21			08a51						08 57			09 10	
Durrington-on-Sea	d	07 59					08 11										08 59			09 13	
Goring-by-Sea	d	08 02					08 14										09 02			09 15	
Angmering 3	d	08 06					08 18		08 31								09 06			09 19	
Littlehampton 4	a						08 27													09 28	
	d			08 11										08 54					09 11		
Ford 4	d	08 12		08 16	08 22									08 58		09 07	09 12		09 16		
Bognor Regis 4	d											08 39									
Barnham	a	08 16		08 20	08 27				08 41			08 45		09 02	08 56	09 11	09 16		09 20		
	d	08 17		08 22	08 27				08 41				08 52	09 03	08 57	09 12	09 17		09 22		
Bognor Regis	a			08 28									08 58			09 18			09 28		
Chichester 4	a	08 24			08 35				08 49					09 10	09 04		09 24				
	d	08 25			08 35				08 49					09 11	09 05		09 25				
Fishbourne (Sussex)	d													09 14							
Bosham	d													09 17							
Nutbourne	d													09 20							
Southbourne	d								08 56					09 23	09 12						
Emsworth	d	08 33							08 59					09 26	09 15		09 33				
Warblington	d													09 29							
Havant	d	08 37			08 46				09 04					09 32	09 19		09 37				
Bedhampton	a													09 34							
Hilsea	a													09 42							
Fratton	a				08 55				09 12					09 46							
Portsmouth & Southsea	a				08 58				09 16					09 50							
Portsmouth Harbour ⛴	a				09 02				09 20												
Cosham	a	08 45													09 26		09 45				
Portchester	a														09 30						
Fareham	a	08 53													09 35		09 53				
Swanwick	a	09 00													09 42						
Southampton Central ⛴	a	09 19													09 59		10 28				

London, Gatwick Airport, Brighton - Sussex Coast, Portsmouth and Southampton

			SN ◇1	SN ◇	GW ◇	SN ◇1	SN ◇	SN ◇1	SN 1	SN ◇	SN ◇	SN ◇	SN ◇		SN ◇1	SN 1	SN ◇	SN ◇	SN ◇1	SN 1		SN ◇1	SN ◇
London Victoria 15 ⊖	d		08 02					08 17							08 32				08 47			09 02	
Clapham Junction 10	d		08 08					08 23							08 38				08 53			09 08	
London Bridge 4 ⊖	d								08 03											08 33			
East Croydon	d		08 18					08 33	08 21						08 48				09 03	08 51		09 18	
Redhill 5	d		08 30						08 44						09 00					09 10		09 30	
Horley	d		08 36						08 51											09 19		09 36	
Gatwick Airport 10 ✈	d		08 40					08 49	08 56						09 09				09 19	09 24		09 40	
Three Bridges 4	a		08 44						09 01						09 14					09 29		09 44	
	d		08 45						09 01						09 14					09 30		09 45	
Crawley	d		08 48						09 05						09 18					09 33		09 48	
Horsham 4	a		08 56						09 17						09 26					09 45		09 56	
	d	09 00	09 05											09 30	09 35						10 00	10 05	
Christs Hospital	d														09 38								
Billingshurst	d		09 13												09 44							10 14	
Pulborough	d		09 19												09 51							10 20	
Amberley	d														09 57								
Arundel	d		09 28												10 02							10 29	
Haywards Heath 3	d							09 05											09 37				
Burgess Hill	d							09 10															
Preston Park	d							09 18															
Brighton 10	d			08 53	09 00	09 03	09 14			09 23						09 33	09 44						09 53
Hove 2	d			08 57	09 04	09 07	09a17	09 22		09 27						09 37	09a47		09 53				09 57
Aldrington	d			08 59						09 29													09 59
Portslade	d			09 01		09 10		09 25		09 31						09 40							10 01
Fishersgate	d			09 03						09 33													10 03
Southwick	d			09 05		09 13				09 35						09 43							10 05
Shoreham-by-Sea	d			09 09	09 13	09 17		09 30		09 39						09 46			10 00				10 09
Lancing	d			09 13		09 21				09 43						09 50			10 04				10 13
East Worthing	d			09 16						09 46													10 16
Worthing 4	a			09 18	09 22	09 25		09 36		09 48						09 54			10 08				10 18
	d			09 19	09 22	09 25		09 37		09 49						09 55			10 08				10 19
West Worthing	d			09a21				09 39		09a51						09 57			10 10				10a21
Durrington-on-Sea	d							09 41								09 59			10 13				
Goring-by-Sea	d							09 44								10 02			10 15				
Angmering 3	d					09 34		09 48								10 06			10 19				
Littlehampton 4	a							09 57											10 28				
	d												09 54					10 11					
Ford 4	d		09 33										09 58		10 07	10 12		10 16				10 34	
Bognor Regis 4	d										09 39												
Barnham	a	09 26	09 38		09 40	09 44					09 45		10 02	09 56	10 11	10 16		10 20			10 26	10 39	
	d	09 27	09 38		09 41	09 45						09 52	10 03	09 57	10 12	10 17		10 22			10 27	10 39	
Bognor Regis	a		09 45									09 58			10 18			10 28				10 46	
Chichester 4	a	09 34			09 48	09 52							10 10	10 04		10 24					10 34		
	d	09 35			09 49	09 53							10 11	10 05		10 25					10 35		
Fishbourne (Sussex)	d												10 14										
Bosham	d												10 17										
Nutbourne	d												10 20										
Southbourne	d					10 00							10 23	10 12									
Emsworth	d					10 03							10 26	10 15		10 33							
Warblington	d												10 29										
Havant	d	09 46			10 00	10 07							10 32	10 19		10 37					10 46		
Bedhampton	a												10 34										
Hilsea	a												10 43										
Fratton	a	09 54				10 16							10 47								10 54		
Portsmouth & Southsea	a	09 58				10 19							10 50								10 58		
Portsmouth Harbour ⛴	a	10 02				10 23															11 02		
Cosham	a				10 06									10 26		10 45							
Portchester	a													10 30									
Fareham	a				10 15									10 35		10 53							
Swanwick	a													10 42		11 00							
Southampton Central ⛴	a				10 40									10 59		11 19							

Table 188

Saturdays

London, Gatwick Airport, Brighton - Sussex Coast, Portsmouth and Southampton

		SN ◇■	SN ◇	SN ◇■	SN ■	SN ◇	SN ◇	SN ◇	SN ◇	SN ◇■		SN ◇■	SN ◇	SN ◇	SN ◇■	SN ■	SN ◇■ A ✠		SN ◇	SN ◇■	SN ◇	SN ◇■	SN ■
London Victoria ⊖	d			09 17						09 32					09 47		10 02					10 17	
Clapham Junction	d			09 23						09 38					09 53		10 08					10 23	
London Bridge ⊖	d				09 03											09 33							10 03
East Croydon	d			09 33	09 21					09 48					10 03	09 51	10 18					10 33	10 21
Redhill	d				09 44					10 00						10 10	10 30						10 44
Horley	d				09 51											10 19	10 36						10 51
Gatwick Airport ✈	d			09 49	09 56					10 09					10 19	10 24	10 40					10 49	10 56
Three Bridges	a				10 01					10 14						10 29	10 44						11 01
	d				10 01					10 14						10 30	10 45						11 01
Crawley	d				10 05					10 18						10 33	10 48						11 05
Horsham	a				10 17					10 26						10 45	10 56						11 17
	d									10 30	10 35						11 00	11 05					
Christs Hospital	d										10 38												
Billingshurst	d										10 44							11 14					
Pulborough	d										10 51							11 20					
Amberley	d										10 57												
Arundel	d										11 02							11 29					
Haywards Heath	d			10 05											10 37							11 05	
Burgess Hill	d			10 10																		11 10	
Preston Park	d			10 18																		11 18	
Brighton	d	10 03	10 14			10 23						10 33	10 44						10 53	11 03	11 14		
Hove	d	10 07	10a17	10 22		10 27						10 37	10a47		10 53				10 57	11 07	11a17	11 22	
Aldrington	d					10 29													10 59				
Portslade	d	10 10		10 25		10 31						10 40							11 01	11 10		11 25	
Fishersgate	d					10 33													11 03				
Southwick	d	10 13				10 35						10 43							11 05	11 13			
Shoreham-by-Sea	d	10 16		10 30		10 39						10 46			11 00				11 09	11 16		11 30	
Lancing	d	10 20				10 43						10 50			11 04				11 13	11 20			
East Worthing	d					10 46													11 16				
Worthing	a	10 24		10 36		10 48						10 54			11 08				11 18	11 24		11 36	
	d	10 25		10 37		10 49						10 55			11 08				11 19	11 25		11 37	
West Worthing	d			10 39		10a51						10 57			11 10				11a21			11 39	
Durrington-on-Sea	d			10 41								10 59			11 13							11 41	
Goring-by-Sea	d			10 44								11 02			11 15							11 44	
Angmering	d	10 31		10 48								11 06			11 19					11 31		11 48	
Littlehampton	a			10 57											11 28							11 57	
	d								10 54					11 11									
Ford	d								10 58		11 07	11 12		11 16				11 34					
Bognor Regis	d						10 39																
Barnham	a	10 42					10 45		11 02	10 56	11 11	11 16		11 20			11 26	11 39		11 42			
	d	10 42						10 52	11 03	10 57	11 12	11 17		11 22			11 27	11 39		11 42			
Bognor Regis	a							10 58			11 18			11 28				11 46					
Chichester	a	10 50							11 10	11 04		11 24					11 34			11 50			
	d	10 50							11 11	11 05		11 25					11 35			11 50			
Fishbourne (Sussex)	d								11 14														
Bosham	d								11 17														
Nutbourne	d								11 20														
Southbourne	d	10 57							11 23	11 12										11 57			
Emsworth	d	11 00							11 26	11 15		11 33								12 00			
Warblington	d								11 29														
Havant	d	11 05							11 32	11 19		11 37					11 46			12 05			
Bedhampton	a								11 34														
Hilsea	a								11 42														
Fratton	a	11 13							11 46								11 54			12 13			
Portsmouth & Southsea	a	11 17							11 50								11 58			12 17			
Portsmouth Harbour ⛴	a	11 21															12 02			12 21			
Cosham	a									11 26		11 45											
Portchester	a									11 30													
Fareham	a									11 35		11 53											
Swanwick	a									11 42													
Southampton Central ⛴	a									11 59		12 28											

A ✠ to Crawley

Table 188

Saturdays

London, Gatwick Airport, Brighton - Sussex Coast, Portsmouth and Southampton

		SN ◇	SN ◇	SN ◇	SN ◇	SN ◇■		SN ■	SN ◇	SN ◇	SN ◇■	SN ■	SN ◇■ A ✠		SN ◇	SN ◇■	SN ◇	SN ◇■	SN ■	SN ◇	SN ◇	SN ◇
London Victoria ⊖	d					10 32					10 47		11 02					11 17				
Clapham Junction	d					10 38					10 53		11 08					11 23				
London Bridge ⊖	d											10 33							11 03			
East Croydon	d					10 48					11 03	10 51	11 18					11 33	11 21			
Redhill	d					11 00						11 10	11 30						11 44			
Horley	d											11 19	11 36						11 51			
Gatwick Airport ✈	d					11 09					11 19	11 24	11 40					11 49	11 56			
Three Bridges	a					11 14						11 29	11 44						12 01			
	d					11 14						11 30	11 45						12 01			
Crawley	d					11 18						11 33	11 48						12 05			
Horsham	a					11 26						11 45	11 56						12 17			
	d					11 30	11 35						12 00	12 05								
Christs Hospital	d						11 38															
Billingshurst	d						11 44							12 14								
Pulborough	d						11 51							12 20								
Amberley	d						11 57															
Arundel	d						12 02							12 29								
Haywards Heath	d										11 37							12 05				
Burgess Hill	d																	12 10				
Preston Park	d																	12 18				
Brighton	d	11 23						11 33	11 44						11 53	12 03	12 14			12 23		
Hove	d	11 27						11 37	11a47		11 53				11 57	12 07	12a17	12 22		12 27		
Aldrington	d	11 29													11 59					12 29		
Portslade	d	11 31						11 40							12 01	12 10		12 25		12 31		
Fishersgate	d	11 33													12 03					12 33		
Southwick	d	11 35						11 43							12 05	12 13				12 35		
Shoreham-by-Sea	d	11 39						11 46			12 00				12 09	12 16		12 30		12 39		
Lancing	d	11 43						11 50			12 04				12 13	12 20				12 43		
East Worthing	d	11 46													12 16					12 46		
Worthing	a	11 48						11 54			12 08				12 18	12 24		12 36		12 48		
	d	11 49						11 55			12 08				12 19	12 25		12 37		12 49		
West Worthing	d	11a51						11 57			12 10				12a21			12 39		12a51		
Durrington-on-Sea	d							11 59			12 13							12 41				
Goring-by-Sea	d							12 02			12 15							12 44				
Angmering	d							12 06			12 19					12 31		12 48				
Littlehampton	a										12 28							12 57				
	d				11 54					12 11												
Ford	d				11 58		12 07	12 12		12 16				12 34								
Bognor Regis	d		11 39																		12 39	
Barnham	a		11 45		12 02	11 56	12 11	12 16		12 20			12 26	12 39		12 42					12 45	
	d			11 52	12 03	11 57	12 12	12 17		12 22			12 27	12 39		12 42						12 52
Bognor Regis	a			11 58			12 18			12 28				12 46								12 58
Chichester	a				12 10	12 04		12 24					12 34			12 50						
	d				12 11	12 05		12 25					12 35			12 50						
Fishbourne (Sussex)	d				12 14																	
Bosham	d				12 17																	
Nutbourne	d				12 20																	
Southbourne	d				12 23	12 12										12 57						
Emsworth	d				12 26	12 15		12 33								13 00						
Warblington	d				12 29																	
Havant	d				12 32	12 19		12 37					12 46			13 05						
Bedhampton	a				12 34																	
Hilsea	a				12 42																	
Fratton	a				12 46								12 54			13 13						
Portsmouth & Southsea	a				12 50								12 58			13 17						
Portsmouth Harbour ⛴	a												13 02			13 21						
Cosham	a					12 26		12 45														
Portchester	a					12 30																
Fareham	a					12 35		12 53														
Swanwick	a					12 42		13 00														
Southampton Central ⛴	a					12 59		13 19														

A ✠ to Crawley

London, Gatwick Airport, Brighton - Sussex Coast, Portsmouth and Southampton

	SN ◇	SN ◇1		SN ◇1	SN ◇	SN ◇	SN ◇1	SN 1	SN ◇1 A ⊼		SN ◇	SN ◇1	SN ◇	SN ◇1	SN 1	SN ◇	SN ◇	SN ◇	SN ◇	SN ◇1		SN 1
London Victoria 15 ⊖ d		11 32					11 47		12 02					12 17						12 32		
Clapham Junction 10 d		11 38					11 53		12 08					12 23						12 38		
London Bridge 4 ⊖ d								11 33							12 03							
East Croydon d		11 48					12 03	11 51	12 18					12 33	12 21					12 48		
Redhill 5 d		12 00						12 10	12 30						12 44					13 00		
Horley d								12 19	12 36						12 51							
Gatwick Airport 10 ✈ d		12 09					12 19	12 24	12 40					12 49	12 56					13 09		
Three Bridges 4 a		12 14						12 29	12 44						13 01					13 14		
d		12 14						12 30	12 45						13 01					13 14		
Crawley d		12 18						12 33	12 48						13 05					13 18		
Horsham 4 a		12 26						12 45	12 56						13 17					13 26		
d		12 30	12 35						13 00	13 05										13 30	13 35	
Christs Hospital d			12 38																		13 38	
Billingshurst d			12 44							13 14											13 44	
Pulborough d			12 51							13 20											13 51	
Amberley d			12 57																		13 57	
Arundel d			13 02							13 29											14 02	
Haywards Heath 3 d							12 37							13 05								
Burgess Hill d														13 10								
Preston Park d														13 18								
Brighton 10 d				12 33	12 44						12 53	13 03	13 14			13 23						13 33
Hove 2 d				12 37	12a47		12 53				12 57	13 07	13a17	13 22		13 27						13 37
Aldrington d											12 59					13 29						
Portslade d				12 40							13 01	13 10		13 25		13 31						13 40
Fishersgate d											13 03					13 33						
Southwick d				12 43							13 05	13 13				13 35						13 43
Shoreham-by-Sea d				12 46			13 00				13 09	13 16		13 30		13 39						13 46
Lancing d				12 50			13 04				13 13	13 20				13 43						13 50
East Worthing d											13 16					13 46						
Worthing 4 a				12 54			13 08				13 18	13 24		13 36		13 48						13 54
d				12 55			13 08				13 19	13 25		13 37		13 49						13 55
West Worthing d				12 57			13 10				13a21			13 39		13a51						13 57
Durrington-on-Sea d				12 59			13 13							13 41								13 59
Goring-by-Sea d				13 02			13 15							13 44								14 02
Angmering 3 d				13 06			13 19					13 31		13 48								14 06
Littlehampton 4 a							13 28							13 57								
d	12 54					13 11													13 54			
Ford 4 d	12 58		13 07	13 12		13 16				13 34									13 58		14 07	14 12
Bognor Regis 4 d																	13 39					
Barnham a	13 02	12 56	13 11	13 16		13 20			13 26	13 39		13 42					13 45		14 02	13 56	14 11	14 16
d	13 03	12 57	13 12	13 17		13 22			13 27	13 39		13 42						13 52	14 03	13 57	14 12	14 17
Bognor Regis a			13 18			13 28				13 46								13 58			14 18	
Chichester 4 a	13 10	13 04		13 24					13 34			13 50							14 10	14 04		14 24
d	13 11	13 05		13 25					13 35			13 50							14 11	14 05		14 25
Fishbourne (Sussex) d	13 14																		14 14			
Bosham d	13 17																		14 17			
Nutbourne d	13 20																		14 20			
Southbourne d	13 23	13 12										13 57							14 23	14 12		
Emsworth d	13 26	13 15		13 33								14 00							14 26	14 15		14 33
Warblington d	13 29																		14 29			
Havant d	13 32	13 19		13 37					13 46			14 05							14 32	14 19		14 37
Bedhampton a	13 34																		14 34			
Hilsea a	13 42																		14 42			
Fratton a	13 46								13 54			14 13							14 46			
Portsmouth & Southsea a	13 50								13 58			14 17							14 50			
Portsmouth Harbour ⛴ a									14 02			14 21										
Cosham a		13 26		13 45																14 26		14 45
Portchester a		13 30																		14 30		
Fareham a		13 35		13 53																14 35		14 53
Swanwick a		13 42		14 02																14 42		15 00
Southampton Central ⛴ a		13 59		14 19																14 59		15 19

A ⊼ to Crawley

London, Gatwick Airport, Brighton - Sussex Coast, Portsmouth and Southampton

	SN ◇	SN ◇	SN ◇1	SN 1	SN ◇1 A ⊼		SN ◇	SN ◇1	SN ◇	SN ◇1	SN 1	SN ◇	SN ◇	SN ◇	SN ◇	SN ◇1		SN ◇1	SN ◇	SN ◇	SN ◇1
London Victoria 15 ⊖ d			12 47		13 02					13 17						13 32					13 47
Clapham Junction 10 d			12 53		13 08					13 23						13 38					13 53
London Bridge 4 ⊖ d				12 33							13 03										
East Croydon d			13 03	12 51	13 18					13 33	13 21					13 48					14 03
Redhill 5 d				13 10	13 30						13 44					14 00					
Horley d				13 19	13 36						13 51										
Gatwick Airport 10 ✈ d			13 19	13 24	13 40					13 49	13 56					14 09					14 19
Three Bridges 4 a				13 29	13 44						14 01					14 14					
d				13 30	13 45						14 01					14 14					
Crawley d				13 33	13 48						14 05					14 18					
Horsham 4 a				13 45	13 56						14 17					14 26					
d					14 00	14 05										14 30	14 35				
Christs Hospital d																	14 38				
Billingshurst d						14 14											14 44				
Pulborough d						14 20											14 51				
Amberley d																	14 57				
Arundel d						14 29											15 02				
Haywards Heath 3 d			13 37							14 05											14 37
Burgess Hill d										14 10											
Preston Park d										14 18											
Brighton 10 d	13 44						13 53	14 03	14 14			14 23						14 33	14 44		
Hove 2 d	13a47		13 53				13 57	14 07	14a17	14 22		14 27						14 37	14a47		14 53
Aldrington d							13 59					14 29									
Portslade d							14 01	14 10		14 25		14 31						14 40			
Fishersgate d							14 03					14 33									
Southwick d							14 05	14 13				14 35						14 43			
Shoreham-by-Sea d			14 00				14 09	14 16		14 30		14 39						14 46			15 00
Lancing d			14 04				14 13	14 20				14 43						14 50			15 04
East Worthing d							14 16					14 46									
Worthing 4 a			14 08				14 18	14 24		14 36		14 48						14 54			15 08
d			14 08				14 19	14 25		14 37		14 49						14 55			15 08
West Worthing d			14 10				14a21			14 39		14a51						14 57			15 10
Durrington-on-Sea d			14 13							14 41								14 59			15 13
Goring-by-Sea d			14 15							14 44								15 02			15 15
Angmering 3 d			14 19					14 31		14 48								15 06			15 19
Littlehampton 4 a			14 28							14 57											15 28
d		14 11													14 54					15 11	
Ford 4 d		14 16				14 34									14 58		15 07	15 12		15 16	
Bognor Regis 4 d													14 39								
Barnham a		14 20			14 26	14 39		14 42					14 45		15 02	14 56	15 11	15 16		15 20	
d		14 22			14 27	14 39		14 42						14 52	15 03	14 57	15 12	15 17		15 22	
Bognor Regis a		14 28				14 46								14 58			15 18			15 28	
Chichester 4 a					14 34			14 50							15 10	15 04		15 24			
d					14 35			14 50							15 11	15 05		15 25			
Fishbourne (Sussex) d															15 14						
Bosham d															15 17						
Nutbourne d															15 20						
Southbourne d								14 57							15 23	15 12					
Emsworth d								15 00							15 26	15 15		15 33			
Warblington d															15 29						
Havant d					14 46			15 05							15 32	15 19		15 37			
Bedhampton a															15 34						
Hilsea a															15 42						
Fratton a					14 54			15 13							15 46						
Portsmouth & Southsea a					14 58			15 17							15 50						
Portsmouth Harbour ⛴ a					15 02			15 21													
Cosham a																15 26		15 45			
Portchester a																15 30					
Fareham a																15 35		15 53			
Swanwick a																15 42					
Southampton Central ⛴ a																15 59		16 28			

A ⊼ to Crawley

Table 188

Saturdays

London, Gatwick Airport, Brighton - Sussex Coast, Portsmouth and Southampton

	SN	SN		SN	SN	SN	SN	SN	SN	SN	SN	SN	SN		SN	SN	SN	SN	SN	SN		SN
	1	◇1		◇	◇1	◇	◇1	1	◇	◇	◇	◇	◇1		1	◇	◇	◇1	1	◇1		◇
		A																		A		
London Victoria 15 ⊖ d		14 02					14 17						14 32					14 47		15 02		
Clapham Junction 10 d		14 08					14 23						14 38					14 53		15 08		
London Bridge 4 ⊖ d	13 33							14 03											14 33			
East Croydon d	13 51	14 18					14 33	14 21					14 48					15 03	14 51	15 18		
Redhill 5 d	14 10	14 30						14 44					15 00						15 10	15 30		
Horley d	14 19	14 36						14 51											15 19	15 36		
Gatwick Airport 10 ✈ d	14 24	14 40					14 49	14 56					15 09					15 19	15 24	15 40		
Three Bridges 4 a	14 29	14 44						15 01					15 14						15 29	15 44		
d	14 30	14 45						15 01					15 14						15 30	15 45		
Crawley d	14 33	14 48						15 05					15 18						15 33	15 48		
Horsham 4 a	14 45	14 56						15 17					15 26						15 45	15 56		
d		15 00	15 05										15 30	15 35						16 00	16 05	
Christs Hospital d														15 38								
Billingshurst d			15 14											15 44							16 14	
Pulborough d			15 20											15 51							16 20	
Amberley d														15 57								
Arundel d			15 29											16 02							16 29	
Haywards Heath 3 d							15 05											15 37				
Burgess Hill d							15 10															
Preston Park d							15 18															
Brighton 10 d				14 53	15 03	15 14			15 23						15 33	15 44						15 53
Hove 2 d				14 57	15 07	15a17	15 22		15 27						15 37	15a47		15 53				15 57
Aldrington d				14 59					15 29													15 59
Portslade d				15 01	15 10		15 25		15 31						15 40							16 01
Fishersgate d				15 03					15 33													16 03
Southwick d				15 05	15 13				15 35						15 43							16 05
Shoreham-by-Sea d				15 09	15 16		15 30		15 39						15 46			16 00				16 09
Lancing d				15 13	15 20				15 43						15 50			16 04				16 13
East Worthing d				15 16					15 46													16 16
Worthing 4 a				15 18	15 24		15 36		15 48						15 54			16 08				16 18
d				15 19	15 25		15 37		15 49						15 55			16 08				16 19
West Worthing d				15a21			15 39		15a51						15 57			16 10				16a21
Durrington-on-Sea d							15 41								15 59			16 13				
Goring-by-Sea d							15 44								16 02			16 15				
Angmering 3 d					15 31		15 48								16 06			16 19				
Littlehampton 4 a							15 58											16 28				
d												15 54					16 11					
Ford 4 d			15 34									15 58		16 07	16 12		16 16				16 34	
Bognor Regis 4 d										15 39												
Barnham a		15 26	15 39		15 42					15 45		16 02	15 56	16 11	16 16		16 20			16 26	16 39	
d		15 27	15 39		15 42						15 52	16 03	15 57	16 12	16 17		16 22			16 27	16 39	
Bognor Regis a			15 46								15 58			16 18			16 28				16 46	
Chichester 4 a		15 34			15 50							16 10	16 04		16 24					16 34		
d		15 35			15 50							16 11	16 05		16 25					16 35		
Fishbourne (Sussex) d												16 14										
Bosham d												16 17										
Nutbourne d												16 20										
Southbourne d					15 57							16 23	16 12									
Emsworth d					16 00							16 26	16 15		16 33							
Warblington d												16 29										
Havant d		15 46			16 05							16 32	16 19		16 37					16 46		
Bedhampton a												16 34										
Hilsea a												16 42										
Fratton a		15 54			16 13							16 46								16 54		
Portsmouth & Southsea a		15 58			16 17							16 50								16 58		
Portsmouth Harbour ⛴ a		16 02			16 21															17 02		
Cosham a													16 26		16 45							
Portchester a													16 30									
Fareham a													16 35		16 53							
Swanwick a													16 42		17 00							
Southampton Central ⛴ a													16 59		17 19							

A to Crawley

Table 188

Saturdays

London, Gatwick Airport, Brighton - Sussex Coast, Portsmouth and Southampton

	SN	SN	SN	SN	SN	SN	SN	SN	SN		SN	SN	SN	SN	SN	SN	GW	SN		SN	SN	SN
	◇1	◇	◇1	1	◇	◇	◇	◇	◇1		◇1	◇	◇	◇1	1	◇	◇	◇1		◇1	◇	◇1
																		A				
London Victoria 15 ⊖ d			15 17						15 32					15 47				16 02				16 17
Clapham Junction 10 d			15 23						15 38					15 53				16 08				16 23
London Bridge 4 ⊖ d				15 03											15 33							
East Croydon d			15 33	15 21					15 48					16 03	15 51			16 18				16 33
Redhill 5 d				15 44					16 00						16 10			16 30				
Horley d				15 51											16 19			16 36				
Gatwick Airport 10 ✈ d			15 49	15 56					16 09					16 19	16 24			16 40				16 49
Three Bridges 4 a				16 01					16 14						16 29			16 44				
d				16 01					16 14						16 30			16 45				
Crawley d				16 05					16 18						16 33			16 48				
Horsham 4 a				16 17					16 26						16 45			16 56				
d									16 30	16 35								17 00	17 05			
Christs Hospital d										16 38												
Billingshurst d										16 44									17 14			
Pulborough d										16 51									17 20			
Amberley d										16 57												
Arundel d										17 02									17 29			
Haywards Heath 3 d			16 05											16 37								17 05
Burgess Hill d			16 10																			17 10
Preston Park d			16 18																			17 18
Brighton 10 d	16 03	16 14			16 23						16 33	16 44				16 53	17 00			17 03	17 14	
Hove 2 d	16 07	16a17	16 22		16 27						16 37	16a47		16 53		16 57	17 04			17 07	17a17	17 22
Aldrington d					16 29											16 59						
Portslade d	16 10		16 25		16 31						16 40					17 01				17 10		17 25
Fishersgate d					16 33											17 03						
Southwick d	16 13				16 35						16 43					17 05				17 13		
Shoreham-by-Sea d	16 16		16 30		16 39						16 46			17 00		17 09	17 13			17 17		17 30
Lancing d	16 20				16 43						16 50			17 04		17 13				17 21		
East Worthing d					16 46											17 16						
Worthing 4 a	16 24		16 36		16 48						16 54			17 08		17 18	17 22			17 25		17 36
d	16 25		16 37		16 49						16 55			17 08		17 19	17 22			17 25		17 37
West Worthing d			16 39		16a51						16 57			17 10		17a21						17 39
Durrington-on-Sea d			16 41								16 59			17 13								17 41
Goring-by-Sea d			16 44								17 02			17 15								17 44
Angmering 3 d	16 31		16 48								17 06			17 19						17 34		17 48
Littlehampton 4 a			16 57											17 28								17 57
d								16 54					17 11									
Ford 4 d								16 58		17 07	17 12		17 16						17 36			
Bognor Regis 4 d						16 39																
Barnham a	16 42					16 45		17 02	16 56	17 11	17 16		17 20				17 37	17 26	17 40	17 43		
d	16 42						16 52	17 03	16 57	17 12	17 17		17 22				17 38	17 27	17 41	17 44		
Bognor Regis a							16 58			17 18			17 28						17 47			
Chichester 4 a	16 50							17 10	17 04		17 24						17 45	17 34		17 51		
d	16 50							17 11	17 05		17 25						17 46	17 35		17 52		
Fishbourne (Sussex) d								17 14														
Bosham d								17 17														
Nutbourne d								17 20														
Southbourne d	16 57							17 23	17 12											17 59		
Emsworth d	17 00							17 26	17 15		17 33									18 02		
Warblington d								17 29														
Havant d	17 05							17 32	17 19		17 37						18 00	17 46		18 06		
Bedhampton a								17 34														
Hilsea a								17 42														
Fratton a	17 13							17 46										17 54		18 15		
Portsmouth & Southsea a	17 17							17 50										17 58		18 18		
Portsmouth Harbour ⛴ a	17 21																	18 02		18 22		
Cosham a									17 26		17 45						18 06					
Portchester a									17 30													
Fareham a									17 35		17 53						18 14					
Swanwick a									17 42													
Southampton Central ⛴ a									17 59		18 28						18 43					

A to Crawley

London, Gatwick Airport, Brighton - Sussex Coast, Portsmouth and Southampton

		SN	SN	SN	SN	SN	SN		SN	SN	SN	SN	SN	SN		SN	SN	SN	SN	SN	SN	SN
		■	◇	◇	◇	◇	◇■		■	◇	◇	◇■	■	◇■		◇	◇■	◇	◇■	■	◇	◇
														A ⌶								
London Victoria ■ ⊖	d						16 32					16 47		17 02					17 17			
Clapham Junction ■	d						16 38					16 53		17 08					17 23			
London Bridge ■ ⊖	d	16 03											16 33							17 03		
East Croydon	d	16 21					16 48					17 03	16 51	17 18					17 33	17 21		
Redhill ■	d	16 44					17 00						17 10	17 30						17 44		
Horley	d	16 51											17 19	17 36						17 51		
Gatwick Airport ■ ✈	d	16 56					17 09					17 19	17 24	17 40					17 49	17 56		
Three Bridges ■	a	17 01					17 14						17 29	17 44						18 01		
	d	17 01					17 14						17 30	17 45						18 01		
Crawley	d	17 05					17 18						17 33	17 48						18 05		
Horsham ■	a	17 17					17 26						17 45	17 56						18 17		
	d						17 30	17 35						18 00	18 05							
Christs Hospital	d							17 38														
Billingshurst	d							17 44							18 14							
Pulborough	d							17 51							18 20							
Amberley	d							17 57														
Arundel	d							18 02							18 29							
Haywards Heath ■	d											17 37							18 05			
Burgess Hill	d																		18 10			
Preston Park	d																		18 18			
Brighton ■	d		17 23						17 33	17 44						17 53	18 03	18 14				
Hove ■	d		17 27						17 37	17a47		17 53				17 57	18 07	18a17	18 22			
Aldrington	d		17 29													17 59						
Portslade	d		17 31						17 40							18 01	18 10		18 25			
Fishersgate	d		17 33													18 03						
Southwick	d		17 35						17 43							18 05	18 13					
Shoreham-by-Sea	d		17 39						17 46			18 00				18 09	18 16		18 30			
Lancing	d		17 43						17 50			18 04				18 13	18 20					
East Worthing	d		17 46													18 16						
Worthing ■	a		17 48						17 54			18 08				18 18	18 24		18 36			
	d		17 49						17 55			18 08				18 19	18 25		18 37			
West Worthing	d		17a51						17 57			18 10				18a21			18 39			
Durrington-on-Sea	d								17 59			18 13							18 41			
Goring-by-Sea	d								18 02			18 15							18 44			
Angmering ■	d								18 06			18 19					18 31		18 48			
Littlehampton ■	a											18 28							18 57			
	d					17 54					18 11											
Ford ■	d					17 58		18 07	18 12		18 16				18 34							
Bognor Regis ■	d			17 39																	18 39	
Barnham	a			17 45		18 02	17 56	18 11	18 16		18 20			18 26	18 39		18 42				18 46	
	d				17 52	18 03	17 57	18 12	18 17		18 22			18 27	18 39		18 42					18 52
Bognor Regis	a				17 58			18 18			18 28				18 46							18 58
Chichester ■	a					18 10	18 04		18 24					18 34			18 50					
	d					18 11	18 05		18 25					18 35			18 50					
Fishbourne (Sussex)	d					18 14																
Bosham	d					18 17																
Nutbourne	d					18 20																
Southbourne	d					18 23	18 12										18 57					
Emsworth	d					18 26	18 15		18 33								19 00					
Warblington	d					18 29																
Havant	d					18 32	18 19		18 37					18 46			19 05					
Bedhampton	a					18 34																
Hilsea	a					18 42																
Fratton	a					18 46								18 54			19 13					
Portsmouth & Southsea	a					18 50								18 58			19 17					
Portsmouth Harbour ⛴	a													19 02			19 21					
Cosham	a						18 26		18 45													
Portchester	a						18 30															
Fareham	a						18 35		18 53													
Swanwick	a						18 42		19 00													
Southampton Central ⛴	a						18 59		19 19													

A ⌶ to Crawley

London, Gatwick Airport, Brighton - Sussex Coast, Portsmouth and Southampton

		SN	SN		SN	SN	SN	SN	SN	SN	SN		SN	SN	SN	SN	SN	SN	SN		SN	SN	SN
		◇	◇■		◇	◇■	◇	◇	◇■	■	◇■		◇	◇■	◇	◇■	■	◇	◇■		■	◇	◇
											A ⌶												
London Victoria ■ ⊖	d		17 32						17 47		18 02					18 17			18 32				
Clapham Junction ■	d		17 38						17 53		18 08					18 23			18 38				
London Bridge ■ ⊖	d									17 33							18 03						
East Croydon	d		17 48						18 03	17 51	18 18					18 33	18 21		18 48				
Redhill ■	d		18 00							18 10	18 30						18 44		19 00				
Horley	d									18 19	18 36						18 51						
Gatwick Airport ■ ✈	d		18 09						18 19	18 24	18 40					18 49	18 56		19 09				
Three Bridges ■	a		18 14							18 29	18 44						19 01		19 14				
	d		18 14							18 30	18 45						19 01		19 14				
Crawley	d		18 18							18 33	18 48						19 05		19 18				
Horsham ■	a		18 26							18 47	18 56						19 17		19 26				
	d		18 30	18 35							19 00	19 05							19 30	19 35			
Christs Hospital	d			18 38																19 38			
Billingshurst	d			18 44								19 14								19 44			
Pulborough	d			18 51								19 20								19 51			
Amberley	d			18 57																19 57			
Arundel	d			19 02								19 29								20 02			
Haywards Heath ■	d								18 37							19 05							
Burgess Hill	d															19 10							
Preston Park	d															19 18							
Brighton ■	d				18 23	18 33	18 44							19 03	19 14						19 29	19 44	
Hove ■	d				18 27	18 37	18a47		18 53					19 07	19a17	19 22					19 33	19a47	
Aldrington	d				18 29									19 09							19 35		
Portslade	d				18 31	18 40			18 56					19 11		19 25					19 37		
Fishersgate	d				18 33									19 13							19 39		
Southwick	d				18 35	18 43								19 15							19 41		
Shoreham-by-Sea	d				18 39	18 46			19 01					19 19		19 30					19 45		
Lancing	d				18 43	18 50			19 05					19 23		19 34					19 49		
East Worthing	d				18 46									19 26							19 52		
Worthing ■	a				18 48	18 54			19 09					19 28		19 38					19 54		
	d				18 49	18 55			19 10					19 29		19 39					19 55		
West Worthing	d				18 51	18 57			19 12					19 31		19 41					19 57		
Durrington-on-Sea	d				18 53	18 59			19 14					19 33		19 43					19 59		
Goring-by-Sea	d				18 56	19 02			19 17					19 36		19 46					20 02		
Angmering ■	d				19 00	19 06			19 21					19 40		19 50					20 06		
Littlehampton ■	a				19 11				19 30							19 58							
	d	18 54						19 11															20 11
Ford ■	d	18 58		19 07		19 12		19 16				19 34		19 46						20 07	20 12		20 16
Bognor Regis ■	d												19 39										
Barnham	a	19 02	18 56	19 11		19 16		19 20			19 26	19 39	19 46	19 50					19 56	20 11	20 16		20 20
	d	19 03	18 57	19 12		19 17		19 22			19 27	19 39		19 51				19 52	19 57	20 12	20 17		20 22
Bognor Regis	a			19 18				19 28				19 46						19 58		20 18			20 28
Chichester ■	a	19 10	19 04			19 24					19 34			19 58					20 04		20 24		
	d	19 11	19 05			19 25					19 35			19 59					20 05		20 25		
Fishbourne (Sussex)	d	19 14																	20 08				
Bosham	d	19 17																	20 11				
Nutbourne	d	19 20																	20 14				
Southbourne	d	19 23	19 12																20 17				
Emsworth	d	19 26	19 15			19 33													20 20		20 33		
Warblington	d	19 29																	20 23				
Havant	d	19 32	19 19			19 37					19 46			20 10					20 26		20 37		
Bedhampton	a	19 34																					
Hilsea	a	19 42																					
Fratton	a	19 46									19 54			20 18									
Portsmouth & Southsea	a	19 50									19 58			20 22									
Portsmouth Harbour ⛴	a										20 02			20 26									
Cosham	a		19 26			19 45													20 32		20 45		
Portchester	a		19 30																20 36				
Fareham	a		19 35			19 53													20 41		20 53		
Swanwick	a		19 42																20 48		21 00		
Southampton Central ⛴	a		19 59			20 28													21 05		21 19		

A ⌶ to Crawley

London, Gatwick Airport, Brighton - Sussex Coast, Portsmouth and Southampton

		SN ◇1	SN 1	SN ◇1 A 🚌		SN ◇1	SN ◇	SN ◇1	SN 1	SN ◇	SN ◇	SN ◇1		SN ◇1	SN ◇	SN ◇	SN ◇1	SN 1	SN ◇1		SN ◇	SN ◇1
London Victoria 15 ⊖	d	18 47		19 02				19 17				19 32					19 47		20 02			
Clapham Junction 10	d	18 53		19 08				19 23				19 38					19 53		20 08			
London Bridge 4 ⊖	d		18 33						19 03									19 33				
East Croydon ⇌	d	19 03	18 51	19 18				19 33	19 21			19 48					20 03	19 51	20 19			
Redhill 5	d		19 10	19 30					19 46			20 00						20 10	20 31			
Horley	d		19 19	19 36					19 52									20 19				
Gatwick Airport 10 ✈	d	19 19	19 24	19 40				19 49	19 56			20 09					20 19	20 24	20 39			
Three Bridges 4	a		19 28	19 44					20 01			20 14						20 29	20 44			
	d		19 30	19 45					20 01			20 14						20 33	20 44			
Crawley	d		19 33	19 48					20 05			20 18						20 36	20 48			
Horsham 4	a		19 45	19 56					20 17			20 26						20 48	20 56			
	d			20 00	20 05							20 30	20 35						21 00	21 05		
Christs Hospital	d												20 38							21 08		
Billingshurst	d				20 14								20 44							21 14		
Pulborough	d				20 20								20 51							21 21		
Amberley	d												20 57							21 27		
Arundel	d				20 29								21 02							21 32		
Haywards Heath 3	d	19 37						20 05									20 37					
Burgess Hill	d							20 10														
Preston Park	d							20 18														
Brighton 10	d					19 56	20 14							20 30	20 44							21 03
Hove 2	d	19 53				20 00	20a18	20 22						20 34	20a48		20 53					21 07
Aldrington	d					20 02								20 36								21 09
Portslade	d	19 56				20 04		20 25						20 38			20 56					21 11
Fishersgate	d					20 06								20 40								21 13
Southwick	d					20 08								20 42								21 15
Shoreham-by-Sea	d	20 01				20 12		20 30						20 46			21 01					21 19
Lancing	d	20 05				20 16		20 34						20 50			21 05					21 23
East Worthing	d					20 19								20 53								21 26
Worthing 4	a	20 09				20 21		20 38						20 55			21 09					21 28
	d	20 09				20 22		20 39						20 56			21 10					21 29
West Worthing	d	20 11				20 24		20 41						20 58			21 12					21 31
Durrington-on-Sea	d	20 14				20 26		20 43						21 00			21 14					21 33
Goring-by-Sea	d	20 16				20 29		20 46						21 03			21 17					21 36
Angmering 3	d	20 20				20 33		20 50						21 07			21 21					21 40
Littlehampton 4	a	20 29						20 58									21 29					
	d															21 07						
Ford 4	d				20 34	20 39							21 07	21 15		21 11				21 37		21 46
Bognor Regis 4	d									20 39											21 39	
Barnham	a			20 26	20 39	20 43				20 45		20 56	21 11	21 19		21 15			21 26	21 41	21 45	21 50
	d			20 27	20 39	20 44					20 52	20 57	21 12	21 20		21 22			21 27	21 42		21 51
Bognor Regis	a				20 46						20 58		21 18			21 28				21 48		
Chichester 4	a			20 34		20 51						21 04		21 27					21 34			21 58
	d			20 35		20 52						21 05		21 28					21 35			21 59
Fishbourne (Sussex)	d					20 55																
Bosham	d											21 09										
Nutbourne	d					21 00																
Southbourne	d					21 02						21 14							21 42			
Emsworth	d					21 05						21 17		21 36					21 45			
Warblington	d											21 20										
Havant	d			20 46		21 10						21 23		21 40					21 49			22 10
Bedhampton	a																					
Hilsea	a																					
Fratton	a			20 54		21 18													21 59			22 18
Portsmouth & Southsea	a			20 58		21 22													22 02			22 22
Portsmouth Harbour ⛴	a			21 02		21 26													22 06			22 26
Cosham	a											21 29		21 46								
Portchester	a											21 33										
Fareham	a											21 38		21 54								
Swanwick	a											21 45		22 01								
Southampton Central ⛴	a											22 02		22 20								

A 🚌 to Crawley

London, Gatwick Airport, Brighton - Sussex Coast, Portsmouth and Southampton

		SN ◇	SN ◇1	SN 1	SN ◇	SN ◇	SN ◇1		SN ◇1	SN ◇1	SN ◇	SN ◇1	SN 1	SN ◇	SN ◇1	SN ◇	SN ◇	SN ◇1	SN 1	SN 1	SN ◇1	SN ◇	SN ◇1
London Victoria 15 ⊖	d		20 17	20 10			20 32					20 47	20 40					21 17	21 10	21 32			
Clapham Junction 10	d		20 23	20 16			20 38					20 53	20 46					21 23	21 16	21 38			
London Bridge 4 ⊖	d																						
East Croydon ⇌	d		20 33	20 28			20 48					21 03	20 58					21 33	21 28	21 48			
Redhill 5	d			20 46			21 00						21 16						21 46	22 00			
Horley	d			20 52									21 25						21 52				
Gatwick Airport 10 ✈	d		20 49	20 57			21 09					21 19	21 29					21 49	21 56	22 09			
Three Bridges 4	a			21 02			21 14						21 33					21 53	22 00	22 14			
	d			21 02			21 14						21 36					21 53	22 01	22 14			
Crawley	d			21 06			21 18						21 39						22 04	22 18			
Horsham 4	a			21 18			21 26						21 52						22 16	22 26			
	d						21 30	21 35												22 27			
Christs Hospital	d							21 38												22 30			
Billingshurst	d							21 44												22 36			
Pulborough	d							21 51												22 43			
Amberley	d							21 57												22 49			
Arundel	d							22 02												22 54			
Haywards Heath 3	d		21 05									21 37						22 06					
Burgess Hill	d		21 10															22 11					
Preston Park	d		21 19																				
Brighton 10	d	21 14								21 33	21 44				22 03	22 14							22 33
Hove 2	d	21a17	21 23							21 37	21a48	21 52			22 07	22a17		22 23					22 37
Aldrington	d									21 39					22 09								22 39
Portslade	d		21 26							21 41		21 55			22 11			22 26					22 41
Fishersgate	d									21 43					22 13								22 43
Southwick	d									21 45					22 15								22 45
Shoreham-by-Sea	d		21 31							21 49		22 00			22 19			22 31					22 49
Lancing	d		21 35							21 53		22 04			22 23			22 35					22 53
East Worthing	d									21 56					22 26								22 56
Worthing 4	a		21 39							21 58		22 08			22 28			22 39					22 58
	d		21 39							21 59		22 08			22 29			22 39					22 59
West Worthing	d		21 41							22 01		22 10			22 31			22 41					23 01
Durrington-on-Sea	d		21 44							22 03		22 13			22 33			22 44					23 03
Goring-by-Sea	d		21 46							22 06		22 15			22 36			22 46					23 06
Angmering 3	d		21 50							22 10		22 19			22 40			22 50					23 10
Littlehampton 4	a		21 59									22 28											23 18
	d								22 08								22 38						23 23
Ford 4	d							22 07	22 12	22 16					22 46		22 42	22 56		23 00			23 27
Bognor Regis 4	d					22 00															←	23 15	
Barnham	a					22 06	21 56	22 11	22 16	22 20					22 50		22 46	23 01		23 04	23 01	23 21	23 31
	d				21 52		21 57	22 12	22 17	22 21				22 22	22 51		22 52	23 06		23 05	23 06		23 32
Bognor Regis	a				21 58			22 18						22 28			22 58	→			23 12		
Chichester 4	a						22 04		22 24	22 28					22 58					23 12			23 39
	d						22 05			22 29					22 59					23 13			
Fishbourne (Sussex)	d						22 08													23 16			
Bosham	d						22 11													23 19			
Nutbourne	d						22 14													23 22			
Southbourne	d						22 17			22 36										23 25			
Emsworth	d						22 20			22 39										23 28			
Warblington	d						22 23													23 31			
Havant	d						22 26			22 43					23 10					23 36			
Bedhampton	a																						
Hilsea	a																						
Fratton	a									22 52					23 18					23 48			
Portsmouth & Southsea	a									22 55					23 22					23 51			
Portsmouth Harbour ⛴	a									22 59					23 26								
Cosham	a						22 33																
Portchester	a																						
Fareham	a						22 41																
Swanwick	a						22 48																
Southampton Central ⛴	a						23 05																

London, Gatwick Airport, Brighton - Sussex Coast, Portsmouth and Southampton

		SN	SN	SN	SN	SN	SN	SN	SN	SN	SN	SN	SN	SN	SN	SN	SN
		◇	◇1	1	◇	◇	◇	◇1	1	1	◇1	◇	◇1	1	◇1	1	1
London Victoria 15 ⊖	d		21 47	21 40				22 17	22 10	22 32			22 47	22 40	23 17	23 10	23 47
Clapham Junction 10	d		21 53	21 46				22 23	22 16	22 38			22 53	22 46	23 23	23 16	23 53
London Bridge 4 ⊖	d																
East Croydon	d		22 03	21 58				22 33	22 28	22 48			23 03	22 58	23 33	23 28	00 06
Redhill 5	d			22 16					22 46	23 01				23 16		23 46	00 25
Horley	d			22 25					22 52					23 26		23 56	00 31
Gatwick Airport 10 ✈	d		22 19	22 29				22 49	22 56	23 09			23 19	23 29	23 51	23 59	00 34
Three Bridges 4	a			22 33				22 54	23 00	23 14				23 34	23 55	00 04	00 39
	d			22 36				22 54	23 01	23 15				23 38	23 56	00 04	00 39
Crawley	d			22 39					23 04	23 18				23 41		00 07	00 43
Horsham 4	a			22 52					23 16	23 26				23 53		00 19	00 55
	d									23 27							
Christs Hospital	d									23 30							
Billingshurst	d									23 36							
Pulborough	d									23 43							
Amberley	d									23 49							
Arundel	d									23 54							
Haywards Heath 3	d		22 37					23 03					23 37		00 05		
Burgess Hill	d							23 08							00 10		
Preston Park	d																
Brighton 10	d	22 44			23 03	23 14						23 44					
Hove 2	d	22a47	22 52		23 07	23a17		23 22				23a47	23 52		00 22		
Aldrington	d				23 09												
Portslade	d		22 55		23 11			23 25					23 55		00s25		
Fishersgate	d				23 13												
Southwick	d				23 15			23 28					23 58		00s28		
Shoreham-by-Sea	d		23 00		23 19			23 31					00 01		00s31		
Lancing	d		23 04		23 23			23 35					00 05		00s35		
East Worthing	d				23 26												
Worthing 4	a		23 08		23 28			23 39					00 09		00s39		
	d		23 08		23 29			23 39									
West Worthing	d		23 10		23a31			23 41							00s41		
Durrington-on-Sea	d		23 13					23 44							00s44		
Goring-by-Sea	d		23 15					23 46							00s46		
Angmering 3	d		23 19					23 50							00s50		
Littlehampton 4	a		23 28														
	d																
Ford 4	d							23 56		23 59					00s56		
Bognor Regis 4	d										←						
Barnham	a							00 01		00 04	00 01				01s01		
	d						23 36	00 09		00 05	00 09						
Bognor Regis	a						23 42	→			00 15						
Chichester 4	a									00 12					01 09		
	d																
Fishbourne (Sussex)	d																
Bosham	d																
Nutbourne	d																
Southbourne	d																
Emsworth	d																
Warblington	d																
Havant	d																
Bedhampton	a																
Hilsea	a																
Fratton	a																
Portsmouth & Southsea	a																
Portsmouth Harbour ⛴	a																
Cosham	a																
Portchester	a																
Fareham	a																
Swanwick	a																
Southampton Central ⛴	a																

London, Gatwick Airport, Brighton - Sussex Coast, Portsmouth and Southampton

		SN	SN	SN	SN	SN	SN	SN	SN	SN	SN	SN	SN	SN	SN	SN	SN	SN	SN	SN	SN	SN	SN
		◇1	1	◇1	◇1	◇	◇	◇1	1	1	◇1	1	◇	◇1	◇1	◇1	◇1	◇1	◇1	◇1	◇1	1	◇1
		A	A	A	A			A	A	A													
London Victoria 15 ⊖	d	22p17	22p32		22p47			23p17	23p10	23p47	00 05										07 02		
Clapham Junction 10	d	22p23	22p38		22p53			23p23	23p16	23p53	00 11										07 08		
London Bridge 4 ⊖	d																					07 37	
East Croydon	d	22p33	22p48		23p03			23p33	23p28	00 06	00 25										07 20	07 55	
Redhill 5	d		23p01						23p46	00 25											07 34	08 13	
Horley	d								23p56	00 31											07 40	08 25	
Gatwick Airport 10 ✈	d	22p49	23p09		23p19			23p51	23p59	00 34	00 44	06 29									07 43	08 29	
Three Bridges 4	a	22p54	23p14					23p55	00 04	00 39	00 48	06 33									07 48	08 33	
	d	22p54	23p15					23p56	00 04	00 39	00 48	06 40									07 48	08 34	
Crawley	d		23p18						00 07	00 43		06 43									07 52	08 37	
Horsham 4	a		23p26						00 19	00 55		06 56									08 04	08 49	
	d		23p27																		08 04		
Christs Hospital	d		23p30																				
Billingshurst	d		23p36																		08 13		
Pulborough	d		23p43																		08 19		
Amberley	d		23p49																				
Arundel	d		23p54																		08 29		
Haywards Heath 3	d	23p03			23b37			00 05			01 02												
Burgess Hill	d	23p08						00 10															
Preston Park	d																						
Brighton 10	d					00 03	00 10				01s16						07 14	07 18		07 48			08 14
Hove 2	d	23p22			23p52	00 07	00a13	00 22			01s24						07 18	07 22		07 52			08 18
Aldrington	d					00 09												07 24		07 54			
Portslade	d	23p25			23p55	00 11		00s25			01s27							07 26		07 56			
Fishersgate	d					00 13												07 28		07 58			
Southwick	d	23p28			23p58	00 15		00s28			01s30							07 30		08 00			
Shoreham-by-Sea	d	23p31			00 01	00 19		00s31			01s33						07 24	07 33		08 03			08 24
Lancing	d	23p35			00 05	00 23		00s35			01s37							07 37		08 07			
East Worthing	d					00 26												07 40		08 10			
Worthing 4	a	23p39			00 09	00 28		00s39			01 41						07 30	07 43		08 13			08 30
	d	23p39				00 29											07 30	07 43		08 13			08 30
West Worthing	d	23p41				00a31		00s41										07 45		08 15			
Durrington-on-Sea	d	23p44						00s44										07 48		08 18			
Goring-by-Sea	d	23p46						00s46										07 50		08 20			
Angmering 3	d	23p50						00s50									07 37	07 54		08 24			08 37
Littlehampton 4	a																						
	d													06 42	07 19	07 29			07 54				
Ford 4	d	23p56	23p59					00s56						06 46	07 23		07 43	08 01	07 58	08 31	08 35		08 43
Bognor Regis 4	d			←																			
Barnham	a	00 01	00 04	00 01				01s01						06 50	07 27	07 37	07 48	08 05	08 02	08 35	08 39		08 48
	d	00 09	00 05	00 09									06 45	06 51	07 28	07 37	07 48	08 06	08 09	08 36	08 40		08 48
Bognor Regis	a	→		00 15									06 51		07 34				08 15		08 46		
Chichester 4	a		00 12					01 09						06 58		07 45	07 56	08 13		08 43			08 56
	d													06 59		07 45	07 56	08 14		08 44			08 56
Fishbourne (Sussex)	d																	08 17					
Bosham	d																	08 20					
Nutbourne	d																	08 23					
Southbourne	d																08 03	08 26					09 03
Emsworth	d															07 53	08 06	08 29		08 52			09 06
Warblington	d																	08 32					
Havant	d													07 10		07 58	08 11	08 35		08 58			09 11
Bedhampton	a																	08 37					
Hilsea	a																						
Fratton	a													07 18			08 19	08 45					09 19
Portsmouth & Southsea	a													07 22			08 23	08 48					09 23
Portsmouth Harbour ⛴	a													07 26			08 27	08 52					09 27
Cosham	a															08 05				09 05			
Portchester	a																						
Fareham	a															08 13				09 13			
Swanwick	a															08 20				09 20			
Southampton Central ⛴	a															08 44				09 44			

A not 22 May

b Previous night, arr. 2330

London, Gatwick Airport, Brighton - Sussex Coast, Portsmouth and Southampton

		SN ◇1	SN ◇1	SN ◇1	SN ◇1	SN ◇1		SN 1	SN ◇1	SN ◇1	SN ◇1	SN ◇1	SN ◇1		SN 1	SN ◇1	SN ◇1	SN ◇1	SN ◇1	GW ◇	SN ◇1		SN 1
London Victoria 15 ⊖	d				08 02	08 17						09 02	09 17						10 02		10 17		
Clapham Junction 10	d				08 08	08 23						09 08	09 23						10 08		10 23		
London Bridge 4 ⊖	d							08 37							09 37								10 37
East Croydon	d				08 18	08 33		08 55				09 18	09 33		09 55				10 18		10 33		10 55
Redhill 5	d				08 32			09 13				09 32			10 13				10 32				11 13
Horley	d				08 38			09 25				09 38			10 25				10 38				11 25
Gatwick Airport 10 ✈	d				08 41	08 49		09 29				09 41	09 49		10 29				10 41		10 49		11 29
Three Bridges 4	a				08 46			09 33				09 46			10 33				10 46				11 33
	d				08 46			09 34				09 46			10 34				10 46				11 34
Crawley	d				08 50			09 37				09 50			10 37				10 50				11 37
Horsham 4	a				08 58			09 49				09 58			10 49				10 58				11 49
	d				08 59							09 59							10 59				
Christs Hospital	d				09 02							10 02							11 02				
Billingshurst	d				09 09							10 09							11 09				
Pulborough	d				09 15							10 15							11 15				
Amberley	d				09 21							10 21							11 21				
Arundel	d				09 27							10 27							11 27				
Haywards Heath 3	d					09 00							10 00								11 00		
Burgess Hill	d					09 06							10 06								11 06		
Preston Park	d																						
Brighton 10	d	08 18		08 48					09 12		09 48					10 12		10 48		11 10			
Hove 2	d	08 22		08 52		09 19			09 22		09 52		10 19			10 22		10 52		11 14	11 19		
Aldrington	d	08 24		08 54					09 24		09 54					10 24		10 54					
Portslade	d	08 26		08 56					09 26		09 56					10 26		10 56					
Fishersgate	d	08 28		08 58					09 28		09 58					10 28		10 58					
Southwick	d	08 30		09 00					09 30		10 00					10 30		11 00					
Shoreham-by-Sea	d	08 33		09 03		09 25			09 33		10 03		10 25			10 33		11 03		11 20	11 25		
Lancing	d	08 37		09 07					09 37		10 07					10 37		11 07					
East Worthing	d	08 40		09 10					09 40		10 10					10 40		11 10					
Worthing 4	a	08 43		09 13		09 31			09 43		10 13		10 31			10 43		11 13		11 26	11 31		
	d	08 43		09 13		09 35	09 37		09 43		10 13		10 35	10 37		10 43		11 13		11 29	11 35	11 37	
West Worthing	d	08 45		09 15			09 39		09 45		10 15			10 39		10 45		11 15				11 39	
Durrington-on-Sea	d	08 48		09 18			09 41		09 48		10 18			10 41		10 48		11 18				11 41	
Goring-by-Sea	d	08 50		09 20			09 44		09 50		10 20			10 44		10 50		11 20				11 44	
Angmering 3	d	08 54		09 24			09 48		09 54		10 24			10 48		10 54		11 24				11 48	
Littlehampton 4	a						09 57							10 57								11 57	
	d		08 54							09 54							10 54						
Ford 4	d	09 01	08 58	09 31	09 35				10 01	09 58	10 31	10 35				11 01	10 58	11 31	11 35				
Bognor Regis 4	d																						
Barnham	a	09 05	09 02	09 35	09 39	09 51			10 05	10 02	10 35	10 39	10 51			11 05	11 02	11 35	11 39	11 45	11 51		
	d	09 06	09 09	09 36	09 40	09 52			10 06	10 09	10 36	10 40	10 52			11 06	11 09	11 36	11 40	11 46	11 52		
Bognor Regis	a		09 15		09 46					10 15		10 46					11 15		11 46				
Chichester 4	a	09 13		09 43		09 59			10 13		10 43		10 59			11 13		11 43		11 53	11 59		
	d	09 14		09 44		10 00			10 14		10 44		11 00			11 14		11 44		11 54	12 00		
Fishbourne (Sussex)	d	09 17							10 17							11 17							
Bosham	d	09 20							10 20							11 20							
Nutbourne	d	09 23							10 23							11 23							
Southbourne	d	09 26				10 07			10 26				11 07			11 26					12 07		
Emsworth	d	09 29		09 52		10 10			10 29		10 52		11 10			11 29		11 52			12 10		
Warblington	d	09 32							10 32							11 32							
Havant	d	09 35		09 58		10 14			10 35		10 58		11 14			11 35		11 58		12 10	12 14		
Bedhampton	a	09 37							10 37							11 37							
Hilsea	a																						
Fratton	a	09 45				10 23			10 45				11 23			11 45					12 23		
Portsmouth & Southsea	a	09 48				10 26			10 50				11 26			11 49					12 26		
Portsmouth Harbour ⛴	a	09 52				10 30			10 54				11 30			11 53					12 30		
Cosham	a			10 06							11 06							12 05		12 16			
Portchester	a																						
Fareham	a			10 14							11 14							12 13		12 31			
Swanwick	a			10 21							11 21							12 20					
Southampton Central ⛴	a			10 44							11 44							12 44		12 53			

London, Gatwick Airport, Brighton - Sussex Coast, Portsmouth and Southampton

		SN ◇1	SN ◇1	SN ◇1	SN ◇1	SN ◇1		SN 1	SN ◇1	SN ◇1	SN ◇1	SN ◇1	SN ◇1		SN 1	SN ◇1	SN ◇1	SN ◇1	SN ◇1	SN ◇1		SN 1
London Victoria 15 ⊖	d				11 02	11 17						12 02	12 17						13 02	13 17		
Clapham Junction 10	d				11 08	11 23						12 08	12 23						13 08	13 23		
London Bridge 4 ⊖	d							11 37							12 37							13 37
East Croydon	d				11 18	11 33		11 55				12 18	12 33		12 55				13 18	13 33		13 55
Redhill 5	d				11 32			12 13				12 32			13 13				13 32			14 13
Horley	d				11 38			12 25				12 38			13 25				13 38			14 25
Gatwick Airport 10 ✈	d				11 41	11 49		12 29				12 41	12 49		13 29				13 41	13 49		14 29
Three Bridges 4	a				11 46			12 33				12 46			13 33				13 46			14 33
	d				11 46			12 34				12 46			13 34				13 46			14 34
Crawley	d				11 50			12 37				12 50			13 37				13 50			14 37
Horsham 4	a				11 58			12 49				12 58			13 49				13 58			14 49
	d				11 59							12 59							13 59			
Christs Hospital	d				12 02							13 02							14 02			
Billingshurst	d				12 09							13 09							14 09			
Pulborough	d				12 15							13 15							14 15			
Amberley	d				12 21							13 21							14 21			
Arundel	d				12 27							13 27							14 27			
Haywards Heath 3	d					12 00							13 00							14 00		
Burgess Hill	d					12 06							13 06							14 06		
Preston Park	d																					
Brighton 10	d	11 13		11 48					12 12		12 48					13 12		13 48				
Hove 2	d	11 22		11 52		12 19			12 22		12 52		13 19			13e22		13 52		14 19		
Aldrington	d	11 24		11 54					12 24		12 54					13 24		13 54				
Portslade	d	11 26		11 56					12 26		12 56					13 26		13 56				
Fishersgate	d	11 28		11 58					12 28		12 58					13 28		13 58				
Southwick	d	11 30		12 00					12 30		13 00					13 30		14 00				
Shoreham-by-Sea	d	11 33		12 03		12 25			12 33		13 03		13 25			13 33		14 03		14 25		
Lancing	d	11 37		12 07					12 37		13 07					13 37		14 07				
East Worthing	d	11 40		12 10					12 40		13 10					13 40		14 10				
Worthing 4	a	11 43		12 13		12 31			12 43		13 13		13 31			13 43		14 13		14 31		
	d	11 43		12 13		12 35	12 37		12 43		13 13		13 35	13 37		13 43		14 13		14 35	14 37	
West Worthing	d	11 45		12 15			12 39		12 45		13 15			13 39		13 45		14 15			14 39	
Durrington-on-Sea	d	11 48		12 18			12 41		12 48		13 18			13 41		13 48		14 18			14 41	
Goring-by-Sea	d	11 50		12 20			12 44		12 50		13 20			13 44		13 50		14 20			14 44	
Angmering 3	d	11 54		12 24			12 48		12 54		13 24			13 48		13 54		14 24			14 48	
Littlehampton 4	a						12 57							13 57							14 57	
	d		11 54							12 54							13 54					
Ford 4	d	12 01	11 58	12 31	12 35				13 01	12 58	13 31	13 35				14 01	13 58	14 31	14 36			
Bognor Regis 4	d																					
Barnham	a	12 05	12 02	12 35	12 39	12 51			13 05	13 02	13 35	13 39	13 51			14 05	14 02	14 35	14 40	14 51		
	d	12 06	12 09	12 36	12 40	12 52			13 06	13 09	13 36	13 40	13 52			14 06	14 09	14 36	14 41	14 52		
Bognor Regis	a		12 15		12 46					13 15		13 46					14 15		14 47			
Chichester 4	a	12 13		12 43		12 59			13 13		13 43		13 59			14 13		14 43		14 59		
	d	12 14		12 44		13 00			13 14		13 44		14 00			14 14		14 44		15 00		
Fishbourne (Sussex)	d	12 17							13 17							14 17						
Bosham	d	12 20							13 20							14 20						
Nutbourne	d	12 23							13 23							14 23						
Southbourne	d	12 26				13 07			13 26				14 07			14 26				15 07		
Emsworth	d	12 29		12 52		13 10			13 29		13 52		14 10			14 29		14 52		15 10		
Warblington	d	12 32							13 32							14 32						
Havant	d	12 35		12 58		13 14			13 35		13 58		14 14			14 35		14 58		15 14		
Bedhampton	a	12 37							13 37							14 37						
Hilsea	a																					
Fratton	a	12 46				13 23			13 45				14 23			14 45				15 23		
Portsmouth & Southsea	a	12 57				13 26			13 48				14 26			14 48				15 26		
Portsmouth Harbour ⛴	a	13 01				13 30			13 52				14 30			14 53				15 30		
Cosham	a			13 05							14 05							15 05				
Portchester	a																					
Fareham	a			13 13							14 13							15 13				
Swanwick	a			13 20							14 20							15 20				
Southampton Central ⛴	a			13 44							14 44							15 44				

London, Gatwick Airport, Brighton - Sussex Coast, Portsmouth and Southampton

		SN ◇1	SN ◇1	SN ◇1	SN ◇1	SN ◇1		SN 1	SN ◇1	SN ◇1	GW ◇	SN ◇1	SN ◇1	SN ◇1		SN 1	SN ◇1	SN ◇1	SN ◇1	SN ◇1	SN ◇1		SN 1
London Victoria 15 ⊖	d				14 02	14 17							15 02	15 17						16 02	16 17		
Clapham Junction 10	d				14 08	14 23							15 08	15 23						16 08	16 23		
London Bridge 4 ⊖	d							14 37								15 37							16 37
East Croydon	d				14 18	14 33		14 55					15 18	15 33		15 55				16 18	16 33		16 55
Redhill 5	d				14 32			15 13					15 32			16 13				16 32			17 13
Horley	d				14 38			15 25					15 38			16 25				16 38			17 25
Gatwick Airport 10 ✈	d				14 41	14 49		15 29					15 41	15 49		16 29				16 41	16 49		17 29
Three Bridges 4	a				14 46			15 33					15 46			16 33				16 46			17 33
	d				14 46			15 34					15 46			16 34				16 46			17 34
Crawley	d				14 50			15 37					15 50			16 37				16 50			17 37
Horsham 4	a				14 58			15 49					15 58			16 49				16 58			17 49
	d				14 59								15 59							16 59			
Christs Hospital	d				15 02								16 02							17 02			
Billingshurst	d				15 09								16 09							17 09			
Pulborough	d				15 15								16 15							17 15			
Amberley	d				15 21								16 21							17 21			
Arundel	d				15 27								16 27							17 27			
Haywards Heath 3	d					15 00								16 00							17 00		
Burgess Hill	d					15 06								16 06							17 06		
Preston Park	d																						
Brighton 10	d	14 12		14 48					15 12		15 46	15 50					16 12		16 48				
Hove 2	d	14 22		14 52		15 19			15 22		15 50	15 54		16 19			16 22		16 52		17 19		
Aldrington	d	14 24		14 54					15 24			15 56					16 24		16 54				
Portslade	d	14 26		14 56					15 26			15 58					16 26		16 56				
Fishersgate	d	14 28		14 58					15 28			16 00					16 28		16 58				
Southwick	d	14 30		15 00					15 30			16 02					16 30		17 00				
Shoreham-by-Sea	d	14 33		15 03		15 25			15 33		15 56	16 05		16 25			16 33		17 03		17 25		
Lancing	d	14 37		15 07					15 37			16 09					16 37		17 07				
East Worthing	d	14 40		15 10					15 40			16 12					16 40		17 10				
Worthing 4	a	14 43		15 13		15 31			15 43		16 03	16 15		16 31			16 43		17 13		17 31		
	d	14 43		15 13		15 35	15 37		15 43		16 08	16 15		16 35	16 37		16 43		17 13		17 35	17 37	
West Worthing	d	14 45		15 15			15 39		15 45			16 17			16 39		16 45		17 15			17 39	
Durrington-on-Sea	d	14 48		15 18			15 41		15 48			16 20			16 41		16 48		17 18			17 41	
Goring-by-Sea	d	14 50		15 20			15 44		15 50			16 22			16 44		16 50		17 20			17 44	
Angmering 3	d	14 54		15 24			15 48		15 54			16 26			16 48		16 54		17 24			17 48	
Littlehampton 4	a						15 57								16 57							17 57	
	d		14 54							15 54								16 54					
Ford 4	d	15 01	14 58	15 31	15 35				16 01	15 58		16 32	16 36				17 01	16 58	17 31	17 35			
Bognor Regis 4	d																						
Barnham	a	15 05	15 02	15 35	15 39	15 51			16 05	16 02	16 25	16 37	16 40	16 51			17 05	17 02	17 35	17 39	17 51		
	d	15 06	15 09	15 36	15 40	15 52			16 06	16 09	16 25	16 37	16 41	16 52			17 06	17 09	17 36	17 40	17 52		
Bognor Regis	a		15 15		15 46					16 15			16 47					17 15		17 46			
Chichester 4	a	15 13		15 43		15 59			16 13		16 33	16 45		16 59			17 13		17 43		17 59		
	d	15 14		15 44		16 00			16 14		16 34	16 45		17 00			17 14		17 44		18 00		
Fishbourne (Sussex)	d	15 17							16 17								17 17						
Bosham	d	15 20							16 20								17 20						
Nutbourne	d	15 23							16 23								17 23						
Southbourne	d	15 26				16 07			16 26					17 07			17 26				18 07		
Emsworth	d	15 29		15 52		16 10			16 29			16 53		17 10			17 29		17 52		18 10		
Warblington	d	15 32							16 32								17 32						
Havant	d	15 35		15 56		16 14			16 35		16 48	16 59		17 14			17 35		17 58		18 14		
Bedhampton	a	15 37							16 37								17 37						
Hilsea	a																						
Fratton	a	15 45				16 23			16 46					17 23			17 46				18 23		
Portsmouth & Southsea	a	15 48				16 26			16 57					17 26			17 57				18 26		
Portsmouth Harbour ⛴	a	15 52				16 30			17 01					17 30			18 01				18 30		
Cosham	a			16 04							16 54	17 06							18 05				
Portchester	a																						
Fareham	a			16 12							17 02	17 15							18 13				
Swanwick	a			16 19								17 23							18 20				
Southampton Central ⛴	a			16 44							17 24	17 49							18 44				

London, Gatwick Airport, Brighton - Sussex Coast, Portsmouth and Southampton

		SN ◇1	SN ◇1	GW ◇	SN ◇1	SN ◇1	SN ◇1		SN 1	SN ◇1	SN ◇1	SN ◇1	SN ◇1	SN ◇1		SN 1	SN ◇1	SN ◇1	SN ◇1	SN ◇1	SN ◇1		SN 1
London Victoria 15 ⊖	d					17 02	17 17						18 02	18 17						19 02	19 17		
Clapham Junction 10	d					17 08	17 23						18 08	18 23						19 08	19 23		
London Bridge 4 ⊖	d								17 37							18 37							19 37
East Croydon	d					17 18	17 33		17 55				18 18	18 33		18 55				19 18	19 33		19 55
Redhill 5	d					17 32			18 13				18 32			19 13				19 32			20 13
Horley	d					17 38			18 25				18 38			19 25				19 38			20 25
Gatwick Airport 10 ✈	d					17 41	17 49		18 29				18 41	18 49		19 29				19 41	19 49		20 29
Three Bridges 4	a					17 46			18 33				18 46			19 33				19 46			20 33
	d					17 46			18 34				18 46			19 34				19 46			20 34
Crawley	d					17 50			18 37				18 50			19 37				19 50			20 37
Horsham 4	a					17 58			18 49				18 58			19 49				19 58			20 49
	d					17 59							18 59							19 59			
Christs Hospital	d					18 02							19 02							20 02			
Billingshurst	d					18 09							19 09							20 09			
Pulborough	d					18 15							19 15							20 15			
Amberley	d					18 21							19 21							20 21			
Arundel	d					18 27							19 27							20 27			
Haywards Heath 3	d						18 00							19 00							20 00		
Burgess Hill	d						18 06							19 06							20 06		
Preston Park	d																						
Brighton 10	d	17 12		17 46	17 50					18 12		18 48					19 12		19 48				
Hove 2	d	17 22		17 50	17 54		18 19			18 22		18 52		19 19			19 22		19 52		20 19		
Aldrington	d	17 24			17 56					18 24		18 54					19 24		19 54				
Portslade	d	17 26			17 58					18 26		18 56					19 26		19 56				
Fishersgate	d	17 28			18 00					18 28		18 58					19 28		19 58				
Southwick	d	17 30			18 02					18 30		19 00					19 30		20 00				
Shoreham-by-Sea	d	17 33		17 56	18 05		18 25			18 33		19 03		19 25			19 33		20 03		20 25		
Lancing	d	17 37			18 09					18 37		19 07					19 37		20 07				
East Worthing	d	17 40			18 12					18 40		19 10					19 40		20 10				
Worthing 4	a	17 43		18 03	18 15		18 31			18 43		19 13		19 31			19 43		20 13		20 31		
	d	17 43		18 08	18 15		18 35	18 37		18 43		19 13		19 35	19 37		19 43		20 13		20 35	20 37	
West Worthing	d	17 45			18 17			18 39		18 45		19 15			19 39		19 45		20 15			20 39	
Durrington-on-Sea	d	17 48			18 20			18 41		18 48		19 18			19 41		19 48		20 18			20 41	
Goring-by-Sea	d	17 50			18 22			18 44		18 50		19 20			19 44		19 50		20 20			20 44	
Angmering 3	d	17 54			18 26			18 48		18 54		19 24			19 48		19 54		20 24			20 48	
Littlehampton 4	a							18 57							19 57							20 57	
	d		17 54								18 54							19 54					
Ford 4	d	18 01	17 58		18 32	18 36				19 01	18 58	19 31	19 35				20 01	19 58	20 31	20 35			
Bognor Regis 4	d																						
Barnham	a	18 05	18 02	18 25	18 37	18 40	18 51			19 05	19 02	19 35	19 39	19 51			20 05	20 02	20 35	20 39	20 52		
	d	18 06	18 09	18 25	18 37	18 41	18 52			19 06	19 09	19 36	19 40	19 52			20 06	20 09	20 36	20 40	20 53		
Bognor Regis	a		18 15			18 47					19 15		19 46					20 15		20 46			
Chichester 4	a	18 13		18 33	18 45		18 59			19 13		19 43		19 59			20 13		20 43		21 00		
	d	18 14		18 34	18 45		19 00			19 14		19 44		20 00			20 14		20 44		21 01		
Fishbourne (Sussex)	d	18 17								19 17							20 17						
Bosham	d	18 20								19 20							20 20						
Nutbourne	d	18 23								19 23							20 23						
Southbourne	d	18 26					19 07			19 26				20 07			20 26				21 08		
Emsworth	d	18 29			18 53		19 10			19 29		19 52		20 10			20 29		20 52		21 11		
Warblington	d	18 32								19 32							20 32						
Havant	d	18 35		18 48	18 58		19 14			19 35		19 58		20 14			20 35		20 58		21 15		
Bedhampton	a	18 37								19 37							20 37						
Hilsea	a																						
Fratton	a	18 46					19 23			19 46				20 23			20 45				21 24		
Portsmouth & Southsea	a	18 57					19 26			19 57				20 26			20 48				21 27		
Portsmouth Harbour ⛴	a	19 01					19 30			20 01				20 30			20 52				21 31		
Cosham	a			18 54	19 05							20 05							21 07				
Portchester	a																						
Fareham	a			19 02	19 13							20 13							21 15				
Swanwick	a				19 22							20 20							21 22				
Southampton Central ⛴	a			19 24	19 48							20 46							21 45				

Table 188

Sundays until 4 September

London, Gatwick Airport, Brighton - Sussex Coast, Portsmouth and Southampton

		SN ◇1	SN ◇1	SN ◇1	SN ◇1	SN ◇1		SN 1	SN ◇1	SN ◇1	GW
London Victoria 15 ⊖	d				20 02	20 17					
Clapham Junction 10	d				20 08	20 23					
London Bridge 4 ⊖	d							20 37			
East Croydon	d				20 18	20 33		20 55			
Redhill 5	d				20 32			21 13			
Horley	d				20 38			21 25			
Gatwick Airport 10 ✈	d				20 41	20 49		21 29			
Three Bridges 4	a				20 46			21 33			
	d				20 46			21 34			
Crawley	d				20 50			21 37			
Horsham 4	a				20 58			21 49			
	d				20 59						
Christs Hospital	d				21 02						
Billingshurst	d				21 09						
Pulborough	d				21 15						
Amberley	d				21 21						
Arundel	d				21 27						
Haywards Heath 3	d					21 00					
Burgess Hill	d					21 06					
Preston Park	d										
Brighton 10	d	20 12		20 48					21 12		21 46
Hove 2	d	20 23		20 52		21 19			21 22		21 50
Aldrington	d	20 25		20 54					21 24		
Portslade	d	20 27		20 56					21 26		
Fishersgate	d	20 29		20 58					21 28		
Southwick	d	20 31		21 00					21 30		
Shoreham-by-Sea	d	20 34		21 03		21 25			21 33		21 56
Lancing	d	20 38		21 07					21 37		
East Worthing	d	20 41		21 10					21 40		
Worthing 4	a	20 43		21 13		21 31			21 43		22 02
	d	20 44		21 13		21 35	21 37		21 43		22 03
West Worthing	d	20 46		21 15			21 39		21 45		
Durrington-on-Sea	d	20 49		21 18			21 41		21 48		
Goring-by-Sea	d	20 51		21 20			21 44		21 50		
Angmering 3	d	20 55		21 24			21 48		21 54		
Littlehampton 4	a						21 57				
	d		20 54							21 54	
Ford 4	d	21 02	20 58	21 31	21 35				22 01	21 58	
Bognor Regis 4	d										
Barnham	a	21 07	21 02	21 35	21 39	21 51			22 05	22 02	22 17
	d	21 07	21 09	21 36	21 40	21 52			22 06	22 09	22 18
Bognor Regis	a		21 15		21 46					22 15	
Chichester 4	a	21 15		21 43		21 59			22 13		22 25
	d	21 15		21 44		22 00			22 14		22 26
Fishbourne (Sussex)	d	21 18							22 17		
Bosham	d	21 21							22 20		
Nutbourne	d	21 25							22 23		
Southbourne	d	21 27				22 07			22 26		
Emsworth	d	21 30		21 52		22 10			22 29		
Warblington	d	21 33							22 32		
Havant	d	21 36		21 58		22 14			22 35		22 47
Bedhampton	a	21 39							22 37		
Hilsea	a										
Fratton	a	21 47				22 23			22 45		22 57
Portsmouth & Southsea	a	21 50				22 26			22 48		23 00
Portsmouth Harbour ⛴	a	21 53				22 30			22 52		23 04
Cosham	a			22 05							
Portchester	a										
Fareham	a			22 13							
Swanwick	a			22 20							
Southampton Central ⛴	a			22 44							

		SN ◇1	SN ◇	SN ◇1	SN ◇1		SN 1	SN ◇	SN ◇	SN ◇1	SN ◇1	SN ◇1
London Victoria 15 ⊖	d			21 02	21 17						22 02	
Clapham Junction 10	d			21 08	21 23						22 08	
London Bridge 4 ⊖	d						21 37					
East Croydon	d			21 18	21 33		21 55				22 18	
Redhill 5	d			21 32			22 13				22 32	
Horley	d			21 38			22 25				22 38	
Gatwick Airport 10 ✈	d			21 41	21 49		22 29				22 41	
Three Bridges 4	a			21 46			22 33				22 46	
	d			21 46			22 34				22 46	
Crawley	d			21 50			22 37				22 50	
Horsham 4	a			21 58			22 49				22 58	
	d			21 59							22 59	
Christs Hospital	d			22 02							23 02	
Billingshurst	d			22 09							23 09	
Pulborough	d			22 15							23 15	
Amberley	d			22 21							23 21	
Arundel	d			22 27							23 27	
Haywards Heath 3	d				22 00							
Burgess Hill	d				22 06							
Preston Park	d											
Brighton 10	d	21 50						22 15				22 40
Hove 2	d	21 54			22 19			22a18				22 44
Aldrington	d	21 56										22 46
Portslade	d	21 58										22 48
Fishersgate	d	22 00										22 50
Southwick	d	22 02										22 52
Shoreham-by-Sea	d	22 05			22 25							22 55
Lancing	d	22 09										22 59
East Worthing	d	22 12										23 02
Worthing 4	a	22 15			22 31							23 05
	d	22 15			22 35	22 37						23 05
West Worthing	d	22 17				22 39						23 07
Durrington-on-Sea	d	22 20				22 41						23 09
Goring-by-Sea	d	22 22				22 44						23 12
Angmering 3	d	22 26				22 48						23 16
Littlehampton 4	a	22 36				22 57						23 24
	d									23 06		23 29
Ford 4	d			22 32						23 10	23 32	23 36
Bognor Regis 4	d		22 12									
Barnham	a		22 18	22 36	22 49					23 14	23 36	23 40
	d			22 37	22 56				22 52	23 15	23 42	23 45
Bognor Regis	a			22 43					22 58	23 21	23 48	
Chichester 4	a				23 03							23 52
	d				23 04							
Fishbourne (Sussex)	d											
Bosham	d				23 08							
Nutbourne	d				23 12							
Southbourne	d				23 14							
Emsworth	d				23 17							
Warblington	d											
Havant	d				23 22							
Bedhampton	a											
Hilsea	a											
Fratton	a				23 32							
Portsmouth & Southsea	a				23 35							
Portsmouth Harbour ⛴	a				23 39							
Cosham	a											
Portchester	a											
Fareham	a											
Swanwick	a											
Southampton Central ⛴	a											

Table 188

Sundays until 4 September

London, Gatwick Airport, Brighton - Sussex Coast, Portsmouth and Southampton

		SN ◇	SN ◇1	SN 1	SN 1	SN ◇1
London Victoria 15 ⊖	d		22 17		23 04	23 17
Clapham Junction 10	d		22 23		23 10	23 23
London Bridge 4 ⊖	d			22 37		
East Croydon	d		22 33	22 55	23 22	23 38
Redhill 5	d			23 13	23 42	
Horley	d			23 25	23 50	
Gatwick Airport 10 ✈	d		22 49	23 29	23 55	00 01
Three Bridges 4	a			23 33	00 01	00 05
	d			23 34	00 01	00 06
Crawley	d			23 37	00 05	
Horsham 4	a			23 49	00 17	
	d					
Christs Hospital	d					
Billingshurst	d					
Pulborough	d					
Amberley	d					
Arundel	d					
Haywards Heath 3	d		23 00			00 15
Burgess Hill	d		23 06			00 20
Preston Park	d					
Brighton 10	d	23 15				
Hove 2	d	23a18	23 25			00 31
Aldrington	d					
Portslade	d		23 28			00s34
Fishersgate	d					
Southwick	d		23 31			00s37
Shoreham-by-Sea	d		23 34			00s40
Lancing	d		23 38			00s44
East Worthing	d					
Worthing 4	a		23 42			00 48
	d					
West Worthing	d					
Durrington-on-Sea	d					
Goring-by-Sea	d					
Angmering 3	d					
Littlehampton 4	a					
	d					
Ford 4	d					
Bognor Regis 4	d					
Barnham	a					
	d					
Bognor Regis	a					
Chichester 4	a					
	d					
Fishbourne (Sussex)	d					
Bosham	d					
Nutbourne	d					
Southbourne	d					
Emsworth	d					
Warblington	d					
Havant	d					
Bedhampton	a					
Hilsea	a					
Fratton	a					
Portsmouth & Southsea	a					
Portsmouth Harbour ⛴	a					
Cosham	a					
Portchester	a					
Fareham	a					
Swanwick	a					
Southampton Central ⛴	a					

London, Gatwick Airport, Brighton - Sussex Coast, Portsmouth and Southampton

Station		SN ◇1	SN 1	SN ◇1	SN ◇1	SN ◇	SN ◇	SN ◇1	SN 1	SN 1	SN ◇1	SN 1	SN ◇	SN ◇1	SN ◇1	SN ◇1	SN ◇1	SN ◇1	SN ◇1	SN ◇1	SN ◇1	SN 1	SN ◇1
London Victoria 15	d	22p17	22p32		22p47			23p17	23p10	23p47	00 05										07 02		
Clapham Junction 10	d	22p23	22p38		22p53			23p23	23p16	23p53	00 11										07 08		
London Bridge 4	d																					07 37	
East Croydon	d	22p33	22p48		23p03			23p33	23p28	00 06	00 25										07 23	07 55	
Redhill 5	d		23p01						23p46	00 25											07 37	08 13	
Horley	d								23p56	00 31											07 43	08 22	
Gatwick Airport 10	d	22p49	23p09		23p19			23p51	23p59	00 34	00 44	06 29									07 47	08 25	
Three Bridges 4	a	22p54	23p14					23p55	00 04	00 39	00 48	06 33									07 51	08 30	
	d	22p54	23p15					23p56	00 04	00 39	00 48	06 40									07 52	08 33	
Crawley	d		23p18						00 07	00 43		06 43									07 55	08 36	
Horsham 4	a		23p26						00 19	00 55		06 56									08 07	08 49	
	d		23p27																		08 08		
Christs Hospital	d		23p30																				
Billingshurst	d		23p36																		08 16		
Pulborough	d		23p43																		08 23		
Amberley	d		23p49																				
Arundel	d		23p54																		08 33		
Haywards Heath 3	d	23p03			23b37			00 05			01 02												
Burgess Hill	d	23p08						00 10															
Preston Park	d																						
Brighton 10	d					00 03	00 10				01s16						07 14	07 22		07 50			08 14
Hove 2	d	23p22			23p52	00 07	00a13	00 22			01s24						07 18	07 26		07 54			08 18
Aldrington	d					00 09												07 28		07 56			
Portslade	d	23p25			23p55	00 11		00s25			01s27							07 30		07 58			
Fishersgate	d					00 13												07 32		08 00			
Southwick	d	23p28			23p58	00 15		00s28			01s30							07 34		08 02			
Shoreham-by-Sea	d	23p31			00 01	00 19		00s31			01s33						07 24	07 37		08 05			08 24
Lancing	d	23p35			00 05	00 23		00s35			01s37							07 41		08 09			
East Worthing	d					00 26												07 44		08 12			
Worthing 4	a	23p39			00 09	00 28		00s39			01 41						07 30	07 47		08 15			08 30
	d	23p39				00 29											07 30	07 47		08 15			08 30
West Worthing	d	23p41				00a31		00s41										07 49		08 17			
Durrington-on-Sea	d	23p44						00s44										07 51		08 20			
Goring-by-Sea	d	23p46						00s46										07 54		08 22			
Angmering 3	d	23p50						00s50									07 37	07 58		08 26			08 37
Littlehampton 4	a																	08 06					
	d													06 42	07 19	07 29		08 11	07 57				
Ford 4	d	23p56	23p59					00s56						06 46	07 23		07 43	08 15	08 01	08 32	08 38		08 43
Bognor Regis 4	d			←																			
Barnham	a	00 01	00 04	00 01				01s01						06 50	07 27	07 37	07 48	08 19	08 08	08 37	08 42		08 48
	d	00 09	00 05	00 09									06 45	06 51	07 28	07 37	07 48	08 20	08 26	08 37	08 43		08 48
Bognor Regis	a	→		00 15									06 51		07 34				08 32		08 49		
Chichester 4	a		00 12					01 09						06 58		07 45	07 56	08 27		08 45			08 56
	d													06 59		07 45	07 56	08 28		08 45			08 56
Fishbourne (Sussex)	d																	08 31					
Bosham	d																	08 34					
Nutbourne	d																	08 37					
Southbourne	d																08 03	08 40					09 03
Emsworth	d															07 53	08 06	08 43		08 53			09 06
Warblington	d																	08 46					
Havant	d													07 10		07 58	08 11	08 49		08 58			09 11
Bedhampton	a																	08 51					
Hilsea	a																						
Fratton	a													07 18			08 19	08 59					09 19
Portsmouth & Southsea	a													07 22			08 23	09 03					09 23
Portsmouth Harbour	a													07 26			08 27	09 07					09 27
Cosham	a															08 05				09 05			
Portchester	a																						
Fareham	a															08 13				09 13			
Swanwick	a															08 20				09 20			
Southampton Central	a															08 44				09 44			

b Previous night, arr. 2330

London, Gatwick Airport, Brighton - Sussex Coast, Portsmouth and Southampton

Station		SN ◇1	SN ◇1	SN ◇1	SN ◇1	SN ◇1		SN 1	SN ◇1	SN ◇1	SN ◇1	SN ◇1	SN ◇1		SN 1	SN ◇1	SN ◇1	SN ◇1	SN ◇1	GW ◇	SN ◇1		SN 1
London Victoria 15	d				08 04	08 17						09 04	09 17						10 04		10 17		
Clapham Junction 10	d				08 10	08 23						09 10	09 23						10 10		10 23		
London Bridge 4	d							08 37							09 37								10 37
East Croydon	d				08 24	08 37		08 55				09 24	09 37		09 55				10 24		10 37		10 55
Redhill 5	d				08 39			09 16				09 39			10 16				10 39				11 16
Horley	d				08 45			09 22				09 45			10 22				10 45				11 22
Gatwick Airport 10	d				08 48	08 56		09 25				09 48	09 56		10 25				10 48		10 56		11 25
Three Bridges 4	a				08 53			09 30				09 53			10 30				10 53				11 30
	d				08 53			09 33				09 53			10 33				10 53				11 33
Crawley	d				08 56			09 37				09 56			10 37				10 56				11 37
Horsham 4	a				09 04			09 49				10 04			10 49				11 04				11 49
	d				09 05							10 05							11 05				
Christs Hospital	d				09 08							10 08							11 08				
Billingshurst	d				09 15							10 15							11 15				
Pulborough	d				09 21							10 21							11 21				
Amberley	d				09 27							10 27							11 27				
Arundel	d				09 33							10 33							11 33				
Haywards Heath 3	d					09 07							10 07								11 07		
Burgess Hill	d					09 12							10 12								11 12		
Preston Park	d																						
Brighton 10	d	08 22		08 50					09 17		09 50					10 17		10 50		11 10			
Hove 2	d	08 26		08 54		09 24			09 27		09 54		10 24			10 27		10 54		11 14	11 24		
Aldrington	d	08 28		08 56					09 29		09 56					10 29		10 56					
Portslade	d	08 30		08 58					09 32		09 58					10 32		10 58					
Fishersgate	d	08 32		09 00					09 34		10 00					10 34		11 00					
Southwick	d	08 34		09 02					09 36		10 02					10 36		11 02					
Shoreham-by-Sea	d	08 37		09 05		09 30			09 39		10 05		10 30			10 39		11 05		11 20	11 30		
Lancing	d	08 41		09 09					09 43		10 09					10 43		11 09					
East Worthing	d	08 44		09 12					09 46		10 12					10 46		11 12					
Worthing 4	a	08 47		09 15		09 36			09 48		10 15		10 36			10 48		11 15		11 26	11 36		
	d	08 47		09 15		09 40	09 42		09 49		10 15		10 40	10 42		10 49		11 15		11 29	11 40	11 42	
West Worthing	d	08 49		09 17			09 44		09 51		10 17			10 44		10 51		11 17				11 44	
Durrington-on-Sea	d	08 51		09 20			09 46		09 53		10 20			10 46		10 53		11 20				11 46	
Goring-by-Sea	d	08 54		09 22			09 49		09 56		10 22			10 49		10 56		11 22				11 49	
Angmering 3	d	08 58		09 26			09 53		10 00		10 26			10 53		11 00		11 26				11 53	
Littlehampton 4	a	09 06					10 02							11 02								12 02	
	d	09 11	08 57							09 57							10 57						
Ford 4	d	09 15	09 01	09 32	09 39				10 06	10 01	10 32	10 38				11 06	11 01	11 32	11 38				
Bognor Regis 4	d																						
Barnham	a	09 19	09 08	09 37	09 43	09 54			10 11	10 08	10 37	10 42	10 54			11 11	11 08	11 37	11 42	11 45	11 54		
	d	09 20	09 26	09 37	09 44	09 55			10 12	10 15	10 37	10 43	10 55			11 12	11 15	11 37	11 43	11 46	11 55		
Bognor Regis	a		09 32		09 50					10 21		10 49					11 21		11 49				
Chichester 4	a	09 27		09 45		10 02			10 19		10 45		11 02			11 19		11 45		11 53	12 02		
	d	09 28		09 45		10 03			10 20		10 45		11 03			11 20		11 45		11 54	12 03		
Fishbourne (Sussex)	d	09 31							10 23							11 23							
Bosham	d	09 34							10 26							11 26							
Nutbourne	d	09 37							10 29							11 29							
Southbourne	d	09 40				10 10			10 32				11 10			11 32					12 10		
Emsworth	d	09 43		09 53		10 13			10 35		10 53		11 13			11 35		11 53			12 13		
Warblington	d	09 46							10 38							11 38							
Havant	d	09 49		09 58		10 17			10 41		10 58		11 17			11 44		11 58		12 10	12 17		
Bedhampton	a	09 51							10 43							11 46							
Hilsea	a																						
Fratton	a	09 59				10 26			10 51				11 26			11 54					12 26		
Portsmouth & Southsea	a	10 03				10 29			10 54				11 29			11 57					12 29		
Portsmouth Harbour	a	10 07				10 35			10 58				11 35			12 01					12 35		
Cosham	a			10 06							11 06							12 05		12 16			
Portchester	a																						
Fareham	a			10 14							11 14							12 13		12 31			
Swanwick	a			10 21							11 21							12 20					
Southampton Central	a			10 44							11 44							12 44		12 53			

Table 188

London, Gatwick Airport, Brighton - Sussex Coast, Portsmouth and Southampton

		SN ◇1	SN ◇1	SN ◇1	SN ◇1 ⊼	SN ◇1		SN 1	SN ◇1	SN ◇1	SN ◇1	SN ◇1 ⊼	SN ◇1		SN 1	SN ◇1	SN ◇1	SN ◇1	SN ◇1 ⊼	SN ◇1		SN 1
London Victoria 15 ⊖	d				11 04	11 17						12 04	12 17						13 04	13 17		
Clapham Junction 10	d				11 10	11 23						12 10	12 23						13 10	13 23		
London Bridge 4 ⊖	d							11 37							12 37							13 37
East Croydon	d				11 24	11 37		11 55				12 24	12 37		12 55				13 24	13 37		13 55
Redhill 5	d				11 39			12 16				12 39			13 16				13 39			14 16
Horley	d				11 45			12 22				12 45			13 22				13 45			14 22
Gatwick Airport 10 ✈	d				11 48	11 56		12 25				12 48	12 56		13 25				13 48	13 56		14 25
Three Bridges 4	a				11 53			12 30				12 53			13 30				13 53			14 30
	d				11 53			12 33				12 53			13 33				13 53			14 33
Crawley	d				11 56			12 37				12 56			13 37				13 56			14 37
Horsham 4	a				12 04			12 49				13 04			13 49				14 04			14 49
	d				12 05							13 05							14 05			
Christs Hospital	d				12 08							13 08							14 08			
Billingshurst	d				12 15							13 15							14 15			
Pulborough	d				12 21							13 21							14 21			
Amberley	d				12 27							13 27							14 27			
Arundel	d				12 33							13 33							14 33			
Haywards Heath 3	d					12 07							13 07							14 07		
Burgess Hill	d					12 12							13 12							14 12		
Preston Park	d																					
Brighton 10	d	11 17		11 50					12 17		12 50					13 17		13 50				
Hove 2	d	11 27		11 54		12 24			12 27		12 54		13 24			13 27		13 54		14 24		
Aldrington	d	11 29		11 56					12 29		12 56					13 29		13 56				
Portslade	d	11 32		11 58					12 32		12 58					13 32		13 58				
Fishersgate	d	11 34		12 00					12 34		13 00					13 34		14 00				
Southwick	d	11 36		12 02					12 36		13 02					13 36		14 02				
Shoreham-by-Sea	d	11 39		12 05		12 30			12 39		13 05		13 30			13 39		14 05		14 30		
Lancing	d	11 43		12 09					12 43		13 09					13 43		14 09				
East Worthing	d	11 46		12 12					12 46		13 12					13 46		14 12				
Worthing 4	a	11 48		12 15		12 36			12 48		13 15		13 36			13 48		14 15		14 36		
	d	11 49		12 15		12 40	12 42		12 49		13 15		13 40	13 42		13 49		14 15		14 40	14 42	
West Worthing	d	11 51		12 17			12 44		12 51		13 17			13 44		13 51		14 17			14 44	
Durrington-on-Sea	d	11 53		12 20			12 46		12 53		13 20			13 46		13 53		14 20			14 46	
Goring-by-Sea	d	11 56		12 22			12 49		12 56		13 22			13 49		13 56		14 22			14 49	
Angmering 3	d	12 00		12 26			12 53		13 00		13 26			13 53		14 00		14 26			14 53	
Littlehampton 4	a						13 02							14 02							15 02	
	d		11 57							12 57							13 57					
Ford 4	d	12 06	12 01	12 32	12 38				13 06	13 01	13 32	13 38				14 06	14 01	14 32	14 38			
Bognor Regis 4	d																					
Barnham	a	12 11	12 08	12 37	12 42	12 54			13 11	13 08	13 37	13 42	13 54			14 11	14 08	14 37	14 42	14 54		
	d	12 12	12 15	12 37	12 43	12 55			13 12	13 15	13 37	13 43	13 55			14 12	14 15	14 37	14 43	14 55		
Bognor Regis	a		12 21		12 49					13 21		13 49					14 21		14 49			
Chichester 4	a	12 19		12 45		13 02			13 19		13 45		14 02			14 19		14 45		15 02		
	d	12 20		12 45		13 03			13 20		13 45		14 03			14 20		14 45		15 03		
Fishbourne (Sussex)	d	12 23							13 23							14 23						
Bosham	d	12 26							13 26							14 26						
Nutbourne	d	12 29							13 29							14 29						
Southbourne	d	12 32				13 10			13 32				14 10			14 32				15 10		
Emsworth	d	12 35		12 53		13 13			13 35		13 53		14 13			14 35		14 53		15 13		
Warblington	d	12 38							13 38							14 38						
Havant	d	12 44		12 58		13 17			13 44		13 58		14 17			14 44		14 58		15 17		
Bedhampton	a	12 46							13 46							14 46						
Hilsea	a																					
Fratton	a	12 54				13 26			13 54				14 26			14 54				15 26		
Portsmouth & Southsea	a	12 57				13 29			13 57				14 29			14 57				15 29		
Portsmouth Harbour ⛴	a	13 01				13 35			14 01				14 35			15 01				15 35		
Cosham	a			13 05							14 05							15 05				
Portchester	a																					
Fareham	a			13 13							14 13							15 13				
Swanwick	a			13 20							14 20							15 20				
Southampton Central ⛴	a			13 44							14 44							15 44				

Table 188

London, Gatwick Airport, Brighton - Sussex Coast, Portsmouth and Southampton

		SN ◇1	SN ◇1	SN ◇1	SN ◇1 ⊼	SN ◇1		SN 1	SN ◇1	SN ◇1	GW ◇	SN ◇1	SN ◇1 ⊼	SN ◇1		SN 1	SN ◇1	SN ◇1	SN ◇1	SN ◇1 ⊼	SN ◇1		SN 1
London Victoria 15 ⊖	d				14 04	14 17							15 04	15 17						16 04	16 17		
Clapham Junction 10	d				14 10	14 23							15 10	15 23						16 10	16 23		
London Bridge 4 ⊖	d							14 37								15 37							16 37
East Croydon	d				14 24	14 37		14 55					15 24	15 37		15 55				16 24	16 37		16 55
Redhill 5	d				14 39			15 16					15 39			16 16				16 39			17 16
Horley	d				14 45			15 22					15 45			16 22				16 45			17 22
Gatwick Airport 10 ✈	d				14 48	14 56		15 25					15 48	15 56		16 25				16 48	16 56		17 25
Three Bridges 4	a				14 53			15 30					15 53			16 30				16 53			17 30
	d				14 53			15 33					15 53			16 33				16 53			17 33
Crawley	d				14 56			15 37					15 56			16 37				16 56			17 37
Horsham 4	a				15 04			15 49					16 04			16 49				17 04			17 49
	d				15 05								16 05							17 05			
Christs Hospital	d				15 08								16 08							17 08			
Billingshurst	d				15 15								16 15							17 15			
Pulborough	d				15 21								16 21							17 21			
Amberley	d				15 27								16 27							17 27			
Arundel	d				15 33								16 33							17 33			
Haywards Heath 3	d					15 07								16 07							17 07		
Burgess Hill	d					15 12								16 12							17 12		
Preston Park	d																						
Brighton 10	d	14 17		14 50					15 17		15 46	15 50					16 17		16 50				
Hove 2	d	14 27		14 54		15 24			15 27		15 50	15 54		16 24			16 27		16 54		17 24		
Aldrington	d	14 29		14 56					15 29			15 56					16 29		16 56				
Portslade	d	14 32		14 58					15 32			15 58					16 32		16 58				
Fishersgate	d	14 34		15 00					15 34			16 00					16 34		17 00				
Southwick	d	14 36		15 02					15 36			16 02					16 36		17 02				
Shoreham-by-Sea	d	14 39		15 05		15 30			15 39		15 56	16 05		16 30			16 39		17 05		17 30		
Lancing	d	14 43		15 09					15 43			16 09					16 43		17 09				
East Worthing	d	14 46		15 12					15 46			16 12					16 46		17 12				
Worthing 4	a	14 48		15 15		15 36			15 48		16 03	16 15		16 36			16 48		17 15		17 36		
	d	14 49		15 15		15 40	15 42		15 49		16 08	16 15		16 40	16 42		16 49		17 15		17 40	17 42	
West Worthing	d	14 51		15 17			15 44		15 51			16 17			16 44		16 51		17 17			17 44	
Durrington-on-Sea	d	14 53		15 20			15 46		15 53			16 20			16 46		16 53		17 20			17 46	
Goring-by-Sea	d	14 56		15 22			15 49		15 56			16 22			16 49		16 56		17 22			17 49	
Angmering 3	d	15 00		15 26			15 53		16 00			16 26			16 53		17 00		17 26			17 53	
Littlehampton 4	a						16 02								17 02							18 02	
	d		14 57							15 57								16 57					
Ford 4	d	15 06	15 01	15 32	15 38				16 06	16 01		16 32	16 38				17 06	17 01	17 32	17 38			
Bognor Regis 4	d																						
Barnham	a	15 11	15 08	15 37	15 42	15 54			16 11	16 08	16 25	16 37	16 42	16 54			17 11	17 08	17 37	17 42	17 54		
	d	15 12	15 15	15 37	15 43	15 55			16 12	16 15	16 25	16 37	16 43	16 55			17 12	17 15	17 37	17 43	17 55		
Bognor Regis	a		15 21		15 49					16 21			16 49					17 21		17 49			
Chichester 4	a	15 19		15 45		16 02			16 19		16 33	16 45		17 02			17 19		17 45		18 02		
	d	15 20		15 45		16 03			16 20		16 34	16 45		17 03			17 20		17 45		18 03		
Fishbourne (Sussex)	d	15 23							16 23								17 23						
Bosham	d	15 26							16 26								17 26						
Nutbourne	d	15 29							16 29								17 29						
Southbourne	d	15 32				16 10			16 32					17 10			17 32				18 10		
Emsworth	d	15 35		15 53		16 13			16 35			16 53		17 13			17 35		17 53		18 13		
Warblington	d	15 38							16 38								17 38						
Havant	d	15 44		15 58		16 17			16 44		16 48	16 58		17 17			17 44		17 58		18 17		
Bedhampton	a	15 46							16 46								17 46						
Hilsea	a																						
Fratton	a	15 54				16 26			16 54					17 26			17 54				18 26		
Portsmouth & Southsea	a	15 57				16 29			16 57					17 29			17 57				18 29		
Portsmouth Harbour ⛴	a	16 01				16 35			17 01					17 35			18 01				18 35		
Cosham	a			16 05							16 54	17 05							18 05				
Portchester	a																						
Fareham	a			16 13							17 02	17 14							18 13				
Swanwick	a			16 20								17 22							18 20				
Southampton Central ⛴	a			16 44							17 24	17 48							18 44				

London, Gatwick Airport, Brighton - Sussex Coast, Portsmouth and Southampton

from 11 September

		SN	SN	GW	SN	SN	SN		SN	SN	SN	SN	SN	SN		SN	SN	SN	SN	SN	SN		SN
		◇1	◇1	◇	◇1	◇1 🛒	◇1		1	◇1	◇1	◇1	◇1 🛒	◇1		1	◇1	◇1	◇1	◇1 🛒	◇1		1
London Victoria 15 ⊖	d					17 04	17 17						18 04	18 17						19 04	19 17		
Clapham Junction 10	d					17 10	17 23						18 10	18 23						19 10	19 23		
London Bridge 4 ⊖	d								17 37							18 37							19 37
East Croydon	d					17 24	17 37		17 55				18 24	18 37		18 55				19 24	19 37		19 55
Redhill 5	d					17 39			18 16				18 39			19 16				19 39			20 16
Horley	d					17 45			18 22				18 45			19 22				19 45			20 22
Gatwick Airport 10 ✈	d					17 48	17 56		18 25				18 48	18 56		19 25				19 48	19 56		20 25
Three Bridges 4	a					17 53			18 30				18 53			19 30				19 53			20 30
	d					17 53			18 33				18 53			19 33				19 53			20 33
Crawley	d					17 56			18 37				18 56			19 37				19 56			20 37
Horsham 4	a					18 04			18 49				19 04			19 49				20 04			20 49
	d					18 05							19 05							20 05			
Christs Hospital	d					18 08							19 08							20 08			
Billingshurst	d					18 15							19 15							20 15			
Pulborough	d					18 21							19 21							20 21			
Amberley	d					18 27							19 27							20 27			
Arundel	d					18 33							19 33							20 33			
Haywards Heath 3	d						18 07							19 07							20 07		
Burgess Hill	d						18 12							19 12							20 12		
Preston Park	d																						
Brighton 10	d	17 17		17 46	17 50					18 17		18 50					19 17		19 50				
Hove 2	d	17 27		17 50	17 54		18 24			18 27		18 54		19 24			19 27		19 54		20 24		
Aldrington	d	17 29			17 56					18 29		18 56					19 29		19 56				
Portslade	d	17 32			17 58					18 32		18 58					19 32		19 58				
Fishersgate	d	17 34			18 00					18 34		19 00					19 34		20 00				
Southwick	d	17 36			18 02					18 36		19 02					19 36		20 02				
Shoreham-by-Sea	d	17 39		17 56	18 05		18 30			18 39		19 05		19 30			19 39		20 05		20 30		
Lancing	d	17 43			18 09					18 43		19 09					19 43		20 09				
East Worthing	d	17 46			18 12					18 46		19 12					19 46		20 12				
Worthing 4	a	17 48		18 03	18 15		18 36			18 48		19 15		19 36			19 48		20 15		20 36		
	d	17 49		18 08	18 15		18 40	18 42		18 49		19 15		19 40	19 42		19 49		20 15		20 40	20 42	
West Worthing	d	17 51			18 17			18 44		18 51		19 17			19 44		19 51		20 17			20 44	
Durrington-on-Sea	d	17 53			18 20			18 46		18 53		19 20			19 46		19 53		20 20			20 46	
Goring-by-Sea	d	17 56			18 22			18 49		18 56		19 22			19 49		19 56		20 22			20 49	
Angmering 3	d	18 00			18 26			18 53		19 00		19 26			19 53		20 00		20 26			20 53	
Littlehampton 4	a							19 02							20 02							21 02	
	d		17 57								18 57							19 57					
Ford 4	d	18 06	18 01		18 32	18 38				19 06	19 01	19 32	19 38				20 06	20 01	20 32	20 38			
Bognor Regis 4	d																						
Barnham	a	18 11	18 08	18 25	18 37	18 42	18 54			19 11	19 08	19 37	19 42	19 54			20 11	20 08	20 37	20 42	20 54		
	d	18 12	18 15	18 25	18 37	18 43	18 55			19 12	19 15	19 37	19 43	19 55			20 12	20 15	20 37	20 43	20 55		
Bognor Regis	a		18 21			18 49					19 21		19 49					20 21		20 49			
Chichester 4	a	18 19		18 33	18 45		19 02			19 19		19 45		20 02			20 19		20 45		21 02		
	d	18 20		18 34	18 45		19 03			19 20		19 45		20 03			20 20		20 45		21 03		
Fishbourne (Sussex)	d	18 23								19 23							20 23						
Bosham	d	18 26								19 26							20 26						
Nutbourne	d	18 29								19 29							20 29						
Southbourne	d	18 32					19 10			19 32				20 10			20 32				21 10		
Emsworth	d	18 35			18 53		19 13			19 35		19 53		20 13			20 35		20 53		21 13		
Warblington	d	18 38								19 38							20 38						
Havant	d	18 44		18 48	18 58		19 17			19 44		19 58		20 17			20 44		20 58		21 17		
Bedhampton	a	18 46								19 46							20 46						
Hilsea	a																						
Fratton	a	18 54					19 26			19 54				20 26			20 54				21 26		
Portsmouth & Southsea	a	18 57					19 29			19 57				20 29			20 57				21 29		
Portsmouth Harbour ⛴	a	19 01					19 35			20 01				20 35			21 01				21 35		
Cosham	a			18 54	19 05							20 05							21 07				
Portchester	a																						
Fareham	a			19 02	19 13							20 13							21 15				
Swanwick	a				19 22							20 20							21 22				
Southampton Central ⛴	a			19 24	19 48							20 46							21 45				

London, Gatwick Airport, Brighton - Sussex Coast, Portsmouth and Southampton

from 11 September

		SN	SN	SN	SN	SN		SN	SN	SN	GW	SN	SN	SN	SN	SN		SN	SN	SN	SN	SN
		◇1	◇1	◇1	◇1	◇1		1	◇1	◇1		◇1	◇	◇1	◇	◇1		1	◇	◇1	◇1	◇1
London Victoria 15 ⊖	d				20 04	20 17								21 04		21 17					22 04	
Clapham Junction 10	d				20 10	20 23								21 10		21 23					22 10	
London Bridge 4 ⊖	d							20 37										21 37				
East Croydon	d				20 24	20 37		20 55						21 24		21 37		21 55			22 24	
Redhill 5	d				20 39			21 16						21 39				22 16			22 39	
Horley	d				20 45			21 22						21 45				22 22			22 45	
Gatwick Airport 10 ✈	d				20 48	20 56		21 25						21 48		21 56		22 25			22 48	
Three Bridges 4	a				20 53			21 30						21 53				22 30			22 53	
	d				20 53			21 33						21 53				22 33			22 53	
Crawley	d				20 56			21 37						21 56				22 37			22 56	
Horsham 4	a				21 04			21 49						22 04				22 49			23 04	
	d				21 05									22 05							23 05	
Christs Hospital	d				21 08									22 08							23 08	
Billingshurst	d				21 15									22 15							23 15	
Pulborough	d				21 21									22 21							23 21	
Amberley	d				21 27									22 27							23 27	
Arundel	d				21 33									22 33							23 33	
Haywards Heath 3	d					21 07										22 07						
Burgess Hill	d					21 12										22 12						
Preston Park	d																					
Brighton 10	d	20 17		20 50					21 17		21 46	21 50			22 15							22 40
Hove 2	d	20 27		20 54		21 24			21 27		21 50	21 54			22a18	22 25						22 44
Aldrington	d	20 29		20 56					21 29			21 56										22 46
Portslade	d	20 32		20 58					21 32			21 58										22 48
Fishersgate	d	20 34		21 00					21 34			22 00										22 50
Southwick	d	20 36		21 02					21 36			22 02										22 52
Shoreham-by-Sea	d	20 39		21 05		21 30			21 39		21 56	22 05				22 31						22 55
Lancing	d	20 43		21 09					21 43			22 09										22 59
East Worthing	d	20 46		21 12					21 46			22 12										23 02
Worthing 4	a	20 48		21 15		21 36			21 48		22 02	22 15				22 37						23 05
	d	20 49		21 15		21 40	21 42		21 49		22 03	22 15				22 41	22 43					23 05
West Worthing	d	20 51		21 17			21 44		21 51			22 17					22 45					23 07
Durrington-on-Sea	d	20 53		21 20			21 46		21 53			22 20					22 47					23 09
Goring-by-Sea	d	20 56		21 22			21 49		21 56			22 22					22 50					23 12
Angmering 3	d	21 00		21 26			21 53		22 00			22 26					22 54					23 16
Littlehampton 4	a						22 02					22 35					23 02					23 24
	d		20 57							21 57										23 06		23 29
Ford 4	d	21 06	21 01	21 32	21 38				22 06	22 01				22 38						23 10	23 38	23 33
Bognor Regis 4	d												22 12									
Barnham	a	21 11	21 08	21 37	21 42	21 54			22 11	22 08	22 17		22 18	22 42		22 55				23 14	23 42	23 37
	d	21 12	21 15	21 37	21 43	21 55			22 12	22 15	22 18			22 43		22 56			22 57	23 15	23 43	23 45
Bognor Regis	a		21 21		21 49					22 21				22 49					23 03	23 21	23 49	
Chichester 4	a	21 19		21 45		22 02			22 19		22 25					23 03						23 52
	d	21 20		21 45		22 03			22 20		22 26					23 04						
Fishbourne (Sussex)	d	21 23							22 23													
Bosham	d	21 26							22 26							23 08						
Nutbourne	d	21 29							22 29							23 12						
Southbourne	d	21 32				22 10			22 32							23 14						
Emsworth	d	21 35		21 53		22 13			22 35							23 17						
Warblington	d	21 38							22 38													
Havant	d	21 44		21 58		22 17			22 44		22 47					23 22						
Bedhampton	a	21 46							22 46													
Hilsea	a																					
Fratton	a	21 54				22 26			22 54		22 57					23 32						
Portsmouth & Southsea	a	21 57				22 29			22 57		23 00					23 35						
Portsmouth Harbour ⛴	a	22 01				22 35			23 01		23 04					23 39						
Cosham	a			22 05																		
Portchester	a																					
Fareham	a			22 13																		
Swanwick	a			22 20																		
Southampton Central ⛴	a			22 44																		

Table 188

Sundays
from 11 September

London, Gatwick Airport, Brighton - Sussex Coast, Portsmouth and Southampton

Station		SN ◇	SN ◇1	SN 1	SN 1	SN ◇1
London Victoria 15	d		22 17		23 04	23 17
Clapham Junction 10	d		22 23		23 10	23 23
London Bridge 4	d			22 37		
East Croydon	d		22 37	22 55	23 22	23 38
Redhill 5	d			23 16	23 42	
Horley	d			23 22	23 50	
Gatwick Airport 10	d		22 56	23 25	23 55	00 01
Three Bridges 4	a			23 30	00 01	00 05
	d			23 33	00 01	00 06
Crawley	d			23 37	00 05	
Horsham 4	a			23 49	00 17	
	d					
Christs Hospital	d					
Billingshurst	d					
Pulborough	d					
Amberley	d					
Arundel	d					
Haywards Heath 3	d		23 07			00 15
Burgess Hill	d		23 12			00 20
Preston Park	d					
Brighton 10	d	23 15				
Hove 2	d	23a18	23 25			00 31
Aldrington	d					
Portslade	d		23 28			00s34
Fishersgate	d					
Southwick	d		23 31			00s37
Shoreham-by-Sea	d		23 34			00s40
Lancing	d		23 38			00s44
East Worthing	d					
Worthing 4	a		23 42			00 48
	d					
West Worthing	d					
Durrington-on-Sea	d					
Goring-by-Sea	d					
Angmering 3	d					
Littlehampton 4	a					
	d					
Ford 4	d					
Bognor Regis 4	d					
Barnham	a					
	d					
Bognor Regis	a					
Chichester 4	a					
	d					
Fishbourne (Sussex)	d					
Bosham	d					
Nutbourne	d					
Southbourne	d					
Emsworth	d					
Warblington	d					
Havant	d					
Bedhampton	a					
Hilsea	a					
Fratton	a					
Portsmouth & Southsea	a					
Portsmouth Harbour	a					
Cosham	a					
Portchester	a					
Fareham	a					
Swanwick	a					
Southampton Central	a					

Table 188

Mondays to Fridays

Southampton, Portsmouth and Sussex Coast - Brighton, Gatwick Airport and London

Miles	Miles	Miles	Station		SN MX ◇1	SN MO ◇1	SN MX 1	SN MO 1	SN MX ◇1	SN MX ◇1	SN ◇1	SN 1	SN 1	SN 1	SN ◇	SN ◇	SN ◇	SN ◇1	SN 1	SN ◇1	SN 1	SN ◇	SN ◇
0	—	—	**Southampton Central**	d		22p52																	
10¾	—	—	Swanwick	d		23p11																	
14½	—	—	Fareham	d		23p17																	
17¾	—	—	Portchester	d																			
20¼	—	—	Cosham	d		23p26																	
—	0	—	**Portsmouth Harbour**	d	22p44					23p15													
—	0¾	—	Portsmouth & Southsea	d	22p48					23p19													
—	1½	—	Fratton	d	22p52					23p23													
—	4¼	—	Hilsea	d	22p56					23p27													
—	7¼	—	Bedhampton	d	23p01					23p33													
24¼	8	—	**Havant**	d	23p05	23p32				23p36				05 01						05 30			
—	8½	—	Warblington	d						23p38													
—	9¾	—	Emsworth	d		23p36				23p41													
—	11¼	—	Southbourne	d						23p44													
—	12¼	—	Nutbourne	d						23p47													
—	14	—	Bosham	d						23p50													
—	15¼	—	Fishbourne (Sussex)	d						23p53													
—	16¾	—	**Chichester 4**	a	23p16	23p44				23p57				05 15						05 40			
—	—	—		d	23p17	23p45			23p52	23p57				05 16						05 41			
0	—	—	**Bognor Regis 4**	d											05 13			05 35				05 49	
3½	23	—	Barnham	a	23p24	23p52			23p59	00 05				05 23	05 19			05 41		05 48		05 55	
—	—	—		d	23p25	23p53			00 01	00 06	04 48			05 24	05 27	05 36		05 42		05 49		05 56	
—	—	—	Bognor Regis	a												05 42							
0	25¾	0	Ford 4	d	23p29				00 05	00 10	04 52				05 31			05 46				06 00	
2	—	2	**Littlehampton 4**	a	23p34	00 01			00 10	00 15	04 57				05 36							06 05	
—	—	—		d	23p39						05 02										05 53		
8	30	—	Angmering 3	d	23p47						05 10			05 33				05 53			06 02		
—	32½	—	Goring-by-Sea	d	23p51						05 14							05 57			06 06		
—	33¼	—	Durrington-on-Sea	d	23p53						05 17							05 59			06 09		
—	34	—	West Worthing	d	23p55						05 19							06 01			06 11		
—	35	—	**Worthing 4**	a	23p58						05 21			05 40				06 04			06 13		
—	—	—		d	23p59						05 22			05 41				06 04			06 14		
—	35¾	—	East Worthing	d	00 01						05 24							06 07					
—	37¼	—	Lancing	d	00 04						05 27			05 45				06 10			06 18		
—	40	—	Shoreham-by-Sea	d	00 08						05 32			05 49				06 14			06 22		
—	41	—	Southwick	d	00 11						05 35							06 17					
—	42	—	Fishersgate	d	00 13						05 37							06 19					
—	42½	—	Portslade	d	00 15						05 39			05 53				06 21			06 27		
—	43½	—	Aldrington	d	00 18						05 41							06 23					
0	44	—	Hove 2	d	00 20						05 44			05 57			05 59	06 26			06 31		06 38
—	45½	—	**Brighton 10**	a	00 25						05 48						06 03	06 30					06 42
—	—	—	Preston Park	d																	06 36		
9¼	—	—	Burgess Hill	a																	06 46		
13	—	—	Haywards Heath 3	a										06 12							06 54		
—	—	2¼	Arundel	d																05 57			
—	—	6	Amberley	d																			
—	—	10¾	Pulborough	d																06 06			
—	—	15¾	Billingshurst	d																06 13			
—	—	20½	Christs Hospital	d																06 19			
—	—	23	**Horsham 4**	a																06 23			
—	—	—		d			23p02	23p03				05 17	05 38						06 10	06 24			
—	—	30	Crawley	d			23p14	23p16				05 29	05 50						06 23	06 37			
21½	—	31½	**Three Bridges 4**	a			23p18	23p19				05 33	05 54	06 21					06 26	06 40			
24¼	—	—	**Gatwick Airport 10**	a			23p22	23p24				05 37	05 58	06 25					06 31	06 52	07 11		
—	—	—		d			23p23	23p25				05 38	06 00	06 26					06 32	06 53	07 12		
25	—	—	Horley	a			23p26	23p28				05 40	06 02						06 35	06 56			
30	—	—	Redhill 5	a			23p36	23p34				05 47	06 13						06 46	07 02			
40½	0	—	**East Croydon**	a			23p54	23p55				06 06	06 30	06 41					07 04	07 14	07 27		
—	10¼	—	London Bridge 4	a																	07 43		
48¼	—	—	Clapham Junction 10	a			00 11	00 11				06 18	06 41	06 51					07 16	07 24			
51	—	61	**London Victoria 15**	a			00 18	00 21				06 25	06 48	07 00					07 23	07 33			

Southampton, Portsmouth and Sussex Coast - Brighton, Gatwick Airport and London

Station		SN ◇	SN [1]	SN ◇[1] (trolley)	SN ◇	SN ◇[1]	SN ◇	SN ◇	SN ◇[1] A (trolley)	SN [1]	SN [1]	SN ◇	SN ◇[1]	SN ◇[1]	SN ◇	SN [1]	SN ◇[1] (trolley)	SN ◇	SN [1]	SN ◇[1] B	SN [1]	SN ◇[1]	SN ◇
Southampton Central ⛴	d																			05 48			
Swanwick	d																			06 06			
Fareham	d																			06 13			
Portchester	d																			06 18			
Cosham	d																			06 23			
Portsmouth Harbour ⛴	d					05 33			05 47					06 04									
Portsmouth & Southsea	d					05 37			05 51					06 08									
Fratton	d					05 41			05 55					06 12									
Hilsea	d					05 45			05 59														
Bedhampton	d					05 50			06 04											06 34			
Havant	d					05 53			06 07					06 20						06 37			
Warblington	d					05 55														06 39			
Emsworth	d					05 58			06 11					06 24						06 42			
Southbourne	d					06 01			06 14					06 27						06 45			
Nutbourne	d					06 03														06 48			
Bosham	d					06 07			06 18											06 51			
Fishbourne (Sussex)	d					06 10			06 21											06 54			
Chichester [4]	a					06 13			06 25					06 34						06 58			
	d					06 14			06 29					06 35						06 59			
Bognor Regis [4]	d	05 55		06 06	06 13			06 22									06 41	06 50			06 57		
Barnham	a	06 02		06 12	06 19	06 21		06 28	06 36					06 42			06 47	06 56		07 07	07 03		
	d	06 02		06 13		06 22	06 27	06 29	06 37					06 43			06 48	06 57		07 11			
Bognor Regis	a						06 33																
Ford [4]	d	06 07				06 26		06 33						06 47			06 52	07 01					
Littlehampton [4]	a							06 38										07 06					
	d									06 31			06 41									07 02	
Angmering [3]	d	06 13				06 32				06 40			06 50	06 56								07 11	
Goring-by-Sea	d	06 17				06 36				06 44			06 54	07 00								07 15	
Durrington-on-Sea	d	06 19				06 39				06 47			06 57	07 03								07 17	
West Worthing	d	06 21				06 41				06 49			06 59	07 05	07 12							07 20	
Worthing [4]	a	06 24				06 43				06 52			07 02	07 07	07 14							07 22	
	d	06 24				06 44				06 52			07 02	07 08	07 15							07 23	
East Worthing	d	06 27				06 46									07 17								
Lancing	d	06 30				06 49				06 57			07 07	07 12	07 20							07 27	
Shoreham-by-Sea	d	06 34				06 53				07 01			07 11	07 16	07 25							07 31	
Southwick	d	06 37				06 56								07 19	07 28								
Fishersgate	d	06 39				06 58									07 30								
Portslade	d	06 41				07 00				07 06			07 16	07 22	07 32							07 36	
Aldrington	d	06 43				07 03									07 34								
Hove [2]	d	06 46				07 05				07 11		07 17	07 20	07 26	07 37							07 41	07 49
Brighton [10]	a	06 50				07 09						07 21		07 30	07 41								07 54
Preston Park	d																						
Burgess Hill	a																					07 51	
Haywards Heath [3]	a									07 30			07 40									07 57	
Arundel	d			06 21													06 58			07 18			
Amberley	d			06 26																			
Pulborough	d			06 32													07 07			07 28			
Billingshurst	d			06 39													07 14			07 35			
Christs Hospital	d			06 45													07 20			07 41			
Horsham [4]	a			06 49					07 03								07 24			07 45			
	d		06 38	06 50					07 04		07 09					07 18	07 25		07 40	07 46			
Crawley	d		06 52	07 04					07 13		07 23					07 31	07 37		07 53	08 00			
Three Bridges [4]	a		06 56	07 07					07 18		07 27					07 34	07 40		07 57	08 05			
Gatwick Airport [10] ✈	a		07 01	07 12							07 32					07 39			08 04			08 12	
	d		07 02	07 14							07 33					07 40			08 05			08 13	
Horley	a		07 04	07 16							07 36					07 42			08 07				
Redhill [5]	a		07 15								07 47					07 53			08 18				
East Croydon	a		07 34	07 31					07 38	07 57	08 02		08 08			08 11	08 00		08 36	08 26		08 29	
London Bridge [4] ⊖	a		07 49							08 13	08 19									08 45			
Clapham Junction [10]	a			07 40					07 48				08 17			08 20	08 10		08 47			08 39	
London Victoria [15] ⊖	a			07 49					07 57				08 26			08 27	08 19		08 56			08 48	

A (trolley) from Three Bridges

B ◇ to Barnham

Southampton, Portsmouth and Sussex Coast - Brighton, Gatwick Airport and London

Station		SN ◇[1]	SN ◇	SN [1]	SN ◇	SN ◇[1] (trolley)	SN ◇[1] A (trolley)	SW [1]	SN ◇[1]	GW (trolley)	SN ◇	SN [1]	SN ◇	SN ◇	SN ◇	SN ◇[1]	SN ◇	SN [1]	SN ◇[1] (trolley)	SN ◇[1] A (trolley)	SW [1]	SN ◇[1]	SN ◇
Southampton Central ⛴	d	06 10						06 21												07 06	07 17		
Swanwick	d	06 27						06 49												07 24	07 44		
Fareham	d	06 34						06 58												07 31	07 53		
Portchester	d	06 40						07 03												07 36	07 58		
Cosham	d	06 44						07 08												07 40	08 03		
Portsmouth Harbour ⛴	d						06 46			07 01						07 20							
Portsmouth & Southsea	d						06 50			07 05						07 24							
Fratton	d						06 54			07 10						07 28							
Hilsea	d						06 58	07a13													08a09		
Bedhampton	d						07 03																
Havant	d	06 53					07 06			07 20						07 36				07 47			
Warblington	d						07 08													07 49			
Emsworth	d	06 57					07 11													07 52			
Southbourne	d	07 00					07 14													07 55			
Nutbourne	d						07 16													07 58			
Bosham	d						07 20													08 01			
Fishbourne (Sussex)	d						07 23													08 04			
Chichester [4]	a	07 07					07 26			07 31						07 47				08 08			
	d	07 08					07 28			07 32						07 47				08 08			
Bognor Regis [4]	d				07 27	07 17									07 36				07 55				
Barnham	a	07 15			07 33	07 23	07 35			07 39					07 42	07 55			08 01	08 16			
	d	07 16				07 24	07 36			07 40	07 39				07 45	07 55			08 02	08 16			
Bognor Regis	a										07 45												
Ford [4]	d	07 20													07 50	08 00			08 06				
Littlehampton [4]	a														07 54								
	d		07 22						07 29					07 45			08 01					08 15	
Angmering [3]	d	07 26	07 30						07 38					07 53		08 06	08 10					08 23	
Goring-by-Sea	d	07 30	07 34						07 42					07 57			08 14					08 27	
Durrington-on-Sea	d	07 33	07 37						07 45					08 00		08 12	08 17					08 30	
West Worthing	d	07 35	07 39						07 47					08 02			08 19					08 32	
Worthing [4]	a	07 37	07 41						07 50	07 56				08 04		08 16	08 21					08 34	
	d	07 38	07 42						07 50	08 00				08 05		08 16	08 22					08 35	
East Worthing	d		07 44											08 07			08 24						
Lancing	d	07 42	07 47						07 54					08 10		08 20	08 27					08 39	
Shoreham-by-Sea	d	07 46	07 52						07 59	08 06				08 15		08 24	08 32					08 43	
Southwick	d	07 49	07 55											08 18		08 27	08 35						
Fishersgate	d		07 57											08 20			08 37						
Portslade	d	07 52	07 59						08 04					08 22		08 31	08 39					08 48	
Aldrington	d		08 01											08 24			08 41						
Hove [2]	d	07 55	08 04						08 08	08 14			08 22	08 27		08 34	08 44					08 52	08 54
Brighton [10]	a	08 00	08 08							08 20			08 26	08 31		08 38	08 48						08 58
Preston Park	d								08 12													08 57	
Burgess Hill	a								08 23													09 07	
Haywards Heath [3]	a								08 28													09 12	
Arundel	d					07 31													08 11				
Amberley	d					07 36													08 16				
Pulborough	d					07 42													08 22				
Billingshurst	d					07 49													08 29				
Christs Hospital	d					07 55													08 35				
Horsham [4]	a					07 59	08 05												08 39	08 45			
	d			07 51		08 09						08 12						08 35	08 49				
Crawley	d			08 06		08 18						08 26						08 47	08 58				
Three Bridges [4]	a			08 09		08 22			08 38			08 29						08 51	09 01				
Gatwick Airport [10] ✈	a			08 14								08 34						08 55	09 06			09 26	
	d			08 15								08 35						08 56	09 07			09 27	
Horley	a			08 17		08 28						08 38						08 59					
Redhill [5]	a			08 28								08 49						09 10					
East Croydon	a			08 50		08 43			08 57			09 10						09 29	09 22			09 42	
London Bridge [4] ⊖	a			09 06																			
Clapham Junction [10]	a					08 52			09 07			09 20						09 39	09 32			09 52	
London Victoria [15] ⊖	a					09 01			09 16			09 27						09 50	09 42			10 00	

A (trolley) from Horsham

Southampton, Portsmouth and Sussex Coast - Brighton, Gatwick Airport and London

Station		SN	SN	SN	SN	SN	SN	SW	SN	SN	SN	SN	SN	SN	SN	SN	SN	SN	SN	SN	SN	SN
		◇	◇	1	◇1	◇	◇1	1	◇	◇1	◇1	◇1	◇	◇	◇	1	◇	◇	◇	◇	◇1	◇1
										bus	A bus	B bus										
Southampton Central	d				07 33			07 51														08 10
Swanwick	d				07 51			08 20														08 28
Fareham	d				07 58			08 28														08 35
Portchester	d							08 33														08 40
Cosham	d				08 07			08 38														08 44
Portsmouth Harbour	d										08 10						08 29					
Portsmouth & Southsea	d						08 03				08 14						08 33					
Fratton	d						08 07				08 18						08 37					
Hilsea	d						08 11	08a45														
Bedhampton	d						08 16															
Havant	d				08 13		08 19				08 27						08 46					08 51
Warblington	d						08 21															08 53
Emsworth	d						08 24				08 31						08 50					08 56
Southbourne	d						08 27										08 53					08 59
Nutbourne	d						08 29															09 01
Bosham	d				08 21																	09 05
Fishbourne (Sussex)	d				08 24																	09 08
Chichester 4	a				08 27		08 35				08 40						09 00					09 11
	d		08 21		08 28		08 36				08 41						09 00			09 06		09 12
Bognor Regis 4	d	08 13				08 32				08 26			08 48					09 06			08 56	
Barnham	a	08 19	08 28		08 35	08 38	08 43			08 32	08 48		08 55				09 08	09 12		09 14	09 02	09 19
	d	08 20	08 29		08 36		08 44		08 45	08 33	08 49						09 08	09 15	09 12		09 03	09 20
Bognor Regis	a								08 51										09 18			
Ford 4	d	08 24	08 33		08 40		08 48			08 37								09 19			09 07	
Littlehampton 4	a		08 38				08 53											09 24				
	d											08 45										
Angmering 3	d	08 30			08 46							08 53					09 17					
Goring-by-Sea	d	08 34										08 57										
Durrington-on-Sea	d	08 37			08 52							09 00										
West Worthing	d	08 39										09 02			09 09							
Worthing 4	a	08 41			08 56							09 04			09 11		09 24					
	d	08 42			08 56							09 05			09 12		09 26					
East Worthing	d	08 44													09 14							
Lancing	d	08 47			09 00							09 09			09 17		09 30					
Shoreham-by-Sea	d	08 52			09 04							09 13			09 22		09 34					
Southwick	d	08 55			09 07										09 25		09 37					
Fishersgate	d	08 57													09 27							
Portslade	d	08 59			09 11							09 18			09 29		09 40					
Aldrington	d	09 01													09 31							
Hove 2	d	09 04			09 14							09 22		09 24	09 34		09 44					
Brighton 10	a	09 08			09 18									09 28	09 38		09 48					
Preston Park	d																					
Burgess Hill	a																					
Haywards Heath 3	a											09 40										
Arundel	d									08 42											09 12	
Amberley	d									08 47											09 17	
Pulborough	d									08 53											09 23	
Billingshurst	d									09 00											09 29	
Christs Hospital	d									09 06											09 36	
Horsham 4	a									09 11	09 16										09 40	09 47
	d			09 00						09 20						09 30					09 51	
Crawley	d			09 13						09 29						09 44					10 00	
Three Bridges 4	a			09 16						09 32						09 48					10 03	
Gatwick Airport 10	a			09 22						09 37		09 55				09 53					10 08	
	d			09 23						09 38		09 56				09 54					10 09	
Horley	a			09 26						09 41						09 56						
Redhill 5	a			09 36						09 47						10 03					10 16	
East Croydon	a			09 54						09 59		10 11				10 24					10 28	
London Bridge 4	a			10 13												10 43						
Clapham Junction 10	a									10 09		10 21									10 37	
London Victoria 15	a									10 16		10 28									10 44	

A bus from Horsham

B bus from Haywards Heath

Southampton, Portsmouth and Sussex Coast - Brighton, Gatwick Airport and London

Station		SN	SN	SN	SN	SN	SN	SN	SW	SN	SN	SN	SN	SN	SN	SN	SN	SN	SN	SN	SN	SN	SN
		◇1	◇	◇	◇	◇1	1	◇	1	◇	◇1	◇1	◇1	◇	◇	◇	1	◇	◇	◇1	◇1	◇1	◇
		A bus																					
Southampton Central	d					08 33			08 44												09 10		
Swanwick	d					08 50			09 11												09 28		
Fareham	d					08 57			09 18												09 37		
Portchester	d								09 23												09 42		
Cosham	d					09 05			09 28												09 46		
Portsmouth Harbour	d							08 51				09 12						09 29					
Portsmouth & Southsea	d							08 55				09 16						09 33					
Fratton	d							08 59				09 20						09 37					
Hilsea	d							09 04	09a33														
Bedhampton	d							09 13															
Havant	d					09 12		09 16				09 30						09 46			09 54		
Warblington	d							09 18															
Emsworth	d					09 16		09 21										09 50			10 00		
Southbourne	d							09 24										09 53			10 03		
Nutbourne	d							09 26															
Bosham	d							09 30															
Fishbourne (Sussex)	d							09 33															
Chichester 4	a					09 24		09 36				09 40						10 00			10 10		
	d					09 25		09 37				09 41						10 00			10 11		
Bognor Regis 4	d									09 39	09 30								10 07	09 56			
Barnham	a					09 32		09 44		09 45	09 36	09 48						10 08	10 13	10 02	10 18		
	d		09 19			09 33		09 45			09 37	09 49		09 52				10 08	10 15	10 03	10 19		
Bognor Regis	a		09 25											09 58									
Ford 4	d					09 37		09 49			09 41								10 19	10 07			
Littlehampton 4	a							09 54											10 24				
	d	09 15											09 45									10 15	
Angmering 3	d	09 23				09 43							09 54					10 17				10 23	
Goring-by-Sea	d	09 27				09 47							09 58									10 27	
Durrington-on-Sea	d	09 30				09 50							10 00									10 30	
West Worthing	d	09 32			09 39	09 52							10 02			10 09						10 32	
Worthing 4	a	09 34			09 41	09 54							10 05			10 11		10 24				10 34	
	d	09 36			09 42	09 56							10 06			10 12		10 26				10 36	
East Worthing	d				09 44											10 14							
Lancing	d				09 47	10 00							10 10			10 17		10 30					
Shoreham-by-Sea	d	09 42			09 52	10 04							10 14			10 22		10 34				10 42	
Southwick	d				09 55	10 07										10 25		10 37					
Fishersgate	d				09 57											10 27							
Portslade	d	09 47			09 59	10 10										10 29		10 40				10 47	
Aldrington	d				10 01											10 31							
Hove 2	d	09 51		09 54	10 04	10 14							10 21		10 24	10 34		10 44				10 51	10 54
Brighton 10	a			09 58	10 08	10 18									10 28	10 38		10 48					10 58
Preston Park	d	09 55																				10 55	
Burgess Hill	a	10 04																				11 03	
Haywards Heath 3	a	10 10											10 35									11 09	
Arundel	d										09 46									10 12			
Amberley	d																			10 17			
Pulborough	d										09 55									10 23			
Billingshurst	d										10 01									10 29			
Christs Hospital	d																			10 36			
Horsham 4	a										10 10	10 16								10 40	10 46		
	d						10 00				10 20						10 30			10 50			
Crawley	d						10 13				10 29						10 43			10 59			
Three Bridges 4	a						10 16				10 32						10 46			11 02			
Gatwick Airport 10	a	10 25					10 22				10 37		10 55				10 52			11 07		11 25	
	d	10 26					10 23				10 38		10 56				10 53			11 08		11 26	
Horley	a						10 26				10 41						10 56						
Redhill 5	a						10 36				10 47						11 02			11 15			
East Croydon	a	10 41					10 54				10 59		11 11				11 24			11 27		11 41	
London Bridge 4	a						11 13										11 43						
Clapham Junction 10	a	10 51									11 09		11 21							11 37		11 51	
London Victoria 15	a	10 58									11 16		11 28							11 45		11 58	

A bus from Haywards Heath

Southampton, Portsmouth and Sussex Coast - Brighton, Gatwick Airport and London

		SN	SN	SN	SN	SW	SN	SN	SN	SN	SN	SN	SN	SN	SN	SN	SN	SN	SN	SN	SN	SN
		◇	◇ 1	1	◇	1	◇	◇ 1	◇ 1	◇ 1	◇	◇	◇	1	◇ 1	◇	◇ 1	◇ 1	◇ 1	◇	◇	◇ 1
Southampton Central ⛴	d		09 33			09 44												10 13				10 33
Swanwick	d		09 50			10 11												10 32				10 50
Fareham	d		09 56			10 18												10 39				10 57
Portchester	d					10 23												10 44				
Cosham	d		10 05			10 28												10 48				11 05
Portsmouth Harbour ⛴	d								10 12						10 29							
Portsmouth & Southsea	d				09 59				10 16						10 33							
Fratton	d				10 04				10 20						10 37							
Hilsea	d				10 08	10a33																
Bedhampton	d				10 13																	
Havant	d		10 11		10 16				10 30						10 46			10 56				11 12
Warblington	d				10 18																	
Emsworth	d		10 15		10 21										10 50			11 00				11 16
Southbourne	d				10 24										10 53			11 03				
Nutbourne	d				10 26																	
Bosham	d				10 30																	
Fishbourne (Sussex)	d				10 33																	
Chichester 4	a		10 23		10 36				10 40						11 00			11 10				11 24
	d		10 25		10 37				10 41						11 00			11 11				11 25
Bognor Regis 4	d						10 39	10 30								11 07	10 56					
Barnham	a		10 32		10 44		10 45	10 36	10 48						11 08	11 13	11 02	11 18				11 32
	d		10 33		10 45			10 37	10 49		10 52				11 08	11 15	11 03	11 19				11 33
Bognor Regis	a										10 58											
Ford 4	d		10 37		10 49			10 41								11 19	11 07					11 37
Littlehampton 4	a				10 54											11 24						
	d									10 45									11 15			
Angmering 3	d		10 43							10 53					11 17				11 23			11 43
Goring-by-Sea	d		10 47							10 57									11 27			11 47
Durrington-on-Sea	d		10 50							11 00									11 30			11 50
West Worthing	d	10 39	10 52							11 02			11 09						11 32		11 39	11 52
Worthing 4	a	10 41	10 54							11 04			11 11		11 24				11 34		11 41	11 54
	d	10 42	10 56							11 06			11 12		11 26				11 36		11 42	11 56
East Worthing	d	10 44											11 14								11 44	
Lancing	d	10 47	11 00							11 10			11 17		11 30						11 47	12 00
Shoreham-by-Sea	d	10 52	11 04							11 14			11 22		11 34				11 42		11 52	12 04
Southwick	d	10 55	11 07										11 25		11 37						11 55	12 07
Fishersgate	d	10 57											11 27								11 57	
Portslade	d	10 59	11 10										11 29		11 40				11 47		11 59	12 10
Aldrington	d	11 01											11 31								12 01	
Hove 2	d	11 04	11 14							11 21		11 24	11 34		11 44				11 51	11 54	12 04	12 14
Brighton 10	a	11 08	11 18									11 28	11 38		11 48					11 58	12 08	12 18
Preston Park	d																		11 55			
Burgess Hill	a																		12 03			
Haywards Heath 3	a									11 35									12 09			
Arundel	d							10 46									11 12					
Amberley	d																11 17					
Pulborough	d							10 55									11 23					
Billingshurst	d							11 01									11 29					
Christs Hospital	d																11 36					
Horsham 4	a							11 10	11 16								11 40	11 46				
	d			11 00				11 20						11 30			11 50					
Crawley	d			11 13				11 29						11 43			11 59					
Three Bridges 4	a			11 16				11 32						11 46			12 02					
Gatwick Airport 10 ✈	a			11 22				11 37		11 55				11 52			12 07		12 25			
	d			11 23				11 38		11 56				11 53			12 08		12 26			
Horley	a			11 26				11 41						11 56								
Redhill 5	a			11 36				11 47						12 02			12 15					
East Croydon 🚊	a			11 54				11 59		12 11				12 24			12 27		12 41			
London Bridge 4 ⊖	a			12 13										12 43								
Clapham Junction 10	a							12 09		12 21							12 37		12 51			
London Victoria 15 ⊖	a							12 18		12 28							12 44		12 58			

Southampton, Portsmouth and Sussex Coast - Brighton, Gatwick Airport and London

		SN	SN	SW	SN	SN	SN	SN	SN	SN	SN	SN	SN	SN	SN	SN	SN	SN	SN	SN	SN	SN	SW
		1	◇ 1	1	◇	◇ 1	◇ 1	◇ 1	◇	◇	◇	1	◇	◇	◇ 1	◇ 1	◇ 1	◇	◇	◇ 1	1	◇	1
Southampton Central ⛴	d			10 44												11 13				11 33			11 44
Swanwick	d			11 11												11 33				11 50			12 11
Fareham	d			11 18												11 40				11 57			12 18
Portchester	d			11 23												11 45							12 23
Cosham	d			11 28												11 49				12 05			12 28
Portsmouth Harbour ⛴	d						11 12						11 29										
Portsmouth & Southsea	d		10 59				11 16						11 33									11 59	
Fratton	d		11 04				11 20						11 37									12 04	
Hilsea	d		11 08	11a33																		12 08	12a33
Bedhampton	d		11 13																			12 13	
Havant	d		11 16				11 30						11 46			11 56				12 12		12 16	
Warblington	d		11 18																			12 18	
Emsworth	d		11 21										11 50			12 00				12 16		12 21	
Southbourne	d		11 24										11 53			12 03						12 24	
Nutbourne	d		11 26																			12 26	
Bosham	d		11 30																			12 30	
Fishbourne (Sussex)	d		11 33																			12 33	
Chichester 4	a		11 36				11 40						12 00			12 10				12 24		12 36	
	d		11 37				11 41						12 00			12 11				12 25		12 37	
Bognor Regis 4	d				11 39	11 30								12 07	11 56								
Barnham	a		11 44		11 45	11 36	11 48						12 08	12 13	12 02	12 18				12 32		12 44	
	d		11 45			11 37	11 49		11 52				12 08	12 15	12 03	12 19				12 33		12 45	
Bognor Regis	a								11 58														
Ford 4	d		11 49			11 41								12 19	12 07					12 37		12 49	
Littlehampton 4	a		11 54											12 24								12 54	
	d							11 45									12 15						
Angmering 3	d							11 53					12 17				12 23			12 43			
Goring-by-Sea	d							11 57									12 27			12 47			
Durrington-on-Sea	d							12 00									12 30			12 50			
West Worthing	d							12 02			12 09						12 32		12 39	12 52			
Worthing 4	a							12 04			12 11		12 24				12 34		12 41	12 54			
	d							12 06			12 12		12 26				12 36		12 42	12 56			
East Worthing	d										12 14								12 44				
Lancing	d							12 10			12 17		12 30						12 47	13 00			
Shoreham-by-Sea	d							12 14			12 22		12 34				12 42		12 52	13 04			
Southwick	d										12 25		12 37						12 55	13 07			
Fishersgate	d										12 27								12 57				
Portslade	d										12 29		12 40				12 47		12 59	13 10			
Aldrington	d										12 31								13 01				
Hove 2	d							12 21		12 24	12 34		12 44				12 51	12 54	13 04	13 14			
Brighton 10	a									12 28	12 38		12 48					12 58	13 08	13 18			
Preston Park	d																12 55						
Burgess Hill	a																13 03						
Haywards Heath 3	a							12 35									13 09						
Arundel	d					11 46									12 12								
Amberley	d														12 17								
Pulborough	d					11 55									12 23								
Billingshurst	d					12 01									12 29								
Christs Hospital	d														12 36								
Horsham 4	a					12 10	12 16								12 40	12 46							
	d	12 00				12 20						12 30			12 50						13 00		
Crawley	d	12 13				12 29						12 44			12 59						13 13		
Three Bridges 4	a	12 16				12 32						12 47			13 02						13 16		
Gatwick Airport 10 ✈	a	12 22				12 37		12 55				12 52			13 07		13 25				13 22		
	d	12 23				12 38		12 56				12 53			13 08		13 26				13 23		
Horley	a	12 26				12 41						12 56									13 26		
Redhill 5	a	12 36				12 47						13 02			13 15						13 36		
East Croydon 🚊	a	12 54				12 59		13 11				13 24			13 27		13 41				13 54		
London Bridge 4 ⊖	a	13 13										13 43									14 13		
Clapham Junction 10	a					13 09		13 21							13 37		13 51						
London Victoria 15 ⊖	a					13 16		13 28							13 44		13 58						

Southampton, Portsmouth and Sussex Coast - Brighton, Gatwick Airport and London

		SN	SN	SN	SN	SN	SN	SN	SN	SN	SN	SN	SN	SN	SN	SN	SN	SN	SN	SW	SN	SN	SN
		◇	◇■	◇■	◇■	◇	◇	◇	■	◇	◇	◇■	◇■	◇■	◇	◇	◇■	■	◇	■	◇	◇■	◇■
Southampton Central	d												12 13				12 33			12 44			
Swanwick	d												12 33				12 50			13 11			
Fareham	d												12 40				12 56			13 18			
Portchester	d												12 45							13 23			
Cosham	d												12 49				13 05			13 28			
Portsmouth Harbour	d			12 12						12 29													13 12
Portsmouth & Southsea	d			12 16						12 33									12 59				13 16
Fratton	d			12 20						12 37									13 04				13 20
Hilsea	d																		13 08	13a33			
Bedhampton	d																		13 13				
Havant	d			12 30						12 46			12 56				13 11		13 16				13 30
Warblington	d																		13 18				
Emsworth	d									12 50			13 00				13 15		13 21				
Southbourne	d									12 53			13 03						13 24				
Nutbourne	d																		13 26				
Bosham	d																		13 30				
Fishbourne (Sussex)	d																		13 33				
Chichester ■	a			12 40						13 00			13 10				13 23		13 36				13 40
	d			12 41						13 00			13 11				13 25		13 37				13 41
Bognor Regis ■	d	12 39	12 30								13 07	12 56									13 39	13 30	
Barnham	a	12 45	12 36	12 48						13 08	13 13	13 02	13 18				13 32		13 44		13 45	13 36	13 48
	d		12 37	12 49		12 52				13 08	13 15	13 03	13 19				13 33		13 45			13 37	13 49
Bognor Regis	a					12 58																	
Ford ■	d		12 41								13 19	13 07					13 37		13 49			13 41	
Littlehampton ■	a										13 24								13 54				
	d				12 45									13 15									
Angmering ■	d				12 53					13 17				13 23			13 43						
Goring-by-Sea	d				12 57									13 27			13 47						
Durrington-on-Sea	d				13 00									13 30			13 50						
West Worthing	d				13 02			13 09						13 32		13 39	13 52						
Worthing ■	a				13 04			13 11		13 24				13 34		13 41	13 54						
	d				13 06			13 12		13 26				13 36		13 42	13 56						
East Worthing	d							13 14								13 44							
Lancing	d				13 10			13 17		13 30						13 47	14 00						
Shoreham-by-Sea	d				13 14			13 22		13 34				13 42		13 52	14 04						
Southwick	d							13 25		13 37						13 55	14 07						
Fishersgate	d							13 27								13 57							
Portslade	d							13 29		13 40				13 47		13 59	14 10						
Aldrington	d							13 31								14 01							
Hove ■	d				13 21		13 24	13 34		13 44				13 51	13 54	14 04	14 14						
Brighton ■	a						13 28	13 38		13 48					13 58	14 08	14 18						
Preston Park	d													13 55									
Burgess Hill	a													14 03									
Haywards Heath ■	a				13 35									14 09									
Arundel	d		12 46									13 12										13 46	
Amberley	d											13 17											
Pulborough	d		12 55									13 23										13 55	
Billingshurst	d		13 01									13 29										14 01	
Christs Hospital	d											13 36											
Horsham ■	a		13 10	13 16								13 40	13 46									14 10	14 16
	d			13 20					13 30				13 50					14 00					14 20
Crawley	d			13 29					13 43				13 59					14 13					14 29
Three Bridges ■	a			13 32					13 46				14 02					14 16					14 32
Gatwick Airport ■	a			13 37	13 55				13 52				14 07	14 25				14 22					14 37
	d			13 38	13 56				13 53				14 08	14 26				14 23					14 38
Horley	a			13 41					13 56									14 26					14 41
Redhill ■	a			13 47					14 02				14 15					14 36					14 47
East Croydon	a			13 59	14 11				14 24				14 27	14 41				14 54					14 59
London Bridge ■	a								14 43									15 13					
Clapham Junction ■	a			14 09	14 21								14 37	14 51									15 09
London Victoria ■	a			14 16	14 28								14 44	14 58									15 20

Southampton, Portsmouth and Sussex Coast - Brighton, Gatwick Airport and London

		SN	SN	SN	SN	SN	SN	SN	SN	SN	SN	SN	SN	SN	SN	SN	SW	SN	SN	SN	SN	SN
		◇■	◇	◇	◇	■	◇■	◇	◇■	◇■	◇■	◇	◇	◇■	■	◇	■	◇	◇■	◇■	◇■	◇
											A ⌶								⌶	B ⌶	A ⌶	
Southampton Central	d									13 13				13 33			13 44					
Swanwick	d									13 33				13 50			14 11					
Fareham	d									13 40				13 56			14 18					
Portchester	d									13 45							14 23					
Cosham	d									13 49				14 05			14 28					
Portsmouth Harbour	d						13 29													14 12		
Portsmouth & Southsea	d						13 33									13 59				14 16		
Fratton	d						13 37									14 04				14 20		
Hilsea	d															14 08	14a33					
Bedhampton	d															14 13						
Havant	d						13 46			13 56				14 11		14 16				14 30		
Warblington	d															14 18						
Emsworth	d						13 50			14 00				14 15		14 21						
Southbourne	d						13 53			14 03						14 24						
Nutbourne	d															14 26						
Bosham	d															14 30						
Fishbourne (Sussex)	d															14 33						
Chichester ■	a						14 00			14 10				14 23		14 36				14 40		
	d						14 00			14 11				14 25		14 37				14 41		
Bognor Regis ■	d							14 07	13 56									14 40	14 30			
Barnham	a						14 08	14 13	14 02	14 18				14 32		14 44		14 46	14 36	14 48		
	d		13 52				14 08	14 15	14 03	14 19				14 33		14 45			14 37	14 49		14 52
Bognor Regis	a		13 58																			14 58
Ford ■	d							14 19	14 07					14 37		14 49			14 41			
Littlehampton ■	a							14 24								14 54						
	d	13 45									14 15										14 45	
Angmering ■	d	13 53					14 17				14 23			14 43							14 53	
Goring-by-Sea	d	13 57									14 27			14 47							14 57	
Durrington-on-Sea	d	14 00									14 30			14 50							15 00	
West Worthing	d	14 02			14 09						14 32		14 39	14 52							15 02	
Worthing ■	a	14 04			14 11		14 24				14 34		14 41	14 54							15 04	
	d	14 06			14 12		14 26				14 36		14 42	14 56							15 06	
East Worthing	d				14 14								14 44									
Lancing	d	14 10			14 17		14 30						14 47	15 00							15 10	
Shoreham-by-Sea	d	14 14			14 22		14 34				14 42		14 52	15 04							15 14	
Southwick	d				14 25		14 37						14 55	15 07								
Fishersgate	d				14 27								14 57									
Portslade	d				14 29		14 40				14 47		14 59	15 10								
Aldrington	d				14 31								15 01									
Hove ■	d	14 21		14 24	14 34		14 44				14 51	14 54	15 04	15 14							15 21	
Brighton ■	a			14 28	14 38		14 48					14 58	15 08	15 18								
Preston Park	d										14 55											
Burgess Hill	a										15 03											
Haywards Heath ■	a	14 35									15 09										15 35	
Arundel	d								14 12										14 46			
Amberley	d								14 17													
Pulborough	d								14 23										14 55			
Billingshurst	d								14 29										15 01			
Christs Hospital	d								14 36													
Horsham ■	a								14 40	14 46									15 10	15 16		
	d					14 30				14 50					15 00					15 20		
Crawley	d					14 43				14 59					15 13					15 29		
Three Bridges ■	a					14 46				15 02					15 16					15 32		
Gatwick Airport ■	a	14 55				14 52				15 07	15 25				15 22					15 37	15 55	
	d	14 56				14 53				15 08	15 26				15 23					15 38	15 56	
Horley	a					14 56									15 26					15 41		
Redhill ■	a					15 02				15 16					15 36					15 47		
East Croydon	a	15 11				15 24				15 28	15 41				15 54					15 59	16 11	
London Bridge ■	a					15 43									16 13							
Clapham Junction ■	a	15 21								15 37	15 51									16 09	16 21	
London Victoria ■	a	15 28								15 46	15 58									16 16	16 28	

A ⌶ from Haywards Heath

B ⌶ from Horsham

Southampton, Portsmouth and Sussex Coast - Brighton, Gatwick Airport and London

		SN	SN	SN	SN	SN	SN	SN	SN	SN	SN	GW	SN	SN	SN	SW	SN	SN	SN	SN	SN	SN	SN
		◇	◇	[1]	◇	◇	◇[1]	◇[1]	◇[1]	◇	◇	[1]	[1]	◇[1]	◇[1]	[1]	◇	◇[1]	◇[1]	◇[1]	◇	◇	◇[1]
							🍴	A 🍴	B 🍴			🍴								B 🍴			
Southampton Central ⛴	d							14 13				14 34		14 26		14 44							
Swanwick	d							14 33								15 11							
Fareham	d							14 40				14 56		15 00		15 18							
Portchester	d							14 45								15 23							
Cosham	d							14 49				15 04				15 28							
Portsmouth Harbour ⛴	d				14 29														15 12				
Portsmouth & Southsea	d				14 33										14 59				15 16				
Fratton	d				14 37										15 04				15 20				
Hilsea	d														15 08	15a33							
Bedhampton	d														15 14								
Havant	d				14 46			14 56				15 11		15 15	15 17				15 30				
Warblington	d														15 19								
Emsworth	d				14 50			15 00							15 22								
Southbourne	d				14 53			15 03							15 25								
Nutbourne	d														15 28								
Bosham	d														15 31								
Fishbourne (Sussex)	d														15 34								
Chichester [4]	a				15 00			15 10				15 21		15 25	15 37				15 41				
	d				15 00			15 11				15 22		15 29	15 38				15 42				
Bognor Regis [4]	d					15 07	14 56										15 39	15 27					
Barnham	a				15 08	15 13	15 02	15 18				15 29		15 36	15 45		15 45	15 33	15 49				
	d				15 08	15 15	15 03	15 19				15 30		15 37	15 46			15 34	15 50		15 53		
Bognor Regis	a																				15 59		
Ford [4]	d					15 19	15 07							15 41	15 50			15 38					
Littlehampton [4]	a					15 24									15 55								
	d								15 15											15 45			15 50
Angmering [3]	d				15 17				15 23					15 47						15 53			16 00
Goring-by-Sea	d								15 27					15 51						15 57			16 04
Durrington-on-Sea	d								15 30					15 54						16 00			16 07
West Worthing	d		15 09						15 32		15 39			15 56						16 02			16 09
Worthing [4]	a		15 11		15 24				15 34		15 41	15 45		15 58						16 04			16 11
	d		15 12		15 26				15 35		15 42	15 50		15 59						16 06			16 12
East Worthing	d		15 14						15 37		15 44												16 14
Lancing	d		15 17		15 30						15 47			16 03						16 10			16 17
Shoreham-by-Sea	d		15 22		15 34				15 43		15 52	15 57		16 07						16 14			16 22
Southwick	d		15 25		15 37						15 55			16 10									16 25
Fishersgate	d		15 27								15 57												16 27
Portslade	d		15 29		15 40				15 48		15 59			16 13									16 29
Aldrington	d		15 31								16 01												16 31
Hove [2]	d	15 24	15 34		15 44				15 52	15 54	16 04	16 08		16 17						16 21		16 24	16 34
Brighton [10]	a	15 28	15 38		15 48					15 58	16 08	16 14		16 21								16 28	16 38
Preston Park	d								15 56														
Burgess Hill	a								16 04														
Haywards Heath [3]	a								16 10											16 34			
Arundel	d						15 12											15 43					
Amberley	d						15 17																
Pulborough	d						15 23											15 52					
Billingshurst	d						15 29											15 58					
Christs Hospital	d						15 36											16 05					
Horsham [4]	a						15 40	15 46										16 10	16 16				
	d			15 30				15 50					16 00						16 20				
Crawley	d			15 43				15 59					16 13						16 29				
Three Bridges [4]	a			15 46				16 02					16 16						16 32				
Gatwick Airport [10] ✈	a			15 52				16 07	16 25				16 22						16 37	16 57			
	d			15 53				16 08	16 26				16 23						16 38	16 58			
Horley	a			15 56									16 26										
Redhill [5]	a			16 02				16 17					16 36						16 46				
East Croydon 🚊	a			16 23				16 30	16 41				16 54						17 01	17 13			
London Bridge [4] ⊖	a			16 43									17 14										
Clapham Junction [10]	a							16 39	16 51										17 10	17 22			
London Victoria [15] ⊖	a							16 46	16 58										17 17	17 29			

A 🍴 from Horsham

B 🍴 from Haywards Heath

Southampton, Portsmouth and Sussex Coast - Brighton, Gatwick Airport and London

		SN	SN	SN	SN	SN	SN	SN	SN	SN	SN	SN	SN	SW	SN	SN	SN	SN	SN	SN	SN	SN
		[1]	◇	◇	◇[1]	◇[1]	◇[1]	◇	◇	◇	◇[1]	[1]	◇[1]	[1]	◇	◇[1]	◇[1]	◇[1]	◇	◇	◇	[1]
					🍴	A 🍴	B 🍴									🍴	A 🍴	B 🍴				
Southampton Central ⛴	d					15 13					15 33			15 44								
Swanwick	d					15 33					15 50			16 11								
Fareham	d					15 40					15 57			16 18								
Portchester	d					15 45								16 23								
Cosham	d					15 49					16 05			16 28								
Portsmouth Harbour ⛴	d		15 29														16 12					
Portsmouth & Southsea	d		15 33										15 59				16 16					
Fratton	d		15 37										16 04				16 20					
Hilsea	d												16 08	16a33								
Bedhampton	d												16 13									
Havant	d		15 46			15 58					16 12		16 16				16 30					
Warblington	d												16 18									
Emsworth	d		15 50			16 02					16 16		16 21				16 34					
Southbourne	d		15 53			16 05							16 24									
Nutbourne	d												16 26									
Bosham	d												16 30									
Fishbourne (Sussex)	d												16 33									
Chichester [4]	a		16 00			16 12					16 24		16 36				16 42					
	d		16 00			16 13					16 25		16 37				16 43					
Bognor Regis [4]	d			16 09	15 56										16 39	16 30						
Barnham	a		16 08	16 15	16 02	16 20					16 32		16 44		16 45	16 36	16 50					
	d		16 08		16 03	16 21		16 24			16 33		16 45			16 37	16 51		16 54			
Bognor Regis	a							16 30											17 00			
Ford [4]	d				16 07						16 37		16 49			16 41						
Littlehampton [4]	a												16 54									
	d						16 15											16 45				
Angmering [3]	d		16 17				16 23				16 43							16 53				
Goring-by-Sea	d						16 27				16 47							16 57				
Durrington-on-Sea	d						16 30				16 50							17 00				
West Worthing	d						16 32			16 39	16 52							17 02			17 09	
Worthing [4]	a		16 24				16 34			16 41	16 54							17 04			17 11	
	d		16 26				16 36			16 42	16 56							17 06			17 12	
East Worthing	d									16 44											17 14	
Lancing	d		16 30							16 47	17 00							17 10			17 17	
Shoreham-by-Sea	d		16 34				16 42			16 52	17 04							17 14			17 22	
Southwick	d		16 37							16 55	17 07										17 25	
Fishersgate	d									16 57											17 27	
Portslade	d		16 40				16 47			16 59	17 10										17 29	
Aldrington	d									17 01											17 31	
Hove [2]	d		16 44				16 51		16 54	17 04	17 14							17 21		17 24	17 34	
Brighton [10]	a		16 48						16 58	17 08	17 18									17 28	17 38	
Preston Park	d																					
Burgess Hill	a						17 01															
Haywards Heath [3]	a						17 09											17 35				
Arundel	d				16 12											16 46						
Amberley	d				16 17																	
Pulborough	d				16 23											16 55						
Billingshurst	d				16 29											17 01						
Christs Hospital	d				16 36											17 08						
Horsham [4]	a				16 40	16 48										17 12	17 18					
	d	16 30				16 52						17 00					17 22					17 30
Crawley	d	16 44				17 01						17 14					17 31					17 44
Three Bridges [4]	a	16 47				17 04						17 17					17 34					17 47
Gatwick Airport [10] ✈	a	16 52				17 09	17 24					17 22					17 41	17 54				17 52
	d	16 53				17 10	17 25					17 23					17 42	17 55				17 53
Horley	a	16 56										17 26										17 56
Redhill [5]	a	17 06				17 17						17 36					17 49					18 06
East Croydon 🚊	a	17 24				17 30	17 40					17 54					18 01	18 11				18 24
London Bridge [4] ⊖	a	17 45										18 16										
Clapham Junction [10]	a					17 39	17 50										18 13	18 21				18 37
London Victoria [15] ⊖	a					17 46	17 58										18 20	18 29				18 44

A 🍴 from Horsham

B 🍴 from Haywards Heath

Southampton, Portsmouth and Sussex Coast - Brighton, Gatwick Airport and London

		SN	SN	SN	SN	SN	SN	SN	SN	SN	SN	SW	SN	SN	SN	SN	SN	SN	SN	SN	SN	SN	SN
		◇	◇1	◇1	◇1	◇	1	◇	◇	◇1	◇	1	◇1	◇1	◇1	◇	◇	1	◇	◇	◇1	◇1	◇1
			⌶	A ⌶	B ⌶										B ⌶								
Southampton Central	d			16 12						16 33		16 44										17 13	
Swanwick	d			16 29						16 50		17 11										17 33	
Fareham	d			16 36						16 57		17 18										17 40	
Portchester	d			16 41								17 23										17 45	
Cosham	d			16 45						17 05		17 28										17 49	
Portsmouth Harbour	d	16 29							16 40					17 12					17 29				
Portsmouth & Southsea	d	16 33							16 46		17 00			17 16					17 33				
Fratton	d	16 37							16 50		17 05			17 20					17 37				
Hilsea	d								16 54		17 09	17a33											
Bedhampton	d										17 14												
Havant	d	16 46		16 52					17 00	17 12	17 17			17 30					17 46			17 56	
Warblington	d								17 02		17 19												
Emsworth	d	16 50		16 56					17 05	17 17	17 22								17 50			18 00	
Southbourne	d	16 53		16 59					17 08		17 25								17 53			18 03	
Nutbourne	d								17 10		17 28												
Bosham	d			17 03					17 14		17 31												
Fishbourne (Sussex)	d								17 17		17 34												
Chichester 4	a	17 00		17 08					17 20	17 25	17 37			17 42					18 00			18 10	
	d	17 00		17 13					17 21	17 25	17 38			17 43					18 00			18 13	
Bognor Regis 4	d		16 56			17 18							17 30			17 51					17 57		
Barnham	a	17 08	17 02	17 20		17 24			17 28	17 33	17 45		17 36	17 50		17 57			18 08		18 03	18 20	
	d	17 08	17 03	17 21		17 25			17 29	17 33	17 46		17 37	17 51					18 08	18 08	18 04	18 21	
Bognor Regis	a																			18 14			
Ford 4	d		17 07			17 29				17 38	17 50		17 41								18 08		
Littlehampton 4	a					17 37					17 55												
	d				17 15										17 45								18 15
Angmering 3	d	17 17			17 23					17 44					17 53				18 18				18 23
Goring-by-Sea	d				17 27					17 48					17 57								18 27
Durrington-on-Sea	d				17 30					17 50					18 00								18 30
West Worthing	d				17 32					17 52					18 02								18 32
Worthing 4	a	17 24			17 34				17 43	17 55					18 04				18 25				18 34
	d	17 26			17 36				17 43	17 56					18 06				18 25				18 35
East Worthing	d								17 46										18 28				
Lancing	d	17 30							17 49	18 00					18 10				18 31				18 39
Shoreham-by-Sea	d	17 34			17 42				17 53	18 04					18 14				18 35				18 43
Southwick	d	17 37							17 56	18 07									18 38				
Fishersgate	d								17 58										18 40				
Portslade	d	17 40			17 47				18 00	18 10									18 42				18 48
Aldrington	d								18 02										18 44				
Hove 2	d	17 44			17 51			18 01	18 05	18 14					18 21		18 24		18 47				18 52
Brighton 10	a	17 48						18 05	18 09	18 18							18 28		18 51				
Preston Park	d																						
Burgess Hill	a				18 03										18 33								
Haywards Heath 3	a				18 10										18 41								19 06
Arundel	d		17 12										17 46								18 13		
Amberley	d		17 17																		18 18		
Pulborough	d		17 23										17 55								18 24		
Billingshurst	d		17 29										18 01								18 30		
Christs Hospital	d		17 36										18 08								18 37		
Horsham 4	a		17 40	17 48									18 12	18 18							18 42	18 48	
	d			17 52			18 00							18 22				18 30				18 52	
Crawley	d			18 01			18 14							18 31				18 44				19 01	
Three Bridges 4	a			18 04			18 17							18 34				18 47				19 04	
Gatwick Airport 10 ✈	a			18 09	18 26		18 22							18 39	18 56			18 52				19 09	19 25
	d			18 10	18 27		18 23							18 40	18 57			18 53				19 10	19 26
Horley	a						18 26											18 56					
Redhill 5	a			18 17			18 36							18 47				19 06				19 17	
East Croydon	a			18 29	18 42		18 54							18 59	19 12			19 24				19 28	19 42
London Bridge 4 ⊖	a																						
Clapham Junction 10	a			18 40	18 52		19 05							19 11	19 21			19 37				19 40	19 52
London Victoria 15 ⊖	a			18 47	18 59		19 13							19 18	19 29			19 44				19 47	19 59

A ⌶ from Horsham B ⌶ from Haywards Heath

Southampton, Portsmouth and Sussex Coast - Brighton, Gatwick Airport and London

		SN	SN	SN	SN	SN	SN	SN	SW	SN	SN	SN	SN	SN	SN	SN	SN	SN	SN	SN	SN	SN	SN
		◇	◇	◇	◇1	1	◇1	1	1	◇	◇	◇	◇	◇1	◇	1	◇1	◇1	◇1	◇	◇1	1	◇1
Southampton Central	d				17 33				17 44								18 11				18 33		
Swanwick	d				17 50				18 11								18 28				18 50		
Fareham	d				17 56				18 18								18 35				18 56		
Portchester	d								18 23								18 40						
Cosham	d				18 05				18 28								18 44				19 05		
Portsmouth Harbour	d													18 28					18 37				
Portsmouth & Southsea	d		17 46					17 59						18 32					18 42				
Fratton	d		17 50					18 04						18 36					18 46				
Hilsea	d		17 54					18 08	18a33										18 50				
Bedhampton	d							18 13															
Havant	d		18 00		18 11			18 16						18 44			18 51		18 56		19 11		
Warblington	d		18 02					18 18											18 58				
Emsworth	d		18 05		18 15			18 21						18 48			18 55		19 01				
Southbourne	d		18 08					18 24						18 51			18 58		19 04				
Nutbourne	d		18 10					18 26											19 07				
Bosham	d		18 14					18 30											19 10				
Fishbourne (Sussex)	d		18 17					18 33											19 13				
Chichester 4	a		18 20		18 24			18 36						18 58			19 05		19 17		19 22		
	d		18 21		18 25			18 37						18 59			19 06		19 17		19 22		
Bognor Regis 4	d	18 19					18 33					18 46			19 03								19 36
Barnham	a	18 25	18 28		18 32		18 39	18 44				18 52		19 06	19 09		19 13		19 25		19 30		19 42
	d		18 29		18 33		18 40	18 45				18 53	18 55	19 07	19 10		19 14		19 25		19 30		19 43
Bognor Regis	a												19 01										
Ford 4	d		18 33				18 44					18 57			19 14		19 18		19 30				19 47
Littlehampton 4	a		18 40									19 02			19 19				19 38				
	d										18 52							19 15					
Angmering 3	d				18 42		18 53				19 00			19 16				19 23			19 40		19 53
Goring-by-Sea	d						18 57				19 04							19 27			19 44		19 57
Durrington-on-Sea	d				18 48		19 00				19 07							19 30			19 46		20 00
West Worthing	d						19 02				19 09							19 32			19 48		20 02
Worthing 4	a				18 52		19 04				19 11			19 23				19 34			19 51		20 04
	d				18 52		19 05				19 12			19 24				19 35			19 52		20 05
East Worthing	d				18 55						19 14			19 26							19 55		
Lancing	d				18 58		19 09				19 17			19 29				19 39			19 58		20 09
Shoreham-by-Sea	d				19 02		19 13				19 22			19 33				19 43			20 02		20 13
Southwick	d				19 05						19 25			19 36							20 05		
Fishersgate	d				19 07						19 27			19 38							20 07		
Portslade	d				19 09		19 18				19 29			19 40				19 48			20 09		20 18
Aldrington	d				19 11						19 31			19 43							20 11		
Hove 2	d			19 00	19 14		19 22			19 24	19 34			19 45				19 52		19 54	20 14		20 22
Brighton 10	a			19 04	19 18					19 28	19 38			19 49						19 58	20 18		
Preston Park	d																						
Burgess Hill	a						19 32																20 32
Haywards Heath 3	a						19 36											20 04					20 37
Arundel	d							18 52									19 23						
Amberley	d																19 28						
Pulborough	d							19 01									19 34						
Billingshurst	d							19 08									19 41						
Christs Hospital	d																19 47						
Horsham 4	a							19 16									19 51						
	d					19 02		19 17								19 32	19 52					20 02	
Crawley	d					19 14		19 26								19 45	20 01					20 14	
Three Bridges 4	a					19 18		19 29								19 49	20 04					20 18	20 47
Gatwick Airport 10 ✈	a					19 22	19 55	19 39								19 55	20 10	20 25				20 22	20 51
	d					19 23	19 56	19 40								19 56	20 11	20 26				20 23	20 53
Horley	a					19 26										19 59						20 26	
Redhill 5	a					19 38		19 47								20 05	20 18					20 36	
East Croydon	a					19 58	20 11	20 00								20 23	20 30	20 41				20 57	21 08
London Bridge 4 ⊖	a																						
Clapham Junction 10	a					20 08	20 20	20 11								20 37	20 40	20 50				21 07	21 18
London Victoria 15 ⊖	a					20 15	20 28	20 20								20 44	20 50	20 58				21 15	21 26

Southampton, Portsmouth and Sussex Coast - Brighton, Gatwick Airport and London

Station		SN ◇	SN ◇	SN ◇	SW 1	SN ◇1	SN ◇	SN 1	SN ◇1	SN ◇1	SN ◇1	SN ◇	SN ◇1	SN 1	SN ◇1	SN ◇	SN ◇	SN ◇	SW 1	SN ◇	SN ◇	SN 1
Southampton Central	d				18 44				19 12				19 33						19 44			
Swanwick	d				19 11				19 29				19 51						20 11			
Fareham	d				19 18				19 36				19 57						20 18			
Portchester	d				19 23				19 41										20 23			
Cosham	d				19 28				19 46				20 06						20 28			
Portsmouth Harbour	d										19 40											
Portsmouth & Southsea	d			18 59		19 32					19 44							19 59		20 32		
Fratton	d			19 04		19 36					19 48							20 04		20 36		
Hilsea	d			19 08	19a33													20 08	20a33			
Bedhampton	d			19 13														20 14				
Havant	d			19 16		19 46			19 52		19 57		20 12					20 17		20 45		
Warblington	d			19 18							19 59							20 19				
Emsworth	d			19 21		19 50			19 56		20 02		20 16					20 22		20 49		
Southbourne	d			19 24		19 53			19 59		20 05							20 25		20 52		
Nutbourne	d			19 26							20 07							20 27				
Bosham	d			19 30							20 11							20 31				
Fishbourne (Sussex)	d			19 33							20 14							20 34				
Chichester 4	a			19 36		20 00			20 06		20 17		20 24					20 37		20 59		
	d			19 40		20 01			20 07		20 18		20 25					20 38		20 59		
Bognor Regis 4	d						20 05								20 33						21 04	
Barnham	a			19 47		20 08	20 11		20 14		20 25		20 32		20 39			20 45		21 07	21 10	
	d			19 48		20 09	20 12		20 15		20 27		20 33		20 40			20 46		21 07	21 11	
Bognor Regis	a																					
Ford 4	d			19 52			20 16		20 19		20 31				20 44			20 50			21 15	
Littlehampton 4	a			19 58			20 21				20 36							20 55			21 20	
	d		19 52							20 15							20 52					
Angmering 3	d		20 00			20 18				20 23			20 42		20 53		21 00			21 16		
Goring-by-Sea	d		20 04							20 27					20 57		21 04					
Durrington-on-Sea	d		20 07							20 30			20 48		21 00		21 07					
West Worthing	d		20 09							20 32					21 02		21 09					
Worthing 4	a		20 11			20 25				20 34			20 52		21 04		21 11			21 23		
	d		20 12			20 25				20 35			20 52		21 05		21 12			21 24		
East Worthing	d		20 14			20 28							20 55				21 14			21 26		
Lancing	d		20 17			20 31				20 39			20 58		21 09		21 17			21 29		
Shoreham-by-Sea	d		20 22			20 35				20 43			21 02		21 13		21 22			21 33		
Southwick	d		20 25			20 38							21 05				21 25			21 36		
Fishersgate	d		20 27			20 40							21 07				21 27			21 38		
Portslade	d		20 29			20 42				20 48			21 09		21 18		21 29			21 40		
Aldrington	d		20 31			20 44							21 11				21 31			21 43		
Hove 2	d	20 24	20 34			20 47				20 52		20 54	21 14		21 22	21 24	21 34			21 45		
Brighton 10	a	20 28	20 38			20 51						20 58	21 18			21 28	21 38			21 49		
Preston Park	d																					
Burgess Hill	a														21 32							
Haywards Heath 3	a									21 05					21 37							
Arundel	d								20 24													
Amberley	d								20 29													
Pulborough	d								20 35													
Billingshurst	d								20 41													
Christs Hospital	d								20 48													
Horsham 4	a								20 52													
	d							20 32	20 52					21 02								21 32
Crawley	d							20 45	21 01					21 14								21 45
Three Bridges 4	a							20 48	21 05					21 18	21 47							21 48
Gatwick Airport 10	a							20 56	21 10	21 25				21 22	21 51							21 55
	d							20 57	21 11	21 26				21 23	21 53							21 56
Horley	a							20 59						21 26								21 59
Redhill 5	a							21 06	21 18					21 36								22 05
East Croydon	a							21 25	21 30	21 41				21 54	22 08							22 24
London Bridge 4	a																					
Clapham Junction 10	a							21 37	21 40	21 51				22 07	22 18							22 37
London Victoria 15	a							21 45	21 50	21 58				22 14	22 26							22 44

Southampton, Portsmouth and Sussex Coast - Brighton, Gatwick Airport and London

Station		SN ◇1	SN ◇1 A	SN ◇1	SN ◇	SN ◇1	SN ◇	SN ◇	SN 1	SN ◇	SN ◇	SN ◇1	SW 1	SN ◇	SN ◇	SN ◇1	SN 1	SN ◇	SN ◇	SN ◇1	SN 1	SN 1	SN ◇
Southampton Central	d	20 11				20 33							20 44			21 13				21 33			
Swanwick	d	20 28				20 50							21 11			21 33				21 51			
Fareham	d	20 35				20 57							21 18			21 40				21 58			
Portchester	d	20 40											21 23			21 45				22 03			
Cosham	d	20 44				21 06							21 28			21 49				22 07			
Portsmouth Harbour	d			20 40													21 40						
Portsmouth & Southsea	d			20 44								21 15					21 44						
Fratton	d			20 48								21 19					21 48						
Hilsea	d											21 23	21a33				21 52						
Bedhampton	d											21 28					21 57						
Havant	d	20 51		20 57		21 12						21 31				21 56	22 00			22 14			
Warblington	d			20 59								21 33								22 16			
Emsworth	d	20 55		21 02		21 16						21 36								22 19			
Southbourne	d	20 58		21 05								21 39								22 22			
Nutbourne	d			21 07								21 41								22 24			
Bosham	d			21 11								21 45								22 28			
Fishbourne (Sussex)	d			21 14								21 48								22 31			
Chichester 4	a	21 05		21 17		21 24						21 51				22 06	22 10			22 34			
	d	21 07		21 18		21 25						21 52				22 07	22 11			22 34		22 40	
Bognor Regis 4	d						21 39							22 00					22 30				
Barnham	a	21 14		21 25		21 32	21 45					21 59		22 06		22 14	22 18		22 36	22 42		22 47	
	d	21 15		21 26		21 33		21 52				22 00				22 15	22 19	22 22	22 37			22 48	
Bognor Regis	a							21 58										22 28					
Ford 4	d	21 19		21 30		21 37						22 04				22 19	22 23		22 41			22 52	
Littlehampton 4	a			21 35												22 24			22 46				
	d		21 15								21 52					22 33							
Angmering 3	d		21 23			21 43					22 00	22 11				22 41							
Goring-by-Sea	d		21 27			21 47					22 04	22 15				22 45							
Durrington-on-Sea	d		21 30			21 50					22 07	22 18				22 47							
West Worthing	d		21 32			21 52					22 09	22 20				22 49							
Worthing 4	a		21 34			21 54					22 11	22 22				22 52							
	d		21 35			21 55					22 12	22 23				22 52							
East Worthing	d					21 57					22 14	22 25				22 55							
Lancing	d		21 39			22 00					22 17	22 28				22 58							
Shoreham-by-Sea	d		21 43			22 04					22 22	22 32				23 02							
Southwick	d					22 07					22 25	22 35				23 05							
Fishersgate	d					22 09					22 27	22 37				23 07							
Portslade	d		21 48			22 11					22 29	22 39				23 09							
Aldrington	d					22 14					22 31	22 42				23 11							
Hove 2	d		21 52		21 54	22 16				22 24	22 34	22 44			22 54	23 14							23 24
Brighton 10	a				21 58	22 21				22 28	22 38	22 48			22 58	23 18							23 28
Preston Park	d																						
Burgess Hill	a		22 03																				
Haywards Heath 3	a		22 10																				
Arundel	d	21 24															22 28					22 57	
Amberley	d	21 29																				23 02	
Pulborough	d	21 35															22 37					23 08	
Billingshurst	d	21 41															22 43					23 14	
Christs Hospital	d	21 48															22 50					23 21	
Horsham 4	a	21 52															22 54					23 25	
	d	21 52							22 02								22 55				23 02	23 25	
Crawley	d	22 01							22 14								23 03				23 14	23 38	
Three Bridges 4	a	22 05							22 18								23 07				23 18	23 42	
Gatwick Airport 10	a	22 10	22 25						22 23												23 22		
	d	22 11	22 26						22 24												23 23		
Horley	a								22 27												23 26		
Redhill 5	a	22 18							22 37												23 36		
East Croydon	a	22 30	22 41						22 55												23 54		
London Bridge 4	a																						
Clapham Junction 10	a	22 40	22 50						23 06												00 11		
London Victoria 15	a	22 50	22 57						23 15												00 18		

A from Haywards Heath

Table 188

Mondays to Fridays

Southampton, Portsmouth and Sussex Coast - Brighton, Gatwick Airport and London

		SN	SW	SN	SN	SN	SN	SN	SN	SN	SN	SW
		◇1	1	◇1	◇	◇	◇1	◇1	◇	◇1	◇1	1
Southampton Central	d		21 44	22 13				22 33				22 44
Swanwick	d		22 11	22 30				22 50				23 11
Fareham	d		22 18	22 37				22 57				23 18
Portchester	d		22 23	22 42								23 23
Cosham	d		22 28	22 47				23 05				23 28
Portsmouth Harbour	d	22 15					22 44				23 15	
Portsmouth & Southsea	d	22 19					22 48				23 19	
Fratton	d	22 23					22 52				23 23	
Hilsea	d	22 27	22a33				22 56				23 27	23a33
Bedhampton	d	22 32					23 01				23 33	
Havant	d	22 35		22 57			23 05	23 12			23 36	
Warblington	d										23 38	
Emsworth	d	22 39		23 01							23 41	
Southbourne	d	22 42		23 04							23 44	
Nutbourne	d										23 47	
Bosham	d										23 50	
Fishbourne (Sussex)	d										23 53	
Chichester 4	a	22 49		23 11			23 16	23 22			23 57	
	d	22 52		23 12			23 17	23 23		23 52	23 57	
Bognor Regis 4	d				23 15							
Barnham	a	22 59		23 19	23 21		23 24	23 30		23 59	00 05	
	d	23 00		23 20			23 25	23 31	23 36	00 01	00 06	
Bognor Regis	a								23 42			
Ford 4	d	23 04					23 29			00 05	00 10	
Littlehampton 4	a			23 31			23 34	23 42		00 10	00 15	
	d						23 39					
Angmering 3	d	23 11					23 47					
Goring-by-Sea	d	23 15					23 51					
Durrington-on-Sea	d	23 17					23 53					
West Worthing	d	23 19					23 55					
Worthing 4	a	23 22					23 58					
	d	23 22					23 59					
East Worthing	d	23 25					00 01					
Lancing	d	23 28					00 04					
Shoreham-by-Sea	d	23 32					00 08					
Southwick	d	23 35					00 11					
Fishersgate	d	23 37					00 13					
Portslade	d	23 39					00 15					
Aldrington	d	23 41					00 18					
Hove 2	d	23 44				23 54	00 20					
Brighton 10	a	23 48				23 58	00 25					
Preston Park	d											
Burgess Hill	a											
Haywards Heath 3	a											
Arundel	d											
Amberley	d											
Pulborough	d											
Billingshurst	d											
Christs Hospital	d											
Horsham 4	a											
	d											
Crawley	d											
Three Bridges 4	a											
Gatwick Airport 10	a											
	d											
Horley	a											
Redhill 5	a											
East Croydon	a											
London Bridge 4	a											
Clapham Junction 10	a											
London Victoria 15	a											

Table 188

Saturdays

Southampton, Portsmouth and Sussex Coast - Brighton, Gatwick Airport and London

		SN	SN	SN	SN	SN	SN	SN	SN	SN	SN	SN	SN	SN	SN	SN	SN	SN	SN	SN	SN	SN	SN
		◇1	1	◇1	◇1	◇1	1	◇1	◇	◇	1	◇1	◇	◇	◇	1	◇1	◇1	◇	◇	◇	◇	◇1
Southampton Central	d																						
Swanwick	d																						
Fareham	d																						
Portchester	d																						
Cosham	d																						
Portsmouth Harbour	d	22p44			23p15																		
Portsmouth & Southsea	d	22p48			23p19			04 56															
Fratton	d	22p52			23p23			05 00															
Hilsea	d	22p56			23p27																		
Bedhampton	d	23p01			23p33																		
Havant	d	23p05			23p36			05 08									05 52						
Warblington	d				23p38																		
Emsworth	d				23p41												05 56						
Southbourne	d				23p44												05 59						
Nutbourne	d				23p47																		
Bosham	d				23p50																		
Fishbourne (Sussex)	d				23p53																		
Chichester 4	a	23p16			23p57			05 19									06 06						
	d	23p17		23p52	23p57			05 19									06 06						06 25
Bognor Regis 4	d								05 13					05 43	06 04				06 13				
Barnham	a	23p24		23p59	00 05			05 27	05 19					05 49	06 10		06 14		06 19				06 32
	d	23p25		00 01	00 06	04 48		05 27	05 31					05 50			06 14		06 20	06 22			06 33
Bognor Regis	a																			06 28			
Ford 4	d	23p29		00 05	00 10	04 52			05 35					05 54			06 19		06 24				06 37
Littlehampton 4	a	23p34		00 10	00 15	04 57			05 40										06 29				
	d	23p39				05 02						05 45						06 15					
Angmering 3	d	23p47				05 10						05 53		06 00				06 23					06 43
Goring-by-Sea	d	23p51				05 14						05 57		06 04				06 27					06 47
Durrington-on-Sea	d	23p53				05 17						06 00		06 07				06 30					06 50
West Worthing	d	23p55				05 19						06 02		06 09				06 32				06 39	06 52
Worthing 4	a	23p58				05 21		05 41				06 04		06 11				06 34				06 41	06 54
	d	23p59				05 22		05 42				06 05		06 12				06 35				06 42	06 56
East Worthing	d	00 01				05 24								06 14								06 44	
Lancing	d	00 04				05 27						06 09		06 17				06 39				06 47	07 00
Shoreham-by-Sea	d	00 08				05 32		05 48				06 13		06 22				06 43				06 52	07 04
Southwick	d	00 11				05 35								06 25								06 55	07 07
Fishersgate	d	00 13				05 37								06 27								06 57	
Portslade	d	00 15				05 39						06 17		06 29				06 47				06 59	07 10
Aldrington	d	00 18				05 41								06 31								07 01	
Hove 2	d	00 20				05 44		05 54		05 56		06 21	06 24	06 34				06 51			06 54	07 04	07 14
Brighton 10	a	00 25				05 48				06 00			06 28	06 38							06 58	07 08	07 18
Preston Park	d																	06 55					
Burgess Hill	a																	07 04					
Haywards Heath 3	a							06 07				06 35						07 09					
Arundel	d																06 23						
Amberley	d																06 28						
Pulborough	d																06 34						
Billingshurst	d																06 41						
Christs Hospital	d																06 47						
Horsham 4	a																06 51						
	d		23p02				05 30				06 00					06 30	06 52						
Crawley	d		23p14				05 43				06 13					06 43	07 01						
Three Bridges 4	a		23p18				05 46	06 20			06 16	06 49				06 46	07 04						
Gatwick Airport 10	a		23p22				05 52	06 24			06 22	06 53				06 52	07 09	07 25					
	d		23p23				05 53	06 25			06 23	06 55				06 53	07 10	07 26					
Horley	a		23p26				05 56				06 26					06 56							
Redhill 5	a		23p36				06 06				06 36					07 02	07 17						
East Croydon	a		23p54				06 24	06 40			06 54	07 10				07 24	07 29	07 41					
London Bridge 4	a						06 43				07 13					07 43							
Clapham Junction 10	a		00 11					06 50				07 20					07 39	07 51					
London Victoria 15	a		00 18					06 57				07 27					07 46	07 58					

Southampton, Portsmouth and Sussex Coast - Brighton, Gatwick Airport and London

		SN	SN	SW	SN	SN	SN	SN	SN	SN	SN	SN	SN	SN	SN	SN	SN	SN	SN	GW	SN	SN	SN
		■	◇	■	◇	◇■	◇■	◇■	◇	◇	◇	■	◇■	◇	◇■	◇■	◇■	◇	◇		◇■	■	◇
Southampton Central	d			05 44												06 13					06 33		
Swanwick	d			06 11												06 33					06 50		
Fareham	d			06 18												06 40					06 56		
Portchester	d			06 23												06 45							
Cosham	d			06 28												06 49					07 05		
Portsmouth Harbour	d						06 12						06 29							06 48			
Portsmouth & Southsea	d		05 59				06 16						06 33							06 54			06 56
Fratton	d		06 04				06 20						06 37							06 58			07 01
Hilsea	d		06 08	06a33																			07 05
Bedhampton	d		06 13																				07 13
Havant	d		06 16				06 30						06 46			06 56				07 08	07 11		07 16
Warblington	d		06 18																				07 18
Emsworth	d		06 21										06 50			07 00					07 15		07 21
Southbourne	d		06 24										06 53			07 03							07 24
Nutbourne	d		06 26																				07 26
Bosham	d		06 30																				07 30
Fishbourne (Sussex)	d		06 33																				07 33
Chichester	a		06 36				06 40						07 00			07 10				07 19	07 23		07 36
	d		06 37				06 41						07 00			07 11				07 20	07 25		07 37
Bognor Regis	d				06 39	06 30								07 07	06 56								
Barnham	a		06 44		06 45	06 36	06 48						07 08	07 13	07 02	07 18				07 27	07 32		07 44
	d		06 45			06 37	06 49		06 52				07 08	07 15	07 03	07 19				07 28	07 33		07 45
Bognor Regis	a								06 58														
Ford	d		06 49			06 41								07 19	07 07						07 37		07 49
Littlehampton	a		06 54											07 24									07 54
	d							06 45									07 15						
Angmering	d							06 55					07 17				07 23				07 43		
Goring-by-Sea	d							06 59									07 27				07 47		
Durrington-on-Sea	d							07 02									07 30				07 50		
West Worthing	d							07 04			07 09						07 32		07 39		07 52		
Worthing	a							07 06			07 11		07 24				07 34		07 41	07 45	07 54		
	d							07 07			07 12		07 26				07 36		07 42	07 50	07 56		
East Worthing	d										07 14								07 44				
Lancing	d							07 11			07 17		07 30						07 47		08 00		
Shoreham-by-Sea	d							07 15			07 22		07 34				07 42		07 52	07 57	08 04		
Southwick	d										07 25		07 37						07 55		08 07		
Fishersgate	d										07 27								07 57				
Portslade	d										07 29		07 40				07 47		07 59		08 10		
Aldrington	d										07 31								08 01				
Hove	d							07 22		07 24	07 34		07 44				07 51	07 54	08 04	08 08	08 14		
Brighton	a									07 28	07 38		07 48					07 58	08 08	08 15	08 18		
Preston Park	d																07 55						
Burgess Hill	a																08 03						
Haywards Heath	a							07 35									08 09						
Arundel	d					06 46									07 12								
Amberley	d														07 17								
Pulborough	d					06 55									07 23								
Billingshurst	d					07 01									07 29								
Christs Hospital	d														07 36								
Horsham	a					07 10	07 16								07 40	07 46							
	d	07 00				07 20						07 30			07 50							08 00	
Crawley	d	07 13				07 29						07 43			07 59							08 13	
Three Bridges	a	07 16				07 32						07 46			08 02							08 16	
Gatwick Airport	a	07 22				07 37		07 55				07 52			08 07		08 25					08 22	
	d	07 23				07 38		07 56				07 53			08 08		08 26					08 23	
Horley	a	07 26				07 41						07 56										08 26	
Redhill	a	07 36				07 47						08 02			08 15							08 36	
East Croydon	a	07 54				07 59		08 11				08 24			08 27		08 41					08 54	
London Bridge	a	08 13										08 43										09 13	
Clapham Junction	a					08 09		08 21							08 37		08 51						
London Victoria	a					08 16		08 28							08 44		08 58						

Southampton, Portsmouth and Sussex Coast - Brighton, Gatwick Airport and London

		SW	SN	SN	SN	SN	SN	SN	SN	SN	SN	SN	SN	SN	SN	SN	SN	SN	SN	SN	SW	SN
		■	◇	◇■	◇■	◇■	◇	◇	◇	■	◇■	◇	◇■	◇■	◇■	◇	◇	◇■	■	◇	■	◇
													🚌	A 🚌								
Southampton Central	d	06 44												07 13				07 33			07 44	
Swanwick	d	07 11												07 33				07 50			08 11	
Fareham	d	07 18												07 40				07 56			08 18	
Portchester	d	07 23												07 45							08 23	
Cosham	d	07 28												07 49				08 05			08 28	
Portsmouth Harbour	d				07 12						07 29											
Portsmouth & Southsea	d				07 16						07 33									07 59		
Fratton	d				07 20						07 37									08 04		
Hilsea	d	07a33																		08 08	08a33	
Bedhampton	d																			08 13		
Havant	d				07 30						07 46			07 56				08 11		08 16		
Warblington	d																			08 18		
Emsworth	d										07 50			08 00				08 15		08 21		
Southbourne	d										07 53			08 03						08 24		
Nutbourne	d																			08 27		
Bosham	d																			08 30		
Fishbourne (Sussex)	d																			08 33		
Chichester	a				07 40						08 00			08 10				08 23		08 36		
	d				07 41						08 00			08 11				08 25		08 37		
Bognor Regis	d		07 39	07 30								08 07	07 56									08 39
Barnham	a		07 45	07 36	07 48						08 08	08 13	08 02	08 18				08 32		08 44		08 45
	d			07 37	07 49		07 52				08 08	08 15	08 03	08 19				08 33		08 45		
Bognor Regis	a						07 58															
Ford	d			07 41								08 19	08 07					08 37		08 49		
Littlehampton	a											08 24								08 54		
	d					07 45									08 15							
Angmering	d					07 53					08 17				08 23			08 43				
Goring-by-Sea	d					07 57									08 27			08 47				
Durrington-on-Sea	d					08 00									08 30			08 50				
West Worthing	d					08 02			08 09						08 32		08 39	08 52				
Worthing	a					08 04			08 11		08 24				08 34		08 41	08 54				
	d					08 06			08 12		08 26				08 36		08 42	08 56				
East Worthing	d								08 14								08 44					
Lancing	d					08 10			08 17		08 30						08 47	09 00				
Shoreham-by-Sea	d					08 14			08 22		08 34				08 42		08 52	09 04				
Southwick	d								08 25		08 37						08 55	09 07				
Fishersgate	d								08 27								08 57					
Portslade	d								08 29		08 40				08 47		08 59	09 10				
Aldrington	d								08 31								09 01					
Hove	d					08 21		08 24	08 34		08 44				08 51	08 54	09 04	09 14				
Brighton	a							08 28	08 38		08 48					08 58	09 08	09 18				
Preston Park	d														08 55							
Burgess Hill	a														09 03							
Haywards Heath	a					08 35									09 09							
Arundel	d			07 46									08 12									
Amberley	d												08 17									
Pulborough	d			07 55									08 23									
Billingshurst	d			08 01									08 29									
Christs Hospital	d												08 36									
Horsham	a			08 10	08 16								08 40	08 46								
	d			08 20						08 30			08 50						09 00			
Crawley	d			08 29						08 43			08 59						09 13			
Three Bridges	a			08 32						08 46			09 02						09 16			
Gatwick Airport	a			08 37		08 55				08 52			09 07		09 25				09 22			
	d			08 38		08 56				08 53			09 08		09 26				09 23			
Horley	a			08 41						08 56									09 26			
Redhill	a			08 47						09 02			09 15						09 36			
East Croydon	a			08 59		09 11				09 24			09 27		09 41				09 54			
London Bridge	a									09 43									10 13			
Clapham Junction	a			09 09		09 21							09 37		09 51							
London Victoria	a			09 16		09 28							09 44		09 58							

A 🚌 from Horsham

Southampton, Portsmouth and Sussex Coast - Brighton, Gatwick Airport and London

		SN	SN	SN	SN	SN	SN	SN	SN	SN	SN	SN	SN	SN	SN	SN	SN	SN	SW	SN	SN	SN	SN
		◇1	◇1	◇1	◇	◇	◇	1	◇1	◇	◇1	◇1	◇1	◇	◇	◇1	1	◇	1	◇	◇1	◇1	◇1
											(trolley)	A (trolley)											
Southampton Central	d											08 13				08 33			08 44				
Swanwick	d											08 33				08 50			09 11				
Fareham	d											08 40				08 56			09 18				
Portchester	d											08 45							09 23				
Cosham	d											08 49				09 05			09 28				
Portsmouth Harbour	d		08 12						08 29													09 12	
Portsmouth & Southsea	d		08 16						08 33									08 59				09 16	
Fratton	d		08 20						08 37									09 04				09 20	
Hilsea	d																	09 08	09a33				
Bedhampton	d																	09 13					
Havant	d		08 30						08 46			08 56				09 11		09 16				09 30	
Warblington	d																	09 18					
Emsworth	d								08 50			09 00				09 15		09 21					
Southbourne	d								08 53			09 03						09 24					
Nutbourne	d																	09 26					
Bosham	d																	09 30					
Fishbourne (Sussex)	d																	09 33					
Chichester 4	a		08 40						09 00			09 10				09 23		09 36				09 40	
	d		08 41						09 00			09 11				09 25		09 37				09 41	
Bognor Regis 4	d	08 30								09 07	08 56									09 39	09 30		
Barnham	a	08 36	08 48						09 08	09 13	09 02	09 18				09 32		09 44		09 45	09 36	09 48	
	d	08 37	08 49		08 52				09 08	09 15	09 03	09 19				09 33		09 45			09 37	09 49	
Bognor Regis	a				08 58																		
Ford 4	d	08 41								09 19	09 07					09 37		09 49			09 41		
Littlehampton 4	a									09 24								09 54					
	d			08 45									09 15										09 45
Angmering 3	d			08 53					09 17				09 23			09 43							09 53
Goring-by-Sea	d			08 57									09 27			09 47							09 57
Durrington-on-Sea	d			09 00									09 30			09 50							10 00
West Worthing	d			09 02			09 09						09 32		09 39	09 52							10 02
Worthing 4	a			09 04			09 11		09 24				09 34		09 41	09 54							10 04
	d			09 06			09 12		09 26				09 36		09 42	09 56							10 06
East Worthing	d						09 14								09 44								
Lancing	d			09 10			09 17		09 30						09 47	10 00							10 10
Shoreham-by-Sea	d			09 14			09 22		09 34				09 42		09 52	10 04							10 14
Southwick	d						09 25		09 37						09 55	10 07							
Fishersgate	d						09 27								09 57								
Portslade	d						09 29		09 40				09 47		09 59	10 10							
Aldrington	d						09 31								10 01								
Hove 2	d			09 21		09 24	09 34		09 44				09 51	09 54	10 04	10 14							10 21
Brighton 10	a					09 28	09 38		09 48					09 58	10 08	10 18							
Preston Park	d												09 55										
Burgess Hill	a												10 03										
Haywards Heath 3	a			09 35									10 09										10 35
Arundel	d	08 46									09 12										09 46		
Amberley	d										09 17												
Pulborough	d	08 55									09 23										09 55		
Billingshurst	d	09 01									09 29										10 01		
Christs Hospital	d										09 36												
Horsham 4	a	09 10	09 16								09 40	09 46									10 10	10 16	
	d	09 20						09 30			09 50						10 00				10 20		
Crawley	d	09 29						09 43			09 59						10 13				10 29		
Three Bridges 4	a	09 32						09 46			10 02						10 16				10 32		
Gatwick Airport 10	a	09 37		09 55				09 52			10 07		10 25				10 22				10 37		10 55
	d	09 38		09 56				09 53			10 08		10 26				10 23				10 38		10 56
Horley	a	09 41						09 56									10 26				10 41		
Redhill 5	a	09 47						10 02			10 15						10 36				10 47		
East Croydon	a	09 59		10 11				10 24			10 27		10 41				10 54				10 59		11 11
London Bridge 4	a							10 43									11 13						
Clapham Junction 10	a	10 09		10 21							10 37		10 51								11 09		11 21
London Victoria 15	a	10 16		10 28							10 44		10 58								11 16		11 28

A (trolley) from Horsham

Southampton, Portsmouth and Sussex Coast - Brighton, Gatwick Airport and London

		SN	SN	SN	SN	SN	SN	SN	SN	SN	SN	SN	SN	SN	SN	SW	SN	SN	SN	SN	SN	SN	SN
		◇	◇	◇	1	◇1	◇	◇1	◇1	◇1	◇	◇	◇1	1	◇	1	◇	◇1	◇1	◇1	◇	◇	◇
								(trolley)	A (trolley)														
Southampton Central	d								09 13				09 33			09 44							
Swanwick	d								09 33				09 50			10 11							
Fareham	d								09 40				09 56			10 18							
Portchester	d								09 45							10 23							
Cosham	d								09 49				10 05			10 28							
Portsmouth Harbour	d					09 29													10 12				
Portsmouth & Southsea	d					09 33									09 59				10 16				
Fratton	d					09 37									10 04				10 20				
Hilsea	d														10 08	10a33							
Bedhampton	d														10 13								
Havant	d					09 46			09 56				10 11		10 16				10 30				
Warblington	d														10 18								
Emsworth	d					09 50			10 00				10 15		10 21								
Southbourne	d					09 53			10 03						10 24								
Nutbourne	d														10 26								
Bosham	d														10 30								
Fishbourne (Sussex)	d														10 33								
Chichester 4	a					10 00			10 10				10 23		10 36				10 40				
	d					10 00			10 11				10 25		10 37				10 41				
Bognor Regis 4	d						10 07	09 56									10 39	10 30					
Barnham	a					10 08	10 13	10 02	10 18				10 32		10 44		10 45	10 36	10 48				
	d	09 52				10 08	10 15	10 03	10 19				10 33		10 45			10 37	10 49		10 52		
Bognor Regis	a	09 58																			10 58		
Ford 4	d						10 19	10 07					10 37		10 49			10 41					
Littlehampton 4	a						10 24								10 54								
	d									10 15										10 45			
Angmering 3	d					10 17				10 23			10 43							10 53			
Goring-by-Sea	d									10 27			10 47							10 57			
Durrington-on-Sea	d									10 30			10 50							11 00			
West Worthing	d			10 09						10 32		10 39	10 52							11 02			11 09
Worthing 4	a			10 11		10 24				10 34		10 41	10 54							11 04			11 11
	d			10 12		10 26				10 36		10 42	10 56							11 06			11 12
East Worthing	d			10 14								10 44											11 14
Lancing	d			10 17		10 30						10 47	11 00							11 10			11 17
Shoreham-by-Sea	d			10 22		10 34				10 42		10 52	11 04							11 14			11 22
Southwick	d			10 25		10 37						10 55	11 07										11 25
Fishersgate	d			10 27								10 57											11 27
Portslade	d			10 29		10 40				10 47		10 59	11 10										11 29
Aldrington	d			10 31								11 01											11 31
Hove 2	d		10 24	10 34		10 44				10 51	10 54	11 04	11 14							11 21		11 24	11 34
Brighton 10	a		10 28	10 38		10 48					10 58	11 08	11 18									11 28	11 38
Preston Park	d									10 55													
Burgess Hill	a									11 03													
Haywards Heath 3	a									11 09										11 35			
Arundel	d							10 12										10 46					
Amberley	d							10 17															
Pulborough	d							10 23										10 55					
Billingshurst	d							10 29										11 01					
Christs Hospital	d							10 36															
Horsham 4	a							10 40	10 46									11 10	11 16				
	d				10 30			10 50						11 00				11 20					
Crawley	d				10 43			10 59						11 13				11 29					
Three Bridges 4	a				10 46			11 02						11 16				11 32					
Gatwick Airport 10	a				10 52			11 07		11 25				11 22				11 37		11 55			
	d				10 53			11 08		11 26				11 23				11 38		11 56			
Horley	a				10 56									11 26				11 41					
Redhill 5	a				11 02			11 15						11 36				11 47					
East Croydon	a				11 24			11 27		11 41				11 54				11 59		12 11			
London Bridge 4	a				11 43									12 13									
Clapham Junction 10	a							11 37		11 51								12 09		12 21			
London Victoria 15	a							11 44		11 58								12 16		12 28			

A (trolley) from Horsham

Southampton, Portsmouth and Sussex Coast - Brighton, Gatwick Airport and London

		SN	SN	SN	SN	SN	SN	SN	SN	SN	SN	SN	SW	SN	SN	SN	SN	SN	SN	SN	SN	SN
		■	◇■	◇	◇■	◇■	◇■	◇	◇	◇■	■	◇	■	◇	◇■	◇■	◇■	◇	◇	◇	■	◇■
					🛒	A 🛒																
Southampton Central ⛴	d					10 13				10 33			10 44									
Swanwick	d					10 33				10 50			11 11									
Fareham	d					10 40				10 56			11 18									
Portchester	d					10 45							11 23									
Cosham	d					10 49				11 05			11 28									
Portsmouth Harbour ⛴	d		10 29													11 12						11 29
Portsmouth & Southsea	d		10 33									10 59				11 16						11 33
Fratton	d		10 37									11 04				11 20						11 37
Hilsea	d											11 08	11a33									
Bedhampton	d											11 13										
Havant	d		10 46			10 56				11 11		11 16				11 30						11 46
Warblington	d											11 18										
Emsworth	d		10 50			11 00				11 15		11 21										11 50
Southbourne	d		10 53			11 03						11 24										11 53
Nutbourne	d											11 26										
Bosham	d											11 30										
Fishbourne (Sussex)	d											11 33										
Chichester 4	a		11 00			11 10				11 23		11 36				11 40						12 00
	d		11 00			11 11				11 25		11 37				11 41						12 00
Bognor Regis 4	d			11 07	10 56									11 39	11 30							
Barnham	a		11 08	11 13	11 02	11 18				11 32		11 44		11 45	11 36	11 48						12 08
	d		11 08	11 15	11 03	11 19				11 33		11 45			11 37	11 49		11 52				12 08
Bognor Regis	a																	11 58				
Ford 4	d			11 19	11 07					11 37		11 49			11 41							
Littlehampton 4	a			11 24								11 54										
	d						11 15										11 45					
Angmering 3	d		11 17				11 23			11 43							11 53					12 17
Goring-by-Sea	d						11 27			11 47							11 57					
Durrington-on-Sea	d						11 30			11 50							12 00					
West Worthing	d						11 32		11 39	11 52							12 02			12 09		
Worthing 4	a		11 24				11 34		11 41	11 54							12 04			12 11		12 24
	d		11 26				11 36		11 42	11 56							12 06			12 12		12 26
East Worthing	d								11 44											12 14		
Lancing	d		11 30						11 47	12 00							12 10			12 17		12 30
Shoreham-by-Sea	d		11 34				11 42		11 52	12 04							12 14			12 22		12 34
Southwick	d		11 37						11 55	12 07										12 25		12 37
Fishersgate	d								11 57											12 27		
Portslade	d		11 40				11 47		11 59	12 10										12 29		12 40
Aldrington	d								12 01											12 31		
Hove 2	d		11 44				11 51	11 54	12 04	12 14							12 21		12 24	12 34		12 44
Brighton 10	a		11 48					11 58	12 08	12 18									12 28	12 38		12 48
Preston Park	d						11 55															
Burgess Hill	a						12 03															
Haywards Heath 3	a						12 09										12 35					
Arundel	d				11 12										11 46							
Amberley	d				11 17																	
Pulborough	d				11 23										11 55							
Billingshurst	d				11 29										12 01							
Christs Hospital	d				11 36																	
Horsham 4	a				11 40	11 46									12 10	12 16						
	d	11 30			11 50						12 00				12 20						12 30	
Crawley	d	11 43			11 59						12 13				12 29						12 43	
Three Bridges 4	a	11 46			12 02						12 16				12 32						12 46	
Gatwick Airport 10 ✈	a	11 52			12 07		12 25				12 22				12 37		12 55				12 52	
	d	11 53			12 08		12 26				12 23				12 38		12 56				12 53	
Horley	a	11 56									12 26				12 41						12 56	
Redhill 5	a	12 02			12 15						12 36				12 47						13 02	
East Croydon	a	12 24			12 27		12 41				12 54				12 59		13 11				13 24	
London Bridge 4 ⊖	a	12 43									13 13										13 43	
Clapham Junction 10	a				12 37		12 51								13 09		13 21					
London Victoria 15 ⊖	a				12 44		12 58								13 16		13 28					

A 🛒 from Horsham

Southampton, Portsmouth and Sussex Coast - Brighton, Gatwick Airport and London

		SN	SN	SN	SN	SN	SN	SN	SN	SN	SW	SN	SN	SN	SN	SN	SN	SN	SN	SN	SN	SN	SN
		◇	◇■	◇■	◇■	◇	◇	◇■	■	◇	■	◇	◇■	◇■	◇■	◇	◇	◇	■	◇■	◇	◇■	◇■
			🛒	A 🛒																		🛒	A 🛒
Southampton Central ⛴	d			11 13				11 33			11 44												12 13
Swanwick	d			11 33				11 50			12 11												12 33
Fareham	d			11 40				11 56			12 18												12 40
Portchester	d			11 45							12 23												12 45
Cosham	d			11 49				12 05			12 28												12 49
Portsmouth Harbour ⛴	d													12 12						12 29			
Portsmouth & Southsea	d									11 59				12 16						12 33			
Fratton	d									12 04				12 20						12 37			
Hilsea	d									12 08	12a33												
Bedhampton	d									12 13													
Havant	d			11 56				12 11		12 16				12 30						12 46			12 56
Warblington	d									12 18													
Emsworth	d			12 00				12 15		12 21										12 50			13 00
Southbourne	d			12 03						12 24										12 53			13 03
Nutbourne	d									12 26													
Bosham	d									12 30													
Fishbourne (Sussex)	d									12 33													
Chichester 4	a			12 10				12 23		12 36				12 40						13 00			13 10
	d			12 11				12 25		12 37				12 41						13 00			13 11
Bognor Regis 4	d	12 07	11 56									12 39	12 30								13 07	12 56	
Barnham	a	12 13	12 02	12 18				12 32		12 44		12 45	12 36	12 48						13 08	13 13	13 02	13 18
	d	12 15	12 03	12 19				12 33		12 45			12 37	12 49		12 52				13 08	13 15	13 03	13 19
Bognor Regis	a															12 58							
Ford 4	d	12 19	12 07					12 37		12 49			12 41								13 19	13 07	
Littlehampton 4	a	12 24								12 54											13 24		
	d				12 15										12 45								
Angmering 3	d				12 23			12 43							12 53					13 17			
Goring-by-Sea	d				12 27			12 47							12 57								
Durrington-on-Sea	d				12 30			12 50							13 00								
West Worthing	d				12 32		12 39	12 52							13 02			13 09					
Worthing 4	a				12 34		12 41	12 54							13 04			13 11		13 24			
	d				12 36		12 42	12 56							13 06			13 12		13 26			
East Worthing	d						12 44											13 14					
Lancing	d						12 47	13 00							13 10			13 17		13 30			
Shoreham-by-Sea	d				12 42		12 52	13 04							13 14			13 22		13 34			
Southwick	d						12 55	13 07										13 25		13 37			
Fishersgate	d						12 57											13 27					
Portslade	d				12 47		12 59	13 10										13 29		13 40			
Aldrington	d						13 01											13 31					
Hove 2	d				12 51	12 54	13 04	13 14							13 21		13 24	13 34		13 44			
Brighton 10	a					12 58	13 08	13 18									13 28	13 38		13 48			
Preston Park	d				12 55																		
Burgess Hill	a				13 03																		
Haywards Heath 3	a				13 09										13 35								
Arundel	d		12 12										12 46									13 12	
Amberley	d		12 17																			13 17	
Pulborough	d		12 23										12 55									13 23	
Billingshurst	d		12 29										13 01									13 29	
Christs Hospital	d		12 36																			13 36	
Horsham 4	a		12 40	12 46									13 10	13 16								13 40	13 46
	d		12 50						13 00				13 20						13 30			13 50	
Crawley	d		12 59						13 13				13 29						13 43			13 59	
Three Bridges 4	a		13 02						13 16				13 32						13 46			14 02	
Gatwick Airport 10 ✈	a		13 07		13 25				13 22				13 37		13 55				13 52			14 07	
	d		13 08		13 26				13 23				13 38		13 56				13 53			14 08	
Horley	a								13 26				13 41						13 56				
Redhill 5	a		13 15						13 36				13 47						14 02			14 15	
East Croydon	a		13 27		13 41				13 54				13 59		14 11				14 24			14 27	
London Bridge 4 ⊖	a								14 13										14 43				
Clapham Junction 10	a		13 37		13 51								14 09		14 21							14 37	
London Victoria 15 ⊖	a		13 44		13 58								14 16		14 28							14 44	

A 🛒 from Horsham

Table 188

Saturdays

Southampton, Portsmouth and Sussex Coast - Brighton, Gatwick Airport and London

		SN	SN		SN	SN	SN	SN	SW	SN	SN	SN	SN		SN	SN	SN	SN	SN	SN	SN	SN	SN		SN
		◇1	◇		◇	◇1	1	◇	1	◇	◇1	◇1	◇1		◇	◇	◇	1	◇1	◇	◇1	◇1	◇1		◇
																					🚌	A 🚌			
Southampton Central	d					12 33			12 44													13 13			
Swanwick	d					12 50			13 11													13 33			
Fareham	d					12 56			13 18													13 40			
Portchester	d								13 23													13 45			
Cosham	d					13 05			13 28													13 49			
Portsmouth Harbour	d											13 12							13 29						
Portsmouth & Southsea	d							12 59				13 16							13 33						
Fratton	d							13 04				13 20							13 37						
Hilsea	d							13 08	13a33																
Bedhampton	d							13 13																	
Havant	d					13 11		13 16				13 30							13 46			13 56			
Warblington	d							13 18																	
Emsworth	d					13 15		13 21											13 50			14 00			
Southbourne	d							13 24											13 53			14 03			
Nutbourne	d							13 26																	
Bosham	d							13 30																	
Fishbourne (Sussex)	d							13 33																	
Chichester [4]	a					13 23		13 36				13 40							14 00			14 10			
	d					13 25		13 37				13 41							14 00			14 11			
Bognor Regis [4]	d									13 39	13 30									14 07	13 56				
Barnham	a					13 32		13 44		13 45	13 36	13 48							14 08	14 13	14 02	14 18			
	d					13 33		13 45			13 37	13 49			13 52				14 08	14 15	14 03	14 19			
Bognor Regis	a														13 58										
Ford [4]	d					13 37		13 49			13 41									14 19	14 07				
Littlehampton [4]	a							13 54												14 24					
	d	13 15											13 45										14 15		
Angmering [3]	d	13 23				13 43							13 53						14 17				14 23		
Goring-by-Sea	d	13 27				13 47							13 57										14 27		
Durrington-on-Sea	d	13 30				13 50							14 00										14 30		
West Worthing	d	13 32			13 39	13 52							14 02				14 09						14 32		
Worthing [4]	a	13 34			13 41	13 54							14 04				14 11		14 24				14 34		
	d	13 36			13 42	13 56							14 06				14 12		14 26				14 36		
East Worthing	d				13 44												14 14								
Lancing	d				13 47	14 00							14 10				14 17		14 30						
Shoreham-by-Sea	d	13 42			13 52	14 04							14 14				14 22		14 34				14 42		
Southwick	d				13 55	14 07											14 25		14 37						
Fishersgate	d				13 57												14 27								
Portslade	d	13 47			13 59	14 10											14 29		14 40				14 47		
Aldrington	d				14 01												14 31								
Hove [2]	d	13 51	13 54		14 04	14 14							14 21			14 24	14 34		14 44				14 51		14 54
Brighton [10]	a		13 58		14 08	14 18										14 28	14 38		14 48						14 58
Preston Park	d	13 55																					14 55		
Burgess Hill	a	14 03																					15 03		
Haywards Heath [3]	a	14 09											14 35										15 09		
Arundel	d										13 46										14 12				
Amberley	d																				14 17				
Pulborough	d										13 55										14 23				
Billingshurst	d										14 01										14 29				
Christs Hospital	d																				14 36				
Horsham [4]	a										14 10	14 16									14 40	14 46			
	d						14 00				14 20							14 30			14 50				
Crawley	d						14 13				14 29							14 43			14 59				
Three Bridges [4]	a						14 16				14 32							14 46			15 02				
Gatwick Airport [10]	a	14 25					14 22				14 37		14 55					14 52			15 07		15 25		
	d	14 26					14 23				14 38		14 56					14 53			15 08		15 26		
Horley	a						14 26				14 41							14 56							
Redhill [5]	a						14 36				14 47							15 02			15 15				
East Croydon	a	14 41					14 54				14 59		15 11					15 24			15 27		15 41		
London Bridge [4]	a						15 13											15 43							
Clapham Junction [10]	a	14 51									15 09		15 21								15 37		15 51		
London Victoria [15]	a	14 58									15 16		15 28								15 44		15 58		

A 🚌 from Horsham

Table 188

Saturdays

Southampton, Portsmouth and Sussex Coast - Brighton, Gatwick Airport and London

		SN	SN	SN	SN	SW	SN	SN	SN		SN	SN	SN	SN	SN	SN	SN	SN	SN		SN	SN	SN	GW	SN
		◇	◇1	1	◇	1	◇	◇1	◇1		◇1	◇	◇	◇	1	◇1	◇	◇1	◇1		◇1	◇	◇	◇	◇1
																		🚌	A 🚌						
Southampton Central	d		13 33			13 44													14 13					14 34	14 26
Swanwick	d		13 50			14 11													14 33						
Fareham	d		13 56			14 18													14 40					14 55	15 00
Portchester	d					14 23													14 45						
Cosham	d		14 05			14 28													14 49					15 03	
Portsmouth Harbour	d								14 12							14 29									
Portsmouth & Southsea	d				13 59				14 16							14 33									
Fratton	d				14 04				14 20							14 37									
Hilsea	d				14 08	14a33																			
Bedhampton	d				14 13																				
Havant	d		14 11		14 16				14 30							14 46			14 56					15 10	15 14
Warblington	d				14 18																				
Emsworth	d		14 15		14 21											14 50			15 00						
Southbourne	d				14 24											14 53			15 03						
Nutbourne	d				14 26																				
Bosham	d				14 30																				
Fishbourne (Sussex)	d				14 33																				
Chichester [4]	a		14 23		14 36				14 40							15 00			15 10					15 21	15 25
	d		14 25		14 37				14 41							15 00			15 11					15 21	15 25
Bognor Regis [4]	d						14 39	14 30									15 07	14 56							
Barnham	a		14 32		14 44		14 45	14 36	14 48							15 08	15 13	15 02	15 18					15 29	15 33
	d		14 33		14 45			14 37	14 49			14 52				15 08	15 15	15 03	15 19					15 29	15 33
Bognor Regis	a											14 58													
Ford [4]	d		14 37		14 49			14 41									15 19	15 07							15 38
Littlehampton [4]	a				14 54												15 24								
	d										14 45										15 15				
Angmering [3]	d		14 43								14 53					15 17					15 23				15 44
Goring-by-Sea	d		14 47								14 57										15 27				15 48
Durrington-on-Sea	d		14 50								15 00										15 30				15 50
West Worthing	d	14 39	14 52								15 02			15 09							15 32		15 39		15 52
Worthing [4]	a	14 41	14 54								15 04			15 11		15 24					15 34		15 41	15 44	15 55
	d	14 42	14 56								15 06			15 12		15 26					15 36		15 42	15 48	15 56
East Worthing	d	14 44												15 14									15 44		
Lancing	d	14 47	15 00								15 10			15 17		15 30							15 47		16 00
Shoreham-by-Sea	d	14 52	15 04								15 14			15 22		15 34					15 42		15 52	15 56	16 04
Southwick	d	14 55	15 07											15 25		15 37							15 55		16 07
Fishersgate	d	14 57												15 27									15 57		
Portslade	d	14 59	15 10											15 29		15 40					15 47		15 59		16 10
Aldrington	d	15 01												15 31									16 01		
Hove [2]	d	15 04	15 14								15 21		15 24	15 34		15 44					15 51	15 54	16 04	16 08	16 14
Brighton [10]	a	15 08	15 18										15 28	15 38		15 48						15 58	16 08	16 14	16 18
Preston Park	d																				15 55				
Burgess Hill	a																				16 03				
Haywards Heath [3]	a										15 35										16 09				
Arundel	d							14 46										15 12							
Amberley	d																	15 17							
Pulborough	d							14 55										15 23							
Billingshurst	d							15 01										15 29							
Christs Hospital	d																	15 36							
Horsham [4]	a							15 10	15 16									15 40	15 46						
	d			15 00				15 20							15 30			15 50							
Crawley	d			15 13				15 29							15 43			15 59							
Three Bridges [4]	a			15 16				15 32							15 46			16 02							
Gatwick Airport [10]	a			15 22				15 37			15 55				15 52			16 07			16 25				
	d			15 23				15 38			15 56				15 53			16 08			16 26				
Horley	a			15 26				15 41							15 56										
Redhill [5]	a			15 36				15 47							16 02			16 15							
East Croydon	a			15 54				15 59			16 11				16 24			16 27			16 41				
London Bridge [4]	a			16 13											16 43										
Clapham Junction [10]	a							16 09			16 21							16 37			16 51				
London Victoria [15]	a							16 16			16 28							16 44			16 58				

A 🚌 from Horsham

Southampton, Portsmouth and Sussex Coast - Brighton, Gatwick Airport and London

		SN	SN	SW	SN	SN	SN	SN	SN	SN	SN	SN	SN	SN	SN	SN	SN	SN	SN	SN	SN	SN	SW
		1	◇	1	◇	◇1	◇1	◇1	◇	◇	◇	1	◇1	◇	◇1 🍴	◇1 A 🍴	◇1	◇	◇	◇1	1	◇	1
Southampton Central ⛴	d			14 44												15 13				15 33			15 44
Swanwick	d			15 11												15 33				15 50			16 11
Fareham	d			15 18												15 40				15 56			16 18
Portchester	d			15 23												15 45							16 23
Cosham	d			15 28												15 49				16 05			16 28
Portsmouth Harbour ⛴	d						15 12						15 29										
Portsmouth & Southsea	d		14 59				15 16						15 33									15 59	
Fratton	d		15 04				15 20						15 37									16 04	
Hilsea	d		15 08	15a33																		16 08	16a33
Bedhampton	d		15 14																			16 13	
Havant	d		15 17				15 30						15 46			15 56				16 11		16 16	
Warblington	d		15 19																			16 18	
Emsworth	d		15 22										15 50			16 00				16 15		16 21	
Southbourne	d		15 25										15 53			16 03						16 24	
Nutbourne	d		15 28																			16 26	
Bosham	d		15 31																			16 30	
Fishbourne (Sussex)	d		15 34																			16 33	
Chichester 4	a		15 37				15 41						16 00			16 10				16 23		16 36	
	d		15 38				15 42						16 00			16 11				16 25		16 37	
Bognor Regis 4	d				15 39	15 30								16 07	15 56								
Barnham	a		15 45		15 45	15 36	15 49						16 08	16 13	16 02	16 18				16 32		16 44	
	d		15 46			15 37	15 50		15 52				16 08	16 15	16 03	16 19				16 33		16 45	
Bognor Regis	a								15 58														
Ford 4	d		15 50			15 41								16 19	16 07					16 37		16 49	
Littlehampton 4	a		15 55											16 24								16 54	
	d							15 45									16 15						
Angmering 3	d							15 53					16 17				16 23			16 43			
Goring-by-Sea	d							15 57									16 27			16 47			
Durrington-on-Sea	d							16 00									16 30			16 50			
West Worthing	d							16 02			16 09						16 32		16 39	16 52			
Worthing 4	a							16 04			16 11		16 24				16 34		16 41	16 54			
	d							16 06			16 12		16 26				16 36		16 42	16 56			
East Worthing	d										16 14								16 44				
Lancing	d							16 10			16 17		16 30						16 47	17 00			
Shoreham-by-Sea	d							16 14			16 22		16 34				16 42		16 52	17 04			
Southwick	d										16 25		16 37						16 55	17 07			
Fishersgate	d										16 27								16 57				
Portslade	d										16 29		16 40				16 47		16 59	17 10			
Aldrington	d										16 31								17 01				
Hove 2	d							16 21		16 24	16 34		16 44				16 51	16 54	17 04	17 14			
Brighton 10	a									16 28	16 38		16 48					16 58	17 08	17 18			
Preston Park	d																16 55						
Burgess Hill	a																17 03						
Haywards Heath 3	a							16 35									17 09						
Arundel	d					15 46									16 12								
Amberley	d														16 17								
Pulborough	d					15 55									16 23								
Billingshurst	d					16 01									16 29								
Christs Hospital	d														16 36								
Horsham 4	a					16 10	16 16								16 40	16 46							
	d	16 00				16 20						16 30			16 50						17 00		
Crawley	d	16 13				16 29						16 43			16 59						17 13		
Three Bridges 4	a	16 16				16 32						16 46			17 02						17 16		
Gatwick Airport 10 ✈	a	16 22				16 37		16 55				16 52			17 07		17 25				17 22		
	d	16 23				16 38		16 56				16 53			17 08		17 26				17 23		
Horley	a	16 26				16 41						16 56									17 26		
Redhill 5	a	16 36				16 47						17 02			17 15						17 36		
East Croydon 🚊	a	16 54				16 59		17 11				17 24			17 27		17 41				17 54		
London Bridge 4 ⊖	a	17 13										17 43									18 13		
Clapham Junction 10	a					17 09		17 21							17 37		17 51						
London Victoria 15 ⊖	a					17 16		17 28							17 44		17 58						

A 🍴 from Horsham

Southampton, Portsmouth and Sussex Coast - Brighton, Gatwick Airport and London

		SN	SN	SN	SN	SN	SN	SN	SN	SN	SN	SN	SN	SN	SN	SN	SN	SN	SN	SW	SN
		◇	◇1	◇1	◇1	◇	◇	◇	1	◇1	◇	◇1 🍴	◇1 A 🍴	◇1	◇	◇	◇1	1	◇	1	◇
Southampton Central ⛴	d												16 13				16 33			16 44	
Swanwick	d												16 33				16 50			17 11	
Fareham	d												16 40				16 56			17 18	
Portchester	d												16 45							17 23	
Cosham	d												16 49				17 05			17 28	
Portsmouth Harbour ⛴	d			16 12						16 29											
Portsmouth & Southsea	d			16 16						16 33									16 59		
Fratton	d			16 20						16 37									17 04		
Hilsea	d																		17 08	17a33	
Bedhampton	d																		17 13		
Havant	d			16 30						16 46			16 56				17 11		17 16		
Warblington	d																		17 18		
Emsworth	d									16 50			17 00				17 15		17 21		
Southbourne	d									16 53			17 03						17 24		
Nutbourne	d																		17 26		
Bosham	d																		17 30		
Fishbourne (Sussex)	d																		17 33		
Chichester 4	a			16 40						17 00			17 10				17 23		17 36		
	d			16 41						17 00			17 11				17 25		17 37		
Bognor Regis 4	d	16 39	16 30								17 07	16 56									17 39
Barnham	a	16 45	16 36	16 48						17 08	17 13	17 02	17 18				17 32		17 44		17 45
	d		16 37	16 49		16 52				17 08	17 15	17 03	17 19				17 33		17 45		
Bognor Regis	a					16 58															
Ford 4	d		16 41								17 19	17 07					17 37		17 49		
Littlehampton 4	a										17 24								17 54		
	d				16 45									17 15							
Angmering 3	d				16 53					17 17				17 23			17 43				
Goring-by-Sea	d				16 57									17 27			17 47				
Durrington-on-Sea	d				17 00									17 30			17 50				
West Worthing	d				17 02			17 09						17 32		17 39	17 52				
Worthing 4	a				17 04			17 11		17 24				17 34		17 41	17 54				
	d				17 06			17 12		17 26				17 36		17 42	17 56				
East Worthing	d							17 14								17 44					
Lancing	d				17 10			17 17		17 30						17 47	18 00				
Shoreham-by-Sea	d				17 14			17 22		17 34				17 42		17 52	18 04				
Southwick	d							17 25		17 37						17 55	18 07				
Fishersgate	d							17 27								17 57					
Portslade	d							17 29		17 40				17 47		17 59	18 10				
Aldrington	d							17 31								18 01					
Hove 2	d				17 21		17 24	17 34		17 44				17 51	17 54	18 04	18 14				
Brighton 10	a						17 28	17 38		17 48					17 58	18 08	18 18				
Preston Park	d													17 55							
Burgess Hill	a													18 03							
Haywards Heath 3	a				17 35									18 09							
Arundel	d		16 46									17 12									
Amberley	d											17 17									
Pulborough	d		16 55									17 23									
Billingshurst	d		17 01									17 29									
Christs Hospital	d											17 36									
Horsham 4	a		17 10	17 16								17 40	17 46								
	d		17 20						17 30			17 50						18 00			
Crawley	d		17 29						17 43			17 59						18 13			
Three Bridges 4	a		17 32						17 46			18 02						18 16			
Gatwick Airport 10 ✈	a		17 37		17 55				17 52			18 07		18 25				18 22			
	d		17 38		17 56				17 53			18 08		18 26				18 23			
Horley	a		17 41						17 56									18 26			
Redhill 5	a		17 47						18 02			18 15						18 36			
East Croydon 🚊	a		17 59		18 11				18 24			18 27		18 41				18 54			
London Bridge 4 ⊖	a								18 43									19 13			
Clapham Junction 10	a		18 09		18 21							18 37		18 51							
London Victoria 15 ⊖	a		18 16		18 28							18 44		18 58							

A 🍴 from Horsham

Southampton, Portsmouth and Sussex Coast - Brighton, Gatwick Airport and London

		SN	SN	SN	SN	SN	SN	SN	SN	SN	SN	SN	SN	SN	SN	SN	SN	SN	SN	SW	SN	SN	SN
		◇1	◇1	◇1	◇	◇	◇	1	◇1	◇	◇1	◇1	◇1	◇	◇	◇1	1	◇1	1	1	◇	◇	◇
Southampton Central	d											17 13				17 33				17 44			
Swanwick	d											17 33				17 50				18 11			
Fareham	d											17 40				17 56				18 18			
Portchester	d											17 45								18 23			
Cosham	d											17 49				18 05				18 28			
Portsmouth Harbour	d		17 12						17 29														
Portsmouth & Southsea	d		17 16						17 33										17 59				
Fratton	d		17 20						17 37										18 04	18a33			
Hilsea	d																		18 08				
Bedhampton	d																		18 13				
Havant	d		17 30						17 46			17 56				18 11			18 16				
Warblington	d																		18 18				
Emsworth	d								17 50			18 00				18 15			18 21				
Southbourne	d								17 53			18 03							18 24				
Nutbourne	d																		18 26				
Bosham	d																		18 30				
Fishbourne (Sussex)	d																		18 33				
Chichester 4	a		17 40						18 00			18 10				18 23			18 36				
	d		17 41						18 00			18 11				18 25			18 37				
Bognor Regis 4	d	17 30								18 07	17 56							18 33			18 39		
Barnham	a	17 36	17 48						18 08	18 13	18 02	18 18				18 32		18 40	18 44		18 46		
	d	17 37	17 49		17 52				18 08	18 15	18 03	18 19				18 33		18 41	18 45			18 52	
Bognor Regis	a				17 58																	18 58	
Ford 4	d	17 41								18 19	18 07					18 37		18 45	18 49				
Littlehampton 4	a									18 24													
	d			17 45									18 15										
Angmering 3	d			17 53					18 17				18 23			18 43		18 53					
Goring-by-Sea	d			17 57									18 27			18 47		18 57					
Durrington-on-Sea	d			18 00									18 30			18 50		19 00					
West Worthing	d			18 02			18 09						18 32		18 39	18 52		19 02					
Worthing 4	a			18 04			18 11		18 24				18 34		18 41	18 54		19 04					
	d			18 06			18 12		18 26				18 36		18 42	18 56		19 06					
East Worthing	d						18 14								18 44								
Lancing	d			18 10			18 17		18 30						18 47	19 00		19 10					
Shoreham-by-Sea	d			18 14			18 22		18 34				18 42		18 52	19 04		19 14					
Southwick	d						18 25		18 37						18 55	19 07							
Fishersgate	d						18 27								18 57								
Portslade	d						18 29		18 40				18 47		18 59	19 10							
Aldrington	d						18 31								19 01								
Hove 2	d			18 21		18 24	18 34		18 44				18 51	18 54	19 04	19 14		19 21					19 24
Brighton 10	a					18 28	18 38		18 48					18 58	19 08	19 18							19 28
Preston Park	d												18 55										
Burgess Hill	a												19 03										
Haywards Heath 3	a			18 35									19 09					19 35					
Arundel	d	17 46									18 12								18 54				
Amberley	d										18 17								18 59				
Pulborough	d	17 55									18 23								19 05				
Billingshurst	d	18 01									18 29								19 11				
Christs Hospital	d										18 36												
Horsham 4	a	18 10	18 16								18 40	18 46							19 20				
	d		18 20					18 32				18 50					19 02		19 21				
Crawley	d		18 29					18 45				18 59					19 14		19 30				
Three Bridges 4	a		18 32					18 48				19 02					19 18		19 33				
Gatwick Airport 10	a		18 37	18 55				18 54				19 07	19 25				19 22	19 55	19 38				
	d		18 38	18 56				18 55				19 08	19 26				19 23	19 56	19 39				
Horley	a		18 41					18 58				19 11					19 26						
Redhill 5	a		18 47					19 04				19 17					19 36		19 47				
East Croydon	a		18 59	19 11				19 24				19 28	19 41				19 54	20 11	19 59				
London Bridge 4	a																						
Clapham Junction 10	a		19 09	19 21				19 37				19 40	19 51				20 08	20 21	20 11				
London Victoria 15	a		19 16	19 28				19 44				19 50	19 58				20 15	20 28	20 20				

Southampton, Portsmouth and Sussex Coast - Brighton, Gatwick Airport and London

		SN	SN	SN	SN	SN	SN	SN	SN	SN	SN	SN	SN	SN	SN	SW	SN	SN	SN	SN	SN	SN
		◇	◇	◇1	1	◇1	◇1	◇	◇	◇1	1	◇1	◇	◇	◇	1	◇	◇1	◇	◇1	◇	1
Southampton Central	d					18 11				18 33						18 44						
Swanwick	d					18 28				18 50						19 11						
Fareham	d					18 35				18 56						19 18						
Portchester	d					18 40										19 23						
Cosham	d					18 44				19 05						19 28						
Portsmouth Harbour	d		18 12	18 29														19 12		19 29		
Portsmouth & Southsea	d		18 16	18 33											18 59			19 16		19 33		
Fratton	d		18 20	18 37											19 04	19a33		19 20		19 37		
Hilsea	d														19 08							
Bedhampton	d														19 13							
Havant	d		18 30	18 46		18 51				19 11					19 16			19 30		19 46		
Warblington	d														19 18							
Emsworth	d		18 34	18 50		18 55				19 15					19 21			19 34				
Southbourne	d		18 37	18 53		18 58									19 24			19 37				
Nutbourne	d														19 26							
Bosham	d														19 30							
Fishbourne (Sussex)	d														19 33							
Chichester 4	a		18 44	19 00		19 05				19 23					19 36			19 44		19 57		
	d		18 45	19 00		19 07				19 25					19 37			19 45		19 59		
Bognor Regis 4	d							19 03				19 33					19 39				20 04	
Barnham	a		18 52	19 08		19 14		19 09		19 32		19 40			19 44		19 46	19 52		20 06	20 10	
	d		18 53	19 08		19 15		19 22		19 33		19 41			19 45			19 53	19 52	20 07	20 11	
Bognor Regis	a																		19 58			
Ford 4	d		18 57			19 19		19 26		19 37		19 45			19 49			19 57			20 15	
Littlehampton 4	a		19 02					19 32							19 55			20 02			20 20	
	d	18 51					19 15							19 52								
Angmering 3	d	19 00		19 17			19 23			19 43		19 53		20 00						20 16		
Goring-by-Sea	d	19 04					19 27					19 57		20 04								
Durrington-on-Sea	d	19 07					19 30			19 49		20 00		20 07								
West Worthing	d	19 09					19 32					20 02		20 09								
Worthing 4	a	19 11		19 24			19 34			19 53		20 04		20 11						20 23		
	d	19 12		19 26			19 35			19 53		20 05		20 12						20 23		
East Worthing	d	19 14								19 56				20 14						20 26		
Lancing	d	19 17		19 30			19 39			19 59		20 09		20 17						20 29		
Shoreham-by-Sea	d	19 22		19 34			19 43			20 03		20 13		20 22						20 33		
Southwick	d	19 25		19 37						20 06				20 25						20 36		
Fishersgate	d	19 27								20 08				20 27						20 38		
Portslade	d	19 29		19 40			19 48			20 10		20 17		20 29						20 40		
Aldrington	d	19 31								20 12				20 31						20 42		
Hove 2	d	19 34		19 44			19 52		19 54	20 15		20 22	20 24	20 34						20 45		
Brighton 10	a	19 38		19 49					19 59	20 19			20 28	20 38						20 49		
Preston Park	d																					
Burgess Hill	a						20 02															
Haywards Heath 3	a						20 10					20 35										
Arundel	d					19 24																
Amberley	d					19 29																
Pulborough	d					19 35																
Billingshurst	d					19 41																
Christs Hospital	d					19 48																
Horsham 4	a					19 52																
	d				19 32	19 52					20 02											20 32
Crawley	d				19 45	20 01					20 14											20 45
Three Bridges 4	a				19 48	20 05					20 18	20 47										20 48
Gatwick Airport 10	a				19 54	20 10	20 25				20 22	20 51										20 56
	d				19 55	20 11	20 26				20 23	20 53										20 57
Horley	a				19 58						20 26											20 59
Redhill 5	a				20 04	20 18					20 36											21 06
East Croydon	a				20 24	20 30	20 41				20 54	21 08										21 24
London Bridge 4	a																					
Clapham Junction 10	a				20 37	20 40	20 51				21 07	21 18										21 37
London Victoria 15	a				20 44	20 50	20 58				21 14	21 26										21 44

Southampton, Portsmouth and Sussex Coast - Brighton, Gatwick Airport and London

		SN	SN	SN	SN	SN	SN	SN	SN	SN	SN	SW	SN	SN	SN	SN	SN	SN	SN	SN	SN	SN	SN
		◇[1]	◇[1]	◇	◇[1]	[1]	◇[1]	◇	◇	◇[1]	◇	[1]	◇	◇[1]	◇	[1]	◇[1]	◇[1] A ⌶		◇	◇[1]	◇	◇
Southampton Central ⛴	d	19 09			19 33							19 44					20 11				20 33		
Swanwick	d	19 28			19 50							20 11					20 28				20 50		
Fareham	d	19 35			19 56							20 18					20 35				20 56		
Portchester	d	19 40										20 23					20 40						
Cosham	d	19 44			20 05							20 28					20 44				21 05		
Portsmouth Harbour ⛴	d													20 28					20 40				
Portsmouth & Southsea	d										19 59			20 32					20 44				
Fratton	d										20 04			20 36					20 48				
Hilsea	d										20 08	20a37							20 52				
Bedhampton	d										20 13												
Havant	d	19 52			20 11						20 16			20 44			20 51		20 58		21 11		
Warblington	d										20 18								21 00				
Emsworth	d	19 56			20 15						20 21			20 48			20 55		21 03		21 15		
Southbourne	d	19 59									20 24			20 51			20 58		21 06				
Nutbourne	d										20 26								21 09				
Bosham	d										20 30								21 12				
Fishbourne (Sussex)	d										20 33								21 15				
Chichester [4]	a	20 06			20 23						20 36			20 58			21 05		21 18		21 23		
	d	20 07			20 25						20 37			20 59			21 07		21 19		21 25		
Bognor Regis [4]	d						20 33	20 39							21 04							21 39	
Barnham	a	20 14			20 32		20 39	20 45			20 44			21 06	21 10		21 14		21 26		21 32	21 45	
	d	20 15			20 33		20 40				20 45		20 52	21 07	21 11		21 15		21 27		21 33		21 52
Bognor Regis	a												20 58										21 58
Ford [4]	d	20 19					20 44				20 49				21 15		21 19		21 31		21 37		
Littlehampton [4]	a										20 55				21 20				21 36				
	d		20 15							20 52								21 15					
Angmering [3]	d		20 23		20 42		20 53			21 00				21 16				21 23			21 43		
Goring-by-Sea	d		20 27				20 57			21 04								21 27			21 47		
Durrington-on-Sea	d		20 30		20 48		21 00			21 07								21 30			21 50		
West Worthing	d		20 32				21 02			21 09								21 32			21 52		
Worthing [4]	a		20 34		20 52		21 04			21 11				21 23				21 34			21 54		
	d		20 35		20 52		21 05			21 12				21 23				21 35			21 55		
East Worthing	d				20 55					21 14				21 26							21 57		
Lancing	d		20 39		20 58		21 09			21 17				21 29				21 39			22 00		
Shoreham-by-Sea	d		20 43		21 02		21 13			21 22				21 33				21 43			22 04		
Southwick	d				21 05					21 25				21 36							22 07		
Fishersgate	d				21 07					21 27				21 38							22 09		
Portslade	d		20 48		21 09		21 18			21 29				21 40				21 48			22 11		
Aldrington	d				21 11					21 31				21 42							22 14		
Hove [2]	d		20 52	20 54	21 14		21 22		21 24	21 34				21 45				21 52		21 54	22 16		
Brighton [10]	a			20 58	21 18				21 28	21 38				21 49						21 58	22 21		
Preston Park	d																						
Burgess Hill	a		21 03															22 03					
Haywards Heath [3]	a		21 11				21 35											22 09					
Arundel	d	20 24															21 24						
Amberley	d	20 29															21 29						
Pulborough	d	20 35															21 35						
Billingshurst	d	20 41															21 41						
Christs Hospital	d	20 48															21 48						
Horsham [4]	a	20 52															21 52						
	d	20 52				21 02										21 32	21 52						
Crawley	d	21 01				21 14										21 45	22 01						
Three Bridges [4]	a	21 05				21 18	21 47									21 48	22 05						
Gatwick Airport [10] ✈	a	21 10	21 26			21 22	21 51									21 56	22 10	22 24					
	d	21 11	21 27			21 23	21 53									21 57	22 11	22 25					
Horley	a					21 26										22 00							
Redhill [5]	a	21 18				21 36										22 06	22 18						
East Croydon 🚌	a	21 30	21 42			21 54	22 08									22 24	22 30	22 40					
London Bridge [4] ⊖	a																						
Clapham Junction [10]	a	21 40	21 51			22 07	22 18									22 37	22 40	22 49					
London Victoria [15] ⊖	a	21 50	21 58			22 15	22 26									22 44	22 50	22 57					

A ⌶ from Haywards Heath

Southampton, Portsmouth and Sussex Coast - Brighton, Gatwick Airport and London

		SN	SN	SN	SN	SW	SN	SN	SN	SN	SN	SN	SN	SN	SN	SN	SN	SW	SN	SN	SN	SN	SN
		[1]	◇	◇[1]	◇[1]	[1]	◇	◇	◇[1]	[1]	◇	◇	◇[1]	[1]	[1]	◇	◇[1]	[1]	◇[1]	◇	◇	◇[1]	◇[1]
Southampton Central ⛴	d					20 44			21 13				21 33					21 44	22 13				22 33
Swanwick	d					21 11			21 33				21 50					22 11	22 31				22 50
Fareham	d					21 18			21 40				21 57					22 18	22 39				23 00
Portchester	d					21 23			21 45				22 02					22 23	22 44				
Cosham	d					21 28			21 49				22 06					22 28	22 48				23 08
Portsmouth Harbour ⛴	d				21 11					21 40							22 15					22 44	
Portsmouth & Southsea	d				21 15					21 44							22 19					22 48	
Fratton	d				21 19					21 48							22 23					22 52	
Hilsea	d				21 23	21a33				21 52							22 27	22a33				22 56	
Bedhampton	d				21 28					21 57							22 32					23 01	
Havant	d				21 31				21 56	22 00			22 13				22 35		22 55			23 05	23 15
Warblington	d				21 33								22 15										
Emsworth	d				21 36								22 18				22 39		22 59				
Southbourne	d				21 39								22 21				22 42		23 02				
Nutbourne	d				21 41								22 23										
Bosham	d				21 45								22 27										
Fishbourne (Sussex)	d				21 48								22 30										
Chichester [4]	a				21 51				22 06	22 10			22 33				22 49		23 09			23 16	23 25
	d				21 52				22 07	22 11			22 34		22 40		22 52		23 09			23 18	23 26
Bognor Regis [4]	d						22 00					22 30								23 15			
Barnham	a				21 59		22 06		22 14	22 18		22 36	22 41		22 47		22 59		23 17	23 21		23 26	23 33
	d				22 00				22 15	22 19	22 22	22 37			22 48		23 00		23 17			23 26	23 34
Bognor Regis	a										22 28												
Ford [4]	d				22 04				22 19	22 23		22 41			22 52		23 04					23 31	
Littlehampton [4]	a								22 24			22 46							23 25			23 35	23 42
	d			21 52					22 33													23 40	
Angmering [3]	d			22 00	22 11				22 41								23 11					23 48	
Goring-by-Sea	d			22 04	22 15				22 45								23 15					23 52	
Durrington-on-Sea	d			22 07	22 18				22 47								23 17					23 54	
West Worthing	d			22 09	22 20				22 49								23 19					23 56	
Worthing [4]	a			22 11	22 22				22 52								23 22					23 59	
	d			22 12	22 23				22 52								23 22					23 59	
East Worthing	d			22 14	22 25				22 55								23 25					00 02	
Lancing	d			22 17	22 28				22 58								23 28					00 05	
Shoreham-by-Sea	d			22 22	22 32				23 02								23 32					00 09	
Southwick	d			22 25	22 35				23 05								23 35					00 12	
Fishersgate	d			22 27	22 37				23 07								23 37					00 14	
Portslade	d			22 29	22 39				23 09								23 39					00 16	
Aldrington	d			22 31	22 42				23 11								23 41					00 18	
Hove [2]	d		22 24	22 34	22 44			22 54	23 14							23 24	23 44				23 54	00 21	
Brighton [10]	a		22 28	22 38	22 48			22 58	23 18							23 28	23 48				23 58	00 25	
Preston Park	d																						
Burgess Hill	a																						
Haywards Heath [3]	a																						
Arundel	d									22 28					22 57								
Amberley	d														23 02								
Pulborough	d									22 37					23 08								
Billingshurst	d									22 43					23 14								
Christs Hospital	d									22 50					23 21								
Horsham [4]	a									22 54					23 25								
	d	22 02								22 55				23 02	23 25								
Crawley	d	22 14								23 03				23 14	23 38								
Three Bridges [4]	a	22 18								23 07				23 18	23 42								
Gatwick Airport [10] ✈	a	22 23												23 22									
	d	22 24												23 23									
Horley	a	22 27												23 26									
Redhill [5]	a	22 37												23 36									
East Croydon 🚌	a	22 55												23 55									
London Bridge [4] ⊖	a																						
Clapham Junction [10]	a	23 06												00 11									
London Victoria [15] ⊖	a	23 14												00 18									

Table 188

Saturdays

Southampton, Portsmouth and Sussex Coast - Brighton, Gatwick Airport and London

		SN ◇	SN ◇1	SN ◇1	SW 1
Southampton Central ⛴	d				22 44
Swanwick	d				23 11
Fareham	d				23 18
Portchester	d				23 23
Cosham	d				23 28
Portsmouth Harbour ⛴	d			23 15	
Portsmouth & Southsea	d			23 19	
Fratton	d			23 23	
Hilsea	d			23 27	23a33
Bedhampton	d			23 33	
Havant	d			23 36	
Warblington	d			23 38	
Emsworth	d			23 41	
Southbourne	d			23 44	
Nutbourne	d			23 47	
Bosham	d			23 50	
Fishbourne (Sussex)	d			23 53	
Chichester 4	a			23 57	
	d		23 52	23 57	
Bognor Regis 4	d				
Barnham	a		23 59	00 05	
	d	23 36	00 01	00 06	
Bognor Regis	a	23 42			
Ford 4	d		00 05	00 10	
Littlehampton 4	a		00 10	00 15	
	d				
Angmering 3	d				
Goring-by-Sea	d				
Durrington-on-Sea	d				
West Worthing	d				
Worthing 4	a				
	d				
East Worthing	d				
Lancing	d				
Shoreham-by-Sea	d				
Southwick	d				
Fishersgate	d				
Portslade	d				
Aldrington	d				
Hove 2	d				
Brighton 10	a				
Preston Park	d				
Burgess Hill	a				
Haywards Heath 3	a				
Arundel	d				
Amberley	d				
Pulborough	d				
Billingshurst	d				
Christs Hospital	d				
Horsham 4	a				
	d				
Crawley	d				
Three Bridges 4	a				
Gatwick Airport 10 ✈	a				
	d				
Horley	a				
Redhill 5	a				
East Croydon 🚋	a				
London Bridge 4 ⊖	a				
Clapham Junction 10	a				
London Victoria 15 ⊖	a				

Table 188

Sundays
until 4 September

Southampton, Portsmouth and Sussex Coast - Brighton, Gatwick Airport and London

		SN ◇1 A	SN 1 A	SN ◇1 A	SN ◇1 A	SN 1	SN ◇1	SN 1	SW 1	SN ◇	SN 1	SN ◇1
Southampton Central ⛴	d								06 35			
Swanwick	d								07 02			
Fareham	d								07 10			
Portchester	d								07 15			
Cosham	d								07 20			
Portsmouth Harbour ⛴	d	22p44			23p15							
Portsmouth & Southsea	d	22p48			23p19							
Fratton	d	22p52			23p23							
Hilsea	d	22p56			23p27				07a26			
Bedhampton	d	23p01			23p33							
Havant	d	23p05			23p36							
Warblington	d				23p38							
Emsworth	d				23p41							
Southbourne	d				23p44							
Nutbourne	d				23p47							
Bosham	d				23p50							
Fishbourne (Sussex)	d				23p53							
Chichester 4	a	23p16			23p57							
	d	23p18		23p52	23p57							
Bognor Regis 4	d											06 52
Barnham	a	23p26		23p59	00 05							06 58
	d	23p26		00 01	00 06		06 06			06 45		06 59
Bognor Regis	a									06 51		
Ford 4	d	23p31		00 05	00 10							07 03
Littlehampton 4	a	23p35		00 10	00 15		06 13					
	d	23p40					06 20					
Angmering 3	d	23p48										
Goring-by-Sea	d	23p52										
Durrington-on-Sea	d	23p54										
West Worthing	d	23p56										
Worthing 4	a	23p59					06 33					
	d	23p59					06 33					
East Worthing	d	00 02										
Lancing	d	00 05					06 37					
Shoreham-by-Sea	d	00 09					06 41					
Southwick	d	00 12					06 44					
Fishersgate	d	00 14										
Portslade	d	00 16					06 48					
Aldrington	d	00 18										
Hove 2	d	00 21					06 51					
Brighton 10	a	00 25					06 55					
Preston Park	d											
Burgess Hill	a											
Haywards Heath 3	a											
Arundel	d											07 08
Amberley	d											07 13
Pulborough	d											07 19
Billingshurst	d											07 26
Christs Hospital	d											07 32
Horsham 4	a											07 37
	d		23p02			06 04		06 34			07 00	07 37
Crawley	d		23p14			06 17		06 47			07 13	07 46
Three Bridges 4	a		23p18			06 20		06 51			07 16	07 50
Gatwick Airport 10 ✈	a		23p22			06 25		06 57			07 22	07 55
	d		23p23					06 58			07 23	07 56
Horley	a		23p26					07 00			07 26	07 58
Redhill 5	a		23p36					07 07			07 36	08 05
East Croydon 🚋	a		23p55					07 26			07 56	08 19
London Bridge 4 ⊖	a										08 13	
Clapham Junction 10	a		00 11					07 40				08 31
London Victoria 15 ⊖	a		00 18					07 48				08 39

		SN ◇1	SN ◇	SN ◇	SN ◇1	SN 1	SN ◇1	SN ◇1	SN ◇1	SN ◇1	SN 1	SN ◇1
Southampton Central ⛴	d											
Swanwick	d											
Fareham	d											
Portchester	d											
Cosham	d											
Portsmouth Harbour ⛴	d							07 05		07 43		
Portsmouth & Southsea	d							07 09		07 47		
Fratton	d							07 13		07 51		
Hilsea	d											
Bedhampton	d							07 21				
Havant	d							07 27		08 00		
Warblington	d							07 29				
Emsworth	d							07 32		08 04		
Southbourne	d							07 35		08 07		
Nutbourne	d							07 38				
Bosham	d							07 41				
Fishbourne (Sussex)	d							07 44				
Chichester 4	a							07 47		08 14		
	d							07 48		08 14		
Bognor Regis 4	d				07 34		07 52					
Barnham	a				07 40		07 58	07 55		08 22		
	d				07 41		07 59	08 02		08 22		
Bognor Regis	a											
Ford 4	d				07 45		08 03	08 06				
Littlehampton 4	a				07 50							
	d	07 14		07 40					08 14			
Angmering 3	d	07 22		07 48				08 12	08 22			
Goring-by-Sea	d	07 26		07 52				08 16	08 26			
Durrington-on-Sea	d	07 29		07 55				08 19	08 29			
West Worthing	d	07 31		07 57				08 21	08 31			
Worthing 4	a	07 33		07 59				08 23	08 33	08 37		
	d	07 35		08 00				08 24		08 41		
East Worthing	d			08 02				08 26				
Lancing	d	07 39		08 05				08 29				
Shoreham-by-Sea	d	07 43		08 09				08 33		08 47		
Southwick	d	07 46		08 12				08 36				
Fishersgate	d			08 14				08 38				
Portslade	d	07 49		08 16				08 40				
Aldrington	d			08 19				08 43				
Hove 2	d	07 54	07 56	08 21				08 45		08 54		09 01
Brighton 10	a		08 00	08 25				08 49				09 05
Preston Park	d											
Burgess Hill	a	08 04								09 04		
Haywards Heath 3	a	08 09								09 09		
Arundel	d						08 08					
Amberley	d						08 13					
Pulborough	d						08 19					
Billingshurst	d						08 26					
Christs Hospital	d						08 32					
Horsham 4	a						08 37					
	d					08 00	08 37				09 00	
Crawley	d					08 13	08 46				09 13	
Three Bridges 4	a					08 16	08 50				09 16	
Gatwick Airport 10 ✈	a	08 22				08 22	08 55			09 22	09 22	
	d	08 23				08 23	08 56			09 23	09 23	
Horley	a					08 26	08 58				09 26	
Redhill 5	a					08 36	09 05				09 36	
East Croydon 🚋	a	08 39				08 56	09 19			09 39	09 56	
London Bridge 4 ⊖	a					09 13					10 13	
Clapham Junction 10	a	08 48					09 31			09 48		
London Victoria 15 ⊖	a	08 55					09 39			09 55		

A not 22 May

until 4 September

Southampton, Portsmouth and Sussex Coast - Brighton, Gatwick Airport and London

Station		SN	SW	SN	SN	SN	SN	SN	GW	SN	SN	SN	SW	SN	SN	SN	SN	SN	SN	SN	SN	SW	SN
		◇1	1	◇1	◇1	◇1	◇1	◇1		1	◇1	◇1	1	◇1	◇1 ⊼	◇1	◇1	◇1	1	◇1	◇1	1	◇1
Southampton Central	d	07 29	07 35						08 31			08 27	08 35								09 29	09 35	
Swanwick	d	07 46	08 02										09 02								09 46	10 02	
Fareham	d	07 53	08 10						08 52			09 02	09 10								09 53	10 10	
Portchester	d		08 15										09 15									10 15	
Cosham	d	08 02	08 20						09 00			09 11	09 20								10 02	10 20	
Portsmouth Harbour	d					08 05		08 43								09 05		09 43					
Portsmouth & Southsea	d					08 09		08 47								09 09		09 47					
Fratton	d					08 13		08 51								09 13		09 51					
Hilsea	d		08a26										09a26									10a26	
Bedhampton	d					08 20										09 20							
Havant	d	08 11				08 27		09 00	09 11			09 17				09 27		10 00			10 11		
Warblington	d					08 29										09 29							
Emsworth	d	08 15				08 32		09 04				09 21				09 32		10 04			10 15		
Southbourne	d					08 35		09 07								09 35		10 07					
Nutbourne	d					08 38										09 38							
Bosham	d					08 41										09 41							
Fishbourne (Sussex)	d					08 44										09 44							
Chichester 4	a	08 23				08 47		09 14	09 22			09 29				09 47		10 14			10 23		
	d	08 23				08 48		09 14	09 22			09 30				09 48		10 14			10 23		
Bognor Regis 4	d			08 34	08 52									09 34	09 52								10 34
Barnham	a	08 31		08 40	08 58	08 55		09 22	09 30			09 37		09 40	09 58	09 55		10 22			10 31		10 40
	d	08 32		08 41	08 59	09 02		09 22	09 30			09 38		09 41	09 59	10 02		10 22			10 32		10 41
Bognor Regis	a																						
Ford 4	d	08 36		08 45	09 03	09 06						09 42		09 45	10 03	10 06					10 36		10 45
Littlehampton 4	a			08 50										09 50									10 50
	d						09 14										10 14						
Angmering 3	d	08 42				09 12	09 22					09 48				10 12	10 22				10 42		
Goring-by-Sea	d	08 46				09 16	09 26					09 52				10 16	10 26				10 46		
Durrington-on-Sea	d	08 49				09 19	09 29					09 55				10 19	10 29				10 49		
West Worthing	d	08 51				09 21	09 31					09 57				10 21	10 31				10 51		
Worthing 4	a	08 53				09 23	09 33	09 37	09 45			09 59				10 23	10 33	10 37			10 53		
	d	08 54				09 24	09 41		09 45			10 00				10 24	10 41				10 54		
East Worthing	d	08 56				09 26						10 02				10 26					10 56		
Lancing	d	08 59				09 29						10 05				10 29					10 59		
Shoreham-by-Sea	d	09 03				09 33	09 47		09 52			10 09				10 33	10 47				11 03		
Southwick	d	09 06				09 36						10 12				10 36					11 06		
Fishersgate	d	09 08				09 38						10 14				10 38					11 08		
Portslade	d	09 10				09 40						10 16				10 40					11 10		
Aldrington	d	09 13				09 43						10 19				10 43					11 13		
Hove 2	d	09 15				09 45	09 54		09 59		10 02	10 21				10 45	10 54			11 01	11 15		
Brighton 10	a	09 19				09 49			10 05		10 06	10 25				10 49				11 05	11 19		
Preston Park	d																						
Burgess Hill	a						10 04										11 04						
Haywards Heath 3	a						10 09										11 09						
Arundel	d				09 08										10 08								
Amberley	d				09 13										10 13								
Pulborough	d				09 19										10 19								
Billingshurst	d				09 26										10 26								
Christs Hospital	d				09 32										10 32								
Horsham 4	a				09 37										10 37								
	d				09 37					10 00					10 37				11 00				
Crawley	d				09 46					10 13					10 46				11 13				
Three Bridges 4	a				09 50					10 16					10 50				11 16				
Gatwick Airport 10 ✈	a				09 55		10 22			10 22					10 55		11 22		11 22				
	d				09 56		10 23			10 23					10 56		11 23		11 23				
Horley	a				09 58					10 26					10 58				11 26				
Redhill 5	a				10 05					10 36					11 05				11 36				
East Croydon	a				10 19		10 39			10 56					11 19		11 39		11 56				
London Bridge 4 ⊖	a									11 13									12 13				
Clapham Junction 10	a				10 31		10 48								11 31		11 48						
London Victoria 15 ⊖	a				10 39		10 55								11 39		11 55						

until 4 September

Southampton, Portsmouth and Sussex Coast - Brighton, Gatwick Airport and London

Station		SN	SN	SN	SN	SN	SN	SN	SW	SN	SN	SN	SN	SN	SN	SN	SN	SW	SN	SN	SN
		◇1 ⊼	◇1	◇1	◇1	1	◇1	◇1	1	◇1	◇1 ⊼	◇1	◇1	◇1	1	◇1	◇1	1	◇1	◇1 ⊼	◇1
Southampton Central	d							10 29	10 35								11 28	11 35			
Swanwick	d							10 46	11 02								11 46	12 02			
Fareham	d							10 53	11 10								11 53	12 10			
Portchester	d								11 15									12 15			
Cosham	d							11 02	11 20								12 02	12 20			
Portsmouth Harbour	d		10 05		10 43							11 05		11 43							12 05
Portsmouth & Southsea	d		10 09		10 47							11 09		11 47							12 09
Fratton	d		10 13		10 51							11 13		11 51							12 13
Hilsea	d								11a26									12a26			
Bedhampton	d		10 20									11 20									12 20
Havant	d		10 27		11 00			11 11				11 27		12 00			12 11				12 27
Warblington	d		10 29									11 29									12 29
Emsworth	d		10 32		11 04			11 15				11 32		12 04			12 15				12 32
Southbourne	d		10 35		11 07							11 35		12 07							12 35
Nutbourne	d		10 38									11 38									12 38
Bosham	d		10 41									11 41									12 41
Fishbourne (Sussex)	d		10 44									11 44									12 44
Chichester 4	a		10 47		11 14			11 23				11 47		12 14			12 23				12 47
	d		10 48		11 14			11 23				11 48		12 14			12 23				12 48
Bognor Regis 4	d	10 52								11 34	11 52								12 34	12 52	
Barnham	a	10 58	10 55		11 22			11 31		11 40	11 58	11 55		12 22			12 31		12 40	12 58	12 55
	d	10 59	11 02		11 22			11 32		11 41	11 59	12 02		12 22			12 32		12 41	12 59	13 02
Bognor Regis	a																				
Ford 4	d	11 03	11 06					11 36		11 45	12 03	12 06					12 36		12 45	13 03	13 06
Littlehampton 4	a									11 50									12 50		
	d			11 14									12 14								
Angmering 3	d		11 12	11 22				11 42				12 12	12 22				12 42				13 12
Goring-by-Sea	d		11 16	11 26				11 46				12 16	12 26				12 46				13 16
Durrington-on-Sea	d		11 19	11 29				11 49				12 19	12 29				12 49				13 19
West Worthing	d		11 21	11 31				11 51				12 21	12 31				12 51				13 21
Worthing 4	a		11 23	11 33	11 37			11 53				12 23	12 33	12 37			12 53				13 23
	d		11 24	11 41				11 54				12 24	12 41				12 54				13 24
East Worthing	d		11 26					11 56				12 26					12 56				13 26
Lancing	d		11 29					11 59				12 29					12 59				13 29
Shoreham-by-Sea	d		11 33	11 47				12 03				12 33	12 47				13 03				13 33
Southwick	d		11 36					12 06				12 36					13 06				13 36
Fishersgate	d		11 38					12 08				12 38					13 08				13 38
Portslade	d		11 40					12 10				12 40					13 10				13 40
Aldrington	d		11 43					12 13				12 43					13 13				13 43
Hove 2	d		11 45	11 54			12 01	12 15				12 45	12 54			13 01	13 15				13 45
Brighton 10	a		11 49				12 05	12 19				12 49				13 05	13 19				13 49
Preston Park	d																				
Burgess Hill	a			12 04									13 04								
Haywards Heath 3	a			12 09									13 09								
Arundel	d	11 08									12 08									13 08	
Amberley	d	11 13									12 13									13 13	
Pulborough	d	11 19									12 19									13 19	
Billingshurst	d	11 26									12 26									13 26	
Christs Hospital	d	11 32									12 32									13 32	
Horsham 4	a	11 37									12 37									13 37	
	d	11 37				12 00					12 37				13 00					13 37	
Crawley	d	11 46				12 13					12 46				13 13					13 46	
Three Bridges 4	a	11 50				12 16					12 50				13 16					13 50	
Gatwick Airport 10 ✈	a	11 55		12 22		12 22					12 55		13 22		13 22					13 55	
	d	11 56		12 23		12 23					12 56		13 23		13 23					13 56	
Horley	a	11 58				12 26					12 58				13 26					13 58	
Redhill 5	a	12 05				12 36					13 05				13 36					14 05	
East Croydon	a	12 19		12 39		12 56					13 19		13 39		13 56					14 19	
London Bridge 4 ⊖	a					13 13									14 13						
Clapham Junction 10	a	12 31		12 48							13 31		13 48							14 31	
London Victoria 15 ⊖	a	12 39		12 55							13 39		13 55							14 39	

Table 188

Sundays

until 4 September

Southampton, Portsmouth and Sussex Coast - Brighton, Gatwick Airport and London

		SN	SN	SN	SN	SN	SW	SN	SN	SN	SN	SN	GW	SN	SN	SN	SW	SN	SN	SN	SN	SN	SN
		◇1	◇1	1	◇1	◇1	1	◇1	◇1 🚲	◇1	◇1	◇1	◇	1	◇1	◇1	1	◇1	◇1 🚲	◇1	◇1	◇1	1
Southampton Central ⛴	d					12 29	12 35						13 08			13 29	13 35						
Swanwick	d					12 46	13 02									13 46	14 02						
Fareham	d					12 53	13 10						13 34			13 53	14 10						
Portchester	d						13 15										14 15						
Cosham	d					13 02	13 20						13 42			14 02	14 20						
Portsmouth Harbour ⛴	d		12 43							13 05		13 43								14 05		14 43	
Portsmouth & Southsea	d		12 47							13 09		13 47								14 09		14 47	
Fratton	d		12 51							13 13		13 51								14 13		14 51	
Hilsea	d						13a26										14a26						
Bedhampton	d									13 20										14 20			
Havant	d		13 00			13 11				13 27		14 00	14 04			14 11				14 27		15 00	
Warblington	d									13 29										14 29			
Emsworth	d		13 04			13 15				13 32		14 04				14 15				14 32		15 04	
Southbourne	d		13 07							13 35		14 07								14 35		15 07	
Nutbourne	d									13 38										14 38			
Bosham	d									13 41										14 41			
Fishbourne (Sussex)	d									13 44										14 44			
Chichester 4	a		13 14			13 23				13 47		14 14	14 19			14 23				14 47		15 14	
	d		13 14			13 23				13 48		14 14	14 19			14 23				14 48		15 14	
Bognor Regis 4	d							13 34	13 52									14 34	14 52				
Barnham	a		13 22			13 31		13 40	13 58	13 55		14 22	14 27			14 31		14 40	14 58	14 55		15 22	
	d		13 22			13 32		13 41	13 59	14 02		14 22	14 27			14 32		14 41	14 59	15 02		15 22	
Bognor Regis	a																						
Ford 4	d					13 36		13 45	14 03	14 06						14 36		14 45	15 03	15 06			
Littlehampton 4	a							13 50										14 50					
	d	13 14									14 14										15 14		
Angmering 3	d	13 22				13 42				14 12	14 22					14 42				15 12	15 22		
Goring-by-Sea	d	13 26				13 46				14 16	14 26					14 46				15 16	15 26		
Durrington-on-Sea	d	13 29				13 49				14 19	14 29					14 49				15 19	15 29		
West Worthing	d	13 31				13 51				14 21	14 31					14 51				15 21	15 31		
Worthing 4	a	13 33	13 37			13 53				14 23	14 33	14 37	14 44			14 53				15 23	15 33	15 37	
	d		13 41			13 54				14 24		14 41	14 45			14 54				15 24		15 41	
East Worthing	d					13 56				14 26						14 56				15 26			
Lancing	d					13 59				14 29						14 59				15 29			
Shoreham-by-Sea	d		13 47			14 03				14 33		14 47	14 51			15 03				15 33		15 47	
Southwick	d					14 06				14 36						15 06				15 36			
Fishersgate	d					14 08				14 38						15 08				15 38			
Portslade	d					14 10				14 40						15 10				15 40			
Aldrington	d					14 13				14 43						15 13				15 43			
Hove 2	d		13 54		14 01	14 15				14 45		14 54	15 00		15 03	15 15				15 45		15 54	
Brighton 10	a				14 05	14 19				14 49			15 06		15 07	15 19				15 49			
Preston Park	d																						
Burgess Hill	a		14 04									15 04										16 04	
Haywards Heath 3	a		14 09									15 09										16 09	
Arundel	d								14 08										15 08				
Amberley	d								14 13										15 13				
Pulborough	d								14 19										15 19				
Billingshurst	d								14 26										15 26				
Christs Hospital	d								14 32										15 32				
Horsham 4	a								14 37										15 37				
	d			14 00					14 37					15 00					15 37				16 00
Crawley	d			14 13					14 46					15 13					15 46				16 13
Three Bridges 4	a			14 16					14 50					15 16					15 50				16 16
Gatwick Airport 10 ✈	a		14 22	14 22					14 55			15 22		15 22					15 55			16 22	16 22
	d		14 23	14 23					14 56			15 23		15 23					15 56			16 23	16 23
Horley	a			14 26					14 58					15 26					15 58				16 26
Redhill 5	a			14 36					15 05					15 36					16 05				16 36
East Croydon 🚊	a		14 39	14 56					15 19			15 39		15 56					16 19			16 39	16 56
London Bridge 4 ⊖	a			15 13										16 13									17 13
Clapham Junction 10	a		14 48						15 31			15 48							16 31			16 48	
London Victoria 15 ⊖	a		14 55						15 39			15 55							16 39			16 55	

Table 188

Sundays

until 4 September

Southampton, Portsmouth and Sussex Coast - Brighton, Gatwick Airport and London

		SN	SN	SW	SN	SN	SN	SN	SN	GW	SN	SN	SN	SW	SN	SN	SN	SN	SN	SN	SN	SN	SW
		◇1	◇1	1	◇1	◇1 🚲	◇1	◇1	◇1	◇	1	◇1	◇1	1	◇1	◇1 🚲	◇1	◇1	◇1	1	◇1	◇1	1
Southampton Central ⛴	d		14 29	14 35						15 22			15 29	15 35								16 29	16 35
Swanwick	d		14 46	15 02									15 46	16 02								16 46	17 02
Fareham	d		14 53	15 10						15 51			15 58	16 10								16 53	17 10
Portchester	d			15 15										16 15									17 15
Cosham	d		15 02	15 20						16 01			16 07	16 20								17 02	17 20
Portsmouth Harbour ⛴	d						15 05		15 43								16 05		16 43				
Portsmouth & Southsea	d						15 09		15 47								16 09		16 47				
Fratton	d						15 13		15 51								16 13		16 51				
Hilsea	d			15a26										16a26									17a26
Bedhampton	d						15 20										16 20						
Havant	d		15 11				15 27		16 00	16 11			16 16				16 27		17 00			17 11	
Warblington	d						15 29										16 29						
Emsworth	d		15 15				15 32		16 04				16 20				16 32		17 04			17 15	
Southbourne	d						15 35		16 07								16 35		17 07				
Nutbourne	d						15 38										16 38						
Bosham	d						15 41										16 41						
Fishbourne (Sussex)	d						15 44										16 44						
Chichester 4	a		15 23				15 47		16 14	16 22			16 28				16 47		17 14			17 23	
	d		15 23				15 48		16 14	16 22			16 28				16 48		17 14			17 23	
Bognor Regis 4	d				15 34	15 52									16 34	16 52							
Barnham	a		15 31		15 40	15 58	15 55		16 22	16 30			16 36		16 40	16 58	16 55		17 22			17 31	
	d		15 32		15 41	15 59	16 02		16 22	16 30			16 38		16 41	16 59	17 02		17 22			17 32	
Bognor Regis	a																						
Ford 4	d		15 36		15 45	16 03	16 06						16 42		16 45	17 03	17 06					17 36	
Littlehampton 4	a				15 50										16 50								
	d							16 14										17 14					
Angmering 3	d		15 42				16 12	16 22					16 48				17 12	17 22				17 42	
Goring-by-Sea	d		15 46				16 16	16 26					16 52				17 16	17 26				17 46	
Durrington-on-Sea	d		15 49				16 19	16 29					16 55				17 19	17 29				17 49	
West Worthing	d		15 51				16 21	16 31					16 57				17 21	17 31				17 51	
Worthing 4	a		15 53				16 23	16 33	16 37	16 45			16 59				17 23	17 33	17 37			17 53	
	d		15 54				16 24		16 41	16 45			17 00				17 24		17 41			17 54	
East Worthing	d		15 56				16 26						17 02				17 26					17 56	
Lancing	d		15 59				16 29						17 05				17 29					17 59	
Shoreham-by-Sea	d		16 03				16 33		16 47	16 52			17 09				17 33		17 47			18 03	
Southwick	d		16 06				16 36						17 12				17 36					18 06	
Fishersgate	d		16 08				16 38						17 14				17 38					18 08	
Portslade	d		16 10				16 40						17 16				17 40					18 10	
Aldrington	d		16 13				16 43						17 19				17 43					18 13	
Hove 2	d	16 01	16 15				16 45		16 54	16 59		17 02	17 22				17 45		17 54		18 01	18 15	
Brighton 10	a	16 05	16 19				16 49			17 05		17 06	17 26				17 49				18 05	18 19	
Preston Park	d																						
Burgess Hill	a								17 04										18 04				
Haywards Heath 3	a								17 09										18 09				
Arundel	d					16 08										17 08							
Amberley	d					16 13										17 13							
Pulborough	d					16 19										17 19							
Billingshurst	d					16 26										17 26							
Christs Hospital	d					16 32										17 32							
Horsham 4	a					16 37										17 37							
	d					16 37					17 00					17 37				18 00			
Crawley	d					16 46					17 13					17 46				18 13			
Three Bridges 4	a					16 50					17 16					17 50				18 16			
Gatwick Airport 10 ✈	a					16 55			17 22		17 22					17 55			18 22	18 22			
	d					16 56			17 23		17 23					17 56			18 23	18 23			
Horley	a					16 58					17 26					17 58				18 26			
Redhill 5	a					17 05					17 36					18 05				18 36			
East Croydon 🚊	a					17 19			17 39		17 56					18 19			18 39	18 56			
London Bridge 4 ⊖	a										18 13									19 13			
Clapham Junction 10	a					17 31			17 48							18 31			18 48				
London Victoria 15 ⊖	a					17 39			17 55							18 39			18 55				

Southampton, Portsmouth and Sussex Coast - Brighton, Gatwick Airport and London

		SN ◇1	SN ◇1	SN ◇1	SN ◇1	SN ◇1	SN 1	SN ◇1	SN ◇1	SW 1	SN ◇1	SN ◇1	SN ◇1	SN ◇1	SN ◇1	SN 1	SN ◇1	SN ◇1	SW 1	SN ◇1	SN ◇1
Southampton Central ⛴	d								17 29	17 35								18 29	18 35		
Swanwick	d								17 46	18 02								18 46	19 02		
Fareham	d								17 53	18 10								18 53	19 10		
Portchester	d									18 15									19 15		
Cosham	d								18 02	18 20								19 02	19 20		
Portsmouth Harbour ⛴	d			17 05		17 43							18 05		18 43						19 05
Portsmouth & Southsea	d			17 09		17 47							18 09		18 47						19 09
Fratton	d			17 13		17 51							18 13		18 51						19 13
Hilsea	d									18a26									19a26		
Bedhampton	d			17 20									18 20								19 20
Havant	d			17 27		18 00			18 11				18 27		19 00			19 11			19 27
Warblington	d			17 29									18 29								19 29
Emsworth	d			17 32		18 04			18 15				18 32		19 04			19 15			19 32
Southbourne	d			17 35		18 07							18 35		19 07						19 35
Nutbourne	d			17 38									18 38								19 38
Bosham	d			17 41									18 41								19 41
Fishbourne (Sussex)	d			17 44									18 44								19 44
Chichester 4	a			17 47		18 14			18 23				18 47		19 14			19 23			19 47
	d			17 48		18 14			18 23				18 48		19 14			19 23			19 48
Bognor Regis 4	d	17 34	17 52								18 34	18 52								19 34	
Barnham	a	17 40	17 58	17 55		18 22			18 31		18 40	18 58	18 55		19 22			19 31		19 40	19 55
	d	17 41	17 59	18 02		18 22			18 32		18 41	18 59	19 02		19 22			19 32		19 41	20 02
Bognor Regis	a																				
Ford 4	d	17 45	18 03	18 06					18 36		18 45	19 03	19 06					19 36		19 45	20 06
Littlehampton 4	a	17 50									18 50									19 50	
	d				18 14									19 14							
Angmering 3	d			18 12	18 22				18 42				19 12	19 22				19 42			20 12
Goring-by-Sea	d			18 16	18 26				18 46				19 16	19 26				19 46			20 16
Durrington-on-Sea	d			18 19	18 29				18 49				19 19	19 29				19 49			20 19
West Worthing	d			18 21	18 31				18 51				19 21	19 31				19 51			20 21
Worthing 4	a			18 23	18 33	18 37			18 53				19 23	19 33	19 37			19 53			20 23
	d			18 24	18 41				18 54				19 24	19 41				19 54			20 24
East Worthing	d			18 26					18 56				19 26					19 56			20 26
Lancing	d			18 29					18 59				19 29					19 59			20 29
Shoreham-by-Sea	d			18 33	18 47				19 03				19 33	19 47				20 03			20 33
Southwick	d			18 36					19 06				19 36					20 06			20 36
Fishersgate	d			18 38					19 08				19 38					20 08			20 38
Portslade	d			18 40					19 10				19 40					20 10			20 40
Aldrington	d			18 43					19 13				19 43					20 13			20 43
Hove 2	d			18 45	18 54			19 01	19 15				19 45	19 54			20 01	20 15			20 45
Brighton 10	a			18 49				19 05	19 19				19 49				20 05	20 19			20 49
Preston Park	d																				
Burgess Hill	a				19 04									20 04							
Haywards Heath 3	a				19 09									20 09							
Arundel	d		18 08									19 08									
Amberley	d		18 13									19 13									
Pulborough	d		18 19									19 19									
Billingshurst	d		18 26									19 26									
Christs Hospital	d		18 32									19 32									
Horsham 4	a		18 37									19 37									
	d		18 37				19 00					19 37				20 00					
Crawley	d		18 46				19 13					19 46				20 13					
Three Bridges 4	a		18 50				19 16					19 50				20 16					
Gatwick Airport 10 ✈	a		18 55		19 22		19 22					19 55		20 22		20 22					
	d		18 56		19 23		19 23					19 56		20 23		20 23					
Horley	a		18 58				19 26					19 58				20 26					
Redhill 5	a		19 05				19 36					20 05				20 36					
East Croydon	a		19 19		19 39		19 56					20 19		20 39		20 56					
London Bridge 4 ⊖	a						20 13									21 13					
Clapham Junction 10	a		19 31		19 48							20 31		20 48							
London Victoria 15 ⊖	a		19 39		19 55							20 39		20 55							

Southampton, Portsmouth and Sussex Coast - Brighton, Gatwick Airport and London

		SN ◇1	SN ◇1	SN 1	SN ◇1	GW ◇	SN ◇1	SW 1	SN ◇1	SN ◇1	SN ◇1	SN ◇1	SN ◇1	SW 1	SN ◇1	SN 1	SN ◇1	SN ◇1	SN ◇	SN ◇1	SN ◇1	SW 1	SN ◇
Southampton Central ⛴	d					19 27	19 30	19 35					20 29	20 35							21 30	21 35	
Swanwick	d							20 02						21 02							21 47	22 02	
Fareham	d					19 50	20 03	20 10					21 02	21 10							21 54	22 10	
Portchester	d							20 15						21 15								22 15	
Cosham	d					19 59	20 12	20 20					21 11	21 20							22 03	22 20	
Portsmouth Harbour ⛴	d		19 43							20 05		20 43						21 05		21 43			
Portsmouth & Southsea	d		19 47							20 09		20 47						21 09		21 47			
Fratton	d		19 51							20 13		20 51						21 13		21 51			
Hilsea	d							20a26						21a26								22a26	
Bedhampton	d									20 20								21 20					
Havant	d		20 00			20 11	20 18			20 27		21 00	21 17					21 27		22 00	22 11		
Warblington	d									20 29								21 29					
Emsworth	d		20 04				20 22			20 32		21 04	21 21					21 32		22 04	22 15		
Southbourne	d		20 07							20 35		21 07						21 35		22 07			
Nutbourne	d									20 38								21 38					
Bosham	d									20 41								21 41					
Fishbourne (Sussex)	d									20 44								21 44					
Chichester 4	a		20 14			20 21	20 30			20 47		21 14	21 29					21 47		22 14	22 23		
	d		20 14			20 22	20 31			20 48		21 14	21 30					21 48		22 14	22 23		
Bognor Regis 4	d								20 34		20 52				21 34		21 52		22 12				
Barnham	a		20 22			20 29	20 38		20 41	20 55	20 58	21 22	21 37		21 40		21 58	21 55	22 18	22 22	22 31		
	d		20 22			20 30	20 39		20 42	20 56	20 59	21 22	21 38		21 41		21 59	22 02		22 23	22 32		22 52
Bognor Regis	a																						22 58
Ford 4	d						20 43		20 46	21 00	21 03	21 27	21 42		21 45		22 03	22 06		22 27	22 36		
Littlehampton 4	a								20 51	21 05		21 31			21 50					22 32			
	d	20 14								21 14		21 42								22 42			
Angmering 3	d	20 22					20 49			21 22		21 52	21 48					22 12		22 50	22 42		
Goring-by-Sea	d	20 26					20 53			21 26		21 56	21 52					22 16		22 54	22 46		
Durrington-on-Sea	d	20 29					20 56			21 29		21 59	21 55					22 19		22 57	22 49		
West Worthing	d	20 31					20 58			21 31		22 01	21 57					22 21		22 59	22 51		
Worthing 4	a	20 33	20 37			20 51	21 00			21 33		22 03	21 59					22 23		23 01	22 53		
	d	20 41				20 51	21 01			21 34		22 04	22 00					22 24		23 02	22 54		
East Worthing	d						21 03			21 36		22 06	22 02					22 26		23 04	22 56		
Lancing	d						21 06			21 39		22 09	22 05					22 29		23 07	22 59		
Shoreham-by-Sea	d	20 47				20 58	21 10			21 43		22 13	22 09					22 33		23 11	23 03		
Southwick	d						21 13			21 46		22 16	22 12					22 36		23 14	23 06		
Fishersgate	d						21 15			21 48		22 18	22 14					22 38		23 16	23 08		
Portslade	d						21 17			21 50		22 20	22 16					22 40		23 18	23 10		
Aldrington	d						21 20			21 53		22 23	22 19					22 43		23 21	23 13		
Hove 2	d	20 54			21 01	21 05	21 22			21 55		22 25	22 21					22 45		23 25	23 15		
Brighton 10	a				21 05	21 10	21 26			21 59		22 29	22 25					22 49		23 29	23 19		
Preston Park	d																						
Burgess Hill	a	21 04																					
Haywards Heath 3	a	21 09																					
Arundel	d										21 08						22 08						
Amberley	d										21 13						22 13						
Pulborough	d										21 19						22 19						
Billingshurst	d										21 26						22 26						
Christs Hospital	d										21 32						22 32						
Horsham 4	a										21 37						22 37						
	d			21 00							21 37					22 00	22 37						
Crawley	d			21 13							21 46					22 13	22 46						
Three Bridges 4	a			21 16							21 50					22 16	22 50						
Gatwick Airport 10 ✈	a	21 22		21 22							21 55					22 22	22 55						
	d	21 23		21 23							21 56					22 23	22 56						
Horley	a			21 26							21 58					22 26	22 58						
Redhill 5	a			21 36							22 05					22 36	23 05						
East Croydon	a	21 39		21 56							22 19					22 56	23 20						
London Bridge 4 ⊖	a			22 13																			
Clapham Junction 10	a	21 48									22 31					23 07	23 31						
London Victoria 15 ⊖	a	21 55									22 39					23 14	23 38						

Table 188

Sundays until 4 September

Southampton, Portsmouth and Sussex Coast - Brighton, Gatwick Airport and London

		SN ◇ 1	SN ◇ 1	SW 1	SN ◇ 1	SN ◇ 1	SN 1
Southampton Central ⛴	d		22 15	22 35		22 52	
Swanwick	d		22 32	23 02		23 11	
Fareham	d		22 39	23 10		23 17	
Portchester	d			23 15			
Cosham	d		22 48	23 20		23 26	
Portsmouth Harbour ⛴	d	22 14			22 43		
Portsmouth & Southsea	d	22 18			22 47		
Fratton	d	22 22			22 51		
Hilsea	d			23a24			
Bedhampton	d	22 32					
Havant	d	22 35	22 54		23 00	23 32	
Warblington	d	22 37					
Emsworth	d	22 40	22 58		23 04	23 36	
Southbourne	d	22 43			23 07		
Nutbourne	d	22 46					
Bosham	d	22 49					
Fishbourne (Sussex)	d	22 52					
Chichester 4	a	22 55	23 06		23 14	23 44	
	d	22 56	23 07		23 14	23 45	
Bognor Regis 4	d						
Barnham	a	23 03	23 14		23 23	23 52	
	d	23 04	23 15		23 24	23 53	
Bognor Regis	a						
Ford 4	d	23 08	23 19		23 28		
Littlehampton 4	a	23 13	23 27		23 33	00 01	
	d						
Angmering 3	d						
Goring-by-Sea	d						
Durrington-on-Sea	d						
West Worthing	d						
Worthing 4	a						
	d						
East Worthing	d						
Lancing	d						
Shoreham-by-Sea	d						
Southwick	d						
Fishersgate	d						
Portslade	d						
Aldrington	d						
Hove 2	d						
Brighton 10	a						
Preston Park	d						
Burgess Hill	a						
Haywards Heath 3	a						
Arundel	d						
Amberley	d						
Pulborough	d						
Billingshurst	d						
Christs Hospital	d						
Horsham 4	a						
	d						23 03
Crawley	d						23 16
Three Bridges 4	a						23 19
Gatwick Airport 10 ✈	a						23 24
	d						23 25
Horley	a						23 28
Redhill 5	a						23 34
East Croydon 🚊	a						23 55
London Bridge 4 ⊖	a						
Clapham Junction 10	a						00 11
London Victoria 15 ⊖	a						00 21

Table 188

Sundays from 11 September

Southampton, Portsmouth and Sussex Coast - Brighton, Gatwick Airport and London

		SN ◇ 1	SN 1	SN ◇ 1	SN ◇ 1	SN 1	SN ◇ 1	SN 1	SW 1	SN ◇	SN 1	SN ◇ 1
Southampton Central ⛴	d								06 35			
Swanwick	d								07 02			
Fareham	d								07 10			
Portchester	d								07 15			
Cosham	d								07 20			
Portsmouth Harbour ⛴	d	22p44			23p15							
Portsmouth & Southsea	d	22p48			23p19							
Fratton	d	22p52			23p23							
Hilsea	d	22p56			23p27				07a26			
Bedhampton	d	23p01			23p33							
Havant	d	23p05			23p36							
Warblington	d				23p38							
Emsworth	d				23p41							
Southbourne	d				23p44							
Nutbourne	d				23p47							
Bosham	d				23p50							
Fishbourne (Sussex)	d				23p53							
Chichester 4	a	23p16			23p57							
	d	23p18		23p52	23p57							
Bognor Regis 4	d											06 58
Barnham	a	23p26		23p59	00 05							07 04
	d	23p26		00 01	00 06		06 06			06 45		07 05
Bognor Regis	a									06 51		
Ford 4	d	23p31		00 05	00 10							07 09
Littlehampton 4	a	23p35		00 10	00 15		06 13					
	d	23p40					06 20					
Angmering 3	d	23p48										
Goring-by-Sea	d	23p52										
Durrington-on-Sea	d	23p54										
West Worthing	d	23p56										
Worthing 4	a	23p59					06 33					
	d	23p59					06 33					
East Worthing	d	00 02										
Lancing	d	00 05					06 37					
Shoreham-by-Sea	d	00 09					06 41					
Southwick	d	00 12					06 44					
Fishersgate	d	00 14										
Portslade	d	00 16					06 48					
Aldrington	d	00 18										
Hove 2	d	00 21					06 51					
Brighton 10	a	00 25					06 55					
Preston Park	d											
Burgess Hill	a											
Haywards Heath 3	a											
Arundel	d											07 14
Amberley	d											07 19
Pulborough	d											07 25
Billingshurst	d											07 31
Christs Hospital	d											07 38
Horsham 4	a											07 42
	d		23p02			06 04		06 34			07 03	07 42
Crawley	d		23p14			06 17		06 47			07 16	07 51
Three Bridges 4	a		23p18			06 20		06 51			07 19	07 54
Gatwick Airport 10 ✈	a		23p22			06 25		06 57			07 24	07 59
	d		23p23					06 58			07 25	08 00
Horley	a		23p26					07 00			07 28	08 02
Redhill 5	a		23p36					07 07			07 34	08 09
East Croydon 🚊	a		23p55					07 26			07 56	08 26
London Bridge 4 ⊖	a										08 13	
Clapham Junction 10	a		00 11					07 40				08 37
London Victoria 15 ⊖	a		00 18					07 48				08 46

		SN ◇ 1	SN ◇	SN ◇	SN ◇ 1	SN 1	SN ◇ 1	SN ◇ 1	SN ◇ 1	SN ◇ 1	SN ◇ 1	SW 1
Southampton Central ⛴	d										07 29	07 35
Swanwick	d										07 46	08 02
Fareham	d										07 53	08 10
Portchester	d											08 15
Cosham	d										08 02	08 20
Portsmouth Harbour ⛴	d							07 14		07 43		
Portsmouth & Southsea	d							07 18		07 47		
Fratton	d							07 22		07 51		
Hilsea	d											08a26
Bedhampton	d							07 30				
Havant	d							07 33		08 00	08 11	
Warblington	d							07 35				
Emsworth	d							07 38		08 04	08 15	
Southbourne	d							07 41		08 07		
Nutbourne	d							07 43				
Bosham	d							07 47				
Fishbourne (Sussex)	d							07 50				
Chichester 4	a							07 53		08 14	08 23	
	d							07 53		08 14	08 23	
Bognor Regis 4	d				07 34		07 58					
Barnham	a				07 40		08 04	08 01		08 22	08 31	
	d				07 41		08 05	08 08		08 22	08 38	
Bognor Regis	a											
Ford 4	d				07 45		08 09	08 12			08 42	
Littlehampton 4	a				07 50							
	d	07 14		07 40					08 14			
Angmering 3	d	07 22		07 48				08 18	08 22		08 48	
Goring-by-Sea	d	07 26		07 52				08 22	08 26		08 52	
Durrington-on-Sea	d	07 29		07 55				08 25	08 29		08 55	
West Worthing	d	07 31		07 57				08 27	08 31		08 57	
Worthing 4	a	07 33		07 59				08 29	08 33	08 37	08 59	
	d	07 35		08 00				08 30	08 41		09 00	
East Worthing	d			08 02				08 32			09 02	
Lancing	d	07 39		08 05				08 35			09 05	
Shoreham-by-Sea	d	07 43		08 09				08 39	08 47		09 09	
Southwick	d	07 46		08 12				08 42			09 12	
Fishersgate	d			08 14				08 44			09 14	
Portslade	d	07 49		08 16				08 46			09 16	
Aldrington	d			08 19				08 49			09 19	
Hove 2	d	07 54	07 56	08 21				08 56	08 54		09 22	
Brighton 10	a		08 00	08 25				09 00			09 26	
Preston Park	d											
Burgess Hill	a	08 04							09 04			
Haywards Heath 3	a	08 09							09 09			
Arundel	d						08 14					
Amberley	d						08 19					
Pulborough	d						08 25					
Billingshurst	d						08 31					
Christs Hospital	d						08 38					
Horsham 4	a						08 42					
	d					08 03	08 42					
Crawley	d					08 16	08 51					
Three Bridges 4	a					08 19	08 54					
Gatwick Airport 10 ✈	a	08 22				08 24	08 59		09 21			
	d	08 23				08 25	09 00		09 23			
Horley	a					08 28	09 02					
Redhill 5	a					08 34	09 09					
East Croydon 🚊	a	08 39				08 56	09 26		09 39			
London Bridge 4 ⊖	a					09 13						
Clapham Junction 10	a	08 54					09 37		09 54			
London Victoria 15 ⊖	a	09 01					09 46		10 01			

Table 188

Sunday

from 11 September

Southampton, Portsmouth and Sussex Coast - Brighton, Gatwick Airport and London

		SN ◇1	SN 1	SN ◇1 🛒	SN ◇1	SN ◇1	SN ◇1	GW	SN ◇1	SW 1	SN ◇1	SN 1	SN ◇1 🛒	SN ◇1	SN ◇1	SN ◇1	SN ◇1	SW 1	SN ◇1	SN 1	SN ◇1 🛒	SN ◇1	SN ◇1
Southampton Central ⛴	d							08 31	08 27	08 35							09 29	09 35					
Swanwick	d									09 02							09 46	10 02					
Fareham	d							08 52	09 02	09 10							09 53	10 10					
Portchester	d									09 15								10 15					
Cosham	d							09 00	09 11	09 20							10 02	10 20					
Portsmouth Harbour ⛴	d				08 14		08 43							09 14		09 43						10 14	
Portsmouth & Southsea	d				08 18		08 47							09 18		09 47						10 18	
Fratton	d				08 22		08 51							09 22		09 51						10 22	
Hilsea	d									09a26								10a26					
Bedhampton	d				08 30									09 30								10 30	
Havant	d				08 33		09 00	09 11	09 17					09 33		10 00	10 11					10 33	
Warblington	d				08 35									09 35								10 35	
Emsworth	d				08 38		09 04		09 21					09 38		10 04	10 15					10 38	
Southbourne	d				08 41		09 07							09 41		10 07						10 41	
Nutbourne	d				08 43									09 43								10 43	
Bosham	d				08 47									09 47								10 47	
Fishbourne (Sussex)	d				08 50									09 50								10 50	
Chichester 4	a				08 53		09 14	09 22	09 29					09 53		10 14	10 23					10 53	
	d				08 53		09 14	09 22	09 30					09 53		10 14	10 23					10 53	
Bognor Regis 4	d	08 36		08 58							09 36		09 58						10 34		10 58		
Barnham	a	08 42		09 04	09 01		09 22	09 30	09 37		09 42		10 04	10 01		10 22	10 31		10 40		11 04	11 01	
	d	08 43		09 05	09 08		09 22	09 30	09 38		09 43		10 05	10 08		10 22	10 38		10 41		11 05	11 08	
Bognor Regis	a																						
Ford 4	d	08 47		09 09	09 12				09 42		09 47		10 09	10 12			10 42		10 45		11 09	11 12	
Littlehampton 4	a	08 52									09 52								10 50				
	d					09 14									10 14								11 14
Angmering 3	d				09 18	09 22			09 48					10 18	10 22		10 48					11 18	11 22
Goring-by-Sea	d				09 22	09 26			09 52					10 22	10 26		10 52					11 22	11 26
Durrington-on-Sea	d				09 25	09 29			09 55					10 25	10 29		10 55					11 25	11 29
West Worthing	d				09 27	09 31			09 57					10 27	10 31		10 57					11 27	11 31
Worthing 4	a				09 29	09 33	09 37	09 45	09 59					10 29	10 33	10 37	10 59					11 29	11 33
	d				09 30	09 41		09 45	10 00					10 30	10 41		11 00					11 30	11 41
East Worthing	d				09 32				10 02					10 32			11 02					11 32	
Lancing	d				09 35				10 05					10 35			11 05					11 35	
Shoreham-by-Sea	d				09 39	09 47		09 52	10 09					10 39	10 47		11 09					11 39	11 47
Southwick	d				09 42				10 12					10 42			11 12					11 42	
Fishersgate	d				09 44				10 14					10 44			11 14					11 44	
Portslade	d				09 46				10 16					10 46			11 16					11 46	
Aldrington	d				09 49				10 19					10 49			11 19					11 49	
Hove 2	d				09 56	09 54		09 59	10 21					10 56	10 54		11 22					11 56	11 54
Brighton 10	a				10 00			10 05	10 25					11 00			11 26					12 00	
Preston Park	d																						
Burgess Hill	a					10 04									11 04								12 04
Haywards Heath 3	a					10 09									11 09								12 09
Arundel	d			09 14									10 14								11 14		
Amberley	d			09 19									10 19								11 19		
Pulborough	d			09 25									10 25								11 25		
Billingshurst	d			09 31									10 31								11 31		
Christs Hospital	d			09 38									10 38								11 38		
Horsham 4	a			09 42									10 42								11 42		
	d		09 03	09 42								10 03	10 42							11 03	11 42		
Crawley	d		09 16	09 51								10 16	10 51							11 16	11 51		
Three Bridges 4	a		09 19	09 54								10 19	10 54							11 19	11 54		
Gatwick Airport 10 ✈	a		09 24	09 59		10 21						10 24	10 59		11 21					11 24	11 59		12 22
	d		09 25	10 00		10 23						10 25	11 00		11 23					11 25	12 00		12 23
Horley	a		09 28	10 02								10 28	11 02							11 28	12 02		
Redhill 5	a		09 34	10 09								10 34	11 09							11 34	12 09		
East Croydon 🚆	a		09 56	10 26		10 39						10 56	11 26		11 39					11 56	12 26		12 39
London Bridge 4 ⊖	a		10 13									11 13								12 13			
Clapham Junction 10	a			10 37		10 54							11 37		11 54						12 37		12 54
London Victoria 15 ⊖	a			10 46		11 01							11 46		12 01						12 46		13 01

from 11 September

Southampton, Portsmouth and Sussex Coast - Brighton, Gatwick Airport and London

		SN ◇1	SN ◇1	SW 1	SN ◇1	SN 1	SN ◇1 🛒	SN ◇1	SN ◇1	SN ◇1	SN ◇1	SW 1	SN ◇1	SN 1	SN ◇1 🛒	SN ◇1	SN ◇1	SN ◇1	SN ◇1	SW 1	SN ◇1	SN 1
Southampton Central ⛴	d		10 29	10 35							11 28	11 35							12 29	12 35		
Swanwick	d		10 46	11 02							11 46	12 02							12 46	13 02		
Fareham	d		10 53	11 10							11 53	12 10							12 53	13 10		
Portchester	d			11 15								12 15								13 15		
Cosham	d		11 02	11 20							12 02	12 20							13 02	13 20		
Portsmouth Harbour ⛴	d	10 43						11 14		11 43						12 14		12 43				
Portsmouth & Southsea	d	10 47						11 18		11 47						12 18		12 47				
Fratton	d	10 51						11 22		11 51						12 22		12 51				
Hilsea	d			11a26								12a26								13a26		
Bedhampton	d							11 30								12 30						
Havant	d	11 00	11 11					11 33		12 00	12 11					12 33		13 00	13 11			
Warblington	d							11 35								12 35						
Emsworth	d	11 04	11 15					11 38		12 04	12 15					12 38		13 04	13 15			
Southbourne	d	11 07						11 41		12 07						12 41		13 07				
Nutbourne	d							11 43								12 43						
Bosham	d							11 47								12 47						
Fishbourne (Sussex)	d							11 50								12 50						
Chichester 4	a	11 14	11 23					11 53		12 14	12 23					12 53		13 14	13 23			
	d	11 14	11 23					11 53		12 14	12 23					12 53		13 14	13 23			
Bognor Regis 4	d				11 34		11 58						12 34		12 58						13 34	
Barnham	a	11 22	11 31		11 40		12 04	12 01		12 22	12 31		12 40		13 04	13 01		13 22	13 31		13 40	
	d	11 22	11 38		11 41		12 05	12 08		12 22	12 38		12 41		13 05	13 08		13 22	13 38		13 41	
Bognor Regis	a																					
Ford 4	d		11 42		11 45		12 09	12 12			12 42		12 45		13 09	13 12			13 42		13 45	
Littlehampton 4	a				11 50								12 50								13 50	
	d								12 14								13 14					
Angmering 3	d		11 48					12 18	12 22		12 48					13 18	13 22		13 48			
Goring-by-Sea	d		11 52					12 22	12 26		12 52					13 22	13 26		13 52			
Durrington-on-Sea	d		11 55					12 25	12 29		12 55					13 25	13 29		13 55			
West Worthing	d		11 57					12 27	12 31		12 57					13 27	13 31		13 57			
Worthing 4	a	11 37	11 59					12 29	12 33	12 37	12 59					13 29	13 33	13 37	13 59			
	d		12 00					12 30	12 41		13 00					13 30	13 41		14 00			
East Worthing	d		12 02					12 32			13 02					13 32			14 02			
Lancing	d		12 05					12 35			13 05					13 35			14 05			
Shoreham-by-Sea	d		12 09					12 39	12 47		13 09					13 39	13 47		14 09			
Southwick	d		12 12					12 42			13 12					13 42			14 12			
Fishersgate	d		12 14					12 44			13 14					13 44			14 14			
Portslade	d		12 16					12 46			13 16					13 46			14 16			
Aldrington	d		12 19					12 49			13 19					13 49			14 19			
Hove 2	d		12 22					12 56	12 54		13 22					13 56	13 54		14 22			
Brighton 10	a		12 26					13 00			13 26					14 00			14 26			
Preston Park	d																					
Burgess Hill	a								13 04								14 04					
Haywards Heath 3	a								13 09								14 09					
Arundel	d						12 14								13 14							
Amberley	d						12 19								13 19							
Pulborough	d						12 25								13 25							
Billingshurst	d						12 31								13 31							
Christs Hospital	d						12 38								13 38							
Horsham 4	a						12 42								13 42							
	d					12 03	12 42							13 03	13 42							14 03
Crawley	d					12 16	12 51							13 16	13 51							14 16
Three Bridges 4	a					12 19	12 54							13 19	13 54							14 19
Gatwick Airport 10 ✈	a					12 24	12 59		13 22					13 24	13 59		14 22					14 24
	d					12 25	13 00		13 23					13 25	14 00		14 23					14 25
Horley	a					12 28	13 02							13 28	14 02							14 28
Redhill 5	a					12 34	13 09							13 34	14 09							14 34
East Croydon 🚆	a					12 56	13 26		13 39					13 56	14 26		14 39					14 56
London Bridge 4 ⊖	a					13 13								14 13								15 13
Clapham Junction 10	a						13 37		13 54						14 37		14 54					
London Victoria 15 ⊖	a						13 46		14 01						14 46		15 01					

Table 188

Sundays
from 11 September

Southampton, Portsmouth and Sussex Coast - Brighton, Gatwick Airport and London

		SN	SN	SN	SN	GW	SN	SW	SN	SN	SN	SN	SN	SN	SN	SW	SN	SN	SN	SN	SN	SN	GW
		◇1 H	◇1	◇1	◇1	◇	◇1	1	◇1	1	◇1 H	◇1	◇1	◇1	◇1	1	◇1	1	◇1 H	◇1	◇1	◇1	◇
Southampton Central	d					13 08	13 29	13 35							14 29	14 35							15 22
Swanwick	d						13 46	14 02							14 46	15 02							
Fareham	d					13 34	13 53	14 10							14 53	15 10							15 51
Portchester	d							14 15								15 15							
Cosham	d					13 42	14 02	14 20							15 02	15 20							16 01
Portsmouth Harbour	d		13 14		13 43							14 14		14 43						15 14		15 43	
Portsmouth & Southsea	d		13 18		13 47							14 18		14 47						15 18		15 47	
Fratton	d		13 22		13 51							14 22		14 51						15 22		15 51	
Hilsea	d							14a26								15a26							
Bedhampton	d		13 30									14 30								15 30			
Havant	d		13 33		14 00	14 04	14 11					14 33		15 00	15 11					15 33		16 00	16 11
Warblington	d		13 35									14 35								15 35			
Emsworth	d		13 38		14 04		14 15					14 38		15 04	15 15					15 38		16 04	
Southbourne	d		13 41		14 07							14 41		15 07						15 41		16 07	
Nutbourne	d		13 43									14 43								15 43			
Bosham	d		13 47									14 47								15 47			
Fishbourne (Sussex)	d		13 50									14 50								15 50			
Chichester 4	a		13 53		14 14	14 19	14 23					14 53		15 14	15 23					15 53		16 14	16 22
	d		13 53		14 14	14 19	14 23					14 53		15 14	15 23					15 53		16 14	16 22
Bognor Regis 4	d	13 58							14 34		14 58						15 34		15 58				
Barnham	a	14 04	14 01		14 22	14 27	14 31		14 40		15 04	15 01		15 22	15 31		15 40		16 04	16 01		16 22	16 30
	d	14 05	14 08		14 22	14 27	14 38		14 41		15 05	15 08		15 22	15 38		15 41		16 05	16 08		16 22	16 30
Bognor Regis	a																						
Ford 4	d	14 09	14 12				14 42		14 45		15 09	15 12			15 42		15 45		16 09	16 12			
Littlehampton 4	a								14 50								15 50						
	d			14 14									15 14								16 14		
Angmering 3	d		14 18	14 22			14 48					15 18	15 22		15 48					16 18	16 22		
Goring-by-Sea	d		14 22	14 26			14 52					15 22	15 26		15 52					16 22	16 26		
Durrington-on-Sea	d		14 25	14 29			14 55					15 25	15 29		15 55					16 25	16 29		
West Worthing	d		14 27	14 31			14 57					15 27	15 31		15 57					16 27	16 31		
Worthing 4	a		14 29	14 33	14 37	14 44	14 59					15 29	15 33	15 37	15 59					16 29	16 33	16 37	16 45
	d		14 30		14 41	14 45	15 00					15 30	15 41		16 00					16 30	16 41		16 45
East Worthing	d		14 32				15 02					15 32			16 02					16 32			
Lancing	d		14 35				15 05					15 35			16 05					16 35			
Shoreham-by-Sea	d		14 39		14 47	14 51	15 09					15 39	15 47		16 09					16 39	16 47		16 52
Southwick	d		14 42				15 12					15 42			16 12					16 42			
Fishersgate	d		14 44				15 14					15 44			16 14					16 44			
Portslade	d		14 46				15 16					15 46			16 16					16 46			
Aldrington	d		14 49				15 19					15 49			16 19					16 49			
Hove 2	d		14 56		14 54	15 00	15 22					15 56	15 54		16 22					16 56	16 54		16 59
Brighton 10	a		15 00			15 06	15 26					16 00			16 26					17 00			17 05
Preston Park	d																						
Burgess Hill	a				15 04								16 04								17 04		
Haywards Heath 3	a				15 09								16 09								17 09		
Arundel	d	14 14									15 14								16 14				
Amberley	d	14 19									15 19								16 19				
Pulborough	d	14 25									15 25								16 25				
Billingshurst	d	14 31									15 31								16 31				
Christs Hospital	d	14 38									15 38								16 38				
Horsham 4	a	14 42									15 42								16 42				
	d	14 42								15 03	15 42							16 03	16 42				
Crawley	d	14 51								15 16	15 51							16 16	16 51				
Three Bridges 4	a	14 54								15 19	15 54							16 19	16 54				
Gatwick Airport 10 ✈	a	14 59			15 22					15 24	15 59		16 22					16 24	16 59		17 22		
	d	15 00			15 23					15 25	16 00		16 23					16 25	17 00		17 23		
Horley	a	15 02								15 28	16 02							16 28	17 02				
Redhill 5	a	15 09								15 34	16 09							16 34	17 09				
East Croydon	a	15 26			15 39					15 56	16 26		16 39					16 56	17 26		17 39		
London Bridge 4 ⊖	a									16 13								17 13					
Clapham Junction 10	a	15 37			15 54						16 37		16 54						17 37		17 54		
London Victoria 15 ⊖	a	15 46			16 01						16 46		17 01						17 46		18 01		

Table 188

Sundays
from 11 September

Southampton, Portsmouth and Sussex Coast - Brighton, Gatwick Airport and London

		SN	SW	SN	SN	SN	SN	SN	SN	SN	SW	SN	SN	SN	SN	SN	SN	SN	SW	SN	SN	SN	SN
		◇1	1	◇1	1	◇1 H	◇1	◇1	◇1	◇1	1	◇1	1	◇1	◇1	◇1	◇1	◇1	1	◇1	1	◇1	◇1
Southampton Central	d	15 29	15 35							16 29	16 35							17 29	17 35				
Swanwick	d	15 46	16 02							16 46	17 02							17 46	18 02				
Fareham	d	15 58	16 10							16 53	17 10							17 53	18 10				
Portchester	d		16 15								17 15								18 15				
Cosham	d	16 07	16 20							17 02	17 20							18 02	18 20				
Portsmouth Harbour	d						16 14		16 43						17 14		17 43						18 14
Portsmouth & Southsea	d						16 18		16 47						17 18		17 47						18 18
Fratton	d						16 22		16 51						17 22		17 51						18 22
Hilsea	d		16a26								17a26								18a26				
Bedhampton	d						16 30								17 30								18 30
Havant	d	16 16					16 33		17 00	17 11					17 33		18 00	18 11					18 33
Warblington	d						16 35								17 35								18 35
Emsworth	d	16 20					16 38		17 04	17 15					17 38		18 04	18 15					18 38
Southbourne	d						16 41		17 07						17 41		18 07						18 41
Nutbourne	d						16 43								17 43								18 43
Bosham	d						16 47								17 47								18 47
Fishbourne (Sussex)	d						16 50								17 50								18 50
Chichester 4	a	16 28					16 53		17 14	17 23					17 53		18 14	18 23					18 53
	d	16 28					16 53		17 14	17 23					17 53		18 14	18 23					18 53
Bognor Regis 4	d			16 34		16 58						17 34		17 58						18 34		18 58	
Barnham	a	16 36		16 40		17 04	17 01		17 22	17 31		17 40		18 04	18 01		18 22	18 31		18 40		19 04	19 01
	d	16 38		16 41		17 05	17 08		17 22	17 38		17 41		18 05	18 08		18 22	18 38		18 41		19 05	19 08
Bognor Regis	a																						
Ford 4	d	16 42		16 45		17 09	17 12			17 42		17 45		18 09	18 12			18 42		18 45		19 09	19 12
Littlehampton 4	a			16 50								17 50								18 50			
	d							17 14								18 14							
Angmering 3	d	16 48					17 18	17 22		17 48					18 18	18 22		18 48					19 18
Goring-by-Sea	d	16 52					17 22	17 26		17 52					18 22	18 26		18 52					19 22
Durrington-on-Sea	d	16 55					17 25	17 29		17 55					18 25	18 29		18 55					19 25
West Worthing	d	16 57					17 27	17 31		17 57					18 27	18 31		18 57					19 27
Worthing 4	a	16 59					17 29	17 33	17 37	17 59					18 29	18 33	18 37	18 59					19 29
	d	17 00					17 30	17 41		18 00					18 30	18 41		19 00					19 30
East Worthing	d	17 02					17 32			18 02					18 32			19 02					19 32
Lancing	d	17 05					17 35			18 05					18 35			19 05					19 35
Shoreham-by-Sea	d	17 09					17 39	17 47		18 09					18 39	18 47		19 09					19 39
Southwick	d	17 12					17 42			18 12					18 42			19 12					19 42
Fishersgate	d	17 14					17 44			18 14					18 44			19 14					19 44
Portslade	d	17 16					17 46			18 16					18 46			19 16					19 46
Aldrington	d	17 19					17 49			18 19					18 49			19 19					19 49
Hove 2	d	17 22					17 56	17 54		18 22					18 56	18 54		19 22					19 56
Brighton 10	a	17 26					18 00			18 26					19 00			19 26					20 00
Preston Park	d																						
Burgess Hill	a							18 04								19 04							
Haywards Heath 3	a							18 09								19 09							
Arundel	d					17 14								18 14								19 14	
Amberley	d					17 19								18 19								19 19	
Pulborough	d					17 25								18 25								19 25	
Billingshurst	d					17 31								18 31								19 31	
Christs Hospital	d					17 38								18 38								19 38	
Horsham 4	a					17 42								18 42								19 42	
	d				17 03	17 42							18 03	18 42							19 03	19 42	
Crawley	d				17 16	17 51							18 16	18 51							19 16	19 51	
Three Bridges 4	a				17 19	17 54							18 19	18 54							19 19	19 54	
Gatwick Airport 10 ✈	a				17 24	17 59		18 22					18 24	18 59		19 22					19 24	19 59	
	d				17 25	18 00		18 23					18 25	19 00		19 23					19 25	20 00	
Horley	a				17 28	18 02							18 28	19 02							19 28	20 02	
Redhill 5	a				17 34	18 09							18 34	19 09							19 34	20 09	
East Croydon	a				17 56	18 26		18 39					18 56	19 26		19 39					19 56	20 26	
London Bridge 4 ⊖	a				18 13								19 13								20 13		
Clapham Junction 10	a					18 37		18 54						19 37		19 54						20 37	
London Victoria 15 ⊖	a					18 46		19 01						19 46		20 01						20 46	

Southampton, Portsmouth and Sussex Coast - Brighton, Gatwick Airport and London

		SN ◇1	SN ◇1	SN ◇1	SW 1	SN ◇1	SN 1	SN ◇1	SN ◇1	SN ◇1	SN ◇1	GW ◇	SN ◇1	SW 1	SN ◇1	SN ◇1	SN 1	SN ◇1	SN ◇1	SN ◇1	SW 1	SN ◇1
Southampton Central ⛴	d			18 29	18 35							19 27	19 30	19 35						20 29	20 35	
Swanwick	d			18 46	19 02									20 02							21 02	
Fareham	d			18 53	19 10							19 50	20 03	20 10						21 02	21 10	
Portchester	d				19 15									20 15							21 15	
Cosham	d			19 02	19 20							19 59	20 12	20 20						21 11	21 20	
Portsmouth Harbour ⛴	d		18 43						19 14		19 43					20 14			20 43			
Portsmouth & Southsea	d		18 47						19 18		19 47					20 18			20 47			
Fratton	d		18 51						19 22		19 51					20 22			20 51			
Hilsea	d				19a26									20a26							21a26	
Bedhampton	d								19 30							20 30						
Havant	d		19 00	19 11					19 33		20 00	20 11	20 18			20 33			21 00	21 17		
Warblington	d								19 35							20 35						
Emsworth	d		19 04	19 15					19 38		20 04		20 22			20 38			21 04	21 21		
Southbourne	d		19 07						19 41		20 07					20 41			21 07			
Nutbourne	d								19 43							20 43						
Bosham	d								19 47							20 47						
Fishbourne (Sussex)	d								19 50							20 50						
Chichester 4	a		19 14	19 23					19 53		20 14	20 21	20 30			20 53			21 14	21 29		
	d		19 14	19 23					19 53		20 14	20 22	20 31			20 53			21 14	21 30		
Bognor Regis 4	d					19 34		19 58							20 34			20 58				21 34
Barnham	a		19 22	19 31		19 40		20 04	20 01		20 22	20 29	20 38		20 41	21 01		21 04	21 22	21 37		21 40
	d		19 22	19 38		19 41		20 05	20 08		20 22	20 30	20 39		20 42	21 02		21 05	21 22	21 38		21 41
Bognor Regis	a																					
Ford 4	d			19 42		19 45		20 09	20 12				20 43		20 46	21 06		21 09	21 27	21 42		21 45
Littlehampton 4	a					19 50									20 51	21 11			21 31			21 50
	d	19 14								20 14						21 15			21 42			
Angmering 3	d	19 22		19 48					20 18	20 22			20 49			21 23			21 52	21 48		
Goring-by-Sea	d	19 26		19 52					20 22	20 26			20 53			21 27			21 56	21 52		
Durrington-on-Sea	d	19 29		19 55					20 25	20 29			20 56			21 30			21 59	21 55		
West Worthing	d	19 31		19 57					20 27	20 31			20 58			21 32			22 01	21 57		
Worthing 4	a	19 33	19 37	19 59					20 29	20 33	20 37	20 51	21 00			21 34			22 03	21 59		
	d	19 41		20 00					20 30	20 41		20 51	21 01			21 35			22 04	22 00		
East Worthing	d			20 02					20 32				21 03			21 37			22 06	22 02		
Lancing	d			20 05					20 35				21 06			21 40			22 09	22 05		
Shoreham-by-Sea	d	19 47		20 09					20 39	20 47		20 58	21 10			21 44			22 13	22 09		
Southwick	d			20 12					20 42				21 13			21 47			22 16	22 12		
Fishersgate	d			20 14					20 44				21 15			21 49			22 18	22 14		
Portslade	d			20 16					20 46				21 17			21 51			22 20	22 16		
Aldrington	d			20 19					20 49				21 20			21 54			22 23	22 19		
Hove 2	d	19 54		20 22					20 56	20 54		21 05	21 22			21 56			22 25	22 21		
Brighton 10	a			20 26					21 00			21 10	21 26			22 00			22 29	22 25		
Preston Park	d																					
Burgess Hill	a	20 04								21 04												
Haywards Heath 3	a	20 09								21 09												
Arundel	d							20 14										21 14				
Amberley	d							20 19										21 19				
Pulborough	d							20 25										21 25				
Billingshurst	d							20 31										21 31				
Christs Hospital	d							20 38										21 38				
Horsham 4	a							20 42										21 42				
	d						20 03	20 42									21 03	21 42				
Crawley	d						20 16	20 51									21 16	21 51				
Three Bridges 4	a						20 19	20 54									21 19	21 54				
Gatwick Airport 10 ✈	a	20 22					20 24	20 59		21 22							21 24	21 59				
	d	20 23					20 25	21 00		21 23							21 25	22 00				
Horley	a						20 28	21 02									21 28	22 02				
Redhill 5	a						20 34	21 09									21 34	22 09				
East Croydon	a	20 39					20 56	21 26		21 39							21 56	22 26				
London Bridge 4 ⊖	a						21 13										22 13					
Clapham Junction 10	a	20 54						21 37		21 54								22 37				
London Victoria 15 ⊖	a	21 01						21 46		22 01								22 46				

Southampton, Portsmouth and Sussex Coast - Brighton, Gatwick Airport and London

		SN 1	SN ◇1	SN ◇1	SN ◇	SN ◇1	SN ◇1	SW 1	SN ◇	SN ◇1	SN ◇1	SW 1	SN ◇1	SN ◇1	SN 1
Southampton Central ⛴	d						21 30	21 35			22 15	22 35		22 52	
Swanwick	d						21 47	22 02			22 32	23 02		23 11	
Fareham	d						21 54	22 10			22 39	23 10		23 17	
Portchester	d							22 15				23 15			
Cosham	d						22 03	22 20			22 48	23 20		23 26	
Portsmouth Harbour ⛴	d			21 14		21 43				22 14			22 43		
Portsmouth & Southsea	d			21 18		21 47				22 18			22 47		
Fratton	d			21 22		21 51				22 22			22 51		
Hilsea	d							22a26				23a24			
Bedhampton	d			21 30						22 32					
Havant	d			21 33		22 00	22 11			22 35	22 54		23 00	23 32	
Warblington	d			21 35						22 37					
Emsworth	d			21 38		22 04	22 15			22 40	22 58		23 04	23 36	
Southbourne	d			21 41		22 07				22 43			23 07		
Nutbourne	d			21 43						22 46					
Bosham	d			21 47						22 49					
Fishbourne (Sussex)	d			21 50						22 52					
Chichester 4	a			21 53		22 14	22 23			22 55	23 06		23 14	23 44	
	d			21 53		22 14	22 23			22 56	23 07		23 14	23 45	
Bognor Regis 4	d		21 58		22 12										
Barnham	a		22 04	22 01	22 18	22 22	22 31			23 03	23 14		23 23	23 52	
	d		22 05	22 08		22 23	22 32		22 57	23 04	23 15		23 24	23 53	
Bognor Regis	a								23 03						
Ford 4	d		22 09	22 12		22 27	22 36			23 08	23 19		23 28		
Littlehampton 4	a					22 32				23 13	23 27		23 33	00 01	
	d					22 42									
Angmering 3	d			22 18		22 50	22 42								
Goring-by-Sea	d			22 22		22 54	22 46								
Durrington-on-Sea	d			22 25		22 57	22 49								
West Worthing	d			22 27		22 59	22 51								
Worthing 4	a			22 29		23 01	22 53								
	d			22 30		23 02	22 54								
East Worthing	d			22 32		23 04	22 56								
Lancing	d			22 35		23 07	22 59								
Shoreham-by-Sea	d			22 39		23 11	23 03								
Southwick	d			22 42		23 14	23 06								
Fishersgate	d			22 44		23 16	23 08								
Portslade	d			22 46		23 18	23 10								
Aldrington	d			22 49		23 21	23 13								
Hove 2	d			22 51		23 25	23 15								
Brighton 10	a			22 56		23 29	23 19								
Preston Park	d														
Burgess Hill	a														
Haywards Heath 3	a														
Arundel	d		22 14												
Amberley	d		22 19												
Pulborough	d		22 25												
Billingshurst	d		22 31												
Christs Hospital	d		22 38												
Horsham 4	a		22 42												
	d	22 03	22 42												23 03
Crawley	d	22 16	22 51												23 16
Three Bridges 4	a	22 19	22 54												23 19
Gatwick Airport 10 ✈	a	22 24	22 59												23 24
	d	22 25	23 00												23 25
Horley	a	22 28	23 02												23 28
Redhill 5	a	22 34	23 09												23 34
East Croydon	a	22 56	23 26												23 55
London Bridge 4 ⊖	a														
Clapham Junction 10	a	23 07	23 38												00 11
London Victoria 15 ⊖	a	23 14	23 46												00 21

London, Haywards Heath and Brighton - Lewes, Seaford, Eastbourne, Hastings and Ashford

Miles	Miles			SN	SN MX	SN MX	SN	SN MX	SN	SN	SN	SN	SN	SN	SN	SN	SN	SN	SN	SN	SN	SN	SN
				◇1 A	◇1	◇	◇1 B	◇1	◇	◇1	◇1	◇	◇	◇	◇		◇1	◇1	◇	◇	◇1	◇1	◇1
—	—	**London Victoria** 15 ⊖	d	22p47	22p47		22p47	00 05															05 32
—	—	Clapham Junction 10	d	22p53	22p53		22p53	00 11															05 38
—	—	**London Bridge** 4 ⊖	d																				
—	—	East Croydon	d	23p03	23p03		23p07	00 24															05 49
—	—	**Gatwick Airport** 10 ✈	d	23p19	23p19		23p29	00 42															06 20
—	0	**Haywards Heath** 3	d	23p30	23p34		23p41	01 06								06 07							06 34
—	3	Wivelsfield 4	d	23p34	23p38		23p45									06 11							06 38
—	6¾	Plumpton	d	23p40	23p44		23p51																
—	9½	Cooksbridge	d																				
0	—	**Brighton** 10	d			23p34					05 12	05 45			06 00					06 18		06 26	
0¾	—	London Road (Brighton)	d			23p37						05 48			06 03							06 29	
1¾	—	Moulsecoomb	d			23p39						05 50			06 05							06 31	
3½	—	Falmer	d			23p43						05 54			06 09							06 35	
8	12¼	**Lewes** 4	a	23p48	23p51	23p49	23p58	01 20			05 23	06 00			06 15	06 22				06 29		06 41	06 49
—	—		d	23p59	23p53	23p56	23p59	01 20			05 23	06 05				06 27				06 30		06 42	06 51
—	15¾	Southease	d																				
—	18½	Newhaven Town ⛴	d			00 04						06 13				06 35							
—	18¾	Newhaven Harbour	d			00 06						06 15				06 37							
—	20¼	Bishopstone	d			00 09						06 18				06 40							
—	21¼	**Seaford**	a			00 12						06 21				06 43							
11	—	Glynde	d																			06 47	06 56
15½	—	Berwick	d		00 02																	06 53	07 02
19¾	—	Polegate	d	00 11	00 07		00 11	01s32			05 35									06 43		06 58	07 07
21¾	—	Hampden Park 4	d	00 15	00 11		00 15	01s36														07 02	07 11
23¾	—	**Eastbourne** 4	a	00 20	00 16		00 20	01 41			05 42									06 50		07 07	07 16
—	—		d		00 22				04 50	05 15				05 53			06 14	06 33		06 54	07 02		07 21
25¾	—	Hampden Park 4	d														06 18				07 06		07 25
28¾	—	Pevensey & Westham	d		00 29					05 22							06 23	06 40			07 11		07 30
29½	—	Pevensey Bay	d																				
31½	—	Normans Bay	d															06 45					
33¼	—	Cooden Beach	d		00 35												06 29				07 17		07 36
34¾	—	Collington	d		00 38												06 32				07 20		07 39
35½	—	**Bexhill** 4	d		00 41				05 05	05 31				06 07			06 34	06 51		07 09	07 22		07 41
39¼	—	**St Leonards Warrior Sq** 4	d		00 47				05 12	05 37				06 14			06 41	06 58		07 16	07 29		07 48
40	0	**Hastings** 4	a		00 50				05 15	05 41				06 18			06 44	07 01		07 19	07 32		07 51
—	—		d						05 21				05 47	06 19						07 20			07 52
—	1	Ore	d						05 23				05 49										07a55
—	3¾	Three Oaks	d										05 55							07 28			
—	5	Doleham	d										05 58										
—	9¼	Winchelsea	d										06 04							07 36			
—	11¼	**Rye**	a						05 44				06 08	06 36						07 39			
—	—		d						05 44				06 08	06 38					07 11	07 41			
—	18	Appledore (Kent)	d						05 53				06 17	06 47					07 20	07 50			
—	21	Ham Street	d						05 58				06 22	06 52					07 25	07 55			
—	26½	**Ashford International**	a						06 06				06 30	07 00					07 33	08 03			

A MO until 5 September

B MO from 12 September

Table 189

London, Haywards Heath and Brighton - Lewes, Seaford, Eastbourne, Hastings and Ashford

		SN	SN	SN	SN	SN	SN	SN		SN	SN	SN	SN	SN	SN	SN	SN	SN		SN	SN	SN	SN	SN	SN
		◇	◇	◇	◇	◇1	1	◇1		◇	◇1	◇	◇1	◇	◇1	◇1	◇	◇		◇	◇1	◇	◇	◇1	◇1
London Victoria 15 ⊖	d												06 47								07 47				08 17
Clapham Junction 10	d												06 53								07 53				08 23
London Bridge 4 ⊖	d																								
East Croydon	d												07 03								08 03				08 33
Gatwick Airport 10 ✈	d												07 19								08 19				08 49
Haywards Heath 3	d						07 10						07 33								08 31				09 10
Wivelsfield 4	d						07 14						07 37								08 35				09 14
Plumpton	d						07 20						07 43								08 41				
Cooksbridge	d						07 24						07 47								08 45				
Brighton 10	d	06 39	06 52	07 00	07 10			07 17		07 25		07 32		07 40	07 52	08 03	08 10	08 22		08 32		08 38	08 45	08 52	
London Road (Brighton)	d	06 42	06 55	07 03	07 13			07 20						07 43	07 55	08 06	08 13	08 25				08 41	08 48	08 55	
Moulsecoomb	d	06 44	06 57	07 05	07 15			07 22						07 45	07 57	08 08	08 15	08 27				08 43	08 50	08 57	
Falmer	d	06 48	07 01	07 09	07 19			07 26						07 49	08 01	08 12	08 19	08 31				08 47	08 54	09 01	
Lewes 4	a	06 54	07 08	07 17	07 26		07 29	07 32		07 38		07 43	07 52	07 56	08 08	08 18	08 26	08 37		08 43	08 50	08 53	09 00	09 07	09 25
	d	06 55	07 10				07 31	07 34				07 44	07 53	07 58	08 09	08 19	08 30			08 44	08 51		09 02	09 09	09 26
Southease	d																								
Newhaven Town ⛴	d	07 03	07 18					07 42						08 06			08 38						09 10		
Newhaven Harbour	d	07 05	07 23					07 44						08 08			08 40						09 12		
Bishopstone	d	07 08	07 26					07 47						08 11			08 43						09 15		
Seaford	a	07 11	07 29					07 50						08 14			08 46						09 18		
Glynde	d						07 36								08 14	08 24								09 14	
Berwick	d						07 42								08 20	08 30								09 20	
Polegate	d						07 47					07 57	08 05		08 25	08 35				08 57	09 03			09 25	09 38
Hampden Park 4	d						07 51						08 09		08 29	08 39					09 07			09 29	09 42
Eastbourne 4	a						07 56					08 04	08 14		08 34	08 44				09 04	09 12			09 34	09 50
	d					07 38						08 09	08 21		08 40					09 09	09 19			09 40	
Hampden Park 4	d					07 42							08 25		08 44						09 23			09 44	
Pevensey & Westham	d					07 47						08 17	08 30		08 49						09 28			09 49	
Pevensey Bay	d					07 49							08 32												
Normans Bay	d					07 53							08 36		08 53									09 53	
Cooden Beach	d					07 56							08 39		08 57						09 34			09 57	
Collington	d					07 59							08 42		09 00						09 37			10 00	
Bexhill 4	d					08 02						08 25	08 45		09 02					09 24	09 39			10 02	
St Leonards Warrior Sq 4	d					08 08						08 32	08 51		09 09					09 32	09 46			10 09	
Hastings 4	a					08 11						08 35	08 55		09 12					09 35	09 49			10 12	
	d					08 12						08 36	08 56		09 13					09 36	09 50			10 13	
Ore	d					08a15							08a59		09a16						09a53			10a16	
Three Oaks	d											08 44													
Doleham	d																								
Winchelsea	d																			09 50					
Rye	a											08 54								09 54					
	d										08 13	08 56								09 56					
Appledore (Kent)	d										08 22	09 05								10 05					
Ham Street	d										08 27	09 10								10 10					
Ashford International	a										08 35	09 18								10 18					

London, Haywards Heath and Brighton - Lewes, Seaford, Eastbourne, Hastings and Ashford

		SN	SN	SN	SN	SN	SN	SN	SN	SN	SN	SN	SN	SN	SN	SN	SN	SN	SN	SN	SN	SN
		◇	◇	◇	◇1	◇	◇1	◇1	◇	◇	◇	◇1	◇	◇1	◇1	◇	◇	◇	◇1	◇	◇1	◇1
					A ⌶			B ⌶				C ⌶			B ⌶				C ⌶			
London Victoria 15 ⊖	d				08 47			09 17				09 47			10 17				10 47			11 17
Clapham Junction 10	d				08 53			09 23				09 53			10 23				10 53			11 23
London Bridge 4 ⊖	d																					
East Croydon	d				09 03			09 33				10 03			10 33				11 03			11 33
Gatwick Airport 10 ✈	d				09 19			09 49				10 19			10 49				11 19			11 49
Haywards Heath 3	d				09 35			10 07				10 35			11 07				11 35			12 07
Wivelsfield 4	d							10 11							11 11							12 11
Plumpton	d				09 44							10 44							11 44			
Cooksbridge	d				09 49																	
Brighton 10	d	09 10	09 22	09 32		09 40	09 52		10 10	10 22	10 32		10 40	10 52		11 10	11 22	11 32		11 40	11 52	
London Road (Brighton)	d	09 13	09 25			09 43	09 55		10 13	10 25			10 43	10 55		11 13	11 25			11 43	11 55	
Moulsecoomb	d	09 15	09 27			09 45	09 57		10 15	10 27			10 45	10 57		11 15	11 27			11 45	11 57	
Falmer	d	09 19	09 31			09 49	10 01		10 19	10 31			10 49	11 01		11 19	11 31			11 49	12 01	
Lewes 4	a	09 25	09 37	09 43	09 53	09 55	10 07	10 22	10 25	10 37	10 43	10 52	10 55	11 07	11 22	11 25	11 37	11 43	11 52	11 55	12 07	12 22
	d	09 29		09 44	09 54	09 58	10 09	10 23	10 28		10 44	10 53	10 58	11 09	11 23	11 28		11 44	11 53	11 58	12 09	12 23
Southease	d	09 35							10 34							11 34						
Newhaven Town ⛴	d	09 39				10 06			10 38				11 06			11 38				12 06		
Newhaven Harbour	d	09 41				10 08			10 40				11 08			11 40				12 08		
Bishopstone	d	09 44				10 11			10 43				11 11			11 43				12 11		
Seaford	a	09 47				10 14			10 46				11 14			11 46				12 14		
Glynde	d						10 14							11 14							12 14	
Berwick	d						10 20							11 20							12 20	
Polegate	d			09 57	10 06		10 25	10 35			10 57	11 05		11 25	11 35			11 57	12 05		12 25	12 35
Hampden Park 4	d						10 29	10 39						11 29	11 39						12 29	12 39
Eastbourne 4	a			10 04	10 14		10 34	10 44			11 04	11 13		11 34	11 44			12 04	12 13		12 34	12 44
	d			10 09	10 20		10 40				11 09	11 19		11 40				12 09	12 19		12 40	
Hampden Park 4	d				10 24		10 44					11 23		11 44					12 23		12 44	
Pevensey & Westham	d				10 29		10 49					11 28		11 49					12 28		12 49	
Pevensey Bay	d																					
Normans Bay	d						10 53							11 53							12 53	
Cooden Beach	d				10 35		10 57					11 34		11 57					12 34		12 57	
Collington	d				10 38		11 00					11 37		12 00					12 37		13 00	
Bexhill 4	d			10 24	10 40		11 02				11 24	11 39		12 02				12 24	12 39		13 02	
St Leonards Warrior Sq 4	d			10 31	10 47		11 09				11 31	11 46		12 09				12 31	12 46		13 09	
Hastings 4	a			10 35	10 50		11 12				11 35	11 49		12 12				12 35	12 49		13 12	
	d			10 36	10 51		11 13				11 36	11 50		12 13				12 36	12 50		13 13	
Ore	d				10a54		11a16					11a53		12a16					12a53		13a16	
Three Oaks	d			10 44														12 44				
Doleham	d																					
Winchelsea	d										11 50											
Rye	a			10 54							11 54							12 54				
	d			10 56							11 56							12 56				
Appledore (Kent)	d			11 05							12 05							13 05				
Ham Street	d			11 10							12 10							13 10				
Ashford International	a			11 18							12 18							13 18				

A ⌶ to Cooksbridge

B ⌶ to Gatwick Airport ⌶ from Haywards Heath to Wivelsfield

C ⌶ to Plumpton

London, Haywards Heath and Brighton - Lewes, Seaford, Eastbourne, Hastings and Ashford

		SN	SN	SN	SN	SN	SN	SN	SN	SN	SN	SN	SN	SN	SN	SN	SN	SN	SN	SN	SN	SN	SN
		◇	◇	◇	◇ 1	◇	◇ 1	◇ 1	◇	◇	◇	◇ 1	◇	◇ 1	◇ 1	◇	◇	◇	◇ 1	◇	◇ 1	◇ 1	◇
London Victoria 15 ⊖	d				11 47			12 17				12 47			13 17				13 47			14 17	
Clapham Junction 10	d				11 53			12 23				12 53			13 23				13 53			14 23	
London Bridge 4 ⊖	d																						
East Croydon	d				12 03			12 33				13 03			13 33				14 03			14 33	
Gatwick Airport 10 ✈	d				12 19			12 49				13 19			13 49				14 19			14 49	
Haywards Heath 3	d				12 35			13 07				13 35			14 07				14 35			15 07	
Wivelsfield 4	d							13 11							14 11							15 11	
Plumpton	d				12 44							13 44							14 44				
Cooksbridge	d																						
Brighton 10	d	12 10	12 22	12 32		12 40	12 52		13 10	13 22	13 32		13 40	13 52		14 10	14 22	14 32		14 40	14 52		15 10
London Road (Brighton)	d	12 13	12 25			12 43	12 55		13 13	13 25			13 43	13 55		14 13	14 25			14 43	14 55		15 13
Moulsecoomb	d	12 15	12 27			12 45	12 57		13 15	13 27			13 45	13 57		14 15	14 27			14 45	14 57		15 15
Falmer	d	12 19	12 31			12 49	13 01		13 19	13 31			13 49	14 01		14 19	14 31			14 49	15 01		15 19
Lewes 4	a	12 25	12 37	12 43	12 52	12 55	13 07	13 22	13 25	13 37	13 43	13 52	13 55	14 07	14 22	14 25	14 37	14 43	14 52	14 55	15 07	15 22	15 25
	d	12 28		12 44	12 53	12 58	13 09	13 23	13 28		13 44	13 53	13 58	14 09	14 23	14 28		14 44	14 53	14 58	15 09	15 23	15 28
Southease	d	12 34							13 34							14 34							15 34
Newhaven Town ⛴	d	12 38				13 06			13 38				14 06			14 38				15 06			15 38
Newhaven Harbour	d	12 40				13 08			13 40				14 08			14 40				15 08			15 40
Bishopstone	d	12 43				13 11			13 43				14 11			14 43				15 11			15 43
Seaford	a	12 46				13 14			13 46				14 14			14 46				15 14			15 46
Glynde	d						13 14							14 14							15 14		
Berwick	d						13 20							14 20							15 20		
Polegate	d			12 57	13 05		13 25	13 35			13 57	14 05		14 25	14 35			14 57	15 05		15 25	15 35	
Hampden Park 4	d						13 29	13 39						14 29	14 39						15 29	15 39	
Eastbourne 4	a			13 04	13 13		13 34	13 44			14 04	14 13		14 34	14 44			15 04	15 13		15 34	15 44	
	d			13 09	13 19		13 40				14 09	14 19		14 40				15 09	15 19		15 40		
Hampden Park 4	d				13 23		13 44					14 23		14 44					15 23		15 44		
Pevensey & Westham	d				13 28		13 49					14 28		14 49					15 28		15 49		
Pevensey Bay	d																		15 30				
Normans Bay	d						13 53							14 53					15 34		15 53		
Cooden Beach	d				13 34		13 57					14 34		14 57					15 37		15 57		
Collington	d				13 37		14 00					14 37		15 00					15 40		16 00		
Bexhill 4	d			13 24	13 39		14 02				14 24	14 39		15 02				15 24	15 43		16 02		
St Leonards Warrior Sq 4	d			13 31	13 46		14 09				14 31	14 46		15 09				15 31	15 49		16 09		
Hastings 4	a			13 35	13 49		14 12				14 35	14 49		15 12				15 35	15 52		16 12		
	d			13 36	13 50		14 13				14 36	14 50		15 13				15 36	15 54		16 13		
Ore	d				13a53		14a16					14a53		15a16					15a57		16a16		
Three Oaks	d										14 44												
Doleham	d																						
Winchelsea	d			13 50														15 50					
Rye	a			13 54							14 54							15 54					
	d			13 56							14 56							15 56					
Appledore (Kent)	d			14 05							15 05							16 05					
Ham Street	d			14 10							15 10							16 10					
Ashford International	a			14 18							15 18							16 18					

London, Haywards Heath and Brighton - Lewes, Seaford, Eastbourne, Hastings and Ashford

		SN	SN	SN	SN	SN	SN	SN	SN	SN	SN	SN	SN	SN	SN	SN	SN	SN	SN	SN	SN	SN	SN
		◇	◇	◇1	◇	◇	◇1	◇1	◇	◇	◇	◇1	◇	◇1	◇	◇1	◇	◇1	◇	◇	◇1	◇	◇1
																A					B		
																✠					✠		
London Victoria 15 ⊖	d			14 47				15 17				15 47				16 17					16 47		
Clapham Junction 10	d			14 53				15 23				15 53				16 23					16 53		
London Bridge 4 ⊖	d																						
East Croydon	d			15 03				15 33				16 03				16 33					17 03		
Gatwick Airport 10 ✈	d			15 19				15 49				16 19				16 49					17 20		
Haywards Heath 3	d			15 35				16 07				16 35				17 06					17 36		
Wivelsfield 4	d			15 39				16 11				16 39				17 10					17 41		
Plumpton	d			15 45								16 45									17 47		
Cooksbridge	d											16 49									17 52		
Brighton 10	d	15 22	15 32		15 40		15 52		16 10	16 22	16 32		16 40	16 52	17 02		17 10	17 20		17 32		17 40	17 52
London Road (Brighton)	d	15 25			15 43		15 55		16 13	16 25			16 43	16 55	17 05		17 13	17 23				17 43	17 55
Moulsecoomb	d	15 27			15 45		15 57		16 15	16 27			16 45	16 57	17 07		17 15	17 25				17 45	17 57
Falmer	d	15 31			15 49		16 01		16 19	16 31			16 49	17 01	17 11		17 19	17 29				17 49	18 01
Lewes 4	a	15 37	15 43	15 52	15 55		16 07	16 22	16 25	16 37	16 43	16 54	16 55	17 07	17 17	17 21	17 25	17 35		17 43	17 56	17 55	18 07
	d		15 44	15 53	15 58		16 09	16 23	16 28		16 44	16 54	16 58	17 09		17 22	17 28	17 36		17 44	17 57	18 01	18 08
Southease	d				16 04				16 34								17 34					18 07	
Newhaven Town ⛴	d				16 08				16 38				17 06				17 38					18 11	
Newhaven Harbour	d				16 10				16 40				17 08				17 40					18 13	
Bishopstone	d				16 13				16 43				17 11				17 43					18 16	
Seaford	a				16 16				16 46				17 14				17 46					18 19	
Glynde	d						16 14							17 14									18 13
Berwick	d						16 20					17 03		17 20		17 31		17 45					18 19
Polegate	d		15 57	16 05			16 25	16 35			16 57	17 08		17 25		17 36		17 50		17 57	18 09		18 24
Hampden Park 4	d						16 29	16 39						17 29		17 40		17 55			18 13		18 28
Eastbourne 4	a		16 04	16 13			16 34	16 44			17 04	17 16		17 34		17 48		18 00		18 04	18 18		18 34
	d		16 09	16 19			16 40				17 09	17 21		17 40						18 09	18 25		18 43
Hampden Park 4	d			16 23			16 44					17 25		17 44							18 29		18 47
Pevensey & Westham	d			16 28			16 49					17 30		17 49							18 34		18 52
Pevensey Bay	d											17 32		17 51									
Normans Bay	d						16 53					17 36		17 55									18 56
Cooden Beach	d			16 34			16 57					17 39		17 58							18 40		19 00
Collington	d			16 37			17 00					17 42		18 01							18 43		19 03
Bexhill 4	d		16 24	16 39			17 02				17 25	17 45		18 04						18 24	18 45		19 05
St Leonards Warrior Sq 4	d		16 31	16 46			17 09				17 31	17 53		18 10						18 31	18 56		19 11
Hastings 4	a		16 35	16 49			17 12				17 35	17 57		18 13						18 34	19 00		19 14
	d		16 36	16 50		17 09	17 13				17 36	17 58		18 14						18 36			19 15
Ore	d			16a53		17 12	17a16					18a01		18a17									19a18
Three Oaks	d		16 44			17 18														18 44			
Doleham	d					17 21																	
Winchelsea	d					17 27					17 50												
Rye	a		16 54			17 30					17 54									18 54			
	d		16 56			17 31					17 56								18 31	18 56			
Appledore (Kent)	d		17 05			17 40					18 05								18 40	19 05			
Ham Street	d		17 10			17 45					18 10								18 45	19 10			
Ashford International	a		17 18			17 53					18 18								18 53	19 18			

A ✠ to Gatwick Airport ✠ from Haywards Heath to Wivelsfield

B ✠ to Cooksbridge

Table 189

Mondays to Fridays

London, Haywards Heath and Brighton - Lewes, Seaford, Eastbourne, Hastings and Ashford

		SN	SN	SN	SN	SN	SN	SN	SN	SN		SN	SN	SN	SN	SN	SN	SN	SN	SN	SN	SN
		1	◇	◇1	◇	◇	◇	◇	◇1	◇1		1	◇	◇	◇	◇1	◇	◇1	◇1	◇	◇	◇1
				A						A						A			B			C
				⚲						⚲						⚲			⚲			⚲
London Victoria 15 ⊖	d			17 35						18 06						18 47			19 17			19 47
Clapham Junction 10	d			17 42						18 12						18 53			19 23			19 53
London Bridge 4 ⊖	d	17 23										18 23										
East Croydon	d	17 36		17 52						18 22		18 37				19 03			19 33			20 03
Gatwick Airport 10 ✈	d			18 07						18 38						19 20			19 49			20 19
Haywards Heath 3	d	18 05		18 18						18 50		19 06				19 34			20 07			20 36
Wivelsfield 4	d	18 09		18 23						18 54		19 11				19 38			20 11			20 40
Plumpton	d			18 29						19 00		19 17				19 44						20 46
Cooksbridge	d			18 33						19 05		19 22				19 49						20 50
Brighton 10	d		18 08		18 17		18 32	18 38	18 51				19 08	19 22	19 32		19 40	19 52		20 10	20 30	
London Road (Brighton)	d		18 11		18 20			18 41	18 54				19 11	19 25			19 43	19 55		20 13		
Moulsecoomb	d		18 13		18 22			18 43	18 56				19 13	19 27			19 45	19 57		20 15		
Falmer	d		18 17		18 26			18 47	19 00				19 17	19 31			19 49	20 01		20 19		
Lewes 4	a	18 20	18 23	18 38	18 32		18 44	18 53	19 06	19 09		19 27	19 23	19 37	19 43	19 53	19 55	20 07	20 22	20 25	20 43	20 55
	d	18 21	18 24	18 38	18 42		18 45	18 54	19 07	19 13	19 16	19 27	19 31		19 44	19 54	19 58	20 09	20 23	20 28	20 44	20 55
Southease	d							19 00					19 37				20 04					
Newhaven Town ⛴	d		18 33		18 50			19 04		19 21			19 41				20 08			20 36		
Newhaven Harbour	d							19 09					19 44				20 10			20 38		
Bishopstone	d		18 37		18 54			19 12		19 29			19 47				20 13			20 41		
Seaford	a		18 40		18 58			19 15		19 34			19 50				20 16			20 44		
Glynde	d	18 26									19 21	19 33						20 14	20 28			
Berwick	d	18 32									19 27	19 39						20 20	20 34			
Polegate	d	18 37		18 51			18 58		19 19		19 32	19 45			19 57	20 06		20 25	20 39		20 57	21 08
Hampden Park 4	d	18 41		18 55							19 36	19 49						20 29	20 43			
Eastbourne 4	a	18 48		19 01			19 05		19 28		19 41	19 56			20 04	20 14		20 34	20 48		21 04	21 15
	d			19 19			19 09				19 51				20 09	20 19					21 09	21 21
Hampden Park 4	d			19 23							19 55					20 23						21 25
Pevensey & Westham	d			19 28			19 17				20 00					20 28						21 30
Pevensey Bay	d																					
Normans Bay	d																					
Cooden Beach	d			19 34							20 06					20 34						21 36
Collington	d			19 37							20 09					20 37						21 39
Bexhill 4	d			19 39			19 25				20 11				20 24	20 39					21 24	21 41
St Leonards Warrior Sq 4	d			19 45			19 32				20 18				20 31	20 46					21 31	21 48
Hastings 4	a			19 48			19 35				20 21				20 34	20 49					21 34	21 53
	d			19 49			19 36				20 22				20 36	20 50					21 35	21 54
Ore	d			19a55							20a27					20a55					21 37	21a57
Three Oaks	d														20 44						21 43	
Doleham	d																				21 46	
Winchelsea	d						19 50														21 52	
Rye	a						19 54								20 54						21 56	
	d					19 31	19 56								20 56						21 56	
Appledore (Kent)	d					19 40	20 05								21 05						22 05	
Ham Street	d					19 45	20 10								21 10						22 10	
Ashford International	a					19 53	20 18								21 18						22 18	

A ⚲ to Cooksbridge
B ⚲ to Gatwick Airport ⚲ from Haywards Heath to Wivelsfield
C ⚲ to Gatwick Airport ⚲ from Haywards Heath to Cooksbridge

London, Haywards Heath and Brighton - Lewes, Seaford, Eastbourne, Hastings and Ashford

		SN ◇	SN ◇1	SN ◇	SN ◇	SN ◇1	SN ◇	SN ◇1		SN ◇	SN ◇	SN ◇1	SN ◇	SN ◇1	SN ◇	SN ◇1	SN ◇
London Victoria 15 ⊖	d		20 17			20 47		21 17				21 47				22 47	
Clapham Junction 10	d		20 23			20 53		21 23				21 53				22 53	
London Bridge 4 ⊖	d																
East Croydon	d		20 33			21 04		21 33				22 03				23 03	
Gatwick Airport 10 ✈	d		20 49			21 19		21 49				22 19				23 19	
Haywards Heath 3	d		21 07			21 37		22 08				22 34				23 34	
Wivelsfield 4	d		21 11			21 41		22 12				22 38				23 38	
Plumpton	d					21 47						22 44				23 44	
Cooksbridge	d																
Brighton 10	d	20 40		21 04	21 30		21 40			22 04	22 28		22 34	23 06	23 28		23 34
London Road (Brighton)	d	20 43		21 07			21 43			22 07			22 37	23 09			23 37
Moulsecoomb	d	20 45		21 09			21 45			22 09			22 39	23 11			23 39
Falmer	d	20 49		21 13			21 49			22 13			22 43	23 15			23 43
Lewes 4	a	20 55	21 22	21 19	21 43	21 54	21 55	22 23		22 19	22 39	22 51	22 49	23 21	23 39	23 51	23 49
	d	21 00	21 23	21 28	21 44	21 55	21 58	22 23		22 28	22 39	22 53	22 56	23 22	23 39	23 53	23 56
Southease	d						22 04						23 02				
Newhaven Town ⛴	d	21 08		21 36			22 08			22 36			23 06				00 04
Newhaven Harbour	d	21 10		21 38			22 10			22 38			23 08				00 06
Bishopstone	d	21 13		21 41			22 13			22 41			23 11				00 09
Seaford	a	21 16		21 44			22 16			22 44			23 14				00 12
Glynde	d		21 28					22 29						23 27			
Berwick	d		21 34					22 34						23 33		00 02	
Polegate	d		21 39		21 57	22 07		22 39			22 52	23 05		23 38	23 52	00 07	
Hampden Park 4	d		21 43					22 43				23 09		23 42		00 11	
Eastbourne 4	a		21 48		22 04	22 15		22 48			23 03	23 14		23 47	23 59	00 16	
	d				22 09	22 21						23 20				00 22	
Hampden Park 4	d					22 25						23 24					
Pevensey & Westham	d					22 30						23 29				00 29	
Pevensey Bay	d																
Normans Bay	d																
Cooden Beach	d					22 36						23 35				00 35	
Collington	d					22 39						23 38				00 38	
Bexhill 4	d				22 23	22 41						23 40				00 41	
St Leonards Warrior Sq 4	d				22 31	22 48						23 47				00 47	
Hastings 4	a				22 34	22 51						23 50				00 50	
	d																
Ore	d																
Three Oaks	d																
Doleham	d																
Winchelsea	d																
Rye	a																
	d																
Appledore (Kent)	d																
Ham Street	d																
Ashford International	a																

Table 189

Saturdays
until 4 June

London, Haywards Heath and Brighton - Lewes, Seaford, Eastbourne, Hastings and Ashford

		SN	SN	SN	SN	SN	SN	SN	SN	SN	SN	SN	SN	SN	SN	SN	SN	SN	SN	SN	SN	SN	SN
		◇[1]	◇	◇[1]	◇	◇[1]	◇[1]	◇	◇	◇[1]	◇	◇[1]	◇[1]	◇	[1]	◇	◇[1]	◇	◇	◇	[1]	◇	◇[1]
London Victoria [15] ⊖	d	22p47		00 05																			
Clapham Junction [10]	d	22p53		00 11																			
London Bridge [4] ⊖	d																						
East Croydon (tram)	d	23p03		00 25																			
Gatwick Airport [10] ✈	d	23p19		00 43											06 11								
Haywards Heath [3]	d	23p34		01 06											06 25						07 33		
Wivelsfield [4]	d	23p38													06 29						07 37		
Plumpton	d	23p44																					
Cooksbridge	d																						
Brighton [10]	d		23p34				05 10	05 52			06 10			06 32		06 40	06 52	07 10	07 22	07 32		07 40	07 52
London Road (Brighton)	d		23p37					05 55			06 13					06 43	06 55	07 13	07 25			07 43	07 55
Moulsecoomb	d		23p39					05 57			06 15					06 45	06 57	07 15	07 27			07 45	07 57
Falmer	d		23p43					06 01			06 19					06 49	07 01	07 19	07 31			07 49	08 01
Lewes [4]	a	23p51	23p49	01 20			05 21	06 07			06 25			06 43	06 40	06 55	07 07	07 25	07 37	07 43	07 48	07 55	08 07
	d	23p53	23p56	01 20			05 21	06 08			06 28			06 44	06 53	06 58	07 09	07 28		07 44	07 53	07 58	08 09
Southease	d																						
Newhaven Town (ferry)	d		00 04					06 16			06 36					07 06		07 36				08 06	
Newhaven Harbour	d		00 06					06 18			06 38					07 08		07 38				08 08	
Bishopstone	d		00 09								06 41					07 11		07 41				08 11	
Seaford	a		00 12					06 23			06 44					07 14		07 44				08 14	
Glynde	d																07 14						08 14
Berwick	d	00 02													07 02		07 20						08 20
Polegate	d	00 07		01s32			05 33							06 57	07 07		07 25			07 57	08 05		08 25
Hampden Park [4]	d	00 11		01s36											07 11		07 29						08 29
Eastbourne [4]	a	00 16		01 41			05 41							07 04	07 16		07 34			08 05	08 13		08 34
	d	00 22				05 38			05 53	06 04		06 18	06 45	07 09	07 21		07 40			08 09	08 19		08 40
Hampden Park [4]	d											06 22			07 25		07 44				08 23		08 44
Pevensey & Westham	d	00 29										06 27			07 30		07 49				08 28		08 49
Pevensey Bay	d																						
Normans Bay	d											06 31					07 53						08 53
Cooden Beach	d	00 35										06 35			07 36		07 57				08 34		08 57
Collington	d	00 38										06 38			07 39		08 00				08 37		09 00
Bexhill [4]	d	00 41				05 52			06 07	06 18		06 40	07 00	07 24	07 41		08 02			08 24	08 39		09 02
St Leonards Warrior Sq [4]	d	00 47				06 00			06 14	06 24		06 49	07 06	07 31	07 48		08 09			08 31	08 46		09 09
Hastings [4]	a	00 50				06 04			06 17	06 28		06 53	07 10	07 35	07 51		08 12			08 35	08 50		09 12
	d				05 20	06 05			06 18	06 28		06 54	07 11	07 36	07 52		08 13			08 36	08 51		09 13
Ore	d				05 23	06a08				06a32		06a57	07a14		07a55		08a16				08a54		09a16
Three Oaks	d				05 29				06 26											08 44			
Doleham	d				05 32																		
Winchelsea	d				05 38									07 50									
Rye	a				05 41				06 36					07 54						08 54			
	d				05 42				06 38					07 56						08 56			
Appledore (Kent)	d				05 51				06 47					08 05						09 05			
Ham Street	d				05 56				06 52					08 10						09 10			
Ashford International	a				06 04				07 00					08 18						09 18			

Table 189

Saturdays
until 4 June

London, Haywards Heath and Brighton - Lewes, Seaford, Eastbourne, Hastings and Ashford

		SN	SN	SN	SN	SN	SN	SN	SN	SN	SN	SN	SN	SN	SN	SN	SN	SN	SN	SN	SN	SN	SN
		◇	◇	◇	◇1	◇	◇1	◇1	◇	◇	◇	◇1	◇	◇1	◇1	◇	◇	◇	◇1	◇	◇1	◇1	◇
London Victoria 15 ⊖	d				07 47			08 17				08 47			09 17				09 47			10 17	
Clapham Junction 10	d				07 53			08 23				08 53			09 23				09 53			10 23	
London Bridge 4 ⊖	d																						
East Croydon	d				08 03			08 33				09 03			09 33				10 03			10 33	
Gatwick Airport 10 ✈	d				08 19			08 49				09 19			09 49				10 19			10 49	
Haywards Heath 3	d				08 35			09 07				09 35			10 07				10 35			11 07	
Wivelsfield 4	d							09 11							10 11							11 11	
Plumpton	d											09 44							10 44				
Cooksbridge	d																						
Brighton 10	d	08 10	08 22	08 32		08 40	08 52		09 10	09 22	09 32		09 40	09 52		10 10	10 22	10 32		10 40	10 52		11 10
London Road (Brighton)	d	08 13	08 25			08 43	08 55		09 13	09 25			09 43	09 55		10 13	10 25			10 43	10 55		11 13
Moulsecoomb	d	08 15	08 27			08 45	08 57		09 15	09 27			09 45	09 57		10 15	10 27			10 45	10 57		11 15
Falmer	d	08 19	08 31			08 49	09 01		09 19	09 31			09 49	10 01		10 19	10 31			10 49	11 01		11 19
Lewes 4	a	08 25	08 37	08 43	08 49	08 55	09 07	09 22	09 25	09 37	09 43	09 52	09 55	10 07	10 22	10 25	10 37	10 43	10 52	10 55	11 07	11 22	11 25
	d	08 28		08 44	08 53	08 58	09 09	09 23	09 28		09 44	09 53	09 58	10 09	10 23	10 28		10 44	10 53	10 58	11 09	11 23	11 28
Southease	d								09 34							10 34							11 34
Newhaven Town ⛴	d	08 36				09 06			09 38				10 06			10 38				11 06			11 38
Newhaven Harbour	d	08 38				09 08			09 40				10 08			10 40				11 08			11 40
Bishopstone	d	08 41				09 11			09 43				10 11			10 43				11 11			11 43
Seaford	a	08 44				09 14			09 46				10 14			10 46				11 14			11 46
Glynde	d						09 14							10 14							11 14		
Berwick	d						09 20							10 20							11 20		
Polegate	d			08 57	09 05		09 25	09 35			09 57	10 05		10 25	10 35			10 57	11 05		11 25	11 35	
Hampden Park 4	d						09 29	09 39						10 29	10 39						11 29	11 39	
Eastbourne 4	a			09 04	09 13		09 34	09 44			10 04	10 13		10 34	10 44			11 04	11 13		11 34	11 44	
	d			09 09	09 19		09 40				10 09	10 19		10 40				11 09	11 19		11 40		
Hampden Park 4	d				09 23		09 44					10 23		10 44					11 23		11 44		
Pevensey & Westham	d				09 28		09 49					10 28		10 49					11 28		11 49		
Pevensey Bay	d																						
Normans Bay	d						09 53							10 53							11 53		
Cooden Beach	d				09 34		09 57					10 34		10 57					11 34		11 57		
Collington	d				09 37		10 00					10 37		11 00					11 37		12 00		
Bexhill 4	d			09 24	09 39		10 02				10 24	10 39		11 02				11 24	11 39		12 02		
St Leonards Warrior Sq 4	d			09 31	09 46		10 09				10 31	10 46		11 09				11 31	11 46		12 09		
Hastings 4	a			09 35	09 49		10 12				10 35	10 49		11 12				11 35	11 49		12 12		
	d			09 36	09 50		10 13				10 36	10 50		11 13				11 36	11 50		12 13		
Ore	d				09a53		10a16					10a53		11a16					11a53		12a16		
Three Oaks	d										10 44												
Doleham	d																						
Winchelsea	d			09 50														11 50					
Rye	a			09 54							10 54							11 54					
	d			09 56							10 56							11 56					
Appledore (Kent)	d			10 05							11 05							12 05					
Ham Street	d			10 10							11 10							12 10					
Ashford International	a			10 18							11 18							12 18					

Table 189

Saturdays
until 4 June

London, Haywards Heath and Brighton - Lewes, Seaford, Eastbourne, Hastings and Ashford

		SN		SN	SN	SN	SN	SN	SN	SN	SN	SN		SN	SN	SN	SN	SN	SN	SN	SN	SN		SN	SN
		◇		◇	◇1	◇	◇1	◇1	◇	◇	◇	◇1		◇	◇1	◇1	◇	◇	◇	◇1	◇	◇1		◇1	◇
London Victoria 15 ⊖	d				10 47			11 17				11 47				12 17				12 47				13 17	
Clapham Junction 10	d				10 53			11 23				11 53				12 23				12 53				13 23	
London Bridge 4 ⊖	d																								
East Croydon	d				11 03			11 33				12 03				12 33				13 03				13 33	
Gatwick Airport 10 ✈	d				11 19			11 49				12 19				12 49				13 19				13 49	
Haywards Heath 3	d				11 35			12 07				12 35				13 07				13 35				14 07	
Wivelsfield 4	d							12 11								13 11								14 11	
Plumpton	d				11 44							12 44								13 44					
Cooksbridge	d																								
Brighton 10	d	11 22		11 32		11 40	11 52		12 10	12 22	12 32			12 40	12 52		13 10	13 22	13 32		13 40	13 52			14 10
London Road (Brighton)	d	11 25				11 43	11 55		12 13	12 25				12 43	12 55		13 13	13 25			13 43	13 55			14 13
Moulsecoomb	d	11 27				11 45	11 57		12 15	12 27				12 45	12 57		13 15	13 27			13 45	13 57			14 15
Falmer	d	11 31				11 49	12 01		12 19	12 31				12 49	13 01		13 19	13 31			13 49	14 01			14 19
Lewes 4	a	11 37		11 43	11 52	11 55	12 07	12 22	12 25	12 37	12 43	12 52		12 55	13 07	13 22	13 25	13 37	13 43	13 52	13 55	14 07		14 22	14 25
	d			11 44	11 53	11 58	12 09	12 23	12 28		12 44	12 53		12 58	13 09	13 23	13 28		13 44	13 53	13 58	14 09		14 23	14 28
Southease	d								12 34								13 34								14 34
Newhaven Town ⛴	d					12 06			12 38					13 06			13 38				14 06				14 38
Newhaven Harbour	d					12 08			12 40					13 08			13 40				14 08				14 40
Bishopstone	d					12 11			12 43					13 11			13 43				14 11				14 43
Seaford	a					12 14			12 46					13 14			13 46				14 14				14 46
Glynde	d						12 14								13 14							14 14			
Berwick	d						12 20								13 20							14 20			
Polegate	d			11 57	12 05		12 25	12 35			12 57	13 05			13 25	13 35			13 57	14 05		14 25		14 35	
Hampden Park 4	d						12 29	12 39							13 29	13 39						14 29		14 39	
Eastbourne 4	a			12 04	12 13		12 34	12 44			13 04	13 13			13 34	13 44			14 04	14 13		14 34		14 44	
	d			12 09	12 19		12 40				13 09	13 19			13 40				14 09	14 19		14 40			
Hampden Park 4	d				12 23		12 44					13 23			13 44					14 23		14 44			
Pevensey & Westham	d				12 28		12 49					13 28			13 49					14 28		14 49			
Pevensey Bay	d																								
Normans Bay	d						12 53								13 53							14 53			
Cooden Beach	d				12 34		12 57					13 34			13 57					14 34		14 57			
Collington	d				12 37		13 00					13 37			14 00					14 37		15 00			
Bexhill 4	d			12 24	12 39		13 02				13 24	13 39			14 02				14 24	14 39		15 02			
St Leonards Warrior Sq 4	d			12 31	12 46		13 09				13 31	13 46			14 09				14 31	14 46		15 09			
Hastings 4	a			12 35	12 49		13 12				13 35	13 49			14 12				14 35	14 49		15 12			
	d			12 36	12 50		13 13				13 36	13 50			14 13				14 36	14 50		15 13			
Ore	d				12a53		13a16					13a53			14a16					14a53		15a16			
Three Oaks	d			12 44															14 44						
Doleham	d																								
Winchelsea	d										13 50														
Rye	a			12 54							13 54								14 54						
	d			12 56							13 56								14 56						
Appledore (Kent)	d			13 05							14 05								15 05						
Ham Street	d			13 10							14 10								15 10						
Ashford International	a			13 18							14 18								15 18						

Table 189

Saturdays
until 4 June

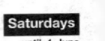

London, Haywards Heath and Brighton - Lewes, Seaford, Eastbourne, Hastings and Ashford

		SN	SN	SN	SN	SN	SN	SN	SN	SN	SN	SN	SN	SN	SN	SN	SN	SN	SN	SN	SN	SN	SN
		◇	◇	◇1	◇	◇1	◇1	◇	◇	◇	◇1	◇	◇1	◇1	◇	◇	◇	◇1	◇	◇1	◇1	◇	◇
London Victoria 15 ⊖	d			13 47			14 17				14 47			15 17				15 47			16 17		
Clapham Junction 10	d			13 53			14 23				14 53			15 23				15 53			16 23		
London Bridge 4 ⊖	d																						
East Croydon	d			14 03			14 33				15 03			15 33				16 03			16 33		
Gatwick Airport 10 ✈	d			14 19			14 49				15 19			15 49				16 19			16 49		
Haywards Heath 3	d			14 35			15 07				15 35			16 07				16 35			17 07		
Wivelsfield 4	d						15 11							16 11							17 11		
Plumpton	d			14 44							15 44							16 44					
Cooksbridge	d																						
Brighton 10	d	14 22	14 32		14 40	14 52		15 10	15 22	15 32		15 40	15 52		16 10	16 22	16 32		16 40	16 52		17 10	17 22
London Road (Brighton)	d	14 25			14 43	14 55		15 13	15 25			15 43	15 55		16 13	16 25			16 43	16 55		17 13	17 25
Moulsecoomb	d	14 27			14 45	14 57		15 15	15 27			15 45	15 57		16 15	16 27			16 45	16 57		17 15	17 27
Falmer	d	14 31			14 49	15 01		15 19	15 31			15 49	16 01		16 19	16 31			16 49	17 01		17 19	17 31
Lewes 4	a	14 37	14 43	14 52	14 55	15 07	15 22	15 25	15 37	15 43	15 52	15 55	16 07	16 22	16 25	16 37	16 43	16 52	16 55	17 07	17 22	17 25	17 37
	d		14 44	14 53	14 58	15 09	15 23	15 28		15 44	15 53	15 58	16 09	16 23	16 28		16 44	16 53	16 58	17 09	17 23	17 28	
Southease	d							15 34							16 34							17 34	
Newhaven Town ⛴	d				15 06			15 38				16 06			16 38				17 06			17 38	
Newhaven Harbour	d				15 08			15 40				16 08			16 40				17 08			17 40	
Bishopstone	d				15 11			15 43				16 11			16 43				17 11			17 43	
Seaford	a				15 14			15 46				16 14			16 46				17 14			17 46	
Glynde	d					15 14							16 14							17 14			
Berwick	d					15 20							16 20							17 20			
Polegate	d		14 57	15 05		15 25	15 35			15 57	16 05		16 25	16 35			16 57	17 05		17 25	17 35		
Hampden Park 4	d					15 29	15 39						16 29	16 39						17 29	17 39		
Eastbourne 4	a		15 04	15 13		15 34	15 44			16 04	16 13		16 34	16 44			17 04	17 13		17 34	17 44		
	d		15 09	15 19		15 40				16 09	16 19		16 40				17 09	17 19		17 40			
Hampden Park 4	d			15 23		15 44					16 23		16 44					17 23		17 44			
Pevensey & Westham	d			15 28		15 49					16 28		16 49					17 28		17 49			
Pevensey Bay	d																						
Normans Bay	d					15 53							16 53							17 53			
Cooden Beach	d			15 34		15 57					16 34		16 57					17 34		17 57			
Collington	d			15 37		16 00					16 37		17 00					17 37		18 00			
Bexhill 4	d		15 24	15 39		16 02				16 24	16 39		17 02				17 24	17 39		18 02			
St Leonards Warrior Sq 4	d		15 31	15 46		16 09				16 31	16 46		17 09				17 31	17 46		18 09			
Hastings 4	a		15 35	15 49		16 12				16 35	16 49		17 12				17 35	17 49		18 12			
	d		15 36	15 50		16 13				16 36	16 50		17 13				17 36	17 50		18 13			
Ore	d			15a53		16a16					16a53		17a16					17a53		18a16			
Three Oaks	d									16 44													
Doleham	d																						
Winchelsea	d		15 50														17 50						
Rye	a		15 54							16 54							17 54						
	d		15 56							16 56							17 56						
Appledore (Kent)	d		16 05							17 05							18 05						
Ham Street	d		16 10							17 10							18 10						
Ashford International	a		16 18							17 18							18 18						

Table 189

Saturdays
until 4 June

London, Haywards Heath and Brighton - Lewes, Seaford, Eastbourne, Hastings and Ashford

		SN	SN	SN	SN	SN	SN	SN	SN	SN	SN	SN	SN	SN	SN	SN	SN	SN	SN	SN	SN	SN
		◇	◇1	◇	◇1	◇1	◇	◇	◇	◇1	◇	◇1	◇1	◇	◇	◇	◇1	◇	◇1	◇1	◇	◇
																				A		
London Victoria 15 ⊖	d		16 47			17 17				17 47			18 17				18 47			19 17		
Clapham Junction 10	d		16 53			17 23				17 53			18 23				18 53			19 23		
London Bridge 4 ⊖	d																					
East Croydon	d		17 03			17 33				18 03			18 33				19 03			19 33		
Gatwick Airport 10 ✈	d		17 19			17 49				18 19			18 49				19 19			19 49		
Haywards Heath 3	d		17 35			18 07				18 35			19 07				19 35			20 07		
Wivelsfield 4	d					18 11							19 11							20 11		
Plumpton	d		17 44							18 44							19 44					
Cooksbridge	d																					
Brighton 10	d	17 32		17 40	17 52		18 10	18 22	18 32		18 40	18 52		19 10	19 22	19 32		19 40	19 52		20 10	20 32
London Road (Brighton)	d			17 43	17 55		18 13	18 25			18 43	18 55		19 13	19 25			19 43	19 55		20 13	
Moulsecoomb	d			17 45	17 57		18 15	18 27			18 45	18 57		19 15	19 27			19 45	19 57		20 15	
Falmer	d			17 49	18 01		18 19	18 31			18 49	19 01		19 19	19 31			19 49	20 01		20 19	
Lewes 4	a	17 43	17 52	17 55	18 07	18 22	18 25	18 37	18 43	18 52	18 55	19 07	19 22	19 25	19 37	19 43	19 52	19 55	20 08	20 22	20 25	20 43
	d	17 44	17 53	17 58	18 09	18 23	18 28		18 44	18 53	18 58	19 09	19 23	19 28		19 44	19 53	19 58	20 09	20 23	20 28	20 44
Southease	d						18 34							19 34								
Newhaven Town ⛴	d			18 06			18 38				19 06			19 38				20 06			20 36	
Newhaven Harbour	d			18 08			18 40				19 08			19 40				20 08			20 38	
Bishopstone	d			18 11			18 43				19 11			19 43				20 11			20 41	
Seaford	a			18 14			18 46				19 14			19 46				20 14			20 44	
Glynde	d				18 14							19 14							20 14	20 28		
Berwick	d				18 20							19 20							20 20	20 34		
Polegate	d	17 57	18 05		18 25	18 35			18 57	19 05		19 25	19 35			19 57	20 05		20 25	20 39		20 57
Hampden Park 4	d				18 29	18 39						19 29	19 39						20 29	20 43		
Eastbourne 4	a	18 04	18 13		18 34	18 44			19 04	19 13		19 34	19 44			20 04	20 13		20 34	20 48		21 04
	d	18 09	18 19		18 40				19 09	19 19		19 40				20 09	20 19			20 54		21 09
Hampden Park 4	d		18 23		18 44					19 23		19 44					20 23					
Pevensey & Westham	d		18 28		18 49					19 28		19 49					20 28			21 01		
Pevensey Bay	d																					
Normans Bay	d				18 53							19 53										
Cooden Beach	d		18 34		18 57					19 34		19 57					20 34			21 07		
Collington	d		18 37		19 00					19 37		20 00					20 37					
Bexhill 4	d	18 24	18 39		19 02				19 24	19 39		20 02				20 24	20 39			21 12		21 23
St Leonards Warrior Sq 4	d	18 31	18 46		19 09				19 31	19 46		20 09				20 31	20 46			21 18		21 30
Hastings 4	a	18 35	18 49		19 12				19 35	19 49		20 12				20 35	20 49			21 21		21 33
	d	18 36	18 50		19 13				19 36	19 50		20 13				20 36	20 50					21 35
Ore	d		18a53		19a16					19a53		20a16					20a53					21 37
Three Oaks	d	18 44														20 44						21 43
Doleham	d																					21 46
Winchelsea	d								19 50													21 52
Rye	a	18 54							19 54							20 54						21 56
	d	18 56							19 56							20 56						21 56
Appledore (Kent)	d	19 05							20 05							21 05						22 05
Ham Street	d	19 10							20 10							21 10						22 10
Ashford International	a	19 18							20 18							21 18						22 18

A ◇ to Haywards Heath

Table 189

Saturdays
until 4 June

London, Haywards Heath and Brighton - Lewes, Seaford, Eastbourne, Hastings and Ashford

		SN	SN	SN	SN	SN	SN	SN	SN	SN	SN	SN	SN	SN	SN	SN	SN
		◇1	◇	◇1	◇	◇	◇1	◇	◇1	◇	◇	◇1	◇	◇1	◇	◇1	◇
London Victoria 15	d	19 47		20 17			20 47		21 17			21 47				22 47	
Clapham Junction 10	d	19 53		20 23			20 53		21 23			21 53				22 53	
London Bridge 4	d																
East Croydon	d	20 03		20 33			21 03		21 33			22 03				23 03	
Gatwick Airport 10	d	20 19		20 49			21 19		21 49			22 19				23 19	
Haywards Heath 3	d	20 35		21 07			21 34		22 08			22 34				23 34	
Wivelsfield 4	d	20 39		21 11			21 38		22 12			22 38				23 38	
Plumpton	d	20 45					21 44					22 44				23 44	
Cooksbridge	d																
Brighton 10	d		20 40		21 04	21 32		21 40		22 04	22 28		22 34	23 06	23 28		23 34
London Road (Brighton)	d		20 43		21 07			21 43		22 07			22 37	23 09			23 37
Moulsecoomb	d		20 45		21 09			21 45		22 09			22 39	23 11			23 39
Falmer	d		20 49		21 13			21 49		22 13			22 43	23 15			23 43
Lewes 4	a	20 52	20 55	21 22	21 19	21 43	21 51	21 55	22 23	22 19	22 39	22 51	22 49	23 21	23 39	23 51	23 49
	d	20 53	20 58	21 23	21 28	21 44	21 53	21 58	22 23	22 28	22 39	22 53	22 56	23 22	23 39	23 53	23 56
Southease	d																
Newhaven Town	d		21 06		21 36			22 06		22 36			23 04				00 04
Newhaven Harbour	d		21 08		21 38			22 08		22 38			23 06				00 06
Bishopstone	d		21 11		21 41			22 11		22 41			23 09				00 09
Seaford	a		21 14		21 44			22 14		22 44			23 12				00 12
Glynde	d			21 28					22 29					23 27			
Berwick	d			21 34					22 34					23 33		00 02	
Polegate	d	21 05		21 39		21 57	22 05		22 39		22 52	23 05		23 38	23 52	00 07	
Hampden Park 4	d			21 43					22 43			23 09		23 42		00 11	
Eastbourne 4	a	21 13		21 48		22 04	22 15		22 48		23 03	23 14		23 47	23 59	00 16	
	d	21 19				22 09	22 21				23 10	23 20				00 22	
Hampden Park 4	d	21 23					22 25					23 24					
Pevensey & Westham	d	21 28					22 30					23 29				00 29	
Pevensey Bay	d																
Normans Bay	d																
Cooden Beach	d	21 34					22 36					23 35				00 35	
Collington	d	21 37					22 39					23 38				00 38	
Bexhill 4	d	21 39				22 23	22 41				23 24	23 40				00 41	
St Leonards Warrior Sq 4	d	21 46				22 30	22 48				23 31	23 47				00 47	
Hastings 4	a	21 49				22 33	22 51				23 34	23 50				00 50	
	d	21 50															
Ore	d	21a53															
Three Oaks	d																
Doleham	d																
Winchelsea	d																
Rye	a																
	d																
Appledore (Kent)	d																
Ham Street	d																
Ashford International	a																

Table 189

Saturdays

11 June to 3 September

London, Haywards Heath and Brighton - Lewes, Seaford, Eastbourne, Hastings and Ashford

		SN	SN	SN	SN	SN	SN	SN	SN	SN	SN	SN
		◇1	◇	◇1	◇	◇1	◇1	◇	◇	◇1	◇	◇1
London Victoria 15 ⊖	d	22p47		00 05								
Clapham Junction 10	d	22p53		00 11								
London Bridge 4 ⊖	d											
East Croydon	d	23p03		00 25								
Gatwick Airport 10 ✈	d	23p19		00 43								
Haywards Heath 3	d	23p34		01 06								
Wivelsfield 4	d	23p38										
Plumpton	d	23p44										
Cooksbridge	d											
Brighton 10	d		23p34				05 10	05 52			06 10	
London Road (Brighton)	d		23p37					05 55			06 13	
Moulsecoomb	d		23p39					05 57			06 15	
Falmer	d		23p43					06 01			06 19	
Lewes 4	a	23p51	23p49	01 20			05 21	06 07			06 25	
	d	23p53	23p56	01 20			05 21	06 08			06 28	
Southease	d											
Newhaven Town	d		00 04					06 16			06 36	
Newhaven Harbour	d		00 06					06 18			06 38	
Bishopstone	d		00 09								06 41	
Seaford	a		00 12					06 23			06 44	
Glynde	d											
Berwick	d	00 02										
Polegate	d	00 07		01s32			05 33					
Hampden Park 4	d	00 11		01s36								
Eastbourne 4	a	00 16		01 41			05 41					
	d	00 22				05 38			05 53	06 04		06 18
Hampden Park 4	d											06 22
Pevensey & Westham	d	00 29										06 27
Pevensey Bay	d											
Normans Bay	d											06 31
Cooden Beach	d	00 35										06 35
Collington	d	00 38										06 38
Bexhill 4	d	00 41				05 52			06 07	06 18		06 40
St Leonards Warrior Sq 4	d	00 47				06 00			06 14	06 24		06 49
Hastings 4	a	00 50				06 04			06 17	06 28		06 53
	d				05 20	06 05			06 18	06 28		06 54
Ore	d				05 23	06a08				06a32		06a57
Three Oaks	d				05 29				06 26			
Doleham	d				05 32							
Winchelsea	d				05 38							
Rye	a				05 41				06 36			
	d				05 42				06 38			
Appledore (Kent)	d				05 51				06 47			
Ham Street	d				05 56				06 52			
Ashford International	a				06 04				07 00			

		SN	SN	SN	SN	SN	SN	SN	SN	SN	SN	SN
		◇1	◇	1	◇	◇1	◇	◇	◇	1	◇	◇1
London Victoria 15 ⊖	d											
Clapham Junction 10	d											
London Bridge 4 ⊖	d											
East Croydon	d											
Gatwick Airport 10 ✈	d			06 11								
Haywards Heath 3	d			06 25						07 33		
Wivelsfield 4	d			06 29						07 37		
Plumpton	d											
Cooksbridge	d											
Brighton 10	d		06 32		06 40	06 52	07 10	07 22	07 32		07 40	07 52
London Road (Brighton)	d				06 43	06 55	07 13	07 25			07 43	07 55
Moulsecoomb	d				06 45	06 57	07 15	07 27			07 45	07 57
Falmer	d				06 49	07 01	07 19	07 31			07 49	08 01
Lewes 4	a		06 43	06 40	06 55	07 07	07 25	07 37	07 43	07 48	07 55	08 07
	d		06 44	06 53	06 58	07 09	07 28		07 44	07 53	07 58	08 09
Southease	d											
Newhaven Town	d				07 06		07 36				08 06	
Newhaven Harbour	d				07 08		07 38				08 08	
Bishopstone	d				07 11		07 41				08 11	
Seaford	a				07 14		07 44				08 14	
Glynde	d					07 14						08 14
Berwick	d			07 02		07 20						08 20
Polegate	d		06 57	07 07		07 25			07 57	08 05		08 25
Hampden Park 4	d			07 11		07 29						08 29
Eastbourne 4	a		07 04	07 16		07 34			08 05	08 13		08 34
	d	06 45	07 09	07 21		07 40			08 09	08 19		08 40
Hampden Park 4	d			07 25		07 44				08 23		08 44
Pevensey & Westham	d			07 30		07 49				08 28		08 49
Pevensey Bay	d											
Normans Bay	d					07 53						08 53
Cooden Beach	d			07 36		07 57				08 34		08 57
Collington	d			07 39		08 00				08 37		09 00
Bexhill 4	d	07 00	07 24	07 41		08 02			08 24	08 39		09 02
St Leonards Warrior Sq 4	d	07 06	07 31	07 48		08 09			08 31	08 46		09 09
Hastings 4	a	07 10	07 35	07 51		08 12			08 35	08 50		09 12
	d	07 11	07 36	07 52		08 13			08 36	08 51		09 13
Ore	d	07a14		07a55		08a16				08a54		09a16
Three Oaks	d								08 44			
Doleham	d											
Winchelsea	d		07 50									
Rye	a		07 54						08 54			
	d		07 56						08 56			
Appledore (Kent)	d		08 05						09 05			
Ham Street	d		08 10						09 10			
Ashford International	a		08 18						09 18			

Table 189

Saturdays

11 June to 3 September

London, Haywards Heath and Brighton - Lewes, Seaford, Eastbourne, Hastings and Ashford

		SN	SN	SN	SN	SN	SN	SN	SN	SN	SN	SN	SN	SN	SN	SN	SN	SN	SN	SN	SN	SN	SN
		◇	◇	◇	◇1	◇	◇1	◇1	◇	◇	◇	◇1	◇	◇1	◇1	◇	◇	◇	◇1	◇	◇1	◇1	◇
London Victoria 15 ⊖	d				07 47			08 17				08 47			09 17				09 47			10 17	
Clapham Junction 10	d				07 53			08 23				08 53			09 23				09 53			10 23	
London Bridge 4 ⊖	d																						
East Croydon	d				08 03			08 33				09 03			09 33				10 03			10 33	
Gatwick Airport 10 ✈	d				08 19			08 49				09 19			09 49				10 19			10 49	
Haywards Heath 3	d				08 35			09 07				09 35			10 07				10 35			11 07	
Wivelsfield 4	d							09 11							10 11							11 11	
Plumpton	d											09 44							10 44				
Cooksbridge	d																						
Brighton 10	d	08 10	08 22	08 32		08 40	08 52		09 10	09 22	09 32		09 40	09 52		10 10	10 22	10 32		10 40	10 52		11 10
London Road (Brighton)	d	08 13	08 25			08 43	08 55		09 13	09 25			09 43	09 55		10 13	10 25			10 43	10 55		11 13
Moulsecoomb	d	08 15	08 27			08 45	08 57		09 15	09 27			09 45	09 57		10 15	10 27			10 45	10 57		11 15
Falmer	d	08 19	08 31			08 49	09 01		09 19	09 31			09 49	10 01		10 19	10 31			10 49	11 01		11 19
Lewes 4	a	08 25	08 37	08 43	08 49	08 55	09 07	09 22	09 25	09 37	09 43	09 52	09 55	10 07	10 22	10 25	10 37	10 43	10 52	10 55	11 07	11 22	11 25
	d	08 28		08 44	08 53	08 58	09 09	09 23	09 28		09 44	09 53	09 58	10 09	10 23	10 28		10 44	10 53	10 58	11 09	11 23	11 28
Southease	d								09 34							10 34							11 34
Newhaven Town	d	08 36				09 06			09 38				10 06			10 38				11 06			11 38
Newhaven Harbour	d	08 38				09 08			09 40				10 08			10 40				11 08			11 40
Bishopstone	d	08 41				09 11			09 43				10 11			10 43				11 11			11 43
Seaford	a	08 44				09 14			09 46				10 14			10 46				11 14			11 46
Glynde	d						09 14							10 14							11 14		
Berwick	d						09 20							10 20							11 20		
Polegate	d			08 57	09 05		09 25	09 35			09 57	10 05		10 25	10 35			10 57	11 05		11 25	11 35	
Hampden Park 4	d						09 29	09 39						10 29	10 39						11 29	11 39	
Eastbourne 4	a			09 04	09 13		09 34	09 44			10 04	10 13		10 34	10 44			11 04	11 13		11 34	11 44	
	d			09 09	09 19		09 40				10 09	10 19		10 40				11 09	11 19		11 40		
Hampden Park 4	d				09 23		09 44					10 23		10 44					11 23		11 44		
Pevensey & Westham	d				09 28		09 49					10 28		10 49					11 28		11 49		
Pevensey Bay	d																						
Normans Bay	d						09 53							10 53							11 53		
Cooden Beach	d				09 34		09 57					10 34		10 57					11 34		11 57		
Collington	d				09 37		10 00					10 37		11 00					11 37		12 00		
Bexhill 4	d			09 24	09 39		10 02				10 24	10 39		11 02				11 24	11 39		12 02		
St Leonards Warrior Sq 4	d			09 31	09 46		10 09				10 31	10 46		11 09				11 31	11 46		12 09		
Hastings 4	a			09 35	09 49		10 12				10 35	10 49		11 12				11 35	11 49		12 12		
	d			09 36	09 50		10 13				10 36	10 50		11 13				11 36	11 50		12 13		
Ore	d				09a53		10a16					10a53		11a16					11a53		12a16		
Three Oaks	d										10 44												
Doleham	d																						
Winchelsea	d			09 50														11 50					
Rye	a			09 54							10 54							11 54					
	d			09 56							10 56							11 56					
Appledore (Kent)	d			10 05							11 05							12 05					
Ham Street	d			10 10							11 10							12 10					
Ashford International	a			10 18							11 18							12 18					

Table 189

Saturdays

11 June to 3 September

London, Haywards Heath and Brighton - Lewes, Seaford, Eastbourne, Hastings and Ashford

		SN		SN	SN	SN	SN	SN	SN	SN	SN	SN		SN	SN	SN	SN	SN	SN	SN	SN	SN		SN	SN
		◇		◇	◇1	◇	◇1	◇1	◇	◇	◇	◇1		◇	◇1	◇1	◇	◇	◇	◇1	◇	◇1		◇1	◇
London Victoria 15 ⊖	d				10 47			11 17				11 47				12 17				12 47				13 17	
Clapham Junction 10	d				10 53			11 23				11 53				12 23				12 53				13 23	
London Bridge 4 ⊖	d																								
East Croydon	d				11 03			11 33				12 03				12 33				13 03				13 33	
Gatwick Airport 10 ✈	d				11 19			11 49				12 19				12 49				13 19				13 49	
Haywards Heath 3	d				11 35			12 07				12 35				13 07				13 35				14 07	
Wivelsfield 4	d							12 11								13 11								14 11	
Plumpton	d				11 44							12 44								13 44					
Cooksbridge	d																								
Brighton 10	d	11 22		11 32		11 40	11 52		12 10	12 22	12 32			12 40	12 52		13 10	13 22	13 32		13 40	13 52			14 10
London Road (Brighton)	d	11 25				11 43	11 55		12 13	12 25				12 43	12 55		13 13	13 25			13 43	13 55			14 13
Moulsecoomb	d	11 27				11 45	11 57		12 15	12 27				12 45	12 57		13 15	13 27			13 45	13 57			14 15
Falmer	d	11 31				11 49	12 01		12 19	12 31				12 49	13 01		13 19	13 31			13 49	14 01			14 19
Lewes 4	a	11 37		11 43	11 52	11 55	12 07	12 22	12 25	12 37	12 43	12 52		12 55	13 07	13 22	13 25	13 37	13 43	13 52	13 55	14 07		14 22	14 25
	d			11 44	11 53	11 58	12 09	12 23	12 28		12 44	12 53		12 58	13 09	13 23	13 28		13 44	13 53	13 58	14 09		14 23	14 28
Southease	d								12 34								13 34								14 34
Newhaven Town ⛴	d					12 06			12 38					13 06			13 38				14 06				14 38
Newhaven Harbour	d					12 08			12 40					13 08			13 40				14 08				14 40
Bishopstone	d					12 11			12 43					13 11			13 43				14 11				14 43
Seaford	a					12 14			12 46					13 14			13 46				14 14				14 46
Glynde	d						12 14								13 14							14 14			
Berwick	d						12 20								13 20							14 20			
Polegate	d			11 57	12 05		12 25	12 35			12 57	13 05			13 25	13 35			13 57	14 05		14 25		14 35	
Hampden Park 4	d						12 29	12 39							13 29	13 39						14 29		14 39	
Eastbourne 4	a			12 04	12 13		12 34	12 44			13 04	13 13			13 34	13 44			14 04	14 13		14 34		14 44	
	d			12 09	12 19		12 40				13 09	13 19			13 40				14 09	14 19		14 40			
Hampden Park 4	d				12 23		12 44					13 23			13 44					14 23		14 44			
Pevensey & Westham	d				12 28		12 49					13 28			13 49					14 28		14 49			
Pevensey Bay	d																								
Normans Bay	d						12 53								13 53							14 53			
Cooden Beach	d				12 34		12 57					13 34			13 57					14 34		14 57			
Collington	d				12 37		13 00					13 37			14 00					14 37		15 00			
Bexhill 4	d			12 24	12 39		13 02				13 24	13 39			14 02				14 24	14 39		15 02			
St Leonards Warrior Sq 4	d			12 31	12 46		13 09				13 31	13 46			14 09				14 31	14 46		15 09			
Hastings 4	a			12 35	12 49		13 12				13 35	13 49			14 12				14 35	14 49		15 12			
	d			12 36	12 50		13 13				13 36	13 50			14 13				14 36	14 50		15 13			
Ore	d				12a53		13a16					13a53			14a16					14a53		15a16			
Three Oaks	d			12 44															14 44						
Doleham	d																								
Winchelsea	d										13 50														
Rye	a			12 54							13 54								14 54						
	d			12 56							13 56								14 56						
Appledore (Kent)	d			13 05							14 05								15 05						
Ham Street	d			13 10							14 10								15 10						
Ashford International	a			13 18							14 18								15 18						

Table 189

Saturdays

11 June to 3 September

London, Haywards Heath and Brighton - Lewes, Seaford, Eastbourne, Hastings and Ashford

		SN	SN	SN	SN	SN	SN	SN	SN	SN	SN	SN	SN	SN	SN	SN	SN	SN	SN	SN	SN	SN	SN
		◇	◇	◇1	◇	◇1	◇1	◇	◇	◇	◇1	◇	◇1	◇1	◇	◇	◇	◇1	◇	◇1	◇1	◇	◇
London Victoria 15 ⊖	d			13 47			14 17				14 47			15 17				15 47			16 17		
Clapham Junction 10	d			13 53			14 23				14 53			15 23				15 53			16 23		
London Bridge 4 ⊖	d																						
East Croydon	d			14 03			14 33				15 03			15 33				16 03			16 33		
Gatwick Airport 10 ✈	d			14 19			14 49				15 19			15 49				16 19			16 49		
Haywards Heath 3	d			14 35			15 07				15 35			16 07				16 35			17 07		
Wivelsfield 4	d						15 11							16 11							17 11		
Plumpton	d			14 44							15 44							16 44					
Cooksbridge	d																						
Brighton 10	d	14 22	14 32		14 40	14 52		15 10	15 22	15 32		15 40	15 52		16 10	16 22	16 32		16 40	16 52		17 10	17 22
London Road (Brighton)	d	14 25			14 43	14 55		15 13	15 25			15 43	15 55		16 13	16 25			16 43	16 55		17 13	17 25
Moulsecoomb	d	14 27			14 45	14 57		15 15	15 27			15 45	15 57		16 15	16 27			16 45	16 57		17 15	17 27
Falmer	d	14 31			14 49	15 01		15 19	15 31			15 49	16 01		16 19	16 31			16 49	17 01		17 19	17 31
Lewes 4	a	14 37	14 43	14 52	14 55	15 07	15 22	15 25	15 37	15 43	15 52	15 55	16 07	16 22	16 25	16 37	16 43	16 52	16 55	17 07	17 22	17 25	17 37
	d		14 44	14 53	14 58	15 09	15 23	15 28		15 44	15 53	15 58	16 09	16 23	16 28		16 44	16 53	16 58	17 09	17 23	17 28	
Southease	d							15 34							16 34							17 34	
Newhaven Town ⛴	d				15 06			15 38				16 06			16 38				17 06			17 38	
Newhaven Harbour	d				15 08			15 40				16 08			16 40				17 08			17 40	
Bishopstone	d				15 11			15 43				16 11			16 43				17 11			17 43	
Seaford	a				15 14			15 46				16 14			16 46				17 14			17 46	
Glynde	d					15 14							16 14							17 14			
Berwick	d					15 20							16 20							17 20			
Polegate	d		14 57	15 05		15 25	15 35			15 57	16 05		16 25	16 35			16 57	17 05		17 25	17 35		
Hampden Park 4	d					15 29	15 39						16 29	16 39						17 29	17 39		
Eastbourne 4	a		15 04	15 13		15 34	15 44			16 04	16 13		16 34	16 44			17 04	17 13		17 34	17 44		
	d		15 09	15 19		15 40				16 09	16 19		16 40				17 09	17 19		17 40			
Hampden Park 4	d			15 23		15 44					16 23		16 44					17 23		17 44			
Pevensey & Westham	d			15 28		15 49					16 28		16 49					17 28		17 49			
Pevensey Bay	d																						
Normans Bay	d					15 53							16 53							17 53			
Cooden Beach	d			15 34		15 57					16 34		16 57					17 34		17 57			
Collington	d			15 37		16 00					16 37		17 00					17 37		18 00			
Bexhill 4	d		15 24	15 39		16 02				16 24	16 39		17 02				17 24	17 39		18 02			
St Leonards Warrior Sq 4	d		15 31	15 46		16 09				16 31	16 46		17 09				17 31	17 46		18 09			
Hastings 4	a		15 35	15 49		16 12				16 35	16 49		17 12				17 35	17 49		18 12			
	d		15 36	15 50		16 13				16 36	16 50		17 13				17 36	17 50		18 13			
Ore	d			15a53		16a16					16a53		17a16					17a53		18a16			
Three Oaks	d									16 44													
Doleham	d																						
Winchelsea	d		15 50														17 50						
Rye	a		15 54							16 54							17 54						
	d		15 56							16 56							17 56						
Appledore (Kent)	d		16 05							17 05							18 05						
Ham Street	d		16 10							17 10							18 10						
Ashford International	a		16 18							17 18							18 18						

Table 189

Saturdays

11 June to 3 September

London, Haywards Heath and Brighton - Lewes, Seaford, Eastbourne, Hastings and Ashford

		SN	SN	SN	SN	SN	SN	SN	SN	SN	SN	SN	SN	SN	SN	SN	SN	SN	SN	SN	SN	SN
		◇	◇1	◇	◇1	◇1	◇	◇	◇	◇1		◇	◇1	◇1	◇	◇	◇	◇1	◇	◇1	◇1	◇
																					A	
London Victoria 15 ⊖	d		16 47			17 17				17 47				18 17				18 47			19 17	
Clapham Junction 10	d		16 53			17 23				17 53				18 23				18 53			19 23	
London Bridge 4 ⊖	d										17 44											
East Croydon	d		17 03			17 33				18 03				18 33				19 03			19 33	
Gatwick Airport 10 ✈	d		17 19			17 49				18 19				18 49				19 19			19 49	
Haywards Heath 3	d		17 35			18 07				18 35				19 07				19 35			20 07	
Wivelsfield 4	d					18 11								19 11							20 11	
Plumpton	d		17 44							18 44								19 44				
Cooksbridge	d																					
Brighton 10	d	17 32		17 40	17 52		18 10	18 22	18 32			18 40	18 52		19 10	19 22	19 32		19 40	19 52		20 10
London Road (Brighton)	d			17 43	17 55		18 13	18 25				18 43	18 55		19 13	19 25			19 43	19 55		20 13
Moulsecoomb	d			17 45	17 57		18 15	18 27				18 45	18 57		19 15	19 27			19 45	19 57		20 15
Falmer	d			17 49	18 01		18 19	18 31				18 49	19 01		19 19	19 31			19 49	20 01		20 19
Lewes 4	a	17 43	17 52	17 55	18 07	18 22	18 25	18 37	18 43	18 52		18 55	19 07	19 22	19 25	19 37	19 43	19 52	19 55	20 08	20 22	20 25
	d	17 44	17 53	17 58	18 09	18 23	18 28		18 44	18 53		18 58	19 09	19 23	19 28		19 44	19 53	19 58	20 09	20 23	20 28
Southease	d						18 34								19 34							
Newhaven Town ⛴	d			18 06			18 38					19 06			19 38				20 06			20 36
Newhaven Harbour	d			18 08			18 40					19 08			19 40				20 08			20 38
Bishopstone	d			18 11			18 43					19 11			19 43				20 11			20 41
Seaford	a			18 14			18 46					19 14			19 46				20 14			20 44
Glynde	d				18 14								19 14							20 14	20 28	
Berwick	d				18 20								19 20							20 20	20 34	
Polegate	d	17 57	18 05		18 25	18 35			18 57	19 05			19 25	19 35			19 57	20 05		20 25	20 39	
Hampden Park 4	d				18 29	18 39							19 29	19 39						20 29	20 43	
Eastbourne 4	a	18 04	18 13		18 34	18 44			19 04	19 13	19 22		19 34	19 44			20 04	20 13		20 34	20 48	
	d	18 09	18 19		18 40				19 09	19 19			19 40				20 09	20 19			20 54	
Hampden Park 4	d		18 23		18 44					19 23			19 44					20 23				
Pevensey & Westham	d		18 28		18 49					19 28			19 49					20 28			21 01	
Pevensey Bay	d																					
Normans Bay	d				18 53								19 53									
Cooden Beach	d		18 34		18 57					19 34			19 57					20 34			21 07	
Collington	d		18 37		19 00					19 37			20 00					20 37				
Bexhill 4	d	18 24	18 39		19 02				19 24	19 39			20 02				20 24	20 39			21 12	
St Leonards Warrior Sq 4	d	18 31	18 46		19 09				19 31	19 46			20 09				20 31	20 46			21 18	
Hastings 4	a	18 35	18 49		19 12				19 35	19 49			20 12				20 35	20 49			21 21	
	d	18 36	18 50		19 13				19 36	19 50			20 13				20 36	20 50				
Ore	d		18a53		19a16					19a53			20a16					20a53				
Three Oaks	d	18 44															20 44					
Doleham	d																					
Winchelsea	d								19 50													
Rye	a	18 54							19 54								20 54					
	d	18 56							19 56								20 56					
Appledore (Kent)	d	19 05							20 05								21 05					
Ham Street	d	19 10							20 10								21 10					
Ashford International	a	19 18							20 18								21 18					

A ◇ to Haywards Heath

Table 189

Saturdays

11 June to 3 September

London, Haywards Heath and Brighton - Lewes, Seaford, Eastbourne, Hastings and Ashford

		SN	SN	SN	SN	SN	SN	SN	SN	SN	SN	SN	SN	SN	SN	SN	SN	SN
		◇	◇ 1	◇	◇ 1	◇	◇	◇ 1	◇	◇ 1	◇	◇	◇ 1	◇	◇ 1	◇	◇ 1	◇
London Victoria (15) ⊖	d		19 47		20 17			20 47		21 17			21 47				22 47	
Clapham Junction (10)	d		19 53		20 23			20 53		21 23			21 53				22 53	
London Bridge (4) ⊖	d																	
East Croydon	d		20 03		20 33			21 03		21 33			22 03				23 03	
Gatwick Airport (10) ✈	d		20 19		20 49			21 19		21 49			22 19				23 19	
Haywards Heath (3)	d		20 35		21 07			21 34		22 08			22 34				23 34	
Wivelsfield (4)	d		20 39		21 11			21 38		22 12			22 38				23 38	
Plumpton	d		20 45					21 44					22 44				23 44	
Cooksbridge	d																	
Brighton (10)	d	20 32		20 40		21 04	21 32		21 40		22 04	22 28		22 34	23 06	23 28		23 34
London Road (Brighton)	d			20 43		21 07			21 43		22 07			22 37	23 09			23 37
Moulsecoomb	d			20 45		21 09			21 45		22 09			22 39	23 11			23 39
Falmer	d			20 49		21 13			21 49		22 13			22 43	23 15			23 43
Lewes (4)	a	20 43	20 52	20 55	21 22	21 19	21 43	21 51	21 55	22 23	22 19	22 39	22 51	22 49	23 21	23 39	23 51	23 49
	d	20 44	20 53	20 58	21 23	21 28	21 44	21 53	21 58	22 23	22 28	22 39	22 53	22 56	23 22	23 39	23 53	23 56
Southease	d																	
Newhaven Town ⛴	d			21 06		21 36			22 06		22 36			23 04				00 04
Newhaven Harbour	d			21 08		21 38			22 08		22 38			23 06				00 06
Bishopstone	d			21 11		21 41			22 11		22 41			23 09				00 09
Seaford	a			21 14		21 44			22 14		22 44			23 12				00 12
Glynde	d				21 28					22 29					23 27			
Berwick	d				21 34					22 34					23 33		00 02	
Polegate	d	20 57	21 05		21 39		21 57	22 05		22 39		22 52	23 05		23 38	23 52	00 07	
Hampden Park (4)	d				21 43					22 43			23 09		23 42		00 11	
Eastbourne (4)	a	21 04	21 13		21 48		22 04	22 15		22 48		23 03	23 14		23 47	23 59	00 16	
	d	21 09	21 19				22 09	22 21				23 10	23 20				00 22	
Hampden Park (4)	d		21 23					22 25					23 24					
Pevensey & Westham	d		21 28					22 30					23 29				00 29	
Pevensey Bay	d																	
Normans Bay	d																	
Cooden Beach	d		21 34					22 36					23 35				00 35	
Collington	d		21 37					22 39					23 38				00 38	
Bexhill (4)	d	21 23	21 39				22 23	22 41				23 24	23 40				00 41	
St Leonards Warrior Sq (4)	d	21 30	21 46				22 30	22 48				23 31	23 47				00 47	
Hastings (4)	a	21 33	21 49				22 33	22 51				23 34	23 50				00 50	
	d	21 35	21 50															
Ore	d	21 37	21a53															
Three Oaks	d	21 43																
Doleham	d	21 46																
Winchelsea	d	21 52																
Rye	a	21 56																
	d	21 56																
Appledore (Kent)	d	22 05																
Ham Street	d	22 10																
Ashford International	a	22 18																

Table 189

Saturdays
from 10 September

London, Haywards Heath and Brighton - Lewes, Seaford, Eastbourne, Hastings and Ashford

		SN	SN	SN	SN	SN	SN	SN	SN	SN	SN	SN	SN	SN	SN	SN	SN	SN	SN	SN	SN	SN	SN
		◇1	◇	◇1	◇	◇1	◇1	◇	◇	◇1	◇	◇1	◇1	◇	1	◇	◇1	◇	◇	◇	1	◇	◇1
London Victoria 15 ⊖	d	22p47		00 05																			
Clapham Junction 10	d	22p53		00 11																			
London Bridge 4 ⊖	d																						
East Croydon	d	23p03		00 25																			
Gatwick Airport 10 ✈	d	23p19		00 43											06 11								
Haywards Heath 3	d	23p34		01 06											06 25						07 33		
Wivelsfield 4	d	23p38													06 29						07 37		
Plumpton	d	23p44																					
Cooksbridge	d																						
Brighton 10	d		23p34				05 10	05 52			06 10			06 32		06 40	06 52	07 10	07 22	07 32		07 40	07 52
London Road (Brighton)	d		23p37					05 55			06 13					06 43	06 55	07 13	07 25			07 43	07 55
Moulsecoomb	d		23p39					05 57			06 15					06 45	06 57	07 15	07 27			07 45	07 57
Falmer	d		23p43					06 01			06 19					06 49	07 01	07 19	07 31			07 49	08 01
Lewes 4	a	23p51	23p49	01 20			05 21	06 07			06 25			06 43	06 40	06 55	07 07	07 25	07 37	07 43	07 48	07 55	08 07
	d	23p53	23p56	01 20			05 21	06 08			06 28			06 44	06 53	06 58	07 09	07 28		07 44	07 53	07 58	08 09
Southease	d																						
Newhaven Town ⛴	d		00 04					06 16			06 36					07 06		07 36				08 06	
Newhaven Harbour	d		00 06					06 18			06 38					07 08		07 38				08 08	
Bishopstone	d		00 09								06 41					07 11		07 41				08 11	
Seaford	a		00 12					06 23			06 44					07 14		07 44				08 14	
Glynde	d																07 14						08 14
Berwick	d	00 02													07 02		07 20						08 20
Polegate	d	00 07		01s32			05 33							06 57	07 07		07 25			07 57	08 05		08 25
Hampden Park 4	d	00 11		01s36											07 11		07 29						08 29
Eastbourne 4	a	00 16		01 41			05 41							07 04	07 16		07 34			08 05	08 13		08 34
	d	00 22				05 38			05 53	06 04		06 18	06 45	07 09	07 21		07 40			08 09	08 19		08 40
Hampden Park 4	d											06 22			07 25		07 44				08 23		08 44
Pevensey & Westham	d	00 29										06 27			07 30		07 49				08 28		08 49
Pevensey Bay	d																						
Normans Bay	d											06 31					07 53						08 53
Cooden Beach	d	00 35										06 35			07 36		07 57				08 34		08 57
Collington	d	00 38										06 38			07 39		08 00				08 37		09 00
Bexhill 4	d	00 41				05 52			06 07	06 18		06 40	07 00	07 24	07 41		08 02			08 24	08 39		09 02
St Leonards Warrior Sq 4	d	00 47				06 00			06 14	06 24		06 49	07 06	07 31	07 48		08 09			08 31	08 46		09 09
Hastings 4	a	00 50				06 04			06 17	06 28		06 53	07 10	07 35	07 51		08 12			08 35	08 50		09 12
	d				05 20	06 05			06 18	06 28		06 54	07 11	07 36	07 52		08 13			08 36	08 51		09 13
Ore	d				05 23	06a08				06a32		06a57	07a14		07a55		08a16				08a54		09a16
Three Oaks	d				05 29				06 26											08 44			
Doleham	d				05 32																		
Winchelsea	d				05 38									07 50									
Rye	a				05 41				06 36					07 54						08 54			
	d				05 42				06 38					07 56						08 56			
Appledore (Kent)	d				05 51				06 47					08 05						09 05			
Ham Street	d				05 56				06 52					08 10						09 10			
Ashford International	a				06 04				07 00					08 18						09 18			

Table 189

Saturdays
from 10 September

London, Haywards Heath and Brighton - Lewes, Seaford, Eastbourne, Hastings and Ashford

		SN	SN	SN	SN	SN	SN	SN	SN	SN	SN	SN	SN	SN	SN	SN	SN	SN	SN	SN	SN	SN	SN
		◇	◇	◇	◇1	◇	◇1	◇1	◇	◇	◇	◇1	◇	◇1	◇1	◇	◇	◇	◇1	◇	◇1	◇1	◇
London Victoria 15 ⊖	d				07 47			08 17				08 47			09 17				09 47			10 17	
Clapham Junction 10	d				07 53			08 23				08 53			09 23				09 53			10 23	
London Bridge 4 ⊖	d																						
East Croydon	d				08 03			08 33				09 03			09 33				10 03			10 33	
Gatwick Airport 10 ✈	d				08 19			08 49				09 19			09 49				10 19			10 49	
Haywards Heath 3	d				08 35			09 07				09 35			10 07				10 35			11 07	
Wivelsfield 4	d							09 11							10 11							11 11	
Plumpton	d											09 44							10 44				
Cooksbridge	d																						
Brighton 10	d	08 10	08 22	08 32		08 40	08 52		09 10	09 22	09 32		09 40	09 52		10 10	10 22	10 32		10 40	10 52		11 10
London Road (Brighton)	d	08 13	08 25			08 43	08 55		09 13	09 25			09 43	09 55		10 13	10 25			10 43	10 55		11 13
Moulsecoomb	d	08 15	08 27			08 45	08 57		09 15	09 27			09 45	09 57		10 15	10 27			10 45	10 57		11 15
Falmer	d	08 19	08 31			08 49	09 01		09 19	09 31			09 49	10 01		10 19	10 31			10 49	11 01		11 19
Lewes 4	a	08 25	08 37	08 43	08 49	08 55	09 07	09 22	09 25	09 37	09 43	09 52	09 55	10 07	10 22	10 25	10 37	10 43	10 52	10 55	11 07	11 22	11 25
	d	08 28		08 44	08 53	08 58	09 09	09 23	09 28		09 44	09 53	09 58	10 09	10 23	10 28		10 44	10 53	10 58	11 09	11 23	11 28
Southease	d								09 34							10 34							11 34
Newhaven Town ⛴	d	08 36				09 06			09 38				10 06			10 38				11 06			11 38
Newhaven Harbour	d	08 38				09 08			09 40				10 08			10 40				11 08			11 40
Bishopstone	d	08 41				09 11			09 43				10 11			10 43				11 11			11 43
Seaford	a	08 44				09 14			09 46				10 14			10 46				11 14			11 46
Glynde	d						09 14							10 14							11 14		
Berwick	d						09 20							10 20							11 20		
Polegate	d			08 57	09 05		09 25	09 35			09 57	10 05		10 25	10 35			10 57	11 05		11 25	11 35	
Hampden Park 4	d						09 29	09 39						10 29	10 39						11 29	11 39	
Eastbourne 4	a			09 04	09 13		09 34	09 44			10 04	10 13		10 34	10 44			11 04	11 13		11 34	11 44	
	d			09 09	09 19		09 40				10 09	10 19		10 40				11 09	11 19		11 40		
Hampden Park 4	d				09 23		09 44					10 23		10 44					11 23		11 44		
Pevensey & Westham	d				09 28		09 49					10 28		10 49					11 28		11 49		
Pevensey Bay	d																						
Normans Bay	d						09 53							10 53							11 53		
Cooden Beach	d				09 34		09 57					10 34		10 57					11 34		11 57		
Collington	d				09 37		10 00					10 37		11 00					11 37		12 00		
Bexhill 4	d			09 24	09 39		10 02				10 24	10 39		11 02				11 24	11 39		12 02		
St Leonards Warrior Sq 4	d			09 31	09 46		10 09				10 31	10 46		11 09				11 31	11 46		12 09		
Hastings 4	a			09 35	09 49		10 12				10 35	10 49		11 12				11 35	11 49		12 12		
	d			09 36	09 50		10 13				10 36	10 50		11 13				11 36	11 50		12 13		
Ore	d				09a53		10a16					10a53		11a16					11a53		12a16		
Three Oaks	d										10 44												
Doleham	d																						
Winchelsea	d			09 50														11 50					
Rye	a			09 54							10 54							11 54					
	d			09 56							10 56							11 56					
Appledore (Kent)	d			10 05							11 05							12 05					
Ham Street	d			10 10							11 10							12 10					
Ashford International	a			10 18							11 18							12 18					

Table 189

Saturdays
from 10 September

London, Haywards Heath and Brighton - Lewes, Seaford, Eastbourne, Hastings and Ashford

		SN		SN	SN	SN	SN	SN	SN	SN	SN	SN		SN	SN	SN	SN	SN	SN	SN	SN	SN		SN	SN
		◇		◇	◇ 1	◇	◇ 1	◇ 1	◇	◇	◇	◇ 1		◇	◇ 1	◇ 1	◇	◇	◇	◇ 1	◇	◇ 1		◇ 1	◇
London Victoria 15 ⊖	d				10 47			11 17				11 47				12 17				12 47				13 17	
Clapham Junction 10	d				10 53			11 23				11 53				12 23				12 53				13 23	
London Bridge 4 ⊖	d																								
East Croydon	d				11 03			11 33				12 03				12 33				13 03				13 33	
Gatwick Airport 10 ✈	d				11 19			11 49				12 19				12 49				13 19				13 49	
Haywards Heath 3	d				11 35			12 07				12 35				13 07				13 35				14 07	
Wivelsfield 4	d							12 11								13 11								14 11	
Plumpton	d				11 44							12 44								13 44					
Cooksbridge	d																								
Brighton 10	d	11 22		11 32		11 40	11 52		12 10	12 22	12 32			12 40	12 52		13 10	13 22	13 32		13 40	13 52			14 10
London Road (Brighton)	d	11 25				11 43	11 55		12 13	12 25				12 43	12 55		13 13	13 25			13 43	13 55			14 13
Moulsecoomb	d	11 27				11 45	11 57		12 15	12 27				12 45	12 57		13 15	13 27			13 45	13 57			14 15
Falmer	d	11 31				11 49	12 01		12 19	12 31				12 49	13 01		13 19	13 31			13 49	14 01			14 19
Lewes 4	a	11 37		11 43	11 52	11 55	12 07	12 22	12 25	12 37	12 43	12 52		12 55	13 07	13 22	13 25	13 37	13 43	13 52	13 55	14 07		14 22	14 25
	d			11 44	11 53	11 58	12 09	12 23	12 28		12 44	12 53		12 58	13 09	13 23	13 28		13 44	13 53	13 58	14 09		14 23	14 28
Southease	d								12 34								13 34								14 34
Newhaven Town	d					12 06			12 38					13 06			13 38				14 06				14 38
Newhaven Harbour	d					12 08			12 40					13 08			13 40				14 08				14 40
Bishopstone	d					12 11			12 43					13 11			13 43				14 11				14 43
Seaford	a					12 14			12 46					13 14			13 46				14 14				14 46
Glynde	d						12 14								13 14							14 14			
Berwick	d						12 20								13 20							14 20			
Polegate	d			11 57	12 05		12 25	12 35			12 57	13 05			13 25	13 35			13 57	14 05		14 25		14 35	
Hampden Park 4	d						12 29	12 39							13 29	13 39						14 29		14 39	
Eastbourne 4	a			12 04	12 13		12 34	12 44			13 04	13 13			13 34	13 44			14 04	14 13		14 34		14 44	
	d			12 09	12 19		12 40				13 09	13 19			13 40				14 09	14 19		14 40			
Hampden Park 4	d				12 23		12 44					13 23			13 44					14 23		14 44			
Pevensey & Westham	d				12 28		12 49					13 28			13 49					14 28		14 49			
Pevensey Bay	d																								
Normans Bay	d						12 53								13 53							14 53			
Cooden Beach	d				12 34		12 57					13 34			13 57					14 34		14 57			
Collington	d				12 37		13 00					13 37			14 00					14 37		15 00			
Bexhill 4	d			12 24	12 39		13 02				13 24	13 39			14 02				14 24	14 39		15 02			
St Leonards Warrior Sq 4	d			12 31	12 46		13 09				13 31	13 46			14 09				14 31	14 46		15 09			
Hastings 4	a			12 35	12 49		13 12				13 35	13 49			14 12				14 35	14 49		15 12			
	d			12 36	12 50		13 13				13 36	13 50			14 13				14 36	14 50		15 13			
Ore	d				12a53		13a16					13a53			14a16					14a53		15a16			
Three Oaks	d			12 44															14 44						
Doleham	d																								
Winchelsea	d										13 50														
Rye	a			12 54							13 54								14 54						
	d			12 56							13 56								14 56						
Appledore (Kent)	d			13 05							14 05								15 05						
Ham Street	d			13 10							14 10								15 10						
Ashford International	a			13 18							14 18								15 18						

Table 189

Saturdays
from 10 September

London, Haywards Heath and Brighton - Lewes, Seaford, Eastbourne, Hastings and Ashford

		SN	SN	SN	SN	SN	SN	SN	SN	SN	SN	SN	SN	SN	SN	SN	SN	SN	SN	SN	SN	SN	SN
		◇	◇	◇1	◇	◇1	◇1	◇	◇	◇	◇1	◇	◇1	◇1	◇	◇	◇	◇1	◇	◇1	◇1	◇	◇
London Victoria 15 ⊖	d			13 47			14 17				14 47			15 17				15 47			16 17		
Clapham Junction 10	d			13 53			14 23				14 53			15 23				15 53			16 23		
London Bridge 4 ⊖	d																						
East Croydon	d			14 03			14 33				15 03			15 33				16 03			16 33		
Gatwick Airport 10 ✈	d			14 19			14 49				15 19			15 49				16 19			16 49		
Haywards Heath 3	d			14 35			15 07				15 35			16 07				16 35			17 07		
Wivelsfield 4	d						15 11							16 11							17 11		
Plumpton	d			14 44							15 44							16 44					
Cooksbridge	d																						
Brighton 10	d	14 22	14 32		14 40	14 52		15 10	15 22	15 32		15 40	15 52		16 10	16 22	16 32		16 40	16 52		17 10	17 22
London Road (Brighton)	d	14 25			14 43	14 55		15 13	15 25			15 43	15 55		16 13	16 25			16 43	16 55		17 13	17 25
Moulsecoomb	d	14 27			14 45	14 57		15 15	15 27			15 45	15 57		16 15	16 27			16 45	16 57		17 15	17 27
Falmer	d	14 31			14 49	15 01		15 19	15 31			15 49	16 01		16 19	16 31			16 49	17 01		17 19	17 31
Lewes 4	a	14 37	14 43	14 52	14 55	15 07	15 22	15 25	15 37	15 43	15 52	15 55	16 07	16 22	16 25	16 37	16 43	16 52	16 55	17 07	17 22	17 25	17 37
	d		14 44	14 53	14 58	15 09	15 23	15 28		15 44	15 53	15 58	16 09	16 23	16 28		16 44	16 53	16 58	17 09	17 23	17 28	
Southease	d							15 34							16 34							17 34	
Newhaven Town ⛴	d				15 06			15 38				16 06			16 38				17 06			17 38	
Newhaven Harbour	d				15 08			15 40				16 08			16 40				17 08			17 40	
Bishopstone	d				15 11			15 43				16 11			16 43				17 11			17 43	
Seaford	a				15 14			15 46				16 14			16 46				17 14			17 46	
Glynde	d					15 14							16 14							17 14			
Berwick	d					15 20							16 20							17 20			
Polegate	d		14 57	15 05		15 25	15 35			15 57	16 05		16 25	16 35			16 57	17 05		17 25	17 35		
Hampden Park 4	d					15 29	15 39						16 29	16 39						17 29	17 39		
Eastbourne 4	a		15 04	15 13		15 34	15 44			16 04	16 13		16 34	16 44			17 04	17 13		17 34	17 44		
	d		15 09	15 19		15 40				16 09	16 19		16 40				17 09	17 19		17 40			
Hampden Park 4	d			15 23		15 44					16 23		16 44					17 23		17 44			
Pevensey & Westham	d			15 28		15 49					16 28		16 49					17 28		17 49			
Pevensey Bay	d																						
Normans Bay	d					15 53							16 53							17 53			
Cooden Beach	d			15 34		15 57					16 34		16 57					17 34		17 57			
Collington	d			15 37		16 00					16 37		17 00					17 37		18 00			
Bexhill 4	d		15 24	15 39		16 02				16 24	16 39		17 02				17 24	17 39		18 02			
St Leonards Warrior Sq 4	d		15 31	15 46		16 09				16 31	16 46		17 09				17 31	17 46		18 09			
Hastings 4	a		15 35	15 49		16 12				16 35	16 49		17 12				17 35	17 49		18 12			
	d		15 36	15 50		16 13				16 36	16 50		17 13				17 36	17 50		18 13			
Ore	d			15a53		16a16					16a53		17a16					17a53		18a16			
Three Oaks	d									16 44													
Doleham	d																						
Winchelsea	d		15 50														17 50						
Rye	a		15 54							16 54							17 54						
	d		15 56							16 56							17 56						
Appledore (Kent)	d		16 05							17 05							18 05						
Ham Street	d		16 10							17 10							18 10						
Ashford International	a		16 18							17 18							18 18						

Table 189

Saturdays
from 10 September

London, Haywards Heath and Brighton - Lewes, Seaford, Eastbourne, Hastings and Ashford

		SN ◇	SN ◇ 1	SN ◇	SN ◇ 1	SN ◇ 1	SN ◇	SN ◇	SN ◇	SN ◇ 1	SN ◇	SN ◇ 1	SN ◇ 1
London Victoria 15 ⊖	d		16 47			17 17				17 47			18 17
Clapham Junction 10	d		16 53			17 23				17 53			18 23
London Bridge 4 ⊖	d												
East Croydon	d		17 03			17 33				18 03			18 33
Gatwick Airport 10 ✈	d		17 19			17 49				18 19			18 49
Haywards Heath 3	d		17 35			18 07				18 35			19 07
Wivelsfield 4	d					18 11							19 11
Plumpton	d		17 44							18 44			
Cooksbridge	d												
Brighton 10	d	17 32		17 40	17 52		18 10	18 22	18 32		18 40	18 52	
London Road (Brighton)	d			17 43	17 55		18 13	18 25			18 43	18 55	
Moulsecoomb	d			17 45	17 57		18 15	18 27			18 45	18 57	
Falmer	d			17 49	18 01		18 19	18 31			18 49	19 01	
Lewes 4	a	17 43	17 52	17 55	18 07	18 22	18 25	18 37	18 43	18 52	18 55	19 07	19 22
	d	17 44	17 53	17 58	18 09	18 23	18 28		18 44	18 53	18 58	19 09	19 23
Southease	d						18 34						
Newhaven Town ⛴	d			18 06			18 38				19 06		
Newhaven Harbour	d			18 08			18 40				19 08		
Bishopstone	d			18 11			18 43				19 11		
Seaford	a			18 14			18 46				19 14		
Glynde	d				18 14							19 14	
Berwick	d				18 20							19 20	
Polegate	d	17 57	18 05		18 25	18 35			18 57	19 05		19 25	19 35
Hampden Park 4	d				18 29	18 39						19 29	19 39
Eastbourne 4	a	18 04	18 13		18 34	18 44			19 04	19 13		19 34	19 44
	d	18 09	18 19		18 40				19 09	19 19		19 40	
Hampden Park 4	d		18 23		18 44					19 23		19 44	
Pevensey & Westham	d		18 28		18 49					19 28		19 49	
Pevensey Bay	d												
Normans Bay	d				18 53							19 53	
Cooden Beach	d		18 34		18 57					19 34		19 57	
Collington	d		18 37		19 00					19 37		20 00	
Bexhill 4	d	18 24	18 39		19 02				19 24	19 39		20 02	
St Leonards Warrior Sq 4	d	18 31	18 46		19 09				19 31	19 46		20 09	
Hastings 4	a	18 35	18 49		19 12				19 35	19 49		20 12	
	d	18 36	18 50		19 13				19 36	19 50		20 13	
Ore	d		18a53		19a16					19a53		20a16	
Three Oaks	d	18 44											
Doleham	d												
Winchelsea	d								19 50				
Rye	a	18 54							19 54				
	d	18 56							19 56				
Appledore (Kent)	d	19 05							20 05				
Ham Street	d	19 10							20 10				
Ashford International	a	19 18							20 18				

		SN ◇	SN ◇	SN ◇	SN ◇ 1	SN ◇	SN ◇ 1	SN ◇ 1 A	SN ◇	SN ◇
London Victoria 15 ⊖	d				18 47			19 17		
Clapham Junction 10	d				18 53			19 23		
London Bridge 4 ⊖	d									
East Croydon	d				19 03			19 33		
Gatwick Airport 10 ✈	d				19 19			19 49		
Haywards Heath 3	d				19 35			20 07		
Wivelsfield 4	d							20 11		
Plumpton	d				19 44					
Cooksbridge	d									
Brighton 10	d	19 10	19 22	19 32		19 40	19 52		20 10	20 32
London Road (Brighton)	d	19 13	19 25			19 43	19 55		20 13	
Moulsecoomb	d	19 15	19 27			19 45	19 57		20 15	
Falmer	d	19 19	19 31			19 49	20 01		20 19	
Lewes 4	a	19 25	19 37	19 43	19 52	19 55	20 08	20 22	20 25	20 43
	d	19 28		19 44	19 53	19 58	20 09	20 23	20 28	20 44
Southease	d	19 34								
Newhaven Town ⛴	d	19 38				20 06			20 36	
Newhaven Harbour	d	19 40				20 08			20 38	
Bishopstone	d	19 43				20 11			20 41	
Seaford	a	19 46				20 14			20 44	
Glynde	d						20 14	20 28		
Berwick	d						20 20	20 34		
Polegate	d			19 57	20 05		20 25	20 39		20 57
Hampden Park 4	d						20 29	20 43		
Eastbourne 4	a			20 04	20 13		20 34	20 48		21 04
	d			20 09	20 19			20 54		21 09
Hampden Park 4	d				20 23					
Pevensey & Westham	d				20 28			21 01		
Pevensey Bay	d									
Normans Bay	d									
Cooden Beach	d				20 34			21 07		
Collington	d				20 37					
Bexhill 4	d			20 24	20 39			21 12		21 23
St Leonards Warrior Sq 4	d			20 31	20 46			21 18		21 30
Hastings 4	a			20 35	20 49			21 21		21 33
	d			20 36	20 50					21 35
Ore	d				20a53					21 37
Three Oaks	d			20 44						21 43
Doleham	d									21 46
Winchelsea	d									21 52
Rye	a			20 54						21 56
	d			20 56						21 56
Appledore (Kent)	d			21 05						22 05
Ham Street	d			21 10						22 10
Ashford International	a			21 18						22 18

A ◇ to Haywards Heath

Table 189

Saturdays
from 10 September

London, Haywards Heath and Brighton - Lewes, Seaford, Eastbourne, Hastings and Ashford

		SN	SN	SN	SN	SN	SN	SN	SN	SN	SN	SN	SN	SN	SN	SN	SN
		◇■	◇	◇■	◇	◇	◇■	◇	◇■	◇	◇	◇■	◇	◇■	◇	◇■	◇
London Victoria ■ ⊖	d	19 47		20 17			20 47		21 17			21 47				22 47	
Clapham Junction ■	d	19 53		20 23			20 53		21 23			21 53				22 53	
London Bridge ■ ⊖	d																
East Croydon	d	20 03		20 33			21 03		21 33			22 03				23 03	
Gatwick Airport ■ ✈	d	20 19		20 49			21 19		21 49			22 19				23 19	
Haywards Heath ■	d	20 35		21 07			21 34		22 08			22 34				23 34	
Wivelsfield ■	d	20 39		21 11			21 38		22 12			22 38				23 38	
Plumpton	d	20 45					21 44					22 44				23 44	
Cooksbridge	d																
Brighton ■	d		20 40		21 04	21 32		21 40		22 04	22 28		22 34	23 06	23 28		23 34
London Road (Brighton)	d		20 43		21 07			21 43		22 07			22 37	23 09			23 37
Moulsecoomb	d		20 45		21 09			21 45		22 09			22 39	23 11			23 39
Falmer	d		20 49		21 13			21 49		22 13			22 43	23 15			23 43
Lewes ■	a	20 52	20 55	21 22	21 19	21 43	21 51	21 55	22 23	22 19	22 39	22 51	22 49	23 21	23 39	23 51	23 49
	d	20 53	20 58	21 23	21 28	21 44	21 53	21 58	22 23	22 28	22 39	22 53	22 56	23 22	23 39	23 53	23 56
Southease	d																
Newhaven Town ⛴	d		21 06		21 36			22 06		22 36			23 04				00 04
Newhaven Harbour	d		21 08		21 38			22 08		22 38			23 06				00 06
Bishopstone	d		21 11		21 41			22 11		22 41			23 09				00 09
Seaford	a		21 14		21 44			22 14		22 44			23 12				00 12
Glynde	d			21 28					22 29					23 27			
Berwick	d			21 34					22 34					23 33		00 02	
Polegate	d	21 05		21 39		21 57	22 05		22 39		22 52	23 05		23 38	23 52	00 07	
Hampden Park ■	d			21 43					22 43			23 09		23 42		00 11	
Eastbourne ■	a	21 13		21 48		22 04	22 15		22 48		23 03	23 14		23 47	23 59	00 16	
	d	21 19				22 09	22 21				23 10	23 20				00 22	
Hampden Park ■	d	21 23					22 25					23 24					
Pevensey & Westham	d	21 28					22 30					23 29				00 29	
Pevensey Bay	d																
Normans Bay	d																
Cooden Beach	d	21 34					22 36					23 35				00 35	
Collington	d	21 37					22 39					23 38				00 38	
Bexhill ■	d	21 39				22 23	22 41				23 24	23 40				00 41	
St Leonards Warrior Sq ■	d	21 46				22 30	22 48				23 31	23 47				00 47	
Hastings ■	a	21 49				22 33	22 51				23 34	23 50				00 50	
	d	21 50															
Ore	d	21a53															
Three Oaks	d																
Doleham	d																
Winchelsea	d																
Rye	a																
	d																
Appledore (Kent)	d																
Ham Street	d																
Ashford International	a																

Table 189

Sundays
until 4 September

London, Haywards Heath and Brighton - Lewes, Seaford, Eastbourne, Hastings and Ashford

		SN	SN	SN	SN	SN	SN	SN	SN	SN	SN	SN	SN	SN	SN	SN	SN	SN	SN	SN	SN	SN	SN
		◇1	◇	◇1	◇	◇1	◇1	◇	◇	◇1	◇	◇	◇	◇1	◇	◇	◇	◇1	◇	◇	◇	◇1	◇
		A	A															B ⚲				B ⚲	
London Victoria 15 ⊖	d	22p47		00 05														08 47				09 47	
Clapham Junction 10	d	22p53		00 11														08 53				09 53	
London Bridge 4 ⊖	d																						
East Croydon 🚋	d	23p03		00 25														09 03				10 03	
Gatwick Airport 10 ✈	d	23p19		00 44														09 19				10 19	
Haywards Heath 3	d	23p34		01 06														09 30				10 30	
Wivelsfield 4	d	23p38																09 34				10 34	
Plumpton	d	23p44																09 40				10 40	
Cooksbridge	d																						
Brighton 10	d		23p34				07 09	07 15		07 43	07 49	08 09	08 20	08 43	08 49	09 09	09 20		09 29	10 09	10 20		10 29
London Road (Brighton)	d		23p37				07 12	07 18		07 46	07 52	08 12		08 46	08 52	09 12			09 32	10 12			10 32
Moulsecoomb	d		23p39				07 14	07 20		07 48	07 54	08 14		08 48	08 54	09 14			09 34	10 14			10 34
Falmer	d		23p43				07 18	07 24		07 52	07 58	08 18		08 52	08 58	09 18			09 38	10 18			10 38
Lewes 4	a	23p51	23p49	01 20			07 24	07 31		07 58	08 04	08 24	08 31	08 58	09 04	09 24	09 31	09 48	09 44	10 24	10 31	10 48	10 44
	d	23p53	23p56	01 20			07 25	07 32		07 59	08 05	08 25	08 32	08 59	09 05	09 25	09 32	09 48	09 52	10 25	10 32	10 48	10 52
Southease	d										08 11				09 11				09 58				10 58
Newhaven Town ⛴	d		00 04					07 40			08 15	08 33			09 15	09 33			10 02	10 33			11 02
Newhaven Harbour	d		00 06					07 42			08 17	08 35			09 17	09 35			10 04	10 35			11 04
Bishopstone	d		00 09					07 45			08 20	08 38			09 20	09 38			10 07	10 38			11 07
Seaford	a		00 12					07 48			08 23	08 41			09 23	09 41			10 10	10 41			11 10
Glynde	d						07 30						08 37				09 37				10 37		
Berwick	d	00 02					07 36						08 43				09 43				10 43		
Polegate	d	00 07		01s32			07 41			08 11			08 49	09 11			09 49	10 01			10 49	11 01	
Hampden Park 4	d	00 11		01s36			07 45						08 53				09 53				10 53		
Eastbourne 4	a	00 16		01 41			07 50			08 19			08 58	09 19			09 58	10 08			10 58	11 08	
	d	00 22				07 26			07 58	08 26			09 02	09 26			10 02	10 15			11 02	11 15	
Hampden Park 4	d					07 30				08 30				09 30				10 19				11 19	
Pevensey & Westham	d	00 29				07 35				08 35				09 35				10 24				11 24	
Pevensey Bay	d																						
Normans Bay	d																						
Cooden Beach	d	00 35				07 41				08 41				09 41				10 30				11 30	
Collington	d	00 38				07 44				08 44				09 44				10 33				11 33	
Bexhill 4	d	00 41				07 47			08 11	08 46			09 16	09 46			10 16	10 35			11 16	11 35	
St Leonards Warrior Sq 4	d	00 47				07 53			08 18	08 53			09 23	09 53			10 23	10 42			11 23	11 42	
Hastings 4	a	00 50				07 56			08 22	08 56			09 26	09 56			10 26	10 45			11 26	11 45	
	d				07 22	07 57			08 22	08 57			09 27	09 57			10 27	10 46			11 27	11 46	
Ore	d				07 24	08a00				09a00				10a00				10a49				11a49	
Three Oaks	d				07 30																		
Doleham	d				07 33																		
Winchelsea	d				07 39																		
Rye	a				07 43				08 39				09 44				10 44				11 44		
	d				07 43				08 41				09 46				10 46				11 46		
Appledore (Kent)	d				07 52				08 50				09 55				10 55				11 55		
Ham Street	d				07 57				08 55				10 00				11 00				12 00		
Ashford International	a				08 06				09 03				10 08				11 08				12 08		

A not 22 May

B ⚲ to Plumpton

Table 189

Sundays

until 4 September

London, Haywards Heath and Brighton - Lewes, Seaford, Eastbourne, Hastings and Ashford

		SN	SN	SN	SN	SN		SN	SN	SN	SN	SN	SN	SN	SN	SN		SN	SN	SN	SN	SN	SN	SN	SN
		◇	◇	◇1	◇	◇		◇	◇1	◇	◇	◇	◇1	◇	◇	◇		◇1	◇	◇	◇	◇1	◇	◇	◇
				A 🚌					A 🚌				B 🚌					B 🚌				B 🚌			
London Victoria 15 ⊖	d			10 47					11 47				12 47					13 47				14 47			
Clapham Junction 10	d			10 53					11 53				12 53					13 53				14 53			
London Bridge 4 ⊖	d																								
East Croydon	d			11 03					12 03				13 03					14 03				15 03			
Gatwick Airport 10 ✈	d			11 19					12 19				13 19					14 19				15 19			
Haywards Heath 3	d			11 30					12 30				13 30					14 30				15 30			
Wivelsfield 4	d			11 34					12 34				13 34					14 34				15 34			
Plumpton	d			11 40					12 40																
Cooksbridge	d																								
Brighton 10	d	11 09	11 20		11 29	12 09		12 20		12 29	13 09	13 20		13 29	14 09	14 20			14 29	15 09	15 20		15 29	16 09	16 20
London Road (Brighton)	d	11 12			11 32	12 12				12 32	13 12			13 32	14 12				14 32	15 12			15 32	16 12	
Moulsecoomb	d	11 14			11 34	12 14				12 34	13 14			13 34	14 14				14 34	15 14			15 34	16 14	
Falmer	d	11 18			11 38	12 18				12 38	13 18			13 38	14 18				14 38	15 18			15 38	16 18	
Lewes 4	a	11 24	11 31	11 48	11 44	12 24		12 31	12 48	12 44	13 24	13 31	13 48	13 44	14 24	14 31		14 48	14 44	15 24	15 31	15 48	15 44	16 24	16 31
	d	11 25	11 32	11 48	11 52	12 25		12 32	12 48	12 52	13 25	13 32	13 48	13 52	14 25	14 32		14 48	14 52	15 25	15 32	15 48	15 52	16 25	16 32
Southease	d				11 58					12 58				13 58					14 58				15 58		
Newhaven Town ⛴	d	11 33			12 02	12 33				13 02	13 33			14 02	14 33				15 02	15 33			16 02	16 33	
Newhaven Harbour	d	11 35			12 04	12 35				13 04	13 35			14 04	14 35				15 04	15 35			16 04	16 35	
Bishopstone	d	11 38			12 07	12 38				13 07	13 38			14 07	14 38				15 07	15 38			16 07	16 38	
Seaford	a	11 41			12 10	12 41				13 10	13 41			14 10	14 41				15 10	15 41			16 10	16 41	
Glynde	d		11 37					12 37				13 37				14 37					15 37				16 37
Berwick	d		11 43					12 43				13 43				14 43					15 43				16 43
Polegate	d		11 49	12 01				12 49	13 01			13 49	14 01			14 49		15 01			15 49	16 01			16 49
Hampden Park 4	d		11 53					12 53				13 53				14 53					15 53				16 53
Eastbourne 4	a		11 58	12 08				12 58	13 08			13 58	14 08			14 58		15 08			15 58	16 08			16 58
	d		12 02	12 15				13 02	13 15			14 02	14 15			15 02		15 15			16 02	16 15			17 02
Hampden Park 4	d			12 19					13 19				14 19					15 19				16 19			
Pevensey & Westham	d			12 24					13 24				14 24					15 24				16 24			
Pevensey Bay	d																								
Normans Bay	d																								
Cooden Beach	d			12 30					13 30				14 30					15 30				16 30			
Collington	d			12 33					13 33				14 33					15 33				16 33			
Bexhill 4	d		12 16	12 35				13 16	13 35			14 16	14 35			15 16		15 35			16 16	16 35			17 16
St Leonards Warrior Sq 4	d		12 23	12 42				13 23	13 42			14 23	14 42			15 23		15 42			16 23	16 42			17 23
Hastings 4	a		12 26	12 45				13 26	13 45			14 26	14 45			15 26		15 45			16 26	16 45			17 26
	d		12 27	12 46				13 27	13 46			14 27	14 46			15 27		15 46			16 27	16 46			17 27
Ore	d			12a49					13a49				14a49					15a49				16a49			
Three Oaks	d																								
Doleham	d																								
Winchelsea	d																								
Rye	a		12 44					13 44				14 44				15 44					16 44				17 44
	d		12 46					13 46				14 46				15 46					16 46				17 46
Appledore (Kent)	d		12 55					13 55				14 55				15 55					16 55				17 55
Ham Street	d		13 00					14 00				15 00				16 00					17 00				18 00
Ashford International	a		13 08					14 08				15 08				16 08					17 08				18 08

A 🚌 to Plumpton

B 🚌 to Wivelsfield

Table 189

Sundays

until 4 September

London, Haywards Heath and Brighton - Lewes, Seaford, Eastbourne, Hastings and Ashford

		SN		SN	SN	SN	SN	SN	SN	SN	SN	SN		SN	SN	SN	SN	SN	SN	SN	SN	SN		SN	SN
		◇1		◇	◇	◇	◇1	◇	◇	◇	◇1	◇		◇	◇	◇1	◇	◇	◇	◇1	◇	◇		◇	◇1
		A					A				A					A				A					
		🚲					🚲				🚲					🚲				🚲					
London Victoria 15 ⊖	d	15 47					16 47				17 47					18 47				19 47					20 47
Clapham Junction 10	d	15 53					16 53				17 53					18 53				19 53					20 53
London Bridge 4 ⊖	d																								
East Croydon	d	16 03					17 03				18 03					19 03				20 03					21 03
Gatwick Airport 10 ✈	d	16 19					17 19				18 19					19 19				20 19					21 19
Haywards Heath 3	d	16 30					17 30				18 30					19 30				20 30					21 30
Wivelsfield 4	d	16 34					17 34				18 34					19 34				20 34					21 34
Plumpton	d	16 40					17 40				18 40					19 40				20 40					21 40
Cooksbridge	d																								
Brighton 10	d			16 29	17 09	17 20		17 29	18 09	18 20		18 29		19 09	19 20		19 29	20 09	20 20		20 29	21 09		21 20	
London Road (Brighton)	d			16 32	17 12			17 32	18 12			18 32		19 12			19 32	20 12			20 32	21 12			
Moulsecoomb	d			16 34	17 14			17 34	18 14			18 34		19 14			19 34	20 14			20 34	21 14			
Falmer	d			16 38	17 18			17 38	18 18			18 38		19 18			19 38	20 18			20 38	21 18			
Lewes 4	a	16 48		16 44	17 24	17 31	17 48	17 44	18 24	18 31	18 48	18 44		19 24	19 31	19 48	19 44	20 24	20 31	20 48	20 44	21 24		21 31	21 48
	d	16 48		16 52	17 25	17 32	17 48	17 52	18 25	18 32	18 48	18 52		19 25	19 32	19 48	19 52	20 25	20 32	20 48	20 52	21 25		21 32	21 48
Southease	d			16 58				17 58				18 58					19 58								
Newhaven Town ⛴	d			17 02	17 33			18 02	18 33			19 02		19 33			20 02	20 33			21 00	21 33			
Newhaven Harbour	d			17 04	17 35			18 04	18 35			19 04		19 35			20 04	20 35			21 04	21 35			
Bishopstone	d			17 07	17 38			18 07	18 38			19 07		19 38			20 07	20 38			21 07	21 38			
Seaford	a			17 10	17 41			18 10	18 41			19 10		19 41			20 10	20 41			21 10	21 41			
Glynde	d					17 37				18 37					19 37				20 37					21 37	
Berwick	d					17 43				18 43					19 43				20 43					21 43	
Polegate	d	17 01				17 49	18 01			18 49	19 01				19 49	20 01			20 49	21 01				21 49	22 01
Hampden Park 4	d					17 53				18 53					19 53				20 53					21 53	
Eastbourne 4	a	17 08				17 58	18 08			18 58	19 08				19 58	20 08			20 58	21 08				21 58	22 08
	d	17 15				18 02	18 15			19 02	19 15				20 02	20 15			21 02	21 15				22 02	22 15
Hampden Park 4	d	17 19					18 19				19 19					20 19				21 19					22 19
Pevensey & Westham	d	17 24					18 24				19 24					20 24				21 24					22 24
Pevensey Bay	d																								
Normans Bay	d																								
Cooden Beach	d	17 30					18 30				19 30					20 30				21 30					22 30
Collington	d	17 33					18 33				19 33					20 33				21 33					22 33
Bexhill 4	d	17 35				18 16	18 35			19 16	19 35				20 16	20 35			21 16	21 35				22 16	22 35
St Leonards Warrior Sq 4	d	17 42				18 23	18 42			19 23	19 42				20 23	20 42			21 23	21 42				22 23	22 42
Hastings 4	a	17 45				18 26	18 45			19 26	19 45				20 26	20 45			21 26	21 45				22 26	22 45
	d	17 46				18 27	18 46			19 27	19 46				20 27	20 46			21 27	21 46					
Ore	d	17a49					18a49				19a49					20a49				21a49					
Three Oaks	d																								
Doleham	d																								
Winchelsea	d																								
Rye	a					18 44				19 44					20 44				21 44						
	d					18 46				19 46					20 46				21 46						
Appledore (Kent)	d					18 55				19 55					20 55				21 55						
Ham Street	d					19 00				20 00					21 00				22 00						
Ashford International	a					19 08				20 08					21 08				22 08						

A 🚲 to Plumpton

Table 189

Sundays
until 4 September

London, Haywards Heath and Brighton - Lewes, Seaford, Eastbourne, Hastings and Ashford

		SN	SN	SN	SN	SN	SN	SN	SN	SN
		◇	◇	◇	◇1	◇	◇	◇	◇1	◇
London Victoria 15 ⊖	d				21 47				22 47	
Clapham Junction 10	d				21 53				22 53	
London Bridge 4 ⊖	d									
East Croydon	d				22 03				23 03	
Gatwick Airport 10 ✈	d				22 19				23 19	
Haywards Heath 3	d				22 30				23 30	
Wivelsfield 4	d				22 34				23 34	
Plumpton	d				22 40				23 40	
Cooksbridge	d									
Brighton 10	d	21 29	22 09	22 20		22 39	23 09	23 20		23 39
London Road (Brighton)	d	21 32	22 12			22 42	23 12			23 42
Moulsecoomb	d	21 34	22 14			22 44	23 14			23 44
Falmer	d	21 38	22 18			22 48	23 18			23 48
Lewes 4	a	21 44	22 24	22 31	22 48	22 54	23 24	23 31	23 48	23 54
	d	21 52	22 25	22 32	22 59	23 03		23 32	23 59	
Southease	d									
Newhaven Town ⛴	d	22 00	22 33			23 11				
Newhaven Harbour	d	22 02	22 35			23 13				
Bishopstone	d	22 05	22 38			23 16				
Seaford	a	22 08	22 41			23 19				
Glynde	d			22 37				23 37		
Berwick	d			22 43				23 43		
Polegate	d			22 49	23 11			23 49	00 11	
Hampden Park 4	d			22 53				23 53	00 15	
Eastbourne 4	a			22 58	23 19			23 58	00 20	
	d				23 26					
Hampden Park 4	d				23 30					
Pevensey & Westham	d				23 35					
Pevensey Bay	d									
Normans Bay	d									
Cooden Beach	d				23 41					
Collington	d				23 44					
Bexhill 4	d				23 46					
St Leonards Warrior Sq 4	d				23 53					
Hastings 4	a				23 56					
	d									
Ore	d									
Three Oaks	d									
Doleham	d									
Winchelsea	d									
Rye	a									
	d									
Appledore (Kent)	d									
Ham Street	d									
Ashford International	a									

Table 189

Sundays
from 11 September

London, Haywards Heath and Brighton - Lewes, Seaford, Eastbourne, Hastings and Ashford

		SN	SN	SN	SN	SN	SN	SN	SN	SN	SN	SN	SN	SN	SN	SN	SN	SN	SN	SN	SN	SN	SN
		◇1	◇	◇1	◇	◇1	◇1	◇	◇	◇1	◇	◇	◇	◇1	◇	◇	◇	◇1	◇	◇	◇	◇1	◇
																		A				A	
																		⚲				⚲	
London Victoria 15 ⊖	d	22p47		00 05														08 47				09 47	
Clapham Junction 10	d	22p53		00 11														08 53				09 53	
London Bridge 4 ⊖	d																						
East Croydon	d	23p03		00 25														09 07				10 07	
Gatwick Airport 10 ✈	d	23p19		00 44														09 29				10 29	
Haywards Heath 3	d	23p34		01 06														09 41				10 41	
Wivelsfield 4	d	23p38																09 45				10 45	
Plumpton	d	23p44																09 51				10 51	
Cooksbridge	d																						
Brighton 10	d		23p34				07 09	07 15		07 43	07 49	08 09	08 20	08 43	08 49	09 09	09 20		09 39	10 09	10 20		10 39
London Road (Brighton)	d		23p37				07 12	07 18		07 46	07 52	08 12		08 46	08 52	09 12			09 42	10 12			10 42
Moulsecoomb	d		23p39				07 14	07 20		07 48	07 54	08 14		08 48	08 54	09 14			09 44	10 14			10 44
Falmer	d		23p43				07 18	07 24		07 52	07 58	08 18		08 52	08 58	09 18			09 48	10 18			10 48
Lewes 4	a	23p51	23p49	01 20			07 24	07 31		07 58	08 04	08 24	08 31	08 58	09 04	09 24	09 31	09 58	09 54	10 24	10 31	10 58	10 54
	d	23p53	23p56	01 20			07 25	07 32		07 59	08 05	08 25	08 32	08 59	09 05	09 25	09 32	09 59	10 03	10 25	10 32	10 59	11 03
Southease	d										08 11				09 11				10 09				11 09
Newhaven Town ⛴	d		00 04					07 40			08 15	08 33			09 15	09 33			10 13	10 33			11 13
Newhaven Harbour	d		00 06					07 42			08 17	08 35			09 17	09 35			10 15	10 35			11 15
Bishopstone	d		00 09					07 45			08 20	08 38			09 20	09 38			10 18	10 38			11 18
Seaford	a		00 12					07 48			08 23	08 41			09 23	09 41			10 21	10 41			11 21
Glynde	d						07 30						08 37				09 37				10 37		
Berwick	d	00 02					07 36						08 43				09 43				10 43		
Polegate	d	00 07		01s32			07 41			08 11			08 49	09 11			09 49	10 11			10 49	11 11	
Hampden Park 4	d	00 11		01s36			07 45						08 53				09 53				10 53		
Eastbourne 4	a	00 16		01 41			07 50			08 19			08 58	09 19			09 58	10 19			10 58	11 19	
	d	00 22				07 26			07 58	08 26			09 02	09 26			10 02	10 26			11 02	11 26	
Hampden Park 4	d					07 30				08 30				09 30				10 30				11 30	
Pevensey & Westham	d	00 29				07 35				08 35				09 35				10 35				11 35	
Pevensey Bay	d																						
Normans Bay	d																						
Cooden Beach	d	00 35				07 41				08 41				09 41				10 41				11 41	
Collington	d	00 38				07 44				08 44				09 44				10 44				11 44	
Bexhill 4	d	00 41				07 47			08 11	08 46			09 16	09 46			10 16	10 46			11 16	11 46	
St Leonards Warrior Sq 4	d	00 47				07 53			08 18	08 53			09 23	09 53			10 23	10 53			11 23	11 53	
Hastings 4	a	00 50				07 56			08 22	08 56			09 26	09 56			10 26	10 56			11 26	11 56	
	d				07 22	07 57			08 22	08 57			09 27	09 57			10 27	10 57			11 27	11 57	
Ore	d				07 24	08a00				09a00				10a00				11a00				12a00	
Three Oaks	d				07 30																		
Doleham	d				07 33																		
Winchelsea	d				07 39																		
Rye	a				07 43				08 39				09 44				10 44				11 44		
	d				07 43				08 41				09 46				10 46				11 46		
Appledore (Kent)	d				07 52				08 50				09 55				10 55				11 55		
Ham Street	d				07 57				08 55				10 00				11 00				12 00		
Ashford International	a				08 06				09 03				10 08				11 08				12 08		

A ⚲ to Plumpton

Table 189

Sundays

from 11 September

London, Haywards Heath and Brighton - Lewes, Seaford, Eastbourne, Hastings and Ashford

		SN	SN	SN	SN	SN	SN	SN	SN	SN	SN	SN	SN	SN	SN	SN	SN	SN	SN	SN	SN	SN	SN
		◇	◇	◇1	◇	◇	◇	◇1	◇	◇	◇	◇1	◇	◇	◇	◇1	◇	◇	◇	◇1	◇	◇	◇
				A				A				B				B				B			
				✠				✠				✠				✠				✠			
London Victoria 15 ⊖	d			10 47				11 47				12 47				13 47				14 47			
Clapham Junction 10	d			10 53				11 53				12 53				13 53				14 53			
London Bridge 4 ⊖	d																						
East Croydon	d			11 07				12 07				13 07				14 07				15 07			
Gatwick Airport 10 ✈	d			11 29				12 29				13 29				14 29				15 29			
Haywards Heath 3	d			11 41				12 41				13 41				14 41				15 41			
Wivelsfield 4	d			11 45				12 45				13 45				14 45				15 45			
Plumpton	d			11 51				12 51															
Cooksbridge	d																						
Brighton 10	d	11 09	11 20		11 39	12 09	12 20		12 39	13 09	13 20		13 39	14 09	14 20		14 39	15 09	15 20		15 39	16 09	16 20
London Road (Brighton)	d	11 12			11 42	12 12			12 42	13 12			13 42	14 12			14 42	15 12			15 42	16 12	
Moulsecoomb	d	11 14			11 44	12 14			12 44	13 14			13 44	14 14			14 44	15 14			15 44	16 14	
Falmer	d	11 18			11 48	12 18			12 48	13 18			13 48	14 18			14 48	15 18			15 48	16 18	
Lewes 4	a	11 24	11 31	11 58	11 54	12 24	12 31	12 58	12 54	13 24	13 31	13 56	13 54	14 24	14 31	14 56	14 54	15 24	15 31	15 56	15 54	16 24	16 31
	d	11 25	11 32	11 59	12 03	12 25	12 32	12 59	13 03	13 25	13 32	13 59	14 03	14 25	14 32	14 59	15 03	15 25	15 32	15 59	16 03	16 25	16 32
Southease	d				12 09				13 09				14 09				15 09				16 09		
Newhaven Town ⛴	d	11 33			12 13	12 33			13 13	13 33			14 13	14 33			15 13	15 33			16 13	16 33	
Newhaven Harbour	d	11 35			12 15	12 35			13 15	13 35			14 15	14 35			15 15	15 35			16 15	16 35	
Bishopstone	d	11 38			12 18	12 38			13 18	13 38			14 18	14 38			15 18	15 38			16 18	16 38	
Seaford	a	11 41			12 21	12 41			13 21	13 41			14 21	14 41			15 21	15 41			16 21	16 41	
Glynde	d		11 37				12 37				13 37				14 37				15 37				16 37
Berwick	d		11 43				12 43				13 43				14 43				15 43				16 43
Polegate	d		11 49	12 11			12 49	13 11			13 49	14 11			14 49	15 11			15 49	16 11			16 49
Hampden Park 4	d		11 53				12 53				13 53				14 53				15 53				16 53
Eastbourne 4	a		11 58	12 19			12 58	13 19			13 58	14 19			14 58	15 19			15 58	16 19			16 58
	d		12 02	12 26			13 02	13 26			14 02	14 26			15 02	15 26			16 02	16 26			17 02
Hampden Park 4	d			12 30				13 30				14 30				15 30				16 30			
Pevensey & Westham	d			12 35				13 35				14 35				15 35				16 35			
Pevensey Bay	d																						
Normans Bay	d																						
Cooden Beach	d			12 41				13 41				14 41				15 41				16 41			
Collington	d			12 44				13 44				14 44				15 44				16 44			
Bexhill 4	d		12 16	12 46			13 16	13 46			14 16	14 46			15 16	15 46			16 16	16 46			17 16
St Leonards Warrior Sq 4	d		12 23	12 53			13 23	13 53			14 23	14 53			15 23	15 53			16 23	16 53			17 23
Hastings 4	a		12 26	12 56			13 26	13 56			14 26	14 56			15 26	15 56			16 26	16 56			17 26
	d		12 27	12 57			13 27	13 57			14 27	14 57			15 27	15 57			16 27	16 57			17 27
Ore	d			13a00				14a00				15a00				16a00				17a00			
Three Oaks	d																						
Doleham	d																						
Winchelsea	d																						
Rye	a		12 44				13 44				14 44				15 44				16 44				17 44
	d		12 46				13 46				14 46				15 46				16 46				17 46
Appledore (Kent)	d		12 55				13 55				14 55				15 55				16 55				17 55
Ham Street	d		13 00				14 00				15 00				16 00				17 00				18 00
Ashford International	a		13 08				14 08				15 08				16 08				17 08				18 08

A ✠ to Plumpton

B ✠ to Wivelsfield

Table 189

Sundays

from 11 September

London, Haywards Heath and Brighton - Lewes, Seaford, Eastbourne, Hastings and Ashford

		SN ◇1 A 🚲		SN ◇	SN ◇	SN ◇	SN ◇1 A 🚲	SN ◇	SN ◇	SN ◇	SN ◇1 A 🚲	SN ◇	
London Victoria 15 ⊖	d	15 47					16 47				17 47		
Clapham Junction 10	d	15 53					16 53				17 53		
London Bridge 4 ⊖	d												
East Croydon 🚋	d	16 07					17 07				18 07		
Gatwick Airport 10 ✈	d	16 29					17 29				18 29		
Haywards Heath 3	d	16 41					17 41				18 41		
Wivelsfield 4	d	16 45					17 45				18 45		
Plumpton	d	16 51					17 51				18 51		
Cooksbridge	d												
Brighton 10	d			16 39	17 09	17 20		17 39	18 09	18 20		18 39	
London Road (Brighton)	d			16 42	17 12			17 42	18 12			18 42	
Moulsecoomb	d			16 44	17 14			17 44	18 14			18 44	
Falmer	d			16 48	17 18			17 48	18 18			18 48	
Lewes 4	a	16 58		16 54	17 24	17 31	17 58	17 54	18 24	18 31	18 58	18 54	
	d	16 59		17 03	17 25	17 32	17 59	18 03	18 25	18 32	18 59	19 03	
Southease	d			17 09				18 09				19 09	
Newhaven Town ⛴	d			17 13	17 33			18 13	18 33			19 13	
Newhaven Harbour	d			17 15	17 35			18 15	18 35			19 15	
Bishopstone	d			17 18	17 38			18 18	18 38			19 18	
Seaford	a			17 21	17 41			18 21	18 41			19 21	
Glynde	d					17 37				18 37			
Berwick	d					17 43				18 43			
Polegate	d	17 11				17 49	18 11			18 49	19 11		
Hampden Park 4	d					17 53				18 53			
Eastbourne 4	a	17 19				17 58	18 19			18 58	19 19		
	d	17 26				18 02	18 26			19 02	19 26		
Hampden Park 4	d	17 30					18 30				19 30		
Pevensey & Westham	d	17 35					18 35				19 35		
Pevensey Bay	d												
Normans Bay	d												
Cooden Beach	d	17 41					18 41				19 41		
Collington	d	17 44					18 44				19 44		
Bexhill 4	d	17 46				18 16	18 46			19 16	19 46		
St Leonards Warrior Sq 4	d	17 53				18 23	18 53			19 23	19 53		
Hastings 4	a	17 56				18 26	18 56			19 26	19 56		
	d	17 57				18 27	18 57			19 27	19 57		
Ore	d	18a00					19a00				20a00		
Three Oaks	d												
Doleham	d												
Winchelsea	d												
Rye	a					18 44				19 44			
	d					18 46				19 46			
Appledore (Kent)	d					18 55				19 55			
Ham Street	d					19 00				20 00			
Ashford International	a					19 08				20 08			

		SN ◇	SN ◇	SN ◇1 A 🚲	SN ◇	SN ◇	SN ◇	SN ◇1 A 🚲	SN ◇	SN ◇		SN ◇	SN ◇1
London Victoria 15 ⊖	d			18 47				19 47					20 47
Clapham Junction 10	d			18 53				19 53					20 53
London Bridge 4 ⊖	d												
East Croydon 🚋	d			19 07				20 07					21 07
Gatwick Airport 10 ✈	d			19 29				20 29					21 29
Haywards Heath 3	d			19 41				20 41					21 41
Wivelsfield 4	d			19 45				20 45					21 45
Plumpton	d			19 51				20 51					21 51
Cooksbridge	d												
Brighton 10	d	19 09	19 20		19 39	20 09	20 20		20 39	21 09		21 20	
London Road (Brighton)	d	19 12			19 42	20 12			20 42	21 12			
Moulsecoomb	d	19 14			19 44	20 14			20 44	21 14			
Falmer	d	19 18			19 48	20 18			20 48	21 18			
Lewes 4	a	19 24	19 31	19 58	19 54	20 24	20 31	20 58	20 54	21 24		21 31	21 58
	d	19 25	19 32	19 59	20 03	20 25	20 32	20 59	21 03	21 25		21 32	21 59
Southease	d				20 09								
Newhaven Town ⛴	d	19 33			20 13	20 33			21 11	21 33			
Newhaven Harbour	d	19 35			20 15	20 35			21 13	21 35			
Bishopstone	d	19 38			20 18	20 38			21 16	21 38			
Seaford	a	19 41			20 21	20 41			21 19	21 41			
Glynde	d		19 37				20 37					21 37	
Berwick	d		19 43				20 43					21 43	
Polegate	d		19 49	20 11			20 49	21 11				21 49	22 11
Hampden Park 4	d		19 53				20 53					21 53	
Eastbourne 4	a		19 58	20 19			20 58	21 19				21 58	22 19
	d		20 02	20 26			21 02	21 26				22 02	22 26
Hampden Park 4	d			20 30				21 30					22 30
Pevensey & Westham	d			20 35				21 35					22 35
Pevensey Bay	d												
Normans Bay	d												
Cooden Beach	d			20 41				21 41					22 41
Collington	d			20 44				21 44					22 44
Bexhill 4	d		20 16	20 46			21 16	21 46				22 16	22 46
St Leonards Warrior Sq 4	d		20 23	20 53			21 23	21 53				22 23	22 53
Hastings 4	a		20 26	20 56			21 26	21 56				22 26	22 56
	d		20 27	20 57			21 27	21 57					
Ore	d			21a00				22a00					
Three Oaks	d												
Doleham	d												
Winchelsea	d												
Rye	a		20 44				21 44						
	d		20 46				21 46						
Appledore (Kent)	d		20 55				21 55						
Ham Street	d		21 00				22 00						
Ashford International	a		21 08				22 08						

A 🚲 to Plumpton

Table 189

Sundays
from 11 September

London, Haywards Heath and Brighton - Lewes, Seaford, Eastbourne, Hastings and Ashford

		SN	SN	SN	SN	SN	SN	SN	SN	SN
		◇	◇	◇	◇1	◇	◇	◇	◇	◇1
London Victoria 15 ⊖	d				21 47					22 47
Clapham Junction 10	d				21 53					22 53
London Bridge 4 ⊖	d									
East Croydon	d				22 07					23 07
Gatwick Airport 10 ✈	d				22 29					23 29
Haywards Heath 3	d				22 41					23 41
Wivelsfield 4	d				22 45					23 45
Plumpton	d				22 51					23 51
Cooksbridge	d									
Brighton 10	d	21 39	22 09	22 20		22 39	23 09	23 20	23 39	
London Road (Brighton)	d	21 42	22 12			22 42	23 12		23 42	
Moulsecoomb	d	21 44	22 14			22 44	23 14		23 44	
Falmer	d	21 48	22 18			22 48	23 18		23 48	
Lewes 4	a	21 54	22 24	22 31	22 58	22 54	23 24	23 31	23 54	23 58
	d	22 03	22 25	22 32	22 59	23 03		23 32		23 59
Southease	d									
Newhaven Town ⛴	d	22 11	22 33			23 11				
Newhaven Harbour	d	22 13	22 35			23 13				
Bishopstone	d	22 16	22 38			23 16				
Seaford	a	22 19	22 41			23 19				
Glynde	d			22 37				23 37		
Berwick	d			22 43				23 43		
Polegate	d			22 49	23 11			23 49		00 11
Hampden Park 4	d			22 53				23 53		00 15
Eastbourne 4	a			22 58	23 19			23 58		00 20
	d				23 26					
Hampden Park 4	d				23 30					
Pevensey & Westham	d				23 35					
Pevensey Bay	d									
Normans Bay	d									
Cooden Beach	d				23 41					
Collington	d				23 44					
Bexhill 4	d				23 46					
St Leonards Warrior Sq 4	d				23 53					
Hastings 4	a				23 56					
	d									
Ore	d									
Three Oaks	d									
Doleham	d									
Winchelsea	d									
Rye	a									
	d									
Appledore (Kent)	d									
Ham Street	d									
Ashford International	a									

Ashford, Hastings, Eastbourne, Seaford and Lewes - Brighton, Haywards Heath and London

Miles	Miles			SN	SN	SN	SN	SN	SN	SN	SN	SN	SN	SN	SN	SN	SN	SN	SN	SN	SN	SN	SN
				MX																			
				◇1	◇	◇1	◇	◇	1	◇1	◇	◇	1	◇	◇1	◇1	◇1	◇	◇	1	◇	◇	◇1
																A (trolley)	A (trolley)						A (trolley)
—	0	**Ashford International**	d																				
—	5½	Ham Street	d																				
—	8½	Appledore (Kent)	d																				
—	15¼	Rye	a																				
—	—		d																				
—	17¼	Winchelsea	d																				
—	21½	Doleham	d																				
—	22¾	Three Oaks	d																				
—	25½	Ore	d																				
0	26½	**Hastings** 4	a																				
—	—		d	23p22					05 07	05 42				05 58			06 15						06 49
0¾	—	**St Leonards Warrior Sq** 4	d	23p24					05 09	05 45				06 01			06 18						06 52
4½	—	**Bexhill** 4	d	23p31					05 16	05 52				06 12			06 26						06 59
5¼	—	Collington	d	23p33					05 18	05 54							06 28						07 01
6¾	—	Cooden Beach	d	23p36					05 21	05 57							06 31						07 04
8½	—	Normans Bay	d																				
10½	—	Pevensey Bay	d																				
11¼	—	Pevensey & Westham	d	23p42					05 27	06 03							06 37						07 10
14¼	—	Hampden Park 4	d	23p47					05 32	06 08				06 24			06 42						07 15
16¼	—	**Eastbourne** 4	a	23p52					05 37	06 13				06 29			06 47						07 20
—	—		d	23p56		05 08	05 32		05 42				06 24	06 37	06 47		06 57			07 14			07 32
18¼	—	Hampden Park 4	d	00 01		05 12	05 36		05 46				06 28		06 51		07 01			07 19			
20¼	—	Polegate	d	00 05		05 16	05 41		05 50				06 33	06 44	06 55		07 05			07 23			07 39
24¼	—	Berwick	d						05 55				06 39		07 00					07 29			07 44
29	—	Glynde	d										06 45		07 06					07 35			
—	0	**Seaford**	d		05 09			05 45				06 30				06 56			07 16			07 33	
—	1	Bishopstone	d		05 11			05 47				06 32				06 58			07 18			07 35	
—	2½	Newhaven Harbour	d		05 14			05 50				06 35				07 01			07 21			07 38	
—	2¾	Newhaven Town (ferry)	d		05 16			05 52				06 37				07 03			07 23			07 40	
—	5½	Southease	d													07 07			07 27			07 44	
32	9	**Lewes** 4	a	00 17	05 25	05 28	05 53	06 01	06 04			06 46	06 50	06 57	07 11	07 14	07 18		07 33	07 41		07 50	07 53
—	—																						
—	—		d	00 18	05 32	05 29	05 54	06 09	06 05		06 26	06 47	06 51	06 59	07 12	07 22		07 23	07 34	07 42	07 45	07 51	07 55
36½	—	Falmer	d	00 25	05 39		06 01	06 16			06 33	06 54		07 06	07 19			07 30	07 41		07 52	07 58	
38¼	—	Moulsecoomb	d	00 28	05 42		06 05	06 19			06 36	06 57		07 10	07 22			07 33	07 44		07 55	08 01	
39¼	—	London Road (Brighton)	d	00 30	05 44		06 07	06 21			06 38	06 59		07 12	07 24			07 35	07 46		07 57	08 03	
40	—	**Brighton** 10	a	00 34	05 48		06 11	06 25			06 42	07 03		07 16	07 28			07 39	07 50		08 01	08 07	
—	11¾	Cooksbridge	d										06 56			07 27				07 48			08 00
—	14½	Plumpton	d			05 37			06 13				07 01			07 32				07 53			08 05
—	18¼	Wivelsfield 4	a										07 07			07 39							08 11
—	21¼	**Haywards Heath** 3	a			05 46			06 23				07 12			07 43				08 02			08 16
—	—	**Gatwick Airport** 10 (airport)	a			05 58			06 40				07 29										
—	—	East Croydon (tram)	a			06 15			06 56				07 45			08 14				08 31			08 46
—	—	**London Bridge** 4 ⊖	a						07 13				08 01							08 52			
—	—	Clapham Junction 10	a			06 25										08 23							09 00
—	—	**London Victoria** 15 ⊖	a			06 32										08 32							09 09

A (trolley) from Lewes

Ashford, Hastings, Eastbourne, Seaford and Lewes - Brighton, Haywards Heath and London

		SN	SN	SN	SN	SN	SN	SN	SN	SN	SN	SN	SN	SN	SN	SN	SN	SN	SN	SN	SN	SN	SN
		◇	◇	◇	◇	◇ 1	◇ 1	◇ 1	◇ 1	◇	◇	◇	◇	◇	◇ 1	◇ 1	◇	◇ 1	◇	◇	◇	◇ 1	◇ 1
						A		A	A						A			A					
						🛒		🛒	🛒						🛒			🛒					
Ashford International	d		06 13	06 39								07 17	07 39							08 32			
Ham Street	d		06 22	06 48								07 26	07 48							08 41			
Appledore (Kent)	d		06 27	06 53								07 31	07 53							08 46			
Rye	a		06 36	07 02								07 40	08 02							08 55			
	d		06 36									07 45								08 55			
Winchelsea	d		06 40									07 48											
Doleham	d		06 46									07 55											
Three Oaks	d		06 50									07 58								09 06			
Ore	d		06 55									08 04				08 22		08 47					09 22
Hastings 4	a		06 58									08 07				08 25		08 50		09 13			09 25
	d		07 12			07 20			07 38			08 10				08 26		08 52		09 14			09 26
St Leonards Warrior Sq 4	d		07 15			07 23			07 40			08 13				08 28		08 54		09 17			09 28
Bexhill 4	d		07 22			07 31			07 47			08 22				08 35		09 01		09 24			09 35
Collington	d					07 33			07 49							08 37		09 03					09 37
Cooden Beach	d					07 36			07 52							08 40		09 06					09 40
Normans Bay	d								07 55							08 43							09 43
Pevensey Bay	d								07 59														
Pevensey & Westham	d					07 42			08 01							08 48		09 13					09 48
Hampden Park 4	d					07 46			08 06							08 52		09 17					09 52
Eastbourne 4	a		07 37			07 51			08 11			08 37				08 57		09 23		09 39			09 57
	d		07 47			07 57	08 04		08 18			08 45			08 56	09 04		09 29		09 47		09 55	10 04
Hampden Park 4	d					08 01	08 08								09 00	09 08						09 59	10 08
Polegate	d		07 54			08 05	08 12		08 25			08 52			09 04	09 12		09 36		09 54		10 03	10 12
Berwick	d					08 11	08 18		08 30							09 18						10 09	10 18
Glynde	d					08 16	08 23		08 36							09 23							10 23
Seaford	d				07 59			08 21						08 57			09 25				09 58		
Bishopstone	d				08 01			08 23						08 59			09 27				10 00		
Newhaven Harbour	d				08 04			08 26						09 02			09 30				10 03		
Newhaven Town ⛴	d	07 49			08 06			08 28						09 04			09 32				10 05		
Southease	d				08 10			08 32									09 36						
Lewes 4	a	07 57	08 07		08 17	08 22	08 29	08 39	08 42			09 07		09 13	09 16	09 29	09 44	09 48		10 07	10 14	10 18	10 29
	d	07 58	08 07		08 19	08 23	08 30	08 48		08 46	08 58	09 07		09 14	09 18	09 29	09 44	09 49	09 58	10 07	10 14	10 19	10 29
Falmer	d	08 05			08 26		08 37			08 53	09 05			09 21		09 36	09 51		10 05		10 21		10 36
Moulsecoomb	d	08 08			08 29		08 40			08 56	09 08			09 24		09 39	09 54		10 08		10 24		10 39
London Road (Brighton)	d	08 10			08 32		08 42			08 58	09 10			09 27		09 42	09 57		10 10		10 27		10 42
Brighton 10	a	08 14	08 20		08 35		08 46			09 02	09 14	09 20		09 30		09 45	10 00		10 14	10 20	10 30		10 45
Cooksbridge	d					08 28									09 23			09 54				10 24	
Plumpton	d					08 33									09 28			09 59				10 29	
Wivelsfield 4	a					08 39		09 00							09 34							10 35	
Haywards Heath 3	a					08 44		09 05							09 38			10 07				10 40	
Gatwick Airport 10 ✈	a					08 56		09 22							09 55			10 25				10 55	
East Croydon 🚊	a					09 14		09 38							10 11			10 41				11 11	
London Bridge 4 ⊖	a																						
Clapham Junction 10	a					09 23		09 48							10 21			10 51				11 21	
London Victoria 15 ⊖	a					09 32		09 58							10 28			10 58				11 28	

A 🛒 from Lewes

Table 189

Mondays to Fridays

Ashford, Hastings, Eastbourne, Seaford and Lewes - Brighton, Haywards Heath and London

		SN	SN	SN	SN	SN	SN	SN	SN	SN	SN	SN	SN	SN	SN	SN	SN	SN	SN	SN	SN	SN	SN
		◇	◇	◇1	◇	◇	◇	◇1	◇1	◇	◇1	◇	◇	◇	◇1	◇1	◇	◇1	◇	◇	◇	◇1	◇1
Ashford International	d	08 52				09 32							10 32							11 32			
Ham Street	d	09 01				09 41							10 41							11 41			
Appledore (Kent)	d	09 06				09 46							10 46							11 46			
Rye	a	09 15				09 55							10 55							11 55			
	d	09 16				09 55							10 55							11 55			
Winchelsea	d	09 19				09 59														11 59			
Doleham	d	09 26																					
Three Oaks	d	09 29											11 06										
Ore	d	09 35		09 50					10 22		10 50					11 22		11 50					12 22
Hastings 4	a	09 38		09 53		10 13			10 25		10 53		11 13			11 25		11 53		12 13			12 25
	d			09 55		10 14			10 26		10 55		11 14			11 26		11 55		12 14			12 26
St Leonards Warrior Sq 4	d			09 57		10 17			10 28		10 57		11 17			11 28		11 57		12 17			12 28
Bexhill 4	d			10 04		10 24			10 35		11 04		11 24			11 35		12 04		12 24			12 35
Collington	d			10 06					10 37		11 06					11 37		12 06					12 37
Cooden Beach	d			10 09					10 40		11 09					11 40		12 09					12 40
Normans Bay	d								10 43							11 43							12 43
Pevensey Bay	d																						
Pevensey & Westham	d			10 15					10 48		11 15					11 48		12 15					12 48
Hampden Park 4	d			10 20					10 52		11 20					11 52		12 20					12 52
Eastbourne 4	a			10 25		10 39			10 57		11 25		11 39			11 57		12 25		12 39			12 57
	d			10 31		10 47		10 58	11 04		11 31		11 47		11 58	12 04		12 31		12 47		12 58	13 04
Hampden Park 4	d							11 02	11 08						12 02	12 08						13 02	13 08
Polegate	d			10 37		10 54		11 06	11 12		11 37		11 54		12 06	12 12		12 37		12 54		13 06	13 12
Berwick	d								11 18							12 18							13 18
Glynde	d								11 23							12 23							13 23
Seaford	d		10 25				10 58			11 25				11 58			12 25				12 58		
Bishopstone	d		10 27				11 00			11 27				12 00			12 27				13 00		
Newhaven Harbour	d		10 30				11 03			11 30				12 03			12 30				13 03		
Newhaven Town ⛴	d		10 32				11 05			11 32				12 05			12 32				13 05		
Southease	d		10 36							11 36							12 36						
Lewes 4	a		10 44	10 49		11 07	11 14	11 19	11 29	11 44	11 49		12 07	12 14	12 19	12 29	12 44	12 49		13 07	13 14	13 19	13 29
	d		10 44	10 50	10 58	11 07	11 14	11 20	11 29	11 44	11 50	11 58	12 07	12 14	12 20	12 29	12 44	12 50	12 58	13 07	13 14	13 20	13 29
Falmer	d		10 51		11 05		11 21		11 36	11 51		12 05		12 21		12 36	12 51		13 05		13 21		13 36
Moulsecoomb	d		10 54		11 08		11 24		11 39	11 54		12 08		12 24		12 39	12 54		13 08		13 24		13 39
London Road (Brighton)	d		10 57		11 10		11 27		11 42	11 57		12 10		12 27		12 42	12 57		13 10		13 27		13 42
Brighton 10	a		11 00		11 14	11 20	11 30		11 45	12 00		12 14	12 20	12 30		12 45	13 00		13 14	13 20	13 30		13 45
Cooksbridge	d																						
Plumpton	d							11 28							12 28							13 28	
Wivelsfield 4	a							11 35							12 35							13 35	
Haywards Heath 3	a			11 05				11 40			12 05				12 40			13 05				13 40	
Gatwick Airport 10 ✈	a			11 25				11 55			12 25				12 55			13 25				13 55	
East Croydon 🚊	a			11 41				12 11			12 41				13 11			13 41				14 11	
London Bridge 4 ⊖	a																						
Clapham Junction 10	a			11 51				12 21			12 51				13 21			13 51				14 21	
London Victoria 15 ⊖	a			11 58				12 28			12 58				13 28			13 58				14 28	

Ashford, Hastings, Eastbourne, Seaford and Lewes - Brighton, Haywards Heath and London

		SN	SN	SN	SN	SN	SN	SN	SN	SN	SN	SN	SN	SN	SN	SN	SN	SN	SN	SN	SN	SN
		◇	◇1	◇	◇	◇	◇1	◇1	◇	◇1	◇	◇	◇	◇1	◇1	◇	◇1	◇	◇	◇	◇1	◇1
										A 🛒				A 🛒			A 🛒				A 🛒	
Ashford International	d				12 32							13 32							14 32			
Ham Street	d				12 41							13 41							14 41			
Appledore (Kent)	d				12 46							13 46							14 46			
Rye	a				12 55							13 55							14 55			
	d				12 55							13 55							14 55			
Winchelsea	d											13 59										
Doleham	d																					
Three Oaks	d				13 06														15 06			
Ore	d		12 50					13 22		13 50					14 22		14 50					15 20
Hastings 4	a		12 53		13 13			13 25		13 53		14 13			14 25		14 53		15 13			15 23
	d		12 55		13 14			13 26		13 55		14 14			14 26		14 55		15 14			15 24
St Leonards Warrior Sq 4	d		12 57		13 17			13 28		13 57		14 17			14 28		14 57		15 17			15 26
Bexhill 4	d		13 04		13 24			13 35		14 04		14 24			14 35		15 04		15 24			15 33
Collington	d		13 06					13 37		14 06					14 37		15 06					15 35
Cooden Beach	d		13 09					13 40		14 09					14 40		15 09					15 38
Normans Bay	d							13 43							14 43							15 41
Pevensey Bay	d																					15 45
Pevensey & Westham	d		13 15					13 48		14 15					14 48		15 15					15 47
Hampden Park 4	d		13 20					13 52		14 20					14 52		15 20					15 52
Eastbourne 4	a		13 25		13 39			13 57		14 25		14 39			14 57		15 25		15 39			15 57
	d		13 31		13 47		13 58	14 04		14 31		14 47		14 58	15 04		15 31		15 47		15 58	16 04
Hampden Park 4	d						14 02	14 08						15 02	15 08						16 02	16 08
Polegate	d		13 37		13 54		14 06	14 12		14 37		14 54		15 06	15 12		15 37		15 54		16 06	16 12
Berwick	d							14 18							15 18							16 18
Glynde	d							14 23							15 23							16 23
Seaford	d	13 25				13 58			14 25				14 58			15 25				15 58		
Bishopstone	d	13 27				14 00			14 27				15 00			15 27				16 00		
Newhaven Harbour	d	13 30				14 03			14 30				15 03			15 30				16 03		
Newhaven Town ⛴	d	13 32				14 05			14 32				15 05			15 32				16 05		
Southease	d	13 36							14 36							15 36						
Lewes 4	a	13 44	13 49		14 07	14 14	14 19	14 29	14 44	14 49		15 07	15 14	15 18	15 29	15 44	15 49		16 07	16 14	16 18	16 29
	d	13 44	13 50	13 58	14 07	14 14	14 20	14 29	14 44	14 50	14 58	15 07	15 14	15 19	15 29	15 44	15 50	15 58	16 07	16 14	16 20	16 29
Falmer	d	13 51		14 05		14 21		14 36	14 51		15 05		15 21		15 36	15 51		16 05		16 21		16 36
Moulsecoomb	d	13 54		14 08		14 24		14 39	14 54		15 08		15 24		15 39	15 54		16 08		16 24		16 39
London Road (Brighton)	d	13 57		14 10		14 27		14 42	14 57		15 10		15 27		15 42	15 57		16 10		16 27		16 42
Brighton 10	a	14 00		14 14	14 20	14 30		14 45	15 00		15 14	15 20	15 30		15 45	16 00		16 14	16 20	16 30		16 45
Cooksbridge	d													15 24							16 25	
Plumpton	d						14 28							15 29							16 30	
Wivelsfield 4	a						14 35							15 35							16 38	
Haywards Heath 3	a		14 05				14 40			15 05				15 40			16 05				16 42	
Gatwick Airport 10 ✈	a		14 25				14 55			15 25				15 55			16 25				16 57	
East Croydon	a		14 41				15 11			15 41				16 11			16 41				17 13	
London Bridge 4 ⊖	a																					
Clapham Junction 10	a		14 51				15 21			15 51				16 21			16 51				17 22	
London Victoria 15 ⊖	a		14 58				15 28			15 58				16 28			16 58				17 29	

A 🛒 from Lewes

Ashford, Hastings, Eastbourne, Seaford and Lewes - Brighton, Haywards Heath and London

		SN	SN	SN	SN	SN	SN	SN	SN	SN	SN	SN	SN	SN	SN	SN	SN	SN	SN	SN	SN	SN	SN
		◇	◇[1]	◇	◇	◇	◇[1]	◇[1]	◇	◇[1]	◇	◇	◇	◇[1]	◇[1]	◇	◇[1]	◇	◇	◇	◇	◇[1]	◇[1]
			A 🛒				A 🛒			A 🛒				A 🛒									
Ashford International	d				15 32							16 32							17 32	17 58			
Ham Street	d				15 41							16 41							17 41	18 07			
Appledore (Kent)	d				15 46							16 46							17 46	18 12			
Rye	a				15 55							16 55							17 55	18 21			
	d				15 55							16 55							17 55				
Winchelsea	d				15 59														17 59				
Doleham	d																						
Three Oaks	d											17 06											
Ore	d		15 48					16 22		16 50					17 22		17 50						18 22
Hastings [4]	a		15 51		16 13			16 25		16 53		17 13			17 25		17 53		18 13				18 25
	d		15 52		16 14			16 26		16 55		17 14			17 26		17 55		18 14				18 26
St Leonards Warrior Sq [4]	d		15 54		16 17			16 28		16 57		17 17			17 28		17 57		18 17				18 28
Bexhill [4]	d		16 01		16 24			16 35		17 04		17 24			17 35		18 04		18 24				18 35
Collington	d		16 03					16 37		17 06					17 37		18 06						18 37
Cooden Beach	d		16 06					16 40		17 09					17 40		18 09						18 40
Normans Bay	d		16 09					16 43							17 43								18 43
Pevensey Bay	d		16 13																				
Pevensey & Westham	d		16 15					16 48		17 15					17 48		18 15						18 48
Hampden Park [4]	d		16 20					16 52		17 20					17 52		18 20						18 52
Eastbourne [4]	a		16 25		16 39			16 57		17 25		17 39			17 57		18 25		18 39				18 57
	d		16 31		16 45		16 58	17 04		17 31		17 45		17 57	18 01		18 31		18 47			18 58	19 04
Hampden Park [4]	d				16 49		17 02	17 08						18 01	18 05							19 02	19 08
Polegate	d		16 37		16 54		17 06	17 12		17 37		17 52		18 05	18 11		18 37		18 54			19 06	19 12
Berwick	d							17 18							18 17								19 18
Glynde	d							17 23							18 22								19 23
Seaford	d	16 25				16 58			17 25				17 58			18 26		18 44			19 02		
Bishopstone	d	16 27				17 00			17 27				18 00			18 28		18 46			19 04		
Newhaven Harbour	d	16 30				17 03			17 30				18 03			18 31							
Newhaven Town ⛴	d	16 32				17 05			17 32				18 05			18 33		18 50			19 08		
Southease	d	16 36							17 36							18 37							
Lewes [4]	a	16 44	16 49		17 07	17 14	17 18	17 29	17 44	17 49		18 04	18 14	18 17	18 28	18 44	18 49	18 59	19 07		19 17	19 20	19 29
	d	16 44	16 50	16 58	17 07	17 14	17 19	17 29	17 44	17 50	17 55	18 07	18 14	18 18	18 28	18 44	18 50	18 59	19 07		19 18	19 21	19 29
Falmer	d	16 51		17 05		17 21		17 36	17 51		18 02		18 21		18 35	18 51		19 06			19 25		19 36
Moulsecoomb	d	16 54		17 08		17 24		17 39	17 54		18 05		18 24		18 38	18 54		19 09			19 28		19 39
London Road (Brighton)	d	16 57		17 10		17 27		17 42	17 57		18 07		18 27		18 41	18 57		19 12			19 30		19 42
Brighton [10]	a	17 00		17 14	17 20	17 30		17 45	18 00		18 11	18 20	18 30		18 44	19 00		19 15	19 21		19 34		19 45
Cooksbridge	d						17 24							18 23								19 26	
Plumpton	d						17 29							18 28			18 58					19 31	
Wivelsfield [4]	a						17 35							18 34			19 06						
Haywards Heath [3]	a		17 05				17 39			18 06				18 38			19 10					19 40	
Gatwick Airport [10] ✈	a		17 24				17 54			18 26				18 56			19 25					19 55	
East Croydon 🚌	a		17 40				18 11			18 42				19 12			19 42					20 11	
London Bridge [4] ⊖	a																						
Clapham Junction [10]	a		17 50				18 21			18 52				19 21			19 52					20 20	
London Victoria [15] ⊖	a		17 58				18 29			18 59				19 29			19 59					20 28	

A 🛒 from Lewes

Ashford, Hastings, Eastbourne, Seaford and Lewes - Brighton, Haywards Heath and London

		SN	SN	SN	SN	SN	SN	SN	SN	SN	SN	SN	SN	SN	SN	SN	SN	SN	SN	SN	SN	SN
		◇	◇1	◇	◇	◇	◇	◇1	◇	◇1	◇	◇	◇1	◇	◇	◇1	◇	◇	◇1	◇	◇1	◇
																A						
Ashford International	d				18 32	18 58					19 32			19 58			20 32					21 32
Ham Street	d				18 41	19 07					19 41			20 07			20 41					21 41
Appledore (Kent)	d				18 46	19 12					19 46			20 12			20 46					21 46
Rye	a				18 55	19 21					19 55			20 21			20 55					21 55
	d				18 55						19 55			20 22			20 55					21 57
Winchelsea	d										19 59											22 00
Doleham	d																					
Three Oaks	d				19 06												21 06					
Ore	d		18 50							19 50			20 22			20 50					21 22	
Hastings 4	a		18 53		19 13					19 54	20 13		20 25	20 39		20 53	21 13				21 25	22 14
	d		18 55		19 14			19 27		19 55	20 14		20 26			20 55	21 14				21 30	22 15
St Leonards Warrior Sq 4	d		18 57		19 17			19 30		19 57	20 17		20 28			20 57	21 17				21 32	22 18
Bexhill 4	d		19 04		19 24			19 37		20 04	20 24		20 35			21 04	21 24				21 39	22 25
Collington	d		19 06					19 39		20 06			20 37			21 06					21 41	
Cooden Beach	d		19 09					19 42		20 09			20 40			21 09					21 44	
Normans Bay	d																					
Pevensey Bay	d																					
Pevensey & Westham	d		19 15					19 48		20 15			20 46			21 15					21 50	
Hampden Park 4	d		19 20					19 52		20 20			20 51			21 20					21 55	
Eastbourne 4	a		19 25		19 44			19 57		20 25	20 39		20 56			21 25	21 39				22 00	22 40
	d		19 31		19 48			20 04		20 31	20 45		21 04			21 31	21 45		22 04		22 15	22 45
Hampden Park 4	d							20 08					21 08						22 08		22 19	
Polegate	d		19 37		19 55			20 12		20 37	20 52		21 12			21 37	21 52		22 12		22 23	22 52
Berwick	d							20 18					21 18						22 18		22 29	
Glynde	d							20 23					21 23						22 23			
Seaford	d	19 19		19 37			19 58		20 28			20 58			21 28			21 58		22 20		
Bishopstone	d	19 21		19 39			20 00		20 30			21 00			21 30			22 00		22 22		
Newhaven Harbour	d	19 24		19 42			20 03		20 33			21 03			21 33			22 03		22 25		
Newhaven Town ⛴	d	19 26		19 44			20 05		20 35			21 05			21 35			22 05		22 27		
Southease	d			19 48					20 39													
Lewes 4	a	19 35	19 49	19 55	20 07		20 14	20 29	20 46	20 49	21 07	21 14	21 29		21 44	21 49	22 07	22 14	22 29	22 35	22 38	23 07
	d	19 38	19 50	19 57	20 08		20 14	20 29	20 53	20 50	21 07	21 14	21 29		21 53	21 50	22 07	22 14	22 29	22 42	22 40	23 07
Falmer	d	19 45		20 04			20 21	20 36	21 00			21 21	21 36		22 00			22 21	22 36	22 49		
Moulsecoomb	d	19 48		20 07			20 24	20 39	21 03			21 24	21 39		22 03			22 24	22 39	22 52		
London Road (Brighton)	d	19 50		20 09			20 27	20 42	21 05			21 27	21 42		22 05			22 27	22 42	22 54		
Brighton 10	a	19 55		20 13	20 20		20 33	20 45	21 09		21 20	21 33	21 45		22 09		22 20	22 31	22 45	22 58		23 20
Cooksbridge	d																					
Plumpton	d									20 58											22 48	
Wivelsfield 4	a		20 05							21 05						22 02					22 54	
Haywards Heath 3	a		20 10							21 09						22 06					22 58	
Gatwick Airport 10 ✈	a		20 25							21 25						22 25					23 12	
East Croydon	a		20 41							21 41						22 41					23 30	
London Bridge 4 ⊖	a																					
Clapham Junction 10	a		20 50							21 51						22 50					23 42	
London Victoria 15 ⊖	a		20 58							21 58						22 57					23 52	

A ⚲ from Lewes

Ashford, Hastings, Eastbourne, Seaford and Lewes - Brighton, Haywards Heath and London

			SN	SN	SN	SN	SN
			◇	◇1	◇	◇	◇1
Ashford International		d			22 32		
Ham Street		d			22 41		
Appledore (Kent)		d			22 46		
Rye		a			22 55		
		d			22 55		
Winchelsea		d			22 58		
Doleham		d			23 05		
Three Oaks		d			23 08		
Ore		d		22 22	23 14		
Hastings 4		a		22 25	23 17		
		d		22 26			23 22
St Leonards Warrior Sq 4		d		22 29			23 24
Bexhill 4		d		22 38			23 31
Collington		d		22 40			23 33
Cooden Beach		d		22 43			23 36
Normans Bay		d		22 46			
Pevensey Bay		d					
Pevensey & Westham		d		22 51			23 42
Hampden Park 4		d		22 55			23 47
Eastbourne 4		a		23 00			23 52
		d		23 05			23 56
Hampden Park 4		d		23 09			00 01
Polegate		d		23 13			00 05
Berwick		d		23 18			
Glynde		d		23 24			
Seaford		d	22 58			23 25	
Bishopstone		d	23 00			23 27	
Newhaven Harbour		d	23 03			23 30	
Newhaven Town	⛴	d	23 05			23 32	
Southease		d					
Lewes 4		a	23 14	23 29		23 40	00 17
		d	23 14	23 30		23 40	00 18
Falmer		d	23 21	23 37		23 47	00 25
Moulsecoomb		d	23 24	23 40		23 50	00 28
London Road (Brighton)		d	23 27	23 42		23 53	00 30
Brighton 10		a	23 31	23 46		23 56	00 34
Cooksbridge		d					
Plumpton		d					
Wivelsfield 4		a					
Haywards Heath 3		a					
Gatwick Airport 10	✈	a					
East Croydon	🚌	a					
London Bridge 4	⊖	a					
Clapham Junction 10		a					
London Victoria 15	⊖	a					

Ashford, Hastings, Eastbourne, Seaford and Lewes - Brighton, Haywards Heath and London

		SN ◇1	SN ◇	SN 1	SN ◇	SN ◇	SN ◇1	SN ◇	SN ◇	SN ◇1		SN ◇1	SN ◇	SN ◇1	SN ◇	SN ◇	SN ◇	SN ◇1	SN ◇1	SN ◇		SN ◇1	SN ◇	SN ◇	SN ◇
Ashford International	d															06 13								07 32	
Ham Street	d															06 22								07 41	
Appledore (Kent)	d															06 27								07 46	
Rye	a															06 36								07 55	
	d															06 51								07 55	
Winchelsea	d															06 54								07 59	
Doleham	d															07 01									
Three Oaks	d															07 04									
Ore	d											06 22		06 50		07 10			07 22			07 50			
Hastings [4]	a											06 25		06 53		07 13			07 25			07 53		08 13	
	d	23p22										06 26		06 55		07 14			07 26			07 55		08 14	
St Leonards Warrior Sq [4]	d	23p24										06 28		06 57		07 17			07 28			07 57		08 17	
Bexhill [4]	d	23p31										06 35		07 04		07 24			07 35			08 04		08 24	
Collington	d	23p33										06 37		07 06					07 37			08 06			
Cooden Beach	d	23p36										06 40		07 09					07 40			08 09			
Normans Bay	d											06 43							07 43						
Pevensey Bay	d																								
Pevensey & Westham	d	23p42										06 48		07 15					07 48			08 15			
Hampden Park [4]	d	23p47										06 52		07 20					07 52			08 20			
Eastbourne [4]	a	23p52										06 57		07 25		07 39			07 57			08 25		08 39	
	d	23p56		05 03	05 48		06 24	06 38		06 58		07 04		07 31		07 47		07 58	08 04			08 31		08 47	
Hampden Park [4]	d	00 01		05 07	05 52		06 28			07 02		07 08						08 02	08 08						
Polegate	d	00 05		05 11	05 57		06 32	06 45		07 06		07 12		07 37		07 54		08 06	08 12			08 37		08 54	
Berwick	d						06 38					07 18							08 18						
Glynde	d						06 43					07 23							08 23						
Seaford	d		05 05			06 28			06 58				07 28				07 58			08 25					08 58
Bishopstone	d		05 07			06 30			07 00				07 30				08 00			08 27					09 00
Newhaven Harbour	d		05 10			06 33			07 03				07 33				08 03			08 30					09 03
Newhaven Town ⛴	d		05 12			06 35			07 05				07 35				08 05			08 32					09 05
Southease	d																			08 36					
Lewes [4]	a	00 17	05 21	05 25	06 10	06 44	06 49	06 57	07 14	07 18		07 29	07 44	07 49		08 07	08 14	08 18	08 29	08 44		08 49		09 07	09 14
	d	00 18	05 28	05 26	06 10	06 44	06 50	06 58	07 14	07 20		07 29	07 44	07 50	07 58	08 07	08 14	08 20	08 29	08 44		08 50	08 58	09 07	09 14
Falmer	d	00 25	05 35		06 18	06 51		07 05	07 21			07 36	07 51		08 05		08 21		08 36	08 51			09 05		09 21
Moulsecoomb	d	00 28	05 38		06 21	06 54		07 09	07 24			07 39	07 54		08 08		08 24		08 39	08 54			09 08		09 24
London Road (Brighton)	d	00 30	05 40		06 24	06 57		07 11	07 27			07 42	07 57		08 10		08 27		08 42	08 57			09 10		09 27
Brighton [10]	a	00 34	05 44		06 27	07 00		07 15	07 30			07 45	08 00		08 14	08 20	08 30		08 45	09 00			09 14	09 20	09 30
Cooksbridge	d																								
Plumpton	d									07 28								08 28							
Wivelsfield [4]	a									07 35								08 35							
Haywards Heath [3]	a			05 40			07 05			07 40				08 05				08 40				09 05			
Gatwick Airport [10] ✈	a			06 03			07 25			07 55				08 25				08 55				09 25			
East Croydon 🚋	a						07 41			08 11				08 41				09 11				09 41			
London Bridge [4] ⊖	a																								
Clapham Junction [10]	a						07 51			08 21				08 51				09 21				09 51			
London Victoria [15] ⊖	a						07 58			08 28				08 58				09 28				09 58			

		SN ◇1	SN ◇1	SN ◇	SN ◇1	SN ◇		SN ◇	SN ◇	SN ◇1	SN ◇1	SN ◇	SN ◇1	SN ◇	SN ◇	SN ◇		SN ◇1	SN ◇1	SN ◇	SN ◇1	SN ◇	SN ◇	SN ◇	SN ◇1
Ashford International	d							08 32							09 32								10 32		
Ham Street	d							08 41							09 41								10 41		
Appledore (Kent)	d							08 46							09 46								10 46		
Rye	a							08 55							09 55								10 55		
	d							08 55							09 55								10 55		
Winchelsea	d														09 59										
Doleham	d																								
Three Oaks	d							09 06															11 06		
Ore	d		08 22		08 50						09 22		09 50						10 22		10 50				
Hastings [4]	a		08 25		08 53			09 13			09 25		09 53		10 13				10 25		10 53		11 13		
	d		08 26		08 55			09 14			09 26		09 55		10 14				10 26		10 55		11 14		
St Leonards Warrior Sq [4]	d		08 28		08 57			09 17			09 28		09 57		10 17				10 28		10 57		11 17		
Bexhill [4]	d		08 35		09 04			09 24			09 35		10 04		10 24				10 35		11 04		11 24		
Collington	d		08 37		09 06						09 37		10 06						10 37		11 06				
Cooden Beach	d		08 40		09 09						09 40		10 09						10 40		11 09				
Normans Bay	d		08 43								09 43								10 43						
Pevensey Bay	d																								
Pevensey & Westham	d		08 48		09 15						09 48		10 15						10 48		11 15				
Hampden Park [4]	d		08 52		09 20						09 52		10 20						10 52		11 20				
Eastbourne [4]	a		08 57		09 25			09 39			09 57		10 25		10 39				10 57		11 25		11 39		
	d	08 58	09 04		09 31			09 47		09 58	10 04		10 31		10 47			10 58	11 04		11 31		11 47		11 58
Hampden Park [4]	d	09 02	09 08							10 02	10 08							11 02	11 08						12 02
Polegate	d	09 06	09 12		09 37			09 54		10 06	10 12		10 37		10 54			11 06	11 12		11 37		11 54		12 06
Berwick	d		09 18								10 18								11 18						
Glynde	d		09 23								10 23								11 23						
Seaford	d			09 25					09 58			10 25				10 58				11 25				11 58	
Bishopstone	d			09 27					10 00			10 27				11 00				11 27				12 00	
Newhaven Harbour	d			09 30					10 03			10 30				11 03				11 30				12 03	
Newhaven Town ⛴	d			09 32					10 05			10 32				11 05				11 32				12 05	
Southease	d			09 36								10 36								11 36					
Lewes [4]	a	09 18	09 29	09 44	09 49			10 07	10 14	10 18	10 29	10 44	10 49		11 07	11 14		11 18	11 29	11 44	11 49		12 07	12 14	12 18
	d	09 20	09 29	09 44	09 50	09 58		10 07	10 14	10 20	10 29	10 44	10 50	10 58	11 07	11 14		11 20	11 29	11 44	11 50	11 58	12 07	12 14	12 20
Falmer	d		09 36	09 51		10 05			10 21		10 36	10 51		11 05		11 21			11 36	11 51		12 05		12 21	
Moulsecoomb	d		09 39	09 54		10 08			10 24		10 39	10 54		11 08		11 24			11 39	11 54		12 08		12 24	
London Road (Brighton)	d		09 42	09 57		10 10			10 27		10 42	10 57		11 10		11 27			11 42	11 57		12 10		12 27	
Brighton [10]	a		09 45	10 00		10 14		10 20	10 30		10 45	11 00		11 14	11 20	11 30			11 45	12 00		12 14	12 20	12 30	
Cooksbridge	d																								
Plumpton	d	09 28								10 28								11 28							12 28
Wivelsfield [4]	a	09 35								10 35								11 35							12 35
Haywards Heath [3]	a	09 40			10 05					10 40			11 05					11 40			12 05				12 40
Gatwick Airport [10] ✈	a	09 55			10 25					10 55			11 25					11 55			12 25				12 55
East Croydon 🚋	a	10 11			10 41					11 11			11 41					12 11			12 41				13 11
London Bridge [4] ⊖	a																								
Clapham Junction [10]	a	10 21			10 51					11 21			11 51					12 21			12 51				13 21
London Victoria [15] ⊖	a	10 28			10 58					11 28			11 58					12 28			12 58				13 28

Table 189

Saturdays
until 4 June

Ashford, Hastings, Eastbourne, Seaford and Lewes - Brighton, Haywards Heath and London

		SN ◇1		SN ◇	SN ◇1	SN ◇	SN ◇	SN ◇	SN ◇1	SN ◇1	SN ◇	SN ◇1		SN ◇	SN ◇	SN ◇	SN ◇1	SN ◇1	SN ◇	SN ◇1	SN ◇	SN ◇		SN ◇	SN ◇1
Ashford International	d						11 32								12 32							13 32			
Ham Street	d						11 41								12 41							13 41			
Appledore (Kent)	d						11 46								12 46							13 46			
Rye	a						11 55								12 55							13 55			
	d						11 55								12 55							13 55			
Winchelsea	d						11 59															13 59			
Doleham	d																								
Three Oaks	d														13 06										
Ore	d	11 22			11 50					12 22		12 50						13 22		13 50					
Hastings 4	a	11 25			11 53		12 13			12 25		12 53			13 13			13 25		13 53		14 13			
	d	11 26			11 55		12 14			12 26		12 55			13 14			13 26		13 55		14 14			
St Leonards Warrior Sq 4	d	11 28			11 57		12 17			12 28		12 57			13 17			13 28		13 57		14 17			
Bexhill 4	d	11 35			12 04		12 24			12 35		13 04			13 24			13 35		14 04		14 24			
Collington	d	11 37			12 06					12 37		13 06						13 37		14 06					
Cooden Beach	d	11 40			12 09					12 40		13 09						13 40		14 09					
Normans Bay	d	11 43								12 43								13 43							
Pevensey Bay	d																								
Pevensey & Westham	d	11 48			12 15					12 48		13 15						13 48		14 15					
Hampden Park 4	d	11 52			12 20					12 52		13 20						13 52		14 20					
Eastbourne 4	a	11 57			12 25		12 39			12 57		13 25			13 39			13 57		14 25		14 39			
	d	12 04			12 31		12 47		12 58	13 04		13 31			13 47		13 58	14 04		14 31		14 47			14 58
Hampden Park 4	d	12 08							13 02	13 08							14 02	14 08							15 02
Polegate	d	12 12			12 37		12 54		13 06	13 12		13 37			13 54		14 06	14 12		14 37		14 54			15 06
Berwick	d	12 18								13 18								14 18							
Glynde	d	12 23								13 23								14 23							
Seaford	d			12 25				12 58			13 25					13 58			14 25					14 58	
Bishopstone	d			12 27				13 00			13 27					14 00			14 27					15 00	
Newhaven Harbour	d			12 30				13 03			13 30					14 03			14 30					15 03	
Newhaven Town ⛴	d			12 32				13 05			13 32					14 05			14 32					15 05	
Southease	d			12 36							13 36								14 36						
Lewes 4	a	12 29		12 44	12 49		13 07	13 14	13 19	13 29	13 44	13 49			14 07	14 14	14 19	14 29	14 44	14 49		15 07		15 14	15 19
	d	12 29		12 44	12 50	12 58	13 07	13 14	13 20	13 29	13 44	13 50		13 58	14 07	14 14	14 20	14 29	14 44	14 50	14 58	15 07		15 14	15 20
Falmer	d	12 36		12 51		13 05		13 21		13 36	13 51			14 05		14 21		14 36	14 51		15 05			15 21	
Moulsecoomb	d	12 39		12 54		13 08		13 24		13 39	13 54			14 08		14 24		14 39	14 54		15 08			15 24	
London Road (Brighton)	d	12 42		12 57		13 10		13 27		13 42	13 57			14 10		14 27		14 42	14 57		15 10			15 27	
Brighton 10	a	12 45		13 00		13 14	13 20	13 30		13 45	14 00			14 14	14 20	14 30		14 45	15 00		15 14	15 20		15 30	
Cooksbridge	d																								
Plumpton	d								13 28								14 28								15 28
Wivelsfield 4	a								13 35								14 35								15 35
Haywards Heath 3	a				13 05				13 40			14 05					14 40			15 05					15 40
Gatwick Airport 10 ✈	a				13 25				13 55			14 25					14 55			15 25					15 55
East Croydon 🚋	a				13 41				14 11			14 41					15 11			15 41					16 11
London Bridge 4 ⊖	a																								
Clapham Junction 10	a				13 51				14 21			14 51					15 21			15 51					16 21
London Victoria 15 ⊖	a				13 58				14 28			14 58					15 28			15 58					16 28

		SN ◇1	SN ◇	SN ◇1	SN ◇	SN ◇	SN ◇	SN ◇1		SN ◇1	SN ◇	SN ◇1	SN ◇	SN ◇	SN ◇	SN ◇1	SN ◇1	SN ◇		SN ◇1	SN ◇	SN ◇	SN ◇	SN ◇1	SN ◇1
Ashford International	d					14 32								15 32								16 32			
Ham Street	d					14 41								15 41								16 41			
Appledore (Kent)	d					14 46								15 46								16 46			
Rye	a					14 55								15 55								16 55			
	d					14 55								15 55								16 55			
Winchelsea	d													15 59											
Doleham	d																								
Three Oaks	d					15 06																17 06			
Ore	d	14 22		14 50						15 22		15 50					16 22			16 50					17 22
Hastings 4	a	14 25		14 53		15 13				15 25		15 53		16 13			16 25			16 53		17 13			17 25
	d	14 26		14 55		15 14				15 26		15 55		16 14			16 26			16 55		17 14			17 26
St Leonards Warrior Sq 4	d	14 28		14 57		15 17				15 28		15 57		16 17			16 28			16 57		17 17			17 28
Bexhill 4	d	14 35		15 04		15 24				15 35		16 04		16 24			16 35			17 04		17 24			17 35
Collington	d	14 37		15 06						15 37		16 06					16 37			17 06					17 37
Cooden Beach	d	14 40		15 09						15 40		16 09					16 40			17 09					17 40
Normans Bay	d	14 43								15 43							16 43								17 43
Pevensey Bay	d																								
Pevensey & Westham	d	14 48		15 15						15 48		16 15					16 48			17 15					17 48
Hampden Park 4	d	14 52		15 20						15 52		16 20					16 52			17 20					17 52
Eastbourne 4	a	14 57		15 25		15 39				15 57		16 25		16 39			16 57			17 25		17 39			17 57
	d	15 04		15 31		15 47		15 58		16 04		16 31		16 47		16 58	17 04			17 31		17 47		17 58	18 04
Hampden Park 4	d	15 08						16 02		16 08						17 02	17 08							18 02	18 08
Polegate	d	15 12		15 37		15 54		16 06		16 12		16 37		16 54		17 06	17 12			17 37		17 54		18 06	18 12
Berwick	d	15 18								16 18							17 18								18 18
Glynde	d	15 23								16 23							17 23								18 23
Seaford	d		15 25				15 58				16 25				16 58			17 25					17 58		
Bishopstone	d		15 27				16 00				16 27				17 00			17 27					18 00		
Newhaven Harbour	d		15 30				16 03				16 30				17 03			17 30					18 03		
Newhaven Town ⛴	d		15 32				16 05				16 32				17 05			17 32					18 05		
Southease	d		15 36								16 36							17 36							
Lewes 4	a	15 29	15 44	15 49		16 07	16 14	16 18		16 29	16 44	16 49		17 07	17 14	17 18	17 29	17 44		17 49		18 07	18 14	18 18	18 29
	d	15 29	15 44	15 50	15 58	16 07	16 14	16 20		16 29	16 44	16 50	16 58	17 07	17 14	17 20	17 29	17 44		17 50	17 58	18 07	18 14	18 20	18 29
Falmer	d	15 36	15 51		16 05		16 21			16 36	16 51		17 05		17 21		17 36	17 51			18 05		18 21		18 36
Moulsecoomb	d	15 39	15 54		16 08		16 24			16 39	16 54		17 08		17 24		17 39	17 54			18 08		18 24		18 39
London Road (Brighton)	d	15 42	15 57		16 10		16 27			16 42	16 57		17 10		17 27		17 42	17 57			18 10		18 27		18 42
Brighton 10	a	15 45	16 00		16 14	16 20	16 30			16 45	17 00		17 14	17 20	17 30		17 45	18 00			18 14	18 20	18 30		18 45
Cooksbridge	d																								
Plumpton	d							16 28								17 28								18 28	
Wivelsfield 4	a							16 35								17 35								18 35	
Haywards Heath 3	a			16 05				16 40				17 05				17 40				18 05				18 40	
Gatwick Airport 10 ✈	a			16 25				16 55				17 25				17 55				18 25				18 55	
East Croydon 🚋	a			16 41				17 11				17 41				18 11				18 41				19 11	
London Bridge 4 ⊖	a																								
Clapham Junction 10	a			16 51				17 21				17 51				18 21				18 51				19 21	
London Victoria 15 ⊖	a			16 58				17 28				17 58				18 28				18 58				19 28	

Table 189

Saturdays
until 4 June

Ashford, Hastings, Eastbourne, Seaford and Lewes - Brighton, Haywards Heath and London

		SN	SN	SN	SN	SN	SN	SN	SN	SN	SN	SN	SN	SN	SN	SN	SN	SN	SN	SN	SN	SN
		◇	◇1	◇	◇	◇	◇1	◇1	◇	◇1	◇	◇	◇	◇1	◇	◇1	◇	◇	◇1	◇	◇1 A ⚓	◇
Ashford International	d				17 32							18 32					19 32					20 32
Ham Street	d				17 41							18 41					19 41					20 41
Appledore (Kent)	d				17 46							18 46					19 46					20 46
Rye	a				17 55							18 55					19 55					20 55
	d				17 55							18 55					19 55					20 55
Winchelsea	d				17 59												19 59					
Doleham	d																					
Three Oaks	d											19 06										21 06
Ore	d		17 50					18 22		18 50				19 22		19 50			20 22		20 50	
Hastings 4	a		17 53		18 13			18 25		18 53		19 13		19 25		19 53	20 13		20 25		20 53	21 13
	d		17 55		18 14			18 26		18 55		19 14		19 26		19 55	20 14		20 26		20 55	21 14
St Leonards Warrior Sq 4	d		17 57		18 17			18 28		18 57		19 17		19 28		19 57	20 17		20 28		20 57	21 17
Bexhill 4	d		18 04		18 24			18 35		19 04		19 24		19 35		20 04	20 24		20 35		21 04	21 24
Collington	d		18 06					18 37		19 06				19 37		20 06			20 37		21 06	
Cooden Beach	d		18 09					18 40		19 09				19 40		20 09			20 40		21 09	
Normans Bay	d							18 43						19 43					20 43			
Pevensey Bay	d																					
Pevensey & Westham	d		18 15					18 48		19 15				19 48		20 15			20 48		21 15	
Hampden Park 4	d		18 20					18 52		19 20				19 52		20 20			20 52		21 20	
Eastbourne 4	a		18 25		18 39			18 57		19 25		19 39		19 57		20 25	20 39		20 57		21 25	21 39
	d		18 31		18 47		18 58	19 04		19 31		19 47		20 04		20 31	20 45		21 04		21 31	21 45
Hampden Park 4	d						19 02	19 08						20 08					21 08			
Polegate	d		18 37		18 54		19 06	19 12		19 37		19 54		20 12		20 37	20 52		21 12		21 37	21 52
Berwick	d							19 18						20 18					21 18			
Glynde	d							19 23						20 23					21 23			
Seaford	d	18 25				18 58			19 25				19 58		20 28			20 58		21 28		
Bishopstone	d	18 27				19 00			19 27				20 00		20 30			21 00		21 30		
Newhaven Harbour	d	18 30				19 03			19 30				20 03		20 33			21 03		21 33		
Newhaven Town ⛴	d	18 32				19 05			19 32				20 05		20 35			21 05		21 35		
Southease	d	18 36							19 36													
Lewes 4	a	18 44	18 49		19 07	19 14	19 18	19 29	19 44	19 49		20 07	20 14	20 29	20 44	20 49	21 07	21 14	21 29	21 44	21 49	22 07
	d	18 44	18 50	18 58	19 07	19 14	19 20	19 29	19 44	19 50	19 58	20 07	20 14	20 29	20 53	20 50	21 07	21 14	21 29	21 53	21 50	22 07
Falmer	d	18 51		19 05		19 21		19 36	19 51		20 05		20 21	20 36	21 00			21 21	21 36	22 00		
Moulsecoomb	d	18 54		19 08		19 24		19 39	19 54		20 08		20 24	20 39	21 03			21 24	21 39	22 03		
London Road (Brighton)	d	18 57		19 10		19 27		19 42	19 57		20 10		20 27	20 42	21 05			21 27	21 42	22 05		
Brighton 10	a	19 00		19 14	19 20	19 30		19 45	20 00		20 14	20 20	20 30	20 45	21 09		21 20	21 30	21 45	22 10		22 20
Cooksbridge	d																					
Plumpton	d						19 28															
Wivelsfield 4	a						19 35			20 02						21 04					22 02	
Haywards Heath 3	a		19 05				19 40			20 07						21 09					22 06	
Gatwick Airport 10 ✈	a		19 25				19 55			20 25						21 26					22 24	
East Croydon 🚋	a		19 41				20 11			20 41						21 42					22 40	
London Bridge 4 ⊖	a																					
Clapham Junction 10	a		19 51				20 21			20 51						21 51					22 49	
London Victoria 15 ⊖	a		19 58				20 28			20 58						21 58					22 57	

A ⚓ from Lewes

Table 189

Saturdays
until 4 June

Ashford, Hastings, Eastbourne, Seaford and Lewes - Brighton, Haywards Heath and London

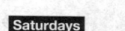

		SN	SN	SN	SN	SN	SN	SN	SN	SN		SN
		◇	◇1	◇	◇1	◇	◇	◇1	◇	◇		◇1
Ashford International	d					21 32			22 32			
Ham Street	d					21 41			22 41			
Appledore (Kent)	d					21 46			22 46			
Rye	a					21 55			22 55			
	d					21 57			22 55			
Winchelsea	d					22 00			22 59			
Doleham	d								23 05			
Three Oaks	d								23 09			
Ore	d		21 22					22 22	23 14			
Hastings 4	a		21 25			22 14		22 25	23 17			
	d		21 26		21 42	22 15		22 26				23 22
St Leonards Warrior Sq 4	d		21 28		21 44	22 18		22 29				23 24
Bexhill 4	d		21 35		21 51	22 25		22 38				23 31
Collington	d		21 37		21 53			22 40				23 33
Cooden Beach	d		21 40		21 56			22 43				23 36
Normans Bay	d							22 46				
Pevensey Bay	d											
Pevensey & Westham	d		21 46		22 02			22 51				23 42
Hampden Park 4	d		21 51		22 07			22 55				23 47
Eastbourne 4	a		21 56		22 12	22 40		23 00				23 52
	d		22 04		22 18	22 45		23 05				23 56
Hampden Park 4	d		22 08					23 09				00 01
Polegate	d		22 12		22 25	22 52		23 13				00 05
Berwick	d		22 18					23 18				
Glynde	d		22 23					23 24				
Seaford	d	21 58		22 20			22 58			23 25		
Bishopstone	d	22 00		22 22			23 00			23 27		
Newhaven Harbour	d	22 03		22 25			23 03			23 30		
Newhaven Town	d	22 05		22 27			23 05			23 32		
Southease	d											
Lewes 4	a	22 14	22 29	22 35	22 38	23 07	23 14	23 29		23 40		00 17
	d	22 14	22 29	22 42	22 40	23 07	23 14	23 30		23 40		00 18
Falmer	d	22 21	22 36	22 49			23 21	23 37		23 47		00 25
Moulsecoomb	d	22 24	22 39	22 52			23 24	23 40		23 50		00 28
London Road (Brighton)	d	22 27	22 42	22 54			23 27	23 42		23 53		00 30
Brighton 10	a	22 31	22 45	22 58		23 20	23 31	23 46		23 56		00 34
Cooksbridge	d											
Plumpton	d				22 48							
Wivelsfield 4	a				22 54							
Haywards Heath 3	a				22 58							
Gatwick Airport 10	a				23 12							
East Croydon	a				23 30							
London Bridge 4	a											
Clapham Junction 10	a				23 42							
London Victoria 15	a				23 52							

Table 189

Saturdays

11 June to 3 September

Ashford, Hastings, Eastbourne, Seaford and Lewes - Brighton, Haywards Heath and London

		SN ◇1	SN ◇	SN 1	SN ◇	SN ◇	SN ◇1	SN ◇	SN ◇	SN ◇1		SN ◇1	SN ◇	SN ◇1	SN ◇	SN ◇	SN ◇	SN ◇1	SN ◇1	SN		SN ◇	SN ◇1	SN ◇	SN ◇
Ashford International	d															06 13									07 32
Ham Street	d															06 22									07 41
Appledore (Kent)	d															06 27									07 46
Rye	a															06 36									07 55
	d															06 51									07 55
Winchelsea	d															06 54									07 59
Doleham	d															07 01									
Three Oaks	d															07 04									
Ore	d											06 22		06 50		07 10			07 22				07 50		
Hastings 4	a											06 25		06 53		07 13			07 25				07 53		08 13
	d	23p22										06 26		06 55		07 14			07 26				07 55		08 14
St Leonards Warrior Sq 4	d	23p24										06 28		06 57		07 17			07 28				07 57		08 17
Bexhill 4	d	23p31										06 35		07 04		07 24			07 35				08 04		08 24
Collington	d	23p33										06 37		07 06					07 37				08 06		
Cooden Beach	d	23p36										06 40		07 09					07 40				08 09		
Normans Bay	d											06 43							07 43						
Pevensey Bay	d																								
Pevensey & Westham	d	23p42										06 48		07 15					07 48				08 15		
Hampden Park 4	d	23p47										06 52		07 20					07 52				08 20		
Eastbourne 4	a	23p52										06 57		07 25		07 39			07 57				08 25		08 39
	d	23p56		05 03	05 48		06 24	06 38		06 58		07 04		07 31		07 47		07 58	08 04	08 22			08 31		08 47
Hampden Park 4	d	00 01		05 07	05 52		06 28			07 02		07 08						08 02	08 08						
Polegate	d	00 05		05 11	05 57		06 32	06 45		07 06		07 12		07 37		07 54		08 06	08 12				08 37		08 54
Berwick	d						06 38					07 18							08 18						
Glynde	d						06 43					07 23							08 23						
Seaford	d		05 05			06 28			06 58				07 28				07 58					08 25			
Bishopstone	d		05 07			06 30			07 00				07 30				08 00					08 27			
Newhaven Harbour	d		05 10			06 33			07 03				07 33				08 03					08 30			
Newhaven Town ⛴	d		05 12			06 35			07 05				07 35				08 05					08 32			
Southease	d																					08 36			
Lewes 4	a	00 17	05 21	05 25	06 10	06 44	06 49	06 57	07 14	07 18		07 29	07 44	07 49		08 07	08 14	08 18	08 29			08 44	08 49		09 07
	d	00 18	05 28	05 26	06 10	06 44	06 50	06 58	07 14	07 20		07 29	07 44	07 50	07 58	08 07	08 14	08 20	08 29			08 44	08 50	08 58	09 07
Falmer	d	00 25	05 35		06 18	06 51		07 05	07 21			07 36	07 51		08 05		08 21		08 36			08 51		09 05	
Moulsecoomb	d	00 28	05 38		06 21	06 54		07 09	07 24			07 39	07 54		08 08		08 24		08 39			08 54		09 08	
London Road (Brighton)	d	00 30	05 40		06 24	06 57		07 11	07 27			07 42	07 57		08 10		08 27		08 42			08 57		09 10	
Brighton 10	a	00 34	05 44		06 27	07 00		07 15	07 30			07 45	08 00		08 14	08 20	08 30		08 45			09 00		09 14	09 20
Cooksbridge	d																								
Plumpton	d									07 28								08 28							
Wivelsfield 4	a									07 35								08 35							
Haywards Heath 3	a			05 40			07 05			07 40				08 05				08 40					09 05		
Gatwick Airport 10 ✈	a			06 03			07 25			07 55				08 25				08 55					09 25		
East Croydon	a						07 41			08 11				08 41				09 11					09 41		
London Bridge 4 ⊖	a																			09 52					
Clapham Junction 10	a						07 51			08 21				08 51				09 21					09 51		
London Victoria 15 ⊖	a						07 58			08 28				08 58				09 28					09 58		

		SN ◇	SN ◇1	SN ◇1	SN ◇	SN ◇1		SN ◇	SN ◇	SN ◇	SN ◇1	SN ◇1	SN ◇	SN ◇1	SN ◇	SN ◇		SN ◇	SN ◇1	SN ◇1	SN ◇	SN ◇1	SN ◇	SN ◇	SN ◇
Ashford International	d								08 32							09 32								10 32	
Ham Street	d								08 41							09 41								10 41	
Appledore (Kent)	d								08 46							09 46								10 46	
Rye	a								08 55							09 55								10 55	
	d								08 55							09 55								10 55	
Winchelsea	d															09 59									
Doleham	d																								
Three Oaks	d								09 06															11 06	
Ore	d			08 22		08 50						09 22		09 50						10 22		10 50			
Hastings 4	a			08 25		08 53			09 13			09 25		09 53		10 13				10 25		10 53		11 13	
	d			08 26		08 55			09 14			09 26		09 55		10 14				10 26		10 55		11 14	
St Leonards Warrior Sq 4	d			08 28		08 57			09 17			09 28		09 57		10 17				10 28		10 57		11 17	
Bexhill 4	d			08 35		09 04			09 24			09 35		10 04		10 24				10 35		11 04		11 24	
Collington	d			08 37		09 06						09 37		10 06						10 37		11 06			
Cooden Beach	d			08 40		09 09						09 40		10 09						10 40		11 09			
Normans Bay	d			08 43								09 43								10 43					
Pevensey Bay	d																								
Pevensey & Westham	d			08 48		09 15						09 48		10 15						10 48		11 15			
Hampden Park 4	d			08 52		09 20						09 52		10 20						10 52		11 20			
Eastbourne 4	a			08 57		09 25			09 39			09 57		10 25		10 39				10 57		11 25		11 39	
	d		08 58	09 04		09 31			09 47		09 58	10 04		10 31		10 47			10 58	11 04		11 31		11 47	
Hampden Park 4	d		09 02	09 08							10 02	10 08							11 02	11 08					
Polegate	d		09 06	09 12		09 37			09 54		10 06	10 12		10 37		10 54			11 06	11 12		11 37		11 54	
Berwick	d			09 18								10 18								11 18					
Glynde	d			09 23								10 23								11 23					
Seaford	d	08 58			09 25					09 58			10 25					10 58			11 25				11 58
Bishopstone	d	09 00			09 27					10 00			10 27					11 00			11 27				12 00
Newhaven Harbour	d	09 03			09 30					10 03			10 30					11 03			11 30				12 03
Newhaven Town ⛴	d	09 05			09 32					10 05			10 32					11 05			11 32				12 05
Southease	d				09 36								10 36								11 36				
Lewes 4	a	09 14	09 18	09 29	09 44	09 49			10 07	10 14	10 18	10 29	10 44	10 49		11 07		11 14	11 18	11 29	11 44	11 49		12 07	12 14
	d	09 14	09 20	09 29	09 44	09 50		09 58	10 07	10 14	10 20	10 29	10 44	10 50	10 58	11 07		11 14	11 20	11 29	11 44	11 50	11 58	12 07	12 14
Falmer	d	09 21		09 36	09 51			10 05		10 21		10 36	10 51		11 05			11 21		11 36	11 51		12 05		12 21
Moulsecoomb	d	09 24		09 39	09 54			10 08		10 24		10 39	10 54		11 08			11 24		11 39	11 54		12 08		12 24
London Road (Brighton)	d	09 27		09 42	09 57			10 10		10 27		10 42	10 57		11 10			11 27		11 42	11 57		12 10		12 27
Brighton 10	a	09 30		09 45	10 00			10 14	10 20	10 30		10 45	11 00		11 14	11 20		11 30		11 45	12 00		12 14	12 20	12 30
Cooksbridge	d																								
Plumpton	d		09 28								10 28								11 28						
Wivelsfield 4	a		09 35								10 35								11 35						
Haywards Heath 3	a		09 40			10 05					10 40			11 05					11 40			12 05			
Gatwick Airport 10 ✈	a		09 55			10 25					10 55			11 25					11 55			12 25			
East Croydon	a		10 11			10 41					11 11			11 41					12 11			12 41			
London Bridge 4 ⊖	a																								
Clapham Junction 10	a		10 21			10 51					11 21			11 51					12 21			12 51			
London Victoria 15 ⊖	a		10 28			10 58					11 28			11 58					12 28			12 58			

Table 189

Saturdays

11 June to 3 September

Ashford, Hastings, Eastbourne, Seaford and Lewes - Brighton, Haywards Heath and London

		SN		SN	SN	SN	SN	SN	SN	SN	SN	SN		SN	SN	SN	SN	SN	SN	SN	SN	SN		SN	SN
		◇ 1		◇ 1	◇	◇ 1	◇	◇	◇	◇ 1	◇ 1	◇		◇ 1	◇	◇	◇	◇ 1	◇ 1	◇	◇ 1	◇		◇	◇
Ashford International	d							11 32								12 32								13 32	
Ham Street	d							11 41								12 41								13 41	
Appledore (Kent)	d							11 46								12 46								13 46	
Rye	a							11 55								12 55								13 55	
	d							11 55								12 55								13 55	
Winchelsea	d							11 59																13 59	
Doleham	d																								
Three Oaks	d															13 06									
Ore	d			11 22		11 50					12 22			12 50					13 22		13 50				
Hastings 4	a			11 25		11 53		12 13			12 25			12 53		13 13			13 25		13 53			14 13	
	d			11 26		11 55		12 14			12 26			12 55		13 14			13 26		13 55			14 14	
St Leonards Warrior Sq 4	d			11 28		11 57		12 17			12 28			12 57		13 17			13 28		13 57			14 17	
Bexhill 4	d			11 35		12 04		12 24			12 35			13 04		13 24			13 35		14 04			14 24	
Collington	d			11 37		12 06					12 37			13 06					13 37		14 06				
Cooden Beach	d			11 40		12 09					12 40			13 09					13 40		14 09				
Normans Bay	d			11 43							12 43								13 43						
Pevensey Bay	d																								
Pevensey & Westham	d			11 48		12 15					12 48			13 15					13 48		14 15				
Hampden Park 4	d			11 52		12 20					12 52			13 20					13 52		14 20				
Eastbourne 4	a			11 57		12 25		12 39			12 57			13 25		13 39			13 57		14 25			14 39	
	d	11 58		12 04		12 31		12 47		12 58	13 04			13 31		13 47		13 58	14 04		14 31			14 47	
Hampden Park 4	d	12 02		12 08						13 02	13 08							14 02	14 08						
Polegate	d	12 06		12 12		12 37		12 54		13 06	13 12			13 37		13 54		14 06	14 12		14 37			14 54	
Berwick	d			12 18							13 18								14 18						
Glynde	d			12 23							13 23								14 23						
Seaford	d				12 25				12 58			13 25					13 58			14 25					14 58
Bishopstone	d				12 27				13 00			13 27					14 00			14 27					15 00
Newhaven Harbour	d				12 30				13 03			13 30					14 03			14 30					15 03
Newhaven Town	d				12 32				13 05			13 32					14 05			14 32					15 05
Southease	d				12 36							13 36								14 36					
Lewes 4	a	12 18		12 29	12 44	12 49		13 07	13 14	13 19	13 29	13 44		13 49		14 07	14 14	14 19	14 29	14 44	14 49			15 07	15 14
	d	12 20		12 29	12 44	12 50	12 58	13 07	13 14	13 20	13 29	13 44		13 50	13 58	14 07	14 14	14 20	14 29	14 44	14 50	14 58		15 07	15 14
Falmer	d			12 36	12 51		13 05		13 21		13 36	13 51			14 05		14 21		14 36	14 51		15 05			15 21
Moulsecoomb	d			12 39	12 54		13 08		13 24		13 39	13 54			14 08		14 24		14 39	14 54		15 08			15 24
London Road (Brighton)	d			12 42	12 57		13 10		13 27		13 42	13 57			14 10		14 27		14 42	14 57		15 10			15 27
Brighton 10	a			12 45	13 00		13 14	13 20	13 30		13 45	14 00			14 14	14 20	14 30		14 45	15 00		15 14		15 20	15 30
Cooksbridge	d																								
Plumpton	d	12 28								13 28								14 28							
Wivelsfield 4	a	12 35								13 35								14 35							
Haywards Heath 3	a	12 40				13 05				13 40				14 05				14 40			15 05				
Gatwick Airport 10	a	12 55				13 25				13 55				14 25				14 55			15 25				
East Croydon	a	13 11				13 41				14 11				14 41				15 11			15 41				
London Bridge 4	a																								
Clapham Junction 10	a	13 21				13 51				14 21				14 51				15 21			15 51				
London Victoria 15	a	13 28				13 58				14 28				14 58				15 28			15 58				

		SN	SN	SN	SN	SN	SN	SN		SN	SN	SN	SN	SN	SN	SN	SN	SN		SN	SN	SN	SN	SN	SN
		◇ 1	◇ 1	◇	◇ 1	◇	◇	◇		◇ 1	◇ 1	◇	◇ 1	◇	◇	◇	◇ 1	◇ 1		◇	◇ 1	◇	◇	◇	◇ 1
Ashford International	d						14 32								15 32								16 32		
Ham Street	d						14 41								15 41								16 41		
Appledore (Kent)	d						14 46								15 46								16 46		
Rye	a						14 55								15 55								16 55		
	d						14 55								15 55								16 55		
Winchelsea	d														15 59										
Doleham	d																								
Three Oaks	d						15 06																17 06		
Ore	d		14 22		14 50						15 22		15 50					16 22			16 50				
Hastings 4	a		14 25		14 53		15 13				15 25		15 53		16 13			16 25			16 53		17 13		
	d		14 26		14 55		15 14				15 26		15 55		16 14			16 26			16 55		17 14		
St Leonards Warrior Sq 4	d		14 28		14 57		15 17				15 28		15 57		16 17			16 28			16 57		17 17		
Bexhill 4	d		14 35		15 04		15 24				15 35		16 04		16 24			16 35			17 04		17 24		
Collington	d		14 37		15 06						15 37		16 06					16 37			17 06				
Cooden Beach	d		14 40		15 09						15 40		16 09					16 40			17 09				
Normans Bay	d		14 43								15 43							16 43							
Pevensey Bay	d																								
Pevensey & Westham	d		14 48		15 15						15 48		16 15					16 48			17 15				
Hampden Park 4	d		14 52		15 20						15 52		16 20					16 52			17 20				
Eastbourne 4	a		14 57		15 25		15 39				15 57		16 25		16 39			16 57			17 25		17 39		
	d	14 58	15 04		15 31		15 47			15 58	16 04		16 31		16 47		16 58	17 04			17 31		17 47		17 58
Hampden Park 4	d	15 02	15 08							16 02	16 08						17 02	17 08							18 02
Polegate	d	15 06	15 12		15 37		15 54			16 06	16 12		16 37		16 54		17 06	17 12			17 37		17 54		18 06
Berwick	d		15 18								16 18							17 18							
Glynde	d		15 23								16 23							17 23							
Seaford	d			15 25				15 58				16 25				16 58				17 25				17 58	
Bishopstone	d			15 27				16 00				16 27				17 00				17 27				18 00	
Newhaven Harbour	d			15 30				16 03				16 30				17 03				17 30				18 03	
Newhaven Town	d			15 32				16 05				16 32				17 05				17 32				18 05	
Southease	d			15 36								16 36								17 36					
Lewes 4	a	15 19	15 29	15 44	15 49		16 07	16 14		16 18	16 29	16 44	16 49		17 07	17 14	17 18	17 29		17 44	17 49		18 07	18 14	18 18
	d	15 20	15 29	15 44	15 50	15 58	16 07	16 14		16 20	16 29	16 44	16 50	16 58	17 07	17 14	17 20	17 29		17 44	17 50	17 58	18 07	18 14	18 20
Falmer	d		15 36	15 51		16 05		16 21			16 36	16 51		17 05		17 21		17 36		17 51		18 05		18 21	
Moulsecoomb	d		15 39	15 54		16 08		16 24			16 39	16 54		17 08		17 24		17 39		17 54		18 08		18 24	
London Road (Brighton)	d		15 42	15 57		16 10		16 27			16 42	16 57		17 10		17 27		17 42		17 57		18 10		18 27	
Brighton 10	a		15 45	16 00		16 14	16 20	16 30			16 45	17 00		17 14	17 20	17 30		17 45		18 00		18 14	18 20	18 30	
Cooksbridge	d																								
Plumpton	d	15 28								16 28							17 28								18 28
Wivelsfield 4	a	15 35								16 35							17 35								18 35
Haywards Heath 3	a	15 40			16 05					16 40			17 05				17 40				18 05				18 40
Gatwick Airport 10	a	15 55			16 25					16 55			17 25				17 55				18 25				18 55
East Croydon	a	16 11			16 41					17 11			17 41				18 11				18 41				19 11
London Bridge 4	a																								
Clapham Junction 10	a	16 21			16 51					17 21			17 51				18 21				18 51				19 21
London Victoria 15	a	16 28			16 58					17 28			17 58				18 28				18 58				19 28

Table 189

Saturdays

11 June to 3 September

Ashford, Hastings, Eastbourne, Seaford and Lewes - Brighton, Haywards Heath and London

		SN	SN	SN	SN	SN	SN	SN	SN	SN	SN	SN	SN	SN	SN	SN	SN	SN	SN	SN	SN	SN
		◇1	◇	◇1	◇	◇	◇	◇1	◇1	◇	◇1	◇	◇	◇	◇1	◇	◇1	◇	◇	◇1	◇	◇1
																						A [trolley]
Ashford International	d					17 32							18 32					19 32				
Ham Street	d					17 41							18 41					19 41				
Appledore (Kent)	d					17 46							18 46					19 46				
Rye	a					17 55							18 55					19 55				
	d					17 55							18 55					19 55				
Winchelsea	d					17 59												19 59				
Doleham	d																					
Three Oaks	d												19 06									
Ore	d	17 22		17 50					18 22		18 50				19 22		19 50			20 22		20 50
Hastings 4	a	17 25		17 53		18 13			18 25		18 53		19 13		19 25		19 53	20 13		20 25		20 53
	d	17 26		17 55		18 14			18 26		18 55		19 14		19 26		19 55	20 14		20 26		20 55
St Leonards Warrior Sq 4	d	17 28		17 57		18 17			18 28		18 57		19 17		19 28		19 57	20 17		20 28		20 57
Bexhill 4	d	17 35		18 04		18 24			18 35		19 04		19 24		19 35		20 04	20 24		20 35		21 04
Collington	d	17 37		18 06					18 37		19 06				19 37		20 06			20 37		21 06
Cooden Beach	d	17 40		18 09					18 40		19 09				19 40		20 09			20 40		21 09
Normans Bay	d	17 43							18 43						19 43					20 43		
Pevensey Bay	d																					
Pevensey & Westham	d	17 48		18 15					18 48		19 15				19 48		20 15			20 48		21 15
Hampden Park 4	d	17 52		18 20					18 52		19 20				19 52		20 20			20 52		21 20
Eastbourne 4	a	17 57		18 25		18 39			18 57		19 25		19 39		19 57		20 25	20 39		20 57		21 25
	d	18 04		18 31		18 47		18 58	19 04		19 31		19 47		20 04		20 31	20 45		21 04		21 31
Hampden Park 4	d	18 08						19 02	19 08						20 08					21 08		
Polegate	d	18 12		18 37		18 54		19 06	19 12		19 37		19 54		20 12		20 37	20 52		21 12		21 37
Berwick	d	18 18							19 18						20 18					21 18		
Glynde	d	18 23							19 23						20 23					21 23		
Seaford	d		18 25				18 58			19 25				19 58		20 28			20 58		21 28	
Bishopstone	d		18 27				19 00			19 27				20 00		20 30			21 00		21 30	
Newhaven Harbour	d		18 30				19 03			19 30				20 03		20 33			21 03		21 33	
Newhaven Town ⛴	d		18 32				19 05			19 32				20 05		20 35			21 05		21 35	
Southease	d		18 36							19 36												
Lewes 4	a	18 29	18 44	18 49		19 07	19 14	19 18	19 29	19 44	19 49		20 07	20 14	20 29	20 44	20 49	21 07	21 14	21 29	21 44	21 49
	d	18 29	18 44	18 50	18 58	19 07	19 14	19 20	19 29	19 44	19 50	19 58	20 07	20 14	20 29	20 53	20 50	21 07	21 14	21 29	21 53	21 50
Falmer	d	18 36	18 51		19 05		19 21		19 36	19 51		20 05		20 21	20 36	21 00			21 21	21 36	22 00	
Moulsecoomb	d	18 39	18 54		19 08		19 24		19 39	19 54		20 08		20 24	20 39	21 03			21 24	21 39	22 03	
London Road (Brighton)	d	18 42	18 57		19 10		19 27		19 42	19 57		20 10		20 27	20 42	21 05			21 27	21 42	22 05	
Brighton 10	a	18 45	19 00		19 14	19 20	19 30		19 45	20 00		20 14	20 20	20 30	20 45	21 09		21 20	21 30	21 45	22 10	
Cooksbridge	d																					
Plumpton	d							19 28														
Wivelsfield 4	a							19 35			20 02						21 04					22 02
Haywards Heath 3	a			19 05				19 40			20 07						21 09					22 06
Gatwick Airport 10 ✈	a			19 25				19 55			20 25						21 26					22 24
East Croydon	a			19 41				20 11			20 41						21 42					22 40
London Bridge 4 ⊖	a																					
Clapham Junction 10	a			19 51				20 21			20 51						21 51					22 49
London Victoria 15 ⊖	a			19 58				20 28			20 58						21 58					22 57

A [trolley] from Lewes

Table 189

Saturdays

11 June to 3 September

Ashford, Hastings, Eastbourne, Seaford and Lewes - Brighton, Haywards Heath and London

		SN	SN	SN	SN	SN	SN	SN	SN	SN	SN	SN
		◇	◇	◇1	◇	◇1	◇	◇	◇1	◇	◇	◇1
Ashford International	d	20 32					21 32			22 32		
Ham Street	d	20 41					21 41			22 41		
Appledore (Kent)	d	20 46					21 46			22 46		
Rye	a	20 55					21 55			22 55		
	d	20 55					21 57			22 55		
Winchelsea	d						22 00			22 59		
Doleham	d									23 05		
Three Oaks	d	21 06								23 09		
Ore	d			21 22					22 22	23 14		
Hastings 4	a	21 13		21 25			22 14		22 25	23 17		
	d	21 14		21 26		21 42	22 15		22 26			23 22
St Leonards Warrior Sq 4	d	21 17		21 28		21 44	22 18		22 29			23 24
Bexhill 4	d	21 24		21 35		21 51	22 25		22 38			23 31
Collington	d			21 37		21 53			22 40			23 33
Cooden Beach	d			21 40		21 56			22 43			23 36
Normans Bay	d								22 46			
Pevensey Bay	d											
Pevensey & Westham	d			21 46		22 02			22 51			23 42
Hampden Park 4	d			21 51		22 07			22 55			23 47
Eastbourne 4	a	21 39		21 56		22 12	22 40		23 00			23 52
	d	21 45		22 04		22 18	22 45		23 05			23 56
Hampden Park 4	d			22 08					23 09			00 01
Polegate	d	21 52		22 12		22 25	22 52		23 13			00 05
Berwick	d			22 18					23 18			
Glynde	d			22 23					23 24			
Seaford	d		21 58		22 20			22 58			23 25	
Bishopstone	d		22 00		22 22			23 00			23 27	
Newhaven Harbour	d		22 03		22 25			23 03			23 30	
Newhaven Town ⛴	d		22 05		22 27			23 05			23 32	
Southease	d											
Lewes 4	a	22 07	22 14	22 29	22 35	22 38	23 07	23 14	23 29		23 40	00 17
	d	22 07	22 14	22 29	22 42	22 40	23 07	23 14	23 30		23 40	00 18
Falmer	d		22 21	22 36	22 49			23 21	23 37		23 47	00 25
Moulsecoomb	d		22 24	22 39	22 52			23 24	23 40		23 50	00 28
London Road (Brighton)	d		22 27	22 42	22 54			23 27	23 42		23 53	00 30
Brighton 10	a	22 20	22 31	22 45	22 58		23 20	23 31	23 46		23 56	00 34
Cooksbridge	d											
Plumpton	d					22 48						
Wivelsfield 4	a					22 54						
Haywards Heath 3	a					22 58						
Gatwick Airport 10 ✈	a					23 12						
East Croydon 🚋	a					23 30						
London Bridge 4 ⊖	a											
Clapham Junction 10	a					23 42						
London Victoria 15 ⊖	a					23 52						

Table 189

Saturdays
from 10 September

Ashford, Hastings, Eastbourne, Seaford and Lewes - Brighton, Haywards Heath and London

		SN	SN	SN	SN	SN	SN	SN	SN	SN	SN	SN	SN	SN	SN	SN	SN	SN	SN	SN	SN	SN	SN
		◇1	◇	1	◇	◇	◇1	◇	◇	◇1	◇1	◇	◇1	◇	◇	◇	◇1	◇1	◇	◇1	◇	◇	◇
Ashford International	d														06 13							07 32	
Ham Street	d														06 22							07 41	
Appledore (Kent)	d														06 27							07 46	
Rye	a														06 36							07 55	
	d														06 51							07 55	
Winchelsea	d														06 54							07 59	
Doleham	d														07 01								
Three Oaks	d														07 04								
Ore	d										06 22		06 50		07 10			07 22		07 50			
Hastings 4	a										06 25		06 53		07 13			07 25		07 53		08 13	
	d	23p22									06 26		06 55		07 14			07 26		07 55		08 14	
St Leonards Warrior Sq 4	d	23p24									06 28		06 57		07 17			07 28		07 57		08 17	
Bexhill 4	d	23p31									06 35		07 04		07 24			07 35		08 04		08 24	
Collington	d	23p33									06 37		07 06					07 37		08 06			
Cooden Beach	d	23p36									06 40		07 09					07 40		08 09			
Normans Bay	d										06 43							07 43					
Pevensey Bay	d																						
Pevensey & Westham	d	23p42									06 48		07 15					07 48		08 15			
Hampden Park 4	d	23p47									06 52		07 20					07 52		08 20			
Eastbourne 4	a	23p52									06 57		07 25		07 39			07 57		08 25		08 39	
	d	23p56		05 03	05 48		06 24	06 38		06 58	07 04		07 31		07 47		07 58	08 04		08 31		08 47	
Hampden Park 4	d	00 01		05 07	05 52		06 28			07 02	07 08						08 02	08 08					
Polegate	d	00 05		05 11	05 57		06 32	06 45		07 06	07 12		07 37		07 54		08 06	08 12		08 37		08 54	
Berwick	d						06 38				07 18							08 18					
Glynde	d						06 43				07 23							08 23					
Seaford	d		05 05			06 28			06 58			07 28				07 58			08 25				08 58
Bishopstone	d		05 07			06 30			07 00			07 30				08 00			08 27				09 00
Newhaven Harbour	d		05 10			06 33			07 03			07 33				08 03			08 30				09 03
Newhaven Town	d		05 12			06 35			07 05			07 35				08 05			08 32				09 05
Southease	d																		08 36				
Lewes 4	a	00 17	05 21	05 25	06 10	06 44	06 49	06 57	07 14	07 18	07 29	07 44	07 49		08 07	08 14	08 18	08 29	08 44	08 49		09 07	09 14
	d	00 18	05 28	05 26	06 10	06 44	06 50	06 58	07 14	07 20	07 29	07 44	07 50	07 58	08 07	08 14	08 20	08 29	08 44	08 50	08 58	09 07	09 14
Falmer	d	00 25	05 35		06 18	06 51		07 05	07 21		07 36	07 51		08 05		08 21		08 36	08 51		09 05		09 21
Moulsecoomb	d	00 28	05 38		06 21	06 54		07 09	07 24		07 39	07 54		08 08		08 24		08 39	08 54		09 08		09 24
London Road (Brighton)	d	00 30	05 40		06 24	06 57		07 11	07 27		07 42	07 57		08 10		08 27		08 42	08 57		09 10		09 27
Brighton 10	a	00 34	05 44		06 27	07 00		07 15	07 30		07 45	08 00		08 14	08 20	08 30		08 45	09 00		09 14	09 20	09 30
Cooksbridge	d																						
Plumpton	d									07 28							08 28						
Wivelsfield 4	a									07 35							08 35						
Haywards Heath 3	a			05 40			07 05			07 40			08 05				08 40			09 05			
Gatwick Airport 10 ✈	a			06 03			07 25			07 55			08 25				08 55			09 25			
East Croydon	a						07 41			08 11			08 41				09 11			09 41			
London Bridge 4 ⊖	a																						
Clapham Junction 10	a						07 51			08 21			08 51				09 21			09 51			
London Victoria 15 ⊖	a						07 58			08 28			08 58				09 28			09 58			

		SN	SN	SN	SN	SN	SN	SN	SN	SN	SN	SN	SN	SN	SN	SN	SN	SN	SN	SN	SN	SN	SN
		◇1	◇1	◇	◇1	◇	◇	◇	◇1	◇1	◇	◇1	◇	◇	◇	◇1	◇1	◇	◇1	◇	◇	◇	◇1
Ashford International	d						08 32							09 32							10 32		
Ham Street	d						08 41							09 41							10 41		
Appledore (Kent)	d						08 46							09 46							10 46		
Rye	a						08 55							09 55							10 55		
	d						08 55							09 55							10 55		
Winchelsea	d													09 59									
Doleham	d																						
Three Oaks	d						09 06														11 06		
Ore	d		08 22		08 50					09 22		09 50					10 22		10 50				
Hastings 4	a		08 25		08 53		09 13			09 25		09 53		10 13			10 25		10 53		11 13		
	d		08 26		08 55		09 14			09 26		09 55		10 14			10 26		10 55		11 14		
St Leonards Warrior Sq 4	d		08 28		08 57		09 17			09 28		09 57		10 17			10 28		10 57		11 17		
Bexhill 4	d		08 35		09 04		09 24			09 35		10 04		10 24			10 35		11 04		11 24		
Collington	d		08 37		09 06					09 37		10 06					10 37		11 06				
Cooden Beach	d		08 40		09 09					09 40		10 09					10 40		11 09				
Normans Bay	d		08 43							09 43							10 43						
Pevensey Bay	d																						
Pevensey & Westham	d		08 48		09 15					09 48		10 15					10 48		11 15				
Hampden Park 4	d		08 52		09 20					09 52		10 20					10 52		11 20				
Eastbourne 4	a		08 57		09 25		09 39			09 57		10 25		10 39			10 57		11 25		11 39		
	d	08 58	09 04		09 31		09 47		09 58	10 04		10 31		10 47		10 58	11 04		11 31		11 47		11 58
Hampden Park 4	d	09 02	09 08						10 02	10 08						11 02	11 08						12 02
Polegate	d	09 06	09 12		09 37		09 54		10 06	10 12		10 37		10 54		11 06	11 12		11 37		11 54		12 06
Berwick	d		09 18							10 18							11 18						
Glynde	d		09 23							10 23							11 23						
Seaford	d			09 25				09 58			10 25				10 58			11 25				11 58	
Bishopstone	d			09 27				10 00			10 27				11 00			11 27				12 00	
Newhaven Harbour	d			09 30				10 03			10 30				11 03			11 30				12 03	
Newhaven Town	d			09 32				10 05			10 32				11 05			11 32				12 05	
Southease	d			09 36							10 36							11 36					
Lewes 4	a	09 18	09 29	09 44	09 49		10 07	10 14	10 18	10 29	10 44	10 49		11 07	11 14	11 18	11 29	11 44	11 49		12 07	12 14	12 18
	d	09 20	09 29	09 44	09 50	09 58	10 07	10 14	10 20	10 29	10 44	10 50	10 58	11 07	11 14	11 20	11 29	11 44	11 50	11 58	12 07	12 14	12 20
Falmer	d		09 36	09 51		10 05		10 21		10 36	10 51		11 05		11 21		11 36	11 51		12 05		12 21	
Moulsecoomb	d		09 39	09 54		10 08		10 24		10 39	10 54		11 08		11 24		11 39	11 54		12 08		12 24	
London Road (Brighton)	d		09 42	09 57		10 10		10 27		10 42	10 57		11 10		11 27		11 42	11 57		12 10		12 27	
Brighton 10	a		09 45	10 00		10 14	10 20	10 30		10 45	11 00		11 14	11 20	11 30		11 45	12 00		12 14	12 20	12 30	
Cooksbridge	d																						
Plumpton	d	09 28							10 28							11 28							12 28
Wivelsfield 4	a	09 35							10 35							11 35							12 35
Haywards Heath 3	a	09 40			10 05				10 40			11 05				11 40			12 05				12 40
Gatwick Airport 10 ✈	a	09 55			10 25				10 55			11 25				11 55			12 25				12 55
East Croydon	a	10 11			10 41				11 11			11 41				12 11			12 41				13 11
London Bridge 4 ⊖	a																						
Clapham Junction 10	a	10 21			10 51				11 21			11 51				12 21			12 51				13 21
London Victoria 15 ⊖	a	10 28			10 58				11 28			11 58				12 28			12 58				13 28

Table 189

Saturdays

from 10 September

Ashford, Hastings, Eastbourne, Seaford and Lewes - Brighton, Haywards Heath and London

		SN		SN	SN	SN	SN	SN	SN	SN	SN	SN		SN	SN	SN	SN	SN	SN	SN	SN	SN		SN	SN
		◇1		◇	◇1	◇	◇	◇	◇1	◇1	◇	◇1		◇	◇	◇	◇1	◇1	◇	◇1	◇	◇		◇	◇1
Ashford International	d						11 32								12 32							13 32			
Ham Street	d						11 41								12 41							13 41			
Appledore (Kent)	d						11 46								12 46							13 46			
Rye	a						11 55								12 55							13 55			
	d						11 55								12 55							13 55			
Winchelsea	d						11 59															13 59			
Doleham	d																								
Three Oaks	d														13 06										
Ore	d	11 22			11 50					12 22		12 50						13 22		13 50					
Hastings [4]	a	11 25			11 53		12 13			12 25		12 53			13 13			13 25		13 53		14 13			
	d	11 26			11 55		12 14			12 26		12 55			13 14			13 26		13 55		14 14			
St Leonards Warrior Sq [4]	d	11 28			11 57		12 17			12 28		12 57			13 17			13 28		13 57		14 17			
Bexhill [4]	d	11 35			12 04		12 24			12 35		13 04			13 24			13 35		14 04		14 24			
Collington	d	11 37			12 06					12 37		13 06						13 37		14 06					
Cooden Beach	d	11 40			12 09					12 40		13 09						13 40		14 09					
Normans Bay	d	11 43								12 43								13 43							
Pevensey Bay	d																								
Pevensey & Westham	d	11 48			12 15					12 48		13 15						13 48		14 15					
Hampden Park [4]	d	11 52			12 20					12 52		13 20						13 52		14 20					
Eastbourne [4]	a	11 57			12 25		12 39			12 57		13 25			13 39			13 57		14 25		14 39			
	d	12 04			12 31		12 47		12 58	13 04		13 31			13 47		13 58	14 04		14 31		14 47			14 58
Hampden Park [4]	d	12 08							13 02	13 08							14 02	14 08							15 02
Polegate	d	12 12			12 37		12 54		13 06	13 12		13 37			13 54		14 06	14 12		14 37		14 54			15 06
Berwick	d	12 18								13 18								14 18							
Glynde	d	12 23								13 23								14 23							
Seaford	d			12 25				12 58			13 25					13 58			14 25					14 58	
Bishopstone	d			12 27				13 00			13 27					14 00			14 27					15 00	
Newhaven Harbour	d			12 30				13 03			13 30					14 03			14 30					15 03	
Newhaven Town ⛴	d			12 32				13 05			13 32					14 05			14 32					15 05	
Southease	d			12 36							13 36								14 36						
Lewes [4]	a	12 29		12 44	12 49		13 07	13 14	13 19	13 29	13 44	13 49			14 07	14 14	14 19	14 29	14 44	14 49		15 07		15 14	15 19
	d	12 29		12 44	12 50	12 58	13 07	13 14	13 20	13 29	13 44	13 50		13 58	14 07	14 14	14 20	14 29	14 44	14 50	14 58	15 07		15 14	15 20
Falmer	d	12 36		12 51		13 05		13 21		13 36	13 51			14 05		14 21		14 36	14 51		15 05			15 21	
Moulsecoomb	d	12 39		12 54		13 08		13 24		13 39	13 54			14 08		14 24		14 39	14 54		15 08			15 24	
London Road (Brighton)	d	12 42		12 57		13 10		13 27		13 42	13 57			14 10		14 27		14 42	14 57		15 10			15 27	
Brighton [10]	a	12 45		13 00		13 14	13 20	13 30		13 45	14 00			14 14	14 20	14 30		14 45	15 00		15 14	15 20		15 30	
Cooksbridge	d																								
Plumpton	d								13 28								14 28								15 28
Wivelsfield [4]	a								13 35								14 35								15 35
Haywards Heath [3]	a				13 05				13 40			14 05					14 40			15 05					15 40
Gatwick Airport [10] ✈	a				13 25				13 55			14 25					14 55			15 25					15 55
East Croydon 🚌	a				13 41				14 11			14 41					15 11			15 41					16 11
London Bridge [4] ⊖	a																								
Clapham Junction [10]	a				13 51				14 21			14 51					15 21			15 51					16 21
London Victoria [15] ⊖	a				13 58				14 28			14 58					15 28			15 58					16 28

		SN	SN	SN	SN	SN	SN	SN		SN	SN	SN	SN	SN	SN	SN	SN	SN		SN	SN	SN	SN	SN	SN
		◇1	◇	◇1	◇	◇	◇	◇1		◇1	◇	◇1	◇	◇	◇	◇1	◇1	◇		◇1	◇	◇	◇	◇1	◇1
Ashford International	d					14 32								15 32								16 32			
Ham Street	d					14 41								15 41								16 41			
Appledore (Kent)	d					14 46								15 46								16 46			
Rye	a					14 55								15 55								16 55			
	d					14 55								15 55								16 55			
Winchelsea	d													15 59											
Doleham	d																								
Three Oaks	d					15 06																17 06			
Ore	d	14 22		14 50						15 22		15 50					16 22			16 50					17 22
Hastings [4]	a	14 25		14 53		15 13				15 25		15 53		16 13			16 25			16 53		17 13			17 25
	d	14 26		14 55		15 14				15 26		15 55		16 14			16 26			16 55		17 14			17 26
St Leonards Warrior Sq [4]	d	14 28		14 57		15 17				15 28		15 57		16 17			16 28			16 57		17 17			17 28
Bexhill [4]	d	14 35		15 04		15 24				15 35		16 04		16 24			16 35			17 04		17 24			17 35
Collington	d	14 37		15 06						15 37		16 06					16 37			17 06					17 37
Cooden Beach	d	14 40		15 09						15 40		16 09					16 40			17 09					17 40
Normans Bay	d	14 43								15 43							16 43								17 43
Pevensey Bay	d																								
Pevensey & Westham	d	14 48		15 15						15 48		16 15					16 48			17 15					17 48
Hampden Park [4]	d	14 52		15 20						15 52		16 20					16 52			17 20					17 52
Eastbourne [4]	a	14 57		15 25		15 39				15 57		16 25		16 39			16 57			17 25		17 39			17 57
	d	15 04		15 31		15 47		15 58		16 04		16 31		16 47		16 58	17 04			17 31		17 47		17 58	18 04
Hampden Park [4]	d	15 08						16 02		16 08						17 02	17 08							18 02	18 08
Polegate	d	15 12		15 37		15 54		16 06		16 12		16 37		16 54		17 06	17 12			17 37		17 54		18 06	18 12
Berwick	d	15 18								16 18							17 18								18 18
Glynde	d	15 23								16 23							17 23								18 23
Seaford	d		15 25				15 58				16 25				16 58			17 25					17 58		
Bishopstone	d		15 27				16 00				16 27				17 00			17 27					18 00		
Newhaven Harbour	d		15 30				16 03				16 30				17 03			17 30					18 03		
Newhaven Town ⛴	d		15 32				16 05				16 32				17 05			17 32					18 05		
Southease	d		15 36								16 36							17 36							
Lewes [4]	a	15 29	15 44	15 49		16 07	16 14	16 18		16 29	16 44	16 49		17 07	17 14	17 18	17 29	17 44		17 49		18 07	18 14	18 18	18 29
	d	15 29	15 44	15 50	15 58	16 07	16 14	16 20		16 29	16 44	16 50	16 58	17 07	17 14	17 20	17 29	17 44		17 50	17 58	18 07	18 14	18 20	18 29
Falmer	d	15 36	15 51		16 05		16 21			16 36	16 51		17 05		17 21		17 36	17 51			18 05		18 21		18 36
Moulsecoomb	d	15 39	15 54		16 08		16 24			16 39	16 54		17 08		17 24		17 39	17 54			18 08		18 24		18 39
London Road (Brighton)	d	15 42	15 57		16 10		16 27			16 42	16 57		17 10		17 27		17 42	17 57			18 10		18 27		18 42
Brighton [10]	a	15 45	16 00		16 14	16 20	16 30			16 45	17 00		17 14	17 20	17 30		17 45	18 00			18 14	18 20	18 30		18 45
Cooksbridge	d																								
Plumpton	d							16 28								17 28								18 28	
Wivelsfield [4]	a							16 35								17 35								18 35	
Haywards Heath [3]	a			16 05				16 40				17 05				17 40				18 05				18 40	
Gatwick Airport [10] ✈	a			16 25				16 55				17 25				17 55				18 25				18 55	
East Croydon 🚌	a			16 41				17 11				17 41				18 11				18 41				19 11	
London Bridge [4] ⊖	a																								
Clapham Junction [10]	a			16 51				17 21				17 51				18 21				18 51				19 21	
London Victoria [15] ⊖	a			16 58				17 28				17 58				18 28				18 58				19 28	

Table 189

Saturdays
from 10 September

Ashford, Hastings, Eastbourne, Seaford and Lewes - Brighton, Haywards Heath and London

		SN	SN	SN	SN	SN	SN	SN	SN	SN	SN	SN	SN	SN	SN	SN	SN	SN	SN	SN	SN	SN
		◇	◇1	◇	◇	◇	◇1	◇1	◇	◇1	◇	◇	◇	◇1	◇	◇1	◇	◇	◇1	◇	◇1 A ⚒	◇
Ashford International	d				17 32							18 32					19 32					20 32
Ham Street	d				17 41							18 41					19 41					20 41
Appledore (Kent)	d				17 46							18 46					19 46					20 46
Rye	a				17 55							18 55					19 55					20 55
	d				17 55							18 55					19 55					20 55
Winchelsea	d				17 59												19 59					
Doleham	d																					
Three Oaks	d											19 06										21 06
Ore	d		17 50					18 22		18 50				19 22		19 50			20 22		20 50	
Hastings 4	a		17 53		18 13			18 25		18 53		19 13		19 25		19 53	20 13		20 25		20 53	21 13
	d		17 55		18 14			18 26		18 55		19 14		19 26		19 55	20 14		20 26		20 55	21 14
St Leonards Warrior Sq 4	d		17 57		18 17			18 28		18 57		19 17		19 28		19 57	20 17		20 28		20 57	21 17
Bexhill 4	d		18 04		18 24			18 35		19 04		19 24		19 35		20 04	20 24		20 35		21 04	21 24
Collington	d		18 06					18 37		19 06				19 37		20 06			20 37		21 06	
Cooden Beach	d		18 09					18 40		19 09				19 40		20 09			20 40		21 09	
Normans Bay	d							18 43						19 43					20 43			
Pevensey Bay	d																					
Pevensey & Westham	d		18 15					18 48		19 15				19 48		20 15			20 48		21 15	
Hampden Park 4	d		18 20					18 52		19 20				19 52		20 20			20 52		21 20	
Eastbourne 4	a		18 25		18 39			18 57		19 25		19 39		19 57		20 25	20 39		20 57		21 25	21 39
	d		18 31		18 47		18 58	19 04		19 31		19 47		20 04		20 31	20 45		21 04		21 31	21 45
Hampden Park 4	d						19 02	19 08						20 08					21 08			
Polegate	d		18 37		18 54		19 06	19 12		19 37		19 54		20 12		20 37	20 52		21 12		21 37	21 52
Berwick	d							19 18						20 18					21 18			
Glynde	d							19 23						20 23					21 23			
Seaford	d	18 25				18 58			19 25				19 58		20 28			20 58		21 28		
Bishopstone	d	18 27				19 00			19 27				20 00		20 30			21 00		21 30		
Newhaven Harbour	d	18 30				19 03			19 30				20 03		20 33			21 03		21 33		
Newhaven Town ⛴	d	18 32				19 05			19 32				20 05		20 35			21 05		21 35		
Southease	d	18 36							19 36													
Lewes 4	a	18 44	18 49		19 07	19 14	19 18	19 29	19 44	19 49		20 07	20 14	20 29	20 44	20 49	21 07	21 14	21 29	21 44	21 49	22 07
	d	18 44	18 50	18 58	19 07	19 14	19 20	19 29	19 44	19 50	19 58	20 07	20 14	20 29	20 53	20 50	21 07	21 14	21 29	21 53	21 50	22 07
Falmer	d	18 51		19 05		19 21		19 36	19 51		20 05		20 21	20 36	21 00			21 21	21 36	22 00		
Moulsecoomb	d	18 54		19 08		19 24		19 39	19 54		20 08		20 24	20 39	21 03			21 24	21 39	22 03		
London Road (Brighton)	d	18 57		19 10		19 27		19 42	19 57		20 10		20 27	20 42	21 05			21 27	21 42	22 05		
Brighton 10	a	19 00		19 14	19 20	19 30		19 45	20 00		20 14	20 20	20 30	20 45	21 09		21 20	21 30	21 45	22 10		22 20
Cooksbridge	d																					
Plumpton	d						19 28															
Wivelsfield 4	a						19 35			20 02						21 04					22 02	
Haywards Heath 3	a		19 05				19 40			20 07						21 09					22 06	
Gatwick Airport 10 ✈	a		19 25				19 55			20 25						21 26					22 24	
East Croydon 🚋	a		19 41				20 11			20 41						21 42					22 40	
London Bridge 4 ⊖	a																					
Clapham Junction 10	a		19 51				20 21			20 51						21 51					22 49	
London Victoria 15 ⊖	a		19 58				20 28			20 58						21 58					22 57	

A ⚒ from Lewes

Table 189

Saturdays
from 10 September

Ashford, Hastings, Eastbourne, Seaford and Lewes - Brighton, Haywards Heath and London

		SN	SN	SN	SN	SN	SN	SN	SN	SN	SN
		◇	◇■1	◇	◇■1	◇	◇	◇■1	◇	◇	◇■1
Ashford International	d					21 32			22 32		
Ham Street	d					21 41			22 41		
Appledore (Kent)	d					21 46			22 46		
Rye	a					21 55			22 55		
	d					21 57			22 55		
Winchelsea	d					22 00			22 59		
Doleham	d								23 05		
Three Oaks	d								23 09		
Ore	d		21 22					22 22	23 14		
Hastings ■4	a		21 25			22 14		22 25	23 17		
	d		21 26		21 42	22 15		22 26			23 22
St Leonards Warrior Sq ■4	d		21 28		21 44	22 18		22 29			23 24
Bexhill ■4	d		21 35		21 51	22 25		22 38			23 31
Collington	d		21 37		21 53			22 40			23 33
Cooden Beach	d		21 40		21 56			22 43			23 36
Normans Bay	d							22 46			
Pevensey Bay	d										
Pevensey & Westham	d		21 46		22 02			22 51			23 42
Hampden Park ■4	d		21 51		22 07			22 55			23 47
Eastbourne ■4	a		21 56		22 12	22 40		23 00			23 52
	d		22 04		22 18	22 45		23 05			23 56
Hampden Park ■4	d		22 08					23 09			00 01
Polegate	d		22 12		22 25	22 52		23 13			00 05
Berwick	d		22 18					23 18			
Glynde	d		22 23					23 24			
Seaford	d	21 58		22 20			22 58			23 25	
Bishopstone	d	22 00		22 22			23 00			23 27	
Newhaven Harbour	d	22 03		22 25			23 03			23 30	
Newhaven Town ⛴	d	22 05		22 27			23 05			23 32	
Southease	d										
Lewes ■4	a	22 14	22 29	22 35	22 38	23 07	23 14	23 29		23 40	00 17
	d	22 14	22 29	22 42	22 40	23 07	23 14	23 30		23 40	00 18
Falmer	d	22 21	22 36	22 49			23 21	23 37		23 47	00 25
Moulsecoomb	d	22 24	22 39	22 52			23 24	23 40		23 50	00 28
London Road (Brighton)	d	22 27	22 42	22 54			23 27	23 42		23 53	00 30
Brighton ■10	a	22 31	22 45	22 58		23 20	23 31	23 46		23 56	00 34
Cooksbridge	d										
Plumpton	d				22 48						
Wivelsfield ■4	a				22 54						
Haywards Heath ■3	a				22 58						
Gatwick Airport ■10 ✈	a				23 12						
East Croydon 🚋	a				23 30						
London Bridge ■4 ⊖	a										
Clapham Junction ■10	a				23 42						
London Victoria ■15 ⊖	a				23 52						

Table 189

Sundays

until 4 September

Ashford, Hastings, Eastbourne, Seaford and Lewes - Brighton, Haywards Heath and London

		SN	SN	SN	SN	SN	SN	SN	SN	SN	SN	SN	SN	SN	SN	SN	SN	SN	SN	SN	SN	SN	SN
		◇1	◇1	◇	◇	◇	◇1	◇	◇	◇	◇1	◇	◇	◇	◇1	◇	◇	◇	◇1	◇	◇	◇	◇1
		A	B				B				B				B				B				B
Ashford International	d												08 15				09 21				10 21		
Ham Street	d												08 24				09 30				10 30		
Appledore (Kent)	d												08 29				09 35				10 35		
Rye	a												08 38				09 44				10 44		
	d												08 40				09 45				10 45		
Winchelsea	d												08 43										
Doleham	d												08 50										
Three Oaks	d												08 53										
Ore	d										08 14		08 59		09 14				10 14				11 14
Hastings 4	a										08 17		09 02		09 17		10 02		10 17		11 02		11 17
	d	23p22									08 18		09 03		09 18		10 03		10 18		11 03		11 18
St Leonards Warrior Sq 4	d	23p24									08 21		09 06		09 21		10 06		10 21		11 06		11 21
Bexhill 4	d	23p31									08 28		09 13		09 28		10 13		10 28		11 13		11 28
Collington	d	23p33									08 30				09 30				10 30				11 30
Cooden Beach	d	23p36									08 33				09 33				10 33				11 33
Normans Bay	d	|																					
Pevensey Bay	d	|																					
Pevensey & Westham	d	23p42									08 39				09 39				10 39				11 39
Hampden Park 4	d	23p47									08 43				09 43				10 43				11 43
Eastbourne 4	a	23p52									08 49		09 29		09 49		10 29		10 49		11 29		11 49
	d	23p56	06 58		07 30		07 55		08 34		08 59		09 34		09 59		10 34		10 59		11 34		11 59
Hampden Park 4	d	00 01	07 02		07 34				08 38				09 38				10 38				11 38		
Polegate	d	00 05	07 06		07 38		08 02		08 42		09 06		09 42		10 06		10 42		11 06		11 42		12 06
Berwick	d	|			07 44				08 48				09 48				10 48				11 48		
Glynde	d	|			07 49				08 53				09 53				10 53				11 53		
Seaford	d	|				07 57		08 27		08 57		09 27		09 57		10 27		10 57		11 27		11 57	
Bishopstone	d	|				07 59		08 29		08 59		09 29		09 59		10 29		10 59		11 29		11 59	
Newhaven Harbour	d	|				08 02		08 32		09 02		09 32		10 02		10 32		11 02		11 32		12 02	
Newhaven Town	d	|				08 04		08 34		09 04		09 34		10 04		10 34		11 04		11 34		12 04	
Southease	d	|				08 08				09 08				10 08				11 08				12 08	
Lewes 4	a	00 17	07 18		07 55	08 15	08 18	08 43	08 59	09 15	09 18	09 43	09 59	10 15	10 18	10 43	10 59	11 15	11 18	11 43	11 59	12 15	12 18
	d	00 18	07 22	07 22	07 56	08 22	08 22	08 44	09 00	09 22	09 22	09 44	10 00	10 22	10 22	10 44	11 00	11 22	11 22	11 44	12 00	12 22	12 22
Falmer	d	00 25		07 29	08 03	08 29		08 51		09 29		09 51		10 29		10 51		11 29		11 51		12 29	
Moulsecoomb	d	00 28		07 32	08 07	08 32		08 54		09 32		09 54		10 32		10 54		11 32		11 54		12 32	
London Road (Brighton)	d	00 30		07 34	08 09	08 34		08 56		09 34		09 56		10 34		10 56		11 34		11 56		12 34	
Brighton 10	a	00 34		07 38	08 13	08 38		09 00	09 12	09 38		10 00	10 12	10 38		11 00	11 12	11 38		12 00	12 12	12 38	
Cooksbridge	d																						
Plumpton	d						08 30				09 30				10 30				11 30				12 30
Wivelsfield 4	a		07 36				08 36				09 36				10 36				11 36				12 36
Haywards Heath 3	a		07 40				08 40				09 40				10 40				11 40				12 40
Gatwick Airport 10 ✈	a		07 52				08 52				09 52				10 52				11 52				12 52
East Croydon	a		08 09				09 09				10 09				11 09				12 09				13 09
London Bridge 4 ⊖	a																						
Clapham Junction 10	a		08 18				09 18				10 18				11 18				12 18				13 18
London Victoria 15 ⊖	a		08 25				09 25				10 25				11 25				12 25				13 25

A not 22 May

B from Lewes

Table 189

Sundays until 4 September

Ashford, Hastings, Eastbourne, Seaford and Lewes - Brighton, Haywards Heath and London

		SN	SN	SN	SN	SN	SN	SN	SN	SN	SN	SN	SN	SN	SN	SN	SN	SN	SN	SN	SN	SN	SN
		◇	◇	◇	◇1	◇	◇	◇	◇1	◇	◇	◇	◇1	◇	◇	◇	◇1	◇	◇	◇	◇1	◇	◇
					A				A				A				A				A		
Ashford International	d		11 21				12 21				13 21				14 21				15 21				16 21
Ham Street	d		11 30				12 30				13 30				14 30				15 30				16 30
Appledore (Kent)	d		11 35				12 35				13 35				14 35				15 35				16 35
Rye	a		11 44				12 44				13 44				14 44				15 44				16 44
	d		11 45				12 45				13 45				14 45				15 45				16 45
Winchelsea	d																						
Doleham	d																						
Three Oaks	d																						
Ore	d				12 14				13 14				14 14				15 14				16 14		
Hastings 4	a		12 02		12 17		13 02		13 17		14 02		14 17		15 02		15 17		16 02		16 17		17 02
	d		12 03		12 18		13 03		13 18		14 03		14 18		15 03		15 18		16 03		16 18		17 03
St Leonards Warrior Sq 4	d		12 06		12 21		13 06		13 21		14 06		14 21		15 06		15 21		16 06		16 21		17 06
Bexhill 4	d		12 13		12 28		13 13		13 28		14 13		14 28		15 13		15 28		16 13		16 28		17 13
Collington	d				12 30				13 30				14 30				15 30				16 30		
Cooden Beach	d				12 33				13 33				14 33				15 33				16 33		
Normans Bay	d																						
Pevensey Bay	d																						
Pevensey & Westham	d				12 39				13 39				14 39				15 39				16 39		
Hampden Park 4	d				12 43				13 43				14 43				15 43				16 43		
Eastbourne 4	a		12 29		12 49		13 29		13 49		14 29		14 49		15 29		15 49		16 29		16 49		17 29
	d		12 34		12 59		13 34		13 59		14 34		14 59		15 34		15 59		16 34		16 59		17 34
Hampden Park 4	d		12 38				13 38				14 38				15 38				16 38				17 38
Polegate	d		12 42		13 06		13 42		14 06		14 42		15 06		15 42		16 06		16 42		17 06		17 42
Berwick	d		12 48				13 48				14 48				15 48				16 48				17 48
Glynde	d		12 53				13 53				14 53				15 53				16 53				17 53
Seaford	d	12 27		12 57		13 27		13 57		14 27		14 57		15 27		15 57		16 27		16 57		17 27	
Bishopstone	d	12 29		12 59		13 29		13 59		14 29		14 59		15 29		15 59		16 29		16 59		17 29	
Newhaven Harbour	d	12 32		13 02		13 32		14 02		14 32		15 02		15 32		16 02		16 32		17 02		17 32	
Newhaven Town	d	12 34		13 04		13 34		14 04		14 34		15 04		15 34		16 04		16 34		17 04		17 34	
Southease	d			13 08				14 08				15 08				16 08				17 08			
Lewes 4	a	12 43	12 59	13 15	13 18	13 43	13 59	14 15	14 18	14 43	14 59	15 15	15 18	15 43	15 59	16 15	16 18	16 43	16 59	17 15	17 18	17 43	17 59
	d	12 44	13 00	13 22	13 22	13 44	14 00	14 22	14 22	14 44	15 00	15 22	15 22	15 44	16 00	16 22	16 22	16 44	17 00	17 22	17 22	17 44	18 00
Falmer	d	12 51		13 29		13 51		14 29		14 51		15 29		15 51		16 29		16 51		17 29		17 51	
Moulsecoomb	d	12 54		13 32		13 54		14 32		14 54		15 32		15 54		16 32		16 54		17 32		17 54	
London Road (Brighton)	d	12 56		13 34		13 56		14 34		14 56		15 34		15 56		16 34		16 56		17 34		17 56	
Brighton 10	a	13 00	13 12	13 38		14 00	14 12	14 38		15 00	15 12	15 38		16 00	16 12	16 38		17 00	17 12	17 38		18 00	18 12
Cooksbridge	d																						
Plumpton	d																16 30				17 30		
Wivelsfield 4	a				13 36				14 36				15 36				16 36				17 36		
Haywards Heath 3	a				13 40				14 40				15 40				16 40				17 40		
Gatwick Airport 10	a				13 52				14 52				15 52				16 52				17 52		
East Croydon	a				14 09				15 09				16 09				17 09				18 09		
London Bridge 4 ⊖	a																						
Clapham Junction 10	a				14 18				15 18				16 18				17 18				18 18		
London Victoria 15 ⊖	a				14 25				15 25				16 25				17 25				18 25		

A from Lewes

Table 189

Sundays
until 4 September

Ashford, Hastings, Eastbourne, Seaford and Lewes - Brighton, Haywards Heath and London

		SN	SN	SN	SN	SN	SN	SN	SN	SN	SN	SN	SN	SN	SN	SN	SN	SN	SN	SN	SN	SN
		◇	◇ 1	◇	◇	◇	◇ 1	◇	◇	◇	◇ 1	◇	◇	◇	◇ 1	◇	◇	◇	◇ 1	◇	◇	◇
			A ⌶																			
Ashford International	d				17 21				18 21				19 21				20 21				21 21	
Ham Street	d				17 30				18 30				19 30				20 30				21 30	
Appledore (Kent)	d				17 35				18 35				19 35				20 35				21 35	
Rye	a				17 44				18 44				19 44				20 44				21 44	
	d				17 45				18 45				19 45				20 45				21 45	
Winchelsea	d																					
Doleham	d																					
Three Oaks	d																					
Ore	d		17 14				18 14				19 14				20 14				21 14			
Hastings 4	a		17 17		18 02		18 17		19 02		19 17		20 02		20 17		21 02		21 17		22 02	
	d		17 18		18 03		18 18		19 03		19 18		20 03		20 18		21 03		21 18		22 03	
St Leonards Warrior Sq 4	d		17 21		18 06		18 21		19 06		19 21		20 06		20 21		21 06		21 21		22 06	
Bexhill 4	d		17 28		18 13		18 28		19 13		19 28		20 13		20 28		21 13		21 28		22 13	
Collington	d		17 30				18 30				19 30				20 30				21 30			
Cooden Beach	d		17 33				18 33				19 33				20 33				21 33			
Normans Bay	d																					
Pevensey Bay	d																					
Pevensey & Westham	d		17 39				18 39				19 39				20 39				21 39			
Hampden Park 4	d		17 43				18 43				19 43				20 43				21 43			
Eastbourne 4	a		17 49		18 29		18 49		19 29		19 49		20 29		20 49		21 29		21 49		22 29	
	d		17 59		18 34		18 59		19 34		19 59		20 34		20 59		21 34		21 59		22 34	
Hampden Park 4	d				18 38				19 38				20 38				21 38				22 38	
Polegate	d		18 06		18 42		19 06		19 42		20 06		20 42		21 06		21 42		22 06		22 42	
Berwick	d				18 48				19 48				20 48				21 48				22 48	
Glynde	d				18 53				19 53				20 53				21 53				22 53	
Seaford	d	17 57		18 27		18 57		19 27		19 57		20 27		20 57		21 27		21 53		22 27		22 53
Bishopstone	d	17 59		18 29		18 59		19 29		19 59		20 29		20 59		21 29		21 55		22 29		22 55
Newhaven Harbour	d	18 02		18 32		19 02		19 32		20 02		20 32		21 02		21 32		21 58		22 32		22 58
Newhaven Town ⛴	d	18 04		18 34		19 04		19 34		20 04		20 34		21 04		21 34		22 00		22 34		23 00
Southease	d	18 08				19 08				20 08												
Lewes 4	a	18 15	18 18	18 43	18 59	19 15	19 18	19 43	19 59	20 15	20 18	20 43	20 59	21 13	21 18	21 43	21 59	22 09	22 18	22 43	22 59	23 09
	d	18 22	18 22	18 44	19 00	19 22	19 22	19 44	20 00	20 22	20 22	20 44	21 00	21 22	21 22	21 44	22 00	22 10	22 19	22 44	23 00	23 10
Falmer	d	18 29		18 51		19 29		19 51		20 29		20 51		21 29		21 51		22 17	22 26	22 51		23 17
Moulsecoomb	d	18 32		18 54		19 32		19 54		20 32		20 54		21 32		21 54		22 20	22 29	22 54		23 20
London Road (Brighton)	d	18 34		18 56		19 34		19 56		20 34		20 56		21 34		21 56		22 22	22 31	22 56		23 22
Brighton 10	a	18 38		19 00	19 12	19 38		20 00	20 12	20 38		21 00	21 12	21 38		22 00	22 12	22 26	22 35	23 00	23 12	23 26
Cooksbridge	d																					
Plumpton	d		18 30				19 30				20 30				21 30							
Wivelsfield 4	a		18 36				19 36				20 36				21 36							
Haywards Heath 3	a		18 40				19 40				20 40				21 40							
Gatwick Airport 10 ✈	a		18 52				19 52				20 52				21 52							
East Croydon 🚌	a		19 09				20 09				21 09				22 09							
London Bridge 4 ⊖	a																					
Clapham Junction 10	a		19 18				20 18				21 18				22 18							
London Victoria 15 ⊖	a		19 25				20 25				21 25				22 25							

A ⌶ from Lewes

Table 189

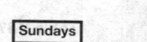

Sundays
until 4 September

Ashford, Hastings, Eastbourne, Seaford and Lewes - Brighton, Haywards Heath and London

Station		SN	SN	SN
		◇1	◇	◇1
Ashford International	d		22 32	
Ham Street	d		22 41	
Appledore (Kent)	d		22 46	
Rye	a		22 55	
	d		22 55	
Winchelsea	d		22 58	
Doleham	d		23 05	
Three Oaks	d		23 08	
Ore	d	22 14	23 14	
Hastings 4	a	22 17	23 17	
	d	22 18		23 22
St Leonards Warrior Sq 4	d	22 21		23 24
Bexhill 4	d	22 28		23 31
Collington	d	22 30		23 33
Cooden Beach	d	22 33		23 36
Normans Bay	d			
Pevensey Bay	d			
Pevensey & Westham	d	22 39		23 42
Hampden Park 4	d	22 43		23 47
Eastbourne 4	a	22 49		23 52
	d	22 59		
Hampden Park 4	d			
Polegate	d	23 06		
Berwick	d			
Glynde	d			
Seaford	d			
Bishopstone	d			
Newhaven Harbour	d			
Newhaven Town ⛴	d			
Southease	d			
Lewes 4	a	23 18		
	d	23 19		
Falmer	d	23 26		
Moulsecoomb	d	23 29		
London Road (Brighton)	d	23 31		
Brighton 10	a	23 35		
Cooksbridge	d			
Plumpton	d			
Wivelsfield 4	a			
Haywards Heath 3	a			
Gatwick Airport 10 ✈	a			
East Croydon 🚋	a			
London Bridge 4 ⊖	a			
Clapham Junction 10	a			
London Victoria 15 ⊖	a			

Table 189

Sundays

from 11 September

Ashford, Hastings, Eastbourne, Seaford and Lewes - Brighton, Haywards Heath and London

		SN	SN	SN	SN	SN	SN	SN	SN	SN
		◇1	◇1	◇	◇	◇	◇1	◇	◇	◇
			A				A			
			🛒				🛒			
Ashford International	d									
Ham Street	d									
Appledore (Kent)	d									
Rye	a									
	d									
Winchelsea	d									
Doleham	d									
Three Oaks	d									
Ore	d									
Hastings 4	a									
	d	23p22								
St Leonards Warrior Sq 4	d	23p24								
Bexhill 4	d	23p31								
Collington	d	23p33								
Cooden Beach	d	23p36								
Normans Bay	d									
Pevensey Bay	d									
Pevensey & Westham	d	23p42								
Hampden Park 4	d	23p47								
Eastbourne 4	a	23p52								
	d	23p56	06 54		07 30		07 55		08 34	
Hampden Park 4	d	00 01	06 58		07 34				08 38	
Polegate	d	00 05	07 02		07 38		08 02		08 42	
Berwick	d				07 44				08 48	
Glynde	d				07 49				08 53	
Seaford	d					07 53		08 27		08 53
Bishopstone	d					07 55		08 29		08 55
Newhaven Harbour	d					07 58		08 32		08 58
Newhaven Town ⛴	d					08 00		08 34		09 00
Southease	d					08 04				09 04
Lewes 4	a	00 17	07 14		07 55	08 11	08 14	08 43	08 59	09 11
	d	00 18	07 20	07 18	07 56	08 18	08 16	08 44	09 00	09 18
Falmer	d	00 25		07 25	08 03	08 25		08 51		09 25
Moulsecoomb	d	00 28		07 28	08 07	08 28		08 54		09 28
London Road (Brighton)	d	00 30		07 30	08 09	08 30		08 56		09 30
Brighton 10	a	00 34		07 34	08 13	08 34		09 00	09 12	09 34
Cooksbridge	d									
Plumpton	d						08 24			
Wivelsfield 4	a		07 32				08 31			
Haywards Heath 3	a		07 36				08 36			
Gatwick Airport 10 ✈	a		07 51				08 51			
East Croydon 🚋	a		08 09				09 09			
London Bridge 4 ⊖	a									
Clapham Junction 10	a		08 24				09 24			
London Victoria 15 ⊖	a		08 31				09 31			

		SN	SN	SN	SN	SN	SN	SN	SN	SN	SN	SN	SN	SN
		◇1	◇	◇	◇	◇1	◇	◇	◇	◇1	◇	◇	◇	◇1
		A				A				A				A
		🛒				🛒				🛒				🛒
Ashford International	d			08 15				09 21				10 21		
Ham Street	d			08 24				09 30				10 30		
Appledore (Kent)	d			08 29				09 35				10 35		
Rye	a			08 38				09 44				10 44		
	d			08 40				09 45				10 45		
Winchelsea	d			08 43										
Doleham	d			08 50										
Three Oaks	d			08 53										
Ore	d	08 14		08 59		09 14				10 14				11 14
Hastings 4	a	08 17		09 02		09 17		10 02		10 17		11 02		11 17
	d	08 18		09 03		09 18		10 03		10 18		11 03		11 18
St Leonards Warrior Sq 4	d	08 21		09 06		09 21		10 06		10 21		11 06		11 21
Bexhill 4	d	08 28		09 13		09 28		10 13		10 28		11 13		11 28
Collington	d	08 30				09 30				10 30				11 30
Cooden Beach	d	08 33				09 33				10 33				11 33
Normans Bay	d													
Pevensey Bay	d													
Pevensey & Westham	d	08 39				09 39				10 39				11 39
Hampden Park 4	d	08 43				09 43				10 43				11 43
Eastbourne 4	a	08 49		09 29		09 49		10 29		10 49		11 29		11 49
	d	08 55		09 34		09 55		10 34		10 55		11 34		11 55
Hampden Park 4	d			09 38				10 38				11 38		
Polegate	d	09 02		09 42		10 02		10 42		11 02		11 42		12 02
Berwick	d			09 48				10 48				11 48		
Glynde	d			09 53				10 53				11 53		
Seaford	d		09 27		09 53		10 27		10 53		11 27		11 53	
Bishopstone	d		09 29		09 55		10 29		10 55		11 29		11 55	
Newhaven Harbour	d		09 32		09 58		10 32		10 58		11 32		11 58	
Newhaven Town ⛴	d		09 34		10 00		10 34		11 00		11 34		12 00	
Southease	d				10 04				11 04				12 04	
Lewes 4	a	09 14	09 43	09 59	10 11	10 14	10 43	10 59	11 11	11 14	11 43	11 59	12 11	12 14
	d	09 16	09 44	10 00	10 18	10 16	10 44	11 00	11 18	11 16	11 44	12 00	12 18	12 16
Falmer	d		09 51		10 25		10 51		11 25		11 51		12 25	
Moulsecoomb	d		09 54		10 28		10 54		11 28		11 54		12 28	
London Road (Brighton)	d		09 56		10 30		10 56		11 30		11 56		12 30	
Brighton 10	a		10 00	10 12	10 34		11 00	11 12	11 34		12 00	12 12	12 34	
Cooksbridge	d													
Plumpton	d	09 24				10 24				11 24				12 24
Wivelsfield 4	a	09 31				10 31				11 31				12 31
Haywards Heath 3	a	09 35				10 35				11 35				12 35
Gatwick Airport 10 ✈	a	09 51				10 51				11 51				12 52
East Croydon 🚋	a	10 09				11 09				12 09				13 09
London Bridge 4 ⊖	a													
Clapham Junction 10	a	10 24				11 24				12 24				13 24
London Victoria 15 ⊖	a	10 31				11 31				12 31				13 31

A 🛒 from Lewes

Table 189

Sundays

from 11 September

Ashford, Hastings, Eastbourne, Seaford and Lewes - Brighton, Haywards Heath and London

		SN	SN	SN	SN	SN		SN	SN	SN	SN	SN	SN	SN	SN	SN		SN	SN	SN	SN	SN	SN	SN	SN
		◇	◇	◇	◇[1] A 🛒	◇		◇	◇	◇[1] A 🛒	◇	◇	◇	◇[1] A 🛒	◇	◇		◇	◇[1] A 🛒	◇	◇	◇	◇[1] A 🛒	◇	◇
Ashford International	d		11 21					12 21				13 21				14 21					15 21				16 21
Ham Street	d		11 30					12 30				13 30				14 30					15 30				16 30
Appledore (Kent)	d		11 35					12 35				13 35				14 35					15 35				16 35
Rye	a		11 44					12 44				13 44				14 44					15 44				16 44
	d		11 45					12 45				13 45				14 45					15 45				16 45
Winchelsea	d																								
Doleham	d																								
Three Oaks	d																								
Ore	d				12 14					13 14				14 14					15 14				16 14		
Hastings [4]	a		12 02		12 17			13 02		13 17		14 02		14 17		15 02			15 17		16 02		16 17		17 02
	d		12 03		12 18			13 03		13 18		14 03		14 18		15 03			15 18		16 03		16 18		17 03
St Leonards Warrior Sq [4]	d		12 06		12 21			13 06		13 21		14 06		14 21		15 06			15 21		16 06		16 21		17 06
Bexhill [4]	d		12 13		12 28			13 13		13 28		14 13		14 28		15 13			15 28		16 13		16 28		17 13
Collington	d				12 30					13 30				14 30					15 30				16 30		
Cooden Beach	d				12 33					13 33				14 33					15 33				16 33		
Normans Bay	d																								
Pevensey Bay	d																								
Pevensey & Westham	d				12 39					13 39				14 39					15 39				16 39		
Hampden Park [4]	d				12 43					13 43				14 43					15 43				16 43		
Eastbourne [4]	a		12 29		12 49			13 29		13 49		14 29		14 49		15 29			15 49		16 29		16 49		17 29
	d		12 34		12 55			13 34		13 55		14 34		14 55		15 34			15 55		16 34		16 55		17 34
Hampden Park [4]	d		12 38					13 38				14 38				15 38					16 38				17 38
Polegate	d		12 42		13 02			13 42		14 02		14 42		15 02		15 42			16 02		16 42		17 02		17 42
Berwick	d		12 48					13 48				14 48				15 48					16 48				17 48
Glynde	d		12 53					13 53				14 53				15 53					16 53				17 53
Seaford	d	12 27		12 53		13 27			13 53		14 27		14 53		15 27			15 53		16 27		16 53		17 27	
Bishopstone	d	12 29		12 55		13 29			13 55		14 29		14 55		15 29			15 55		16 29		16 55		17 29	
Newhaven Harbour	d	12 32		12 58		13 32			13 58		14 32		14 58		15 32			15 58		16 32		16 58		17 32	
Newhaven Town ⛴	d	12 34		13 00		13 34			14 00		14 34		15 00		15 34			16 00		16 34		17 00		17 34	
Southease	d			13 04					14 04				15 04					16 04				17 04			
Lewes [4]	a	12 43	12 59	13 11	13 14	13 43		13 59	14 11	14 14	14 43	14 59	15 11	15 14	15 43	15 59		16 11	16 14	16 43	16 59	17 11	17 14	17 43	17 59
	d	12 44	13 00	13 18	13 16	13 44		14 00	14 18	14 16	14 44	15 00	15 18	15 16	15 44	16 00		16 18	16 16	16 44	17 00	17 18	17 16	17 44	18 00
Falmer	d	12 51		13 25		13 51			14 25		14 51		15 25		15 51			16 25		16 51		17 25		17 51	
Moulsecoomb	d	12 54		13 28		13 54			14 28		14 54		15 28		15 54			16 28		16 54		17 28		17 54	
London Road (Brighton)	d	12 56		13 30		13 56			14 30		14 56		15 30		15 56			16 30		16 56		17 30		17 56	
Brighton [10]	a	13 00	13 12	13 34		14 00		14 12	14 34		15 00	15 12	15 34		16 00	16 12		16 34		17 00	17 12	17 34		18 00	18 12
Cooksbridge	d																								
Plumpton	d																		16 24				17 24		
Wivelsfield [4]	a				13 31					14 31				15 31					16 31				17 31		
Haywards Heath [3]	a				13 35					14 35				15 35					16 35				17 35		
Gatwick Airport [10] ✈	a				13 52					14 52				15 52					16 52				17 52		
East Croydon 🚊	a				14 09					15 09				16 09					17 09				18 09		
London Bridge [4] ⊖	a																								
Clapham Junction [10]	a				14 24					15 24				16 24					17 24				18 24		
London Victoria [15] ⊖	a				14 31					15 31				16 31					17 31				18 31		

A 🛒 from Lewes

Table 189

Sundays

from 11 September

Ashford, Hastings, Eastbourne, Seaford and Lewes - Brighton, Haywards Heath and London

		SN ◇	SN ◇1 A 🚌	SN ◇	SN ◇	SN ◇	SN ◇1	SN ◇	SN ◇	SN ◇	SN ◇1	SN ◇	SN ◇	SN ◇	SN ◇1	SN ◇	SN ◇	SN ◇	SN ◇1	SN ◇	SN ◇	SN ◇
Ashford International	d				17 21				18 21				19 21				20 21				21 21	
Ham Street	d				17 30				18 30				19 30				20 30				21 30	
Appledore (Kent)	d				17 35				18 35				19 35				20 35				21 35	
Rye	a				17 44				18 44				19 44				20 44				21 44	
	d				17 45				18 45				19 45				20 45				21 45	
Winchelsea	d																					
Doleham	d																					
Three Oaks	d																					
Ore	d		17 14				18 14				19 14				20 14				21 14			
Hastings 4	a		17 17		18 02		18 17		19 02		19 17		20 02		20 17		21 02		21 17		22 02	
	d		17 18		18 03		18 18		19 03		19 18		20 03		20 18		21 03		21 18		22 03	
St Leonards Warrior Sq 4	d		17 21		18 06		18 21		19 06		19 21		20 06		20 21		21 06		21 21		22 06	
Bexhill 4	d		17 28		18 13		18 28		19 13		19 28		20 13		20 28		21 13		21 28		22 13	
Collington	d		17 30				18 30				19 30				20 30				21 30			
Cooden Beach	d		17 33				18 33				19 33				20 33				21 33			
Normans Bay	d																					
Pevensey Bay	d																					
Pevensey & Westham	d		17 39				18 39				19 39				20 39				21 39			
Hampden Park 4	d		17 43				18 43				19 43				20 43				21 43			
Eastbourne 4	a		17 49		18 29		18 49		19 29		19 49		20 29		20 49		21 29		21 49		22 29	
	d		17 55		18 34		18 55		19 34		19 55		20 34		20 55		21 34		21 59		22 34	
Hampden Park 4	d				18 38				19 38				20 38				21 38				22 38	
Polegate	d		18 02		18 42		19 02		19 42		20 02		20 42		21 02		21 42		22 06		22 42	
Berwick	d				18 48				19 48				20 48				21 48				22 48	
Glynde	d				18 53				19 53				20 53				21 53				22 53	
Seaford	d	17 53		18 27		18 53		19 27		19 53		20 27		20 53		21 27		21 53		22 27		22 53
Bishopstone	d	17 55		18 29		18 55		19 29		19 55		20 29		20 55		21 29		21 55		22 29		22 55
Newhaven Harbour	d	17 58		18 32		18 58		19 32		19 58		20 32		20 58		21 32		21 58		22 32		22 58
Newhaven Town ⛴	d	18 00		18 34		19 00		19 34		20 00		20 34		21 00		21 34		22 00		22 34		23 00
Southease	d	18 04				19 04				20 04												
Lewes 4	a	18 11	18 14	18 43	18 59	19 11	19 14	19 43	19 59	20 11	20 14	20 43	20 59	21 09	21 14	21 43	21 59	22 09	22 18	22 43	22 59	23 09
	d	18 18	18 16	18 44	19 00	19 18	19 16	19 44	20 00	20 18	20 16	20 44	21 00	21 18	21 16	21 44	22 00	22 10	22 19	22 44	23 00	23 10
Falmer	d	18 25		18 51		19 25		19 51		20 25		20 51		21 25		21 51		22 17	22 26	22 51		23 17
Moulsecoomb	d	18 28		18 54		19 28		19 54		20 28		20 54		21 28		21 54		22 20	22 29	22 54		23 20
London Road (Brighton)	d	18 30		18 56		19 30		19 56		20 30		20 56		21 30		21 56		22 22	22 31	22 56		23 22
Brighton 10	a	18 34		19 00	19 12	19 34		20 00	20 12	20 34		21 00	21 12	21 34		22 00	22 12	22 26	22 35	23 00	23 12	23 26
Cooksbridge	d																					
Plumpton	d		18 24				19 24				20 24				21 24							
Wivelsfield 4	a		18 31				19 31				20 31				21 31							
Haywards Heath 3	a		18 35				19 35				20 35				21 35							
Gatwick Airport 10 ✈	a		18 52				19 52				20 52				21 52							
East Croydon 🚋	a		19 09				20 09				21 09				22 09							
London Bridge 4 ⊖	a																					
Clapham Junction 10	a		19 24				20 24				21 24				22 24							
London Victoria 15 ⊖	a		19 31				20 31				21 31				22 31							

A 🚌 from Lewes

Table 189

Sundays
from 11 September

Ashford, Hastings, Eastbourne, Seaford and Lewes - Brighton, Haywards Heath and London

		SN	SN	SN
		◇1	◇	◇1
Ashford International	d		22 32	
Ham Street	d		22 41	
Appledore (Kent)	d		22 46	
Rye	a		22 55	
	d		22 55	
Winchelsea	d		22 58	
Doleham	d		23 05	
Three Oaks	d		23 08	
Ore	d	22 14	23 14	
Hastings 4	a	22 17	23 17	
	d	22 18		23 22
St Leonards Warrior Sq 4	d	22 21		23 24
Bexhill 4	d	22 28		23 31
Collington	d	22 30		23 33
Cooden Beach	d	22 33		23 36
Normans Bay	d			
Pevensey Bay	d			
Pevensey & Westham	d	22 39		23 42
Hampden Park 4	d	22 43		23 47
Eastbourne 4	a	22 49		23 52
	d	22 59		
Hampden Park 4	d			
Polegate	d	23 06		
Berwick	d			
Glynde	d			
Seaford	d			
Bishopstone	d			
Newhaven Harbour	d			
Newhaven Town ⛴	d			
Southease	d			
Lewes 4	a	23 18		
	d	23 19		
Falmer	d	23 26		
Moulsecoomb	d	23 29		
London Road (Brighton)	d	23 31		
Brighton 10	a	23 35		
Cooksbridge	d			
Plumpton	d			
Wivelsfield 4	a			
Haywards Heath 3	a			
Gatwick Airport 10 ✈	a			
East Croydon 🚋	a			
London Bridge 4 ⊖	a			
Clapham Junction 10	a			
London Victoria 15 ⊖	a			

Route Diagram for Table 194

HIGH SPEED SERVICES

DM-12/10
Design BAJS

© 2010 Network Rail.
All rights reserved

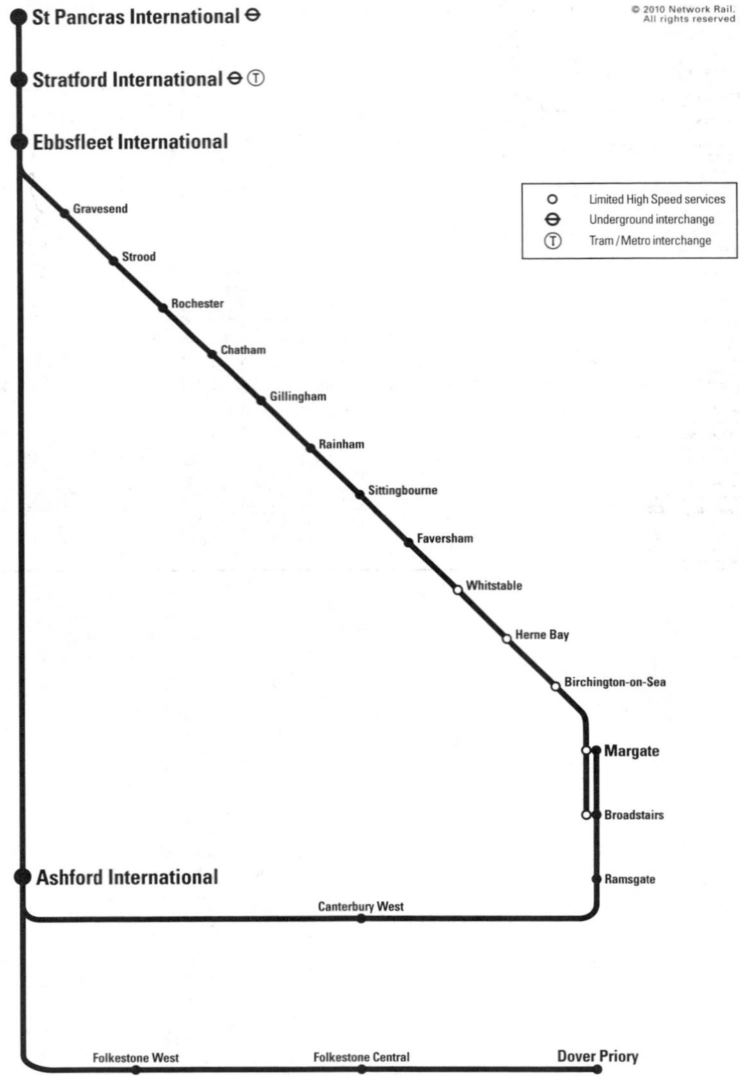

St Pancras International - Kent High Speed Domestic Services

Miles	Miles	Miles			SE	SE	SE	SE MO	SE MX	SE MX	SE	SE	SE	SE	SE	SE	SE	SE	SE	SE	SE	SE	SE	SE
—	—	—	**St Pancras International** [15] ⊖	d	22p55	23p12	23p25	23p42	23p55	00 12	06 25	06 40	06 55	07 10	07 25	07 40	07 55	08 10	08 22	08 40	08 58	09 10	09 25	09 37
6	6	6	**Stratford International** ⊖	d	23p02	23p19	23p32	23p49	00 02	00 19	06 32	06 47	07 02	07 17	07 32	07 47	08 02	08 17	08 29	08 47	09 05	09 17	09 32	09 44
22¾	22¾	22¾	**Ebbsfleet International**	a	23p12	23p30	23p42	23p59	00 12	00 30	06 42	06 58	07 12	07 28	07 42	07 59	08 12	08 29	08 39	08 59	09 15	09 28	09 42	09 55
—	—	—		d	23p13	23p31	23p43	00 01	00 13	00 31	06 42	06 59	07 13	07 29	07 43	08 00	08 13	08 30	08 43	09 00	09 16	09 29	09 43	09 56
24¾	—	—	Gravesend [4]	d	23p18		23p48		00 18		06 46		07 21		07 48		08 18		08 48		09 21		09 48	
32	—	—	Strood [4]	d	23p28		23p58		00 28		06 57		07 31		07 58		08 28		08 58		09 31		09 58	
—	—	—	Maidstone West	d							07a12													
33	—	—	Rochester [4]	d	23p33		00 03		00 33				07 36		08 03		08 33		09 03		09 36		10 03	
33½	—	—	Chatham [4]	d	23p35		00 05		00 35				07 38		08 05		08 35		09 05		09 38		10 05	
35¼	—	—	Gillingham (Kent) [4]	d	23p40		00 10		00 40				07 43		08 10		08 40		09 10		09 43		10 10	
38¼	—	—	Rainham (Kent)	d	23p45		00 15		00 45				07 48		08 15		08 45		09 15		09 48		10 15	
44	—	—	Sittingbourne [4]	d	23p53		00 23		00 53				07 57		08 23		08 53		09 23		09 55		10 23	
51¾	—	—	**Faversham** [2]	a	00 03		00 33		01 03				08 05		08 33		09 03		09 33		10 03		10 33	
58¾	—	—	Whitstable	d																				
62½	—	—	Herne Bay	d																				
70½	—	—	Birchington-on-Sea	d																				
73½	—	—	Margate [4]	d																				
76¾	—	—	**Broadstairs**	a																				
—	56	56	**Ashford International**	a		23p50		00 20		00 50		07 18		07 48		08 20		08 50		09 20		09 48		10 15
—	—	—		d		23p52						07 22		07 50		08 22		08 52		09 22		09 52		10 22
—	69¼	—	Folkestone West	d		00 05								08 03				09 05				10 05		
—	70	—	Folkestone Central	d		00 08								08 06				09 08				10 08		
—	77¼	—	**Dover Priory** [4]	a		00 20								08 18				09 20				10 20		
—	—	70¼	**Canterbury West** [4]	a								07 38				08 38				09 38				10 38
—	—	—		d								07 39				08 39				09 39				10 39
—	—	87¾	Ramsgate [4]	d								08 01				08 59				09 59				10 59
—	—	87¾	Broadstairs	d								08 06				09 05				10 05				11 05
—	—	91	**Margate** [4]	a								08 11				09 10				10 10				11 10

		SE	SE	SE	SE	SE	SE	SE	SE	SE	SE	SE	SE	SE	SE	SE	SE	SE	SE	SE	SE	SE
St Pancras International [15] ⊖	d	09 55	10 12	10 28	10 42	10 52	11 12	11 25	11 42	11 55	12 12	12 25	12 42	12 52	13 12	13 25	13 42	13 55	14 12	14 25	14 42	14 55
Stratford International ⊖	d	10 02	10 19	10 35	10 49	10 59	11 19	11 32	11 49	12 02	12 19	12 35	12 49	12 58	13 19	13 32	13 49	14 02	14 19	14 32	14 49	15 02
Ebbsfleet International	a	10 12	10 30	10 45	11 00	11 09	11 30	11 42	12 00	12 12	12 30	12 45	13 00	13 08	13 30	13 42	14 00	14 12	14 30	14 42	15 00	15 12
	d	10 13	10 31	10 46	11 01	11 13	11 31	11 43	12 01	12 13	12 31	12 46	13 01	13 13	13 31	13 43	14 01	14 13	14 31	14 43	15 01	15 13
Gravesend [4]	d	10 18		10 51		11 18		11 48		12 18		12 51		13 18		13 48		14 18		14 48		15 18
Strood [4]	d	10 28		11 01		11 28		11 58		12 28		13 01		13 28		13 58		14 28		14 58		15 28
Maidstone West	d																					
Rochester [4]	d	10 33		11 06		11 33		12 03		12 33		13 06		13 33		14 03		14 33		15 03		15 33
Chatham [4]	d	10 35		11 08		11 35		12 05		12 35		13 08		13 35		14 05		14 35		15 05		15 35
Gillingham (Kent) [4]	d	10 40		11 13		11 40		12 10		12 40		13 13		13 40		14 10		14 40		15 10		15 40
Rainham (Kent)	d	10 45		11 18		11 45		12 15		12 45		13 18		13 45		14 15		14 45		15 15		15 45
Sittingbourne [4]	d	10 53		11 25		11 53		12 23		12 53		13 25		13 53		14 23		14 53		15 23		15 53
Faversham [2]	a	11 03		11 33		12 03		12 33		13 03		13 33		14 03		14 33		15 03		15 33		16 03
Whitstable	d																					
Herne Bay	d																					
Birchington-on-Sea	d																					
Margate [4]	d																					
Broadstairs	a																					
Ashford International	a		10 50		11 20		11 50		12 20		12 50		13 20		13 50		14 20		14 50		15 20	
	d		10 52		11 22		11 52		12 22		12 52		13 22		13 52		14 22		14 52		15 22	
Folkestone West	d		11 05				12 05				13 05				14 05				15 05			
Folkestone Central	d		11 08				12 08				13 08				14 08				15 08			
Dover Priory [4]	a		11 20				12 20				13 20				14 20				15 20			
Canterbury West [4]	a				11 38				12 38				13 38				14 38				15 38	
	d				11 39				12 39				13 39				14 39				15 39	
Ramsgate [4]	d				11 59				12 59				13 59				14 59				15 59	
Broadstairs	d				12 05				13 05				14 05				15 05				16 05	
Margate [4]	a				12 10				13 10				14 10				15 10				16 10	

		SE	SE	SE	SE	SE	SE	SE	SE	SE		SE	SE	SE	SE		SE	SE	SE	SE		SE	SE
St Pancras International [15] ⊖	d	15 12	15 25	15 42	15 55	16 10	16 25	16 42	16 55	17 10		17 14	17 18	17 27	17 40		17 44	17 48	17 55	18 10		18 14	18 18
Stratford International ⊖	d	15 19	15 32	15 49	16 02	16 17	16 32	16 49	17 02	17 17		17 21	17 25	17 38	17 47		17 51	17 55	18 02	18 17		18 21	18 25
Ebbsfleet International	a	15 30	15 42	16 00	16 12	16 28	16 42	17 00	17 12				17 35	17 48				18 05	18 12				18 35
	d	15 31	15 43	16 01	16 13	16 29	16 43	17 01	17 13					17 49					18 13				
Gravesend [4]	d		15 48		16 18		16 48		17 18			17 36					18 06					18 38	
Strood [4]	d		15 58		16 28		16 58		17 28			17 46					18 16					18 49	
Maidstone West	d											18a02					18a32					19a05	
Rochester [4]	d		16 03		16 33		17 03		17 33					18 05					18 31				
Chatham [4]	d		16 05		16 35		17 05		17 35					18 08					18 34				
Gillingham (Kent) [4]	d		16 10		16 40		17 10		17 40					18 13					18 39				
Rainham (Kent)	d		16 15		16 45		17 15		17 45					18 18					18 44				
Sittingbourne [4]	d		16 23		16 53		17 23		17 55					18 25					18 52				
Faversham [2]	a		16 33		17 03		17 33		18 03					18 33					19 00				
Whitstable	d													18 43					19 09				
Herne Bay	d													18 49					19 15				
Birchington-on-Sea	d													18 58					19 24				
Margate [4]	d													19 04					19 30				
Broadstairs	a													19 10					19 36				
Ashford International	a	15 50		16 20		16 48		17 20		17 46					18 16					18 46			
	d	15 52		16 22		16 52		17 23		17 50	17 53				18 20	18 23				18 50	18 53		
Folkestone West	d	16 05				17 05				18 03					18 33					19 05			
Folkestone Central	d	16 08				17 08				18 06					18 36					19 08			
Dover Priory [4]	a	16 20				17 20				18 18					18 48					19 20			
Canterbury West [4]	a			16 38				17 39			18 09					18 39					19 09		
	d			16 39				17 40			18 10					18 40					19 10		
Ramsgate [4]	d			16 59				17 59			18 29					18 59					19 31		
Broadstairs	d			17 05				18 05			18 35					19 05					19 36		
Margate [4]	a			17 10				18 10			18 40					19 10					19 41		

St Pancras International - Kent High Speed Domestic Services

		SE	SE		SE	SE	SE	SE	SE		SE	SE	SE	SE	SE	SE	SE	SE	SE	SE		SE	SE	SE	SE
St Pancras International 15 ⊖	d	18 25	18 40		18 48	18 55	19 12	19 25	19 42		19 55	20 12	20 25	20 42	20 55	21 12	21 25	21 42	21 55	22 12		22 25	22 42	22 55	23 12
Stratford International ⊖	d	18 32	18 47		18 55	19 02	19 19	19 32	19 49		20 02	20 19	20 32	20 49	21 02	21 19	21 32	21 49	22 02	22 19		22 32	22 49	23 02	23 19
Ebbsfleet International	a	18 42			19 05	19 12	19 30	19 42	20 00		20 12	20 30	20 42	21 00	21 12	21 30	21 42	22 00	22 12	22 30		22 42	23 00	23 12	23 30
	d	18 43				19 13	19 31	19 45	20 01		20 13	20 31	20 43	21 01	21 13	21 31	21 43	22 01	22 13	22 31		22 43	23 01	23 13	23 31
Gravesend 4	d					19 20		19 51			20 18		20 48		21 18		21 48		22 18			22 48		23 18	
Strood 4	d					19 30		20 01			20 28		20 58		21 28		21 58		22 28			22 58		23 28	
Maidstone West	d																								
Rochester 4	d	19 03				19 35		20 08			20 33		21 03		21 33		22 03		22 33			23 03		23 33	
Chatham 4	d	19 07				19 38		20 10			20 35		21 05		21 35		22 05		22 35			23 05		23 35	
Gillingham (Kent) 4	d	19 13				19 43		20 15			20 40		21 10		21 40		22 10		22 40			23 10		23 40	
Rainham (Kent)	d	19 18				19 48		20 20			20 45		21 15		21 45		22 15		22 45			23 15		23 45	
Sittingbourne 4	d	19 28				19 58		20 27			20 53		21 23		21 53		22 23		22 53			23 23		23 53	
Faversham 2	a	19 36				20 07		20 36			21 03		21 33		22 03		22 33		23 03			23 33		00 03	
Whitstable	d	19 46																							
Herne Bay	d	19 52																							
Birchington-on-Sea	d	20 01																							
Margate 4	d	20 07																							
Broadstairs	a	20 14																							
Ashford International	a		19 16				19 50		20 20			20 50		21 20		21 50		22 20		22 50			23 20		23 50
	d		19 20	19 23			19 53		20 22			20 52		21 22		21 52		22 22		22 52			23 22		23 52
Folkestone West	d		19 33				20 06					21 05				22 05				23 05					00 05
Folkestone Central	d		19 36				20 09					21 08				22 08				23 08					00 08
Dover Priory 4	a		19 47				20 21					21 20				22 20				23 20					00 20
Canterbury West 4	a			19 39					20 38					21 38				22 38					23 38		
	d			19 40					20 39					21 39				22 39					23 39		
Ramsgate 4	d			19 59					21 00					21 59				22 59					23a59		
Broadstairs	d			20 05					21 05					22 05				23 05							
Margate 4	a			20 10					21 11					22 10				23 10							

		SE	SE
St Pancras International 15 ⊖	d	23 25	23 55
Stratford International ⊖	d	23 32	00 02
Ebbsfleet International	a	23 42	00 12
	d	23 43	00 13
Gravesend 4	d	23 48	00 18
Strood 4	d	23 58	00 28
Maidstone West	d		
Rochester 4	d	00 03	00 33
Chatham 4	d	00 05	00 35
Gillingham (Kent) 4	d	00 10	00 40
Rainham (Kent)	d	00 15	00 45
Sittingbourne 4	d	00 23	00 53
Faversham 2	a	00 33	01 03
Whitstable	d		
Herne Bay	d		
Birchington-on-Sea	d		
Margate 4	d		
Broadstairs	a		
Ashford International	a		
	d		
Folkestone West	d		
Folkestone Central	d		
Dover Priory 4	a		
Canterbury West 4	a		
	d		
Ramsgate 4	d		
Broadstairs	d		
Margate 4	a		

Saturdays

		SE	SE	SE	SE	SE	SE	SE	SE	SE	SE		SE	SE	SE	SE	SE	SE	SE	SE	SE	SE		SE	SE
St Pancras International 15 ⊖	d	22p55	23p12	23p25	23p55	00 12	06 12	06 40	06 55	07 12	07 28		07 42	07 52	08 12	08 25	08 42	08 52	09 10	09 25	09 37	09 55		10 12	10 28
Stratford International ⊖	d	23p02	23p19	23p32	00 02	00 19	06 19	06 47	07 06	07 19	07 35		07 49	07 58	08 19	08 32	08 49	08 58	09 17	09 32	09 44	10 02		10 19	10 35
Ebbsfleet International	a	23p12	23p30	23p42	00 12	00 30	06 30	06 58	07 16	07 30	07 45		08 00	08 08	08 30	08 42	09 00	09 08	09 28	09 42	09 55	10 12		10 30	10 45
	d	23p13	23p31	23p43	00 13	00 31	06 31	06 59	07 17	07 31	07 46		08 01	08 13	08 31	08 43	09 01	09 13	09 29	09 43	09 56	10 13		10 31	10 46
Gravesend 4	d	23p18		23p48	00 18				07 21		07 51			08 18		08 48		09 18		09 48		10 18			10 51
Strood 4	d	23p28		23p58	00 28				07 31		08 01			08 28		08 58		09 28		09 58		10 28			11 01
Maidstone West	d																								
Rochester 4	d	23p33		00 03	00 33				07 36		08 06			08 33		09 03		09 33		10 03		10 33			11 06
Chatham 4	d	23p35		00 05	00 35				07 38		08 08			08 35		09 05		09 35		10 05		10 35			11 08
Gillingham (Kent) 4	d	23p40		00 10	00 40				07 43		08 13			08 40		09 10		09 40		10 10		10 40			11 13
Rainham (Kent)	d	23p45		00 15	00 45				07 48		08 18			08 45		09 15		09 45		10 15		10 45			11 18
Sittingbourne 4	d	23p53		00 23	00 53				07 55		08 25			08 53		09 23		09 53		10 23		10 53			11 25
Faversham 2	a	00 03		00 33	01 03				08 04		08 33			09 03		09 33		10 03		10 33		11 03			11 34
Whitstable	d																								
Herne Bay	d																								
Birchington-on-Sea	d																								
Margate 4	d																								
Broadstairs	a																								
Ashford International	a		23p50			00 50	06 50	07 18		07 51			08 20		08 50		09 20		09 48		10 15			10 50	
	d		23p52				06 52	07 22		07 52			08 22		08 52		09 22		09 52		10 22			10 52	
Folkestone West	d		00 05				07 05			08 05					09 05				10 05					11 05	
Folkestone Central	d		00 08				07 08			08 08					09 08				10 08					11 08	
Dover Priory 4	a		00 20				07 20			08 20					09 20				10 20					11 20	
Canterbury West 4	a							07 38					08 38				09 38				10 38				
	d							07 39					08 39				09 39				10 39				
Ramsgate 4	d							07 59					08 59				09 59				10 59				
Broadstairs	d							08 05					09 05				10 05				11 05				
Margate 4	a							08 10					09 10				10 10				11 10				

Table 194

Saturdays

St Pancras International - Kent High Speed Domestic Services

		SE	SE	SE	SE	SE	SE	SE	SE	SE	SE	SE	SE	SE	SE	SE	SE	SE	SE	SE	SE	SE	SE
St Pancras International [15] ⊖	d	10 42	10 52	11 12	11 28	11 42	11 55	12 12	12 25	12 42	12 55	13 12	13 25	13 42	13 55	14 12	14 25	14 42	14 55	15 12	15 25	15 42	15 55
Stratford International ⊖	d	10 49	10 58	11 19	11 35	11 49	12 02	12 19	12 36	12 49	13 06	13 19	13 32	13 49	14 02	14 19	14 32	14 49	15 02	15 19	15 32	15 49	16 02
Ebbsfleet International	a	11 00	11 08	11 30	11 45	12 00	12 12	12 30	12 46	13 00	13 16	13 30	13 42	14 00	14 12	14 30	14 42	15 00	15 12	15 30	15 42	16 00	16 12
	d	11 01	11 13	11 31	11 46	12 01	12 13	12 31	12 47	13 01	13 17	13 31	13 43	14 01	14 13	14 31	14 43	15 01	15 13	15 31	15 43	16 01	16 13
Gravesend [4]	d		11 18		11 51		12 18		12 51		13 22		13 48		14 18		14 48		15 18		15 48		16 18
Strood [4]	d		11 28		12 01		12 28		13 01		13 32		13 58		14 28		14 58		15 28		15 58		16 28
Maidstone West	d																						
Rochester [4]	d		11 33		12 06		12 33		13 06		13 37		14 03		14 33		15 03		15 33		16 03		16 33
Chatham [4]	d		11 35		12 08		12 35		13 08		13 39		14 05		14 35		15 05		15 35		16 05		16 35
Gillingham (Kent) [4]	d		11 40		12 13		12 40		13 13		13 44		14 10		14 40		15 10		15 40		16 10		16 40
Rainham (Kent)	d		11 45		12 18		12 45		13 18		13 49		14 15		14 45		15 15		15 45		16 15		16 45
Sittingbourne [4]	d		11 53		12 25		12 53		13 25		13 56		14 23		14 53		15 23		15 53		16 23		16 53
Faversham [2]	a		12 03		12 33		13 03		13 34		14 04		14 33		15 03		15 33		16 03		16 33		17 03
Whitstable	d																						
Herne Bay	d																						
Birchington-on-Sea	d																						
Margate [4]	d																						
Broadstairs	a																						
Ashford International	a	11 20		11 50		12 20		12 50		13 20		13 50		14 20		14 50		15 20		15 50		16 20	
	d	11 22		11 52		12 22		12 52		13 22		13 52		14 22		14 52		15 22		15 52		16 22	
Folkestone West	d			12 05				13 05				14 05				15 05				16 05			
Folkestone Central	d			12 08				13 08				14 08				15 08				16 08			
Dover Priory [4]	a			12 20				13 20				14 20				15 20				16 20			
Canterbury West [4]	a	11 38				12 38				13 38				14 38				15 38				16 38	
	d	11 39				12 39				13 39				14 39				15 39				16 39	
Ramsgate [4]	d	11 59				12 59				13 59				14 59				15 59				16 59	
Broadstairs	d	12 05				13 05				14 05				15 05				16 05				17 05	
Margate [4]	a	12 10				13 10				14 10				15 10				16 10				17 10	

		SE	SE	SE	SE	SE	SE	SE	SE	SE	SE	SE	SE	SE	SE	SE	SE	SE	SE	SE	SE	SE	SE
St Pancras International [15] ⊖	d	16 10	16 25	16 42	16 55	17 12	17 25	17 42	17 55	18 12	18 25	18 42	18 55	19 12	19 25	19 42	19 55	20 12	20 25	20 42	20 55	21 12	21 25
Stratford International ⊖	d	16 17	16 32	16 49	17 02	17 19	17 32	17 49	18 02	18 19	18 32	18 49	19 02	19 19	19 32	19 49	20 02	20 19	20 32	20 49	21 02	21 19	21 32
Ebbsfleet International	a	16 28	16 42	17 00	17 12	17 30	17 42	18 00	18 12	18 30	18 42	19 00	19 12	19 30	19 42	20 00	20 12	20 30	20 42	21 00	21 12	21 30	21 42
	d	16 29	16 43	17 01	17 13	17 31	17 43	18 01	18 13	18 31	18 43	19 01	19 13	19 31	19 43	20 01	20 13	20 31	20 43	21 01	21 13	21 31	21 43
Gravesend [4]	d		16 48		17 18		17 48		18 18		18 48		19 18		19 48		20 18		20 48		21 18		21 48
Strood [4]	d		16 58		17 28		17 58		18 28		18 58		19 28		19 58		20 28		20 58		21 28		21 58
Maidstone West	d																						
Rochester [4]	d		17 03		17 33		18 03		18 33		19 03		19 33		20 03		20 33		21 03		21 33		22 03
Chatham [4]	d		17 05		17 35		18 05		18 35		19 05		19 35		20 05		20 35		21 05		21 35		22 05
Gillingham (Kent) [4]	d		17 10		17 40		18 10		18 40		19 10		19 40		20 10		20 40		21 10		21 40		22 10
Rainham (Kent)	d		17 15		17 45		18 15		18 45		19 15		19 45		20 15		20 45		21 15		21 45		22 15
Sittingbourne [4]	d		17 23		17 53		18 23		18 53		19 23		19 53		20 23		20 53		21 23		21 53		22 23
Faversham [2]	a		17 33		18 03		18 33		19 03		19 33		20 03		20 33		21 03		21 33		22 03		22 31
Whitstable	d																						
Herne Bay	d																						
Birchington-on-Sea	d																						
Margate [4]	d																						
Broadstairs	a																						
Ashford International	a	16 48		17 20		17 50		18 20		18 50		19 20		19 50		20 20		20 50		21 20		21 50	
	d	16 52		17 22		17 52		18 22		18 52		19 22		19 52		20 22		20 52		21 22		21 52	
Folkestone West	d	17 05				18 05				19 05				20 05				21 05				22 05	
Folkestone Central	d	17 08				18 08				19 08				20 08				21 08				22 08	
Dover Priory [4]	a	17 20				18 20				19 20				20 20				21 20				22 20	
Canterbury West [4]	a			17 38				18 38				19 38				20 38				21 38			
	d			17 39				18 39				19 39				20 39				21 39			
Ramsgate [4]	d			17 59				18 59				19 59				20 59				21 59			
Broadstairs	d			18 05				19 05				20 05				21 05				22 05			
Margate [4]	a			18 10				19 10				20 10				21 10				22 10			

		SE	SE	SE	SE	SE	SE	SE	SE	SE
St Pancras International [15] ⊖	d	21 42	21 55	22 12	22 25	22 42	22 55	23 12	23 25	23 55
Stratford International ⊖	d	21 49	22 02	22 19	22 32	22 49	23 02	23 19	23 32	00 02
Ebbsfleet International	a	22 00	22 12	22 30	22 42	23 00	23 12	23 30	23 42	00 12
	d	22 01	22 13	22 31	22 43	23 01	23 13	23 31	23 43	00 13
Gravesend [4]	d		22 18		22 48		23 18		23 48	00 18
Strood [4]	d		22 28		22 58		23 28		23 58	00 28
Maidstone West	d									
Rochester [4]	d		22 33		23 03		23 33		00 03	00 33
Chatham [4]	d		22 35		23 05		23 35		00 05	00 35
Gillingham (Kent) [4]	d		22 40		23 10		23 40		00 10	00 40
Rainham (Kent)	d		22 45		23 15		23 45		00 15	00 45
Sittingbourne [4]	d		22 53		23 23		23 53		00 23	00 53
Faversham [2]	a		23 01		23 31		00 01		00 31	01 01
Whitstable	d									
Herne Bay	d									
Birchington-on-Sea	d									
Margate [4]	d									
Broadstairs	a									
Ashford International	a	22 20		22 50		23 20		23 50		
	d	22 22		22 52		23 22		23 52		
Folkestone West	d			23 05				00 05		
Folkestone Central	d			23 08				00 08		
Dover Priory [4]	a			23 20				00 20		
Canterbury West [4]	a	22 38				23 38				
	d	22 39				23 39				
Ramsgate [4]	d	22 59				23a59				
Broadstairs	d	23 05								
Margate [4]	a	23 10								

Table 194

Sundays

St Pancras International - Kent High Speed Domestic Services

		SE A	SE A	SE A	SE A	SE	SE	SE	SE	SE	SE		SE	SE	SE	SE	SE	SE	SE	SE	SE	SE		SE	SE
St Pancras International [15] ⊖	d	22p55	23p12	23p25	23p55	00 12	08 42	08 52	09 10	09 25	09 37		09 55	10 12	10 28	10 42	10 52	11 12	11 25	11 42	11 52	12 12		12 25	12 42
Stratford International ⊖	d	23p02	23p19	23p32	00 02	00 19	08 49	08 58	09 17	09 32	09 44		10 02	10 19	10 35	10 49	10 58	11 19	11 32	11 49	11 58	12 19		12 36	12 49
Ebbsfleet International	a	23p12	23p30	23p42	00 12	00 30	09 00	09 08	09 28	09 42	09 55		10 12	10 30	10 45	11 00	11 09	11 30	11 42	12 00	12 08	12 30		12 46	13 00
	d	23p13	23p31	23p43	00 13	00 31	09 01	09 13	09 29	09 43	09 56		10 13	10 31	10 46	11 01	11 14	11 31	11 43	12 01	12 13	12 31		12 47	13 01
Gravesend [4]	d	23p18		23p48	00 18			09 18		09 48			10 18		10 51		11 18		11 48		12 18			12 51	
Strood [4]	d	23p28		23p58	00 28			09 28		09 58			10 28		11 01		11 28		11 58		12 28			13 01	
Maidstone West	d																								
Rochester [4]	d	23p33		00 03	00 33			09 33		10 03			10 33		11 06		11 33		12 03		12 33			13 06	
Chatham [4]	d	23p35		00 05	00 35			09 35		10 05			10 35		11 08		11 35		12 05		12 35			13 08	
Gillingham (Kent) [4]	d	23p40		00 10	00 40			09 40		10 10			10 40		11 13		11 40		12 10		12 40			13 13	
Rainham (Kent)	d	23p45		00 15	00 45			09 45		10 15			10 45		11 18		11 45		12 15		12 45			13 18	
Sittingbourne [4]	d	23p53		00 23	00 53			09 53		10 23			10 53		11 25		11 53		12 23		12 53			13 25	
Faversham [2]	a	00 01		00 31	01 01			10 01		10 33			11 03		11 33		12 03		12 33		13 01			13 33	
Whitstable	d																								
Herne Bay	d																								
Birchington-on-Sea	d																								
Margate [4]	d																								
Broadstairs	a																								
Ashford International	a		23p50			00 50	09 20		09 48		10 15			10 50		11 20		11 50		12 20		12 50			13 20
	d		23p52				09 22		09 52		10 22			10 52		11 22		11 52		12 22		12 52			13 22
Folkestone West	d		00 05						10 05					11 05				12 05				13 05			
Folkestone Central	d		00 08						10 08					11 08				12 08				13 08			
Dover Priory [4]	a		00 20						10 20					11 20				12 20				13 20			
Canterbury West [4]	a						09 38				10 38					11 38				12 38					13 38
	d						09 39				10 39					11 39				12 39					13 39
Ramsgate [4]	d						09 59				10 59					11 59				12 59					13 59
Broadstairs	d						10 05				11 05					12 05				13 05					14 05
Margate [4]	a						10 10				11 10					12 10				13 10					14 10

		SE	SE	SE	SE	SE	SE	SE	SE		SE	SE	SE	SE	SE	SE	SE	SE	SE	SE		SE	SE	SE	SE
St Pancras International [15] ⊖	d	12 55	13 12	13 25	13 42	13 55	14 12	14 25	14 42		14 55	15 12	15 25	15 42	15 55	16 10	16 25	16 42	16 55	17 12		17 25	17 42	17 55	18 12
Stratford International ⊖	d	13 02	13 19	13 32	13 49	14 02	14 19	14 32	14 49		15 02	15 19	15 32	15 49	16 02	16 17	16 32	16 49	17 02	17 19		17 32	17 49	18 02	18 19
Ebbsfleet International	a	13 12	13 30	13 42	14 00	14 12	14 30	14 42	15 00		15 12	15 30	15 42	16 00	16 12	16 28	16 42	17 00	17 12	17 30		17 42	18 00	18 12	18 30
	d	13 13	13 31	13 43	14 01	14 13	14 31	14 43	15 01		15 13	15 31	15 43	16 01	16 13	16 29	16 43	17 01	17 13	17 31		17 43	18 01	18 13	18 31
Gravesend [4]	d	13 18		13 48		14 18		14 48			15 18		15 48		16 18		16 48		17 18			17 48		18 18	
Strood [4]	d	13 28		13 58		14 28		14 58			15 28		15 58		16 28		16 58		17 28			17 58		18 28	
Maidstone West	d																								
Rochester [4]	d	13 33		14 03		14 33		15 03			15 33		16 03		16 33		17 03		17 33			18 03		18 33	
Chatham [4]	d	13 35		14 05		14 35		15 05			15 35		16 05		16 35		17 05		17 35			18 05		18 35	
Gillingham (Kent) [4]	d	13 40		14 10		14 40		15 10			15 40		16 10		16 40		17 10		17 40			18 10		18 40	
Rainham (Kent)	d	13 45		14 15		14 45		15 15			15 45		16 15		16 45		17 15		17 45			18 15		18 45	
Sittingbourne [4]	d	13 53		14 23		14 53		15 23			15 53		16 23		16 53		17 23		17 53			18 23		18 53	
Faversham [2]	a	14 03		14 33		15 03		15 33			16 03		16 33		17 03		17 33		18 03			18 33		19 03	
Whitstable	d																								
Herne Bay	d																								
Birchington-on-Sea	d																								
Margate [4]	d																								
Broadstairs	a																								
Ashford International	a		13 50		14 20		14 50		15 20			15 50		16 20		16 48		17 20		17 50			18 20		18 50
	d		13 52		14 22		14 52		15 22			15 52		16 22		16 52		17 22		17 52			18 22		18 52
Folkestone West	d		14 05				15 05					16 05				17 05				18 05					19 05
Folkestone Central	d		14 08				15 08					16 08				17 08				18 08					19 08
Dover Priory [4]	a		14 20				15 20					16 20				17 20				18 20					19 20
Canterbury West [4]	a				14 38				15 38					16 38				17 38					18 38		
	d				14 39				15 39					16 39				17 39					18 39		
Ramsgate [4]	d				14 59				15 59					16 59				17 59					18 59		
Broadstairs	d				15 05				16 05					17 05				18 05					19 05		
Margate [4]	a				15 10				16 10					17 10				18 10					19 10		

		SE	SE	SE	SE	SE	SE		SE	SE	SE	SE	SE	SE	SE	SE	SE	SE		SE	SE	SE	SE	SE	SE
St Pancras International [15] ⊖	d	18 28	18 42	18 55	19 12	19 25	19 42		19 55	20 12	20 25	20 42	20 55	21 12	21 25	21 42	21 55	22 12		22 25	22 42	22 55	23 12	23 25	23 42
Stratford International ⊖	d	18 35	18 49	19 02	19 19	19 32	19 49		20 02	20 19	20 32	20 49	21 02	21 19	21 32	21 49	22 02	22 19		22 32	22 49	23 02	23 19	23 32	23 49
Ebbsfleet International	a	18 45	19 00	19 12	19 30	19 42	20 00		20 12	20 30	20 42	21 00	21 12	21 30	21 42	22 01	22 12	22 30		22 42	23 00	23 12	23 30	23 42	23 59
	d	18 46	19 01	19 13	19 31	19 43	20 01		20 13	20 31	20 43	21 01	21 13	21 31	21 43	22 01	22 13	22 31		22 43	23 01	23 13	23 31	23 43	00 01
Gravesend [4]	d	18 51		19 18		19 48			20 18		20 48		21 18		21 48		22 18			22 48		23 18		23 48	
Strood [4]	d	19 01		19 28		19 58			20 28		20 58		21 28		21 58		22 28			22 58		23 28		23 58	
Maidstone West	d																								
Rochester [4]	d	19 06		19 33		20 03			20 33		21 03		21 33		22 03		22 33			23 03		23 33		00 03	
Chatham [4]	d	19 08		19 35		20 05			20 35		21 05		21 35		22 05		22 35			23 05		23 35		00 05	
Gillingham (Kent) [4]	d	19 13		19 40		20 10			20 40		21 10		21 40		22 10		22 40			23 10		23 40		00 10	
Rainham (Kent)	d	19 18		19 45		20 15			20 45		21 15		21 45		22 15		22 45			23 15		23 45		00 15	
Sittingbourne [4]	d	19 25		19 53		20 23			20 53		21 23		21 53		22 23		22 53			23 23		23 53		00 23	
Faversham [2]	a	19 34		20 03		20 33			21 03		21 33		22 03		22 33		23 03			23 31		00 03		00 33	
Whitstable	d																								
Herne Bay	d																								
Birchington-on-Sea	d																								
Margate [4]	d																								
Broadstairs	a																								
Ashford International	a		19 20		19 50		20 20			20 50		21 20		21 50		22 21		22 50			23 20		23 50		00 20
	d		19 22		19 52		20 22			20 52		21 22		21 52		22 22		22 52			23 22		23 52		
Folkestone West	d				20 05					21 05				22 05				23 05					00 05		
Folkestone Central	d				20 08					21 08				22 08				23 08					00 08		
Dover Priory [4]	a				20 20					21 20				22 20				23 20					00 20		
Canterbury West [4]	a		19 38				20 38					21 38				22 38					23 38				
	d		19 39				20 39					21 39				22 39					23 39				
Ramsgate [4]	d		19 59				20 59					21 59				22 59					23a59				
Broadstairs	d		20 05				21 05					22 05				23 05									
Margate [4]	a		20 10				21 10					22 10				23 10									

A not 22 May

Table 194

Mondays to Fridays

Kent - St Pancras International High Speed Domestic Services

Miles	Miles	Miles			SE	SE	SE	SE	SE	SE	SE	SE	SE	SE		SE	SE	SE	SE	SE	SE	SE	SE	SE	SE
—	—	0	Margate [4]	d							05 47											06 44			
—	—	3¼	Broadstairs	d							05 54											06 50			
—	—	5½	Ramsgate [4]	d			05 00				06 00						06 26					06 56			
—	0	—	**Dover Priory**	d					05 44			06 12						06 38					07 08		
—	7¼	—	Folkestone Central	d					05 56			06 24						06 50					07 20		
—	8	—	Folkestone West	d					05 58			06 26						06 52					07 22		
—	21¼	—	**Ashford International**	a			05 41		06 11		06 36	06 39					07 03	07 06				07 32	07 35		
—	—	—																							
—	—	—		d	05 13		05 43		06 13		06 43						07 13					07 43			
0	—	—	**Broadstairs**	d										06 00						06 30					07 00
3¼	—	—	Margate [4]	d										06 05						06 35					07 05
6¼	—	—	Birchington-on-Sea	d										06 10						06 40					07 10
14¼	—	—	Herne Bay	d										06 19						06 49					07 19
18¼	—	—	Whitstable	d										06 25						06 55					07 25
25	—	—	**Faversham [2]**	a										06 33						07 03					07 33
—	—	—		d		04 56		05 28		05 58				06 34						07 04					07 34
32¾	—	—	Sittingbourne [4]	d		05 07		05 37		06 06				06 42						07 12					07 42
38½	—	—	Rainham (Kent)	d		05 15		05 45		06 14				06 50						07 20					07 50
41½	—	—	Gillingham (Kent) [4]	d		05 20		05 50		06 19				06 55						07 25					07 55
43¼	—	—	Chatham [4]	d		05 24		05 54		06 24				07 00						07 30					08 00
43¾	—	—	Rochester [4]	d		05 27		05 57		06 26				07 02						07 32					08 02
—	—	—	Maidstone West	d												06 56					07 26				
44¾	—	—	Strood [4]	d		05 32		06 02		06 32						07 12					07 42				
52	—	—	Gravesend	d		05 43		06 13		06 43						07 22					07 52				
54	54½	68¼	**Ebbsfleet International**	a	05 32	05 47	06 02	06 17	06 32	06 47				07 17		07 25				07 47					08 17
—	—	—		d	05 33	05 48	06 03	06 18	06 33	06 48			07 06	07 18		07 25			07 34	07 48				08 04	08 18
70¾	71¼	85	**Stratford International** ⊖	a	05 44	05 59	06 15	06 29	06 44	06 59	07 11		07 18	07 29		07 37	07 41		07 45	07 59	08 06	08 11		08 15	08 29
76¾	77¼	91	**St Pancras International [4]** ⊖	a	05 51	06 06	06 23	06 36	06 53	07 07	07 18		07 25	07 36		07 44	07 48		07 52	08 06	08 13	08 19		08 22	08 36

			SE	SE	SE	SE	SE	SE	SE	SE	SE	SE		SE	SE	SE	SE	SE	SE	SE	SE	SE	SE		SE
Margate [4]	d							07 49				08 53					09 53				10 53				
Broadstairs	d							07 55				08 59					09 59				10 59				
Ramsgate [4]	d			07 26				08 01				09 05					10 05				11 05				
Dover Priory	d				07 38					08 44					09 44				10 44				11 44		
Folkestone Central	d				07 50					08 56					09 56				10 56				11 56		
Folkestone West	d				07 52					08 58					09 58				10 58				11 58		
Ashford International	a			08 03	08 06			08 41		09 11		09 41			10 11		10 41		11 11		11 41		12 11		
	d			08 13				08 43		09 13		09 43			10 13		10 43		11 13		11 43		12 13		
Broadstairs	d																								
Margate [4]	d																								
Birchington-on-Sea	d																								
Herne Bay	d																								
Whitstable	d																								
Faversham [2]	a																								
	d						07 58		08 28		08 58			09 28		09 58		10 28		10 58		11 28			11 58
Sittingbourne [4]	d						08 06		08 37		09 07			09 37		10 07		10 37		11 07		11 37			12 07
Rainham (Kent)	d						08 14		08 45		09 15			09 45		10 15		10 45		11 15		11 45			12 15
Gillingham (Kent) [4]	d						08 19		08 50		09 20			09 50		10 20		10 50		11 20		11 50			12 20
Chatham [4]	d						08 24		08 54		09 24			09 54		10 24		10 54		11 24		11 54			12 24
Rochester [4]	d						08 26		08 57		09 27			09 57		10 27		10 57		11 27		11 57			12 27
Maidstone West	d		07 56																						
Strood [4]	d		08 12				08 32		09 02		09 32			10 02		10 32		11 02		11 32		12 02			12 32
Gravesend	d		08 22				08 43		09 13		09 43			10 12		10 43		11 13		11 43		12 13			12 43
Ebbsfleet International	a		08 26				08 47	09 02	09 17	09 32	09 47	10 02		10 16	10 32	10 47	11 02	11 17	11 32	11 47	12 02	12 17	12 32		12 47
	d		08 26			08 34	08 48	09 03	09 18	09 33	09 48	10 03		10 17	10 33	10 48	11 03	11 18	11 33	11 48	12 03	12 21	12 33		12 48
Stratford International ⊖	a		08 36	08 41		08 45	08 59	09 14	09 29	09 44	09 59	10 14		10 27	10 44	10 59	11 14	11 29	11 44	11 59	12 14	12 32	12 45		12 59
St Pancras International [4] ⊖	a		08 43	08 48		08 52	09 07	09 21	09 40	09 51	10 06	10 21		10 38	10 51	11 06	11 21	11 36	11 51	12 06	12 21	12 39	12 54		13 06

		SE	SE	SE	SE	SE	SE	SE	SE	SE		SE	SE	SE	SE	SE	SE	SE	SE	SE	SE		SE	SE	SE
Margate [4]	d	11 53				12 53				13 53					14 53				15 53					16 53	
Broadstairs	d	11 59				12 59				13 59					14 59				15 59					16 59	
Ramsgate [4]	d	12 05				13 05				14 05					15 05				16 05					17 05	
Dover Priory	d			12 44				13 44					14 44				15 44				16 44				
Folkestone Central	d			12 56				13 56					14 56				15 56				16 56				
Folkestone West	d			12 58				13 58					14 58				15 58				16 58				
Ashford International	a	12 41		13 11		13 41		14 11		14 41			15 11		15 41		16 11		16 41		17 11			17 41	
	d	12 43		13 13		13 43		14 13		14 43			15 13		15 43		16 13		16 43		17 13			17 43	
Broadstairs	d																								
Margate [4]	d																								
Birchington-on-Sea	d																								
Herne Bay	d																								
Whitstable	d																								
Faversham [2]	a																								
	d		12 28		12 58		13 28		13 58			14 28		14 58		15 28		15 58		16 28			16 58		17 28
Sittingbourne [4]	d		12 37		13 07		13 37		14 07			14 37		15 07		15 37		16 07		16 37			17 07		17 37
Rainham (Kent)	d		12 45		13 15		13 45		14 15			14 45		15 15		15 45		16 15		16 45			17 15		17 45
Gillingham (Kent) [4]	d		12 50		13 20		13 50		14 20			14 50		15 20		15 50		16 20		16 50			17 20		17 50
Chatham [4]	d		12 54		13 24		13 54		14 24			14 54		15 24		15 54		16 24		16 54			17 24		17 54
Rochester [4]	d		12 57		13 27		13 57		14 27			14 57		15 27		15 57		16 27		16 57			17 27		17 57
Maidstone West	d																								
Strood [4]	d		13 02		13 32		14 02		14 32			15 02		15 32		16 02		16 32		17 02			17 32		18 02
Gravesend	d		13 13		13 43		14 13		14 43			15 13		15 43		16 13		16 43		17 12			17 42		18 13
Ebbsfleet International	a	13 02	13 17	13 32	13 47	14 02	14 17	14 32	14 47	15 02		15 17	15 32	15 47	16 02	16 17	16 32	16 47	17 02	17 16	17 32		17 46	18 02	18 17
	d	13 03	13 21	13 33	13 48	14 03	14 18	14 33	14 48	15 03		15 18	15 33	15 48	16 03	16 18	16 33	16 51	17 03	17 17	17 33		17 47	18 03	18 18
Stratford International ⊖	a	13 14	13 32	13 44	13 59	14 14	14 29	14 44	14 59	15 14		15 29	15 44	15 59	16 14	16 28	16 44	17 02	17 14	17 27	17 44		17 57	18 14	18 29
St Pancras International [4] ⊖	a	13 21	13 39	13 51	14 06	14 21	14 40	14 51	15 06	15 21		15 36	15 51	16 06	16 21	16 39	16 51	17 09	17 21	17 38	17 51		18 08	18 21	18 36

Table 194 **Mondays to Fridays**

Kent - St Pancras International
High Speed Domestic Services

		SE	SE	SE	SE	SE	SE	SE		SE	SE	SE	SE	SE	SE	SE	SE	SE	SE		SE	SE	SE		
Margate 4	d			17 53				18 53					19 53				20 53					21 53			
Broadstairs	d			17 59				18 59					19 59				20 59					21 59			
Ramsgate 4	d			18 05				19 05					20 05				21 05					22 05			
Dover Priory	d	17 44				18 44					19 44				20 44				21 44				22 44		
Folkestone Central	d	17 56				18 56					19 56				20 56				21 56				22 56		
Folkestone West	d	17 58				18 58					19 58				20 58				21 58				22 58		
Ashford International	a	18 11		18 41		19 11		19 41			20 12		20 44		21 11		21 41		22 11			22 41	23 11		
	d	18 13		18 43		19 13		19 43			20 13		20 47		21 13		21 43		22 13			22 43	23 13		
Broadstairs	d																								
Margate 4	d																								
Birchington-on-Sea	d																								
Herne Bay	d																								
Whitstable	d																								
Faversham 2	a																								
	d		17 58		18 28					19 28		19 58		20 28		20 58		21 28			21 58				
Sittingbourne 4	d		18 07		18 37					19 37		20 07		20 37		21 07		21 37			22 07				
Rainham (Kent)	d		18 15		18 45					19 45		20 15		20 45		21 15		21 45			22 15				
Gillingham (Kent) 4	d		18 20		18 50					19 50		20 20		20 50		21 20		21 50			22 20				
Chatham 4	d		18 24		18 54					19 54		20 24		20 54		21 24		21 54			22 24				
Rochester 4	d		18 27		18 57					19 57		20 27		20 57		21 27		21 57			22 27				
Maidstone West	d						19 13																		
Strood 4	d		18 32		19 02		19 32			20 02		20 32		21 02		21 32		22 02			22 32				
Gravesend	d		18 43		19 12		19 43			20 12		20 43		21 13		21 43		22 12			22 43				
Ebbsfleet International	a	18 32	18 47	19 02	19 16	19 32	19 47	20 02		20 16	20 32	20 47	21 06	21 17	21 32	21 47	22 02	22 16	22 32		22 47	23 02	23 32		
	d	18 33	18 51	19 03	19 17	19 33	19 50	20 03		20 17	20 33	20 48	21 07	21 21	21 33	21 48	22 03	22 17	22 33		22 48	23 03	23 33		
Stratford International ⊖	a	18 44	19 02	19 14	19 27	19 44	20 01	20 14		20 27	20 44	20 59	21 18	21 32	21 44	21 59	22 14	22 27	22 44		22 59	23 14	23 44		
St Pancras International 4 ⊖	a	18 51	19 09	19 21	19 38	19 51	20 08	20 21		20 38	20 51	21 06	21 25	21 39	21 51	22 06	22 21	22 38	22 51		23 06	23 21	23 51		

Saturdays

		SE	SE	SE	SE	SE	SE	SE	SE	SE	SE		SE	SE	SE	SE	SE	SE	SE	SE	SE	SE		SE	SE
Margate 4	d						05 53				06 53					07 53				08 53					09 53
Broadstairs	d						05 59				06 59					07 59				08 59					09 59
Ramsgate 4	d		05 05				06 05				07 05					08 05				09 05					10 05
Dover Priory	d				05 44				06 44					07 44				08 44				09 44			
Folkestone Central	d				05 56				06 56					07 56				08 56				09 56			
Folkestone West	d				05 58				06 58					07 58				08 58				09 58			
Ashford International	a		05 41		06 11		06 41		07 11		07 41			08 11		08 41		09 11		09 41		10 11			10 41
	d	05 13	05 43		06 13		06 43		07 13		07 43			08 13		08 43		09 13		09 43		10 13			10 43
Broadstairs	d																								
Margate 4	d																								
Birchington-on-Sea	d																								
Herne Bay	d																								
Whitstable	d																								
Faversham 2	a																								
	d			05 28		05 58		06 28		06 58			07 28		07 58		08 28		08 58		09 28			09 58	
Sittingbourne 4	d			05 37		06 07		06 37		07 07			07 37		08 07		08 37		09 07		09 37			10 07	
Rainham (Kent)	d			05 45		06 15		06 45		07 15			07 45		08 15		08 45		09 15		09 45			10 15	
Gillingham (Kent) 4	d			05 50		06 20		06 50		07 20			07 50		08 20		08 50		09 20		09 50			10 20	
Chatham 4	d			05 54		06 24		06 54		07 24			07 54		08 24		08 54		09 24		09 54			10 24	
Rochester 4	d			05 57		06 27		06 57		07 27			07 57		08 27		08 57		09 27		09 57			10 27	
Maidstone West	d																								
Strood 4	d			06 02		06 32		07 02		07 32			08 02		08 32		09 02		09 32		10 02			10 32	
Gravesend	d			06 13		06 43		07 13		07 43			08 13		08 43		09 13		09 43		10 12			10 43	
Ebbsfleet International	a	05 32	06 02	06 17	06 32	06 47	07 02	07 17	07 32	07 47	08 02		08 17	08 32	08 47	09 02	09 17	09 32	09 47	10 02	10 16	10 32		10 47	11 02
	d	05 33	06 03	06 18	06 33	06 48	07 03	07 18	07 33	07 48	08 03		08 18	08 33	08 48	09 03	09 18	09 33	09 48	10 03	10 17	10 33		10 48	11 03
Stratford International ⊖	a	05 44	06 14	06 29	06 44	06 59	07 14	07 29	07 44	07 59	08 14		08 29	08 44	08 59	09 14	09 29	09 44	09 59	10 14	10 27	10 44		10 59	11 14
St Pancras International 4 ⊖	a	05 51	06 21	06 36	06 51	07 06	07 21	07 36	07 51	08 06	08 21		08 36	08 51	09 06	09 21	09 36	09 51	10 06	10 21	10 38	10 51		11 06	11 21

		SE	SE	SE	SE	SE	SE	SE	SE		SE	SE	SE	SE	SE	SE	SE	SE	SE	SE		SE	SE	SE	SE
Margate 4	d				10 53				11 53					12 53				13 53					14 53		
Broadstairs	d				10 59				11 59					12 59				13 59					14 59		
Ramsgate 4	d				11 05				12 05					13 05				14 05					15 05		
Dover Priory	d		10 44				11 44					12 44				13 44				14 44					15 44
Folkestone Central	d		10 56				11 56					12 56				13 56				14 56					15 56
Folkestone West	d		10 58				11 58					12 58				13 58				14 58					15 58
Ashford International	a		11 11		11 41		12 11		12 41			13 11		13 41		14 11		14 41		15 11			15 41		16 11
	d		11 13		11 43		12 13		12 43			13 13		13 43		14 13		14 43		15 13			15 43		16 13
Broadstairs	d																								
Margate 4	d																								
Birchington-on-Sea	d																								
Herne Bay	d																								
Whitstable	d																								
Faversham 2	a																								
	d	10 28		10 58		11 28		11 58			12 28		12 58		13 28		13 58		14 28			14 58		15 28	
Sittingbourne 4	d	10 37		11 07		11 37		12 07			12 37		13 07		13 37		14 07		14 37			15 07		15 37	
Rainham (Kent)	d	10 45		11 15		11 45		12 15			12 45		13 15		13 45		14 15		14 45			15 15		15 45	
Gillingham (Kent) 4	d	10 50		11 20		11 50		12 20			12 50		13 20		13 50		14 20		14 50			15 20		15 50	
Chatham 4	d	10 54		11 24		11 54		12 24			12 54		13 24		13 54		14 24		14 54			15 24		15 54	
Rochester 4	d	10 57		11 27		11 57		12 27			12 57		13 27		13 57		14 27		14 57			15 27		15 57	
Maidstone West	d																								
Strood 4	d	11 02		11 32		12 02		12 32			13 02		13 32		14 02		14 32		15 02			15 32		16 02	
Gravesend	d	11 13		11 43		12 13		12 43			13 13		13 43		14 13		14 43		15 13			15 43		16 13	
Ebbsfleet International	a	11 17	11 32	11 47	12 02	12 17	12 32	12 47	13 02		13 17	13 32	13 47	14 02	14 17	14 32	14 47	15 02	15 17	15 32		15 47	16 02	16 17	16 32
	d	11 18	11 33	11 48	12 03	12 18	12 33	12 48	13 03		13 18	13 33	13 48	14 03	14 18	14 33	14 51	15 03	15 18	15 33		15 48	16 03	16 18	16 33
Stratford International ⊖	a	11 29	11 44	11 59	12 14	12 29	12 45	12 59	13 14		13 29	13 44	13 59	14 14	14 29	14 44	15 02	15 14	15 29	15 44		15 59	16 14	16 29	16 44
St Pancras International 4 ⊖	a	11 36	11 51	12 06	12 21	12 36	12 54	13 06	13 21		13 36	13 51	14 06	14 21	14 40	14 51	15 09	15 21	15 36	15 51		16 06	16 21	16 37	16 51

Table 194

Saturdays

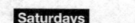

Kent - St Pancras International
High Speed Domestic Services

		SE	SE	SE	SE	SE	SE		SE	SE	SE	SE	SE	SE	SE	SE	SE	SE		SE	SE	SE	SE	SE	SE
Margate 4	d		15 53				16 53					17 53				18 53					19 53				20 53
Broadstairs	d		15 59				16 59					17 59				18 59					19 59				20 59
Ramsgate 4	d		16 05				17 05					18 05				19 05					20 05				21 05
Dover Priory	d				16 44					17 44				18 44				19 44					20 44		
Folkestone Central	d				16 56					17 56				18 56				19 56					20 56		
Folkestone West	d				16 58					17 58				18 58				19 58					20 58		
Ashford International	a		16 41		17 11		17 41			18 11		18 41		19 11		19 41		20 11			20 41		21 11		21 41
	d		16 43		17 13		17 43			18 13		18 43		19 13		19 43		20 13			20 47		21 13		21 43
Broadstairs	d																								
Margate 4	d																								
Birchington-on-Sea	d																								
Herne Bay	d																								
Whitstable	d																								
Faversham 2	a																								
	d	15 58		16 28		16 58			17 28		17 58		18 28		18 58		19 28			19 58		20 28		20 58	
Sittingbourne 4	d	16 07		16 37		17 07			17 37		18 07		18 37		19 07		19 37			20 07		20 37		21 07	
Rainham (Kent)	d	16 15		16 45		17 15			17 45		18 15		18 45		19 15		19 45			20 15		20 45		21 15	
Gillingham (Kent) 4	d	16 20		16 50		17 20			17 50		18 20		18 50		19 20		19 50			20 20		20 50		21 20	
Chatham 4	d	16 24		16 54		17 24			17 54		18 24		18 54		19 24		19 54			20 24		20 54		21 24	
Rochester 4	d	16 27		16 57		17 27			17 57		18 27		18 57		19 27		19 57			20 27		20 57		21 27	
Maidstone West	d																								
Strood 4	d	16 32		17 02		17 32			18 02		18 32		19 02		19 32		20 02			20 32		21 02		21 32	
Gravesend	d	16 43		17 12		17 43			18 13		18 43		19 12		19 43		20 12			20 43		21 13		21 43	
Ebbsfleet International	a	16 47	17 02	17 16	17 32	17 47	18 02		18 17	18 32	18 47	19 02	19 16	19 32	19 47	20 02	20 16	20 32		20 47	21 06	21 17	21 32	21 47	22 02
	d	16 51	17 03	17 17	17 33	17 48	18 03		18 18	18 33	18 51	19 03	19 17	19 33	19 48	20 03	20 17	20 33		20 51	21 07	21 25	21 33	21 48	22 03
Stratford International ⊖	a	17 02	17 14	17 27	17 44	17 59	18 14		18 29	18 44	19 02	19 14	19 27	19 44	19 59	20 14	20 27	20 44		21 02	21 18	21 35	21 44	21 59	22 14
St Pancras International 4 ⊖	a	17 09	17 21	17 38	17 51	18 06	18 21		18 36	18 51	19 09	19 21	19 38	19 51	20 06	20 21	20 38	20 51		21 09	21 25	21 42	21 51	22 06	22 21

		SE	SE	SE	SE		SE
Margate 4	d				21 53		
Broadstairs	d				21 59		
Ramsgate 4	d				22 05		
Dover Priory	d		21 44				22 44
Folkestone Central	d		21 56				22 56
Folkestone West	d		21 58				22 58
Ashford International	a		22 11		22 41		23 11
	d		22 13		22 43		23 13
Broadstairs	d						
Margate 4	d						
Birchington-on-Sea	d						
Herne Bay	d						
Whitstable	d						
Faversham 2	a						
	d	21 28		21 58			
Sittingbourne 4	d	21 37		22 07			
Rainham (Kent)	d	21 45		22 15			
Gillingham (Kent) 4	d	21 50		22 20			
Chatham 4	d	21 54		22 24			
Rochester 4	d	21 57		22 27			
Maidstone West	d						
Strood 4	d	22 02		22 32			
Gravesend	d	22 13		22 43			
Ebbsfleet International	a	22 17	22 32	22 47	23 02		23 32
	d	22 18	22 33	22 48	23 03		23 33
Stratford International ⊖	a	22 29	22 44	22 59	23 14		23 44
St Pancras International 4 ⊖	a	22 36	22 51	23 06	23 21		23 51

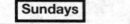

Sundays

		SE	SE	SE	SE	SE	SE	SE	SE	SE	SE		SE	SE	SE	SE	SE	SE	SE	SE	SE	SE		SE	SE
Margate 4	d					07 53				08 53					09 53				10 53					11 53	
Broadstairs	d					07 59				08 59					09 59				10 59					11 59	
Ramsgate 4	d					08 05				09 05					10 05				11 05					12 05	
Dover Priory	d			07 44				08 44					09 44				10 44				11 44				
Folkestone Central	d			07 56				08 56					09 56				10 56				11 56				
Folkestone West	d			07 58				08 58					09 58				10 58				11 58				
Ashford International	a			08 11		08 41		09 11		09 41			10 11		10 41		11 11		11 41		12 11			12 41	
	d			08 13		08 43		09 13		09 43			10 13		10 43		11 13		11 43		12 13			12 43	
Broadstairs	d																								
Margate 4	d																								
Birchington-on-Sea	d																								
Herne Bay	d																								
Whitstable	d																								
Faversham 2	a																								
	d	06 58	07 28		07 58		08 28		08 58		09 28			09 58		10 28		10 58		11 28		11 58			12 28
Sittingbourne 4	d	07 07	07 37		08 07		08 37		09 07		09 37			10 07		10 37		11 07		11 37		12 07			12 37
Rainham (Kent)	d	07 15	07 45		08 15		08 45		09 15		09 45			10 15		10 45		11 15		11 45		12 15			12 45
Gillingham (Kent) 4	d	07 20	07 50		08 20		08 50		09 20		09 50			10 20		10 50		11 20		11 50		12 20			12 50
Chatham 4	d	07 24	07 54		08 24		08 54		09 24		09 54			10 24		10 54		11 24		11 54		12 24			12 54
Rochester 4	d	07 27	07 57		08 27		08 57		09 27		09 57			10 27		10 57		11 27		11 57		12 27			12 57
Maidstone West	d																								
Strood 4	d	07 32	08 02		08 32		09 02		09 32		10 02			10 32		11 02		11 32		12 02		12 32			13 02
Gravesend	d	07 43	08 13		08 43		09 13		09 43		10 13			10 43		11 13		11 43		12 13		12 43			13 13
Ebbsfleet International	a	07 47	08 17	08 32	08 47	09 02	09 17	09 32	09 47	10 02	10 17		10 32	10 47	11 02	11 17	11 32	11 47	12 02	12 17	12 32	12 47		13 02	13 17
	d	07 48	08 18	08 33	08 48	09 03	09 18	09 33	09 48	10 03	10 22		10 33	10 48	11 03	11 18	11 33	11 48	12 03	12 18	12 33	12 48		13 03	13 21
Stratford International ⊖	a	07 59	08 29	08 44	08 59	09 14	09 29	09 44	09 59	10 14	10 33		10 44	10 59	11 14	11 29	11 44	11 59	12 14	12 29	12 45	12 59		13 14	13 32
St Pancras International 4 ⊖	a	08 06	08 36	08 51	09 06	09 21	09 40	09 51	10 06	10 21	10 40		10 51	11 06	11 21	11 36	11 51	12 06	12 21	12 36	12 54	13 06		13 21	13 39

Table 194

Sundays

Kent - St Pancras International High Speed Domestic Services

		SE	SE	SE	SE	SE	SE	SE	SE		SE	SE	SE	SE	SE	SE	SE	SE	SE	SE		SE	SE	SE	SE
Margate 4	d			12 53				13 53					14 53				15 53					16 53			
Broadstairs	d			12 59				13 59					14 59				15 59					16 59			
Ramsgate 4	d			13 05				14 05					15 05				16 05					17 05			
Dover Priory	d	12 44				13 44					14 44				15 44				16 44					17 44	
Folkestone Central	d	12 56				13 56					14 56				15 56				16 56					17 56	
Folkestone West	d	12 58				13 58					14 58				15 58				16 58					17 58	
Ashford International	a	13 11		13 41		14 11		14 41			15 11		15 41		16 11		16 41		17 11			17 41		18 11	
	d	13 13		13 43		14 13		14 43			15 13		15 43		16 13		16 43		17 13			17 43		18 13	
Broadstairs	d																								
Margate 4	d																								
Birchington-on-Sea	d																								
Herne Bay	d																								
Whitstable	d																								
Faversham 2	a																								
	d		12 58		13 28		13 58		14 28			14 58		15 28		15 58		16 28		16 58			17 28		17 58
Sittingbourne 4	d		13 07		13 37		14 07		14 37			15 07		15 37		16 07		16 37		17 07			17 37		18 07
Rainham (Kent)	d		13 15		13 45		14 15		14 45			15 15		15 45		16 15		16 45		17 15			17 45		18 15
Gillingham (Kent) 4	d		13 20		13 50		14 20		14 50			15 20		15 50		16 20		16 50		17 20			17 50		18 20
Chatham 4	d		13 24		13 54		14 24		14 54			15 24		15 54		16 24		16 54		17 24			17 54		18 24
Rochester 4	d		13 27		13 57		14 27		14 57			15 27		15 57		16 27		16 57		17 27			17 57		18 27
Maidstone West	d																								
Strood 4	d		13 32		14 02		14 32		15 02			15 32		16 02		16 32		17 02		17 32			18 02		18 32
Gravesend	d		13 43		14 13		14 43		15 13			15 43		16 13		16 43		17 12		17 43			18 12		18 43
Ebbsfleet International	a	13 32	13 47	14 02	14 17	14 32	14 47	15 02	15 17		15 32	15 47	16 02	16 17	16 32	16 47	17 02	17 16	17 32	17 47		18 02	18 16	18 32	18 47
	d	13 33	13 48	14 03	14 18	14 33	14 51	15 03	15 18		15 33	15 48	16 03	16 18	16 33	16 51	17 03	17 17	17 33	17 48		18 03	18 17	18 33	18 51
Stratford International ⊖	a	13 44	13 59	14 14	14 29	14 44	15 02	15 14	15 29		15 44	15 59	16 14	16 29	16 44	17 02	17 14	17 27	17 44	17 59		18 14	18 27	18 44	19 02
St Pancras International 4 ⊖	a	13 51	14 06	14 21	14 40	14 51	15 09	15 21	15 36		15 51	16 06	16 21	16 36	16 51	17 09	17 21	17 38	17 51	18 09		18 21	18 41	18 51	19 09

		SE	SE	SE	SE	SE	SE		SE	SE	SE	SE	SE	SE	SE	SE	SE	SE		SE					
Margate 4	d	17 53				18 53					19 53				20 53					21 53					
Broadstairs	d	17 59				18 59					19 59				20 59					21 59					
Ramsgate 4	d	18 05				19 05					20 05				21 05					22 05					
Dover Priory	d			18 44					19 44				20 44				21 44								
Folkestone Central	d			18 56					19 56				20 56				21 56								
Folkestone West	d			18 58					19 58				20 58				21 58								
Ashford International	a	18 41		19 11		19 41			20 11		20 41		21 11		21 41		22 11			22 41					
	d	18 43		19 13		19 43			20 13		20 47		21 13		21 43		22 13			22 43					
Broadstairs	d																								
Margate 4	d																								
Birchington-on-Sea	d																								
Herne Bay	d																								
Whitstable	d																								
Faversham 2	a																								
	d		18 28		18 58		19 28			19 58		20 28		20 58		21 28		21 58							
Sittingbourne 4	d		18 37		19 07		19 37			20 07		20 37		21 07		21 37		22 07							
Rainham (Kent)	d		18 45		19 15		19 45			20 15		20 45		21 15		21 45		22 15							
Gillingham (Kent) 4	d		18 50		19 20		19 50			20 20		20 50		21 20		21 50		22 20							
Chatham 4	d		18 54		19 24		19 54			20 24		20 54		21 24		21 54		22 24							
Rochester 4	d		18 57		19 27		19 57			20 27		20 57		21 27		21 57		22 27							
Maidstone West	d																								
Strood 4	d		19 02		19 32		20 02			20 32		21 02		21 32		22 02		22 32							
Gravesend	d		19 13		19 43		20 12			20 43		21 13		21 43		22 13		22 43							
Ebbsfleet International	a	19 02	19 17	19 32	19 47	20 02	20 16		20 32	20 47	21 06	21 17	21 32	21 47	22 02	22 17	22 32	22 47		23 02					
	d	19 03	19 18	19 33	19 51	20 03	20 17		20 33	20 48	21 07	21 25	21 33	21 48	22 03	22 18	22 33	22 48		23 03					
Stratford International ⊖	a	19 14	19 29	19 44	20 02	20 14	20 27		20 44	20 59	21 18	21 35	21 44	21 59	22 14	22 29	22 44	22 59		23 14					
St Pancras International 4 ⊖	a	19 21	19 36	19 51	20 12	20 21	20 38		20 51	21 06	21 25	21 42	21 51	22 06	22 21	22 36	22 51	23 06		23 21					

Network Diagram for Tables 195, 196 | also 199★

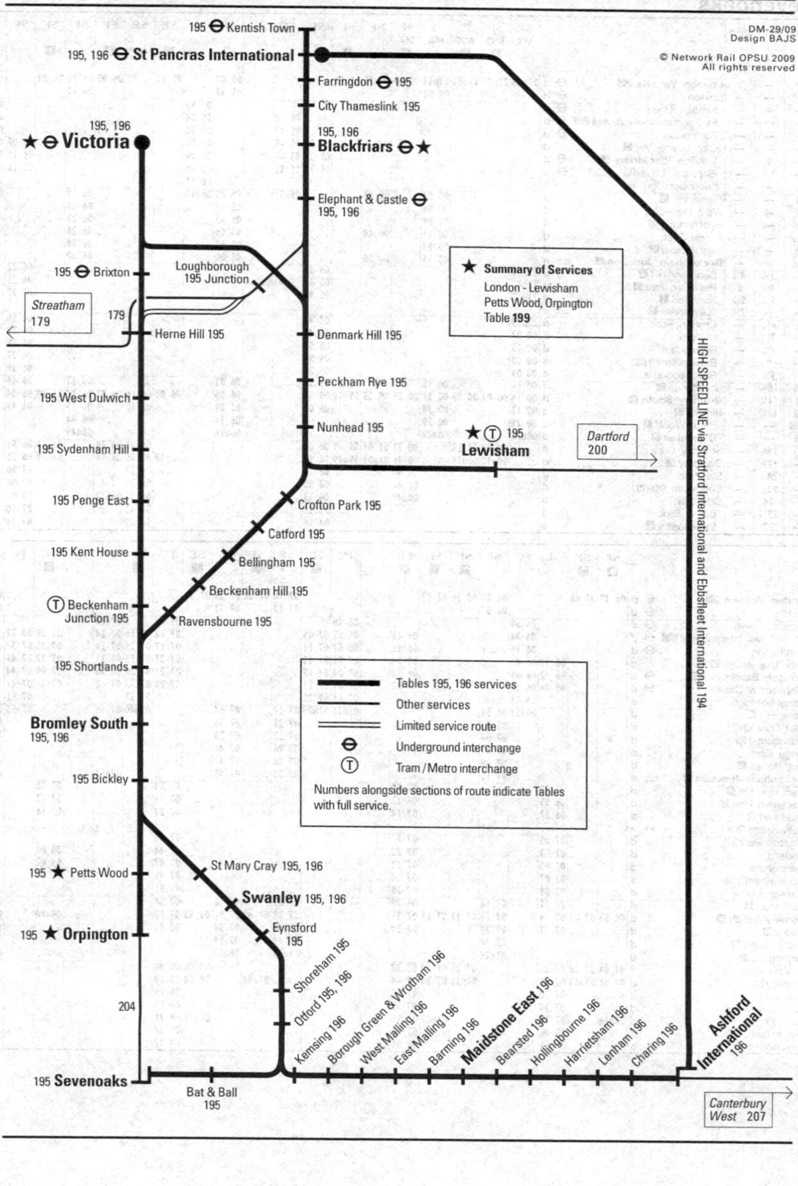

London - Catford, Beckenham Junction, Bromley South, Orpington, Otford and Sevenoaks

Miles	Miles	Miles			SE	SE	SE	SE	SE	SE	SE	SE	FC		SE	FC	SE	SE	SE	SE	SE	SE	FC		SE
					MX	MO	MX	MX	MX																
						1	1		1		1						1		1		1				
0	—	0	**London Victoria** 15 ⊖	d	23p43	23p45	23p52	23p55	00 07	00 35	05 22				05 40		05 52		06 07	06 10	06 22				06 30
3¼	—	—	Brixton ⊖	d				00 02							05 47					06 17					06 37
—	—	—	Kentish Town ⊖	d												05 50							06 08		
—	—	—	St Pancras International 15 ⊖	d									05 38			05 54							06 12		
—	—	—	Farringdon ⊖	d									05 42			05 58							06 17		
—	—	—	City Thameslink 3	d								05 26	05 45			06 01						06 07	06 21		
—	0	—	**London Blackfriars** 3 ⊖	d								05 28	05 48			06 06						06 10	06 24		
—	1¼	—	Elephant & Castle ⊖	d								05 32	05 51			06 09						06 16	06 27		
—	—	—	Loughborough Jn	d												06 13							06 31		
4	—	—	Herne Hill 4	d				00 04		00 43			05a57		05 49	06a16				06 19			06a34		06 39
5	—	—	West Dulwich	d				00 06							05 51					06 21					06 41
5¾	—	—	Sydenham Hill	d				00 08							05 53					06 23					06 43
7¼	—	—	Penge East	d				00 11		00 48					05 56					06 26					06 46
7¾	—	—	Kent House 4	d				00 13							05 58					06 28					06 48
8¾	—	—	**Beckenham Junction** 4	d				00 15		00 50					06 00					06 30					06 50
—	3¾	4¼	Denmark Hill 4	d	23p52							05 39										06 22			
—	4½	5	Peckham Rye 4	d	23p55							05 41										06 25			
—	5¼	5¾	Nunhead 4	d	23p57							05 44										06 27			
—	—	7½	Lewisham 4	a																					
—	6½	—	Crofton Park	d	23p59							05 47										06 30			
—	7½	—	Catford	d	00 03							05 49										06 33			
—	8¼	—	Bellingham	d	00 05							05 52										06 35			
—	9	—	Beckenham Hill	d	00 07							05 54										06 37			
—	9¾	—	Ravensbourne	d	00 09							05 56										06 39			
10	10½	—	Shortlands 4	d	00 11			00 18				05 58			06 03					06 33		06 41			06 54
11	11½	—	**Bromley South** 4	d	00 14	00 02	00 09	00 21	00 25	00 55	05 39	06 01			06 06		06 09	06 16	06 23	06 37	06 39	06 44			06 57
12	12½	—	Bickley 4	d	00 17			00 24				06 03			06 09			06 18		06 39		06 47			07 00
13¾	—	—	Petts Wood 4	d	00 21			00 29							06 14					06 44					07 04
15	—	—	**Orpington** 4	d	00a25			00a32							06a18					06a49					07a08
—	14¾	—	St Mary Cray	d		00 08	00 15		00 31	01 01	05 45	06 08						06 23	06 30		06 45	06 51			
—	17½	—	**Swanley** 4	d		00a12	00a19		00 36	01a05	05a49	06 12					06a19	06 28	06 34		06a49	06 56			
—	20½	—	Eynsford	d					00 40			06 17						06 32				07 00			
—	22¾	—	Shoreham (Kent)	d					00 44			06 20						06 36				07 04			
—	24	—	Otford 4	d					00a47			06 23						06 39	06a42			07 07			
—	25¾	—	Bat & Ball	d								06 26						06 42				07 10			
—	27	—	**Sevenoaks** 4	a								06 29						06 45				07 14			

		SE	SE	SE	FC	SE	SE	SE	FC		FC	FC	SE	SE	SE	SE	FC	FC	FC		FC	FC	SE	SE	SE
		1	1				1	1	1			1		1		1		1			1				1
London Victoria 15 ⊖	d	06 37	06 45			06 50	06 58	07 07					07 10	07 22	07 25	07 36							07 40	07 43	07 52
Brixton ⊖	d					06 57							07 17		07 32								07 47		
Kentish Town ⊖	d				06 30						06 48						07 08		07 20						
St Pancras International 15 ⊖	d				06 34				06 46		06 52	07 06					07 12	07 16	07 24		07 28	07 32			
Farringdon ⊖	d				06 39				06 51		06 57	07 11					07 17	07 21	07 29		07 33	07 37			
City Thameslink 3	d			06 39	06 43				06 54		07 01	07 15					07 21	07 25	07 33		07 37	07 41			
London Blackfriars 3 ⊖	d			06 42	06 46				06 58		07 04	07 18					07 24	07 28	07 36		07 40	07 44			
Elephant & Castle ⊖	d			06 46	06 49				07 02		07 07	07 21					07 28	07 33	07 40		07 44	07 47			
Loughborough Jn	d				06 53						07 11	07 25						07 37				07 51			
Herne Hill 4	d				06a57	06 59					07a15	07a29	07 19		07 34			07a40	07 46			07a55	07 49		
West Dulwich	d					07 02							07 21		07 36								07 51		
Sydenham Hill	d					07 04							07 23		07 38								07 53		
Penge East	d					07 07							07 26		07 41								07 56		
Kent House 4	d					07 09							07 28		07 43								07 58		
Beckenham Junction 4	d					07 11							07 30		07 45				07a53				08 00		
Denmark Hill 4	d			06 52					07 09								07 34				07 50			07 53	
Peckham Rye 4	d			06 55					07 12								07 36				07 53			07 56	
Nunhead 4	d			06 57					07 14								07 39				07 56			07 59	
Lewisham 4	a																							08 07	
Crofton Park	d			07 00					07 17								07 42								
Catford	d			07 03					07 20								07 44				08 00				
Bellingham	d			07 05					07 22								07 47				08 02				
Beckenham Hill	d			07 07					07 24								07 49								
Ravensbourne	d			07 09					07 26								07 51								
Shortlands 4	d			07 11		07 14			07 28				07 33		07 48		07 54						08 03		
Bromley South 4	d	06 58	07 02	07 14		07 17	07 19	07 23	07 31				07 38	07 40	07 51	07 53	07 57				08a10		08 06		08a09
Bickley 4	d			07 17		07 20			07 34				07 40		07 54		08 00						08 09		
Petts Wood 4	d					07 24							07 49		07 59								08 14		
Orpington 4	d					07a28							07a53		08a02								08a19		
St Mary Cray	d	07 04	07 08	07 21			07 25	07 30	07 38							08 00	08 04								
Swanley 4	d	07 08	07a12	07 26			07a29	07 34	07 44					07a48		08 04	08 10								
Eynsford	d			07 30					07 48								08 15								
Shoreham (Kent)	d			07 34					07 52								08 18								
Otford 4	d	07a16		07 37				07a42	07 55							08a12	08 21								
Bat & Ball	d			07 40					07 58								08 24								
Sevenoaks 4	a			07 43					08 01								08 27								

Table 195

Mondays to Fridays

London - Catford, Beckenham Junction, Bromley South, Orpington, Otford and Sevenoaks

		SE	SE 1	SE 1	FC		FC	FC	SE	SE	FC	SE 1	SE	SE 1	FC 1		FC 1	SE	SE	FC	FC 1	FC	FC	FC	SE 1
London Victoria 15 ⊖	d	07 55	07 58	08 07					08 09	08 10		08 22	08 25	08 37				08 39	08 40						08 52
Brixton ⊖	d	08 02								08 17			08 32						08 47						
Kentish Town ⊖	d						07 40										08 19					08 35		08 51	
St Pancras International 15 ⊖	d				07 38		07 44	07 52			08 12				08 16		08 24			08 28	08 32	08 40	08 44	08 56	
Farringdon ⊖	d				07 43		07 49	07 57			08 17				08 21		08 29			08 33	08 37	08 45	08 49	09 01	
City Thameslink 3	d				07 47		07 53	08 01			08 21				08 25		08 33			08 37	08 41	08 49	08 53	09 05	
London Blackfriars 3 ⊖	d				07 50		07 56	08 04			08 24				08 28		08 36			08 40	08 44	08 52	08 56	09 08	
Elephant & Castle ⊖	d				07 54		08 00	08 07			08 27				08 32					08 44	08 47	08 56	09 00	09 12	
Loughborough Jn.	d							08 11			08 31										08 51		09 04	09 16	
Herne Hill 4	d	08 04						08a15		08 19	08a36		08 34				08a45		08 48		08a57		09a08	09a21	
West Dulwich	d	08 06								08 21			08 36						08 51						
Sydenham Hill	d	08 08								08 23			08 38						08 53						
Penge East	d	08 11								08 26			08 41						08 56						
Kent House 4	d	08 13								08 28			08 43						08 58						
Beckenham Junction 4	d	08 15								08 30			08 45						09 00						
Denmark Hill 4	d				08 00		08 09		08 18						08 38			08 48		08 52		09 02			
Peckham Rye 4	d				08 03		08 12		08 21						08 41			08 51		08 55					
Nunhead 4	d				08 06		08 14		08 23						08 43			08 53		08 57					
Lewisham 4	a								08 30									09 01							
Crofton Park	d				08 09		08 17								08 46					09 00					
Catford	d				08 12		08 20								08 49					09 03		09 09			
Bellingham	d				08 15		08 22								08 51					09 05					
Beckenham Hill	d				08 17		08 24								08 53					09 07					
Ravensbourne	d				08 19		08 26								08 55					09 09					
Shortlands 4	d				08 22		08 30			08 33			08 48		08 57				09 03	09 11					
Bromley South 4	d	08 22	08 27	08 23	08 25		08 33			08 36		08a39	08 51	08 53	09 00				09 07	09 14		09 18			09a08
Bickley 4	d	08 24			08 28		08 35			08 39			08 54		09 03				09 09	09 17		09 20			
Petts Wood 4	d	08 29			08 32					08 44			08 59						09 14						
Orpington 4	d	08a32			08a35					08a47			09a02						09a17						
St Mary Cray	d		08 33	08 30			08 40							09 00	09 07					09 21		09 25			
Swanley 4	d		08a38	08 34			08 44							09 04	09 12					09 26		09 36			
Eynsford	d						08 49								09 16					09 30		09 40			
Shoreham (Kent)	d						08 52								09 20					09 34		09 44			
Otford 4	d			08a42			08 55							09a12	09 23					09 37		09 47			
Bat & Ball	d						08 58								09 26					09 40		09 50			
Sevenoaks 4	a						09 01								09 29					09 45		09 53			

			SE	SE 1	SE 1	SE	SE	FC	FC	SE 1	SE		SE 1	SE	SE	FC	FC	FC	SE 1	SE	SE 1		SE 1	SE	SE
London Victoria 15 ⊖	d		08 55	08 58	09 07	09 09	09 10			09 22	09 25		09 37	09 39	09 40				09 52	09 55	09 58		10 07	10 09	10 10
Brixton ⊖	d		09 02				09 17				09 32				09 47					10 02					10 17
Kentish Town ⊖	d								09 11							09 26		09 43							
St Pancras International 15 ⊖	d							09 00	09 16							09 30	09 34	09 48							
Farringdon ⊖	d							09 05	09 21							09 35	09 39	09 53							
City Thameslink 3	d							09 09	09 25							09 39	09 43	09 57							
London Blackfriars 3 ⊖	d							09 12	09 28							09 42	09 46	10 00							
Elephant & Castle ⊖	d							09 16	09 31							09 46	09 49	10 03							
Loughborough Jn.	d								09 35								09 53	10 07							
Herne Hill 4	d		09 04				09 19		09a39		09 34				09 49		09a57	10a11		10 04					10 19
West Dulwich	d		09 06				09 21				09 36				09 51					10 06					10 21
Sydenham Hill	d		09 08				09 23				09 38				09 53					10 08					10 23
Penge East	d		09 11				09 26				09 41				09 56					10 11					10 26
Kent House 4	d		09 13				09 28				09 43				09 58					10 13					10 28
Beckenham Junction 4	d		09 15				09 30				09 45				10 00					10 15					10 30
Denmark Hill 4	d					09 18		09 22						09 48		09 52								10 18	
Peckham Rye 4	d					09 21		09 25						09 51		09 55								10 21	
Nunhead 4	d					09 23		09 27						09 53		09 57								10 23	
Lewisham 4	a					09 31								10 01										10 31	
Crofton Park	d							09 30								10 00									
Catford	d							09 33								10 03									
Bellingham	d							09 35								10 05									
Beckenham Hill	d							09 37								10 07									
Ravensbourne	d							09 39								10 09									
Shortlands 4	d		09 18				09 33	09 41			09 48				10 03	10 11				10 18					10 33
Bromley South 4	d		09 21	09 19	09 23		09 36	09 44		09a38	09 52		09 53		10 07	10 14			10a08	10 21	10 19		10 23		10 36
Bickley 4	d		09 24				09 39	09 47			09 54				10 09	10 17				10 24					10 39
Petts Wood 4	d		09 29				09 44				09 59				10 14					10 29					10 44
Orpington 4	d		09a33				09a47				10a02				10a17					10a32					10a47
St Mary Cray	d			09 25				09 51					10 00			10 21					10 25				
Swanley 4	d			09a29	09 33			09 56					10 04			10 26					10a29		10 33		
Eynsford	d							10 00								10 30									
Shoreham (Kent)	d							10 04								10 34									
Otford 4	d				09a41			10 07					10a12			10 37							10a41		
Bat & Ball	d							10 10								10 40									
Sevenoaks 4	a							10 13								10 43									

London - Catford, Beckenham Junction, Bromley South, Orpington, Otford and Sevenoaks

		FC	FC	FC	SE 1	SE	SE 1		SE	SE	FC	FC	FC	SE 1	SE	SE 1	SE 1		SE	SE	FC		FC	FC
London Victoria 15 ⊖	d				10 22	10 25	10 37		10 39	10 40				10 52	10 55	10 58	11 07		11 09	11 10		and at the same minutes past each hour until		
Brixton ⊖	d					10 32				10 47					11 02					11 17				
Kentish Town ⊖	d	09 54	10 00	10 13							10 26	10 30	10 43								10 56		14 56	15 00
St Pancras International 15 ⊖	d	10 00	10 04	10 18							10 30	10 34	10 48								11 00		15 00	15 04
Farringdon ⊖	d	10 05	10 09	10 23							10 35	10 39	10 53								11 05		15 05	15 09
City Thameslink 3	d	10 09	10 13	10 27							10 39	10 43	10 57								11 09		15 09	15 13
London Blackfriars 3 ⊖	d	10 12	10 16	10 30							10 42	10 46	11 00								11 12		15 12	15 16
Elephant & Castle ⊖	d	10 16	10 19	10 33							10 46	10 49	11 03								11 16		15 16	15 19
Loughborough Jn.	d		10 23	10 37								10 53	11 07											15 23
Herne Hill 4	d		10a27	10a41		10 34				10 49		10a57	11a11		11 04					11 19				15a27
West Dulwich	d					10 36				10 51					11 06					11 21				
Sydenham Hill	d					10 38				10 53					11 08					11 23				
Penge East	d					10 41				10 56					11 11					11 26				
Kent House 4	d					10 43				10 58					11 13					11 28				
Beckenham Junction 4	d					10 45				11 00					11 15					11 30				
Denmark Hill 4	d	10 22							10 48		10 52								11 18		11 22		15 22	
Peckham Rye 4	d	10 25							10 51		10 55								11 21		11 25		15 25	
Nunhead 4	d	10 27							10 53		10 57								11 23		11 27		15 27	
Lewisham 4	a								11 01										11 31					
Crofton Park	d	10 30									11 00										11 30		15 30	
Catford	d	10 33									11 03										11 33		15 33	
Bellingham	d	10 35									11 05										11 35		15 35	
Beckenham Hill	d	10 37									11 07										11 37		15 37	
Ravensbourne	d	10 39									11 09										11 39		15 39	
Shortlands 4	d	10 41				10 48				11 03	11 11				11 18					11 33	11 41		15 41	
Bromley South 4	d	10 44			10a38	10 51	10 53			11 06	11 14			11a08	11 21	11 19	11 23			11 36	11 44		15 44	
Bickley 4	d	10 47				10 54				11 09	11 17				11 24					11 39	11 47		15 47	
Petts Wood 4	d					10 59				11 14					11 29					11 44				
Orpington 4	d					11a02				11a17					11a32					11a47				
St Mary Cray	d	10 51					11 00				11 21					11 25					11 51		15 51	
Swanley 4	d	10 56					11 04				11 26					11a29	11 33				11 56		15 56	
Eynsford	d	11 00									11 30										12 00		16 00	
Shoreham (Kent)	d	11 04									11 34										12 04		16 04	
Otford 4	d	11 07					11a12				11 37						11a41				12 07		16 07	
Bat & Ball	d	11 10									11 40										12 10		16 10	
Sevenoaks 4	a	11 13									11 43										12 13		16 13	

		FC	SE 1		SE	SE 1	SE	SE	FC	FC	FC	SE 1	SE		SE	SE 1	SE 1	SE	SE	FC	FC	SE 1	SE		SE 1
London Victoria 15 ⊖	d		15 22		15 25	15 37	15 39	15 40				15 52			15 55	15 58	16 07	16 09	16 10			16 22	16 25		16 28
Brixton ⊖	d				15 32			15 47							16 02				16 17				16 32		
Kentish Town ⊖	d	15 13							15 26	15 30	15 43									15 56	16 00				
St Pancras International 15 ⊖	d	15 18							15 30	15 34	15 48									16 00	16 04				
Farringdon ⊖	d	15 23							15 35	15 39	15 53									16 05	16 09				
City Thameslink 3	d	15 27							15 39	15 43	15 57									16 09	16 13				
London Blackfriars 3 ⊖	d	15 30							15 42	15 46	16 00									16 12	16 16				
Elephant & Castle ⊖	d	15 33							15 46	15 49	16 03									16 16	16 19				
Loughborough Jn.	d	15 37								15 53	16 07										16 23				
Herne Hill 4	d	15a41			15 34			15 49		15a57	16a11				16 04				16 19		16a27		16 34		
West Dulwich	d				15 36			15 51							16 06				16 21				16 36		
Sydenham Hill	d				15 38			15 53							16 08				16 23				16 38		
Penge East	d				15 41			15 56							16 11				16 26				16 41		
Kent House 4	d				15 43			15 58							16 13				16 28				16 43		
Beckenham Junction 4	d				15 45			16 00					16 12		16 15				16 30				16 45		
Denmark Hill 4	d						15 48		15 52									16 18		16 22					
Peckham Rye 4	d						15 51		15 55									16 21		16 25					
Nunhead 4	d						15 53		15 57									16 23		16 27					
Lewisham 4	a						16 01											16 31							
Crofton Park	d								16 00											16 30					
Catford	d								16 03											16 33					
Bellingham	d								16 05											16 35					
Beckenham Hill	d								16 07											16 37					
Ravensbourne	d								16 09											16 39					
Shortlands 4	d				15 48			16 03	16 11						16 18				16 33	16 41			16 48		
Bromley South 4	d		15a38		15 51	15 53		16 06	16 14			16a08			16 21	16 19	16 23		16 36	16 44		16a38	16 51		16 49
Bickley 4	d				15 54			16 09	16 17						16 24				16 39	16 47			16 54		
Petts Wood 4	d				15 59			16 14							16 29				16 44				16 59		
Orpington 4	d				16a02			16a17							16a32				16a49				17a04		
St Mary Cray	d					16 00			16 21							16 25				16 51					16 55
Swanley 4	d					16 04			16 26							16a29	16 33			16 56					16a59
Eynsford	d								16 30											17 00					
Shoreham (Kent)	d								16 34											17 04					
Otford 4	d					16a12			16 37								16a41			17 07					
Bat & Ball	d								16 40											17 10					
Sevenoaks 4	a								16 43											17 14					

Table 195

Mondays to Fridays

London - Catford, Beckenham Junction, Bromley South, Orpington, Otford and Sevenoaks

		SE 1	FC	FC	SE	SE	FC	FC	FC 1		FC	SE 1	SE 1	SE	SE	SE	SE 1	SE	FC		FC	FC 1	FC	SE 1	SE 1
London Victoria 15 ⊖	d	16 37			16 39	16 40						16 57	16 58	17 00	17 04	17 04	17 12	17 15						17 27	17 28
Brixton ⊖	d					16 47								17 07				17 22							
Kentish Town ⊖	d		16 09	16 13			16 24	16 30			16 46										16 58		17 14		
St Pancras International 15 ⊖	d		16 14	16 18			16 28	16 34	16 40		16 52								16 58		17 02	17 14	17 18		
Farringdon ⊖	d		16 19	16 23			16 33	16 39	16 45		16 57								17 03		17 07	17 19	17 23		
City Thameslink 3	d		16 23	16 27			16 37	16 43	16 49		17 01								17 07		17 11	17 23	17 27		
London Blackfriars 3 ⊖	d		16 26	16 30			16 42	16 46	16 52		17 04								17 10		17 14	17 26	17 30		
Elephant & Castle ⊖	d		16 30	16 33			16 46	16 49	16 56		17 08								17 14		17 18	17 30	17 34		
Loughborough Jn	d			16 37				16 53	17 00		17 12										17 22		17 38		
Herne Hill 4	d			16a41		16 49		16a57	17 06		17a15			17 09				17 24			17a25	17 36	17a41		
West Dulwich	d					16 51			17 09					17 12				17 27							
Sydenham Hill	d					16 53			17 11					17 14				17 29							
Penge East	d					16 56			17 14					17 17				17 32							
Kent House 4	d					16 58			17 16					17 19				17 34							
Beckenham Junction 4	d					17 00			17a20					17 21				17 37							
Denmark Hill 4	d		16 39		16 48		16 52								17 13				17 20						
Peckham Rye 4	d		16 42		16 51		16 55								17 16				17 23						
Nunhead 4	d		16 44		16 53		16 57								17 18				17 26						
Lewisham 4	a				16 58										17 23										
Crofton Park	d		16 47				17 00												17 29						
Catford	d		16 50				17 03												17 32						
Bellingham	d		16 52				17 05												17 35						
Beckenham Hill	d		16 54				17 07												17 37						
Ravensbourne	d		16 56				17 09												17 39						
Shortlands 4	d		16 58			17 03	17 11							17 25				17 40	17 43						
Bromley South 4	d	16 53	17 01			17 06	17 14					17a13	17 19	17 28		17 24	17 28	17 43	17 46			17 48		17a43	17 50
Bickley 4	d		17 04			17 09	17 17							17 30				17 45				17 50			
Petts Wood 4	d		17 08			17 14								17 35				17 50							
Orpington 4	d		17a15			17a19								17a40				17a55							
St Mary Cray	d	17 00					17 21									17 30	17 35					17 55			17 57
Swanley 4	d	17 04					17 30									17a34	17 39		17 55			17a59			18 01
Eynsford	d						17 34												18 00						
Shoreham (Kent)	d						17 38												18 03						
Otford 4	d	17a12					17 41						17a35				17a47		18 06						18a09
Bat & Ball	d						17 44												18 14						
Sevenoaks 4	a						17 49												18 23						

		SE	SE	SE 1	FC		FC	FC 1	SE	FC	SE 1	SE	SE 1	SE	SE 1		FC 1	FC	FC	FC	SE	SE	SE 1	SE 1	SE 1
London Victoria 15 ⊖	d	17 30	17 34	17 42					17 45		17 54	17 56	17 57	18 00	18 03						18 15	18 18	18 18	18 24	18 27
Brixton ⊖	d	17 37							17 52					18 07							18 22				
Kentish Town ⊖	d				17 18		17 28											17 44	17 48	18 00					
St Pancras International 15 ⊖	d				17 22		17 32	17 36		17 44							17 58	17 48	17 52	18 04					
Farringdon ⊖	d				17 27		17 37	17 41		17 49							18 03	17 53	17 57	18 09					
City Thameslink 3	d				17 31		17 41	17 45		17 53							18 07	17 57	18 01	18 13					
London Blackfriars 3 ⊖	d				17 36		17 44	17 48		17 56							18 10	18 00	18 04	18 16					
Elephant & Castle ⊖	d				17 40		17 48	17 52		18 00							18 14	18 05	18 08	18 20					
Loughborough Jn	d						17 52												18 12	18 24					
Herne Hill 4	d	17 39					17a55		17 54	18 06				18 09			18 21		18a16	18a27	18 24				
West Dulwich	d	17 42							17 57	18 09				18 12							18 27				
Sydenham Hill	d	17 44							17 59	18 11				18 14							18 29				
Penge East	d	17 47							18 02	18 14				18 17							18 32				
Kent House 4	d	17 49							18 04	18a18				18 19							18 34				
Beckenham Junction 4	d	17 51							18 06					18 21							18 36				
Denmark Hill 4	d		17 43		17 47							18 06						18 15				18 28			
Peckham Rye 4	d		17 46		17 50							18 09						18 18				18 32			
Nunhead 4	d		17 49		17 52							18 11						18 20				18 34			
Lewisham 4	a		17 55									18 17										18 42			
Crofton Park	d				17 55													18 23							
Catford	d				17 58													18 26							
Bellingham	d				18 01													18 29							
Beckenham Hill	d				18 03													18 31							
Ravensbourne	d				18 05													18 33							
Shortlands 4	d	17 55			18 07				18 10					18 25				18 35			18 39				
Bromley South 4	d	17 58		17 59	18 10			18 11	18 15		18 19		18a14	18 28	18 24		18 31	18 38			18 42		18 39	18 46	18a43
Bickley 4	d	18 00			18 12				18 18					18 31				18 40			18 45				
Petts Wood 4	d	18 05							18 26					18 36							18 54				
Orpington 4	d	18a10							18a32					18a41							18a59				
St Mary Cray	d			18 06	18 22			18 18			18 25						18 38	18 45					18 45	18 52	
Swanley 4	d			18 11	18 26			18 22			18a29						18a42	18 53					18 50	18a56	
Eynsford	d				18 31													18 57							
Shoreham (Kent)	d				18 34													19 01							
Otford 4	d			18a19	18 38			18a30							18a42			19 04					18a58		
Bat & Ball	d				18 41													19 07							
Sevenoaks 4	a				18 50													19 14							

London - Catford, Beckenham Junction, Bromley South, Orpington, Otford and Sevenoaks

Station			SE	SE	SE	FC	FC	SE	FC	FC	FC		SE	SE	SE	SE	SE	SE	FC	FC	FC		SE	SE	SE
					1				1				1	1		1							1		
London Victoria 15 ⊖	d		18 30	18 39	18 42			18 45					18 57	18 58	19 00	19 07	19 09	19 10					19 22	19 25	19 28
Brixton ⊖	d		18 37					18 52							19 07			19 17						19 32	
Kentish Town ⊖	d						18 20			18 34									18 54						
St Pancras International 15 ⊖	d					18 12	18 24		18 30	18 38	18 48								19 00	19 04	19 18				
Farringdon ⊖	d					18 17	18 29		18 35	18 43	18 53								19 05	19 09	19 23				
City Thameslink 3	d					18 21	18 33		18 39	18 47	18 57								19 09	19 13	19 27				
London Blackfriars 3 ⊖	d					18 24	18 36		18 42	18 50	19 00								19 12	19 16	19 30				
Elephant & Castle ⊖	d					18 28	18 40		18 46	18 54	19 04								19 16	19 19	19 33				
Loughborough Jn.	d						18 44			18 58	19 08									19 23	19 37				
Herne Hill 4	d		18 39				18a47	18 54		19a01	19a11				19 09			19 19		19a27	19a41			19 34	
West Dulwich	d		18 42					18 56							19 12			19 21						19 36	
Sydenham Hill	d		18 44					18 58							19 14			19 23						19 38	
Penge East	d		18 47					19 01							19 17			19 26						19 41	
Kent House 4	d		18 49					19 03							19 19			19 28						19 43	
Beckenham Junction 4	d		18 51					19 06							19 21			19 30						19 45	
Denmark Hill 4	d			18 48		18 34			18 52								19 18		19 22						
Peckham Rye 4	d			18 51		18 38			18 55								19 21		19 25						
Nunhead 4	d			18 54		18 40			18 57								19 23		19 27						
Lewisham 4	a			19 02													19 31								
Crofton Park	d					18 43			19 00										19 30						
Catford	d					18 46			19 03										19 33						
Bellingham	d					18 49			19 05										19 35						
Beckenham Hill	d					18 51			19 07										19 37						
Ravensbourne	d					18 53			19 09										19 39						
Shortlands 4	d		18 55			18 57		19 09	19 13						19 25			19 33	19 41					19 48	
Bromley South 4	d		18 58		18 59	19 00		19 12	19 16				19a13	19 19	19 28	19 27		19 36	19 44				19a38	19 51	19 49
Bickley 4	d		19 00			19 03		19 15	19 19						19 30			19 39	19 47					19 54	
Petts Wood 4	d		19 07					19 20							19 35			19 44						19 59	
Orpington 4	d		19a12					19a25							19a38			19a48						20a02	
St Mary Cray	d				19 06	19 10			19 23					19 25					19 51						19 55
Swanley 4	d				19 11	19 15			19 28					19a29		19 36			19 56						19a59
Eynsford	d					19 19			19 32										20 00						
Shoreham (Kent)	d					19 23			19 36										20 04						
Otford 4	d				19a19	19 26			19 39							19a44			20 07						
Bat & Ball	d					19 29			19 42										20 10						
Sevenoaks 4	a					19 37			19 50										20 13						

Station		SE	SE	SE	FC	FC	FC		SE	SE	SE	SE	SE	FC	FC	FC	SE		SE	SE	FC	FC	SE	SE	SE
		1							1			1					1			1			1		1
London Victoria 15 ⊖	d	19 37	19 39	19 40					19 52	19 55	19 58	20 07	20 10				20 22		20 25	20 37			20 52	20 55	20 58
Brixton ⊖	d			19 47						20 02			20 17						20 32					21 02	
Kentish Town ⊖	d				19 26									19 56							20 26	20 30			
St Pancras International 15 ⊖	d				19 30	19 34	19 48							20 00	20 04	20 18					20 30	20 36			
Farringdon ⊖	d				19 35	19 39	19 53							20 05	20 09	20 23					20 35	20 40			
City Thameslink 3	d				19 39	19 43	19 57							20 09	20 13	20 27					20 39	20 43			
London Blackfriars 3 ⊖	d				19 42	19 46	20 00							20 12	20 16	20 30					20 42	20 46			
Elephant & Castle ⊖	d				19 46	19 49	20 03							20 16	20 19	20 33					20 46	20 49			
Loughborough Jn.	d					19 53	20 07								20 23	20 37						20 53			
Herne Hill 4	d			19 49		19a57	20a11			20 04			20 19		20a27	20a41			20 34			20a57		21 04	
West Dulwich	d			19 51						20 06			20 21						20 36					21 06	
Sydenham Hill	d			19 53						20 08			20 23						20 38					21 08	
Penge East	d			19 56						20 11			20 26						20 41					21 11	
Kent House 4	d			19 58						20 13			20 28						20 43					21 13	
Beckenham Junction 4	d			20 00						20 15			20 30						20 45					21 15	
Denmark Hill 4	d		19 48		19 52									20 22							20 52				
Peckham Rye 4	d		19 51		19 55									20 25							20 55				
Nunhead 4	d		19 53		19 57									20 27							20 57				
Lewisham 4	a		20 01																						
Crofton Park	d				20 00									20 30							21 00				
Catford	d				20 03									20 33							21 03				
Bellingham	d				20 05									20 35							21 05				
Beckenham Hill	d				20 07									20 37							21 07				
Ravensbourne	d				20 09									20 39							21 09				
Shortlands 4	d			20 03	20 11					20 18			20 33	20 41					20 48		21 11			21 18	
Bromley South 4	d	19 53		20 06	20 14				20a08	20 21	20 19	20 23	20 36	20 44			20a38		20 51	20 53	21 14		21a09	21 21	21 19
Bickley 4	d			20 09	20 17					20 24			20 39	20 47					20 54		21 17			21 24	
Petts Wood 4	d			20 14						20 29			20 44						20 59					21 29	
Orpington 4	d			20a18						20a32			20a47						21a02					21a32	
St Mary Cray	d	20 00			20 21						20 25			20 51						21 00	21 21				21 25
Swanley 4	d	20 04			20 26						20a29	20 33		20 56						21 04	21 26				21a29
Eynsford	d				20 30									21 00							21 30				
Shoreham (Kent)	d				20 34									21 04							21 34				
Otford 4	d	20a12			20 37							20a41		21 07						21a12	21 37				
Bat & Ball	d				20 40									21 10							21 40				
Sevenoaks 4	a				20 43									21 13							21 43				

London - Catford, Beckenham Junction, Bromley South, Orpington, Otford and Sevenoaks

		SE [1]	FC		FC	SE [1]	SE	FC	SE	SE [1]	SE	FC	SE [1]		SE	SE [1]	SE	SE	SE [1]	SE	SE [1]	SE	SE [1]		SE
London Victoria [15] ⊖	d	21 07				21 22	21 25		21 43	21 52	21 55		22 07		22 13	22 22	22 25	22 43	22 52	22 55	23 07	23 13	23 22		23 25
Brixton ⊖	d						21 32				22 02						22 32			23 02					23 32
Kentish Town ⊖	d		20 56		21 00			21 30				22 00													
St Pancras International [15] ⊖	d		21 00		21 06			21 36				22 06													
Farringdon ⊖	d		21 05		21 10			21 40				22 10													
City Thameslink [3]	d		21 09		21 13			21 43				22 13													
London Blackfriars [3] ⊖	d		21 12		21 16			21 46				22 16													
Elephant & Castle ⊖	d		21 16		21 19			21 49				22 19													
Loughborough Jn	d				21 23			21 53				22 23													
Herne Hill [4]	d				21a27		21 34	21a57			22 04	22a27					22 34			23 04					23 34
West Dulwich	d						21 36				22 06						22 36			23 06					23 36
Sydenham Hill	d						21 38				22 08						22 38			23 08					23 38
Penge East	d						21 41				22 11						22 41			23 11					23 41
Kent House [4]	d						21 43				22 13						22 43			23 13					23 43
Beckenham Junction [4]	d						21 45				22 15						22 45			23 15					23 45
Denmark Hill [4]	d		21 22						21 52						22 22			22 52				23 22			
Peckham Rye [4]	d		21 25						21 55						22 25			22 55				23 25			
Nunhead [4]	d		21 27						21 57						22 27			22 57				23 27			
Lewisham [4]	a																								
Crofton Park	d		21 30						22 00						22 30			23 00				23 30			
Catford	d		21 33						22 03						22 33			23 03				23 33			
Bellingham	d		21 35						22 05						22 35			23 05				23 35			
Beckenham Hill	d		21 37						22 07						22 37			23 07				23 37			
Ravensbourne	d		21 39						22 09						22 39			23 09				23 39			
Shortlands [4]	d		21 41				21 48		22 11		22 18				22 41		22 48	23 11		23 18		23 41			23 48
Bromley South [4]	d	21 23	21 44			21a38	21 51		22 14	22 09	22 21		22 23		22 44	22a38	22 51	23 14	23 09	23 21	23 23	23 44	23a38		23 51
Bickley [4]	d		21 47				21 54		22 17		22 24				22 47		22 54	23 17		23 24		23 47			23 54
Petts Wood [4]	d						21 59				22 29						22 59	23 21		23 29		23 54			23 59
Orpington [4]	d						22a02				22a32						23a02	23a25		23a32		23a57			00a02
St Mary Cray	d	21 30	21 51						22 21	22 15			22 30		22 51				23 15		23 30				
Swanley [4]	d	21 34	21 56						22 26	22a19			22 34		22 56				23a19		23 34				
Eynsford	d		22 00						22 30						23 00										
Shoreham (Kent)	d		22 04						22 34						23 04										
Otford [4]	d	21a42	22 07						22 37				22a42		23 07						23a42				
Bat & Ball	d		22 10						22 40						23 10										
Sevenoaks [4]	a		22 13						22 43						23 13										

		SE	SE [1]	SE
London Victoria [15] ⊖	d	23 43	23 52	23 55
Brixton ⊖	d			00 02
Kentish Town ⊖	d			
St Pancras International [15] ⊖	d			
Farringdon ⊖	d			
City Thameslink [3]	d			
London Blackfriars [3] ⊖	d			
Elephant & Castle ⊖	d			
Loughborough Jn	d			
Herne Hill [4]	d			00 04
West Dulwich	d			00 06
Sydenham Hill	d			00 08
Penge East	d			00 11
Kent House [4]	d			00 13
Beckenham Junction [4]	d			00 15
Denmark Hill [4]	d	23 52		
Peckham Rye [4]	d	23 55		
Nunhead [4]	d	23 57		
Lewisham [4]	a			
Crofton Park	d	23 59		
Catford	d	00 03		
Bellingham	d	00 05		
Beckenham Hill	d	00 07		
Ravensbourne	d	00 09		
Shortlands [4]	d	00 11		00 18
Bromley South [4]	d	00 14	00 09	00 21
Bickley [4]	d	00 17		00 24
Petts Wood [4]	d	00 21		00 29
Orpington [4]	d	00a25		00a32
St Mary Cray	d		00 15	
Swanley [4]	d		00a19	
Eynsford	d			
Shoreham (Kent)	d			
Otford [4]	d			
Bat & Ball	d			
Sevenoaks [4]	a			

Table 195

Saturdays

London - Catford, Beckenham Junction, Bromley South, Orpington, Otford and Sevenoaks

		SE	SE 1	SE	SE 1	SE	SE 1	SE	SE 1	SE		SE 1	SE	SE	SE	SE 1	SE 1	SE	SE	SE 1		SE	SE 1	SE	SE
London Victoria 15 ⊖	d	23p43	23p52	23p55	00 07	00 35	05 22	05 55	06 07	06 13		06 22	06 25	06 43	06 55	06 58	07 07	07 10	07 13	07 22		07 25	07 37	07 39	07 40
Brixton ⊖	d			00 02				06 02					06 32		07 02			07 17				07 32			07 47
Kentish Town ⊖	d																								
St Pancras International 15 ⊖	d																								
Farringdon ⊖	d																								
City Thameslink 3	d																								
London Blackfriars 3 ⊖	d																								
Elephant & Castle ⊖	d																								
Loughborough Jn	d																								
Herne Hill 4	d			00 04		00 43		06 04					06 34		07 04			07 19				07 34			07 49
West Dulwich	d			00 06				06 06					06 36		07 06			07 21				07 36			07 51
Sydenham Hill	d			00 08				06 08					06 38		07 08			07 23				07 38			07 53
Penge East	d			00 11		00 48		06 11					06 41		07 11			07 26				07 41			07 56
Kent House 4	d			00 13				06 13					06 43		07 13			07 28				07 43			07 58
Beckenham Junction 4	d			00 15		00 50		06 15					06 45		07 15			07 30				07 45			08 00
Denmark Hill 4	d	23p52								06 22				06 52					07 22					07 48	
Peckham Rye 4	d	23p55								06 25				06 55					07 25					07 51	
Nunhead 4	d	23p57								06 27				06 57					07 27					07 53	
Lewisham 4	a																							08 02	
Crofton Park	d	23p59								06 30				07 00					07 30						
Catford	d	00 03								06 33				07 03					07 33						
Bellingham	d	00 05								06 35				07 05					07 35						
Beckenham Hill	d	00 07								06 37				07 07					07 37						
Ravensbourne	d	00 09								06 39				07 09					07 39						
Shortlands 4	d	00 11		00 18				06 18		06 41			06 48	07 11	07 18			07 33	07 41			07 48			08 03
Bromley South 4	d	00 14	00 09	00 21	00 25	00 55	05 39	06 21	06 23	06 44		06 39	06 51	07 14	07 21	07 19	07 23	07 36	07 44	07a38		07 51	07 53		08 06
Bickley 4	d	00 17		00 24				06 24		06 47			06 54	07 17	07 24			07 39	07 47			07 54			08 09
Petts Wood 4	d	00 21		00 29				06 29					06 59		07 29			07 44				07 59			08 14
Orpington 4	d	00a25		00a32				06a32					07a02		07a32			07a47				08a02			08a17
St Mary Cray	d		00 15		00 31	01 01	05 45		06 30	06 51		06 45		07 21		07 25	07 30		07 51				08 00		
Swanley 4	d		00a19		00 36	01a05	05a49		06 34	06 56		06a49		07 26		07a29	07 34		07 56				08 04		
Eynsford	d				00 40					07 00				07 30					08 00						
Shoreham (Kent)	d				00 44					07 04				07 34					08 04						
Otford 4	d				00a47				06a42	07 07				07 37			07a42		08 07				08a12		
Bat & Ball	d									07 10				07 40					08 10						
Sevenoaks 4	a									07 13				07 43					08 13						

		SE	SE 1	SE	SE 1	SE 1		SE	SE	SE	SE 1	SE	SE 1	SE		SE		SE	SE	SE 1	SE	SE 1	SE 1	SE
London Victoria 15 ⊖	d	07 43	07 52	07 55	07 58	08 07		08 09	08 10	08 13	08 22	08 25	08 37	08 39		18 39		18 40	18 43	18 52	18 55	18 58	19 07	19 09
Brixton ⊖	d			08 02					08 17			08 32						18 47			19 02			
Kentish Town ⊖	d																							
St Pancras International 15 ⊖	d																							
Farringdon ⊖	d																							
City Thameslink 3	d																							
London Blackfriars 3 ⊖	d																							
Elephant & Castle ⊖	d																							
Loughborough Jn	d																							
Herne Hill 4	d			08 04					08 19			08 34						18 49			19 04			
West Dulwich	d			08 06					08 21			08 36						18 51			19 06			
Sydenham Hill	d			08 08					08 23			08 38						18 53			19 08			
Penge East	d			08 11					08 26			08 41						18 56			19 11			
Kent House 4	d			08 13					08 28			08 43			and at			18 58			19 13			
Beckenham Junction 4	d			08 15					08 30			08 45			the same			19 00			19 15			
Denmark Hill 4	d	07 52						08 18		08 22				08 48	minutes	18 48			18 52					19 18
Peckham Rye 4	d	07 55						08 21		08 25				08 51	past	18 51			18 55					19 21
Nunhead 4	d	07 57						08 23		08 27				08 53	each	18 53			18 57					19 23
Lewisham 4	a							08 31						09 01	hour until	19 01								19 31
Crofton Park	d	08 00								08 30									19 00					
Catford	d	08 03								08 33									19 03					
Bellingham	d	08 05								08 35									19 05					
Beckenham Hill	d	08 07								08 37									19 07					
Ravensbourne	d	08 09								08 39									19 09					
Shortlands 4	d	08 11		08 18					08 33	08 41		08 48						19 03	19 11		19 18			
Bromley South 4	d	08 14	08a08	08 21	08 19	08 23			08 36	08 44	08a38	08 51	08 53					19 06	19 14	19a08	19 21	19 19	19 23	
Bickley 4	d	08 17		08 24					08 39	08 47		08 54						19 09	19 17		19 24			
Petts Wood 4	d			08 29					08 44			08 59						19 14			19 29			
Orpington 4	d			08a32					08a47			09a02						19a17			19a32			
St Mary Cray	d	08 21			08 25					08 51			09 00						19 21			19 25		
Swanley 4	d	08 26			08a29	08 33				08 56			09 04						19 26			19a29	19 33	
Eynsford	d	08 30								09 00									19 30					
Shoreham (Kent)	d	08 34								09 04									19 34					
Otford 4	d	08 37				08a41				09 07			09a12						19 37				19a41	
Bat & Ball	d	08 40								09 10									19 40					
Sevenoaks 4	a	08 43								09 13									19 43					

Table 195

Saturdays

London - Catford, Beckenham Junction, Bromley South, Orpington, Otford and Sevenoaks

		SE	SE		SE 1	SE	SE 1	SE	SE	SE	SE 1	SE	SE 1		SE 1	SE	SE	SE 1	SE	SE	SE 1	SE	SE 1		SE
London Victoria 15 ⊖	d	19 10	19 13		19 22	19 25	19 37	19 39	19 40	19 43	19 52	19 55	19 58		20 07	20 10	20 13	20 22	20 25	20 43	20 52	20 55	21 07		21 13
Brixton ⊖	d	19 17				19 32			19 47			20 02				20 17			20 32			21 02			
Kentish Town ⊖	d																								
St Pancras International 15 ⊖	d																								
Farringdon ⊖	d																								
City Thameslink 3	d																								
London Blackfriars 3 ⊖	d																								
Elephant & Castle ⊖	d																								
Loughborough Jn	d																								
Herne Hill 4	d	19 19				19 34			19 49			20 04				20 19			20 34			21 04			
West Dulwich	d	19 21				19 36			19 51			20 06				20 21			20 36			21 06			
Sydenham Hill	d	19 23				19 38			19 53			20 08				20 23			20 38			21 08			
Penge East	d	19 26				19 41			19 56			20 11				20 26			20 41			21 11			
Kent House 4	d	19 28				19 43			19 58			20 13				20 28			20 43			21 13			
Beckenham Junction 4	d	19 30				19 45			20 00			20 15				20 30			20 45			21 15			
Denmark Hill 4	d		19 22					19 48		19 52							20 22			20 52					21 22
Peckham Rye 4	d		19 25					19 51		19 55							20 25			20 55					21 25
Nunhead 4	d		19 27					19 53		19 57							20 27			20 57					21 27
Lewisham 4	a							20 01																	
Crofton Park	d		19 30							20 00							20 30			21 00					21 30
Catford	d		19 33							20 03							20 33			21 03					21 33
Bellingham	d		19 35							20 05							20 35			21 05					21 35
Beckenham Hill	d		19 37							20 07							20 37			21 07					21 37
Ravensbourne	d		19 39							20 09							20 39			21 09					21 39
Shortlands 4	d	19 33	19 41			19 48			20 03	20 11		20 18				20 33	20 41		20 48	21 11		21 18			21 41
Bromley South 4	d	19 36	19 44		19a38	19 51	19 53		20 06	20 14	20a08	20 21	20 19		20 23	20 36	20 44	20a38	20 51	21 14	21 09	21 21	21 23		21 44
Bickley 4	d	19 39	19 47			19 54			20 09	20 17		20 24				20 39	20 47		20 54	21 17		21 24			21 47
Petts Wood 4	d	19 44				19 59			20 14			20 29				20 44			20 59			21 29			
Orpington 4	d	19a48				20a02			20a18			20a32				20a47			21a02			21a32			
St Mary Cray	d		19 51				20 00			20 21			20 25		20 30		20 51			21 21	21 15		21 30		21 51
Swanley 4	d		19 56				20 04			20 26			20a29		20 34		20 56			21 26	21a19		21 34		21 56
Eynsford	d		20 00							20 30							21 00			21 30					22 00
Shoreham (Kent)	d		20 04							20 34							21 04			21 34					22 04
Otford 4	d		20 07				20a12			20 37					20a42		21 07			21 37			21a42		22 07
Bat & Ball	d		20 10							20 40							21 10			21 40					22 10
Sevenoaks 4	a		20 13							20 43							21 13			21 43					22 13

		SE 1	SE	SE	SE 1	SE	SE 1	SE	SE 1		SE	SE	SE 1	SE	SE 1	SE	SE 1	SE	SE		SE 1	SE			
London Victoria 15 ⊖	d	21 22	21 25	21 43	21 52	21 55	22 07	22 13	22 22		22 25	22 43	22 52	22 55	23 07	23 13	23 22	23 25	23 43		23 52	23 55			
Brixton ⊖	d		21 32			22 02					22 32			23 02				23 32				00 02			
Kentish Town ⊖	d																								
St Pancras International 15 ⊖	d																								
Farringdon ⊖	d																								
City Thameslink 3	d																								
London Blackfriars 3 ⊖	d																								
Elephant & Castle ⊖	d																								
Loughborough Jn	d																								
Herne Hill 4	d		21 34			22 04					22 34			23 04				23 34				00 04			
West Dulwich	d		21 36			22 06					22 36			23 06				23 36				00 06			
Sydenham Hill	d		21 38			22 08					22 38			23 08				23 38				00 08			
Penge East	d		21 41			22 11					22 41			23 11				23 41				00 11			
Kent House 4	d		21 43			22 13					22 43			23 13				23 43				00 13			
Beckenham Junction 4	d		21 45			22 15					22 45			23 15				23 45				00 15			
Denmark Hill 4	d			21 52				22 22				22 52				23 22			23 52						
Peckham Rye 4	d			21 55				22 25				22 55				23 25			23 55						
Nunhead 4	d			21 57				22 27				22 57				23 27			23 57						
Lewisham 4	a																								
Crofton Park	d			22 00				22 30				23 00				23 30			23 58						
Catford	d			22 03				22 33				23 03				23 33			00 03						
Bellingham	d			22 05				22 35				23 05				23 35			00 05						
Beckenham Hill	d			22 07				22 37				23 07				23 37			00 07						
Ravensbourne	d			22 09				22 39				23 09				23 39			00 09						
Shortlands 4	d		21 48	22 11		22 18		22 41			22 48	23 11		23 18		23 41		23 48	00 11			00 18			
Bromley South 4	d	21a38	21 51	22 14	22 09	22 21	22 23	22 44	22a38		22 51	23 14	23 09	23 21	23 23	23 44	23a38	23 51	00 14		00 09	00 21			
Bickley 4	d		21 54	22 17		22 24		22 47			22 54	23 17		23 24		23 47		23 54	00 17			00 24			
Petts Wood 4	d		21 59			22 29					22 59	23 22		23 29		23 52		23 59	00 22			00 29			
Orpington 4	d		22a02			22a32					23a02	23a25		23a32		23a55		00a02	00a25			00a32			
St Mary Cray	d			22 21	22 15		22 30	22 51					23 15		23 30						00 15				
Swanley 4	d			22 26	22a19		22 34	22 56					23a19		23 34						00a19				
Eynsford	d			22 30				23 00																	
Shoreham (Kent)	d			22 34				23 04																	
Otford 4	d			22 37			22a42	23 07							23a42										
Bat & Ball	d			22 40				23 10																	
Sevenoaks 4	a			22 43				23 13																	

Table 195

Sundays

London - Catford, Beckenham Junction, Bromley South, Orpington, Otford and Sevenoaks

		SE	SE	SE	SE	SE	SE	SE	SE	SE		SE	SE	SE
			1		1		1		1			1		
		A	A	A										
London Victoria 15 ⊖	d	23p43	23p52	23p55	00 07	00 35	07 24	07 39	07 45	07 51		08 05	08 09	08 21
Brixton ⊖	d			00 02						07 58				08 28
Kentish Town ⊖	d													
St Pancras International 15 ⊖	d													
Farringdon ⊖	d													
City Thameslink 3	d													
London Blackfriars 3 ⊖	d													
Elephant & Castle ⊖	d													
Loughborough Jn	d													
Herne Hill 4	d			00 04		00 43				08 00				08 30
West Dulwich	d			00 06						08 02				08 32
Sydenham Hill	d			00 08						08 04				08 34
Penge East	d			00 11		00 48				08 07				08 37
Kent House 4	d			00 13						08 09				08 39
Beckenham Junction 4	d			00 15		00 50				08 11				08 41
Denmark Hill 4	d	23p52						07 48					08 18	
Peckham Rye 4	d	23p55						07 51					08 21	
Nunhead 4	d	23p57						07 53					08 23	
Lewisham 4	a													
Crofton Park	d	23p58						07 56					08 26	
Catford	d	00 03						07 59					08 29	
Bellingham	d	00 05						08 01					08 31	
Beckenham Hill	d	00 07						08 03					08 33	
Ravensbourne	d	00 09						08 05					08 35	
Shortlands 4	d	00 11		00 18				08 07		08 14			08 37	08 44
Bromley South 4	d	00 14	00 09	00 21	00 25	00 55	07 44	08 10	08 01	08 18		08a21	08 40	08 48
Bickley 4	d	00 17		00 24				08 13		08 20			08 43	08 50
Petts Wood 4	d	00 22		00 29						08 25				08 55
Orpington 4	d	00a25		00a32						08a28				08a58
St Mary Cray	d		00 15		00 31	01 01	07 50	08 17	08 08				08 47	
Swanley 4	d		00a19		00 36	01a05	07a54	08 22	08 12				08 52	
Eynsford	d				00 40			08 26					08 56	
Shoreham (Kent)	d				00 44			08 30					09 00	
Otford 4	d				00a47			08 33	08a20				09 03	
Bat & Ball	d							08 36					09 06	
Sevenoaks 4	a							08 39					09 09	

and at the same minutes past each hour until

		SE	SE	SE	SE	SE	SE	SE	SE	SE
			1		1		1			
London Victoria 15 ⊖	d	22 21	22 24	22 39	22 45	22 51	23 05	23 09	23 21	23 45
Brixton ⊖	d	22 28				22 58			23 28	
Kentish Town ⊖	d									
St Pancras International 15 ⊖	d									
Farringdon ⊖	d									
City Thameslink 3	d									
London Blackfriars 3 ⊖	d									
Elephant & Castle ⊖	d									
Loughborough Jn	d									
Herne Hill 4	d	22 30				23 00			23 30	
West Dulwich	d	22 32				23 02			23 32	
Sydenham Hill	d	22 34				23 04			23 34	
Penge East	d	22 37				23 07			23 37	
Kent House 4	d	22 39				23 09			23 39	
Beckenham Junction 4	d	22 41				23 11			23 41	
Denmark Hill 4	d			22 48				23 18		
Peckham Rye 4	d			22 51				23 21		
Nunhead 4	d			22 53				23 23		
Lewisham 4	a									
Crofton Park	d			22 56				23 26		
Catford	d			22 59				23 29		
Bellingham	d			23 01				23 31		
Beckenham Hill	d			23 03				23 33		
Ravensbourne	d			23 05				23 35		
Shortlands 4	d	22 44		23 07		23 14		23 37	23 44	
Bromley South 4	d	22 48	22 44	23 10	23 01	23 18	23a21	23 40	23 48	00 02
Bickley 4	d	22 50		23 13		23 20		23 43	23 50	
Petts Wood 4	d	22 55		23 22		23 25		23 52	23 55	
Orpington 4	d	22a58		23a26		23a29		23a56	23a59	
St Mary Cray	d		22 50		23 08					00 08
Swanley 4	d		22a54		23 12					00a12
Eynsford	d									
Shoreham (Kent)	d									
Otford 4	d				23a20					
Bat & Ball	d									
Sevenoaks 4	a									

A not 22 May

Sevenoaks, Otford, Orpington, Bromley South, Beckenham Junction and Catford - London

Miles	Miles	Miles			SE MO 1	SE MX 1	SE MO 1	SE MX 1	SE	SE	SE	SE	FC		SE	SE	FC	SE	SE 1	SE 1	SE	SE 1	FC		SE
—	0	—	**Sevenoaks** 4	d														05 40							
—	1¼	—	Bat & Ball	d														05 43							
—	3	—	Otford 4	d														05 46				06 15			
—	4¼	—	Shoreham (Kent)	d														05 49							
—	6½	—	Eynsford	d														05 53							
—	9½	—	**Swanley** 4	d	23p32			00 10		04 33								05 58		06 02		06 25			
—	12¼	—	St Mary Cray	d	23p36			00 14		04 37								06 02		06 06					
0	—	—	**Orpington** 4	d					04 34		04 55	05 10			05 34	05 40					06 10				
1¼	—	—	Petts Wood 4	d					04 37		04 58	05 13			05 37	05 43					06 13				
3	14½	—	Bickley 4	d					04 41	04 41	05 02	05 17			05 41	05 47		06 06			06 17				
4	15½	—	**Bromley South** 4	d	23p43	23p51	00 13	00 20	04 44	04 50	05 05	05 20			05 44	05 50		06 10	06 12	06 15	06 20	06 33			
5	16½	—	Shortlands 4	d					04 47	04 53	05 08	05 23			05 47	05 53		06 13			06 23				
—	17¼	—	Ravensbourne	d					04 49						05 49			06 15							
—	18	—	Beckenham Hill	d					04 51						05 51			06 17							
—	18¾	—	Bellingham	d					04 53						05 53			06 19							
—	19½	—	Catford	d					04 56						05 56			06 22							
—	20½	—	Crofton Park	d					04 58						05 58			06 25							
—	—	0	Lewisham 4	d																					
—	21¾	1¾	Nunhead 4	d					05 01						06 01			06 27							
—	22½	2½	Peckham Rye 4	d					05 04						06 04			06 30							
—	23¼	3¼	Denmark Hill 4	d					05 07						06 07			06 33							
6¼	—	—	**Beckenham Junction** 4	d						04 56	05 11	05 26				05 56					06 26				06 40
7¼	—	—	Kent House 4	d						04 58	05 13	05 28				05 58					06 28				06 42
7¾	—	—	Penge East	d						05 00	05 15	05 30				06 00					06 30				06 44
9¼	—	—	Sydenham Hill	d						05 03	05 18	05 33				06 03					06 33				06 47
10	—	—	West Dulwich	d						05 05	05 20	05 35				06 05					06 35				06 49
11	—	—	Herne Hill 4	d						05 08	05 23	05 38	05 54			06 08	06 16				06 38	06 43	06 46		06 52
—	—	—	Loughborough Jn	d													06 19						06 49		
—	25¾	—	Elephant & Castle	⊖ d					05 13		05 29		06 00		06 13		06 24	06 40					06 54		
—	27	—	**London Blackfriars** 3	⊖ d					05 17		05 33		06 04		06 17		06 30	06 48					07 00		
—	—	—	City Thameslink 3	a					05 19		05 35		06 06		06 19		06 32	06 50					07 02		
—	—	—	Farringdon	⊖ a									06 10				06 36	06 54					07 06		
—	—	—	St Pancras International 15	⊖ a									06 13				06 39	06 57					07 09		
—	—	—	Kentish Town	⊖ a									06 18				06 44	07 02							
11	—	—	Brixton	⊖ d						05 10		05 40				06 10					06 40				06 54
15	—	7½	**London Victoria** 15	⊖ a	00 02	00 07	00 29	00 38		05 17		05 47				06 18			06 28	06 31	06 47	06 51			07 03

		SE	FC	SE	SE 1	SE 1	SE	SE 1	SE 1		SE 1	SE	SE	FC	SE	SE	SE 1	SE 1	SE		SE 1	SE	FC 1	FC	SE
Sevenoaks 4	d			06 13												06 42									
Bat & Ball	d			06 16												06 48									
Otford 4	d			06 19				06 38	06 46							06 51		07 01			07 14				
Shoreham (Kent)	d			06 22												06 54									
Eynsford	d			06 26												06 58									
Swanley 4	d			06 31	06 35			06 48	06 54		06 57					07 03		07 10			07 22	07 23			
St Mary Cray	d			06 35	06 39						07 01					07 07						07 27			
Orpington 4	d						06 40								06 58				07 08						
Petts Wood 4	d						06 43								07 01				07 11						
Bickley 4	d			06 39			06 47								07 05	07 11			07 16						
Bromley South 4	d			06 42	06 46	06 50	06 50	06 57	07 02		07 08				07 08	07 14	07 16	07 20	07 20		07 31	07 34			07 34
Shortlands 4	d			06 45			06 53								07 11	07 17			07 23						07 36
Ravensbourne	d			06 47												07 19									
Beckenham Hill	d			06 49												07 21									
Bellingham	d			06 51												07 23									
Catford	d			06 54												07 26									
Crofton Park	d			06 57												07 29									
Lewisham 4	d	06 41											07 15												
Nunhead 4	d			06 59									07 20			07 31									
Peckham Rye 4	d	06 47		07 02									07 23			07 34									
Denmark Hill 4	d	06 50		07 05									07 29			07 37									
Beckenham Junction 4	d						06 56					07 08			07 14				07 26						07 39
Kent House 4	d						06 58					07 11			07 17				07 28						07 42
Penge East	d						07 00					07 14			07 19				07 30						07 44
Sydenham Hill	d						07 03					07 17			07 22				07 33						07 47
West Dulwich	d						07 05					07 19			07 24				07 35						07 49
Herne Hill 4	d		06 57				07 08					07 22		07 24	07 31				07 38				07 41	07 46	07 52
Loughborough Jn.	d		07 00											07 27	07 34									07 49	
Elephant & Castle	⊖ d		07 06	07 12				07 16						07 32	07 38	07 44							07 48	07 54	
London Blackfriars 3	⊖ d		07 12	07 18				07 24						07 36	07 42	07 48							07 54	07 58	
City Thameslink 3	a		07 14	07 20				07 26						07 38	07 44	07 50							07 56	08 00	
Farringdon	⊖ a		07 18	07 24				07 30						07 42	07 48	07 54							08 00	08 03	
St Pancras International 15	⊖ a		07 21	07 27				07 33						07 45	07 51	07 57							08 03	08 07	
Kentish Town	⊖ a			07 32												08 02								08 14	
Brixton	⊖ d						07 10					07 24							07 40						07 54
London Victoria 15	⊖ a	07 04			07 07	07 09	07 19		07 22		07 30	07 33	07 42				07 38	07 43	07 49		07 53	07 55			08 03

Sevenoaks, Otford, Orpington, Bromley South, Beckenham Junction and Catford - London

		SE	SE	SE	SE		SE	FC	SE	SE	SE	SE	SE	SE	FC		SE	SE	SE	SE	SE	SE	FC	SE	SE
					1		1			1	1	1							1	1	1	1			
Sevenoaks 4	d			07 11														07 36							
Bat & Ball	d			07 14														07 39							
Otford 4	d			07 18	07 23						07 38							07 43			07 56				
Shoreham (Kent)	d			07 21														07 46							
Eynsford	d			07 24														07 49							
Swanley 4	d			07 30	07 32					07 40	07 47							07 54	07 55	08 02	08 05				
St Mary Cray	d			07 34						07 45								07 59	08 00	08 06					
Orpington 4	d	07 28							07 38					07 47											
Petts Wood 4	d	07 31							07 41					07 50											
Bickley 4	d	07 35		07 39					07 46					07 55				08 03							
Bromley South 4	d	07 38		07 42	07 40		07 49		07 50	07 53	07 57			07 58			08 04	08 08	08 06	08 12	08 13	08 16			
Shortlands 4	d	07 41		07 44					07 53					08 00			08 06	08 10							
Ravensbourne	d			07 47														08 13							
Beckenham Hill	d			07 49														08 15							
Bellingham	d			07 51										08 05				08 17							
Catford	d			07 53										08 08				08 20							
Crofton Park	d			07 56										08 10											
Lewisham 4	d		07 46										08 05												08 25
Nunhead 4	d		07 51	07 58									08 11	08 14											08 30
Peckham Rye 4	d		07 54	08 01									08 13	08 16											08 33
Denmark Hill 4	d		07 59	08 04									08 17	08 19				08 26		08 30					08 36
Beckenham Junction 4	d	07 44							07 56			07 59					08 10							08 22	
Kent House 4	d	07 47							07 58			08 02					08 12							08 24	
Penge East	d	07 49							08 00			08 04					08 14							08 26	
Sydenham Hill	d	07 52							08 03			08 07					08 17							08 29	
West Dulwich	d	07 54							08 05			08 09					08 19							08 31	
Herne Hill 4	d	07 57						08 01	08 08			08 12			08 20		08 23						08 31	08 34	
Loughborough Jn.	d	08 00						08 04				08 16			08 23								08 35		
Elephant & Castle ⊖	d	08 05		08 13	08 00			08 09				08 21		08 25	08 28			08 35	08 31				08 40		
London Blackfriars 3 ⊖	d	08 09		08 17	08 04			08 13				08 25		08 29	08 33			08 42	08 37				08 46		
City Thameslink 3	a	08 11		08 19	08 06			08 15				08 27		08 31	08 35			08 44	08 39				08 48		
Farringdon ⊖	a	08 15		08 23	08 10			08 19				08 30		08 35	08 39			08 48	08 43				08 52		
St Pancras International 15 ⊖	a	08 19		08 27	08 13			08 23				08 35		08 39	08 43			08 51	08 47				08 55		
Kentish Town ⊖	a							08 28							08 48			08 58					09 00		
Brixton ⊖	d								08 10								08 25							08 36	
London Victoria 15 ⊖	a		08 11				08 09		08 20	08 17	08 23		08 29				08 35			08 42	08 36	08 39		08 45	08 49

			SE	SE	SE	SE	SE	FC	SE	SE	SE		FC	FC	SE	SE	SE	SE	SE	SE	SE		FC	SE	SE
			1			1	1		1				1			1		1			1				
Sevenoaks 4	d				07 53													08 24							08 43
Bat & Ball	d				07 56													08 27							08 46
Otford 4	d				08 00	08 09												08 31			08 46				08 49
Shoreham (Kent)	d				08 03													08 34							08 52
Eynsford	d				08 06													08 37							08 56
Swanley 4	d				08 11		08 22											08 42			08 54				09 01
St Mary Cray	d				08 16		08 27											08 46			08 58				09 05
Orpington 4	d			08 10						08 26							08 40			08 47				08 55	
Petts Wood 4	d			08 13						08 29							08 43			08 50				08 58	
Bickley 4	d			08 17	08 20					08 33							08 47	08 51		08 55				09 02	09 09
Bromley South 4	d		08 18	08 22	08 26	08 25	08 33			08 36					08 44	08 50	08 50	08 54		08 58	09 05			09 05	09 12
Shortlands 4	d		08 20	08 24	08 29					08 39					08 46		08 53	08 56		09 00				09 08	09 15
Ravensbourne	d		08 23												08 49					09 03					09 17
Beckenham Hill	d		08 25												08 51					09 05					09 19
Bellingham	d		08 27		08 33										08 53			09 01		09 07					09 21
Catford	d		08 30		08 36										08 56			09 04		09 09					09 24
Crofton Park	d				08 39										08 58					09 12					09 26
Lewisham 4	d										08 46								09 06						
Nunhead 4	d				08 41						08 52				09 01				09 11	09 14					09 29
Peckham Rye 4	d		08 36		08 44						08 55				09 04			09 09	09 14	09 17					09 31
Denmark Hill 4	d		08 39		08 47						09 02				09 07			09 12	09 17	09 19					09 34
Beckenham Junction 4	d			08 28						08 42							08 56							09 11	
Kent House 4	d			08 30					08 42	08 45							08 58							09 13	
Penge East	d								08 44	08 47							09 00							09 15	
Sydenham Hill	d								08 47	08 50							09 03							09 18	
West Dulwich	d			08 35					08 49	08 52							09 05							09 20	
Herne Hill 4	d			08 39				08 47	08 52	08 54			08 57	09 02			09 08						09 20	09 23	
Loughborough Jn.	d							08 50	08 55					09 05									09 23		
Elephant & Castle ⊖	d		08 45		08 54			08 58	09 02				09 06	09 10	09 14			09 20		09 26			09 30		09 42
London Blackfriars 3 ⊖	d		08 50		08 58			09 02	09 06				09 10	09 14	09 18			09 26		09 30			09 34		09 46
City Thameslink 3	a		08 52		09 00			09 04	09 08				09 12	09 16	09 20			09 27		09 32			09 36		09 48
Farringdon ⊖	a		08 56		09 04			09 08	09 12				09 16	09 20	09 24			09 32		09 36			09 40		09 52
St Pancras International 15 ⊖	a		08 59		09 07			09 11	09 15				09 19	09 23	09 27			09 35		09 39			09 43		09 55
Kentish Town ⊖	a				09 14			09 16							09 34					09 46			09 49		10 00
Brixton ⊖	d			08 41						08 57							09 10							09 25	
London Victoria 15 ⊖	a			08 50		08 53	08 53			09 06	09 11					09 09	09 19		09 29		09 23			09 34	

Sevenoaks, Otford, Orpington, Bromley South, Beckenham Junction and Catford - London

Station		SE 1	SE 1	FC	SE	SE 1	SE		FC	SE	FC	SE	SE 1	SE	SE 1	SE	FC		SE	FC	SE	SE 1	SE 1	SE	SE
Sevenoaks 4	d											09 13									09 42				
Bat & Ball	d											09 16									09 46				
Otford 4	d					09 17						09 21			09 46						09 50				
Shoreham (Kent)	d											09 24									09 53				
Eynsford	d											09 28									09 56				
Swanley 4	d	09 05				09 26						09 33			09 54						10 01	10 05			
St Mary Cray	d	09 09										09 37			09 58						10 05	10 09			
Orpington 4	d				09 10					09 25				09 40					09 55					10 10	
Petts Wood 4	d				09 13					09 28				09 43					09 58					10 13	
Bickley 4	d				09 17					09 32		09 42		09 47					10 02		10 10			10 17	
Bromley South 4	d	09 15	09 20		09 20	09 34				09 35		09 45	09 50	09 50	10 05				10 05		10 15	10 15	10 20	10 20	
Shortlands 4	d				09 23					09 38		09 48		09 53					10 08		10 18			10 23	
Ravensbourne	d											09 50									10 20				
Beckenham Hill	d											09 52									10 22				
Bellingham	d											09 54									10 24				
Catford	d											09 57									10 27				
Crofton Park	d											09 59									10 29				
Lewisham 4 ⛴	d						09 38									10 08									10 38
Nunhead 4	d						09 43					10 02				10 13					10 32				10 43
Peckham Rye 4	d						09 45					10 04				10 15					10 34				10 45
Denmark Hill 4	d						09 49					10 07				10 19					10 37				10 49
Beckenham Junction 4 ⛴	d				09 26					09 41				09 56					10 11					10 26	
Kent House 4	d				09 28					09 43				09 58					10 13					10 28	
Penge East	d				09 30					09 45				10 00					10 15					10 30	
Sydenham Hill	d				09 33					09 48				10 03					10 18					10 33	
West Dulwich	d				09 35					09 50				10 05					10 20					10 35	
Herne Hill 4	d			09 35	09 38				09 47	09 53	10 01			10 08			10 16		10 23	10 31				10 38	
Loughborough Jn.	d			09 39					09 50		10 04						10 19			10 34					
Elephant & Castle ⊖	d			09 46					09 55		10 09	10 14					10 24			10 39	10 44				
London Blackfriars 3 ⊖	d			09 50					10 00		10 13	10 18					10 30			10 43	10 48				
City Thameslink 3	a			09 52					10 02		10 15	10 20					10 32			10 45	10 50				
Farringdon ⊖	a			09 56					10 06		10 19	10 24					10 35			10 49	10 54				
St Pancras International 15 ⊖	a			09 59					10 09		10 22	10 27					10 39			10 52	10 57				
Kentish Town ⊖	a			10 06					10 14		10 27	10 34					10 44			10 57	11 03				
Brixton ⊖	d				09 40					09 55				10 10					10 25					10 40	
London Victoria 15 ⊖	a	09 38	09 43		09 49	09 51	10 00			10 02			10 07	10 17	10 21	10 28			10 32			10 41	10 37	10 47	10 58

Station		FC	SE		SE 1	SE	SE 1	FC	SE	SE	FC	SE	SE 1		SE	SE 1	SE 1	FC	and at the same minutes past each hour until	FC	SE	SE		FC
Sevenoaks 4	d		10 02									10 32												
Bat & Ball	d		10 05									10 35												
Otford 4	d		10 08		10 17							10 38	10 46											
Shoreham (Kent)	d		10 11									10 41												
Eynsford	d		10 15									10 45												
Swanley 4	d		10 20		10 26							10 50	10 54			11 05								
St Mary Cray	d		10 24									10 54	10 58			11 09								
Orpington 4	d					10 25			10 40						10 55						15 10			
Petts Wood 4	d					10 28			10 43						10 58						15 13			
Bickley 4	d		10 28			10 32			10 47			10 58			11 02						15 17			
Bromley South 4	d		10 31		10 35	10 35	10 50		10 50			11 01	11 05		11 05	11 15	11 20				15 20			
Shortlands 4	d		10 34			10 38			10 53			11 04			11 08						15 23			
Ravensbourne	d		10 36									11 06												
Beckenham Hill	d		10 38									11 08												
Bellingham	d		10 40									11 10												
Catford	d		10 43									11 13												
Crofton Park	d		10 45									11 15												
Lewisham 4 ⛴	d									11 08												15 38		
Nunhead 4	d		10 48							11 13		11 18										15 43		
Peckham Rye 4	d		10 50							11 15		11 20										15 45		
Denmark Hill 4	d		10 54							11 19		11 24										15 49		
Beckenham Junction 4 ⛴	d					10 41			10 56						11 11						15 26			
Kent House 4	d					10 43			10 58						11 13						15 28			
Penge East	d					10 45			11 00						11 15						15 30			
Sydenham Hill	d					10 48			11 03						11 18						15 33			
West Dulwich	d					10 50			11 05						11 20						15 35			
Herne Hill 4	d	10 46				10 53		11 01	11 08		11 16				11 23			11 31		15 31	15 38			15 46
Loughborough Jn.	d	10 49						11 04			11 19							11 34		15 34				15 49
Elephant & Castle ⊖	d	10 54	11 00					11 09			11 24	11 30						11 39		15 39				15 54
London Blackfriars 3 ⊖	d	11 00	11 04					11 13			11 30	11 34						11 43		15 43				16 00
City Thameslink 3	a	11 02	11 06					11 15			11 32	11 36						11 45		15 45				16 02
Farringdon ⊖	a	11 06	11 10					11 19			11 36	11 40						11 49		15 49				16 06
St Pancras International 15 ⊖	a	11 09	11 13					11 22			11 39	11 43						11 52		15 52				16 09
Kentish Town ⊖	a	11 14	11 20					11 27			11 44	11 50						11 57		15 57				16 14
Brixton ⊖	d					10 55			11 10						11 25						15 40			
London Victoria 15 ⊖	a				10 51	11 02	11 07		11 17	11 28			11 21		11 32	11 37	11 37				15 47	15 58		

Sevenoaks, Otford, Orpington, Bromley South, Beckenham Junction and Catford - London

		SE	SE 1	SE	SE 1	FC	SE	SE	FC		SE 1	SE 1	SE	SE	SE 1	FC	SE	SE	FC		SE 1	SE 1	SE	FC 1	SE
Sevenoaks 4	d	15 02									15 32										16 02				16 22
Bat & Ball	d	15 05									15 35										16 05				16 25
Otford 4	d	15 08	15 17								15 38	15 46									16 08	16 17			16 28
Shoreham (Kent)	d	15 11									15 41										16 11				
Eynsford	d	15 15									15 45										16 15				
Swanley 4	d	15 20	15 26								15 50	15 54		16 05							16 20	16 26			16 37
St Mary Cray	d	15 24									15 54	15 58		16 09							16 24				16 41
Orpington 4	d			15 25			15 40						15 55				16 10						16 25		
Petts Wood 4	d			15 28			15 43						15 58				16 13						16 28		
Bickley 4	d	15 28		15 32			15 47				15 58		16 02				16 17				16 28		16 32		
Bromley South 4	d	15 31	15 35	15 35	15 50		15 50				16 01	16 05	16 05	16 15	16 20		16 20				16 31	16 35	16 35		16 47
Shortlands 4	d	15 34		15 38			15 53				16 04		16 08				16 23				16 34		16 38		
Ravensbourne	d	15 36									16 06										16 36				
Beckenham Hill	d	15 38									16 08										16 38				
Bellingham	d	15 40									16 10										16 40				16 52
Catford	d	15 43									16 13										16 43				16 55
Crofton Park	d	15 45									16 15										16 45				
Lewisham 4 ⇌	d							16 08										16 38							
Nunhead 4	d	15 48						16 13			16 18							16 43			16 48				16 59
Peckham Rye 4	d	15 50						16 15			16 20							16 45			16 50				17 02
Denmark Hill 4	d	15 54						16 19			16 24							16 49			16 54				17 05
Beckenham Junction 4 ⇌	d			15 41			15 56						16 11				16 26						16 41		
Kent House 4	d			15 43			15 58						16 13				16 28						16 43		
Penge East	d			15 45			16 00						16 15				16 30						16 45		
Sydenham Hill	d			15 48			16 03						16 18				16 33						16 48		
West Dulwich	d			15 50			16 05						16 20				16 35						16 50		
Herne Hill 4	d			15 53		16 01	16 08		16 16				16 23			16 31	16 38		16 50				16 53	17 01	
Loughborough Jn.	d					16 04			16 19							16 34			16 53						
Elephant & Castle ⊖	d	16 00				16 09			16 24		16 30					16 39			17 00		17 04			17 08	17 12
London Blackfriars 3 ⊖	d	16 04				16 14			16 30		16 38					16 44			17 04		17 08			17 12	17 16
City Thameslink 3	a	16 06				16 16			16 32		16 40					16 46			17 06		17 10			17 14	17 18
Farringdon ⊖	a	16 10				16 19			16 35		16 43					16 49			17 09		17 13			17 17	17 23
St Pancras International 15 ⊖	a	16 13				16 23			16 39		16 47					16 53			17 13		17 17			17 21	17 27
Kentish Town ⊖	a	16 20				16 28			16 44							16 58			17 18						17 32
Brixton ⊖	d			15 55			16 10						16 25				16 40						16 55		
London Victoria 15 ⊖	a		15 51	16 02	16 07		16 17	16 28				16 21	16 32	16 37	16 38		16 47	17 01				16 51	17 04		

		SE 1	SE	SE	FC		SE	SE 1	SE	SE 1	SE 1	FC	SE	SE 1	SE		FC	SE 1	SE 1	SE	SE 1	SE 1	SE 1	FC	SE
Sevenoaks 4	d						16 32											17 02							
Bat & Ball	d						16 35											17 05							
Otford 4	d						16 38	16 46										17 08	17 17						
Shoreham (Kent)	d						16 41											17 11							
Eynsford	d						16 45											17 15							
Swanley 4	d						16 50	16 54		17 05								17 20	17 26			17 35			
St Mary Cray	d						16 54	16 58		17 09								17 24				17 39			
Orpington 4	d		16 40						16 55				17 10							17 24	17 34				17 40
Petts Wood 4	d		16 43						16 58				17 13							17 28	17 37				17 43
Bickley 4	d		16 47				16 58		17 02				17 17					17 28		17 32	17 42				17 47
Bromley South 4	d	16 50	16 50				17 01	17 05	17 05	17 15	17 20		17 20					17 31	17 35	17 35	17 45	17 46	17 50		17 50
Shortlands 4	d		16 53				17 04		17 08				17 23					17 34		17 38					17 53
Ravensbourne	d						17 06											17 36							
Beckenham Hill	d						17 08											17 38							
Bellingham	d						17 10											17 40							
Catford	d						17 13											17 43							
Crofton Park	d						17 15											17 45							
Lewisham 4 ⇌	d			17 08											17 38										
Nunhead 4	d			17 13			17 18								17 43			17 48							
Peckham Rye 4	d			17 15			17 20								17 45			17 50							
Denmark Hill 4	d			17 19			17 24								17 49			17 54							
Beckenham Junction 4 ⇌	d		16 56						17 11				17 26	17 30						17 41	17 49				17 56
Kent House 4	d		16 58						17 13				17 28	17 33						17 43					17 58
Penge East	d		17 00						17 15				17 30	17 35						17 45					18 00
Sydenham Hill	d		17 03						17 18				17 33	17 38						17 48					18 03
West Dulwich	d		17 05						17 20				17 35	17 40						17 50					18 05
Herne Hill 4	d		17 08		17 20				17 23			17 31	17 38	17 43			17 48			17 53				18 06	18 09
Loughborough Jn.	d				17 23							17 34		17 46			17 51							18 09	
Elephant & Castle ⊖	d				17 28		17 34					17 39		17 52			17 56	18 00			18 05			18 14	
London Blackfriars 3 ⊖	d				17 32		17 40					17 46		17 56			18 00	18 06			18 10			18 18	
City Thameslink 3	a				17 34		17 42					17 48		17 58			18 02	18 08			18 12			18 20	
Farringdon ⊖	a				17 37		17 45					17 51		18 01			18 05	18 11			18 15			18 23	
St Pancras International 15 ⊖	a				17 41		17 49					17 55		18 05			18 09	18 15			18 19			18 27	
Kentish Town ⊖	a				17 46							18 00					18 14							18 32	
Brixton ⊖	d		17 10						17 25				17 40							17 55					18 11
London Victoria 15 ⊖	a	17 07	17 18	17 28				17 21	17 33	17 38	17 37		17 48		17 59				17 53	18 03		18 08	18 07		18 18

Table 195

Sevenoaks, Otford, Orpington, Bromley South, Beckenham Junction and Catford - London

		SE	FC	SE [1]	SE [1]	SE	SE [1]	SE [1]	FC	SE	SE	FC	SE [1]	SE [1]	SE	SE	SE [1]	FC	SE	SE	FC	SE
Sevenoaks [4]	d			17 32									18 02			18 18						18 32
Bat & Ball	d			17 35									18 05			18 21						18 35
Otford [4]	d			17 38	17 46								18 08	18 17		18 24						18 38
Shoreham (Kent)	d			17 41									18 11			18 27						18 41
Eynsford	d			17 45									18 15			18 31						18 45
Swanley [4]	d			17 50	17 54		18 05						18 20	18 26		18 36						18 50
St Mary Cray	d			17 54	17 58		18 09						18 24			18 40						18 54
Orpington [4]	d					17 55				18 09					18 25				18 40			
Petts Wood [4]	d					17 58				18 12					18 28				18 43			
Bickley [4]	d			17 58		18 02				18 17			18 28		18 32				18 47			18 58
Bromley South [4]	d			18 01	18 05	18 05	18 15	18 20		18 20			18 31	18 35	18 35	18 46	18 50		18 50			19 01
Shortlands [4]	d			18 04		18 08				18 23			18 34		18 38				18 53			19 04
Ravensbourne	d			18 06									18 36									19 06
Beckenham Hill	d			18 08									18 38									19 08
Bellingham	d			18 10									18 40									19 10
Catford	d			18 13									18 43									19 13
Crofton Park	d			18 15									18 45									19 15
Lewisham [4]	d	18 08									18 38									19 08		
Nunhead [4]	d	18 13		18 18							18 43		18 48							19 13		19 18
Peckham Rye [4]	d	18 15		18 20							18 45		18 50							19 15		19 20
Denmark Hill [4]	d	18 19		18 23							18 49		18 54			18 59				19 19		19 24
Beckenham Junction [4]	d					18 11				18 26					18 41				18 56			
Kent House [4]	d					18 13				18 28					18 43				18 58			
Penge East	d					18 15				18 30					18 45				19 00			
Sydenham Hill	d					18 18				18 33					18 48				19 03			
West Dulwich	d					18 20				18 35					18 50				19 05			
Herne Hill [4]	d		18 20			18 24			18 31	18 38		18 48			18 53			19 01	19 08		19 17	
Loughborough Jn.	d		18 23						18 34			18 51						19 04			19 20	
Elephant & Castle ⊖	d		18 28	18 32					18 40			18 56	19 00					19 09			19 25	19 30
London Blackfriars [3] ⊖	d		18 32	18 36					18 44			19 00	19 06					19 18			19 30	19 34
City Thameslink [3]	a		18 34	18 38					18 46			19 02	19 08					19 20			19 32	19 36
Farringdon ⊖	a		18 37	18 41					18 49			19 05	19 11					19 23			19 36	19 40
St Pancras International [15] ⊖	a		18 41	18 45					18 53			19 09	19 15					19 27			19 39	19 43
Kentish Town ⊖	a		18 46									19 14						19 32			19 44	19 50
Brixton ⊖	d					18 26				18 40					18 55				19 10			
London Victoria [15] ⊖	a	18 29			18 21	18 33	18 37	18 37		18 48	18 58			18 53	19 03	19 13	19 07		19 17	19 28		

		SE [1]	SE	SE	SE	SE [1]	SE [1]	FC	SE	FC	SE	SE [1]	SE	SE [1]	FC	SE	FC	SE	SE [1]	SE	SE	SE [1]	SE [1]
Sevenoaks [4]	d			18 45							19 02							19 32			19 45		
Bat & Ball	d			18 48							19 05							19 35			19 48		
Otford [4]	d	18 46		18 51							19 08	19 17						19 38	19 46		19 51		
Shoreham (Kent)	d			18 54							19 11							19 41			19 54		
Eynsford	d			18 58							19 15							19 45			19 58		
Swanley [4]	d	18 54		19 03	19 05						19 20	19 26						19 50	19 54		20 03	20 05	
St Mary Cray	d	18 58			19 09						19 24							19 54	19 58			20 09	
Orpington [4]	d		18 55						19 10				19 25			19 40				19 55			
Petts Wood [4]	d		18 58						19 13				19 28			19 43				19 58			
Bickley [4]	d		19 02						19 17		19 28		19 32			19 47		19 58		20 02			
Bromley South [4]	d	19 05	19 05	19 11	19 15	19 17	19 20		19 20		19 31	19 35	19 35	19 50		19 50		20 01	20 05	20 05	20a11	20 15	20 20
Shortlands [4]	d		19 08						19 23		19 34		19 38			19 53		20 04		20 08			
Ravensbourne	d										19 36							20 06					
Beckenham Hill	d										19 38							20 08					
Bellingham	d										19 40							20 10					
Catford	d										19 43							20 13					
Crofton Park	d										19 45							20 15					
Lewisham [4]	d																						
Nunhead [4]	d										19 48							20 18					
Peckham Rye [4]	d										19 50							20 20					
Denmark Hill [4]	d			19 28							19 54							20 24					
Beckenham Junction [4]	d		19 11						19 26				19 41			19 56				20 11			
Kent House [4]	d		19 13						19 28				19 43			19 58				20 13			
Penge East	d		19 15						19 30				19 45			20 00				20 15			
Sydenham Hill	d		19 18						19 33				19 48			20 03				20 18			
West Dulwich	d		19 20						19 35				19 50			20 05				20 20			
Herne Hill [4]	d		19 23					19 31	19 38	19 47			19 53		20 05	20 08	20 16			20 23			
Loughborough Jn.	d							19 34		19 50					20 08		20 19						
Elephant & Castle ⊖	d							19 39		19 55	20 00				20 13		20 24	20 30					
London Blackfriars [3] ⊖	d							19 46		20 00	20 04				20 18		20 30	20 34					
City Thameslink [3]	a							19 48		20 02	20 06				20 20		20 32	20 36					
Farringdon ⊖	a							19 52		20 06	20 10				20 24		20 36	20 40					
St Pancras International [15] ⊖	a							19 55		20 09	20 13				20 27		20 39	20 43					
Kentish Town ⊖	a							20 00		20 14	20 20				20 32		20 44	20 50					
Brixton ⊖	d		19 25						19 40				19 55			20 10				20 25			
London Victoria [15] ⊖	a	19 21	19 32	19 43	19 37	19 35	19 37		19 47			19 51	20 02	20 07		20 17			20 21	20 32		20 37	20 38

Sevenoaks, Otford, Orpington, Bromley South, Beckenham Junction and Catford - London

		FC	SE		FC	SE	SE 1	SE 1	FC	SE	SE	SE 1	FC		FC	SE	SE	SE 1	SE 1	FC	SE	SE	SE 1		SE
Sevenoaks 4	d					20 02					20 32						21 02					21 32			
Bat & Ball	d					20 05					20 35						21 05					21 35			
Otford 4	d					20 08	20 16				20 38						21 08	21 16				21 38			
Shoreham (Kent)	d					20 11					20 41						21 11					21 41			
Eynsford	d					20 15					20 45						21 15					21 45			
Swanley 4	d					20 20	20 24				20 50	21 10					21 20	21 24				21 50	22 10		
St Mary Cray	d					20 24	20 28				20 54	21 14					21 24	21 28				21 54	22 14		
Orpington 4	d		20 10							20 40						21 10					21 40				22 10
Petts Wood 4	d		20 13							20 43						21 13					21 43				22 13
Bickley 4	d		20 17			20 28				20 47	20 58					21 17	21 28				21 47	21 58			22 17
Bromley South 4	d		20 20			20 31	20 35	20 50		20 50	21 01	21 20				21 20	21 31	21 35	21 50		21 50	22 01	22 20		22 20
Shortlands 4	d		20 23			20 34				20 53	21 04					21 23	21 34				21 53	22 04			22 23
Ravensbourne	d					20 36					21 06						21 36					22 06			
Beckenham Hill	d					20 38					21 08						21 38					22 08			
Bellingham	d					20 40					21 10						21 40					22 10			
Catford	d					20 43					21 13						21 43					22 13			
Crofton Park	d					20 45					21 15						21 45					22 15			
Lewisham 4	d																								
Nunhead 4	d					20 48					21 18						21 48					22 18			
Peckham Rye 4	d					20 50					21 20						21 50					22 20			
Denmark Hill 4	d					20 54					21 23						21 53					22 23			
Beckenham Junction 4	d		20 26							20 56						21 26					21 56				22 26
Kent House 4	d		20 28							20 58						21 28					21 58				22 28
Penge East	d		20 30							21 00						21 30					22 00				22 30
Sydenham Hill	d		20 33							21 03						21 33					22 03				22 33
West Dulwich	d		20 35							21 05						21 35					22 05				22 35
Herne Hill 4	d	20 35	20 38		20 46				21 05	21 08			21 16		21 35	21 38				21 54	22 08				22 38
Loughborough Jn.	d	20 38			20 49				21 08				21 19		21 38					21 57					
Elephant & Castle ⊖	d	20 43			20 54	21 00			21 13				21 24		21 43					22 02					
London Blackfriars 3 ⊖	d	20 48			21 00	21 04			21 18				21 30		21 48					22 08					
City Thameslink 3	a	20 50			21 02	21 06			21 20				21 32		21 50					22 10					
Farringdon ⊖	a	20 54			21 06	21 10			21 24				21 36		21 54					22 14					
St Pancras International 15 ⊖	a	20 57			21 09	21 13			21 27				21 39		21 57					22 17					
Kentish Town ⊖	a	21 02			21 14	21 20			21 32				21 44		22 02					22 22					
Brixton ⊖	d		20 40							21 10						21 40					22 10				22 40
London Victoria 15 ⊖	a		20 47				20 51	21 07		21 17	21 33	21 37				21 47	22 03	21 51	22 07		22 17	22 33	22 37		22 47

		SE	SE 1	SE 1	SE	SE	SE 1	SE	SE 1		SE 1
Sevenoaks 4	d	22 02				22 32					
Bat & Ball	d	22 05				22 35					
Otford 4	d	22 08	22 16			22 38			23 16		
Shoreham (Kent)	d	22 11				22 41					
Eynsford	d	22 15				22 45					
Swanley 4	d	22 20	22 24			22 50	23 10		23 24		
St Mary Cray	d	22 24	22 28			22 54	23 14		23 28		
Orpington 4	d				22 40			23 10			
Petts Wood 4	d				22 43			23 13			
Bickley 4	d	22 28			22 47	22 58		23 17			
Bromley South 4	d	22 31	22 35	22 50	22 50	23 01	23 20	23 20	23 35		23 51
Shortlands 4	d	22 34			22 53	23 04		23 23			
Ravensbourne	d	22 36				23 06					
Beckenham Hill	d	22 38				23 08					
Bellingham	d	22 40				23 10					
Catford	d	22 43				23 13					
Crofton Park	d	22 45				23 15					
Lewisham 4	d										
Nunhead 4	d	22 48				23 18					
Peckham Rye 4	d	22 50				23 20					
Denmark Hill 4	d	22 53				23 23					
Beckenham Junction 4	d				22 56			23 26			
Kent House 4	d				22 58			23 28			
Penge East	d				23 00			23 30			
Sydenham Hill	d				23 03			23 33			
West Dulwich	d				23 05			23 35			
Herne Hill 4	d				23 08			23 38			
Loughborough Jn.	d										
Elephant & Castle ⊖	d										
London Blackfriars 3 ⊖	d										
City Thameslink 3	a										
Farringdon ⊖	a										
St Pancras International 15 ⊖	a										
Kentish Town ⊖	a										
Brixton ⊖	d				23 10			23 40			
London Victoria 15 ⊖	a	23 03	22 51	23 07	23 17	23 33	23 37	23 47	23 51		00 07

Table 195

Saturdays

Sevenoaks, Otford, Orpington, Bromley South, Beckenham Junction and Catford - London

		SE [1]	SE [1]	SE	SE [1]	SE	SE	SE [1]	SE	SE [1]		SE	SE	SE [1]	SE	SE	SE [1]	SE [1]	SE	SE		SE [1]	SE	
Sevenoaks [4]	d						05 55						06 25							06 55				and at the same minutes past each hour until
Bat & Ball	d						05 58						06 28							06 58				
Otford [4]	d						06 01	06 16					06 31	06 46						07 01		07 17		
Shoreham (Kent)	d						06 04						06 34							07 04				
Eynsford	d						06 08						06 38							07 08				
Swanley [4]	d		00 10		06 05		06 13	06 24					06 43	06 54			07 05			07 13		07 26		
St Mary Cray	d		00 14		06 09		06 17	06 28					06 47	06 58			07 09			07 17				
Orpington [4]	d			05 44		06 10			06 25			06 40				06 55			07 10					
Petts Wood [4]	d			05 47		06 13			06 28			06 43				06 58			07 13					
Bickley [4]	d			05 51		06 17	06 21		06 32			06 47	06 51			07 02			07 17	07 21				
Bromley South [4]	d	23p51	00 20	05 54	06 16	06 20	06 24	06 35	06 35	06 50		06 50	06 54	07 05		07 05	07 15	07 20	07 20	07 24		07 35		
Shortlands [4]	d			05 57		06 23	06 27		06 38			06 53	06 57			07 08			07 23	07 27				
Ravensbourne	d			05 59			06 29						06 59							07 29				
Beckenham Hill	d			06 01			06 31						07 01							07 31				
Bellingham	d			06 03			06 33						07 03							07 33				
Catford	d			06 06			06 36						07 06							07 36				
Crofton Park	d			06 08			06 38						07 08							07 38				
Lewisham [4]	d														07 08								07 38	
Nunhead [4]	d			06 11			06 41						07 11		07 15					07 41			07 45	
Peckham Rye [4]	d			06 13			06 43						07 13		07 17					07 43			07 47	
Denmark Hill [4]	d			06 17			06 47						07 17		07 21					07 47			07 51	
Beckenham Junction [4]	d					06 26			06 41			06 56				07 11			07 26					
Kent House [4]	d					06 28			06 43			06 58				07 13			07 28					
Penge East	d					06 30			06 45			07 00				07 15			07 30					
Sydenham Hill	d					06 33			06 48			07 03				07 18			07 33					
West Dulwich	d					06 35			06 50			07 05				07 20			07 35					
Herne Hill [4]	d					06 38			06 53			07 08				07 23			07 38					
Loughborough Jn.	d																							
Elephant & Castle ⊖	d																							
London Blackfriars [3] ⊖	d																							
City Thameslink [3]	a																							
Farringdon ⊖	a																							
St Pancras International [15] ⊖	a																							
Kentish Town ⊖	a																							
Brixton ⊖	d					06 40			06 55			07 10				07 25			07 40					
London Victoria [15] ⊖	a	00 07	00 38	06 26	06 37	06 47	06 56	06 51	07 02	07 07		07 17	07 26	07 21	07 30	07 32	07 37	07 37	07 47	07 56		07 51	08 00	

		SE	SE	SE [1]	SE	SE		SE [1]	SE	SE	SE [1]	SE [1]	SE	SE	SE [1]	SE		SE [1]	SE	SE	SE [1]	SE	SE [1]	SE [1]	SE
Sevenoaks [4]	d					18 25								18 55						19 25					
Bat & Ball	d					18 28								18 58						19 28					
Otford [4]	d					18 31		18 46						19 01	19 17					19 31	19 46				
Shoreham (Kent)	d					18 34								19 04						19 34					
Eynsford	d					18 38								19 08						19 38					
Swanley [4]	d					18 43		18 54			19 05			19 13	19 26					19 43	19 54		20 05		
St Mary Cray	d					18 47		18 58			19 09			19 17						19 47	19 58		20 09		
Orpington [4]	d		18 25		18 40					18 55			19 10			19 25			19 40			19 55			20 10
Petts Wood [4]	d		18 28		18 43					18 58			19 13			19 28			19 43			19 58			20 13
Bickley [4]	d		18 32		18 47	18 51				19 02			19 17	19 21		19 32			19 47	19 51		20 02			20 17
Bromley South [4]	d		18 35	18 50	18 50	18 54		19 05		19 05	19 15	19 20	19 20	19 24	19 35	19 35		19 50	19 50	19 54	20 05	20 05	20 15	20 20	20 20
Shortlands [4]	d		18 38		18 53	18 57				19 08			19 23	19 27		19 38			19 53	19 57		20 08			20 23
Ravensbourne	d					18 59								19 29						19 59					
Beckenham Hill	d					19 01								19 31						20 01					
Bellingham	d					19 03								19 33						20 03					
Catford	d					19 06								19 36						20 06					
Crofton Park	d					19 08								19 38						20 08					
Lewisham [4]	d	18 38							19 08																
Nunhead [4]	d	18 45				19 11			19 15					19 41						20 11					
Peckham Rye [4]	d	18 47				19 13			19 17					19 43						20 13					
Denmark Hill [4]	d	18 51				19 17			19 21					19 47						20 17					
Beckenham Junction [4]	d		18 41		18 56					19 11			19 26			19 41			19 56			20 11			20 26
Kent House [4]	d		18 43		18 58					19 13			19 28			19 43			19 58			20 13			20 28
Penge East	d		18 45		19 00					19 15			19 30			19 45			20 00			20 15			20 30
Sydenham Hill	d		18 48		19 03					19 18			19 33			19 48			20 03			20 18			20 33
West Dulwich	d		18 50		19 05					19 20			19 35			19 50			20 05			20 20			20 35
Herne Hill [4]	d		18 53		19 08					19 23			19 38			19 53			20 08			20 23			20 38
Loughborough Jn.	d																								
Elephant & Castle ⊖	d																								
London Blackfriars [3] ⊖	d																								
City Thameslink [3]	a																								
Farringdon ⊖	a																								
St Pancras International [15] ⊖	a																								
Kentish Town ⊖	a																								
Brixton ⊖	d		18 55		19 10					19 25			19 40			19 55			20 10			20 25			20 40
London Victoria [15] ⊖	a	19 00	19 02	19 07	19 17	19 26		19 21	19 30	19 32	19 37	19 37	19 47	19 56	19 51	20 02		20 07	20 17	20 26	20 21	20 32	20 37	20 37	20 47

Table 195

Saturdays

Sevenoaks, Otford, Orpington, Bromley South, Beckenham Junction and Catford - London

		SE		SE 1	SE	SE	SE 1	SE 1	SE	SE	SE 1	SE		SE	SE 1	SE 1	SE	SE	SE 1	SE	SE	SE 1	SE	SE 1	SE 1
Sevenoaks 4	d	19 55				20 25				20 55				21 25				21 55			22 25				
Bat & Ball	d	19 58				20 28				20 58				21 28				21 58			22 28				
Otford 4	d	20 01				20 31	20 46			21 01				21 31	21 46			22 01			22 31			23 16	
Shoreham (Kent)	d	20 04				20 34				21 04				21 34				22 04			22 34				
Eynsford	d	20 08				20 38				21 08				21 38				22 08			22 38				
Swanley 4	d	20 13				20 43	20 54	21 10		21 13				21 43	21 54	22 10		22 13			22 43	23 10		23 24	
St Mary Cray	d	20 17				20 47	20 58	21 14		21 17				21 47	21 58	22 14		22 17			22 47	23 14		23 28	
Orpington 4	d				20 40				21 10			21 40					22 10			22 40			23 10		
Petts Wood 4	d				20 43				21 13			21 43					22 13			22 43			23 13		
Bickley 4	d	20 21			20 47	20 51			21 17	21 21		21 47		21 51			22 17	22 21		22 47	22 51		23 17		
Bromley South 4	d	20 24		20 50	20 50	20 54	21 05	21 20	21 20	21 24	21 50	21 50		21 54	22 05	22 20	22 20	22 24	22 50	22 50	22 54	23 20	23 20	23 35	23 50
Shortlands 4	d	20 27			20 53	20 57			21 23	21 27		21 53		21 57			22 23	22 27		22 53	22 57		23 23		
Ravensbourne	d	20 29				20 59				21 29				21 59				22 29			22 59				
Beckenham Hill	d	20 31				21 01				21 31				22 01				22 31			23 01				
Bellingham	d	20 33				21 03				21 33				22 03				22 33			23 03				
Catford	d	20 36				21 06				21 36				22 06				22 36			23 06				
Crofton Park	d	20 38				21 08				21 38				22 08				22 38			23 08				
Lewisham 4 ⇌	d																								
Nunhead 4	d	20 41				21 11				21 41				22 11				22 41			23 11				
Peckham Rye 4	d	20 43				21 13				21 43				22 13				22 43			23 13				
Denmark Hill 4	d	20 47				21 17				21 47				22 17				22 47			23 17				
Beckenham Junction 4 ⇌	d				20 56				21 26			21 56					22 26			22 56			23 26		
Kent House 4	d				20 58				21 28			21 58					22 28			22 58			23 28		
Penge East	d				21 00				21 30			22 00					22 30			23 00			23 30		
Sydenham Hill	d				21 03				21 33			22 03					22 33			23 03			23 33		
West Dulwich	d				21 05				21 35			22 05					22 35			23 05			23 35		
Herne Hill 4	d				21 08				21 38			22 08					22 38			23 08			23 38		
Loughborough Jn.	d																								
Elephant & Castle ⊖	d																								
London Blackfriars 3 ⊖	d																								
City Thameslink 3	a																								
Farringdon ⊖	a																								
St Pancras International 15 ⊖	a																								
Kentish Town ⊖	a																								
Brixton ⊖	d				21 10				21 40			22 10					22 40			23 10			23 40		
London Victoria 15 ⊖	a	20 56		21 07	21 17	21 26	21 21	21 37	21 47	21 56	22 07	22 17		22 26	22 21	22 37	22 47	22 56	23 07	23 17	23 26	23 37	23 47	23 51	00 07

Table 195

Sundays

Sevenoaks, Otford, Orpington, Bromley South, Beckenham Junction and Catford - London

		SE 1 A	SE	SE	SE	SE 1	SE	SE	SE 1	SE 1		SE	SE	SE 1	SE	SE		SE	SE 1		SE 1	SE	SE 1	
Sevenoaks 4	d												07 54			08 24		22 24				22 54		
Bat & Ball	d												07 57			08 27		22 27				22 57		
Otford 4	d								07 43				08 00			08 30		22 30	22 43			23 00		
Shoreham (Kent)	d												08 03			08 33		22 33				23 03		
Eynsford	d												08 07			08 37		22 37				23 07		
Swanley 4	d					07 32			07 51				08 12	08 32		08 42		22 42	22 51			23 12	23 32	
St Mary Cray	d					07 36			07 55				08 16	08 36		08 46		22 46	22 55			23 16	23 36	
Orpington 4	d		06 43	07 06	07 13		07 36	07 43				08 06			08 36									
Petts Wood 4	d		06 46	07 09	07 16		07 39	07 46				08 09			08 39									
Bickley 4	d		06 50	07 13	07 20		07 43	07 50				08 13	08 20		08 43	08 50		22 50				23 20		
Bromley South 4	d	23p50	06 53	07 16	07 23	07 43	07 46	07 53	08 02	08 13		08 16	08 23	08 43	08 46	08 53		22 53	23 02		23 13	23 23	23 43	
Shortlands 4	d		06 56	07 19	07 26		07 49	07 56				08 19	08 26		08 49	08 56		22 56				23 26		
Ravensbourne	d		06 58		07 28			07 58					08 28			08 58		22 58				23 28		
Beckenham Hill	d		07 00		07 30			08 00					08 30			09 00	and at	23 00				23 30		
Bellingham	d		07 02		07 32			08 02					08 32			09 02	the same	23 02				23 32		
Catford	d		07 05		07 35			08 05					08 35			09 05	minutes	23 05				23 35		
Crofton Park	d		07 07		07 37			08 07					08 37			09 07	past	23 07				23 37		
Lewisham 4	d																each							
Nunhead 4	d		07 10		07 40			08 10					08 40			09 10	hour until	23 10				23 40		
Peckham Rye 4	d		07 12		07 42			08 12					08 42			09 12		23 12				23 42		
Denmark Hill 4	d		07 16		07 46			08 16					08 46			09 16		23 16				23 46		
Beckenham Junction 4	d			07 22			07 52					08 22			08 52									
Kent House 4	d			07 24			07 54					08 24			08 54									
Penge East	d			07 26			07 56					08 26			08 56									
Sydenham Hill	d			07 29			07 59					08 29			08 59									
West Dulwich	d			07 31			08 01					08 31			09 01									
Herne Hill 4	d			07 34			08 04					08 34			09 04									
Loughborough Jn.	d																							
Elephant & Castle ⊖	d																							
London Blackfriars 3 ⊖	d																							
City Thameslink 3	a																							
Farringdon ⊖	a																							
St Pancras International 15 ⊖	a																							
Kentish Town ⊖	a																							
Brixton ⊖	d			07 36			08 06					08 36			09 06									
London Victoria 15 ⊖	a	00 07	07 25	07 43	07 55	08 03	08 13	08 25	08 18	08 29		08 43	08 55	09 02	09 13	09 25		23 25	23 18		23 29	23 55	00 02	

A not 22 May

London - Maidstone East and Ashford International

Miles	Miles	Miles			SE MO 1	SE MX 1	SE MX 1	SE 1	SE 1	SE 1	SE 1	SE 1	SE 1		SE 1	SE 1	SE 1	SE 1	SE 1	SE 1	SE 1	SE 1	SE 1		SE 1
0	—	—	**London Victoria** 15 ⊖	d	22p45	23p07	00 07		06 07	06 37	07 07	07 36	08 07		08 37	09 07	09 37	10 07	10 37	11 07	11 37	12 07	12 37		13 07
—	0	—	**London Blackfriars** 3 ⊖195	d																					
—	1¼	—	Elephant & Castle ⊖195	d																					
11	11½	—	Bromley South 4 195	d	23p01	23p23	00 25		06 23	06 58	07 23	07 53	08 23		08 53	09 23	09 53	10 23	10 53	11 23	11 53	12 23	12 53		13 23
14¾	—	—	St Mary Cray 195	d	23p08	23p30	00 31		06 30	07 04	07 30	08 00	08 30		09 00		10 00		11 00		12 00		13 00		
17½	—	—	Swanley 4 195	d	23p12	23p34	00 36		06 34	07 08	07 34	08 04	08 34		09 04	09 33	10 04	10 33	11 04	11 33	12 04	12 33	13 04		13 33
24	—	—	Otford 4 195	d	23p20	23p42	00 47		06 42	07 16	07 42	08 12	08 42		09 12	09 41	10 12	10 41	11 12	11 41	12 12	12 41	13 12		13 41
27	—	—	Kemsing	d		23p47	00 52		06 47	07 21	07 47	08 17	08 47		09 17		10 17		11 17		12 17		13 17		
29½	—	—	Borough Green & Wrotham	d	23p28	23p52	00 56		06 52	07 26	07 52	08 22	08 52		09 22	09 48	10 22	10 48	11 22	11 48	12 22	12 48	13 22		13 48
34¾	—	—	West Malling	d	23p34	23p58	01 03		06 58	07 32	07 58	08 28	08 58		09 28	09 55	10 28	10 55	11 28	11 55	12 28	12 55	13 28		13 55
35¾	—	—	East Malling	d	23p37	00 01	01 06		07 01	07 35	08 01	08 31	09 01		09 31		10 31		11 31		12 31		13 31		
37½	—	—	Barming	d	23p41	00 05	01 09		07 05	07 39	08 05	08 35	09 05		09 35		10 35		11 35		12 35		13 35		
40	—	—	**Maidstone East** 4	a	23p45	00 09	01 13		07 09	07 43	08 09	08 39	09 09		09 39	10 02	10 39	11 02	11 39	12 02	12 39	13 02	13 39		14 02
—	—	—		d	23p46	00 10	01 14	06 34	07 10	07 44	08 10	08 40	09 10		09 40	10 03	10 40	11 03	11 40	12 03	12 40	13 03	13 40		14 03
42¾	—	—	Bearsted	d	23p51	00 15	01 19	06 39	07 15	07 49	08 15	08 45	09 15		09 45	10 08	10 45	11 08	11 45	12 08	12 45	13 08	13 45		14 08
45	—	—	Hollingbourne	d	23p54	00 18	01 22	06 42	07 18	07 52	08 18	08 48	09 18		09 48		10 48		11 48		12 48		13 48		
47½	—	—	Harrietsham	d	23p58	00 22	01 26	06 46	07 22	07 56	08 22	08 52	09 22		09 52		10 52		11 52		12 52		13 52		
49¼	—	—	Lenham	d	00 01	00 25	01 29	06 49	07 25	07 59	08 25	08 55	09 25		09 55		10 55		11 55		12 55		13 55		
53¼	—	—	Charing	d	00 06	00 30	01 34	06 54	07 30	08 04	08 30	09 00	09 30		10 00		11 00		12 00		13 00		14 00		
59¼	—	56	**Ashford International**	a	00 15	00 39	01 43	07 02	07 39	08 13	08 39	09 09	09 39		10 09	10 27	11 09	11 27	12 09	12 27	13 09	13 27	14 09		14 27
—	—	—		d																					

		SE 1	SE 1	SE 1	SE 1	SE 1	SE 1	SE 1	SE 1		SE 1	SE 1	SE 1	FC 1	SE 1	SE 1	SE 1	SE 1	SE 1		SE 1	SE 1	SE 1	SE 1	SE 1
London Victoria 15 ⊖	d	13 37	14 07	14 37	15 07	15 37	16 07	16 37	16 58		17 12	17 28	17 42		18 03	18 18	18 42	19 07	19 37		20 07	20 37	21 07	22 07	23 07
London Blackfriars 3 ⊖195	d													17 48											
Elephant & Castle ⊖195	d													17 52											
Bromley South 4 195	d	13 53	14 23	14 53	15 23	15 53	16 23	16 53	17 19		17 28	17 50	17 59	18 11	18 24	18 39	18 59	19 27	19 53		20 23	20 53	21 23	22 23	23 23
St Mary Cray 195	d	14 00		15 00		16 00		17 00			17 35	17 57	18 06	18 18		18 45	19 06		20 00			21 00	21 30	22 30	23 30
Swanley 4 195	d	14 04	14 33	15 04	15 33	16 04	16 33	17 04			17 39	18 01	18 11	18 22		18 50	19 11	19 36	20 04		20 33	21 04	21 34	22 34	23 34
Otford 4 195	d	14 12	14 41	15 12	15 41	16 12	16 41	17 12	17 35		17 48	18 10	18 19	18 31	18 43	18 58	19 19	19 44	20 12		20 41	21 12	21 42	22 42	23 42
Kemsing	d	14 17		15 17		16 17		17 17			17 53		18 24	18 36		19 03	19 24		20 17			21 17	21 47	22 47	23 47
Borough Green & Wrotham	d	14 22	14 48	15 22	15 48	16 22	16 48	17 22	17 43		17 57	18 17	18 29	18 41	18 51	19 08	19 29	19 51	20 22		20 48	21 22	21 52	22 52	23 52
West Malling	d	14 28	14 55	15 28	15 55	16 28	16 55	17 28	17 49		18 04	18 24	18 35	18 47	18 57	19 14	19 35	19 57	20 28		20 55	21 28	21 58	22 58	23 58
East Malling	d	14 31		15 31		16 31		17 31			18 07		18 38	18 50		19 17	19 38		20 31			21 31	22 01	23 01	00 01
Barming	d	14 35		15 35		16 35		17 35			18 10		18 42	18 54		19 21	19 42		20 35			21 35	22 05	23 05	00 05
Maidstone East 4	a	14 39	15 02	15 39	16 02	16 39	17 02	17 39	17 56		18 14	18 33	18 46	18 58	19 04	19 25	19 46	20 04	20 39		21 02	21 39	22 09	23 09	00 09
	d	14 40	15 03	15 40	16 03	16 40	17 03	17 40	17 57		18 15		18 47	18 59	19 06	19 26	19 47	20 05	20 40		21 03	21 40	22 10	23 10	00 10
Bearsted	d	14 45	15 08	15 45	16 08	16 45	17 08	17 45	18 02		18 20		18 52	19 04	19 11	19 31	19 52	20 10	20 45		21 08	21 45	22 15	23 15	00 15
Hollingbourne	d	14 48		15 48	16 11	16 48	17 11	17 48	18 06		18 24		18 55	19 08	19 15	19 34	19 55	20 13	20 48		21 11	21 48	22 18	23 18	00 18
Harrietsham	d	14 52		15 52	16 15	16 52	17 15	17 52	18 09		18 27		18 59	19 11	19 18	19 38	19 59	20 17	20 52		21 15	21 52	22 22	23 22	00 22
Lenham	d	14 55		15 55	16 18	16 55	17 18	17 55	18 13		18 31		19 02	19 15	19 22	19 41	20 02	20 20	20 55		21 18	21 55	22 25	23 25	00 25
Charing	d	15 00		16 00	16 23	17 00	17 23	18 00	18 18		18 36		19 07	19 20	19 27	19 46	20 07	20 25	21 00		21 23	22 00	22 30	23 30	00 30
Ashford International	a	15 09	15 30	16 09	16 32	17 09	17 34	18 11	18 28		18 47		19 18	19 32	19 39	19 58	20 18	20 34	21 09		21 32	22 09	22 39	23 39	00 39
	d																								

Saturdays

		SE 1	SE 1	SE 1	SE 1	SE 1	SE 1	SE 1	SE 1	SE 1		SE 1	SE 1	SE 1	SE 1	SE 1	SE 1	SE 1	SE 1	SE 1		SE 1	SE 1	SE 1	SE 1
London Victoria 15 ⊖	d	23p07	00 07		06 07	07 07	07 37	08 07	08 37	09 07		09 37	10 07	10 37	11 07	11 37	12 07	12 37	13 07	13 37		14 07	14 37	15 07	15 37
London Blackfriars 3 ⊖195	d																								
Elephant & Castle ⊖195	d																								
Bromley South 4 195	d	23p23	00 25		06 23	07 23	07 53	08 23	08 53	09 23		09 53	10 23	10 53	11 23	11 53	12 23	12 53	13 23	13 53		14 23	14 53	15 23	15 53
St Mary Cray 195	d	23p30	00 31		06 30	07 30	08 00		09 00			10 00		11 00		12 00		13 00		14 00			15 00		16 00
Swanley 4 195	d	23p34	00 36		06 34	07 34	08 04	08 33	09 04	09 33		10 04	10 33	11 04	11 33	12 04	12 33	13 04	13 33	14 04		14 33	15 04	15 33	16 04
Otford 4 195	d	23p42	00 47		06 42	07 42	08 12	08 41	09 12	09 41		10 12	10 41	11 12	11 41	12 12	12 41	13 12	13 41	14 12		14 41	15 12	15 41	16 12
Kemsing	d	23p47	00 52		06 47	07 47	08 17		09 17			10 17		11 17		12 17		13 17		14 17			15 17		16 17
Borough Green & Wrotham	d	23p52	00 56		06 52	07 52	08 22	08 48	09 22	09 48		10 22	10 48	11 22	11 48	12 22	12 48	13 22	13 48	14 22		14 48	15 22	15 48	16 22
West Malling	d	23p58	01 03		06 58	07 58	08 28	08 55	09 28	09 55		10 28	10 55	11 28	11 55	12 28	12 55	13 28	13 55	14 28		14 55	15 28	15 55	16 28
East Malling	d	00 01	01 06		07 01	08 01	08 31		09 31			10 31		11 31		12 31		13 31		14 31			15 31		16 31
Barming	d	00 05	01 09		07 05	08 05	08 35		09 35			10 35		11 35		12 35		13 35		14 35			15 35		16 35
Maidstone East 4	a	00 09	01 13		07 09	08 09	08 39	09 02	09 39	10 02		10 39	11 02	11 39	12 02	12 39	13 02	13 39	14 02	14 39		15 02	15 39	16 02	16 39
	d	00 10	01 14	06 10	07 10	08 10	08 40	09 03	09 40	10 03		10 40	11 03	11 40	12 03	12 40	13 03	13 40	14 03	14 40		15 03	15 40	16 03	16 40
Bearsted	d	00 15	01 19	06 15	07 15	08 15	08 45	09 08	09 45	10 08		10 45	11 08	11 45	12 08	12 45	13 08	13 45	14 08	14 45		15 08	15 45	16 08	16 45
Hollingbourne	d	00 18	01 22	06 18	07 18	08 18	08 48		09 48			10 48		11 48		12 48		13 48		14 48			15 48		16 48
Harrietsham	d	00 22	01 26	06 22	07 22	08 22	08 52		09 52			10 52		11 52		12 52		13 52		14 52			15 52		16 52
Lenham	d	00 25	01 29	06 25	07 25	08 25	08 55		09 55			10 55		11 55		12 55		13 55		14 55			15 55		16 55
Charing	d	00 30	01 34	06 30	07 30	08 30	09 00		10 00			11 00		12 00		13 00		14 00		15 00			16 00		17 00
Ashford International	a	00 39	01 43	06 39	07 39	08 39	09 09	09 27	10 09	10 27		11 09	11 27	12 09	12 27	13 09	13 27	14 09	14 27	15 09		15 27	16 09	16 27	17 09
	d																								

Table 196

Saturdays

London - Maidstone East and Ashford International

			SE 1	SE 1	SE 1	SE 1	SE 1	SE 1	SE 1	SE 1	SE 1	SE 1	SE 1	SE 1
London Victoria 15	⊖	d	16 07	16 37	17 07	17 37	18 07	18 37	19 07	19 37	20 07	21 07	22 07	23 07
London Blackfriars 3	⊖195	d												
Elephant & Castle	⊖195	d												
Bromley South 4	195	d	16 23	16 53	17 23	17 53	18 23	18 53	19 23	19 53	20 23	21 23	22 23	23 23
St Mary Cray	195	d		17 00		18 00		19 00		20 00	20 30	21 30	22 30	23 30
Swanley 4	195	d	16 33	17 04	17 33	18 04	18 33	19 04	19 33	20 04	20 34	21 34	22 34	23 34
Otford 4	195	d	16 41	17 12	17 41	18 12	18 41	19 12	19 41	20 12	20 42	21 42	22 42	23 42
Kemsing		d		17 17		18 17		19 17		20 17	20 47	21 47	22 47	23 47
Borough Green & Wrotham		d	16 48	17 22	17 48	18 22	18 48	19 22	19 48	20 22	20 52	21 52	22 52	23 52
West Malling		d	16 55	17 28	17 55	18 28	18 55	19 28	19 55	20 28	20 58	21 58	22 58	23 58
East Malling		d		17 31		18 31		19 31		20 31	21 01	22 01	23 01	00 01
Barming		d		17 35		18 35		19 35		20 35	21 05	22 05	23 05	00 05
Maidstone East 4		a	17 02	17 39	18 02	18 39	19 02	19 39	20 02	20 39	21 09	22 09	23 09	00 09
		d	17 03	17 40	18 03	18 40	19 03	19 40	20 03	20 40	21 10	22 10	23 10	00 10
Bearsted		d	17 08	17 45	18 08	18 45	19 08	19 45	20 08	20 45	21 15	22 15	23 15	00 15
Hollingbourne		d		17 48		18 48		19 48		20 48	21 18	22 18	23 18	00 18
Harrietsham		d		17 52		18 52		19 52		20 52	21 22	22 22	23 22	00 22
Lenham		d		17 55		18 55		19 55		20 55	21 25	22 25	23 25	00 25
Charing		d		18 00		19 00		20 00		21 00	21 30	22 30	23 30	00 30
Ashford International		a	17 27	18 09	18 27	19 09	19 27	20 09	20 27	21 09	21 39	22 39	23 39	00 39
		d												

Sundays

			SE 1 A	SE 1	SE 1	SE 1	SE 1	SE 1	SE 1	SE 1	SE 1	SE 1	SE 1	SE 1	SE 1	SE 1	SE 1	SE 1	SE 1	SE 1
London Victoria 15	⊖	d	23p07	00 07	07 45	08 45	09 45	10 45	11 45	12 45	13 45	14 45	15 45	16 45	17 45	18 45	19 45	20 45	21 45	22 45
London Blackfriars 3	⊖195	d																		
Elephant & Castle	⊖195	d																		
Bromley South 4	195	d	23p23	00 25	08 01	09 01	10 01	11 01	12 01	13 01	14 01	15 01	16 01	17 01	18 01	19 01	20 01	21 01	22 01	23 01
St Mary Cray	195	d	23p30	00 31	08 08	09 08	10 08	11 08	12 08	13 08	14 08	15 08	16 08	17 08	18 08	19 08	20 08	21 08	22 08	23 08
Swanley 4	195	d	23p34	00 36	08 12	09 12	10 12	11 12	12 12	13 12	14 12	15 12	16 12	17 12	18 12	19 12	20 12	21 12	22 12	23 12
Otford 4	195	d	23p42	00 47	08 20	09 20	10 20	11 20	12 20	13 20	14 20	15 20	16 20	17 20	18 20	19 20	20 20	21 20	22 20	23 20
Kemsing		d	23p47	00 52																
Borough Green & Wrotham		d	23p52	00 56	08 28	09 28	10 28	11 28	12 28	13 28	14 28	15 28	16 28	17 28	18 28	19 28	20 28	21 28	22 28	23 28
West Malling		d	23p58	01 03	08 34	09 34	10 34	11 34	12 34	13 34	14 34	15 34	16 34	17 34	18 34	19 34	20 34	21 34	22 34	23 34
East Malling		d	00 01	01 06	08 37	09 37	10 37	11 37	12 37	13 37	14 37	15 37	16 37	17 37	18 37	19 37	20 37	21 37	22 37	23 37
Barming		d	00 05	01 09	08 41	09 41	10 41	11 41	12 41	13 41	14 41	15 41	16 41	17 41	18 41	19 41	20 41	21 41	22 41	23 41
Maidstone East 4		a	00 09	01 13	08 45	09 45	10 45	11 45	12 45	13 45	14 45	15 45	16 45	17 45	18 45	19 45	20 45	21 45	22 45	23 45
		d	00 10	01 14	08 46	09 46	10 46	11 46	12 46	13 46	14 46	15 46	16 46	17 46	18 46	19 46	20 46	21 46	22 46	23 46
Bearsted		d	00 15	01 19	08 51	09 51	10 51	11 51	12 51	13 51	14 51	15 51	16 51	17 51	18 51	19 51	20 51	21 51	22 51	23 51
Hollingbourne		d	00 18	01 22	08 54	09 54	10 54	11 54	12 54	13 54	14 54	15 54	16 54	17 54	18 54	19 54	20 54	21 54	22 54	23 54
Harrietsham		d	00 22	01 26	08 58	09 58	10 58	11 58	12 58	13 58	14 58	15 58	16 58	17 58	18 58	19 58	20 58	21 58	22 58	23 58
Lenham		d	00 25	01 29	09 01	10 01	11 01	12 01	13 01	14 01	15 01	16 01	17 01	18 01	19 01	20 01	21 01	22 01	23 01	00 01
Charing		d	00 30	01 34	09 06	10 06	11 06	12 06	13 06	14 06	15 06	16 06	17 06	18 06	19 06	20 06	21 06	22 06	23 06	00 06
Ashford International		a	00 39	01 43	09 15	10 15	11 15	12 15	13 15	14 15	15 15	16 15	17 15	18 15	19 15	20 15	21 15	22 15	23 15	00 15
		d																		

A not 22 May

Ashford International and Maidstone East to London

Miles	Miles	Miles				SE [1]	SE [1]	SE [1]	SE [1]	SE [1]	SE [1]	SE [1]	SE [1]	SE [1]	SE [1]	SE [1]	SE [1]	SE [1]	SE [1]	SE [1]	SE [1]	SE [1]	SE [1]	SE [1]
14¼	—	0	**Ashford International**		a																			
—	—	—			d	05 20	05 44	05 50	06 03	06 16	06 25	06 40	06 58	07 15	07 47	08 26	08 47	09 30	09 47	10 30	10 47	11 30	11 47	12 30
20¼	—	—	Charing		d	05 28	05 53	05 58	06 11	06 24	06 33	06 48	07 06	07 23	07 55	08 34	08 55		09 55		10 55		11 55	
24¼	—	—	Lenham		d	05 33	05 58	06 03	06 16	06 29	06 38	06 53	07 11	07 28	08 00	08 39	09 00		10 00		11 00		12 00	
26	—	—	Harrietsham		d	05 36	06 01	06 06	06 19	06 32	06 41	06 56	07 14	07 31	08 03	08 42	09 03		10 03		11 03		12 03	
28½	—	—	Hollingbourne		d	05 40	06 04	06 10	06 23	06 36	06 45	07 00	07 18	07 35	08 07	08 46	09 07		10 07		11 07		12 07	
30¾	—	—	Bearsted		d	05 43	06 09	06 13	06 26	06 39	06 48	07 03	07 21	07 38	08 11	08 49	09 11	09 48	10 11	10 48	11 11	11 48	12 11	12 48
33½	—	—	**Maidstone East [4]**		a	05 48	06 14	06 20	06 31	06 44	06 53	07 08	07 26	07 43	08 17	08 54	09 17	09 53	10 17	10 53	11 17	11 53	12 17	12 53
—	—	—			d	05 49	06 15	06 20	06 32	06 45	06 54	07 09	07 27	07 44	08 18	08 55	09 18	09 55	10 18	10 55	11 18	11 55	12 18	12 55
36	—	—	Barming		d	05 54		06 25	06 37	06 50	06 59	07 14	07 32	07 49	08 23		09 23		10 23		11 23		12 23	
37¾	—	—	East Malling		d	05 57		06 29	06 41	06 54	07 03	07 18	07 36		08 26		09 26		10 26		11 26		12 26	
38¾	—	—	West Malling		d	06 00	06 22	06 31	06 44	06 57	07 06	07 21	07 39	07 54	08 29	09 02	09 29	10 02	10 29	11 02	11 29	12 02	12 29	13 02
44	—	—	Borough Green & Wrotham		d	06 07	06 30	06 38	06 51	07 04	07 13	07 28	07 46	08 01	08 36	09 09	09 36	10 09	10 36	11 09	11 36	12 09	12 36	13 09
46½	—	—	Kemsing		d				06 55	07 08	07 17	07 32	07 50		08 40		09 40		10 40		11 40		12 40	
49½	—	—	Otford [4]	195	a	06 15	06 38	06 46	07 00	07 13	07 22	07 37	07 55	08 09	08 46	09 17	09 46	10 17	10 46	11 17	11 46	12 17	12 46	13 17
56	—	—	Swanley [4]	195	a	06 24	06 47	06 54	07 09	07 22	07 31	07 46	08 04		08 54	09 25	09 54	10 25	10 54	11 25	11 54	12 25	12 54	13 25
58¾	—	—	St Mary Cray	195	a										08 58		09 58		10 58		11 58		12 58	
62½	0	—	Bromley South [4]	195	a	06 33	06 56	07 02	07 19	07 30	07 40	07 57	08 13	08 25	09 04	09 34	10 04	10 34	11 04	11 34	12 04	12 34	13 04	13 34
—	10¼	—	Elephant & Castle	⊖195	a		07 15				07 59													
—	11½	—	**London Blackfriars [3]**	⊖195	a		07 22				08 04													
73½	—	—	**London Victoria [15]**	⊖	a	06 51		07 22	07 43	07 53		08 23	08 36	08 53	09 23	09 51	10 21	10 51	11 21	11 51	12 21	12 51	13 21	13 51

			SE [1]	SE [1]	SE [1]	SE [1]	SE [1]	SE [1]	SE [1]	SE [1]	SE [1]	SE [1]	SE [1]	SE [1]	SE [1]	SE [1]	SE [1]	SE [1]	SE [1]	SE [1]
Ashford International		a																		
		d	12 47	13 30	13 47	14 30	14 47	15 24	15 47	16 26	16 47	17 26	17 49		18 26	18 49	19 19	20 17	21 17	22 17
Charing		d	12 55		13 55		14 55	15 32	15 55	16 34	16 55	17 34	17 57		18 34	18 57	19 27	20 25	21 25	22 25
Lenham		d	13 00		14 00		15 00	15 37	16 00	16 39	17 00	17 39	18 02		18 39	19 02	19 32	20 30	21 30	22 30
Harrietsham		d	13 03		14 03		15 03	15 40	16 03	16 42	17 03	17 42	18 05		18 42	19 05	19 35	20 33	21 33	22 33
Hollingbourne		d	13 07		14 07		15 07	15 44	16 07	16 46	17 07	17 46	18 09		18 46	19 09	19 39	20 37	21 37	22 37
Bearsted		d	13 11	13 48	14 11	14 48	15 11	15 48	16 11	16 49	17 11	17 49	18 12		18 49	19 12	19 42	20 41	21 41	22 41
Maidstone East [4]		a	13 17	13 53	14 17	14 53	15 17	15 53	16 17	16 54	17 17	17 54	18 17		18 54	19 17	19 47	20 47	21 47	22 47
		d	13 18	13 55	14 18	14 55	15 18	15 55	16 18	16 55	17 18	17 55	18 18	18 40	18 55	19 18	19 48	20 48	21 48	22 48
Barming		d	13 23		14 23		15 23		16 23		17 23		18 23			19 23	19 53	20 53	21 53	22 53
East Malling		d	13 26		14 26		15 26		16 26		17 26		18 26			19 26	19 56	20 56	21 56	22 56
West Malling		d	13 29	14 02	14 29	15 02	15 29	16 02	16 29	17 02	17 29	18 02	18 29	18 47	19 02	19 29	19 59	20 59	21 59	22 59
Borough Green & Wrotham		d	13 36	14 09	14 36	15 09	15 36	16 09	16 36	17 09	17 36	18 09	18 36	18 54	19 09	19 36	20 06	21 06	22 06	23 06
Kemsing		d	13 40		14 40		15 40		16 40		17 40		18 40			19 40	20 10	21 10	22 10	23 10
Otford [4]	195	a	13 46	14 17	14 46	15 17	15 46	16 17	16 46	17 17	17 46	18 17	18 46		19 17	19 46	20 16	21 16	22 16	23 16
Swanley [4]	195	a	13 54	14 25	14 54	15 25	15 54	16 25	16 54	17 25	17 54	18 25	18 54		19 25	19 54	20 24	21 24	22 24	23 24
St Mary Cray	195	a	13 58		14 58		15 58		16 58		17 58		18 58			19 58	20 28	21 28	22 28	23 28
Bromley South [4]	195	a	14 04	14 34	15 04	15 34	16 04	16 34	17 04	17 34	18 05	18 34	19 04	19 16	19 34	20 04	20 34	21 34	22 34	23 34
Elephant & Castle	⊖195	a																		
London Blackfriars [3]	⊖195	a																		
London Victoria [15]	⊖	a	14 21	14 51	15 21	15 51	16 21	16 51	17 21	17 53	18 21	18 53	19 21	19 35	19 51	20 21	20 51	21 51	22 51	23 51

Saturdays

			SE [1]	SE [1]	SE [1]	SE [1]	SE [1]	SE [1]	SE [1]	SE [1]	SE [1]	SE [1]	SE [1]	SE [1]	SE [1]	SE [1]	SE [1]	SE [1]	SE [1]	SE [1]	SE [1]	SE [1]	SE [1]	SE [1]
Ashford International		a																						
		d	05 20	05 47	06 30	06 47	07 30	07 47	08 30	08 47	09 30	09 47	10 30	10 47	11 30	11 47	12 30	12 47	13 30	13 47	14 30	14 47	15 30	15 47
Charing		d	05 28	05 55		06 55		07 55		08 55		09 55		10 55		11 55		12 55		13 55		14 55		15 55
Lenham		d	05 33	06 00		07 00		08 00		09 00		10 00		11 00		12 00		13 00		14 00		15 00		16 00
Harrietsham		d	05 36	06 03		07 03		08 03		09 03		10 03		11 03		12 03		13 03		14 03		15 03		16 03
Hollingbourne		d	05 40	06 07		07 07		08 07		09 07		10 07		11 07		12 07		13 07		14 07		15 07		16 07
Bearsted		d	05 43	06 11	06 48	07 11	07 48	08 11	08 48	09 11	09 48	10 11	10 48	11 11	11 48	12 11	12 48	13 11	13 48	14 11	14 48	15 11	15 48	16 11
Maidstone East [4]		a	05 48	06 17	06 53	07 17	07 53	08 17	08 53	09 17	09 53	10 17	10 53	11 17	11 53	12 17	12 53	13 17	13 53	14 17	14 53	15 17	15 53	16 17
		d	05 49	06 18	06 55	07 18	07 55	08 18	08 55	09 18	09 55	10 18	10 55	11 18	11 55	12 18	12 55	13 18	13 55	14 18	14 55	15 18	15 55	16 18
Barming		d	05 54	06 23		07 23		08 23		09 23		10 23		11 23		12 23		13 23		14 23		15 23		16 23
East Malling		d	05 58	06 26		07 26		08 26		09 26		10 26		11 26		12 26		13 26		14 26		15 26		16 26
West Malling		d	06 01	06 29	07 02	07 29	08 02	08 29	09 02	09 29	10 02	10 29	11 02	11 29	12 02	12 29	13 02	13 29	14 02	14 29	15 02	15 29	16 02	16 29
Borough Green & Wrotham		d	06 08	06 36	07 09	07 36	08 09	08 36	09 09	09 36	10 09	10 36	11 09	11 36	12 09	12 36	13 09	13 36	14 09	14 36	15 09	15 36	16 09	16 36
Kemsing		d		06 40		07 40		08 40		09 40		10 40		11 40		12 40		13 40		14 40		15 40		16 40
Otford [4]	195	a	06 16	06 46	07 17	07 46	08 17	08 46	09 17	09 46	10 17	10 46	11 17	11 46	12 17	12 46	13 17	13 46	14 17	14 46	15 17	15 46	16 17	16 46
Swanley [4]	195	a	06 24	06 54	07 25	07 54	08 25	08 54	09 25	09 54	10 25	10 54	11 25	11 54	12 25	12 54	13 25	13 54	14 25	14 54	15 25	15 54	16 25	16 54
St Mary Cray	195	a	06 28	06 58		07 58		08 58		09 58		10 58		11 58		12 58		13 58		14 58		15 58		16 58
Bromley South [4]	195	a	06 34	07 04	07 34	08 04	08 34	09 04	09 34	10 04	10 34	11 04	11 34	12 04	12 34	13 04	13 34	14 04	14 34	15 04	15 34	16 04	16 34	17 04
Elephant & Castle	⊖195	a																						
London Blackfriars [3]	⊖195	a																						
London Victoria [15]	⊖	a	06 51	07 21	07 51	08 21	08 51	09 21	09 51	10 21	10 51	11 21	11 51	12 21	12 51	13 21	13 51	14 21	14 51	15 21	15 51	16 21	16 51	17 21

Table 196

Saturdays

Ashford International and Maidstone East to London

			SE 1	SE 1	SE 1	SE 1	SE 1	SE 1	SE 1	SE 1	SE 1
Ashford International		a									
		d	16 30	16 47	17 30	17 47	18 30	18 47	19 47	20 47	22 17
Charing		d		16 55		17 55		18 55	19 55	20 55	22 25
Lenham		d		17 00		18 00		19 00	20 00	21 00	22 30
Harrietsham		d		17 03		18 03		19 03	20 03	21 03	22 33
Hollingbourne		d		17 07		18 07		19 07	20 07	21 07	22 37
Bearsted		d	16 48	17 11	17 48	18 11	18 48	19 11	20 11	21 11	22 41
Maidstone East 4		a	16 53	17 17	17 53	18 17	18 53	19 17	20 17	21 17	22 47
		d	16 55	17 18	17 55	18 18	18 55	19 18	20 18	21 18	22 48
Barming		d		17 23		18 23		19 23	20 23	21 23	22 53
East Malling		d		17 26		18 26		19 26	20 26	21 26	22 56
West Malling		d	17 02	17 29	18 02	18 29	19 02	19 29	20 29	21 29	22 59
Borough Green & Wrotham		d	17 09	17 36	18 09	18 36	19 09	19 36	20 36	21 36	23 06
Kemsing		d		17 40		18 40		19 40	20 40	21 40	23 10
Otford 4	195	a	17 17	17 46	18 17	18 46	19 17	19 46	20 46	21 46	23 16
Swanley 4	195	a	17 25	17 54	18 25	18 54	19 25	19 54	20 54	21 54	23 24
St Mary Cray	195	a		17 58		18 58		19 58	20 58	21 58	23 28
Bromley South 4	195	a	17 34	18 04	18 34	19 04	19 34	20 04	21 04	22 04	23 34
Elephant & Castle	⊖195	a									
London Blackfriars 3	⊖195	a									
London Victoria 15	⊖	a	17 51	18 21	18 51	19 21	19 51	20 21	21 21	22 21	23 51

Sundays

			SE 1	SE 1	SE 1	SE 1	SE 1	SE 1	SE 1	SE 1	SE 1	SE 1	SE 1	SE 1	SE 1	SE 1	SE 1	SE 1
Ashford International		a																
		d	06 47	07 47	08 47	09 47	10 47	11 47	12 47	13 47	14 47	15 47	16 47	17 47	18 47	19 47	20 47	21 47
Charing		d	06 55	07 55	08 55	09 55	10 55	11 55	12 55	13 55	14 55	15 55	16 55	17 55	18 55	19 55	20 55	21 55
Lenham		d	07 00	08 00	09 00	10 00	11 00	12 00	13 00	14 00	15 00	16 00	17 00	18 00	19 00	20 00	21 00	22 00
Harrietsham		d	07 03	08 03	09 03	10 03	11 03	12 03	13 03	14 03	15 03	16 03	17 03	18 03	19 03	20 03	21 03	22 03
Hollingbourne		d	07 07	08 07	09 07	10 07	11 07	12 07	13 07	14 07	15 07	16 07	17 07	18 07	19 07	20 07	21 07	22 07
Bearsted		d	07 11	08 11	09 11	10 11	11 11	12 11	13 11	14 11	15 11	16 11	17 11	18 11	19 11	20 11	21 11	22 11
Maidstone East 4		a	07 16	08 16	09 16	10 16	11 16	12 16	13 16	14 16	15 16	16 16	17 16	18 16	19 16	20 16	21 16	22 16
		d	07 16	08 16	09 16	10 16	11 16	12 16	13 16	14 16	15 16	16 16	17 16	18 16	19 16	20 16	21 16	22 16
Barming		d	07 21	08 21	09 21	10 21	11 21	12 21	13 21	14 21	15 21	16 21	17 21	18 21	19 21	20 21	21 21	22 21
East Malling		d	07 25	08 25	09 25	10 25	11 25	12 25	13 25	14 25	15 25	16 25	17 25	18 25	19 25	20 25	21 25	22 25
West Malling		d	07 28	08 28	09 28	10 28	11 28	12 28	13 28	14 28	15 28	16 28	17 28	18 28	19 28	20 28	21 28	22 28
Borough Green & Wrotham		d	07 35	08 35	09 35	10 35	11 35	12 35	13 35	14 35	15 35	16 35	17 35	18 35	19 35	20 35	21 35	22 35
Kemsing		d																
Otford 4	195	a	07 43	08 43	09 43	10 43	11 43	12 43	13 43	14 43	15 43	16 43	17 43	18 43	19 43	20 43	21 43	22 43
Swanley 4	195	a	07 51	08 51	09 51	10 51	11 51	12 51	13 51	14 51	15 51	16 51	17 51	18 51	19 51	20 51	21 51	22 51
St Mary Cray	195	a	07 55	08 55	09 55	10 55	11 55	12 55	13 55	14 55	15 55	16 55	17 55	18 55	19 55	20 55	21 55	22 55
Bromley South 4	195	a	08 02	09 02	10 02	11 02	12 02	13 02	14 02	15 02	16 02	17 02	18 02	19 02	20 02	21 02	22 02	23 02
Elephant & Castle	⊖195	a																
London Blackfriars 3	⊖195	a																
London Victoria 15	⊖	a	08 18	09 18	10 18	11 18	12 18	13 18	14 18	15 18	16 18	17 18	18 18	19 18	20 18	21 18	22 18	23 18

London - Lewisham, Hither Green, Petts Wood and Orpington (Summary of Services)

		SE MX	SE MX	SE MO [1]	SE MX [1]	SE MO	SE MX	SE MO	SE MX	SE MX		SE MO	SE MX	SE MX	SE MX	SE	SE	SE	SE	SE		SE	FC [1]	SE	SE
London Charing Cross [4] ⊖	d		23p36	23p38	23p45	23p46		23p50	23p52			23p56	00 02	00 05	00 10	00 15	00 48	04 50	04 56	05 02		05 20			05 26
London Waterloo (East) [4] ⊖	d		23p39	23p41	23p48	23p49		23p53	23p55			23p59	00 05	00 08	00 13	00 18	00 51	04 53	04 59	05 05		05 23			05 29
London Cannon Street [4] ⊖	d																								
London Blackfriars [3] ⊖	d																						05 24		
London Bridge [4] ⊖	d		23p44	23p46	23p53	23p54		23p58	23p59			00 04	00 10	00 13	00 18	00 23	00 56	04a57	05 04	05 10		05a27	05a30		05 34
London Victoria [15] ⊖	d	23p25					23p43			23p55															
New Cross [4] ⊖	d							00 04	00 05				00 15	00 18		00 28	01 01		05 09	05 15				05 31	05 39
St Johns	d								00 07															05 33	
Lewisham [4]	a		23p51			00 02		00 07	00 10			00 11	00 19	00 22		00 32	01 05		05 13	05 19				05 35	05 43
Hither Green [4]	a		23p56			00 07						00 16		00 26			01 09		05 17						05 47
Petts Wood [4]	a	23p59	00 08			00 20	00 21			00 29					00 40		01 22								
Orpington [4]	a	00 02	00 12	00 01	00 08	00 23	00 25			00 32					00 43		01 25								

		SE [1]	SE	SE	SE	SE		FC [1]	SE	SE	SE	SE	SE	SE	SE	SE		FC [1]	SE [1]	SE	SE	SE	SE	SE [1]	SE
London Charing Cross [4] ⊖	d	05 30	05 32	05 36	05 39				05 47		05 52	05 56	06 02	06 06		06 09			06 15		06 17		06 26	06 30	
London Waterloo (East) [4] ⊖	d	05 33	05 35	05 39	05 42				05 50		05 55	05 59	06 05	06 09		06 12			06 18		06 20		06 29	06 33	
London Cannon Street [4] ⊖	d									05 52					06 12							06 27			
London Blackfriars [3] ⊖	d							05 44										06 14							
London Bridge [4] ⊖	d	05 39	05 42	05 44	05 47			05a50	05 55	05a55	05a59	06 04	06 10	06 14	06a15	06 17		06a20	06 24		06 26	06a30	06 34	06 38	
London Victoria [15] ⊖	d					05 40														06 10					06 30
New Cross [4] ⊖	d		05 48		05 52				06 01			06 09	06 15								06 32		06 40		
St Johns	d								06 03												06 34				
Lewisham [4]	a		05 51	05 52	05 56				06 05			06 13	06 19	06 22		06 26					06 37		06 43		
Hither Green [4]	a			05 56								06 17		06 27									06 48		
Petts Wood [4]	a			06 08		06 14								06 39						06 44					07 04
Orpington [4]	a	05 54		06 11		06 18								06 42					06 40	06 49				06 53	07 08

		SE		FC [1]	SE	SE	SE [1]	SE	SE	FC [1]	SE	SE		SE	SE [1]	SE	SE	SE	SE	SE	FC [1]	SE		SE [1]	SE
London Charing Cross [4] ⊖	d	06 32			06 36	06 39	06 45		06 47		06 52			06 56	07 00		07 02	07 06						07 10	07 12
London Waterloo (East) [4] ⊖	d	06 35			06 39	06 42	06 48		06 50		06 55			06 59	07 03		07 05	07 09						07 13	07 15
London Cannon Street [4] ⊖	d							06 50				07 00								07 10		07 13			
London Blackfriars [3] ⊖	d			06 34						06 50											07 08				
London Bridge [4] ⊖	d	06 40		06a41	06 44	06 47	06 53	06 54	06 55	06a56	06a59	07 04		07 05	07 08		07 10	07 14		07 14	07a15	07a16		07a18	07 21
London Victoria [15] ⊖	d															06 50			07 09						
New Cross [4] ⊖	d	06 46						06 59	07 02			07 09								07 20					
St Johns	d							07 01	07 04			07 11								07 22					
Lewisham [4]	a	06 49			06 53	06 56		07 04	07 07			07 14					07 18		07 24	07 26					07 29
Hither Green [4]	a				06 58			07 08						07 18				07 23		07 31					
Petts Wood [4]	a				07 10			07 21								07 24		07 36							
Orpington [4]	a				07 13		07 09	07 25							07 25	07 28		07 40							

		SE [1]	SE	SE	SE	SE	SE	SE		SE	SE [1]	SE	SE	SE	FC [1]	SE	SE	SE		SE	SE [1]	SE	SE [1]	SE	SE
London Charing Cross [4] ⊖	d	07 15	07 17					07 26			07 29					07 36		07 39			07 40	07 44			
London Waterloo (East) [4] ⊖	d	07 18	07 20					07 29			07 32					07 39		07 42			07 43	07 47			
London Cannon Street [4] ⊖	d			07 20		07 24	07 27			07 30			07 32	07 36			07 41			07 44			07 47		07 51
London Blackfriars [3] ⊖	d														07 32										
London Bridge [4] ⊖	d	07 23	07a24	07 24		07 28	07a30	07 34		07 34	07 38		07a36	07 40	07a41	07 44	07 45	07 47		07a47	07a48	07a51	07 51		07 55
London Victoria [15] ⊖	d				07 10							07 25												07 40	
New Cross [4] ⊖	d					07 33				07 39							07 50								08 00
St Johns	d					07 35				07 41															
Lewisham [4]	a					07 38				07 44				07 48			07 54	07 56							08 04
Hither Green [4]	a			07 34				07 45								07 53	07 58								08 10
Petts Wood [4]	a				07 49							07 59				08 06								08 14	08 23
Orpington [4]	a	07 38		07 48	07 53						07 53	08 02				08 09							08 08	08 19	08 26

		SE	SE	SE		SE [1]	SE	SE	SE	SE [1]	SE	FC	SE	SE		SE	SE	FC [1]	SE	SE	SE	SE [1]	SE	SE	
London Charing Cross [4] ⊖	d		07 48			07 52			07 59	08 00				08 03		08 05			08 11			08 13		08 15	
London Waterloo (East) [4] ⊖	d		07 51			07 55			08 02	08 03				08 06		08 08			08 14			08 16		08 18	
London Cannon Street [4] ⊖	d			07 54			07 56	08 00					08 05				08 10						08 16		
London Blackfriars [3] ⊖	d											07 50						08 10							
London Bridge [4] ⊖	d		07 56	07 58		08a00	08a00	08 04	08a06	08 09			08a08	08 11		08 13	08 14	08a16	08 19			08a20	08 20	08a22	
London Victoria [15] ⊖	d	07 43									07 55									08 09	08 10				
New Cross [4] ⊖	d			08 04				08 09									08 20						09a38		
St Johns	d			08 06				08 11									08 22								
Lewisham [4]	a	08 07		08 10				08 14						08 18			08 25		08 28	08 30					
Hither Green [4]	a															08 23	08 29								
Petts Wood [4]	a										08 29	08 32				08 36					08 44				
Orpington [4]	a		08 12							08 25	08 32	08 35				08 39					08 47				

London - Lewisham, Hither Green, Petts Wood and Orpington (Summary of Services)

		SE	SE 1	SE	SE	SE	SE	SE 1	SE	SE		SE 1	SE	SE	SE	SE 1	SE	SE	SE	SE		SE	SE	SE	SE
London Charing Cross 4	⊖ d		08 17	08 20		08 23		08 27	08 31			08 33			08 37		08 41					08 44		08 49	08 49
London Waterloo (East) 4	⊖ d		08 20	08 23		08 26		08 30	08 34			08 36			08 40		08 44					08 47		08 52	08 52
London Cannon Street 4	⊖ d	08 19			08 25		08 30			08 36				08 39		08 42				08 47			08 51		
London Blackfriars 3	⊖ d																								
London Bridge 4	⊖ d	08 23	08 25	08 29	08a28	08 31	08 34	08 35	08 39	08a39		08 41		08 43	08 45	08 46	08 49			08 51		08a52	08 55	08 57	08 57
London Victoria 15	⊖ d												08 25					08 39	08 40						
New Cross 4	⊖ d	08 29				08 38	08 41							08 49						10a08			09 00		
St Johns	d	08 31				08 40	08 43							08 51									09 02		
Lewisham 4	a	08 33				08 43	08 45		08 48					08 54			08 56	09 01					09 05		
Hither Green 4	a	08 38		08 41										08 59	08 55								09 10	09 08	
Petts Wood 4	a	08 51											08 59		09 08				09 14				09 23		
Orpington 4	a	08 54	08 41					08 53				08 57	09 02		09 11	09 07			09 17				09 26		09 22

		SE	SE 1	SE	SE	SE		SE	SE 1	SE	SE	SE	FC 1	SE	SE	SE		SE	SE	SE 1	SE 1	SE	SE	SE	FC 1
London Charing Cross 4	⊖ d		08 53		08 55				09 00		09 02			09 06		09 11				09 13			09 17		
London Waterloo (East) 4	⊖ d		08 56		08 58				09 03		09 05			09 09		09 14				09 16			09 20		
London Cannon Street 4	⊖ d	08 54		08 56		09 00		09 03				09 07			09 09				09 15		09 18			09 20	
London Blackfriars 3	⊖ d												09 00												09 16
London Bridge 4	⊖ d	08 58	09 01	09a00	09 03	09 04		09a06	09 08		09 10	09a10	09a11	09 14	09 14	09 19			09 19	09a20	09 22		09a24	09 25	09a26
London Victoria 15	⊖ d									08 55								09 09				09 10			
New Cross 4	⊖ d	09 04				09 09									09 19				10a38					09 29	
St Johns	d	09 06				09 11									09 21									09 31	
Lewisham 4	a	09 09				09 14					09 18				09 24	09 28		09 31						09 34	
Hither Green 4	a				09 14									09 23	09 28									09 38	
Petts Wood 4	a									09 29				09 36								09 44		09 51	
Orpington 4	a		09 20						09 26	09 33				09 39							09 40	09 47		09 55	

		SE		SE	SE	SE	SE 1	SE	SE	SE	FC 1	SE		SE	SE	SE	SE 1	SE	SE 1	SE	SE	SE		FC 1	SE
London Charing Cross 4	⊖ d				09 26		09 30		09 32			09 36			09 39		09 40		09 45		09 47				
London Waterloo (East) 4	⊖ d				09 29		09 33		09 35			09 39			09 42		09 43		09 48		09 50				
London Cannon Street 4	⊖ d	09 24		09 27		09 30				09 37				09 40				09 47				09 50			09 54
London Blackfriars 3	⊖ d										09 34													09 50	
London Bridge 4	⊖ d	09 28		09a30	09 34	09 34	09 39		09 40	09a40	09a41	09 44		09 44	09 47		09a48	09 51	09 53		09a54	09 54		09a56	09 58
London Victoria 15	⊖ d							09 25								09 39				09 40					
New Cross 4	⊖ d	09 33				09 39								09 49				11a08				09 59			10 03
St Johns	d	09 35				09 41								09 51								10 01			10 05
Lewisham 4	a	09 38				09 44			09 49					09 54	09 56	10 01						10 04			10 08
Hither Green 4	a				09 43							09 53		09 58								10 08			
Petts Wood 4	a							09 59				10 06								10 14		10 21			
Orpington 4	a						09 55	10 02				10 09							10 08	10 17		10 24			

		SE	SE	SE	SE 1	SE	SE	SE		FC 1	SE	SE	SE	SE	SE 1	SE	SE 1	SE		SE	SE	FC 1	SE	SE	SE
London Charing Cross 4	⊖ d		09 56		10 00		10 02				10 06		10 09		10 10		10 15			10 17					10 26
London Waterloo (East) 4	⊖ d		09 59		10 03		10 05				10 09		10 12		10 13		10 18			10 20					10 29
London Cannon Street 4	⊖ d	09 57		10 00				10 07				10 10				10 17					10 20		10 24	10 27	
London Blackfriars 3	⊖ d									10 05												10 20			
London Bridge 4	⊖ d	10a00	10 04	10 04	10 09		10 10	10a10		10a11	10 14	10 14	10 17		10a18	10 21	10 23			10a24	10 24	10a26	10 28	10a30	10 34
London Victoria 15	⊖ d					09 55								10 09				10 10							
New Cross 4	⊖ d			10 09								10 19				11a38					10 29		10 33		
St Johns	d			10 11								10 21									10 31		10 35		
Lewisham 4	a			10 14			10 19					10 24	10 26	10 31							10 34		10 38		
Hither Green 4	a		10 13								10 23	10 28									10 38				10 43
Petts Wood 4	a					10 29					10 36							10 44			10 51				
Orpington 4	a				10 25	10 32					10 39						10 38	10 47			10 54				

		SE	SE 1	SE		SE	SE	FC 1	SE	SE	SE	SE	SE 1	SE		SE 1	SE	SE	SE	FC 1	SE	SE	SE	SE	
London Charing Cross 4	⊖ d		10 30			10 32			10 36		10 39		10 40			10 45		10 47					10 56		
London Waterloo (East) 4	⊖ d		10 33			10 35			10 39		10 42		10 43			10 48		10 50					10 59		
London Cannon Street 4	⊖ d	10 30					10 37			10 40				10 47					10 50		10 54	10 57		11 00	
London Blackfriars 3	⊖ d							10 35												10 50					
London Bridge 4	⊖ d	10 34	10 39			10 40	10a40	10a41	10 44	10 44	10 47		10a48	10 51		10 53		10a54	10 54	10a56	10 58	11a00	11 04	11 04	
London Victoria 15	⊖ d			10 25								10 39					10 40								
New Cross 4	⊖ d	10 39								10 49				12a08					10 59		11 03			11 09	
St Johns	d	10 41								10 51									11 01		11 05			11 11	
Lewisham 4	a	10 44				10 49				10 54	10 56	11 01							11 04		11 08			11 14	
Hither Green 4	a								10 53	10 58									11 08				11 13		
Petts Wood 4	a			10 59					11 06								11 14		11 21						
Orpington 4	a		10 55	11 02					11 09							11 08	11 17		11 24						

		SE 1	SE	SE	SE	FC 1	SE	SE	SE	SE		SE 1	SE	SE 1	SE	SE	SE	FC 1	SE	SE		SE	SE	SE 1	SE
London Charing Cross 4	⊖ d	11 00		11 02			11 06		11 09			11 10		11 15		11 17						11 26		11 30	
London Waterloo (East) 4	⊖ d	11 03		11 05			11 09		11 12			11 13		11 18		11 20						11 29		11 33	
London Cannon Street 4	⊖ d				11 07			11 10					11 17				11 20		11 24	11 27			11 30		
London Blackfriars 3	⊖ d					11 05												11 20							
London Bridge 4	⊖ d	11 09		11 10	11a10	11a11	11 14	11 14	11 17			11a18	11 21	11 23		11a24	11 24	11a26	11 28	11a30		11 34	11 34	11 39	
London Victoria 15	⊖ d		10 55							11 09					11 10										11 25
New Cross 4	⊖ d							11 19					12a38				11 29		11 33				11 39		
St Johns	d							11 21									11 31		11 35				11 41		
Lewisham 4	a			11 19				11 24	11 26	11 31							11 33		11 38				11 44		
Hither Green 4	a						11 23	11 28									11 38					11 43			
Petts Wood 4	a		11 29				11 36								11 44		11 51								11 59
Orpington 4	a	11 25	11 32				11 39							11 38	11 47		11 54							11 55	12 02

London - Lewisham, Hither Green, Petts Wood and Orpington (Summary of Services)

		SE	SE	FC 1	SE	SE		SE	SE	SE 1	SE	SE 1	SE	SE	SE	FC 1		SE	SE	SE	SE	SE 1	SE	SE	SE
London Charing Cross 4 ⊖	d	11 32			11 36			11 39		11 40		11 45		11 47						11 56		12 00		12 02	
London Waterloo (East) 4 ⊖	d	11 35			11 39			11 42		11 43		11 48		11 50						11 59		12 03		12 05	
London Cannon Street 4 ⊖	d		11 37			11 40					11 47				11 50			11 54	11 57		12 00				12 07
London Blackfriars 3 ⊖	d			11 35												11 50									
London Bridge 4 ⊖	d	11 40	11a40	11a41	11 44	11 44		11 47		11a48	11 51	11 53		11a54	11 54	11a56		11 58	12a00	12 04	12 04	12 09		12 10	12a10
London Victoria 15 ⊖	d								11 39				11 40										11 55		
New Cross 4 ⊖	d					11 49					13a08				11 59			12 03			12 09				
St Johns	d					11 51									12 01			12 05			12 11				
Lewisham 4	a	11 49				11 54		11 56	12 01						12 03			12 08			12 14			12 19	
Hither Green 4	a				11 53	11 58									12 08					12 13					
Petts Wood 4	a				12 06								12 14		12 21								12 29		
Orpington 4	a				12 09							12 08	12 17		12 24							12 25	12 32		

		FC 1		SE	SE	SE	SE	SE 1	SE	SE 1	SE	SE		SE	FC 1	SE	SE	SE	SE	SE 1	SE	SE		SE	FC 1
London Charing Cross 4 ⊖	d			12 06		12 09		12 10		12 15		12 17						12 26		12 30		12 32			
London Waterloo (East) 4 ⊖	d			12 09		12 12		12 13		12 18		12 20						12 29		12 33		12 35			
London Cannon Street 4 ⊖	d				12 10				12 17					12 20		12 24	12 27		12 30					12 37	
London Blackfriars 3 ⊖	d	12 05													12 20										12 35
London Bridge 4 ⊖	d	12a11		12 14	12 14	12 17		12a18	12 21	12 23		12a24		12 24	12a26	12 28	12a30	12 34	12 34	12 39		12 40		12a40	12a41
London Victoria 15 ⊖	d						12 09				12 10										12 25				
New Cross 4 ⊖	d				12 19				13a38					12 29		12 33			12 39						
St Johns	d				12 21									12 31		12 35			12 41						
Lewisham 4	a				12 24	12 26	12 31							12 34		12 38			12 44			12 49			
Hither Green 4	a			12 23	12 28									12 38				12 43							
Petts Wood 4	a			12 36							12 44			12 51							12 59				
Orpington 4	a			12 39						12 38	12 47			12 54						12 55	13 02				

		SE	SE	SE	SE	SE 1	SE	SE 1		SE	SE	SE	FC 1	SE	SE	SE	SE	SE 1		SE	SE	SE	FC 1	SE	SE
London Charing Cross 4 ⊖	d	12 36		12 39		12 40		12 45			12 47					12 56		13 00			13 02			13 06	
London Waterloo (East) 4 ⊖	d	12 39		12 42		12 43		12 48			12 50					12 59		13 03			13 05			13 09	
London Cannon Street 4 ⊖	d		12 40				12 47					12 50		12 54	12 57		13 00					13 07			13 10
London Blackfriars 3 ⊖	d												12 50										13 05		
London Bridge 4 ⊖	d	12 44	12 44	12 47		12a48	12 51	12 53			12a54	12 54	12a56	12 58	13a00	13 04	13 04	13 09			13 10	13a10	13a11	13 14	13 14
London Victoria 15 ⊖	d				12 39					12 40										12 55					
New Cross 4 ⊖	d		12 49				14a08					12 59		13 03			13 09								13 19
St Johns	d		12 51									13 01		13 05			13 11								13 21
Lewisham 4	a		12 54	12 56	13 01							13 03		13 08			13 14				13 19				13 24
Hither Green 4	a	12 53	12 58									13 08				13 13								13 23	13 28
Petts Wood 4	a	13 06								13 14		13 21								13 29				13 36	
Orpington 4	a	13 09						13 08		13 17		13 24						13 25		13 32				13 39	

		SE	SE	SE 1		SE	SE 1	SE	SE	SE	FC 1	SE	SE	SE		SE	SE 1	SE	SE	SE	FC 1	SE	SE	SE	
London Charing Cross 4 ⊖	d	13 09		13 10			13 15		13 17					13 26			13 30		13 32			13 36		13 39	
London Waterloo (East) 4 ⊖	d	13 12		13 13			13 18		13 20					13 29			13 33		13 35			13 39		13 42	
London Cannon Street 4 ⊖	d					13 17				13 20		13 24	13 27			13 30				13 37			13 40		
London Blackfriars 3 ⊖	d										13 20										13 35				
London Bridge 4 ⊖	d	13 17		13a18		13 21	13 23		13a24	13 24	13a26	13 28	13a30	13 34		13 34	13 39		13 40	13a40	13a41	13 44	13 44	13 47	
London Victoria 15 ⊖	d		13 09					13 10										13 25							
New Cross 4 ⊖	d					14a38				13 29		13 33				13 39							13 49		
St Johns	d									13 31		13 35				13 41							13 51		
Lewisham 4	a	13 26	13 31							13 34		13 38				13 44			13 49				13 54	13 56	
Hither Green 4	a									13 38				13 43								13 53	13 58		
Petts Wood 4	a							13 44		13 51								13 59				14 06			
Orpington 4	a						13 38	13 47		13 54							13 55	14 02				14 09			

		SE	SE 1	SE	SE 1	SE	SE	SE	FC 1	SE		SE	SE	SE	SE 1	SE	SE	SE	FC 1	SE		SE	SE	SE	SE 1
London Charing Cross 4 ⊖	d		13 40		13 45		13 47						13 56		14 00		14 02			14 06			14 09		14 10
London Waterloo (East) 4 ⊖	d		13 43		13 48		13 50						13 59		14 03		14 05			14 09			14 12		14 13
London Cannon Street 4 ⊖	d			13 47				13 50		13 54		13 57		14 00				14 07				14 10			
London Blackfriars 3 ⊖	d								13 50										14 05						
London Bridge 4 ⊖	d		13a48	13 51	13 53		13a54	13 54	13a56	13 58		14a00	14 04	14 04	14 09		14 10	14a10	14a11	14 14		14 14	14 17		14a18
London Victoria 15 ⊖	d	13 39				13 40										13 55								14 09	
New Cross 4 ⊖	d			15a08				13 59		14 03				14 09								14 19			
St Johns	d							14 01		14 05				14 11								14 21			
Lewisham 4	a	14 01						14 04		14 08				14 14			14 19					14 24	14 26	14 31	
Hither Green 4	a							14 08					14 13							14 23		14 28			
Petts Wood 4	a					14 14		14 21								14 29				14 36					
Orpington 4	a				14 08	14 17		14 24							14 25	14 32				14 39					

		SE	SE 1	SE	SE	SE		FC 1	SE	SE	SE	SE	SE 1	SE	SE	SE		FC 1	SE	SE	SE	SE	SE 1	SE	SE 1
London Charing Cross 4 ⊖	d		14 15		14 17						14 26		14 30		14 32				14 36		14 39		14 40		14 45
London Waterloo (East) 4 ⊖	d		14 18		14 20						14 29		14 33		14 35				14 39		14 42		14 43		14 48
London Cannon Street 4 ⊖	d	14 17				14 20			14 24	14 27		14 30				14 37				14 40				14 47	
London Blackfriars 3 ⊖	d							14 20										14 35							
London Bridge 4 ⊖	d	14 21	14 23		14a24	14 24		14a26	14 28	14a30	14 34	14 34	14 39		14 40	14a40		14a41	14 44	14 44	14 47		14a48	14 51	14 53
London Victoria 15 ⊖	d			14 10										14 25								14 39			
New Cross 4 ⊖	d	15a38				14 29			14 33			14 39								14 49				16a08	
St Johns	d					14 31			14 35			14 41								14 51					
Lewisham 4	a					14 34			14 38			14 44			14 49					14 54	14 56	15 01			
Hither Green 4	a					14 38					14 43								14 53	14 58					
Petts Wood 4	a			14 44		14 51								14 59					15 06						
Orpington 4	a		14 38	14 47		14 54							14 55	15 02					15 09						15 08

Table 199

Mondays to Fridays

London - Lewisham, Hither Green, Petts Wood and Orpington (Summary of Services)

	SE		SE	SE	FC [1]	SE	SE	SE	SE	SE [1]	SE		SE	SE	FC [1]	SE	SE	SE	SE	SE [1]	SE		SE [1]	SE
London Charing Cross [4] ⊖ d			14 47					14 56		15 00			15 02			15 06		15 09		15 10			15 15	
London Waterloo (East) [4] ⊖ d			14 50					14 59		15 03			15 05			15 09		15 12		15 13			15 18	
London Cannon Street [4] ⊖ d				14 50		14 54	14 57		15 00					15 07			15 10				15 17			
London Blackfriars [3] ⊖ d					14 50										15 05									
London Bridge [4] ⊖ d			14a54	14 54	14a56	14 58	15a00	15 04	15 04	15 09			15 10	15a10	15a11	15 14	15 14	15 17		15a18	15 21		15 23	
London Victoria [15] ⊖ d	14 40										14 55								15 09					15 10
New Cross [4] ⊖ d				14 59		15 03			15 09								15 19				16a38			
St Johns d				15 01		15 05			15 11								15 21							
Lewisham [4] a				15 04		15 08			15 14				15 19				15 24	15 26	15 31					
Hither Green [4] a				15 08				15 13								15 23	15 28							
Petts Wood [4] a	15 14			15 21							15 29					15 36								15 44
Orpington [4] a	15 17			15 24						15 25	15 32					15 39							15 38	15 47

	SE	SE	FC [1]	SE	SE	SE	SE		SE [1]	SE	SE	SE	FC [1]	SE	SE	SE	SE		SE [1]	SE	SE [1]	SE	SE	SE
London Charing Cross [4] ⊖ d	15 17					15 26			15 30		15 32			15 36		15 39			15 40		15 45		15 47	
London Waterloo (East) [4] ⊖ d	15 20					15 29			15 33		15 35			15 39		15 42			15 43		15 48		15 50	
London Cannon Street [4] ⊖ d		15 20		15 24	15 27		15 30					15 37			15 40					15 47				15 50
London Blackfriars [3] ⊖ d			15 20										15 35											
London Bridge [4] ⊖ d	15a24	15 24	15a26	15 28	15a30	15 34	15 34		15 39		15 40	15a40	15a41	15 44	15 44	15 47			15a48	15 51	15 53		15a54	15 54
London Victoria [15] ⊖ d										15 25							15 39					15 40		
New Cross [4] ⊖ d		15 29		15 33			15 39								15 49					17a11				15 59
St Johns d		15 31		15 35			15 41								15 51									16 01
Lewisham [4] a		15 34		15 38			15 44				15 49				15 54	15 56	16 01							16 03
Hither Green [4] a		15 38				15 43								15 53	15 58									16 08
Petts Wood [4] a		15 51								15 59				16 06								16 14		16 21
Orpington [4] a		15 54							15 55	16 02				16 09							16 08	16 17		16 24

	FC [1]	SE	SE		SE	SE	SE [1]	SE	SE	SE	FC [1]	SE	SE		SE	SE	SE	SE [1]	SE	SE [1]	SE	FC [1]	SE	
London Charing Cross [4] ⊖ d					15 56		16 00		16 02			16 06			16 09			16 10		16 15			16 20	
London Waterloo (East) [4] ⊖ d					15 59		16 03		16 05			16 09			16 12			16 13		16 18			16 23	
London Cannon Street [4] ⊖ d		15 54	15 57			16 00				16 07			16 10						16 17		16 20			
London Blackfriars [3] ⊖ d	15 50										16 05											16 20		
London Bridge [4] ⊖ d	15a56	15 58	16a00		16 04	16 04	16 09		16 10	16a10	16a11	16 14	16 14		16 17			16a18	16 21	16a22	16 24	16a26	16a28	
London Victoria [15] ⊖ d								15 55								16 09	16 10							
New Cross [4] ⊖ d		16 03				16 10							16 20						17a39		16 30			
St Johns d		16 05				16 12							16 22								16 32			
Lewisham [4] a		16 08				16 14			16 19				16 24		16 26	16 31					16 34			
Hither Green [4] a					16 13							16 23	16 29								16 39			
Petts Wood [4] a								16 29				16 36					16 44				16 51			
Orpington [4] a							16 25	16 32				16 39					16 49				16 57			

	SE	SE	SE	SE	SE [1]	SE	SE	SE	SE		FC	FC [1]	SE	SE [1]	SE	SE	SE	SE	SE		SE [1]	SE [1]	SE	SE
London Charing Cross [4] ⊖ d			16 26		16 28		16 30		16 32					16 37	16 39						16 41		16 42	16 45
London Waterloo (East) [4] ⊖ d			16 29		16 31		16 33		16 35					16 40	16 42						16 44		16 45	16 48
London Cannon Street [4] ⊖ d	16 24	16 27		16 30				16 35					16 39			16 42			16 44			16 46		
London Blackfriars [3] ⊖ d											16 26	16 36												
London Bridge [4] ⊖ d	16 28	16a30	16 34	16 34	16 36		16 38	16a38	16 40			16a42	16 43	16a44	16a46	16 46			16a47		16a48	16a49	16 51	16a52
London Victoria [15] ⊖ d						16 25											16 39	16 40						
New Cross [4] ⊖ d	16 34			16 40									16 49			16 52								
St Johns d	16 36			16 42									16 51											
Lewisham [4] a	16 38			16 44			16 47						16 53			16 55	16 58						17 00	
Hither Green [4] a			16 43						16 49				16 58										17 05	
Petts Wood [4] a						16 59			17 03		17 08							17 14					17 18	
Orpington [4] a					16 52	17 04			17 06		17 15							17 19					17 24	

	SE	SE	SE	SE	SE		SE	SE [1]	SE	SE	SE [1]	SE	SE [1]	SE	SE		SE	SE	SE [1]	SE	SE	SE	SE	SE
London Charing Cross [4] ⊖ d		16 49		16 51			16 55	16 57				16 59	17 01				17 03			17 06		17 10		17 12
London Waterloo (East) [4] ⊖ d		16 52		16 54			16 58	16a59				17 02	17 04				17 06			17 09		17 13		17 15
London Cannon Street [4] ⊖ d	16 51		16 54		16 56				16 58		17 02			17 04	17 06				17 08		17 12		17 16	
London Blackfriars [3] ⊖ d																								
London Bridge [4] ⊖ d	16 55	16 57	16a57	16 59	17 00		17a02		17 02		17a05	17a06	17a08	17 08	17a09		17 11		17a11	17 14	17 16	17 19	17a19	17 21
London Victoria [15] ⊖ d										17 00								17 04						
New Cross [4] ⊖ d	17 01								17 08					17 14							17 22			
St Johns d	17 03								17 10												17 24			
Lewisham [4] a	17 05			17 07					17 12					17 17			17 20	17 23			17 26			17 30
Hither Green [4] a		17 07							17 17								17 25			18 21		17 28		
Petts Wood [4] a					17 24					17 35							17 38							
Orpington [4] a					17 27					17 40							17 44							

	SE [1]		SE	SE	SE	SE [1]	SE	SE [1]	SE	SE [1]	SE		SE	SE [1]	SE	SE	SE	SE	SE	SE	SE [1]		SE	SE
London Charing Cross [4] ⊖ d	17 14				17 17	17 19			17 21	17 23					17 26	17 29		17 30		17 32			17 34	
London Waterloo (East) [4] ⊖ d	17a17				17 20	17a21			17 24	17 26					17 29	17 32		17a32		17 35			17 37	
London Cannon Street [4] ⊖ d			17 19				17 21	17 24			17 26		17 28	17 30					17 34		17 37			
London Blackfriars [3] ⊖ d																								
London Bridge [4] ⊖ d			17 23		17a24		17 25	17a27	17a28	17a30	17 30		17a31	17a33	17 35	17a36			17 39	17 41	17a40		17 43	
London Victoria [15] ⊖ d				17 15													17 30							17 34
New Cross [4] ⊖ d							17 31				17 36								17 45					
St Johns d							17 33												17 47					
Lewisham [4] a							17 35				17 39				17 43				17 49				17 52	17 55
Hither Green [4] a							17 40								17 48					17 51				
Petts Wood [4] a			17 43	17 50											18 01		18 05							
Orpington [4] a			17 47	17 55											18 07		18 10							

Table 199

Mondays to Fridays

London - Lewisham, Hither Green, Petts Wood and Orpington (Summary of Services)

		SE	SE	SE	SE 1	SE	SE 1	SE		SE	SE 1	SE	SE	SE	SE 1	SE	SE	SE		SE	SE	SE	SE 1	SE	SE
London Charing Cross 4 ⊖	d			17 39	17 41			17 43			17 45		17 47			17 50	17 52			17 54	17 56		17 59		
London Waterloo (East) 4 ⊖	d			17 42	17a43			17 46			17 48		17 50			17 53	17a54			17 57	17 59		18a01		
London Cannon Street 4 ⊖	d	17 39	17 41			17 43	17 45			17 47		17 50			17 52			17 56						18 00	18 02
London Blackfriars 3 ⊖	d																								
London Bridge 4 ⊖	d	17a42	17 45	17a46		17 47	17a48	17a50		17 51	17a52	17a53	17 55		17a55	17a57		18 00		18 02	18 04			18a03	18 06
London Victoria 15 ⊖	d													17 45								17 56			
New Cross 4 ⊖	d					17 53				17 58								18 06							
St Johns	d					17 55												18 08							
Lewisham 4	a					17 58				18 01			18 04					18 10			18 13	18 17			
Hither Green 4	a					18 03							18 09							18 12					
Petts Wood 4	a		18 08										18 23	18 26											18 28
Orpington 4	a		18 11										18 29	18 32											18 32

		SE	SE	SE 1		SE	SE 1	SE	SE 1	SE	SE	SE	SE 1	SE		SE	SE	SE	SE	SE	FC 1	SE 1	SE	SE	
London Charing Cross 4 ⊖	d		18 01	18 03				18 05	18 07			18 09		18 12		18 12	18 14			18 18		18 21			
London Waterloo (East) 4 ⊖	d		18 04	18a05				18 08	18 10			18 12		18 15		18 15	18 17			18 21		18a23			
London Cannon Street 4 ⊖	d					18 04	18 08			18 10	18 12		18 14					18 18	18 21				18 23		
London Blackfriars 3 ⊖	d																				18 20				
London Bridge 4 ⊖	d		18a08			18 08	18a11	18a12	18a14	18 14	18a15	18 17	18a17	18a20		18 21	18 23	18 23	18a24	18 26	18a27		18 27		
London Victoria 15 ⊖	d	18 00																						18 15	
New Cross 4 ⊖	d					18 14				18 20						19a38		18 28							
St Johns	d					18 16												18 30							
Lewisham 4	a					18 19				18 23		18 26						18 33		18 35					
Hither Green 4	a					18 24						18 31					18 35								
Petts Wood 4	a	18 35										18 43											18 49	18 53	
Orpington 4	a	18 41										18 49											18 53	18 59	

		SE	SE	SE	SE 1	SE	SE	SE 1	SE	SE		SE 1	SE	SE	SE	SE	SE 1	SE 1	SE	SE		SE	SE 1	SE	SE
London Charing Cross 4 ⊖	d			18 23			18 27		18 30			18 32	18 34		18 37	18 39		18 41					18 45		
London Waterloo (East) 4 ⊖	d			18 26			18 30		18 33			18 35	18 37		18 40	18 42		18 44					18 48		
London Cannon Street 4 ⊖	d	18 25			18 28	18 30		18 32		18 34				18 40			18 44					18 46		18 48	
London Blackfriars 3 ⊖	d																								
London Bridge 4 ⊖	d	18 29		18a31	18a31	18a33	18a34	18a35	18 38	18 38		18a39	18a41	18 44	18 46	18 48	18a47	18 50				18a49	18a52	18 52	
London Victoria 15 ⊖	d		18 18																18 30	18 39					18 45
New Cross 4 ⊖	d	18 35								18 44				18 50		18 55									
St Johns	d	18 37								18 46				18 52											
Lewisham 4	a	18 40	18 42							18 48				18 54		18 59				19 02					
Hither Green 4	a	18 45							18 48						18 55										
Petts Wood 4	a								19 02										19 06					19 13	19 19
Orpington 4	a								19 06									19 06	19 12					19 19	19 25

		FC 1	SE	SE	SE	SE		SE	SE	SE	SE 1	SE	SE 1	SE	SE	FC 1		SE	SE	SE	SE	SE 1	SE	SE 1	SE
London Charing Cross 4 ⊖	d			18 48		18 52			18 56		19 00			19 02				19 06		19 09		19 10		19 15	
London Waterloo (East) 4 ⊖	d			18 51		18 55			18 59		19 03			19 05				19 09		19 12		19 13		19 18	
London Cannon Street 4 ⊖	d		18 50		18 54			18 57		19 00			19 04		19 07				19 10				19 17		
London Blackfriars 3 ⊖	d	18 46														19 05									
London Bridge 4 ⊖	d	18a54	18 54	18 57	18 58	18a59		19a00	19 04	19 04	19 09		19a07	19 10	19a10	19a11		19 14	19 14	19 17		19a18	19a20	19 23	
London Victoria 15 ⊖	d											19 00									19 09				19 10
New Cross 4 ⊖	d		19 00		19 05					19 09									19 19						
St Johns	d		19 02		19 07					19 11									19 21						
Lewisham 4	a		19 04	19 06	19 10					19 14				19 19					19 24	19 26	19 31				
Hither Green 4	a		19 09						19 14									19 23	19 28						
Petts Wood 4	a											19 35						19 37							19 44
Orpington 4	a										19 27	19 38						19 43						19 38	19 48

		SE		SE	FC 1	SE	SE	SE	SE	SE 1	SE	SE		SE	FC 1	SE	SE	SE	SE	SE 1	SE	SE 1		SE	SE
London Charing Cross 4 ⊖	d	19 17						19 26		19 30		19 32				19 36		19 39		19 40		19 45			19 47
London Waterloo (East) 4 ⊖	d	19 20						19 29		19 33		19 35				19 39		19 42		19 43		19 48			19 50
London Cannon Street 4 ⊖	d			19 20		19 24	19 27		19 30					19 37			19 40				19 47				
London Blackfriars 3 ⊖	d				19 20										19 35										
London Bridge 4 ⊖	d	19a24		19 24	19a26	19 28	19a30	19 34	19 34	19 39		19 40		19a40	19a41	19 44	19 44	19 47		19a48	19a50	19 53			19a54
London Victoria 15 ⊖	d										19 25								19 39					19 40	
New Cross 4 ⊖	d			19 29		19 33			19 39								19 49								
St Johns	d			19 31		19 35			19 41								19 51								
Lewisham 4	a			19 33		19 38			19 44			19 49					19 55	19 56	20 01						
Hither Green 4	a			19 38				19 43								19 53	19 59								
Petts Wood 4	a			19 51							19 59					20 06								20 14	
Orpington 4	a			19 54						19 55	20 02					20 09						20 08		20 18	

		SE	FC 1	SE	SE	SE	SE	SE 1		SE	SE	FC 1	SE	SE	SE	SE 1	SE	SE 1		SE	SE	SE	SE	SE	SE 1
London Charing Cross 4 ⊖	d					19 56		20 00			20 02		20 06		20 09	20 10		20 15				20 17	20 22		20 30
London Waterloo (East) 4 ⊖	d					19 59		20 03			20 05		20 09		20 12	20 13		20 18				20 20	20 25		20 33
London Cannon Street 4 ⊖	d	19 50		19 54	19 57		20 00							20 10			20 17				20 20			20 27	
London Blackfriars 3 ⊖	d		19 50									20 05													
London Bridge 4 ⊖	d	19 54	19a56	19 58	20a00	20 04	20 04	20 09			20 10	20a11	20 14	20 14	20 17	20a18	20a20	20 23			20 24	20 25	20 30	20a30	20 39
London Victoria 15 ⊖	d									19 55										20 10					
New Cross 4 ⊖	d	19 59		20 03			20 09							20 19							20 29	20 32	20 35		
St Johns	d	20 01		20 05			20 11							20 21							20 31	20 34			
Lewisham 4	a	20 04		20 08			20 14				20 19			20 25	20 26						20 34	20 36	20 38		
Hither Green 4	a	20 08				20 13							20 23	20 29							20 38		20 44		
Petts Wood 4	a	20 21								20 29			20 36							20 44	20 51				
Orpington 4	a	20 24						20 25		20 32			20 39					20 38		20 47	20 54				20 55

Table 199

Mondays to Fridays

London - Lewisham, Hither Green, Petts Wood and Orpington (Summary of Services)

		SE	SE	FC 1		SE	SE	SE 1	SE	SE 1	SE	SE	SE	SE 1		SE	SE	FC 1	SE	SE	SE 1	SE	SE	SE	
London Charing Cross 4 ⊖	d		20 32			20 36	20 39	20 40		20 45	20 47	20 52		21 00			21 02		21 06	21 09	21 10	21 17	21 22	21 26	
London Waterloo (East) 4 ⊖	d		20 35			20 39	20 42	20 43		20 48	20 50	20 55		21 03			21 05		21 09	21 12	21 13	21 20	21 25	21 29	
London Cannon Street 4 ⊖	d								20 47				20 57												
London Blackfriars 3 ⊖	d			20 35														21 05							
London Bridge 4 ⊖	d		20 40	20a41		20 44	20 47	20a48	20a50	20 53	20 55	21 00	21a00	21 09			21 10	21a11	21 14	21 17	21 19	21 25	21 30	21a33	
London Victoria 15 ⊖	d	20 25														20 55									
New Cross 4 ⊖	d		20 45								21 00	21 05					21 15					21 30	21 35		
St Johns	d										21 02											21 32			
Lewisham 4	a		20 49				20 56				21 05	21 09					21 19		21 21	21 26		21 35	21 39		
Hither Green 4	a					20 53						21 13							21 26				21 43		
Petts Wood 4	a	20 59				21 06										21 29			21 38						
Orpington 4	a	21 02				21 09				21 08				21 25		21 32			21 42		21 34				

		SE 1	SE	SE	FC 1	SE	SE	SE 1	SE 1	SE		SE	SE	SE 1	SE	SE	FC 1	SE	SE	SE 1		SE	SE	SE	SE 1
London Charing Cross 4 ⊖	d	21 30		21 32		21 36	21 39	21 40	21 45	21 47		21 52	21 56	22 00		22 02		22 06	22 09	22 10		22 17	22 22	22 26	22 30
London Waterloo (East) 4 ⊖	d	21 33		21 35		21 39	21 42	21 43	21 48	21 50		21 55	21 59	22 03		22 05		22 09	22 12	22 13		22 20	22 25	22 29	22 33
London Cannon Street 4 ⊖	d																								
London Blackfriars 3 ⊖	d				21 35												22 05								
London Bridge 4 ⊖	d	21 39		21 40	21a41	21 44	21 47	21a48	21 53	21 55		22 00	22a03	22 09		22 10	22a11	22 14	22 17	22 19		22 25	22 30	22a33	22 39
London Victoria 15 ⊖	d		21 25												21 55										
New Cross 4 ⊖	d			21 45						22 00		22 05				22 15						22 30	22 35		
St Johns	d									22 02												22 32			
Lewisham 4	a			21 49		21 51	21 56			22 05		22 09				22 19		22 21	22 26			22 35	22 39		
Hither Green 4	a					21 56						22 13						22 26					22 43		
Petts Wood 4	a		21 59			22 08									22 29			22 38							
Orpington 4	a	21 55	22 02			22 12			22 08					22 25	22 32			22 42		22 34					22 54

		SE	SE	SE	SE	SE 1		SE 1	SE	SE	SE	SE 1	SE	SE	SE	SE		SE	SE 1	SE	SE	SE	SE 1	SE	SE
London Charing Cross 4 ⊖	d		22 32	22 36	22 39	22 40		22 45	22 47	22 52	22 56	23 00			23 02	23 06		23 09	23 10	23 17	23 22	23 26	23 30		
London Waterloo (East) 4 ⊖	d		22 35	22 39	22 42	22 43		22 48	22 50	22 55	22 59	23 03			23 05	23 09		23 12	23 13	23 20	23 25	23 29	23 33		
London Cannon Street 4 ⊖	d																								
London Blackfriars 3 ⊖	d																								
London Bridge 4 ⊖	d		22 40	22 44	22 47	22a48		22 53	22 55	23 00	23a03	23 09			23 10	23 14		23 17	23 19	23 25	23 30	23a33	23 39		
London Victoria 15 ⊖	d	22 25											22 43	22 55										23 13	23 25
New Cross 4 ⊖	d		22 45						23 00	23 05					23 15					23 30	23 35				
St Johns	d								23 02											23 32					
Lewisham 4	a		22 49	22 51	22 56				23 05	23 09					23 19	23 21		23 26		23 35	23 39				
Hither Green 4	a			22 56						23 13						23 26					23 43				
Petts Wood 4	a	22 59		23 08									23 21	23 29		23 38								23 51	23 59
Orpington 4	a	23 02		23 12				23 08				23 24	23 25	23 32		23 42			23 34				23 54	23 57	00 02

		SE		SE	SE	SE 1	SE 1	SE	SE	SE	SE
London Charing Cross 4 ⊖	d	23 32		23 36	23 39	23 40	23 45		23 52		23 56
London Waterloo (East) 4 ⊖	d	23 35		23 39	23 42	23 43	23 48		23 55		23 59
London Cannon Street 4 ⊖	d										
London Blackfriars 3 ⊖	d										
London Bridge 4 ⊖	d	23 40		23 44	23 47	23a48	23 53		23 59		00a03
London Victoria 15 ⊖	d							23 43		23 55	
New Cross 4 ⊖	d	23 45							00 05		
St Johns	d								00 07		
Lewisham 4	a	23 49		23 51	23 56				00 10		
Hither Green 4	a			23 56							
Petts Wood 4	a			00 08				00 21		00 29	
Orpington 4	a			00 12			00 08	00 25		00 32	

Saturdays

		SE	SE	SE 1	SE	SE	SE	SE	SE	SE		SE	SE	SE	SE	SE	SE	SE	SE	SE		SE	SE	SE 1	SE
London Charing Cross 4 ⊖	d		23p36	23p45		23p52		00 02	00 05	00 10		00 15	00 48	04 52	05 22	05 26	05 32	05 36	05 39	05 47		05 52	05 56	06 00	
London Waterloo (East) 4 ⊖	d		23p39	23p48		23p55		00 05	00 08	00 13		00 18	00 51	04 55	05 25	05 29	05 35	05 39	05 42	05 50		05 55	05 59	06 03	
London Cannon Street 4 ⊖	d																								
London Blackfriars 3 ⊖	d																								
London Bridge 4 ⊖	d		23p44	23p53		23p59		00 10	00 13	00 18		00 23	00 56	05 00	05 30	05a33	05 40	05 44	05 47	05 55		06 00	06a03	06 08	
London Victoria 15 ⊖	d	23p25			23p43		23p55																		05 55
New Cross 4 ⊖	d					00 05		00 15	00 18			00 28	01 01	05 05	05 35		05 45			06 00		06 05			
St Johns	d					00 07														06 02					
Lewisham 4	a		23p51			00 10		00 19	00 22			00 32	01 05	05 09	05 39		05 49	05 52	05 56	06 05		06 09			
Hither Green 4	a		23p56						00 26				01 09	05 13	05 43			05 57				06 13			
Petts Wood 4	a	23p59	00 08		00 21		00 29			00 40			01 22					06 09							06 29
Orpington 4	a	00 02	00 12	00 08	00 25		00 32			00 43			01 25					06 12						06 23	06 32

Table 199

London - Lewisham, Hither Green, Petts Wood and Orpington (Summary of Services)

		SE	SE	SE	SE	SE		SE	SE	SE	SE	SE	SE	SE	SE	SE 1		SE	SE	SE	SE	SE	SE	SE	SE
London Charing Cross 4	⊖ d	06 02	06 06	06 09	06 17	06 22			06 26	06 32	06 36	06 39	06 47	06 52	06 56	07 00			07 02	07 06	07 09		07 17	07 22	07 26
London Waterloo (East) 4	⊖ d	06 05	06 09	06 12	06 20	06 25			06 29	06 35	06 39	06 42	06 50	06 55	06 59	07 03			07 05	07 09	07 12		07 20	07 25	07 29
London Cannon Street 4	⊖ d																								
London Blackfriars 3	⊖ d																								
London Bridge 4	⊖ d	06 10	06 14	06 17	06 25	06 30			06a33	06 40	06 44	06 47	06 55	07 00	07a03	07 08			07 10	07 14	07 17		07 25	07 30	07a33
London Victoria 15	⊖ d							06 25										06 55				07 10			
New Cross 4	⊖ d	06 15			06 30	06 35				06 45			07 00	07 05					07 15				07 30	07 35	
St Johns	d				06 32								07 02										07 32		
Lewisham 4	a	06 19	06 22	06 26	06 35	06 39				06 49	06 52	06 56	07 05	07 08					07 19	07 22	07 26		07 35	07 39	
Hither Green 4	a		06 27			06 43					06 57			07 14						07 27				07 44	
Petts Wood 4	a		06 39					06 59			07 09							07 29		07 39		07 44			
Orpington 4	a		06 42					07 02			07 12					07 23		07 32		07 42		07 47			

		SE 1		SE	SE	SE	SE	SE	SE 1	SE	SE	SE		SE	SE	SE 1	SE	SE	SE	SE	SE	SE		SE	SE
London Charing Cross 4	⊖ d	07 30			07 32	07 36	07 39		07 45		07 47	07 52		07 56		08 00		08 02		08 06		08 09			
London Waterloo (East) 4	⊖ d	07 33			07 35	07 39	07 42		07 48		07 50	07 55		07 59		08 03		08 05		08 09		08 12			
London Cannon Street 4	⊖ d														08 00				08 07		08 10				08 17
London Blackfriars 3	⊖ d																								
London Bridge 4	⊖ d	07 38			07 40	07 44	07 47		07 53		07a54	08 00		08a03	08 04	08 08		08 10	08a10	08 14	08 14	08 17			08 21
London Victoria 15	⊖ d			07 25				07 39		07 40							07 55							08 09	
New Cross 4	⊖ d				07 45							08 05			08 09			08 15			08 19				09a38
St Johns	d														08 11						08 21				
Lewisham 4	a				07 49	07 52	07 56	08 02				08 08			08 13			08 19			08 24	08 26		08 31	
Hither Green 4	a					07 57						08 14								08 23	08 28				
Petts Wood 4	a			07 59		08 09				08 14							08 29			08 36					
Orpington 4	a	07 54		08 02		08 12			08 08	08 17						08 23	08 32			08 39					

		SE 1	SE	SE	SE	SE	SE	SE		SE	SE 1	SE	SE	SE	SE	SE	SE	SE		SE 1	SE	SE 1	SE	SE	SE
London Charing Cross 4	⊖ d	08 15		08 17				08 26			08 30		08 32		08 36		08 39			08 40		08 45		08 47	
London Waterloo (East) 4	⊖ d	08 18		08 20				08 29			08 33		08 35		08 39		08 42			08 43		08 48		08 50	
London Cannon Street 4	⊖ d				08 20	08 24	08 27			08 30				08 37		08 40					08 47				08 50
London Blackfriars 3	⊖ d																								
London Bridge 4	⊖ d	08 23		08a24	08 24	08 28	08a30	08 34		08 34	08 39		08 40	08a40	08 44	08 44	08 47			08a48	08 51	08 53		08a54	08 54
London Victoria 15	⊖ d		08 10									08 25						08 39					08 40		
New Cross 4	⊖ d				08 29	08 33				08 39						08 49					10a08				08 59
St Johns	d				08 31	08 35				08 41						08 51									09 01
Lewisham 4	a				08 34	08 38				08 44			08 49			08 54	08 56	09 01							09 04
Hither Green 4	a				08 38			08 43							08 53	08 58									09 08
Petts Wood 4	a		08 44		08 51							08 59			09 06								09 14		09 21
Orpington 4	a	08 38	08 47		08 54						08 55	09 02			09 09							09 08	09 17		09 24

		SE	SE	SE		SE	SE 1	SE	SE	SE	SE	SE	SE	SE		SE 1		SE 1	SE	SE 1	SE	SE	SE	
London Charing Cross 4	⊖ d			08 56			09 00		09 02		09 06		09 09			09 10		18 10		18 15		18 17		
London Waterloo (East) 4	⊖ d			08 59			09 03		09 05		09 09		09 12			09 13	and at the same minutes past each hour until	18 13		18 18		18 20		
London Cannon Street 4	⊖ d	08 54	08 57			09 00				09 07		09 10							18 17				18 20	
London Blackfriars 3	⊖ d																							
London Bridge 4	⊖ d	08 58	09a00	09 04		09 04	09 09		09 10	09a10	09 14	09 14	09 17			09a18		18a18	18a20	18 23		18a24	18 24	
London Victoria 15	⊖ d							08 55						09 09							18 10			
New Cross 4	⊖ d	09 03				09 09						09 19											18 29	
St Johns	d	09 05				09 11						09 21											18 31	
Lewisham 4	a	09 08				09 14			09 19			09 24	09 26	09 31									18 34	
Hither Green 4	a			09 13							09 23	09 28											18 38	
Petts Wood 4	a							09 29			09 36										18 44		18 51	
Orpington 4	a						09 25	09 32			09 39									18 38	18 47		18 54	

		SE	SE	SE	SE	SE 1	SE	SE	SE	SE		SE	SE	SE	SE 1	SE	SE 1	SE	SE	SE		SE	SE	SE	SE
London Charing Cross 4	⊖ d			18 26		18 30		18 32		18 36			18 39		18 40		18 45		18 47					18 56	
London Waterloo (East) 4	⊖ d			18 29		18 33		18 35		18 39			18 42		18 43		18 48		18 50					18 59	
London Cannon Street 4	⊖ d	18 24	18 27		18 30				18 37			18 40				18 47				18 50		18 54	18 57		19 00
London Blackfriars 3	⊖ d																								
London Bridge 4	⊖ d	18 28	18a30	18 34	18 34	18 39		18 40	18a40	18 44		18 44	18 47		18a48	18a50	18 53		18a54	18 54		18 58	19a00	19 04	19 04
London Victoria 15	⊖ d						18 25							18 39				18 40							
New Cross 4	⊖ d	18 33			18 39							18 49								18 59		19 03			19 09
St Johns	d	18 35			18 41							18 51								19 01		19 05			19 11
Lewisham 4	a	18 38			18 44			18 49				18 54	18 56	19 01						19 04		19 08			19 14
Hither Green 4	a			18 43						18 53		18 58								19 08				19 13	
Petts Wood 4	a						18 59			19 06								19 14		19 21					
Orpington 4	a					18 55	19 02			19 09							19 08	19 17		19 24					

		SE 1	SE	SE	SE	SE		SE	SE	SE	SE 1	SE 1	SE	SE	SE	SE		SE	SE 1	SE	SE	SE	SE	SE	SE
London Charing Cross 4	⊖ d	19 00		19 02		19 06			19 09		19 10	19 15		19 17				19 26	19 30		19 32	19 36	19 39		
London Waterloo (East) 4	⊖ d	19 03		19 05		19 09			19 12		19 13	19 18		19 20				19 29	19 33		19 35	19 39	19 42		
London Cannon Street 4	⊖ d				19 07			19 10							19 24	19 27									
London Blackfriars 3	⊖ d																								
London Bridge 4	⊖ d	19 09		19 10	19a10	19 14		19 14	19 17		19a18	19 23		19 25	19 28	19a30		19 34	19 39		19 40	19 44	19 47		
London Victoria 15	⊖ d		18 55							19 09			19 10							19 25				19 39	19 40
New Cross 4	⊖ d							19 19						19 30	19 33						19 45				
St Johns	d							19 21						19 32	19 35										
Lewisham 4	a			19 19				19 24	19 26	19 31				19 35	19 38						19 49	19 51	19 56	20 01	
Hither Green 4	a					19 23		19 28										19 43				19 56			
Petts Wood 4	a		19 29			19 36							19 44							19 59		20 08			20 14
Orpington 4	a	19 25	19 32			19 39						19 38	19 48						19 55	20 02		20 12			20 18

Table 199

Saturdays

London - Lewisham, Hither Green, Petts Wood and Orpington (Summary of Services)

		SE 1		SE	SE	SE 1	SE	SE	SE	SE	SE	SE 1		SE	SE	SE	SE 1	SE	SE	SE	SE	SE		SE 1	SE
London Charing Cross 4 ⊖	d	19 40		19 47	19 52	19 55		19 56	20 02	20 06	20 09	20 10			20 17	20 22	20 25		20 26	20 32	20 36	20 39		20 40	20 47
London Waterloo (East) 4 ⊖	d	19 43		19 50	19 55	19 58		19 59	20 05	20 09	20 12	20 13			20 20	20 25	20 28		20 29	20 35	20 39	20 42		20 43	20 50
London Cannon Street 4 ⊖	d																								
London Blackfriars 3 ⊖	d																								
London Bridge 4 ⊖	d	19a48		19 55	20 00	20 03		20a04	20 10	20 14	20 17	20 19			20 25	20 30	20 33		20a34	20 40	20 44	20 47		20 49	20 55
London Victoria 15 ⊖	d						19 55							20 10				20 25							
New Cross 4 ⊖	d			20 00	20 05				20 15						20 30	20 35				20 45					21 00
St Johns	d			20 02											20 32										21 02
Lewisham 4	a			20 05	20 09				20 19	20 21	20 26				20 35	20 39				20 49	20 51	20 56			21 05
Hither Green 4	a				20 13					20 26						20 43					20 56				
Petts Wood 4	a						20 29			20 38				20 44				20 59			21 08				
Orpington 4	a					20 18	20 32			20 42		20 34		20 47			20 48	21 02			21 12			21 04	

		SE	SE 1	SE	SE	SE	SE	SE		SE 1	SE	SE	SE 1	SE	SE	SE	SE	SE		SE 1	SE	SE	SE 1	SE	SE
London Charing Cross 4 ⊖	d	20 52	20 55		20 56	21 02	21 06	21 09		21 10	21 17	21 22	21 25		21 26	21 32	21 36	21 39		21 40	21 47	21 52	21 55		21 56
London Waterloo (East) 4 ⊖	d	20 55	20 58		20 59	21 05	21 09	21 12		21 13	21 20	21 25	21 28		21 29	21 35	21 39	21 42		21 43	21 50	21 55	21 58		21 59
London Cannon Street 4 ⊖	d																								
London Blackfriars 3 ⊖	d																								
London Bridge 4 ⊖	d	21 00	21 03		21a04	21 10	21 14	21 17		21 19	21 25	21 30	21 33		21a34	21 40	21 44	21 47		21 49	21 55	22 00	22 03		22a04
London Victoria 15 ⊖	d			20 55										21 25										21 55	
New Cross 4 ⊖	d	21 05				21 15					21 30	21 35				21 45					22 00	22 05			
St Johns	d										21 32										22 02				
Lewisham 4	a	21 09				21 19	21 21	21 26			21 35	21 39				21 49	21 51	21 56			22 05	22 09			
Hither Green 4	a	21 13					21 26					21 43					21 56					22 13			
Petts Wood 4	a			21 29			21 38							21 59			22 08							22 29	
Orpington 4	a		21 18	21 32			21 42			21 34			21 48	22 02			22 12			22 04			22 18	22 32	

		SE	SE	SE		SE 1	SE	SE	SE 1	SE	SE	SE	SE	SE		SE 1	SE	SE	SE 1	SE	SE	SE	SE	SE	
London Charing Cross 4 ⊖	d	22 02	22 06	22 09		22 10	22 17	22 22	22 25		22 26	22 32	22 36	22 39		22 40	22 47	22 52	22 55			22 56	23 02	23 06	
London Waterloo (East) 4 ⊖	d	22 05	22 09	22 12		22 13	22 20	22 25	22 28		22 29	22 35	22 39	22 42		22 43	22 50	22 55	22 58			22 59	23 05	23 09	
London Cannon Street 4 ⊖	d																								
London Blackfriars 3 ⊖	d																								
London Bridge 4 ⊖	d	22 10	22 14	22 17		22 19	22 25	22 30	22 33		22a34	22 40	22 44	22 47		22 49	22 55	23 00	23 03			23a04	23 10	23 14	
London Victoria 15 ⊖	d									22 25										22 43	22 55				
New Cross 4 ⊖	d	22 15					22 30	22 35				22 45					23 00	23 05					23 15		
St Johns	d						22 32										23 02								
Lewisham 4	a	22 19	22 21	22 26			22 35	22 39				22 49	22 51	22 56			23 05	23 09					23 19	23 21	
Hither Green 4	a		22 26					22 43					22 56					23 13						23 26	
Petts Wood 4	a		22 38							22 59			23 08							23 22	23 29			23 38	
Orpington 4	a		22 42			22 34			22 48	23 02			23 12			23 04			23 18	23 25	23 32			23 42	

		SE	SE 1	SE	SE 1	SE	SE	SE	SE	SE		SE	SE 1	SE 1	SE	SE	SE	SE							
London Charing Cross 4 ⊖	d	23 09	23 10	23 22	23 25			23 26	23 32	23 36		23 39	23 40	23 45		23 52		23 56							
London Waterloo (East) 4 ⊖	d	23 12	23 13	23 25	23 28			23 29	23 35	23 39		23 42	23 43	23 48		23 55		23 59							
London Cannon Street 4 ⊖	d																								
London Blackfriars 3 ⊖	d																								
London Bridge 4 ⊖	d	23 17	23 19	23 30	23 33			23a34	23 40	23 44		23 47	23 49	23 53		23 59		00a04							
London Victoria 15 ⊖	d					23 13	23 25								23 43		23 55								
New Cross 4 ⊖	d			23 35					23 45							00 05									
St Johns	d															00 07									
Lewisham 4	a	23 26		23 39					23 49	23 51		23 55				00 10									
Hither Green 4	a			23 43						23 56															
Petts Wood 4	a					23 52	23 59			00 08					00 22		00 29								
Orpington 4	a		23 34		23 48	23 55	00 02			00 12			00 04	00 08	00 25		00 32								

Sundays

		SE A	SE A	SE 1 A	SE 1 A	SE A	SE A	SE A	SE	SE		SE	SE	SE	SE	SE	SE	SE	SE	SE		SE	SE	SE 1	SE
London Charing Cross 4 ⊖	d		23p36	23p40	23p45		23p52		00 02	00 05		00 10	00 15	00 48	07 30	07 35	07 46	07 50		07 56		08 00	08 05	08 08	08 10
London Waterloo (East) 4 ⊖	d		23p39	23p43	23p48		23p55		00 05	00 08		00 13	00 18	00 51	07 33	07 38	07 49	07 53		07 59		08 03	08 08	08 11	08 13
London Cannon Street 4 ⊖	d																								
London Blackfriars 3 ⊖	d																								
London Bridge 4 ⊖	d		23p44	23p49	23p53		23p59		00 10	00 13		00 18	00 23	00 56	07a37	07 43	07 54	07 58		08 04		08a07	08 13	08 16	08 18
London Victoria 15 ⊖	d	23p25				23p43		23p55											07 51						
New Cross 4 ⊖	d						00 05		00 15	00 18			00 28	01 01		07 49		08 04					08 19		
St Johns	d						00 07									07 51							08 21		
Lewisham 4	a		23p51				00 10		00 19	00 22			00 32	01 05		07 53	08 02	08 07		08 11			08 23		08 27
Hither Green 4	a		23p56							00 26				01 09			08 07			08 16					
Petts Wood 4	a	23p59	00 08			00 22		00 29				00 40		01 22			08 20		08 25						
Orpington 4	a	00 02	00 12	00 04	00 08	00 25		00 32				00 43		01 25			08 23		08 28					08 31	

A not 22 May

Sundays

London - Lewisham, Hither Green, Petts Wood and Orpington (Summary of Services)

		SE	SE	SE 1	SE	SE		SE	SE	SE 1	SE	SE	SE	SE	SE	SE		SE	SE 1	SE	SE	SE	SE 1	SE	SE
London Charing Cross 4	⊖ d	08 16	08 20	08 23		08 26		08 30	08 35	08 38	08 40	08 46	08 50		08 56	09 00		09 05	09 08	09 10	09 16	09 20	09 23		09 26
London Waterloo (East) 4	⊖ d	08 19	08 23	08 26		08 29		08 33	08 38	08 41	08 43	08 49	08 53		08 59	09 03		09 08	09 11	09 13	09 19	09 23	09 26		09 29
London Cannon Street 4	⊖ d																								
London Blackfriars 3	⊖ d																								
London Bridge 4	⊖ d	08 24	08 28	08 31		08 34		08a37	08 43	08 46	08 48	08 54	08 58		09 04	09a07		09 13	09 16	09 18	09 24	09 28	09 31		09 34
London Victoria 15	⊖ d				08 21									08 51										09 21	
New Cross 4	⊖ d		08 34						08 49				09 04					09 19				09 34			
St Johns	d								08 51									09 21							
Lewisham 4	a	08 32	08 37			08 41			08 53		08 57	09 02	09 07		09 11			09 23		09 27	09 32	09 37			09 41
Hither Green 4	a	08 37				08 46						09 07			09 16						09 37				09 46
Petts Wood 4	a	08 50			08 55							09 20		09 25							09 50			09 55	
Orpington 4	a	08 53		08 46	08 58					09 01		09 23		09 28					09 31		09 53		09 46	09 58	

		SE		SE	SE 1	SE	SE	SE	SE 1		SE 1		SE	SE	SE	SE	SE 1	SE	SE	SE	SE 1		SE	SE
London Charing Cross 4	⊖ d	09 30		09 35	09 38	09 40	09 46	09 50	09 53		19 53			19 56	20 00	20 05	20 08	20 10	20 16	20 20	20 23			20 26
London Waterloo (East) 4	⊖ d	09 33		09 38	09 41	09 43	09 49	09 53	09 56	and at	19 56			19 59	20 03	20 08	20 11	20 13	20 19	20 23	20 26			20 29
London Cannon Street 4	⊖ d									the same														
London Blackfriars 3	⊖ d									minutes														
London Bridge 4	⊖ d	09a37		09 43	09 46	09 48	09 54	09 58	10 01	past	20 01			20 04	20a07	20 13	20 16	20 18	20 24	20 28	20 31			20 34
London Victoria 15	⊖ d									each			19 51										20 21	
New Cross 4	⊖ d			09 49				10 04		hour until						20 19				20 34				
St Johns	d			09 51												20 21								
Lewisham 4	a			09 53		09 57	10 02	10 07						20 11		20 23		20 27	20 32	20 37				20 41
Hither Green 4	a						10 07							20 16					20 37					20 46
Petts Wood 4	a						10 20						20 25						20 50				20 55	
Orpington 4	a				10 01		10 23		10 16		20 16		20 28				20 31		20 53		20 46		20 58	

		SE	SE	SE 1	SE	SE	SE	SE		SE	SE	SE	SE 1	SE	SE	SE	SE 1	SE		SE	SE	SE	SE 1	SE	SE
London Charing Cross 4	⊖ d	20 30	20 35	20 38	20 40	20 46	20 50			20 56	21 00	21 05	21 08	21 10	21 16	21 20	21 23			21 26	21 30	21 35	21 38	21 40	21 46
London Waterloo (East) 4	⊖ d	20 33	20 38	20 41	20 43	20 49	20 53			20 59	21 03	21 08	21 11	21 13	21 19	21 23	21 26			21 29	21 33	21 38	21 41	21 43	21 49
London Cannon Street 4	⊖ d																								
London Blackfriars 3	⊖ d																								
London Bridge 4	⊖ d	20a37	20 43	20 46	20 48	20 54	20 58			21 04	21a07	21 13	21 16	21 18	21 24	21 28	21 31			21 34	21a37	21 43	21 46	21 48	21 54
London Victoria 15	⊖ d							20 51										21 21							
New Cross 4	⊖ d		20 49				21 04					21 19				21 34						21 49			
St Johns	d		20 51									21 21										21 51			
Lewisham 4	a		20 53		20 57	21 02	21 07			21 11		21 23		21 27	21 32	21 37				21 41		21 53		21 57	22 02
Hither Green 4	a					21 07				21 16					21 37					21 46					22 07
Petts Wood 4	a					21 20		21 25							21 50			21 55							22 20
Orpington 4	a			21 01		21 23		21 28					21 31		21 53		21 46	21 58					22 01		22 23

		SE	SE	SE		SE	SE	SE 1	SE	SE	SE	SE 1	SE	SE		SE	SE	SE 1	SE	SE	SE	SE	SE	SE	
London Charing Cross 4	⊖ d	21 50		21 56		22 00	22 05	22 08	22 10	22 16	22 20	22 23		22 26		22 30	22 35	22 38	22 40	22 46		22 50		22 56	
London Waterloo (East) 4	⊖ d	21 53		21 59		22 03	22 08	22 11	22 13	22 19	22 23	22 26		22 29		22 33	22 38	22 41	22 43	22 49		22 53		22 59	
London Cannon Street 4	⊖ d																								
London Blackfriars 3	⊖ d																								
London Bridge 4	⊖ d	21 58		22 04		22a07	22 13	22 16	22 18	22 24	22 28	22 31		22 34		22a37	22 43	22 46	22 48	22 54		22 58		23 04	
London Victoria 15	⊖ d		21 51										22 21								22 39		22 51		
New Cross 4	⊖ d	22 04					22 19				22 34						22 49					23 04			
St Johns	d						22 21										22 51								
Lewisham 4	a	22 07		22 11			22 23		22 27	22 32	22 37			22 41			22 53		22 57	23 02		23 07		23 11	
Hither Green 4	a			22 16						22 37				22 46						23 07				23 16	
Petts Wood 4	a		22 25							22 50			22 55							23 20	23 22		23 25		
Orpington 4	a		22 28					22 31		22 53		22 46	22 58					23 01		23 23	23 26		23 29		

		SE	SE	SE 1	SE	SE	SE	SE 1	SE	SE		SE	SE	SE	SE 1	SE	SE	SE
London Charing Cross 4	⊖ d	23 00	23 05	23 08	23 10	23 16	23 20	23 23				23 26	23 30	23 35	23 38	23 46	23 50	23 56
London Waterloo (East) 4	⊖ d	23 03	23 08	23 11	23 13	23 19	23 23	23 26				23 29	23 33	23 38	23 41	23 49	23 53	23 59
London Cannon Street 4	⊖ d																	
London Blackfriars 3	⊖ d																	
London Bridge 4	⊖ d	23a07	23 13	23 16	23 18	23 24	23 28	23 31				23 34	23a37	23 43	23 46	23 54	23 58	00 04
London Victoria 15	⊖ d								23 09	23 21								
New Cross 4	⊖ d		23 19				23 34							23 49			00 04	
St Johns	d		23 21											23 51				
Lewisham 4	a		23 23		23 26	23 32	23 37					23 41		23 53		00 02	00 07	00 11
Hither Green 4	a					23 37						23 46				00 07		00 16
Petts Wood 4	a					23 50			23 52	23 55						00 20		
Orpington 4	a			23 31		23 53		23 46	23 56	23 59					00 01	00 23		

Orpington, Petts Wood, Hither Green and Lewisham - London (Summary of Services)

		SE MX ■1	SE	SE	SE	SE	FC ■1	SE	SE	SE		SE	SE	SE	FC ■1	SE	SE	SE	SE	SE ■1		SE	FC ■1	SE	SE
Orpington ■4	d	23p37	04 34	04 55		05 10				05 20						05 34	05 40			05 54					
Petts Wood ■4	d		04 37	04 58		05 13				05 23						05 37	05 43								
Hither Green ■4	d				05 08			05 23		05 35			05 38												
Lewisham ■4	d				05 13			05 28				05 39	05 43	05 50					05 56					06 09	
St Johns	d											05 41												06 11	
New Cross ■4	⊖ d				05 16			05 31		05 40		05 43	05 46	05 53										06 13	
London Victoria ■15	⊖ a					05 47											06 18								
London Bridge ■4	⊖ d	23p53			05 22		05 34	05 37	05 42	05 46		05 49	05 53	05 59	06 02			06 02	06 06	06 10		06 13	06 16	06 19	06 20
London Blackfriars ■3	⊖ a		05 17	05 33			05 41								06 10	06 17							06 23		
London Cannon Street ■4	⊖ a							05 41										06 06							06 24
London Waterloo (East) ■4	⊖ d	23p58			05 27				05 47	05 50		05 53	05 57	06 04					06 10	06 15		06 18		06 24	
London Charing Cross ■4	⊖ a	00 01			05 30				05 50	05 53		05 56	06 01	06 07					06 13	06 18		06 21		06 27	

		SE	SE ■1	SE	SE	SE		SE	SE	SE	SE ■1	SE ■1	SE	SE	FC ■1	SE		SE	SE	SE	SE ■1	SE	FC ■1	SE	SE
Orpington ■4	d		06 09			06 01		06 10			06 20	06 24							06 22	06 40					
Petts Wood ■4	d					06 04		06 13											06 25	06 43					
Hither Green ■4	d	06 08				06 16				06 22									06 38						
Lewisham ■4	d	06 13			06 20	06 22			06 25	06 27				06 35		06 39		06 41	06 43					06 48	06 50
St Johns	d									06 29						06 41								06 50	
New Cross ■4	⊖ d	06 16				06 25				06 31				06 38		06 43								06 52	
London Victoria ■15	⊖ a							06 47										07 04		07 19					
London Bridge ■4	⊖ d	06 22	06 25	06 28	06 29	06 32			06 34	06 37	06 38	06 40	06 43	06 44	06 46	06 49			06 52		06 55	06 57	06 58	07 00	07 01
London Blackfriars ■3	⊖ a														06 52								07 04		
London Cannon Street ■4	⊖ a			06 32							06 42			06 48								07 03		07 05	
London Waterloo (East) ■4	⊖ d	06 27	06 30		06 33	06 36			06 40	06 42		06 45	06 49			06 54			06 57		07 00				07 06
London Charing Cross ■4	⊖ a	06 30	06 33		06 36	06 39			06 43	06 45		06 49	06 52			06 57			07 02		07 05				07 11

		SE		SE	SE	SE	SE	SE ■1	SE ■1	SE	SE	SE		SE	SE	SE	SE	SE	SE ■1	SE ■1	SE	FC ■1		SE	SE
Orpington ■4	d						06 43	06 54						06 52	06 58			07 03		07 04	07 08				
Petts Wood ■4	d						06 46							06 55	07 01			07 06			07 11				
Hither Green ■4	d			06 56	06 51		06 58							07 08				07 19						07 11	07 16
Lewisham ■4	d	06 55			06 57	07 01	07 04				07 08					07 11	07 15	07 25						07 17	
St Johns	d				06 59																			07 19	
New Cross ■4	⊖ d				07 01	07 04					07 11													07 21	
London Victoria ■15	⊖ a																07 42				07 49				
London Bridge ■4	⊖ d	07 04		07 07	07 08	07 10		07 10	07 15	07 15	07 18	07 18		07 19		07 21			07 21	07 23		07 24		07 27	07 27
London Blackfriars ■3	⊖ a														07 42							07 30			
London Cannon Street ■4	⊖ a				07 14	07 16				07 21	07 23			07 25					07 27	07 29				07 33	
London Waterloo (East) ■4	⊖ d	07 10		07 12			07 17	07 15	07 20			07 23				07 26		07 37							07 32
London Charing Cross ■4	⊖ a	07 15		07 17			07 22	07 20	07 25			07 28				07 31		07 42							07 37

		SE	SE ■1	SE	SE	SE	SE ■1	SE		SE ■1	SE	SE	SE	SE	SE	SE	SE ■1	SE ■1		SE	SE	SE	SE ■1	SE	SE ■1
Orpington ■4	d		07 14					07 11												07 22	07 28				
Petts Wood ■4	d							07 15												07 25	07 31				
Hither Green ■4	d							07 28							07 32	07 36				07 39					
Lewisham ■4	d	07 20		07 22							07 30	07 35			07 38					07 44		07 46			
St Johns	d			07 24											07 40										
New Cross ■4	⊖ d	07 23		07 26								07 38			07 42										
London Victoria ■15	⊖ a																					08 11			
London Bridge ■4	⊖ d	07 29	07 30	07 34	07 34	07 36	07 37	07 38			07 42	07 44	07 45	07 46	07 48	07 48	07 51	07 52		07 54			07 54	07 58	
London Blackfriars ■3	⊖ a																				08 08				
London Cannon Street ■4	⊖ a	07 35		07 39		07 42		07 44				07 50		07 52	07 54			07 57					07 59	08 04	
London Waterloo (East) ■4	⊖ d		07 35		07 39		07 42			07 45	07 47		07 51			07 53	07 56			07 59					08 01
London Charing Cross ■4	⊖ a		07 40		07 44		07 47			07 50	07 52		07 56			07 58	08 01			08 04					08 06

		SE	SE	SE		SE	SE ■1 ⚲	SE	SE	SE	SE	SE	SE	SE		SE ■1	SE	SE	SE	SE ■1	SE	SE ■1	SE	SE ■1	
Orpington ■4	d		07 33	07 38													07 42	07 47							
Petts Wood ■4	d		07 36	07 41													07 45	07 50							
Hither Green ■4	d		07 49										07 52				07 57				08 02				
Lewisham ■4	d					07 48		07 50	07 55				07 57				08 03		08 05						
St Johns	d					07 50							08 00												
New Cross ■4	⊖ d					07 53			07 58				08 02												
London Victoria ■15	⊖ a			08 20															08 29						
London Bridge ■4	⊖ d	07 58	08 00			08 02		08 02	08 04	08 06		08 06	08 09			08 10				08 12	08 14	08 14	08 18		
London Blackfriars ■3	⊖ a																	08 29							
London Cannon Street ■4	⊖ a		08 06			08 08			08 10	08 12			08 15							08 19		08 20	08 24		
London Waterloo (East) ■4	⊖ d	08 03					08 05	08 07			08 09	08 11		08 13		08 15	08 17				08 19			08 21	
London Charing Cross ■4	⊖ a	08 08					08 08	08 12			08 14	08 16		08 18		08 20	08 22				08 24			08 26	

Orpington, Petts Wood, Hither Green and Lewisham - London (Summary of Services)

		SE	SE	SE	SE	SE	SE 1 ✕	SE	SE	SE		SE	SE	SE	SE 1	SE	SE	SE	SE 1	SE		SE 1	SE 1	SE	SE
Orpington 4	d		07 52	07 57												08 01		08 10							
Petts Wood 4	d		07 55	08 00												08 04		08 13							
Hither Green 4	d												08 12			08 17				08 22					
Lewisham 4	d				08 08	08 11		08 15					08 17			08 23	08 25								
St Johns	d				08 12								08 21												
New Cross 4 ⊖	d				08 14			08 18					08 23											07 20	
London Victoria 15 ⊖	a																08 49	08 50							
London Bridge 4 ⊖	d	08 18	08 20		08 22	08 22	08 24	08 26		08 26		08 28	08 30		08 30				08 33	08 34		08 34		08 38	08 38
London Blackfriars 3 ⊖	a																								
London Cannon Street 4 ⊖	a		08 26		08 28		08 30	08 32				08 35	08 36						08 40			08 41			
London Waterloo (East) 4 ⊖	d	08 23		08 25		08 27			08 29	08 31				08 33	08 35	08 37				08 39			08 41	08 43	08 43
London Charing Cross 4 ⊖	a	08 28		08 30		08 32			08 34	08 36				08 39	08 40	08 42				08 44			08 46	08 48	08 48

		SE	SE	SE	SE 1	SE		SE	SE	SE	SE	SE	SE	SE	SE	SE 1		SE 1	SE	SE 1	SE	SE 1	SE	SE	SE
Orpington 4	d		08 13										08 21	08 26										08 32	08 40
Petts Wood 4	d		08 16										08 24	08 29										08 35	08 43
Hither Green 4	d											08 32	08 37						08 42						
Lewisham 4	d			08 28		08 31		08 35				08 37			08 46						08 48				
St Johns	d			08 30								08 40									08 50				
New Cross 4 ⊖	d			08 32				08 38				08 42									08 52				
London Victoria 15 ⊖	a													09 06	09 11										09 19
London Bridge 4 ⊖	d	08 39	08 40	08 42		08 42		08 44	08 46		08 46	08 50				08 50		08 51	08 54	08 56	08 58		08 58	09 00	
London Blackfriars 3 ⊖	a																								
London Cannon Street 4 ⊖	a	08 44	08 46	08 48				08 50	08 52			08 55						08 57		09 02	09 04			09 06	
London Waterloo (East) 4 ⊖	d				08 45	08 47				08 49	08 51		08 53			08 55			08 59			09 01	09 03		
London Charing Cross 4 ⊖	a				08 50	08 52				08 54	08 56		08 58			09 00			09 04			09 04	09 08		

		SE		SE	SE 1	SE	SE	SE	SE	FC 1	SE	SE 1		SE 1	SE 1	SE	SE	SE	SE	SE	SE	SE 1		SE	SE
Orpington 4	d															08 43	08 47			08 52	08 55	09 04			
Petts Wood 4	d															08 46	08 50			08 55	08 58				
Hither Green 4	d					08 50		08 55								08 59				09 08				09 14	
Lewisham 4	d	08 52				08 55					08 59					09 04		09 06							09 15
St Johns	d					08 57					09 01					09 07									09 17
New Cross 4 ⊖	d					08 59			07 50		09 03					09 09									09 19
London Victoria 15 ⊖	a																	09 29			09 34				
London Bridge 4 ⊖	d	09 01		09 02	09 04	09 06		09 06	09 08	09 09	09 10	09 12		09 12	09 15	09 18			09 18	09 21		09 23		09 24	09 26
London Blackfriars 3 ⊖	a									09 21							09 30								
London Cannon Street 4 ⊖	a			09 08	09 10	09 12			09 14		09 18	09 18				09 23						09 28			09 32
London Waterloo (East) 4 ⊖	d	09 06					09 08	09 11						09 17	09 20				09 23	09 26				09 29	
London Charing Cross 4 ⊖	a	09 12					09 13	09 16						09 22	09 25				09 28	09 31				09 34	

		SE 1	SE	SE	SE	SE	SE	SE		SE	SE 1	SE	SE 1	SE	SE	FC 1	SE	SE		SE	SE	SE 1	SE	SE	FC 1
Orpington 4	d	09 09			09 03	09 10					09 24						09 21	09 25				09 39			
Petts Wood 4	d				09 06	09 13											09 24	09 28							
Hither Green 4	d				09 19									09 28			09 37				09 42				
Lewisham 4	d			09 20	09 24		09 26			09 29				09 34	09 38								09 45	09 50	
St Johns	d				09 26					09 31				09 36									09 47		
New Cross 4 ⊖	d		08 20		09 28					09 33				09 38									09 49		
London Victoria 15 ⊖	a					09 49									10 00			10 02							
London Bridge 4 ⊖	d	09 27	09 30	09 30	09 34		09 35	09 38		09 39	09 41	09 42	09 44	09 45		09 46	09 49			09 51	09 52	09 55	09 55	09 58	10 00
London Blackfriars 3 ⊖	a															09 53									10 08
London Cannon Street 4 ⊖	a		09 36		09 40					09 45		09 48		09 51						09 57			10 00		
London Waterloo (East) 4 ⊖	d	09 32		09 35			09 40	09 43			09 46		09 49				09 54				09 57	10 00		10 03	
London Charing Cross 4 ⊖	a	09 37		09 40			09 45	09 48			09 51		09 54				09 59				10 00	10 03		10 06	

		SE	SE	SE		SE	SE	SE	SE 1	SE	SE 1	SE	SE	FC 1		SE	SE	SE	SE	SE	SE 1	SE	FC 1	SE	
Orpington 4	d		09 33	09 40					09 54							09 51	09 55				10 09				
Petts Wood 4	d		09 36	09 43												09 54	09 58								
Hither Green 4	d		09 49									09 58				10 07			10 12						
Lewisham 4	d		09 54			09 56		09 59				10 04	10 08							10 14		10 20			
St Johns	d		09 56					10 01				10 06								10 16					
New Cross 4 ⊖	d	08 49	09 58					10 03				10 08								10 18				09 19	
London Victoria 15 ⊖	a			10 17									10 28				10 32								
London Bridge 4 ⊖	d	10 01	10 04			10 05	10 08	10 09	10 11	10 11	10 13	10 14		10 16		10 19		10 21	10 22	10 24	10 25	10 28	10 30	10 31	
London Blackfriars 3 ⊖	a													10 23									10 37		
London Cannon Street 4 ⊖	a	10 04	10 08					10 13		10 15		10 19						10 24		10 28				10 36	
London Waterloo (East) 4 ⊖	d					10 10	10 13		10 15		10 18					10 24			10 27		10 30	10 33			
London Charing Cross 4 ⊖	a					10 13	10 16		10 19		10 22					10 27			10 30		10 33	10 36			

Table 199

Mondays to Fridays

Orpington, Petts Wood, Hither Green and Lewisham - London (Summary of Services)

		SE	SE	SE	SE	SE	SE 1	SE	SE 1	SE		SE	FC 1	SE	SE	SE	SE	SE	SE 1	SE		FC 1	SE	SE	SE
Orpington 4	d	10 03	10 10				10 24							10 21	10 25				10 39					10 33	10 40
Petts Wood 4	d	10 06	10 13											10 24	10 28									10 36	10 43
Hither Green 4	d	10 19								10 28				10 37			10 42							10 49	
Lewisham 4	d	10 24		10 26		10 29				10 34		10 38						10 44		10 50				10 54	
St Johns	d	10 26				10 31				10 36								10 46						10 56	
New Cross 4	d	10 28				10 33				10 38								10 48					09 49	10 58	
London Victoria 15	a		10 47									10 58			11 02										11 17
London Bridge 4	d	10 34		10 35	10 38	10 39	10 41	10 41	10 43	10 45			10 45	10 49		10 51	10 52	10 54	10 55	10 58		11 00	11 01	11 04	
London Blackfriars 3	a												10 52									11 07			
London Cannon Street 4	a	10 38				10 43		10 45		10 50						10 54		10 58					11 06	11 08	
London Waterloo (East) 4	d			10 40	10 43		10 45		10 49					10 54			10 57		11 00	11 03					
London Charing Cross 4	a			10 43	10 46		10 49		10 52					10 57			11 00		11 03	11 06					

		SE	SE	SE	SE 1	SE		SE 1	SE	SE	FC 1	SE	SE	SE	SE	SE		SE 1	SE	FC 1	SE	SE	SE	SE	SE
Orpington 4	d				10 54							10 51	10 55					11 09				11 03	11 10		
Petts Wood 4	d											10 54	10 58									11 06	11 13		
Hither Green 4	d								10 58			11 07			11 12							11 19			
Lewisham 4	d	10 56		10 59					11 04	11 08						11 14			11 20			11 24		11 26	
St Johns	d			11 01					11 06							11 16						11 26			
New Cross 4	d			11 03					11 08							11 18					10 19	11 28			
London Victoria 15	a									11 28			11 32										11 47		
London Bridge 4	d	11 05	11 08	11 09	11 11	11 11		11 13	11 15		11 15	11 19		11 21	11 22	11 24		11 25	11 28	11 30	11 31	11 34		11 35	11 38
London Blackfriars 3	a										11 22									11 37					
London Cannon Street 4	a			11 13		11 15			11 19					11 24		11 28					11 36	11 38			
London Waterloo (East) 4	d	11 10	11 13		11 15			11 19				11 24			11 27			11 30	11 33					11 40	11 43
London Charing Cross 4	a	11 13	11 16		11 19			11 22				11 27			11 30			11 33	11 36					11 43	11 46

		SE		SE 1	SE	SE 1	SE	SE	FC 1	SE	SE	SE		SE	SE	SE 1	SE	FC 1	SE	SE	SE	SE		SE	SE
Orpington 4	d			11 24						11 21	11 25					11 39				11 33	11 40				
Petts Wood 4	d									11 24	11 28									11 36	11 43				
Hither Green 4	d						11 28			11 37				11 42						11 49					
Lewisham 4	d	11 29					11 34	11 38							11 44		11 50			11 54		11 56			11 59
St Johns	d	11 31					11 36								11 46					11 56					12 01
New Cross 4	d	11 33					11 38								11 48				10 49	11 58					12 03
London Victoria 15	a							11 58			12 02										12 17				
London Bridge 4	d	11 39		11 41	11 41	11 43	11 45		11 45	11 49		11 51		11 52	11 54	11 55	11 58	12 00	12 01	12 04		12 05		12 08	12 09
London Blackfriars 3	a								11 52									12 07							
London Cannon Street 4	a	11 43			11 45		11 49					11 54			11 58				12 04	12 08					12 13
London Waterloo (East) 4	d			11 45		11 49				11 54				11 57		12 00	12 03					12 10		12 13	
London Charing Cross 4	a			11 49		11 52				11 57				12 00		12 03	12 06					12 13		12 16	

		SE 1	SE	SE 1	SE	SE	FC 1	SE		SE	SE	SE	SE	SE 1	SE	FC 1	SE	SE		SE	SE	SE	SE	SE 1	SE
Orpington 4	d	11 54						11 51		11 55				12 09				12 03		12 10				12 24	
Petts Wood 4	d							11 54		11 58								12 06		12 13					
Hither Green 4	d				11 58			12 07				12 12						12 19							
Lewisham 4	d				12 04	12 08							12 14		12 20			12 24			12 26		12 29		
St Johns	d				12 06								12 16					12 26					12 31		
New Cross 4	d				12 08								12 18				11 19	12 28					12 33		
London Victoria 15	a					12 28				12 32										12 47					
London Bridge 4	d	12 11	12 11	12 13	12 15		12 15	12 19			12 21	12 22	12 24	12 25	12 28	12 30	12 31	12 34			12 35	12 38	12 39	12 41	12 41
London Blackfriars 3	a						12 22									12 37									
London Cannon Street 4	a		12 15		12 19						12 24		12 28				12 36	12 38					12 43		12 45
London Waterloo (East) 4	d	12 15		12 19				12 24				12 27		12 30	12 33						12 40	12 43		12 45	
London Charing Cross 4	a	12 19		12 22				12 27				12 30		12 33	12 36						12 43	12 46		12 49	

		SE 1	SE	SE		FC 1	SE	SE	SE	SE	SE	SE 1	SE	FC 1		SE	SE	SE	SE	SE	SE	SE 1	SE	SE 1	
Orpington 4	d						12 21	12 25				12 39					12 33	12 40				12 54			
Petts Wood 4	d						12 24	12 28									12 36	12 43							
Hither Green 4	d		12 28				12 37			12 42							12 49								
Lewisham 4	d		12 34	12 38							12 44		12 50				12 54		12 56		12 59				
St Johns	d		12 36								12 46						12 56				13 01				
New Cross 4	d		12 38								12 48					11 49	12 58				13 03				
London Victoria 15	a			12 58				13 02										13 17							
London Bridge 4	d	12 43	12 45			12 45	12 49		12 51	12 52	12 54	12 55	12 58	13 00		13 01	13 04		13 05	13 08	13 09	13 11	13 11	13 13	
London Blackfriars 3	a					12 52								13 07											
London Cannon Street 4	a		12 49						12 54		12 58					13 06	13 08				13 13		13 15		
London Waterloo (East) 4	d	12 49					12 54			12 57		13 00	13 03						13 10	13 13		13 15		13 19	
London Charing Cross 4	a	12 52					12 57			13 00		13 03	13 06						13 13	13 16		13 19		13 22	

		SE	SE	FC 1	SE	SE	SE	SE	SE	SE 1		SE	FC 1	SE	SE	SE	SE	SE	SE	SE 1		SE	SE 1	SE	SE
Orpington 4	d				12 51	12 55				13 09					13 03	13 10				13 24					
Petts Wood 4	d				12 54	12 58									13 06	13 13									
Hither Green 4	d	12 58			13 07			13 12							13 19									13 28	
Lewisham 4	d	13 04	13 08						13 14			13 20			13 24		13 26		13 29					13 34	13 38
St Johns	d	13 06							13 16						13 26				13 31					13 36	
New Cross 4	d	13 08							13 18					12 19	13 28				13 33					13 38	
London Victoria 15	a		13 28			13 32										13 47									13 58
London Bridge 4	d	13 15		13 15	13 19		13 21	13 22	13 24	13 25		13 28	13 30	13 31	13 34		13 35	13 38	13 39	13 41		13 41	13 43	13 45	
London Blackfriars 3	a			13 22									13 37												
London Cannon Street 4	a	13 19					13 24		13 28					13 36	13 38				13 43			13 45		13 49	
London Waterloo (East) 4	d				13 24			13 27		13 30		13 33					13 40	13 43		13 45			13 49		
London Charing Cross 4	a				13 27			13 30		13 33		13 36					13 43	13 46		13 49			13 52		

Orpington, Petts Wood, Hither Green and Lewisham - London (Summary of Services)

		FC 1	SE	SE	SE	SE		SE	SE 1	SE	FC 1	SE	SE	SE	SE	SE		SE	SE 1	SE	SE 1	SE	SE	FC 1	SE
Orpington 4	d		13 21	13 25					13 39				13 33	13 40					13 54						13 51
Petts Wood 4	d		13 24	13 28									13 36	13 43											13 54
Hither Green 4	d		13 37			13 42							13 49									13 58			14 07
Lewisham 4	d							13 44		13 50			13 54		13 56			13 59				14 04	14 08		
St Johns	d							13 46					13 56					14 01				14 06			
New Cross 4	d							13 48				12 49	13 58					14 03				14 08			
London Victoria 15	a			14 02										14 17									14 28		
London Bridge 4	d	13 45	13 49		13 51	13 52		13 54	13 55	13 58	14 00	14 01	14 04		14 05	14 08		14 09	14 11	14 11	14 13	14 15		14 15	14 19
London Blackfriars 3	a	13 52									14 07													14 22	
London Cannon Street 4	a				13 54			13 58				14 06	14 08					14 13		14 15		14 19			
London Waterloo (East) 4	d		13 54			13 57			14 00	14 03					14 10	14 13			14 15		14 19				14 24
London Charing Cross 4	a		13 57			14 00			14 03	14 06					14 13	14 16			14 19		14 22				14 27

		SE		SE	SE	SE	SE 1	SE	FC 1	SE	SE	SE		SE	SE	SE	SE 1	SE	SE 1	SE	SE	FC 1		SE	SE
Orpington 4	d	13 55					14 09				14 03	14 10					14 24							14 21	14 25
Petts Wood 4	d	13 58									14 06	14 13												14 24	14 28
Hither Green 4	d				14 12						14 19									14 28				14 37	
Lewisham 4	d					14 14		14 20			14 24			14 26		14 29				14 34	14 38				
St Johns	d					14 16					14 26					14 31				14 36					
New Cross 4	d					14 18				13 19	14 28					14 33				14 38					
London Victoria 15	a	14 32										14 47									14 58				15 02
London Bridge 4	d			14 21	14 22	14 24	14 25	14 28	14 30	14 31	14 34			14 35	14 38	14 39	14 41	14 41	14 43	14 45		14 45		14 49	
London Blackfriars 3	a								14 37													14 52			
London Cannon Street 4	a			14 24		14 28				14 36	14 38					14 43		14 45		14 49					
London Waterloo (East) 4	d				14 27		14 30	14 33						14 40	14 43		14 45		14 49					14 54	
London Charing Cross 4	a				14 30		14 33	14 36						14 43	14 46		14 49		14 52					14 57	

		SE	SE	SE	SE 1	SE	FC 1	SE		SE	SE	SE	SE	SE	SE 1	SE	SE 1	SE		SE	FC 1	SE	SE	SE	SE
Orpington 4	d				14 39					14 33	14 40				14 54							14 51	14 55		
Petts Wood 4	d									14 36	14 43											14 54	14 58		
Hither Green 4	d		14 42							14 49								14 58				15 07			15 12
Lewisham 4	d			14 44		14 50				14 54		14 56		14 59				15 04		15 08					
St Johns	d			14 46						14 56				15 01				15 06							
New Cross 4	d			14 48				13 49		14 58				15 03				15 08							
London Victoria 15	a										15 17									15 28			15 32		
London Bridge 4	d	14 51	14 52	14 54	14 55	14 58	15 00	15 01		15 04		15 05	15 08	15 09	15 11	15 11	15 13	15 15			15 15	15 19		15 21	15 22
London Blackfriars 3	a						15 07														15 22				
London Cannon Street 4	a	14 54		14 58				15 06		15 08				15 13		15 15		15 19						15 24	
London Waterloo (East) 4	d		14 57		15 00	15 03						15 10	15 13		15 15		15 19					15 24			15 27
London Charing Cross 4	a		15 00		15 03	15 06						15 13	15 16		15 19		15 22					15 27			15 30

		SE	SE 1	SE		FC 1	SE	SE	SE	SE	SE	SE	SE 1	SE		SE 1	SE	SE	FC 1	SE	SE	SE	SE	SE	
Orpington 4	d		15 09					15 03	15 10				15 24							15 21	15 25				
Petts Wood 4	d							15 06	15 13											15 24	15 28				
Hither Green 4	d							15 19									15 28			15 37			15 42		
Lewisham 4	d	15 14		15 20				15 24		15 26		15 29					15 34	15 38						15 44	
St Johns	d	15 16						15 26				15 31					15 36							15 46	
New Cross 4	d	15 18					14 19	15 28				15 33					15 38							15 48	
London Victoria 15	a								15 47									15 58			16 02				
London Bridge 4	d	15 24	15 25	15 28		15 30	15 31	15 34		15 35	15 38	15 39	15 41	15 41		15 43	15 45		15 45	15 50		15 51	15 53	15 54	
London Blackfriars 3	a					15 37													15 52						
London Cannon Street 4	a	15 28					15 36	15 38				15 43		15 45			15 49					15 54		15 58	
London Waterloo (East) 4	d		15 30	15 33						15 40	15 43		15 46			15 49				15 55			15 58		
London Charing Cross 4	a		15 33	15 36						15 43	15 46		15 49			15 52				15 58			16 01		

		SE 1	SE	FC 1	SE	SE	SE	SE	SE	SE		SE 1	SE	SE 1	SE	SE	FC 1	SE	SE	SE		SE	SE	SE 1	SE
Orpington 4	d	15 39				15 33	15 40					15 54						15 51	15 55					16 08	
Petts Wood 4	d					15 36	15 43											15 54	15 58						
Hither Green 4	d					15 49									15 58			16 07				16 12			
Lewisham 4	d		15 50			15 54		15 56	15 59						16 04	16 08							16 14		16 20
St Johns	d					15 56			16 01						16 06								16 16		
New Cross 4	d				14 49	15 58			16 03						16 08								16 18		
London Victoria 15	a						16 17									16 28			16 32						
London Bridge 4	d	15 55	15 58	16 00	16 01	16 04		16 05	16 09	16 09		16 12	16 12	16 14	16 15		16 16	16 19		16 21		16 22	16 24	16 25	16 29
London Blackfriars 3	a			16 07													16 25								
London Cannon Street 4	a				16 06	16 08			16 13				16 16		16 19					16 24			16 28		
London Waterloo (East) 4	d	16 00	16 03					16 10		16 14		16 17		16 20				16 25				16 28		16 30	16 34
London Charing Cross 4	a	16 03	16 06					16 13		16 18		16 20		16 24				16 28				16 31		16 33	16 37

		SE	SE	SE	SE	SE		SE	SE	SE 1	SE	SE	SE	SE 1	SE	SE		SE	SE	SE	SE 1	SE	SE	SE	SE
Orpington 4	d			16 03	16 10					16 25					16 21	16 25					16 39			16 33	16 40
Petts Wood 4	d			16 06	16 13										16 24	16 28								16 36	16 43
Hither Green 4	d			16 19								16 28			16 37				16 42					16 50	
Lewisham 4	d			16 24		16 26			16 29			16 34	16 38							16 44		16 50			
St Johns	d			16 26					16 31			16 36								16 46					
New Cross 4	d	15 19		16 28					16 33			16 38								16 48			15 49		
London Victoria 15	a				16 47								17 01			17 04									17 18
London Bridge 4	d	16 31	16 32	16 34		16 35		16 38	16 39	16 42	16 42	16 45		16 46	16 49			16 51	16 52	16 54	16 56	16 59	17 01	17 02	
London Blackfriars 3	a																								
London Cannon Street 4	a	16 36		16 38					16 43		16 46	16 49						16 54		16 58			17 05		
London Waterloo (East) 4	d		16 38			16 40		16 43		16 49				16 53	16 55				16 57		17 01	17 04		17 07	
London Charing Cross 4	a		16 42			16 44		16 46		16 52				16 56	16 58				17 00		17 04	17 07		17 10	

Orpington, Petts Wood, Hither Green and Lewisham - London (Summary of Services)

		SE		SE	SE	SE	SE	SE	SE 1	SE	SE 1	SE		SE	SE	SE	SE	SE	FC 1	SE 1	SE	SE		SE	SE
Orpington 4	d							16 51	16 54							16 55				17 09				17 03	17 10
Petts Wood 4	d							16 54								16 58								17 06	17 13
Hither Green 4	d	16 50		16 56				17 09				17 00		17 07										17 19	
Lewisham 4	d				16 56	16 59						17 05			17 08			17 14			17 20			17 24	
St Johns	d	16 54				17 01						17 09						17 16						17 26	
New Cross 4 ⊖	d	16 56				17 03						17 11						17 18				16 20		17 28	
London Victoria 15 ⊖	a														17 28	17 33									17 48
London Bridge 4 ⊖	d	17 04		17 06	17 07	17 09	17 09		17 12	17 13	17 18	17 19		17 22			17 22	17 25	17 27	17 28	17 30	17 31		17 34	
London Blackfriars 3 ⊖	a																		17 35						
London Cannon Street 4 ⊖	a	17 09			17 11	17 15				17 17		17 24					17 26	17 29		17 32		17 36		17 38	
London Waterloo (East) 4 ⊖	d			17 11			17 14	17 25	17 16		17 23			17 29							17 35				
London Charing Cross 4 ⊖	a			17 15			17 18	17 29	17 20		17 26			17 33							17 38				

		SE	SE	SE	SE	SE 1	SE	SE		SE	SE 1	SE	SE	SE 1	SE	SE	SE	SE 1		SE	SE	SE	SE	SE	SE
Orpington 4	d	17 13				17 24						17 20	17 24	17 34				17 39					17 37	17 40	
Petts Wood 4	d											17 24	17 28	17 37									17 40	17 43	
Hither Green 4	d							17 28				17 38				17 42							17 53		
Lewisham 4	d		17 27		17 30			17 35		17 38							17 44			17 50		17 56			
St Johns	d							17 37									17 46						17 57		
New Cross 4 ⊖	d				17 33			17 39									17 48				16 49		17 59		
London Victoria 15 ⊖	a									17 59			18 03											18 18	
London Bridge 4 ⊖	d		17 36	17 38	17 39	17 42	17 42	17 45			17 45	17 49			17 52	17 54	17 55	17 58		18 00	18 03	18 04	18 06		18 07
London Blackfriars 3 ⊖	a													18 09											
London Cannon Street 4 ⊖	a				17 44		17 46	17 49							17 56		17 59			18 04	18 07		18 11		
London Waterloo (East) 4 ⊖	d	17 37	17 41	17 43		17 47					17 50	17 54				17 59		18 03				18 09			18 13
London Charing Cross 4 ⊖	a	17 40	17 44	17 46		17 50					17 53	17 57				18 03		18 06				18 12			18 16

		SE	SE 1	FC 1		SE	SE	SE	SE 1	SE	SE	SE	SE	SE		SE 1	SE	SE	SE	SE	SE	SE	SE	SE	
Orpington 4	d		17 54							17 50		17 55				18 09				18 03	18 09				
Petts Wood 4	d									17 54		17 58								18 06	18 12				
Hither Green 4	d						17 58			18 07			18 12						18 21	18 19					
Lewisham 4	d	17 59					18 05	18 08						18 14			18 20			18 24		18 26	18 29		
St Johns	d						18 07							18 16						18 26					
New Cross 4 ⊖	d	18 02					18 09				17 08			18 18						18 28			18 32		
London Victoria 15 ⊖	a							18 29				18 33									18 48				
London Bridge 4 ⊖	d	18 09	18 10	18 13		18 13	18 16		18 16	18 19	18 21		18 23	18 24		18 25	18 28	18 31	18 33	18 34		18 36	18 38	18 38	
London Blackfriars 3 ⊖	a			18 21																					
London Cannon Street 4 ⊖	a	18 13				18 17	18 20				18 24			18 29				18 35		18 38			18 42		
London Waterloo (East) 4 ⊖	d		18 15						18 21	18 24			18 28			18 30	18 33		18 38			18 42		18 45	
London Charing Cross 4 ⊖	a		18 18						18 25	18 27			18 31			18 35	18 37		18 41			18 45		18 48	

		SE 1	SE 1	SE	SE	SE	FC 1	SE	SE	SE		SE	SE	SE 1	SE	FC 1	SE	SE	SE	SE		SE	SE	SE 1	SE
Orpington 4	d	18 24						18 21	18 25									18 33	18 40					18 54	
Petts Wood 4	d							18 24	18 28									18 36	18 43						
Hither Green 4	d				18 28			18 37				18 42						18 49							
Lewisham 4	d				18 35	18 38							18 45		18 50			18 54		18 56			18 59		
St Johns	d				18 37								18 47					18 56							
New Cross 4 ⊖	d				18 39								18 49					18 58					19 03		
London Victoria 15 ⊖	a					18 58			19 03										19 17						
London Bridge 4 ⊖	d	18 41	18 43	18 43	18 46		18 46	18 49		18 51		18 53	18 55	18 55	18 58	19 00	19 01	19 05		19 05		19 08	19 09	19 10	19 12
London Blackfriars 3 ⊖	a						18 55									19 09									
London Cannon Street 4 ⊖	a			18 47	18 51					18 54			18 59				19 06	19 10					19 13		19 16
London Waterloo (East) 4 ⊖	d	18 46	18 49					18 54				18 58		19 00	19 03					19 10		19 13		19 15	
London Charing Cross 4 ⊖	a	18 49	18 52					18 57				19 01		19 04	19 06					19 13		19 16		19 18	

		SE 1	SE	SE	FC 1	SE		SE	SE	SE	SE 1	SE	SE	FC 1	SE	SE		SE	SE	SE	SE 1	SE	SE 1	SE	FC 1
Orpington 4	d					18 50		18 55			19 08				19 03	19 10					19 24				
Petts Wood 4	d					18 54		18 58							19 06	19 13									
Hither Green 4	d		18 59			19 07			19 12						19 19									19 28	
Lewisham 4	d		19 05	19 08						19 14			19 20		19 24			19 26	19 29					19 34	
St Johns	d		19 07							19 16					19 26									19 36	
New Cross 4 ⊖	d		19 09							19 18		18 14			19 28				19 32					19 38	
London Victoria 15 ⊖	a			19 28				19 32								19 47									
London Bridge 4 ⊖	d	19 13	19 15		19 17	19 19			19 22	19 24	19 25	19 28	19 28	19 30	19 34			19 35	19 38	19 38	19 41	19 41	19 43	19 45	19 45
London Blackfriars 3 ⊖	a				19 22									19 37											19 52
London Cannon Street 4 ⊖	a		19 20							19 28		19 33			19 38				19 43			19 45		19 49	
London Waterloo (East) 4 ⊖	d	19 18				19 24			19 27		19 30		19 33					19 40		19 43	19 46		19 49		
London Charing Cross 4 ⊖	a	19 21				19 27			19 30		19 33		19 36					19 43		19 46	19 49		19 52		

		SE		SE	SE	SE 1	SE	SE	SE	SE	FC 1	SE		SE	SE 1	SE	SE 1	FC 1	SE	SE	SE	SE 1		SE	SE
Orpington 4	d			19 21	19 25	19 39	19 40								19 54					19 51	19 55	20 09			20 10
Petts Wood 4	d			19 24	19 28		19 43													19 54	19 58				20 13
Hither Green 4	d			19 37				19 42												20 07					
Lewisham 4	d	19 38		19 43				19 48				19 52		19 56					20 08	20 13					
St Johns	d	19 40																	20 10						
New Cross 4 ⊖	d	19 42						19 51	18 35			19 56							20 12					19 00	
London Victoria 15 ⊖	a				20 02		20 17														20 32				20 47
London Bridge 4 ⊖	d	19 49		19 52		19 55		19 58	19 59	19 59	20 00	20 04		20 06	20 11	20 11	20 13	20 15	20 19	20 22		20 25		20 28	
London Blackfriars 3 ⊖	a										20 07							20 22							
London Cannon Street 4 ⊖	a								20 03	20 03						20 15								20 31	
London Waterloo (East) 4 ⊖	d	19 54		19 57		20 00		20 03				20 09		20 11	20 16		20 19		20 24	20 27		20 30			
London Charing Cross 4 ⊖	a	19 57		20 00		20 03		20 06				20 12		20 14	20 19		20 22		20 27	20 30		20 33			

Orpington, Petts Wood, Hither Green and Lewisham - London (Summary of Services)

		SE	FC 1	SE	SE	SE 1	SE	SE 1		FC 1	SE	SE	SE	SE	FC 1	SE	SE	SE 1		SE	SE 1	FC 1	SE	SE	SE 1
Orpington 4	d					20 24						20 21	20 40					20 53						20 51	21 09
Petts Wood 4	d											20 24	20 43											20 54	
Hither Green 4	d	20 12										20 38		20 42										21 07	
Lewisham 4	d	20 18		20 22	20 26						20 38	20 43		20 48		20 53	20 56						21 08	21 13	
St Johns	d										20 40												21 10		
New Cross 4	⊖ d	20 21		20 26							20 42			20 51		20 56							21 12		
London Victoria 15	⊖ a												21 17												
London Bridge 4	⊖ d	20 28	20 30	20 34	20 36	20 40	20 41	20 43		20 45	20 49	20 52		20 58	21 00	21 04	21 06	21 09		21 11	21 14	21 15	21 19	21 22	21 25
London Blackfriars 3	⊖ a		20 37							20 52					21 07							21 22			
London Cannon Street 4	⊖ a						20 45																		
London Waterloo (East) 4	⊖ d	20 33		20 39	20 41	20 45		20 48			20 54	20 57		21 03		21 09	21 11	21 14		21 16	21 19		21 24	21 27	21 30
London Charing Cross 4	⊖ a	20 36		20 42	20 44	20 48		20 51			20 57	21 00		21 06		21 12	21 14	21 18		21 19	21 22		21 27	21 30	21 33

		SE	SE	FC 1		SE	SE	SE 1	SE	SE 1	FC 1	SE	SE	SE		SE	SE	SE	SE 1	SE	SE 1	SE	SE	SE 1	
Orpington 4	d	21 10						21 23					21 21	21 40					21 53				21 51	22 09	
Petts Wood 4	d	21 13											21 24	21 43									21 54		
Hither Green 4	d		21 12										21 37			21 42							22 07		
Lewisham 4	d		21 18			21 23	21 26					21 38	21 43			21 48	21 53	21 56				22 08	22 13		
St Johns	d											21 40										22 10			
New Cross 4	⊖ d		21 21			21 26						21 42				21 51	21 56					22 12			
London Victoria 15	⊖ a	21 47												22 17											
London Bridge 4	⊖ d		21 28	21 30		21 34	21 36	21 39	21 41	21 44	21 45	21 49	21 52			21 58	22 02	22 05	22 09	22 11	22 14	22 19	22 22	22 25	
London Blackfriars 3	⊖ a			21 37							21 52														
London Cannon Street 4	⊖ a																								
London Waterloo (East) 4	⊖ d		21 33			21 39	21 41	21 44	21 46	21 49		21 54	21 57			22 03	22 07	22 10	22 14	22 16	22 19	22 24	22 27	22 30	
London Charing Cross 4	⊖ a		21 36			21 42	21 44	21 48	21 49	21 52		21 57	22 00			22 06	22 10	22 13	22 18	22 19	22 22	22 27	22 30	22 33	

		SE	SE	SE	SE	SE 1	SE	SE 1	SE	SE		SE	SE	SE	SE	SE 1	SE	SE 1	SE	SE		SE 1	SE	SE	SE
Orpington 4	d	22 10				22 23				22 21		22 40				22 53				22 51		23 09	23 10		
Petts Wood 4	d	22 13								22 24		22 43								22 54			23 13		
Hither Green 4	d		22 12							22 37			22 42							23 07				23 12	
Lewisham 4	d		22 18	22 23	22 26				22 38	22 43			22 48	22 53	22 56				23 08	23 13				23 18	23 23
St Johns	d								22 40										23 10						
New Cross 4	⊖ d		22 21	22 26					22 42				22 51	22 56					23 12					23 21	23 26
London Victoria 15	⊖ a	22 47										23 17											23 47		
London Bridge 4	⊖ d		22 28	22 32	22 35	22 39	22 41	22 44	22 49	22 52			22 58	23 02	23 05	23 09	23 11	23 14	23 19	23 22		23 25		23 28	23 32
London Blackfriars 3	⊖ a																								
London Cannon Street 4	⊖ a																								
London Waterloo (East) 4	⊖ d		22 33	22 37	22 40	22 44	22 46	22 49	22 54	22 57			23 03	23 07	23 10	23 14	23 16	23 19	23 24	23 27		23 30		23 33	23 37
London Charing Cross 4	⊖ a		22 36	22 40	22 43	22 48	22 49	22 52	22 57	23 00			23 06	23 10	23 13	23 18	23 19	23 22	23 27	23 30		23 33		23 36	23 40

		SE	SE	SE	SE 1
Orpington 4	d			23 21	23 37
Petts Wood 4	d			23 24	
Hither Green 4	d			23 37	
Lewisham 4	d	23 26		23 43	
St Johns	d				
New Cross 4	⊖ d				
London Victoria 15	⊖ a				
London Bridge 4	⊖ d	23 35	23 41	23 50	23 53
London Blackfriars 3	⊖ a				
London Cannon Street 4	⊖ a				
London Waterloo (East) 4	⊖ d	23 40	23 46	23 55	23 58
London Charing Cross 4	⊖ a	23 43	23 49	23 59	00 01

Saturdays

		SE 1	SE	SE	SE	SE	SE	SE	SE	SE		SE	SE	SE	SE	SE	SE 1	SE	SE	SE		SE	SE	SE	SE
Orpington 4	d	23p37	05 44									05 51	06 10				06 24			06 21		06 25	06 40		
Petts Wood 4	d		05 47									05 54	06 13							06 24		06 28	06 43		
Hither Green 4	d					05 42						06 07		06 12						06 37				06 42	
Lewisham 4	d				05 39	05 48	05 50	05 56	06 02			06 13		06 18	06 20	06 26		06 32		06 43				06 48	06 50
St Johns	d				05 41				06 04									06 34							
New Cross 4	⊖ d				05 43	05 51			06 06					06 21				06 36						06 51	
London Victoria 15	⊖ a		06 26										06 47									07 02	07 17		
London Bridge 4	⊖ d	23p53		05 45	05 49	05 57	05 59	06 05	06 12	06 15		06 21		06 27	06 29	06 35	06 39	06 42	06 45	06 51				06 57	06 59
London Blackfriars 3	⊖ a																								
London Cannon Street 4	⊖ a																								
London Waterloo (East) 4	⊖ d	23p58		05 50	05 53	06 02	06 04	06 10	06 17	06 20		06 26		06 32	06 34	06 40	06 44	06 47	06 50	06 56				07 02	07 04
London Charing Cross 4	⊖ a	00 01		05 53	05 56	06 05	06 07	06 13	06 20	06 25		06 29		06 35	06 37	06 43	06 47	06 50	06 55	06 59				07 05	07 07

Table 199

Saturdays

Orpington, Petts Wood, Hither Green and Lewisham - London (Summary of Services)

		SE	SE 1	SE	SE	SE		SE	SE	SE 1	SE	SE	SE	SE	SE 1	SE		SE	SE	SE	SE	SE	SE 1	SE	SE
Orpington 4	d		06 54					06 51	06 55	07 09	07 10				07 24				07 21		07 25		07 39		
Petts Wood 4	d							06 54	06 58		07 13								07 24		07 28				
Hither Green 4	d							07 07				07 12							07 37			07 42			
Lewisham 4	d	06 56		07 02	07 08			07 13				07 18	07 20	07 26				07 32		07 38				07 50	
St Johns	d			07 04														07 34							
New Cross 4	d			07 06								07 21						07 36							
London Victoria 15	a				07 30				07 32		07 47									08 00	08 02				
London Bridge 4	d	07 05	07 09	07 12		07 15		07 21		07 24		07 27	07 29	07 35	07 39	07 41		07 42	07 49			07 52	07 55	07 58	08 01
London Blackfriars 3	a																								
London Cannon Street 4	a															07 45									08 04
London Waterloo (East) 4	d	07 10	07 14	07 17		07 20		07 26		07 29		07 32	07 34	07 40	07 44			07 47	07 54			07 57	08 00	08 03	
London Charing Cross 4	a	07 13	07 17	07 20		07 25		07 29		07 33		07 35	07 40	07 43	07 48			07 50	07 57			08 00	08 03	08 06	

		SE		SE	SE	SE	SE	SE 1	SE	SE 1	SE	SE		SE	SE	SE	SE	SE	SE 1	SE	SE	SE		SE	SE
Orpington 4	d	07 33		07 40				07 54				07 51			07 55				08 09			08 03		08 10	
Petts Wood 4	d	07 36		07 43								07 54			07 58							08 06		08 13	
Hither Green 4	d	07 49									07 58	08 07					08 12					08 19			
Lewisham 4	d	07 54			07 56	07 59	07 59				08 04			08 08				08 14		08 20		08 24			08 26
St Johns	d	07 56					08 01				08 06							08 16				08 26			
New Cross 4	d	07 58					08 03				08 08							08 18				08 28			
London Victoria 15	a			08 17										08 30	08 32									08 47	
London Bridge 4	d	08 04			08 05	08 08	08 09	08 11	08 11	08 14	08 15	08 19				08 21	08 22	08 24	08 25	08 28	08 31	08 34			08 35
London Blackfriars 3	a																								
London Cannon Street 4	a	08 08					08 13		08 15		08 19					08 24		08 28			08 34	08 38			
London Waterloo (East) 4	d				08 10	08 13		08 15		08 19		08 24					08 27		08 30	08 33					08 40
London Charing Cross 4	a				08 13	08 16		08 19		08 22		08 27					08 30		08 33	08 36					08 43

		SE	SE	SE 1	SE	SE 1	SE	SE		SE	SE	SE	SE	SE	SE 1	SE	SE	SE		SE	SE	SE	SE	SE 1	SE
Orpington 4	d			08 24				08 21			08 25				08 39			08 33		08 40				08 54	
Petts Wood 4	d							08 24			08 28							08 36		08 43					
Hither Green 4	d						08 28	08 37					08 42					08 49							
Lewisham 4	d		08 29				08 34			08 38				08 44		08 50		08 54			08 56		08 59		
St Johns	d		08 31				08 36							08 46				08 56					09 01		
New Cross 4	d		08 33				08 38							08 48				08 58					09 03		
London Victoria 15	a									09 00	09 02									09 17					
London Bridge 4	d	08 38	08 39	08 41	08 41	08 44	08 45	08 49				08 51	08 52	08 54	08 55	08 58	09 01	09 04			09 05	09 08	09 09	09 11	09 11
London Blackfriars 3	a																								
London Cannon Street 4	a		08 43		08 45		08 49					08 54		08 58			09 04	09 08					09 13		09 15
London Waterloo (East) 4	d	08 43		08 45		08 49		08 54					08 57		09 00	09 03					09 10	09 13		09 15	
London Charing Cross 4	a	08 46		08 49		08 52		08 57					09 00		09 03	09 06					09 13	09 16		09 19	

		SE 1	SE	SE		SE	SE	SE	SE	SE	SE 1	SE	SE	SE		SE	SE	SE	SE	SE 1	SE	SE 1	SE	SE	
Orpington 4	d			08 51			08 55				09 09			09 03		09 10				09 24				09 21	
Petts Wood 4	d			08 54			08 58							09 06		09 13								09 24	
Hither Green 4	d		08 58	09 07					09 12					09 19									09 28	09 37	
Lewisham 4	d		09 04			09 08				09 14		09 20		09 24			09 26		09 29				09 34		
St Johns	d		09 06							09 16				09 26					09 31				09 36		
New Cross 4	d		09 08							09 18			08 19	09 28					09 33				09 38		
London Victoria 15	a					09 30	09 32									09 47									
London Bridge 4	d	09 14	09 15	09 19				09 21	09 22	09 24	09 25	09 28	09 31	09 34			09 35	09 38	09 39	09 41	09 41	09 44	09 45	09 49	
London Blackfriars 3	a																								
London Cannon Street 4	a		09 19					09 24		09 28			09 34	09 38					09 43		09 45		09 49		
London Waterloo (East) 4	d	09 19		09 24					09 27		09 30	09 33					09 40	09 43		09 45		09 49		09 54	
London Charing Cross 4	a	09 22		09 27					09 30		09 33	09 36					09 43	09 46		09 49		09 52		09 57	

		SE	SE	SE	SE	SE	SE 1	SE	SE	and at the same minutes past each hour until	SE		SE	SE	SE	SE	SE	SE 1	SE	SE 1	SE		SE	SE
Orpington 4	d		09 25				09 39						17 33	17 40				17 54					17 51	
Petts Wood 4	d		09 28										17 36	17 43									17 54	
Hither Green 4	d				09 42								17 49								17 58		18 07	
Lewisham 4	d	09 38				09 44		09 50					17 54		17 56		17 59				18 04			18 08
St Johns	d					09 46							17 56				18 01				18 06			
New Cross 4	d					09 48			08 49		16 49		17 58				18 03				18 08			
London Victoria 15	a	10 00	10 02											18 17										18 30
London Bridge 4	d			09 51	09 52	09 54	09 55	09 58	10 01		18 01		18 04		18 05	18 08	18 09	18 11	18 11	18 14	18 15		18 19	
London Blackfriars 3	a																							
London Cannon Street 4	a			09 54		09 58			10 04		18 04		18 08				18 13		18 15		18 19			
London Waterloo (East) 4	d				09 57		10 00	10 03							18 10	18 13		18 15		18 19			18 24	
London Charing Cross 4	a				10 00		10 03	10 06							18 13	18 16		18 19		18 22			18 27	

		SE	SE	SE	SE	SE 1	SE	SE		SE	SE	SE	SE	SE	SE 1	SE	SE 1	SE		SE	SE	SE	SE	SE	SE
Orpington 4	d	17 55				18 09				18 03	18 10				18 24					18 21		18 25			
Petts Wood 4	d	17 58								18 06	18 13									18 24		18 28			
Hither Green 4	d			18 12						18 19								18 28		18 37				18 42	
Lewisham 4	d				18 14		18 20			18 24		18 26		18 29				18 34			18 38				18 44
St Johns	d				18 16					18 26				18 31				18 36							18 46
New Cross 4	d				18 18			17 19		18 28				18 33				18 38							18 48
London Victoria 15	a	18 32									18 47										19 00	19 02			
London Bridge 4	d		18 21	18 22	18 24	18 25	18 28	18 31		18 34		18 35	18 38	18 39	18 41	18 41	18 44	18 45		18 49			18 51	18 52	18 54
London Blackfriars 3	a																								
London Cannon Street 4	a		18 24		18 28			18 34		18 38				18 43		18 45		18 49					18 54		18 58
London Waterloo (East) 4	d			18 27		18 30	18 33					18 40	18 43		18 45		18 49			18 54				18 57	
London Charing Cross 4	a			18 30		18 33	18 36					18 43	18 46		18 49		18 52			18 57				19 00	

Orpington, Petts Wood, Hither Green and Lewisham - London (Summary of Services)

		SE [1]	SE	SE		SE	SE	SE	SE	SE	SE	SE [1]	SE	SE [1]		SE	SE	SE	SE	SE [1]	SE	SE	SE	SE
Orpington [4]	d	18 39	18 40									18 54						18 51	18 55	19 09	19 10			
Petts Wood [4]	d		18 43															18 54	18 58		19 13			
Hither Green [4]	d															18 58		19 07					19 12	
Lewisham [4]	d			18 50					18 56		18 59					19 04	19 08	19 12				19 14	19 18	
St Johns	d										19 01					19 06						19 16		
New Cross [4] ⊖	d					17 49	18 19	18 49			19 03					19 08						19 18		19 19
London Victoria [15] ⊖	a		19 17														19 30		19 32		19 47			
London Bridge [4] ⊖	d	18 55		18 58		19 01	19a30	20a00	19 05	19 08	19 09	19 11	19 11	19 14		19 15		19 21		19 25		19a24	19 28	20a30
London Blackfriars [3] ⊖	a																							
London Cannon Street [4] ⊖	a					19 04					19 13		19 15			19 19								
London Waterloo (East) [4] ⊖	d	19 00		19 03					19 10	19 13		19 15		19 19				19 26		19 30			19 32	
London Charing Cross [4] ⊖	a	19 03		19 06					19 13	19 16		19 19		19 22				19 29		19 33			19 35	

		SE	SE	SE	SE [1]	SE	SE	SE	SE [1]	SE		SE	SE	SE	SE	SE [1]	SE	SE	SE	SE [1]		SE	SE	SE	SE
Orpington [4]	d				19 28		19 21	19 25	19 39	19 40						19 58		19 51	19 55	20 09		20 10			
Petts Wood [4]	d						19 24	19 28		19 43								19 54	19 58			20 13			
Hither Green [4]	d						19 37					19 42						20 07					20 12		
Lewisham [4]	d	19 20	19 26			19 38	19 43					19 48	19 53	19 56			20 08	20 13					20 18	20 23	20 26
St Johns	d					19 40											20 10								
New Cross [4] ⊖	d	19 23				19 42						19 51	19 56				20 12						20 21	20 26	
London Victoria [15] ⊖	a							20 02		20 17									20 32			20 47			
London Bridge [4] ⊖	d	19 34	19 37	19 41	19 44	19 49	19 52		19 55			19 58	20 04	20 06	20 11	20 14	20 19	20 22		20 25			20 28	20 34	20 36
London Blackfriars [3] ⊖	a																								
London Cannon Street [4] ⊖	a																								
London Waterloo (East) [4] ⊖	d	19 39	19 42	19 46	19 48	19 54	19 57		20 00			20 04	20 09	20 11	20 16	20 18	20 24	20 27		20 30			20 34	20 39	20 41
London Charing Cross [4] ⊖	a	19 42	19 45	19 49	19 51	19 58	20 00		20 03			20 07	20 12	20 14	20 19	20 21	20 28	20 30		20 33			20 37	20 42	20 44

		SE	SE [1]	SE	SE	SE [1]		SE	SE	SE	SE	SE	SE [1]	SE	SE	SE [1]		SE	SE	SE	SE	SE	SE [1]	SE	SE
Orpington [4]	d		20 28		20 21	20 39		20 40					20 58		20 51	21 09		21 10					21 28		21 21
Petts Wood [4]	d				20 24			20 43							20 54			21 13							21 24
Hither Green [4]	d				20 37				20 42						21 07				21 12						21 37
Lewisham [4]	d			20 38	20 43				20 48	20 53	20 56			21 08	21 13				21 18	21 23	21 26			21 38	21 43
St Johns	d			20 40										21 10										21 40	
New Cross [4] ⊖	d			20 42					20 51	20 56				21 12					21 21	21 26				21 42	
London Victoria [15] ⊖	a							21 17										21 47							
London Bridge [4] ⊖	d	20 41	20 44	20 49	20 52	20 55			20 58	21 04	21 06	21 11	21 14	21 19	21 22	21 25			21 28	21 34	21 36	21 41	21 44	21 49	21 52
London Blackfriars [3] ⊖	a																								
London Cannon Street [4] ⊖	a																								
London Waterloo (East) [4] ⊖	d	20 46	20 48	20 54	20 57	21 00			21 04	21 09	21 11	21 16	21 18	21 24	21 27	21 30			21 34	21 39	21 41	21 46	21 48	21 54	21 57
London Charing Cross [4] ⊖	a	20 49	20 51	20 58	21 00	21 03			21 07	21 12	21 14	21 19	21 21	21 28	21 30	21 33			21 37	21 42	21 44	21 49	21 51	21 58	22 00

		SE [1]		SE	SE	SE	SE	SE	SE [1]	SE	SE	SE [1]		SE	SE	SE	SE	SE	SE [1]	SE	SE	SE [1]		SE	SE
Orpington [4]	d	21 39		21 40					21 58		21 51	22 09		22 10					22 28		22 21	22 39		22 40	
Petts Wood [4]	d			21 43							21 54			22 13							22 24			22 43	
Hither Green [4]	d				21 42						22 07				22 12						22 37				22 42
Lewisham [4]	d				21 48	21 53	21 56			22 08	22 13				22 18	22 23	22 26			22 38	22 43				22 48
St Johns	d									22 10										22 40					
New Cross [4] ⊖	d				21 51	21 56				22 12					22 21	22 26				22 42					22 51
London Victoria [15] ⊖	a			22 17										22 47										23 17	
London Bridge [4] ⊖	d	21 55			21 58	22 02	22 05	22 11	22 14	22 19	22 22	22 25			22 28	22 32	22 35	22 41	22 44	22 49	22 52	22 55			22 58
London Blackfriars [3] ⊖	a																								
London Cannon Street [4] ⊖	a																								
London Waterloo (East) [4] ⊖	d	22 00			22 04	22 07	22 10	22 16	22 18	22 24	22 27	22 30			22 34	22 37	22 40	22 46	22 48	22 54	22 57	23 00			23 04
London Charing Cross [4] ⊖	a	22 03			22 07	22 10	22 13	22 19	22 21	22 28	22 30	22 33			22 37	22 40	22 43	22 49	22 51	22 58	23 00	23 03			23 07

		SE	SE	SE	SE [1]	SE	SE	SE [1]		SE	SE	SE	SE	SE	SE	SE [1]
Orpington [4]	d				22 58		22 51	23 09		23 10					23 21	23 37
Petts Wood [4]	d						22 54			23 13					23 24	
Hither Green [4]	d						23 07				23 12				23 37	
Lewisham [4]	d	22 53	22 56			23 08	23 13				23 18	23 23	23 26		23 43	
St Johns	d					23 10										
New Cross [4] ⊖	d	22 56				23 12					23 21	23 26				
London Victoria [15] ⊖	a									23 47						
London Bridge [4] ⊖	d	23 02	23 05	23 11	23 14	23 19	23 22	23 25			23 28	23 32	23 35	23 41	23 50	23 53
London Blackfriars [3] ⊖	a															
London Cannon Street [4] ⊖	a															
London Waterloo (East) [4] ⊖	d	23 07	23 10	23 16	23 18	23 24	23 27	23 30			23 34	23 37	23 40	23 46	23 55	23 58
London Charing Cross [4] ⊖	a	23 10	23 13	23 20	23 21	23 27	23 30	23 33			23 37	23 40	23 43	23 49	23 58	00 01

Table 199

Sundays

Orpington, Petts Wood, Hither Green and Lewisham - London (Summary of Services)

		SE 1 A	SE	SE	SE	SE	SE	SE	SE	SE 1		SE	SE	SE	SE	SE 1	SE	SE	SE	SE		SE 1	SE	SE	SE
Orpington 4	d	23p37	06 43	07 06				07 10	07 13	07 29		07 36				07 43			07 40	07 43		07 59	08 06		
Petts Wood 4	d		06 46	07 09				07 13	07 16			07 39							07 43	07 46			08 09		
Hither Green 4	d						07 12	07 26							07 42				07 56						
Lewisham 4	d				07 08		07 18	07 31					07 38		07 48		07 52	07 56	08 01					08 08	
St Johns	d																07 54								
New Cross 4 ⊖	d				07 11								07 41				07 56							08 11	
London Victoria 15 ⊖	a		07 25	07 43					07 55			08 13								08 25			08 43		
London Bridge 4 ⊖	d	23p53			07 20	07 23	07 26	07 40		07 45			07 50	07 53	07 56	07 59	08 04	08 07	08 10			08 15		08 20	08 23
London Blackfriars 3 ⊖	a																								
London Cannon Street 4 ⊖	a																								
London Waterloo (East) 4 ⊖	d	23p58			07 25	07 28	07 31	07 45		07 50			07 55	07 58	08 01	08 04	08 08	08 11	08 15			08 20		08 25	08 28
London Charing Cross 4 ⊖	a	00 01			07 28	07 31	07 34	07 48		07 53			07 58	08 01	08 04	08 07	08 11	08 14	08 18			08 23		08 28	08 31

		SE	SE	SE	SE	SE 1		SE	SE	SE	SE	SE 1	SE	SE	SE	SE 1		SE	SE	SE	SE	SE 1		SE 1
Orpington 4	d				08 10	08 29		08 36				08 43			08 40	08 59		09 06				09 13	and at the same minutes past each hour until	19 13
Petts Wood 4	d				08 13			08 39							08 43			09 09						
Hither Green 4	d	08 12			08 26						08 42				08 56						09 12			
Lewisham 4	d	08 18	08 22	08 26	08 31				08 38		08 48		08 52	08 56	09 01				09 08		09 18			
St Johns	d		08 24										08 54											
New Cross 4 ⊖	d		08 26						08 41				08 56						09 11					
London Victoria 15 ⊖	a							09 13										09 43						
London Bridge 4 ⊖	d	08 26	08 34	08 37	08 40	08 45			08 50	08 53	08 56	08 59	09 04	09 07	09 10	09 15			09 20	09 23	09 26	09 29		19 29
London Blackfriars 3 ⊖	a																							
London Cannon Street 4 ⊖	a																							
London Waterloo (East) 4 ⊖	d	08 31	08 38	08 41	08 45	08 50			08 55	08 58	09 01	09 04	09 08	09 11	09 15	09 20			09 25	09 28	09 31	09 34		19 34
London Charing Cross 4 ⊖	a	08 34	08 41	08 44	08 49	08 53			08 58	09 01	09 04	09 07	09 11	09 14	09 18	09 23			09 28	09 31	09 34	09 37		19 37

		SE		SE	SE	SE 1	SE	SE	SE	SE	SE 1	SE		SE	SE	SE 1	SE	SE	SE	SE	SE	SE		SE	SE 1
Orpington 4	d				19 10	19 29	19 36				19 43				19 40	19 59	20 06							20 10	20 29
Petts Wood 4	d				19 13		19 39								19 43		20 09							20 13	
Hither Green 4	d				19 26					19 42					19 56					20 12				20 26	
Lewisham 4	d	19 22		19 26	19 31			19 38		19 48		19 52		19 56	20 01			20 08		20 18	20 22	20 26		20 31	
St Johns	d	19 24										19 54									20 24				
New Cross 4 ⊖	d	19 26						19 41				19 56						20 11			20 26				
London Victoria 15 ⊖	a						20 13										20 43								
London Bridge 4 ⊖	d	19 34		19 37	19 40	19 45		19 50	19 53	19 56	19 59	20 04		20 07	20 10	20 15		20 20	20 23	20 26	20 34	20 37		20 40	20 45
London Blackfriars 3 ⊖	a																								
London Cannon Street 4 ⊖	a																								
London Waterloo (East) 4 ⊖	d	19 38		19 41	19 45	19 50		19 55	19 58	20 01	20 04	20 08		20 11	20 15	20 20		20 25	20 28	20 31	20 38	20 41		20 45	20 50
London Charing Cross 4 ⊖	a	19 41		19 44	19 49	19 53		19 58	20 01	20 04	20 07	20 11		20 14	20 18	20 23		20 28	20 31	20 34	20 41	20 44		20 49	20 53

		SE	SE	SE	SE	SE 1	SE	SE		SE	SE 1	SE	SE	SE	SE	SE	SE	SE		SE 1	SE	SE	SE	SE	SE 1
Orpington 4	d	20 36				20 43				20 40	20 59	21 06						21 10		21 29	21 36				21 43
Petts Wood 4	d	20 39								20 43		21 09						21 13			21 39				
Hither Green 4	d				20 42					20 56					21 12			21 26						21 42	
Lewisham 4	d		20 38		20 48		20 52	20 56		21 01			21 08		21 18	21 22	21 26	21 31				21 38		21 48	
St Johns	d						20 54									21 24									
New Cross 4 ⊖	d		20 41				20 56						21 11			21 26						21 41			
London Victoria 15 ⊖	a	21 13										21 43									22 13				
London Bridge 4 ⊖	d		20 50	20 53	20 56	20 59	21 04	21 07		21 10	21 15		21 20	21 23	21 26	21 34	21 37	21 40		21 45		21 50	21 53	21 56	21 59
London Blackfriars 3 ⊖	a																								
London Cannon Street 4 ⊖	a																								
London Waterloo (East) 4 ⊖	d		20 55	20 58	21 01	21 04	21 08	21 11		21 15	21 20		21 25	21 28	21 31	21 38	21 41	21 45		21 50		21 55	21 58	22 01	22 04
London Charing Cross 4 ⊖	a		20 58	21 01	21 04	21 07	21 11	21 14		21 18	21 23		21 28	21 31	21 34	21 41	21 44	21 49		21 53		21 58	22 01	22 04	22 07

		SE	SE	SE		SE 1	SE	SE	SE	SE	SE	SE	SE	SE 1		SE	SE	SE	SE	SE 1	SE	SE	SE	SE 1	
Orpington 4	d			21 40		21 59	22 06						22 10	22 29		22 36				22 43			22 40	22 59	
Petts Wood 4	d			21 43			22 09						22 13			22 39							22 43		
Hither Green 4	d			21 56						22 12			22 26						22 42				22 56		
Lewisham 4	d	21 52	21 56	22 01				22 08		22 18	22 22	22 26	22 31				22 38		22 48		22 52	22 56	23 01		
St Johns	d	21 54									22 24										22 54				
New Cross 4 ⊖	d	21 56						22 11			22 26						22 41				22 56				
London Victoria 15 ⊖	a						22 43									23 13									
London Bridge 4 ⊖	d	22 04	22 07	22 10		22 15		22 20	22 23	22 26	22 34	22 37	22 40	22 45			22 50	22 53	22 56	22 59	23 04	23 07	23 10	23 15	
London Blackfriars 3 ⊖	a																								
London Cannon Street 4 ⊖	a																								
London Waterloo (East) 4 ⊖	d	22 08	22 11	22 15		22 20		22 25	22 28	22 31	22 38	22 41	22 45	22 50			22 55	22 58	23 01	23 04	23 08	23 11	23 15	23 20	
London Charing Cross 4 ⊖	a	22 11	22 14	22 18		22 23		22 28	22 31	22 34	22 41	22 44	22 49	22 53			22 58	23 01	23 04	23 07	23 11	23 14	23 18	23 23	

A not 22 May

		SE	SE	SE	SE	SE	SE
Orpington 4	d						23 10
Petts Wood 4	d						23 13
Hither Green 4	d			23 12			23 26
Lewisham 4	d	23 08		23 18	23 22	23 26	23 31
St Johns	d				23 24		
New Cross 4 ⊖	d	23 11			23 26		
London Victoria 15 ⊖	a						
London Bridge 4 ⊖	d	23 20	23 23	23 26	23 34	23 37	23 40
London Blackfriars 3 ⊖	a						
London Cannon Street 4 ⊖	a						
London Waterloo (East) 4 ⊖	d	23 25	23 28	23 31	23 38	23 41	23 45
London Charing Cross 4 ⊖	a	23 28	23 31	23 34	23 41	23 44	23 49

Network Diagram for Tables 200, 203, 204

also 199★

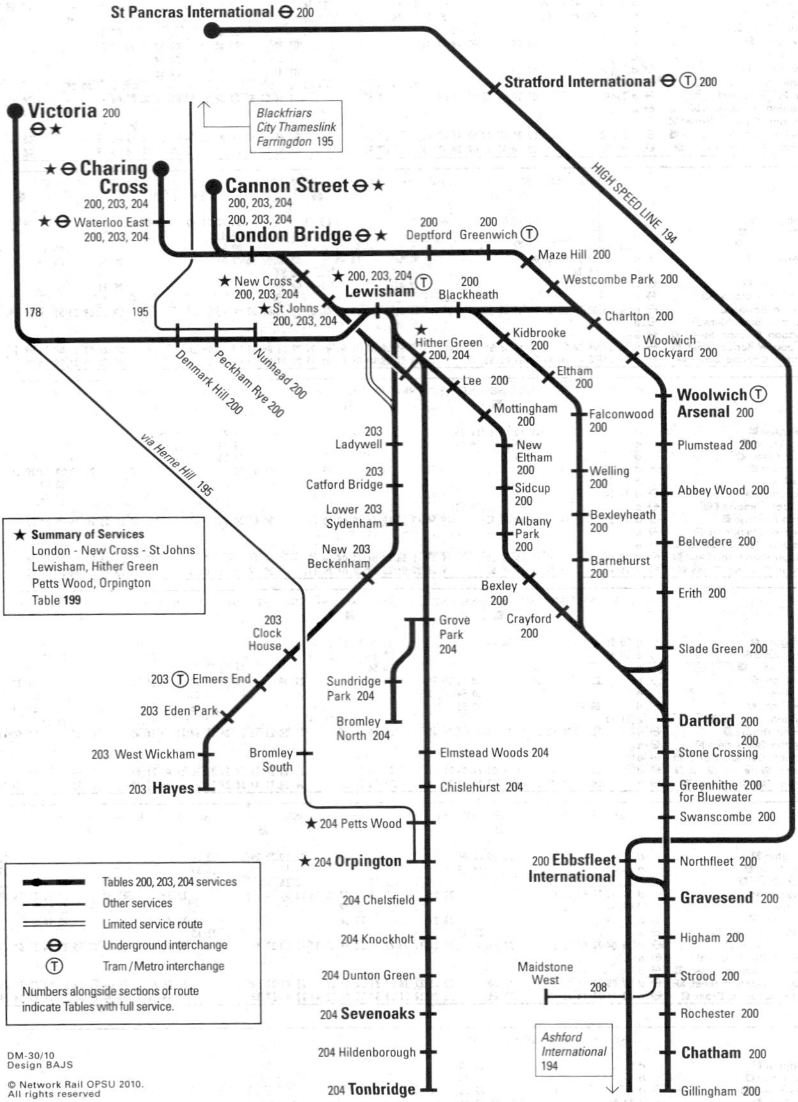

DM-30/10
Design BAJS

© Network Rail OPSU 2010.
All rights reserved

Table 200

London - Dartford and Gillingham

Mondays to Fridays

Miles	Miles	Miles	Miles	Miles			SE MX	SE MO	SE	SE MX	SE MO	SE MO	SE MX	SE MO	SE MX		SE MO	SE MX	SE MX	SE MX	SE MO	SE MO	SE MX	SE MX	SE MX
—	—	—	—	0	**St Pancras Int'l** [15] ⊖	d			23p25										23p55						
—	—	—	—	6	**Stratford International** ⊖ ⛴	d			23p32										00 02						
—	—	—	—	22¾	**Ebbsfleet International**	d			23p43										00 13						
0	—	0	0	—	**London Charing Cross** [4] ⊖	d	22p39	22p40		23p09	23p10	23p20	23p22	23p26	23p26		23p30	23p32		23p39	23p50	23p56	23p56	00 02	00 05
0¾	—	0¾	0¾	—	**London Waterloo (East)** [4] ⊖	d	22p42	22p43		23p12	23p13	23p23	23p25	23p29	23p29		23p33	23p35		23p42	23p53	23p59	23p59	00 05	00 08
—	0	—	—	—	**London Cannon Street** [4] ⊖	d																			
1¾	1¾	1¾	1¾	—	**London Bridge** [4] ⊖	d	22p47	22p48		23p17	23p18	23p28	23p30	23p34	23p34		23p38	23p40		23p47	23p58	00 04	00 04	00 10	00 13
—	3¾	—	—	—	Deptford	d									23p40		23p44						00 10		
—	4¼	—	—	—	Greenwich [4] ⛴	d									23p42		23p46						00 12		
—	5¼	—	—	—	Maze Hill	d									23p45		23p49						00 15		
—	5¾	—	—	—	Westcombe Park	d									23p47		23p51						00 17		
—	—	—	—	0	**London Victoria** [15] ⊖	d																			
—	—	—	—	4¼	Denmark Hill [4]	d																			
—	—	—	—	5	Peckham Rye [4]	d																			
—	—	—	—	5¾	Nunhead [4]	d																			
—	—	4¾	4¾	—	New Cross [4] ⊖	d						23p34	23p35					23p45			00 04			00 15	00 18
—	—	5½	5½	—	St Johns	d																			
6	—	6	6	7½	Lewisham [4] ⛴	d	22p56	22p57		23p26	23p27	23p38	23p39	23p42				23p49		23p56	00 08	00 12		00 19	00 22
7	—	7	—	8½	Blackheath [4]	d	22p59	23p00		23p29	23p30	23p40						23p52		23p59	00 10			00 22	
—	—	8	—	9½	Kidbrooke	d						23p43						23p55			00 13			00 25	
—	—	9	—	10½	Eltham	d						23p47						23p58			00 17			00 28	
—	—	10¼	—	11¾	Falconwood	d						23p49						00 01			00 19			00 31	
—	—	11¼	—	12¾	Welling	d						23p52						00 03			00 22			00 33	
—	—	12¾	—	14¼	Bexleyheath	d						23p54						00 06			00 24			00 36	
—	—	14	—	15½	Barnehurst [4]	d						23p57						00 08			00 27			00 38	
—	—	—	7¼	—	Hither Green [4]	d							23p44	23p46								00 16			00 27
—	—	—	8	—	Lee	d							23p46	23p48								00 18			00 29
—	—	—	9½	—	Mottingham	d							23p49	23p51								00 21			00 32
—	—	—	10½	—	New Eltham	d							23p51	23p53								00 23			00 34
—	—	—	12	—	Sidcup [4]	d							23p55	23p57								00 27			00 38
—	—	—	13	—	Albany Park	d							23p57	23p59								00 29			00 40
—	—	—	14	—	Bexley	d							23p59	00 01								00 31			00 42
—	—	—	15½	—	Crayford	d							00 03	00 04								00 34			00 46
9	6½	—	—	—	Charlton [4]	d	23p03	23p04		23p33	23p34				23p50		23p54			00 03			00 20		
10	7½	—	—	—	Woolwich Dockyard	d									23p53		23p57						00 23		
10¾	8¼	—	—	—	**Woolwich Arsenal** [4] ⛴	d	23p09	23p10		23p39	23p40				23p56		23p59			00 09			00 26		
11¼	8¾	—	—	—	Plumstead	d									23p58		00 02						00 28		
12¾	10¼	—	—	—	Abbey Wood	d	23p13	23p14		23p43	23p44				00 01		00 05			00 13			00 31		
14¼	11¾	—	—	—	Belvedere	d									00 03		00 07						00 33		
15½	13	—	—	—	Erith	d									00 06		00 10						00 36		
16¾	14¼	—	—	—	Slade Green [4]	d									00 09		00 14						00 39		
18¾	16¼	17	17¼	18½	**Dartford** [4]	a	23p24	23p24		23p54	23p54	00 03	00 08	00 09	00 14		00 19	00 16		00 24	00 33	00 39	00 44	00 46	00 51
—	—	—	—	—		d	23p25	23p25		23p55	23p55									00 25					
20¾	—	—	19¼	—	Stone Crossing	d	23p29	23p29		23p58	23p59									00 29					
21½	—	—	20	—	Greenhithe for Bluewater	d	23p31	23p31		23p59	00 01									00 31					
22¾	—	—	21¼	—	Swanscombe	d	23p34	23p34		00 04	00 04									00 34					
23½	—	—	22	—	Northfleet	d	23p36	23p36		00 06	00 06									00 36					
25½	—	—	24	24¾	**Gravesend** [4]	d	23p40	23p40	23p48	00 10	00 10								00 18	00 40					
30	—	—	28½	29¼	Higham	d	23p46	23p46		00 16	00 16									00 46					
32¾	—	—	31¼	32	Strood [4]	d	23p52	23p52	23p58	00 22	00 22								00 28	00 52					
—	—	—	—	—	Maidstone West	d																			
33¾	—	—	32¼	33	Rochester [4]	d	23p56	23p56	00 03	00 26	00 26								00 33	00 56					
34½	—	—	32¾	33½	**Chatham** [4]	d	23p58	23p58	00 05	00 28	00 28								00 35	00 58					
36	—	—	34½	35¼	**Gillingham (Kent)** [4]	a	00 03	00 03	00 09	00 33	00 33								00 39	01 03					

		SE	SE	SE	SE	SE	SE	SE	SE	SE		SE	SE	SE	SE	SE	SE	SE	SE	SE		SE	SE	SE
St Pancras Int'l [15] ⊖	d												06 25					06 55						07 25
Stratford International ⊖ ⛴	d												06 32					07 02						07 32
Ebbsfleet International	d												06 42					07 13						07 43
London Charing Cross [4] ⊖	d	00 15		04 50	04 56	05 02	05 20	05 26	05 32	05 39		05 52		05 56	06 02	06 09			06 26	06 32		06 39	06 52	
London Waterloo (East) [4] ⊖	d	00 18		04 53	04 59	05 05	05 23	05 29	05 35	05 42		05 55		05 59	06 05	06 12			06 29	06 35		06 42	06 55	
London Cannon Street [4] ⊖	d																06 27							
London Bridge [4] ⊖	d	00 23		04 58	05 04	05 10	05 28	05 34	05 42	05 47		06 01		06 04	06 10	06 17	06 31		06 34	06 40		06 47	07 00	
Deptford	d			05 04			05 34					06 07					06 37						07 07	
Greenwich [4] ⛴	d			05 06			05 36					06 09					06 39						07 09	
Maze Hill	d			05 09			05 39					06 12					06 42						07 12	
Westcombe Park	d			05 11			05 41					06 14					06 44						07 14	
London Victoria [15] ⊖	d																							
Denmark Hill [4]	d																							
Peckham Rye [4]	d																							
Nunhead [4]	d																							
New Cross [4] ⊖	d	00 28			05 09	05 15		05 39	05 48	05 52				06 09	06 15				06 40	06 46				
St Johns	d																							
Lewisham [4] ⛴	d	00 33			05 13	05 19		05 43	05 52	05 56				06 13	06 19	06 26			06 44	06 50		06 56		
Blackheath [4]	d	00 35				05 22			05 54	05 59					06 22	06 29				06 53		06 59		
Kidbrooke	d					05 25			05 57						06 25					06 56				
Eltham	d					05 28			06 00						06 28					06 59				
Falconwood	d					05 31			06 03						06 31					07 01				
Welling	d					05 33			06 05						06 33					07 04				
Bexleyheath	d					05 36			06 08						06 36					07 06				
Barnehurst [4]	d					05 38			06 10						06 38					07 11				
Hither Green [4]	d				05 18			05 48						06 18					06 48					
Lee	d				05 20			05 50						06 20					06 50					
Mottingham	d				05 23			05 53						06 23					06 53					
New Eltham	d				05 25			05 55						06 25					06 55					
Sidcup [4]	d				05 29			05 59						06 29					06 59					
Albany Park	d				05 31			06 01						06 31					07 01					
Bexley	d				05 33			06 03						06 33					07 03					
Crayford	d				05 36			06 06						06 36					07 06					
Charlton [4]	d	00 40		05 14			05 44			06 03		06 17				06 33	06 47					07 03	07 17	
Woolwich Dockyard	d			05 17			05 47					06 20					06 50						07 20	
Woolwich Arsenal [4] ⛴	d	00 45		05 20			05 50			06 09		06 23				06 39	06 53					07 09	07 23	
Plumstead	d	00 47		05 22			05 52					06 25					06 55						07 25	
Abbey Wood	d	00 50		05 25			05 55			06 13		06 28				06 43	06 58					07 13	07 28	
Belvedere	d	00 53		05 27			05 57					06 30					07 00						07 30	
Erith	d	00 55		05 30			06 00					06 33					07 03						07 33	
Slade Green [4]	d	00 58		05 34			06 04			06 19		06 37					07 07						07 37	
Dartford [4]	a	01 03		05 38	05 41	05 45	06 08	06 11	06 17	06 24		06 44		06 41	06 45	06 54	07 12		07 11	07 18		07 23	07 46	
	d	01 03	05 25		05 42	05 55		06 12		06 25				06 42		06 55			07 12			07 25		
Stone Crossing	d				05 46			06 16						06 46					07 16					
Greenhithe for Bluewater	d	01 08	05 30		05 48	06 00		06 18		06 30				06 48		07 00			07 18			07 30		
Swanscombe	d				05 51			06 21						06 51					07 21					
Northfleet	d				05 53			06 23						06 53					07 23					
Gravesend [4]	d	01 15	05 37		05a57	06 07		06a27		06 38			06 46	06 59		07a06		07 21	07 27			07 37		07 48
Higham	d	01 21	05 43			06 13				06 44				07 05								07 43		
Strood [4]	d	01 26	05 48			06 18				06 49			06 57	07b17				07 31	07a37			07 48		07 58
Maidstone West	d												07a12											
Rochester [4]	d	01 32	05 52			06 22				06 53				07 21				07 36				07 52		08 03
Chatham [4]	d	01 35	05 55			06 25				06 56				07 24				07 38				07 55		08 05
Gillingham (Kent) [4]	a	01 41	05 59			06 29				07 00				07 28				07 42				07 59		08 09

London - Dartford and Gillingham

Station		SE	SE	SE	SE	SE	SE		SE	SE	SE	SE	SE	SE	SE	SE	SE		SE	SE	SE	SE	SE	SE	SE
St Pancras Int'l 15 ⊖	d										07 55											08 22			
Stratford International ⊖	d										08 02											08 29			
Ebbsfleet International	d										08 13											08 43			
London Charing Cross 4 ⊖	d	06 56	07 02				07 12					07 26				07 39							07 59		08 03
London Waterloo (East) 4 ⊖	d	06 59	07 05				07 15					07 29				07 42							08 02		08 06
London Cannon Street 4 ⊖	d				07 10	07 13			07 24	07 27			07 32	07 36	07 41				07 44	07 54	07 56			08 05	
London Bridge 4 ⊖	d	07 05	07 10		07 14	07 17	07 21		07 28	07 31		07 34	07 37	07 40	07 45	07 47			07 48	07 58	08 01		08 07	08 09	08 11
Deptford	d					07 23							07 43						07 54		08 07			08 15	
Greenwich 4	d					07 25				07 38			07 45						07 59		08 09			08 19	
Maze Hill	d					07 28							07 48						08 02		08 12			08 22	
Westcombe Park	d					07 30							07 50						08 04		08 14			08 24	
London Victoria 15 ⊖	d			07 09													07 43								
Denmark Hill 4	d																07 53								
Peckham Rye 4	d																07 56								
Nunhead 4	d																07 59								
New Cross 4 ⊖	d				07 20				07 33						07 50					08 04					
St Johns	d				07 22				07 35											08 06					
Lewisham 4	d		07 18	07 27	07 27		07 30		07 38					07 49	07 54	07 56	08 08			08 11					08 19
Blackheath 4	d		07 21	07 29			07 32		07 41					07 52		07 59	08 10			08 13					08 22
Kidbrooke	d		07 24						07 44					07 55						08 16					08 25
Eltham	d		07 27						07 47					07 58						08 20					08 28
Falconwood	d		07 29						07 50					08 01						08 22					08 31
Welling	d		07 32						07 52					08 03						08 25					08 33
Bexleyheath	d		07 34						07 55					08 06						08 27					08 36
Barnehurst 4	d		07 37	07 40					07 59					08 08						08 30					08 38
Hither Green 4	d	07 18			07 31							07 45			07 59										
Lee	d	07 20			07 33							07 47			08 01										
Mottingham	d	07 23			07 36							07 50			08 04										
New Eltham	d	07 26			07 39							07 53			08 07								08 21		
Sidcup 4	d	07 29			07 42							07 56			08 13								08 25		
Albany Park	d	07 31			07 44							07 58			08 15								08 27		
Bexley	d	07 34			07 47							08 01			08 17								08 29		
Crayford	d	07 37	07a46		07 50				08a08			08 05			08 21								08 33		
Charlton 4	d					07 33	07 37			07 44			07 53		08a50	08 04			08 07		08 17			08 27	
Woolwich Dockyard	d					07 36							07 56						08 10		08 20			08 30	
Woolwich Arsenal 4	d					07 39	07 43			07 49			07 59			08 09			08 13		08 23			08 33	
Plumstead	d					07 41							08 01						08 15		08 25			08 35	
Abbey Wood	d					07 44	07 48			07 53			08 04			08 13			08 18		08 28			08 38	
Belvedere	d					07 46							08 06						08 20		08 30			08 40	
Erith	d					07 49							08 09						08 23		08 33			08 43	
Slade Green 4	d				07a57	07 52				07a59			08a12			08 20			08a26	08a35	08 37			08a45	
Dartford 4	a	07 42		07 48		07 57	07 59					08 11		08 15		08 25	08 27				08 42		08 38		08 45
	d	07 43					08 00					08 12				08 25							08 39		
Stone Crossing	d	07 47										08 16											08 43		
Greenhithe for Bluewater	d	07 49					08 05					08 18				08 30							08 45		
Swanscombe	d	07 52										08 21											08 48		
Northfleet	d	07 54										08 23											08 50		
Gravesend 4	d	07a58					08 12				08 18	08a27				08 37						08 48	08a55		
Higham	d						08 18									08 43									
Strood 4	d						08 23				08 28					08 48						08 58			
Maidstone West	d																								
Rochester 4	d						08 27				08 33					08 52						09 03			
Chatham 4	d						08 30				08 35					08 55						09 05			
Gillingham (Kent) 4	a						08 35				08 39					08 59						09 09			

Station		SE	SE		SE	SE	SE	SE	SE	SE	SE	SE	SE		SE	SE	SE	SE	SE	SE	SE	SE	SE		SE
St Pancras Int'l 15 ⊖	d						08 58														09 25				
Stratford International ⊖	d						09 05														09 32				
Ebbsfleet International	d						09 16														09 43				
London Charing Cross 4 ⊖	d		08 11					08 20		08 23	08 31				08 41			08 49				08 55	09 02		
London Waterloo (East) 4 ⊖	d		08 14					08 23		08 26	08 34				08 44			08 52				08 58	09 05		
London Cannon Street 4 ⊖	d	08 10				08 16			08 25			08 36	08 39				08 47		08 54	08 56					09 07
London Bridge 4 ⊖	d	08 14	08 19			08 20		08 29	08 29	08 31	08 39	08 40	08 43		08 49		08 51	08 57	08 58	09 01		09 03	09 10		09 11
Deptford	d					08 27			08 35			08 46					08 57			09 07					09 17
Greenwich 4	d					08 29			08 39			08 49					08 59			09 09					09 19
Maze Hill	d					08 32			08 42			08 52					09 02			09 12					09 22
Westcombe Park	d					08 34			08 44			08 54					09 04			09 14					09 24
London Victoria 15 ⊖	d				08 09											08 39									
Denmark Hill 4	d				08 18											08 48									
Peckham Rye 4	d				08 21											08 51									
Nunhead 4	d				08 23											08 53									
New Cross 4 ⊖	d	08 20								08 38			08 49						09 04						
St Johns	d	08 22								08 40			08 51						09 06						
Lewisham 4	d	08 25	08 28		08 32					08 43	08 49		08 54		08 56	09 02			09 09				09 19		
Blackheath 4	d		08 31		08 34					08 46	08 52				08 59	09 04			09 12				09 22		
Kidbrooke	d				08 37					08 49	08 55					09 07			09 15				09 25		
Eltham	d				08 41					08 52	08 58					09 11			09 18				09 28		
Falconwood	d				08 43					08 55	09 01					09 13			09 21				09 31		
Welling	d				08 46					08 57	09 03					09 16			09 23				09 33		
Bexleyheath	d				08 48					09 00	09 06					09 18			09 26				09 36		
Barnehurst 4	d				08 51					09 04	09 08					09 21			09a28				09 38		
Hither Green 4	d	08 29						08 44					08 59					09 09				09 15			
Lee	d	08 31						08 46					09 01					09 11				09 17			
Mottingham	d	08 34						08 49					09 04					09 14				09 20			
New Eltham	d	08 37						08 51					09 06					09 16				09 22			
Sidcup 4	d	08 40						08 55					09 10					09a19				09 26			
Albany Park	d	08 42						08 57					09 12									09 28			
Bexley	d	08 45						08 59					09 14									09 30			
Crayford	d	08 48						09 03					09 18									09 33			
Charlton 4	d	09a13	08 35			08 37			08 47			08 57	09a45		09 03		09 07			09 17					09 27
Woolwich Dockyard	d					08 40			08 50			09 00					09 10			09 20					09 30
Woolwich Arsenal 4	d		08 40			08 43			08 53			09 03			09 09		09 13			09 23					09 33
Plumstead	d					08 45			08 55			09 05					09 15			09 25					09 35
Abbey Wood	d		08 45			08 48			08 58			09 08			09 13		09 18			09 28					09 38
Belvedere	d					08 50			09 00			09 10					09 20			09 30					09 40
Erith	d					08 53			09 03			09 13					09 23			09 33					09 43
Slade Green 4	d					08a57			09 07	09a09		09a15					09a26			09 37					09a45
Dartford 4	a		08 54		08 58			09 08	09 12		09 15				09 24	09 28				09 42		09 38	09 45		
	d		08 55					09 09							09 25							09 38			
Stone Crossing	d							09 13														09 42			
Greenhithe for Bluewater	d		09 00					09 15							09 30							09 45			
Swanscombe	d							09 18														09 48			
Northfleet	d							09 20														09 50			
Gravesend 4	d		09 07				09 21	09a25							09 37						09 48	09a55			
Higham	d		09 13												09 43										
Strood 4	d		09 18				09 31								09 48						09 58				
Maidstone West	d																								
Rochester 4	d		09 22				09 36								09 52						10 03				
Chatham 4	d		09 25				09 38								09 55						10 05				
Gillingham (Kent) 4	a		09 29				09 42								09 59						10 09				

London - Dartford and Gillingham

		SE	SE	SE	SE	SE	SE	SE	SE		SE	SE	SE	SE	SE	SE	SE	SE	SE		SE	SE	SE	SE	SE
St Pancras Int'l	d						09 55											10 28						
Stratford International	d						10 02											10 35						
Ebbsfleet International	d						10 13											10 46						
London Charing Cross	d	09 11						09 26		09 32			09 39							09 56	10 02			10 09
London Waterloo (East)	d	09 14						09 29		09 35			09 42							09 59	10 05			10 12
London Cannon Street	d	09 09			09 15	09 24	09 27					09 37	09 40			09 47	09 54	09 57					10 07	10 10	
London Bridge	d	09 14	09 19		09 19	09 28	09 31		09 34		09 40	09 41	09 44	09 47		09 51	09 58	10 01			10 04	10 10	10 11	10 14	10 17
Deptford	d				09 25		09 37					09 47				09 57		10 07					10 17		
Greenwich	d				09 29		09 39					09 49				09 59		10 09					10 19		
Maze Hill	d				09 32		09 42					09 52				10 02		10 12					10 22		
Westcombe Park	d				09 34		09 44					09 54				10 04		10 14					10 24		
London Victoria	d			09 09											09 39										
Denmark Hill	d			09 18											09 48										
Peckham Rye	d			09 21											09 51										
Nunhead	d			09 23											09 53										
New Cross	d	09 19				09 33							09 49				10 03							10 19	
St Johns	d	09 21				09 35							09 51				10 05							10 21	
Lewisham	d	09 24	09 29	09 32		09 38					09 49		09 54	09 56	10 02		10 08					10 19		10 24	10 26
Blackheath	d		09 31	09 34		09 41					09 52			09 59	10 04		10 11					10 22			10 29
Kidbrooke	d			09 37		09 44					09 55				10 07		10 14					10 25			
Eltham	d			09 41		09 47					09 58				10 11		10 17					10 28			
Falconwood	d			09 43		09 50					10 01				10 13		10 20					10 31			
Welling	d			09 46		09 52					10 03				10 16		10 22					10 33			
Bexleyheath	d			09 48		09 55					10 06				10 18		10 25					10 36			
Barnehurst	d			09 51		09a57					10 08				10 21		10a27					10 38			
Hither Green	d	09 29							09 44				09 59								10 14			10 29	
Lee	d	09 31							09 46				10 01								10 16			10 31	
Mottingham	d	09 34							09 49				10 04								10 19			10 34	
New Eltham	d	09 36							09 51				10 06								10 21			10 36	
Sidcup	d	09 40							09 55				10 10								10 25			10 40	
Albany Park	d	09 42							09 57				10 12								10 27			10 42	
Bexley	d	09 44							09 59				10 14								10 29			10 44	
Crayford	d	09 48							10 03				10 18								10 33			10 48	
Charlton	d	10a15	09 37		09 40		09 47					09 57	10a45	10 03		10 07		10 17					10 27	11a15	10 33
Woolwich Dockyard	d				09 43		09 50					10 00				10 10		10 20					10 30		
Woolwich Arsenal	d		09 42		09 46		09 53					10 03		10 09		10 13		10 23					10 33		10 39
Plumstead	d				09 48		09 55					10 05				10 15		10 25					10 35		
Abbey Wood	d		09 46		09 51		09 58					10 08		10 13		10 18		10 28					10 38		10 43
Belvedere	d				09 53		10 00					10 10				10 20		10 30					10 40		
Erith	d				09 56		10 03					10 13				10 23		10 33					10 43		
Slade Green	d				09a59		10 07					10a15				10a26		10 37					10a45		
Dartford	a		09 54	09 58			10 12		10 08		10 15			10 24	10 28			10 42			10 38	10 45			10 54
	d		09 55						10 09					10 25							10 39				10 55
Stone Crossing	d								10 13												10 43				
Greenhithe for Bluewater	d		10 00						10 15					10 30							10 45				11 00
Swanscombe	d								10 18												10 48				
Northfleet	d								10 20												10 50				
Gravesend	d		10 07					10 18	10a25					10 37					10 51		10a55				11 07
Higham	d		10 13											10 43											11 13
Strood	d		10 18					10 28						10 48					11 01						11 18
Maidstone West	d																								
Rochester	d		10 22					10 33						10 52					11 06						11 22
Chatham	d		10 25					10 35						10 55					11 08						11 25
Gillingham (Kent)	a		10 29					10 39						10 59					11 12						11 29

		SE	SE	SE	SE		SE	SE	SE	SE	SE	SE	SE	SE	SE		SE	SE	SE	SE	SE	SE	SE	SE	SE
St Pancras Int'l	d						10 52											11 25							
Stratford International	d						10 59											11 32							
Ebbsfleet International	d						11 13											11 43							
London Charing Cross	d							10 26	10 32			10 39							10 56	11 02			11 09		
London Waterloo (East)	d							10 29	10 35			10 42							10 59	11 05			11 12		
London Cannon Street	d		10 17	10 24	10 27					10 37	10 40			10 47	10 54		10 57				11 07	11 10			11 17
London Bridge	d		10 21	10 28	10 31			10 34	10 40	10 41	10 44	10 47		10 51	10 58		11 01		11 04	11 10	11 11	11 14	11 17		11 21
Deptford	d		10 27		10 37					10 47				10 57			11 07				11 17				11 27
Greenwich	d		10 29		10 39					10 49				10 59			11 09				11 19				11 29
Maze Hill	d		10 32		10 42					10 52				11 02			11 12				11 22				11 32
Westcombe Park	d		10 34		10 44					10 54				11 04			11 14				11 24				11 34
London Victoria	d	10 09											10 39											11 09	
Denmark Hill	d	10 18											10 48											11 18	
Peckham Rye	d	10 21											10 51											11 21	
Nunhead	d	10 23											10 53											11 23	
New Cross	d			10 33							10 49				11 03							11 19			
St Johns	d			10 35							10 51				11 05							11 21			
Lewisham	d	10 32		10 38					10 49		10 54	10 56	11 02		11 08					11 19		11 24	11 26	11 32	
Blackheath	d	10 34		10 41					10 52			10 59	11 04		11 11					11 22			11 29	11 34	
Kidbrooke	d	10 37		10 44					10 55				11 07		11 14					11 25				11 37	
Eltham	d	10 41		10 47					10 58				11 11		11 17					11 28				11 41	
Falconwood	d	10 43		10 50					11 01				11 13		11 20					11 31				11 43	
Welling	d	10 46		10 52					11 03				11 16		11 22					11 33				11 46	
Bexleyheath	d	10 48		10 55					11 06				11 18		11 25					11 36				11 48	
Barnehurst	d	10 51		10a57					11 08				11 21		11a27					11 38				11 51	
Hither Green	d							10 44			10 59								11 14			11 29			
Lee	d							10 46			11 01								11 16			11 31			
Mottingham	d							10 49			11 04								11 19			11 34			
New Eltham	d							10 51			11 06								11 21			11 36			
Sidcup	d							10 55			11 10								11 25			11 40			
Albany Park	d							10 57			11 12								11 27			11 42			
Bexley	d							10 59			11 14								11 29			11 44			
Crayford	d							11 03			11 18								11 33			11 48			
Charlton	d		10 37		10 47					10 57	11a45	11 03		11 07			11 17				11 27	12a15	11 33		11 37
Woolwich Dockyard	d		10 40		10 50					11 00				11 10			11 20				11 30				11 40
Woolwich Arsenal	d		10 43		10 53					11 03		11 09		11 13			11 23				11 33		11 39		11 43
Plumstead	d		10 45		10 55					11 05				11 15			11 25				11 35				11 45
Abbey Wood	d		10 48		10 58					11 08		11 13		11 18			11 28				11 38		11 43		11 48
Belvedere	d		10 50		11 00					11 10				11 20			11 30				11 40				11 50
Erith	d		10 53		11 03					11 13				11 23			11 33				11 43				11 53
Slade Green	d		10a56		11 07					11a15				11a26			11 37				11a45				11a56
Dartford	a	10 58			11 12			11 08	11 15			11 24	11 28				11 42		11 38	11 45			11 54	11 58	
	d							11 09				11 25							11 39				11 55		
Stone Crossing	d							11 13											11 43						
Greenhithe for Bluewater	d							11 15				11 30							11 45				12 00		
Swanscombe	d							11 18											11 48						
Northfleet	d							11 20											11 50						
Gravesend	d						11 18	11a25				11 37						11 48	11a55				12 07		
Higham	d											11 43											12 13		
Strood	d						11 28					11 48						11 58					12 18		
Maidstone West	d																								
Rochester	d						11 33					11 52						12 03					12 22		
Chatham	d						11 35					11 55						12 05					12 25		
Gillingham (Kent)	a						11 39					11 59						12 09					12 29		

London - Dartford and Gillingham

			SE	SE	SE	SE	SE	SE	SE	SE	SE		SE	SE	SE	SE	SE	SE	SE	SE	SE		SE	SE	SE
St Pancras Int'l 15 ⊖	d				11 55											12 25									
Stratford International ⊖	d				12 02											12 35									
Ebbsfleet International	d				12 13											12 46									
London Charing Cross 4 ⊖	d					11 26	11 32			11 39							11 56	12 02			12 09				
London Waterloo (East) 4 ⊖	d					11 29	11 35			11 42							11 59	12 05			12 12				
London Cannon Street 4 ⊖	d		11 24	11 27				11 37	11 40				11 47	11 54	11 57				12 07	12 10				12 17	12 24
London Bridge 4 ⊖	d		11 28	11 31		11 34	11 40	11 41	11 44	11 47			11 51	11 58	12 01		12 04	12 10	12 11	12 14	12 17			12 21	12 28
Deptford	d			11 37				11 47					11 57		12 07				12 17					12 27	
Greenwich 4	d			11 39				11 49					11 59		12 09				12 19					12 29	
Maze Hill	d			11 42				11 52					12 02		12 12				12 22					12 32	
Westcombe Park	d			11 44				11 54					12 04		12 14				12 24					12 34	
London Victoria 15 ⊖	d										11 39												12 09		
Denmark Hill 4	d										11 48												12 18		
Peckham Rye 4	d										11 51												12 21		
Nunhead 4	d										11 53												12 23		
New Cross 4 ⊖	d		11 33						11 49					12 03						12 19					12 33
St Johns	d		11 35						11 51					12 05						12 21					12 35
Lewisham 4	d		11 38				11 49		11 54	11 56	12 02			12 08				12 19		12 24	12 26		12 32		12 38
Blackheath 4	d		11 41				11 52			11 59	12 04			12 11				12 22			12 29		12 34		12 41
Kidbrooke	d		11 44				11 55				12 07			12 14				12 25					12 37		12 44
Eltham	d		11 47				11 58				12 11			12 17				12 28					12 41		12 47
Falconwood	d		11 50				12 01				12 13			12 20				12 31					12 43		12 50
Welling	d		11 52				12 03				12 16			12 22				12 33					12 46		12 52
Bexleyheath	d		11 55				12 06				12 18			12 25				12 36					12 48		12 55
Barnehurst 4	d		11a57				12 08				12 21			12a27				12 38					12 51		12a57
Hither Green 4	d					11 44			11 59								12 14			12 29					
Lee	d					11 46			12 01								12 16			12 31					
Mottingham	d					11 49			12 04								12 19			12 34					
New Eltham	d					11 51			12 06								12 21			12 36					
Sidcup 4	d					11 55			12 10								12 25			12 40					
Albany Park	d					11 57			12 12								12 27			12 42					
Bexley	d					11 59			12 14								12 29			12 44					
Crayford	d					12 03			12 18								12 33			12 48					
Charlton 4	d			11 47				11 57	12a45	12 03			12 07		12 17				12 27	13a15	12 33			12 37	
Woolwich Dockyard	d			11 50				12 00					12 10		12 20				12 30					12 40	
Woolwich Arsenal 4	d			11 53				12 03		12 09			12 13		12 23				12 33		12 39			12 43	
Plumstead	d			11 55				12 05					12 15		12 25				12 35					12 45	
Abbey Wood	d			11 58				12 08		12 13			12 18		12 28				12 38		12 43			12 48	
Belvedere	d			12 00				12 10					12 20		12 30				12 40					12 50	
Erith	d			12 03				12 13					12 23		12 33				12 43					12 53	
Slade Green 4	d			12 07				12a15					12a26		12 37				12a45					12a56	
Dartford 4	a			12 12		12 08	12 15			12 24	12 28				12 42		12 38	12 45			12 54		12 58		
	d					12 09				12 25							12 39				12 55				
Stone Crossing	d					12 13											12 43								
Greenhithe for Bluewater	d					12 15				12 30							12 45				13 00				
Swanscombe	d					12 18											12 48								
Northfleet	d					12 20											12 50								
Gravesend 4	d				12 18	12a25				12 37						12 51	12a55				13 07				
Higham	d									12 43											13 13				
Strood 4	d				12 28					12 48						13 01					13 18				
Maidstone West	d																								
Rochester 4	d				12 33					12 52						13 06					13 22				
Chatham 4	d				12 35					12 55						13 08					13 25				
Gillingham (Kent) 4	a				12 39					12 59						13 12					13 29				

		SE	SE	SE	SE	SE	SE		SE	SE	SE	SE	SE	SE	SE	SE	SE		SE	SE	SE	SE	SE	SE	SE
St Pancras Int'l 15 ⊖	d		12 52											13 25											13 55
Stratford International ⊖	d		12 58											13 32											14 02
Ebbsfleet International	d		13 13											13 43											14 13
London Charing Cross 4 ⊖	d			12 26	12 32				12 39						12 56	13 02				13 09					
London Waterloo (East) 4 ⊖	d			12 29	12 35				12 42						12 59	13 05				13 12					
London Cannon Street 4 ⊖	d	12 27				12 37	12 40				12 47	12 54	12 57				13 07		13 10			13 17	13 24	13 27	
London Bridge 4 ⊖	d	12 31		12 34	12 40	12 41	12 44		12 47		12 51	12 58	13 01		13 04	13 10	13 11		13 14	13 17		13 21	13 28	13 31	
Deptford	d	12 37				12 47					12 57		13 07				13 17					13 27		13 37	
Greenwich 4	d	12 39				12 49					12 59		13 09				13 19					13 29		13 39	
Maze Hill	d	12 42				12 52					13 02		13 12				13 22					13 32		13 42	
Westcombe Park	d	12 44				12 54					13 04		13 14				13 24					13 34		13 44	
London Victoria 15 ⊖	d									12 39											13 09				
Denmark Hill 4	d									12 48											13 18				
Peckham Rye 4	d									12 51											13 21				
Nunhead 4	d									12 53											13 23				
New Cross 4 ⊖	d						12 49					13 03							13 19				13 33		
St Johns	d						12 51					13 05							13 21				13 35		
Lewisham 4	d				12 49		12 54		12 56	13 02		13 08				13 19			13 24	13 26	13 32		13 38		
Blackheath 4	d				12 52				12 59	13 04		13 11				13 22				13 29	13 34		13 41		
Kidbrooke	d				12 55					13 07		13 14				13 25					13 37		13 44		
Eltham	d				12 58					13 11		13 17				13 28					13 41		13 47		
Falconwood	d				13 01					13 13		13 20				13 31					13 43		13 50		
Welling	d				13 03					13 16		13 22				13 33					13 46		13 52		
Bexleyheath	d				13 06					13 18		13 25				13 36					13 48		13 55		
Barnehurst 4	d				13 08					13 21		13a27				13 38					13 51		13a57		
Hither Green 4	d			12 44			12 59								13 14				13 29						
Lee	d			12 46			13 01								13 16				13 31						
Mottingham	d			12 49			13 04								13 19				13 34						
New Eltham	d			12 51			13 06								13 21				13 36						
Sidcup 4	d			12 55			13 10								13 25				13 40						
Albany Park	d			12 57			13 12								13 27				13 42						
Bexley	d			12 59			13 14								13 29				13 44						
Crayford	d			13 03			13 18								13 33				13 48						
Charlton 4	d	12 47				12 57	13a45		13 03		13 07		13 17				13 27		14a15	13 33		13 37		13 47	
Woolwich Dockyard	d	12 50				13 00					13 10		13 20				13 30					13 40		13 50	
Woolwich Arsenal 4	d	12 53				13 03			13 09		13 13		13 23				13 33			13 39		13 43		13 53	
Plumstead	d	12 55				13 05					13 15		13 25				13 35					13 45		13 55	
Abbey Wood	d	12 58				13 08			13 13		13 18		13 28				13 38			13 43		13 48		13 58	
Belvedere	d	13 00				13 10					13 20		13 30				13 40					13 50		14 00	
Erith	d	13 03				13 13					13 23		13 33				13 43					13 53		14 03	
Slade Green 4	d	13 07				13a15					13a26		13 37				13a45					13a56		14 07	
Dartford 4	a	13 12		13 08	13 15				13 24	13 28			13 42		13 38	13 45				13 54	13 58			14 12	
	d			13 09					13 25						13 39					13 55					
Stone Crossing	d			13 13											13 43										
Greenhithe for Bluewater	d			13 15					13 30						13 45					14 00					
Swanscombe	d			13 18											13 48										
Northfleet	d			13 20											13 50										
Gravesend 4	d		13 18	13a25					13 37					13 48	13a55					14 07					14 18
Higham	d								13 43											14 13					
Strood 4	d		13 28						13 48					13 58						14 18					14 28
Maidstone West	d																								
Rochester 4	d		13 33						13 52					14 03						14 22					14 33
Chatham 4	d		13 35						13 55					14 05						14 25					14 35
Gillingham (Kent) 4	a		13 39						13 59					14 09						14 29					14 39

Table 200

Mondays to Fridays

London - Dartford and Gillingham

		SE	SE		SE	SE	SE	SE	SE	SE	SE	SE	SE		SE	SE	SE	SE	SE	SE	SE	SE	SE		SE
St Pancras Int'l 15 ⊖	d											14 25											14 55		
Stratford International ⊖	d											14 32											15 02		
Ebbsfleet International	d											14 43											15 13		
London Charing Cross 4 ⊖	d	13 26	13 32				13 39						13 56		14 02			14 09							14 26
London Waterloo (East) 4 ⊖	d	13 29	13 35				13 42						13 59		14 05			14 12							14 29
London Cannon Street 4 ⊖	d				13 37	13 40			13 47	13 54	13 57					14 07	14 10			14 17	14 24	14 27			
London Bridge 4 ⊖	d	13 34	13 40		13 41	13 44	13 47		13 51	13 58	14 01		14 04		14 10	14 11	14 14	14 17		14 21	14 28	14 31			14 34
Deptford	d				13 47				13 57		14 07					14 17				14 27		14 37			
Greenwich 4	d				13 49				13 59		14 09					14 19				14 29		14 39			
Maze Hill	d				13 52				14 02		14 12					14 22				14 32		14 42			
Westcombe Park	d				13 54				14 04		14 14					14 24				14 34		14 44			
London Victoria 15 ⊖	d							13 39											14 09						
Denmark Hill 4	d							13 48											14 18						
Peckham Rye 4	d							13 51											14 21						
Nunhead 4	d							13 53											14 23						
New Cross 4 ⊖	d					13 49				14 03							14 19				14 33				
St Johns	d					13 51				14 05							14 21				14 35				
Lewisham 4	d		13 49			13 54	13 56	14 02		14 08					14 19		14 24	14 26	14 32		14 38				
Blackheath 4	d		13 52				13 59	14 04		14 11					14 22			14 29	14 34		14 41				
Kidbrooke	d		13 55					14 07		14 14					14 25				14 37		14 44				
Eltham	d		13 58					14 11		14 17					14 28				14 41		14 47				
Falconwood	d		14 01					14 13		14 20					14 31				14 43		14 50				
Welling	d		14 03					14 16		14 22					14 33				14 46		14 52				
Bexleyheath	d		14 06					14 18		14 25					14 36				14 48		14 55				
Barnehurst 4	d		14 08					14 21		14a27					14 38				14 51		14a57				
Hither Green 4	d	13 44				13 59							14 14				14 29								14 44
Lee	d	13 46				14 01							14 16				14 31								14 46
Mottingham	d	13 49				14 04							14 19				14 34								14 49
New Eltham	d	13 51				14 06							14 21				14 36								14 51
Sidcup 4	d	13 55				14 10							14 25				14 40								14 55
Albany Park	d	13 57				14 12							14 27				14 42								14 57
Bexley	d	13 59				14 14							14 29				14 44								14 59
Crayford	d	14 03				14 18							14 33				14 48								15 03
Charlton 4	d				13 57	14a45	14 03		14 07		14 17					14 27	15a15	14 33		14 37		14 47			
Woolwich Dockyard	d				14 00				14 10		14 20					14 30				14 40		14 50			
Woolwich Arsenal 4	d				14 03		14 09		14 13		14 23					14 33		14 39		14 43		14 53			
Plumstead	d				14 05				14 15		14 25					14 35				14 45		14 55			
Abbey Wood	d				14 08		14 13		14 18		14 28					14 38		14 43		14 48		14 58			
Belvedere	d				14 10				14 20		14 30					14 40				14 50		15 00			
Erith	d				14 13				14 23		14 33					14 43				14 53		15 03			
Slade Green 4	d				14a15				14a26		14 37					14a45				14a56		15 07			
Dartford 4	a	14 08	14 15				14 24	14 28			14 42		14 38		14 45			14 54	14 58			15 12			15 08
	d	14 09					14 25						14 39					14 55							15 09
Stone Crossing	d	14 13											14 43												15 13
Greenhithe for Bluewater	d	14 15					14 30						14 45					15 00							15 15
Swanscombe	d	14 18											14 48												15 18
Northfleet	d	14 20											14 50												15 20
Gravesend 4	d	14a25					14 37					14 48	14a55					15 07					15 18		15a25
Higham	d						14 43											15 13							
Strood 4	d						14 48					14 58						15 18					15 28		
Maidstone West	d																								
Rochester 4	d						14 52					15 03						15 22					15 33		
Chatham 4	d						14 55					15 05						15 25					15 35		
Gillingham (Kent) 4	a						14 59					15 09						15 29					15 39		

		SE	SE	SE	SE	SE	SE	SE	SE		SE	SE	SE	SE	SE	SE	SE	SE	SE		SE	SE	SE	SE	SE
St Pancras Int'l 15 ⊖	d										15 25											15 55			
Stratford International ⊖	d										15 32											16 02			
Ebbsfleet International	d										15 43											16 13			
London Charing Cross 4 ⊖	d	14 32			14 39							14 56	15 02			15 09							15 26	15 32	
London Waterloo (East) 4 ⊖	d	14 35			14 42							14 59	15 05			15 12							15 29	15 35	
London Cannon Street 4 ⊖	d		14 37	14 40			14 47	14 54	14 57					15 07	15 10			15 17	15 24		15 27				15 37
London Bridge 4 ⊖	d	14 40	14 41	14 44	14 47		14 51	14 58	15 01			15 04	15 10	15 11	15 14	15 17		15 21	15 28		15 31		15 34	15 40	15 41
Deptford	d		14 47				14 57		15 07					15 17				15 27			15 37				15 47
Greenwich 4	d		14 49				14 59		15 09					15 19				15 29			15 39				15 49
Maze Hill	d		14 52				15 02		15 12					15 22				15 32			15 42				15 52
Westcombe Park	d		14 54				15 04		15 14					15 24				15 34			15 44				15 54
London Victoria 15 ⊖	d					14 39											15 09								
Denmark Hill 4	d					14 48											15 18								
Peckham Rye 4	d					14 51											15 21								
Nunhead 4	d					14 53											15 23								
New Cross 4 ⊖	d			14 49				15 03							15 19				15 33						
St Johns	d			14 51				15 05							15 21				15 35						
Lewisham 4	d	14 49		14 54	14 56	15 02		15 08					15 19		15 24	15 26	15 32		15 38					15 49	
Blackheath 4	d	14 52			14 59	15 04		15 11					15 22			15 29	15 34		15 41					15 52	
Kidbrooke	d	14 55				15 07		15 14					15 25				15 37		15 44					15 55	
Eltham	d	14 58				15 11		15 17					15 28				15 41		15 47					15 58	
Falconwood	d	15 01				15 13		15 20					15 31				15 43		15 50					16 01	
Welling	d	15 03				15 16		15 22					15 33				15 46		15 52					16 03	
Bexleyheath	d	15 06				15 18		15 25					15 36				15 48		15 55					16 06	
Barnehurst 4	d	15 08				15 21		15a27					15 38				15 51		15a57					16 08	
Hither Green 4	d			14 59								15 14			15 29								15 44		
Lee	d			15 01								15 16			15 31								15 46		
Mottingham	d			15 04								15 19			15 34								15 49		
New Eltham	d			15 06								15 21			15 36								15 51		
Sidcup 4	d			15 10								15 25			15 40								15 55		
Albany Park	d			15 12								15 27			15 42								15 57		
Bexley	d			15 14								15 29			15 44								15 59		
Crayford	d			15 18								15 33			15 48								16 03		
Charlton 4	d		14 57	15a45	15 03		15 07		15 17					15 27	16a15	15 33		15 37			15 47				15 57
Woolwich Dockyard	d		15 00				15 10		15 20					15 30				15 40			15 50				16 00
Woolwich Arsenal 4	d		15 03		15 09		15 13		15 23					15 33		15 39		15 43			15 53				16 03
Plumstead	d		15 05				15 15		15 25					15 35				15 45			15 55				16 05
Abbey Wood	d		15 08		15 13		15 18		15 28					15 38		15 43		15 48			15 58				16 08
Belvedere	d		15 10				15 20		15 30					15 40				15 50			16 00				16 10
Erith	d		15 13				15 23		15 33					15 43				15 53			16 03				16 13
Slade Green 4	d		15a15				15a26		15 37					15a45				15a56			16 07				16a15
Dartford 4	a	15 15			15 24	15 28			15 42			15 38	15 45			15 54	15 58				16 12		16 08	16 15	
	d				15 25							15 39				15 55							16 09		
Stone Crossing	d											15 43											16 13		
Greenhithe for Bluewater	d				15 30							15 45				16 00							16 15		
Swanscombe	d											15 48											16 18		
Northfleet	d											15 50											16 20		
Gravesend 4	d				15 37						15 48	15a55				16 07					16 18	16a25			
Higham	d				15 43											16 13									
Strood 4	d				15 48						15 58					16 18						16 28			
Maidstone West	d																								
Rochester 4	d				15 52						16 03					16 22						16 33			
Chatham 4	d				15 55						16 05					16 25						16 35			
Gillingham (Kent) 4	a				15 59						16 09					16 29						16 39			

London - Dartford and Gillingham

		SE	SE	SE	SE		SE	SE	SE	SE	SE	SE	SE	SE	SE		SE	SE	SE	SE	SE	SE	SE	SE	SE
St Pancras Int'l 15 ⊖	d								16 25											16 55					
Stratford International ⊖ ⛴	d								16 32											17 02					
Ebbsfleet International	d								16 43											17 13					
London Charing Cross 4 ⊖	d		15 39							15 56	16 02			16 09							16 26	16 30			
London Waterloo (East) 4 ⊖	d		15 42							15 59	16 05			16 12							16 29	16 33			
London Cannon Street 4 ⊖	d	15 40			15 47		15 54	15 57				16 07	16 10				16 17	16 24	16 27				16 35	16 39	16 42
London Bridge 4 ⊖	d	15 44	15 47		15 51		15 58	16 01		16 04	16 10	16 11	16 14	16 17			16 21	16 28	16 31		16 34	16 38	16 39	16 43	16 46
Deptford	d				15 57			16 07				16 17					16 27		16 37				16 45		
Greenwich 4 ⛴	d				15 59			16 09				16 20					16 30		16 40				16 48		
Maze Hill	d				16 02			16 12				16 23					16 33		16 43				16 51		
Westcombe Park	d				16 04			16 14				16 25					16 35		16 45				16 53		
London Victoria 15 ⊖	d			15 39											16 09										
Denmark Hill 4	d			15 48											16 18										
Peckham Rye 4	d			15 51											16 21										
Nunhead 4	d			15 53											16 23										
New Cross 4 ⊖	d	15 49					16 03						16 20					16 34						16 49	16 52
St Johns	d	15 51					16 05						16 22					16 36						16 51	
Lewisham 4 ⛴	d	15 54	15 56	16 02			16 08				16 19		16 25	16 27	16 32			16 39				16 49		16 54	16 56
Blackheath 4	d		15 59	16 04			16 11				16 22			16 29	16 34			16 42				16 53			16 59
Kidbrooke	d			16 07			16 14				16 25				16 37			16 45				16 56			17 02
Eltham	d			16 11			16 17				16 29				16 41			16 48				16 59			17 06
Falconwood	d			16 13			16 20				16 31				16 43			16 51				17 02			17 08
Welling	d			16 16			16 22				16 34				16 46			16 53				17 04			17 11
Bexleyheath	d			16 18			16 25				16 36				16 48			16 56				17 07			17 13
Barnehurst 4	d			16 21			16b33				16 39				16 51			17 01				17 11			17 17
Hither Green 4	d	15 59								16 14			16 29								16 44			16 58	
Lee	d	16 01								16 16			16 31								16 46			17 00	
Mottingham	d	16 04								16 19			16 34								16 49			17 03	
New Eltham	d	16 06								16 21			16 37								16 51			17 06	
Sidcup 4	d	16 10								16 25			16 40								16 55			17 09	
Albany Park	d	16 12								16 27			16 42								16 57			17 11	
Bexley	d	16 14								16 29			16 45								16 59			17 14	
Crayford	d	16 18								16 33			16 48								17 03			17 17	17a32
Charlton 4	d	16a45	16 03		16 07			16 17				16 27	17a15	16 34			16 37		16 47				16 56	17a45	
Woolwich Dockyard	d				16 10			16 20				16 30					16 40		16 50				16 59		
Woolwich Arsenal 4 ⛴	d		16 09		16 13			16 23				16 33		16 39			16 43		16 53				17 02		
Plumstead	d				16 15			16 25				16 35					16 45		16 55				17 04		
Abbey Wood	d		16 13		16 18			16 28				16 39		16 43			16 48		16 59				17 07		
Belvedere	d				16 20			16 30				16 41					16 51		17 01				17 10		
Erith	d				16 23			16 33				16 44					16 53		17 04				17 12		
Slade Green 4	d				16a26			16 37				16a48					16a56	17a12	17 07				17 15		
Dartford 4	a		16 24	16 28			16 42	16 45		16 38	16 48			16 54	17 00				17 14		17 08	17 23	17 22		
	d		16 25							16 39				16 55							17 09				
Stone Crossing	d									16 43											17 13				
Greenhithe for Bluewater	d		16 30							16 45				17 00							17 15				
Swanscombe	d									16 48											17 18				
Northfleet	d									16 50											17 20				
Gravesend 4	d		16 37						16 48	16a55				17 07						17 18	17a27				
Higham	d		16 43											17 13											
Strood 4	d		16 48						16 58					17 18						17 28					
Maidstone West	d																								
Rochester 4	d		16 52						17 03					17 22						17 33					
Chatham 4	d		16 55						17 05					17 25						17 35					
Gillingham (Kent) 4	a		16 59						17 09					17 31						17 39					

			SE	SE	SE	SE	SE	SE	SE	SE	SE		SE	SE	SE	SE	SE	SE	SE	SE	SE		SE	SE	SE
St Pancras Int'l 15 ⊖	d		17 14																	17 44					
Stratford International ⊖ ⛴	d		17 21																	17 51					
Ebbsfleet International	d																								
London Charing Cross 4 ⊖	d					16 45	16 49		16 51		16 55					17 06	17 10		17 12		17 17				
London Waterloo (East) 4 ⊖	d					16 48	16 52		16 54		16 58					17 09	17 13		17 15		17 20				
London Cannon Street 4 ⊖	d			16 44				16 54		16 58			17 04	17 06				17 16					17 21	17 26	17 28
London Bridge 4 ⊖	d			16 48		16 53	16 57	16 58	16 59	17 02	17 04		17 08	17 10		17 14	17 19	17 20	17 21		17 26		17 25	17 30	17 32
Deptford	d					16 59		17 04								17 20		17 26							
Greenwich 4 ⛴	d			16 56		17 02		17 07						17 18		17 23		17 29							17 40
Maze Hill	d					17 05		17 10								17 26		17 32							
Westcombe Park	d					17 07		17 12								17 28		17 34							
London Victoria 15 ⊖	d				16 39										17 04										
Denmark Hill 4	d				16 48										17 13										
Peckham Rye 4	d				16 51										17 16										
Nunhead 4	d				16 53										17 18										
New Cross 4 ⊖	d									17 08			17 14										17 31	17 36	
St Johns	d									17 10													17 33		
Lewisham 4 ⛴	d				17 02				17 08	17 13			17 18		17 25				17 30				17 36	17 40	
Blackheath 4	d				17 04				17 10				17 22		17 28				17 34					17 43	
Kidbrooke	d				17 07				17 13				17 25		17 31				17 37					17 46	
Eltham	d				17 11				17 17				17 29		17 34				17 40					17 50	
Falconwood	d				17 13				17 19				17 31		17 37				17 43					17 52	
Welling	d				17 16				17 22				17 34		17 39				17 45					17 55	
Bexleyheath	d				17 18				17 24				17 36		17 42				17 48					17 58	
Barnehurst 4	d				17 21				17 27				17 41		17 45				17 51					18 02	
Hither Green 4	d						17 07			17 18							17 29						17 41		
Lee	d						17 09			17 20							17 31						17 43		
Mottingham	d						17 12			17 23							17 34						17 46		
New Eltham	d						17 15			17 26	17 20						17 36				17 42		17 48		
Sidcup 4	d						17a20			17 30	17 26						17a41				17 47		17 52		
Albany Park	d									17 32	17 28										17 49		17 54		
Bexley	d									17 35	17 30										17 52		17 57		
Crayford	d									17 39	17 34										17 55		18a00		
Charlton 4	d			17 02		17 10		17 15		18a05				17 24		17 30		17 37							17 46
Woolwich Dockyard	d					17 13		17 18								17 33		17 40							
Woolwich Arsenal 4 ⛴	d			17 07		17 16		17 21						17 29		17 36		17 43							17 51
Plumstead	d					17 18		17 23								17 38		17 45							
Abbey Wood	d			17 11		17 21		17 26						17 33		17 42		17 48							17 55
Belvedere	d					17 24		17 29								17 44		17 51							
Erith	d					17 26		17 31								17 47		17 53							
Slade Green 4	d					17a29		17 34					17a52			17a49		17 56						18a12	
Dartford 4	a			17 26	17 31			17 43	17 38		17 39			17 44	17 54			18 06	18 00		18 00				18 06
	d			17 28							17 40			17 47							18 02				18 08
Stone Crossing	d										17 44														18 12
Greenhithe for Bluewater	d			17 33							17 46			17 52							18 07				18 14
Swanscombe	d										17 49														18 17
Northfleet	d										17 51														18 19
Gravesend 4	d		17 36	17 40							17a57			18 00						18 06	18b19				18a27
Higham	d			17 46										18 06							18 25				
Strood 4	d		17 46	17 52										18 12						18 16	18a33				
Maidstone West	d		18a02																	18a32					
Rochester 4	d			17 57										18 20											
Chatham 4	d			18 00										18 23											
Gillingham (Kent) 4	a			18 07										18 30											

Table 200

Mondays to Fridays

London - Dartford and Gillingham

		SE	SE	SE	SE	SE	SE		SE	SE	SE	SE	SE	SE	SE	SE	SE		SE	SE	SE	SE	SE	SE	SE
St Pancras Int'l 15 ⊖	d											18 14													
Stratford International ⊖	d											18 21													
Ebbsfleet International	d																								
London Charing Cross 4 ⊖	d	17 29	17 30	17 32		17 34	17 39							17 50	17 52	17 54	17 56					18 01			18 12
London Waterloo (East) 4 ⊖	d	17 32	17 33	17 35		17 37	17 42							17 53	17 55	17 57	17 59					18 04			18 15
London Cannon Street 4 ⊖	d				17 39					17 43	17 47		17 50						18 00		18 04		18 10	18 12	
London Bridge 4 ⊖	d	17 37		17 41	17 43	17 43	17 48			17 47	17 51		17 54	17 58		18 02	18 04		18 04		18 08	18 10	18 14	18 16	18 21
Deptford	d	17 43			17 49									18 04					18 10						18 27
Greenwich 4	d	17 46			17 52								18 02	18 07					18 13					18 24	18 29
Maze Hill	d	17 49			17 55									18 10					18 16						18 32
Westcombe Park	d	17 51			17 57									18 12					18 18						18 34
London Victoria 15 ⊖	d								17 34											17 56					
Denmark Hill 4	d								17 43											18 06					
Peckham Rye 4	d								17 46											18 09					
Nunhead 4	d								17 49											18 11					
New Cross 4 ⊖	d									17 53	17 58										18 14		18 20		
St Johns	d									17 55											18 16				
Lewisham 4	d					17 53			17 56	17 59	18 02						18 14			18 18	18 20		18 24		
Blackheath 4	d		17 49			17 56			18 00		18 05				18 09		18 17			18 23			18 27		
Kidbrooke	d		17 52			17 59			18 03		18 08				18 12		18 20			18 26			18 30		
Eltham	d		17 56			18 02			18 06		18 12				18 16		18 23			18 30			18 34		
Falconwood	d		17 58			18 05			18 09		18 14				18 19		18 26			18 32			18 36		
Welling	d		18 01			18 07			18 11		18 17				18 21		18 28			18 35			18 39		
Bexleyheath	d		18 04			18 10			18 14		18 20				18 24		18 31			18 38			18 42		
Barnehurst 4	d		18 07			18 12			18 16		18 23				18 27		18a36			18 41			18a47		
Hither Green 4	d			17 51						18 03						18 12					18 25				
Lee	d			17 53						18 05						18 14					18 27				
Mottingham	d			17 56						18 08						18 17					18 30				
New Eltham	d			17 59			18 04			18 11						18 20					18 32	18 26			
Sidcup 4	d			18a04			18 08			18 15						18a24					18 36	18 30			
Albany Park	d						18 10			18 17											18 38	18 32			
Bexley	d						18 13			18 20											18 40	18 35			
Crayford	d						18 16			18a23	18a34										18 44	18 38			
Charlton 4	d	17 53			18 00								18 08	18 15					18 21		19a10			18 30	18 37
Woolwich Dockyard	d	17 56			18 03									18 18					18 24						18 40
Woolwich Arsenal 4	d	17 59			18 06								18 13	18 21					18 27					18 35	18 43
Plumstead	d	18 01			18 08									18 23					18 29						18 45
Abbey Wood	d	18 05			18 11								18 17	18 26					18 32					18 40	18 48
Belvedere	d	18 07			18 14									18 29					18 35						18 50
Erith	d	18 10			18 16									18 31					18 37						18 53
Slade Green 4	d	18a14			18 19	18a22								18a36					18 41						18a55
Dartford 4	a		18 16		18 27		18 21		18 25				18 29		18 36				18 48	18 53		18 43		18 52	
	d						18 22						18 31									18 44		18 54	
Stone Crossing	d																					18 48			
Greenhithe for Bluewater	d						18 27						18 36									18 50		18 59	
Swanscombe	d																					18 53			
Northfleet	d																					18 55			
Gravesend 4	d						18 34					18 38	18a45									19 02		19a09	
Higham	d						18 40															19 08			
Strood 4	d						18 45					18 49										19 14			
Maidstone West	d											19a05													
Rochester 4	d						18 51															19 19			
Chatham 4	d						18 54															19 22			
Gillingham (Kent) 4	a						19 02															19 30			

		SE	SE		SE	SE	SE	SE	SE	SE	SE	SE	SE		SE	SE	SE	SE	SE	SE	SE	SE	SE		SE
St Pancras Int'l 15 ⊖	d							18 55															19 25		
Stratford International ⊖	d							19 02															19 32		
Ebbsfleet International	d							19 13															19 45		
London Charing Cross 4 ⊖	d	18 14			18 18				18 23				18 34		18 37	18 39				18 48					18 56
London Waterloo (East) 4 ⊖	d	18 17			18 21				18 26				18 37		18 40	18 42				18 51					18 59
London Cannon Street 4 ⊖	d		18 21			18 25	18 25			18 30		18 34						18 46	18 50		18 54	18 57			
London Bridge 4 ⊖	d	18 23	18 25		18 26	18 29	18 29		18 32	18 34		18 38	18 42		18 46	18 48		18 50	18 54	18 57	18 58	19 01			19 04
Deptford	d		18 31										18 48					18 56				19 07			
Greenwich 4	d		18 34							18 42			18 51					18 59				19 10			
Maze Hill	d		18 37										18 54					19 02				19 13			
Westcombe Park	d		18 39										18 56					19 04				19 15			
London Victoria 15 ⊖	d										18 18						18 39								
Denmark Hill 4	d										18 28						18 48								
Peckham Rye 4	d										18 32						18 51								
Nunhead 4	d										18 34						18 54								
New Cross 4 ⊖	d					18 35	18 35					18 44				18 55			19 00		19 05				
St Johns	d					18 37	18 37					18 46							19 02		19 07				
Lewisham 4	d				18 36	18 41	18 41				18 43	18 49				18 59	19 03		19 05	19 07	19 11				
Blackheath 4	d				18 39						18 46	18 52				19 02	19 06			19 10	19 14				
Kidbrooke	d				18 42						18 49	18 55				19 05	19 09				19 17				
Eltham	d				18 46						18 53	18 59				19 09	19 13				19 21				
Falconwood	d				18 48						18 55	19 01				19 11	19 16				19 23				
Welling	d				18 51						18 58	19 04				19 14	19 18				19 26				
Bexleyheath	d				18 54						19 01	19 07				19 16	19 21				19 29				
Barnehurst 4	d				18 57						19 04	19a12				19a21	19 25				19a34				
Hither Green 4	d	18 35				18 46	18 46									18 56				19 09						19 14
Lee	d	18 37				18 48	18 48									18 58				19 11						19 16
Mottingham	d	18 40				18 51	18 51									19 01				19 14						19 19
New Eltham	d	18 43				18 53	18 54		18 48						19 04				19 17						19 22
Sidcup 4	d	18 47				18 57	18 58		18 51						19 08				19 20						19 25
Albany Park	d	18 49				18 59	19 00		18 53						19 10				19 22						19 27
Bexley	d	18 51				19 01	19 03		18 56						19 13				19 25						19 30
Crayford	d	18a54				19a05	19 10		18 59						19 16				19 29						19 33
Charlton 4	d		18 41				19a40			18 48			18 59					19 06	20a10	19 15		19 18			
Woolwich Dockyard	d		18 44										19 02					19 09				19 21			
Woolwich Arsenal 4	d		18 47							18 53			19 05					19 12		19 20		19 24			
Plumstead	d		18 49										19 07					19 14				19 26			
Abbey Wood	d		18 53							18 57			19 10					19 17		19 24		19 29			
Belvedere	d		18 55										19 13					19 19				19 32			
Erith	d		18 58										19 15					19 22				19 34			
Slade Green 4	d		19 01										19 18					19a26				19 37			
Dartford 4	a		19 09		19 06				19 04	19 09	19 13		19 28		19 21		19 34			19 34		19 44			19 38
	d								19 05	19 10					19 22					19 35					19 39
Stone Crossing	d								19 09	19 14					19 26										19 43
Greenhithe for Bluewater	d								19 11	19 16					19 29					19 40					19 46
Swanscombe	d								19 14	19 19					19 32										19 49
Northfleet	d								19 16	19 21					19 34										19 51
Gravesend 4	d							19 20	19a24	19 26					19 38					19 47			19 51		19a57
Higham	d									19 32					19 44					19 53					
Strood 4	d							19 30		19 38					19a53					19 58			20 01		
Maidstone West	d																								
Rochester 4	d							19 35		19 45										20 03			20 08		
Chatham 4	d							19 38		19 48										20 05			20 10		
Gillingham (Kent) 4	a							19 42		19 55										20 13			20 14		

London - Dartford and Gillingham

Station		SE	SE	SE	SE	SE	SE	SE	SE	SE	SE	SE	SE	SE	SE	SE	SE	SE	SE	SE	SE	SE	SE
St Pancras Int'l 15 ⊖	d									19 55													
Stratford International ⊖ ⇌	d									20 02													
Ebbsfleet International	d									20 13													
London Charing Cross 4 ⊖	d	19 02			19 09						19 26	19 32			19 39						19 56	20 02	
London Waterloo (East) 4 ⊖	d	19 05			19 12						19 29	19 35			19 42						19 59	20 05	
London Cannon Street 4 ⊖	d		19 07	19 10			19 17	19 24	19 27				19 37	19 40			19 47	19 54	19 57				20 10
London Bridge 4 ⊖	d	19 10	19 11	19 14	19 17		19 21	19 28	19 31		19 34	19 40	19 41	19 44	19 47		19 51	19 58	20 01		20 04	20 10	20 14
Deptford	d		19 17				19 27		19 37				19 47				19 57		20 07				
Greenwich 4 ⇌	d		19 19				19 29		19 39				19 49				19 59		20 09				
Maze Hill	d		19 22				19 32		19 42				19 52				20 02		20 12				
Westcombe Park	d		19 24				19 34		19 44				19 54				20 04		20 14				
London Victoria 15 ⊖	d					19 09										19 39							
Denmark Hill 4	d					19 18										19 48							
Peckham Rye 4	d					19 21										19 51							
Nunhead 4	d					19 23										19 53							
New Cross 4 ⊖	d			19 19				19 33						19 49				20 03					20 19
St Johns	d			19 21				19 35						19 51				20 05					20 21
Lewisham 4 ⇌	d	19 19		19 24	19 26	19 32		19 38				19 49		19 55	19 56	20 02		20 08				20 19	20 25
Blackheath 4	d	19 22			19 29	19 34		19 41				19 52			19 59	20 04		20 11				20 22	
Kidbrooke	d	19 25				19 37		19 44				19 55				20 07		20 14				20 25	
Eltham	d	19 29				19 41		19 47				19 58				20 11		20 17				20 28	
Falconwood	d	19 31				19 43		19 50				20 01				20 13		20 20				20 31	
Welling	d	19 34				19 46		19 52				20 03				20 16		20 22				20 33	
Bexleyheath	d	19 36				19 48		19 55				20 06				20 18		20 25				20 36	
Barnehurst 4	d	19 39				19 51		19a57				20 08				20 21		20a27				20 38	
Hither Green 4	d			19 29							19 44			20 00							20 14		20 30
Lee	d			19 31							19 46			20 02							20 16		20 32
Mottingham	d			19 34							19 49			20 05							20 19		20 35
New Eltham	d			19 36							19 51			20 07							20 21		20 37
Sidcup 4	d			19 40							19 55			20 11							20 25		20 41
Albany Park	d			19 42							19 57			20 13							20 27		20 43
Bexley	d			19 44							19 59			20 15							20 29		20 45
Crayford	d			19 48							20 03			20 18							20 33		20 48
Charlton 4	d		19 27		19 33		19 37		19 47				19 57		20 03		20 07		20 17				
Woolwich Dockyard	d		19 30				19 40		19 50				20 00				20 10		20 20				
Woolwich Arsenal 4 ⇌	d		19 33		19 39		19 43		19 53				20 03		20 09		20 13		20 23				
Plumstead	d		19 35				19 45		19 55				20 05				20 15		20 25				
Abbey Wood	d		19 38		19 43		19 48		19 58				20 08		20 13		20 18		20 28				
Belvedere	d		19 40				19 50		20 00				20 10				20 20		20 30				
Erith	d		19 43				19 53		20 03				20 13				20 23		20 33				
Slade Green 4	d		19a45				19a55		20 07				20a15				20a25		20 37				
Dartford 4	a	19 48		19 53	19 55	19 58			20 13		20 08	20 15		20 23	20 25	20 28			20 43		20 38	20 45	20 53
	d				19 55						20 09				20 25						20 39		
Stone Crossing	d										20 13										20 43		
Greenhithe for Bluewater	d				20 00						20 15				20 30						20 45		
Swanscombe	d										20 18										20 48		
Northfleet	d										20 20										20 50		
Gravesend 4	d				20 07					20 18	20a25				20 37					20 48	20a55		
Higham	d				20 13										20 43								
Strood 4	d				20 18					20 28					20 48					20 58			
Maidstone West	d																						
Rochester 4	d				20 22					20 33					20 52					21 03			
Chatham 4	d				20 25					20 35					20 55					21 05			
Gillingham (Kent) 4	a				20 29					20 39					20 59					21 09			

Station		SE	SE	SE	SE	SE	SE	SE	SE	SE	SE	SE	SE	SE	SE	SE	SE	SE	SE	SE	SE	SE	SE
St Pancras Int'l 15 ⊖	d			20 55						21 25						21 55						22 25	
Stratford International ⊖ ⇌	d			21 02						21 32						22 02						22 32	
Ebbsfleet International	d			21 13						21 43						22 13						22 43	
London Charing Cross 4 ⊖	d	20 09			20 22		20 32	20 39			20 52		21 02	21 09			21 22	21 26	21 32	21 39			21 52
London Waterloo (East) 4 ⊖	d	20 12			20 25		20 35	20 42			20 55		21 05	21 12			21 25	21 29	21 35	21 42			21 55
London Cannon Street 4 ⊖	d		20 17			20 27			20 47			20 57											
London Bridge 4 ⊖	d	20 17	20 21		20 30	20 31	20 40	20 47	20 51		21 00	21 01	21 10	21 17	21 20		21 30	21 34	21 40	21 47	21 50		22 00
Deptford	d		20 27			20 37			20 57			21 07			21 26			21 40			21 56		
Greenwich 4 ⇌	d		20 29			20 39			20 59			21 09			21 28			21 42			21 58		
Maze Hill	d		20 32			20 42			21 02			21 12			21 31			21 45			22 01		
Westcombe Park	d		20 34			20 44			21 04			21 14			21 33			21 47			22 03		
London Victoria 15 ⊖	d																						
Denmark Hill 4	d																						
Peckham Rye 4	d																						
Nunhead 4	d																						
New Cross 4 ⊖	d				20 35		20 45				21 05		21 15				21 35		21 45				22 05
St Johns	d																						
Lewisham 4 ⇌	d	20 26			20 39		20 49	20 56			21 09		21 19	21 26			21 39		21 49	21 56			22 09
Blackheath 4	d	20 29					20 52	20 59					21 22	21 29					21 52	21 59			
Kidbrooke	d						20 55						21 25						21 55				
Eltham	d						20 58						21 28						21 58				
Falconwood	d						21 01						21 31						22 01				
Welling	d						21 03						21 33						22 03				
Bexleyheath	d						21 06						21 36						22 06				
Barnehurst 4	d						21 08						21 38						22 08				
Hither Green 4	d				20 44						21 14						21 44						22 14
Lee	d				20 46						21 16						21 46						22 16
Mottingham	d				20 49						21 19						21 49						22 19
New Eltham	d				20 51						21 21						21 51						22 21
Sidcup 4	d				20 55						21 25						21 55						22 25
Albany Park	d				20 57						21 27						21 57						22 27
Bexley	d				20 59						21 29						21 59						22 29
Crayford	d				21 03						21 33						22 03						22 33
Charlton 4	d	20 33	20 37			20 47		21 03	21 07			21 17		21 33	21 36			21 50		22 03	22 06		
Woolwich Dockyard	d		20 40			20 50			21 10			21 20			21 39			21 53			22 09		
Woolwich Arsenal 4 ⇌	d	20 39	20 43			20 53		21 09	21 13			21 23		21 39	21 42			21 56		22 09	22 12		
Plumstead	d		20 45			20 55			21 15			21 25			21 44			21 58			22 14		
Abbey Wood	d	20 43	20 48			20 58		21 13	21 18			21 28		21 43	21 47			22 01		22 13	22 17		
Belvedere	d		20 50			21 00			21 20			21 30			21 50			22 03			22 20		
Erith	d		20 53			21 03			21 23			21 33			21 52			22 06			22 22		
Slade Green 4	d		20 57			21 07			21 27			21 37			21 56			22 09			22 26		
Dartford 4	a	20 54	21 02		21 08	21 12	21 15	21 24	21 32		21 38	21 42	21 45	21 54	22 00		22 08	22 14	22 16	22 24	22 30		22 38
	d	20 55			21 09			21 25			21 39			21 55			22 09			22 25			22 39
Stone Crossing	d				21 13						21 43						22 13						22 43
Greenhithe for Bluewater	d	21 00			21 15			21 30			21 45			22 00			22 15			22 30			22 45
Swanscombe	d				21 18						21 48						22 18						22 48
Northfleet	d				21 20						21 50						22 20						22 50
Gravesend 4	d	21 07		21 18	21a25			21 37		21 48	21a55			22 07		22 18	22a25			22 37		22 48	22a55
Higham	d	21 13						21 43						22 13						22 43			
Strood 4	d	21 18		21 28				21 48		21 58				22 18		22 28				22 48		22 58	
Maidstone West	d																						
Rochester 4	d	21 22		21 33				21 52		22 03				22 22		22 33				22 52		23 03	
Chatham 4	d	21 25		21 35				21 55		22 05				22 25		22 35				22 55		23 05	
Gillingham (Kent) 4	a	21 29		21 39				21 59		22 09				22 29		22 39				22 59		23 09	

Table 200

Mondays to Fridays

London - Dartford and Gillingham

		SE	SE	SE	SE	SE	SE	SE	SE	SE	SE	SE	SE	SE	SE	SE	SE	SE	SE	SE	SE	SE
St Pancras Int'l 15 ⊖	d					22 55									23 25					23 55		
Stratford International ⊖ ⛴	d					23 02									23 32					00 02		
Ebbsfleet International	d					23 13									23 43					00 13		
London Charing Cross 4 ⊖	d	21 56	22 02	22 09			22 22	22 26	22 32	22 39		22 52	22 56	23 02		23 09	23 22	23 26	23 32		23 39	23 56
London Waterloo (East) 4 ⊖	d	21 59	22 05	22 12			22 25	22 29	22 35	22 42		22 55	22 59	23 05		23 12	23 25	23 29	23 35		23 42	23 59
London Cannon Street 4 ⊖	d																					
London Bridge 4 ⊖	d	22 04	22 10	22 17	22 20		22 30	22 34	22 40	22 47	22 50	23 00	23 04	23 10		23 17	23 30	23 34	23 40		23 47	00 04
Deptford	d	22 10			22 26			22 40			22 56		23 10					23 40				00 10
Greenwich 4 ⛴	d	22 12			22 28			22 42			22 58		23 12					23 42				00 12
Maze Hill	d	22 15			22 31			22 45			23 01		23 15					23 45				00 15
Westcombe Park	d	22 17			22 33			22 47			23 03		23 17					23 47				00 17
London Victoria 15 ⊖	d																					
Denmark Hill 4	d																					
Peckham Rye 4	d																					
Nunhead 4	d																					
New Cross 4 ⊖	d		22 15				22 35		22 45			23 05		23 15			23 35		23 45			
St Johns	d																					
Lewisham 4 ⛴	d		22 19	22 26			22 39		22 49	22 56		23 09		23 19		23 26	23 39		23 49		23 56	
Blackheath 4	d		22 22	22 29					22 52	22 59				23 22		23 29			23 52		23 59	
Kidbrooke	d		22 25						22 55					23 25					23 55			
Eltham	d		22 28						22 58					23 28					23 58			
Falconwood	d		22 31						23 01					23 31					00 01			
Welling	d		22 33						23 03					23 33					00 03			
Bexleyheath	d		22 36						23 06					23 36					00 06			
Barnehurst 4	d		22 38						23 08					23 38					00 08			
Hither Green 4	d						22 44					23 14					23 44					
Lee	d						22 46					23 16					23 46					
Mottingham	d						22 49					23 19					23 49					
New Eltham	d						22 51					23 21					23 51					
Sidcup 4	d						22 55					23 25					23 55					
Albany Park	d						22 57					23 27					23 57					
Bexley	d						22 59					23 29					23 59					
Crayford	d						23 03					23 33					00 03					
Charlton 4	d	22 20		22 33	22 36			22 50		23 03	23 06		23 20			23 33		23 50			00 03	00 20
Woolwich Dockyard	d	22 23			22 39			22 53			23 09		23 23					23 53				00 23
Woolwich Arsenal 4 ⛴	d	22 26		22 39	22 42			22 56		23 09	23 12		23 26			23 39		23 56			00 09	00 26
Plumstead	d	22 28			22 44			22 58			23 14		23 28					23 58				00 28
Abbey Wood	d	22 31		22 43	22 47			23 01		23 13	23 17		23 31			23 43		00 01			00 13	00 31
Belvedere	d	22 33			22 50			23 03			23 20		23 33					00 03				00 33
Erith	d	22 36			22 52			23 06			23 22		23 36					00 06				00 36
Slade Green 4	d	22 39			22 56			23 09			23 26		23 39					00 09				00 39
Dartford 4	a	22 44	22 46	22 54	23 00		23 08	23 14	23 16	23 24	23 30	23 38	23 44	23 46		23 54	00 08	00 14	00 16		00 24	00 44
	d			22 55			23 09			23 25						23 55					00 25	
Stone Crossing	d						23 13			23 29						23 58					00 29	
Greenhithe for Bluewater	d			23 00			23 15			23 31						23 59					00 31	
Swanscombe	d						23 18			23 34						00 04					00 34	
Northfleet	d						23 20			23 36						00 06					00 36	
Gravesend 4	d			23 07		23 18	23a25			23 40					23 48	00 10				00 18	00 40	
Higham	d			23 13						23 46						00 16					00 46	
Strood 4	d			23 18		23 28				23 52					23 58	00 22				00 28	00 52	
Maidstone West	d																					
Rochester 4	d			23 22		23 33				23 56					00 03	00 26				00 33	00 56	
Chatham 4	d			23 25		23 35				23 58					00 05	00 28				00 35	00 58	
Gillingham (Kent) 4	a			23 29		23 39				00 03					00 09	00 33				00 39	01 03	

Table 200

London - Dartford and Gillingham

		SE	SE	SE	SE	SE	SE	SE	SE	SE		SE	SE	SE	SE	SE	SE	SE	SE	SE		SE	SE	SE	SE
St Pancras Int'l 15 ⊖	d		23p25					23p55																	
Stratford International ⊖ ⛴	d		23p32					00 02																	
Ebbsfleet International	d		23p43					00 13																	
London Charing Cross 4 ⊖	d	22p39		23p09	23p22	23p26	23p32		23p39	23p56		00 02	00 05	00 15	04 52		05 22	05 26	05 32	05 39		05 52	05 56	06 02	06 09
London Waterloo (East) 4 ⊖	d	22p42		23p12	23p25	23p29	23p35		23p42	23p59		00 05	00 08	00 18	04 55		05 25	05 29	05 35	05 42		05 55	05 59	06 05	06 12
London Cannon Street 4 ⊖	d																								
London Bridge 4 ⊖	d	22p47		23p17	23p30	23p34	23p40		23p47	00 04		00 10	00 13	00 23	05 00		05 30	05 34	05 40	05 47		06 00	06 04	06 10	06 17
Deptford	d					23p40				00 10								05 40					06 10		
Greenwich 4 ⛴	d					23p42				00 12								05 42					06 12		
Maze Hill	d					23p45				00 15								05 45					06 15		
Westcombe Park	d					23p47				00 17								05 47					06 17		
London Victoria 15 ⊖	d																								
Denmark Hill 4	d																								
Peckham Rye 4	d																								
Nunhead 4	d																								
New Cross 4 ⊖	d				23p35		23p45					00 15	00 18	00 28	05 05		05 35		05 45			06 05		06 15	
St Johns	d																								
Lewisham 4 ⛴	d	22p56		23p26	23p39		23p49		23p56			00 19	00 22	00 33	05 09		05 39		05 49	05 56		06 09		06 19	06 26
Blackheath 4	d	22p59		23p29			23p52		23p59			00 22		00 35					05 52	05 59				06 22	06 29
Kidbrooke	d						23p55					00 25							05 55					06 25	
Eltham	d						23p58					00 28							05 58					06 28	
Falconwood	d						00 01					00 31							06 01					06 31	
Welling	d						00 03					00 33							06 03					06 33	
Bexleyheath	d						00 06					00 36							06 06					06 36	
Barnehurst 4	d						00 08					00 38							06 08					06 38	
Hither Green 4	d				23p44								00 27		05 14		05 44					06 14			
Lee	d				23p46								00 29		05 16		05 46					06 16			
Mottingham	d				23p49								00 32		05 19		05 49					06 19			
New Eltham	d				23p51								00 34		05 21		05 51					06 21			
Sidcup 4	d				23p55								00 38		05 25		05 55					06 25			
Albany Park	d				23p57								00 40		05 27		05 57					06 27			
Bexley	d				23p59								00 42		05 29		05 59					06 29			
Crayford	d				00 03								00 46		05 33		06 03					06 33			
Charlton 4	d	23p03		23p33		23p50			00 03	00 20				00 40				05 50		06 03			06 20		06 33
Woolwich Dockyard	d					23p53				00 23								05 53					06 23		
Woolwich Arsenal 4 ⛴	d	23p09		23p39		23p56			00 09	00 26				00 45				05 56		06 09			06 26		06 39
Plumstead	d					23p58				00 28				00 47				05 58					06 28		
Abbey Wood	d	23p13		23p43		00 01			00 13	00 31				00 50				06 01		06 13			06 31		06 43
Belvedere	d					00 03				00 33				00 53				06 03					06 33		
Erith	d					00 06				00 36				00 55				06 06					06 36		
Slade Green 4	d					00 09				00 39				00 58				06 09					06 39		
Dartford 4	a	23p24		23p54	00 08	00 14	00 16		00 24	00 44		00 46	00 51	01 03	05 38		06 08	06 14	06 16	06 24		06 38	06 44	06 46	06 54
	d	23p25		23p55					00 25					01 03	05 39	05 55	06 09			06 25		06 39			06 55
Stone Crossing	d	23p29		23p58					00 29						05 43		06 13					06 43			
Greenhithe for Bluewater	d	23p31		23p59					00 31					01 08	05 45	06 00	06 15			06 30		06 45			07 00
Swanscombe	d	23p34		00 04					00 34						05 48		06 18					06 48			
Northfleet	d	23p36		00 06					00 36						05 50		06 20					06 50			
Gravesend 4	d	23p40	23p48	00 10				00 18	00 40					01 15	05a55	06 07	06a25			06 37		06a55			07 07
Higham	d	23p46		00 16					00 46					01 21		06 13				06 43					07 13
Strood 4	d	23p52	23p58	00 22				00 28	00 52					01 26		06 18				06 48					07 18
Maidstone West	d																								
Rochester 4	d	23p56	00 03	00 26				00 33	00 56					01 32		06 22				06 52					07 22
Chatham 4	d	23p58	00 05	00 28				00 35	00 58					01 35		06 25				06 55					07 25
Gillingham (Kent) 4	a	00 03	00 09	00 33				00 39	01 03					01 41		06 29				06 59					07 29

		SE	SE	SE	SE	SE		SE	SE	SE	SE	SE	SE	SE	SE	SE		SE	SE	SE	SE	SE	SE	SE	SE
St Pancras Int'l 15 ⊖	d	06 55						07 28					07 52							08 25					
Stratford International ⊖ ⛴	d	07 06						07 35					07 58							08 32					
Ebbsfleet International	d	07 17						07 46					08 13							08 43					
London Charing Cross 4 ⊖	d		06 22	06 26	06 32	06 39			06 52	06 56	07 02	07 09		07 22	07 26	07 32		07 39			07 52	07 56	08 02		
London Waterloo (East) 4 ⊖	d		06 25	06 29	06 35	06 42			06 55	06 59	07 05	07 12		07 25	07 29	07 35		07 42			07 55	07 59	08 05		
London Cannon Street 4 ⊖	d																							08 07	08 10
London Bridge 4 ⊖	d		06 30	06 34	06 40	06 47			07 00	07 04	07 10	07 17		07 30	07 34	07 40		07 47			08 00	08 04	08 10	08 11	08 14
Deptford	d			06 40						07 10					07 40							08 10		08 17	
Greenwich 4 ⛴	d			06 42						07 12					07 42							08 12		08 19	
Maze Hill	d			06 45						07 15					07 45							08 15		08 22	
Westcombe Park	d			06 47						07 17					07 47							08 17		08 24	
London Victoria 15 ⊖	d																		07 39						
Denmark Hill 4	d																		07 48						
Peckham Rye 4	d																		07 51						
Nunhead 4	d																		07 53						
New Cross 4 ⊖	d		06 35		06 45				07 05		07 15			07 35		07 45					08 05		08 15		08 19
St Johns	d																								08 21
Lewisham 4 ⛴	d		06 39		06 49	06 56			07 09		07 19	07 26		07 39		07 49		07 56	08 02		08 09		08 19		08 24
Blackheath 4	d				06 52	06 59					07 22	07 29				07 52		07 59	08 04				08 22		
Kidbrooke	d				06 55						07 25					07 55			08 07				08 25		
Eltham	d				06 58						07 28					07 58			08 11				08 28		
Falconwood	d				07 01						07 31					08 01			08 13				08 31		
Welling	d				07 03						07 33					08 03			08 16				08 33		
Bexleyheath	d				07 06						07 36					08 06			08 18				08 36		
Barnehurst 4	d				07 08						07 38					08 08			08 21				08 38		
Hither Green 4	d		06 44						07 14					07 44							08 14				08 29
Lee	d		06 46						07 16					07 46							08 16				08 31
Mottingham	d		06 49						07 19					07 49							08 19				08 34
New Eltham	d		06 51						07 21					07 51							08 21				08 36
Sidcup 4	d		06 55						07 25					07 55							08 25				08 40
Albany Park	d		06 57						07 27					07 57							08 27				08 42
Bexley	d		06 59						07 29					07 59							08 29				08 44
Crayford	d		07 03						07 33					08 03							08 33				08 48
Charlton 4	d			06 50		07 03				07 20		07 33			07 50			08 03				08 20		08 27	09a15
Woolwich Dockyard	d			06 53						07 23					07 53							08 23		08 30	
Woolwich Arsenal 4 ⛴	d			06 56		07 09				07 26		07 39			07 56			08 09				08 26		08 33	
Plumstead	d			06 58						07 28					07 58							08 28		08 35	
Abbey Wood	d			07 01		07 13				07 31		07 43			08 01			08 13				08 31		08 38	
Belvedere	d			07 03						07 33					08 03							08 33		08 40	
Erith	d			07 06						07 36					08 06							08 36		08 43	
Slade Green 4	d			07 09						07 39					08 09							08 39		08a45	
Dartford 4	a		07 08	07 14	07 16	07 24			07 38	07 44	07 46	07 54		08 08	08 14	08 16		08 24	08 29		08 38	08 44	08 46		
	d		07 09			07 25			07 39			07 55		08 09				08 25			08 39				
Stone Crossing	d		07 13						07 43					08 13							08 43				
Greenhithe for Bluewater	d		07 15			07 30			07 45			08 00		08 15				08 30			08 45				
Swanscombe	d		07 18						07 48					08 18							08 48				
Northfleet	d		07 20						07 50					08 20							08 50				
Gravesend 4	d	07 21	07a25			07 37		07 51	07a55			08 07	08 18	08a25				08 37		08 48	08a55				
Higham	d					07 43						08 13						08 43							
Strood 4	d	07 31				07 48		08 01				08 18	08 28					08 48		08 58					
Maidstone West	d																								
Rochester 4	d	07 36				07 52		08 06				08 22	08 33					08 52		09 03					
Chatham 4	d	07 38				07 55		08 08				08 25	08 35					08 55		09 05					
Gillingham (Kent) 4	a	07 42				07 59		08 12				08 29	08 39					08 59		09 09					

Table 200

London - Dartford and Gillingham

		SE		SE	SE	SE	SE	SE	SE	SE	SE	SE		SE	SE	SE	SE	SE	SE	SE	SE	SE		SE	SE
St Pancras Int'l 15 ⊖	d							08 52											09 25						
Stratford International ⊖ ⛴	d							08 58											09 32						
Ebbsfleet International	d							09 13											09 43						
London Charing Cross 4 ⊖	d	08 09							08 26	08 32				08 39						08 56	09 02				09 09
London Waterloo (East) 4 ⊖	d	08 12							08 29	08 35				08 42						08 59	09 05				09 12
London Cannon Street 4 ⊖	d				08 17	08 24	08 27				08 37	08 40				08 47	08 54	08 57				09 07		09 10	
London Bridge 4 ⊖	d	08 17			08 21	08 28	08 31		08 34	08 40	08 41	08 44		08 47		08 51	08 58	09 01		09 04	09 10	09 11		09 14	09 17
Deptford	d				08 27		08 37				08 47					08 57		09 07				09 17			
Greenwich 4 ⛴	d				08 29		08 39				08 49					08 59		09 09				09 19			
Maze Hill	d				08 32		08 42				08 52					09 02		09 12				09 22			
Westcombe Park	d				08 34		08 44				08 54					09 04		09 14				09 24			
London Victoria 15 ⊖	d			08 09											08 39										
Denmark Hill 4	d			08 18											08 48										
Peckham Rye 4	d			08 21											08 51										
Nunhead 4	d			08 23											08 53										
New Cross 4 ⊖	d					08 33						08 49					09 03							09 19	
St Johns	d					08 35						08 51					09 05							09 21	
Lewisham 4 ⛴	d	08 26		08 32		08 38				08 49		08 54		08 56	09 02		09 08				09 19			09 24	09 26
Blackheath 4	d	08 29		08 34		08 41				08 52				08 59	09 04		09 11				09 22				09 29
Kidbrooke	d			08 37		08 44				08 55					09 07		09 14				09 25				
Eltham	d			08 41		08 47				08 58					09 11		09 17				09 28				
Falconwood	d			08 43		08 50				09 01					09 13		09 20				09 31				
Welling	d			08 46		08 52				09 03					09 16		09 22				09 33				
Bexleyheath	d			08 48		08 55				09 06					09 18		09 25				09 36				
Barnehurst 4	d			08 51		08a57				09 08					09 21		09a27				09 38				
Hither Green 4	d								08 44			08 59								09 14				09 29	
Lee	d								08 46			09 01								09 16				09 31	
Mottingham	d								08 49			09 04								09 19				09 34	
New Eltham	d								08 51			09 06								09 21				09 36	
Sidcup 4	d								08 55			09 10								09 25				09 40	
Albany Park	d								08 57			09 12								09 27				09 42	
Bexley	d								08 59			09 14								09 29				09 44	
Crayford	d								09 03			09 18								09 33				09 48	
Charlton 4	d	08 33			08 37		08 47				08 57	09a45		09 03		09 07		09 17				09 27		10a15	09 33
Woolwich Dockyard	d				08 40		08 50				09 00					09 10		09 20				09 30			
Woolwich Arsenal 4 ⛴	d	08 39			08 43		08 53				09 03			09 09		09 13		09 23				09 33			09 39
Plumstead	d				08 45		08 55				09 05					09 15		09 25				09 35			
Abbey Wood	d	08 43			08 48		08 58				09 08			09 13		09 18		09 28				09 38			09 43
Belvedere	d				08 50		09 00				09 10					09 20		09 30				09 40			
Erith	d				08 53		09 03				09 13					09 23		09 33				09 43			
Slade Green 4	d				08a56		09 07				09a15					09a26		09 37				09a45			
Dartford 4	a	08 54		08 58			09 12		09 08	09 15				09 24	09 28			09 42		09 38	09 45				09 54
	d	08 55							09 09					09 25						09 39					09 55
Stone Crossing	d								09 13											09 43					
Greenhithe for Bluewater	d	09 00							09 15					09 30						09 45					10 00
Swanscombe	d								09 18											09 48					
Northfleet	d								09 20											09 50					
Gravesend 4	d	09 07						09 18	09a25					09 37					09 48	09a55					10 07
Higham	d	09 13												09 43											10 13
Strood 4	d	09 18						09 28						09 48					09 58						10 18
Maidstone West	d																								
Rochester 4	d	09 22						09 33						09 52					10 03						10 22
Chatham 4	d	09 25						09 35						09 55					10 05						10 25
Gillingham (Kent) 4	a	09 29						09 39						09 59					10 09						10 29

		SE	SE	SE	SE	SE	SE	SE		SE	SE	SE	SE	SE	SE	SE	SE	SE		SE	SE	SE	SE	SE	SE
St Pancras Int'l 15 ⊖	d					09 55											10 28								
Stratford International ⊖ ⛴	d					10 02											10 35								
Ebbsfleet International	d					10 13											10 46								
London Charing Cross 4 ⊖	d						09 26	09 32				09 39						09 56		10 02			10 09		
London Waterloo (East) 4 ⊖	d						09 29	09 35				09 42						09 59		10 05			10 12		
London Cannon Street 4 ⊖	d		09 17	09 24	09 27					09 37	09 40			09 47	09 54	09 57					10 07	10 10			10 17
London Bridge 4 ⊖	d		09 21	09 28	09 31		09 34	09 40		09 41	09 44	09 47		09 51	09 58	10 01		10 04		10 10	10 11	10 14	10 17		10 21
Deptford	d		09 27		09 37					09 47				09 57		10 07					10 17				10 27
Greenwich 4 ⛴	d		09 29		09 39					09 49				09 59		10 09					10 19				10 29
Maze Hill	d		09 32		09 42					09 52				10 02		10 12					10 22				10 32
Westcombe Park	d		09 34		09 44					09 54				10 04		10 14					10 24				10 34
London Victoria 15 ⊖	d	09 09											09 39											10 09	
Denmark Hill 4	d	09 18											09 48											10 18	
Peckham Rye 4	d	09 21											09 51											10 21	
Nunhead 4	d	09 23											09 53											10 23	
New Cross 4 ⊖	d			09 33							09 49				10 03							10 19			
St Johns	d			09 35							09 51				10 05							10 21			
Lewisham 4 ⛴	d	09 32		09 38				09 49			09 54	09 56	10 02		10 08					10 19		10 24	10 26	10 32	
Blackheath 4	d	09 34		09 41				09 52				09 59	10 04		10 11					10 22			10 29	10 34	
Kidbrooke	d	09 37		09 44				09 55					10 07		10 14					10 25				10 37	
Eltham	d	09 41		09 47				09 58					10 11		10 17					10 28				10 41	
Falconwood	d	09 43		09 50				10 01					10 13		10 20					10 31				10 43	
Welling	d	09 46		09 52				10 03					10 16		10 22					10 33				10 46	
Bexleyheath	d	09 48		09 55				10 06					10 18		10 25					10 36				10 48	
Barnehurst 4	d	09 51		09a57				10 08					10 21		10a27					10 38				10 51	
Hither Green 4	d						09 44				09 59							10 14				10 29			
Lee	d						09 46				10 01							10 16				10 31			
Mottingham	d						09 49				10 04							10 19				10 34			
New Eltham	d						09 51				10 06							10 21				10 36			
Sidcup 4	d						09 55				10 10							10 25				10 40			
Albany Park	d						09 57				10 12							10 27				10 42			
Bexley	d						09 59				10 14							10 29				10 44			
Crayford	d						10 03				10 18							10 33				10 48			
Charlton 4	d		09 37		09 47					09 57	10a45	10 03		10 07		10 17					10 27	11a15	10 33		10 37
Woolwich Dockyard	d		09 40		09 50					10 00				10 10		10 20					10 30				10 40
Woolwich Arsenal 4 ⛴	d		09 43		09 53					10 03		10 09		10 13		10 23					10 33		10 39		10 43
Plumstead	d		09 45		09 55					10 05				10 15		10 25					10 35				10 45
Abbey Wood	d		09 48		09 58					10 08		10 13		10 18		10 28					10 38		10 43		10 48
Belvedere	d		09 50		10 00					10 10				10 20		10 30					10 40				10 50
Erith	d		09 53		10 03					10 13				10 23		10 33					10 43				10 53
Slade Green 4	d		09a56		10 07					10a15				10a26		10 37					10a45				10a56
Dartford 4	a	09 58			10 12		10 08	10 15				10 24	10 28			10 42		10 38		10 45			10 54	10 58	
	d						10 09					10 25						10 39					10 55		
Stone Crossing	d						10 13											10 43							
Greenhithe for Bluewater	d						10 15					10 30						10 45					11 00		
Swanscombe	d						10 18											10 48							
Northfleet	d						10 20											10 50							
Gravesend 4	d					10 18	10a25					10 37					10 51	10a55					11 07		
Higham	d											10 43											11 13		
Strood 4	d					10 28						10 48					11 01						11 18		
Maidstone West	d																								
Rochester 4	d					10 33						10 52					11 06						11 22		
Chatham 4	d					10 35						10 55					11 08						11 25		
Gillingham (Kent) 4	a					10 39						10 59					11 12						11 29		

Table 200

Saturdays

London - Dartford and Gillingham

			SE	SE	SE		SE	SE	SE	SE	SE	SE	SE	SE	SE		SE	SE	SE	SE	SE	SE	SE	SE	SE	
St Pancras Int'l 15	⊖	d			10 52												11 28									
Stratford International	⊖ ⛴	d			10 58												11 35									
Ebbsfleet International		d			11 13												11 46									
London Charing Cross 4	⊖	d					10 26	10 32			10 39							10 56	11 02			11 09				
London Waterloo (East) 4	⊖	d					10 29	10 35			10 42							10 59	11 05			11 12				
London Cannon Street 4	⊖	d	10 24	10 27					10 37	10 40			10 47	10 54	10 57					11 07	11 10			11 17	11 24	
London Bridge 4	⊖	d	10 28	10 31			10 34	10 40	10 41	10 44	10 47		10 51	10 58	11 01			11 04	11 10	11 11	11 14	11 17		11 21	11 28	
Deptford		d		10 37					10 47				10 57		11 07					11 17				11 27		
Greenwich 4	⛴	d		10 39					10 49				10 59		11 09					11 19				11 29		
Maze Hill		d		10 42					10 52				11 02		11 12					11 22				11 32		
Westcombe Park		d		10 44					10 54				11 04		11 14					11 24				11 34		
London Victoria 15	⊖	d										10 39											11 09			
Denmark Hill 4		d										10 48											11 18			
Peckham Rye 4		d										10 51											11 21			
Nunhead 4		d										10 53											11 23			
New Cross 4	⊖	d	10 33							10 49				11 03							11 19				11 33	
St Johns		d	10 35							10 51				11 05							11 21				11 35	
Lewisham 4	⛴	d	10 38					10 49		10 54	10 56	11 02		11 08					11 19		11 24	11 26	11 32		11 38	
Blackheath 4		d	10 41					10 52			10 59	11 04		11 11					11 22			11 29	11 34		11 41	
Kidbrooke		d	10 44					10 55				11 07		11 14					11 25				11 37		11 44	
Eltham		d	10 47					10 58				11 11		11 17					11 28				11 41		11 47	
Falconwood		d	10 50					11 01				11 13		11 20					11 31				11 43		11 50	
Welling		d	10 52					11 03				11 16		11 22					11 33				11 46		11 52	
Bexleyheath		d	10 55					11 06				11 18		11 25					11 36				11 48		11 55	
Barnehurst 4		d	10a57					11 08				11 21		11a27					11 38				11 51		11a57	
Hither Green 4		d					10 44			10 59								11 14			11 29					
Lee		d					10 46			11 01								11 16			11 31					
Mottingham		d					10 49			11 04								11 19			11 34					
New Eltham		d					10 51			11 06								11 21			11 36					
Sidcup 4		d					10 55			11 10								11 25			11 40					
Albany Park		d					10 57			11 12								11 27			11 42					
Bexley		d					10 59			11 14								11 29			11 44					
Crayford		d					11 03			11 18								11 33			11 48					
Charlton 4		d		10 47					10 57	11a45	11 03		11 07		11 17					11 27	12a15	11 33		11 37		
Woolwich Dockyard		d		10 50					11 00				11 10		11 20					11 30				11 40		
Woolwich Arsenal 4	⛴	d		10 53					11 03		11 09		11 13		11 23					11 33		11 39		11 43		
Plumstead		d		10 55					11 05				11 15		11 25					11 35				11 45		
Abbey Wood		d		10 58					11 08		11 13		11 18		11 28					11 38		11 43		11 48		
Belvedere		d		11 00					11 10				11 20		11 30					11 40				11 50		
Erith		d		11 03					11 13				11 23		11 33					11 43				11 53		
Slade Green 4		d		11 07					11a15				11a26		11 37					11a45				11a56		
Dartford 4		a		11 12			11 08	11 15			11 24	11 28			11 42			11 38	11 45			11 54	11 58			
		d					11 09				11 25							11 39				11 55				
Stone Crossing		d					11 13											11 43								
Greenhithe for Bluewater		d					11 15				11 30							11 45				12 00				
Swanscombe		d					11 18											11 48								
Northfleet		d					11 20											11 50								
Gravesend 4		d			11 18		11a25				11 37						11 51	11a55				12 07				
Higham		d									11 43											12 13				
Strood 4		d			11 28						11 48						12 01					12 18				
Maidstone West		d																								
Rochester 4		d			11 33						11 52						12 06					12 22				
Chatham 4		d			11 35						11 55						12 08					12 25				
Gillingham (Kent) 4		a			11 39						11 59						12 12					12 29				

			SE	SE	SE	SE	SE	SE	SE	SE	SE		SE	SE	SE	SE	SE	SE	SE	SE	SE		SE	SE	SE	SE
St Pancras Int'l 15	⊖	d		11 55											12 25											12 55
Stratford International	⊖ ⛴	d		12 02											12 36											13 06
Ebbsfleet International		d		12 13											12 47											13 17
London Charing Cross 4	⊖	d			11 26	11 32			11 39							11 56	12 02			12 09						
London Waterloo (East) 4	⊖	d			11 29	11 35			11 42							11 59	12 05			12 12						
London Cannon Street 4	⊖	d	11 27				11 37	11 40			11 47		11 54	11 57				12 07	12 10				12 17	12 24	12 27	
London Bridge 4	⊖	d	11 31		11 34	11 40	11 41	11 44	11 47		11 51		11 58	12 01		12 04	12 10	12 11	12 14	12 17			12 21	12 28	12 31	
Deptford		d	11 37				11 47				11 57			12 07				12 17					12 27		12 37	
Greenwich 4	⛴	d	11 39				11 49				11 59			12 09				12 19					12 29		12 39	
Maze Hill		d	11 42				11 52				12 02			12 12				12 22					12 32		12 42	
Westcombe Park		d	11 44				11 54				12 04			12 14				12 24					12 34		12 44	
London Victoria 15	⊖	d								11 39											12 09					
Denmark Hill 4		d								11 48											12 18					
Peckham Rye 4		d								11 51											12 21					
Nunhead 4		d								11 53											12 23					
New Cross 4	⊖	d						11 49					12 03						12 19					12 33		
St Johns		d						11 51					12 05						12 21					12 35		
Lewisham 4	⛴	d				11 49		11 54	11 56	12 02			12 08				12 19		12 24	12 26	12 32			12 38		
Blackheath 4		d				11 52			11 59	12 04			12 11				12 22			12 29	12 34			12 41		
Kidbrooke		d				11 55				12 07			12 14				12 25				12 37			12 44		
Eltham		d				11 58				12 11			12 17				12 28				12 41			12 47		
Falconwood		d				12 01				12 13			12 20				12 31				12 43			12 50		
Welling		d				12 03				12 16			12 22				12 33				12 46			12 52		
Bexleyheath		d				12 06				12 18			12 25				12 36				12 48			12 55		
Barnehurst 4		d				12 08				12 21			12a27				12 38				12 51			12a57		
Hither Green 4		d			11 44			11 59								12 14			12 29							
Lee		d			11 46			12 01								12 16			12 31							
Mottingham		d			11 49			12 04								12 19			12 34							
New Eltham		d			11 51			12 06								12 21			12 36							
Sidcup 4		d			11 55			12 10								12 25			12 40							
Albany Park		d			11 57			12 12								12 27			12 42							
Bexley		d			11 59			12 14								12 29			12 44							
Crayford		d			12 03			12 18								12 33			12 48							
Charlton 4		d	11 47				11 57	12a45	12 03		12 07			12 17				12 27	13a15	12 33			12 37		12 47	
Woolwich Dockyard		d	11 50				12 00				12 10			12 20				12 30					12 40		12 50	
Woolwich Arsenal 4	⛴	d	11 53				12 03		12 09		12 13			12 23				12 33		12 39			12 43		12 53	
Plumstead		d	11 55				12 05				12 15			12 25				12 35					12 45		12 55	
Abbey Wood		d	11 58				12 08		12 13		12 18			12 28				12 38		12 43			12 48		12 58	
Belvedere		d	12 00				12 10				12 20			12 30				12 40					12 50		13 00	
Erith		d	12 03				12 13				12 23			12 33				12 43					12 53		13 03	
Slade Green 4		d	12 07				12a15				12a26			12 37				12a45					12a56		13 07	
Dartford 4		a	12 12		12 08	12 15			12 24	12 28				12 42		12 38	12 45			12 54	12 58				13 12	
		d			12 09				12 25							12 39				12 55						
Stone Crossing		d			12 13											12 43										
Greenhithe for Bluewater		d			12 15				12 30							12 45				13 00						
Swanscombe		d			12 18											12 48										
Northfleet		d			12 20											12 50										
Gravesend 4		d		12 18	12a25				12 37						12 51	12a55				13 07						13 22
Higham		d							12 43											13 13						
Strood 4		d		12 28					12 48						13 01					13 18						13 32
Maidstone West		d																								
Rochester 4		d		12 33					12 52						13 06					13 22						13 37
Chatham 4		d		12 35					12 55						13 08					13 25						13 39
Gillingham (Kent) 4		a		12 39					12 59						13 12					13 29						13 43

Table 200

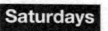

London - Dartford and Gillingham

		SE	SE	SE	SE	SE		SE	SE	SE	SE	SE	SE	SE	SE	SE		SE	SE	SE	SE	SE	SE	SE	SE
St Pancras Int'l 15 ⊖	d											13 25											13 55		
Stratford International ⊖ ⛴	d											13 32											14 02		
Ebbsfleet International	d											13 43											14 13		
London Charing Cross 4 ⊖	d	12 26	12 32			12 39							12 56	13 02				13 09						13 26	13 32
London Waterloo (East) 4 ⊖	d	12 29	12 35			12 42							12 59	13 05				13 12						13 29	13 35
London Cannon Street 4 ⊖	d			12 37	12 40				12 47	12 54	12 57				13 07	13 10				13 17	13 24	13 27			
London Bridge 4 ⊖	d	12 34	12 40	12 41	12 44	12 47			12 51	12 58	13 01		13 04	13 10	13 11	13 14		13 17		13 21	13 28	13 31		13 34	13 40
Deptford	d			12 47					12 57		13 07				13 17					13 27		13 37			
Greenwich 4 ⛴	d			12 49					12 59		13 09				13 19					13 29		13 39			
Maze Hill	d			12 52					13 02		13 12				13 22					13 32		13 42			
Westcombe Park	d			12 54					13 04		13 14				13 24					13 34		13 44			
London Victoria 15 ⊖	d							12 39											13 09						
Denmark Hill 4	d							12 48											13 18						
Peckham Rye 4	d							12 51											13 21						
Nunhead 4	d							12 53											13 23						
New Cross 4 ⊖	d				12 49					13 03						13 19					13 33				
St Johns	d				12 51					13 05						13 21					13 35				
Lewisham 4 ⛴	d		12 49		12 54	12 56		13 02		13 08				13 19		13 24		13 26	13 32		13 38				13 49
Blackheath 4	d		12 52			12 59		13 04		13 11				13 22				13 29	13 34		13 41				13 52
Kidbrooke	d		12 55					13 07		13 14				13 25					13 37		13 44				13 55
Eltham	d		12 58					13 11		13 17				13 28					13 41		13 47				13 58
Falconwood	d		13 01					13 13		13 20				13 31					13 43		13 50				14 01
Welling	d		13 03					13 16		13 22				13 33					13 46		13 52				14 03
Bexleyheath	d		13 06					13 18		13 25				13 36					13 48		13 55				14 06
Barnehurst 4	d		13 08					13 21		13a27				13 38					13 51		13a57				14 08
Hither Green 4	d	12 44			12 59								13 14			13 29								13 44	
Lee	d	12 46			13 01								13 16			13 31								13 46	
Mottingham	d	12 49			13 04								13 19			13 34								13 49	
New Eltham	d	12 51			13 06								13 21			13 36								13 51	
Sidcup 4	d	12 55			13 10								13 25			13 40								13 55	
Albany Park	d	12 57			13 12								13 27			13 42								13 57	
Bexley	d	12 59			13 14								13 29			13 44								13 59	
Crayford	d	13 03			13 18								13 33			13 48								14 03	
Charlton 4	d			12 57	13a45	13 03			13 07		13 17				13 27	14a15		13 33		13 37		13 47			
Woolwich Dockyard	d			13 00					13 10		13 20				13 30					13 40		13 50			
Woolwich Arsenal 4 ⛴	d			13 03		13 09			13 13		13 23				13 33			13 39		13 43		13 53			
Plumstead	d			13 05					13 15		13 25				13 35					13 45		13 55			
Abbey Wood	d			13 08		13 13			13 18		13 28				13 38			13 43		13 48		13 58			
Belvedere	d			13 10					13 20		13 30				13 40					13 50		14 00			
Erith	d			13 13					13 23		13 33				13 43					13 53		14 03			
Slade Green 4	d			13a15					13a26		13 37				13a45					13a56		14 07			
Dartford 4	a	13 08	13 15			13 24		13 28			13 42		13 38	13 45				13 54	13 58			14 12		14 08	14 15
	d	13 09				13 25							13 39					13 55						14 09	
Stone Crossing	d	13 13											13 43											14 13	
Greenhithe for Bluewater	d	13 15				13 30							13 45					14 00						14 15	
Swanscombe	d	13 18											13 48											14 18	
Northfleet	d	13 20											13 50											14 20	
Gravesend 4	d	13a25				13 37						13 48	13a55					14 07					14 18	14a25	
Higham	d					13 43												14 13							
Strood 4	d					13 48						13 58						14 18					14 28		
Maidstone West	d																								
Rochester 4	d					13 52						14 03						14 22					14 33		
Chatham 4	d					13 55						14 05						14 25					14 35		
Gillingham (Kent) 4	a					13 59						14 09						14 29					14 39		

		SE		SE	SE	SE	SE	SE	SE	SE	SE	SE		SE	SE	SE	SE	SE	SE	SE	SE	SE		SE	SE
St Pancras Int'l 15 ⊖	d									14 25											14 55				
Stratford International ⊖ ⛴	d									14 32											15 02				
Ebbsfleet International	d									14 43											15 13				
London Charing Cross 4 ⊖	d				13 39						13 56	14 02				14 09						14 26		14 32	
London Waterloo (East) 4 ⊖	d				13 42						13 59	14 05				14 12						14 29		14 35	
London Cannon Street 4 ⊖	d	13 37		13 40			13 47	13 54	13 57					14 07	14 10			14 17	14 24	14 27					14 37
London Bridge 4 ⊖	d	13 41		13 44	13 47		13 51	13 58	14 01		14 04	14 10		14 11	14 14	14 17		14 21	14 28	14 31		14 34		14 40	14 41
Deptford	d	13 47					13 57		14 07					14 17				14 27		14 37					14 47
Greenwich 4 ⛴	d	13 49					13 59		14 09					14 19				14 29		14 39					14 49
Maze Hill	d	13 52					14 02		14 12					14 22				14 32		14 42					14 52
Westcombe Park	d	13 54					14 04		14 14					14 24				14 34		14 44					14 54
London Victoria 15 ⊖	d					13 39											14 09								
Denmark Hill 4	d					13 48											14 18								
Peckham Rye 4	d					13 51											14 21								
Nunhead 4	d					13 53											14 23								
New Cross 4 ⊖	d			13 49				14 03							14 19				14 33						
St Johns	d			13 51				14 05							14 21				14 35						
Lewisham 4 ⛴	d			13 54	13 56	14 02		14 08				14 19			14 24	14 26	14 32		14 38					14 49	
Blackheath 4	d				13 59	14 04		14 11				14 22				14 29	14 34		14 41					14 52	
Kidbrooke	d					14 07		14 14				14 25					14 37		14 44					14 55	
Eltham	d					14 11		14 17				14 28					14 41		14 47					14 58	
Falconwood	d					14 13		14 20				14 31					14 43		14 50					15 01	
Welling	d					14 16		14 22				14 33					14 46		14 52					15 03	
Bexleyheath	d					14 18		14 25				14 36					14 48		14 55					15 06	
Barnehurst 4	d					14 21		14a27				14 38					14 51		14a57					15 08	
Hither Green 4	d			13 59							14 14				14 29							14 44			
Lee	d			14 01							14 16				14 31							14 46			
Mottingham	d			14 04							14 19				14 34							14 49			
New Eltham	d			14 06							14 21				14 36							14 51			
Sidcup 4	d			14 10							14 25				14 40							14 55			
Albany Park	d			14 12							14 27				14 42							14 57			
Bexley	d			14 14							14 29				14 44							14 59			
Crayford	d			14 18							14 33				14 48							15 03			
Charlton 4	d	13 57		14a45	14 03		14 07		14 17					14 27	15a15	14 33		14 37		14 47					14 57
Woolwich Dockyard	d	14 00					14 10		14 20					14 30				14 40		14 50					15 00
Woolwich Arsenal 4 ⛴	d	14 03			14 09		14 13		14 23					14 33		14 39		14 43		14 53					15 03
Plumstead	d	14 05					14 15		14 25					14 35				14 45		14 55					15 05
Abbey Wood	d	14 08			14 13		14 18		14 28					14 38		14 43		14 48		14 58					15 08
Belvedere	d	14 10					14 20		14 30					14 40				14 50		15 00					15 10
Erith	d	14 13					14 23		14 33					14 43				14 53		15 03					15 13
Slade Green 4	d	14a15					14a26		14 37					14a45				14a56		15 07					15a15
Dartford 4	a				14 24	14 28			14 42		14 38	14 45				14 54	14 58			15 12		15 08		15 15	
	d				14 25						14 39					14 55						15 09			
Stone Crossing	d										14 43											15 13			
Greenhithe for Bluewater	d				14 30						14 45					15 00						15 15			
Swanscombe	d										14 48											15 18			
Northfleet	d										14 50											15 20			
Gravesend 4	d				14 37					14 48	14a55					15 07					15 18	15a25			
Higham	d				14 43											15 13									
Strood 4	d				14 48					14 58						15 18					15 28				
Maidstone West	d																								
Rochester 4	d				14 52					15 03						15 22					15 33				
Chatham 4	d				14 55					15 05						15 25					15 35				
Gillingham (Kent) 4	a				14 59					15 09						15 29					15 39				

Table 200 **Saturdays**

London - Dartford and Gillingham

		SE	SE	SE	SE	SE	SE	SE		SE	SE	SE	SE	SE	SE	SE	SE	SE		SE	SE	SE	SE	SE	SE
St Pancras Int'l 15 ⊖	d							15 25												15 55					
Stratford International ⊖	d							15 32												16 02					
Ebbsfleet International	d							15 43												16 13					
London Charing Cross 4 ⊖	d		14 39							14 56	15 02			15 09							15 26	15 32			15 39
London Waterloo (East) 4 ⊖	d		14 42							14 59	15 05			15 12							15 29	15 35			15 42
London Cannon Street 4 ⊖	d	14 40			14 47	14 54	14 57					15 07	15 10			15 17	15 24	15 27					15 37	15 40	
London Bridge 4 ⊖	d	14 44	14 47		14 51	14 58	15 01			15 04	15 10	15 11	15 14	15 17		15 21	15 28	15 31			15 34	15 40	15 41	15 44	15 47
Deptford	d				14 57		15 07					15 17				15 27		15 37					15 47		
Greenwich 4	d				14 59		15 09					15 19				15 29		15 39					15 49		
Maze Hill	d				15 02		15 12					15 22				15 32		15 42					15 52		
Westcombe Park	d				15 04		15 14					15 24				15 34		15 44					15 54		
London Victoria 15 ⊖	d			14 39											15 09										
Denmark Hill 4	d			14 48											15 18										
Peckham Rye 4	d			14 51											15 21										
Nunhead 4	d			14 53											15 23										
New Cross 4 ⊖	d	14 49				15 03							15 19				15 33							15 49	
St Johns	d	14 51				15 05							15 21				15 35							15 51	
Lewisham 4	d	14 54	14 56	15 02		15 08					15 19		15 24	15 26	15 32		15 38					15 49		15 54	15 56
Blackheath 4	d		14 59	15 04		15 11					15 22			15 29	15 34		15 41					15 52			15 59
Kidbrooke	d			15 07		15 14					15 25				15 37		15 44					15 55			
Eltham	d			15 11		15 17					15 28				15 41		15 47					15 58			
Falconwood	d			15 13		15 20					15 31				15 43		15 50					16 01			
Welling	d			15 16		15 22					15 33				15 46		15 52					16 03			
Bexleyheath	d			15 18		15 25					15 36				15 48		15 55					16 06			
Barnehurst 4	d			15 21		15a27					15 38				15 51		15a57					16 08			
Hither Green 4	d	14 59								15 14			15 29								15 44			15 59	
Lee	d	15 01								15 16			15 31								15 46			16 01	
Mottingham	d	15 04								15 19			15 34								15 49			16 04	
New Eltham	d	15 06								15 21			15 36								15 51			16 06	
Sidcup 4	d	15 10								15 25			15 40								15 55			16 10	
Albany Park	d	15 12								15 27			15 42								15 57			16 12	
Bexley	d	15 14								15 29			15 44								15 59			16 14	
Crayford	d	15 18								15 33			15 48								16 03			16 18	
Charlton 4	d	15a45	15 03		15 07		15 17					15 27	16a15	15 33		15 37		15 47					15 57	16a45	16 03
Woolwich Dockyard	d				15 10		15 20					15 30				15 40		15 50					16 00		
Woolwich Arsenal 4	d		15 09		15 13		15 23					15 33		15 39		15 43		15 53					16 03		16 09
Plumstead	d				15 15		15 25					15 35				15 45		15 55					16 05		
Abbey Wood	d		15 13		15 18		15 28					15 38		15 43		15 48		15 58					16 08		16 13
Belvedere	d				15 20		15 30					15 40				15 50		16 00					16 10		
Erith	d				15 23		15 33					15 43				15 53		16 03					16 13		
Slade Green 4	d				15a26		15 37					15a45				15a56		16 07					16a15		
Dartford 4	a		15 24	15 28			15 42			15 38	15 45			15 54	15 58			16 12			16 08	16 15			16 24
	d		15 25							15 39				15 55							16 09				16 25
Stone Crossing	d									15 43											16 13				
Greenhithe for Bluewater	d		15 30							15 45				16 00							16 15				16 30
Swanscombe	d									15 48											16 18				
Northfleet	d									15 50											16 20				
Gravesend 4	d		15 37					15 48		15a55				16 07						16 18	16a25				16 37
Higham	d		15 43											16 13											16 43
Strood 4	d		15 48					15 58						16 18						16 28					16 48
Maidstone West	d																								
Rochester 4	d		15 52					16 03						16 22						16 33					16 52
Chatham 4	d		15 55					16 05						16 25						16 35					16 55
Gillingham (Kent) 4	a		15 59					16 09						16 29						16 39					16 59

		SE	SE	SE		SE	SE	SE	SE	SE	SE	SE	SE	SE		SE	SE	SE	SE	SE	SE	SE	SE	SE	
St Pancras Int'l 15 ⊖	d						16 25											16 55							
Stratford International ⊖	d						16 32											17 02							
Ebbsfleet International	d						16 43											17 13							
London Charing Cross 4 ⊖	d							15 56	16 02			16 09							16 26	16 32			16 39		
London Waterloo (East) 4 ⊖	d							15 59	16 05			16 12							16 29	16 35			16 42		
London Cannon Street 4 ⊖	d		15 47	15 54		15 57				16 07	16 10			16 17		16 24	16 27				16 37	16 40			
London Bridge 4 ⊖	d		15 51	15 58		16 01		16 04	16 10	16 11	16 14	16 17		16 21		16 28	16 31		16 34	16 40	16 41	16 44	16 47		
Deptford	d		15 57			16 07				16 17				16 27			16 37				16 47				
Greenwich 4	d		15 59			16 09				16 19				16 29			16 39				16 49				
Maze Hill	d		16 02			16 12				16 22				16 32			16 42				16 52				
Westcombe Park	d		16 04			16 14				16 24				16 34			16 44				16 54				
London Victoria 15 ⊖	d	15 39											16 09											16 39	
Denmark Hill 4	d	15 48											16 18											16 48	
Peckham Rye 4	d	15 51											16 21											16 51	
Nunhead 4	d	15 53											16 23											16 53	
New Cross 4 ⊖	d			16 03							16 19					16 33						16 49			
St Johns	d			16 05							16 21					16 35						16 51			
Lewisham 4	d	16 02		16 08					16 19		16 24	16 26	16 32			16 38				16 49		16 54	16 56	17 02	
Blackheath 4	d	16 04		16 11					16 22			16 29	16 34			16 41				16 52			16 59	17 04	
Kidbrooke	d	16 07		16 14					16 25				16 37			16 44				16 55				17 07	
Eltham	d	16 11		16 17					16 28				16 41			16 47				16 58				17 11	
Falconwood	d	16 13		16 20					16 31				16 43			16 50				17 01				17 13	
Welling	d	16 16		16 22					16 33				16 46			16 52				17 03				17 16	
Bexleyheath	d	16 18		16 25					16 36				16 48			16 55				17 06				17 18	
Barnehurst 4	d	16 21		16a27					16 38				16 51			16a57				17 08				17 21	
Hither Green 4	d							16 14			16 29								16 44			16 59			
Lee	d							16 16			16 31								16 46			17 01			
Mottingham	d							16 19			16 34								16 49			17 04			
New Eltham	d							16 21			16 36								16 51			17 06			
Sidcup 4	d							16 25			16 40								16 55			17 10			
Albany Park	d							16 27			16 42								16 57			17 12			
Bexley	d							16 29			16 44								16 59			17 14			
Crayford	d							16 33			16 48								17 03			17 18			
Charlton 4	d		16 07			16 17				16 27	17a15	16 33		16 37			16 47				16 57	17a45	17 03		
Woolwich Dockyard	d		16 10			16 20				16 30				16 40			16 50				17 00				
Woolwich Arsenal 4	d		16 13			16 23				16 33		16 39		16 43			16 53				17 03		17 09		
Plumstead	d		16 15			16 25				16 35				16 45			16 55				17 05				
Abbey Wood	d		16 18			16 28				16 38		16 43		16 48			16 58				17 08		17 13		
Belvedere	d		16 20			16 30				16 40				16 50			17 00				17 10				
Erith	d		16 23			16 33				16 43				16 53			17 03				17 13				
Slade Green 4	d		16a26			16 37				16a45				16a56			17 07				17a15				
Dartford 4	a	16 28				16 42		16 38	16 45			16 54	16 58				17 12		17 08	17 15			17 24	17 28	
	d							16 39				16 55							17 09				17 25		
Stone Crossing	d							16 43											17 13						
Greenhithe for Bluewater	d							16 45				17 00							17 15				17 30		
Swanscombe	d							16 48											17 18						
Northfleet	d							16 50											17 20						
Gravesend 4	d						16 48	16a55				17 07						17 18	17a25				17 37		
Higham	d											17 13											17 43		
Strood 4	d						16 58					17 18						17 28					17 48		
Maidstone West	d																								
Rochester 4	d						17 03					17 22						17 33					17 52		
Chatham 4	d						17 05					17 25						17 35					17 55		
Gillingham (Kent) 4	a						17 09					17 29						17 39					17 59		

Table 200

Saturdays

London - Dartford and Gillingham

		SE	SE	SE	SE	SE	SE	SE	SE	SE		SE	SE	SE	SE	SE	SE	SE	SE	SE		SE	SE	SE	SE
St Pancras Int'l	d				17 25											17 55									
Stratford International	d				17 32											18 02									
Ebbsfleet International	d				17 43											18 13									
London Charing Cross	d					16 56	17 02			17 09							17 26	17 32				17 39			
London Waterloo (East)	d					16 59	17 05			17 12							17 29	17 35				17 42			
London Cannon Street	d	16 47	16 54	16 57				17 07	17 10				17 17	17 24	17 27				17 37	17 40				17 47	17 54
London Bridge	d	16 51	16 58	17 01		17 04	17 10	17 11	17 14	17 17			17 21	17 28	17 31		17 34	17 40	17 41	17 44		17 47		17 51	17 58
Deptford	d	16 57		17 07				17 17					17 27		17 37				17 47					17 57	
Greenwich	d	16 59		17 09				17 19					17 29		17 39				17 49					17 59	
Maze Hill	d	17 02		17 12				17 22					17 32		17 42				17 52					18 02	
Westcombe Park	d	17 04		17 14				17 24					17 34		17 44				17 54					18 04	
London Victoria	d											17 09											17 39		
Denmark Hill	d											17 18											17 48		
Peckham Rye	d											17 21											17 51		
Nunhead	d											17 23											17 53		
New Cross	d		17 03						17 19					17 33						17 49					18 03
St Johns	d		17 05						17 21					17 35						17 51					18 05
Lewisham	d		17 08				17 19		17 24	17 26		17 32		17 38				17 49		17 54		17 56	18 02		18 08
Blackheath	d		17 11				17 22			17 29		17 34		17 41				17 52				17 59	18 04		18 11
Kidbrooke	d		17 14				17 25					17 37		17 44				17 55					18 07		18 14
Eltham	d		17 17				17 28					17 41		17 47				17 58					18 11		18 17
Falconwood	d		17 20				17 31					17 43		17 50				18 01					18 13		18 20
Welling	d		17 22				17 33					17 46		17 52				18 03					18 16		18 22
Bexleyheath	d		17 25				17 36					17 48		17 55				18 06					18 18		18 25
Barnehurst	d		17a27				17 38					17 51		17a57				18 08					18 21		18a27
Hither Green	d					17 14			17 29								17 44			17 59					
Lee	d					17 16			17 31								17 46			18 01					
Mottingham	d					17 19			17 34								17 49			18 04					
New Eltham	d					17 21			17 36								17 51			18 06					
Sidcup	d					17 25			17 40								17 55			18 10					
Albany Park	d					17 27			17 42								17 57			18 12					
Bexley	d					17 29			17 44								17 59			18 14					
Crayford	d					17 33			17 48								18 03			18 18					
Charlton	d	17 07		17 17				17 27	18a15	17 33			17 37		17 47				17 57	18a45		18 03		18 07	
Woolwich Dockyard	d	17 10		17 20				17 30					17 40		17 50				18 00					18 10	
Woolwich Arsenal	d	17 13		17 23				17 33		17 39			17 43		17 53				18 03			18 09		18 13	
Plumstead	d	17 15		17 25				17 35					17 45		17 55				18 05					18 15	
Abbey Wood	d	17 18		17 28				17 38		17 43			17 48		17 58				18 08			18 13		18 18	
Belvedere	d	17 20		17 30				17 40					17 50		18 00				18 10					18 20	
Erith	d	17 23		17 33				17 43					17 53		18 03				18 13					18 23	
Slade Green	d	17a26		17 37				17a45					17a56		18 07				18a15					18a26	
Dartford	a			17 42		17 38	17 45			17 54		17 58			18 12		18 08	18 15				18 24	18 28		
	d					17 39				17 55							18 09					18 25			
Stone Crossing	d					17 43											18 13								
Greenhithe for Bluewater	d					17 45				18 00							18 15					18 30			
Swanscombe	d					17 48											18 18								
Northfleet	d					17 50											18 20								
Gravesend	d				17 48	17a55				18 07						18 18	18a25					18 37			
Higham	d									18 13												18 43			
Strood	d				17 58					18 18						18 28						18 48			
Maidstone West	d																								
Rochester	d				18 03					18 22						18 33						18 52			
Chatham	d				18 05					18 25						18 35						18 55			
Gillingham (Kent)	a				18 09					18 29						18 39						18 59			

		SE	SE	SE	SE	SE		SE	SE	SE	SE	SE	SE	SE	SE	SE		SE	SE	SE	SE	SE	SE	SE	SE
St Pancras Int'l	d		18 25											18 55											19 25
Stratford International	d		18 32											19 02											19 32
Ebbsfleet International	d		18 43											19 13											19 43
London Charing Cross	d			17 56	18 02				18 09						18 26	18 32				18 39					
London Waterloo (East)	d			17 59	18 05				18 12						18 29	18 35				18 42					
London Cannon Street	d	17 57				18 07		18 10			18 17	18 24	18 27					18 37	18 40			18 47	18 54	18 57	
London Bridge	d	18 01		18 04	18 10	18 11		18 14	18 17		18 21	18 28	18 31		18 34	18 40		18 41	18 44	18 47		18 51	18 58	19 01	
Deptford	d	18 07				18 17					18 27		18 37					18 47				18 57		19 07	
Greenwich	d	18 09				18 19					18 29		18 39					18 49				18 59		19 09	
Maze Hill	d	18 12				18 22					18 32		18 42					18 52				19 02		19 12	
Westcombe Park	d	18 14				18 24					18 34		18 44					18 54				19 04		19 14	
London Victoria	d									18 09											18 39				
Denmark Hill	d									18 18											18 48				
Peckham Rye	d									18 21											18 51				
Nunhead	d									18 23											18 53				
New Cross	d							18 19				18 33							18 49				19 03		
St Johns	d							18 21				18 35							18 51				19 05		
Lewisham	d				18 19			18 24	18 26	18 32		18 38				18 49			18 54	18 56	19 02		19 08		
Blackheath	d				18 22				18 29	18 34		18 41				18 52				18 59	19 04		19 11		
Kidbrooke	d				18 25					18 37		18 44				18 55					19 07		19 14		
Eltham	d				18 28					18 41		18 47				18 58					19 11		19 17		
Falconwood	d				18 31					18 43		18 50				19 01					19 13		19 20		
Welling	d				18 33					18 46		18 52				19 03					19 16		19 22		
Bexleyheath	d				18 36					18 48		18 55				19 06					19 18		19 25		
Barnehurst	d				18 38					18 51		18a57				19 08					19 21		19a27		
Hither Green	d			18 14				18 29							18 44				18 59						
Lee	d			18 16				18 31							18 46				19 01						
Mottingham	d			18 19				18 34							18 49				19 04						
New Eltham	d			18 21				18 36							18 51				19 06						
Sidcup	d			18 25				18 40							18 55				19 10						
Albany Park	d			18 27				18 42							18 57				19 12						
Bexley	d			18 29				18 44							18 59				19 14						
Crayford	d			18 33				18 48							19 03				19 18						
Charlton	d	18 17				18 27		19a15	18 33		18 37		18 47					18 57	19a45	19 03		19 07		19 17	
Woolwich Dockyard	d	18 20				18 30					18 40		18 50					19 00				19 10		19 20	
Woolwich Arsenal	d	18 23				18 33			18 39		18 43		18 53					19 03		19 09		19 13		19 23	
Plumstead	d	18 25				18 35					18 45		18 55					19 05				19 15		19 25	
Abbey Wood	d	18 28				18 38			18 43		18 48		18 58					19 08		19 13		19 18		19 28	
Belvedere	d	18 30				18 40					18 50		19 00					19 10				19 20		19 30	
Erith	d	18 33				18 43					18 53		19 03					19 13				19 23		19 33	
Slade Green	d	18 37				18a45					18a56		19 07					19a15				19a26		19 37	
Dartford	a	18 42		18 38	18 45				18 54	18 58			19 12		19 08	19 15				19 24	19 28			19 42	
	d			18 39					18 55						19 09					19 25					
Stone Crossing	d			18 43											19 13										
Greenhithe for Bluewater	d			18 45					19 00						19 15					19 30					
Swanscombe	d			18 48											19 18										
Northfleet	d			18 50											19 20										
Gravesend	d		18 48	18a55					19 07					19 18	19a25					19 37					19 48
Higham	d								19 13											19 43					
Strood	d		18 58						19 18					19 28						19 48					19 58
Maidstone West	d																								
Rochester	d		19 03						19 22					19 33						19 52					20 03
Chatham	d		19 05						19 25					19 35						19 55					20 05
Gillingham (Kent)	a		19 09						19 29					19 39						19 59					20 09

Table 200

Saturdays

London - Dartford and Gillingham

Station		SE		SE	SE	SE	SE	SE	SE	SE	SE	SE		SE	SE	SE	SE	SE	SE	SE	SE	SE		SE	SE
St Pancras Int'l 15 ⊖	d										19 55							20 25							20 55
Stratford International ⊖	d										20 02							20 32							21 02
Ebbsfleet International	d										20 13							20 43							21 13
London Charing Cross 4 ⊖	d	18 56		19 02			19 09					19 26		19 32	19 39				19 52	19 56	20 02	20 09			
London Waterloo (East) 4 ⊖	d	18 59		19 05			19 12					19 29		19 35	19 42				19 55	19 59	20 05	20 12			
London Cannon Street 4 ⊖	d				19 07	19 10			19 24	19 27															
London Bridge 4 ⊖	d	19 04		19 10	19 11	19 14	19 17		19 28	19 31		19 34		19 40	19 47		19 50		20 00	20 05	20 10	20 17		20 20	
Deptford	d				19 17					19 37							19 56			20 11				20 26	
Greenwich 4	d				19 19					19 39							19 58			20 13				20 28	
Maze Hill	d				19 22					19 42							20 01			20 16				20 31	
Westcombe Park	d				19 24					19 44							20 03			20 18				20 33	
London Victoria 15 ⊖	d							19 09								19 39									
Denmark Hill 4	d							19 18								19 48									
Peckham Rye 4	d							19 21								19 51									
Nunhead 4	d							19 23								19 53									
New Cross 4 ⊖	d					19 19			19 33					19 45					20 05		20 15				
St Johns	d					19 21			19 35																
Lewisham 4	d			19 19		19 24	19 26	19 32	19 38					19 49	19 56	20 02			20 09		20 19	20 26			
Blackheath 4	d			19 22			19 29	19 34	19 41					19 52	19 59	20 04					20 22	20 29			
Kidbrooke	d			19 25				19 37	19 44					19 55		20 07					20 25				
Eltham	d			19 28				19 41	19 47					19 58		20 11					20 28				
Falconwood	d			19 31				19 43	19 50					20 01		20 13					20 31				
Welling	d			19 33				19 46	19 52					20 03		20 16					20 33				
Bexleyheath	d			19 36				19 48	19 55					20 06		20 18					20 36				
Barnehurst 4	d			19 38				19 51	19a57					20 08		20 21					20 38				
Hither Green 4	d	19 14				19 29						19 44							20 14						
Lee	d	19 16				19 31						19 46							20 16						
Mottingham	d	19 19				19 34						19 49							20 19						
New Eltham	d	19 21				19 36						19 51							20 21						
Sidcup 4	d	19 25				19 40						19 55							20 25						
Albany Park	d	19 27				19 42						19 57							20 27						
Bexley	d	19 29				19 44						19 59							20 29						
Crayford	d	19 33				19 48						20 03							20 33						
Charlton 4	d				19 27	20a15	19 33			19 47					20 03		20 06			20 20		20 33		20 36	
Woolwich Dockyard	d				19 30					19 50							20 09			20 23				20 39	
Woolwich Arsenal 4	d				19 33		19 39			19 53					20 09		20 12			20 26		20 39		20 42	
Plumstead	d				19 35					19 55							20 14			20 28				20 44	
Abbey Wood	d				19 38		19 43			19 58					20 13		20 17			20 31		20 43		20 47	
Belvedere	d				19 40					20 00							20 20			20 34				20 50	
Erith	d				19 43					20 03							20 22			20 36				20 52	
Slade Green 4	d				19 46					20 07							20 26			20 39				20 56	
Dartford 4	a	19 38		19 45	19 52		19 54	19 58		20 12		20 08		20 15	20 24	20 28	20 31		20 38	20 44	20 46	20 54		21 01	
	d	19 39					19 55					20 09			20 25				20 39			20 55			
Stone Crossing	d	19 43										20 13							20 43						
Greenhithe for Bluewater	d	19 45					20 00					20 15			20 30				20 45			21 00			
Swanscombe	d	19 48										20 18							20 48						
Northfleet	d	19 50										20 20							20 50						
Gravesend 4	d	19a55					20 07				20 18	20a25			20 37			20 48	20a55			21 07			21 18
Higham	d						20 13								20 43							21 13			
Strood 4	d						20 18				20 28				20 48			20 58				21 18			21 28
Maidstone West	d																								
Rochester 4	d						20 22				20 33				20 52			21 03				21 22			21 33
Chatham 4	d						20 25				20 35				20 55			21 05				21 25			21 35
Gillingham (Kent) 4	a						20 29				20 39				20 59			21 09				21 29			21 39

Station		SE	SE	SE	SE	SE	SE	SE		SE	SE	SE	SE	SE	SE	SE	SE	SE		SE	SE	SE	SE	SE	SE
St Pancras Int'l 15 ⊖	d						21 25						21 55									22 25			
Stratford International ⊖	d						21 32						22 02									22 32			
Ebbsfleet International	d						21 43						22 13									22 43			
London Charing Cross 4 ⊖	d	20 22	20 26	20 32	20 39			20 52		20 56	21 02	21 09		21 22	21 26	21 32	21 39	21 52		21 56	22 02		22 09	22 22	22 26
London Waterloo (East) 4 ⊖	d	20 25	20 29	20 35	20 42			20 55		20 59	21 05	21 12		21 25	21 29	21 35	21 42	21 55		21 59	22 05		22 12	22 25	22 29
London Cannon Street 4 ⊖	d																								
London Bridge 4 ⊖	d	20 30	20 35	20 40	20 47	20 50		21 00		21 05	21 10	21 17		21 30	21 35	21 40	21 47	22 00		22 05	22 10		22 17	22 30	22 35
Deptford	d		20 41			20 56				21 11					21 41					22 11					22 41
Greenwich 4	d		20 43			20 58				21 13					21 43					22 13					22 43
Maze Hill	d		20 46			21 01				21 16					21 46					22 16					22 46
Westcombe Park	d		20 48			21 03				21 18					21 48					22 18					22 48
London Victoria 15 ⊖	d																								
Denmark Hill 4	d																								
Peckham Rye 4	d																								
Nunhead 4	d																								
New Cross 4 ⊖	d	20 35		20 45				21 05			21 15			21 35		21 45		22 05			22 15			22 35	
St Johns	d																								
Lewisham 4	d	20 39		20 49	20 56			21 09			21 19	21 26		21 39		21 49	21 56	22 09			22 19		22 26	22 39	
Blackheath 4	d			20 52	20 59						21 22	21 29				21 52	21 59				22 22		22 29		
Kidbrooke	d			20 55							21 25					21 55					22 25				
Eltham	d			20 58							21 28					21 58					22 28				
Falconwood	d			21 01							21 31					22 01					22 31				
Welling	d			21 03							21 33					22 03					22 33				
Bexleyheath	d			21 06							21 36					22 06					22 36				
Barnehurst 4	d			21 08							21 38					22 08					22 38				
Hither Green 4	d	20 44						21 14						21 44				22 14						22 44	
Lee	d	20 46						21 16						21 46				22 16						22 46	
Mottingham	d	20 49						21 19						21 49				22 19						22 49	
New Eltham	d	20 51						21 21						21 51				22 21						22 51	
Sidcup 4	d	20 55						21 25						21 55				22 25						22 55	
Albany Park	d	20 57						21 27						21 57				22 27						22 57	
Bexley	d	20 59						21 29						21 59				22 29						22 59	
Crayford	d	21 03						21 33						22 03				22 33						23 03	
Charlton 4	d		20 50		21 03	21 06				21 20		21 33			21 50		22 03			22 20			22 33		22 50
Woolwich Dockyard	d		20 53			21 09				21 23					21 53					22 23					22 53
Woolwich Arsenal 4	d		20 56		21 09	21 12				21 26		21 39			21 56		22 09			22 26			22 39		22 56
Plumstead	d		20 58			21 14				21 28					21 58					22 28					22 58
Abbey Wood	d		21 01		21 13	21 17				21 31		21 43			22 01		22 13			22 31			22 43		23 01
Belvedere	d		21 04			21 20				21 34					22 04					22 34					23 04
Erith	d		21 06			21 22				21 36					22 06					22 36					23 06
Slade Green 4	d		21 09			21 26				21 39					22 09					22 39					23 09
Dartford 4	a	21 08	21 14	21 16	21 24	21 31		21 38		21 44	21 46	21 54		22 08	22 14	22 16	22 24	22 38		22 44	22 46		22 54	23 08	23 14
	d	21 09			21 25			21 39				21 55		22 09			22 25						22 55		
Stone Crossing	d	21 13						21 43						22 13			22 29						22 59		
Greenhithe for Bluewater	d	21 15			21 30			21 45				22 00		22 15			22 31						23 01		
Swanscombe	d	21 18						21 48						22 18			22 34						23 04		
Northfleet	d	21 20						21 50						22 20			22 36						23 06		
Gravesend 4	d	21a25			21 37		21 48	21a55				22 07	22 18	22a25			22 40					22 48	23 10		
Higham	d				21 43							22 13					22 46						23 16		
Strood 4	d				21 48		21 58					22 18	22 28				22 52					22 58	23 22		
Maidstone West	d																								
Rochester 4	d				21 52		22 03					22 22	22 33				22 56					23 03	23 26		
Chatham 4	d				21 55		22 05					22 25	22 35				22 58					23 05	23 28		
Gillingham (Kent) 4	a				21 59		22 09					22 29	22 39				23 03					23 09	23 33		

Table 200

Saturdays

London - Dartford and Gillingham

		SE	SE	SE		SE	SE	SE	SE	SE	SE	SE	SE	SE		SE	SE
St Pancras Int'l 15 ⊖	d		22 55						23 25					23 55			
Stratford International ⊖	d		23 02						23 32					00 02			
Ebbsfleet International	d		23 13						23 43					00 13			
London Charing Cross 4 ⊖	d	22 32		22 39		22 52	22 56	23 02		23 09	23 22	23 26	23 32			23 39	23 56
London Waterloo (East) 4 ⊖	d	22 35		22 42		22 55	22 59	23 05		23 12	23 25	23 29	23 35			23 42	23 59
London Cannon Street 4 ⊖	d																
London Bridge 4 ⊖	d	22 40		22 47		23 00	23 05	23 10		23 17	23 30	23 35	23 40			23 47	00 05
Deptford	d						23 11					23 41					00 11
Greenwich 4	d						23 13					23 43					00 13
Maze Hill	d						23 16					23 46					00 16
Westcombe Park	d						23 18					23 48					00 18
London Victoria 15 ⊖	d																
Denmark Hill 4	d																
Peckham Rye 4	d																
Nunhead 4	d																
New Cross 4 ⊖	d	22 45				23 05		23 15			23 35		23 45				
St Johns	d																
Lewisham 4	d	22 49		22 56		23 09		23 19		23 26	23 39		23 49			23 56	
Blackheath 4	d	22 52		22 59				23 22		23 29			23 52			23 58	
Kidbrooke	d	22 55						23 25					23 55				
Eltham	d	22 58						23 28					23 58				
Falconwood	d	23 01						23 31					00 01				
Welling	d	23 03						23 33					00 03				
Bexleyheath	d	23 06						23 36					00 06				
Barnehurst 4	d	23 08						23 38					00 08				
Hither Green 4	d					23 14					23 44						
Lee	d					23 16					23 46						
Mottingham	d					23 19					23 49						
New Eltham	d					23 21					23 51						
Sidcup 4	d					23 25					23 55						
Albany Park	d					23 27					23 57						
Bexley	d					23 29					23 59						
Crayford	d					23 33					00 03						
Charlton 4	d			23 03			23 20			23 33		23 50				00 03	00 20
Woolwich Dockyard	d						23 23					23 53					00 23
Woolwich Arsenal 4	d			23 09			23 26			23 39		23 56				00 09	00 26
Plumstead	d						23 28					23 58					00 28
Abbey Wood	d			23 13			23 31			23 43		00 01				00 13	00 31
Belvedere	d						23 34					00 04					00 34
Erith	d						23 36					00 06					00 36
Slade Green 4	d						23 39					00 09					00 39
Dartford 4	a	23 16		23 24		23 38	23 44	23 46		23 54	00 08	00 14	00 16			00 24	00 44
	d			23 25						23 55						00 25	
Stone Crossing	d			23 29						23 58						00 29	
Greenhithe for Bluewater	d			23 31						23 59						00 31	
Swanscombe	d			23 34						00 04						00 34	
Northfleet	d			23 36						00 06						00 36	
Gravesend 4	d		23 18	23 40					23 48	00 10				00 18		00 40	
Higham	d			23 46						00 16						00 46	
Strood 4	d		23 28	23 52					23 58	00 22				00 28		00 52	
Maidstone West	d																
Rochester 4	d		23 33	23 56					00 03	00 26				00 33		00 56	
Chatham 4	d		23 35	23 58					00 05	00 28				00 35		00 58	
Gillingham (Kent) 4	a		23 39	00 03					00 09	00 33				00 39		01 03	

Table 200

Sundays

London - Dartford and Gillingham

	SE A	SE A	SE A	SE A	SE A	SE A	SE A	SE A	SE A
St Pancras Int'l 15 ⊖ d		23p25					23p55		
Stratford International ⊖ d		23p32					00 02		
Ebbsfleet International d		23p43					00 13		
London Charing Cross 4 ⊖ d	22p39		23p09	23p22	23p26	23p32		23p39	23p56
London Waterloo (East) 4 ⊖ d	22p42		23p12	23p25	23p29	23p35		23p42	23p59
London Cannon Street 4 ⊖ d									
London Bridge 4 ⊖ d	22p47		23p17	23p30	23p35	23p40		23p47	00 05
Deptford d					23p41				00 11
Greenwich 4 d					23p43				00 13
Maze Hill d					23p46				00 16
Westcombe Park d					23p48				00 18
London Victoria 15 ⊖ d									
Denmark Hill 4 d									
Peckham Rye 4 d									
Nunhead 4 d									
New Cross 4 ⊖ d				23p35		23p45			
St Johns d									
Lewisham 4 d	22p56		23p26	23p39		23p49		23p56	
Blackheath 4 d	22p59		23p29			23p52		23p58	
Kidbrooke d						23p55			
Eltham d						23p58			
Falconwood d						00 01			
Welling d						00 03			
Bexleyheath d						00 06			
Barnehurst 4 d						00 08			
Hither Green 4 d				23p44					
Lee d				23p46					
Mottingham d				23p49					
New Eltham d				23p51					
Sidcup 4 d				23p55					
Albany Park d				23p57					
Bexley d				23p59					
Crayford d				00 03					
Charlton 4 d	23p03		23p33		23p50			00 03	00 20
Woolwich Dockyard d					23p53				00 23
Woolwich Arsenal 4 d	23p09		23p39		23p56			00 09	00 26
Plumstead d					23p58				00 28
Abbey Wood d	23p13		23p43		00 01			00 13	00 31
Belvedere d					00 04				00 34
Erith d					00 06				00 36
Slade Green 4 d					00 09				00 39
Dartford 4 a	23p24		23p54	00 08	00 14	00 16		00 24	00 44
d	23p25		23p55					00 25	
Stone Crossing d	23p29		23p58					00 29	
Greenhithe for Bluewater d	23p31		23p59					00 31	
Swanscombe d	23p34		00 04					00 34	
Northfleet d	23p36		00 06					00 36	
Gravesend 4 d	23p40	23p48	00 10				00 18	00 40	
Higham d	23p46		00 16					00 46	
Strood 4 d	23p52	23p58	00 22				00 28	00 52	
Maidstone West d									
Rochester 4 d	23p56	00 03	00 26				00 33	00 56	
Chatham 4 d	23p58	00 05	00 28				00 35	00 58	
Gillingham (Kent) 4 a	00 03	00 09	00 33				00 39	01 03	

	SE	SE	SE	SE	SE	SE	SE	SE	SE	SE	SE	SE	SE
St Pancras Int'l 15 ⊖ d												08 52	
Stratford International ⊖ d												08 58	
Ebbsfleet International d												09 13	
London Charing Cross 4 ⊖ d	00 02	00 05	00 15		07 30		07 50	07 56	08 00	08 10	08 20		08 26
London Waterloo (East) 4 ⊖ d	00 05	00 08	00 18		07 33		07 53	07 59	08 03	08 13	08 23		08 29
London Cannon Street 4 ⊖ d													
London Bridge 4 ⊖ d	00 10	00 13	00 23		07 38		07 58	08 04	08 08	08 18	08 28		08 34
Deptford d					07 44				08 14				
Greenwich 4 d					07 46				08 16				
Maze Hill d					07 49				08 19				
Westcombe Park d					07 51				08 21				
London Victoria 15 ⊖ d													
Denmark Hill 4 d													
Peckham Rye 4 d													
Nunhead 4 d													
New Cross 4 ⊖ d	00 15	00 18	00 28				08 04				08 34		
St Johns d													
Lewisham 4 d	00 19	00 22	00 33				08 08	08 12		08 27	08 38		08 42
Blackheath 4 d	00 22		00 35				08 10			08 30	08 40		
Kidbrooke d	00 25						08 13				08 43		
Eltham d	00 28						08 17				08 47		
Falconwood d	00 31						08 19				08 49		
Welling d	00 33						08 22				08 52		
Bexleyheath d	00 36						08 24				08 54		
Barnehurst 4 d	00 38						08 27				08 57		
Hither Green 4 d		00 27						08 16					08 46
Lee d		00 29						08 18					08 48
Mottingham d		00 32						08 21					08 51
New Eltham d		00 34						08 23					08 53
Sidcup 4 d		00 38						08 27					08 57
Albany Park d		00 40						08 29					08 59
Bexley d		00 42						08 31					09 01
Crayford d		00 46						08 34					09 04
Charlton 4 d			00 40		07 54				08 24	08 34			
Woolwich Dockyard d					07 57				08 27				
Woolwich Arsenal 4 d			00 45		08 00				08 30	08 40			
Plumstead d			00 47		08 02				08 32				
Abbey Wood d			00 50		08 05				08 35	08 44			
Belvedere d			00 53		08 07				08 37				
Erith d			00 55		08 10				08 40				
Slade Green 4 d			00 58		08 14				08 44				
Dartford 4 a	00 46	00 51	01 03		08 19		08 33	08 39	08 49	08 54	09 03		09 09
d			01 03	07 55		08 25		08 40		08 55			09 10
Stone Crossing d				07 59		08 29		08 44					09 14
Greenhithe for Bluewater d			01 08	08 01		08 31		08 46		09 00			09 16
Swanscombe d				08 04		08 34		08 49					09 19
Northfleet d				08 06		08 36		08 51					09 21
Gravesend 4 d			01 15	08 10		08 40		08a55		09 07		09 18	09a25
Higham d			01 21	08 16		08 46				09 13			
Strood 4 d			01 26	08 22		08 52				09 18		09 28	
Maidstone West d													
Rochester 4 d			01 32	08 26		08 56				09 23		09 33	
Chatham 4 d			01 35	08 28		08 58				09 26		09 35	
Gillingham (Kent) 4 a			01 41	08 33		09 03				09 30		09 39	

A not 22 May

	SE	SE	SE	SE	SE	SE	SE	SE	SE
St Pancras Int'l 15 ⊖ d				09 25					
Stratford International ⊖ d				09 32					
Ebbsfleet International d				09 43					
London Charing Cross 4 ⊖ d	08 30	08 40	08 50		08 56	09 00	09 10		09 20
London Waterloo (East) 4 ⊖ d	08 33	08 43	08 53		08 59	09 03	09 13		09 23
London Cannon Street 4 ⊖ d									
London Bridge 4 ⊖ d	08 38	08 48	08 58		09 04	09 08	09 18	09 23	09 28
Deptford d	08 44					09 14		09 29	
Greenwich 4 d	08 46					09 16		09 31	
Maze Hill d	08 49					09 19		09 34	
Westcombe Park d	08 51					09 21		09 36	
London Victoria 15 ⊖ d									
Denmark Hill 4 d									
Peckham Rye 4 d									
Nunhead 4 d									
New Cross 4 ⊖ d			09 04						09 34
St Johns d									
Lewisham 4 d		08 57	09 08		09 12		09 27		09 38
Blackheath 4 d		09 00	09 10				09 30		09 40
Kidbrooke d			09 13						09 43
Eltham d			09 17						09 47
Falconwood d			09 19						09 49
Welling d			09 22						09 52
Bexleyheath d			09 24						09 54
Barnehurst 4 d			09 27						09 57
Hither Green 4 d					09 16				
Lee d					09 18				
Mottingham d					09 21				
New Eltham d					09 23				
Sidcup 4 d					09 27				
Albany Park d					09 29				
Bexley d					09 31				
Crayford d					09 34				
Charlton 4 d	08 54	09 04				09 24	09 34	09 39	
Woolwich Dockyard d	08 57					09 27		09 42	
Woolwich Arsenal 4 d	09 00	09 10				09 30	09 40	09 45	
Plumstead d	09 02					09 32		09a47	
Abbey Wood d	09 05	09 14				09 35	09 44		
Belvedere d	09 07					09 37			
Erith d	09 10					09 40			
Slade Green 4 d	09 14					09 44			
Dartford 4 a	09 19	09 24	09 33		09 39	09 49	09 54		10 03
d		09 25			09 40		09 55		
Stone Crossing d					09 44				
Greenhithe for Bluewater d		09 30			09 46		10 00		
Swanscombe d					09 49				
Northfleet d					09 51				
Gravesend 4 d		09 37		09 48	09a55		10 07		
Higham d		09 43					10 13		
Strood 4 d		09 48		09 58			10 18		
Maidstone West d									
Rochester 4 d		09 52		10 03			10 23		
Chatham 4 d		09 55		10 05			10 26		
Gillingham (Kent) 4 a		10 02		10 09			10 30		

	SE	SE	SE	SE	SE	SE	SE	SE	SE	SE	SE	SE	SE
St Pancras Int'l 15 ⊖ d	09 55						10 28						10 52
Stratford International ⊖ d	10 02						10 35						10 58
Ebbsfleet International d	10 13						10 46						11 14
London Charing Cross 4 ⊖ d		09 26	09 30	09 40		09 50		09 56	10 00	10 10		10 20	
London Waterloo (East) 4 ⊖ d		09 29	09 33	09 43		09 53		09 59	10 03	10 13		10 23	
London Cannon Street 4 ⊖ d													
London Bridge 4 ⊖ d		09 34	09 38	09 48	09 53	09 58		10 04	10 08	10 18	10 23	10 28	
Deptford d			09 44		09 59				10 14		10 29		
Greenwich 4 d			09 46		10 01				10 16		10 31		
Maze Hill d			09 49		10 04				10 19		10 34		
Westcombe Park d			09 51		10 06				10 21		10 36		
London Victoria 15 ⊖ d													
Denmark Hill 4 d													
Peckham Rye 4 d													
Nunhead 4 d													
New Cross 4 ⊖ d						10 04						10 34	
St Johns d													
Lewisham 4 d		09 42		09 57		10 08		10 12		10 27		10 38	
Blackheath 4 d				10 00		10 10				10 30		10 40	
Kidbrooke d						10 13						10 43	
Eltham d						10 17						10 47	
Falconwood d						10 19						10 49	
Welling d						10 22						10 52	
Bexleyheath d						10 24						10 54	
Barnehurst 4 d						10 27						10 57	
Hither Green 4 d		09 46						10 16					
Lee d		09 48						10 18					
Mottingham d		09 51						10 21					
New Eltham d		09 53						10 23					
Sidcup 4 d		09 57						10 27					
Albany Park d		09 59						10 29					
Bexley d		10 01						10 31					
Crayford d		10 04						10 34					
Charlton 4 d			09 54	10 04	10 09				10 24	10 34	10 39		
Woolwich Dockyard d			09 57		10 12				10 27		10 42		
Woolwich Arsenal 4 d			10 00	10 10	10 15				10 30	10 40	10 45		
Plumstead d			10 02		10a17				10 32		10a47		
Abbey Wood d			10 05	10 14					10 35	10 44			
Belvedere d			10 07						10 37				
Erith d			10 10						10 40				
Slade Green 4 d			10 14						10 44				
Dartford 4 a		10 09	10 19	10 24		10 33		10 39	10 49	10 54		11 03	
d		10 10		10 25				10 40		10 55			
Stone Crossing d		10 14						10 44					
Greenhithe for Bluewater d		10 16		10 30				10 46		11 00			
Swanscombe d		10 19						10 49					
Northfleet d		10 21						10 51					
Gravesend 4 d	10 18	10a25		10 37			10 51	10a55		11 07			11 18
Higham d				10 43						11 13			
Strood 4 d	10 28			10 48			11 01			11 18			11 28
Maidstone West d													
Rochester 4 d	10 33			10 52			11 06			11 23			11 33
Chatham 4 d	10 35			10 55			11 08			11 26			11 35
Gillingham (Kent) 4 a	10 39			11 02			11 12			11 30			11 39

Table 200

Sundays

London - Dartford and Gillingham

		SE		SE	SE	SE	SE	SE	SE	SE	SE	SE		SE	SE	SE	SE	SE	SE	SE	SE	SE		SE	SE
St Pancras Int'l 15 ⊖	d							11 25							11 52						12 25				
Stratford International ⊖	d							11 32							11 58						12 36				
Ebbsfleet International	d							11 43							12 13						12 47				
London Charing Cross 4 ⊖	d	10 26		10 30	10 40		10 50		10 56	11 00	11 10			11 20		11 26	11 30	11 40		11 50		11 56		12 00	12 10
London Waterloo (East) 4 ⊖	d	10 29		10 33	10 43		10 53		10 59	11 03	11 13			11 23		11 29	11 33	11 43		11 53		11 59		12 03	12 13
London Cannon Street 4 ⊖	d																								
London Bridge 4 ⊖	d	10 34		10 38	10 48	10 53	10 58		11 04	11 08	11 18	11 23		11 28		11 34	11 38	11 48	11 53	11 58		12 04		12 08	12 18
Deptford	d			10 44		10 59				11 14		11 29					11 44		11 59					12 14	
Greenwich 4	d			10 46		11 01				11 16		11 31					11 46		12 01					12 16	
Maze Hill	d			10 49		11 04				11 19		11 34					11 49		12 04					12 19	
Westcombe Park	d			10 51		11 06				11 21		11 36					11 51		12 06					12 21	
London Victoria 15 ⊖	d																								
Denmark Hill 4	d																								
Peckham Rye 4	d																								
Nunhead 4	d																								
New Cross 4 ⊖	d						11 04							11 34						12 04					
St Johns	d																								
Lewisham 4	d	10 42			10 57		11 08		11 12		11 27			11 38		11 42		11 57		12 08		12 12			12 27
Blackheath 4	d				11 00		11 10				11 30			11 40				12 00		12 10					12 30
Kidbrooke	d						11 13							11 43						12 13					
Eltham	d						11 17							11 47						12 17					
Falconwood	d						11 19							11 49						12 19					
Welling	d						11 22							11 52						12 22					
Bexleyheath	d						11 24							11 54						12 24					
Barnehurst 4	d						11 27							11 57						12 27					
Hither Green 4	d	10 46							11 16							11 46						12 16			
Lee	d	10 48							11 18							11 48						12 18			
Mottingham	d	10 51							11 21							11 51						12 21			
New Eltham	d	10 53							11 23							11 53						12 23			
Sidcup 4	d	10 57							11 27							11 57						12 27			
Albany Park	d	10 59							11 29							11 59						12 29			
Bexley	d	11 01							11 31							12 01						12 31			
Crayford	d	11 04							11 34							12 04						12 34			
Charlton 4	d			10 54	11 04	11 09				11 24	11 34	11 39					11 54	12 04	12 09					12 24	12 34
Woolwich Dockyard	d			10 57		11 12				11 27		11 42					11 57		12 12					12 27	
Woolwich Arsenal 4	d			11 00	11 10	11 15				11 30	11 40	11 45					12 00	12 10	12 15					12 30	12 40
Plumstead	d			11 02		11a17				11 32		11a47					12 02		12a17					12 32	
Abbey Wood	d			11 05	11 14					11 35	11 44						12 05	12 14						12 35	12 44
Belvedere	d			11 07						11 37							12 07							12 37	
Erith	d			11 10						11 40							12 10							12 40	
Slade Green 4	d			11 14						11 44							12 14							12 44	
Dartford 4	a	11 09		11 19	11 24		11 33		11 39	11 49	11 54			12 03		12 09	12 19	12 24		12 33		12 39		12 49	12 54
	d	11 10			11 25				11 40		11 55					12 10		12 25				12 40			12 55
Stone Crossing	d	11 14							11 44							12 14						12 44			
Greenhithe for Bluewater	d	11 16			11 30				11 46		12 00					12 16		12 30				12 46			13 00
Swanscombe	d	11 19							11 49							12 19						12 49			
Northfleet	d	11 21							11 51							12 21						12 51			
Gravesend 4	d	11a25			11 37			11 48	11a55		12 07				12 18	12a25		12 37			12 51	12a55			13 07
Higham	d				11 43						12 13							12 43							13 13
Strood 4	d				11 48			11 58			12 18				12 28			12 48			13 01				13 18
Maidstone West	d																								
Rochester 4	d				11 52			12 03			12 23				12 33			12 52			13 06				13 23
Chatham 4	d				11 55			12 05			12 26				12 35			12 55			13 08				13 26
Gillingham (Kent) 4	a				12 02			12 09			12 30				12 39			13 02			13 12				13 30

		SE	SE	SE	SE	SE	SE	SE		SE	SE	SE	SE	SE	SE	SE	SE	SE		SE	SE	SE	SE	SE	SE
St Pancras Int'l 15 ⊖	d			12 55							13 25						13 55							14 25	
Stratford International ⊖	d			13 02							13 32						14 02							14 32	
Ebbsfleet International	d			13 13							13 43						14 13							14 43	
London Charing Cross 4 ⊖	d		12 20		12 26	12 30	12 40			12 50		12 56	13 00	13 10		13 20		13 26		13 30	13 40		13 50		13 56
London Waterloo (East) 4 ⊖	d		12 23		12 29	12 33	12 43			12 53		12 59	13 03	13 13		13 23		13 29		13 33	13 43		13 53		13 59
London Cannon Street 4 ⊖	d																								
London Bridge 4 ⊖	d	12 23	12 28		12 34	12 38	12 48	12 53		12 58		13 04	13 08	13 18	13 23	13 28		13 34		13 38	13 48	13 53	13 58		14 04
Deptford	d	12 29				12 44		12 59					13 14		13 29					13 44		13 59			
Greenwich 4	d	12 31				12 46		13 01					13 16		13 31					13 46		14 01			
Maze Hill	d	12 34				12 49		13 04					13 19		13 34					13 49		14 04			
Westcombe Park	d	12 36				12 51		13 06					13 21		13 36					13 51		14 06			
London Victoria 15 ⊖	d																								
Denmark Hill 4	d																								
Peckham Rye 4	d																								
Nunhead 4	d																								
New Cross 4 ⊖	d		12 34							13 04						13 34							14 04		
St Johns	d																								
Lewisham 4	d		12 38		12 42		12 57			13 08		13 12		13 27		13 38		13 42			13 57		14 08		14 12
Blackheath 4	d		12 40				13 00			13 10				13 30		13 40					14 00		14 10		
Kidbrooke	d		12 43							13 13						13 43							14 13		
Eltham	d		12 47							13 17						13 47							14 17		
Falconwood	d		12 49							13 19						13 49							14 19		
Welling	d		12 52							13 22						13 52							14 22		
Bexleyheath	d		12 54							13 24						13 54							14 24		
Barnehurst 4	d		12 57							13 27						13 57							14 27		
Hither Green 4	d				12 46							13 16						13 46							14 16
Lee	d				12 48							13 18						13 48							14 18
Mottingham	d				12 51							13 21						13 51							14 21
New Eltham	d				12 53							13 23						13 53							14 23
Sidcup 4	d				12 57							13 27						13 57							14 27
Albany Park	d				12 59							13 29						13 59							14 29
Bexley	d				13 01							13 31						14 01							14 31
Crayford	d				13 04							13 34						14 04							14 34
Charlton 4	d	12 39				12 54	13 04	13 09					13 24	13 34	13 39					13 54	14 04	14 09			
Woolwich Dockyard	d	12 42				12 57		13 12					13 27		13 42					13 57		14 12			
Woolwich Arsenal 4	d	12 45				13 00	13 10	13 15					13 30	13 40	13 45					14 00	14 10	14 15			
Plumstead	d	12a47				13 02		13a17					13 32		13a47					14 02		14a17			
Abbey Wood	d					13 05	13 14						13 35	13 44						14 05	14 14				
Belvedere	d					13 07							13 37							14 07					
Erith	d					13 10							13 40							14 10					
Slade Green 4	d					13 14							13 44							14 14					
Dartford 4	a		13 03		13 09	13 19	13 24			13 33		13 39	13 49	13 54		14 03		14 09		14 19	14 24		14 33		14 39
	d				13 10		13 25					13 40		13 55				14 10			14 25				14 40
Stone Crossing	d				13 14							13 44						14 14							14 44
Greenhithe for Bluewater	d				13 16		13 30					13 46		14 00				14 16			14 30				14 46
Swanscombe	d				13 19							13 49						14 19							14 49
Northfleet	d				13 21							13 51						14 21							14 51
Gravesend 4	d			13 18	13a25		13 37				13 48	13a55		14 07			14 18	14a25			14 37			14 48	14a55
Higham	d						13 43							14 13							14 43				
Strood 4	d			13 28			13 48				13 58			14 18			14 28				14 48			14 58	
Maidstone West	d																								
Rochester 4	d			13 33			13 52				14 03			14 23			14 33				14 52			15 03	
Chatham 4	d			13 35			13 55				14 05			14 26			14 35				14 55			15 05	
Gillingham (Kent) 4	a			13 39			14 02				14 09			14 30			14 39				15 02			15 09	

Table 200

Sundays

London - Dartford and Gillingham

		SE	SE	SE		SE	SE	SE	SE	SE	SE	SE	SE	SE		SE	SE	SE	SE	SE	SE	SE	SE	SE	
St Pancras Int'l 15 ⊖	d						14 55						15 25							15 55					
Stratford International ⊖	d						15 02						15 32							16 02					
Ebbsfleet International	d						15 13						15 43							16 13					
London Charing Cross 4 ⊖	d	14 00	14 10			14 20		14 26	14 30	14 40		14 50		14 56		15 00	15 10		15 20		15 26	15 30	15 40		
London Waterloo (East) 4 ⊖	d	14 03	14 13			14 23		14 29	14 33	14 43		14 53		14 59		15 03	15 13		15 23		15 29	15 33	15 43		
London Cannon Street 4 ⊖	d																								
London Bridge 4 ⊖	d	14 08	14 18	14 23		14 28		14 34	14 38	14 48	14 53	14 58		15 04		15 08	15 18	15 23	15 28		15 34	15 38	15 48	15 53	
Deptford	d	14 14		14 29					14 44		14 59					15 14		15 29				15 44		15 59	
Greenwich 4	d	14 16		14 31					14 46		15 01					15 16		15 31				15 46		16 01	
Maze Hill	d	14 19		14 34					14 49		15 04					15 19		15 34				15 49		16 04	
Westcombe Park	d	14 21		14 36					14 51		15 06					15 21		15 36				15 51		16 06	
London Victoria 15 ⊖	d																								
Denmark Hill 4	d																								
Peckham Rye 4	d																								
Nunhead 4	d																								
New Cross 4 ⊖	d					14 34						15 04							15 34						
St Johns	d																								
Lewisham 4	d		14 27			14 38		14 42		14 57		15 08		15 12			15 27		15 38		15 42		15 57		
Blackheath 4	d		14 30			14 40				15 00		15 10					15 30		15 40				16 00		
Kidbrooke	d					14 43						15 13							15 43						
Eltham	d					14 47						15 17							15 47						
Falconwood	d					14 49						15 19							15 49						
Welling	d					14 52						15 22							15 52						
Bexleyheath	d					14 54						15 24							15 54						
Barnehurst 4	d					14 57						15 27							15 57						
Hither Green 4	d							14 46						15 16							15 46				
Lee	d							14 48						15 18							15 48				
Mottingham	d							14 51						15 21							15 51				
New Eltham	d							14 53						15 23							15 53				
Sidcup 4	d							14 57						15 27							15 57				
Albany Park	d							14 59						15 29							15 59				
Bexley	d							15 01						15 31							16 01				
Crayford	d							15 04						15 34							16 04				
Charlton 4	d	14 24	14 34	14 39					14 54	15 04	15 09					15 24	15 34	15 39				15 54	16 04	16 09	
Woolwich Dockyard	d	14 27		14 42					14 57		15 12					15 27		15 42				15 57		16 12	
Woolwich Arsenal 4	d	14 30	14 40	14 45					15 00	15 10	15 15					15 30	15 40	15 45				16 00	16 10	16 15	
Plumstead	d	14 32		14a47					15 02		15a17					15 32		15a47				16 02		16a17	
Abbey Wood	d	14 35	14 44						15 05	15 14						15 35	15 44					16 05	16 14		
Belvedere	d	14 37							15 07							15 37						16 07			
Erith	d	14 40							15 10							15 40						16 10			
Slade Green 4	d	14 44							15 14							15 44						16 14			
Dartford 4	a	14 49	14 54			15 03		15 09	15 19	15 24		15 33		15 39		15 49	15 54		16 03		16 09	16 19	16 24		
	d		14 55					15 10		15 25				15 40			15 55				16 10		16 25		
Stone Crossing	d							15 14						15 44							16 14				
Greenhithe for Bluewater	d		15 00					15 16		15 30				15 46			16 00				16 16		16 30		
Swanscombe	d							15 19						15 49							16 19				
Northfleet	d							15 21						15 51							16 21				
Gravesend 4	d		15 07				15 18	15a25		15 37			15 48	15a55			16 07			16 18	16a25		16 37		
Higham	d		15 13							15 43							16 13						16 43		
Strood 4	d		15 18				15 28			15 48			15 58				16 18			16 28			16 48		
Maidstone West	d																								
Rochester 4	d		15 23				15 33			15 52			16 03				16 23			16 33			16 52		
Chatham 4	d		15 26				15 35			15 55			16 05				16 26			16 35			16 55		
Gillingham (Kent) 4	a		15 30				15 39			16 02			16 09				16 30			16 39			17 02		

		SE	SE	SE	SE	SE	SE	SE	SE	SE		SE	SE	SE	SE	SE	SE	SE	SE	SE		SE	SE	SE	SE
St Pancras Int'l 15 ⊖	d		16 25						16 55							17 25							17 55		
Stratford International ⊖	d		16 32						17 02							17 32							18 02		
Ebbsfleet International	d		16 43						17 13							17 43							18 13		
London Charing Cross 4 ⊖	d	15 50		15 56	16 00	16 10		16 20		16 26		16 30	16 40		16 50		16 56	17 00	17 10			17 20		17 26	17 30
London Waterloo (East) 4 ⊖	d	15 53		15 59	16 03	16 13		16 23		16 29		16 33	16 43		16 53		16 59	17 03	17 13			17 23		17 29	17 33
London Cannon Street 4 ⊖	d																								
London Bridge 4 ⊖	d	15 58		16 04	16 08	16 18	16 23	16 28		16 34		16 38	16 48	16 53	16 58		17 04	17 08	17 18	17 23		17 28		17 34	17 38
Deptford	d				16 14		16 29					16 44		16 59				17 14		17 29					17 44
Greenwich 4	d				16 16		16 31					16 46		17 01				17 16		17 31					17 46
Maze Hill	d				16 19		16 34					16 49		17 04				17 19		17 34					17 49
Westcombe Park	d				16 21		16 36					16 51		17 06				17 21		17 36					17 51
London Victoria 15 ⊖	d																								
Denmark Hill 4	d																								
Peckham Rye 4	d																								
Nunhead 4	d																								
New Cross 4 ⊖	d	16 04						16 34							17 04							17 34			
St Johns	d																								
Lewisham 4	d	16 08		16 12		16 27		16 38		16 42			16 57		17 08		17 12		17 27			17 38		17 42	
Blackheath 4	d	16 10				16 30		16 40					17 00		17 10				17 30			17 40			
Kidbrooke	d	16 13						16 43							17 13							17 43			
Eltham	d	16 17						16 47							17 17							17 47			
Falconwood	d	16 19						16 49							17 19							17 49			
Welling	d	16 22						16 52							17 22							17 52			
Bexleyheath	d	16 24						16 54							17 24							17 54			
Barnehurst 4	d	16 27						16 57							17 27							17 57			
Hither Green 4	d			16 16						16 46							17 16							17 46	
Lee	d			16 18						16 48							17 18							17 48	
Mottingham	d			16 21						16 51							17 21							17 51	
New Eltham	d			16 23						16 53							17 23							17 53	
Sidcup 4	d			16 27						16 57							17 27							17 57	
Albany Park	d			16 29						16 59							17 29							17 59	
Bexley	d			16 31						17 01							17 31							18 01	
Crayford	d			16 34						17 04							17 34							18 04	
Charlton 4	d				16 24	16 34	16 39					16 54	17 04	17 09				17 24	17 34	17 39					17 54
Woolwich Dockyard	d				16 27		16 42					16 57		17 12				17 27		17 42					17 57
Woolwich Arsenal 4	d				16 30	16 40	16 45					17 00	17 10	17 15				17 30	17 40	17 45					18 00
Plumstead	d				16 32		16a47					17 02		17a17				17 32		17a47					18 02
Abbey Wood	d				16 35	16 44						17 05	17 14					17 35	17 44						18 05
Belvedere	d				16 37							17 07						17 37							18 07
Erith	d				16 40							17 10						17 40							18 10
Slade Green 4	d				16 44							17 14						17 44							18 14
Dartford 4	a	16 33		16 39	16 49	16 54		17 03		17 09		17 19	17 24		17 33		17 39	17 49	17 54			18 03		18 09	18 19
	d			16 40		16 55				17 10			17 25				17 40		17 55					18 10	
Stone Crossing	d			16 44						17 14							17 44							18 14	
Greenhithe for Bluewater	d			16 46		17 00				17 16			17 30				17 46		18 00					18 16	
Swanscombe	d			16 49						17 19							17 49							18 19	
Northfleet	d			16 51						17 21							17 51							18 21	
Gravesend 4	d		16 48	16a55		17 07			17 18	17a25			17 37			17 48	17a55		18 07				18 18	18a25	
Higham	d					17 13							17 43						18 13						
Strood 4	d		16 58			17 18			17 28				17 48			17 58			18 18				18 28		
Maidstone West	d																								
Rochester 4	d		17 03			17 23			17 33				17 52			18 03			18 23				18 33		
Chatham 4	d		17 05			17 26			17 35				17 55			18 05			18 26				18 35		
Gillingham (Kent) 4	a		17 09			17 30			17 39				18 02			18 09			18 30				18 39		

Table 200

Sundays

London - Dartford and Gillingham

Station		SE	SE	SE	SE	SE	SE	SE	SE	SE	SE	SE	SE	SE	SE	SE	SE	SE	SE	SE	SE	SE	SE
St Pancras Int'l	d				18 28						18 55								19 25				
Stratford International	d				18 35						19 02								19 32				
Ebbsfleet International	d				18 46						19 13								19 43				
London Charing Cross	d	17 40		17 50		17 56	18 00	18 10		18 20		18 26	18 30	18 40		18 50	18 56	19 00		19 10	19 20	19 26	19 30
London Waterloo (East)	d	17 43		17 53		17 59	18 03	18 13		18 23		18 29	18 33	18 43		18 53	18 59	19 03		19 13	19 23	19 29	19 33
London Cannon Street	d																						
London Bridge	d	17 48	17 53	17 58		18 04	18 08	18 18	18 23	18 28		18 34	18 38	18 48	18 53	18 58	19 04	19 08		19 18	19 28	19 34	19 38
Deptford	d		17 59				18 14		18 29				18 44		18 59			19 14					19 44
Greenwich	d		18 01				18 16		18 31				18 46		19 01			19 16					19 46
Maze Hill	d		18 04				18 19		18 34				18 49		19 04			19 19					19 49
Westcombe Park	d		18 06				18 21		18 36				18 51		19 06			19 21					19 51
London Victoria	d																						
Denmark Hill	d																						
Peckham Rye	d																						
Nunhead	d																						
New Cross	d			18 04						18 34						19 04					19 34		
St Johns	d																						
Lewisham	d	17 57		18 08		18 12		18 27		18 38		18 42		18 57		19 08	19 12			19 27	19 38	19 42	
Blackheath	d	18 00		18 10				18 30		18 40				19 00		19 10				19 30	19 40		
Kidbrooke	d			18 13						18 43						19 13					19 43		
Eltham	d			18 17						18 47						19 17					19 47		
Falconwood	d			18 19						18 49						19 19					19 49		
Welling	d			18 22						18 52						19 22					19 52		
Bexleyheath	d			18 24						18 54						19 24					19 54		
Barnehurst	d			18 27						18 57						19 27					19 57		
Hither Green	d					18 16						18 46					19 16					19 46	
Lee	d					18 18						18 48					19 18					19 48	
Mottingham	d					18 21						18 51					19 21					19 51	
New Eltham	d					18 23						18 53					19 23					19 53	
Sidcup	d					18 27						18 57					19 27					19 57	
Albany Park	d					18 29						18 59					19 29					19 59	
Bexley	d					18 31						19 01					19 31					20 01	
Crayford	d					18 34						19 04					19 34					20 04	
Charlton	d	18 04	18 09				18 24	18 34	18 39				18 54	19 04	19 09			19 24		19 34			19 54
Woolwich Dockyard	d		18 12				18 27		18 42				18 57		19 12			19 27					19 57
Woolwich Arsenal	d	18 10	18 15				18 30	18 40	18 45				19 00	19 10	19 15			19 30		19 40			20 00
Plumstead	d		18a17				18 32		18a47				19 02		19a17			19 32					20 02
Abbey Wood	d	18 14					18 35	18 44					19 05	19 14				19 35		19 44			20 05
Belvedere	d						18 37						19 07					19 37					20 07
Erith	d						18 40						19 10					19 40					20 10
Slade Green	d						18 44						19 14					19 44					20 14
Dartford	a	18 24		18 33		18 39	18 49	18 54		19 03		19 09	19 19	19 24		19 33	19 39	19 49		19 54	20 03	20 09	20 19
	d	18 25				18 40		18 55				19 10		19 25						19 55			
Stone Crossing	d					18 44						19 14		19 29						19 59			
Greenhithe for Bluewater	d	18 30				18 46		19 00				19 16		19 31						20 01			
Swanscombe	d					18 49						19 19		19 34						20 04			
Northfleet	d					18 51						19 21		19 36						20 06			
Gravesend	d	18 37			18 51	18a55		19 07			19 18	19a25		19 40					19 48	20 10			
Higham	d	18 43						19 13						19 46						20 16			
Strood	d	18 48			19 01			19 18			19 28			19 52					19 58	20 22			
Maidstone West	d																						
Rochester	d	18 52			19 06			19 23			19 33			19 56					20 03	20 26			
Chatham	d	18 55			19 08			19 26			19 35			19 58					20 05	20 28			
Gillingham (Kent)	a	19 02			19 12			19 30			19 39			20 03					20 09	20 33			

Table 200

Sundays

London - Dartford and Gillingham

		SE	SE		SE		SE	SE	SE	SE	SE	SE	SE	SE	SE		SE
St Pancras Int'l 15 ⊖	d	19 55		and at the same minutes past each hour until						23 25							
Stratford International ⊖ ⛴	d	20 02								23 32							
Ebbsfleet International	d	20 13								23 43							
London Charing Cross 4 ⊖	d		19 40		22 40		22 50	22 56	23 00		23 10	23 20	23 26	23 30	23 50		23 56
London Waterloo (East) 4 ⊖	d		19 43		22 43		22 53	22 59	23 03		23 13	23 23	23 29	23 33	23 53		23 59
London Cannon Street 4 ⊖	d																
London Bridge 4 ⊖	d		19 48		22 48		22 58	23 04	23 08		23 18	23 28	23 34	23 38	23 58		00 04
Deptford	d								23 14					23 44			
Greenwich 4 ⛴	d								23 16					23 46			
Maze Hill	d								23 19					23 49			
Westcombe Park	d								23 21					23 51			
London Victoria 15 ⊖	d																
Denmark Hill 4	d																
Peckham Rye 4	d																
Nunhead 4	d																
New Cross 4 ⊖	d						23 04					23 34			00 04		
St Johns	d																
Lewisham 4 ⛴	d		19 57		22 57		23 08	23 12			23 27	23 38	23 42		00 08		00 12
Blackheath 4	d		20 00		23 00		23 10				23 30	23 40			00 10		
Kidbrooke	d						23 13					23 43			00 13		
Eltham	d						23 17					23 47			00 17		
Falconwood	d						23 19					23 49			00 19		
Welling	d						23 22					23 52			00 22		
Bexleyheath	d						23 24					23 54			00 24		
Barnehurst 4	d						23 27					23 57			00 27		
Hither Green 4	d							23 16					23 46				00 16
Lee	d							23 18					23 48				00 18
Mottingham	d							23 21					23 51				00 21
New Eltham	d							23 23					23 53				00 23
Sidcup 4	d							23 27					23 57				00 27
Albany Park	d							23 29					23 59				00 29
Bexley	d							23 31					00 01				00 31
Crayford	d							23 34					00 04				00 34
Charlton 4	d		20 04		23 04				23 24		23 34			23 54			
Woolwich Dockyard	d								23 27					23 57			
Woolwich Arsenal 4 ⛴	d		20 10		23 10				23 30		23 40			23 59			
Plumstead	d								23 32					00 02			
Abbey Wood	d		20 14		23 14				23 35		23 44			00 05			
Belvedere	d								23 37					00 07			
Erith	d								23 40					00 10			
Slade Green 4	d								23 44					00 14			
Dartford 4	a		20 24		23 24		23 33	23 39	23 49		23 54	00 03	00 09	00 19	00 33		00 39
	d		20 25		23 25						23 55						
Stone Crossing	d		20 29		23 29						23 59						
Greenhithe for Bluewater	d		20 31		23 31						00 01						
Swanscombe	d		20 34		23 34						00 04						
Northfleet	d		20 36		23 36						00 06						
Gravesend 4	d	20 18	20 40		23 40					23 48	00 10						
Higham	d		20 46		23 46						00 16						
Strood 4	d	20 28	20 52		23 52					23 58	00 22						
Maidstone West	d																
Rochester 4	d	20 33	20 56		23 56					00 03	00 26						
Chatham 4	d	20 35	20 58		23 58					00 05	00 28						
Gillingham (Kent) 4	a	20 39	21 03		00 03					00 09	00 33						

Gillingham and Dartford - London

Miles	Miles	Miles	Miles	Miles			SE	SE	SE	SE	SE	SE	SE	SE	SE		SE	SE	SE	SE	SE	SE	SE	SE	SE
0	—	—	0	0	**Gillingham (Kent)** 4	d	04 09			04 34		04 54			05 20				05 24	05 45					
1¾	—	—	1¾	1¾	**Chatham** 4	d	04 13			04 38		04 58			05 24				05 28	05 49					
2¼	—	—	2¼	2¼	Rochester 4	d	04 15			04 40		05 00			05 27				05 30	05 51					
—	—	—	—	—	Maidstone West	d																			
3¼	—	—	3¼	3¼	Strood 4	d	04 20			04 45		05 05			05 32				05 35						
6	—	—	6	6	Higham	d	04 25			04 50		05 10							05 40						
10½	—	—	10½	10½	**Gravesend** 4	d	04 33			04 58		05 18		05 28	05 43				05 48						
12½	—	—	12½	—	Northfleet	d				05 02				05 32											
13¼	—	—	13¼	—	Swanscombe	d				05 04				05 34											
14½	—	—	14½	—	Greenhithe for Bluewater	d	04 38			05 07		05 23		05 37					05 53						
15¼	—	—	15¼	—	Stone Crossing	d				05 09				05 39											
17¼	0	0	17¼	0	**Dartford** 4	a	04 43			05 13		05 28		05 43					05 58						
—	—	—	—	—		d	04 44		05 01	05 14	05 22	05 29	05 31	05 44			05 52	05 56	05 59		06 01		06 13	06 16	
19¼	2	—	—	—	Slade Green 4	d			05 05				05 35								06 05			06 20	
20½	3¼	—	—	—	Erith	d			05 08				05 38								06 08			06 23	
21¾	4½	—	—	—	Belvedere	d			05 10				05 40								06 10			06 25	
23¼	6	—	—	—	Abbey Wood	d			05 13			05 38	05 43						06 08		06 13			06 28	
24¾	7½	—	—	—	Plumstead	d			05 16				05 46								06 16			06 31	
25¼	8	—	—	—	**Woolwich Arsenal** 4	d			05 19			05 43	05 49						06 13		06 19			06 34	
26	8¾	—	—	—	Woolwich Dockyard	d			05 22				05 52								06 22			06 37	
27	9¾	—	—	—	Charlton 4	d			05 25			05 47	05 55						06 17		06 25			06 40	
—	—	—	19	—	Crayford	d	04 48			05 18				05 48				06 01							
—	—	—	20½	—	Bexley	d	04 51			05 21				05 51				06 04							
—	—	—	21½	—	Albany Park	d	04 54			05 24				05 54				06 07							
—	—	—	22½	—	Sidcup 4	d	04 57			05 27				05 57				06 10							
—	—	—	24	—	New Eltham	d	05 00			05 30				06 00				06 13							
—	—	—	25	—	Mottingham	d	05 02			05 32				06 02				06 16							
—	—	—	26½	—	Lee	d	05 05			05 35				06 05				06 19							
—	—	—	27¼	—	Hither Green 4	d	05 08	05 23		05 38				06 08				06 22							
—	—	3	—	3	Barnehurst 4	d					05 29						05 59					06 14	06 20		
—	—	4¼	—	4¼	Bexleyheath	d					05 31						06 01					06 16	06 22		
—	—	5¾	—	5¾	Welling	d					05 34						06 04					06 19	06 25		
—	—	6¾	—	6¾	Falconwood	d					05 37						06 07					06 22	06 28		
—	—	8	—	8	Eltham	d					05 40						06 10					06 25	06 31		
—	—	9	—	9	Kidbrooke	d					05 43						06 13					06 28	06 34		
29	—	10	—	10	Blackheath 4	d					05 46	05 52					06 16		06 22			06 31	06 37		
30	—	11	28½	11	Lewisham 4	d	05 13	05 28		05 43	05 50	05 56		06 13			06 20	06 27	06 25			06 35	06 41		06 48
—	—	11½	29	—	St Johns	d												06 29							06 50
—	—	12¼	29¾	—	New Cross 4	⊖ d	05 16	05 31		05 46	05 53			06 16				06 31				06 38			06 52
—	—	—	—	12¾	Nunhead 4	d																			
—	—	—	—	13½	Peckham Rye 4	d																	06 47		
—	—	—	—	14¼	Denmark Hill 4	d																	06 50		
—	—	—	—	18½	**London Victoria** 15	⊖ a																	07 04		
—	10½	—	—	—	Westcombe Park	d			05 27				05 57								06 27			06 42	
—	11	—	—	—	Maze Hill	d			05 29				05 59								06 29			06 44	
—	12	—	—	—	Greenwich 4	d			05 32				06 02								06 32			06 47	
—	12½	—	—	—	**Deptford**	a			05 34				06 04								06 34			06 49	
34¼	15½	15¼	32¾	—	London Bridge 4	⊖ a	05 22	05 36	05 41	05 52	05 58	06 05	06 12	06 22			06 28	06 37	06 34	06 27	06 42	06 43		06 56	06 58
—	16¼	—	—	—	**London Cannon Street** 4	⊖ a		05 41												06 32		06 48		07 03	07 05
35¼	—	16¼	33¾	—	**London Waterloo (East)** 4	⊖ a	05 26		05 46	05 57	06 03	06 10	06 17	06 26			06 33	06 41	06 39		06 48				
—	—	—	—	—	**London Charing Cross** 4	⊖ a	05 30		05 50	06 01	06 07	06 13	06 21	06 30			06 36	06 45	06 43		06 52				
—	—	—	—	12½	**Ebbsfleet International**	a									05 47										
—	—	—	—	29¼	**Stratford International** ⊖	a									05 59										
—	—	—	—	35¼	**St Pancras Int'l** 15	⊖ a									06 06										

			SE	SE	SE	SE	SE	SE	SE	SE	SE		SE	SE	SE	SE	SE	SE 1	SE	SE	SE		SE	SE	SE
Gillingham (Kent) 4	d			05 50	05 54						06 07						06 19	06 34							
Chatham 4	d			05 54	05 58						06 11						06 24	06 38							
Rochester 4	d			05 57	06 00						06 13						06 26	06 41							
Maidstone West	d																								
Strood 4	d			06 02	06 05						06 18						06 32								
Higham	d				06 10						06 23														
Gravesend 4	d		06 05	06 13	06 18						06 31					06 34	06 43							06 47	
Northfleet	d		06 09													06 38								06 51	
Swanscombe	d		06 11													06 40								06 53	
Greenhithe for Bluewater	d		06 14		06 23						06 37					06 43								06 56	
Stone Crossing	d		06 16													06 45								06 58	
Dartford 4	a		06 20		06 28						06 41					06 49								07 02	
	d		06 21		06 29		06 31		06 31	06 39	06 42					06 50							07 00	07 03	
Slade Green 4	d								06 36											06 55					
Erith	d								06 39											06 57					
Belvedere	d								06 41											07 00					
Abbey Wood	d				06 38				06 44		06 51									07 03				07 12	
Plumstead	d								06 47											07 06					
Woolwich Arsenal 4	d				06 43				06 50		06 56									07 09				07 17	
Woolwich Dockyard	d								06 53											07 12					
Charlton 4	d				06 47				06 56											07 15				07 22	
Crayford	d					06 30	06 35								06 50	06 55									
Bexley	d					06 33	06 38								06 53	06 58									
Albany Park	d					06 36	06 41								06 56	07 01									
Sidcup 4	d					06 39	06 44								06 59	07 04									
New Eltham	d					06 43	06 47								07 02	07 07									
Mottingham	d					06 45	06 50								07 05	07 10									
Lee	d					06 48	06 53								07 08	07 13									
Hither Green 4	d					06 51	06 56							07 08	07 11	07 16									07 28
Barnehurst 4	d		06 28					06 39		06 49			06 53								07 00		07 08		
Bexleyheath	d		06 31					06 41		06 52			06 56								07 03		07 11		
Welling	d		06 34					06 44		06 55			06 59								07 06		07 14		
Falconwood	d		06 37					06 47		06 57			07 01								07 08		07 16		
Eltham	d		06 40					06 50		07 00			07 04								07 11		07 19		
Kidbrooke	d		06 43					06 53		07 03			07 07								07 14		07 22		
Blackheath 4	d		06 47		06 52			06 57		07 08	07 05		07 11								07 18		07 27		
Lewisham 4	d		06 50		06 55	06 57		07 01		07 11	07 08		07 15		07 17				07 20		07 22		07 30		
St Johns	d					06 59									07 19						07 24				
New Cross 4	⊖ d					07 01		07 04			07 11				07 21				07 23		07 26				
Nunhead 4	d												07 20												
Peckham Rye 4	d												07 23												
Denmark Hill 4	d												07 29												
London Victoria 15	⊖ a												07 42												
Westcombe Park	d								06 58											07 17					
Maze Hill	d								07 00											07 19					
Greenwich 4	d								07 03											07 23				07 28	
Deptford	a								07 05											07 25					
London Bridge 4	⊖ a		07 00		07 03	07 07	07 06	07 09	07 14	07 20	07 17			07 18	07 26	07 26		07 20	07 28	07 33	07 33		07 40	07 35	07 37
London Cannon Street 4	⊖ a					07 14		07 16	07 21		07 23			07 25	07 33			07 27	07 35		07 39			07 42	07 44
London Waterloo (East) 4	⊖ a		07 05		07 09		07 11			07 25						07 31				07 38			07 46		
London Charing Cross 4	⊖ a		07 11		07 15		07 17			07 31						07 37				07 44			07 52		
Ebbsfleet International	a			06 17													06 47								
Stratford International ⊖	a			06 29													06 59								
St Pancras Int'l 15	⊖ a			06 36													07 07								

Gillingham and Dartford - London

		SE	SE	SE	SE	SE	SE		SE	SE	SE	SE	SE	SE	SE	SE	SE		SE	SE	SE	SE	SE	SE	SE
						1																			
Gillingham (Kent) 4	d				06 38	07 04																			
Chatham 4	d				06 42	07 08																			
Rochester 4	d				06 44	07 11																			
Maidstone West	d																		06 56						
Strood 4	d				06 49							06 57							07 12						
Higham	d				06 54							07 02													
Gravesend 4	d				07 02							07 09					07 17		07 22						
Northfleet	d																07 21								
Swanscombe	d																07 23								
Greenhithe for Bluewater	d				07 07							07 16					07 26								
Stone Crossing	d																07 28								
Dartford 4	a				07 12							07 21					07 33								
	d		07 05		07 12		07 17				07 20	07 23			07 25		07 34				07 36				07 40
Slade Green 4	d		07 09						07 19						07 29								07 39		
Erith	d		07 12						07 22						07 32								07 42		
Belvedere	d		07 14						07 24						07 34								07 44		
Abbey Wood	d		07 18						07 28			07 34			07 38								07 48		
Plumstead	d		07 21						07 31						07 41								07 51		
Woolwich Arsenal 4	d		07 24						07 34			07 39			07 44								07 54		
Woolwich Dockyard	d		07 26						07 36						07 46								07 56		
Charlton 4	d		07 30						07 40			07 44			07 50								08 00		
Crayford	d			07 10	07 17											07 30	07 38								
Bexley	d			07 13	07 20											07 33	07 41								
Albany Park	d			07 16	07 22											07 36	07 44								
Sidcup 4	d			07 19	07 25											07 39	07 47					07 51			
New Eltham	d			07 23	07 28											07 43	07 50					07 54			
Mottingham	d			07 25	07 31											07 45						07 56			
Lee	d			07 28	07 34											07 48						07 59			
Hither Green 4	d			07 32	07 36								07 49			07 52						08 02			
Barnehurst 4	d	07 13					07 24				07 28			07 33						07 38	07 44				07 48
Bexleyheath	d	07 16					07 26				07 31			07 36						07 41	07 46				07 51
Welling	d	07 19					07 29				07 34			07 39						07 44	07 49				07 54
Falconwood	d	07 21					07 32				07 36			07 41						07 46	07 52				07 56
Eltham	d	07 24					07 35				07 39			07 44						07 49	07 55				07 59
Kidbrooke	d	07 27					07 38				07 42			07 47						07 52	07 58				08 02
Blackheath 4	d	07 31					07 42				07 47			07 51						07 57	08 02				08 07
Lewisham 4	d	07 35		07 38			07 46			07 48	07 50			07 55		07 57					08 05			08 08	08 11
St Johns	d			07 40						07 50						08 00								08 12	
New Cross 4 ⊖	d	07 38		07 42						07 53				07 58		08 02								08 14	
Nunhead 4	d						07 51														08 11				
Peckham Rye 4	d						07 54														08 13				
Denmark Hill 4	d						07 59														08 17				
London Victoria 15 ⊖	a						08 11														08 29				
Westcombe Park	d		07 32						07 42						07 52								08 02		
Maze Hill	d		07 34						07 44						07 54								08 04		
Greenwich 4	d		07 37						07 47			07 51			07 57								08 07		
Deptford	a		07 39						07 49						07 59								08 09		
London Bridge 4 ⊖	a	07 43	07 45	07 47	07 47	07 51			07 57	08 01	08 00	07 57	07 59	08 03	08 05	08 08	08 05					08 13	08 16	08 20	08 20
London Cannon Street 4 ⊖	a	07 50	07 52	07 54		07 57				08 08		08 04	08 06	08 10	08 12	08 15								08 28	
London Waterloo (East) 4 ⊖	a				07 52				08 02		08 06						08 10			08 12		08 18	08 22		08 26
London Charing Cross 4 ⊖	a				07 58				08 08		08 12						08 16			08 18		08 24	08 28		08 32
Ebbsfleet International	a																		07 25						
Stratford International ⊖	a																		07 37						
St Pancras Int'l 15 ⊖	a																		07 44						

		SE	SE		SE	SE	SE	SE	SE	SE	SE	SE	SE		SE	SE	SE	SE	SE	SE	SE	SE	SE		SE
								1														1	1		
Gillingham (Kent) 4	d						07 12	07 19													07 38	07 46	08 04		
Chatham 4	d						07 16	07 24													07 42	07 50	08 08		
Rochester 4	d						07 18														07 44		08 11		
Maidstone West	d																07 26								
Strood 4	d	07 18					07 23										07 42				07 49				
Higham	d	07 23					07 28														07 54				
Gravesend 4	d	07 31					07 36									07 48	07 52				08 02				
Northfleet	d						07 40									07 52									
Swanscombe	d						07 42									07 54									
Greenhithe for Bluewater	d	07 37					07 45									07 57					08 08				
Stone Crossing	d						07 47									07 59									
Dartford 4	a	07 42					07 51									08 03					08 12				
	d	07 43			07 45		07 52			07 56					08 02	08 04			08 06		08 13				
Slade Green 4	d				07 50							07 59							08 10						08 17
Erith	d				07 52							08 02							08 13						
Belvedere	d				07 55							08 04							08 15						
Abbey Wood	d	07 52			07 58							08 08				08 14			08 18						
Plumstead	d				08 01							08 11							08 21						
Woolwich Arsenal 4	d	07 57			08 05							08 14				08 19			08 24						
Woolwich Dockyard	d				08 07							08 16							08 27						
Charlton 4	d	08 02			08 11							08 20				08 24			08 30						
Crayford	d					07 50	07 56													08 10	08 17				
Bexley	d					07 53	07 59													08 13	08 20				
Albany Park	d					07 56	08 02													08 16	08 23				
Sidcup 4	d					07 59	08 05				08 11									08 19	08 26				
New Eltham	d					08 03	08 09				08 14									08 23	08 30				
Mottingham	d					08 05					08 16									08 25					
Lee	d					08 08					08 19									08 28					
Hither Green 4	d					08 12					08 22									08 32					
Barnehurst 4	d		07 53						07 58	08 04					08 09			08 13							08 24
Bexleyheath	d		07 56						08 01	08 06					08 11			08 16							08 27
Welling	d		07 59						08 04	08 09					08 14			08 19							08 30
Falconwood	d		08 01						08 06	08 12					08 17			08 21							08 32
Eltham	d		08 04						08 09	08 15					08 20			08 24							08 35
Kidbrooke	d		08 07						08 12	08 18					08 23			08 27							08 38
Blackheath 4	d		08 11						08 17	08 22					08 27			08 31							08 42
Lewisham 4	d		08 15			08 17				08 25			08 28		08 31			08 35		08 37					08 46
St Johns	d					08 21							08 30							08 40					
New Cross 4 ⊖	d		08 18			08 23							08 32					08 38		08 42					
Nunhead 4	d									08 30															08 52
Peckham Rye 4	d									08 33															08 55
Denmark Hill 4	d									08 36															09 02
London Victoria 15 ⊖	a									08 49															09 11
Westcombe Park	d				08 13							08 22							08 32						
Maze Hill	d				08 15							08 24							08 34						
Greenwich 4	d	08 11			08 19							08 27				08 31			08 37						
Deptford	a				08 21							08 29							08 39						
London Bridge 4 ⊖	a	08 17	08 25		08 27	08 29	08 25	08 10			08 33	08 37	08 41		08 40	08 38		08 43	08 45	08 49	08 45	08 32	08 49		
London Cannon Street 4 ⊖	a	08 24	08 32		08 35	08 36		08 19					08 48			08 44		08 50	08 52	08 55		08 40	08 57		
London Waterloo (East) 4 ⊖	a						08 30		08 32		08 38	08 42			08 46						08 50				
London Charing Cross 4 ⊖	a						08 36		08 39		08 44	08 48			08 52						08 56				
Ebbsfleet International	a																								
Stratford International ⊖	a																08 06								
St Pancras Int'l 15 ⊖	a																08 13								

Table 200

Gillingham and Dartford - London

Mondays to Fridays

		SE	SE	SE	SE	SE	SE	SE	SE		SE	SE	SE	SE	SE	SE	SE	SE	SE [1]		SE	SE	SE	SE	SE
Gillingham (Kent) [4]	d																08 08	08 19	08 24						
Chatham [4]	d																08 12	08 24	08 28						
Rochester [4]	d																08 14	08 26	08 31						
Maidstone West	d											07 56													
Strood [4]	d								07 58		07 58	08 12					08 19	08 32							
Higham	d								08 03		08 03						08 24								
Gravesend [4]	d						08 06		08c17		08c17	08 22					08 33	08 43							
Northfleet	d						08 10										08 37								
Swanscombe	d						08 12										08 39								
Greenhithe for Bluewater	d						08 15		08 23		08 24						08 42								
Stone Crossing	d						08 17										08 44								
Dartford [4]	a						08 21		08 27		08 29						08 49								
	d						08 22	08 24	08 29		08 31					08 38	08 49						08 52		
Slade Green [4]	d		08 17				08 27						08 31								08 39				
Erith	d		08 19										08 33								08 41				
Belvedere	d		08 22										08 36								08 44				
Abbey Wood	d		08 25				08 34						08 39								08 47				
Plumstead	d		08 28										08 42								08 50				
Woolwich Arsenal [4] ⛴	d		08 31				08 40						08 45								08 53				
Woolwich Dockyard	d		08 34										08 47								08 56				
Charlton [4]	d		08 37			08 37	08 45						08 50								08 59				09 07
Crayford	d				08 28	09b07			08 34		08 36						08 54								09 37
Bexley	d				08 31	09 10			08 37		08 39						08 57								09 40
Albany Park	d				08 34	09 13			08 40		08 41						09 00								09 43
Sidcup [4]	d	08 31			08 37	09 16			08 43		08 44						09 03								09 46
New Eltham	d	08 34			08 41	09 19			08 46		08 47						09 06								09 49
Mottingham	d	08 36			08 43	09 21			08 49		08 50						09 08								09 51
Lee	d	08 39			08 46	09 24			08 52		08 53						09 11								09 54
Hither Green [4]	d	08 42			08 50	09 28			08 55		08 55				08 59		09 14							09 19	09 58
Barnehurst [4]	d							08 30						08 37		08 45							08 59		
Bexleyheath	d							08 33						08 40		08 47							09 01		
Welling	d							08 36						08 43		08 50							09 04		
Falconwood	d							08 38						08 45		08 53							09 07		
Eltham	d							08 41						08 48		08 56							09 10		
Kidbrooke	d							08 44						08 51		08 59							09 13		
Blackheath [4]	d							08 48						08 55		09 02							09 16		
Lewisham [4] ⛴	d			08 48	08 55	09 34		08 52						08 59	09 04	09 06						09 15	09 20	09 24	10 04
St Johns	d			08 50	08 57	09 36								09 01	09 07							09 17		09 26	10 06
New Cross [4] ⊖	d			08 52	08 59	09 38								09 03	09 09							09 19		09 28	10 08
Nunhead [4]	d															09 11									
Peckham Rye [4]	d															09 14									
Denmark Hill [4]	d															09 17									
London Victoria [15] ⊖	a															09 29									
Westcombe Park	d		08 39										08 52								09 01				
Maze Hill	d		08 41										08 54								09 03				
Greenwich [4] ⛴	d		08 45				08 51						08 58								09 07				
Deptford	a		08 47										09 00								09 09				
London Bridge [4] ⊖	a	08 52	08 56	08 57	09 05	09 44	09 00	09 00	09 05		09 05		09 07	09 09	09 17		09 23		09 11		09 17	09 25	09 29	09 33	10 14
London Cannon Street [4] ⊖	a			09 04	09 12	09 51	09 08						09 14	09 18	09 23				09 18			09 32		09 40	10 19
London Waterloo (East) [4] ⊖	a	08 58	09 02					09 05	09 10		09 10						09 28				09 22		09 34		
London Charing Cross [4] ⊖	a	09 04	09 08					09 12	09 16		09 16						09 34				09 28		09 40		
Ebbsfleet International	a											08 26						08 47							
Stratford International ⊖ ⛴	a											08 36						08 59							
St Pancras Int'l [15] ⊖	a											08 43						09 07							

		SE	SE	SE	SE		SE	SE	SE	SE	SE	SE	SE	SE	SE		SE	SE	SE	SE	SE	SE	SE	SE	SE
Gillingham (Kent) [4]	d									08 50							08 54						09 20		
Chatham [4]	d									08 54							08 58						09 24		
Rochester [4]	d									08 57							09 00						09 27		
Maidstone West	d																								
Strood [4]	d									09 02							09 05						09 32		
Higham	d																09 10								
Gravesend [4]	d		08 48						09 02	09 13							09 18					09 32	09 43		
Northfleet	d								09 06													09 36			
Swanscombe	d								09 08													09 38			
Greenhithe for Bluewater	d		08 53						09 11								09 22					09 41			
Stone Crossing	d								09 13													09 43			
Dartford [4]	a		08 58						09 17								09 27					09 47			
	d		08 58		09 01		09 08		09 18			09 22					09 28		09 31	09 38		09 48			09 52
Slade Green [4]	d	08 54			09 05			09 15							09 25				09 35		09 45				
Erith	d	08 56			09 08			09 18							09 28				09 38		09 48				
Belvedere	d	08 59			09 10			09 20							09 30				09 40		09 50				
Abbey Wood	d	09 02	09 07		09 13			09 23							09 33		09 37		09 43		09 53				
Plumstead	d	09 05			09 16			09 26							09 36				09 46		09 56				
Woolwich Arsenal [4] ⛴	d	09 08	09 12		09 19			09 29							09 39		09 43		09 49		09 59				
Woolwich Dockyard	d	09 10			09 22			09 32							09 42				09 52		10 02				
Charlton [4]	d	09 13	09 17		09 25			09 35						09 40	09 45		09 47		09 55		10 05				
Crayford	d								09 22					10 07								09 52			
Bexley	d								09 25					10 10								09 55			
Albany Park	d								09 28					10 13								09 58			
Sidcup [4]	d								09 31					10 16								10 01			
New Eltham	d								09 34					10 19								10 04			
Mottingham	d								09 36					10 21								10 06			
Lee	d								09 39					10 24								10 09			
Hither Green [4]	d								09 42				09 49	10 28								10 12			
Barnehurst [4]	d			09 08			09 16					09 29						09 38		09 46					09 59
Bexleyheath	d			09 10			09 19					09 31						09 40		09 49					10 01
Welling	d			09 13			09 22					09 34						09 43		09 52					10 04
Falconwood	d			09 16			09 24					09 37						09 46		09 54					10 07
Eltham	d			09 19			09 27					09 40						09 49		09 57					10 10
Kidbrooke	d			09 22			09 30					09 43						09 52		10 00					10 13
Blackheath [4]	d		09 21	09 25			09 34					09 46					09 52	09 55		10 04					10 16
Lewisham [4] ⛴	d		09 26	09 29			09 38				09 45	09 50	09 54	10 34			09 56	09 59		10 08				10 14	10 20
St Johns	d			09 31							09 47		09 56	10 36				10 01						10 16	
New Cross [4] ⊖	d			09 33							09 49		09 58	10 38				10 03						10 18	
Nunhead [4]	d						09 43													10 13					
Peckham Rye [4]	d						09 45													10 15					
Denmark Hill [4]	d						09 49													10 19					
London Victoria [15] ⊖	a						10 00													10 28					
Westcombe Park	d	09 15			09 27			09 37							09 47				09 57		10 07				
Maze Hill	d	09 17			09 29			09 39							09 49				09 59		10 09				
Greenwich [4] ⛴	d	09 21			09 32			09 42							09 52				10 02		10 12				
Deptford	a	09 23			09 34			09 44							09 54				10 04		10 14				
London Bridge [4] ⊖	a	09 29	09 34	09 38	09 41			09 50	09 52		09 54	09 58	10 04	10 44	10 00		10 05	10 08	10 11		10 20	10 22		10 24	10 28
London Cannon Street [4] ⊖	a	09 36		09 45	09 48			09 57			10 00		10 08	10 50	10 04			10 13	10 15		10 24			10 28	
London Waterloo (East) [4] ⊖	a		09 39						09 56			10 02					10 09					10 26			10 32
London Charing Cross [4] ⊖	a		09 45						10 00			10 06					10 13					10 30			10 36
Ebbsfleet International	a									09 17													09 47		
Stratford International ⊖ ⛴	a									09 29													09 59		
St Pancras Int'l [15] ⊖	a									09 40													10 06		

Gillingham and Dartford - London

			SE	SE	SE	SE	SE	SE	SE	SE	SE		SE	SE	SE	SE	SE	SE	SE	SE	SE		SE	SE	SE
Gillingham (Kent) 4	d					09 24							09 50						09 54						
Chatham 4	d					09 28							09 54						09 58						
Rochester 4	d					09 30							09 57						10 00						
Maidstone West	d																								
Strood 4	d					09 35							10 02						10 05						
Higham	d					09 40													10 10						
Gravesend 4	d					09 48					10 02		10 12						10 18						10 32
Northfleet	d										10 06														10 36
Swanscombe	d										10 08														10 38
Greenhithe for Bluewater	d					09 53					10 11								10 23						10 41
Stone Crossing	d										10 13														10 43
Dartford 4	a					09 58					10 17								10 28						10 47
	d					09 59		10 01	10 08		10 18				10 22				10 29		10 31		10 38		10 48
Slade Green 4	d				09 55			10 05		10 15								10 25			10 35			10 45	
Erith	d				09 58			10 08		10 18								10 28			10 38			10 48	
Belvedere	d				10 00			10 10		10 20								10 30			10 40			10 50	
Abbey Wood	d				10 03	10 07		10 13		10 23								10 33	10 38		10 43			10 53	
Plumstead	d				10 06			10 16		10 26								10 36			10 46			10 56	
Woolwich Arsenal 4	d				10 09	10 12		10 19		10 29								10 39	10 43		10 49			10 59	
Woolwich Dockyard	d				10 12			10 22		10 32								10 42			10 52			11 02	
Charlton 4	d			10 07	10 15	10 17		10 25		10 35							10 37	10 45	10 47		10 55			11 05	
Crayford	d			10 37							10 22						11 07								10 52
Bexley	d			10 40							10 25						11 10								10 55
Albany Park	d			10 43							10 28						11 13								10 58
Sidcup 4	d			10 46							10 31						11 16								11 01
New Eltham	d			10 49							10 34						11 19								11 04
Mottingham	d			10 51							10 36						11 21								11 06
Lee	d			10 54							10 39						11 24								11 09
Hither Green 4	d		10 19	10 58							10 42					10 49	11 28								11 12
Barnehurst 4	d						10 08		10 16						10 29					10 38			10 46		
Bexleyheath	d						10 10		10 19						10 31					10 40			10 49		
Welling	d						10 13		10 22						10 34					10 43			10 52		
Falconwood	d						10 16		10 24						10 37					10 46			10 54		
Eltham	d						10 19		10 27						10 40					10 49			10 57		
Kidbrooke	d						10 22		10 30						10 43					10 52			11 00		
Blackheath 4	d					10 21	10 25		10 34						10 46				10 52	10 55			11 04		
Lewisham 4	d		10 24	11 04		10 26	10 29		10 38					10 44	10 50	10 54	11 34		10 56	10 59			11 08		
St Johns	d		10 26	11 06			10 31							10 46		10 56	11 36			11 01					
New Cross 4 ⊖	d		10 28	11 08			10 33							10 48		10 58	11 38			11 03					
Nunhead 4	d								10 43														11 13		
Peckham Rye 4	d								10 45														11 15		
Denmark Hill 4	d								10 49														11 19		
London Victoria 15 ⊖	a								10 58														11 28		
Westcombe Park	d				10 17			10 27		10 37								10 47			10 57			11 07	
Maze Hill	d				10 19			10 29		10 39								10 49			10 59			11 09	
Greenwich 4	d				10 22			10 32		10 42								10 52			11 02			11 12	
Deptford	a				10 24			10 34		10 44								10 54			11 04			11 14	
London Bridge 4 ⊖	a		10 34	11 14	10 30	10 35	10 38	10 41		10 50	10 52			10 54	10 58	11 04	11 44	11 00	11 05	11 08	11 11			11 20	11 22
London Cannon Street 4 ⊖	a		10 38	11 19	10 36		10 43	10 45		10 54				10 58		11 08	11 49	11 06		11 13	11 15			11 24	
London Waterloo (East) 4 ⊖	a					10 39					10 56				11 02				11 09						11 26
London Charing Cross 4 ⊖	a					10 43					11 00				11 06				11 13						11 30
Ebbsfleet International	a												10 16												
Stratford International ⊖	a												10 27												
St Pancras Int'l 15 ⊖	a												10 38												

		SE	SE	SE	SE	SE	SE		SE	SE	SE	SE	SE	SE	SE	SE	SE		SE	SE	SE	SE	SE	SE	SE
Gillingham (Kent) 4	d	10 20							10 24						10 50						10 54			
Chatham 4	d	10 24							10 28						10 54						10 58			
Rochester 4	d	10 27							10 30						10 57						11 00			
Maidstone West	d																								
Strood 4	d	10 32							10 35						11 02						11 05			
Higham	d								10 40												11 10			
Gravesend 4	d	10 43							10 48					11 02	11 13						11 18			
Northfleet	d													11 06											
Swanscombe	d													11 08											
Greenhithe for Bluewater	d								10 53					11 11							11 23			
Stone Crossing	d													11 13											
Dartford 4	a								10 58					11 17							11 28			
	d			10 52					10 59		11 01	11 08		11 18			11 22					11 29		11 31	11 38
Slade Green 4	d						10 55				11 05		11 15								11 25			11 35	
Erith	d						10 58				11 08		11 18								11 28			11 38	
Belvedere	d						11 00				11 10		11 20								11 30			11 40	
Abbey Wood	d						11 03		11 08		11 13		11 23								11 33	11 38		11 43	
Plumstead	d						11 06				11 16		11 26								11 36			11 46	
Woolwich Arsenal 4	d						11 09		11 13		11 19		11 29								11 39	11 43		11 49	
Woolwich Dockyard	d						11 12				11 22		11 32								11 42			11 52	
Charlton 4	d					11 07	11 15		11 17		11 25		11 35							11 37	11 45	11 47		11 55	
Crayford	d					11 37								11 22						12b07					
Bexley	d					11 40								11 25						12 10					
Albany Park	d					11 43								11 28						12 13					
Sidcup 4	d					11 46								11 31						12 16					
New Eltham	d					11 49								11 34						12 19					
Mottingham	d					11 51								11 36						12 21					
Lee	d					11 54								11 39						12 24					
Hither Green 4	d				11 19	11 58								11 42					11 49	12 28					
Barnehurst 4	d			10 59						11 08		11 16					11 29						11 38		11 46
Bexleyheath	d			11 01						11 10		11 19					11 31						11 40		11 49
Welling	d			11 04						11 13		11 22					11 34						11 43		11 52
Falconwood	d			11 07						11 16		11 24					11 37						11 46		11 54
Eltham	d			11 10						11 19		11 27					11 40						11 49		11 57
Kidbrooke	d			11 13						11 22		11 30					11 43						11 52		12 00
Blackheath 4	d			11 16					11 22	11 25		11 34					11 46					11 52	11 55		12 04
Lewisham 4	d		11 14	11 20	11 24	12 04			11 26	11 29		11 38				11 44	11 50		11 54	12 34		11 56	11 59		12 08
St Johns	d		11 16		11 26	12 06				11 31						11 46			11 56	12 36			12 01		
New Cross 4 ⊖	d		11 18		11 28	12 08				11 33						11 48			11 58	12 38			12 03		
Nunhead 4	d											11 43													12 13
Peckham Rye 4	d											11 45													12 15
Denmark Hill 4	d											11 49													12 19
London Victoria 15 ⊖	a											11 58													12 28
Westcombe Park	d						11 17				11 27		11 37								11 47			11 57	
Maze Hill	d						11 19				11 29		11 39								11 49			11 59	
Greenwich 4	d						11 22				11 32		11 42								11 52			12 02	
Deptford	a						11 24				11 34		11 44								11 54			12 04	
London Bridge 4 ⊖	a		11 24	11 28	11 34	12 14	11 30		11 35	11 38	11 41		11 50	11 52		11 54	11 58		12 04	12 44	12 00	12 05	12 08	12 11	
London Cannon Street 4 ⊖	a		11 28		11 38	12 19	11 36			11 43	11 45		11 54			11 58			12 08	12 49	12 04		12 13	12 15	
London Waterloo (East) 4 ⊖	a			11 32					11 39					11 56			12 02					12 09			
London Charing Cross 4 ⊖	a			11 36					11 43					12 00			12 06					12 13			
Ebbsfleet International	a	10 47													11 17										
Stratford International ⊖	a	10 59													11 29										
St Pancras Int'l 15 ⊖	a	11 06													11 36										

Gillingham and Dartford - London

		SE	SE		SE	SE	SE	SE	SE	SE	SE	SE	SE		SE	SE	SE	SE	SE	SE	SE	SE	SE		SE
Gillingham (Kent) 4	d				11 20						11 24							11 50							11 54
Chatham 4	d				11 24						11 28							11 54							11 58
Rochester 4	d				11 27						11 30							11 57							12 00
Maidstone West	d																								
Strood 4	d				11 32						11 35							12 02							12 05
Higham	d										11 40														12 10
Gravesend 4	d		11 32		11 43						11 48						12 02	12 13							12 18
Northfleet	d		11 36														12 06								
Swanscombe	d		11 38														12 08								
Greenhithe for Bluewater	d		11 41								11 53						12 11								12 23
Stone Crossing	d		11 43														12 13								
Dartford 4	a		11 47								11 58						12 17								12 28
	d		11 48				11 52				11 59		12 01		12 08		12 18		12 22						12 29
Slade Green 4	d	11 45								11 55			12 05			12 15							12 25		
Erith	d	11 48								11 58			12 08			12 18							12 28		
Belvedere	d	11 50								12 00			12 10			12 20							12 30		
Abbey Wood	d	11 53								12 03	12 08		12 13			12 23							12 33		12 38
Plumstead	d	11 56								12 06			12 16			12 26							12 36		
Woolwich Arsenal 4	d	11 59								12 09	12 13		12 19			12 29							12 39		12 43
Woolwich Dockyard	d	12 02								12 12			12 22			12 32							12 42		
Charlton 4	d	12 05							12 07	12 15	12 17		12 25			12 35						12 37	12 45		12 47
Crayford	d		11 52						12 37								12 22					13 07			
Bexley	d		11 55						12 40								12 25					13 10			
Albany Park	d		11 58						12 43								12 28					13 13			
Sidcup 4	d		12 01						12 46								12 31					13 16			
New Eltham	d		12 04						12 49								12 34					13 19			
Mottingham	d		12 06						12 51								12 36					13 21			
Lee	d		12 09						12 54								12 39					13 24			
Hither Green 4	d		12 12					12 19	12 58								12 42				12 49	13 28			
Barnehurst 4	d						11 59					12 08			12 16				12 29						
Bexleyheath	d						12 01					12 10			12 19				12 31						
Welling	d						12 04					12 13			12 22				12 34						
Falconwood	d						12 07					12 16			12 24				12 37						
Eltham	d						12 10					12 19			12 27				12 40						
Kidbrooke	d						12 13					12 22			12 30				12 43						
Blackheath 4	d						12 16				12 22	12 25			12 34				12 46						12 52
Lewisham 4	d					12 14	12 20	12 24	13 04		12 26	12 29			12 38				12 44	12 50	12 54	13 34			12 56
St Johns	d					12 16		12 26	13 06			12 31							12 46		12 56	13 36			
New Cross 4 ⊖	d					12 18		12 28	13 08			12 33							12 48		12 58	13 38			
Nunhead 4	d														12 43										
Peckham Rye 4	d														12 45										
Denmark Hill 4	d														12 49										
London Victoria 15 ⊖	a														12 58										
Westcombe Park	d	12 07								12 17			12 27			12 37							12 47		
Maze Hill	d	12 09								12 19			12 29			12 39							12 49		
Greenwich 4	d	12 12								12 22			12 32			12 42							12 52		
Deptford	a	12 14								12 24			12 34			12 44							12 54		
London Bridge 4 ⊖	a	12 20	12 22			12 24	12 28	12 34	13 14	12 30	12 35	12 38	12 41			12 50	12 52		12 54	12 58	13 04	13 44	13 00		13 05
London Cannon Street 4 ⊖	a	12 24				12 28		12 38	13 19	12 36		12 43	12 45			12 54			12 58		13 08	13 49	13 06		
London Waterloo (East) 4 ⊖	a		12 26				12 32				12 39						12 56			13 02					13 09
London Charing Cross 4 ⊖	a		12 30				12 36				12 43						13 00			13 06					13 13
Ebbsfleet International	a				11 47													12 17							
Stratford International ⊖	a				11 59													12 32							
St Pancras Int'l 15 ⊖	a				12 06													12 39							

		SE	SE	SE	SE	SE	SE	SE	SE		SE	SE	SE	SE	SE	SE	SE	SE	SE		SE	SE	SE	SE	SE
Gillingham (Kent) 4	d						12 20							12 24							12 50				
Chatham 4	d						12 24							12 28							12 54				
Rochester 4	d						12 27							12 30							12 57				
Maidstone West	d																								
Strood 4	d						12 32							12 35							13 02				
Higham	d													12 40											
Gravesend 4	d					12 32	12 43							12 48					13 02		13 13				
Northfleet	d					12 36													13 06						
Swanscombe	d					12 38													13 08						
Greenhithe for Bluewater	d					12 41								12 53					13 11						
Stone Crossing	d					12 43													13 13						
Dartford 4	a					12 47								12 58					13 17						
	d		12 31	12 38		12 48			12 52					12 59		13 01	13 08		13 18				13 22		
Slade Green 4	d		12 35		12 45								12 55			13 05		13 15							
Erith	d		12 38		12 48								12 58			13 08		13 18							
Belvedere	d		12 40		12 50								13 00			13 10		13 20							
Abbey Wood	d		12 43		12 53								13 03	13 08		13 13		13 23							
Plumstead	d		12 46		12 56								13 06			13 16		13 26							
Woolwich Arsenal 4	d		12 49		12 59								13 09	13 13		13 19		13 29							
Woolwich Dockyard	d		12 52		13 02								13 12			13 22		13 32							
Charlton 4	d		12 55		13 05							13 07	13 15	13 17		13 25		13 35							13 37
Crayford	d					12 52						13 37							13 22						14 07
Bexley	d					12 55						13 40							13 25						14 10
Albany Park	d					12 58						13 43							13 28						14 13
Sidcup 4	d					13 01						13 46							13 31						14 16
New Eltham	d					13 04						13 49							13 34						14 19
Mottingham	d					13 06						13 51							13 36						14 21
Lee	d					13 09						13 54							13 39						14 24
Hither Green 4	d					13 12					13 19	13 58							13 42					13 49	14 28
Barnehurst 4	d	12 38		12 46					12 59						13 08		13 16						13 29		
Bexleyheath	d	12 40		12 49					13 01						13 10		13 19						13 31		
Welling	d	12 43		12 52					13 04						13 13		13 22						13 34		
Falconwood	d	12 46		12 54					13 07						13 16		13 24						13 37		
Eltham	d	12 49		12 57					13 10						13 19		13 27						13 40		
Kidbrooke	d	12 52		13 00					13 13						13 22		13 30						13 43		
Blackheath 4	d	12 55		13 04					13 16					13 22	13 25		13 34						13 46		
Lewisham 4	d	12 59		13 08				13 14	13 20		13 24	14 04		13 26	13 29		13 38					13 44	13 50	13 54	14 34
St Johns	d	13 01						13 16			13 26	14 06			13 31							13 46		13 56	14 36
New Cross 4 ⊖	d	13 03						13 18			13 28	14 08			13 33							13 48		13 58	14 38
Nunhead 4	d			13 13													13 43								
Peckham Rye 4	d			13 15													13 45								
Denmark Hill 4	d			13 19													13 49								
London Victoria 15 ⊖	a			13 28													13 58								
Westcombe Park	d		12 57		13 07								13 17			13 27		13 37							
Maze Hill	d		12 59		13 09								13 19			13 29		13 39							
Greenwich 4	d		13 02		13 12								13 22			13 32		13 42							
Deptford	a		13 04		13 14								13 24			13 34		13 44							
London Bridge 4 ⊖	a	13 08	13 11		13 20	13 22		13 24	13 28		13 34	14 14	13 30	13 35	13 38	13 41		13 50	13 52			13 54	13 58	14 04	14 44
London Cannon Street 4 ⊖	a	13 13	13 15		13 24			13 28			13 38	14 19	13 36		13 43	13 45		13 54				13 58		14 08	14 49
London Waterloo (East) 4 ⊖	a					13 26			13 32					13 39					13 56				14 02		
London Charing Cross 4 ⊖	a					13 30			13 36					13 43					14 00				14 06		
Ebbsfleet International	a						12 47														13 17				
Stratford International ⊖	a						12 59														13 32				
St Pancras Int'l 15 ⊖	a						13 06														13 39				

Gillingham and Dartford - London

Station		SE	SE	SE	SE		SE	SE	SE	SE	SE	SE	SE	SE	SE		SE	SE	SE	SE	SE	SE	SE	SE	SE
Gillingham (Kent) 4	d		12 54							13 20							13 24						13 50		
Chatham 4	d		12 58							13 24							13 28						13 54		
Rochester 4	d		13 00							13 27							13 30						13 57		
Maidstone West	d																								
Strood 4	d		13 05							13 32							13 35						14 02		
Higham	d		13 10														13 40								
Gravesend 4	d		13 18						13 32	13 43							13 48					14 02	14 13		
Northfleet	d								13 36													14 06			
Swanscombe	d								13 38													14 08			
Greenhithe for Bluewater	d		13 23						13 41								13 53					14 11			
Stone Crossing	d								13 43													14 13			
Dartford 4	a		13 28						13 47								13 58					14 17			
	d		13 29		13 31		13 38		13 48			13 52					13 59		14 01	14 08		14 18			14 22
Slade Green 4	d	13 25			13 35			13 45							13 55				14 05		14 15				
Erith	d	13 28			13 38			13 48							13 58				14 08		14 18				
Belvedere	d	13 30			13 40			13 50							14 00				14 10		14 20				
Abbey Wood	d	13 33	13 38		13 43			13 53							14 03		14 08		14 13		14 23				
Plumstead	d	13 36			13 46			13 56							14 06				14 16		14 26				
Woolwich Arsenal 4 ⛴	d	13 39	13 43		13 49			13 59							14 09		14 13		14 19		14 29				
Woolwich Dockyard	d	13 42			13 52			14 02							14 12				14 22		14 32				
Charlton 4	d	13 45	13 47		13 55			14 05						14 07	14 15		14 17		14 25		14 35				
Crayford	d								13 52					14 37								14 22			
Bexley	d								13 55					14 40								14 25			
Albany Park	d								13 58					14 43								14 28			
Sidcup 4	d								14 01					14 46								14 31			
New Eltham	d								14 04					14 49								14 34			
Mottingham	d								14 06					14 51								14 36			
Lee	d								14 09					14 54								14 39			
Hither Green 4	d								14 12				14 19	14 58								14 42			
Barnehurst 4	d			13 38			13 46					13 59						14 08		14 16					14 29
Bexleyheath	d			13 40			13 49					14 01						14 10		14 19					14 31
Welling	d			13 43			13 52					14 04						14 13		14 22					14 34
Falconwood	d			13 46			13 54					14 07						14 16		14 24					14 37
Eltham	d			13 49			13 57					14 10						14 19		14 27					14 40
Kidbrooke	d			13 52			14 00					14 13						14 22		14 30					14 43
Blackheath 4	d		13 52	13 55			14 04					14 16					14 22	14 25		14 34					14 46
Lewisham 4 ⛴	d		13 56	13 59			14 08				14 14	14 20	14 24	15 04			14 26	14 29		14 38				14 44	14 50
St Johns	d			14 01							14 16		14 26	15 06				14 31						14 46	
New Cross 4 ⊖	d			14 03							14 18		14 28	15 08				14 33						14 48	
Nunhead 4	d						14 13													14 43					
Peckham Rye 4	d						14 15													14 45					
Denmark Hill 4	d						14 19													14 49					
London Victoria 15 ⊖	a						14 28													14 58					
Westcombe Park	d	13 47			13 57			14 07							14 17				14 27		14 37				
Maze Hill	d	13 49			13 59			14 09							14 19				14 29		14 39				
Greenwich 4 ⛴	d	13 52			14 02			14 12							14 22				14 32		14 42				
Deptford	a	13 54			14 04			14 14							14 24				14 34		14 44				
London Bridge 4 ⊖	a	14 00	14 05	14 08	14 11			14 20	14 22		14 24	14 28	14 34	15 14	14 30		14 35	14 38	14 41		14 50	14 52		14 54	14 58
London Cannon Street 4 ⊖	a	14 06		14 13	14 15			14 24			14 28		14 38	15 19	14 36			14 43	14 45		14 54			14 58	
London Waterloo (East) 4 ⊖	a		14 09						14 26			14 32					14 39					14 56			15 02
London Charing Cross 4 ⊖	a		14 13						14 30			14 36					14 43					15 00			15 06
Ebbsfleet International	a									13 47													14 17		
Stratford International ⊖ ⛴	a									13 59													14 29		
St Pancras Int'l 15 ⊖	a									14 06													14 40		

Station			SE	SE	SE	SE	SE	SE	SE	SE	SE		SE	SE	SE	SE	SE	SE	SE	SE	SE		SE	SE	SE
Gillingham (Kent) 4	d					13 54							14 20						14 24						
Chatham 4	d					13 58							14 24						14 28						
Rochester 4	d					14 00							14 27						14 30						
Maidstone West	d																								
Strood 4	d					14 05							14 32						14 35						
Higham	d					14 10													14 40						
Gravesend 4	d					14 18					14 32		14 43						14 48						15 02
Northfleet	d										14 36														15 06
Swanscombe	d										14 38														15 08
Greenhithe for Bluewater	d					14 23					14 41								14 53						15 11
Stone Crossing	d										14 43														15 13
Dartford 4	a					14 28					14 47								14 58						15 17
	d					14 29		14 31	14 38		14 48				14 52				14 59		15 01		15 08		15 18
Slade Green 4	d				14 25			14 35		14 45								14 55			15 05			15 15	
Erith	d				14 28			14 38		14 48								14 58			15 08			15 18	
Belvedere	d				14 30			14 40		14 50								15 00			15 10			15 20	
Abbey Wood	d				14 33	14 38		14 43		14 53								15 03	15 08		15 13			15 23	
Plumstead	d				14 36			14 46		14 56								15 06			15 16			15 26	
Woolwich Arsenal 4 ⛴	d				14 39	14 43		14 49		14 59								15 09	15 13		15 19			15 29	
Woolwich Dockyard	d				14 42			14 52		15 02								15 12			15 22			15 32	
Charlton 4	d			14 37	14 45	14 47		14 55		15 05							15 07	15 15	15 17		15 25			15 35	
Crayford	d			15 07							14 52						15 37								15 22
Bexley	d			15 10							14 55						15 40								15 25
Albany Park	d			15 13							14 58						15 43								15 28
Sidcup 4	d			15 16							15 01						15 46								15 31
New Eltham	d			15 19							15 04						15 49								15 34
Mottingham	d			15 21							15 06						15 51								15 36
Lee	d			15 24							15 09						15 54								15 39
Hither Green 4	d		14 49	15 28							15 12					15 19	15 58								15 42
Barnehurst 4	d						14 38		14 46						14 59					15 08			15 16		
Bexleyheath	d						14 40		14 49						15 01					15 10			15 19		
Welling	d						14 43		14 52						15 04					15 13			15 22		
Falconwood	d						14 46		14 54						15 07					15 16			15 24		
Eltham	d						14 49		14 57						15 10					15 19			15 27		
Kidbrooke	d						14 52		15 00						15 13					15 22			15 30		
Blackheath 4	d					14 52	14 55		15 04						15 16				15 22	15 25			15 34		
Lewisham 4 ⛴	d		14 54	15 34		14 56	14 59		15 08					15 14	15 20	15 24	16 04		15 26	15 29			15 38		
St Johns	d		14 56	15 36			15 01							15 16		15 26	16 06			15 31					
New Cross 4 ⊖	d		14 58	15 38			15 03							15 18		15 28	16 08			15 33					
Nunhead 4	d								15 13														15 43		
Peckham Rye 4	d								15 15														15 45		
Denmark Hill 4	d								15 19														15 49		
London Victoria 15 ⊖	a								15 28														15 58		
Westcombe Park	d				14 47			14 57		15 07								15 17			15 27			15 37	
Maze Hill	d				14 49			14 59		15 09								15 19			15 29			15 39	
Greenwich 4 ⛴	d				14 52			15 02		15 12								15 22			15 32			15 42	
Deptford	a				14 54			15 04		15 14								15 24			15 34			15 44	
London Bridge 4 ⊖	a		15 04	15 44	15 00	15 05	15 08	15 11		15 20	15 22			15 24	15 28	15 34	16 15	15 30	15 35	15 38	15 41			15 50	15 52
London Cannon Street 4 ⊖	a		15 08	15 49	15 06		15 13	15 15		15 24				15 28		15 38	16 19	15 36		15 43	15 45			15 54	
London Waterloo (East) 4 ⊖	a					15 09					15 26				15 32				15 39						15 57
London Charing Cross 4 ⊖	a					15 13					15 30				15 36				15 43						16 01
Ebbsfleet International	a												14 47												
Stratford International ⊖ ⛴	a												14 59												
St Pancras Int'l 15 ⊖	a												15 06												

Table 200

Mondays to Fridays

Gillingham and Dartford - London

		SE	SE	SE	SE	SE	SE		SE	SE	SE	SE	SE	SE	SE	SE	SE		SE	SE	SE	SE	SE	SE	SE
Gillingham (Kent) 4	d	14 50							14 54						15 20							15 24			
Chatham 4	d	14 54							14 58						15 24							15 28			
Rochester 4	d	14 57							15 00						15 27							15 30			
Maidstone West	d																								
Strood 4	d	15 02							15 05						15 32							15 35			
Higham	d								15 10													15 40			
Gravesend 4	d	15 13							15 18					15 32	15 43							15 48			
Northfleet	d													15 36											
Swanscombe	d													15 38											
Greenhithe for Bluewater	d								15 23					15 41								15 53			
Stone Crossing	d													15 43											
Dartford 4	a								15 28					15 47								15 58			
	d			15 22					15 29		15 31	15 38		15 48			15 52					15 59		16 01	16 08
Slade Green 4	d						15 25				15 35		15 45								15 55			16 05	
Erith	d						15 28				15 38		15 48								15 58			16 08	
Belvedere	d						15 30				15 40		15 50								16 00			16 10	
Abbey Wood	d						15 33		15 38		15 43		15 53								16 03	16 08		16 13	
Plumstead	d						15 36				15 46		15 56								16 06			16 16	
Woolwich Arsenal 4	d						15 39		15 43		15 49		15 59								16 09	16 13		16 19	
Woolwich Dockyard	d						15 42				15 52		16 02								16 12			16 22	
Charlton 4	d					15 37	15 45		15 47		15 55		16 05							16 07	16 15	16 17		16 25	
Crayford	d					16 07								15 52						16 37					
Bexley	d					16 10								15 55						16 40					
Albany Park	d					16 13								15 58						16 43					
Sidcup 4	d					16 16								16 01						16 46					
New Eltham	d					16 19								16 04						16 49					
Mottingham	d					16 21								16 06						16 51					
Lee	d					16 24								16 09						16 54					
Hither Green 4	d				15 49	16 28								16 12					16 19	17 00					
Barnehurst 4	d			15 29						15 38		15 46					15 59						16 08		16 16
Bexleyheath	d			15 31						15 40		15 49					16 01						16 10		16 19
Welling	d			15 34						15 43		15 52					16 04						16 13		16 22
Falconwood	d			15 37						15 46		15 54					16 07						16 16		16 24
Eltham	d			15 40						15 49		15 57					16 10						16 19		16 27
Kidbrooke	d			15 43						15 52		16 00					16 13						16 22		16 30
Blackheath 4	d			15 46					15 52	15 55		16 04					16 16					16 22	16 25		16 34
Lewisham 4	d		15 44	15 50	15 54	16 34			15 56	15 59		16 08				16 14	16 20		16 24	17 05		16 26	16 29		16 38
St Johns	d		15 46		15 56	16 36				16 01						16 16			16 26	17 09			16 31		
New Cross 4	d		15 48		15 58	16 38				16 03						16 18			16 28	17 11			16 33		
Nunhead 4	d											16 13													16 43
Peckham Rye 4	d											16 15													16 45
Denmark Hill 4	d											16 19													16 49
London Victoria 15	a											16 28													17 01
Westcombe Park	d						15 47				15 57		16 07								16 17			16 27	
Maze Hill	d						15 49				15 59		16 09								16 19			16 29	
Greenwich 4	d						15 52				16 02		16 12								16 22			16 32	
Deptford	a						15 54				16 04		16 14								16 24			16 34	
London Bridge 4	a		15 54	15 58	16 04	16 44	16 00		16 05	16 09	16 12		16 20	16 22		16 24	16 29		16 34	17 18	16 30	16 35	16 39	16 42	
London Cannon Street 4	a		15 58		16 08	16 49	16 06			16 13	16 16		16 24			16 28			16 38	17 24	16 36		16 43	16 46	
London Waterloo (East) 4	a			16 02					16 09					16 27			16 33					16 39			
London Charing Cross 4	a			16 06					16 13					16 31			16 37					16 44			
Ebbsfleet International	a	15 17													15 47										
Stratford International	a	15 29													15 59										
St Pancras Int'l 15	a	15 36													16 06										

		SE	SE		SE	SE	SE	SE	SE	SE	SE	SE	SE		SE	SE	SE	SE	SE	SE	SE	SE	SE		SE
Gillingham (Kent) 4	d				15 50						15 54									16 20			16 24		
Chatham 4	d				15 54						15 58									16 24			16 28		
Rochester 4	d				15 57						16 00									16 27			16 30		
Maidstone West	d																								
Strood 4	d				16 02						16 05									16 32			16 35		
Higham	d										16 10												16 40		
Gravesend 4	d		16 02		16 13						16 18								16 32	16 43			16 48		
Northfleet	d		16 06																16 36						
Swanscombe	d		16 08																16 38						
Greenhithe for Bluewater	d		16 11								16 23								16 41				16 53		
Stone Crossing	d		16 13																16 43						
Dartford 4	a		16 17								16 28								16 48				16 58		
	d		16 18				16 22				16 29		16 31		16 38	16 42			16 52				16 59		
Slade Green 4	d	16 15								16 25			16 35				16 44				16 55				
Erith	d	16 18								16 28			16 38				16 46				16 58				
Belvedere	d	16 20								16 30			16 40				16 49				17 00				
Abbey Wood	d	16 23								16 33	16 38		16 43				16 52				17 03		17 08		
Plumstead	d	16 26								16 36			16 46				16 55				17 06				
Woolwich Arsenal 4	d	16 29								16 39	16 43		16 49				16 58				17 09		17 13		
Woolwich Dockyard	d	16 32								16 42			16 52				17 00				17 12				
Charlton 4	d	16 35							16 37	16 45	16 47		16 55				17 03				17 15		17 17		
Crayford	d		16 22						17 07							16 46									
Bexley	d		16 25						17 10							16 49									
Albany Park	d		16 28						17 13							16 52									
Sidcup 4	d		16 31					16 38	17 16							16 55									
New Eltham	d		16 34					16 41	17 19							16 58									
Mottingham	d		16 36					16 43	17 21							17 00									
Lee	d		16 39					16 46	17 24							17 03									
Hither Green 4	d		16 42					16 50	17 28							17 07						17 19			
Barnehurst 4	d						16 29					16 38			16 46				16 59						17 08
Bexleyheath	d						16 31					16 40			16 49				17 01						17 10
Welling	d						16 34					16 43			16 52				17 04						17 13
Falconwood	d						16 37					16 46			16 54				17 07						17 16
Eltham	d						16 40					16 49			16 57				17 10						17 19
Kidbrooke	d						16 43					16 52			17 00				17 13						17 22
Blackheath 4	d						16 46				16 52	16 55			17 04				17 16				17 22		17 25
Lewisham 4	d					16 44	16 50		17 35		16 56	16 59			17 08			17 14	17 20			17 24	17 27		17 30
St Johns	d					16 46		16 54	17 37			17 01						17 16				17 26			
New Cross 4	d					16 48		16 56	17 39			17 03						17 18				17 28			17 33
Nunhead 4	d														17 13										
Peckham Rye 4	d														17 15										
Denmark Hill 4	d														17 19										
London Victoria 15	a														17 28										
Westcombe Park	d	16 37								16 47			16 57				17 05				17 17				
Maze Hill	d	16 39								16 49			16 59				17 07				17 19				
Greenwich 4	d	16 42								16 52			17 02				17 11				17 22				
Deptford	a	16 44								16 54			17 04				17 13				17 24				
London Bridge 4	a	16 50	16 52			16 54	16 58	17 04	17 45	17 01	17 07	17 09	17 13			17 21	17 21	17 24	17 29		17 31	17 34	17 35		17 39
London Cannon Street 4	a	16 54				16 58		17 09	17 49	17 05	17 11	17 15	17 17				17 26	17 29			17 36	17 38			17 44
London Waterloo (East) 4	a		16 56				17 03									17 28			17 34				17 40		
London Charing Cross 4	a		17 00				17 07									17 33			17 38				17 44		
Ebbsfleet International	a				16 17															16 47					
Stratford International	a				16 28															17 02					
St Pancras Int'l 15	a				16 39															17 09					

Gillingham and Dartford - London

		SE	SE	SE	SE	SE	SE	SE	SE		SE	SE	SE	SE	SE	SE	SE	SE	SE		SE	SE	SE	SE	SE
Gillingham (Kent) 4	d				16 50									16 54							17 20				
Chatham 4	d				16 54									16 58							17 24				
Rochester 4	d				16 57									17 00							17 27				
Maidstone West	d																								
Strood 4	d				17 02									17 05							17 32				
Higham	d													17 10											
Gravesend 4	d			17 02	17 12									17 18					17 32		17 42				
Northfleet	d			17 06															17 36						
Swanscombe	d			17 08															17 38						
Greenhithe for Bluewater	d			17 11										17 23					17 41						
Stone Crossing	d			17 13															17 43						
Dartford 4	a			17 17										17 28					17 47						
	d	17 01	17 08	17 18			17 22							17 28		17 31	17 38		17 48				17 52		
Slade Green 4	d	17 05										17 15	17 25			17 35		17 45						17 55	
Erith	d	17 08										17 18	17 28			17 38		17 48						17 57	
Belvedere	d	17 10										17 20	17 30			17 40		17 50						18 00	
Abbey Wood	d	17 13										17 23	17 33	17 38		17 43		17 53						18 03	
Plumstead	d	17 16										17 26	17 36			17 46		17 56						18 06	
Woolwich Arsenal 4	d	17 19										17 29	17 39	17 43		17 49		17 59						18 09	
Woolwich Dockyard	d	17 22										17 32	17 42			17 52		18 02						18 11	
Charlton 4	d	17 25									17 30	17 35	17 45	17 47		17 55		18 05						18 14	
Crayford	d			17 22					17 37		18 01								17 52						
Bexley	d			17 25					17 40		18 04								17 55						
Albany Park	d			17 28					17 43		18 07								17 58						
Sidcup 4	d			17 31					17 46		18 10								18 01						
New Eltham	d			17 34					17 49		18 13								18 04						
Mottingham	d			17 36					17 51		18 15								18 06						
Lee	d			17 39					17 54		18 18								18 09						
Hither Green 4	d			17 42				17 53	17 58		18 21								18 12						18 19
Barnehurst 4	d		17 16				17 29								17 38		17 46						17 59		
Bexleyheath	d		17 19				17 31								17 40		17 49						18 01		
Welling	d		17 22				17 34								17 43		17 52						18 04		
Falconwood	d		17 24				17 37								17 46		17 54						18 07		
Eltham	d		17 27				17 40								17 49		17 57						18 10		
Kidbrooke	d		17 30				17 43								17 52		18 00						18 13		
Blackheath 4	d		17 34				17 46							17 52	17 55		18 04						18 16		
Lewisham 4	d		17 38			17 44	17 50		18 05					17 56	17 59		18 08					18 14	18 20		18 24
St Johns	d					17 46		17 57	18 07													18 16			18 26
New Cross 4 ⊖	d					17 48		17 59	18 09						18 02							18 18			18 28
Nunhead 4	d		17 43														18 13								
Peckham Rye 4	d		17 45														18 15								
Denmark Hill 4	d		17 49														18 19								
London Victoria 15 ⊖	a		17 59														18 29								
Westcombe Park	d	17 27										17 37	17 47			17 57		18 07						18 16	
Maze Hill	d	17 29										17 39	17 49			17 59		18 09						18 18	
Greenwich 4	d	17 32										17 42	17 52			18 02		18 12						18 22	
Deptford	a	17 34										17 44	17 54			18 04		18 14						18 24	
London Bridge 4 ⊖	a	17 42		17 53		17 55	18 00	18 06	18 16		18 33	17 52	18 03	18 04	18 09	18 13		18 20	18 22			18 24	18 28	18 31	18 34
London Cannon Street 4 ⊖	a	17 46				17 59	18 04	18 11	18 20			17 56	18 07		18 13	18 17		18 24				18 29		18 35	18 38
London Waterloo (East) 4 ⊖	a			17 58							18 37			18 08					18 27				18 32		
London Charing Cross 4 ⊖	a			18 03							18 41			18 12					18 31				18 37		
Ebbsfleet International	a				17 16																17 46				
Stratford International ⊖	a				17 27																17 57				
St Pancras Int'l 15 ⊖	a				17 38																18 08				

		SE	SE	SE	SE		SE	SE	SE	SE	SE	SE	SE	SE	SE		SE	SE	SE	SE	SE	SE	SE	SE	SE
Gillingham (Kent) 4	d	17 24								17 50					17 54							18 20			
Chatham 4	d	17 28								17 54					17 58							18 24			
Rochester 4	d	17 30								17 57					18 00							18 27			
Maidstone West	d																								
Strood 4	d	17 35								18 02					18 05							18 32			
Higham	d	17 40													18 10										
Gravesend 4	d	17 48							18 02	18 13					18 18						18 32	18 43			
Northfleet	d								18 06												18 36				
Swanscombe	d								18 08												18 38				
Greenhithe for Bluewater	d	17 53							18 11						18 23						18 41				
Stone Crossing	d								18 13												18 43				
Dartford 4	a	17 58							18 17						18 28						18 47				
	d	17 59		18 01			18 08		18 18			18 22			18 29			18 31		18 38	18 48				18 52
Slade Green 4	d			18 05				18 15					18 25					18 35						18 51	
Erith	d			18 08				18 18					18 28					18 38						18 53	
Belvedere	d			18 10				18 20					18 30					18 40						18 56	
Abbey Wood	d	18 08		18 13				18 23					18 33		18 38			18 43						18 59	
Plumstead	d			18 16				18 26					18 36					18 46						19 02	
Woolwich Arsenal 4	d	18 13		18 19				18 29					18 39		18 43			18 49						19 05	
Woolwich Dockyard	d			18 22				18 32					18 42					18 52						19 07	
Charlton 4	d	18 17		18 25				18 35					18 45		18 47			18 55						19 10	
Crayford	d								18 22										18 37		18 52				
Bexley	d								18 25										18 40		18 55				
Albany Park	d								18 28										18 43		18 58				
Sidcup 4	d				18 20				18 31										18 46		19 01				
New Eltham	d				18 23				18 34										18 49		19 04				
Mottingham	d								18 36										18 51		19 06				
Lee	d								18 39										18 54		19 09				
Hither Green 4	d				18 28				18 42					18 49					18 59		19 12				
Barnehurst 4	d		18 10				18 16					18 29					18 38			18 46					18 59
Bexleyheath	d		18 12				18 19					18 31					18 40			18 49					19 01
Welling	d		18 15				18 22					18 34					18 43			18 52					19 04
Falconwood	d		18 18				18 24					18 37					18 46			18 54					19 07
Eltham	d		18 20				18 27					18 40					18 49			18 57					19 10
Kidbrooke	d		18 23				18 30					18 43					18 52			19 00					19 13
Blackheath 4	d	18 22					18 34					18 46			18 52		18 55			19 04					19 16
Lewisham 4	d	18 26	18 29		18 35		18 38				18 45	18 50		18 54	18 56		18 59		19 05	19 08			19 14		19 20
St Johns	d				18 37						18 47			18 56					19 07				19 16		
New Cross 4 ⊖	d		18 32		18 39						18 49			18 58			19 03		19 09				19 18		
Nunhead 4	d						18 43													19 13					
Peckham Rye 4	d						18 45													19 15					
Denmark Hill 4	d						18 49													19 19					
London Victoria 15 ⊖	a						18 58													19 28					
Westcombe Park	d			18 27				18 37					18 47					18 57						19 12	
Maze Hill	d			18 29				18 39					18 49					18 59						19 14	
Greenwich 4	d			18 32				18 42					18 52					19 02						19 18	
Deptford	a			18 34				18 44					18 54					19 04						19 20	
London Bridge 4 ⊖	a	18 35	18 38	18 43	18 46			18 50	18 52		18 55	18 58	19 00	19 04	19 05		19 08	19 11	19 15		19 22		19 24	19 27	19 28
London Cannon Street 4 ⊖	a		18 42	18 47	18 51			18 54			18 59		19 06	19 10			19 13	19 16	19 20				19 28	19 33	
London Waterloo (East) 4 ⊖	a	18 41							18 57			19 02			19 09						19 26				19 32
London Charing Cross 4 ⊖	a	18 45							19 01			19 06			19 13						19 30				19 36
Ebbsfleet International	a									18 17												18 47			
Stratford International ⊖	a									18 29												19 02			
St Pancras Int'l 15 ⊖	a									18 36												19 09			

Table 200

Mondays to Fridays

Gillingham and Dartford - London

Station		SE	SE	SE	SE	SE	SE	SE	SE	SE	SE	SE	SE	SE	SE	SE	SE	SE	SE	SE	SE	SE
Gillingham (Kent) 4	d		18 24						18 50			18 54						19 24				19 50
Chatham 4	d		18 28						18 54			18 58						19 28				19 54
Rochester 4	d		18 30						18 57			19 00						19 30				19 57
Maidstone West	d														19 13							
Strood 4	d		18 35						19 02			19 05			19 32			19 35				20 02
Higham	d		18 40									19 10						19 40				
Gravesend 4	d		18 48					19 02	19 12			19 18		19 32	19 43			19 48			20 02	20 12
Northfleet	d							19 06						19 36							20 06	
Swanscombe	d							19 08						19 38							20 08	
Greenhithe for Bluewater	d		18 53					19 11				19 23		19 41				19 53			20 11	
Stone Crossing	d							19 13						19 43							20 13	
Dartford 4	a		18 58					19 17				19 28		19 47				19 58			20 17	
	d		18 59		19 01		19 15	19 18			19 22	19 29	19 31	19 48			19 55	19 59	20 01	20 16	20 18	
Slade Green 4	d				19 05		19 20			19 20			19 35			19 50			20 05	20 20		
Erith	d				19 08		19 23			19 23			19 38			19 53			20 08	20 23		
Belvedere	d				19 10		19 25			19 25			19 40			19 55			20 10	20 25		
Abbey Wood	d		19 08		19 13		19 28			19 28		19 38	19 43			19 58		20 08	20 13	20 28		
Plumstead	d				19 16		19 31			19 31			19 46			20 01			20 16	20 31		
Woolwich Arsenal 4	d		19 13		19 19		19 34			19 34		19 43	19 49			20 04		20 13	20 19	20 34		
Woolwich Dockyard	d				19 22		19 37			19 37			19 52			20 07			20 22	20 37		
Charlton 4	d		19 17		19 25		19 40			19 40		19 47	19 55			20 10		20 17	20 25	20 40		
Crayford	d					19 07		19 22						19 52							20 22	
Bexley	d					19 10		19 25						19 55							20 25	
Albany Park	d					19 13		19 28						19 58							20 28	
Sidcup 4	d					19 16		19 31						20 01							20 31	
New Eltham	d					19 19		19 34						20 04							20 34	
Mottingham	d					19 21		19 36						20 06							20 36	
Lee	d					19 24		19 39						20 09							20 39	
Hither Green 4	d	19 19				19 28		19 42						20 12							20 42	
Barnehurst 4	d			19 08							19 30						20 02					
Bexleyheath	d			19 10							19 32						20 04					
Welling	d			19 13							19 35						20 07					
Falconwood	d			19 16							19 38						20 10					
Eltham	d			19 19							19 41						20 12					
Kidbrooke	d			19 22							19 44						20 15					
Blackheath 4	d		19 22	19 25							19 48	19 52					20 19	20 22				
Lewisham 4	d	19 24	19 26	19 29		19 34		19 48			19 52	19 56		20 18			20 22	20 26			20 48	
St Johns	d	19 26				19 36																
New Cross 4	d	19 28		19 32		19 38		19 51			19 56			20 21			20 26				20 51	
Nunhead 4	d																					
Peckham Rye 4	d																					
Denmark Hill 4	d																					
London Victoria 15	a																					
Westcombe Park	d				19 27		19 42			19 42			19 57			20 12			20 27	20 42		
Maze Hill	d				19 29		19 44			19 44			19 59			20 14			20 29	20 44		
Greenwich 4	d				19 32		19 47			19 47			20 02			20 17			20 32	20 47		
Deptford	a				19 34		19 49			19 49			20 04			20 19			20 34	20 49		
London Bridge 4	a	19 34	19 35	19 38	19 41	19 44	19 59	19 57		19 59	20 03	20 06	20 11	20 27		20 27	20 33	20 36	20 41	20 57	20 57	
London Cannon Street 4	a	19 38		19 43	19 45	19 49	20 03			20 03			20 15			20 31			20 45			
London Waterloo (East) 4	a		19 39					20 02			20 08	20 11		20 32			20 38	20 40			21 02	
London Charing Cross 4	a		19 43					20 06			20 12	20 14		20 36			20 42	20 44			21 06	
Ebbsfleet International	a								19 16						19 47							20 16
Stratford International	a								19 27						20 01							20 27
St Pancras Int'l 15	a								19 38						20 08							20 38

Station		SE	SE	SE	SE	SE	SE	SE	SE	SE	SE	SE	SE	SE	SE	SE	SE	SE	SE	SE	SE	SE	SE
Gillingham (Kent) 4	d		19 54				20 20		20 24				20 50		20 54				21 20		21 24		
Chatham 4	d		19 58				20 24		20 28				20 54		20 58				21 24		21 28		
Rochester 4	d		20 00				20 27		20 30				20 57		21 00				21 27		21 30		
Maidstone West	d																						
Strood 4	d		20 05				20 32		20 35				21 02		21 05				21 32		21 35		
Higham	d		20 10						20 40						21 10						21 40		
Gravesend 4	d		20 18			20 32	20 43		20 48			21 02	21 13		21 18			21 32	21 43		21 48		22 02
Northfleet	d					20 36						21 06						21 36					22 06
Swanscombe	d					20 38						21 08						21 38					22 08
Greenhithe for Bluewater	d		20 23			20 41			20 53			21 11			21 23			21 41			21 53		22 11
Stone Crossing	d					20 43						21 13						21 43					22 13
Dartford 4	a		20 28			20 47			20 58			21 17			21 28			21 47			21 58		22 17
	d	20 25	20 29	20 31	20 46	20 48		20 55	20 59	21 01	21 16	21 18		21 25	21 29	21 31	21 46	21 48		21 55	21 59	22 01	22 18
Slade Green 4	d			20 35	20 50					21 05	21 20					21 35	21 50					22 05	
Erith	d			20 38	20 53					21 08	21 23					21 38	21 53					22 08	
Belvedere	d			20 40	20 55					21 10	21 25					21 40	21 55					22 10	
Abbey Wood	d		20 38	20 43	20 58				21 08	21 13	21 28				21 38	21 43	21 58				22 08	22 13	
Plumstead	d			20 46	21 01					21 16	21 31					21 46	22 01					22 16	
Woolwich Arsenal 4	d		20 43	20 49	21 04				21 13	21 19	21 34				21 43	21 49	22 04				22 13	22 19	
Woolwich Dockyard	d			20 52	21 07					21 22	21 37					21 52	22 07					22 22	
Charlton 4	d		20 47	20 55	21 10				21 17	21 25	21 40				21 47	21 55	22 10				22 17	22 25	
Crayford	d					20 52						21 22						21 52					22 22
Bexley	d					20 55						21 25						21 55					22 25
Albany Park	d					20 58						21 28						21 58					22 28
Sidcup 4	d					21 01						21 31						22 01					22 31
New Eltham	d					21 04						21 34						22 04					22 34
Mottingham	d					21 06						21 36						22 06					22 36
Lee	d					21 09						21 39						22 09					22 39
Hither Green 4	d					21 12						21 42						22 12					22 42
Barnehurst 4	d	20 32						21 02						21 32						22 02			
Bexleyheath	d	20 34						21 04						21 34						22 04			
Welling	d	20 37						21 07						21 37						22 07			
Falconwood	d	20 40						21 10						21 40						22 10			
Eltham	d	20 42						21 12						21 42						22 12			
Kidbrooke	d	20 45						21 15						21 45						22 15			
Blackheath 4	d	20 49	20 52					21 19	21 22					21 49	21 52					22 19	22 22		
Lewisham 4	d	20 53	20 56			21 18		21 23	21 26			21 48		21 53	21 56			22 18		22 23	22 26		22 48
St Johns	d																						
New Cross 4	d	20 56				21 21		21 26				21 51		21 56				22 21		22 26			22 51
Nunhead 4	d																						
Peckham Rye 4	d																						
Denmark Hill 4	d																						
London Victoria 15	a																						
Westcombe Park	d			20 57	21 12					21 27	21 42					21 57	22 12					22 27	
Maze Hill	d			20 59	21 14					21 29	21 44					21 59	22 14					22 29	
Greenwich 4	d			21 02	21 17					21 32	21 47					22 02	22 17					22 32	
Deptford	a			21 04	21 19					21 34	21 49					22 04	22 19					22 34	
London Bridge 4	a	21 03	21 06	21 11	21 27	21 27		21 33	21 36	21 41	21 57	21 57		22 01	22 05	22 11	22 27	22 27		22 31	22 35	22 41	22 57
London Cannon Street 4	a																						
London Waterloo (East) 4	a	21 08	21 10	21 15		21 32		21 38	21 40	21 45		22 02		22 06	22 09	22 15		22 32		22 36	22 39	22 45	23 02
London Charing Cross 4	a	21 12	21 14	21 19		21 36		21 42	21 44	21 49		22 06		22 10	22 13	22 19		22 36		22 40	22 43	22 49	23 06
Ebbsfleet International	a						20 47						21 17						21 47				
Stratford International	a						20 59						21 32						21 59				
St Pancras Int'l 15	a						21 06						21 39						22 06				

Gillingham and Dartford - London

Station		SE	SE	SE	SE	SE	SE	SE	SE	SE	SE
Gillingham (Kent) [4]	d	21 50		21 54			22 20		22 24		22 54
Chatham [4]	d	21 54		21 58			22 24		22 28		22 58
Rochester [4]	d	21 57		22 00			22 27		22 30		23 00
Maidstone West	d										
Strood [4]	d	22 02		22 05			22 32		22 35		23 05
Higham	d			22 10					22 40		23 10
Gravesend [4]	d	22 12		22 18		22 32	22 43		22 48		23 18
Northfleet	d					22 36					
Swanscombe	d					22 38					
Greenhithe for Bluewater	d			22 23		22 41			22 53		23 23
Stone Crossing	d					22 43					
Dartford [4]	a			22 28		22 47			22 58		23 28
	d		22 25	22 29	22 31	22 48		22 55	22 59	23 01	
Slade Green [4]	d				22 35					23 05	
Erith	d				22 38					23 08	
Belvedere	d				22 40					23 10	
Abbey Wood	d			22 38	22 43				23 08	23 13	
Plumstead	d				22 46					23 16	
Woolwich Arsenal [4] ⛴	d			22 43	22 49				23 13	23 19	
Woolwich Dockyard	d				22 52					23 22	
Charlton [4]	d			22 47	22 55				23 17	23 25	
Crayford	d					22 52					
Bexley	d					22 55					
Albany Park	d					22 58					
Sidcup [4]	d					23 01					
New Eltham	d					23 04					
Mottingham	d					23 06					
Lee	d					23 09					
Hither Green [4]	d					23 12					
Barnehurst [4]	d		22 32					23 02			
Bexleyheath	d		22 34					23 04			
Welling	d		22 37					23 07			
Falconwood	d		22 40					23 10			
Eltham	d		22 42					23 12			
Kidbrooke	d		22 45					23 15			
Blackheath [4]	d		22 49	22 52				23 19	23 22		
Lewisham [4] ⛴	d		22 53	22 56		23 18		23 23	23 26		
St Johns	d										
New Cross [4] ⊖	d		22 56			23 21		23 26			
Nunhead [4]	d										
Peckham Rye [4]	d										
Denmark Hill [4]	d										
London Victoria [15] ⊖	a										
Westcombe Park	d				22 57					23 27	
Maze Hill	d				22 59					23 29	
Greenwich [4] ⛴	d				23 02					23 32	
Deptford	a				23 04					23 34	
London Bridge [4] ⊖	a		23 01	23 05	23 11	23 27		23 31	23 35	23 41	
London Cannon Street [4] ⊖	a										
London Waterloo (East) [4] ⊖	a		23 06	23 09	23 15	23 32		23 36	23 39	23 45	
London Charing Cross [4] ⊖	a		23 10	23 13	23 19	23 36		23 40	23 43	23 49	
Ebbsfleet International	a	22 16					22 47				
Stratford International ⊖ ⛴	a	22 27					22 59				
St Pancras Int'l [15] ⊖	a	22 38					23 06				

Table 200

Gillingham and Dartford - London

		SE	SE	SE	SE	SE	SE	SE	SE	SE		SE	SE	SE	SE	SE	SE	SE	SE	SE		SE	SE	SE	SE
Gillingham (Kent) [4]	d				04 48				05 18				05 50		05 54				06 20			06 24			
Chatham [4]	d				04 52				05 22				05 54		05 58				06 24			06 28			
Rochester [4]	d				04 54				05 24				05 57		06 00				06 27			06 30			
Maidstone West	d																								
Strood [4]	d				04 59				05 29				06 02		06 05				06 32			06 35			
Higham	d				05 04				05 34						06 10							06 40			
Gravesend [4]	d				05 12				05 42			06 02	06 13		06 18			06 32	06 43			06 48			07 02
Northfleet	d				05 15				05 45			06 06						06 36							07 06
Swanscombe	d				05 17				05 47			06 08						06 38							07 08
Greenhithe for Bluewater	d				05 21				05 51			06 11			06 23			06 41				06 53			07 11
Stone Crossing	d				05 23				05 53			06 13						06 43							07 13
Dartford [4]	a				05 27				05 57			06 17			06 28			06 47				06 58			07 17
	d	05 05	05 18	05 22	05 29	05 35	05 48	05 52	05 59	06 05		06 18		06 22	06 29	06 35	06 38	06 48		06 52		06 59	07 01	07 08	07 18
Slade Green [4]	d	05 10				05 40				06 10						06 40							07 05		
Erith	d	05 12				05 42				06 12						06 42							07 08		
Belvedere	d	05 15				05 45				06 15						06 45							07 10		
Abbey Wood	d	05 18			05 38	05 48			06 08	06 18					06 38	06 48						07 08	07 13		
Plumstead	d	05 21				05 51				06 21						06 51							07 16		
Woolwich Arsenal [4]	d	05 24			05 43	05 54			06 13	06 24					06 43	06 54						07 13	07 19		
Woolwich Dockyard	d	05 26				05 56				06 26						06 56							07 22		
Charlton [4]	d	05 29			05 47	05 59			06 17	06 29					06 47	06 59						07 17	07 25		
Crayford	d		05 22				05 52					06 22						06 52							07 22
Bexley	d		05 25				05 55					06 25						06 55							07 25
Albany Park	d		05 28				05 58					06 28						06 58							07 28
Sidcup [4]	d		05 31				06 01					06 31						07 01							07 31
New Eltham	d		05 34				06 04					06 34						07 04							07 34
Mottingham	d		05 36				06 06					06 36						07 06							07 36
Lee	d		05 39				06 09					06 39						07 09							07 39
Hither Green [4]	d		05 42				06 12					06 42						07 12							07 42
Barnehurst [4]	d			05 29				05 59						06 29			06 46			06 59				07 16	
Bexleyheath	d			05 31				06 01						06 31			06 49			07 01				07 19	
Welling	d			05 34				06 04						06 34			06 52			07 04				07 22	
Falconwood	d			05 37				06 07						06 37			06 54			07 07				07 24	
Eltham	d			05 40				06 10						06 40			06 57			07 10				07 27	
Kidbrooke	d			05 43				06 13						06 43			07 00			07 13				07 30	
Blackheath [4]	d			05 46	05 52			06 16	06 22					06 46	06 52		07 04			07 16		07 22		07 34	
Lewisham [4]	d		05 48	05 50	05 56		06 18	06 20	06 26			06 48		06 50	06 56		07 08	07 18		07 20		07 26		07 38	
St Johns	d																								
New Cross [4] ⊖	d		05 51				06 21					06 51						07 21							
Nunhead [4]	d																07 15							07 45	
Peckham Rye [4]	d																07 17							07 47	
Denmark Hill [4]	d																07 21							07 51	
London Victoria [15] ⊖	a																07 30							08 00	
Westcombe Park	d	05 31				06 01				06 31						07 01							07 27		
Maze Hill	d	05 33				06 03				06 33						07 03							07 29		
Greenwich [4]	d	05 37				06 07				06 37						07 07							07 32		
Deptford	a	05 39				06 09				06 39						07 09							07 34		
London Bridge [4] ⊖	a	05 45	05 56	05 59	06 05	06 15	06 26	06 29	06 35	06 45		06 56		06 59	07 05	07 15		07 26		07 29		07 35	07 41		07 52
London Cannon Street [4] ⊖	a																						07 45		
London Waterloo (East) [4] ⊖	a	05 49	06 01	06 03	06 09	06 19	06 31	06 33	06 39	06 49		07 01		07 03	07 09	07 19		07 31		07 33		07 39			07 56
London Charing Cross [4] ⊖	a	05 53	06 05	06 07	06 13	06 25	06 35	06 37	06 43	06 55		07 05		07 07	07 13	07 25		07 35		07 40		07 43			08 00
Ebbsfleet International	a												06 17						06 47						
Stratford International ⊖	a												06 29						06 59						
St Pancras Int'l [15] ⊖	a												06 36						07 06						

		SE	SE	SE	SE	SE		SE	SE	SE	SE	SE	SE	SE	SE	SE		SE	SE	SE	SE	SE	SE	SE	SE
Gillingham (Kent) [4]	d	06 50				06 54								07 20						07 24					
Chatham [4]	d	06 54				06 58								07 24						07 28					
Rochester [4]	d	06 57				07 00								07 27						07 30					
Maidstone West	d																								
Strood [4]	d	07 02				07 05								07 32						07 35					
Higham	d					07 10														07 40					
Gravesend [4]	d	07 13				07 18							07 32	07 43						07 48					
Northfleet	d												07 36												
Swanscombe	d												07 38												
Greenhithe for Bluewater	d					07 23							07 41							07 53					
Stone Crossing	d												07 43												
Dartford [4]	a					07 28							07 47							07 58					
	d		07 22			07 29			07 31		07 38		07 48			07 52				07 59		08 01		08 08	
Slade Green [4]	d			07 25					07 35			07 45						07 55				08 05			08 15
Erith	d			07 28					07 38			07 48						07 58				08 08			08 18
Belvedere	d			07 30					07 40			07 50						08 00				08 10			08 20
Abbey Wood	d			07 33		07 38			07 43			07 53						08 03		08 08		08 13			08 23
Plumstead	d			07 36					07 46			07 56						08 06				08 16			08 26
Woolwich Arsenal [4]	d			07 39		07 43			07 49			07 59						08 09		08 13		08 19			08 29
Woolwich Dockyard	d			07 42					07 52			08 02						08 12				08 22			08 32
Charlton [4]	d			07 45		07 47			07 55			08 05						08 15		08 17		08 25			08 35
Crayford	d									07 37			07 52										08 07		
Bexley	d									07 40			07 55										08 10		
Albany Park	d									07 43			07 58										08 13		
Sidcup [4]	d									07 46			08 01										08 16		
New Eltham	d									07 49			08 04										08 19		
Mottingham	d									07 51			08 06										08 21		
Lee	d									07 54			08 09										08 24		
Hither Green [4]	d				07 49					07 58			08 12						08 19				08 28		
Barnehurst [4]	d		07 29					07 38			07 46					07 59					08 08			08 16	
Bexleyheath	d		07 31					07 40			07 49					08 01					08 10			08 19	
Welling	d		07 34					07 43			07 52					08 04					08 13			08 22	
Falconwood	d		07 37					07 46			07 54					08 07					08 16			08 24	
Eltham	d		07 40					07 49			07 57					08 10					08 19			08 27	
Kidbrooke	d		07 43					07 52			08 00					08 13					08 22			08 30	
Blackheath [4]	d		07 46			07 52		07 55			08 04					08 16				08 22	08 25			08 34	
Lewisham [4]	d		07 50		07 54	07 56		07 59		08 04	08 08				08 14	08 20			08 24	08 26	08 29		08 34	08 38	
St Johns	d				07 56			08 01		08 06					08 16				08 26		08 31		08 36		
New Cross [4] ⊖	d				07 58			08 03		08 08					08 18				08 28		08 33		08 38		
Nunhead [4]	d										08 15													08 45	
Peckham Rye [4]	d										08 17													08 47	
Denmark Hill [4]	d										08 21													08 51	
London Victoria [15] ⊖	a										08 30													09 00	
Westcombe Park	d			07 47					07 57			08 07						08 17				08 27			08 37
Maze Hill	d			07 49					07 59			08 09						08 19				08 29			08 39
Greenwich [4]	d			07 52					08 02			08 12						08 22				08 32			08 42
Deptford	a			07 54					08 04			08 14						08 24				08 34			08 44
London Bridge [4] ⊖	a		07 58	08 00	08 04	08 05		08 08	08 11	08 14		08 20	08 22		08 24	08 28		08 30	08 34	08 35	08 38	08 41	08 44		08 50
London Cannon Street [4] ⊖	a			08 04	08 08			08 13	08 15	08 19		08 24			08 28			08 34	08 38		08 43	08 45	08 49		08 54
London Waterloo (East) [4] ⊖	a		08 02			08 09							08 26			08 32				08 39					
London Charing Cross [4] ⊖	a		08 06			08 13							08 30			08 36				08 43					
Ebbsfleet International	a	07 17												07 47											
Stratford International ⊖	a	07 29												07 59											
St Pancras Int'l [15] ⊖	a	07 36												08 06											

Table 200

Gillingham and Dartford - London

		SE		SE	SE	SE	SE	SE	SE	SE	SE	SE		SE	SE	SE	SE	SE	SE	SE	SE	SE		SE	SE
Gillingham (Kent) 4	d			07 50							07 54							08 20							08 24
Chatham 4	d			07 54							07 58							08 24							08 28
Rochester 4	d			07 57							08 00							08 27							08 30
Maidstone West	d																								
Strood 4	d			08 02							08 05							08 32							08 35
Higham	d										08 10														08 40
Gravesend 4	d	08 02		08 13							08 18						08 32	08 43							08 48
Northfleet	d	08 06															08 36								
Swanscombe	d	08 08															08 38								
Greenhithe for Bluewater	d	08 11									08 23						08 41								08 53
Stone Crossing	d	08 13															08 43								
Dartford 4	a	08 17									08 28						08 47								08 58
	d	08 18				08 22					08 29			08 31	08 38		08 48			08 52					08 59
Slade Green 4	d									08 25				08 35		08 45								08 55	
Erith	d									08 28				08 38		08 48								08 58	
Belvedere	d									08 30				08 40		08 50								09 00	
Abbey Wood	d									08 33	08 38			08 43		08 53								09 03	09 08
Plumstead	d									08 36				08 46		08 56								09 06	
Woolwich Arsenal 4 ⛴	d									08 39	08 43			08 49		08 59								09 09	09 13
Woolwich Dockyard	d									08 42				08 52		09 02								09 12	
Charlton 4	d								08 37	08 45	08 47			08 55		09 05						09 07		09 15	09 17
Crayford	d	08 22						08 37	09 07								08 52					09 37			
Bexley	d	08 25						08 40	09 10								08 55					09 40			
Albany Park	d	08 28						08 43	09 13								08 58					09 43			
Sidcup 4	d	08 31						08 46	09 16								09 01					09 46			
New Eltham	d	08 34						08 49	09 19								09 04					09 49			
Mottingham	d	08 36						08 51	09 21								09 06					09 51			
Lee	d	08 39						08 54	09 24								09 09					09 54			
Hither Green 4	d	08 42					08 49	08 58	09 28								09 12				09 19	09 58			
Barnehurst 4	d					08 29						08 38			08 46					08 59					
Bexleyheath	d					08 31						08 40			08 49					09 01					
Welling	d					08 34						08 43			08 52					09 04					
Falconwood	d					08 37						08 46			08 54					09 07					
Eltham	d					08 40						08 49			08 57					09 10					
Kidbrooke	d					08 43						08 52			09 00					09 13					
Blackheath 4	d					08 46					08 52	08 55			09 04					09 16					09 22
Lewisham 4 ⛴	d				08 44	08 50	08 54	09 04	09 34		08 56	08 59			09 08				09 14	09 20	09 24	10 04			09 26
St Johns	d				08 46		08 56	09 06	09 36			09 01							09 16		09 26	10 06			
New Cross 4 ⊖	d				08 48		08 58	09 08	09 38			09 03							09 18		09 28	10 08			
Nunhead 4	d														09 15										
Peckham Rye 4	d														09 17										
Denmark Hill 4	d														09 21										
London Victoria 15 ⊖	a														09 30										
Westcombe Park	d									08 47				08 57		09 07								09 17	
Maze Hill	d									08 49				08 59		09 09								09 19	
Greenwich 4 ⛴	d									08 52				09 02		09 12								09 22	
Deptford	a									08 54				09 04		09 14								09 24	
London Bridge 4 ⊖	a	08 52			08 54	08 58	09 04	09 14	09 44	09 00	09 05	09 08		09 11		09 20	09 22		09 24	09 28	09 34	10 14		09 30	09 35
London Cannon Street 4 ⊖	a				08 58		09 08	09 19	09 49	09 04		09 13		09 15		09 24			09 28		09 38	10 19		09 34	
London Waterloo (East) 4 ⊖	a	08 56				09 02					09 09						09 26			09 32					09 39
London Charing Cross 4 ⊖	a	09 00				09 06					09 13						09 30			09 36					09 43
Ebbsfleet International	a			08 17														08 47							
Stratford International ⊖ ⛴	a			08 29														08 59							
St Pancras Int'l 15 ⊖	a			08 36														09 06							

		SE	SE	SE	SE	SE	SE	SE		SE	SE	SE	SE	SE	SE	SE	SE	SE		SE	SE	SE	SE	SE	SE
Gillingham (Kent) 4	d						08 50							08 54							09 20				
Chatham 4	d						08 54							08 58							09 24				
Rochester 4	d						08 57							09 00							09 27				
Maidstone West	d																								
Strood 4	d						09 02							09 05							09 32				
Higham	d													09 10											
Gravesend 4	d					09 02	09 13							09 18						09 32	09 43				
Northfleet	d					09 06														09 36					
Swanscombe	d					09 08														09 38					
Greenhithe for Bluewater	d					09 11								09 23						09 41					
Stone Crossing	d					09 13														09 43					
Dartford 4	a					09 17								09 28						09 47					
	d		09 01	09 08		09 18				09 22				09 29		09 31	09 38			09 48			09 52		
Slade Green 4	d		09 05		09 15								09 25			09 35		09 45							
Erith	d		09 08		09 18								09 28			09 38		09 48							
Belvedere	d		09 10		09 20								09 30			09 40		09 50							
Abbey Wood	d		09 13		09 23								09 33	09 38		09 43		09 53							
Plumstead	d		09 16		09 26								09 36			09 46		09 56							
Woolwich Arsenal 4 ⛴	d		09 19		09 29								09 39	09 43		09 49		09 59							
Woolwich Dockyard	d		09 22		09 32								09 42			09 52		10 02							
Charlton 4	d		09 25		09 35							09 37	09 45	09 47		09 55		10 05							10 07
Crayford	d					09 22						10 07								09 52					10 37
Bexley	d					09 25						10 10								09 55					10 40
Albany Park	d					09 28						10 13								09 58					10 43
Sidcup 4	d					09 31						10 16								10 01					10 46
New Eltham	d					09 34						10 19								10 04					10 49
Mottingham	d					09 36						10 21								10 06					10 51
Lee	d					09 39						10 24								10 09					10 54
Hither Green 4	d					09 42					09 49	10 28								10 12				10 19	10 58
Barnehurst 4	d	09 08		09 16						09 29					09 38		09 46						09 59		
Bexleyheath	d	09 10		09 19						09 31					09 40		09 49						10 01		
Welling	d	09 13		09 22						09 34					09 43		09 52						10 04		
Falconwood	d	09 16		09 24						09 37					09 46		09 54						10 07		
Eltham	d	09 19		09 27						09 40					09 49		09 57						10 10		
Kidbrooke	d	09 22		09 30						09 43					09 52		10 00						10 13		
Blackheath 4	d	09 25		09 34						09 46				09 52	09 55		10 04						10 16		
Lewisham 4 ⛴	d	09 29		09 38				09 44		09 50	09 54	10 34		09 56	09 59		10 08					10 14	10 20	10 24	11 04
St Johns	d	09 31						09 46			09 56	10 36			10 01							10 16		10 26	11 06
New Cross 4 ⊖	d	09 33						09 48			09 58	10 38			10 03							10 18		10 28	11 08
Nunhead 4	d			09 45													10 15								
Peckham Rye 4	d			09 47													10 17								
Denmark Hill 4	d			09 51													10 21								
London Victoria 15 ⊖	a			10 00													10 30								
Westcombe Park	d		09 27		09 37								09 47			09 57		10 07							
Maze Hill	d		09 29		09 39								09 49			09 59		10 09							
Greenwich 4 ⛴	d		09 32		09 42								09 52			10 02		10 12							
Deptford	a		09 34		09 44								09 54			10 04		10 14							
London Bridge 4 ⊖	a	09 38	09 41		09 50	09 52		09 54		09 58	10 04	10 44	10 00	10 05	10 08	10 11		10 20		10 22		10 24	10 28	10 34	11 14
London Cannon Street 4 ⊖	a	09 43	09 45		09 54			09 58			10 08	10 49	10 04		10 13	10 15		10 24				10 28		10 38	11 19
London Waterloo (East) 4 ⊖	a					09 56				10 02				10 09						10 26			10 32		
London Charing Cross 4 ⊖	a					10 00				10 06				10 13						10 30			10 36		
Ebbsfleet International	a						09 17														09 47				
Stratford International ⊖ ⛴	a						09 29														09 59				
St Pancras Int'l 15 ⊖	a						09 36														10 06				

Table 200

Saturdays

Gillingham and Dartford - London

Station		SE	SE	SE	SE	SE	SE	SE	SE	SE	SE	SE	SE	SE	SE	SE	SE	SE	SE	SE	SE	SE
Gillingham (Kent) 4	d		09 24						09 50						09 54						10 20	
Chatham 4	d		09 28						09 54						09 58						10 24	
Rochester 4	d		09 30						09 57						10 00						10 27	
Maidstone West	d																					
Strood 4	d		09 35						10 02						10 05						10 32	
Higham	d		09 40												10 10							
Gravesend 4	d		09 48					10 02	10 12						10 18					10 32	10 43	
Northfleet	d							10 06												10 36		
Swanscombe	d							10 08												10 38		
Greenhithe for Bluewater	d		09 53					10 11							10 23					10 41		
Stone Crossing	d							10 13												10 43		
Dartford 4	a		09 58					10 17							10 28					10 47		
	d		09 59		10 01	10 08		10 18			10 22				10 29		10 31	10 38		10 48		
Slade Green 4	d	09 55			10 05		10 15							10 25			10 35		10 45			
Erith	d	09 58			10 08		10 18							10 28			10 38		10 48			
Belvedere	d	10 00			10 10		10 20							10 30			10 40		10 50			
Abbey Wood	d	10 03	10 08		10 13		10 23							10 33	10 38		10 43		10 53			
Plumstead	d	10 06			10 16		10 26							10 36			10 46		10 56			
Woolwich Arsenal 4 ⇌	d	10 09	10 13		10 19		10 29							10 39	10 43		10 49		10 59			
Woolwich Dockyard	d	10 12			10 22		10 32							10 42			10 52		11 02			
Charlton 4	d	10 15	10 17		10 25		10 35						10 37	10 45	10 47		10 55		11 05			
Crayford	d							10 22					11 07							10 52		
Bexley	d							10 25					11 10							10 55		
Albany Park	d							10 28					11 13							10 58		
Sidcup 4	d							10 31					11 16							11 01		
New Eltham	d							10 34					11 19							11 04		
Mottingham	d							10 36					11 21							11 06		
Lee	d							10 39					11 24							11 09		
Hither Green 4	d							10 42				10 49	11 28							11 12		
Barnehurst 4	d			10 08		10 16					10 29					10 38		10 46				
Bexleyheath	d			10 10		10 19					10 31					10 40		10 49				
Welling	d			10 13		10 22					10 34					10 43		10 52				
Falconwood	d			10 16		10 24					10 37					10 46		10 54				
Eltham	d			10 19		10 27					10 40					10 49		10 57				
Kidbrooke	d			10 22		10 30					10 43					10 52		11 00				
Blackheath 4	d		10 22	10 25		10 34					10 46				10 52	10 55		11 04				
Lewisham 4 ⇌	d		10 26	10 29		10 38				10 44	10 50	10 54	11 34		10 56	10 59		11 08				11 14
St Johns	d			10 31						10 46		10 56	11 36			11 01						11 16
New Cross 4 ⊖	d			10 33						10 48		10 58	11 38			11 03						11 18
Nunhead 4	d					10 45												11 15				
Peckham Rye 4	d					10 47												11 17				
Denmark Hill 4	d					10 51												11 21				
London Victoria 15 ⊖	a					11 00												11 30				
Westcombe Park	d	10 17			10 27		10 37							10 47			10 57		11 07			
Maze Hill	d	10 19			10 29		10 39							10 49			10 59		11 09			
Greenwich 4 ⇌	d	10 22			10 32		10 42							10 52			11 02		11 12			
Deptford	a	10 24			10 34		10 44							10 54			11 04		11 14			
London Bridge 4 ⊖	a	10 30	10 35	10 38	10 41		10 50	10 52		10 54	10 58	11 04	11 44	11 00	11 05	11 08	11 11		11 20	11 22		11 24
London Cannon Street 4 ⊖	a	10 34		10 43	10 45		10 54			10 58		11 08	11 49	11 04		11 13	11 15		11 24			11 28
London Waterloo (East) 4 ⊖	a		10 39					10 56			11 02				11 09					11 26		
London Charing Cross 4 ⊖	a		10 43					11 00			11 06				11 13					11 30		
Ebbsfleet International	a								10 16												10 47	
Stratford International ⊖ ⇌	a								10 27												10 59	
St Pancras Int'l 15 ⊖	a								10 38												11 06	

Station		SE	SE	SE	SE	SE	SE	SE	SE	SE	SE	SE	SE	SE	SE	SE	SE	SE	SE	SE	SE	SE	SE
Gillingham (Kent) 4	d					10 24						10 50						10 54					
Chatham 4	d					10 28						10 54						10 58					
Rochester 4	d					10 30						10 57						11 00					
Maidstone West	d																						
Strood 4	d					10 35						11 02						11 05					
Higham	d					10 40												11 10					
Gravesend 4	d					10 48					11 02	11 13						11 18					11 32
Northfleet	d										11 06												11 36
Swanscombe	d										11 08												11 38
Greenhithe for Bluewater	d					10 53					11 11							11 23					11 41
Stone Crossing	d										11 13												11 43
Dartford 4	a					10 58					11 17							11 28					11 47
	d	10 52				10 59		11 01	11 08		11 18			11 22				11 29		11 31	11 38		11 48
Slade Green 4	d				10 55			11 05		11 15							11 25			11 35		11 45	
Erith	d				10 58			11 08		11 18							11 28			11 38		11 48	
Belvedere	d				11 00			11 10		11 20							11 30			11 40		11 50	
Abbey Wood	d				11 03	11 08		11 13		11 23							11 33	11 38		11 43		11 53	
Plumstead	d				11 06			11 16		11 26							11 36			11 46		11 56	
Woolwich Arsenal 4 ⇌	d				11 09	11 13		11 19		11 29							11 39	11 43		11 49		11 59	
Woolwich Dockyard	d				11 12			11 22		11 32							11 42			11 52		12 02	
Charlton 4	d			11 07	11 15	11 17		11 25		11 35						11 37	11 45	11 47		11 55		12 05	
Crayford	d			11 37							11 22					12 07							11 52
Bexley	d			11 40							11 25					12 10							11 55
Albany Park	d			11 43							11 28					12 13							11 58
Sidcup 4	d			11 46							11 31					12 16							12 01
New Eltham	d			11 49							11 34					12 19							12 04
Mottingham	d			11 51							11 36					12 21							12 06
Lee	d			11 54							11 39					12 24							12 09
Hither Green 4	d		11 19	11 58							11 42				11 49	12 28							12 12
Barnehurst 4	d	10 59					11 08		11 16					11 29					11 38		11 46		
Bexleyheath	d	11 01					11 10		11 19					11 31					11 40		11 49		
Welling	d	11 04					11 13		11 22					11 34					11 43		11 52		
Falconwood	d	11 07					11 16		11 24					11 37					11 46		11 54		
Eltham	d	11 10					11 19		11 27					11 40					11 49		11 57		
Kidbrooke	d	11 13					11 22		11 30					11 43					11 52		12 00		
Blackheath 4	d	11 16				11 22	11 25		11 34					11 46				11 52	11 55		12 04		
Lewisham 4 ⇌	d	11 20	11 24	12 04		11 26	11 29		11 38				11 44	11 50	11 54	12 34		11 56	11 59		12 08		
St Johns	d		11 26	12 06			11 31						11 46		11 56	12 36			12 01				
New Cross 4 ⊖	d		11 28	12 08			11 33						11 48		11 58	12 38			12 03				
Nunhead 4	d								11 45												12 15		
Peckham Rye 4	d								11 47												12 17		
Denmark Hill 4	d								11 51												12 21		
London Victoria 15 ⊖	a								12 00												12 30		
Westcombe Park	d				11 17			11 27		11 37							11 47			11 57		12 07	
Maze Hill	d				11 19			11 29		11 39							11 49			11 59		12 09	
Greenwich 4 ⇌	d				11 22			11 32		11 42							11 52			12 02		12 12	
Deptford	a				11 24			11 34		11 44							11 54			12 04		12 14	
London Bridge 4 ⊖	a	11 28	11 34	12 14	11 30	11 35	11 38	11 41		11 50	11 52		11 54	11 58	12 04	12 44	12 00	12 05	12 08	12 11		12 20	12 22
London Cannon Street 4 ⊖	a		11 38	12 19	11 34		11 43	11 45		11 54			11 58		12 08	12 49	12 04		12 13	12 15		12 24	
London Waterloo (East) 4 ⊖	a	11 32				11 39					11 56			12 02				12 09					12 26
London Charing Cross 4 ⊖	a	11 36				11 43					12 00			12 06				12 13					12 30
Ebbsfleet International	a											11 17											
Stratford International ⊖ ⇌	a											11 29											
St Pancras Int'l 15 ⊖	a											11 36											

Table 200

Saturdays

Gillingham and Dartford - London

		SE	SE	SE	SE	SE		SE	SE	SE	SE	SE	SE	SE	SE	SE		SE	SE	SE	SE	SE	SE	SE	SE
Gillingham (Kent) 4	d	11 20							11 24						11 50							11 54			
Chatham 4	d	11 24							11 28						11 54							11 58			
Rochester 4	d	11 27							11 30						11 57							12 00			
Maidstone West	d																								
Strood 4	d	11 32							11 35						12 02							12 05			
Higham	d								11 40													12 10			
Gravesend 4	d	11 43							11 48					12 02	12 13							12 18			
Northfleet	d													12 06											
Swanscombe	d													12 08											
Greenhithe for Bluewater	d								11 53					12 11								12 23			
Stone Crossing	d													12 13											
Dartford 4	a								11 58					12 17								12 28			
	d			11 52					11 59		12 01	12 08		12 18				12 22				12 29		12 31	12 38
Slade Green 4	d							11 55			12 05		12 15								12 25			12 35	
Erith	d							11 58			12 08		12 18								12 28			12 38	
Belvedere	d							12 00			12 10		12 20								12 30			12 40	
Abbey Wood	d							12 03	12 08		12 13		12 23								12 33	12 38		12 43	
Plumstead	d							12 06			12 16		12 26								12 36			12 46	
Woolwich Arsenal 4	d							12 09	12 13		12 19		12 29								12 39	12 43		12 49	
Woolwich Dockyard	d							12 12			12 22		12 32								12 42			12 52	
Charlton 4	d					12 07		12 15	12 17		12 25		12 35							12 37	12 45	12 47		12 55	
Crayford	d					12 37								12 22						13 07					
Bexley	d					12 40								12 25						13 10					
Albany Park	d					12 43								12 28						13 13					
Sidcup 4	d					12 46								12 31						13 16					
New Eltham	d					12 49								12 34						13 19					
Mottingham	d					12 51								12 36						13 21					
Lee	d					12 54								12 39						13 24					
Hither Green 4	d				12 19	12 58								12 42					12 49	13 28					
Barnehurst 4	d			11 59						12 08		12 16						12 29					12 38		12 46
Bexleyheath	d			12 01						12 10		12 19						12 31					12 40		12 49
Welling	d			12 04						12 13		12 22						12 34					12 43		12 52
Falconwood	d			12 07						12 16		12 24						12 37					12 46		12 54
Eltham	d			12 10						12 19		12 27						12 40					12 49		12 57
Kidbrooke	d			12 13						12 22		12 30						12 43					12 52		13 00
Blackheath 4	d			12 16					12 22	12 25		12 34						12 46				12 52	12 55		13 04
Lewisham 4	d		12 14	12 20	12 24	13 04			12 26	12 29		12 38				12 44		12 50	12 54	13 34		12 56	12 59		13 08
St Johns	d		12 16		12 26	13 06				12 31						12 46			12 56	13 36			13 01		
New Cross 4 ⊖	d		12 18		12 28	13 08				12 33						12 48			12 58	13 38			13 03		
Nunhead 4	d											12 45													13 15
Peckham Rye 4	d											12 47													13 17
Denmark Hill 4	d											12 51													13 21
London Victoria 15 ⊖	a											13 00													13 30
Westcombe Park	d							12 17			12 27		12 37								12 47			12 57	
Maze Hill	d							12 19			12 29		12 39								12 49			12 59	
Greenwich 4	d							12 22			12 32		12 42								12 52			13 02	
Deptford	a							12 24			12 34		12 44								12 54			13 04	
London Bridge 4 ⊖	a		12 24	12 28	12 34	13 14		12 30	12 35	12 38	12 41		12 50	12 52		12 54		12 58	13 04	13 44	13 00	13 05	13 08	13 11	
London Cannon Street 4 ⊖	a		12 28		12 38	13 19		12 34		12 43	12 45		12 54			12 58			13 08	13 49	13 04		13 13	13 15	
London Waterloo (East) 4 ⊖	a			12 32					12 39					12 56				13 02				13 09			
London Charing Cross 4 ⊖	a			12 36					12 43					13 00				13 06				13 13			
Ebbsfleet International	a	11 47													12 17										
Stratford International ⊖	a	11 59													12 29										
St Pancras Int'l 15 ⊖	a	12 06													12 36										

		SE		SE	SE	SE	SE	SE	SE	SE	SE	SE		SE	SE	SE	SE	SE	SE	SE	SE	SE		SE	SE
Gillingham (Kent) 4	d				12 20						12 24							12 50							12 54
Chatham 4	d				12 24						12 28							12 54							12 58
Rochester 4	d				12 27						12 30							12 57							13 00
Maidstone West	d																								
Strood 4	d				12 32						12 35							13 02							13 05
Higham	d										12 40														13 10
Gravesend 4	d			12 32	12 43						12 48						13 02	13 13							13 18
Northfleet	d			12 36													13 06								
Swanscombe	d			12 38													13 08								
Greenhithe for Bluewater	d			12 41							12 53						13 11								13 23
Stone Crossing	d			12 43													13 13								
Dartford 4	a			12 47							12 58						13 17								13 28
	d			12 48			12 52				12 59			13 01	13 08		13 18			13 22					13 29
Slade Green 4	d	12 45								12 55				13 05		13 15								13 25	
Erith	d	12 48								12 58				13 08		13 18								13 28	
Belvedere	d	12 50								13 00				13 10		13 20								13 30	
Abbey Wood	d	12 53								13 03	13 08			13 13		13 23								13 33	13 38
Plumstead	d	12 56								13 06				13 16		13 26								13 36	
Woolwich Arsenal 4	d	12 59								13 09	13 13			13 19		13 29								13 39	13 43
Woolwich Dockyard	d	13 02								13 12				13 22		13 32								13 42	
Charlton 4	d	13 05							13 07	13 15	13 17			13 25		13 35						13 37		13 45	13 47
Crayford	d			12 52					13 37								13 22					14 07			
Bexley	d			12 55					13 40								13 25					14 10			
Albany Park	d			12 58					13 43								13 28					14 13			
Sidcup 4	d			13 01					13 46								13 31					14 16			
New Eltham	d			13 04					13 49								13 34					14 19			
Mottingham	d			13 06					13 51								13 36					14 21			
Lee	d			13 09					13 54								13 39					14 24			
Hither Green 4	d			13 12				13 19	13 58								13 42				13 49	14 28			
Barnehurst 4	d						12 59					13 08			13 16					13 29					
Bexleyheath	d						13 01					13 10			13 19					13 31					
Welling	d						13 04					13 13			13 22					13 34					
Falconwood	d						13 07					13 16			13 24					13 37					
Eltham	d						13 10					13 19			13 27					13 40					
Kidbrooke	d						13 13					13 22			13 30					13 43					
Blackheath 4	d						13 16				13 22	13 25			13 34					13 46					13 52
Lewisham 4	d					13 14	13 20	13 24	14 04		13 26	13 29			13 38				13 44	13 50	13 54	14 34			13 56
St Johns	d					13 16		13 26	14 06			13 31							13 46		13 56	14 36			
New Cross 4 ⊖	d					13 18		13 28	14 08			13 33							13 48		13 58	14 38			
Nunhead 4	d														13 45										
Peckham Rye 4	d														13 47										
Denmark Hill 4	d														13 51										
London Victoria 15 ⊖	a														14 00										
Westcombe Park	d	13 07								13 17				13 27		13 37								13 47	
Maze Hill	d	13 09								13 19				13 29		13 39								13 49	
Greenwich 4	d	13 12								13 22				13 32		13 42								13 52	
Deptford	a	13 14								13 24				13 34		13 44								13 54	
London Bridge 4 ⊖	a	13 20		13 22		13 24	13 28	13 34	14 14	13 30	13 35	13 38		13 41		13 50	13 52		13 54	13 58	14 04	14 44		14 00	14 05
London Cannon Street 4 ⊖	a	13 24				13 28		13 38	14 19	13 34		13 43		13 45		13 54			13 58		14 08	14 49		14 04	
London Waterloo (East) 4 ⊖	a			13 26			13 33				13 39						13 56			14 02					14 09
London Charing Cross 4 ⊖	a			13 30			13 36				13 43						14 00			14 06					14 13
Ebbsfleet International	a				12 47													13 17							
Stratford International ⊖	a				12 59													13 29							
St Pancras Int'l 15 ⊖	a				13 06													13 36							

Table 200

Saturdays

Gillingham and Dartford - London

		SE	SE	SE	SE	SE	SE	SE		SE	SE	SE	SE	SE	SE	SE	SE	SE		SE	SE	SE	SE	SE	SE
Gillingham (Kent) [4]	d						13 20							13 24							13 50				
Chatham [4]	d						13 24							13 28							13 54				
Rochester [4]	d						13 27							13 30							13 57				
Maidstone West	d																								
Strood [4]	d						13 32							13 35							14 02				
Higham	d													13 40											
Gravesend [4]	d					13 32	13 43							13 48						14 02	14 13				
Northfleet	d					13 36														14 06					
Swanscombe	d					13 38														14 08					
Greenhithe for Bluewater	d					13 41								13 53						14 11					
Stone Crossing	d					13 43														14 13					
Dartford [4]	a					13 47								13 58						14 17					
	d		13 31	13 38		13 48				13 52				13 59		14 01	14 08			14 18			14 22		
Slade Green [4]	d		13 35		13 45								13 55			14 05		14 15							
Erith	d		13 38		13 48								13 58			14 08		14 18							
Belvedere	d		13 40		13 50								14 00			14 10		14 20							
Abbey Wood	d		13 43		13 53								14 03	14 08		14 13		14 23							
Plumstead	d		13 46		13 56								14 06			14 16		14 26							
Woolwich Arsenal [4]	d		13 49		13 59								14 09	14 13		14 19		14 29							
Woolwich Dockyard	d		13 52		14 02								14 12			14 22		14 32							
Charlton [4]	d		13 55		14 05							14 07	14 15	14 17		14 25		14 35							14 37
Crayford	d					13 52						14 37								14 22					15 07
Bexley	d					13 55						14 40								14 25					15 10
Albany Park	d					13 58						14 43								14 28					15 13
Sidcup [4]	d					14 01						14 46								14 31					15 16
New Eltham	d					14 04						14 49								14 34					15 19
Mottingham	d					14 06						14 51								14 36					15 21
Lee	d					14 09						14 54								14 39					15 24
Hither Green [4]	d					14 12					14 19	14 58								14 42				14 49	15 28
Barnehurst [4]	d	13 38		13 46						13 59					14 08		14 16						14 29		
Bexleyheath	d	13 40		13 49						14 01					14 10		14 19						14 31		
Welling	d	13 43		13 52						14 04					14 13		14 22						14 34		
Falconwood	d	13 46		13 54						14 07					14 16		14 24						14 37		
Eltham	d	13 49		13 57						14 10					14 19		14 27						14 40		
Kidbrooke	d	13 52		14 00						14 13					14 22		14 30						14 43		
Blackheath [4]	d	13 55		14 04						14 16				14 22	14 25		14 34						14 46		
Lewisham [4]	d	13 59		14 08				14 14		14 20	14 24	15 04		14 26	14 29		14 38					14 44	14 50	14 54	15 34
St Johns	d	14 01						14 16			14 26	15 06			14 31							14 46		14 56	15 36
New Cross [4]	d	14 03						14 18			14 28	15 08			14 33							14 48		14 58	15 38
Nunhead [4]	d			14 15													14 45								
Peckham Rye [4]	d			14 17													14 47								
Denmark Hill [4]	d			14 21													14 51								
London Victoria [15]	a			14 30													15 00								
Westcombe Park	d		13 57		14 07								14 17			14 27		14 37							
Maze Hill	d		13 59		14 09								14 19			14 29		14 39							
Greenwich [4]	d		14 02		14 12								14 22			14 32		14 42							
Deptford	a		14 04		14 14								14 24			14 34		14 44							
London Bridge [4]	a	14 08	14 11		14 20	14 22		14 24		14 28	14 34	15 14	14 30	14 35	14 38	14 41		14 50		14 52		14 54	14 58	15 04	15 44
London Cannon Street [4]	a	14 13	14 15		14 24			14 28			14 38	15 19	14 34		14 43	14 45		14 54				14 58		15 08	15 49
London Waterloo (East) [4]	a					14 26				14 32				14 39						14 56			15 02		
London Charing Cross [4]	a					14 30				14 36				14 43						15 00			15 06		
Ebbsfleet International	a						13 47														14 17				
Stratford International	a						13 59														14 29				
St Pancras Int'l [15]	a						14 06														14 40				

		SE	SE	SE		SE	SE	SE	SE	SE	SE	SE	SE	SE		SE	SE	SE	SE	SE	SE	SE	SE	SE	
Gillingham (Kent) [4]	d		13 54							14 20							14 24						14 50		
Chatham [4]	d		13 58							14 24							14 28						14 54		
Rochester [4]	d		14 00							14 27							14 30						14 57		
Maidstone West	d																								
Strood [4]	d		14 05							14 32							14 35						15 02		
Higham	d		14 10														14 40								
Gravesend [4]	d		14 18						14 32	14 43							14 48					15 02	15 13		
Northfleet	d								14 36													15 06			
Swanscombe	d								14 38													15 08			
Greenhithe for Bluewater	d		14 23						14 41								14 53					15 11			
Stone Crossing	d								14 43													15 13			
Dartford [4]	a		14 28						14 47								14 58					15 17			
	d		14 29			14 31	14 38		14 48			14 52					14 59		15 01	15 08		15 18			
Slade Green [4]	d	14 25				14 35		14 45								14 55			15 05		15 15				
Erith	d	14 28				14 38		14 48								14 58			15 08		15 18				
Belvedere	d	14 30				14 40		14 50								15 00			15 10		15 20				
Abbey Wood	d	14 33	14 38			14 43		14 53								15 03	15 08		15 13		15 23				
Plumstead	d	14 36				14 46		14 56								15 06			15 16		15 26				
Woolwich Arsenal [4]	d	14 39	14 43			14 49		14 59								15 09	15 13		15 19		15 29				
Woolwich Dockyard	d	14 42				14 52		15 02								15 12			15 22		15 32				
Charlton [4]	d	14 45	14 47			14 55		15 05						15 07		15 15	15 17		15 25		15 35				
Crayford	d								14 52					15 37								15 22			
Bexley	d								14 55					15 40								15 25			
Albany Park	d								14 58					15 43								15 28			
Sidcup [4]	d								15 01					15 46								15 31			
New Eltham	d								15 04					15 49								15 34			
Mottingham	d								15 06					15 51								15 36			
Lee	d								15 09					15 54								15 39			
Hither Green [4]	d								15 12				15 19	15 58								15 42			
Barnehurst [4]	d			14 38			14 46					14 59						15 08		15 16					
Bexleyheath	d			14 40			14 49					15 01						15 10		15 19					
Welling	d			14 43			14 52					15 04						15 13		15 22					
Falconwood	d			14 46			14 54					15 07						15 16		15 24					
Eltham	d			14 49			14 57					15 10						15 19		15 27					
Kidbrooke	d			14 52			15 00					15 13						15 22		15 30					
Blackheath [4]	d		14 52	14 55			15 04					15 16					15 22	15 25		15 34					
Lewisham [4]	d		14 56	14 59			15 08				15 14	15 20	15 24	16 04			15 26	15 29		15 38				15 44	
St Johns	d			15 01							15 16		15 26	16 06				15 31						15 46	
New Cross [4]	d			15 03							15 18		15 28	16 08				15 33						15 48	
Nunhead [4]	d						15 15													15 45					
Peckham Rye [4]	d						15 17													15 47					
Denmark Hill [4]	d						15 21													15 51					
London Victoria [15]	a						15 30													16 00					
Westcombe Park	d	14 47				14 57		15 07								15 17			15 27		15 37				
Maze Hill	d	14 49				14 59		15 09								15 19			15 29		15 39				
Greenwich [4]	d	14 52				15 02		15 12								15 22			15 32		15 42				
Deptford	a	14 54				15 04		15 14								15 24			15 34		15 44				
London Bridge [4]	a	15 00	15 05	15 08		15 11		15 20	15 22		15 24	15 28	15 34	16 14		15 30	15 35	15 38	15 41		15 50	15 52		15 54	
London Cannon Street [4]	a	15 04		15 13		15 15		15 24			15 28		15 38	16 19		15 34		15 43	15 45		15 54			15 58	
London Waterloo (East) [4]	a		15 09						15 26			15 32					15 39					15 56			
London Charing Cross [4]	a		15 13						15 30			15 36					15 43					16 00			
Ebbsfleet International	a									14 47													15 17		
Stratford International	a									15 02													15 29		
St Pancras Int'l [15]	a									15 09													15 36		

Table 200

Saturdays

Gillingham and Dartford - London

Station		SE	SE	SE	SE	SE	SE	SE	SE	SE		SE	SE	SE	SE	SE	SE	SE	SE	SE		SE	SE	SE	SE
Gillingham (Kent) 4	d					14 54							15 20						15 24						
Chatham 4	d					14 58							15 24						15 28						
Rochester 4	d					15 00							15 27						15 30						
Maidstone West	d																								
Strood 4	d					15 05							15 32						15 35						
Higham	d					15 10													15 40						
Gravesend 4	d					15 18						15 32	15 43						15 48						16 02
Northfleet	d											15 36													16 06
Swanscombe	d											15 38													16 08
Greenhithe for Bluewater	d					15 23						15 41							15 53						16 11
Stone Crossing	d											15 43													16 13
Dartford 4	a					15 28						15 47							15 58						16 17
	d	15 22				15 29		15 31	15 38			15 48			15 52				15 59			16 01	16 08		16 18
Slade Green 4	d				15 25			15 35		15 45								15 55				16 05		16 15	
Erith	d				15 28			15 38		15 48								15 58				16 08		16 18	
Belvedere	d				15 30			15 40		15 50								16 00				16 10		16 20	
Abbey Wood	d				15 33	15 38		15 43		15 53								16 03	16 08			16 13		16 23	
Plumstead	d				15 36			15 46		15 56								16 06				16 16		16 26	
Woolwich Arsenal 4	d				15 39	15 43		15 49		15 59								16 09	16 13			16 19		16 29	
Woolwich Dockyard	d				15 42			15 52		16 02								16 12				16 22		16 32	
Charlton 4	d			15 37	15 45	15 47		15 55		16 05							16 07	16 15	16 17			16 25		16 35	
Crayford	d			16 07								15 52					16 37								16 22
Bexley	d			16 10								15 55					16 40								16 25
Albany Park	d			16 13								15 58					16 43								16 28
Sidcup 4	d			16 16								16 01					16 46								16 31
New Eltham	d			16 19								16 04					16 49								16 34
Mottingham	d			16 21								16 06					16 51								16 36
Lee	d			16 24								16 09					16 54								16 39
Hither Green 4	d		15 49	16 28								16 12				16 19	16 58								16 42
Barnehurst 4	d	15 29					15 38		15 46						15 59					16 08			16 16		
Bexleyheath	d	15 31					15 40		15 49						16 01					16 10			16 19		
Welling	d	15 34					15 43		15 52						16 04					16 13			16 22		
Falconwood	d	15 37					15 46		15 54						16 07					16 16			16 24		
Eltham	d	15 40					15 49		15 57						16 10					16 19			16 27		
Kidbrooke	d	15 43					15 52		16 00						16 13					16 22			16 30		
Blackheath 4	d	15 46				15 52	15 55		16 04						16 16				16 22	16 25			16 34		
Lewisham 4	d	15 50	15 54	16 34		15 56	15 59		16 08					16 14	16 20	16 24	17 04		16 26	16 29			16 38		
St Johns	d		15 56	16 36			16 01							16 16		16 26	17 06			16 31					
New Cross 4 ⊖	d		15 58	16 38			16 03							16 18		16 28	17 08			16 33					
Nunhead 4	d								16 15														16 45		
Peckham Rye 4	d								16 17														16 47		
Denmark Hill 4	d								16 21														16 51		
London Victoria 15 ⊖	a								16 30														17 00		
Westcombe Park	d				15 47			15 57		16 07								16 17				16 27		16 37	
Maze Hill	d				15 49			15 59		16 09								16 19				16 29		16 39	
Greenwich 4	d				15 52			16 02		16 12								16 22				16 32		16 42	
Deptford	a				15 54			16 04		16 14								16 24				16 34		16 44	
London Bridge 4 ⊖	a	15 58	16 04	16 44	16 00	16 05	16 08	16 11		16 20		16 22		16 24	16 28	16 34	17 14	16 30	16 35	16 38		16 41		16 50	16 52
London Cannon Street 4 ⊖	a		16 08	16 49	16 04		16 13	16 15		16 24				16 28		16 38	17 19	16 34		16 43		16 45		16 54	
London Waterloo (East) 4 ⊖	a	16 02				16 09						16 26			16 32				16 39						16 56
London Charing Cross 4 ⊖	a	16 06				16 13						16 30			16 36				16 43						17 00
Ebbsfleet International	a												15 47												
Stratford International ⊖	a												15 59												
St Pancras Int'l 15 ⊖	a												16 06												

Station		SE	SE	SE	SE	SE		SE	SE	SE	SE	SE	SE	SE	SE	SE		SE	SE	SE	SE	SE	SE	SE	SE
Gillingham (Kent) 4	d	15 50							15 54						16 20							16 24			
Chatham 4	d	15 54							15 58						16 24							16 28			
Rochester 4	d	15 57							16 00						16 27							16 30			
Maidstone West	d																								
Strood 4	d	16 02							16 05						16 32							16 35			
Higham	d								16 10													16 40			
Gravesend 4	d	16 13							16 18					16 32	16 43							16 48			
Northfleet	d													16 36											
Swanscombe	d													16 38											
Greenhithe for Bluewater	d								16 23					16 41								16 53			
Stone Crossing	d													16 43											
Dartford 4	a								16 28					16 47								16 58			
	d			16 22					16 29		16 31	16 38		16 48				16 52				16 59		17 01	17 08
Slade Green 4	d							16 25			16 35		16 45								16 55			17 05	
Erith	d							16 28			16 38		16 48								16 58			17 08	
Belvedere	d							16 30			16 40		16 50								17 00			17 10	
Abbey Wood	d							16 33	16 38		16 43		16 53								17 03	17 08		17 13	
Plumstead	d							16 36			16 46		16 56								17 06			17 16	
Woolwich Arsenal 4	d							16 39	16 43		16 49		16 59								17 09	17 13		17 19	
Woolwich Dockyard	d							16 42			16 52		17 02								17 12			17 22	
Charlton 4	d					16 37		16 45	16 47		16 55		17 05							17 07	17 15	17 17		17 25	
Crayford	d					17 07								16 52						17 37					
Bexley	d					17 10								16 55						17 40					
Albany Park	d					17 13								16 58						17 43					
Sidcup 4	d					17 16								17 01						17 46					
New Eltham	d					17 19								17 04						17 49					
Mottingham	d					17 21								17 06						17 51					
Lee	d					17 24								17 09						17 54					
Hither Green 4	d				16 49	17 28								17 12					17 19	17 58					
Barnehurst 4	d			16 29						16 38		16 46						16 59					17 08		17 16
Bexleyheath	d			16 31						16 40		16 49						17 01					17 10		17 19
Welling	d			16 34						16 43		16 52						17 04					17 13		17 22
Falconwood	d			16 37						16 46		16 54						17 07					17 16		17 24
Eltham	d			16 40						16 49		16 57						17 10					17 19		17 27
Kidbrooke	d			16 43						16 52		17 00						17 13					17 22		17 30
Blackheath 4	d			16 46					16 52	16 55		17 04						17 16				17 22	17 25		17 34
Lewisham 4	d		16 44	16 50	16 54	17 34			16 56	16 59		17 08				17 14		17 20	17 24	18 04		17 26	17 29		17 38
St Johns	d		16 46		16 56	17 36				17 01						17 16			17 26	18 06			17 31		
New Cross 4 ⊖	d		16 48		16 58	17 38				17 03						17 18			17 28	18 08			17 33		
Nunhead 4	d											17 15													17 45
Peckham Rye 4	d											17 17													17 47
Denmark Hill 4	d											17 21													17 51
London Victoria 15 ⊖	a											17 30													18 00
Westcombe Park	d							16 47			16 57		17 07								17 17			17 27	
Maze Hill	d							16 49			16 59		17 09								17 19			17 29	
Greenwich 4	d							16 52			17 02		17 12								17 22			17 32	
Deptford	a							16 54			17 04		17 14								17 24			17 34	
London Bridge 4 ⊖	a		16 54	16 58	17 04	17 44		17 00	17 05	17 08	17 11		17 20	17 22		17 24		17 28	17 34	18 14	17 30	17 35	17 38	17 41	
London Cannon Street 4 ⊖	a		16 58		17 08	17 49		17 04		17 13	17 15		17 24			17 28			17 38	18 19	17 34		17 43	17 45	
London Waterloo (East) 4 ⊖	a			17 02					17 09					17 26				17 32				17 39			
London Charing Cross 4 ⊖	a			17 06					17 13					17 30				17 36				17 43			
Ebbsfleet International	a	16 17													16 47										
Stratford International ⊖	a	16 29													17 02										
St Pancras Int'l 15 ⊖	a	16 37													17 09										

Table 200

Saturdays

Gillingham and Dartford - London

		SE		SE	SE	SE	SE	SE	SE	SE	SE	SE		SE	SE	SE	SE	SE	SE	SE	SE	SE		SE	SE
Gillingham (Kent)	d				16 50						16 54							17 20							17 24
Chatham	d				16 54						16 58							17 24							17 28
Rochester	d				16 57						17 00							17 27							17 30
Maidstone West	d																								
Strood	d				17 02						17 05							17 32							17 35
Higham	d										17 10														17 40
Gravesend	d			17 02	17 12						17 18						17 32	17 43							17 48
Northfleet	d			17 06													17 36								
Swanscombe	d			17 08													17 38								
Greenhithe for Bluewater	d			17 11							17 23						17 41								17 53
Stone Crossing	d			17 13													17 43								
Dartford	a			17 17							17 28						17 47								17 58
	d			17 18			17 22				17 29			17 31	17 38		17 48			17 52					17 59
Slade Green	d	17 15								17 25				17 35		17 45								17 55	
Erith	d	17 18								17 28				17 38		17 48								17 58	
Belvedere	d	17 20								17 30				17 40		17 50								18 00	
Abbey Wood	d	17 23								17 33	17 38			17 43		17 53								18 03	18 08
Plumstead	d	17 26								17 36				17 46		17 56								18 06	
Woolwich Arsenal	d	17 29								17 39	17 43			17 49		17 59								18 09	18 13
Woolwich Dockyard	d	17 32								17 42				17 52		18 02								18 12	
Charlton	d	17 35							17 37	17 45	17 47			17 55		18 05						18 07		18 15	18 17
Crayford	d			17 22					18 07								17 52					18 37			
Bexley	d			17 25					18 10								17 55					18 40			
Albany Park	d			17 28					18 13								17 58					18 43			
Sidcup	d			17 31					18 16								18 01					18 46			
New Eltham	d			17 34					18 19								18 04					18 49			
Mottingham	d			17 36					18 21								18 06					18 51			
Lee	d			17 39					18 24								18 09					18 54			
Hither Green	d			17 42				17 49	18 28								18 12				18 19	18 58			
Barnehurst	d						17 29					17 38			17 46					17 59					
Bexleyheath	d						17 31					17 40			17 49					18 01					
Welling	d						17 34					17 43			17 52					18 04					
Falconwood	d						17 37					17 46			17 54					18 07					
Eltham	d						17 40					17 49			17 57					18 10					
Kidbrooke	d						17 43					17 52			18 00					18 13					
Blackheath	d						17 46				17 52	17 55			18 04					18 16					18 22
Lewisham	d					17 44	17 50	17 54	18 34		17 56	17 59			18 08				18 14	18 20	18 24	19 04			18 26
St Johns	d					17 46		17 56	18 36			18 01							18 16		18 26	19 06			
New Cross	d					17 48		17 58	18 38			18 03							18 18		18 28	19 08			
Nunhead	d														18 15										
Peckham Rye	d														18 17										
Denmark Hill	d														18 21										
London Victoria	a														18 30										
Westcombe Park	d	17 37								17 47				17 57		18 07								18 17	
Maze Hill	d	17 39								17 49				17 59		18 09								18 19	
Greenwich	d	17 42								17 52				18 02		18 12								18 22	
Deptford	a	17 44								17 54				18 04		18 14								18 24	
London Bridge	a	17 50		17 52		17 54	17 58	18 04	18 44	18 00	18 05	18 08		18 11		18 20	18 22		18 24	18 28	18 34	19 14		18 30	18 35
London Cannon Street	a	17 54				17 58		18 08	18 49	18 04		18 13		18 15		18 24			18 28		18 38	19 19		18 34	
London Waterloo (East)	a			17 56			18 02				18 09						18 26			18 32					18 39
London Charing Cross	a			18 00			18 06				18 13						18 30			18 36					18 43
Ebbsfleet International	a				17 16													17 47							
Stratford International	a				17 27													17 59							
St Pancras Int'l	a				17 38													18 06							

		SE	SE	SE	SE	SE	SE	SE		SE	SE	SE	SE	SE	SE	SE	SE	SE		SE	SE	SE	SE	SE	SE
Gillingham (Kent)	d						17 50					17 54					18 20				18 24			18 50	
Chatham	d						17 54					17 58					18 24				18 28			18 54	
Rochester	d						17 57					18 00					18 27				18 30			18 57	
Maidstone West	d																								
Strood	d						18 02					18 05					18 32				18 35			19 02	
Higham	d											18 10									18 40				
Gravesend	d					18 02	18 13					18 18				18 32	18 43				18 48		19 02	19 12	
Northfleet	d					18 06										18 36							19 06		
Swanscombe	d					18 08										18 38							19 08		
Greenhithe for Bluewater	d					18 11						18 23				18 41					18 53		19 11		
Stone Crossing	d					18 13										18 43							19 13		
Dartford	a					18 17						18 28				18 47					18 58		19 17		
	d		18 01	18 08		18 18				18 22		18 29		18 31	18 38	18 48				18 52	18 59	19 01	19 18		
Slade Green	d		18 05		18 15						18 25			18 35				18 55				19 05			19 25
Erith	d		18 08		18 18						18 28			18 38				18 58				19 08			19 28
Belvedere	d		18 10		18 20						18 30			18 40				19 00				19 10			19 30
Abbey Wood	d		18 13		18 23						18 33	18 38		18 43				19 03			19 08	19 13			19 33
Plumstead	d		18 16		18 26						18 36			18 46				19 06				19 16			19 36
Woolwich Arsenal	d		18 19		18 29						18 39	18 43		18 49				19 09			19 13	19 19			19 39
Woolwich Dockyard	d		18 22		18 32						18 42			18 52				19 12				19 22			19 42
Charlton	d		18 25		18 35						18 45	18 47		18 55				19 15			19 17	19 25			19 45
Crayford	d					18 22										18 52							19 22		
Bexley	d					18 25										18 55							19 25		
Albany Park	d					18 28										18 58							19 28		
Sidcup	d					18 31										19 01							19 31		
New Eltham	d					18 34										19 04							19 34		
Mottingham	d					18 36										19 06							19 36		
Lee	d					18 39										19 09							19 39		
Hither Green	d					18 42										19 12							19 42		
Barnehurst	d	18 08		18 16						18 29			18 38		18 46					18 59					
Bexleyheath	d	18 10		18 19						18 31			18 40		18 49					19 01					
Welling	d	18 13		18 22						18 34			18 43		18 52					19 04					
Falconwood	d	18 16		18 24						18 37			18 46		18 54					19 07					
Eltham	d	18 19		18 27						18 40			18 49		18 57					19 10					
Kidbrooke	d	18 22		18 30						18 43			18 52		19 00					19 13					
Blackheath	d	18 25		18 34						18 46		18 52	18 55		19 04					19 16	19 22				
Lewisham	d	18 29		18 38				18 44		18 50		18 56	18 59		19 08	19 18				19 20	19 26		19 48		
St Johns	d	18 31						18 46					19 01												
New Cross	d	18 33						18 48					19 03							19 23			19 51		
Nunhead	d			18 45											19 15										
Peckham Rye	d			18 47											19 17										
Denmark Hill	d			18 51											19 21										
London Victoria	a			19 00											19 30										
Westcombe Park	d		18 27		18 37						18 47			18 57				19 17				19 27			19 47
Maze Hill	d		18 29		18 39						18 49			18 59				19 19				19 29			19 49
Greenwich	d		18 32		18 42						18 52			19 02				19 22				19 32			19 52
Deptford	a		18 34		18 44						18 54			19 04				19 24				19 34			19 54
London Bridge	a	18 38	18 41		18 50	18 52		18 54		18 58	19 00	19 05	19 08	19 11		19 27		19 30		19 33	19 36	19 41	19 57		20 00
London Cannon Street	a	18 43	18 45		18 54			18 58			19 04		19 13	19 15											
London Waterloo (East)	a					18 56				19 02		19 09				19 32				19 39	19 42	19 45	20 04		
London Charing Cross	a					19 00				19 06		19 13				19 35				19 42	19 45	19 49	20 07		
Ebbsfleet International	a						18 17										18 47							19 16	
Stratford International	a						18 29										19 02							19 27	
St Pancras Int'l	a						18 36										19 09							19 38	

Table 200

Saturdays

Gillingham and Dartford - London

		SE	SE	SE		SE	SE	SE	SE	SE	SE	SE	SE	SE		SE	SE	SE	SE	SE	SE	SE	SE	SE
Gillingham (Kent) 4	d		18 54				19 20			19 24			19 50			19 54			20 20		20 24			20 50
Chatham 4	d		18 58				19 24			19 28			19 54			19 58			20 24		20 28			20 54
Rochester 4	d		19 00				19 27			19 30			19 57			20 00			20 27		20 30			20 57
Maidstone West	d																							
Strood 4	d		19 05				19 32			19 35			20 02			20 05			20 32		20 35			21 02
Higham	d		19 10							19 40						20 10					20 40			
Gravesend 4	d		19 18			19 32	19 43			19 48		20 02	20 12			20 18		20 32	20 43		20 48		21 02	21 13
Northfleet	d					19 36						20 06						20 36					21 06	
Swanscombe	d					19 38						20 08						20 38					21 08	
Greenhithe for Bluewater	d		19 23			19 41				19 53		20 11				20 23		20 41			20 53		21 11	
Stone Crossing	d					19 43						20 13						20 43					21 13	
Dartford 4	a		19 28			19 47				19 58		20 17				20 28		20 47			20 58		21 17	
	d	19 25	19 29	19 31		19 48			19 55	19 59	20 01	20 18		20 25		20 29	20 31	20 48		20 55	20 59	21 01	21 18	
Slade Green 4	d			19 35				19 55			20 05						20 35					21 05		
Erith	d			19 38				19 58			20 08						20 38					21 08		
Belvedere	d			19 40				20 00			20 10						20 40					21 10		
Abbey Wood	d		19 38	19 43				20 03		20 08	20 13					20 38	20 43				21 08	21 13		
Plumstead	d			19 46				20 06			20 16						20 46					21 16		
Woolwich Arsenal 4 ⛴	d		19 43	19 49				20 09		20 13	20 19					20 43	20 49				21 13	21 19		
Woolwich Dockyard	d			19 52				20 12			20 22						20 52					21 22		
Charlton 4	d		19 47	19 55				20 15		20 17	20 25					20 47	20 55				21 17	21 25		
Crayford	d					19 52						20 22						20 52					21 22	
Bexley	d					19 55						20 25						20 55					21 25	
Albany Park	d					19 58						20 28						20 58					21 28	
Sidcup 4	d					20 01						20 31						21 01					21 31	
New Eltham	d					20 04						20 34						21 04					21 34	
Mottingham	d					20 06						20 36						21 06					21 36	
Lee	d					20 09						20 39						21 09					21 39	
Hither Green 4	d					20 12						20 42						21 12					21 42	
Barnehurst 4	d	19 32							20 02					20 32						21 02				
Bexleyheath	d	19 34							20 04					20 34						21 04				
Welling	d	19 37							20 07					20 37						21 07				
Falconwood	d	19 40							20 10					20 40						21 10				
Eltham	d	19 42							20 12					20 42						21 12				
Kidbrooke	d	19 45							20 15					20 45						21 15				
Blackheath 4	d	19 49	19 52						20 19	20 22				20 49		20 52				21 19	21 22			
Lewisham 4 ⛴	d	19 53	19 56			20 18			20 23	20 26		20 48		20 53		20 56		21 18		21 23	21 26		21 48	
St Johns	d																							
New Cross 4 ⊖	d	19 56				20 21			20 26			20 51		20 56				21 21		21 26			21 51	
Nunhead 4	d																							
Peckham Rye 4	d																							
Denmark Hill 4	d																							
London Victoria 15 ⊖	a																							
Westcombe Park	d			19 57				20 17			20 27						20 57					21 27		
Maze Hill	d			19 59				20 19			20 29						20 59					21 29		
Greenwich 4 ⛴	d			20 02				20 22			20 32						21 02					21 32		
Deptford	a			20 04				20 24			20 34						21 04					21 34		
London Bridge 4 ⊖	a	20 03	20 06	20 11		20 27		20 30	20 33	20 36	20 41	20 57		21 03		21 06	21 11	21 27		21 33	21 36	21 41	21 57	
London Cannon Street 4 ⊖	a																							
London Waterloo (East) 4 ⊖	a	20 08	20 10	20 15		20 34			20 38	20 40	20 45	21 04		21 08		21 10	21 15	21 34		21 38	21 40	21 45	22 04	
London Charing Cross 4 ⊖	a	20 12	20 14	20 19		20 37			20 42	20 44	20 49	21 07		21 12		21 14	21 19	21 37		21 42	21 44	21 49	22 07	
Ebbsfleet International	a						19 47						20 16						20 47					21 17
Stratford International ⊖ ⛴	a						19 59						20 27						21 02					21 35
St Pancras Int'l 15 ⊖	a						20 06						20 38						21 09					21 42

		SE	SE	SE	SE	SE	SE	SE	SE	SE		SE	SE	SE	SE	SE	SE	SE	SE	SE		SE
Gillingham (Kent) 4	d		20 54			21 20		21 24				21 50		21 54			22 20		22 24			22 54
Chatham 4	d		20 58			21 24		21 28				21 54		21 58			22 24		22 28			22 58
Rochester 4	d		21 00			21 27		21 30				21 57		22 00			22 27		22 30			23 00
Maidstone West	d																					
Strood 4	d		21 05			21 32		21 35				22 02		22 05			22 32		22 35			23 05
Higham	d		21 10					21 40						22 10					22 40			23 10
Gravesend 4	d		21 18		21 32	21 43		21 48		22 02		22 13		22 18		22 32	22 43		22 48			23 18
Northfleet	d				21 36					22 06						22 36						
Swanscombe	d				21 38					22 08						22 38						
Greenhithe for Bluewater	d		21 23		21 41			21 53		22 11				22 23		22 41			22 53			23 23
Stone Crossing	d				21 43					22 13						22 43						
Dartford 4	a		21 28		21 47			21 58		22 17				22 28		22 47			22 58			23 28
	d	21 25	21 29	21 31	21 48		21 55	21 59	22 01	22 18			22 25	22 29	22 31	22 48		22 55	22 59	23 01		
Slade Green 4	d			21 35					22 05						22 35					23 05		
Erith	d			21 38					22 08						22 38					23 08		
Belvedere	d			21 40					22 10						22 40					23 10		
Abbey Wood	d		21 38	21 43				22 08	22 13					22 38	22 43				23 08	23 13		
Plumstead	d			21 46					22 16						22 46					23 16		
Woolwich Arsenal 4 ⛴	d		21 43	21 49				22 13	22 19					22 43	22 49				23 13	23 19		
Woolwich Dockyard	d			21 52					22 22						22 52					23 22		
Charlton 4	d		21 47	21 55				22 17	22 25					22 47	22 55				23 17	23 25		
Crayford	d				21 52					22 22						22 52						
Bexley	d				21 55					22 25						22 55						
Albany Park	d				21 58					22 28						22 58						
Sidcup 4	d				22 01					22 31						23 01						
New Eltham	d				22 04					22 34						23 04						
Mottingham	d				22 06					22 36						23 06						
Lee	d				22 09					22 39						23 09						
Hither Green 4	d				22 12					22 42						23 12						
Barnehurst 4	d	21 32					22 02						22 32					23 02				
Bexleyheath	d	21 34					22 04						22 34					23 04				
Welling	d	21 37					22 07						22 37					23 07				
Falconwood	d	21 40					22 10						22 40					23 10				
Eltham	d	21 42					22 12						22 42					23 12				
Kidbrooke	d	21 45					22 15						22 45					23 15				
Blackheath 4	d	21 49	21 52				22 19	22 22					22 49	22 52				23 19	23 22			
Lewisham 4 ⛴	d	21 53	21 56		22 18		22 23	22 26		22 48			22 53	22 56		23 18		23 23	23 26			
St Johns	d																					
New Cross 4 ⊖	d	21 56			22 21		22 26			22 51			22 56			23 21		23 26				
Nunhead 4	d																					
Peckham Rye 4	d																					
Denmark Hill 4	d																					
London Victoria 15 ⊖	a																					
Westcombe Park	d			21 57					22 27						22 57					23 27		
Maze Hill	d			21 59					22 29						22 59					23 29		
Greenwich 4 ⛴	d			22 02					22 32						23 02					23 32		
Deptford	a			22 04					22 34						23 04					23 34		
London Bridge 4 ⊖	a	22 01	22 05	22 11	22 27		22 31	22 35	22 41	22 57			23 01	23 05	23 11	23 27		23 31	23 35	23 41		
London Cannon Street 4 ⊖	a																					
London Waterloo (East) 4 ⊖	a	22 06	22 09	22 15	22 34		22 36	22 39	22 45	23 04			23 06	23 09	23 15	23 34		23 36	23 39	23 45		
London Charing Cross 4 ⊖	a	22 10	22 13	22 19	22 37		22 40	22 43	22 49	23 07			23 10	23 13	23 20	23 37		23 40	23 43	23 49		
Ebbsfleet International	a					21 47						22 17					22 47					
Stratford International ⊖ ⛴	a					21 59						22 29					22 59					
St Pancras Int'l 15 ⊖	a					22 06						22 36					23 06					

Table 200

Sundays

Gillingham and Dartford - London

		SE	SE	SE	SE	SE	SE	SE	SE	SE		SE	SE	SE	SE	SE	SE	SE	SE	SE		SE	SE	SE	SE
Gillingham (Kent) 4	d							06 45					07 15	07 20				07 45	07 50						08 15
Chatham 4	d							06 49					07 19	07 24				07 49	07 54						08 19
Rochester 4	d							06 51					07 21	07 27				07 51	07 57						08 21
Maidstone West	d																								
Strood 4	d							06 56					07 26	07 32				07 56	08 02						08 26
Higham	d							07 01					07 31					08 01							08 31
Gravesend 4	d							07 09					07 39	07 43				08 09	08 13						08 39
Northfleet	d							07 12					07 42					08 12							08 42
Swanscombe	d							07 14					07 44					08 14							08 44
Greenhithe for Bluewater	d							07 18					07 48					08 18							08 48
Stone Crossing	d							07 20					07 50					08 20							08 50
Dartford 4	a							07 24					07 54					08 24							08 54
	d	06 40	06 43	06 48	07 10	07 13	07 18	07 29	07 40	07 43		07 48	07 59		08 10	08 13	08 18	08 29				08 40	08 43	08 48	08 59
Slade Green 4	d		06 48			07 18				07 48						08 18							08 48		
Erith	d		06 50			07 20				07 50						08 20							08 50		
Belvedere	d		06 53			07 23				07 53						08 23							08 53		
Abbey Wood	d		06 56			07 26		07 38		07 56			08 08			08 26		08 38					08 56		09 08
Plumstead	d		06 59			07 29				07 59						08 29				08 47			08 59		
Woolwich Arsenal 4	d		07 02			07 32		07 43		08 02			08 13			08 32		08 43		08 50			09 02		09 13
Woolwich Dockyard	d		07 04			07 34				08 04						08 34				08 52			09 04		
Charlton 4	d		07 07			07 37		07 47		08 07			08 17			08 37		08 47		08 55			09 07		09 17
Crayford	d			06 52			07 22					07 52					08 22							08 52	
Bexley	d			06 55			07 25					07 55					08 25							08 55	
Albany Park	d			06 58			07 28					07 58					08 28							08 58	
Sidcup 4	d			07 01			07 31					08 01					08 31							09 01	
New Eltham	d			07 04			07 34					08 04					08 34							09 04	
Mottingham	d			07 06			07 36					08 06					08 36							09 06	
Lee	d			07 09			07 39					08 09					08 39							09 09	
Hither Green 4	d			07 12			07 42					08 12					08 42							09 12	
Barnehurst 4	d	06 47			07 17				07 47						08 17							08 47			
Bexleyheath	d	06 49			07 19				07 49						08 19							08 49			
Welling	d	06 52			07 22				07 52						08 22							08 52			
Falconwood	d	06 55			07 25				07 55						08 25							08 55			
Eltham	d	06 58			07 28				07 58						08 28							08 58			
Kidbrooke	d	07 01			07 31				08 01						08 31							09 01			
Blackheath 4	d	07 04			07 34			07 52	08 04				08 22		08 34			08 52				09 04			09 22
Lewisham 4	d	07 08		07 18	07 38		07 48	07 56	08 08			08 18	08 26		08 38		08 48	08 56				09 08		09 18	09 26
St Johns	d																								
New Cross 4 ⊖	d	07 11			07 41				08 11						08 41							09 11			
Nunhead 4	d																								
Peckham Rye 4	d																								
Denmark Hill 4	d																								
London Victoria 15 ⊖	a																								
Westcombe Park	d		07 09			07 39				08 09						08 39				08 57			09 09		
Maze Hill	d		07 11			07 41				08 11						08 41				08 59			09 11		
Greenwich 4	d		07 15			07 45				08 15						08 45				09 03			09 15		
Deptford	a		07 17			07 47				08 17						08 47				09 05			09 17		
London Bridge 4 ⊖	a	07 19	07 23	07 26	07 49	07 53	07 56	08 06	08 19	08 23		08 26	08 36		08 49	08 53	08 56	09 06		09 11		09 19	09 23	09 26	09 36
London Cannon Street 4 ⊖	a																								
London Waterloo (East) 4 ⊖	a	07 25	07 27	07 30	07 55	07 57	08 00	08 11	08 25	08 27		08 30	08 41		08 55	08 57	09 00	09 11				09 25	09 27	09 30	09 41
London Charing Cross 4 ⊖	a	07 28	07 31	07 34	07 58	08 01	08 04	08 14	08 28	08 31		08 34	08 44		08 58	09 01	09 04	09 14				09 28	09 31	09 34	09 44
Ebbsfleet International	a													07 47					08 17						
Stratford International ⊖	a													07 59					08 29						
St Pancras Int'l 15 ⊖	a													08 06					08 36						

		SE	SE	SE	SE	SE		SE	SE	SE	SE	SE	SE	SE	SE	SE		SE	SE	SE	SE	SE	SE	SE	SE
Gillingham (Kent) 4	d	08 20						08 50	08 54					09 20	09 24						09 50	09 54			
Chatham 4	d	08 24						08 54	08 58					09 24	09 28						09 54	09 58			
Rochester 4	d	08 27						08 57	09 00					09 27	09 30						09 57	10 00			
Maidstone West	d																								
Strood 4	d	08 32						09 02	09 05					09 32	09 35						10 02	10 05			
Higham	d								09 10						09 40							10 10			
Gravesend 4	d	08 43				09 02		09 13	09 18				09 32	09 43	09 48					10 02	10 13	10 18			
Northfleet	d					09 06							09 36							10 06					
Swanscombe	d					09 08							09 38							10 08					
Greenhithe for Bluewater	d					09 11			09 23				09 41		09 53					10 11		10 23			
Stone Crossing	d					09 13							09 43							10 13					
Dartford 4	a					09 17			09 28				09 47		09 58					10 17		10 28			
	d			09 10	09 13	09 18			09 29		09 40	09 43	09 48		09 59			10 10	10 13	10 18		10 29		10 40	10 43
Slade Green 4	d				09 18							09 48							10 18						10 48
Erith	d				09 20							09 50							10 20						10 50
Belvedere	d				09 23							09 53							10 23						10 53
Abbey Wood	d				09 26				09 38			09 56			10 08				10 26			10 38			10 56
Plumstead	d		09 17		09 29					09 47		09 59				10 17			10 29				10 47		10 59
Woolwich Arsenal 4	d		09 20		09 32				09 43	09 50		10 02			10 13	10 20			10 32			10 43	10 50		11 02
Woolwich Dockyard	d		09 22		09 34					09 52		10 04				10 22			10 34				10 52		11 04
Charlton 4	d		09 25		09 37				09 47	09 55		10 07			10 17	10 25			10 37			10 47	10 55		11 07
Crayford	d					09 22							09 52							10 22					
Bexley	d					09 25							09 55							10 25					
Albany Park	d					09 28							09 58							10 28					
Sidcup 4	d					09 31							10 01							10 31					
New Eltham	d					09 34							10 04							10 34					
Mottingham	d					09 36							10 06							10 36					
Lee	d					09 39							10 09							10 39					
Hither Green 4	d					09 42							10 12							10 42					
Barnehurst 4	d			09 17							09 47							10 17						10 47	
Bexleyheath	d			09 19							09 49							10 19						10 49	
Welling	d			09 22							09 52							10 22						10 52	
Falconwood	d			09 25							09 55							10 25						10 55	
Eltham	d			09 28							09 58							10 28						10 58	
Kidbrooke	d			09 31							10 01							10 31						11 01	
Blackheath 4	d			09 34					09 52		10 04				10 22			10 34				10 52		11 04	
Lewisham 4	d			09 38		09 48			09 56		10 08		10 18		10 26			10 38		10 48		10 56		11 08	
St Johns	d																								
New Cross 4 ⊖	d			09 41							10 11							10 41						11 11	
Nunhead 4	d																								
Peckham Rye 4	d																								
Denmark Hill 4	d																								
London Victoria 15 ⊖	a																								
Westcombe Park	d		09 27		09 39					09 57		10 09				10 27			10 39				10 57		11 09
Maze Hill	d		09 29		09 41					09 59		10 11				10 29			10 41				10 59		11 11
Greenwich 4	d		09 33		09 45					10 03		10 15				10 33			10 45				11 03		11 15
Deptford	a		09 35		09 47					10 05		10 17				10 35			10 47				11 05		11 17
London Bridge 4 ⊖	a		09 41	09 49	09 53	09 56			10 06	10 11	10 19	10 23	10 26		10 36	10 41		10 49	10 53	10 56		11 06	11 11	11 19	11 23
London Cannon Street 4 ⊖	a																								
London Waterloo (East) 4 ⊖	a			09 55	09 57	10 00			10 11		10 25	10 27	10 30		10 41			10 55	10 57	11 00		11 11		11 25	11 27
London Charing Cross 4 ⊖	a			09 58	10 01	10 04			10 14		10 28	10 31	10 34		10 44			10 58	11 01	11 04		11 14		11 28	11 31
Ebbsfleet International	a	08 47						09 17						09 47							10 17				
Stratford International ⊖	a	08 59						09 29						09 59							10 33				
St Pancras Int'l 15 ⊖	a	09 06						09 40						10 06							10 40				

Table 200

Sundays

Gillingham and Dartford - London

Station		SE		SE	SE	SE	SE	SE	SE	SE	SE	SE		SE	SE	SE	SE	SE	SE	SE	SE	SE		SE	SE
Gillingham (Kent) 4	d			10 20	10 24					10 50	10 54						11 20	11 24						11 50	11 54
Chatham 4	d			10 24	10 28					10 54	10 58						11 24	11 28						11 54	11 58
Rochester 4	d			10 27	10 30					10 57	11 00						11 27	11 30						11 57	12 00
Maidstone West	d																								
Strood 4	d			10 32	10 35					11 02	11 05						11 32	11 35						12 02	12 05
Higham	d				10 40						11 10							11 40							12 10
Gravesend 4	d	10 32		10 43	10 48				11 02	11 13	11 18					11 32	11 43	11 48				12 02		12 13	12 18
Northfleet	d	10 36							11 06							11 36						12 06			
Swanscombe	d	10 38							11 08							11 38						12 08			
Greenhithe for Bluewater	d	10 41			10 53				11 11		11 23					11 41		11 53				12 11			12 23
Stone Crossing	d	10 43							11 13							11 43						12 13			
Dartford 4	a	10 47			10 58				11 17		11 28					11 47		11 58				12 17			12 28
	d	10 48			10 59		11 10	11 13	11 18		11 29			11 40	11 43	11 48		11 59		12 10	12 13	12 18			12 29
Slade Green 4	d							11 18							11 48						12 18				
Erith	d							11 20							11 50						12 20				
Belvedere	d							11 23							11 53						12 23				
Abbey Wood	d				11 08			11 26			11 38				11 56			12 08			12 26				12 38
Plumstead	d					11 17		11 29				11 47			11 59				12 17		12 29				
Woolwich Arsenal 4	d				11 13	11 20		11 32			11 43	11 50			12 02			12 13	12 20		12 32				12 43
Woolwich Dockyard	d					11 22		11 34				11 52			12 04				12 22		12 34				
Charlton 4	d				11 17	11 25		11 37			11 47	11 55			12 07			12 17	12 25		12 37				12 47
Crayford	d	10 52							11 22							11 52						12 22			
Bexley	d	10 55							11 25							11 55						12 25			
Albany Park	d	10 58							11 28							11 58						12 28			
Sidcup 4	d	11 01							11 31							12 01						12 31			
New Eltham	d	11 04							11 34							12 04						12 34			
Mottingham	d	11 06							11 36							12 06						12 36			
Lee	d	11 09							11 39							12 09						12 39			
Hither Green 4	d	11 12							11 42							12 12						12 42			
Barnehurst 4	d						11 17							11 47						12 17					
Bexleyheath	d						11 19							11 49						12 19					
Welling	d						11 22							11 52						12 22					
Falconwood	d						11 25							11 55						12 25					
Eltham	d						11 28							11 58						12 28					
Kidbrooke	d						11 31							12 01						12 31					
Blackheath 4	d				11 22		11 34				11 52			12 04				12 22		12 34					12 52
Lewisham 4	d	11 18			11 26		11 38		11 48		11 56			12 08		12 18		12 26		12 38		12 48			12 56
St Johns	d																								
New Cross 4 ⊖	d						11 41							12 11						12 41					
Nunhead 4	d																								
Peckham Rye 4	d																								
Denmark Hill 4	d																								
London Victoria 15 ⊖	a																								
Westcombe Park	d					11 27		11 39				11 57			12 09				12 27		12 39				
Maze Hill	d					11 29		11 41				11 59			12 11				12 29		12 41				
Greenwich 4	d					11 33		11 45				12 03			12 15				12 33		12 45				
Deptford	a					11 35		11 47				12 05			12 17				12 35		12 47				
London Bridge 4 ⊖	a	11 26			11 36	11 41	11 49	11 53	11 56		12 06	12 11		12 19	12 23	12 26		12 36	12 41	12 49	12 53	12 56			13 06
London Cannon Street 4 ⊖	a																								
London Waterloo (East) 4 ⊖	a	11 30			11 41		11 55	11 57	12 00		12 11			12 25	12 27	12 30		12 41		12 55	12 57	13 00			13 11
London Charing Cross 4 ⊖	a	11 34			11 44		11 58	12 01	12 04		12 14			12 28	12 31	12 34		12 44		12 58	13 01	13 04			13 14
Ebbsfleet International	a			10 47						11 17							11 47							12 17	
Stratford International ⊖	a			10 59						11 29							11 59							12 29	
St Pancras Int'l 15 ⊖	a			11 06						11 36							12 06							12 36	

Station		SE	SE	SE	SE	SE	SE	SE		SE	SE	SE	SE	SE	SE	SE	SE	SE		SE	SE	SE	SE	SE	SE
Gillingham (Kent) 4	d					12 20	12 24						12 50	12 54						13 20	13 24				
Chatham 4	d					12 24	12 28						12 54	12 58						13 24	13 28				
Rochester 4	d					12 27	12 30						12 57	13 00						13 27	13 30				
Maidstone West	d																								
Strood 4	d					12 32	12 35						13 02	13 05						13 32	13 35				
Higham	d						12 40							13 10							13 40				
Gravesend 4	d				12 32	12 43	12 48					13 02	13 13	13 18				13 32		13 43	13 48				14 02
Northfleet	d				12 36							13 06						13 36							14 06
Swanscombe	d				12 38							13 08						13 38							14 08
Greenhithe for Bluewater	d				12 41		12 53					13 11		13 23				13 41			13 53				14 11
Stone Crossing	d				12 43							13 13						13 43							14 13
Dartford 4	a				12 47		12 58					13 17		13 28				13 47			13 58				14 17
	d		12 40	12 43	12 48		12 59			13 10	13 13	13 18		13 29		13 40	13 43	13 48			13 59		14 10	14 13	14 18
Slade Green 4	d			12 48							13 18						13 48							14 18	
Erith	d			12 50							13 20						13 50							14 20	
Belvedere	d			12 53							13 23						13 53							14 23	
Abbey Wood	d			12 56			13 08				13 26			13 38			13 56				14 08			14 26	
Plumstead	d	12 47		12 59				13 17			13 29				13 47		13 59					14 17		14 29	
Woolwich Arsenal 4	d	12 50		13 02			13 13	13 20			13 32			13 43	13 50		14 02				14 13	14 20		14 32	
Woolwich Dockyard	d	12 52		13 04				13 22			13 34				13 52		14 04					14 22		14 34	
Charlton 4	d	12 55		13 07			13 17	13 25			13 37			13 47	13 55		14 07				14 17	14 25		14 37	
Crayford	d				12 52							13 22						13 52							14 22
Bexley	d				12 55							13 25						13 55							14 25
Albany Park	d				12 58							13 28						13 58							14 28
Sidcup 4	d				13 01							13 31						14 01							14 31
New Eltham	d				13 04							13 34						14 04							14 34
Mottingham	d				13 06							13 36						14 06							14 36
Lee	d				13 09							13 39						14 09							14 39
Hither Green 4	d				13 12							13 42						14 12							14 42
Barnehurst 4	d		12 47							13 17						13 47							14 17		
Bexleyheath	d		12 49							13 19						13 49							14 19		
Welling	d		12 52							13 22						13 52							14 22		
Falconwood	d		12 55							13 25						13 55							14 25		
Eltham	d		12 58							13 28						13 58							14 28		
Kidbrooke	d		13 01							13 31						14 01							14 31		
Blackheath 4	d		13 04				13 22			13 34				13 52		14 04					14 22		14 34		
Lewisham 4	d		13 08		13 18		13 26			13 38		13 48		13 56		14 08		14 18			14 26		14 38		14 48
St Johns	d																								
New Cross 4 ⊖	d		13 11							13 41						14 11							14 41		
Nunhead 4	d																								
Peckham Rye 4	d																								
Denmark Hill 4	d																								
London Victoria 15 ⊖	a																								
Westcombe Park	d	12 57		13 09				13 27			13 39				13 57		14 09					14 27		14 39	
Maze Hill	d	12 59		13 11				13 29			13 41				13 59		14 11					14 29		14 41	
Greenwich 4	d	13 03		13 15				13 33			13 45				14 03		14 15					14 33		14 45	
Deptford	a	13 05		13 17				13 35			13 47				14 05		14 17					14 35		14 47	
London Bridge 4 ⊖	a	13 11	13 19	13 23	13 26		13 36	13 41		13 49	13 53	13 56		14 06	14 11	14 19	14 23	14 26			14 36	14 41	14 49	14 53	14 56
London Cannon Street 4 ⊖	a																								
London Waterloo (East) 4 ⊖	a		13 25	13 27	13 30		13 41			13 55	13 57	14 00		14 11		14 25	14 27	14 30			14 41		14 55	14 57	15 00
London Charing Cross 4 ⊖	a		13 28	13 31	13 34		13 44			13 58	14 01	14 04		14 14		14 28	14 31	14 34			14 44		14 58	15 01	15 04
Ebbsfleet International	a					12 47							13 17							13 47					
Stratford International ⊖	a					12 59							13 32							13 59					
St Pancras Int'l 15 ⊖	a					13 06							13 39							14 06					

Table 200

Sundays

Gillingham and Dartford - London

		SE	SE	SE	SE	SE	SE	SE	SE	SE	SE	SE	SE	SE	SE	SE	SE	SE	SE	SE	SE	SE
Gillingham (Kent) 4	d	13 50	13 54					14 20	14 24					14 50	14 54					15 20	15 24	
Chatham 4	d	13 54	13 58					14 24	14 28					14 54	14 58					15 24	15 28	
Rochester 4	d	13 57	14 00					14 27	14 30					14 57	15 00					15 27	15 30	
Maidstone West	d																					
Strood 4	d	14 02	14 05					14 32	14 35					15 02	15 05					15 32	15 35	
Higham	d		14 10						14 40						15 10						15 40	
Gravesend 4	d	14 13	14 18				14 32	14 43	14 48				15 02	15 13	15 18				15 32	15 43	15 48	
Northfleet	d						14 36						15 06						15 36			
Swanscombe	d						14 38						15 08						15 38			
Greenhithe for Bluewater	d		14 23				14 41		14 53				15 11		15 23				15 41		15 53	
Stone Crossing	d						14 43						15 13						15 43			
Dartford 4	a		14 28				14 47		14 58				15 17		15 28				15 47		15 58	
	d		14 29		14 40	14 43	14 48		14 59		15 10	15 13	15 18		15 29		15 40	15 43	15 48		15 59	
Slade Green 4	d					14 48						15 18						15 48				
Erith	d					14 50						15 20						15 50				
Belvedere	d					14 53						15 23						15 53				
Abbey Wood	d		14 38			14 56			15 08			15 26			15 38			15 56			16 08	
Plumstead	d			14 47		14 59				15 17		15 29				15 47		15 59				16 17
Woolwich Arsenal 4 ⛴	d		14 43	14 50		15 02			15 13	15 20		15 32			15 43	15 50		16 02			16 13	16 20
Woolwich Dockyard	d			14 52		15 04				15 22		15 34				15 52		16 04				16 22
Charlton 4	d		14 47	14 55		15 07			15 17	15 25		15 37			15 47	15 55		16 07			16 17	16 25
Crayford	d						14 52						15 22						15 52			
Bexley	d						14 55						15 25						15 55			
Albany Park	d						14 58						15 28						15 58			
Sidcup 4	d						15 01						15 31						16 01			
New Eltham	d						15 04						15 34						16 04			
Mottingham	d						15 06						15 36						16 06			
Lee	d						15 09						15 39						16 09			
Hither Green 4	d						15 12						15 42						16 12			
Barnehurst 4	d				14 47						15 17						15 47					
Bexleyheath	d				14 49						15 19						15 49					
Welling	d				14 52						15 22						15 52					
Falconwood	d				14 55						15 25						15 55					
Eltham	d				14 58						15 28						15 58					
Kidbrooke	d				15 01						15 31						16 01					
Blackheath 4	d		14 52		15 04				15 22		15 34				15 52		16 04				16 22	
Lewisham 4 ⛴	d		14 56		15 08		15 18		15 26		15 38		15 48		15 56		16 08		16 18		16 26	
St Johns	d																					
New Cross 4 ⊖	d				15 11						15 41						16 11					
Nunhead 4	d																					
Peckham Rye 4	d																					
Denmark Hill 4	d																					
London Victoria 15 ⊖	a																					
Westcombe Park	d			14 57		15 09				15 27		15 39				15 57		16 09				16 27
Maze Hill	d			14 59		15 11				15 29		15 41				15 59		16 11				16 29
Greenwich 4 ⛴	d			15 03		15 15				15 33		15 45				16 03		16 15				16 33
Deptford	a			15 05		15 17				15 35		15 47				16 05		16 17				16 35
London Bridge 4 ⊖	a		15 06	15 11	15 19	15 23	15 26		15 36	15 41	15 49	15 53	15 56		16 06	16 11	16 19	16 23	16 26		16 36	16 41
London Cannon Street 4 ⊖	a																					
London Waterloo (East) 4 ⊖	a		15 11		15 25	15 27	15 30		15 41		15 55	15 57	16 00		16 11		16 25	16 27	16 30		16 41	
London Charing Cross 4 ⊖	a		15 14		15 28	15 31	15 34		15 44		15 58	16 01	16 04		16 14		16 28	16 31	16 34		16 44	
Ebbsfleet International	a	14 17						14 47						15 17						15 47		
Stratford International ⊖ ⛴	a	14 29						15 02						15 29						15 59		
St Pancras Int'l 15 ⊖	a	14 40						15 09						15 36						16 06		

		SE	SE	SE	SE	SE	SE	SE	SE	SE	SE	SE	SE	SE	SE	SE	SE	SE	SE	SE	SE	SE	SE
Gillingham (Kent) 4	d				15 50	15 54					16 20	16 24					16 50	16 54					17 20
Chatham 4	d				15 54	15 58					16 24	16 28					16 54	16 58					17 24
Rochester 4	d				15 57	16 00					16 27	16 30					16 57	17 00					17 27
Maidstone West	d																						
Strood 4	d				16 02	16 05					16 32	16 35					17 02	17 05					17 32
Higham	d					16 10						16 40						17 10					
Gravesend 4	d			16 02	16 13	16 18				16 32	16 43	16 48				17 02	17 12	17 18				17 32	17 43
Northfleet	d			16 06						16 36						17 06						17 36	
Swanscombe	d			16 08						16 38						17 08						17 38	
Greenhithe for Bluewater	d			16 11		16 23				16 41		16 53				17 11		17 23				17 41	
Stone Crossing	d			16 13						16 43						17 13						17 43	
Dartford 4	a			16 17		16 28				16 47		16 58				17 17		17 28				17 47	
	d	16 10	16 13	16 18		16 29		16 40	16 43	16 48		16 59		17 10	17 13	17 18		17 29		17 40	17 43	17 48	
Slade Green 4	d		16 18						16 48						17 18						17 48		
Erith	d		16 20						16 50						17 20						17 50		
Belvedere	d		16 23						16 53						17 23						17 53		
Abbey Wood	d		16 26			16 38			16 56			17 08			17 26			17 38			17 56		
Plumstead	d		16 29				16 47		16 59				17 17		17 29				17 47		17 59		
Woolwich Arsenal 4 ⛴	d		16 32			16 43	16 50		17 02			17 13	17 20		17 32			17 43	17 50		18 02		
Woolwich Dockyard	d		16 34				16 52		17 04				17 22		17 34				17 52		18 04		
Charlton 4	d		16 37			16 47	16 55		17 07			17 17	17 25		17 37			17 47	17 55		18 07		
Crayford	d			16 22						16 52						17 22						17 52	
Bexley	d			16 25						16 55						17 25						17 55	
Albany Park	d			16 28						16 58						17 28						17 58	
Sidcup 4	d			16 31						17 01						17 31						18 01	
New Eltham	d			16 34						17 04						17 34						18 04	
Mottingham	d			16 36						17 06						17 36						18 06	
Lee	d			16 39						17 09						17 39						18 09	
Hither Green 4	d			16 42						17 12						17 42						18 12	
Barnehurst 4	d	16 17						16 47						17 17						17 47			
Bexleyheath	d	16 19						16 49						17 19						17 49			
Welling	d	16 22						16 52						17 22						17 52			
Falconwood	d	16 25						16 55						17 25						17 55			
Eltham	d	16 28						16 58						17 28						17 58			
Kidbrooke	d	16 31						17 01						17 31						18 01			
Blackheath 4	d	16 34				16 52		17 04				17 22		17 34				17 52		18 04			
Lewisham 4 ⛴	d	16 38		16 48		16 56		17 08		17 18		17 26		17 38		17 48		17 56		18 08		18 18	
St Johns	d																						
New Cross 4 ⊖	d	16 41						17 11						17 41						18 11			
Nunhead 4	d																						
Peckham Rye 4	d																						
Denmark Hill 4	d																						
London Victoria 15 ⊖	a																						
Westcombe Park	d		16 39				16 57		17 09				17 27		17 39				17 57		18 09		
Maze Hill	d		16 41				16 59		17 11				17 29		17 41				17 59		18 11		
Greenwich 4 ⛴	d		16 45				17 03		17 15				17 33		17 45				18 03		18 15		
Deptford	a		16 47				17 05		17 17				17 35		17 47				18 05		18 17		
London Bridge 4 ⊖	a	16 49	16 53	16 56		17 06	17 11	17 19	17 23	17 26		17 36	17 41	17 49	17 53	17 56		18 06	18 11	18 19	18 23	18 26	
London Cannon Street 4 ⊖	a																						
London Waterloo (East) 4 ⊖	a	16 55	16 57	17 00		17 11		17 25	17 27	17 30		17 41		17 55	17 57	18 00		18 11		18 25	18 27	18 30	
London Charing Cross 4 ⊖	a	16 58	17 01	17 04		17 14		17 28	17 31	17 34		17 44		17 58	18 01	18 04		18 14		18 28	18 31	18 34	
Ebbsfleet International	a				16 17						16 47						17 16						17 47
Stratford International ⊖ ⛴	a				16 29						17 02						17 27						17 59
St Pancras Int'l 15 ⊖	a				16 36						17 09						17 38						18 09

Table 200

Sundays

Gillingham and Dartford - London

		SE	SE	SE	SE	SE		SE	SE	SE	SE	SE	SE	SE	SE	SE		SE	SE	SE	SE	SE	SE	SE	SE
Gillingham (Kent) [4]	d	17 24						17 50	17 54				18 20	18 24					18 50	18 54				19 20	19 24
Chatham [4]	d	17 28						17 54	17 58				18 24	18 28					18 54	18 58				19 24	19 28
Rochester [4]	d	17 30						17 57	18 00				18 27	18 30					18 57	19 00				19 27	19 30
Maidstone West	d																								
Strood [4]	d	17 35						18 02	18 05				18 32	18 35					19 02	19 05				19 32	19 35
Higham	d	17 40							18 10					18 40						19 10					19 40
Gravesend [4]	d	17 48				18 02		18 12	18 18			18 32	18 43	18 48				19 02	19 13	19 18			19 32	19 43	19 48
Northfleet	d					18 06						18 36						19 06					19 36		
Swanscombe	d					18 08						18 38						19 08					19 38		
Greenhithe for Bluewater	d	17 53				18 11			18 23			18 41		18 53				19 11		19 23			19 41		19 53
Stone Crossing	d					18 13						18 43						19 13					19 43		
Dartford [4]	a	17 58				18 17			18 28			18 47		18 58				19 17		19 28			19 47		19 58
	d	17 59		18 10	18 13	18 18			18 29	18 40	18 43	18 48		18 59	19 10	19 13		19 18		19 29	19 40	19 43	19 48		19 59
Slade Green [4]	d				18 18						18 48					19 18						19 48			
Erith	d				18 20						18 50					19 20						19 50			
Belvedere	d				18 23						18 53					19 23						19 53			
Abbey Wood	d	18 08			18 26				18 38		18 56			19 08		19 26				19 38		19 56			20 08
Plumstead	d		18 17		18 29						18 59					19 29						19 59			
Woolwich Arsenal [4]	d	18 13	18 20		18 32				18 43		19 02			19 13		19 32				19 43		20 02			20 13
Woolwich Dockyard	d		18 22		18 34						19 04					19 34						20 04			
Charlton [4]	d	18 17	18 25		18 37				18 47		19 07			19 17		19 37				19 47		20 07			20 17
Crayford	d					18 22						18 52						19 22					19 52		
Bexley	d					18 25						18 55						19 25					19 55		
Albany Park	d					18 28						18 58						19 28					19 58		
Sidcup [4]	d					18 31						19 01						19 31					20 01		
New Eltham	d					18 34						19 04						19 34					20 04		
Mottingham	d					18 36						19 06						19 36					20 06		
Lee	d					18 39						19 09						19 39					20 09		
Hither Green [4]	d					18 42						19 12						19 42					20 12		
Barnehurst [4]	d			18 17						18 47					19 17						19 47				
Bexleyheath	d			18 19						18 49					19 19						19 49				
Welling	d			18 22						18 52					19 22						19 52				
Falconwood	d			18 25						18 55					19 25						19 55				
Eltham	d			18 28						18 58					19 28						19 58				
Kidbrooke	d			18 31						19 01					19 31						20 01				
Blackheath [4]	d	18 22		18 34					18 52	19 04				19 22	19 34					19 52	20 04				20 22
Lewisham [4]	d	18 26		18 38		18 48			18 56	19 08		19 18		19 26	19 38			19 48		19 56	20 08		20 18		20 26
St Johns	d																								
New Cross [4] ⊖	d			18 41						19 11					19 41						20 11				
Nunhead [4]	d																								
Peckham Rye [4]	d																								
Denmark Hill [4]	d																								
London Victoria [15] ⊖	a																								
Westcombe Park	d		18 27		18 39						19 09					19 39						20 09			
Maze Hill	d		18 29		18 41						19 11					19 41						20 11			
Greenwich [4]	d		18 33		18 45						19 15					19 45						20 15			
Deptford	a		18 35		18 47						19 17					19 47						20 17			
London Bridge [4] ⊖	a	18 36	18 41	18 49	18 53	18 56			19 06	19 19	19 23	19 26		19 36	19 49	19 53		19 56		20 06	20 19	20 23	20 26		20 36
London Cannon Street [4] ⊖	a																								
London Waterloo (East) [4] ⊖	a	18 41		18 55	18 57	19 00			19 11	19 25	19 27	19 30		19 41	19 55	19 57		20 00		20 11	20 25	20 27	20 30		20 41
London Charing Cross [4] ⊖	a	18 44		18 58	19 01	19 04			19 14	19 28	19 31	19 34		19 44	19 58	20 01		20 04		20 14	20 28	20 31	20 34		20 44
Ebbsfleet International	a							18 16					18 47						19 17					19 47	
Stratford International ⊖	a							18 27					19 02						19 29					20 02	
St Pancras Int'l [15] ⊖	a							18 41					19 09						19 36					20 12	

		SE		SE	SE	SE	SE	SE	SE	SE	SE	SE		SE	SE	SE	SE	SE	SE	SE	SE	SE		SE	SE
Gillingham (Kent) [4]	d					19 45	19 50				20 15	20 20					20 45	20 50				21 15		21 20	
Chatham [4]	d					19 49	19 54				20 19	20 24					20 49	20 54				21 19		21 24	
Rochester [4]	d					19 51	19 57				20 21	20 27					20 51	20 57				21 21		21 27	
Maidstone West	d																								
Strood [4]	d					19 56	20 02				20 26	20 32					20 56	21 02				21 26		21 32	
Higham	d					20 01					20 31						21 01					21 31			
Gravesend [4]	d					20 09	20 12				20 39	20 43					21 09	21 13				21 39		21 43	
Northfleet	d					20 12					20 42						21 12					21 42			
Swanscombe	d					20 14					20 44						21 14					21 44			
Greenhithe for Bluewater	d					20 18					20 48						21 18					21 48			
Stone Crossing	d					20 20					20 50						21 20					21 50			
Dartford [4]	a					20 24					20 54						21 24					21 54			
	d	20 10		20 13	20 18	20 29		20 40	20 43	20 48	20 59			21 10	21 13	21 18	21 29		21 40	21 43	21 48	21 59			22 10
Slade Green [4]	d			20 18					20 48						21 18					21 48					
Erith	d			20 20					20 50						21 20					21 50					
Belvedere	d			20 23					20 53						21 23					21 53					
Abbey Wood	d			20 26		20 38			20 56		21 08				21 26		21 38			21 56		22 08			
Plumstead	d			20 29					20 59						21 29					21 59					
Woolwich Arsenal [4]	d			20 32		20 43			21 02		21 13				21 32		21 43			22 02		22 13			
Woolwich Dockyard	d			20 34					21 04						21 34					22 04					
Charlton [4]	d			20 37		20 47			21 07		21 17				21 37		21 47			22 07		22 17			
Crayford	d				20 22					20 52						21 22					21 52				
Bexley	d				20 25					20 55						21 25					21 55				
Albany Park	d				20 28					20 58						21 28					21 58				
Sidcup [4]	d				20 31					21 01						21 31					22 01				
New Eltham	d				20 34					21 04						21 34					22 04				
Mottingham	d				20 36					21 06						21 36					22 06				
Lee	d				20 39					21 09						21 39					22 09				
Hither Green [4]	d				20 42					21 12						21 42					22 12				
Barnehurst [4]	d	20 17						20 47						21 17					21 47						22 17
Bexleyheath	d	20 19						20 49						21 19					21 49						22 19
Welling	d	20 22						20 52						21 22					21 52						22 22
Falconwood	d	20 25						20 55						21 25					21 55						22 25
Eltham	d	20 28						20 58						21 28					21 58						22 28
Kidbrooke	d	20 31						21 01						21 31					22 01						22 31
Blackheath [4]	d	20 34				20 52		21 04			21 22			21 34			21 52		22 04			22 22			22 34
Lewisham [4]	d	20 38			20 48	20 56		21 08		21 18	21 26			21 38		21 48	21 56		22 08		22 18	22 26			22 38
St Johns	d																								
New Cross [4] ⊖	d	20 41						21 11						21 41					22 11						22 41
Nunhead [4]	d																								
Peckham Rye [4]	d																								
Denmark Hill [4]	d																								
London Victoria [15] ⊖	a																								
Westcombe Park	d			20 39					21 09						21 39					22 09					
Maze Hill	d			20 41					21 11						21 41					22 11					
Greenwich [4]	d			20 45					21 15						21 45					22 15					
Deptford	a			20 47					21 17						21 47					22 17					
London Bridge [4] ⊖	a	20 49		20 53	20 56	21 06		21 19	21 23	21 26	21 36			21 49	21 53	21 56	22 06		22 19	22 23	22 26	22 36			22 49
London Cannon Street [4] ⊖	a																								
London Waterloo (East) [4] ⊖	a	20 55		20 57	21 00	21 11		21 25	21 27	21 30	21 41			21 55	21 57	22 00	22 11		22 25	22 27	22 30	22 41			22 55
London Charing Cross [4] ⊖	a	20 58		21 01	21 04	21 14		21 28	21 31	21 34	21 44			21 58	22 01	22 04	22 14		22 28	22 31	22 34	22 44			22 58
Ebbsfleet International	a						20 16					20 47						21 17						21 47	
Stratford International ⊖	a						20 27					20 59						21 35						21 59	
St Pancras Int'l [15] ⊖	a						20 38					21 06						21 42						22 06	

Table 200

Sundays

Gillingham and Dartford - London

			SE	SE	SE	SE	SE	SE	SE		SE	SE
Gillingham (Kent) 4		d			21 45	21 50					22 15	22 20
Chatham 4		d			21 49	21 54					22 19	22 24
Rochester 4		d			21 51	21 57					22 21	22 27
Maidstone West		d										
Strood 4		d			21 56	22 02					22 26	22 32
Higham		d			22 01						22 31	
Gravesend 4		d			22 09	22 13					22 39	22 43
Northfleet		d			22 12						22 42	
Swanscombe		d			22 14						22 44	
Greenhithe for Bluewater		d			22 18						22 48	
Stone Crossing		d			22 20						22 50	
Dartford 4		a			22 24						22 54	
		d	22 13	22 18	22 29		22 40	22 43	22 48		22 59	
Slade Green 4		d	22 18					22 48				
Erith		d	22 20					22 50				
Belvedere		d	22 23					22 53				
Abbey Wood		d	22 26		22 38			22 56			23 08	
Plumstead		d	22 29					22 59				
Woolwich Arsenal 4	⛴	d	22 32		22 43			23 02			23 13	
Woolwich Dockyard		d	22 34					23 04				
Charlton 4		d	22 37		22 47			23 07			23 17	
Crayford		d		22 22					22 52			
Bexley		d		22 25					22 55			
Albany Park		d		22 28					22 58			
Sidcup 4		d		22 31					23 01			
New Eltham		d		22 34					23 04			
Mottingham		d		22 36					23 06			
Lee		d		22 39					23 09			
Hither Green 4		d		22 42					23 12			
Barnehurst 4		d					22 47					
Bexleyheath		d					22 49					
Welling		d					22 52					
Falconwood		d					22 55					
Eltham		d					22 58					
Kidbrooke		d					23 01					
Blackheath 4		d			22 52		23 04				23 22	
Lewisham 4	⛴	d		22 48	22 56		23 08		23 18		23 26	
St Johns		d										
New Cross 4	⊖	d					23 11					
Nunhead 4		d										
Peckham Rye 4		d										
Denmark Hill 4		d										
London Victoria 15	⊖	a										
Westcombe Park		d	22 39					23 09				
Maze Hill		d	22 41					23 11				
Greenwich 4	⛴	d	22 45					23 15				
Deptford		a	22 47					23 17				
London Bridge 4	⊖	a	22 53	22 56	23 06		23 19	23 23	23 26		23 36	
London Cannon Street 4	⊖	a										
London Waterloo (East) 4	⊖	a	22 57	23 00	23 11		23 25	23 27	23 30		23 41	
London Charing Cross 4	⊖	a	23 01	23 04	23 14		23 28	23 31	23 34		23 44	
Ebbsfleet International		a				22 17						22 47
Stratford International	⊖ ⛴	a				22 29						22 59
St Pancras Int'l 15	⊖	a				22 36						23 06

London - Hayes (Kent) via Catford Bridge

Mondays to Fridays

Miles	Miles			SE MO	SE MX	SE	SE	SE	SE	SE	SE	SE		SE	SE	SE	SE	SE	SE	SE	SE	SE		SE	
0	—	London Charing Cross 4 ⊖	d	23p35	23p52		05 47	06 17	06 47		07 17			07 44		08 15		08 44			09 17			09 47	
0¾	—	London Waterloo (East) 4 ⊖	d	23p38	23p55		05 50	06 20	06 50		07 20			07 47		08 18		08 47			09 20			09 50	
—	0	London Cannon Street 4 ⊖	d							07 00		07 30			08 00		08 30		09 00	09 03		09 30			
1¾	0¾	London Bridge 4 ⊖	d	23p43	23p59		05 55	06 26	06 55	07 04	07 25	07 34		07 53	08 04	08 23	08 34	08 53	09 04	09 07	09 25	09 34		09 55	
4¾	—	New Cross 4 ⊖	d	23p49	00 05	05 31	06 01	06 32	07 02	07 09		07 39			08 09		08 41		09 09			09 39			
5½	—	St Johns	d	23p51	00 07	05 33	06 03	06 34	07 04	07 11		07 41			08 11		08 43		09 11			09 41			
6	—	Lewisham 4	d	23p54	00 10	05 36	06 06	06 38	07 08	07 16		07 44			08 17		08 46		09 14			09 44			
6¾	—	Ladywell	d	23p57	00 13	05 39	06 09	06 41	07 11	07 19	07 34	07 47		08 04	08 20	08 34	08 49	09 04	09 17	09 22	09 34	09 47		10 04	
7½	—	Catford Bridge	d	23p59	00 15	05 41	06 11	06 43	07 13	07 21	07 36	07 49		08 06	08 22	08 36	08 51	09 06	09 19	09 24	09 36	09 49		10 06	
9	—	Lower Sydenham	d	00 02	00 18	05 44	06 14	06 46	07 16	07 24	07 39	07 52		08 09	08 25	08 39	08 54	09 09	09 22	09 27	09 39	09 52		10 09	
9½	—	New Beckenham 4	d	00 04	00 20	05 46	06 16	06 48	07 18	07 26	07 41	07 54		08 11	08 27	08 41	08 56	09 11	09 24	09a29	09 41	09 54		10 11	
10¼	—	Clock House	d	00 06	00 23	05 48	06 18	06 50	07 20	07 29	07 43	07 57		08 13	08 29	08 43	08 58	09 13	09 27		09 43	09 57		10 13	
11	—	Elmers End 4	d	00 09	00 25	05 51	06 21	06 53	07 23	07 31	07 46	07 59		08 16	08 32	08 46	09 01	09 16	09 29		09 46	09 59		10 16	
12½	—	Eden Park	d	00 12	00 29	05 54	06 24	06 56	07 26	07 35	07 49	08 03		08 19	08 35	08 49	09 04	09 19	09 33		09 49	10 03		10 19	
13¼	—	West Wickham	d	00 15	00 31	05 57	06 27	06 59	07 29	07 37	07 52	08 05		08 22	08 38	08 52	09 07	09 22	09 35		09 52	10 05		10 22	
14½	—	Hayes (Kent)	a	00 18	00 34	06 00	06 30	07 02	07 32	07 40	07 56	08 08		08 25	08 41	08 55	09 10	09 25	09 38		09 55	10 08		10 25	

		SE		SE	SE	SE	SE	SE		SE	SE	SE	SE	SE	SE	SE	SE	SE		SE	SE	SE	SE	SE
London Charing Cross 4 ⊖	d				15 17		15 47			16 20		16 39		16 59		17 21		17 43			18 05		18 27	
London Waterloo (East) 4 ⊖	d				15 20		15 50			16 23		16 42		17 02		17 24		17 46			18 08		18 30	
London Cannon Street 4 ⊖	d	10 00		15 00		15 30		16 00			16 30		16 51		17 12		17 34			17 56		18 18		18 40
London Bridge 4 ⊖	d	10 04		15 04	15 25	15 34	15 55	16 04		16 29	16 34	16 47	16 55	17 07	17 16	17 29	17 39	17 52		18 00	18 13	18 23	18 35	18 44
New Cross 4 ⊖	d	10 09	and at	15 09		15 39		16 10			16 40		17 01		17 22		17 45			18 06		18 28		18 50
St Johns	d	10 11	the same	15 11		15 41		16 12			16 42		17 03		17 24		17 47			18 08		18 30		18 52
Lewisham 4	d	10 14	minutes	15 14		15 44		16 15			16 45		17 06		17 27		17 50			18 11		18 33		18 55
Ladywell	d	10 17	past	15 17	15 34	15 47	16 04	16 18		16 38	16 48	16 57	17 09	17 17	17 30	17 40	17 53	18 01		18 14	18 23	18 36	18 45	18 58
Catford Bridge	d	10 19	each	15 19	15 36	15 49	16 06	16 20		16 40	16 50	16 59	17 11	17 19	17 32	17 42	17 55	18 03		18 16	18 25	18 38	18 47	19 00
Lower Sydenham	d	10 22	hour until	15 22	15 39	15 52	16 09	16 23		16 43	16 53	17 02	17 14	17 22	17 35	17 45	17 58	18 06		18 19	18 28	18 41	18 50	19 03
New Beckenham 4	d	10 24		15 24	15 41	15 54	16 11	16 25		16 45	16 55	17 04	17 16	17 24	17 37	17 47	18 00	18 08		18 21	18 30	18 43	18 52	19 05
Clock House	d	10 27		15 27	15 43	15 57	16 13	16 27		16 48	16 57	17 07	17 18	17 27	17 39	17 49	18 02	18 11		18 23	18 33	18 46	18 55	19 07
Elmers End 4	d	10 29		15 29	15 46	15 59	16 16	16 30		16 51	17 00	17 10	17 21	17 30	17 42	17 52	18 05	18 14		18 26	18 36	18 49	18 58	19 10
Eden Park	d	10 33		15 33	15 49	16 03	16 19	16 34		16 54	17 04	17 13	17 25	17 33	17 46	17 56	18 09	18 17		18 30	18 39	18 52	19 01	19 14
West Wickham	d	10 35		15 35	15 52	16 05	16 22	16 36		16 57	17 06	17 16	17 27	17 36	17 48	17 58	18 11	18 20		18 32	18 42	18 55	19 04	19 16
Hayes (Kent)	a	10 38		15 38	15 55	16 08	16 25	16 42		17 02	17 12	17 21	17 32	17 42	17 54	18 03	18 16	18 26		18 38	18 47	19 00	19 10	19 22

		SE	SE	SE	SE		SE	SE	SE	SE		SE	SE
London Charing Cross 4 ⊖	d	18 52		19 17			19 47		20 17	20 47		23 17	23 52
London Waterloo (East) 4 ⊖	d	18 55		19 20			19 50		20 20	20 50		23 20	23 55
London Cannon Street 4 ⊖	d		19 00		19 30			20 00					
London Bridge 4 ⊖	d	19 00	19 04	19 25	19 34		19 55	20 04	20 25	20 55		23 25	23 59
New Cross 4 ⊖	d		19 09		19 39			20 09	20 32	21 00		23 30	00 05
St Johns	d		19 11		19 41			20 11	20 34	21 02	and	23 32	00 07
Lewisham 4	d		19 14		19 44			20 14	20 37	21 05	every 30	23 35	00 10
Ladywell	d	19 09	19 17	19 34	19 47		20 04	20 17	20 40	21 08	minutes	23 38	00 13
Catford Bridge	d	19 11	19 19	19 36	19 49		20 06	20 19	20 42	21 10	until	23 40	00 15
Lower Sydenham	d	19 14	19 22	19 39	19 52		20 09	20 22	20 45	21 13		23 43	00 18
New Beckenham 4	d	19 16	19 24	19 41	19 54		20 11	20 24	20 47	21 15		23 45	00 20
Clock House	d	19 19	19 27	19 43	19 57		20 13	20 27	20 50	21 18		23 48	00 23
Elmers End 4	d	19 22	19 29	19 46	19 59		20 16	20 29	20 52	21 20		23 50	00 25
Eden Park	d	19 25	19 33	19 49	20 03		20 19	20 33	20 56	21 24		23 54	00 29
West Wickham	d	19 28	19 35	19 52	20 05		20 22	20 35	20 58	21 26		23 56	00 31
Hayes (Kent)	a	19 33	19 39	19 55	20 09		20 25	20 39	21 01	21 29		23 59	00 34

Saturdays

		SE	SE		SE	SE	SE	SE	SE		SE	SE		SE	SE		SE		SE
London Charing Cross 4 ⊖	d	23p52	05 47		07 17	07 47		08 17			08 47				19 17		22 47		23 52
London Waterloo (East) 4 ⊖	d	23p55	05 50		07 20	07 50		08 20			08 50				19 20		22 50		23 55
London Cannon Street 4 ⊖	d						08 00		08 30			09 00		19 00					
London Bridge 4 ⊖	d	23p59	05 55		07 25	07 55	08 04	08 25	08 34		08 55	09 04		19 04	19 25		22 55		23 59
New Cross 4 ⊖	d	00 05	06 00		07 30		08 09		08 39			09 09	and at	19 09	19 30		23 00		00 05
St Johns	d	00 07	06 02	and	07 32		08 11		08 41			09 11	the same	19 11	19 32	and	23 02		00 07
Lewisham 4	d	00 10	06 05	every 30	07 35		08 14		08 44			09 14	minutes	19 14	19 35	every 30	23 05		00 10
Ladywell	d	00 13	06 08	minutes	07 38	08 04	08 17	08 34	08 47		09 04	09 17	past	19 17	19 38	minutes	23 08		00 13
Catford Bridge	d	00 15	06 10	until	07 40	08 06	08 19	08 36	08 49		09 06	09 19	each	19 19	19 40	until	23 10		00 15
Lower Sydenham	d	00 18	06 13		07 43	08 09	08 22	08 39	08 52		09 09	09 22	hour until	19 22	19 43		23 13		00 18
New Beckenham 4	d	00 20	06 15		07 45	08 11	08 24	08 41	08 54		09 11	09 24		19 24	19 45		23 15		00 20
Clock House	d	00 23	06 18		07 48	08 13	08 27	08 43	08 57		09 13	09 27		19 27	19 48		23 18		00 23
Elmers End 4	d	00 25	06 20		07 50	08 16	08 29	08 46	08 59		09 16	09 29		19 29	19 50		23 20		00 25
Eden Park	d	00 29	06 24		07 54	08 19	08 33	08 49	09 03		09 19	09 33		19 33	19 54		23 24		00 29
West Wickham	d	00 31	06 26		07 56	08 22	08 35	08 52	09 05		09 22	09 35		19 35	19 56		23 26		00 31
Hayes (Kent)	a	00 34	06 29		07 59	08 25	08 41	08 55	09 08		09 25	09 38		19 38	19 59		23 29		00 34

		SE A	SE		SE	SE
London Charing Cross 4 ⊖	d	23p52	07 35		23 05	23 35
London Waterloo (East) 4 ⊖	d	23p55	07 38		23 08	23 38
London Cannon Street 4 ⊖	d					
London Bridge 4 ⊖	d	23p59	07 43		23 13	23 43
New Cross 4 ⊖	d	00 05	07 49		23 19	23 49
St Johns	d	00 07	07 51	and	23 21	23 51
Lewisham 4	d	00 10	07 54	every 30	23 24	23 54
Ladywell	d	00 13	07 57	minutes	23 27	23 57
Catford Bridge	d	00 15	07 59	until	23 29	23 59
Lower Sydenham	d	00 18	08 02		23 32	00 02
New Beckenham 4	d	00 20	08 04		23 34	00 04
Clock House	d	00 23	08 06		23 36	00 06
Elmers End 4	d	00 25	08 09		23 39	00 09
Eden Park	d	00 29	08 12		23 42	00 12
West Wickham	d	00 31	08 15		23 45	00 15
Hayes (Kent)	a	00 34	08 18		23 48	00 18

A not 22 May

Table 203

Mondays to Fridays

Hayes (Kent) - London via Catford Bridge

Miles	Miles			SE	SE	SE	SE	SE	SE	SE	SE	SE		SE	SE	SE	SE	SE	SE	SE	SE	SE	SE		SE
0	—	**Hayes (Kent)**	d	05 15	05 45	06 15	06 23	06 45	06 55	07 13	07 23	07 33		07 43	07 53	08 03	08 13	08 23	08 33	08 50	09 08	09 20	09 38		09 50
1¼	—	West Wickham	d	05 18	05 48	06 18	06 26	06 48	06 58	07 16	07 26	07 36		07 46	07 56	08 06	08 16	08 26	08 36	08 53	09 11	09 23	09 41		09 53
2	—	Eden Park	d	05 20	05 50	06 20	06 28	06 50	07 00	07 18	07 28	07 38		07 48	07 58	08 08	08 18	08 28	08 38	08 55	09 13	09 25	09 43		09 55
3½	—	Elmers End 4 ⛴	d	05 24	05 54	06 24	06 32	06 54	07 04	07 22	07 32	07 42		07 52	08 02	08 12	08 22	08 32	08 42	08 59	09 17	09 29	09 47		09 59
4¼	—	Clock House	d	05 26	05 56	06 26	06 34	06 56	07 06	07 24	07 34	07 44		07 54	08 04	08 14	08 24	08 34	08 44	09 01	09 19	09 31	09 49		10 01
5	—	New Beckenham 4	d	05 28	05 58	06 28	06 37	06 59	07 09	07 27	07 37	07 47		07 57	08 07	08 17	08 27	08 37	08 47	09 04	09 21	09 34	09 51		10 03
5½	—	Lower Sydenham	d	05 30	06 00	06 30	06 39	07 01	07 11	07 29	07 39	07 49		07 59	08 09	08 19	08 29	08 39	08 49	09 06	09 23	09 36	09 53		10 05
7	—	**Catford Bridge**	d	05 33	06 03	06 33	06 42	07 04	07 14	07 32	07 42	07 52		08 02	08 12	08 22	08 32	08 42	08 52	09 09	09 26	09 39	09 56		10 08
7¾	—	Ladywell	d	05 35	06 05	06 35	06 44	07 06	07 16	07 34	07 44	07 54		08 04	08 14	08 24	08 34	08 44	08 54	09 11	09 28	09 41	09 58		10 10
8½	—	**Lewisham 4** ⛴	d	05 39	06 09	06 39	06 48		07 20		07 48			08 08		08 28		08 48		09 15		09 45			10 14
9	—	St Johns	a	05 41	06 11	06 41	06 50				07 50			08 12		08 30		08 50		09 17		09 47			10 16
9¾	—	New Cross 4 ⊖	a	05 43	06 13	06 43	06 52		07 23		07 52			08 14		08 32		08 52		09 19		09 49			10 18
12¾	0	**London Bridge 4** ⊖	a	05 48	06 18	06 48	06 58	07 17	07 28	07 44	08 01			08 20		08 41		08 57		09 25	09 37	09 54	10 07		10 24
—	0¾	**London Cannon Street 4** ⊖	a				07 05		07 35		08 08			08 28		08 48		09 04		09 32		10 00			10 28
13¾	—	**London Waterloo (East) 4** ⊖	a	05 53	06 24	06 53		07 22		07 50		08 08			08 28		08 48		09 07		09 42		10 12		
14½	—	**London Charing Cross 4** ⊖	a	05 56	06 27	06 57		07 28		07 56		08 14			08 34		08 54		09 13		09 48		10 16		

		SE	SE		SE	SE	SE	SE		SE	SE	SE	SE	SE	SE	SE	SE	SE		SE	SE	SE	SE	
Hayes (Kent)	d	10 08	10 20	and at the same minutes past each hour until	15 20	15 38	15 50			16 08	16 20	16 38	16 50	17 08	17 20	17 37	17 47	18 08		18 21	18 38	18 50	19 05	
West Wickham	d	10 11	10 23		15 23	15 41	15 53			16 11	16 23	16 41	16 53	17 11	17 23	17 40	17 50	18 11		18 24	18 41	18 53	19 08	
Eden Park	d	10 13	10 25		15 25	15 43	15 55			16 13	16 25	16 43	16 55	17 13	17 25	17 42	17 52	18 13		18 26	18 43	18 55	19 10	
Elmers End 4 ⛴	d	10 17	10 29		15 29	15 47	15 59			16 17	16 29	16 47	16 59	17 17	17 29	17 46	17 56	18 17		18 30	18 47	18 59	19 17	
Clock House	d	10 19	10 31		15 31	15 49	16 01			16 19	16 31	16 49	17 01	17 19	17 31	17 48	17 58	18 19		18 32	18 49	19 01	19 19	
New Beckenham 4	d	10 21	10 33		15 33	15 51	16 03	16 15		16 21	16 33	16 51	17 03	17 21	17 33	17 50	18 00	18 21		18 34	18 51	19 03	19 21	
Lower Sydenham	d	10 23	10 35		15 35	15 53	16 05	16 17		16 23	16 35	16 53	17 05	17 23	17 35	17 52	18 02	18 23		18 36	18 53	19 05	19 23	
Catford Bridge	d	10 26	10 38		15 38	15 56	16 08	16 20		16 26	16 38	16 56	17 08	17 26	17 38	17 55	18 05	18 26		18 39	18 56	19 08	19 26	
Ladywell	d	10 28	10 40		15 40	15 58	16 10	16 22		16 28	16 40	16 58	17 10	17 28	17 40	17 57	18 07	18 28		18 41	18 58	19 10	19 28	
Lewisham 4 ⛴	d		10 44		15 44		16 14				16 44		17 14		17 44		18 14			18 45		19 14		
St Johns	a		10 46		15 46		16 16				16 46		17 16		17 46		18 16			18 47		19 16		
New Cross 4 ⊖	a		10 48		15 48		16 18				16 48		17 18		17 48		18 18			18 49		19 18		
London Bridge 4 ⊖	a	10 37	10 54		15 54	16 09	16 24	16 32		16 37	16 54	17 08	17 24	17 38	17 55	18 07	18 24	18 38		18 55	19 07	19 24	19 37	
London Cannon Street 4 ⊖	a		10 58		15 58		16 28				16 58		17 29		17 59		18 29			18 59		19 28		
London Waterloo (East) 4 ⊖	a	10 42				16 13		16 37		16 42		17 13		17 42		18 12		18 44			19 12		19 42	
London Charing Cross 4 ⊖	a	10 46				16 18		16 42		16 46		17 18		17 46		18 16		18 48			19 16		19 46	

		SE		SE
Hayes (Kent)	d	19 14	and every 30 minutes until	22 44
West Wickham	d	19 17		22 47
Eden Park	d	19 19		22 49
Elmers End 4 ⛴	d	19 23		22 53
Clock House	d	19 25		22 55
New Beckenham 4	d	19 27		22 57
Lower Sydenham	d	19 29		22 59
Catford Bridge	d	19 32		23 02
Ladywell	d	19 34		23 04
Lewisham 4 ⛴	d	19 38		23 08
St Johns	a	19 40		23 10
New Cross 4 ⊖	a	19 42		23 12
London Bridge 4 ⊖	a	19 49		23 19
London Cannon Street 4 ⊖	a			
London Waterloo (East) 4 ⊖	a	19 53		23 23
London Charing Cross 4 ⊖	a	19 57		23 27

Saturdays

		SE	SE		SE	SE	SE	SE	SE		SE		SE	SE	SE		SE		SE
Hayes (Kent)	d	05 15	05 38	and every 30 minutes until	07 08	07 36	07 50	08 08	08 20		08 38	and at the same minutes past each hour until	18 38	18 50	19 14	and every 30 minutes until	22 14		22 44
West Wickham	d	05 18	05 41		07 11	07 39	07 53	08 11	08 23		08 41		18 41	18 53	19 17		22 17		22 47
Eden Park	d	05 20	05 43		07 13	07 41	07 55	08 13	08 25		08 43		18 43	18 55	19 19		22 19		22 49
Elmers End 4 ⛴	d	05 24	05 47		07 17	07 45	07 59	08 17	08 29		08 47		18 47	18 59	19 23		22 23		22 53
Clock House	d	05 26	05 49		07 19	07 47	08 01	08 19	08 31		08 49		18 49	19 01	19 25		22 25		22 55
New Beckenham 4	d	05 28	05 51		07 21	07 49	08 03	08 21	08 33		08 51		18 51	19 03	19 27		22 27		22 57
Lower Sydenham	d	05 30	05 53		07 23	07 51	08 05	08 23	08 35		08 53		18 53	19 05	19 29		22 29		22 59
Catford Bridge	d	05 33	05 56		07 26	07 54	08 08	08 26	08 38		08 56		18 56	19 08	19 32		22 32		23 02
Ladywell	d	05 35	05 58		07 28	07 56	08 10	08 28	08 40		08 58		18 58	19 10	19 34		22 34		23 04
Lewisham 4 ⛴	d	05 39	06 02		07 32	07 59	08 14		08 44					19 14	19 38		22 38		23 08
St Johns	a	05 41	06 04		07 34		08 16		08 46					19 16	19 40		22 40		23 10
New Cross 4 ⊖	a	05 43	06 06		07 36		08 18		08 48					19 18	19 42		22 42		23 12
London Bridge 4 ⊖	a	05 48	06 12		07 42	08 07	08 24	08 37	08 54		09 07		19 07	19 24	19 49		22 49		23 19
London Cannon Street 4 ⊖	a						08 28		08 58										
London Waterloo (East) 4 ⊖	a	05 53	06 16		07 46	08 12		08 42			09 12		19 12		19 53		22 53		23 23
London Charing Cross 4 ⊖	a	05 56	06 20		07 50	08 16		08 46			09 16		19 16		19 58		22 58		23 27

Sundays

		SE		SE
Hayes (Kent)	d	07 28	and every 30 minutes until	22 58
West Wickham	d	07 31		23 01
Eden Park	d	07 33		23 03
Elmers End 4 ⛴	d	07 37		23 07
Clock House	d	07 39		23 09
New Beckenham 4	d	07 41		23 11
Lower Sydenham	d	07 43		23 13
Catford Bridge	d	07 46		23 16
Ladywell	d	07 48		23 18
Lewisham 4 ⛴	d	07 52		23 22
St Johns	a	07 54		23 24
New Cross 4 ⊖	a	07 56		23 26
London Bridge 4 ⊖	a	08 03		23 33
London Cannon Street 4 ⊖	a			
London Waterloo (East) 4 ⊖	a	08 08		23 38
London Charing Cross 4 ⊖	a	08 11		23 41

London - Grove Park, Bromley North, Orpington, Sevenoaks and Tonbridge

Miles	Miles			SE MO ■1	SE MX ■1	SE MX	SE MX	SE MO ■1	SE MX ■1	SE MX ■1	SE MX	SE MO		SE MX	SE MX	SE MX	SE	SE ■1	SE	SE	SE	SE		SE ■1	SE
0	—	**London Charing Cross** ■4 ⊖	d	23p23	23p30		23p36	23p38	23p40	23p45		23p46			00 10		00 48	05 30	05 36			06 06		06 15	
0¾	—	**London Waterloo (East)** ■4 ⊖	d	23p26	23p33		23p39	23p41	23p43	23p48		23p49			00 13		00 51	05 33	05 39			06 09		06 18	
—	—	**London Cannon Street** ■4 ⊖	d																						
1¾	—	**London Bridge** ■4 ⊖	d	23p31	23p39		23p44	23p46	23p49	23p53		23p54			00 18		00 56	05 39	05 44			06 14		06 24	
4¾	—	New Cross ■4 ⊖	d														01 01								
5½	—	St Johns	d																						
6	—	**Lewisham** ■4 ⛴	d				23p52					00 03					01 05		05 52			06 23			
7¼	—	Hither Green ■4	d				23p56					00 07					01 09		05 56			06 27			
9	0	**Grove Park** ■4	d				23p59				00 07	00 11			00 31	00 37	01 13		06 00		06 16	06 30			06 36
—	1¼	Sundridge Park	d								00 10					00 40					06 19				06 39
—	1¾	**Bromley North**	a								00 12					00 42					06 21				06 41
10¼	—	Elmstead Woods	d				00 03					00 14			00 34		01 16		06 03			06 33			
11¼	—	Chislehurst	d				00 05					00 17			00 37		01 19		06 05			06 36			
12¾	—	Petts Wood ■4	d			23p59	00 08					00 20		00 29	00 40		01 22		06 08	06 14		06 39			
13¾	—	**Orpington** ■4	a	23p46	23p54	00 02	00 12	00 01		00 08		00 23		00 32	00 43		01 25	05 54	06 11	06 18		06 42		06 40	
—	—		d	23p46	23p54			00 02		00 09					00 43			05 55	06 12			06 44		06 40	
15¼	—	Chelsfield ■3	d	23p49	23p57										00 46			05 58	06 15			06 47			
16½	—	Knockholt	d																06 18			06 50			
20½	—	Dunton Green	d																06 23			06 55			
22	—	**Sevenoaks** ■4	a	23p57	00 05			00 11	00 11	00 18					00 54			06 05	06 26			06 59		06 49	
—	—		d	23p57	00 05			00 12	00 12	00 19					00 54			06 06						06 50	
27	—	Hildenborough	d		00 11										01 00			06 12							
29½	—	**Tonbridge** ■4	a	00 05	00 15			00 20	00 20	00 27					01 04			06 16						06 58	

		SE	SE ■1	SE	SE	SE ■1	SE	SE		SE ■1	SE	SE	SE	SE ■1	SE ■1	SE	SE ■1	SE		SE	SE	SE ■1	SE	SE ■1	SE
London Charing Cross ■4 ⊖	d		06 30		06 36	06 45				07 00			07 06	07 10	07 15		07 29						07 36	07 40	07 48
London Waterloo (East) ■4 ⊖	d		06 33		06 39	06 48				07 03			07 09	07 13	07 18		07 32						07 39	07 43	07 51
London Cannon Street ■4 ⊖	d							06 50								07 20						07 47			
London Bridge ■4 ⊖	d		06 38		06 44	06 53		06 54		07 08			07 14	07 19	07 23	07 24	07 38					07 51	07 44	07 49	07 56
New Cross ■4 ⊖	d							06 59																	
St Johns	d							07 01																	
Lewisham ■4 ⛴	d				06 53			07 04																	
Hither Green ■4	d				06 58			07 08					07 23			07 35							07 53		
Grove Park ■4	d				07 02		07 06	07 12				07 25	07 27			07 38		07 46					07 57		
Sundridge Park	d						07 09					07 28						07 49							
Bromley North	a						07 11					07 30						07 51							
Elmstead Woods	d				07 05			07 15					07 30			07 41							08 00		
Chislehurst	d				07 07			07 18					07 33			07 44							08 03		
Petts Wood ■4	d	06 44		07 04	07 10			07 21			07 24		07 36							07 49	07 59		08 06		
Orpington ■4	a	06 49	06 53	07 08	07 13	07 09		07 25		07 25	07 28		07 40		07 38	07 48	07 53			07 53	08 02	08 08	08 09		08 12
	d		06 54		07 14	07 10				07 26			07 42		07 39		07 54					08 09	08 12		
Chelsfield ■3	d				07 17								07 45				07 57						08 15		
Knockholt	d				07 20								07 48				08 00								
Dunton Green	d				07 25								07 53										08 21		
Sevenoaks ■4	a		07 03		07 28	07 19				07 35			08 00	07 42	07 48		08 06					08 18	08 24	08 11	
	d		07 03			07 19				07 35				07 43	07 49		08 07					08 19		08 12	
Hildenborough	d		07 09							07 41							08 13								
Tonbridge ■4	a		07 14			07 27				07 45				07 51	07 58		08 17					08 27		08 20	

		SE	SE	SE		SE ■1	SE ■1	SE	SE	SE	SE ■1	SE ■1	SE	SE		SE ■1	SE ■1	SE	SE	SE ■1	SE	SE	SE	SE
London Charing Cross ■4 ⊖	d					07 52	08 00			08 05	08 13	08 17				08 27	08 33				08 37			08 49
London Waterloo (East) ■4 ⊖	d					07 55	08 03			08 08	08 16	08 20				08 30	08 36				08 40			08 52
London Cannon Street ■4 ⊖	d			07 51										08 19						08 42				
London Bridge ■4 ⊖	d			07 55		08 01	08 09			08 13	08 21	08 25		08 23		08 35	08 41			08 46	08 45			08 57
New Cross ■4 ⊖	d			08 00										08 29										
St Johns	d													08 31										
Lewisham ■4 ⛴	d			08 05										08 34										
Hither Green ■4	d			08 10						08 23				08 38							08 55			
Grove Park ■4	d	08 06		08 14				08 26		08 27				08 42				08 46			08 59	09 07		
Sundridge Park	d	08 09						08 29										08 49				09 10		
Bromley North	a	08 11						08 31										08 51				09 12		
Elmstead Woods	d			08 17						08 30				08 45							09 02			
Chislehurst	d			08 20						08 32				08 48							09 05			
Petts Wood ■4	d		08 14	08 23					08 29	08 36			08 44	08 51					08 59		09 08		09 14	
Orpington ■4	a		08 19	08 26			08 25		08 32	08 39		08 41	08 47	08 54		08 53	08 57		09 02	09 07	09 11		09 17	09 22
	d						08 26			08 45		08 42				08 54	08 58			09 07	09 12			
Chelsfield ■3	d									08 48											09 15			
Knockholt	d									08 51											09 18			
Dunton Green	d									08 56											09 23			
Sevenoaks ■4	a					08 27	08 35			08 59	08 44	08 51				09 03	09 07			09 17	09 26			
	d					08 28	08 35				08 45	08 52				09 03	09 07			09 17				
Hildenborough	d						08 41									09 09								
Tonbridge ■4	a					08 36	08 47				08 53	09 00				09 13	09 18			09 25				

London - Grove Park, Bromley North, Orpington, Sevenoaks and Tonbridge

		SE 1	SE	SE 1	SE	SE	SE 1	SE 1	SE	SE		SE	SE 1	SE	SE	SE 1	SE 1	SE	SE	SE		SE 1	SE	SE	SE 1
London Charing Cross 4 ⊖	d	08 53		09 00		09 06	09 13						09 30		09 36	09 40	09 45					10 00		10 06	10 10
London Waterloo (East) 4 ⊖	d	08 56		09 03		09 09	09 16						09 33		09 39	09 43	09 48					10 03		10 09	10 13
London Cannon Street 4 ⊖	d		08 51					09 18				09 20								09 50					
London Bridge 4 ⊖	d	09 01	08 55	09 08		09 14	09 21	09 22				09 25	09 39		09 44	09 49	09 53			09 54		10 09		10 14	10 19
New Cross 4 ⊖	d		09 00									09 29								09 59					
St Johns	d		09 02									09 31								10 01					
Lewisham 4	d		09 06									09 34								10 04					
Hither Green 4	d		09 10			09 23						09 38			09 53					10 08				10 23	
Grove Park 4	d		09 14			09 27			09 37			09 42			09 57			10 07		10 12				10 27	
Sundridge Park	d								09 40									10 10							
Bromley North	a								09 42									10 12							
Elmstead Woods	d		09 17			09 30						09 45			10 00					10 15				10 30	
Chislehurst	d		09 20			09 33						09 48			10 03					10 18				10 33	
Petts Wood 4	d		09 23		09 29	09 36				09 44		09 51		09 59	10 06				10 14	10 21			10 29	10 36	
Orpington 4	a	09 20	09 26	09 26	09 33	09 39		09 40		09 47		09 55	09 55	10 02	10 09		10 08		10 17	10 24		10 25	10 32	10 39	
	d	09 21		09 26		09 42		09 41					09 56		10 12		10 09					10 26		10 42	
Chelsfield 3	d					09 45									10 15									10 45	
Knockholt	d					09 48									10 18									10 48	
Dunton Green	d					09 53									10 23									10 53	
Sevenoaks 4	a	09 30		09 35		09 57	09 43	09 50					10 05		10 26	10 11	10 18					10 35		10 56	10 41
	d	09 31		09 35			09 44	09 50					10 05			10 12	10 19					10 35			10 42
Hildenborough	d			09 41									10 11									10 41			
Tonbridge 4	a	09 40		09 46			09 52	09 58					10 15			10 20	10 27					10 45			10 50

		SE 1	SE	SE	SE	SE 1		SE	SE	SE 1	SE 1	SE	SE	SE	SE 1	SE		SE	SE 1	SE 1	SE	SE	SE	SE 1	SE
London Charing Cross 4 ⊖	d	10 15				10 30			10 36	10 40	10 45				11 00			11 06	11 10	11 15				11 30	
London Waterloo (East) 4 ⊖	d	10 18				10 33			10 39	10 43	10 48				11 03			11 09	11 13	11 18				11 33	
London Cannon Street 4 ⊖	d				10 20									10 50									11 20		
London Bridge 4 ⊖	d	10 23			10 24	10 39			10 44	10 49	10 53			10 54	11 09			11 14	11 19	11 23			11 24	11 39	
New Cross 4 ⊖	d				10 29									10 59									11 29		
St Johns	d				10 31									11 01									11 31		
Lewisham 4	d				10 34									11 04									11 34		
Hither Green 4	d				10 38				10 53					11 08				11 23					11 38		
Grove Park 4	d		10 37		10 42				10 57			11 07		11 12				11 27			11 37		11 42		
Sundridge Park	d		10 40									11 10									11 40				
Bromley North	a		10 42									11 12									11 42				
Elmstead Woods	d				10 45				11 00					11 15				11 30					11 45		
Chislehurst	d				10 48				11 03					11 18				11 33					11 48		
Petts Wood 4	d			10 44	10 51			10 59	11 06				11 14	11 21		11 29		11 36				11 44	11 51		11 59
Orpington 4	a	10 38		10 47	10 54	10 55		11 02	11 09		11 08		11 17	11 24	11 25	11 32		11 39		11 38		11 47	11 54	11 55	12 02
	d	10 39				10 56			11 12		11 09				11 26			11 42		11 39				11 56	
Chelsfield 3	d								11 15									11 45							
Knockholt	d								11 18									11 48							
Dunton Green	d								11 23									11 53							
Sevenoaks 4	a	10 48				11 05			11 26	11 11	11 18				11 35			11 56	11 41	11 48				12 05	
	d	10 49				11 05				11 12	11 19				11 35				11 42	11 49				12 05	
Hildenborough	d					11 11									11 41									12 11	
Tonbridge 4	a	10 57				11 15				11 20	11 27				11 45				11 50	11 57				12 15	

		SE		SE 1	SE 1	SE	SE	SE	SE 1	SE	SE	SE 1		SE 1	SE	SE	SE	SE 1	SE	SE	SE 1	SE 1		SE	SE
London Charing Cross 4 ⊖	d	11 36		11 40	11 45				12 00		12 06	12 10		12 15				12 30		12 36	12 40	12 45			
London Waterloo (East) 4 ⊖	d	11 39		11 43	11 48				12 03		12 09	12 13		12 18				12 33		12 39	12 43	12 48			
London Cannon Street 4 ⊖	d							11 50									12 20								
London Bridge 4 ⊖	d	11 44		11 49	11 53			11 54	12 09		12 14	12 19		12 23			12 24	12 39		12 44	12 49	12 53			
New Cross 4 ⊖	d							11 59									12 29								
St Johns	d							12 01									12 31								
Lewisham 4	d							12 04									12 34								
Hither Green 4	d	11 53						12 08			12 23						12 38			12 53					
Grove Park 4	d	11 57				12 07		12 12			12 27				12 37		12 42			12 57				13 07	
Sundridge Park	d					12 10									12 40									13 10	
Bromley North	a					12 12									12 42									13 12	
Elmstead Woods	d	12 00						12 15			12 30						12 45			13 00					
Chislehurst	d	12 03						12 18			12 33						12 48			13 03					
Petts Wood 4	d	12 06					12 14	12 21		12 29	12 36					12 44	12 51		12 59	13 06					13 14
Orpington 4	a	12 09			12 08		12 17	12 24	12 25	12 32	12 39			12 38		12 47	12 54	12 55	13 02	13 09		13 08			13 17
	d	12 12			12 09				12 26		12 42			12 39				12 56		13 12		13 09			
Chelsfield 3	d	12 15									12 45									13 15					
Knockholt	d	12 18									12 48									13 18					
Dunton Green	d	12 23									12 53									13 23					
Sevenoaks 4	a	12 26		12 11	12 18				12 35		12 56	12 41		12 48				13 05		13 26	13 11	13 18			
	d			12 12	12 19				12 35			12 42		12 49				13 05			13 12	13 19			
Hildenborough	d								12 41									13 11							
Tonbridge 4	a			12 20	12 27				12 45			12 50		12 57				13 15			13 20	13 27			

London - Grove Park, Bromley North, Orpington, Sevenoaks and Tonbridge

Station		SE	SE [1]	SE	SE	SE [1]	SE [1]	SE		SE	SE	SE [1]	SE	SE	SE [1]	SE [1]	SE	SE		SE	SE [1]	SE	SE	SE [1]	SE [1]
London Charing Cross [4] ⊖	d		13 00		13 06	13 10	13 15					13 30		13 36	13 40	13 45					14 00		14 06	14 10	14 15
London Waterloo (East) [4] ⊖	d		13 03		13 09	13 13	13 18					13 33		13 39	13 43	13 48					14 03		14 09	14 13	14 18
London Cannon Street [4] ⊖	d	12 50									13 20									13 50					
London Bridge [4] ⊖	d	12 54	13 09		13 14	13 19	13 23				13 24	13 39		13 44	13 49	13 53				13 54	14 09		14 14	14 19	14 23
New Cross [4] ⊖	d	12 59									13 29									13 59					
St Johns	d	13 01									13 31									14 01					
Lewisham [4]	d	13 04									13 34									14 04					
Hither Green [4]	d	13 08			13 23						13 38			13 53						14 08			14 23		
Grove Park [4]	d	13 12			13 27			13 37			13 42			13 57			14 07			14 12			14 27		
Sundridge Park	d							13 40									14 10								
Bromley North	a							13 42									14 12								
Elmstead Woods	d	13 15			13 30						13 45			14 00						14 15			14 30		
Chislehurst	d	13 18			13 33						13 48			14 03						14 18			14 33		
Petts Wood [4]	d	13 21		13 29	13 36					13 44	13 51		13 59	14 06				14 14		14 21		14 29	14 36		
Orpington [4]	a	13 24	13 25	13 32	13 39		13 38			13 47	13 54	13 55	14 02	14 09		14 08		14 17		14 24	14 25	14 32	14 39		14 38
	d		13 26		13 42		13 39					13 56		14 12		14 09					14 26		14 42		14 39
Chelsfield [3]	d				13 45									14 15									14 45		
Knockholt	d				13 48									14 18									14 48		
Dunton Green	d				13 53									14 23									14 53		
Sevenoaks [4]	a		13 35		13 56	13 41	13 48					14 05		14 26	14 11	14 18					14 35		14 56	14 41	14 48
	d		13 35			13 42	13 49					14 05			14 12	14 19					14 35			14 42	14 49
Hildenborough	d		13 41									14 11									14 41				
Tonbridge [4]	a		13 45			13 50	13 57					14 15			14 20	14 27					14 45			14 50	14 57

Station		SE	SE	SE		SE [1]	SE	SE	SE [1]	SE [1]	SE	SE	SE	SE [1]		SE	SE	SE [1]	SE [1]	SE	SE	SE	SE [1]	SE	
London Charing Cross [4] ⊖	d					14 30		14 36	14 40	14 45				15 00			15 06	15 10	15 15				15 30		
London Waterloo (East) [4] ⊖	d					14 33		14 39	14 43	14 48				15 03			15 09	15 13	15 18				15 33		
London Cannon Street [4] ⊖	d			14 20									14 50									15 20			
London Bridge [4] ⊖	d			14 24		14 39		14 44	14 49	14 53			14 54	15 09			15 14	15 19	15 23			15 24	15 39		
New Cross [4] ⊖	d			14 29									14 59									15 29			
St Johns	d			14 31									15 01									15 31			
Lewisham [4]	d			14 34									15 04									15 34			
Hither Green [4]	d			14 38				14 53					15 08				15 23					15 38			
Grove Park [4]	d	14 37		14 42				14 57			15 07		15 12				15 27			15 37		15 42			
Sundridge Park	d	14 40									15 10									15 40					
Bromley North	a	14 42									15 12									15 42					
Elmstead Woods	d			14 45				15 00					15 15				15 30					15 45			
Chislehurst	d			14 48				15 03					15 18				15 33					15 48			
Petts Wood [4]	d		14 44	14 51			14 59	15 06				15 14	15 21			15 29	15 36				15 44	15 51		15 59	
Orpington [4]	a		14 47	14 54		14 55	15 02	15 09		15 08		15 17	15 24	15 25		15 32	15 39		15 38		15 47	15 54	15 55	16 02	
	d					14 56		15 12		15 09				15 26			15 42		15 39				15 56		
Chelsfield [3]	d							15 15									15 45								
Knockholt	d							15 18									15 48								
Dunton Green	d							15 23									15 53								
Sevenoaks [4]	a					15 05		15 26	15 11	15 18				15 35			15 56	15 41	15 48				16 05		
	d					15 05			15 12	15 19				15 35				15 42	15 49				16 05		
Hildenborough	d					15 11								15 41									16 11		
Tonbridge [4]	a					15 16			15 20	15 27				15 45				15 50	15 57				16 15		

Station		SE	SE [1]	SE [1]	SE	SE	SE	SE [1]	SE	SE		SE [1]	SE [1]	SE	SE	SE [1]	SE	SE	SE	SE [1]		SE [1]	SE	SE	SE
London Charing Cross [4] ⊖	d	15 36	15 40	15 45				16 00		16 06		16 10	16 15			16 28			16 32	16 37		16 41			16 42
London Waterloo (East) [4] ⊖	d	15 39	15 43	15 48				16 03		16 09		16 13	16 18			16 31			16 35	16 40		16 44			16 45
London Cannon Street [4] ⊖	d						15 50										16 20								
London Bridge [4] ⊖	d	15 44	15 49	15 53			15 54	16 09		16 14		16 19	16 23			16 36	16 24		16 40	16 45		16 49			16 51
New Cross [4] ⊖	d						15 59										16 30								
St Johns	d						16 01										16 32								
Lewisham [4]	d						16 04										16 35								17 01
Hither Green [4]	d	15 53					16 08			16 23							16 39		16 50						17 06
Grove Park [4]	d	15 57			16 07		16 12			16 27				16 37			16 43		16 54				16 57		17 10
Sundridge Park	d				16 10									16 40									17 00		
Bromley North	a				16 12									16 42									17 02		
Elmstead Woods	d	16 00					16 15			16 30							16 46		16 57						17 13
Chislehurst	d	16 03					16 18			16 33							16 48		17 00						17 15
Petts Wood [4]	d	16 06				16 14	16 21		16 29	16 36					16 44		16 51	16 59	17 03					17 14	17 19
Orpington [4]	a	16 09		16 08		16 17	16 24	16 25	16 32	16 39					16 49	16 52	16 57	17 04	17 06					17 19	17 24
	d	16 12		16 09				16 26		16 42						16 53			17 07						
Chelsfield [3]	d	16 15								16 45									17 10						
Knockholt	d	16 18								16 48									17 13						
Dunton Green	d	16 23								16 53									17 18						
Sevenoaks [4]	a	16 26	16 11	16 18				16 35		16 58		16 42	16 46			17 02			17 23	17 09		17 13			
	d		16 12	16 19				16 35				16 43	16 47			17 03				17 10		17 14			
Hildenborough	d							16 41								17 09									
Tonbridge [4]	a		16 20	16 27				16 45				16 51	16 55			17 13				17 18		17 22			

London - Grove Park, Bromley North, Orpington, Sevenoaks and Tonbridge

Station		SE ■1	SE	SE ■1	SE ■1	SE		SE	SE	SE ■1	SE	SE ■1	SE ■1	SE	SE	SE		SE ■1	SE	SE	SE ■1	SE ■1	SE	SE	SE ■1
London Charing Cross ■4 ⊖	d	16 57			17 01				17 03	17 14			17 23			17 26		17 41				17 45		17 47	17 59
London Waterloo (East) ■4 ⊖	d	17 00			17 04				17 06	17 18			17 26			17 29		17 44				17 48		17 50	18 02
London Cannon Street ■4 ⊖	d		16 56	17 02							17 19	17 24								17 41	17 45				
London Bridge ■4 ⊖	d		17 00	17 06	17 09				17 11		17 23	17 28	17 31			17 35				17 45	17 49	17 53		17 55	
New Cross ■4 ⊖	d																								
St Johns	d																								
Lewisham ■4	d								17 21							17 44								18 05	
Hither Green ■4	d								17 26							17 49								18 10	
Grove Park ■4	d		17 15			17 17			17 30		17 35			17 40		17 53				17 59			18 03	18 14	
Sundridge Park	d					17 20								17 43									18 06		
Bromley North	a					17 22								17 45									18 08		
Elmstead Woods	d		17 18						17 33		17 38					17 56				18 02				18 17	
Chislehurst	d		17 21						17 35		17 40					17 58				18 05				18 20	
Petts Wood ■4	d		17 24					17 35	17 39		17 44				17 50	18 02			18 05	18 08				18 23	
Orpington ■4	a		17 27					17 40	17 44		17 47				17 55	18 07			18 10	18 11				18 29	
	d		17 28								17 50									18 12					
Chelsfield ■3	d		17 31		17 28						17 53		17 50							18 15		18 12			
Knockholt	d		17 34								17 56									18 18					
Dunton Green	d		17 39								18 01									18 23					
Sevenoaks ■4	a	17 27	17 44	17 31	17 37					17 45	18 07	17 53	17 59					18 11		18 28	18 15	18 21			18 29
	d	17 27		17 32	17 37					17 46		17 54	17 59					18 11			18 16	18 21			18 30
Hildenborough	d				17 43							18 00	18 05									18 27			
Tonbridge ■4	a	17 35		17 40	17 48					17 54		18 04	18 09					18 19			18 24	18 32			18 38

Station		SE		SE	SE ■1	SE ■1	SE	SE	SE	SE ■1	SE	SE ■1		SE	SE	SE	SE ■1	SE ■1	SE	SE	SE ■1	SE ■1		SE	SE
London Charing Cross ■4 ⊖	d					18 07			18 09	18 21						18 30	18 32	18 41			18 45				
London Waterloo (East) ■4 ⊖	d					18 10			18 12	18 24						18 33	18 35	18 44			18 48				
London Cannon Street ■4 ⊖	d			18 02	18 08						18 23	18 32								18 48		19 04			
London Bridge ■4 ⊖	d			18 06	18 12	18 15			18 17		18 27	18 36				18 38	18 40	18 50		18 52	18 53	19 09			
New Cross ■4 ⊖	d																								
St Johns	d																								
Lewisham ■4	d								18 27																
Hither Green ■4	d								18 31							18 49									
Grove Park ■4	d			18 20			18 23		18 35		18 41			18 45		18 53				19 05				19 08	
Sundridge Park	d						18 26							18 48										19 11	
Bromley North	a						18 28							18 50										19 13	
Elmstead Woods	d			18 23					18 38		18 44					18 56				19 08					
Chislehurst	d			18 25					18 40		18 46					18 58				19 10					
Petts Wood ■4	d	18 26		18 29				18 36	18 44		18 50				18 54	19 03			19 07	19 14					19 20
Orpington ■4	a	18 32		18 32				18 41	18 49		18 53				18 59	19 06		19 06	19 12	19 19					19 25
	d			18 34							18 58					19 12		19 07							
Chelsfield ■3	d			18 37		18 34					19 01					19 15	18 58								
Knockholt	d			18 40							19 04					19 18									
Dunton Green	d			18 45							19 09					19 23									
Sevenoaks ■4	a			18 50	18 37	18 42				18 52	19 15	19 00				19 28	19 06	19 16			19 20	19 32			
	d				18 38	18 43				18 52		19 00					19 06	19 17			19 21	19 33			
Hildenborough	d				18 44	18 49											19 12					19 40			
Tonbridge ■4	a				18 48	18 54				19 00		19 08					19 17	19 25			19 29	19 44			

Station		SE ■1	SE	SE	SE ■1	SE ■1	SE	SE		SE	SE ■1	SE	SE	SE	SE ■1	SE ■1	SE	SE		SE ■1	SE	SE	SE	SE ■1	SE ■1
London Charing Cross ■4 ⊖	d	19 00		19 06	19 10	19 15					19 30			19 36	19 40	19 45				20 00			20 06	20 10	20 15
London Waterloo (East) ■4 ⊖	d	19 03		19 09	19 13	19 18					19 33			19 39	19 43	19 48				20 03			20 09	20 13	20 18
London Cannon Street ■4 ⊖	d									19 20								19 50							
London Bridge ■4 ⊖	d	19 09		19 14	19 19	19 23				19 24	19 39			19 44	19 49	19 53		19 54		20 09			20 14	20 19	20 23
New Cross ■4 ⊖	d									19 29								19 59							
St Johns	d									19 31								20 01							
Lewisham ■4	d									19 34								20 04							
Hither Green ■4	d			19 23						19 38				19 53				20 08					20 23		
Grove Park ■4	d			19 27			19 32			19 42		19 52		19 57				20 12			20 17		20 27		
Sundridge Park	d						19 35					19 55									20 20				
Bromley North	a						19 37					19 57									20 22				
Elmstead Woods	d			19 30						19 45				20 00				20 15					20 30		
Chislehurst	d			19 33						19 48				20 03				20 18					20 33		
Petts Wood ■4	d		19 35	19 38				19 44		19 51			19 59	20 06			20 14	20 21				20 29	20 36		
Orpington ■4	a	19 27	19 38	19 43		19 38		19 48		19 54	19 55		20 02	20 09		20 08	20 18	20 24		20 25		20 32	20 39		20 38
	d	19 28		19 44		19 39					19 56			20 12		20 09				20 26			20 42		20 39
Chelsfield ■3	d	19 31		19 47										20 15									20 45		
Knockholt	d			19 50										20 18									20 48		
Dunton Green	d			19 55										20 23									20 53		
Sevenoaks ■4	a	19 38		19 58	19 41	19 48					20 05			20 26	20 11	20 18				20 35			20 56	20 41	20 48
	d	19 39			19 42	19 49					20 05				20 12	20 19				20 35				20 42	20 49
Hildenborough	d	19 45									20 11									20 41					
Tonbridge ■4	a	19 50			19 53	19 57					20 15				20 20	20 27				20 45				20 50	20 57

London - Grove Park, Bromley North, Orpington, Sevenoaks and Tonbridge

		SE	SE	SE		SE 1	SE	SE	SE 1	SE 1	SE 1	SE	SE	SE		SE 1	SE 1	SE	SE	SE	SE 1	SE 1	SE 1	SE	
London Charing Cross 4	⊖ d					20 30		20 36	20 40	20 45	21 00			21 06		21 10	21 30			21 36	21 40	21 45	22 00		
London Waterloo (East) 4	⊖ d					20 33		20 39	20 43	20 48	21 03			21 09		21 13	21 33			21 39	21 43	21 48	22 03		
London Cannon Street 4	⊖ d			20 20																					
London Bridge 4	⊖ d			20 24		20 39		20 44	20 49	20 53	21 09			21 14		21 19	21 39			21 44	21 49	21 53	22 09		
New Cross 4	⊖ d			20 29																					
St Johns	d			20 31																					
Lewisham 4	⇌ d			20 34										21 22						21 52					
Hither Green 4	d			20 38				20 53						21 26						21 56					
Grove Park 4	d	20 37		20 42				20 57				21 07		21 30				21 37		22 00				22 07	
Sundridge Park	d	20 40										21 10						21 40						22 10	
Bromley North	a	20 42										21 12						21 42						22 12	
Elmstead Woods	d			20 45				21 00						21 33						22 03					
Chislehurst	d			20 48				21 03						21 35						22 05					
Petts Wood 4	d		20 44	20 51			20 59	21 06					21 29	21 38					21 59	22 08					
Orpington 4	a		20 47	20 54		20 55	21 02	21 09		21 08	21 25		21 32	21 42		21 34	21 55		22 02	22 12		22 08	22 25		
	d					20 56		21 12		21 09	21 26			21 43		21 35	21 56					22 09	22 26		
Chelsfield 3	d							21 15						21 46			21 59						22 29		
Knockholt	d							21 18						21 49											
Dunton Green	d							21 23						21 54											
Sevenoaks 4	a					21 05		21 26	21 11	21 18	21 35			21 57		21 44	22 06				22 11	22 18	22 36		
	d					21 05			21 12	21 19	21 35					21 44	22 07				22 12	22 19	22 37		
Hildenborough	d					21 11					21 41						22 13						22 43		
Tonbridge 4	a					21 15			21 20	21 27	21 45					21 52	22 17				22 20	22 27	22 47		

		SE	SE	SE 1	SE 1	SE	SE	SE	SE 1	SE 1		SE 1	SE	SE	SE	SE 1	SE 1	SE	SE	SE		SE 1	SE 1		
London Charing Cross 4	⊖ d		22 06	22 10	22 30			22 36	22 40	22 45		23 00			23 06	23 10	23 30			23 36		23 40	23 45		
London Waterloo (East) 4	⊖ d		22 09	22 13	22 33			22 39	22 43	22 48		23 03			23 09	23 13	23 33			23 39		23 43	23 48		
London Cannon Street 4	⊖ d																								
London Bridge 4	⊖ d		22 14	22 19	22 39			22 44	22 49	22 53		23 09			23 14	23 19	23 39			23 44		23 49	23 53		
New Cross 4	⊖ d																								
St Johns	d																								
Lewisham 4	⇌ d		22 22					22 52							23 22					23 52					
Hither Green 4	d		22 26					22 56							23 26					23 56					
Grove Park 4	d		22 30			22 37		23 00					23 07		23 30			23 37		23 59					
Sundridge Park	d					22 40							23 10					23 40							
Bromley North	a					22 42							23 12					23 42							
Elmstead Woods	d		22 33					23 03							23 33					00 03					
Chislehurst	d		22 35					23 05							23 35					00 05					
Petts Wood 4	d	22 29	22 38				22 59	23 08						23 29	23 38				23 59	00 08					
Orpington 4	a	22 32	22 42	22 34	22 54		23 02	23 12		23 08		23 24		23 32	23 42	23 34	23 54		00 02	00 12			00 08		
	d			22 35	22 54					23 09		23 24				23 35	23 54						00 09		
Chelsfield 3	d				22 57							23 27					23 57								
Knockholt	d																								
Dunton Green	d																								
Sevenoaks 4	a			22 44	23 05				23 11	23 18		23 35				23 44	00 05					00 11	00 18		
	d			22 44	23 05				23 12	23 19		23 35				23 44	00 05					00 12	00 19		
Hildenborough	d				23 11							23 41					00 11								
Tonbridge 4	a			22 52	23 15				23 20	23 27		23 45				23 52	00 15					00 20	00 27		

Saturdays

		SE 1	SE	SE	SE 1	SE 1	SE	SE	SE	SE		SE	SE	SE 1	SE	SE	SE	SE	SE	SE		SE 1	SE	SE	SE
London Charing Cross 4	⊖ d	23p30		23p36	23p40	23p45			00 10			00 48	05 36	06 00			06 06			06 36		07 00			07 06
London Waterloo (East) 4	⊖ d	23p33		23p39	23p43	23p48			00 13			00 51	05 39	06 03			06 09			06 39		07 03			07 09
London Cannon Street 4	⊖ d																								
London Bridge 4	⊖ d	23p39		23p44	23p49	23p53			00 18			00 56	05 44	06 08			06 14			06 44		07 08			07 14
New Cross 4	⊖ d											01 01													
St Johns	d																								
Lewisham 4	⇌ d			23p52								01 05	05 53				06 23			06 53					07 23
Hither Green 4	d			23p56								01 09	05 57				06 27			06 57					07 27
Grove Park 4	d			23p59			00 07		00 31	00 37		01 13	06 01		06 07		06 31	06 37		07 01			07 07		07 31
Sundridge Park	d						00 10			00 40					06 10			06 40					07 10		
Bromley North	a						00 12			00 42					06 12			06 42					07 12		
Elmstead Woods	d			00 03					00 34			01 16	06 04				06 34			07 04					07 34
Chislehurst	d			00 05					00 37			01 19	06 06				06 36			07 06					07 36
Petts Wood 4	d		23p59	00 08				00 29	00 40			01 22	06 09			06 29	06 39		06 59	07 09				07 29	07 39
Orpington 4	a	23p54	00 02	00 12		00 08		00 32	00 43			01 25	06 12	06 23		06 32	06 42		07 02	07 12		07 23		07 32	07 42
	d	23p54				00 09			00 43				06 13	06 24			06 43			07 13		07 24			07 43
Chelsfield 3	d	23p57							00 46				06 16				06 46			07 16					07 46
Knockholt	d												06 19				06 49			07 19					07 49
Dunton Green	d												06 24				06 54			07 24					07 54
Sevenoaks 4	a	00 05			00 11	00 18			00 54				06 27	06 33			06 57			07 27		07 33			07 57
	d	00 05			00 12	00 19			00 54					06 33								07 33			
Hildenborough	d	00 11							01 00					06 39								07 39			
Tonbridge 4	a	00 15			00 20	00 27			01 04					06 43								07 43			

Table 204

Saturdays

London - Grove Park, Bromley North, Orpington, Sevenoaks and Tonbridge

Station		SE	SE	SE 1	SE	SE		SE 1	SE	SE	SE 1	SE	SE	SE 1	SE	SE		SE	SE 1	SE	SE	SE 1	SE 1	SE	SE
London Charing Cross 4 ⊖	d			07 30		07 36		07 45			08 00		08 06	08 15					08 30		08 36	08 40	08 45		
London Waterloo (East) 4 ⊖	d			07 33		07 39		07 48			08 03		08 09	08 18					08 33		08 39	08 43	08 48		
London Cannon Street 4 ⊖	d																	08 20							
London Bridge 4 ⊖	d			07 38		07 44		07 53			08 08		08 14	08 23				08 24	08 39		08 44	08 49	08 53		
New Cross 4 ⊖	d																	08 29							
St Johns	d																	08 31							
Lewisham 4	d					07 53												08 34							
Hither Green 4	d					07 57							08 23					08 38			08 53				
Grove Park 4	d	07 37				08 01			08 07				08 27		08 37			08 42			08 57			09 07	
Sundridge Park	d	07 40							08 10						08 40									09 10	
Bromley North	a	07 42							08 12						08 42									09 12	
Elmstead Woods	d					08 04							08 30					08 45			09 00				
Chislehurst	d					08 06							08 33					08 48			09 03				
Petts Wood 4	d		07 44		07 59	08 09				08 14		08 29	08 36			08 44		08 51		08 59	09 06				09 14
Orpington 4	a		07 47	07 54	08 02	08 12		08 08		08 17	08 23	08 32	08 39	08 38		08 47		08 54	08 55	09 02	09 09		09 08		09 17
	d			07 54		08 13		08 09			08 24		08 42	08 39					08 56		09 12		09 09		
Chelsfield 3	d					08 16							08 45								09 15				
Knockholt	d					08 19							08 48								09 18				
Dunton Green	d					08 24							08 53								09 23				
Sevenoaks 4	a			08 02		08 27		08 18			08 33		08 56	08 48					09 05		09 26	09 11	09 18		
	d			08 03				08 19			08 33			08 49					09 05			09 12	09 19		
Hildenborough	d			08 09							08 39								09 11						
Tonbridge 4	a			08 14				08 27			08 43			08 57					09 15			09 20	09 27		

Station		SE		SE 1	SE	SE	SE 1	SE 1	SE	SE	SE	SE 1		SE	SE	SE 1	SE 1	SE	SE	SE	SE 1	SE		SE	SE 1
London Charing Cross 4 ⊖	d			09 00		09 06	09 10	09 15				09 30			09 36	09 40	09 45				10 00			10 06	10 10
London Waterloo (East) 4 ⊖	d			09 03		09 09	09 13	09 18				09 33			09 39	09 43	09 48				10 03			10 09	10 13
London Cannon Street 4 ⊖	d	08 50									09 20									09 50					
London Bridge 4 ⊖	d	08 54		09 09		09 14	09 19	09 23			09 24	09 39			09 44	09 49	09 53			09 54	10 09			10 14	10 19
New Cross 4 ⊖	d	08 59									09 29									09 59					
St Johns	d	09 01									09 31									10 01					
Lewisham 4	d	09 04									09 34									10 04					
Hither Green 4	d	09 08				09 23					09 38				09 53					10 08				10 23	
Grove Park 4	d	09 12				09 27			09 37		09 42				09 57			10 07		10 12				10 27	
Sundridge Park	d								09 40									10 10							
Bromley North	a								09 42									10 12							
Elmstead Woods	d	09 15				09 30					09 45				10 00					10 15				10 30	
Chislehurst	d	09 18				09 33					09 48				10 03					10 18				10 33	
Petts Wood 4	d	09 21			09 29	09 36				09 44	09 51			09 59	10 06				10 14	10 21		10 29		10 36	
Orpington 4	a	09 24		09 25	09 32	09 39		09 38		09 47	09 54	09 55		10 02	10 09		10 08		10 17	10 24	10 25	10 32		10 39	
	d			09 26		09 42		09 39				09 56			10 12		10 09				10 26			10 42	
Chelsfield 3	d					09 45									10 15									10 45	
Knockholt	d					09 48									10 18									10 48	
Dunton Green	d					09 53									10 23									10 53	
Sevenoaks 4	a			09 35		09 56	09 41	09 48				10 05			10 26	10 11	10 18				10 35			10 56	10 41
	d			09 35			09 42	09 49				10 05				10 12	10 19				10 35				10 42
Hildenborough	d			09 41								10 11									10 41				
Tonbridge 4	a			09 45			09 50	09 57				10 15				10 20	10 27				10 45				10 50

Station		SE 1	SE	SE	SE	SE 1	SE	SE		SE 1	SE 1	SE	SE	SE	SE 1	SE	SE	SE 1		SE 1	SE	SE	SE	SE 1	SE
London Charing Cross 4 ⊖	d	10 15				10 30		10 36		10 40	10 45				11 00		11 06	11 10		11 15				11 30	
London Waterloo (East) 4 ⊖	d	10 18				10 33		10 39		10 43	10 48				11 03		11 09	11 13		11 18				11 33	
London Cannon Street 4 ⊖	d				10 20									10 50									11 20		
London Bridge 4 ⊖	d	10 23			10 24	10 39		10 44		10 49	10 53			10 54	11 09		11 14	11 19		11 23			11 24	11 39	
New Cross 4 ⊖	d				10 29									10 59									11 29		
St Johns	d				10 31									11 01									11 31		
Lewisham 4	d				10 34									11 04									11 34		
Hither Green 4	d				10 38			10 53						11 08			11 23						11 38		
Grove Park 4	d		10 37		10 42			10 57				11 07		11 12			11 27				11 37		11 42		
Sundridge Park	d		10 40									11 10									11 40				
Bromley North	a		10 42									11 12									11 42				
Elmstead Woods	d				10 45			11 00						11 15			11 30						11 45		
Chislehurst	d				10 48			11 03						11 18			11 33						11 48		
Petts Wood 4	d			10 44	10 51		10 59	11 06					11 14	11 21		11 29	11 36					11 44	11 51		11 59
Orpington 4	a	10 38		10 47	10 54	10 55	11 02	11 09			11 08		11 17	11 24	11 25	11 32	11 39			11 38		11 47	11 54	11 55	12 02
	d	10 39				10 56		11 12			11 09				11 26		11 42			11 39				11 56	
Chelsfield 3	d							11 15									11 45								
Knockholt	d							11 18									11 48								
Dunton Green	d							11 23									11 53								
Sevenoaks 4	a	10 48				11 05		11 26		11 11	11 18				11 35		11 56	11 41		11 48				12 05	
	d	10 49				11 05				11 12	11 19				11 35			11 42		11 49				12 05	
Hildenborough	d					11 11									11 41									12 11	
Tonbridge 4	a	10 57				11 15				11 20	11 27				11 45			11 50		11 57				12 15	

Table 204

Saturdays

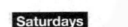

London - Grove Park, Bromley North, Orpington, Sevenoaks and Tonbridge

Station		SE	SE [1]	SE [1]		SE	SE	SE	SE [1]	SE	SE	SE [1]	SE [1]	SE		SE	SE	SE [1]	SE	SE	SE [1]	SE [1]	SE	SE	
London Charing Cross [4] ⊖	d	11 36	11 40	11 45					12 00		12 06	12 10	12 15					12 30		12 36	12 40	12 45			
London Waterloo (East) [4] ⊖	d	11 39	11 43	11 48					12 03		12 09	12 13	12 18					12 33		12 39	12 43	12 48			
London Cannon Street [4] ⊖	d							11 50									12 20								
London Bridge [4] ⊖	d	11 44	11 49	11 53				11 54	12 09		12 14	12 19	12 23				12 24	12 39		12 44	12 49	12 53			
New Cross [4] ⊖	d							11 59									12 29								
St Johns	d							12 01									12 31								
Lewisham [4]	d							12 04									12 34								
Hither Green [4]	d	11 53						12 08			12 23						12 38			12 53					
Grove Park [4]	d	11 57				12 07		12 12			12 27			12 37			12 42			12 57			13 07		
Sundridge Park	d					12 10								12 40									13 10		
Bromley North	a					12 12								12 42									13 12		
Elmstead Woods	d	12 00						12 15			12 30						12 45			13 00					
Chislehurst	d	12 03						12 18			12 33						12 48			13 03					
Petts Wood [4]	d	12 06					12 14	12 21		12 29	12 36					12 44	12 51		12 59	13 06				13 14	
Orpington [4]	a	12 09		12 08			12 17	12 24	12 25	12 32	12 39		12 38			12 47	12 54	12 55	13 02	13 09		13 08		13 17	
	d	12 12		12 09					12 26		12 42		12 39					12 56		13 12		13 09			
Chelsfield [3]	d	12 15									12 45									13 15					
Knockholt	d	12 18									12 48									13 18					
Dunton Green	d	12 23									12 53									13 23					
Sevenoaks [4]	a	12 26	12 11	12 18					12 35		12 56	12 41	12 48					13 05		13 26	13 11	13 18			
	d		12 12	12 19					12 35			12 42	12 49					13 05			13 12	13 19			
Hildenborough	d								12 41									13 11							
Tonbridge [4]	a		12 20	12 27					12 45			12 50	12 57					13 15			13 20	13 27			

Station		SE	SE [1]	SE	SE	SE [1]	SE [1]	SE	SE	SE		SE [1]	SE	SE	SE [1]	SE [1]	SE	SE	SE	SE [1]		SE	SE	SE [1]	SE [1]
London Charing Cross [4] ⊖	d		13 00		13 06	13 10	13 15					13 30		13 36	13 40	13 45				14 00			14 06	14 10	14 15
London Waterloo (East) [4] ⊖	d		13 03		13 09	13 13	13 18					13 33		13 39	13 43	13 48				14 03			14 09	14 13	14 18
London Cannon Street [4] ⊖	d	12 50								13 20									13 50						
London Bridge [4] ⊖	d	12 54	13 09		13 14	13 19	13 23			13 24		13 39		13 44	13 49	13 53			13 54	14 09			14 14	14 19	14 23
New Cross [4] ⊖	d	12 59								13 29									13 59						
St Johns	d	13 01								13 31									14 01						
Lewisham [4]	d	13 04								13 34									14 04						
Hither Green [4]	d	13 08			13 23					13 38				13 53					14 08				14 23		
Grove Park [4]	d	13 12			13 27			13 37		13 42				13 57			14 07		14 12				14 27		
Sundridge Park	d							13 40									14 10								
Bromley North	a							13 42									14 12								
Elmstead Woods	d	13 15			13 30					13 45				14 00					14 15				14 30		
Chislehurst	d	13 18			13 33					13 48				14 03					14 18				14 33		
Petts Wood [4]	d	13 21		13 29	13 36				13 44	13 51			13 59	14 06				14 14	14 21			14 29	14 36		
Orpington [4]	a	13 24	13 25	13 32	13 39		13 38		13 47	13 54		13 55	14 02	14 09		14 08		14 17	14 24	14 25		14 32	14 39		14 38
	d		13 26		13 42		13 39					13 56		14 12		14 09				14 26			14 42		14 39
Chelsfield [3]	d				13 45									14 15									14 45		
Knockholt	d				13 48									14 18									14 48		
Dunton Green	d				13 53									14 23									14 53		
Sevenoaks [4]	a		13 35		13 56	13 41	13 48					14 05		14 26	14 11	14 18				14 35			14 56	14 41	14 48
	d		13 35			13 42	13 49					14 05			14 12	14 19				14 35				14 42	14 49
Hildenborough	d		13 41									14 11								14 41					
Tonbridge [4]	a		13 45			13 50	13 57					14 15			14 20	14 27				14 45				14 50	14 57

Station		SE	SE	SE	SE [1]	SE		SE	SE [1]	SE [1]	SE	SE	SE	SE [1]	SE	SE		SE [1]	SE [1]	SE	SE	SE	SE [1]	SE	SE
London Charing Cross [4] ⊖	d				14 30			14 36	14 40	14 45				15 00		15 06		15 10	15 15				15 30		15 36
London Waterloo (East) [4] ⊖	d				14 33			14 39	14 43	14 48				15 03		15 09		15 13	15 18				15 33		15 39
London Cannon Street [4] ⊖	d			14 20									14 50									15 20			
London Bridge [4] ⊖	d			14 24	14 39			14 44	14 49	14 53			14 54	15 09		15 14		15 19	15 23			15 24	15 39		15 44
New Cross [4] ⊖	d			14 29									14 59									15 29			
St Johns	d			14 31									15 01									15 31			
Lewisham [4]	d			14 34									15 04									15 34			
Hither Green [4]	d			14 38				14 53					15 08			15 23						15 38			15 53
Grove Park [4]	d	14 37		14 42				14 57			15 07		15 12			15 27				15 37		15 42			15 57
Sundridge Park	d	14 40									15 10									15 40					
Bromley North	a	14 42									15 12									15 42					
Elmstead Woods	d			14 45				15 00					15 15			15 30						15 45			16 00
Chislehurst	d			14 48				15 03					15 18			15 33						15 48			16 03
Petts Wood [4]	d		14 44	14 51		14 59		15 06				15 14	15 21		15 29	15 36					15 44	15 51		15 59	16 06
Orpington [4]	a		14 47	14 54	14 55	15 02		15 09		15 08		15 17	15 24	15 25	15 32	15 39			15 38		15 47	15 54	15 55	16 02	16 09
	d				14 56			15 12		15 09				15 26		15 42			15 39				15 56		16 12
Chelsfield [3]	d							15 15								15 45									16 15
Knockholt	d							15 18								15 48									16 18
Dunton Green	d							15 23								15 53									16 23
Sevenoaks [4]	a				15 05			15 26	15 11	15 18				15 35		15 56		15 41	15 48				16 05		16 26
	d				15 05				15 12	15 19				15 35				15 42	15 49				16 05		
Hildenborough	d				15 11									15 41									16 11		
Tonbridge [4]	a				15 15				15 20	15 27				15 45				15 50	15 57				16 15		

Table 204

Saturdays

London - Grove Park, Bromley North, Orpington, Sevenoaks and Tonbridge

		SE 1		SE 1	SE	SE	SE	SE 1	SE	SE	SE 1	SE 1		SE	SE	SE	SE 1	SE	SE	SE 1	SE 1	SE		SE	SE
London Charing Cross 4 ⊖	d	15 40		15 45				16 00		16 06	16 10	16 15					16 30		16 36	16 40	16 45				
London Waterloo (East) 4 ⊖	d	15 43		15 48				16 03		16 09	16 13	16 18					16 33		16 39	16 43	16 48				
London Cannon Street 4 ⊖	d						15 50									16 20									16 50
London Bridge 4 ⊖	d	15 49		15 53			15 54	16 09		16 14	16 19	16 23				16 24	16 39		16 44	16 49	16 53				16 54
New Cross 4 ⊖	d						15 59									16 29									16 59
St Johns	d						16 01									16 31									17 01
Lewisham 4	d						16 04									16 34									17 04
Hither Green 4	d						16 08			16 23						16 38			16 53						17 08
Grove Park 4	d				16 07		16 12			16 27				16 37		16 42			16 57			17 07			17 12
Sundridge Park	d				16 10									16 40								17 10			
Bromley North	a				16 12									16 42								17 12			
Elmstead Woods	d						16 15			16 30						16 45			17 00						17 15
Chislehurst	d						16 18			16 33						16 48			17 03						17 18
Petts Wood 4	d					16 14	16 21		16 29	16 36					16 44	16 51		16 59	17 06					17 14	17 21
Orpington 4	a			16 08		16 17	16 24	16 25	16 32	16 39		16 38			16 47	16 54	16 55	17 02	17 09		17 08			17 17	17 24
	d			16 09				16 26		16 42		16 39					16 56		17 12		17 09				
Chelsfield 3	d									16 45									17 15						
Knockholt	d									16 48									17 18						
Dunton Green	d									16 53									17 23						
Sevenoaks 4	a	16 11		16 18				16 35		16 56	16 41	16 48					17 05		17 26	17 11	17 18				
	d	16 12		16 19				16 35			16 42	16 49					17 05			17 12	17 19				
Hildenborough	d							16 41									17 11								
Tonbridge 4	a	16 20		16 27				16 45			16 50	16 57					17 15			17 20	17 27				

		SE 1	SE	SE	SE 1	SE 1	SE	SE		SE	SE 1	SE	SE	SE 1	SE 1	SE	SE	SE		SE 1	SE	SE	SE 1	SE 1	SE
London Charing Cross 4 ⊖	d	17 00		17 06	17 10	17 15					17 30		17 36	17 40	17 45					18 00		18 06	18 10	18 15	
London Waterloo (East) 4 ⊖	d	17 03		17 09	17 13	17 18					17 33		17 39	17 43	17 48					18 03		18 09	18 13	18 18	
London Cannon Street 4 ⊖	d									17 20								17 50							
London Bridge 4 ⊖	d	17 09		17 14	17 19	17 23				17 24	17 39		17 44	17 49	17 53			17 54		18 09		18 14	18 19	18 23	
New Cross 4 ⊖	d									17 29								17 59							
St Johns	d									17 31								18 01							
Lewisham 4	d									17 34								18 04							
Hither Green 4	d			17 23						17 38			17 53					18 08				18 23			
Grove Park 4	d			17 27			17 37			17 42			17 57			18 07		18 12				18 27			18 37
Sundridge Park	d						17 40									18 10									18 40
Bromley North	a						17 42									18 12									18 42
Elmstead Woods	d			17 30						17 45			18 00					18 15				18 30			
Chislehurst	d			17 33						17 48			18 03					18 18				18 33			
Petts Wood 4	d		17 29	17 36				17 44		17 51		17 59	18 06				18 14	18 21			18 29	18 36			
Orpington 4	a	17 25	17 32	17 39		17 38		17 47		17 54	17 55	18 02	18 09		18 08		18 17	18 24		18 25	18 32	18 39		18 38	
	d	17 26		17 42		17 39					17 56		18 12		18 09					18 26		18 42		18 39	
Chelsfield 3	d			17 45									18 15									18 45			
Knockholt	d			17 48									18 18									18 48			
Dunton Green	d			17 53									18 23									18 53			
Sevenoaks 4	a	17 35		17 56	17 41	17 48					18 05		18 26	18 11	18 18					18 35		18 56	18 41	18 48	
	d	17 35			17 42	17 49					18 05			18 12	18 19					18 35			18 42	18 49	
Hildenborough	d	17 41									18 11									18 41					
Tonbridge 4	a	17 45			17 50	17 57					18 15			18 20	18 27					18 45			18 50	18 58	

		SE	SE	SE 1		SE	SE	SE 1	SE 1	SE	SE	SE	SE 1	SE		SE	SE 1	SE 1	SE	SE	SE 1	SE	SE	SE 1	
London Charing Cross 4 ⊖	d			18 30			18 36	18 40	18 45				19 00			19 06	19 10	19 15			19 30		19 36	19 40	
London Waterloo (East) 4 ⊖	d			18 33			18 39	18 43	18 48				19 03			19 09	19 13	19 18			19 33		19 39	19 43	
London Cannon Street 4 ⊖	d		18 20									18 50													
London Bridge 4 ⊖	d		18 24	18 39			18 44	18 49	18 53			18 54	19 09			19 14	19 19	19 23			19 39		19 44	19 49	
New Cross 4 ⊖	d		18 29									18 59													
St Johns	d		18 31									19 01													
Lewisham 4	d		18 34									19 04											19 52		
Hither Green 4	d		18 38				18 53					19 09				19 23							19 56		
Grove Park 4	d		18 42				18 57			19 07		19 12				19 27			19 37				20 00		
Sundridge Park	d									19 10									19 40						
Bromley North	a									19 12									19 42						
Elmstead Woods	d		18 45				19 00					19 15				19 30							20 03		
Chislehurst	d		18 48				19 03					19 18				19 33							20 05		
Petts Wood 4	d	18 44	18 51			18 59	19 06				19 14	19 21		19 29		19 36				19 44		19 59	20 08		
Orpington 4	a	18 47	18 54	18 55		19 02	19 09		19 08		19 17	19 24	19 25	19 32		19 39		19 38		19 48	19 55	20 02	20 12		
	d			18 56			19 12		19 09				19 26			19 42		19 39			19 56		20 13		
Chelsfield 3	d						19 15									19 45							20 16		
Knockholt	d						19 18									19 48							20 19		
Dunton Green	d						19 23									19 53							20 24		
Sevenoaks 4	a			19 05			19 26	19 11	19 18				19 35			19 56	19 41	19 49			20 05		20 27	20 11	
	d			19 05				19 12	19 19				19 35				19 42	19 49			20 05			20 12	
Hildenborough	d			19 11									19 41								20 11				
Tonbridge 4	a			19 15				19 20	19 27				19 45				19 50	19 58			20 15			20 20	

Table 204

Saturdays

London - Grove Park, Bromley North, Orpington, Sevenoaks and Tonbridge

		SE 1	SE	SE	SE	SE	SE 1	SE	SE	SE 1		SE	SE	SE 1	SE 1	SE	SE	SE	SE 1	SE 1		SE	SE	SE	SE 1
London Charing Cross 4 ⊖	d	19 55				20 06	20 10			20 25			20 36	20 40	20 55			21 06	21 10	21 25				21 36	21 40
London Waterloo (East) 4 ⊖	d	19 58				20 09	20 13			20 28			20 39	20 43	20 58			21 09	21 13	21 28				21 39	21 43
London Cannon Street 4 ⊖	d																								
London Bridge 4 ⊖	d	20 03				20 14	20 19			20 33			20 44	20 49	21 03			21 14	21 19	21 33				21 44	21 49
New Cross 4 ⊖	d																								
St Johns	d																								
Lewisham 4	d					20 22							20 52					21 22						21 52	
Hither Green 4	d					20 26							20 56					21 26						21 56	
Grove Park 4	d		20 07			20 30		20 37					21 00			21 07		21 30				21 37		22 00	
Sundridge Park	d		20 10					20 40								21 10						21 40			
Bromley North	a		20 12					20 42								21 12						21 42			
Elmstead Woods	d					20 33							21 03					21 33						22 03	
Chislehurst	d					20 35							21 05					21 35						22 05	
Petts Wood 4	d			20 14	20 29	20 38			20 44			20 59	21 08				21 29	21 38					21 59	22 08	
Orpington 4	a	20 18		20 18	20 32	20 42	20 34		20 47	20 48		21 02	21 12	21 04	21 18		21 32	21 42	21 34	21 48			22 02	22 12	22 04
	d	20 21				20 43	20 35			20 51			21 13	21 05	21 21			21 43	21 35	21 51					22 05
Chelsfield 3	d					20 46							21 16					21 46							
Knockholt	d					20 49							21 19					21 49							
Dunton Green	d					20 54							21 24					21 54							
Sevenoaks 4	a	20 30				20 57	20 44			21 00			21 27	21 14	21 30			21 57	21 44	22 00					22 14
	d	20 31					20 44			21 01				21 14	21 31				21 44	22 01					22 14
Hildenborough	d									21 07										22 07					
Tonbridge 4	a	20 39					20 52			21 11				21 22	21 39				21 52	22 11					22 22

		SE 1	SE	SE	SE	SE 1		SE 1	SE	SE	SE	SE 1	SE 1	SE	SE	SE		SE 1	SE 1	SE	SE	SE	SE 1	SE 1	
London Charing Cross 4 ⊖	d	21 55			22 06	22 10		22 25			22 36	22 40	22 55			23 06		23 10	23 25			23 36	23 40	23 45	
London Waterloo (East) 4 ⊖	d	21 58			22 09	22 13		22 28			22 39	22 43	22 58			23 09		23 13	23 28			23 39	23 43	23 48	
London Cannon Street 4 ⊖	d																								
London Bridge 4 ⊖	d	22 03			22 14	22 19		22 33			22 44	22 49	23 03			23 14		23 19	23 33			23 44	23 49	23 53	
New Cross 4 ⊖	d																								
St Johns	d																								
Lewisham 4	d				22 22						22 52					23 22						23 52			
Hither Green 4	d				22 26						22 56					23 26						23 56			
Grove Park 4	d		22 07		22 30				22 37		23 00			23 07		23 30				23 37		23 59			
Sundridge Park	d		22 10						22 40					23 10						23 40					
Bromley North	a		22 12						22 42					23 12						23 42					
Elmstead Woods	d				22 33						23 03					23 33						00 03			
Chislehurst	d				22 35						23 05					23 35						00 05			
Petts Wood 4	d			22 29	22 38					22 59	23 08				23 29	23 38					23 59	00 08			
Orpington 4	a	22 18		22 32	22 42	22 34		22 48		23 02	23 12	23 04	23 18		23 32	23 42		23 34	23 48		00 02	00 12	00 04	00 08	
	d	22 21				22 35		22 49				23 05	23 19					23 35	23 49				00 05	00 09	
Chelsfield 3	d							22 52											23 52						
Knockholt	d																								
Dunton Green	d																								
Sevenoaks 4	a	22 30				22 44		22 59				23 14	23 28					23 44	23 59				00 14	00 18	
	d	22 31				22 44		23 00				23 14	23 28					23 44	23 59				00 14	00 19	
Hildenborough	d							23 06											00 06						
Tonbridge 4	a	22 39				22 52		23 10				23 22	23 36					23 52	00 10				00 22	00 27	

Sundays

		SE 1 A	SE A	SE A	SE 1 A	SE 1 A	SE	SE A	SE	SE		SE	SE	SE	SE 1	SE	SE 1	SE	SE 1	SE	SE		SE 1	SE	SE 1
London Charing Cross 4 ⊖	d	23p25		23p36	23p40	23p45			00 10			00 48	07 46		08 08	08 16	08 23		08 38	08 46			09 08	09 16	09 23
London Waterloo (East) 4 ⊖	d	23p28		23p39	23p43	23p48			00 13			00 51	07 49		08 11	08 19	08 26		08 41	08 49			09 11	09 19	09 26
London Cannon Street 4 ⊖	d																								
London Bridge 4 ⊖	d	23p33		23p44	23p49	23p53			00 18			00 56	07 54		08 16	08 24	08 31		08 46	08 54			09 16	09 24	09 31
New Cross 4 ⊖	d											01 01													
St Johns	d																								
Lewisham 4	d			23p52								01 05	08 03			08 33				09 03				09 33	
Hither Green 4	d			23p56								01 09	08 07			08 37				09 07				09 37	
Grove Park 4	d			23p59			00 07		00 31	00 37		01 13	08 11			08 41				09 11				09 41	
Sundridge Park	d						00 10			00 40															
Bromley North	a						00 12			00 42															
Elmstead Woods	d			00 03					00 34			01 16	08 14			08 44				09 14				09 44	
Chislehurst	d			00 05					00 37			01 18	08 17			08 47				09 17				09 47	
Petts Wood 4	d		23p59	00 08				00 29	00 40			01 22	08 20	08 25		08 50		08 55		09 20	09 25			09 50	
Orpington 4	a	23p48	00 02	00 12	00 04	00 08		00 32	00 43			01 25	08 23	08 28	08 31	08 53	08 46	08 58	09 01	09 23	09 28		09 31	09 53	09 46
	d	23p49			00 05	00 09			00 43						08 32	08 54	08 46		09 02				09 32	09 54	09 46
Chelsfield 3	d	23p52							00 46							08 57								09 57	
Knockholt	d															09 00								10 00	
Dunton Green	d															09 05								10 05	
Sevenoaks 4	a	23p59			00 14	00 18			00 54						08 41	09 08	08 55		09 11				09 41	10 08	09 55
	d	23p59			00 14	00 19			00 54						08 42		08 56		09 12				09 42		09 56
Hildenborough	d	00 06							01 00						08 48								09 48		
Tonbridge 4	a	00 10			00 22	00 27			01 04						08 52		09 04		09 20				09 52		10 04

A not 22 May

London - Grove Park, Bromley North, Orpington, Sevenoaks and Tonbridge

		SE	SE 1	SE	SE 1		SE 1		SE	SE 1	SE	SE 1	SE	SE 1	SE	SE	SE 1		SE	SE 1	SE	SE 1	SE	SE
London Charing Cross 4 ⊖	d		09 38	09 46	09 53	and at the same minutes past each hour until	19 53			20 08	20 16	20 23		20 38	20 46		21 08		21 16	21 23		21 38	21 46	
London Waterloo (East) 4 ⊖	d		09 41	09 49	09 56		19 56			20 11	20 19	20 26		20 41	20 49		21 11		21 19	21 26		21 41	21 49	
London Cannon Street 4 ⊖	d																							
London Bridge 4 ⊖	d		09 46	09 54	10 01		20 01			20 16	20 24	20 31		20 46	20 54		21 16		21 24	21 31		21 46	21 54	
New Cross 4 ⊖	d																							
St Johns	d																							
Lewisham 4	d			10 03							20 33				21 03				21 33				22 03	
Hither Green 4	d			10 07							20 37				21 07				21 37				22 07	
Grove Park 4	d			10 11							20 41				21 11				21 41				22 11	
Sundridge Park	d																							
Bromley North	a																							
Elmstead Woods	d			10 14							20 44				21 14				21 44				22 14	
Chislehurst	d			10 17							20 47				21 17				21 47				22 17	
Petts Wood 4	d	09 55		10 20					20 25		20 50		20 55		21 20	21 25			21 50		21 55		22 20	22 25
Orpington 4	a	09 58	10 01	10 23	10 16		20 16		20 28	20 31	20 53	20 46	20 58	21 01	21 23	21 28	21 31		21 53	21 46	21 58	22 01	22 23	22 28
	d		10 02		10 16		20 16			20 32	20 54	20 46		21 02			21 32		21 54	21 46		22 02		
Chelsfield 3	d										20 57								21 57					
Knockholt	d										21 00								22 00					
Dunton Green	d										21 05								22 05					
Sevenoaks 4	a		10 11		10 25		20 25			20 41	21 08	20 55		21 11			21 41		22 08	21 55		22 11		
	d		10 12		10 26		20 26			20 42		20 56		21 12			21 42			21 56		22 12		
Hildenborough	d									20 48							21 48							
Tonbridge 4	a		10 20		10 34		20 34			20 52		21 04		21 20			21 52			22 04		22 20		

		SE 1	SE	SE 1		SE	SE 1	SE	SE	SE 1	SE	SE 1	SE	SE 1		SE
London Charing Cross 4 ⊖	d	22 08	22 16	22 23			22 38	22 46		23 08	23 16	23 23		23 38		23 46
London Waterloo (East) 4 ⊖	d	22 11	22 19	22 26			22 41	22 49		23 11	23 19	23 26		23 41		23 49
London Cannon Street 4 ⊖	d															
London Bridge 4 ⊖	d	22 16	22 24	22 31			22 46	22 54		23 16	23 24	23 31		23 46		23 54
New Cross 4 ⊖	d															
St Johns	d															
Lewisham 4	d		22 33					23 03			23 33					00 03
Hither Green 4	d		22 37					23 07			23 37					00 07
Grove Park 4	d		22 41					23 11			23 41					00 11
Sundridge Park	d															
Bromley North	a															
Elmstead Woods	d		22 44					23 14			23 44					00 14
Chislehurst	d		22 47					23 17			23 47					00 17
Petts Wood 4	d		22 50			22 55		23 20	23 25		23 50		23 55			00 20
Orpington 4	a	22 31	22 53	22 46		22 58	23 01	23 23	23 29	23 31	23 53	23 46	23 59	00 01		00 23
	d	22 32		22 46			23 02			23 32		23 46		00 02		
Chelsfield 3	d			22 49								23 49				
Knockholt	d															
Dunton Green	d															
Sevenoaks 4	a	22 41		22 57			23 11			23 41		23 57		00 11		
	d	22 42		22 57			23 12			23 42		23 57		00 12		
Hildenborough	d	22 48								23 48						
Tonbridge 4	a	22 52		23 05			23 20			23 52		00 05		00 20		

Table 204

Tonbridge, Sevenoaks, Orpington, Bromley North, Grove Park - London

Miles	Miles			SE MX [1]	SE MX	SE	SE	SE	SE [1]	SE	SE [1]	SE		SE	SE	SE [1]	SE [1]	SE [1]	SE	SE	SE	SE		SE [1]	SE [1]
0	—	**Tonbridge** [4]	d	23p14			04 56		05 31		05 50					06 00	06 06	06 19						06 32	06 40
2½	—	Hildenborough	d	23p18			05 00		05 35							06 04		06 23						06 36	
7½	—	**Sevenoaks** [4]	a	23p24			05 06		05 42		05 58					06 10	06 14	06 30						06 43	06 48
—	—		d	23p25			05 07		05 43		05 59				06 02	06 11	06 15	06 32				06 36		06 44	06 49
1½	—	Dunton Green	d												06 05							06 39			
5½	—	Knockholt	d												06 10							06 44			
6¾	—	Chelsfield [3]	d	23p32			05 14		05 50						06 13							06 47			
8¼	—	**Orpington** [4]	a	23p36			05 18		05 54		06 08				06 16	06 19	06 23					06 50		06 53	
—	—		d	23p37		05 10	05 20	05 40	05 54	06 01	06 09	06 10			06 22	06 20	06 24		06 40		06 43	06 52		06 54	
9¼	—	Petts Wood [4]	d			05a13	05 23	05a43		06 04		06a13			06 25				06a43		06 46	06 55			
10¾	—	Chislehurst	d				05 26			06 07					06 28						06 49	06 58			
11¾	—	Elmstead Woods	d				05 28			06 09					06 30						06 51	07 00			
—	0	**Bromley North**	d		00 23									06 25						06 45					
—	0½	Sundridge Park	d		00 25									06 27						06 47					
13	1¾	**Grove Park** [4]	d		00a28		05 31			06 12				06a30	06 34					06a50	06 54	07 04			
14¾	—	Hither Green [4]	d				05 35			06 16					06 38						06 58	07 08			
16	—	**Lewisham** [4] ⇌	d							06 22					06 43						07 04				
16½	—	St Johns	a																						
17¼	—	New Cross [4] ⊖	a				05 40			06 25															
20¼	—	**London Bridge** [4] ⊖	a	23p53			05 45		06 09	06 31	06 24				06 51	06 38	06 39	06 54				07 18		07 09	07 14
—	—	**London Cannon Street** [4] ⊖	a													06 42						07 25			
21¼	—	**London Waterloo (East)** [4] ⊖	a	23p57			05 50		06 14	06 36	06 29				06 56		06 44	06 59			07 16			07 14	07 19
22	—	**London Charing Cross** [4] ⊖	a	00 01			05 53		06 18	06 39	06 33				07 02		06 49	07 05			07 22			07 20	07 25

		SE [1]	SE	SE	SE	SE	SE [1]	SE [1]		SE	SE	SE	SE [1]	SE [1]	SE [1]	SE	SE	SE		SE	SE [1]	SE [1]	SE [1]	SE	SE
Tonbridge [4]	d	06 44					06 51	07 02					07 11	07 15	07 22						07 31	07 35	07 42		
Hildenborough	d						06 55						07 15	07 19							07 35	07 39			
Sevenoaks [4]	a	06 52					07 02	07 10					07 22	07 26	07 31						07 42	07 46	07 50		
	d	06 53				06 56	07 03	07 11				07 17	07 23	07 27	07 32					07 37	07 43	07 47	07 51		
Dunton Green	d					06 59						07 20								07 40					
Knockholt	d					07 04						07 25								07 45					
Chelsfield [3]	d					07 07						07 28	07 32							07 48	07 52				
Orpington [4]	a	07 02				07 10	07 13					07 31								07 51					
	d	07 04	07 03	07 08		07 11	07 14			07 22		07 33				07 38	07 42			07 52				07 57	08 01
Petts Wood [4]	d		07 06	07a11		07 15				07 25		07 36				07a41	07 45			07 55				08 00	08 04
Chislehurst	d		07 09			07 18				07 28		07 39					07 48			07 59				08 03	08 07
Elmstead Woods	d		07 11			07 20				07 31		07 41					07 50			08 01				08 06	08 10
Bromley North	d				07 15						07 35							07 55							
Sundridge Park	d				07 17						07 37							07 57							
Grove Park [4]	d		07 15		07a20	07 24				07 34	07a40	07 45					07 53	08a00		08 05				08 09	08 13
Hither Green [4]	d		07 19			07 28				07 39		07 49					07 57								08 17
Lewisham [4] ⇌	d		07 25							07 44							08 03								08 23
St Johns	a																								
New Cross [4] ⊖	a																								
London Bridge [4] ⊖	a	07 22				07 37	07 29	07 36		07 53		07 59	07 50	07 53						08 18	08 09	08 13			
London Cannon Street [4] ⊖	a	07 29				07 44						08 06		07 59						08 26		08 20			
London Waterloo (East) [4] ⊖	a		07 36				07 34	07 41		07 58			07 55		08 00		08 16				08 14		08 20	08 24	08 36
London Charing Cross [4] ⊖	a		07 42				07 40	07 47		08 04			08 01		08 06		08 22				08 20		08 26	08 30	08 42

		SE	SE	SE		SE [1]	SE [1]	SE [1]	SE	SE	SE	SE	SE [1]	SE [1]		SE [1]	SE	SE	SE	SE	SE [1]	SE [1]	SE	SE [1]	
Tonbridge [4]	d					07 51	07 59	08 03					08 11	08 15		08 22					08 35	08 40		08 44	
Hildenborough	d					07 55							08 15	08 19							08 39			08 48	
Sevenoaks [4]	a					08 02	08 07	08 11					08 22	08 26		08 30					08 45	08 48		08 54	
	d			07 57		08 03	08 07	08 11				08 17	08 23	08 27		08 31				08 37	08 45	08 49		08 55	
Dunton Green	d			08 00								08 20								08 40					
Knockholt	d			08 05								08 25								08 45					
Chelsfield [3]	d			08 08		08 12						08 28	08 32							08 48	08 53				
Orpington [4]	a			08 12								08 31								08 51				09 03	
	d	08 10		08 13					08 21	08 26		08 32					08 40	08 43		08 52			08 55	09 04	
Petts Wood [4]	d	08a13		08 16					08 24	08a29		08 35					08a43	08 46		08 55			08a58		
Chislehurst	d			08 20					08 27			08 39						08 49		08 58					
Elmstead Woods	d			08 22					08 29			08 41						08 51		09 00					
Bromley North	d		08 15								08 35								08 55						
Sundridge Park	d		08 17								08 37								08 57						
Grove Park [4]	d		08a20	08 26					08 33		08a40	08 45						08 55	09a00	09 04					
Hither Green [4]	d								08 37									08 59		09 08					
Lewisham [4] ⇌	d																	09 04							
St Johns	a																	09 07							
New Cross [4] ⊖	a																	09 09							
London Bridge [4] ⊖	a			08 39		08 29	08 33					08 59	08 49	08 55				09 17		09 20	09 11	09 14		09 22	
London Cannon Street [4] ⊖	a			08 46			08 41					09 06		09 02				09 23						09 28	
London Waterloo (East) [4] ⊖	a					08 34		08 40	08 52				08 54			09 00				09 25	09 16	09 19			
London Charing Cross [4] ⊖	a					08 40		08 46	08 58				09 00			09 04				09 31	09 22	09 25			

Tonbridge, Sevenoaks, Orpington, Bromley North, Grove Park - London

		SE	SE 1	SE	SE	SE	SE 1	SE 1	SE	SE	SE 1	SE	SE	SE	SE 1	SE 1	SE	SE	SE 1	SE	SE	SE	SE 1
Tonbridge 4	d		08 50				09 02	09 10			09 20				09 32	09 40			09 50				10 02
Hildenborough	d						09 06								09 36								10 06
Sevenoaks 4	a		08 58				09 13	09 18			09 28				09 43	09 48			09 58				10 13
	d		08 59			09 06	09 14	09 19			09 29			09 36	09 44	09 49			09 59			10 06	10 14
Dunton Green	d					09 09								09 39								10 09	
Knockholt	d					09 14								09 44								10 14	
Chelsfield 3	d					09 17								09 47								10 17	
Orpington 4	a		09 08			09 20	09 24				09 38			09 50	09 53				10 08			10 20	10 23
	d	09 03	09 09	09 10		09 21	09 24		09 25	09 33	09 39	09 40		09 51	09 54		09 55	10 03	10 09	10 10		10 21	10 24
Petts Wood 4	d	09 06		09a13		09 24			09a28	09 36		09a43		09 54			09a58	10 06		10a13		10 24	
Chislehurst	d	09 09				09 27				09 39				09 57				10 09				10 27	
Elmstead Woods	d	09 11				09 30				09 41				09 59				10 11				10 29	
Bromley North	d				09 23								09 53								10 23		
Sundridge Park	d				09 25								09 55								10 25		
Grove Park 4	d	09 15			09a28	09 33				09 45			09a58	10 03				10 15			10a28	10 33	
Hither Green 4	d	09 19				09 37				09 49				10 07				10 19				10 37	
Lewisham 4	d	09 24								09 54								10 24					
St Johns	a	09 26								09 56								10 26					
New Cross 4 ⊖	a	09 28								09 58								10 28					
London Bridge 4 ⊖	a	09 33	09 26			09 49	09 40	09 43		10 04	09 55			10 19	10 10	10 13		10 34	10 25			10 49	10 40
London Cannon Street 4 ⊖	a	09 40								10 08								10 38					
London Waterloo (East) 4 ⊖	a		09 31			09 53	09 45	09 48			09 59			10 23	10 15	10 18			10 29			10 53	10 45
London Charing Cross 4 ⊖	a		09 37			09 59	09 51	09 54			10 03			10 27	10 19	10 22			10 33			10 57	10 49

		SE 1	SE	SE	SE 1	SE	SE	SE	SE 1	SE 1	SE	SE	SE 1	SE	SE	SE	SE 1	SE 1	SE	SE	SE 1	SE	SE
Tonbridge 4	d	10 10			10 20				10 32	10 40			10 50				11 02	11 10			11 20		
Hildenborough	d								10 36								11 06						
Sevenoaks 4	a	10 18			10 28				10 43	10 48			10 58				11 13	11 18			11 28		
	d	10 19			10 29			10 36	10 44	10 49			10 59			11 06	11 14	11 19			11 29		
Dunton Green	d							10 39								11 09							
Knockholt	d							10 44								11 14							
Chelsfield 3	d							10 47								11 17							
Orpington 4	a				10 38			10 50	10 53				11 08			11 20	11 23				11 38		
	d		10 25	10 33	10 39	10 40		10 51	10 54		10 55	11 03	11 09	11 10		11 21	11 24		11 25	11 33	11 39	11 40	
Petts Wood 4	d		10a28	10 36		10a43		10 54			10a58	11 06		11a13		11 24			11a28	11 36		11a43	
Chislehurst	d			10 39				10 57				11 09				11 27				11 39			
Elmstead Woods	d			10 41				10 59				11 11				11 29				11 41			
Bromley North	d						10 53								11 23								11 53
Sundridge Park	d						10 55								11 25								11 55
Grove Park 4	d			10 45			10a58	11 03				11 15			11a28	11 33				11 45			11a58
Hither Green 4	d			10 49				11 07				11 19				11 37				11 49			
Lewisham 4	d			10 54								11 24								11 54			
St Johns	a			10 56								11 26								11 56			
New Cross 4 ⊖	a			10 58								11 28								11 58			
London Bridge 4 ⊖	a	10 43		11 04	10 55			11 19	11 10	11 13		11 34	11 25			11 49	11 40	11 43		12 04	11 55		
London Cannon Street 4 ⊖	a			11 08								11 38								12 08			
London Waterloo (East) 4 ⊖	a	10 48			10 59			11 23	11 15	11 18			11 29			11 53	11 45	11 48			11 59		
London Charing Cross 4 ⊖	a	10 52			11 03			11 27	11 19	11 22			11 33			11 57	11 49	11 52			12 03		

		SE	SE 1	SE 1	SE	SE	SE 1	SE	SE	SE	SE 1	SE 1	SE	SE	SE 1	SE	SE	SE	SE 1	SE 1	SE	SE
Tonbridge 4	d		11 32	11 40			11 50				12 02	12 10			12 20				12 32	12 40		
Hildenborough	d		11 36								12 06								12 36			
Sevenoaks 4	a		11 43	11 48			11 58				12 13	12 18			12 28				12 43	12 48		
	d	11 36	11 44	11 49			11 59			12 06	12 14	12 19			12 29			12 36	12 44	12 49		
Dunton Green	d	11 39								12 09								12 39				
Knockholt	d	11 44								12 14								12 44				
Chelsfield 3	d	11 47								12 17								12 47				
Orpington 4	a	11 50	11 53				12 08			12 20	12 23				12 38			12 50	12 53			
	d	11 51	11 54		11 55	12 03	12 09	12 10		12 21	12 24		12 25	12 33	12 39	12 40		12 51	12 54		12 55	13 03
Petts Wood 4	d	11 54			11a58	12 06		12a13		12 24			12a28	12 36		12a43		12 54			12a58	13 06
Chislehurst	d	11 57				12 09				12 27				12 39				12 57				13 09
Elmstead Woods	d	11 59				12 11				12 29				12 41				12 59				13 11
Bromley North	d								12 23								12 53					
Sundridge Park	d								12 25								12 55					
Grove Park 4	d	12 03				12 15			12a28	12 33				12 45			12a58	13 03				13 15
Hither Green 4	d	12 07				12 19				12 37				12 49				13 07				13 19
Lewisham 4	d					12 24								12 54								13 24
St Johns	a					12 26								12 56								13 26
New Cross 4 ⊖	a					12 28								12 58								13 28
London Bridge 4 ⊖	a	12 19	12 10	12 13		12 34	12 25			12 49	12 40	12 43		13 04	12 55			13 19	13 10	13 13		13 34
London Cannon Street 4 ⊖	a					12 38								13 08								13 38
London Waterloo (East) 4 ⊖	a	12 23	12 15	12 18			12 29			12 53	12 45	12 48			12 59			13 23	13 15	13 18		
London Charing Cross 4 ⊖	a	12 27	12 19	12 22			12 33			12 57	12 49	12 52			13 03			13 27	13 19	13 22		

Tonbridge, Sevenoaks, Orpington, Bromley North, Grove Park - London

		SE 1	SE	SE	SE	SE 1	SE 1	SE		SE	SE 1	SE	SE	SE	SE 1	SE 1	SE	SE		SE 1	SE	SE	SE	SE 1	SE 1
Tonbridge [4]	d	12 50				13 02	13 10				13 20				13 32	13 40				13 50				14 02	14 10
Hildenborough	d					13 06									13 36									14 06	
Sevenoaks [4]	a	12 58				13 13	13 18				13 28				13 43	13 48				13 58				14 13	14 18
	d	12 59			13 06	13 14	13 19				13 29			13 36	13 44	13 49				13 59			14 06	14 14	14 19
Dunton Green	d				13 09									13 39									14 09		
Knockholt	d				13 14									13 44									14 14		
Chelsfield [3]	d				13 17									13 47									14 17		
Orpington [4]	a	13 08			13 20	13 23					13 38			13 50	13 53					14 08			14 20	14 23	
	d	13 09	13 10		13 21	13 24		13 25		13 33	13 39	13 40		13 51	13 54		13 55	14 03		14 09	14 10		14 21	14 24	
Petts Wood [4]	d		13a13		13 24			13a28		13 36		13a43		13 54			13a58	14 06			14a13		14 24		
Chislehurst	d				13 27					13 39				13 57				14 09					14 27		
Elmstead Woods	d				13 29					13 41				13 59				14 11					14 29		
Bromley North	d			13 23									13 53									14 23			
Sundridge Park	d			13 25									13 55									14 25			
Grove Park [4]	d			13a28	13 33					13 45			13a58	14 03				14 15				14a28	14 33		
Hither Green [4]	d				13 37					13 49				14 07				14 19					14 37		
Lewisham [4]	d									13 54								14 24							
St Johns	a									13 56								14 26							
New Cross [4]	a									13 58								14 28							
London Bridge [4]	a	13 25			13 49	13 40	13 43			14 04	13 55			14 19	14 10	14 13		14 34		14 25			14 49	14 40	14 43
London Cannon Street [4]	a									14 08								14 38							
London Waterloo (East) [4]	a	13 29			13 53	13 45	13 48				13 59			14 23	14 15	14 18				14 29			14 53	14 45	14 48
London Charing Cross [4]	a	13 33			13 57	13 49	13 52				14 03			14 27	14 19	14 22				14 33			14 57	14 49	14 52

		SE	SE	SE 1		SE	SE	SE	SE 1	SE 1	SE	SE	SE 1	SE		SE	SE	SE 1	SE 1	SE	SE	SE 1	SE	SE	
Tonbridge [4]	d			14 20					14 32	14 40			14 50					15 02	15 10			15 20			
Hildenborough	d								14 36									15 06							
Sevenoaks [4]	a			14 28					14 43	14 48			14 58					15 13	15 18			15 28			
	d			14 29				14 36	14 44	14 49			14 59				15 06	15 14	15 19			15 29			
Dunton Green	d							14 39									15 09								
Knockholt	d							14 44									15 14								
Chelsfield [3]	d							14 47									15 17								
Orpington [4]	a			14 38				14 50	14 53				15 08				15 20	15 23				15 38			
	d	14 25	14 33	14 39		14 40		14 51	14 54		14 55	15 03	15 09	15 10			15 21	15 24		15 25	15 33	15 39	15 40		
Petts Wood [4]	d	14a28	14 36			14a43		14 54			14a58	15 06		15a13			15 24			15a28	15 36		15a43		
Chislehurst	d		14 39					14 57				15 09					15 27				15 39				
Elmstead Woods	d		14 41					14 59				15 11					15 29				15 41				
Bromley North	d						14 53									15 23								15 53	
Sundridge Park	d						14 55									15 25								15 55	
Grove Park [4]	d		14 45				14a58	15 03				15 15				15a28	15 33				15 45			15a58	
Hither Green [4]	d		14 49					15 07				15 19					15 37				15 49				
Lewisham [4]	d		14 54									15 24									15 54				
St Johns	a		14 56									15 26									15 56				
New Cross [4]	a		14 58									15 28									15 58				
London Bridge [4]	a		15 04	14 55				15 19	15 10	15 13		15 34	15 25				15 49	15 40	15 43		16 04	15 55			
London Cannon Street [4]	a		15 08									15 38									16 08				
London Waterloo (East) [4]	a			14 59				15 23	15 15	15 18			15 29				15 55	15 45	15 48			15 59			
London Charing Cross [4]	a			15 03				15 27	15 19	15 22			15 33				15 58	15 49	15 52			16 03			

		SE	SE 1	SE 1	SE	SE	SE 1	SE	SE	SE		SE 1	SE 1	SE	SE	SE 1	SE	SE	SE	SE 1		SE 1	SE	SE	SE
Tonbridge [4]	d		15 32	15 40			15 50					16 02	16 10			16 20				16 32		16 40			
Hildenborough	d		15 36									16 06								16 36					
Sevenoaks [4]	a		15 43	15 48			15 58					16 13	16 18			16 28				16 43		16 48			
	d	15 36	15 44	15 49			15 59			16 06		16 14	16 19			16 29			16 36	16 44		16 52			
Dunton Green	d	15 39								16 09									16 39						
Knockholt	d	15 44								16 14									16 44						
Chelsfield [3]	d	15 47								16 17		16 21							16 47						
Orpington [4]	a	15 50	15 53				16 07			16 20		16 24				16 38			16 50	16 53					
	d	15 51	15 54		15 55	16 03	16 08	16 10		16 21		16 25		16 25	16 33	16 39	16 40		16 51	16 54			16 55		17 03
Petts Wood [4]	d	15 54			15a58	16 06		16a13		16 24				16a28	16 36		16a43		16 54				16a58		17 06
Chislehurst	d	15 57				16 09				16 27					16 39				16 57						17 09
Elmstead Woods	d	15 59				16 11				16 29					16 41				16 59						17 11
Bromley North	d								16 23									16 47						17 07	
Sundridge Park	d								16 25									16 49						17 09	
Grove Park [4]	d	16 03				16 15			16a28	16 33					16 45			16a52	17 03					17a12	17 15
Hither Green [4]	d	16 07				16 19				16 37					16 50				17 09						17 19
Lewisham [4]	d					16 24																			17 24
St Johns	a					16 26																			17 26
New Cross [4]	a					16 28																			17 28
London Bridge [4]	a	16 19	16 11	16 14		16 34	16 25			16 48		16 42	16 46		17 01	16 56				17 11		17 17			17 34
London Cannon Street [4]	a					16 38																			17 38
London Waterloo (East) [4]	a	16 24	16 16	16 20			16 29			16 54		16 48	16 52		17 06	17 00			17 24	17 16		17 22			
London Charing Cross [4]	a	16 28	16 20	16 24			16 33			16 58		16 52	16 56		17 10	17 04			17 29	17 20		17 26			

Tonbridge, Sevenoaks, Orpington, Bromley North, Grove Park - London

		SE [1]	SE	SE	SE	SE		SE [1]	SE [1]	SE	SE	SE [1]	SE	SE	SE	SE [1]		SE [1]	SE	SE	SE [1]	SE	SE	SE	SE [1]
Tonbridge [4]	d	16 50						17 02	17 10			17 20				17 32		17 40			17 50				18 02
Hildenborough	d							17 06								17 36									18 06
Sevenoaks [4]	a	16 58						17 13	17 18			17 28				17 43		17 48			17 58				18 13
	d	16 59				17 05		17 14	17 19			17 29			17 35	17 44		17 49			17 59			18 06	18 14
Dunton Green	d					17 08									17 38									18 09	
Knockholt	d					17 13									17 43									18 14	
Chelsfield [3]	d					17 16									17 46									18 17	
Orpington [4]	a	17 08				17 19		17 23				17 38			17 49	17 53					18 08			18 20	18 23
	d	17 09	17 10	17 13		17 20		17 24		17 24	17 37	17 39	17 40		17 50	17 54			17 55	18 03	18 09	18 09		18 21	18 24
Petts Wood [4]	d		17a13			17 24				17a27	17 40		17a43		17 54				17a58	18 06		18a12		18 24	
Chislehurst	d					17 27					17 43				17 57					18 09				18 27	
Elmstead Woods	d					17 29					17 45				17 59					18 11				18 29	
Bromley North	d				17 27									17 50									18 13		
Sundridge Park	d				17 29									17 52									18 15		
Grove Park [4]	d				17a32	17 34					17 49			17a55	18 03					18 15			18a18	18 33	
Hither Green [4]	d					17 38					17 53				18 07					18 19				18 37	
Lewisham [4]	d																			18 24					
St Johns	a										17 57									18 26					
New Cross [4] ⊖	a										17 59									18 28					
London Bridge [4] ⊖	a	17 27				17 49		17 41	17 44		18 06	17 58			18 18	18 09		18 16		18 34	18 25			18 48	18 40
London Cannon Street [4] ⊖	a	17 32									18 11									18 38					
London Waterloo (East) [4] ⊖	a			17 36		17 53		17 46	17 50			18 02			18 23	18 14		18 20			18 29			18 53	18 45
London Charing Cross [4] ⊖	a			17 40		17 57		17 50	17 53			18 06			18 27	18 18		18 25			18 35			18 57	18 49

		SE [1]		SE [1]	SE	SE	SE	SE	SE	SE	SE [1]	SE [1]		SE	SE	SE [1]	SE	SE	SE	SE [1]	SE [1]	SE		SE [1]	SE
Tonbridge [4]	d	18 10		18 23							18 32	18 40				18 50				19 02	19 10			19 20	
Hildenborough	d										18 36									19 06					
Sevenoaks [4]	a	18 18		18 31							18 43	18 48				18 59				19 13	19 18			19 28	
	d	18 19		18 32						18 35	18 44	18 49				18 59			19 06	19 14	19 19			19 29	
Dunton Green	d									18 38									19 09						
Knockholt	d									18 43									19 14						
Chelsfield [3]	d									18 46									19 17						
Orpington [4]	a									18 49	18 53					19 08			19 20	19 23				19 38	
	d				18 25		18 33	18 40		18 50	18 54			18 55	19 03	19 08	19 10		19 21	19 24		19 25		19 39	19 40
Petts Wood [4]	d				18a28		18 36	18a43		18 54				18a58	19 06		19a13		19 24			19a28			19a43
Chislehurst	d						18 39			18 57					19 09				19 27						
Elmstead Woods	d						18 41			18 59					19 11				19 29						
Bromley North	d					18 33			18 55									19 18							
Sundridge Park	d					18 35			18 57									19 20							
Grove Park [4]	d					18a38	18 45		19a00	19 03					19 15			19a23	19 33						
Hither Green [4]	d						18 49			19 07					19 19				19 37						
Lewisham [4]	d						18 54								19 24				19 43						
St Johns	a						18 56								19 26										
New Cross [4] ⊖	a						18 58								19 28										
London Bridge [4] ⊖	a	18 43		18 55			19 04			19 19	19 10	19 13			19 34	19 25			19 52	19 40	19 43			19 54	
London Cannon Street [4] ⊖	a						19 10								19 38										
London Waterloo (East) [4] ⊖	a	18 48		18 59						19 23	19 14	19 17				19 29			19 56	19 45	19 48			19 59	
London Charing Cross [4] ⊖	a	18 52		19 04						19 27	19 18	19 21				19 33			20 00	19 49	19 52			20 03	

		SE	SE	SE [1]	SE [1]	SE	SE [1]	SE		SE	SE	SE [1]	SE [1]	SE	SE	SE	SE	SE [1]		SE [1]	SE [1]	SE	SE	SE	SE [1]
Tonbridge [4]	d			19 32	19 40		19 51					20 02	20 10					20 32		20 40	20 50				21 02
Hildenborough	d			19 36								20 06						20 36							21 06
Sevenoaks [4]	a			19 43	19 48		19 59					20 13	20 18					20 43		20 48	20 58				21 13
	d		19 36	19 44	19 49		20 00				20 06	20 14	20 19				20 35	20 44		20 49	20 59			21 05	21 14
Dunton Green	d		19 39								20 09						20 38							21 08	
Knockholt	d		19 44								20 14						20 43							21 13	
Chelsfield [3]	d		19 47								20 17						20 46							21 16	
Orpington [4]	a		19 50	19 53			20 08				20 20	20 23					20 49	20 52			21 08			21 19	21 22
	d		19 51	19 54		19 55	20 09			20 10	20 21	20 24			20 40		20 51	20 53			21 09	21 10		21 21	21 23
Petts Wood [4]	d		19 54			19a58				20a13	20 24				20a43		20 54					21a13		21 24	
Chislehurst	d		19 57								20 27						20 57							21 27	
Elmstead Woods	d		19 59								20 29						20 59							21 29	
Bromley North	d	19 42						20 02						20 27		20 53							21 23		
Sundridge Park	d	19 44						20 04						20 29		20 55							21 25		
Grove Park [4]	d	19a47	20 03					20a07			20 34			20a32		20a58	21 03						21a28	21 33	
Hither Green [4]	d		20 07								20 38						21 07							21 37	
Lewisham [4]	d		20 13								20 43						21 13							21 43	
St Johns	a																								
New Cross [4] ⊖	a																								
London Bridge [4] ⊖	a		20 22	20 10	20 13		20 24				20 52	20 39	20 42				21 22	21 08		21 13	21 24			21 52	21 38
London Cannon Street [4] ⊖	a																								
London Waterloo (East) [4] ⊖	a		20 26	20 15	20 18		20 29				20 56	20 44	20 47				21 26	21 13		21 18	21 29			21 56	21 43
London Charing Cross [4] ⊖	a		20 30	20 19	20 22		20 33				21 00	20 48	20 51				21 30	21 18		21 22	21 33			22 00	21 48

Tonbridge, Sevenoaks, Orpington, Bromley North, Grove Park - London

		SE [1]	SE	SE		SE	SE [1]	SE [1]	SE [1]	SE	SE	SE	SE [1]	SE [1]		SE	SE	SE	SE [1]	SE [1]	SE [1]	SE	SE	SE
Tonbridge [4]	d	21 10					21 32	21 40	21 50				22 02	22 10					22 31	22 40	22 50			
Hildenborough	d						21 36						22 06						22 35					
Sevenoaks [4]	a	21 18					21 43	21 48	21 58				22 13	22 18					22 41	22 48	22 58			
	d	21 19				21 35	21 44	21 49	21 59			22 05	22 14	22 19					22 42	22 49	22 59			
Dunton Green	d					21 38						22 08												
Knockholt	d					21 43						22 13												
Chelsfield [3]	d					21 46						22 16							22 49					
Orpington [4]	a					21 49	21 52		22 08			22 19	22 22						22 52		23 08			
	d		21 40			21 51	21 53		22 09	22 10		22 21	22 23			22 40		22 51	22 53		23 09	23 10		23 21
Petts Wood [4]	d		21a43			21 54				22a13		22 24				22a43		22 54				23a13		23 24
Chislehurst	d					21 57						22 27						22 57						23 27
Elmstead Woods	d					21 59						22 29						22 59						23 29
Bromley North	d			21 53							22 23						22 53						23 23	
Sundridge Park	d			21 55							22 25						22 55						23 25	
Grove Park [4]	d			21a58		22 03					22a28	22 33					22a58	23 03					23a28	23 33
Hither Green [4]	d					22 07						22 37						23 07						23 37
Lewisham [4]	d					22 13						22 43						23 13						23 43
St Johns	a																							
New Cross [4]	a																							
London Bridge [4]	a	21 43				22 22	22 08	22 13	22 24			22 52	22 38	22 43				23 22	23 08	23 13	23 24			23 50
London Cannon Street [4]	a																							
London Waterloo (East) [4]	a	21 48				22 26	22 13	22 18	22 29			22 56	22 43	22 48				23 26	23 13	23 18	23 29			23 54
London Charing Cross [4]	a	21 52				22 30	22 18	22 22	22 33			23 00	22 48	22 52				23 30	23 18	23 22	23 33			23 59

		SE [1]	SE
Tonbridge [4]	d	23 14	
Hildenborough	d	23 18	
Sevenoaks [4]	a	23 24	
	d	23 25	
Dunton Green	d		
Knockholt	d		
Chelsfield [3]	d	23 32	
Orpington [4]	a	23 36	
	d	23 37	
Petts Wood [4]	d		
Chislehurst	d		
Elmstead Woods	d		
Bromley North	d		23 53
Sundridge Park	d		23 55
Grove Park [4]	d		23a58
Hither Green [4]	d		
Lewisham [4]	d		
St Johns	a		
New Cross [4]	a		
London Bridge [4]	a	23 53	
London Cannon Street [4]	a		
London Waterloo (East) [4]	a	23 57	
London Charing Cross [4]	a	00 01	

Saturdays

		SE [1]	SE	SE	SE	SE	SE	SE [1]	SE	SE		SE	SE	SE [1]	SE	SE [1]	SE	SE	SE	SE [1]		SE	SE	SE [1]	SE
Tonbridge [4]	d	23p14						06 02						06 32		06 50				07 02				07 20	
Hildenborough	d	23p18						06 06						06 36						07 06					
Sevenoaks [4]	a	23p24						06 13						06 43		06 58				07 13				07 28	
	d	23p25		05 36			06 06	06 14					06 36	06 44		06 59			07 06	07 14				07 29	
Dunton Green	d			05 39			06 09						06 39						07 09						
Knockholt	d			05 44			06 14						06 44						07 14						
Chelsfield [3]	d	23p32		05 47			06 17						06 47						07 17						
Orpington [4]	a	23p36		05 50			06 20	06 23					06 50	06 53		07 08			07 20	07 23				07 38	
	d	23p37		05 51	06 10		06 21	06 24	06 25	06 40			06 51	06 54	06 55	07 09	07 10		07 21	07 24		07 25	07 33	07 39	07 40
Petts Wood [4]	d			05 54	06a13		06 24		06a28	06a43			06 54		06a58		07a13		07 24			07a28	07 36		07a43
Chislehurst	d			05 57			06 27						06 57						07 27				07 39		
Elmstead Woods	d			05 59			06 29						06 59						07 29				07 41		
Bromley North	d		00 23			06 23						06 53						07 23							
Sundridge Park	d		00 25			06 25						06 55						07 25							
Grove Park [4]	d		00a28	06 03		06a28	06 33					06a58	07 03					07a28	07 33				07 45		
Hither Green [4]	d			06 07			06 37						07 07						07 37				07 49		
Lewisham [4]	d			06 13			06 43						07 13										07 54		
St Johns	a																						07 56		
New Cross [4]	a																						07 58		
London Bridge [4]	a	23p53		06 21			06 51	06 39					07 21	07 09		07 24			07 49	07 39			08 04	07 55	
London Cannon Street [4]	a																						08 08		
London Waterloo (East) [4]	a	23p57		06 25			06 55	06 43					07 25	07 13		07 29			07 53	07 43				07 59	
London Charing Cross [4]	a	00 01		06 29			06 59	06 47					07 29	07 17		07 33			07 57	07 48				08 03	

Table 204

Saturdays

Tonbridge, Sevenoaks, Orpington, Bromley North, Grove Park - London

		SE	SE	SE [1]	SE [1]	SE		SE	SE [1]	SE	SE	SE	SE [1]	SE [1]	SE	SE		SE [1]	SE	SE	SE	SE [1]	SE [1]	SE	SE
Tonbridge [4]	d			07 32	07 40				07 50				08 02	08 10				08 20				08 32	08 40		
Hildenborough	d			07 36									08 06									08 36			
Sevenoaks [4]	a			07 43	07 48				07 58				08 13	08 18				08 28				08 43	08 48		
	d		07 36	07 44	07 49				07 59			08 06	08 14	08 19				08 29			08 36	08 44	08 49		
Dunton Green	d		07 39									08 09									08 39				
Knockholt	d		07 44									08 14									08 44				
Chelsfield [3]	d		07 47									08 17									08 47				
Orpington [4]	a		07 50	07 53					08 08			08 20	08 23					08 38			08 50	08 53			
	d		07 51	07 54		07 55		08 03	08 09	08 10		08 21	08 24		08 25	08 33		08 39	08 40		08 51	08 54		08 55	09 03
Petts Wood [4]	d		07 54			07a58		08 06		08a13		08 24			08a28	08 36			08a43		08 54			08a58	09 06
Chislehurst	d		07 57					08 09				08 27				08 39					08 57				09 09
Elmstead Woods	d		07 59					08 11				08 29				08 41					08 59				09 11
Bromley North	d	07 53									08 23									08 53					
Sundridge Park	d	07 55									08 25									08 55					
Grove Park [4]	d	07a58	08 03					08 15			08a28	08 33				08 45				08a58	09 03				09 15
Hither Green [4]	d		08 07					08 19				08 37				08 49					09 07				09 19
Lewisham [4]	d							08 24								08 54									09 24
St Johns	a							08 26								08 56									09 26
New Cross [4] ⊖	a							08 28								08 58									09 28
London Bridge [4] ⊖	a		08 19	08 10	08 13			08 34	08 25			08 49	08 40	08 43		09 04		08 55			09 19	09 10	09 13		09 34
London Cannon Street [4] ⊖	a							08 38								09 08									09 38
London Waterloo (East) [4] ⊖	a		08 23	08 15	08 19				08 29			08 53	08 45	08 49				08 59			09 23	09 15	09 19		
London Charing Cross [4] ⊖	a		08 27	08 19	08 22				08 33			08 57	08 49	08 52				09 03			09 27	09 19	09 22		

		SE [1]		SE	SE	SE	SE [1]	SE [1]	SE	SE	SE [1]	SE		SE	SE	SE [1]	SE [1]	SE	SE	SE [1]	SE	SE		SE	SE [1]
Tonbridge [4]	d	08 50					09 02	09 10			09 20					09 32	09 40			09 50					10 02
Hildenborough	d						09 06									09 36									10 06
Sevenoaks [4]	a	08 58					09 13	09 18			09 28					09 43	09 48			09 58					10 13
	d	08 59				09 06	09 14	09 19			09 29				09 36	09 44	09 49			09 59				10 06	10 14
Dunton Green	d					09 09									09 39									10 09	
Knockholt	d					09 14									09 44									10 14	
Chelsfield [3]	d					09 17									09 47									10 17	
Orpington [4]	a	09 08				09 20	09 23				09 38				09 50	09 53				10 08				10 20	10 23
	d	09 09		09 10		09 21	09 24		09 25	09 33	09 39	09 40			09 51	09 54		09 55	10 03	10 09	10 10			10 21	10 24
Petts Wood [4]	d			09a13		09 24			09a28	09 36		09a43			09 54			09a58	10 06		10a13			10 24	
Chislehurst	d					09 27				09 39					09 57				10 09					10 27	
Elmstead Woods	d					09 29				09 41					09 59				10 11					10 29	
Bromley North	d				09 23									09 53								10 23			
Sundridge Park	d				09 25									09 55								10 25			
Grove Park [4]	d				09a28	09 33				09 45				09a58	10 03				10 15			10a28		10 33	
Hither Green [4]	d					09 37				09 49					10 07				10 19					10 37	
Lewisham [4]	d									09 54									10 24						
St Johns	a									09 56									10 26						
New Cross [4] ⊖	a									09 58									10 28						
London Bridge [4] ⊖	a	09 25				09 49	09 40	09 43		10 04	09 55				10 19	10 10	10 13		10 34	10 25				10 49	10 40
London Cannon Street [4] ⊖	a									10 08									10 38						
London Waterloo (East) [4] ⊖	a	09 29				09 53	09 45	09 49			09 59				10 23	10 15	10 19			10 29				10 53	10 45
London Charing Cross [4] ⊖	a	09 33				09 57	09 49	09 52			10 03				10 27	10 19	10 22			10 33				10 57	10 49

		SE [1]	SE	SE	SE [1]	SE	SE	SE		SE [1]	SE [1]	SE	SE	SE [1]	SE	SE	SE	SE [1]		SE [1]	SE	SE	SE [1]	SE	SE
Tonbridge [4]	d	10 10			10 20					10 32	10 40			10 50				11 02		11 10			11 20		
Hildenborough	d									10 36								11 06							
Sevenoaks [4]	a	10 18			10 28					10 43	10 48			10 58				11 13		11 18			11 28		
	d	10 19			10 29			10 36		10 44	10 49			10 59			11 06	11 14		11 19			11 29		
Dunton Green	d							10 39									11 09								
Knockholt	d							10 44									11 14								
Chelsfield [3]	d							10 47									11 17								
Orpington [4]	a				10 38			10 50		10 53				11 08			11 20	11 23					11 38		
	d		10 25	10 33	10 39	10 40		10 51		10 54		10 55	11 03	11 09	11 10		11 21	11 24			11 25	11 33	11 39	11 40	
Petts Wood [4]	d		10a28	10 36		10a43		10 54				10a58	11 06		11a13		11 24				11a28	11 36		11a43	
Chislehurst	d			10 39				10 57					11 09				11 27					11 39			
Elmstead Woods	d			10 41				10 59					11 11				11 29					11 41			
Bromley North	d						10 53									11 23									11 53
Sundridge Park	d						10 55									11 25									11 55
Grove Park [4]	d			10 45			10a58	11 03					11 15			11a28	11 33					11 45			11a58
Hither Green [4]	d			10 49				11 07					11 19				11 37					11 49			
Lewisham [4]	d			10 54									11 24									11 54			
St Johns	a			10 56									11 26									11 56			
New Cross [4] ⊖	a			10 58									11 28									11 58			
London Bridge [4] ⊖	a	10 43		11 04	10 55			11 19		11 10	11 13		11 34	11 25			11 49	11 40		11 43		12 04	11 55		
London Cannon Street [4] ⊖	a			11 08									11 38									12 08			
London Waterloo (East) [4] ⊖	a	10 49			10 59			11 23		11 15	11 19			11 29			11 53	11 45		11 49			11 59		
London Charing Cross [4] ⊖	a	10 52			11 03			11 27		11 19	11 22			11 33			11 57	11 49		11 52			12 03		

Table 204

Saturdays

Tonbridge, Sevenoaks, Orpington, Bromley North, Grove Park - London

		SE	SE [1]	SE [1]	SE	SE	SE [1]	SE	SE	SE	SE [1]	SE [1]	SE	SE	SE [1]	SE	SE	SE	SE [1]	SE [1]	SE	SE
Tonbridge [4]	d		11 32	11 40			11 50				12 02	12 10			12 20				12 32	12 40		
Hildenborough	d		11 36								12 06								12 36			
Sevenoaks [4]	a		11 43	11 48			11 58				12 13	12 18			12 28				12 43	12 48		
	d	11 36	11 44	11 49			11 59			12 06	12 14	12 19			12 29			12 36	12 44	12 49		
Dunton Green	d	11 39								12 09								12 39				
Knockholt	d	11 44								12 14								12 44				
Chelsfield [3]	d	11 47								12 17								12 47				
Orpington [4]	a	11 50	11 53				12 08			12 20	12 23				12 38			12 50	12 53			
	d	11 51	11 54		11 55	12 03	12 09	12 10		12 21	12 24		12 25	12 33	12 39	12 40		12 51	12 54		12 55	13 03
Petts Wood [4]	d	11 54			11a58	12 06		12a13		12 24			12a28	12 36		12a43		12 54			12a58	13 06
Chislehurst	d	11 57				12 09				12 27				12 39				12 57				13 09
Elmstead Woods	d	11 59				12 11				12 29				12 41				12 59				13 11
Bromley North	d								12 23								12 53					
Sundridge Park	d								12 25								12 55					
Grove Park [4]	d	12 03				12 15			12a28	12 33				12 45			12a58	13 03				13 15
Hither Green [4]	d	12 07				12 19				12 37				12 49				13 07				13 19
Lewisham [4]	d					12 24								12 54								13 24
St Johns	a					12 26								12 56								13 26
New Cross [4] ⊖	a					12 28								12 58								13 28
London Bridge [4] ⊖	a	12 19	12 10	12 13		12 34	12 25			12 49	12 40	12 43		13 04	12 55			13 19	13 10	13 13		13 34
London Cannon Street [4] ⊖	a					12 38								13 08								13 38
London Waterloo (East) [4] ⊖	a	12 23	12 15	12 19			12 29			12 53	12 45	12 49			12 59			13 23	13 15	13 19		
London Charing Cross [4] ⊖	a	12 27	12 19	12 22			12 33			12 57	12 49	12 52			13 03			13 27	13 19	13 22		

		SE [1]	SE	SE	SE	SE [1]	SE [1]	SE	SE	SE [1]	SE	SE	SE	SE [1]	SE [1]	SE	SE	SE [1]	SE	SE	SE	SE [1]	SE [1]
Tonbridge [4]	d	12 50				13 02	13 10			13 20				13 32	13 40			13 50				14 02	14 10
Hildenborough	d					13 06								13 36								14 06	
Sevenoaks [4]	a	12 58				13 13	13 18			13 28				13 43	13 48			13 58				14 13	14 18
	d	12 59			13 06	13 14	13 19			13 29			13 36	13 44	13 49			13 59			14 06	14 14	14 19
Dunton Green	d				13 09								13 39								14 09		
Knockholt	d				13 14								13 44								14 14		
Chelsfield [3]	d				13 17								13 47								14 17		
Orpington [4]	a	13 08			13 20	13 23				13 38			13 50	13 53				14 08			14 20	14 23	
	d	13 09	13 10		13 21	13 24		13 25	13 33	13 39	13 40		13 51	13 54		13 55	14 03	14 09	14 10		14 21	14 24	
Petts Wood [4]	d		13a13		13 24			13a28	13 36		13a43		13 54			13a58	14 06		14a13		14 24		
Chislehurst	d				13 27				13 39				13 57				14 09				14 27		
Elmstead Woods	d				13 29				13 41				13 59				14 11				14 29		
Bromley North	d			13 23								13 53								14 23			
Sundridge Park	d			13 25								13 55								14 25			
Grove Park [4]	d			13a28	13 33				13 45			13a58	14 03				14 15			14a28	14 33		
Hither Green [4]	d				13 37				13 49				14 07				14 19				14 37		
Lewisham [4]	d								13 54								14 24						
St Johns	a								13 56								14 26						
New Cross [4] ⊖	a								13 58								14 28						
London Bridge [4] ⊖	a	13 25			13 49	13 40	13 43		14 04	13 55			14 19	14 10	14 13		14 34	14 25			14 49	14 40	14 43
London Cannon Street [4] ⊖	a								14 08								14 38						
London Waterloo (East) [4] ⊖	a	13 29			13 53	13 45	13 49			13 59			14 23	14 15	14 19			14 29			14 53	14 45	14 49
London Charing Cross [4] ⊖	a	13 33			13 57	13 49	13 52			14 03			14 27	14 19	14 22			14 33			14 57	14 49	14 52

		SE	SE	SE [1]	SE	SE	SE	SE [1]	SE [1]	SE	SE	SE [1]	SE	SE	SE	SE [1]	SE [1]	SE	SE	SE [1]	SE	SE	SE
Tonbridge [4]	d			14 20				14 32	14 40			14 50				15 02	15 10			15 20			
Hildenborough	d							14 36								15 06							
Sevenoaks [4]	a			14 28				14 43	14 48			14 58				15 13	15 18			15 28			
	d			14 29			14 36	14 44	14 49			14 59			15 06	15 14	15 19			15 29			15 36
Dunton Green	d						14 39								15 09								15 39
Knockholt	d						14 44								15 14								15 44
Chelsfield [3]	d						14 47								15 17								15 47
Orpington [4]	a			14 38			14 50	14 53				15 08			15 20	15 23				15 38			15 50
	d	14 25	14 33	14 39	14 40		14 51	14 54		14 55	15 03	15 09	15 10		15 21	15 24		15 25	15 33	15 39	15 40		15 51
Petts Wood [4]	d	14a28	14 36		14a43		14 54			14a58	15 06		15a13		15 24			15a28	15 36		15a43		15 54
Chislehurst	d		14 39				14 57				15 09				15 27				15 39				15 57
Elmstead Woods	d		14 41				14 59				15 11				15 29				15 41				15 59
Bromley North	d					14 53								15 23								15 53	
Sundridge Park	d					14 55								15 25								15 55	
Grove Park [4]	d		14 45			14a58	15 03				15 15			15a28	15 33				15 45			15a58	16 03
Hither Green [4]	d		14 49				15 07				15 19				15 37				15 49				16 07
Lewisham [4]	d		14 54								15 24								15 54				
St Johns	a		14 56								15 26								15 56				
New Cross [4] ⊖	a		14 58								15 28								15 58				
London Bridge [4] ⊖	a		15 04	14 55			15 19	15 10	15 13		15 34	15 25			15 49	15 40	15 43		16 04	15 55			16 19
London Cannon Street [4] ⊖	a		15 08								15 38								16 08				
London Waterloo (East) [4] ⊖	a			14 59			15 23	15 15	15 19			15 29			15 53	15 45	15 49			15 59			16 23
London Charing Cross [4] ⊖	a			15 03			15 27	15 19	15 22			15 33			15 57	15 49	15 52			16 03			16 27

Table 204

Saturdays

Tonbridge, Sevenoaks, Orpington, Bromley North, Grove Park - London

Station		SE [1]		SE [1]	SE	SE	SE [1]	SE	SE	SE	SE [1]	SE [1]		SE	SE	SE [1]	SE	SE	SE	SE [1]	SE [1]	SE		SE	SE [1]
Tonbridge [4]	d	15 32		15 40			15 50				16 02	16 10				16 20				16 32	16 40				16 50
Hildenborough	d	15 36									16 06									16 36					
Sevenoaks [4]	a	15 43		15 48			15 58				16 13	16 18				16 28				16 43	16 48				16 58
	d	15 44		15 49			15 59			16 06	16 14	16 19				16 29			16 36	16 44	16 49				16 59
Dunton Green	d									16 09									16 39						
Knockholt	d									16 14									16 44						
Chelsfield [3]	d									16 17									16 47						
Orpington [4]	a	15 53					16 08			16 20	16 23					16 38			16 50	16 53					17 08
	d	15 54			15 55	16 03	16 09	16 10		16 21	16 24			16 25	16 33	16 39	16 40		16 51	16 54		16 55		17 03	17 09
Petts Wood [4]	d				15a58	16 06		16a13		16 24				16a28	16 36		16a43		16 54			16a58		17 06	
Chislehurst	d					16 09				16 27					16 39				16 57					17 09	
Elmstead Woods	d					16 11				16 29					16 41				16 59					17 11	
Bromley North	d								16 23									16 53							
Sundridge Park	d								16 25									16 55							
Grove Park [4]	d					16 15			16a28	16 33					16 45			16a58	17 03					17 15	
Hither Green [4]	d					16 19				16 37					16 49				17 07					17 19	
Lewisham [4]	d					16 24									16 54									17 24	
St Johns	a					16 26									16 56									17 26	
New Cross [4] ⊖	a					16 28									16 58									17 28	
London Bridge [4] ⊖	a	16 10		16 13		16 34	16 25			16 49	16 40	16 43			17 04	16 55			17 19	17 10	17 13			17 34	17 25
London Cannon Street [4] ⊖	a					16 38									17 08									17 38	
London Waterloo (East) [4] ⊖	a	16 15		16 19			16 29			16 53	16 45	16 49				16 59			17 23	17 15	17 19				17 29
London Charing Cross [4] ⊖	a	16 19		16 22			16 33			16 57	16 49	16 52				17 03			17 27	17 19	17 22				17 33

Station		SE	SE	SE	SE [1]	SE [1]	SE	SE		SE [1]	SE	SE	SE	SE [1]	SE [1]	SE	SE	SE [1]		SE	SE	SE	SE [1]	SE [1]	SE
Tonbridge [4]	d				17 02	17 10				17 20				17 32	17 40			17 50					18 02	18 10	
Hildenborough	d				17 06									17 36									18 06		
Sevenoaks [4]	a				17 13	17 18				17 28				17 43	17 48			17 58					18 13	18 18	
	d			17 06	17 14	17 19				17 29			17 36	17 44	17 49			17 59				18 06	18 14	18 19	
Dunton Green	d			17 09									17 39									18 09			
Knockholt	d			17 14									17 44									18 14			
Chelsfield [3]	d			17 17									17 47									18 17			
Orpington [4]	a			17 20	17 23					17 38			17 50	17 53				18 08				18 20	18 23		
	d	17 10		17 21	17 24		17 25	17 33		17 39	17 40		17 51	17 54		17 55	18 03	18 09		18 10		18 21	18 24		18 25
Petts Wood [4]	d	17a13		17 24			17a28	17 36			17a43		17 54			17a58	18 06			18a13		18 24			18a28
Chislehurst	d			17 27				17 39					17 57				18 09					18 27			
Elmstead Woods	d			17 29				17 41					17 59				18 11					18 29			
Bromley North	d		17 23									17 53									18 23				
Sundridge Park	d		17 25									17 55									18 25				
Grove Park [4]	d		17a28	17 33				17 45				17a58	18 03				18 15				18a28	18 33			
Hither Green [4]	d			17 37				17 49					18 07				18 19					18 37			
Lewisham [4]	d							17 54									18 24								
St Johns	a							17 56									18 26								
New Cross [4] ⊖	a							17 58									18 28								
London Bridge [4] ⊖	a			17 49	17 40	17 43		18 04		17 55			18 19	18 10	18 13		18 34	18 25				18 49	18 40	18 43	
London Cannon Street [4] ⊖	a							18 08									18 38								
London Waterloo (East) [4] ⊖	a			17 53	17 45	17 49				17 59			18 23	18 15	18 19			18 29				18 53	18 45	18 49	
London Charing Cross [4] ⊖	a			17 57	17 49	17 52				18 03			18 27	18 19	18 22			18 33				18 57	18 49	18 52	

Station		SE [1]	SE	SE		SE	SE [1]	SE [1]	SE	SE [1]	SE	SE	SE	SE		SE [1]	SE [1]	SE	SE	SE	SE	SE [1]	SE [1]	SE	
Tonbridge [4]	d	18 20					18 32	18 40		18 50						19 10	19 18					19 40	19 50		
Hildenborough	d						18 36										19 22								
Sevenoaks [4]	a	18 28					18 43	18 48		18 58						19 18	19 28					19 48	19 58		
	d	18 29				18 36	18 44	18 49		18 59			19 06			19 19	19 29			19 36		19 49	19 59		
Dunton Green	d					18 39							19 09							19 39					
Knockholt	d					18 44							19 14							19 44					
Chelsfield [3]	d					18 47							19 17							19 47					
Orpington [4]	a	18 38				18 50	18 53			19 08			19 20			19 27	19 38			19 50		19 57	20 08		
	d	18 39	18 40			18 51	18 54		18 55	19 09	19 10		19 21	19 25		19 28	19 39	19 40		19 51	19 55	19 58	20 09	20 10	
Petts Wood [4]	d		18a43			18 54			18a58		19a13		19 24	19a28				19a43		19 54	19a58			20a13	
Chislehurst	d					18 57							19 27							19 57					
Elmstead Woods	d					18 59							19 29							19 59					
Bromley North	d			18 53								19 23							19 53						
Sundridge Park	d			18 55								19 25							19 55						
Grove Park [4]	d			18a58		19 03						19a28	19 33						19a58	20 03					
Hither Green [4]	d					19 07							19 37							20 07					
Lewisham [4]	d					19 12							19 43							20 13					
St Johns	a																								
New Cross [4] ⊖	a																								
London Bridge [4] ⊖	a	18 55				19 21	19 10	19 13		19 24			19 52			19 43	19 54			20 22		20 13	20 24		
London Cannon Street [4] ⊖	a																								
London Waterloo (East) [4] ⊖	a	18 59				19 25	19 15	19 19		19 29			19 56			19 48	19 59			20 26		20 18	20 29		
London Charing Cross [4] ⊖	a	19 03				19 29	19 19	19 22		19 33			20 00			19 51	20 03			20 30		20 21	20 33		

Table 204

Saturdays

Tonbridge, Sevenoaks, Orpington, Bromley North, Grove Park - London

		SE	SE	SE [1]	SE [1]	SE	SE	SE	SE [1]	SE [1]		SE	SE	SE	SE [1]	SE [1]	SE	SE	SE	SE [1]		SE [1]	SE	SE	SE
Tonbridge [4]	d			20 10	20 18				20 40	20 50					21 10	21 18				21 40		21 50			
Hildenborough	d				20 22											21 22									
Sevenoaks [4]	a			20 18	20 28				20 48	20 58					21 18	21 28				21 48		21 58			
	d		20 06	20 19	20 29			20 36	20 49	20 59				21 06	21 19	21 29			21 36	21 49		21 59			22 06
Dunton Green	d		20 09					20 39						21 09					21 39						22 09
Knockholt	d		20 14					20 44						21 14					21 44						22 14
Chelsfield [3]	d		20 17					20 47						21 17					21 47						22 17
Orpington [4]	a		20 20	20 27	20 38			20 50	20 57	21 08				21 20	21 27	21 38			21 50	21 57		22 08			22 20
	d		20 21	20 28	20 39	20 40		20 51	20 58	21 09		21 10		21 21	21 28	21 39	21 40		21 51	21 58		22 09	22 10		22 21
Petts Wood [4]	d		20 24			20a43		20 54				21a13		21 24			21a43		21 54				22a13		22 24
Chislehurst	d		20 27					20 57						21 27					21 57						22 27
Elmstead Woods	d		20 29					20 59						21 29					21 59						22 29
Bromley North	d	20 23					20 53						21 23					21 53						22 23	
Sundridge Park	d	20 25					20 55						21 25					21 55						22 25	
Grove Park [4]	d	20a28	20 33				20a58	21 03					21a28	21 33				21a58	22 03					22a28	22 33
Hither Green [4]	d		20 37					21 07						21 37					22 07						22 37
Lewisham [4]	d		20 43					21 13						21 43					22 13						22 43
St Johns	a																								
New Cross [4] ⊖	a																								
London Bridge [4] ⊖	a		20 52	20 43	20 54			21 22	21 13	21 24				21 52	21 43	21 54			22 22	22 13		22 24			22 52
London Cannon Street [4] ⊖	a																								
London Waterloo (East) [4] ⊖	a		20 56	20 48	20 59			21 26	21 18	21 29				21 56	21 48	21 59			22 26	22 18		22 29			22 56
London Charing Cross [4] ⊖	a		21 00	20 51	21 03			21 30	21 21	21 33				22 00	21 51	22 03			22 30	22 21		22 33			23 00

		SE [1]	SE [1]	SE	SE	SE		SE [1]	SE [1]	SE	SE	SE	SE [1]	SE
Tonbridge [4]	d	22 10	22 18					22 40	22 50				23 14	
Hildenborough	d		22 22										23 18	
Sevenoaks [4]	a	22 18	22 28					22 48	22 58				23 24	
	d	22 19	22 29					22 49	22 59				23 25	
Dunton Green	d													
Knockholt	d													
Chelsfield [3]	d												23 32	
Orpington [4]	a	22 27	22 38					22 57	23 08				23 36	
	d	22 28	22 39	22 40		22 51		22 58	23 09	23 10		23 21	23 37	
Petts Wood [4]	d			22a43		22 54				23a13		23 24		
Chislehurst	d					22 57						23 27		
Elmstead Woods	d					22 59						23 29		
Bromley North	d				22 53						23 23			23 53
Sundridge Park	d				22 55						23 25			23 55
Grove Park [4]	d				22a58	23 03					23a28	23 33		23a58
Hither Green [4]	d					23 07						23 37		
Lewisham [4]	d					23 13						23 43		
St Johns	a													
New Cross [4] ⊖	a													
London Bridge [4] ⊖	a	22 43	22 54			23 22		23 13	23 24			23 50	23 53	
London Cannon Street [4] ⊖	a													
London Waterloo (East) [4] ⊖	a	22 48	22 59			23 26		23 18	23 29			23 54	23 57	
London Charing Cross [4] ⊖	a	22 51	23 03			23 30		23 21	23 33			23 58	00 01	

Sundays

		SE [1] A	SE	SE	SE	SE [1]	SE	SE	SE [1]	SE [1]		SE	SE	SE [1]	SE	SE	SE [1]	SE [1]	SE	SE		SE [1]		SE [1]
Tonbridge [4]	d	23p14				07 10			07 23	07 39				08 10			08 25	08 39				08 55		18 55
Hildenborough	d	23p18								07 43								08 43						
Sevenoaks [4]	a	23p24				07 18			07 31	07 49				08 18			08 33	08 49				09 03		19 03
	d	23p25				07 19			07 32	07 49				08 19		08 25	08 33	08 49				09 03		19 03
Dunton Green	d															08 28								
Knockholt	d															08 33								
Chelsfield [3]	d	23p32							07 39							08 36								
Orpington [4]	a	23p36				07 28			07 42	07 58				08 28		08 39	08 42	08 58				09 12	and at the same minutes past each hour until	19 12
	d	23p37		07 06	07 10	07 29	07 36	07 40	07 43	07 59		08 06	08 10	08 29	08 36	08 40	08 43	08 59	09 06	09 10		09 13		19 13
Petts Wood [4]	d			07a09	07 13		07a39	07 43				08a09	08 13		08a39	08 43			09a09	09 13				
Chislehurst	d				07 16			07 46					08 16			08 46				09 16				
Elmstead Woods	d				07 18			07 48					08 18			08 48				09 18				
Bromley North	d		00 23																					
Sundridge Park	d		00 25																					
Grove Park [4]	d		00a28		07 22			07 52					08 22			08 52				09 22				
Hither Green [4]	d				07 26			07 56					08 26			08 56				09 26				
Lewisham [4]	d				07 31			08 01					08 31			09 01				09 31				
St Johns	a																							
New Cross [4] ⊖	a																							
London Bridge [4] ⊖	a	23p53			07 39	07 44		08 09	07 58	08 14			08 39	08 44		09 09	08 58	09 14		09 39		09 28		19 28
London Cannon Street [4] ⊖	a																							
London Waterloo (East) [4] ⊖	a	23p57			07 44	07 49		08 14	08 03	08 19			08 44	08 49		09 14	09 03	09 19		09 44		09 33		19 33
London Charing Cross [4] ⊖	a	00 01			07 48	07 53		08 18	08 07	08 23			08 49	08 53		09 18	09 07	09 23		09 49		09 37		19 37

A not 22 May

Table 204

Sundays

Tonbridge, Sevenoaks, Orpington, Bromley North, Grove Park - London

		SE 1	SE	SE	SE 1	SE 1		SE	SE	SE 1	SE	SE	SE 1	SE 1	SE	SE		SE 1	SE	SE	SE 1	SE 1	SE	SE	SE 1
Tonbridge 4	d	19 10			19 25	19 39				20 10			20 25	20 39				21 10			21 25	21 39			22 10
Hildenborough	d					19 43								20 43								21 43			
Sevenoaks 4	a	19 18			19 33	19 49				20 18			20 33	20 49				21 18			21 33	21 49			22 18
	d	19 19		19 25	19 33	19 49				20 19		20 25	20 33	20 49				21 19		21 25	21 33	21 49			22 19
Dunton Green	d			19 28								20 28								21 28					
Knockholt	d			19 33								20 33								21 33					
Chelsfield 3	d			19 36								20 36								21 36					
Orpington 4	a	19 28		19 39	19 42	19 58				20 28		20 39	20 42	20 58				21 28		21 39	21 42	21 58			22 28
	d	19 29	19 36	19 40	19 43	19 59		20 06	20 10	20 29	20 36	20 40	20 43	20 59	21 06	21 10		21 29	21 36	21 40	21 43	21 59	22 06	22 10	22 29
Petts Wood 4	d		19a39	19 43				20a09	20 13		20a39	20 43			21a09	21 13			21a39	21 43			22a09	22 13	
Chislehurst	d			19 46					20 16			20 46				21 16				21 46				22 16	
Elmstead Woods	d			19 48					20 18			20 48				21 18				21 48				22 18	
Bromley North	d																								
Sundridge Park	d																								
Grove Park 4	d			19 52					20 22			20 52				21 22				21 52				22 22	
Hither Green 4	d			19 56					20 26			20 56				21 26				21 56				22 26	
Lewisham 4	d			20 01					20 31			21 01				21 31				22 01				22 31	
St Johns	a																								
New Cross 4 ⊖	a																								
London Bridge 4 ⊖	a	19 44		20 09	19 58	20 14			20 39	20 44		21 09	20 58	21 14		21 39		21 44		22 09	21 58	22 14		22 39	22 44
London Cannon Street 4 ⊖	a																								
London Waterloo (East) 4 ⊖	a	19 49		20 14	20 03	20 19			20 44	20 49		21 14	21 03	21 19		21 44		21 49		22 14	22 03	22 19		22 44	22 49
London Charing Cross 4 ⊖	a	19 53		20 18	20 07	20 23			20 49	20 53		21 18	21 07	21 23		21 49		21 53		22 18	22 07	22 23		22 49	22 53

		SE		SE	SE 1	SE 1	SE
Tonbridge 4	d				22 25	22 39	
Hildenborough	d					22 43	
Sevenoaks 4	a				22 33	22 49	
	d			22 25	22 33	22 49	
Dunton Green	d			22 28			
Knockholt	d			22 33			
Chelsfield 3	d			22 36			
Orpington 4	a			22 39	22 42	22 58	
	d	22 36		22 40	22 43	22 59	23 10
Petts Wood 4	d	22a39		22 43			23 13
Chislehurst	d			22 46			23 16
Elmstead Woods	d			22 48			23 18
Bromley North	d						
Sundridge Park	d						
Grove Park 4	d			22 52			23 22
Hither Green 4	d			22 56			23 26
Lewisham 4	d			23 01			23 31
St Johns	a						
New Cross 4 ⊖	a						
London Bridge 4 ⊖	a			23 09	22 58	23 14	23 39
London Cannon Street 4 ⊖	a						
London Waterloo (East) 4 ⊖	a			23 14	23 03	23 19	23 44
London Charing Cross 4 ⊖	a			23 18	23 07	23 23	23 49

Network Diagram for Tables 206, 207, 208

DM-31/10(2)
Design BAJS

© 2010 Network Rail.
All rights reserved

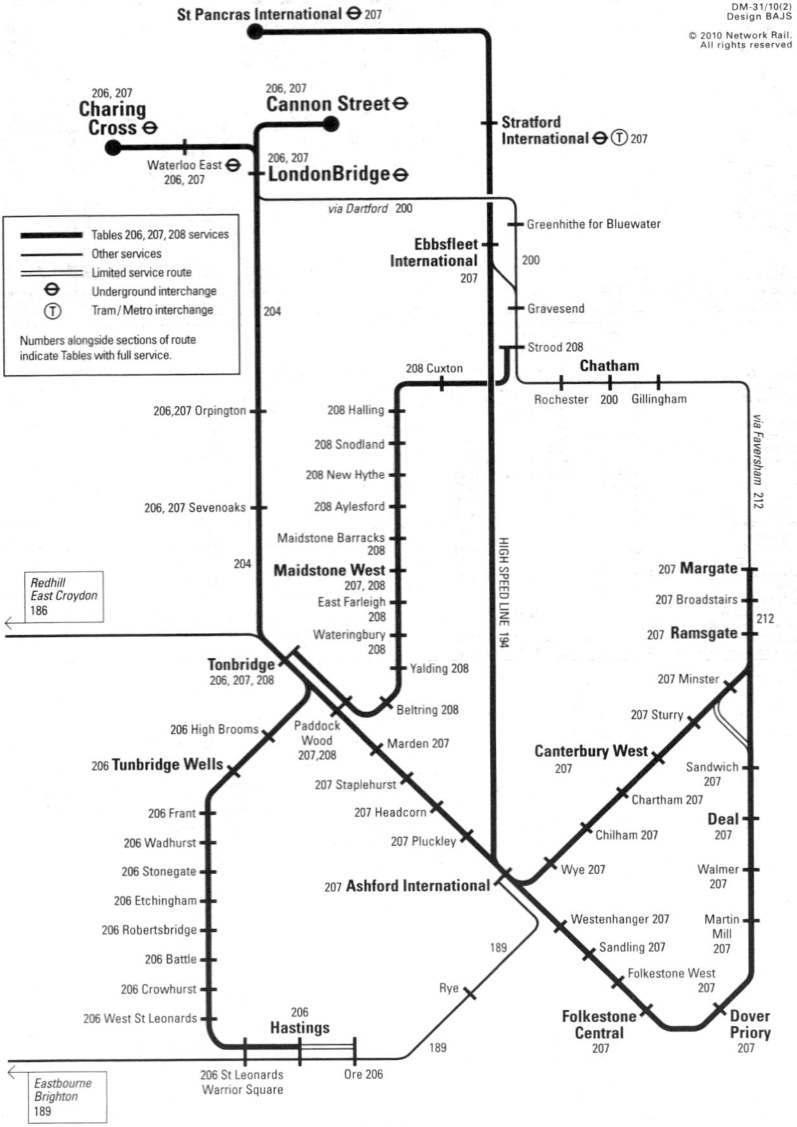

London and Tonbridge - Tunbridge Wells and Hastings

Miles			SE MO [1]	SE MX [1]	SE MO [1]	SE MX [1]	SE MX [1]	SE [1]	SE [1]	SE [1]	SE [1]		SE [1]	SE [1]	SE [1]	SE [1]	SE [1]	SE [1]	SE [1]	SE [1]	SE [1]		SE [1]	SE [1]	SE [1]
—	**London Charing Cross [4]**	⊖ d	22p23	22p45	23p23	23p30	23p45							06 15		06 45	07 00	07 15	07 29		08 00		08 17	08 27	
0¾	**London Waterloo (East) [4]**	⊖ d	22p26	22p48	23p26	23p33	23p48							06 18		06 48	07 03	07 18	07 32		08 03		08 20	08 30	
—	**London Cannon Street [4]**	⊖ d																		07 47					08 42
1¾	**London Bridge [4]**	⊖ d	22p31	22p53	23p31	23p39	23p53							06 24		06 53	07 08	07 23	07 38	07 51	08 09		08 25	08 35	08 46
13¾	Orpington [4]	d	22p46	23p09	23p46	23p54	00 09							06 40		07 10	07 26	07 39	07 54	08 09	08 26		08 42	08 54	09 07
22	Sevenoaks [4]	d	22p57	23p19	23p57	00 05	00 19							06 50		07 19	07 35	07 49	08 07	08 19	08 35		08 52	09 03	09 17
29½	**Tonbridge [4]**	a	23p05	23p27	00 05	00 15	00 27							06 58		07 27	07 45	07 58	08 17	08 27	08 47		09 00	09 13	09 25
—		d	23p06	23p28	00 06	00 16	00 27	05 00	05 31	06 07	06 20		06 35	06 58	07 11	07 31	07 46	07 59	08 17	08 27	08 48		09 00	09 16	09 26
33	High Brooms	d	23p12	23p35	00 12	00 22	00 34	05 06	05 37	06 13	06 26		06 41	07 04	07 17	07 37	07 55	08 05	08 23	08 34	08 54		09 06	09 23	09 35
34½	**Tunbridge Wells [4]**	a	23p15	23p39	00 15	00 26	00 38	05 10	05 40	06 17	06 30		06 44	07 08	07 22	07 41	08 02	08 08	08 28	08 40	08 58		09 10	09 27	09 39
—		d	23p17	23p40	00 17		00 40			06 18			06 46			07 42		08 13		08 49			09 14		09 42
36¾	Frant	d	23p22	23p45	00 22		00 45			06 23			06 51			07 47		08 18					09 19		
39¼	Wadhurst	d	23p27	23p50	00 27		00 50			06 28			06 57			07 52		08 24		08 57			09 25		09 50
43¼	Stonegate	d	23p33	23p56	00 33		00 56			06 34			07 03			07 58		08 30					09 31		
47½	Etchingham	d	23p38	00 01	00 38		01 00			06 38			07 08			08 02		08 34		09 05			09 36		
49¼	Robertsbridge	d	23p42	00 05	00 42		01 04			06 42			07 13			08 06		08 38		09 09			09 40		
55½	Battle	d	23p50	00 13	00 50		01 12			06 50			07 21			08 15		08 46		09 17			09 48		10 06
57½	Crowhurst	d	23p53	00 16	00 53		01 15			06 54			07 24			08 18		08 49					09 51		
60¾	West St Leonards	d	23p58	00 21	00 58		01 20			06 59			07 31			08 23		08 54					09 57		
—	St Leonards Warrior Sq [4]	d	00 01	00 25	01 01		01 23			07 02			07 34			08 26		08 57		09 28			10 00		10 16
62½	**Hastings [4]**	a	00 04	00 28	01 04		01 26			07 06			07 38			08 30		09 01		09 32			10 03		10 20
63½	Ore	a								07 10															

		SE [1]	SE [1]	SE [1]	SE [1]	SE [1]	SE [1]		SE [1]	SE [1]	SE [1]	SE [1]	SE [1]	SE [1]	SE [1]	SE [1]	SE [1]		SE [1]	SE [1]	SE [1]	SE [1]	SE [1]	SE [1]	SE [1]
London Charing Cross [4]	⊖ d	09 00		09 30	09 45	10 00	10 15		10 30	10 45	11 00	11 15	11 30	11 45	12 00	12 15	12 30		12 45	13 00	13 15	13 30	13 45	14 00	14 15
London Waterloo (East) [4]	⊖ d	09 03		09 33	09 48	10 03	10 18		10 33	10 48	11 03	11 18	11 33	11 48	12 03	12 18	12 33		12 48	13 03	13 18	13 33	13 48	14 03	14 18
London Cannon Street [4]	⊖ d		09 18																						
London Bridge [4]	⊖ d	09 08	09 22	09 39	09 53	10 09	10 23		10 39	10 53	11 09	11 23	11 39	11 53	12 09	12 23	12 39		12 53	13 09	13 23	13 39	13 53	14 09	14 23
Orpington [4]	d	09 26	09 41	09 56	10 09	10 26	10 39		10 56	11 09	11 26	11 39	11 56	12 09	12 26	12 39	12 56		13 09	13 26	13 39	13 56	14 09	14 26	14 39
Sevenoaks [4]	d	09 35	09 50	10 05	10 19	10 35	10 49		11 05	11 19	11 35	11 49	12 05	12 19	12 35	12 49	13 05		13 19	13 35	13 49	14 05	14 19	14 35	14 49
Tonbridge [4]	a	09 46	09 58	10 15	10 27	10 45	10 57		11 15	11 27	11 45	11 57	12 15	12 27	12 45	12 57	13 15		13 27	13 45	13 57	14 15	14 27	14 45	14 57
	d	09 46	09 59	10 16	10 28	10 46	11 01		11 16	11 28	11 46	11 58	12 16	12 28	12 46	12 58	13 16		13 28	13 46	13 58	14 16	14 28	14 46	14 58
High Brooms	d	09 53	10 05	10 23	10 35	10 54	11 07		11 23	11 35	11 53	12 05	12 23	12 35	12 53	13 05	13 23		13 35	13 53	14 05	14 23	14 35	14 53	15 05
Tunbridge Wells [4]	a	09 57	10 09	10 27	10 39	10 57	11 11		11 27	11 39	11 57	12 09	12 27	12 39	12 57	13 09	13 27		13 39	13 57	14 09	14 27	14 39	14 57	15 09
	d		10 13		10 40		11 12			11 40		12 10		12 40		13 10			13 40		14 10		14 40		15 10
Frant	d		10 18				11 17					12 15				13 15					14 15				15 15
Wadhurst	d		10 22		10 48		11 22			11 48		12 19		12 48		13 20			13 48		14 20		14 48		15 20
Stonegate	d		10 28				11 28					12 25				13 26					14 26				15 26
Etchingham	d		10 33				11 32					12 30				13 31					14 31				15 31
Robertsbridge	d		10 37				11 36					12 34				13 35					14 35				15 35
Battle	d		10 45		11 04		11 44			12 04		12 41		13 04		13 43			14 04		14 43		15 04		15 43
Crowhurst	d		10 48				11 48					12 45				13 46					14 46				15 46
West St Leonards	d		10 53				11 53					12 50				13 51					14 51				15 51
St Leonards Warrior Sq [4]	d		10 57		11 14		11 56			12 15		12 53		13 15		13 55			14 15		14 55		15 15		15 55
Hastings [4]	a		11 00		11 17		12 00			12 18		12 57		13 18		13 59			14 18		14 59		15 18		15 59
Ore	a																								

		SE [1]	SE [1]		SE [1]	SE [1]	SE [1]	SE [1]	SE [1]	SE [1]	SE [1]	SE [1]	SE [1]		SE [1]	SE [1]	SE [1]	SE [1]		SE [1]	SE [1]	SE [1]	SE [1]		SE [1]
London Charing Cross [4]	⊖ d	14 30	14 45		15 00	15 15	15 30	15 45	16 00	16 15	16 28	16 41			17 01	17 19	17 23			17 45	18 03	18 07			18 32
London Waterloo (East) [4]	⊖ d	14 33	14 48		15 03	15 18	15 33	15 48	16 03	16 18	16 31	16 44			17 04	17 22	17 26			17 48	18 06	18 10			18 35
London Cannon Street [4]	⊖ d												17 02					17 37					18 28		
London Bridge [4]	⊖ d	14 39	14 53		15 09	15 23	15 39	15 53	16 09	16 23	16 36	16 49	17 06		17 09		17 31	17 42		17 53		18 15	18 32		18 40
Orpington [4]	d	14 56	15 09		15 26	15 39	15 56	16 09	16 26		16 53														
Sevenoaks [4]	d	15 05	15 19		15 35	15 49	16 05	16 19	16 35	16 47	17 03	17 14	17 32		17 37		17 59			18 21		18 43			19 06
Tonbridge [4]	a	15 16	15 27		15 45	15 57	16 15	16 27	16 45	16 55	17 13	17 22	17 40		17 48		18 09			18 32		18 54			19 17
	d	15 16	15 28		15 46	15 58	16 16	16 28	16 46	16 55	17 13	17 22	17 41		17 48		18 11			18 32		18 54			19 17
High Brooms	d	15 23	15 35		15 53	16 05	16 23	16 35	16 53	17 01	17 21	17 28	17 47		17 54	18 04	18 17	18 21		18 38	18 47	19 00	19 09		19 23
Tunbridge Wells [4]	a	15 27	15 39		15 57	16 09	16 27	16 39	16 59	17 05	17 26	17 32	17 50		18 00	18 08	18 22	18 24		18 44	18 50	19 06	19 13		19 29
	d		15 40			16 14		16 40		17 05		17 38	17 52			18 08		18 29	18 33		18 56		19 20		
Frant	d					16 19		16 45		17 10			17 57			18 13			18 38		19 01		19 25		
Wadhurst	d		15 48			16 25		16 49		17 15		17 46	18 02			18 18		18 37	18 43		19 06		19 30		
Stonegate	d					16 31		16 55		17 21			18 08			18 24			18 49		19 12		19 36		
Etchingham	d					16 35		17 00		17 25		17 55	18 13			18 28		18 46	18 54		19 16		19 41		
Robertsbridge	d					16 39		17 04		17 29		17 59	18 17			18 32			18 58		19 20		19 45		
Battle	d		16 04			16 47		17 12		17 37		18 07	18 25			18 40		18 56	19 06		19 28		19 53		
Crowhurst	d					16 50		17 15		17 40			18 28			18 43			19 09		19 32		19 56		
West St Leonards	d		16 12			16 55		17 21		17 45			18 34			18 48			19 15		19 37		20 01		
St Leonards Warrior Sq [4]	d		16 15			16 58		17 24		17 48		18 17	18 37			18 51		19 06	19 18		19 41		20 05		
Hastings [4]	a		16 18			17 01		17 28		17 55		18 24	18 43			18 54		19 12	19 23		19 46		20 08		
Ore	a															19 00							20 15		

London and Tonbridge - Tunbridge Wells and Hastings

			SE 1	SE 1	SE 1	SE 1	SE 1	SE 1	SE 1	SE 1	SE 1	SE 1	SE 1	SE 1	SE 1	SE 1	SE 1	SE 1	SE 1	SE 1
London Charing Cross 4	⊖	d	18 45		19 15	19 30	19 45	20 00	20 15	20 30	20 45	21 00	21 30	21 45	22 00	22 30	22 45	23 00	23 30	23 45
London Waterloo (East) 4	⊖	d	18 48		19 18	19 33	19 48	20 03	20 18	20 33	20 48	21 03	21 33	21 48	22 03	22 33	22 48	23 03	23 33	23 48
London Cannon Street 4	⊖	d		19 04																
London Bridge 4	⊖	d	18 53	19 09	19 23	19 39	19 53	20 09	20 23	20 39	20 53	21 09	21 39	21 53	22 09	22 39	22 53	23 09	23 39	23 53
Orpington 4		d			19 39	19 56	20 09	20 26	20 39	20 56	21 09	21 26	21 56	22 09	22 26	22 54	23 09	23 24	23 54	00 09
Sevenoaks 4		d	19 21	19 33	19 49	20 05	20 19	20 35	20 49	21 05	21 19	21 35	22 07	22 19	22 37	23 05	23 19	23 35	00 05	00 19
Tonbridge 4		a	19 29	19 44	19 57	20 15	20 27	20 45	20 57	21 15	21 27	21 45	22 17	22 27	22 47	23 15	23 27	23 45	00 15	00 27
		d	19 30	19 45	19 58	20 16	20 28	20 46	20 58	21 16	21 28	21 46	22 17	22 28	22 47	23 16	23 28	23 46	00 16	00 27
High Brooms		d	19 36	19 53	20 05	20 23	20 35	20 53	21 05	21 23	21 35	21 53	22 24	22 35	22 54	23 22	23 35	23 52	00 22	00 34
Tunbridge Wells 4		a	19 39	19 56	20 09	20 27	20 39	20 57	21 09	21 27	21 39	21 57	22 27	22 39	22 58	23 26	23 39	23 56	00 26	00 38
		d	19 41	19 57	20 11		20 40		21 10		21 40			22 40			23 40			00 40
Frant		d	19 46	20 02	20 16		20 45		21 15		21 45			22 45			23 45			00 45
Wadhurst		d	19 50	20 07	20 21		20 50		21 20		21 50			22 50			23 50			00 50
Stonegate		d	19 56	20 13	20 27		20 56		21 26		21 56			22 56			23 56			00 56
Etchingham		d	20 01	20 18	20 32		21 01		21 31		22 01			23 01			00 01			01 00
Robertsbridge		d	20 05	20 22	20 36		21 05		21 36		22 05			23 05			00 05			01 04
Battle		d	20 13	20 29	20 44		21 13		21 44		22 13			23 13			00 13			01 12
Crowhurst		d	20 16		20 47		21 16		21 47		22 16			23 16			00 16			01 15
West St Leonards		d	20 21		20 53		21 21		21 52		22 21			23 21			00 21			01 20
St Leonards Warrior Sq 4		d	20 25	20 39	20 56		21 25		21 56		22 25			23 25			00 25			01 23
Hastings 4		a	20 30	20 43	21 00		21 29		21 59		22 29			23 29			00 28			01 26
Ore		a																		

Saturdays

			SE 1	SE 1	SE 1	SE 1	SE 1	SE 1	SE 1	SE 1	SE 1	SE 1	SE 1	SE 1	SE 1	SE 1	SE 1	SE 1	SE 1	SE 1	SE 1	SE 1	SE 1	SE 1
London Charing Cross 4	⊖	d	22p45	23p30	23p45				07 45	08 15	08 30	08 45	09 00	09 15	09 30	09 45	10 00	10 15	10 30	10 45	11 00	11 15	11 30	11 45
London Waterloo (East) 4	⊖	d	22p48	23p33	23p48				07 48	08 18	08 33	08 48	09 03	09 18	09 33	09 48	10 03	10 18	10 33	10 48	11 03	11 18	11 33	11 48
London Cannon Street 4	⊖	d																						
London Bridge 4	⊖	d	22p53	23p39	23p53				07 53	08 23	08 39	08 53	09 09	09 23	09 39	09 53	10 09	10 23	10 39	10 53	11 09	11 23	11 39	11 53
Orpington 4		d	23p09	23p54	00 09				08 09	08 39	08 56	09 09	09 26	09 39	09 56	10 09	10 26	10 39	10 56	11 09	11 26	11 39	11 56	12 09
Sevenoaks 4		d	23p19	00 05	00 19				08 19	08 49	09 05	09 19	09 35	09 49	10 05	10 19	10 35	10 49	11 05	11 19	11 35	11 49	12 05	12 19
Tonbridge 4		a	23p27	00 15	00 27				08 27	08 57	09 15	09 27	09 45	09 57	10 15	10 27	10 45	10 57	11 15	11 27	11 45	11 57	12 15	12 27
		d	23p28	00 16	00 27	06 58	07 28	07 58	08 28	08 58	09 16	09 28	09 46	09 58	10 16	10 28	10 46	10 58	11 16	11 28	11 46	11 58	12 16	12 28
High Brooms		d	23p35	00 22	00 34	07 05	07 35	08 05	08 35	09 05	09 23	09 35	09 53	10 05	10 23	10 35	10 53	11 05	11 23	11 35	11 53	12 05	12 23	12 35
Tunbridge Wells 4		a	23p39	00 26	00 38	07 09	07 39	08 09	08 39	09 09	09 27	09 39	09 57	10 09	10 27	10 39	10 57	11 09	11 27	11 39	11 57	12 09	12 27	12 39
		d	23p40		00 40	07 10		08 10	08 40	09 10		09 40		10 10		10 40		11 10		11 40		12 10		12 40
Frant		d	23p45		00 45	07 15		08 15	08 45	09 15				10 15				11 15				12 15		
Wadhurst		d	23p50		00 50	07 20		08 20	08 50	09 20		09 48		10 20		10 48		11 20		11 48		12 20		12 48
Stonegate		d	23p56		00 56	07 26		08 26	08 56	09 26				10 26				11 26				12 26		
Etchingham		d	00 01		01 00	07 31		08 31	09 01	09 31				10 31				11 31				12 31		
Robertsbridge		d	00 05		01 04	07 35		08 35	09 05	09 35				10 35				11 35				12 35		
Battle		d	00 13		01 12	07 43		08 43	09 13	09 43		10 04		10 43		11 04		11 43		12 04		12 43		13 04
Crowhurst		d	00 16		01 15	07 46		08 46	09 16	09 46				10 46				11 46				12 46		
West St Leonards		d	00 21		01 20	07 51		08 51	09 21	09 51				10 51				11 51				12 51		
St Leonards Warrior Sq 4		d	00 25		01 23	07 55		08 55	09 25	09 55		10 15		10 55		11 15		11 55		12 15		12 55		13 15
Hastings 4		a	00 28		01 26	07 59		08 59	09 29	09 59		10 18		10 59		11 18		11 59		12 18		12 59		13 18
Ore		a																						

			SE 1	SE 1	SE 1	SE 1	SE 1	SE 1	SE 1	SE 1	SE 1	SE 1	SE 1	SE 1	SE 1	SE 1	SE 1	SE 1	SE 1	SE 1	SE 1	SE 1	SE 1	SE 1
London Charing Cross 4	⊖	d	12 00	12 15	12 30	12 45	13 00	13 15	13 30	13 45	14 00	14 15	14 30	14 45	15 00	15 15	15 30	15 45	16 00	16 15	16 30	16 45	17 00	17 15
London Waterloo (East) 4	⊖	d	12 03	12 18	12 33	12 48	13 03	13 18	13 33	13 48	14 03	14 18	14 33	14 48	15 03	15 18	15 33	15 48	16 03	16 18	16 33	16 48	17 03	17 18
London Cannon Street 4	⊖	d																						
London Bridge 4	⊖	d	12 09	12 23	12 39	12 53	13 09	13 23	13 39	13 53	14 09	14 23	14 39	14 53	15 09	15 23	15 39	15 53	16 09	16 23	16 39	16 53	17 09	17 23
Orpington 4		d	12 26	12 39	12 56	13 09	13 26	13 39	13 56	14 09	14 26	14 39	14 56	15 09	15 26	15 39	15 56	16 09	16 26	16 39	16 56	17 09	17 26	17 39
Sevenoaks 4		d	12 35	12 49	13 05	13 19	13 35	13 49	14 05	14 19	14 35	14 49	15 05	15 19	15 35	15 49	16 05	16 19	16 35	16 49	17 05	17 19	17 35	17 49
Tonbridge 4		a	12 45	12 57	13 15	13 27	13 45	13 57	14 15	14 27	14 45	14 57	15 15	15 27	15 45	15 57	16 15	16 27	16 45	16 57	17 15	17 27	17 45	17 57
		d	12 46	12 58	13 16	13 28	13 46	13 58	14 16	14 28	14 46	14 58	15 16	15 28	15 46	15 58	16 16	16 28	16 46	16 58	17 16	17 28	17 46	17 58
High Brooms		d	12 53	13 05	13 23	13 35	13 53	14 05	14 23	14 35	14 53	15 05	15 23	15 35	15 53	16 05	16 23	16 35	16 53	17 05	17 23	17 35	17 53	18 05
Tunbridge Wells 4		a	12 57	13 09	13 27	13 39	13 57	14 09	14 27	14 39	14 57	15 09	15 27	15 39	15 57	16 09	16 27	16 39	16 57	17 09	17 27	17 39	17 57	18 09
		d		13 10		13 40		14 10		14 40		15 10		15 40		16 10		16 40		17 10		17 40		18 10
Frant		d		13 15				14 15				15 15				16 15				17 15				18 15
Wadhurst		d		13 20		13 48		14 20		14 48		15 20		15 48		16 20		16 48		17 20		17 48		18 20
Stonegate		d		13 26				14 26				15 26				16 26				17 26				18 26
Etchingham		d		13 31				14 31				15 31				16 31				17 31				18 31
Robertsbridge		d		13 35				14 35				15 35				16 35				17 35				18 35
Battle		d		13 43		14 04		14 43		15 04		15 43		16 04		16 43		17 04		17 43		18 04		18 43
Crowhurst		d		13 46				14 46				15 46				16 46				17 46				18 46
West St Leonards		d		13 51				14 51				15 51				16 51				17 51				18 51
St Leonards Warrior Sq 4		d		13 55		14 15		14 55		15 15		15 55		16 15		16 55		17 15		17 55		18 15		18 55
Hastings 4		a		13 59		14 18		14 59		15 18		15 59		16 18		16 59		17 18		17 59		18 18		18 59
Ore		a																						

Table 206

Saturdays

London and Tonbridge - Tunbridge Wells and Hastings

		SE 1	SE 1	SE 1	SE 1	SE 1	SE 1	SE 1	SE 1	SE 1	SE 1	SE 1	SE 1	SE 1	SE 1	SE 1	SE 1	SE 1	SE 1
London Charing Cross 4 ⊖	d	17 30	17 45	18 00	18 15	18 30	18 45	19 00	19 15	19 30	19 55	20 25	20 55	21 25	21 55	22 25	22 55	23 25	23 45
London Waterloo (East) 4 ⊖	d	17 33	17 48	18 03	18 18	18 33	18 48	19 03	19 18	19 33	19 58	20 28	20 58	21 28	21 58	22 28	22 58	23 28	23 48
London Cannon Street 4 ⊖	d																		
London Bridge 4 ⊖	d	17 39	17 53	18 09	18 23	18 39	18 53	19 09	19 23	19 39	20 03	20 33	21 03	21 33	22 03	22 33	23 03	23 33	23 53
Orpington 4	d	17 56	18 09	18 26	18 39	18 56	19 09	19 26	19 39	19 56	20 21	20 51	21 21	21 51	22 21	22 49	23 19	23 49	00 09
Sevenoaks 4	d	18 05	18 19	18 35	18 49	19 05	19 19	19 35	19 49	20 05	20 31	21 01	21 31	22 01	22 31	23 00	23 28	23 59	00 19
Tonbridge 4	a	18 15	18 27	18 45	18 58	19 15	19 27	19 45	19 58	20 15	20 39	21 11	21 39	22 11	22 39	23 10	23 36	00 10	00 27
	d	18 16	18 28	18 46	18 58	19 16	19 28	19 46	19 58	20 16	20 40	21 11	21 40	22 11	22 40	23 11	23 37	00 11	00 27
High Brooms	d	18 23	18 35	18 53	19 05	19 23	19 35	19 53	20 05	20 23	20 46	21 19	21 46	22 19	22 46	23 17	23 43	00 17	00 34
Tunbridge Wells 4	a	18 27	18 39	18 57	19 09	19 27	19 39	19 57	20 09	20 27	20 50	21 23	21 50	22 23	22 50	23 21	23 47	00 21	00 38
	d		18 40		19 10		19 40		20 10		20 51		21 51		22 51		23 48		00 39
Frant	d				19 15				20 15		20 56		21 56		22 56		23 53		00 44
Wadhurst	d		18 48		19 20		19 48		20 20		21 01		22 01		23 01		23 58		00 49
Stonegate	d				19 26				20 26		21 07		22 07		23 07		00 04		00 55
Etchingham	d				19 31				20 31		21 12		22 12		23 12		00 09		00 59
Robertsbridge	d				19 35				20 35		21 16		22 16		23 16		00 13		01 03
Battle	d		19 04		19 43		20 04		20 43		21 24		22 24		23 24		00 21		01 11
Crowhurst	d				19 46				20 46		21 27		22 27		23 27		00 24		01 15
West St Leonards	d				19 51				20 51		21 32		22 32		23 33		00 29		01 20
St Leonards Warrior Sq 4	d		19 15		19 55		20 15		20 55		21 36		22 36		23 36		00 33		01 23
Hastings 4	a		19 18		19 59		20 18		20 59		21 39		22 39		23 39		00 36		01 26
Ore	a																		

Sundays

		SE 1 A	SE 1 A	SE 1 A	SE 1	SE 1	SE 1	SE 1	SE 1	SE 1	SE 1	SE 1	SE 1	SE 1	SE 1	SE 1	SE 1	SE 1	SE 1	SE 1	SE 1	SE 1	SE 1
London Charing Cross 4 ⊖	d	22p55	23p25	23p45		08 23		09 23	09 53	10 23	10 53	11 23	11 53	12 23	12 53	13 23	13 53	14 23	14 53	15 23	15 53	16 23	16 53
London Waterloo (East) 4 ⊖	d	22p58	23p28	23p48		08 26		09 26	09 56	10 26	10 56	11 26	11 56	12 26	12 56	13 26	13 56	14 26	14 56	15 26	15 56	16 26	16 56
London Cannon Street 4 ⊖	d																						
London Bridge 4 ⊖	d	23p03	23p33	23p53		08 31		09 31	10 01	10 31	11 01	11 31	12 01	12 31	13 01	13 31	14 01	14 31	15 01	15 31	16 01	16 31	17 01
Orpington 4	d	23p19	23p49	00 09		08 46		09 46	10 16	10 46	11 16	11 46	12 16	12 46	13 16	13 46	14 16	14 46	15 16	15 46	16 16	16 46	17 16
Sevenoaks 4	d	23p28	23p59	00 19		08 56		09 56	10 26	10 56	11 26	11 56	12 26	12 56	13 26	13 56	14 26	14 56	15 26	15 56	16 26	16 56	17 26
Tonbridge 4	a	23p36	00 10	00 27		09 04		10 04	10 34	11 04	11 34	12 04	12 34	13 04	13 34	14 04	14 34	15 04	15 34	16 04	16 34	17 04	17 34
	d	23p37	00 11	00 27	08 25	09 04	09 34	10 04	10 34	11 04	11 34	12 04	12 34	13 04	13 34	14 04	14 34	15 04	15 34	16 04	16 34	17 04	17 34
High Brooms	d	23p43	00 17	00 34	08 31	09 10	09 40	10 10	10 40	11 10	11 40	12 10	12 40	13 10	13 40	14 10	14 40	15 10	15 40	16 10	16 40	17 10	17 40
Tunbridge Wells 4	a	23p47	00 21	00 38	08 35	09 14	09 44	10 14	10 44	11 14	11 44	12 14	12 44	13 14	13 44	14 14	14 44	15 14	15 44	16 14	16 44	17 14	17 44
	d	23p48		00 39		09 15	09 45	10 15	10 45	11 15	11 45	12 15	12 45	13 15	13 45	14 15	14 45	15 15	15 45	16 15	16 45	17 15	17 45
Frant	d	23p53		00 44		09 20		10 20		11 20		12 20		13 20		14 20		15 20		16 20		17 20	
Wadhurst	d	23p58		00 49		09 25	09 52	10 25	10 52	11 25	11 52	12 25	12 52	13 25	13 52	14 25	14 52	15 25	15 52	16 25	16 52	17 25	17 52
Stonegate	d	00 04		00 55		09 31		10 31		11 31		12 31		13 31		14 31		15 31		16 31		17 31	
Etchingham	d	00 09		00 59		09 36		10 36		11 36		12 36		13 36		14 36		15 36		16 36		17 36	
Robertsbridge	d	00 13		01 03		09 40		10 40		11 40		12 40		13 40		14 40		15 40		16 40		17 40	
Battle	d	00 21		01 11		09 48	10 08	10 48	11 08	11 48	12 08	12 48	13 08	13 48	14 08	14 48	15 08	15 48	16 08	16 48	17 08	17 48	18 08
Crowhurst	d	00 24		01 15		09 51		10 51		11 51		12 51		13 51		14 51		15 51		16 51		17 51	
West St Leonards	d	00 29		01 20		09 56		10 56		11 56		12 56		13 56		14 56		15 56		16 56		17 56	
St Leonards Warrior Sq 4	d	00 33		01 23		10 00	10 18	11 00	11 18	12 00	12 18	13 00	13 18	14 00	14 18	15 00	15 18	16 00	16 18	17 00	17 18	18 00	18 18
Hastings 4	a	00 36		01 26		10 03	10 21	11 03	11 21	12 03	12 21	13 03	13 21	14 03	14 21	15 03	15 21	16 03	16 21	17 03	17 21	18 03	18 21
Ore	a																						

		SE 1	SE 1	SE 1	SE 1	SE 1	SE 1	SE 1	SE 1	SE 1	SE 1
London Charing Cross 4 ⊖	d	17 23	17 53	18 23	18 53	19 23	19 53	20 23	21 23	22 23	23 23
London Waterloo (East) 4 ⊖	d	17 26	17 56	18 26	18 56	19 26	19 56	20 26	21 26	22 26	23 26
London Cannon Street 4 ⊖	d										
London Bridge 4 ⊖	d	17 31	18 01	18 31	19 01	19 31	20 01	20 31	21 31	22 31	23 31
Orpington 4	d	17 46	18 16	18 46	19 16	19 46	20 16	20 46	21 46	22 46	23 46
Sevenoaks 4	d	17 56	18 26	18 56	19 26	19 56	20 26	20 56	21 56	22 57	23 57
Tonbridge 4	a	18 04	18 34	19 04	19 34	20 04	20 34	21 04	22 04	23 05	00 05
	d	18 04	18 34	19 04	19 34	20 04	20 34	21 04	22 04	23 06	00 06
High Brooms	d	18 10	18 40	19 10	19 40	20 10	20 40	21 10	22 10	23 12	00 12
Tunbridge Wells 4	a	18 14	18 44	19 14	19 44	20 14	20 44	21 14	22 14	23 15	00 15
	d	18 15	18 45	19 15	19 45	20 15		21 15	22 15	23 17	00 17
Frant	d	18 20		19 20		20 20		21 20	22 20	23 22	00 22
Wadhurst	d	18 25	18 52	19 25	19 52	20 25		21 25	22 25	23 27	00 27
Stonegate	d	18 31		19 31		20 31		21 31	22 31	23 33	00 33
Etchingham	d	18 36		19 36		20 36		21 36	22 36	23 38	00 38
Robertsbridge	d	18 40		19 40		20 40		21 40	22 40	23 42	00 42
Battle	d	18 48	19 08	19 48	20 08	20 48		21 48	22 48	23 50	00 50
Crowhurst	d	18 51		19 51		20 51		21 51	22 51	23 53	00 53
West St Leonards	d	18 56		19 56		20 56		21 56	22 56	23 58	00 58
St Leonards Warrior Sq 4	d	19 00	19 18	20 00	20 18	21 00		22 00	23 00	00 01	01 01
Hastings 4	a	19 03	19 21	20 03	20 21	21 03		22 03	23 03	00 04	01 04
Ore	a										

A not 22 May

Hastings and Tunbridge Wells - Tonbridge and London

Miles			SE MX [1]	SE [1]	SE [1]	SE [1]	SE [1]	SE [1]	SE [1]	SE [1]	SE [1]		SE [1]	SE [1] A ⊥	SE [1]	SE [1]	SE [1] A ⊥	SE [1]	SE [1]	SE [1]	SE [1]		SE [1]	SE [1]	SE [1]
0	Ore	d												06 12			06 37							07 40	
1	**Hastings [4]**	d	22p10			05 17		05 37	05 48		06 03			06 20	06 28		06 41		07 01		07 25			07 44	
1¾	St Leonards Warrior Sq [4]	d	22p13			05 20		05 40	05 51		06 06			06 23	06 31		06 44		07 04		07 28			07 47	
2¾	West St Leonards	d	22p16			05 23		05 43			06 09				06 34		06 47		07 07		07 31			07 50	
6	Crowhurst	d	22p22			05 29		05 49			06 15				06 40		06 53		07 13		07 37			07 56	
8	Battle	d	22p26			05 33		05 53	06 01		06 19			06 33	06 44		06 57		07 17		07 41			08 00	
14¼	Robertsbridge	d	22p33			05 40		06 00			06 27			06 40			07 05		07 25		07 48			08 07	
16	Etchingham	d	22p37			05 44		06 04	06 10		06 31			06 44	06 53		07 09		07 29		07 52			08 11	
19¾	Stonegate	d	22p42			05 49		06 09			06 36			06 50			07 14		07 34		07 57			08 17	
24¼	Wadhurst	d	22p49			05 56		06 16	06 21		06 43			06 57	07 04		07 21		07 41		08 04			08 24	
26¾	Frant	d	22p53			06 00		06 20			06 47			07 01			07 25		07 45		08 08			08 28	
29	**Tunbridge Wells [4]**	a	22p58			06 06		06 25	06 29		06 53			07 06	07 11		07 31		07 51		08 13			08 33	
—		d	22p59	05 21	05 50	06 09	06 21	06 34		06 40	06 56		07 00	07 16		07 20	07 36	07 40	07 56	08 00	08 18		08 25	08 40	08 51
30½	High Brooms	d	23p02	05 24	05 53	06 12	06 24	06 37		06 44	07 00		07 04	07 20		07 24	07 40	07 44	08 00	08 04	08 22		08 28	08 43	08 54
34	**Tonbridge [4]**	a	23p08	05 30	05 59	06 18	06 30	06 44		06 50			07 10			07 30		07 50		08 10			08 34	08 49	09 00
41½	Sevenoaks [4]	a	23p24	05 42	06 10	06 30	06 43	06 52		07 02			07 22			07 42		08 02		08 22			08 45	08 58	09 13
49¾	Orpington [4]	a	23p36	05 54	06 19		06 53	07 02		07 13														09 08	09 24
61¾	**London Bridge [4]** ⊖	a	23p53	06 09	06 38	06 54	07 09	07 22		07 29			07 50			08 09	08 24	08 29		08 49	09 03		09 11	09 26	09 40
—	**London Cannon Street [4]** ⊖	a			06 42			07 29									08 30				09 10				
62¾	**London Waterloo (East) [4]** ⊖	a	23p57	06 14		06 59	07 14			07 34	07 44		07 55	08 04		08 14		08 34	08 44	08 54			09 16	09 31	09 45
63½	**London Charing Cross [4]** ⊖	a	00 01	06 18		07 05	07 20			07 40	07 50		08 01	08 08		08 20		08 40	08 50	09 00			09 22	09 37	09 51

		SE [1]	SE [1]	SE [1]	SE [1]	SE [1]	SE [1]		SE [1]	SE [1]	SE [1]	SE [1]	SE [1]	SE [1]	SE [1]	SE [1]	SE [1]		SE [1]	SE [1]	SE [1]	SE [1]	SE [1]	SE [1]	SE [1]
Ore	d																								
Hastings [4]	d	08 15		08 47		09 29			09 50		10 31		10 50		11 31		11 50			12 31		12 50		13 31	
St Leonards Warrior Sq [4]	d	08 18		08 50		09 32			09 53		10 34		10 53		11 34		11 53			12 34		12 53		13 34	
West St Leonards	d	08 21		08 53					09 56				10 56				11 56					12 56			
Crowhurst	d	08 27		08 58					10 02				11 02				12 02					13 02			
Battle	d	08 31		09 02		09 42			10 06		10 44		11 06		11 44		12 06			12 44		13 06		13 44	
Robertsbridge	d	08 38		09 09					10 13				11 13				12 13					13 13			
Etchingham	d	08 42		09 13					10 17				11 17				12 17					13 17			
Stonegate	d	08 47		09 18					10 23				11 23				12 23					13 23			
Wadhurst	d	08 54		09 25		09 58			10 30		11 00		11 29		12 00		12 29			13 00		13 29		14 00	
Frant	d	08 58		09 29					10 34				11 33				12 33					13 33			
Tunbridge Wells [4]	a	09 03		09 34		10 05			10 39		11 07		11 38		12 07		12 38			13 07		13 38		14 07	
	d	09 09	09 21	09 39	09 51	10 09	10 21		10 39	10 51	11 09	11 21	11 39	11 51	12 09	12 21	12 39		12 51	13 09	13 21	13 39	13 51	14 09	14 21
High Brooms	d	09 12	09 24	09 42	09 54	10 12	10 24		10 43	10 54	11 12	11 24	11 42	11 54	12 12	12 24	12 42		12 54	13 12	13 24	13 42	13 54	14 12	14 24
Tonbridge [4]	a	09 18	09 30	09 48	10 00	10 18	10 30		10 49	11 00	11 18	11 30	11 48	12 00	12 18	12 30	12 48		13 00	13 18	13 30	13 48	14 00	14 18	14 30
Sevenoaks [4]	a	09 28	09 43	09 58	10 13	10 28	10 43		10 58	11 13	11 28	11 43	11 58	12 13	12 28	12 43	12 58		13 13	13 28	13 43	13 58	14 13	14 28	14 43
Orpington [4]	a	09 38	09 53	10 08	10 23	10 38	10 53		11 08	11 23	11 38	11 53	12 08	12 23	12 38	12 53	13 08		13 23	13 38	13 53	14 08	14 23	14 38	14 53
London Bridge [4] ⊖	a	09 55	10 10	10 25	10 40	10 55	11 10		11 25	11 40	11 55	12 10	12 25	12 40	12 55	13 10	13 25		13 40	13 55	14 10	14 25	14 40	14 55	15 10
London Cannon Street [4] ⊖	a																								
London Waterloo (East) [4] ⊖	a	09 59	10 15	10 29	10 45	10 59	11 15		11 29	11 45	11 59	12 15	12 29	12 45	12 59	13 15	13 29		13 45	13 59	14 15	14 29	14 45	14 59	15 15
London Charing Cross [4] ⊖	a	10 03	10 19	10 33	10 49	11 03	11 19		11 33	11 49	12 03	12 19	12 33	12 49	13 03	13 19	13 33		13 49	14 03	14 19	14 33	14 49	15 03	15 19

		SE [1]	SE [1]		SE [1]	SE [1]	SE [1]	SE [1]	SE [1]	SE [1]	SE [1]	SE [1]	SE [1]		SE [1]	SE [1]	SE [1]	SE [1]	SE [1]	SE [1]	SE [1]	SE [1]	SE [1]		SE [1]
Ore	d																								
Hastings [4]	d	13 50			14 31		14 50		15 31		15 45		16 19			16 50		17 19		17 50		18 19			18 46
St Leonards Warrior Sq [4]	d	13 53			14 34		14 53		15 34		15 48		16 21			16 53		17 22		17 53		18 22			18 49
West St Leonards	d	13 56					14 56				15 51		16 25			16 56		17 25		17 56		18 25			18 52
Crowhurst	d	14 02					15 02				15 57		16 30			17 02		17 31		18 02		18 31			18 58
Battle	d	14 06			14 44		15 06		15 44		16 01		16 34			17 06		17 35		18 06		18 35			19 02
Robertsbridge	d	14 13					15 13				16 08		16 41			17 13		17 42		18 13		18 44			19 09
Etchingham	d	14 17					15 17				16 12		16 45			17 17		17 46		18 17		18 47			19 12
Stonegate	d	14 23					15 23				16 17		16 50			17 23		17 52		18 23		18 53			19 18
Wadhurst	d	14 29			15 00		15 29		16 00		16 24		16 57			17 29		17 59		18 29		18 59			19 24
Frant	d	14 33					15 33				16 28		17 01			17 33		18 03		18 33		19 03			19 28
Tunbridge Wells [4]	a	14 38			15 07		15 38		16 07		16 33		17 06			17 38		18 08		18 39		19 08			19 33
	d	14 39	14 51		15 09	15 21	15 39	15 51	16 09	16 21	16 36	16 51	17 06		17 21	17 39	17 49	18 13	18 19	18 39	18 51	19 09	19 21		19 38
High Brooms	d	14 42	14 54		15 12	15 24	15 42	15 54	16 12	16 24	16 39	16 55	17 10		17 24	17 42	17 52	18 16	18 22	18 42	18 54	19 12	19 24		19 41
Tonbridge [4]	a	14 48	15 00		15 18	15 30	15 48	16 00	16 18	16 30	16 46	17 01	17 16		17 30	17 49	17 59	18 22	18 28	18 50	19 00	19 18	19 30		19 47
Sevenoaks [4]	a	14 58	15 13		15 28	15 43	15 58	16 13	16 28	16 43	16 58	17 13	17 28		17 43	17 58	18 13	18 31	18 43	18 59	19 13	19 28	19 43		19 59
Orpington [4]	a	15 08	15 23		15 38	15 53	16 07	16 24	16 38	16 53	17 08	17 23	17 38		17 53	18 08	18 23		18 53	19 08	19 23	19 38	19 53		20 08
London Bridge [4] ⊖	a	15 25	15 40		15 55	16 11	16 25	16 42	16 56	17 11	17 27	17 41	17 58		18 09	18 25	18 40	18 55	19 10	19 25	19 40	19 54	20 10		20 24
London Cannon Street [4] ⊖	a										17 32														
London Waterloo (East) [4] ⊖	a	15 29	15 45		15 59	16 16	16 29	16 48	17 00	17 16		17 46	18 02		18 14	18 29	18 45	18 59	19 14	19 29	19 45	19 59	20 15		20 29
London Charing Cross [4] ⊖	a	15 33	15 49		16 03	16 20	16 33	16 52	17 04	17 20		17 50	18 06		18 18	18 35	18 49	19 04	19 18	19 33	19 49	20 03	20 19		20 33

A ⊥ from Hastings

Table 206

Mondays to Fridays

Hastings and Tunbridge Wells - Tonbridge and London

		SE 1	SE 1	SE 1	SE 1	SE 1	SE 1	SE 1	SE 1		SE 1	SE 1	SE 1
Ore	d												
Hastings 4	d			19 50			20 50				21 50	22 10	
St Leonards Warrior Sq 4	d			19 53			20 53				21 53	22 13	
West St Leonards	d			19 56			20 56				21 56	22 16	
Crowhurst	d			20 02			21 02				22 02	22 22	
Battle	d			20 06			21 06				22 06	22 26	
Robertsbridge	d			20 14			21 14				22 14	22 33	
Etchingham	d			20 17			21 17				22 17	22 37	
Stonegate	d			20 23			21 23				22 23	22 42	
Wadhurst	d			20 29			21 29				22 29	22 49	
Frant	d			20 33			21 33				22 33	22 53	
Tunbridge Wells 4	a			20 38			21 38				22 38	22 58	
	d	19 51	20 21	20 39	20 51	21 21	21 39	21 51	22 21		22 39	22 59	23 33
High Brooms	d	19 54	20 24	20 42	20 54	21 24	21 42	21 54	22 24		22 42	23 02	23 36
Tonbridge 4	a	20 00	20 30	20 48	21 00	21 30	21 48	22 00	22 30		22 48	23 08	23 42
Sevenoaks 4	a	20 13	20 43	20 58	21 13	21 43	21 58	22 13	22 41		22 58	23 24	
Orpington 4	a	20 23	20 52	21 08	21 22	21 52	22 08	22 22	22 52		23 08	23 36	
London Bridge 4 ⊖	a	20 39	21 08	21 24	21 38	22 08	22 24	22 38	23 08		23 24	23 53	
London Cannon Street 4 ⊖	a												
London Waterloo (East) 4 ⊖	a	20 44	21 13	21 29	21 43	22 13	22 29	22 43	23 13		23 29	23 57	
London Charing Cross 4 ⊖	a	20 48	21 18	21 33	21 48	22 18	22 33	22 48	23 18		23 33	00 01	

Saturdays

		SE 1	SE	SE 1	SE 1	SE 1	SE 1	SE 1	SE 1	SE 1		SE 1	SE 1	SE 1	SE 1	SE 1	SE 1	SE 1	SE 1	SE 1		SE 1	SE 1	SE 1	SE 1
Ore	d																								
Hastings 4	d	22p10		05 50	06 20		06 50		07 20			07 50		08 20		08 50		09 31		09 50			10 31		10 50
St Leonards Warrior Sq 4	d	22p13		05 53	06 23		06 53		07 23			07 53		08 23		08 53		09 34		09 53			10 34		10 53
West St Leonards	d	22p16		05 56	06 26		06 56		07 26			07 56		08 26		08 56				09 56					10 56
Crowhurst	d	22p22		06 02	06 32		07 02		07 32			08 02		08 32		09 02				10 02					11 02
Battle	d	22p26		06 06	06 36		07 06		07 36			08 06		08 36		09 06		09 44		10 06			10 44		11 06
Robertsbridge	d	22p33		06 13	06 43		07 13		07 44			08 13		08 44		09 14				10 13					11 13
Etchingham	d	22p37		06 17	06 47		07 17		07 47			08 17		08 47		09 17				10 17					11 17
Stonegate	d	22p42		06 23	06 53		07 23		07 53			08 23		08 53		09 23				10 23					11 23
Wadhurst	d	22p49		06 29	06 59		07 29		07 59			08 29		08 59		09 29		10 00		10 29			11 00		11 29
Frant	d	22p53		06 33	07 03		07 33		08 03			08 33		09 03		09 33				10 33					11 33
Tunbridge Wells 4	a	22p58		06 38	07 08		07 38		08 08			08 38		09 08		09 38		10 07		10 38			11 07		11 38
	d	22p59	05 48	06 39	07 09	07 21	07 39	07 51	08 09	08 21		08 39	08 51	09 09	09 21	09 39	09 51	10 09	10 21	10 39		10 51	11 09	11 21	11 39
High Brooms	d	23p02	05 51	06 42	07 12	07 24	07 42	07 54	08 12	08 24		08 42	08 54	09 12	09 24	09 42	09 54	10 12	10 24	10 42		10 54	11 12	11 24	11 42
Tonbridge 4	a	23p08	05 57	06 48	07 18	07 30	07 48	08 00	08 18	08 30		08 48	09 00	09 18	09 30	09 48	10 00	10 18	10 30	10 48		11 00	11 18	11 30	11 48
Sevenoaks 4	a	23p24		06 58	07 28	07 43	07 58	08 13	08 28	08 43		08 58	09 13	09 28	09 43	09 58	10 13	10 28	10 43	10 58		11 13	11 28	11 43	11 58
Orpington 4	a	23p36		07 08	07 38	07 53	08 08	08 23	08 38	08 53		09 08	09 23	09 38	09 53	10 08	10 23	10 38	10 53	11 08		11 23	11 38	11 53	12 08
London Bridge 4 ⊖	a	23p53		07 24	07 55	08 10	08 25	08 40	08 55	09 10		09 25	09 40	09 55	10 10	10 25	10 40	10 55	11 10	11 25		11 40	11 55	12 10	12 25
London Cannon Street 4 ⊖	a																								
London Waterloo (East) 4 ⊖	a	23p57		07 29	07 59	08 15	08 29	08 45	08 59	09 15		09 29	09 45	09 59	10 15	10 29	10 45	10 59	11 15	11 29		11 45	11 59	12 15	12 29
London Charing Cross 4 ⊖	a	00 01		07 33	08 03	08 19	08 33	08 49	09 03	09 19		09 33	09 49	10 03	10 19	10 33	10 49	11 03	11 19	11 33		11 49	12 03	12 19	12 33

		SE 1	SE 1	SE 1	SE 1	SE 1		SE 1	SE 1	SE 1	SE 1	SE 1	SE 1	SE 1	SE 1	SE 1		SE 1	SE 1	SE 1	SE 1	SE 1	SE 1	SE 1	SE 1
Ore	d																								
Hastings 4	d		11 31		11 50			12 31		12 50		13 31		13 50		14 31			14 50		15 31		15 50		16 31
St Leonards Warrior Sq 4	d		11 34		11 53			12 34		12 53		13 34		13 53		14 34			14 53		15 34		15 53		16 34
West St Leonards	d				11 56					12 56				13 56					14 56				15 56		
Crowhurst	d				12 02					13 02				14 02					15 02				16 02		
Battle	d		11 44		12 06			12 44		13 06		13 44		14 06		14 44			15 06		15 44		16 06		16 44
Robertsbridge	d				12 13					13 13				14 13					15 13				16 13		
Etchingham	d				12 17					13 17				14 17					15 17				16 17		
Stonegate	d				12 23					13 23				14 23					15 23				16 23		
Wadhurst	d		12 00		12 29			13 00		13 29		14 00		14 29		15 00			15 29		16 00		16 29		17 00
Frant	d				12 33					13 33				14 33					15 33				16 33		
Tunbridge Wells 4	a		12 07		12 38			13 07		13 38		14 07		14 38		15 07			15 38		16 07		16 38		17 07
	d	11 51	12 09	12 21	12 39	12 51		13 09	13 21	13 39	13 51	14 09	14 21	14 39	14 51	15 09		15 21	15 39	15 51	16 09	16 21	16 39	16 51	17 09
High Brooms	d	11 54	12 12	12 24	12 42	12 54		13 12	13 24	13 42	13 54	14 12	14 24	14 42	14 54	15 12		15 24	15 42	15 54	16 12	16 24	16 42	16 54	17 12
Tonbridge 4	a	12 00	12 18	12 30	12 48	13 00		13 18	13 30	13 48	14 00	14 18	14 30	14 48	15 00	15 18		15 30	15 48	16 00	16 18	16 30	16 48	17 00	17 18
Sevenoaks 4	a	12 13	12 28	12 43	12 58	13 13		13 28	13 43	13 58	14 13	14 28	14 43	14 58	15 13	15 28		15 43	15 58	16 13	16 28	16 43	16 58	17 13	17 28
Orpington 4	a	12 23	12 38	12 53	13 08	13 23		13 38	13 53	14 08	14 23	14 38	14 53	15 08	15 23	15 38		15 53	16 08	16 23	16 38	16 53	17 08	17 23	17 38
London Bridge 4 ⊖	a	12 40	12 55	13 10	13 25	13 40		13 55	14 10	14 25	14 40	14 55	15 10	15 25	15 40	15 55		16 10	16 25	16 40	16 55	17 10	17 25	17 40	17 55
London Cannon Street 4 ⊖	a																								
London Waterloo (East) 4 ⊖	a	12 45	12 59	13 15	13 29	13 45		13 59	14 15	14 29	14 45	14 59	15 15	15 29	15 45	15 59		16 15	16 29	16 45	16 59	17 15	17 29	17 45	17 59
London Charing Cross 4 ⊖	a	12 49	13 03	13 19	13 33	13 49		14 03	14 19	14 33	14 49	15 03	15 19	15 33	15 49	16 03		16 19	16 33	16 49	17 03	17 19	17 33	17 49	18 03

Table 206

Saturdays

Hastings and Tunbridge Wells - Tonbridge and London

		SE [1]		SE [1]	SE [1]	SE [1]	SE [1]	SE [1]	SE [1]	SE [1]	SE [1]	SE [1]		SE [1]	SE [1]	SE [1]	SE [1]	SE [1]	SE [1]
Ore	d																		
Hastings [4]	d			16 50		17 20		17 50		18 50		19 50			20 50		21 50	22 10	
St Leonards Warrior Sq [4]	d			16 53		17 23		17 53		18 53		19 53			20 53		21 53	22 13	
West St Leonards	d			16 56		17 26		17 56		18 56		19 56			20 56		21 56	22 16	
Crowhurst	d			17 02		17 32		18 02		19 02		20 02			21 02		22 02	22 22	
Battle	d			17 06		17 36		18 06		19 06		20 06			21 06		22 06	22 26	
Robertsbridge	d			17 13		17 44		18 13		19 13		20 13			21 13		22 13	22 33	
Etchingham	d			17 17		17 47		18 17		19 17		20 17			21 17		22 17	22 37	
Stonegate	d			17 23		17 53		18 23		19 23		20 23			21 23		22 23	22 42	
Wadhurst	d			17 29		17 59		18 29		19 29		20 29			21 29		22 29	22 49	
Frant	d			17 33		18 03		18 33		19 33		20 33			21 33		22 33	22 53	
Tunbridge Wells [4]	a			17 38		18 08		18 38		19 38		20 38			21 38		22 38	22 58	
	d	17 21		17 39	17 51	18 09	18 21	18 39	19 08	19 39	20 08	20 39		21 05	21 39	22 05	22 39	22 59	23 33
High Brooms	d	17 24		17 42	17 54	18 12	18 24	18 42	19 11	19 42	20 11	20 42		21 08	21 42	22 08	22 42	23 02	23 36
Tonbridge [4]	a	17 30		17 48	18 00	18 18	18 30	18 48	19 17	19 48	20 17	20 48		21 14	21 48	22 14	22 48	23 08	23 45
Sevenoaks [4]	a	17 43		17 58	18 13	18 28	18 43	18 58	19 28	19 58	20 28	20 58		21 28	21 58	22 28	22 58	23 24	
Orpington [4]	a	17 53		18 08	18 23	18 38	18 53	19 08	19 38	20 08	20 38	21 08		21 38	22 08	22 38	23 08	23 36	
London Bridge [4] ⊖	a	18 10		18 25	18 40	18 55	19 10	19 24	19 54	20 24	20 54	21 24		21 54	22 24	22 54	23 24	23 53	
London Cannon Street [4] ⊖	a																		
London Waterloo (East) [4] ⊖	a	18 15		18 29	18 45	18 59	19 15	19 29	19 59	20 29	20 59	21 29		21 59	22 29	22 59	23 29	23 57	
London Charing Cross [4] ⊖	a	18 19		18 33	18 49	19 03	19 19	19 33	20 03	20 33	21 03	21 33		22 03	22 33	23 03	23 33	00 01	

Sundays

		SE [1] A	SE [1]	SE [1]	SE [1]	SE [1]	SE [1]	SE [1]	SE [1]	SE [1]		SE [1]	SE [1]	SE [1]	SE [1]	SE [1]	SE [1]	SE [1]	SE [1]	SE [1]		SE [1]	SE [1]	SE [1]	SE [1]
Ore	d																								
Hastings [4]	d	22p10	07 27		08 27	09 08	09 27	10 08	10 27	11 08		11 27	12 08	12 27	13 08	13 27	14 08	14 27	15 08	15 27		16 08	16 27	17 08	17 27
St Leonards Warrior Sq [4]	d	22p13	07 29		08 29	09 11	09 29	10 11	10 29	11 11		11 29	12 11	12 29	13 11	13 29	14 11	14 29	15 11	15 29		16 11	16 29	17 11	17 29
West St Leonards	d	22p16	07 33		08 33		09 33		10 33			11 33		12 33		13 33		14 33		15 33			16 33		17 33
Crowhurst	d	22p22	07 38		08 38		09 38		10 38			11 38		12 38		13 38		14 38		15 38			16 38		17 38
Battle	d	22p26	07 43		08 43	09 21	09 43	10 21	10 43	11 21		11 43	12 21	12 43	13 21	13 43	14 21	14 43	15 21	15 43		16 21	16 43	17 21	17 43
Robertsbridge	d	22p33	07 50		08 50		09 50		10 50			11 50		12 50		13 50		14 50		15 50			16 50		17 50
Etchingham	d	22p37	07 53		08 53		09 53		10 53			11 53		12 53		13 53		14 53		15 53			16 53		17 53
Stonegate	d	22p42	07 59		08 59		09 59		10 59			11 59		12 59		13 59		14 59		15 59			16 59		17 59
Wadhurst	d	22p49	08 05		09 05	09 37	10 05	10 37	11 05	11 37		12 05	12 37	13 05	13 37	14 05	14 37	15 05	15 37	16 05		16 37	17 05	17 37	18 05
Frant	d	22p53	08 09		09 09		10 09		11 09			12 09		13 09		14 09		15 09		16 09			17 09		18 09
Tunbridge Wells [4]	a	22p58	08 14		09 14	09 44	10 14	10 44	11 14	11 44		12 14	12 44	13 14	13 44	14 14	14 44	15 14	15 44	16 14		16 44	17 14	17 44	18 14
	d	22p59	08 15	08 45	09 15	09 45	10 15	10 45	11 15	11 45		12 15	12 45	13 15	13 45	14 15	14 45	15 15	15 45	16 15		16 45	17 15	17 45	18 15
High Brooms	d	23p02	08 18	08 48	09 18	09 48	10 18	10 48	11 18	11 48		12 18	12 48	13 18	13 48	14 18	14 48	15 18	15 48	16 18		16 48	17 18	17 48	18 18
Tonbridge [4]	a	23p08	08 24	08 54	09 24	09 54	10 24	10 54	11 24	11 54		12 24	12 54	13 24	13 54	14 24	14 54	15 24	15 54	16 24		16 54	17 24	17 54	18 24
Sevenoaks [4]	a	23p24	08 33	09 03	09 33	10 03	10 33	11 03	11 33	12 03		12 33	13 03	13 33	14 03	14 33	15 03	15 33	16 03	16 33		17 03	17 33	18 03	18 33
Orpington [4]	a	23p36	08 42	09 12	09 42	10 12	10 42	11 12	11 42	12 12		12 42	13 12	13 42	14 12	14 42	15 12	15 42	16 12	16 42		17 12	17 42	18 12	18 42
London Bridge [4] ⊖	a	23p53	08 58	09 28	09 58	10 28	10 58	11 28	11 58	12 28		12 58	13 28	13 58	14 28	14 58	15 28	15 58	16 28	16 58		17 28	17 58	18 28	18 58
London Cannon Street [4] ⊖	a																								
London Waterloo (East) [4] ⊖	a	23p57	09 03	09 33	10 03	10 33	11 03	11 33	12 03	12 33		13 03	13 33	14 03	14 33	15 03	15 33	16 03	16 33	17 03		17 33	18 03	18 33	19 03
London Charing Cross [4] ⊖	a	00 01	09 07	09 37	10 07	10 37	11 07	11 37	12 07	12 37		13 07	13 37	14 07	14 37	15 07	15 37	16 07	16 37	17 07		17 37	18 07	18 37	19 07

		SE [1]	SE [1]	SE [1]	SE [1]	SE [1]		SE [1]	SE [1]
Ore	d								
Hastings [4]	d	18 08	18 27	19 27		20 27		21 27	22 27
St Leonards Warrior Sq [4]	d	18 11	18 29	19 29		20 29		21 29	22 29
West St Leonards	d		18 33	19 33		20 33		21 33	22 33
Crowhurst	d		18 38	19 38		20 38		21 38	22 38
Battle	d	18 21	18 43	19 43		20 43		21 43	22 43
Robertsbridge	d		18 50	19 50		20 50		21 50	22 50
Etchingham	d		18 53	19 53		20 53		21 53	22 53
Stonegate	d		18 59	19 59		20 59		21 59	22 59
Wadhurst	d	18 37	19 05	20 05		21 05		22 05	23 05
Frant	d		19 09	20 09		21 09		22 09	23 09
Tunbridge Wells [4]	a	18 44	19 14	20 14		21 14		22 14	23 14
	d	18 45	19 15	20 15	20 53	21 15		22 15	23 15
High Brooms	d	18 48	19 18	20 18	20 56	21 18		22 18	23 18
Tonbridge [4]	a	18 54	19 24	20 24	21 02	21 24		22 24	23 24
Sevenoaks [4]	a	19 03	19 33	20 33		21 33		22 33	
Orpington [4]	a	19 12	19 42	20 42		21 42		22 42	
London Bridge [4] ⊖	a	19 28	19 58	20 58		21 58		22 58	
London Cannon Street [4] ⊖	a								
London Waterloo (East) [4] ⊖	a	19 33	20 03	21 03		22 03		23 03	
London Charing Cross [4] ⊖	a	19 37	20 07	21 07		22 07		23 07	

A not 22 May

London and Tonbridge - Ashford International, Folkestone, Dover, Canterbury West, Ramsgate and Margate

Miles	Miles	Miles	Miles			SE MX 1	SE MO 1	SE MX 1	SE	SE MO 1	SE MX 1		SE MO 1	SE MO	SE MX 1	SE MX 1	SE MO 1	SE MX 1		SE MX	SE 1	SE	SE 1
—	—	—	0	**St Pancras Intl.** 15 ⊖	d				23p12					23p42						00 12			
—	—	—	6	**Stratford International** ⊖	d				23p19					23p49						00 19			
—	—	—	22¾	**Ebbsfleet International**	d				23p31					00 01						00 31			
0	—	—	—	**London Charing Cross** 4 ⊖	d	21p40	22p08	22p10		22p38	22p40		23p08			23p10	23p38	23p40					
0¾	—	—	—	**London Waterloo (East)** 4 ⊖	d	21p43	22p11	22p13		22p41	22p43		23p11			23p13	23p41	23p43					
—	—	—	—	**London Cannon Street** 4 ⊖	d																		
1¾	—	—	—	**London Bridge** 4 ⊖	d	21p49	22p16	22p19		22p46	22p49		23p16			23p19	23p46	23p49					
13¾	—	—	—	Orpington 4	d		22p32	22p35		23p02			23p32			23p35	00 02						
22	—	—	—	Sevenoaks 4	d	22p12	22p42	22p44		23p12	23p12		23p42			23p44	00 12	00 12					
29½	—	—	—	**Tonbridge** 4	a	22p20	22p52	22p52		23p20	23p20		23p52			23p52	00 20	00 20					
—	—	—	—		d	22p20	22p52	22p53		23p20	23p20		23p52			23p53	00 20	00 20			04 50		
34¾	—	—	—	Paddock Wood 4	d	22p28	23p00	23p00		23p28	23p28		23p59			23p59	00 28	00 28			04 58	05 42	
—	—	—	—	Maidstone West 4 194	a																	06 01	
39½	—	—	—	Marden	d	22p33	23p05	23p06		23p33	23p33		00 05			00 06	00 33	00 33			05 03		
41¾	—	—	—	Staplehurst	d	22p37	23p09	23p10		23p37	23p37		00 09			00 10	00 37	00 37			05 07		
45¼	—	—	—	Headcorn	d	22p43	23p15	23p15		23p43	23p43		00 15			00 15	00 43	00 43			05 13		
50½	—	—	—	Pluckley	d	22p49		23p21		23p49	23p49					00 21	00 49	00 49			05 19		
56	0	—	56	**Ashford International**	a	22p56	23p26	23p29	23p50	23p56	23p56		00 26	00 20		00 29	00 56	00 56		00 50	05 26		
—	—	—	—		d	23p00	23p30	23p32	23p52	00 01	00 01	00 03			00 03	00 32		01 00	01 03		05 30		06 02
—	4¼	—	—	Wye	d							00 09			00 09				01 09				
—	9	—	—	Chilham	d							00 15			00 15				01 15				
—	11	—	—	Chartham	d							00 19			00 19				01 19				
—	14¼	—	—	**Canterbury West** 4	d							00 25			00 25				01a24				
—	16½	—	—	Sturry	d							00 29			00 29								
64¼	—	—	—	Westenhanger	d	23p08	23p38	23p41			00 09					00 41		01 08			05 38		06 10
65½	—	—	—	Sandling	d	23p11	23p41	23p43		00 11	00 12					00 43		01 11			05 41		06 13
69¼	—	—	—	Folkestone West	d	23p17	23p47	23p49	00 05	00 17	00 18					00 49		01 17			05 47		06 19
70	—	—	—	**Folkestone Central**	d	23p20	23p50	23p52	00 08	00 19	00 21					00 52		01 20			05 50		06 22
77¼	—	—	—	**Dover Priory** 4	a	23p31	00 01	00 05	00 20	00 30	00 32					01 03		01 31			06 01		06 33
—	—	—	—		d	23p32	00 02	00 06													06 02		
82¼	—	—	—	Martin Mill	d	23p41	00 11	00 15													06 11		
85	—	—	—	Walmer	d	23p45	00 15	00 19													06 15		
86½	—	—	—	**Deal**	d	23p49	00 19	00 23													06 19		
90¾	—	—	—	Sandwich	d	23p56	00 26	00 30													06 26		
—	25½	4¾	—	Minster 4	d							00 41			00 41								
99	29½	—	—	**Ramsgate** 4	a	00 08	00 38	00 42				00 47			00 47						06 38		
101¼	31¾	—	—	Broadstairs	a																		
104½	35	—	—	**Margate** 4	a																		

		SE	SE 1	SE 1	SE 1	SE	SE	SE 1	SE	SE	SE 1	SE	SE 1	SE	SE 1		SE	SE	SE 1		SE	SE 1	
St Pancras Intl. 15 ⊖	d						06 25		06 40	07 10				07 40				08 10			08 40		
Stratford International ⊖	d						06 32		06 47	07 17				07 47				08 17			08 47		
Ebbsfleet International	d						06 42		06 59	07 29				08 00				08 30			09 00		
London Charing Cross 4 ⊖	d				05 30						06 30				07 10				07 40			08 13	
London Waterloo (East) 4 ⊖	d				05 33						06 33				07 13				07 43			08 16	
London Cannon Street 4 ⊖	d																						
London Bridge 4 ⊖	d				05 39						06 38				07 19				07 49			08 21	
Orpington 4	d				05 55						06 54												
Sevenoaks 4	d				06 06						07 03				07 43				08 12			08 45	
Tonbridge 4	a				06 16						07 14				07 51				08 20			08 53	
	d				06 20						07 14				07 51				08 20			08 53	
Paddock Wood 4	d	06 20			06 28	06 50					07 22	07 40			07 59		08 10		08 28			09 01	
Maidstone West 4 194	a	06 39				07 09	07 12					07 59					08 29						
Marden	d				06 33						07 27				08 04				08 33			09 06	
Staplehurst	d				06 37						07 31				08 08				08 37			09 10	
Headcorn	d				06 43						07 37				08 14				08 43			09 16	
Pluckley	d				06 49						07 43				08 20				08 49			09 22	
Ashford International	a				06 58				07 18	07 48	07 51			08 20	08 27			08 50	08 57		09 20	09 29	
	d		06 30	06 33	07 00			07 03	07 22	07 50	07 52		07 58	08 22	08 31	08 34		08 52	09 00	09 03	09 22	09 33	09 36
Wye	d			06 39				07 09			07 58					08 40				09 09			09 42
Chilham	d			06 45				07 15			08 04					08 46							09 48
Chartham	d			06 49				07 19			08 08					08 50							09 52
Canterbury West 4	d			06 55				07a24	07 39		08 15			08 39		08a55				09 22	09 39		09a57
Sturry	d			06 59					07 44		08 19									09 26			
Westenhanger	d		06 38		07 08								08 08		08 39				09 08			09 41	
Sandling	d		06 41		07 11								08 11		08 42				09 11			09 44	
Folkestone West	d		06 47		07 17					08 03			08 17		08 47			09 05	09 17			09 49	
Folkestone Central	d		06 50		07 20					08 06			08 20		08 50			09 08	09 20			09 52	
Dover Priory 4	a		07 00		07 31					08 18			08 31		09 01			09 20	09 31			10 03	
	d		07 07		07 50								08 32						09 32				
Martin Mill	d		07 16		07 59								08 41						09 41				
Walmer	d		07 20		08 04								08 45						09 45				
Deal	d		07 25		08 08								08 49						09 49				
Sandwich	d		07 31		08 16								08 56						09 56				
Minster 4	d			07 11					07 55		08 31									09 38			
Ramsgate 4	a		07 43	07 17	08 29				08 00		08 37		09 08	08 57					10 08	09 44	09 59		
Broadstairs	a								08 06					09 04							10 04		
Margate 4	a								08 11					09 10							10 10		

London and Tonbridge - Ashford International, Folkestone, Dover, Canterbury West, Ramsgate and Margate

		SE	SE	SE 1		SE 1	SE	SE 1		SE	SE	SE 1		SE	SE 1		SE	SE	SE 1		SE	SE 1	
St Pancras Intl. 15 ⊖	d		09 10				09 37				10 12			10 42				11 12			11 42		
Stratford International ⊖	d		09 17				09 44				10 19			10 49				11 19			11 49		
Ebbsfleet International	d		09 29				09 56				10 31			11 01				11 31			12 01		
London Charing Cross 4 ⊖	d			08 33		08 53		09 13				09 40			10 10				10 40			11 10	
London Waterloo (East) 4 ⊖	d			08 36		08 56		09 16				09 43			10 13				10 43			11 13	
London Cannon Street 4 ⊖	d																						
London Bridge 4 ⊖	d			08 41		09 01		09 21				09 49			10 19				10 49			11 19	
Orpington 4	d			08 58		09 21																	
Sevenoaks 4	d			09 07		09 31		09 44				10 12			10 42				11 12			11 42	
Tonbridge 4	a			09 18		09 40		09 52				10 20			10 50				11 20			11 50	
	d	09 03		09 20		09 42		09 52		10 03		10 20			10 50		11 03		11 20			11 50	
Paddock Wood 4	d	09 10		09 28				10 00		10 10		10 28			10 58		11 10		11 28			11 58	
Maidstone West 4 194	a	09 29								10 29							11 30						
Marden	d			09 33				10 05				10 33			11 03				11 33			12 03	
Staplehurst	d			09 37				10 09				10 37			11 07				11 37			12 07	
Headcorn	d			09 43				10 15				10 43			11 13				11 43			12 13	
Pluckley	d			09 49				10 21				10 49			11 19				11 49			12 19	
Ashford International	a		09 48	09 56		10 12	10 15	10 28			10 50	10 56		11 20	11 26			11 50	11 56		12 20	12 26	
	d		09 52	10 00	10 03		10 22	10 32	10 34		10 52	11 00	11 03	11 22	11 30	11 33		11 52	12 00	12 03	12 22	12 30	12 33
Wye	d				10 09				10 40				11 09			11 39				12 09			12 39
Chilham	d								10 46							11 45							12 45
Chartham	d								10 50							11 49							12 49
Canterbury West 4	d				10 22		10 39		10a55				11 22	11 39		11a54				12 22	12 39		12a54
Sturry	d				10 26								11 26							12 26			
Westenhanger	d			10 08				10 40				11 08			11 38				12 08			12 38	
Sandling	d			10 11				10 43				11 11			11 41				12 11			12 41	
Folkestone West	d		10 05	10 17				10 48			11 05	11 17			11 47			12 05	12 17			12 47	
Folkestone Central	d		10 08	10 20				10 51			11 08	11 20			11 50			12 08	12 20			12 50	
Dover Priory 4	a		10 20	10 31				11 02			11 20	11 31			12 01			12 20	12 31			13 01	
	d			10 32								11 32							12 32				
Martin Mill	d			10 41								11 41							12 41				
Walmer	d			10 45								11 45							12 45				
Deal	d			10 49								11 49							12 49				
Sandwich	d			10 56								11 56							12 56				
Minster 4	d				10 38								11 38							12 38			
Ramsgate 4	a			11 08	10 44		10 59					12 08	11 44	11 59					13 08	12 44	12 59		
Broadstairs	a						11 04							12 04							13 04		
Margate 4	a						11 10							12 10							13 10		

		SE	SE	SE 1		SE	SE 1		SE	SE	SE 1		SE	SE 1		SE	SE	SE 1		SE	SE 1	
St Pancras Intl. 15 ⊖	d		12 12			12 42				13 12			13 42				14 12			14 42		
Stratford International ⊖	d		12 19			12 49				13 19			13 49				14 19			14 49		
Ebbsfleet International	d		12 31			13 01				13 31			14 01				14 31			15 01		
London Charing Cross 4 ⊖	d			11 40			12 10				12 40			13 10				13 40			14 10	
London Waterloo (East) 4 ⊖	d			11 43			12 13				12 43			13 13				13 43			14 13	
London Cannon Street 4 ⊖	d																					
London Bridge 4 ⊖	d			11 49			12 19				12 49			13 19				13 49			14 19	
Orpington 4	d																					
Sevenoaks 4	d			12 12			12 42				13 12			13 42				14 12			14 42	
Tonbridge 4	a			12 20			12 50				13 20			13 50				14 20			14 50	
	d	12 03		12 20			12 50		13 03		13 20			13 50		14 03		14 20			14 50	
Paddock Wood 4	d	12 10		12 28			12 58		13 10		13 28			13 58		14 10		14 28			14 58	
Maidstone West 4 194	a	12 29							13 29							14 29						
Marden	d			12 33			13 03				13 33			14 03				14 33			15 03	
Staplehurst	d			12 37			13 07				13 37			14 07				14 37			15 07	
Headcorn	d			12 43			13 13				13 43			14 13				14 43			15 13	
Pluckley	d			12 49			13 19				13 49			14 19				14 49			15 19	
Ashford International	a		12 50	12 56		13 20	13 26			13 50	13 56		14 20	14 26			14 50	14 56		15 20	15 26	
	d		12 52	13 00	13 03	13 22	13 30	13 33		13 52	14 00	14 03	14 22	14 30	14 33		14 52	15 00	15 03	15 22	15 30	15 33
Wye	d				13 09			13 39				14 09			14 39				15 09			15 39
Chilham	d							13 45							14 45							15 45
Chartham	d							13 49							14 49							15 49
Canterbury West 4	d				13 22	13 39		13a54				14 22	14 39		14a54				15 22	15 39		15a54
Sturry	d				13 26							14 26							15 26			
Westenhanger	d			13 08			13 38				14 08			14 38				15 08			15 38	
Sandling	d			13 11			13 41				14 11			14 41				15 11			15 41	
Folkestone West	d		13 05	13 17			13 47			14 05	14 17			14 47			15 05	15 17			15 47	
Folkestone Central	d		13 08	13 20			13 50			14 08	14 20			14 50			15 08	15 20			15 50	
Dover Priory 4	a		13 20	13 31			14 01			14 20	14 31			15 01			15 20	15 31			16 01	
	d			13 32							14 32							15 32			16 02	
Martin Mill	d			13 41							14 41							15 41			16 11	
Walmer	d			13 45							14 45							15 45			16 15	
Deal	d			13 49							14 49							15 49			16 19	
Sandwich	d			13 56							14 56							15 56			16 26	
Minster 4	d				13 38							14 38						16 07	15 38			
Ramsgate 4	a			14 08	13 44	13 59					15 08	14 44	14 59					16 14	15 44	15 59	16 38	
Broadstairs	a					14 04							15 04							16 04		
Margate 4	a					14 10							15 10							16 10		

London and Tonbridge - Ashford International, Folkestone, Dover, Canterbury West, Ramsgate and Margate

		SE	SE	SE ■1		SE	SE ■1		SE	SE		SE ■1		SE	SE ■1		SE	SE		SE ■1			SE ■1	SE ■1	SE
St Pancras Intl. ■15 ⊖	d		15 12			15 42				16 10				16 42				17 10							
Stratford International ⊖	d		15 19			15 49				16 17				16 49				17 17							
Ebbsfleet International	d		15 31			16 01				16 29				17 01											
London Charing Cross ■4 ⊖	d			14 40			15 10					15 40			16 10					16 37					
London Waterloo (East) ■4 ⊖	d			14 43			15 13					15 43			16 13					16 40					
London Cannon Street ■4 ⊖	d																						16 46	17 08	
London Bridge ■4 ⊖	d			14 49			15 19					15 49			16 19					16 45			16 50	17 12	
Orpington ■4	d																								
Sevenoaks ■4	d			15 12			15 42					16 12			16 43					17 10					
Tonbridge ■4	a			15 20			15 50					16 20			16 51					17 18					
	d	15 03		15 20			15 50		16 03			16 20			16 51					17 18					
Paddock Wood ■4	d	15 10		15 28			15 58		16 10			16 28			16 59		17 02			17 26					17 30
Maidstone West ■4 194	a	15 29							16 29								17 21								17 49
Marden	d			15 33			16 03					16 33			17 04					17 32					
Staplehurst	d			15 37			16 07					16 37			17 08					17 36					
Headcorn	d			15 43			16 13					16 43			17 14					17 42					
Pluckley	d			15 49			16 19					16 49			17 20					17 48					
Ashford International	a		15 50	15 56		16 20	16 26			16 48		16 56		17 20	17 27			17 46		17 56					
	d		15 52	16 00	16 03	16 22	16 30	16 35		16 52		17 00	17 03	17 23	17 31	17 35		17 50	17 53	18 00	18 03				
Wye	d				16 09			16 41					17 09			17 41					18 09				
Chilham	d							16 47					17 15			17 47					18 15				
Chartham	d							16 51					17 19			17 51					18 19				
Canterbury West ■4	d				16 22	16 39		16a56					17 25	17 40		17a58			18 10		18 25				
Sturry	d				16 26								17 29								18 29				
Westenhanger	d			16 08			16 38					17 08			17 39					18 08					
Sandling	d			16 11			16 41					17 11			17 42					18 11					
Folkestone West	d		16 05	16 17			16 47			17 05		17 17			17 47			18 03		18 17					
Folkestone Central	d		16 08	16 20			16 50			17 08		17 20			17 50			18 06		18 20					
Dover Priory ■4	a		16 20	16 31			17 01			17 20		17 31			18 01			18 18		18 31					
	d			16 32			17 02					17 32			18 02					18 32					
Martin Mill	d			16 41			17 11					17 41			18 11					18 41					
Walmer	d			16 45			17 15					17 45			18 15					18 45					
Deal	d			16 49			17 19					17 49			18 19					18 49					
Sandwich	d			16 56			17 26					17 56			18 26					18 56					
Minster ■4	d			17 07	16 38								17 41								18 41				
Ramsgate ■4	a			17 14	16 44	16 59	17 38					18 08	17 47	17 59	18 40				18 29	19 10	18 49				
Broadstairs	a					17 04								18 04					18 34						
Margate ■4	a					17 10								18 10					18 40				18 31	18 55	

		SE ■1	SE	SE	SE		SE		SE ■1	SE ■1	SE ■1	SE	SE	SE		SE ■1	SE ■1		SE ■1	SE	SE ■1	SE	SE	SE	
St Pancras Intl. ■15 ⊖	d		17 14	17 27	17 40							17 44	17 55	18 10								18 14	18 25	18 40	
Stratford International ⊖	d		17 21	17 38	17 47							17 51	18 02	18 17								18 21	18 32	18 47	
Ebbsfleet International	d			17 49									18 13										18 43		
London Charing Cross ■4 ⊖	d	16 57							17 14								17 41				17 59				
London Waterloo (East) ■4 ⊖	d	17 00							17 18								17 44				18 02				
London Cannon Street ■4 ⊖	d									17 24	17 30					17 45			17 52						
London Bridge ■4 ⊖	d									17 28	17 34					17 49			17 56						
Orpington ■4	d																								
Sevenoaks ■4	d	17 27							17 46	17 54						18 16	18 11				18 30				
Tonbridge ■4	a	17 35							17 54	18 04						18 24	18 19				18 38				
	d	17 36							17 54	18 05						18 25	18 20				18 39				
Paddock Wood ■4	d	17 43					17 52		18 02	18 12						18 32	18 28			18 42	18 46				
Maidstone West ■4 194	a		18 02				18 11					18 32								19 01		19 05			
Marden	d	17 49							18 08	18 18						18 38	18 33				18 52				
Staplehurst	d	17 53							18 12	18 22						18 42	18 37				18 56				
Headcorn	d	17 59							18 18	18 28						18 48	18 43				19 02				
Pluckley	d	18 05								18 34						18 54	18 49								
Ashford International	a	18 15			18 16				18 30	18 42				18 46		19 01	18 58				19 16			19 16	
	d				18 20	18 23			18 32	18 44				18 50	18 53	19 03	19 04							19 20	19 23
Wye	d								18 38							19 09									
Chilham	d								18 44							19 15									
Chartham	d								18 48							19 19									
Canterbury West ■4	d					18 40			18 54						19 10	19 25									19 40
Sturry	d								18 59							19 29									
Westenhanger	d									18 53							19 12								
Sandling	d									18 55							19 15								
Folkestone West	d				18 33					19 01				19 05			19 21							19 33	
Folkestone Central	d				18 36					19 04				19 08			19 24							19 36	
Dover Priory ■4	a				18 48					19 15				19 20			19 35							19 47	
	d									19 17							19 36								
Martin Mill	d									19 26							19 45								
Walmer	d									19 30							19 49								
Deal	d									19 34							19 53								
Sandwich	d									19 41							20 00								
Minster ■4	d								19 10							19 41									
Ramsgate ■4	a					18 59			19 19	19 55					19 30	19 49	20 14								19 59
Broadstairs	a					19 04									19 36										20 04
Margate ■4	a			19 03		19 10					19 23		19 29		19 41				19 42				20 06		20 10

London and Tonbridge - Ashford International, Folkestone, Dover, Canterbury West, Ramsgate and Margate

		SE 1	SE 1		SE 1	SE	SE 1	SE 1	SE	SE 1		SE	SE
St Pancras Intl. 15 ⊖	d								19 12				19 42
Stratford International ⊖	d								19 19				19 49
Ebbsfleet International	d								19 31				20 01
London Charing Cross 4 ⊖	d				18 21					18 41			
London Waterloo (East) 4 ⊖	d				18 24					18 44			
London Cannon Street 4 ⊖	d	18 08	18 14				18 32	18 44					
London Bridge 4 ⊖	d	18 12	18 18				18 36	18 48		18 50			
Orpington 4	d									19 07			
Sevenoaks 4	d	18 38			18 52		19 00			19 17			
Tonbridge 4	a	18 48			19 00		19 08			19 25			
	d	18 49			19 01		19 09			19 25			
Paddock Wood 4	d	18 56			19 09	19 12	19 17			19 33		19 42	
Maidstone West 4 194	a					19 31						20 01	
Marden	d	19 02					19 23			19 38			
Staplehurst	d	19 06			19 17		19 27			19 42			
Headcorn	d	19 12			19 23		19 33			19 48			
Pluckley	d	19 18					19 39			19 54			
Ashford International	a	19 27			19 35		19 49		19 50	20 02			20 20
	d	19 29			19 37				19 53	20 06	20 08		20 22
Wye	d	19 36									20 14		
Chilham	d	19 42											
Chartham	d	19 45											
Canterbury West 4	d	19 52									20 27		20 39
Sturry	d	19 56									20 31		
Westenhanger	d				19 45					20 14			
Sandling	d				19 48					20 17			
Folkestone West	d				19 54				20 06	20 23			
Folkestone Central	d				19 57				20 09	20 26			
Dover Priory 4	a				20 08				20 21	20 37			
	d				20 09					20 38			
Martin Mill	d				20 18					20 47			
Walmer	d				20 23					20 51			
Deal	d				20 27					20 55			
Sandwich	d				20 34					21 02			
Minster 4	d	20 08									20 43		
Ramsgate 4	a	20 18			20 48					21 16	20 52		20 59
Broadstairs	a												21 05
Margate 4	a		20 02					20 35					21 11

			SE 1		SE	SE 1		SE	SE	SE 1	SE
St Pancras Intl. 15 ⊖	d				20 12				20 42		21 12
Stratford International ⊖	d				20 19				20 49		21 19
Ebbsfleet International	d				20 31				21 01		21 31
London Charing Cross 4 ⊖	d		19 10			19 40				20 10	
London Waterloo (East) 4 ⊖	d		19 13			19 43				20 13	
London Cannon Street 4 ⊖	d										
London Bridge 4 ⊖	d		19 19			19 49				20 19	
Orpington 4	d										
Sevenoaks 4	d		19 42			20 12				20 42	
Tonbridge 4	a		19 53			20 20				20 50	
	d		19 54			20 20		20 33		20 50	
Paddock Wood 4	d		20 01			20 28		20 40		20 58	
Maidstone West 4 194	a							20 59			
Marden	d		20 07			20 33				21 03	
Staplehurst	d		20 11			20 37				21 07	
Headcorn	d		20 17			20 43				21 13	
Pluckley	d		20 23			20 49				21 19	
Ashford International	a		20 31		20 50	20 56			21 20	21 26	21 50
	d		20 37	20 40	20 52	21 00	21 03		21 22	21 30	21 52
Wye	d			20 46			21 09				
Chilham	d			20 52			21 15				
Chartham	d			20 56			21 19				
Canterbury West 4	d			21a02			21 25		21 39		
Sturry	d						21 29				
Westenhanger	d		20 45			21 08				21 38	
Sandling	d		20 48			21 11				21 41	
Folkestone West	d		20 54		21 05	21 17				21 47	22 05
Folkestone Central	d		20 57		21 08	21 20				21 50	22 08
Dover Priory 4	a		21 09		21 20	21 31				22 01	22 20
	d					21 32					
Martin Mill	d					21 41					
Walmer	d					21 45					
Deal	d					21 49					
Sandwich	d					21 56					
Minster 4	d						21 41				
Ramsgate 4	a					22 08	21 47		21 59		
Broadstairs	a								22 04		
Margate 4	a								22 10		

		SE 1		SE	SE	SE 1	SE	SE 1		SE	
St Pancras Intl. 15 ⊖	d				21 42		22 12				
Stratford International ⊖	d				21 49		22 19				
Ebbsfleet International	d				22 01		22 31				
London Charing Cross 4 ⊖	d	20 40				21 10		21 40			
London Waterloo (East) 4 ⊖	d	20 43				21 13		21 43			
London Cannon Street 4 ⊖	d										
London Bridge 4 ⊖	d	20 49				21 19		21 49			
Orpington 4	d					21 35					
Sevenoaks 4	d	21 12				21 44		22 12			
Tonbridge 4	a	21 20				21 52		22 20			
	d	21 20		21 33		21 53		22 20		22 33	
Paddock Wood 4	d	21 28		21 40		22 00		22 28		22 40	
Maidstone West 4 194	a			21 59						22 59	
Marden	d	21 33				22 06		22 33			
Staplehurst	d	21 37				22 10		22 37			
Headcorn	d	21 43				22 15		22 43			
Pluckley	d	21 49				22 21		22 49			
Ashford International	a	21 56			22 20	22 29	22 50	22 56			
	d	22 00	22 03		22 22	22 32	22 52	23 00	23 03		
Wye	d		22 09						23 09		
Chilham	d		22 15						23 15		
Chartham	d		22 19						23 19		
Canterbury West 4	d		22 25		22 39				23 25		
Sturry	d		22 29						23 29		
Westenhanger	d	22 08				22 41		23 08			
Sandling	d	22 11				22 43		23 11			
Folkestone West	d	22 17				22 49	23 05	23 17			
Folkestone Central	d	22 20				22 52	23 08	23 20			
Dover Priory 4	a	22 31				23 03	23 20	23 31			
	d	22 32						23 32			
Martin Mill	d	22 41						23 41			
Walmer	d	22 45						23 45			
Deal	d	22 49						23 49			
Sandwich	d	22 56						23 56			
Minster 4	d		22 41						23 41		
Ramsgate 4	a	23 08	22 47		22 59			00 08	23 47		
Broadstairs	a				23 04						
Margate 4	a				23 10						

		SE	SE 1	SE	SE 1		SE 1	SE 1	
St Pancras Intl. 15 ⊖	d	22 42		23 12					
Stratford International ⊖	d	22 49		23 19					
Ebbsfleet International	d	23 01		23 31					
London Charing Cross 4 ⊖	d		22 10		22 40		23 10	23 40	
London Waterloo (East) 4 ⊖	d		22 13		22 43		23 13	23 43	
London Cannon Street 4 ⊖	d								
London Bridge 4 ⊖	d		22 19		22 49		23 19	23 49	
Orpington 4	d		22 35				23 35		
Sevenoaks 4	d		22 44		23 12		23 44	00 12	
Tonbridge 4	a		22 52		23 20		23 52	00 20	
	d		22 53		23 20		23 53	00 20	
Paddock Wood 4	d		23 00		23 28		23 59	00 28	
Maidstone West 4 194	a								
Marden	d		23 06		23 33		00 06	00 33	
Staplehurst	d		23 10		23 37		00 10	00 37	
Headcorn	d		23 15		23 43		00 15	00 43	
Pluckley	d		23 21		23 49		00 21	00 49	
Ashford International	a	23 20	23 29	23 50	23 56		00 29	00 56	
	d	23 22	23 32	23 52	00 01	00 03	00 32	01 00	01 03
Wye	d					00 09			01 09
Chilham	d					00 15			01 15
Chartham	d					00 19			01 19
Canterbury West 4	d	23 39				00 25			01a24
Sturry	d					00 29			
Westenhanger	d		23 41		00 09		00 41	01 08	
Sandling	d		23 43		00 12		00 43	01 11	
Folkestone West	d		23 49	00 05	00 18		00 49	01 17	
Folkestone Central	d		23 52	00 08	00 21		00 52	01 20	
Dover Priory 4	a		00 05	00 20	00 32		01 03	01 31	
	d		00 06						
Martin Mill	d		00 15						
Walmer	d		00 19						
Deal	d		00 23						
Sandwich	d		00 30						
Minster 4	d					00 41			
Ramsgate 4	a	23 59	00 42			00 47			
Broadstairs	a								
Margate 4	a								

Table 207

Saturdays

London and Tonbridge - Ashford International, Folkestone, Dover, Canterbury West, Ramsgate and Margate

		SE 1	SE 1	SE	SE 1	SE 1	SE 1	SE 1	SE	SE 1		SE	SE 1	SE 1	SE	SE 1	SE	SE 1	SE	SE 1		SE	SE 1	SE 1	SE
St Pancras Intl. 15 ⊖	d			23p12					00 12						06 12		06 40					07 12			07 42
Stratford International ⊖	d			23p19					00 19						06 19		06 47					07 19			07 49
Ebbsfleet International	d			23p31					00 31						06 31		06 59					07 31			08 01
London Charing Cross 4 ⊖	d	21p40	22p10		22p40		23p10	23p40										06 00							
London Waterloo (East) 4 ⊖	d	21p43	22p13		22p43		23p13	23p43										06 03							
London Cannon Street 4 ⊖	d																								
London Bridge 4 ⊖	d	21p49	22p19		22p49		23p19	23p49										06 08							
Orpington 4	d		22p35				23p35											06 24							
Sevenoaks 4	d	22p12	22p44		23p12		23p44	00 12										06 33							
Tonbridge 4	a	22p20	22p52		23p20		23p52	00 20										06 43							
	d	22p20	22p53		23p20		23p53	00 20				06 03				06 20		06 50	07 03						
Paddock Wood 4	d	22p28	23p00		23p28		23p59	00 28				06 10				06 28		06 58	07 10						
Maidstone West 4 194	a											06 29							07 29						
Marden	d	22p33	23p06		23p33		00 06	00 33								06 33		07 03							
Staplehurst	d	22p37	23p10		23p37		00 10	00 37								06 37		07 07							
Headcorn	d	22p43	23p15		23p43		00 15	00 43								06 43		07 13							
Pluckley	d	22p49	23p21		23p49		00 21	00 49								06 49		07 19							
Ashford International	a	22p56	23p29	23p50	23p56		00 29	00 56	00 50						06 50	06 56	07 18	07 26				07 51			08 20
	d	23p00	23p32	23p52	00 01	00 03	00 32	01 00		01 03			06 30	06 33	06 52	07 03	07 22	07 30		07 33		07 52	08 00	08 03	08 22
Wye	d					00 09				01 09				06 39		07 09				07 39				08 09	
Chilham	d					00 15				01 15				06 45						07 45					
Chartham	d					00 19				01 19				06 49						07 49					
Canterbury West 4	d					00 25				01a24				06a54		07 22	07 39			07a54				08 22	08 39
Sturry	d					00 29										07 26								08 26	
Westenhanger	d	23p08	23p41		00 09		00 41	01 08					06 38					07 38					08 08		
Sandling	d	23p11	23p43		00 12		00 43	01 11					06 41					07 41					08 11		
Folkestone West	d	23p17	23p49	00 05	00 18		00 49	01 17					06 47		07 05			07 47				08 05	08 17		
Folkestone Central	d	23p20	23p52	00 08	00 21		00 52	01 20					06 50		07 08			07 50				08 08	08 20		
Dover Priory 4	a	23p31	00 05	00 20	00 32		01 03	01 31					07 01		07 20			08 01				08 20	08 31		
	d	23p32	00 06										07 02					08 02							
Martin Mill	d	23p41	00 15										07 11					08 11							
Walmer	d	23p45	00 19										07 15					08 15							
Deal	d	23p49	00 23										07 19					08 19							
Sandwich	d	23p56	00 30										07 26					08 26							
Minster 4	d					00 41										07 38								08 38	
Ramsgate 4	a	00 08	00 42			00 47							07 38			07 44	07 59	08 38						08 44	08 59
Broadstairs	a																08 04								09 04
Margate 4	a																08 10								09 10

		SE 1		SE	SE	SE		SE 1	SE 1	SE	SE 1		SE	SE	SE 1	SE 1		SE	SE 1		SE	SE	SE 1	SE 1	SE
St Pancras Intl. 15 ⊖	d				08 12					08 42				09 10				09 37				10 12			10 42
Stratford International ⊖	d				08 19					08 49				09 17				09 44				10 19			10 49
Ebbsfleet International	d				08 31					09 01				09 29				09 56				10 31			11 01
London Charing Cross 4 ⊖	d	07 00							07 30		08 00					08 40			09 10					09 40	
London Waterloo (East) 4 ⊖	d	07 03							07 33		08 03					08 43			09 13					09 43	
London Cannon Street 4 ⊖	d																								
London Bridge 4 ⊖	d	07 08							07 38		08 08					08 49			09 19					09 49	
Orpington 4	d	07 24							07 54		08 24														
Sevenoaks 4	d	07 33							08 03		08 33					09 12			09 42					10 12	
Tonbridge 4	a	07 43							08 14		08 43					09 20			09 50					10 20	
	d	07 50		08 03					08 20		08 50		09 03			09 20			09 50		10 03			10 20	
Paddock Wood 4	d	07 58		08 10					08 28		08 58		09 10			09 28			09 58		10 10			10 28	
Maidstone West 4 194	a			08 29									09 29								10 29				
Marden	d	08 03							08 33		09 03					09 33			10 03					10 33	
Staplehurst	d	08 07							08 37		09 07					09 37			10 07					10 37	
Headcorn	d	08 13							08 43		09 13					09 43			10 13					10 43	
Pluckley	d	08 19							08 49		09 19					09 49			10 19					10 49	
Ashford International	a	08 29			08 50				08 56	09 20	09 26			09 48		09 56		10 15	10 26			10 50		10 56	11 20
	d	08 32	08 35		08 52	08 52		09 00	09 03	09 22	09 30	09 33		09 52	10 00	10 03		10 22	10 30	10 33		10 52	11 00	11 03	11 22
Wye	d		08 41						09 09			09 39				10 09				10 39				11 09	
Chilham	d		08 47									09 45								10 45					
Chartham	d		08 51									09 49								10 49					
Canterbury West 4	d		08a56						09 22	09 39		09a54				10 22		10 39		10a54				11 22	11 39
Sturry	d								09 26							10 26								11 26	
Westenhanger	d	08 41						09 08			09 38				10 08				10 38				11 08		
Sandling	d	08 43						09 11			09 41				10 11				10 41				11 11		
Folkestone West	d	08 49			09 05	09 05		09 17			09 47			10 05	10 17				10 47			11 05	11 17		
Folkestone Central	d	08 52			09 08	09 08		09 20			09 50			10 08	10 20				10 50			11 08	11 20		
Dover Priory 4	a	09 03			09 20	09 20		09 31			10 01			10 20	10 31				11 01			11 20	11 31		
	d	09 08									10 02								11 02						
Martin Mill	d	09 17									10 11								11 11						
Walmer	d	09 21									10 15								11 15						
Deal	d	09 25									10 19								11 19						
Sandwich	d	09 32									10 26								11 26						
Minster 4	d								09 38							10 38								11 38	
Ramsgate 4	a	09 44							09 48	09 59	10 38					10 44		10 59	11 38					11 44	11 59
Broadstairs	a									10 04								11 04							12 04
Margate 4	a									10 10								11 10							12 10

Table 207

London and Tonbridge - Ashford International, Folkestone, Dover, Canterbury West, Ramsgate and Margate

Station		SE ■1		SE	SE	SE ■1	SE ■1	SE	SE ■1		SE	SE	SE ■1	SE ■1	SE	SE ■1		SE	SE	SE ■1	SE ■1	SE
St Pancras Intl. ■15 ⊖	d				11 12			11 42				12 12			12 42				13 12			13 42
Stratford International ⊖	d				11 19			11 49				12 19			12 49				13 19			13 49
Ebbsfleet International	d				11 31			12 01				12 31			13 01				13 31			14 01
London Charing Cross ■4 ⊖	d	10 10					10 40		11 10					11 40		12 10					12 40	
London Waterloo (East) ■4 ⊖	d	10 13					10 43		11 13					11 43		12 13					12 43	
London Cannon Street ■4 ⊖	d																					
London Bridge ■4 ⊖	d	10 19					10 49		11 19					11 49		12 19					12 49	
Orpington ■4	d																					
Sevenoaks ■4	d	10 42					11 12		11 42					12 12		12 42					13 12	
Tonbridge ■4	a	10 50					11 20		11 50					12 20		12 50					13 20	
	d	10 50		11 03			11 20		11 50		12 03			12 20		12 50		13 03			13 20	
Paddock Wood ■4	d	10 58		11 10			11 28		11 58		12 10			12 28		12 58		13 10			13 28	
Maidstone West ■4 194	a			11 29							12 29							13 29				
Marden	d	11 03					11 33		12 03					12 33		13 03					13 33	
Staplehurst	d	11 07					11 37		12 07					12 37		13 07					13 37	
Headcorn	d	11 13					11 43		12 13					12 43		13 13					13 43	
Pluckley	d	11 19					11 49		12 19					12 49		13 19					13 49	
Ashford International	a	11 26			11 50		11 56	12 20	12 26			12 50		12 56	13 20	13 26			13 50		13 56	14 20
	d	11 30	11 33		11 52	12 00	12 03	12 22	12 30	12 33		12 52	13 00	13 03	13 22	13 30	13 33		13 52	14 00	14 03	14 22
Wye	d		11 39				12 09			12 39				13 09			13 39				14 09	
Chilham	d		11 45							12 45							13 45					
Chartham	d		11 49							12 49							13 49					
Canterbury West ■4	d		11a54				12 22	12 39		12a54				13 22	13 39		13a54				14 22	14 39
Sturry	d						12 26							13 26							14 26	
Westenhanger	d	11 38				12 08			12 38				13 08			13 38				14 08		
Sandling	d	11 41				12 11			12 41				13 11			13 41				14 11		
Folkestone West	d	11 47			12 05	12 17			12 47			13 05	13 17			13 47			14 05	14 17		
Folkestone Central	d	11 50			12 08	12 20			12 50			13 08	13 20			13 50			14 08	14 20		
Dover Priory ■4	a	12 01			12 20	12 31			13 01			13 20	13 31			14 01			14 20	14 31		
	d	12 02							13 02							14 02						
Martin Mill	d	12 11							13 11							14 11						
Walmer	d	12 15							13 15							14 15						
Deal	d	12 19							13 19							14 19						
Sandwich	d	12 26							13 26							14 26						
Minster ■4	d						12 38							13 38							14 38	
Ramsgate ■4	a	12 38					12 44	12 59	13 38					13 44	13 59	14 38					14 44	14 59
Broadstairs	a							13 04							14 04							15 04
Margate ■4	a							13 10							14 10							15 10

Station		SE ■1		SE	SE	SE ■1	SE ■1	SE	SE ■1		SE	SE	SE ■1	SE ■1	SE	SE ■1		SE	SE	SE ■1	SE ■1	SE
St Pancras Intl. ■15 ⊖	d				14 12			14 42				15 12			15 42				16 10			16 42
Stratford International ⊖	d				14 19			14 49				15 19			15 49				16 17			16 49
Ebbsfleet International	d				14 31			15 01				15 31			16 01				16 29			17 01
London Charing Cross ■4 ⊖	d	13 10					13 40		14 10					14 40		15 10					15 40	
London Waterloo (East) ■4 ⊖	d	13 13					13 43		14 13					14 43		15 13					15 43	
London Cannon Street ■4 ⊖	d																					
London Bridge ■4 ⊖	d	13 19					13 49		14 19					14 49		15 19					15 49	
Orpington ■4	d																					
Sevenoaks ■4	d	13 42					14 12		14 42					15 12		15 42					16 12	
Tonbridge ■4	a	13 50					14 20		14 50					15 20		15 50					16 20	
	d	13 50		14 03			14 20		14 50		15 03			15 20		15 50		16 03			16 20	
Paddock Wood ■4	d	13 58		14 10			14 28		14 58		15 10			15 28		15 58		16 10			16 28	
Maidstone West ■4 194	a			14 29							15 29							16 29				
Marden	d	14 03					14 33		15 03					15 33		16 03					16 33	
Staplehurst	d	14 07					14 37		15 07					15 37		16 07					16 37	
Headcorn	d	14 13					14 43		15 13					15 43		16 13					16 43	
Pluckley	d	14 19					14 49		15 19					15 49		16 19					16 49	
Ashford International	a	14 26			14 50		14 56	15 20	15 26			15 50		15 56	16 20	16 26			16 48		16 56	17 20
	d	14 30	14 33		14 52	15 00	15 03	15 22	15 30	15 33		15 52	16 00	16 03	16 22	16 30	16 33		16 52	17 00	17 03	17 22
Wye	d		14 39				15 09			15 39				16 09			16 39				17 09	
Chilham	d		14 45							15 45							16 45					
Chartham	d		14 49							15 49							16 49					
Canterbury West ■4	d		14a54				15 22	15 39		15a54				16 22	16 39		16a54				17 22	17 39
Sturry	d						15 26							16 26							17 26	
Westenhanger	d	14 38				15 08			15 38				16 08			16 38				17 08		
Sandling	d	14 41				15 11			15 41				16 11			16 41				17 11		
Folkestone West	d	14 47			15 05	15 17			15 47			16 05	16 17			16 47			17 05	17 17		
Folkestone Central	d	14 50			15 08	15 20			15 50			16 08	16 20			16 50			17 08	17 20		
Dover Priory ■4	a	15 01			15 20	15 31			16 01			16 20	16 31			17 01			17 20	17 31		
	d	15 02							16 02							17 02						
Martin Mill	d	15 11							16 11							17 11						
Walmer	d	15 15							16 15							17 15						
Deal	d	15 19							16 19							17 19						
Sandwich	d	15 26							16 26							17 26						
Minster ■4	d						15 38							16 38							17 38	
Ramsgate ■4	a	15 38					15 44	15 59	16 38					16 44	16 59	17 38					17 44	17 59
Broadstairs	a							16 04							17 04							18 04
Margate ■4	a							16 10							17 10							18 10

Table 207

Saturdays

London and Tonbridge - Ashford International, Folkestone, Dover, Canterbury West, Ramsgate and Margate

	SE ■1		SE	SE	SE ■1	SE ■1		SE	SE ■1		SE	SE	SE ■1	SE ■1	SE	SE ■1		SE	SE	SE ■1	SE ■1	SE	SE ■	SE
St Pancras Intl. ■15 ⊖ d				17 12				17 42				18 12			18 42				19 12			19 42		
Stratford International ⊖ d				17 19				17 49				18 19			18 49				19 19			19 49		
Ebbsfleet International d				17 31				18 01				18 31			19 01				19 31			20 01		
London Charing Cross ■4 ⊖ d	16 10					16 40			17 10					17 40		18 10					18 40		19 10	
London Waterloo (East) ■4 ⊖ d	16 13					16 43			17 13					17 43		18 13					18 43		19 13	
London Cannon Street ■4 ⊖ d																								
London Bridge ■4 ⊖ d	16 19					16 49			17 19					17 49		18 19					18 49		19 19	
Orpington ■4 d																								
Sevenoaks ■4 d	16 42					17 12			17 42					18 12		18 42					19 12		19 42	
Tonbridge ■4 a	16 50					17 20			17 50					18 20		18 50					19 20		19 50	
d	16 50		17 03			17 20			17 50		18 03			18 20		18 50		19 03			19 20		19 50	20 03
Paddock Wood ■4 d	16 58		17 10			17 28			17 58		18 10			18 28		18 58		19 10			19 28		19 58	20 10
Maidstone West ■4 194 a			17 29								18 29							19 29						20 29
Marden d	17 03					17 33			18 03					18 33		19 03					19 33		20 03	
Staplehurst d	17 07					17 37			18 07					18 37		19 07					19 37		20 07	
Headcorn d	17 13					17 43			18 13					18 43		19 13					19 43		20 13	
Pluckley d	17 19					17 49			18 19					18 49		19 19					19 49		20 19	
Ashford International a	17 26			17 50		17 56		18 20	18 26			18 50		18 56	19 20	19 26			19 50		19 56	20 20	20 26	
d	17 30	17 33		17 52	18 00	18 03		18 22	18 30	18 33		18 52	19 00	19 03	19 22	19 30			19 52	20 00	20 03	20 22	20 30	
Wye d		17 39				18 09				18 39				19 09							20 09			
Chilham d		17 45								18 45				19 15							20 15			
Chartham d		17 49								18 49				19 19							20 19			
Canterbury West ■4 d		17a54				18 22		18 39		18a54				19 25	19 39						20 25	20 39		
Sturry d						18 26								19 29							20 29			
Westenhanger d	17 38				18 08				18 38				19 08			19 38				20 08			20 38	
Sandling d	17 41				18 11				18 41				19 11			19 41				20 11			20 41	
Folkestone West d	17 47			18 05	18 17				18 47			19 05	19 17			19 47			20 05	20 17			20 47	
Folkestone Central d	17 50			18 08	18 20				18 50			19 08	19 20			19 50			20 08	20 20			20 50	
Dover Priory ■4 a	18 01			18 20	18 31				19 01			19 20	19 31			20 01			20 20	20 31			21 01	
d	18 02								19 02							20 02							21 02	
Martin Mill d	18 11								19 11							20 11							21 11	
Walmer d	18 15								19 15							20 15							21 15	
Deal d	18 19								19 19							20 19							21 19	
Sandwich d	18 26								19 26							20 26							21 26	
Minster ■4 d						18 38								19 41							20 41			
Ramsgate ■4 a	18 38					18 44		18 59	19 38					19 47	19 59	20 38					20 47	20 59	21 38	
Broadstairs a								19 04							20 04							21 04		
Margate ■4 a								19 10							20 10							21 10		

	SE	SE ■1		SE ■1	SE	SE ■1	SE	SE	SE ■1	SE ■1	SE	SE ■1		SE	SE	SE ■1	SE ■1	SE	SE ■1	SE	SE ■1	SE ■1		SE ■1
St Pancras Intl. ■15 ⊖ d	20 12				20 42			21 12			21 42				22 12			22 42		23 12				
Stratford International ⊖ d	20 19				20 49			21 19			21 49				22 19			22 49		23 19				
Ebbsfleet International d	20 31				21 01			21 31			22 01				22 31			23 01		23 31				
London Charing Cross ■4 ⊖ d				19 40		20 10				20 40		21 10					21 40		22 10		22 40	23 10		23 40
London Waterloo (East) ■4 ⊖ d				19 43		20 13				20 43		21 13					21 43		22 13		22 43	23 13		23 43
London Cannon Street ■4 ⊖ d																								
London Bridge ■4 ⊖ d				19 49		20 19				20 49		21 19					21 49		22 19		22 49	23 19		23 49
Orpington ■4 d						20 35				21 05		21 35					22 05		22 35		23 05	23 35		00 05
Sevenoaks ■4 d				20 12		20 44				21 14		21 44					22 14		22 44		23 14	23 44		00 14
Tonbridge ■4 a				20 20		20 52				21 22		21 52					22 22		22 52		23 22	23 52		00 22
d				20 20		20 53	21 03			21 23		21 53		22 03			22 23		22 53		23 23	23 53		00 23
Paddock Wood ■4 d				20 28		21 00	21 10			21 30		22 00		22 10			22 30		23 00		23 30	23 59		00 30
Maidstone West ■4 194 a							21 29							22 29										
Marden d				20 33		21 05				21 35		22 05					22 35		23 05		23 35	00 05		00 35
Staplehurst d				20 37		21 09				21 39		22 09					22 39		23 09		23 39	00 09		00 39
Headcorn d				20 43		21 14				21 44		22 14					22 44		23 14		23 44	00 14		00 44
Pluckley d				20 49		21 20				21 50		22 20					22 50		23 20		23 50	00 20		00 50
Ashford International a	20 50			20 56	21 20	21 28		21 50		21 58	22 20	22 28			22 50		22 58	23 20	23 28	23 50	23 58	00 28		00 58
d	20 52	21 00		21 03	21 22	21 31		21 52	22 00	22 03	22 22	22 31			22 52	23 00	23 03	23 22	23 31	23 52	00 03	00 31		01 01
Wye d				21 09						22 09							23 09				00 09			
Chilham d				21 15						22 15							23 15				00 15			
Chartham d				21 19						22 19							23 19				00 19			
Canterbury West ■4 d				21 25	21 39					22 25	22 39						23 25	23 39			00 25			
Sturry d				21 29						22 29							23 29				00 29			
Westenhanger d		21 08				21 40			22 08			22 40				23 08			23 40			00 40		01 10
Sandling d		21 11				21 42			22 11			22 42				23 11			23 42			00 42		01 12
Folkestone West d	21 05	21 17				21 47		22 05	22 17			22 47			23 05	23 17			23 47	00 05		00 47		01 17
Folkestone Central d	21 08	21 20				21 50		22 08	22 20			22 50			23 08	23 20			23 50	00 08		00 50		01 20
Dover Priory ■4 a	21 20	21 31				22 01		22 20	22 31			23 01			23 20	23 31			00 01	00 20		01 01		01 31
d						22 02						23 02							00 02					
Martin Mill d						22 11						23 11							00 11					
Walmer d						22 15						23 15							00 15					
Deal d						22 19						23 19							00 19					
Sandwich d						22 26						23 26							00 26					
Minster ■4 d				21 41						22 41							23 41				00 41			
Ramsgate ■4 a				21 47	21 59	22 38				22 48	22 59	23 38					23 47	23 59	00 38		00 47			
Broadstairs a					22 04						23 04													
Margate ■4 a					22 10						23 10													

Table 207

Sundays

London and Tonbridge - Ashford International, Folkestone, Dover, Canterbury West, Ramsgate and Margate

		SE	SE	SE	SE	SE	SE	SE	SE	SE		SE	SE	SE	SE	SE	SE	SE		SE		SE	SE	SE	SE
		1		1	1	1		1				1	1	1	1			1				1	1		
		A	A	A	A	A																			
St Pancras Intl. 15 ⊖	d		23p12				00 12										08 42			09 10					09 37
Stratford International ⊖	d		23p19				00 19										08 49			09 17					09 44
Ebbsfleet International	d		23p31				00 31										09 01			09 29					09 56
London Charing Cross 4 ⊖	d	22p10		22p40	23p10	23p40												08 08					08 38		
London Waterloo (East) 4 ⊖	d	22p13		22p43	23p13	23p43												08 11					08 41		
London Cannon Street 4 ⊖	d																								
London Bridge 4 ⊖	d	22p19		22p49	23p19	23p49												08 16					08 46		
Orpington 4	d	22p35		23p05	23p35	00 05												08 32					09 02		
Sevenoaks 4	d	22p44		23p14	23p44	00 14												08 42					09 12		
Tonbridge 4	a	22p52		23p22	23p52	00 22												08 52					09 20		
	d	22p53		23p23	23p53	00 23			06 26						08 20			08 52					09 20		
Paddock Wood 4	d	23p00		23p30	23p59	00 30			06 34	07 34					08 28	08 34		09 00					09 28	09 34	
Maidstone West 4 194	a								06 53	07 53						08 53								09 53	
Marden	d	23p05		23p35	00 05	00 35									08 33			09 05					09 33		
Staplehurst	d	23p09		23p39	00 09	00 39									08 37			09 09					09 37		
Headcorn	d	23p14		23p44	00 14	00 44									08 43			09 15					09 43		
Pluckley	d	23p20		23p50	00 20	00 50									08 49								09 49		
Ashford International	a	23p28	23p50	23p58	00 28	00 58	00 50								08 56		09 20	09 26		09 48			09 56		10 15
	d	23p31	23p52	00 03	00 31	01 01		01 04				08 30	08 33	09 00	09 03		09 22	09 30	09 33	09 52		10 00	10 03		10 22
Wye	d			00 09				01 10					08 39		09 09				09 39				10 09		
Chilham	d			00 15				01 16					08 45						09 45						
Chartham	d			00 19				01 20					08 49						09 49						
Canterbury West 4	d			00 25				01a25					08a54		09 22		09 39		09a54				10 22		10 39
Sturry	d			00 29											09 26								10 26		
Westenhanger	d	23p40			00 40	01 10						08 38		09 08				09 38				10 08			
Sandling	d	23p42			00 42	01 12						08 41		09 11				09 41				10 11			
Folkestone West	d	23p47	00 05		00 47	01 17						08 47		09 17				09 47		10 05		10 17			
Folkestone Central	d	23p50	00 08		00 50	01 20						08 50		09 19				09 50		10 08		10 19			
Dover Priory 4	a	00 01	00 20		01 01	01 31						09 01		09 30				10 01		10 20		10 30			
	d	00 02										09 02						10 02							
Martin Mill	d	00 11										09 11						10 11							
Walmer	d	00 15										09 15						10 15							
Deal	d	00 19										09 19						10 19							
Sandwich	d	00 26										09 26						10 26							
Minster 4	d			00 41											09 38								10 38		
Ramsgate 4	a	00 38		00 47								09 38			09 44		09 59	10 38					10 44		10 59
Broadstairs	a																10 04								11 04
Margate 4	a																10 10								11 10

		SE		SE	SE	SE		SE	SE	SE		SE	SE	SE	SE	SE		SE		SE	SE	SE	SE	SE	
		1			1	1				1			1	1				1			1	1			
St Pancras Intl. 15 ⊖	d			10 12					10 42			11 12				11 42				12 12				12 42	
Stratford International ⊖	d			10 19					10 49			11 19				11 49				12 19				12 49	
Ebbsfleet International	d			10 31					11 01			11 31				12 01				12 31				13 01	
London Charing Cross 4 ⊖	d	09 08				09 38				10 08				10 38				11 08				11 38			
London Waterloo (East) 4 ⊖	d	09 11				09 41				10 11				10 41				11 11				11 41			
London Cannon Street 4 ⊖	d																								
London Bridge 4 ⊖	d	09 16				09 46				10 16				10 46				11 16				11 46			
Orpington 4	d	09 32				10 02				10 32				11 02				11 32				12 02			
Sevenoaks 4	d	09 42				10 12				10 42				11 12				11 42				12 12			
Tonbridge 4	a	09 52				10 20				10 52				11 20				11 52				12 20			
	d	09 52				10 20				10 52				11 20				11 52				12 20			
Paddock Wood 4	d	10 00				10 28		10 34		11 00				11 28	11 34			12 00				12 28	12 34		
Maidstone West 4 194	a							10 53							11 53								12 53		
Marden	d	10 05				10 33				11 05				11 33				12 05				12 33			
Staplehurst	d	10 09				10 37				11 09				11 37				12 09				12 37			
Headcorn	d	10 15				10 43				11 15				11 43				12 15				12 43			
Pluckley	d					10 49								11 49								12 49			
Ashford International	a	10 26		10 50		10 56			11 20	11 26		11 50		11 56		12 20		12 26		12 50		12 56		13 20	
	d	10 30	10 33	10 52	11 00	11 03			11 22	11 30	11 33	11 52	12 00	12 03		12 22		12 30	12 33	12 52	13 00	13 03		13 22	
Wye	d		10 39			11 09					11 39			12 09					12 39			13 09			
Chilham	d		10 45								11 45								12 45						
Chartham	d		10 49								11 49								12 49						
Canterbury West 4	d		10a54			11 22			11 39		11a54			12 22		12 39			12a54			13 22		13 39	
Sturry	d					11 26								12 26								13 26			
Westenhanger	d	10 38			11 08					11 38			12 08					12 38			13 08				
Sandling	d	10 41			11 11					11 41			12 11					12 41			13 11				
Folkestone West	d	10 47		11 05	11 17					11 47		12 05	12 17					12 47		13 05	13 17				
Folkestone Central	d	10 50		11 08	11 19					11 50		12 08	12 19					12 50		13 08	13 19				
Dover Priory 4	a	11 01		11 20	11 30					12 01		12 20	12 30					13 01		13 20	13 30				
	d	11 02								12 02								13 02							
Martin Mill	d	11 11								12 11								13 11							
Walmer	d	11 15								12 15								13 15							
Deal	d	11 19								12 19								13 19							
Sandwich	d	11 26								12 26								13 26							
Minster 4	d					11 38								12 38								13 38			
Ramsgate 4	a	11 38				11 44			11 59	12 38				12 44		12 59		13 38				13 44		13 59	
Broadstairs	a								12 04							13 04								14 04	
Margate 4	a								12 10							13 10								14 10	

A not 22 May

Table 207

Sundays

London and Tonbridge - Ashford International, Folkestone, Dover, Canterbury West, Ramsgate and Margate

	SE [1]		SE	SE [1]	SE [1]	SE	SE	SE [1]		SE	SE [1]	SE [1]	SE	SE	SE [1]		SE	SE [1]	SE [1]	SE	SE
St Pancras Intl. [15] ⊖ d			13 12				13 42			14 12				14 42			15 12				15 42
Stratford International ⊖ d			13 19				13 49			14 19				14 49			15 19				15 49
Ebbsfleet International d			13 31				14 01			14 31				15 01			15 31				16 01
London Charing Cross [4] ⊖ d	12 08				12 38			13 08				13 38			14 08				14 38		
London Waterloo (East) [4] ⊖ d	12 11				12 41			13 11				13 41			14 11				14 41		
London Cannon Street [4] ⊖ d																					
London Bridge [4] ⊖ d	12 16				12 46			13 16				13 46			14 16				14 46		
Orpington [4] d	12 32				13 02			13 32				14 02			14 32				15 02		
Sevenoaks [4] d	12 42				13 12			13 42				14 12			14 42				15 12		
Tonbridge [4] a	12 52				13 20			13 52				14 20			14 52				15 20		
d	12 52				13 20			13 52				14 20			14 52				15 20		
Paddock Wood [4] d	13 00				13 28	13 34		14 00				14 28	14 34		15 00				15 28	15 34	
Maidstone West [4] 194 a						13 53							14 53							15 53	
Marden d	13 05				13 33			14 05				14 33			15 05				15 33		
Staplehurst d	13 09				13 37			14 09				14 37			15 09				15 37		
Headcorn d	13 15				13 43			14 15				14 43			15 15				15 43		
Pluckley d					13 49							14 49							15 49		
Ashford International a	13 26		13 50		13 56		14 20	14 26		14 50		14 56		15 20	15 26		15 50		15 56		16 20
d	13 30	13 33	13 52	14 00	14 03		14 22	14 30	14 33	14 52	15 00	15 03		15 22	15 30	15 33	15 52	16 00	16 03		16 22
Wye d		13 39			14 09				14 39			15 09				15 39			16 09		
Chilham d		13 45							14 45							15 45					
Chartham d		13 49							14 49							15 49					
Canterbury West [4] d		13a54			14 22		14 39		14a54			15 22		15 39		15a54			16 22		16 39
Sturry d					14 26							15 26							16 26		
Westenhanger d	13 38			14 08				14 38			15 08				15 38			16 08			
Sandling d	13 41			14 11				14 41			15 11				15 41			16 11			
Folkestone West d	13 47		14 05	14 17				14 47		15 05	15 17				15 47		16 05	16 17			
Folkestone Central d	13 50		14 08	14 19				14 50		15 08	15 19				15 50		16 08	16 19			
Dover Priory [4] a	14 01		14 20	14 30				15 01		15 20	15 30				16 01		16 20	16 30			
d	14 02							15 02							16 02						
Martin Mill d	14 11							15 11							16 11						
Walmer d	14 15							15 15							16 15						
Deal d	14 19							15 19							16 19						
Sandwich d	14 26							15 26							16 26						
Minster [4] d					14 38							15 38							16 38		
Ramsgate [4] a	14 38				14 44		14 59	15 38				15 44		15 59	16 38				16 44		16 59
Broadstairs a							15 04							16 04							17 04
Margate [4] a							15 10							16 10							17 10

	SE [1]		SE	SE [1]	SE [1]	SE	SE	SE [1]		SE	SE [1]	SE [1]	SE	SE	SE [1]	SE	SE [1]	SE [1]	SE	SE	SE [1]	SE
St Pancras Intl. [15] ⊖ d			16 10				16 42			17 12				17 42		18 12				18 42		19 12
Stratford International ⊖ d			16 17				16 49			17 19				17 49		18 19				18 49		19 19
Ebbsfleet International d			16 29				17 01			17 31				18 01		18 31				19 01		19 31
London Charing Cross [4] ⊖ d	15 08				15 38			16 08				16 38			17 08			17 38			18 08	
London Waterloo (East) [4] ⊖ d	15 11				15 41			16 11				16 41			17 11			17 41			18 11	
London Cannon Street [4] ⊖ d																						
London Bridge [4] ⊖ d	15 16				15 46			16 16				16 46			17 16			17 46			18 16	
Orpington [4] d	15 32				16 02			16 32				17 02			17 32			18 02			18 32	
Sevenoaks [4] d	15 42				16 12			16 42				17 12			17 42			18 12			18 42	
Tonbridge [4] a	15 52				16 20			16 52				17 20			17 52			18 20			18 52	
d	15 52				16 20			16 52				17 20			17 52			18 20			18 52	
Paddock Wood [4] d	16 00				16 28	16 34		17 00				17 28	17 34		18 00			18 28	18 34		19 00	
Maidstone West [4] 194 a						16 53							17 53						18 53			
Marden d	16 05				16 33			17 05				17 33			18 05			18 33			19 05	
Staplehurst d	16 09				16 37			17 09				17 37			18 09			18 37			19 09	
Headcorn d	16 15				16 43			17 15				17 43			18 15			18 43			19 15	
Pluckley d					16 49							17 49						18 49				
Ashford International a	16 26		16 48		16 56		17 20	17 26		17 50		17 56		18 20	18 26	18 50		18 56		19 20	19 26	19 50
d	16 30	16 33	16 52	17 00	17 03		17 22	17 30	17 33	17 52	18 00	18 03		18 22	18 30	18 52	19 00	19 03		19 22	19 30	19 52
Wye d		16 39			17 09				17 39			18 09						19 09				
Chilham d		16 45							17 45			18 15						19 15				
Chartham d		16 49							17 49			18 19						19 19				
Canterbury West [4] d		16a54			17 22		17 39		17a54			18 25		18 39				19 25		19 39		
Sturry d					17 26							18 29						19 29				
Westenhanger d	16 38			17 08				17 38			18 08				18 38		19 08				19 38	
Sandling d	16 41			17 11				17 41			18 11				18 41		19 11				19 41	
Folkestone West d	16 47		17 05	17 17				17 47		18 05	18 17				18 47	19 05	19 17				19 47	20 05
Folkestone Central d	16 50		17 08	17 19				17 50		18 08	18 19				18 50	19 08	19 19				19 50	20 08
Dover Priory [4] a	17 01		17 20	17 30				18 01		18 20	18 30				19 01	19 20	19 30				20 01	20 20
d	17 02							18 02							19 02						20 02	
Martin Mill d	17 11							18 11							19 11						20 11	
Walmer d	17 15							18 15							19 15						20 15	
Deal d	17 19							18 19							19 19						20 19	
Sandwich d	17 26							18 26							19 26						20 26	
Minster [4] d					17 38							18 41						19 41				
Ramsgate [4] a	17 38				17 44		17 59	18 38				18 47		18 59	19 38			19 47		19 59	20 38	
Broadstairs a							18 04							19 04						20 04		
Margate [4] a							18 10							19 10						20 10		

Table 207

Sundays

London and Tonbridge - Ashford International, Folkestone, Dover, Canterbury West, Ramsgate and Margate

		SE 1	SE 1	SE	SE	SE 1		SE	SE 1	SE 1	SE	SE	SE 1	SE	SE 1	SE 1		SE	SE	SE 1	SE	SE 1	SE 1	SE	SE 1
St Pancras Intl. 15 ⊖	d				19 42			20 12				20 42		21 12					21 42		22 12			22 42	
Stratford International ⊖	d				19 49			20 19				20 49		21 19					21 49		22 19			22 49	
Ebbsfleet International	d				20 01			20 31				21 01		21 31					22 01		22 31			23 01	
London Charing Cross 4 ⊖	d		18 38			19 08				19 38			20 08			20 38				21 08			21 38		22 08
London Waterloo (East) 4 ⊖	d		18 41			19 11				19 41			20 11			20 41				21 11			21 41		22 11
London Cannon Street 4 ⊖	d																								
London Bridge 4 ⊖	d		18 46			19 16				19 46			20 16			20 46				21 16			21 46		22 16
Orpington 4	d		19 02			19 32				20 02			20 32			21 02				21 32			22 02		22 32
Sevenoaks 4	d		19 12			19 42				20 12			20 42			21 12				21 42			22 12		22 42
Tonbridge 4	a		19 20			19 52				20 20			20 52			21 20				21 52			22 20		22 52
	d		19 20			19 52				20 20			20 52			21 20				21 52			22 20		22 52
Paddock Wood 4	d		19 28	19 34		20 00				20 28	20 34		21 00			21 28		21 34		22 00			22 28		23 00
Maidstone West 4 194	a			19 53							20 53							21 53							
Marden	d		19 33			20 05				20 33			21 05			21 33				22 05			22 33		23 05
Staplehurst	d		19 37			20 09				20 37			21 09			21 37				22 09			22 37		23 09
Headcorn	d		19 43			20 15				20 43			21 15			21 43				22 15			22 43		23 15
Pluckley	d		19 49							20 49						21 49							22 49		
Ashford International	a		19 56		20 20	20 26		20 50		20 56		21 20	21 26	21 50		21 56			22 21	22 26	22 50		22 56	23 20	23 26
	d	20 00	20 03		20 22	20 30		20 52	21 00	21 03		21 22	21 30	21 52	22 00	22 03			22 22	22 30	22 52	23 00	23 03	23 22	23 30
Wye	d		20 09							21 09						22 09							23 09		
Chilham	d		20 15							21 15						22 15							23 15		
Chartham	d		20 19							21 19						22 19							23 19		
Canterbury West 4	d		20 25		20 39					21 25		21 39				22 25			22 39				23 25	23 39	
Sturry	d		20 29							21 29						22 29							23 29		
Westenhanger	d	20 08				20 38			21 08				21 38		22 08					22 38		23 08			23 38
Sandling	d	20 11				20 41			21 11				21 41		22 11					22 41		23 11			23 41
Folkestone West	d	20 17				20 47		21 05	21 17				21 47	22 05	22 17					22 47	23 05	23 17			23 47
Folkestone Central	d	20 19				20 50		21 08	21 19				21 50	22 08	22 19					22 50	23 08	23 19			23 50
Dover Priory 4	a	20 30				21 01		21 20	21 30				22 01	22 20	22 30					23 01	23 20	23 30			00 01
	d					21 02							22 02							23 02					00 02
Martin Mill	d					21 11							22 11							23 11					00 11
Walmer	d					21 15							22 15							23 15					00 15
Deal	d					21 19							22 19							23 19					00 19
Sandwich	d					21 26							22 26							23 26					00 26
Minster 4	d		20 41							21 41						22 41							23 41		
Ramsgate 4	a		20 47		20 59	21 38				21 47		21 59	22 38			22 47			22 59	23 38			23 47	23 59	00 38
Broadstairs	a				21 04							22 04							23 04						
Margate 4	a				21 10							22 10							23 10						

		SE		SE 1	SE 1	SE 1	SE
St Pancras Intl. 15 ⊖	d	23 12					23 42
Stratford International ⊖	d	23 19					23 49
Ebbsfleet International	d	23 31					00 01
London Charing Cross 4 ⊖	d			22 38	23 08	23 38	
London Waterloo (East) 4 ⊖	d			22 41	23 11	23 41	
London Cannon Street 4 ⊖	d						
London Bridge 4 ⊖	d			22 46	23 16	23 46	
Orpington 4	d			23 02	23 32	00 02	
Sevenoaks 4	d			23 12	23 42	00 12	
Tonbridge 4	a			23 20	23 52	00 20	
	d			23 20	23 52	00 20	
Paddock Wood 4	d			23 28	23 59	00 28	
Maidstone West 4 194	a						
Marden	d			23 33	00 05	00 33	
Staplehurst	d			23 37	00 09	00 37	
Headcorn	d			23 43	00 15	00 43	
Pluckley	d			23 49		00 49	
Ashford International	a	23 50		23 56	00 26	00 56	00 20
	d	23 52		00 01			
Wye	d						
Chilham	d						
Chartham	d						
Canterbury West 4	d						
Sturry	d						
Westenhanger	d						
Sandling	d			00 11			
Folkestone West	d	00 05		00 17			
Folkestone Central	d	00 08		00 19			
Dover Priory 4	a	00 20		00 30			
	d						
Martin Mill	d						
Walmer	d						
Deal	d						
Sandwich	d						
Minster 4	d						
Ramsgate 4	a						
Broadstairs	a						
Margate 4	a						

Table 207

Mondays to Fridays

Margate, Ramsgate, Canterbury West, Dover, Folkestone, Ashford International - Tonbridge and London

Miles	Miles	Miles	Miles			SE MX 1	SE	SE	SE 1	SE 1	SE	SE 1	SE	SE 1		SE	SE	SE 1	SE 1	SE 1	SE	SE	SE 1	SE
0	0	—	—	**Margate 4**	d																05 47			
3¼	3¼	—	—	Broadstairs	d																05 54			
5½	5½	—	—	**Ramsgate 4**	d	21p22					05 00			04 50				05 36		05 28	06 00			
—	9½	0	—	Minster 4	d						05 06							05 42						
13¾	—	4¾	—	Sandwich	d	21p34								05 02						05 40				
18	—	—	—	**Deal**	d	21p40								05 08						05 46				
19½	—	—	—	Walmer	d	21p43								05 11						05 49				
22¼	—	—	—	Martin Mill	d	21p48								05 16						05 54				
27¼	—	—	—	**Dover Priory 4**	a	21p56								05 24						06 02				
—	—	—	—		d	21p57			04 37					05 26		05 44			05 45	06 04		06 12		
34½	—	—	—	**Folkestone Central**	d	22p09			04 49					05 38		05 56				06 16		06 24		
35¼	—	—	—	Folkestone West	d	22p11			04 51					05 40		05 58				06 18		06 26		
39	—	—	—	Sandling	d	22p16			04 56					05 45						06 23				
40¼	—	—	—	Westenhanger	d	22p19			04 59					05 48						06 26				
—	18½	—	—	Sturry	d						05 18							05 54						
—	20¾	—	—	**Canterbury West 4**	d						05 25	05 36						06 00			06 20			
—	24	—	—	Chartham	d							05 41						06 05						
—	26	—	—	Chilham	d							05 44						06 08						
—	30¾	—	—	Wye	d							05 51						06 15						
48½	35	—	0	**Ashford International**	a	22p28			05 08		05 41	05 57		05 57		06 11		06 21		06 35	06 36	06 39		
—	—	—	—																					
—	—	—	—		d	22p33	05 13		05 13	05 29	05 43			06 03		06 13		06 24		06 38	06 43		06 44	
54	—	—	—	Pluckley	d	22p39			05 19	05 35				06 09				06 30		06 44			06 50	
59¼	—	—	—	Headcorn	d	22p46			05 26	05 42				06 16				06 37		06 51			06 57	
62¾	—	—	—	Staplehurst	d	22p51			05 31	05 47				06 21				06 42		06 56			07 02	
65	—	—	—	Marden	d	22p55			05 35	05 51				06 25				06 46		07 00			07 07	
—	—	—	—	Maidstone West 4 194	d			05 18					05 56				06 26							06 56
69¾	—	—	—	Paddock Wood 4	d	23p01		05a37	05 42	05 58			06a15	06 32			06a45	06 53		07 07			07 13	
75	—	—	—	**Tonbridge 4**	a	23p10			05 49	06 05				06 39				07 01		07 14			07 21	
—	—	—	—		d	23p14			05 50	06 06				06 40				07 02		07 15			07 22	
82¼	—	—	—	Sevenoaks 4	a	23p24			05 58	06 14				06 48				07 10		07 26			07 31	
90¾	—	—	—	Orpington 4	a	23p36			06 08	06 23														
102¾	—	—	—	**London Bridge 4** ⊖	a	23p53			06 24	06 39				07 14				07 36	07 51	07 53				
—	—	—	—	**London Cannon Street 4** ⊖	a														07 57	07 59				
103¾	—	—	—	**London Waterloo (East) 4** ⊖	a	23p57			06 29	06 44				07 19				07 41					08 00	
104½	—	—	—	**London Charing Cross 4** ⊖	a	00 01			06 33	06 49				07 25				07 47					08 06	
—	—	—	33¼	**Ebbsfleet International**	a		05 32				06 02					06 32								07 25
—	—	—	50	**Stratford International** ⊖	a		05 44				06 15					06 44					07 11			07 36
—	—	—	56	**St Pancras Intl. 15** ⊖	a		05 51				06 23					06 53					07 18			07 43

		SE	SE 1	SE 1	SE	SE	SE 1	SE 1	SE	SE		SE 1	SE	SE	SE 1	SE 1	SE 1	SE 1	SE 1	SE		SE	SE	SE
Margate 4	d												06 44											
Broadstairs	d												06 50											
Ramsgate 4	d		06 10		06 26		06 14	06 40					06 56			06 59	06 49	07 10	07 19			07 26		
Minster 4	d		06 16					06 46										07 16						
Sandwich	d						06 26										07 01							
Deal	d						06 32										07 07							
Walmer	d						06 35										07 10							
Martin Mill	d						06 40										07 15							
Dover Priory 4	a						06 48										07 23							
	d			06 24		06 38	06 49							07 08			07 24						07 38	
Folkestone Central	d			06 36		06 50	07 01					07 12		07 20			07 36						07 50	
Folkestone West	d			06 38		06 52	07 03					07 14		07 22			07 38						07 52	
Sandling	d			06 43			07 08					07 19					07 43							
Westenhanger	d			06 46			07 11					07 22					07 46							
Sturry	d		06 28					06 58										07 28						
Canterbury West 4	d		06 33		06 46			07 03					07 16					07 36				07 46		
Chartham	d		06 38					07 08										07 41						
Chilham	d		06 41					07 11										07 44						
Wye	d		06 48					07 18										07 51						
Ashford International	a		06 56	06 55	07 03	07 06	07 20	07 24				07 31	07 32	07 35			07 55	07 58				08 03	08 06	
	d		06 57	07 03	07 13		07 22	07 28				07 38	07 43		07 45		08 03					08 13		
Pluckley	d		07 04	07 09			07 28					07 44			07 51		08 09							
Headcorn	d		07 11	07 16			07 35	07 39				07 51			07 58		08 16							
Staplehurst	d		07 16	07 22			07 40	07 44				07 56			08 03		08 21							
Marden	d		07 20	07 26			07 44	07 48				08 00			08 07		08 25							
Maidstone West 4 194	d	07 01							07 26	07 41										07 56				08 18
Paddock Wood 4	d	07a20	07 27	07 33			07 51	07 55		08a00		08 07			08 14		08 31							08 37
Tonbridge 4	a		07 34	07 41			07 58	08 02				08 14			08 21		08 39							08 45
	d		07 35	07 42			07 59	08 03				08 15			08 22		08 40							
Sevenoaks 4	a		07 46	07 50			08 07	08 11				08 26			08 30		08 48							
Orpington 4	a																							
London Bridge 4 ⊖	a		08 13				08 33					08 55				08 49	09 14		09 11					
London Cannon Street 4 ⊖	a		08 20				08 41					09 02				08 57			09 18					
London Waterloo (East) 4 ⊖	a			08 20				08 40							09 00		09 19							
London Charing Cross 4 ⊖	a			08 26				08 46							09 04		09 25							
Ebbsfleet International	a																			08 26				
Stratford International ⊖	a				07 41				08 06				08 11							08 36		08 41		
St Pancras Intl. 15 ⊖	a				07 48				08 13				08 19							08 43		08 48		

Margate, Ramsgate, Canterbury West, Dover, Folkestone, Ashford International - Tonbridge and London

		SE 1	SE 1	SE	SE 1	SE 1	SE		SE	SE 1	SE 1	SE	SE 1	SE 1	SE	SE	SE 1	SE 1		SE	SE 1	SE 1	SE	SE	
Margate 4	d			07 49								08 53								09 53					
Broadstairs	d			07 55								08 59								09 59					
Ramsgate 4	d	07 22		08 01	07 40	08 16				08 05	08 40	09 05					09 22	09 40		10 05					
Minster 4	d			08 07	07 53					08 16	08 46							09 46							
Sandwich	d	07 34			08 01					08 25							09 34								
Deal	d	07 40			08 07					08 31							09 40								
Walmer	d	07 43			08 10					08 34							09 43								
Martin Mill	d	07 48			08 15					08 38							09 48								
Dover Priory 4	a	07 56			08 23					08 47							09 56								
	d	07 57			08 24		08 44			08 57			09 24		09 44		09 57				10 24		10 44		
Folkestone Central	d	08 09			08 36		08 56			09 09			09 36		09 56		10 09				10 36		10 56		
Folkestone West	d	08 11			08 38		08 58			09 11			09 38		09 58		10 11				10 38		10 58		
Sandling	d	08 16			08 43					09 16			09 43				10 16				10 43				
Westenhanger	d	08 19			08 46					09 19			09 46				10 19				10 46				
Sturry	d			08 19							08 58							09 58							
Canterbury West 4	d		08 00	08 25		08 36					09 07	09 25		09 36				10 07		10 25		10 36			
Chartham	d		08 05			08 41								09 41								10 41			
Chilham	d		08 08			08 44								09 44								10 44			
Wye	d		08 15			08 51					09 19			09 51				10 19				10 51			
Ashford International	a	08 28	08 21	08 41	08 55	08 58	09 11			09 28	09 25	09 41	09 55	09 58	10 11		10 28	10 25		10 41	10 55	10 58	11 11		
	d	08 33		08 43	09 03		09 13			09 33		09 43	10 03		10 13		10 33			10 43	11 03		11 13		
Pluckley	d	08 39			09 09					09 39			10 09				10 39				11 09				
Headcorn	d	08 46			09 16					09 46			10 16				10 46				11 16				
Staplehurst	d	08 51			09 21					09 51			10 21				10 51				11 21				
Marden	d	08 55			09 25					09 55			10 25				10 55				11 25				
Maidstone West 4 194	d								09 28							10 28								11 28	
Paddock Wood 4	d	09 01			09 31				09 47	10 01			10 31			10 47	11 01				11 31			11 47	
Tonbridge 4	a	09 09			09 39				09 57	10 09			10 39			10 55	11 09				11 39			11 55	
	d	09 10			09 40					10 10			10 40				11 10				11 40				
Sevenoaks 4	a	09 18			09 48					10 18			10 48				11 18				11 48				
Orpington 4	a																								
London Bridge 4 ⊖	a	09 43			10 13					10 43			11 13				11 43				12 13				
London Cannon Street 4 ⊖	a																								
London Waterloo (East) 4 ⊖	a	09 48			10 18					10 48			11 18				11 48				12 18				
London Charing Cross 4 ⊖	a	09 54			10 22					10 52			11 22				11 52				12 22				
Ebbsfleet International	a			09 02			09 32					10 02			10 32					11 02			11 32		
Stratford International ⊖	a			09 14			09 44					10 14			10 44					11 14			11 44		
St Pancras Intl. 15 ⊖	a			09 21			09 51					10 21			10 51					11 21			11 51		

		SE 1	SE 1	SE	SE 1	SE 1		SE	SE	SE 1	SE 1	SE	SE 1	SE 1	SE	SE		SE 1	SE 1	SE	SE 1	SE 1	SE	SE	
Margate 4	d			10 53								11 53								12 53					
Broadstairs	d			10 59								11 59								12 59					
Ramsgate 4	d	10 22	10 40	11 05						11 22	11 40	12 05						12 22	12 40	13 05					
Minster 4	d		10 46								11 46								12 46						
Sandwich	d	10 34								11 34								12 34							
Deal	d	10 40								11 40								12 40							
Walmer	d	10 43								11 43								12 43							
Martin Mill	d	10 48								11 48								12 48							
Dover Priory 4	a	10 56								11 56								12 56							
	d	10 57			11 24			11 44		11 57			12 24		12 44			12 57			13 24		13 44		
Folkestone Central	d	11 09			11 36			11 56		12 09			12 36		12 56			13 09			13 36		13 56		
Folkestone West	d	11 11			11 38			11 58		12 11			12 38		12 58			13 11			13 38		13 58		
Sandling	d	11 16			11 43					12 16			12 43					13 16			13 43				
Westenhanger	d	11 19			11 46					12 19			12 46					13 19			13 46				
Sturry	d		10 58								11 58								12 58						
Canterbury West 4	d		11 07	11 25		11 36					12 07	12 25		12 36					13 07	13 25		13 36			
Chartham	d					11 41								12 41								13 41			
Chilham	d					11 44								12 44								13 44			
Wye	d		11 19			11 51					12 19			12 51					13 19			13 51			
Ashford International	a	11 28	11 25	11 41	11 55	11 58		12 11		12 28	12 25	12 41	12 55	12 58	13 11			13 28	13 25	13 41	13 55	13 58	14 11		
	d	11 33		11 43	12 03			12 13		12 33		12 43	13 03		13 13			13 33		13 43	14 03		14 13		
Pluckley	d	11 39			12 09					12 39			13 09					13 39			14 09				
Headcorn	d	11 46			12 16					12 46			13 16					13 46			14 16				
Staplehurst	d	11 51			12 21					12 51			13 21					13 51			14 21				
Marden	d	11 55			12 25					12 55			13 25					13 55			14 25				
Maidstone West 4 194	d								12 28							13 28								14 28	
Paddock Wood 4	d	12 01			12 31				12 47	13 01			13 31			13 47		14 01			14 31			14 47	
Tonbridge 4	a	12 09			12 39				12 58	13 09			13 39			13 55		14 09			14 39			14 55	
	d	12 10			12 40					13 10			13 40					14 10			14 40				
Sevenoaks 4	a	12 18			12 48					13 18			13 48					14 18			14 48				
Orpington 4	a																								
London Bridge 4 ⊖	a	12 43			13 13					13 43			14 13					14 43			15 13				
London Cannon Street 4 ⊖	a																								
London Waterloo (East) 4 ⊖	a	12 48			13 18					13 48			14 18					14 48			15 18				
London Charing Cross 4 ⊖	a	12 52			13 22					13 52			14 22					14 52			15 22				
Ebbsfleet International	a			12 02				12 32				13 02			13 32					14 02			14 32		
Stratford International ⊖	a			12 14				12 45				13 14			13 44					14 14			14 44		
St Pancras Intl. 15 ⊖	a			12 21				12 54				13 21			13 51					14 21			14 51		

Table 207

Mondays to Fridays

Margate, Ramsgate, Canterbury West, Dover, Folkestone, Ashford International - Tonbridge and London

		SE [1]	SE [1]		SE	SE [1]	SE [1]	SE	SE	SE [1]	SE [1]	SE	SE [1]	SE [1]		SE	SE	SE [1]	SE [1]	SE	SE	SE [1]	SE [1]	SE	
Margate [4]	d				13 53							14 53								15 53					
Broadstairs	d				13 59							14 59								15 59					
Ramsgate [4]	d	13 22	13 40		14 05					14 22	14 40	15 05						15 22	15 40	16 05		15 50			
Minster [4]	d		13 46								14 46								15 46						
Sandwich	d	13 34								14 34								15 34				16 02			
Deal	d	13 40								14 40								15 40				16 08			
Walmer	d	13 43								14 43								15 43				16 11			
Martin Mill	d	13 48								14 48								15 48				16 16			
Dover Priory [4]	a	13 56								14 56								15 56				16 24			
	d	13 57				14 24		14 44		14 57			15 24			15 44		15 57				16 24		16 44	
Folkestone Central	d	14 09				14 36		14 56		15 09			15 36			15 56		16 09				16 36		16 56	
Folkestone West	d	14 11				14 38		14 58		15 11			15 38			15 58		16 11				16 38		16 58	
Sandling	d	14 16				14 43				15 16			15 43					16 16				16 43			
Westenhanger	d	14 19				14 46				15 19			15 46					16 19				16 46			
Sturry	d		13 58								14 58								15 58						
Canterbury West [4]	d		14 07		14 25		14 36				15 04	15 25		15 36					16 04	16 25			16 36		
Chartham	d						14 41							15 41									16 41		
Chilham	d						14 44							15 44									16 44		
Wye	d		14 19				14 51				15 16			15 51					16 16				16 51		
Ashford International	a	14 28	14 25		14 41	14 55	14 58	15 11		15 28	15 22	15 41	15 55	15 58		16 11		16 28	16 22	16 41		16 55	16 58	17 11	
	d	14 33			14 43	15 03		15 13		15 33		15 43	16 03			16 13		16 33		16 43		17 03		17 13	
Pluckley	d	14 39				15 09				15 39			16 09					16 39				17 09			
Headcorn	d	14 46				15 16				15 46			16 16					16 46				17 16			
Staplehurst	d	14 51				15 21				15 51			16 21					16 51				17 21			
Marden	d	14 55				15 25				15 55			16 25					16 55				17 25			
Maidstone West [4] 194	d								15 28								16 33				16 58				
Paddock Wood [4]	d	15 01				15 31			15 47	16 01			16 31				16a52	17 01			17a17	17 31			
Tonbridge [4]	a	15 09				15 39			15 55	16 09			16 39					17 09				17 39			
	d	15 10				15 40				16 10			16 40					17 10				17 40			
Sevenoaks [4]	a	15 18				15 48				16 18			16 48					17 18				17 48			
Orpington [4]	a																								
London Bridge [4] ⊖	a	15 43				16 14				16 46			17 17					17 44				18 16			
London Cannon Street [4] ⊖	a																								
London Waterloo (East) [4] ⊖	a	15 48				16 20				16 52			17 22					17 50				18 20			
London Charing Cross [4] ⊖	a	15 52				16 24				16 56			17 26					17 53				18 25			
Ebbsfleet International	a				15 02			15 32				16 02				16 32				17 02				17 32	
Stratford International ⊖	a				15 14			15 44				16 14				16 44				17 14				17 44	
St Pancras Intl. [15] ⊖	a				15 21			15 51				16 21				16 51				17 21				17 51	

		SE	SE [1]	SE [1]	SE	SE [1]	SE [1]	SE	SE	SE [1]	SE [1]		SE	SE	SE [1]	SE [1]	SE	SE	SE	SE [1]	SE [1]		SE	SE	
Margate [4]	d				16 53								17 53										18 53		
Broadstairs	d				16 59								17 59										18 59		
Ramsgate [4]	d		16 22	16 40	17 05	16 50				17 22	17 40		18 05		17 50					18 22	18 40		19 05		
Minster [4]	d			16 46							17 46										18 46				
Sandwich	d		16 34			17 02				17 34					18 02					18 34					
Deal	d		16 40			17 08				17 40					18 08					18 40					
Walmer	d		16 43			17 11				17 43					18 11					18 43					
Martin Mill	d		16 48			17 16				17 48					18 16					18 48					
Dover Priory [4]	a		16 56			17 24				17 56					18 24					18 56					
	d		16 57			17 24		17 44		17 57					18 24		18 44			18 57					
Folkestone Central	d		17 09			17 36		17 56		18 09					18 36		18 56			19 09					
Folkestone West	d		17 11			17 38		17 58		18 11					18 38		18 58			19 11					
Sandling	d		17 16			17 43				18 16					18 43					19 16					
Westenhanger	d		17 19			17 46				18 19					18 46					19 19					
Sturry	d			16 58							17 58										18 58				
Canterbury West [4]	d			17 04	17 25		17 36				18 04		18 25			18 36					19 07		19 25		
Chartham	d						17 41									18 41									
Chilham	d						17 44									18 44									
Wye	d			17 16			17 51				18 16					18 51					19 19				
Ashford International	a		17 28	17 22	17 41	17 55	17 58	18 11		18 28	18 23		18 41		18 55	18 58	19 11			19 28	19 25		19 41		
	d		17 33		17 43	18 03		18 13		18 33			18 43		19 03		19 13			19 33			19 43		
Pluckley	d		17 39			18 09				18 39					19 09					19 39					
Headcorn	d		17 46			18 16				18 46					19 16					19 46					
Staplehurst	d		17 51			18 21				18 51					19 21					19 51					
Marden	d		17 55			18 25				18 55					19 25					19 55					
Maidstone West [4] 194	d	17 28							18 18					18 48				19 13	19 18					19 58	
Paddock Wood [4]	d	17a47	18 01			18 31			18a37	19 01				19a07	19 31				19a37	20 01				20 17	
Tonbridge [4]	a		18 09			18 39				19 09					19 39					20 09				20 25	
	d		18 10			18 40				19 10					19 40					20 10					
Sevenoaks [4]	a		18 18			18 48				19 18					19 48					20 18					
Orpington [4]	a																								
London Bridge [4] ⊖	a		18 43			19 13				19 43					20 13					20 42					
London Cannon Street [4] ⊖	a																								
London Waterloo (East) [4] ⊖	a		18 48			19 17				19 48					20 18					20 47					
London Charing Cross [4] ⊖	a		18 52			19 21				19 52					20 22					20 51					
Ebbsfleet International	a				18 02			18 32					19 02				19 32	19 47					20 02		
Stratford International ⊖	a				18 14			18 44					19 14				19 44	20 01					20 14		
St Pancras Intl. [15] ⊖	a				18 21			18 51					19 21				19 51	20 08					20 21		

Margate, Ramsgate, Canterbury West, Dover, Folkestone, Ashford International - Tonbridge and London

	SE 1	SE 1	SE	SE 1	SE 1	SE	SE		SE 1	SE 1	SE	SE 1	SE 1	SE	SE	SE 1	SE 1		SE	SE 1	SE	SE 1	SE	SE 1
Margate 4 d						19 53								20 53							21 53			
Broadstairs d						19 59								20 59							21 59			
Ramsgate 4 d				19 22	19 40	20 05						20 22	20 40	21 05						21 22	22 05	22 24		22 45
Minster 4 d					19 46								20 46									22 30		
Sandwich d				19 34								20 34								21 34				22 57
Deal d				19 40								20 40								21 40				23 03
Walmer d				19 43								20 43								21 43				23 06
Martin Mill d				19 48								20 48								21 48				23 11
Dover Priory 4 a				19 56								20 56								21 56				23 19
d	19 24		19 44	19 57					20 24		20 44	20 57				21 24			21 44	21 57			22 44	23 24
Folkestone Central d	19 36		19 56	20 09					20 36		20 56	21 09				21 36			21 56	22 09			22 56	23 36
Folkestone West d	19 38		19 58	20 11					20 38		20 58	21 11				21 38			21 58	22 11			22 58	23 38
Sandling d	19 43			20 16					20 43			21 16				21 43				22 16				23 43
Westenhanger d	19 46			20 19					20 46			21 19				21 46				22 19				23 46
Sturry d					19 58								20 58									22 42		
Canterbury West 4 d		19 36			20 07	20 25				20 36			21 07	21 25			21 36				22 25	22 47		
Chartham d		19 41								20 41							21 41					22 52		
Chilham d		19 44								20 44							21 44					22 55		
Wye d		19 51			20 19					20 51			21 19				21 51					23 02		
Ashford International a	19 55	19 58	20 12	20 28	20 25	20 44			20 55	20 58	21 11	21 28	21 25	21 41		21 55	21 58		22 11	22 28	22 41	23 08	23 11	23 55
d	20 03		20 13	20 33		20 47			21 03		21 13	21 33		21 43		22 03			22 13	22 33	22 43		23 13	
Pluckley d	20 09			20 39					21 09			21 39				22 09				22 39				
Headcorn d	20 16			20 46					21 16			21 46				22 16				22 46				
Staplehurst d	20 21			20 51					21 21			21 51				22 21				22 51				
Marden d	20 25			20 55					21 25			21 55				22 25				22 55				
Maidstone West 4 194 d							20 58								21 58									
Paddock Wood 4 d	20 31			21 01			21 17		21 31			22 01			22 17	22 31				23 01				
Tonbridge 4 a	20 39			21 09			21 25		21 39			22 09			22 25	22 39				23 10				
d	20 40			21 10					21 40			22 10				22 40								
Sevenoaks 4 a	20 48			21 18					21 48			22 18				22 48								
Orpington 4 a																								
London Bridge 4 ⊖ a	21 13			21 43					22 13			22 43				23 13								
London Cannon Street 4 ⊖ a																								
London Waterloo (East) 4 ⊖ a	21 18			21 48					22 18			22 48				23 18								
London Charing Cross 4 ⊖ a	21 22			21 52					22 22			22 52				23 22								
Ebbsfleet International a			20 32			21 06					21 32			22 02					22 32		23 02		23 32	
Stratford International ⊖ a			20 44			21 18					21 44			22 14					22 44		23 14		23 44	
St Pancras Intl. 15 ⊖ a			20 51			21 25					21 51			22 21					22 51		23 21		23 51	

Saturdays

	SE 1	SE	SE 1	SE	SE	SE	SE 1	SE 1	SE		SE 1	SE	SE 1	SE	SE 1	SE	SE 1	SE 1	SE		SE 1	SE	SE 1	SE
Margate 4 d									05 53							06 53								07 53
Broadstairs d									05 59							06 59								07 59
Ramsgate 4 d	21p22			05 05			05 32		06 05		05 50		06 22		06 40	07 05	06 50				07 22		07 40	08 05
Minster 4 d							05 38								06 46								07 46	
Sandwich d	21p34										06 02		06 34				07 02				07 34			
Deal d	21p40										06 08		06 40				07 08				07 40			
Walmer d	21p43										06 11		06 43				07 11				07 43			
Martin Mill d	21p48										06 16		06 48				07 16				07 48			
Dover Priory 4 a	21p56										06 24		06 56				07 24				07 56			
d	21p57		04 50		05 44			05 50			06 24	06 44	06 57				07 24		07 44		07 57			
Folkestone Central d	22p09		05 02		05 56			06 02			06 36	06 56	07 09				07 36		07 56		08 09			
Folkestone West d	22p11		05 04		05 58			06 04			06 38	06 58	07 11				07 38		07 58		08 11			
Sandling d	22p16		05 09					06 09			06 43		07 16				07 43				08 16			
Westenhanger d	22p19		05 12					06 12			06 46		07 19				07 46				08 19			
Sturry d							05 50								06 58								07 58	
Canterbury West 4 d				05 25			05 56		06 25						07 03	07 25		07 36					08 07	08 25
Chartham d							06 01								07 08			07 41						
Chilham d							06 04								07 11			07 44						
Wye d							06 11								07 18			07 51					08 19	
Ashford International a	22p28		05 21	05 41	06 11		06 17	06 21	06 41		06 55	07 11	07 28		07 24	07 41	07 55	07 58	08 11		08 28		08 25	08 41
d	22p33	05 13	05 25	05 43	06 13		06 25		06 43		07 03	07 13			07 33	07 43	08 03		08 13				08 33	08 43
Pluckley d	22p39		05 31				06 31				07 09				07 39		08 09						08 39	
Headcorn d	22p46		05 38				06 38				07 16				07 46		08 16						08 46	
Staplehurst d	22p51		05 43				06 43				07 21				07 51		08 21						08 51	
Marden d	22p55		05 47				06 47				07 25				07 55		08 25						08 55	
Maidstone West 4 194 d						06 28								07 28								08 28		
Paddock Wood 4 d	23p01		05 53			06 47	06 53				07 31			07 47	08 01		08 31					08 47	09 01	
Tonbridge 4 a	23p10		06 01			06 55	07 01				07 39			07 55	08 09		08 39					08 55	09 09	
d	23p14		06 02				07 02				07 40				08 10		08 40						09 10	
Sevenoaks 4 a	23p24		06 13				07 13				07 48				08 18		08 48						09 18	
Orpington 4 a	23p36		06 23				07 23																	
London Bridge 4 ⊖ a	23p53		06 39				07 39				08 13				08 43		09 13						09 43	
London Cannon Street 4 ⊖ a																								
London Waterloo (East) 4 ⊖ a	23p57		06 43				07 43				08 19				08 49		09 19						09 49	
London Charing Cross 4 ⊖ a	00 01		06 47				07 48				08 22				08 52		09 22						09 52	
Ebbsfleet International a		05 32		06 02	06 32				07 02			07 32				08 02			08 32					09 02
Stratford International ⊖ a		05 44		06 14	06 44				07 14			07 44				08 14			08 44					09 14
St Pancras Intl. 15 ⊖ a		05 51		06 21	06 51				07 21			07 51				08 21			08 51					09 21

Table 207 | **Saturdays**

Margate, Ramsgate, Canterbury West, Dover, Folkestone, Ashford International - Tonbridge and London

		SE [1]	SE [1]	SE	SE [1]	SE	SE [1]	SE	SE [1]	SE [1]	SE	SE [1]	SE	SE [1]	SE	SE [1]	SE [1]	SE	SE [1]	SE	SE [1]	SE
Margate [4]	d							08 53							09 53							10 53
Broadstairs	d							08 59							09 59							10 59
Ramsgate [4]	d	07 50			08 22		08 40	09 05	08 50			09 22		09 40	10 05	09 50			10 22		10 40	11 05
Minster [4]	d						08 46							09 46							10 46	
Sandwich	d	08 02			08 34				09 02			09 34				10 02			10 34			
Deal	d	08 08			08 40				09 08			09 40				10 08			10 40			
Walmer	d	08 11			08 43				09 11			09 43				10 11			10 43			
Martin Mill	d	08 16			08 48				09 16			09 48				10 16			10 48			
Dover Priory [4]	a	08 24			08 56				09 24			09 56				10 24			10 56			
	d	08 24		08 44	08 57				09 24		09 44	09 57				10 24		10 44	10 57			
Folkestone Central	d	08 36		08 56	09 09				09 36		09 56	10 09				10 36		10 56	11 09			
Folkestone West	d	08 38		08 58	09 11				09 38		09 58	10 11				10 38		10 58	11 11			
Sandling	d	08 43			09 16				09 43			10 16				10 43			11 16			
Westenhanger	d	08 46			09 19				09 46			10 19				10 46			11 19			
Sturry	d						08 58							09 58							10 58	
Canterbury West [4]	d		08 36				09 07	09 25		09 36				10 07	10 25		10 36				11 07	11 25
Chartham	d		08 41							09 41							10 41					
Chilham	d		08 44							09 44							10 44					
Wye	d		08 51				09 19			09 51				10 19			10 51				11 19	
Ashford International	a	08 55	08 58	09 11	09 28		09 25	09 41	09 55	09 58	10 11	10 28		10 25	10 41	10 55	10 58	11 11	11 28		11 25	11 41
	d	09 03		09 13			09 33	09 43	10 03		10 13			10 33	10 43	11 03		11 13			11 33	11 43
Pluckley	d	09 09					09 39		10 09					10 39		11 09					11 39	
Headcorn	d	09 16					09 46		10 16					10 46		11 16					11 46	
Staplehurst	d	09 21					09 51		10 21					10 51		11 21					11 51	
Marden	d	09 25					09 55		10 25					10 55		11 25					11 55	
Maidstone West [4] 194	d					09 28							10 28							11 28		
Paddock Wood [4]	d	09 31				09 47	10 01		10 31				10 47	11 01		11 31				11 47	12 01	
Tonbridge [4]	a	09 39				09 55	10 09		10 39				10 55	11 09		11 39				11 55	12 09	
	d	09 40					10 10		10 40					11 10		11 40					12 10	
Sevenoaks [4]	a	09 48					10 18		10 48					11 18		11 48					12 18	
Orpington [4]	a																					
London Bridge [4] ⊖	a	10 13					10 43		11 13					11 43		12 13					12 43	
London Cannon Street [4] ⊖	a																					
London Waterloo (East) [4] ⊖	a	10 19					10 49		11 19					11 49		12 19					12 49	
London Charing Cross [4] ⊖	a	10 22					10 52		11 22					11 52		12 22					12 52	
Ebbsfleet International	a			09 32				10 02			10 32				11 02			11 32				12 02
Stratford International ⊖	a			09 44				10 14			10 44				11 14			11 44				12 14
St Pancras Intl. [15] ⊖	a			09 51				10 21			10 51				11 21			11 51				12 21

		SE [1]	SE [1]	SE	SE [1]	SE	SE [1]	SE	SE [1]	SE [1]	SE	SE [1]	SE	SE [1]	SE	SE [1]	SE [1]	SE	SE [1]	SE	SE [1]	SE
Margate [4]	d							11 53							12 53							13 53
Broadstairs	d							11 59							12 59							13 59
Ramsgate [4]	d	10 50			11 22		11 40	12 05	11 50			12 22		12 40	13 05	12 50			13 22		13 40	14 05
Minster [4]	d						11 46							12 46							13 46	
Sandwich	d	11 02			11 34				12 02			12 34				13 02			13 34			
Deal	d	11 08			11 40				12 08			12 40				13 08			13 40			
Walmer	d	11 11			11 43				12 11			12 43				13 11			13 43			
Martin Mill	d	11 16			11 48				12 16			12 48				13 16			13 48			
Dover Priory [4]	a	11 24			11 56				12 24			12 56				13 24			13 56			
	d	11 24		11 44	11 57				12 24		12 44	12 57				13 24		13 44	13 57			
Folkestone Central	d	11 36		11 56	12 09				12 36		12 56	13 09				13 36		13 56	14 09			
Folkestone West	d	11 38		11 58	12 11				12 38		12 58	13 11				13 38		13 58	14 11			
Sandling	d	11 43			12 16				12 43			13 16				13 43			14 16			
Westenhanger	d	11 46			12 19				12 46			13 19				13 46			14 19			
Sturry	d						11 58							12 58							13 58	
Canterbury West [4]	d		11 36				12 07	12 25		12 36				13 07	13 25		13 36				14 07	14 25
Chartham	d		11 41							12 41							13 41					
Chilham	d		11 44							12 44							13 44					
Wye	d		11 51				12 19			12 51				13 19			13 51				14 19	
Ashford International	a	11 55	11 58	12 11	12 28		12 25	12 41	12 55	12 58	13 11	13 28		13 25	13 41	13 55	13 58	14 11	14 28		14 25	14 41
	d	12 03		12 13			12 33	12 43	13 03		13 13			13 33	13 43	14 03		14 13			14 33	14 43
Pluckley	d	12 09					12 39		13 09					13 39		14 09					14 39	
Headcorn	d	12 16					12 46		13 16					13 46		14 16					14 46	
Staplehurst	d	12 21					12 51		13 21					13 51		14 21					14 51	
Marden	d	12 25					12 55		13 25					13 55		14 25					14 55	
Maidstone West [4] 194	d					12 28							13 28							14 28		
Paddock Wood [4]	d	12 31				12 47	13 01		13 31				13 47	14 01		14 31				14 47	15 01	
Tonbridge [4]	a	12 39				12 55	13 09		13 39				13 55	14 09		14 39				14 55	15 09	
	d	12 40					13 10		13 40					14 10		14 40					15 10	
Sevenoaks [4]	a	12 48					13 18		13 48					14 18		14 48					15 18	
Orpington [4]	a																					
London Bridge [4] ⊖	a	13 13					13 43		14 13					14 43		15 13					15 43	
London Cannon Street [4] ⊖	a																					
London Waterloo (East) [4] ⊖	a	13 19					13 49		14 19					14 49		15 19					15 49	
London Charing Cross [4] ⊖	a	13 22					13 52		14 22					14 52		15 22					15 52	
Ebbsfleet International	a			12 32				13 02			13 32				14 02			14 32				15 02
Stratford International ⊖	a			12 45				13 14			13 44				14 14			14 44				15 14
St Pancras Intl. [15] ⊖	a			12 54				13 21			13 51				14 21			14 51				15 21

Table 207

Saturdays

Margate, Ramsgate, Canterbury West, Dover, Folkestone, Ashford International - Tonbridge and London

		SE [1]	SE [1]	SE	SE [1]	SE	SE [1]	SE	SE [1]	SE [1]	SE	SE [1]	SE	SE [1]	SE	SE [1]	SE [1]	SE	SE [1]	SE	SE [1]	SE
Margate [4]	d							14 53							15 53							16 53
Broadstairs	d							14 59							15 59							16 59
Ramsgate [4]	d	13 50			14 22		14 40	15 05	14 50			15 22		15 40	16 05	15 50			16 22		16 40	17 05
Minster [4]	d						14 46							15 46							16 46	
Sandwich	d	14 02			14 34				15 02			15 34				16 02			16 34			
Deal	d	14 08			14 40				15 08			15 40				16 08			16 40			
Walmer	d	14 11			14 43				15 11			15 43				16 11			16 43			
Martin Mill	d	14 16			14 48				15 16			15 48				16 16			16 48			
Dover Priory [4]	a	14 24			14 56				15 24			15 56				16 24			16 56			
	d	14 24		14 44	14 57				15 24		15 44	15 57				16 24		16 44	16 57			
Folkestone Central	d	14 36		14 56	15 09				15 36		15 56	16 09				16 36		16 56	17 09			
Folkestone West	d	14 38		14 58	15 11				15 38		15 58	16 11				16 38		16 58	17 11			
Sandling	d	14 43			15 16				15 43			16 16				16 43			17 16			
Westenhanger	d	14 46			15 19				15 46			16 19				16 46			17 19			
Sturry	d						14 58							15 58							16 58	
Canterbury West [4]	d		14 36				15 07	15 25		15 36				16 07	16 25		16 36				17 07	17 25
Chartham	d		14 41							15 41							16 41					
Chilham	d		14 44							15 44							16 44					
Wye	d		14 51				15 19			15 51				16 19			16 51				17 19	
Ashford International	a	14 55	14 58	15 11	15 28		15 25	15 41	15 55	15 58	16 11	16 28		16 25	16 41	16 55	16 58	17 11	17 28		17 25	17 41
	d	15 03		15 13			15 33	15 43	16 03		16 13			16 33	16 43	17 03		17 13			17 33	17 43
Pluckley	d	15 09					15 39		16 09					16 39		17 09					17 39	
Headcorn	d	15 16					15 46		16 16					16 46		17 16					17 46	
Staplehurst	d	15 21					15 51		16 21					16 51		17 21					17 51	
Marden	d	15 25					15 55		16 25					16 55		17 25					17 55	
Maidstone West [4] 194	d					15 28							16 28							17 28		
Paddock Wood [4]	d	15 31				15 47	16 01		16 31				16 47	17 01		17 31				17 47	18 01	
Tonbridge [4]	a	15 39				15 55	16 09		16 39				16 55	17 09		17 39				17 55	18 09	
	d	15 40					16 10		16 40					17 10		17 40					18 10	
Sevenoaks [4]	a	15 48					16 18		16 48					17 18		17 48					18 18	
Orpington [4]	a																					
London Bridge [4] ⊖	a	16 13					16 43		17 13					17 43		18 13					18 43	
London Cannon Street [4] ⊖	a																					
London Waterloo (East) [4] ⊖	a	16 19					16 49		17 19					17 49		18 19					18 49	
London Charing Cross [4] ⊖	a	16 22					16 52		17 22					17 52		18 22					18 52	
Ebbsfleet International	a			15 32				16 02			16 32				17 02			17 32				18 02
Stratford International ⊖	a			15 44				16 14			16 44				17 14			17 44				18 14
St Pancras Intl. [15] ⊖	a			15 51				16 21			16 51				17 21			17 51				18 21

		SE [1]	SE [1]	SE	SE [1]	SE	SE [1]	SE	SE [1]	SE [1]	SE	SE [1]	SE	SE [1]	SE	SE [1]	SE [1]	SE	SE [1]	SE	SE [1]	SE	SE [1]
Margate [4]	d							17 53							18 53							19 53	
Broadstairs	d							17 59							18 59							19 59	
Ramsgate [4]	d	16 50			17 22		17 40	18 05	17 50			18 22		18 40	19 05	18 50			19 22		19 40	20 05	19 50
Minster [4]	d						17 46							18 46							19 46		
Sandwich	d	17 02			17 34				18 02			18 34				19 02			19 34				20 02
Deal	d	17 08			17 40				18 08			18 40				19 08			19 40				20 08
Walmer	d	17 11			17 43				18 11			18 43				19 11			19 43				20 11
Martin Mill	d	17 16			17 48				18 16			18 48				19 16			19 48				20 16
Dover Priory [4]	a	17 24			17 56				18 24			18 56				19 24			19 56				20 24
	d	17 24		17 44	17 57				18 24		18 44	18 57				19 24		19 44	19 57				20 24
Folkestone Central	d	17 36		17 56	18 09				18 36		18 56	19 09				19 36		19 56	20 09				20 36
Folkestone West	d	17 38		17 58	18 11				18 38		18 58	19 11				19 38		19 58	20 11				20 38
Sandling	d	17 43			18 16				18 43			19 16				19 43			20 16				20 43
Westenhanger	d	17 46			18 19				18 46			19 19				19 46			20 19				20 46
Sturry	d						17 58							18 58							19 58		
Canterbury West [4]	d		17 36				18 07	18 25		18 36				19 07	19 25		19 36				20 04	20 25	
Chartham	d		17 41							18 41							19 41				20 09		
Chilham	d		17 44							18 44							19 44				20 12		
Wye	d		17 51				18 19			18 51				19 19			19 51				20 19		
Ashford International	a	17 55	17 58	18 11	18 28		18 25	18 41	18 55	18 58	19 11	19 28		19 25	19 41	19 55	19 58	20 11	20 28		20 25	20 41	20 55
	d	18 03		18 13			18 33	18 43	19 03		19 13			19 33	19 43	20 03		20 13			20 33	20 47	21 03
Pluckley	d	18 09					18 39		19 09					19 39		20 09					20 39		21 09
Headcorn	d	18 16					18 46		19 16					19 46		20 16					20 46		21 16
Staplehurst	d	18 21					18 51		19 21					19 51		20 21					20 51		21 21
Marden	d	18 25					18 55		19 25					19 55		20 25					20 55		21 25
Maidstone West [4] 194	d					18 28							19 28							20 28			
Paddock Wood [4]	d	18 31				18 47	19 01		19 31				19 47	20 01		20 31				20 47	21 01		21 31
Tonbridge [4]	a	18 39				18 55	19 09		19 39				19 55	20 09		20 39				20 55	21 09		21 39
	d	18 40					19 10		19 40					20 10		20 40					21 10		21 40
Sevenoaks [4]	a	18 48					19 18		19 48					20 18		20 48					21 18		21 48
Orpington [4]	a						19 27		19 57					20 27		20 57					21 27		21 57
London Bridge [4] ⊖	a	19 13					19 43		20 13					20 43		21 13					21 43		22 13
London Cannon Street [4] ⊖	a																						
London Waterloo (East) [4] ⊖	a	19 19					19 48		20 18					20 48		21 18					21 48		22 18
London Charing Cross [4] ⊖	a	19 22					19 51		20 21					20 51		21 21					21 51		22 21
Ebbsfleet International	a			18 32				19 02			19 32				20 02			20 32				21 06	
Stratford International ⊖	a			18 44				19 14			19 44				20 14			20 44				21 18	
St Pancras Intl. [15] ⊖	a			18 51				19 21			19 51				20 21			20 51				21 25	

Table 207

Saturdays

Margate, Ramsgate, Canterbury West, Dover, Folkestone, Ashford International - Tonbridge and London

		SE	SE 1	SE		SE 1	SE	SE 1	SE	SE	SE 1	SE	SE 1	SE		SE 1
Margate 4	d						20 53					21 53				
Broadstairs	d						20 59					21 59				
Ramsgate 4	d		20 22			20 40	21 05	20 50			21 22	22 05	22 24			22 45
Minster 4	d					20 46							22 30			
Sandwich	d		20 34					21 02			21 34					22 57
Deal	d		20 40					21 08			21 40					23 03
Walmer	d		20 43					21 11			21 43					23 06
Martin Mill	d		20 48					21 16			21 48					23 11
Dover Priory 4	a		20 56					21 24			21 56					23 19
	d	20 44	20 57					21 24	21 44		21 57			22 44		23 24
Folkestone Central	d	20 56	21 09					21 36	21 56		22 09			22 56		23 36
Folkestone West	d	20 58	21 11					21 38	21 58		22 11			22 58		23 38
Sandling	d		21 16					21 43			22 16					23 43
Westenhanger	d		21 19					21 46			22 19					23 46
Sturry	d					20 58							22 42			
Canterbury West 4	d					21 04	21 25					22 25	22 47			
Chartham	d					21 09							22 52			
Chilham	d					21 12							22 55			
Wye	d					21 19							23 02			
Ashford International	a	21 11	21 28			21 25	21 41	21 55	22 11		22 28	22 41	23 08	23 11		23 55
	d	21 13				21 33	21 43	22 03	22 13		22 33	22 43		23 13		
Pluckley	d					21 39		22 09			22 39					
Headcorn	d					21 46		22 16			22 46					
Staplehurst	d					21 51		22 21			22 51					
Marden	d					21 55		22 25			22 55					
Maidstone West 4 194	d			21 28						22 28						
Paddock Wood 4	d			21 47		22 01		22 31		22 47	23 01					
Tonbridge 4	a			21 55		22 09		22 39		22 55	23 10					
	d					22 10		22 40								
Sevenoaks 4	a					22 18		22 48								
Orpington 4	a					22 27		22 57								
London Bridge 4 ⊖	a					22 43		23 13								
London Cannon Street 4 ⊖	a															
London Waterloo (East) 4 ⊖	a					22 48		23 18								
London Charing Cross 4 ⊖	a					22 51		23 21								
Ebbsfleet International	a	21 32					22 02		22 32			23 02		23 32		
Stratford International ⊖	a	21 44					22 14		22 44			23 14		23 44		
St Pancras Intl. 15 ⊖	a	21 51					22 21		22 51			23 21		23 51		

Sundays

		SE 1 A	SE 1	SE	SE 1	SE 1	SE	SE 1	SE	SE 1		SE 1	SE	SE	SE 1	SE	SE 1	SE 1	SE	SE		SE 1	SE 1	SE	SE 1
Margate 4	d												07 53						08 53						
Broadstairs	d												07 59						08 59						
Ramsgate 4	d	21p22						06 50		07 23		07 40	08 05		07 50		08 23	08 40	09 05			08 50			09 23
Minster 4	d	⟆										07 46						08 46							
Sandwich	d	21p34						07 02		07 35					08 02		08 35					09 02			09 35
Deal	d	21p40						07 08		07 41					08 08		08 41					09 08			09 41
Walmer	d	21p43						07 11		07 44					08 11		08 44					09 11			09 44
Martin Mill	d	21p48						07 16		07 49					08 16		08 49					09 16			09 49
Dover Priory 4	a	21p56						07 24		07 57					08 24		08 57					09 24			09 57
	d	21p57						07 24	07 44	07 58					08 24	08 44	08 58					09 24		09 44	09 58
Folkestone Central	d	22p09						07 36	07 56	08 10					08 36	08 56	09 10					09 36		09 56	10 10
Folkestone West	d	22p11						07 38	07 58	08 12					08 38	08 58	09 12					09 38		09 58	10 12
Sandling	d	22p16						07 43		08 17					08 43		09 17					09 43			10 17
Westenhanger	d	22p19						07 46							08 46							09 46			
Sturry	d	⟆										07 58						08 58							
Canterbury West 4	d	⟆										08 04	08 25					09 04	09 25				09 36		
Chartham	d	⟆										08 09						09 09					09 41		
Chilham	d	⟆										08 12						09 12					09 44		
Wye	d	⟆										08 19						09 19					09 51		
Ashford International	a	22p28						07 55	08 11	08 28		08 25	08 41		08 55	09 11	09 28	09 25	09 41			09 55	09 58	10 11	10 28
	d	22p33	06 33		07 03	07 33		08 03	08 13			08 33	08 43		09 03	09 13		09 33	09 43			10 03		10 13	
Pluckley	d	22p39	06 39			07 39						08 39						09 39							
Headcorn	d	22p46	06 46		07 14	07 46		08 14				08 46			09 14			09 46				10 14			
Staplehurst	d	22p51	06 51		07 19	07 51		08 19				08 51			09 19			09 51				10 19			
Marden	d	22p55	06 55		07 23	07 55		08 23				08 55			09 23			09 55				10 23			
Maidstone West 4 194	d	⟆		07 03			08 03							09 03						10 03					
Paddock Wood 4	d	23p01	07 01	07a22	07 29	08 01	08a22	08 29				09 01		09a22	09 29			10 01		10a22		10 29			
Tonbridge 4	a	23p10	07 09		07 38	08 09		08 38				09 09			09 38			10 09				10 38			
	d	23p14	07 10		07 39	08 10		08 39				09 10			09 39			10 10				10 39			
Sevenoaks 4	a	23p24	07 18		07 49	08 18		08 49				09 18			09 49			10 18				10 49			
Orpington 4	a	23p36	07 28		07 58	08 28		08 58				09 28			09 58			10 28				10 58			
London Bridge 4 ⊖	a	23p53	07 44		08 14	08 44		09 14				09 44			10 14			10 44				11 14			
London Cannon Street 4 ⊖	a	⟆																							
London Waterloo (East) 4 ⊖	a	23p57	07 49		08 19	08 49		09 19				09 49			10 19			10 49				11 19			
London Charing Cross 4 ⊖	a	00 01	07 53		08 23	08 53		09 23				09 53			10 23			10 53				11 23			
Ebbsfleet International	a								08 32				09 02			09 32			10 02					10 32	
Stratford International ⊖	a								08 44				09 14			09 44			10 14					10 44	
St Pancras Intl. 15 ⊖	a								08 51				09 21			09 51			10 21					10 51	

A not 22 May

Table 207

Sundays

Margate, Ramsgate, Canterbury West, Dover, Folkestone, Ashford International - Tonbridge and London

		SE [1]	SE	SE	SE [1]	SE [1]		SE	SE [1]	SE [1]	SE	SE	SE [1]	SE [1]	SE	SE [1]		SE [1]	SE	SE	SE [1]	SE [1]	SE	SE [1]	SE [1]
Margate [4]	d		09 53								10 53								11 53						
Broadstairs	d		09 59								10 59								11 59						
Ramsgate [4]	d	09 40	10 05		09 50				10 23	10 40	11 05		10 50			11 23		11 40	12 05		11 50			12 23	12 40
Minster [4]	d	09 46								10 46								11 46							12 46
Sandwich	d				10 02				10 35				11 02			11 35					12 02			12 35	
Deal	d				10 08				10 41				11 08			11 41					12 08			12 41	
Walmer	d				10 11				10 44				11 11			11 44					12 11			12 44	
Martin Mill	d				10 16				10 49				11 16			11 49					12 16			12 49	
Dover Priory [4]	a				10 24				10 57				11 24			11 57					12 24			12 57	
	d				10 24			10 44	10 58				11 24		11 44	11 58					12 24		12 44	12 58	
Folkestone Central	d				10 36			10 56	11 10				11 36		11 56	12 10					12 36		12 56	13 10	
Folkestone West	d				10 38			10 58	11 12				11 38		11 58	12 12					12 38		12 58	13 12	
Sandling	d				10 43				11 17				11 43			12 17					12 43			13 17	
Westenhanger	d				10 46								11 46								12 46				
Sturry	d	09 58								10 58								11 58							12 58
Canterbury West [4]	d	10 07	10 25			10 36				11 07	11 25			11 36				12 07	12 25			12 36			13 07
Chartham	d					10 41								11 41								12 41			
Chilham	d					10 44								11 44								12 44			
Wye	d	10 19				10 51				11 19				11 51				12 19				12 51			13 19
Ashford International	a	10 25	10 41		10 55	10 58		11 11	11 28	11 25	11 41		11 55	11 58	12 11	12 28		12 25	12 41		12 55	12 58	13 11	13 28	13 25
	d	10 33	10 43		11 03			11 13		11 33	11 43		12 03		12 13			12 33	12 43		13 03		13 13		13 33
Pluckley	d	10 39								11 39								12 39							13 39
Headcorn	d	10 46			11 14					11 46			12 14					12 46			13 14				13 46
Staplehurst	d	10 51			11 19					11 51			12 19					12 51			13 19				13 51
Marden	d	10 55			11 23					11 55			12 23					12 55			13 23				13 55
Maidstone West [4] 194	d			11 03								12 03								13 03					
Paddock Wood [4]	d	11 01		11a22	11 29					12 01		12a22	12 29					13 01		13a22	13 29				14 01
Tonbridge [4]	a	11 09			11 38					12 09			12 38					13 09			13 38				14 09
	d	11 10			11 39					12 10			12 39					13 10			13 39				14 10
Sevenoaks [4]	a	11 18			11 49					12 18			12 49					13 18			13 49				14 18
Orpington [4]	a	11 28			11 58					12 28			12 58					13 28			13 58				14 28
London Bridge [4] ⊖	a	11 44			12 14					12 44			13 14					13 44			14 14				14 44
London Cannon Street [4] ⊖	a																								
London Waterloo (East) [4] ⊖	a	11 49			12 19					12 49			13 19					13 49			14 19				14 49
London Charing Cross [4] ⊖	a	11 53			12 23					12 53			13 23					13 53			14 23				14 53
Ebbsfleet International	a		11 02					11 32			12 02				12 32				13 02				13 32		
Stratford International ⊖	a		11 14					11 44			12 14				12 45				13 14				13 44		
St Pancras Intl. [15] ⊖	a		11 21					11 51			12 21				12 54				13 21				13 51		

		SE		SE	SE [1]	SE [1]	SE	SE [1]	SE [1] A 🛒	SE	SE	SE [1]	SE [1]		SE	SE [1]	SE [1]	SE	SE	SE [1]	SE [1]	SE	SE [1]		SE [1]
Margate [4]	d	12 53								13 53								14 53							
Broadstairs	d	12 59								13 59								14 59							
Ramsgate [4]	d	13 05			12 50			13 23	13 40	14 05		13 50				14 23	14 40	15 05		14 50			15 23		15 40
Minster [4]	d								13 46								14 46								15 46
Sandwich	d				13 02			13 35				14 02				14 35				15 02			15 35		
Deal	d				13 08			13 41				14 08				14 41				15 08			15 41		
Walmer	d				13 11			13 44				14 11				14 44				15 11			15 44		
Martin Mill	d				13 16			13 49				14 16				14 49				15 16			15 49		
Dover Priory [4]	a				13 24			13 57				14 24				14 57				15 24			15 57		
	d				13 24		13 44	13 58				14 24			14 44	14 58				15 24		15 44	15 58		
Folkestone Central	d				13 36		13 56	14 10				14 36			14 56	15 10				15 36		15 56	16 10		
Folkestone West	d				13 38		13 58	14 12				14 38			14 58	15 12				15 38		15 58	16 12		
Sandling	d				13 43			14 17				14 43				15 17				15 43			16 17		
Westenhanger	d				13 46							14 46								15 46					
Sturry	d								13 58								14 58								15 58
Canterbury West [4]	d	13 25				13 36			14 07	14 25			14 36				15 07	15 25			15 36				16 07
Chartham	d					13 41							14 41								15 41				
Chilham	d					13 44							14 44								15 44				
Wye	d					13 51			14 19				14 51				15 19				15 51				16 19
Ashford International	a	13 41			13 55	13 58	14 11	14 28	14 25	14 41		14 55	14 58		15 11	15 28	15 25	15 41		15 55	15 58	16 11	16 28		16 25
	d	13 43			14 03		14 13		14 33	14 43		15 03			15 13		15 33	15 43		16 03		16 13			16 33
Pluckley	d								14 39								15 39								16 39
Headcorn	d				14 14				14 46			15 14					15 46			16 14					16 46
Staplehurst	d				14 19				14 51			15 19					15 51			16 19					16 51
Marden	d				14 23				14 55			15 23					15 55			16 23					16 55
Maidstone West [4] 194	d			14 03							15 03								16 03						
Paddock Wood [4]	d			14a22	14 29				15 01		15a22	15 29					16 01		16a22	16 29					17 01
Tonbridge [4]	a				14 38				15 09			15 38					16 09			16 38					17 09
	d				14 39				15 10			15 39					16 10			16 39					17 10
Sevenoaks [4]	a				14 49				15 18			15 49					16 18			16 49					17 18
Orpington [4]	a				14 58				15 28			15 58					16 28			16 58					17 28
London Bridge [4] ⊖	a				15 14				15 44			16 14					16 44			17 14					17 44
London Cannon Street [4] ⊖	a																								
London Waterloo (East) [4] ⊖	a				15 19				15 49			16 19					16 49			17 19					17 49
London Charing Cross [4] ⊖	a				15 23				15 53			16 23					16 53			17 23					17 53
Ebbsfleet International	a	14 02					14 32			15 02					15 32			16 02				16 32			
Stratford International ⊖	a	14 14					14 44			15 14					15 44			16 14				16 44			
St Pancras Intl. [15] ⊖	a	14 21					14 51			15 21					15 51			16 21				16 51			

A 🛒 from Ashford International

Table 207

Sundays

Margate, Ramsgate, Canterbury West, Dover, Folkestone, Ashford International - Tonbridge and London

		SE	SE	SE	SE	SE	SE	SE	SE		SE	SE	SE	SE	SE	SE	SE	SE	SE	SE		SE	SE	SE	SE
				[1]	[1]		[1]	[1]				[1]	[1]		[1]	[1]			[1]	[1]			[1]	[1]	
Margate [4]	d	15 53							16 53								17 53								18 53
Broadstairs	d	15 59							16 59								17 59								18 59
Ramsgate [4]	d	16 05		15 50			16 23	16 40	17 05			16 50			17 23	17 40	18 05		17 50				18 23	18 40	19 05
Minster [4]	d							16 46								17 46								18 46	
Sandwich	d			16 02			16 35					17 02			17 35				18 02				18 35		
Deal	d			16 08			16 41					17 08			17 41				18 08				18 41		
Walmer	d			16 11			16 44					17 11			17 44				18 11				18 44		
Martin Mill	d			16 16			16 49					17 16			17 49				18 16				18 49		
Dover Priory [4]	a			16 24			16 57					17 24			17 57				18 24				18 57		
	d			16 24		16 44	16 58					17 24		17 44	17 58				18 24			18 44	18 58		
Folkestone Central	d			16 36		16 56	17 10					17 36		17 56	18 10				18 36			18 56	19 10		
Folkestone West	d			16 38		16 58	17 12					17 38		17 58	18 12				18 38			18 58	19 12		
Sandling	d			16 43			17 17					17 43			18 17				18 43				19 17		
Westenhanger	d			16 46								17 46							18 46						
Sturry	d							16 58								17 58								18 58	
Canterbury West [4]	d	16 25			16 36			17 07	17 25				17 36			18 07	18 25			18 36				19 04	19 25
Chartham	d				16 41								17 41							18 41				19 09	
Chilham	d				16 44								17 44							18 44				19 12	
Wye	d				16 51			17 19					17 51			18 19				18 51				19 19	
Ashford International	a	16 41		16 55	16 58	17 11	17 28	17 25	17 41			17 55	17 58	18 11	18 28	18 25	18 41		18 55	18 58		19 11	19 28	19 25	19 41
	d	16 43		17 03		17 13		17 33	17 43			18 03		18 13		18 33	18 43		19 03			19 13		19 33	19 43
Pluckley	d							17 39								18 39								19 39	
Headcorn	d			17 14				17 46				18 14				18 46			19 14					19 46	
Staplehurst	d			17 19				17 51				18 19				18 51			19 19					19 51	
Marden	d			17 23				17 55				18 23				18 55			19 23					19 55	
Maidstone West [4] 194	d		17 03								18 03							19 03							
Paddock Wood [4]	d		17a22	17 29				18 01			18a22	18 29				19 01		19a22	19 29					20 01	
Tonbridge [4]	a			17 38				18 09				18 38				19 09			19 38					20 09	
	d			17 39				18 10				18 39				19 10			19 39					20 10	
Sevenoaks [4]	a			17 49				18 18				18 49				19 18			19 49					20 18	
Orpington [4]	a			17 58				18 28				18 58				19 28			19 58					20 28	
London Bridge [4] ⊖	a			18 14				18 44				19 14				19 44			20 14					20 44	
London Cannon Street [4] ⊖	a																								
London Waterloo (East) [4] ⊖	a			18 19				18 49				19 19				19 49			20 19					20 49	
London Charing Cross [4] ⊖	a			18 23				18 53				19 23				19 53			20 23					20 53	
Ebbsfleet International	a	17 02				17 32			18 02					18 32			19 02					19 32			20 02
Stratford International ⊖	a	17 14				17 44			18 14					18 44			19 14					19 44			20 14
St Pancras Intl. [15] ⊖	a	17 21				17 51			18 21					18 51			19 21					19 51			20 21

		SE	SE	SE	SE	SE		SE	SE	SE	SE	SE	SE	SE	SE	SE		SE	SE	SE	SE				
			[1]		[1]	[1]				[1]		[1]	[1]			[1]			[1]		[1]				
Margate [4]	d							19 53						20 53						21 53					
Broadstairs	d							19 59						20 59						21 59					
Ramsgate [4]	d		18 50		19 23	19 40		20 05		19 50		20 23	20 40	21 05		20 50			21 40	22 05	21 50				
Minster [4]	d					19 46							20 46						21 46						
Sandwich	d		19 02		19 35					20 02		20 35				21 02					22 02				
Deal	d		19 08		19 41					20 08		20 41				21 08					22 08				
Walmer	d		19 11		19 44					20 11		20 44				21 11					22 11				
Martin Mill	d		19 16		19 49					20 16		20 49				21 16					22 16				
Dover Priory [4]	a		19 24		19 57					20 24		20 57				21 24					22 24				
	d		19 24	19 44	19 58					20 24	20 44	20 58				21 24		21 44			22 24				
Folkestone Central	d		19 36	19 56	20 10					20 36	20 56	21 10				21 36		21 56			22 36				
Folkestone West	d		19 38	19 58	20 12					20 38	20 58	21 12				21 38		21 58			22 38				
Sandling	d		19 43		20 17					20 43		21 17				21 43					22 43				
Westenhanger	d		19 46							20 46						21 46					22 46				
Sturry	d					19 58							20 58						21 58						
Canterbury West [4]	d					20 04		20 25					21 04	21 25					22 04	22 25					
Chartham	d					20 09							21 09						22 09						
Chilham	d					20 12							21 12						22 12						
Wye	d					20 19							21 19						22 19						
Ashford International	a		19 55	20 11	20 28	20 25		20 41		20 55	21 11	21 28	21 25	21 41		21 55		22 11	22 25	22 41	22 55				
	d		20 03	20 13		20 33		20 47		21 03	21 13		21 33	21 43		22 03		22 13		22 43					
Pluckley	d					20 39							21 39												
Headcorn	d		20 14			20 46				21 14			21 46			22 14									
Staplehurst	d		20 19			20 51				21 19			21 51			22 19									
Marden	d		20 23			20 55				21 23			21 55			22 23									
Maidstone West [4] 194	d	20 03							21 03						22 03										
Paddock Wood [4]	d	20a22	20 29			21 01			21a22	21 29			22 01		22 23	22 29									
Tonbridge [4]	a		20 38			21 09				21 38			22 09		22 32	22 38									
	d		20 39			21 10				21 39			22 10			22 39									
Sevenoaks [4]	a		20 49			21 18				21 49			22 18			22 49									
Orpington [4]	a		20 58			21 28				21 58			22 28			22 58									
London Bridge [4] ⊖	a		21 14			21 44				22 14			22 44			23 14									
London Cannon Street [4] ⊖	a																								
London Waterloo (East) [4] ⊖	a		21 19			21 49				22 19			22 49			23 19									
London Charing Cross [4] ⊖	a		21 23			21 53				22 23			22 53			23 23									
Ebbsfleet International	a			20 32				21 06			21 32			22 02				22 32		23 02					
Stratford International ⊖	a			20 44				21 18			21 44			22 14				22 44		23 14					
St Pancras Intl. [15] ⊖	a			20 51				21 25			21 51			22 21				22 51		23 21					

Strood - Maidstone West and Paddock Wood

Miles				SE	SE	SE	SE	SE	SE	SE	SE	SE	SE	SE	SE	SE	SE	SE	SE	SE	SE	SE	SE	SE
—	St Pancras International		d					06 25																
—	Stratford International		d					06 32																
—	Ebbsfleet International		d					06 42																
—	Gravesend		d					06 46																
0	**Strood** ■4		d	04 55	05 33	06 03	06 35	06 57	07 18	07 55	08 35	09 05	09 35	10 05	10 35	11 05	11 35	12 05	12 35	13 05	13 35	14 05	14 35	15 05
2¼	Cuxton		d	04 59	05 37	06 07	06 39		07 22	07 59	08 39	09 09	09 39	10 09	10 39	11 09	11 39	12 09	12 39	13 09	13 39	14 09	14 39	15 09
4	Halling		d	05 02	05 40	06 10	06 42		07 25	08 02	08 42	09 12	09 42	10 12	10 42	11 12	11 42	12 12	12 42	13 12	13 42	14 12	14 42	15 12
5½	Snodland		d	05 05	05 43	06 13	06 45		07 28	08 05	08 45	09 15	09 45	10 15	10 45	11 15	11 45	12 15	12 45	13 15	13 45	14 15	14 45	15 15
7	New Hythe		d	05 08	05 46	06 16	06 48		07 31	08 08	08 48	09 18	09 48	10 18	10 48	11 18	11 48	12 18	12 48	13 18	13 48	14 18	14 48	15 18
7¾	Aylesford		d	05 10	05 48	06 18	06 50		07 33	08 10	08 50	09 20	09 50	10 20	10 50	11 20	11 50	12 20	12 50	13 20	13 50	14 20	14 50	15 20
11	Maidstone Barracks		d	05 15	05 53	06 23	06 55		07 38	08 15	08 55	09 25	09 55	10 25	10 55	11 25	11 55	12 25	12 55	13 25	13 55	14 25	14 55	15 25
11¼	**Maidstone West** ■4	194	a	05 17	05 55	06 25	07 00	07 12	07 40	08 17	08 57	09 27	09 57	10 27	10 57	11 27	11 57	12 27	12 57	13 27	13 57	14 27	14 57	15 27
—			d	05 18	05 56	06 26	07 01		07 41	08 18		09 28		10 28		11 28		12 28		13 28		14 28		15 28
13	East Farleigh		d	05 21	05 59	06 29	07 04		07 44	08 21		09 31		10 31		11 31		12 31		13 31		14 31		15 31
16	Wateringbury		d	05 26	06 04	06 34	07 09		07 49	08 26		09 36		10 36		11 36		12 36		13 36		14 36		15 36
17¾	Yalding		d	05 30	06 08	06 38	07 13		07 53	08 30		09 40		10 40		11 40		12 40		13 40		14 40		15 40
19½	Beltring		d	05 33	06 11	06 41	07 16		07 56	08 33		09 43		10 43		11 43		12 43		13 43		14 43		15 43
21¼	**Paddock Wood** ■4		a	05 37	06 15	06 45	07 20		08 00	08 37		09 47		10 47		11 47		12 47		13 47		14 47		15 47
26½	Tonbridge ■4		a							08 45		09 57		10 55		11 55		12 58		13 55		14 55		15 55

			SE	SE	SE	SE	SE	SE	SE	SE	SE	SE	SE	SE	SE	SE	SE	SE	SE
St Pancras International		d					17 14		17 44		18 14								
Stratford International		d					17 21		17 51		18 21								
Ebbsfleet International		d																	
Gravesend		d					17 36		18 06		18 38								
Strood ■4		d	15 35	16 10	16 35	17 05	17 46	17 55	18 16	18 25	18 49	18 55	19 35	20 05	20 35	21 05	21 35	22 05	22 35
Cuxton		d	15 39	16 14	16 39	17 09		17 59		18 29		18 59	19 39	20 09	20 39	21 09	21 39	22 09	22 39
Halling		d	15 42	16 17	16 42	17 12		18 02		18 32		19 02	19 42	20 12	20 42	21 12	21 42	22 12	22 42
Snodland		d	15 45	16 20	16 45	17 15		18 05		18 35		19 05	19 45	20 15	20 45	21 15	21 45	22 15	22 45
New Hythe		d	15 48	16 23	16 48	17 18		18 08		18 38		19 08	19 48	20 18	20 48	21 18	21 48	22 18	22 48
Aylesford		d	15 50	16 25	16 50	17 20		18 10		18 40		19 10	19 50	20 20	20 50	21 20	21 50	22 20	22 50
Maidstone Barracks		d	15 55	16 30	16 55	17 25		18 15		18 45		19 15	19 55	20 25	20 55	21 25	21 55	22 25	22 55
Maidstone West ■4	194	a	15 57	16 32	16 57	17 27	18 02	18 17	18 32	18 47	19 05	19 17	19 57	20 27	20 57	21 27	21 57	22 27	22 57
		d		16 33	16 58	17 28		18 18		18 48		19 18	19 58		20 58		21 58		
East Farleigh		d		16 36	17 01	17 31		18 21		18 51		19 21	20 01		21 01		22 01		
Wateringbury		d		16 41	17 06	17 36		18 26		18 56		19 26	20 06		21 06		22 06		
Yalding		d		16 45	17 10	17 40		18 30		19 00		19 30	20 10		21 10		22 10		
Beltring		d		16 48	17 13	17 43		18 33		19 03		19 33	20 13		21 13		22 13		
Paddock Wood ■4		a		16 52	17 17	17 47		18 37		19 07		19 37	20 17		21 17		22 17		
Tonbridge ■4		a											20 25		21 25		22 25		

Saturdays

			SE	SE	SE	SE	SE	SE	SE	SE	SE	SE	SE	SE	SE	SE	SE	SE	SE	SE	SE	SE	SE	SE
St Pancras International		d																						
Stratford International		d																						
Ebbsfleet International		d																						
Gravesend		d																						
Strood ■4		d	06 05	06 35	07 05	07 35	08 05	08 35	09 05	09 35	10 05	10 35	11 05	11 35	12 05	12 35	13 05	13 35	14 05	14 35	15 05	15 35	16 05	16 35
Cuxton		d	06 09	06 39	07 09	07 39	08 09	08 39	09 09	09 39	10 09	10 39	11 09	11 39	12 09	12 39	13 09	13 39	14 09	14 39	15 09	15 39	16 09	16 39
Halling		d	06 12	06 42	07 12	07 42	08 12	08 42	09 12	09 42	10 12	10 42	11 12	11 42	12 12	12 42	13 12	13 42	14 12	14 42	15 12	15 42	16 12	16 42
Snodland		d	06 15	06 45	07 15	07 45	08 15	08 45	09 15	09 45	10 15	10 45	11 15	11 45	12 15	12 45	13 15	13 45	14 15	14 45	15 15	15 45	16 15	16 45
New Hythe		d	06 18	06 48	07 18	07 48	08 18	08 48	09 18	09 48	10 18	10 48	11 18	11 48	12 18	12 48	13 18	13 48	14 18	14 48	15 18	15 48	16 18	16 48
Aylesford		d	06 20	06 50	07 20	07 50	08 20	08 50	09 20	09 50	10 20	10 50	11 20	11 50	12 20	12 50	13 20	13 50	14 20	14 50	15 20	15 50	16 20	16 50
Maidstone Barracks		d	06 25	06 55	07 25	07 55	08 25	08 55	09 25	09 55	10 25	10 55	11 25	11 55	12 25	12 55	13 25	13 55	14 25	14 55	15 25	15 55	16 25	16 55
Maidstone West ■4	194	a	06 27	06 57	07 27	07 57	08 27	08 57	09 27	09 57	10 27	10 57	11 27	11 57	12 27	12 57	13 27	13 57	14 27	14 57	15 27	15 57	16 27	16 57
		d	06 28		07 28		08 28		09 28		10 28		11 28		12 28		13 28		14 28		15 28		16 28	
East Farleigh		d	06 31		07 31		08 31		09 31		10 31		11 31		12 31		13 31		14 31		15 31		16 31	
Wateringbury		d	06 36		07 36		08 36		09 36		10 36		11 36		12 36		13 36		14 36		15 36		16 36	
Yalding		d	06 40		07 40		08 40		09 40		10 40		11 40		12 40		13 40		14 40		15 40		16 40	
Beltring		d	06 43		07 43		08 43		09 43		10 43		11 43		12 43		13 43		14 43		15 43		16 43	
Paddock Wood ■4		a	06 47		07 47		08 47		09 47		10 47		11 47		12 47		13 47		14 47		15 47		16 47	
Tonbridge ■4		a	06 55		07 55		08 55		09 55		10 55		11 55		12 55		13 55		14 55		15 55		16 55	

			SE	SE	SE	SE	SE	SE	SE	SE	SE	SE	SE	SE
St Pancras International		d												
Stratford International		d												
Ebbsfleet International		d												
Gravesend		d												
Strood ■4		d	17 05	17 35	18 05	18 35	19 05	19 35	20 05	20 35	21 05	21 35	22 05	22 35
Cuxton		d	17 09	17 39	18 09	18 39	19 09	19 39	20 09	20 39	21 09	21 39	22 09	22 39
Halling		d	17 12	17 42	18 12	18 42	19 12	19 42	20 12	20 42	21 12	21 42	22 12	22 42
Snodland		d	17 15	17 45	18 15	18 45	19 15	19 45	20 15	20 45	21 15	21 45	22 15	22 45
New Hythe		d	17 18	17 48	18 18	18 48	19 18	19 48	20 18	20 48	21 18	21 48	22 18	22 48
Aylesford		d	17 20	17 50	18 20	18 50	19 20	19 50	20 20	20 50	21 20	21 50	22 20	22 50
Maidstone Barracks		d	17 25	17 55	18 25	18 55	19 25	19 55	20 25	20 55	21 25	21 55	22 25	22 55
Maidstone West ■4	194	a	17 27	17 57	18 27	18 57	19 27	19 57	20 27	20 57	21 27	21 57	22 27	22 57
		d	17 28		18 28		19 28		20 28		21 28		22 28	
East Farleigh		d	17 31		18 31		19 31		20 31		21 31		22 31	
Wateringbury		d	17 36		18 36		19 36		20 36		21 36		22 36	
Yalding		d	17 40		18 40		19 40		20 40		21 40		22 40	
Beltring		d	17 43		18 43		19 43		20 43		21 43		22 43	
Paddock Wood ■4		a	17 47		18 47		19 47		20 47		21 47		22 47	
Tonbridge ■4		a	17 55		18 55		19 55		20 55		21 55		22 55	

Table 208

Sundays

Strood - Maidstone West and Paddock Wood

			SE	SE	SE	SE	SE	SE	SE	SE	SE		SE	SE	SE	SE	SE	SE	SE
St Pancras International		d																	
Stratford International		d																	
Ebbsfleet International		d																	
Gravesend		d																	
Strood 4		d	06 35	07 35	08 35	09 35	10 35	11 35	12 35	13 35	14 35		15 35	16 35	17 35	18 35	19 35	20 35	21 35
Cuxton		d	06 39	07 39	08 39	09 39	10 39	11 39	12 39	13 39	14 39		15 39	16 39	17 39	18 39	19 39	20 39	21 39
Halling		d	06 42	07 42	08 42	09 42	10 42	11 42	12 42	13 42	14 42		15 42	16 42	17 42	18 42	19 42	20 42	21 42
Snodland		d	06 45	07 45	08 45	09 45	10 45	11 45	12 45	13 45	14 45		15 45	16 45	17 45	18 45	19 45	20 45	21 45
New Hythe		d	06 48	07 48	08 48	09 48	10 48	11 48	12 48	13 48	14 48		15 48	16 48	17 48	18 48	19 48	20 48	21 48
Aylesford		d	06 50	07 50	08 50	09 50	10 50	11 50	12 50	13 50	14 50		15 50	16 50	17 50	18 50	19 50	20 50	21 50
Maidstone Barracks		d	06 55	07 55	08 55	09 55	10 55	11 55	12 55	13 55	14 55		15 55	16 55	17 55	18 55	19 55	20 55	21 55
Maidstone West 4	194	a	06 57	07 57	08 57	09 57	10 57	11 57	12 57	13 57	14 57		15 57	16 57	17 57	18 57	19 57	20 57	21 57
		d	07 03	08 03	09 03	10 03	11 03	12 03	13 03	14 03	15 03		16 03	17 03	18 03	19 03	20 03	21 03	22 03
East Farleigh		d	07 07	08 07	09 07	10 07	11 07	12 07	13 07	14 07	15 07		16 07	17 07	18 07	19 07	20 07	21 07	22 07
Wateringbury		d	07 12	08 12	09 12	10 12	11 12	12 12	13 12	14 12	15 12		16 12	17 12	18 12	19 12	20 12	21 12	22 12
Yalding		d	07 15	08 15	09 15	10 15	11 15	12 15	13 15	14 15	15 15		16 15	17 15	18 15	19 15	20 15	21 15	22 15
Beltring		d	07 18	08 18	09 18	10 18	11 18	12 18	13 18	14 18	15 18		16 18	17 18	18 18	19 18	20 18	21 18	22 18
Paddock Wood 4		a	07 22	08 22	09 22	10 22	11 22	12 22	13 22	14 22	15 22		16 22	17 22	18 22	19 22	20 22	21 22	22 22
Tonbridge 4		a																	22 32

Paddock Wood and Maidstone West - Strood

Miles			SE	SE	SE	SE	SE	SE	SE	SE	SE		SE	SE	SE	SE	SE	SE	SE	SE	SE		SE	SE	SE
0	Tonbridge [4]	d											09 03		10 03		11 03		12 03		13 03			14 03	
5¼	**Paddock Wood [4]**	d	05 42	06 20		06 50			07 40	08 10			09 10		10 10		11 11		12 10		13 10			14 10	
7	Beltring	d	05 46	06 24		06 54			07 44	08 14			09 14		10 14		11 15		12 14		13 14			14 14	
8¾	Yalding	d	05 49	06 27		06 57			07 48	08 18			09 18		10 18		11 19		12 18		13 18			14 18	
10½	Wateringbury	d	05 52	06 30		07 00			07 51	08 21			09 21		10 21		11 22		12 21		13 21			14 21	
13½	East Farleigh	d	05 56	06 34		07 04			07 55	08 25			09 25		10 25		11 26		12 25		13 25			14 25	
15¼	**Maidstone West [4]** 194	a	06 01	06 39		07 09			07 59	08 29			09 29		10 29		11 30		12 29		13 29			14 29	
—		d	06 02	06 40	06 56	07 10	07 26	07 56	08 02	08 32	09 02		09 32	10 02	10 32	11 02	11 32	12 02	12 32	13 02	13 32		14 02	14 32	15 02
15½	Maidstone Barracks	d	06 04	06 42		07 12			08 04	08 34	09 04		09 34	10 04	10 34	11 04	11 34	12 04	12 34	13 04	13 34		14 04	14 34	15 04
18¾	Aylesford	d	06 09	06 47		07 17			08 09	08 39	09 09		09 39	10 09	10 39	11 09	11 39	12 09	12 39	13 09	13 39		14 09	14 39	15 09
19½	New Hythe	d	06 11	06 49		07 19			08 11	08 41	09 11		09 41	10 11	10 41	11 11	11 41	12 11	12 41	13 11	13 41		14 11	14 41	15 11
21	Snodland	d	06 14	06 52		07 22			08 14	08 44	09 14		09 44	10 14	10 44	11 14	11 44	12 14	12 44	13 14	13 44		14 14	14 44	15 14
22½	Halling	d	06 17	06 55		07 25			08 17	08 47	09 17		09 47	10 17	10 47	11 17	11 47	12 17	12 47	13 17	13 47		14 17	14 47	15 17
24¼	Cuxton	d	06 20	06 58		07 28			08 20	08 50	09 20		09 50	10 20	10 50	11 20	11 50	12 20	12 50	13 20	13 50		14 20	14 50	15 20
26½	**Strood [4]**	a	06 24	07 14	07 11	07 32	07 41	08 11	08 24	08 54	09 24		09 54	10 24	10 54	11 24	11 54	12 24	12 54	13 24	13 54		14 24	14 54	15 24
—	Gravesend	d			07 22		07 52	08 22																	
—	Ebbsfleet International	d			07 25			08 26																	
—	Stratford International	d			07 37		08 07	08 37																	
—	St Pancras International	a			07 44		08 13	08 43																	

		SE	SE	SE	SE	SE	SE		SE	SE	SE	SE	SE	SE	SE	SE	SE		SE
Tonbridge [4]	d	15 03		16 03										20 33		21 33			22 33
Paddock Wood [4]	d	15 10		16 10	17 02	17 30	17 52		18 42		19 12	19 42		20 40		21 40			22 40
Beltring	d	15 14		16 14	17 06	17 34	17 56		18 46		19 16	19 46		20 44		21 44			22 44
Yalding	d	15 18		16 18	17 09	17 37	17 59		18 50		19 20	19 49		20 48		21 48			22 48
Wateringbury	d	15 21		16 21	17 12	17 40	18 02		18 53		19 23	19 52		20 51		21 51			22 51
East Farleigh	d	15 25		16 25	17 16	17 44	18 06		18 57		19 27	19 56		20 55		21 55			22 55
Maidstone West [4] 194	a	15 29		16 29	17 21	17 49	18 11		19 01		19 31	20 01		20 59		21 59			22 59
	d	15 44	16 02	16 32	17 22	17 50	18 18		19 02	19 13	19 32	20 02	20 32	21 02	21 32	22 02	22 32		23 02
Maidstone Barracks	d	15 46	16 04	16 34	17 24	17 52	18 20		19 04		19 34	20 04	20 34	21 04	21 34	22 04	22 34		23 04
Aylesford	d	15 51	16 09	16 39	17 29	17 57	18 25		19 09		19 39	20 09	20 39	21 09	21 39	22 09	22 39		23 09
New Hythe	d	15 53	16 11	16 41	17 31	17 59	18 27		19 11		19 41	20 11	20 41	21 11	21 41	22 11	22 41		23 11
Snodland	d	15 56	16 14	16 44	17 34	18 02	18 30		19 14		19 44	20 14	20 44	21 14	21 44	22 14	22 44		23 14
Halling	d	15 59	16 17	16 47	17 37	18 05	18 33		19 17		19 47	20 17	20 47	21 17	21 47	22 17	22 47		23 17
Cuxton	d	16 02	16 20	16 50	17 40	18 08	18 36		19 20		19 50	20 20	20 50	21 20	21 50	22 20	22 50		23 20
Strood [4]	a	16 06	16 24	16 54	17 44	18 12	18 40		19 24	19 30	19 54	20 24	20 54	21 24	21 54	22 24	22 54		23 24
Gravesend	d									19 43									
Ebbsfleet International	d									19 50									
Stratford International	d									20 02									
St Pancras International	a									20 08									

Saturdays

		SE	SE	SE	SE	SE	SE	SE	SE	SE		SE	SE	SE	SE	SE	SE	SE	SE	SE		SE	SE	SE	SE
Tonbridge [4]	d	06 03		07 03		08 03		09 03		10 03			11 03		12 03		13 03		14 03			15 03		16 03	
Paddock Wood [4]	d	06 10		07 10		08 10		09 10		10 10			11 10		12 10		13 10		14 10			15 10		16 10	
Beltring	d	06 14		07 14		08 14		09 14		10 14			11 14		12 14		13 14		14 14			15 14		16 14	
Yalding	d	06 18		07 18		08 18		09 18		10 18			11 18		12 18		13 18		14 18			15 18		16 18	
Wateringbury	d	06 21		07 21		08 21		09 21		10 21			11 21		12 21		13 21		14 21			15 21		16 21	
East Farleigh	d	06 25		07 25		08 25		09 25		10 25			11 25		12 25		13 25		14 25			15 25		16 25	
Maidstone West [4] 194	a	06 29		07 29		08 29		09 29		10 29			11 29		12 29		13 29		14 29			15 29		16 29	
	d	06 32	07 02	07 32	08 02	08 32	09 02	09 32	10 02	10 32		11 02	11 32	12 02	12 32	13 02	13 32	14 02	14 32	15 02		15 32	16 02	16 32	17 02
Maidstone Barracks	d	06 34	07 04	07 34	08 04	08 34	09 04	09 34	10 04	10 34		11 04	11 34	12 04	12 34	13 04	13 34	14 04	14 34	15 04		15 34	16 04	16 34	17 04
Aylesford	d	06 39	07 09	07 39	08 09	08 39	09 09	09 39	10 09	10 39		11 09	11 39	12 09	12 39	13 09	13 39	14 09	14 39	15 09		15 39	16 09	16 39	17 09
New Hythe	d	06 41	07 11	07 41	08 11	08 41	09 11	09 41	10 11	10 41		11 11	11 41	12 11	12 41	13 11	13 41	14 11	14 41	15 11		15 41	16 11	16 41	17 11
Snodland	d	06 44	07 14	07 44	08 14	08 44	09 14	09 44	10 14	10 44		11 14	11 44	12 14	12 44	13 14	13 44	14 14	14 44	15 14		15 44	16 14	16 44	17 14
Halling	d	06 47	07 17	07 47	08 17	08 47	09 17	09 47	10 17	10 47		11 17	11 47	12 17	12 47	13 17	13 47	14 17	14 47	15 17		15 47	16 17	16 47	17 17
Cuxton	d	06 50	07 20	07 50	08 20	08 50	09 20	09 50	10 20	10 50		11 20	11 50	12 20	12 50	13 20	13 50	14 20	14 50	15 20		15 50	16 20	16 50	17 20
Strood [4]	a	06 54	07 24	07 54	08 24	08 54	09 24	09 54	10 24	10 54		11 24	11 54	12 24	12 54	13 24	13 54	14 24	14 54	15 24		15 54	16 24	16 54	17 24
Gravesend	d																								
Ebbsfleet International	d																								
Stratford International	d																								
St Pancras International	a																								

		SE	SE	SE	SE	SE		SE	SE	SE	SE	SE	SE	SE
Tonbridge [4]	d	17 03		18 03		19 03			20 03		21 03		22 03	
Paddock Wood [4]	d	17 10		18 10		19 10			20 10		21 10		22 10	
Beltring	d	17 14		18 14		19 14			20 14		21 14		22 14	
Yalding	d	17 18		18 18		19 18			20 18		21 18		22 18	
Wateringbury	d	17 21		18 21		19 21			20 21		21 21		22 21	
East Farleigh	d	17 25		18 25		19 25			20 25		21 25		22 25	
Maidstone West [4] 194	a	17 29		18 29		19 29			20 29		21 29		22 29	
	d	17 32	18 02	18 32	19 02	19 32		20 02	20 32	21 02	21 32	22 02	22 32	23 02
Maidstone Barracks	d	17 34	18 04	18 34	19 04	19 34		20 04	20 34	21 04	21 34	22 04	22 34	23 04
Aylesford	d	17 39	18 09	18 39	19 09	19 39		20 09	20 39	21 09	21 39	22 09	22 39	23 09
New Hythe	d	17 41	18 11	18 41	19 11	19 41		20 11	20 41	21 11	21 41	22 11	22 41	23 11
Snodland	d	17 44	18 14	18 44	19 14	19 44		20 14	20 44	21 14	21 44	22 14	22 44	23 14
Halling	d	17 47	18 17	18 47	19 17	19 47		20 17	20 47	21 17	21 47	22 17	22 47	23 17
Cuxton	d	17 50	18 20	18 50	19 20	19 50		20 20	20 50	21 20	21 50	22 20	22 50	23 20
Strood [4]	a	17 54	18 24	18 54	19 24	19 54		20 24	20 54	21 24	21 54	22 24	22 54	23 24
Gravesend	d													
Ebbsfleet International	d													
Stratford International	d													
St Pancras International	a													

Table 208

Sundays

Paddock Wood and Maidstone West - Strood

			SE	SE	SE	SE	SE	SE	SE	SE	SE		SE	SE	SE	SE	SE	SE	SE
Tonbridge 4		d	06 26																
Paddock Wood 4		d	06 34	07 34	08 34	09 34	10 34	11 34	12 34	13 34	14 34		15 34	16 34	17 34	18 34	19 34	20 34	21 34
Beltring		d	06 38	07 38	08 38	09 38	10 38	11 38	12 38	13 38	14 38		15 38	16 38	17 38	18 38	19 38	20 38	21 38
Yalding		d	06 41	07 41	08 41	09 41	10 41	11 41	12 41	13 41	14 41		15 41	16 41	17 41	18 41	19 41	20 41	21 41
Wateringbury		d	06 44	07 44	08 44	09 44	10 44	11 44	12 44	13 44	14 44		15 44	16 44	17 44	18 44	19 44	20 44	21 44
East Farleigh		d	06 48	07 48	08 48	09 48	10 48	11 48	12 48	13 48	14 48		15 48	16 48	17 48	18 48	19 48	20 48	21 48
Maidstone West 4	194	a	06 53	07 53	08 53	09 53	10 53	11 53	12 53	13 53	14 53		15 53	16 53	17 53	18 53	19 53	20 53	21 53
		d	07 00	08 00	09 02	10 02	11 02	12 02	13 02	14 02	15 02		16 02	17 02	18 02	19 02	20 00	21 00	22 00
Maidstone Barracks		d	07 02	08 02	09 04	10 04	11 04	12 04	13 04	14 04	15 04		16 04	17 04	18 04	19 04	20 02	21 02	22 02
Aylesford		d	07 07	08 07	09 09	10 09	11 09	12 09	13 09	14 09	15 09		16 09	17 09	18 09	19 09	20 07	21 07	22 07
New Hythe		d	07 09	08 09	09 11	10 11	11 11	12 11	13 11	14 11	15 11		16 11	17 11	18 11	19 11	20 09	21 09	22 09
Snodland		d	07 12	08 12	09 14	10 14	11 14	12 14	13 14	14 14	15 14		16 14	17 14	18 14	19 14	20 12	21 12	22 12
Halling		d	07 15	08 15	09 17	10 17	11 17	12 17	13 17	14 17	15 17		16 17	17 17	18 17	19 17	20 15	21 15	22 15
Cuxton		d	07 18	08 18	09 20	10 20	11 20	12 20	13 20	14 20	15 20		16 20	17 20	18 20	19 20	20 18	21 18	22 18
Strood 4		a	07 22	08 22	09 24	10 24	11 24	12 24	13 24	14 24	15 24		16 24	17 24	18 24	19 24	20 22	21 22	22 22
Gravesend		d																	
Ebbsfleet International		d																	
Stratford International		d																	
St Pancras International		a																	

Network Diagram for Table 212

DM-32/09
Design BAJS

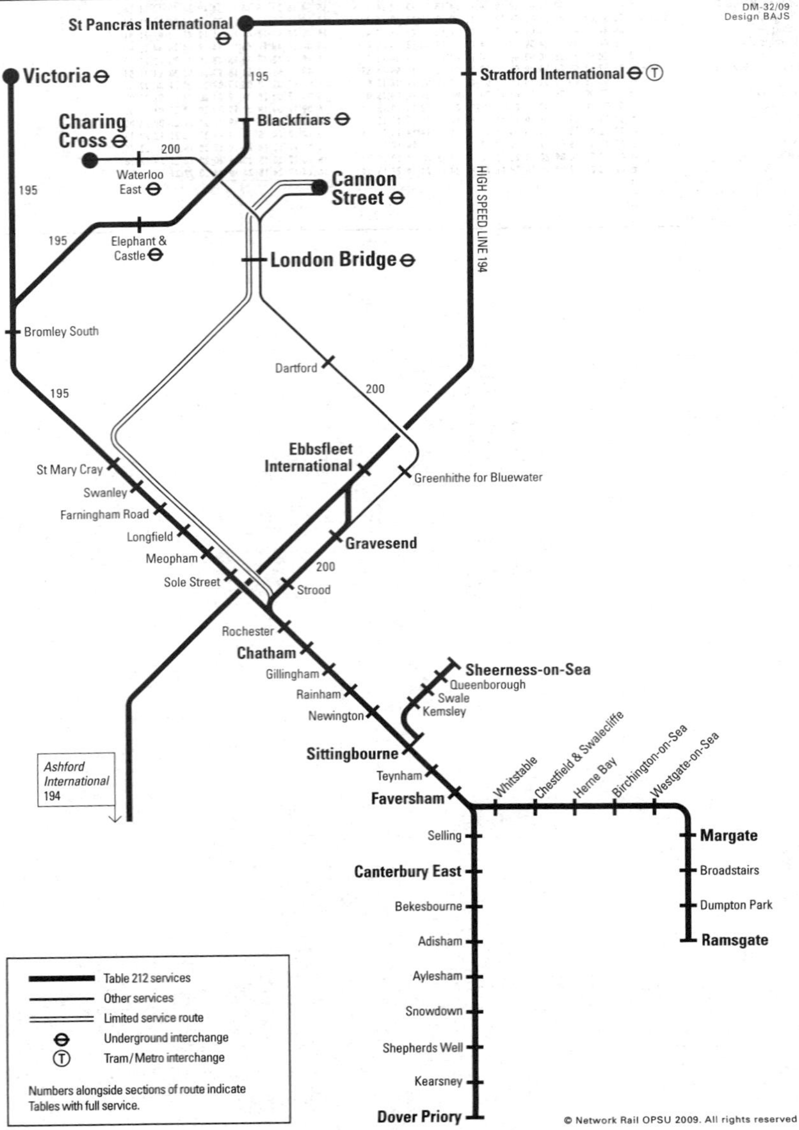

© Network Rail OPSU 2009. All rights reserved

London - Medway, Sheerness-on-Sea, Dover and Ramsgate

Miles	Miles	Miles	Miles	Miles			SE MO 1		SE MX 1		SE	SE MX 1	SE MO 1	SE MX	SE		SE MX 1	SE MX	SE MO	SE MO	SE MX	SE MO 1	SE MX 1	SE MX 1	SE MX
—	—	—	—	0	**St Pancras Internatnl 15** ⊖	d					22p55				23p25					23p42	23p55				
—	—	—	—	6	**Stratford International** ⊖	d					23p02				23p32					23p49	00 02				
—	—	—	—	22¾	**Ebbsfleet International**	d					23p13				23p43					00 01	00 13				
0	0	—	—	—	**London Victoria 15** ⊖	d	22p05		22p22			22p52	23p05				23p22					23p45	23p52	00 10	
—	—	—	—	—	**London Blackfriars 3** ⊖	d																			
—	—	—	—	—	Elephant & Castle ⊖	d																			
11	11	—	—	—	Bromley South 4	d	22p22		22p39			23p09	23p22				23p39					00 02	00 09		
14¾	14¾	—	—	—	St Mary Cray	d						23p15										00 08	00 15		
17½	17½	—	—	—	Swanley 4	d						23p19										00 12	00 19		
20½	20½	—	—	—	Farningham Road	d						23p24										00 17	00 24		
23½	23½	—	—	—	Longfield	d			22p52			23p28					23p52					00 21	00 28		
26	26	—	—	—	Meopham	d			22p57			23p32					23p57					00 25	00 32		
27	27	—	—	—	Sole Street	d						23p35										00 28	00 35		
—	—	—	0	—	**London Charing Cross 4** ⊖	d												23p09	23p10						23p39
—	—	—	0¾	—	**London Waterloo (East) 4** ⊖	d												23p12	23p13						23p42
—	—	—	—	—	**London Cannon Street 4** ⊖	d																			
—	—	—	1¾	—	**London Bridge 4** ⊖	d												23p17	23p18						23p47
—	—	—	18¾	—	Dartford 4	d												23p55	23p55						00 25
—	—	—	21½	—	Greenhithe for Bluewater	d												23p59	00 01						00 31
—	—	—	25½	24¾	Gravesend 4	d					23p18				23p48			00 10	00 10		00 18				00 40
—	—	—	32¾	32	Strood 4	d					23p28				23p58			00 22	00 22		00 28				00 52
33¾	33¾	—	33¾	33	Rochester 4	d	22p46		23p09		23p33	23p45	23p46		00 03		00 09	00 26	00 26		00 33	00 37	00 45	00 49	00 56
34¼	34¼	—	34¼	33½	**Chatham 4**	d	22p48		23p12		23p35	23p47	23p48		00 05		00 12	00 28	00 28		00 35	00 40	00 47	00 52	00 58
36	36	—	36	35¼	**Gillingham (Kent) 4**	d	22p53		23p17		23p40	23p52	23p53		00 10		00 17	00a33	00a33		00 40	00 44	00a52	00 57	01a03
39	39	—	—	38¼	Rainham (Kent)	d	22p57		23p21		23p45	23p56	23p57		00 15		00 21				00 45	00 49		01 01	
41½	41½	—	—	40¾	Newington	d						00 01										00 53		01 05	
44¾	44¾	0	—	44	**Sittingbourne 4**	a	23p04		23p28		23p52	00 06	00 04		00 22		00 28				00 52	00 58		01 10	
—	—	—	—	—		d	23p05		23p29		23p53	00 07	00 05	00 15	00 23		00 29				00 53	00 58		01 11	
—	—	2	—	—	Kemsley	d								00 20											
—	—	4	—	—	Swale	d								00 23											
—	—	6	—	—	Queenborough	d								00 27											
—	—	8	—	—	**Sheerness-on-Sea**	a								00 32											
47½	47½	—	—	46¾	Teynham	d			23p33								00 33					01 03		01 15	
52	52	—	—	51¾	**Faversham 2**	a	23p13		23p39		00 03	00 15	00 13		00 33		00 39				01 03	01 09		01 23	
—	—	—	—	—																					
—	—	—	—	—		d	23p17	23p19	23p43	23p45			00 17				00 43							01 24	
—	55¼	—	—	—	Selling	d		23p24		23p50															
—	61¾	—	—	—	**Canterbury East 4**	d		23p33		23p59															
—	64¾	—	—	—	Bekesbourne	d		23p37																	
—	67¾	—	—	—	Adisham	d		23p42																	
—	68¾	—	—	—	Aylesham	d		23p44		00 07															
—	69¾	—	—	—	Snowdown	d		23p47																	
—	71¾	—	—	—	Shepherds Well	d		23p51																	
—	75	—	—	—	Kearsney	d		23p55																	
—	77¼	—	—	—	**Dover Priory 4**	a		00 01		00 18															
59	—	—	—	—	Whitstable	d	23p25		23p51				00 25				00 51							01 32	
60½	—	—	—	—	Chestfield & Swalecliffe	d	23p28		23p54				00 28				00 54							01 35	
62¾	—	—	—	—	**Herne Bay**	d	23p32		23p58				00 32				00 58							01 39	
70¾	—	—	—	—	Birchington-on-Sea	d	23p41		00 07				00 41				01 07							01 48	
72½	—	—	—	—	Westgate-on-Sea	d	23p45		00 11				00 45				01 11							01 52	
73¾	—	—	—	—	**Margate 4**	d	23p49		00 15				00 49				01 15							01 56	
77	—	—	—	—	Broadstairs	d	23p54		00 20				00 54				01 20							02 01	
78¼	—	—	—	—	Dumpton Park	d	23p57		00 23				00 57				01 23							02 04	
79¼	—	—	—	—	**Ramsgate 4**	a	00 01		00 26				01 00				01 26							02 07	

London - Medway, Sheerness-on-Sea, Dover and Ramsgate

		SE	SE	SE	SE	SE	SE	SE	SE	SE	SE	SE	SE	SE	SE	SE	SE	SE	SE	SE	SE	SE
		MX																				
						1		1			1		1		1	1				1		
St Pancras Internatnl 15 ⊖	d	00 12																06 25				
Stratford International ⊖	d	00 19																06 32				
Ebbsfleet International	d	00 31																06 42				
London Victoria 15 ⊖	d		00 35										05 22			05 52				06 22		
London Blackfriars 3 ⊖	d																					
Elephant & Castle ⊖	d																					
Bromley South 4	d		00 55										05 39			06 09				06 39		
St Mary Cray	d		01 01										05 45							06 45		
Swanley 4	d		01 05										05 49			06 19				06 49		
Farningham Road	d		01 10										05 54							06 54		
Longfield	d		01 14										05 58			06 25				06 58		
Meopham	d		01 18										06 02			06 29				07 02		
Sole Street	d												06 05							07 05		
London Charing Cross 4 ⊖	d			00 15													05 39				05 56	
London Waterloo (East) 4 ⊖	d			00 18													05 42				05 59	
London Cannon Street 4 ⊖	d																					
London Bridge 4 ⊖	d			00 23													05 47				06 04	
Dartford 4	d			01 03					05 25								06 25				06 42	
Greenhithe for Bluewater	d			01 08					05 30								06 30				06 48	
Gravesend 4	d			01 15					05 37								06 38	06 46			06 59	
Strood 4	d			01 26					05 48								06 49	06a56			07 17	
Rochester 4	d		01 29	01 32					05 52				06 15			06 41	06 53			07 15	07 21	
Chatham 4	d		01 31	01 35					05 55				06 17			06 44	06 56			07 17	07 24	
Gillingham (Kent) 4	d		01a35	01a41	05 00			05 47	05a59				06 22			06 48	07a00			07 22	07a28	
Rainham (Kent)	d				05 04			05 51					06 26			06 53				07 26		
Newington	d				05 08			05 55					06 30			06 57				07 30		
Sittingbourne 4	a							06 00					06 35			07 02				07 37		
	d						05 33	06 01		06 03		06 22	06 36	06 53		07 02			07 09	07 38		07 45
Kemsley	d				05 15		05 38			06 08		06 27		06 58					07 14			07 50
Swale	d				05 18		05 43			06 11		06 30		07 01					07 17			07 53
Queenborough	d				05 22		05 47			06 15		06 35		07 05					07 22			07 57
Sheerness-on-Sea	a				05 27		05 51			06 20		06 40		07 10					07 27			08 02
Teynham	d							06 05					06 40			07 07				07 42		
Faversham 2	a							06 11					06 46			07 13				07 48		
	d					05 15		06 12			06 15		06 47		07 05	07 13				07 49		
Selling	d					05 20		06 17							07 09							
Canterbury East 4	d					05 29		06 26							07 18							
Bekesbourne	d					05 33		06 30							07 23							
Adisham	d					05 38		06 35							07 27							
Aylesham	d					05 40		06 37							07 29							
Snowdown	d					05 43		06 40							07 32							
Shepherds Well	d					05 47		06 44							07 35							
Kearsney	d					05 51		06 48							07 40							
Dover Priory 4	a					05 56		06 53							07 45							
Whitstable	d										06 23		06 55			07 21				07 57		
Chestfield & Swalecliffe	d										06 26		06 58			07 24				08 00		
Herne Bay	d										06 30		07 02			07 28				08 04		
Birchington-on-Sea	d										06 39		07 11			07 37				08 12		
Westgate-on-Sea	d										06 43		07 15			07 41				08 16		
Margate 4	d										06 49		07 19			07 45				08 20		
Broadstairs	d										06 54		07 24			07 50				08 25		
Dumpton Park	d										06 57		07 27			07 53				08 28		
Ramsgate 4	a										07 02		07 30			07 56				08 31		

Table 212

Mondays to Fridays

London - Medway, Sheerness-on-Sea, Dover and Ramsgate

		SE	SE	SE [1]	SE [1]	SE	SE [1]		SE	SE	SE	SE [1]	SE [1]		SE	SE	SE		SE	SE [1]		SE	SE [1]	SE	SE
St Pancras Internatnl [15] ⊖	d	06 55									07 25								07 55						08 22
Stratford International ⊖	d	07 02									07 32								08 02						08 29
Ebbsfleet International	d	07 13									07 43								08 13						08 43
London Victoria [15] ⊖	d				06 45		06 58		07 09				07 22			07 43				07 52			07 58		
London Blackfriars [3] ⊖	d																								
Elephant & Castle ⊖	d																								
Bromley South [4]	d				07 02		07 19						07 40							08 09			08 27		
St Mary Cray	d				07 08		07 25																08 33		
Swanley [4]	d				07 13		07 29						07 49										08 38		
Farningham Road	d				07 18		07 34																08 43		
Longfield	d				07 22		07 38						07 55							08 22			08 47		
Meopham	d				07 26		07 42						07 59							08 27			08 51		
Sole Street	d				07 28		07 45																08 54		
London Charing Cross [4] ⊖	d		06 26			06 39									07 12							07 39			
London Waterloo (East) [4] ⊖	d		06 29			06 42									07 15							07 42			
London Cannon Street [4] ⊖	d																								
London Bridge [4] ⊖	d		06 34			06 47									07 21							07 47			
Dartford [4]	d		07 12			07 25			07a48						08 00	08a27						08 25			
Greenhithe for Bluewater	d		07 18			07 30									08 05							08 30			
Gravesend [4]	d	07 21	07 27			07 37					07 48				08 12				08 18			08 37			08 48
Strood [4]	d	07 31	07a37			07 48					07 58				08 23				08 28			08 48			08 58
Rochester [4]	d	07 36			07 40	07 52	07 56				08 03		08 11		08 27				08 33	08 39		08 52	09a07		09 03
Chatham [4]	d	07 38			07 43	07 55	07 59				08 05		08 13		08 30				08 35	08 42		08 55			09 05
Gillingham (Kent) [4]	d	07 43			07 48	07a59	08a03				08 10		08 18		08a35				08 40	08 47		08a59			09 10
Rainham (Kent)	d	07 48			07 52						08 15		08 22						08 45	08 51					09 15
Newington	d				07 56								08 26							08 55					
Sittingbourne [4]	a	07 57			08 01						08 22		08 31						08 52	09 00					09 22
	d	07 57			08 02					08 13	08 23		08 32				08 40		08 53	09 01				09 10	09 23
Kemsley	d									08 18							08 45							09 15	
Swale	d									08 21							08 48							09 18	
Queenborough	d									08 25							08 52							09 22	
Sheerness-on-Sea	a									08 30							08 57							09 27	
Teynham	d				08 06								08 36												
Faversham [2]	a	08 05			08 12						08 33		08 42						09 03	09 09					09 33
	d			07 51	08 13							08 16	08 46	08 49						09 13	09 15				
Selling	d			07 55	08 18									08 53											
Canterbury East [4]	d			08 05	08 27									09 02							09 29				
Bekesbourne	d			08 10	08 31									09 07											
Adisham	d			08 14	08 36									09 11											
Aylesham	d			08 17	08 38									09 13											
Snowdown	d			08 19	08 41									09 16											
Shepherds Well	d			08 23	08 45									09 20											
Kearsney	d			08 28	08 49									09 24											
Dover Priory [4]	a			08 35	08 54									09 29							09 50				
Whitstable	d											08 24	08 54							09 21					
Chestfield & Swalecliffe	d											08 27	08 57												
Herne Bay	d											08 31	09 01							09 26					
Birchington-on-Sea	d											08 40	09 10							09 35					
Westgate-on-Sea	d											08 44	09 14												
Margate [4]	d											08 48	09 18							09 41					
Broadstairs	d											08 53	09 23							09 46					
Dumpton Park	d											08 56	09 26												
Ramsgate [4]	a											08 59	09 29							09 51					

London - Medway, Sheerness-on-Sea, Dover and Ramsgate

		SE [1]			SE	SE	SE	SE [1]		SE	SE [1]	SE	SE		SE [1]		SE	SE	SE	SE [1]		SE	SE [1]		SE
St Pancras Internatnl [15] ⊖	d						08 58						09 25						09 55						
Stratford International ⊖	d						09 05						09 32						10 02						
Ebbsfleet International	d						09 16						09 43						10 13						
London Victoria [15] ⊖	d	08 22						08 52			08 58				09 22					09 52			09 58		
London Blackfriars [3] ⊖	d																								
Elephant & Castle ⊖	d																								
Bromley South [4]	d	08 39						09 09			09 19				09 39					10 09			10 19		
St Mary Cray	d										09 25												10 25		
Swanley [4]	d										09 29												10 29		
Farningham Road	d										09 34												10 34		
Longfield	d	08 52						09 22			09 38				09 52					10 22			10 38		
Meopham	d	08 57						09 27			09 42				09 57					10 27			10 42		
Sole Street	d										09 45												10 45		
London Charing Cross [4] ⊖	d				08 11					08 41							09 11					09 39			
London Waterloo (East) [4] ⊖	d				08 14					08 44							09 14					09 42			
London Cannon Street [4] ⊖	d																								
London Bridge [4] ⊖	d				08 19					08 49							09 19					09 47			
Dartford [4]	d				08 55					09 25							09 55					10 25			
Greenhithe for Bluewater	d				09 00					09 30							10 00					10 30			
Gravesend [4]	d				09 07		09 21			09 37			09 48				10 07		10 18			10 37			
Strood [4]	d				09 18		09 31			09 48			09 58				10 18		10 28			10 48			
Rochester [4]	d	09 09			09 22		09 36	09 39		09 52	09 56		10 03		10 09		10 22		10 33	10 39		10 52	10 56		
Chatham [4]	d	09 12			09 25		09 38	09 42		09 55	09 59		10 05		10 12		10 25		10 35	10 42		10 55	10 59		
Gillingham (Kent) [4]	d	09 17			09a29		09 43	09 47		09a59	10a03		10 10		10 17		10a29		10 40	10 47		10a59	11a03		
Rainham (Kent)	d	09 21					09 48	09 51					10 15		10 21				10 45	10 51					
Newington	d							09 55												10 55					
Sittingbourne [4]	a	09 28					09 55	10 01					10 22		10 28				10 52	11 00					
	d	09 29				09 40	09 55	10 01				10 10	10 23		10 29			10 40	10 53	11 01					11 10
Kemsley	d					09 45						10 15						10 45							11 15
Swale	d					09 48						10 18						10 48							11 18
Queenborough	d					09 52						10 22						10 52							11 22
Sheerness-on-Sea	a					09 57						10 27						10 57							11 27
Teynham	d	09 33													10 33										
Faversham [2]	a	09 39					10 03	10 09					10 33		10 39				11 03	11 09					
	d	09 43	09 45					10 13	10 15						10 43	10 45				11 13	11 15				
Selling	d		09 50													10 50									
Canterbury East [4]	d		09 59						10 29							10 59					11 29				
Bekesbourne	d		10 03													11 03									
Adisham	d		10 08													11 08									
Aylesham	d		10 10													11 10									
Snowdown	d		10 13													11 13									
Shepherds Well	d		10 17													11 17									
Kearsney	d		10 21													11 21									
Dover Priory [4]	a		10 26						10 50							11 26					11 50				
Whitstable	d	09 51						10 21							10 51					11 21					
Chestfield & Swalecliffe	d	09 54													10 54										
Herne Bay	d	09 58						10 26							10 58					11 26					
Birchington-on-Sea	d	10 07						10 35							11 07					11 35					
Westgate-on-Sea	d	10 11													11 11										
Margate [4]	d	10 15						10 41							11 15					11 41					
Broadstairs	d	10 20						10 46							11 20					11 46					
Dumpton Park	d	10 23													11 23										
Ramsgate [4]	a	10 26						10 51							11 26					11 51					

London - Medway, Sheerness-on-Sea, Dover and Ramsgate

		SE	SE [1]		SE	SE	SE	SE [1]		SE	SE [1]	SE	SE	SE [1]		SE	SE	SE	SE [1]		SE	SE [1]	SE
St Pancras Internatnl [15] ⊖	d	10 28					10 52						11 25					11 55					
Stratford International ⊖	d	10 35					10 59						11 32					12 02					
Ebbsfleet International	d	10 46					11 13						11 43					12 13					
London Victoria [15] ⊖	d		10 22					10 52			10 58			11 22					11 52			11 58	
London Blackfriars [3] ⊖	d																						
Elephant & Castle ⊖	d																						
Bromley South [4]	d		10 39					11 09			11 19			11 39					12 09			12 19	
St Mary Cray	d										11 25											12 25	
Swanley [4]	d										11 29											12 29	
Farningham Road	d										11 34											12 34	
Longfield	d		10 52					11 22			11 38			11 52					12 22			12 38	
Meopham	d		10 57					11 27			11 42			11 57					12 27			12 42	
Sole Street	d										11 45											12 45	
London Charing Cross [4] ⊖	d				10 09					10 39						11 09					11 39		
London Waterloo (East) [4] ⊖	d				10 12					10 42						11 12					11 42		
London Cannon Street [4] ⊖	d																						
London Bridge [4] ⊖	d				10 17					10 47						11 17					11 47		
Dartford [4]	d				10 55					11 25						11 55					12 25		
Greenhithe for Bluewater	d				11 00					11 30						12 00					12 30		
Gravesend [4]	d	10 51			11 07		11 18			11 37			11 48			12 07		12 18			12 37		
Strood [4]	d	11 01			11 18		11 28			11 48			11 58			12 18		12 28			12 48		
Rochester [4]	d	11 06	11 09		11 22		11 33	11 39		11 52	11 56		12 03	12 09		12 22		12 33	12 39		12 52	12 56	
Chatham [4]	d	11 08	11 12		11 25		11 35	11 42		11 55	11 59		12 05	12 12		12 25		12 35	12 42		12 55	12 59	
Gillingham (Kent) [4]	d	11 13	11 17		11a29		11 40	11 47		11a59	12a03		12 10	12 17		12a29		12 40	12 47		12a59	13a03	
Rainham (Kent)	d	11 18	11 21				11 45	11 51					12 15	12 21				12 45	12 51				
Newington	d							11 55											12 55				
Sittingbourne [4]	a	11 25	11 29				11 52	12 00					12 22	12 28				12 52	13 00				
	d	11 25	11 29			11 40	11 53	12 01				12 10	12 23	12 29			12 40	12 53	13 01				13 10
Kemsley	d					11 45						12 15					12 45						13 15
Swale	d					11 48						12 18					12 48						13 18
Queenborough	d					11 52						12 22					12 52						13 22
Sheerness-on-Sea	a					11 57						12 27					12 57						13 27
Teynham	d		11 33											12 33									
Faversham [2]	a	11 33	11 39				12 03	12 09					12 33	12 39				13 03	13 09				
	d		11 43	11 45				12 13	12 15					12 43	12 45				13 13	13 15			
Selling	d			11 50											12 50								
Canterbury East [4]	d			11 59					12 29						12 59					13 29			
Bekesbourne	d			12 03											13 03								
Adisham	d			12 08											13 08								
Aylesham	d			12 10											13 10								
Snowdown	d			12 13											13 13								
Shepherds Well	d			12 17											13 17								
Kearsney	d			12 21											13 21								
Dover Priory [4]	a			12 26					12 50						13 26					13 50			
Whitstable	d		11 51					12 21						12 51					13 21				
Chestfield & Swalecliffe	d		11 54											12 54									
Herne Bay	d		11 58					12 26						12 58					13 26				
Birchington-on-Sea	d		12 07					12 35						13 07					13 35				
Westgate-on-Sea	d		12 11											13 11									
Margate [4]	d		12 15					12 41						13 15					13 41				
Broadstairs	d		12 20					12 46						13 20					13 46				
Dumpton Park	d		12 23											13 23									
Ramsgate [4]	a		12 26					12 51						13 26					13 51				

London - Medway, Sheerness-on-Sea, Dover and Ramsgate

		SE	SE [1]		SE	SE	SE	SE [1]		SE	SE [1]	SE	SE	SE [1]		SE	SE	SE	SE [1]		SE	SE [1]	SE
St Pancras Internatnl [15] ⊖	d	12 25					12 52						13 25					13 55					
Stratford International ⊖	d	12 35					12 58						13 32					14 02					
Ebbsfleet International	d	12 46					13 13						13 43					14 13					
London Victoria [15] ⊖	d		12 22					12 52			12 58			13 22					13 52			13 58	
London Blackfriars [3] ⊖	d																						
Elephant & Castle ⊖	d																						
Bromley South [4]	d		12 39					13 09			13 19			13 39					14 09			14 19	
St Mary Cray	d										13 25											14 25	
Swanley [4]	d										13 29											14 29	
Farningham Road	d										13 34											14 34	
Longfield	d		12 52					13 22			13 38			13 52					14 22			14 38	
Meopham	d		12 57					13 27			13 42			13 57					14 27			14 42	
Sole Street	d										13 45											14 45	
London Charing Cross [4] ⊖	d				12 09					12 39						13 09					13 39		
London Waterloo (East) [4] ⊖	d				12 12					12 42						13 12					13 42		
London Cannon Street [4] ⊖	d																						
London Bridge [4] ⊖	d				12 17					12 47						13 17					13 47		
Dartford [4]	d				12 55					13 25						13 55					14 25		
Greenhithe for Bluewater	d				13 00					13 30						14 00					14 30		
Gravesend [4]	d	12 51			13 07		13 18			13 37			13 48			14 07		14 18			14 37		
Strood [4]	d	13 01			13 18		13 28			13 48			13 58			14 18		14 28			14 48		
Rochester [4]	d	13 06	13 09		13 22		13 33	13 39		13 52	13 56		14 03	14 09		14 22		14 33	14 39		14 52	14 56	
Chatham [4]	d	13 08	13 12		13 25		13 35	13 42		13 55	13 59		14 05	14 12		14 25		14 35	14 42		14 55	14 59	
Gillingham (Kent) [4]	d	13 13	13 17		13a29		13 40	13 47		13a59	14a03		14 10	14 17		14a29		14 40	14 47		14a59	15a03	
Rainham (Kent)	d	13 18	13 21				13 45	13 51					14 15	14 21				14 45	14 51				
Newington	d							13 55											14 55				
Sittingbourne [4]	a	13 25	13 29				13 52	14 00					14 22	14 28				14 52	15 00				
	d	13 25	13 29			13 40	13 53	14 01				14 10	14 23	14 29			14 40	14 53	15 01				15 10
Kemsley	d					13 45						14 15					14 45						15 15
Swale	d					13 48						14 18					14 48						15 18
Queenborough	d					13 52						14 22					14 52						15 22
Sheerness-on-Sea	a					13 57						14 27					14 57						15 27
Teynham	d		13 33											14 33									
Faversham [2]	a	13 33	13 39				14 03	14 09					14 33	14 39				15 03	15 09				
	d		13 43	13 45				14 13	14 15					14 43	14 45				15 13	15 15			
Selling	d			13 50											14 50								
Canterbury East [4]	d			13 59					14 29						14 59					15 29			
Bekesbourne	d			14 03											15 03								
Adisham	d			14 08											15 08								
Aylesham	d			14 10											15 10								
Snowdown	d			14 13											15 13								
Shepherds Well	d			14 17											15 17					15 39			
Kearsney	d			14 21											15 21								
Dover Priory [4]	a			14 26					14 50						15 26					15 48			
Whitstable	d		13 51					14 21						14 51					15 21				
Chestfield & Swalecliffe	d		13 54											14 54									
Herne Bay	d		13 58					14 26						14 58					15 26				
Birchington-on-Sea	d		14 07					14 35						15 07					15 35				
Westgate-on-Sea	d		14 11											15 11									
Margate [4]	d		14 15					14 41						15 15					15 41				
Broadstairs	d		14 20					14 46						15 20					15 46				
Dumpton Park	d		14 23											15 23									
Ramsgate [4]	a		14 26					14 51						15 26					15 51				

Table 212

Mondays to Fridays

London - Medway, Sheerness-on-Sea, Dover and Ramsgate

		SE		SE 1		SE	SE	SE	SE 1		SE	SE 1		SE	SE	SE 1		SE	SE	SE	SE 1			SE	SE 1
St Pancras Internatnl 15 ⊖	d	14 25						14 55							15 25					15 55					
Stratford International ⊖	d	14 32						15 02							15 32					16 02					
Ebbsfleet International	d	14 43						15 13							15 43					16 13					
London Victoria 15 ⊖	d			14 22					14 52			14 58				15 22					15 52				15 58
London Blackfriars 3 ⊖	d																								
Elephant & Castle ⊖	d																								
Bromley South 4	d			14 39					15 09			15 19				15 39					16 09				16 19
St Mary Cray	d											15 25													16 25
Swanley 4	d											15 29													16 29
Farningham Road	d											15 34													16 34
Longfield	d			14 52					15 22			15 38				15 52					16 22				16 38
Meopham	d			14 57					15 27			15 42				15 57					16 27				16 42
Sole Street	d											15 45													16 45
London Charing Cross 4 ⊖	d					14 09					14 39							15 09						15 39	
London Waterloo (East) 4 ⊖	d					14 12					14 42							15 12						15 42	
London Cannon Street 4 ⊖	d																								
London Bridge 4 ⊖	d					14 17					14 47							15 17						15 47	
Dartford 4	d					14 55					15 25							15 55						16 25	
Greenhithe for Bluewater	d					15 00					15 30							16 00						16 30	
Gravesend 4	d	14 48				15 07		15 18			15 37				15 48			16 07		16 18				16 37	
Strood 4	d	14 58				15 18		15 28			15 48				15 58			16 18		16 28				16 48	
Rochester 4	d	15 03		15 09		15 22		15 33	15 39		15 52	15 56			16 03	16 09		16 22		16 33	16 39			16 52	16 56
Chatham 4	d	15 05		15 12		15 25		15 35	15 42		15 55	15 59			16 05	16 12		16 25		16 35	16 42			16 55	16 59
Gillingham (Kent) 4	d	15 10		15 17		15a29		15 40	15 47		15a59	16a03			16 10	16 17		16a29		16 40	16 47			16a59	17a03
Rainham (Kent)	d	15 15		15 21				15 45	15 51						16 15	16 21				16 45	16 51				
Newington	d								15 55												16 55				
Sittingbourne 4	a	15 22		15 29				15 52	16 00						16 22	16 28				16 52	17 00				
	d	15 23		15 29			15 40	15 53	16 01					16 10	16 23	16 29			16 40	16 53	17 01				
Kemsley	d						15 45							16 15					16 45						
Swale	d						15 48							16 18					16 48						
Queenborough	d						15 52							16 22					16 52						
Sheerness-on-Sea	a						15 57							16 27					16 57						
Teynham	d			15 33												16 33					17 05				
Faversham 2	a	15 33		15 39				16 03	16 09						16 33	16 39				17 03	17 11				
	d			15 43	15 45				16 13	16 15						16 43	16 45				17 15	17 19			
Selling	d				15 50					16 19							16 50					17 23			
Canterbury East 4	d				15 59					16 28							16 59					17 32			
Bekesbourne	d				16 03					16 33							17 03								
Adisham	d				16 08					16 37							17 08								
Aylesham	d				16 10					16 39							17 10					17 40			
Snowdown	d				16 13												17 13								
Shepherds Well	d				16 17					16 44							17 17					17 45			
Kearsney	d				16 21												17 21								
Dover Priory 4	a				16 27					16 52							17 26					17 53			
Whitstable	d			15 51					16 21							16 51					17 23				
Chestfield & Swalecliffe	d			15 54					16 24							16 54					17 26				
Herne Bay	d			15 58					16 28							16 58					17 30				
Birchington-on-Sea	d			16 07					16 37							17 07					17 39				
Westgate-on-Sea	d			16 11					16 41							17 11					17 43				
Margate 4	d			16 15					16 45							17 15					17 47				
Broadstairs	d			16 20					16 50							17 20					17 52				
Dumpton Park	d			16 23					16 53							17 23					17 55				
Ramsgate 4	a			16 26					16 56							17 26					17 58				

London - Medway, Sheerness-on-Sea, Dover and Ramsgate

		SE	SE	SE 1		SE	SE 1	SE	SE 1	SE	SE 1		SE	SE	SE	SE 1	SE	SE	SE	SE 1		SE 1	SE 1
St Pancras Internatnl 15 ⊖	d		16 25							16 55				17 14	17 18				17 27				
Stratford International ⊖	d		16 32							17 02				17 21	17 25				17 38				
Ebbsfleet International	d		16 43							17 13					17a35				17 49				
London Victoria 15 ⊖	d			16 22			16 28				16 57		17 04							17 27		17 54	
London Blackfriars 3 ⊖	d																						
Elephant & Castle ⊖	d																						
Bromley South 4	d			16 39			16 49				17 13		17 24							17 44		18 19	
St Mary Cray	d						16 55						17 30									18 25	
Swanley 4	d						16 59						17 34									18 30	
Farningham Road	d						17 04						17 39									18 35	
Longfield	d			16 52			17 08						17 43										
Meopham	d			16 57			17 12						17 47									18 41	
Sole Street	d						17 15						17 50									18 44	
London Charing Cross 4 ⊖	d					16 09																	
London Waterloo (East) 4 ⊖	d					16 12																	
London Cannon Street 4 ⊖	d								16 46							17 08	16 44						17 30
London Bridge 4 ⊖	d					16 17			16 50							17 12	16 48						17 34
Dartford 4	d					16 55											17 28						
Greenhithe for Bluewater	d					17 00											17 33						
Gravesend 4	d		16 48			17 07				17 18				17 36			17 40						
Strood 4	d		16 58			17 18				17 28				17a46			17 52						
Rochester 4	d		17 03	17 10		17 22	17a27		17 29	17 34	17 40		18a02			17 49	17 57		18 05	18 10		18a56	18 15
Chatham 4	d		17 05	17 13		17 25			17 32	17 37	17 43					17 52	18 00		18 08	18 13			18 18
Gillingham (Kent) 4	d		17 10	17 18		17a31			17 37	17 43	17 48					17 57	18a07		18 13	18 18			18 24
Rainham (Kent)	d		17 15	17 23					17 42	17 48	17 53					18 02			18 18	18 23			18 29
Newington	d			17 27							17 57					18 06							18 33
Sittingbourne 4	a		17 22	17 32					17 49	17 56	18 02					18 11			18 25	18 30			18 38
	d	17 10	17 23	17 33				17 40	17 50	17 57	18 03					18 12		18 15	18 25	18 31			18 39
Kemsley	d	17 15						17 45										18 20					
Swale	d	17 18						17 48										18 23					
Queenborough	d	17 22						17 52										18 27					
Sheerness-on-Sea	a	17 27						17 57										18 32					
Teynham	d			17 37							18 07					18 16				18 35			
Faversham 2	a		17 33	17 43					17 58	18 05	18 13					18 22			18 33	18 41			18 47
	d			17 47	17 49				17 59		18 17	18 19				18 24			18 35	18 45	18 50		18 51
Selling	d				17 54							18 23									18 54		
Canterbury East 4	d				18 03							18 32									19 04		
Bekesbourne	d				18 07																19 08		
Adisham	d				18 12																19 12		
Aylesham	d				18 14							18 40									19 15		
Snowdown	d				18 17																19 17		
Shepherds Well	d				18 21							18 45									19 21		
Kearsney	d				18 25																19 25		
Dover Priory 4	a				18 32							18 55									19 32		
Whitstable	d			17 55					18 08		18 25					18 32			18 43	18 54			19 00
Chestfield & Swalecliffe	d			17 58					18 11		18 28					18 35				18 57			19 03
Herne Bay	d			18 02					18 15		18 32					18 39			18 49	19 01			19 07
Birchington-on-Sea	d			18 11					18 24		18 41					18 48			18 58	19 10			19 16
Westgate-on-Sea	d			18 15					18 27		18 45					18 52				19 13			19 19
Margate 4	d			18 19					18 31		18 49					18 57			19 04	19 18			19 24
Broadstairs	d			18 24					18 37		18 54					19 02			19a10	19 24			19 30
Dumpton Park	d			18 27					18 40		18 57					19 05				19 27			19 33
Ramsgate 4	a			18 34					18 47		19 02					19 12				19 36			19 40

London - Medway, Sheerness-on-Sea, Dover and Ramsgate

		SE	SE	SE		SE	SE	SE	SE ■1	SE ■1	SE	SE	SE		SE	SE ■1	SE	SE ■1	SE ■1	SE	SE	SE	
St Pancras Internatnl ■15 ⊖	d		17 44			17 48		17 55				18 14	18 18				18 25				18 48		
Stratford International ⊖	d		17 51			17 55		18 02				18 21	18 25				18 32				18 55		
Ebbsfleet International	d					18a05		18 13					18a35				18 43				19a05		
London Victoria ■15 ⊖	d									17 57								18 24	18 27				
London Blackfriars ■3 ⊖	d																						
Elephant & Castle ⊖	d																						
Bromley South ■4	d									18 15								18 46	18 44				
St Mary Cray	d																	18 52					
Swanley ■4	d																	18 57					
Farningham Road	d																	19 02					
Longfield	d									18 28								19 06					
Meopham	d																	19 11					
Sole Street	d																	19 13					
London Charing Cross ■4 ⊖	d			17 17							17 39									18 01			
London Waterloo (East) ■4 ⊖	d			17 20							17 42									18 04			
London Cannon Street ■4 ⊖	d	17 06							17 52							18 14							
London Bridge ■4 ⊖	d	17 10		17 26					17 56		17 48					18 18				18 10			
Dartford ■4	d	17 47		18 02							18 22									18 44			
Greenhithe for Bluewater	d	17 52		18 07							18 27									18 50			
Gravesend ■4	d	18 00	18 06	18 19							18 34	18 38								19 02			
Strood ■4	d	18 12	18a16	18a33							18 45	18a49								19 14			
Rochester ■4	d	18 20						18 31	18 38	18 43	18 51						19 03	19 24	19 12	19 19			
Chatham ■4	d	18 23						18 34	18 41	18 46	18 54					19 01	19 07	19 27	19 15	19 22			
Gillingham (Kent) ■4	d	18a30						18 39	18 46	18 51	19a02					19 07	19 13	19a34	19 20	19a30			
Rainham (Kent)	d							18 44	18 51	18 56						19 12	19 18		19 25				
Newington	d									19 00						19 16							
Sittingbourne ■4	a							18 51	18 58	19 05						19 21	19 27		19 32				
	d						18 44	18 52	18 59	19 06					19 10	19 22	19 28		19 33			19 40	
Kemsley	d						18 49								19 15							19 45	
Swale	d						18 54								19 18							19 48	
Queenborough	d						18 58								19 22							19 52	
Sheerness-on-Sea	a						19 02								19 27							19 57	
Teynham	d								19 03	19 10									19 37				
Faversham ■2	a							19 00	19 09	19 16						19 30	19 36		19 43				
	d							19 01	19 10	19 20 / 19 22						19 31	19 38		19 47 / 19 49				
Selling	d									19 26									19 54				
Canterbury East ■4	d									19 36									20 03				
Bekesbourne	d																		20 07				
Adisham	d																		20 12				
Aylesham	d																		20 14				
Snowdown	d																		20 17				
Shepherds Well	d																		20 21				
Kearsney	d																		20 25				
Dover Priory ■4	a									19 54									20 32				
Whitstable	d							19 09	19 19	19 28						19 39	19 46		19 55				
Chestfield & Swalecliffe	d								19 22	19 31						19 42			19 58				
Herne Bay	d							19 15	19 26	19 35						19 46	19 52		20 02				
Birchington-on-Sea	d							19 24	19 35	19 44						19 55	20 01		20 11				
Westgate-on-Sea	d								19 38	19 48						19 59			20 15				
Margate ■4	d							19 30	19 42	19a55						20 03	20 07		20 19				
Broadstairs	d							19a36	19a50							20 09	20a14		20 25				
Dumpton Park	d															20 12			20 28				
Ramsgate ■4	a															20 19			20 35				

London - Medway, Sheerness-on-Sea, Dover and Ramsgate

		SE 1	SE	SE 1		SE	SE	SE 1	SE	SE		SE	SE 1		SE	SE	SE	SE	SE 1			SE	SE	SE	SE
St Pancras Internatnl 15 ⊖	d		18 55									19 25						19 55							20 25
Stratford International ⊖	d		19 02									19 32						20 02							20 32
Ebbsfleet International	d		19 13									19 45						20 13							20 43
London Victoria 15 ⊖	d			18 57				18 58					19 22			19 28			19 52				19 58		
London Blackfriars 3 ⊖	d																								
Elephant & Castle ⊖	d																								
Bromley South 4	d			19 14				19 19					19 39			19 49			20 09				20 19		
St Mary Cray	d							19 25								19 55							20 25		
Swanley 4	d							19 29								19 59							20 29		
Farningham Road	d							19 34								20 04							20 34		
Longfield	d							19 39					19 52			20 08			20 22				20 38		
Meopham	d							19 43					19 57			20 12			20 27				20 42		
Sole Street	d							19 46								20 15							20 45		
London Charing Cross 4 ⊖	d						18 37		18 48						19 09							19 39			
London Waterloo (East) 4 ⊖	d						18 40		18 51						19 12							19 42			
London Cannon Street 4 ⊖	d	18 44				18 30																			
London Bridge 4 ⊖	d	18 48				18 34	18 46		18 57						19 17							19 47			
Dartford 4	d					19 10	19 22		19 35						19 55							20 25			
Greenhithe for Bluewater	d					19 16	19 29		19 40						20 00							20 30			
Gravesend 4	d		19 20			19 26	19 38		19 47			19 51			20 07			20 18				20 37			20 48
Strood 4	d		19 30			19 38	19a53		19 58			20 01			20 18			20 28				20 48			20 58
Rochester 4	d	19 29	19 35	19 40		19 45		19 56	20 03			20 08	20 13		20 22	20 26		20 33	20 39			20 52	20 56		21 03
Chatham 4	d	19 32	19 38	19 43		19 48		19 59	20 05			20 10	20 16		20 25	20 29		20 35	20 42			20 55	20 59		21 05
Gillingham (Kent) 4	d	19 37	19 43	19 49		19a55		20a06	20a13			20 15	20 21		20a29	20a33		20 40	20 47			20a59	21a03		21 10
Rainham (Kent)	d	19 42	19 48	19 54								20 20	20 25					20 45	20 51						21 15
Newington	d	19 46		19 58															20 55						
Sittingbourne 4	a	19 51	19 57	20 03								20 27	20 32					20 52	21 00						21 22
	d	19 52	19 58	20 03						20 10		20 27	20 33				20 40	20 53	21 01					21 10	21 23
Kemsley	d									20 15							20 45							21 15	
Swale	d									20 18							20 48							21 18	
Queenborough	d									20 22							20 52							21 22	
Sheerness-on-Sea	a									20 27							20 57							21 27	
Teynham	d	19 56											20 37												
Faversham 2	a	20 02	20 07	20 11								20 36	20 43					21 03	21 09						21 33
	d	20 04		20 15	20 17								20 47	20 49					21 13	21 15					
Selling	d				20 21									20 54						21 19					
Canterbury East 4	d				20 30									21 03						21 28					
Bekesbourne	d				20 35									21 07						21 33					
Adisham	d				20 39									21 12						21 37					
Aylesham	d				20 41									21 14						21 39					
Snowdown	d													21 17											
Shepherds Well	d				20 46									21 21						21 44					
Kearsney	d													21 25											
Dover Priory 4	a				20 56									21 32						21 52					
Whitstable	d	20 12		20 23									20 55						21 21						
Chestfield & Swalecliffe	d	20 15		20 26									20 58						21 24						
Herne Bay	d	20 19		20 30									21 02						21 28						
Birchington-on-Sea	d	20 28		20 39									21 11						21 37						
Westgate-on-Sea	d	20 32		20 43									21 15						21 41						
Margate 4	d	20 36		20 47									21 19						21 45						
Broadstairs	d	20 42		20 52									21 24						21 50						
Dumpton Park	d	20 45		20 55									21 27						21 53						
Ramsgate 4	a	20 52		21 02									21 34						21 56						

Table 212

London - Medway, Sheerness-on-Sea, Dover and Ramsgate

		SE ■1	SE	SE	SE	SE ■1	SE	SE ■1	SE	SE ■1	SE	SE	SE	SE ■1	SE	SE	SE ■1	SE	SE
St Pancras Internatnl ■15 ⊖	d				20 55				21 25				21 55			22 25			
Stratford International ⊖	d				21 02				21 32				22 02			22 32			
Ebbsfleet International	d				21 13				21 43				22 13			22 43			
London Victoria ■15 ⊖	d	20 22				20 52		20 58		21 22				21 52			22 22		
London Blackfriars ■3 ⊖	d																		
Elephant & Castle ⊖	d																		
Bromley South ■4	d	20 39				21 09		21 19		21 39				22 09			22 39		
St Mary Cray	d							21 25						22 15					
Swanley ■4	d							21 29						22 19					
Farningham Road	d							21 34						22 24					
Longfield	d	20 52				21 22		21 38		21 52				22 28			22 52		
Meopham	d	20 57				21 27		21 42		21 57				22 32			22 57		
Sole Street	d							21 45						22 35					
London Charing Cross ■4 ⊖	d		20 09				20 39				21 09				21 39			22 09	
London Waterloo (East) ■4 ⊖	d		20 12				20 42				21 12				21 42			22 12	
London Cannon Street ■4 ⊖	d																		
London Bridge ■4 ⊖	d		20 17				20 47				21 17				21 47			22 17	
Dartford ■4	d		20 55				21 25				21 55				22 25			22 55	
Greenhithe for Bluewater	d		21 00				21 30				22 00				22 30			23 00	
Gravesend ■4	d		21 07		21 18		21 37		21 48		22 07		22 18		22 37	22 48		23 07	
Strood ■4	d		21 18		21 28		21 48		21 58		22 18		22 28		22 48	22 58		23 18	
Rochester ■4	d	21 09	21 22		21 33	21 39	21 52	21 56	22 03	22 09	22 22		22 33	22 45	22 52	23 03	23 09	23 22	
Chatham ■4	d	21 12	21 25		21 35	21 42	21 55	21 59	22 05	22 12	22 25		22 35	22 47	22 55	23 05	23 12	23 25	
Gillingham (Kent) ■4	d	21 17	21a29		21 40	21 47	21a59	22a03	22 10	22 17	22a29		22 40	22 52	22a59	23 10	23 17	23a29	
Rainham (Kent)	d	21 21			21 45	21 51			22 15	22 21			22 45	22 56		23 15	23 21		
Newington	d					21 55								23 00					
Sittingbourne ■4	a	21 28			21 53	22 00			22 22	22 28			22 52	23 05		23 22	23 28		
	d	21 29		21 40	21 53	22 01			22 23	22 29		22 40	22 53	23 06		23 23	23 29		23 32
Kemsley	d			21 45								22 45							23 37
Swale	d			21 48								22 48							23 40
Queenborough	d			21 52								22 52							23 44
Sheerness-on-Sea	a			21 57								22 57							23 49
Teynham	d	21 33								22 33							23 33		
Faversham ■2	a	21 39			22 03	22 09			22 33	22 39			23 03	23 17		23 33	23 39		
	d	21 43 / 21 45				22 13 / 22 15				22 43 / 22 45							23 43 / 23 45		
Selling	d	21 50				22 19				22 50							23 50		
Canterbury East ■4	d	21 59				22 28				22 59							23 59		
Bekesbourne	d	22 03				22 33				23 03									
Adisham	d	22 08				22 37				23 08									
Aylesham	d	22 10				22 39				23 10							00 07		
Snowdown	d	22 13								23 13									
Shepherds Well	d	22 17				22 44				23 17									
Kearsney	d	22 21								23 21									
Dover Priory ■4	a	22 26				22 52				23 26							00 18		
Whitstable	d	21 51				22 21				22 51							23 51		
Chestfield & Swalecliffe	d	21 54				22 24				22 54							23 54		
Herne Bay	d	21 58				22 28				22 58							23 58		
Birchington-on-Sea	d	22 07				22 37				23 07							00 07		
Westgate-on-Sea	d	22 11				22 41				23 11							00 11		
Margate ■4	d	22 15				22 45				23 15							00 15		
Broadstairs	d	22 20				22 50				23 20							00 20		
Dumpton Park	d	22 23				22 53				23 23							00 23		
Ramsgate ■4	a	22 26				22 56				23 26							00 26		

London - Medway, Sheerness-on-Sea, Dover and Ramsgate

Station		SE	SE 1	SE	SE	SE 1	SE	SE	SE 1	SE
St Pancras Internatnl 15 ⊖	d	22 55			23 25			23 55		
Stratford International ⊖	d	23 02			23 32			00 02		
Ebbsfleet International	d	23 13			23 43			00 13		
London Victoria 15 ⊖	d		22 52			23 22			23 52	
London Blackfriars 3 ⊖	d									
Elephant & Castle ⊖	d									
Bromley South 4	d		23 09			23 39			00 09	
St Mary Cray	d		23 15						00 15	
Swanley 4	d		23 19						00 19	
Farningham Road	d		23 24						00 24	
Longfield	d		23 28			23 52			00 28	
Meopham	d		23 32			23 57			00 32	
Sole Street	d		23 35						00 35	
London Charing Cross 4 ⊖	d			22 39			23 09			23 39
London Waterloo (East) 4 ⊖	d			22 42			23 12			23 42
London Cannon Street 4 ⊖	d									
London Bridge 4 ⊖	d			22 47			23 17			23 47
Dartford 4	d			23 25			23 55			00 25
Greenhithe for Bluewater	d			23 31			23 59			00 31
Gravesend 4	d	23 18		23 40	23 48		00 10	00 18		00 40
Strood 4	d	23 28		23 52	23 58		00 22	00 28		00 52
Rochester 4	d	23 33	23 45	23 56	00 03	00 09	00 26	00 33	00 45	00 56
Chatham 4	d	23 35	23 47	23 58	00 05	00 12	00 28	00 35	00 47	00 58
Gillingham (Kent) 4	d	23 40	23 52	00a03	00 10	00 17	00a33	00 40	00a52	01a03
Rainham (Kent)	d	23 45	23 56		00 15	00 21		00 45		
Newington	d		00 01							
Sittingbourne 4	a	23 52	00 06		00 22	00 28		00 52		
	d	23 53	00 07		00 23	00 29		00 53		
Kemsley	d									
Swale	d									
Queenborough	d									
Sheerness-on-Sea	a									
Teynham	d					00 33				
Faversham 2	a	00 03	00 15		00 33	00 39		01 03		
	d					00 43				
Selling	d									
Canterbury East 4	d									
Bekesbourne	d									
Adisham	d									
Aylesham	d									
Snowdown	d									
Shepherds Well	d									
Kearsney	d									
Dover Priory 4	a									
Whitstable	d					00 51				
Chestfield & Swalecliffe	d					00 54				
Herne Bay	d					00 58				
Birchington-on-Sea	d					01 07				
Westgate-on-Sea	d					01 11				
Margate 4	d					01 15				
Broadstairs	d					01 20				
Dumpton Park	d					01 23				
Ramsgate 4	a					01 26				

Table 212

Saturdays

London - Medway, Sheerness-on-Sea, Dover and Ramsgate

		SE ■1		SE	SE ■1	SE	SE	SE ■1	SE	SE		SE ■1	SE ■1	SE	SE	SE	SE	SE ■1	SE	SE ■1		SE ■1	SE	SE	SE
St Pancras Internatnl ■15 ⊖	d			22p55			23p25			23p55					00 12										
Stratford International ⊖	d			23p02			23p32			00 02					00 19										
Ebbsfleet International	d			23p13			23p43			00 13					00 31										
London Victoria ■15 ⊖	d	22p22			22p52			23p22				23p52	00 10			00 35						05 22			
London Blackfriars ■3 ⊖	d																								
Elephant & Castle ⊖	d																								
Bromley South ■4	d	22p39			23p09			23p39				00 09				00 55						05 39			
St Mary Cray	d				23p15							00 15				01 01						05 45			
Swanley ■4	d				23p19							00 19				01 05						05 49			
Farningham Road	d				23p24							00 24				01 10						05 54			
Longfield	d	22p52			23p28			23p52				00 28				01 14						05 58			
Meopham	d	22p57			23p32			23p57				00 32				01 18						06 02			
Sole Street	d				23p35							00 35										06 05			
London Charing Cross ■4 ⊖	d								23p09					23p39			00 15							05 39	
London Waterloo (East) ■4 ⊖	d								23p12					23p42			00 18							05 42	
London Cannon Street ■4 ⊖	d																								
London Bridge ■4 ⊖	d								23p17					23p47			00 23							05 47	
Dartford ■4	d								23p55					00 25			01 03						05 55	06 25	
Greenhithe for Bluewater	d								23p59					00 31			01 08						06 00	06 30	
Gravesend ■4	d			23p18			23p48		00 10	00 18				00 40			01 15						06 07	06 37	
Strood ■4	d			23p28			23p58		00 22	00 28				00 52			01 26						06 18	06 48	
Rochester ■4	d	23p09		23p33	23p45		00 03	00 09	00 26	00 33		00 45	00 49	00 56		01 29	01 32					06 15	06 22	06 52	
Chatham ■4	d	23p12		23p35	23p47		00 05	00 12	00 28	00 35		00 47	00 52	00 58		01 31	01 35					06 17	06 25	06 55	
Gillingham (Kent) ■4	d	23p17		23p40	23p52		00 10	00 17	00a33	00 40		00a52	00 57	01a03		01a35	01a41	05 47				06 22	06a29	06a59	
Rainham (Kent)	d	23p21		23p45	23p56		00 15	00 21		00 45			01 01					05 51				06 26			
Newington	d				00 01								01 05					05 55				06 30			
Sittingbourne ■4	a	23p28		23p52	00 06		00 22	00 28		00 52			01 10					06 00				06 35			
	d	23p29		23p53	00 07	00 15	00 23	00 29		00 53			01 11					06 01	06 10			06 36			06 40
Kemsley	d					00 20													06 15						06 45
Swale	d					00 23													06 18						06 48
Queenborough	d					00 27													06 22						06 52
Sheerness-on-Sea	a					00 32													06 27						06 57
Teynham	d	23p33						00 33					01 15					06 05				06 40			
Faversham ■2	a	23p39		00 03	00 15		00 33	00 39		01 03			01 23					06 11				06 46			
	d	23p43	23p45					00 43					01 24					06 12		06 17		06 47			
Selling	d		23p50															06 17							
Canterbury East ■4	d		23p59															06 26							
Bekesbourne	d																	06 30							
Adisham	d																	06 35							
Aylesham	d		00 07															06 37							
Snowdown	d																	06 40							
Shepherds Well	d																	06 44							
Kearsney	d																	06 48							
Dover Priory ■4	a		00 18															06 53							
Whitstable	d	23p51						00 51					01 32							06 25		06 55			
Chestfield & Swalecliffe	d	23p54						00 54					01 35							06 28		06 58			
Herne Bay	d	23p58						00 58					01 39							06 32		07 02			
Birchington-on-Sea	d	00 07						01 07					01 48							06 41		07 11			
Westgate-on-Sea	d	00 11						01 11					01 52							06 45		07 15			
Margate ■4	d	00 15						01 15					01 56							06 49		07 19			
Broadstairs	d	00 20						01 20					02 01							06 54		07 24			
Dumpton Park	d	00 23						01 23					02 04							06 57		07 27			
Ramsgate ■4	a	00 26						01 26					02 07							07 00		07 30			

Table 212

London - Medway, Sheerness-on-Sea, Dover and Ramsgate

		SE 1	SE	SE 1	SE	SE		SE	SE	SE 1	SE 1	SE	SE	SE 1	SE 1	SE 1			SE	SE	SE	SE 1		SE	SE 1
St Pancras Internatnl 15 ⊖	d							06 55					07 28								07 52				
Stratford International ⊖	d							07 06					07 35								07 58				
Ebbsfleet International	d							07 17					07 46								08 13				
London Victoria 15 ⊖	d			06 22						06 58						07 22						07 52			07 58
London Blackfriars 3 ⊖	d																								
Elephant & Castle ⊖	d																								
Bromley South 4	d			06 39						07 19						07 39						08 09			08 19
St Mary Cray	d			06 45						07 25															08 25
Swanley 4	d			06 49						07 29															08 29
Farningham Road	d			06 54						07 34															08 34
Longfield	d			06 58						07 38						07 52						08 22			08 38
Meopham	d			07 02						07 42						07 57						08 27			08 42
Sole Street	d			07 05						07 45															08 45
London Charing Cross 4 ⊖	d				06 09				06 39										07 09					07 39	
London Waterloo (East) 4 ⊖	d				06 12				06 42										07 12					07 42	
London Cannon Street 4 ⊖	d																								
London Bridge 4 ⊖	d				06 17				06 47										07 17					07 47	
Dartford 4	d				06 55				07 25										07 55					08 25	
Greenhithe for Bluewater	d				07 00				07 30										08 00					08 30	
Gravesend 4	d				07 07			07 21	07 37				07 51						08 07		08 18			08 37	
Strood 4	d				07 18			07 31	07 48				08 01						08 18		08 28			08 48	
Rochester 4	d			07 15	07 22			07 36	07 52	07 56			08 06			08 09			08 22		08 33	08 39		08 52	08 56
Chatham 4	d			07 17	07 25			07 38	07 55	07 59			08 08			08 12			08 25		08 35	08 42		08 55	08 59
Gillingham (Kent) 4	d			07 22	07a29			07 43	07a59	08a03			08 13			08 17			08a29		08 40	08 47		08a59	09a03
Rainham (Kent)	d			07 26				07 48					08 18			08 21					08 45	08 51			
Newington	d			07 30												08 25						08 55			
Sittingbourne 4	a			07 35				07 55					08 25			08 30					08 52	09 00			
	d		07 10	07 36		07 40		07 55				08 10	08 25			08 31				08 40	08 53	09 01			
Kemsley	d		07 15			07 45						08 15								08 45					
Swale	d		07 18			07 48						08 18								08 48					
Queenborough	d		07 22			07 52						08 22								08 52					
Sheerness-on-Sea	a		07 27			07 57						08 27								08 57					
Teynham	d			07 40												08 35									
Faversham 2	a			07 46				08 04					08 33			08 41					09 03	09 09			
	d	06 50		07 47							07 50			08 13	08 15	08 45	08 50					09 13	09 15		
Selling	d	06 55									07 55						08 55								
Canterbury East 4	d	07 04									08 04				08 29		09 04						09 29		
Bekesbourne	d	07 08									08 08						09 08								
Adisham	d	07 13									08 13						09 13								
Aylesham	d	07 15									08 15						09 15								
Snowdown	d	07 18									08 18						09 18								
Shepherds Well	d	07 22									08 22						09 22								
Kearsney	d	07 26									08 26						09 26								
Dover Priory 4	a	07 31									08 31				08 48		09 31						09 48		
Whitstable	d			07 55										08 21		08 53						09 21			
Chestfield & Swalecliffe	d			07 58												08 56									
Herne Bay	d			08 02										08 26		09 00						09 26			
Birchington-on-Sea	d			08 11										08 35		09 09						09 35			
Westgate-on-Sea	d			08 15												09 13									
Margate 4	d			08 19										08 41		09 17						09 41			
Broadstairs	d			08 24										08 46		09 22						09 46			
Dumpton Park	d			08 27												09 25									
Ramsgate 4	a			08 30										08 51		09 28						09 51			

Table 212

Saturdays

London - Medway, Sheerness-on-Sea, Dover and Ramsgate

		SE	SE		SE 1	SE	SE	SE		SE 1	SE	SE 1	SE	SE		SE 1	SE	SE	SE		SE 1	SE
St Pancras Internatnl 15 ⊖	d		08 25					08 52						09 25					09 55			
Stratford International ⊖	d		08 32					08 58						09 32					10 02			
Ebbsfleet International	d		08 43					09 13						09 43					10 13			
London Victoria 15 ⊖	d				08 22					08 52		08 58				09 22					09 52	
London Blackfriars 3 ⊖	d																					
Elephant & Castle ⊖	d																					
Bromley South 4	d				08 39					09 09		09 19				09 39					10 09	
St Mary Cray	d											09 25										
Swanley 4	d											09 29										
Farningham Road	d											09 34										
Longfield	d				08 52					09 22		09 38				09 52					10 22	
Meopham	d				08 57					09 27		09 42				09 57					10 27	
Sole Street	d											09 45										
London Charing Cross 4 ⊖	d					08 09					08 39						09 09					09 39
London Waterloo (East) 4 ⊖	d					08 12					08 42						09 12					09 42
London Cannon Street 4 ⊖	d																					
London Bridge 4 ⊖	d					08 17					08 47						09 17					09 47
Dartford 4	d					08 55					09 25						09 55					10 25
Greenhithe for Bluewater	d					09 00					09 30						10 00					10 30
Gravesend 4	d		08 48			09 07		09 18			09 37			09 48			10 07		10 18			10 37
Strood 4	d		08 58			09 18		09 28			09 48			09 58			10 18		10 28			10 48
Rochester 4	d		09 03		09 09	09 22		09 33		09 39	09 52	09 56		10 03		10 09	10 22		10 33		10 39	10 52
Chatham 4	d		09 05		09 12	09 25		09 35		09 42	09 55	09 59		10 05		10 12	10 25		10 35		10 42	10 55
Gillingham (Kent) 4	d		09 10		09 17	09a29		09 40		09 47	09a59	10a03		10 10		10 17	10a29		10 40		10 47	10a59
Rainham (Kent)	d		09 15		09 21			09 45		09 51				10 15		10 21			10 45		10 51	
Newington	d									09 55											10 55	
Sittingbourne 4	a		09 22		09 28			09 52		10 00				10 22		10 28			10 52		11 00	
	d	09 10	09 23		09 29		09 40	09 53		10 01			10 10	10 23		10 29		10 40	10 53		11 01	
Kemsley	d	09 15					09 45						10 15					10 45				
Swale	d	09 18					09 48						10 18					10 48				
Queenborough	d	09 22					09 52						10 22					10 52				
Sheerness-on-Sea	a	09 27					09 57						10 27					10 57				
Teynham	d				09 33											10 33						
Faversham 2	a		09 33		09 39			10 03		10 09				10 33		10 39			11 03		11 09	
	d			09 43	09 45				10 13	10 15					10 43	10 45				11 13	11 15	
Selling	d				09 50											10 50						
Canterbury East 4	d				09 59					10 29						10 59					11 29	
Bekesbourne	d				10 03											11 03						
Adisham	d				10 08											11 08						
Aylesham	d				10 10											11 10						
Snowdown	d				10 13											11 13						
Shepherds Well	d				10 17											11 17						
Kearsney	d				10 21											11 21						
Dover Priory 4	a				10 27					10 48						11 27					11 48	
Whitstable	d			09 51					10 21						10 51					11 21		
Chestfield & Swalecliffe	d			09 54											10 54							
Herne Bay	d			09 58					10 26						10 58					11 26		
Birchington-on-Sea	d			10 07					10 35						11 07					11 35		
Westgate-on-Sea	d			10 11											11 11							
Margate 4	d			10 15					10 41						11 15					11 41		
Broadstairs	d			10 20					10 46						11 20					11 46		
Dumpton Park	d			10 23											11 23							
Ramsgate 4	a			10 26					10 51						11 26					11 51		

Table 212

London - Medway, Sheerness-on-Sea, Dover and Ramsgate

		SE ■1	SE	SE	SE ■1	SE	SE	SE		SE ■1	SE	SE ■1	SE	SE	SE ■1	SE		SE	SE	SE ■1	SE
St Pancras Internatnl ■15 ⊖	d			10 28				10 52						11 28					11 55		
Stratford International ⊖	d			10 35				10 58						11 35					12 02		
Ebbsfleet International	d			10 46				11 13						11 46					12 13		
London Victoria ■15 ⊖	d	09 58			10 22					10 52		10 58			11 22					11 52	
London Blackfriars ■3 ⊖	d																				
Elephant & Castle ⊖	d																				
Bromley South ■4	d	10 19			10 39					11 09		11 19			11 39					12 09	
St Mary Cray	d	10 25										11 25									
Swanley ■4	d	10 29										11 29									
Farningham Road	d	10 34										11 34									
Longfield	d	10 38			10 52					11 22		11 38			11 52					12 22	
Meopham	d	10 42			10 57					11 27		11 42			11 57					12 27	
Sole Street	d	10 45										11 45									
London Charing Cross ■4 ⊖	d					10 09					10 39					11 09					11 39
London Waterloo (East) ■4 ⊖	d					10 12					10 42					11 12					11 42
London Cannon Street ■4 ⊖	d																				
London Bridge ■4 ⊖	d					10 17					10 47					11 17					11 47
Dartford ■4	d					10 55					11 25					11 55					12 25
Greenhithe for Bluewater	d					11 00					11 30					12 00					12 30
Gravesend ■4	d			10 51		11 07		11 18			11 37			11 51		12 07			12 18		12 37
Strood ■4	d			11 01		11 18		11 28			11 48			12 01		12 18			12 28		12 48
Rochester ■4	d	10 56		11 06	11 09	11 22		11 33		11 39	11 52	11 56		12 06	12 09	12 22			12 33	12 39	12 52
Chatham ■4	d	10 59		11 08	11 12	11 25		11 35		11 42	11 55	11 59		12 08	12 12	12 25			12 35	12 42	12 55
Gillingham (Kent) ■4	d	11a03		11 13	11 17	11a29		11 40		11 47	11a59	12a03		12 13	12 17	12a29			12 40	12 47	12a59
Rainham (Kent)	d			11 18	11 21			11 45		11 51				12 18	12 21				12 45	12 51	
Newington	d									11 55										12 55	
Sittingbourne ■4	a			11 25	11 29			11 52		12 00				12 25	12 28				12 52	13 00	
	d		11 10	11 25	11 29		11 40	11 53		12 01			12 10	12 25	12 29			12 40	12 53	13 01	
Kemsley	d		11 15				11 45						12 15					12 45			
Swale	d		11 18				11 48						12 18					12 48			
Queenborough	d		11 22				11 52						12 22					12 52			
Sheerness-on-Sea	a		11 27				11 57						12 27					12 57			
Teynham	d				11 33										12 33						
Faversham ■2	a			11 34	11 39			12 03		12 09				12 33	12 39				13 03	13 09	
	d				11 43 / 11 45					12 13 / 12 15					12 43 / 12 45					13 13 / 13 15	
Selling	d				11 50										12 50						
Canterbury East ■4	d				11 59					12 29					12 59					13 29	
Bekesbourne	d				12 03										13 03						
Adisham	d				12 08										13 08						
Aylesham	d				12 10										13 10						
Snowdown	d				12 13										13 13						
Shepherds Well	d				12 17										13 17						
Kearsney	d				12 21										13 21						
Dover Priory ■4	a				12 27					12 48					13 27					13 48	
Whitstable	d				11 51					12 21					12 51					13 21	
Chestfield & Swalecliffe	d				11 54										12 54						
Herne Bay	d				11 58					12 26					12 58					13 26	
Birchington-on-Sea	d				12 07					12 35					13 07					13 35	
Westgate-on-Sea	d				12 11										13 11						
Margate ■4	d				12 15					12 41					13 15					13 41	
Broadstairs	d				12 20					12 46					13 20					13 46	
Dumpton Park	d				12 23										13 23						
Ramsgate ■4	a				12 26					12 51					13 26					13 51	

Table 212

Saturdays

London - Medway, Sheerness-on-Sea, Dover and Ramsgate

		SE 1	SE	SE	SE 1			SE	SE	SE	SE 1		SE	SE 1	SE	SE		SE 1		SE	SE	SE	SE 1		SE
St Pancras Internatnl 15 ⊖	d			12 25						12 55						13 25						13 55			
Stratford International ⊖	d			12 36						13 06						13 32						14 02			
Ebbsfleet International	d			12 47						13 17						13 43						14 13			
London Victoria 15 ⊖	d	11 58			12 22						12 52			12 58				13 22					13 52		
London Blackfriars 3 ⊖	d																								
Elephant & Castle ⊖	d																								
Bromley South 4	d	12 19			12 39						13 09			13 19				13 39					14 09		
St Mary Cray	d	12 25												13 25											
Swanley 4	d	12 29												13 29											
Farningham Road	d	12 34												13 34											
Longfield	d	12 38			12 52						13 22			13 38				13 52					14 22		
Meopham	d	12 42			12 57						13 27			13 42				13 57					14 27		
Sole Street	d	12 45												13 45											
London Charing Cross 4 ⊖	d							12 09					12 39							13 09					13 39
London Waterloo (East) 4 ⊖	d							12 12					12 42							13 12					13 42
London Cannon Street 4 ⊖	d																								
London Bridge 4 ⊖	d							12 17					12 47							13 17					13 47
Dartford 4	d							12 55					13 25							13 55					14 25
Greenhithe for Bluewater	d							13 00					13 30							14 00					14 30
Gravesend 4	d			12 51				13 07		13 22			13 37			13 48				14 07		14 18			14 37
Strood 4	d			13 01				13 18		13 32			13 48			13 58				14 18		14 28			14 48
Rochester 4	d	12 56		13 06	13 09			13 22		13 37	13 39		13 52	13 56		14 03		14 09		14 22		14 33	14 39		14 52
Chatham 4	d	12 59		13 08	13 12			13 25		13 39	13 42		13 55	13 59		14 05		14 12		14 25		14 35	14 42		14 55
Gillingham (Kent) 4	d	13a03		13 13	13 17			13a29		13 44	13 47		13a59	14a03		14 10		14 17		14a29		14 40	14 47		14a59
Rainham (Kent)	d			13 18	13 21					13 49	13 51					14 15		14 21				14 45	14 51		
Newington	d										13 55												14 55		
Sittingbourne 4	a			13 25	13 29					13 56	14 00					14 22		14 28				14 52	15 00		
	d		13 10	13 25	13 29				13 40	13 56	14 01				14 10	14 23		14 29			14 40	14 53	15 01		
Kemsley	d		13 15						13 45						14 15						14 45				
Swale	d		13 18						13 48						14 18						14 48				
Queenborough	d		13 22						13 52						14 22						14 52				
Sheerness-on-Sea	a		13 27						13 57						14 27						14 57				
Teynham	d				13 33													14 33							
Faversham 2	a			13 34	13 39					14 04	14 09					14 33		14 39				15 03	15 09		
	d				13 43	13 45					14 13	14 15						14 43	14 45				15 13	15 15	
Selling	d					13 50													14 50						
Canterbury East 4	d					13 59						14 29							14 59					15 29	
Bekesbourne	d					14 03													15 03						
Adisham	d					14 08													15 08						
Aylesham	d					14 10													15 10						
Snowdown	d					14 13													15 13						
Shepherds Well	d					14 17													15 17						
Kearsney	d					14 21													15 21						
Dover Priory 4	a					14 27						14 48							15 27					15 48	
Whitstable	d				13 51						14 21							14 51					15 21		
Chestfield & Swalecliffe	d				13 54													14 54							
Herne Bay	d				13 58						14 26							14 58					15 26		
Birchington-on-Sea	d				14 07						14 35							15 07					15 35		
Westgate-on-Sea	d				14 11													15 11							
Margate 4	d				14 15						14 41							15 15					15 41		
Broadstairs	d				14 20						14 46							15 20					15 46		
Dumpton Park	d				14 23													15 23							
Ramsgate 4	a				14 26						14 51							15 26					15 51		

Table 212

Saturdays

London - Medway, Sheerness-on-Sea, Dover and Ramsgate

		SE [1]		SE	SE	SE [1]	SE	SE	SE	SE [1]		SE	SE [1]	SE	SE	SE [1]	SE	SE	SE		SE [1]
St Pancras Internatnl [15] ⊖	d				14 25				14 55						15 25				15 55		
Stratford International ⊖	d				14 32				15 02						15 32				16 02		
Ebbsfleet International	d				14 43				15 13						15 43				16 13		
London Victoria [15] ⊖	d	13 58				14 22				14 52			14 58			15 22					15 52
London Blackfriars [3] ⊖	d																				
Elephant & Castle ⊖	d																				
Bromley South [4]	d	14 19				14 39				15 09			15 19			15 39					16 09
St Mary Cray	d	14 25											15 25								
Swanley [4]	d	14 29											15 29								
Farningham Road	d	14 34											15 34								
Longfield	d	14 38				14 52				15 22			15 38			15 52					16 22
Meopham	d	14 42				14 57				15 27			15 42			15 57					16 27
Sole Street	d	14 45											15 45								
London Charing Cross [4] ⊖	d						14 09					14 39					15 09				
London Waterloo (East) [4] ⊖	d						14 12					14 42					15 12				
London Cannon Street [4] ⊖	d																				
London Bridge [4] ⊖	d						14 17					14 47					15 17				
Dartford [4]	d						14 55					15 25					15 55				
Greenhithe for Bluewater	d						15 00					15 30					16 00				
Gravesend [4]	d				14 48		15 07		15 18			15 37			15 48		16 07		16 18		
Strood [4]	d				14 58		15 18		15 28			15 48			15 58		16 18		16 28		
Rochester [4]	d	14 56			15 03	15 09	15 22		15 33	15 39		15 52	15 56		16 03	16 09	16 22		16 33		16 39
Chatham [4]	d	14 59			15 05	15 12	15 25		15 35	15 42		15 55	15 59		16 05	16 12	16 25		16 35		16 42
Gillingham (Kent) [4]	d	15a03			15 10	15 17	15a29		15 40	15 47		15a59	16a03		16 10	16 17	16a29		16 40		16 47
Rainham (Kent)	d				15 15	15 21			15 45	15 51					16 15	16 21			16 45		16 51
Newington	d									15 55											16 55
Sittingbourne [4]	a				15 22	15 29			15 52	16 00					16 22	16 28			16 52		17 00
	d			15 10	15 23	15 29		15 40	15 53	16 01				16 10	16 23	16 29		16 40	16 53		17 01
Kemsley	d			15 15				15 45						16 15				16 45			
Swale	d			15 18				15 48						16 18				16 48			
Queenborough	d			15 22				15 52						16 22				16 52			
Sheerness-on-Sea	a			15 27				15 57						16 27				16 57			
Teynham	d					15 33										16 33					
Faversham [2]	a				15 33	15 39			16 03	16 09					16 33	16 39			17 03		17 09
	d					15 43 / 15 45				16 13 / 16 15						16 43 / 16 45					17 13 / 17 15
Selling	d					15 50										16 50					
Canterbury East [4]	d					15 59				16 29						16 59					17 29
Bekesbourne	d					16 03										17 03					
Adisham	d					16 08										17 08					
Aylesham	d					16 10										17 10					
Snowdown	d					16 13										17 13					
Shepherds Well	d					16 17										17 17					
Kearsney	d					16 21										17 21					
Dover Priory [4]	a					16 27				16 48						17 27					17 48
Whitstable	d					15 51				16 21						16 51					17 21
Chestfield & Swalecliffe	d					15 54										16 54					
Herne Bay	d					15 58				16 26						16 58					17 26
Birchington-on-Sea	d					16 07				16 35						17 07					17 35
Westgate-on-Sea	d					16 11										17 11					
Margate [4]	d					16 15				16 41						17 15					17 41
Broadstairs	d					16 20				16 46						17 20					17 46
Dumpton Park	d					16 23										17 23					
Ramsgate [4]	a					16 26				16 51						17 26					17 51

Table 212

Saturdays

London - Medway, Sheerness-on-Sea, Dover and Ramsgate

		SE	SE [1]	SE	SE	SE [1]		SE		SE	SE	SE [1]		SE	SE [1]	SE	SE	SE [1]			SE	SE	SE	SE [1]	
St Pancras Internatnl [15] ⊖	d				16 25						16 55						17 25						17 55		
Stratford International ⊖	d				16 32						17 02						17 32						18 02		
Ebbsfleet International	d				16 43						17 13						17 43						18 13		
London Victoria [15] ⊖	d		15 58			16 22						16 52			16 58			17 22						17 52	
London Blackfriars [3] ⊖	d																								
Elephant & Castle ⊖	d																								
Bromley South [4]	d		16 19			16 39						17 09			17 19			17 39						18 09	
St Mary Cray	d		16 25												17 25										
Swanley [4]	d		16 29												17 29										
Farningham Road	d		16 34												17 34										
Longfield	d		16 38			16 52						17 22			17 38			17 52						18 22	
Meopham	d		16 42			16 57						17 27			17 42			17 57						18 27	
Sole Street	d		16 45												17 45										
London Charing Cross [4] ⊖	d	15 39						16 09						16 39							17 09				
London Waterloo (East) [4] ⊖	d	15 42						16 12						16 42							17 12				
London Cannon Street [4] ⊖	d																								
London Bridge [4] ⊖	d	15 47						16 17						16 47							17 17				
Dartford [4]	d	16 25						16 55						17 25							17 55				
Greenhithe for Bluewater	d	16 30						17 00						17 30							18 00				
Gravesend [4]	d	16 37			16 48			17 07			17 18			17 37			17 48				18 07		18 18		
Strood [4]	d	16 48			16 58			17 18			17 28			17 48			17 58				18 18		18 28		
Rochester [4]	d	16 52	16 56		17 03	17 09		17 22			17 33	17 39		17 52	17 56		18 03	18 09			18 22		18 33	18 39	
Chatham [4]	d	16 55	16 59		17 05	17 12		17 25			17 35	17 42		17 55	17 59		18 05	18 12			18 25		18 35	18 42	
Gillingham (Kent) [4]	d	16a59	17a03		17 10	17 17		17a29			17 40	17 47		17a59	18a03		18 10	18 17			18a29		18 40	18 47	
Rainham (Kent)	d				17 15	17 21					17 45	17 51					18 15	18 21					18 45	18 51	
Newington	d											17 55												18 55	
Sittingbourne [4]	a				17 22	17 29					17 52	18 00					18 22	18 29					18 52	19 00	
	d			17 10	17 23	17 29				17 40	17 53	18 01				18 10	18 23	18 29				18 40	18 53	19 01	
Kemsley	d			17 15						17 45						18 15						18 45			
Swale	d			17 18						17 48						18 18						18 48			
Queenborough	d			17 22						17 52						18 22						18 52			
Sheerness-on-Sea	a			17 27						17 57						18 27						18 57			
Teynham	d					17 33												18 33							
Faversham [2]	a				17 33	17 39					18 03	18 09					18 33	18 39					19 03	19 09	
	d					17 43	17 45					18 13	18 15					18 43	18 45					19 13	19 15
Selling	d						17 50												18 50						
Canterbury East [4]	d						17 59						18 29						18 59						19 29
Bekesbourne	d						18 03												19 03						
Adisham	d						18 08												19 08						
Aylesham	d						18 10												19 10						
Snowdown	d						18 13												19 13						
Shepherds Well	d						18 17												19 17						
Kearsney	d						18 21												19 21						
Dover Priory [4]	a						18 27						18 48						19 27						19 48
Whitstable	d					17 51						18 21						18 51						19 21	
Chestfield & Swalecliffe	d					17 54												18 54							
Herne Bay	d					17 58						18 26						18 58						19 26	
Birchington-on-Sea	d					18 07						18 35						19 07						19 35	
Westgate-on-Sea	d					18 11												19 11							
Margate [4]	d					18 15						18 41						19 15						19 41	
Broadstairs	d					18 20						18 46						19 20						19 46	
Dumpton Park	d					18 23												19 23							
Ramsgate [4]	a					18 26						18 51						19 26						19 51	

Table 212

Saturdays

London - Medway, Sheerness-on-Sea, Dover and Ramsgate

		SE	SE ■1	SE	SE		SE ■1		SE	SE	SE	SE ■1		SE	SE ■1		SE	SE	SE ■1		SE	SE	SE	SE ■1	
St Pancras Internatnl ■15 ⊖	d				18 25						18 55							19 25					19 55		
Stratford International ⊖	d				18 32						19 02							19 32					20 02		
Ebbsfleet International	d				18 43						19 13							19 43					20 13		
London Victoria ■15 ⊖	d		17 58				18 22					18 52			18 58				19 22					19 52	
London Blackfriars ■3 ⊖	d																								
Elephant & Castle ⊖	d																								
Bromley South ■4	d		18 19				18 39					19 09			19 19				19 39					20 09	
St Mary Cray	d		18 25												19 25										
Swanley ■4	d		18 29												19 29										
Farningham Road	d		18 34												19 34										
Longfield	d		18 38				18 52					19 22			19 38				19 52					20 22	
Meopham	d		18 42				18 57					19 27			19 42				19 57					20 27	
Sole Street	d		18 45												19 45										
London Charing Cross ■4 ⊖	d	17 39							18 09					18 39							19 09				
London Waterloo (East) ■4 ⊖	d	17 42							18 12					18 42							19 12				
London Cannon Street ■4 ⊖	d																								
London Bridge ■4 ⊖	d	17 47							18 17					18 47							19 17				
Dartford ■4	d	18 25							18 55					19 25							19 55				
Greenhithe for Bluewater	d	18 30							19 00					19 30							20 00				
Gravesend ■4	d	18 37			18 48				19 07		19 18			19 37				19 48			20 07		20 18		
Strood ■4	d	18 48			18 58				19 18		19 28			19 48				19 58			20 18		20 28		
Rochester ■4	d	18 52	18 56		19 03		19 09		19 22		19 33	19 39		19 52	19 56			20 03	20 09		20 22		20 33	20 39	
Chatham ■4	d	18 55	18 59		19 05		19 12		19 25		19 35	19 42		19 55	19 59			20 05	20 12		20 25		20 35	20 42	
Gillingham (Kent) ■4	d	18a59	19a03		19 10		19 17		19a29		19 40	19 47		19a59	20a03			20 10	20 17		20a29		20 40	20 47	
Rainham (Kent)	d				19 15		19 21				19 45	19 51						20 15	20 21				20 45	20 51	
Newington	d											19 55												20 55	
Sittingbourne ■4	a				19 22		19 28				19 52	20 00						20 22	20 28				20 52	21 00	
	d			19 10	19 23		19 29			19 40	19 53	20 01					20 10	20 23	20 29			20 40	20 53	21 01	
Kemsley	d			19 15						19 45							20 15					20 45			
Swale	d			19 18						19 48							20 18					20 48			
Queenborough	d			19 22						19 52							20 22					20 52			
Sheerness-on-Sea	a			19 27						19 57							20 27					20 57			
Teynham	d						19 33												20 33						
Faversham ■2	a				19 33		19 39				20 03	20 09						20 33	20 39				21 03	21 09	
	d						19 43	19 45				20 13	20 15						20 43	20 45				21 13	21 15
Selling	d							19 50												20 50					
Canterbury East ■4	d							19 59					20 29							20 59					21a26
Bekesbourne	d							20 03												21 03					
Adisham	d							20 08												21 08					
Aylesham	d							20 10												21 10					
Snowdown	d							20 13												21 13					
Shepherds Well	d							20 17												21 17					
Kearsney	d							20 21												21 21					
Dover Priory ■4	a							20 27					20 48							21 27					
Whitstable	d						19 51					20 21							20 51					21 21	
Chestfield & Swalecliffe	d						19 54												20 54						
Herne Bay	d						19 58					20 26							20 58					21 26	
Birchington-on-Sea	d						20 07					20 35							21 07					21 35	
Westgate-on-Sea	d						20 11												21 11						
Margate ■4	d						20 15					20 41							21 15					21 41	
Broadstairs	d						20 20					20 46							21 20					21 46	
Dumpton Park	d						20 23												21 23						
Ramsgate ■4	a						20 26					20 51							21 26					21 51	

Table 212

Saturdays

London - Medway, Sheerness-on-Sea, Dover and Ramsgate

		SE	SE 1	SE	SE 1		SE	SE	SE	SE 1	SE	SE	SE 1		SE	SE	SE	SE 1	SE	SE	SE 1	
St Pancras Internatnl 15 ⊖	d			20 25					20 55			21 25					21 55			22 25		
Stratford International ⊖	d			20 32					21 02			21 32					22 02			22 32		
Ebbsfleet International	d			20 43					21 13			21 43					22 13			22 43		
London Victoria 15 ⊖	d		19 58		20 22					20 52			21 22					21 52			22 22	
London Blackfriars 3 ⊖	d																					
Elephant & Castle ⊖	d																					
Bromley South 4	d		20 19		20 39					21 09			21 39					22 09			22 39	
St Mary Cray	d		20 25							21 15								22 15				
Swanley 4	d		20 29							21 19								22 19				
Farningham Road	d		20 34							21 24								22 24				
Longfield	d		20 38		20 52					21 28			21 52					22 28			22 52	
Meopham	d		20 42		20 57					21 32			21 57					22 32			22 57	
Sole Street	d		20 45							21 35								22 35				
London Charing Cross 4 ⊖	d	19 39					20 09				20 39				21 09				21 39			
London Waterloo (East) 4 ⊖	d	19 42					20 12				20 42				21 12				21 42			
London Cannon Street 4 ⊖	d																					
London Bridge 4 ⊖	d	19 47					20 17				20 47				21 17				21 47			
Dartford 4	d	20 25					20 55				21 25				21 55				22 25			
Greenhithe for Bluewater	d	20 30					21 00				21 30				22 00				22 31			
Gravesend 4	d	20 37		20 48			21 07		21 18		21 37	21 48			22 07		22 18		22 40	22 48		
Strood 4	d	20 48		20 58			21 18		21 28		21 48	21 58			22 18		22 28		22 52	22 58		
Rochester 4	d	20 52	20 56	21 03	21 09		21 22		21 33	21 45	21 52	22 03	22 09		22 22		22 33	22 45	22 56	23 03	23 09	
Chatham 4	d	20 55	20 59	21 05	21 12		21 25		21 35	21 47	21 55	22 05	22 12		22 25		22 35	22 47	22 58	23 05	23 12	
Gillingham (Kent) 4	d	20a59	21a03	21 10	21 17		21a29		21 40	21 52	21a59	22 10	22 17		22a29		22 40	22 52	23a03	23 10	23 17	
Rainham (Kent)	d			21 15	21 21				21 45	21 56		22 15	22 21				22 45	22 56		23 15	23 21	
Newington	d									22 00								23 00				
Sittingbourne 4	a			21 22	21 28				21 52	22 05		22 22	22 28				22 52	23 05		23 22	23 28	
	d			21 23	21 29			21 40	21 53	22 06		22 23	22 29			22 40	22 53	23 06		23 23	23 29	
Kemsley	d							21 45								22 45						
Swale	d							21 48								22 48						
Queenborough	d							21 52								22 52						
Sheerness-on-Sea	a							21 57								22 57						
Teynham	d				21 33								22 33								23 33	
Faversham 2	a			21 33	21 39				22 03	22 14		22 31	22 39				23 01	23 14		23 31	23 39	
	d				21 43	21 45				22 15			22 43	22 45							23 43	23 45
Selling	d					21 50								22 50								23 50
Canterbury East 4	d					21 59				22a26				22 59								23 59
Bekesbourne	d					22 03								23 03								
Adisham	d					22 08								23 08								
Aylesham	d					22 10								23 10								00 07
Snowdown	d					22 13								23 13								
Shepherds Well	d					22 17								23 17								
Kearsney	d					22 21								23 21								
Dover Priory 4	a					22 27								23 27								00 18
Whitstable	d				21 51								22 51								23 51	
Chestfield & Swalecliffe	d				21 54								22 54								23 54	
Herne Bay	d				21 58								22 58								23 58	
Birchington-on-Sea	d				22 07								23 07								00 07	
Westgate-on-Sea	d				22 11								23 11								00 11	
Margate 4	d				22 15								23 15								00 15	
Broadstairs	d				22 20								23 20								00 20	
Dumpton Park	d				22 23								23 23								00 23	
Ramsgate 4	a				22 26								23 26								00 26	

Table 212

Saturdays

London - Medway, Sheerness-on-Sea, Dover and Ramsgate

		SE	SE	SE	SE 1	SE	SE	SE 1	SE	SE	SE 1	SE
St Pancras Internatnl 15 ⊖	d			22 55			23 25			23 55		
Stratford International ⊖	d			23 02			23 32			00 02		
Ebbsfleet International	d			23 13			23 43			00 13		
London Victoria 15 ⊖	d				22 52			23 22			23 52	
London Blackfriars 3 ⊖	d											
Elephant & Castle ⊖	d											
Bromley South 4	d				23 09			23 39			00 09	
St Mary Cray	d				23 15						00 15	
Swanley 4	d				23 19						00 19	
Farningham Road	d				23 24						00 24	
Longfield	d				23 28			23 52			00 28	
Meopham	d				23 32			23 57			00 32	
Sole Street	d				23 35						00 35	
London Charing Cross 4 ⊖	d	22 09				22 39			23 09			23 39
London Waterloo (East) 4 ⊖	d	22 12				22 42			23 12			23 42
London Cannon Street 4 ⊖	d											
London Bridge 4 ⊖	d	22 17				22 47			23 17			23 47
Dartford 4	d	22 55				23 25			23 55			00 25
Greenhithe for Bluewater	d	23 01				23 31			23 59			00 31
Gravesend 4	d	23 10		23 18		23 40	23 48		00 10	00 18		00 40
Strood 4	d	23 22		23 28		23 52	23 58		00 22	00 28		00 52
Rochester 4	d	23 26		23 33	23 45	23 56	00 03	00 09	00 26	00 33	00 45	00 56
Chatham 4	d	23 28		23 35	23 47	23 58	00 05	00 12	00 28	00 35	00 47	00 58
Gillingham (Kent) 4	d	23a33		23 40	23 52	00a03	00 10	00 17	00a33	00 40	00a52	01a03
Rainham (Kent)	d			23 45	23 56		00 15	00 21		00 45		
Newington	d				00 01							
Sittingbourne 4	a			23 52	00 06		00 22	00 28		00 52		
	d		23 32	23 53	00 07		00 23	00 29		00 53		
Kemsley	d		23 37									
Swale	d		23 40									
Queenborough	d		23 44									
Sheerness-on-Sea	a		23 49									
Teynham	d							00 33				
Faversham 2	a			00 01	00 16		00 31	00 39		01 01		
	d							00 43				
Selling	d											
Canterbury East 4	d											
Bekesbourne	d											
Adisham	d											
Aylesham	d											
Snowdown	d											
Shepherds Well	d											
Kearsney	d											
Dover Priory 4	a											
Whitstable	d							00 51				
Chestfield & Swalecliffe	d							00 54				
Herne Bay	d							00 58				
Birchington-on-Sea	d							01 07				
Westgate-on-Sea	d							01 11				
Margate 4	d							01 15				
Broadstairs	d							01 20				
Dumpton Park	d							01 23				
Ramsgate 4	a							01 26				

Table 212

Sundays

London - Medway, Sheerness-on-Sea, Dover and Ramsgate

Station		SE [1] A	SE A	SE [1] A	SE	SE A	SE [1] A	SE A	SE A	SE [1] A	SE [1]	SE A	SE	SE	SE	SE	SE [1]	SE	SE [1]	SE	SE
St Pancras Internatnl [15] ⊖	d		22p55			23p25			23p55				00 12								
Stratford International ⊖	d		23p02			23p32			00 02				00 19								
Ebbsfleet International	d		23p13			23p43			00 13				00 31								
London Victoria [15] ⊖	d	22p22		22p52			23p22			23p52	00 10			00 35			07 24		08 05		
London Blackfriars [3] ⊖	d																				
Elephant & Castle ⊖	d																				
Bromley South [4]	d	22p39		23p09			23p39			00 09				00 55			07 44		08 22		
St Mary Cray	d			23p15						00 15				01 01			07 50				
Swanley [4]	d			23p19						00 19				01 05			07 54				
Farningham Road	d			23p24						00 24				01 10			07 59				
Longfield	d	22p52		23p28			23p52			00 28				01 14			08 03				
Meopham	d	22p57		23p32			23p57			00 32				01 18			08 07				
Sole Street	d			23p35						00 35							08 10				
London Charing Cross [4] ⊖	d							23p09				23p39			00 15						
London Waterloo (East) [4] ⊖	d							23p12				23p42			00 18						
London Cannon Street [4] ⊖	d																				
London Bridge [4] ⊖	d							23p17				23p47			00 23						
Dartford [4]	d							23p55				00 25			01 03			07 55		08 25	
Greenhithe for Bluewater	d							23p59				00 31			01 08			08 01		08 31	
Gravesend [4]	d		23p18			23p48		00 10	00 18			00 40			01 15			08 10		08 40	
Strood [4]	d		23p28			23p58		00 22	00 28			00 52			01 26			08 22		08 52	
Rochester [4]	d	23p09	23p33	23p45		00 03	00 09	00 26	00 33	00 45	00 49	00 56		01 29	01 32		08 20	08 26	08 46	08 56	
Chatham [4]	d	23p12	23p35	23p47		00 05	00 12	00 28	00 35	00 47	00 52	00 58		01 31	01 35		08 22	08 28	08 48	08 58	
Gillingham (Kent) [4]	d	23p17	23p40	23p52		00 10	00 17	00a33	00 40	00a52	00 57	01a03		01a35	01a41		08 27	08a33	08 53	09a03	
Rainham (Kent)	d	23p21	23p45	23p56		00 15	00 21		00 45		01 01						08 31		08 57		
Newington	d			00 01							01 05						08 35				
Sittingbourne [4]	a	23p28	23p52	00 06		00 22	00 28		00 52		01 10						08 40		09 04		
	d	23p29	23p53	00 07	00 15	00 23	00 29		00 53		01 11					08 10	08 41		09 05		09 10
Kemsley	d				00 20											08 15					09 15
Swale	d				00 23											08 18					09 18
Queenborough	d				00 27											08 22					09 22
Sheerness-on-Sea	a				00 32											08 27					09 27
Teynham	d	23p33					00 33				01 15						08 45				
Faversham [2]	a	23p39	00 01	00 16		00 31	00 39		01 01		01 23						08 51		09 13		
	d	23p43 23p45					00 43				01 24						08 52		09 17 09 19		
Selling	d	23p50																	09 24		
Canterbury East [4]	d	23p59															09a04		09 33		
Bekesbourne	d																		09 37		
Adisham	d																		09 42		
Aylesham	d	00 07																	09 44		
Snowdown	d																		09 47		
Shepherds Well	d																		09 51		
Kearsney	d																		09 55		
Dover Priory [4]	a	00 18																	10 00		
Whitstable	d	23p51					00 51				01 32								09 25		
Chestfield & Swalecliffe	d	23p54					00 54				01 35								09 28		
Herne Bay	d	23p58					00 58				01 39								09 32		
Birchington-on-Sea	d	00 07					01 07				01 48								09 41		
Westgate-on-Sea	d	00 11					01 11				01 52								09 45		
Margate [4]	d	00 15					01 15				01 56								09 49		
Broadstairs	d	00 20					01 20				02 01								09 54		
Dumpton Park	d	00 23					01 23				02 04								09 57		
Ramsgate [4]	a	00 26					01 26				02 07								10 00		

A not 22 May

Table 212

Sundays

London - Medway, Sheerness-on-Sea, Dover and Ramsgate

		SE 1	SE	SE	SE 1			SE	SE	SE	SE 1	SE	SE	SE 1		SE		SE	SE	SE 1	SE	SE	SE 1		SE
St Pancras Internatnl 15 ⊖	d			08 52						09 25			09 55						10 28			10 52			
Stratford International ⊖	d			08 58						09 32			10 02						10 35			10 58			
Ebbsfleet International	d			09 13						09 43			10 13						10 46			11 14			
London Victoria 15 ⊖	d	08 24			09 05						09 24			10 05						10 24			11 05		
London Blackfriars 3 ⊖	d																								
Elephant & Castle ⊖	d																								
Bromley South 4	d	08 44			09 22						09 44			10 22						10 44			11 22		
St Mary Cray	d	08 50									09 50									10 50					
Swanley 4	d	08 54									09 54									10 54					
Farningham Road	d	08 59									09 59									10 59					
Longfield	d	09 03									10 03									11 03					
Meopham	d	09 07									10 07									11 07					
Sole Street	d	09 10									10 10									11 10					
London Charing Cross 4 ⊖	d		08 10					08 40				09 10				09 40					10 10				10 40
London Waterloo (East) 4 ⊖	d		08 13					08 43				09 13				09 43					10 13				10 43
London Cannon Street 4 ⊖	d																								
London Bridge 4 ⊖	d		08 18					08 48				09 18				09 48					10 18				10 48
Dartford 4	d		08 55					09 25				09 55				10 25					10 55				11 25
Greenhithe for Bluewater	d		09 00					09 30				10 00				10 30					11 00				11 30
Gravesend 4	d		09 07	09 18				09 37		09 48		10 07	10 18			10 37			10 51		11 07	11 18			11 37
Strood 4	d		09 18	09 28				09 48		09 58		10 18	10 28			10 48			11 01		11 18	11 28			11 48
Rochester 4	d	09 20	09 23	09 33	09 46			09 52		10 03	10 20	10 23	10 33	10 46		10 52			11 06	11 20	11 23	11 33	11 46		11 52
Chatham 4	d	09 22	09 26	09 35	09 48			09 55		10 05	10 22	10 26	10 35	10 48		10 55			11 08	11 22	11 26	11 35	11 48		11 55
Gillingham (Kent) 4	d	09 27	09a30	09 40	09 53			10a02		10 10	10 27	10a30	10 40	10 53		11a02			11 13	11 27	11a30	11 40	11 53		12a02
Rainham (Kent)	d	09 31		09 45	09 57					10 15	10 31		10 45	10 57					11 18	11 31		11 45	11 57		
Newington	d	09 35									10 35									11 35					
Sittingbourne 4	a	09 40		09 52	10 04					10 22	10 40		10 52	11 04					11 25	11 40		11 52	12 04		
	d	09 41		09 53	10 05				10 10	10 23	10 41		10 53	11 05				11 10	11 25	11 41		11 53	12 05		
Kemsley	d								10 15									11 15							
Swale	d								10 18									11 18							
Queenborough	d								10 22									11 22							
Sheerness-on-Sea	a								10 27									11 27							
Teynham	d	09 45									10 45									11 45					
Faversham 2	a	09 51		10 01	10 13					10 33	10 51		11 03	11 13					11 33	11 51		12 03	12 13		
	d	09 52			10 17	10 19					10 52			11 17	11 19					11 52			12 17	12 19	
Selling	d					10 24									11 24									12 24	
Canterbury East 4	d	10a04				10 33					11a04				11 33					12a04				12 33	
Bekesbourne	d					10 37									11 37									12 37	
Adisham	d					10 42									11 42									12 42	
Aylesham	d					10 44									11 44									12 44	
Snowdown	d					10 47									11 47									12 47	
Shepherds Well	d					10 51									11 51									12 51	
Kearsney	d					10 55									11 55									12 55	
Dover Priory 4	a					11 00									12 00									13 00	
Whitstable	d				10 25									11 25									12 25		
Chestfield & Swalecliffe	d				10 28									11 28									12 28		
Herne Bay	d				10 32									11 32									12 32		
Birchington-on-Sea	d				10 41									11 41									12 41		
Westgate-on-Sea	d				10 45									11 45									12 45		
Margate 4	d				10 49									11 49									12 49		
Broadstairs	d				10 54									11 54									12 54		
Dumpton Park	d				10 57									11 57									12 57		
Ramsgate 4	a				11 00									12 00									13 00		

Table 212

Sundays

London - Medway, Sheerness-on-Sea, Dover and Ramsgate

		SE		SE	SE [1]	SE [1]	SE	SE	SE [1]		SE	SE		SE	SE [1]	SE	SE	SE [1]		SE	SE	SE		SE [1]	SE
St Pancras Internatnl [15] ⊖	d			11 25				11 52						12 25			12 55					13 25			
Stratford International ⊖	d			11 32				11 58						12 36			13 02					13 32			
Ebbsfleet International	d			11 43				12 13						12 47			13 13					13 43			
London Victoria [15] ⊖	d					11 24			12 05						12 24			13 05						13 24	
London Blackfriars [3] ⊖	d																								
Elephant & Castle ⊖	d																								
Bromley South [4]	d					11 44			12 22						12 44			13 22						13 44	
St Mary Cray	d					11 50									12 50									13 50	
Swanley [4]	d					11 54									12 54									13 54	
Farningham Road	d					11 59									12 59									13 59	
Longfield	d					12 03									13 03									14 03	
Meopham	d					12 07									13 07									14 07	
Sole Street	d					12 10									13 10									14 10	
London Charing Cross [4] ⊖	d						11 10				11 40					12 10				12 40					13 10
London Waterloo (East) [4] ⊖	d						11 13				11 43					12 13				12 43					13 13
London Cannon Street [4] ⊖	d																								
London Bridge [4] ⊖	d						11 18				11 48					12 18				12 48					13 18
Dartford [4]	d						11 55				12 25					12 55				13 25					13 55
Greenhithe for Bluewater	d						12 00				12 30					13 00				13 30					14 00
Gravesend [4]	d			11 48			12 07	12 18			12 37			12 51		13 07	13 18			13 37		13 48			14 07
Strood [4]	d			11 58			12 18	12 28			12 48			13 01		13 18	13 28			13 48		13 58			14 18
Rochester [4]	d			12 03		12 20	12 23	12 33	12 46		12 52			13 06	13 20	13 23	13 33	13 46		13 52		14 03		14 20	14 23
Chatham [4]	d			12 05		12 22	12 26	12 35	12 48		12 55			13 08	13 22	13 26	13 35	13 48		13 55		14 05		14 22	14 26
Gillingham (Kent) [4]	d			12 10		12 27	12a30	12 40	12 53		13a02			13 13	13 27	13a30	13 40	13 53		14a02		14 10		14 27	14a30
Rainham (Kent)	d			12 15		12 31		12 45	12 57					13 18	13 31		13 45	13 57				14 15		14 31	
Newington	d					12 35									13 35									14 35	
Sittingbourne [4]	a			12 22		12 40		12 52	13 04					13 25	13 40		13 52	14 04				14 22		14 40	
	d	12 10		12 23		12 41		12 53	13 05			13 10		13 25	13 41		13 53	14 05			14 10	14 23		14 41	
Kemsley	d	12 15										13 15									14 15				
Swale	d	12 18										13 18									14 18				
Queenborough	d	12 22										13 22									14 22				
Sheerness-on-Sea	a	12 27										13 27									14 27				
Teynham	d					12 45									13 45									14 45	
Faversham [2]	a			12 33		12 51		13 01	13 13					13 33	13 51		14 03	14 13				14 33		14 51	
	d				12 19	12 52			13 17	13 19					13 52			14 17	14 19					14 52	
Selling	d				12 24					13 24									14 24						
Canterbury East [4]	d				12 33	13a04				13 33					14a04				14 33					15a04	
Bekesbourne	d				12 37					13 37									14 37						
Adisham	d				12 42					13 42									14 42						
Aylesham	d				12 44					13 44									14 44						
Snowdown	d				12 47					13 47									14 47						
Shepherds Well	d				12 51					13 51									14 51						
Kearsney	d				12 55					13 55									14 55						
Dover Priory [4]	a				13 00					14 00									15 00						
Whitstable	d								13 25									14 25							
Chestfield & Swalecliffe	d								13 28									14 28							
Herne Bay	d								13 32									14 32							
Birchington-on-Sea	d								13 41									14 41							
Westgate-on-Sea	d								13 45									14 45							
Margate [4]	d								13 49									14 49							
Broadstairs	d								13 54									14 54							
Dumpton Park	d								13 57									14 57							
Ramsgate [4]	a								14 00									15 00							

Table 212

Sundays

London - Medway, Sheerness-on-Sea, Dover and Ramsgate

		SE	SE ■1		SE	SE	SE	SE ■1		SE	SE	SE ■1		SE	SE	SE	SE ■1	SE		SE	SE ■1		SE	SE	SE
St Pancras Internatnl ■15 ⊖	d	13 55					14 25				14 55					15 25				15 55					16 25
Stratford International ⊖	d	14 02					14 32				15 02					15 32				16 02					16 32
Ebbsfleet International	d	14 13					14 43				15 13					15 43				16 13					16 43
London Victoria ■15 ⊖	d		14 05					14 24				15 05					15 24				16 05				
London Blackfriars ■3 ⊖	d																								
Elephant & Castle ⊖	d																								
Bromley South ■4	d		14 22					14 44				15 22					15 44				16 22				
St Mary Cray	d							14 50									15 50								
Swanley ■4	d							14 54									15 54								
Farningham Road	d							14 59									15 59								
Longfield	d							15 03									16 03								
Meopham	d							15 07									16 07								
Sole Street	d							15 10									16 10								
London Charing Cross ■4 ⊖	d				13 40					14 10				14 40				15 10					15 40		
London Waterloo (East) ■4 ⊖	d				13 43					14 13				14 43				15 13					15 43		
London Cannon Street ■4 ⊖	d																								
London Bridge ■4 ⊖	d				13 48					14 18				14 48				15 18					15 48		
Dartford ■4	d				14 25					14 55				15 25				15 55					16 25		
Greenhithe for Bluewater	d				14 30					15 00				15 30				16 00					16 30		
Gravesend ■4	d	14 18			14 37		14 48			15 07	15 18			15 37		15 48		16 07		16 18			16 37		16 48
Strood ■4	d	14 28			14 48		14 58			15 18	15 28			15 48		15 58		16 18		16 28			16 48		16 58
Rochester ■4	d	14 33	14 46		14 52		15 03	15 20		15 23	15 33	15 46		15 52		16 03	16 20	16 23		16 33	16 46		16 52		17 03
Chatham ■4	d	14 35	14 48		14 55		15 05	15 22		15 26	15 35	15 48		15 55		16 05	16 22	16 26		16 35	16 48		16 55		17 05
Gillingham (Kent) ■4	d	14 40	14 53		15a02		15 10	15 27		15a30	15 40	15 53		16a02		16 10	16 27	16a30		16 40	16 53		17a02		17 10
Rainham (Kent)	d	14 45	14 57				15 15	15 31			15 45	15 57				16 15	16 31			16 45	16 57				17 15
Newington	d							15 35									16 35								
Sittingbourne ■4	a	14 52	15 04				15 22	15 40			15 52	16 04				16 22	16 40			16 52	17 04				17 22
	d	14 53	15 05			15 10	15 23	15 41			15 53	16 05			16 10	16 23	16 41			16 53	17 05			17 10	17 23
Kemsley	d					15 15									16 15									17 15	
Swale	d					15 18									16 18									17 18	
Queenborough	d					15 22									16 22									17 22	
Sheerness-on-Sea	a					15 27									16 27									17 27	
Teynham	d							15 45									16 45								
Faversham ■2	a	15 03	15 13				15 33	15 51			16 03	16 13				16 33	16 51			17 03	17 13				17 33
	d		15 17	15 19				15 52				16 17	16 19				16 52				17 17	17 19			
Selling	d			15 24									16 24									17 24			
Canterbury East ■4	d			15 33				16a04					16 33				17a04					17 33			
Bekesbourne	d			15 37									16 37									17 37			
Adisham	d			15 42									16 42									17 42			
Aylesham	d			15 44									16 44									17 44			
Snowdown	d			15 47									16 47									17 47			
Shepherds Well	d			15 51									16 51									17 51			
Kearsney	d			15 55									16 55									17 55			
Dover Priory ■4	a			16 00									17 00									18 00			
Whitstable	d		15 25									16 25									17 25				
Chestfield & Swalecliffe	d		15 28									16 28									17 28				
Herne Bay	d		15 32									16 32									17 32				
Birchington-on-Sea	d		15 41									16 41									17 41				
Westgate-on-Sea	d		15 45									16 45									17 45				
Margate ■4	d		15 49									16 49									17 49				
Broadstairs	d		15 54									16 54									17 54				
Dumpton Park	d		15 57									16 57									17 57				
Ramsgate ■4	a		16 00									17 00									18 00				

Table 212

Sundays

London - Medway, Sheerness-on-Sea, Dover and Ramsgate

Station		SE 1	SE	SE		SE 1	SE	SE	SE	SE 1	SE	SE	SE 1		SE	SE	SE	SE 1	SE	SE	SE 1	SE
St Pancras Internatnl 15 ⊖	d			16 55					17 25			17 55					18 28			18 55		
Stratford International ⊖	d			17 02					17 32			18 02					18 35			19 02		
Ebbsfleet International	d			17 13					17 43			18 13					18 46			19 13		
London Victoria 15 ⊖	d	16 24				17 05				17 24			18 05					18 24			19 05	
London Blackfriars 3 ⊖	d																					
Elephant & Castle ⊖	d																					
Bromley South 4	d	16 44				17 22				17 44			18 22					18 44			19 22	
St Mary Cray	d	16 50								17 50								18 50				
Swanley 4	d	16 54								17 54								18 54				
Farningham Road	d	16 59								17 59								18 59				
Longfield	d	17 03								18 03								19 03				
Meopham	d	17 07								18 07								19 07				
Sole Street	d	17 10								18 10								19 10				
London Charing Cross 4 ⊖	d		16 10				16 40				17 10				17 40				18 10			18 40
London Waterloo (East) 4 ⊖	d		16 13				16 43				17 13				17 43				18 13			18 43
London Cannon Street 4 ⊖	d																					
London Bridge 4 ⊖	d		16 18				16 48				17 18				17 48				18 18			18 48
Dartford 4	d		16 55				17 25				17 55				18 25				18 55			19 25
Greenhithe for Bluewater	d		17 00				17 30				18 00				18 30				19 00			19 31
Gravesend 4	d		17 07	17 18			17 37		17 48		18 07	18 18			18 37		18 51		19 07	19 18		19 40
Strood 4	d		17 18	17 28			17 48		17 58		18 18	18 28			18 48		19 01		19 18	19 28		19 52
Rochester 4	d	17 20	17 23	17 33		17 46	17 52		18 03	18 20	18 23	18 33	18 46		18 52		19 06	19 20	19 23	19 33	19 46	19 56
Chatham 4	d	17 22	17 26	17 35		17 48	17 55		18 05	18 22	18 26	18 35	18 48		18 55		19 08	19 22	19 26	19 35	19 48	19 58
Gillingham (Kent) 4	d	17 27	17a30	17 40		17 53	18a02		18 10	18 27	18a30	18 40	18 53		19a02		19 13	19 27	19a30	19 40	19 53	20a03
Rainham (Kent)	d	17 31		17 45		17 57			18 15	18 31		18 45	18 57				19 18	19 31		19 45	19 57	
Newington	d	17 35								18 35								19 35				
Sittingbourne 4	a	17 40		17 52		18 04			18 22	18 40		18 52	19 04				19 25	19 40		19 52	20 04	
	d	17 41		17 53		18 05		18 10	18 23	18 41		18 53	19 05			19 10	19 25	19 41		19 53	20 05	
Kemsley	d							18 15								19 15						
Swale	d							18 18								19 18						
Queenborough	d							18 22								19 22						
Sheerness-on-Sea	a							18 27								19 27						
Teynham	d	17 45								18 45								19 45				
Faversham 2	a	17 51		18 03		18 13			18 33	18 51		19 03	19 13				19 34	19 51		20 03	20 13	
	d	17 52				18 17 / 18 19				18 52			19 17 / 19 19								20 17 / 20 19	
Selling	d					18 24							19 24								20 24	
Canterbury East 4	d	18a04				18 33				19a04			19 33								20 33	
Bekesbourne	d					18 37							19 37								20 37	
Adisham	d					18 42							19 42								20 42	
Aylesham	d					18 44							19 44								20 44	
Snowdown	d					18 47							19 47								20 47	
Shepherds Well	d					18 51							19 51								20 51	
Kearsney	d					18 55							19 55								20 55	
Dover Priory 4	a					19 00							20 00								21 00	
Whitstable	d					18 25							19 25								20 25	
Chestfield & Swalecliffe	d					18 28							19 28								20 28	
Herne Bay	d					18 32							19 32								20 32	
Birchington-on-Sea	d					18 41							19 41								20 41	
Westgate-on-Sea	d					18 45							19 45								20 45	
Margate 4	d					18 49							19 49								20 49	
Broadstairs	d					18 54							19 54								20 54	
Dumpton Park	d					18 57							19 57								20 57	
Ramsgate 4	a					19 00							20 00								21 00	

Table 212

Sundays

London - Medway, Sheerness-on-Sea, Dover and Ramsgate

		SE	SE	SE 1	SE	SE	SE 1		SE	SE	SE	SE 1	SE	SE	SE 1		SE	SE	SE	SE 1	SE	SE
St Pancras Internatnl 15 ⊖	d		19 25			19 55					20 25			20 55					21 25			21 55
Stratford International ⊖	d		19 32			20 02					20 32			21 02					21 32			22 02
Ebbsfleet International	d		19 43			20 13					20 43			21 13					21 43			22 13
London Victoria 15 ⊖	d			19 24			20 05					20 24			21 05					21 24		
London Blackfriars 3 ⊖	d																					
Elephant & Castle ⊖	d																					
Bromley South 4	d			19 44			20 22					20 44			21 22					21 44		
St Mary Cray	d			19 50								20 50								21 50		
Swanley 4	d			19 54								20 54								21 54		
Farningham Road	d			19 59								20 59								21 59		
Longfield	d			20 03								21 03								22 03		
Meopham	d			20 07								21 07								22 07		
Sole Street	d			20 10								21 10								22 10		
London Charing Cross 4 ⊖	d				19 10				19 40				20 10				20 40				21 10	
London Waterloo (East) 4 ⊖	d				19 13				19 43				20 13				20 43				21 13	
London Cannon Street 4 ⊖	d																					
London Bridge 4 ⊖	d				19 18				19 48				20 18				20 48				21 18	
Dartford 4	d				19 55				20 25				20 55				21 25				21 55	
Greenhithe for Bluewater	d				20 01				20 31				21 01				21 31				22 01	
Gravesend 4	d		19 48		20 10	20 18			20 40		20 48		21 10	21 18			21 40		21 48		22 10	22 18
Strood 4	d		19 58		20 22	20 28			20 52		20 58		21 22	21 28			21 52		21 58		22 22	22 28
Rochester 4	d		20 03	20 20	20 26	20 33	20 46		20 56		21 03	21 20	21 26	21 33	21 46		21 56		22 03	22 20	22 26	22 33
Chatham 4	d		20 05	20 22	20 28	20 35	20 48		20 58		21 05	21 22	21 28	21 35	21 48		21 58		22 05	22 22	22 28	22 35
Gillingham (Kent) 4	d		20 10	20 27	20a33	20 40	20 53		21a03		21 10	21 27	21a33	21 40	21 53		22a03		22 10	22 27	22a33	22 40
Rainham (Kent)	d		20 15	20 31		20 45	20 57				21 15	21 31		21 45	21 57				22 15	22 31		22 45
Newington	d			20 35								21 35								22 35		
Sittingbourne 4	a		20 22	20 40		20 52	21 04				21 22	21 40		21 52	22 04				22 22	22 40		22 52
	d	20 10	20 23	20 41		20 53	21 05			21 10	21 23	21 41		21 53	22 05			22 10	22 23	22 41		22 53
Kemsley	d	20 15								21 15								22 15				
Swale	d	20 18								21 18								22 18				
Queenborough	d	20 22								21 22								22 22				
Sheerness-on-Sea	a	20 27								21 27								22 27				
Teynham	d			20 45								21 45								22 45		
Faversham 2	a		20 33	20 51		21 03	21 13				21 33	21 51		22 03	22 13				22 33	22 51		23 03
	d						21 17	21 19							22 17	22 19						
Selling	d							21 24								22 24						
Canterbury East 4	d							21 33								22 33						
Bekesbourne	d							21 37								22 37						
Adisham	d							21 42								22 42						
Aylesham	d							21 44								22 44						
Snowdown	d							21 47								22 47						
Shepherds Well	d							21 51								22 51						
Kearsney	d							21 55								22 55						
Dover Priory 4	a							22 00								23 00						
Whitstable	d						21 25								22 25							
Chestfield & Swalecliffe	d						21 28								22 28							
Herne Bay	d						21 32								22 32							
Birchington-on-Sea	d						21 41								22 41							
Westgate-on-Sea	d						21 45								22 45							
Margate 4	d						21 49								22 49							
Broadstairs	d						21 54								22 54							
Dumpton Park	d						21 57								22 57							
Ramsgate 4	a						22 00								23 00							

Table 212

Sundays

London - Medway, Sheerness-on-Sea, Dover and Ramsgate

		SE [1]		SE	SE	SE	SE [1]	SE	SE	SE [1]	SE	SE	SE	SE	SE [1]
St Pancras Internatnl [15] ⊖	d					22 25			22 55			23 25		23 42	
Stratford International ⊖	d					22 32			23 02			23 32		23 49	
Ebbsfleet International	d					22 43			23 13			23 43		00 01	
London Victoria [15] ⊖	d	22 05					22 24			23 05					23 45
London Blackfriars [3] ⊖	d														
Elephant & Castle ⊖	d														
Bromley South [4]	d	22 22					22 44			23 22					00 02
St Mary Cray	d						22 50								00 08
Swanley [4]	d						22 54								00 12
Farningham Road	d						22 59								00 17
Longfield	d						23 03								00 21
Meopham	d						23 07								00 25
Sole Street	d						23 10								00 28
London Charing Cross [4] ⊖	d			21 40				22 10			22 40		23 10		
London Waterloo (East) [4] ⊖	d			21 43				22 13			22 43		23 13		
London Cannon Street [4] ⊖	d														
London Bridge [4] ⊖	d			21 48				22 18			22 48		23 18		
Dartford [4]	d			22 25				22 55			23 25		23 55		
Greenhithe for Bluewater	d			22 31				23 01			23 31		00 01		
Gravesend [4]	d			22 40		22 48		23 10	23 18		23 40	23 48	00 10		
Strood [4]	d			22 52		22 58		23 22	23 28		23 52	23 58	00 22		
Rochester [4]	d	22 46		22 56		23 03	23 20	23 26	23 33	23 46	23 56	00 03	00 26		00 37
Chatham [4]	d	22 48		22 58		23 05	23 22	23 28	23 35	23 48	23 58	00 05	00 28		00 40
Gillingham (Kent) [4]	d	22 53		23a03		23 10	23 27	23a33	23 40	23 53	00a03	00 10	00a33		00 44
Rainham (Kent)	d	22 57				23 15	23 31		23 45	23 57		00 15			00 49
Newington	d						23 35								00 53
Sittingbourne [4]	a	23 04				23 22	23 40		23 52	00 04		00 22			00 58
	d	23 05			23 10	23 23	23 41		23 53	00 05		00 23			00 58
Kemsley	d				23 15										
Swale	d				23 18										
Queenborough	d				23 22										
Sheerness-on-Sea	a				23 27										
Teynham	d						23 45								01 03
Faversham [2]	a	23 13				23 31	23 51		00 03	00 13		00 33			01 09
	d	23 17	23 19							00 17					
Selling	d		23 24												
Canterbury East [4]	d		23 33												
Bekesbourne	d		23 37												
Adisham	d		23 42												
Aylesham	d		23 44												
Snowdown	d		23 47												
Shepherds Well	d		23 51												
Kearsney	d		23 55												
Dover Priory [4]	a		00 01												
Whitstable	d	23 25								00 25					
Chestfield & Swalecliffe	d	23 28								00 28					
Herne Bay	d	23 32								00 32					
Birchington-on-Sea	d	23 41								00 41					
Westgate-on-Sea	d	23 45								00 45					
Margate [4]	d	23 49								00 49					
Broadstairs	d	23 54								00 54					
Dumpton Park	d	23 57								00 57					
Ramsgate [4]	a	00 01								01 00					

Ramsgate, Dover, Sheerness-on-Sea and Medway - London

Miles	Miles	Miles	Miles	Miles			SE MO [1]	SE MX [1]	SE MX [1]	SE MO [1]	SE MX [1]	SE MX	SE	SE	SE		SE	SE	SE	SE [1]	SE [1]	SE	SE	SE	SE [1]
0	—	—	—	—	**Ramsgate [4]**	d		22p04		22p34	23p04										04 36				
1	—	—	—	—	Dumpton Park	d		22p07		22p37	23p07										04 39				
2¼	—	—	—	—	Broadstairs	d		22p10		22p40	23p10										04 42				
5½	—	—	—	—	**Margate [4]**	d		22p16		22p45	23p16										04 47				
6¾	—	—	—	—	Westgate-on-Sea	d		22p20		22p49	23p20										04 50				
8½	—	—	—	—	Birchington-on-Sea	d		22p23		22p52	23p23										04 54				
16¼	—	—	—	—	**Herne Bay**	d		22p32		23p01	23p32										05 03				
18½	—	—	—	—	Chestfield & Swalecliffe	d		22p36		23p05	23p36										05 06				
20½	—	—	—	—	Whitstable	d		22p39		23p08	23p39										05 10				
—	0	—	—	—	**Dover Priory [4]**	d			22p45																04 42
—	2¼	—	—	—	Kearsney	d																			04 46
—	5½	—	—	—	Shepherds Well	d																			04 51
—	7½	—	—	—	Snowdown	d																			04 55
—	8½	—	—	—	Aylesham	d																			04 57
—	9½	—	—	—	Adisham	d																			05 00
—	12½	—	—	—	Bekesbourne	d																			05 04
—	15½	—	—	—	**Canterbury East [4]**	d			23p02																05 09
—	22	—	—	—	Selling	d																			05 18
27¼	25¼	—	—	0	**Faversham [2]**	a		22p48	23p13	23p17	23p48										05 18				05 23
—	—	—	—	—		d	22p34	22p52	23p14	23p21	23p52							04 56			05 19		05 28		05 34
31¾	29¾	—	—	4½	Teynham	d	22p40	22p58			23p58														05 40
—	—	0	—	—	**Sheerness-on-Sea**	d						23p53													
—	—	2	—	—	Queenborough	d						23p57													
—	—	4	—	—	Swale	d						00 01													
—	—	6	—	—	Kemsley	d						00 05													
34½	32½	8	—	7¼	**Sittingbourne [4]**	a	22p44	23p02	23p21	23p28	00 02	00 10						05 06			05 26		05 36		05 44
—	—	—	—	—		d	22p45	23p03	23p22	23p29	00 03							05 07			05 27		05 37		05 45
37¾	35¾	—	—	10½	Newington	d	22p50		23p27		00 08														05 50
40¼	38¼	—	—	13	Rainham (Kent)	d	22p54	23p10	23p31	23p36	00 12							05 15			05 35		05 45		05 55
43¼	41¼	—	0	16	**Gillingham (Kent) [4]**	d	22p59	23p15	23p36	23p41	00a17		04 09	04 34	04 54			05 20	05 24	05 30	05 40	05 45	05 50	05 54	06 02
45	43	—	1¾	17¾	**Chatham [4]**	d	23p04	23p20	23p41	23p46			04 13	04 38	04 58			05 24	05 28	05 34	05 44	05 49	05 54	05 58	06 06
45½	43½	—	2¼	18¼	Rochester [4]	d	23p06	23p22	23p43	23p48			04 15	04 40	05 00			05 27	05 30	05 36	05 47	05 51	05 57	06 00	06 09
—	—	—	3¼	19¼	Strood [4]	a							04 20	04 45	05 05			05 31	05 35				06 01	06 05	
—	—	—	10½	26½	Gravesend [4]	a							04 32	04 57	05 17			05 42	05 47				06 12	06 17	
—	—	—	14½	—	Greenhithe for Bluewater	a							04 38	05 07	05 23				05 53					06 23	
—	—	—	17¼	—	Dartford [4]	a							04 43	05 13	05 28				05 58					06 28	
—	—	—	34¼	—	**London Bridge [4]** ⊖	a							05 22	05 52	06 05				06 34			06 27		07 03	
—	—	—	—	—	**London Cannon Street [4]** ⊖	a																06 32			
—	—	—	35¼	—	**London Waterloo (East) [4]** ⊖	a							05 26	05 57	06 10				06 39					07 09	
—	—	—	36	—	**London Charing Cross [4]** ⊖	a							05 30	06 01	06 13				06 43					07 15	
52¼	50¼	—	—	—	Sole Street	d	23p17		23p54											05 47					06 19
53¼	51¼	—	—	—	Meopham	d	23p19	23p33	23p56											05 49					06 22
55¾	53¾	—	—	—	Longfield	d	23p23	23p37	23p59											05 53					06 26
58¾	56¾	—	—	—	Farningham Road	d	23p27		00 04											05 57					06 29
61¾	59¾	—	—	—	Swanley [4]	a	23p32		00 09											06 02					06 34
64½	62½	—	—	—	St Mary Cray	a	23p36		00 14											06 06					06 39
68¼	66¼	—	—	—	Bromley South [4]	a	23p42	23p51	00 20	00 13										06 14	06 12				06 45
—	—	—	—	—	Elephant & Castle ⊖	a																			
—	—	—	—	—	**London Blackfriars [3]** ⊖	a																			
79¼	77¼	—	—	—	**London Victoria [15]** ⊖	a	00 02	00 07	00 38	00 29										06 31	06 28				07 07
—	—	—	—	28½	**Ebbsfleet International**	a											05 32	05 47					06 17		
—	—	—	—	45¼	**Stratford International** ⊖	a											05 44	05 59					06 29		
—	—	—	—	51¼	**St Pancras Internatnl [15]** ⊖	a											05 51	06 06					06 36		

Table 212

Mondays to Fridays

Ramsgate, Dover, Sheerness-on-Sea and Medway - London

		SE [1]	SE	SE	SE [1]	SE	SE	SE [1]	SE [1]	SE	SE [1]	SE	SE [1]	SE	SE	SE [1]	SE	SE [1]	SE [1]	SE [1]	SE	SE
Ramsgate [4]	d				05 06						05 40							06 09				
Dumpton Park	d				05 09						05 43							06 12				
Broadstairs	d				05 12						05 46			06 00				06 15	06 20			06 30
Margate [4]	d				05 17						05 51			06 05				06 20	06 25			06 35
Westgate-on-Sea	d				05 20						05 54							06 23	06 28			
Birchington-on-Sea	d				05 24						05 58			06 10				06 27	06 32			06 40
Herne Bay	d				05 33						06 07			06 19				06 36	06 41			06 49
Chestfield & Swalecliffe	d				05 36						06 10							06 39	06 44			
Whitstable	d				05 40						06 14			06 25				06 43	06 48			06 55
Dover Priory [4]	d	05 05											05 45							06 19		
Kearsney	d	05 09											05 50							06 23		
Shepherds Well	d	05 14											05 55							06 28		
Snowdown	d	05 18											05 59							06 32		
Aylesham	d	05 20											06 02							06 34		
Adisham	d	05 23											06 04							06 37		
Bekesbourne	d	05 27											06 09							06 41		
Canterbury East [4]	d	05 32											06 15							06 46		
Selling	d	05 41											06 24							06 55		
Faversham [2]	a	05 46			05 48						06 22		06 29	06 33				06 51	06 56	07 00		07 03
	d				05 49	05 58			06 08		06 23		06 37	06 34				06 52	06 57			07 04
Teynham	d				05 55				06 14				06 43									
Sheerness-on-Sea	d		05 31				05 57								06 29						06 46	
Queenborough	d		05 35				06 01								06 35						06 50	
Swale	d		05 39				06 05								06 39						06 54	
Kemsley	d		05 43				06 09								06 42						06 58	
Sittingbourne [4]	a		05 48		05 59	06 06	06 14		06 18		06 30		06 47	06 41	06 47			07 00	07 05		07 05	07 11
	d				06 00	06 06			06 19		06 31		06 48	06 42				07 01	07 06			07 12
Newington	d				06 05				06 24				06 54									
Rainham (Kent)	d				06 10	06 14			06 29		06 39		06 59	06 50				07 09	07 14			07 20
Gillingham (Kent) [4]	d			06 07	06 15	06 19		06 24	06 34	06 38	06 44	06 50	07 04	06 55		07 08	07 12	07 15	07 19			07 25
Chatham [4]	d			06 11	06 19	06 24		06 28	06 38	06 42	06 48	06 54	07 08	07 00		07 12	07 16	07 20	07 24			07 30
Rochester [4]	d			06 13	06 22	06 26		06 31	06 41	06 44		06 57	07 11	07 02		07 15	07 18					07 32
Strood [4]	a			06 18		06 31				06 49							07 23					
Gravesend [4]	a			06 30		06 42				07 01							07 35					
Greenhithe for Bluewater	a			06 36						07 07							07 45					
Dartford [4]	a			06 41						07 12							07 51					
London Bridge [4] ⊖	a			07 17					07 20	07 47			07 51				08 25		08 09			
London Cannon Street [4] ⊖	a			07 23					07 27				07 57						08 17			
London Waterloo (East) [4] ⊖	a									07 52							08 30					
London Charing Cross [4] ⊖	a									07 58							08 36					
Sole Street	d							06 41				07 07				07 25						
Meopham	d							06 44				07 10				07 28						
Longfield	d							06 48				07 14						07 35				
Farningham Road	d							06 51				07 17				07 33						
Swanley [4]	a							06 56				07 22				07 38						
St Mary Cray	a							07 01				07 27				07 44						
Bromley South [4]	a				06 49			07 07			07 15	07 33				07 52		07 49				
Elephant & Castle ⊖	a																					
London Blackfriars [3] ⊖	a																					
London Victoria [15] ⊖	a				07 09			07 30			07 38	07 55				08 17		08 09				
Ebbsfleet International	a					06 47								07 17								07 47
Stratford International ⊖	a					06 59								07 29								07 59
St Pancras Internatnl [15] ⊖	a					07 07								07 36								08 06

Ramsgate, Dover, Sheerness-on-Sea and Medway - London

		SE	SE	SE	SE	SE	SE		SE	SE	SE	SE	SE	SE	SE	SE	SE		SE	SE	SE	SE	SE	SE	SE
		1		1	1	1			1		1	1			1		1			1	1	1			
Ramsgate 4	d			06 32							06 59				07 06		07 19					07 36			
Dumpton Park	d			06 35							07 02				07 09		07 22					07 39			
Broadstairs	d			06 38		06 48				07 00	07 05				07 12		07 25					07 42			
Margate 4	d			06 43		06 53				07 05	07 10				07 17		07 30					07 47			
Westgate-on-Sea	d			06 46		06 56					07 14				07 20		07 33					07 50			
Birchington-on-Sea	d			06 50		07 00				07 10	07 17				07 24		07 37					07 54			
Herne Bay	d			06 59		07 09				07 19	07 26				07 33		07 46					08 03			
Chestfield & Swalecliffe	d			07 02		07 12					07 30				07 36		07 49					08 06			
Whitstable	d			07 06		07 16				07 25	07 33				07 40		07 53					08 10			
Dover Priory 4	d				06 39							07 04									07 35				
Kearsney	d				06 43							07 08									07 39				
Shepherds Well	d				06 48							07 13									07 44				
Snowdown	d				06 52							07 17									07 48				
Aylesham	d				06 54							07 19									07 50				
Adisham	d				06 57							07 22									07 53				
Bekesbourne	d				07 01							07 26									07 57				
Canterbury East 4	d				07 06							07 31									08 02				
Selling	d				07 15							07 40									08 11				
Faversham 2	a			07 14	07 20	07 24				07 33	07 41	07 45			07 48		08 01				08 16	08 18			
	d			07 16		07 25				07 34	07 43				07 49	07 58	08 02				08 22		08 28		
Teynham	d			07 22											07 55										
Sheerness-on-Sea	d						07 16						07 35						08 07					08 36	
Queenborough	d						07 22						07 39						08 11					08 40	
Swale	d						07 26						07 43						08 15					08 44	
Kemsley	d						07 29						07 47						08 19					08 48	
Sittingbourne 4	a			07 26		07 32	07 34			07 41	07 50		07 52		07 59	08 05	08 09		08 25		08 29		08 36	08 56	
	d			07 27		07 33				07 42	07 51				08 00	08 06	08 10				08 30		08 37		
Newington	d			07 32											08 05						08 35				
Rainham (Kent)	d			07 37		07 41				07 50	07 59				08 10	08 14	08 18				08 40		08 45		
Gillingham (Kent) 4	d	07 33	07 38	07 42		07 46			07 50	07 55	08 04			08 08	08 15	08 19	08 24			08 32	08 45		08 50		08 54
Chatham 4	d	07 37	07 42	07 46		07 50			07 54	08 00	08 08			08 12	08 19	08 24	08 28			08 36	08 50		08 54		08 58
Rochester 4	d	07 40	07 44						07 56	08 02	08 11			08 14	08 22	08 26	08 31			08 39	08 52		08 57		09 00
Strood 4	a		07 49											08 19		08 31							09 01		09 05
Gravesend 4	a		08 01											08 31		08 42							09 12		09 17
Greenhithe for Bluewater	a		08 07											08 42											09 22
Dartford 4	a		08 12											08 49											09 27
London Bridge 4 ⊖	a		08 45			08 31					08 49			09 23			09 11								10 05
London Cannon Street 4 ⊖	a					08 38					08 57						09 18								
London Waterloo (East) 4 ⊖	a		08 50											09 28											10 09
London Charing Cross 4 ⊖	a		08 56											09 34											10 13
Sole Street	d								08 07											08 49					
Meopham	d	07 51							08 09						08 33					08 52	09 03				
Longfield	d	07 55							08 13						08 37					08 56	09 07				
Farningham Road	d								08 17											08 59					
Swanley 4	a	08 01							08 22											09 04					
St Mary Cray	a	08 06							08 26											09 09					
Bromley South 4	a	08 12		08 15					08 33						08 50					09 15	09 20				
Elephant & Castle ⊖	a																								
London Blackfriars 3 ⊖	a																								
London Victoria 15 ⊖	a	08 42		08 39					08 53						09 09					09 38	09 43				
Ebbsfleet International	a									08 17						08 47							09 17		
Stratford International ⊖	a									08 29						08 59							09 29		
St Pancras Internatnl 15 ⊖	a									08 36						09 07							09 40		

Table 212

Mondays to Fridays

Ramsgate, Dover, Sheerness-on-Sea and Medway - London

Station		SE	SE		SE	SE	SE	SE	SE	SE	SE	SE	SE		SE	SE	SE	SE	SE	SE	SE	SE	SE		SE
		1	1					1	1	1					1	1				1	1	1			
Ramsgate 4	d		08 06							08 40						09 04						09 40			
Dumpton Park	d		08 09													09 07									
Broadstairs	d		08 12							08 45						09 10						09 45			
Margate 4	d		08 17							08 50						09 16						09 50			
Westgate-on-Sea	d		08 20													09 20									
Birchington-on-Sea	d		08 24							08 55						09 23						09 55			
Herne Bay	d		08 33							09 04						09 32						10 04			
Chestfield & Swalecliffe	d		08 36													09 36									
Whitstable	d		08 40							09 09						09 39						10 09			
Dover Priory 4	d	08 05							08 45						09 05						09 45				
Kearsney	d	08 09													09 09										
Shepherds Well	d	08 14													09 14										
Snowdown	d	08 18													09 18										
Aylesham	d	08 20													09 20										
Adisham	d	08 23													09 23										
Bekesbourne	d	08 27													09 27										
Canterbury East 4	d	08 32							09 02						09 32						10 02				
Selling	d	08 41													09 41										
Faversham 2	a	08 46	08 48						09 14	09 18					09 46	09 48					10 14	10 18			
	d		08 52		08 58					09 22	09 28					09 52	09 58					10 22	10 28		
Teynham	d		08 58													09 58									
Sheerness-on-Sea	d					09 02						09 32						10 02							10 32
Queenborough	d					09 06						09 36						10 06							10 36
Swale	d					09 10						09 40						10 10							10 40
Kemsley	d					09 14						09 44						10 14							10 44
Sittingbourne 4	a		09 02		09 06	09 19				09 29	09 36	09 49				10 02	10 06	10 19				10 29	10 36		10 49
	d		09 03		09 07					09 30	09 37					10 03	10 07					10 30	10 37		
Newington	d									09 35												10 35			
Rainham (Kent)	d		09 10		09 15					09 40	09 45					10 10	10 15					10 40	10 45		
Gillingham (Kent) 4	d		09 15		09 20		09 24	09 32		09 45	09 50		09 54			10 15	10 20		10 24	10 32		10 45	10 50		
Chatham 4	d		09 20		09 24		09 28	09 36		09 50	09 54		09 58			10 20	10 24		10 28	10 36		10 50	10 54		
Rochester 4	d		09 22		09 27		09 30	09 39		09 52	09 57		10 00			10 22	10 27		10 30	10 39		10 52	10 57		
Strood 4	a				09 31		09 35				10 01		10 05				10 31		10 35				11 01		
Gravesend 4	a				09 42		09 47				10 12		10 17				10 42		10 47				11 12		
Greenhithe for Bluewater	a						09 53						10 23						10 53						
Dartford 4	a						09 58						10 28						10 58						
London Bridge 4 ⊖	a						10 35						11 05						11 35						
London Cannon Street 4 ⊖	a																								
London Waterloo (East) 4 ⊖	a						10 39						11 09						11 39						
London Charing Cross 4 ⊖	a						10 43						11 13						11 43						
Sole Street	d							09 49												10 49					
Meopham	d		09 33					09 52		10 03						10 33				10 52		11 03			
Longfield	d		09 37					09 56		10 07						10 37				10 56		11 07			
Farningham Road	d							09 59												10 59					
Swanley 4	a							10 04												11 04					
St Mary Cray	a							10 09												11 09					
Bromley South 4	a		09 50					10 15		10 20						10 50				11 15		11 20			
Elephant & Castle ⊖	a																								
London Blackfriars 3 ⊖	a																								
London Victoria 15 ⊖	a		10 07					10 41		10 37						11 07				11 37		11 37			
Ebbsfleet International	a				09 47						10 16						10 47						11 17		
Stratford International ⊖	a				09 59						10 27						10 59						11 29		
St Pancras Internatnl 15 ⊖	a				10 06						10 38						11 06						11 36		

Ramsgate, Dover, Sheerness-on-Sea and Medway - London

		SE	SE 1	SE 1	SE	SE	SE	SE 1	SE 1	SE 1		SE	SE	SE	SE 1	SE 1	SE	SE	SE	SE 1		SE 1	SE 1	SE	SE
Ramsgate 4	d			10 04						10 40						11 04							11 40		
Dumpton Park	d			10 07												11 07									
Broadstairs	d			10 10						10 45						11 10							11 45		
Margate 4	d			10 16						10 50						11 16							11 50		
Westgate-on-Sea	d			10 20												11 20									
Birchington-on-Sea	d			10 23						10 55						11 23							11 55		
Herne Bay	d			10 32						11 04						11 32							12 04		
Chestfield & Swalecliffe	d			10 36												11 36									
Whitstable	d			10 39						11 09						11 39							12 09		
Dover Priory 4	d		10 05						10 45						11 05							11 45			
Kearsney	d		10 09												11 09										
Shepherds Well	d		10 14												11 14										
Snowdown	d		10 18												11 18										
Aylesham	d		10 20												11 20										
Adisham	d		10 23												11 23										
Bekesbourne	d		10 27												11 27										
Canterbury East 4	d		10 32						11 02						11 32							12 02			
Selling	d		10 41												11 41										
Faversham 2	a		10 46	10 48					11 14	11 18					11 46	11 48						12 14	12 18		
	d		10 52		10 58				11 22			11 28			11 52		11 58					12 22		12 28	
Teynham	d		10 58												11 58										
Sheerness-on-Sea	d					11 02							11 32					12 02							12 32
Queenborough	d					11 06							11 36					12 06							12 36
Swale	d					11 10							11 40					12 10							12 40
Kemsley	d					11 14							11 44					12 14							12 44
Sittingbourne 4	a		11 02		11 06	11 19			11 29			11 36	11 49		12 02		12 06	12 19				12 29		12 36	12 49
	d		11 03		11 07				11 30			11 37			12 03		12 07					12 30		12 37	
Newington	d								11 35													12 35			
Rainham (Kent)	d		11 10		11 15				11 40			11 45			12 10		12 15					12 40		12 45	
Gillingham (Kent) 4	d	10 54	11 15		11 20		11 24	11 32	11 45			11 50		11 54	12 15		12 20		12 24	12 32		12 45		12 50	
Chatham 4	d	10 58	11 20		11 24		11 28	11 36	11 50			11 54		11 58	12 20		12 24		12 28	12 36		12 50		12 54	
Rochester 4	d	11 00	11 22		11 27		11 30	11 39	11 52			11 57		12 00	12 22		12 27		12 30	12 39		12 52		12 57	
Strood 4	a	11 05			11 31		11 35					12 01		12 05			12 31		12 35					13 01	
Gravesend 4	a	11 17			11 42		11 47					12 12		12 17			12 42		12 47					13 12	
Greenhithe for Bluewater	a	11 23					11 53							12 23					12 53						
Dartford 4	a	11 28					11 58							12 28					12 58						
London Bridge 4 ⊖	a	12 05					12 35							13 05					13 35						
London Cannon Street 4 ⊖	a																								
London Waterloo (East) 4 ⊖	a	12 09					12 39							13 09					13 39						
London Charing Cross 4 ⊖	a	12 13					12 43							13 13					13 43						
Sole Street	d							11 49												12 49					
Meopham	d		11 33					11 52	12 03						12 33					12 52		13 03			
Longfield	d		11 37					11 56	12 07						12 37					12 56		13 07			
Farningham Road	d							11 59												12 59					
Swanley 4	a							12 04												13 04					
St Mary Cray	a							12 09												13 09					
Bromley South 4	a		11 50					12 15	12 20						12 50					13 15		13 20			
Elephant & Castle ⊖	a																								
London Blackfriars 3 ⊖	a																								
London Victoria 15 ⊖	a		12 07					12 37	12 37						13 07					13 37		13 37			
Ebbsfleet International	a				11 47							12 17					12 47							13 17	
Stratford International ⊖	a				11 59							12 32					12 59							13 32	
St Pancras Internatnl 15 ⊖	a				12 06							12 39					13 06							13 39	

Ramsgate, Dover, Sheerness-on-Sea and Medway - London

		SE	SE [1]	SE [1]	SE	SE	SE	SE [1]	SE [1]	SE [1]	SE	SE	SE	SE [1]	SE [1]	SE	SE	SE	SE [1]	SE [1]	SE [1]	SE	SE
Ramsgate [4]	d			12 04						12 40					13 04						13 40		
Dumpton Park	d			12 07											13 07								
Broadstairs	d			12 10						12 45					13 10						13 45		
Margate [4]	d			12 16						12 50					13 16						13 50		
Westgate-on-Sea	d			12 20											13 20								
Birchington-on-Sea	d			12 23						12 55					13 23						13 55		
Herne Bay	d			12 32						13 04					13 32						14 04		
Chestfield & Swalecliffe	d			12 36											13 36								
Whitstable	d			12 39						13 09					13 39						14 09		
Dover Priory [4]	d		12 05						12 45					13 05						13 45			
Kearsney	d		12 09											13 09									
Shepherds Well	d		12 14											13 14									
Snowdown	d		12 18											13 18									
Aylesham	d		12 20											13 20									
Adisham	d		12 23											13 23									
Bekesbourne	d		12 27											13 27									
Canterbury East [4]	d		12 32						13 02					13 32						14 02			
Selling	d		12 41											13 41									
Faversham [2]	a		12 46	12 48					13 14	13 18				13 46	13 48					14 14	14 18		
	d			12 52	12 58					13 22	13 28				13 52	13 58					14 22	14 28	
Teynham	d			12 58											13 58								
Sheerness-on-Sea	d					13 02						13 32					14 02						14 32
Queenborough	d					13 06						13 36					14 06						14 36
Swale	d					13 10						13 40					14 10						14 40
Kemsley	d					13 14						13 44					14 14						14 44
Sittingbourne [4]	a			13 02	13 06	13 19				13 29	13 36	13 49			14 02	14 06	14 19				14 29	14 36	14 49
	d			13 03	13 07					13 30	13 37				14 03	14 07					14 30	14 37	
Newington	d									13 35											14 35		
Rainham (Kent)	d			13 10	13 15					13 40	13 45				14 10	14 15					14 40	14 45	
Gillingham (Kent) [4]	d	12 54		13 15	13 20		13 24	13 32		13 45	13 50		13 54		14 15	14 20		14 24	14 32		14 45	14 50	
Chatham [4]	d	12 58		13 20	13 24		13 28	13 36		13 50	13 54		13 58		14 20	14 24		14 28	14 36		14 50	14 54	
Rochester [4]	d	13 00		13 22	13 27		13 30	13 39		13 52	13 57		14 00		14 22	14 27		14 30	14 39		14 52	14 57	
Strood [4]	a	13 05			13 31		13 35				14 01		14 05			14 31		14 35				15 01	
Gravesend [4]	a	13 17			13 42		13 47				14 12		14 17			14 42		14 47				15 12	
Greenhithe for Bluewater	a	13 23					13 53						14 23					14 53					
Dartford [4]	a	13 28					13 58						14 28					14 58					
London Bridge [4] ⊖	a	14 05					14 35						15 05					15 35					
London Cannon Street [4] ⊖	a																						
London Waterloo (East) [4] ⊖	a	14 09					14 39						15 09					15 39					
London Charing Cross [4] ⊖	a	14 13					14 43						15 13					15 43					
Sole Street	d							13 49											14 49				
Meopham	d			13 33				13 52		14 03					14 33				14 52		15 03		
Longfield	d			13 37				13 56		14 07					14 37				14 56		15 07		
Farningham Road	d							13 59											14 59				
Swanley [4]	a							14 04											15 04				
St Mary Cray	a							14 09											15 09				
Bromley South [4]	a			13 50				14 15		14 20					14 50				15 15		15 20		
Elephant & Castle ⊖	a																						
London Blackfriars [3] ⊖	a																						
London Victoria [15] ⊖	a			14 07				14 37		14 37					15 07				15 37		15 37		
Ebbsfleet International	a				13 47						14 17					14 47						15 17	
Stratford International ⊖	a				13 59						14 29					14 59						15 29	
St Pancras Internatnl [15] ⊖	a				14 06						14 40					15 06						15 36	

Table 212

Ramsgate, Dover, Sheerness-on-Sea and Medway - London

		SE		SE 1	SE 1	SE	SE	SE	SE	SE 1	SE 1	SE		SE	SE	SE 1	SE 1	SE	SE	SE	SE 1	SE 1	SE 1		SE
Ramsgate 4	d				14 04						14 40						15 04						15 34		
Dumpton Park	d				14 07												15 07						15 37		
Broadstairs	d				14 10						14 45						15 10						15 40		
Margate 4	d				14 16						14 50						15 16						15 46		
Westgate-on-Sea	d				14 20												15 20						15 50		
Birchington-on-Sea	d				14 23						14 55						15 23						15 53		
Herne Bay	d				14 32						15 04						15 32						16 02		
Chestfield & Swalecliffe	d				14 36												15 36						16 06		
Whitstable	d				14 39						15 09						15 39						16 09		
Dover Priory 4	d			14 05						14 45						15 05						15 39			
Kearsney	d			14 09												15 09						15 43			
Shepherds Well	d			14 14												15 14						15 48			
Snowdown	d			14 18												15 18									
Aylesham	d			14 20												15 20						15 52			
Adisham	d			14 23												15 23						15 55			
Bekesbourne	d			14 27												15 27									
Canterbury East 4	d			14 32						15 02						15 32						16 02			
Selling	d			14 41												15 41						16 11			
Faversham 2	a			14 46	14 48					15 14	15 18					15 46	15 48					16 16	16 18		
	d			14 52		14 58				15 22		15 28				15 52		15 58				16 22			16 28
Teynham	d			14 58												15 58									
Sheerness-on-Sea	d						15 02							15 32					16 02						
Queenborough	d						15 06							15 36					16 06						
Swale	d						15 10							15 40					16 10						
Kemsley	d						15 14							15 44					16 14						
Sittingbourne 4	a			15 02		15 06	15 19			15 29		15 36		15 55		16 02		16 06	16 19			16 29			16 36
	d			15 03		15 07				15 30		15 37				16 03		16 07				16 30			16 37
Newington	d									15 35												16 35			
Rainham (Kent)	d			15 10		15 15				15 40		15 45				16 10		16 15				16 40			16 45
Gillingham (Kent) 4	d	14 54		15 15		15 20		15 24	15 32	15 45		15 50			15 54	16 15		16 20		16 24	16 32	16 45			16 50
Chatham 4	d	14 58		15 20		15 24		15 28	15 36	15 50		15 54			15 58	16 20		16 24		16 28	16 36	16 50			16 54
Rochester 4	d	15 00		15 22		15 27		15 30	15 39	15 52		15 57			16 00	16 22		16 27		16 30	16 39	16 52			16 57
Strood 4	a	15 05				15 31		15 35				16 01			16 05			16 31		16 35					17 01
Gravesend 4	a	15 17				15 42		15 47				16 12			16 17			16 42		16 47					17 12
Greenhithe for Bluewater	a	15 23						15 53							16 23					16 53					
Dartford 4	a	15 28						15 58							16 28					16 58					
London Bridge 4 ⊖	a	16 05						16 35							17 07					17 35					
London Cannon Street 4 ⊖	a														17 11										
London Waterloo (East) 4 ⊖	a	16 09						16 39												17 40					
London Charing Cross 4 ⊖	a	16 13						16 44												17 44					
Sole Street	d								15 49												16 49				
Meopham	d			15 33					15 52	16 03						16 33					16 52	17 03			
Longfield	d			15 37					15 56	16 07						16 37					16 56	17 07			
Farningham Road	d								15 59												16 59				
Swanley 4	a								16 04												17 04				
St Mary Cray	a								16 09												17 09				
Bromley South 4	a			15 50					16 15	16 20						16 50					17 15	17 20			
Elephant & Castle ⊖	a																								
London Blackfriars 3 ⊖	a																								
London Victoria 15 ⊖	a			16 07					16 37	16 38						17 07					17 38	17 37			
Ebbsfleet International	a					15 47						16 17						16 47							17 16
Stratford International ⊖	a					15 59						16 28						17 02							17 27
St Pancras Internatnl 15 ⊖	a					16 06						16 39						17 09							17 38

Table 212

Mondays to Fridays

Ramsgate, Dover, Sheerness-on-Sea and Medway - London

Station		SE	SE	SE [1]	SE [1]	SE [1]	SE	SE	SE		SE [1]	SE [1]	SE [1]	SE	SE	SE	SE [1]	SE [1]	SE		SE	SE	SE	SE [1]	SE [1]
Ramsgate [4]	d					16 04							16 34					17 04							17 34
Dumpton Park	d					16 07							16 37					17 07							17 37
Broadstairs	d					16 10							16 40					17 10							17 40
Margate [4]	d					16 16							16 46					17 16							17 46
Westgate-on-Sea	d					16 20							16 50					17 20							17 50
Birchington-on-Sea	d					16 23							16 53					17 23							17 53
Herne Bay	d					16 32							17 02					17 32							18 02
Chestfield & Swalecliffe	d					16 36							17 06					17 36							18 06
Whitstable	d					16 39							17 09					17 39							18 09
Dover Priory [4]	d				16 05							16 39					17 05							17 39	
Kearsney	d				16 09							16 43					17 09							17 43	
Shepherds Well	d				16 14							16 48					17 14							17 48	
Snowdown	d				16 18												17 18								
Aylesham	d				16 20							16 52					17 20							17 52	
Adisham	d				16 23							16 55					17 23							17 55	
Bekesbourne	d				16 27												17 27								
Canterbury East [4]	d				16 32							17 02					17 32							18 02	
Selling	d				16 41							17 11					17 41							18 11	
Faversham [2]	a				16 46	16 48						17 16	17 18				17 46	17 48						18 16	18 18
	d					16 52	16 58						17 22	17 28				17 52	17 58						18 22
Teynham	d					16 58												17 58							
Sheerness-on-Sea	d	16 32						17 02							17 32						18 02				
Queenborough	d	16 36						17 06							17 36						18 06				
Swale	d	16 40						17 10							17 40						18 10				
Kemsley	d	16 44						17 14							17 44						18 14				
Sittingbourne [4]	a	16 49				17 02	17 06	17 19					17 29	17 36	17 52			18 02	18 06		18 19				18 29
	d					17 03	17 07						17 30	17 37				18 03	18 07						18 30
Newington	d												17 35												18 35
Rainham (Kent)	d					17 10	17 15						17 40	17 45				18 10	18 15						18 40
Gillingham (Kent) [4]	d		16 54	17 02		17 15	17 20		17 24		17 32		17 45	17 50		17 54		18 15	18 20			18 24	18 32		18 45
Chatham [4]	d		16 58	17 06		17 20	17 24		17 28		17 36		17 50	17 54		17 58		18 20	18 24			18 28	18 36		18 50
Rochester [4]	d		17 00	17 09		17 22	17 27		17 30		17 39		17 52	17 57		18 00		18 22	18 27			18 30	18 39		18 52
Strood [4]	a		17 05				17 31		17 35					18 02		18 05			18 31			18 35			
Gravesend [4]	a		17 17				17 42		17 47					18 13		18 17			18 42			18 47			
Greenhithe for Bluewater	a		17 23						17 53							18 23						18 53			
Dartford [4]	a		17 28						17 58							18 28						18 58			
London Bridge [4] ⊖	a		18 04						18 35							19 05						19 35			
London Cannon Street [4] ⊖	a																								
London Waterloo (East) [4] ⊖	a		18 08						18 41							19 09						19 39			
London Charing Cross [4] ⊖	a		18 12						18 45							19 13						19 43			
Sole Street	d			17 19							17 49												18 49		
Meopham	d			17 22		17 33					17 52		18 03					18 33					18 52		19 03
Longfield	d			17 26		17 37					17 56		18 07					18 37					18 56		19 07
Farningham Road	d			17 29							17 59												18 59		
Swanley [4]	a			17 34							18 04												19 04		
St Mary Cray	a			17 39							18 09												19 09		
Bromley South [4]	a			17 45		17 50					18 15		18 20					18 50					19 15		19 20
Elephant & Castle ⊖	a																								
London Blackfriars [3] ⊖	a																								
London Victoria [15] ⊖	a			18 08		18 07					18 37		18 37					19 07					19 37		19 37
Ebbsfleet International	a						17 46							18 17					18 47						
Stratford International ⊖	a						17 57							18 29					19 02						
St Pancras Internatnl [15] ⊖	a						18 08							18 36					19 09						

Table 212

Ramsgate, Dover, Sheerness-on-Sea and Medway - London

		SE	SE	SE	SE	SE		SE	SE	SE	SE	SE	SE	SE	SE	SE		SE	SE	SE	SE	SE	SE	SE	SE
					1	1			1	1	1				1	1						1	1		
Ramsgate 4	d					18 04					18 34					19 04							19 24		
Dumpton Park	d					18 07					18 37					19 07							19 27		
Broadstairs	d					18 10					18 40					19 10							19 30		
Margate 4	d					18 16					18 46					19 16							19 35		
Westgate-on-Sea	d					18 20					18 50					19 20							19 38		
Birchington-on-Sea	d					18 23					18 53					19 23							19 42		
Herne Bay	d					18 32					19 02					19 32							19 51		
Chestfield & Swalecliffe	d					18 36					19 06					19 36							19 55		
Whitstable	d					18 39					19 09					19 39							19 58		
Dover Priory 4	d				18 05					18 39					19 05							19 40			
Kearsney	d				18 09					18 43					19 09										
Shepherds Well	d				18 14					18 48					19 14										
Snowdown	d				18 18										19 18										
Aylesham	d				18 20					18 52					19 20										
Adisham	d				18 23					18 55					19 23										
Bekesbourne	d				18 27										19 27										
Canterbury East 4	d				18 32					19 02					19 32							19 57			
Selling	d				18 41					19 11					19 41										
Faversham 2	a				18 46	18 48				19 16	19 18				19 46	19 48						20 08	20 10		
	d	18 28			18 52					19 22			19 28		19 52				19 58			20 14		20 28	
Teynham	d				18 58										19 58										
Sheerness-on-Sea	d		18 37									19 16						19 46		20 02					20 32
Queenborough	d		18 41									19 23						19 53		20 06					20 36
Swale	d		18 45									19 27						19 57		20 10					20 40
Kemsley	d		18 49									19 31						20 01		20 14					20 44
Sittingbourne 4	a	18 36	18 54		19 02					19 29		19 36	19 36		20 02			20 06	20 06	20 19		20 21		20 36	20 49
	d	18 37			19 03					19 30			19 37		20 03				20 07			20 22		20 37	
Newington	d									19 35												20 27			
Rainham (Kent)	d	18 45			19 10					19 40			19 45		20 10				20 15			20 31		20 45	
Gillingham (Kent) 4	d	18 50		18 54	19 15			19 24		19 45			19 50	19 54	20 15				20 20		20 24	20 36		20 50	
Chatham 4	d	18 54		18 58	19 20			19 28		19 50			19 54	19 58	20 20				20 24		20 28	20 41		20 54	
Rochester 4	d	18 57		19 00	19 22			19 30	19 39	19 52			19 57	20 00	20 22				20 27		20 30	20 43		20 57	
Strood 4	a	19 01		19 05				19 35					20 01	20 05					20 31		20 35			21 01	
Gravesend 4	a	19 12		19 17				19 47					20 12	20 17					20 42		20 47			21 12	
Greenhithe for Bluewater	a			19 23				19 53						20 23							20 53				
Dartford 4	a			19 28				19 58						20 28							20 58				
London Bridge 4 ⊖	a			20 06				20 36						21 06							21 36				
London Cannon Street 4 ⊖	a																								
London Waterloo (East) 4 ⊖	a			20 11				20 40						21 10							21 40				
London Charing Cross 4 ⊖	a			20 14				20 44						21 14							21 44				
Sole Street	d								19 49													20 54			
Meopham	d				19 33				19 52	20 03					20 33							20 56			
Longfield	d				19 37				19 56	20 07					20 37							21 00			
Farningham Road	d								19 59													21 04			
Swanley 4	a								20 04													21 09			
St Mary Cray	a								20 09													21 14			
Bromley South 4	a				19 50				20 15	20 20					20 50							21 20			
Elephant & Castle ⊖	a																								
London Blackfriars 3 ⊖	a																								
London Victoria 15 ⊖	a				20 07				20 37	20 38					21 07							21 37			
Ebbsfleet International	a	19 16											20 16						20 47					21 17	
Stratford International ⊖	a	19 27											20 27						20 59					21 32	
St Pancras Internatnl 15 ⊖	a	19 38											20 38						21 06					21 39	

Ramsgate, Dover, Sheerness-on-Sea and Medway - London

		SE		SE 1	SE 1	SE	SE	SE	SE 1	SE	SE	SE		SE 1	SE 1	SE	SE	SE	SE 1	SE 1	SE	SE 1		SE	SE 1
Ramsgate 4	d				20 04										21 04							22 04			
Dumpton Park	d				20 07										21 07							22 07			
Broadstairs	d				20 10										21 10							22 10			
Margate 4	d				20 16										21 16							22 16			
Westgate-on-Sea	d				20 20										21 20							22 20			
Birchington-on-Sea	d				20 23										21 23							22 23			
Herne Bay	d				20 32										21 32							22 32			
Chestfield & Swalecliffe	d				20 36										21 36							22 36			
Whitstable	d				20 39										21 39							22 39			
Dover Priory 4	d			20 05					20 45					21 05					21 45	22 05					22 45
Kearsney	d			20 09										21 09						22 09					
Shepherds Well	d			20 14										21 14						22 14					
Snowdown	d			20 18										21 18						22 18					
Aylesham	d			20 20										21 20						22 20					
Adisham	d			20 23										21 23						22 23					
Bekesbourne	d			20 27										21 27						22 27					
Canterbury East 4	d			20 32					21 02					21 32					22 02	22 32					23 02
Selling	d			20 41										21 41						22 41					
Faversham 2	a			20 46	20 48				21 13					21 46	21 48				22 13	22 46		22 48			23 13
	d			20 52		20 58			21 14	21 28				21 52		21 58			22 14			22 52			23 14
Teynham	d			20 58										21 58								22 58			
Sheerness-on-Sea	d						21 02					21 32					22 02							23 02	
Queenborough	d						21 06					21 36					22 06							23 06	
Swale	d						21 10					21 40					22 10							23 10	
Kemsley	d						21 14					21 44					22 14							23 14	
Sittingbourne 4	a			21 02		21 06	21 19		21 21	21 36				22 02		22 06	22 19		22 21			23 02		23 19	23 21
	d			21 03		21 07			21 22	21 37				22 03		22 07			22 22			23 03			23 22
Newington	d								21 27			21 51							22 27						23 27
Rainham (Kent)	d			21 10		21 15			21 31	21 45		21 55		22 10		22 15			22 31			23 10			23 31
Gillingham (Kent) 4	d	20 54		21 15		21 20		21 24	21 36	21 50	21 54	22a02		22 15		22 20		22 24	22 36		22 54	23 15			23 36
Chatham 4	d	20 58		21 20		21 24		21 28	21 41	21 54	21 58			22 20		22 24		22 28	22 41		22 58	23 20			23 41
Rochester 4	d	21 00		21 22		21 27		21 30	21 43	21 57	22 00			22 22		22 27		22 30	22 43		23 00	23 22			23 43
Strood 4	a	21 05				21 31		21 35		22 01	22 05					22 31		22 35			23 05				
Gravesend 4	a	21 17				21 42		21 47		22 12	22 17					22 42		22 47			23 17				
Greenhithe for Bluewater	a	21 23						21 53			22 23							22 53			23 23				
Dartford 4	a	21 28						21 58			22 28							22 58			23 28				
London Bridge 4 ⊖	a	22 05						22 35			23 05							23 35							
London Cannon Street 4 ⊖	a																								
London Waterloo (East) 4 ⊖	a	22 09						22 39			23 09							23 39							
London Charing Cross 4 ⊖	a	22 13						22 43			23 13							23 43							
Sole Street	d								21 54										22 54						23 54
Meopham	d			21 33					21 56					22 33					22 56			23 33			23 56
Longfield	d			21 37					22 00					22 37					23 00			23 37			23 59
Farningham Road	d								22 04										23 04						00 04
Swanley 4	a								22 09										23 09						00 09
St Mary Cray	a								22 14										23 14						00 14
Bromley South 4	a			21 50					22 20					22 50					23 20			23 51			00 20
Elephant & Castle ⊖	a																								
London Blackfriars 3 ⊖	a																								
London Victoria 15 ⊖	a			22 07					22 37					23 07					23 37			00 07			00 38
Ebbsfleet International	a					21 47				22 16						22 47									
Stratford International ⊖	a					21 59				22 27						22 59									
St Pancras Internatnl 15 ⊖	a					22 06				22 38						23 06									

Ramsgate, Dover, Sheerness-on-Sea and Medway - London

		SE 1	SE 1	SE
Ramsgate 4	d		23 04	
Dumpton Park	d		23 07	
Broadstairs	d		23 10	
Margate 4	d		23 16	
Westgate-on-Sea	d		23 20	
Birchington-on-Sea	d		23 23	
Herne Bay	d		23 32	
Chestfield & Swalecliffe	d		23 36	
Whitstable	d		23 39	
Dover Priory 4	d	23 05		
Kearsney	d	23 09		
Shepherds Well	d	23 14		
Snowdown	d	23 18		
Aylesham	d	23 20		
Adisham	d	23 23		
Bekesbourne	d	23 27		
Canterbury East 4	d	23 32		
Selling	d	23 41		
Faversham 2	a	23 46	23 48	
	d		23 52	
Teynham	d		23 58	
Sheerness-on-Sea	d			23 53
Queenborough	d			23 57
Swale	d			00 01
Kemsley	d			00 05
Sittingbourne 4	a		00 02	00 10
	d		00 03	
Newington	d		00 08	
Rainham (Kent)	d		00 12	
Gillingham (Kent) 4	d		00a17	
Chatham 4	d			
Rochester 4	d			
Strood 4	a			
Gravesend 4	a			
Greenhithe for Bluewater	a			
Dartford 4	a			
London Bridge 4 ⊖	a			
London Cannon Street 4 ⊖	a			
London Waterloo (East) 4 ⊖	a			
London Charing Cross 4 ⊖	a			
Sole Street	d			
Meopham	d			
Longfield	d			
Farningham Road	d			
Swanley 4	a			
St Mary Cray	a			
Bromley South 4	a			
Elephant & Castle ⊖	a			
London Blackfriars 3 ⊖	a			
London Victoria 15 ⊖	a			
Ebbsfleet International	a			
Stratford International ⊖	a			
St Pancras Internatnl 15 ⊖	a			

Table 212

Saturdays

Ramsgate, Dover, Sheerness-on-Sea and Medway - London

		SE 1	SE 1	SE 1	SE	SE	SE	SE 1	SE	SE		SE	SE 1	SE 1	SE	SE	SE 1	SE 1	SE 1	SE		SE	SE	SE 1	SE 1
Ramsgate 4	d	22p04		23p04				04 32						05 04					05 40						06 04
Dumpton Park	d	22p07		23p07										05 07											06 07
Broadstairs	d	22p10		23p10				04 37						05 10					05 45						06 10
Margate 4	d	22p16		23p16				04 42						05 16					05 50						06 16
Westgate-on-Sea	d	22p20		23p20										05 20											06 20
Birchington-on-Sea	d	22p23		23p23				04 47						05 23					05 55						06 23
Herne Bay	d	22p32		23p32				04 56						05 32					06 04						06 32
Chestfield & Swalecliffe	d	22p36		23p36										05 36											06 36
Whitstable	d	22p39		23p39				05 01						05 39					06 09						06 39
Dover Priory 4	d		22p45										05 05					05 45						06 05	
Kearsney	d												05 09											06 09	
Shepherds Well	d												05 14											06 14	
Snowdown	d												05 18											06 18	
Aylesham	d												05 20											06 20	
Adisham	d												05 23											06 23	
Bekesbourne	d												05 27											06 27	
Canterbury East 4	d		23p02										05 32					06 02						06 32	
Selling	d												05 41											06 41	
Faversham 2	a	22p48	23p13	23p48				05 09					05 46	05 48				06 14	06 18					06 46	06 48
	d	22p52	23p14	23p52				05 09		05 28			05 52		05 58			06 22		06 28				06 52	
Teynham	d	22p58		23p58									05 58											06 58	
Sheerness-on-Sea	d				23p53																	06 32			
Queenborough	d				23p57																	06 36			
Swale	d				00 01																	06 40			
Kemsley	d				00 05																	06 44			
Sittingbourne 4	a	23p02	23p21	00 02	00 10			05 17		05 36			06 02		06 06			06 29		06 36		06 49		07 02	
	d	23p03	23p22	00 03				05 17		05 37			06 03		06 07			06 30		06 37				07 03	
Newington	d		23p27	00 08				05 23										06 35							
Rainham (Kent)	d	23p10	23p31	00 12				05 27		05 45			06 10		06 15			06 40		06 45				07 10	
Gillingham (Kent) 4	d	23p15	23p36	00a17		04 48	05 18	05 32		05 50		05 54	06 15		06 20	06 24	06 32	06 45		06 50			06 54	07 15	
Chatham 4	d	23p20	23p41			04 52	05 22	05 36		05 54		05 58	06 20		06 24	06 28	06 36	06 50		06 54			06 58	07 20	
Rochester 4	d	23p22	23p43			04 54	05 24	05 39		05 57		06 00	06 22		06 27	06 30	06 39	06 52		06 57			07 00	07 22	
Strood 4	a					04 59	05 29			06 01		06 05			06 31	06 35				07 01			07 05		
Gravesend 4	a					05 11	05 41			06 12		06 17			06 42	06 47				07 12			07 17		
Greenhithe for Bluewater	a					05 20	05 50					06 23				06 53							07 23		
Dartford 4	a					05 27	05 57					06 28				06 58							07 28		
London Bridge 4 ⊖	a					06 05	06 35					07 05				07 35							08 05		
London Cannon Street 4 ⊖	a																								
London Waterloo (East) 4 ⊖	a					06 09	06 39					07 09				07 39							08 09		
London Charing Cross 4 ⊖	a					06 13	06 43					07 13				07 43							08 13		
Sole Street	d		23p54					05 49									06 49								
Meopham	d	23p33	23p56					05 52					06 33				06 52	07 03						07 33	
Longfield	d	23p37	23p59					05 56					06 37				06 56	07 07						07 37	
Farningham Road	d		00 04					06 00									06 59								
Swanley 4	a		00 09					06 05									07 04								
St Mary Cray	a		00 14					06 09									07 09								
Bromley South 4	a	23p51	00 20					06 15					06 50				07 15	07 20						07 50	
Elephant & Castle ⊖	a																								
London Blackfriars 3 ⊖	a																								
London Victoria 15 ⊖	a	00 07	00 38					06 37					07 07				07 37	07 37						08 07	
Ebbsfleet International	a								05 32	06 17					06 47					07 17					
Stratford International ⊖	a								05 44	06 29					06 59					07 29					
St Pancras Internatnl 15 ⊖	a								05 51	06 36					07 06					07 36					

Table 212

Saturdays

Ramsgate, Dover, Sheerness-on-Sea and Medway - London

		SE	SE	SE	SE 1	SE 1	SE 1		SE	SE	SE	SE 1	SE 1	SE	SE	SE	SE 1		SE 1	SE 1	SE	SE	SE		
Ramsgate [4]	d						06 40						07 04							07 40					
Dumpton Park	d												07 07												
Broadstairs	d						06 45						07 10							07 45					
Margate [4]	d						06 50						07 16							07 50					
Westgate-on-Sea	d												07 20												
Birchington-on-Sea	d						06 55						07 23							07 55					
Herne Bay	d						07 04						07 32							08 04					
Chestfield & Swalecliffe	d												07 36												
Whitstable	d						07 09						07 39							08 09					
Dover Priory [4]	d					06 45						07 05							07 45						
Kearsney	d											07 09													
Shepherds Well	d											07 14													
Snowdown	d											07 18													
Aylesham	d											07 20													
Adisham	d											07 23													
Bekesbourne	d											07 27													
Canterbury East [4]	d					07 02						07 32							08 02						
Selling	d											07 41													
Faversham [2]	a					07 14	07 18					07 46	07 48						08 14	08 18					
	d	06 58					07 22		07 28				07 52	07 58						08 22	08 28				
Teynham	d												07 58												
Sheerness-on-Sea	d		07 02							07 32					08 02							08 32			
Queenborough	d		07 06							07 36					08 06							08 36			
Swale	d		07 10							07 40					08 10							08 40			
Kemsley	d		07 14							07 44					08 14							08 44			
Sittingbourne [4]	a	07 06	07 19				07 29		07 36	07 49			08 02	08 06	08 19					08 29	08 36	08 49			
	d	07 07					07 30		07 37				08 03	08 07						08 30	08 37				
Newington	d						07 35													08 35					
Rainham (Kent)	d	07 15					07 40		07 45				08 10	08 15						08 40	08 45				
Gillingham (Kent) [4]	d	07 20		07 24	07 32		07 45		07 50		07 54		08 15	08 20		08 24	08 32			08 45	08 50		08 54		
Chatham [4]	d	07 24		07 28	07 36		07 50		07 54		07 58		08 20	08 24		08 28	08 36			08 50	08 54		08 58		
Rochester [4]	d	07 27		07 30	07 39		07 52		07 57		08 00		08 22	08 27		08 30	08 39			08 52	08 57		09 00		
Strood [4]	a	07 31		07 35					08 01		08 05			08 31		08 35					09 01		09 05		
Gravesend [4]	a	07 42		07 47					08 12		08 17			08 42		08 47					09 12		09 17		
Greenhithe for Bluewater	a			07 53							08 23					08 53							09 23		
Dartford [4]	a			07 58							08 28					08 58							09 28		
London Bridge [4] ⊖	a			08 35							09 05					09 35							10 05		
London Cannon Street [4] ⊖	a																								
London Waterloo (East) [4] ⊖	a			08 39							09 09					09 39							10 09		
London Charing Cross [4] ⊖	a			08 43							09 13					09 43							10 13		
Sole Street	d				07 49												08 49								
Meopham	d				07 52		08 03						08 33				08 52			09 03					
Longfield	d				07 56		08 07						08 37				08 56			09 07					
Farningham Road	d				07 59												08 59								
Swanley [4]	a				08 04												09 04								
St Mary Cray	a				08 09												09 09								
Bromley South [4]	a				08 15		08 20						08 50				09 15			09 20					
Elephant & Castle ⊖	a																								
London Blackfriars [3] ⊖	a																								
London Victoria [15] ⊖	a				08 37		08 37						09 07				09 37			09 37					
Ebbsfleet International	a	07 47							08 17					08 47							09 17				
Stratford International ⊖	a	07 59							08 29					08 59							09 29				
St Pancras Internatnl [15] ⊖	a	08 06							08 36					09 06							09 36				

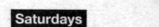

Ramsgate, Dover, Sheerness-on-Sea and Medway - London

Station		SE [1]	SE [1]	SE	SE	SE	SE [1]	SE [1]	SE [1]	SE	SE	SE	SE [1]	SE [1]	SE	SE	SE	SE [1]	SE [1]	SE [1]	SE
Ramsgate [4]	d		08 04						08 40					09 04						09 40	
Dumpton Park	d		08 07											09 07							
Broadstairs	d		08 10						08 45					09 10						09 45	
Margate [4]	d		08 16						08 50					09 16						09 50	
Westgate-on-Sea	d		08 20											09 20							
Birchington-on-Sea	d		08 23						08 55					09 23						09 55	
Herne Bay	d		08 32						09 04					09 32						10 04	
Chestfield & Swalecliffe	d		08 36											09 36							
Whitstable	d		08 39						09 09					09 39						10 09	
Dover Priory [4]	d	08 05						08 45					09 05						09 45		
Kearsney	d	08 09											09 09								
Shepherds Well	d	08 14											09 14								
Snowdown	d	08 18											09 18								
Aylesham	d	08 20											09 20								
Adisham	d	08 23											09 23								
Bekesbourne	d	08 27											09 27								
Canterbury East [4]	d	08 32						09 02					09 32						10 02		
Selling	d	08 41											09 41								
Faversham [2]	a	08 46	08 48					09 14	09 18				09 46	09 48					10 14	10 18	
	d		08 52	08 58					09 22	09 28				09 52	09 58					10 22	10 28
Teynham	d		08 58											09 58							
Sheerness-on-Sea	d				09 02						09 32					10 02					
Queenborough	d				09 06						09 36					10 06					
Swale	d				09 10						09 40					10 10					
Kemsley	d				09 14						09 44					10 14					
Sittingbourne [4]	a		09 02	09 06	09 19				09 29	09 36	09 49			10 02	10 06	10 19				10 29	10 36
	d		09 03	09 07					09 30	09 37				10 03	10 07					10 30	10 37
Newington	d								09 35											10 35	
Rainham (Kent)	d		09 10	09 15					09 40	09 45				10 10	10 15					10 40	10 45
Gillingham (Kent) [4]	d		09 15	09 20		09 24	09 32		09 45	09 50		09 54		10 15	10 20		10 24	10 32		10 45	10 50
Chatham [4]	d		09 20	09 24		09 28	09 36		09 50	09 54		09 58		10 20	10 24		10 28	10 36		10 50	10 54
Rochester [4]	d		09 22	09 27		09 30	09 39		09 52	09 57		10 00		10 22	10 27		10 30	10 39		10 52	10 57
Strood [4]	a			09 31		09 35				10 01		10 05			10 31		10 35				11 01
Gravesend [4]	a			09 42		09 47				10 12		10 17			10 42		10 47				11 12
Greenhithe for Bluewater	a					09 53						10 23					10 53				
Dartford [4]	a					09 58						10 28					10 58				
London Bridge [4] ⊖	a					10 35						11 05					11 35				
London Cannon Street [4] ⊖	a																				
London Waterloo (East) [4] ⊖	a					10 39						11 09					11 39				
London Charing Cross [4] ⊖	a					10 43						11 13					11 43				
Sole Street	d						09 49											10 49			
Meopham	d		09 33				09 52		10 03					10 33				10 52		11 03	
Longfield	d		09 37				09 56		10 07					10 37				10 56		11 07	
Farningham Road	d						09 59											10 59			
Swanley [4]	a						10 04											11 04			
St Mary Cray	a						10 09											11 09			
Bromley South [4]	a		09 50				10 15		10 20					10 50				11 15		11 20	
Elephant & Castle ⊖	a																				
London Blackfriars [3] ⊖	a																				
London Victoria [15] ⊖	a		10 07				10 37		10 37					11 07				11 37		11 37	
Ebbsfleet International	a			09 47						10 16					10 47						11 17
Stratford International ⊖	a			09 59						10 27					10 59						11 29
St Pancras Internatnl [15] ⊖	a			10 06						10 38					11 06						11 36

Table 212

Saturdays

Ramsgate, Dover, Sheerness-on-Sea and Medway - London

		SE	SE	SE [1]	SE [1]	SE	SE	SE	SE [1]	SE [1]	SE [1]		SE	SE	SE	SE [1]	SE [1]	SE	SE	SE	SE [1]			SE [1]	SE [1]
Ramsgate [4]	d				10 04						10 40						11 04								11 40
Dumpton Park	d				10 07												11 07								
Broadstairs	d				10 10						10 45						11 10								11 45
Margate [4]	d				10 16						10 50						11 16								11 50
Westgate-on-Sea	d				10 20												11 20								
Birchington-on-Sea	d				10 23						10 55						11 23								11 55
Herne Bay	d				10 32						11 04						11 32								12 04
Chestfield & Swalecliffe	d				10 36												11 36								
Whitstable	d				10 39						11 09						11 39								12 09
Dover Priory [4]	d			10 05						10 45						11 05								11 45	
Kearsney	d			10 09												11 09									
Shepherds Well	d			10 14												11 14									
Snowdown	d			10 18												11 18									
Aylesham	d			10 20												11 20									
Adisham	d			10 23												11 23									
Bekesbourne	d			10 27												11 27									
Canterbury East [4]	d			10 32						11 02						11 32								12 02	
Selling	d			10 41												11 41									
Faversham [2]	a			10 46	10 48					11 14	11 18					11 46	11 48							12 14	12 18
	d			10 52		10 58				11 22			11 28			11 52		11 58						12 22	
Teynham	d			10 58												11 58									
Sheerness-on-Sea	d	10 32					11 02							11 32					12 02						
Queenborough	d	10 36					11 06							11 36					12 06						
Swale	d	10 40					11 10							11 40					12 10						
Kemsley	d	10 44					11 14							11 44					12 14						
Sittingbourne [4]	a	10 49		11 02		11 06	11 19			11 29			11 36	11 49		12 02		12 06	12 19					12 29	
	d			11 03		11 07				11 30			11 37			12 03		12 07						12 30	
Newington	d									11 35														12 35	
Rainham (Kent)	d			11 10		11 15				11 40			11 45			12 10		12 15						12 40	
Gillingham (Kent) [4]	d		10 54	11 15		11 20		11 24	11 32	11 45			11 50		11 54	12 15		12 20		12 24	12 32			12 45	
Chatham [4]	d		10 58	11 20		11 24		11 28	11 36	11 50			11 54		11 58	12 20		12 24		12 28	12 36			12 50	
Rochester [4]	d		11 00	11 22		11 27		11 30	11 39	11 52			11 57		12 00	12 22		12 27		12 30	12 39			12 52	
Strood [4]	a		11 05			11 31		11 35					12 01		12 05			12 31		12 35					
Gravesend [4]	a		11 17			11 42		11 47					12 12		12 17			12 42		12 47					
Greenhithe for Bluewater	a		11 23					11 53							12 23					12 53					
Dartford [4]	a		11 28					11 58							12 28					12 58					
London Bridge [4] ⊖	a		12 05					12 35							13 05					13 35					
London Cannon Street [4] ⊖	a																								
London Waterloo (East) [4] ⊖	a		12 09					12 39							13 09					13 39					
London Charing Cross [4] ⊖	a		12 13					12 43							13 13					13 43					
Sole Street	d								11 49												12 49				
Meopham	d			11 33					11 52	12 03						12 33					12 52			13 03	
Longfield	d			11 37					11 56	12 07						12 37					12 56			13 07	
Farningham Road	d								11 59												12 59				
Swanley [4]	a								12 04												13 04				
St Mary Cray	a								12 09												13 09				
Bromley South [4]	a			11 50					12 15	12 20						12 50					13 15			13 20	
Elephant & Castle ⊖	a																								
London Blackfriars [3] ⊖	a																								
London Victoria [15] ⊖	a			12 07					12 37	12 37						13 07					13 37			13 37	
Ebbsfleet International	a					11 47							12 17					12 47							
Stratford International ⊖	a					11 59							12 29					12 59							
St Pancras Internatnl [15] ⊖	a					12 06							12 36					13 06							

Table 212

Saturdays

Ramsgate, Dover, Sheerness-on-Sea and Medway - London

		SE	SE	SE	SE 1	SE 1	SE		SE	SE	SE 1	SE 1	SE 1	SE	SE	SE	SE 1	SE 1		SE	SE	SE	SE 1	SE 1	SE 1
Ramsgate 4	d					12 04							12 40					13 04							13 40
Dumpton Park	d					12 07												13 07							
Broadstairs	d					12 10							12 45					13 10							13 45
Margate 4	d					12 16							12 50					13 16							13 50
Westgate-on-Sea	d					12 20												13 20							
Birchington-on-Sea	d					12 23							12 55					13 23							13 55
Herne Bay	d					12 32							13 04					13 32							14 04
Chestfield & Swalecliffe	d					12 36												13 36							
Whitstable	d					12 39							13 09					13 39							14 09
Dover Priory 4	d				12 05							12 45					13 05							13 45	
Kearsney	d				12 09												13 09								
Shepherds Well	d				12 14												13 14								
Snowdown	d				12 18												13 18								
Aylesham	d				12 20												13 20								
Adisham	d				12 23												13 23								
Bekesbourne	d				12 27												13 27								
Canterbury East 4	d				12 32							13 02					13 32							14 02	
Selling	d				12 41												13 41								
Faversham 2	a				12 46	12 48						13 14	13 18				13 46	13 48						14 14	14 18
	d	12 28			12 52		12 58					13 22		13 28			13 52			13 58				14 22	
Teynham	d				12 58												13 58								
Sheerness-on-Sea	d		12 32						13 02						13 32						14 02				
Queenborough	d		12 36						13 06						13 36						14 06				
Swale	d		12 40						13 10						13 40						14 10				
Kemsley	d		12 44						13 14						13 44						14 14				
Sittingbourne 4	a	12 36	12 49		13 02		13 06		13 19			13 29		13 36	13 49		14 02			14 06	14 19			14 29	
	d	12 37			13 03		13 07					13 30		13 37			14 03			14 07				14 30	
Newington	d											13 35												14 35	
Rainham (Kent)	d	12 45			13 10		13 15					13 40		13 45			14 10			14 15				14 40	
Gillingham (Kent) 4	d	12 50		12 54	13 15		13 20			13 24	13 32	13 45		13 50		13 54	14 15			14 20		14 24	14 32	14 45	
Chatham 4	d	12 54		12 58	13 20		13 24			13 28	13 36	13 50		13 54		13 58	14 20			14 24		14 28	14 36	14 50	
Rochester 4	d	12 57		13 00	13 22		13 27			13 30	13 39	13 52		13 57		14 00	14 22			14 27		14 30	14 39	14 52	
Strood 4	a	13 01		13 05			13 31			13 35				14 01		14 05				14 31		14 35			
Gravesend 4	a	13 12		13 17			13 42			13 47				14 12		14 17				14 42		14 47			
Greenhithe for Bluewater	a			13 23						13 53						14 23						14 53			
Dartford 4	a			13 28						13 58						14 28						14 58			
London Bridge 4 ⊖	a			14 05						14 35						15 05						15 35			
London Cannon Street 4 ⊖	a																								
London Waterloo (East) 4 ⊖	a			14 09						14 39						15 09						15 39			
London Charing Cross 4 ⊖	a			14 13						14 43						15 13						15 43			
Sole Street	d										13 49												14 49		
Meopham	d				13 33						13 52	14 03					14 33						14 52		15 03
Longfield	d				13 37						13 56	14 07					14 37						14 56		15 07
Farningham Road	d										13 59												14 59		
Swanley 4	a										14 04												15 04		
St Mary Cray	a										14 09												15 09		
Bromley South 4	a				13 50						14 15	14 20					14 50						15 15		15 20
Elephant & Castle ⊖	a																								
London Blackfriars 3 ⊖	a																								
London Victoria 15 ⊖	a				14 07						14 37	14 37					15 07						15 37		15 37
Ebbsfleet International	a	13 17					13 47							14 17						14 47					
Stratford International ⊖	a	13 29					13 59							14 29						15 02					
St Pancras Internatnl 15 ⊖	a	13 36					14 06							14 40						15 09					

Table 212

Saturdays

Ramsgate, Dover, Sheerness-on-Sea and Medway - London

		SE	SE	SE		SE ■1	SE ■1	SE	SE	SE	SE ■1	SE ■1	SE ■1	SE		SE	SE	SE ■1	SE ■1	SE	SE	SE	SE ■1	SE ■1	SE ■1
Ramsgate ■4	d						14 04						14 40						15 04						15 40
Dumpton Park	d						14 07												15 07						
Broadstairs	d						14 10						14 45						15 10						15 45
Margate ■4	d						14 16						14 50						15 16						15 50
Westgate-on-Sea	d						14 20												15 20						
Birchington-on-Sea	d						14 23						14 55						15 23						15 55
Herne Bay	d						14 32						15 04						15 32						16 04
Chestfield & Swalecliffe	d						14 36												15 36						
Whitstable	d						14 39						15 09						15 39						16 09
Dover Priory ■4	d					14 05						14 45						15 05						15 45	
Kearsney	d					14 09												15 09							
Shepherds Well	d					14 14												15 14							
Snowdown	d					14 18												15 18							
Aylesham	d					14 20												15 20							
Adisham	d					14 23												15 23							
Bekesbourne	d					14 27												15 27							
Canterbury East ■4	d					14 32						15 02						15 32						16 02	
Selling	d					14 41												15 41							
Faversham ■2	a					14 46	14 48					15 14	15 18					15 46	15 48					16 14	16 18
	d	14 28					14 52	14 58					15 22	15 28					15 52	15 58					16 22
Teynham	d						14 58												15 58						
Sheerness-on-Sea	d		14 32						15 02							15 32					16 02				
Queenborough	d		14 36						15 06							15 36					16 06				
Swale	d		14 40						15 10							15 40					16 10				
Kemsley	d		14 44						15 14							15 44					16 14				
Sittingbourne ■4	a	14 36	14 49				15 02	15 06	15 19				15 29	15 36		15 49			16 02	16 06	16 19				16 29
	d	14 37					15 03	15 07					15 30	15 37					16 03	16 07					16 30
Newington	d												15 35												16 35
Rainham (Kent)	d	14 45					15 10	15 15					15 40	15 45					16 10	16 15					16 40
Gillingham (Kent) ■4	d	14 50		14 54			15 15	15 20		15 24	15 32		15 45	15 50			15 54		16 15	16 20		16 24	16 32		16 45
Chatham ■4	d	14 54		14 58			15 20	15 24		15 28	15 36		15 50	15 54			15 58		16 20	16 24		16 28	16 36		16 50
Rochester ■4	d	14 57		15 00			15 22	15 27		15 30	15 39		15 52	15 57			16 00		16 22	16 27		16 30	16 39		16 52
Strood ■4	a	15 01		15 05				15 31		15 35				16 01			16 05			16 31		16 35			
Gravesend ■4	a	15 12		15 17				15 42		15 47				16 12			16 17			16 42		16 47			
Greenhithe for Bluewater	a			15 23						15 53							16 23					16 53			
Dartford ■4	a			15 28						15 58							16 28					16 58			
London Bridge ■4 ⊖	a			16 05						16 35							17 05					17 35			
London Cannon Street ■4 ⊖	a																								
London Waterloo (East) ■4 ⊖	a			16 09						16 39							17 09					17 39			
London Charing Cross ■4 ⊖	a			16 13						16 43							17 13					17 43			
Sole Street	d										15 49												16 49		
Meopham	d						15 33				15 52		16 03						16 33				16 52		17 03
Longfield	d						15 37				15 56		16 07						16 37				16 56		17 07
Farningham Road	d										15 59												16 59		
Swanley ■4	a										16 04												17 04		
St Mary Cray	a										16 09												17 09		
Bromley South ■4	a						15 50				16 15		16 20						16 50				17 15		17 20
Elephant & Castle ⊖	a																								
London Blackfriars ■3 ⊖	a																								
London Victoria ■15 ⊖	a						16 07				16 37		16 37						17 07				17 37		17 37
Ebbsfleet International	a	15 17						15 47						16 17						16 47					
Stratford International ⊖	a	15 29						15 59						16 29						17 02					
St Pancras Internatnl ■15 ⊖	a	15 36						16 06						16 37						17 09					

Table 212

Saturdays

Ramsgate, Dover, Sheerness-on-Sea and Medway - London

		SE	SE	SE	SE	SE	SE	SE	SE	SE		SE	SE	SE	SE	SE	SE	SE	SE	SE		SE	SE
					1	1				1		1	1				1	1					1
Ramsgate 4	d					16 04							16 40					17 04					
Dumpton Park	d					16 07												17 07					
Broadstairs	d					16 10							16 45					17 10					
Margate 4	d					16 16							16 50					17 16					
Westgate-on-Sea	d					16 20												17 20					
Birchington-on-Sea	d					16 23							16 55					17 23					
Herne Bay	d					16 32							17 04					17 32					
Chestfield & Swalecliffe	d					16 36												17 36					
Whitstable	d					16 39							17 09					17 39					
Dover Priory 4	d				16 05							16 45					17 05						
Kearsney	d				16 09												17 09						
Shepherds Well	d				16 14												17 14						
Snowdown	d				16 18												17 18						
Aylesham	d				16 20												17 20						
Adisham	d				16 23												17 23						
Bekesbourne	d				16 27												17 27						
Canterbury East 4	d				16 32							17 02					17 32						
Selling	d				16 41												17 41						
Faversham 2	a				16 46	16 48						17 14	17 18				17 46	17 48					
	d	16 28			16 52		16 58					17 22		17 28			17 52		17 58				
Teynham	d				16 58												17 58						
Sheerness-on-Sea	d		16 32					17 02							17 32					18 02			
Queenborough	d		16 36					17 06							17 36					18 06			
Swale	d		16 40					17 10							17 40					18 10			
Kemsley	d		16 44					17 14							17 44					18 14			
Sittingbourne 4	a	16 36	16 49		17 02		17 06	17 19				17 29		17 36	17 49		18 02		18 06	18 19			
	d	16 37			17 03		17 07					17 30		17 37			18 03		18 07				
Newington	d											17 35											
Rainham (Kent)	d	16 45			17 10		17 15					17 40		17 45			18 10		18 15				
Gillingham (Kent) 4	d	16 50		16 54	17 15		17 20		17 24	17 32		17 45		17 50		17 54	18 15		18 20			18 24	18 32
Chatham 4	d	16 54		16 58	17 20		17 24		17 28	17 36		17 50		17 54		17 58	18 20		18 24			18 28	18 36
Rochester 4	d	16 57		17 00	17 22		17 27		17 30	17 39		17 52		17 57		18 00	18 22		18 27			18 30	18 39
Strood 4	a	17 01		17 05			17 31		17 35					18 01		18 05			18 31			18 35	
Gravesend 4	a	17 12		17 17			17 42		17 47					18 12		18 17			18 42			18 47	
Greenhithe for Bluewater	a			17 23					17 53							18 23						18 53	
Dartford 4	a			17 28					17 58							18 28						18 58	
London Bridge 4 ⊖	a			18 05					18 35							19 05						19 36	
London Cannon Street 4 ⊖	a																						
London Waterloo (East) 4 ⊖	a			18 09					18 39							19 09						19 42	
London Charing Cross 4 ⊖	a			18 13					18 43							19 13						19 45	
Sole Street	d									17 49													18 49
Meopham	d				17 33					17 52		18 03					18 33						18 52
Longfield	d				17 37					17 56		18 07					18 37						18 56
Farningham Road	d									17 59													18 59
Swanley 4	a									18 04													19 04
St Mary Cray	a									18 09													19 09
Bromley South 4	a				17 50					18 15		18 20					18 50						19 15
Elephant & Castle ⊖	a																						
London Blackfriars 3 ⊖	a																						
London Victoria 15 ⊖	a				18 07					18 37		18 37					19 07						19 37
Ebbsfleet International	a	17 16					17 47							18 17					18 47				
Stratford International ⊖	a	17 27					17 59							18 29					19 02				
St Pancras Internatnl 15 ⊖	a	17 38					18 06							18 36					19 09				

Table 212

Saturdays

Ramsgate, Dover, Sheerness-on-Sea and Medway - London

		SE 1	SE 1	SE	SE	SE	SE 1	SE 1	SE	SE	SE	SE 1	SE 1	SE 1	SE	SE	SE	SE 1	SE 1	SE	SE
Ramsgate 4	d		17 40					18 04						18 40					19 04		
Dumpton Park	d							18 07											19 07		
Broadstairs	d		17 45					18 10						18 45					19 10		
Margate 4	d		17 50					18 16						18 50					19 16		
Westgate-on-Sea	d							18 20											19 20		
Birchington-on-Sea	d		17 55					18 23						18 55					19 23		
Herne Bay	d		18 04					18 32						19 04					19 32		
Chestfield & Swalecliffe	d							18 36											19 36		
Whitstable	d		18 09					18 39						19 09					19 39		
Dover Priory 4	d	17 45					18 05						18 45					19 05			
Kearsney	d						18 09											19 09			
Shepherds Well	d						18 14											19 14			
Snowdown	d						18 18											19 18			
Aylesham	d						18 20											19 20			
Adisham	d						18 23											19 23			
Bekesbourne	d						18 27											19 27			
Canterbury East 4	d	18 02					18 32						19 02					19 32			
Selling	d						18 41											19 41			
Faversham 2	a	18 14	18 18				18 46	18 48					19 14	19 18				19 46	19 48		
	d	18 22		18 28			18 52		18 58				19 22		19 28			19 52		19 58	
Teynham	d						18 58											19 58			
Sheerness-on-Sea	d				18 32					19 02						19 32					20 02
Queenborough	d				18 36					19 06						19 36					20 06
Swale	d				18 40					19 10						19 40					20 10
Kemsley	d				18 44					19 14						19 44					20 14
Sittingbourne 4	a	18 29		18 36	18 49		19 02		19 06	19 19			19 29		19 36	19 49		20 02		20 06	20 19
	d	18 30		18 37			19 03		19 07				19 30		19 37			20 03		20 07	
Newington	d	18 35											19 35								
Rainham (Kent)	d	18 40		18 45			19 10		19 15				19 40		19 45			20 10		20 15	
Gillingham (Kent) 4	d	18 45		18 50		18 54	19 15		19 20		19 24	19 32	19 45		19 50		19 54	20 15		20 20	
Chatham 4	d	18 50		18 54		18 58	19 20		19 24		19 28	19 36	19 50		19 54		19 58	20 20		20 24	
Rochester 4	d	18 52		18 57		19 00	19 22		19 27		19 30	19 39	19 52		19 57		20 00	20 22		20 27	
Strood 4	a			19 01		19 05			19 31		19 35				20 01		20 05			20 31	
Gravesend 4	a			19 12		19 17			19 42		19 47				20 12		20 17			20 42	
Greenhithe for Bluewater	a					19 23					19 53						20 23				
Dartford 4	a					19 28					19 58						20 28				
London Bridge 4 ⊖	a					20 06					20 36						21 06				
London Cannon Street 4 ⊖	a																				
London Waterloo (East) 4 ⊖	a					20 10					20 40						21 10				
London Charing Cross 4 ⊖	a					20 14					20 44						21 14				
Sole Street	d											19 49									
Meopham	d	19 03					19 33					19 52	20 03					20 33			
Longfield	d	19 07					19 37					19 56	20 07					20 37			
Farningham Road	d											19 59									
Swanley 4	a											20 04									
St Mary Cray	a											20 09									
Bromley South 4	a	19 20					19 50					20 15	20 20					20 50			
Elephant & Castle ⊖	a																				
London Blackfriars 3 ⊖	a																				
London Victoria 15 ⊖	a	19 37					20 07					20 37	20 37					21 07			
Ebbsfleet International	a			19 16					19 47						20 16					20 47	
Stratford International ⊖	a			19 27					19 59						20 27					21 02	
St Pancras Internatnl 15 ⊖	a			19 38					20 06						20 38					21 09	

Table 212

Saturdays

Ramsgate, Dover, Sheerness-on-Sea and Medway - London

		SE	SE [1]	SE		SE	SE	SE [1]	SE [1]	SE	SE	SE	SE [1]	SE		SE	SE [1]	SE [1]	SE	SE	SE	SE [1]	SE [1]	SE	
Ramsgate [4]	d								20 04									21 04							
Dumpton Park	d								20 07									21 07							
Broadstairs	d								20 10									21 10							
Margate [4]	d								20 16									21 16							
Westgate-on-Sea	d								20 20									21 20							
Birchington-on-Sea	d								20 23									21 23							
Herne Bay	d								20 32									21 32							
Chestfield & Swalecliffe	d								20 36									21 36							
Whitstable	d								20 39									21 39							
Dover Priory [4]	d							20 05									21 05						22 05		
Kearsney	d							20 09									21 09						22 09		
Shepherds Well	d							20 14									21 14						22 14		
Snowdown	d							20 18									21 18						22 18		
Aylesham	d							20 20									21 20						22 20		
Adisham	d							20 23									21 23						22 23		
Bekesbourne	d							20 27									21 27						22 27		
Canterbury East [4]	d							20 32									21 32					22 02	22 32		
Selling	d							20 41									21 41						22 41		
Faversham [2]	a							20 46	20 48								21 46	21 48				22 13	22 46		
	d		20 14	20 28				20 52		20 58			21 14	21 28			21 52		21 58			22 14			
Teynham	d							20 58									21 58								
Sheerness-on-Sea	d					20 32					21 02									22 02					
Queenborough	d					20 36					21 06									22 06					
Swale	d					20 40					21 10									22 10					
Kemsley	d					20 44					21 14									22 14					
Sittingbourne [4]	a		20 21	20 36		20 49		21 02		21 06	21 19		21 21	21 36			22 02		22 06	22 19		22 21			
	d		20 22	20 37				21 03		21 07			21 22	21 37			22 03		22 07			22 22			
Newington	d		20 27										21 27									22 27			
Rainham (Kent)	d		20 31	20 45				21 10		21 15			21 31	21 45			22 10		22 15			22 31			
Gillingham (Kent) [4]	d	20 24	20 36	20 50			20 54	21 15		21 20		21 24	21 36	21 50		21 54	22 15		22 20		22 24	22 36		22 54	
Chatham [4]	d	20 28	20 41	20 54			20 58	21 20		21 24		21 28	21 41	21 54		21 58	22 20		22 24		22 28	22 41		22 58	
Rochester [4]	d	20 30	20 43	20 57			21 00	21 22		21 27		21 30	21 43	21 57		22 00	22 22		22 27		22 30	22 43		23 00	
Strood [4]	a	20 35		21 01			21 05			21 31		21 35		22 01		22 05			22 31		22 35			23 05	
Gravesend [4]	a	20 47		21 12			21 17			21 42		21 47		22 12		22 17			22 42		22 47			23 17	
Greenhithe for Bluewater	a	20 53					21 23					21 53				22 23					22 53			23 23	
Dartford [4]	a	20 58					21 28					21 58				22 28					22 58			23 28	
London Bridge [4] ⊖	a	21 36					22 05					22 35				23 05					23 35				
London Cannon Street [4] ⊖	a																								
London Waterloo (East) [4] ⊖	a	21 40					22 09					22 39				23 09					23 39				
London Charing Cross [4] ⊖	a	21 44					22 13					22 43				23 13					23 43				
Sole Street	d		20 54										21 54									22 54			
Meopham	d		20 56					21 33					21 56				22 33					22 56			
Longfield	d		21 00					21 37					22 00				22 37					23 00			
Farningham Road	d		21 04										22 04									23 04			
Swanley [4]	a		21 09										22 09									23 09			
St Mary Cray	a		21 14										22 14									23 14			
Bromley South [4]	a		21 20					21 50					22 20				22 50					23 20			
Elephant & Castle ⊖	a																								
London Blackfriars [3] ⊖	a																								
London Victoria [15] ⊖	a		21 37					22 07					22 37				23 07					23 37			
Ebbsfleet International	a			21 17						21 47				22 17					22 47						
Stratford International ⊖	a			21 35						21 59				22 29					22 59						
St Pancras Internatnl [15] ⊖	a			21 42						22 06				22 36					23 06						

Table 212

Saturdays

Ramsgate, Dover, Sheerness-on-Sea and Medway - London

		SE [1]	SE	SE [1]	SE [1]	SE
Ramsgate [4]	d	22 04			23 04	
Dumpton Park	d	22 07			23 07	
Broadstairs	d	22 10			23 10	
Margate [4]	d	22 16			23 16	
Westgate-on-Sea	d	22 20			23 20	
Birchington-on-Sea	d	22 23			23 23	
Herne Bay	d	22 32			23 32	
Chestfield & Swalecliffe	d	22 36			23 36	
Whitstable	d	22 39			23 39	
Dover Priory [4]	d			23 05		
Kearsney	d			23 09		
Shepherds Well	d			23 14		
Snowdown	d			23 18		
Aylesham	d			23 20		
Adisham	d			23 23		
Bekesbourne	d			23 27		
Canterbury East [4]	d			23 32		
Selling	d			23 41		
Faversham [2]	a	22 48		23 46	23 49	
	d	22 52			23 52	
Teynham	d	22 58			23 58	
Sheerness-on-Sea	d		23 02			23 53
Queenborough	d		23 06			23 57
Swale	d		23 10			00 01
Kemsley	d		23 14			00 05
Sittingbourne [4]	a	23 02	23 19		00 02	00 10
	d	23 03			00 03	
Newington	d				00 08	
Rainham (Kent)	d	23 10			00 12	
Gillingham (Kent) [4]	d	23 15			00a17	
Chatham [4]	d	23 20				
Rochester [4]	d	23 22				
Strood [4]	a					
Gravesend [4]	a					
Greenhithe for Bluewater	a					
Dartford [4]	a					
London Bridge [4] ⊖	a					
London Cannon Street [4] ⊖	a					
London Waterloo (East) [4] ⊖	a					
London Charing Cross [4] ⊖	a					
Sole Street	d					
Meopham	d	23 33				
Longfield	d	23 37				
Farningham Road	d					
Swanley [4]	a					
St Mary Cray	a					
Bromley South [4]	a	23 50				
Elephant & Castle ⊖	a					
London Blackfriars [3] ⊖	a					
London Victoria [15] ⊖	a	00 07				
Ebbsfleet International	a					
Stratford International ⊖	a					
St Pancras Internatnl [15] ⊖	a					

Table 212

Sundays

Ramsgate, Dover, Sheerness-on-Sea and Medway - London

		SE	SE	SE	SE	SE	SE	SE	SE	SE		SE	SE	SE	SE	SE	SE	SE	SE	SE		SE	SE	SE	
		1	1			1			1				1			1	1			1					
		A	A	A																					
Ramsgate 4	d	22p04	23p04						06 34								07 34								
Dumpton Park	d	22p07	23p07						06 37								07 37								
Broadstairs	d	22p10	23p10						06 40								07 40								
Margate 4	d	22p16	23p16						06 45								07 45								
Westgate-on-Sea	d	22p20	23p20						06 49								07 49								
Birchington-on-Sea	d	22p23	23p23						06 52								07 52								
Herne Bay	d	22p32	23p32						07 01								08 01								
Chestfield & Swalecliffe	d	22p36	23p36						07 05								08 05								
Whitstable	d	22p39	23p39						07 08								08 08								
Dover Priory 4	d															07 34									
Kearsney	d															07 38									
Shepherds Well	d															07 43									
Snowdown	d															07 47									
Aylesham	d															07 49									
Adisham	d															07 52									
Bekesbourne	d															07 56									
Canterbury East 4	d															08 01									
Selling	d															08 10									
Faversham 2	a	22p48	23p49						07 17							08 15	08 17								
	d	22p52	23p52			06 34		06 58	07 21			07 28	07 34		07 58	08 21		08 28		08 34			08 58		
Teynham	d	22p58	23p58			06 40							07 40							08 40					
Sheerness-on-Sea	d			23p53																		08 42			
Queenborough	d			23p57																		08 46			
Swale	d			00 01																		08 50			
Kemsley	d			00 05																		08 54			
Sittingbourne 4	a	23p02	00 02	00 10		06 44		07 06	07 28			07 36	07 44		08 06	08 28		08 36		08 44		08 59	09 06		
	d	23p03	00 03			06 45		07 07	07 29			07 37	07 45		08 07	08 29		08 37		08 45			09 07		
Newington	d		00 08			06 50							07 50							08 50					
Rainham (Kent)	d	23p10	00 12			06 54		07 15	07 36			07 45	07 54		08 15	08 36		08 45		08 54			09 15		
Gillingham (Kent) 4	d	23p15	00a17		06 45	06 59	07 15	07 20	07 41	07 45		07 50	07 59	08 15	08 20	08 41		08 50	08 54	08 59			09 20	09 24	
Chatham 4	d	23p20			06 49	07 04	07 19	07 24	07 46	07 49		07 54	08 04	08 19	08 24	08 46		08 54	08 58	09 04			09 24	09 28	
Rochester 4	d	23p22			06 51	07 06	07 21	07 27	07 48	07 51		07 57	08 06	08 21	08 27	08 48		08 57	09 00	09 06			09 27	09 30	
Strood 4	a				06 56		07 26	07 31		07 56		08 01		08 26	08 31			09 01	09 05				09 31	09 35	
Gravesend 4	a				07 08		07 38	07 42		08 08		08 12		08 38	08 42			09 12	09 17				09 42	09 47	
Greenhithe for Bluewater	a				07 17		07 47			08 17				08 47					09 23					09 53	
Dartford 4	a				07 24		07 54			08 24				08 54					09 28					09 58	
London Bridge 4 ⊖	a				08 06		08 36			09 06				09 36					10 06					10 36	
London Cannon Street 4 ⊖	a																								
London Waterloo (East) 4 ⊖	a				08 11		08 41			09 11				09 41					10 11					10 41	
London Charing Cross 4 ⊖	a				08 14		08 44			09 14				09 44					10 14					10 44	
Sole Street	d					07 17							08 17							09 17					
Meopham	d	23p33				07 19							08 19							09 19					
Longfield	d	23p37				07 23							08 23							09 23					
Farningham Road	d					07 27							08 27							09 27					
Swanley 4	a					07 32							08 32							09 32					
St Mary Cray	a					07 36							08 36							09 36					
Bromley South 4	a	23p50				07 42			08 13				08 42			09 13				09 42					
Elephant & Castle ⊖	a																								
London Blackfriars 3 ⊖	a																								
London Victoria 15 ⊖	a	00 07				08 03			08 29				09 02			09 29				10 02					
Ebbsfleet International	a							07 47				08 17			08 47			09 17					09 47		
Stratford International ⊖	a							07 59				08 29			08 59			09 29					09 59		
St Pancras Internatnl 15 ⊖	a							08 06				08 36			09 06			09 40					10 06		

A not 22 May

Table 212

Sundays

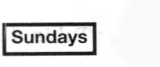

Ramsgate, Dover, Sheerness-on-Sea and Medway - London

		SE 1	SE 1	SE	SE	SE 1	SE		SE	SE	SE 1	SE 1	SE	SE	SE 1	SE	SE		SE	SE 1	SE 1	SE	SE	SE 1	SE
Ramsgate 4	d		08 34									09 34									10 34				
Dumpton Park	d		08 37									09 37									10 37				
Broadstairs	d		08 40									09 40									10 40				
Margate 4	d		08 45									09 45									10 45				
Westgate-on-Sea	d		08 49									09 49									10 49				
Birchington-on-Sea	d		08 52									09 52									10 52				
Herne Bay	d		09 01									10 01									11 01				
Chestfield & Swalecliffe	d		09 05									10 05									11 05				
Whitstable	d		09 08									10 08									11 08				
Dover Priory 4	d	08 34									09 34									10 34					
Kearsney	d	08 38									09 38									10 38					
Shepherds Well	d	08 43									09 43									10 43					
Snowdown	d	08 47									09 47									10 47					
Aylesham	d	08 49									09 49									10 49					
Adisham	d	08 52									09 52									10 52					
Bekesbourne	d	08 56									09 56									10 56					
Canterbury East 4	d	09 01				09 22					10 01				10 22					11 01				11 22	
Selling	d	09 10									10 10									11 10					
Faversham 2	a	09 15	09 17			09 33					10 15	10 17			10 33					11 15	11 17			11 33	
	d		09 21	09 28		09 34			09 58			10 21	10 28		10 34		10 58				11 21	11 28		11 34	
Teynham	d					09 40									10 40									11 40	
Sheerness-on-Sea	d						09 42									10 42									11 42
Queenborough	d						09 46									10 46									11 46
Swale	d						09 50									10 50									11 50
Kemsley	d						09 54									10 54									11 54
Sittingbourne 4	a		09 28	09 36		09 44	09 59		10 06			10 28	10 36		10 44	10 59	11 06				11 28	11 36		11 44	11 59
	d		09 29	09 37		09 45			10 07			10 29	10 37		10 45		11 07				11 29	11 37		11 45	
Newington	d					09 50									10 50									11 50	
Rainham (Kent)	d		09 36	09 45		09 54			10 15			10 36	10 45		10 54		11 15				11 36	11 45		11 54	
Gillingham (Kent) 4	d		09 41	09 50	09 54	09 59			10 20	10 24		10 41	10 50	10 54	10 59		11 20		11 24		11 41	11 50	11 54	11 59	
Chatham 4	d		09 46	09 54	09 58	10 04			10 24	10 28		10 46	10 54	10 58	11 04		11 24		11 28		11 46	11 54	11 58	12 04	
Rochester 4	d		09 48	09 57	10 00	10 06			10 27	10 30		10 48	10 57	11 00	11 06		11 27		11 30		11 48	11 57	12 00	12 06	
Strood 4	a			10 01	10 05				10 31	10 35			11 01	11 05			11 31		11 35			12 01	12 05		
Gravesend 4	a			10 12	10 17				10 42	10 47			11 12	11 17			11 42		11 47			12 12	12 17		
Greenhithe for Bluewater	a				10 23					10 53				11 23					11 53				12 23		
Dartford 4	a				10 28					10 58				11 28					11 58				12 28		
London Bridge 4 ⊖	a				11 06					11 36				12 06					12 36				13 06		
London Cannon Street 4 ⊖	a																								
London Waterloo (East) 4 ⊖	a				11 11					11 41				12 11					12 41				13 11		
London Charing Cross 4 ⊖	a				11 14					11 44				12 14					12 44				13 14		
Sole Street	d					10 17									11 17									12 17	
Meopham	d					10 19									11 19									12 19	
Longfield	d					10 23									11 23									12 23	
Farningham Road	d					10 27									11 27									12 27	
Swanley 4	a					10 32									11 32									12 32	
St Mary Cray	a					10 36									11 36									12 36	
Bromley South 4	a		10 13			10 42						11 13			11 42						12 13			12 42	
Elephant & Castle ⊖	a																								
London Blackfriars 3 ⊖	a																								
London Victoria 15 ⊖	a		10 29			11 02						11 29			12 02						12 29			13 02	
Ebbsfleet International	a			10 17					10 47				11 17				11 47					12 17			
Stratford International ⊖	a			10 33					10 59				11 29				11 59					12 29			
St Pancras Internatnl 15 ⊖	a			10 40					11 06				11 36				12 06					12 36			

Table 212

Sundays

Ramsgate, Dover, Sheerness-on-Sea and Medway - London

		SE	SE	SE 1	SE 1	SE	SE	SE 1	SE	SE	SE	SE 1	SE 1	SE	SE	SE 1	SE	SE	SE	SE 1	SE 1	SE
Ramsgate 4	d				11 34								12 34								13 34	
Dumpton Park	d				11 37								12 37								13 37	
Broadstairs	d				11 40								12 40								13 40	
Margate 4	d				11 45								12 45								13 45	
Westgate-on-Sea	d				11 49								12 49								13 49	
Birchington-on-Sea	d				11 52								12 52								13 52	
Herne Bay	d				12 01								13 01								14 01	
Chestfield & Swalecliffe	d				12 05								13 05								14 05	
Whitstable	d				12 08								13 08								14 08	
Dover Priory 4	d			11 34								12 34								13 34		
Kearsney	d			11 38								12 38								13 38		
Shepherds Well	d			11 43								12 43								13 43		
Snowdown	d			11 47								12 47								13 47		
Aylesham	d			11 49								12 49								13 49		
Adisham	d			11 52								12 52								13 52		
Bekesbourne	d			11 56								12 56								13 56		
Canterbury East 4	d			12 01				12 22				13 01				13 22				14 01		
Selling	d			12 10								13 10								14 10		
Faversham 2	a			12 15	12 17			12 33				13 15	13 17			13 33				14 15	14 17	
	d	11 58		12 21		12 28		12 34		12 58		13 21		13 28		13 34		13 58		14 21		14 28
Teynham	d							12 40								13 40						
Sheerness-on-Sea	d								12 42								13 42					
Queenborough	d								12 46								13 46					
Swale	d								12 50								13 50					
Kemsley	d								12 54								13 54					
Sittingbourne 4	a	12 06		12 28		12 36		12 44	12 59	13 06		13 28		13 36		13 44	13 59	14 06		14 28		14 36
	d	12 07		12 29		12 37		12 45		13 07		13 29		13 37		13 45		14 07		14 29		14 37
Newington	d							12 50								13 50						
Rainham (Kent)	d	12 15		12 36		12 45		12 54		13 15		13 36		13 45		13 54		14 15		14 36		14 45
Gillingham (Kent) 4	d	12 20	12 24	12 41		12 50	12 54	12 59		13 20	13 24	13 41		13 50	13 54	13 59		14 20	14 24	14 41		14 50
Chatham 4	d	12 24	12 28	12 46		12 54	12 58	13 04		13 24	13 28	13 46		13 54	13 58	14 04		14 24	14 28	14 46		14 54
Rochester 4	d	12 27	12 30	12 48		12 57	13 00	13 06		13 27	13 30	13 48		13 57	14 00	14 06		14 27	14 30	14 48		14 57
Strood 4	a	12 31	12 35			13 01	13 05			13 31	13 35			14 01	14 05			14 31	14 35			15 01
Gravesend 4	a	12 42	12 47			13 12	13 17			13 42	13 47			14 12	14 17			14 42	14 47			15 12
Greenhithe for Bluewater	a		12 53				13 23				13 53				14 23				14 53			
Dartford 4	a		12 58				13 28				13 58				14 28				14 58			
London Bridge 4 ⊖	a		13 36				14 06				14 36				15 06				15 36			
London Cannon Street 4 ⊖	a																					
London Waterloo (East) 4 ⊖	a		13 41				14 11				14 41				15 11				15 41			
London Charing Cross 4 ⊖	a		13 44				14 14				14 44				15 14				15 44			
Sole Street	d							13 17								14 17						
Meopham	d							13 19								14 19						
Longfield	d							13 23								14 23						
Farningham Road	d							13 27								14 27						
Swanley 4	a							13 32								14 32						
St Mary Cray	a							13 36								14 36						
Bromley South 4	a			13 13				13 42				14 13				14 42				15 13		
Elephant & Castle ⊖	a																					
London Blackfriars 3 ⊖	a																					
London Victoria 15 ⊖	a			13 29				14 02				14 29				15 02				15 29		
Ebbsfleet International	a	12 47				13 17				13 47				14 17				14 47				15 17
Stratford International ⊖	a	12 59				13 32				13 59				14 29				15 02				15 29
St Pancras Internatnl 15 ⊖	a	13 06				13 39				14 06				14 40				15 09				15 36

Table 212

Sundays

Ramsgate, Dover, Sheerness-on-Sea and Medway - London

		SE	SE 1	SE	SE	SE	SE 1	SE 1	SE	SE		SE 1	SE	SE	SE	SE 1	SE 1	SE	SE	SE 1		SE	SE	SE
Ramsgate 4	d							14 34									15 34							
Dumpton Park	d							14 37									15 37							
Broadstairs	d							14 40									15 40							
Margate 4	d							14 45									15 45							
Westgate-on-Sea	d							14 49									15 49							
Birchington-on-Sea	d							14 52									15 52							
Herne Bay	d							15 01									16 01							
Chestfield & Swalecliffe	d							15 05									16 05							
Whitstable	d							15 08									16 08							
Dover Priory 4	d						14 34									15 34								
Kearsney	d						14 38									15 38								
Shepherds Well	d						14 43									15 43								
Snowdown	d						14 47									15 47								
Aylesham	d						14 49									15 49								
Adisham	d						14 52									15 52								
Bekesbourne	d						14 56									15 56								
Canterbury East 4	d		14 22				15 01					15 22				16 01				16 22				
Selling	d						15 10									16 10								
Faversham 2	a		14 33				15 15	15 17				15 33				16 15	16 17			16 33				
	d		14 34		14 58			15 21	15 28			15 34		15 58			16 21	16 28		16 34			16 58	
Teynham	d		14 40									15 40								16 40				
Sheerness-on-Sea	d			14 42									15 42									16 42		
Queenborough	d			14 46									15 46									16 46		
Swale	d			14 50									15 50									16 50		
Kemsley	d			14 54									15 54									16 54		
Sittingbourne 4	a		14 44	14 59	15 06			15 28	15 36			15 44	15 59	16 06			16 28	16 36		16 44		16 59	17 06	
	d		14 45		15 07			15 29	15 37			15 45		16 07			16 29	16 37		16 45			17 07	
Newington	d		14 50									15 50								16 50				
Rainham (Kent)	d		14 54		15 15			15 36	15 45			15 54		16 15			16 36	16 45		16 54			17 15	
Gillingham (Kent) 4	d	14 54	14 59		15 20	15 24		15 41	15 50	15 54		15 59		16 20	16 24		16 41	16 50	16 54	16 59			17 20	17 24
Chatham 4	d	14 58	15 04		15 24	15 28		15 46	15 54	15 58		16 04		16 24	16 28		16 46	16 54	16 58	17 04			17 24	17 28
Rochester 4	d	15 00	15 06		15 27	15 30		15 48	15 57	16 00		16 06		16 27	16 30		16 48	16 57	17 00	17 06			17 27	17 30
Strood 4	a	15 05			15 31	15 35			16 01	16 05				16 31	16 35			17 01	17 05				17 31	17 35
Gravesend 4	a	15 17			15 42	15 47			16 12	16 17				16 42	16 47			17 12	17 17				17 42	17 47
Greenhithe for Bluewater	a	15 23				15 53				16 23					16 53				17 23					17 53
Dartford 4	a	15 28				15 58				16 28					16 58				17 28					17 58
London Bridge 4 ⊖	a	16 06				16 36				17 06					17 36				18 06					18 36
London Cannon Street 4 ⊖	a																							
London Waterloo (East) 4 ⊖	a	16 11				16 41				17 11					17 41				18 11					18 41
London Charing Cross 4 ⊖	a	16 14				16 44				17 14					17 44				18 14					18 44
Sole Street	d		15 17									16 17								17 17				
Meopham	d		15 19									16 19								17 19				
Longfield	d		15 23									16 23								17 23				
Farningham Road	d		15 27									16 27								17 27				
Swanley 4	a		15 32									16 32								17 32				
St Mary Cray	a		15 36									16 36								17 36				
Bromley South 4	a		15 42					16 13				16 42					17 13			17 42				
Elephant & Castle ⊖	a																							
London Blackfriars 3 ⊖	a																							
London Victoria 15 ⊖	a		16 02					16 29				17 02					17 29			18 02				
Ebbsfleet International	a				15 47				16 17					16 47				17 16					17 47	
Stratford International ⊖	a				15 59				16 29					17 02				17 27					17 59	
St Pancras Internatnl 15 ⊖	a				16 06				16 36					17 09				17 38					18 09	

Table 212

Sundays

Ramsgate, Dover, Sheerness-on-Sea and Medway - London

		SE 1	SE 1	SE	SE	SE 1		SE	SE	SE	SE 1	SE 1	SE	SE	SE 1	SE		SE	SE		SE 1	SE 1	SE	SE	SE 1
Ramsgate 4	d		16 34									17 34										18 34			
Dumpton Park	d		16 37									17 37										18 37			
Broadstairs	d		16 40									17 40										18 40			
Margate 4	d		16 45									17 45										18 45			
Westgate-on-Sea	d		16 49									17 49										18 49			
Birchington-on-Sea	d		16 52									17 52										18 52			
Herne Bay	d		17 01									18 01										19 01			
Chestfield & Swalecliffe	d		17 05									18 05										19 05			
Whitstable	d		17 08									18 08										19 08			
Dover Priory 4	d	16 34									17 34										18 34				
Kearsney	d	16 38									17 38										18 38				
Shepherds Well	d	16 43									17 43										18 43				
Snowdown	d	16 47									17 47										18 47				
Aylesham	d	16 49									17 49										18 49				
Adisham	d	16 52									17 52										18 52				
Bekesbourne	d	16 56									17 56										18 56				
Canterbury East 4	d	17 01				17 22					18 01				18 22						19 01				19 22
Selling	d	17 10									18 10										19 10				
Faversham 2	a	17 15	17 17			17 33					18 15	18 17			18 33						19 15	19 17			19 33
	d		17 21	17 28		17 34			17 58			18 21	18 28		18 34			18 58				19 21		19 28	19 34
Teynham	d					17 40									18 40										19 40
Sheerness-on-Sea	d							17 42								18 42									
Queenborough	d							17 46								18 46									
Swale	d							17 50								18 50									
Kemsley	d							17 54								18 54									
Sittingbourne 4	a		17 28	17 36		17 44		17 59	18 06			18 28	18 36		18 44	18 59		19 06				19 28		19 36	19 44
	d		17 29	17 37		17 45			18 07			18 29	18 37		18 45			19 07				19 29		19 37	19 45
Newington	d					17 50									18 50										19 50
Rainham (Kent)	d		17 36	17 45		17 54			18 15			18 36	18 45		18 54			19 15				19 36		19 45	19 54
Gillingham (Kent) 4	d		17 41	17 50	17 54	17 59			18 20	18 24		18 41	18 50	18 54	18 59			19 20	19 24			19 41	19 45	19 50	19 59
Chatham 4	d		17 46	17 54	17 58	18 04			18 24	18 28		18 46	18 54	18 58	19 04			19 24	19 28			19 46	19 49	19 54	20 04
Rochester 4	d		17 48	17 57	18 00	18 06			18 27	18 30		18 48	18 57	19 00	19 06			19 27	19 30			19 48	19 51	19 57	20 06
Strood 4	a			18 01	18 05				18 31	18 35			19 01	19 05				19 31	19 35				19 56	20 01	
Gravesend 4	a			18 12	18 17				18 42	18 47			19 12	19 17				19 42	19 47				20 08	20 12	
Greenhithe for Bluewater	a				18 23					18 53				19 23					19 53				20 17		
Dartford 4	a				18 28					18 58				19 28					19 58				20 24		
London Bridge 4 ⊖	a				19 06					19 36				20 06					20 36				21 06		
London Cannon Street 4 ⊖	a																								
London Waterloo (East) 4 ⊖	a				19 11					19 41				20 11					20 41				21 11		
London Charing Cross 4 ⊖	a				19 14					19 44				20 14					20 44				21 14		
Sole Street	d					18 17									19 17										20 17
Meopham	d					18 19									19 19										20 19
Longfield	d					18 23									19 23										20 23
Farningham Road	d					18 27									19 27										20 27
Swanley 4	a					18 32									19 32										20 32
St Mary Cray	a					18 36									19 36										20 36
Bromley South 4	a		18 13			18 42						19 13			19 42							20 13			20 42
Elephant & Castle ⊖	a																								
London Blackfriars 3 ⊖	a																								
London Victoria 15 ⊖	a		18 29			19 02						19 29			20 02							20 29			21 02
Ebbsfleet International	a			18 16					18 47				19 17					19 47						20 16	
Stratford International ⊖	a			18 27					19 02				19 29					20 02						20 27	
St Pancras Internatnl 15 ⊖	a			18 41					19 09				19 36					20 12						20 38	

Table 212

Sundays

Ramsgate, Dover, Sheerness-on-Sea and Medway - London

		SE		SE	SE	SE 1	SE 1	SE	SE	SE 1	SE	SE		SE	SE 1	SE 1	SE	SE	SE 1	SE	SE	SE		SE 1	SE 1
Ramsgate 4	d						19 34									20 34									21 34
Dumpton Park	d						19 37									20 37									21 37
Broadstairs	d						19 40									20 40									21 40
Margate 4	d						19 45									20 45									21 45
Westgate-on-Sea	d						19 49									20 49									21 49
Birchington-on-Sea	d						19 52									20 52									21 52
Herne Bay	d						20 01									21 01									22 01
Chestfield & Swalecliffe	d						20 05									21 05									22 05
Whitstable	d						20 08									21 08									22 08
Dover Priory 4	d					19 34									20 34									21 34	
Kearsney	d					19 38									20 38									21 38	
Shepherds Well	d					19 43									20 43									21 43	
Snowdown	d					19 47									20 47									21 47	
Aylesham	d					19 49									20 49									21 49	
Adisham	d					19 52									20 52									21 52	
Bekesbourne	d					19 56									20 56									21 56	
Canterbury East 4	d					20 01									21 01									22 01	
Selling	d					20 10									21 10									22 10	
Faversham 2	a					20 15	20 17								21 15	21 17								22 15	22 17
	d				19 58	20 21			20 28	20 34				20 58	21 21			21 28	21 34			21 58		22 21	
Teynham	d									20 40									21 40						
Sheerness-on-Sea	d	19 42									20 42									21 42					
Queenborough	d	19 46									20 46									21 46					
Swale	d	19 50									20 50									21 50					
Kemsley	d	19 54									20 54									21 54					
Sittingbourne 4	a	19 59			20 06	20 28			20 36	20 44	20 59			21 06	21 28			21 36	21 44	21 59		22 06		22 28	
	d				20 07	20 29			20 37	20 45				21 07	21 29			21 37	21 45			22 07		22 29	
Newington	d									20 50									21 50						
Rainham (Kent)	d				20 15	20 36			20 45	20 54				21 15	21 36			21 45	21 54			22 15		22 36	
Gillingham (Kent) 4	d			20 15	20 20	20 41		20 45	20 50	20 59		21 15		21 20	21 41		21 45	21 50	21 59		22 15	22 20		22 41	
Chatham 4	d			20 19	20 24	20 46		20 49	20 54	21 04		21 19		21 24	21 46		21 49	21 54	22 04		22 19	22 24		22 46	
Rochester 4	d			20 21	20 27	20 48		20 51	20 57	21 06		21 21		21 27	21 48		21 51	21 57	22 06		22 21	22 27		22 48	
Strood 4	a			20 26	20 31			20 56	21 01			21 26		21 31			21 56	22 01			22 26	22 31			
Gravesend 4	a			20 38	20 42			21 08	21 12			21 38		21 42			22 08	22 12			22 38	22 42			
Greenhithe for Bluewater	a			20 47				21 17				21 47					22 17				22 47				
Dartford 4	a			20 54				21 24				21 54					22 24				22 54				
London Bridge 4 ⊖	a			21 36				22 06				22 36					23 06				23 36				
London Cannon Street 4 ⊖	a																								
London Waterloo (East) 4 ⊖	a			21 41				22 11				22 41					23 11				23 41				
London Charing Cross 4 ⊖	a			21 44				22 14				22 44					23 14				23 44				
Sole Street	d									21 17									22 17						
Meopham	d									21 19									22 19						
Longfield	d									21 23									22 23						
Farningham Road	d									21 27									22 27						
Swanley 4	a									21 32									22 32						
St Mary Cray	a									21 36									22 36						
Bromley South 4	a					21 13				21 42					22 13				22 42					23 13	
Elephant & Castle ⊖	a																								
London Blackfriars 3 ⊖	a																								
London Victoria 15 ⊖	a					21 29				22 02					22 29				23 02					23 29	
Ebbsfleet International	a				20 47				21 17					21 47				22 17				22 47			
Stratford International ⊖	a				20 59				21 35					21 59				22 29				22 59			
St Pancras Internatnl 15 ⊖	a				21 06				21 42					22 06				22 36				23 06			

Table 212

Sundays

Ramsgate, Dover, Sheerness-on-Sea and Medway - London

		SE [1]	SE [1]	SE	SE [1]	SE
Ramsgate [4]	d				22 34	
Dumpton Park	d				22 37	
Broadstairs	d				22 40	
Margate [4]	d				22 45	
Westgate-on-Sea	d				22 49	
Birchington-on-Sea	d				22 52	
Herne Bay	d				23 01	
Chestfield & Swalecliffe	d				23 05	
Whitstable	d				23 08	
Dover Priory [4]	d		22 34			
Kearsney	d		22 38			
Shepherds Well	d		22 43			
Snowdown	d		22 47			
Aylesham	d		22 49			
Adisham	d		22 52			
Bekesbourne	d		22 56			
Canterbury East [4]	d		23 01			
Selling	d		23 10			
Faversham [2]	a		23 15		23 17	
	d	22 34			23 21	
Teynham	d	22 40				
Sheerness-on-Sea	d			22 42		23 42
Queenborough	d			22 46		23 46
Swale	d			22 50		23 50
Kemsley	d			22 54		23 54
Sittingbourne [4]	a	22 44		22 59	23 28	23 59
	d	22 45			23 29	
Newington	d	22 50				
Rainham (Kent)	d	22 54			23 36	
Gillingham (Kent) [4]	d	22 59			23 41	
Chatham [4]	d	23 04			23 46	
Rochester [4]	d	23 06			23 48	
Strood [4]	a					
Gravesend [4]	a					
Greenhithe for Bluewater	a					
Dartford [4]	a					
London Bridge [4] ⊖	a					
London Cannon Street [4] ⊖	a					
London Waterloo (East) [4] ⊖	a					
London Charing Cross [4] ⊖	a					
Sole Street	d	23 17				
Meopham	d	23 19				
Longfield	d	23 23				
Farningham Road	d	23 27				
Swanley [4]	a	23 32				
St Mary Cray	a	23 36				
Bromley South [4]	a	23 42			00 13	
Elephant & Castle ⊖	a					
London Blackfriars [3] ⊖	a					
London Victoria [15] ⊖	a	00 02			00 29	
Ebbsfleet International	a					
Stratford International ⊖	a					
St Pancras Internatnl [15] ⊖	a					

Network Diagram for Tables 216, 217, 218, 219, 221, 222

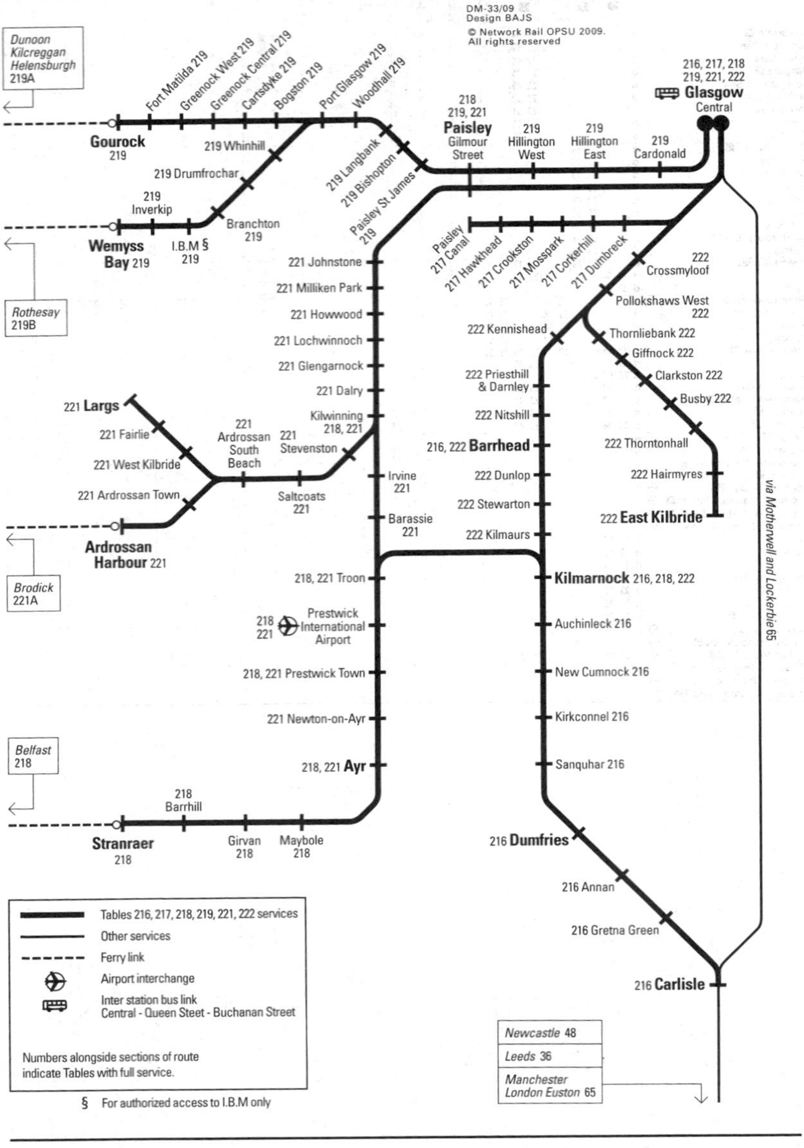

§ For authorized access to I.B.M only

Table 216

Mondays to Saturdays

Glasgow Central and Kilmarnock - Dumfries and Carlisle

Miles	Miles				SR MO A	SR MO B 🚌	SR MO B 🚌	SR MX	SR	SR	SR SO	SR SX	SR
0	—	**Glasgow Central** 15	65,222	d	22p12			23p12					07 08
7½	—	Barrhead	222	d	22p23			23p32					07 23
24¼	74½	**Kilmarnock** 3	218,222	a	22p48			23p59					07 48
—	—			d	22p49	22p55	22p55	23p59					07 48
38	89¼	Auchinleck		d	23p06		23p25	00 18					08 05
45½	96¾	New Cumnock		d	23p14		23p45	00 29					08 13
52¾	104½	Kirkconnel		d	23p23		23p59	00 39					08 22
56	107¾	Sanquhar		d	23p28		00 10	00 44					08 26
82¼	135	**Dumfries**		d	23p56	00 15	01 00	01a17	04 56	06 17	07 43	07 45	08 57
97¾	150½	Annan		d	00 11	00 40	01 25		05 11	06 32	07 58	08 00	09 12
105½	158	Gretna Green		d	00 20	00 50	01 35		05 20	06 41	08 07	08 09	09 22
115½	168	**Carlisle** 8	65	a	00 34	01 15	02 00		05 33	06 54	08 20	08 22	09 37
—	—	Newcastle 8	48	a						08 57		10 00	11 07

Miles	Miles				SR	SR SO	SR	SR SO	SR	SR	SR SO	SR	SR SO	SR SX	SR SO
0	—	**Glasgow Central** 15	65,222	d	08 37		10 12		12 12	13 12			16 12	16 12	
7½	—	Barrhead	222	d	08 49								16 23	16 23	
24¼	74½	**Kilmarnock** 3	218,222	a	09 18		10 47		12 47	13 47			16 49	16 49	
—	—			d	09 18		10 49		12 48	13 49			16 49	16 49	
38	89¼	Auchinleck		d	09 35		11 05		13 04	14 05			17 06	17 06	
45½	96¾	New Cumnock		d	09 43		11 14		13 13	14 14			17 14	17 14	
52¾	104½	Kirkconnel		d	09 52		11 22		13 21	14 22			17 23	17 23	
56	107¾	Sanquhar		d	09 57		11 27		13 26	14 27			17 28	17 28	
82¼	135	**Dumfries**		d	10 23	11 02	11 57	13 10	13 54	14 55	16 02	17 07	17 56	17 56	18 41
97¾	150½	Annan		d	10 38	11 17	12 13	13 25	14 10	15 11	16 17	17 22	18 11	18 11	18 56
105½	158	Gretna Green		d	10 47	11 26	12 21	13 34	14 18	15 19	16 26	17 31	18 20	18 20	19 05
115½	168	**Carlisle** 8	65	a	11 02	11 39	12 35	13 52	14 32	15 34	16 39	17 44	18 35	18 35	19 18
—	—	Newcastle 8	48	a					15 54				20 11	20 12	

			SR	SR	SR SO	SR SX	SR SO	SR SX
Glasgow Central 15	65,222	d	17 42	19 12		21 12	22 12	23 12
Barrhead	222	d	17 54	19 24		21 23	22 23	23 32
Kilmarnock 3	218,222	a	18 22	19 50		21 50	22 50	23 59
		d	18 25	19 51		21 51	22 51	23 59
Auchinleck		d	18 42	20 07		22 08	23 07	00 18
New Cumnock		d	18 51	20 16		22 16	23 16	00 29
Kirkconnel		d	18 59	20 24		22 25	23 24	00 39
Sanquhar		d	19 04	20 29		22 30	23 29	00 44
Dumfries		d	19 33	20 57	22 13	22 58	23 57	01a17
Annan		d	19 48	21 12	22 28	23 13	00 12	
Gretna Green		d	19 57	21 21	22 37	23 22	00 21	
Carlisle 8	65	a	20 11	21 43	22 50	23 35	00 34	
Newcastle 8	48	a						

Sundays

			SR C	SR D 🚌	SR E	SR D 🚌	SR E	SR E	SR D 🚌	SR D 🚌	SR D 🚌	SR E	SR E	SR D 🚌	SR D 🚌
Glasgow Central 15	65,222	d	22p12					15 12					22 12		
Barrhead	222	d	22p23					15 26					22 23		
Kilmarnock 3	218,222	a	22p50					15 52					22 48		
		d	22p51					15 53	16 00	16 00			22 49	22 55	22 55
Auchinleck		d	23p07					16 10		16 30			23 06		23 25
New Cumnock		d	23p16					16 18		16 50			23 14		23 45
Kirkconnel		d	23p24					16 27		17 05			23 23		23 59
Sanquhar		d	23p29					16 32		17 15			23 28		00 10
Dumfries		d	23p57	12 46	13 00	14 41	15 01	17 00	17 20	18 05	18 36	19 01	23 56	00 15	01 00
Annan		d	00 12	13 11	13 15	15 06	15 16	17 15	17 45	18 30	19 01	19 16	00 11	00 40	01 25
Gretna Green		d	00 21	13 21	13 24	15 16	15 25	17 24	17 55	18 40	19 11	19 25	00 20	00 50	01 35
Carlisle 8	65	a	00 34	13 46	13 37	15 41	15 38	17 37	18 20	19 05	19 36	19 38	00 34	01 15	02 00
Newcastle 8	48	a													

A Until 4 July, MO from 12 September
B From 11 July until 5 September
C not 22 May
D from 10 July until 4 September
E until 3 July, from 11 September

Carlisle and Dumfries - Kilmarnock and Glasgow Central

Mondays to Saturdays

Miles	Miles				SR	SR	SR	SR SO	SR SX	SR SO	SR	SR SO	SR
—	—	Newcastle 8	48	d				06 30	06 47				
0	0	**Carlisle** 8	65	d		05 27	06 08	08 15	08 15	09 55	11 15	12 20	13 12
9¾	9¾	Gretna Green		d		05 38	06 19	08 26	08 26	10 06	11 27	12 31	13 23
17½	17½	Annan		d		05 47	06 27	08 34	08 34	10 14	11 35	12 40	13 31
33	33	**Dumfries**		d	05 46	06a04	06 46	08 53	08 53	10a32	11 54	12a57	13 48
59¼	59¼	Sanquhar		d	06 12		07 12	09 19	09 19		12 20		14 16
62½	62½	Kirkconnel		d	06 17		07 17	09 24	09 24		12 25		14 21
69¾	69¾	New Cumnock		d	06 26		07 26	09 33	09 33		12 34		14 30
77¼	77¼	Auchinleck		d	06 34		07 34	09 41	09 41		12 42		14 38
91	91	**Kilmarnock** 3	218,222	a	06 51		07 51	09 58	09 58		12 59		14 55
—	—			d	06 52		07 53	09 59	09 59		13 00		15 00
107¾	—	Barrhead	222	d	07 18		08 20	10 21	10 21				
115¼	—	**Glasgow Central** 15	65,222	a	07 31		08 37	10 37	10 37		13 33		15 33

Miles	Miles				SR SO	SR	SR	SR SO	SR	SR	SR SO	SR	SR
—	—	Newcastle 8	48	d		13 22				17 16			
0	0	**Carlisle** 8	65	d	14 22	15 12	16 17	17 12	17 55	19 17	20 22	21 12	23 06
9¾	9¾	Gretna Green		d	14 33	15 23	16 28	17 23	18 06	19 28	20 33	21 23	23 17
17½	17½	Annan		d	14 41	15 31	16 36	17 31	18 14	19 37	20 41	21 31	23 25
33	33	**Dumfries**		d	14a59	15 50	16a54	17a49	18 31	19 55	20a59	21 50	23a43
59¼	59¼	Sanquhar		d		16 16			18 57	20 21		22 16	
62½	62½	Kirkconnel		d		16 21			19 02	20 26		22 21	
69¾	69¾	New Cumnock		d		16 30			19 13	20 35		22 30	
77¼	77¼	Auchinleck		d		16 38			19 21	20 44		22 38	
91	91	**Kilmarnock** 3	218,222	a		16 55			19 38	21 00		22 55	
—	—			d		16 57			20 00	21 01		22 57	
107¾	—	Barrhead	222	d		17 22			20 21	21 21		23 22	
115¼	—	**Glasgow Central** 15	65,222	a		17 35			20 34	21 36		23 35	

Sundays

			SR A 🚌	SR B	SR A 🚌	SR B	SR A 🚌	SR A 🚌	SR B	SR A 🚌	SR B	SR A 🚌
Newcastle 8	48	d										
Carlisle 8	65	d	12 46	13 12	13 30	15 12	15 12	18 20	19 12	19 05	21 22	21 22
Gretna Green		d	13 10	13 23	13 55	15 23	15 37	18 45	19 23	19 30	21 33	21 47
Annan		d	13 20	13 31	14 05	15 31	15 47	18 55	19 31	19 40	21 41	21 57
Dumfries		d	13 45	13 50	14 30	15a49	16a12	19 20	19 50	20 05	21a59	22a22
Sanquhar		d	14 30	14 16				20 05	20 16			
Kirkconnel		d	14 45	14 21				20 20	20 21			
New Cumnock		d	15 00	14 30				20 35	20 30			
Auchinleck		d	15 20	14 38				20 55	20 38			
Kilmarnock 3	218,222	a	15 50	14 55	15 50			21 25	20 55	21 25		
		d		14 57					20 57			
Barrhead	222	d		15 21					21 21			
Glasgow Central 15	65,222	a		15 36					21 35			

A from 10 July until 4 September
B until 3 July, from 11 September

For connections to London Euston please refer to Table 65

Table 217

Mondays to Saturdays

Glasgow Central - Paisley Canal

Miles			SR SO	SR	SR	SR	SR	SR	SR	SR	SR	SR	SR	SR	SR	SR	SR	SR	SR	SR	SR	SR	SR
0	**Glasgow Central 15**	d	00 08	06 08	06 38	07 08	07 38	08 08	08 37	09 08	09 38	10 08	10 38	11 08	11 38	12 08	12 38	13 08	13 38	14 08	14 38	15 08	15 38
1¾	Dumbreck	d	00 14	06 14	06 43	07 14	07 44	08 14	08 43	09 14	09 44	10 14	10 44	11 14	11 44	12 14	12 44	13 14	13 44	14 14	14 44	15 14	15 44
3¼	Corkerhill	d	00 16	06 16	06 45	07 16	07 46	08 16	08 45	09 16	09 46	10 16	10 46	11 16	11 46	12 16	12 46	13 16	13 46	14 16	14 46	15 16	15 46
3¾	Mosspark	d	00 18	06 18	06 47	07 18	07 48	08 18	08 47	09 18	09 48	10 18	10 48	11 18	11 48	12 18	12 48	13 18	13 48	14 18	14 48	15 18	15 48
4½	Crookston	d	00 20	06 20	06 49	07 20	07 50	08 20	08 49	09 20	09 50	10 20	10 50	11 20	11 50	12 20	12 50	13 20	13 50	14 20	14 50	15 20	15 50
6½	Hawkhead	d	00 23	06 23	06 53	07 23	07 53	08 23	08 53	09 23	09 53	10 23	10 53	11 23	11 53	12 23	12 53	13 23	13 53	14 23	14 53	15 23	15 53
7	**Paisley Canal**	a	00 26	06 26	06 56	07 26	07 56	08 26	08 56	09 26	09 56	10 26	10 56	11 26	11 56	12 26	12 56	13 26	13 56	14 26	14 56	15 26	15 56

		SR	SR	SR	SR	SR	SR	SR	SR	SR	SR	SR	SR	SR	SR	SR
Glasgow Central 15	d	16 08	16 38	17 08	17 38	18 08	18 38	19 08	19 38	20 08	20 38	21 08	21 38	22 08	22 38	23 08
Dumbreck	d	16 14	16 44	17 14	17 44	18 14	18 44	19 14	19 44	20 14	20 44	21 14	21 44	22 14	22 44	23 14
Corkerhill	d	16 16	16 46	17 16	17 46	18 16	18 46	19 16	19 46	20 16	20 46	21 16	21 46	22 16	22 45	23 16
Mosspark	d	16 18	16 48	17 18	17 48	18 18	18 48	19 18	19 48	20 18	20 48	21 18	21 48	22 18	22 47	23 18
Crookston	d	16 20	16 50	17 20	17 50	18 20	18 50	19 20	19 50	20 20	20 50	21 20	21 50	22 20	22 49	23 20
Hawkhead	d	16 23	16 53	17 23	17 53	18 23	18 53	19 23	19 53	20 23	20 53	21 23	21 53	22 23	22 53	23 23
Paisley Canal	a	16 26	16 56	17 26	17 56	18 26	18 56	19 26	19 56	20 26	20 56	21 26	21 56	22 26	22 56	23 26

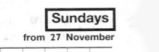

Sundays

from 27 November

		SR	SR	SR	SR	SR A	SR A	SR A	SR A	SR A
Glasgow Central 15	d	09 37	10 37	11 37	12 37					
Dumbreck	d	09 43	10 43	11 43	12 43	13 37	14 37	15 37	16 37	17 37
Corkerhill	d	09 45	10 45	11 45	12 45	13 43	14 43	15 43	16 43	17 43
Mosspark	d	09 47	10 47	11 47	12 47	13 45	14 45	15 45	16 45	17 45
Crookston	d	09 49	10 49	11 49	12 49	13 47	14 47	15 47	16 47	17 47
Hawkhead	d	09 52	10 52	11 52	12 52	13 49	14 49	15 49	16 49	17 49
Paisley Canal	a	09 55	10 55	11 55	12 55	13 52	14 52	15 52	16 52	17 52

A 27 November, 4 December

Table 217

Mondays to Saturdays

Paisley Canal - Glasgow Central

Miles			SR	SR	SR	SR	SR	SR	SR	SR	SR	SR	SR	SR	SR	SR	SR	SR	SR	SR	SR	SR	SR
0	**Paisley Canal**	d	06 29	07 00	07 30	08 00	08 30	09 00	09 30	10 00	10 30	11 00	11 30	12 00	12 30	13 00	13 30	14 00	14 30	15 00	15 30	16 00	16 30
0½	Hawkhead	d	06 32	07 03	07 33	08 03	08 33	09 03	09 33	10 03	10 33	11 03	11 33	12 03	12 33	13 03	13 33	14 03	14 33	15 03	15 33	16 03	16 33
2½	Crookston	d	06 35	07 06	07 36	08 06	08 36	09 06	09 36	10 06	10 36	11 06	11 36	12 06	12 36	13 06	13 36	14 06	14 36	15 06	15 36	16 06	16 36
3¼	Mosspark	d	06 37	07 08	07 38	08 08	08 38	09 08	09 38	10 08	10 38	11 08	11 38	12 08	12 38	13 08	13 38	14 08	14 38	15 08	15 38	16 08	16 38
3¾	Corkerhill	d	06 39	07 10	07 40	08 10	08 40	09 10	09 40	10 10	10 40	11 10	11 40	12 10	12 40	13 10	13 40	14 10	14 40	15 10	15 40	16 10	16 40
5¼	Dumbreck	d	06 42	07 13	07 44	08 13	08 43	09 13	09 43	10 13	10 43	11 13	11 43	12 13	12 43	13 13	13 43	14 13	14 43	15 13	15 43	16 13	16 43
7	**Glasgow Central 15**	a	06 49	07 20	07 52	08 21	08 53	09 19	09 49	10 19	10 49	11 19	11 49	12 19	12 49	13 19	13 49	14 19	14 49	15 19	15 49	16 19	16 49

		SR	SR	SR	SR	SR	SR	SR	SR	SR	SR	SR	SR SX	SR SO	SR SX	SR SO
Paisley Canal	d	17 00	17 30	18 00	18 30	19 00	19 30	20 00	20 30	21 00	21 30	22 00	22 30	22 30	23 00	23 00
Hawkhead	d	17 03	17 33	18 03	18 33	19 03	19 33	20 03	20 33	21 03	21 33	22 03	22 33	22 33	23 03	23 03
Crookston	d	17 06	17 36	18 06	18 36	19 06	19 36	20 06	20 36	21 06	21 36	22 06	22 36	22 36	23 06	23 06
Mosspark	d	17 08	17 38	18 08	18 38	19 08	19 38	20 08	20 38	21 08	21 38	22 08	22 38	22 38	23 08	23 08
Corkerhill	d	17 10	17 40	18 10	18 40	19 10	19 40	20 10	20 40	21 10	21 40	22 10	22 40	22 40	23 10	23 10
Dumbreck	d	17 13	17 43	18 13	18 43	19 13	19 43	20 13	20 43	21 13	21 43	22 13	22 43	22 43	23 13	23 13
Glasgow Central 15	a	17 19	17 53	18 19	18 49	19 19	19 50	20 19	20 49	21 19	21 49	22 19	22 49	22 50	23 19	23 20

Sundays

from 27 November

		SR	SR	SR	SR	SR	SR	SR	SR	SR
Paisley Canal	d	09 00	10 00	11 00	12 00	13 00	14 00	15 00	16 00	17 00
Hawkhead	d	09 03	10 03	11 03	12 03	13 03	14 03	15 03	16 03	17 03
Crookston	d	09 06	10 06	11 06	12 06	13 06	14 06	15 06	16 06	17 06
Mosspark	d	09 08	10 08	11 08	12 08	13 08	14 08	15 08	16 08	17 08
Corkerhill	d	09 10	10 10	11 10	12 09	13 09	14 09	15 09	16 09	17 09
Dumbreck	d	09 13	10 13	11 13	12 12	13 12	14 12	15 12	16 12	17 12
Glasgow Central 15	a	09 19	10 19	11 19	12 19	13 19	14 19	15 19	16 19	17 19

A 27 November, 4 December

Table 218

Mondays to Saturdays

Glasgow Central and Kilmarnock - Girvan, Stranraer and Belfast

Miles	Miles			SR MX	SR	SR ◇	SR ◇	SR	SR ◇	SR	SR SO	SR SX	SR	SR	SR	SR	SR SO	SR SX
0	—	**Glasgow Cen.** 15 219,221,222	d	22p12		06 30	08 07		11 42		15 12	15 12		17 12				22 12
7¼	—	Paisley Gilmour St. 219,221	d						11 53									
—	—	Kilwinning 221	d						12 11									
—	0	**Kilmarnock** 3 222	a	22p50		07 22	08 47				15 49	15 48		17 50				22 50
—	—		d	23p10		07 33	09 07	11 05		13 34	16 03	16 03	17 04	18 09	19 05	21 10	23 10	23 10
35	10¾	Troon 221	d	23p22		07 47	09 21	11 18		13 46	16 16	16 16	17 16	18 21	19 17	21 22	23 22	23 22
37¾	11¾	Prestwick Int. Airport 221	d	23p27		07 52	09 26	11 22		13 51	16 20	16 20	17 21	18 26	19 21	21 27	23 27	23 27
38¼	12½	Prestwick Town 221	d	23p29		07 54	09 28	11 24		13 53	16 22	16 22	17 23	18 28	19 23	21 29	23 29	23 29
41½	15½	**Ayr** 221	a	23p36		07 59	09 33	11 30	12 29	14 00	16 30	16 30	17 30	18 36	19 30	21 34	23 36	23 36
—	—		d	23p38	05 45	08 00	09 34	11 31	12 32	14 01	16 30	16 30	17 31	18 38	19 31	21 35	23 37	23 38
50½	24½	Maybole	d	23p49	05 56	08 11	09 45	11 42	12 43	14 12	16 42	16 42	17 42	18 49	19 42	21 46	23 48	23 49
62¾	36½	**Girvan**	d	00 08	06a12	08 26	10 00	11a58	12 58	14a28	16a58	16a58	17 57	19a05	19 57	22 07	00 08	00 08
75	51¼	Barrhill	d	00 27		08 45	10 19		13 18				18 16		20 22	22 27	00 27	00 27
101	77¼	**Stranraer**	a	01 01		09 21	10 57		13 54				18 52		20 58	23 01	01 01	01 01
—	—	Stranraer Harbour §	d				12 00		14 30				19 55			23 30		
—	—	Belfast Port §	a				15 00		16 30				22 05			02 30		

Sundays

		SR A	SR	SR	SR	SR ◇	SR ◇
Glasgow Cen. 15 219,221,222	d		08 12	09 12	10 12	11 42	16 25
Paisley Gilmour St. 219,221	d					11 53	16 39
Kilwinning 221	d					12 11	16 56
Kilmarnock 3 222	a		08 52	09 52	10 52		
	d	23p10	08 59	10 00	11 00		
Troon 221	d	23p22	09 12	10 14	11 13		
Prestwick Int. Airport 221	d	23p27	09 16	10 18	11 18		
Prestwick Town 221	d	23p29	09 18	10 20	11 20		
Ayr 221	a	23p36	09 29	10 26	11 26	12 29	17 17
	d	23p37				12 32	17 19
Maybole	d	23p48				12 43	17 30
Girvan	d	00c08				12 58	17 47
Barrhill	d	00 27				13 18	18 06
Stranraer	a	01 01				13 54	18 42
Stranraer Harbour §	d					14 30	19 55
Belfast Port §	a					16 30	22 05

§ Stena HSS and shipping services operated by Stena Line

A not 22 May

Belfast, Stranraer and Girvan - Kilmarnock and Glasgow Central

Mondays to Saturdays

Miles	Miles			SR MX ◇	SR SX	SR SO	SR ◇	SR ◇	SR	SR ◇	SR	SR ◇	SR	SR	SR ◇	SR ◇	SR SX ◇
—	—	Belfast Port §	d							07 30		11 45			17 00		
—	—	Stranraer Harbour §	a							10 20		13 45			19 20		
0	—	**Stranraer**	d	23p12			07 09	10 05		12 40		14 43			19 45	21 12	23 12
26	—	Barrhill	d	23p48			07 43	10 45		13 19		15 17			20 21	21 46	23 48
38¼	—	**Girvan**	d	00 06	06 20	06 20	08 01	11 03	12 06	13 37	14 40	15 36	17 33	19 33	20 39	22 05	00 06
50½	—	Maybole	d	00 22	06 36	06 36	08 25	11 19	12 22	13 53	14 56	15 52	17 56	19 56	20 55	22 21	00 22
59¼	—	**Ayr**	a	00 34	06 48	06 48	08 35	11 35	12 34	14 05	15 08	16 04	18 08	20 08	21 07	22 33	00 34
—	—		d		06 50	06 50	08 36	11 36	12 36	14 18	15 18	16 06	18 17	20 18	21 08	22 34	
62½	—	Prestwick Town 221	a		06 55	06 55	08 41		12 41	14 23	15 23	16 11	18 23	20 23	21 13	22 39	
63	—	Prestwick Int. Airport 221	a		06 57	06 57	08 43		12 43	14 25	15 25	16 13	18 25	20 25	21 15		
63¼	0	Troon 221	a		07 02	07 02	08 48		12 48	14 30	15 30	16 18	18 30	20 30	21 20	22 44	
—	10¾	**Kilmarnock** 3	a		07 18	07 18	09 04		13 04	14 53	15 46	16 34	18 46	20 46	21 37		
—	—		d		07 22	07 22	09 27				15 57				22 00		
—	—	Glengarnock	d														
74¼	—	Kilwinning 221	a					11 51								22 53	
93¾	—	Paisley Gilmour St. 219,221	a					12 15								23 14	
101	—	**Glasgow Cen.** 15 219,221,222	a		08 00	08 09	10 05	12 32			16 33				22 34	23 25	

Sundays

		SR ◇	SR ◇	SR ◇
Belfast Port §	d	07 30	11 45	17 00
Stranraer Harbour §	a	10 20	13 45	19 20
Stranraer	d	10 40	14 40	19 45
Barrhill	d	11 14	15 14	20 19
Girvan	d	11 32	15 32	20 37
Maybole	d	11 48	15 48	20 53
Ayr	a	12 00	15 59	21 04
	d	12 00	15 59	21 04
Prestwick Town 221	a			
Prestwick Int. Airport 221	a			
Troon 221	a			
Kilmarnock 3	a			21 26
	d			21 31
Glengarnock	d			
Kilwinning 221	a	12 15	16 14	
Paisley Gilmour St. 219,221	a	12 36	16 38	
Glasgow Cen. 15 219,221,222	a	12 51	16 49	22 05

§ Stena HSS and shipping services operated by Stena Line

Glasgow Central - Wemyss Bay and Gourock

Miles	Miles			SR MX	SR MO	SR MX	SR	SR	SR	SR	SR	SR		SR	SR	SR	SR	SR	SR	SR	SR	SR		SR	SR
0	0	**Glasgow Central** 15 221	d	23p20		23p50	05 55	06 05	06 25	06 32	06 55	07 04		07 25	07 35	07 50	08 05	08 28	08 36	08 50	09 05	09 25		09 35	09 50
3¾	3¾	Cardonald	d	23p27		23p57				06 39		07 12		07 32	07 42		08 12		08 42		09 12			09 42	
4½	4½	Hillington East	d	23p29		23p59		06 13		06 41		07 14		07 34	07 44		08 14		08 44		09 14			09 44	
5	5	Hillington West	d	23p31		00 01	06 03	06 15		06 43	07 03	07 16		07 36	07 46	07 58	08 16		08 46		09 16			09 46	
7¼	7¼	Paisley Gilmour Street 221 ✈	a	23p35		00 05	06 07	06 19	06 35	06 47	07 07	07 20		07 40	07 50	08 02	08 20	08 37	08 50	09 00	09 19	09 35		09 50	10 01
—	—		d	23p36	23p35	00 05	06 07	06 19	06 36	06 47	07 07	07 20		07 40	07 51	08 02	08 20	08 38	08 50	09 01	09 20	09 36		09 50	10 01
8	8	Paisley St James	d	23p38	23p40	00 07			06 38			07 22			07 53		08 22		08 52		09 22			09 52	
12¼	12¼	Bishopton	d	23p44	23p46	00 13	06 13	06 25	06 44	06 53	07 13	07 28		07 46	07 59	08 08	08 28	08 44	08 58	09 07	09 28	09 42		09 58	10 07
16¼	16¼	Langbank	d	23p49	23p51	00 19			06 49			07 34			08 04		08 34		09 04		09 34			10 04	
19	19	Woodhall	d	23p53	23p55	00 23		06 33	06 53	07 01		07 38		07 54	08 08		08 38		09 08		09 38			10 08	
20¼	20¼	Port Glasgow	d	23p56	23p58	00 26	06 23	06 36	06 56	07 04	07 23	07 41		07 57	08 11	08 18	08 41	08 53	09 11	09 16	09 41	09 51		10 11	10 16
—	22½	Whinhill	d					06 40		07 08						08 22				09 21					10 21
—	23	Drumfrochar	d					06 43		07 11						08 25				09 23					10 23
—	24¾	Branchton	d					06 46		07 14						08 28				09 26					10 26
—	25½	I.B.M. §	d					06 48		07 16						08 30				09 29					10 29
—	28¾	Inverkip	d					06 53		07 25						08 35				09 34					10 34
—	31	**Wemyss Bay**	a					06 58		07 30						08 40				09 40					10 40
21¼	—	Bogston	d	23p58	00 01	00 28			06 58		07 25	07 43		07 59	08 13		08 43		09 13		09 43			10 13	
22	—	Cartsdyke	d	00 02	00 03	00 30	06 26		07 01		07 27	07 45		08 01	08 16		08 45		09 15		09 45			10 15	
23	—	Greenock Central	d	00 03	00 05	00 32	06 28		07 03		07 29	07 47		08 03	08 18		08 47	08 58	09 17		09 47	09 56		10 17	
23¾	—	Greenock West	d	00 05	00 07	00 35	06 31		07 05		07 32	07 50		08 06	08 20		08 50	09 01	09 20		09 50	09 59		10 20	
25	—	Fort Matilda	d	00 08	00 10	00 38			07 08		07 35	07 53		08 09	08 23		08 53	09 04	09 23		09 53	10 02		10 23	
26¼	—	**Gourock**	a	00 12	00 14	00 42	06 36		07 13		07 39	07 57		08 13	08 28		08 57	09 09	09 27		09 58	10 06		10 27	

		SR	SR	SR	SR	SR	SR	SR		SR	SR	SR	SR	SR	SR	SR	SR	SR		SR	SR	SR	SR	SR	SR
Glasgow Central 15 221	d	10 05	10 25	10 35	10 50	11 05	11 25	11 35		11 50	12 05	12 25	12 35	12 50	13 05	13 25	13 35	13 50		14 05	14 25	14 35	14 50	15 05	15 25
Cardonald	d	10 12		10 42		11 12		11 42			12 12		12 42		13 12		13 42			14 12		14 42		15 12	
Hillington East	d	10 14		10 44		11 14		11 44			12 14		12 44		13 14		13 44			14 14		14 44		15 14	
Hillington West	d	10 16		10 46		11 16		11 46			12 16		12 46		13 16		13 46			14 16		14 46		15 16	
Paisley Gilmour Street 221 ✈	a	10 20	10 35	10 50	11 00	11 19	11 35	11 50		12 00	12 20	12 35	12 50	13 00	13 20	13 35	13 50	14 00		14 20	14 35	14 50	15 00	15 19	15 35
	d	10 20	10 36	10 50	11 01	11 20	11 36	11 50		12 01	12 20	12 36	12 50	13 01	13 20	13 36	13 50	14 01		14 20	14 36	14 50	15 01	15 20	15 36
Paisley St James	d	10 22		10 52		11 22		11 52			12 22		12 52		13 22		13 52			14 22		14 52		15 22	
Bishopton	d	10 28	10 42	10 58	11 07	11 28	11 42	11 58		12 07	12 28	12 42	12 58	13 07	13 28	13 42	13 58	14 07		14 28	14 42	14 58	15 07	15 28	15 42
Langbank	d	10 34		11 04		11 34		12 04			12 34		13 04		13 34		14 04			14 34		15 04		15 34	
Woodhall	d	10 38		11 08		11 38		12 08			12 38		13 08		13 38		14 08			14 38		15 08		15 38	
Port Glasgow	d	10 41	10 51	11 11	11 16	11 41	11 51	12 11		12 16	12 41	12 51	13 11	13 16	13 41	13 51	14 11	14 16		14 41	14 51	15 11	15 16	15 41	15 51
Whinhill	d				11 21					12 21				13 21				14 21					15 21		
Drumfrochar	d				11 23					12 23				13 23				14 23					15 23		
Branchton	d				11 26					12 26				13 26				14 26					15 26		
I.B.M. §	d				11 29					12 29				13 29				14 29					15 29		
Inverkip	d				11 34					12 34				13 34				14 34					15 34		
Wemyss Bay	a				11 40					12 40				13 40				14 40					15 40		
Bogston	d	10 43		11 13		11 43		12 13			12 43		13 13		13 43		14 13			14 43		15 13		15 43	
Cartsdyke	d	10 45		11 15		11 45		12 15			12 45		13 15		13 45		14 15			14 45		15 15		15 45	
Greenock Central	d	10 47	10 56	11 17		11 47	11 56	12 17			12 47	12 56	13 17		13 47	13 56	14 17			14 47	14 56	15 17		15 47	15 56
Greenock West	d	10 50	10 59	11 20		11 50	11 59	12 20			12 50	12 59	13 20		13 50	13 59	14 20			14 50	14 59	15 20		15 50	15 59
Fort Matilda	d	10 53	11 02	11 23		11 53	12 02	12 23			12 53	13 02	13 23		13 53	14 02	14 23			14 53	15 02	15 23		15 53	16 02
Gourock	a	10 57	11 06	11 27		11 57	12 06	12 27			12 57	13 06	13 27		13 57	14 06	14 27			14 57	15 06	15 27		15 57	16 06

		SR	SR	SR		SR	SR	SR	SR	SR	SR	SR	SR	SR		SR	SR	SR	SR	SR	SR	SR	SR	SR	
Glasgow Central 15 221	d	15 35	15 50	16 05		16 23	16 33	16 55	17 05	17 15	17 25	17 40	17 55	18 05		18 25	18 35	18 50	19 05	19 25	19 40	19 50	20 05	20 35	
Cardonald	d	15 42		16 12		16 30	16 42		17 12	17 22		17 47		18 12			18 42		19 12		19 47		20 12	20 42	
Hillington East	d	15 44		16 14		16 32	16 44		17 14	17 24		17 49		18 14			18 44		19 14		19 49		20 14	20 44	
Hillington West	d	15 46	15 58	16 16		16 34	16 46	17 02	17 16			17 51		18 16			18 46		19 15		19 51		20 15	20 46	
Paisley Gilmour Street 221 ✈	a	15 50	16 02	16 20		16 38	16 49	17 06	17 20	17 29	17 37	17 55	18 05	18 20		18 35	18 50	19 01	19 19	19 35	19 55	20 00	20 21	20 50	
	d	15 50	16 02	16 20		16 38	16 49	17 06	17 21	17 29	17 37	17 55	18 06	18 20		18 36	18 50	19 01	19 20	19 36	19 55	20 01	20 21	20 50	
Paisley St James	d	15 52		16 22		16 40			17 23			17 57		18 22			18 52		19 22		19 57		20 23	20 52	
Bishopton	d	15 58	16 08	16 28		16 46	16 55	17 13	17 29	17 35		18 03	18 10	18 28		18 42	18 58	19 07	19 28	19 42	20 03	20 07	20 29	20 58	
Langbank	d	16 04		16 34		16 52			17 34			18 09		18 34			19 04		19 34		20 09		20 35	21 04	
Woodhall	d	16 08		16 38		16 56			17 38			18 12		18 38			19 08		19 38		20 13		20 39	21 08	
Port Glasgow	d	16 11	16 18	16 41		16 59	17 05	17 23	17 41	17 45	17 51	18 14	18 21	18 41		18 51	19 11	19 16	19 41	19 51	20 16	20 18	20 42	21 11	
Whinhill	d		16 22				17 09			17 49			18 25					19 21			20 20			21 15	
Drumfrochar	d		16 25				17 12			17 52			18 28					19 23			20 23			21 18	
Branchton	d		16 28				17 15			17 55			18 31					19 26			20 26			21 21	
I.B.M. §	d		16 30							17 57			18 33					19 29			20 28			21 23	
Inverkip	d		16 35				17 20			18 02			18 38					19 34			20 33			21 28	
Wemyss Bay	a		16 40				17 26			18 08			18 44					19 40			20 38			21 34	
Bogston	d	16 13		16 43		17 01		17 25	17 43			18 18		18 43			19 13		19 43				20 44		
Cartsdyke	d	16 15		16 45		17 03		17 27	17 46			18 20		18 45			19 15		19 45			20 21	20 46		
Greenock Central	d	16 17		16 47		17 05		17 29	17 48		17 56	18 22		18 47		18 56	19 17		19 47	19 56		20 23	20 48		
Greenock West	d	16 20		16 50		17 08		17 32	17 50		17 58	18 25		18 50		18 59	19 20		19 50	19 59		20 26	20 51		
Fort Matilda	d	16 23		16 53		17 11		17 35	17 53		18 01	18 28		18 53		19 02	19 23		19 53	20 02		20 29	20 54		
Gourock	a	16 27		16 57		17 15		17 39	17 57		18 06	18 32		18 57		19 06	19 27		19 57	20 06		20 34	20 58		

§ For authorised access to and from I.B.M. only

Table 219

Mondays to Saturdays

Glasgow Central - Wemyss Bay and Gourock

		SR	SR	SR	SR	SR	SR	SR	SR	SR
Glasgow Central 15 221	d	20 50	21 05	21 35	21 50	22 05	22 35	22 50	23 20	23 50
Cardonald	d		21 12	21 42		22 12	22 42		23 27	23 57
Hillington East	d		21 14	21 44		22 14	22 44		23 29	23 59
Hillington West	d		21 16	21 46		22 16	22 46		23 31	00 01
Paisley Gilmour Street .. 221 ⇜	a	21 00	21 20	21 50	22 00	22 20	22 50	23 00	23 35	00 05
	d	21 01	21 20	21 50	22 01	22 20	22 50	23 01	23 36	00 05
Paisley St James	d		21 22	21 52		22 22	22 52		23 38	00 07
Bishopton	d	21 07	21 28	21 58	22 07	22 28	22 58	23 07	23 44	00 13
Langbank	d		21 34	22 04		22 34	23 04		23 49	00 19
Woodhall	d		21 38	22 08		22 38	23 08		23 53	00 23
Port Glasgow	d	21 16	21 41	22 11	22 16	22 41	23 11	23 16	23 56	00 26
Whinhill	d			22 15			23 15			
Drumfrochar	d			22 18			23 18			
Branchton	d			22 21			23 21			
I.B.M. §	d			22 23			23 23			
Inverkip	d			22 28			23 28			
Wemyss Bay	a			22 34			23 34			
Bogston	d		21 43			22 43			23 58	00 28
Cartsdyke	d	21 20	21 45		22 20	22 45		23 20	00 02	00 30
Greenock Central	d	21 22	21 47		22 22	22 47		23 22	00 03	00 32
Greenock West	d	21 24	21 50		22 24	22 50		23 24	00 05	00 35
Fort Matilda	d	21 27	21 53		22 29	22 53		23 29	00 08	00 38
Gourock	a	21 32	21 57		22 33	22 57		23 33	00 12	00 42

Sundays

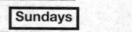

until 20 November

		SR A	SR A	SR	SR	SR	SR	SR	SR	SR	SR
Glasgow Central 15 221	d	23p20	23p50								
Cardonald	d	23p27	23p57								
Hillington East	d	23p29	23p59								
Hillington West	d	23p31	00 01								
Paisley Gilmour Street .. 221 ⇜	a	23p35	00 05								
	d	23p36	00 05	07 35	07 59	08 35	09 05	09 35	10 05	10 36	11 05
Paisley St James	d	23p38	00 07	07 40	08 04	08 40	09 10	09 40	10 10	10 41	11 10
Bishopton	d	23p44	00 13	07 46	08 10	08 46	09 16	09 46	10 16	10 47	11 16
Langbank	d	23p49	00 19			08 51		09 51		10 52	
Woodhall	d	23p53	00 23	07 53		08 55		09 55		10 56	
Port Glasgow	d	23p56	00 26	07 56	08 19	08 58	09 25	09 58	10 25	10 59	11 25
Whinhill	d				08 24		09 30		10 30		11 30
Drumfrochar	d				08 26		09 32		10 32		11 32
Branchton	d				08 29		09 35		10 35		11 35
I.B.M. §	d				08 32		09 38		10 38		11 38
Inverkip	d				08 37		09 43		10 43		11 43
Wemyss Bay	a				08 42		09 48		10 48		11 48
Bogston	d	23p58	00 28	07 58		09 00		10 00		11 01	
Cartsdyke	d	00 02	00 30	08 01		09 03		10 03		11 04	
Greenock Central	d	00 03	00 32	08 03		09 05		10 05		11 06	
Greenock West	d	00 05	00 35	08 05		09 07		10 07		11 08	
Fort Matilda	d	00 08	00 38			09 10		10 10		11 11	
Gourock	a	00 12	00 42	08 10		09 14		10 14		11 16	

		SR	SR	SR	SR	SR	SR	SR	SR	SR	SR	SR	SR
Glasgow Central 15 221	d	11 20	11 50	12 20	12 50	13 20	13 50	14 20	14 50	15 20	15 50	16 20	16 50
Cardonald	d	11 27		12 27		13 27		14 27		15 27		16 27	
Hillington East	d	11 29	11 58	12 29	12 58	13 29	13 58	14 29	14 58	15 29	15 58	16 29	16 58
Hillington West	d	11 31		12 31	13 00	13 31		14 31		15 31		16 31	
Paisley Gilmour Street .. 221 ⇜	a	11 35	12 03	12 35	13 03	13 35	14 03	14 35	15 03	15 35	16 03	16 35	17 03
	d	11 35	12 03	12 35	13 03	13 35	14 03	14 35	15 03	15 35	16 03	16 35	17 03
Paisley St James	d	11 37		12 37		13 37		14 37		15 37		16 37	
Bishopton	d	11 43	12 09	12 43	13 09	13 43	14 09	14 43	15 09	15 43	16 09	16 43	17 09
Langbank	d	11 49		12 49		13 49		14 49		15 49		16 49	
Woodhall	d	11 53		12 53		13 53		14 53		15 53		16 53	
Port Glasgow	d	11 56	12 19	12 56	13 19	13 56	14 19	14 56	15 19	15 56	16 19	16 56	17 19
Whinhill	d		12 23		13 23		14 23		15 23		16 23		17 23
Drumfrochar	d		12 26		13 26		14 26		15 26		16 26		17 26
Branchton	d		12 29		13 29		14 29		15 29		16 29		17 29
I.B.M. §	d		12 31		13 31		14 31		15 31		16 31		17 31
Inverkip	d		12 36		13 36		14 36		15 36		16 36		17 36
Wemyss Bay	a		12 43		13 42		14 42		15 42		16 42		17 42
Bogston	d	11 58		12 58		13 58		14 58		15 58		16 58	
Cartsdyke	d	12 00		13 00		14 00		15 00		16 00		17 00	
Greenock Central	d	12 02		13 02		14 02		15 02		16 02		17 02	
Greenock West	d	12 05		13 05		14 05		15 05		16 05		17 05	
Fort Matilda	d	12 08		13 08		14 08		15 08		16 08		17 08	
Gourock	a	12 12		13 12		14 12		15 12		16 12		17 12	

		SR	SR	SR	SR	SR	SR	SR	SR	SR	SR
Glasgow Central 15 221	d	17 20	17 50	18 20	18 50	19 20	19 50	20 20			
Cardonald	d	17 27		18 27		19 27		20 27			
Hillington East	d	17 29	17 58	18 29	18 58	19 29	19 58	20 29			
Hillington West	d	17 31		18 31		19 31		20 31			
Paisley Gilmour Street .. 221 ⇜	a	17 35	18 03	18 35	19 03	19 35	20 03	20 35			
	d	17 35	18 03	18 35	19 03	19 35	20 03	20 35	21 35	22 35	23 35
Paisley St James	d	17 37		18 37		19 37		20 37	21 40	22 40	23 40
Bishopton	d	17 43	18 09	18 43	19 09	19 43	20 09	20 43	21 46	22 46	23 46
Langbank	d	17 49		18 49		19 49		20 49	21 51	22 51	23 51
Woodhall	d	17 53		18 53		19 53		20 53	21 55	22 55	23 55
Port Glasgow	d	17 56	18 19	18 56	19 19	19 56	20 19	20 56	21 58	22 58	23 58
Whinhill	d		18 23		19 23		20 23				
Drumfrochar	d		18 26		19 26		20 26				
Branchton	d		18 29		19 29		20 29				
I.B.M. §	d		18 31		19 31		20 31				
Inverkip	d		18 36		19 36		20 36				
Wemyss Bay	a		18 42		19 42		20 42				
Bogston	d	17 58		18 58		19 58		20 58	22 00	23 00	00 01
Cartsdyke	d	18 00		19 00		20 00		21 00	22 03	23 03	00 03
Greenock Central	d	18 02		19 02		20 02		21 02	22 05	23 05	00 05
Greenock West	d	18 05		19 05		20 05		21 05	22 07	23 07	00 07
Fort Matilda	d	18 08		19 08		20 08		21 08	22 10	23 10	00 10
Gourock	a	18 12		19 12		20 12		21 12	22 14	23 14	00 14

§ For authorised access to and from I.B.M. only

A not 22 May

Table 219

Sundays

from 27 November

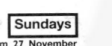

Glasgow Central - Wemyss Bay and Gourock

			SR	SR	SR	SR	SR	SR	SR	SR	SR	SR	SR	SR	SR	SR	SR	SR	SR	SR	SR	SR	SR	SR
Glasgow Central 15	221	d	23p20	23p50											11 20	11 35	11 50	12 20	12 35	12 50	13 20	13 35	13 50	14 20
Cardonald		d	23p27	23p57											11 27	11 42		12 27	12 42		13 27	13 42		14 27
Hillington East		d	23p29	23p59											11 29	11 44	11 58	12 29	12 44	12 58	13 29	13 44	13 58	14 29
Hillington West		d	23p31	00 01											11 31	11 46		12 31	12 49	13 00	13 31	13 46		14 31
Paisley Gilmour Street	221 ✈	a	23p35	00 05											11 35	11 50	12 03	12 35	12 52	13 03	13 35	13 51	14 03	14 35
		d	23p36	00 05	07 35	07 59	08 35	09 05	09 35	09 50	10 05	10 36	10 51	11 05	11 35	11 51	12 03	12 35	12 53	13 03	13 35	13 51	14 03	14 35
Paisley St James		d	23p38	00 07	07 40	08 04	08 40	09 10	09 40	09 52	10 10	10 41	10 53	11 10	11 37	11 53		12 37	12 55		13 37	13 53		14 37
Bishopton		d	23p44	00 13	07 46	08 10	08 46	09 16	09 46	09 58	10 16	10 47	10 59	11 16	11 43	11 59	12 09	12 43	13 01	13 09	13 43	13 59	14 09	14 43
Langbank		d	23p49	00 19			08 51		09 51	10 04		10 52	11 05		11 49	12 05		12 49	13 06		13 49	14 05		14 49
Woodhall		d	23p53	00 23	07 53		08 55		09 55	10 08		10 56	11 09		11 53	12 09		12 53	13 10		13 53	14 09		14 53
Port Glasgow		d	23p56	00 26	07 56	08 19	08 58	09 25	09 58	10 11	10 25	10 59	11 12	11 25	11 56	12 12	12 19	12 56	13 13	13 19	13 56	14 12	14 19	14 56
Whinhill		d				08 24		09 30			10 30			11 30			12 23			13 23			14 23	
Drumfrochar		d				08 26		09 32			10 32			11 32			12 26			13 26			14 26	
Branchton		d				08 29		09 35			10 35			11 35			12 29			13 29			14 29	
I.B.M. §		d				08 32		09 38			10 38			11 38			12 31			13 31			14 31	
Inverkip		d				08 37		09 43			10 43			11 43			12 36			13 36			14 36	
Wemyss Bay		a				08 42		09 48			10 48			11 48			12 43			13 42			14 42	
Bogston		d	23p58	00 28	07 58		09 00		10 00	10 13		11 01	11 14		11 58	12 14		12 58	13 15		13 58	14 12		14 58
Cartsdyke		d	00 02	00 30	08 01		09 03		10 03	10 15		11 04	11 16		12 00	12 16		13 00	13 18		14 00	14 14		15 00
Greenock Central		d	00 03	00 32	08 03		09 05		10 05	10 17		11 06	11 18		12 02	12 18		13 02	13 20		14 02	14 16		15 02
Greenock West		d	00 05	00 35	08 05		09 07		10 07	10 20		11 08	11 21		12 05	12 21		13 05	13 22		14 05	14 19		15 05
Fort Matilda		d	00 08	00 38			09 10		10 10	10 23		11 11	11 24		12 08	12 24		13 08	13 25		14 08	14 22		15 08
Gourock		a	00 12	00 42	08 10		09 14		10 14	10 27		11 16	11 27		12 12	12 27		13 12	13 29		14 12	14 27		15 12

			SR	SR	SR	SR	SR	SR	SR	SR	SR	SR	SR	SR	SR	SR	SR	SR	SR	SR	SR
Glasgow Central 15	221	d	14 35	14 50	15 20	15 33	15 50	16 20	16 35	16 50	17 20	17 35	17 50	18 20	18 50	19 20	19 50	20 20			
Cardonald		d	14 42		15 27	15 40		16 27	16 42		17 27	17 42		18 27		19 27		20 27			
Hillington East		d	14 44	14 58	15 29	15 42	15 58	16 29	16 44	16 58	17 29	17 44	17 58	18 29	18 58	19 29	19 58	20 29			
Hillington West		d	14 47		15 31	15 44		16 31	16 48		17 31	17 47		18 31		19 31		20 31			
Paisley Gilmour Street	221 ✈	a	14 51	15 03	15 35	15 48	16 03	16 35	16 51	17 03	17 35	17 51	18 03	18 35	19 03	19 35	20 03	20 35			
		d	14 51	15 03	15 35	15 48	16 03	16 35	16 52	17 03	17 35	17 51	18 03	18 35	19 03	19 35	20 03	20 35	21 35	22 35	23 35
Paisley St James		d	14 53		15 37	15 50		16 37	16 54		17 37	17 53		18 37		19 37		20 37	21 40	22 40	23 40
Bishopton		d	14 59	15 09	15 43	15 56	16 09	16 43	17 00	17 09	17 43	17 59	18 09	18 43	19 09	19 43	20 09	20 43	21 46	22 46	23 46
Langbank		d	15 05		15 49	16 02		16 49	17 05		17 49	18 05		18 49		19 49		20 49	21 51	22 51	23 51
Woodhall		d	15 09		15 53	16 06		16 53	17 09		17 53	18 09		18 53		19 53		20 53	21 55	22 55	23 55
Port Glasgow		d	15 12	15 19	15 56	16 09	16 19	16 56	17 12	17 19	17 56	18 12	18 19	18 56	19 19	19 56	20 19	20 56	21 58	22 58	23 58
Whinhill		d		15 23			16 23			17 23			18 23		19 23		20 23				
Drumfrochar		d		15 26			16 26			17 26			18 26		19 26		20 26				
Branchton		d		15 29			16 29			17 29			18 29		19 29		20 29				
I.B.M. §		d		15 31			16 31			17 31			18 31		19 31		20 31				
Inverkip		d		15 36			16 36			17 36			18 36		19 36		20 36				
Wemyss Bay		a		15 42			16 42			17 42			18 42		19 42		20 42				
Bogston		d	15 13		15 58	16 11		16 58	17 13		17 58	18 13		18 58		19 58		20 58	22 00	23 00	00 01
Cartsdyke		d	15 15		16 00	16 13		17 00	17 16		18 00	18 15		19 00		20 00		21 00	22 03	23 03	00 03
Greenock Central		d	15 17		16 02	16 15		17 02	17 18		18 02	18 17		19 02		20 02		21 02	22 05	23 05	00 05
Greenock West		d	15 20		16 05	16 18		17 05	17 20		18 05	18 20		19 05		20 05		21 05	22 07	23 07	00 07
Fort Matilda		d	15 23		16 08	16 21		17 08	17 23		18 08	18 23		19 08		20 08		21 08	22 10	23 10	00 10
Gourock		a	15 27		16 12	16 25		17 12	17 28		18 12	18 27		19 12		20 12		21 12	22 14	23 14	00 14

§ For authorised access to and from I.B.M. only

Gourock and Wemyss Bay - Glasgow Central

Miles	Miles			SR MX	SR	SR	SR SX	SR SO	SR SX	SR SX	SR SO	SR	SR SX	SR SO	SR SX	SR	SR	SR SX	SR	SR	SR	SR	SR
0	—	**Gourock**	d	23p20	05 20	06 05	06 22	06 35	06 44	07 06	07 06		07 22	07 36	07 47	07 52		08 09	08 24	08 36		09 06	09 23
1¼	—	Fort Matilda	d	23p23	05 23	06 08	06 25	06 38	06 47	07 09	07 09		07 25	07 39		07 55		08 12	08 27	08 39		09 09	09 26
2½	—	Greenock West	d	23p26	05 26	06 11	06 28	06 41	06 50	07 12	07 12		07 28	07 42	07 52	07 58		08 15	08 30	08 42		09 12	09 29
3¼	—	Greenock Central	d	23p29	05 29	06 14	06 31	06 44	06 53	07 15	07 15		07 31	07 45	07 55	08 01		08 18	08 33	08 45		09 15	09 32
4¼	—	Cartsdyke	d	23p31	05 31	06 16	06 33	06 46	06 55	07 17	07 17		07 33	07 47		08 03			08 35	08 47		09 17	
5	—	Bogston	d	23p33	05 33		06 35	06 48	06 57	07 19	07 19		07 35	07 49		08 05			08 37	08 49		09 19	
—	0	**Wemyss Bay**	d									07 13					07 51				08 50		
—	2¼	Inverkip	d									07 18					07 55				08 54		
—	4¾	I.B.M. §	d									07 23					08 00				08 59		
—	6¼	Branchton	d									07 25					08 03				09 02		
—	8	Drumfrochar	d									07 28					08 05				09 04		
—	8½	Whinhill	d									07 30					08 08				09 07		
6	10¾	Port Glasgow	d	23p36	05 36	06 19	06 38	06 51	07 00	07 22	07 22	07 35	07 38	07 52	07 59	08 08	08 12	08 22	08 40	08 52	09 11	09 22	09 36
7¼	12	Woodhall	d	23p38	05 38		06 40	06 53	07 02		07 24	07 37	07 40	07 54		08 10	08 15		08 42	08 54		09 24	
10	14¾	Langbank	d	23p43	05 43		06 45	06 58	07 07		07 29		07 45	07 59			08 19		08 47	08 59		09 29	
14	18	Bishopton	d	23p48	05 48	06 28	06 50	07 03	07 12	07 31	07 34	07 45	07 50	08 04	08 08	08 19	08 25	08 31	08 52	09 04	09 20	09 34	09 45
18¼	22¼	Paisley St James	d	23p54	05 54	06 34	06 56	07 09	07 18		07 40		07 56	08 10			08 30		08 58	09 10		09 40	
19	23	Paisley Gilmour Street 221 ⇜	a	23p56	05 55	06 36	06 58	07 11	07 20	07 37	07 42	07 51	07 58	08 12	08 14	08 25	08 33	08 37	09 00	09 11	09 26	09 42	09 51
—	—		d	23p57	05 56	06 37	06 59	07 12	07 21	07 38	07 43	07 52	07 59	08 13	08 14	08 26	08 33	08 38	09 01	09 12	09 27	09 43	09 52
21¼	25¼	Hillington West	d	00 01	05 59	06 40	07 02	07 15	07 24	07 41	07 46	07 55	08 02	08 16	08 18	08 29			09 04	09 15		09 46	
21¾	25¾	Hillington East	d	00 02	06 01	06 42	07 04	07 17	07 26	07 43	07 48	07 57	08 04	08 18	08 20	08 31			09 06	09 17		09 48	
22½	26½	Cardonald	d	00 04	06 03	06 44	07 06	07 19	07 28	07 45	07 50	07 59	08 06	08 20	08 22	08 33			09 08	09 19		09 50	
26½	31	**Glasgow Central** 15 221	a	00 12	06 12	06 52	07 14	07 27	07 36	07 53	07 58	08 07	08 14	08 29	08 30	08 42	08 44	08 49	09 16	09 28	09 38	09 58	10 03

		SR	SR	SR	SR	SR	SR	SR	SR	SR	SR	SR	SR	SR	SR	SR	SR	SR	SR	SR	SR	SR	SR
Gourock	d	09 36		10 06	10 23	10 36		11 06	11 23	11 36		12 06	12 23	12 36		13 06	13 23	13 36		14 06	14 23	14 36	
Fort Matilda	d	09 39		10 09	10 26	10 39		11 09	11 26	11 39		12 09	12 26	12 39		13 09	13 26	13 39		14 09	14 26	14 39	
Greenock West	d	09 42		10 12	10 29	10 42		11 12	11 29	11 42		12 12	12 29	12 42		13 12	13 29	13 42		14 12	14 29	14 42	
Greenock Central	d	09 45		10 15	10 32	10 45		11 15	11 32	11 45		12 15	12 32	12 45		13 15	13 32	13 45		14 15	14 32	14 45	
Cartsdyke	d	09 47		10 17		10 47		11 17		11 47		12 17		12 47		13 17		13 47		14 17		14 47	
Bogston	d	09 49		10 19		10 49		11 19		11 49		12 19		12 49		13 19		13 49		14 19		14 49	
Wemyss Bay	d		09 50				10 55				11 50				12 50				13 50				14 50
Inverkip	d		09 54				10 59				11 54				12 54				13 54				14 54
I.B.M. §	d		09 59				11 04				11 59				12 59				13 59				14 59
Branchton	d		10 02				11 07				12 02				13 02				14 02				15 02
Drumfrochar	d		10 04				11 09				12 04				13 04				14 04				15 04
Whinhill	d		10 07				11 12				12 07				13 07				14 07				15 07
Port Glasgow	d	09 52	10 11	10 22	10 36	10 52	11 16	11 22	11 36	11 52	12 11	12 22	12 36	12 52	13 11	13 22	13 36	13 52	14 11	14 22	14 36	14 52	15 11
Woodhall	d	09 54		10 24		10 54		11 24		11 54		12 24		12 54		13 24		13 54		14 24		14 54	
Langbank	d	09 59		10 29		10 59		11 29		11 59		12 29		12 59		13 29		13 59		14 29		14 59	
Bishopton	d	10 04	10 20	10 34	10 45	11 04	11 25	11 34	11 45	12 04	12 20	12 34	12 45	13 04	13 20	13 34	13 45	14 04	14 20	14 34	14 45	15 04	15 20
Paisley St James	d	10 10		10 40		11 10		11 40		12 10		12 40		13 10		13 40		14 10		14 40		15 10	
Paisley Gilmour Street 221 ⇜	a	10 12	10 26	10 42	10 51	11 12	11 31	11 42	11 51	12 12	12 26	12 43	12 51	13 12	13 26	13 43	13 51	14 12	14 26	14 42	14 51	15 12	15 26
	d	10 13	10 27	10 43	10 52	11 13	11 32	11 43	11 52	12 13	12 27	12 43	12 52	13 13	13 27	13 43	13 52	14 13	14 27	14 43	14 52	15 13	15 27
Hillington West	d	10 16		10 46		11 16		11 46		12 16		12 46		13 16		13 46		14 16		14 46		15 16	
Hillington East	d	10 18		10 48		11 18		11 48		12 18		12 48		13 18		13 48		14 18		14 48		15 18	
Cardonald	d	10 20		10 50		11 20		11 50		12 20		12 50		13 20		13 50		14 20		14 50		15 20	
Glasgow Central 15 221	a	10 28	10 38	10 58	11 03	11 28	11 43	11 58	12 03	12 28	12 38	12 58	13 03	13 28	13 38	13 58	14 03	14 28	14 38	14 58	15 03	15 28	15 38

		SR	SR SO	SR SX	SR	SR	SR	SR	SR SO	SR SX	SR	SR	SR SX	SR SO	SR	SR SX	SR SO	SR	SR	SR	SR	SR
Gourock	d	15 06	15 23	15 23	15 36		16 06	16 23	16 36	16 36		17 06	17 23	17 23	17 48			18 06	18 23		18 40	
Fort Matilda	d	15 09	15 26	15 26	15 39		16 09	16 26	16 39	16 39		17 09	17 26	17 26	17 51			18 09	18 26		18 43	
Greenock West	d	15 12	15 29	15 29	15 42		16 12	16 29	16 42	16 42		17 12	17 29	17 29	17 54			18 12	18 29		18 46	
Greenock Central	d	15 15	15 32	15 32	15 45		16 15	16 32	16 45	16 45		17 15	17 32	17 32	17 57			18 15	18 32		18 49	
Cartsdyke	d	15 17			15 47		16 17		16 47	16 47		17 17			17 59			18 17			18 51	
Bogston	d	15 19			15 49		16 19		16 49	16 49		17 19			18 01			18 19			18 53	
Wemyss Bay	d					15 55					16 45					17 49	17 49			18 26		18 55
Inverkip	d					15 59					16 49					17 53	17 53			18 30		18 59
I.B.M. §	d					16 04					16 54					18 02	18 02			18 39		19 04
Branchton	d					16 07					16 57					18 05	18 05			18 41		19 07
Drumfrochar	d					16 09					16 59					18 07	18 07			18 44		19 09
Whinhill	d					16 12					17 02					18 10	18 10			18 46		19 12
Port Glasgow	d	15 22	15 36	15 36	15 52	16 16	16 22	16 36	16 52	16 52	17 06	17 22	17 36	17 36	18 04	18 14	18 14	18 22	18 36	18 51	18 56	19 16
Woodhall	d	15 24			15 54		16 24		16 54	16 54		17 24			18 06			18 24			18 58	
Langbank	d	15 29			15 59		16 29		16 59	16 59		17 29			18 11			18 29			19 03	
Bishopton	d	15 34	15 45	15 45	16 04	16 25	16 34	16 45	17 04	17 04	17 15	17 34	17 45	17 45	18 16	18 23	18 23	18 34	18 45	19 00	19 08	19 25
Paisley St James	d	15 40			16 10		16 40		17 10	17 10		17 40			18 22			18 40			19 14	
Paisley Gilmour Street 221 ⇜	a	15 42	15 51	15 51	16 12	16 31	16 42	16 51	17 11	17 11	17 21	17 43	17 51	17 51	18 24	18 30	18 30	18 42	18 51	19 06	19 16	19 31
	d	15 43	15 52	15 52	16 13	16 32	16 43	16 52	17 12	17 12	17 22	17 43	17 52	17 52	18 25	18 31	18 31	18 43	18 52	19 06	19 17	19 32
Hillington West	d	15 46	15 55	15 55	16 16		16 46	16 56	17 15	17 15		17 47			18 28			18 46			19 20	
Hillington East	d	15 48			16 18		16 48		17 17	17 17		17 49			18 30			18 48			19 22	
Cardonald	d	15 50			16 20		16 50		17 19	17 19		17 51			18 32			18 50			19 24	
Glasgow Central 15 221	a	15 58	16 05	16 06	16 28	16 45	16 58	17 05	17 28	17 29	17 34	17 58	18 03	18 05	18 40	18 43	18 44	18 58	19 04	19 17	19 32	19 44

§ For authorised access to and from I.B.M. only

Table 219

Gourock and Wemyss Bay - Glasgow Central

		SR	SR	SR	SR	SR	SR	SR	SR	SR	SR SX	SR SO	SR	SR	SR SO	SR SX	SR SO
Gourock	d	19 06	19 22	19 45		20 20	20 47		21 24	21 45			22 20		23 17	23 20	
Fort Matilda	d	19 09	19 25	19 48		20 23	20 50		21 27	21 48			22 23		23 20	23 23	
Greenock West	d	19 12	19 28	19 51		20 26	20 53		21 30	21 51			22 26		23 23	23 26	
Greenock Central	d	19 15	19 31	19 54		20 29	20 56		21 33	21 54			22 29		23 26	23 29	
Cartsdyke	d	19 17	19 33	19 56		20 31	20 58		21 35	21 56			22 31		23 28	23 31	
Bogston	d	19 19	19 35			20 33			21 37				22 33		23 30	23 33	
Wemyss Bay	d				19 45			20 44			21 44	21 50		22 44			23 40
Inverkip	d				19 48			20 48			21 48	21 54		22 48			23 44
I.B.M. §	d				19 53			20 53			21 53	21 59		22 53			23 49
Branchton	d				19 56			20 56			21 56	22 02		22 56			23 52
Drumfrochar	d				19 58			20 58			21 58	22 04		22 58			23 54
Whinhill	d				20 01			21 01			22 01	22 07		23 01			23 57
Port Glasgow	d	19 22	19 38	19 59	20 06	20 36	21 01	21 06	21 40	21 59	22 06	22 11	22 36	23 06	23 33	23 36	00 01
Woodhall	d	19 24	19 40		20 08	20 38		21 08	21 42		22 08	22 14	22 38	23 08	23 35	23 38	
Langbank	d	19 29	19 45		20 13	20 43		21 13	21 47		22 13	22 18	22 43	23 13	23 40	23 43	
Bishopton	d	19 34	19 50	20 08	20 18	20 48	21 10	21 18	21 52	22 08	22 18	22 24	22 48	23 18	23 45	23 48	00 10
Paisley St James	d	19 40	19 56		20 24	20 54		21 24	21 58		22 24	22 29	22 54	23 24	23 51	23 54	
Paisley Gilmour Street 221 ✈	a	19 42	19 58	20 14	20 26	20 56	21 17	21 26	22 00	22 14	22 26	22 32	22 56	23 26	23 53	23 56	00 16
	d	19 43	19 59	20 15	20 27	20 56	21 18	21 27	22 01	22 15	22 27	22 32	22 57	23 27	23 54	23 57	
Hillington West	d	19 46	20 02		20 30	21 00		21 30	22 04		22 30	22 35	23 00	23 30	23 57	00 01	
Hillington East	d	19 48	20 04		20 32	21 02		21 32	22 06		22 32	22 37	23 02	23 32	23 58	00 02	
Cardonald	d	19 50	20 06		20 34	21 04		21 34	22 08		22 34	22 39	23 04	23 34	00 01	00 04	
Glasgow Central 15 221	a	19 58	20 14	20 26	20 43	21 12	21 29	21 42	22 15	22 26	22 42	22 46	23 14	23 42	00 08	00 12	

Sundays

until 20 November

		SR A	SR A	SR	SR	SR	SR	SR	SR	SR	SR	SR	SR	SR	SR	SR	SR	SR	SR	SR	SR	SR	SR
Gourock	d	23p17		08 23		09 23		10 23		11 23		12 23		13 23		14 23		15 23		16 23		17 23	
Fort Matilda	d	23p20		08 26		09 26		10 26		11 26		12 26		13 26		14 26		15 26		16 26		17 26	
Greenock West	d	23p23		08 29		09 29		10 29		11 29		12 29		13 29		14 29		15 29		16 29		17 29	
Greenock Central	d	23p26		08 32		09 32		10 32		11 32		12 32		13 32		14 32		15 32		16 32		17 32	
Cartsdyke	d	23p28		08 34		09 34		10 34		11 34		12 34		13 34		14 34		15 34		16 34		17 34	
Bogston	d	23p30		08 36		09 36		10 36		11 36		12 36		13 36		14 36		15 36		16 36		17 36	
Wemyss Bay	d		23p40		08 51		09 53		10 55		11 53		12 50		13 50		14 50		15 55		16 50		17 50
Inverkip	d		23p44		08 55		09 57		10 59		11 57		12 54		13 54		14 54		15 59		16 54		17 54
I.B.M. §	d		23p49		09 00		10 02		11 04		12 02		12 59		13 59		14 59		16 04		16 59		17 59
Branchton	d		23p52		09 03		10 05		11 07		12 05		13 02		14 02		15 02		16 07		17 02		18 02
Drumfrochar	d		23p54		09 05		10 07		11 09		12 07		13 04		14 04		15 04		16 09		17 04		18 04
Whinhill	d		23p57		09 08		10 10		11 12		12 10		13 07		14 07		15 07		16 12		17 07		18 07
Port Glasgow	d	23p33	00 01	08 39	09 12	09 39	10 14	10 39	11 16	11 39	12 14	12 39	13 11	13 39	14 11	14 39	15 11	15 39	16 16	16 39	17 11	17 39	18 11
Woodhall	d	23p35		08 41		09 41		10 41		11 41		12 41		13 41		14 41		15 41		16 41		17 41	
Langbank	d	23p40		08 46		09 46		10 46		11 46		12 46		13 46		14 46		15 46		16 46		17 46	
Bishopton	d	23p45	00 10	08 51	09 21	09 51	10 23	10 51	11 26	11 51	12 23	12 51	13 20	13 51	14 20	14 51	15 20	15 51	16 25	16 51	17 20	17 51	18 20
Paisley St James	d	23p51		08 58	09 28	09 58	10 30	10 58		11 57		12 57		13 57		14 57		15 57		16 57		17 57	
Paisley Gilmour Street 221 ✈	a	23p53	00 16	09 00	09 30	10 00	10 31	10 59	11 30	11 59	12 29	12 59	13 26	13 59	14 26	14 59	15 26	15 59	16 31	16 59	17 26	17 59	18 26
	d	23p54							11 31	12 00	12 30	13 00	13 27	14 00	14 27	15 00	15 27	16 00	16 32	17 00	17 27	18 00	18 27
Hillington West	d	23p57								12 03		13 03		14 03		15 03		16 03		17 03		18 03	
Hillington East	d	23p58							11 35	12 05	12 34	13 05	13 31	14 05	14 31	15 05	15 31	16 05	16 36	17 05	17 31	18 05	18 31
Cardonald	d	00 01								12 07		13 07		14 07		15 07		16 07		17 07		18 07	
Glasgow Central 15 221	a	00 08							11 45	12 15	12 42	13 15	13 40	14 15	14 40	15 15	15 40	16 15	16 45	17 15	17 40	18 15	18 40

		SR	SR	SR	SR	SR	SR	SR	SR
Gourock	d	18 23		19 23		20 23		21 23	22 23
Fort Matilda	d	18 26		19 26		20 26		21 26	22 26
Greenock West	d	18 29		19 29		20 29		21 29	22 29
Greenock Central	d	18 32		19 32		20 32		21 32	22 32
Cartsdyke	d	18 34		19 34		20 34		21 34	22 34
Bogston	d	18 36		19 36		20 36		21 36	22 36
Wemyss Bay	d		18 55		19 50		20 50		
Inverkip	d		18 59		19 54		20 54		
I.B.M. §	d		19 04		19 59		20 59		
Branchton	d		19 07		20 02		21 02		
Drumfrochar	d		19 09		20 04		21 04		
Whinhill	d		19 12		20 07		21 07		
Port Glasgow	d	18 39	19 16	19 39	20 11	20 39	21 11	21 39	22 39
Woodhall	d	18 41		19 41		20 41		21 41	22 41
Langbank	d	18 46		19 46		20 46		21 46	22 46
Bishopton	d	18 51	19 25	19 51	20 20	20 51	21 20	21 51	22 51
Paisley St James	d	18 57		19 57		20 57		21 58	22 58
Paisley Gilmour Street 221 ✈	a	18 59	19 31	19 59	20 26	20 59	21 26	22 00	23 00
	d	19 00	19 32	20 00	20 27	21 00			
Hillington West	d	19 03		20 03		21 03			
Hillington East	d	19 05	19 36	20 05	20 31	21 05			
Cardonald	d	19 07		20 07		21 07			
Glasgow Central 15 221	a	19 15	19 44	20 15	20 40	21 15			

§ For authorised access to and from I.B.M. only

A not 22 May

Table 219

Sundays

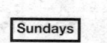

from 27 November

Gourock and Wemyss Bay - Glasgow Central

			SR	SR	SR	SR	SR	SR	SR	SR	SR		SR	SR	SR	SR	SR	SR	SR	SR	SR		SR	SR	SR	SR
Gourock		d	23p17		08 23		09 23	09 36		10 23	10 36			11 23	11 36		12 23	12 36		13 23	13 36			14 23	14 36	
Fort Matilda		d	23p20		08 26		09 26	09 39		10 26	10 39			11 26	11 39		12 26	12 39		13 26	13 39			14 26	14 39	
Greenock West		d	23p23		08 29		09 29	09 42		10 29	10 42			11 29	11 42		12 29	12 42		13 29	13 42			14 29	14 42	
Greenock Central		d	23p26		08 32		09 32	09 45		10 32	10 45			11 32	11 45		12 32	12 45		13 32	13 45			14 32	14 45	
Cartsdyke		d	23p28		08 34		09 34	09 47		10 34	10 47			11 34	11 47		12 34	12 47		13 34	13 47			14 34	14 47	
Bogston		d	23p30		08 36		09 36	09 49		10 36	10 49			11 36	11 49		12 36	12 49		13 36	13 49			14 36	14 49	
Wemyss Bay		d		23p40		08 51			09 53				10 55			11 53			12 50				13 50			14 50
Inverkip		d		23p44		08 55			09 57				10 59			11 57			12 54				13 54			14 54
I.B.M. §		d		23p49		09 00			10 02				11 04			12 02			12 59				13 59			14 59
Branchton		d		23p52		09 03			10 05				11 07			12 05			13 02				14 02			15 02
Drumfrochar		d		23p54		09 05			10 07				11 09			12 07			13 04				14 04			15 04
Whinhill		d		23p57		09 08			10 10				11 12			12 10			13 07				14 07			15 07
Port Glasgow		d	23p33	00 01	08 39	09 12	09 39	09 52	10 14	10 39	10 52		11 16	11 39	11 52	12 14	12 39	12 52	13 11	13 39	13 52		14 11	14 39	14 52	15 11
Woodhall		d	23p35		08 41		09 41	09 54		10 41	10 54			11 41	11 54		12 41	12 54		13 41	13 54			14 41	14 54	
Langbank		d	23p40		08 46		09 46	09 59		10 46	10 59			11 46	11 59		12 46	12 59		13 46	13 59			14 46	14 59	
Bishopton		d	23p45	00 10	08 51	09 21	09 51	10 04	10 23	10 51	11 04		11 26	11 51	12 04	12 23	12 51	13 04	13 20	13 51	14 04		14 20	14 51	15 04	15 20
Paisley St James		d	23p51		08 58	09 28	09 58	10 10	10 30	10 58	11 10			11 57	12 10		12 57	13 10		13 57	14 10			14 57	15 10	
Paisley Gilmour Street	221 ⇌	a	23p53	00 16	09 00	09 30	10 00	10 12	10 31	10 59	11 12		11 30	11 59	12 12	12 29	12 59	13 12	13 26	13 59	14 12		14 26	14 59	15 12	15 26
		d	23p54								11 13		11 31	12 00	12 13	12 30	13 00	13 13	13 27	14 00	14 14		14 27	15 00	15 13	15 27
Hillington West		d	23p57								11 16			12 03	12 16		13 03	13 18		14 03	14 16			15 03	15 16	
Hillington East		d	23p58								11 18		11 35	12 05	12 18	12 34	13 05	13 20	13 31	14 05	14 18		14 31	15 05	15 18	15 31
Cardonald		d	00 01								11 20			12 07	12 20		13 07	13 22		14 07	14 20			15 07	15 20	
Glasgow Central 15	221	a	00 08								11 28		11 45	12 15	12 28	12 42	13 15	13 30	13 40	14 15	14 28		14 40	15 15	15 28	15 40

			SR	SR	SR	SR	SR		SR	SR	SR	SR	SR	SR	SR	SR	SR		SR	SR	SR					
Gourock		d	15 23	15 36		16 23	16 36			17 23	17 36		18 23		19 23		20 23			21 23	22 23					
Fort Matilda		d	15 26	15 39		16 26	16 39			17 26	17 39		18 26		19 26		20 26			21 26	22 26					
Greenock West		d	15 29	15 42		16 29	16 42			17 29	17 42		18 29		19 29		20 29			21 29	22 29					
Greenock Central		d	15 32	15 45		16 32	16 45			17 32	17 45		18 32		19 32		20 32			21 32	22 32					
Cartsdyke		d	15 34	15 47		16 34	16 47			17 34	17 47		18 34		19 34		20 34			21 34	22 34					
Bogston		d	15 36	15 49		16 36	16 49			17 36	17 49		18 36		19 36		20 36			21 36	22 36					
Wemyss Bay		d			15 55				16 50			17 50		18 55		19 50			20 50							
Inverkip		d			15 59				16 54			17 54		18 59		19 54			20 54							
I.B.M. §		d			16 04				16 59			17 59		19 04		19 59			20 59							
Branchton		d			16 07				17 02			18 02		19 07		20 02			21 02							
Drumfrochar		d			16 09				17 04			18 04		19 09		20 04			21 04							
Whinhill		d			16 12				17 07			18 07		19 12		20 07			21 07							
Port Glasgow		d	15 39	15 52	16 16	16 39	16 52		17 11	17 39	17 52	18 11	18 39	19 16	19 39	20 11	20 39		21 11	21 39	22 39					
Woodhall		d	15 41	15 54		16 41	16 54			17 41	17 54		18 41		19 41		20 41			21 41	22 41					
Langbank		d	15 46	15 59		16 46	16 59			17 46	17 59		18 46		19 46		20 46			21 46	22 46					
Bishopton		d	15 51	16 04	16 25	16 51	17 04		17 20	17 51	18 04	18 20	18 51	19 25	19 51	20 20	20 51		21 20	21 51	22 51					
Paisley St James		d	15 57	16 10		16 57	17 10			17 57	18 10		18 57		19 57		20 57			21 58	22 58					
Paisley Gilmour Street	221 ⇌	a	15 59	16 12	16 31	16 59	17 12		17 26	17 59	18 12	18 26	18 59	19 31	19 59	20 26	20 59		21 26	22 00	23 00					
		d	16 00	16 13	16 32	17 00	17 13		17 27	18 00	18 13	18 27	19 00	19 32	20 00	20 27	21 00									
Hillington West		d	16 03	16 16		17 03	17 16			18 03	18 16		19 03		20 03		21 03									
Hillington East		d	16 05	16 18	16 36	17 05	17 18		17 31	18 05	18 18	18 31	19 05	19 36	20 05	20 31	21 05									
Cardonald		d	16 07	16 20		17 07	17 20			18 07	18 20		19 07		20 07		21 07									
Glasgow Central 15	221	a	16 15	16 28	16 45	17 15	17 28		17 40	18 15	18 28	18 40	19 15	19 44	20 15	20 40	21 15									

§ For authorised access to and from I.B.M. only

Table 219A — **SHIPPING SERVICES** — **Mondays to Saturdays**

Glasgow and Gourock - Kilcreggan and Helensburgh Pier

Operated by Clyde Marine Transport Ltd on behalf of Strathclyde Partnership for Transport.

		SX	SX		A	B			
Glasgow Central 15	219 d	*05 55*	*06 25*	*07 04*	*07 35*	*07 35*	*09 05*	*10 35*	*11 25*
Paisley Gilmour Street	219 d	*06 07*	*06 36*	*07 20*	*07 51*	*07 51*	*09 20*	*10 50*	*11 36*
Gourock	219 a	*06 36*	*07 13*	*07 57*	*08 28*	*08 28*	*09 58*	*11 27*	*12 06*
Gourock	d	**07 00**	**07 30**	**08 05**	**08 35**	**08 50**	**10 05**	**11 35**	**12 25**
Dunoon	a								
Kilcreggan	a	**07 12**	**07 42**	**08 17**		**09 02**	**10 20**	**11 47**	**12 37**
Helensburgh Pier	a				**09 05**		**10 45**		

							D	E
Glasgow Central 15	219 d	*13 25*	*14 35*	*15 25*	*15 35*	*16 23*	*17 25*	*17 25*
Paisley Gilmour Street	219 d	*13 36*	*14 50*	*15 36*	*15 50*	*16 38*	*17 37*	*17 37*
Gourock	219 a	*14 06*	*15 27*	*16 06*	*16 27*	*17 15*	*18 06*	*18 06*
Gourock	d	**14 15**	**15 45**	**16 15**	**16 50**	**17 25**	**18 10**	**18 10**
Dunoon	a							
Kilcreggan	a	**14 30**	**15 57**	**16 27**	**17 03**	**17 37**	**18 25**	**18 25**
Helensburgh Pier	a	**14 55**					**18 50**	

Sundays

Until 9 October only

		C	C			
Glasgow Central 15	219 d	*10 08*	*10 08*	*11 20*	*13 20*	*15 20*
Paisley Gilmour Street	219 d	*10 36*	*10 36*	*11 35*	*13 35*	*15 35*
Gourock	219 a	*11 16*	*11 16*	*12 12*	*14 12*	*16 12*
Gourock	d	**11 25**	**11 55**	**13 05**	**14 35**	**16 25**
Dunoon	a					
Kilcreggan	a	**11 37**			**14 50**	**16 37**
Helensburgh Pier	a		**12 25**	**13 35**	**15 20**	

Glasgow Central 15	219 d	
Paisley Gilmour Street	219 d	
Gourock	219 a	
Gourock	d	
Dunoon	a	
Kilcreggan	a	
Helensburgh Pier	a	

A Until 15 October
B From 17 October
C Connecting Bus Service From Glasgow Central to Paisley arr. 1028
D Until 15 October. Should the train be late in arriving the ferry will be held a maximum of 15 minutes until 1825.
E From 17 October. Should the train be late in arriving the ferry will be held a maximum of 15 minutes until 1825.

GOUROCK/DUNOON

This route is currently being tendered by the Scottish Government and is subject to change or withdrawal at short notice. Please check the Caledonian MacBrayne website for information prior to sailing at www.calmac.co.uk or telephone 08000 66 5000 for full details. Caledonian MacBrayne apologise for any inconvenience caused.

Helensburgh Pier and Kilgreggan - Gourock and Glasgow

Operated by Clyde Marine Transport Ltd on behalf of Strathclyde Partnership for Transport.

		SX	SX		A	B			
Helensburgh Pier	⛴ d					**09 10**	**10 50**		
Kilcreggan	⛴ d	**07 15**	**07 50**	**08 20**	**09 10**	**09 40**	**11 15**	**11 50**	**12 45**
Dunoon	⛴ d								
Gourock	⛴ a	**07 27**	**08 02**	**08 32**	**09 22**	**09 52**	**11 27**	**12 02**	**12 57**
Gourock	219 d	*07 47*	*08 08*	*09 06*	*09 36*	*10 06*	*11 36*	*12 23*	*13 06*
Paisley Gilmour Street	219 a	*08 14*	*08 36*	*09 42*	*10 12*	*10 42*	*12 12*	*12 51*	*13 43*
Glasgow Central 15	219 a	*08 30*	*08 48*	*09 58*	*10 28*	*10 58*	*12 28*	*13 03*	*13 58*

							A	B
Helensburgh Pier	⛴ d	**15 00**						**18 55**
Kilcreggan	⛴ d	**15 30**	**16 00**	**16 30**	**17 05**	**17 40**	**18 30**	**19 20**
Dunoon	⛴ d							
Gourock	⛴ a	**15 42**	**16 12**	**16 42**	**17 17**	**17 52**	**18 42**	**19 32**
Gourock	219 d	*16 06*	*16 23*	*17 06*	*17 23*	*18 06*	*19 06*	*19 45*
Paisley Gilmour Street	219 a	*16 42*	*16 51*	*17 43*	*17 51*	*18 42*	*19 42*	*20 14*
Glasgow Central 15	219 a	*16 58*	*17 05*	*17 58*	*18b03*	*18 58*	*19 58*	*20 26*

Sundays

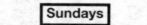

Until 9 October only

Helensburgh Pier	⛴ d		**12 30**	**13 40**	**15 25**	
Kilcreggan	⛴ d	**11 40**			**15 55**	**16 40**
Dunoon	⛴ d					
Gourock	⛴ a	**11 52**	**13 00**	**14 10**	**16 03**	**16 52**
Gourock	219 d	*12 23*	*13 23*	*14 23*	*16 23*	*17 23*
Paisley Gilmour Street	219 a	*12 59*	*13 59*	*14 59*	*16 59*	*17 59*
Glasgow Central 15	219 a	*13 15*	*14 15*	*15 15*	*17 15*	*18 15*

Helensburgh Pier	⛴ d	
Kilcreggan	⛴ d	
Dunoon	⛴ d	
Gourock	⛴ a	
Gourock	219 d	
Paisley Gilmour Street	219 a	
Glasgow Central 15	219 a	

A From 17 October　**B** Until 15 October　**b** Arrives 1805 on Saturdays

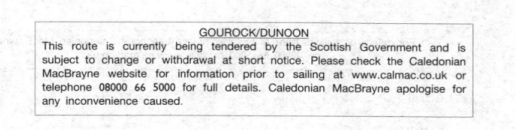

GOUROCK/DUNOON

This route is currently being tendered by the Scottish Government and is subject to change or withdrawal at short notice. Please check the Caledonian MacBrayne website for information prior to sailing at www.calmac.co.uk or telephone 08000 66 5000 for full details. Caledonian MacBrayne apologise for any inconvenience caused.

SHIPPING SERVICES

Mondays to Saturdays

Until 22 October

Glasgow and Wemyss Bay - Rothesay (Bute)

Operated by Caledonian MacBrayne Ltd

		SX														FSO
Glasgow Central 15	219 d	*06 05*	*06 32*	*07 50*	*08 50*	*09 50*	*10 50*	*11 50*	*12 50*	*13 50*	*14 50*	*15 50*	*16 33*	*17 15*	*17 55*	*18 50*	*19 40*
Paisley Gilmour Street	219 d	*06 19*	*06 47*	*08 02*	*09 01*	*10 01*	*11 01*	*12 01*	*13 01*	*14 01*	*15 01*	*16 02*	*16 49*	*17 29*	*18 06*	*19 01*	*19 55*
Wemyss Bay	219 a	*06 58*	*07 30*	*08 40*	*09 40*	*10 40*	*11 40*	*12 40*	*13 40*	*14 40*	*15 40*	*16 40*	*17 26*	*18 08*	*18 44*	*19 40*	*20 38*
Wemyss Bay	d	**07 15**	**08 00**	**08 45**	**10 15**	**11 00**	**12 00**	**13 05**	**14 05**	**15 00**	**16 00**	**16 45**	**17 30**	**18 15**	**19 00**	**19 45**	**20 45**
Rothesay	a	**07 50**	**08 35**	**09 20**	**10 50**	**11 35**	**12 35**	**13 40**	**14 40**	**15 35**	**16 35**	**17 20**	**18 05**	**18 50**	**19 35**	**20 20**	**21 20**

Sundays

Until 16 October

		E	E	E	E								
Glasgow Central 15	219 d	*07 25*	*08 35*	*09 35*	*10 35*	*11 50*	*12 50*	*13 50*	*14 50*	*15 50*	*16 50*	*17 50*	*18 50*
Paisley Gilmour Street	219 d	*07 59*	*09 05*	*10 05*	*11 05*	*12 03*	*13 03*	*14 03*	*15 03*	*16 03*	*17 03*	*18 03*	*19 03*
Wemyss Bay	219 a	*08 42*	*09 48*	*10 48*	*11 48*	*12 43*	*13 42*	*14 42*	*15 42*	*16 42*	*17 42*	*18 42*	*19 42*
Wemyss Bay	d	**08 45**	**10 15**	**11 00**	**12 00**	**13 00**	**13 50**	**15 00**	**16 00**	**17 30**	**18 15**	**19 00**	**19 45**
Rothesay	a	**09 20**	**10 50**	**11 35**	**12 35**	**13 35**	**14 25**	**15 35**	**16 35**	**18 05**	**18 50**	**19 35**	**20 20**

Mondays to Saturdays

Until 22 October

		SX															FSO	SO A
Rothesay	d	**06 25**	**07 00**	**08 00**	**08 45**	**10 10**	**11 00**	**12 00**	**13 00**	**14 00**	**15 00**	**16 00**	**16 45**	**17 30**	**18 15**	**19 00**	**19 45**	**21 10**
Wemyss Bay	a	**07 00**	**07 35**	**08 35**	**09 20**	**10 45**	**11 35**	**12 35**	**13 35**	**14 35**	**15 35**	**16 35**	**17 20**	**18 05**	**18 50**	**19 35**	**20 20**	**21 45**
Wemyss Bay	219 d	*07 13*	*07 51*	*08 50*	*09 50*	*10 55*	*11 50*	*12 50*	*13 50*	*14 50*	*15 55*	*16 45*	*17 49*	*18 26*	*18 55*	*19 45*	*20 44*	*21 50*
Paisley Gilmour Street	219 a	*07 51*	*08 33*	*09 26*	*10 26*	*11 31*	*12 26*	*13 26*	*14 26*	*15 26*	*16 31*	*17 21*	*18 30*	*19 06*	*19 31*	*20 26*	*21 26*	*22 32*
Glasgow Central 15	219 a	*08 07*	*08 44*	*09 38*	*10 38*	*11 43*	*12 38*	*13 38*	*14 38*	*15 38*	*16 45*	*17 34*	*18b43*	*19 17*	*19 44*	*20 43*	*21 42*	*22 46*

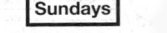

Sundays

Until 16 October

		H											H
Rothesay	d	**08 00**	**10 10**	**11 00**	**12 00**	**13 00**	**14 00**	**15 10**	**16 00**	**16 45**	**18 15**	**19 00**	**19 45**
Wemyss Bay	a	**08 35**	**10 45**	**11 35**	**12 35**	**13 35**	**14 35**	**15 45**	**16 35**	**17 20**	**18 50**	**19 35**	**20 20**
Wemyss Bay	219 d	*08 51*	*10 55*	*11 53*	*12 50*	*13 50*	*14 50*	*15 55*	*16 50*	*17 50*	*18 55*	*19 50*	*20 50*
Paisley Gilmour Street	219 a	*09 30*	*11 30*	*12 29*	*13 26*	*14 26*	*15 26*	*16 31*	*17 26*	*18 26*	*19 31*	*20 26*	*21 26*
Glasgow Central 15	219 a	*10 00*	*11 45*	*12 42*	*13 40*	*14 40*	*15 40*	*16 45*	*17 40*	*18 40*	*19 44*	*20 40*	*21 57*

A From 4 June to 20 August
b Arrives 1844 on Saturdays
E Connecting bus service from Glasgow to Paisley
H Connecting bus service from Paisley to Glasgow

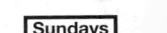

For details of sailings from 23 October please telephone Caledonian MacBrayne on 08000 66 5000 or visit www.calmac.co.uk

Network Diagram for Tables 220, 223, 224, 226, 232

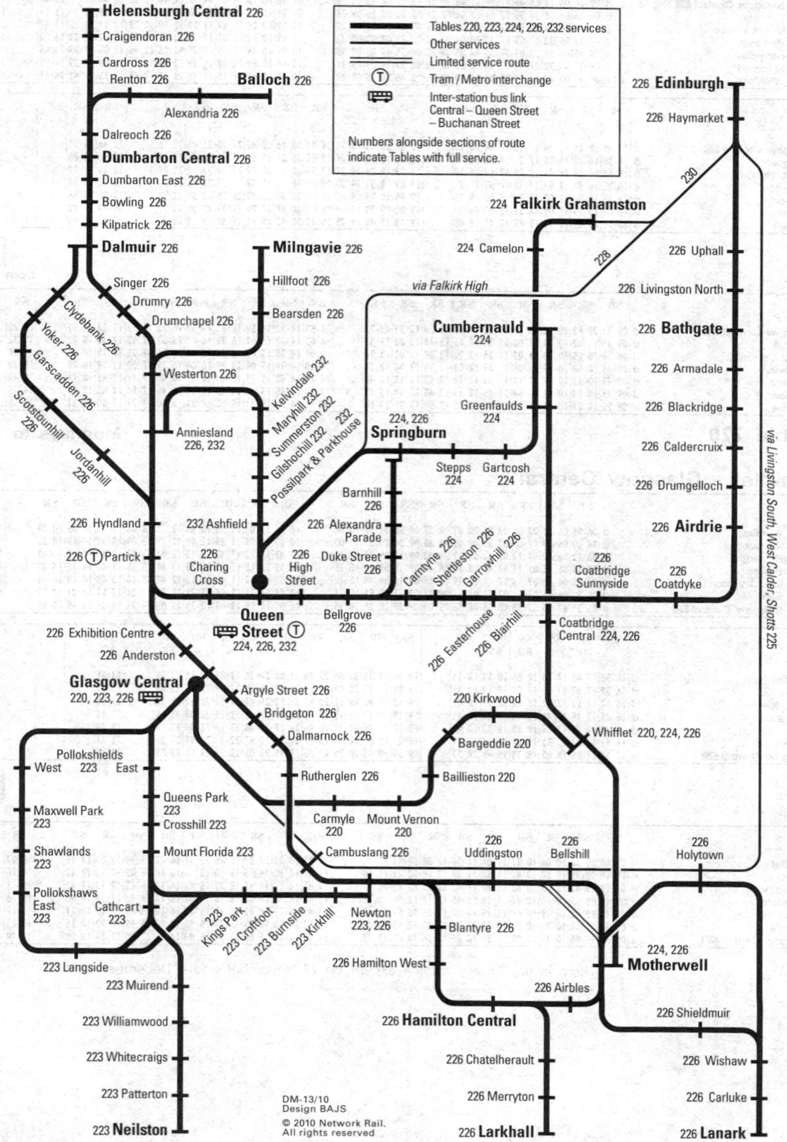

Table 220

Mondays to Saturdays

Glasgow Central - Whifflet

Miles			SR SO	SR	SR	SR	SR	SR SO	SR SX	SR	SR	SR	SR	SR	SR	SR	SR	SR	SR	SR	SR	SR	SR
0	**Glasgow Central** 15	d	00 16	06 16	06 46	07 16	07 46	08 16	08 17	08 43	09 16	09 46	10 16	10 46	11 16	11 46	12 16	12 46	13 16	13 46	14 16	14 46	15 16
5½	Carmyle	d	00 26	06 26	06 56	07 26	07 56	08 26	08 26	08 56	09 26	09 56	10 26	10 56	11 26	11 56	12 26	12 56	13 26	13 56	14 26	14 56	15 26
6¾	Mount Vernon	d	00 29	06 29	06 59	07 29	07 59	08 29	08 29	08 59	09 29	09 59	10 29	10 59	11 29	11 59	12 29	12 59	13 29	13 59	14 29	14 59	15 29
8	Baillieston	d	00 32	06 32	07 02	07 32	08 02	08 32	08 32	09 02	09 32	10 02	10 32	11 02	11 32	12 02	12 32	13 02	13 32	14 02	14 32	15 02	15 32
9¼	Bargeddie	d	00 35	06 35	07 05	07 35	08 05	08 35	08 35	09 05	09 35	10 05	10 35	11 05	11 35	12 05	12 35	13 05	13 35	14 05	14 35	15 05	15 35
10	Kirkwood	d	00 39	06 39	07 09	07 39	08 09	08 39	08 39	09 09	09 39	10 09	10 39	11 09	11 39	12 09	12 39	13 09	13 39	14 09	14 39	15 09	15 39
12½	**Whifflet**	a	00 45	06 47	07 15	07 47	08 15	08 45	08 48	09 15	09 45	10 15	10 45	11 15	11 45	12 15	12 45	13 15	13 45	14 15	14 45	15 15	15 45

		SR	SR	SR	SR	SR	SR	SR	SR SX	SR SO	SR	SR	SR	SR	SR	SR	SR	SR
Glasgow Central 15	d	15 46	16 16	16 46	17 16	17 46	18 16	18 46	19 13	19 16	19 46	20 16	20 46	21 16	21 46	22 16	22 46	23 16
Carmyle	d	15 56	16 26	16 56	17 26	17 56	18 26	18 56	19 26	19 26	19 56	20 26	20 56	21 26	21 56	22 26	22 56	23 26
Mount Vernon	d	15 59	16 29	16 59	17 29	17 59	18 29	18 59	19 29	19 29	19 59	20 29	20 59	21 29	21 59	22 29	22 59	23 29
Baillieston	d	16 02	16 32	17 02	17 32	18 02	18 32	19 02	19 32	19 32	20 02	20 32	21 02	21 32	22 02	22 32	23 02	23 32
Bargeddie	d	16 05	16 35	17 05	17 35	18 05	18 35	19 05	19 35	19 35	20 05	20 35	21 05	21 35	22 05	22 36	23 05	23 35
Kirkwood	d	16 09	16 39	17 09	17 39	18 09	18 39	19 09	19 39	19 39	20 09	20 39	21 09	21 39	22 09	22 39	23 09	23 39
Whifflet	a	16 15	16 45	17 15	17 45	18 15	18 45	19 15	19 45	19 45	20 15	20 45	21 15	21 45	22 15	22 46	23 15	23 45

Sundays

from 27 November

		SR	SR	SR	SR	SR	SR	SR	SR	SR	SR	SR	SR	SR	SR	SR	SR	SR	SR	SR
Glasgow Central 15	d	09 22	09 52	10 22	10 52	11 22	11 53	12 24	12 52	13 22	13 52	14 22	14 52	15 22	15 52	16 22	16 52	17 22	17 52	18 22
Carmyle	d	09 33	10 02	10 33	11 02	11 33	12 03	12 33	13 02	13 33	14 02	14 33	15 02	15 33	16 02	16 33	17 02	17 33	18 02	18 32
Mount Vernon	d	09 36	10 05	10 36	11 05	11 36	12 06	12 36	13 05	13 36	14 05	14 36	15 05	15 36	16 05	16 36	17 05	17 36	18 05	18 36
Baillieston	d	09 39	10 08	10 39	11 08	11 39	12 09	12 39	13 08	13 39	14 08	14 39	15 08	15 39	16 08	16 39	17 08	17 39	18 08	18 39
Bargeddie	d	09 42	10 11	10 42	11 11	11 42	12 12	12 42	13 11	13 42	14 11	14 42	15 11	15 42	16 11	16 42	17 11	17 42	18 11	18 42
Kirkwood	d	09 45	10 14	10 45	11 14	11 45	12 15	12 45	13 14	13 45	14 14	14 45	15 14	15 45	16 14	16 45	17 14	17 45	18 14	18 45
Whifflet	a	09 50	10 21	10 50	11 21	11 50	12 21	12 50	13 21	13 50	14 21	14 50	15 21	15 50	16 21	16 50	17 21	17 50	18 21	18 50

Table 220

Mondays to Saturdays

Whifflet - Glasgow Central

Miles			SR	SR	SR	SR	SR	SR	SR	SR	SR	SR	SR	SR	SR	SR	SR	SR	SR	SR	SR	SR	SR
0	**Whifflet**	d	06 06	06 37	07 06	07 36	08 07	08 37	09 06	09 36	10 06	10 36	11 06	11 36	12 06	12 36	13 06	13 36	14 06	14 36	15 06	15 36	16 06
2½	Kirkwood	d	06 09	06 39	07 09	07 39	08 09	08 39	09 09	09 39	10 09	10 39	11 09	11 39	12 09	12 39	13 09	13 39	14 09	14 39	15 09	15 39	16 09
3¼	Bargeddie	d	06 12	06 42	07 12	07 42	08 12	08 42	09 12	09 42	10 12	10 42	11 12	11 42	12 12	12 42	13 12	13 42	14 12	14 42	15 12	15 42	16 12
4½	Baillieston	d	06 15	06 45	07 15	07 45	08 15	08 45	09 15	09 45	10 15	10 45	11 15	11 45	12 15	12 45	13 15	13 45	14 15	14 45	15 15	15 45	16 15
5¾	Mount Vernon	d	06 18	06 48	07 18	07 48	08 18	08 48	09 18	09 48	10 18	10 48	11 18	11 48	12 18	12 48	13 18	13 48	14 18	14 48	15 18	15 48	16 18
7	Carmyle	d	06 21	06 51	07 21	07 51	08 21	08 51	09 21	09 51	10 21	10 51	11 21	11 51	12 21	12 51	13 21	13 51	14 21	14 51	15 21	15 51	16 21
12½	**Glasgow Central** 15	a	06 35	07 06	07 35	08 05	08 36	09 06	09 37	10 05	10 35	11 05	11 35	12 05	12 35	13 05	13 35	14 05	14 35	15 05	15 35	16 05	16 35

		SR	SR	SR	SR SO	SR SX	SR	SR	SR	SR	SR	SR	SR	SR	SR	SR SX	SR SO
Whifflet	d	16 36	17 06	17 36	18 06	18 12	18 36	19 06	19 36	20 06	20 36	21 06	21 36	22 07	22 36	23 06	23 06
Kirkwood	d	16 39	17 09	17 39	18 09	18 14	18 39	19 09	19 39	20 09	20 39	21 09	21 39	22 09	22 39	23 09	23 09
Bargeddie	d	16 42	17 12	17 42	18 12	18 17	18 42	19 12	19 42	20 12	20 42	21 12	21 42	22 12	22 42	23 12	23 12
Baillieston	d	16 45	17 15	17 45	18 15	18 20	18 45	19 15	19 45	20 15	20 45	21 15	21 45	22 15	22 45	23 15	23 15
Mount Vernon	d	16 48	17 18	17 48	18 18	18 23	18 48	19 18	19 48	20 18	20 48	21 18	21 48	22 18	22 48	23 18	23 18
Carmyle	d	16 51	17 21	17 51	18 21	18 26	18 51	19 21	19 51	20 21	20 51	21 21	21 51	22 21	22 51	23 21	23 21
Glasgow Central 15	a	17 05	17 35	18 05	18 35	18 40	19 05	19 35	20 05	20 35	21 05	21 35	22 05	22 38	23 05	23 35	23 37

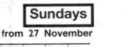

Sundays

from 27 November

		SR	SR	SR	SR	SR	SR	SR	SR	SR	SR	SR	SR	SR	SR	SR	SR	SR	SR	SR
Whifflet	d	09 06	09 36	10 06	10 37	11 06	11 36	12 06	12 39	13 06	13 37	14 06	14 37	15 06	15 37	16 07	16 39	17 07	17 39	18 07
Kirkwood	d	09 10	09 39	10 10	10 40	11 10	11 39	12 10	12 42	13 10	13 40	14 10	14 40	15 10	15 40	16 10	16 42	17 10	17 42	18 10
Bargeddie	d	09 13	09 42	10 13	10 43	11 13	11 42	12 13	12 45	13 13	13 43	14 13	14 43	15 13	15 43	16 13	16 45	17 13	17 45	18 13
Baillieston	d	09 16	09 45	10 16	10 46	11 16	11 45	12 16	12 48	13 16	13 46	14 16	14 46	15 16	15 46	16 16	16 48	17 16	17 48	18 16
Mount Vernon	d	09 19	09 48	10 19	10 49	11 19	11 48	12 19	12 51	13 19	13 49	14 19	14 49	15 19	15 49	16 19	16 51	17 19	17 51	18 19
Carmyle	d	09 22	09 52	10 22	10 53	11 22	11 52	12 22	12 55	13 22	13 53	14 22	14 53	15 22	15 53	16 23	16 55	17 23	17 55	18 23
Glasgow Central 15	a	09 37	10 06	10 35	11 07	11 36	12 05	12 34	13 08	13 37	14 06	14 37	15 08	15 39	16 08	16 36	17 08	17 36	18 08	18 40

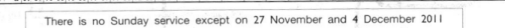

There is no Sunday service except on 27 November and 4 December 2011

Glasgow Central - Ardrossan, Largs and Ayr

Miles	Miles	Miles				SR SO	SR MSX	SR MX	SR SO	SR MSX	SR MX	SR	SR	SR		SR ◇ A	SR	SR	SR	SR	SR	SR ◇ A	SR SX	SR		SR
0	0	—	**Glasgow Central** 15	219	d	23p15	23p15	23p30	23p45	23p45	00 15	06 00	06 15	06 30		06 30	06 45	07 00	07 15	07 30	08 00	08 07	08 15	08 30		08 34
7¼	7¼	—	Paisley Gilmour Street	219	a	23p25	23p25	23p40	23p55	23p55	00 25	06 10	06 25	06 40			06 55	07 10	07 25	07 40	08 10		08 25	08 41		08 45
—	—	—			d	23p26	23p26	23p41	23p56	23p56	00 26	06 11	06 26	06 41			06 56	07 11	07 26	07 41	08 11		08 26	08 41		08 45
10¾	10¾	—	Johnstone		d	23p30	23p30	23p45	23p59	23p59	00 30	06 13	06 30	06 45			07 00	07 15	07 31	07 45	08 15		08 30	08 46		08 50
11½	11½	—	Milliken Park		d	23p33	23p33		00 03	00 03			06 33				07 03		07 34				08 33			08 52
13	13	—	Howwood		d	23p36	23p36		00 06	00 06			06 36				07 06		07 37				08 36			
16½	16½	—	Lochwinnoch		d	23p40	23p40		00 10	00 10			06 40						07 41				08 40			08 57
20½	20½	—	Glengarnock		d	23p45	23p45		00 15	00 15			06 45				07 13		07 46		08 24		08 45	08 55		09 02
23¼	23¼	—	Dalry		d	23p49	23p49		00 19	00 19			06 49				07 17		07 50		08 28		08 49	08 59		09 06
26¾	26¾	—	Kilwinning		d	23p54	23p54	23p59	00 23	00 23	00 42	06 27	06 54	06 59			07 23	07 29	07 54	08 00	08 33		08 54	09 03		09 11
—	29	—	Stevenston		d	23p57	23p57		00 27	00 27			06 57				07 27		07 58				08 57			09 14
—	30¼	—	Saltcoats		d	23p59	23p59		00 29	00 29			07 00				07 29		08 00				09 00			09 17
—	31¼	—	Ardrossan South Beach		d	00 02	00 02		00 31	00a32			07 02				07 31		08 02				09a02			09 19
—	—	31¾	Ardrossan Town		d	00a06											07 35									09 23
—	—	32¼	**Ardrossan Harbour**		a												07 37									09 25
—	35¾	—	West Kilbride		d		00 08		00 37				07 08						08 08							
—	39¾	—	Fairlie		d		00 14		00 43				07 13						08 14							
—	42¾	—	**Largs**		a		00 19		00 49				07 20						08 20							
30	—	—	Irvine		d			00 03			00 47	06 31		07 03				07 33		08 04	08 37			09 07		
33¾	—	—	Barassie		d			00 08			00 51			07 07						08 09	08 42			09 12		
35	—	—	Troon		d			00 11			00 54	06 37		07 10		07 47		07 39		08 12	08 45	09 21		09 15		
37¾	—	—	Prestwick Int. Airport ✈		d			00 15			00 58	06 41		07 14		07 52		07 43		08 16	08 49	09 26		09 19		
38¼	—	—	Prestwick Town		d			00 17			01 00	06 43		07 16		07 54		07 45		08 18	08 51	09 28		09 21		
40¼	—	—	Newton-on-Ayr		d			00 20			01 04			07 19						08 21	08 54			09 24		
41½	—	—	**Ayr**		a			00 25			01 11	06 52		07 24		07 59		07 52		08 26	08 58	09 33		09 27		

			SR	SR	SR	SR	SR	SR	SR	SR		SR	SR B	SR	SR	SR	SR ◇ A	SR	SR	SR		SR	SR	SR	SR	SR B
Glasgow Central 15	219	d	08 45	09 00	09 15	09 30	09 45	10 00	10 15	10 30		10 45		11 00	11 15	11 30	11 42	11 45	12 00	12 15		12 30	12 45	13 00	13 15	
Paisley Gilmour Street	219	a	08 55	09 10	09 25	09 40	09 56	10 10	10 25	10 40		10 55		11 10	11 25	11 40	11 52	11 55	12 09	12 25		12 40	12 55	13 10	13 25	
		d	08 56	09 11	09 26	09 41	09 57	10 11	10 26	10 41		10 56		11 11	11 26	11 41	11 53	11 56	12 10	12 26		12 41	12 56	13 11	13 26	
Johnstone		d	09 00	09 17	09 30	09 45	10 01	10 15	10 30	10 45		11 00		11 15	11 30	11 45		12 01	12 14	12 30		12 45	13 00	13 15	13 30	
Milliken Park		d	09 03		09 33		10 04		10 33			11 03			11 33			12 03		12 33			13 03		13 33	
Howwood		d			09 36				10 36						11 36					12 36					13 36	
Lochwinnoch		d			09 40				10 40						11 40					12 40					13 40	
Glengarnock		d	09 11		09 45	09 54	10 12		10 45	10 55		11 11			11 45			12 11		12 45			13 11		13 45	
Dalry		d			09 49		10 16	10 26	10 49						11 49					12 49			13 15		13 49	
Kilwinning		d	09 18	09 31	09 54	10 01	10 21	10 31	10 54	11 01		11 18		11 29	11 54	11 59	12 11	12 18	12 27	12 54		12 59	13 20	13 29	13 54	
Stevenston		d	09 21		09 57		10 24		10 57			11 21			11 57			12 22		12 57			13 23		13 57	
Saltcoats		d	09 24		10 00		10 27		11 00			11 24			12 00			12 24		13 00			13 26		14 00	
Ardrossan South Beach		d	09 26		10 02		10 29		11 02			11 26			12 02			12 26		13 02			13 28		14 02	
Ardrossan Town		d			10 06				11 06						12 06					13 06					14 06	
Ardrossan Harbour		a			10 08				11 08						12 09					13 09					14 09	
West Kilbride		d	09 31				10 34					11 32						12 32					13 34			
Fairlie		d	09 35				10 39					11 37						12 38					13 39			
Largs		a	09 44				10 47					11 44						12 44					13 46			
Irvine		d		09 35		10 05		10 35		11 05				11 33		12 03			12 33			13 03		13 33		
Barassie		d				10 10				11 10						12 08						13 08				
Troon		d		09 41		10 13		10 41		11 13			11 18	11 39		12 11			12 39			13 11		13 39		13 46
Prestwick Int. Airport ✈		d		09 45		10 17		10 45		11 17			11 22	11 43		12 15			12 43			13 15		13 43		13 51
Prestwick Town		d		09 47		10 19		10 47		11 19			11 24	11 45		12 17			12 45			13 17		13 45		13 53
Newton-on-Ayr		d				10 22				11 22						12 20						13 20				
Ayr		a		09 53		10 26		10 54		11 26			11 30	11 52		12 24	12 29		12 52			13 24		13 52		14 00

			SR	SR	SR	SR		SR	SR	SR	SR C	SR	SR	SR	SR	SR		SR	SR	SR D	SR	SR C	SR SX	SR	SR SX	SR SO
Glasgow Central 15	219	d	13 30	13 45	14 00	14 15		14 30	14 45	15 00	15 12	15 15	15 30	15 45	16 00	16 18		16 30	16 50		17 00	17 12	17 13	17 20	17 30	17 30
Paisley Gilmour Street	219	a	13 40	13 55	14 10	14 25		14 40	14 55	15 10		15 25	15 40	15 55	16 10	16 27		16 40	17 00		17 10			17 31		17 40
		d	13 41	13 56	14 11	14 26		14 41	14 56	15 11		15 26	15 41	15 56	16 11	16 28		16 41	17 01		17 11		17u24	17 32	17u41	17 41
Johnstone		d	13 45	14 00	14 15	14 30		14 45	15 00	15 15		15 30	15 45	16 00	16 15	16 32		16 45	17 05		17 15			17 36		17 45
Milliken Park		d		14 03		14 33			15 03			15 33		16 03		16 35			17 08					17 39		
Howwood		d				14 36						15 36				16 38			17 11							
Lochwinnoch		d				14 40						15 40				16 42					17 21					
Glengarnock		d		14 11		14 45			15 11			15 45		16 11		16 47			17 18		17 26		17 35			
Dalry		d			14 26	14 49						15 49				16 51			17 22		17 30			17 49		
Kilwinning		d	13 59	14 18	14 31	14 54		14 59	15 18	15 29		15 54	15 59	16 18	16 29	16 56		17 00	17 26		17 35		17 42	17 54		17 59
Stevenston		d		14 21		14 57			15 21			15 57		16 21		17 01			17 30					17 57		
Saltcoats		d		14 24		15 00			15 24			16 00		16 24		17 09			17 32					18 00		
Ardrossan South Beach		d		14 26		15 01			15 26			16 02		16 26		17 11			17 36					18 02		
Ardrossan Town		d				15 06						16 06							17 39							
Ardrossan Harbour		a				15 09						16 09							17 45							
West Kilbride		d		14 32					15 32					16 32		17 17								18 08		
Fairlie		d		14 37					15 37					16 37		17 22								18 13		
Largs		a		14 44					15 44					16 44		17 28								18 20		
Irvine		d	14 03		14 35			15 03		15 33			16 03		16 33			17 04			17 39		17 46		18 00	18 03
Barassie		d	14 08					15 09					16 08					17 08			17 44				18 04	18 08
Troon		d	14 11		14 41			15 12		15 39	16 16		16 11		16 39			17 11		17 16	17 47	18 21	17 52		18 07	18 11
Prestwick Int. Airport ✈		d	14 15		14 45			15 16		15 43	16 20		16 15		16 43			17 15		17 21	17 51	18 26	17 56		18 11	18 15
Prestwick Town		d	14 17		14 47			15 18		15 45	16 22		16 17		16 45			17 17		17 23	17 53	18 28	17 58		18 13	18 17
Newton-on-Ayr		d	14 20					15 21					16 20					17 21			17 56				18 17	18 20
Ayr		a	14 24		14 54			15 24		15 52	16 30		16 24		16 52			17 25		17 30	18 00	18 36	18 05		18 21	18 24

A To Stranraer
B From Kilmarnock to Girvan
C To Girvan
D From Kilmarnock to Stranraer

Glasgow Central - Ardrossan, Largs and Ayr

Station		d/a	SR	SR	SR	SR	SR	SR	SR A	SR	SR	SR	SR	SR	SR	SR	SR	SR A	SR	SR	SR	SR	SR
Glasgow Central 15	219	d	17 35	17 45	18 00	18 15	18 30	18 45		19 00	19 15	19 30	19 45	20 00	20 15	20 30	20 45		21 00	21 15	21 30	21 45	22 00
Paisley Gilmour Street	219	a	17 47	17 55	18 10	18 25	18 40	18 55		19 10	19 25	19 40	19 57	20 10	20 25	20 40	20 55		21 10	21 25	21 40	21 55	22 10
		d	17 47	17 56	18 11	18 26	18 41	18 56		19 11	19 26	19 41	19 57	20 11	20 26	20 41	20 56		21 11	21 26	21 41	21 56	22 11
Johnstone		d	17 53	18 00	18 15	18 30	18 45	19 00		19 15	19 30	19 45	20 02	20 15	20 30	20 45	21 00		21 15	21 30	21 45	22 02	22 15
Milliken Park		d	17 56	18 03		18 33		19 03			19 33		20 04		20 33		21 03			21 33		22 04	
Howwood		d	17 59			18 36					19 36				20 36					21 36			
Lochwinnoch		d	18 03			18 40					19 40				20 40					21 40			
Glengarnock		d	18 08	18 11		18 45		19 11			19 45		20 12		20 45		21 11			21 45		22 12	
Dalry		d	18 12	18 15	18 26	18 49	18 57				19 49				20 49					21 49			
Kilwinning		d	18 16	18 20	18 31	18 54	19 02	19 18		19 29	19 54	20 00	20 19	20 29	20 54	20 59	21 18		21 29	21 53	21 59	22 19	22 29
Stevenston		d	18 20	18 23		18 57		19 21			19 57		20 23		20 57		21 21			21 57		22 21	
Saltcoats		d	18 22	18 26		19 00		19 24			20 00		20 24		21 00		21 24			22 00		22 24	
Ardrossan South Beach		d	18 24	18 28		19 02		19 26			20 02		20 26		21 02		21 26			22 02		22 26	
Ardrossan Town		d	18a27			19 06					20 06				21 06					22 06			
Ardrossan Harbour		a				19 09					20 09				21 09					22 09			
West Kilbride		d		18 34				19 32					20 32				21 32					22 32	
Fairlie		d		18 39				19 39					20 37				21 37					22 37	
Largs		a		18 48				19 44					20 44				21 44					22 44	
Irvine		d			18 35		19 06			19 33		20 04		20 33		21 03			21 33		22 03		22 33
Barassie		d			18 40		19 11					20 09				21 08					22 08		
Troon		d			18 43		19 14		19 17	19 39		20 12		20 39		21 11		21 22	21 39		22 11		22 39
Prestwick Int. Airport ✈		d			18 47		19 18		19 21	19 43		20 16		20 43		21 15		21 27	21 43		22 15		22 43
Prestwick Town		d			18 49		19 20		19 23	19 45		20 18		20 45		21 17		21 29	21 45		22 17		22 45
Newton-on-Ayr		d			18 52		19 23					20 21				21 20					22 20		
Ayr		a			18 56		19 26		19 30	19 52		20 25		20 52		21 24		21 34	21 52		22 24		22 52

Station		d/a	SR SX B	SR	SR	SR	SR SO A	SR	SR FO	SR FX	SR	SR FO	SR FSX
Glasgow Central 15	219	d	22 12	22 15	22 30	22 45		23 00	23 15	23 15	23 30	23 45	23 45
Paisley Gilmour Street	219	a		22 25	22 40	22 55		23 10	23 25	23 25	23 40	23 55	23 55
		d		22 26	22 41	22 56		23 11	23 26	23 26	23 41	23 56	23 56
Johnstone		d		22 30	22 45	23 00		23 15	23 30	23 30	23 45	23 59	23 59
Milliken Park		d		22 33		23 03			23 33	23 33		00 03	00 03
Howwood		d		22 36					23 36	23 36		00 06	00 06
Lochwinnoch		d		22 40					23 40	23 40		00 10	00 10
Glengarnock		d		22 45		23 11			23 45	23 45		00 15	00 15
Dalry		d		22 49					23 49	23 49		00 19	00 19
Kilwinning		d		22 56	23 00	23 18		23 27	23 54	23 54	23 59	00 23	00 23
Stevenston		d		23 00		23 21			23 57	23 57		00 27	00 27
Saltcoats		d		23 02		23 24			23 59	23 59		00 29	00 29
Ardrossan South Beach		d		23 04		23 26			00 02	00 02		00 31	00a32
Ardrossan Town		d		23a07					00a06				
Ardrossan Harbour		a											
West Kilbride		d				23 32				00 08		00 37	
Fairlie		d				23 37				00 14		00 43	
Largs		a				23 44				00 19		00 49	
Irvine		d			23 04			23 33			00 03		
Barassie		d			23 09						00 08		
Troon		d	23 22		23 12		23 22	23 39			00 11		
Prestwick Int. Airport ✈		d	23 27		23 16		23 27	23 43			00 15		
Prestwick Town		d	23 29		23 18		23 29	23 45			00 17		
Newton-on-Ayr		d			23 21						00 20		
Ayr		a	23 36		23 24		23 36	23 52			00 25		

Sundays

until 25 September

Station		d/a	SR C	SR C	SR	SR	SR	SR	SR	SR	SR	SR	SR	SR	SR	SR	SR	SR ◇ B	SR	SR	SR	SR	SR	SR
Glasgow Central 15	219	d	23p15	23p30	08 12				09 12				10 12			11 15	11 30	11 42	11 45	12 00	12 30	12 42	13 00	13 30
Paisley Gilmour Street	219	a	23p25	23p40												11 25	11 40	11 52	11 58	12 10	12 40	12 55	13 10	13 40
		d	23p26	23p41		08 51	09 11	09 41		09 54	10 11	10 41		10 55	11 11	11 26	11 41	11 53	11 58	12 11	12 41	12 56	13 11	13 41
Johnstone		d	23p30	23p45		08 55	09 15	09 45		09 57	10 15	10 45		10 59	11 15	11 30	11 45		12 03	12 15	12 45	13 00	13 15	13 45
Milliken Park		d	23p33			08 58				10 01				11 02		11 33			12 05			13 03		
Howwood		d	23p36							10 04				11 05					12 08			13 06		
Lochwinnoch		d	23p40							10 08				11 09					12 12			13 10		
Glengarnock		d	23p45			09 06				10 13				11 14					12 17			13 15		
Dalry		d	23p49			09 10				10 17				11 18					12 21			13 19		
Kilwinning		d	23p54	23p59		09 15	09 29	09 59		10 22	10 29	10 59		11 23	11 29	11 46	11 59	12 11	12 26	12 30	12 59	13 23	13 29	13 59
Stevenston		d	23p57			09 18				10 24				11 26		11 49			12 30			13 27		
Saltcoats		d	23p59			09 21				10 28				11 29		11 52			12 32			13 29		
Ardrossan South Beach		d	00 02			09 23				10 29				11 31		11 54			12 34			13 31		
Ardrossan Town		d				09 27										11 59								
Ardrossan Harbour		a				09 30										12 02								
West Kilbride		d	00 08							10 35				11 37					12 40			13 37		
Fairlie		d	00 14							10 41				11 42					12 46			13 43		
Largs		a	00 19							10 47				11 48					12 51			13 48		
Irvine		d		00 03			09 33	10 03			10 33	11 03			11 33		12 03			12 34	13 03		13 33	14 03
Barassie		d		00 08			09 38				10 38				11 38					12 39			13 38	
Troon		d		00 11	09 12		09 41	10 09	10 14		10 41	11 09	11 13		11 41		12 09			12 42	13 09		13 41	14 09
Prestwick Int. Airport ✈		d		00 15	09 16		09 45	10 13	10 18		10 45	11 13	11 18		11 45		12 13			12 46	13 13		13 45	14 13
Prestwick Town		d		00 17	09 18		09 47	10 15	10 20		10 47	11 15	11 20		11 47		12 15			12 48	13 15		13 47	14 15
Newton-on-Ayr		d		00 20																				
Ayr		a		00 25	09 29		09 54	10 22	10 26		10 54	11 22	11 26		11 54		12 22	12 29		12 54	13 22		13 54	14 22

A From Kilmarnock to Stranraer

B To Stranraer

C not 22 May

Table 221

Sundays

until 25 September

Glasgow Central - Ardrossan, Largs and Ayr

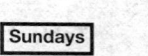

			SR	SR	SR	SR	SR		SR	SR	SR	SR	SR ◇ A	SR	SR	SR	SR		SR	SR	SR	SR	SR	SR	SR	SR
Glasgow Central 15	219	d	13 42	14 00	14 05	14 30	14 42		15 00	15 30	15 42	16 00	16 25	16 30	16 42	16 55	17 00		17 30	17 42	18 00	18 30	18 42	19 00	19 42	20 00
Paisley Gilmour Street	219	a	13 54	14 10	14 15	14 40	14 54		15 10	15 40	15 53	16 10	16 38	16 41	16 55	17 06	17 10		17 40	17 54	18 10	18 40	18 53	19 10	19 53	20 10
		d	13 54	14 11	14 16	14 41	14 54		15 11	15 41	15 53	16 11	16 39	16 41	16 55	17 07	17 12		17 41	17 54	18 11	18 41	18 53	19 11	19 53	20 11
Johnstone		d	13 59	14 15	14 20	14 45	14 59		15 15	15 45	15 58	16 15		16 46	17 00	17 11	17 17		17 45	17 59	18 15	18 45	18 58	19 15	19 58	20 15
Milliken Park		d	14 01		14 23		15 01				16 00				17 02	17 14				18 01			19 00		20 00	
Howwood		d	14 04				15 04				16 03				17 05					18 04			19 03		20 03	
Lochwinnoch		d	14 08				15 08				16 07				17 09					18 08			19 07		20 07	
Glengarnock		d	14 13				15 13				16 12				17 14					18 13			19 12		20 12	
Dalry		d	14 17				15 17				16 16				17 18					18 17			19 16		20 16	
Kilwinning		d	14 22	14 29	14 37	14 59	15 22		15 29	16 00	16 20	16 29	16 56	17 00	17 23	17 28	17 31		17 59	18 22	18 29	18 59	19 21	19 29	20 21	20 29
Stevenston		d	14 26		14 41		15 26				16 24				17 27	17 31				18 26			19 25		20 25	
Saltcoats		d	14 28		14 43		15 28				16 26				17 29	17 34				18 28			19 27		20 27	
Ardrossan South Beach		d	14 30		14 45		15 30				16 28				17 31	17 36				18 30			19 29		20 29	
Ardrossan Town		d			14 49											17 40										
Ardrossan Harbour		a			14 52											17 43										
West Kilbride		d	14 36				15 36				16 34				17 37					18 36			19 35		20 35	
Fairlie		d	14 42				15 42				16 40				17 43					18 42			19 41		20 41	
Largs		a	14 47				15 47				16 47				17 48					18 47			19 47		20 47	
Irvine		d		14 33		15 03			15 33	16 04		16 33		17 04			17 35		18 03		18 33	19 03		19 33		20 33
Barassie		d		14 38					15 38			16 38					17 40				18 38			19 38		20 38
Troon		d		14 41		15 09			15 41	16 10		16 41		17 10			17 43		18 09		18 41	19 09		19 41		20 41
Prestwick Int. Airport ✈		d		14 45		15 13			15 45	16 14		16 45		17 14			17 47		18 13		18 45	19 13		19 45		20 45
Prestwick Town		d		14 47		15 15			15 47	16 17		16 47		17 16			17 49		18 15		18 47	19 15		19 47		20 47
Newton-on-Ayr		d																								
Ayr		a		14 54		15 22			15 54	16 22		16 54	17 17	17 24			17 54		18 22		18 54	19 22		19 54		20 54

			SR		SR	SR	SR	SR	SR
Glasgow Central 15	219	d	20 42		21 00				
Paisley Gilmour Street	219	a	20 53		21 10				
		d	20 53		21 11	21 56	22 11	22 53	23 11
Johnstone		d	20 58		21 15	22 00	22 15	22 58	23 15
Milliken Park		d	21 00			22 02		23 00	
Howwood		d	21 03			22 05		23 03	
Lochwinnoch		d	21 07			22 09		23 07	
Glengarnock		d	21 12			22 14		23 12	
Dalry		d	21 16			22 18		23 16	
Kilwinning		d	21 24		21 29	22 23	22 29	23 26	23 29
Stevenston		d	21 28			22 27		23 29	
Saltcoats		d	21 30			22 29		23 32	
Ardrossan South Beach		d	21 32			22 31		23 34	
Ardrossan Town		d							
Ardrossan Harbour		a							
West Kilbride		d	21 38			22 38		23 40	
Fairlie		d	21 44			22 42		23 45	
Largs		a	21 49			22 50		23 51	
Irvine		d			21 33		22 33		23 33
Barassie		d			21 38		22 38		23 38
Troon		d			21 41		22 41		23 41
Prestwick Int. Airport ✈		d			21 45		22 45		23 45
Prestwick Town		d			21 47		22 47		23 47
Newton-on-Ayr		d							
Ayr		a			21 54		22 54		23 54

Sundays

2 October to 20 November

			SR	SR	SR	SR	SR	SR	SR	SR	SR		SR	SR	SR	SR ◇ A	SR	SR	SR	SR	SR		SR	SR	SR	SR
Glasgow Central 15	219	d	23p15	23p30	08 12			09 12			10 12				11 15	11 42	11 45	12 00	12 42	13 00	13 42		14 00	14 05	14 42	15 00
Paisley Gilmour Street	219	a	23p25	23p40											11 25	11 52	11 58	12 10	12 55	13 10	13 54		14 10	14 15	14 54	15 10
		d	23p26	23p41		08 51	09 11		09 54	10 11			10 55	11 11	11 26	11 53	11 58	12 11	12 56	13 11	13 54		14 11	14 16	14 54	15 11
Johnstone		d	23p30	23p45		08 55	09 15		09 57	10 15			10 59	11 15	11 30		12 03	12 15	13 00	13 15	13 59		14 15	14 20	14 59	15 15
Milliken Park		d	23p33			08 58			10 01				11 02		11 33		12 05		13 03		14 01			14 23	15 01	
Howwood		d	23p36						10 04				11 05				12 08		13 06		14 04				15 04	
Lochwinnoch		d	23p40						10 08				11 09				12 12		13 10		14 08				15 08	
Glengarnock		d	23p45			09 06			10 13				11 14				12 17		13 15		14 13				15 13	
Dalry		d	23p49			09 10			10 17				11 18				12 21		13 19		14 17				15 17	
Kilwinning		d	23p54	23p59		09 15	09 29		10 22	10 29			11 23	11 29	11 46	12 11	12 26	12 30	13 23	13 29	14 22		14 29	14 37	15 22	15 29
Stevenston		d	23p57			09 18			10 24				11 26		11 49		12 30		13 27		14 26			14 41	15 26	
Saltcoats		d	23p59			09 21			10 28				11 29		11 52		12 32		13 29		14 28			14 43	15 28	
Ardrossan South Beach		d	00 02			09 23			10 29				11 31		11 54		12 34		13 31		14 30			14 45	15 30	
Ardrossan Town		d				09 27									11 59									14 49		
Ardrossan Harbour		a				09 30									12 02									14 52		
West Kilbride		d	00 08						10 35				11 37				12 40		13 37		14 36				15 36	
Fairlie		d	00 14						10 41				11 42				12 46		13 43		14 42				15 42	
Largs		a	00 19						10 47				11 48				12 51		13 48		14 47				15 47	
Irvine		d		00 03			09 33			10 33				11 33				12 34		13 33			14 33			15 33
Barassie		d		00 08			09 38			10 38				11 38				12 39		13 38			14 38			15 38
Troon		d		00 11	09 12		09 41	10 14		10 41	11 13			11 41				12 42		13 41			14 41			15 41
Prestwick Int. Airport ✈		d		00 15	09 16		09 45	10 18		10 45	11 18			11 45				12 46		13 45			14 45			15 45
Prestwick Town		d		00 17	09 18		09 47	10 20		10 47	11 20			11 47				12 48		13 47			14 47			15 47
Newton-on-Ayr		d		00 20																						
Ayr		a		00 25	09 29		09 54	10 26		10 54	11 26			11 54		12 29		12 54		13 54			14 54			15 54

A To Stranraer

Table 221

Sundays

2 October to 20 November

Glasgow Central - Ardrossan, Largs and Ayr

		SR	SR	SR	SR	SR		SR	SR	SR	SR	SR	SR	SR	SR	SR		SR	SR	SR	SR				
				◇ A																					
Glasgow Central 15	219 d	15 42	16 00	16 25	16 42	16 55		17 00	17 42	18 00	18 42	19 00	19 42	20 00	20 42	21 00									
Paisley Gilmour Street	219 a	15 53	16 10	16 38	16 55	17 06		17 10	17 54	18 10	18 53	19 10	19 53	20 10	20 53	21 10									
	d	15 53	16 11	16 39	16 55	17 07		17 12	17 54	18 11	18 53	19 11	19 53	20 11	20 53	21 11		21 56	22 11	22 53	23 11				
Johnstone	d	15 58	16 15		17 00	17 11		17 17	17 59	18 15	18 58	19 15	19 58	20 15	20 58	21 15		22 00	22 15	22 58	23 15				
Milliken Park	d	16 00			17 02	17 14			18 01		19 00		20 00		21 00			22 02		23 00					
Howwood	d	16 03			17 05				18 04		19 03		20 03		21 03			22 05		23 03					
Lochwinnoch	d	16 07			17 09				18 08		19 07		20 07		21 07			22 09		23 07					
Glengarnock	d	16 12			17 14				18 13		19 12		20 12		21 12			22 14		23 12					
Dalry	d	16 16			17 18				18 17		19 16		20 16		21 16			22 18		23 16					
Kilwinning	d	16 20	16 29	16 56	17 23	17 28		17 31	18 22	18 29	19 21	19 29	20 21	20 29	21 24	21 29		22 23	22 29	23 26	23 29				
Stevenston	d	16 24			17 27	17 31			18 26		19 25		20 25		21 28			22 27		23 29					
Saltcoats	d	16 26			17 29	17 34			18 28		19 27		20 27		21 30			22 29		23 32					
Ardrossan South Beach	d	16 28			17 31	17 36			18 30		19 29		20 29		21 32			22 31		23 34					
Ardrossan Town	d					17 40																			
Ardrossan Harbour	a					17 43																			
West Kilbride	d	16 34			17 37				18 36		19 35		20 35		21 38			22 38		23 40					
Fairlie	d	16 40			17 43				18 42		19 41		20 41		21 44			22 42		23 45					
Largs	a	16 47			17 48				18 47		19 47		20 47		21 49			22 50		23 51					
Irvine	d		16 33					17 35		18 33		19 33		20 33		21 33			22 33		23 33				
Barassie	d		16 38					17 40		18 38		19 38		20 38		21 38			22 38		23 38				
Troon	d		16 41					17 43		18 41		19 41		20 41		21 41			22 41		23 41				
Prestwick Int. Airport ✈	d		16 45					17 47		18 45		19 45		20 45		21 45			22 45		23 45				
Prestwick Town	d		16 47					17 49		18 47		19 47		20 47		21 47			22 47		23 47				
Newton-on-Ayr	d																								
Ayr	a		16 54	17 17				17 54		18 54		19 54		20 54		21 54			22 54		23 54				

Sundays

from 27 November

		SR	SR	SR	SR	SR	SR	SR	SR	SR		SR	SR	SR	SR	SR	SR	SR	SR	SR		SR	SR	SR	SR
																		◇ A							
Glasgow Central 15	219 d	23p15	23p30	08 12				09 12					10 12			11 15	11 30	11 42	11 45	12 00		12 30	12 42	13 00	13 30
Paisley Gilmour Street	219 a	23p25	23p40													11 25	11 40	11 52	11 58	12 10		12 40	12 55	13 10	13 40
	d	23p26	23p41		08 51	09 11	09 41		09 54	10 11		10 41		10 55	11 11	11 26	11 41	11 53	11 58	12 11		12 41	12 56	13 11	13 41
Johnstone	d	23p30	23p45		08 55	09 15	09 45		09 57	10 15		10 45		10 59	11 15	11 30	11 45		12 03	12 15		12 45	13 00	13 15	13 45
Milliken Park	d	23p33			08 58				10 01					11 02		11 33			12 05				13 03		
Howwood	d	23p36							10 04					11 05					12 08				13 06		
Lochwinnoch	d	23p40							10 08					11 09					12 12				13 10		
Glengarnock	d	23p45			09 06				10 13					11 14					12 17				13 15		
Dalry	d	23p49			09 10				10 17					11 18					12 21				13 19		
Kilwinning	d	23p54	23p59		09 15	09 29	09 59		10 22	10 29		10 59		11 23	11 29	11 46	11 59	12 11	12 26	12 30		12 59	13 23	13 29	13 59
Stevenston	d	23p57			09 18				10 24					11 26		11 49			12 30				13 27		
Saltcoats	d	23p59			09 21				10 28					11 29		11 52			12 32				13 29		
Ardrossan South Beach	d	00 02			09 23				10 29					11 31		11 54			12 34				13 31		
Ardrossan Town	d				09 27											11 59									
Ardrossan Harbour	a				09 30											12 02									
West Kilbride	d	00 08							10 35					11 37					12 40				13 37		
Fairlie	d	00 14							10 41					11 42					12 46				13 43		
Largs	a	00 19							10 47					11 48					12 51				13 48		
Irvine	d		00 03			09 33	10 03			10 33		11 03			11 33		12 03			12 34		13 03		13 33	14 03
Barassie	d		00 08			09 38				10 38					11 38					12 39				13 38	
Troon	d		00 11	09 12		09 41	10 09	10 14		10 41		11 09	11 13		11 41		12 09			12 42		13 09		13 41	14 09
Prestwick Int. Airport ✈	d		00 15	09 16		09 45	10 13	10 18		10 45		11 13	11 18		11 45		12 13			12 46		13 13		13 45	14 13
Prestwick Town	d		00 17	09 18		09 47	10 15	10 20		10 47		11 15	11 20		11 47		12 15			12 48		13 15		13 47	14 15
Newton-on-Ayr	d		00 20																						
Ayr	a		00 25	09 29		09 54	10 22	10 26		10 54		11 22	11 26		11 54		12 22	12 29		12 54		13 22		13 54	14 22

		SR	SR	SR	SR	SR		SR	SR	SR	SR	SR	SR	SR	SR	SR		SR	SR	SR	SR	SR	SR	SR	SR
												◇ A													
Glasgow Central 15	219 d	13 42	14 00	14 05	14 30	14 42		15 00	15 30	15 42	16 00	16 25	16 30	16 42	16 55	17 00		17 30	17 42	18 00	18 42	19 00	19 42	20 00	20 42
Paisley Gilmour Street	219 a	13 54	14 10	14 15	14 40	14 54		15 10	15 40	15 53	16 10	16 38	16 41	16 55	17 06	17 10		17 40	17 54	18 10	18 53	19 10	19 53	20 10	20 53
	d	13 54	14 11	14 16	14 41	14 54		15 11	15 41	15 53	16 11	16 39	16 41	16 55	17 07	17 12		17 41	17 54	18 11	18 53	19 11	19 53	20 11	20 53
Johnstone	d	13 59	14 15	14 20	14 45	14 59		15 15	15 45	15 58	16 15		16 46	17 00	17 11	17 17		17 45	17 59	18 15	18 58	19 15	19 58	20 15	20 58
Milliken Park	d	14 01		14 23		15 01				16 00				17 02	17 14				18 01		19 00		20 00		21 00
Howwood	d	14 04				15 04				16 03				17 05					18 04		19 03		20 03		21 03
Lochwinnoch	d	14 08				15 08				16 07				17 09					18 08		19 07		20 07		21 07
Glengarnock	d	14 13				15 13				16 12				17 14					18 13		19 12		20 12		21 12
Dalry	d	14 17				15 17				16 16				17 18					18 17		19 16		20 16		21 16
Kilwinning	d	14 22	14 29	14 37	14 59	15 22		15 29	16 00	16 20	16 29	16 56	17 00	17 23	17 28	17 31		17 59	18 22	18 29	19 21	19 29	20 21	20 29	21 24
Stevenston	d	14 26		14 41		15 26				16 24				17 27	17 31				18 26		19 25		20 25		21 28
Saltcoats	d	14 28		14 43		15 28				16 26				17 29	17 34				18 28		19 27		20 27		21 30
Ardrossan South Beach	d	14 30		14 45		15 30				16 28				17 31	17 36				18 30		19 29		20 29		21 32
Ardrossan Town	d			14 49											17 40										
Ardrossan Harbour	a			14 52											17 43										
West Kilbride	d	14 36				15 36				16 34				17 37					18 36		19 35		20 35		21 38
Fairlie	d	14 42				15 42				16 40				17 43					18 42		19 41		20 41		21 44
Largs	a	14 47				15 47				16 47				17 48					18 47		19 47		20 47		21 49
Irvine	d		14 33		15 03			15 33	16 04		16 33		17 04			17 35		18 03		18 33		19 33		20 33	
Barassie	d		14 38					15 38			16 38					17 40				18 38		19 38		20 38	
Troon	d		14 41		15 09			15 41	16 10		16 41		17 10			17 43		18 09		18 41		19 41		20 41	
Prestwick Int. Airport ✈	d		14 45		15 13			15 45	16 14		16 45		17 14			17 47		18 13		18 45		19 45		20 45	
Prestwick Town	d		14 47		15 15			15 47	16 17		16 47		17 16			17 49		18 15		18 47		19 47		20 47	
Newton-on-Ayr	d																								
Ayr	a		14 54		15 22			15 54	16 22		16 54	17 17	17 24			17 54		18 22		18 54		19 54		20 54	

A To Stranraer

Table 221

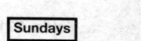

Sundays
from 27 November

Glasgow Central - Ardrossan, Largs and Ayr

			SR		SR	SR	SR	SR
Glasgow Central 15	219	d	21 00					
Paisley Gilmour Street	219	a	21 10					
		d	21 11		21 56	22 11	22 53	23 11
Johnstone		d	21 15		22 00	22 15	22 58	23 15
Milliken Park		d			22 02		23 00	
Howwood		d			22 05		23 03	
Lochwinnoch		d			22 09		23 07	
Glengarnock		d			22 14		23 12	
Dalry		d			22 18		23 16	
Kilwinning		d	21 29		22 23	22 29	23 26	23 29
Stevenston		d			22 27		23 29	
Saltcoats		d			22 29		23 32	
Ardrossan South Beach		d			22 31		23 34	
Ardrossan Town		d						
Ardrossan Harbour		a						
West Kilbride		d			22 38		23 40	
Fairlie		d			22 42		23 45	
Largs		a			22 50		23 51	
Irvine		d	21 33			22 33		23 33
Barassie		d	21 38			22 38		23 38
Troon		d	21 41			22 41		23 41
Prestwick Int. Airport	✈	d	21 45			22 45		23 45
Prestwick Town		d	21 47			22 47		23 47
Newton-on-Ayr		d						
Ayr		a	21 54			22 54		23 54

Ayr, Largs and Ardrossan - Glasgow Central

Miles	Miles	Miles			SR	SR	SR	SR	SR	SR SX	SR SX A	SR SO A	SR SX		SR SO	SR SX	SR SX	SR	SR SX	SR SO	SR SX	SR SX	SR		SR SO
0	—	—	**Ayr**	d	05 12	05 40	06 13	06 43		06 57	06 50	06 50	07 13		07 13	07 25		07 43			07 58		08 13		
1¼	—	—	Newton-on-Ayr	d	05 15	05 43	06 16	06 46					07 16		07 16						08 01		08 16		
3¼	—	—	Prestwick Town	d	05 18	05 46	06 19	06 49		07 02	06 55	06 55	07 19		07 19	07 30		07 48			08 03		08 19		
3¾	—	—	Prestwick Int. Airport ✈	d	05 20	05 48	06 21	06 51		07 04	06 57	06 57	07 21		07 21	07 32		07 50			08 05		08 21		
6½	—	—	Troon	d	05 24	05 52	06 25	06 55		07 08	07 02	07 02	07 25		07 25	07 36		07 54			08 09		08 25		
7¾	—	—	Barassie	d	05 26	05 54	06 27	06 57		07 10			07 27		07 27	07 38					08 11		08 27		
11½	—	—	Irvine	d	05 31	05 59	06 32	07 02		07 15			07 32		07 32	07 43		08 00			08 16		08 32		
—	0	—	**Largs**	d					06 41								07 25		07 42	07 42					
—	3	—	Fairlie	d					06 46								07 30		07 47	07 47					
—	7	—	West Kilbride	d					06 51								07 35		07 52	07 52					
—	—	0	**Ardrossan Harbour**	d																		08 11			08 29
—	—	0½	Ardrossan Town	d																		08 14			08 31
—	11½	1	Ardrossan South Beach	d					06 57								07 41		07 58	07 58		08 16			08 33
—	12½	2	Saltcoats	d					07 02								07 43		08 00	08 00		08 18			08 35
—	13¾	3¼	Stevenston	d					07 05								07 46		08 03	08 03		08 21			08 37
14¾	16	5½	Kilwinning	d	05 36	06 04	06 37	07 07	07 10	07 20			07 37		07 37		07 50	08 04	08 08	08 08	08 20	08 25	08 34		08 41
18½	19¾	9¼	Dalry	d	05 40	06 08			07 14	07 24			07 41		07 41		07 55		08 12	08 12		08 30			08 46
21	22¼	11¾	Glengarnock	d	05 44	06 12			07 18	07 28					07 45	07 52			08 16	08 16		08 34			08 50
25	26¼	15¾	Lochwinnoch	d	05 49	06 17				07 33					07 50		08 01		08 21	08 21		08 39			08 55
28½	29¾	19¼	Howwood	d	05 53	06 21				07 37					07 54	07 59						08 43			08 59
30	31¼	20¾	Milliken Park	d	05 56	06 24			07 26	07 40					07 57		08 06		08 26	08 26		08 46			09 02
30¾	32	21½	Johnstone	d	05 59	06 27	06 50	07 20	07 29	07 43			07 52		08 00	08 03	08 09	08 18	08 29	08 29	08 34	08 48	08 50		09 05
34¼	35½	25	Paisley Gilmour Street 219	a	06 03	06 31	06 55	07 25	07 34	07 47			07 57		08 04	08 07	08 13	08 22	08 35	08 35	08 42	08 53	08 56		09 09
—	—	—		d	06 04	06 32	06 55	07 25	07 34	07 48			07 57		08 05	08 08	08 13	08 23	08 35	08 35	08 43	08 53	08 56		09 10
41½	42¾	32¼	**Glasgow Central** 15 219	a	06 15	06 43	07 07	07 38	07 47	07 59	08 00	08 09	08 09		08 16	08 19	08 24	08 34	08 46	08 47	08 55	09 04	09 07		09 22

		SR SX	SR	SR SO	SR ◇ B	SR	SR	SR	SR		SR	SR	SR	SR	SR	SR	SR ◇ B	SR	SR		SR	SR	SR C	SR	SR
Ayr	d		08 43		08 36	09 13		09 43			10 13		10 43		11 13		11 36	11 43			12 13		12 36	12 43	
Newton-on-Ayr	d					09 16					10 16				11 16						12 16				
Prestwick Town	d		08 48		08 41	09 19		09 48			10 19		10 48		11 19			11 48			12 19		12 41	12 47	
Prestwick Int. Airport ✈	d		08 50		08 43	09 21		09 50			10 21		10 50		11 21			11 50			12 21		12 43	12 49	
Troon	d		08 54		08 48	09 25		09 54			10 25		10 54		11 25			11 54			12 25		12a48	12 53	
Barassie	d					09 27					10 27				11 27						12 27				
Irvine	d		08 59			09 32		09 59			10 32		10 59		11 32			11 59			12 32			12 58	
Largs	d	08 28		08 51					09 53					10 53					11 53						12 53
Fairlie	d	08 33		08 56					09 58					10 58					11 58						12 58
West Kilbride	d	08 38		09 01					10 03					11 03					12 05						13 05
Ardrossan Harbour	d						09 30					10 28				11 28						12 28			
Ardrossan Town	d						09 33					10 31				11 31						12 31			
Ardrossan South Beach	d	08 44		09 07			09 35		10 09			10 34		11 09		11 34			12 11			12 33			13 11
Saltcoats	d	08 46		09 09			09 37		10 11			10 36		11 11		11 36			12 13			12 35			13 13
Stevenston	d	08 49		09 12			09 40		10 14			10 39		11 14		11 39			12 16			12 38			13 16
Kilwinning	d	08 53	09 04	09 16		09 37	09 45	10 04	10 18		10 38	10 43	11 04	11 18	11 37	11 43	11 51	12 04	12 20		12 37	12 43		13 03	13 20
Dalry	d	08 57				09 41	09 49					10 47				11 47						12 47			
Glengarnock	d	09 01		09 22			09 53		10 25			10 51		11 25		11 51			12 26			12 51			13 26
Lochwinnoch	d			09 27			09 58					10 56				11 56						12 56			
Howwood	d			09 31				10 16				11 00				12 00						13 00			
Milliken Park	d	09 09		09 32			10 03		10 33			11 03		11 33		12 03			12 34			13 03			13 34
Johnstone	d	09 12	09 18	09 35		09 52	10 06	10 20	10 35		10 50	11 06	11 18	11 35	11 50	12 06		12 18	12 37		12 50	13 06		13 18	13 37
Paisley Gilmour Street 219	a	09 16	09 23	09 39		09 57	10 10	10 24	10 40		10 55	11 10	11 23	11 39	11 55	12 10	12 15	12 23	12 41		12 55	13 10		13 23	13 41
	d	09 17	09 24	09 40		09 57	10 11	10 25	10 41		10 55	11 11	11 23	11 39	11 55	12 11	12 15	12 24	12 42		12 55	13 11		13 24	13 42
Glasgow Central 15 219	a	09 31	09 36	09 53	10 05	10 09	10 22	10 36	10 52		11 07	11 22	11 36	11 52	12 07	12 22	12 32	12 35	12 52		13 07	13 22		13 35	13 52

		SR	SR	SR SO	SR SX		SR	SR SO	SR SX	SR ◇ D	SR	SR	SR	SR	SR		SR A	SR	SR	SR ◇ D	SR	SR	SR	SR	SR
Ayr	d	13 13		13 43	13 43			14 13	14 13	14 18		14 43		15 13			15 18	15 43		16 06	16 13		16 43		17 13
Newton-on-Ayr	d	13 16						14 16	14 16					15 16							16 16		16 46		17 16
Prestwick Town	d	13 19		13 48	13 48			14 19	14 19	14 23		14 48		15 19			15 23	15 48		16 11	16 19		16 49		17 19
Prestwick Int. Airport ✈	d	13 21		13 50	13 50			14 21	14 21	14 25		14 50		15 21			15 25	15 50		16 13	16 21		16 51		17 21
Troon	d	13 24		13 54	13 54			14 25	14 25	14a30		14 54		15 25			15 30	15 54		16a18	16 25		16 55		17 25
Barassie	d	13 26						14 27	14 27					15 27							16 27				17 27
Irvine	d	13 31		13 59	13 59			14 32	14 32			14 59		15 32				15 59			16 32		17 00		17 32
Largs	d						13 53						14 53						15 53					16 50	
Fairlie	d						13 58						14 58						15 58					16 55	
West Kilbride	d						14 03						15 03						16 03					17 00	
Ardrossan Harbour	d		13 28								14 28				15 28							16 28			
Ardrossan Town	d		13 31								14 31				15 31							16 31			
Ardrossan South Beach	d		13 34				14 09				14 33		15 09		15 34				16 09			16 34		17 06	
Saltcoats	d		13 36				14 11				14 35		15 11		15 36				16 11			16 36		17 08	
Stevenston	d		13 39				14 14				14 38		15 14		15 39				16 14			16 39		17 11	
Kilwinning	d	13 36	13 43	14 04	14 04		14 18	14 37	14 37		14 42	15 04	15 18	15 37	15 43			16 04	16 18		16 37	16 43	17 05	17 15	17 36
Dalry	d		13 47								14 47				15 47							16 47		17 20	17 41
Glengarnock	d		13 51				14 25				14 51		15 25	15 43	15 51				16 25		16 43	16 51		17 24	
Lochwinnoch	d		13 56								14 56				15 56							16 56		17 29	
Howwood	d		14 00								15 00				16 00							17 00			
Milliken Park	d		14 03				14 33				15 03		15 33		16 03				16 33			17 03		17 34	
Johnstone	d	13 49	14 06	14 18	14 18		14 35	14 50	14 50		15 05	15 18	15 35	15 52	16 06			16 18	16 35		16 52	17 06	17 19	17 36	17 52
Paisley Gilmour Street 219	a	13 55	14 10	14 22	14 22		14 40	14 55	14 55		15 10	15 24	15 40	15 57	16 10			16 22	16 40		16 57	17 10	17 23	17 41	17 58
	d	13 55	14 11	14 23	14 23		14 40	14 55	14 55		15 10	15 25	15 40	15 57	16 11			16 23	16 41		16 57	17 11	17 24	17 41	17 58
Glasgow Central 15 219	a	14 07	14 24	14 34	14 35		14 52	15 06	15 07		15 22	15 36	15 52	16 09	16 25		16 33	16 34	16 52		17 09	17 22	17 36	17 55	18 09

A From Girvan
B From Stranraer
C From Girvan to Kilmarnock
D From Stranraer to Kilmarnock

Table 221

Mondays to Saturdays

Ayr, Largs and Ardrossan - Glasgow Central

			SR	SR SX	SR SO	SR	SR	SR A	SR	SR	SR	SR	SR	SR	SR	SR A	SR SX	SR SO	SR	SR	SR	SR	SR ◇ B
Ayr		d		17 43	17 43		18 13	18 17	18 43		19 13		19 43		20 13	20 18			20 43		21 13		21 08
Newton-on-Ayr		d					18 16				19 16				20 16						21 16		
Prestwick Town		d		17 48	17 48		18 19	18 23	18 48		19 19		19 48		20 19	20 23			20 48		21 19		21 13
Prestwick Int. Airport	✈	d		17 50	17 50		18 21	18 25	18 50		19 21		19 50		20 21	20 25			20 50		21 21		21 15
Troon		d		17 54	17 54		18 25	18a30	18 54		19 25		19 54		20 25	20a30			20 54		21 25		21 20
Barassie		d					18 27				19 27				20 27						21 27		
Irvine		d		17 59	17 59		18 32		18 59		19 32		19 59		20 32				20 59		21 32		
Largs		d	17 35							18 53				19 53						20 53			
Fairlie		d	17 40							18 58				19 58						20 58			
West Kilbride		d	17 45							19 03				20 03						21 03			
Ardrossan Harbour		d				18 00						19 28					20 33	20 33				21 28	
Ardrossan Town		d				18 03						19 30					20 35	20 35				21 31	
Ardrossan South Beach		d	17 51			18 06				19 09		19 34		20 09			20 38	20 38		21 09		21 34	
Saltcoats		d	17 53			18 08				19 11		19 36		20 11			20 40	20 40		21 11		21 36	
Stevenston		d	17 56			18 11				19 14		19 39		20 14			20 43	20 43		21 14		21 39	
Kilwinning		d	18 00	18 04	18 04	18 16	18 37		19 04	19 18	19 37	19 43	20 04	20 18	20 36		20 47	20 47	21 04	21 18	21 37	21 43	
Dalry		d	18 05	18 09	18 09		18 41					19 47					20 51	20 51			21 41	21 47	
Glengarnock		d		18 13	18 13	18 23				19 25		19 51		20 25			20 55	20 55		21 25		21 51	
Lochwinnoch		d		18 18	18 18							19 56					21 00	21 00				21 56	
Howwood		d	18 14			18 30						20 00					21 04	21 04				22 00	
Milliken Park		d				18 33				19 33		20 03		20 33			21 07	21 07		21 33		22 03	
Johnstone		d	18 18	18 24	18 24	18 35	18 52		19 18	19 35	19 50	20 06	20 18	20 35	20 50		21 10	21 10	21 18	21 35	21 52	22 06	
Paisley Gilmour Street	219	a	18 22	18 28	18 28	18 40	18 57		19 23	19 40	19 57	20 10	20 25	20 40	20 55		21 14	21 14	21 22	21 40	21 57	22 10	
		d	18 23	18 29	18 29	18 40	18 57		19 23	19 40	19 57	20 11	20 25	20 40	20 55		21 15	21 15	21 23	21 40	21 57	22 11	
Glasgow Central 15	219	a	18 34	18 41	18 42	18 52	19 08		19 34	19 53	20 08	20 22	20 36	20 52	21 07		21 26	21 27	21 34	21 52	22 09	22 22	22 34

			SR	SR	SR	SR ◇ B	SR	SR
Ayr		d	21 43		22 13	22 34		23 00
Newton-on-Ayr		d			22 16			23 03
Prestwick Town		d	21 48		22 19	22 39		23 06
Prestwick Int. Airport	✈	d	21 50		22 21			23 08
Troon		d	21 54		22 25	22 44		23 12
Barassie		d			22 27			23 14
Irvine		d	21 59		22 32			23 19
Largs		d		21 53			22 53	
Fairlie		d		21 58			22 58	
West Kilbride		d		22 03			23 03	
Ardrossan Harbour		d						
Ardrossan Town		d						
Ardrossan South Beach		d		22 09			23 09	
Saltcoats		d		22 11			23 11	
Stevenston		d		22 14			23 14	
Kilwinning		d	22 04	22 18	22 37	22 53	23 18	23 24
Dalry		d	22 09	22 23	22 41			23 28
Glengarnock		d		22 27			23 24	23 32
Lochwinnoch		d					23 29	
Howwood		d					23 33	
Milliken Park		d		22 35			23 36	
Johnstone		d	22 20	22 37	22 52		23 39	23 43
Paisley Gilmour Street	219	a	22 24	22 42	22 57	23 14	23 43	23 47
		d	22 25	22 42	22 57	23 14	23 44	23 48
Glasgow Central 15	219	a	22 36	22 54	23 09	23 25	23 54	23 58

Sundays

until 25 September

			SR	SR	SR	SR	SR	SR	SR	SR	SR	SR	SR	SR	SR	SR ◇ B	SR	SR	SR	SR	SR	SR	SR	SR
Ayr		d	08 19	08 43		09 19	09 25	09 43		10 19	10 27	10 43		11 13	11 43	12 00		12 13		12 43		13 13	13 43	
Newton-on-Ayr		d																						
Prestwick Town		d	08 24	08 48		09 24	09 30	09 48		10 24	10 32	10 48		11 18	11 48			12 18		12 48		13 18	13 48	
Prestwick Int. Airport	✈	d	08 27	08 50		09 26	09 32	09 50		10 26	10 34	10 50		11 20	11 50			12 20		12 50		13 20	13 50	
Troon		d	08 32	08 54		09 32	09 36	09 54		10 32	10 38	10 54		11 24	11 54			12 24		12 54		13 24	13 54	
Barassie		d		08 56				09 56				10 56			11 56					12 56			13 56	
Irvine		d		09 01			09 42	10 01			10 43	11 01		11 29	12 01			12 29		13 01		13 29	14 01	
Largs		d			08 55				09 57				10 53				11 53				12 56			13 53
Fairlie		d			09 00				10 02				10 58				11 58				13 01			13 58
West Kilbride		d			09 05				10 07				11 03				12 03				13 06			14 03
Ardrossan Harbour		d																	12 35					
Ardrossan Town		d																						
Ardrossan South Beach		d			09 11				10 13				11 09				12 09		12 40		13 12			14 09
Saltcoats		d			09 13				10 15				11 11				12 11		12 42		13 14			14 11
Stevenston		d			09 16				10 18				11 14				12 14		12 45		13 17			14 14
Kilwinning		d		09 06	09 20		09 47	10 06	10 22		10 48	11 06	11 18	11 34	12 06	12 15	12 18	12 34	12 49	13 06	13 21	13 34	14 06	14 18
Dalry		d			09 25				10 27				11 23				12 23				13 25			14 23
Glengarnock		d			09 29				10 31				11 27				12 27				13 29			14 27
Lochwinnoch		d			09 34				10 36				11 32				12 32				13 34			14 32
Howwood		d			09 38				10 40				11 36				12 36				13 38			14 36
Milliken Park		d			09 41				10 43				11 39				12 39		13 02		13 41			14 39
Johnstone		d		09 19	09 43		10 01	10 19	10 45		10 59	11 19	11 41	11 51	12 19		12 42	12 51	13 04	13 19	13 44	13 51	14 19	14 41
Paisley Gilmour Street	219	a		09 24	09 49		10 05	10 24	10 50		11 02	11 25	11 46	11 55	12 24	12 36	12 46	12 55	13 09	13 24	13 48	13 55	14 24	14 46
		d										11 26	11 46	11 56	12 24	12 36	12 47	12 56	13 10	13 24	13 48	13 56	14 24	14 46
Glasgow Central 15	219	a	09 36			10 40				11 36		11 36	11 58	12 06	12 36	12 51	12 58	13 06	13 22	13 36	14 03	14 06	14 36	14 58

A From Girvan to Kilmarnock

B From Stranraer

Table 221

Sundays

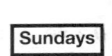

until 25 September

Ayr, Largs and Ardrossan - Glasgow Central

		SR	SR	SR	SR	SR		SR	SR	SR	SR	SR	SR	SR	SR	SR		SR	SR	SR	SR	SR	SR	SR	SR
									◇ A																
Ayr	d	14 13	14 43			15 13		15 43	15 59		16 13	16 43		17 13	17 43				18 13	18 43		19 13	19 43		
Newton-on-Ayr	d																								
Prestwick Town	d	14 18	14 48			15 18		15 48			16 18	16 48		17 18	17 48				18 18	18 48		19 18	19 48		
Prestwick Int. Airport ✈	d	14 20	14 50			15 20		15 50			16 20	16 50		17 20	17 50				18 20	18 50		19 20	19 50		
Troon	d	14 24	14 54			15 24		15 54			16 24	16 54		17 24	17 54				18 24	18 54		19 24	19 54		
Barassie	d		14 56					15 56				16 56			17 56					18 56			19 56		
Irvine	d	14 29	15 01			15 29		16 01			16 29	17 01		17 29	18 01				18 29	19 01		19 29	20 01		
Largs	d				14 53					15 53			16 53					17 53			18 53			19 53	
Fairlie	d				14 58					15 58			16 58					18 00			18 58			19 58	
West Kilbride	d				15 03					16 03			17 03					18 05			19 03			20 03	
Ardrossan Harbour	d			15 04												18 00									20 31
Ardrossan Town	d																								
Ardrossan South Beach	d			15 09	15 09					16 09			17 09			18 05		18 11			19 09			20 09	20 36
Saltcoats	d			15 11	15 11					16 11			17 11			18 07		18 13			19 11			20 11	20 38
Stevenston	d			15 14	15 14					16 14			17 14			18 10		18 16			19 14			20 14	20 41
Kilwinning	d	14 34	15 06	15 18	15 23	15 34		16 06	16 14	16 19	16 34	17 06	17 18	17 34	18 06	18 14		18 20	18 34	19 06	19 18	19 34	20 06	20 18	20 45
Dalry	d				15 27					16 23			17 23					18 24			19 23			20 23	
Glengarnock	d				15 31					16 27			17 27					18 28			19 27			20 27	
Lochwinnoch	d				15 36					16 32			17 32					18 33			19 32			20 32	
Howwood	d				15 40					16 36			17 36					18 37			19 36			20 36	
Milliken Park	d			15 31	15 43					16 39			17 39			18 27		18 40			19 39			20 39	20 58
Johnstone	d	14 48	15 19	15 33	15 46	15 48		16 19		16 42	16 50	17 19	17 41	17 51	18 19	18 29		18 43	18 48	19 19	19 41	19 48	20 19	20 41	21 00
Paisley Gilmour Street 219	a	14 52	15 24	15 38	15 50	15 52		16 24	16 38	16 46	16 54	17 24	17 46	17 55	18 24	18 37		18 47	18 52	19 24	19 46	19 52	20 24	20 46	21 05
	d	14 53	15 24	15 39	15 51	15 53		16 24	16 38	16 47	16 55	17 24	17 46	17 56	18 24	18 38		18 48	18 53	19 24	19 47	19 53	20 24	20 47	21 06
Glasgow Central 15 219	a	15 06	15 36	15 50	16 01	16 06		16 36	16 49	16 58	17 06	17 36	17 58	18 07	18 36	18 48		18 58	19 04	19 36	19 58	20 04	20 36	20 58	21 17

		SR		SR	SR	SR	SR	SR	SR
					◇ A				
Ayr	d	20 43			21 04	21 43		23 00	
Newton-on-Ayr	d								
Prestwick Town	d	20 48				21 48		23 05	
Prestwick Int. Airport ✈	d	20 50				21 50		23 07	
Troon	d	20 54				21 54		23 11	
Barassie	d	20 56				21 56		23 13	
Irvine	d	21 01				22 01		23 18	
Largs	d			20 53			21 53		23 01
Fairlie	d			20 58			21 58		23 06
West Kilbride	d			21 03			22 03		23 11
Ardrossan Harbour	d								
Ardrossan Town	d								
Ardrossan South Beach	d			21 09			22 09		23 17
Saltcoats	d			21 11			22 11		23 19
Stevenston	d			21 14			22 14		23 22
Kilwinning	d	21 06		21 22		22 06	22 18	23 22	23 28
Dalry	d			21 27			22 23		23 32
Glengarnock	d			21 31			22 27		23 36
Lochwinnoch	d			21 36			22 32		23 41
Howwood	d			21 40			22 36		23 45
Milliken Park	d			21 43			22 39		23 48
Johnstone	d	21 19		21 45		22 19	22 41	23 38	23 51
Paisley Gilmour Street 219	a	21 24		21 50		22 24	22 46	23 42	23 55
	d								
Glasgow Central 15 219	a				22 05				

Sundays

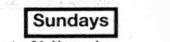

2 October to 20 November

		SR	SR	SR	SR	SR	SR	SR	SR	SR		SR	SR	SR	SR	SR	SR	SR	SR	SR		SR	SR	SR	SR
										◇ A													◇ A		
Ayr	d	08 19	09 19	09 43		10 19	10 43		11 43	12 00				12 43		13 43		14 43				15 43	15 59		16 43
Newton-on-Ayr	d																								
Prestwick Town	d	08 24	09 24	09 48		10 24	10 48		11 48					12 48		13 48		14 48				15 48			16 48
Prestwick Int. Airport ✈	d	08 27	09 26	09 50		10 26	10 50		11 50					12 50		13 50		14 50				15 50			16 50
Troon	d	08 32	09 32	09 54		10 32	10 54		11 54					12 54		13 54		14 54				15 54			16 54
Barassie	d			09 56			10 56		11 56					12 56		13 56		14 56				15 56			16 56
Irvine	d			10 01			11 01		12 01					13 01		14 01		15 01				16 01			17 01
Largs	d				09 57			10 53				11 53			12 56		13 53			14 53				15 53	
Fairlie	d				10 02			10 58				11 58			13 01		13 58			14 58				15 58	
West Kilbride	d				10 07			11 03				12 03			13 06		14 03			15 03				16 03	
Ardrossan Harbour	d												12 35						15 04						
Ardrossan Town	d																								
Ardrossan South Beach	d				10 13			11 09				12 09	12 40		13 12		14 09		15 09	15 09				16 09	
Saltcoats	d				10 15			11 11				12 11	12 42		13 14		14 11		15 11	15 11				16 11	
Stevenston	d				10 18			11 14				12 14	12 45		13 17		14 14		15 14	15 14				16 14	
Kilwinning	d			10 06	10 22		11 06	11 18	12 06	12 15		12 18	12 49	13 06	13 21	14 06	14 18	15 06	15 18	15 23		16 06	16 14	16 19	17 06
Dalry	d				10 27			11 23				12 23			13 25		14 23			15 27				16 23	
Glengarnock	d				10 31			11 27				12 27			13 29		14 27			15 31				16 27	
Lochwinnoch	d				10 36			11 32				12 32			13 34		14 32			15 36				16 32	
Howwood	d				10 40			11 36				12 36			13 38		14 36			15 40				16 36	
Milliken Park	d				10 43			11 39				12 39	13 02		13 41		14 39		15 31	15 43				16 39	
Johnstone	d			10 19	10 45		11 19	11 41	12 19			12 42	13 04	13 19	13 44	14 19	14 41	15 19	15 33	15 46		16 19		16 42	17 19
Paisley Gilmour Street 219	a			10 24	10 50		11 25	11 46	12 24	12 36		12 46	13 09	13 24	13 48	14 24	14 46	15 24	15 38	15 50		16 24	16 38	16 46	17 24
	d						11 26	11 46	12 24	12 36		12 47	13 10	13 24	13 48	14 24	14 46	15 24	15 39	15 51		16 24	16 38	16 47	17 24
Glasgow Central 15 219	a	09 36	10 40			11 36	11 36	11 58	12 36	12 51		12 58	13 22	13 36	14 03	14 36	14 58	15 36	15 50	16 01		16 36	16 49	16 58	17 36

A From Stranraer

Table 221

Sundays
2 October to 20 November

Ayr, Largs and Ardrossan - Glasgow Central

			SR	SR	SR	SR	SR	SR	SR	SR	SR	SR	SR	SR ◇ A	SR	SR	SR	SR
Ayr		d		17 43			18 43		19 43			20 43		21 04	21 43		23 00	
Newton-on-Ayr		d																
Prestwick Town		d		17 48			18 48		19 48			20 48			21 48		23 05	
Prestwick Int. Airport ✈		d		17 50			18 50		19 50			20 50			21 50		23 07	
Troon		d		17 54			18 54		19 54			20 54			21 54		23 11	
Barassie		d		17 56			18 56		19 56			20 56			21 56		23 13	
Irvine		d		18 01			19 01		20 01			21 01			22 01		23 18	
Largs		d	16 53			17 53		18 53		19 53			20 53			21 53		23 01
Fairlie		d	16 58			18 00		18 58		19 58			20 58			21 58		23 06
West Kilbride		d	17 03			18 05		19 03		20 03			21 03			22 03		23 11
Ardrossan Harbour		d			18 00						20 31							
Ardrossan Town		d																
Ardrossan South Beach		d	17 09		18 05	18 11		19 09		20 09	20 36		21 09			22 09		23 17
Saltcoats		d	17 11		18 07	18 13		19 11		20 11	20 38		21 11			22 11		23 19
Stevenston		d	17 14		18 10	18 16		19 14		20 14	20 41		21 14			22 14		23 22
Kilwinning		d	17 18	18 06	18 14	18 20	19 06	19 18	20 06	20 18	20 45	21 06	21 22		22 06	22 18	23 22	23 28
Dalry		d	17 23			18 24		19 23		20 23			21 27			22 23		23 32
Glengarnock		d	17 27			18 28		19 27		20 27			21 31			22 27		23 36
Lochwinnoch		d	17 32			18 33		19 32		20 32			21 36			22 32		23 41
Howwood		d	17 36			18 37		19 36		20 36			21 40			22 36		23 45
Milliken Park		d	17 39		18 27	18 40		19 39		20 39	20 58		21 43			22 39		23 48
Johnstone		d	17 41	18 19	18 29	18 43	19 19	19 41	20 19	20 41	21 00	21 19	21 45		22 19	22 41	23 38	23 51
Paisley Gilmour Street	219	a	17 46	18 24	18 37	18 47	19 24	19 46	20 24	20 46	21 05	21 24	21 50		22 24	22 46	23 42	23 55
		d	17 46	18 24	18 38	18 48	19 24	19 47	20 24	20 47	21 06							
Glasgow Central 15	219	a	17 58	18 36	18 48	18 58	19 36	19 58	20 36	20 58	21 17			22 05				

Sundays
from 27 November

			SR	SR	SR	SR	SR	SR	SR	SR	SR	SR	SR	SR ◇ A	SR	SR	SR	SR	SR	SR	SR	SR	SR	SR
Ayr		d	08 19	09 19	09 25	09 43		10 19	10 27	10 43		11 13	11 43	12 00		12 13		12 43		13 13	13 43		14 13	14 43
Newton-on-Ayr		d																						
Prestwick Town		d	08 24	09 24	09 30	09 48		10 24	10 32	10 48		11 18	11 48			12 18		12 48		13 18	13 48		14 18	14 48
Prestwick Int. Airport ✈		d	08 27	09 26	09 32	09 50		10 26	10 34	10 50		11 20	11 50			12 20		12 50		13 20	13 50		14 20	14 50
Troon		d	08 32	09 32	09 36	09 54		10 32	10 38	10 54		11 24	11 54			12 24		12 54		13 24	13 54		14 24	14 54
Barassie		d				09 56				10 56			11 56					12 56			13 56			14 56
Irvine		d			09 42	10 01			10 43	11 01		11 29	12 01			12 29		13 01		13 29	14 01		14 29	15 01
Largs		d					09 57				10 53				11 53				12 56			13 53		
Fairlie		d					10 02				10 58				11 58				13 01			13 58		
West Kilbride		d					10 07				11 03				12 03				13 06			14 03		
Ardrossan Harbour		d															12 35							
Ardrossan Town		d																						
Ardrossan South Beach		d					10 13				11 09				12 09		12 40		13 12			14 09		
Saltcoats		d					10 15				11 11				12 11		12 42		13 14			14 11		
Stevenston		d					10 18				11 14				12 14		12 45		13 17			14 14		
Kilwinning		d			09 47	10 06	10 22		10 48	11 06	11 18	11 34	12 06	12 15	12 18	12 34	12 49	13 06	13 21	13 34	14 06	14 18	14 34	15 06
Dalry		d					10 27				11 23				12 23				13 25			14 23		
Glengarnock		d					10 31				11 27				12 27				13 29			14 27		
Lochwinnoch		d					10 36				11 32				12 32				13 34			14 32		
Howwood		d					10 40				11 36				12 36				13 38			14 36		
Milliken Park		d					10 43				11 39				12 39		13 02		13 41			14 39		
Johnstone		d			10 01	10 19	10 45		10 59	11 19	11 41	11 51	12 19		12 42	12 51	13 04	13 19	13 44	13 51	14 19	14 41	14 48	15 19
Paisley Gilmour Street	219	a			10 05	10 24	10 50		11 02	11 25	11 46	11 55	12 24	12 36	12 46	12 55	13 09	13 24	13 48	13 55	14 24	14 46	14 52	15 24
		d								11 26	11 46	11 56	12 24	12 36	12 47	12 56	13 10	13 24	13 48	13 56	14 24	14 46	14 53	15 24
Glasgow Central 15	219	a	09 36	10 40				11 36		11 36	11 58	12 06	12 36	12 51	12 58	13 06	13 22	13 36	14 03	14 06	14 36	14 58	15 06	15 36

			SR	SR	SR	SR	SR ◇ A	SR	SR	SR	SR	SR	SR	SR	SR	SR	SR	SR	SR	SR	SR	SR	SR ◇ A	SR
Ayr		d			15 13	15 43	15 59		16 13	16 43		17 13	17 43			18 43		19 43			20 43		21 04	21 43
Newton-on-Ayr		d																						
Prestwick Town		d			15 18	15 48			16 18	16 48		17 18	17 48			18 48		19 48			20 48			21 48
Prestwick Int. Airport ✈		d			15 20	15 50			16 20	16 50		17 20	17 50			18 50		19 50			20 50			21 50
Troon		d			15 24	15 54			16 24	16 54		17 24	17 54			18 54		19 54			20 54			21 54
Barassie		d				15 56				16 56			17 56			18 56		19 56			20 56			21 56
Irvine		d			15 29	16 01			16 29	17 01		17 29	18 01			19 01		20 01			21 01			22 01
Largs		d		14 53				15 53			16 53				17 53		18 53		19 53			20 53		
Fairlie		d		14 58				15 58			16 58				18 00		18 58		19 58			20 58		
West Kilbride		d		15 03				16 03			17 03				18 05		19 03		20 03			21 03		
Ardrossan Harbour		d	15 04											18 00						20 31				
Ardrossan Town		d																						
Ardrossan South Beach		d	15 09	15 09				16 09			17 09			18 05	18 11		19 09		20 09	20 36		21 09		
Saltcoats		d	15 11	15 11				16 11			17 11			18 07	18 13		19 11		20 11	20 38		21 11		
Stevenston		d	15 14	15 14				16 14			17 14			18 10	18 16		19 14		20 14	20 41		21 14		
Kilwinning		d	15 18	15 23	15 34	16 06	16 14	16 19	16 34	17 06	17 18	17 34	18 06	18 14	18 20	19 06	19 18	20 06	20 18	20 45	21 06	21 22		22 06
Dalry		d		15 27				16 23			17 23				18 24		19 23		20 23			21 27		
Glengarnock		d		15 31				16 27			17 27				18 28		19 27		20 27			21 31		
Lochwinnoch		d		15 36				16 32			17 32				18 33		19 32		20 32			21 36		
Howwood		d		15 40				16 36			17 36				18 37		19 36		20 36			21 40		
Milliken Park		d	15 31	15 43				16 39			17 39			18 27	18 40		19 39		20 39	20 58		21 43		
Johnstone		d	15 33	15 46	15 48	16 19		16 42	16 50	17 19	17 41	17 51	18 19	18 29	18 43	19 19	19 41	20 19	20 41	21 00	21 19	21 45		22 19
Paisley Gilmour Street	219	a	15 38	15 50	15 52	16 24	16 38	16 46	16 54	17 24	17 46	17 55	18 24	18 37	18 47	19 24	19 46	20 24	20 46	21 05	21 24	21 50		22 24
		d	15 39	15 51	15 53	16 24	16 38	16 47	16 55	17 24	17 46	17 56	18 24	18 38	18 48	19 24	19 47	20 24	20 47	21 06				
Glasgow Central 15	219	a	15 50	16 01	16 06	16 36	16 49	16 58	17 06	17 36	17 58	18 07	18 36	18 48	18 58	19 36	19 58	20 36	20 58	21 17			22 05	

A From Stranraer

Table 221

Sundays
from 27 November

Ayr, Largs and Ardrossan - Glasgow Central

			SR		SR	SR
Ayr		d			23 00	
Newton-on-Ayr		d				
Prestwick Town		d			23 05	
Prestwick Int. Airport ✈		d			23 07	
Troon		d			23 11	
Barassie		d			23 13	
Irvine		d			23 18	
Largs		d	21 53			23 01
Fairlie		d	21 58			23 06
West Kilbride		d	22 03			23 11
Ardrossan Harbour		d				
Ardrossan Town		d				
Ardrossan South Beach		d	22 09			23 17
Saltcoats		d	22 11			23 19
Stevenston		d	22 14			23 22
Kilwinning		d	22 18		23 22	23 28
Dalry		d	22 23			23 32
Glengarnock		d	22 27			23 36
Lochwinnoch		d	22 32			23 41
Howwood		d	22 36			23 45
Milliken Park		d	22 39			23 48
Johnstone		d	22 41		23 38	23 51
Paisley Gilmour Street	219	a	22 46		23 42	23 55
		d				
Glasgow Central 15	219	a				

Table 221A SHIPPING SERVICES

Mondays to Saturdays

Until 22 October

Glasgow and Ardrossan - Brodick (Arran)

Operated by Caledonian MacBrayne Ltd

							FO
Glasgow Central	221	d	*08 34*	*11 15*	*14 15*	*16 50*	*19 15*
Paisley Gilmour Street	221	d	*08 45*	*11 26*	*14 26*	*17 01*	*19 26*
Ardrossan Harbour	221	a	*09 25*	*12 09*	*15 09*	*17 45*	*20 09*
Ardrossan Harbour		d	**09 45**	**12 30**	**15 15**	**18 00**	**20 30**
Brodick		a	**10 40**	**13 25**	**16 10**	**18 55**	**21 25**

Sundays

Until 16 October

			C			
Glasgow Central	221	d	*08 20*	*11 15*	*14 05*	*16 55*
Paisley Gilmour Street	221	d	*08 51*	*11 26*	*14 16*	*17 07*
Ardrossan Harbour	221	a	*09 30*	*12 02*	*14 52*	*17 43*
Ardrossan Harbour		d	**09 45**	**12 30**	**15 15**	**18 00**
Brodick		a	**10 40**	**13 25**	**16 10**	**18 55**

Mondays to Saturdays

Until 22 October

Brodick		d	**08 20**	**11 05**	**13 50**	**16 40**	**19 20**
Ardrossan Harbour		a	**09 15**	**12 00**	**14 45**	**17 35**	**20 15**
Ardrossan Harbour	221	d	*09 30*	*12 28*	*15 28*	*18 00*	*20 33*
Paisley Gilmour Street	221	a	*10 10*	*13 10*	*16 10*	*18 40*	*21 14*
Glasgow Central	221	a	*10 22*	*13 22*	*16 25*	*18 52*	*21b26*

Sundays

Until 16 October

Brodick		d	**11 05**	**13 50**	**16 40**	**19 20**
Ardrossan Harbour		a	**12 00**	**14 45**	**17 35**	**20 15**
Ardrossan Harbour	221	d	*12 35*	*15 04*	*18 00*	*20 31*
Paisley Gilmour Street	221	a	*13 09*	*15 38*	*18 37*	*21 05*
Glasgow Central	221	a	*13 22*	*15 50*	*18 48*	*21 17*

C Connecting bus service from Glasgow to Paisley

b Arrives 2127 on Saturdays

For details of sailings from 23 October please telephone Caledonian MacBrayne on 08000 66 5000 or visit www.calmac.co.uk

Table 222

Mondays to Saturdays

Glasgow Central - East Kilbride, Barrhead and Kilmarnock

Miles	Miles			SR SO	SR SO	SR	SR ◇ A	SR	SR	SR B	SR SX	SR SO		SR SX	SR	SR SX	SR SO	SR	SR ◇ A	SR SX	SR SO	SR		SR C	SR
0	0	**Glasgow Central 15**	d	00 12	00 18	06 13	06 30	06 48	06 54	07 08	07 12	07 18		07 22	07 37	07 43	07 48	07 52	08 07	08 17	08 18	08 24		08 37	08 48
2¼	2¼	Crossmyloof	d	00 18	00 24	06 19	06 36	06 54	07 00		07 19	07 24		07 29		07 49	07 54	07 58		08 23	08 24	08 30			08 56
3¼	3¼	Pollokshaws West	d	00 21	00 27	06 22	06 39	06 57	07 03		07 21	07 27		07 32		07 52	07 57	08 01		08 26	08 27	08 34			08 58
—	4¼	Thornliebank	d		00 30	06 25		07 00			07 24	07 30				07 55	08 00			08 29	08 30				09 01
—	5¼	Giffnock	d		00 33	06 28		07 03			07 27	07 33				07 58	08 03			08 32	08 33				09 04
—	6½	Clarkston	d		00 37	06 32		07 07			07 31	07 37				08 02	08 07			08 36	08 37				09 08
—	7¼	Busby	d		00 40	06 35		07 10			07 36	07 40				08 08	08 10			08 39	08 40				09 11
—	8½	Thorntonhall	d		00 43	06 38											08 13			08 42					09 14
—	10	Hairmyres	d		00 46	06 41		07 16			07 41	07 45				08 14	08 16			08 45	08 45				09 18
—	11½	**East Kilbride**	a		00 50	06 45		07 19			07 50	07 49				08 17	08 20			08 49	08 49				09 21
4½	—	Kennishead	d	00 24			06 42		07 06					07 35				08 04				08 37			
5	—	Priesthill & Darnley	d	00 26			06 44		07 08					07 37				08 06				08 39			
5¾	—	Nitshill	d	00 29			06 47		07 11					07 40				08 09				08 42			
7½	—	**Barrhead**	d	00 32			06 51		07a14	07 23				07a43	07 49			08a12	08 21			08a45		08 49	
16½	—	Dunlop	d	00 44			07 03			07 35					08 01				08 33					09 01	
18¾	—	Stewarton	d	00 48			07 07			07 39					08 05				08 37					09 05	
22	—	Kilmaurs	d	00 53			07 12			07 44					08 10				08 41					09 10	
24¼	—	**Kilmarnock 3**	a	00 59			07 22			07 48					08 16				08 47					09 18	

		SR	SR	SR	SR	SR	SR	SR		SR C	SR	SR	SR	SR	SR	SR	SR	SR		SR	SR	SR	SR B	SR	SR
Glasgow Central 15	d	08 57	09 12	09 18	09 27	09 42	09 48	09 57		10 12	10 18	10 27	10 42	10 48	10 57	11 12	11 18	11 27		11 42	11 48	11 57	12 12	12 18	12 27
Crossmyloof	d	09 03		09 24	09 33		09 54	10 03			10 24	10 33		10 54	11 03		11 24	11 33			11 54	12 03		12 24	12 33
Pollokshaws West	d	09 06		09 27	09 36		09 57	10 06			10 27	10 36		10 57	11 06		11 27	11 36			11 57	12 06		12 27	12 36
Thornliebank	d			09 30			10 00				10 30			11 00			11 30				12 00			12 30	
Giffnock	d			09 33			10 03				10 33			11 03			11 33				12 03			12 33	
Clarkston	d			09 37			10 07				10 37			11 07			11 37				12 07			12 37	
Busby	d			09 40			10 10				10 40			11 10			11 40				12 10			12 40	
Thorntonhall	d						10 13							11 13							12 13				
Hairmyres	d			09 45			10 16				10 45			11 16			11 45				12 16			12 45	
East Kilbride	a			09 50			10 20				10 49			11 20			11 49				12 20			12 49	
Kennishead	d	09 09			09 39			10 09				10 39			11 09			11 39				12 09			12 39
Priesthill & Darnley	d	09 11			09 41			10 11				10 41			11 11			11 41				12 11			12 41
Nitshill	d	09 14			09 44			10 14				10 44			11 14			11 44				12 14			12 44
Barrhead	d	09a17			09a48	09 54		10a17				10a47	10 53		11a17			11a47		11 53		12a17			12a47
Dunlop	d					10 06							11 05			11 35				12 05					
Stewarton	d		09 38			10 10				10 38			11 09			11 39				12 10			12 38		
Kilmaurs	d					10 14							11 13			11 44				12 13					
Kilmarnock 3	a		09 47			10 21				10 47			11 20			11 50				12 20			12 47		

		SR	SR	SR		SR C	SR	SR	SR	SR	SR	SR	SR	SR		SR	SR	SR	SR D	SR	SR	SR	SR	SR	
Glasgow Central 15	d	12 42	12 48	12 57		13 12	13 18	13 27	13 42	13 48	13 57	14 12	14 18	14 27		14 42	14 48	14 57	15 12	15 18	15 27	15 42	15 48	15 57	
Crossmyloof	d		12 54	13 03			13 24	13 33		13 54	14 03		14 24	14 33			14 54	15 03		15 24	15 33		15 54	16 03	
Pollokshaws West	d		12 57	13 06			13 27	13 36		13 57	14 06		14 27	14 36			14 57	15 06		15 27	15 36		15 57	16 06	
Thornliebank	d		13 00				13 30			14 00			14 30				15 00			15 30			16 00		
Giffnock	d		13 03				13 33			14 03			14 33				15 03			15 33			16 03		
Clarkston	d		13 07				13 37			14 07			14 37				15 07			15 37			16 07		
Busby	d		13 10				13 40			14 10			14 40				15 10			15 40			16 11		
Thorntonhall	d		13 13							14 13							15 13						16 14		
Hairmyres	d		13 16				13 45			14 16			14 45				15 16			15 45			16 17		
East Kilbride	a		13 20				13 49			14 20			14 49				15 20			15 49			16 21		
Kennishead	d			13 09				13 39			14 09			14 39				15 09			15 39			16 09	
Priesthill & Darnley	d			13 11				13 41			14 11			14 41				15 11			15 41			16 11	
Nitshill	d			13 14				13 44			14 14			14 44				15 14			15 44			16 14	
Barrhead	d	12 54		13a17				13a47	13 53		14a17			14a47		14 53		15a17			15a47	15 53		16a17	
Dunlop	d	13 06							14 05			14 34				15 05			15 33			16 05			
Stewarton	d	13 10				13 38			14 10			14 39				15 10			15 37			16 10			
Kilmaurs	d	13 14							14 13			14 43				15 13			15 42			16 14			
Kilmarnock 3	a	13 20				13 47			14 20			14 49				15 20			15 48			16 21			

		SR B	SR	SR	SR	SR	SR	SR SX	SR D	SR SO		SR SX	SR	SR SX	SR C	SR SO	SR SX	SR	SR SX	SR		SR	SR	SR	SR
Glasgow Central 15	d	16 12	16 18	16 27	16 42	16 48	16 57	17 01	17 12	17 18		17 21	17 27	17 32	17 42	17 48	17 48	17 57	18 03	18 12		18 18	18 27	18 42	18 48
Crossmyloof	d		16 25	16 33		16 54	17 03	17 07		17 24			17 33	17 38		17 54	17 55	18 03	18 09			18 25	18 34		18 54
Pollokshaws West	d		16 27	16 36		16 57	17 06	17 10		17 27			17 36	17 41		17 57	17 57	18 06	18 12			18 27	18 37		18 57
Thornliebank	d		16 30			17 00		17 13		17 30				17 44		18 00	18 00		18 15			18 30			19 00
Giffnock	d		16 33			17 03		17 16		17 33				17 47		18 03	18 03		18 18			18 33			19 03
Clarkston	d		16 37			17 07		17 20		17 37		17 34		17 51		18 07	18 07		18 22			18 37			19 07
Busby	d		16 40			17 10		17 23		17 40		17 38		17 54		18 10	18 10		18 25			18 40			19 10
Thorntonhall	d		16 43			17 13				17 43				17 57		18 13			18 28						19 13
Hairmyres	d		16 47			17 16		17 28		17 46		17 44		18 00		18 16	18 17		18 32			18 46			19 16
East Kilbride	a		16 50			17 20		17 32		17 50		17 47		18 04		18 20	18 20		18 35			18 50			19 20
Kennishead	d			16 39			17 09						17 39					18 09					18 40		
Priesthill & Darnley	d			16 41			17 11						17 41					18 11					18 42		
Nitshill	d			16 44			17 14						17 44					18 14					18 45		
Barrhead	d	16 23		16a47	16 53		17a17		17 23				17a47		17 54			18a17		18 23			18a48	18 54	
Dunlop	d	16 35			17 05				17 35						18 07					18 35				19 06	
Stewarton	d	16 39			17 09				17 40						18 11					18 39				19 10	
Kilmaurs	d	16 44			17 14				17 43						18 16					18 42				19 15	
Kilmarnock 3	a	16 49			17 20				17 50						18 22					18 50				19 21	

A To Stranraer
B To Newcastle
C To Carlisle
D To Girvan

Table 222

Mondays to Saturdays

Glasgow Central - East Kilbride, Barrhead and Kilmarnock

		SR	SR A	SR	SR	SR		SR	SR	SR	SR	SR	SR	SR	SR	SR A		SR	SR	SR	SR B	SR			
Glasgow Central 15	d	18 57	19 12	19 18	19 33	19 48		20 12	20 18	20 33	20 48	21 12	21 18	21 33	21 48	22 12		22 18	22 33	22 48	23 12	23 18			
Crossmyloof	d	19 03		19 24	19 39	19 54			20 24	20 39	20 54		21 24	21 39	21 54			22 24	22 39	22 54	23 18	23 24			
Pollokshaws West	d	19 06		19 27	19 42	19 57			20 27	20 42	20 57		21 27	21 42	21 57			22 27	22 42	22 57	23 21	23 27			
Thornliebank	d			19 30		20 00			20 30		21 00		21 30		22 00			22 30		23 00		23 30			
Giffnock	d			19 33		20 03			20 33		21 03		21 33		22 03			22 33		23 03		23 33			
Clarkston	d			19 37		20 07			20 37		21 07		21 37		22 07			22 37		23 07		23 37			
Busby	d			19 40		20 10			20 40		21 10		21 40		22 10			22 40		23 10		23 40			
Thorntonhall	d					20 13					21 13				22 13					23 13		23 43			
Hairmyres	d			19 45		20 16			20 45		21 16		21 45		22 16			22 45		23 16		23 46			
East Kilbride	a			19 49		20 20			20 49		21 20		21 49		22 20			22 49		23 20		23 50			
Kennishead	d	19 09			19 45					20 45				21 45					22 45		23 24				
Priesthill & Darnley	d	19 11			19 47					20 47				21 47					22 47		23 26				
Nitshill	d	19 14			19 50					20 50				21 50					22 50		23 29				
Barrhead	d	19a17	19 24		19 54			20 25		20 53		21 23		21 53		22 23			22 54		23 32				
Dunlop	d		19 36		20 06					21 05		21 35		22 05		22 35			23 06		23 44				
Stewarton	d		19 40		20 10			20 39		21 10		21 39		22 10		22 39			23 10		23 48				
Kilmaurs	d		19 44		20 13					21 13		21 44		22 13		22 44			23 13		23 53				
Kilmarnock 3	a		19 50		20 20			20 49		21 20		21 50		22 20		22 50			23 20		23 59				

Sundays

		SR C	SR	SR	SR C	SR	SR	SR C	SR	SR		SR	SR	SR	SR	SR	SR	SR	SR	SR		SR	SR	SR	SR
Glasgow Central 15	d	08 12	08 18	08 48	09 12	09 18	09 48	10 12	10 18	10 48		11 12	11 18	11 48	12 12	12 18	12 48	13 12	13 18	13 48		14 12	14 18	14 48	15 12
Crossmyloof	d		08 24	08 54		09 24	09 54		10 24	10 54			11 24	11 54		12 24	12 54		13 24	13 54			14 24	14 54	
Pollokshaws West	d	08 20	08 27	08 57	09 20	09 27	09 57	10 20	10 27	10 57		11 20	11 27	11 57	12 20	12 27	12 57	13 20	13 27	13 57		14 20	14 27	14 57	15 20
Thornliebank	d		08 30	09 00		09 30	10 00		10 30	11 00			11 30	12 00		12 30	13 00		13 30	14 00			14 30	15 00	
Giffnock	d		08 33	09 03		09 33	10 03		10 33	11 03			11 33	12 03		12 33	13 03		13 33	14 03			14 33	15 03	
Clarkston	d		08 37	09 07		09 37	10 07		10 37	11 07			11 37	12 07		12 37	13 07		13 37	14 07			14 37	15 07	
Busby	d		08 40	09 10		09 40	10 10		10 40	11 10			11 40	12 10		12 40	13 10		13 40	14 10			14 40	15 10	
Thorntonhall	d			09 13			10 13			11 13				12 13			13 13			14 13				15 13	
Hairmyres	d		08 45	09 16		09 45	10 16		10 45	11 16			11 45	12 16		12 45	13 16		13 45	14 16			14 45	15 16	
East Kilbride	a		08 49	09 20		09 49	10 20		10 49	11 20			11 49	12 20		12 49	13 20		13 49	14 20			14 49	15 20	
Kennishead	d																								
Priesthill & Darnley	d																								
Nitshill	d																								
Barrhead	d	08 26			09 26			10 26				11 26			12 26			13 26				14 26			15 26
Dunlop	d	08 38			09 38			10 38				11 38			12 38			13 38				14 38			15 38
Stewarton	d	08 42			09 42			10 42				11 42			12 42			13 42				14 42			15 42
Kilmaurs	d	08 46			09 46			10 46				11 46			12 46			13 46				14 46			15 46
Kilmarnock 3	a	08 52			09 52			10 52				11 52			12 52			13 52				14 52			15 52

		SR	SR	SR	SR	SR		SR	SR	SR	SR	SR	SR	SR	SR	SR		SR	SR	SR	SR	SR A	SR	SR	SR
Glasgow Central 15	d	15 18	15 48	16 12	16 18	16 48		17 12	17 18	17 48	18 12	18 18	18 48	19 12	19 18	19 48		20 18	20 48	21 18	21 48	22 12	22 18	22 48	23 18
Crossmyloof	d	15 24	15 54		16 24	16 54			17 24	17 54		18 24	18 54		19 24	19 54		20 24	20 54	21 24	21 54		22 24	22 54	23 24
Pollokshaws West	d	15 27	15 57	16 20	16 27	16 57		17 20	17 27	17 57	18 20	18 27	18 57	19 20	19 27	19 57		20 27	20 57	21 27	21 57		22 27	22 57	23 27
Thornliebank	d	15 30	16 00		16 30	17 00			17 30	18 00		18 30	19 00		19 30	20 00		20 30	21 00	21 30	22 00		22 30	23 00	23 30
Giffnock	d	15 33	16 03		16 33	17 03			17 33	18 03		18 33	19 03		19 33	20 03		20 33	21 03	21 33	22 03		22 33	23 03	23 33
Clarkston	d	15 37	16 07		16 37	17 07			17 37	18 07		18 37	19 07		19 37	20 07		20 37	21 07	21 37	22 07		22 37	23 07	23 37
Busby	d	15 40	16 10		16 40	17 10			17 40	18 10		18 40	19 10		19 40	20 10		20 40	21 10	21 40	22 10		22 40	23 10	23 40
Thorntonhall	d		16 13			17 13				18 13			19 13			20 13			21 13		22 13			23 13	23 43
Hairmyres	d	15 45	16 16		16 45	17 16			17 45	18 16		18 45	19 16		19 45	20 16		20 45	21 16	21 45	22 16		22 45	23 16	23 46
East Kilbride	a	15 49	16 20		16 49	17 20			17 49	18 20		18 49	19 20		19 49	20 20		20 49	21 20	21 49	22 20		22 49	23 20	23 50
Kennishead	d																								
Priesthill & Darnley	d																								
Nitshill	d																								
Barrhead	d			16 26				17 26			18 26			19 26								22 23			
Dunlop	d			16 38				17 38			18 38			19 38								22 35			
Stewarton	d			16 42				17 42			18 42			19 42								22 39			
Kilmaurs	d			16 46				17 46			18 46			19 46								22 44			
Kilmarnock 3	a			16 52				17 52			18 52			19 52								22 48			

A To Carlisle

B To Dumfries

C To Ayr

Kilmarnock, Barrhead and East Kilbride - Glasgow Central

Miles	Miles			SR	SR	SR SX	SR	SR	SR A	SR SX	SR SO	SR	SR SX B	SR SO B	SR SX	SR SX	SR	SR C	SR SX	SR SO	SR SX	SR	SR
0	—	**Kilmarnock** 3	d		05 22		06 22		06 52				07 22	07 22				07 53					08 23
2¼	—	Kilmaurs	d		05 26		06 26		06 56				07 26	07 27				07 57					08 27
5½	—	Stewarton	d		05 31		06 31		07 02				07 32	07 32				08 03					08 32
7¾	—	Dunlop	d		05 36		06 36		07 06				07 36	07 37				08 08					08 37
16¾	—	**Barrhead**	d		05 47		06 47		07 18	07 25	07 28		07 47	07 48		07 57		08 20		08 28	08 28		08 49
18½	—	Nitshill	d		05 50		06 50			07 28	07 31			07 51		08 00				08 31	08 31		
19½	—	Priesthill & Darnley	d		05 52		06 52			07 30	07 33			07 53		08 02				08 33	08 33		
20	—	Kennishead	d		05 54		06 54			07 32	07 35			07 55		08 04				08 35	08 35		
—	0	**East Kilbride**	d	23p56		06 17		06 56				07 25			07 42		07 58		08 10			08 26	
—	1½	Hairmyres	d	23p59		06 20		06 59				07 29			07 46		08 01		08 17			08 30	
—	3	Thorntonhall	d	00 03		06 24		07 03				07 32					08 05					08 33	
—	4¼	Busby	d	00 06		06 27		07 06				07 36					08 08		08 22			08 36	
—	5	Clarkston	d	00 09		06 30		07 09				07 39			07 54		08 11		08 25			08 39	
—	6¼	Giffnock	d	00 12		06 33		07 12				07 42					08 15		08 28			08 42	
—	7¼	Thornliebank	d	00 14		06 35		07 14				07 45					08 18		08 30			08 45	
21¼	8¼	Pollokshaws West	d	00 17	05 57	06 38	06 57	07 17		07 35	07 38	07 48		07 58		08 07	08 21		08 35	08 38	08 38	08 48	
22¼	9¼	Crossmyloof	d	00 20	06 00	06 41	07 00	07 20		07 38	07 41	07 51		08 01		08 10	08 24		08 38	08 41	08 41	08 51	
24¼	11½	**Glasgow Central** 15	a	00 26	06 08	06 49	07 08	07 27	07 31	07 45	07 47	07 57	08 00	08 09	08 09	08 16	08 30	08 37	08 45	08 47	08 49	08 58	09 01

		SR	SR	SR	SR	SR	SR ◇ D	SR	SR	NT E	SR	SR	SR	SR	SR	SR	SR	SR	SR	SR	SR	SR	SR
Kilmarnock 3	d			08 58			09 27			09 59			10 28			10 58			11 27			11 57	
Kilmaurs	d			09 02			09 31			10 03			10 32			11 02			11 31			12 01	
Stewarton	d			09 07			09 36			10 08			10 36			11 07			11 36			12 06	
Dunlop	d			09 12			09 41			10 13			10 42			11 12			11 41			12 11	
Barrhead	d	08 58		09 23	09 28		09 53	09 58		10 21	10 28		10 53	10 58			11 28		11 52	11 58			12 28
Nitshill	d	09 01			09 31			10 01			10 31			11 01			11 31			12 01			12 31
Priesthill & Darnley	d	09 03			09 33			10 03			10 33			11 03			11 33			12 03			12 33
Kennishead	d	09 05			09 35			10 05			10 35			11 05			11 35			12 05			12 35
East Kilbride	d		08 56			09 27			09 56			10 27			10 56			11 27			11 56		
Hairmyres	d		09 00			09 30			09 59			10 30			10 59			11 30			11 59		
Thorntonhall	d		09 03						10 03						11 03						12 03		
Busby	d		09 06			09 35			10 06			10 35			11 06			11 35			12 06		
Clarkston	d		09 09			09 38			10 09			10 38			11 09			11 38			12 09		
Giffnock	d		09 12			09 42			10 12			10 42			11 12			11 42			12 12		
Thornliebank	d		09 15			09 44			10 14			10 44			11 14			11 44			12 14		
Pollokshaws West	d	09 08	09 18		09 38	09 47		10 08	10 17		10 38	10 47		11 08	11 17		11 38	11 47		12 08	12 17		12 38
Crossmyloof	d	09 11	09 21		09 41	09 51		10 11	10 21		10 41	10 51		11 11	11 21		11 41	11 51		12 11	12 21		12 41
Glasgow Central 15	a	09 17	09 27	09 36	09 47	09 57	10 05	10 17	10 27	10 37	10 47	10 57	11 06	11 17	11 27	11 34	11 47	11 57	12 05	12 17	12 27	12 33	12 47

		SR	SR	SR	SR	SR C	SR	SR	SR	SR	SR	SR	SR	SR	SR	SR	SR	SR C	SR	SR	SR	SR
Kilmarnock 3	d		12 27			13 00			13 27			13 57			14 27			15 00			15 27	
Kilmaurs	d		12 31						13 31			14 01			14 31						15 31	
Stewarton	d		12 36			13 07			13 36			14 06			14 36			15 07			15 36	
Dunlop	d		12 41						13 41			14 11			14 41						15 41	
Barrhead	d		12 52	12 58			13 28		13 52	13 58			14 28		14 52	14 58			15 28		15 52	15 58
Nitshill	d			13 01			13 31			14 01			14 31			15 01			15 31			16 01
Priesthill & Darnley	d			13 03			13 33			14 03			14 33			15 03			15 33			16 03
Kennishead	d			13 05			13 35			14 05			14 35			15 05			15 35			16 05
East Kilbride	d	12 27			12 56			13 27			13 56			14 27			14 56			15 27		
Hairmyres	d	12 30			12 59			13 30			13 59			14 30			14 59			15 30		
Thorntonhall	d				13 03						14 03						15 03					
Busby	d	12 35			13 06			13 35			14 06			14 35			15 06			15 35		
Clarkston	d	12 38			13 09			13 38			14 09			14 38			15 09			15 38		
Giffnock	d	12 42			13 12			13 42			14 12			14 42			15 12			15 42		
Thornliebank	d	12 44			13 14			13 44			14 14			14 44			15 14			15 44		
Pollokshaws West	d	12 47		13 08	13 17		13 38	13 47		14 08	14 17		14 38	14 47		15 08	15 17		15 38	15 47		16 08
Crossmyloof	d	12 50		13 11	13 20		13 41	13 51		14 11	14 20		14 41	14 50		15 11	15 20		15 41	15 50		16 11
Glasgow Central 15	a	12 57	13 05	13 17	13 27	13 33	13 47	13 57	14 05	14 17	14 27	14 33	14 47	14 57	15 05	15 17	15 27	15 33	15 47	15 57	16 05	16 17

		SR	SR B	SR	SR	SR	SR	SR	NT E	SR	SR	SR	SR	SR SO	SR SX	SR	SR	SR SO	SR SX	SR	SR	SR	SR
Kilmarnock 3	d		15 57			16 27			16 57			17 27				17 57				18 27			18 57
Kilmaurs	d		16 01			16 31			17 01			17 31				18 01				18 31			19 01
Stewarton	d		16 06			16 36			17 06			17 36				18 06				18 36			19 06
Dunlop	d		16 11			16 41			17 11			17 41				18 11				18 41			19 11
Barrhead	d			16 28		16 51	16 58		17 22	17 28		17 52	17 58			18 21	18 28			18 52	18 58		19 22
Nitshill	d			16 31			17 01			17 31			18 01				18 31				19 01		
Priesthill & Darnley	d			16 33			17 03			17 33			18 03				18 33				19 03		
Kennishead	d			16 35			17 05			17 35			18 05				18 35				19 05		
East Kilbride	d	15 56			16 27			16 56			17 25			17 56	17 55			18 27	18 27			18 56	
Hairmyres	d	15 59			16 30			16 59			17 31			17 59	18 03			18 30	18 35			18 59	
Thorntonhall	d	16 03						17 03						18 03	18 07							19 03	
Busby	d	16 06			16 35			17 06			17 36			18 06	18 10			18 35	18 40			19 06	
Clarkston	d	16 09			16 38			17 09			17 39			18 09	18 13			18 38	18 43			19 09	
Giffnock	d	16 12			16 42			17 12			17 42			18 12	18 16			18 42	18 47			19 12	
Thornliebank	d	16 14			16 44			17 14			17 45			18 14	18 18			18 44	18 50			19 14	
Pollokshaws West	d	16 17		16 38	16 47		17 08	17 17		17 38	17 48		18 08	18 17	18 23		18 38	18 47	18 53		19 08	19 17	
Crossmyloof	d	16 20		16 41	16 50		17 11	17 21		17 41	17 50		18 11	18 20	18 26		18 41	18 50	18 56		19 11	19 20	
Glasgow Central 15	a	16 26	16 33	16 47	16 57	17 05	17 17	17 27	17 35	17 47	17 57	18 05	18 17	18 27	18 32	18 36	18 47	18 57	19 03	19 07	19 19	19 27	19 35

A From Dumfries
B From Girvan
C From Carlisle
D From Stranraer
E From Newcastle

Table 222

Mondays to Saturdays

Kilmarnock, Barrhead and East Kilbride - Glasgow Central

		SR	SR	SR	SR	SR	SR	SR	SR	NT	SR	SR	SR	SR	SR	SR	SR	SR	SR	SR
						A				B				◇ C				A		
Kilmarnock 3	d			19 27		20 00		20 27		21 01		21 27		22 00		22 27		22 57		
Kilmaurs	d			19 31				20 31				21 31				22 31		23 01		
Stewarton	d			19 36		20 07		20 36		21 08		21 36		22 07		22 36		23 06		
Dunlop	d			19 41				20 41				21 41				22 41		23 11		
Barrhead	d	19 28		19 52		20 21		20 52		21 21		21 52		22 21		22 52		23 22		
Nitshill	d	19 31		19 55				20 55				21 55				22 55				
Priesthill & Darnley	d	19 33		19 57				20 57				21 57				22 57				
Kennishead	d	19 35		19 59				20 59				21 59				22 59				
East Kilbride	d		19 27		19 56		20 27		20 56		21 27		21 56		22 27		22 56		23 27	23 56
Hairmyres	d		19 30		19 59		20 30		20 59		21 30		21 59		22 30		22 59		23 30	23 59
Thorntonhall	d				20 03				21 03				22 03				23 03			00 03
Busby	d		19 35		20 06		20 35		21 06		21 35		22 06		22 35		23 06		23 35	00 06
Clarkston	d		19 38		20 09		20 38		21 09		21 38		22 09		22 38		23 09		23 38	00 09
Giffnock	d		19 42		20 12		20 42		21 12		21 42		22 12		22 42		23 12		23 42	00 12
Thornliebank	d		19 44		20 14		20 44		21 14		21 44		22 14		22 44		23 14		23 44	00 14
Pollokshaws West	d	19 38	19 47	20 02	20 17		20 47	21 02	21 17		21 47	22 02	22 17		22 47	23 02	23 17		23 47	00 17
Crossmyloof	d	19 41	19 50	20 05	20 20		20 50	21 05	21 20		21 50	22 05	22 20		22 50	23 05	23 20		23 50	00 20
Glasgow Central 15	a	19 47	19 57	20 13	20 27	20 34	20 57	21 13	21 27	21 36	21 57	22 13	22 27	22 34	22 57	23 13	23 27	23 35	23 56	00 26

Sundays

		SR	SR	SR	SR	SR	SR	SR	SR	SR	SR	SR	SR	SR	SR	SR	SR	SR	SR	SR	SR	SR	SR
		D			E			E			E												A
Kilmarnock 3	d				08 57			09 57			10 57			11 57			12 57			13 57			14 57
Kilmaurs	d				09 01			10 01			11 01			12 01			13 01			14 01			15 01
Stewarton	d				09 06			10 06			11 06			12 06			13 06			14 06			15 06
Dunlop	d				09 11			10 11			11 11			12 11			13 11			14 11			15 11
Barrhead	d				09 21			10 23			11 21			12 21			13 21			14 21			15 21
Nitshill	d																						
Priesthill & Darnley	d																						
Kennishead	d																						
East Kilbride	d	23p56	08 27	08 56		09 27	09 56		10 27	10 56		11 27	11 56		12 27	12 56		13 27	13 56		14 27	14 56	
Hairmyres	d	23p59	08 30	08 59		09 30	09 59		10 30	10 59		11 30	11 59		12 30	12 59		13 30	13 59		14 30	14 59	
Thorntonhall	d	00 03		09 03			10 03			11 03			12 03			13 03			14 03			15 03	
Busby	d	00 06	08 35	09 06		09 35	10 06		10 35	11 06		11 35	12 06		12 35	13 06		13 35	14 06		14 35	15 06	
Clarkston	d	00 09	08 38	09 09		09 38	10 09		10 38	11 09		11 38	12 09		12 38	13 09		13 38	14 09		14 38	15 09	
Giffnock	d	00 12	08 42	09 12		09 42	10 12		10 42	11 12		11 42	12 12		12 42	13 12		13 42	14 12		14 42	15 12	
Thornliebank	d	00 14	08 44	09 14		09 44	10 14		10 44	11 14		11 44	12 14		12 44	13 14		13 44	14 14		14 44	15 14	
Pollokshaws West	d	00 17	08 47	09 17	09 27	09 47	10 17	10 29	10 47	11 17	11 27	11 47	12 17	12 27	12 47	13 17	13 27	13 47	14 17	14 27	14 47	15 17	15 27
Crossmyloof	d	00 20	08 50	09 20		09 50	10 20		10 50	11 20		11 50	12 20		12 50	13 20		13 50	14 20		14 50	15 20	
Glasgow Central 15	a	00 26	08 57	09 26	09 36	09 56	10 26	10 40	10 56	11 26	11 36	11 56	12 26	12 36	12 56	13 26	13 36	13 56	14 26	14 36	14 56	15 26	15 36

		SR	SR	SR	SR	SR	SR	SR	SR	SR	SR	SR	SR	SR	SR	SR	SR	SR	SR	SR	SR	SR	SR
																			A		◇ C		
Kilmarnock 3	d			15 57			16 57			17 57			18 57			19 57			20 57		21 31		
Kilmaurs	d			16 01			17 01			18 01			19 01			20 01			21 01				
Stewarton	d			16 06			17 06			18 06			19 06			20 06			21 06				
Dunlop	d			16 11			17 11			18 11			19 11			20 11			21 11				
Barrhead	d			16 21			17 21			18 21			19 21			20 21			21 21				
Nitshill	d																						
Priesthill & Darnley	d																						
Kennishead	d																						
East Kilbride	d	15 27	15 56		16 27	16 56		17 27	17 56		18 27	18 56		19 27	19 56		20 27	20 56		21 27		21 56	22 27
Hairmyres	d	15 30	15 59		16 30	16 59		17 30	17 59		18 30	18 59		19 30	19 59		20 30	20 59		21 30		21 59	22 30
Thorntonhall	d		16 03			17 03			18 03			19 03			20 03			21 03				22 03	
Busby	d	15 35	16 06		16 35	17 06		17 35	18 06		18 35	19 06		19 35	20 06		20 35	21 06		21 35		22 06	22 35
Clarkston	d	15 38	16 09		16 38	17 09		17 38	18 09		18 38	19 09		19 38	20 09		20 38	21 09		21 38		22 09	22 38
Giffnock	d	15 42	16 12		16 42	17 12		17 42	18 12		18 42	19 12		19 42	20 12		20 42	21 12		21 42		22 12	22 42
Thornliebank	d	15 44	16 14		16 44	17 14		17 44	18 14		18 44	19 14		19 44	20 14		20 44	21 14		21 44		22 14	22 44
Pollokshaws West	d	15 47	16 17	16 27	16 47	17 17	17 27	17 47	18 17	18 27	18 47	19 17	19 27	19 47	20 17	20 27	20 47	21 17		21 47		22 17	22 47
Crossmyloof	d	15 50	16 20		16 50	17 20		17 50	18 20		18 50	19 20		19 50	20 20		20 50	21 20		21 50		22 20	22 50
Glasgow Central 15	a	15 56	16 26	16 36	16 56	17 26	17 36	17 56	18 26	18 36	18 56	19 26	19 36	19 56	20 26	20 36	20 56	21 26	21 35	21 56	22 05	22 26	22 56

		SR	SR	SR
Kilmarnock 3	d			
Kilmaurs	d			
Stewarton	d			
Dunlop	d			
Barrhead	d			
Nitshill	d			
Priesthill & Darnley	d			
Kennishead	d			
East Kilbride	d	22 56	23 27	23 56
Hairmyres	d	22 59	23 30	23 59
Thorntonhall	d	23 03		00 03
Busby	d	23 06	23 35	00 06
Clarkston	d	23 09	23 38	00 09
Giffnock	d	23 12	23 42	00 12
Thornliebank	d	23 14	23 44	00 14
Pollokshaws West	d	23 17	23 47	00 17
Crossmyloof	d	23 20	23 50	00 20
Glasgow Central 15	a	23 26	23 56	00 26

A From Carlisle
B From Newcastle
C From Stranraer
D not 22 May
E From Ayr

Glasgow Central, Cathcart Circle, Neilston and Newton

Miles	Miles	Miles			SR	SR	SR	SR	SR	SR	SR	SR	SR		SR	SR	SR	SR	SR	SR	SR	SR	SR		SR
0	0	0	**Glasgow Central** 15 226	d	06 15	06 17	06 20	06 34	06 36	06 50	07 00	07 03	07 07		07 14	07 20	07 29	07 35	07 45	07 48	07 54	07 56	08 01		08 10
2¼	—	—	Pollokshields West	d	06 21				06 42			07 09			07 20				07 51		08 00				08 16
2¾	—	—	Maxwell Park	d	06 23				06 44			07 11			07 22				07 53		08 02				08 18
3½	—	—	Shawlands	d	06 25				06 46			07 13			07 24				07 55		08 04				08 20
3¾	—	—	Pollokshaws East	d	06 26				06 47			07 14			07 25				07 56		08 05				08 21
4¼	—	—	Langside	d	06 28				06 49			07 17			07 27				07 58		08 07				08 23
—	1¾	1¾	Pollokshields East	d		06 22	06 25	06 39		06 55	07 05		07 12			07 25	07 34	07 40				08 01	08 06		
—	2¼	2¼	Queens Park	d		06 23	06 26	06 40		06 56	07 06		07 13			07 26	07 35	07 41				08 02	08 07		
—	2½	2½	Crosshill	d		06 25	06 28	06 42		06 58	07 08		07 15			07 28	07 37	07 43				08 04	08 09		
—	3¼	3¼	Mount Florida	d		06 27	06 30	06 44		07 00	07 10		07 17			07 30	07 39	07 45				08 06	08 11		
5¼	—	4	Cathcart	d	06a31	06 29		06 46		07a03	07 12		07 21		07a30		07 41	07a47			08a10		08 13		08a26
—	—	4¾	Muirend	d		06 32		06 49			07 15		07 24				07 44			07 58			08 16		
—	—	6	Williamwood	d		06 35		06 52			07 18		07 27				07 47			08 01			08 19		
—	—	6¾	Whitecraigs	d		06 37		06 54			07 20		07 29				07 49			08 03			08 21		
—	—	7¾	Patterton	d		06 40		06 57			07 23		07 32				07 52			08 06			08 24		
—	—	11¾	**Neilston**	a		06 46		07 03			07 29		07 38				07 58			08 12			08 30		
5¾	4½	—	Kings Park	d			06 33		06 53			07 21				07 33			08 03			08 09			
6	4¾	—	Croftfoot	d			06 35		06 55			07 23				07 35			08 05			08 11			
7	5¾	—	Burnside	d			06 38		06 58			07 25				07 38			08 08			08 14			
8½	7¼	—	Kirkhill	a			06 41		07 01			07 28				07 41			08 11			08 17			
10	8¾	—	**Newton** 226	a			06 44		07 04			07 31				07 44			08 14			08 20			

		SR	SR	SR	SR	SR	SR	SR	SR		SR	SR	SR	SR	SR	SR	SR	SR	SR		SR		SR	SR
Glasgow Central 15 226	d	08 12	08 15	08 20	08 26	08 33	08 39	08 46	08 50		09 07	09 14	09 19	09 35	09 45	09 50	10 05	10 15	10 20	and at the same minutes past each hour until	14 20		14 35	14 45
Pollokshields West	d					08 39		08 53				09 20			09 51			10 21						14 51
Maxwell Park	d					08 41		08 55				09 22			09 53			10 23						14 53
Shawlands	d					08 43		08 57				09 24			09 55			10 25						14 55
Pollokshaws East	d					08 44		08 58				09 25			09 56			10 26						14 56
Langside	d					08 46		09 00				09 27			09 58			10 28						14 58
Pollokshields East	d	08 17	08 21	08 25	08 31		08 44		08 55		09 12		09 25	09 40		09 55	10 10		10 25		14 25		14 40	
Queens Park	d	08 18	08 22	08 26	08 32		08 45		08 57		09 13		09 26	09 41		09 56	10 11		10 26		14 26		14 41	
Crosshill	d	08 20	08 24	08 28	08 34		08 47		08 59		09 15		09 28	09 43		09 58	10 13		10 28		14 28		14 43	
Mount Florida	d	08 22	08 26	08 30	08 36		08 49		09 01		09 17		09 30	09 45		10 00	10 15		10 30		14 30		14 45	
Cathcart	d	08a24	08a28		08 38	08a49	08 51		09a03		09 19	09a30		09 47		10a03	10 17	10a31					14 47	
Muirend	d				08 41		08 54				09 22			09 50			10 20						14 50	
Williamwood	d				08 44		08 57				09 25			09 53			10 23						14 53	
Whitecraigs	d				08 46		08 59				09 27			09 55			10 25						14 55	
Patterton	d				08 49		09 02				09 30			09 58			10 28						14 58	
Neilston	a				08 55		09 08				09 36			10 04			10 34						15 04	
Kings Park	d			08 33				09 04					09 33		10 03				10 33		14 33			15 03
Croftfoot	d			08 35				09 06					09 35		10 05				10 35		14 35			15 05
Burnside	d			08 38				09 09					09 38		10 08				10 38		14 38			15 08
Kirkhill	a			08 41				09 12					09 41		10 11				10 41		14 41			15 11
Newton 226	a			08 44				09 15					09 45		10 14				10 44		14 44			15 14

		SR	SR	SR	SR	SR	SR	SR		SR	SR	SR	SR	SR	SR	SR	SR	SR		SR	SR	SR	SR	SR	SR
Glasgow Central 15 226	d	14 50	15 05	15 15	15 20	15 35	15 45	15 50		16 05	16 15	16 20	16 35	16 45	16 50	16 59	17 05	17 08		17 14	17 18	17 23	17 29	17 38	17 45
Pollokshields West	d			15 21			15 51				16 21			16 51			17 11					17 29			17 51
Maxwell Park	d			15 23			15 53				16 23			16 53			17 13					17 32			17 53
Shawlands	d			15 25			15 55				16 25			16 55			17 15					17 34			17 55
Pollokshaws East	d			15 26			15 56				16 26			16 56			17 16					17 35			17 56
Langside	d			15 28			15 58				16 28			16 58			17 18					17 37			17 58
Pollokshields East	d	14 55	15 10		15 25	15 40		15 55		16 10		16 25	16 40		16 55	17 04		17 13			17 23		17 34	17 43	
Queens Park	d	14 56	15 11		15 26	15 41		15 57		16 11		16 27	16 41		16 56	17 05		17 14			17 24		17 35	17 44	
Crosshill	d	14 58	15 13		15 28	15 43		16 03		16 13		16 29	16 43		16 58	17 07		17 16			17 26		17 37	17 46	
Mount Florida	d	15 00	15 15		15 30	15 45		16 05		16 15		16 31	16 45		17 00	17 09		17 18			17 28		17 39	17 48	
Cathcart	d	15a03	15 17	15a31		15 47		16a06		16 17	16a31		16 47		17a03	17 11	17a21				17 30	17a40		17 50	
Muirend	d		15 20			15 50				16 20			16 50			17 14				17 25	17 33			17 53	
Williamwood	d		15 23			15 53				16 23			16 53			17 17				17 28	17 36			17 56	
Whitecraigs	d		15 25			15 55				16 25			16 55			17 19				17 30	17 38			17 58	
Patterton	d		15 28			15 58				16 28			16 58			17 22				17 33	17 41			18 01	
Neilston	a		15 34			16 04				16 36			17 04			17 28				17 39	17 47			18 07	
Kings Park	d				15 33		16 03					16 34		17 03				17 21					17 42		18 03
Croftfoot	d				15 35		16 05					16 36		17 05				17 23					17 44		18 05
Burnside	d				15 38		16 08					16 38		17 08				17 26					17 47		18 08
Kirkhill	a				15 41		16 11					16 41		17 11				17 29					17 50		18 11
Newton 226	a				15 45		16 15					16 45		17 14				17 32					17 53		18 14

		SR	SR	SR		SR	SR	SR	SR	SR	SR	SR		SR		SR	SR	SR	SR	SR	SR	SR FO		
Glasgow Central 15 226	d	17 50	18 07	18 15		18 20	18 35	18 45	18 50	19 05	19 15	19 20	and at the same minutes past each hour until	22 20		22 35	22 45	22 50	23 05	23 15	23 20	23 50		
Pollokshields West	d			18 21				18 51			19 21						22 51			23 21				
Maxwell Park	d			18 23				18 53			19 23						22 53			23 23				
Shawlands	d			18 25				18 55			19 25						22 55			23 25				
Pollokshaws East	d			18 26				18 56			19 26						22 56			23 26				
Langside	d			18 28				18 58			19 28						22 58			23 28				
Pollokshields East	d	17 55	18 12			18 25	18 40		18 55	19 10		19 25		22 25		22 40		22 55	23 10		23 25	23 55		
Queens Park	d	17 57	18 13			18 27	18 41		18 56	19 11		19 26		22 26		22 41		22 56	23 11		23 26	23 56		
Crosshill	d	17 59	18 15			18 29	18 43		18 58	19 13		19 28		22 28		22 43		22 58	23 13		23 28	23 58		
Mount Florida	d	18 01	18 17			18 31	18 45		19 00	19 15		19 30		22 30		22 45		23 00	23 15		23 30	23 59		
Cathcart	d	18a03	18 19	18a31			18 47		19a03	19 17	19a31					22 47		23a03	23 17	23a31				
Muirend	d		18 22				18 50			19 20						22 50			23 20					
Williamwood	d		18 25				18 53			19 23						22 53			23 23					
Whitecraigs	d		18 27				18 55			19 25						22 55			23 25					
Patterton	d		18 30				18 58			19 28						22 58			23 28					
Neilston	a		18 36				19 04			19 34						23 04			23 34					
Kings Park	d					18 34		19 03				19 33		22 33			23 03				23 33	00 03		
Croftfoot	d					18 36		19 05				19 35		22 35			23 05				23 35	00 05		
Burnside	d					18 38		19 08				19 38		22 38			23 08				23 38	00 08		
Kirkhill	a					18 41		19 11				19 41		22 41			23 11				23 41	00 11		
Newton 226	a					18 45		19 14				19 44		22 44			23 14				23 45	00 14		

Table 223

Saturdays

Glasgow Central, Cathcart Circle, Neilston and Newton

			SR	SR	SR	SR	SR	SR	SR	SR	SR		SR	SR	SR	SR	SR	SR	SR	SR	SR		SR	SR	SR	SR
Glasgow Central 15	226	d	23p50	00 05	00 20	06 15	06 17	06 20	06 34	06 45	07 06		07 20	07 35	07 45	08 05	08 20	08 35	08 45	08 50	09 05		09 14	09 20	09 35	09 45
Pollokshields West		d			00 26	06 21				06 51					07 51				08 51				09 20			09 51
Maxwell Park		d			00 28	06 23				06 53					07 53				08 53				09 22			09 53
Shawlands		d			00 30	06 25				06 55					07 55				08 55				09 24			09 55
Pollokshaws East		d			00 31	06 26				06 56					07 56				08 56				09 25			09 56
Langside		d			00 33	06 28				06 58					07 58				08 58				09 27			09 58
Pollokshields East		d	23p55	00 10			06 22	06 25	06 39		07 11		07 25	07 40		08 10	08 25	08 40		08 55	09 10			09 25	09 40	
Queens Park		d	23p56	00 11			06 23	06 26	06 40		07 12		07 26	07 41		08 11	08 26	08 41		08 56	09 11			09 26	09 41	
Crosshill		d	23p58	00 13			06 25	06 28	06 42		07 14		07 28	07 43		08 13	08 28	08 43		08 58	09 13			09 28	09 43	
Mount Florida		d	23p59	00 15			06 27	06 30	06 44		07 16		07 30	07 45		08 15	08 30	08 45		09 00	09 15			09 30	09 45	
Cathcart		d		00 17	00a36	06a31	06 29		06 46		07 18			07 47		08 17		08 47		09a03	09 17		09a30		09 47	
Muirend		d		00 20			06 32		06 49		07 21			07 50		08 20		08 50			09 20				09 50	
Williamwood		d		00 23			06 35		06 52		07 24			07 53		08 23		08 53			09 23				09 53	
Whitecraigs		d		00 25			06 37		06 54		07 26			07 55		08 25		08 55			09 25				09 55	
Patterton		d		00 28			06 40		06 57		07 29			07 58		08 28		08 58			09 28				09 58	
Neilston		a		00 34			06 46		07 03		07 35			08 04		08 34		09 04			09 34				10 04	
Kings Park		d	00 03					06 33		07 03			07 33		08 03		08 33		09 03					09 33		10 03
Croftfoot		d	00 05					06 35		07 05			07 35		08 05		08 35		09 05					09 35		10 05
Burnside		d	00 08					06 38		07 08			07 38		08 08		08 38		09 08					09 38		10 08
Kirkhill		a	00 11					06 41		07 11			07 41		08 11		08 41		09 11					09 41		10 11
Newton	226	a	00 14					06 44		07 14			07 44		08 14		08 44		09 15					09 45		10 14

			SR	SR	SR	SR		SR		SR	SR	SR	SR	SR	SR	SR	SR	SR		SR	SR	SR	SR	SR	SR
Glasgow Central 15	226	d	09 50	10 05	10 15	10 20	and at the same minutes past each hour until	14 20		14 35	14 45	14 50	15 05	15 15	15 20	15 35	15 45	15 50		16 05	16 15	16 20	16 35	16 45	16 50
Pollokshields West		d			10 21						14 51			15 21			15 51				16 21			16 51	
Maxwell Park		d			10 23						14 53			15 23			15 53				16 23			16 53	
Shawlands		d			10 25						14 55			15 25			15 55				16 25			16 55	
Pollokshaws East		d			10 26						14 56			15 26			15 56				16 26			16 56	
Langside		d			10 28						14 58			15 28			15 58				16 28			16 58	
Pollokshields East		d	09 55	10 10		10 25		14 25		14 40		14 55	15 10		15 25	15 40		15 55		16 10		16 25	16 40		16 55
Queens Park		d	09 56	10 11		10 26		14 26		14 41		14 56	15 11		15 26	15 41		15 57		16 11		16 27	16 41		16 56
Crosshill		d	09 58	10 13		10 28		14 28		14 43		14 58	15 13		15 28	15 43		15 59		16 13		16 29	16 43		16 58
Mount Florida		d	10 00	10 15		10 30		14 30		14 45		15 00	15 15		15 30	15 45		16 02		16 15		16 31	16 45		17 00
Cathcart		d	10a03	10 17	10a31					14 47		15a03	15 17	15a31		15 47		16a04		16 17	16a31		16 47		17a03
Muirend		d		10 20						14 50			15 20			15 50				16 20			16 50		
Williamwood		d		10 23						14 53			15 23			15 53				16 23			16 53		
Whitecraigs		d		10 25						14 55			15 25			15 55				16 25			16 55		
Patterton		d		10 28						14 58			15 28			15 58				16 28			16 58		
Neilston		a		10 34						15 04			15 34			16 04				16 36			17 04		
Kings Park		d				10 33		14 33			15 03				15 33		16 03					16 34		17 03	
Croftfoot		d				10 35		14 35			15 05				15 35		16 05					16 36		17 05	
Burnside		d				10 38		14 38			15 08				15 38		16 08					16 38		17 08	
Kirkhill		a				10 41		14 41			15 11				15 41		16 11					16 41		17 11	
Newton	226	a				10 44		14 44			15 14				15 45		16 15					16 45		17 14	

			SR	SR	SR		SR	SR	SR	SR	SR	SR	SR	SR	SR		SR		SR	SR	SR
Glasgow Central 15	226	d	17 07	17 15	17 20		17 35	17 45	17 50	18 07	18 15	18 20	18 35	18 45	18 50		19 05	and at the same minutes past each hour until	23 05	23 15	23 20
Pollokshields West		d		17 21				17 51			18 21			18 51						23 21	
Maxwell Park		d		17 23				17 53			18 23			18 53						23 23	
Shawlands		d		17 25				17 55			18 25			18 55						23 25	
Pollokshaws East		d		17 26				17 56			18 26			18 56						23 26	
Langside		d		17 28				17 58			18 28			18 58						23 28	
Pollokshields East		d	17 12		17 25		17 40		17 55	18 12		18 25	18 40		18 55		19 10		23 10		23 25
Queens Park		d	17 13		17 26		17 41		17 56	18 13		18 26	18 41		18 56		19 11		23 11		23 26
Crosshill		d	17 15		17 28		17 43		17 58	18 15		18 28	18 43		18 58		19 13		23 13		23 28
Mount Florida		d	17 17		17 30		17 45		18 00	18 17		18 30	18 45		19 00		19 15		23 15		23 30
Cathcart		d	17 19	17a31			17 47		18a03	18 19	18a31		18 47		19a03		19 17		23 17	23a31	
Muirend		d	17 22				17 50			18 22			18 50				19 20		23 20		
Williamwood		d	17 25				17 53			18 25			18 53				19 23		23 23		
Whitecraigs		d	17 27				17 55			18 27			18 55				19 25		23 25		
Patterton		d	17 30				17 58			18 30			18 58				19 28		23 28		
Neilston		a	17 36				18 04			18 36			19 04				19 34		23 34		
Kings Park		d			17 33			18 03				18 33		19 03							23 33
Croftfoot		d			17 35			18 05				18 35		19 05							23 35
Burnside		d			17 38			18 08				18 38		19 08							23 38
Kirkhill		a			17 41			18 11				18 41		19 11							23 41
Newton	226	a			17 44			18 14				18 44		19 14							23 45

Sundays

			SR	SR	SR	SR	SR	SR		SR		SR	SR	SR	SR	SR		SR	SR
Glasgow Central 15	226	d	08 23	08 34	08 53	09 08	09 23	09 34	and at the same minutes past each hour until	12 34		12 59	13 08	13 23	13 34	13 53	and at the same minutes past each hour until	22 53	23 08
Pollokshields West		d		08 40				09 40		12 40					13 40				
Maxwell Park		d		08 42				09 42		12 42					13 42				
Shawlands		d		08 44				09 44		12 44					13 44				
Pollokshaws East		d		08 45				09 45		12 45					13 45				
Langside		d		08 47				09 47		12 47					13 47				
Pollokshields East		d	08 28		08 58	09 13	09 28					13 04	13 13	13 28		13 58		22 58	23 13
Queens Park		d	08 29		08 59	09 14	09 29					13 05	13 14	13 29		13 59		22 59	23 14
Crosshill		d	08 31		09 01	09 16	09 31					13 07	13 16	13 31		14 01		23 01	23 16
Mount Florida		d	08 33		09 03	09 18	09 33					13 09	13 18	13 33		14 03		23 03	23 18
Cathcart		d	08 35		09 05		09 35					13 11		13 35		14 05		23 05	
Muirend		d	08 38		09 08		09 38					13 14		13 38		14 08		23 08	
Williamwood		d	08 41		09 11		09 41					13 17		13 41		14 11		23 11	
Whitecraigs		d	08 43		09 13		09 43					13 19		13 43		14 13		23 13	
Patterton		d	08 46		09 16		09 46					13 22		13 46		14 16		23 16	
Neilston		a	08 52		09 22		09 52					13 28		13 52		14 22		23 22	
Kings Park		d		08 51		09 21		09 52		12 52			13 21		13 52				23 21
Croftfoot		d		08 53		09 23		09 54		12 54			13 23		13 54				23 23
Burnside		d		08 56		09 26		09 57		12 57			13 26		13 57				23 26
Kirkhill		a		08 59		09 29		10 00		13 00			13 29		14 00				23 29
Newton	226	a		09 02		09 32		10 03		13 03			13 32		14 03				23 32

Newton, Neilston, Cathcart Circle and Glasgow Central

Miles	Miles	Miles			SR	SR	SR	SR	SR	SR	SR	SR	SR		SR	SR	SR	SR	SR	SR	SR	SR	SR		SR
0	0	—	**Newton**	226 d		06 20		06 50			07 15					07 41		07 51							08 21
1½	1½	—	Kirkhill	d		06 23		06 53			07 18					07 44		07 54							08 24
2¾	2¾	—	Burnside	d		06 26		06 56			07 21					07 47		07 57							08 27
3¾	3¾	—	Croftfoot	d		06 30		06 58			07 23					07 49		07 59							08 29
4¼	4¼	—	Kings Park	d		06 32		07 00			07 25					07 51		08 02							08 31
—	—	—	**Neilston**	d			06 30			07 00			07 24				07 41			07 56	08 06				
—	—	3¾	Patterton	d			06 36			07 06			07 30				07 47			08 02	08 12				
—	—	4¾	Whitecraigs	d			06 39			07 09			07 33				07 50			08 05	08 15				
—	—	5½	Williamwood	d			06 41			07 11			07 35				07 52			08 08	08 17				
—	—	7	Muirend	d			06 44			07 14			07 38				07 55			08 11	08 20				
4¾	—	7¾	Cathcart	d	06 31		06 47		07 03	07 17		07 32	07 41		07 47		07 58		08 10	08 14		08 26	08 24		
—	5½	8½	Mount Florida	d	06 33		06 49	07 04		07 19		07 34	07 43			07 55	08 01		08 12	08 17		08 28			08 35
—	6	9	Crosshill	d	06 35		06 51	07 06		07 21		07 36	07 45			07 57	08 03		08 14	08 19		08 30			08 37
—	6½	9½	Queens Park	d	06 37		06 53	07 08		07 23		07 38	07 47			07 59	08 05		08 16	08 21		08 32			08 39
—	6¾	9¾	Pollokshields East	d	06 38		06 54	07 09		07 24		07 39	07 48			08 00	08 07		08 18	08 23	08 29	08 33			08 40
5¾	—	—	Langside	d		06 37			07 05		07 29				07 50			08 06					08 27		
6¼	—	—	Pollokshaws East	d		06 39			07 07		07 31				07 52			08 08					08 29		
6¾	—	—	Shawlands	d		06 42			07 09		07 33				07 54			08 10					08 31		
7½	—	—	Maxwell Park	d		06 44			07 11		07 35				07 56			08 12					08 33		
8	—	—	Pollokshields West	d		06 48			07 14		07 37				07 58			08 14					08 35		
10	8¾	11¾	**Glasgow Central** 15	226 a	06 43	06 54	06 59	07 14	07 20	07 29	07 43	07 47	07 55		08 04	08 07	08 12	08 21	08 23	08 28	08 34	08 39	08 41		08 47

		SR	SR	SR	SR	SR	SR	SR	SR	SR		SR	SR	SR	SR	SR		SR	SR		SR	SR	SR	SR
Newton	226 d				08 33			08 59				09 20		09 50			and at the same minutes past each hour until				15 20		15 50	
Kirkhill	d				08 36			09 02				09 23		09 53							15 23		15 53	
Burnside	d				08 39			09 05				09 26		09 56							15 26		15 56	
Croftfoot	d				08 42			09 07				09 28		09 58							15 28		15 58	
Kings Park	d				08 44			09 10				09 30		10 00							15 30		16 00	
Neilston	d		08 20			08 43			09 04				09 30			10 00		15 00				15 30		
Patterton	d		08 26			08 49			09 10				09 36			10 06		15 06				15 36		
Whitecraigs	d		08 29			08 52			09 13				09 39			10 09		15 09				15 39		
Williamwood	d		08 31			08 54			09 15				09 41			10 11		15 11				15 41		
Muirend	d		08 35			08 57			09 18				09 44			10 14		15 14				15 44		
Cathcart	d	08 33	08 38	08 49		09 00	09 03		09 21	09 32			09 47		10 03	10 17		15 17	15 32			15 47		16 06
Mount Florida	d		08 41	08 52		09 02		09 14	09 23	09 34			09 49	10 04		10 19		15 19	15 34			15 49	16 04	
Crosshill	d		08 43	08 54		09 04		09 16	09 25	09 36			09 51	10 06		10 21		15 21	15 36			15 51	16 06	
Queens Park	d		08 45	08 56		09 06		09 18	09 27	09 38			09 53	10 08		10 23		15 23	15 38			15 53	16 08	
Pollokshields East	d		08 47	08 58		09 07		09 19	09 28	09 39			09 54	10 09		10 24		15 24	15 39			15 54	16 09	
Langside	d	08 36			08 49		09 06					09 35			10 05						15 35			16 09
Pollokshaws East	d	08 38			08 51		09 08					09 37			10 07						15 37			16 11
Shawlands	d	08 40			08 54		09 10					09 39			10 09						15 39			16 13
Maxwell Park	d	08 42			08 56		09 12					09 41			10 11						15 41			16 15
Pollokshields West	d	08 45			09 00		09 15					09 44			10 14						15 44			16 18
Glasgow Central 15	226 a	08 51	08 53	09 03	09 06	09 12	09 22	09 24	09 33	09 44		09 50	09 59	10 14	10 20	10 29		15 29	15 44		15 50	15 59	16 14	16 24

		SR	SR	SR	SR	SR		SR	SR	SR	SR	SR	SR	SR	SR	SR		SR	SR	SR	SR	SR	SR	SR	SR
Newton	226 d			16 20		16 50						17 20			17 50						18 20		18 50		
Kirkhill	d			16 23		16 53						17 23			17 53						18 23		18 53		
Burnside	d			16 26		16 56						17 26			17 56						18 26		18 56		
Croftfoot	d			16 28		16 58						17 28			17 58						18 28		18 58		
Kings Park	d			16 30		17 00						17 30			18 00						18 30		19 00		
Neilston	d	16 00			16 30				16 53		17 14			17 39				17 54	18 04			18 30			19 00
Patterton	d	16 06			16 36				16 59		17 20			17 45				18 00	18 10			18 36			19 06
Whitecraigs	d	16 09			16 39				17 02		17 23			17 48				18 03	18 13			18 39			19 09
Williamwood	d	16 11			16 41				17 04		17 25			17 50				18 05	18 15			18 41			19 11
Muirend	d	16 14			16 44				17 07		17 28			17 53				18 08	18 18			18 44			19 14
Cathcart	d	16 17	16 32		16 47			17 03	17 10	17 21	17 31		17 41	17 56		18 03		18 11	18 21	18 32		18 47		19 03	19 17
Mount Florida	d	16 19	16 34		16 49	17 04			17 12	17 23	17 33		17 43	17 58	18 04			18 13	18 23	18 34		18 49	19 04		19 19
Crosshill	d	16 21	16 36		16 51	17 06			17 14	17 25	17 35		17 45	18 00	18 06			18 15	18 25	18 36		18 51	19 06		19 21
Queens Park	d	16 23	16 38		16 53	17 08			17 16	17 27	17 37		17 47	18 02	18 08			18 17	18 27	18 38		18 53	19 08		19 23
Pollokshields East	d	16 24	16 39		16 54	17 09			17 17	17 29	17 38		17 48	18 03	18 09			18 18	18 28	18 39		18 54	19 09		19 24
Langside	d			16 35				17 05				17 35				18 05					18 35			19 05	
Pollokshaws East	d			16 37				17 07				17 37				18 07					18 37			19 07	
Shawlands	d			16 39				17 09				17 39				18 09					18 39			19 09	
Maxwell Park	d			16 41				17 11				17 41				18 11					18 41			19 11	
Pollokshields West	d			16 44				17 14				17 44				18 14					18 44			19 14	
Glasgow Central 15	226 a	16 29	16 44	16 50	16 59	17 15		17 20	17 22	17 37	17 43	17 50	17 55	18 08	18 14	18 20		18 25	18 34	18 44	18 50	18 59	19 14	19 21	19 29

		SR		SR	SR	SR	SR	SR	SR	SR		SR		SR
Newton	226 d			19 20		19 50				20 20	and at the same minutes past each hour until	23 20		
Kirkhill	d			19 23		19 53				20 23		23 23		
Burnside	d			19 26		19 56				20 26		23 26		
Croftfoot	d			19 28		19 58				20 28		23 28		
Kings Park	d			19 30		20 00				20 30		23 30		
Neilston	d				19 30			20 00						23 30
Patterton	d				19 36			20 06						23 36
Whitecraigs	d				19 39			20 09						23 39
Williamwood	d				19 41			20 11						23 41
Muirend	d				19 44			20 14						23 44
Cathcart	d	19 32			19 47		20 03	20 17	20 32					23 47
Mount Florida	d	19 34			19 49	20 04		20 19	20 34					23 49
Crosshill	d	19 36			19 51	20 06		20 21	20 36					23 51
Queens Park	d	19 38			19 53	20 08		20 23	20 38					23 53
Pollokshields East	d	19 39			19 54	20 09		20 24	20 39					23 54
Langside	d			19 35			20 05			20 35		23 35		
Pollokshaws East	d			19 37			20 07			20 37		23 37		
Shawlands	d			19 39			20 09			20 39		23 39		
Maxwell Park	d			19 41			20 11			20 41		23 41		
Pollokshields West	d			19 44			20 14			20 44		23 44		
Glasgow Central 15	226 a	19 44		19 51	19 59	20 15	20 20	20 29	20 44	20 50		23 50		23 59

Table 223

Saturdays

Newton, Neilston, Cathcart Circle and Glasgow Central

		SR	SR	SR	SR	SR	SR	SR	SR	SR		SR	SR	SR	SR	SR	SR	SR		SR		SR	SR	SR
Newton	226 d			06 20		06 50		07 20		07 50			08 20		08 50				and at the same minutes past each hour until			15 20		15 50
Kirkhill	d			06 23		06 53		07 23		07 53			08 23		08 53							15 23		15 53
Burnside	d			06 26		06 56		07 26		07 56			08 26		08 56							15 26		15 56
Croftfoot	d			06 30		06 58		07 28		07 58			08 28		08 58							15 28		15 58
Kings Park	d			06 32		07 00		07 30		08 00			08 30		09 00							15 30		16 00
Neilston	d				06 30		07 00		07 30			07 56		08 30			09 00						15 30	
Patterton	d				06 36		07 06		07 36			08 02		08 36			09 06						15 36	
Whitecraigs	d				06 39		07 09		07 39			08 05		08 39			09 09						15 39	
Williamwood	d				06 41		07 11		07 41			08 08		08 41			09 11						15 41	
Muirend	d				06 44		07 14		07 44			08 11		08 44			09 14						15 44	
Cathcart	d	00 36	06 31		06 47		07 17		07 47			08 14		08 47		09 03	09 17	09 32		15 32			15 47	
Mount Florida	d	00 38	06 33		06 49	07 04	07 19		07 49	08 04		08 17		08 49	09 04		09 19	09 34		15 34			15 49	16 04
Crosshill	d	00 40	06 35		06 51	07 06	07 21		07 51	08 06		08 19		08 51	09 06		09 21	09 36		15 36			15 51	16 06
Queens Park	d	00 42	06 37		06 53	07 08	07 23		07 53	08 08		08 21		08 53	09 08		09 23	09 38		15 38			15 53	16 08
Pollokshields East	d	00 43	06 38		06 54	07 09	07 24		07 54	08 09		08 23		08 54	09 09		09 24	09 39		15 39			15 54	16 09
Langside	d			06 37				07 35					08 35			09 05						15 35		
Pollokshaws East	d			06 39				07 37					08 37			09 07						15 37		
Shawlands	d			06 42				07 39					08 39			09 09						15 39		
Maxwell Park	d			06 44				07 41					08 41			09 11						15 41		
Pollokshields West	d			06 48				07 44					08 44			09 14						15 44		
Glasgow Central 15	226 a	00 48	06 43	06 54	06 59	07 14	07 29	07 50	07 59	08 14		08 28	08 50	08 59	09 14	09 20	09 29	09 44		15 44		15 50	15 59	16 14

		SR	SR	SR	SR	SR	SR		SR	SR	SR	SR	SR	SR	SR	SR	SR		SR	SR	SR	SR	SR	SR	SR
Newton	226 d				16 20		16 50					17 20		17 50					18 20		18 50				19 20
Kirkhill	d				16 23		16 53					17 23		17 53					18 23		18 53				19 23
Burnside	d				16 26		16 56					17 26		17 56					18 26		18 56				19 26
Croftfoot	d				16 28		16 58					17 28		17 58					18 28		18 58				19 28
Kings Park	d				16 30		17 00					17 30		18 00					18 30		19 00				19 30
Neilston	d		16 00			16 30				17 00			17 30			18 00				18 30			19 00		
Patterton	d		16 06			16 36				17 06			17 36			18 06				18 36			19 06		
Whitecraigs	d		16 09			16 39				17 09			17 39			18 09				18 39			19 09		
Williamwood	d		16 11			16 41				17 11			17 41			18 11				18 41			19 11		
Muirend	d		16 14			16 44				17 14			17 44			18 14				18 44			19 14		
Cathcart	d	16 04	16 17	16 32		16 47			17 03	17 17	17 32		17 47		18 03	18 17	18 32			18 47		19 03	19 17	19 32	
Mount Florida	d		16 19	16 34		16 49	17 04			17 19	17 34		17 49	18 04		18 19	18 34			18 49	19 04		19 19	19 34	
Crosshill	d		16 21	16 36		16 51	17 06			17 21	17 36		17 51	18 06		18 21	18 36			18 51	19 06		19 21	19 36	
Queens Park	d		16 23	16 38		16 53	17 08			17 23	17 38		17 53	18 08		18 23	18 38			18 53	19 08		19 23	19 38	
Pollokshields East	d		16 24	16 39		16 54	17 09			17 24	17 39		17 54	18 09		18 24	18 39			18 54	19 09		19 24	19 39	
Langside	d	16 07			16 35				17 05			17 35			18 05				18 35			19 05			19 35
Pollokshaws East	d	16 09			16 37				17 07			17 37			18 07				18 37			19 07			19 37
Shawlands	d	16 11			16 39				17 09			17 39			18 09				18 39			19 09			19 39
Maxwell Park	d	16 13			16 41				17 11			17 41			18 11				18 41			19 11			19 41
Pollokshields West	d	16 16			16 44				17 14			17 44			18 14				18 44			19 14			19 44
Glasgow Central 15	226 a	16 22	16 29	16 44	16 50	16 59	17 14		17 20	17 29	17 44	17 50	17 59	18 14	18 20	18 29	18 44		18 50	18 59	19 14	19 20	19 29	19 44	19 51

		SR	SR		SR	SR	SR	SR		SR	SR
Newton	226 d		19 50					20 20	and at the same minutes past each hour until	23 20	
Kirkhill	d		19 53					20 23		23 23	
Burnside	d		19 56					20 26		23 26	
Croftfoot	d		19 58					20 28		23 28	
Kings Park	d		20 00					20 30		23 30	
Neilston	d	19 30				20 00					23 30
Patterton	d	19 36				20 06					23 36
Whitecraigs	d	19 39				20 09					23 39
Williamwood	d	19 41				20 11					23 41
Muirend	d	19 44				20 14					23 44
Cathcart	d	19 47			20 03	20 17	20 32				23 47
Mount Florida	d	19 49	20 04			20 19	20 34				23 49
Crosshill	d	19 51	20 06			20 21	20 36				23 51
Queens Park	d	19 53	20 08			20 23	20 38				23 53
Pollokshields East	d	19 54	20 09			20 24	20 39				23 54
Langside	d				20 05			20 35		23 35	
Pollokshaws East	d				20 07			20 37		23 37	
Shawlands	d				20 09			20 39		23 39	
Maxwell Park	d				20 11			20 41		23 41	
Pollokshields West	d				20 14			20 44		23 44	
Glasgow Central 15	226 a	19 59	20 15		20 20	20 29	20 44	20 50		23 50	23 59

Sundays

		SR	SR	SR	SR		SR	SR	SR		SR	SR	SR	SR	SR
Newton	226 d		09 09		09 39	and at the same minutes past each hour until	21 39		22 09			22 39		23 09	
Kirkhill	d		09 12		09 42		21 42		22 12			22 42		23 12	
Burnside	d		09 15		09 45		21 45		22 15			22 45		23 15	
Croftfoot	d		09 17		09 47		21 47		22 17			22 47		23 17	
Kings Park	d		09 19		09 49		21 49		22 19			22 49		23 19	
Neilston	d	08 48		09 19				21 48			22 19		22 48		23 19
Patterton	d	08 54		09 25				21 54			22 25		22 54		23 25
Whitecraigs	d	08 57		09 28				21 57			22 28		22 57		23 28
Williamwood	d	08 59		09 30				21 59			22 30		22 59		23 30
Muirend	d	09 02		09 33				22 02			22 33		23 02		23 33
Cathcart	d	09 05		09 36				22 05			22 36		23 05		23 36
Mount Florida	d	09 07		09 38	09 53		21 53	22 07			22 38	22 53	23 07		23 38
Crosshill	d	09 09		09 40	09 55		21 55	22 09			22 40	22 55	23 09		23 40
Queens Park	d	09 11		09 42	09 57		21 57	22 11			22 42	22 57	23 11		23 42
Pollokshields East	d	09 12		09 43	09 58		21 58	22 12			22 43	22 58	23 12		23 43
Langside	d		09 23						22 23					23 23	
Pollokshaws East	d		09 25						22 25					23 25	
Shawlands	d		09 27						22 27					23 27	
Maxwell Park	d		09 29						22 29					23 29	
Pollokshields West	d		09 31						22 31					23 31	
Glasgow Central 15	226 a	09 17	09 38	09 48	10 03		22 03	22 17	22 37		22 48	23 03	23 17	23 37	23 48

Table 224

Mondays to Saturdays

Motherwell and Glasgow Queen Street - Cumbernauld and Falkirk Grahamston

Miles	Miles			SR MX	SR	SR SX	SR	SR	SR	SR SX	SR	SR	SR	SR	SR SX	SR SO	SR
—	0	**Motherwell**	226 d			06 11				07 07		07 35			08 37	08 37	
—	4½	Whifflet	d									07 43			08 43	08 45	
—	5¼	**Coatbridge Central**	d			06 21		06 45		07 17		07 46			08 46	08 48	
0	—	**Glasgow Queen Street** 10	d	23p51	05 51		06 21		06 51		07 21		07 52	08 23			08 51
1¼	—	Springburn	d	23p55	05 55		06 25		06 55		07 26		07 55	08 25			08 55
5¼	—	Stepps	d	00 02	06 02		06 32		07 02		07 33		08 02	08 32			09 02
7¾	—	Gartcosh	d	00 06	06 06		06 36		07 06		07 37		08 06	08 36			09 06
13¼	11	Greenfaulds	d	00 14	06 14		06 44	06 52	07 14		07 45	07 52	08 14	08 44	08 52	08 55	09 14
14	11¾	**Cumbernauld**	d	00a18	06a18		06 46	06a57	07a18		07 47	07a57	08a19	08 46	09a01	09a01	09a20
22½	—	Camelon	d				06 57				08 04			09 04			
24	—	**Falkirk Grahamston**	a				07 03				08 11			09 10			

		SR	SR	SR	SR	SR	SR	SR	SR	SR	SR	SR	SR	SR	SR
Motherwell	226 d		09 37			10 37			11 37			12 37			13 37
Whifflet	d		09 45			10 45			11 45			12 45			13 45
Coatbridge Central	d		09 48			10 48			11 48			12 48			13 48
Glasgow Queen Street 10	d	09 21		09 52	10 21		10 51	11 21		11 51	12 22		12 51	13 21	
Springburn	d	09 25		09 55	10 25		10 55	11 25		11 55	12 25		12 55	13 25	
Stepps	d	09 32		10 02	10 32		11 02	11 32		12 02	12 32		13 02	13 32	
Gartcosh	d	09 36		10 06	10 36		11 06	11 36		12 06	12 36		13 06	13 36	
Greenfaulds	d	09 44	09 55	10 14	10 44	10 55	11 14	11 44	11 55	12 14	12 44	12 55	13 14	13 44	13 55
Cumbernauld	d	09 46	10a01	10a19	10 46	11a01	11a18	11 46	12a01	12a18	12 46	13a01	13a18	13 46	14a01
Camelon	d	10 04			11 04			12 04			13 04			14 04	
Falkirk Grahamston	a	10 10			11 10			12 10			13 10			14 10	

		SR	SR	SR	SR	SR	SR	SR	SR SX	SR SX	SR SO	SR	SR SX	SR	SR SX
Motherwell	226 d			14 37			15 37					16 37	16 46		
Whifflet	d			14 45			15 45					16 45			
Coatbridge Central	d			14 48			15 48					16 49	16 56		
Glasgow Queen Street 10	d	13 51	14 21		14 51	15 21		15 54	15 51	16 22	16 22			16 51	17 03
Springburn	d	13 55	14 25		14 55	15 25		15 56		16 25	16 25			16 55	
Stepps	d	14 02	14 32		15 02	15 32		16 02		16 32	16 32			17 02	
Gartcosh	d	14 06	14 36		15 06	15 36		16 06		16 36	16 36			17 06	
Greenfaulds	d	14 14	14 44	14 55	15 14	15 44	15 55	16 14		16 44	16 44	16 55		17 15	
Cumbernauld	d	14a18	14 46	15a01	15a19	15 46	16a01	16a21		16 46	16 46	17a01		17a20	
Camelon	d		15 04			16 04			16 27	17 01	17 07				17 30
Falkirk Grahamston	a		15 10			16 10			16 33	17 04	17 12				17 32

		SR SX	SR SX	SR	SR	SR	SR SX	SR	SR	SR	SR	SR	SR	SR	SR	SR	SR
Motherwell	226 d	17 13			17 37		17 58		18 37			19 37			20 37		
Whifflet	d				17 46				18 45			19 45			20 45		
Coatbridge Central	d	17 22			17 49		18 07		18 48			19 48			20 48		
Glasgow Queen Street 10	d		17 33	17 22		17 51		18 23		18 51	19 21		19 51	20 21		20 51	21 21
Springburn	d			17 25		17 55		18 25		18 55	19 27		19 56	20 25		20 55	21 25
Stepps	d			17 32		18 02		18 32		19 02	19 34		20 03	20 32		21 02	21 32
Gartcosh	d			17 36		18 06		18 36		19 06	19 37		20 07	20 36		21 06	21 36
Greenfaulds	d			17 44	17 56	18 14		18 44	18 55	19 14	19 45	19 55	20 15	20 44	20 55	21 14	21 44
Cumbernauld	d			17 46	18a01	18a19		18 46	19a01	19a18	19a50	20a01	20 17	20a48	21a01	21 16	21a48
Camelon	d		17 58	18 04				19 04					20 34			21 27	
Falkirk Grahamston	a		18 01	18 10				19 10					20 40			21 33	

		SR	SR	SR	SR	SR	SR
Motherwell	226 d	21 37					
Whifflet	d	21 45					
Coatbridge Central	d	21 48					
Glasgow Queen Street 10	d		21 51	22 21	22 51	23 21	23 51
Springburn	d		21 55	22 26	22 55	23 25	23 55
Stepps	d		22 02	22 33	23 02	23 32	00 02
Gartcosh	d		22 05	22 37	23 06	23 36	00 06
Greenfaulds	d	21 56	22 15	22 45	23 14	23 44	00 14
Cumbernauld	d	22a01	22 16	22a49	23 16	23a48	00a18
Camelon	d		22 27		23 29		
Falkirk Grahamston	a		22 34		23 36		

Sundays

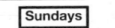

until 20 November

		SR A	SR	SR	SR	SR	SR	SR	SR	SR	SR	SR	SR
Motherwell	226 d												
Whifflet	d												
Coatbridge Central	d												
Glasgow Queen Street 10	d	23p51	08 19	09 22	10 21	11 21	12 23	13 21	14 21	15 21	16 21	17 21	18 23
Springburn	d	23p55	08 24	09 25	10 25	11 25	12 25	13 25	14 25	15 25	16 25	17 25	18 25
Stepps	d	00 02	08 30	09 32	10 32	11 32	12 32	13 32	14 32	15 32	16 32	17 32	18 32
Gartcosh	d	00 06	08 34	09 36	10 36	11 36	12 36	13 36	14 36	15 36	16 36	17 36	18 36
Greenfaulds	d	00 14	08 42	09 44	10 44	11 44	12 43	13 44	14 44	15 44	16 44	17 44	18 44
Cumbernauld	d	00a18	08a46	09a49	10a48	11a48	12a50	13a48	14a48	15a48	16a48	17a48	18a50
Camelon	d												
Falkirk Grahamston	a												

A not 22 May

Table 224

Sundays
until 20 November

Motherwell and Glasgow Queen Street - Cumbernauld and Falkirk Grahamston

	SR		SR				SR		SR															
Motherwell 226 d																								
Whifflet d																								
Coatbridge Central d																								
Glasgow Queen Street 10 d	19 22		20 21				21 26		22 25															
Springburn d	19 25		20 25				21 30		22 30															
Stepps d	19 32		20 32				21 37		22 37															
Gartcosh d	19 36		20 36				21 41		22 41															
Greenfaulds d	19 44		20 44				21 49		22 49															
Cumbernauld d	19a49		20a48				21a53		22a52															
Camelon d																								
Falkirk Grahamston a																								

Sundays
from 27 November

	SR	SR	SR		SR	SR		SR	SR		SR		SR	SR		SR	SR		SR		SR		SR	SR
Motherwell 226 d																								
Whifflet d																								
Coatbridge Central d																								
Glasgow Queen Street 10 d	23p51	08 19	08 42		09 22	09 51		10 21	10 51		11 21		11 51	12 23		12 52	13 21		13 51		14 21		14 51	15 21
Springburn d	23p55	08 24	08 47		09 25	09 56		10 25	10 56		11 25		11 56	12 25		12 57	13 25		13 55		14 25		14 55	15 25
Stepps d	00 02	08 30	08 54		09 32	10 02		10 32	11 02		11 32		12 02	12 32		13 04	13 32		14 02		14 32		15 02	15 32
Gartcosh d	00 06	08 34	08 58		09 36	10 06		10 36	11 06		11 36		12 06	12 36		13 07	13 36		14 06		14 36		15 06	15 36
Greenfaulds d	00 14	08 42	09 06		09 44	10 14		10 44	11 14		11 44		12 14	12 43		13 15	13 44		14 14		14 44		15 14	15 44
Cumbernauld d	00a18	08a46	09a09		09a49	10a18		10a48	11a18		11a48		12a20	12a50		13a20	13a48		14a18		14a48		15a18	15a48
Camelon d																								
Falkirk Grahamston a																								

		SR	SR		SR		SR		SR	SR		SR		SR				SR		SR				
Motherwell 226 d																								
Whifflet d																								
Coatbridge Central d																								
Glasgow Queen Street 10 d		15 54	16 21		16 52		17 21		17 51	18 23		19 22		20 21				21 26		22 25				
Springburn d		16 00	16 25		16 56		17 25		17 55	18 25		19 25		20 25				21 30		22 30				
Stepps d		16 07	16 32		17 03		17 32		18 02	18 32		19 32		20 32				21 37		22 37				
Gartcosh d		16 11	16 36		17 07		17 36		18 06	18 36		19 36		20 36				21 41		22 41				
Greenfaulds d		16 19	16 44		17 15		17 44		18 14	18 44		19 44		20 44				21 49		22 49				
Cumbernauld d		16a22	16a48		17a19		17a48		18a18	18a50		19a49		20a48				21a53		22a52				
Camelon d																								
Falkirk Grahamston a																								

Falkirk Grahamston and Cumbernauld - Glasgow Queen Street and Motherwell

Miles	Miles			SR	SR	SR	SR	SR	SR	SR SX	SR	SR SO		SR SX	SR	SR	SR	SR	SR	SR	SR	SR		SR	SR
0	—	**Falkirk Grahamston**	d	05 42			06 44				07 42					08 42			09 42			10 42			
1½	—	Camelon	d	05 44			06 46				07 44					08 44			09 44			10 44			
10	—	**Cumbernauld**	d	05 58	06 28		06 58	07 08	07 28		07 58	08 10		08 10	08 30	08 58	09 10	09 28	09 58	10 10	10 28	10 58		11 10	11 28
10¾	0¾	Greenfaulds	d	05 59	06 29		06 59	07 10	07 29		07 59	08 12		08 12	08 31	08 59	09 12	09 29	09 59	10 12	10 29	10 59		11 12	11 29
16¼	—	Gartcosh	d	06 06	06 36		07 06		07 36		08 06				08 38	09 06		09 36	10 06		10 36	11 06			11 36
18¾	—	Stepps	d	06 10	06 40		07 10		07 40		08 10				08 42	09 10		09 40	10 10		10 40	11 10			11 40
22¾	—	Springburn	d	06 16	06 46		07 16		07 46		08 16				08 48	09 16		09 46	10 16		10 46	11 16			11 46
24	—	**Glasgow Queen Street** 10	a	06 25	06 55		07 29		07 55		08 28				08 59	09 25		09 56	10 25		10 55	11 25			11 55
—	6¼	**Coatbridge Central**	d			06 40		07 20		07 39		08 20		08 20			09 20			10 20				11 20	
—	7¼	Whifflet	d			06 42		07 22		07 41		08 22		08 24			09 22			10 22				11 22	
—	11¾	**Motherwell** 226	a			06 51		07 30		07 48		08 32		08 32			09 32			10 32				11 32	

		SR	SR	SR	SR	SR	SR	SR		SR SX	SR SO	SR	SR	SR	SR SX	SR B	SR	SR		SR	SR	SR	SR	SR SX	SR
Falkirk Grahamston	d	11 42			12 42			13 42					14 42				15 42				16 42				17 42
Camelon	d	11 44			12 44			13 44					14 44				15 44				16 44				17 44
Cumbernauld	d	12 00	12 10	12 28	12 58	13 10	13 28	13 58		14 10	14 10	14 28	14 58	15 10	15 28	15 28	15 59	16 10		16 28	16 58	17 10	17 28		17 58
Greenfaulds	d	12 01	12 12	12 29	12 59	13 12	13 29	13 59		14 12	14 12	14 29	14 59	15 12	15 29	15 29	16 01	16 12		16 29	16 59	17 12	17 29		17 59
Gartcosh	d	12 08		12 36	13 06		13 36	14 06				14 36	15 06		15 36	15 36	16 06			16 36	17 06		17 36		18 06
Stepps	d	12 12		12 40	13 10		13 40	14 10				14 40	15 10		15 40	15 40	16 10			16 40	17 10		17 40		18 10
Springburn	d	12 18		12 46	13 16		13 46	14 16				14 46	15 16		15 46	15 46	16 16			16 46	17 16		17 46		18 16
Glasgow Queen Street 10	a	12 27		12 55	13 25		13 55	14 25				14 55	15 25		15 55	15 57	16 26			16 58	17 27		17 56		18 27
Coatbridge Central	d		12 20			13 20				14 18	14 20			15 20				16 20				17 18		17 32	
Whifflet	d		12 22			13 22				14 22	14 22			15 24				16 22				17 22		17 34	
Motherwell 226	a		12 32			13 32				14 32	14 32			15 32				16 32				17 32		17 40	

		SR SX	SR	SR		SR SX	SR	SR	SR	SR	SR	SR	SR	SR		SR	SR	SR	SR	SR	SR
Falkirk Grahamston	d						18 45			19 42						21 11			22 11		23 12
Camelon	d						18 47			19 44						21 14			22 14		23 14
Cumbernauld	d		18 10	18 28			19 01	19 10	19 28	19 58	20 10	20 28	20 58	21 10		21 28	21 58	22 10	22 28	22 58	23 28
Greenfaulds	d		18 12	18 29			19 02	19 12	19 29	19 59	20 12	20 29	20 59	21 12		21 29	21 59	22 12	22 29	22 59	23 29
Gartcosh	d			18 36			19 09		19 36	20 06		20 36	21 06			21 36	22 06		22 36	23 06	23 36
Stepps	d			18 40			19 13		19 40	20 10		20 40	21 10			21 40	22 10		22 40	23 10	23 40
Springburn	d			18 46			19 19		19 46	20 16		20 46	21 16			21 46	22 16		22 46	23 16	23 46
Glasgow Queen Street 10	a			18 55			19 29		19 55	20 26		20 55	21 25			21 55	22 26		22 55	23 26	23 55
Coatbridge Central	d	17 56	18 20			18 39		19 20			20 20			21 20				22 18			
Whifflet	d	18 00	18 22			18 41		19 22			20 22			21 22				22 22			
Motherwell 226	a	18 08	18 32			18 49		19 32			20 32			21 32				22 32			

Sundays

until 20 November

		SR	SR	SR	SR	SR	SR	SR	SR	SR		SR	SR	SR	SR	SR	SR
Falkirk Grahamston	d																
Camelon	d																
Cumbernauld	d	08 55	09 58	10 58	11 58	12 58	13 58	14 58	15 58	16 58		17 58	18 58	19 58	21 03	22 02	23 01
Greenfaulds	d	08 56	09 59	10 59	11 59	12 59	13 59	14 59	15 59	16 59		17 59	18 59	19 59	21 05	22 03	23 03
Gartcosh	d	09 03	10 06	11 06	12 06	13 06	14 06	15 06	16 06	17 06		18 06	19 06	20 06	21 11	22 08	23 10
Stepps	d	09 07	10 10	11 10	12 10	13 10	14 10	15 10	16 10	17 10		18 10	19 10	20 10	21 15	22 12	23 14
Springburn	d	09 13	10 16	11 16	12 16	13 17	14 16	15 16	16 16	17 16		18 16	19 16	20 16	21 21	22 18	23 20
Glasgow Queen Street 10	a	09 22	10 25	11 25	12 25	13 26	14 26	15 25	16 25	17 25		18 26	19 26	20 26	21 30	22 29	23 28
Coatbridge Central	d																
Whifflet	d																
Motherwell 226	a																

Sundays

from 27 November

		SR	SR	SR	SR	SR	SR	SR	SR	SR		SR	SR	SR	SR	SR	SR	SR	SR	SR		SR	SR	SR	SR
Falkirk Grahamston	d																								
Camelon	d																								
Cumbernauld	d	08 55	09 28	09 58	10 28	10 58	11 26	11 58	12 29	12 58		13 28	13 58	14 28	14 58	15 32	15 58	16 29	16 58	17 28		17 58	18 28	18 58	19 58
Greenfaulds	d	08 56	09 29	09 59	10 29	10 59	11 28	11 59	12 31	12 59		13 29	13 59	14 29	14 59	15 34	15 59	16 30	16 59	17 29		17 59	18 29	18 59	19 59
Gartcosh	d	09 03	09 36	10 06	10 36	11 06	11 35	12 06	12 38	13 06		13 36	14 06	14 36	15 06	15 41	16 06	16 37	17 06	17 36		18 06	18 36	19 06	20 06
Stepps	d	09 07	09 40	10 10	10 40	11 10	11 39	12 10	12 42	13 10		13 40	14 10	14 40	15 10	15 45	16 10	16 41	17 10	17 40		18 10	18 40	19 10	20 10
Springburn	d	09 13	09 46	10 16	10 46	11 16	11 45	12 16	12 48	13 17		13 46	14 16	14 46	15 16	15 51	16 16	16 47	17 16	17 46		18 16	18 46	19 16	20 16
Glasgow Queen Street 10	a	09 22	09 55	10 25	10 55	11 25	11 54	12 25	12 58	13 26		13 57	14 26	14 58	15 25	15 59	16 25	16 58	17 25	17 57		18 26	18 57	19 26	20 26
Coatbridge Central	d																								
Whifflet	d																								
Motherwell 226	a																								

		SR	SR	SR
Falkirk Grahamston	d			
Camelon	d			
Cumbernauld	d	21 03	22 02	23 01
Greenfaulds	d	21 05	22 03	23 03
Gartcosh	d	21 11	22 08	23 10
Stepps	d	21 15	22 12	23 14
Springburn	d	21 21	22 18	23 20
Glasgow Queen Street 10	a	21 30	22 29	23 28
Coatbridge Central	d			
Whifflet	d			
Motherwell 226	a			

B until 24 September, SO from 1 October

Network Diagram for Tables 225, 228, 229, 230, 238, 240, 242

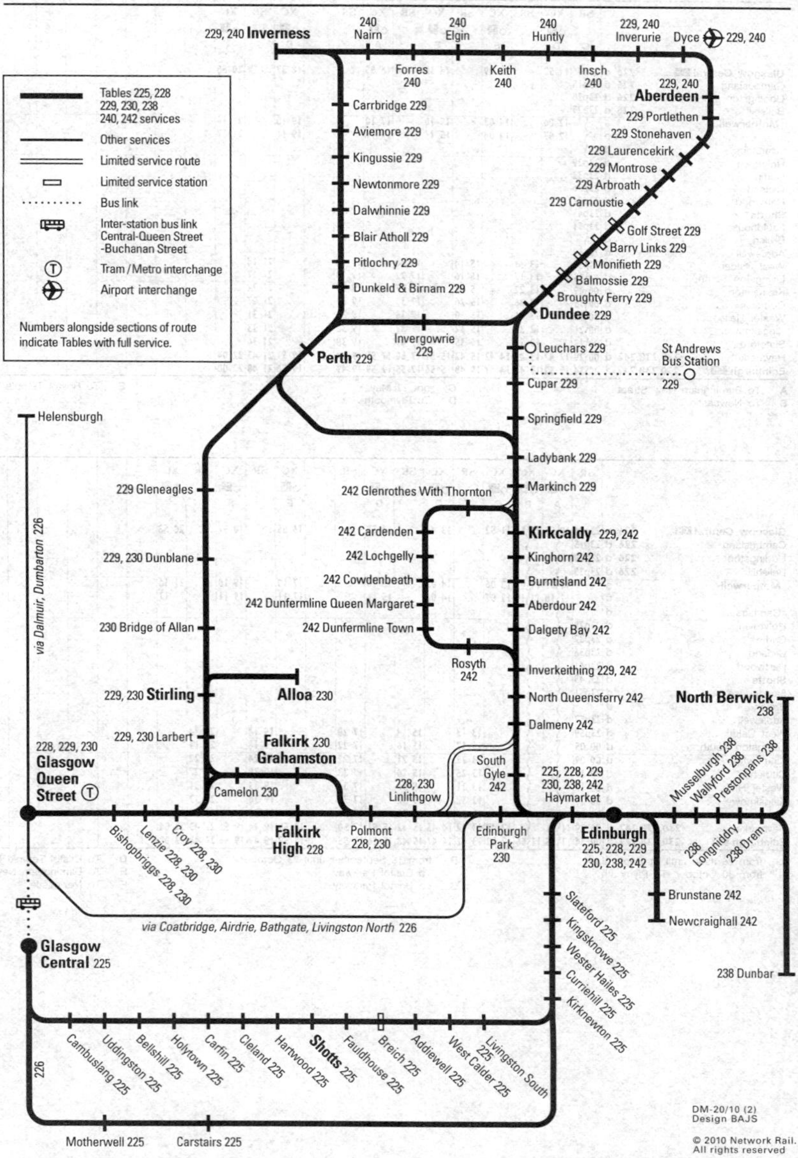

DM-20/10 (2)
Design BAJS

© 2010 Network Rail.
All rights reserved

Table 225

Sundays until 19 June

Glasgow Central, Motherwell, Carstairs and Shotts - Edinburgh

		SR	XC	SR	XC	SR	XC	SR	XC	SR	XC	SR	XC
			◇■		◇■		◇■		◇■		◇■		◇■
		C	D		E		E		A		B		
Glasgow Central ■ 226	d	23p06	11 52		13 49		14 55		16 55		18 57		20 58
Cambuslang 226	d	23p15											
Uddingston 226	d	23p20											
Bellshill 226	d	23p25											
Motherwell	a		12 06		14 03		15 10		17 10		19 10		21 16
	d		12 07		14 04		15 11		17 11		19 11		21 17
Carstairs	d												
Holytown	d	23p29											
Carfin	d	23p32											
Cleland	d	23p36											
Hartwood	d	23p41											
Shotts	d	23p45											
Fauldhouse	d	23p51											
Breich	d												
Addiewell	d	23p57											
West Calder	d	23p59		13 13		15 14		17 20		19 14		21 14	
Livingston South	d	00 05		13 17		15 16		17 22		19 18		21 17	
Kirknewton	d	00 09		13 22		15 21		17 27		19 24		21 22	
Curriehill	d	00 15		13 26		15 26		17 33		19 30		21 27	
Wester Hailes	d	00 18		13 31		15 30		17 36		19 33		21 31	
Kingsknowe	d	00 21		13 32		15 32		17 39		19 36		21 33	
Slateford	d	00 23		13 36		15 35		17 41		19 38		21 36	
Haymarket 230,238,242	d	00 29	12 47	13 42	14 43	15 42	15 51	17 50	17 55	19 44	19 51	21 43	22 04
Edinburgh ■ 230,238,242	a	00 34	12 52	13 47	14 47	15 48	15 56	17 55	17 59	19 49	19 56	21 48	22 08

A To Birmingham New Street
B To Newcastle
C not 22 May
D To Plymouth
E To Bristol Temple Meads

Sundays until 26 June

		SR	XC	XC	XC	SR	XC	SR	XC	SR	XC	SR	XC	SR	XC
			◇■	◇■	◇■		◇■		◇■		◇■		◇■		◇■
			A	B	C		C		D		E		F		
Glasgow Central ■ 226	d	23p06	10 55	10 55	11 52		13 49		14 55		16 55		18 57		20 58
Cambuslang 226	d	23p15													
Uddingston 226	d	23p20													
Bellshill 226	d	23p25													
Motherwell	a		11 09	11 09	12 06		14 03		15 10		17 10		19 10		21 16
	d		11 10	11 10	12 07		14 04		15 11		17 11		19 11		21 17
Carstairs	d														
Holytown	d	23p29													
Carfin	d	23p32													
Cleland	d	23p36													
Hartwood	d	23p41													
Shotts	d	23p45													
Fauldhouse	d	23p51													
Breich	d														
Addiewell	d	23p57													
West Calder	d	23p59				13 13		15 14		17 20		19 14		21 14	
Livingston South	d	00 05				13 17		15 16		17 22		19 18		21 17	
Kirknewton	d	00 09				13 22		15 21		17 27		19 24		21 22	
Curriehill	d	00 15				13 26		15 26		17 33		19 30		21 27	
Wester Hailes	d	00 18				13 31		15 30		17 36		19 33		21 31	
Kingsknowe	d	00 21				13 32		15 32		17 39		19 36		21 33	
Slateford	d	00 23				13 36		15 35		17 41		19 38		21 36	
Haymarket 230,238,242	d	00 29	11 51		12 47	13 42	14 43	15 42	15 51	17 50	17 55	19 44	19 51	21 43	22 04
Edinburgh ■ 230,238,242	a	00 34	11 55	11 56	12 52	13 47	14 47	15 48	15 56	17 55	17 59	19 49	19 56	21 48	22 08

A from 26 June until 11 September, from 30 October. To Plymouth
B from 18 September until 23 October. To Bristol Parkway
C To Bristol Parkway
D To Bristol Temple Meads
E To Birmingham New Street
F To Newcastle

Lanark, Coatbridge, Motherwell, Larkhall, Hamilton, Edinburgh and Bathgate, Airdrie and Springburn - Glasgow - Milngavie, Dalmuir, Balloch and Helensburgh

Miles	Miles	Miles	Miles	Miles			SR MO	SR MX	SR MO	SR MX	SR MX	SR MO	SR MX	SR MX	SR MX	SR MX A	SR B	SR	SR	SR	SR	SR	SR	SR
0	—	—	—	—	**Lanark**	d																		
8½	—	—	—	—	Carluke	d																		
13	—	—	—	—	Wishaw	d																		
16½	—	—	—	—	Holytown	d										23p59								
15	—	—	—	—	Shieldmuir	d																		
—	—	—	—	0	**Coatbridge Central**	d																		
—	—	—	—	1	Whifflet	d																		
16¼	0	0	—	5½	**Motherwell**	a																		
—	—	—	—	—		d	22p40																06 16	
—	3	—	—	—	Bellshill	d										00 02							06 22	
20½	5½	—	—	—	Uddingston	d										00 06							06 26	
—	—	0¾	—	—	Airbles	d	22p42																	
—	—	—	—	0	**Larkhall**	d															06 07			
—	—	—	—	1½	Merryton	d															06 09			
—	—	—	—	2¾	Chatelherault	d															06 12			
—	—	3	—	5¼	**Hamilton Central**	d	22p47														06 16			
—	—	3¾	—	0	Hamilton West	d	22p50														06 18			
—	—	5¾	—	—	Blantyre	d	22p53														06 22			
22½	—	8¼	—	—	Newton	d	22p57																	
24	9	—	—	—	Cambuslang	d	23p01									00 12							06 31	
25¾	10¾	—	—	—	Rutherglen	d	23p04														06 29		06 34	
26½	11½	—	—	—	Dalmarnock	d																	06 36	
27	12	—	—	—	Bridgeton	d	23p07																06 38	
—	—	—	0	—	**Edinburgh**	d				22p19		22p40	22p51	23p37	23p51		04 50							
—	—	—	1¼	—	Haymarket	d				22p23		22p44	22p55	23p42	23p55									
—	—	—	3¾	—	Edinburgh Park	d				22p30		22p49	23p00	23p47	23p59									
—	—	—	12½	—	Uphall	d				22p38		22p57	23p08	23p55	00 08									
—	—	—	15½	—	Livingston North	d				22p41		23p00	23p11	23p59	00 11									
—	—	—	18½	—	**Bathgate**	a				22p46		23p05	23p16	00 04	00 16									
—	—	—	—	—		d				22p47		23p06	23p17							05 36		05 51		
—	—	—	21	—	Armadale	d				22p51		23p10	23p21							05 40		05 55		
—	—	—	23¼	—	Blackridge	d				22p55		23p14	23p25							05 43		05 58		
—	—	—	28¾	—	Caldercruix	d				23p01		23p20	23p31							05 50		06 05		
—	—	—	31¾	—	Drumgelloch	d				23p05		23p24	23p35							05 53		06 08		
—	—	—	33¼	—	**Airdrie**	d			22p58	23p12		23p28	23p38					05 35		05 57		06 12		06 27
—	—	—	34½	—	Coatdyke	d			23p00	23p14		23p30	23p40					05 37		05 59		06 14		06 29
—	—	—	35¼	—	Coatbridge Sunnyside	d			23p02	23p16		23p32	23p43					05 39		06 01		06 16		06 31
—	—	—	35¾	—	Blairhill	d			23p05	23p19		23p35	23p45					05 42		06 04		06 19		06 34
—	—	—	38½	—	Easterhouse	d			23p09	23p23		23p39	23p49					05 46		06 08		06 23		06 38
—	—	—	39½	—	Garrowhill	d			23p11	23p25		23p41	23p52					05 48		06 10		06 25		06 40
—	—	—	40¾	—	Shettleston	d			23p14	23p28		23p44	23p54					05 51		06 13		06 28		06 43
—	—	—	41½	—	Carntyne	d			23p16	23p30		23p46	23p56					05 53		06 15		06 30		06 45
—	—	—	—	0	**Springburn**	d		23p09			23p39													
—	—	—	—	0¾	Barnhill	d		23p10			23p40													
—	—	—	—	1½	Alexandra Parade	d		23p13			23p43													
—	—	—	—	1¾	Duke Street	d		23p15			23p45													
—	—	—	43¼	2¼	Bellgrove	d		23p17	23p19	23p33	23p47	23p49	23p59					05 56		06 18		06 33		06 48
—	—	—	43¾	2¾	High Street	d		23p19	23p21	23p35	23p49	23p51	00 02					05 58		06 20		06 35		06 50
—	—	—	44¼	3¼	**Glasgow Queen St LL** 10	a		23p21	23p23	23p37	23p51	23p53	00 04					06 00		06 22		06 37		06 52
—	—	—	—	—		d		23p23	23p24	23p45	23p53	23p54	00 04					06 01		06 23		06 40		06 53
—	—	—	45	4	Charing Cross	d		23p25	23p27	23p47	23p55	23p57	00 06					06 03		06 25		06 42		06 55
28¼	13¼	—	—	—	Argyle Street	d															06 34		06 42	
28¾	13¾	—	—	—	**Glasgow Central LL** 15	a	23p14									00b23					06 37		06 46	
—	—	—	—	—		d	23p14														06 37		06 46	
29¼	14¼	—	—	—	Anderston	d															06 39		06 48	
29¾	14¾	—	—	—	Exhibition Centre	d	23p18														06 41		06 50	
31	16	—	47	6	Partick	d	23p22	23p29	23p32	23p51	23p59	00 01	00 11					06 07		06 29	06 44	06 47	06 54	06 59
31½	16½	0	47½	6½	Hyndland	d	23p24	23p32	23p34	23p53	00 02	00 03	00 13					06 10		06 32	06 47	06 49	06 56	07 02
—	—	0½	—	—	Jordanhill	d	23p26			23p55	00 04	00 05	00 15					06 12					06 58	
—	—	1½	—	—	Scotstounhill	d	23p28			23p58	00 06	00 07	00 17					06 14					07 00	
—	—	2	—	—	Garscadden	d	23p30			23p59	00a08	00 09	00a19					06 17				06 53	07 02	
—	—	3	—	—	Yoker	d	23p33			00 02		00 12						06 19					07 05	
—	—	4	—	—	Clydebank	d	23p35			00 04								06 21					07 07	
32½	17½	—	48½	7½	Anniesland	d		23p35	23p37											06 35	06 50			07 05
33¾	18¾	—	49¾	8¾	Westerton	d		23p38	23p40								05 56			06 38	06 53			07 08
35	—	—	—	—	Bearsden	d																		
35¾	—	—	—	—	Hillfoot	d																		
37¼	—	—	—	—	**Milngavie**	a																		
—	20	—	51	10	Drumchapel	d		23p40	23p42											06 40	06 55			07 10
—	20¾	—	51¾	10¾	Drumry	d		23p42	23p44											06 42	06 57			07 12
—	21¾	—	52¾	11¾	Singer	d		23p45	23p47											06 45	07 00			07 15
—	22¼	5¼	53½	12½	**Dalmuir**	a	23p39	23p47	23p49	00 08		00 16					06 03	06 24		06 47	07 02	06 58	07 12	07 17
—	—	—	—	—		d	23p39	23p48	23p50	00 08							06 04	06 24	06 30	06 48		06 59		07 17
—	—	—	54¾	13¾	Kilpatrick	d	23p41	23p51											06 32	06 51				07 20
—	—	—	56½	15½	Bowling	d	23p44	23p54											06 35	06 54				07 23
—	—	—	59¼	18¼	Dumbarton East	d	23p49	23p58	23p58	00 15								06 32	06 40	06 58		07 06		07 27
—	—	—	60	19	Dumbarton Central	d	23p51	23p59	23p59	00 18								06 34	06 42	07 00		07 09		07 28
—	—	—	60¾	19¾	Dalreoch	d	23p52	00 02	00 01	00 19								06 35	06 43	07 02		07 10		07 31
—	—	—	—	20¾	Renton	d	23p55	00 05										06 38		07 05				07 34
—	—	—	—	22	Alexandria	d	23p58	00 07										06 41		07 07				07 35
—	—	—	—	23	**Balloch**	a	00 01	00 10										06 43		07 10				07 40
—	—	—	63½	—	Cardross	d			00 06	00 24									06 48			07 15		
—	—	—	67¼	—	Craigendoran	d			00 11	00 29									06 53			07 20		
—	—	—	68¼	—	**Helensburgh Central**	a			00 14	00 32							06c26		06 56			07 23		

A From Edinburgh
B To Fort William
b Glasgow Central High Level
c Helensburgh Upper

Lanark, Coatbridge, Motherwell, Larkhall, Hamilton, Edinburgh and Bathgate, Airdrie and Springburn - Glasgow - Milngavie, Dalmuir, Balloch and Helensburgh

		SR	SR	SR	SR	SR	SR	SR	SR	SR A	SR	SR	SR	SR	SR	SR	SR	SR	SR	SR	SR	SR ◇ B
Lanark	d						06 23												07 22			
Carluke	d						06 33												07 32			
Wishaw	d						06 38												07 37			
Holytown	d									06 58												
Shieldmuir	d						06 42												07 41			
Coatbridge Central	d								06 40													
Whifflet	d								06 42													
Motherwell	a						06 46		06 51										07 44			
	d	06 20					06 46		06 51						07 17		07 20		07 44			
Bellshill	d						06 51			07 02					07 22							
Uddingston	d						06 56			07 12					07 26							
Airbles	d	06 22							06 54								07 22					
Larkhall	d			06 37								07 07										
Merryton	d			06 39								07 09										
Chatelherault	d			06 42								07 12										
Hamilton Central	d	06 27		06 46					06 59			07 16					07 27					
Hamilton West	d	06 30		06 48					07 01			07 18					07 30					
Blantyre	d	06 33		06 52					07 05			07 22					07 33					
Newton	d	06 37							07 09			07 26					07 37					
Cambuslang	d	06 41					07 01		07 12	07 17					07 31		07 41					
Rutherglen	d	06 45		06 58			07 03		07 16			07 30			07 35		07 45		07 56			
Dalmarnock	d	06 47					07 05		07 18						07 37		07 47					
Bridgeton	d	06 49					07 07		07 20						07 39		07 49					
Edinburgh	d					06 08							06 21	06 37						06 48	07 07	
Haymarket	d					06 11							06 25	06 41						06 52	07 11	
Edinburgh Park	d					06 16							06 30	06 46						06 58	07 16	
Uphall	d					06 24							06 38	06 54						07 05	07 24	
Livingston North	d					06 29							06 41	06 58						07 08	07 28	
Bathgate	a					06 33							06 46	07 02						07 13	07 32	
	d				06 21	06 34							06 47	07 04						07 17	07 34	
Armadale	d				06 25								06 51							07 21		
Blackridge	d				06 28								06 55							07 25		
Caldercruix	d				06 35								07 01							07 31		
Drumgelloch	d				06 38	06 46							07 05	07 16						07 35	07 46	
Airdrie	d				06 42	06 50		06 57					07 12	07 20		07 27				07 42	07 50	
Coatdyke	d				06 44			06 59					07 14	07 22		07 29				07 44	07 52	
Coatbridge Sunnyside	d				06 46	06 53		07 01					07 16	07 24		07 31				07 46	07 54	
Blairhill	d				06 49			07 04					07 19	07 27		07 34				07 49	07 57	
Easterhouse	d				06 53			07 08					07 23			07 38				07 53		
Garrowhill	d				06 55			07 10					07 25			07 40				07 55		
Shettleston	d				06 58			07 13					07 28			07 43				07 58		
Carntyne	d				07 00			07 15					07 30			07 45				08 00		
Springburn	d		06 49								07 19							07 49				
Barnhill	d		06 50								07 20							07 50				
Alexandra Parade	d		06 53								07 23							07 53				
Duke Street	d		06 55								07 25							07 55				
Bellgrove	d		06 57		07 03			07 18			07 27		07 33			07 48		07 57		08 03		
High Street	d		06 59		07 05	07 10		07 20			07 29		07 35	07 40		07 50		07 59		08 05	08 10	
Glasgow Queen St LL 10	a		07 01		07 07	07 12		07 22			07 31		07 37	07 42		07 52		08 01		08 07	08 12	
	d		07 02		07 10	07 13		07 23			07 32		07 40	07 43		07 53		08 03		08 10	08 13	08c21
Charing Cross	d		07 04		07 12	07 16		07 25			07 34		07 42	07 46		07 55		08 05		08 12	08 16	
Argyle Street	d	06 53		07 03			07 11		07 23			07 35			07 43		07 53		08 04			
Glasgow Central LL 15	a	06 56		07 07			07 14		07 26	07b29		07 37			07 46		07 56		08 05			
	d	06 58		07 07			07 16		07 28			07 38			07 46		08 00		08 07			
Anderston	d	06 59		07 08			07 17		07 29			07 39			07 48		08 01		08 09			
Exhibition Centre	d	07 01		07 10			07 19		07 31			07 41			07 50		08 03		08 11			
Partick	d	07 05	07 08	07 14	07 17	07 20	07 23	07 29	07 35		07 38	07 45	07 47	07 50	07 53	07 59	08 07	08 08	08 14	08 17	08 20	
Hyndland	d	07 08	07 10	07 16	07 19	07 23	07 25	07 32	07 38		07 40	07 47	07 49	07 53	07 55	08 02	08 09	08 10	08 17	08 19	08 23	
Jordanhill	d		07 12				07 27				07 42				07 57			08 12				
Scotstounhill	d		07 15				07 30				07 45				08 00			08 14				
Garscadden	d		07 17				07 32				07 47				08 02			08 17				
Yoker	d		07 19				07 35				07 49				08 04			08 19				
Clydebank	d		07 21				07 37				07 51				08 06			08 21				
Anniesland	d	07 11		07 19		07 26		07 35	07 41			07 50		07 56		08 05	08 12		08 20		08 26	
Westerton	d	07 14		07 22		07 29		07 38	07 44			07 53		07 59		08 08	08 18		08 26		08 30	
Bearsden	d	07 16				07 31			07 46					08 01			08 21				08 32	
Hillfoot	d	07 17				07 32			07 48					08 03			08 23				08 33	
Milngavie	a	07 22				07 37			07 52					08 07			08 29				08 39	
Drumchapel	d			07 25				07 40				07 56				08 10			08 28			
Drumry	d			07 27				07 42				07 58				08 12			08 30			
Singer	d			07 29				07 45				08 00				08 15			08 33			
Dalmuir	a		07 26	07 32	07 29		07 41	07 47			07 56	08 03	07 59		08 11	08 17		08 28	08 35	08 28		08 39
	d				07 29			07 48					07 59			08 18				08 29		08 39
Kilpatrick	d							07 51								08 21						
Bowling	d							07 54								08 24						
Dumbarton East	d				07 36			07 58					08 06			08 28				08 36		
Dumbarton Central	d				07 39			08 00					08 09			08 30				08 39		08 48
Dalreoch	d				07 40			08 02					08 10			08 32				08 40		
Renton	d							08 05								08 35						
Alexandria	d							08 07								08 37						
Balloch	a							08 10								08 40						
Cardross	d				07 45								08 15							08 45		
Craigendoran	d				07 50								08 20							08 50		
Helensburgh Central	a				07 54								08 24							08 55		09e03

A From Edinburgh
B To Oban
b Glasgow Central High Level
c Glasgow Queen St High Level
e Helensburgh Upper

Lanark, Coatbridge, Motherwell, Larkhall, Hamilton, Edinburgh and Bathgate, Airdrie and Springburn - Glasgow - Milngavie, Dalmuir, Balloch and Helensburgh

		SR	SR	SR	SR	SR	SR	SR	SR	SR	SR	SR	SR	SR	SR	SR	SR	SR	SR	SR	SR	SR	SR
												A			◇ B								
Lanark	d						07 47										08 23						
Carluke	d						07 57					08 13					08 33						
Wishaw	d						08 04					08 21					08 38						
Holytown	d																						
Shieldmuir	d						08 07					08 23					08 42						
Coatbridge Central	d				07 39																		
Whifflet	d				07 41																		
Motherwell	a				07 48		08 13					08 26					08 46						
	d		07 47		07 50		08 13				08 18	08 27		08 20			08 46				08 48		08 50
Bellshill	d		07 53								08 24										08 54		
Uddingston	d		07 58				08 19				08 28	08 33									09 00		
Airbles	d				07 52									08 22									08 52
Larkhall	d	07 37								08 07								08 37					
Merryton	d	07 39								08 09								08 39					
Chatelherault	d	07 42								08 12								08 42					
Hamilton Central	d	07 46			07 57					08 15				08 27				08 46					08 57
Hamilton West	d	07 48			08 00					08 18				08 30				08 48					09 00
Blantyre	d	07 52			08 03					08 21				08 33				08 52					09 03
Newton	d	07 56			08 07					08 26				08 37				08 56					09 07
Cambuslang	d	08 00	08 05		08 11					08 30	08 33			08 41							09 05		09 11
Rutherglen	d	08 04	08 10		08 15		08 26				08 37			08 46			08 56	09 00			09 09		09 16
Dalmarnock	d	08 06	08 12		08 17						08 39			08 48							09 11		09 17
Bridgeton	d	08 08	08 14		08 19						08 41			08 51							09 13		09 19
Edinburgh	d							07 21	07 37										07 54	08 07			
Haymarket	d							07 25	07 42										07 57	08 10			
Edinburgh Park	d							07 30	07 47										08 02	08 16			
Uphall	d							07 38	07 55										08 09	08 24			
Livingston North	d							07 41	07 58										08 12	08 28			
Bathgate	a							07 46	08 03										08 17	08 33			
	d							07 47	08 04										08 17	08 34			
Armadale	d							07 51											08 21				
Blackridge	d							07 55											08 25				
Caldercruix	d							08 01											08 31				
Drumgelloch	d							08 05	08 16										08 35	08 46			
Airdrie	d			07 57				08 12	08 20				08 27						08 42	08 50		08 57	
Coatdyke	d			07 59				08 14	08 22				08 29						08 44			08 59	
Coatbridge Sunnyside	d			08 01				08 16	08 24				08 31						08 46	08 53		09 01	
Blairhill	d			08 04				08 19	08 27				08 34						08 49			09 04	
Easterhouse	d			08 08				08 23					08 38						08 53			09 08	
Garrowhill	d			08 10				08 25					08 40						08 55			09 10	
Shettleston	d			08 13				08 28					08 43						08 58			09 13	
Carntyne	d			08 15				08 30					08 45						09 00			09 15	
Springburn	d					08 19										08 49							
Barnhill	d					08 20										08 50							
Alexandra Parade	d					08 23										08 53							
Duke Street	d					08 25										08 55							
Bellgrove	d			08 18		08 27		08 33					08 48			08 57			09 03			09 18	
High Street	d			08 20		08 29		08 35	08 40				08 50			08 59			09 05	09 10		09 20	
Glasgow Queen St LL 10 ⛴	a			08 22		08 31		08 37	08 42				08 52			09 01			09 07	09 13		09 22	
	d			08 23		08 32		08 40	08 44				08 53		09b07	09 02			09 10	09 13		09 23	
Charing Cross	d			08 25		08 34		08 42	08 46				08 55			09 04			09 12	09 15		09 25	
Argyle Street	d	08 12	08 18		08 23		08 32			08 36	08 45	08 47		08 55			09 01	09 05			09 17		09 24
Glasgow Central LL 15	a	08 15	08 20		08 27		08 33			08 37	08 46	08 48		08 56			09 03	09 07			09 18		09 26
	d	08 18	08 21		08 28		08 35			08 39	08 46	08 48		08 59			09 03	09 08			09 18		09 28
Anderston	d	08 19	08a22		08 30		08 38			08a42	08 48	08 51		09 00			09 05	09 09			09 20		09 29
Exhibition Centre	d	08 21			08 32		08 41				08 50	08 54		09 02			09 07	09 11			09 22		09 31
Partick ⛴	d	08 24		08 29	08 36	08 39	08 44	08 47	08 50		08 54	08 57	08 59	09 06		09 09	09 12	09 15	09 17	09 21	09 25	09 29	09 35
Hyndland	d	08 27		08 32	08 38	08 41	08 47	08 49	08 53		08 56	08 59	09 02	09 09		09 11	09 14	09 17	09 19	09 23	09 27	09 32	09 38
Jordanhill	d	08 28				08 43					08 58	09 01				09 12	09 17				09 29		
Scotstounhill	d	08 30				08 45					09 00	09 03				09 15	09 19				09 32		
Garscadden	d	08 32				08 47					09 02	09a06				09 18	09a21				09 35		
Yoker	d	08 35				08 50					09 05					09 20					09 37		
Clydebank	d	08 37				08 52					09 07					09 22					09 39		
Anniesland	d			08 35	08 41		08 50		08 56				09 05	09 12				09 20		09 26		09 35	09 41
Westerton	d			08 38	08 44		08 53		08 59				09 08	09 15				09 23		09 29		09 38	09 44
Bearsden	d				08 46				09 01					09 17						09 32			09 46
Hillfoot	d				08 48				09 02					09 19						09 33			09 47
Milngavie	a				08 52				09 07					09 23						09 37			09 52
Drumchapel	d			08 40			08 55						09 10					09 26				09 40	
Drumry	d			08 42			08 57						09 12					09 28				09 42	
Singer	d			08 45			09 00						09 15					09 30				09 45	
Dalmuir	a	08 43		08 48		08 56	09 02	08 59			09 11		09 17		09 23	09 26		09 33	09 29		09 43	09 47	
	d			08 48				08 59					09 18		09 24				09 29			09 48	
Kilpatrick	d			08 51									09 21									09 51	
Bowling	d			08 54									09 24									09 54	
Dumbarton East	d			08 58				09 06					09 28						09 36			09 58	
Dumbarton Central	d			09 00				09 09					09 30		09 36				09 39			10 00	
Dalreoch	d			09 02				09 10					09 32						09 40			10 02	
Renton	d			09 05									09 35									10 05	
Alexandria	d			09 07									09 37									10 07	
Balloch	a			09 10									09 40									10 10	
Cardross	d							09 15											09 45				
Craigendoran	d							09 20											09 50				
Helensburgh Central	a							09 24							09c50				09 55				

A From Carstairs
B until 23 September. To Mallaig
b Glasgow Queen St High Level
c Helensburgh Upper

Lanark, Coatbridge, Motherwell, Larkhall, Hamilton, Edinburgh and Bathgate, Airdrie and Springburn - Glasgow - Milngavie, Dalmuir, Balloch and Helensburgh

		SR	SR	SR	SR	SR	SR	SR	SR	SR	SR	SR	SR	SR	SR	SR	SR	SR	SR	SR	SR	SR
									A													
Lanark	d												09 23								
Carluke	d												09 33								
Wishaw	d												09 38								
Holytown	d								09 32													
Shieldmuir	d												09 42								
Coatbridge Central	d																					
Whifflet	d																					
Motherwell	a												09 46								
	d					09 16		09 20						09 47		09 50					10 16	
Bellshill	d					09 22			09 36					09 53							10 22	
Uddingston	d					09 26			09 41					09 57							10 26	
Airbles	d							09 22								09 52						
Larkhall	d		09 07								09 37							10 07				
Merryton	d		09 09								09 39							10 09				
Chatelherault	d		09 12								09 42							10 12				
Hamilton Central	d		09 16					09 28			09 46					09 57		10 16				
Hamilton West	d		09 18					09 31			09 48					10 00		10 18				
Blantyre	d		09 22					09 34			09 52					10 03		10 22				
Newton	d							09 40								10 07		10 26				
Cambuslang	d					09 31		09 43						10 02		10 11					10 31	
Rutherglen	d		09 29			09 36		09 48			09 59			10 06		10 15		10 30			10 34	
Dalmarnock	d					09 38		09 50						10 08		10 17					10 36	
Bridgeton	d					09 40		09 52						10 10		10 19					10 38	
Edinburgh	d			08 21	08 37							08 48	09 07						09 18	09 37		
Haymarket	d			08 25	08 41							08 52	09 11						09 22	09 41		
Edinburgh Park	d			08 30	08 47							08 57	09 17						09 27	09 46		
Uphall	d			08 38	08 55							09 05	09 25						09 35	09 54		
Livingston North	d			08 41	08 58							09 08	09 29						09 38	09 58		
Bathgate	a			08 46	09 03							09 13	09 33						09 43	10 03		
	d			08 47	09 04							09 17	09 34						09 47	10 04		
Armadale	d			08 51								09 21							09 51			
Blackridge	d			08 55								09 25							09 55			
Caldercruix	d			09 01								09 31							10 01			
Drumgelloch	d			09 05	09 16							09 35	09 47						10 05	10 16		
Airdrie	d			09 12	09 20		09 27					09 42	09 51		09 57				10 12	10 20		10 27
Coatdyke	d			09 14			09 29					09 44			09 59				10 14			10 29
Coatbridge Sunnyside	d			09 16	09 23		09 31					09 46	09 54		10 01				10 16	10 23		10 31
Blairhill	d			09 19			09 34					09 49			10 04				10 19			10 34
Easterhouse	d			09 23			09 38					09 53			10 08				10 23			10 38
Garrowhill	d			09 25			09 40					09 55			10 10				10 25			10 40
Shettleston	d			09 28			09 43					09 58			10 13				10 28			10 43
Carntyne	d			09 30			09 45					10 00			10 15				10 30			10 45
Springburn	d	09 19								09 49							10 19					
Barnhill	d	09 20								09 50							10 20					
Alexandra Parade	d	09 23								09 53							10 23					
Duke Street	d	09 25								09 55							10 25					
Bellgrove	d	09 27		09 33			09 48			09 57		10 03			10 18		10 27		10 33			10 48
High Street	d	09 29		09 35	09 40		09 50			09 59		10 05	10 10		10 20		10 29		10 35	10 41		10 50
Glasgow Queen St LL 10 ⛴	a	09 31		09 37	09 42		09 52			10 01		10 07	10 13		10 22		10 31		10 37	10 43		10 52
	d	09 32		09 40	09 43		09 53			10 02		10 10	10 14		10 23		10 32		10 41	10 43		10 53
Charing Cross	d	09 34		09 42	09 46		09 55			10 04		10 12	10 16		10 25		10 34		10 43	10 45		10 55
Argyle Street	d		09 35			09 44		09 54			10 04			10 14		10 23		10 36			10 42	
Glasgow Central LL 15	a		09 37			09 46		09 56	09b57		10 07			10 16		10 26		10 37			10 46	
	d		09 37			09 47		09 58			10 07			10 19		10 28		10 38			10 46	
Anderston	d		09 39			09 48		09 59			10 09			10 20		10 29		10 39			10 48	
Exhibition Centre	d		09 41			09 50		10 01			10 11			10 22		10 31		10 41			10 50	
Partick ⛴	d	09 39	09 44	09 47	09 50	09 54	09 59	10 05		10 09	10 14	10 17	10 20	10 26	10 29	10 35	10 39	10 45	10 47	10 50	10 53	10 59
Hyndland	d	09 41	09 47	09 49	09 52	09 56	10 02	10 08		10 11	10 17	10 19	10 22	10 28	10 32	10 38	10 41	10 47	10 49	10 53	10 55	11 02
Jordanhill	d	09 43				09 58				10 13				10 30			10 43				10 57	
Scotstounhill	d	09 45				10 00				10 15				10 33			10 45				11 00	
Garscadden	d	09 47				10 02				10 17				10 36			10 47				11 02	
Yoker	d	09 50				10 05				10 20				10 38			10 50				11 05	
Clydebank	d	09 52				10 07				10 22				10 40			10 52				11 07	
Anniesland	d		09 50		09 55		10 05	10 11			10 20		10 25		10 35	10 41		10 50		10 56		11 05
Westerton	d		09 53		09 58		10 08	10 14			10 23		10 28		10 38	10 44		10 53		10 59		11 08
Bearsden	d				10 01			10 16					10 31			10 46				11 01		
Hillfoot	d				10 03			10 18					10 33			10 47				11 02		
Milngavie	a				10 06			10 22					10 37			10 52				11 07		
Drumchapel	d		09 55				10 10				10 25				10 40			10 55				11 10
Drumry	d		09 57				10 12				10 27				10 42			10 57				11 12
Singer	d		10 00				10 15				10 30				10 45			11 00				11 15
Dalmuir	a	09 56	10 02	09 59		10 11	10 17			10 26	10 32	10 29		10 44	10 47		10 56	11 02	11 00		11 11	11 17
	d			09 59			10 18					10 29			10 48				11 00			11 18
Kilpatrick	d						10 21								10 51							11 21
Bowling	d						10 24								10 54							11 24
Dumbarton East	d			10 06			10 28					10 36			10 58				11 06			11 28
Dumbarton Central	d			10 09			10 30					10 39			11 00				11 09			11 30
Dalreoch	d			10 10			10 32					10 40			11 02				11 11			11 32
Renton	d						10 35								11 05							11 35
Alexandria	d						10 37								11 07							11 37
Balloch	a						10 40								11 10							11 40
Cardross	d			10 15								10 45							11 16			
Craigendoran	d			10 20								10 51							11 21			
Helensburgh Central	a			10 23								10 54							11 24			

A From Edinburgh
b Glasgow Central High Level

Lanark, Coatbridge, Motherwell, Larkhall, Hamilton, Edinburgh and Bathgate, Airdrie and Springburn - Glasgow - Milngavie, Dalmuir, Balloch and Helensburgh

		SR	SR	SR	SR	SR	SR	SR	SR	SR	SR	SR	SR	SR	SR	SR	SR	SR	SR	SR	SR	SR	SR
			A															A					◇ B
Lanark	d	09 53						10 22									10 53						
Carluke	d	10 04						10 32									11 03						
Wishaw	d	10 08						10 37									11 08						
Holytown	d	10 13	10 32														11 13	11 30					
Shieldmuir	d							10 41															
Coatbridge Central	d																						
Whifflet	d																						
Motherwell	a	10 20						10 45									11 20						
	d	10 20						10 46		10 50					11 16		11 20						
Bellshill	d		10 35					10 52							11 22			11 34					
Uddingston	d		10 40					10 56							11 26			11 38					
Airbles	d	10 23								10 52							11 22						
Larkhall	d				10 37							11 07								11 37			
Merryton	d				10 39							11 09								11 39			
Chatelherault	d				10 42							11 12								11 42			
Hamilton Central	d	10 28			10 46					10 57		11 16					11 27			11 46			
Hamilton West	d	10 30			10 48					11 00		11 18					11 30			11 48			
Blantyre	d	10 34			10 52					11 03		11 22					11 33			11 52			
Newton	d	10 38								11 07							11 37						
Cambuslang	d	10 41						11 01		11 11					11 31		11 41						
Rutherglen	d	10 45			10 59			11 05		11 15		11 29			11 36		11 46			11 59			
Dalmarnock	d	10 49						11 07		11 17					11 38		11 48						
Bridgeton	d	10 51						11 09		11 19					11 40		11 50						
Edinburgh	d					09 48	10 07						10 21	10 37							10 48	11 07	
Haymarket	d					09 52	10 10						10 25	10 41							10 52	11 11	
Edinburgh Park	d					09 57	10 16						10 30	10 46							10 57	11 17	
Uphall	d					10 05	10 24						10 38	10 54							11 05	11 25	
Livingston North	d					10 09	10 28						10 41	10 58							11 08	11 29	
Bathgate	a					10 13	10 33						10 47	11 04							11 13	11 33	
	d					10 17	10 34						10 47	11 04							11 17	11 36	
Armadale	d					10 21							10 51								11 21		
Blackridge	d					10 25							10 55								11 25		
Caldercruix	d					10 31							11 01								11 31		
Drumgelloch	d					10 35	10 46						11 05	11 16							11 35	11 48	
Airdrie	d					10 42	10 50		10 57				11 12	11 20		11 27					11 42	11 52	
Coatdyke	d					10 44			10 59				11 14			11 29					11 44		
Coatbridge Sunnyside	d					10 46	10 53		11 01				11 16	11 23		11 31					11 46	11 55	
Blairhill	d					10 49			11 04				11 19			11 34					11 49		
Easterhouse	d					10 53			11 08				11 23			11 38					11 53		
Garrowhill	d					10 55			11 10				11 25			11 40					11 55		
Shettleston	d					10 58			11 13				11 28			11 43					11 58		
Carntyne	d					11 00			11 15				11 30			11 45					12 00		
Springburn	d			10 49							11 19								11 49				
Barnhill	d			10 50							11 20								11 50				
Alexandra Parade	d			10 53							11 23								11 53				
Duke Street	d			10 55							11 25								11 55				
Bellgrove	d			10 57		11 03			11 18		11 27		11 33			11 48			11 57		12 03		
High Street	d			10 59		11 05	11 10		11 20		11 29		11 35	11 41		11 50			11 59		12 05	12 11	
Glasgow Queen St LL 10 ⇌	a			11 01		11 07	11 12		11 22		11 31		11 37	11 43		11 52			12 01		12 07	12 13	
	d			11 02		11 10	11 13		11 23		11 32		11 40	11 43		11 53			12 02		12 10	12 14	12c21
Charing Cross	d			11 04		11 12	11 15		11 25		11 34		11 42	11 46		11 55			12 04		12 12	12 16	
Argyle Street	d	10 55			11 04			11 13		11 23		11 34			11 44		11 53			12 05			
Glasgow Central LL 15	a	10 56	10b55		11 07			11 16		11 26		11 37			11 46		11 57	11b57		12 07			
	d	10 58			11 07			11 16		11 28		11 37			11 46		11 58			12 07			
Anderston	d	10 59			11 09			11 18		11 29		11 39			11 48		12 00			12 09			
Exhibition Centre	d	11 01			11 11			11 20		11 31		11 41			11 50		12 02			12 11			
Partick ⇌	d	11 05		11 09	11 15	11 17	11 20	11 24	11 29	11 35	11 39	11 44	11 47	11 50	11 53	11 59	12 05		12 08	12 14	12 17	12 20	
Hyndland	d	11 08		11 11	11 17	11 20	11 23	11 26	11 32	11 38	11 41	11 47	11 49	11 52	11 55	12 02	12 08		12 10	12 17	12 19	12 23	
Jordanhill	d			11 13				11 28			11 43				11 57				12 12				
Scotstounhill	d			11 15				11 31			11 45				12 00				12 15				
Garscadden	d			11 17				11 32			11 47				12 02				12 17				
Yoker	d			11 20				11 35			11 50				12 04				12 19				
Clydebank	d			11 22				11 37			11 52				12 06				12 21				
Anniesland	d	11 11			11 20		11 26		11 35	11 41		11 50		11 55		12 05	12 11			12 20		12 26	
Westerton	d	11 14			11 23		11 29		11 38	11 44		11 53		11 58		12 08	12 14			12 23		12 29	
Bearsden	d	11 16					11 31			11 46				12 00			12 16					12 32	
Hillfoot	d	11 18					11 33			11 47				12 01			12 18					12 34	
Milngavie	a	11 24					11 37			11 52				12 07			12 22					12 37	
Drumchapel	d				11 25				11 40			11 55				12 10				12 25			
Drumry	d				11 27				11 42			11 57				12 12				12 27			
Singer	d				11 30				11 45			12 00				12 15				12 30			
Dalmuir	a			11 26	11 32	11 29		11 41	11 47		11 56	12 02	11 59		12 11	12 17			12 26	12 32	12 29		12 38
	d					11 29			11 48				11 59			12 18					12 29		12 42
Kilpatrick	d								11 51							12 21							
Bowling	d								11 54							12 24							
Dumbarton East	d					11 36			11 58				12 06			12 28					12 36		
Dumbarton Central	d					11 39			12 00				12 09			12 30					12 39		12 48
Dalreoch	d					11 40			12 02				12 10			12 32					12 40		
Renton	d								12 05							12 35							
Alexandria	d								12 07							12 37							
Balloch	a								12 10							12 40							
Cardross	d					11 45							12 15								12 45		
Craigendoran	d					11 50							12 20								12 50		
Helensburgh Central	a					11 53							12 24								12 53		13e03

A From Edinburgh
B To Oban
b Glasgow Central High Level
c Glasgow Queen St High Level
e Helensburgh Upper

Lanark, Coatbridge, Motherwell, Larkhall, Hamilton, Edinburgh and Bathgate, Airdrie and Springburn - Glasgow - Milngavie, Dalmuir, Balloch and Helensburgh

		SR	SR	SR	SR	SR	SR	SR	SR	SR	SR	SR	SR	SR	SR	SR	SR	SR	SR	SR	SR	SR	SR
												A											
Lanark	d	11 24									11 53						12 23						
Carluke	d	11 32									12 03						12 33						
Wishaw	d	11 38									12 08						12 41						
Holytown	d										12 13	12 30											
Shieldmuir	d	11 42															12 45						
Coatbridge Central	d																						
Whifflet	d																						
Motherwell	a	11 46									12 20						12 48						
	d	11 46		11 50					12 16		12 20						12 48		12 50				
Bellshill	d	11 52							12 22			12 34					12 54						
Uddingston	d	11 57							12 26			12 38					12 58						
Airbles	d			11 52							12 22								12 52				
Larkhall	d					12 07								12 37							13 07		
Merryton	d					12 09								12 39							13 09		
Chatelherault	d					12 12								12 42							13 12		
Hamilton Central	d			11 57		12 16					12 28			12 46					12 57		13 16		
Hamilton West	d			12 00		12 18					12 30			12 48					13 00		13 18		
Blantyre	d			12 03		12 22					12 34			12 52					13 03		13 22		
Newton	d			12 07							12 38								13 07				
Cambuslang	d	12 02		12 11					12 31		12 41						13 03		13 11				
Rutherglen	d	12 06		12 15		12 29			12 34		12 45			12 59			13 06		13 15		13 29		
Dalmarnock	d	12 08		12 17					12 36		12 48						13 08		13 17				
Bridgeton	d	12 10		12 19					12 38		12 50						13 10		13 19				
Edinburgh	d						11 21	11 37							11 51	12 07						12 21	12 37
Haymarket	d						11 25	11 41							11 55	12 11						12 25	12 41
Edinburgh Park	d						11 30	11 46							12 00	12 16						12 30	12 45
Uphall	d						11 40	11 55							12 08	12 27						12 38	12 54
Livingston North	d						11 43	11 57							12 11	12 30						12 41	12 58
Bathgate	a						11 48	12 03							12 16	12 35						12 47	13 02
	d						11 49	12 03							12 17	12 36						12 47	13 04
Armadale	d						11 53								12 21							12 51	
Blackridge	d						11 57								12 25							12 55	
Caldercruix	d						12 03								12 31							13 01	
Drumgelloch	d						12 07	12 17							12 35	12 49						13 05	13 16
Airdrie	d		11 57				12 12	12 20		12 27					12 42	12 52		12 57				13 12	13 20
Coatdyke	d		11 59				12 14			12 29					12 44			12 59				13 14	
Coatbridge Sunnyside	d		12 01				12 16	12 23		12 31					12 46	12 56		13 01				13 16	13 23
Blairhill	d		12 04				12 19			12 34					12 49			13 04				13 19	
Easterhouse	d		12 08				12 23			12 38					12 53			13 08				13 23	
Garrowhill	d		12 10				12 25			12 40					12 55			13 10				13 25	
Shettleston	d		12 13				12 28			12 43					12 58			13 13				13 28	
Carntyne	d		12 15				12 30			12 45					13 00			13 15				13 30	
Springburn	d				12 19								12 49							13 19			
Barnhill	d				12 20								12 50							13 20			
Alexandra Parade	d				12 23								12 53							13 23			
Duke Street	d				12 25								12 55							13 25			
Bellgrove	d		12 18		12 27		12 33			12 48			12 57		13 03			13 18		13 27		13 33	
High Street	d		12 20		12 29		12 36	12 40		12 50			12 59		13 05	13 11		13 20		13 29		13 35	13 41
Glasgow Queen St LL 10 ⇌	a		12 22		12 31		12 38	12 42		12 52			13 01		13 08	13 13		13 22		13 31		13 37	13 43
	d		12 23		12 32		12 40	12 43		12 53			13 02		13 10	13 13		13 23		13 32		13 41	13 43
Charing Cross	d		12 25		12 34		12 42	12 46		12 55			13 04		13 12	13 15		13 25		13 34		13 43	13 45
Argyle Street	d	12 14		12 23		12 35			12 42		12 54			13 05			13 14		13 23		13 34		
Glasgow Central LL 15	a	12 16		12 26		12 37			12 46		12 56	12b55		13 07			13 16		13 26		13 37		
	d	12 18		12 28		12 37			12 46		12 58			13 07			13 18		13 28		13 37		
Anderston	d	12 20		12 30		12 39			12 48		12 59			13 09			13 19		13 29		13 39		
Exhibition Centre	d	12 22		12 32		12 41			12 50		13 01			13 11			13 21		13 31		13 41		
Partick ⇌	d	12 26	12 29	12 35	12 39	12 44	12 47	12 50	12 53	12 59	13 05		13 08	13 14	13 17	13 20	13 25	13 29	13 35	13 38	13 44	13 47	13 50
Hyndland	d	12 28	12 32	12 38	12 41	12 47	12 49	12 52	12 55	13 02	13 08		13 10	13 17	13 19	13 22	13 27	13 32	13 38	13 40	13 47	13 49	13 53
Jordanhill	d	12 30			12 43				12 57				13 12				13 29			13 42			
Scotstounhill	d	12 32			12 45				13 00				13 15				13 31			13 45			
Garscadden	d	12 35			12 47				13 02				13 17				13 33			13 47			
Yoker	d	12 37			12 50				13 04				13 19				13 35			13 49			
Clydebank	d	12 39			12 52				13 06				13 21				13 37			13 51			
Anniesland	d		12 35	12 41		12 50		12 55		13 05	13 11			13 20		13 25		13 35	13 41		13 50		13 56
Westerton	d		12 38	12 44		12 53		12 58		13 08	13 14			13 23		13 28		13 38	13 44		13 53		13 59
Bearsden	d			12 46				13 01			13 16					13 31			13 46				14 01
Hillfoot	d			12 48				13 02			13 18					13 32			13 47				14 02
Milngavie	a			12 52				13 07			13 22					13 37			13 52				14 07
Drumchapel	d		12 40			12 55				13 10				13 25				13 40			13 55		
Drumry	d		12 42			12 57				13 12				13 27				13 42			13 57		
Singer	d		12 45			13 00				13 15				13 30				13 45			14 00		
Dalmuir	a	12 43	12 47		12 56	13 02	12 59		13 11	13 17			13 26	13 32	13 29		13 42	13 47		13 56	14 02	13 59	
	d		12 48				12 59			13 18					13 29			13 48				13 59	
Kilpatrick	d		12 51							13 21								13 51					
Bowling	d		12 54							13 24								13 54					
Dumbarton East	d		12 58				13 06			13 28					13 36			13 58				14 06	
Dumbarton Central	d		13 00				13 09			13 30					13 39			14 00				14 10	
Dalreoch	d		13 02				13 10			13 32					13 40			14 02				14 11	
Renton	d		13 05							13 35								14 05					
Alexandria	d		13 07							13 37								14 07					
Balloch	a		13 10							13 40								14 10					
Cardross	d						13 15								13 45							14 16	
Craigendoran	d						13 20								13 50							14 21	
Helensburgh Central	a						13 23								13 53							14 24	

A From Edinburgh
b Glasgow Central High Level

Lanark, Coatbridge, Motherwell, Larkhall, Hamilton, Edinburgh and Bathgate, Airdrie and Springburn - Glasgow - Milngavie, Dalmuir, Balloch and Helensburgh

		SR	SR	SR	SR A	SR	SR	SR	SR	SR	SR	SR	SR	SR	SR	SR	SR	SR	SR	SR A	SR	SR
Lanark	d			12 53						13 23									13 53			
Carluke	d			13 03						13 33									14 03			
Wishaw	d			13 08						13 40									14 08			
Holytown	d			13 13	13 31														14 13	14 30		
Shieldmuir	d									13 43												
Coatbridge Central	d																					
Whifflet	d																					
Motherwell	a			13 19						13 47									14 19			
	d	13 16		13 20						13 48		13 50					14 16		14 20			
Bellshill	d	13 22			13 34					13 54							14 22			14 34		
Uddingston	d	13 26			13 39					13 59							14 26			14 38		
Airbles	d			13 22								13 52							14 22			
Larkhall	d						13 37							14 07								14 37
Merryton	d						13 39							14 09								14 39
Chatelherault	d						13 42							14 12								14 42
Hamilton Central	d			13 27			13 46					13 57		14 16					14 27			14 46
Hamilton West	d			13 30			13 48					14 00		14 18					14 30			14 48
Blantyre	d			13 33			13 52					14 03		14 22					14 33			14 52
Newton	d			13 37								14 07							14 37			
Cambuslang	d	13 31		13 41						14 04		14 11					14 31		14 41			
Rutherglen	d	13 34		13 45			13 59			14 06		14 15		14 29			14 36		14 45			14 59
Dalmarnock	d	13 36		13 47						14 08		14 17					14 38		14 47			
Bridgeton	d	13 38		13 49						14 10		14 19					14 40		14 49			
Edinburgh	d							12 48	13 07						13 21	13 37						
Haymarket	d							12 52	13 11						13 25	13 43						
Edinburgh Park	d							12 57	13 17						13 30	13 47						
Uphall	d							13 05	13 26						13 38	13 55						
Livingston North	d							13 08	13 28						13 41	13 59						
Bathgate	a							13 13	13 33						13 46	14 03						
	d							13 17	13 33						13 47	14 04						
Armadale	d							13 21							13 51							
Blackridge	d							13 25							13 55							
Caldercruix	d							13 31							14 01							
Drumgelloch	d							13 35	13 47						14 05	14 16						
Airdrie	d		13 27					13 42	13 50		13 57				14 12	14 22		14 27				
Coatdyke	d		13 29					13 44			13 59				14 14			14 29				
Coatbridge Sunnyside	d		13 31					13 46	13 53		14 01				14 16	14 25		14 31				
Blairhill	d		13 34					13 49			14 04				14 19			14 34				
Easterhouse	d		13 38					13 53			14 08				14 23			14 38				
Garrowhill	d		13 40					13 55			14 10				14 25			14 40				
Shettleston	d		13 43					13 58			14 13				14 28			14 43				
Carntyne	d		13 45					14 00			14 15				14 30			14 45				
Springburn	d					13 49							14 19								14 49	
Barnhill	d					13 50							14 20								14 50	
Alexandra Parade	d					13 53							14 23								14 53	
Duke Street	d					13 55							14 25								14 55	
Bellgrove	d		13 48			13 57		14 03			14 18		14 27		14 33			14 48			14 57	
High Street	d		13 50			13 59		14 05	14 11		14 20		14 29		14 35	14 41		14 50			15 00	
Glasgow Queen St LL	a		13 52			14 01		14 07	14 13		14 22		14 31		14 37	14 43		14 52			15 02	
	d		13 53			14 02		14 11	14 14		14 23		14 32		14 40	14 43		14 53			15 03	
Charing Cross	d		13 55			14 04		14 13	14 16		14 25		14 34		14 42	14 46		14 55			15 05	
Argyle Street	d	13 42		13 53			14 04			14 14		14 23		14 35			14 43		14 53			15 04
Glasgow Central LL	a	13 44		13 56	13b55		14 07			14 16		14 26		14 37			14 46		14 56	14b55		15 07
	d	13 46		13 58			14 07			14 16		14 28		14 37			14 46		15 00			15 07
Anderston	d	13 48		13 59			14 09			14 18		14 29		14 39			14 48		15 01			15 09
Exhibition Centre	d	13 50		14 01			14 11			14 20		14 31		14 41			14 50		15 03			15 11
Partick	d	13 53	13 59	14 05		14 09	14 14	14 17	14 20	14 24	14 29	14 35	14 38	14 44	14 47	14 50	14 54	14 59	15 07		15 09	15 14
Hyndland	d	13 55	14 02	14 08		14 11	14 17	14 19	14 23	14 26	14 32	14 38	14 40	14 47	14 49	14 53	14 56	15 02	15 09		15 11	15 17
Jordanhill	d	13 57				14 13				14 28			14 42				14 58				15 13	
Scotstounhill	d	14 00				14 15				14 30			14 45				15 00				15 16	
Garscadden	d	14 02				14 17				14 31			14 47				15 02				15 18	
Yoker	d	14 05				14 20				14 34			14 49				15 05				15 20	
Clydebank	d	14 07				14 22				14 36			14 51				15 09				15 22	
Anniesland	d		14 05	14 11			14 20		14 26		14 35	14 41		14 50		14 56		15 05	15 12			15 20
Westerton	d		14 08	14 14			14 23		14 29		14 38	14 44		14 53		14 59		15 08	15 16			15 23
Bearsden	d			14 16					14 31			14 46				15 01			15 19			
Hillfoot	d			14 17					14 32			14 47				15 02			15 21			
Milngavie	a			14 22					14 37			14 52				15 07			15 24			
Drumchapel	d		14 10				14 25				14 40			14 55				15 10				15 25
Drumry	d		14 12				14 27				14 42			14 57				15 12				15 27
Singer	d		14 15				14 30				14 45			15 00				15 15				15 30
Dalmuir	a	14 11	14 17			14 26	14 32	14 29		14 42	14 47		14 56	15 02	14 59		15 14	15 17			15 26	15 32
	d		14 18					14 29			14 49				14 59			15 18				
Kilpatrick	d		14 21								14 51							15 21				
Bowling	d		14 24								14 54							15 24				
Dumbarton East	d		14 28					14 36			14 59				15 06			15 28				
Dumbarton Central	d		14 30					14 39			15 01				15 09			15 30				
Dalreoch	d		14 32					14 40			15 02				15 10			15 32				
Renton	d		14 35								15 05							15 35				
Alexandria	d		14 37								15 07							15 37				
Balloch	a		14 40								15 10							15 40				
Cardross	d							14 45							15 15							
Craigendoran	d							14 51							15 20							
Helensburgh Central	a							14 54							15 26							

A From Edinburgh

b Glasgow Central High Level

Lanark, Coatbridge, Motherwell, Larkhall, Hamilton, Edinburgh and Bathgate, Airdrie and Springburn - Glasgow - Milngavie, Dalmuir, Balloch and Helensburgh

		SR	SR	SR	SR	SR	SR	SR	SR	SR	SR	SR	SR	SR A	SR	SR	SR	SR	SR	SR	SR	SR	SR
Lanark	d			14 23									14 53						15 23				
Carluke	d			14 33									15 03						15 33				
Wishaw	d			14 38									15 08						15 39				
Holytown	d												15 13	15 30									
Shieldmuir	d			14 42															15 42				
Coatbridge Central	d																						
Whifflet	d																						
Motherwell	a			14 46									15 19						15 46				
	d			14 46		14 50					15 16		15 20						15 47		15 50		
Bellshill	d			14 52							15 22			15 34					15 53				
Uddingston	d			14 56							15 26			15 38					15 57				
Airbles	d					14 52							15 23								15 52		
Larkhall	d							15 07								15 37							16 07
Merryton	d							15 09								15 39							16 09
Chatelherault	d							15 12								15 42							16 12
Hamilton Central	d					14 57		15 16					15 27			15 46					15 58		16 16
Hamilton West	d					15 00		15 18					15 30			15 48					16 01		16 18
Blantyre	d					15 03		15 22					15 33			15 52					16 04		16 22
Newton	d					15 08							15 37								16 08		16 26
Cambuslang	d			15 01		15 11					15 31		15 41						16 02		16 12		
Rutherglen	d			15 04		15 15		15 29			15 34		15 45			15 59			16 06		16 16		16 30
Dalmarnock	d			15 06		15 17					15 36		15 47						16 08		16 18		
Bridgeton	d			15 08		15 19					15 38		15 49						16 10		16 20		
Edinburgh	d	13 51	14 10						14 21	14 37							14 48	15 07					
Haymarket	d	13 55	14 14						14 25	14 42							14 52	15 11					
Edinburgh Park	d	14 00	14 20						14 30	14 47							15 00	15 17					
Uphall	d	14 08	14 28						14 38	14 54							15 09	15 25					
Livingston North	d	14 11	14 31						14 41	14 59							15 12	15 29					
Bathgate	a	14 16	14 36						14 47	15 03							15 17	15 33					
	d	14 17	14 36						14 47	15 04							15 17	15 35					
Armadale	d	14 21							14 51								15 21						
Blackridge	d	14 25							14 55								15 25						
Caldercruix	d	14 31							15 01								15 31						
Drumgelloch	d	14 35	14 49						15 05	15 16							15 35	15 47					
Airdrie	d	14 42	14 52		14 57				15 12	15 20		15 27					15 42	15 51		15 57			
Coatdyke	d	14 44			14 59				15 14			15 29					15 44			15 59			
Coatbridge Sunnyside	d	14 46	14 55		15 01				15 16	15 23		15 31					15 46	15 54		16 01			
Blairhill	d	14 49			15 04				15 19			15 34					15 49			16 04			
Easterhouse	d	14 53			15 08				15 23			15 38					15 53			16 08			
Garrowhill	d	14 55			15 10				15 25			15 40					15 55			16 10			
Shettleston	d	14 58			15 13				15 28			15 43					15 58			16 13			
Carntyne	d	15 00			15 15				15 30			15 45					16 00			16 15			
Springburn	d						15 19								15 50							16 22	
Barnhill	d						15 20								15 51							16 23	
Alexandra Parade	d						15 23								15 54							16 26	
Duke Street	d						15 25								15 56							16 28	
Bellgrove	d	15 03			15 19		15 27		15 33			15 48			15 58		16 03			16 18		16 30	
High Street	d	15 05	15 12		15 21		15 29		15 35	15 41		15 50			16 00		16 05	16 10		16 20		16 32	
Glasgow Queen St LL	a	15 07	15 14		15 23		15 31		15 37	15 43		15 52			16 02		16 07	16 12		16 22		16 34	
	d	15 10	15 15		15 23		15 32		15 40	15 44		15 53			16 03		16 10	16 13		16 23		16 34	
Charing Cross	d	15 12	15 17		15 25		15 34		15 42	15 46		15 55			16 05		16 12	16 15		16 25		16 36	
Argyle Street	d			15 12		15 23		15 36			15 42		15 53			16 04			16 13		16 24		16 35
Glasgow Central LL	a			15 16		15 26		15 37			15 46		15 56	15b56		16 07			16 16		16 26		16 37
	d			15 16		15 28		15 38			15 46		15 58			16 07			16 18		16 28		16 38
Anderston	d			15 18		15 29		15 39			15 48		15 59			16 09			16 20		16 29		16 39
Exhibition Centre	d			15 20		15 31		15 41			15 50		16 01			16 11			16 22		16 31		16 41
Partick	d	15 17	15 21	15 24	15 29	15 35	15 39	15 45	15 47	15 50	15 54	15 59	16 05		16 09	16 14	16 17	16 20	16 25	16 29	16 35	16 40	16 45
Hyndland	d	15 19	15 23	15 26	15 32	15 38	15 41	15 47	15 49	15 53	15 56	16 02	16 07		16 11	16 17	16 19	16 22	16 27	16 32	16 38	16 42	16 47
Jordanhill	d			15 28			15 43				15 58				16 13				16 29			16 44	
Scotstounhill	d			15 31			15 45				16 00				16 16				16 32			16 47	
Garscadden	d			15 33			15 47				16 03				16 18				16 34			16 49	
Yoker	d			15 35			15 50				16 05				16 20				16 36			16 51	
Clydebank	d			15 37			15 52				16 07				16 22				16 38			16 53	
Anniesland	d		15 26		15 35	15 43		15 50		15 56		16 05	16 10			16 20		16 25		16 35	16 41		16 50
Westerton	d		15 29		15 38	15 46		15 53		15 59		16 08	16 13			16 23		16 28		16 38	16 44		16 53
Bearsden	d		15 31			15 49				16 01			16 16					16 31			16 46		
Hillfoot	d		15 33			15 50				16 02			16 18					16 33			16 47		
Milngavie	a		15 38			15 55				16 07			16 22					16 36			16 52		
Drumchapel	d				15 40			15 55				16 10				16 25				16 40			16 55
Drumry	d				15 42			15 57				16 12				16 27				16 42			16 57
Singer	d				15 45			16 00				16 15				16 30				16 45			17 00
Dalmuir	a	15 29		15 41	15 47		15 56	16 02	15 59		16 11	16 17			16 26	16 32	16 29		16 43	16 47		16 57	17 02
	d	15 29			15 48				15 59			16 18					16 29			16 48			
Kilpatrick	d				15 51							16 21								16 51			
Bowling	d				15 54							16 24								16 54			
Dumbarton East	d	15 36			15 58				16 06			16 28					16 36			16 58			
Dumbarton Central	d	15 39			16 00				16 09			16 30					16 39			17 00			
Dalreoch	d	15 45			16 02				16 10			16 32					16 40			17 02			
Renton	d				16 05							16 35								17 05			
Alexandria	d				16 07							16 37								17 07			
Balloch	a				16 10							16 40								17 10			
Cardross	d	15 49							16 15								16 45						
Craigendoran	d	15 54							16 20								16 50						
Helensburgh Central	a	15 58							16 24								16 54						

A From Edinburgh

Table 226

Mondays to Fridays

Lanark, Coatbridge, Motherwell, Larkhall, Hamilton, Edinburgh and Bathgate, Airdrie and Springburn - Glasgow - Milngavie, Dalmuir, Balloch and Helensburgh

		SR	SR	SR	SR	SR	SR	SR	SR	SR	SR	SR	SR	SR	SR	SR	SR	SR	SR	SR	SR	SR
							A															
Lanark	d					15 53						16 23									16 53	
Carluke	d					16 03						16 34									17 03	
Wishaw	d					16 08						16 39									17 08	
Holytown	d					16 13	16 33															
Shieldmuir	d											16 43									17 12	
Coatbridge Central	d																					
Whifflet	d																					
Motherwell	a					16 19						16 46									17 16	
	d			16 16		16 20						16 46			16 50						17 16	
Bellshill	d			16 22			16 35					16 52									17 23	
Uddingston	d			16 26			16 40					16 56									17 27	
Airbles	d					16 22									16 52							
Larkhall	d								16 37									17 06				
Merryton	d								16 39									17 08				
Chatelherault	d								16 42									17 11				
Hamilton Central	d					16 28			16 46						16 58			17 15				
Hamilton West	d					16 30			16 48						17 00			17 17				
Blantyre	d					16 34			16 52						17 04			17 21				
Newton	d					16 38									17 08							
Cambuslang	d			16 31		16 41						17 01			17 11						17 31	
Rutherglen	d			16 34		16 46			16 59			17 06			17 16			17 29			17 34	
Dalmarnock	d			16 36		16 48						17 08			17 18						17 36	
Bridgeton	d			16 38		16 50						17 10			17 20						17 38	
Edinburgh	d	15 20	15 37							15 49	16 07								16 20	16 41		
Haymarket	d	15 25	15 42							15 53	16 12								16 25	16 44		
Edinburgh Park	d	15 30	15 46							16 00	16 16								16 30	16 49		
Uphall	d	15 38	15 54							16 08	16 24								16 38	16 56		
Livingston North	d	15 41	15 58							16 11	16 28								16 41	17 00		
Bathgate	a	15 46	16 02							16 16	16 32								16 47	17 04		
	d	15 47	16 04							16 17	16 34								16 47	17 05		
Armadale	d	15 51								16 21									16 51			
Blackridge	d	15 55								16 25									16 55			
Caldercruix	d	16 01								16 31									17 01			
Drumgelloch	d	16 05	16 16							16 35	16 46								17 05	17 17		
Airdrie	d	16 12	16 20		16 27					16 42	16 50			16 57					17 12	17 21		17 27
Coatdyke	d	16 14			16 29					16 44				16 59					17 14			17 29
Coatbridge Sunnyside	d	16 16	16 23		16 31					16 46	16 53			17 01					17 16	17 24		17 31
Blairhill	d	16 19			16 34					16 49				17 04					17 19			17 34
Easterhouse	d	16 23			16 38					16 53				17 08					17 23			17 38
Garrowhill	d	16 25			16 40					16 55				17 10					17 25			17 40
Shettleston	d	16 28			16 43					16 58				17 13					17 28			17 43
Carntyne	d	16 30			16 45					17 00				17 15					17 30			17 45
Springburn	d							16 52									17 22					
Barnhill	d							16 53									17 23					
Alexandra Parade	d							16 56									17 26					
Duke Street	d							16 58									17 28					
Bellgrove	d	16 33			16 48			17 00		17 03			17 15	17 18		17 27	17 30		17 33			17 48
High Street	d	16 35	16 40		16 50			17 02		17 05	17 11		17 17	17 20		17 29	17 32		17 35	17 41		17 50
Glasgow Queen St LL	a	16 37	16 42		16 52			17 04		17 07	17 13		17 19	17 22		17 31	17 34		17 37	17 43		17 53
	d	16 40	16 43		16 53			17 04		17 11	17 14		17 20	17 23		17 31	17 34		17 40	17 44		17 53
Charing Cross	d	16 42	16 45		16 55			17 06		17 13	17 16		17 22	17 25		17 34	17 36		17 42	17 46		17 55
Argyle Street	d			16 42		16 54			17 05			17 14			17 24			17 34			17 42	
Glasgow Central LL	a			16 46		16 56	16b57		17 07			17 16			17 26			17 36			17 46	
	d			16 46		16 58			17 07			17 16			17 28			17 38			17 47	
Anderston	d			16 48		16 59			17 09			17 18			17 29			17 39			17 48	
Exhibition Centre	d			16 50		17 01			17 11			17 20			17 31			17 41			17 50	
Partick	d	16 47	16 50	16 53	16 59	17 05		17 10	17 14	17 18	17 20	17 23	17 27	17 29	17 35	17 38	17 40	17 45	17 47	17 50	17 54	18 00
Hyndland	d	16 49	16 53	16 55	17 02	17 08		17 12	17 17	17 20	17 22	17 25		17 32	17 38		17 42	17 47	17 49	17 53	17 56	18 02
Jordanhill	d			16 57				17 14				17 27					17 44				17 58	
Scotstounhill	d			17 00				17 17				17 30					17 47				18 00	
Garscadden	d			17 02				17 19				17 32					17 49				18 02	
Yoker	d			17 04				17 21				17 34					17 51				18 04	
Clydebank	d			17 06				17 23				17 36					17 53				18 06	
Anniesland	d		16 56		17 05	17 12			17 20		17 25			17 35	17 41			17 50		17 56		18 05
Westerton	d		16 59		17 08	17 15			17 23		17 28			17 38	17 44			17 53		17 59		18 08
Bearsden	d		17 01			17 17					17 31				17 46					18 01		
Hillfoot	d		17 02			17 18					17 32				17 47					18 03		
Milngavie	a		17 07			17 23					17 37				17 52					18 07		
Drumchapel	d				17 10				17 25					17 40				17 55				18 10
Drumry	d				17 12				17 27					17 42				17 57				18 12
Singer	d				17 15				17 30					17 45				18 00				18 14
Dalmuir	a	16 59		17 11	17 17			17 27	17 32	17 30		17 41		17 47			17 58	18 02	17 59		18 11	18 18
	d	16 59			17 18					17 30				17 51					17 59			18 18
Kilpatrick	d				17 21									17 53								18 21
Bowling	d				17 24									17 56								18 24
Dumbarton East	d	17 06			17 28					17 37				18 01					18 06			18 28
Dumbarton Central	d	17 09			17 30					17 40			17 46	18 04		17 59			18 09			18 30
Dalreoch	d	17 10			17 32					17 41			17 48	18 05		18 01			18 10			18 32
Renton	d				17 35											18 04						18 35
Alexandria	d				17 37											18 06						18 37
Balloch	a				17 40											18 09						18 40
Cardross	d	17 15								17 46			17 53	18 09					18 15			
Craigendoran	d	17 20								17 51			17 58	18 17					18 20			
Helensburgh Central	a	17 24								17 54			18 01	18 20					18 25			

A From Edinburgh

b Glasgow Central High Level

Lanark, Coatbridge, Motherwell, Larkhall, Hamilton, Edinburgh and Bathgate, Airdrie and Springburn - Glasgow - Milngavie, Dalmuir, Balloch and Helensburgh

		SR	SR	SR	SR	SR	SR	SR	SR	SR	SR	SR	SR	SR	SR	SR	SR	SR	SR	SR	SR	SR	SR
			A					◇ B											A				
Lanark	d								17 23														
Carluke	d								17 33														
Wishaw	d								17 39														
Holytown	d		17 30																				
Shieldmuir	d								17 43														
Coatbridge Central	d					17 32							17 56										
Whifflet	d					17 34							18 00										
Motherwell	a					17 40			17 47				18 08										
	d	17 20				17 40			17 47				18 11					18 20					
Bellshill	d		17 33						17 53				18 17						18 41				
Uddingston	d		17 38						17 57				18 21										
Airbles	d	17 22				17 43												18 22					
Larkhall	d										17 48					18 05					18 37		
Merryton	d										17 50					18 07					18 39		
Chatelherault	d										17 53					18 14					18 42		
Hamilton Central	d	17 27				17 48					17 57					18 18		18 27			18 46		
Hamilton West	d	17 30				17 50					18 00					18 21		18 30			18 48		
Blantyre	d	17 33				17 54					18 04					18 24		18 33			18 52		
Newton	d	17 37									18 08							18 37					
Cambuslang	d	17 41	17 44						18 02		18 11					18 31		18 41	18 52				
Rutherglen	d	17 45				18 02			18 06		18 15		18 29			18 34		18 45			18 59		
Dalmarnock	d	17 47							18 08		18 17					18 36		18 47					
Bridgeton	d	17 49							18 10		18 19					18 38		18 49					
Edinburgh	d				16 48		17 07							17 22	17 37							17 51	18 06
Haymarket	d				16 52		17 11							17 26	17 42							17 56	18 11
Edinburgh Park	d				16 57		17 16							17 31	17 48							18 01	18 16
Uphall	d				17 05		17 27							17 39	17 56							18 09	18 24
Livingston North	d				17 08		17 30							17 42	17 59							18 12	18 28
Bathgate	a				17 14		17 35							17 46	18 04							18 17	18 34
	d				17 17		17 35							17 47	18 05							18 17	18 35
Armadale	d				17 21									17 51								18 21	
Blackridge	d				17 25									17 55								18 25	
Caldercruix	d				17 31									18 01								18 31	
Drumgelloch	d				17 35		17 48							18 05	18 17							18 35	18 46
Airdrie	d				17 42		17 51			17 57				18 12	18 21		18 27					18 42	18 51
Coatdyke	d				17 44					17 59				18 14			18 29					18 44	
Coatbridge Sunnyside	d				17 46		17 55			18 01				18 16	18 24		18 31					18 46	18 53
Blairhill	d				17 49					18 04				18 19			18 34					18 49	
Easterhouse	d				17 53					18 08				18 23			18 38					18 53	
Garrowhill	d				17 55					18 10				18 25			18 40					18 55	
Shettleston	d				17 58					18 13				18 28			18 43					18 58	
Carntyne	d				18 00					18 15				18 30			18 45					19 00	
Springburn	d			17 49								18 19								18 49			
Barnhill	d			17 50								18 20								18 50			
Alexandra Parade	d			17 53								18 23								18 53			
Duke Street	d			17 55								18 25								18 55			
Bellgrove	d			17 57	18 03					18 18		18 27		18 33			18 48			18 57		19 03	
High Street	d			17 59	18 05		18 10			18 20		18 29		18 35	18 40		18 50			18 59		19 05	19 12
Glasgow Queen St LL	a			18 01	18 07		18 12			18 22		18 31		18 37	18 42		18 52			19 01		19 07	19 14
	d			18 02	18 10		18 14	18c21		18 23		18 32		18 40	18 43		18 53			19 02		19 10	19 14
Charing Cross	d			18 04	18 12		18 17			18 25		18 34		18 42	18 46		18 55			19 04		19 12	19 17
Argyle Street	d	17 53				18 07			18 14		18 23		18 34			18 42		18 53			19 04		
Glasgow Central LL	a	17 56	17b57			18 08			18 16		18 26		18 37			18 46		18 56	19b03		19 07		
	d	17 58				18 11			18 17		18 28		18 37			18 46		18 58			19 07		
Anderston	d	17 59				18 13			18 18		18 29		18 39			18 48		18 59			19 09		
Exhibition Centre	d	18 01				18 15			18 20		18 31		18 41			18 50		19 01			19 11		
Partick	d	18 05		18 09	18 16	18 18	18 21		18 24	18 29	18 35	18 39	18 44	18 47	18 50	18a53	19 00	19 05		19 09	19 14	19 17	19 21
Hyndland	d	18 07		18 11	18 18	18 20	18 24		18 26	18 32	18 37	18 41	18 47	18 49	18 53		19 03	19 08		19 11	19 17	19 19	19 23
Jordanhill	d			18 13					18 28			18 43		18 51						19 13		19 21	19 25
Scotstounhill	d			18 15					18 31			18 45		18 54						19 15		19 24	19 27
Garscadden	d			18 17					18 32			18a47		18 56						19a17		19 26	19a30
Yoker	d			18 20					18 34					18 58								19 28	
Clydebank	d			18 22					18 36					19 00								19 30	
Anniesland	d	18 10				18 23	18 27			18 35	18 40		18 50		18 56		19 06	19 11			19 20		
Westerton	d	18 13				18 26	18 30			18 38	18 43		18 53		18 59		19 09	19 14			19 23		
Bearsden	d	18 16					18 32				18 46				19 02			19 17					
Hillfoot	d	18 17					18 34				18 47				19 03			19 18					
Milngavie	a	18 22					18 38				18 52				19 07			19 22					
Drumchapel	d					18 29				18 40			18 55				19 11				19 25		
Drumry	d					18 31				18 42			18 57				19 13				19 27		
Singer	d					18 33				18 45			19 00				19 16				19 30		
Dalmuir	a			18 26	18 29	18 36		18 38	18 41	18 47			19 02	19 04			19 18				19 32	19 34	
	d				18 29			18 38		18 48				19 04			19 18					19 34	
Kilpatrick	d									18 51							19 21						
Bowling	d									18 54							19 24						
Dumbarton East	d				18 36					18 58				19 12			19 28					19 42	
Dumbarton Central	d				18 39			18 47		19 00				19 14			19 30					19 44	
Dalreoch	d				18 40					19 02				19 15			19 32					19 45	
Renton	d									19 05							19 35						
Alexandria	d									19 07							19 37						
Balloch	a									19 10							19 40						
Cardross	d				18 45									19 20								19 50	
Craigendoran	d				18 50									19 25								19 55	
Helensburgh Central	a				18 53			19e02						19 28								19 58	

A From Edinburgh

B To Oban

b Glasgow Central High Level

c Glasgow Queen St High Level

e Helensburgh Upper

Table 226

Lanark, Coatbridge, Motherwell, Larkhall, Hamilton, Edinburgh and Bathgate, Airdrie and Springburn - Glasgow - Milngavie, Dalmuir, Balloch and Helensburgh

		SR	SR	SR	SR A	SR	SR	SR	SR	SR	SR	SR	SR	SR	SR	SR	SR	SR	SR	SR	SR	SR	SR
Lanark	d	18 23									18 53				19 23								19 53
Carluke	d	18 33									19 03				19 33								20 03
Wishaw	d	18 38									19 08				19 40								20 08
Holytown	d				19 00						19 13												20 13
Shieldmuir	d	18 42													19 43								
Coatbridge Central	d			18 39																			
Whifflet	d			18 41																			
Motherwell	a	18 46		18 49							19 19				19 47								20 19
	d	18 46		18 50					19 16		19 20				19 48		19 50				20 19		20 20
Bellshill	d	18 52			19 03				19 22						19 54						20 24		
Uddingston	d	18 56			19 06				19 26						19 58						20 29		
Airbles	d			18 52							19 22						19 52						20 22
Larkhall	d					19 07						19 37						20 07					
Merryton	d					19 09						19 39						20 09					
Chatelherault	d					19 12						19 42						20 12					
Hamilton Central	d			18 57		19 16					19 27	19 46					19 57	20 16					20 27
Hamilton West	d			19 00		19 18					19 30	19 48					20 00	20 18					20 30
Blantyre	d			19 03		19 22					19 33	19 52					20 03	20 22					20 33
Newton	d			19 07							19 37	19 56					20 06						20 37
Cambuslang	d	19 01		19 11	19 16				19 31		19 41				20 03		20 09				20 33		20 41
Rutherglen	d	19 05		19 16		19 29			19 34		19 45	20 00			20 05		20 14	20 29			20 40		20 45
Dalmarnock	d	19 07		19 18					19 36		19 47				20 07		20 16				20 42		20 47
Bridgeton	d	19 09		19 20					19 38		19 49				20 09		20 18				20 44		20 49
Edinburgh	d						18 20	18 37					18 48	19 07					19 21	19 39			
Haymarket	d						18 24	18 42					18 52	19 11					19 24	19 41			
Edinburgh Park	d						18 30	18 46					18 57	19 18					19 30	19 47			
Uphall	d						18 38	18 55					19 05	19 26					19 38	19 54			
Livingston North	d						18 41	18 57					19 08	19 29					19 44	19 58			
Bathgate	a						18 46	19 03					19 13	19 34					19 48	20 04			
	d						18 47	19 03					19 17						19 49				
Armadale	d						18 51						19 21						19 53				
Blackridge	d						18 55						19 25						19 56				
Caldercruix	d						19 01						19 31						20 03				
Drumgelloch	d						19 05	19 17					19 35						20 06				
Airdrie	d						19 12	19 20					19 42						20 13				
Coatdyke	d						19 14						19 44						20 15				
Coatbridge Sunnyside	d						19 16	19 23					19 46						20 17				
Blairhill	d						19 19						19 49						20 20				
Easterhouse	d						19 23						19 53						20 24				
Garrowhill	d						19 25						19 55						20 26				
Shettleston	d						19 28						19 58						20 29				
Carntyne	d						19 30						20 00						20 31				
Springburn	d		19 09							19 39						20 09						20 39	
Barnhill	d		19 10							19 40						20 10						20 40	
Alexandra Parade	d		19 13							19 43						20 13						20 43	
Duke Street	d		19 15							19 45						20 15						20 45	
Bellgrove	d		19 17				19 33			19 47			20 03			20 17			20 34			20 47	
High Street	d		19 19				19 35	19 40		19 49			20 05			20 19			20 36			20 49	
Glasgow Queen St LL 10 ⛴	a		19 21				19 37	19 42		19 51			20 07			20 21			20 38			20 51	
	d		19 23				19 40	19 43		19 53			20 10			20 23			20 40			20 53	
Charing Cross	d		19 25				19 42	19 45		19 55			20 12			20 25			20 42			20 55	
Argyle Street	d	19 13		19 24		19 35			19 42		19 53	20 06			20 13		20 23	20 34			20 46		20 53
Glasgow Central LL 15	a	19 15		19 26	19b29	19 37			19 46		19 56	20 07			20 16		20 26	20 37			20 48		20 56
	d	19 17		19 28		19 37			19 46		19 58	20 08			20 16		20 28	20 37			20 49		20 58
Anderston	d	19 19		19 29		19 39			19 48		19 59	20 09			20 18		20 29	20 39			20 51		20 59
Exhibition Centre	d	19 21		19 31		19 41			19 50		20 01	20 11			20 20		20 31	20 41			20 53		21 01
Partick ⛴	d	19a24	19 29	19 35		19 44	19 47	19 50	19a53	19 59	20 05	20 15	20 17		20a23	20 29	20 35	20 44	20 48		20a56	20 59	21 05
Hyndland	d		19 32	19 38		19 47	19 49	19 52		20 03	20 08	20 17	20 19			20 33	20 38	20 47	20 50			21 02	21 08
Jordanhill	d						19 51	19 54					20 21						20 52				
Scotstounhill	d						19 54	19 57					20 24						20 54				
Garscadden	d						19 56	19a59					20 26						20 56				
Yoker	d						19 58						20 28						20 58				
Clydebank	d						20 00						20 30						21 00				
Anniesland	d		19 35	19 41		19 50				20 06	20 11	20 20				20 36	20 41	20 50				21 05	21 11
Westerton	d		19 38	19 44		19 53				20 09	20 14	20 23				20 39	20 44	20 53				21 08	21 14
Bearsden	d			19 46							20 17						20 46						21 16
Hillfoot	d			19 48							20 18						20 47						21 18
Milngavie	a			19 52							20 22						20 52						21 25
Drumchapel	d		19 40			19 55				20 11		20 25				20 41		20 55				21 10	
Drumry	d		19 42			19 57				20 13		20 27				20 43		20 57				21 12	
Singer	d		19 45			20 00				20 16		20 30				20 46		21 00				21 15	
Dalmuir	a		19 47			20 02	20 04			20 18		20 32	20 34			20 48		21 02	21 04			21 18	
	d		19 48				20 04			20 18			20 34			20 48			21 04			21 18	
Kilpatrick	d		19 51							20 21						20 51						21 21	
Bowling	d		19 54							20 24						20 54						21 24	
Dumbarton East	d		19 58				20 12			20 28			20 42			20 58			21 11			21 28	
Dumbarton Central	d		20 00				20 14			20 30			20 44			21 00			21 14			21 30	
Dalreoch	d		20 02				20 15			20 32			20 45			21 02			21 15			21 32	
Renton	d		20 05							20 35						21 05						21 35	
Alexandria	d		20 07							20 37						21 07						21 37	
Balloch	a		20 10							20 40						21 10						21 40	
Cardross	d						20 20						20 50						21 20				
Craigendoran	d						20 25						20 55						21 25				
Helensburgh Central	a						20 28						20 58						21 28				

A From Edinburgh

b Glasgow Central High Level

Table 226

Lanark, Coatbridge, Motherwell, Larkhall, Hamilton, Edinburgh and Bathgate, Airdrie and Springburn - Glasgow - Milngavie, Dalmuir, Balloch and Helensburgh

		SR A	SR	SR	SR	SR	SR	SR	SR	SR	SR	SR	SR	SR	SR	SR	SR	SR	SR	SR	SR	SR
Lanark	d				20 23							20 53			21 23							21 53
Carluke	d				20 33							21 03			21 33							22 03
Wishaw	d				20 38							21 08			21 39							22 08
Holytown	d	20 30										21 13										22 13
Shieldmuir	d				20 42										21 42							
Coatbridge Central	d																					
Whifflet	d																					
Motherwell	a				20 46							21 19			21 46							22 19
	d				20 47		20 50			21 15		21 20			21 47		21 50			22 16		22 20
Bellshill	d	20 34			20 53					21 22					21 53					22 22		
Uddingston	d	20 38			20 57					21 26					21 57					22 27		
Airbles	d						20 52					21 22					21 52					22 22
Larkhall	d		20 37					21 07					21 37					22 07				
Merryton	d		20 39					21 09					21 39					22 09				
Chatelherault	d		20 42					21 12					21 42					22 12				
Hamilton Central	d		20 46				20 57	21 16				21 27	21 46				21 57	22 16				22 27
Hamilton West	d		20 48				21 00	21 18				21 30	21 48				22 00	22 18				22 30
Blantyre	d		20 52				21 03	21 22				21 33	21 52				22 03	22 22				22 33
Newton	d						21 07					21 37					22 07					22 37
Cambuslang	d				21 02		21 11			21 32		21 41			22 02		22 11			22 32		22 41
Rutherglen	d		20 59		21 04		21 16	21 29		21 36		21 45	22 01		22 04		22 15	22 30		22 35		22 45
Dalmarnock	d				21 06		21 18			21 38		21 47			22 06		22 17			22 37		22 47
Bridgeton	d				21 08		21 20			21 40		21 49			22 08		22 19			22 39		22 49
Edinburgh	d			19 51					20 21					20 50					21 21			
Haymarket	d			19 55					20 25					20 54					21 25			
Edinburgh Park	d			20 00					20 30					21 00					21 30			
Uphall	d			20 08					20 38					21 08					21 38			
Livingston North	d			20 17					20 41					21 11					21 41			
Bathgate	a			20 21					20 46					21 16					21 46			
	d			20 22					20 47					21 17					21 47			
Armadale	d			20 26					20 51					21 21					21 51			
Blackridge	d			20 29					20 55					21 25					21 55			
Caldercruix	d			20 36					21 01					21 31					22 01			
Drumgelloch	d			20 39					21 05					21 35					22 05			
Airdrie	d			20 43					21 12					21 42					22 12			
Coatdyke	d			20 45					21 14					21 44					22 14			
Coatbridge Sunnyside	d			20 47					21 16					21 46					22 16			
Blairhill	d			20 50					21 19					21 49					22 19			
Easterhouse	d			20 54					21 23					21 53					22 23			
Garrowhill	d			20 56					21 25					21 55					22 25			
Shettleston	d			20 59					21 28					21 58					22 28			
Carntyne	d			21 01					21 30					22 00					22 30			
Springburn	d					21 09					21 39					22 09					22 39	
Barnhill	d					21 10					21 40					22 10					22 40	
Alexandra Parade	d					21 13					21 43					22 13					22 43	
Duke Street	d					21 15					21 45					22 15					22 45	
Bellgrove	d			21 04		21 17			21 33		21 47			22 03		22 17			22 33		22 47	
High Street	d			21 06		21 19			21 35		21 49			22 05		22 19			22 35		22 49	
Glasgow Queen St LL 10 ⛴	a			21 08		21 21			21 37		21 51			22 07		22 21			22 37		22 51	
	d			21 10		21 23			21 40		21 53			22 10		22 23			22 40		22 53	
Charing Cross	d			21 12		21 25			21 42		21 55			22 12		22 25			22 42		22 55	
Argyle Street	d		21 04		21 13		21 24	21 34		21 44		21 53	22 06		22 12		22 23	22 35		22 43		22 53
Glasgow Central LL 15	a	20b57	21 07		21 16		21 26	21 37		21 46		21 56	22 07		22 16		22 26	22 37		22 46		22 56
	d		21 07		21 16		21 28	21 37		21 46		21 58	22 07		22 16		22 28	22 37		22 46		22 58
Anderston	d		21 09		21 18		21 29	21 39		21 48		21 59	22 09		22 18		22 29	22 39		22 48		22 59
Exhibition Centre	d		21 11		21 20		21 31	21 41		21 50		22 01	22 11		22 20		22 31	22 41		22 50		23 01
Partick ⛴	d		21 14	21 17	21a23	21 29	21 35	21 44	21 47	21a53	21 59	22 05	22 14	22 17	22a23	22 30	22 35	22 44	22 47	22a54	22 59	23 05
Hyndland	d		21 17	21 19		21 32	21 38	21 47	21 49		22 03	22 08	22 17	22 19		22 33	22 38	22 47	22 49		23 03	23 08
Jordanhill	d			21 21					21 51					22 21					22 51			
Scotstounhill	d			21 24					21 54					22 24					22 54			
Garscadden	d			21 26					21 56					22 26					22 56			
Yoker	d			21 28					21 58					22 28					22 58			
Clydebank	d			21 30					22 00					22 30					23 00			
Anniesland	d		21 20			21 35	21 41	21 50			22 06	22 11	22 20			22 36	22 41	22 50			23 06	23 11
Westerton	d		21 23			21 38	21 44	21 53			22 09	22 14	22 23			22 39	22 44	22 53			23 09	23 14
Bearsden	d						21 46					22 17					22 46					23 17
Hillfoot	d						21 47					22 18					22 47					23 18
Milngavie	a						21 52					22 22					22 52					23 22
Drumchapel	d		21 25			21 40		21 55			22 11		22 25			22 41		22 55			23 11	
Drumry	d		21 27			21 42		21 57			22 13		22 27			22 43		22 57			23 13	
Singer	d		21 30			21 45		22 00			22 16		22 30			22 46		23 00			23 16	
Dalmuir	a		21 32	21 34		21 47		22 02	22 03		22 18		22 32	22 34		22 48		23 02	23 04		23 18	
	d			21 34		21 48			22 04		22 18			22 34		22 48			23 04		23 18	
Kilpatrick	d					21 51					22 21					22 51					23 21	
Bowling	d					21 54					22 24					22 54					23 24	
Dumbarton East	d			21 42		21 58			22 11		22 28			22 42		22 58			23 12		23 28	
Dumbarton Central	d			21 44		22 00			22 13		22 30			22 44		23 00			23 14		23 30	
Dalreoch	d			21 45		22 02			22 15		22 32			22 45		23 02			23 15		23 32	
Renton	d					22 05					22 35					23 05					23 35	
Alexandria	d					22 07					22 37					23 07					23 37	
Balloch	a					22 10					22 40					23 10					23 40	
Cardross	d			21 50					22 20					22 50					23 20			
Craigendoran	d			21 55					22 25					22 55					23 25			
Helensburgh Central	a			21 58					22 28					22 58					23 28			

A From Edinburgh

b Glasgow Central High Level

Lanark, Coatbridge, Motherwell, Larkhall, Hamilton, Edinburgh and Bathgate, Airdrie and Springburn - Glasgow - Milngavie, Dalmuir, Balloch and Helensburgh

		SR A	SR	SR	SR	SR	SR	SR	SR	SR FX	SR FO	SR FO	SR	SR	SR	SR FO	SR	SR A
Lanark	d				22 23													
Carluke	d				22 34													
Wishaw	d				22 39													
Holytown	d	22 33																23 59
Shieldmuir	d				22 42													
Coatbridge Central	d																	
Whifflet	d																	
Motherwell	a				22 46													
	d				22 46		22 50					23 20						
Bellshill	d	22 36			22 52													00 02
Uddingston	d	22 41			22 56													00 06
Airbles	d						22 52					23 22						
Larkhall	d		22 37					23 07								23 37		
Merryton	d		22 39					23 09								23 39		
Chatelherault	d		22 42					23 12								23 42		
Hamilton Central	d		22 46				22 57	23 16				23 27				23 46		
Hamilton West	d		22 48				23 00	23 18				23 30				23 48		
Blantyre	d		22 52				23 03	23 22				23 33				23 52		
Newton	d						23 07					23 37						
Cambuslang	d				23 01		23 11					23 41						00 12
Rutherglen	d		22 59		23 05		23 15	23 29				23 45				00 01		
Dalmarnock	d				23 07		23 17					23 47						
Bridgeton	d				23 09		23 19					23 49						
Edinburgh	d			21 51					22 19				22 51	23 07	23 37		23 51	
Haymarket	d			21 55					22 23				22 55	23 11	23 42		23 55	
Edinburgh Park	d			22 00					22 30				23 00	23 16	23 47		23 59	
Uphall	d			22 08					22 38				23 08	23 24	23 55		00 08	
Livingston North	d			22 11					22 41				23 11	23 27	23 59		00 11	
Bathgate	a			22 16					22 46				23 16	23 32	00 04		00 16	
	d			22 17					22 47				23 17	23 33				
Armadale	d			22 21					22 51				23 21	23 37				
Blackridge	d			22 25					22 55				23 25	23 41				
Caldercruix	d			22 31					23 01				23 31	23 47				
Drumgelloch	d			22 35					23 05				23 35	23 51				
Airdrie	d			22 42					23 12				23 38	23a54				
Coatdyke	d			22 44					23 14				23 40					
Coatbridge Sunnyside	d			22 46					23 16				23 43					
Blairhill	d			22 49					23 19				23 45					
Easterhouse	d			22 53					23 23				23 49					
Garrowhill	d			22 55					23 25				23 52					
Shettleston	d			22 58					23 28				23 54					
Carntyne	d			23 00					23 30				23 56					
Springburn	d					23 09				23 39	23 39							
Barnhill	d					23 10				23 40	23 40							
Alexandra Parade	d					23 13				23 43	23 43							
Duke Street	d					23 15				23 45	23 45							
Bellgrove	d			23 03		23 17			23 33	23 47	23 47		23 59					
High Street	d			23 05		23 19			23 35	23 49	23 49		00 02					
Glasgow Queen St LL	a			23 07		23 21			23 37	23 51	23 51		00 04					
	d			23 10		23 23			23 45	23 53	23 53		00 04					
Charing Cross	d			23 12		23 25			23 47	23 55	23 55		00 06					
Argyle Street	d		23 04		23 12		23 23	23 34				23 53				00 06		
Glasgow Central LL	a	22b55	23 07		23 16		23 26	23 37				23 56				00 07		00b23
	d		23 07		23 16		23 28	23 37				23 58				00 07		
Anderston	d		23 09		23 18		23 29	23 39				23 59				00 09		
Exhibition Centre	d		23 11		23 20		23 31	23 41				00 01				00 11		
Partick	d		23 14	23 17	23 24	23 29	23 35	23 44	23 51	23 59	23 59	00 05	00 11			00 14		
Hyndland	d		23 17	23 19	23 26	23 32	23 38	23 47	23 53	00 02	00 02	00 08	00 13			00 17		
Jordanhill	d			23 21	23 28			23 49	23 55	00 04			00 15					
Scotstounhill	d			23 24	23 30			23 51	23 58	00 06			00 17					
Garscadden	d			23 25	23a32			23a53	23 59	00a08			00a19					
Yoker	d			23 27					00 02									
Clydebank	d			23 29					00 04									
Anniesland	d		23 20			23 35	23 41				00 05	00 12				00 20		
Westerton	d		23 23			23 38	23 44				00 08	00 15				00 23		
Bearsden	d						23 46					00 17						
Hillfoot	d						23 47					00 18						
Milngavie	a						23 52					00 23						
Drumchapel	d		23 25			23 40					00 10					00 25		
Drumry	d		23 27			23 42					00 12					00 27		
Singer	d		23 30			23 45					00 15					00 30		
Dalmuir	a		23 32	23 33		23 47			00 08		00 17					00 32		
	d			23 33		23 48			00 08		00 18							
Kilpatrick	d					23 51					00 21							
Bowling	d					23 54					00 24							
Dumbarton East	d			23 41		23 58			00 15		00 28							
Dumbarton Central	d			23 43		23 59			00 18		00 30							
Dalreoch	d			23 44		00 02			00 19		00 32							
Renton	d					00 05					00 35							
Alexandria	d					00 07					00 37							
Balloch	a					00 10					00 40							
Cardross	d			23 49					00 24									
Craigendoran	d			23 54					00 29									
Helensburgh Central	a			23 58					00 32									

A From Edinburgh
b Glasgow Central High Level

Lanark, Coatbridge, Motherwell, Larkhall, Hamilton, Edinburgh and Bathgate, Airdrie and Springburn - Glasgow - Milngavie, Dalmuir, Balloch and Helensburgh

		SR	SR	SR	SR	SR	SR	SR	SR	SR A	SR B	SR	SR	SR	SR	SR	SR	SR	SR	SR	SR	SR	SR
Lanark	d																					06 23	
Carluke	d																					06 33	
Wishaw	d																					06 38	
Holytown	d									23p59													
Shieldmuir	d																					06 42	
Coatbridge Central	d																						
Whifflet	d																						
Motherwell	a																					06 46	
	d				23p20												06 16		06 20			06 46	
Bellshill	d									00 02							06 22					06 51	
Uddingston	d									00 06							06 26					06 56	
Airbles	d				23p22														06 22				
Larkhall	d							23p37							06 07					06 37			
Merryton	d							23p39							06 09					06 39			
Chatelherault	d							23p42							06 12					06 42			
Hamilton Central	d				23p27			23p46							06 16				06 27	06 46			
Hamilton West	d				23p30			23p48							06 18				06 30	06 48			
Blantyre	d				23p33			23p52							06 22				06 33	06 52			
Newton	d				23p37														06 37				
Cambuslang	d				23p41					00 12							06 31		06 41			07 01	
Rutherglen	d				23p45			00 01							06 29		06 34		06 45	06 58		07 03	
Dalmarnock	d				23p47												06 36		06 47			07 05	
Bridgeton	d				23p49												06 38		06 49			07 07	
Edinburgh	d		22p19			22p51	23p37		23p51		04 50												
Haymarket	d		22p23			22p55	23p42		23p55														
Edinburgh Park	d		22p30			23p00	23p47		23p59														
Uphall	d		22p38			23p08	23p55		00 08														
Livingston North	d		22p41			23p11	23p59		00 11														
Bathgate	a		22p46			23p16	00 04		00 16														
	d		22p47			23p17								05 36		05 51					06 21		
Armadale	d		22p51			23p21								05 40		05 55					06 25		
Blackridge	d		22p55			23p25								05 43		05 58					06 28		
Caldercruix	d		23p01			23p31								05 50		06 05					06 35		
Drumgelloch	d		23p05			23p35								05 53		06 08					06 38		
Airdrie	d		23p12			23p38						05 35		05 57		06 12					06 42		
Coatdyke	d		23p14			23p40						05 37		05 59		06 14					06 44		
Coatbridge Sunnyside	d		23p16			23p43						05 39		06 01		06 16					06 46		
Blairhill	d		23p19			23p45						05 42		06 04		06 19					06 49		
Easterhouse	d		23p23			23p49						05 46		06 08		06 23					06 53		
Garrowhill	d		23p25			23p52						05 48		06 10		06 25					06 55		
Shettleston	d		23p28			23p54						05 51		06 13		06 28					06 58		
Carntyne	d		23p30			23p56						05 53		06 15		06 30					07 00		
Springburn	d	23p09		23p39														06 39					07 09
Barnhill	d	23p10		23p40														06 40					07 10
Alexandra Parade	d	23p13		23p43														06 43					07 13
Duke Street	d	23p15		23p45														06 45					07 15
Bellgrove	d	23p17	23p33	23p47		23p59						05 56		06 18		06 33		06 47			07 03		07 17
High Street	d	23p19	23p35	23p49		00 02						05 58		06 20		06 35		06 49			07 05		07 19
Glasgow Queen St LL	a	23p21	23p37	23p51		00 04						06 00		06 22		06 37		06 51			07 07		07 21
	d	23p23	23p45	23p53		00 04						06 01		06 23		06 40		06 53			07 10		07 23
Charing Cross	d	23p25	23p47	23p55		00 06						06 03		06 25		06 42		06 55			07 12		07 25
Argyle Street	d				23p53			00 06							06 34		06 42		06 53	07 03		07 11	
Glasgow Central LL	a				23p56			00 07		00b23					06 37		06 46		06 56	07 07		07 14	
	d				23p58			00 07							06 37		06 46		06 58	07 07		07 16	
Anderston	d				23p59			00 09							06 39		06 48		06 59	07 08		07 17	
Exhibition Centre	d				00 01			00 11							06 41		06 50		07 01	07 10		07 19	
Partick	d	23p29	23p51	23p59	00 05	00 11		00 14				06 07		06 29	06 44	06 47	06 54	06 59	07 05	07 14	07 17	07 23	07 29
Hyndland	d	23p32	23p53	00 02	00 08	00 13		00 17				06 10		06 32	06 47	06 49	06 56	07 02	07 08	07 16	07 19	07 25	07 32
Jordanhill	d		23p55			00 15						06 12					06 58					07 27	
Scotstounhill	d		23p58			00 17						06 14					07 00					07 30	
Garscadden	d		23p59			00a19						06 17				06 53	07 02					07 32	
Yoker	d		00 02									06 19					07 05					07 35	
Clydebank	d		00 04									06 21					07 07					07 37	
Anniesland	d	23p35		00 05	00 12			00 20						06 35	06 50			07 05	07 11	07 19			07 35
Westerton	d	23p38		00 08	00 15			00 23			05 56			06 38	06 53			07 08	07 14	07 22			07 38
Bearsden	d				00 17														07 16				
Hillfoot	d				00 18														07 17				
Milngavie	a				00 23														07 22				
Drumchapel	d	23p40		00 10				00 25						06 40	06 55			07 10		07 25			07 40
Drumry	d	23p42		00 12				00 27						06 42	06 57			07 12		07 27			07 42
Singer	d	23p45		00 15				00 30						06 45	07 00			07 15		07 29			07 45
Dalmuir	a	23p47	00 08	00 17				00 32			06 03	06 24		06 47	07 02	06 58	07 11	07 17		07 32	07 29	07 41	07 47
	d	23p48	00 08	00 18							06 04	06 24	06 30	06 48		06 59		07 18			07 29		07 48
Kilpatrick	d	23p51		00 21									06 32	06 51				07 21					07 51
Bowling	d	23p54		00 24									06 35	06 54				07 24					07 54
Dumbarton East	d	23p58	00 15	00 28								06 32	06 40	06 58		07 06		07 28			07 36		07 58
Dumbarton Central	d	23p59	00 18	00 30								06 34	06 42	07 00		07 09		07 30			07 39		08 00
Dalreoch	d	00 02	00 19	00 32								06 35	06 43	07 02		07 10		07 32			07 40		08 02
Renton	d	00 05		00 35								06 38		07 05				07 35					08 05
Alexandria	d	00 07		00 37								06 41		07 07				07 37					08 07
Balloch	a	00 10		00 40								06 43		07 10				07 40					08 10
Cardross	d		00 24										06 48			07 15					07 45		
Craigendoran	d		00 29										06 53			07 20					07 50		
Helensburgh Central	a		00 32								06c26		06 56			07 23					07 55		

A From Edinburgh
B To Fort William
b Glasgow Central High Level
c Helensburgh Upper

Table 226

Saturdays

Lanark, Coatbridge, Motherwell, Larkhall, Hamilton, Edinburgh and Bathgate, Airdrie and Springburn - Glasgow - Milngavie, Dalmuir, Balloch and Helensburgh

Station		SR	SR	SR	SR	SR	SR	SR	SR	SR	SR	SR	SR	SR	SR	SR	SR	SR	SR	SR	SR	SR	SR
			A								◇ B		C										
Lanark	d											07 23								07 53			
Carluke	d											07 33								08 03			
Wishaw	d											07 38								08 08			
Holytown	d		06 58										07 58							08 13			
Shieldmuir	d											07 42											
Coatbridge Central	d	06 40																					
Whifflet	d	06 42																					
Motherwell	a	06 51										07 46								08 19			
	d	06 51				07 16		07 20				07 47			07 50			08 16		08 20			
Bellshill	d		07 02			07 22						07 53	08 02					08 22					
Uddingston	d		07 12			07 26						07 57	08 05					08 26					
Airbles	d	06 54						07 22							07 52					08 22			
Larkhall	d			07 07					07 37							08 07					08 37		
Merryton	d			07 09					07 39							08 09					08 39		
Chatelherault	d			07 12					07 42							08 12					08 42		
Hamilton Central	d	06 59		07 16				07 27	07 46						07 57	08 15				08 27	08 46		
Hamilton West	d	07 01		07 18				07 30	07 48						08 00	08 18				08 30	08 48		
Blantyre	d	07 05		07 22				07 33	07 52						08 03	08 21				08 33	08 52		
Newton	d	07 09		07 26				07 37							08 07					08 37			
Cambuslang	d	07 12	07 17			07 32		07 41				08 02			08 11			08 31		08 41			
Rutherglen	d	07 16		07 30		07 35		07 46	07 59			08 04			08 16	08 30		08 34		08 47	08 59		
Dalmarnock	d	07 18				07 39		07 48				08 06			08 18			08 36		08 49			
Bridgeton	d	07 20				07 41		07 50				08 08			08 20			08 38		08 51			
Edinburgh	d				06 21					06 48							07 21					07 54	
Haymarket	d				06 25					06 52							07 25					07 57	
Edinburgh Park	d				06 30					06 58							07 30					08 02	
Uphall	d				06 38					07 05							07 38					08 09	
Livingston North	d				06 41					07 08							07 41					08 12	
Bathgate	a				06 46					07 13							07 46					08 17	
	d				06 47					07 17							07 47					08 17	08 34
Armadale	d				06 51					07 21							07 51					08 21	
Blackridge	d				06 55					07 25							07 55					08 25	
Caldercruix	d				07 01					07 31							08 01					08 31	
Drumgelloch	d				07 05					07 35							08 05					08 35	08 46
Airdrie	d				07 12					07 42							08 12					08 42	08 50
Coatdyke	d				07 14					07 44							08 14					08 44	
Coatbridge Sunnyside	d				07 16					07 46							08 16					08 46	08 53
Blairhill	d				07 19					07 49							08 19					08 49	
Easterhouse	d				07 23					07 53							08 23					08 53	
Garrowhill	d				07 25					07 55							08 25					08 55	
Shettleston	d				07 28					07 58							08 28					08 58	
Carntyne	d				07 30					08 00							08 30					09 00	
Springburn	d						07 39							08 09					08 39				
Barnhill	d						07 40							08 10					08 40				
Alexandra Parade	d						07 43							08 13					08 43				
Duke Street	d						07 45							08 15					08 45				
Bellgrove	d				07 33		07 47			08 03				08 17			08 33		08 47			09 03	
High Street	d				07 35		07 49			08 05				08 19			08 35		08 50			09 05	09 10
Glasgow Queen St LL 10	a				07 37		07 51			08 07				08 21			08 37		08 52			09 07	09 13
	d				07 40		07 53			08 10	08c21			08 23			08 40		08 53			09 10	09 13
Charing Cross	d				07 42		07 55			08 12				08 25			08 42		08 56			09 12	09 15
Argyle Street	d	07 23		07 35		07 44		07 53	08 04			08 13			08 24	08 36		08 42		08 55	09 04		
Glasgow Central LL 15	a	07 26	07b29	07 37		07 46		07 56	08 07			08 16	08b24		08 27	08 37		08 46		08 56	09 07		
	d	07 28		07 38		07 46		07 58	08 07			08 16			08 28	08 37		08 46		08 59	09 07		
Anderston	d	07 29		07 39		07 48		07 59	08 09			08 18			08 29	08 39		08 48		09 00	09 09		
Exhibition Centre	d	07 31		07 41		07 50		08 01	08 11			08 20			08 31	08 41		08 50		09 02	09 11		
Partick	d	07 35		07 45	07 47	07 53	07 59	08 05	08 14	08 17		08 23		08 29	08 35	08 45	08 47	08 54	09 00	09 06	09 14	09 17	09 20
Hyndland	d	07 38		07 47	07 49	07 55	08 02	08 08	08 17	08 19		08 25		08 32	08 38	08 47	08 49	08 56	09 02	09 09	09 17	09 19	09 22
Jordanhill	d					07 57						08 27						08 58					
Scotstounhill	d					08 00						08 30						09 00					
Garscadden	d					08 02						08 32						09 02					
Yoker	d					08 04						08 34						09 05					
Clydebank	d					08 06						08 36						09 07					
Anniesland	d	07 41		07 50			08 05	08 11	08 20					08 35	08 41	08 50			09 05	09 12	09 20		09 25
Westerton	d	07 44		07 53			08 08	08 14	08 23					08 38	08 44	08 53			09 08	09 15	09 23		09 28
Bearsden	d	07 46						08 16							08 46					09 17			09 31
Hillfoot	d	07 48						08 17							08 47					09 20			09 32
Milngavie	a	07 52						08 22							08 52					09 23			09 37
Drumchapel	d			07 56			08 10		08 25					08 40		08 55			09 10		09 25		
Drumry	d			07 58			08 12		08 27					08 42		08 57			09 12		09 27		
Singer	d			08 00			08 15		08 30					08 45		09 00			09 15		09 30		
Dalmuir	a			08 03	07 59	08 11	08 17		08 32	08 28	08 39	08 41		08 47		09 02	08 59	09 11	09 17		09 32	09 29	
	d				07 59		08 18			08 29	08 39			08 48			08 59		09 18			09 29	
Kilpatrick	d						08 21							08 51					09 21				
Bowling	d						08 24							08 54					09 24				
Dumbarton East	d				08 06		08 28			08 36				08 58			09 06		09 28			09 36	
Dumbarton Central	d				08 09		08 30			08 39	08 48			09 00			09 09		09 30			09 39	
Dalreoch	d				08 10		08 32			08 40				09 02			09 10		09 32			09 40	
Renton	d						08 35							09 05					09 35				
Alexandria	d						08 37							09 07					09 37				
Balloch	a						08 40							09 10					09 40				
Cardross	d				08 15					08 45							09 15					09 45	
Craigendoran	d				08 20					08 50							09 20					09 50	
Helensburgh Central	a				08 24					08 55	09e03						09 24					09 55	

A From Edinburgh
B To Oban
C From Newcraighall
b Glasgow Central High Level
c Glasgow Queen St High Level
e Helensburgh Upper

Table 226

Saturdays

Lanark, Coatbridge, Motherwell, Larkhall, Hamilton, Edinburgh and Bathgate, Airdrie and Springburn - Glasgow - Milngavie, Dalmuir, Balloch and Helensburgh

Station		SR	SR	SR	SR	SR	SR	SR	SR	SR	SR	SR	SR	SR	SR	SR	SR	SR	SR	SR	SR	SR
												A								◇ B		
Lanark	d	08 23									08 53						09 23					
Carluke	d	08 33									09 03						09 33					
Wishaw	d	08 38									09 08						09 38					
Holytown	d										09 13	09 32										
Shieldmuir	d	08 42															09 42					
Coatbridge Central	d																					
Whifflet	d																					
Motherwell	a	08 45									09 22						09 46					
	d	08 45		08 50					09 16		09 22						09 47		09 50			
Bellshill	d	08 50							09 22			09 36					09 53					
Uddingston	d	08 57							09 26			09 41					09 57					
Airbles	d			08 52							09 25								09 52			
Larkhall	d					09 07								09 37								10 07
Merryton	d					09 09								09 39								10 09
Chatelherault	d					09 12								09 42								10 12
Hamilton Central	d			08 57		09 16					09 30			09 46					09 57			10 16
Hamilton West	d			09 00		09 18					09 32			09 48					10 00			10 18
Blantyre	d			09 03		09 22					09 36			09 52					10 03			10 22
Newton	d			09 07							09 40								10 07			10 26
Cambuslang	d	09 02		09 11					09 31		09 43						10 02		10 11			
Rutherglen	d	09 06		09 16		09 29			09 34		09 47			09 59			10 05		10 15			10 30
Dalmarnock	d	09 08		09 17					09 36		09 49						10 07		10 17			
Bridgeton	d	09 10		09 19					09 38		09 51						10 09		10 19			
Edinburgh	d						08 21	08 37							08 48	09 07						
Haymarket	d						08 25	08 41							08 52	09 11						
Edinburgh Park	d						08 30	08 47							08 57	09 17						
Uphall	d						08 38	08 55							09 05	09 25						
Livingston North	d						08 41	08 58							09 08	09 29						
Bathgate	a						08 46	09 03							09 13	09 33						
	d						08 47	09 04							09 17	09 34						
Armadale	d						08 51								09 21							
Blackridge	d						08 55								09 25							
Caldercruix	d						09 01								09 31							
Drumgelloch	d						09 05	09 16							09 35	09 47						
Airdrie	d						09 12	09 20		09 27					09 42	09 51		09 57				
Coatdyke	d						09 14			09 29					09 44			09 59				
Coatbridge Sunnyside	d						09 16	09 23		09 31					09 46	09 54		10 01				
Blairhill	d						09 19			09 34					09 49			10 04				
Easterhouse	d						09 23			09 38					09 53			10 08				
Garrowhill	d						09 25			09 40					09 55			10 10				
Shettleston	d						09 28			09 43					09 58			10 13				
Carntyne	d						09 30			09 45					10 00			10 15				
Springburn	d		09 09		09 19								09 49								10 19	
Barnhill	d		09 10		09 20								09 50								10 20	
Alexandra Parade	d		09 13		09 23								09 53								10 23	
Duke Street	d		09 15		09 25								09 55								10 25	
Bellgrove	d		09 17		09 27		09 33			09 48			09 57		10 03			10 18			10 27	
High Street	d		09 19		09 29		09 35	09 40		09 50			09 59		10 05	10 10		10 20			10 29	
Glasgow Queen St LL 10	a		09 23		09 31		09 37	09 42		09 52			10 01		10 07	10 13		10 22			10 31	
	d		09 23		09 32		09 40	09 43		09 53			10 02		10 10	10 14		10 23		10c37	10 32	
Charing Cross	d		09 25		09 34		09 42	09 46		09 55			10 04		10 12	10 16		10 25			10 34	
Argyle Street	d	09 13		09 24		09 34			09 42		09 54			10 04			10 14		10 23			10 36
Glasgow Central LL 15	a	09 16		09 26		09 37			09 44		09 56	09b57		10 07			10 16		10 26			10 37
	d	09 18		09 28		09 37			09 47		09 58			10 07			10 19		10 28			10 38
Anderston	d	09 20		09 29		09 39			09 48		09 59			10 09			10 20		10 29			10 39
Exhibition Centre	d	09 22		09 31		09 41			09 50		10 01			10 11			10 22		10 31			10 41
Partick	d	09 25	09 29	09 35	09 39	09 44	09 47	09 50	09 54	09 59	10 05		10 09	10 14	10 17	10 20	10 26	10 29	10 35		10 39	10 45
Hyndland	d	09 27	09 32	09 38	09 41	09 47	09 49	09 52	09 56	10 02	10 08		10 11	10 17	10 19	10 22	10 28	10 32	10 38		10 41	10 47
Jordanhill	d	09 29			09 43				09 58				10 13				10 30				10 43	
Scotstounhill	d	09 32			09 45				10 00				10 15				10 33				10 45	
Garscadden	d	09 35			09 47				10 02				10 17				10 36				10 47	
Yoker	d	09 37			09 50				10 05				10 20				10 38				10 50	
Clydebank	d	09 39			09 52				10 07				10 22				10 40				10 52	
Anniesland	d		09 35	09 41		09 50		09 55		10 05	10 11			10 20		10 25		10 35	10 41			10 50
Westerton	d		09 38	09 44		09 53		09 58		10 08	10 14			10 23		10 28		10 38	10 44			10 53
Bearsden	d			09 46				10 01			10 16					10 31			10 46			
Hillfoot	d			09 47				10 03			10 18					10 33			10 47			
Milngavie	a			09 52				10 06			10 22					10 37			10 52			
Drumchapel	d		09 40			09 55				10 10				10 25				10 40				10 55
Drumry	d		09 42			09 57				10 12				10 27				10 42				10 57
Singer	d		09 45			10 00				10 15				10 30				10 45				11 00
Dalmuir	a	09 43	09 47		09 56	10 02	09 59		10 11	10 17			10 26	10 32	10 29		10 44	10 47		10 52	10 56	11 02
	d		09 48				09 59			10 18					10 29			10 48		10 52		
Kilpatrick	d		09 51							10 21								10 51				
Bowling	d		09 54							10 24								10 54				
Dumbarton East	d		09 58				10 06			10 28					10 36			10 58				
Dumbarton Central	d		10 00				10 09			10 30					10 39			11 00		11 05		
Dalreoch	d		10 02				10 10			10 32					10 40			11 02				
Renton	d		10 05							10 35								11 05				
Alexandria	d		10 07							10 37								11 07				
Balloch	a		10 10							10 40								11 10				
Cardross	d						10 15								10 45							
Craigendoran	d						10 20								10 51							
Helensburgh Central	a						10 23								10 54					11e20		

A From Edinburgh
B until 29 October. To Ob…
b Glasgow Central High Level

Lanark, Coatbridge, Motherwell, Larkhall, Hamilton, Edinburgh and Bathgate, Airdrie and Springburn - Glasgow - Milngavie, Dalmuir, Balloch and Helensburgh

		SR	SR	SR	SR	SR	SR A	SR	SR	SR	SR	SR	SR	SR	SR	SR	SR	SR	SR	SR	SR	SR A	SR
Lanark	d					09 53						10 21									10 53		
Carluke	d					10 04						10 31									11 03		
Wishaw	d					10 08						10 38									11 08		
Holytown	d					10 13	10 32														11 13	11 30	
Shieldmuir	d											10 42											
Coatbridge Central	d																						
Whifflet	d																						
Motherwell	a					10 20						10 46									11 20		
	d			10 16		10 20						10 47		10 50					11 16		11 20		
Bellshill	d			10 22			10 35					10 53							11 22			11 34	
Uddingston	d			10 26			10 40					10 57							11 26			11 38	
Airbles	d					10 23								10 52							11 22		
Larkhall	d								10 37							11 07							
Merryton	d								10 39							11 09							
Chatelherault	d								10 42							11 12							
Hamilton Central	d					10 28			10 46					10 57		11 16					11 27		
Hamilton West	d					10 30			10 48					11 00		11 18					11 30		
Blantyre	d					10 34			10 52					11 03		11 22					11 33		
Newton	d					10 38								11 07							11 37		
Cambuslang	d			10 31		10 41						11 02		11 11					11 31		11 41		
Rutherglen	d			10 35		10 45			10 59			11 06		11 15		11 29			11 36		11 46		
Dalmarnock	d			10 37		10 49						11 08		11 17					11 38		11 48		
Bridgeton	d			10 39		10 51						11 10		11 19					11 40		11 50		
Edinburgh	d	09 18	09 37							09 48	10 07						10 21	10 37					
Haymarket	d	09 22	09 41							09 52	10 10						10 25	10 41					
Edinburgh Park	d	09 27	09 46							09 57	10 16						10 30	10 46					
Uphall	d	09 35	09 54							10 05	10 24						10 38	10 54					
Livingston North	d	09 38	09 58							10 09	10 28						10 41	10 58					
Bathgate	a	09 43	10 03							10 13	10 33						10 47	11 04					
	d	09 47	10 04							10 17	10 34						10 47	11 04					
Armadale	d	09 51								10 21							10 51						
Blackridge	d	09 55								10 25							10 55						
Caldercruix	d	10 01								10 31							11 01						
Drumgelloch	d	10 05	10 16							10 35	10 46						11 05	11 16					
Airdrie	d	10 12	10 20		10 27					10 42	10 50		10 57				11 12	11 20		11 27			
Coatdyke	d	10 14			10 29					10 44			10 59				11 14			11 29			
Coatbridge Sunnyside	d	10 16	10 23		10 31					10 46	10 53		11 01				11 16	11 23		11 31			
Blairhill	d	10 19			10 34					10 49			11 04				11 19			11 34			
Easterhouse	d	10 23			10 38					10 53			11 08				11 23			11 38			
Garrowhill	d	10 25			10 40					10 55			11 10				11 25			11 40			
Shettleston	d	10 28			10 43					10 58			11 13				11 28			11 43			
Carntyne	d	10 30			10 45					11 00			11 15				11 30			11 45			
Springburn	d							10 49							11 19								11 49
Barnhill	d							10 50							11 20								11 50
Alexandra Parade	d							10 53							11 23								11 53
Duke Street	d							10 55							11 25								11 55
Bellgrove	d	10 33			10 48			10 57		11 03			11 18		11 27		11 33			11 48			11 57
High Street	d	10 35	10 41		10 50			10 59		11 05	11 10		11 20		11 29		11 35	11 41		11 50			11 59
Glasgow Queen St LL 10	a	10 37	10 43		10 52			11 01		11 07	11 12		11 22		11 31		11 37	11 43		11 52			12 01
	d	10 41	10 43		10 53			11 02		11 10	11 13		11 23		11 32		11 40	11 43		11 53			12 02
Charing Cross	d	10 43	10 45		10 55			11 04		11 12	11 15		11 25		11 34		11 42	11 46		11 55			12 04
Argyle Street	d			10 43		10 55			11 04			11 14		11 23		11 34			11 44		11 53		
Glasgow Central LL 15	a			10 45		10 56	10b55		11 07			11 16		11 26		11 37			11 46		11 57	11b57	
	d			10 46		10 58			11 07			11 16		11 28		11 37			11 46		11 58		
Anderston	d			10 48		10 59			11 09			11 18		11 29		11 39			11 48		12 00		
Exhibition Centre	d			10 50		11 01			11 11			11 20		11 31		11 41			11 50		12 02		
Partick	d	10 47	10 50	10 53	10 59	11 05		11 09	11 15	11 17	11 20	11 24	11 29	11 35	11 39	11 44	11 47	11 50	11 53	11 59	12 05		12 08
Hyndland	d	10 49	10 53	10 55	11 02	11 08		11 11	11 17	11 20	11 23	11 26	11 32	11 38	11 41	11 47	11 49	11 52	11 55	12 02	12 08		12 10
Jordanhill	d			10 57				11 13				11 28			11 43				11 57				12 12
Scotstounhill	d			11 00				11 15				11 31			11 45				12 00				12 15
Garscadden	d			11 02				11 17				11 32			11 47				12 02				12 17
Yoker	d			11 05				11 20				11 35			11 50				12 04				12 19
Clydebank	d			11 07				11 22				11 37			11 52				12 06				12 21
Anniesland	d		10 56		11 05	11 11			11 20		11 26		11 35	11 41		11 50		11 55		12 05	12 11		
Westerton	d		10 59		11 08	11 14			11 23		11 29		11 38	11 44		11 53		11 58		12 08	12 14		
Bearsden	d		11 01			11 16					11 31			11 46				12 00			12 16		
Hillfoot	d		11 02			11 18					11 33			11 47				12 01			12 18		
Milngavie	a		11 07			11 24					11 37			11 52				12 07			12 22		
Drumchapel	d				11 10				11 25				11 40			11 55				12 10			
Drumry	d				11 12				11 27				11 42			11 57				12 12			
Singer	d				11 15				11 30				11 45			12 00				12 15			
Dalmuir	a	11 00		11 11	11 17			11 26	11 32	11 29		11 41	11 47		11 56	12 02	11 59		12 11	12 17			12 26
	d	11 00			11 18					11 29			11 48				11 59			12 18			
Kilpatrick	d				11 21								11 51							12 21			
Bowling	d				11 24								11 54							12 24			
Dumbarton East	d	11 06			11 28					11 36			11 58				12 06			12 28			
Dumbarton Central	d	11 09			11 30					11 39			12 00				12 09			12 30			
Dalreoch	d	11 11			11 32					11 40			12 02				12 10			12 32			
Renton	d				11 35								12 05							12 35			
Alexandria	d				11 37								12 07							12 37			
Balloch	a				11 40								12 10							12 40			
Cardross	d	11 16								11 45							12 15						
Craigendoran	d	11 21								11 50							12 20						
Helensburgh Central	a	11 24								11 53							12 24						

A From Edinburgh
b Glasgow Central High Level

Lanark, Coatbridge, Motherwell, Larkhall, Hamilton, Edinburgh and Bathgate, Airdrie and Springburn - Glasgow - Milngavie, Dalmuir, Balloch and Helensburgh

		SR	SR	SR	SR ◇ A	SR	SR	SR	SR	SR	SR	SR	SR	SR	SR	SR B	SR	SR	SR	SR	SR	SR
Lanark	d					11 21									11 53						12 23	
Carluke	d					11 31									12 03						12 33	
Wishaw	d					11 37									12 08						12 41	
Holytown	d														12 13	12 30						
Shieldmuir	d					11 42															12 45	
Coatbridge Central	d																					
Whifflet	d																					
Motherwell	a					11 46									12 19						12 48	
	d					11 47		11 50					12 16		12 20						12 48	
Bellshill	d					11 53							12 22			12 34					12 54	
Uddingston	d					12 00							12 26			12 38					12 58	
Airbles	d							11 52							12 22							
Larkhall	d	11 37								12 07								12 37				
Merryton	d	11 39								12 09								12 39				
Chatelherault	d	11 42								12 12								12 42				
Hamilton Central	d	11 46						11 57		12 16					12 28			12 46				
Hamilton West	d	11 48						12 00		12 18					12 30			12 48				
Blantyre	d	11 52						12 03		12 22					12 34			12 52				
Newton	d							12 07							12 38							
Cambuslang	d					12 05		12 11					12 31		12 41						13 03	
Rutherglen	d	11 59				12 06		12 16		12 29			12 34		12 46			12 59			13 06	
Dalmarnock	d					12 08		12 18					12 36		12 48						13 08	
Bridgeton	d					12 10		12 20					12 38		12 51						13 10	
Edinburgh	d		10 48	11 07							11 21	11 37							11 51	12 11		
Haymarket	d		10 52	11 11							11 25	11 41							11 55	12 14		
Edinburgh Park	d		10 57	11 17							11 30	11 46							12 00	12 19		
Uphall	d		11 05	11 25							11 40	11 55							12 08	12 27		
Livingston North	d		11 08	11 29							11 43	11 57							12 11	12 30		
Bathgate	a		11 13	11 33							11 48	12 03							12 16	12 35		
	d		11 17	11 36							11 49	12 03							12 17	12 36		
Armadale	d		11 21								11 53								12 21			
Blackridge	d		11 25								11 57								12 25			
Caldercruix	d		11 31								12 03								12 31			
Drumgelloch	d		11 35	11 48							12 07	12 17							12 35	12 49		
Airdrie	d		11 42	11 52			11 57				12 12	12 20		12 27					12 42	12 52		12 57
Coatdyke	d		11 44				11 59				12 14			12 29					12 44			12 59
Coatbridge Sunnyside	d		11 46	11 55			12 01				12 16	12 23		12 31					12 46	12 56		13 01
Blairhill	d		11 49				12 04				12 19			12 34					12 49			13 04
Easterhouse	d		11 53				12 08				12 23			12 38					12 53			13 08
Garrowhill	d		11 55				12 10				12 25			12 40					12 55			13 10
Shettleston	d		11 58				12 13				12 28			12 43					12 58			13 13
Carntyne	d		12 00				12 15				12 30			12 45					13 00			13 15
Springburn	d								12 19								12 49					
Barnhill	d								12 20								12 50					
Alexandra Parade	d								12 23								12 53					
Duke Street	d								12 25								12 55					
Bellgrove	d		12 03				12 18		12 27		12 33			12 48			12 57		13 03			13 18
High Street	d		12 05	12 11			12 20		12 29		12 36	12 40		12 50			12 59		13 05	13 11		13 20
Glasgow Queen St LL 10	a		12 07	12 13			12 22		12 31		12 38	12 42		12 52			13 01		13 08	13 13		13 22
	d		12 10	12 14	12b21		12 23		12 32		12 40	12 43		12 53			13 02		13 10	13 13		13 23
Charing Cross	d		12 12	12 16			12 25		12 34		12 42	12 46		12 55			13 04		13 12	13 15		13 25
Argyle Street	d	12 05				12 14		12 23		12 35			12 42		12 55			13 05			13 14	
Glasgow Central LL 15	a	12 07				12 16		12 26		12 37			12 46		12 56	12e55		13 07			13 18	
	d	12 07				12 18		12 28		12 37			12 46		12 58			13 07			13 18	
Anderston	d	12 09				12 20		12 30		12 39			12 48		12 59			13 09			13 19	
Exhibition Centre	d	12 11				12 22		12 32		12 41			12 50		13 01			13 11			13 21	
Partick	d	12 14	12 17	12 20		12 26	12 29	12 35	12 39	12 44	12 47	12 50	12 53	12 59	13 05		13 08	13 14	13 17	13 20	13 25	13 29
Hyndland	d	12 17	12 19	12 23		12 28	12 32	12 38	12 41	12 47	12 49	12 52	12 55	13 02	13 08		13 10	13 17	13 19	13 22	13 27	13 32
Jordanhill	d					12 30			12 43				12 57				13 12				13 29	
Scotstounhill	d					12 32			12 45				13 00				13 15				13 31	
Garscadden	d					12 35			12 47				13 02				13 17				13 33	
Yoker	d					12 37			12 50				13 04				13 19				13 35	
Clydebank	d					12 39			12 52				13 06				13 21				13 37	
Anniesland	d	12 20		12 26			12 35	12 41		12 50		12 55		13 05	13 11			13 20		13 25		13 35
Westerton	d	12 23		12 29			12 38	12 44		12 53		12 58		13 08	13 14			13 23		13 28		13 38
Bearsden	d			12 32				12 46				13 01			13 16					13 31		
Hillfoot	d			12 34				12 48				13 02			13 18					13 32		
Milngavie	a			12 37				12 52				13 07			13 22					13 37		
Drumchapel	d	12 25					12 40			12 55				13 10				13 25				13 40
Drumry	d	12 27					12 42			12 57				13 12				13 27				13 42
Singer	d	12 30					12 45			13 00				13 15				13 30				13 45
Dalmuir	a	12 32	12 29		12 38	12 43	12 47		12 56	13 02	12 59		13 11	13 17			13 26	13 32	13 29		13 42	13 47
	d		12 29		12 42		12 48				12 59			13 18					13 29			13 48
Kilpatrick	d						12 51							13 21								13 51
Bowling	d						12 54							13 24								13 54
Dumbarton East	d		12 36				12 58				13 06			13 28					13 36			13 58
Dumbarton Central	d		12 39		12 48		13 00				13 09			13 30					13 39			14 00
Dalreoch	d		12 40				13 02				13 10			13 32					13 40			14 02
Renton	d						13 05							13 35								14 05
Alexandria	d						13 07							13 37								14 07
Balloch	a						13 10							13 40								14 10
Cardross	d		12 45								13 15								13 45			
Craigendoran	d		12 50								13 20								13 50			
Helensburgh Central	a		12 53		13c03						13 23								13 53			

A To Oban
B From Edinburgh
b Glasgow Queen St High Level
c Helensburgh Upper
e Glasgow Central High Level

Table 226

Saturdays

Lanark, Coatbridge, Motherwell, Larkhall, Hamilton, Edinburgh and Bathgate, Airdrie and Springburn - Glasgow - Milngavie, Dalmuir, Balloch and Helensburgh

		SR	SR	SR	SR	SR	SR	SR	SR	SR A	SR	SR	SR	SR	SR	SR	SR	SR	SR	SR	SR	SR	SR
Lanark	d								12 53						13 23								
Carluke	d								13 03						13 33								
Wishaw	d								13 08						13 40								
Holytown	d								13 13	13 31													
Shieldmuir	d														13 43								
Coatbridge Central	d																						
Whifflet	d																						
Motherwell	a								13 19						13 47								
	d	12 50					13 16		13 20						13 48		13 50					14 16	
Bellshill	d						13 22			13 34					13 54							14 22	
Uddingston	d						13 26			13 39					14 00							14 26	
Airbles	d	12 52							13 22								13 52						
Larkhall	d			13 07								13 37							14 07				
Merryton	d			13 09								13 39							14 09				
Chatelherault	d			13 12								13 42							14 12				
Hamilton Central	d	12 57		13 16					13 27			13 46					13 57		14 16				
Hamilton West	d	13 00		13 18					13 30			13 48					14 00		14 18				
Blantyre	d	13 03		13 22					13 33			13 52					14 03		14 22				
Newton	d	13 07							13 37								14 07						
Cambuslang	d	13 11					13 31		13 41						14 05		14 11					14 31	
Rutherglen	d	13 15		13 29			13 34		13 45			13 59			14 06		14 15		14 29			14 36	
Dalmarnock	d	13 17					13 36		13 47						14 08		14 17					14 38	
Bridgeton	d	13 19					13 38		13 49						14 10		14 19					14 40	
Edinburgh	d				12 21	12 37							12 48	13 07						13 21	13 37		
Haymarket	d				12 25	12 41							12 52	13 11						13 25	13 43		
Edinburgh Park	d				12 30	12 45							12 57	13 17						13 30	13 47		
Uphall	d				12 38	12 54							13 05	13 26						13 38	13 55		
Livingston North	d				12 41	12 58							13 08	13 28						13 41	13 59		
Bathgate	a				12 47	13 02							13 13	13 33						13 46	14 03		
	d				12 47	13 04							13 17	13 33						13 47	14 04		
Armadale	d				12 51								13 21							13 51			
Blackridge	d				12 55								13 25							13 55			
Caldercruix	d				13 01								13 31							14 01			
Drumgelloch	d				13 05	13 16							13 35	13 47						14 05	14 16		
Airdrie	d				13 12	13 20		13 27					13 42	13 50		13 57				14 12	14 22		14 27
Coatdyke	d				13 14			13 29					13 44			13 59				14 14			14 29
Coatbridge Sunnyside	d				13 16	13 23		13 31					13 46	13 53		14 01				14 16	14 25		14 31
Blairhill	d				13 19			13 34					13 49			14 04				14 19			14 34
Easterhouse	d				13 23			13 38					13 53			14 08				14 23			14 38
Garrowhill	d				13 25			13 40					13 55			14 10				14 25			14 40
Shettleston	d				13 28			13 43					13 58			14 13				14 28			14 43
Carntyne	d				13 30			13 45					14 00			14 15				14 30			14 45
Springburn	d		13 19								13 49							14 19					
Barnhill	d		13 20								13 50							14 20					
Alexandra Parade	d		13 23								13 53							14 23					
Duke Street	d		13 25								13 55							14 25					
Bellgrove	d		13 27		13 33			13 48			13 57		14 03			14 18		14 27		14 33			14 48
High Street	d		13 29		13 35	13 41		13 50			13 59		14 05	14 11		14 20		14 29		14 35	14 41		14 50
Glasgow Queen St LL 10	a		13 31		13 37	13 43		13 52			14 01		14 07	14 13		14 22		14 31		14 37	14 43		14 52
	d		13 32		13 41	13 43		13 53			14 02		14 11	14 14		14 23		14 32		14 40	14 43		14 53
Charing Cross	d		13 34		13 43	13 45		13 55			14 04		14 13	14 16		14 25		14 34		14 42	14 46		14 55
Argyle Street	d	13 23		13 34			13 42		13 53			14 04			14 14		14 23		14 35			14 43	
Glasgow Central LL 15	a	13 26		13 37			13 44		13 56	13b55		14 07			14 16		14 26		14 37			14 45	
	d	13 28		13 37			13 46		13 58			14 07			14 16		14 28		14 37			14 48	
Anderston	d	13 29		13 39			13 48		13 59			14 09			14 18		14 29		14 39			14 49	
Exhibition Centre	d	13 31		13 41			13 50		14 01			14 11			14 20		14 31		14 41			14 51	
Partick	d	13 35	13 38	13 44	13 47	13 50	13 53	13 59	14 05		14 09	14 14	14 17	14 20	14 24	14 29	14 35	14 38	14 44	14 47	14 50	14 55	14 59
Hyndland	d	13 38	13 40	13 47	13 49	13 53	13 55	14 02	14 08		14 11	14 17	14 19	14 23	14 26	14 32	14 38	14 40	14 47	14 49	14 53	14 58	15 02
Jordanhill	d		13 42				13 57				14 13				14 28			14 42				15 00	
Scotstounhill	d		13 45				14 00				14 15				14 30			14 45				15 03	
Garscadden	d		13 47				14 02				14 17				14 31			14 47				15 05	
Yoker	d		13 49				14 05				14 20				14 34			14 49				15 07	
Clydebank	d		13 51				14 07				14 22				14 36			14 51				15 09	
Anniesland	d	13 41		13 50		13 56		14 05	14 11			14 20		14 26		14 35	14 41		14 50		14 56		15 05
Westerton	d	13 44		13 53		13 59		14 08	14 14			14 23		14 29		14 38	14 44		14 53		14 59		15 08
Bearsden	d	13 46				14 01			14 16					14 31			14 46				15 01		
Hillfoot	d	13 47				14 02			14 17					14 32			14 47				15 02		
Milngavie	a	13 52				14 07			14 22					14 37			14 52				15 07		
Drumchapel	d			13 55				14 10				14 25				14 40			14 55				15 10
Drumry	d			13 57				14 12				14 27				14 42			14 57				15 12
Singer	d			14 00				14 15				14 30				14 45			15 00				15 15
Dalmuir	a		13 56	14 02	13 59		14 11	14 17			14 26	14 32	14 29		14 42	14 47		14 56	15 02	14 59		15 13	15 17
	d				13 59			14 18					14 29			14 49				14 59			15 18
Kilpatrick	d							14 21								14 51							15 21
Bowling	d							14 24								14 54							15 24
Dumbarton East	d				14 06			14 28					14 36			14 59				15 07			15 28
Dumbarton Central	d				14 10			14 30					14 39			15 01				15 09			15 30
Dalreoch	d				14 11			14 32					14 40			15 02				15 10			15 32
Renton	d							14 35								15 05							15 35
Alexandria	d							14 37								15 07							15 37
Balloch	a							14 40								15 10							15 40
Cardross	d				14 16								14 45							15 15			
Craigendoran	d				14 21								14 51							15 20			
Helensburgh Central	a				14 24								14 54							15 26			

A From Edinburgh

b Glasgow Central High Level

Table 226

Saturdays

Lanark, Coatbridge, Motherwell, Larkhall, Hamilton, Edinburgh and Bathgate, Airdrie and Springburn - Glasgow - Milngavie, Dalmuir, Balloch and Helensburgh

		SR	SR A	SR	SR	SR	SR	SR	SR	SR	SR	SR	SR	SR	SR	SR	SR	SR A	SR	SR	SR	SR	SR
Lanark	d	13 53						14 23									14 53						15 23
Carluke	d	14 03						14 32									15 03						15 33
Wishaw	d	14 08						14 41									15 08						15 40
Holytown	d	14 13	14 30														15 13	15 30					
Shieldmuir	d							14 45															15 43
Coatbridge Central	d																						
Whifflet	d																						
Motherwell	a	14 19						14 48									15 19						15 47
	d	14 20						14 49		14 50					15 16		15 20						15 48
Bellshill	d		14 34					14 55							15 22			15 34					15 54
Uddingston	d		14 38					14 59							15 26			15 38					15 58
Airbles	d	14 22								14 52							15 22						
Larkhall	d				14 37							15 07								15 37			
Merryton	d				14 39							15 09								15 39			
Chatelherault	d				14 42							15 12								15 42			
Hamilton Central	d	14 27			14 46					14 57		15 16					15 27			15 46			
Hamilton West	d	14 30			14 48					15 00		15 18					15 30			15 48			
Blantyre	d	14 33			14 52					15 03		15 22					15 33			15 52			
Newton	d	14 37								15 07							15 37						
Cambuslang	d	14 41						15 04		15 11					15 31		15 41						16 03
Rutherglen	d	14 45			14 59			15 08		15 15		15 29			15 34		15 45			15 59			16 06
Dalmarnock	d	14 47						15 10		15 17					15 36		15 47						16 08
Bridgeton	d	14 49						15 12		15 19					15 38		15 49						16 10
Edinburgh	d					13 51	14 10						14 21	14 37							14 48	15 07	
Haymarket	d					13 55	14 14						14 25	14 42							14 52	15 11	
Edinburgh Park	d					14 00	14 20						14 30	14 47							15 00	15 17	
Uphall	d					14 08	14 28						14 38	14 54							15 09	15 25	
Livingston North	d					14 11	14 31						14 41	14 59							15 12	15 29	
Bathgate	a					14 16	14 36						14 47	15 03							15 17	15 33	
	d					14 17	14 36						14 47	15 04							15 17	15 35	
Armadale	d					14 21							14 51								15 21		
Blackridge	d					14 25							14 55								15 25		
Caldercruix	d					14 31							15 01								15 31		
Drumgelloch	d					14 35	14 49						15 05	15 16							15 35	15 47	
Airdrie	d					14 42	14 52		14 57				15 12	15 20		15 27					15 42	15 51	
Coatdyke	d					14 44			14 59				15 14			15 29					15 44		
Coatbridge Sunnyside	d					14 46	14 55		15 01				15 16	15 23		15 31					15 46	15 54	
Blairhill	d					14 49			15 04				15 19			15 34					15 49		
Easterhouse	d					14 53			15 08				15 23			15 38					15 53		
Garrowhill	d					14 55			15 10				15 25			15 40					15 55		
Shettleston	d					14 58			15 13				15 28			15 43					15 58		
Carntyne	d					15 00			15 15				15 30			15 45					16 00		
Springburn	d			14 49							15 19								15 50				
Barnhill	d			14 50							15 20								15 51				
Alexandra Parade	d			14 53							15 23								15 54				
Duke Street	d			14 55							15 25								15 56				
Bellgrove	d			14 57		15 03			15 19		15 27		15 33			15 48			15 58		16 03		
High Street	d			15 00		15 05	15 12		15 21		15 29		15 35	15 41		15 50			16 00		16 05	16 10	
Glasgow Queen St LL 10	a			15 02		15 07	15 14		15 23		15 31		15 37	15 43		15 52			16 02		16 07	16 12	
	d			15 03		15 10	15 15		15 23		15 32		15 40	15 44		15 53			16 03		16 10	16 13	
Charing Cross	d			15 05		15 12	15 17		15 25		15 34		15 42	15 46		15 55			16 05		16 12	16 15	
Argyle Street	d	14 53			15 04			15 16		15 23		15 36			15 42		15 53			16 04			16 14
Glasgow Central LL 15	a	14 56	14b55		15 07			15 19		15 26		15 37			15 46		15 56	15b56		16 07			16 16
	d	15 00			15 07			15 19		15 28		15 38			15 46		15 58			16 07			16 18
Anderston	d	15 01			15 09			15 21		15 29		15 39			15 48		15 59			16 09			16 20
Exhibition Centre	d	15 03			15 11			15 23		15 31		15 41			15 50		16 01			16 11			16 22
Partick	d	15 07		15 09	15 14	15 17	15 21	15 27	15 29	15 35	15 39	15 45	15 47	15 50	15 54	15 59	16 05		16 09	16 14	16 17	16 20	16 25
Hyndland	d	15 09		15 11	15 17	15 19	15 23	15 29	15 32	15 38	15 41	15 47	15 49	15 53	15 56	16 02	16 07		16 11	16 17	16 19	16 22	16 27
Jordanhill	d			15 13				15 31			15 43				15 58				16 13				16 29
Scotstounhill	d			15 16				15 33			15 45				16 00				16 16				16 32
Garscadden	d			15 18				15 35			15 47				16 03				16 18				16 34
Yoker	d			15 20				15 38			15 50				16 05				16 20				16 36
Clydebank	d			15 22				15 40			15 52				16 07				16 22				16 38
Anniesland	d	15 12			15 20		15 26		15 35	15 43		15 50		15 56		16 05	16 10			16 20		16 25	
Westerton	d	15 16			15 23		15 29		15 38	15 46		15 53		15 59		16 08	16 13			16 23		16 28	
Bearsden	d	15 19					15 31			15 49				16 01			16 16					16 31	
Hillfoot	d	15 21					15 33			15 50				16 02			16 17					16 33	
Milngavie	a	15 24					15 38			15 55				16 07			16 22					16 36	
Drumchapel	d				15 25				15 40			15 55				16 10				16 25			
Drumry	d				15 27				15 42			15 57				16 12				16 27			
Singer	d				15 30				15 45			16 00				16 15				16 30			
Dalmuir	a			15 26	15 32	15 29		15 44	15 47		15 56	16 02	15 59		16 11	16 17			16 26	16 32	16 29		16 43
	d					15 29			15 48				15 59			16 18					16 29		
Kilpatrick	d								15 51							16 21							
Bowling	d								15 54							16 24							
Dumbarton East	d					15 36			15 58				16 06			16 28					16 36		
Dumbarton Central	d					15 39			16 00				16 09			16 30					16 39		
Dalreoch	d					15 40			16 02				16 10			16 32					16 40		
Renton	d								16 05							16 35							
Alexandria	d								16 07							16 37							
Balloch	a								16 10							16 40							
Cardross	d					15 45							16 15								16 45		
Craigendoran	d					15 50							16 20								16 50		
Helensburgh Central	a					15 54							16 24								[illegible]		

A From Edinburgh

Lanark, Coatbridge, Motherwell, Larkhall, Hamilton, Edinburgh and Bathgate, Airdrie and Springburn - Glasgow - Milngavie, Dalmuir, Balloch and Helensburgh

		SR	SR	SR	SR	SR	SR	SR	SR	SR	SR A	SR	SR	SR	SR	SR	SR	SR	SR	SR	SR	SR
Lanark	d									15 53						16 23						
Carluke	d									16 03						16 33						
Wishaw	d									16 08						16 40						
Holytown	d									16 13	16 33											
Shieldmuir	d															16 44						
Coatbridge Central	d																					
Whifflet	d																					
Motherwell	a									16 19						16 48						
	d		15 50					16 16		16 20						16 49		16 50				
Bellshill	d							16 22			16 35					16 55						
Uddingston	d							16 26			16 40					16 59						
Airbles	d		15 52							16 22								16 52				
Larkhall	d				16 07								16 37							17 07		
Merryton	d				16 09								16 39							17 09		
Chatelherault	d				16 12								16 42							17 12		
Hamilton Central	d		15 58		16 16					16 28			16 46					16 58		17 16		
Hamilton West	d		16 01		16 18					16 30			16 48					17 00		17 18		
Blantyre	d		16 04		16 22					16 34			16 52					17 04		17 22		
Newton	d		16 08		16 26					16 38								17 08				
Cambuslang	d		16 12					16 31		16 41						17 04		17 11				
Rutherglen	d		16 15		16 30			16 34		16 46			16 59			17 06		17 16		17 30		
Dalmarnock	d		16 17					16 36		16 48						17 08		17 18				
Bridgeton	d		16 19					16 38		16 50						17 10		17 20				
Edinburgh	d					15 20	15 37							15 49	16 07						16 20	16 41
Haymarket	d					15 25	15 42							15 53	16 12						16 25	16 44
Edinburgh Park	d					15 30	15 46							16 00	16 16						16 30	16 49
Uphall	d					15 38	15 54							16 08	16 24						16 38	16 56
Livingston North	d					15 41	15 58							16 11	16 28						16 41	17 00
Bathgate	a					15 46	16 02							16 16	16 32						16 47	17 04
	d					15 47	16 04							16 17	16 34						16 47	17 05
Armadale	d					15 51								16 21							16 51	
Blackridge	d					15 55								16 25							16 55	
Caldercruix	d					16 01								16 31							17 01	
Drumgelloch	d					16 05	16 16							16 35	16 46						17 05	17 17
Airdrie	d	15 57				16 12	16 20		16 27					16 42	16 50		16 57				17 12	17 21
Coatdyke	d	15 59				16 14			16 29					16 44			16 59				17 14	
Coatbridge Sunnyside	d	16 01				16 16	16 23		16 31					16 46	16 53		17 01				17 16	17 24
Blairhill	d	16 04				16 19			16 34					16 49			17 04				17 19	
Easterhouse	d	16 08				16 23			16 38					16 53			17 08				17 23	
Garrowhill	d	16 10				16 25			16 40					16 55			17 10				17 25	
Shettleston	d	16 13				16 28			16 43					16 58			17 13				17 28	
Carntyne	d	16 15				16 30			16 45					17 00			17 15				17 30	
Springburn	d			16 19								16 49							17 19			
Barnhill	d			16 20								16 50							17 20			
Alexandra Parade	d			16 23								16 53							17 23			
Duke Street	d			16 25								16 55							17 25			
Bellgrove	d	16 18		16 27		16 33			16 48			16 57		17 03			17 18		17 27		17 33	
High Street	d	16 20		16 29		16 35	16 40		16 50			16 59		17 05	17 11		17 20		17 29		17 35	17 41
Glasgow Queen St LL 10	a	16 22		16 31		16 37	16 42		16 52			17 01		17 07	17 13		17 22		17 31		17 37	17 43
	d	16 23		16 32		16 40	16 43		16 53			17 02		17 11	17 14		17 23		17 32		17 40	17 44
Charing Cross	d	16 25		16 34		16 42	16 45		16 55			17 04		17 13	17 16		17 25		17 34		17 42	17 46
Argyle Street	d		16 23		16 35			16 42		16 54			17 05			17 15		17 24		17 35		
Glasgow Central LL 15	a		16 26		16 37			16 46		16 56	16b57		17 07			17 17		17 26		17 37		
	d		16 28		16 38			16 46		16 58			17 07			17 17		17 28		17 38		
Anderston	d		16 29		16 39			16 48		16 59			17 09			17 19		17 29		17 39		
Exhibition Centre	d		16 31		16 41			16 50		17 01			17 11			17 21		17 31		17 41		
Partick	d	16 29	16 35	16 38	16 45	16 47	16 50	16 53	16 59	17 05		17 08	17 14	17 18	17 20	17 24	17 29	17 35	17 38	17 45	17 47	17 50
Hyndland	d	16 32	16 38	16 40	16 47	16 49	16 53	16 55	17 02	17 08		17 10	17 17	17 20	17 22	17 26	17 32	17 38	17 40	17 47	17 49	17 53
Jordanhill	d			16 42				16 57				17 12				17 28			17 42			
Scotstounhill	d			16 45				17 00				17 15				17 31			17 45			
Garscadden	d			16 47				17 02				17 17				17 33			17 47			
Yoker	d			16 49				17 04				17 19				17 34			17 49			
Clydebank	d			16 51				17 06				17 21				17 36			17 51			
Anniesland	d	16 35	16 41		16 50		16 56		17 05	17 12			17 20		17 25		17 35	17 41		17 50		17 56
Westerton	d	16 38	16 44		16 53		16 59		17 08	17 15			17 23		17 28		17 38	17 44		17 53		17 59
Bearsden	d		16 46				17 01			17 17					17 31			17 46				18 01
Hillfoot	d		16 48				17 02			17 18					17 32			17 47				18 03
Milngavie	a		16 52				17 07			17 23					17 37			17 52				18 07
Drumchapel	d	16 40			16 55				17 10				17 25				17 40			17 55		
Drumry	d	16 42			16 57				17 12				17 27				17 42			17 57		
Singer	d	16 45			17 00				17 15				17 30				17 45			18 00		
Dalmuir	a	16 47		16 56	17 02	16 59		17 11	17 17			17 26	17 32	17 30		17 41	17 47		17 56	18 02	17 59	
	d	16 48				16 59			17 18					17 30			17 48				17 59	
Kilpatrick	d	16 51							17 21								17 51					
Bowling	d	16 54							17 24								17 54					
Dumbarton East	d	16 58				17 06			17 28					17 37			17 58				18 06	
Dumbarton Central	d	17 00				17 09			17 30					17 40			18 00				18 09	
Dalreoch	d	17 02				17 10			17 32					17 41			18 02				18 10	
Renton	d	17 05							17 35								18 05					
Alexandria	d	17 07							17 37								18 07					
Balloch	a	17 10							17 40								18 10					
Cardross	d					17 15								17 46							18 15	
Craigendoran	d					17 20								17 51							18 20	
Helensburgh Central	a					17 24								17 54							18 25	

A From Edinburgh
b Glasgow Central High Level

Lanark, Coatbridge, Motherwell, Larkhall, Hamilton, Edinburgh and Bathgate, Airdrie and Springburn - Glasgow - Milngavie, Dalmuir, Balloch and Helensburgh

		SR	SR	SR	SR A	SR	SR	SR	SR	SR ◇ B	SR	SR	SR	SR	SR	SR	SR	SR	SR	SR	SR	SR	SR
Lanark	d			16 53							17 23									17 53			
Carluke	d			17 03							17 33									18 03			
Wishaw	d			17 08							17 40									18 08			
Holytown	d			17 13	17 30															18 13			
Shieldmuir	d										17 43												
Coatbridge Central	d																						
Whifflet	d																						
Motherwell	a			17 19							17 47									18 19			
	d	17 16		17 20							17 48		17 50					18 16		18 20			
Bellshill	d	17 22			17 33						17 56							18 22					
Uddingston	d	17 26			17 38						18 00							18 26					
Airbles	d			17 22									17 52							18 22			
Larkhall	d							17 37							18 07							18 37	
Merryton	d							17 39							18 09							18 39	
Chatelherault	d							17 42							18 12							18 42	
Hamilton Central	d			17 27				17 46					17 57		18 16					18 27		18 46	
Hamilton West	d			17 30				17 48					18 00		18 18					18 30		18 48	
Blantyre	d			17 33				17 52					18 03		18 22					18 33		18 52	
Newton	d			17 37									18 07							18 37			
Cambuslang	d	17 31		17 41	17 44						18 05		18 11					18 31		18 41			
Rutherglen	d	17 34		17 45				17 59			18 06		18 15		18 30			18 34		18 45		18 59	
Dalmarnock	d	17 36		17 47							18 08		18 17					18 36		18 47			
Bridgeton	d	17 38		17 49							18 10		18 19					18 38		18 49			
Edinburgh	d						16 48		17 07							17 22	17 37						17 51
Haymarket	d						16 52		17 11							17 26	17 42						17 56
Edinburgh Park	d						16 57		17 16							17 31	17 48						18 01
Uphall	d						17 05		17 27							17 39	17 56						18 09
Livingston North	d						17 08		17 30							17 42	17 59						18 12
Bathgate	a						17 14		17 35							17 46	18 04						18 17
	d						17 17		17 35							17 47	18 05						18 17
Armadale	d						17 21									17 51							18 21
Blackridge	d						17 25									17 55							18 25
Caldercruix	d						17 31									18 01							18 31
Drumgelloch	d						17 35		17 48							18 05	18 17						18 35
Airdrie	d		17 27				17 42		17 51			17 57				18 12	18 21		18 27				18 42
Coatdyke	d		17 29				17 44					17 59				18 14			18 29				18 44
Coatbridge Sunnyside	d		17 31				17 46		17 55			18 01				18 16	18 24		18 31				18 46
Blairhill	d		17 34				17 49					18 04				18 19			18 34				18 49
Easterhouse	d		17 38				17 53					18 08				18 23			18 38				18 53
Garrowhill	d		17 40				17 55					18 10				18 25			18 40				18 55
Shettleston	d		17 43				17 58					18 13				18 28			18 43				18 58
Carntyne	d		17 45				18 00					18 15				18 30			18 45				19 00
Springburn	d					17 49								18 19							18 49		
Barnhill	d					17 50								18 20							18 50		
Alexandra Parade	d					17 53								18 23							18 53		
Duke Street	d					17 55								18 25							18 55		
Bellgrove	d		17 48			17 57	18 03					18 18		18 27		18 33			18 48		18 57		19 03
High Street	d		17 50			17 59	18 05		18 10			18 20		18 29		18 35	18 40		18 50		18 59		19 05
Glasgow Queen St LL 10	a		17 53			18 01	18 07		18 12			18 22		18 31		18 37	18 42		18 52		19 01		19 07
	d		17 53			18 02	18 10		18 14	18c21		18 23		18 32		18 40	18 43		18 53		19 02		19 10
Charing Cross	d		17 55			18 04	18 12		18 17			18 25		18 34		18 42	18 46		18 55		19 04		19 12
Argyle Street	d	17 42		17 53				18 04			18 14		18 23		18 35			18 42		18 53		19 04	
Glasgow Central LL 15	a	17 46		17 54	17b57			18 07			18 16		18 26		18 37			18 46		18 56		19 07	
	d	17 47		17 58				18 11			18 17		18 28		18 37			18 46		18 58		19 07	
Anderston	d	17 48		17 59				18 13			18 18		18 29		18 39			18 48		18 59		19 09	
Exhibition Centre	d	17 50		18 01				18 15			18 20		18 31		18 41			18 50		19 01		19 11	
Partick	d	17 54	18 00	18 05		18 09	18 16	18 18	18 21		18 25	18 29	18 35	18 39	18 44	18 47	18 50	18a53	19 00	19 05	19 09	19 14	19 17
Hyndland	d	17 56	18 02	18 07		18 11	18 18	18 20	18 24		18 27	18 32	18 37	18 41	18 47	18 49	18 53		19 03	19 08	19 11	19 17	19 19
Jordanhill	d	17 58				18 13					18 29			18 43		18 51					19 13		19 21
Scotstounhill	d	18 00				18 15					18 30			18 45		18 54					19 15		19 24
Garscadden	d	18 02				18 17					18 32			18a47		18 56					19a17		19 26
Yoker	d	18 04				18 20					18 36					18 58							19 28
Clydebank	d	18 06				18 22					18 38					19 00							19 30
Anniesland	d		18 05	18 10				18 23	18 27			18 35	18 40		18 50		18 56		19 06	19 11		19 20	
Westerton	d		18 08	18 13				18 26	18 30			18 38	18 43		18 53		18 59		19 09	19 14		19 23	
Bearsden	d			18 16					18 32				18 46				19 02			19 17			
Hillfoot	d			18 17					18 34				18 47				19 03			19 18			
Milngavie	a			18 22					18 38				18 52				19 07			19 22			
Drumchapel	d		18 10					18 29				18 40			18 55				19 11			19 25	
Drumry	d		18 12					18 31				18 42			18 57				19 13			19 27	
Singer	d		18 14					18 33				18 45			19 00				19 16			19 30	
Dalmuir	a	18 11	18 18			18 26	18 29	18 36		18 38	18 44	18 47			19 02	19 04			19 18			19 32	19 34
	d		18 18				18 29			18 38		18 48				19 04			19 18				19 34
Kilpatrick	d		18 21									18 51							19 21				
Bowling	d		18 24									18 54							19 24				
Dumbarton East	d		18 28				18 36					18 58				19 12			19 28				19 42
Dumbarton Central	d		18 30				18 39			18 47		19 00				19 14			19 30				19 44
Dalreoch	d		18 32				18 40					19 02				19 15			19 32				19 45
Renton	d		18 35									19 05							19 35				
Alexandria	d		18 37									19 07							19 37				
Balloch	a		18 40									19 10							19 40				
Cardross	d						18 45									19 20							19 50
Craigendoran	d						18 50									19 25							19 55
Helensburgh Central	a						18 53			19e02						19 28							19 58

A From Edinburgh
B To Oban
b Glasgow Central High Level
c Glasgow Queen St High Level
e Helensburgh Upper

Table 226

Saturdays

Lanark, Coatbridge, Motherwell, Larkhall, Hamilton, Edinburgh and Bathgate, Airdrie and Springburn - Glasgow - Milngavie, Dalmuir, Balloch and Helensburgh

		SR	SR	SR	SR	SR A	SR	SR	SR	SR	SR	SR	SR	SR	SR	SR	SR	SR	SR	SR	SR	SR
Lanark	d		18 23									18 53				19 23						
Carluke	d		18 33									19 03				19 33						
Wishaw	d		18 40									19 08				19 40						
Holytown	d					19 00						19 13										
Shieldmuir	d		18 44													19 43						
Coatbridge Central	d																					
Whifflet	d																					
Motherwell	a		18 48									19 19				19 47						
	d		18 48		18 50					19 16		19 20				19 48		19 50				20 18
Bellshill	d		18 54			19 03				19 22						19 54						20 24
Uddingston	d		18 58			19 06				19 26						20 00						20 28
Airbles	d				18 52							19 22						19 52				
Larkhall	d						19 07						19 37						20 07			
Merryton	d						19 09						19 39						20 09			
Chatelherault	d						19 12						19 42						20 12			
Hamilton Central	d				18 57		19 16					19 27	19 46					19 57	20 16			
Hamilton West	d				19 00		19 18					19 30	19 48					20 00	20 18			
Blantyre	d				19 03		19 22					19 33	19 52					20 03	20 22			
Newton	d				19 07							19 37	19 56					20 07				
Cambuslang	d		19 03		19 11	19 16				19 31		19 41				20 05		20 11				20 33
Rutherglen	d		19 06		19 16		19 29			19 34		19 45	20 00			20 07		20 16	20 29			20 39
Dalmarnock	d		19 08		19 18					19 36		19 47				20 09		20 18				20 41
Bridgeton	d		19 10		19 20					19 38		19 49				20 11		20 20				20 43
Edinburgh	d	18 06						18 20	18 37					18 48	19 07					19 21	19 39	
Haymarket	d	18 11						18 24	18 42					18 52	19 11					19 24	19 41	
Edinburgh Park	d	18 16						18 30	18 46					18 57	19 18					19 30	19 47	
Uphall	d	18 24						18 38	18 55					19 05	19 26					19 38	19 54	
Livingston North	d	18 28						18 41	18 57					19 08	19 29					19 44	19 58	
Bathgate	a	18 34						18 46	19 03					19 13	19 34					19 48	20 04	
	d	18 35						18 47	19 03					19 17						19 49		
Armadale	d							18 51						19 21						19 53		
Blackridge	d							18 55						19 25						19 56		
Caldercruix	d							19 01						19 31						20 03		
Drumgelloch	d	18 46						19 05	19 17					19 35						20 06		
Airdrie	d	18 51						19 12	19 20					19 42						20 13		
Coatdyke	d							19 14						19 44						20 15		
Coatbridge Sunnyside	d	18 53						19 16	19 23					19 46						20 17		
Blairhill	d							19 19						19 49						20 20		
Easterhouse	d							19 23						19 53						20 24		
Garrowhill	d							19 25						19 55						20 26		
Shettleston	d							19 28						19 58						20 29		
Carntyne	d							19 30						20 00						20 31		
Springburn	d			19 09							19 39						20 09					
Barnhill	d			19 10							19 40						20 10					
Alexandra Parade	d			19 13							19 43						20 13					
Duke Street	d			19 15							19 45						20 15					
Bellgrove	d			19 17				19 33			19 47			20 03			20 17			20 34		
High Street	d	19 12		19 19				19 35	19 40		19 49			20 05			20 19			20 36		
Glasgow Queen St LL	a	19 14		19 21				19 37	19 42		19 51			20 07			20 21			20 38		
	d	19 14		19 23				19 40	19 43		19 53			20 10			20 23			20 40		
Charing Cross	d	19 17		19 25				19 42	19 45		19 55			20 12			20 25			20 42		
Argyle Street	d		19 13		19 24		19 35			19 42		19 53	20 06			20 15		20 24	20 34			20 46
Glasgow Central LL	a		19 17		19 26	19b29	19 37			19 46		19 56	20 07			20 18		20 26	20 37			20 48
	d		19 17		19 28		19 37			19 46		19 58	20 08			20 18		20 28	20 37			20 49
Anderston	d		19 19		19 29		19 39			19 48		19 59	20 09			20 20		20 29	20 39			20 51
Exhibition Centre	d		19 21		19 31		19 41			19 50		20 01	20 11			20 22		20 31	20 41			20 53
Partick	d	19 21	19a24	19 29	19 35		19 44	19 47	19 50	19a53	19 59	20 05	20 15	20 17		20a25	20 29	20 35	20 44	20 48		20a56
Hyndland	d	19 23		19 32	19 38		19 47	19 49	19 52		20 03	20 08	20 17	20 19			20 33	20 38	20 47	20 50		
Jordanhill	d	19 25						19 51	19 54					20 21						20 52		
Scotstounhill	d	19 27						19 54	19 57					20 24						20 54		
Garscadden	d	19a30						19 56	19a59					20 26						20 56		
Yoker	d							19 58						20 28						20 58		
Clydebank	d							20 00						20 30						21 00		
Anniesland	d			19 35	19 41		19 50				20 06	20 11	20 20				20 36	20 41	20 50			
Westerton	d			19 38	19 44		19 53				20 09	20 14	20 23				20 39	20 44	20 53			
Bearsden	d				19 46							20 17						20 46				
Hillfoot	d				19 47							20 18						20 47				
Milngavie	a				19 52							20 22						20 52				
Drumchapel	d			19 40			19 55				20 11		20 25				20 41		20 55			
Drumry	d			19 42			19 57				20 13		20 27				20 43		20 57			
Singer	d			19 45			20 00				20 16		20 30				20 46		21 00			
Dalmuir	a			19 47			20 02	20 04			20 18		20 32	20 34			20 48		21 02	21 04		
	d			19 48				20 04			20 18			20 34			20 48			21 04		
Kilpatrick	d			19 51							20 21						20 51					
Bowling	d			19 54							20 24						20 54					
Dumbarton East	d			19 58				20 12			20 28			20 42			20 58			21 11		
Dumbarton Central	d			20 00				20 14			20 30			20 44			21 00			21 14		
Dalreoch	d			20 02				20 15			20 32			20 45			21 02			21 15		
Renton	d			20 05							20 35						21 05					
Alexandria	d			20 07							20 37						21 07					
Balloch	a			20 10							20 40						21 10					
Cardross	d							20 20						20 50						21 20		
Craigendoran	d							20 25						20 55						21 25		
Helensburgh Central	a							20 28						20 58						21 28		

A From Edinburgh

b Glasgow Central High Level

Table 226

Saturdays

Lanark, Coatbridge, Motherwell, Larkhall, Hamilton, Edinburgh and Bathgate, Airdrie and Springburn - Glasgow - Milngavie, Dalmuir, Balloch and Helensburgh

		SR	SR	SR A	SR	SR	SR	SR	SR	SR	SR	SR	SR	SR	SR	SR	SR	SR	SR	SR	SR	SR	SR
Lanark	d		19 53				20 23							20 53			21 23						
Carluke	d		20 03				20 33							21 03			21 33						
Wishaw	d		20 08				20 38							21 08			21 39						
Holytown	d		20 13	20 24										21 13									
Shieldmuir	d						20 41										21 42						
Coatbridge Central	d																						
Whifflet	d																						
Motherwell	a		20 19				20 45							21 19			21 46						
	d		20 20				20 46		20 50			21 15		21 20			21 47		21 50			22 16	
Bellshill	d			20 28			20 52					21 22					21 53					22 22	
Uddingston	d			20 31			20 56					21 26					21 57					22 26	
Airbles	d		20 22						20 52					21 22					21 52				
Larkhall	d				20 37					21 07					21 37					22 07			
Merryton	d				20 39					21 09					21 39					22 09			
Chatelherault	d				20 42					21 12					21 42					22 12			
Hamilton Central	d		20 27		20 46				20 58	21 16				21 27	21 46				21 57	22 16			
Hamilton West	d		20 30		20 48				21 00	21 18				21 30	21 48				22 00	22 18			
Blantyre	d		20 33		20 52				21 04	21 22				21 33	21 52				22 03	22 22			
Newton	d		20 37						21 08					21 37					22 07				
Cambuslang	d		20 41				21 01		21 11			21 32		21 41			22 02		22 11			22 31	
Rutherglen	d		20 45		20 59		21 04		21 15	21 29		21 36		21 45	22 01		22 05		22 15	22 30		22 34	
Dalmarnock	d		20 47				21 06		21 17			21 38		21 47			22 07		22 17			22 36	
Bridgeton	d		20 49				21 08		21 19			21 40		21 49			22 09		22 19			22 38	
Edinburgh	d					19 51					20 21					20 50					21 21		
Haymarket	d					19 55					20 25					20 54					21 25		
Edinburgh Park	d					20 00					20 30					21 00					21 30		
Uphall	d					20 08					20 38					21 08					21 38		
Livingston North	d					20 17					20 41					21 11					21 41		
Bathgate	a					20 21					20 46					21 16					21 46		
	d					20 22					20 47					21 17					21 47		
Armadale	d					20 26					20 51					21 21					21 51		
Blackridge	d					20 29					20 55					21 25					21 55		
Caldercruix	d					20 36					21 01					21 31					22 01		
Drumgelloch	d					20 39					21 05					21 35					22 05		
Airdrie	d					20 43					21 12					21 42					22 12		
Coatdyke	d					20 45					21 14					21 44					22 14		
Coatbridge Sunnyside	d					20 47					21 16					21 46					22 16		
Blairhill	d					20 50					21 19					21 49					22 19		
Easterhouse	d					20 54					21 23					21 53					22 23		
Garrowhill	d					20 56					21 25					21 55					22 25		
Shettleston	d					20 59					21 28					21 58					22 28		
Carntyne	d					21 01					21 30					22 00					22 30		
Springburn	d	20 39						21 09					21 39					22 09					22 39
Barnhill	d	20 40						21 10					21 40					22 10					22 40
Alexandra Parade	d	20 43						21 13					21 43					22 13					22 43
Duke Street	d	20 45						21 15					21 45					22 15					22 45
Bellgrove	d	20 47				21 04		21 17			21 33		21 47			22 03		22 17			22 33		22 47
High Street	d	20 49				21 06		21 19			21 35		21 49			22 05		22 19			22 35		22 49
Glasgow Queen St LL	a	20 51				21 08		21 21			21 37		21 51			22 07		22 21			22 37		22 51
	d	20 53				21 10		21 23			21 40		21 53			22 10		22 23			22 40		22 53
Charing Cross	d	20 55				21 12		21 25			21 42		21 55			22 12		22 25			22 42		22 55
Argyle Street	d		20 53		21 04		21 12		21 23	21 34		21 44		21 53	22 06		22 13		22 23	22 35		22 42	
Glasgow Central LL	a		20 56	20b47	21 07		21 15		21 26	21 37		21 46		21 56	22 07		22 16		22 26	22 37		22 46	
	d		20 58		21 07		21 16		21 28	21 37		21 46		21 58	22 07		22 16		22 28	22 37		22 46	
Anderston	d		20 59		21 09		21 17		21 29	21 39		21 48		21 59	22 09		22 18		22 29	22 39		22 48	
Exhibition Centre	d		21 01		21 11		21 19		21 31	21 41		21 50		22 01	22 11		22 20		22 31	22 41		22 50	
Partick	d	20 59	21 05		21 14	21 17	21a23	21 29	21 35	21 44	21 47	21a53	21 59	22 05	22 14	22 17	22a24	22 30	22 35	22 44	22 47	22a53	22 59
Hyndland	d	21 02	21 08		21 17	21 19		21 32	21 38	21 47	21 49		22 03	22 08	22 17	22 19		22 33	22 38	22 47	22 49		23 03
Jordanhill	d					21 21					21 51					22 21					22 51		
Scotstounhill	d					21 24					21 54					22 24					22 54		
Garscadden	d					21 26					21 56					22 26					22 56		
Yoker	d					21 28					21 58					22 28					22 58		
Clydebank	d					21 30					22 00					22 30					23 00		
Anniesland	d	21 05	21 11		21 20			21 35	21 41	21 50			22 06	22 11	22 20			22 36	22 41	22 50			23 06
Westerton	d	21 08	21 14		21 23			21 38	21 44	21 53			22 09	22 14	22 23			22 39	22 44	22 53			23 09
Bearsden	d		21 16						21 46					22 17					22 46				
Hillfoot	d		21 18						21 47					22 18					22 47				
Milngavie	a		21 25						21 52					22 22					22 52				
Drumchapel	d	21 10			21 25			21 40		21 55			22 11		22 25			22 41		22 55			23 11
Drumry	d	21 12			21 27			21 42		21 57			22 13		22 27			22 43		22 57			23 13
Singer	d	21 15			21 30			21 45		22 00			22 16		22 30			22 46		23 00			23 16
Dalmuir	a	21 18			21 32	21 34		21 47		22 02	22 03		22 18		22 32	22 34		22 48		23 02	23 04		23 18
	d	21 18				21 34		21 48			22 04		22 18			22 34		22 48			23 04		23 18
Kilpatrick	d	21 21						21 51					22 21					22 51					23 21
Bowling	d	21 24						21 54					22 24					22 54					23 24
Dumbarton East	d	21 28				21 42		21 58			22 11		22 28			22 42		22 58			23 12		23 28
Dumbarton Central	d	21 30				21 44		22 00			22 13		22 30			22 44		23 00			23 14		23 30
Dalreoch	d	21 32				21 45		22 02			22 15		22 32			22 45		23 02			23 15		23 32
Renton	d	21 35						22 05					22 35					23 05					23 35
Alexandria	d	21 37						22 07					22 37					23 07					23 37
Balloch	a	21 40						22 10					22 40					23 10					23 40
Cardross	d					21 50					22 20					22 50					23 20		
Craigendoran	d					21 55					22 25					22 55					23 25		
Helensburgh Central	a					21 58					22 28					22 58					23 28		

A From Edinburgh

b Glasgow Central High Level

Table 226

Lanark, Coatbridge, Motherwell, Larkhall, Hamilton, Edinburgh and Bathgate, Airdrie and Springburn - Glasgow - Milngavie, Dalmuir, Balloch and Helensburgh

		SR	SR A	SR	SR	SR	SR	SR	SR	SR	SR	SR	SR	SR	SR	SR A
Lanark	d	21 53				22 23										
Carluke	d	22 03				22 33										
Wishaw	d	22 08				22 39										
Holytown	d	22 13	22 33													23 59
Shieldmuir	d					22 42										
Coatbridge Central	d															
Whifflet	d															
Motherwell	a	22 19				22 46										
	d	22 20				22 47		22 50								
Bellshill	d		22 36			22 53										00 02
Uddingston	d		22 41			22 57										00 06
Airbles	d	22 22						22 52								
Larkhall	d			22 37					23 07							
Merryton	d			22 39					23 09							
Chatelherault	d			22 42					23 12							
Hamilton Central	d	22 27		22 46				22 57	23 16							
Hamilton West	d	22 30		22 48				23 00	23 18							
Blantyre	d	22 33		22 52				23 03	23 22							
Newton	d	22 37						23 07								
Cambuslang	d	22 41				23 02		23 11								00 12
Rutherglen	d	22 45		22 59		23 05		23 15	23 29							
Dalmarnock	d	22 47				23 07		23 17								
Bridgeton	d	22 49				23 09		23 19								
Edinburgh	d				21 51					22 19		22 51	23 07	23 37	23 51	
Haymarket	d				21 55					22 23		22 55	23 11	23 42	23 55	
Edinburgh Park	d				22 00					22 30		23 00	23 16	23 47	23 59	
Uphall	d				22 08					22 38		23 08	23 24	23 55	00 08	
Livingston North	d				22 11					22 41		23 11	23 27	23 59	00 11	
Bathgate	a				22 16					22 46		23 16	23 32	00 04	00 16	
	d				22 17					22 47		23 17	23 33			
Armadale	d				22 21					22 51		23 21	23 37			
Blackridge	d				22 25					22 55		23 25	23 41			
Caldercruix	d				22 31					23 01		23 31	23 47			
Drumgelloch	d				22 35					23 05		23 35	23 51			
Airdrie	d				22 42					23 12		23 38	23a54			
Coatdyke	d				22 44					23 14		23 40				
Coatbridge Sunnyside	d				22 46					23 16		23 43				
Blairhill	d				22 49					23 19		23 45				
Easterhouse	d				22 53					23 23		23 49				
Garrowhill	d				22 55					23 25		23 52				
Shettleston	d				22 58					23 28		23 54				
Carntyne	d				23 00					23 30		23 56				
Springburn	d						23 09				23 39					
Barnhill	d						23 10				23 40					
Alexandra Parade	d						23 13				23 43					
Duke Street	d						23 15				23 45					
Bellgrove	d				23 03		23 17			23 33	23 47	23 59				
High Street	d				23 05		23 19			23 35	23 49	00 02				
Glasgow Queen St LL 10 ⛴	a				23 07		23 21			23 37	23 51	00 04				
	d				23 10		23 23			23 45	23 53	00 04				
Charing Cross	d				23 12		23 25			23 47	23 55	00 06				
Argyle Street	d	22 53		23 04		23 13		23 23	23 34							
Glasgow Central LL 15	a	22 56	22b55	23 07		23 17		23 26	23 37							00b23
	d	22 58		23 07		23 17		23 28	23 37							
Anderston	d	22 59		23 09		23 19		23 29	23 39							
Exhibition Centre	d	23 01		23 11		23 21		23 31	23 41							
Partick ⛴	d	23 05		23 14	23 17	23 25	23 29	23 35	23 44	23 51	23 59	00 11				
Hyndland	d	23 08		23 17	23 19	23 27	23 32	23 38	23 47	23 53	00 02	00 13				
Jordanhill	d				23 21	23 29			23 49	23 55	00 04	00 15				
Scotstounhill	d				23 24	23 31			23 51	23 58	00 06	00 17				
Garscadden	d				23 25	23a33			23a53	23 59	00a08	00a19				
Yoker	d				23 27					00 02						
Clydebank	d				23 29					00 04						
Anniesland	d	23 11		23 20			23 35	23 41								
Westerton	d	23 14		23 23			23 38	23 44								
Bearsden	d	23 17						23 46								
Hillfoot	d	23 18						23 47								
Milngavie	a	23 22						23 52								
Drumchapel	d			23 25			23 40									
Drumry	d			23 27			23 42									
Singer	d			23 30			23 45									
Dalmuir	a			23 32	23 33		23 47			00 08						
	d				23 33		23 48			00 08						
Kilpatrick	d						23 51									
Bowling	d						23 54									
Dumbarton East	d				23 41		23 58			00 15						
Dumbarton Central	d				23 43		23 59			00 18						
Dalreoch	d				23 44		00 02			00 19						
Renton	d						00 05									
Alexandria	d						00 07									
Balloch	a						00 10									
Cardross	d				23 49					00 24						
Craigendoran	d				23 54					00 29						
Helensburgh Central	a				23 58					00 32						

A From Edinburgh
b Glasgow Central High Level

Lanark, Coatbridge, Motherwell, Larkhall, Hamilton, Edinburgh and Bathgate, Airdrie and Springburn - Glasgow - Milngavie, Dalmuir, Balloch and Helensburgh

		SR A	SR A	SR A	SR A	SR A	SR A	SR B	SR	SR	SR	SR	SR	SR	SR	SR	SR ◇ C	SR	SR	SR	SR	SR	SR
Lanark	d																						
Carluke	d																						
Wishaw	d																						
Holytown	d							23p59															
Shieldmuir	d																						
Coatbridge Central	d																						
Whifflet	d																						
Motherwell	a																						
	d												08 36	08 40		09 10				09 36	09 40		10 06
Bellshill	d							00 02					08 42							09 42			10 12
Uddingston	d							00 06					08 46							09 46			10 18
Airbles	d													08 42		09 12					09 42		
Larkhall	d																		09 25				
Merryton	d																		09 27				
Chatelherault	d																		09 30				
Hamilton Central	d													08 47		09 17			09 34		09 47		
Hamilton West	d													08 50		09 20			09 36		09 50		
Blantyre	d													08 53		09 23			09 40		09 53		
Newton	d													08 57		09 27					09 57		
Cambuslang	d							00 12					08 51	09 01		09 31				09 51	10 01		10 23
Rutherglen	d												08 54	09 04		09 34			09 48	09 54	10 04		10 26
Dalmarnock	d																						
Bridgeton	d												08 57	09 07		09 37				09 57	10 07		10 29
Edinburgh	d		22p19		22p51	23p37	23p51											08 37					
Haymarket	d		22p23		22p55	23p42	23p55											08 41					
Edinburgh Park	d		22p30		23p00	23p47	23p59											08 46					
Uphall	d		22p38		23p08	23p55	00 08											08 57					
Livingston North	d		22p41		23p11	23p59	00 11											09 00					
Bathgate	a		22p46		23p16	00 04	00 16											09 06					
	d		22p47		23p17							08 06						09 06					
Armadale	d		22p51		23p21							08 10						09 10					
Blackridge	d		22p55		23p25							08 14						09 14					
Caldercruix	d		23p01		23p31							08 20						09 20					
Drumgelloch	d		23p05		23p35							08 24						09 24					
Airdrie	d		23p12		23p38					07 58		08 28			08 58			09 28				09 58	
Coatdyke	d		23p14		23p40					08 00		08 30			09 00			09 30				10 00	
Coatbridge Sunnyside	d		23p16		23p43					08 02		08 32			09 02			09 32				10 02	
Blairhill	d		23p19		23p45					08 05		08 35			09 05			09 35				10 05	
Easterhouse	d		23p23		23p49					08 09		08 39			09 09			09 39				10 09	
Garrowhill	d		23p25		23p52					08 11		08 41			09 11			09 41				10 11	
Shettleston	d		23p28		23p54					08 14		08 44			09 14			09 44				10 14	
Carntyne	d		23p30		23p56					08 16		08 46			09 16			09 46				10 16	
Springburn	d	23p09		23p39																			
Barnhill	d	23p10		23p40																			
Alexandra Parade	d	23p13		23p43																			
Duke Street	d	23p15		23p45																			
Bellgrove	d	23p17	23p33	23p47	23p59					08 19		08 49			09 19			09 49				10 19	
High Street	d	23p19	23p35	23p49	00 02					08 21		08 51			09 21			09 51				10 21	
Glasgow Queen St LL 10 ⛴	a	23p21	23p37	23p51	00 04					08 23		08 53			09 23			09 54				10 23	
	d	23p23	23p45	23p53	00 04					08 24		08 54			09 24		09c55	09 54				10 24	
Charing Cross	d	23p25	23p47	23p55	00 06					08 27		08 57			09 27			09 57				10 27	
Argyle Street	d																			10 01	10 11		10 33
Glasgow Central LL 15	a							00b23					09 04	09 14		09 44			09 56	10 04	10 14		10 34
	d												09 04	09 14		09 44			09 57	10 04	10 14		10 34
Anderston	d																						
Exhibition Centre	d												09 08	09 18		09 48			10 01	10 08	10 18		10 38
Partick ⛴	d	23p29	23p51	23p59	00 11					08 32		09 02	09 12	09 22	09 32	09 52		10 02	10a05	10 12	10 22	10 32	10 42
Hyndland	d	23p32	23p53	00 02	00 13					08 34		09 04	09 16	09 24	09 34	09 54		10 04		10 15	10 24	10 34	10 45
Jordanhill	d		23p55	00 04	00 15									09 26		09 56					10 26		
Scotstounhill	d		23p58	00 06	00 17									09 28		09 58					10 28		
Garscadden	d		23p59	00a08	00a19									09 30		10 00					10 30		
Yoker	d		00 02						08 33		09 03			09 33		10 03					10 33		
Clydebank	d		00 04						08 35		09 05			09 35		10 05					10 35		
Anniesland	d	23p35								08 37		09 07	09 19		09 37			10 07		10 18		10 37	10 48
Westerton	d	23p38								08 40		09 10	09 22		09 40			10 10		10 21		10 40	10 51
Bearsden	d												09 25							10 25			10 55
Hillfoot	d												09 27							10 27			10 57
Milngavie	a												09 30							10 30			11 00
Drumchapel	d	23p40								08 42		09 12			09 42			10 13				10 42	
Drumry	d	23p42								08 44		09 14			09 44			10 15				10 44	
Singer	d	23p45								08 47		09 17			09 47			10 17				10 47	
Dalmuir	a	23p47	00 08						08 38	08 49	09 08	09 19		09 39	09 49	10 09	10 12	10 20			10 39	10 49	
	d	23p48	00 08						08 39	08 50	09 09	09 20		09 39	09 50	10 09	10 16	10 20			10 39	10 50	
Kilpatrick	d	23p51							08 41		09 11			09 41		10 11					10 41		
Bowling	d	23p54							08 44		09 14			09 44		10 14					10 44		
Dumbarton East	d	23p58	00 15						08 49	08 58	09 19	09 28		09 49	09 58	10 19		10 28			10 49	10 58	
Dumbarton Central	d	23p59	00 18						08 51	09 00	09 21	09 30		09 51	10 00	10 21	10 25	10 30			10 51	11 00	
Dalreoch	d	00 02	00 19						08 52	09 01	09 22	09 31		09 52	10 01	10 22		10 31			10 52	11 01	
Renton	d	00 05							08 55		09 25			09 55		10 25					10 55		
Alexandria	d	00 07							08 58		09 28			09 58		10 28					10 58		
Balloch	a	00 10							09 00		09 30			10 00		10 30					11 00		
Cardross	d		00 24							09 06		09 36			10 06			10 36				11 06	
Craigendoran	d		00 29							09 11		09 41			10 11			10 41				11 11	
Helensburgh Central	a		00 32							09 14		09 44			10 14		10e37	10 44				11 14	

A not 22 May
B not 22 May. From Edinburgh
C To Oban
b Glasgow Central High Level
c Glasgow Queen St High Level
e Helensburgh Upper

Table 226

Sundays
until 19 June

Lanark, Coatbridge, Motherwell, Larkhall, Hamilton, Edinburgh and Bathgate, Airdrie and Springburn - Glasgow - Milngavie, Dalmuir, Balloch and Helensburgh

		SR	SR	SR	SR	SR	SR	SR	SR	SR	SR	SR	SR ◇ A	SR	SR	SR	SR	SR	SR	SR	SR	SR	SR
Lanark	d				10 12							11 12								12 12			
Carluke	d				10 22							11 22								12 22			
Wishaw	d				10 27							11 27								12 27			
Holytown	d																						
Shieldmuir	d				10 31							11 31								12 31			
Coatbridge Central	d																						
Whifflet	d																						
Motherwell	a				10 34							11 34								12 34			
	d	10 10			10 36	10 40		11 10	11 10			11 36		11 40		12 07	12 10			12 36	12 40		13 06
Bellshill	d				10 42			11 16				11 42				12 13				12 42			13 12
Uddingston	d				10 47			11 20				11 46				12 17				12 46			13 16
Airbles	d	10 12				10 42			11 12					11 42			12 12				12 42		
Larkhall	d			10 25							11 25								12 25				
Merryton	d			10 27							11 27								12 27				
Chatelherault	d			10 30							11 30								12 30				
Hamilton Central	d	10 17		10 34		10 47			11 17		11 34			11 47			12 17		12 34		12 47		
Hamilton West	d	10 20		10 36		10 50			11 20		11 36			11 50			12 20		12 36		12 50		
Blantyre	d	10 23		10 40		10 53			11 23		11 40			11 53			12 23		12 40		12 53		
Newton	d	10 27				10 57			11 27					11 57			12 27				12 57		
Cambuslang	d	10 31			10 52	11 01		11 25	11 31			11 51		12 01		12 22	12 31			12 51	13 01		13 21
Rutherglen	d	10 34		10 48	10 56	11 06		11 29	11 34		11 48	11 53		12 07		12 25	12 35		12 46	12 54	13 04		13 24
Dalmarnock	d																						
Bridgeton	d	10 37			10 59	11 09		11 32	11 37			11 56		12 10		12 28	12 38			12 57	13 07		13 27
Edinburgh	d		09 37							10 40								11 40				12 08	
Haymarket	d		09 41							10 44								11 44				12 12	
Edinburgh Park	d		09 46							10 49								11 49				12 17	
Uphall	d		09 57							10 57								11 57				12 25	
Livingston North	d		10 00							11 00								12 00				12 28	
Bathgate	a		10 05							11 05								12 05				12 33	
	d		10 06							11 06								12 06				12 36	
Armadale	d		10 10							11 10								12 10				12 40	
Blackridge	d		10 14							11 14								12 14				12 44	
Caldercruix	d		10 20							11 20								12 20				12 50	
Drumgelloch	d		10 24							11 24								12 24				12 54	
Airdrie	d		10 28				10 58			11 28					11 58			12 28				12 58	
Coatdyke	d		10 30				11 00			11 30					12 00			12 30				13 00	
Coatbridge Sunnyside	d		10 32				11 02			11 32					12 02			12 32				13 02	
Blairhill	d		10 35				11 05			11 35					12 05			12 35				13 05	
Easterhouse	d		10 39				11 09			11 39					12 09			12 39				13 09	
Garrowhill	d		10 41				11 11			11 41					12 11			12 41				13 11	
Shettleston	d		10 44				11 14			11 44					12 14			12 44				13 14	
Carntyne	d		10 46				11 16			11 46					12 16			12 46				13 16	
Springburn	d																						
Barnhill	d																						
Alexandra Parade	d																						
Duke Street	d																						
Bellgrove	d		10 49				11 19			11 49					12 19			12 49				13 19	
High Street	d		10 51				11 21			11 51					12 21			12 51				13 21	
Glasgow Queen St LL 10 ⇌	a		10 54				11 23			11 53					12 23			12 53				13 23	
	d		10 54				11 24			11 54			12b20		12 24			12 54				13 24	
Charing Cross	d		10 57				11 27			11 57					12 27			12 57				13 27	
Argyle Street	d	10 41		10 53	11 02	11 12		11 35	11 41		11 53	12 01		12 13		12 32	12 42		12 52	13 01	13 11		13 31
Glasgow Central LL 15	a	10 44		10 57	11 04	11 14		11 36	11 44		11 57	12 04		12 14		12 34	12 44		12 55	13 04	13 14		13 34
	d	10 44		10 57	11 04	11 14		11 36	11 44		11 57	12 04		12 14		12 34	12 44		12 56	13 04	13 14		13 34
Anderston	d																						
Exhibition Centre	d	10 48		11 01	11 08	11 18		11 40	11 48		12 01	12 08		12 18		12 38	12 48		13 01	13 08	13 18		13 38
Partick ⇌	d	10 52	11 02	11a05	11 12	11 22	11 32	11 43	11 52	12 02	12a04	12 12		12 22	12 32	12 42	12 52	13 02	13a04	13 12	13 22	13 32	13 42
Hyndland	d	10 54	11 04		11 15	11 24	11 34	11 45	11 54	12 04		12 15		12 24	12 34	12 45	12 54	13 04		13 15	13 24	13 34	13 45
Jordanhill	d	10 56				11 26			11 56					12 26			12 56				13 26		
Scotstounhill	d	10 58				11 28			11 58					12 28			12 58				13 28		
Garscadden	d	11 00				11 30			12 00					12 30			13 00				13 30		
Yoker	d	11 03				11 33			12 03					12 33			13 03				13 33		
Clydebank	d	11 05				11 35			12 05					12 35			13 05				13 35		
Anniesland	d		11 07		11 18		11 37	11 48		12 07		12 18			12 37	12 48		13 07		13 18		13 37	13 48
Westerton	d		11 10		11 21		11 40	11 51		12 10		12 21			12 40	12 51		13 10		13 21		13 40	13 51
Bearsden	d				11 25			11 55				12 25				12 55				13 25			13 55
Hillfoot	d				11 27			11 57				12 27				12 57				13 27			13 57
Milngavie	a				11 30			12 00				12 30				13 00				13 30			14 00
Drumchapel	d		11 12				11 42			12 12					12 42			13 12				13 42	
Drumry	d		11 14				11 44			12 14					12 44			13 14				13 44	
Singer	d		11 17				11 47			12 17					12 47			13 17				13 47	
Dalmuir	a	11 09	11 19			11 39	11 49		12 09	12 19			12 34	12 39	12 49		13 09	13 19			13 39	13 49	
	d	11 09	11 20			11 39	11 50		12 09	12 20			12 34	12 39	12 50		13 09	13 20			13 39	13 50	
Kilpatrick	d	11 11				11 41			12 11					12 41			13 11				13 41		
Bowling	d	11 14				11 44			12 14					12 44			13 14				13 44		
Dumbarton East	d	11 19	11 28			11 49	11 58		12 19	12 28				12 49	12 58		13 19	13 28			13 49	13 58	
Dumbarton Central	d	11 21	11 30			11 51	12 00		12 21	12 30			12 44	12 51	13 00		13 21	13 30			13 51	14 00	
Dalreoch	d	11 22	11 31			11 52	12 01		12 22	12 31				12 52	13 01		13 22	13 31			13 52	14 01	
Renton	d	11 25				11 55			12 25					12 55			13 25				13 55		
Alexandria	d	11 28				11 58			12 28					12 58			13 28				13 58		
Balloch	a	11 30				12 00			12 30					13 00			13 30				14 00		
Cardross	d		11 36				12 06			12 36					13 06			13 36				14 06	
Craigendoran	d		11 41				12 11			12 41					13 11			13 41				14 11	
Helensburgh Central	a		11 44				12 14			12 44			12c59		13 14			13 44				14 14	

A To Oban b Glasgow Queen St High Level c Helensburgh Upper

Table 226

Sundays
until 19 June

Lanark, Coatbridge, Motherwell, Larkhall, Hamilton, Edinburgh and Bathgate, Airdrie and Springburn - Glasgow - Milngavie, Dalmuir, Balloch and Helensburgh

		SR	SR	SR	SR	SR	SR	SR	SR	SR	SR	SR	SR	SR	SR	SR	SR	SR	SR	SR	SR	SR
Lanark	d				13 12							14 12							15 12			
Carluke	d				13 22							14 22							15 22			
Wishaw	d				13 27							14 27							15 28			
Holytown	d																					
Shieldmuir	d				13 30							14 31							15 31			
Coatbridge Central	d																					
Whifflet	d																					
Motherwell	a				13 36							14 34							15 34			
	d	13 10			13 36	13 40		14 06	14 10			14 34	14 40		15 06	15 10			15 35	15 40		16 06
Bellshill	d				13 42			14 12				14 40			15 12				15 41			16 12
Uddingston	d				13 48			14 16				14 44			15 16				15 45			16 16
Airbles	d	13 12				13 42			14 12				14 42			15 12				15 42		
Larkhall	d			13 25							14 25							15 25				
Merryton	d			13 27							14 27							15 27				
Chatelherault	d			13 30							14 30							15 30				
Hamilton Central	d	13 17		13 34		13 47			14 17		14 34		14 47			15 17		15 34		15 47		
Hamilton West	d	13 20		13 36		13 50			14 20		14 36		14 50			15 20		15 36		15 50		
Blantyre	d	13 23		13 40		13 53			14 23		14 40		14 53			15 23		15 40		15 53		
Newton	d	13 27				13 57			14 27				14 57			15 27				15 57		
Cambuslang	d	13 31			13 53	14 01		14 21	14 31			14 49	15 01		15 21	15 31			15 50	16 01		16 21
Rutherglen	d	13 35		13 49	13 56	14 05		14 24	14 34		14 48	14 53	15 06		15 24	15 34		15 48	15 53	16 05		16 24
Dalmarnock	d																					
Bridgeton	d	13 38			13 59	14 08		14 27	14 37			14 57	15 09		15 27	15 37			15 56	16 09		16 27
Edinburgh	d		12 40				13 11			13 40				14 06			14 40				15 08	
Haymarket	d		12 44				13 15			13 44				14 10			14 44				15 12	
Edinburgh Park	d		12 49				13 20			13 49				14 15			14 49				15 19	
Uphall	d		12 57				13 28			13 57				14 27			14 57				15 27	
Livingston North	d		13 00				13 31			14 00				14 30			15 00				15 30	
Bathgate	a		13 05				13 36			14 05				14 35			15 05				15 35	
	d		13 06				13 36			14 06				14 36			15 06				15 36	
Armadale	d		13 10				13 40			14 10				14 40			15 10				15 40	
Blackridge	d		13 14				13 44			14 14				14 44			15 14				15 44	
Caldercruix	d		13 20				13 50			14 20				14 50			15 20				15 50	
Drumgelloch	d		13 24				13 54			14 24				14 54			15 24				15 54	
Airdrie	d		13 28				13 58			14 28				14 58			15 28				15 58	
Coatdyke	d		13 30				14 00			14 30				15 00			15 30				16 00	
Coatbridge Sunnyside	d		13 32				14 02			14 32				15 02			15 32				16 02	
Blairhill	d		13 35				14 05			14 35				15 05			15 35				16 05	
Easterhouse	d		13 39				14 09			14 39				15 09			15 39				16 09	
Garrowhill	d		13 41				14 11			14 41				15 11			15 41				16 11	
Shettleston	d		13 44				14 14			14 44				15 14			15 44				16 14	
Carntyne	d		13 46				14 16			14 46				15 16			15 46				16 16	
Springburn	d																					
Barnhill	d																					
Alexandra Parade	d																					
Duke Street	d																					
Bellgrove	d		13 49				14 19			14 49				15 19			15 49				16 19	
High Street	d		13 51				14 21			14 51				15 21			15 51				16 21	
Glasgow Queen St LL 10 ⇌	a		13 53				14 24			14 53				15 23			15 53				16 23	
	d		13 54				14 24			14 54				15 24			15 54				16 24	
Charing Cross	d		13 57				14 27			14 57				15 27			15 57				16 27	
Argyle Street	d	13 42		13 54	14 03	14 11		14 31	14 41		14 53	15 01	15 12		15 31	15 41		15 53	16 00	16 12		16 31
Glasgow Central LL 15	a	13 44		13 57	14 06	14 14		14 34	14 44		14 57	15 04	15 13		15 34	15 44		15 57	16 03	16 14		16 34
	d	13 44		13 57	14 06	14 14		14 34	14 44		14 57	15 04	15 13		15 34	15 44		15 57	16 04	16 14		16 34
Anderston	d																					
Exhibition Centre	d	13 48		14 01	14 10	14 18		14 38	14 48		15 01	15 08	15 17		15 38	15 48		16 01	16 08	16 18		16 38
Partick ⇌	d	13 52	14 02	14a04	14 13	14 22	14 32	14 42	14 52	15 02	15a04	15 12	15 21	15 32	15 42	15 52	16 02	16a04	16 12	16 22	16 32	16 42
Hyndland	d	13 54	14 04		14 15	14 24	14 34	14 45	14 54	15 04		15 15	15 23	15 34	15 45	15 54	16 04		16 15	16 24	16 34	16 45
Jordanhill	d	13 56				14 26			14 56				15 25			15 56				16 26		
Scotstounhill	d	13 58				14 28			14 58				15 27			15 58				16 28		
Garscadden	d	14 00				14 30			15 00				15 29			16 00				16 30		
Yoker	d	14 03				14 33			15 03				15 32			16 03				16 33		
Clydebank	d	14 05				14 35			15 05				15 34			16 05				16 35		
Anniesland	d		14 07		14 18		14 37	14 48		15 07		15 18		15 37	15 48		16 07		16 18		16 37	16 48
Westerton	d		14 10		14 21		14 40	14 51		15 10		15 21		15 40	15 51		16 10		16 21		16 40	16 51
Bearsden	d				14 25			14 55				15 25			15 55				16 25			16 55
Hillfoot	d				14 27			14 57				15 27			15 57				16 27			16 57
Milngavie	a				14 30			15 00				15 30			16 00				16 30			17 00
Drumchapel	d		14 12				14 42			15 12				15 42			16 12				16 42	
Drumry	d		14 14				14 44			15 14				15 44			16 14				16 44	
Singer	d		14 17				14 47			15 17				15 47			16 17				16 47	
Dalmuir	a	14 09	14 19			14 39	14 50		15 09	15 19			15 38	15 49		16 09	16 19			16 39	16 49	
	d	14 09	14 20			14 39	14 50		15 09	15 20			15 38	15 50		16 09	16 20			16 39	16 50	
Kilpatrick	d	14 11				14 41			15 11				15 41			16 11				16 41		
Bowling	d	14 14				14 44			15 14				15 44			16 14				16 44		
Dumbarton East	d	14 19	14 28			14 49	14 58		15 19	15 28			15 48	15 57		16 19	16 28			16 49	16 57	
Dumbarton Central	d	14 21	14 30			14 51	15 00		15 21	15 30			15 50	16 00		16 21	16 30			16 51	17 00	
Dalreoch	d	14 22	14 31			14 52	15 01		15 22	15 31			15 52	16 01		16 22	16 31			16 52	17 01	
Renton	d	14 25				14 55			15 25				15 55			16 25				16 55		
Alexandria	d	14 28				14 58			15 28				15 57			16 28				16 58		
Balloch	a	14 30				15 01			15 30				16 00			16 30				17 00		
Cardross	d		14 36				15 06			15 36				16 06			16 36				17 06	
Craigendoran	d		14 41				15 11			15 41				16 11			16 41				17 11	
Helensburgh Central	a		14 44				15 14			15 44				[illegible]			[illegible]				[illegible]	

Lanark, Coatbridge, Motherwell, Larkhall, Hamilton, Edinburgh and Bathgate, Airdrie and Springburn - Glasgow - Milngavie, Dalmuir, Balloch and Helensburgh

		SR	SR	SR	SR	SR	SR	SR	SR	SR	SR	SR	SR ◇ A	SR	SR	SR	SR	SR	SR	SR	SR	SR	SR
Lanark	d				16 12							17 12								18 14			
Carluke	d				16 22							17 22								18 23			
Wishaw	d				16 27							17 27								18 28			
Holytown	d																						
Shieldmuir	d				16 31							17 31								18 32			
Coatbridge Central	d																						
Whifflet	d																						
Motherwell	a				16 34							17 34								18 36			
	d	16 10			16 34	16 40		17 06	17 10			17 34		17 40		18 06	18 10			18 36	18 40		19 06
Bellshill	d				16 40			17 12				17 40				18 12				18 42			19 12
Uddingston	d				16 44			17 16				17 44				18 16				18 46			19 16
Airbles	d	16 12				16 42			17 12					17 42			18 12				18 42		
Larkhall	d			16 25							17 25								18 25				
Merryton	d			16 27							17 27								18 27				
Chatelherault	d			16 30							17 30								18 30				
Hamilton Central	d	16 17		16 34		16 47			17 17		17 34			17 47			18 17		18 34		18 47		
Hamilton West	d	16 20		16 36		16 50			17 20		17 36			17 50			18 20		18 36		18 50		
Blantyre	d	16 23		16 40		16 53			17 23		17 40			17 53			18 23		18 40		18 53		
Newton	d	16 27				16 57			17 27					17 57			18 27				18 57		
Cambuslang	d	16 31			16 49	17 01		17 21	17 31			17 49		18 01		18 21	18 31			18 51	19 01		19 21
Rutherglen	d	16 34		16 48	16 53	17 06		17 24	17 34		17 48	17 54		18 04		18 24	18 34		18 48	18 54	19 06		19 24
Dalmarnock	d																						
Bridgeton	d	16 37			16 57	17 09		17 27	17 37			17 57		18 08		18 27	18 37			18 57	19 09		19 27
Edinburgh	d		15 40				16 10			16 40					17 07			17 39				18 10	
Haymarket	d		15 44				16 14			16 44					17 11			17 44				18 14	
Edinburgh Park	d		15 49				16 19			16 49					17 16			17 49				18 19	
Uphall	d		15 57				16 27			16 57					17 25			17 57				18 27	
Livingston North	d		16 00				16 30			17 00					17 28			18 00				18 30	
Bathgate	a		16 05				16 36			17 05					17 33			18 05				18 35	
	d		16 06				16 36			17 06					17 36			18 06				18 36	
Armadale	d		16 10				16 40			17 10					17 40			18 10				18 40	
Blackridge	d		16 14				16 44			17 14					17 44			18 14				18 44	
Caldercruix	d		16 20				16 50			17 20					17 50			18 20				18 50	
Drumgelloch	d		16 24				16 54			17 24					17 54			18 24				18 54	
Airdrie	d		16 28				16 58			17 28					17 58			18 28				18 58	
Coatdyke	d		16 30				17 00			17 30					18 00			18 30				19 00	
Coatbridge Sunnyside	d		16 32				17 02			17 32					18 02			18 32				19 02	
Blairhill	d		16 35				17 05			17 35					18 05			18 35				19 05	
Easterhouse	d		16 39				17 09			17 39					18 09			18 39				19 09	
Garrowhill	d		16 41				17 11			17 41					18 11			18 41				19 11	
Shettleston	d		16 44				17 14			17 44					18 14			18 44				19 14	
Carntyne	d		16 46				17 16			17 46					18 16			18 46				19 16	
Springburn	d																						
Barnhill	d																						
Alexandra Parade	d																						
Duke Street	d																						
Bellgrove	d		16 49				17 19			17 49					18 19			18 49				19 19	
High Street	d		16 51				17 21			17 51					18 21			18 51				19 21	
Glasgow Queen St LL 10	a		16 53				17 24			17 53					18 23			18 53				19 24	
	d		16 54				17 24			17 54			18b20		18 24			18 54				19 24	
Charing Cross	d		16 57				17 27			17 57					18 27			18 57				19 27	
Argyle Street	d	16 41		16 53	17 01	17 12		17 31	17 41		17 53	18 01		18 12									
Glasgow Central LL 15	a	16 44		16 57	17 04	17 14		17 34	17 44		17 57	18 04		18 14		18 34	18 44		18 56	19 04	19 14		19 34
	d	16 44		16 57	17 04	17 14		17 34	17 44		17 57	18 05		18 14		18 34	18 44		18 57	19 04	19 14		19 34
Anderston	d																						
Exhibition Centre	d	16 48		17 01	17 09	17 18		17 38	17 48		18 01	18 09		18 18		18 38	18 48		19 01	19 08	19 18		19 38
Partick	d	16 52	17 02	17a04	17 13	17 22	17 32	17 42	17 52	18 02	18a04	18 13		18 22	18 32	18 42	18 52	19 02	19a04	19 11	19 22	19 32	19 42
Hyndland	d	16 54	17 04		17 15	17 24	17 34	17 45	17 54	18 04		18 16		18 24	18 34	18 46	18 54	19 04		19 13	19 24	19 34	19 46
Jordanhill	d	16 56				17 26			17 56					18 26			18 56				19 26		
Scotstounhill	d	16 58				17 28			17 58					18 28			18 58				19 28		
Garscadden	d	17 00				17 30			18 00					18 30			19 00				19 30		
Yoker	d	17 03				17 33			18 03					18 33			19 03				19 33		
Clydebank	d	17 05				17 35			18 05					18 35			19 05				19 35		
Anniesland	d		17 07		17 18		17 37	17 48		18 07		18 19			18 37	18 49		19 07		19 19		19 37	19 49
Westerton	d		17 10		17 21		17 40	17 51		18 10		18 22			18 40	18 52		19 10		19 22		19 40	19 52
Bearsden	d				17 25			17 55				18 25				18 55				19 25			19 55
Hillfoot	d				17 27			17 57				18 27				18 57				19 27			19 57
Milngavie	a				17 30			18 00				18 30				19 00				19 30			20 00
Drumchapel	d		17 12				17 42			18 12					18 42			19 12				19 42	
Drumry	d		17 14				17 44			18 14					18 44			19 14				19 44	
Singer	d		17 17				17 47			18 17					18 47			19 17				19 47	
Dalmuir	a	17 09	17 19			17 39	17 50		18 09	18 19			18 34	18 39	18 49		19 09	19 19			19 39	19 50	
	d	17 09	17 20			17 39	17 50		18 09	18 20			18 34	18 39	18 50		19 09	19 20			19 39	19 50	
Kilpatrick	d	17 11				17 41			18 11					18 41			19 11				19 41		
Bowling	d	17 14				17 44			18 14					18 44			19 14				19 44		
Dumbarton East	d	17 19	17 28			17 49	17 58		18 19	18 28				18 49	18 58		19 19	19 28			19 49	19 58	
Dumbarton Central	d	17 21	17 30			17 51	18 00		18 21	18 30			18 44	18 51	19 00		19 21	19 30			19 51	20 00	
Dalreoch	d	17 22	17 31			17 52	18 01		18 22	18 31				18 52	19 01		19 22	19 31			19 52	20 01	
Renton	d	17 25				17 55			18 25					18 55			19 25				19 55		
Alexandria	d	17 28				17 58			18 28					18 58			19 28				19 58		
Balloch	a	17 30				18 00			18 30					19 00			19 30				20 00		
Cardross	d		17 36				18 06			18 36					19 06			19 36				20 06	
Craigendoran	d		17 41				18 11			18 40					19 11			19 41				20 11	
Helensburgh Central	a		17 44				18 14			18 44			18c59		19 14			19 44				20 14	

A To Oban

b Glasgow Queen St High Level

c Helensburgh Upper

Lanark, Coatbridge, Motherwell, Larkhall, Hamilton, Edinburgh and Bathgate, Airdrie and Springburn - Glasgow - Milngavie, Dalmuir, Balloch and Helensburgh

		SR	SR	SR	SR	SR	SR	SR	SR	SR	SR	SR	SR	SR	SR	SR	SR	SR	SR	SR	SR	SR
Lanark	d					19 12								20 12							21 12	
Carluke	d					19 22								20 23							21 23	
Wishaw	d					19 27								20 30							21 28	
Holytown	d																					
Shieldmuir	d					19 31								20 34							21 32	
Coatbridge Central	d																					
Whifflet	d																					
Motherwell	a					19 34								20 37							21 35	
	d	19 10				19 34	19 40		20 06	20 10				20 37	20 40		21 06	21 10			21 36	21 40
Bellshill	d					19 40			20 12					20 43			21 12				21 42	
Uddingston	d					19 44			20 19					20 47			21 16				21 46	
Airbles	d	19 12					19 42			20 12					20 42			21 12				21 42
Larkhall	d				19 25								20 25							21 25		
Merryton	d				19 27								20 27							21 27		
Chatelherault	d				19 30								20 30							21 30		
Hamilton Central	d	19 17			19 34		19 47			20 17			20 34		20 47			21 17		21 34		21 47
Hamilton West	d	19 20			19 36		19 50			20 20			20 36		20 50			21 20		21 36		21 50
Blantyre	d	19 23			19 40		19 53			20 23			20 40		20 53			21 23		21 40		21 53
Newton	d	19 27					19 57			20 27					20 57			21 28				21 57
Cambuslang	d	19 31				19 49	20 01		20 24	20 31				20 52	21 01		21 21	21 32			21 51	22 01
Rutherglen	d	19 34			19 49	19 53	20 04		20 27	20 34			20 48	20 56	21 04		21 25	21 35		21 48	21 54	22 06
Dalmarnock	d																					
Bridgeton	d	19 37				19 57	20 07		20 30	20 37				20 59	21 07		21 28	21 38			21 57	22 09
Edinburgh	d		18 40	19 10							19 40	20 08							20 40			
Haymarket	d		18 44	19 14							19 44	20 12							20 44			
Edinburgh Park	d		18 49	19 19							19 49	20 17							20 49			
Uphall	d		18 57	19 27							19 57	20 25							20 57			
Livingston North	d		19 00	19 30							20 00	20 28							21 00			
Bathgate	a		19 05	19 35							20 05	20 33							21 05			
	d		19 06								20 06								21 06			
Armadale	d		19 10								20 10								21 10			
Blackridge	d		19 14								20 14								21 14			
Caldercruix	d		19 20								20 20								21 20			
Drumgelloch	d		19 24								20 24								21 24			
Airdrie	d		19 28					19 58			20 28					20 58			21 28			
Coatdyke	d		19 30					20 00			20 30					21 00			21 30			
Coatbridge Sunnyside	d		19 32					20 02			20 32					21 02			21 32			
Blairhill	d		19 35					20 05			20 35					21 05			21 35			
Easterhouse	d		19 39					20 09			20 39					21 09			21 39			
Garrowhill	d		19 41					20 11			20 41					21 11			21 41			
Shettleston	d		19 44					20 14			20 44					21 14			21 44			
Carntyne	d		19 46					20 16			20 46					21 16			21 46			
Springburn	d																					
Barnhill	d																					
Alexandra Parade	d																					
Duke Street	d																					
Bellgrove	d		19 49					20 19			20 49					21 19			21 49			
High Street	d		19 51					20 21			20 51					21 21			21 51			
Glasgow Queen St LL 10	a		19 53					20 23			20 54					21 23			21 53			
	d		19 54					20 24			20 54					21 24			21 54			
Charing Cross	d		19 57					20 27			20 57					21 27			21 57			
Argyle Street	d																					
Glasgow Central LL 15	a	19 44			19 57	20 04	20 14		20 34	20 44			20 57	21 04	21 14		21 34	21 44		21 56	22 04	22 14
	d	19 44			19 57	20 04	20 14		20 34	20 44			20 58	21 04	21 14		21 34	21 44		21 57	22 04	22 14
Anderston	d																					
Exhibition Centre	d	19 48			20 01	20 08	20 18		20 38	20 48			21 01	21 08	21 18		21 38	21 48		22 01	22 08	22 18
Partick	d	19 52	20 02		20a04	20 12	20 22	20 32	20 42	20 52	21 02		21a05	21 12	21 22	21 32	21 42	21 52	22 02	22a04	22 12	22 22
Hyndland	d	19 54	20 04			20 16	20 24	20 34	20 46	20 54	21 04			21 16	21 24	21 34	21 46	21 54	22 04		22 16	22 24
Jordanhill	d	19 56					20 26			20 56					21 26			21 56				22 26
Scotstounhill	d	19 58					20 28			20 58					21 28			21 58				22 28
Garscadden	d	20 00					20 30			21 00					21 30			22 00				22 30
Yoker	d	20 03					20 33			21 03					21 33			22 03				22 33
Clydebank	d	20 05					20 35			21 05					21 35			22 05				22 35
Anniesland	d		20 07			20 19		20 37	20 49		21 07			21 19		21 37	21 49		22 07		22 19	
Westerton	d		20 10			20 22		20 40	20 52		21 10			21 22		21 40	21 52		22 10		22 22	
Bearsden	d					20 25			20 55					21 25			21 55				22 25	
Hillfoot	d					20 27			20 57					21 27			21 57				22 27	
Milngavie	a					20 30			21 00					21 30			22 00				22 30	
Drumchapel	d		20 12					20 42			21 12					21 42			22 12			
Drumry	d		20 14					20 44			21 14					21 44			22 14			
Singer	d		20 17					20 47			21 17					21 47			22 17			
Dalmuir	a	20 09	20 19				20 39	20 49		21 09	21 20				21 39	21 49		22 09	22 19			22 39
	d	20 09	20 20				20 39	20 50		21 09	21 20				21 39	21 50		22 09	22 20			22 39
Kilpatrick	d	20 11					20 41			21 11					21 41			22 11				22 41
Bowling	d	20 14					20 44			21 14					21 44			22 14				22 44
Dumbarton East	d	20 19	20 28				20 49	20 58		21 19	21 28				21 49	21 58		22 19	22 28			22 49
Dumbarton Central	d	20 21	20 30				20 51	21 00		21 21	21 30				21 51	22 00		22 21	22 30			22 51
Dalreoch	d	20 22	20 31				20 52	21 01		21 22	21 31				21 52	22 01		22 22	22 31			22 52
Renton	d	20 25					20 55			21 25					21 55			22 25				22 55
Alexandria	d	20 28					20 58			21 28					21 58			22 28				22 58
Balloch	a	20 30					21 01			21 30					22 00			22 30				23 00
Cardross	d		20 36					21 06			21 36					22 06			22 36			
Craigendoran	d		20 41					21 11			21 41					22 11			22 41			
Helensburgh Central	a		20 44					21 14			21 45					22 14			22 44			

Table 226

Sundays until 19 June

Lanark, Coatbridge, Motherwell, Larkhall, Hamilton, Edinburgh and Bathgate, Airdrie and Springburn - Glasgow - Milngavie, Dalmuir, Balloch and Helensburgh

		SR	SR	SR	SR	SR	SR	SR	SR	SR	SR	SR	SR
Lanark	d						22 12						
Carluke	d						22 23						
Wishaw	d						22 28						
Holytown	d												
Shieldmuir	d						22 32						
Coatbridge Central	d												
Whifflet	d												
Motherwell	a						22 35						
	d		22 06	22 10			22 36	22 40		23 06	23 10		
Bellshill	d		22 12				22 42			23 12			
Uddingston	d		22 15				22 46			23 16			
Airbles	d			22 12				22 42			23 12		
Larkhall	d					22 25							
Merryton	d					22 27							
Chatelherault	d					22 30							
Hamilton Central	d			22 17		22 34		22 47			23 17		
Hamilton West	d			22 20		22 36		22 50			23 20		
Blantyre	d			22 23		22 40		22 53			23 23		
Newton	d			22 27				22 57			23 27		
Cambuslang	d		22 20	22 31			22 51	23 01		23 21	23 31		
Rutherglen	d		22 23	22 34		22 48	22 54	23 04		23 24	23 34		
Dalmarnock	d												
Bridgeton	d		22 27	22 37			22 57	23 07		23 27	23 37		
Edinburgh	d				21 38							22 40	23 18
Haymarket	d				21 42							22 44	23 22
Edinburgh Park	d				21 47							22 49	23 27
Uphall	d				21 55							22 57	23 35
Livingston North	d				21 58							23 00	23 38
Bathgate	a				22 03							23 05	23 43
	d				22 06							23 06	
Armadale	d				22 10							23 10	
Blackridge	d				22 14							23 14	
Caldercruix	d				22 20							23 20	
Drumgelloch	d				22 24							23 24	
Airdrie	d	21 58			22 28				22 58			23 28	
Coatdyke	d	22 00			22 30				23 00			23 30	
Coatbridge Sunnyside	d	22 02			22 32				23 02			23 32	
Blairhill	d	22 05			22 35				23 05			23 35	
Easterhouse	d	22 09			22 39				23 09			23 39	
Garrowhill	d	22 11			22 41				23 11			23 41	
Shettleston	d	22 14			22 44				23 14			23 44	
Carntyne	d	22 16			22 46				23 16			23 46	
Springburn	d												
Barnhill	d												
Alexandra Parade	d												
Duke Street	d												
Bellgrove	d	22 19			22 49				23 19			23 49	
High Street	d	22 21			22 51				23 21			23 51	
Glasgow Queen St LL	a	22 23			22 53				23 23			23 53	
	d	22 24			22 54				23 24			23 54	
Charing Cross	d	22 27			22 57				23 27			23 57	
Argyle Street	d												
Glasgow Central LL	a		22 34	22 44		22 57	23 04	23 14		23 34	23 44		
	d		22 34	22 44		22 57	23 04	23 14		23 34	23 44		
Anderston	d												
Exhibition Centre	d		22 38	22 48		23 01	23 08	23 18		23 38	23 48		
Partick	d	22 32	22 42	22 52	23 02	23a04	23 12	23 22	23 32	23 42	23 52	00 01	
Hyndland	d	22 34	22 46	22 54	23 04		23 16	23 24	23 34	23 44	23 54	00 03	
Jordanhill	d			22 56				23 26		23 46	23 56	00 05	
Scotstounhill	d			22 58				23 28		23 48	23 58	00 07	
Garscadden	d			23 00				23 30		23a50	00a01	00 09	
Yoker	d			23 03				23 33				00 12	
Clydebank	d			23 05				23 35					
Anniesland	d	22 37	22 49		23 07		23 19		23 37				
Westerton	d	22 40	22 52		23 10		23 22		23 40				
Bearsden	d		22 55				23 25						
Hillfoot	d		22 57				23 27						
Milngavie	a		23 00				23 30						
Drumchapel	d	22 42			23 12				23 42				
Drumry	d	22 44			23 14				23 44				
Singer	d	22 47			23 17				23 47				
Dalmuir	a	22 49		23 09	23 19			23 39	23 49			00 16	
	d	22 50		23 09	23 20			23 39	23 50				
Kilpatrick	d			23 11				23 41					
Bowling	d			23 14				23 44					
Dumbarton East	d	22 58		23 19	23 28			23 49	23 58				
Dumbarton Central	d	23 00		23 21	23 30			23 51	23 59				
Dalreoch	d	23 01		23 22	23 31			23 52	00 01				
Renton	d			23 25				23 55					
Alexandria	d			23 28				23 58					
Balloch	a			23 30				00 01					
Cardross	d	23 06			23 36				00 06				
Craigendoran	d	23 11			23 41				00 11				
Helensburgh Central	a	23 14			23 44				00 14				

Table 226

Sundays 26 June to 30 October

Lanark, Coatbridge, Motherwell, Larkhall, Hamilton, Edinburgh and Bathgate, Airdrie and Springburn - Glasgow - Milngavie, Dalmuir, Balloch and Helensburgh

		SR	SR	SR	SR	SR	SR	SR	SR	SR	SR	SR	SR	SR	SR	SR	SR	SR	SR	SR	SR	SR	SR
								A					◇ B					◇ C					
Lanark	d																						
Carluke	d																						
Wishaw	d																						
Holytown	d							23p59															
Shieldmuir	d																						
Coatbridge Central	d																						
Whifflet	d																						
Motherwell	a																						
	d													08 36	08 40		09 10				09 36	09 40	
Bellshill	d							00 02						08 42							09 42		
Uddingston	d							00 06						08 46							09 46		
Airbles	d														08 42		09 12					09 42	
Larkhall	d																			09 25			
Merryton	d																			09 27			
Chatelherault	d																			09 30			
Hamilton Central	d														08 47		09 17			09 34		09 47	
Hamilton West	d														08 50		09 20			09 36		09 50	
Blantyre	d														08 53		09 23			09 40		09 53	
Newton	d														08 57		09 27					09 57	
Cambuslang	d							00 12						08 51	09 01		09 31				09 51	10 01	
Rutherglen	d													08 54	09 04		09 34			09 48	09 54	10 04	
Dalmarnock	d																						
Bridgeton	d													08 57	09 07		09 37				09 57	10 07	
Edinburgh	d		22p19		22p51	23p37	23p51						08ʃ10						08 37				
Haymarket	d		22p23		22p55	23p42	23p55						08u14						08 41				
Edinburgh Park	d		22p30		23p00	23p47	23p59												08 46				
Uphall	d		22p38		23p08	23p55	00 08												08 57				
Livingston North	d		22p41		23p11	23p59	00 11												09 00				
Bathgate	a		22p46		23p16	00 04	00 16												09 06				
	d		22p47		23p17							08 06							09 06				
Armadale	d		22p51		23p21							08 10							09 10				
Blackridge	d		22p55		23p25							08 14							09 14				
Caldercruix	d		23p01		23p31							08 20							09 20				
Drumgelloch	d		23p05		23p35							08 24							09 24				
Airdrie	d		23p12		23p38					07 58		08 28				08 58			09 28				09 58
Coatdyke	d		23p14		23p40					08 00		08 30				09 00			09 30				10 00
Coatbridge Sunnyside	d		23p16		23p43					08 02		08 32				09 02			09 32				10 02
Blairhill	d		23p19		23p45					08 05		08 35				09 05			09 35				10 05
Easterhouse	d		23p23		23p49					08 09		08 39				09 09			09 39				10 09
Garrowhill	d		23p25		23p52					08 11		08 41				09 11			09 41				10 11
Shettleston	d		23p28		23p54					08 14		08 44				09 14			09 44				10 14
Carntyne	d		23p30		23p56					08 16		08 46				09 16			09 46				10 16
Springburn	d	23p09		23p39																			
Barnhill	d	23p10		23p40																			
Alexandra Parade	d	23p13		23p43																			
Duke Street	d	23p15		23p45																			
Bellgrove	d	23p17	23p33	23p47	23p59					08 19		08 49				09 19			09 49				10 19
High Street	d	23p19	23p35	23p49	00 02					08 21		08 51				09 21			09 51				10 21
Glasgow Queen St LL	a	23p21	23p37	23p51	00 04					08 23		08 53				09 23			09 54				10 23
	d	23p23	23p45	23p53	00 04					08 24		08 54				09 24		09e55	09 54				10 24
Charing Cross	d	23p25	23p47	23p55	00 06					08 27		08 57				09 27			09 57				10 27
Argyle Street	d																				10 01	10 11	
Glasgow Central LL	a							00b23						09 04	09 14		09 44			09 56	10 04	10 14	
	d													09 04	09 14		09 44			09 57	10 04	10 14	
Anderston	d																						
Exhibition Centre	d													09 08	09 18		09 48			10 01	10 08	10 18	
Partick	d	23p29	23p51	23p59	00 11					08 32		09 02		09 12	09 22	09 32	09 52		10 02	10a05	10 12	10 22	10 32
Hyndland	d	23p32	23p53	00 02	00 13					08 34		09 04		09 16	09 24	09 34	09 54		10 04		10 15	10 24	10 34
Jordanhill	d		23p55	00 04	00 15										09 26		09 56					10 26	
Scotstounhill	d		23p58	00 06	00 17										09 28		09 58					10 28	
Garscadden	d		23p59	00a08	00a19										09 30		10 00					10 30	
Yoker	d		00 02						08 33		09 03				09 33		10 03					10 33	
Clydebank	d		00 04						08 35		09 05				09 35		10 05					10 35	
Anniesland	d	23p35								08 37		09 07		09 19		09 37			10 07		10 18		10 37
Westerton	d	23p38								08 40		09 10		09 22		09 40			10 10		10 21		10 40
Bearsden	d													09 25							10 25		
Hillfoot	d													09 27							10 27		
Milngavie	a													09 30							10 30		
Drumchapel	d	23p40								08 42		09 12				09 42			10 13				10 42
Drumry	d	23p42								08 44		09 14				09 44			10 15				10 44
Singer	d	23p45								08 47		09 17				09 47			10 17				10 47
Dalmuir	a	23p47	00 08						08 38	08 49	09 08	09 19			09 39	09 49	10 09	10ʃ12	10 20			10 39	10 49
	d	23p48	00 08						08 39	08 50	09 09	09 20	09u27		09 39	09 50	10 09	10ʃ16	10 20			10 39	10 50
Kilpatrick	d	23p51							08 41		09 11				09 41		10 11					10 41	
Bowling	d	23p54							08 44		09 14				09 44		10 14					10 44	
Dumbarton East	d	23p58	00 15						08 49	08 58	09 19	09 28			09 49	09 58	10 19		10 28			10 49	10 58
Dumbarton Central	d	23p59	00 18						08 51	09 00	09 21	09 30			09 51	10 00	10 21	10ʃ25	10 30			10 51	11 00
Dalreoch	d	00 02	00 19						08 52	09 01	09 22	09 31			09 52	10 01	10 22		10 31			10 52	11 01
Renton	d	00 05							08 55		09 25				09 55		10 25					10 55	
Alexandria	d	00 07							08 58		09 28				09 58		10 28					10 58	
Balloch	a	00 10							09 00		09 30				10 00		10 30					11 00	
Cardross	d		00 24							09 06		09 36				10 06			10 36				11 06
Craigendoran	d		00 29							09 11		09 41				10 11			10 41				11 11
Helensburgh Central	a		00 32							09 14		09 44	09c49			10 14		10c37	10 44				11 14

A From Edinburgh
B from 26 June until [illegible]
C from 26 June until 25 September. To O[illegible]

Lanark, Coatbridge, Motherwell, Larkhall, Hamilton, Edinburgh and Bathgate, Airdrie and Springburn - Glasgow - Milngavie, Dalmuir, Balloch and Helensburgh

		SR	SR	SR	SR	SR	SR	SR	SR	SR	SR	SR	SR	SR	SR	SR	SR	SR	SR	SR	SR	SR	SR
														◇ A									
Lanark	d					10 12							11 12								12 12		
Carluke	d					10 22							11 22								12 22		
Wishaw	d					10 27							11 27								12 27		
Holytown	d																						
Shieldmuir	d					10 31							11 31								12 31		
Coatbridge Central	d																						
Whifflet	d																						
Motherwell	a					10 34							11 34								12 34		
	d	10 06	10 10			10 36	10 40		11 10	11 10			11 36		11 40		12 07	12 10			12 36	12 40	
Bellshill	d	10 12				10 42			11 16				11 42				12 13				12 42		
Uddingston	d	10 18				10 47			11 20				11 46				12 17				12 46		
Airbles	d		10 12				10 42			11 12					11 42			12 12				12 42	
Larkhall	d				10 25							11 25								12 25			
Merryton	d				10 27							11 27								12 27			
Chatelherault	d				10 30							11 30								12 30			
Hamilton Central	d		10 17		10 34		10 47			11 17		11 34			11 47			12 17		12 34		12 47	
Hamilton West	d		10 20		10 36		10 50			11 20		11 36			11 50			12 20		12 36		12 50	
Blantyre	d		10 23		10 40		10 53			11 23		11 40			11 53			12 23		12 40		12 53	
Newton	d		10 27				10 57			11 27					11 57			12 27				12 57	
Cambuslang	d	10 23	10 31			10 52	11 01		11 25	11 31			11 51		12 01		12 22	12 31			12 51	13 01	
Rutherglen	d	10 26	10 34		10 48	10 56	11 06		11 29	11 34		11 48	11 53		12 07		12 25	12 35		12 46	12 54	13 04	
Dalmarnock	d																						
Bridgeton	d	10 29	10 37			10 59	11 09		11 32	11 37			11 56		12 10		12 28	12 38			12 57	13 07	
Edinburgh	d			09 37							10 40								11 40				12 08
Haymarket	d			09 41							10 44								11 44				12 12
Edinburgh Park	d			09 46							10 49								11 49				12 17
Uphall	d			09 57							10 57								11 57				12 25
Livingston North	d			10 00							11 00								12 00				12 28
Bathgate	a			10 05							11 05								12 05				12 33
	d			10 06							11 06								12 06				12 36
Armadale	d			10 10							11 10								12 10				12 40
Blackridge	d			10 14							11 14								12 14				12 44
Caldercruix	d			10 20							11 20								12 20				12 50
Drumgelloch	d			10 24							11 24								12 24				12 54
Airdrie	d			10 28				10 58			11 28					11 58			12 28				12 58
Coatdyke	d			10 30				11 00			11 30					12 00			12 30				13 00
Coatbridge Sunnyside	d			10 32				11 02			11 32					12 02			12 32				13 02
Blairhill	d			10 35				11 05			11 35					12 05			12 35				13 05
Easterhouse	d			10 39				11 09			11 39					12 09			12 39				13 09
Garrowhill	d			10 41				11 11			11 41					12 11			12 41				13 11
Shettleston	d			10 44				11 14			11 44					12 14			12 44				13 14
Carntyne	d			10 46				11 16			11 46					12 16			12 46				13 16
Springburn	d																						
Barnhill	d																						
Alexandra Parade	d																						
Duke Street	d																						
Bellgrove	d			10 49				11 19			11 49					12 19			12 49				13 19
High Street	d			10 51				11 21			11 51					12 21			12 51				13 21
Glasgow Queen St LL 10	a			10 54				11 23			11 53					12 23			12 53				13 23
	d			10 54				11 24			11 54			12b20		12 24			12 54				13 24
Charing Cross	d			10 57				11 27			11 57					12 27			12 57				13 27
Argyle Street	d	10 33	10 41		10 53	11 02	11 12		11 35	11 41		11 53	12 01		12 13		12 32	12 42		12 52	13 01	13 11	
Glasgow Central LL 15	a	10 34	10 44		10 57	11 04	11 14		11 36	11 44		11 57	12 04		12 14		12 34	12 44		12 55	13 04	13 14	
	d	10 34	10 44		10 57	11 04	11 14		11 36	11 44		11 57	12 04		12 14		12 34	12 44		12 56	13 04	13 14	
Anderston	d																						
Exhibition Centre	d	10 38	10 48		11 01	11 08	11 18		11 40	11 48		12 01	12 08		12 18		12 38	12 48		13 01	13 08	13 18	
Partick	d	10 42	10 52	11 02	11a05	11 12	11 22	11 32	11 43	11 52	12 02	12a04	12 12		12 22	12 32	12 42	12 52	13 02	13a04	13 12	13 22	13 32
Hyndland	d	10 45	10 54	11 04		11 15	11 24	11 34	11 45	11 54	12 04		12 15		12 24	12 34	12 45	12 54	13 04		13 15	13 24	13 34
Jordanhill	d		10 56				11 26			11 56					12 26			12 56				13 26	
Scotstounhill	d		10 58				11 28			11 58					12 28			12 58				13 28	
Garscadden	d		11 00				11 30			12 00					12 30			13 00				13 30	
Yoker	d		11 03				11 33			12 03					12 33			13 03				13 33	
Clydebank	d		11 05				11 35			12 05					12 35			13 05				13 35	
Anniesland	d	10 48		11 07		11 18		11 37	11 48		12 07		12 18			12 37	12 48		13 07		13 18		13 37
Westerton	d	10 51		11 10		11 21		11 40	11 51		12 10		12 21			12 40	12 51		13 10		13 21		13 40
Bearsden	d	10 55				11 25			11 55				12 25				12 55				13 25		
Hillfoot	d	10 57				11 27			11 57				12 27				12 57				13 27		
Milngavie	a	11 00				11 30			12 00				12 30				13 00				13 30		
Drumchapel	d			11 12				11 42			12 12					12 42			13 12				13 42
Drumry	d			11 14				11 44			12 14					12 44			13 14				13 44
Singer	d			11 17				11 47			12 17					12 47			13 17				13 47
Dalmuir	a		11 09	11 19			11 39	11 49		12 09	12 19			12 34	12 39	12 49		13 09	13 19			13 39	13 49
	d		11 09	11 20			11 39	11 50		12 09	12 20			12 34	12 39	12 50		13 09	13 20			13 39	13 50
Kilpatrick	d		11 11				11 41			12 11					12 41			13 11				13 41	
Bowling	d		11 14				11 44			12 14					12 44			13 14				13 44	
Dumbarton East	d		11 19	11 28			11 49	11 58		12 19	12 28				12 49	12 58		13 19	13 28			13 49	13 58
Dumbarton Central	d		11 21	11 30			11 51	12 00		12 21	12 30			12 44	12 51	13 00		13 21	13 30			13 51	14 00
Dalreoch	d		11 22	11 31			11 52	12 01		12 22	12 31				12 52	13 01		13 22	13 31			13 52	14 01
Renton	d		11 25				11 55			12 25					12 55			13 25				13 55	
Alexandria	d		11 28				11 58			12 28					12 58			13 28				13 58	
Balloch	a		11 30				12 00			12 30					13 00			13 30				14 00	
Cardross	d			11 36				12 06			12 36					13 06			13 36				14 06
Craigendoran	d			11 41				12 11			12 41					13 11			13 41				14 11
Helensburgh Central	a			11 44				12 14			12 44			12c59		13 14			13 44				14 14

A To Oban

b Glasgow Queen St High Level

c Helensburgh Upper

Lanark, Coatbridge, Motherwell, Larkhall, Hamilton, Edinburgh and Bathgate, Airdrie and Springburn - Glasgow - Milngavie, Dalmuir, Balloch and Helensburgh

		SR	SR	SR	SR	SR	SR	SR	SR	SR	SR	SR	SR	SR	SR	SR	SR	SR	SR	SR	SR	SR
Lanark	d					13 12							14 12							15 12		
Carluke	d					13 22							14 22							15 22		
Wishaw	d					13 27							14 27							15 28		
Holytown	d																					
Shieldmuir	d					13 30							14 31							15 31		
Coatbridge Central	d																					
Whifflet	d																					
Motherwell	a					13 36							14 34							15 34		
	d	13 06	13 10			13 36	13 40		14 06	14 10			14 34	14 40		15 06	15 10			15 35	15 40	
Bellshill	d	13 12				13 42			14 12				14 40			15 12				15 41		
Uddingston	d	13 16				13 48			14 16				14 44			15 16				15 45		
Airbles	d		13 12				13 42			14 12				14 42			15 12				15 42	
Larkhall	d				13 25							14 25							15 25			
Merryton	d				13 27							14 27							15 27			
Chatelherault	d				13 30							14 30							15 30			
Hamilton Central	d		13 17		13 34		13 47			14 17		14 34		14 47			15 17		15 34		15 47	
Hamilton West	d		13 20		13 36		13 50			14 20		14 36		14 50			15 20		15 36		15 50	
Blantyre	d		13 23		13 40		13 53			14 23		14 40		14 53			15 23		15 40		15 53	
Newton	d		13 27				13 57			14 27				14 57			15 27				15 57	
Cambuslang	d	13 21	13 31			13 53	14 01		14 21	14 31			14 49	15 01		15 21	15 31			15 50	16 01	
Rutherglen	d	13 24	13 35		13 49	13 56	14 05		14 24	14 34		14 48	14 53	15 06		15 24	15 34		15 48	15 53	16 05	
Dalmarnock	d																					
Bridgeton	d	13 27	13 38			13 59	14 08		14 27	14 37			14 57	15 09		15 27	15 37			15 56	16 09	
Edinburgh	d			12 40				13 11			13 40				14 06			14 40				15 08
Haymarket	d			12 44				13 15			13 44				14 10			14 44				15 12
Edinburgh Park	d			12 49				13 20			13 49				14 15			14 49				15 19
Uphall	d			12 57				13 28			13 57				14 27			14 57				15 27
Livingston North	d			13 00				13 31			14 00				14 30			15 00				15 30
Bathgate	a			13 05				13 36			14 05				14 35			15 05				15 35
	d			13 06				13 36			14 06				14 36			15 06				15 36
Armadale	d			13 10				13 40			14 10				14 40			15 10				15 40
Blackridge	d			13 14				13 44			14 14				14 44			15 14				15 44
Caldercruix	d			13 20				13 50			14 20				14 50			15 20				15 50
Drumgelloch	d			13 24				13 54			14 24				14 54			15 24				15 54
Airdrie	d			13 28				13 58			14 28				14 58			15 28				15 58
Coatdyke	d			13 30				14 00			14 30				15 00			15 30				16 00
Coatbridge Sunnyside	d			13 32				14 02			14 32				15 02			15 32				16 02
Blairhill	d			13 35				14 05			14 35				15 05			15 35				16 05
Easterhouse	d			13 39				14 09			14 39				15 09			15 39				16 09
Garrowhill	d			13 41				14 11			14 41				15 11			15 41				16 11
Shettleston	d			13 44				14 14			14 44				15 14			15 44				16 14
Carntyne	d			13 46				14 16			14 46				15 16			15 46				16 16
Springburn	d																					
Barnhill	d																					
Alexandra Parade	d																					
Duke Street	d																					
Bellgrove	d			13 49				14 19			14 49				15 19			15 49				16 19
High Street	d			13 51				14 21			14 51				15 21			15 51				16 21
Glasgow Queen St LL 10	a			13 53				14 24			14 53				15 23			15 53				16 23
	d			13 54				14 24			14 54				15 24			15 54				16 24
Charing Cross	d			13 57				14 27			14 57				15 27			15 57				16 27
Argyle Street	d	13 31	13 42		13 54	14 03	14 11		14 31	14 41		14 53	15 01	15 12		15 31	15 41		15 53	16 00	16 12	
Glasgow Central LL 15	a	13 34	13 44		13 57	14 06	14 14		14 34	14 44		14 57	15 04	15 13		15 34	15 44		15 57	16 03	16 14	
	d	13 34	13 44		13 57	14 06	14 14		14 34	14 44		14 57	15 04	15 13		15 34	15 44		15 57	16 04	16 14	
Anderston	d																					
Exhibition Centre	d	13 38	13 48		14 01	14 10	14 18		14 38	14 48		15 01	15 08	15 17		15 38	15 48		16 01	16 08	16 18	
Partick	d	13 42	13 52	14 02	14a04	14 13	14 22	14 32	14 42	14 52	15 02	15a04	15 12	15 21	15 32	15 42	15 52	16 02	16a04	16 12	16 22	16 32
Hyndland	d	13 45	13 54	14 04		14 15	14 24	14 34	14 45	14 54	15 04		15 15	15 23	15 34	15 45	15 54	16 04		16 15	16 24	16 34
Jordanhill	d		13 56				14 26			14 56				15 25			15 56				16 26	
Scotstounhill	d		13 58				14 28			14 58				15 27			15 58				16 28	
Garscadden	d		14 00				14 30			15 00				15 29			16 00				16 30	
Yoker	d		14 03				14 33			15 03				15 32			16 03				16 33	
Clydebank	d		14 05				14 35			15 05				15 34			16 05				16 35	
Anniesland	d	13 48		14 07		14 18		14 37	14 48		15 07		15 18		15 37	15 48		16 07		16 18		16 37
Westerton	d	13 51		14 10		14 21		14 40	14 51		15 10		15 21		15 40	15 51		16 10		16 21		16 40
Bearsden	d	13 55				14 25			14 55				15 25			15 55				16 25		
Hillfoot	d	13 57				14 27			14 57				15 27			15 57				16 27		
Milngavie	a	14 00				14 30			15 00				15 30			16 00				16 30		
Drumchapel	d			14 12				14 42			15 12				15 42			16 12				16 42
Drumry	d			14 14				14 44			15 14				15 44			16 14				16 44
Singer	d			14 17				14 47			15 17				15 47			16 17				16 47
Dalmuir	a		14 09	14 19			14 39	14 50		15 09	15 19			15 38	15 49		16 09	16 19			16 39	16 49
	d		14 09	14 20			14 39	14 50		15 09	15 20			15 38	15 50		16 09	16 20			16 39	16 50
Kilpatrick	d		14 11				14 41			15 11				15 41			16 11				16 41	
Bowling	d		14 14				14 44			15 14				15 44			16 14				16 44	
Dumbarton East	d		14 19	14 28			14 49	14 58		15 19	15 28			15 48	15 57		16 19	16 28			16 49	16 57
Dumbarton Central	d		14 21	14 30			14 51	15 00		15 21	15 30			15 50	16 00		16 21	16 30			16 51	17 00
Dalreoch	d		14 22	14 31			14 52	15 01		15 22	15 31			15 52	16 01		16 22	16 31			16 52	17 01
Renton	d		14 25				14 55			15 25				15 55			16 25				16 55	
Alexandria	d		14 28				14 58			15 28				15 57			16 28				16 58	
Balloch	a		14 30				15 01			15 30				16 00			16 30				17 00	
Cardross	d			14 36				15 06			15 36				16 06			16 36				17 06
Craigendoran	d			14 41				15 11			15 41				16 11			16 41				17 11
Helensburgh Central	a			14 44				15 14			15 44				16 14			16 44				17 14

Table 226

Sundays
26 June to 30 October

Lanark, Coatbridge, Motherwell, Larkhall, Hamilton, Edinburgh and Bathgate, Airdrie and Springburn - Glasgow - Milngavie, Dalmuir, Balloch and Helensburgh

		SR	SR	SR	SR	SR	SR	SR	SR	SR	SR	SR	SR	SR	SR	SR	SR	SR	SR	SR	SR	SR	SR
														◇ A									
Lanark	d					16 12							17 12								18 14		
Carluke	d					16 22							17 22								18 23		
Wishaw	d					16 27							17 27								18 28		
Holytown	d																						
Shieldmuir	d					16 31							17 31								18 32		
Coatbridge Central	d																						
Whifflet	d																						
Motherwell	a					16 34							17 34								18 36		
	d	16 06	16 10			16 34	16 40		17 06	17 10			17 34		17 40		18 06	18 10			18 36	18 40	
Bellshill	d	16 12				16 40			17 12				17 40				18 12				18 42		
Uddingston	d	16 16				16 44			17 16				17 44				18 16				18 46		
Airbles	d		16 12				16 42			17 12					17 42			18 12				18 42	
Larkhall	d				16 25							17 25								18 25			
Merryton	d				16 27							17 27								18 27			
Chatelherault	d				16 30							17 30								18 30			
Hamilton Central	d		16 17		16 34		16 47			17 17		17 34			17 47			18 17		18 34		18 47	
Hamilton West	d		16 20		16 36		16 50			17 20		17 36			17 50			18 20		18 36		18 50	
Blantyre	d		16 23		16 40		16 53			17 23		17 40			17 53			18 23		18 40		18 53	
Newton	d		16 27				16 57			17 27					17 57			18 27				18 57	
Cambuslang	d	16 21	16 31			16 49	17 01		17 21	17 31			17 49		18 01		18 21	18 31			18 51	19 01	
Rutherglen	d	16 24	16 34		16 48	16 53	17 06		17 24	17 34		17 48	17 54		18 04		18 24	18 34		18 48	18 54	19 06	
Dalmarnock	d																						
Bridgeton	d	16 27	16 37			16 57	17 09		17 27	17 37			17 57		18 08		18 27	18 37			18 57	19 09	
Edinburgh	d			15 40				16 10			16 40					17 07			17 39				18 10
Haymarket	d			15 44				16 14			16 44					17 11			17 44				18 14
Edinburgh Park	d			15 49				16 19			16 49					17 16			17 49				18 19
Uphall	d			15 57				16 27			16 57					17 25			17 57				18 27
Livingston North	d			16 00				16 30			17 00					17 28			18 00				18 30
Bathgate	a			16 05				16 36			17 05					17 33			18 05				18 35
	d			16 06				16 36			17 06					17 36			18 06				18 36
Armadale	d			16 10				16 40			17 10					17 40			18 10				18 40
Blackridge	d			16 14				16 44			17 14					17 44			18 14				18 44
Caldercruix	d			16 20				16 50			17 20					17 50			18 20				18 50
Drumgelloch	d			16 24				16 54			17 24					17 54			18 24				18 54
Airdrie	d			16 28				16 58			17 28					17 58			18 28				18 58
Coatdyke	d			16 30				17 00			17 30					18 00			18 30				19 00
Coatbridge Sunnyside	d			16 32				17 02			17 32					18 02			18 32				19 02
Blairhill	d			16 35				17 05			17 35					18 05			18 35				19 05
Easterhouse	d			16 39				17 09			17 39					18 09			18 39				19 09
Garrowhill	d			16 41				17 11			17 41					18 11			18 41				19 11
Shettleston	d			16 44				17 14			17 44					18 14			18 44				19 14
Carntyne	d			16 46				17 16			17 46					18 16			18 46				19 16
Springburn	d																						
Barnhill	d																						
Alexandra Parade	d																						
Duke Street	d																						
Bellgrove	d			16 49				17 19			17 49					18 19			18 49				19 19
High Street	d			16 51				17 21			17 51					18 21			18 51				19 21
Glasgow Queen St LL 10	a			16 53				17 24			17 53					18 23			18 53				19 24
	d			16 54				17 24			17 54			18b20		18 24			18 54				19 24
Charing Cross	d			16 57				17 27			17 57					18 27			18 57				19 27
Argyle Street	d	16 31	16 41		16 53	17 01	17 12		17 31	17 41		17 53	18 01		18 12								
Glasgow Central LL 15	a	16 34	16 44		16 57	17 04	17 14		17 34	17 44		17 57	18 04		18 14		18 34	18 44		18 56	19 04	19 14	
	d	16 34	16 44		16 57	17 04	17 14		17 34	17 44		17 57	18 05		18 14		18 34	18 44		18 57	19 04	19 14	
Anderston	d																						
Exhibition Centre	d	16 38	16 48		17 01	17 09	17 18		17 38	17 48		18 01	18 09		18 18		18 38	18 48		19 01	19 08	19 18	
Partick	d	16 42	16 52	17 02	17a04	17 13	17 22	17 32	17 42	17 52	18 02	18a04	18 13		18 22	18 32	18 42	18 52	19 02	19a04	19 11	19 22	19 32
Hyndland	d	16 45	16 54	17 04		17 15	17 24	17 34	17 45	17 54	18 04		18 16		18 24	18 34	18 46	18 54	19 04		19 13	19 24	19 34
Jordanhill	d		16 56				17 26			17 56					18 26			18 56				19 26	
Scotstounhill	d		16 58				17 28			17 58					18 28			18 58				19 28	
Garscadden	d		17 00				17 30			18 00					18 30			19 00				19 30	
Yoker	d		17 03				17 33			18 03					18 33			19 03				19 33	
Clydebank	d		17 05				17 35			18 05					18 35			19 05				19 35	
Anniesland	d	16 48		17 07		17 18		17 37	17 48		18 07		18 19			18 37	18 49		19 07		19 19		19 37
Westerton	d	16 51		17 10		17 21		17 40	17 51		18 10		18 22			18 40	18 52		19 10		19 22		19 40
Bearsden	d	16 55				17 25			17 55				18 25				18 55				19 25		
Hillfoot	d	16 57				17 27			17 57				18 27				18 57				19 27		
Milngavie	a	17 00				17 30			18 00				18 30				19 00				19 30		
Drumchapel	d			17 12				17 42			18 12					18 42			19 12				19 42
Drumry	d			17 14				17 44			18 14					18 44			19 14				19 44
Singer	d			17 17				17 47			18 17					18 47			19 17				19 47
Dalmuir	a		17 09	17 19			17 39	17 50		18 09	18 19			18 34	18 39	18 49		19 09	19 19			19 39	19 50
	d		17 09	17 20			17 39	17 50		18 09	18 20			18 34	18 39	18 50		19 09	19 20			19 39	19 50
Kilpatrick	d		17 11				17 41			18 11					18 41			19 11				19 41	
Bowling	d		17 14				17 44			18 14					18 44			19 14				19 44	
Dumbarton East	d		17 19	17 28			17 49	17 58		18 19	18 28				18 49	18 58		19 19	19 28			19 49	19 58
Dumbarton Central	d		17 21	17 30			17 51	18 00		18 21	18 30			18 44	18 51	19 00		19 21	19 30			19 51	20 00
Dalreoch	d		17 22	17 31			17 52	18 01		18 22	18 31				18 52	19 01		19 22	19 31			19 52	20 01
Renton	d		17 25				17 55			18 25					18 55			19 25				19 55	
Alexandria	d		17 28				17 58			18 28					18 58			19 28				19 58	
Balloch	a		17 30				18 00			18 30					19 00			19 30				20 00	
Cardross	d			17 36				18 06			18 36					19 06			19 36				20 06
Craigendoran	d			17 41				18 11			18 40					19 11			19 41				20 11
Helensburgh Central	a			17 44				18 14			18 44			18c59		19 14			19 44				20 14

A To Oban

b Glasgow Queen St High Level

c Helensburgh Upper

Table 226

Sundays
26 June to 30 October

Lanark, Coatbridge, Motherwell, Larkhall, Hamilton, Edinburgh and Bathgate, Airdrie and Springburn - Glasgow - Milngavie, Dalmuir, Balloch and Helensburgh

		SR	SR	SR	SR	SR	SR	SR	SR	SR	SR	SR	SR	SR	SR	SR	SR	SR	SR	SR	SR	SR
Lanark	d						19 12								20 12							21 12
Carluke	d						19 22								20 23							21 23
Wishaw	d						19 27								20 30							21 28
Holytown	d																					
Shieldmuir	d						19 31								20 34							21 32
Coatbridge Central	d																					
Whifflet	d																					
Motherwell	a						19 34								20 37							21 35
	d	19 06	19 10				19 34	19 40		20 06	20 10				20 37	20 40		21 06	21 10			21 36
Bellshill	d	19 12					19 40			20 12					20 43			21 12				21 42
Uddingston	d	19 16					19 44			20 19					20 47			21 16				21 46
Airbles	d		19 12					19 42			20 12					20 42			21 12			
Larkhall	d					19 25								20 25							21 25	
Merryton	d					19 27								20 27							21 27	
Chatelherault	d					19 30								20 30							21 30	
Hamilton Central	d		19 17			19 34		19 47			20 17			20 34		20 47			21 17		21 34	
Hamilton West	d		19 20			19 36		19 50			20 20			20 36		20 50			21 20		21 36	
Blantyre	d		19 23			19 40		19 53			20 23			20 40		20 53			21 23		21 40	
Newton	d		19 27					19 57			20 27					20 57			21 28			
Cambuslang	d	19 21	19 31				19 49	20 01		20 24	20 31				20 52	21 01		21 21	21 32			21 51
Rutherglen	d	19 24	19 34			19 49	19 53	20 04		20 27	20 34			20 48	20 56	21 04		21 25	21 35		21 48	21 54
Dalmarnock	d																					
Bridgeton	d	19 27	19 37				19 57	20 07		20 30	20 37				20 59	21 07		21 28	21 38			21 57
Edinburgh	d			18 40	19 10							19 40	20 08							20 40		
Haymarket	d			18 44	19 14							19 44	20 12							20 44		
Edinburgh Park	d			18 49	19 19							19 49	20 17							20 49		
Uphall	d			18 57	19 27							19 57	20 25							20 57		
Livingston North	d			19 00	19 30							20 00	20 28							21 00		
Bathgate	a			19 05	19 35							20 05	20 33							21 05		
	d			19 06								20 06								21 06		
Armadale	d			19 10								20 10								21 10		
Blackridge	d			19 14								20 14								21 14		
Caldercruix	d			19 20								20 20								21 20		
Drumgelloch	d			19 24								20 24								21 24		
Airdrie	d			19 28					19 58			20 28					20 58			21 28		
Coatdyke	d			19 30					20 00			20 30					21 00			21 30		
Coatbridge Sunnyside	d			19 32					20 02			20 32					21 02			21 32		
Blairhill	d			19 35					20 05			20 35					21 05			21 35		
Easterhouse	d			19 39					20 09			20 39					21 09			21 39		
Garrowhill	d			19 41					20 11			20 41					21 11			21 41		
Shettleston	d			19 44					20 14			20 44					21 14			21 44		
Carntyne	d			19 46					20 16			20 46					21 16			21 46		
Springburn	d																					
Barnhill	d																					
Alexandra Parade	d																					
Duke Street	d																					
Bellgrove	d			19 49					20 19			20 49					21 19			21 49		
High Street	d			19 51					20 21			20 51					21 21			21 51		
Glasgow Queen St LL 10	a			19 53					20 23			20 54					21 23			21 53		
	d			19 54					20 24			20 54					21 24			21 54		
Charing Cross	d			19 57					20 27			20 57					21 27			21 57		
Argyle Street	d																					
Glasgow Central LL 15	a	19 34	19 44			19 57	20 04	20 14		20 34	20 44			20 57	21 04	21 14		21 34	21 44		21 56	22 04
	d	19 34	19 44			19 57	20 04	20 14		20 34	20 44			20 58	21 04	21 14		21 34	21 44		21 57	22 04
Anderston	d																					
Exhibition Centre	d	19 38	19 48			20 01	20 08	20 18		20 38	20 48			21 01	21 08	21 18		21 38	21 48		22 01	22 08
Partick	d	19 42	19 52	20 02		20a04	20 12	20 22	20 32	20 42	20 52	21 02		21a05	21 12	21 22	21 32	21 42	21 52	22 02	22a04	22 12
Hyndland	d	19 46	19 54	20 04			20 16	20 24	20 34	20 46	20 54	21 04			21 16	21 24	21 34	21 46	21 54	22 04		22 16
Jordanhill	d		19 56					20 26			20 56					21 26			21 56			
Scotstounhill	d		19 58					20 28			20 58					21 28			21 58			
Garscadden	d		20 00					20 30			21 00					21 30			22 00			
Yoker	d		20 03					20 33			21 03					21 33			22 03			
Clydebank	d		20 05					20 35			21 05					21 35			22 05			
Anniesland	d	19 49		20 07			20 19		20 37	20 49		21 07			21 19		21 37	21 49		22 07		22 19
Westerton	d	19 52		20 10			20 22		20 40	20 52		21 10			21 22		21 40	21 52		22 10		22 22
Bearsden	d	19 55					20 25			20 55					21 25			21 55				22 25
Hillfoot	d	19 57					20 27			20 57					21 27			21 57				22 27
Milngavie	a	20 00					20 30			21 00					21 30			22 00				22 30
Drumchapel	d			20 12					20 42			21 12					21 42			22 12		
Drumry	d			20 14					20 44			21 14					21 44			22 14		
Singer	d			20 17					20 47			21 17					21 47			22 17		
Dalmuir	a		20 09	20 19				20 39	20 49		21 09	21 20				21 39	21 49		22 09	22 19		
	d		20 09	20 20				20 39	20 50		21 09	21 20				21 39	21 50		22 09	22 20		
Kilpatrick	d		20 11					20 41			21 11					21 41			22 11			
Bowling	d		20 14					20 44			21 14					21 44			22 14			
Dumbarton East	d		20 19	20 28				20 49	20 58		21 19	21 28				21 49	21 58		22 19	22 28		
Dumbarton Central	d		20 21	20 30				20 51	21 00		21 21	21 30				21 51	22 00		22 21	22 30		
Dalreoch	d		20 22	20 31				20 52	21 01		21 22	21 31				21 52	22 01		22 22	22 31		
Renton	d		20 25					20 55			21 25					21 55			22 25			
Alexandria	d		20 28					20 58			21 28					21 58			22 28			
Balloch	a		20 30					21 01			21 30					22 00			22 30			
Cardross	d			20 36					21 06			21 36					22 06			22 36		
Craigendoran	d			20 41					21 11			21 41					22 11			22 41		
Helensburgh Central	a			20 44					21 14			21 45					22 14			22 44		

Sundays

26 June to 30 October

Lanark, Coatbridge, Motherwell, Larkhall, Hamilton, Edinburgh and Bathgate, Airdrie and Springburn - Glasgow - Milngavie, Dalmuir, Balloch and Helensburgh

		SR	SR	SR	SR	SR	SR	SR	SR	SR		SR	SR	SR	SR
Lanark	d							22 12							
Carluke	d							22 23							
Wishaw	d							22 28							
Holytown	d														
Shieldmuir	d							22 32							
Coatbridge Central	d														
Whifflet	d														
Motherwell	a							22 35							
	d	21 40		22 06	22 10			22 36	22 40			23 06	23 10		
Bellshill	d			22 12				22 42				23 12			
Uddingston	d			22 15				22 46				23 16			
Airbles	d	21 42			22 12				22 42				23 12		
Larkhall	d						22 25								
Merryton	d						22 27								
Chatelherault	d						22 30								
Hamilton Central	d	21 47			22 17		22 34		22 47				23 17		
Hamilton West	d	21 50			22 20		22 36		22 50				23 20		
Blantyre	d	21 53			22 23		22 40		22 53				23 23		
Newton	d	21 57			22 27				22 57				23 27		
Cambuslang	d	22 01		22 20	22 31			22 51	23 01			23 21	23 31		
Rutherglen	d	22 06		22 23	22 34		22 48	22 54	23 04			23 24	23 34		
Dalmarnock	d														
Bridgeton	d	22 09		22 27	22 37			22 57	23 07			23 27	23 37		
Edinburgh	d					21 38								22 40	23 18
Haymarket	d					21 42								22 44	23 22
Edinburgh Park	d					21 47								22 49	23 27
Uphall	d					21 55								22 57	23 35
Livingston North	d					21 58								23 00	23 38
Bathgate	a					22 03								23 05	23 43
	d					22 06								23 06	
Armadale	d					22 10								23 10	
Blackridge	d					22 14								23 14	
Caldercruix	d					22 20								23 20	
Drumgelloch	d					22 24								23 24	
Airdrie	d		21 58			22 28				22 58				23 28	
Coatdyke	d		22 00			22 30				23 00				23 30	
Coatbridge Sunnyside	d		22 02			22 32				23 02				23 32	
Blairhill	d		22 05			22 35				23 05				23 35	
Easterhouse	d		22 09			22 39				23 09				23 39	
Garrowhill	d		22 11			22 41				23 11				23 41	
Shettleston	d		22 14			22 44				23 14				23 44	
Carntyne	d		22 16			22 46				23 16				23 46	
Springburn	d														
Barnhill	d														
Alexandra Parade	d														
Duke Street	d														
Bellgrove	d		22 19			22 49				23 19				23 49	
High Street	d		22 21			22 51				23 21				23 51	
Glasgow Queen St LL 10	a		22 23			22 53				23 23				23 53	
	d		22 24			22 54				23 24				23 54	
Charing Cross	d		22 27			22 57				23 27				23 57	
Argyle Street	d														
Glasgow Central LL 15	a	22 14		22 34	22 44		22 57	23 04	23 14			23 34	23 44		
	d	22 14		22 34	22 44		22 57	23 04	23 14			23 34	23 44		
Anderston	d														
Exhibition Centre	d	22 18		22 38	22 48		23 01	23 08	23 18			23 38	23 48		
Partick	d	22 22	22 32	22 42	22 52	23 02	23a04	23 12	23 22	23 32		23 42	23 52	00 01	
Hyndland	d	22 24	22 34	22 46	22 54	23 04		23 16	23 24	23 34		23 44	23 54	00 03	
Jordanhill	d	22 26			22 56				23 26			23 46	23 56	00 05	
Scotstounhill	d	22 28			22 58				23 28			23 48	23 58	00 07	
Garscadden	d	22 30			23 00				23 30			23a50	00a01	00 09	
Yoker	d	22 33			23 03				23 33					00 12	
Clydebank	d	22 35			23 05				23 35						
Anniesland	d		22 37	22 49		23 07		23 19		23 37					
Westerton	d		22 40	22 52		23 10		23 22		23 40					
Bearsden	d			22 55				23 25							
Hillfoot	d			22 57				23 27							
Milngavie	a			23 00				23 30							
Drumchapel	d		22 42			23 12				23 42					
Drumry	d		22 44			23 14				23 44					
Singer	d		22 47			23 17				23 47					
Dalmuir	a	22 39	22 49		23 09	23 19			23 39	23 49				00 16	
	d	22 39	22 50		23 09	23 20			23 39	23 50					
Kilpatrick	d	22 41			23 11				23 41						
Bowling	d	22 44			23 14				23 44						
Dumbarton East	d	22 49	22 58		23 19	23 28			23 49	23 58					
Dumbarton Central	d	22 51	23 00		23 21	23 30			23 51	23 59					
Dalreoch	d	22 52	23 01		23 22	23 31			23 52	00 01					
Renton	d	22 55			23 25				23 55						
Alexandria	d	22 58			23 28				23 58						
Balloch	a	23 00			23 30				00 01						
Cardross	d		23 06			23 36				00 06					
Craigendoran	d		23 11			23 41				00 11					
Helensburgh Central	a		23 14			23 44				00 14					

6 November to 27 November

Lanark, Coatbridge, Motherwell, Larkhall, Hamilton, Edinburgh and Bathgate, Airdrie and Springburn - Glasgow - Milngavie, Dalmuir, Balloch and Helensburgh

		SR	SR	SR	SR	SR	SR	SR A	SR	SR		SR	SR	SR	SR	SR	SR B	SR B	SR	SR		SR	SR B	SR	SR B
Lanark	d																								
Carluke	d																								
Wishaw	d																								
Holytown	d							23p59																	
Shieldmuir	d																								
Coatbridge Central	d																								
Whifflet	d																								
Motherwell	a																								
	d													08 36	08 40				09 10					09 36	
Bellshill	d							00 02						08 42										09 42	
Uddingston	d							00 06						08 46										09 46	
Airbles	d														08 42				09 12						
Larkhall	d																					09 25			
Merryton	d																					09 27			
Chatelherault	d																					09 30			
Hamilton Central	d														08 47				09 17			09 34			
Hamilton West	d														08 50				09 20			09 36			
Blantyre	d														08 53				09 23			09 40			
Newton	d														08 57				09 27						
Cambuslang	d							00 12						08 51	09 01				09 31					09 51	
Rutherglen	d													08 54	09 04				09 34			09 48		09 54	
Dalmarnock	d																								
Bridgeton	d													08 57	09 07				09 37					09 57	
Edinburgh	d		22p19		22p51	23p37	23p51													08 37					
Haymarket	d		22p23		22p55	23p42	23p55													08 41					
Edinburgh Park	d		22p30		23p00	23p47	23p59													08 46					
Uphall	d		22p38		23p08	23p55	00 08													08 57					
Livingston North	d		22p41		23p11	23p59	00 11													09 00					
Bathgate	a		22p46		23p16	00 04	00 16													09 06					
	d		22p47		23p17								08 06							09 06					
Armadale	d		22p51		23p21								08 10							09 10					
Blackridge	d		22p55		23p25								08 14							09 14					
Caldercruix	d		23p01		23p31								08 20							09 20					
Drumgelloch	d		23p05		23p35								08 24							09 24					
Airdrie	d		23p12		23p38					07 58			08 28			08 58		09 13		09 28					09 38
Coatdyke	d		23p14		23p40					08 00			08 30			09 00		09 15		09 30					09 45
Coatbridge Sunnyside	d		23p16		23p43					08 02			08 32			09 02		09 17		09 32					09 47
Blairhill	d		23p19		23p45					08 05			08 35			09 05		09 20		09 35					09 50
Easterhouse	d		23p23		23p49					08 09			08 39			09 09		09 24		09 39					09 54
Garrowhill	d		23p25		23p52					08 11			08 41			09 11		09 26		09 41					09 56
Shettleston	d		23p28		23p54					08 14			08 44			09 14		09 29		09 44					09 59
Carntyne	d		23p30		23p56					08 16			08 46			09 16		09 31		09 46					10 01
Springburn	d	23p09		23p39													09 19						09 49		
Barnhill	d	23p10		23p40													09 20						09 50		
Alexandra Parade	d	23p13		23p43													09 23						09 53		
Duke Street	d	23p15		23p45													09 25						09 55		
Bellgrove	d	23p17	23p33	23p47	23p59					08 19			08 49			09 19	09 27	09 34		09 49			09 57		10 04
High Street	d	23p19	23p35	23p49	00 02					08 21			08 51			09 21	09 29	09 36		09 51			09 59		10 06
Glasgow Queen St LL 10	a	23p21	23p37	23p51	00 04					08 23			08 53			09 23	09 31	09 39		09 54			10 01		10 09
	d	23p23	23p45	23p53	00 04					08 24			08 54			09 24	09 31	09 39		09 54			10 01		10 09
Charing Cross	d	23p25	23p47	23p55	00 06					08 27			08 57			09 27	09 33	09 42		09 57			10 03		10 12
Argyle Street	d																							10 01	
Glasgow Central LL 15	a							00b23						09 04	09 14				09 44			09 56		10 04	
	d													09 04	09 14				09 44			09 57		10 04	
Anderston	d																								
Exhibition Centre	d													09 08	09 18				09 48			10 01		10 08	
Partick	d	23p29	23p51	23p59	00 11					08 32			09 02	09 12	09 22	09 32	09 37	09 46	09 52	10 02		10a05	10 08	10 12	10 17
Hyndland	d	23p32	23p53	00 02	00 13					08 34			09 04	09 16	09 24	09 34	09 39	09 48	09 54	10 04			10 10	10 15	10 19
Jordanhill	d		23p55	00 04	00 15										09 26		09 41		09 56				10 12		
Scotstounhill	d		23p58	00 06	00 17										09 28		09 43		09 58				10 14		
Garscadden	d		23p59	00a08	00a19										09 30		09 46		10 00				10 17		
Yoker	d		00 02						08 33			09 03			09 33		09 48		10 03				10 19		
Clydebank	d		00 04						08 35			09 05			09 35		09 50		10 05				10 21		
Anniesland	d	23p35								08 37			09 07	09 19		09 37		09 51		10 07				10 18	10 22
Westerton	d	23p38								08 40			09 10	09 22		09 40		09 54		10 10				10 21	10 25
Bearsden	d													09 25										10 25	
Hillfoot	d													09 27										10 27	
Milngavie	a													09 30										10 30	
Drumchapel	d	23p40								08 42			09 12			09 42		09 57		10 13					10 27
Drumry	d	23p42								08 44			09 14			09 44		09 59		10 15					10 29
Singer	d	23p45								08 47			09 17			09 47		10 02		10 17					10 32
Dalmuir	a	23p47	00 08						08 38	08 49		09 08	09 19		09 39	09 49	09 53	10 04	10 09	10 20			10 24		10 34
	d	23p48	00 08						08 39	08 50		09 09	09 20		09 39	09 50			10 09	10 20					
Kilpatrick	d	23p51							08 41			09 11			09 41				10 11						
Bowling	d	23p54							08 44			09 14			09 44				10 14						
Dumbarton East	d	23p58	00 15						08 49	08 58		09 19	09 28		09 49	09 58			10 19	10 28					
Dumbarton Central	d	23p59	00 18						08 51	09 00		09 21	09 30		09 51	10 00			10 21	10 30					
Dalreoch	d	00 02	00 19						08 52	09 01		09 22	09 31		09 52	10 01			10 22	10 31					
Renton	d	00 05							08 55			09 25			09 55				10 25						
Alexandria	d	00 07							08 58			09 28			09 58				10 28						
Balloch	a	00 10							09 00			09 30			10 00				10 30						
Cardross	d		00 24							09 06			09 36			10 06				10 36					
Craigendoran	d		00 29							09 11			09 41			10 11				10 41					
Helensburgh Central	a		00 32							09 14			09 44			10 14				10 44					

A From Edinburgh

B 27 November

b Glasgow Central High Level

Table 226

6 November to 27 November

Lanark, Coatbridge, Motherwell, Larkhall, Hamilton, Edinburgh and Bathgate, Airdrie and Springburn - Glasgow - Milngavie, Dalmuir, Balloch and Helensburgh

		SR	SR	SR A	SR	SR A	SR	SR	SR	SR A	SR	SR A	SR	SR	SR A	SR	SR A	SR	SR	SR	SR A	SR	SR A
Lanark	d										10 12											11 12	
Carluke	d										10 22											11 22	
Wishaw	d										10 27											11 27	
Holytown	d																						
Shieldmuir	d										10 31											11 31	
Coatbridge Central	d																						
Whifflet	d																						
Motherwell	a										10 34											11 34	
	d	09 40			10 06		10 10				10 36		10 40			11 10		11 10				11 36	
Bellshill	d				10 12						10 42					11 16						11 42	
Uddingston	d				10 18						10 47					11 20						11 46	
Airbles	d	09 42					10 12						10 42					11 12					
Larkhall	d								10 25											11 25			
Merryton	d								10 27											11 27			
Chatelherault	d								10 30											11 30			
Hamilton Central	d	09 47					10 17		10 34				10 47					11 17		11 34			
Hamilton West	d	09 50					10 20		10 36				10 50					11 20		11 36			
Blantyre	d	09 53					10 23		10 40				10 53					11 23		11 40			
Newton	d	09 57					10 27						10 57					11 27					
Cambuslang	d	10 01			10 23		10 31				10 52		11 01			11 25		11 31				11 51	
Rutherglen	d	10 04			10 26		10 34		10 48		10 56		11 06			11 29		11 34		11 48		11 53	
Dalmarnock	d																						
Bridgeton	d	10 07			10 29		10 37				10 59		11 09			11 32		11 37				11 56	
Edinburgh	d							09 37											10 40				
Haymarket	d							09 41											10 44				
Edinburgh Park	d							09 46											10 49				
Uphall	d							09 57											10 57				
Livingston North	d							10 00											11 00				
Bathgate	a							10 05											11 05				
	d							10 06											11 06				
Armadale	d							10 10											11 10				
Blackridge	d							10 14											11 14				
Caldercruix	d							10 20											11 20				
Drumgelloch	d							10 24											11 24				
Airdrie	d		09 58			10 13		10 28				10 38		10 58			11 13		11 28				11 38
Coatdyke	d		10 00			10 15		10 30				10 45		11 00			11 15		11 30				11 45
Coatbridge Sunnyside	d		10 02			10 17		10 32				10 47		11 02			11 17		11 32				11 47
Blairhill	d		10 05			10 20		10 35				10 50		11 05			11 20		11 35				11 50
Easterhouse	d		10 09			10 24		10 39				10 54		11 09			11 24		11 39				11 54
Garrowhill	d		10 11			10 26		10 41				10 56		11 11			11 26		11 41				11 56
Shettleston	d		10 14			10 29		10 44				10 59		11 14			11 29		11 44				11 59
Carntyne	d		10 16			10 31		10 46				11 01		11 16			11 31		11 46				12 01
Springburn	d			10 19						10 49					11 19						11 49		
Barnhill	d			10 20						10 50					11 20						11 50		
Alexandra Parade	d			10 23						10 53					11 23						11 53		
Duke Street	d			10 25						10 55					11 25						11 55		
Bellgrove	d		10 19	10 27		10 34		10 49		10 57		11 04		11 19	11 27		11 34		11 49		11 57		12 04
High Street	d		10 21	10 29		10 36		10 51		10 59		11 06		11 21	11 29		11 36		11 51		11 59		12 06
Glasgow Queen St LL	a		10 23	10 31		10 39		10 54		11 01		11 09		11 23	11 31		11 39		11 53		12 01		12 09
	d		10 24	10 31		10 39		10 54		11 01		11 09		11 24	11 31		11 39		11 54		12 01		12 09
Charing Cross	d		10 27	10 33		10 42		10 57		11 03		11 12		11 27	11 33		11 42		11 57		12 03		12 12
Argyle Street	d	10 11			10 33		10 41		10 53		11 02		11 12			11 35		11 41		11 53		12 01	
Glasgow Central LL	a	10 14			10 34		10 44		10 57		11 04		11 14			11 36		11 44		11 57		12 04	
	d	10 14			10 34		10 44		10 57		11 04		11 14			11 36		11 44		11 57		12 04	
Anderston	d																						
Exhibition Centre	d	10 18			10 38		10 48		11 01		11 08		11 18			11 40		11 48		12 01		12 08	
Partick	d	10 22	10 32	10 37	10 42	10 47	10 52	11 02	11a05	11 07	11 12	11 16	11 22	11 32	11 37	11 43	11 47	11 52	12 02	12a04	12 09	12 12	12 17
Hyndland	d	10 24	10 34	10 39	10 45	10 49	10 54	11 04		11 09	11 15	11 18	11 24	11 34	11 39	11 45	11 49	11 54	12 04		12 11	12 15	12 19
Jordanhill	d	10 26		10 41			10 56			11 11			11 26		11 41			11 56			12 13		
Scotstounhill	d	10 28		10 43			10 58			11 13			11 28		11 43			11 58			12 15		
Garscadden	d	10 30		10 46			11 00			11 16			11 30		11 46			12 00			12 18		
Yoker	d	10 33		10 48			11 03			11 18			11 33		11 48			12 03			12 20		
Clydebank	d	10 35		10 50			11 05			11 20			11 35		11 50			12 05			12 22		
Anniesland	d		10 37		10 48	10 52		11 07			11 18	11 22		11 37		11 48	11 52		12 07			12 18	12 22
Westerton	d		10 40		10 51	10 55		11 10			11 21	11 24		11 40		11 51	11 55		12 10			12 21	12 25
Bearsden	d				10 55						11 25					11 55						12 25	
Hillfoot	d				10 57						11 27					11 57						12 27	
Milngavie	a				11 00						11 30					12 00						12 30	
Drumchapel	d		10 42			10 57		11 12				11 26		11 42			11 57		12 12				12 27
Drumry	d		10 44			10 59		11 14				11 28		11 44			11 59		12 14				12 29
Singer	d		10 47			11 02		11 17				11 32		11 47			12 02		12 17				12 32
Dalmuir	a	10 39	10 49	10 53		11 04	11 09	11 19		11 24		11 33	11 39	11 49	11 53		12 04	12 09	12 19		12 25		12 34
	d	10 39	10 50				11 09	11 20					11 39	11 50				12 09	12 20				
Kilpatrick	d	10 41					11 11						11 41					12 11					
Bowling	d	10 44					11 14						11 44					12 14					
Dumbarton East	d	10 49	10 58				11 19	11 28					11 49	11 58				12 19	12 28				
Dumbarton Central	d	10 51	11 00				11 21	11 30					11 51	12 00				12 21	12 30				
Dalreoch	d	10 52	11 01				11 22	11 31					11 52	12 01				12 22	12 31				
Renton	d	10 55					11 25						11 55					12 25					
Alexandria	d	10 58					11 28						11 58					12 28					
Balloch	a	11 00					11 30						12 00					12 30					
Cardross	d		11 06					11 36						12 06					12 36				
Craigendoran	d		11 11					11 41						12 11					12 41				
Helensburgh Central	a		11 14					11 44						12 14					12 44				

A 27 November

Table 226

6 November to 27 November

Lanark, Coatbridge, Motherwell, Larkhall, Hamilton, Edinburgh and Bathgate, Airdrie and Springburn - Glasgow - Milngavie, Dalmuir, Balloch and Helensburgh

		SR	SR	SR A	SR	SR A	SR	SR	SR	SR A	SR	SR A	SR	SR	SR A	SR	SR A	SR	SR	SR	SR A	SR
Lanark	d										12 12											13 12
Carluke	d										12 22											13 22
Wishaw	d										12 27											13 27
Holytown	d																					
Shieldmuir	d										12 31											13 30
Coatbridge Central	d																					
Whifflet	d																					
Motherwell	a										12 34											13 36
	d	11 40			12 07		12 10				12 36		12 40			13 06		13 10				13 36
Bellshill	d				12 13						12 42					13 12						13 42
Uddingston	d				12 17						12 46					13 16						13 48
Airbles	d	11 42					12 12						12 42					13 12				
Larkhall	d								12 25											13 25		
Merryton	d								12 27											13 27		
Chatelherault	d								12 30											13 30		
Hamilton Central	d	11 47					12 17		12 34				12 47					13 17		13 34		
Hamilton West	d	11 50					12 20		12 36				12 50					13 20		13 36		
Blantyre	d	11 53					12 23		12 40				12 53					13 23		13 40		
Newton	d	11 57					12 27						12 57					13 27				
Cambuslang	d	12 01			12 22		12 31				12 51		13 01			13 21		13 31				13 53
Rutherglen	d	12 07			12 25		12 35		12 46		12 54		13 04			13 24		13 35		13 49		13 56
Dalmarnock	d																					
Bridgeton	d	12 10			12 28		12 38				12 57		13 07			13 27		13 38				13 59
Edinburgh	d							11 40						12 08					12 40			
Haymarket	d							11 44						12 12					12 44			
Edinburgh Park	d							11 49						12 17					12 49			
Uphall	d							11 57						12 25					12 57			
Livingston North	d							12 00						12 28					13 00			
Bathgate	a							12 05						12 33					13 05			
	d							12 06						12 36					13 06			
Armadale	d							12 10						12 40					13 10			
Blackridge	d							12 14						12 44					13 14			
Caldercruix	d							12 20						12 50					13 20			
Drumgelloch	d							12 24						12 54					13 24			
Airdrie	d		11 58			12 13		12 28				12 43		12 58			13 13		13 28			
Coatdyke	d		12 00			12 15		12 30				12 45		13 00			13 15		13 30			
Coatbridge Sunnyside	d		12 02			12 17		12 32				12 47		13 02			13 17		13 32			
Blairhill	d		12 05			12 20		12 35				12 50		13 05			13 20		13 35			
Easterhouse	d		12 09			12 24		12 39				12 54		13 09			13 24		13 39			
Garrowhill	d		12 11			12 26		12 41				12 56		13 11			13 26		13 41			
Shettleston	d		12 14			12 29		12 44				12 59		13 14			13 29		13 44			
Carntyne	d		12 16			12 31		12 46				13 01		13 16			13 31		13 46			
Springburn	d			12 19						12 49					13 19						13 49	
Barnhill	d			12 20						12 50					13 20						13 50	
Alexandra Parade	d			12 23						12 53					13 23						13 53	
Duke Street	d			12 25						12 55					13 25						13 55	
Bellgrove	d		12 19	12 27		12 34		12 49		12 57		13 04		13 19	13 27		13 34		13 49		13 57	
High Street	d		12 21	12 29		12 36		12 51		12 59		13 06		13 21	13 29		13 36		13 51		13 59	
Glasgow Queen St LL	a		12 23	12 31		12 39		12 53		13 01		13 09		13 23	13 31		13 39		13 53		14 01	
	d		12 24	12 31		12 39		12 54		13 01		13 09		13 24	13 31		13 39		13 54		14 01	
Charing Cross	d		12 27	12 33		12 42		12 57		13 03		13 12		13 27	13 33		13 42		13 57		14 03	
Argyle Street	d	12 13			12 32		12 42		12 52		13 01		13 11			13 31		13 42		13 54		14 03
Glasgow Central LL	a	12 14			12 34		12 44		12 55		13 04		13 14			13 34		13 44		13 57		14 06
	d	12 14			12 34		12 44		12 56		13 04		13 14			13 34		13 44		13 57		14 06
Anderston	d																					
Exhibition Centre	d	12 18			12 38		12 48		13 01		13 08		13 18			13 38		13 48		14 01		14 10
Partick	d	12 22	12 32	12 37	12 42	12 47	12 52	13 02	13a04	13 07	13 12	13 17	13 22	13 32	13 37	13 42	13 47	13 52	14 02	14a04	14 09	14 13
Hyndland	d	12 24	12 34	12 39	12 45	12 49	12 54	13 04		13 09	13 15	13 19	13 24	13 34	13 39	13 45	13 49	13 54	14 04		14 11	14 15
Jordanhill	d	12 26		12 41			12 56			13 11			13 26		13 41			13 56			14 13	
Scotstounhill	d	12 28		12 43			12 58			13 13			13 28		13 43			13 58			14 14	
Garscadden	d	12 30		12 46			13 00			13 16			13 30		13 46			14 00			14 17	
Yoker	d	12 33		12 48			13 03			13 18			13 33		13 48			14 03			14 20	
Clydebank	d	12 35		12 50			13 05			13 20			13 35		13 50			14 05			14 22	
Anniesland	d		12 37		12 48	12 52		13 07			13 18	13 22		13 37		13 48	13 52		14 07			14 18
Westerton	d		12 40		12 51	12 55		13 10			13 21	13 25		13 40		13 51	13 55		14 10			14 21
Bearsden	d				12 55						13 25					13 55						14 25
Hillfoot	d				12 57						13 27					13 57						14 27
Milngavie	a				13 00						13 30					14 00						14 30
Drumchapel	d		12 42			12 57		13 12				13 27		13 42			13 57		14 12			
Drumry	d		12 44			12 59		13 14				13 29		13 44			13 59		14 14			
Singer	d		12 47			13 02		13 17				13 32		13 47			14 02		14 17			
Dalmuir	a	12 39	12 49	12 53		13 04	13 09	13 19		13 24		13 34	13 39	13 49	13 53		14 04	14 09	14 19		14 25	
	d	12 39	12 50				13 09	13 20					13 39	13 50				14 09	14 20			
Kilpatrick	d	12 41					13 11						13 41					14 11				
Bowling	d	12 44					13 14						13 44					14 14				
Dumbarton East	d	12 49	12 58				13 19	13 28					13 49	13 58				14 19	14 28			
Dumbarton Central	d	12 51	13 00				13 21	13 30					13 51	14 00				14 21	14 30			
Dalreoch	d	12 52	13 01				13 22	13 31					13 52	14 01				14 22	14 31			
Renton	d	12 55					13 25						13 55					14 25				
Alexandria	d	12 58					13 28						13 58					14 28				
Balloch	a	13 00					13 30						14 00					14 30				
Cardross	d		13 06					13 36						14 06					14 36			
Craigendoran	d		13 11					13 41						14 11					14 41			
Helensburgh Central	a		13 14					13 44						14 14					14 44			

A 27 November

Lanark, Coatbridge, Motherwell, Larkhall, Hamilton, Edinburgh and Bathgate, Airdrie and Springburn - Glasgow - Milngavie, Dalmuir, Balloch and Helensburgh

		SR A	SR	SR	SR A	SR	SR A	SR	SR	SR	SR A	SR	SR A	SR	SR	SR A	SR	SR A	SR	SR	SR	SR A	SR
Lanark	d											14 12											15 12
Carluke	d											14 22											15 22
Wishaw	d											14 27											15 28
Holytown	d																						
Shieldmuir	d											14 31											15 31
Coatbridge Central	d																						
Whifflet	d																						
Motherwell	a											14 34											15 34
	d		13 40			14 06		14 10				14 34		14 40			15 06		15 10				15 35
Bellshill	d					14 12						14 40					15 12						15 41
Uddingston	d					14 16						14 44					15 16						15 45
Airbles	d		13 42					14 12						14 42					15 12				
Larkhall	d									14 25											15 25		
Merryton	d									14 27											15 27		
Chatelherault	d									14 30											15 30		
Hamilton Central	d		13 47					14 17		14 34				14 47					15 17		15 34		
Hamilton West	d		13 50					14 20		14 36				14 50					15 20		15 36		
Blantyre	d		13 53					14 23		14 40				14 53					15 23		15 40		
Newton	d		13 57					14 27						14 57					15 27				
Cambuslang	d		14 01			14 21		14 31				14 49		15 01			15 21		15 31				15 50
Rutherglen	d		14 05			14 24		14 34		14 48		14 53		15 06			15 24		15 34		15 48		15 53
Dalmarnock	d																						
Bridgeton	d		14 08			14 27		14 37				14 57		15 09			15 27		15 37				15 56
Edinburgh	d			13 11					13 40						14 06					14 40			
Haymarket	d			13 15					13 44						14 10					14 44			
Edinburgh Park	d			13 20					13 49						14 15					14 49			
Uphall	d			13 28					13 57						14 27					14 57			
Livingston North	d			13 31					14 00						14 30					15 00			
Bathgate	a			13 36					14 05						14 35					15 05			
	d			13 36					14 06						14 36					15 06			
Armadale	d			13 40					14 10						14 40					15 10			
Blackridge	d			13 44					14 14						14 44					15 14			
Caldercruix	d			13 50					14 20						14 50					15 20			
Drumgelloch	d			13 54					14 24						14 54					15 24			
Airdrie	d	13 43		13 58			14 13		14 28				14 43		14 58			15 13		15 28			
Coatdyke	d	13 45		14 00			14 15		14 30				14 45		15 00			15 15		15 30			
Coatbridge Sunnyside	d	13 47		14 02			14 17		14 32				14 47		15 02			15 17		15 32			
Blairhill	d	13 50		14 05			14 20		14 35				14 50		15 05			15 20		15 35			
Easterhouse	d	13 54		14 09			14 24		14 39				14 54		15 09			15 24		15 39			
Garrowhill	d	13 56		14 11			14 26		14 41				14 56		15 11			15 26		15 41			
Shettleston	d	13 59		14 14			14 29		14 44				14 59		15 14			15 29		15 44			
Carntyne	d	14 01		14 16			14 31		14 46				15 01		15 16			15 31		15 46			
Springburn	d				14 18						14 49					15 19						15 48	
Barnhill	d				14 19						14 50					15 20						15 49	
Alexandra Parade	d				14 22						14 53					15 23						15 52	
Duke Street	d				14 24						14 55					15 25						15 54	
Bellgrove	d	14 04		14 19	14 26		14 34		14 49		14 57		15 04		15 19	15 27		15 34		15 49		15 56	
High Street	d	14 06		14 21	14 28		14 36		14 51		14 59		15 06		15 21	15 29		15 36		15 51		15 58	
Glasgow Queen St LL	a	14 09		14 24	14 30		14 39		14 53		15 01		15 09		15 23	15 31		15 39		15 53		16 00	
	d	14 09		14 24	14 30		14 39		14 54		15 01		15 09		15 24	15 31		15 39		15 54		16 00	
Charing Cross	d	14 12		14 27	14 32		14 42		14 57		15 05		15 12		15 27	15 33		15 42		15 57		16 02	
Argyle Street	d		14 11			14 31		14 41		14 53		15 01		15 12			15 31		15 41		15 53		16 00
Glasgow Central LL	a		14 14			14 34		14 44		14 57		15 04		15 13			15 34		15 44		15 57		16 03
	d		14 14			14 34		14 44		14 57		15 04		15 13			15 34		15 44		15 57		16 04
Anderston	d																						
Exhibition Centre	d		14 18			14 38		14 48		15 01		15 08		15 17			15 38		15 48		16 01		16 08
Partick	d	14 17	14 22	14 32	14 36	14 42	14 47	14 52	15 02	15a04	15 09	15 12	15 17	15 21	15 32	15 37	15 42	15 47	15 52	16 02	16a04	16 08	16 12
Hyndland	d	14 19	14 24	14 34	14 38	14 45	14 49	14 54	15 04		15 11	15 15	15 19	15 23	15 34	15 39	15 45	15 49	15 54	16 04		16 10	16 15
Jordanhill	d		14 26		14 40			14 56			15 13			15 25		15 41			15 56			16 12	
Scotstounhill	d		14 28		14 42			14 58			15 14			15 27		15 43			15 58			16 14	
Garscadden	d		14 30		14 45			15 00			15 17			15 29		15 46			16 00			16 17	
Yoker	d		14 33		14 47			15 03			15 20			15 32		15 48			16 03			16 19	
Clydebank	d		14 35		14 49			15 05			15 22			15 34		15 50			16 05			16 21	
Anniesland	d	14 22		14 37		14 48	14 52		15 07			15 18	15 22		15 37		15 48	15 52		16 07			16 18
Westerton	d	14 25		14 40		14 51	14 55		15 10			15 21	15 25		15 40		15 51	15 55		16 10			16 21
Bearsden	d					14 55						15 25					15 55						16 25
Hillfoot	d					14 57						15 27					15 57						16 27
Milngavie	a					15 00						15 30					16 00						16 30
Drumchapel	d	14 27		14 42			14 57		15 12				15 27		15 42			15 57		16 12			
Drumry	d	14 29		14 44			14 59		15 14				15 29		15 44			15 59		16 14			
Singer	d	14 32		14 47			15 02		15 17				15 32		15 47			16 02		16 17			
Dalmuir	a	14 34	14 39	14 50	14 52		15 04	15 09	15 19		15 25		15 34	15 38	15 49	15 53		16 04	16 09	16 19		16 25	
	d		14 39	14 50				15 09	15 20					15 38	15 50				16 09	16 20			
Kilpatrick	d		14 41					15 11						15 41					16 11				
Bowling	d		14 44					15 14						15 44					16 14				
Dumbarton East	d		14 49	14 58				15 19	15 28					15 48	15 57				16 19	16 28			
Dumbarton Central	d		14 51	15 00				15 21	15 30					15 50	16 00				16 21	16 30			
Dalreoch	d		14 52	15 01				15 22	15 31					15 52	16 01				16 22	16 31			
Renton	d		14 55					15 25						15 55					16 25				
Alexandria	d		14 58					15 28						15 57					16 28				
Balloch	a		15 01					15 30						16 00					16 30				
Cardross	d			15 06					15 36						16 06					16 36			
Craigendoran	d			15 11					15 41						16 11					16 41			
Helensburgh Central	a			15 14					15 44						16 14					16 44			

A 27 November

Lanark, Coatbridge, Motherwell, Larkhall, Hamilton, Edinburgh and Bathgate, Airdrie and Springburn - Glasgow - Milngavie, Dalmuir, Balloch and Helensburgh

		SR A	SR	SR	SR A	SR	SR A	SR	SR	SR	SR A	SR	SR A	SR	SR	SR A	SR	SR A	SR	SR	SR	SR A
Lanark	d											16 12										
Carluke	d											16 22										
Wishaw	d											16 27										
Holytown	d																					
Shieldmuir	d											16 31										
Coatbridge Central	d																					
Whifflet	d																					
Motherwell	a											16 34										
	d		15 40			16 06		16 10				16 34		16 40			17 06		17 10			
Bellshill	d					16 12						16 40					17 12					
Uddingston	d					16 16						16 44					17 16					
Airbles	d		15 42					16 12						16 42					17 12			
Larkhall	d									16 25											17 25	
Merryton	d									16 27											17 27	
Chatelherault	d									16 30											17 30	
Hamilton Central	d		15 47					16 17		16 34				16 47					17 17		17 34	
Hamilton West	d		15 50					16 20		16 36				16 50					17 20		17 36	
Blantyre	d		15 53					16 23		16 40				16 53					17 23		17 40	
Newton	d		15 57					16 27						16 57					17 27			
Cambuslang	d		16 01			16 21		16 31				16 49		17 01			17 21		17 31			
Rutherglen	d		16 05			16 24		16 34		16 48		16 53		17 06			17 24		17 34		17 48	
Dalmarnock	d																					
Bridgeton	d		16 09			16 27		16 37				16 57		17 09			17 27		17 37			
Edinburgh	d			15 08					15 40						16 10					16 40		
Haymarket	d			15 12					15 44						16 14					16 44		
Edinburgh Park	d			15 19					15 49						16 19					16 49		
Uphall	d			15 27					15 57						16 27					16 57		
Livingston North	d			15 30					16 00						16 30					17 00		
Bathgate	a			15 35					16 05						16 36					17 05		
	d			15 36					16 06						16 36					17 06		
Armadale	d			15 40					16 10						16 40					17 10		
Blackridge	d			15 44					16 14						16 44					17 14		
Caldercruix	d			15 50					16 20						16 50					17 20		
Drumgelloch	d			15 54					16 24						16 54					17 24		
Airdrie	d	15 43		15 58			16 13		16 28				16 43		16 58			17 13		17 28		
Coatdyke	d	15 45		16 00			16 15		16 30				16 45		17 00			17 15		17 30		
Coatbridge Sunnyside	d	15 47		16 02			16 17		16 32				16 47		17 02			17 17		17 32		
Blairhill	d	15 50		16 05			16 20		16 35				16 50		17 05			17 20		17 35		
Easterhouse	d	15 54		16 09			16 24		16 39				16 54		17 09			17 24		17 39		
Garrowhill	d	15 56		16 11			16 26		16 41				16 56		17 11			17 26		17 41		
Shettleston	d	15 59		16 14			16 29		16 44				16 59		17 14			17 29		17 44		
Carntyne	d	16 01		16 16			16 31		16 46				17 01		17 16			17 31		17 46		
Springburn	d				16 19						16 49					17 19						17 49
Barnhill	d				16 20						16 50					17 20						17 50
Alexandra Parade	d				16 23						16 53					17 23						17 53
Duke Street	d				16 25						16 55					17 25						17 55
Bellgrove	d	16 04		16 19	16 27		16 34		16 49		16 57		17 04		17 19	17 27		17 34		17 49		17 57
High Street	d	16 06		16 21	16 29		16 36		16 51		16 59		17 06		17 21	17 29		17 36		17 51		17 59
Glasgow Queen St LL	a	16 09		16 23	16 31		16 39		16 53		17 01		17 09		17 24	17 31		17 39		17 53		18 01
	d	16 09		16 24	16 31		16 39		16 54		17 01		17 09		17 24	17 31		17 39		17 54		18 01
Charing Cross	d	16 12		16 27	16 33		16 42		16 57		17 03		17 12		17 27	17 33		17 42		17 57		18 03
Argyle Street	d		16 12			16 31		16 41		16 53		17 01		17 12			17 31		17 41		17 53	
Glasgow Central LL	a		16 14			16 34		16 44		16 57		17 04		17 14			17 34		17 44		17 57	
	d		16 14			16 34		16 44		16 57		17 04		17 14			17 34		17 44		17 57	
Anderston	d																					
Exhibition Centre	d		16 18			16 38		16 48		17 01		17 09		17 18			17 38		17 48		18 01	
Partick	d	16 17	16 22	16 32	16 37	16 42	16 47	16 52	17 02	17a04	17 09	17 13	17 17	17 22	17 32	17 37	17 42	17 47	17 52	18 02	18a04	18 10
Hyndland	d	16 19	16 24	16 34	16 39	16 45	16 49	16 54	17 04		17 11	17 15	17 19	17 24	17 34	17 39	17 45	17 49	17 54	18 04		18 12
Jordanhill	d		16 26		16 41			16 56			17 13			17 26		17 41			17 56			18 14
Scotstounhill	d		16 28		16 43			16 58			17 15			17 28		17 43			17 58			18 16
Garscadden	d		16 30		16 46			17 00			17 18			17 30		17 46			18 00			18 19
Yoker	d		16 33		16 48			17 03			17 20			17 33		17 48			18 03			18 21
Clydebank	d		16 35		16 50			17 05			17 22			17 35		17 50			18 05			18 23
Anniesland	d	16 22		16 37		16 48	16 52		17 07			17 18	17 22		17 37		17 48	17 52		18 07		
Westerton	d	16 25		16 40		16 51	16 55		17 10			17 21	17 25		17 40		17 51	17 55		18 10		
Bearsden	d					16 55						17 25					17 55					
Hillfoot	d					16 57						17 27					17 57					
Milngavie	a					17 00						17 30					18 00					
Drumchapel	d	16 27		16 42			16 57		17 12				17 27		17 42			17 57		18 12		
Drumry	d	16 29		16 44			16 59		17 14				17 29		17 44			17 59		18 14		
Singer	d	16 32		16 47			17 02		17 17				17 32		17 47			18 02		18 17		
Dalmuir	a	16 34	16 39	16 49	16 53		17 04	17 09	17 19		17 25		17 34	17 39	17 50	17 53		18 04	18 09	18 19		18 26
	d		16 39	16 50				17 09	17 20					17 39	17 50				18 09	18 20		
Kilpatrick	d		16 41					17 11						17 41					18 11			
Bowling	d		16 44					17 14						17 44					18 14			
Dumbarton East	d		16 49	16 57				17 19	17 28					17 49	17 58				18 19	18 28		
Dumbarton Central	d		16 51	17 00				17 21	17 30					17 51	18 00				18 21	18 30		
Dalreoch	d		16 52	17 01				17 22	17 31					17 52	18 01				18 22	18 31		
Renton	d		16 55					17 25						17 55					18 25			
Alexandria	d		16 58					17 28						17 58					18 28			
Balloch	a		17 00					17 30						18 00					18 30			
Cardross	d			17 06					17 36						18 06					18 36		
Craigendoran	d			17 11					17 41						18 11					18 40		
Helensburgh Central	a			17 14					17 44						18 14					18 44		

A 27 November

Lanark, Coatbridge, Motherwell, Larkhall, Hamilton, Edinburgh and Bathgate, Airdrie and Springburn - Glasgow - Milngavie, Dalmuir, Balloch and Helensburgh

		SR	SR	SR	SR	SR	SR	SR	SR	SR	SR	SR	SR	SR	SR	SR	SR	SR	SR	SR	SR	SR	SR
			◇ A	B																			
Lanark	d	17 12									18 14								19 12				
Carluke	d	17 22									18 23								19 22				
Wishaw	d	17 27									18 28								19 27				
Holytown	d																						
Shieldmuir	d	17 31									18 32								19 31				
Coatbridge Central	d																						
Whifflet	d																						
Motherwell	a	17 34									18 36								19 34				
	d	17 34			17 40		18 06	18 10			18 36	18 40		19 06	19 10				19 34	19 40		20 06	20 10
Bellshill	d	17 40					18 12				18 42			19 12					19 40			20 12	
Uddingston	d	17 44					18 16				18 46			19 16					19 44			20 19	
Airbles	d				17 42			18 12				18 42			19 12					19 42			20 12
Larkhall	d									18 25								19 25					
Merryton	d									18 27								19 27					
Chatelherault	d									18 30								19 30					
Hamilton Central	d				17 47			18 17		18 34		18 47			19 17			19 34		19 47			20 17
Hamilton West	d				17 50			18 20		18 36		18 50			19 20			19 36		19 50			20 20
Blantyre	d				17 53			18 23		18 40		18 53			19 23			19 40		19 53			20 23
Newton	d				17 57			18 27				18 57			19 27					19 57			20 27
Cambuslang	d	17 49			18 01		18 21	18 31			18 51	19 01		19 21	19 31				19 49	20 01		20 24	20 31
Rutherglen	d	17 54			18 04		18 24	18 34		18 48	18 54	19 06		19 24	19 34			19 49	19 53	20 04		20 27	20 34
Dalmarnock	d																						
Bridgeton	d	17 57			18 08		18 27	18 37			18 57	19 09		19 27	19 37				19 57	20 07		20 30	20 37
Edinburgh	d					17 07			17 39				18 10			18 40	19 10						
Haymarket	d					17 11			17 44				18 14			18 44	19 14						
Edinburgh Park	d					17 16			17 49				18 19			18 49	19 19						
Uphall	d					17 25			17 57				18 27			18 57	19 27						
Livingston North	d					17 28			18 00				18 30			19 00	19 30						
Bathgate	a					17 33			18 05				18 35			19 05	19 35						
	d					17 36			18 06				18 36			19 06							
Armadale	d					17 40			18 10				18 40			19 10							
Blackridge	d					17 44			18 14				18 44			19 14							
Caldercruix	d					17 50			18 20				18 50			19 20							
Drumgelloch	d					17 54			18 24				18 54			19 24							
Airdrie	d			17 43		17 58			18 28				18 58			19 28					19 58		
Coatdyke	d			17 45		18 00			18 30				19 00			19 30					20 00		
Coatbridge Sunnyside	d			17 47		18 02			18 32				19 02			19 32					20 02		
Blairhill	d			17 50		18 05			18 35				19 05			19 35					20 05		
Easterhouse	d			17 54		18 09			18 39				19 09			19 39					20 09		
Garrowhill	d			17 56		18 11			18 41				19 11			19 41					20 11		
Shettleston	d			17 59		18 14			18 44				19 14			19 44					20 14		
Carntyne	d			18 01		18 16			18 46				19 16			19 46					20 16		
Springburn	d																						
Barnhill	d																						
Alexandra Parade	d																						
Duke Street	d																						
Bellgrove	d			18 04		18 19			18 49				19 19			19 49					20 19		
High Street	d			18 06		18 21			18 51				19 21			19 51					20 21		
Glasgow Queen St LL 10	a			18 09		18 23			18 53				19 24			19 53					20 23		
	d		18b20	18 09		18 24			18 54				19 24			19 54					20 24		
Charing Cross	d			18 12		18 27			18 57				19 27			19 57					20 27		
Argyle Street	d	18 01			18 12																		
Glasgow Central LL 15	a	18 04			18 14		18 34	18 44		18 56	19 04	19 14		19 34	19 44			19 57	20 04	20 14		20 34	20 44
	d	18 05			18 14		18 34	18 44		18 57	19 04	19 14		19 34	19 44			19 57	20 04	20 14		20 34	20 44
Anderston	d																						
Exhibition Centre	d	18 09			18 18		18 38	18 48		19 01	19 08	19 18		19 38	19 48			20 01	20 08	20 18		20 38	20 48
Partick	d	18 13		18 17	18 22	18 32	18 42	18 52	19 02	19a04	19 11	19 22	19 32	19 42	19 52	20 02		20a04	20 12	20 22	20 32	20 42	20 52
Hyndland	d	18 16		18 19	18 24	18 34	18 46	18 54	19 04		19 13	19 24	19 34	19 46	19 54	20 04			20 16	20 24	20 34	20 46	20 54
Jordanhill	d				18 26			18 56				19 26			19 56					20 26			20 56
Scotstounhill	d				18 28			18 58				19 28			19 58					20 28			20 58
Garscadden	d				18 30			19 00				19 30			20 00					20 30			21 00
Yoker	d				18 33			19 03				19 33			20 03					20 33			21 03
Clydebank	d				18 35			19 05				19 35			20 05					20 35			21 05
Anniesland	d	18 19		18 26		18 37	18 49		19 07		19 19		19 37	19 49		20 07			20 19		20 37	20 49	
Westerton	d	18 22		18 33		18 40	18 52		19 10		19 22		19 40	19 52		20 10			20 22		20 40	20 52	
Bearsden	d	18 25					18 55				19 25			19 55					20 25			20 55	
Hillfoot	d	18 27					18 57				19 27			19 57					20 27			20 57	
Milngavie	a	18 30					19 00				19 30			20 00					20 30			21 00	
Drumchapel	d			18 35		18 42			19 12				19 42			20 12					20 42		
Drumry	d			18 37		18 44			19 14				19 44			20 14					20 44		
Singer	d			18 40		18 47			19 17				19 47			20 17					20 47		
Dalmuir	a		18 34	18 42	18 39	18 49		19 09	19 19			19 39	19 50		20 09	20 19				20 39	20 49		21 09
	d		18 34		18 39	18 50		19 09	19 20			19 39	19 50		20 09	20 20				20 39	20 50		21 09
Kilpatrick	d				18 41			19 11				19 41			20 11					20 41			21 11
Bowling	d				18 44			19 14				19 44			20 14					20 44			21 14
Dumbarton East	d				18 49	18 58		19 19	19 28			19 49	19 58		20 19	20 28				20 49	20 58		21 19
Dumbarton Central	d		18 44		18 51	19 00		19 21	19 30			19 51	20 00		20 21	20 30				20 51	21 00		21 21
Dalreoch	d				18 52	19 01		19 22	19 31			19 52	20 01		20 22	20 31				20 52	21 01		21 22
Renton	d				18 55			19 25				19 55			20 25					20 55			21 25
Alexandria	d				18 58			19 28				19 58			20 28					20 58			21 28
Balloch	a				19 00			19 30				20 00			20 30					21 01			21 30
Cardross	d					19 06			19 36				20 06			20 36					21 06		
Craigendoran	d					19 11			19 41				20 11			20 41					21 11		
Helensburgh Central	a		18c59			19 14			19 44				20 14			20 44					21 14		

A To Oban
B 27 November
b Glasgow Queen St High Level
c Helensburgh Upper

Lanark, Coatbridge, Motherwell, Larkhall, Hamilton, Edinburgh and Bathgate, Airdrie and Springburn - Glasgow - Milngavie, Dalmuir, Balloch and Helensburgh

		SR	SR	SR	SR	SR	SR	SR	SR	SR	SR	SR	SR	SR	SR	SR	SR	SR	SR	SR	SR	SR	SR
Lanark	d				20 12							21 12							22 12				
Carluke	d				20 23							21 23							22 23				
Wishaw	d				20 30							21 28							22 28				
Holytown	d																						
Shieldmuir	d				20 34							21 32							22 32				
Coatbridge Central	d																						
Whifflet	d																						
Motherwell	a				20 37							21 35							22 35				
	d				20 37	20 40		21 06	21 10			21 36	21 40		22 06	22 10			22 36	22 40		23 06	23 10
Bellshill	d				20 43			21 12				21 42			22 12				22 42			23 12	
Uddingston	d				20 47			21 16				21 46			22 15				22 46			23 16	
Airbles	d					20 42			21 12				21 42			22 12				22 42			23 12
Larkhall	d			20 25							21 25							22 25					
Merryton	d			20 27							21 27							22 27					
Chatelherault	d			20 30							21 30							22 30					
Hamilton Central	d			20 34		20 47			21 17		21 34		21 47			22 17		22 34		22 47			23 17
Hamilton West	d			20 36		20 50			21 20		21 36		21 50			22 20		22 36		22 50			23 20
Blantyre	d			20 40		20 53			21 23		21 40		21 53			22 23		22 40		22 53			23 23
Newton	d					20 57			21 28				21 57			22 27				22 57			23 27
Cambuslang	d				20 52	21 01		21 21	21 32			21 51	22 01		22 20	22 31			22 51	23 01		23 21	23 31
Rutherglen	d			20 48	20 56	21 04		21 25	21 35		21 48	21 54	22 06		22 23	22 34		22 48	22 54	23 04		23 24	23 34
Dalmarnock	d																						
Bridgeton	d				20 59	21 07		21 28	21 38			21 57	22 09		22 27	22 37			22 57	23 07		23 27	23 37
Edinburgh	d	19 40	20 08							20 40							21 38						
Haymarket	d	19 44	20 12							20 44							21 42						
Edinburgh Park	d	19 49	20 17							20 49							21 47						
Uphall	d	19 57	20 25							20 57							21 55						
Livingston North	d	20 00	20 28							21 00							21 58						
Bathgate	a	20 05	20 33							21 05							22 03						
	d	20 06								21 06							22 06						
Armadale	d	20 10								21 10							22 10						
Blackridge	d	20 14								21 14							22 14						
Caldercruix	d	20 20								21 20							22 20						
Drumgelloch	d	20 24								21 24							22 24						
Airdrie	d	20 28					20 58			21 28				21 58			22 28				22 58		
Coatdyke	d	20 30					21 00			21 30				22 00			22 30				23 00		
Coatbridge Sunnyside	d	20 32					21 02			21 32				22 02			22 32				23 02		
Blairhill	d	20 35					21 05			21 35				22 05			22 35				23 05		
Easterhouse	d	20 39					21 09			21 39				22 09			22 39				23 09		
Garrowhill	d	20 41					21 11			21 41				22 11			22 41				23 11		
Shettleston	d	20 44					21 14			21 44				22 14			22 44				23 14		
Carntyne	d	20 46					21 16			21 46				22 16			22 46				23 16		
Springburn	d																						
Barnhill	d																						
Alexandra Parade	d																						
Duke Street	d																						
Bellgrove	d	20 49					21 19			21 49				22 19			22 49				23 19		
High Street	d	20 51					21 21			21 51				22 21			22 51				23 21		
Glasgow Queen St LL 10	a	20 54					21 23			21 53				22 23			22 53				23 23		
	d	20 54					21 24			21 54				22 24			22 54				23 24		
Charing Cross	d	20 57					21 27			21 57				22 27			22 57				23 27		
Argyle Street	d																						
Glasgow Central LL 15	a			20 57	21 04	21 14		21 34	21 44		21 56	22 04	22 14		22 34	22 44		22 57	23 04	23 14		23 34	23 44
	d			20 58	21 04	21 14		21 34	21 44		21 57	22 04	22 14		22 34	22 44		22 57	23 04	23 14		23 34	23 44
Anderston	d																						
Exhibition Centre	d			21 01	21 08	21 18		21 38	21 48		22 01	22 08	22 18		22 38	22 48		23 01	23 08	23 18		23 38	23 48
Partick	d	21 02		21a05	21 12	21 22	21 32	21 42	21 52	22 02	22a04	22 12	22 22	22 32	22 42	22 52	23 02	23a04	23 12	23 22	23 32	23 42	23 52
Hyndland	d	21 04			21 16	21 24	21 34	21 46	21 54	22 04		22 16	22 24	22 34	22 46	22 54	23 04		23 16	23 24	23 34	23 44	23 54
Jordanhill	d					21 26			21 56				22 26			22 56				23 26		23 46	23 56
Scotstounhill	d					21 28			21 58				22 28			22 58				23 28		23 48	23 58
Garscadden	d					21 30			22 00				22 30			23 00				23 30		23a50	00a01
Yoker	d					21 33			22 03				22 33			23 03				23 33			
Clydebank	d					21 35			22 05				22 35			23 05				23 35			
Anniesland	d	21 07			21 19		21 37	21 49		22 07		22 19		22 37	22 49		23 07		23 19		23 37		
Westerton	d	21 10			21 22		21 40	21 52		22 10		22 22		22 40	22 52		23 10		23 22		23 40		
Bearsden	d				21 25			21 55				22 25			22 55				23 25				
Hillfoot	d				21 27			21 57				22 27			22 57				23 27				
Milngavie	a				21 30			22 00				22 30			23 00				23 30				
Drumchapel	d	21 12					21 42			22 12				22 42			23 12				23 42		
Drumry	d	21 14					21 44			22 14				22 44			23 14				23 44		
Singer	d	21 17					21 47			22 17				22 47			23 17				23 47		
Dalmuir	a	21 20				21 39	21 49		22 09	22 19			22 39	22 49		23 09	23 19			23 39	23 49		
	d	21 20				21 39	21 50		22 09	22 20			22 39	22 50		23 09	23 20			23 39	23 50		
Kilpatrick	d					21 41			22 11				22 41			23 11				23 41			
Bowling	d					21 44			22 14				22 44			23 14				23 44			
Dumbarton East	d	21 28				21 49	21 58		22 19	22 28			22 49	22 58		23 19	23 28			23 49	23 58		
Dumbarton Central	d	21 30				21 51	22 00		22 21	22 30			22 51	23 00		23 21	23 30			23 51	23 59		
Dalreoch	d	21 31				21 52	22 01		22 22	22 31			22 52	23 01		23 22	23 31			23 52	00 01		
Renton	d					21 55			22 25				22 55			23 25				23 55			
Alexandria	d					21 58			22 28				22 58			23 28				23 58			
Balloch	a					22 00			22 30				23 00			23 30				00 01			
Cardross	d	21 36					22 06			22 36				23 06			23 36				00 06		
Craigendoran	d	21 41					22 11			22 41				23 11			23 41				00 11		
Helensburgh Central	a	21 45					22 14			22 44				23 14			23 44				[illegible]		

Lanark, Coatbridge, Motherwell, Larkhall, Hamilton, Edinburgh and Bathgate, Airdrie and Springburn - Glasgow - Milngavie, Dalmuir, Balloch and Helensburgh

		SR	SR
Lanark	d		
Carluke	d		
Wishaw	d		
Holytown	d		
Shieldmuir	d		
Coatbridge Central	d		
Whifflet	d		
Motherwell	a		
	d		
Bellshill	d		
Uddingston	d		
Airbles	d		
Larkhall	d		
Merryton	d		
Chatelherault	d		
Hamilton Central	d		
Hamilton West	d		
Blantyre	d		
Newton	d		
Cambuslang	d		
Rutherglen	d		
Dalmarnock	d		
Bridgeton	d		
Edinburgh	d	22 40	23 18
Haymarket	d	22 44	23 22
Edinburgh Park	d	22 49	23 27
Uphall	d	22 57	23 35
Livingston North	d	23 00	23 38
Bathgate	a	23 05	23 43
	d	23 06	
Armadale	d	23 10	
Blackridge	d	23 14	
Caldercruix	d	23 20	
Drumgelloch	d	23 24	
Airdrie	d	23 28	
Coatdyke	d	23 30	
Coatbridge Sunnyside	d	23 32	
Blairhill	d	23 35	
Easterhouse	d	23 39	
Garrowhill	d	23 41	
Shettleston	d	23 44	
Carntyne	d	23 46	
Springburn	d		
Barnhill	d		
Alexandra Parade	d		
Duke Street	d		
Bellgrove	d	23 49	
High Street	d	23 51	
Glasgow Queen St LL 10 ⛴	a	23 53	
	d	23 54	
Charing Cross	d	23 57	
Argyle Street	d		
Glasgow Central LL 15	a		
	d		
Anderston	d		
Exhibition Centre	d		
Partick ⛴	d	00 01	
Hyndland	d	00 03	
Jordanhill	d	00 05	
Scotstounhill	d	00 07	
Garscadden	d	00 09	
Yoker	d	00 12	
Clydebank	d		
Anniesland	d		
Westerton	d		
Bearsden	d		
Hillfoot	d		
Milngavie	a		
Drumchapel	d		
Drumry	d		
Singer	d		
Dalmuir	a	00 16	
	d		
Kilpatrick	d		
Bowling	d		
Dumbarton East	d		
Dumbarton Central	d		
Dalreoch	d		
Renton	d		
Alexandria	d		
Balloch	a		
Cardross	d		
Craigendoran	d		
Helensburgh Central	a		

Lanark, Coatbridge, Motherwell, Larkhall, Hamilton, Edinburgh and Bathgate, Airdrie and Springburn - Glasgow - Milngavie, Dalmuir, Balloch and Helensburgh

		SR	SR	SR	SR	SR	SR	SR A	SR	SR	SR	SR	SR	SR	SR	SR	SR	SR	SR	SR	SR	SR	SR
Lanark	d																						
Carluke	d																						
Wishaw	d																						
Holytown	d							23p59															
Shieldmuir	d																						
Coatbridge Central	d																						
Whifflet	d																						
Motherwell	a																						
	d												08 36	08 40				09 10				09 36	
Bellshill	d							00 02					08 42									09 42	
Uddingston	d							00 06					08 46									09 46	
Airbles	d													08 42				09 12					
Larkhall	d																			09 25			
Merryton	d																			09 27			
Chatelherault	d																			09 30			
Hamilton Central	d													08 47				09 17		09 34			
Hamilton West	d													08 50				09 20		09 36			
Blantyre	d													08 53				09 23		09 40			
Newton	d													08 57				09 27					
Cambuslang	d							00 12					08 51	09 01				09 31				09 51	
Rutherglen	d												08 54	09 04				09 34		09 48		09 54	
Dalmarnock	d																						
Bridgeton	d												08 57	09 07				09 37				09 57	
Edinburgh	d		22p19		22p51	23p37	23p51												08 37				
Haymarket	d		22p23		22p55	23p42	23p55												08 41				
Edinburgh Park	d		22p30		23p00	23p47	23p59												08 46				
Uphall	d		22p38		23p08	23p55	00 08												08 57				
Livingston North	d		22p41		23p11	23p59	00 11												09 00				
Bathgate	a		22p46		23p16	00 04	00 16												09 06				
	d		22p47		23p17							08 06							09 06				
Armadale	d		22p51		23p21							08 10							09 10				
Blackridge	d		22p55		23p25							08 14							09 14				
Caldercruix	d		23p01		23p31							08 20							09 20				
Drumgelloch	d		23p05		23p35							08 24							09 24				
Airdrie	d		23p12		23p38					07 58		08 28			08 58		09 13		09 28				09 38
Coatdyke	d		23p14		23p40					08 00		08 30			09 00		09 15		09 30				09 45
Coatbridge Sunnyside	d		23p16		23p43					08 02		08 32			09 02		09 17		09 32				09 47
Blairhill	d		23p19		23p45					08 05		08 35			09 05		09 20		09 35				09 50
Easterhouse	d		23p23		23p49					08 09		08 39			09 09		09 24		09 39				09 54
Garrowhill	d		23p25		23p52					08 11		08 41			09 11		09 26		09 41				09 56
Shettleston	d		23p28		23p54					08 14		08 44			09 14		09 29		09 44				09 59
Carntyne	d		23p30		23p56					08 16		08 46			09 16		09 31		09 46				10 01
Springburn	d	23p09		23p39												09 19					09 49		
Barnhill	d	23p10		23p40												09 20					09 50		
Alexandra Parade	d	23p13		23p43												09 23					09 53		
Duke Street	d	23p15		23p45												09 25					09 55		
Bellgrove	d	23p17	23p33	23p47	23p59					08 19		08 49			09 19	09 27	09 34		09 49		09 57		10 04
High Street	d	23p19	23p35	23p49	00 02					08 21		08 51			09 21	09 29	09 36		09 51		09 59		10 06
Glasgow Queen St LL 10 ⛴	a	23p21	23p37	23p51	00 04					08 23		08 53			09 23	09 31	09 39		09 54		10 01		10 09
	d	23p23	23p45	23p53	00 04					08 24		08 54			09 24	09 31	09 39		09 54		10 01		10 09
Charing Cross	d	23p25	23p47	23p55	00 06					08 27		08 57			09 27	09 33	09 42		09 57		10 03		10 12
Argyle Street	d																					10 01	
Glasgow Central LL 15	a							00b23					09 04	09 14				09 44		09 56		10 04	
	d												09 04	09 14				09 44		09 57		10 04	
Anderston	d																						
Exhibition Centre	d												09 08	09 18				09 48		10 01		10 08	
Partick ⛴	d	23p29	23p51	23p59	00 11					08 32		09 02	09 12	09 22	09 32	09 37	09 46	09 52	10 02	10a05	10 08	10 12	10 17
Hyndland	d	23p32	23p53	00 02	00 13					08 34		09 04	09 16	09 24	09 34	09 39	09 48	09 54	10 04		10 10	10 15	10 19
Jordanhill	d		23p55	00 04	00 15									09 26		09 41		09 56			10 12		
Scotstounhill	d		23p58	00 06	00 17									09 28		09 43		09 58			10 14		
Garscadden	d		23p59	00a08	00a19									09 30		09 46		10 00			10 17		
Yoker	d		00 02						08 33		09 03			09 33		09 48		10 03			10 19		
Clydebank	d		00 04						08 35		09 05			09 35		09 50		10 05			10 21		
Anniesland	d	23p35								08 37		09 07	09 19		09 37		09 51		10 07			10 18	10 22
Westerton	d	23p38								08 40		09 10	09 22		09 40		09 54		10 10			10 21	10 25
Bearsden	d												09 25									10 25	
Hillfoot	d												09 27									10 27	
Milngavie	a												09 30									10 30	
Drumchapel	d	23p40								08 42		09 12			09 42		09 57		10 13				10 27
Drumry	d	23p42								08 44		09 14			09 44		09 59		10 15				10 29
Singer	d	23p45								08 47		09 17			09 47		10 02		10 17				10 32
Dalmuir	a	23p47	00 08						08 38	08 49	09 08	09 19		09 39	09 49	09 53	10 04	10 09	10 20		10 24		10 34
	d	23p48	00 08						08 39	08 50	09 09	09 20		09 39	09 50			10 09	10 20				
Kilpatrick	d	23p51							08 41		09 11			09 41				10 11					
Bowling	d	23p54							08 44		09 14			09 44				10 14					
Dumbarton East	d	23p58	00 15						08 49	08 58	09 19	09 28		09 49	09 58			10 19	10 28				
Dumbarton Central	d	23p59	00 18						08 51	09 00	09 21	09 30		09 51	10 00			10 21	10 30				
Dalreoch	d	00 02	00 19						08 52	09 01	09 22	09 31		09 52	10 01			10 22	10 31				
Renton	d	00 05							08 55		09 25			09 55				10 25					
Alexandria	d	00 07							08 58		09 28			09 58				10 28					
Balloch	a	00 10							09 00		09 30			10 00				10 30					
Cardross	d		00 24							09 06		09 36			10 06				10 36				
Craigendoran	d		00 29							09 11		09 41			10 11				10 41				
Helensburgh Central	a		00 32							09 14		09 44			10 14				10 44				

A From Edinburgh

b Glasgow Central High Level

Table 226

Sundays from 4 December

Lanark, Coatbridge, Motherwell, Larkhall, Hamilton, Edinburgh and Bathgate, Airdrie and Springburn - Glasgow - Milngavie, Dalmuir, Balloch and Helensburgh

		SR	SR	SR	SR	SR	SR	SR	SR	SR	SR	SR	SR	SR	SR	SR	SR	SR	SR	SR	SR	SR	SR
Lanark	d										10 12											11 12	
Carluke	d										10 22											11 22	
Wishaw	d										10 27											11 27	
Holytown	d																						
Shieldmuir	d										10 31											11 31	
Coatbridge Central	d																						
Whifflet	d																						
Motherwell	a										10 34											11 34	
	d	09 40			10 06		10 10				10 36		10 40			11 10		11 10				11 36	
Bellshill	d				10 12						10 42					11 16						11 42	
Uddingston	d				10 18						10 47					11 20						11 46	
Airbles	d	09 42					10 12						10 42					11 12					
Larkhall	d								10 25											11 25			
Merryton	d								10 27											11 27			
Chatelherault	d								10 30											11 30			
Hamilton Central	d	09 47					10 17		10 34				10 47					11 17		11 34			
Hamilton West	d	09 50					10 20		10 36				10 50					11 20		11 36			
Blantyre	d	09 53					10 23		10 40				10 53					11 23		11 40			
Newton	d	09 57					10 27						10 57					11 27					
Cambuslang	d	10 01			10 23		10 31				10 52		11 01			11 25		11 31				11 51	
Rutherglen	d	10 04			10 26		10 34		10 48		10 56		11 06			11 29		11 34		11 48		11 53	
Dalmarnock	d																						
Bridgeton	d	10 07			10 29		10 37				10 59		11 09			11 32		11 37				11 56	
Edinburgh	d							09 37											10 40				
Haymarket	d							09 41											10 44				
Edinburgh Park	d							09 46											10 49				
Uphall	d							09 57											10 57				
Livingston North	d							10 00											11 00				
Bathgate	a							10 05											11 05				
	d							10 06											11 06				
Armadale	d							10 10											11 10				
Blackridge	d							10 14											11 14				
Caldercruix	d							10 20											11 20				
Drumgelloch	d							10 24											11 24				
Airdrie	d		09 58			10 13		10 28				10 38		10 58			11 13		11 28				11 38
Coatdyke	d		10 00			10 15		10 30				10 45		11 00			11 15		11 30				11 45
Coatbridge Sunnyside	d		10 02			10 17		10 32				10 47		11 02			11 17		11 32				11 47
Blairhill	d		10 05			10 20		10 35				10 50		11 05			11 20		11 35				11 50
Easterhouse	d		10 09			10 24		10 39				10 54		11 09			11 24		11 39				11 54
Garrowhill	d		10 11			10 26		10 41				10 56		11 11			11 26		11 41				11 56
Shettleston	d		10 14			10 29		10 44				10 59		11 14			11 29		11 44				11 59
Carntyne	d		10 16			10 31		10 46				11 01		11 16			11 31		11 46				12 01
Springburn	d			10 19						10 49					11 19						11 49		
Barnhill	d			10 20						10 50					11 20						11 50		
Alexandra Parade	d			10 23						10 53					11 23						11 53		
Duke Street	d			10 25						10 55					11 25						11 55		
Bellgrove	d		10 19	10 27		10 34		10 49		10 57		11 04		11 19	11 27		11 34		11 49		11 57		12 04
High Street	d		10 21	10 29		10 36		10 51		10 59		11 06		11 21	11 29		11 36		11 51		11 59		12 06
Glasgow Queen St LL	a		10 23	10 31		10 39		10 54		11 01		11 09		11 23	11 31		11 39		11 53		12 01		12 09
	d		10 24	10 31		10 39		10 54		11 01		11 09		11 24	11 31		11 39		11 54		12 01		12 09
Charing Cross	d		10 27	10 33		10 42		10 57		11 03		11 12		11 27	11 33		11 42		11 57		12 03		12 12
Argyle Street	d	10 11			10 33		10 41		10 53		11 02		11 12			11 35		11 41		11 53		12 01	
Glasgow Central LL	a	10 14			10 34		10 44		10 57		11 04		11 14			11 36		11 44		11 57		12 04	
	d	10 14			10 34		10 44		10 57		11 04		11 14			11 36		11 44		11 57		12 04	
Anderston	d																						
Exhibition Centre	d	10 18			10 38		10 48		11 01		11 08		11 18			11 40		11 48		12 01		12 08	
Partick	d	10 22	10 32	10 37	10 42	10 47	10 52	11 02	11a05	11 07	11 12	11 16	11 22	11 32	11 37	11 43	11 47	11 52	12 02	12a04	12 09	12 12	12 17
Hyndland	d	10 24	10 34	10 39	10 45	10 49	10 54	11 04		11 09	11 15	11 18	11 24	11 34	11 39	11 45	11 49	11 54	12 04		12 11	12 15	12 19
Jordanhill	d	10 26		10 41			10 56			11 11			11 26		11 41			11 56			12 13		
Scotstounhill	d	10 28		10 43			10 58			11 13			11 28		11 43			11 58			12 15		
Garscadden	d	10 30		10 46			11 00			11 16			11 30		11 46			12 00			12 18		
Yoker	d	10 33		10 48			11 03			11 18			11 33		11 48			12 03			12 20		
Clydebank	d	10 35		10 50			11 05			11 20			11 35		11 50			12 05			12 22		
Anniesland	d		10 37		10 48	10 52		11 07			11 18	11 22		11 37		11 48	11 52		12 07			12 18	12 22
Westerton	d		10 40		10 51	10 55		11 10			11 21	11 24		11 40		11 51	11 55		12 10			12 21	12 25
Bearsden	d				10 55						11 25					11 55						12 25	
Hillfoot	d				10 57						11 27					11 57						12 27	
Milngavie	a				11 00						11 30					12 00						12 30	
Drumchapel	d		10 42			10 57		11 12				11 26		11 42			11 57		12 12				12 27
Drumry	d		10 44			10 59		11 14				11 28		11 44			11 59		12 14				12 29
Singer	d		10 47			11 02		11 17				11 32		11 47			12 02		12 17				12 32
Dalmuir	a	10 39	10 49	10 53		11 04	11 09	11 19		11 24		11 33	11 39	11 49	11 53		12 04	12 09	12 19		12 25		12 34
	d	10 39	10 50				11 09	11 20					11 39	11 50				12 09	12 20				
Kilpatrick	d	10 41					11 11						11 41					12 11					
Bowling	d	10 44					11 14						11 44					12 14					
Dumbarton East	d	10 49	10 58				11 19	11 28					11 49	11 58				12 19	12 28				
Dumbarton Central	d	10 51	11 00				11 21	11 30					11 51	12 00				12 21	12 30				
Dalreoch	d	10 52	11 01				11 22	11 31					11 52	12 01				12 22	12 31				
Renton	d	10 55					11 25						11 55					12 25					
Alexandria	d	10 58					11 28						11 58					12 28					
Balloch	a	11 00					11 30						12 00					12 30					
Cardross	d		11 06					11 36						12 06					12 36				
Craigendoran	d		11 11					11 41						12 11					12 41				
Helensburgh Central	a		11 14					11 44						12 14					12 44				

Table 226

Sundays from 4 December

Lanark, Coatbridge, Motherwell, Larkhall, Hamilton, Edinburgh and Bathgate, Airdrie and Springburn - Glasgow - Milngavie, Dalmuir, Balloch and Helensburgh

		SR	SR	SR	SR	SR	SR	SR	SR	SR	SR	SR	SR	SR	SR	SR	SR	SR	SR	SR	SR	SR
Lanark	d										12 12											13 12
Carluke	d										12 22											13 22
Wishaw	d										12 27											13 27
Holytown	d																					
Shieldmuir	d										12 31											13 30
Coatbridge Central	d																					
Whifflet	d																					
Motherwell	a										12 34											13 36
	d	11 40			12 07		12 10				12 36		12 40			13 06		13 10				13 36
Bellshill	d				12 13						12 42					13 12						13 42
Uddingston	d				12 17						12 46					13 16						13 48
Airbles	d	11 42					12 12						12 42					13 12				
Larkhall	d								12 25											13 25		
Merryton	d								12 27											13 27		
Chatelherault	d								12 30											13 30		
Hamilton Central	d	11 47					12 17		12 34				12 47					13 17		13 34		
Hamilton West	d	11 50					12 20		12 36				12 50					13 20		13 36		
Blantyre	d	11 53					12 23		12 40				12 53					13 23		13 40		
Newton	d	11 57					12 27						12 57					13 27				
Cambuslang	d	12 01			12 22		12 31				12 51		13 01			13 21		13 31				13 53
Rutherglen	d	12 07			12 25		12 35		12 46		12 54		13 04			13 24		13 35		13 49		13 56
Dalmarnock	d																					
Bridgeton	d	12 10			12 28		12 38				12 57		13 07			13 27		13 38				13 59
Edinburgh	d							11 40						12 08					12 40			
Haymarket	d							11 44						12 12					12 44			
Edinburgh Park	d							11 49						12 17					12 49			
Uphall	d							11 57						12 25					12 57			
Livingston North	d							12 00						12 28					13 00			
Bathgate	a							12 05						12 33					13 05			
	d							12 06						12 36					13 06			
Armadale	d							12 10						12 40					13 10			
Blackridge	d							12 14						12 44					13 14			
Caldercruix	d							12 20						12 50					13 20			
Drumgelloch	d							12 24						12 54					13 24			
Airdrie	d		11 58			12 13		12 28				12 43		12 58			13 13		13 28			
Coatdyke	d		12 00			12 15		12 30				12 45		13 00			13 15		13 30			
Coatbridge Sunnyside	d		12 02			12 17		12 32				12 47		13 02			13 17		13 32			
Blairhill	d		12 05			12 20		12 35				12 50		13 05			13 20		13 35			
Easterhouse	d		12 09			12 24		12 39				12 54		13 09			13 24		13 39			
Garrowhill	d		12 11			12 26		12 41				12 56		13 11			13 26		13 41			
Shettleston	d		12 14			12 29		12 44				12 59		13 14			13 29		13 44			
Carntyne	d		12 16			12 31		12 46				13 01		13 16			13 31		13 46			
Springburn	d			12 19						12 49					13 19						13 49	
Barnhill	d			12 20						12 50					13 20						13 50	
Alexandra Parade	d			12 23						12 53					13 23						13 53	
Duke Street	d			12 25						12 55					13 25						13 55	
Bellgrove	d		12 19	12 27		12 34		12 49		12 57		13 04		13 19	13 27		13 34		13 49		13 57	
High Street	d		12 21	12 29		12 36		12 51		12 59		13 06		13 21	13 29		13 36		13 51		13 59	
Glasgow Queen St LL	a		12 23	12 31		12 39		12 53		13 01		13 09		13 23	13 31		13 39		13 53		14 01	
	d		12 24	12 31		12 39		12 54		13 01		13 09		13 24	13 31		13 39		13 54		14 01	
Charing Cross	d		12 27	12 33		12 42		12 57		13 03		13 12		13 27	13 33		13 42		13 57		14 03	
Argyle Street	d	12 13			12 32		12 42		12 52		13 01		13 11			13 31		13 42		13 54		14 03
Glasgow Central LL	a	12 14			12 34		12 44		12 55		13 04		13 14			13 34		13 44		13 57		14 06
	d	12 14			12 34		12 44		12 56		13 04		13 14			13 34		13 44		13 57		14 06
Anderston	d																					
Exhibition Centre	d	12 18			12 38		12 48		13 01		13 08		13 18			13 38		13 48		14 01		14 10
Partick	d	12 22	12 32	12 37	12 42	12 47	12 52	13 02	13a04	13 07	13 12	13 17	13 22	13 32	13 37	13 42	13 47	13 52	14 02	14a04	14 09	14 13
Hyndland	d	12 24	12 34	12 39	12 45	12 49	12 54	13 04		13 09	13 15	13 19	13 24	13 34	13 39	13 45	13 49	13 54	14 04		14 11	14 15
Jordanhill	d	12 26		12 41			12 56			13 11			13 26		13 41			13 56			14 13	
Scotstounhill	d	12 28		12 43			12 58			13 13			13 28		13 43			13 58			14 14	
Garscadden	d	12 30		12 46			13 00			13 16			13 30		13 46			14 00			14 17	
Yoker	d	12 33		12 48			13 03			13 18			13 33		13 48			14 03			14 20	
Clydebank	d	12 35		12 50			13 05			13 20			13 35		13 50			14 05			14 22	
Anniesland	d		12 37		12 48	12 52		13 07			13 18	13 22		13 37		13 48	13 52		14 07			14 18
Westerton	d		12 40		12 51	12 55		13 10			13 21	13 25		13 40		13 51	13 55		14 10			14 21
Bearsden	d				12 55						13 25					13 55						14 25
Hillfoot	d				12 57						13 27					13 57						14 27
Milngavie	a				13 00						13 30					14 00						14 30
Drumchapel	d		12 42			12 57		13 12				13 27		13 42			13 57		14 12			
Drumry	d		12 44			12 59		13 14				13 29		13 44			13 59		14 14			
Singer	d		12 47			13 02		13 17				13 32		13 47			14 02		14 17			
Dalmuir	a	12 39	12 49	12 53		13 04	13 09	13 19		13 24		13 34	13 39	13 49	13 53		14 04	14 09	14 19		14 25	
	d	12 39	12 50				13 09	13 20					13 39	13 50				14 09	14 20			
Kilpatrick	d	12 41					13 11						13 41					14 11				
Bowling	d	12 44					13 14						13 44					14 14				
Dumbarton East	d	12 49	12 58				13 19	13 28					13 49	13 58				14 19	14 28			
Dumbarton Central	d	12 51	13 00				13 21	13 30					13 51	14 00				14 21	14 30			
Dalreoch	d	12 52	13 01				13 22	13 31					13 52	14 01				14 22	14 31			
Renton	d	12 55					13 25						13 55					14 25				
Alexandria	d	12 58					13 28						13 58					14 28				
Balloch	a	13 00					13 30						14 00					14 30				
Cardross	d		13 06					13 36						14 06					14 36			
Craigendoran	d		13 11					13 41						14 11					14 41			
Helensburgh Central	a		13 14					13 44						14 14					14 44			

Lanark, Coatbridge, Motherwell, Larkhall, Hamilton, Edinburgh and Bathgate, Airdrie and Springburn - Glasgow - Milngavie, Dalmuir, Balloch and Helensburgh

		SR	SR	SR	SR	SR	SR	SR	SR	SR	SR	SR	SR	SR	SR	SR	SR	SR	SR	SR	SR	SR	SR
Lanark	d											14 12											15 12
Carluke	d											14 22											15 22
Wishaw	d											14 27											15 28
Holytown	d																						
Shieldmuir	d											14 31											15 31
Coatbridge Central	d																						
Whifflet	d																						
Motherwell	a											14 34											15 34
	d		13 40			14 06		14 10				14 34		14 40			15 06		15 10				15 35
Bellshill	d					14 12						14 40					15 12						15 41
Uddingston	d					14 16						14 44					15 16						15 45
Airbles	d		13 42					14 12						14 42					15 12				
Larkhall	d									14 25											15 25		
Merryton	d									14 27											15 27		
Chatelherault	d									14 30											15 30		
Hamilton Central	d		13 47					14 17		14 34				14 47					15 17		15 34		
Hamilton West	d		13 50					14 20		14 36				14 50					15 20		15 36		
Blantyre	d		13 53					14 23		14 40				14 53					15 23		15 40		
Newton	d		13 57					14 27						14 57					15 27				
Cambuslang	d		14 01			14 21		14 31				14 49		15 01			15 21		15 31				15 50
Rutherglen	d		14 05			14 24		14 34		14 48		14 53		15 06			15 24		15 34		15 48		15 53
Dalmarnock	d																						
Bridgeton	d		14 08			14 27		14 37				14 57		15 09			15 27		15 37				15 56
Edinburgh	d			13 11					13 40						14 06					14 40			
Haymarket	d			13 15					13 44						14 10					14 44			
Edinburgh Park	d			13 20					13 49						14 15					14 49			
Uphall	d			13 28					13 57						14 27					14 57			
Livingston North	d			13 31					14 00						14 30					15 00			
Bathgate	a			13 36					14 05						14 35					15 05			
	d			13 36					14 06						14 36					15 06			
Armadale	d			13 40					14 10						14 40					15 10			
Blackridge	d			13 44					14 14						14 44					15 14			
Caldercruix	d			13 50					14 20						14 50					15 20			
Drumgelloch	d			13 54					14 24						14 54					15 24			
Airdrie	d	13 43		13 58			14 13		14 28				14 43		14 58			15 13		15 28			
Coatdyke	d	13 45		14 00			14 15		14 30				14 45		15 00			15 15		15 30			
Coatbridge Sunnyside	d	13 47		14 02			14 17		14 32				14 47		15 02			15 17		15 32			
Blairhill	d	13 50		14 05			14 20		14 35				14 50		15 05			15 20		15 35			
Easterhouse	d	13 54		14 09			14 24		14 39				14 54		15 09			15 24		15 39			
Garrowhill	d	13 56		14 11			14 26		14 41				14 56		15 11			15 26		15 41			
Shettleston	d	13 59		14 14			14 29		14 44				14 59		15 14			15 29		15 44			
Carntyne	d	14 01		14 16			14 31		14 46				15 01		15 16			15 31		15 46			
Springburn	d				14 18						14 49					15 19						15 48	
Barnhill	d				14 19						14 50					15 20						15 49	
Alexandra Parade	d				14 22						14 53					15 23						15 52	
Duke Street	d				14 24						14 55					15 25						15 54	
Bellgrove	d	14 04		14 19	14 26		14 34		14 49		14 57		15 04		15 19	15 27		15 34		15 49		15 56	
High Street	d	14 06		14 21	14 28		14 36		14 51		14 59		15 06		15 21	15 29		15 36		15 51		15 58	
Glasgow Queen St LL 10	a	14 09		14 24	14 30		14 39		14 53		15 01		15 09		15 23	15 31		15 39		15 53		16 00	
	d	14 09		14 24	14 30		14 39		14 54		15 01		15 09		15 24	15 31		15 39		15 54		16 00	
Charing Cross	d	14 12		14 27	14 32		14 42		14 57		15 05		15 12		15 27	15 33		15 42		15 57		16 02	
Argyle Street	d		14 11			14 31		14 41		14 53		15 01		15 12			15 31		15 41		15 53		16 00
Glasgow Central LL 15	a		14 14			14 34		14 44		14 57		15 04		15 13			15 34		15 44		15 57		16 03
	d		14 14			14 34		14 44		14 57		15 04		15 13			15 34		15 44		15 57		16 04
Anderston	d																						
Exhibition Centre	d		14 18			14 38		14 48		15 01		15 08		15 17			15 38		15 48		16 01		16 08
Partick	d	14 17	14 22	14 32	14 36	14 42	14 47	14 52	15 02	15a04	15 09	15 12	15 17	15 21	15 32	15 37	15 42	15 47	15 52	16 02	16a04	16 08	16 12
Hyndland	d	14 19	14 24	14 34	14 38	14 45	14 49	14 54	15 04		15 11	15 15	15 19	15 23	15 34	15 39	15 45	15 49	15 54	16 04		16 10	16 15
Jordanhill	d		14 26		14 40			14 56			15 13			15 25		15 41			15 56			16 12	
Scotstounhill	d		14 28		14 42			14 58			15 14			15 27		15 43			15 58			16 14	
Garscadden	d		14 30		14 45			15 00			15 17			15 29		15 46			16 00			16 17	
Yoker	d		14 33		14 47			15 03			15 20			15 32		15 48			16 03			16 19	
Clydebank	d		14 35		14 49			15 05			15 22			15 34		15 50			16 05			16 21	
Anniesland	d	14 22		14 37		14 48	14 52		15 07			15 18	15 22		15 37		15 48	15 52		16 07			16 18
Westerton	d	14 25		14 40		14 51	14 55		15 10			15 21	15 25		15 40		15 51	15 55		16 10			16 21
Bearsden	d					14 55						15 25					15 55						16 25
Hillfoot	d					14 57						15 27					15 57						16 27
Milngavie	a					15 00						15 30					16 00						16 30
Drumchapel	d	14 27		14 42			14 57		15 12				15 27		15 42			15 57		16 12			
Drumry	d	14 29		14 44			14 59		15 14				15 29		15 44			15 59		16 14			
Singer	d	14 32		14 47			15 02		15 17				15 32		15 47			16 02		16 17			
Dalmuir	a	14 34	14 39	14 50	14 52		15 04	15 09	15 19		15 25		15 34	15 38	15 49	15 53		16 04	16 09	16 19		16 25	
	d		14 39	14 50				15 09	15 20					15 38	15 50				16 09	16 20			
Kilpatrick	d		14 41					15 11						15 41					16 11				
Bowling	d		14 44					15 14						15 44					16 14				
Dumbarton East	d		14 49	14 58				15 19	15 28					15 48	15 57				16 19	16 28			
Dumbarton Central	d		14 51	15 00				15 21	15 30					15 50	16 00				16 21	16 30			
Dalreoch	d		14 52	15 01				15 22	15 31					15 52	16 01				16 22	16 31			
Renton	d		14 55					15 25						15 55					16 25				
Alexandria	d		14 58					15 28						15 57					16 28				
Balloch	a		15 01					15 30						16 00					16 30				
Cardross	d			15 06					15 36						16 06					16 36			
Craigendoran	d			15 11					15 41						16 11					16 41			
Helensburgh Central	a			15 14					15 44						16 14					16 44			

Lanark, Coatbridge, Motherwell, Larkhall, Hamilton, Edinburgh and Bathgate, Airdrie and Springburn - Glasgow - Milngavie, Dalmuir, Balloch and Helensburgh

		SR	SR	SR	SR	SR	SR	SR	SR	SR	SR	SR	SR	SR	SR	SR	SR	SR	SR	SR	SR	SR
Lanark	d											16 12										
Carluke	d											16 22										
Wishaw	d											16 27										
Holytown	d																					
Shieldmuir	d											16 31										
Coatbridge Central	d																					
Whifflet	d																					
Motherwell	a											16 34										
	d		15 40			16 06		16 10				16 34		16 40			17 06		17 10			
Bellshill	d					16 12						16 40					17 12					
Uddingston	d					16 16						16 44					17 16					
Airbles	d		15 42					16 12						16 42					17 12			
Larkhall	d									16 25											17 25	
Merryton	d									16 27											17 27	
Chatelherault	d									16 30											17 30	
Hamilton Central	d		15 47					16 17		16 34				16 47					17 17		17 34	
Hamilton West	d		15 50					16 20		16 36				16 50					17 20		17 36	
Blantyre	d		15 53					16 23		16 40				16 53					17 23		17 40	
Newton	d		15 57					16 27						16 57					17 27			
Cambuslang	d		16 01			16 21		16 31				16 49		17 01			17 21		17 31			
Rutherglen	d		16 05			16 24		16 34		16 48		16 53		17 06			17 24		17 34		17 48	
Dalmarnock	d																					
Bridgeton	d		16 09			16 27		16 37				16 57		17 09			17 27		17 37			
Edinburgh	d			15 08					15 40						16 10					16 40		
Haymarket	d			15 12					15 44						16 14					16 44		
Edinburgh Park	d			15 19					15 49						16 19					16 49		
Uphall	d			15 27					15 57						16 27					16 57		
Livingston North	d			15 30					16 00						16 30					17 00		
Bathgate	a			15 35					16 05						16 36					17 05		
	d			15 36					16 06						16 36					17 06		
Armadale	d			15 40					16 10						16 40					17 10		
Blackridge	d			15 44					16 14						16 44					17 14		
Caldercruix	d			15 50					16 20						16 50					17 20		
Drumgelloch	d			15 54					16 24						16 54					17 24		
Airdrie	d	15 43		15 58			16 13		16 28				16 43		16 58			17 13		17 28		
Coatdyke	d	15 45		16 00			16 15		16 30				16 45		17 00			17 15		17 30		
Coatbridge Sunnyside	d	15 47		16 02			16 17		16 32				16 47		17 02			17 17		17 32		
Blairhill	d	15 50		16 05			16 20		16 35				16 50		17 05			17 20		17 35		
Easterhouse	d	15 54		16 09			16 24		16 39				16 54		17 09			17 24		17 39		
Garrowhill	d	15 56		16 11			16 26		16 41				16 56		17 11			17 26		17 41		
Shettleston	d	15 59		16 14			16 29		16 44				16 59		17 14			17 29		17 44		
Carntyne	d	16 01		16 16			16 31		16 46				17 01		17 16			17 31		17 46		
Springburn	d				16 19						16 49					17 19						17 49
Barnhill	d				16 20						16 50					17 20						17 50
Alexandra Parade	d				16 23						16 53					17 23						17 53
Duke Street	d				16 25						16 55					17 25						17 55
Bellgrove	d	16 04		16 19	16 27		16 34		16 49		16 57		17 04		17 19	17 27		17 34		17 49		17 57
High Street	d	16 06		16 21	16 29		16 36		16 51		16 59		17 06		17 21	17 29		17 36		17 51		17 59
Glasgow Queen St LL 10	a	16 09		16 23	16 31		16 39		16 53		17 01		17 09		17 24	17 31		17 39		17 53		18 01
	d	16 09		16 24	16 31		16 39		16 54		17 01		17 09		17 24	17 31		17 39		17 54		18 01
Charing Cross	d	16 12		16 27	16 33		16 42		16 57		17 03		17 12		17 27	17 33		17 42		17 57		18 03
Argyle Street	d		16 12			16 31		16 41		16 53		17 01		17 12			17 31		17 41		17 53	
Glasgow Central LL 15	a		16 14			16 34		16 44		16 57		17 04		17 14			17 34		17 44		17 57	
	d		16 14			16 34		16 44		16 57		17 04		17 14			17 34		17 44		17 57	
Anderston	d																					
Exhibition Centre	d		16 18			16 38		16 48		17 01		17 09		17 18			17 38		17 48		18 01	
Partick	d	16 17	16 22	16 32	16 37	16 42	16 47	16 52	17 02	17a04	17 09	17 13	17 17	17 22	17 32	17 37	17 42	17 47	17 52	18 02	18a04	18 10
Hyndland	d	16 19	16 24	16 34	16 39	16 45	16 49	16 54	17 04		17 11	17 15	17 19	17 24	17 34	17 39	17 45	17 49	17 54	18 04		18 12
Jordanhill	d		16 26		16 41			16 56			17 13			17 26		17 41			17 56			18 14
Scotstounhill	d		16 28		16 43			16 58			17 15			17 28		17 43			17 58			18 16
Garscadden	d		16 30		16 46			17 00			17 18			17 30		17 46			18 00			18 19
Yoker	d		16 33		16 48			17 03			17 20			17 33		17 48			18 03			18 21
Clydebank	d		16 35		16 50			17 05			17 22			17 35		17 50			18 05			18 23
Anniesland	d	16 22		16 37		16 48	16 52		17 07			17 18	17 22		17 37		17 48	17 52		18 07		
Westerton	d	16 25		16 40		16 51	16 55		17 10			17 21	17 25		17 40		17 51	17 55		18 10		
Bearsden	d					16 55						17 25					17 55					
Hillfoot	d					16 57						17 27					17 57					
Milngavie	a					17 00						17 30					18 00					
Drumchapel	d	16 27		16 42			16 57		17 12				17 27		17 42			17 57		18 12		
Drumry	d	16 29		16 44			16 59		17 14				17 29		17 44			17 59		18 14		
Singer	d	16 32		16 47			17 02		17 17				17 32		17 47			18 02		18 17		
Dalmuir	a	16 34	16 39	16 49	16 53		17 04	17 09	17 19		17 25		17 34	17 39	17 50	17 53		18 04	18 09	18 19		18 26
	d		16 39	16 50				17 09	17 20					17 39	17 50				18 09	18 20		
Kilpatrick	d		16 41					17 11						17 41					18 11			
Bowling	d		16 44					17 14						17 44					18 14			
Dumbarton East	d		16 49	16 57				17 19	17 28					17 49	17 58				18 19	18 28		
Dumbarton Central	d		16 51	17 00				17 21	17 30					17 51	18 00				18 21	18 30		
Dalreoch	d		16 52	17 01				17 22	17 31					17 52	18 01				18 22	18 31		
Renton	d		16 55					17 25						17 55					18 25			
Alexandria	d		16 58					17 28						17 58					18 28			
Balloch	a		17 00					17 30						18 00					18 30			
Cardross	d			17 06					17 36						18 06					18 36		
Craigendoran	d			17 11					17 41						18 11					18 40		
Helensburgh Central	a			17 14					17 44						18 14					18 44		

Table 226

Sundays from 4 December

Lanark, Coatbridge, Motherwell, Larkhall, Hamilton, Edinburgh and Bathgate, Airdrie and Springburn - Glasgow - Milngavie, Dalmuir, Balloch and Helensburgh

		SR	SR	SR	SR	SR	SR	SR	SR	SR	SR	SR	SR	SR	SR	SR	SR	SR	SR	SR	SR	SR	SR
			◇ A																				
Lanark	d	17 12									18 14								19 12				
Carluke	d	17 22									18 23								19 22				
Wishaw	d	17 27									18 28								19 27				
Holytown	d																						
Shieldmuir	d	17 31									18 32								19 31				
Coatbridge Central	d																						
Whifflet	d																						
Motherwell	a	17 34									18 36								19 34				
	d	17 34			17 40		18 06	18 10			18 36	18 40		19 06	19 10				19 34	19 40		20 06	20 10
Bellshill	d	17 40					18 12				18 42			19 12					19 40			20 12	
Uddingston	d	17 44					18 16				18 46			19 16					19 44			20 19	
Airbles	d				17 42			18 12				18 42			19 12					19 42			20 12
Larkhall	d									18 25								19 25					
Merryton	d									18 27								19 27					
Chatelherault	d									18 30								19 30					
Hamilton Central	d				17 47			18 17		18 34		18 47			19 17			19 34		19 47			20 17
Hamilton West	d				17 50			18 20		18 36		18 50			19 20			19 36		19 50			20 20
Blantyre	d				17 53			18 23		18 40		18 53			19 23			19 40		19 53			20 23
Newton	d				17 57			18 27				18 57			19 27					19 57			20 27
Cambuslang	d	17 49			18 01		18 21	18 31			18 51	19 01		19 21	19 31				19 49	20 01		20 24	20 31
Rutherglen	d	17 54			18 04		18 24	18 34		18 48	18 54	19 06		19 24	19 34			19 49	19 53	20 04		20 27	20 34
Dalmarnock	d																						
Bridgeton	d	17 57			18 08		18 27	18 37			18 57	19 09		19 27	19 37				19 57	20 07		20 30	20 37
Edinburgh	d					17 07			17 39				18 10			18 40	19 10						
Haymarket	d					17 11			17 44				18 14			18 44	19 14						
Edinburgh Park	d					17 16			17 49				18 19			18 49	19 19						
Uphall	d					17 25			17 57				18 27			18 57	19 27						
Livingston North	d					17 28			18 00				18 30			19 00	19 30						
Bathgate	a					17 33			18 05				18 35			19 05	19 35						
	d					17 36			18 06				18 36			19 06							
Armadale	d					17 40			18 10				18 40			19 10							
Blackridge	d					17 44			18 14				18 44			19 14							
Caldercruix	d					17 50			18 20				18 50			19 20							
Drumgelloch	d					17 54			18 24				18 54			19 24							
Airdrie	d			17 43		17 58			18 28				18 58			19 28					19 58		
Coatdyke	d			17 45		18 00			18 30				19 00			19 30					20 00		
Coatbridge Sunnyside	d			17 47		18 02			18 32				19 02			19 32					20 02		
Blairhill	d			17 50		18 05			18 35				19 05			19 35					20 05		
Easterhouse	d			17 54		18 09			18 39				19 09			19 39					20 09		
Garrowhill	d			17 56		18 11			18 41				19 11			19 41					20 11		
Shettleston	d			17 59		18 14			18 44				19 14			19 44					20 14		
Carntyne	d			18 01		18 16			18 46				19 16			19 46					20 16		
Springburn	d																						
Barnhill	d																						
Alexandra Parade	d																						
Duke Street	d																						
Bellgrove	d			18 04		18 19			18 49				19 19			19 49					20 19		
High Street	d			18 06		18 21			18 51				19 21			19 51					20 21		
Glasgow Queen St LL	a			18 09		18 23			18 53				19 24			19 53					20 23		
	d		18b20	18 09		18 24			18 54				19 24			19 54					20 24		
Charing Cross	d			18 12		18 27			18 57				19 27			19 57					20 27		
Argyle Street	d	18 01			18 12																		
Glasgow Central LL	a	18 04			18 14		18 34	18 44		18 56	19 04	19 14		19 34	19 44			19 57	20 04	20 14		20 34	20 44
	d	18 05			18 14		18 34	18 44		18 57	19 04	19 14		19 34	19 44			19 57	20 04	20 14		20 34	20 44
Anderston	d																						
Exhibition Centre	d	18 09			18 18		18 38	18 48		19 01	19 08	19 18		19 38	19 48			20 01	20 08	20 18		20 38	20 48
Partick	d	18 13		18 17	18 22	18 32	18 42	18 52	19 02	19a04	19 11	19 22	19 32	19 42	19 52	20 02		20a04	20 12	20 22	20 32	20 42	20 52
Hyndland	d	18 16		18 19	18 24	18 34	18 46	18 54	19 04		19 13	19 24	19 34	19 46	19 54	20 04			20 16	20 24	20 34	20 46	20 54
Jordanhill	d				18 26			18 56				19 26			19 56					20 26			20 56
Scotstounhill	d				18 28			18 58				19 28			19 58					20 28			20 58
Garscadden	d				18 30			19 00				19 30			20 00					20 30			21 00
Yoker	d				18 33			19 03				19 33			20 03					20 33			21 03
Clydebank	d				18 35			19 05				19 35			20 05					20 35			21 05
Anniesland	d	18 19		18 26		18 37	18 49		19 07		19 19		19 37	19 49		20 07			20 19		20 37	20 49	
Westerton	d	18 22		18 33		18 40	18 52		19 10		19 22		19 40	19 52		20 10			20 22		20 40	20 52	
Bearsden	d	18 25					18 55				19 25			19 55					20 25			20 55	
Hillfoot	d	18 27					18 57				19 27			19 57					20 27			20 57	
Milngavie	a	18 30					19 00				19 30			20 00					20 30			21 00	
Drumchapel	d			18 35		18 42			19 12				19 42			20 12					20 42		
Drumry	d			18 37		18 44			19 14				19 44			20 14					20 44		
Singer	d			18 40		18 47			19 17				19 47			20 17					20 47		
Dalmuir	a		18 34	18 42	18 39	18 49		19 09	19 19			19 39	19 50		20 09	20 19				20 39	20 49		21 09
	d		18 34		18 39	18 50		19 09	19 20			19 39	19 50		20 09	20 20				20 39	20 50		21 09
Kilpatrick	d				18 41			19 11				19 41			20 11					20 41			21 11
Bowling	d				18 44			19 14				19 44			20 14					20 44			21 14
Dumbarton East	d				18 49	18 58		19 19	19 28			19 49	19 58		20 19	20 28				20 49	20 58		21 19
Dumbarton Central	d		18 44		18 51	19 00		19 21	19 30			19 51	20 00		20 21	20 30				20 51	21 00		21 21
Dalreoch	d				18 52	19 01		19 22	19 31			19 52	20 01		20 22	20 31				20 52	21 01		21 22
Renton	d				18 55			19 25				19 55			20 25					20 55			21 25
Alexandria	d				18 58			19 28				19 58			20 28					20 58			21 28
Balloch	a				19 00			19 30				20 00			20 30					21 01			21 30
Cardross	d					19 06			19 36				20 06			20 36					21 06		
Craigendoran	d					19 11			19 41				20 11			20 41					21 11		
Helensburgh Central	a		18c59			19 14			19 44				20 14			20 44					21 14		

A To Oban

b Glasgow Queen St High Level

c Helensburgh Upper

Table 226

Sundays from 4 December

Lanark, Coatbridge, Motherwell, Larkhall, Hamilton, Edinburgh and Bathgate, Airdrie and Springburn - Glasgow - Milngavie, Dalmuir, Balloch and Helensburgh

		SR	SR	SR	SR	SR	SR	SR	SR	SR	SR	SR	SR	SR	SR	SR	SR	SR	SR	SR	SR	SR	SR
Lanark	d				20 12							21 12							22 12				
Carluke	d				20 23							21 23							22 23				
Wishaw	d				20 30							21 28							22 28				
Holytown	d																						
Shieldmuir	d				20 34							21 32							22 32				
Coatbridge Central	d																						
Whifflet	d																						
Motherwell	a				20 37							21 35							22 35				
	d				20 37	20 40		21 06	21 10			21 36	21 40		22 06	22 10			22 36	22 40		23 06	23 10
Bellshill	d				20 43			21 12				21 42			22 12				22 42			23 12	
Uddingston	d				20 47			21 16				21 46			22 15				22 46			23 16	
Airbles	d					20 42			21 12				21 42			22 12				22 42			23 12
Larkhall	d			20 25							21 25							22 25					
Merryton	d			20 27							21 27							22 27					
Chatelherault	d			20 30							21 30							22 30					
Hamilton Central	d			20 34		20 47			21 17		21 34		21 47			22 17		22 34		22 47			23 17
Hamilton West	d			20 36		20 50			21 20		21 36		21 50			22 20		22 36		22 50			23 20
Blantyre	d			20 40		20 53			21 23		21 40		21 53			22 23		22 40		22 53			23 23
Newton	d					20 57			21 28				21 57			22 27				22 57			23 27
Cambuslang	d				20 52	21 01		21 21	21 32			21 51	22 01		22 20	22 31			22 51	23 01		23 21	23 31
Rutherglen	d			20 48	20 56	21 04		21 25	21 35		21 48	21 54	22 06		22 23	22 34		22 48	22 54	23 04		23 24	23 34
Dalmarnock	d																						
Bridgeton	d				20 59	21 07		21 28	21 38			21 57	22 09		22 27	22 37			22 57	23 07		23 27	23 37
Edinburgh	d	19 40	20 08							20 40							21 38						
Haymarket	d	19 44	20 12							20 44							21 42						
Edinburgh Park	d	19 49	20 17							20 49							21 47						
Uphall	d	19 57	20 25							20 57							21 55						
Livingston North	d	20 00	20 28							21 00							21 58						
Bathgate	a	20 05	20 33							21 05							22 03						
	d	20 06								21 06							22 06						
Armadale	d	20 10								21 10							22 10						
Blackridge	d	20 14								21 14							22 14						
Caldercruix	d	20 20								21 20							22 20						
Drumgelloch	d	20 24								21 24							22 24						
Airdrie	d	20 28					20 58			21 28				21 58			22 28				22 58		
Coatdyke	d	20 30					21 00			21 30				22 00			22 30				23 00		
Coatbridge Sunnyside	d	20 32					21 02			21 32				22 02			22 32				23 02		
Blairhill	d	20 35					21 05			21 35				22 05			22 35				23 05		
Easterhouse	d	20 39					21 09			21 39				22 09			22 39				23 09		
Garrowhill	d	20 41					21 11			21 41				22 11			22 41				23 11		
Shettleston	d	20 44					21 14			21 44				22 14			22 44				23 14		
Carntyne	d	20 46					21 16			21 46				22 16			22 46				23 16		
Springburn	d																						
Barnhill	d																						
Alexandra Parade	d																						
Duke Street	d																						
Bellgrove	d	20 49					21 19			21 49				22 19			22 49				23 19		
High Street	d	20 51					21 21			21 51				22 21			22 51				23 21		
Glasgow Queen St LL	a	20 54					21 23			21 53				22 23			22 53				23 23		
	d	20 54					21 24			21 54				22 24			22 54				23 24		
Charing Cross	d	20 57					21 27			21 57				22 27			22 57				23 27		
Argyle Street	d																						
Glasgow Central LL	a			20 57	21 04	21 14		21 34	21 44		21 56	22 04	22 14		22 34	22 44		22 57	23 04	23 14		23 34	23 44
	d			20 58	21 04	21 14		21 34	21 44		21 57	22 04	22 14		22 34	22 44		22 57	23 04	23 14		23 34	23 44
Anderston	d																						
Exhibition Centre	d			21 01	21 08	21 18		21 38	21 48		22 01	22 08	22 18		22 38	22 48		23 01	23 08	23 18		23 38	23 48
Partick	d	21 02		21a05	21 12	21 22	21 32	21 42	21 52	22 02	22a04	22 12	22 22	22 32	22 42	22 52	23 02	23a04	23 12	23 22	23 32	23 42	23 52
Hyndland	d	21 04			21 16	21 24	21 34	21 46	21 54	22 04		22 16	22 24	22 34	22 46	22 54	23 04		23 16	23 24	23 34	23 44	23 54
Jordanhill	d					21 26			21 56				22 26			22 56				23 26		23 46	23 56
Scotstounhill	d					21 28			21 58				22 28			22 58				23 28		23 48	23 58
Garscadden	d					21 30			22 00				22 30			23 00				23 30		23a50	00a01
Yoker	d					21 33			22 03				22 33			23 03				23 33			
Clydebank	d					21 35			22 05				22 35			23 05				23 35			
Anniesland	d	21 07			21 19		21 37	21 49		22 07		22 19		22 37	22 49		23 07		23 19		23 37		
Westerton	d	21 10			21 22		21 40	21 52		22 10		22 22		22 40	22 52		23 10		23 22		23 40		
Bearsden	d				21 25			21 55				22 25			22 55				23 25				
Hillfoot	d				21 27			21 57				22 27			22 57				23 27				
Milngavie	a				21 30			22 00				22 30			23 00				23 30				
Drumchapel	d	21 12					21 42			22 12				22 42			23 12				23 42		
Drumry	d	21 14					21 44			22 14				22 44			23 14				23 44		
Singer	d	21 17					21 47			22 17				22 47			23 17				23 47		
Dalmuir	a	21 20				21 39	21 49		22 09	22 19			22 39	22 49		23 09	23 19			23 39	23 49		
	d	21 20				21 39	21 50		22 09	22 20			22 39	22 50		23 09	23 20			23 39	23 50		
Kilpatrick	d					21 41			22 11				22 41			23 11				23 41			
Bowling	d					21 44			22 14				22 44			23 14				23 44			
Dumbarton East	d	21 28				21 49	21 58		22 19	22 28			22 49	22 58		23 19	23 28			23 49	23 58		
Dumbarton Central	d	21 30				21 51	22 00		22 21	22 30			22 51	23 00		23 21	23 30			23 51	23 59		
Dalreoch	d	21 31				21 52	22 01		22 22	22 31			22 52	23 01		23 22	23 31			23 52	00 01		
Renton	d					21 55			22 25				22 55			23 25				23 55			
Alexandria	d					21 58			22 28				22 58			23 28				23 58			
Balloch	a					22 00			22 30				23 00			23 30				00 01			
Cardross	d	21 36					22 06			22 36				23 06			23 36				00 06		
Craigendoran	d	21 41					22 11			22 41				23 11			23 41				00 11		
Helensburgh Central	a	21 45					22 14			22 44				23 14			23 44				00 14		

Table 226

Sundays from 4 December

Lanark, Coatbridge, Motherwell, Larkhall, Hamilton, Edinburgh and Bathgate, Airdrie and Springburn - Glasgow - Milngavie, Dalmuir, Balloch and Helensburgh

Station		SR	SR
Lanark	d		
Carluke	d		
Wishaw	d		
Holytown	d		
Shieldmuir	d		
Coatbridge Central	d		
Whifflet	d		
Motherwell	a		
	d		
Bellshill	d		
Uddingston	d		
Airbles	d		
Larkhall	d		
Merryton	d		
Chatelherault	d		
Hamilton Central	d		
Hamilton West	d		
Blantyre	d		
Newton	d		
Cambuslang	d		
Rutherglen	d		
Dalmarnock	d		
Bridgeton	d		
Edinburgh	d	22 40	23 18
Haymarket	d	22 44	23 22
Edinburgh Park	d	22 49	23 27
Uphall	d	22 57	23 35
Livingston North	d	23 00	23 38
Bathgate	a	23 05	23 43
	d	23 06	
Armadale	d	23 10	
Blackridge	d	23 14	
Caldercruix	d	23 20	
Drumgelloch	d	23 24	
Airdrie	d	23 28	
Coatdyke	d	23 30	
Coatbridge Sunnyside	d	23 32	
Blairhill	d	23 35	
Easterhouse	d	23 39	
Garrowhill	d	23 41	
Shettleston	d	23 44	
Carntyne	d	23 46	
Springburn	d		
Barnhill	d		
Alexandra Parade	d		
Duke Street	d		
Bellgrove	d	23 49	
High Street	d	23 51	
Glasgow Queen St LL	a	23 53	
	d	23 54	
Charing Cross	d	23 57	
Argyle Street	d		
Glasgow Central LL	a		
	d		
Anderston	d		
Exhibition Centre	d		
Partick	d	00 01	
Hyndland	d	00 03	
Jordanhill	d	00 05	
Scotstounhill	d	00 07	
Garscadden	d	00 09	
Yoker	d	00 12	
Clydebank	d		
Anniesland	d		
Westerton	d		
Bearsden	d		
Hillfoot	d		
Milngavie	a		
Drumchapel	d		
Drumry	d		
Singer	d		
Dalmuir	a	00 16	
	d		
Kilpatrick	d		
Bowling	d		
Dumbarton East	d		
Dumbarton Central	d		
Dalreoch	d		
Renton	d		
Alexandria	d		
Balloch	a		
Cardross	d		
Craigendoran	d		
Helensburgh Central	a		

Helensburgh, Balloch, Dalmuir and Milngavie - Glasgow - Springburn, Airdrie, Bathgate and Edinburgh, Hamilton, Larkhall, Motherwell, Coatbridge and Lanark

Miles	Miles	Miles	Miles	Miles	Station		SR MX	SR MO	SR MX	SR MX	SR MX	SR MX	SR	SR	SR		SR	SR	SR	SR	SR	SR	SR	SR	SR
								A				A						B							
0	—	—	—	—	**Helensburgh Central**	d		22b37	22p40		23p10	23b24													
1¼	—	—	—	—	Craigendoran	d			22p43		23p13														
4¼	—	—	—	—	Cardross	d			22p48		23p18														
—	0	—	—	—	**Balloch**	d				22p53															
—	1	—	—	—	Alexandria	d				22p55															
—	2¼	—	—	—	Renton	d				22p58															
8	3¾	—	—	—	Dalreoch	d			22p53	23p01	23p23														
8¾	4	—	—	—	Dumbarton Central	d			22p55	23p02	23p25														
9	4¾	—	—	—	Dumbarton East	d			22p57	23p04	23p27														
11¾	7½	—	—	—	Bowling	d				23p09															
13½	9¼	—	—	—	Kilpatrick	d				23p12															
14¾	10½	0	0	—	**Dalmuir**	a		23p02	23p05	23p15	23p35	23p49													
—	—	—	—	—		d	23p01	23p04	23p05	23p16	23p35	23p51					05 47					06 01			06 16
15½	11¼	—	0¾	—	Singer	d	23p03			23p18												06 03			06 18
16½	12¼	—	1¾	—	Drumry	d	23p05			23p20												06 05			06 20
17¼	13	—	2½	—	Drumchapel	d	23p08			23p23												06 08			06 23
—	—	—	—	0	**Milngavie**	d																			
—	—	—	—	1½	Hillfoot	d																			
—	—	—	—	2¼	Bearsden	d																			
18½	14¼	—	3¾	3½	Westerton	d	23p10	23p13		23p25		23p56										06 10			06 25
19¾	15½	—	5	4¾	Anniesland	d	23p14			23p28												06 14			06 28
—	—	1¼	—	—	Clydebank	d			23p07		23p37						05 49								
—	—	2¼	—	—	Yoker	d			23p09		23p39						05 51								
—	—	3¼	—	—	Garscadden	d			23p13		23p43				05 42		05 54			06 00	06 08		06 13	06 17	
—	—	3¾	—	—	Scotstounhill	d			23p15		23p45				05 44		05 56			06 01	06 10		06 15	06 19	
—	—	4¾	—	—	Jordanhill	d			23p17		23p47				05 46		05 58			06 03	06 12		06 18	06 21	
20¾	16½	5¼	6	5¾	Hyndland	d	23p17		23p21	23p31	23p49				05 48		06 01			06 05	06 14	06 17	06 20	06 22	06 31
21¼	17	—	6½	6¼	Partick	d	23p20		23p23	23p34	23p52				05 51		06 04			06 10	06 17	06 20	06 22	06 25	06 34
—	—	—	8¼	7½	Exhibition Centre	d	23p23													06 13		06 23		06 28	
—	—	—	8¾	8	Anderston	d	23p25													06 15		06 25		06 30	
—	—	—	8¾	8½	**Glasgow Central LL**	a	23p26													06 17		06 26		06 32	
—	—	—	—	—		d	23p27											06e16		06 17		06 27		06 32	
—	—	—	9¼	9	Argyle Street	d	23p29													06 19		06 29		06 34	
23¼	19	—	—	—	Charing Cross	d			23p27	23p38	23p56				05 55		06 08				06 21		06 26		06 38
24	19¾	—	—	—	**Glasgow Queen St LL**	a			23p29	23p40	23p59				05 57		06 10				06 23		06 28		06 40
—	—	—	—	—		d			23p30	23p44	23p59				05 58		06 12				06 24		06 29		06 42
24½	20¼	—	—	—	High Street	d			23p32	23p46	00 02				06 00		06 14				06 26		06 31		06 44
25	20¾	—	—	—	Bellgrove	d			23p34	23p49	00 04				06 02		06 16				06 28		06 33		06 46
—	21¼	—	—	—	Duke Street	d															06 30				
—	21½	—	—	—	Alexandra Parade	d															06 31				
—	22¼	—	—	—	Barnhill	d															06 34				
—	23	—	—	—	**Springburn**	a															06 36				
26¼	—	—	—	—	Carntyne	d			23p37	23p52	00 07				06 05		06 19						06 36		06 49
27½	—	—	—	—	Shettleston	d			23p40	23p55	00 10				06 08		06 22						06 39		06 52
28¾	—	—	—	—	Garrowhill	d			23p42	23p57	00 12				06 10		06 24						06 41		06 54
29¼	—	—	—	—	Easterhouse	d			23p45	23p59	00 15				06 13		06 27						06 44		06 57
32½	—	—	—	—	Blairhill	d			23p49	00 04	00 19				06 17		06 31						06 48		07 01
33	—	—	—	—	Coatbridge Sunnyside	d			23p51	00 06	00 21				06 19		06 33						06 50		07 03
34	—	—	—	—	Coatdyke	d			23p54	00 09	00 24				06 22		06 36						06 53		07 06
35	—	—	—	—	**Airdrie**	d			23p57	00a12	00a27				06 25		06 45						06 56		07a09
36½	—	—	—	—	Drumgelloch	d			23p59						06 28		06 48						06 59		
39½	—	—	—	—	Caldercruix	d			00 03						06 32								07 03		
45	—	—	—	—	Blackridge	d			00 09						06 38								07 09		
47¼	—	—	—	—	Armadale	d			00 13						06 41								07 13		
49¾	—	—	—	—	**Bathgate**	a			00 17						06 45		07 00						07 17		
—	—	—	—	—		d							05 44	06 18	06 47		07 02						07 18		
52¾	—	—	—	—	Livingston North	d							05 48	06 22	06 50		07 06						07 22		
55¾	—	—	—	—	Uphall	d							05 51	06 25	06 53		07 09						07 25		
64½	—	—	—	—	Edinburgh Park	a							05 59	06 36	07 02		07 19						07 33		
67	—	—	—	—	Haymarket	a							06 05	06 41	07 07		07 24						07 38		
68¼	—	—	—	—	**Edinburgh**	a		00 13				00 50	06 10	06 46	07 13		07 29						07 43		
—	—	—	10½	10¼	Bridgeton	d														06 22				06 37	
—	—	—	11	10¾	Dalmarnock	d														06 24				06 39	
—	—	—	11¾	11½	Rutherglen	d	23p34													06 25		06 34		06 41	
—	—	—	13½	13¼	Cambuslang	d												06 25		06 30				06 45	
—	—	0	—	14¾	Newton	d																		06 49	
—	—	2½	—	—	Blantyre	d	23p44															06 44		06 53	
—	—	4½	—	—	Hamilton West	d	23p47															06 47		06 56	
0	—	5¼	—	—	**Hamilton Central**	d	23p50															06 50		06 59	
2¼	—	—	—	—	Chatelherault	d	23p53															06 53			
3¾	—	—	—	—	Merryton	d	23p56															06 56			
5¼	—	—	—	—	**Larkhall**	a	00 01															06 59			
0	—	7½	—	—	Airbles	d																		07 04	
—	—	—	17	16¾	Uddingston	d												06 30		06 35					
—	—	—	19½	—	Bellshill	d												06 35		06 40					
—	0	8¼	22½	21	**Motherwell**	a														06 45				07 06	
—	—	—	—	—		d													06 37	06 47				07 07	
—	4½	—	—	—	Whifflet	a																		07 15	
—	5¼	—	—	—	**Coatbridge Central**	a																		07 21	
—	—	—	—	22½	Shieldmuir	d														06 49					
—	—	—	—	—	Holytown	d												06a39	06 43						
—	—	—	—	24¼	Wishaw	d													06 49	06 53					
—	—	—	—	28¾	Carluke	d													06 55	06 59					
—	—	—	—	37¼	**Lanark**	a													07 07	07 14					

A From Fort William
B To Edinburgh
b Helensburgh Upper, previous night
e Glasgow Central High Level

Helensburgh, Balloch, Dalmuir and Milngavie - Glasgow - Springburn, Airdrie, Bathgate and Edinburgh, Hamilton, Larkhall, Motherwell, Coatbridge and Lanark

Station		SR	SR	SR	SR	SR	SR	SR	SR A	SR	SR	SR	SR	SR	SR	SR	SR	SR	SR	SR	SR	SR
Helensburgh Central	d			06 10								06 40							07 10			
Craigendoran	d			06 13								06 43							07 13			
Cardross	d			06 18								06 48							07 18			
Balloch	d							06 23								06 53						
Alexandria	d							06 25								06 55						
Renton	d							06 28								06 58						
Dalreoch	d			06 23				06 31				06 53				07 01			07 23			
Dumbarton Central	d			06 25				06 32				06 55				07 02			07 25			
Dumbarton East	d			06 27				06 34				06 57				07 04			07 27			
Bowling	d							06 39								07 09						
Kilpatrick	d							06 42								07 12						
Dalmuir	a			06 34				06 45				07 04				07 15			07 34			
	d	06 24		06 35	06 31			06 46		06 53		07 05	07 01			07 16	07 23		07 35	07 31	07 38	
Singer	d				06 33			06 48					07 03			07 18				07 33		
Drumry	d				06 35			06 50					07 05			07 20				07 35		
Drumchapel	d				06 38			06 53					07 08			07 23				07 38		
Milngavie	d						06 42				06 56				07 12			07 27				07 42
Hillfoot	d						06 45				06 59				07 15			07 30				07 45
Bearsden	d						06 47				07 01				07 17			07 32				07 49
Westerton	d				06 40		06 50	06 55			07 05		07 10		07 20	07 25		07 35		07 40		07 52
Anniesland	d				06 44		06 53	06 58			07 08		07 14		07 23	07 28		07 38		07 44		07 55
Clydebank	d	06 26								06 55							07 25				07 40	
Yoker	d	06 28								06 57							07 27				07 42	
Garscadden	d	06 31				06 46				07 01				07 16			07 31				07 46	
Scotstounhill	d	06 33				06 48				07 03				07 18			07 33				07 48	
Jordanhill	d	06 35				06 50				07 05				07 20			07 35				07 50	
Hyndland	d	06 37	06 41	06 44	06 47	06 52	06 56	07 01		07 07	07 11	07 14	07 17	07 22	07 26	07 31	07 37	07 41	07 44	07 47	07 52	07 58
Partick ⛴	d	06 40	06 43	06 46	06 49	06 55	06 59	07 04		07 10	07 14	07 17	07 20	07 25	07 29	07 34	07 40	07 44	07 47	07 50	07 55	08 00
Exhibition Centre	d	06 43			06 52		07 02			07 13			07 23		07 32		07 43			07 53		08 03
Anderston	d	06 45			06 54		07 04			07 15			07 25		07 34		07 45			07 55		08 05
Glasgow Central LL 15	a	06 46			06 55		07 05			07 16			07 26		07 35		07 46			07 56		08 07
	d	06 48			06 57		07 07		07b13	07 17			07 27		07 37		07 47			07 57		08 09
Argyle Street	d	06 50			06 58		07 09			07 19			07 29		07 39		07 49			07 59		08 11
Charing Cross	d		06 49	06 54		06 59		07 08			07 19	07 24		07 29		07 38		07 49	07 54		07 59	
Glasgow Queen St LL 10 ⛴	a		06 51	06 56		07 01		07 10			07 21	07 26		07 31		07 40		07 51	07 56		08 01	
	d		06 54	06 57		07 02		07 12			07 24	07 28		07 32		07 42		07 54	07 58		08 02	
High Street	d		06 56	07 00		07 04		07 14			07 26	07 30		07 34		07 44		07 56	08 00		08 04	
Bellgrove	d			07 01		07 06		07 16				07 32		07 36		07 46			08 01		08 06	
Duke Street	d					07 08								07 38							08 08	
Alexandra Parade	d					07 09								07 39							08 09	
Barnhill	d					07 12								07 42							08 12	
Springburn	a					07 14								07 44							08 14	
Carntyne	d			07 05				07 19				07 36				07 49			08 05			
Shettleston	d			07 07				07 22				07 38				07 52			08 07			
Garrowhill	d			07 10				07 24				07 41				07 54			08 10			
Easterhouse	d			07 12				07 27				07 43				07 57			08 12			
Blairhill	d			07 16				07 31				07 47				08 01			08 16			
Coatbridge Sunnyside	d		07 09	07 19				07 33			07 38	07 50				08 03		08 09	08 19			
Coatdyke	d			07 21				07 36				07 52				08 06			08 21			
Airdrie	d		07 15	07 24				07a39			07 45	07 55				08a09		08 15	08 24			
Drumgelloch	d		07 18	07 27							07 48	07 58						08 18	08 27			
Caldercruix	d			07 31								08 02							08 31			
Blackridge	d			07 37								08 08							08 37			
Armadale	d			07 41								08 12							08 41			
Bathgate	a		07 29	07 46							08 00	08 16						08 30	08 45			
	d		07 31	07 46							08 02	08 17						08 31	08 46			
Livingston North	d		07 36	07 50							08 06	08 21						08 36	08 51			
Uphall	d		07 39	07 53							08 09	08 24						08 39	08 54			
Edinburgh Park	a		07 53	08 01							08 16	08 33						08 47	09 03			
Haymarket	a		07 57	08 08							08 23	08 38						08 52	09 08			
Edinburgh	a		08 02	08 14							08 29	08 43						08 58	09 13			
Bridgeton	d	06 53					07 12			07 22					07 42		07 52					08 14
Dalmarnock	d	06 55					07 14			07 24					07 44		07 54					08 16
Rutherglen	d	06 57			07 03		07 17			07 26			07 34		07 46		07 56			08 05		08 18
Cambuslang	d	07 01					07 21		07 23	07 31					07 50		08 00					08 22
Newton	d						07 24								07 54							08 26
Blantyre	d				07 12		07 28						07 44		07 58					08 14		08 30
Hamilton West	d				07 15		07 31						07 47		08 01					08 17		08 33
Hamilton Central	d				07 17		07 34						07 50		08 03					08 20		08 35
Chatelherault	d				07 21								07 53							08 23		
Merryton	d				07 24								07 56							08 26		
Larkhall	a				07 27								07 59							08 29		
Airbles	d						07 39								08 08							08 40
Uddingston	d	07 06							07 29	07 35							08 05					
Bellshill	d	07 10							07 34	07 40							08 10					
Motherwell	a	07 18					07 41			07 46					08 11		08 17					08 43
	d									07 46												
Whifflet	a																					
Coatbridge Central	a																					
Shieldmuir	d									07 50												
Holytown	d								07a38													
Wishaw	d									07 53												
Carluke	d									08 00												
Lanark	a									08 15												

A To Edinburgh
b Glasgow Central High Level

Helensburgh, Balloch, Dalmuir and Milngavie - Glasgow - Springburn, Airdrie, Bathgate and Edinburgh, Hamilton, Larkhall, Motherwell, Coatbridge and Lanark

Station		SR	SR A	SR	SR	SR	SR	SR B	SR	SR	SR	SR	SR	SR	SR	SR	SR	SR	SR	SR	SR	SR A	SR
Helensburgh Central	d				07 34			07e42					08 00	07 54			08 10						
Craigendoran	d				07 37								08 03	07 57			08 13						
Cardross	d				07 42			07 50					08 08	08 02			08 18						
Balloch	d	07 23							07 53												08 23		
Alexandria	d	07 25							07 55												08 25		
Renton	d	07 28							07 58												08 28		
Dalreoch	d	07 31			07 47				08 01					08 07			08 23				08 31		
Dumbarton Central	d	07 32			07 49			07 56	08 03				08 14	08 09			08 25				08 32		
Dumbarton East	d	07 34			07 51									08 11			08 27				08 34		
Bowling	d	07 39			07 56												08 30				08 39		
Kilpatrick	d	07 42			07 59												08 32				08 42		
Dalmuir	a	07 45			08 02				08 12					08 18			08 34				08 45		
	d	07 46		07 53	08 02		08 00		08 12	08 08				08 18	08 23		08 35	08 31	08 39		08 46		08 53
Singer	d	07 48					08 02	08 07						08 21				08 33			08 48		
Drumry	d	07 50					08 04							08 24				08 35			08 50		
Drumchapel	d	07 54					08 07							08 26				08 38			08 53		
Milngavie	d					07 58					08 10	08 18				08 29				08 42			
Hillfoot	d					08 01					08 13	08 21				08 32				08 45			
Bearsden	d					08 02					08 16	08 24				08 34				08 47			
Westerton	d	07 56				08 05	08 11				08 19			08 29		08 37		08 42		08 50	08 55		
Anniesland	d	07 59				08 10	08 15				08 23			08 32		08 40		08 46		08 53	08 58		
Clydebank	d			07 55	08 05					08 10					08 25				08 40				08 55
Yoker	d			07 57						08 12					08 27				08 42				08 57
Garscadden	d			08 01						08 16					08 31				08 46				09 01
Scotstounhill	d			08 03						08 18			08 27		08 33				08 48				09 03
Jordanhill	d			08 05						08 21					08 35				08 50				09 05
Hyndland	d	08 02		08 07	08 11	08 13	08 18			08 24	08 26		08 33	08 35	08 37	08 43	08 44	08 47	08 52	08 56	09 01		09 08
Partick ⛴	d	08 05		08 10	08 14	08 16	08 20		08 22	08 26	08 29		08 35	08 37	08 40	08 45	08 47	08 50	08 55	08 59	09 04		09 10
Exhibition Centre	d			08 13		08 19	08 23				08 32				08 43			08 53		09 02			09 13
Anderston	d			08 15		08 21	08 25				08 34				08 45			08 55		09 04			09 15
Glasgow Central LL 15	a			08 16		08 23	08 26				08 35				08 47			08 57		09 06			09 16
	d		08c18	08 17		08 23	08 26				08 37				08 47			08 57		09 07		09c18	09 17
Argyle Street	d			08 19		08 24	08 28				08 39				08 49			08 59		09 08			09 19
Charing Cross	d	08 09			08 19				08 27	08 31		08 35	08 40	08 42		08 49	08 54		08 59		09 08		
Glasgow Queen St LL 10 ⛴	a	08 12			08 21			08f37	08 29	08 33		08 37	08 42	08 44		08 51	08 56		09 01		09 10		
	d	08 12			08 24				08 29	08 33		08 38	08 42	08 44		08 54	08 58		09 02		09 12		
High Street	d	08 14			08 27				08 31	08 35		08 40	08 44	08a47		08 56	09 00		09 04		09 14		
Bellgrove	d	08 16			08 29				08 33	08 37			08 46				09 02		09 06		09 16		
Duke Street	d								08 35	08 42									09 08				
Alexandra Parade	d								08 37	08 43									09 09				
Barnhill	d								08 40	08 46									09 12				
Springburn	a								08 42	08 48									09 14				
Carntyne	d	08 19			08 32								08 49				09 06				09 19		
Shettleston	d	08 22			08 35								08 52				09 09				09 22		
Garrowhill	d	08 24			08 37								08 54				09 11				09 24		
Easterhouse	d	08 27			08 40								08 57				09 14				09 27		
Blairhill	d	08 31			08 44								09 01				09 18				09 31		
Coatbridge Sunnyside	d	08 33			08 46							08 52	09 03			09 12	09 20				09 33		
Coatdyke	d	08 36			08 49								09 06				09 23				09 36		
Airdrie	d	08 44			08a52							08 57	09a09			09 16	09 26				09a39		
Drumgelloch	d	08 47										09 00				09 19	09 29						
Caldercruix	d											09 04					09 33						
Blackridge	d											09 10					09 39						
Armadale	d											09 14					09 42						
Bathgate	a	09 00										09 18				09 32	09 46						
	d	09 01										09 18				09 32	09 47						
Livingston North	d	09 06										09 22				09 36	09 50						
Uphall	d	09 09										09 25				09 40	09 53						
Edinburgh Park	a	09 18										09 33				09 48	10 01						
Haymarket	a	09 22										09 38				09 52	10 08						
Edinburgh	a	09 27										09 43				09 57	10 14						
Bridgeton	d			08 22		08 26					08 42				08 52					09 11			09 22
Dalmarnock	d			08 24		08 28					08 44				08 54					09 13			09 24
Rutherglen	d			08 26		08 31	08 34				08 46				08 56			09 04		09 16			09 27
Cambuslang	d			08 31							08 51				09 01					09 20			09 31
Newton	d										08 54									09 24			
Blantyre	d						08 44				08 58							09 14		09 28			
Hamilton West	d						08 47				09 01							09 17		09 31			
Hamilton Central	d						08 50				09 04							09 20		09 33			
Chatelherault	d						08 53											09 23					
Merryton	d						08 56											09 26					
Larkhall	a						08 59											09 29					
Airbles	d										09 09									09 38			
Uddingston	d		08 30	08 36											09 05							09 30	09 35
Bellshill	d		08 34	08 41											09 10							09 34	09 40
Motherwell	a			08 46		08 46					09 13				09 16					09 42			09 47
	d			08 47											09 16					09 42			
Whifflet	a																						
Coatbridge Central	a																						
Shieldmuir	d			08 50											09 20								
Holytown	d		08a38																	09 48		09a38	
Wishaw	d			08 53											09 23					09 54			
Carluke	d			09 00											09 30					10 00			
Lanark	a			09 12											09 42					10 15			

A To Edinburgh
B From Arrochar & Tarbet
c Glasgow Central High Level
e Helensburgh [illegible]
f Glasgow Queen St High Level

Helensburgh, Balloch, Dalmuir and Milngavie - Glasgow - Springburn, Airdrie, Bathgate and Edinburgh, Hamilton, Larkhall, Motherwell, Coatbridge and Lanark

		SR	SR	SR	SR	SR	SR	SR	SR	SR	SR	SR	SR	SR	SR	SR	SR	SR	SR	SR	SR	SR
															A							
Helensburgh Central	d		08 40							09 10								09 40				
Craigendoran	d		08 43							09 13								09 43				
Cardross	d		08 48							09 18								09 48				
Balloch	d						08 53							09 23								09 53
Alexandria	d						08 55							09 25								09 55
Renton	d						08 58							09 28								09 58
Dalreoch	d		08 53				09 01			09 23				09 31				09 53				10 01
Dumbarton Central	d		08 55				09 02			09 25				09 32				09 55				10 02
Dumbarton East	d		08 57				09 04			09 27				09 34				09 57				10 04
Bowling	d						09 09							09 39								10 09
Kilpatrick	d						09 12							09 42								10 12
Dalmuir	a		09 04				09 15			09 34				09 45				10 04				10 15
	d		09 05	09 01	09 08		09 16	09 23		09 35	09 31	09 38		09 46		09 53		10 05	10 01	10 08		10 16
Singer	d			09 03			09 18				09 33			09 48					10 03			10 18
Drumry	d			09 05			09 20				09 35			09 50					10 05			10 20
Drumchapel	d			09 08			09 23				09 38			09 53					10 08			10 23
Milngavie	d	08 57				09 12			09 28				09 42				09 57				10 12	
Hillfoot	d	09 00				09 15			09 31				09 45				10 00				10 15	
Bearsden	d	09 02				09 17			09 33				09 47				10 02				10 17	
Westerton	d	09 05		09 10		09 20	09 25		09 36		09 40		09 50	09 55			10 05		10 10		10 20	10 25
Anniesland	d	09 08		09 14		09 23	09 28		09 39		09 44		09 53	09 58			10 08		10 14		10 23	10 28
Clydebank	d				09 10			09 25				09 40				09 55				10 10		
Yoker	d				09 12			09 27				09 42				09 57				10 12		
Garscadden	d				09 16			09 31				09 46				10 01				10 16		
Scotstounhill	d				09 18			09 33				09 48				10 03				10 18		
Jordanhill	d				09 20			09 35				09 50				10 05				10 20		
Hyndland	d	09 12	09 14	09 17	09 22	09 26	09 31	09 37	09 42	09 44	09 47	09 52	09 56	10 01		10 07	10 12	10 14	10 17	10 22	10 26	10 31
Partick	d	09 14	09 17	09 20	09 25	09 29	09 34	09 40	09 44	09 47	09 50	09 55	09 59	10 04		10 10	10 14	10 17	10 20	10 25	10 29	10 34
Exhibition Centre	d			09 23		09 32		09 43			09 53		10 02			10 13			10 23		10 32	
Anderston	d			09 25		09 34		09 45			09 55		10 04			10 15			10 25		10 34	
Glasgow Central LL	a			09 26		09 35		09 46			09 56		10 05			10 16			10 26		10 36	
	d			09 27		09 37		09 47			09 57		10 07		10b18	10 17			10 27		10 37	
Argyle Street	d			09 29		09 38		09 49			09 59		10 09			10 19			10 29		10 39	
Charing Cross	d	09 19	09 24		09 29		09 38		09 49	09 54		09 59		10 08			10 19	10 24		10 29		10 38
Glasgow Queen St LL	a	09 21	09 26		09 31		09 40		09 51	09 56		10 01		10 10			10 21	10 26		10 31		10 40
	d	09 24	09 28		09 32		09 42		09 54	09 58		10 02		10 12			10 24	10 28		10 32		10 42
High Street	d	09 26	09 30		09 34		09 44		09 57	10 00		10 04		10 14			10 26	10 30		10 34		10 44
Bellgrove	d		09 32		09 36		09 46			10 02		10 06		10 16				10 32		10 36		10 46
Duke Street	d				09 38							10 08								10 38		
Alexandra Parade	d				09 39							10 09								10 39		
Barnhill	d				09 42							10 12								10 42		
Springburn	a				09 44							10 14								10 44		
Carntyne	d		09 35				09 49			10 05				10 19				10 35				10 49
Shettleston	d		09 38				09 52			10 08				10 22				10 40				10 52
Garrowhill	d		09 40				09 54			10 10				10 24				10 42				10 54
Easterhouse	d		09 43				09 57			10 13				10 27				10 45				10 57
Blairhill	d		09 47				10 01			10 17				10 31				10 49				11 01
Coatbridge Sunnyside	d	09 39	09 49				10 03		10 09	10 19				10 33			10 39	10 51				11 03
Coatdyke	d		09 52				10 06			10 22				10 36				10 54				11 06
Airdrie	d	09 44	09 55				10a09		10 15	10 25				10a39			10 44	10 56				11a09
Drumgelloch	d	09 47	09 58						10 18	10 28							10 47	10 59				
Caldercruix	d		10 02							10 32								11 03				
Blackridge	d		10 08							10 38								11 09				
Armadale	d		10 11							10 41								11 13				
Bathgate	a	10 00	10 15						10 29	10 45							11 00	11 17				
	d	10 01	10 17						10 32	10 47							11 01	11 17				
Livingston North	d	10 06	10 20						10 35	10 50							11 06	11 20				
Uphall	d	10 09	10 23						10 38	10 53							11 09	11 23				
Edinburgh Park	a	10 17	10 31						10 47	11 01							11 17	11 31				
Haymarket	a	10 22	10 37						10 52	11 06							11 22	11 37				
Edinburgh	a	10 28	10 43						10 57	11 14							11 27	11 43				
Bridgeton	d					09 41		09 52					10 12			10 22					10 42	
Dalmarnock	d					09 43		09 54					10 14			10 24					10 44	
Rutherglen	d			09 34		09 46		09 56			10 04		10 17			10 26			10 34		10 46	
Cambuslang	d					09 50		10 00					10 22			10 31					10 50	
Newton	d					09 53							10 25								10 54	
Blantyre	d			09 44		09 57					10 14		10 29						10 44		10 58	
Hamilton West	d			09 47		10 00					10 17		10 32						10 47		11 01	
Hamilton Central	d			09 50		10 03					10 20		10 35						10 50		11 03	
Chatelherault	d			09 53							10 23								10 53			
Merryton	d			09 56							10 26								10 56			
Larkhall	a			09 59							10 29								10 59			
Airbles	d					10 08							10 40								11 08	
Uddingston	d							10 05							10 28	10 35						
Bellshill	d							10 10							10 33	10 40						
Motherwell	a					10 11		10 16					10 42			10 47					11 11	
	d							10 16					10 43									
Whifflet	a																					
Coatbridge Central	a																					
Shieldmuir	d							10 20														
Holytown	d												10 49		10a37							
Wishaw	d							10 26					10 54									
Carluke	d							10 32					11 01									
Lanark	a							10 44					11 13									

A To Edinburgh
b Glasgow Central High Level

Helensburgh, Balloch, Dalmuir and Milngavie - Glasgow - Springburn, Airdrie, Bathgate and Edinburgh, Hamilton, Larkhall, Motherwell, Coatbridge and Lanark

		SR	SR	SR	SR	SR	SR	SR	SR	SR	SR	SR	SR	SR	SR	SR	SR	SR	SR	SR	SR	SR	SR
									A					◇ B									
Helensburgh Central	d			10 10								10 39		10c44						11 10			
Craigendoran	d			10 13								10 42								11 13			
Cardross	d			10 18								10 47								11 18			
Balloch	d							10 22									10 53						
Alexandria	d							10 24									10 55						
Renton	d							10 27									10 58						
Dalreoch	d			10 23				10 30				10 52					11 01			11 23			
Dumbarton Central	d			10 25				10 31				10 54		10 58			11 02			11 25			
Dumbarton East	d			10 27				10 33				10 56					11 04			11 27			
Bowling	d							10 38									11 09						
Kilpatrick	d							10 41									11 12						
Dalmuir	a			10 34				10 44				11 03		11 07			11 15			11 34			
	d	10 23		10 35	10 31	10 38		10 46		10 53		11 05	11 00	11 07	11 08		11 16	11 23		11 35	11 31	11 38	
Singer	d				10 33			10 48					11 02				11 18				11 33		
Drumry	d				10 35			10 50					11 04				11 20				11 35		
Drumchapel	d				10 38			10 53					11 07				11 23				11 38		
Milngavie	d		10 27				10 42				10 57					11 12			11 27				11 42
Hillfoot	d		10 30				10 45				11 00					11 15			11 30				11 45
Bearsden	d		10 32				10 47				11 02					11 17			11 32				11 47
Westerton	d		10 35		10 40		10 50	10 55			11 05		11 10			11 20	11 25		11 35		11 40		11 50
Anniesland	d		10 38		10 44		10 53	10 58			11 08		11 14			11 23	11 28		11 38		11 44		11 53
Clydebank	d	10 25				10 40				10 55					11 10			11 25				11 40	
Yoker	d	10 27				10 42				10 57					11 12			11 27				11 42	
Garscadden	d	10 31				10 46				11 01					11 16			11 31				11 46	
Scotstounhill	d	10 33				10 48				11 03					11 18			11 33				11 48	
Jordanhill	d	10 35				10 50				11 07					11 20			11 35				11 50	
Hyndland	d	10 37	10 41	10 44	10 47	10 52	10 56	11 01		11 09	11 11	11 15	11 17		11 22	11 26	11 31	11 37	11 41	11 44	11 47	11 52	11 56
Partick	d	10 40	10 44	10 47	10 50	10 55	10 59	11 04		11 11	11 14	11 17	11 20		11 25	11 29	11 34	11 40	11 44	11 47	11 50	11 55	11 59
Exhibition Centre	d	10 43			10 53		11 02			11 14			11 23			11 32		11 43			11 53		12 02
Anderston	d	10 45			10 55		11 04			11 16			11 25			11 34		11 45			11 55		12 04
Glasgow Central LL	a	10 46			10 56		11 05			11 17			11 26			11 37		11 46			11 56		12 05
	d	10 47			10 57		11 07		11b18	11 18			11 27			11 37		11 47			11 58		12 07
Argyle Street	d	10 48			10 59		11 08			11 19			11 29			11 39		11 49			11 59		12 08
Charing Cross	d		10 49	10 54		10 59		11 09			11 19	11 24			11 29		11 38		11 49	11 54		11 59	
Glasgow Queen St LL	a		10 51	10 56		11 01		11 10			11 21	11 26		11e30	11 31		11 40		11 51	11 56		12 01	
	d		10 54	10 58		11 02		11 11			11 24	11 28			11 32		11 42		11 54	11 58		12 02	
High Street	d		10 56	11 00		11 04		11 13			11 26	11 30			11 34		11 44		11 56	12 00		12 04	
Bellgrove	d			11 02		11 06		11 16				11 32			11 36		11 46			12 02		12 06	
Duke Street	d					11 08									11 38							12 08	
Alexandra Parade	d					11 09									11 39							12 09	
Barnhill	d					11 12									11 42							12 12	
Springburn	a					11 14									11 44							12 14	
Carntyne	d			11 05				11 19				11 35					11 49			12 06			
Shettleston	d			11 08				11 22				11 38					11 52			12 08			
Garrowhill	d			11 10				11 24				11 40					11 54			12 11			
Easterhouse	d			11 13				11 27				11 43					11 57			12 13			
Blairhill	d			11 17				11 31				11 47					12 01			12 17			
Coatbridge Sunnyside	d		11 10	11 19				11 33			11 39	11 49					12 03		12 09	12 20			
Coatdyke	d			11 22				11 36				11 52					12 06			12 22			
Airdrie	d		11 14	11 25				11a39			11 44	11 55					12a10		12 15	12 25			
Drumgelloch	d		11 17	11 28							11 47	11 58							12 18	12 28			
Caldercruix	d			11 32								12 02								12 32			
Blackridge	d			11 38								12 08								12 38			
Armadale	d			11 41								12 11								12 42			
Bathgate	a		11 30	11 45							12 00	12 16							12 30	12 46			
	d		11 31	11 47							12 01	12 17							12 31	12 47			
Livingston North	d		11 36	11 50							12 06	12 21							12 35	12 51			
Uphall	d		11 39	11 53							12 09	12 24							12 38	12 54			
Edinburgh Park	a		11 47	12 02							12 18	12 32							12 47	13 02			
Haymarket	a		11 52	12 07							12 23	12 37							12 52	13 07			
Edinburgh	a		11 57	12 13							12 28	12 43							12 58	13 13			
Bridgeton	d	10 51					11 11			11 22						11 42		11 52					12 11
Dalmarnock	d	10 53					11 13			11 24						11 44		11 54					12 13
Rutherglen	d	10 55			11 04		11 16			11 27			11 34			11 46		11 56			12 06		12 16
Cambuslang	d	11 00					11 20			11 31						11 50		12 00					12 20
Newton	d						11 23									11 54							12 23
Blantyre	d				11 14		11 27						11 45			11 58					12 15		12 27
Hamilton West	d				11 17		11 30						11 48			12 01					12 18		12 30
Hamilton Central	d				11 20		11 33						11 50			12 03					12 20		12 33
Chatelherault	d				11 23								11 54								12 24		
Merryton	d				11 26								11 57								12 27		
Larkhall	a				11 29								12 00								12 30		
Airbles	d						11 38									12 08							12 38
Uddingston	d	11 04							11 30	11 35								12 05					
Bellshill	d	11 09							11 35	11 40								12 09					
Motherwell	a	11 16					11 40			11 48						12 11		12 16					12 40
	d	11 17					11 41											12 16					12 41
Whifflet	a																						
Coatbridge Central	a																						
Shieldmuir	d	11 21																12 20					
Holytown	d						11 48		11a39														12 48
Wishaw	d	11 24					11 53											12 22					12 53
Carluke	d	11 31					12 00											12 30					13 00
Lanark	a	11 42					12 12											12 42					13 12

A To Edinburgh
B From Mallaig
b Glasgow Central High Level
c Helensburgh Upper
e Glasgow Queen St High Level

Helensburgh, Balloch, Dalmuir and Milngavie - Glasgow - Springburn, Airdrie, Bathgate and Edinburgh, Hamilton, Larkhall, Motherwell, Coatbridge and Lanark

Station		SR	SR A	SR	SR	SR	SR	SR	SR	SR	SR	SR	SR	SR	SR	SR	SR	SR A	SR	SR	SR	SR	SR
Helensburgh Central	d					11 40							12 10								12 40		
Craigendoran	d					11 43							12 13								12 43		
Cardross	d					11 48							12 18								12 48		
Balloch	d	11 23								11 53							12 23						
Alexandria	d	11 25								11 55							12 25						
Renton	d	11 28								11 58							12 28						
Dalreoch	d	11 31				11 53				12 01			12 23				12 31				12 53		
Dumbarton Central	d	11 32				11 55				12 02			12 25				12 32				12 55		
Dumbarton East	d	11 34				11 57				12 04			12 27				12 34				12 57		
Bowling	d	11 39								12 09							12 39						
Kilpatrick	d	11 42								12 12							12 42						
Dalmuir	a	11 45				12 04				12 15			12 34				12 45				13 04		
	d	11 46		11 53		12 05	12 01	12 08		12 16	12 23		12 35	12 31	12 38		12 46		12 53		13 05	13 01	13 08
Singer	d	11 48					12 03			12 18				12 33			12 48					13 03	
Drumry	d	11 50					12 05			12 20				12 35			12 50					13 05	
Drumchapel	d	11 53					12 08			12 23				12 38			12 53					13 08	
Milngavie	d				11 57				12 12			12 27				12 42				12 57			
Hillfoot	d				12 00				12 15			12 30				12 45				13 00			
Bearsden	d				12 02				12 17			12 32				12 47				13 02			
Westerton	d	11 55			12 05		12 10		12 20	12 25		12 35		12 40		12 50	12 55			13 05		13 10	
Anniesland	d	11 58			12 08		12 14		12 23	12 28		12 38		12 44		12 53	12 58			13 08		13 14	
Clydebank	d			11 55				12 10			12 25				12 40				12 55				13 10
Yoker	d			11 57				12 12			12 27				12 42				12 57				13 12
Garscadden	d			12 01				12 16			12 31				12 46				13 01				13 16
Scotstounhill	d			12 03				12 18			12 33				12 48				13 03				13 18
Jordanhill	d			12 05				12 20			12 35				12 50				13 05				13 20
Hyndland	d	12 01		12 07	12 11	12 14	12 17	12 22	12 26	12 31	12 37	12 41	12 44	12 47	12 52	12 56	13 01		13 07	13 11	13 14	13 17	13 22
Partick ⇌	d	12 04		12 10	12 14	12 17	12 20	12 25	12 29	12 34	12 40	12 44	12 47	12 50	12 55	12 59	13 04		13 10	13 14	13 17	13 20	13 25
Exhibition Centre	d			12 13			12 23		12 32		12 43			12 53		13 02			13 13			13 23	
Anderston	d			12 15			12 25		12 34		12 45			12 55		13 04			13 15			13 25	
Glasgow Central LL	a			12 16			12 26		12 35		12 46			12 56		13 05			13 16			13 26	
	d		12b18	12 17			12 27		12 37		12 47			12 57		13 07		13b18	13 17			13 27	
Argyle Street	d			12 19			12 29		12 38		12 49			12 59		13 08			13 19			13 29	
Charing Cross	d	12 09			12 19	12 24		12 29		12 38		12 49	12 54		12 59		13 08			13 19	13 24		13 29
Glasgow Queen St LL ⇌	a	12 10			12 21	12 26		12 31		12 40		12 51	12 56		13 01		13 10			13 21	13 26		13 31
	d	12 12			12 24	12 28		12 32		12 42		12 54	12 58		13 02		13 12			13 24	13 28		13 32
High Street	d	12 14			12 26	12 30		12 34		12 44		12 56	13 00		13 04		13 14			13 26	13 30		13 34
Bellgrove	d	12 16				12 32		12 36		12 46			13 02		13 06		13 16				13 32		13 36
Duke Street	d							12 38							13 08								13 38
Alexandra Parade	d							12 39							13 09								13 39
Barnhill	d							12 42							13 12								13 42
Springburn	a							12 44							13 14								13 44
Carntyne	d	12 19				12 35				12 49			13 05				13 19				13 36		
Shettleston	d	12 22				12 38				12 52			13 08				13 22				13 38		
Garrowhill	d	12 24				12 40				12 54			13 10				13 24				13 41		
Easterhouse	d	12 27				12 43				12 57			13 13				13 27				13 43		
Blairhill	d	12 31				12 47				13 01			13 17				13 31				13 47		
Coatbridge Sunnyside	d	12 33			12 39	12 49				13 03		13 09	13 19				13 33			13 39	13 50		
Coatdyke	d	12 36				12 52				13 06			13 22				13 36				13 52		
Airdrie	d	12a39			12 44	12 55				13a09		13 14	13 25				13a39			13 44	13 55		
Drumgelloch	d				12 47	12 58						13 17	13 28							13 47	13 58		
Caldercruix	d					13 02							13 32								14 02		
Blackridge	d					13 08							13 38								14 08		
Armadale	d					13 11							13 41								14 12		
Bathgate	a				13 00	13 15						13 30	13 46							14 00	14 16		
	d				13 01	13 17						13 31	13 47							14 01	14 17		
Livingston North	d				13 06	13 20						13 36	13 50							14 06	14 21		
Uphall	d				13 09	13 23						13 39	13 53							14 09	14 24		
Edinburgh Park	a				13 17	13 31						13 47	14 02							14 17	14 33		
Haymarket	a				13 22	13 37						13 52	14 07							14 22	14 38		
Edinburgh	a				13 28	13 43						13 58	14 14							14 28	14 44		
Bridgeton	d			12 22					12 41		12 52					13 11			13 22				
Dalmarnock	d			12 24					12 43		12 54					13 13			13 24				
Rutherglen	d			12 26			12 34		12 46		12 56			13 04		13 16			13 26			13 34	
Cambuslang	d			12 31					12 50		13 01					13 20			13 31				
Newton	d								12 53							13 23							
Blantyre	d						12 45		12 58					13 14		13 28						13 44	
Hamilton West	d						12 48		13 01					13 17		13 31						13 47	
Hamilton Central	d						12 50		13 03					13 20		13 33						13 50	
Chatelherault	d						12 54							13 23								13 53	
Merryton	d						12 57							13 26								13 56	
Larkhall	a						13 00							13 29								13 59	
Airbles	d								13 07							13 38							
Uddingston	d		12 30	12 35							13 05							13 30	13 35				
Bellshill	d		12 35	12 40							13 10							13 35	13 40				
Motherwell	a			12 48					13 11		13 16					13 41			13 48				
	d										13 16					13 41							
Whifflet	a																						
Coatbridge Central	a																						
Shieldmuir	d										13 20												
Holytown	d		12a39													13 48		13a39					
Wishaw	d										13 23					13 53							
Carluke	d										13 30					14 00							
Lanark	a										13 42					14 12							

A To Edinburgh

b Glasgow Central High Level

Helensburgh, Balloch, Dalmuir and Milngavie - Glasgow - Springburn, Airdrie, Bathgate and Edinburgh, Hamilton, Larkhall, Motherwell, Coatbridge and Lanark

Station		SR	SR	SR	SR	SR	SR	SR	SR	SR	SR A	SR	SR	SR	SR	SR	SR	SR	SR	SR	SR	SR
Helensburgh Central	d					13 10								13 40							14 10	
Craigendoran	d					13 13								13 43							14 13	
Cardross	d					13 18								13 48							14 18	
Balloch	d		12 53							13 23								13 53				
Alexandria	d		12 55							13 25								13 55				
Renton	d		12 58							13 28								13 58				
Dalreoch	d		13 01			13 23				13 31				13 53				14 01			14 23	
Dumbarton Central	d		13 02			13 25				13 32				13 55				14 02			14 25	
Dumbarton East	d		13 04			13 27				13 34				13 57				14 04			14 27	
Bowling	d		13 09							13 39								14 09				
Kilpatrick	d		13 12							13 42								14 12				
Dalmuir	a		13 15			13 34				13 45				14 04				14 15			14 34	
	d		13 16	13 23		13 35	13 31	13 38		13 46		13 53		14 05	14 01	14 08		14 16	14 23		14 35	14 31
Singer	d		13 18				13 33			13 48					14 03			14 18				14 33
Drumry	d		13 20				13 35			13 50					14 05			14 20				14 35
Drumchapel	d		13 23				13 38			13 53					14 08			14 23				14 38
Milngavie	d	13 12			13 27				13 42				13 57				14 12			14 27		
Hillfoot	d	13 15			13 30				13 45				14 00				14 15			14 30		
Bearsden	d	13 17			13 32				13 47				14 02				14 17			14 32		
Westerton	d	13 20	13 25		13 35		13 40		13 50	13 55			14 05		14 10		14 20	14 25		14 35		14 40
Anniesland	d	13 23	13 28		13 38		13 44		13 53	13 58			14 08		14 14		14 23	14 28		14 38		14 44
Clydebank	d			13 25				13 40				13 55				14 10			14 25			
Yoker	d			13 27				13 42				13 57				14 12			14 27			
Garscadden	d			13 31				13 46				14 01				14 16			14 31			
Scotstounhill	d			13 33				13 48				14 03				14 18			14 33			
Jordanhill	d			13 35				13 50				14 05				14 20			14 35			
Hyndland	d	13 26	13 31	13 37	13 41	13 44	13 47	13 52	13 56	14 01		14 07	14 11	14 14	14 17	14 22	14 26	14 31	14 37	14 41	14 44	14 47
Partick ⇌	d	13 29	13 34	13 40	13 44	13 47	13 50	13 55	13 59	14 04		14 10	14 14	14 17	14 20	14 25	14 29	14 34	14 40	14 44	14 47	14 50
Exhibition Centre	d	13 32		13 43			13 53		14 02			14 13			14 23		14 32		14 43			14 53
Anderston	d	13 34		13 45			13 55		14 04			14 15			14 25		14 34		14 45			14 55
Glasgow Central LL	a	13 35		13 46			13 56		14 05			14 16			14 26		14 35		14 46			14 56
	d	13 36		13 47			13 57		14 07		14b18	14 17			14 27		14 36		14 47			14 57
Argyle Street	d	13 38		13 49			13 59		14 08			14 19			14 29		14 38		14 49			14 59
Charing Cross	d		13 38		13 49	13 54		13 59		14 08			14 19	14 24		14 29		14 38		14 49	14 54	
Glasgow Queen St LL ⇌	a		13 40		13 51	13 56		14 01		14 10			14 21	14 26		14 31		14 40		14 51	14 56	
	d		13 42		13 54	13 58		14 02		14 12			14 24	14 28		14 32		14 42		14 54	14 58	
High Street	d		13 44		13 56	14 01		14 04		14 14			14 26	14 30		14 34		14 44		14 56	15 01	
Bellgrove	d		13 46			14 03		14 06		14 16				14 32		14 36		14 46			15 03	
Duke Street	d							14 08								14 38						
Alexandra Parade	d							14 09								14 39						
Barnhill	d							14 12								14 42						
Springburn	a							14 14								14 44						
Carntyne	d		13 49			14 06				14 19				14 36				14 50			15 06	
Shettleston	d		13 52			14 10				14 22				14 38				14 52			15 09	
Garrowhill	d		13 54			14 12				14 24				14 41				14 55			15 12	
Easterhouse	d		13 57			14 15				14 27				14 43				14 57			15 14	
Blairhill	d		14 01			14 19				14 31				14 47				15 01			15 18	
Coatbridge Sunnyside	d		14 03		14 09	14 21				14 33			14 39	14 50				15 04		15 09	15 21	
Coatdyke	d		14 06			14 24				14 36				14 52				15 06			15 23	
Airdrie	d		14a09		14 14	14 26				14a39			14 44	14 55				15a09		15 14	15 26	
Drumgelloch	d				14 17	14 29							14 47	14 58						15 17	15 29	
Caldercruix	d					14 33								15 02							15 33	
Blackridge	d					14 39								15 08							15 39	
Armadale	d					14 43								15 12							15 43	
Bathgate	a				14 29	14 47							14 59	15 16						15 30	15 47	
	d				14 30	14 47							15 00	15 17						15 30	15 48	
Livingston North	d				14 34	14 51							15 04	15 21						15 35	15 51	
Uphall	d				14 37	14 54							15 07	15 24						15 38	15 54	
Edinburgh Park	a				14 46	15 02							15 17	15 34						15 47	16 02	
Haymarket	a				14 51	15 07							15 21	15 39						15 52	16 08	
Edinburgh	a				14 57	15 12							15 27	15 44						15 57	16 14	
Bridgeton	d	13 41		13 52					14 11			14 22					14 41		14 52			
Dalmarnock	d	13 43		13 54					14 13			14 24					14 43		14 54			
Rutherglen	d	13 46		13 56			14 04		14 16			14 26			14 34		14 46		14 55			15 06
Cambuslang	d	13 50		14 00					14 20			14 31					14 50		15 00			
Newton	d	13 53							14 23								14 53					
Blantyre	d	13 57					14 14		14 28						14 44		14 57					15 14
Hamilton West	d	14 00					14 17		14 31						14 47		15 00					15 17
Hamilton Central	d	14 03					14 20		14 33						14 50		15 03					15 20
Chatelherault	d						14 23								14 53							15 23
Merryton	d						14 26								14 56							15 26
Larkhall	a						14 29								14 59							15 29
Airbles	d	14 08							14 38								15 08					
Uddingston	d			14 05							14 30	14 35							15 05			
Bellshill	d			14 09							14 36	14 40							15 09			
Motherwell	a	14 11		14 16					14 41			14 46					15 11		15 15			
	d			14 16					14 42										15 16			
Whifflet	a																					
Coatbridge Central	a																					
Shieldmuir	d			14 20															15 22			
Holytown	d								14 48		14a40											
Wishaw	d			14 23					14 53										15 25			
Carluke	d			14 30					15 00										15 32			
Lanark	a			14 43					15 12										15 42			

A To Edinburgh

b Glasgow Central High Level

Table 226

Helensburgh, Balloch, Dalmuir and Milngavie - Glasgow - Springburn, Airdrie, Bathgate and Edinburgh, Hamilton, Larkhall, Motherwell, Coatbridge and Lanark

		SR	SR	SR	SR	SR	SR	SR	SR	SR	SR	SR	SR	SR	SR	SR	SR	SR	SR	SR	SR	SR	SR
					A			◇ B										◇ C				A	
Helensburgh Central	d							14c39	14 40							15 10		15c15					
Craigendoran	d								14 46							15 13							
Cardross	d								14 52							15 18							
Balloch	d			14 23									14 53								15 23		
Alexandria	d			14 25									14 55								15 25		
Renton	d			14 28									14 58								15 28		
Dalreoch	d			14 31					14 57				15 01			15 23					15 31		
Dumbarton Central	d			14 32				14 52	14 58				15 02			15 25		15 28			15 32		
Dumbarton East	d			14 34					15 00				15 04			15 27					15 34		
Bowling	d			14 39									15 09								15 39		
Kilpatrick	d			14 42									15 12								15 42		
Dalmuir	a			14 45				15 04	15 08				15 15			15 34		15 37			15 45		
	d	14 38		14 46		14 53		15 04	15 08	15 00	15 11		15 16	15 23		15 35	15 30	15 37	15 38		15 46		15 53
Singer	d			14 48						15 02			15 18				15 32				15 48		
Drumry	d			14 50						15 04			15 20				15 34				15 50		
Drumchapel	d			14 53						15 07			15 23				15 37				15 53		
Milngavie	d		14 42				14 57					15 12			15 27					15 42			
Hillfoot	d		14 45				15 00					15 15			15 30					15 45			
Bearsden	d		14 47				15 02					15 17			15 33					15 49			
Westerton	d		14 50	14 55			15 05			15 09		15 20	15 25		15 36		15 39	15 43		15 52	15 55		
Anniesland	d		14 53	14 59			15 08			15 14		15 23	15 28		15 39		15 43			15 55	15 58		
Clydebank	d	14 40				14 55					15 13			15 25					15 40				15 55
Yoker	d	14 42				14 57					15 15			15 27					15 42				15 57
Garscadden	d	14 46				15 01					15 18			15 31					15 46				16 00
Scotstounhill	d	14 48				15 03					15 20			15 33					15 48				16 02
Jordanhill	d	14 50				15 05					15 22			15 35					15 50				16 04
Hyndland	d	14 52	14 55	15 02		15 07	15 11		15 14	15 17	15 24	15 26	15 31	15 37	15 42	15 44	15 47		15 52	15 57	16 01		16 07
Partick	d	14 55	14 58	15 04		15 10	15 14		15 17	15 20	15 26	15 29	15 34	15 40	15 44	15 47	15 50		15 55	16 00	16 04		16 09
Exhibition Centre	d		15 01			15 13				15 23		15 32		15 43			15 53			16 03			16 12
Anderston	d		15 03			15 15				15 25		15 34		15 45			15 55			16 05			16 15
Glasgow Central LL	a		15 04			15 16				15 26		15 37		15 46			15 56			16 07			16 16
	d		15 07		15b18	15 17				15 27		15 37		15 47			15 57			16 08		16b18	16 17
Argyle Street	d		15 09			15 19				15 29		15 39		15 48			15 59			16 10			16 18
Charing Cross	d	14 59		15 09			15 19		15 24		15 30		15 38		15 48	15 54			15 59		16 08		
Glasgow Queen St LL	a	15 01		15 11			15 21	15e30	15 26		15 32		15 40		15 50	15 56		16e00	16 01		16 11		
	d	15 02		15 11			15 24		15 28		15 33		15 42		15 51	15 58			16 02		16 11		
High Street	d	15 04		15 13			15 26		15 30		15 35		15 44		15 53	16 00			16 04		16 13		
Bellgrove	d	15 06		15 15					15 32		15 37		15 46			16 02			16 06		16 15		
Duke Street	d	15 08									15 39								16 08				
Alexandra Parade	d	15 09									15 40								16 09				
Barnhill	d	15 12									15 43								16 12				
Springburn	a	15 14									15 45								16 14				
Carntyne	d			15 19					15 35				15 49			16 05					16 19		
Shettleston	d			15 21					15 38				15 52			16 08					16 21		
Garrowhill	d			15 24					15 40				15 54			16 10					16 24		
Easterhouse	d			15 26					15 43				15 57			16 13					16 26		
Blairhill	d			15 30					15 47				16 01			16 17					16 30		
Coatbridge Sunnyside	d			15 33			15 39		15 49				16 03		16 09	16 19					16 33		
Coatdyke	d			15 35					15 52				16 06			16 22					16 35		
Airdrie	d			15a38			15 44		15 55				16a09		16 14	16 25					16a39		
Drumgelloch	d						15 47		15 58						16 17	16 28							
Caldercruix	d								16 02							16 32							
Blackridge	d								16 08							16 38							
Armadale	d								16 11							16 41							
Bathgate	a						16 00		16 15						16 30	16 45							
	d						16 01		16 17						16 31	16 47							
Livingston North	d						16 06		16 20						16 36	16 50							
Uphall	d						16 09		16 24						16 39	16 53							
Edinburgh Park	a						16 17		16 32						16 48	17 02							
Haymarket	a						16 22		16 37						16 52	17 14							
Edinburgh	a						16 29		16 43						16 57	17 19							
Bridgeton	d		15 12			15 22						15 42		15 51						16 13			16 21
Dalmarnock	d		15 14			15 24						15 44		15 53						16 15			16 23
Rutherglen	d		15 16			15 26				15 34		15 46		15 55			16 06			16 17			16 25
Cambuslang	d		15 20			15 31						15 50		16 00						16 21			16 30
Newton	d		15 24									15 54								16 25			
Blantyre	d		15 28							15 44		15 58					16 15			16 29			
Hamilton West	d		15 31							15 47		16 01					16 18			16 32			
Hamilton Central	d		15 33							15 50		16 03					16 20			16 34			
Chatelherault	d									15 54							16 24						
Merryton	d									15 57							16 27						
Larkhall	a									16 00							16 30						
Airbles	d		15 38									16 08								16 39			
Uddingston	d				15 31	15 35								16 04								16 30	16 34
Bellshill	d				15 34	15 40								16 09								16 34	16 40
Motherwell	a		15 41			15 47						16 11		16 15						16 42			16 49
	d		15 41											16 16						16 46			
Whifflet	a																			16 53			
Coatbridge Central	a																			16 58			
Shieldmuir	d													16 20									
Holytown	d		15 48		15a39																	16a38	
Wishaw	d		15 54											16 23									
Carluke	d		16 00											16 30									
Lanark	a		16 13											16 42									

A To Edinburgh
B From Mallaig
C until 23 September. From Oban
b Glasgow Central High Level
c Helensburgh Upper
e Glasgow Queen St High Level

Helensburgh, Balloch, Dalmuir and Milngavie - Glasgow - Springburn, Airdrie, Bathgate and Edinburgh, Hamilton, Larkhall, Motherwell, Coatbridge and Lanark

		SR	SR	SR	SR	SR	SR	SR	SR	SR	SR	SR	SR	SR	SR	SR	SR	SR	SR	SR	SR	SR
																		A	B			
Helensburgh Central	d			15 40						16 10							16 40					
Craigendoran	d			15 43						16 13							16 43					
Cardross	d			15 48						16 18							16 48					
Balloch	d						15 53							16 23								16 53
Alexandria	d						15 55							16 25								16 55
Renton	d						15 58							16 28								16 58
Dalreoch	d			15 53			16 01			16 23				16 31			16 53					17 01
Dumbarton Central	d			15 55			16 02			16 25				16 32			16 55					17 02
Dumbarton East	d			15 57			16 04			16 27				16 34			16 57					17 04
Bowling	d						16 09							16 39								17 09
Kilpatrick	d						16 12							16 42								17 12
Dalmuir	a			16 04			16 15			16 34				16 45			17 04					17 15
	d		16 01	16 05	16 08		16 16	16 23		16 35	16 31	16 38		16 46	16 53		17 05		17 01	17 08		17 16
Singer	d		16 03				16 18				16 33			16 48					17 03			17 18
Drumry	d		16 05				16 20				16 35			16 50					17 05			17 20
Drumchapel	d		16 08	16 12			16 23				16 38			16 53					17 08			17 23
Milngavie	d	15 57				16 12			16 27				16 42			16 57					17 13	
Hillfoot	d	16 00				16 15			16 30				16 45			17 00					17 16	
Bearsden	d	16 02				16 17			16 32				16 47			17 02					17 18	
Westerton	d	16 05	16 10			16 20	16 25		16 35		16 40		16 50	16 55		17 05			17 10		17 21	17 25
Anniesland	d	16 08	16 14			16 23	16 28		16 38		16 44		16 53	16 58		17 08			17 14		17 24	17 28
Clydebank	d				16 10			16 25				16 40			16 55					17 10		
Yoker	d				16 12			16 27				16 42			16 57					17 12		
Garscadden	d				16 16			16 31				16 46			17 01					17 16		
Scotstounhill	d				16 18			16 33				16 48			17 03					17 18		
Jordanhill	d				16 21			16 35				16 51			17 05					17 20		
Hyndland	d	16 11	16 17	16 20	16 23	16 26	16 32	16 37	16 41	16 44	16 47	16 52	16 56	17 01	17 07	17 11	17 14		17 17	17 21	17 26	17 31
Partick	d	16 14	16 20	16 22	16 25	16 29	16 35	16 40	16 44	16 47	16 50	16 55	16 59	17 04	17 10	17 14	17 17		17 20	17 25	17 29	17 34
Exhibition Centre	d		16 23			16 32		16 43			16 53		17 04		17 13				17 23		17 34	
Anderston	d		16 25			16 34		16 45			16 55		17 06		17 15				17 25		17 37	
Glasgow Central LL	a		16 27			16 35		16 46			16 56		17 09		17 17				17 26		17 39	
	d		16 27			16 37		16 47			16 57		17 09		17 18			17b20	17 27		17 39	
Argyle Street	d		16 29			16 38		16 48			16 59		17 10		17 21				17 28		17 40	
Charing Cross	d	16 19		16 26	16 29		16 39		16 49	16 54		16 59		17 08		17 19	17 24			17 29		17 38
Glasgow Queen St LL	a	16 21		16 28	16 31		16 41		16 51	16 56		17 01		17 10		17 21	17 26			17 31		17 40
	d	16 22		16 29	16 32		16 42		16 52	16 58		17 02		17 12		17 22	17 28			17 32		17 42
High Street	d	16 24		16 31	16 34		16 44		16 54	17 00		17 04		17 14		17 25	17 30			17 34		17 44
Bellgrove	d			16 33	16 36		16 46			17 02		17 06		17 16			17 32			17 36		17 46
Duke Street	d				16 38							17 08								17 38		
Alexandra Parade	d				16 39							17 09								17 39		
Barnhill	d				16 42							17 12								17 42		
Springburn	a				16 44							17 14								17 44		
Carntyne	d			16 36			16 49			17 06				17 19			17 36					17 49
Shettleston	d			16 39			16 52			17 08				17 22			17 38					17 52
Garrowhill	d			16 41			16 54			17 11				17 24			17 41					17 54
Easterhouse	d			16 44			16 57			17 13				17 27			17 43					17 57
Blairhill	d	16 35		16 48			17 01		17 05	17 17				17 31		17 39	17 47					18 01
Coatbridge Sunnyside	d	16 38		16 50			17 03		17 08	17 20				17 33		17 42	17 50					18 03
Coatdyke	d	16 40		16 53			17 06		17 10	17 22				17 36		17 44	17 52					18 06
Airdrie	d	16 44		16 56			17a09		17 14	17 25				17a39		17 47	17 55					18a09
Drumgelloch	d	16 47		16 59					17 17	17 28						17 50	17 58					
Caldercruix	d			17 03						17 32							18 02					
Blackridge	d			17 09						17 38							18 08					
Armadale	d			17 12						17 42							18 12					
Bathgate	a	17 00		17 16					17 30	17 46						18 02	18 16					
	d	17 01		17 17					17 31	17 46						18 04	18 17					
Livingston North	d	17 06		17 21					17 36	17 50						18 08	18 20					
Uphall	d	17 09		17 24					17 39	17 53						18 11	18 23					
Edinburgh Park	a	17 18		17 32					17 47	18 01						18 17	18 32					
Haymarket	a	17 23		17 37					17 56	18 06						18 25	18 37					
Edinburgh	a	17 29		17 43					18 02	18 12						18 32	18 43					
Bridgeton	d					16 41		16 51					17 14		17 24				17 31		17 44	
Dalmarnock	d					16 43		16 53					17 16		17 26				17 33		17 46	
Rutherglen	d		16 35			16 46		16 56			17 04		17 20		17 28				17 36		17 49	
Cambuslang	d					16 50		17 00			17 08		17 25		17 32				17 40		17 53	
Newton	d					16 53							17 27		17 36						17 56	
Blantyre	d		16 45			16 58					17 14		17 32		17 40						18 00	
Hamilton West	d		16 48			17 01					17 17		17 35		17 43						18 03	
Hamilton Central	d		16 50			17 03					17 20		17 38		17 50						18 06	
Chatelherault	d		16 54								17 23		17 41								18 09	
Merryton	d		16 57								17 26		17 44								18 12	
Larkhall	a		17 00								17 29		17 47								18 15	
Airbles	d					17 08									17 55							
Uddingston	d							17 04											17 44			
Bellshill	d							17 09										17 34	17 49			
Motherwell	a					17 11		17 15							17 57				18 01			
	d					17 13									17 58				18 01			
Whifflet	a					17 20									18 05							
Coatbridge Central	a					17 22									18 07							
Shieldmuir	d																		18 05			
Holytown	d																	17a40				
Wishaw	d																		18 11			
Carluke	d																		18a18			
Lanark	a																					

A To Edinburgh
B To Carstairs
b Glasgow Central High Level

Table 226

Mondays to Fridays

Helensburgh, Balloch, Dalmuir and Milngavie - Glasgow - Springburn, Airdrie, Bathgate and Edinburgh, Hamilton, Larkhall, Motherwell, Coatbridge and Lanark

		SR	SR	SR	SR	SR	SR	SR	SR A	SR	SR	SR	SR	SR	SR	SR	SR	SR	SR	SR	SR	SR A	SR
Helensburgh Central	d			17 10								17 40							18 10				
Craigendoran	d			17 13								17 43							18 13				
Cardross	d			17 18								17 48							18 18				
Balloch	d							17 23								17 53					18 23		
Alexandria	d							17 25								17 55					18 25		
Renton	d							17 28								17 58					18 29		
Dalreoch	d			17 23				17 31				17 53				18 01			18 23		18 32		
Dumbarton Central	d			17 25				17 32				17 55				18 02			18 25		18 33		
Dumbarton East	d			17 27				17 34				17 57				18 04			18 27		18 35		
Bowling	d							17 39								18 09					18 40		
Kilpatrick	d							17 42								18 12					18 43		
Dalmuir	a			17 34				17 45				18 04				18 15			18 35		18 46		
	d	17 23		17 35	17 31	17 38		17 46		17 53		18 05	18 01	18 07		18 16	18 23	18 31	18 35		18 47		
Singer	d				17 33			17 48					18 03			18 18		18 33			18 49		
Drumry	d				17 35			17 50					18 05			18 20		18 35			18 51		
Drumchapel	d				17 38			17 53					18 08			18 23		18 38			18 54		
Milngavie	d		17 28				17 42				17 57				18 12					18 42			
Hillfoot	d		17 31				17 45				18 00				18 15					18 45			
Bearsden	d		17 33				17 47				18 02				18 17					18 47			
Westerton	d		17 36		17 40		17 50	17 55			18 05		18 10		18 20	18 25		18 40		18 50	18 56		
Anniesland	d		17 39		17 44		17 53	17 58			18 08		18 14		18 23	18 28		18 44		18 53	19 00		
Clydebank	d	17 25				17 40				17 55				18 09			18 25		18 37				
Yoker	d	17 27				17 42				17 57				18 11			18 27		18 39				
Garscadden	d	17 31				17 46				18 00				18 14			18 31		18 43				
Scotstounhill	d	17 33				17 48				18 02				18 16			18 33		18 45				
Jordanhill	d	17 35				17 50				18 03				18 18			18 35		18 47				
Hyndland	d	17 37	17 41	17 44	17 47	17 52	17 56	18 01		18 05	18 11	18 14	18 17	18 22	18 26	18 31	18 37	18 47	18 51	18 56	19 03		
Partick	d	17 40	17 44	17 47	17 50	17 55	17 59	18 04		18 08	18 14	18 17	18 20	18 25	18 29	18 34	18 40	18 50	18 53	18 59	19 05		19 11
Exhibition Centre	d	17 43			17 53		18 02			18 11			18 23		18 32		18 43	18 53		19 02			19 14
Anderston	d	17 45			17 55		18 04			18 13			18 25		18 34		18 45	18 55		19 04			19 16
Glasgow Central LL	a	17 46			17 56		18 05			18 15			18 26		18 35		18 46	18 56		19 05			19 17
	d	17 47			17 57		18 06		18b14	18 15			18 27		18 37		18 47	18 57		19 07		19b15	19 18
Argyle Street	d	17 49			17 59		18 08			18 17			18 29		18 38		18 48	18 59		19 08			19 19
Charing Cross	d		17 49	17 54		17 59		18 08			18 18	18 24		18 29		18 38			18 57		19 09		
Glasgow Queen St LL	a		17 51	17 56		18 01		18 10			18 20	18 26		18 31		18 40			18 59		19 11		
	d		17 54	17 58		18 02		18 12			18 23	18 28		18 32		18 45			19 00		19 14		
High Street	d		17 56	18 00		18 04		18 14			18 26	18 30		18 34		18 47			19 02		19 16		
Bellgrove	d			18 02		18 06		18 16			18 28	18 32		18 36		18 49			19 04		19 19		
Duke Street	d					18 08								18 38		18 51					19 21		
Alexandra Parade	d					18 09								18 39		18 52					19 22		
Barnhill	d					18 12								18 42		18 55					19 25		
Springburn	a					18 14								18 44		18 57					19 27		
Carntyne	d			18 06				18 19				18 36							19 07				
Shettleston	d			18 08				18 22				18 38							19 10				
Garrowhill	d			18 11				18 24				18 41							19 12				
Easterhouse	d			18 13				18 27				18 43							19 15				
Blairhill	d			18 17				18 31				18 47							19 19				
Coatbridge Sunnyside	d		18 09	18 20				18 33			18 39	18 50							19 21				
Coatdyke	d			18 22				18 36				18 52							19 24				
Airdrie	d		18 14	18 25				18a39			18 44	18 55							19 27				
Drumgelloch	d		18 17	18 28							18 47	18 58							19 30				
Caldercruix	d			18 32								19 02							19 34				
Blackridge	d			18 38								19 08							19 40				
Armadale	d			18 42								19 12							19 43				
Bathgate	a		18 30	18 46							19 00	19 16							19 47				
	d		18 31	18 47							19 01	19 17							19 49				
Livingston North	d		18 35	18 50							19 06	19 20							19 53				
Uphall	d		18 38	18 53							19 09	19 23							19 56				
Edinburgh Park	a		18 47	19 02							19 17	19 32							20 04				
Haymarket	a		18 52	19 08							19 22	19 37							20 09				
Edinburgh	a		18 58	19 14							19 28	19 45							20 14				
Bridgeton	d	17 52					18 11			18 20					18 41		18 51			19 11			19 22
Dalmarnock	d	17 54					18 13			18 22					18 43		18 53			19 13			19 24
Rutherglen	d	17 56			18 04		18 16			18 23			18 34		18 46		18 55	19 04		19 16			19 26
Cambuslang	d	18 01					18 20		18 23	18 28					18 50		19 00			19 20			19 31
Newton	d						18 23								18 53					19 23			
Blantyre	d				18 14		18 27						18 44		18 58			19 15		19 27			
Hamilton West	d				18 17		18 30						18 47		19 01			19 18		19 30			
Hamilton Central	d				18 20		18 33						18 50		19 03			19 20		19 33			
Chatelherault	d				18 23								18 53					19 24					
Merryton	d				18 26								18 56					19 27					
Larkhall	a				18 29								18 59					19 30					
Airbles	d						18 38								19 08					19 38			
Uddingston	d	18 05							18 29	18 33							19 04					19 30	19 35
Bellshill	d	18 10							18 34	18 37							19 09					19 35	19 40
Motherwell	a	18 16					18 41			18 44					19 11		19 16			19 39			19 48
	d						18 43										19 17			19 40			
Whifflet	a																						
Coatbridge Central	a																						
Shieldmuir	d																19 21						
Holytown	d						18 49		18a38											19 48		19a39	
Wishaw	d						18 55										19 24			19 54			
Carluke	d						19 01										19 31			20 02			
Lanark	a						19 14										19 41			20 15			

A To Edinburgh

b Glasgow Central High Level

Table 226

Mondays to Fridays

Helensburgh, Balloch, Dalmuir and Milngavie - Glasgow - Springburn, Airdrie, Bathgate and Edinburgh, Hamilton, Larkhall, Motherwell, Coatbridge and Lanark

		SR	SR	SR	SR	SR	SR	SR	SR	SR	SR	SR	SR	SR	SR	SR	SR	SR	SR	SR	SR A	SR	SR
Helensburgh Central	d		18 40					19 10					19 40					20 10					
Craigendoran	d		18 43					19 13					19 43					20 13					
Cardross	d		18 48					19 18					19 48					20 18					
Balloch	d				18 53					19 23					19 53					20 23			
Alexandria	d				18 55					19 25					19 55					20 25			
Renton	d				18 58					19 28					19 58					20 28			
Dalreoch	d		18 53		19 01			19 23		19 31			19 53		20 01			20 23		20 31			
Dumbarton Central	d		18 55		19 02			19 25		19 32			19 55		20 02			20 25		20 32			
Dumbarton East	d		18 57		19 04			19 27		19 34			19 57		20 04			20 27		20 34			
Bowling	d				19 09					19 39					20 09					20 39			
Kilpatrick	d				19 12					19 42					20 12					20 42			
Dalmuir	a		19 05		19 15			19 35		19 45			20 05		20 15			20 35		20 45			
	d	19 01	19 05		19 16		19 31	19 35		19 46		20 01	20 05		20 16		20 31	20 35		20 46			21 00
Singer	d	19 03			19 18		19 33			19 48		20 03			20 18		20 33			20 48			21 02
Drumry	d	19 05			19 20		19 35			19 50		20 05			20 20		20 35			20 50			21 04
Drumchapel	d	19 08			19 23		19 38			19 53		20 08			20 23		20 38			20 53			21 07
Milngavie	d			19 12					19 42					20 12					20 42				
Hillfoot	d			19 15					19 45					20 15					20 45				
Bearsden	d			19 17					19 47					20 17					20 47				
Westerton	d	19 10		19 20	19 25		19 40		19 50	19 55		20 10		20 20	20 25		20 40		20 50	20 55			21 09
Anniesland	d	19 14		19 23	19 30		19 44		19 54	19 59		20 14		20 22	20 30		20 44		20 53	20 59			21 14
Clydebank	d		19 07					19 37					20 07					20 37					
Yoker	d		19 09					19 39					20 09					20 39					
Garscadden	d		19 13					19 43					20 13					20 43					
Scotstounhill	d		19 15					19 45					20 15					20 45					
Jordanhill	d		19 17					19 47					20 17					20 47					
Hyndland	d	19 17	19 21	19 25	19 33		19 47	19 51	19 56	20 02		20 17	20 21	20 25	20 33		20 47	20 51	20 56	21 02			21 17
Partick	d	19 20	19 23	19 29	19 35	19 40	19 50	19 53	19 59	20 04	20 10	20 20	20 23	20 28	20 35	20 40	20 50	20 53	20 59	21 04		21 10	21 20
Exhibition Centre	d	19 23		19 32		19 43	19 53		20 02		20 13	20 23		20 32		20 43	20 53		21 02			21 13	21 23
Anderston	d	19 25		19 34		19 45	19 55		20 04		20 15	20 25		20 34		20 45	20 55		21 04			21 15	21 25
Glasgow Central LL	a	19 26		19 35		19 46	19 56		20 05		20 16	20 26		20 35		20 46	20 56		21 05			21 16	21 26
	d	19 27		19 37		19 47	19 57		20 07		20 17	20 27		20 36		20 47	20 57		21 07		21b18	21 17	21 27
Argyle Street	d	19 29		19 39		19 49	19 59		20 08		20 19	20 29		20 38		20 49	20 59		21 08			21 19	21 29
Charing Cross	d		19 27		19 39			19 57		20 08			20 27		20 40			20 57		21 08			
Glasgow Queen St LL	a		19 29		19 41			19 59		20 10			20 29		20 42			20 59		21 11			
	d		19 30		19 44			20 00		20 14			20 30		20 44			21 00		21 14			
High Street	d		19 32		19 46			20 02		20 16			20 32		20 46			21 02		21 16			
Bellgrove	d		19 34		19 49			20 04		20 19			20 34		20 49			21 04		21 19			
Duke Street	d				19 51					20 21					20 51					21 21			
Alexandra Parade	d				19 52					20 22					20 52					21 22			
Barnhill	d				19 55					20 25					20 55					21 25			
Springburn	a				19 57					20 27					20 57					21 27			
Carntyne	d		19 37					20 07					20 37					21 07					
Shettleston	d		19 40					20 10					20 40					21 10					
Garrowhill	d		19 42					20 12					20 42					21 12					
Easterhouse	d		19 45					20 15					20 45					21 15					
Blairhill	d		19 49					20 19					20 49					21 19					
Coatbridge Sunnyside	d		19 51					20 21					20 51					21 21					
Coatdyke	d		19 54					20 24					20 54					21 24					
Airdrie	d		19 57					20 27					20 57					21 27					
Drumgelloch	d		20 00					20 30					21 00					21 30					
Caldercruix	d		20 04					20 34					21 04					21 34					
Blackridge	d		20 10					20 40					21 10					21 40					
Armadale	d		20 13					20 43					21 13					21 43					
Bathgate	a		20 17					20 47					21 17					21 47					
	d		20 18					20 49					21 19					21 49					
Livingston North	d		20 23					20 53					21 23					21 53					
Uphall	d		20 26					20 56					21 26					21 56					
Edinburgh Park	a		20 34					21 04					21 34					22 04					
Haymarket	a		20 38					21 09					21 39					22 09					
Edinburgh	a		20 43					21 14					21 44					22 14					
Bridgeton	d			19 42		19 52			20 11		20 22			20 41		20 52			21 11			21 22	
Dalmarnock	d			19 44		19 54			20 13		20 24			20 43		20 54			21 13			21 24	
Rutherglen	d	19 34		19 46		19 56	20 04		20 16		20 26	20 34		20 46		20 55	21 04		21 16			21 26	21 34
Cambuslang	d			19 50		20 01			20 20		20 31			20 50		21 00			21 20			21 31	
Newton	d			19 54					20 23					20 54					21 24				
Blantyre	d	19 44		19 58			20 12		20 27			20 44		20 58			21 14		21 28				21 44
Hamilton West	d	19 47		20 01			20 15		20 30			20 47		21 01			21 17		21 31				21 47
Hamilton Central	d	19 49		20 04			20 20		20 33			20 50		21 03			21 20		21 33				21 50
Chatelherault	d	19 53					20 23					20 53					21 23						21 53
Merryton	d	19 56					20 26					20 56					21 26						21 56
Larkhall	a	19 59					20 31					20 59					21 29						21 59
Airbles	d			20 09					20 38					21 08					21 38				
Uddingston	d					20 05					20 35					21 05					21 30	21 35	
Bellshill	d					20 10					20 40					21 09					21 36	21 40	
Motherwell	a			20 12		20 16			20 41		20 47			21 11		21 15			21 41			21 47	
	d					20 16			20 41							21 16			21 43				
Whifflet	a																						
Coatbridge Central	a																						
Shieldmuir	d					20 20										21 19							
Holytown	d								20 48										21 48		21a40		
Wishaw	d					20 23			20 53							21 24			21 53				
Carluke	d					20 30			21 00							21 33			22 00				
Lanark	a					20 42			21 12							21 44			22 14				

A To Edinburgh

Helensburgh, Balloch, Dalmuir and Milngavie - Glasgow - Springburn, Airdrie, Bathgate and Edinburgh, Hamilton, Larkhall, Motherwell, Coatbridge and Lanark

		SR	SR	SR	SR	SR	SR	SR	SR	SR	SR	SR	SR	SR	SR	SR	SR	SR	SR	SR	SR	SR
			◇ A																B			
Helensburgh Central	d	20 40	20b40					21 10					21 40					22 10				
Craigendoran	d	20 43						21 13					21 43					22 13				
Cardross	d	20 48						21 18					21 48					22 18				
Balloch	d				20 53					21 23					21 53						22 23	
Alexandria	d				20 55					21 25					21 55						22 25	
Renton	d				20 59					21 28					21 58						22 28	
Dalreoch	d	20 53			21 01			21 23		21 31			21 53		22 01			22 23			22 31	
Dumbarton Central	d	20 55	20 59		21 02			21 25		21 32			21 55		22 02			22 25			22 32	
Dumbarton East	d	20 57			21 04			21 27		21 34			21 57		22 04			22 27			22 34	
Bowling	d				21 09					21 39					22 09						22 39	
Kilpatrick	d				21 12					21 42					22 12						22 42	
Dalmuir	a	21 04	21 08		21 15			21 35		21 45			22 05		22 15			22 35			22 45	
	d	21 05	21 08		21 16		21 31	21 35		21 46		22 01	22 05		22 16		22 31	22 35			22 46	
Singer	d				21 18		21 33			21 48		22 03			22 18		22 33				22 48	
Drumry	d				21 20		21 35			21 50		22 05			22 20		22 35				22 50	
Drumchapel	d				21 23		21 38			21 53		22 08			22 23		22 38				22 53	
Milngavie	d			21 12					21 42					22 12						22 42		
Hillfoot	d			21 15					21 45					22 15						22 45		
Bearsden	d			21 17					21 47					22 17						22 47		
Westerton	d			21 20	21 26		21 40		21 50	21 55		22 10		22 20	22 25		22 40			22 50	22 55	
Anniesland	d			21 23	21 29		21 44		21 53	22 00		22 14		22 23	22 30		22 44			22 53	23 00	
Clydebank	d	21 07						21 37					22 07					22 37				
Yoker	d	21 09						21 39					22 09					22 39				
Garscadden	d	21 13						21 43					22 13					22 43				
Scotstounhill	d	21 15						21 45					22 15					22 45				
Jordanhill	d	21 17						21 47					22 17					22 47				
Hyndland	d	21 21		21 27	21 32		21 47	21 51	21 56	22 03		22 17	22 21	22 26	22 33		22 47	22 51		22 56	23 03	
Partick	d	21 23		21 30	21 34	21 40	21 50	21 53	21 59	22 05	22 10	22 20	22 23	22 29	22 35	22 40	22 50	22 53		22 59	23 05	23 10
Exhibition Centre	d			21 33		21 43	21 53		22 02		22 13	22 23		22 32		22 43	22 53			23 02		23 13
Anderston	d			21 35		21 45	21 55		22 04		22 15	22 25		22 34		22 45	22 55			23 04		23 15
Glasgow Central LL 15	a			21 37		21 46	21 56		22 05		22 16	22 26		22 35		22 46	22 56			23 05		23 16
	d			21 37		21 47	21 57		22 07		22 17	22 27		22 37		22 47	22 57		23e06	23 07		23 17
Argyle Street	d			21 39		21 49	21 59		22 08		22 19	22 29		22 39		22 49	22 59			23 09		23 19
Charing Cross	d	21 27			21 39			21 57		22 10			22 27		22 40			22 57			23 10	
Glasgow Queen St LL 10	a	21 29	21c31		21 42			21 59		22 12			22 29		22 42			22 59			23 12	
	d	21 30			21 44			22 00		22 14			22 30		22 44			23 00			23 14	
High Street	d	21 32			21 46			22 02		22 16			22 32		22 46			23 02			23 16	
Bellgrove	d	21 34			21 49			22 04		22 19			22 34		22 49			23 04			23 19	
Duke Street	d				21 51					22 21					22 51						23 21	
Alexandra Parade	d				21 52					22 22					22 52						23 22	
Barnhill	d				21 55					22 25					22 55						23 25	
Springburn	a				21 57					22 27					22 57						23 27	
Carntyne	d	21 37						22 07					22 37					23 07				
Shettleston	d	21 40						22 10					22 40					23 10				
Garrowhill	d	21 42						22 12					22 42					23 12				
Easterhouse	d	21 45						22 15					22 45					23 15				
Blairhill	d	21 49						22 19					22 49					23 19				
Coatbridge Sunnyside	d	21 51						22 21					22 51					23 21				
Coatdyke	d	21 54						22 24					22 54					23 24				
Airdrie	d	21 57						22 27					22 57					23 27				
Drumgelloch	d	22 00						22 30					23 00					23 30				
Caldercruix	d	22 04						22 34					23 04					23 34				
Blackridge	d	22 10						22 40					23 10					23 40				
Armadale	d	22 13						22 43					23 13					23 43				
Bathgate	a	22 17						22 47					23 17					23 47				
	d	22 19						22 49					23 17									
Livingston North	d	22 23						22 53					23 22									
Uphall	d	22 26						22 56					23 25									
Edinburgh Park	a	22 34						23 05					23 33									
Haymarket	a	22 39						23 09					23 38									
Edinburgh	a	22 44						23 14					23 43									
Bridgeton	d			21 42		21 52			22 11		22 22			22 42		22 52				23 12		23 22
Dalmarnock	d			21 44		21 54			22 13		22 24			22 44		22 54				23 14		23 24
Rutherglen	d			21 47		21 56	22 04		22 16		22 26	22 34		22 46		22 56	23 04			23 16		23 26
Cambuslang	d			21 51		22 01			22 20		22 31			22 50		23 01			23 15	23 20		23 31
Newton	d			21 54					22 23					22 54						23 24		
Blantyre	d			21 58			22 14		22 28			22 44		22 58			23 14			23 28		
Hamilton West	d			22 01			22 17		22 31			22 47		23 01			23 17			23 31		
Hamilton Central	d			22 04			22 20		22 33			22 50		23 03			23 20			23 33		
Chatelherault	d						22 23					22 53					23 23					
Merryton	d						22 26					22 56					23 26					
Larkhall	a						22 29					22 59					23 29					
Airbles	d			22 09					22 38					23 08						23 38		
Uddingston	d					22 05					22 35					23 05			23 20			23 35
Bellshill	d					22 10					22 40					23 10			23 25			23 40
Motherwell	a			22 11		22 16			22 41		22 48			23 11		23 16				23 41		23 46
	d					22 16			22 41							23 16						
Whifflet	a								22 49													
Coatbridge Central	a								22 51													
Shieldmuir	d					22 20										23 20						
Holytown	d																		23a29			
Wishaw	d					22 23										23 23						
Carluke	d					22 30										23 30						
Lanark	a					22 42										23 42						

A From Mallaig
B To Edinburgh
b Helensburgh Upper
c Glasgow Queen St High Level
e Glasgow Central High Level

Helensburgh, Balloch, Dalmuir and Milngavie - Glasgow - Springburn, Airdrie, Bathgate and Edinburgh, Hamilton, Larkhall, Motherwell, Coatbridge and Lanark

		SR	SR	SR	SR	SR	SR	SR	SR	SR
				FX	FO	FO	FO		FO	A
Helensburgh Central	d		22 40					23 10		23b24
Craigendoran	d		22 43					23 13		
Cardross	d		22 48					23 18		
Balloch	d			22 53	22 53					
Alexandria	d			22 55	22 55					
Renton	d			22 58	22 58					
Dalreoch	d		22 53	23 01	23 01			23 23		
Dumbarton Central	d		22 55	23 02	23 02			23 25		
Dumbarton East	d		22 57	23 04	23 04			23 27		
Bowling	d			23 09	23 09					
Kilpatrick	d			23 12	23 12					
Dalmuir	a		23 05	23 15	23 15			23 35		23 49
	d	23 01	23 05	23 16	23 16		23 31	23 35		23 51
Singer	d	23 03		23 18	23 18		23 33			
Drumry	d	23 05		23 20	23 20		23 35			
Drumchapel	d	23 08		23 23	23 23		23 38			
Milngavie	d								23 42	
Hillfoot	d								23 45	
Bearsden	d								23 47	
Westerton	d	23 10		23 25	23 25		23 40		23 50	23 56
Anniesland	d	23 14		23 28	23 28		23 44		23 53	
Clydebank	d		23 07					23 37		
Yoker	d		23 09					23 39		
Garscadden	d		23 13					23 43		
Scotstounhill	d		23 15					23 45		
Jordanhill	d		23 17					23 47		
Hyndland	d	23 17	23 21	23 31	23 31		23 47	23 49	23 56	
Partick	d	23 20	23 23	23 34	23 34	23 40	23 50	23 52	23 59	
Exhibition Centre	d	23 23				23 43	23 53		00 02	
Anderston	d	23 25				23 45	23 55		00 04	
Glasgow Central LL 15	a	23 26				23 46	23 56		00 05	
	d	23 27				23 47	23 57		00 07	
Argyle Street	d	23 29				23 49	23 59		00 09	
Charing Cross	d		23 27	23 38	23 38			23 56		
Glasgow Queen St LL 10	a		23 29	23 40	23 40			23 59		
	d		23 30	23 44	23 44			23 59		
High Street	d		23 32	23 46	23 46			00 02		
Bellgrove	d		23 34	23 49	23 49			00 04		
Duke Street	d				23 51					
Alexandra Parade	d				23 52					
Barnhill	d				23 55					
Springburn	a				23 57					
Carntyne	d		23 37	23 52				00 07		
Shettleston	d		23 40	23 55				00 10		
Garrowhill	d		23 42	23 57				00 12		
Easterhouse	d		23 45	23 59				00 15		
Blairhill	d		23 49	00 04				00 19		
Coatbridge Sunnyside	d		23 51	00 06				00 21		
Coatdyke	d		23 54	00 09				00 24		
Airdrie	d		23 57	00a12				00a27		
Drumgelloch	d		23 59							
Caldercruix	d		00 03							
Blackridge	d		00 09							
Armadale	d		00 13							
Bathgate	a		00 17							
	d									
Livingston North	d									
Uphall	d									
Edinburgh Park	a									
Haymarket	a									
Edinburgh	a									00 50
Bridgeton	d					23 52			00 12	
Dalmarnock	d					23 54			00 14	
Rutherglen	d	23 34				23 57	00 04		00 16	
Cambuslang	d					00 01			00 20	
Newton	d								00 24	
Blantyre	d	23 44					00 15		00 28	
Hamilton West	d	23 47					00 18		00 31	
Hamilton Central	d	23 50					00 21		00 33	
Chatelherault	d	23 53					00 24			
Merryton	d	23 56					00 27			
Larkhall	a	00 01					00 30			
Airbles	d								00 38	
Uddingston	d					00 05				
Bellshill	d					00 10				
Motherwell	a					00 16			00 41	
	d					00 16				
Whifflet	a									
Coatbridge Central	a									
Shieldmuir	d					00 20				
Holytown	d									
Wishaw	d					00 23				
Carluke	d					00 30				
Lanark	a					00 42				

A From Fort William
b Helensburgh Upper

Table 226

Helensburgh, Balloch, Dalmuir and Milngavie - Glasgow - Springburn, Airdrie, Bathgate and Edinburgh, Hamilton, Larkhall, Motherwell, Coatbridge and Lanark

		SR	SR	SR	SR	SR	SR	SR	SR	SR	SR	SR	SR	SR	SR	SR	SR	SR	SR	SR	SR	SR	SR
							A		B					A									
Helensburgh Central	d		22p40			23p10			23c24												06 10		
Craigendoran	d		22p43			23p13															06 13		
Cardross	d		22p48			23p18															06 18		
Balloch	d																						
Alexandria	d																						
Renton	d																						
Dalreoch	d		22p53			23p23															06 23		
Dumbarton Central	d		22p55			23p25															06 25		
Dumbarton East	d		22p57			23p27															06 27		
Bowling	d																						
Kilpatrick	d																						
Dalmuir	a		23p05			23p35			23p49												06 34		
	d	23p01	23p05		23p31	23p35			23p51				05 48			06 01			06 16	06 23	06 35	06 31	
Singer	d	23p03			23p33											06 03			06 18			06 33	
Drumry	d	23p05			23p35											06 05			06 20			06 35	
Drumchapel	d	23p08			23p38											06 08			06 23			06 38	
Milngavie	d							23p42															06 42
Hillfoot	d							23p45															06 45
Bearsden	d							23p47															06 47
Westerton	d	23p10			23p40			23p50	23p56							06 10			06 25			06 40	06 50
Anniesland	d	23p14			23p44			23p53								06 14			06 28			06 44	06 53
Clydebank	d		23p07			23p37							05 50							06 25			
Yoker	d		23p09			23p39							05 52							06 27			
Garscadden	d		23p13			23p43						05 42	05 55		06 00		06 13	06 20		06 31			
Scotstounhill	d		23p15			23p45						05 44	05 57		06 01		06 15	06 22		06 33			
Jordanhill	d		23p17			23p47						05 46	05 59		06 03		06 18	06 24		06 35			
Hyndland	d	23p17	23p21		23p47	23p49		23p56				05 48	06 01		06 05	06 17	06 20	06 26	06 31	06 37	06 44	06 47	06 56
Partick ⇌	d	23p20	23p23	23p40	23p50	23p52		23p59				05 51	06 04		06 10	06 20	06 22	06 29	06 34	06 40	06 46	06 50	06 59
Exhibition Centre	d	23p23		23p43	23p53			00 02							06 13	06 23		06 32		06 43		06 53	07 02
Anderston	d	23p25		23p45	23p55			00 04							06 15	06 25		06 34		06 45		06 55	07 04
Glasgow Central LL	a	23p26		23p46	23p56			00 05							06 17	06 26		06 35		06 46		06 56	07 05
	d	23p27		23p47	23p57		00b06	00 07						06b16	06 17	06 27		06 37		06 47		06 57	07 07
Argyle Street	d	23p29		23p49	23p59			00 09							06 19	06 29		06 39		06 49		06 58	07 09
Charing Cross	d		23p27			23p56						05 55	06 08				06 26		06 38		06 54		
Glasgow Queen St LL ⇌	a		23p29			23p59						05 57	06 10				06 28		06 40		06 56		
	d		23p30			23p59						05 58	06 15				06 29		06 44		06 57		
High Street	d		23p32			00 02						06 00	06 17				06 31		06 46		07 00		
Bellgrove	d		23p34			00 04						06 02	06 19				06 33		06 49		07 01		
Duke Street	d												06 21						06 51				
Alexandra Parade	d												06 22						06 52				
Barnhill	d												06 25						06 55				
Springburn	a												06 27						06 57				
Carntyne	d		23p37			00 07						06 05					06 36				07 05		
Shettleston	d		23p40			00 10						06 08					06 39				07 07		
Garrowhill	d		23p42			00 12						06 10					06 41				07 10		
Easterhouse	d		23p45			00 15						06 13					06 44				07 12		
Blairhill	d		23p49			00 19						06 17					06 48				07 16		
Coatbridge Sunnyside	d		23p51			00 21						06 19					06 50				07 19		
Coatdyke	d		23p54			00 24						06 22					06 53				07 21		
Airdrie	d		23p57			00a27						06 25					06 56				07 24		
Drumgelloch	d		23p59									06 28					06 59				07 27		
Caldercruix	d		00 03									06 32					07 03				07 31		
Blackridge	d		00 09									06 38					07 09				07 37		
Armadale	d		00 13									06 41					07 13				07 41		
Bathgate	a		00 17									06 45					07 17				07 46		
	d									05 48	06 18	06 47					07 18				07 46		
Livingston North	d									05 52	06 22	06 50					07 22				07 50		
Uphall	d									05 55	06 25	06 53					07 25				07 53		
Edinburgh Park	a									06 03	06 36	07 02					07 33				08 01		
Haymarket	a									06 08	06 41	07 07					07 42				08 08		
Edinburgh	a								00 50	06 13	06 46	07 13					07 47				08 14		
Bridgeton	d			23p52				00 12							06 22			06 42		06 52			07 12
Dalmarnock	d			23p54				00 14							06 24			06 44		06 54			07 14
Rutherglen	d	23p34		23p57	00 04			00 16							06 25	06 34		06 46		06 56		07 03	07 16
Cambuslang	d			00 01			00 15	00 20						06 25	06 30			06 50		07 01			07 20
Newton	d							00 24										06 54					07 24
Blantyre	d	23p44			00 15			00 28								06 44		06 58				07 11	07 28
Hamilton West	d	23p47			00 18			00 31								06 47		07 01				07 14	07 31
Hamilton Central	d	23p50			00 21			00 33								06 50		07 03				07 17	07 33
Chatelherault	d	23p53			00 24											06 53						07 20	
Merryton	d	23p56			00 27											06 56						07 23	
Larkhall	a	00 01			00 30											06 59						07 26	
Airbles	d							00 38										07 08					07 38
Uddingston	d			00 05			00 20							06 30	06 35					07 05			
Bellshill	d			00 10			00 25							06 35	06 40					07 10			
Motherwell	a			00 16				00 41							06 45			07 11		07 17			07 41
	d			00 16											06 47								07 41
Whifflet	a																						
Coatbridge Central	a																						
Shieldmuir	d			00 20											06 49								
Holytown	d						00a29							06a39									07 48
Wishaw	d			00 23											06 53								07 53
Carluke	d			00 30											06 59								08 00
Lanark	a			00 42											07 14								08 13

A To Edinburgh
B From Fort William
b Glasgow Central High Level
c Helensburgh Upper, previous night

Table 226

Helensburgh, Balloch, Dalmuir and Milngavie - Glasgow - Springburn, Airdrie, Bathgate and Edinburgh, Hamilton, Larkhall, Motherwell, Coatbridge and Lanark

		SR	SR	SR	SR	SR	SR	SR	SR	SR	SR	SR	SR	SR	SR	SR	SR	SR	SR	SR	SR	SR	SR
			A													A							
Helensburgh Central	d					06 40						07 10							07 40				
Craigendoran	d					06 43						07 13							07 43				
Cardross	d					06 48						07 18							07 48				
Balloch	d	06 23							06 53						07 23							07 53	
Alexandria	d	06 25							06 55						07 25							07 55	
Renton	d	06 28							06 58						07 28							07 58	
Dalreoch	d	06 31				06 53			07 01			07 23			07 31				07 53			08 01	
Dumbarton Central	d	06 32				06 55			07 02			07 25			07 32				07 55			08 02	
Dumbarton East	d	06 34				06 57			07 04			07 27			07 34				07 57			08 04	
Bowling	d	06 39							07 09						07 39							08 09	
Kilpatrick	d	06 42							07 12						07 42							08 12	
Dalmuir	a	06 45				07 04			07 15			07 34			07 45				08 04			08 15	
	d	06 46		06 53		07 05	07 01		07 16	07 23		07 35	07 31		07 46		07 53		08 05	08 01		08 16	08 23
Singer	d	06 48					07 03		07 18				07 33		07 48					08 03		08 18	
Drumry	d	06 50					07 05		07 20				07 35		07 50					08 05		08 20	
Drumchapel	d	06 53					07 08		07 23				07 38		07 53					08 08		08 23	
Milngavie	d							07 12						07 42							08 12		
Hillfoot	d							07 15						07 45							08 15		
Bearsden	d							07 17						07 47							08 17		
Westerton	d	06 55					07 10	07 20	07 25				07 40	07 50	07 55					08 10	08 20	08 25	
Anniesland	d	06 58					07 14	07 23	07 28				07 44	07 53	07 58					08 14	08 23	08 28	
Clydebank	d			06 55						07 25							07 55						08 25
Yoker	d			06 57						07 27							07 57						08 27
Garscadden	d			07 01						07 31							08 01						08 31
Scotstounhill	d			07 03						07 33							08 03						08 33
Jordanhill	d			07 05						07 35							08 05						08 35
Hyndland	d	07 01		07 07		07 14	07 17	07 26	07 31	07 37		07 44	07 47	07 56	08 01		08 07		08 14	08 17	08 26	08 31	08 37
Partick ⇌	d	07 04		07 10	07 14	07 17	07 20	07 29	07 34	07 40	07 44	07 47	07 50	07 59	08 04		08 10	08 14	08 17	08 20	08 29	08 34	08 40
Exhibition Centre	d			07 13			07 23	07 32		07 43			07 53	08 02			08 13			08 23	08 32		08 43
Anderston	d			07 15			07 25	07 34		07 45			07 55	08 04			08 15			08 25	08 34		08 45
Glasgow Central LL	a			07 16			07 26	07 35		07 46			07 56	08 05			08 16			08 26	08 35		08 46
	d		07b13	07 17			07 27	07 37		07 47			07 57	08 07		08b18	08 17			08 27	08 37		08 47
Argyle Street	d			07 19			07 29	07 38		07 49			07 59	08 09			08 19			08 29	08 38		08 49
Charing Cross	d	07 08			07 19	07 24			07 38		07 49	07 54			08 08			08 19	08 24			08 38	
Glasgow Queen St LL ⇌	a	07 10			07 21	07 26			07 40		07 51	07 56			08 10			08 21	08 26			08 40	
	d	07 15			07 24	07 28			07 44		07 54	07 58			08 15			08 24	08 28			08 44	
High Street	d	07 17			07 26	07 30			07 46		07 56	08 00			08 17			08 27	08 30			08 46	
Bellgrove	d	07 19				07 32			07 49			08 01			08 19				08 32			08 49	
Duke Street	d	07 21							07 51						08 21							08 51	
Alexandra Parade	d	07 22							07 52						08 22							08 52	
Barnhill	d	07 25							07 55						08 25							08 55	
Springburn	a	07 27							07 57						08 27							08 57	
Carntyne	d					07 36						08 05							08 35				
Shettleston	d					07 38						08 07							08 38				
Garrowhill	d					07 41						08 10							08 40				
Easterhouse	d					07 43						08 12							08 43				
Blairhill	d					07 47						08 16							08 47				
Coatbridge Sunnyside	d				07 38	07 50					08 09	08 19						08 39	08 49				
Coatdyke	d					07 52						08 21							08 52				
Airdrie	d				07 45	07 55					08 15	08 24						08 44	08 55				
Drumgelloch	d				07 48	07 58					08 18	08 27						08 47	08 58				
Caldercruix	d					08 02						08 31							09 02				
Blackridge	d					08 08						08 37							09 08				
Armadale	d					08 12						08 41							09 11				
Bathgate	a				08 00	08 16					08 30	08 45						09 00	09 15				
	d				08 02	08 17					08 31	08 46						09 01	09 17				
Livingston North	d				08 06	08 21					08 36	08 51						09 06	09 20				
Uphall	d				08 09	08 24					08 39	08 54						09 09	09 23				
Edinburgh Park	a				08 16	08 33					08 47	09 03						09 18	09 31				
Haymarket	a				08 23	08 38					08 52	09 08						09 22	09 37				
Edinburgh	a				08 29	08 43					08 58	09 13						09 27	09 43				
Bridgeton	d			07 22				07 41		07 52				08 12			08 22				08 41		08 52
Dalmarnock	d			07 24				07 43		07 54				08 14			08 24				08 43		08 54
Rutherglen	d			07 26			07 34	07 46		07 55			08 05	08 16			08 26			08 34	08 46		08 56
Cambuslang	d		07 23	07 31				07 50		08 00				08 20			08 31				08 50		09 01
Newton	d							07 54						08 24							08 54		
Blantyre	d						07 44	07 58					08 14	08 28						08 44	08 58		
Hamilton West	d						07 47	08 01					08 17	08 31						08 47	09 01		
Hamilton Central	d						07 50	08 03					08 20	08 33						08 50	09 03		
Chatelherault	d						07 53						08 23							08 53			
Merryton	d						07 56						08 26							08 56			
Larkhall	a						07 59						08 29							08 59			
Airbles	d							08 08						08 38							09 08		
Uddingston	d		07 29	07 35						08 05						08 30	08 35						09 05
Bellshill	d		07 34	07 40						08 10						08 34	08 40						09 10
Motherwell	a			07 46				08 11		08 16				08 41			08 49				09 11		09 19
	d									08 16				08 41									09 19
Whifflet	a																						
Coatbridge Central	a																						
Shieldmuir	d									08 20													09 23
Holytown	d		07a38											08 47		08a38							
Wishaw	d									08 23				08 53									09 25
Carluke	d									08 30				09 00									09 33
Lanark	a									08 42				09 12									09 43

A To Edinburgh
b Glasgow Central High Level

Helensburgh, Balloch, Dalmuir and Milngavie - Glasgow - Springburn, Airdrie, Bathgate and Edinburgh, Hamilton, Larkhall, Motherwell, Coatbridge and Lanark

		SR	SR	SR	SR	SR	SR	SR	SR	SR	SR	SR	SR	SR	SR	SR	SR	SR	SR	SR	SR	SR
								A														
Helensburgh Central	d		08 10								08 40							09 10				
Craigendoran	d		08 13								08 43							09 13				
Cardross	d		08 18								08 48							09 18				
Balloch	d						08 23								08 53							09 23
Alexandria	d						08 25								08 55							09 25
Renton	d						08 28								08 58							09 28
Dalreoch	d		08 23				08 31				08 53				09 01			09 23				09 31
Dumbarton Central	d		08 25				08 32				08 55				09 02			09 25				09 32
Dumbarton East	d		08 27				08 34				08 57				09 04			09 27				09 34
Bowling	d						08 39								09 09							09 39
Kilpatrick	d						08 42								09 12							09 42
Dalmuir	a		08 34				08 45				09 04				09 15			09 34				09 45
	d		08 35	08 31			08 46		08 53		09 05	09 01	09 08		09 16	09 23		09 35	09 31	09 38		09 46
Singer	d			08 33			08 48					09 03			09 18				09 33			09 48
Drumry	d			08 35			08 50					09 05			09 20				09 35			09 50
Drumchapel	d			08 38			08 53					09 08			09 23				09 38			09 53
Milngavie	d					08 42				08 57				09 12			09 28				09 42	
Hillfoot	d					08 45				09 00				09 15			09 31				09 45	
Bearsden	d					08 47				09 02				09 18			09 33				09 47	
Westerton	d			08 40		08 50	08 55			09 05		09 10		09 21	09 25		09 36		09 40		09 50	09 55
Anniesland	d			08 44		08 53	08 58			09 08		09 14		09 24	09 28		09 39		09 44		09 53	09 58
Clydebank	d								08 55				09 10			09 25				09 40		
Yoker	d								08 57				09 12			09 27				09 42		
Garscadden	d				08 46				09 01				09 16			09 31				09 46		
Scotstounhill	d				08 48				09 03				09 18			09 33				09 48		
Jordanhill	d				08 50				09 05				09 20			09 35				09 50		
Hyndland	d		08 44	08 47	08 52	08 56	09 01		09 08	09 12	09 14	09 17	09 22	09 27	09 31	09 37	09 42	09 44	09 47	09 52	09 56	10 01
Partick	d	08 44	08 47	08 50	08 55	08 59	09 04		09 10	09 14	09 17	09 20	09 25	09 30	09 34	09 40	09 44	09 47	09 50	09 55	09 59	10 04
Exhibition Centre	d			08 53		09 02			09 13			09 23		09 33		09 43			09 53		10 02	
Anderston	d			08 55		09 04			09 15			09 25		09 35		09 45			09 55		10 04	
Glasgow Central LL	a			08 56		09 05			09 16			09 26		09 36		09 46			09 56		10 05	
	d			08 57		09 07		09b18	09 17			09 27		09 37		09 47			09 57		10 07	
Argyle Street	d			08 59		09 08			09 19			09 29		09 38		09 49			09 59		10 09	
Charing Cross	d	08 49	08 54		08 59		09 08			09 19	09 24		09 29		09 38		09 49	09 54		09 59		10 08
Glasgow Queen St LL	a	08 51	08 56		09 01		09 10			09 21	09 26		09 31		09 40		09 51	09 56		10 01		10 10
	d	08 54	08 58		09 02		09 12			09 24	09 28		09 32		09 42		09 54	09 58		10 02		10 12
High Street	d	08 56	09 00		09 04		09 14			09 26	09 30		09 34		09 44		09 57	10 00		10 04		10 14
Bellgrove	d		09 02		09 06		09 16				09 32		09 36		09 46			10 02		10 06		10 16
Duke Street	d				09 08								09 38							10 08		
Alexandra Parade	d				09 09								09 39							10 09		
Barnhill	d				09 12								09 42							10 12		
Springburn	a				09 14								09 44							10 14		
Carntyne	d		09 06				09 19				09 35				09 49			10 05				10 19
Shettleston	d		09 09				09 22				09 38				09 52			10 08				10 22
Garrowhill	d		09 11				09 24				09 40				09 54			10 10				10 24
Easterhouse	d		09 14				09 27				09 43				09 57			10 13				10 27
Blairhill	d		09 18				09 31				09 47				10 01			10 17				10 31
Coatbridge Sunnyside	d	09 12	09 20				09 33			09 39	09 49				10 03		10 09	10 19				10 33
Coatdyke	d		09 23				09 36				09 52				10 06			10 22				10 36
Airdrie	d	09 16	09 26				09a39			09 44	09 55				10a09		10 15	10 25				10a39
Drumgelloch	d	09 19	09 29							09 47	09 58						10 18	10 28				
Caldercruix	d		09 33								10 02							10 32				
Blackridge	d		09 39								10 08							10 38				
Armadale	d		09 42								10 11							10 41				
Bathgate	a	09 32	09 46							10 00	10 15						10 29	10 45				
	d	09 32	09 47							10 01	10 17						10 32	10 47				
Livingston North	d	09 37	09 50							10 06	10 20						10 35	10 50				
Uphall	d	09 40	09 53							10 09	10 23						10 38	10 53				
Edinburgh Park	a	09 48	10 01							10 17	10 31						10 47	11 01				
Haymarket	a	09 52	10 08							10 22	10 37						10 52	11 06				
Edinburgh	a	09 57	10 14							10 28	10 43						10 57	11 14				
Bridgeton	d					09 11			09 22					09 41		09 52					10 12	
Dalmarnock	d					09 13			09 24					09 43		09 54					10 14	
Rutherglen	d			09 04		09 16			09 27			09 34		09 46		09 56			10 04		10 16	
Cambuslang	d					09 20			09 31					09 50		10 00					10 22	
Newton	d					09 24								09 54							10 25	
Blantyre	d			09 15		09 28						09 44		09 58					10 14		10 29	
Hamilton West	d			09 18		09 31						09 47		10 01					10 17		10 32	
Hamilton Central	d			09 20		09 33						09 50		10 03					10 20		10 35	
Chatelherault	d			09 24								09 53							10 23			
Merryton	d			09 27								09 56							10 26			
Larkhall	a			09 30								09 59							10 29			
Airbles	d					09 38								10 08							10 40	
Uddingston	d							09 30	09 35							10 05						
Bellshill	d							09 34	09 40							10 10						
Motherwell	a					09 41			09 47					10 11		10 16					10 43	
	d					09 41										10 16					10 43	
Whifflet	a																					
Coatbridge Central	a																					
Shieldmuir	d															10 20						
Holytown	d					09 48		09a38													10 48	
Wishaw	d					09 53										10 26					10 53	
Carluke	d					10 00										10 32					11 02	
Lanark	a					10 14										10 44					11 14	

A To Edinburgh
b Glasgow Central High Level

Helensburgh, Balloch, Dalmuir and Milngavie - Glasgow - Springburn, Airdrie, Bathgate and Edinburgh, Hamilton, Larkhall, Motherwell, Coatbridge and Lanark

		SR	SR	SR	SR	SR	SR	SR	SR	SR	SR	SR	SR	SR	SR	SR	SR	SR	SR	SR	SR	SR	SR
		A															A					◇ B	
Helensburgh Central	d				09 40							10 10								10 39		10c44	
Craigendoran	d				09 43							10 13								10 42			
Cardross	d				09 48							10 18								10 47			
Balloch	d								09 53							10 22							
Alexandria	d								09 55							10 24							
Renton	d								09 58							10 27							
Dalreoch	d				09 53				10 01			10 23				10 30				10 52			
Dumbarton Central	d				09 55				10 02			10 25				10 31				10 54		10 58	
Dumbarton East	d				09 57				10 04			10 27				10 33				10 56			
Bowling	d								10 09							10 38							
Kilpatrick	d								10 12							10 41							
Dalmuir	a				10 04				10 15			10 34				10 44				11 03		11 07	
	d		09 53		10 05	10 01	10 08		10 16	10 23		10 35	10 31	10 38		10 46		10 53		11 05	11 00	11 07	11 08
Singer	d					10 03			10 18				10 33			10 48					11 02		
Drumry	d					10 05			10 20				10 35			10 50					11 04		
Drumchapel	d					10 08			10 23				10 38			10 53					11 07		
Milngavie	d			09 57				10 12			10 27				10 42				10 57				
Hillfoot	d			10 00				10 15			10 30				10 45				11 00				
Bearsden	d			10 02				10 17			10 32				10 47				11 02				
Westerton	d			10 05		10 10		10 20	10 25		10 35		10 40		10 50	10 55			11 05		11 10		
Anniesland	d			10 08		10 14		10 23	10 28		10 38		10 44		10 53	10 58			11 08		11 14		
Clydebank	d		09 55				10 10			10 25				10 40				10 55					11 10
Yoker	d		09 57				10 12			10 27				10 42				10 57					11 12
Garscadden	d		10 01				10 16			10 31				10 46				11 01					11 16
Scotstounhill	d		10 03				10 18			10 33				10 48				11 03					11 18
Jordanhill	d		10 05				10 20			10 35				10 50				11 07					11 20
Hyndland	d		10 07	10 12	10 14	10 17	10 22	10 26	10 31	10 37	10 41	10 44	10 47	10 52	10 56	11 01		11 09	11 11	11 15	11 17		11 22
Partick	d		10 10	10 14	10 17	10 20	10 25	10 29	10 34	10 40	10 44	10 47	10 50	10 55	10 59	11 04		11 11	11 14	11 17	11 20		11 25
Exhibition Centre	d		10 13			10 23		10 32		10 43			10 53		11 02			11 14			11 23		
Anderston	d		10 15			10 25		10 34		10 45			10 55		11 04			11 16			11 25		
Glasgow Central LL	a		10 16			10 26		10 36		10 46			10 56		11 05			11 17			11 26		
	d	10b18	10 17			10 27		10 37		10 47			10 57		11 07		11b18	11 18			11 27		
Argyle Street	d		10 19			10 29		10 39		10 48			10 59		11 08			11 19			11 29		
Charing Cross	d			10 19	10 24		10 29		10 38		10 49	10 54		10 59		11 09			11 19	11 24			11 29
Glasgow Queen St LL	a			10 21	10 26		10 31		10 40		10 51	10 56		11 01		11 10			11 21	11 26		11e30	11 31
	d			10 24	10 28		10 32		10 42		10 54	10 58		11 02		11 11			11 24	11 28			11 32
High Street	d			10 26	10 30		10 34		10 44		10 56	11 00		11 04		11 13			11 26	11 30			11 34
Bellgrove	d				10 32		10 36		10 46			11 02		11 06		11 16				11 32			11 36
Duke Street	d						10 38							11 08									11 38
Alexandra Parade	d						10 39							11 09									11 39
Barnhill	d						10 42							11 12									11 42
Springburn	a						10 44							11 14									11 44
Carntyne	d				10 35				10 49			11 05				11 19				11 35			
Shettleston	d				10 40				10 52			11 08				11 22				11 38			
Garrowhill	d				10 42				10 54			11 10				11 24				11 40			
Easterhouse	d				10 45				10 57			11 13				11 27				11 43			
Blairhill	d				10 49				11 01			11 17				11 31				11 47			
Coatbridge Sunnyside	d			10 39	10 51				11 03		11 10	11 19				11 33			11 39	11 49			
Coatdyke	d				10 54				11 06			11 22				11 36				11 52			
Airdrie	d			10 44	10 56				11a09		11 14	11 25				11a39			11 44	11 55			
Drumgelloch	d			10 47	10 59						11 17	11 28							11 47	11 58			
Caldercruix	d				11 03							11 32								12 02			
Blackridge	d				11 09							11 38								12 08			
Armadale	d				11 13							11 41								12 11			
Bathgate	a			11 00	11 17						11 30	11 45							12 00	12 16			
	d			11 01	11 17						11 31	11 47							12 01	12 17			
Livingston North	d			11 06	11 20						11 36	11 50							12 06	12 21			
Uphall	d			11 09	11 23						11 39	11 53							12 09	12 24			
Edinburgh Park	a			11 17	11 31						11 47	12 02							12 18	12 32			
Haymarket	a			11 22	11 37						11 52	12 07							12 23	12 37			
Edinburgh	a			11 27	11 43						11 57	12 13							12 28	12 43			
Bridgeton	d		10 22					10 42		10 51					11 11			11 22					
Dalmarnock	d		10 24					10 44		10 53					11 13			11 24					
Rutherglen	d		10 26			10 34		10 46		10 55			11 04		11 16			11 27			11 34		
Cambuslang	d		10 31					10 50		11 00					11 20			11 31					
Newton	d							10 54							11 23								
Blantyre	d					10 44		10 58					11 14		11 27						11 45		
Hamilton West	d					10 47		11 01					11 17		11 30						11 48		
Hamilton Central	d					10 50		11 03					11 20		11 33						11 50		
Chatelherault	d					10 53							11 23								11 54		
Merryton	d					10 56							11 26								11 57		
Larkhall	a					10 59							11 29								12 00		
Airbles	d							11 08							11 38								
Uddingston	d	10 28	10 35							11 04							11 30	11 35					
Bellshill	d	10 33	10 40							11 09							11 35	11 40					
Motherwell	a		10 46					11 11		11 16					11 40			11 47					
	d									11 16					11 41								
Whifflet	a																						
Coatbridge Central	a																						
Shieldmuir	d									11 20													
Holytown	d	10a37													11 48		11a39						
Wishaw	d									11 23					11 53								
Carluke	d									11 30					12 00								
Lanark	a									11 42					12 12								

A To Edinburgh
B From Mallaig
b Glasgow Central High Level
c Helensburgh Upper
e Glasgow Queen St High Level

Table 226

Saturdays

Helensburgh, Balloch, Dalmuir and Milngavie - Glasgow - Springburn, Airdrie, Bathgate and Edinburgh, Hamilton, Larkhall, Motherwell, Coatbridge and Lanark

		SR	SR	SR	SR	SR	SR	SR	SR	SR	SR A	SR	SR	SR	SR	SR	SR	SR	SR	SR	SR	SR
Helensburgh Central	d					11 10								11 40							12 10	
Craigendoran	d					11 13								11 43							12 13	
Cardross	d					11 18								11 48							12 18	
Balloch	d		10 53							11 23								11 53				
Alexandria	d		10 55							11 25								11 55				
Renton	d		10 58							11 28								11 58				
Dalreoch	d		11 01			11 23				11 31				11 53				12 01			12 23	
Dumbarton Central	d		11 02			11 25				11 32				11 55				12 02			12 25	
Dumbarton East	d		11 04			11 27				11 34				11 57				12 04			12 27	
Bowling	d		11 09							11 39								12 09				
Kilpatrick	d		11 12							11 42								12 12				
Dalmuir	a		11 15			11 34				11 45				12 04				12 15			12 34	
	d		11 16	11 23		11 35	11 31	11 38		11 46		11 53		12 05	12 01	12 08		12 16	12 23		12 35	12 31
Singer	d		11 18				11 33			11 48					12 03			12 18				12 33
Drumry	d		11 20				11 35			11 50					12 05			12 20				12 35
Drumchapel	d		11 23				11 38			11 53					12 08			12 23				12 38
Milngavie	d	11 12			11 27				11 42				11 57				12 12			12 27		
Hillfoot	d	11 15			11 30				11 45				12 00				12 15			12 30		
Bearsden	d	11 17			11 32				11 47				12 02				12 17			12 32		
Westerton	d	11 20	11 25		11 35		11 40		11 50	11 55			12 05		12 10		12 20	12 25		12 35		12 40
Anniesland	d	11 23	11 28		11 38		11 44		11 53	11 58			12 08		12 14		12 23	12 28		12 38		12 44
Clydebank	d			11 25				11 40				11 55				12 10			12 25			
Yoker	d			11 27				11 42				11 57				12 12			12 27			
Garscadden	d			11 31				11 46				12 01				12 16			12 31			
Scotstounhill	d			11 33				11 48				12 03				12 18			12 33			
Jordanhill	d			11 35				11 50				12 05				12 20			12 35			
Hyndland	d	11 26	11 31	11 37	11 41	11 44	11 47	11 52	11 56	12 01		12 07	12 11	12 14	12 17	12 22	12 26	12 31	12 37	12 41	12 44	12 47
Partick	d	11 29	11 34	11 40	11 44	11 47	11 50	11 55	11 59	12 04		12 10	12 14	12 17	12 20	12 25	12 29	12 34	12 40	12 44	12 47	12 50
Exhibition Centre	d	11 32		11 43			11 53		12 02			12 13			12 23		12 32		12 43			12 53
Anderston	d	11 34		11 45			11 55		12 04			12 15			12 25		12 34		12 45			12 55
Glasgow Central LL 15	a	11 37		11 46			11 56		12 05			12 16			12 26		12 35		12 46			12 56
	d	11 37		11 47			11 58		12 07		12b18	12 17			12 27		12 37		12 47			12 57
Argyle Street	d	11 39		11 49			11 59		12 08			12 19			12 29		12 38		12 48			12 59
Charing Cross	d		11 38		11 49	11 54		11 59		12 09			12 19	12 24		12 29		12 38		12 49	12 54	
Glasgow Queen St LL 10	a		11 40		11 51	11 56		12 01		12 10			12 21	12 26		12 31		12 40		12 51	12 56	
	d		11 42		11 54	11 58		12 02		12 12			12 24	12 28		12 32		12 42		12 54	12 58	
High Street	d		11 44		11 56	12 00		12 04		12 14			12 26	12 30		12 34		12 44		12 56	13 00	
Bellgrove	d		11 46			12 02		12 06		12 16				12 32		12 36		12 46			13 02	
Duke Street	d							12 08								12 38						
Alexandra Parade	d							12 09								12 39						
Barnhill	d							12 12								12 42						
Springburn	a							12 14								12 44						
Carntyne	d		11 49			12 06				12 19				12 35				12 49			13 05	
Shettleston	d		11 52			12 08				12 22				12 38				12 52			13 08	
Garrowhill	d		11 54			12 11				12 24				12 40				12 54			13 10	
Easterhouse	d		11 57			12 13				12 27				12 43				12 57			13 13	
Blairhill	d		12 01			12 17				12 31				12 47				13 01			13 17	
Coatbridge Sunnyside	d		12 03		12 09	12 20				12 33			12 39	12 49				13 03		13 09	13 19	
Coatdyke	d		12 06			12 22				12 36				12 52				13 06			13 22	
Airdrie	d		12a10		12 15	12 25				12a39			12 44	12 55				13a09		13 14	13 25	
Drumgelloch	d				12 18	12 28							12 47	12 58						13 17	13 28	
Caldercruix	d					12 32								13 02							13 32	
Blackridge	d					12 38								13 08							13 38	
Armadale	d					12 42								13 11							13 41	
Bathgate	a				12 30	12 46							13 00	13 15						13 30	13 46	
	d				12 31	12 47							13 01	13 17						13 31	13 47	
Livingston North	d				12 35	12 51							13 06	13 20						13 36	13 50	
Uphall	d				12 38	12 54							13 09	13 23						13 39	13 53	
Edinburgh Park	a				12 47	13 02							13 17	13 31						13 47	14 02	
Haymarket	a				12 52	13 07							13 22	13 37						13 52	14 07	
Edinburgh	a				12 58	13 13							13 27	13 43						13 58	14 14	
Bridgeton	d	11 42		11 52					12 11			12 22					12 41		12 51			
Dalmarnock	d	11 44		11 54					12 13			12 24					12 43		12 53			
Rutherglen	d	11 46		11 56			12 06		12 16			12 26			12 34		12 46		12 56			13 04
Cambuslang	d	11 50		12 01					12 20			12 31					12 50		13 01			
Newton	d	11 54							12 23								12 53					
Blantyre	d	11 58					12 15		12 27						12 45		12 58					13 14
Hamilton West	d	12 01					12 18		12 30						12 48		13 01					13 17
Hamilton Central	d	12 03					12 20		12 33						12 50		13 03					13 20
Chatelherault	d						12 24								12 54							13 23
Merryton	d						12 27								12 57							13 26
Larkhall	a						12 30								13 00							13 29
Airbles	d	12 08							12 38								13 07					
Uddingston	d			12 05							12 30	12 35							13 05			
Bellshill	d			12 10							12 35	12 40							13 10			
Motherwell	a	12 11		12 16					12 40			12 48					13 11		13 16			
	d			12 16					12 41										13 16			
Whifflet	a																					
Coatbridge Central	a																					
Shieldmuir	d			12 20															13 20			
Holytown	d								12 48		12a39											
Wishaw	d			12 23					12 53										13 23			
Carluke	d			12 30					13 00										13 31			
Lanark	a			12 42					13 12										13 42			

A To Edinburgh

b Glasgow Central High Level

Table 226

Saturdays

Helensburgh, Balloch, Dalmuir and Milngavie - Glasgow - Springburn, Airdrie, Bathgate and Edinburgh, Hamilton, Larkhall, Motherwell, Coatbridge and Lanark

		SR	SR	SR	SR A	SR	SR	SR	SR	SR	SR	SR	SR	SR	SR	SR	SR	SR	SR	SR A	SR	SR	SR
Helensburgh Central	d							12 40							13 10								13 40
Craigendoran	d							12 43							13 13								13 43
Cardross	d							12 48							13 18								13 48
Balloch	d			12 23								12 53							13 23				
Alexandria	d			12 25								12 55							13 25				
Renton	d			12 28								12 58							13 28				
Dalreoch	d			12 31				12 53				13 01			13 23				13 31				13 53
Dumbarton Central	d			12 32				12 55				13 02			13 25				13 32				13 55
Dumbarton East	d			12 34				12 57				13 04			13 27				13 34				13 57
Bowling	d			12 39								13 09							13 39				
Kilpatrick	d			12 42								13 12							13 42				
Dalmuir	a			12 45				13 04				13 15			13 34				13 45				14 04
	d	12 38		12 46		12 53		13 05	13 01	13 08		13 16	13 23		13 35	13 31	13 38		13 46		13 53		14 05
Singer	d			12 48					13 03			13 18				13 33			13 48				
Drumry	d			12 50					13 05			13 20				13 35			13 50				
Drumchapel	d			12 53					13 08			13 23				13 38			13 53				
Milngavie	d		12 42				12 57				13 12			13 27				13 42				13 57	
Hillfoot	d		12 45				13 00				13 15			13 30				13 45				14 00	
Bearsden	d		12 47				13 02				13 17			13 32				13 47				14 02	
Westerton	d		12 50	12 55			13 05		13 10		13 20	13 25		13 35		13 40		13 50	13 55			14 05	
Anniesland	d		12 53	12 58			13 08		13 14		13 23	13 28		13 38		13 44		13 53	13 58			14 08	
Clydebank	d	12 40				12 55				13 10			13 25				13 40				13 55		
Yoker	d	12 42				12 57				13 12			13 27				13 42				13 57		
Garscadden	d	12 46				13 01				13 16			13 31				13 46				14 01		
Scotstounhill	d	12 48				13 03				13 18			13 33				13 48				14 03		
Jordanhill	d	12 50				13 05				13 20			13 35				13 50				14 05		
Hyndland	d	12 52	12 56	13 01		13 07	13 11	13 14	13 17	13 22	13 26	13 31	13 37	13 41	13 44	13 47	13 52	13 56	14 01		14 07	14 11	14 14
Partick	d	12 55	12 59	13 04		13 10	13 14	13 17	13 20	13 25	13 29	13 34	13 40	13 44	13 47	13 50	13 55	13 59	14 04		14 10	14 14	14 17
Exhibition Centre	d		13 02			13 13			13 23		13 32		13 43			13 53		14 02			14 13		
Anderston	d		13 04			13 15			13 25		13 34		13 45			13 55		14 04			14 15		
Glasgow Central LL 15	a		13 05			13 16			13 26		13 35		13 46			13 56		14 05			14 16		
	d		13 07		13b18	13 17			13 27		13 36		13 47			13 57		14 07		14b18	14 17		
Argyle Street	d		13 08			13 19			13 29		13 38		13 48			13 59		14 09			14 19		
Charing Cross	d	12 59		13 08			13 19	13 24		13 29		13 38		13 49	13 54		13 59		14 08			14 19	14 24
Glasgow Queen St LL 10	a	13 01		13 10			13 21	13 26		13 31		13 40		13 51	13 56		14 01		14 10			14 21	14 26
	d	13 02		13 12			13 24	13 28		13 32		13 42		13 54	13 58		14 02		14 12			14 24	14 28
High Street	d	13 04		13 14			13 26	13 30		13 34		13 44		13 56	14 01		14 04		14 14			14 26	14 30
Bellgrove	d	13 06		13 16				13 32		13 36		13 46			14 03		14 06		14 16				14 32
Duke Street	d	13 08								13 38							14 08						
Alexandra Parade	d	13 09								13 39							14 09						
Barnhill	d	13 12								13 42							14 12						
Springburn	a	13 14								13 44							14 14						
Carntyne	d			13 19				13 36				13 49			14 06				14 19				14 36
Shettleston	d			13 22				13 38				13 52			14 10				14 22				14 38
Garrowhill	d			13 24				13 41				13 54			14 12				14 24				14 41
Easterhouse	d			13 27				13 43				13 57			14 15				14 27				14 43
Blairhill	d			13 31				13 47				14 01			14 19				14 31				14 47
Coatbridge Sunnyside	d			13 33			13 39	13 50				14 03		14 09	14 21				14 33			14 39	14 50
Coatdyke	d			13 36				13 52				14 06			14 24				14 36				14 52
Airdrie	d			13a39			13 44	13 55				14a09		14 14	14 26				14a39			14 44	14 55
Drumgelloch	d						13 47	13 58						14 17	14 29							14 47	14 58
Caldercruix	d							14 02							14 33								15 02
Blackridge	d							14 08							14 39								15 08
Armadale	d							14 12							14 43								15 12
Bathgate	a						14 00	14 16						14 29	14 47							14 59	15 16
	d						14 01	14 17						14 30	14 47							15 00	15 17
Livingston North	d						14 06	14 21						14 34	14 51							15 04	15 21
Uphall	d						14 09	14 24						14 37	14 54							15 07	15 24
Edinburgh Park	a						14 17	14 33						14 46	15 02							15 17	15 34
Haymarket	a						14 22	14 38						14 51	15 07							15 21	15 39
Edinburgh	a						14 28	14 44						14 57	15 12							15 27	15 44
Bridgeton	d		13 11			13 22					13 41		13 51					14 12			14 22		
Dalmarnock	d		13 13			13 24					13 43		13 53					14 14			14 24		
Rutherglen	d		13 16			13 26			13 34		13 46		13 56			14 04		14 16			14 26		
Cambuslang	d		13 20			13 31					13 50		14 00					14 20			14 31		
Newton	d		13 23								13 53							14 24					
Blantyre	d		13 28						13 44		13 57					14 14		14 28					
Hamilton West	d		13 31						13 47		14 00					14 17		14 31					
Hamilton Central	d		13 33						13 50		14 03					14 20		14 33					
Chatelherault	d								13 53							14 23							
Merryton	d								13 56							14 26							
Larkhall	a								13 59							14 29							
Airbles	d		13 38								14 08							14 38					
Uddingston	d				13 30	13 35							14 04							14 30	14 35		
Bellshill	d				13 35	13 40							14 10							14 36	14 40		
Motherwell	a		13 41			13 48					14 11		14 16					14 41			14 48		
	d		13 41										14 16					14 41					
Whifflet	a																						
Coatbridge Central	a																						
Shieldmuir	d												14 20										
Holytown	d		13 48		13a39													14 48		14a40			
Wishaw	d		13 53										14 23					14 53					
Carluke	d		14 00										14 30					15 00					
Lanark	a		14 12										14 42					15 12					

A To Edinburgh

b Glasgow Central High Level

Table 226

Helensburgh, Balloch, Dalmuir and Milngavie - Glasgow - Springburn, Airdrie, Bathgate and Edinburgh, Hamilton, Larkhall, Motherwell, Coatbridge and Lanark

		SR	SR	SR	SR	SR	SR	SR	SR	SR	SR	SR	SR	SR	SR	SR	SR	SR	SR	SR	SR	SR	SR
													A					◇ B					
Helensburgh Central	d							14 10								14 39		14c39					
Craigendoran	d							14 13								14 42							
Cardross	d							14 18								14 47							
Balloch	d				13 53							14 23									14 53		
Alexandria	d				13 55							14 25									14 55		
Renton	d				13 58							14 28									14 58		
Dalreoch	d				14 01			14 23				14 31				14 52					15 01		
Dumbarton Central	d				14 02			14 25				14 32				14 54		14 58			15 02		
Dumbarton East	d				14 04			14 27				14 34				14 56					15 04		
Bowling	d				14 09							14 39									15 09		
Kilpatrick	d				14 12							14 42									15 12		
Dalmuir	a				14 15			14 34				14 45				15 03		15 07			15 15		
	d	14 01	14 08		14 16	14 23		14 35	14 31	14 38		14 46		14 53		15 05	15 00	15 07	15 08		15 16	15 23	
Singer	d	14 03			14 18				14 33			14 48					15 02				15 18		
Drumry	d	14 05			14 20				14 35			14 50					15 04				15 20		
Drumchapel	d	14 08			14 23				14 38			14 53					15 07				15 23		
Milngavie	d			14 12			14 27				14 42				14 57					15 12			15 27
Hillfoot	d			14 15			14 30				14 45				15 00					15 15			15 30
Bearsden	d			14 17			14 32				14 47				15 02					15 17			15 33
Westerton	d	14 10		14 20	14 25		14 35		14 40		14 50	14 55			15 05		15 09			15 20	15 25		15 36
Anniesland	d	14 14		14 23	14 28		14 38		14 44		14 53	14 59			15 08		15 14			15 23	15 28		15 39
Clydebank	d		14 10			14 25				14 40				14 55					15 10			15 25	
Yoker	d		14 12			14 27				14 42				14 57					15 12			15 27	
Garscadden	d		14 16			14 31				14 46				15 01					15 16			15 31	
Scotstounhill	d		14 18			14 33				14 48				15 03					15 18			15 33	
Jordanhill	d		14 20			14 35				14 50				15 05					15 20			15 35	
Hyndland	d	14 17	14 22	14 26	14 31	14 37	14 41	14 44	14 47	14 52	14 56	15 02		15 07	15 11	15 14	15 17		15 22	15 26	15 31	15 37	15 42
Partick	d	14 20	14 25	14 29	14 34	14 40	14 44	14 47	14 50	14 55	14 58	15 04		15 10	15 14	15 17	15 20		15 25	15 29	15 34	15 40	15 44
Exhibition Centre	d	14 23		14 32		14 43			14 53		15 01			15 13			15 23			15 32		15 43	
Anderston	d	14 25		14 34		14 45			14 55		15 03			15 15			15 25			15 34		15 45	
Glasgow Central LL 15	a	14 26		14 35		14 46			14 56		15 04			15 16			15 26			15 37		15 46	
	d	14 27		14 36		14 47			14 57		15 07		15b18	15 17			15 27			15 37		15 47	
Argyle Street	d	14 29		14 38		14 49			14 59		15 09			15 19			15 29			15 39		15 48	
Charing Cross	d		14 29		14 38		14 49	14 54		14 59		15 09			15 19	15 24			15 29		15 38		15 48
Glasgow Queen St LL 10	a		14 31		14 40		14 51	14 56		15 01		15 11			15 21	15 26		15e30	15 31		15 40		15 50
	d		14 32		14 42		14 54	14 58		15 02		15 11			15 24	15 28			15 32		15 42		15 51
High Street	d		14 34		14 44		14 56	15 01		15 04		15 13			15 26	15 30			15 34		15 44		15 53
Bellgrove	d		14 36		14 46			15 03		15 06		15 15				15 32			15 36		15 46		
Duke Street	d		14 38							15 08									15 38				
Alexandra Parade	d		14 39							15 09									15 39				
Barnhill	d		14 42							15 12									15 42				
Springburn	a		14 44							15 14									15 44				
Carntyne	d				14 50			15 06				15 19				15 35					15 49		
Shettleston	d				14 52			15 09				15 21				15 38					15 52		
Garrowhill	d				14 55			15 12				15 24				15 40					15 54		
Easterhouse	d				14 57			15 14				15 26				15 43					15 57		
Blairhill	d				15 01			15 18				15 30				15 47					16 01		
Coatbridge Sunnyside	d				15 04		15 09	15 21				15 33			15 39	15 49					16 03		16 09
Coatdyke	d				15 06			15 23				15 35				15 52					16 06		
Airdrie	d				15a09		15 14	15 26				15a38			15 44	15 55					16a09		16 14
Drumgelloch	d						15 17	15 29							15 47	15 58							16 17
Caldercruix	d							15 33								16 02							
Blackridge	d							15 39								16 08							
Armadale	d							15 43								16 11							
Bathgate	a						15 30	15 47							16 00	16 15							16 30
	d						15 30	15 48							16 01	16 17							16 31
Livingston North	d						15 35	15 51							16 06	16 20							16 36
Uphall	d						15 38	15 54							16 09	16 24							16 39
Edinburgh Park	a						15 47	16 02							16 17	16 32							16 48
Haymarket	a						15 52	16 08							16 22	16 37							16 52
Edinburgh	a						15 57	16 14							16 29	16 43							16 57
Bridgeton	d			14 41		14 52					15 12			15 22						15 42		15 51	
Dalmarnock	d			14 43		14 54					15 14			15 24						15 44		15 53	
Rutherglen	d	14 34		14 46		14 56			15 06		15 16			15 26			15 34			15 46		15 55	
Cambuslang	d			14 50		15 00					15 20			15 31						15 50		16 00	
Newton	d			14 53							15 24									15 54			
Blantyre	d	14 44		14 57					15 14		15 28						15 44			15 58			
Hamilton West	d	14 47		15 00					15 17		15 31						15 47			16 01			
Hamilton Central	d	14 50		15 03					15 20		15 33						15 50			16 03			
Chatelherault	d	14 53							15 23								15 54						
Merryton	d	14 56							15 26								15 57						
Larkhall	a	14 59							15 29								16 00						
Airbles	d			15 08							15 38									16 08			
Uddingston	d					15 05							15 31	15 35								16 04	
Bellshill	d					15 10							15 34	15 40								16 09	
Motherwell	a			15 11		15 18					15 41			15 48						16 11		16 15	
	d					15 18					15 41											16 16	
Whifflet	a																						
Coatbridge Central	a																						
Shieldmuir	d					15 22																16 20	
Holytown	d										15 48		15a39										
Wishaw	d					15 25					15 53											16 23	
Carluke	d					15 32					16 00											16 30	
Lanark	a					15 42					16 12											16 42	

A To Edinburgh
B From Mallaig
b Glasgow Central High Level
c Helensburgh Upper
e Glasgow Queen St High Level

Helensburgh, Balloch, Dalmuir and Milngavie - Glasgow - Springburn, Airdrie, Bathgate and Edinburgh, Hamilton, Larkhall, Motherwell, Coatbridge and Lanark

		SR	SR	SR	SR	SR	SR	SR	SR	SR	SR	SR	SR	SR	SR	SR	SR	SR	SR	SR	SR	SR
							A															A
Helensburgh Central	d	15 10								15 40							16 10					
Craigendoran	d	15 13								15 43							16 13					
Cardross	d	15 18								15 48							16 18					
Balloch	d					15 23								15 53							16 23	
Alexandria	d					15 25								15 55							16 25	
Renton	d					15 28								15 58							16 28	
Dalreoch	d	15 23				15 31				15 53				16 01			16 23				16 31	
Dumbarton Central	d	15 25				15 32				15 55				16 02			16 25				16 32	
Dumbarton East	d	15 27				15 34				15 57				16 04			16 27				16 34	
Bowling	d					15 39								16 09							16 39	
Kilpatrick	d					15 42								16 12							16 42	
Dalmuir	a	15 34				15 45				16 04				16 15			16 34				16 45	
	d	15 35	15 30	15 38		15 46		15 53		16 05	16 01	16 08		16 16	16 23		16 35	16 31	16 38		16 46	
Singer	d		15 32			15 48					16 03			16 18				16 33			16 48	
Drumry	d		15 34			15 50					16 05			16 20				16 35			16 50	
Drumchapel	d		15 37			15 53					16 08			16 23				16 38			16 53	
Milngavie	d				15 42				15 57				16 12			16 27				16 42		
Hillfoot	d				15 45				16 00				16 15			16 30				16 45		
Bearsden	d				15 49				16 02				16 17			16 32				16 47		
Westerton	d		15 39		15 52	15 55			16 05		16 10		16 20	16 25		16 35		16 40		16 50	16 55	
Anniesland	d		15 43		15 55	15 58			16 08		16 14		16 23	16 28		16 38		16 44		16 53	16 58	
Clydebank	d			15 40				15 55				16 10			16 25				16 40			
Yoker	d			15 42				15 57				16 12			16 27				16 42			
Garscadden	d			15 46				16 00				16 16			16 31				16 46			
Scotstounhill	d			15 48				16 02				16 18			16 33				16 48			
Jordanhill	d			15 50				16 04				16 21			16 35				16 51			
Hyndland	d	15 44	15 47	15 52	15 57	16 01		16 07	16 11	16 14	16 17	16 23	16 26	16 32	16 37	16 41	16 44	16 47	16 53	16 56	17 01	
Partick	d	15 47	15 50	15 55	16 00	16 04		16 09	16 14	16 17	16 20	16 25	16 29	16 35	16 40	16 44	16 47	16 50	16 55	16 59	17 04	
Exhibition Centre	d		15 53		16 03			16 12			16 23		16 32		16 43			16 53		17 02		
Anderston	d		15 55		16 05			16 15			16 25		16 34		16 45			16 55		17 04		
Glasgow Central LL 15	a		15 56		16 07			16 16			16 26		16 35		16 46			16 56		17 05		
	d		15 57		16 07		16b18	16 17			16 27		16 37		16 47			16 57		17 07		17b18
Argyle Street	d		15 59		16 09			16 19			16 29		16 38		16 48			16 59		17 08		
Charing Cross	d	15 54		15 59		16 08			16 19	16 24		16 29		16 39		16 49	16 54		16 59		17 08	
Glasgow Queen St LL 10	a	15 56		16 01		16 11			16 21	16 26		16 31		16 41		16 51	16 56		17 01		17 10	
	d	15 58		16 02		16 11			16 24	16 29		16 32		16 42		16 54	16 58		17 02		17 12	
High Street	d	16 00		16 04		16 13			16 26	16 31		16 34		16 44		16 56	17 00		17 04		17 14	
Bellgrove	d	16 02		16 06		16 15				16 33		16 36		16 46			17 02		17 06		17 16	
Duke Street	d			16 08								16 38							17 08			
Alexandra Parade	d			16 09								16 39							17 09			
Barnhill	d			16 12								16 42							17 12			
Springburn	a			16 14								16 44							17 14			
Carntyne	d	16 05				16 19				16 36				16 49			17 06				17 19	
Shettleston	d	16 08				16 21				16 39				16 52			17 08				17 22	
Garrowhill	d	16 10				16 24				16 41				16 54			17 11				17 24	
Easterhouse	d	16 13				16 26				16 44				16 57			17 13				17 27	
Blairhill	d	16 17				16 30				16 48				17 01			17 17				17 31	
Coatbridge Sunnyside	d	16 19				16 33			16 38	16 50				17 03		17 08	17 20				17 33	
Coatdyke	d	16 22				16 35				16 53				17 06			17 22				17 36	
Airdrie	d	16 25				16a39			16 44	16 56				17a09		17 14	17 25				17a39	
Drumgelloch	d	16 28							16 47	16 59						17 17	17 28					
Caldercruix	d	16 32								17 03							17 32					
Blackridge	d	16 38								17 09							17 38					
Armadale	d	16 41								17 12							17 42					
Bathgate	a	16 45							17 00	17 16						17 30	17 46					
	d	16 47							17 01	17 17						17 31	17 46					
Livingston North	d	16 50							17 06	17 21						17 36	17 50					
Uphall	d	16 53							17 09	17 24						17 39	17 53					
Edinburgh Park	a	17 02							17 18	17 32						17 47	18 01					
Haymarket	a	17 07							17 23	17 37						17 52	18 06					
Edinburgh	a	17 14							17 29	17 43						17 57	18 12					
Bridgeton	d				16 12			16 22					16 41		16 51					17 11		
Dalmarnock	d				16 14			16 24					16 43		16 53					17 13		
Rutherglen	d		16 06		16 16			16 26			16 34		16 46		16 56			17 04		17 16		
Cambuslang	d				16 20			16 31					16 50		17 00			17 08		17 20		
Newton	d				16 24								16 54							17 23		
Blantyre	d		16 15		16 28						16 44		16 58					17 14		17 27		
Hamilton West	d		16 18		16 31						16 47		17 01					17 17		17 30		
Hamilton Central	d		16 20		16 33						16 50		17 03					17 20		17 33		
Chatelherault	d		16 24								16 53							17 23				
Merryton	d		16 27								16 56							17 26				
Larkhall	a		16 30								16 59							17 29				
Airbles	d				16 38								17 08							17 38		
Uddingston	d						16 30	16 35							17 04							17 30
Bellshill	d						16 34	16 40							17 10							17 34
Motherwell	a				16 41			16 49					17 11		17 16					17 40		
	d				16 41										17 17					17 41		
Whifflet	a																					
Coatbridge Central	a																					
Shieldmuir	d														17 20							
Holytown	d				16 48		16a38													17 48		17a39
Wishaw	d				16 53										17 24					17 53		
Carluke	d				17 02										17 30					18 00		
Lanark	a				17 15										17 42					18 12		

A To Edinburgh
b Glasgow Central High Level

Table 226

Saturdays

Helensburgh, Balloch, Dalmuir and Milngavie - Glasgow - Springburn, Airdrie, Bathgate and Edinburgh, Hamilton, Larkhall, Motherwell, Coatbridge and Lanark

		SR	SR	SR	SR	SR	SR	SR	SR	SR	SR	SR	SR	SR	SR	SR	SR	SR	SR	SR	SR	SR	SR
																A							
Helensburgh Central	d			16 40							17 10								17 40				
Craigendoran	d			16 43							17 13								17 43				
Cardross	d			16 48							17 18								17 48				
Balloch	d							16 53							17 23								17 53
Alexandria	d							16 55							17 25								17 55
Renton	d							16 58							17 28								17 58
Dalreoch	d			16 53				17 01			17 23				17 31				17 53				18 01
Dumbarton Central	d			16 55				17 02			17 25				17 32				17 55				18 02
Dumbarton East	d			16 57				17 04			17 27				17 34				17 57				18 04
Bowling	d							17 09							17 39								18 09
Kilpatrick	d							17 12							17 42								18 12
Dalmuir	a			17 04				17 15			17 34				17 45				18 04				18 15
	d	16 53		17 05	17 01	17 08		17 16	17 23		17 35	17 31	17 38		17 46		17 53		18 05	18 01	18 07		18 16
Singer	d				17 03			17 18				17 33			17 48					18 03			18 18
Drumry	d				17 05			17 20				17 35			17 50					18 05			18 20
Drumchapel	d				17 08			17 23				17 38			17 53					18 08			18 23
Milngavie	d		16 57				17 13			17 28				17 42				17 57				18 12	
Hillfoot	d		17 00				17 16			17 31				17 45				18 00				18 15	
Bearsden	d		17 02				17 18			17 33				17 47				18 02				18 17	
Westerton	d		17 05		17 10		17 21	17 25		17 36		17 40		17 50	17 55			18 05		18 10		18 20	18 25
Anniesland	d		17 08		17 13		17 24	17 28		17 39		17 44		17 53	17 58			18 08		18 14		18 23	18 28
Clydebank	d	16 55				17 10			17 25				17 40				17 55				18 09		
Yoker	d	16 57				17 12			17 27				17 42				17 57				18 11		
Garscadden	d	17 01				17 16			17 31				17 46				18 00				18 14		
Scotstounhill	d	17 03				17 18			17 33				17 48				18 02				18 16		
Jordanhill	d	17 05				17 20			17 35				17 50				18 04				18 18		
Hyndland	d	17 07	17 11	17 14	17 17	17 22	17 26	17 31	17 37	17 41	17 44	17 47	17 52	17 56	18 01		18 06	18 11	18 14	18 17	18 22	18 26	18 31
Partick	d	17 10	17 14	17 17	17 20	17 25	17 29	17 34	17 40	17 44	17 47	17 50	17 55	17 59	18 04		18 08	18 14	18 17	18 20	18 25	18 29	18 34
Exhibition Centre	d	17 13			17 23		17 32		17 43			17 53		18 02			18 11			18 23		18 32	
Anderston	d	17 15			17 25		17 34		17 45			17 55		18 04			18 13			18 25		18 34	
Glasgow Central LL	a	17 16			17 26		17 35		17 46			17 56		18 05			18 15			18 26		18 35	
	d	17 17			17 27		17 37		17 47			17 57		18 07		18b18	18 16			18 27		18 37	
Argyle Street	d	17 19			17 29		17 38		17 48			17 59		18 08			18 18			18 29		18 38	
Charing Cross	d		17 19	17 24		17 29		17 38		17 49	17 54		17 59		18 08			18 18	18 24		18 29		18 38
Glasgow Queen St LL	a		17 21	17 26		17 31		17 40		17 51	17 56		18 01		18 10			18 20	18 26		18 31		18 40
	d		17 24	17 28		17 32		17 42		17 54	17 58		18 02		18 12			18 23	18 28		18 32		18 45
High Street	d		17 26	17 30		17 34		17 44		17 56	18 00		18 04		18 14			18 26	18 30		18 34		18 47
Bellgrove	d			17 32		17 36		17 46			18 02		18 06		18 16			18 28	18 32		18 36		18 49
Duke Street	d					17 38							18 08								18 38		18 51
Alexandra Parade	d					17 39							18 09								18 39		18 52
Barnhill	d					17 42							18 12								18 42		18 55
Springburn	a					17 44							18 14								18 44		18 57
Carntyne	d			17 36				17 49			18 06				18 19				18 36				
Shettleston	d			17 38				17 52			18 08				18 22				18 38				
Garrowhill	d			17 41				17 54			18 11				18 24				18 41				
Easterhouse	d			17 43				17 57			18 13				18 27				18 43				
Blairhill	d			17 47				18 01			18 17				18 31				18 47				
Coatbridge Sunnyside	d		17 42	17 50				18 03		18 09	18 20				18 33			18 39	18 50				
Coatdyke	d			17 52				18 06			18 22				18 36				18 52				
Airdrie	d		17 47	17 55				18a09		18 14	18 25				18a39			18 44	18 55				
Drumgelloch	d		17 50	17 58						18 17	18 28							18 47	18 58				
Caldercruix	d			18 02							18 32								19 02				
Blackridge	d			18 08							18 38								19 08				
Armadale	d			18 12							18 42								19 12				
Bathgate	a		18 02	18 16						18 30	18 46							19 00	19 16				
	d		18 04	18 17						18 31	18 47							19 01	19 17				
Livingston North	d		18 08	18 20						18 35	18 50							19 06	19 20				
Uphall	d		18 11	18 23						18 38	18 53							19 09	19 23				
Edinburgh Park	a		18 17	18 32						18 47	19 02							19 17	19 32				
Haymarket	a		18 25	18 37						18 52	19 08							19 22	19 37				
Edinburgh	a		18 32	18 43						18 58	19 14							19 28	19 45				
Bridgeton	d	17 22					17 41		17 51					18 11			18 21					18 41	
Dalmarnock	d	17 24					17 43		17 53					18 13			18 23					18 43	
Rutherglen	d	17 26			17 34		17 46		17 56			18 04		18 16			18 25			18 34		18 46	
Cambuslang	d	17 31					17 50		18 00					18 20		18 27	18 30					18 50	
Newton	d						17 54							18 23								18 53	
Blantyre	d				17 44		17 58					18 14		18 28						18 44		18 58	
Hamilton West	d				17 47		18 01					18 17		18 31						18 47		19 01	
Hamilton Central	d				17 49		18 03					18 20		18 33						18 50		19 03	
Chatelherault	d				17 53							18 23								18 53			
Merryton	d				17 56							18 26								18 56			
Larkhall	a				17 59							18 29								18 59			
Airbles	d						18 08							18 38								19 08	
Uddingston	d	17 35							18 04							18 29	18 34						
Bellshill	d	17 40							18 10							18 34	18 39						
Motherwell	a	17 48					18 11		18 16					18 40			18 48					19 11	
	d								18 16					18 40									
Whifflet	a																						
Coatbridge Central	a																						
Shieldmuir	d								18 20														
Holytown	d													18 48		18a38							
Wishaw	d								18 23					18 53									
Carluke	d								18 30					19 00									
Lanark	a								18 42					19 12									

A To Edinburgh

b Glasgow Central High Level

Table 226

Saturdays

Helensburgh, Balloch, Dalmuir and Milngavie - Glasgow - Springburn, Airdrie, Bathgate and Edinburgh, Hamilton, Larkhall, Motherwell, Coatbridge and Lanark

		SR	SR	SR	SR	SR	SR	SR	SR	SR	SR	SR	SR	SR	SR	SR	SR	SR	SR	SR	SR	SR
							◇ A ⚭	B														
Helensburgh Central	d			18 10			18b34				18 40					19 10					19 40	
Craigendoran	d			18 13							18 43					19 13					19 43	
Cardross	d			18 18							18 48					19 18					19 48	
Balloch	d					18 23							18 53					19 23				
Alexandria	d					18 25							18 55					19 25				
Renton	d					18 29							18 58					19 28				
Dalreoch	d			18 23		18 32					18 53		19 01			19 23		19 31			19 53	
Dumbarton Central	d			18 25		18 33	18 47				18 55		19 02			19 25		19 32			19 55	
Dumbarton East	d			18 27		18 35					18 57		19 04			19 27		19 34			19 57	
Bowling	d					18 40							19 09					19 39				
Kilpatrick	d					18 43							19 12					19 42				
Dalmuir	a			18 35		18 46	18 56				19 05		19 15			19 35		19 45			20 05	
	d	18 23	18 31	18 35		18 47	18 56			19 01	19 05		19 16		19 31	19 35		19 46		20 01	20 05	
Singer	d		18 33			18 49				19 03			19 18		19 33			19 48		20 03		
Drumry	d		18 35			18 51				19 05			19 20		19 35			19 50		20 05		
Drumchapel	d		18 38			18 54				19 08			19 23		19 38			19 53		20 08		
Milngavie	d				18 42							19 12					19 42					20 12
Hillfoot	d				18 45							19 15					19 45					20 15
Bearsden	d				18 47							19 17					19 47					20 17
Westerton	d		18 40		18 51	18 56				19 10		19 20	19 25		19 40		19 50	19 55		20 10		20 20
Anniesland	d		18 44		18 54	19 00				19 14		19 23	19 30		19 44		19 54	19 59		20 14		20 22
Clydebank	d	18 25		18 37							19 07					19 37					20 07	
Yoker	d	18 27		18 39							19 09					19 39					20 09	
Garscadden	d	18 31		18 43							19 13					19 43					20 13	
Scotstounhill	d	18 33		18 45							19 15					19 45					20 15	
Jordanhill	d	18 35		18 47							19 17					19 47					20 17	
Hyndland	d	18 37	18 47	18 51	18 56	19 03				19 17	19 21	19 25	19 33		19 47	19 51	19 56	20 02		20 17	20 21	20 25
Partick	d	18 40	18 50	18 53	18 59	19 05			19 11	19 20	19 23	19 29	19 35	19 40	19 50	19 53	19 59	20 04	20 10	20 20	20 23	20 28
Exhibition Centre	d	18 43	18 53		19 02				19 14	19 23		19 32		19 43	19 53		20 02		20 13	20 23		20 32
Anderston	d	18 45	18 55		19 04				19 16	19 25		19 34		19 45	19 55		20 04		20 15	20 25		20 34
Glasgow Central LL	a	18 46	18 56		19 05				19 17	19 26		19 35		19 46	19 56		20 05		20 16	20 26		20 35
	d	18 47	18 57		19 07			19e18	19 18	19 27		19 37		19 47	19 57		20 07		20 17	20 27		20 36
Argyle Street	d	18 48	18 59		19 08				19 19	19 29		19 39		19 49	19 59		20 08		20 19	20 29		20 38
Charing Cross	d			18 57		19 09					19 27		19 39			19 57		20 08			20 27	
Glasgow Queen St LL	a			18 59		19 11	19c20				19 29		19 41			19 59		20 10			20 29	
	d			19 00		19 14					19 30		19 44			20 00		20 14			20 30	
High Street	d			19 02		19 16					19 32		19 46			20 02		20 16			20 32	
Bellgrove	d			19 04		19 19					19 34		19 49			20 04		20 19			20 34	
Duke Street	d					19 21							19 51					20 21				
Alexandra Parade	d					19 22							19 52					20 22				
Barnhill	d					19 25							19 55					20 25				
Springburn	a					19 27							19 57					20 27				
Carntyne	d			19 07							19 37					20 07					20 37	
Shettleston	d			19 10							19 40					20 10					20 40	
Garrowhill	d			19 12							19 42					20 12					20 42	
Easterhouse	d			19 15							19 45					20 15					20 45	
Blairhill	d			19 19							19 49					20 19					20 49	
Coatbridge Sunnyside	d			19 21							19 51					20 21					20 51	
Coatdyke	d			19 24							19 54					20 24					20 54	
Airdrie	d			19 27							19 57					20 27					20 57	
Drumgelloch	d			19 30							20 00					20 30					21 00	
Caldercruix	d			19 34							20 04					20 34					21 04	
Blackridge	d			19 40							20 10					20 40					21 10	
Armadale	d			19 43							20 13					20 43					21 13	
Bathgate	a			19 47							20 17					20 47					21 17	
	d			19 49							20 18					20 49					21 19	
Livingston North	d			19 53							20 23					20 53					21 23	
Uphall	d			19 56							20 26					20 56					21 26	
Edinburgh Park	a			20 04							20 34					21 04					21 34	
Haymarket	a			20 09							20 38					21 09					21 39	
Edinburgh	a			20 14							20 43					21 14					21 44	
Bridgeton	d	18 51			19 11				19 22			19 42		19 52			20 11		20 22			20 41
Dalmarnock	d	18 53			19 13				19 24			19 44		19 54			20 13		20 24			20 43
Rutherglen	d	18 55	19 04		19 16				19 26	19 34		19 46		19 56	20 04		20 16		20 26	20 34		20 46
Cambuslang	d	19 00			19 20				19 31			19 50		20 01			20 20		20 31			20 50
Newton	d				19 23							19 54					20 23					20 54
Blantyre	d		19 15		19 27					19 44		19 58			20 14		20 27			20 45		20 58
Hamilton West	d		19 18		19 30					19 47		20 01			20 17		20 30			20 48		21 01
Hamilton Central	d		19 20		19 33					19 49		20 04			20 20		20 33			20 50		21 03
Chatelherault	d		19 24							19 53					20 23					20 54		
Merryton	d		19 27							19 56					20 26					20 57		
Larkhall	a		19 30							19 59					20 29					21 00		
Airbles	d				19 38							20 09					20 38					21 08
Uddingston	d	19 04						19 30	19 35					20 05					20 35			
Bellshill	d	19 09						19 35	19 40					20 10					20 40			
Motherwell	a	19 16			19 39				19 48			20 12		20 16			20 41		20 48			21 11
	d	19 17			19 40									20 16			20 41					
Whifflet	a																					
Coatbridge Central	a																					
Shieldmuir	d	19 21												20 20								
Holytown	d				19 47			19a39									20 48					
Wishaw	d	19 24			19 52									20 23			20 53					
Carluke	d	19 31			19 59									20 30			21 00					
Lanark	a	19 41			20 12									20 42			21 12					

A until 29 October. From Oban

B To Edinburgh

b Helensburgh Upper

e Glasgow Central High Level

Helensburgh, Balloch, Dalmuir and Milngavie - Glasgow - Springburn, Airdrie, Bathgate and Edinburgh, Hamilton, Larkhall, Motherwell, Coatbridge and Lanark

		SR	SR	SR	SR	SR	SR	SR	SR	SR	SR	SR	SR	SR	SR	SR	SR	SR	SR	SR	SR	SR	SR
								A				◇ B											
Helensburgh Central	d				20 10						20 40	20c40					21 10					21 40	
Craigendoran	d				20 13						20 43						21 13					21 43	
Cardross	d				20 18						20 48						21 18					21 48	
Balloch	d	19 53					20 23							20 53					21 23				
Alexandria	d	19 55					20 25							20 55					21 25				
Renton	d	19 58					20 28							20 59					21 28				
Dalreoch	d	20 01			20 23		20 31				20 53			21 01			21 23		21 31			21 53	
Dumbarton Central	d	20 02			20 25		20 32				20 55	20 59		21 02			21 25		21 32			21 55	
Dumbarton East	d	20 04			20 27		20 34				20 57			21 04			21 27		21 34			21 57	
Bowling	d	20 09					20 39							21 09					21 39				
Kilpatrick	d	20 12					20 42							21 12					21 42				
Dalmuir	a	20 15			20 35		20 45				21 04	21 08		21 15			21 35		21 45			22 05	
	d	20 16		20 31	20 35		20 46			21 00	21 05	21 08		21 16		21 31	21 35		21 46		22 01	22 05	
Singer	d	20 18		20 33			20 48			21 02				21 18		21 33			21 48		22 03		
Drumry	d	20 20		20 35			20 50			21 04				21 20		21 35			21 50		22 05		
Drumchapel	d	20 23		20 38			20 53			21 07				21 23		21 38			21 53		22 08		
Milngavie	d					20 42							21 12					21 42					22 12
Hillfoot	d					20 45							21 15					21 45					22 15
Bearsden	d					20 47							21 17					21 47					22 17
Westerton	d	20 25		20 40		20 50	20 55			21 09			21 20	21 26		21 40		21 50	21 55		22 10		22 20
Anniesland	d	20 30		20 44		20 53	20 59			21 14			21 23	21 29		21 44		21 53	22 00		22 14		22 23
Clydebank	d				20 37						21 07						21 37					22 07	
Yoker	d				20 39						21 09						21 39					22 09	
Garscadden	d				20 43						21 13						21 43					22 13	
Scotstounhill	d				20 45						21 15						21 45					22 15	
Jordanhill	d				20 47						21 17						21 47					22 17	
Hyndland	d	20 33		20 47	20 51	20 55	21 02			21 17	21 21		21 27	21 32		21 47	21 51	21 57	22 03		22 17	22 21	22 26
Partick	d	20 35	20 40	20 50	20 53	20 59	21 04		21 10	21 20	21 23		21 30	21 34	21 40	21 50	21 53	21 59	22 05	22 10	22 20	22 23	22 29
Exhibition Centre	d		20 43	20 53		21 02			21 13	21 23			21 33		21 43	21 53		22 02		22 13	22 23		22 32
Anderston	d		20 45	20 55		21 04			21 15	21 25			21 35		21 45	21 55		22 04		22 15	22 25		22 34
Glasgow Central LL	a		20 46	20 56		21 05			21 16	21 26			21 37		21 46	21 56		22 05		22 16	22 26		22 35
	d		20 47	20 57		21 07		21b18	21 17	21 27			21 37		21 47	21 57		22 07		22 17	22 27		22 37
Argyle Street	d		20 49	20 59		21 08			21 19	21 29			21 39		21 49	21 59		22 08		22 19	22 29		22 39
Charing Cross	d	20 40			20 57		21 08				21 27			21 39			21 57		22 10			22 27	
Glasgow Queen St LL	a	20 42			20 59		21 11				21 29	21e31		21 42			21 59		22 12			22 29	
	d	20 44			21 00		21 14				21 30			21 44			22 00		22 14			22 30	
High Street	d	20 46			21 02		21 16				21 32			21 46			22 02		22 16			22 32	
Bellgrove	d	20 49			21 04		21 19				21 34			21 49			22 04		22 19			22 34	
Duke Street	d	20 51					21 21							21 51					22 21				
Alexandra Parade	d	20 52					21 22							21 52					22 22				
Barnhill	d	20 55					21 25							21 55					22 25				
Springburn	a	20 57					21 27							21 57					22 27				
Carntyne	d				21 07						21 37						22 07					22 37	
Shettleston	d				21 10						21 40						22 10					22 40	
Garrowhill	d				21 12						21 42						22 12					22 42	
Easterhouse	d				21 15						21 45						22 15					22 45	
Blairhill	d				21 19						21 49						22 19					22 49	
Coatbridge Sunnyside	d				21 21						21 51						22 21					22 51	
Coatdyke	d				21 24						21 54						22 24					22 54	
Airdrie	d				21 27						21 57						22 27					22 57	
Drumgelloch	d				21 30						22 00						22 30					23 00	
Caldercruix	d				21 34						22 04						22 34					23 04	
Blackridge	d				21 40						22 10						22 40					23 10	
Armadale	d				21 43						22 13						22 43					23 13	
Bathgate	a				21 47						22 17						22 47					23 17	
	d				21 49						22 19						22 49					23 17	
Livingston North	d				21 53						22 23						22 53					23 22	
Uphall	d				21 56						22 26						22 56					23 25	
Edinburgh Park	a				22 04						22 34						23 05					23 33	
Haymarket	a				22 09						22 39						23 09					23 38	
Edinburgh	a				22 14						22 44						23 14					23 43	
Bridgeton	d		20 52			21 11			21 22				21 42		21 52			22 11		22 22			22 42
Dalmarnock	d		20 54			21 13			21 24				21 44		21 54			22 13		22 24			22 44
Rutherglen	d		20 56	21 04		21 16			21 26	21 34			21 47		21 56	22 04		22 16		22 26	22 34		22 46
Cambuslang	d		21 01			21 20			21 31				21 51		22 01			22 20		22 31			22 50
Newton	d					21 23							21 54					22 23					22 54
Blantyre	d			21 14		21 28				21 44			21 58			22 14		22 28			22 44		22 58
Hamilton West	d			21 17		21 31				21 47			22 01			22 17		22 31			22 47		23 01
Hamilton Central	d			21 20		21 33				21 50			22 04			22 20		22 33			22 50		23 03
Chatelherault	d			21 23						21 53						22 23					22 53		
Merryton	d			21 26						21 56						22 26					22 56		
Larkhall	a			21 29						21 59						22 29					22 59		
Airbles	d					21 38							22 09					22 38					23 08
Uddingston	d		21 05					21 30	21 35						22 05					22 35			
Bellshill	d		21 10					21 36	21 40						22 10					22 40			
Motherwell	a		21 16			21 41			21 48				22 11		22 16			22 41		22 49			23 11
	d		21 16			21 41									22 16			22 41					
Whifflet	a																	22 46					
Coatbridge Central	a																	22 51					
Shieldmuir	d		21 20												22 20								
Holytown	d					21 48		21a40															
Wishaw	d		21 23			21 53									22 23								
Carluke	d		21 30			22 00									22 30								
Lanark	a		21 42			22 12									22 42								

A To Edinburgh
B From Mallaig
b Glasgow Central High Level
c Helensburgh Upper
e Glasgow Queen St High Level

Helensburgh, Balloch, Dalmuir and Milngavie - Glasgow - Springburn, Airdrie, Bathgate and Edinburgh, Hamilton, Larkhall, Motherwell, Coatbridge and Lanark

		SR	SR	SR	SR	SR	SR	SR	SR	SR	SR	SR	SR
						A							
Helensburgh Central	d				22 10						22 40		23 10
Craigendoran	d				22 13						22 43		23 13
Cardross	d				22 18						22 48		23 18
Balloch	d	21 53						22 23				22 53	
Alexandria	d	21 55						22 25				22 55	
Renton	d	21 58						22 28				22 58	
Dalreoch	d	22 01			22 23			22 31			22 53	23 01	23 23
Dumbarton Central	d	22 02			22 25			22 32			22 55	23 02	23 25
Dumbarton East	d	22 04			22 27			22 34			22 57	23 04	23 27
Bowling	d	22 09						22 39				23 09	
Kilpatrick	d	22 12						22 42				23 12	
Dalmuir	a	22 15			22 35			22 45			23 05	23 15	23 35
	d	22 16		22 31	22 35			22 46		23 01	23 05	23 16	23 35
Singer	d	22 18		22 33				22 48		23 03		23 18	
Drumry	d	22 20		22 35				22 50		23 05		23 20	
Drumchapel	d	22 23		22 38				22 53		23 08		23 23	
Milngavie	d						22 42						
Hillfoot	d						22 45						
Bearsden	d						22 47						
Westerton	d	22 25		22 40			22 50	22 55		23 10		23 25	
Anniesland	d	22 30		22 44			22 53	23 00		23 14		23 28	
Clydebank	d				22 37						23 07		23 37
Yoker	d				22 39						23 09		23 39
Garscadden	d				22 43						23 13		23 43
Scotstounhill	d				22 45						23 15		23 45
Jordanhill	d				22 47						23 17		23 47
Hyndland	d	22 33		22 47	22 51		22 56	23 03		23 17	23 21	23 31	23 49
Partick	d	22 35	22 40	22 50	22 53		22 59	23 05	23 10	23 20	23 23	23 34	23 52
Exhibition Centre	d		22 43	22 53			23 02		23 13	23 23			
Anderston	d		22 45	22 55			23 04		23 15	23 25			
Glasgow Central LL	a		22 46	22 56			23 05		23 16	23 26			
	d		22 47	22 57		23b06	23 07		23 17	23 27			
Argyle Street	d		22 49	22 59			23 09		23 19	23 29			
Charing Cross	d	22 40			22 57			23 10			23 27	23 38	23 56
Glasgow Queen St LL	a	22 42			22 59			23 12			23 29	23 40	23 59
	d	22 44			23 00			23 14			23 30	23 44	23 59
High Street	d	22 46			23 02			23 16			23 32	23 46	00 02
Bellgrove	d	22 49			23 04			23 19			23 34	23 49	00 04
Duke Street	d	22 51						23 21					
Alexandra Parade	d	22 52						23 22					
Barnhill	d	22 55						23 25					
Springburn	a	22 57						23 27					
Carntyne	d				23 07						23 37	23 52	00 07
Shettleston	d				23 10						23 40	23 55	00 10
Garrowhill	d				23 12						23 42	23 57	00 12
Easterhouse	d				23 15						23 45	23 59	00 15
Blairhill	d				23 19						23 49	00 04	00 19
Coatbridge Sunnyside	d				23 21						23 51	00 06	00 21
Coatdyke	d				23 24						23 54	00 09	00 24
Airdrie	d				23 27						23 57	00a12	00a27
Drumgelloch	d				23 30						23 59		
Caldercruix	d				23 34						00 03		
Blackridge	d				23 40						00 09		
Armadale	d				23 43						00 13		
Bathgate	a				23 47						00 17		
	d												
Livingston North	d												
Uphall	d												
Edinburgh Park	a												
Haymarket	a												
Edinburgh	a												
Bridgeton	d		22 52				23 12		23 22				
Dalmarnock	d		22 54				23 14		23 24				
Rutherglen	d		22 56	23 04			23 16		23 26	23 34			
Cambuslang	d		23 01			23 15	23 20		23 31				
Newton	d						23 24						
Blantyre	d			23 14			23 28			23 44			
Hamilton West	d			23 17			23 31			23 47			
Hamilton Central	d			23 20			23 33			23 50			
Chatelherault	d			23 23						23 53			
Merryton	d			23 26						23 56			
Larkhall	a			23 29						00 01			
Airbles	d						23 38						
Uddingston	d		23 05			23 20			23 35				
Bellshill	d		23 10			23 25			23 40				
Motherwell	a		23 16				23 41		23 46				
	d		23 16										
Whifflet	a												
Coatbridge Central	a												
Shieldmuir	d		23 20										
Holytown	d					23a29							
Wishaw	d		23 23										
Carluke	d		23 30										
Lanark	a		23 42										

A To Edinburgh
b Glasgow Central High Level

Table 226

Sundays until 19 June

Helensburgh, Balloch, Dalmuir and Milngavie - Glasgow - Springburn, Airdrie, Bathgate and Edinburgh, Hamilton, Larkhall, Motherwell, Coatbridge and Lanark

		SR A	SR A	SR A	SR A	SR	SR	SR	SR	SR	SR	SR	SR	SR	SR	SR	SR	SR	SR	SR	SR	SR	SR
Helensburgh Central	d		22p40		23p10				07 55			08 25				08 55			09 25				
Craigendoran	d		22p43		23p13				07 58			08 28				08 58			09 28				
Cardross	d		22p48		23p18				08 03			08 33				09 03			09 33				
Balloch	d			22p53						08 09			08 39				09 09			09 39			
Alexandria	d			22p55						08 11			08 41				09 11			09 41			
Renton	d			22p58						08 14			08 44				09 14			09 44			
Dalreoch	d		22p53	23p01	23p23				08 08	08 17		08 38	08 47			09 08	09 17		09 38	09 47			
Dumbarton Central	d		22p55	23p02	23p25				08 10	08 18		08 40	08 48			09 10	09 18		09 40	09 48			
Dumbarton East	d		22p57	23p04	23p27				08 12	08 20		08 42	08 50			09 12	09 20		09 42	09 50			
Bowling	d			23p09						08 25			08 55				09 25			09 55			
Kilpatrick	d			23p12						08 28			08 58				09 28			09 58			
Dalmuir	a		23p05	23p15	23p35				08 19	08 31		08 49	09 01			09 19	09 31		09 49	10 01			
	d	23p01	23p05	23p16	23p35		07 40	08 01	08 20	08 31		08 50	09 01			09 20	09 31		09 50	10 01			
Singer	d	23p03		23p18			07 42		08 22			08 52				09 22			09 52				
Drumry	d	23p05		23p20			07 45		08 25			08 55				09 25			09 55				
Drumchapel	d	23p08		23p23			07 47		08 27			08 57				09 27			09 57				
Milngavie	d													09 11				09 41			10 11		
Hillfoot	d													09 14				09 44			10 14		
Bearsden	d													09 16				09 46			10 16		
Westerton	d	23p10		23p25			07 50		08 30			09 00		09 19		09 30		09 49	10 00		10 19		
Anniesland	d	23p14		23p28			07 53		08 33			09 03		09 22		09 33		09 52	10 03		10 22		
Clydebank	d		23p07		23p37			08 03		08 33			09 03				09 33			10 03			
Yoker	d		23p09		23p39			08 05		08 35			09 05				09 35			10 05			
Garscadden	d		23p13		23p43			08 09		08 39			09 09				09 39			10 09			
Scotstounhill	d		23p15		23p45			08 11		08 41			09 11				09 41			10 11			
Jordanhill	d		23p17		23p47			08 13		08 43			09 13				09 43			10 13			
Hyndland	d	23p17	23p21	23p31	23p49		07 55	08 15	08 35	08 45	08 55	09 05	09 15	09 25		09 35	09 45	09 55	10 05	10 15	10 25		
Partick	d	23p20	23p23	23p34	23p52		07 58	08 18	08 38	08 48	08 58	09 08	09 18	09 28	09 34	09 38	09 48	09 58	10 08	10 18	10 28	10 34	
Exhibition Centre	d	23p23						08 21		08 51	09 01		09 21	09 31	09 37		09 51	10 01		10 21	10 31	10 37	
Anderston	d	23p25																					
Glasgow Central LL	a	23p26						08 23		08 53	09 03		09 23	09 33	09 39		09 53	10 03		10 23	10 33	10 39	
	d	23p27						08 24		08 54	09 04		09 24	09 34	09 40		09 54	10 04		10 23	10 34	10 40	
Argyle Street	d	23p29															09 55	10 06		10 25	10 36	10 42	
Charing Cross	d		23p27	23p38	23p56		08 03		08 43			09 13				09 43			10 13				
Glasgow Queen St LL	a		23p29	23p40	23p59		08 05		08 45			09 15				09 45			10 15				
	d		23p30	23p44	23p59		08 05		08 45			09 15				09 45			10 15				
High Street	d		23p32	23p46	00 02		08 07		08 47			09 17				09 47			10 17				
Bellgrove	d		23p34	23p49	00 04		08 09		08 49			09 19				09 49			10 19				
Duke Street	d																						
Alexandra Parade	d																						
Barnhill	d																						
Springburn	a																						
Carntyne	d		23p37	23p52	00 07		08 13		08 53			09 23				09 53			10 23				
Shettleston	d		23p40	23p55	00 10		08 15		08 55			09 25				09 55			10 25				
Garrowhill	d		23p42	23p57	00 12		08 18		08 58			09 28				09 58			10 28				
Easterhouse	d		23p45	23p59	00 15		08 20		09 00			09 30				10 00			10 30				
Blairhill	d		23p49	00 04	00 19		08 24		09 04			09 34				10 04			10 34				
Coatbridge Sunnyside	d		23p51	00 06	00 21		08 27		09 07			09 37				10 07			10 37				
Coatdyke	d		23p54	00 09	00 24		08 29		09 09			09 39				10 09			10 39				
Airdrie	d		23p57	00a12	00a27		08 32		09 12			09a42				10 12			10a42				
Drumgelloch	d		23p59				08 35		09 15							10 15							
Caldercruix	d		00 03				08 39		09 19							10 19							
Blackridge	d		00 09				08 45		09 25							10 25							
Armadale	d		00 13				08 49		09 29							10 29							
Bathgate	a		00 17				08 53		09 33							10 33							
	d					07 55	08 54		09 34							10 34							11 05
Livingston North	d					07 59	08 59		09 39							10 38							11 09
Uphall	d					08 02	09 02		09 42							10 41							11 12
Edinburgh Park	a					08 10	09 10		09 52							10 49							11 20
Haymarket	a					08 20	09 20		10 02							10 55							11 25
Edinburgh	a					08 25	09 25		10 07							11 00							11 30
Bridgeton	d							08 29		08 59	09 09		09 29	09 39			09 58	10 09		10 28	10 39		
Dalmarnock	d																						
Rutherglen	d	23p34						08 32		09 02	09 12		09 32	09 42	09 47		10 01	10 12		10 30	10 42	10 45	
Cambuslang	d							08 36		09 06	09 16		09 36	09 48			10 04	10 16		10 34	10 46		
Newton	d									09 09			09 39				10 09			10 38			
Blantyre	d	23p44								09 13			09 43		09 57		10 13			10 42		10 57	
Hamilton West	d	23p47								09 16			09 46		10 00		10 16			10 46		11 00	
Hamilton Central	d	23p50								09 20			09 50		10 03		10 20			10 50		11 03	
Chatelherault	d	23p53													10 06							11 06	
Merryton	d	23p56													10 09							11 09	
Larkhall	a	00 01													10 12							11 12	
Airbles	d									09 25			09 55				10 25			10 55			
Uddingston	d							08 40			09 20			09 53				10 20			10 50		
Bellshill	d							08 45			09 25			09 57				10 25			10 55		
Motherwell	a							08 53		09 27	09 33		09 57	10 03			10 27	10 33		10 57	11 03		
	d										09 33							10 33					
Whifflet	a																						
Coatbridge Central	a																						
Shieldmuir	d										09 37							10 37					
Holytown	d																						
Wishaw	d										09 40							10 40					
Carluke	d										09 47							10 47					
Lanark	a										09 59							10 59					

A not 22 May

Table 226

Sundays until 19 June

Helensburgh, Balloch, Dalmuir and Milngavie - Glasgow - Springburn, Airdrie, Bathgate and Edinburgh, Hamilton, Larkhall, Motherwell, Coatbridge and Lanark

		SR	SR	SR	SR	SR	SR	SR	SR	SR	SR	SR	SR	SR	SR	SR	SR	SR	SR	SR	SR	SR	SR
Helensburgh Central	d	09 55			10 25					10 55			11 25				11 55			12 25			
Craigendoran	d	09 58			10 28					10 58			11 28				11 58			12 28			
Cardross	d	10 03			10 33					11 03			11 33				12 03			12 33			
Balloch	d		10 09			10 39					11 09			11 39				12 09			12 39		
Alexandria	d		10 11			10 41					11 11			11 41				12 11			12 41		
Renton	d		10 14			10 44					11 14			11 44				12 14			12 44		
Dalreoch	d	10 08	10 17		10 38	10 47				11 08	11 17		11 38	11 47			12 08	12 17		12 38	12 47		
Dumbarton Central	d	10 10	10 18		10 40	10 48				11 10	11 18		11 40	11 48			12 10	12 18		12 40	12 48		
Dumbarton East	d	10 12	10 20		10 42	10 50				11 12	11 20		11 42	11 50			12 12	12 20		12 42	12 50		
Bowling	d		10 25			10 55					11 25			11 55				12 25			12 55		
Kilpatrick	d		10 28			10 58					11 28			11 58				12 28			12 58		
Dalmuir	a	10 19	10 31		10 49	11 01				11 19	11 31		11 49	12 01			12 19	12 31		12 49	13 01		
	d	10 20	10 31		10 50	11 01				11 20	11 31		11 50	12 01			12 20	12 31		12 50	13 01		
Singer	d	10 22			10 52					11 22			11 52				12 22			12 52			
Drumry	d	10 25			10 55					11 25			11 55				12 25			12 55			
Drumchapel	d	10 27			10 57					11 27			11 57				12 27			12 57			
Milngavie	d			10 41			11 11					11 41			12 11				12 41			13 11	
Hillfoot	d			10 44			11 14					11 44			12 14				12 44			13 14	
Bearsden	d			10 46			11 16					11 46			12 16				12 46			13 16	
Westerton	d	10 30		10 49	11 00		11 19			11 30		11 49	12 00		12 19		12 30		12 49	13 00		13 19	
Anniesland	d	10 33		10 52	11 03		11 22			11 33		11 52	12 03		12 22		12 33		12 52	13 03		13 22	
Clydebank	d		10 33			11 03					11 33			12 03				12 33			13 03		
Yoker	d		10 35			11 05					11 35			12 05				12 35			13 05		
Garscadden	d		10 39			11 09					11 39			12 09				12 39			13 09		
Scotstounhill	d		10 41			11 11					11 41			12 11				12 41			13 11		
Jordanhill	d		10 43			11 13					11 43			12 13				12 43			13 13		
Hyndland	d	10 35	10 45	10 55	11 05	11 15	11 25			11 35	11 45	11 55	12 05	12 15	12 25		12 35	12 45	12 55	13 05	13 15	13 25	
Partick	d	10 38	10 48	10 58	11 08	11 18	11 28	11 34		11 38	11 48	11 58	12 08	12 18	12 28	12 34	12 38	12 48	12 58	13 08	13 18	13 28	13 34
Exhibition Centre	d		10 51	11 01		11 21	11 31	11 37			11 51	12 01		12 21	12 31	12 37		12 51	13 01		13 21	13 31	13 37
Anderston	d																						
Glasgow Central LL	a		10 53	11 03		11 23	11 33	11 39			11 53	12 03		12 23	12 33	12 39		12 53	13 03		13 23	13 33	13 39
	d		10 54	11 04		11 24	11 34	11 40			11 54	12 04		12 24	12 34	12 40		12 54	13 04		13 24	13 34	13 40
Argyle Street	d		10 56	11 06		11 26	11 36	11 42			11 56	12 06		12 25	12 36	12 41		12 56	13 06		13 26	13 36	13 42
Charing Cross	d	10 43			11 13					11 43			12 13				12 43			13 13			
Glasgow Queen St LL	a	10 45			11 15					11 45			12 15				12 45			13 15			
	d	10 45			11 15					11 45			12 15				12 45			13 15			
High Street	d	10 47			11 17					11 47			12 17				12 47			13 17			
Bellgrove	d	10 49			11 19					11 49			12 19				12 49			13 19			
Duke Street	d																						
Alexandra Parade	d																						
Barnhill	d																						
Springburn	a																						
Carntyne	d	10 53			11 23					11 53			12 23				12 53			13 23			
Shettleston	d	10 55			11 25					11 55			12 25				12 55			13 25			
Garrowhill	d	10 58			11 28					11 58			12 28				12 58			13 28			
Easterhouse	d	11 00			11 30					12 00			12 30				13 00			13 30			
Blairhill	d	11 04			11 34					12 04			12 34				13 04			13 34			
Coatbridge Sunnyside	d	11 07			11 37					12 07			12 37				13 07			13 37			
Coatdyke	d	11 09			11 39					12 09			12 39				13 09			13 39			
Airdrie	d	11 12			11a42					12 12			12 42				13 12			13 42			
Drumgelloch	d	11 15								12 15			12 45				13 15			13 45			
Caldercruix	d	11 19								12 19			12 49				13 19			13 49			
Blackridge	d	11 25								12 25			12 55				13 25			13 55			
Armadale	d	11 29								12 29			12 59				13 29			13 59			
Bathgate	a	11 33								12 33			13 03				13 33			14 03			
	d	11 34							12 05	12 34			13 04				13 34			14 04			
Livingston North	d	11 38							12 09	12 38			13 09				13 38			14 09			
Uphall	d	11 41							12 12	12 41			13 12				13 41			14 12			
Edinburgh Park	a	11 49							12 20	12 49			13 21				13 49			14 20			
Haymarket	a	11 54							12 25	12 54			13 25				13 54			14 24			
Edinburgh	a	11 59							12 30	12 59			13 30				13 59			14 29			
Bridgeton	d		10 59	11 09		11 29	11 39				11 59	12 09		12 29	12 39			12 59	13 09		13 29	13 39	
Dalmarnock	d																						
Rutherglen	d		11 02	11 12		11 31	11 44	11 47			12 05	12 12		12 32	12 42	12 46		13 02	13 12		13 32	13 43	13 51
Cambuslang	d		11 06	11 16		11 35	11 48				12 09	12 16		12 35	12 46			13 06	13 16		13 35	13 46	
Newton	d		11 09			11 39					12 12			12 39				13 09			13 39		
Blantyre	d		11 13			11 43		11 55			12 16			12 43		12 54		13 13			13 43		13 59
Hamilton West	d		11 16			11 46		11 58			12 19			12 46		12 57		13 16			13 46		14 02
Hamilton Central	d		11 20			11 50		12 01			12 23			12 50		13 00		13 20			13 50		14 04
Chatelherault	d							12 05								13 03							14 08
Merryton	d							12 08								13 06							14 11
Larkhall	a							12 13								13 09							14 14
Airbles	d		11 25			11 55					12 28			12 55				13 25			13 55		
Uddingston	d			11 20			11 53					12 20			12 50				13 20			13 50	
Bellshill	d			11 25			11 57					12 25			12 55				13 25			13 55	
Motherwell	a		11 27	11 33		11 57	12 03				12 30	12 33		12 57	13 03			13 27	13 33		13 57	14 06	
	d			11 33								12 33							13 33				
Whifflet	a																						
Coatbridge Central	a																						
Shieldmuir	d			11 37								12 37							13 37				
Holytown	d																						
Wishaw	d			11 40								12 40							13 40				
Carluke	d			11 47								12 47							13 47				
Lanark	a			11 59								12 59							13 59				

until 19 June

Helensburgh, Balloch, Dalmuir and Milngavie - Glasgow - Springburn, Airdrie, Bathgate and Edinburgh, Hamilton, Larkhall, Motherwell, Coatbridge and Lanark

		SR	SR	SR	SR	SR	SR	SR	SR	SR	SR	SR	SR	SR	SR	SR	SR	SR	SR	SR	SR	SR
														◇ A								
Helensburgh Central	d	12 55			13 25				13 55			14 25		14b39			14 55			15 25		
Craigendoran	d	12 58			13 28				13 58			14 28					14 58			15 28		
Cardross	d	13 03			13 33				14 03			14 33					15 03			15 33		
Balloch	d		13 09			13 39				14 09			14 39					15 09			15 39	
Alexandria	d		13 11			13 41				14 11			14 41					15 11			15 41	
Renton	d		13 14			13 44				14 14			14 44					15 14			15 44	
Dalreoch	d	13 08	13 17		13 38	13 47			14 08	14 17		14 38	14 47				15 08	15 17		15 38	15 47	
Dumbarton Central	d	13 10	13 18		13 40	13 48			14 10	14 18		14 40	14 48	14 56			15 10	15 18		15 40	15 48	
Dumbarton East	d	13 12	13 20		13 42	13 50			14 12	14 20		14 42	14 50				15 12	15 20		15 42	15 50	
Bowling	d		13 25			13 55				14 25			14 55					15 25			15 55	
Kilpatrick	d		13 28			13 58				14 28			14 58					15 28			15 58	
Dalmuir	a	13 20	13 31		13 49	14 01			14 19	14 31		14 49	15 01	15 05			15 19	15 31		15 49	16 01	
	d	13 20	13 31		13 50	14 01			14 20	14 31		14 50	15 01	15 05			15 20	15 31		15 50	16 01	
Singer	d	13 22			13 52				14 22			14 52					15 22			15 52		
Drumry	d	13 25			13 55				14 25			14 55					15 25			15 55		
Drumchapel	d	13 27			13 57				14 27			14 57					15 27			15 57		
Milngavie	d			13 41			14 11				14 41				15 11				15 41			16 11
Hillfoot	d			13 44			14 14				14 44				15 14				15 44			16 14
Bearsden	d			13 46			14 16				14 46				15 16				15 46			16 16
Westerton	d	13 30		13 49	14 00		14 19		14 30		14 49	15 00			15 19		15 30		15 49	16 00		16 19
Anniesland	d	13 33		13 52	14 03		14 22		14 33		14 52	15 03			15 22		15 33		15 52	16 03		16 22
Clydebank	d		13 33			14 03				14 33			15 03					15 33			16 03	
Yoker	d		13 35			14 05				14 35			15 05					15 35			16 05	
Garscadden	d		13 39			14 09				14 39			15 09					15 39			16 09	
Scotstounhill	d		13 41			14 11				14 41			15 11					15 41			16 11	
Jordanhill	d		13 43			14 13				14 43			15 13					15 43			16 13	
Hyndland	d	13 35	13 45	13 55	14 05	14 15	14 25		14 35	14 45	14 55	15 05	15 15		15 25		15 35	15 45	15 55	16 05	16 15	16 25
Partick	d	13 38	13 48	13 58	14 08	14 18	14 28	14 34	14 38	14 48	14 58	15 08	15 18		15 28	15 34	15 38	15 48	15 58	16 08	16 18	16 28
Exhibition Centre	d		13 51	14 01		14 21	14 31	14 37		14 51	15 01		15 21		15 31	15 37		15 51	16 01		16 21	16 31
Anderston	d																					
Glasgow Central LL 15	a		13 53	14 03		14 23	14 33	14 39		14 53	15 03		15 23		15 33	15 39		15 53	16 03		16 23	16 33
	d		13 54	14 04		14 24	14 34	14 40		14 54	15 04		15 24		15 34	15 43		15 54	16 04		16 24	16 34
Argyle Street	d		13 56	14 06		14 26	14 36	14 41		14 56	15 06		15 26		15 36	15 45		15 56	16 06		16 26	16 36
Charing Cross	d	13 43			14 13				14 43			15 13					15 43			16 13		
Glasgow Queen St LL 10	a	13 45			14 15				14 45			15 15		15c31			15 45			16 15		
	d	13 45			14 15				14 45			15 15					15 45			16 15		
High Street	d	13 47			14 17				14 47			15 17					15 47			16 17		
Bellgrove	d	13 49			14 19				14 49			15 19					15 49			16 19		
Duke Street	d																					
Alexandra Parade	d																					
Barnhill	d																					
Springburn	a																					
Carntyne	d	13 53			14 23				14 53			15 23					15 53			16 23		
Shettleston	d	13 55			14 25				14 55			15 25					15 55			16 25		
Garrowhill	d	13 58			14 28				14 58			15 28					15 58			16 28		
Easterhouse	d	14 00			14 30				15 00			15 30					16 00			16 30		
Blairhill	d	14 04			14 34				15 04			15 34					16 04			16 34		
Coatbridge Sunnyside	d	14 07			14 37				15 07			15 37					16 07			16 37		
Coatdyke	d	14 09			14 39				15 09			15 39					16 09			16 39		
Airdrie	d	14 12			14 42				15 12			15 42					16 12			16 42		
Drumgelloch	d	14 15			14 45				15 15			15 45					16 15			16 45		
Caldercruix	d	14 19			14 49				15 19			15 49					16 19			16 49		
Blackridge	d	14 25			14 55				15 25			15 55					16 25			16 55		
Armadale	d	14 29			14 59				15 29			15 59					16 29			16 59		
Bathgate	a	14 33			15 03				15 33			16 03					16 33			17 03		
	d	14 34			15 04				15 34			16 04					16 34			17 04		
Livingston North	d	14 38			15 09				15 38			16 09					16 38			17 09		
Uphall	d	14 41			15 12				15 41			16 12					16 41			17 12		
Edinburgh Park	a	14 49			15 20				15 49			16 20					16 50			17 20		
Haymarket	a	14 54			15 24				15 54			16 24					16 54			17 24		
Edinburgh	a	14 59			15 29				15 59			16 29					16 59			17 29		
Bridgeton	d		13 59	14 09		14 29	14 39			14 59	15 09		15 29		15 39			15 59	16 09		16 29	16 39
Dalmarnock	d																					
Rutherglen	d		14 05	14 12		14 32	14 43	14 47		15 03	15 14		15 32		15 42	15 50		16 03	16 12		16 32	16 44
Cambuslang	d		14 09	14 16		14 36	14 47			15 07	15 18		15 36		15 46			16 07	16 16		16 36	16 50
Newton	d		14 12			14 39				15 10			15 39					16 11			16 39	
Blantyre	d		14 16			14 43		14 56		15 14			15 43			15 58		16 15			16 43	
Hamilton West	d		14 19			14 46		14 59		15 17			15 46			16 02		16 18			16 46	
Hamilton Central	d		14 23			14 50		15 02		15 21			15 50			16 05		16 21			16 50	
Chatelherault	d							15 06								16 08						
Merryton	d							15 09								16 11						
Larkhall	a							15 12								16 14						
Airbles	d		14 28			14 55				15 26			15 55					16 26			16 55	
Uddingston	d			14 20			14 52				15 22				15 51				16 20			16 54
Bellshill	d			14 25			14 56				15 27				15 55				16 25			16 59
Motherwell	a		14 30	14 33		14 57	15 04			15 28	15 33		15 57		16 03			16 28	16 33		16 57	17 05
	d			14 33							15 34								16 33			
Whifflet	a																					
Coatbridge Central	a																					
Shieldmuir	d			14 37							15 37								16 37			
Holytown	d																					
Wishaw	d			14 40							15 41								16 40			
Carluke	d			14 47							15 47								16 47			
Lanark	a			14 59							15 59								16 59			

A From Mallaig   b Helensburgh Upper   c Glasgow Queen St High Level

Helensburgh, Balloch, Dalmuir and Milngavie - Glasgow - Springburn, Airdrie, Bathgate and Edinburgh, Hamilton, Larkhall, Motherwell, Coatbridge and Lanark

		SR	SR	SR	SR	SR	SR	SR	SR	SR	SR	SR	SR	SR	SR	SR	SR	SR	SR	SR	SR	SR	SR
																					◇ A		
Helensburgh Central	d		15 55			16 25				16 55			17 25				17 55			18 25	18b33		
Craigendoran	d		15 58			16 28				16 58			17 28				17 58			18 28			
Cardross	d		16 03			16 33				17 03			17 33				18 03			18 33			
Balloch	d			16 09			16 39				17 09			17 39				18 09				18 39	
Alexandria	d			16 11			16 41				17 11			17 41				18 11				18 41	
Renton	d			16 14			16 44				17 14			17 44				18 14				18 44	
Dalreoch	d		16 08	16 17		16 38	16 47			17 08	17 17		17 38	17 47			18 08	18 17		18 38		18 48	
Dumbarton Central	d		16 10	16 18		16 40	16 48			17 10	17 18		17 40	17 48			18 10	18 18		18 40	18 47	18 49	
Dumbarton East	d		16 12	16 20		16 42	16 50			17 12	17 20		17 42	17 50			18 12	18 20		18 42		18 51	
Bowling	d			16 25			16 55				17 25			17 55				18 25				18 56	
Kilpatrick	d			16 28			16 58				17 28			17 58				18 28				18 59	
Dalmuir	a		16 19	16 31		16 49	17 01			17 19	17 31		17 49	18 01			18 19	18 31		18 49	18 56	19 02	
	d		16 20	16 31		16 50	17 01			17 20	17 31		17 50	18 01			18 20	18 31		18 50	18 56	19 02	
Singer	d		16 22			16 52				17 22			17 52				18 22			18 52			
Drumry	d		16 25			16 55				17 25			17 55				18 25			18 55			
Drumchapel	d		16 27			16 57				17 27			17 57				18 27			18 57			
Milngavie	d				16 41			17 11				17 41			18 11				18 41				19 11
Hillfoot	d				16 44			17 14				17 44			18 14				18 44				19 14
Bearsden	d				16 46			17 16				17 46			18 16				18 46				19 16
Westerton	d		16 30		16 49	17 00		17 19		17 30		17 49	18 00		18 19		18 30		18 49	19 00			19 19
Anniesland	d		16 33		16 52	17 03		17 22		17 33		17 52	18 03		18 22		18 33		18 52	19 03			19 22
Clydebank	d			16 33			17 03				17 33			18 03				18 33				19 03	
Yoker	d			16 35			17 05				17 35			18 05				18 35				19 05	
Garscadden	d			16 39			17 09				17 39			18 09				18 39				19 10	
Scotstounhill	d			16 41			17 11				17 41			18 11				18 41				19 12	
Jordanhill	d			16 43			17 13				17 43			18 13				18 43				19 13	
Hyndland	d		16 35	16 45	16 55	17 05	17 15	17 25		17 35	17 45	17 55	18 05	18 15	18 25		18 35	18 45	18 55	19 05		19 15	19 25
Partick	d	16 34	16 38	16 48	16 58	17 08	17 18	17 28	17 34	17 38	17 48	17 58	18 08	18 18	18 28	18 34	18 38	18 48	18 58	19 08		19 18	19 28
Exhibition Centre	d	16 37		16 51	17 01		17 21	17 31	17 37		17 51	18 01		18 21	18 31	18 37		18 51	19 01			19 21	19 31
Anderston	d																						
Glasgow Central LL 15	a	16 39		16 53	17 03		17 23	17 33	17 39		17 53	18 03		18 23	18 33	18 39		18 53	19 03			19 24	19 33
	d	16 40		16 54	17 04		17 24	17 34	17 40		17 54	18 04		18 24	18 34	18 40		18 54	19 04			19 24	19 34
Argyle Street	d	16 46		16 56	17 06		17 26	17 36	17 41		17 56	18 06											
Charing Cross	d		16 43			17 13				17 43			18 13				18 43			19 13			
Glasgow Queen St LL 10	a		16 45			17 15				17 45			18 15				18 45			19 15	19c15		
	d		16 45			17 15				17 45			18 15				18 45			19 15			
High Street	d		16 47			17 17				17 47			18 17				18 47			19 17			
Bellgrove	d		16 49			17 19				17 49			18 19				18 49			19 19			
Duke Street	d																						
Alexandra Parade	d																						
Barnhill	d																						
Springburn	a																						
Carntyne	d		16 53			17 23				17 53			18 23				18 53			19 23			
Shettleston	d		16 55			17 25				17 55			18 25				18 55			19 25			
Garrowhill	d		16 58			17 28				17 58			18 28				18 58			19 28			
Easterhouse	d		17 00			17 30				18 00			18 30				19 00			19 30			
Blairhill	d		17 04			17 34				18 04			18 34				19 04			19 34			
Coatbridge Sunnyside	d		17 07			17 37				18 07			18 37				19 07			19 37			
Coatdyke	d		17 09			17 39				18 09			18 39				19 09			19 39			
Airdrie	d		17 12			17 42				18 12			18 42				19 12			19a42			
Drumgelloch	d		17 15			17 45				18 15			18 45				19 15						
Caldercruix	d		17 19			17 49				18 19			18 49				19 19						
Blackridge	d		17 25			17 55				18 25			18 55				19 25						
Armadale	d		17 29			17 59				18 29			18 59				19 29						
Bathgate	a		17 33			18 03				18 33			19 03				19 33						
	d		17 34			18 04				18 34			19 04				19 34						
Livingston North	d		17 38			18 09				18 38			19 09				19 38						
Uphall	d		17 41			18 12				18 41			19 12				19 41						
Edinburgh Park	a		17 49			18 20				18 49			19 20				19 49						
Haymarket	a		17 58			18 24				18 54			19 24				19 54						
Edinburgh	a		18 03			18 30				18 59			19 29				19 59						
Bridgeton	d			16 59	17 09		17 29	17 39			17 59	18 09		18 29	18 39			18 59	19 09			19 29	19 37
Dalmarnock	d																						
Rutherglen	d	16 51		17 03	17 13		17 32	17 42	17 46		18 02	18 12		18 32	18 42	18 47		19 03	19 12			19 32	19 40
Cambuslang	d			17 07	17 17		17 36	17 46			18 06	18 16		18 36	18 46			19 07	19 16			19 36	19 44
Newton	d			17 10			17 39				18 09			18 39				19 10				19 39	
Blantyre	d	16 59		17 14			17 43		17 56		18 13			18 43		18 57		19 14				19 43	
Hamilton West	d	17 02		17 17			17 46		17 59		18 16			18 46		19 00		19 17				19 46	
Hamilton Central	d	17 04		17 20			17 50		18 02		18 20			18 50		19 02		19 20				19 50	
Chatelherault	d	17 08							18 05							19 06							
Merryton	d	17 11							18 08							19 09							
Larkhall	a	17 14							18 12							19 12							
Airbles	d			17 25			17 55				18 25			18 55				19 25				19 55	
Uddingston	d				17 21			17 50				18 20			18 50				19 20				19 49
Bellshill	d				17 26			17 55				18 25			18 55				19 25				19 55
Motherwell	a			17 27	17 33		17 57	18 02			18 27	18 33		18 57	19 03			19 27	19 33			19 57	20 03
	d				17 33							18 33							19 33				
Whifflet	a																						
Coatbridge Central	a																						
Shieldmuir	d				17 37							18 37							19 37				
Holytown	d																						
Wishaw	d				17 40							18 40							19 40				
Carluke	d				17 47							18 47							19 47				
Lanark	a				17 59							18 59							19 59				

A From Oban   b Helensburgh Upper   c Glasgow Queen St High Level

Table 226

Sundays
until 19 June

Helensburgh, Balloch, Dalmuir and Milngavie - Glasgow - Springburn, Airdrie, Bathgate and Edinburgh, Hamilton, Larkhall, Motherwell, Coatbridge and Lanark

		SR	SR	SR	SR	SR	SR	SR	SR	SR	SR	SR	SR	SR	SR	SR	SR	SR	SR	SR	SR	SR
															◇ A ⊣							
Helensburgh Central	d		18 55			19 25				19 55			20 25		20b40			20 55			21 25	
Craigendoran	d		18 58			19 28				19 58			20 28					20 58			21 28	
Cardross	d		19 03			19 33				20 03			20 33					21 03			21 33	
Balloch	d			19 09			19 39				20 09			20 38					21 09			21 39
Alexandria	d			19 11			19 41				20 11			20 40					21 11			21 41
Renton	d			19 14			19 44				20 14			20 43					21 14			21 44
Dalreoch	d		19 08	19 17		19 38	19 47			20 08	20 17		20 38	20 46				21 08	21 17		21 38	21 47
Dumbarton Central	d		19 10	19 18		19 40	19 48			20 10	20 18		20 40	20 47	20 53			21 10	21 18		21 40	21 48
Dumbarton East	d		19 12	19 20		19 42	19 50			20 12	20 20		20 42	20 49				21 12	21 20		21 42	21 50
Bowling	d			19 25			19 55				20 25			20 54					21 25			21 55
Kilpatrick	d			19 28			19 58				20 28			20 57					21 28			21 58
Dalmuir	a		19 20	19 31		19 49	20 01			20 19	20 31		20 49	21 00	21 03			21 19	21 31		21 49	22 01
	d		19 20	19 31		19 50	20 01			20 20	20 31		20 50	21 01	21 03			21 20	21 31		21 50	22 01
Singer	d		19 22			19 52				20 22			20 52					21 22			21 52	
Drumry	d		19 25			19 55				20 25			20 55					21 25			21 55	
Drumchapel	d		19 27			19 57				20 27			20 57					21 27			21 57	
Milngavie	d				19 41			20 11				20 41				21 11				21 41		
Hillfoot	d				19 44			20 14				20 44				21 14				21 44		
Bearsden	d				19 46			20 16				20 46				21 16				21 46		
Westerton	d		19 30		19 49	20 00		20 19		20 30		20 49	21 00			21 19		21 30		21 49	22 00	
Anniesland	d		19 33		19 52	20 03		20 22		20 33		20 52	21 03			21 22		21 33		21 52	22 03	
Clydebank	d			19 33			20 03				20 33			21 03					21 33			22 03
Yoker	d			19 35			20 05				20 35			21 05					21 35			22 05
Garscadden	d			19 39			20 09				20 39			21 09					21 39			22 09
Scotstounhill	d			19 41			20 11				20 41			21 11					21 41			22 11
Jordanhill	d			19 43			20 13				20 43			21 13					21 43			22 13
Hyndland	d		19 35	19 45	19 55	20 05	20 15	20 25		20 35	20 45	20 55	21 05	21 15		21 25		21 35	21 45	21 55	22 05	22 15
Partick ⛴	d	19 34	19 38	19 48	19 58	20 08	20 18	20 28	20 34	20 38	20 48	20 58	21 08	21 18		21 28	21 34	21 38	21 48	21 58	22 08	22 18
Exhibition Centre	d	19 37		19 51	20 01		20 21	20 31	20 37		20 51	21 01		21 21		21 31	21 37		21 51	22 01		22 21
Anderston	d																					
Glasgow Central LL 10	a	19 39		19 53	20 03		20 23	20 33	20 39		20 53	21 03		21 23		21 33	21 39		21 53	22 03		22 23
	d	19 40		19 54	20 04		20 24	20 34	20 40		20 54	21 04		21 24		21 34	21 40		21 54	22 04		22 24
Argyle Street	d																					
Charing Cross	d		19 43			20 13				20 43			21 13					21 43			22 13	
Glasgow Queen St LL 10 ⛴	a		19 45			20 15				20 45			21 15		21c19			21 45			22 15	
	d		19 45			20 15				20 45			21 15					21 45			22 15	
High Street	d		19 47			20 17				20 47			21 17					21 47			22 17	
Bellgrove	d		19 49			20 19				20 49			21 19					21 49			22 19	
Duke Street	d																					
Alexandra Parade	d																					
Barnhill	d																					
Springburn	a																					
Carntyne	d		19 53			20 23				20 53			21 23					21 53			22 23	
Shettleston	d		19 55			20 25				20 55			21 25					21 55			22 25	
Garrowhill	d		19 58			20 28				20 58			21 28					21 58			22 28	
Easterhouse	d		20 00			20 30				21 00			21 30					22 00			22 30	
Blairhill	d		20 04			20 34				21 04			21 34					22 04			22 34	
Coatbridge Sunnyside	d		20 07			20 37				21 07			21 37					22 07			22 37	
Coatdyke	d		20 09			20 39				21 09			21 39					22 09			22 39	
Airdrie	d		20 12			20a42				21 12			21a42					22 12			22a42	
Drumgelloch	d		20 15							21 15								22 15				
Caldercruix	d		20 19							21 19								22 19				
Blackridge	d		20 25							21 25								22 25				
Armadale	d		20 29							21 29								22 29				
Bathgate	a		20 33							21 33								22 33				
	d		20 34							21 34								22 34				
Livingston North	d		20 38							21 39								22 39				
Uphall	d		20 41							21 42								22 42				
Edinburgh Park	a		20 49							21 50								22 50				
Haymarket	a		20 54							21 54								22 55				
Edinburgh	a		20 59							21 59								23 00				
Bridgeton	d			19 59	20 09		20 29	20 37			20 57	21 09		21 29		21 37			21 59	22 08		22 29
Dalmarnock	d																					
Rutherglen	d	19 46		20 02	20 14		20 32	20 40	20 46		21 00	21 12		21 32		21 40	21 47		22 02	22 11		22 32
Cambuslang	d			20 06	20 18		20 36	20 44			21 04	21 16		21 36		21 44			22 06	22 15		22 36
Newton	d			20 09			20 39				21 08			21 39					22 09			22 39
Blantyre	d	19 56		20 13			20 43		20 54		21 13			21 43			21 54		22 13			22 43
Hamilton West	d	19 59		20 16			20 46		20 58		21 16			21 46			21 57		22 16			22 46
Hamilton Central	d	20 02		20 20			20 50		21 02		21 20			21 50			22 01		22 20			22 50
Chatelherault	d	20 05							21 05								22 04					
Merryton	d	20 08							21 08								22 07					
Larkhall	a	20 12							21 13								22 12					
Airbles	d			20 25			20 55				21 25			21 55					22 25			22 55
Uddingston	d				20 22			20 49				21 20				21 49				22 19		
Bellshill	d				20 27			20 55				21 25				21 55				22 24		
Motherwell	a			20 27	20 33		20 57	21 04			21 27	21 33		21 57		22 03			22 27	22 32		22 57
	d				20 33							21 33								22 32		
Whifflet	a																					
Coatbridge Central	a																					
Shieldmuir	d				20 37							21 37								22 36		
Holytown	d																					
Wishaw	d				20 40							21 40								22 39		
Carluke	d				20 47							21 47								22 44		
Lanark	a				20 59							21 59								22 58		

A From Mallaig

b Helensburgh Upper

c Glasgow Queen St High Level

Table 226

Sundays
until 19 June

Helensburgh, Balloch, Dalmuir and Milngavie - Glasgow - Springburn, Airdrie, Bathgate and Edinburgh, Hamilton, Larkhall, Motherwell, Coatbridge and Lanark

		SR	SR	SR	SR	SR	SR	SR	SR	SR
									▣ A ⊡	
Helensburgh Central	d			21 55			22 25		22b37	
Craigendoran	d			21 58			22 28			
Cardross	d			22 03			22 33			
Balloch	d				22 09			22 39		23 09
Alexandria	d				22 11			22 41		23 11
Renton	d				22 14			22 44		23 14
Dalreoch	d			22 08	22 17		22 38	22 47		23 17
Dumbarton Central	d			22 10	22 18		22 40	22 48		23 18
Dumbarton East	d			22 12	22 20		22 42	22 50		23 20
Bowling	d				22 25			22 55		23 25
Kilpatrick	d				22 28			22 58		23 28
Dalmuir	a			22 19	22 31		22 49	23 01	23 02	23 31
	d			22 20	22 31		22 50	23 01	23 04	23 31
Singer	d			22 22			22 52			
Drumry	d			22 25			22 55			
Drumchapel	d			22 27			22 57			
Milngavie	d	22 11				22 41				
Hillfoot	d	22 14				22 44				
Bearsden	d	22 16				22 46				
Westerton	d	22 19		22 30		22 49	23 00		23 13	
Anniesland	d	22 22		22 33		22 52	23 03			
Clydebank	d				22 33			23 03		23 33
Yoker	d				22 35			23a05		23a35
Garscadden	d				22 39					
Scotstounhill	d				22 41					
Jordanhill	d				22 43					
Hyndland	d	22 25		22 35	22 45	22 55	23 05			
Partick ⛴	d	22 28	22 34	22 38	22 48	22 58	23 08			
Exhibition Centre	d	22 31	22 37		22 51	23 01				
Anderston	d									
Glasgow Central LL 10	a	22 33	22 39		22 53	23 03				
	d	22 34	22 40		22 54	23 04				
Argyle Street	d									
Charing Cross	d			22 43			23 13			
Glasgow Queen St LL 10 ⛴	a			22 45			23 15			
	d			22 45			23 15			
High Street	d			22 47			23 17			
Bellgrove	d			22 49			23 19			
Duke Street	d									
Alexandra Parade	d									
Barnhill	d									
Springburn	a									
Carntyne	d			22 53			23 23			
Shettleston	d			22 55			23 25			
Garrowhill	d			22 58			23 28			
Easterhouse	d			23 00			23 30			
Blairhill	d			23 04			23 34			
Coatbridge Sunnyside	d			23 07			23 37			
Coatdyke	d			23 09			23 39			
Airdrie	d			23 12			23a42			
Drumgelloch	d			23 15						
Caldercruix	d			23 19						
Blackridge	d			23 25						
Armadale	d			23 29						
Bathgate	a			23 33						
	d									
Livingston North	d									
Uphall	d									
Edinburgh Park	a									
Haymarket	a									
Edinburgh	a								00 13	
Bridgeton	d	22 39			22 59	23 09				
Dalmarnock	d									
Rutherglen	d	22 42	22 47		23 02	23 12				
Cambuslang	d	22 46			23 06	23 16				
Newton	d				23 09					
Blantyre	d		22 55		23 13					
Hamilton West	d		22 58		23 16					
Hamilton Central	d		23 02		23 20					
Chatelherault	d		23 05							
Merryton	d		23 08							
Larkhall	a		23 11							
Airbles	d				23 25					
Uddingston	d	22 50				23 20				
Bellshill	d	22 55				23 25				
Motherwell	a	23 03			23 27	23 33				
	d									
Whifflet	a									
Coatbridge Central	a									
Shieldmuir	d									
Holytown	d									
Wishaw	d									
Carluke	d									
Lanark	a									

A From Fort William

b Helensburgh Upper

Helensburgh, Balloch, Dalmuir and Milngavie - Glasgow - Springburn, Airdrie, Bathgate and Edinburgh, Hamilton, Larkhall, Motherwell, Coatbridge and Lanark

Station		SR	SR	SR	SR	SR	SR	SR	SR	SR	SR	SR	SR	SR	SR	SR	SR	SR	SR	SR	SR	SR	SR
Helensburgh Central	d		22p40		23p10				07 55			08 25				08 55			09 25				
Craigendoran	d		22p43		23p13				07 58			08 28				08 58			09 28				
Cardross	d		22p48		23p18				08 03			08 33				09 03			09 33				
Balloch	d			22p53						08 09			08 39				09 09			09 39			
Alexandria	d			22p55						08 11			08 41				09 11			09 41			
Renton	d			22p58						08 14			08 44				09 14			09 44			
Dalreoch	d		22p53	23p01	23p23				08 08	08 17		08 38	08 47			09 08	09 17		09 38	09 47			
Dumbarton Central	d		22p55	23p02	23p25				08 10	08 18		08 40	08 48			09 10	09 18		09 40	09 48			
Dumbarton East	d		22p57	23p04	23p27				08 12	08 20		08 42	08 50			09 12	09 20		09 42	09 50			
Bowling	d			23p09						08 25			08 55				09 25			09 55			
Kilpatrick	d			23p12						08 28			08 58				09 28			09 58			
Dalmuir	a		23p05	23p15	23p35				08 19	08 31		08 49	09 01			09 19	09 31		09 49	10 01			
	d	23p01	23p05	23p16	23p35		07 40	08 01	08 20	08 31		08 50	09 01			09 20	09 31		09 50	10 01			
Singer	d	23p03		23p18			07 42		08 22			08 52				09 22			09 52				
Drumry	d	23p05		23p20			07 45		08 25			08 55				09 25			09 55				
Drumchapel	d	23p08		23p23			07 47		08 27			08 57				09 27			09 57				
Milngavie	d													09 11				09 41			10 11		
Hillfoot	d													09 14				09 44			10 14		
Bearsden	d													09 16				09 46			10 16		
Westerton	d	23p10		23p25			07 50		08 30			09 00		09 19		09 30		09 49	10 00		10 19		
Anniesland	d	23p14		23p28			07 53		08 33			09 03		09 22		09 33		09 52	10 03		10 22		
Clydebank	d		23p07		23p37			08 03		08 33			09 03				09 33			10 03			
Yoker	d		23p09		23p39			08 05		08 35			09 05				09 35			10 05			
Garscadden	d		23p13		23p43			08 09		08 39			09 09				09 39			10 09			
Scotstounhill	d		23p15		23p45			08 11		08 41			09 11				09 41			10 11			
Jordanhill	d		23p17		23p47			08 13		08 43			09 13				09 43			10 13			
Hyndland	d	23p17	23p21	23p31	23p49		07 55	08 15	08 35	08 45	08 55	09 05	09 15	09 25		09 35	09 45	09 55	10 05	10 15	10 25		
Partick	d	23p20	23p23	23p34	23p52		07 58	08 18	08 38	08 48	08 58	09 08	09 18	09 28	09 34	09 38	09 48	09 58	10 08	10 18	10 28	10 34	
Exhibition Centre	d	23p23						08 21		08 51	09 01		09 21	09 31	09 37		09 51	10 01		10 21	10 31	10 37	
Anderston	d	23p25																					
Glasgow Central LL	a	23p26						08 23		08 53	09 03		09 23	09 33	09 39		09 53	10 03		10 23	10 33	10 39	
	d	23p27						08 24		08 54	09 04		09 24	09 34	09 40		09 54	10 04		10 23	10 34	10 40	
Argyle Street	d	23p29															09 55	10 06		10 25	10 36	10 42	
Charing Cross	d		23p27	23p38	23p56		08 03		08 43			09 13				09 43			10 13				
Glasgow Queen St LL	a		23p29	23p40	23p59		08 05		08 45			09 15				09 45			10 15				
	d		23p30	23p44	23p59		08 05		08 45			09 15				09 45			10 15				
High Street	d		23p32	23p46	00 02		08 07		08 47			09 17				09 47			10 17				
Bellgrove	d		23p34	23p49	00 04		08 09		08 49			09 19				09 49			10 19				
Duke Street	d																						
Alexandra Parade	d																						
Barnhill	d																						
Springburn	a																						
Carntyne	d		23p37	23p52	00 07		08 13		08 53			09 23				09 53			10 23				
Shettleston	d		23p40	23p55	00 10		08 15		08 55			09 25				09 55			10 25				
Garrowhill	d		23p42	23p57	00 12		08 18		08 58			09 28				09 58			10 28				
Easterhouse	d		23p45	23p59	00 15		08 20		09 00			09 30				10 00			10 30				
Blairhill	d		23p49	00 04	00 19		08 24		09 04			09 34				10 04			10 34				
Coatbridge Sunnyside	d		23p51	00 06	00 21		08 27		09 07			09 37				10 07			10 37				
Coatdyke	d		23p54	00 09	00 24		08 29		09 09			09 39				10 09			10 39				
Airdrie	d		23p57	00a12	00a27		08 32		09 12			09a42				10 12			10a42				
Drumgelloch	d		23p59				08 35		09 15							10 15							
Caldercruix	d		00 03				08 39		09 19							10 19							
Blackridge	d		00 09				08 45		09 25							10 25							
Armadale	d		00 13				08 49		09 29							10 29							
Bathgate	a		00 17				08 53		09 33							10 33							
	d					07 55	08 54		09 34							10 34							11 05
Livingston North	d					07 59	08 59		09 39							10 38							11 09
Uphall	d					08 02	09 02		09 42							10 41							11 12
Edinburgh Park	a					08 10	09 10		09 52							10 49							11 20
Haymarket	a					08 20	09 20		10 02							10 55							11 25
Edinburgh	a					08 25	09 25		10 07							11 00							11 30
Bridgeton	d							08 29		08 59	09 09		09 29	09 39			09 58	10 09		10 28	10 39		
Dalmarnock	d																						
Rutherglen	d	23p34						08 32		09 02	09 12		09 32	09 42	09 47		10 01	10 12		10 30	10 42	10 45	
Cambuslang	d							08 36		09 06	09 16		09 36	09 48			10 04	10 16		10 34	10 46		
Newton	d									09 09			09 39				10 09			10 38			
Blantyre	d	23p44								09 13			09 43		09 57		10 13			10 42		10 57	
Hamilton West	d	23p47								09 16			09 46		10 00		10 16			10 46		11 00	
Hamilton Central	d	23p50								09 20			09 50		10 03		10 20			10 50		11 03	
Chatelherault	d	23p53													10 06							11 06	
Merryton	d	23p56													10 09							11 09	
Larkhall	a	00 01													10 12							11 12	
Airbles	d									09 25			09 55				10 25			10 55			
Uddingston	d							08 40			09 20			09 53				10 20			10 50		
Bellshill	d							08 45			09 25			09 57				10 25			10 55		
Motherwell	a							08 53		09 27	09 33		09 57	10 03			10 27	10 33		10 57	11 03		
	d										09 33							10 33					
Whifflet	a																						
Coatbridge Central	a																						
Shieldmuir	d										09 37							10 37					
Holytown	d																						
Wishaw	d										09 40							10 40					
Carluke	d										09 47							10 47					
Lanark	a										09 59							10 59					

Helensburgh, Balloch, Dalmuir and Milngavie - Glasgow - Springburn, Airdrie, Bathgate and Edinburgh, Hamilton, Larkhall, Motherwell, Coatbridge and Lanark

Station		SR	SR	SR	SR	SR	SR	SR	SR	SR	SR	SR	SR	SR	SR	SR	SR	SR	SR	SR	SR	SR	SR
Helensburgh Central	d	09 55			10 25					10 55			11 25				11 55			12 25			
Craigendoran	d	09 58			10 28					10 58			11 28				11 58			12 28			
Cardross	d	10 03			10 33					11 03			11 33				12 03			12 33			
Balloch	d		10 09			10 39					11 09			11 39				12 09			12 39		
Alexandria	d		10 11			10 41					11 11			11 41				12 11			12 41		
Renton	d		10 14			10 44					11 14			11 44				12 14			12 44		
Dalreoch	d	10 08	10 17		10 38	10 47				11 08	11 17		11 38	11 47			12 08	12 17		12 38	12 47		
Dumbarton Central	d	10 10	10 18		10 40	10 48				11 10	11 18		11 40	11 48			12 10	12 18		12 40	12 48		
Dumbarton East	d	10 12	10 20		10 42	10 50				11 12	11 20		11 42	11 50			12 12	12 20		12 42	12 50		
Bowling	d		10 25			10 55					11 25			11 55				12 25			12 55		
Kilpatrick	d		10 28			10 58					11 28			11 58				12 28			12 58		
Dalmuir	a	10 19	10 31		10 49	11 01				11 19	11 31		11 49	12 01			12 19	12 31		12 49	13 01		
	d	10 20	10 31		10 50	11 01				11 20	11 31		11 50	12 01			12 20	12 31		12 50	13 01		
Singer	d	10 22			10 52					11 22			11 52				12 22			12 52			
Drumry	d	10 25			10 55					11 25			11 55				12 25			12 55			
Drumchapel	d	10 27			10 57					11 27			11 57				12 27			12 57			
Milngavie	d			10 41			11 11					11 41			12 11				12 41			13 11	
Hillfoot	d			10 44			11 14					11 44			12 14				12 44			13 14	
Bearsden	d			10 46			11 16					11 46			12 16				12 46			13 16	
Westerton	d	10 30		10 49	11 00		11 19			11 30		11 49	12 00		12 19		12 30		12 49	13 00		13 19	
Anniesland	d	10 33		10 52	11 03		11 22			11 33		11 52	12 03		12 22		12 33		12 52	13 03		13 22	
Clydebank	d		10 33			11 03					11 33			12 03				12 33			13 03		
Yoker	d		10 35			11 05					11 35			12 05				12 35			13 05		
Garscadden	d		10 39			11 09					11 39			12 09				12 39			13 09		
Scotstounhill	d		10 41			11 11					11 41			12 11				12 41			13 11		
Jordanhill	d		10 43			11 13					11 43			12 13				12 43			13 13		
Hyndland	d	10 35	10 45	10 55	11 05	11 15	11 25			11 35	11 45	11 55	12 05	12 15	12 25		12 35	12 45	12 55	13 05	13 15	13 25	
Partick	d	10 38	10 48	10 58	11 08	11 18	11 28	11 34		11 38	11 48	11 58	12 08	12 18	12 28	12 34	12 38	12 48	12 58	13 08	13 18	13 28	13 34
Exhibition Centre	d		10 51	11 01		11 21	11 31	11 37			11 51	12 01		12 21	12 31	12 37		12 51	13 01		13 21	13 31	13 37
Anderston	d																						
Glasgow Central LL	a		10 53	11 03		11 23	11 33	11 39			11 53	12 03		12 23	12 33	12 39		12 53	13 03		13 23	13 33	13 39
	d		10 54	11 04		11 24	11 34	11 40			11 54	12 04		12 24	12 34	12 40		12 54	13 04		13 24	13 34	13 40
Argyle Street	d		10 56	11 06		11 26	11 36	11 42			11 56	12 06		12 25	12 36	12 41		12 56	13 06		13 26	13 36	13 42
Charing Cross	d	10 43			11 13					11 43			12 13				12 43			13 13			
Glasgow Queen St LL	a	10 45			11 15					11 45			12 15				12 45			13 15			
	d	10 45			11 15					11 45			12 15				12 45			13 15			
High Street	d	10 47			11 17					11 47			12 17				12 47			13 17			
Bellgrove	d	10 49			11 19					11 49			12 19				12 49			13 19			
Duke Street	d																						
Alexandra Parade	d																						
Barnhill	d																						
Springburn	a																						
Carntyne	d	10 53			11 23					11 53			12 23				12 53			13 23			
Shettleston	d	10 55			11 25					11 55			12 25				12 55			13 25			
Garrowhill	d	10 58			11 28					11 58			12 28				12 58			13 28			
Easterhouse	d	11 00			11 30					12 00			12 30				13 00			13 30			
Blairhill	d	11 04			11 34					12 04			12 34				13 04			13 34			
Coatbridge Sunnyside	d	11 07			11 37					12 07			12 37				13 07			13 37			
Coatdyke	d	11 09			11 39					12 09			12 39				13 09			13 39			
Airdrie	d	11 12			11a42					12 12			12 42				13 12			13 42			
Drumgelloch	d	11 15								12 15			12 45				13 15			13 45			
Caldercruix	d	11 19								12 19			12 49				13 19			13 49			
Blackridge	d	11 25								12 25			12 55				13 25			13 55			
Armadale	d	11 29								12 29			12 59				13 29			13 59			
Bathgate	a	11 33								12 33			13 03				13 33			14 03			
	d	11 34							12 05	12 34			13 04				13 34			14 04			
Livingston North	d	11 38							12 09	12 38			13 09				13 38			14 09			
Uphall	d	11 41							12 12	12 41			13 12				13 41			14 12			
Edinburgh Park	a	11 49							12 20	12 49			13 21				13 49			14 20			
Haymarket	a	11 54							12 25	12 54			13 25				13 54			14 24			
Edinburgh	a	11 59							12 30	12 59			13 30				13 59			14 29			
Bridgeton	d		10 59	11 09		11 29	11 39				11 59	12 09		12 29	12 39			12 59	13 09		13 29	13 39	
Dalmarnock	d																						
Rutherglen	d		11 02	11 12		11 31	11 44	11 47			12 05	12 12		12 32	12 42	12 46		13 02	13 12		13 32	13 43	13 51
Cambuslang	d		11 06	11 16		11 35	11 48				12 09	12 16		12 35	12 46			13 06	13 16		13 35	13 46	
Newton	d		11 09			11 39					12 12			12 39				13 09			13 39		
Blantyre	d		11 13			11 43		11 55			12 16			12 43		12 54		13 13			13 43		13 59
Hamilton West	d		11 16			11 46		11 58			12 19			12 46		12 57		13 16			13 46		14 02
Hamilton Central	d		11 20			11 50		12 01			12 23			12 50		13 00		13 20			13 50		14 04
Chatelherault	d							12 05								13 03							14 08
Merryton	d							12 08								13 06							14 11
Larkhall	a							12 13								13 09							14 14
Airbles	d		11 25			11 55					12 28			12 55				13 25			13 55		
Uddingston	d			11 20			11 53					12 20			12 50				13 20			13 50	
Bellshill	d			11 25			11 57					12 25			12 55				13 25			13 55	
Motherwell	a		11 27	11 33		11 57	12 03				12 30	12 33		12 57	13 03			13 27	13 33		13 57	14 06	
	d			11 33								12 33							13 33				
Whifflet	a																						
Coatbridge Central	a																						
Shieldmuir	d			11 37								12 37							13 37				
Holytown	d																						
Wishaw	d			11 40								12 40							13 40				
Carluke	d			11 47								12 47							13 47				
Lanark	a			11 59								12 59							13 59				

Table 226

Sundays
26 June to 30 October

Helensburgh, Balloch, Dalmuir and Milngavie - Glasgow - Springburn, Airdrie, Bathgate and Edinburgh, Hamilton, Larkhall, Motherwell, Coatbridge and Lanark

		SR		SR	SR	SR	SR	SR	SR	SR	SR	SR		SR	SR	SR ◇ A	SR	SR	SR	SR	SR	SR		SR	SR
Helensburgh Central	d	12 55				13 25				13 55				14 25		14b39			14 55			15 25			
Craigendoran	d	12 58				13 28				13 58				14 28					14 58			15 28			
Cardross	d	13 03				13 33				14 03				14 33					15 03			15 33			
Balloch	d			13 09			13 39				14 09				14 39					15 09				15 39	
Alexandria	d			13 11			13 41				14 11				14 41					15 11				15 41	
Renton	d			13 14			13 44				14 14				14 44					15 14				15 44	
Dalreoch	d	13 08		13 17		13 38	13 47			14 08	14 17			14 38	14 47				15 08	15 17		15 38		15 47	
Dumbarton Central	d	13 10		13 18		13 40	13 48			14 10	14 18			14 40	14 48	14 56			15 10	15 18		15 40		15 48	
Dumbarton East	d	13 12		13 20		13 42	13 50			14 12	14 20			14 42	14 50				15 12	15 20		15 42		15 50	
Bowling	d			13 25			13 55				14 25				14 55					15 25				15 55	
Kilpatrick	d			13 28			13 58				14 28				14 58					15 28				15 58	
Dalmuir	a	13 20		13 31		13 49	14 01			14 19	14 31			14 49	15 01	15 05			15 19	15 31		15 49		16 01	
	d	13 20		13 31		13 50	14 01			14 20	14 31			14 50	15 01	15 05			15 20	15 31		15 50		16 01	
Singer	d	13 22				13 52				14 22				14 52					15 22			15 52			
Drumry	d	13 25				13 55				14 25				14 55					15 25			15 55			
Drumchapel	d	13 27				13 57				14 27				14 57					15 27			15 57			
Milngavie	d				13 41			14 11				14 41					15 11				15 41				16 11
Hillfoot	d				13 44			14 14				14 44					15 14				15 44				16 14
Bearsden	d				13 46			14 16				14 46					15 16				15 46				16 16
Westerton	d	13 30			13 49	14 00		14 19		14 30		14 49		15 00			15 19		15 30		15 49	16 00			16 19
Anniesland	d	13 33			13 52	14 03		14 22		14 33		14 52		15 03			15 22		15 33		15 52	16 03			16 22
Clydebank	d			13 33			14 03				14 33				15 03					15 33				16 03	
Yoker	d			13 35			14 05				14 35				15 05					15 35				16 05	
Garscadden	d			13 39			14 09				14 39				15 09					15 39				16 09	
Scotstounhill	d			13 41			14 11				14 41				15 11					15 41				16 11	
Jordanhill	d			13 43			14 13				14 43				15 13					15 43				16 13	
Hyndland	d	13 35		13 45	13 55	14 05	14 15	14 25		14 35	14 45	14 55		15 05	15 15		15 25		15 35	15 45	15 55	16 05		16 15	16 25
Partick	d	13 38		13 48	13 58	14 08	14 18	14 28	14 34	14 38	14 48	14 58		15 08	15 18		15 28	15 34	15 38	15 48	15 58	16 08		16 18	16 28
Exhibition Centre	d			13 51	14 01		14 21	14 31	14 37		14 51	15 01			15 21		15 31	15 37		15 51	16 01			16 21	16 31
Anderston	d																								
Glasgow Central LL	a			13 53	14 03		14 23	14 33	14 39		14 53	15 03			15 23		15 33	15 39		15 53	16 03			16 23	16 33
	d			13 54	14 04		14 24	14 34	14 40		14 54	15 04			15 24		15 34	15 43		15 54	16 04			16 24	16 34
Argyle Street	d			13 56	14 06		14 26	14 36	14 41		14 56	15 06			15 26		15 36	15 45		15 56	16 06			16 26	16 36
Charing Cross	d	13 43				14 13				14 43				15 13					15 43			16 13			
Glasgow Queen St LL	a	13 45				14 15				14 45				15 15		15c31			15 45			16 15			
	d	13 45				14 15				14 45				15 15					15 45			16 15			
High Street	d	13 47				14 17				14 47				15 17					15 47			16 17			
Bellgrove	d	13 49				14 19				14 49				15 19					15 49			16 19			
Duke Street	d																								
Alexandra Parade	d																								
Barnhill	d																								
Springburn	a																								
Carntyne	d	13 53				14 23				14 53				15 23					15 53			16 23			
Shettleston	d	13 55				14 25				14 55				15 25					15 55			16 25			
Garrowhill	d	13 58				14 28				14 58				15 28					15 58			16 28			
Easterhouse	d	14 00				14 30				15 00				15 30					16 00			16 30			
Blairhill	d	14 04				14 34				15 04				15 34					16 04			16 34			
Coatbridge Sunnyside	d	14 07				14 37				15 07				15 37					16 07			16 37			
Coatdyke	d	14 09				14 39				15 09				15 39					16 09			16 39			
Airdrie	d	14 12				14 42				15 12				15 42					16 12			16 42			
Drumgelloch	d	14 15				14 45				15 15				15 45					16 15			16 45			
Caldercruix	d	14 19				14 49				15 19				15 49					16 19			16 49			
Blackridge	d	14 25				14 55				15 25				15 55					16 25			16 55			
Armadale	d	14 29				14 59				15 29				15 59					16 29			16 59			
Bathgate	a	14 33				15 03				15 33				16 03					16 33			17 03			
	d	14 34				15 04				15 34				16 04					16 34			17 04			
Livingston North	d	14 38				15 09				15 38				16 09					16 38			17 09			
Uphall	d	14 41				15 12				15 41				16 12					16 41			17 12			
Edinburgh Park	a	14 49				15 20				15 49				16 20					16 50			17 20			
Haymarket	a	14 54				15 24				15 54				16 24					16 54			17 24			
Edinburgh	a	14 59				15 29				15 59				16 29					16 59			17 29			
Bridgeton	d			13 59	14 09		14 29	14 39			14 59	15 09			15 29		15 39			15 59	16 09			16 29	16 39
Dalmarnock	d																								
Rutherglen	d			14 05	14 12		14 32	14 43	14 47		15 03	15 14			15 32		15 42	15 50		16 03	16 12			16 32	16 44
Cambuslang	d			14 09	14 16		14 36	14 47			15 07	15 18			15 36		15 46			16 07	16 16			16 36	16 50
Newton	d			14 12			14 39				15 10				15 39					16 11				16 39	
Blantyre	d			14 16			14 43		14 56		15 14				15 43			15 58		16 15				16 43	
Hamilton West	d			14 19			14 46		14 59		15 17				15 46			16 02		16 18				16 46	
Hamilton Central	d			14 23			14 50		15 02		15 21				15 50			16 05		16 21				16 50	
Chatelherault	d								15 06									16 08							
Merryton	d								15 09									16 11							
Larkhall	a								15 12									16 14							
Airbles	d			14 28			14 55				15 26				15 55					16 26				16 55	
Uddingston	d				14 20			14 52				15 22					15 51				16 20				16 54
Bellshill	d				14 25			14 56				15 27					15 55				16 25				16 59
Motherwell	a			14 30	14 33		14 57	15 04			15 28	15 33			15 57		16 03			16 28	16 33			16 57	17 05
	d				14 33							15 34									16 33				
Whifflet	a																								
Coatbridge Central	a																								
Shieldmuir	d				14 37							15 37									16 37				
Holytown	d																								
Wishaw	d				14 40							15 41									16 40				
Carluke	d				14 47							15 47									16 47				
Lanark	a				14 59							15 59									16 59				

A From Mallaig b Helensburgh Upper c Glasgow Queen St High Level

Table 226

Sundays
26 June to 30 October

Helensburgh, Balloch, Dalmuir and Milngavie - Glasgow - Springburn, Airdrie, Bathgate and Edinburgh, Hamilton, Larkhall, Motherwell, Coatbridge and Lanark

		SR	SR	SR	SR	SR	SR	SR		SR	SR	SR	SR	SR	SR	SR	SR	SR		SR	SR	SR	SR ◇ A	SR	SR
Helensburgh Central	d		15 55			16 25					16 55			17 25				17 55				18 25	18b33		
Craigendoran	d		15 58			16 28					16 58			17 28				17 58				18 28			
Cardross	d		16 03			16 33					17 03			17 33				18 03				18 33			
Balloch	d			16 09			16 39					17 09			17 39					18 09				18 39	
Alexandria	d			16 11			16 41					17 11			17 41					18 11				18 41	
Renton	d			16 14			16 44					17 14			17 44					18 14				18 44	
Dalreoch	d		16 08	16 17		16 38	16 47				17 08	17 17		17 38	17 47			18 08		18 17		18 38		18 48	
Dumbarton Central	d		16 10	16 18		16 40	16 48				17 10	17 18		17 40	17 48			18 10		18 18		18 40	18 47	18 49	
Dumbarton East	d		16 12	16 20		16 42	16 50				17 12	17 20		17 42	17 50			18 12		18 20		18 42		18 51	
Bowling	d			16 25			16 55					17 25			17 55					18 25				18 56	
Kilpatrick	d			16 28			16 58					17 28			17 58					18 28				18 59	
Dalmuir	a		16 19	16 31		16 49	17 01				17 19	17 31		17 49	18 01			18 19		18 31		18 49	18 56	19 02	
	d		16 20	16 31		16 50	17 01				17 20	17 31		17 50	18 01			18 20		18 31		18 50	18 56	19 02	
Singer	d		16 22			16 52					17 22			17 52				18 22				18 52			
Drumry	d		16 25			16 55					17 25			17 55				18 25				18 55			
Drumchapel	d		16 27			16 57					17 27			17 57				18 27				18 57			
Milngavie	d				16 41			17 11					17 41			18 11					18 41				19 11
Hillfoot	d				16 44			17 14					17 44			18 14					18 44				19 14
Bearsden	d				16 46			17 16					17 46			18 16					18 46				19 16
Westerton	d		16 30		16 49	17 00		17 19			17 30		17 49	18 00		18 19		18 30			18 49	19 00			19 19
Anniesland	d		16 33		16 52	17 03		17 22			17 33		17 52	18 03		18 22		18 33			18 52	19 03			19 22
Clydebank	d			16 33			17 03					17 33			18 03					18 33				19 03	
Yoker	d			16 35			17 05					17 35			18 05					18 35				19 05	
Garscadden	d			16 39			17 09					17 39			18 09					18 39				19 10	
Scotstounhill	d			16 41			17 11					17 41			18 11					18 41				19 12	
Jordanhill	d			16 43			17 13					17 43			18 13					18 43				19 13	
Hyndland	d		16 35	16 45	16 55	17 05	17 15	17 25			17 35	17 45	17 55	18 05	18 15	18 25		18 35		18 45	18 55	19 05		19 15	19 25
Partick	d	16 34	16 38	16 48	16 58	17 08	17 18	17 28		17 34	17 38	17 48	17 58	18 08	18 18	18 28	18 34	18 38		18 48	18 58	19 08		19 18	19 28
Exhibition Centre	d	16 37		16 51	17 01		17 21	17 31		17 37		17 51	18 01		18 21	18 31	18 37			18 51	19 01			19 21	19 31
Anderston	d																								
Glasgow Central LL	a	16 39		16 53	17 03		17 23	17 33		17 39		17 53	18 03		18 23	18 33	18 39			18 53	19 03			19 24	19 33
	d	16 40		16 54	17 04		17 24	17 34		17 40		17 54	18 04		18 24	18 34	18 40			18 54	19 04			19 24	19 34
Argyle Street	d	16 46		16 56	17 06		17 26	17 36		17 41		17 56	18 06												
Charing Cross	d		16 43			17 13					17 43			18 13				18 43				19 13			
Glasgow Queen St LL	a		16 45			17 15					17 45			18 15				18 45				19 15	19c15		
	d		16 45			17 15					17 45			18 15				18 45				19 15			
High Street	d		16 47			17 17					17 47			18 17				18 47				19 17			
Bellgrove	d		16 49			17 19					17 49			18 19				18 49				19 19			
Duke Street	d																								
Alexandra Parade	d																								
Barnhill	d																								
Springburn	a																								
Carntyne	d		16 53			17 23					17 53			18 23				18 53				19 23			
Shettleston	d		16 55			17 25					17 55			18 25				18 55				19 25			
Garrowhill	d		16 58			17 28					17 58			18 28				18 58				19 28			
Easterhouse	d		17 00			17 30					18 00			18 30				19 00				19 30			
Blairhill	d		17 04			17 34					18 04			18 34				19 04				19 34			
Coatbridge Sunnyside	d		17 07			17 37					18 07			18 37				19 07				19 37			
Coatdyke	d		17 09			17 39					18 09			18 39				19 09				19 39			
Airdrie	d		17 12			17 42					18 12			18 42				19 12				19a42			
Drumgelloch	d		17 15			17 45					18 15			18 45				19 15							
Caldercruix	d		17 19			17 49					18 19			18 49				19 19							
Blackridge	d		17 25			17 55					18 25			18 55				19 25							
Armadale	d		17 29			17 59					18 29			18 59				19 29							
Bathgate	a		17 33			18 03					18 33			19 03				19 33							
	d		17 34			18 04					18 34			19 04				19 34							
Livingston North	d		17 38			18 09					18 38			19 09				19 38							
Uphall	d		17 41			18 12					18 41			19 12				19 41							
Edinburgh Park	a		17 49			18 20					18 49			19 20				19 49							
Haymarket	a		17 58			18 24					18 54			19 24				19 54							
Edinburgh	a		18 03			18 30					18 59			19 29				19 59							
Bridgeton	d			16 59	17 09		17 29	17 39				17 59	18 09		18 29	18 39				18 59	19 09			19 29	19 37
Dalmarnock	d																								
Rutherglen	d	16 51		17 03	17 13		17 32	17 42		17 46		18 02	18 12		18 32	18 42	18 47			19 03	19 12			19 32	19 40
Cambuslang	d			17 07	17 17		17 36	17 46				18 06	18 16		18 36	18 46				19 07	19 16			19 36	19 44
Newton	d			17 10			17 39					18 09			18 39					19 10				19 39	
Blantyre	d	16 59		17 14			17 43			17 56		18 13			18 43		18 57			19 14				19 43	
Hamilton West	d	17 02		17 17			17 46			17 59		18 16			18 46		19 00			19 17				19 46	
Hamilton Central	d	17 04		17 20			17 50			18 02		18 20			18 50		19 02			19 20				19 50	
Chatelherault	d	17 08								18 05							19 06								
Merryton	d	17 11								18 08							19 09								
Larkhall	a	17 14								18 12							19 12								
Airbles	d			17 25			17 55					18 25			18 55					19 25				19 55	
Uddingston	d				17 21			17 50					18 20			18 50					19 20				19 49
Bellshill	d				17 26			17 55					18 25			18 55					19 25				19 55
Motherwell	a			17 27	17 33		17 57	18 02				18 27	18 33		18 57	19 03				19 27	19 33			19 57	20 03
	d				17 33								18 33								19 33				
Whifflet	a																								
Coatbridge Central	a																								
Shieldmuir	d				17 37								18 37								19 37				
Holytown	d																								
Wishaw	d				17 40								18 40								19 40				
Carluke	d				17 47								18 47								19 47				
Lanark	a				17 59								18 59								19 59				

A from 26 June until 25 September. From Oban b Helensburgh Upper c Glasgow Queen St High Level

Helensburgh, Balloch, Dalmuir and Milngavie - Glasgow - Springburn, Airdrie, Bathgate and Edinburgh, Hamilton, Larkhall, Motherwell, Coatbridge and Lanark

		SR	SR	SR	SR	SR	SR	SR	SR	SR	SR	SR	SR	SR	SR	SR	SR	SR	SR	SR	SR	SR
							◇ A									◇ B ✕						
Helensburgh Central	d		18 55			19 25	19b29				19 55			20 25		20b40			20 55			21 25
Craigendoran	d		18 58			19 28					19 58			20 28					20 58			21 28
Cardross	d		19 03			19 33					20 03			20 33					21 03			21 33
Balloch	d			19 09				19 39				20 09			20 38					21 09		
Alexandria	d			19 11				19 41				20 11			20 40					21 11		
Renton	d			19 14				19 44				20 14			20 43					21 14		
Dalreoch	d		19 08	19 17		19 38		19 47			20 08	20 17		20 38	20 46				21 08	21 17		21 38
Dumbarton Central	d		19 10	19 18		19 40		19 48			20 10	20 18		20 40	20 47	20 53			21 10	21 18		21 40
Dumbarton East	d		19 12	19 20		19 42		19 50			20 12	20 20		20 42	20 49				21 12	21 20		21 42
Bowling	d			19 25				19 55				20 25			20 54					21 25		
Kilpatrick	d			19 28				19 58				20 28			20 57					21 28		
Dalmuir	a		19 20	19 31		19 49	19s55	20 01			20 19	20 31		20 49	21 00	21 03			21 19	21 31		21 49
	d		19 20	19 31		19 50		20 01			20 20	20 31		20 50	21 01	21 03			21 20	21 31		21 50
Singer	d		19 22			19 52					20 22			20 52					21 22			21 52
Drumry	d		19 25			19 55					20 25			20 55					21 25			21 55
Drumchapel	d		19 27			19 57					20 27			20 57					21 27			21 57
Milngavie	d				19 41				20 11				20 41				21 11				21 41	
Hillfoot	d				19 44				20 14				20 44				21 14				21 44	
Bearsden	d				19 46				20 16				20 46				21 16				21 46	
Westerton	d		19 30		19 49	20 00			20 19		20 30		20 49	21 00			21 19		21 30		21 49	22 00
Anniesland	d		19 33		19 52	20 03			20 22		20 33		20 52	21 03			21 22		21 33		21 52	22 03
Clydebank	d			19 33				20 03				20 33			21 03					21 33		
Yoker	d			19 35				20 05				20 35			21 05					21 35		
Garscadden	d			19 39				20 09				20 39			21 09					21 39		
Scotstounhill	d			19 41				20 11				20 41			21 11					21 41		
Jordanhill	d			19 43				20 13				20 43			21 13					21 43		
Hyndland	d		19 35	19 45	19 55	20 05		20 15	20 25		20 35	20 45	20 55	21 05	21 15		21 25		21 35	21 45	21 55	22 05
Partick	d	19 34	19 38	19 48	19 58	20 08		20 18	20 28	20 34	20 38	20 48	20 58	21 08	21 18		21 28	21 34	21 38	21 48	21 58	22 08
Exhibition Centre	d	19 37		19 51	20 01			20 21	20 31	20 37		20 51	21 01		21 21		21 31	21 37		21 51	22 01	
Anderston	d																					
Glasgow Central LL 15	a	19 39		19 53	20 03			20 23	20 33	20 39		20 53	21 03		21 23		21 33	21 39		21 53	22 03	
	d	19 40		19 54	20 04			20 24	20 34	20 40		20 54	21 04		21 24		21 34	21 40		21 54	22 04	
Argyle Street	d																					
Charing Cross	d		19 43			20 13					20 43			21 13					21 43			22 13
Glasgow Queen St LL 10	a		19 45			20 15					20 45			21 15		21c19			21 45			22 15
	d		19 45			20 15					20 45			21 15					21 45			22 15
High Street	d		19 47			20 17					20 47			21 17					21 47			22 17
Bellgrove	d		19 49			20 19					20 49			21 19					21 49			22 19
Duke Street	d																					
Alexandra Parade	d																					
Barnhill	d																					
Springburn	a																					
Carntyne	d		19 53			20 23					20 53			21 23					21 53			22 23
Shettleston	d		19 55			20 25					20 55			21 25					21 55			22 25
Garrowhill	d		19 58			20 28					20 58			21 28					21 58			22 28
Easterhouse	d		20 00			20 30					21 00			21 30					22 00			22 30
Blairhill	d		20 04			20 34					21 04			21 34					22 04			22 34
Coatbridge Sunnyside	d		20 07			20 37					21 07			21 37					22 07			22 37
Coatdyke	d		20 09			20 39					21 09			21 39					22 09			22 39
Airdrie	d		20 12			20a42					21 12			21a42					22 12			22a42
Drumgelloch	d		20 15								21 15								22 15			
Caldercruix	d		20 19								21 19								22 19			
Blackridge	d		20 25								21 25								22 25			
Armadale	d		20 29								21 29								22 29			
Bathgate	a		20 33								21 33								22 33			
	d		20 34								21 34								22 34			
Livingston North	d		20 38								21 39								22 39			
Uphall	d		20 41								21 42								22 42			
Edinburgh Park	a		20 49								21 50								22 50			
Haymarket	a		20 54				21s03				21 54								22 55			
Edinburgh	a		20 59				21 09				21 59								23 00			
Bridgeton	d			19 59	20 09			20 29	20 37			20 57	21 09		21 29		21 37			21 59	22 08	
Dalmarnock	d																					
Rutherglen	d	19 46		20 02	20 14			20 32	20 40	20 46		21 00	21 12		21 32		21 40	21 47		22 02	22 11	
Cambuslang	d			20 06	20 18			20 36	20 44			21 04	21 16		21 36		21 44			22 06	22 15	
Newton	d			20 09				20 39				21 08			21 39					22 09		
Blantyre	d	19 56		20 13				20 43		20 54		21 13			21 43			21 54		22 13		
Hamilton West	d	19 59		20 16				20 46		20 58		21 16			21 46			21 57		22 16		
Hamilton Central	d	20 02		20 20				20 50		21 02		21 20			21 50			22 01		22 20		
Chatelherault	d	20 05								21 05								22 04				
Merryton	d	20 08								21 08								22 07				
Larkhall	a	20 12								21 13								22 12				
Airbles	d			20 25				20 55				21 25			21 55					22 25		
Uddingston	d				20 22				20 49				21 20				21 49				22 19	
Bellshill	d				20 27				20 55				21 25				21 55				22 24	
Motherwell	a			20 27	20 33			20 57	21 04			21 27	21 33		21 57		22 03			22 27	22 32	
	d				20 33								21 33								22 32	
Whifflet	a																					
Coatbridge Central	a																					
Shieldmuir	d				20 37								21 37								22 36	
Holytown	d																					
Wishaw	d				20 40								21 40								22 39	
Carluke	d				20 47								21 47								22 44	
Lanark	a				20 59								21 59								22 58	

A from 26 June until 28 August. From Oban
B From Mallaig
b Helensburgh Upper
c Glasgow Queen St High Level

Helensburgh, Balloch, Dalmuir and Milngavie - Glasgow - Springburn, Airdrie, Bathgate and Edinburgh, Hamilton, Larkhall, Motherwell, Coatbridge and Lanark

		SR	SR	SR	SR	SR	SR	SR	SR	SR	SR
										A	
Helensburgh Central	d				21 55			22 25		22b37	
Craigendoran	d				21 58			22 28			
Cardross	d				22 03			22 33			
Balloch	d	21 39				22 09			22 39		23 09
Alexandria	d	21 41				22 11			22 41		23 11
Renton	d	21 44				22 14			22 44		23 14
Dalreoch	d	21 47			22 08	22 17		22 38	22 47		23 17
Dumbarton Central	d	21 48			22 10	22 18		22 40	22 48		23 18
Dumbarton East	d	21 50			22 12	22 20		22 42	22 50		23 20
Bowling	d	21 55				22 25			22 55		23 25
Kilpatrick	d	21 58				22 28			22 58		23 28
Dalmuir	a	22 01			22 19	22 31		22 49	23 01	23 02	23 31
	d	22 01			22 20	22 31		22 50	23 01	23 04	23 31
Singer	d				22 22			22 52			
Drumry	d				22 25			22 55			
Drumchapel	d				22 27			22 57			
Milngavie	d		22 11				22 41				
Hillfoot	d		22 14				22 44				
Bearsden	d		22 16				22 46				
Westerton	d		22 19		22 30		22 49	23 00		23 13	
Anniesland	d		22 22		22 33		22 52	23 03			
Clydebank	d	22 03				22 33			23 03		23 33
Yoker	d	22 05				22 35			23a05		23a35
Garscadden	d	22 09				22 39					
Scotstounhill	d	22 11				22 41					
Jordanhill	d	22 13				22 43					
Hyndland	d	22 15	22 25		22 35	22 45	22 55	23 05			
Partick	d	22 18	22 28	22 34	22 38	22 48	22 58	23 08			
Exhibition Centre	d	22 21	22 31	22 37		22 51	23 01				
Anderston	d										
Glasgow Central LL 15	a	22 23	22 33	22 39		22 53	23 03				
	d	22 24	22 34	22 40		22 54	23 04				
Argyle Street	d										
Charing Cross	d				22 43			23 13			
Glasgow Queen St LL 10	a				22 45			23 15			
	d				22 45			23 15			
High Street	d				22 47			23 17			
Bellgrove	d				22 49			23 19			
Duke Street	d										
Alexandra Parade	d										
Barnhill	d										
Springburn	a										
Carntyne	d				22 53			23 23			
Shettleston	d				22 55			23 25			
Garrowhill	d				22 58			23 28			
Easterhouse	d				23 00			23 30			
Blairhill	d				23 04			23 34			
Coatbridge Sunnyside	d				23 07			23 37			
Coatdyke	d				23 09			23 39			
Airdrie	d				23 12			23a42			
Drumgelloch	d				23 15						
Caldercruix	d				23 19						
Blackridge	d				23 25						
Armadale	d				23 29						
Bathgate	a				23 33						
	d										
Livingston North	d										
Uphall	d										
Edinburgh Park	a										
Haymarket	a										
Edinburgh	a									00 13	
Bridgeton	d	22 29	22 39			22 59	23 09				
Dalmarnock	d										
Rutherglen	d	22 32	22 42	22 47		23 02	23 12				
Cambuslang	d	22 36	22 46			23 06	23 16				
Newton	d	22 39				23 09					
Blantyre	d	22 43		22 55		23 13					
Hamilton West	d	22 46		22 58		23 16					
Hamilton Central	d	22 50		23 02		23 20					
Chatelherault	d			23 05							
Merryton	d			23 08							
Larkhall	a			23 11							
Airbles	d	22 55				23 25					
Uddingston	d		22 50				23 20				
Bellshill	d		22 55				23 25				
Motherwell	a	22 57	23 03			23 27	23 33				
	d										
Whifflet	a										
Coatbridge Central	a										
Shieldmuir	d										
Holytown	d										
Wishaw	d										
Carluke	d										
Lanark	a										

A From Fort William
b Helensburgh Upper

Table 226

Sundays
6 November to 27 November

Helensburgh, Balloch, Dalmuir and Milngavie - Glasgow - Springburn, Airdrie, Bathgate and Edinburgh, Hamilton, Larkhall, Motherwell, Coatbridge and Lanark

		SR	SR	SR	SR	SR	SR	SR	SR	SR	SR	SR	SR A	SR	SR B	SR	SR B	SR	SR	SR	SR B	SR	SR B
Helensburgh Central	d		22p40		23p10				07 55			08 25							08 55				
Craigendoran	d		22p43		23p13				07 58			08 28							08 58				
Cardross	d		22p48		23p18				08 03			08 33							09 03				
Balloch	d			22p53						08 09				08 39						09 09			
Alexandria	d			22p55						08 11				08 41						09 11			
Renton	d			22p58						08 14				08 44						09 14			
Dalreoch	d		22p53	23p01	23p23				08 08	08 17		08 38		08 47					09 08	09 17			
Dumbarton Central	d		22p55	23p02	23p25				08 10	08 18		08 40		08 48					09 10	09 18			
Dumbarton East	d		22p57	23p04	23p27				08 12	08 20		08 42		08 50					09 12	09 20			
Bowling	d			23p09						08 25				08 55						09 25			
Kilpatrick	d			23p12						08 28				08 58						09 28			
Dalmuir	a		23p05	23p15	23p35				08 19	08 31		08 49		09 01					09 19	09 31			
	d	23p01	23p05	23p16	23p35		07 40	08 01	08 20	08 31		08 50		09 01	09 05		09 15		09 20	09 31	09 35		09 45
Singer	d	23p03		23p18			07 42		08 22			08 52			09 07				09 22		09 37		
Drumry	d	23p05		23p20			07 45		08 25			08 55			09 09				09 25		09 39		
Drumchapel	d	23p08		23p23			07 47		08 27			08 57			09 12				09 27		09 42		
Milngavie	d															09 11						09 41	
Hillfoot	d															09 14						09 44	
Bearsden	d															09 16						09 46	
Westerton	d	23p10		23p25			07 50		08 30			09 00			09 14	09 19			09 30		09 44	09 49	
Anniesland	d	23p14		23p28			07 53		08 33			09 03			09 17	09 22			09 33		09 47	09 52	
Clydebank	d		23p07		23p37			08 03		08 33				09 03			09 17			09 33			09 47
Yoker	d		23p09		23p39			08 05		08 35				09 05			09 19			09 35			09 49
Garscadden	d		23p13		23p43			08 09		08 39				09 09			09 22			09 39			09 52
Scotstounhill	d		23p15		23p45			08 11		08 41				09 11			09 24			09 41			09 54
Jordanhill	d		23p17		23p47			08 13		08 43				09 13			09 26			09 43			09 56
Hyndland	d	23p17	23p21	23p31	23p49		07 55	08 15	08 35	08 45	08 55	09 05		09 15	09 20	09 25	09 28		09 35	09 45	09 50	09 55	09 59
Partick	d	23p20	23p23	23p34	23p52		07 58	08 18	08 38	08 48	08 58	09 08		09 18	09 22	09 28	09 30	09 34	09 38	09 48	09 52	09 58	10 01
Exhibition Centre	d	23p23						08 21		08 51	09 01			09 21		09 31		09 37		09 51		10 01	
Anderston	d	23p25																					
Glasgow Central LL	a	23p26						08 23		08 53	09 03			09 23		09 33		09 39		09 53		10 03	
	d	23p27						08 24		08 54	09 04		09b22	09 24		09 34		09 40		09 54		10 04	
Argyle Street	d	23p29																		09 55		10 06	
Charing Cross	d		23p27	23p38	23p56		08 03		08 43			09 13			09 26		09 34		09 43		09 56		10 05
Glasgow Queen St LL	a		23p29	23p40	23p59		08 05		08 45			09 15			09 28		09 36		09 45		09 58		10 07
	d		23p30	23p44	23p59		08 05		08 45			09 15			09 29		09 37		09 45		09 59		10 07
High Street	d		23p32	23p46	00 02		08 07		08 47			09 17			09 31		09 39		09 47		10 01		10 09
Bellgrove	d		23p34	23p49	00 04		08 09		08 49			09 19			09 33		09 41		09 49		10 03		10 11
Duke Street	d														09 35						10 05		
Alexandra Parade	d														09 36						10 06		
Barnhill	d														09 39						10 09		
Springburn	a														09 41						10 11		
Carntyne	d		23p37	23p52	00 07		08 13		08 53			09 23					09 44		09 53				10 15
Shettleston	d		23p40	23p55	00 10		08 15		08 55			09 25					09 47		09 55				10 17
Garrowhill	d		23p42	23p57	00 12		08 18		08 58			09 28					09 49		09 58				10 20
Easterhouse	d		23p45	23p59	00 15		08 20		09 00			09 30					09 52		10 00				10 22
Blairhill	d		23p49	00 04	00 19		08 24		09 04			09 34					09 56		10 04				10 26
Coatbridge Sunnyside	d		23p51	00 06	00 21		08 27		09 07			09 37					09 58		10 07				10 29
Coatdyke	d		23p54	00 09	00 24		08 29		09 09			09 39					10 01		10 09				10 31
Airdrie	d		23p57	00a12	00a27		08 32		09 12			09a42					10a04		10 12				10a34
Drumgelloch	d		23p59				08 35		09 15										10 15				
Caldercruix	d		00 03				08 39		09 19										10 19				
Blackridge	d		00 09				08 45		09 25										10 25				
Armadale	d		00 13				08 49		09 29										10 29				
Bathgate	a		00 17				08 53		09 33										10 33				
	d					07 55	08 54		09 34										10 34				
Livingston North	d					07 59	08 59		09 39										10 38				
Uphall	d					08 02	09 02		09 42										10 41				
Edinburgh Park	a					08 10	09 10		09 52										10 49				
Haymarket	a					08 20	09 20		10 02										10 55				
Edinburgh	a					08 25	09 25		10 07										11 00				
Bridgeton	d							08 29		08 59	09 09			09 29		09 39				09 58		10 09	
Dalmarnock	d																						
Rutherglen	d	23p34						08 32		09 02	09 12			09 32		09 42		09 47		10 01		10 12	
Cambuslang	d							08 36		09 06	09 16			09 36		09 48				10 04		10 16	
Newton	d									09 09				09 39						10 09			
Blantyre	d	23p44								09 13				09 43				09 57		10 13			
Hamilton West	d	23p47								09 16				09 46				10 00		10 16			
Hamilton Central	d	23p50								09 20				09 50				10 03		10 20			
Chatelherault	d	23p53																10 06					
Merryton	d	23p56																10 09					
Larkhall	a	00 01																10 12					
Airbles	d									09 25				09 55						10 25			
Uddingston	d							08 40			09 20					09 53						10 20	
Bellshill	d							08 45			09 25					09 57						10 25	
Motherwell	a							08 53		09 27	09 33			09 57		10 03				10 27		10 33	
	d										09 33											10 33	
Whifflet	a												09 50										
Coatbridge Central	a																						
Shieldmuir	d										09 37											10 37	
Holytown	d												09a59										
Wishaw	d										09 40											10 40	
Carluke	d										09 47											10 47	
Lanark	a										09 59											10 59	

A 27 November. To Shotts   B 27 November   b Glasgow Central High Level

Table 226

Sundays
6 November to 27 November

Helensburgh, Balloch, Dalmuir and Milngavie - Glasgow - Springburn, Airdrie, Bathgate and Edinburgh, Hamilton, Larkhall, Motherwell, Coatbridge and Lanark

		SR	SR	SR A	SR	SR B	SR	SR B	SR	SR	SR	SR B	SR	SR B	SR	SR	SR A	SR	SR B	SR	SR B	SR	SR
Helensburgh Central	d	09 25								09 55					10 25								10 55
Craigendoran	d	09 28								09 58					10 28								10 58
Cardross	d	09 33								10 03					10 33								11 03
Balloch	d				09 39						10 09							10 39					
Alexandria	d				09 41						10 11							10 41					
Renton	d				09 44						10 14							10 44					
Dalreoch	d	09 38			09 47					10 08	10 17				10 38			10 47					11 08
Dumbarton Central	d	09 40			09 48					10 10	10 18				10 40			10 48					11 10
Dumbarton East	d	09 42			09 50					10 12	10 20				10 42			10 50					11 12
Bowling	d				09 55						10 25							10 55					
Kilpatrick	d				09 58						10 28							10 58					
Dalmuir	a	09 49			10 01					10 19	10 31				10 49			11 01					11 19
	d	09 50			10 01	10 05		10 15		10 20	10 31	10 35		10 45	10 50			11 01	11 05		11 15		11 20
Singer	d	09 52				10 07				10 22		10 37			10 52				11 07				11 22
Drumry	d	09 55				10 09				10 25		10 39			10 55				11 09				11 25
Drumchapel	d	09 57				10 12				10 27		10 42			10 57				11 12				11 27
Milngavie	d						10 11						10 41							11 11			
Hillfoot	d						10 14						10 44							11 14			
Bearsden	d						10 16						10 46							11 16			
Westerton	d	10 00				10 14	10 19			10 30		10 44	10 49		11 00				11 14	11 19			11 30
Anniesland	d	10 03				10 17	10 22			10 33		10 47	10 52		11 03				11 17	11 22			11 33
Clydebank	d				10 03			10 17			10 33			10 47				11 03			11 17		
Yoker	d				10 05			10 19			10 35			10 49				11 05			11 19		
Garscadden	d				10 09			10 22			10 39			10 52				11 09			11 22		
Scotstounhill	d				10 11			10 24			10 41			10 54				11 11			11 24		
Jordanhill	d				10 13			10 26			10 43			10 56				11 13			11 26		
Hyndland	d	10 05			10 15	10 20	10 25	10 28		10 35	10 45	10 50	10 55	10 59	11 05			11 15	11 20	11 25	11 28		11 35
Partick	d	10 08			10 18	10 22	10 28	10 30	10 34	10 38	10 48	10 52	10 58	11 01	11 08			11 18	11 22	11 28	11 30	11 34	11 38
Exhibition Centre	d				10 21		10 31		10 37		10 51		11 01					11 21		11 31		11 37	
Anderston	d																						
Glasgow Central LL	a				10 23		10 33		10 39		10 53		11 03					11 23		11 33		11 39	
	d			10b22	10 23		10 34		10 40		10 54		11 04				11b22	11 24		11 34		11 40	
Argyle Street	d				10 25		10 36		10 42		10 56		11 06					11 26		11 36		11 42	
Charing Cross	d	10 13				10 26		10 35		10 43		10 56		11 05	11 13				11 26		11 34		11 43
Glasgow Queen St LL	a	10 15				10 28		10 37		10 45		10 58		11 07	11 15				11 28		11 36		11 45
	d	10 15				10 29		10 37		10 45		10 59		11 07	11 15				11 29		11 37		11 45
High Street	d	10 17				10 31		10 39		10 47		11 01		11 09	11 17				11 31		11 39		11 47
Bellgrove	d	10 19				10 33		10 41		10 49		11 03		11 11	11 19				11 33		11 41		11 49
Duke Street	d					10 35						11 05							11 35				
Alexandra Parade	d					10 36						11 06							11 36				
Barnhill	d					10 39						11 09							11 39				
Springburn	a					10 41						11 11							11 41				
Carntyne	d	10 23						10 45		10 53				11 15	11 23						11 44		11 53
Shettleston	d	10 25						10 47		10 55				11 17	11 25						11 47		11 55
Garrowhill	d	10 28						10 50		10 58				11 20	11 28						11 49		11 58
Easterhouse	d	10 30						10 52		11 00				11 22	11 30						11 52		12 00
Blairhill	d	10 34						10 56		11 04				11 26	11 34						11 56		12 04
Coatbridge Sunnyside	d	10 37						10 59		11 07				11 29	11 37						11 58		12 07
Coatdyke	d	10 39						11 01		11 09				11 31	11 39						12 01		12 09
Airdrie	d	10a42						11a04		11 12				11a34	11a42						12a04		12 12
Drumgelloch	d									11 15													12 15
Caldercruix	d									11 19													12 19
Blackridge	d									11 25													12 25
Armadale	d									11 29													12 29
Bathgate	a									11 33													12 33
	d		11 05							11 34						12 05							12 34
Livingston North	d		11 09							11 38						12 09							12 38
Uphall	d		11 12							11 41						12 12							12 41
Edinburgh Park	a		11 20							11 49						12 20							12 49
Haymarket	a		11 25							11 54						12 25							12 54
Edinburgh	a		11 30							11 59						12 30							12 59
Bridgeton	d				10 28		10 39				10 59		11 09					11 29		11 39			
Dalmarnock	d																						
Rutherglen	d				10 30		10 42		10 45		11 02		11 12					11 31		11 44		11 47	
Cambuslang	d				10 34		10 46				11 06		11 16					11 35		11 48			
Newton	d				10 38						11 09							11 39					
Blantyre	d				10 42				10 57		11 13							11 43				11 55	
Hamilton West	d				10 46				11 00		11 16							11 46				11 58	
Hamilton Central	d				10 50				11 03		11 20							11 50				12 01	
Chatelherault	d								11 06													12 05	
Merryton	d								11 09													12 08	
Larkhall	a								11 12													12 13	
Airbles	d				10 55						11 25							11 55					
Uddingston	d						10 50						11 20							11 53			
Bellshill	d						10 55						11 25							11 57			
Motherwell	a				10 57		11 03				11 27		11 33					11 57		12 03			
	d												11 33										
Whifflet	a			10 50													11 50						
Coatbridge Central	a																						
Shieldmuir	d												11 37										
Holytown	d			10a59													11a59						
Wishaw	d												11 40										
Carluke	d												11 47										
Lanark	a												11 59										

A 27 November. To Shotts   B 27 November

Helensburgh, Balloch, Dalmuir and Milngavie - Glasgow - Springburn, Airdrie, Bathgate and Edinburgh, Hamilton, Larkhall, Motherwell, Coatbridge and Lanark

		SR	SR A	SR	SR A	SR	SR	SR A	SR B	SR	SR A	SR	SR	SR	SR A	SR	SR A	SR	SR B	SR	SR A	SR
Helensburgh Central	d					11 25							11 55					12 25				
Craigendoran	d					11 28							11 58					12 28				
Cardross	d					11 33							12 03					12 33				
Balloch	d	11 09					11 39							12 09						12 39		
Alexandria	d	11 11					11 41							12 11						12 41		
Renton	d	11 14					11 44							12 14						12 44		
Dalreoch	d	11 17				11 38	11 47						12 08	12 17				12 38		12 47		
Dumbarton Central	d	11 18				11 40	11 48						12 10	12 18				12 40		12 48		
Dumbarton East	d	11 20				11 42	11 50						12 12	12 20				12 42		12 50		
Bowling	d	11 25					11 55							12 25						12 55		
Kilpatrick	d	11 28					11 58							12 28						12 58		
Dalmuir	a	11 31				11 49	12 01						12 19	12 31				12 49		13 01		
	d	11 31	11 35		11 45	11 50	12 01	12 05			12 15		12 20	12 31	12 35		12 45	12 50		13 01	13 05	
Singer	d		11 37			11 52		12 07					12 22		12 37			12 52			13 07	
Drumry	d		11 39			11 55		12 09					12 25		12 39			12 55			13 09	
Drumchapel	d		11 42			11 57		12 12					12 27		12 42			12 57			13 12	
Milngavie	d			11 41						12 11						12 41						13 11
Hillfoot	d			11 44						12 14						12 44						13 14
Bearsden	d			11 46						12 16						12 46						13 16
Westerton	d		11 44	11 49		12 00		12 14		12 19			12 30		12 44	12 49		13 00			13 14	13 19
Anniesland	d		11 47	11 52		12 03		12 17		12 22			12 33		12 47	12 52		13 03			13 17	13 22
Clydebank	d	11 33			11 47		12 03				12 17			12 33			12 47			13 03		
Yoker	d	11 35			11 49		12 05				12 19			12 35			12 49			13 05		
Garscadden	d	11 39			11 52		12 09				12 22			12 39			12 52			13 09		
Scotstounhill	d	11 41			11 54		12 11				12 24			12 41			12 54			13 11		
Jordanhill	d	11 43			11 56		12 13				12 26			12 43			12 56			13 13		
Hyndland	d	11 45	11 50	11 55	11 59	12 05	12 15	12 20		12 25	12 28		12 35	12 45	12 50	12 55	12 58	13 05		13 15	13 20	13 25
Partick	d	11 48	11 52	11 58	12 01	12 08	12 18	12 22		12 28	12 30	12 34	12 38	12 48	12 52	12 58	13 00	13 08		13 18	13 22	13 28
Exhibition Centre	d	11 51		12 01			12 21			12 31		12 37		12 51		13 01				13 21		13 31
Anderston	d																					
Glasgow Central LL	a	11 53		12 03			12 23			12 33		12 39		12 53		13 03				13 23		13 33
	d	11 54		12 04			12 24		12b24	12 34		12 40		12 54		13 04			13b22	13 24		13 34
Argyle Street	d	11 56		12 06			12 25			12 36		12 41		12 56		13 06				13 26		13 36
Charing Cross	d		11 56		12 05	12 13		12 26			12 34		12 43		12 56		13 04	13 13			13 26	
Glasgow Queen St LL	a		11 58		12 07	12 15		12 28			12 36		12 45		12 58		13 06	13 15			13 28	
	d		11 59		12 07	12 15		12 29			12 37		12 45		12 59		13 07	13 15			13 29	
High Street	d		12 01		12 09	12 17		12 31			12 39		12 47		13 01		13 09	13 17			13 31	
Bellgrove	d		12 03		12 11	12 19		12 33			12 41		12 49		13 03		13 11	13 19			13 33	
Duke Street	d		12 05					12 35							13 05						13 35	
Alexandra Parade	d		12 06					12 36							13 06						13 36	
Barnhill	d		12 09					12 39							13 09						13 39	
Springburn	a		12 11					12 41							13 11						13 41	
Carntyne	d				12 15	12 23					12 44		12 53				13 14	13 23				
Shettleston	d				12 17	12 25					12 47		12 55				13 17	13 25				
Garrowhill	d				12 20	12 28					12 49		12 58				13 19	13 28				
Easterhouse	d				12 22	12 30					12 52		13 00				13 22	13 30				
Blairhill	d				12 26	12 34					12 56		13 04				13 26	13 34				
Coatbridge Sunnyside	d				12 29	12 37					12 58		13 07				13 28	13 37				
Coatdyke	d				12 31	12 39					13 01		13 09				13 31	13 39				
Airdrie	d				12a34	12 42					13a04		13 12				13a34	13 42				
Drumgelloch	d					12 45							13 15					13 45				
Caldercruix	d					12 49							13 19					13 49				
Blackridge	d					12 55							13 25					13 55				
Armadale	d					12 59							13 29					13 59				
Bathgate	a					13 03							13 33					14 03				
	d					13 04							13 34					14 04				
Livingston North	d					13 09							13 38					14 09				
Uphall	d					13 12							13 41					14 12				
Edinburgh Park	a					13 21							13 49					14 20				
Haymarket	a					13 25							13 54					14 24				
Edinburgh	a					13 30							13 59					14 29				
Bridgeton	d	11 59		12 09			12 29			12 39				12 59		13 09				13 29		13 39
Dalmarnock	d																					
Rutherglen	d	12 05		12 12			12 32			12 42		12 46		13 02		13 12				13 32		13 43
Cambuslang	d	12 09		12 16			12 35			12 46				13 06		13 16				13 35		13 46
Newton	d	12 12					12 39							13 09						13 39		
Blantyre	d	12 16					12 43					12 54		13 13						13 43		
Hamilton West	d	12 19					12 46					12 57		13 16						13 46		
Hamilton Central	d	12 23					12 50					13 00		13 20						13 50		
Chatelherault	d											13 03										
Merryton	d											13 06										
Larkhall	a											13 09										
Airbles	d	12 28					12 55							13 25						13 55		
Uddingston	d			12 20						12 50						13 20						13 50
Bellshill	d			12 25						12 55						13 25						13 55
Motherwell	a	12 30		12 33			12 57			13 03				13 27		13 33				13 57		14 06
	d			12 33												13 33						
Whifflet	a								12 50										13 50			
Coatbridge Central	a																					
Shieldmuir	d			12 37												13 37						
Holytown	d								12a59										13a59			
Wishaw	d			12 40												13 40						
Carluke	d			12 47												13 47						
Lanark	a			12 59												13 59						

A 27 November

B 27 November. To Shotts

b Glasgow Central High Level

Helensburgh, Balloch, Dalmuir and Milngavie - Glasgow - Springburn, Airdrie, Bathgate and Edinburgh, Hamilton, Larkhall, Motherwell, Coatbridge and Lanark

		SR A	SR	SR	SR	SR A	SR	SR A	SR	SR B	SR	SR A	SR	SR A	SR	SR	SR	SR A	SR	SR A	SR	SR B	SR
Helensburgh Central	d			12 55					13 25							13 55					14 25		
Craigendoran	d			12 58					13 28							13 58					14 28		
Cardross	d			13 03					13 33							14 03					14 33		
Balloch	d				13 09						13 39						14 09						14 39
Alexandria	d				13 11						13 41						14 11						14 41
Renton	d				13 14						13 44						14 14						14 44
Dalreoch	d			13 08	13 17				13 38		13 47					14 08	14 17				14 38		14 47
Dumbarton Central	d			13 10	13 18				13 40		13 48					14 10	14 18				14 40		14 48
Dumbarton East	d			13 12	13 20				13 42		13 50					14 12	14 20				14 42		14 50
Bowling	d				13 25						13 55						14 25						14 55
Kilpatrick	d				13 28						13 58						14 28						14 58
Dalmuir	a			13 20	13 31				13 49		14 01					14 19	14 31				14 49		15 01
	d	13 15		13 20	13 31	13 35		13 45	13 50		14 01	14 05		14 15		14 20	14 31	14 35		14 45	14 50		15 01
Singer	d			13 22		13 37			13 52			14 07				14 22		14 37			14 52		
Drumry	d			13 25		13 39			13 55			14 09				14 25		14 39			14 55		
Drumchapel	d			13 27		13 42			13 57			14 12				14 27		14 42			14 57		
Milngavie	d						13 41						14 11						14 41				
Hillfoot	d						13 44						14 14						14 44				
Bearsden	d						13 46						14 16						14 46				
Westerton	d			13 30		13 44	13 49		14 00			14 14	14 19			14 30		14 44	14 49		15 00		
Anniesland	d			13 33		13 47	13 52		14 03			14 17	14 22			14 33		14 47	14 52		15 03		
Clydebank	d	13 17			13 33			13 47			14 03			14 17			14 33			14 47			15 03
Yoker	d	13 19			13 35			13 49			14 05			14 19			14 35			14 49			15 05
Garscadden	d	13 22			13 39			13 52			14 09			14 22			14 39			14 52			15 09
Scotstounhill	d	13 24			13 41			13 54			14 11			14 24			14 41			14 54			15 11
Jordanhill	d	13 26			13 43			13 56			14 13			14 26			14 43			14 56			15 13
Hyndland	d	13 28		13 35	13 45	13 50	13 55	13 58	14 05		14 15	14 20	14 25	14 28		14 35	14 45	14 50	14 55	14 58	15 05		15 15
Partick	d	13 30	13 34	13 38	13 48	13 52	13 58	14 00	14 08		14 18	14 22	14 28	14 30	14 34	14 38	14 48	14 52	14 58	15 00	15 08		15 18
Exhibition Centre	d		13 37		13 51		14 01				14 21		14 31		14 37		14 51		15 01				15 21
Anderston	d																						
Glasgow Central LL	a		13 39		13 53		14 03				14 23		14 33		14 39		14 53		15 03				15 23
	d		13 40		13 54		14 04			14b22	14 24		14 34		14 40		14 54		15 04			15b22	15 24
Argyle Street	d		13 42		13 56		14 06				14 26		14 36		14 41		14 56		15 06				15 26
Charing Cross	d	13 34		13 43		13 56		14 04	14 13			14 26		14 34		14 43		14 56		15 04	15 13		
Glasgow Queen St LL	a	13 36		13 45		13 58		14 06	14 15			14 28		14 36		14 45		14 58		15 06	15 15		
	d	13 37		13 45		13 59		14 07	14 15			14 29		14 37		14 45		14 59		15 07	15 15		
High Street	d	13 39		13 47		14 01		14 09	14 17			14 31		14 39		14 47		15 01		15 09	15 17		
Bellgrove	d	13 41		13 49		14 03		14 11	14 19			14 33		14 41		14 49		15 03		15 11	15 19		
Duke Street	d					14 05						14 35						15 05					
Alexandra Parade	d					14 06						14 36						15 06					
Barnhill	d					14 09						14 39						15 09					
Springburn	a					14 11						14 41						15 11					
Carntyne	d	13 44		13 53				14 14	14 23					14 44		14 53				15 14	15 23		
Shettleston	d	13 47		13 55				14 17	14 25					14 47		14 55				15 17	15 25		
Garrowhill	d	13 49		13 58				14 19	14 28					14 49		14 58				15 19	15 28		
Easterhouse	d	13 52		14 00				14 22	14 30					14 52		15 00				15 22	15 30		
Blairhill	d	13 56		14 04				14 26	14 34					14 56		15 04				15 26	15 34		
Coatbridge Sunnyside	d	13 58		14 07				14 28	14 37					14 58		15 07				15 28	15 37		
Coatdyke	d	14 01		14 09				14 31	14 39					15 01		15 09				15 31	15 39		
Airdrie	d	14a04		14 12				14a34	14 42					15a04		15 12				15a34	15 42		
Drumgelloch	d			14 15					14 45							15 15					15 45		
Caldercruix	d			14 19					14 49							15 19					15 49		
Blackridge	d			14 25					14 55							15 25					15 55		
Armadale	d			14 29					14 59							15 29					15 59		
Bathgate	a			14 33					15 03							15 33					16 03		
	d			14 34					15 04							15 34					16 04		
Livingston North	d			14 38					15 09							15 38					16 09		
Uphall	d			14 41					15 12							15 41					16 12		
Edinburgh Park	a			14 49					15 20							15 49					16 20		
Haymarket	a			14 54					15 24							15 54					16 24		
Edinburgh	a			14 59					15 29							15 59					16 29		
Bridgeton	d				13 59		14 09				14 29		14 39				14 59		15 09				15 29
Dalmarnock	d																						
Rutherglen	d		13 51		14 05		14 12				14 32		14 43		14 47		15 03		15 14				15 32
Cambuslang	d				14 09		14 16				14 36		14 47				15 07		15 18				15 36
Newton	d				14 12						14 39						15 10						15 39
Blantyre	d		13 59		14 16						14 43				14 56		15 14						15 43
Hamilton West	d		14 02		14 19						14 46				14 59		15 17						15 46
Hamilton Central	d		14 04		14 23						14 50				15 02		15 21						15 50
Chatelherault	d		14 08												15 06								
Merryton	d		14 11												15 09								
Larkhall	a		14 14												15 12								
Airbles	d				14 28						14 55						15 26						15 55
Uddingston	d						14 20						14 52						15 22				
Bellshill	d						14 25						14 56						15 27				
Motherwell	a				14 30		14 33				14 57		15 04				15 28		15 33				15 57
	d						14 33												15 34				
Whifflet	a									14 50												15 50	
Coatbridge Central	a																						
Shieldmuir	d						14 37												15 37				
Holytown	d									14a59												15a59	
Wishaw	d						14 40												15 41				
Carluke	d						14 47												15 47				
Lanark	a						14 59												15 59				

A 27 November

B 27 November. To Shotts

b Glasgow Central High Level

Table 226

Sundays

6 November to 27 November

Helensburgh, Balloch, Dalmuir and Milngavie - Glasgow - Springburn, Airdrie, Bathgate and Edinburgh, Hamilton, Larkhall, Motherwell, Coatbridge and Lanark

		SR A	SR	SR A	SR	SR	SR	SR A	SR	SR A	SR	SR B	SR	SR A	SR	SR A	SR	SR	SR	SR A	SR	SR A
Helensburgh Central	d					14 55					15 25							15 55				
Craigendoran	d					14 58					15 28							15 58				
Cardross	d					15 03					15 33							16 03				
Balloch	d						15 09						15 39						16 09			
Alexandria	d						15 11						15 41						16 11			
Renton	d						15 14						15 44						16 14			
Dalreoch	d					15 08	15 17				15 38		15 47					16 08	16 17			
Dumbarton Central	d					15 10	15 18				15 40		15 48					16 10	16 18			
Dumbarton East	d					15 12	15 20				15 42		15 50					16 12	16 20			
Bowling	d						15 25						15 55						16 25			
Kilpatrick	d						15 28						15 58						16 28			
Dalmuir	a					15 19	15 31				15 49		16 01					16 19	16 31			
	d	15 05		15 15		15 20	15 31	15 35		15 45	15 50		16 01	16 05		16 15		16 20	16 31	16 35		16 45
Singer	d	15 07				15 22		15 37			15 52			16 07				16 22		16 37		
Drumry	d	15 09				15 25		15 39			15 55			16 09				16 25		16 39		
Drumchapel	d	15 12				15 27		15 42			15 57			16 12				16 27		16 42		
Milngavie	d		15 11						15 41						16 11						16 41	
Hillfoot	d		15 14						15 44						16 14						16 44	
Bearsden	d		15 16						15 46						16 16						16 46	
Westerton	d	15 14	15 19			15 30		15 44	15 49		16 00			16 14	16 19			16 30		16 44	16 49	
Anniesland	d	15 17	15 22			15 33		15 47	15 52		16 03			16 17	16 22			16 33		16 47	16 52	
Clydebank	d			15 17			15 33			15 47			16 03			16 17			16 33			16 47
Yoker	d			15 19			15 35			15 49			16 05			16 19			16 35			16 49
Garscadden	d			15 22			15 39			15 52			16 09			16 22			16 39			16 52
Scotstounhill	d			15 24			15 41			15 54			16 11			16 24			16 41			16 54
Jordanhill	d			15 26			15 43			15 56			16 13			16 26			16 43			16 56
Hyndland	d	15 20	15 25	15 28		15 35	15 45	15 50	15 55	15 58	16 05		16 15	16 20	16 25	16 28		16 35	16 45	16 50	16 55	16 59
Partick	d	15 22	15 28	15 30	15 34	15 38	15 48	15 52	15 58	16 00	16 08		16 18	16 22	16 28	16 30	16 34	16 38	16 48	16 52	16 58	17 01
Exhibition Centre	d		15 31		15 37		15 51		16 01				16 21		16 31		16 37		16 51		17 01	
Anderston	d																					
Glasgow Central LL	a		15 33		15 39		15 53		16 03				16 23		16 33		16 39		16 53		17 03	
	d		15 34		15 43		15 54		16 04			16b22	16 24		16 34		16 40		16 54		17 04	
Argyle Street	d		15 36		15 45		15 56		16 06				16 26		16 36		16 46		16 56		17 06	
Charing Cross	d	15 26		15 34		15 43		15 56		16 04	16 13			16 26		16 34		16 43		16 56		17 05
Glasgow Queen St LL	a	15 28		15 36		15 45		15 58		16 06	16 15			16 28		16 36		16 45		16 58		17 07
	d	15 29		15 37		15 45		15 59		16 07	16 15			16 29		16 37		16 45		16 59		17 07
High Street	d	15 31		15 39		15 47		16 01		16 09	16 17			16 31		16 39		16 47		17 01		17 09
Bellgrove	d	15 33		15 41		15 49		16 03		16 11	16 19			16 33		16 41		16 49		17 03		17 11
Duke Street	d	15 35						16 05						16 35						17 05		
Alexandra Parade	d	15 36						16 06						16 36						17 06		
Barnhill	d	15 39						16 09						16 39						17 09		
Springburn	a	15 41						16 11						16 41						17 11		
Carntyne	d			15 44		15 53				16 14	16 23					16 44		16 53				17 15
Shettleston	d			15 47		15 55				16 17	16 25					16 47		16 55				17 17
Garrowhill	d			15 49		15 58				16 19	16 28					16 49		16 58				17 20
Easterhouse	d			15 52		16 00				16 22	16 30					16 52		17 00				17 22
Blairhill	d			15 56		16 04				16 26	16 34					16 56		17 04				17 26
Coatbridge Sunnyside	d			15 58		16 07				16 28	16 37					16 58		17 07				17 29
Coatdyke	d			16 01		16 09				16 31	16 39					17 01		17 09				17 31
Airdrie	d			16a04		16 12				16a34	16 42					17a04		17 12				17a34
Drumgelloch	d					16 15					16 45							17 15				
Caldercruix	d					16 19					16 49							17 19				
Blackridge	d					16 25					16 55							17 25				
Armadale	d					16 29					16 59							17 29				
Bathgate	a					16 33					17 03							17 33				
	d					16 34					17 04							17 34				
Livingston North	d					16 38					17 09							17 38				
Uphall	d					16 41					17 12							17 41				
Edinburgh Park	a					16 50					17 20							17 49				
Haymarket	a					16 54					17 24							17 58				
Edinburgh	a					16 59					17 29							18 03				
Bridgeton	d		15 39				15 59		16 09				16 29		16 39				16 59		17 09	
Dalmarnock	d																					
Rutherglen	d		15 42		15 50		16 03		16 12				16 32		16 44		16 51		17 03		17 13	
Cambuslang	d		15 46				16 07		16 16				16 36		16 50				17 07		17 17	
Newton	d						16 11						16 39						17 10			
Blantyre	d				15 58		16 15						16 43				16 59		17 14			
Hamilton West	d				16 02		16 18						16 46				17 02		17 17			
Hamilton Central	d				16 05		16 21						16 50				17 04		17 20			
Chatelherault	d				16 08												17 08					
Merryton	d				16 11												17 11					
Larkhall	a				16 14												17 14					
Airbles	d						16 26						16 55						17 25			
Uddingston	d		15 51						16 20						16 54						17 21	
Bellshill	d		15 55						16 25						16 59						17 26	
Motherwell	a		16 03				16 28		16 33				16 57		17 05				17 27		17 33	
	d								16 33												17 33	
Whifflet	a											16 50										
Coatbridge Central	a																					
Shieldmuir	d								16 37												17 37	
Holytown	d											16a59										
Wishaw	d								16 40												17 40	
Carluke	d								16 47												17 47	
Lanark	a								16 59												17 59	

A 27 November

B 27 November. To Shotts

b Glasgow Central High Level

Table 226

Sundays

6 November to 27 November

Helensburgh, Balloch, Dalmuir and Milngavie - Glasgow - Springburn, Airdrie, Bathgate and Edinburgh, Hamilton, Larkhall, Motherwell, Coatbridge and Lanark

		SR	SR A	SR	SR B	SR	SR B	SR	SR	SR	SR B	SR	SR B	SR	SR A	SR	SR	SR	SR	SR	SR	SR	SR
Helensburgh Central	d	16 25							16 55					17 25					17 55			18 25	
Craigendoran	d	16 28							16 58					17 28					17 58			18 28	
Cardross	d	16 33							17 03					17 33					18 03			18 33	
Balloch	d			16 39						17 09						17 39				18 09			18 39
Alexandria	d			16 41						17 11						17 41				18 11			18 41
Renton	d			16 44						17 14						17 44				18 14			18 44
Dalreoch	d	16 38		16 47					17 08	17 17				17 38		17 47			18 08	18 17		18 38	18 48
Dumbarton Central	d	16 40		16 48					17 10	17 18				17 40		17 48			18 10	18 18		18 40	18 49
Dumbarton East	d	16 42		16 50					17 12	17 20				17 42		17 50			18 12	18 20		18 42	18 51
Bowling	d			16 55						17 25						17 55				18 25			18 56
Kilpatrick	d			16 58						17 28						17 58				18 28			18 59
Dalmuir	a	16 49		17 01					17 19	17 31				17 49		18 01			18 19	18 31		18 49	19 02
	d	16 50		17 01	17 05		17 15		17 20	17 31	17 35		17 45	17 50		18 01			18 20	18 31		18 50	19 02
Singer	d	16 52			17 07				17 22		17 37			17 52					18 22			18 52	
Drumry	d	16 55			17 09				17 25		17 39			17 55					18 25			18 55	
Drumchapel	d	16 57			17 12				17 27		17 42			17 57					18 27			18 57	
Milngavie	d					17 11						17 41					18 11				18 41		
Hillfoot	d					17 14						17 44					18 14				18 44		
Bearsden	d					17 16						17 46					18 16				18 46		
Westerton	d	17 00			17 14	17 19			17 30		17 44	17 49		18 00			18 19		18 30		18 49	19 00	
Anniesland	d	17 03			17 17	17 22			17 33		17 47	17 52		18 03			18 22		18 33		18 52	19 03	
Clydebank	d			17 03			17 17			17 33			17 47			18 03				18 33			19 03
Yoker	d			17 05			17 19			17 35			17 49			18 05				18 35			19 05
Garscadden	d			17 09			17 22			17 39			17 52			18 09				18 39			19 10
Scotstounhill	d			17 11			17 24			17 41			17 54			18 11				18 41			19 12
Jordanhill	d			17 13			17 26			17 43			17 56			18 13				18 43			19 13
Hyndland	d	17 05		17 15	17 20	17 25	17 28		17 35	17 45	17 50	17 55	17 58	18 05		18 15	18 25		18 35	18 45	18 55	19 05	19 15
Partick	d	17 08		17 18	17 22	17 28	17 30	17 34	17 38	17 48	17 52	17 58	18 00	18 08		18 18	18 28	18 34	18 38	18 48	18 58	19 08	19 18
Exhibition Centre	d			17 21		17 31		17 37		17 51		18 01				18 21	18 31	18 37		18 51	19 01		19 21
Anderston	d																						
Glasgow Central LL	a			17 23		17 33		17 39		17 53		18 03				18 23	18 33	18 39		18 53	19 03		19 24
	d		17b22	17 24		17 34		17 40		17 54		18 04			18b22	18 24	18 34	18 40		18 54	19 04		19 24
Argyle Street	d			17 26		17 36		17 41		17 56		18 06											
Charing Cross	d	17 13			17 26		17 34		17 43		17 56		18 04	18 13					18 43			19 13	
Glasgow Queen St LL	a	17 15			17 28		17 36		17 45		17 58		18 06	18 15					18 45			19 15	
	d	17 15			17 29		17 37		17 45		17 59		18 07	18 15					18 45			19 15	
High Street	d	17 17			17 31		17 39		17 47		18 01		18 09	18 17					18 47			19 17	
Bellgrove	d	17 19			17 33		17 41		17 49		18 03		18 11	18 19					18 49			19 19	
Duke Street	d				17 35						18 05												
Alexandra Parade	d				17 36						18 06												
Barnhill	d				17 39						18 09												
Springburn	a				17 41						18 11												
Carntyne	d	17 23					17 44		17 53				18 14	18 23					18 53			19 23	
Shettleston	d	17 25					17 47		17 55				18 17	18 25					18 55			19 25	
Garrowhill	d	17 28					17 49		17 58				18 19	18 28					18 58			19 28	
Easterhouse	d	17 30					17 52		18 00				18 22	18 30					19 00			19 30	
Blairhill	d	17 34					17 56		18 04				18 26	18 34					19 04			19 34	
Coatbridge Sunnyside	d	17 37					17 58		18 07				18 28	18 37					19 07			19 37	
Coatdyke	d	17 39					18 01		18 09				18 31	18 39					19 09			19 39	
Airdrie	d	17 42					18a04		18 12				18a34	18 42					19 12			19a42	
Drumgelloch	d	17 45							18 15					18 45					19 15				
Caldercruix	d	17 49							18 19					18 49					19 19				
Blackridge	d	17 55							18 25					18 55					19 25				
Armadale	d	17 59							18 29					18 59					19 29				
Bathgate	a	18 03							18 33					19 03					19 33				
	d	18 04							18 34					19 04					19 34				
Livingston North	d	18 09							18 38					19 09					19 38				
Uphall	d	18 12							18 41					19 12					19 41				
Edinburgh Park	a	18 20							18 49					19 20					19 49				
Haymarket	a	18 24							18 54					19 24					19 54				
Edinburgh	a	18 30							18 59					19 29					19 59				
Bridgeton	d			17 29		17 39				17 59		18 09				18 29	18 39			18 59	19 09		19 29
Dalmarnock	d																						
Rutherglen	d			17 32		17 42		17 46		18 02		18 12				18 32	18 42	18 47		19 03	19 12		19 32
Cambuslang	d			17 36		17 46				18 06		18 16				18 36	18 46			19 07	19 16		19 36
Newton	d			17 39						18 09						18 39				19 10			19 39
Blantyre	d			17 43				17 56		18 13						18 43		18 57		19 14			19 43
Hamilton West	d			17 46				17 59		18 16						18 46		19 00		19 17			19 46
Hamilton Central	d			17 50				18 02		18 20						18 50		19 02		19 20			19 50
Chatelherault	d							18 05										19 06					
Merryton	d							18 08										19 09					
Larkhall	a							18 12										19 12					
Airbles	d			17 55						18 25						18 55				19 25			19 55
Uddingston	d					17 50						18 20					18 50				19 20		
Bellshill	d					17 55						18 25					18 55				19 25		
Motherwell	a			17 57		18 02				18 27		18 33				18 57	19 03			19 27	19 33		19 57
	d											18 33									19 33		
Whifflet	a		17 50												18 50								
Coatbridge Central	a																						
Shieldmuir	d											18 37									19 37		
Holytown	d		17a59												18a59								
Wishaw	d											18 40									19 40		
Carluke	d											18 47									19 47		
Lanark	a											18 59									19 59		

A 27 November. To Shotts

B [illegible]

Table 226

Sundays

6 November to 27 November

Helensburgh, Balloch, Dalmuir and Milngavie - Glasgow - Springburn, Airdrie, Bathgate and Edinburgh, Hamilton, Larkhall, Motherwell, Coatbridge and Lanark

		SR	SR	SR	SR	SR	SR	SR	SR	SR	SR	SR	SR	SR	SR	SR	SR	SR	SR	SR	SR	SR	SR
																◇ A							
Helensburgh Central	d			18 55			19 25				19 55			20 25		20b40			20 55			21 25	
Craigendoran	d			18 58			19 28				19 58			20 28					20 58			21 28	
Cardross	d			19 03			19 33				20 03			20 33					21 03			21 33	
Balloch	d				19 09			19 39				20 09			20 38					21 09			21 39
Alexandria	d				19 11			19 41				20 11			20 40					21 11			21 41
Renton	d				19 14			19 44				20 14			20 43					21 14			21 44
Dalreoch	d			19 08	19 17		19 38	19 47			20 08	20 17		20 38	20 46				21 08	21 17		21 38	21 47
Dumbarton Central	d			19 10	19 18		19 40	19 48			20 10	20 18		20 40	20 47	20 53			21 10	21 18		21 40	21 48
Dumbarton East	d			19 12	19 20		19 42	19 50			20 12	20 20		20 42	20 49				21 12	21 20		21 42	21 50
Bowling	d				19 25			19 55				20 25			20 54					21 25			21 55
Kilpatrick	d				19 28			19 58				20 28			20 57					21 28			21 58
Dalmuir	a			19 20	19 31		19 49	20 01			20 19	20 31		20 49	21 00	21 03			21 19	21 31		21 49	22 01
	d			19 20	19 31		19 50	20 01			20 20	20 31		20 50	21 01	21 03			21 20	21 31		21 50	22 01
Singer	d			19 22			19 52				20 22			20 52					21 22			21 52	
Drumry	d			19 25			19 55				20 25			20 55					21 25			21 55	
Drumchapel	d			19 27			19 57				20 27			20 57					21 27			21 57	
Milngavie	d	19 11				19 41			20 11				20 41				21 11				21 41		
Hillfoot	d	19 14				19 44			20 14				20 44				21 14				21 44		
Bearsden	d	19 16				19 46			20 16				20 46				21 16				21 46		
Westerton	d	19 19		19 30		19 49	20 00		20 19		20 30		20 49	21 00			21 19		21 30		21 49	22 00	
Anniesland	d	19 22		19 33		19 52	20 03		20 22		20 33		20 52	21 03			21 22		21 33		21 52	22 03	
Clydebank	d				19 33			20 03				20 33			21 03					21 33			22 03
Yoker	d				19 35			20 05				20 35			21 05					21 35			22 05
Garscadden	d				19 39			20 09				20 39			21 09					21 39			22 09
Scotstounhill	d				19 41			20 11				20 41			21 11					21 41			22 11
Jordanhill	d				19 43			20 13				20 43			21 13					21 43			22 13
Hyndland	d	19 25		19 35	19 45	19 55	20 05	20 15	20 25		20 35	20 45	20 55	21 05	21 15		21 25		21 35	21 45	21 55	22 05	22 15
Partick ⇌	d	19 28	19 34	19 38	19 48	19 58	20 08	20 18	20 28	20 34	20 38	20 48	20 58	21 08	21 18		21 28	21 34	21 38	21 48	21 58	22 08	22 18
Exhibition Centre	d	19 31	19 37		19 51	20 01		20 21	20 31	20 37		20 51	21 01		21 21		21 31	21 37		21 51	22 01		22 21
Anderston	d																						
Glasgow Central LL 15	a	19 33	19 39		19 53	20 03		20 23	20 33	20 39		20 53	21 03		21 23		21 33	21 39		21 53	22 03		22 23
	d	19 34	19 40		19 54	20 04		20 24	20 34	20 40		20 54	21 04		21 24		21 34	21 40		21 54	22 04		22 24
Argyle Street	d																						
Charing Cross	d			19 43			20 13				20 43			21 13					21 43			22 13	
Glasgow Queen St LL 10 ⇌	a			19 45			20 15				20 45			21 15		21c19			21 45			22 15	
	d			19 45			20 15				20 45			21 15					21 45			22 15	
High Street	d			19 47			20 17				20 47			21 17					21 47			22 17	
Bellgrove	d			19 49			20 19				20 49			21 19					21 49			22 19	
Duke Street	d																						
Alexandra Parade	d																						
Barnhill	d																						
Springburn	a																						
Carntyne	d			19 53			20 23				20 53			21 23					21 53			22 23	
Shettleston	d			19 55			20 25				20 55			21 25					21 55			22 25	
Garrowhill	d			19 58			20 28				20 58			21 28					21 58			22 28	
Easterhouse	d			20 00			20 30				21 00			21 30					22 00			22 30	
Blairhill	d			20 04			20 34				21 04			21 34					22 04			22 34	
Coatbridge Sunnyside	d			20 07			20 37				21 07			21 37					22 07			22 37	
Coatdyke	d			20 09			20 39				21 09			21 39					22 09			22 39	
Airdrie	d			20 12			20a42				21 12			21a42					22 12			22a42	
Drumgelloch	d			20 15							21 15								22 15				
Caldercruix	d			20 19							21 19								22 19				
Blackridge	d			20 25							21 25								22 25				
Armadale	d			20 29							21 29								22 29				
Bathgate	a			20 33							21 33								22 33				
	d			20 34							21 34								22 34				
Livingston North	d			20 38							21 39								22 39				
Uphall	d			20 41							21 42								22 42				
Edinburgh Park	a			20 49							21 50								22 50				
Haymarket	a			20 54							21 54								22 55				
Edinburgh	a			20 59							21 59								23 00				
Bridgeton	d	19 37			19 59	20 09		20 29	20 37			20 57	21 09		21 29		21 37			21 59	22 08		22 29
Dalmarnock	d																						
Rutherglen	d	19 40	19 46		20 02	20 14		20 32	20 40	20 46		21 00	21 12		21 32		21 40	21 47		22 02	22 11		22 32
Cambuslang	d	19 44			20 06	20 18		20 36	20 44			21 04	21 16		21 36		21 44			22 06	22 15		22 36
Newton	d				20 09			20 39				21 08			21 39					22 09			22 39
Blantyre	d		19 56		20 13			20 43		20 54		21 13			21 43			21 54		22 13			22 43
Hamilton West	d		19 59		20 16			20 46		20 58		21 16			21 46			21 57		22 16			22 46
Hamilton Central	d		20 02		20 20			20 50		21 02		21 20			21 50			22 01		22 20			22 50
Chatelherault	d		20 05							21 05								22 04					
Merryton	d		20 08							21 08								22 07					
Larkhall	a		20 12							21 13								22 12					
Airbles	d				20 25			20 55				21 25			21 55					22 25			22 55
Uddingston	d	19 49				20 22			20 49				21 20				21 49				22 19		
Bellshill	d	19 55				20 27			20 55				21 25				21 55				22 24		
Motherwell	a	20 03			20 27	20 33		20 57	21 04			21 27	21 33		21 57		22 03			22 27	22 32		22 57
	d					20 33							21 33								22 32		
Whifflet	a																						
Coatbridge Central	a																						
Shieldmuir	d					20 37							21 37								22 36		
Holytown	d																						
Wishaw	d					20 40							21 40								22 39		
Carluke	d					20 47							21 47								22 44		
Lanark	a					20 59							21 59								22 58		

A From Mallaig

b Helensburgh Upper

c Glasgow Queen St High Level

Helensburgh, Balloch, Dalmuir and Milngavie - Glasgow - Springburn, Airdrie, Bathgate and Edinburgh, Hamilton, Larkhall, Motherwell, Coatbridge and Lanark

		SR	SR	SR	SR	SR	SR	SR	SR	SR
									A	
Helensburgh Central	d			21 55			22 25		22b37	
Craigendoran	d			21 58			22 28			
Cardross	d			22 03			22 33			
Balloch	d				22 09			22 39		23 09
Alexandria	d				22 11			22 41		23 11
Renton	d				22 14			22 44		23 14
Dalreoch	d			22 08	22 17		22 38	22 47		23 17
Dumbarton Central	d			22 10	22 18		22 40	22 48		23 18
Dumbarton East	d			22 12	22 20		22 42	22 50		23 20
Bowling	d				22 25			22 55		23 25
Kilpatrick	d				22 28			22 58		23 28
Dalmuir	a			22 19	22 31		22 49	23 01	23 02	23 31
	d			22 20	22 31		22 50	23 01	23 04	23 31
Singer	d			22 22			22 52			
Drumry	d			22 25			22 55			
Drumchapel	d			22 27			22 57			
Milngavie	d	22 11				22 41				
Hillfoot	d	22 14				22 44				
Bearsden	d	22 16				22 46				
Westerton	d	22 19		22 30		22 49	23 00		23 13	
Anniesland	d	22 22		22 33		22 52	23 03			
Clydebank	d				22 33			23 03		23 33
Yoker	d				22 35			23a05		23a35
Garscadden	d				22 39					
Scotstounhill	d				22 41					
Jordanhill	d				22 43					
Hyndland	d	22 25		22 35	22 45	22 55	23 05			
Partick ⇌	d	22 28	22 34	22 38	22 48	22 58	23 08			
Exhibition Centre	d	22 31	22 37		22 51	23 01				
Anderston	d									
Glasgow Central LL 15	a	22 33	22 39		22 53	23 03				
	d	22 34	22 40		22 54	23 04				
Argyle Street	d									
Charing Cross	d			22 43			23 13			
Glasgow Queen St LL 10 ⇌	a			22 45			23 15			
	d			22 45			23 15			
High Street	d			22 47			23 17			
Bellgrove	d			22 49			23 19			
Duke Street	d									
Alexandra Parade	d									
Barnhill	d									
Springburn	a									
Carntyne	d			22 53			23 23			
Shettleston	d			22 55			23 25			
Garrowhill	d			22 58			23 28			
Easterhouse	d			23 00			23 30			
Blairhill	d			23 04			23 34			
Coatbridge Sunnyside	d			23 07			23 37			
Coatdyke	d			23 09			23 39			
Airdrie	d			23 12			23a42			
Drumgelloch	d			23 15						
Caldercruix	d			23 19						
Blackridge	d			23 25						
Armadale	d			23 29						
Bathgate	a			23 33						
	d									
Livingston North	d									
Uphall	d									
Edinburgh Park	a									
Haymarket	a									
Edinburgh	a								00 13	
Bridgeton	d	22 39			22 59	23 09				
Dalmarnock	d									
Rutherglen	d	22 42	22 47		23 02	23 12				
Cambuslang	d	22 46			23 06	23 16				
Newton	d				23 09					
Blantyre	d		22 55		23 13					
Hamilton West	d		22 58		23 16					
Hamilton Central	d		23 02		23 20					
Chatelherault	d		23 05							
Merryton	d		23 08							
Larkhall	a		23 11							
Airbles	d				23 25					
Uddingston	d	22 50				23 20				
Bellshill	d	22 55				23 25				
Motherwell	a	23 03			23 27	23 33				
	d									
Whifflet	a									
Coatbridge Central	a									
Shieldmuir	d									
Holytown	d									
Wishaw	d									
Carluke	d									
Lanark	a									

A From Fort William

b Helensburgh Upper

Table 226

Sundays from 4 December

Helensburgh, Balloch, Dalmuir and Milngavie - Glasgow - Springburn, Airdrie, Bathgate and Edinburgh, Hamilton, Larkhall, Motherwell, Coatbridge and Lanark

		SR	SR	SR	SR	SR	SR	SR	SR	SR	SR	SR	SR A	SR	SR	SR	SR	SR	SR	SR	SR	SR	SR
Helensburgh Central	d		22p40		23p10				07 55			08 25							08 55				
Craigendoran	d		22p43		23p13				07 58			08 28							08 58				
Cardross	d		22p48		23p18				08 03			08 33							09 03				
Balloch	d			22p53						08 09				08 39						09 09			
Alexandria	d			22p55						08 11				08 41						09 11			
Renton	d			22p58						08 14				08 44						09 14			
Dalreoch	d		22p53	23p01	23p23				08 08	08 17		08 38		08 47					09 08	09 17			
Dumbarton Central	d		22p55	23p02	23p25				08 10	08 18		08 40		08 48					09 10	09 18			
Dumbarton East	d		22p57	23p04	23p27				08 12	08 20		08 42		08 50					09 12	09 20			
Bowling	d			23p09						08 25				08 55						09 25			
Kilpatrick	d			23p12						08 28				08 58						09 28			
Dalmuir	a		23p05	23p15	23p35				08 19	08 31		08 49		09 01					09 19	09 31			
	d	23p01	23p05	23p16	23p35		07 40	08 01	08 20	08 31		08 50		09 01	09 05		09 15		09 20	09 31	09 35		09 45
Singer	d	23p03		23p18			07 42		08 22			08 52			09 07				09 22		09 37		
Drumry	d	23p05		23p20			07 45		08 25			08 55			09 09				09 25		09 39		
Drumchapel	d	23p08		23p23			07 47		08 27			08 57			09 12				09 27		09 42		
Milngavie	d															09 11						09 41	
Hillfoot	d															09 14						09 44	
Bearsden	d															09 16						09 46	
Westerton	d	23p10		23p25			07 50		08 30			09 00			09 14	09 19			09 30		09 44	09 49	
Anniesland	d	23p14		23p28			07 53		08 33			09 03			09 17	09 22			09 33		09 47	09 52	
Clydebank	d		23p07		23p37			08 03		08 33				09 03			09 17			09 33			09 47
Yoker	d		23p09		23p39			08 05		08 35				09 05			09 19			09 35			09 49
Garscadden	d		23p13		23p43			08 09		08 39				09 09			09 22			09 39			09 52
Scotstounhill	d		23p15		23p45			08 11		08 41				09 11			09 24			09 41			09 54
Jordanhill	d		23p17		23p47			08 13		08 43				09 13			09 26			09 43			09 56
Hyndland	d	23p17	23p21	23p31	23p49		07 55	08 15	08 35	08 45	08 55	09 05		09 15	09 20	09 25	09 28		09 35	09 45	09 50	09 55	09 59
Partick	d	23p20	23p23	23p34	23p52		07 58	08 18	08 38	08 48	08 58	09 08		09 18	09 22	09 28	09 30	09 34	09 38	09 48	09 52	09 58	10 01
Exhibition Centre	d	23p23						08 21		08 51	09 01			09 21		09 31		09 37		09 51		10 01	
Anderston	d	23p25																					
Glasgow Central LL 15	a	23p26						08 23		08 53	09 03			09 23		09 33		09 39		09 53		10 03	
	d	23p27						08 24		08 54	09 04		09b22	09 24		09 34		09 40		09 54		10 04	
Argyle Street	d	23p29																		09 55		10 06	
Charing Cross	d		23p27	23p38	23p56		08 03		08 43			09 13			09 26		09 34		09 43		09 56		10 05
Glasgow Queen St LL 10	a		23p29	23p40	23p59		08 05		08 45			09 15			09 28		09 36		09 45		09 58		10 07
	d		23p30	23p44	23p59		08 05		08 45			09 15			09 29		09 37		09 45		09 59		10 07
High Street	d		23p32	23p46	00 02		08 07		08 47			09 17			09 31		09 39		09 47		10 01		10 09
Bellgrove	d		23p34	23p49	00 04		08 09		08 49			09 19			09 33		09 41		09 49		10 03		10 11
Duke Street	d														09 35						10 05		
Alexandra Parade	d														09 36						10 06		
Barnhill	d														09 39						10 09		
Springburn	a														09 41						10 11		
Carntyne	d		23p37	23p52	00 07		08 13		08 53			09 23					09 44		09 53				10 15
Shettleston	d		23p40	23p55	00 10		08 15		08 55			09 25					09 47		09 55				10 17
Garrowhill	d		23p42	23p57	00 12		08 18		08 58			09 28					09 49		09 58				10 20
Easterhouse	d		23p45	23p59	00 15		08 20		09 00			09 30					09 52		10 00				10 22
Blairhill	d		23p49	00 04	00 19		08 24		09 04			09 34					09 56		10 04				10 26
Coatbridge Sunnyside	d		23p51	00 06	00 21		08 27		09 07			09 37					09 58		10 07				10 29
Coatdyke	d		23p54	00 09	00 24		08 29		09 09			09 39					10 01		10 09				10 31
Airdrie	d		23p57	00a12	00a27		08 32		09 12			09a42					10a04		10 12				10a34
Drumgelloch	d		23p59				08 35		09 15										10 15				
Caldercruix	d		00 03				08 39		09 19										10 19				
Blackridge	d		00 09				08 45		09 25										10 25				
Armadale	d		00 13				08 49		09 29										10 29				
Bathgate	a		00 17				08 53		09 33										10 33				
	d					07 55	08 54		09 34										10 34				
Livingston North	d					07 59	08 59		09 39										10 38				
Uphall	d					08 02	09 02		09 42										10 41				
Edinburgh Park	a					08 10	09 10		09 52										10 49				
Haymarket	a					08 20	09 20		10 02										10 55				
Edinburgh	a					08 25	09 25		10 07										11 00				
Bridgeton	d							08 29		08 59	09 09			09 29		09 39				09 58		10 09	
Dalmarnock	d																						
Rutherglen	d	23p34						08 32		09 02	09 12			09 32		09 42		09 47		10 01		10 12	
Cambuslang	d							08 36		09 06	09 16			09 36		09 48				10 04		10 16	
Newton	d									09 09				09 39						10 09			
Blantyre	d	23p44								09 13				09 43				09 57		10 13			
Hamilton West	d	23p47								09 16				09 46				10 00		10 16			
Hamilton Central	d	23p50								09 20				09 50				10 03		10 20			
Chatelherault	d	23p53																10 06					
Merryton	d	23p56																10 09					
Larkhall	a	00 01																10 12					
Airbles	d									09 25				09 55						10 25			
Uddingston	d							08 40			09 20					09 53						10 20	
Bellshill	d							08 45			09 25					09 57						10 25	
Motherwell	a							08 53		09 27	09 33			09 57		10 03				10 27		10 33	
	d										09 33											10 33	
Whifflet	a												09 50										
Coatbridge Central	a																						
Shieldmuir	d										09 37											10 37	
Holytown	d												09a59										
Wishaw	d										09 40											10 40	
Carluke	d										09 47											10 47	
Lanark	a										09 59											10 59	

A To Shotts

b Glasgow Central High Level

Table 226

Sundays from 4 December

Helensburgh, Balloch, Dalmuir and Milngavie - Glasgow - Springburn, Airdrie, Bathgate and Edinburgh, Hamilton, Larkhall, Motherwell, Coatbridge and Lanark

		SR	SR	SR A	SR	SR	SR	SR	SR	SR	SR	SR	SR	SR	SR	SR	SR A	SR	SR	SR	SR	SR	SR
Helensburgh Central	d	09 25								09 55					10 25								10 55
Craigendoran	d	09 28								09 58					10 28								10 58
Cardross	d	09 33								10 03					10 33								11 03
Balloch	d				09 39						10 09							10 39					
Alexandria	d				09 41						10 11							10 41					
Renton	d				09 44						10 14							10 44					
Dalreoch	d	09 38			09 47					10 08	10 17				10 38			10 47					11 08
Dumbarton Central	d	09 40			09 48					10 10	10 18				10 40			10 48					11 10
Dumbarton East	d	09 42			09 50					10 12	10 20				10 42			10 50					11 12
Bowling	d				09 55						10 25							10 55					
Kilpatrick	d				09 58						10 28							10 58					
Dalmuir	a	09 49			10 01					10 19	10 31				10 49			11 01					11 19
	d	09 50			10 01	10 05		10 15		10 20	10 31	10 35		10 45	10 50			11 01	11 05		11 15		11 20
Singer	d	09 52				10 07				10 22		10 37			10 52				11 07				11 22
Drumry	d	09 55				10 09				10 25		10 39			10 55				11 09				11 25
Drumchapel	d	09 57				10 12				10 27		10 42			10 57				11 12				11 27
Milngavie	d						10 11						10 41							11 11			
Hillfoot	d						10 14						10 44							11 14			
Bearsden	d						10 16						10 46							11 16			
Westerton	d	10 00				10 14	10 19			10 30		10 44	10 49		11 00				11 14	11 19			11 30
Anniesland	d	10 03				10 17	10 22			10 33		10 47	10 52		11 03				11 17	11 22			11 33
Clydebank	d				10 03			10 17			10 33			10 47				11 03			11 17		
Yoker	d				10 05			10 19			10 35			10 49				11 05			11 19		
Garscadden	d				10 09			10 22			10 39			10 52				11 09			11 22		
Scotstounhill	d				10 11			10 24			10 41			10 54				11 11			11 24		
Jordanhill	d				10 13			10 26			10 43			10 56				11 13			11 26		
Hyndland	d	10 05			10 15	10 20	10 25	10 28		10 35	10 45	10 50	10 55	10 59	11 05			11 15	11 20	11 25	11 28		11 35
Partick	d	10 08			10 18	10 22	10 28	10 30	10 34	10 38	10 48	10 52	10 58	11 01	11 08			11 18	11 22	11 28	11 30	11 34	11 38
Exhibition Centre	d				10 21		10 31		10 37		10 51		11 01					11 21		11 31		11 37	
Anderston	d																						
Glasgow Central LL 15	a				10 23		10 33		10 39		10 53		11 03					11 23		11 33		11 39	
	d			10b22	10 23		10 34		10 40		10 54		11 04				11b22	11 24		11 34		11 40	
Argyle Street	d				10 25		10 36		10 42		10 56		11 06					11 26		11 36		11 42	
Charing Cross	d	10 13				10 26		10 35		10 43		10 56		11 05	11 13				11 26		11 34		11 43
Glasgow Queen St LL 10	a	10 15				10 28		10 37		10 45		10 58		11 07	11 15				11 28		11 36		11 45
	d	10 15				10 29		10 37		10 45		10 59		11 07	11 15				11 29		11 37		11 45
High Street	d	10 17				10 31		10 39		10 47		11 01		11 09	11 17				11 31		11 39		11 47
Bellgrove	d	10 19				10 33		10 41		10 49		11 03		11 11	11 19				11 33		11 41		11 49
Duke Street	d					10 35						11 05							11 35				
Alexandra Parade	d					10 36						11 06							11 36				
Barnhill	d					10 39						11 09							11 39				
Springburn	a					10 41						11 11							11 41				
Carntyne	d	10 23						10 45		10 53				11 15	11 23						11 44		11 53
Shettleston	d	10 25						10 47		10 55				11 17	11 25						11 47		11 55
Garrowhill	d	10 28						10 50		10 58				11 20	11 28						11 49		11 58
Easterhouse	d	10 30						10 52		11 00				11 22	11 30						11 52		12 00
Blairhill	d	10 34						10 56		11 04				11 26	11 34						11 56		12 04
Coatbridge Sunnyside	d	10 37						10 59		11 07				11 29	11 37						11 58		12 07
Coatdyke	d	10 39						11 01		11 09				11 31	11 39						12 01		12 09
Airdrie	d	10a42						11a04		11 12				11a34	11a42						12a04		12 12
Drumgelloch	d									11 15													12 15
Caldercruix	d									11 19													12 19
Blackridge	d									11 25													12 25
Armadale	d									11 29													12 29
Bathgate	a									11 33													12 33
	d		11 05							11 34						12 05							12 34
Livingston North	d		11 09							11 38						12 09							12 38
Uphall	d		11 12							11 41						12 12							12 41
Edinburgh Park	a		11 20							11 49						12 20							12 49
Haymarket	a		11 25							11 54						12 25							12 54
Edinburgh	a		11 30							11 59						12 30							12 59
Bridgeton	d				10 28		10 39				10 59		11 09					11 29		11 39			
Dalmarnock	d																						
Rutherglen	d				10 30		10 42		10 45		11 02		11 12					11 31		11 44		11 47	
Cambuslang	d				10 34		10 46				11 06		11 16					11 35		11 48			
Newton	d				10 38						11 09							11 39					
Blantyre	d				10 42				10 57		11 13							11 43				11 55	
Hamilton West	d				10 46				11 00		11 16							11 46				11 58	
Hamilton Central	d				10 50				11 03		11 20							11 50				12 01	
Chatelherault	d								11 06													12 05	
Merryton	d								11 09													12 08	
Larkhall	a								11 12													12 13	
Airbles	d				10 55						11 25							11 55					
Uddingston	d						10 50						11 20							11 53			
Bellshill	d						10 55						11 25							11 57			
Motherwell	a				10 57		11 03				11 27		11 33					11 57		12 03			
	d												11 33										
Whifflet	a			10 50													11 50						
Coatbridge Central	a																						
Shieldmuir	d												11 37										
Holytown	d			10a59													11a59						
Wishaw	d												11 40										
Carluke	d												11 47										
Lanark	a												11 59										

A To Shotts

Helensburgh, Balloch, Dalmuir and Milngavie - Glasgow - Springburn, Airdrie, Bathgate and Edinburgh, Hamilton, Larkhall, Motherwell, Coatbridge and Lanark

		SR	SR	SR	SR	SR	SR	SR	SR A	SR	SR	SR	SR	SR	SR	SR	SR	SR	SR A	SR	SR	SR
Helensburgh Central	d					11 25							11 55					12 25				
Craigendoran	d					11 28							11 58					12 28				
Cardross	d					11 33							12 03					12 33				
Balloch	d	11 09					11 39							12 09						12 39		
Alexandria	d	11 11					11 41							12 11						12 41		
Renton	d	11 14					11 44							12 14						12 44		
Dalreoch	d	11 17				11 38	11 47						12 08	12 17				12 38		12 47		
Dumbarton Central	d	11 18				11 40	11 48						12 10	12 18				12 40		12 48		
Dumbarton East	d	11 20				11 42	11 50						12 12	12 20				12 42		12 50		
Bowling	d	11 25					11 55							12 25						12 55		
Kilpatrick	d	11 28					11 58							12 28						12 58		
Dalmuir	a	11 31				11 49	12 01						12 19	12 31				12 49		13 01		
	d	11 31	11 35		11 45	11 50	12 01	12 05			12 15		12 20	12 31	12 35		12 45	12 50		13 01	13 05	
Singer	d		11 37			11 52		12 07					12 22		12 37			12 52			13 07	
Drumry	d		11 39			11 55		12 09					12 25		12 39			12 55			13 09	
Drumchapel	d		11 42			11 57		12 12					12 27		12 42			12 57			13 12	
Milngavie	d			11 41						12 11						12 41						13 11
Hillfoot	d			11 44						12 14						12 44						13 14
Bearsden	d			11 46						12 16						12 46						13 16
Westerton	d		11 44	11 49		12 00		12 14		12 19			12 30		12 44	12 49		13 00			13 14	13 19
Anniesland	d		11 47	11 52		12 03		12 17		12 22			12 33		12 47	12 52		13 03			13 17	13 22
Clydebank	d	11 33			11 47		12 03				12 17			12 33			12 47			13 03		
Yoker	d	11 35			11 49		12 05				12 19			12 35			12 49			13 05		
Garscadden	d	11 39			11 52		12 09				12 22			12 39			12 52			13 09		
Scotstounhill	d	11 41			11 54		12 11				12 24			12 41			12 54			13 11		
Jordanhill	d	11 43			11 56		12 13				12 26			12 43			12 56			13 13		
Hyndland	d	11 45	11 50	11 55	11 59	12 05	12 15	12 20		12 25	12 28		12 35	12 45	12 50	12 55	12 58	13 05		13 15	13 20	13 25
Partick	d	11 48	11 52	11 58	12 01	12 08	12 18	12 22		12 28	12 30	12 34	12 38	12 48	12 52	12 58	13 00	13 08		13 18	13 22	13 28
Exhibition Centre	d	11 51		12 01			12 21			12 31		12 37		12 51		13 01				13 21		13 31
Anderston	d																					
Glasgow Central LL	a	11 53		12 03			12 23			12 33		12 39		12 53		13 03				13 23		13 33
	d	11 54		12 04			12 24		12b24	12 34		12 40		12 54		13 04			13b22	13 24		13 34
Argyle Street	d	11 56		12 06			12 25			12 36		12 41		12 56		13 06				13 26		13 36
Charing Cross	d		11 56		12 05	12 13		12 26			12 34		12 43		12 56		13 04	13 13			13 26	
Glasgow Queen St LL	a		11 58		12 07	12 15		12 28			12 36		12 45		12 58		13 06	13 15			13 28	
	d		11 59		12 07	12 15		12 29			12 37		12 45		12 59		13 07	13 15			13 29	
High Street	d		12 01		12 09	12 17		12 31			12 39		12 47		13 01		13 09	13 17			13 31	
Bellgrove	d		12 03		12 11	12 19		12 33			12 41		12 49		13 03		13 11	13 19			13 33	
Duke Street	d		12 05					12 35							13 05						13 35	
Alexandra Parade	d		12 06					12 36							13 06						13 36	
Barnhill	d		12 09					12 39							13 09						13 39	
Springburn	a		12 11					12 41							13 11						13 41	
Carntyne	d				12 15	12 23					12 44		12 53				13 14	13 23				
Shettleston	d				12 17	12 25					12 47		12 55				13 17	13 25				
Garrowhill	d				12 20	12 28					12 49		12 58				13 19	13 28				
Easterhouse	d				12 22	12 30					12 52		13 00				13 22	13 30				
Blairhill	d				12 26	12 34					12 56		13 04				13 26	13 34				
Coatbridge Sunnyside	d				12 29	12 37					12 58		13 07				13 28	13 37				
Coatdyke	d				12 31	12 39					13 01		13 09				13 31	13 39				
Airdrie	d				12a34	12 42					13a04		13 12				13a34	13 42				
Drumgelloch	d					12 45							13 15					13 45				
Caldercruix	d					12 49							13 19					13 49				
Blackridge	d					12 55							13 25					13 55				
Armadale	d					12 59							13 29					13 59				
Bathgate	a					13 03							13 33					14 03				
	d					13 04							13 34					14 04				
Livingston North	d					13 09							13 38					14 09				
Uphall	d					13 12							13 41					14 12				
Edinburgh Park	a					13 21							13 49					14 20				
Haymarket	a					13 25							13 54					14 24				
Edinburgh	a					13 30							13 59					14 29				
Bridgeton	d	11 59		12 09			12 29			12 39				12 59		13 09				13 29		13 39
Dalmarnock	d																					
Rutherglen	d	12 05		12 12			12 32			12 42		12 46		13 02		13 12				13 32		13 43
Cambuslang	d	12 09		12 16			12 35			12 46				13 06		13 16				13 35		13 46
Newton	d	12 12					12 39							13 09						13 39		
Blantyre	d	12 16					12 43					12 54		13 13						13 43		
Hamilton West	d	12 19					12 46					12 57		13 16						13 46		
Hamilton Central	d	12 23					12 50					13 00		13 20						13 50		
Chatelherault	d											13 03										
Merryton	d											13 06										
Larkhall	a											13 09										
Airbles	d	12 28					12 55							13 25						13 55		
Uddingston	d			12 20						12 50						13 20						13 50
Bellshill	d			12 25						12 55						13 25						13 55
Motherwell	a	12 30		12 33			12 57			13 03				13 27		13 33				13 57		14 06
	d			12 33												13 33						
Whifflet	a								12 50										13 50			
Coatbridge Central	a																					
Shieldmuir	d			12 37												13 37						
Holytown	d								12a59										13a59			
Wishaw	d			12 40												13 40						
Carluke	d			12 47												13 47						
Lanark	a			12 59												13 59						

A To Shotts

b Glasgow Central High Level

Helensburgh, Balloch, Dalmuir and Milngavie - Glasgow - Springburn, Airdrie, Bathgate and Edinburgh, Hamilton, Larkhall, Motherwell, Coatbridge and Lanark

		SR	SR	SR	SR	SR	SR	SR	SR	SR A	SR	SR	SR	SR	SR	SR	SR	SR	SR	SR	SR	SR A	SR
Helensburgh Central	d			12 55					13 25							13 55					14 25		
Craigendoran	d			12 58					13 28							13 58					14 28		
Cardross	d			13 03					13 33							14 03					14 33		
Balloch	d				13 09						13 39						14 09						14 39
Alexandria	d				13 11						13 41						14 11						14 41
Renton	d				13 14						13 44						14 14						14 44
Dalreoch	d			13 08	13 17				13 38		13 47					14 08	14 17				14 38		14 47
Dumbarton Central	d			13 10	13 18				13 40		13 48					14 10	14 18				14 40		14 48
Dumbarton East	d			13 12	13 20				13 42		13 50					14 12	14 20				14 42		14 50
Bowling	d				13 25						13 55						14 25						14 55
Kilpatrick	d				13 28						13 58						14 28						14 58
Dalmuir	a			13 20	13 31				13 49		14 01					14 19	14 31				14 49		15 01
	d	13 15		13 20	13 31	13 35		13 45	13 50		14 01	14 05		14 15		14 20	14 31	14 35		14 45	14 50		15 01
Singer	d			13 22		13 37			13 52			14 07				14 22		14 37			14 52		
Drumry	d			13 25		13 39			13 55			14 09				14 25		14 39			14 55		
Drumchapel	d			13 27		13 42			13 57			14 12				14 27		14 42			14 57		
Milngavie	d						13 41						14 11						14 41				
Hillfoot	d						13 44						14 14						14 44				
Bearsden	d						13 46						14 16						14 46				
Westerton	d			13 30		13 44	13 49		14 00			14 14	14 19			14 30		14 44	14 49		15 00		
Anniesland	d			13 33		13 47	13 52		14 03			14 17	14 22			14 33		14 47	14 52		15 03		
Clydebank	d	13 17			13 33			13 47			14 03			14 17			14 33			14 47			15 03
Yoker	d	13 19			13 35			13 49			14 05			14 19			14 35			14 49			15 05
Garscadden	d	13 22			13 39			13 52			14 09			14 22			14 39			14 52			15 09
Scotstounhill	d	13 24			13 41			13 54			14 11			14 24			14 41			14 54			15 11
Jordanhill	d	13 26			13 43			13 56			14 13			14 26			14 43			14 56			15 13
Hyndland	d	13 28		13 35	13 45	13 50	13 55	13 58	14 05		14 15	14 20	14 25	14 28		14 35	14 45	14 50	14 55	14 58	15 05		15 15
Partick	d	13 30	13 34	13 38	13 48	13 52	13 58	14 00	14 08		14 18	14 22	14 28	14 30	14 34	14 38	14 48	14 52	14 58	15 00	15 08		15 18
Exhibition Centre	d		13 37		13 51		14 01				14 21		14 31		14 37		14 51		15 01				15 21
Anderston	d																						
Glasgow Central LL	a		13 39		13 53		14 03				14 23		14 33		14 39		14 53		15 03				15 23
	d		13 40		13 54		14 04			14b22	14 24		14 34		14 40		14 54		15 04			15b22	15 24
Argyle Street	d		13 42		13 56		14 06				14 26		14 36		14 41		14 56		15 06				15 26
Charing Cross	d	13 34		13 43		13 56		14 04	14 13			14 26		14 34		14 43		14 56		15 04	15 13		
Glasgow Queen St LL	a	13 36		13 45		13 58		14 06	14 15			14 28		14 36		14 45		14 58		15 06	15 15		
	d	13 37		13 45		13 59		14 07	14 15			14 29		14 37		14 45		14 59		15 07	15 15		
High Street	d	13 39		13 47		14 01		14 09	14 17			14 31		14 39		14 47		15 01		15 09	15 17		
Bellgrove	d	13 41		13 49		14 03		14 11	14 19			14 33		14 41		14 49		15 03		15 11	15 19		
Duke Street	d					14 05						14 35						15 05					
Alexandra Parade	d					14 06						14 36						15 06					
Barnhill	d					14 09						14 39						15 09					
Springburn	a					14 11						14 41						15 11					
Carntyne	d	13 44		13 53				14 14	14 23					14 44		14 53				15 14	15 23		
Shettleston	d	13 47		13 55				14 17	14 25					14 47		14 55				15 17	15 25		
Garrowhill	d	13 49		13 58				14 19	14 28					14 49		14 58				15 19	15 28		
Easterhouse	d	13 52		14 00				14 22	14 30					14 52		15 00				15 22	15 30		
Blairhill	d	13 56		14 04				14 26	14 34					14 56		15 04				15 26	15 34		
Coatbridge Sunnyside	d	13 58		14 07				14 28	14 37					14 58		15 07				15 28	15 37		
Coatdyke	d	14 01		14 09				14 31	14 39					15 01		15 09				15 31	15 39		
Airdrie	d	14a04		14 12				14a34	14 42					15a04		15 12				15a34	15 42		
Drumgelloch	d			14 15					14 45							15 15					15 45		
Caldercruix	d			14 19					14 49							15 19					15 49		
Blackridge	d			14 25					14 55							15 25					15 55		
Armadale	d			14 29					14 59							15 29					15 59		
Bathgate	a			14 33					15 03							15 33					16 03		
	d			14 34					15 04							15 34					16 04		
Livingston North	d			14 38					15 09							15 38					16 09		
Uphall	d			14 41					15 12							15 41					16 12		
Edinburgh Park	a			14 49					15 20							15 49					16 20		
Haymarket	a			14 54					15 24							15 54					16 24		
Edinburgh	a			14 59					15 29							15 59					16 29		
Bridgeton	d				13 59		14 09				14 29		14 39				14 59		15 09				15 29
Dalmarnock	d																						
Rutherglen	d		13 51		14 05		14 12				14 32		14 43		14 47		15 03		15 14				15 32
Cambuslang	d				14 09		14 16				14 36		14 47				15 07		15 18				15 36
Newton	d				14 12						14 39						15 10						15 39
Blantyre	d		13 59		14 16						14 43				14 56		15 14						15 43
Hamilton West	d		14 02		14 19						14 46				14 59		15 17						15 46
Hamilton Central	d		14 04		14 23						14 50				15 02		15 21						15 50
Chatelherault	d		14 08												15 06								
Merryton	d		14 11												15 09								
Larkhall	a		14 14												15 12								
Airbles	d				14 28						14 55						15 26						15 55
Uddingston	d						14 20						14 52						15 22				
Bellshill	d						14 25						14 56						15 27				
Motherwell	a				14 30		14 33				14 57		15 04				15 28		15 33				15 57
	d						14 33												15 34				
Whifflet	a									14 50												15 50	
Coatbridge Central	a																						
Shieldmuir	d						14 37												15 37				
Holytown	d									14a59												15a59	
Wishaw	d						14 40												15 41				
Carluke	d						14 47												15 47				
Lanark	a						14 59												15 59				

A To Shotts

b Glasgow Central High Level

Table 226

Sundays
from 4 December

Helensburgh, Balloch, Dalmuir and Milngavie - Glasgow - Springburn, Airdrie, Bathgate and Edinburgh, Hamilton, Larkhall, Motherwell, Coatbridge and Lanark

		SR	SR	SR	SR	SR	SR	SR	SR	SR	SR	SR A	SR	SR	SR	SR	SR	SR	SR	SR	SR	SR
Helensburgh Central	d					14 55					15 25							15 55				
Craigendoran	d					14 58					15 28							15 58				
Cardross	d					15 03					15 33							16 03				
Balloch	d						15 09						15 39						16 09			
Alexandria	d						15 11						15 41						16 11			
Renton	d						15 14						15 44						16 14			
Dalreoch	d					15 08	15 17				15 38		15 47					16 08	16 17			
Dumbarton Central	d					15 10	15 18				15 40		15 48					16 10	16 18			
Dumbarton East	d					15 12	15 20				15 42		15 50					16 12	16 20			
Bowling	d						15 25						15 55						16 25			
Kilpatrick	d						15 28						15 58						16 28			
Dalmuir	a					15 19	15 31				15 49		16 01					16 19	16 31			
	d	15 05		15 15		15 20	15 31	15 35		15 45	15 50		16 01	16 05		16 15		16 20	16 31	16 35		16 45
Singer	d	15 07				15 22		15 37			15 52			16 07				16 22		16 37		
Drumry	d	15 09				15 25		15 39			15 55			16 09				16 25		16 39		
Drumchapel	d	15 12				15 27		15 42			15 57			16 12				16 27		16 42		
Milngavie	d		15 11						15 41						16 11						16 41	
Hillfoot	d		15 14						15 44						16 14						16 44	
Bearsden	d		15 16						15 46						16 16						16 46	
Westerton	d	15 14	15 19			15 30		15 44	15 49		16 00			16 14	16 19			16 30		16 44	16 49	
Anniesland	d	15 17	15 22			15 33		15 47	15 52		16 03			16 17	16 22			16 33		16 47	16 52	
Clydebank	d			15 17			15 33			15 47			16 03			16 17			16 33			16 47
Yoker	d			15 19			15 35			15 49			16 05			16 19			16 35			16 49
Garscadden	d			15 22			15 39			15 52			16 09			16 22			16 39			16 52
Scotstounhill	d			15 24			15 41			15 54			16 11			16 24			16 41			16 54
Jordanhill	d			15 26			15 43			15 56			16 13			16 26			16 43			16 56
Hyndland	d	15 20	15 25	15 28		15 35	15 45	15 50	15 55	15 58	16 05		16 15	16 20	16 25	16 28		16 35	16 45	16 50	16 55	16 59
Partick ⇌	d	15 22	15 28	15 30	15 34	15 38	15 48	15 52	15 58	16 00	16 08		16 18	16 22	16 28	16 30	16 34	16 38	16 48	16 52	16 58	17 01
Exhibition Centre	d		15 31		15 37		15 51		16 01				16 21		16 31		16 37		16 51		17 01	
Anderston	d																					
Glasgow Central LL	a		15 33		15 39		15 53		16 03				16 23		16 33		16 39		16 53		17 03	
	d		15 34		15 43		15 54		16 04			16b22	16 24		16 34		16 40		16 54		17 04	
Argyle Street	d		15 36		15 45		15 56		16 06				16 26		16 36		16 46		16 56		17 06	
Charing Cross	d	15 26		15 34		15 43		15 56		16 04	16 13			16 26		16 34		16 43		16 56		17 05
Glasgow Queen St LL ⇌	a	15 28		15 36		15 45		15 58		16 06	16 15			16 28		16 36		16 45		16 58		17 07
	d	15 29		15 37		15 45		15 59		16 07	16 15			16 29		16 37		16 45		16 59		17 07
High Street	d	15 31		15 39		15 47		16 01		16 09	16 17			16 31		16 39		16 47		17 01		17 09
Bellgrove	d	15 33		15 41		15 49		16 03		16 11	16 19			16 33		16 41		16 49		17 03		17 11
Duke Street	d	15 35						16 05						16 35						17 05		
Alexandra Parade	d	15 36						16 06						16 36						17 06		
Barnhill	d	15 39						16 09						16 39						17 09		
Springburn	a	15 41						16 11						16 41						17 11		
Carntyne	d			15 44		15 53				16 14	16 23					16 44		16 53				17 15
Shettleston	d			15 47		15 55				16 17	16 25					16 47		16 55				17 17
Garrowhill	d			15 49		15 58				16 19	16 28					16 49		16 58				17 20
Easterhouse	d			15 52		16 00				16 22	16 30					16 52		17 00				17 22
Blairhill	d			15 56		16 04				16 26	16 34					16 56		17 04				17 26
Coatbridge Sunnyside	d			15 58		16 07				16 28	16 37					16 58		17 07				17 29
Coatdyke	d			16 01		16 09				16 31	16 39					17 01		17 09				17 31
Airdrie	d			16a04		16 12				16a34	16 42					17a04		17 12				17a34
Drumgelloch	d					16 15					16 45							17 15				
Caldercruix	d					16 19					16 49							17 19				
Blackridge	d					16 25					16 55							17 25				
Armadale	d					16 29					16 59							17 29				
Bathgate	a					16 33					17 03							17 33				
	d					16 34					17 04							17 34				
Livingston North	d					16 38					17 09							17 38				
Uphall	d					16 41					17 12							17 41				
Edinburgh Park	a					16 50					17 20							17 49				
Haymarket	a					16 54					17 24							17 58				
Edinburgh	a					16 59					17 29							18 03				
Bridgeton	d		15 39				15 59		16 09				16 29		16 39				16 59		17 09	
Dalmarnock	d																					
Rutherglen	d		15 42		15 50		16 03		16 12				16 32		16 44		16 51		17 03		17 13	
Cambuslang	d		15 46				16 07		16 16				16 36		16 50				17 07		17 17	
Newton	d						16 11						16 39						17 10			
Blantyre	d				15 58		16 15						16 43				16 59		17 14			
Hamilton West	d				16 02		16 18						16 46				17 02		17 17			
Hamilton Central	d				16 05		16 21						16 50				17 04		17 20			
Chatelherault	d				16 08												17 08					
Merryton	d				16 11												17 11					
Larkhall	a				16 14												17 14					
Airbles	d						16 26						16 55						17 25			
Uddingston	d		15 51						16 20						16 54						17 21	
Bellshill	d		15 55						16 25						16 59						17 26	
Motherwell	a		16 03				16 28		16 33				16 57		17 05				17 27		17 33	
	d								16 33												17 33	
Whifflet	a											16 50										
Coatbridge Central	a																					
Shieldmuir	d								16 37												17 37	
Holytown	d											16a59										
Wishaw	d								16 40												17 40	
Carluke	d								16 47												17 47	
Lanark	a								16 59												17 59	

A To Shotts

b Glasgow Central High Level

Table 226

Sundays
from 4 December

Helensburgh, Balloch, Dalmuir and Milngavie - Glasgow - Springburn, Airdrie, Bathgate and Edinburgh, Hamilton, Larkhall, Motherwell, Coatbridge and Lanark

		SR	SR A	SR	SR	SR	SR	SR	SR	SR	SR	SR	SR	SR	SR A	SR	SR	SR	SR	SR	SR	SR	SR
Helensburgh Central	d	16 25							16 55					17 25					17 55			18 25	
Craigendoran	d	16 28							16 58					17 28					17 58			18 28	
Cardross	d	16 33							17 03					17 33					18 03			18 33	
Balloch	d			16 39						17 09						17 39				18 09			18 39
Alexandria	d			16 41						17 11						17 41				18 11			18 41
Renton	d			16 44						17 14						17 44				18 14			18 44
Dalreoch	d	16 38		16 47					17 08	17 17				17 38		17 47			18 08	18 17		18 38	18 48
Dumbarton Central	d	16 40		16 48					17 10	17 18				17 40		17 48			18 10	18 18		18 40	18 49
Dumbarton East	d	16 42		16 50					17 12	17 20				17 42		17 50			18 12	18 20		18 42	18 51
Bowling	d			16 55						17 25						17 55				18 25			18 56
Kilpatrick	d			16 58						17 28						17 58				18 28			18 59
Dalmuir	a	16 49		17 01					17 19	17 31				17 49		18 01			18 19	18 31		18 49	19 02
	d	16 50		17 01	17 05		17 15		17 20	17 31	17 35		17 45	17 50		18 01			18 20	18 31		18 50	19 02
Singer	d	16 52			17 07				17 22		17 37			17 52					18 22			18 52	
Drumry	d	16 55			17 09				17 25		17 39			17 55					18 25			18 55	
Drumchapel	d	16 57			17 12				17 27		17 42			17 57					18 27			18 57	
Milngavie	d					17 11						17 41					18 11				18 41		
Hillfoot	d					17 14						17 44					18 14				18 44		
Bearsden	d					17 16						17 46					18 16				18 46		
Westerton	d	17 00			17 14	17 19			17 30		17 44	17 49		18 00			18 19		18 30		18 49	19 00	
Anniesland	d	17 03			17 17	17 22			17 33		17 47	17 52		18 03			18 22		18 33		18 52	19 03	
Clydebank	d			17 03			17 17			17 33			17 47			18 03				18 33			19 03
Yoker	d			17 05			17 19			17 35			17 49			18 05				18 35			19 05
Garscadden	d			17 09			17 22			17 39			17 52			18 09				18 39			19 10
Scotstounhill	d			17 11			17 24			17 41			17 54			18 11				18 41			19 12
Jordanhill	d			17 13			17 26			17 43			17 56			18 13				18 43			19 13
Hyndland	d	17 05		17 15	17 20	17 25	17 28		17 35	17 45	17 50	17 55	17 58	18 05		18 15	18 25		18 35	18 45	18 55	19 05	19 15
Partick ⇌	d	17 08		17 18	17 22	17 28	17 30	17 34	17 38	17 48	17 52	17 58	18 00	18 08		18 18	18 28	18 34	18 38	18 48	18 58	19 08	19 18
Exhibition Centre	d			17 21		17 31		17 37		17 51		18 01				18 21	18 31	18 37		18 51	19 01		19 21
Anderston	d																						
Glasgow Central LL	a			17 23		17 33		17 39		17 53		18 03				18 23	18 33	18 39		18 53	19 03		19 24
	d		17b22	17 24		17 34		17 40		17 54		18 04			18b22	18 24	18 34	18 40		18 54	19 04		19 24
Argyle Street	d			17 26		17 36		17 41		17 56		18 06											
Charing Cross	d	17 13			17 26		17 34		17 43		17 56		18 04	18 13					18 43			19 13	
Glasgow Queen St LL ⇌	a	17 15			17 28		17 36		17 45		17 58		18 06	18 15					18 45			19 15	
	d	17 15			17 29		17 37		17 45		17 59		18 07	18 15					18 45			19 15	
High Street	d	17 17			17 31		17 39		17 47		18 01		18 09	18 17					18 47			19 17	
Bellgrove	d	17 19			17 33		17 41		17 49		18 03		18 11	18 19					18 49			19 19	
Duke Street	d				17 35						18 05												
Alexandra Parade	d				17 36						18 06												
Barnhill	d				17 39						18 09												
Springburn	a				17 41						18 11												
Carntyne	d	17 23					17 44		17 53				18 14	18 23					18 53			19 23	
Shettleston	d	17 25					17 47		17 55				18 17	18 25					18 55			19 25	
Garrowhill	d	17 28					17 49		17 58				18 19	18 28					18 58			19 28	
Easterhouse	d	17 30					17 52		18 00				18 22	18 30					19 00			19 30	
Blairhill	d	17 34					17 56		18 04				18 26	18 34					19 04			19 34	
Coatbridge Sunnyside	d	17 37					17 58		18 07				18 28	18 37					19 07			19 37	
Coatdyke	d	17 39					18 01		18 09				18 31	18 39					19 09			19 39	
Airdrie	d	17 42					18a04		18 12				18a34	18 42					19 12			19a42	
Drumgelloch	d	17 45							18 15					18 45					19 15				
Caldercruix	d	17 49							18 19					18 49					19 19				
Blackridge	d	17 55							18 25					18 55					19 25				
Armadale	d	17 59							18 29					18 59					19 29				
Bathgate	a	18 03							18 33					19 03					19 33				
	d	18 04							18 34					19 04					19 34				
Livingston North	d	18 09							18 38					19 09					19 38				
Uphall	d	18 12							18 41					19 12					19 41				
Edinburgh Park	a	18 20							18 49					19 20					19 49				
Haymarket	a	18 24							18 54					19 24					19 54				
Edinburgh	a	18 30							18 59					19 29					19 59				
Bridgeton	d			17 29		17 39				17 59		18 09				18 29	18 39			18 59	19 09		19 29
Dalmarnock	d																						
Rutherglen	d			17 32		17 42		17 46		18 02		18 12				18 32	18 42	18 47		19 03	19 12		19 32
Cambuslang	d			17 36		17 46				18 06		18 16				18 36	18 46			19 07	19 16		19 36
Newton	d			17 39						18 09						18 39				19 10			19 39
Blantyre	d			17 43				17 56		18 13						18 43		18 57		19 14			19 43
Hamilton West	d			17 46				17 59		18 16						18 46		19 00		19 17			19 46
Hamilton Central	d			17 50				18 02		18 20						18 50		19 02		19 20			19 50
Chatelherault	d							18 05										19 06					
Merryton	d							18 08										19 09					
Larkhall	a							18 12										19 12					
Airbles	d			17 55						18 25						18 55				19 25			19 55
Uddingston	d					17 50						18 20					18 50				19 20		
Bellshill	d					17 55						18 25					18 55				19 25		
Motherwell	a			17 57		18 02				18 27		18 33				18 57	19 03			19 27	19 33		19 57
	d											18 33									19 33		
Whifflet	a		17 50												18 50								
Coatbridge Central	a																						
Shieldmuir	d											18 37									19 37		
Holytown	d		17a59												18a59								
Wishaw	d											18 40									19 40		
Carluke	d											18 47									19 47		
Lanark	a											18 59									19 59		

A To Shotts

b Glasgow Central High Level

Sundays
from 4 December

Helensburgh, Balloch, Dalmuir and Milngavie - Glasgow - Springburn, Airdrie, Bathgate and Edinburgh, Hamilton, Larkhall, Motherwell, Coatbridge and Lanark

		SR	SR	SR	SR	SR	SR	SR	SR	SR	SR	SR	SR	SR	SR	SR ◇ A	SR	SR	SR	SR	SR	SR	SR
Helensburgh Central	d			18 55			19 25				19 55			20 25		20b40			20 55			21 25	
Craigendoran	d			18 58			19 28				19 58			20 28					20 58			21 28	
Cardross	d			19 03			19 33				20 03			20 33					21 03			21 33	
Balloch	d				19 09			19 39				20 09			20 38					21 09			21 39
Alexandria	d				19 11			19 41				20 11			20 40					21 11			21 41
Renton	d				19 14			19 44				20 14			20 43					21 14			21 44
Dalreoch	d			19 08	19 17		19 38	19 47			20 08	20 17		20 38	20 46				21 08	21 17		21 38	21 47
Dumbarton Central	d			19 10	19 18		19 40	19 48			20 10	20 18		20 40	20 47	20 53			21 10	21 18		21 40	21 48
Dumbarton East	d			19 12	19 20		19 42	19 50			20 12	20 20		20 42	20 49				21 12	21 20		21 42	21 50
Bowling	d				19 25			19 55				20 25			20 54					21 25			21 55
Kilpatrick	d				19 28			19 58				20 28			20 57					21 28			21 58
Dalmuir	a			19 20	19 31		19 49	20 01			20 19	20 31		20 49	21 00	21 03			21 19	21 31		21 49	22 01
	d			19 20	19 31		19 50	20 01			20 20	20 31		20 50	21 01	21 03			21 20	21 31		21 50	22 01
Singer	d			19 22			19 52				20 22			20 52					21 22			21 52	
Drumry	d			19 25			19 55				20 25			20 55					21 25			21 55	
Drumchapel	d			19 27			19 57				20 27			20 57					21 27			21 57	
Milngavie	d	19 11				19 41			20 11				20 41				21 11				21 41		
Hillfoot	d	19 14				19 44			20 14				20 44				21 14				21 44		
Bearsden	d	19 16				19 46			20 16				20 46				21 16				21 46		
Westerton	d	19 19		19 30		19 49	20 00		20 19		20 30		20 49	21 00			21 19		21 30		21 49	22 00	
Anniesland	d	19 22		19 33		19 52	20 03		20 22		20 33		20 52	21 03			21 22		21 33		21 52	22 03	
Clydebank	d				19 33			20 03				20 33			21 03					21 33			22 03
Yoker	d				19 35			20 05				20 35			21 05					21 35			22 05
Garscadden	d				19 39			20 09				20 39			21 09					21 39			22 09
Scotstounhill	d				19 41			20 11				20 41			21 11					21 41			22 11
Jordanhill	d				19 43			20 13				20 43			21 13					21 43			22 13
Hyndland	d	19 25		19 35	19 45	19 55	20 05	20 15	20 25		20 35	20 45	20 55	21 05	21 15		21 25		21 35	21 45	21 55	22 05	22 15
Partick	d	19 28	19 34	19 38	19 48	19 58	20 08	20 18	20 28	20 34	20 38	20 48	20 58	21 08	21 18		21 28	21 34	21 38	21 48	21 58	22 08	22 18
Exhibition Centre	d	19 31	19 37		19 51	20 01		20 21	20 31	20 37		20 51	21 01		21 21		21 31	21 37		21 51	22 01		22 21
Anderston	d																						
Glasgow Central LL 15	a	19 33	19 39		19 53	20 03		20 23	20 33	20 39		20 53	21 03		21 23		21 33	21 39		21 53	22 03		22 23
	d	19 34	19 40		19 54	20 04		20 24	20 34	20 40		20 54	21 04		21 24		21 34	21 40		21 54	22 04		22 24
Argyle Street	d																						
Charing Cross	d			19 43			20 13				20 43			21 13					21 43			22 13	
Glasgow Queen St LL 10	a			19 45			20 15				20 45			21 15		21c19			21 45			22 15	
	d			19 45			20 15				20 45			21 15					21 45			22 15	
High Street	d			19 47			20 17				20 47			21 17					21 47			22 17	
Bellgrove	d			19 49			20 19				20 49			21 19					21 49			22 19	
Duke Street	d																						
Alexandra Parade	d																						
Barnhill	d																						
Springburn	a																						
Carntyne	d			19 53			20 23				20 53			21 23					21 53			22 23	
Shettleston	d			19 55			20 25				20 55			21 25					21 55			22 25	
Garrowhill	d			19 58			20 28				20 58			21 28					21 58			22 28	
Easterhouse	d			20 00			20 30				21 00			21 30					22 00			22 30	
Blairhill	d			20 04			20 34				21 04			21 34					22 04			22 34	
Coatbridge Sunnyside	d			20 07			20 37				21 07			21 37					22 07			22 37	
Coatdyke	d			20 09			20 39				21 09			21 39					22 09			22 39	
Airdrie	d			20 12			20a42				21 12			21a42					22 12			22a42	
Drumgelloch	d			20 15							21 15								22 15				
Caldercruix	d			20 19							21 19								22 19				
Blackridge	d			20 25							21 25								22 25				
Armadale	d			20 29							21 29								22 29				
Bathgate	a			20 33							21 33								22 33				
	d			20 34							21 34								22 34				
Livingston North	d			20 38							21 39								22 39				
Uphall	d			20 41							21 42								22 42				
Edinburgh Park	a			20 49							21 50								22 50				
Haymarket	a			20 54							21 54								22 55				
Edinburgh	a			20 59							21 59								23 00				
Bridgeton	d	19 37			19 59	20 09		20 29	20 37			20 57	21 09		21 29		21 37			21 59	22 08		22 29
Dalmarnock	d																						
Rutherglen	d	19 40	19 46		20 02	20 14		20 32	20 40	20 46		21 00	21 12		21 32		21 40	21 47		22 02	22 11		22 32
Cambuslang	d	19 44			20 06	20 18		20 36	20 44			21 04	21 16		21 36		21 44			22 06	22 15		22 36
Newton	d				20 09			20 39				21 08			21 39					22 09			22 39
Blantyre	d		19 56		20 13			20 43		20 54		21 13			21 43			21 54		22 13			22 43
Hamilton West	d		19 59		20 16			20 46		20 58		21 16			21 46			21 57		22 16			22 46
Hamilton Central	d		20 02		20 20			20 50		21 02		21 20			21 50			22 01		22 20			22 50
Chatelherault	d		20 05							21 05								22 04					
Merryton	d		20 08							21 08								22 07					
Larkhall	a		20 12							21 13								22 12					
Airbles	d				20 25			20 55				21 25			21 55					22 25			22 55
Uddingston	d	19 49				20 22			20 49				21 20				21 49				22 19		
Bellshill	d	19 55				20 27			20 55				21 25				21 55				22 24		
Motherwell	a	20 03			20 27	20 33		20 57	21 04			21 27	21 33		21 57		22 03			22 27	22 32		22 57
	d					20 33							21 33								22 32		
Whifflet	a																						
Coatbridge Central	a																						
Shieldmuir	d					20 37							21 37								22 36		
Holytown	d																						
Wishaw	d					20 40							21 40								22 39		
Carluke	d					20 47							21 47								22 44		
Lanark	a					20 59							21 59								22 58		

A From Mallaig
b Helensburgh Upper
c Glasgow Queen St High Level

from 4 December

Helensburgh, Balloch, Dalmuir and Milngavie - Glasgow - Springburn, Airdrie, Bathgate and Edinburgh, Hamilton, Larkhall, Motherwell, Coatbridge and Lanark

		SR	SR	SR	SR	SR	SR	SR	SR A	SR
Helensburgh Central	d			21 55			22 25		22b37	
Craigendoran	d			21 58			22 28			
Cardross	d			22 03			22 33			
Balloch	d				22 09			22 39		23 09
Alexandria	d				22 11			22 41		23 11
Renton	d				22 14			22 44		23 14
Dalreoch	d			22 08	22 17		22 38	22 47		23 17
Dumbarton Central	d			22 10	22 18		22 40	22 48		23 18
Dumbarton East	d			22 12	22 20		22 42	22 50		23 20
Bowling	d				22 25			22 55		23 25
Kilpatrick	d				22 28			22 58		23 28
Dalmuir	a			22 19	22 31		22 49	23 01	23 02	23 31
	d			22 20	22 31		22 50	23 01	23 04	23 31
Singer	d			22 22			22 52			
Drumry	d			22 25			22 55			
Drumchapel	d			22 27			22 57			
Milngavie	d	22 11				22 41				
Hillfoot	d	22 14				22 44				
Bearsden	d	22 16				22 46				
Westerton	d	22 19		22 30		22 49	23 00		23 13	
Anniesland	d	22 22		22 33		22 52	23 03			
Clydebank	d				22 33			23 03		23 33
Yoker	d				22 35			23a05		23a35
Garscadden	d				22 39					
Scotstounhill	d				22 41					
Jordanhill	d				22 43					
Hyndland	d	22 25		22 35	22 45	22 55	23 05			
Partick	d	22 28	22 34	22 38	22 48	22 58	23 08			
Exhibition Centre	d	22 31	22 37		22 51	23 01				
Anderston	d									
Glasgow Central LL 15	a	22 33	22 39		22 53	23 03				
	d	22 34	22 40		22 54	23 04				
Argyle Street	d									
Charing Cross	d			22 43			23 13			
Glasgow Queen St LL 10	a			22 45			23 15			
	d			22 45			23 15			
High Street	d			22 47			23 17			
Bellgrove	d			22 49			23 19			
Duke Street	d									
Alexandra Parade	d									
Barnhill	d									
Springburn	a									
Carntyne	d			22 53			23 23			
Shettleston	d			22 55			23 25			
Garrowhill	d			22 58			23 28			
Easterhouse	d			23 00			23 30			
Blairhill	d			23 04			23 34			
Coatbridge Sunnyside	d			23 07			23 37			
Coatdyke	d			23 09			23 39			
Airdrie	d			23 12			23a42			
Drumgelloch	d			23 15						
Caldercruix	d			23 19						
Blackridge	d			23 25						
Armadale	d			23 29						
Bathgate	a			23 33						
	d									
Livingston North	d									
Uphall	d									
Edinburgh Park	a									
Haymarket	a									
Edinburgh	a								00 13	
Bridgeton	d	22 39			22 59	23 09				
Dalmarnock	d									
Rutherglen	d	22 42	22 47		23 02	23 12				
Cambuslang	d	22 46			23 06	23 16				
Newton	d				23 09					
Blantyre	d		22 55		23 13					
Hamilton West	d		22 58		23 16					
Hamilton Central	d		23 02		23 20					
Chatelherault	d		23 05							
Merryton	d		23 08							
Larkhall	a		23 11							
Airbles	d				23 25					
Uddingston	d	22 50				23 20				
Bellshill	d	22 55				23 25				
Motherwell	a	23 03			23 27	23 33				
	d									
Whifflet	a									
Coatbridge Central	a									
Shieldmuir	d									
Holytown	d									
Wishaw	d									
Carluke	d									
Lanark	a									

A From Fort William
b Helensburgh Upper

Network Diagram for Tables 227, 239

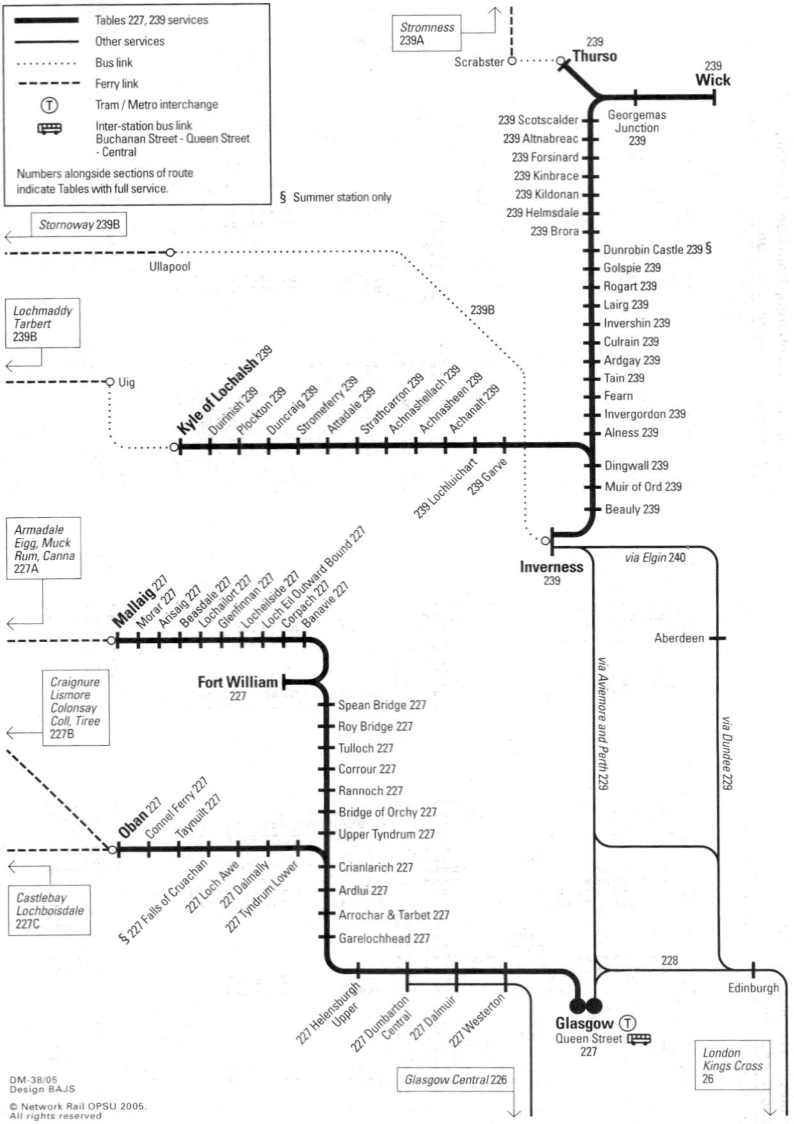

DM-38/05
Design BAJS

© Network Rail OPSU 2005.
All rights reserved

Table 227

Mondays to Saturdays

until 24 September

Glasgow Queen Street - Oban, Fort William and Mallaig

Miles	Miles			SR	SR	WR	SR		SR SX	SR SO	SR			SR	
				[R]											
					◇		◇		◇	◇	◇			◇	
				🛏			🛒		🛒	🛒	🛒			🛒	
—	—	Edinburgh 228	d	04 50											
0	0	**Glasgow Queen St.** 10 226 ⛴	d				08 21		09 07	10 37	12 21			18 21	
5½	5½	Westerton 226	d	05 56											
10	10	Dalmuir 226	d	06 04			08 39		09 24	10 52	12 42			18 38	
16½	16½	Dumbarton Central 226	d				08 48		09 36	11 05	12 48			18 47	
25½	25½	Helensburgh Upper	a	06 26			09 03		09 50	11 20	13 03			19 02	
—	—		d	06 29			09 06		09 52	11 22	13 06			19 04	
32¼	32¼	Garelochhead	d	06 42			09 17		10 04	11 34	13 17			19 16	
43	43	Arrochar & Tarbet	d	07 08			09 37		10 26	11 54	13 37			19 36	
51	51	Ardlui	d	07x22			09 53		10x39	12 08	13 53			19 51	
59¾	59¾	**Crianlarich**	a	07 43			10 09		10 55	12 24	14 09			20 08	
—	—														
—	—		d	07 44			10 15	10 21	10 58	12 26	14 15	14 21		20 14	20 17
64¾	—	Tyndrum Lower	d				10 24			12 35	14 24			20 23	
76¾	—	Dalmally	d				10 42			12 57	14 42			20 41	
79½	—	Loch Awe	d				10 47			13 02	14 47			20 46	
83½	—	Falls of Cruachan §	d				10x52			13x07	14x52			20x51	
88½	—	Taynuilt	d				11 03			13 18	15 03			21 02	
95¼	—	Connel Ferry	d				11 14			13 29	15 14			21 13	
101½	—	**Oban**	a				11 27			13 42	15 27			21 26	
—	64½	Upper Tyndrum	d	07 57				10 32	11 09			14 32			20 28
—	72¼	Bridge of Orchy	d	08 14				10 46	11 23			14 46			20 42
—	87¾	Rannoch	d	08 45				11 08	11 45			15 09			21 07
—	95	Corrour	d	08x58				11 20	11 57			15 21			21 19
—	105	Tulloch	d	09 18				11 36	12 13			15 38			21 35
—	110¾	Roy Bridge	d	09x29				11 46	12 23			15 48			21 45
—	114	Spean Bridge	d	09 37				11 54	12 30			15 56			21 52
—	122¾	**Fort William**	a	09 54				12 07	12 43			16 09			22 05
—	—		d		08 30	10 18		12 12	12 48			16 19			22 14
—	125	Banavie	d		08 36			12 18	12 54			16 25			22 20
—	126	Corpach	d		08 42			12 23	12 59			16 30			22 25
—	129	Loch Eil Outward Bound	d		08 49	10 37		12 29	13 05			16 36			22 31
—	132¾	Locheilside	d		08x54			12x34	13x10			16x41			22x36
—	139¼	Glenfinnan	d		09 05	11 21		12 46	13 21			16 54			22 47
—	148½	Lochailort	d		09x20			13x01	13x37			17x10			23x03
—	153¼	Beasdale	d		09x29			13x10	13x46			17x19			23x12
—	156¾	Arisaig	d		09 38	11 59		13 18	13 54			17 27			23 20
—	161¼	Morar	d		09 46			13 26	14 02			17 35			23 28
—	164¼	**Mallaig**	a		09 53	12 22		13 34	14 09			17 43			23 35

§ Summer station only

Mondays to Saturdays

from 26 September

		SR	SR	WR	SR		SR SO	SR SO	SR			SR	
		[R]											
			◇		◇		◇	◇	◇			◇	
							A	B					
		🛏			🛒		🛒	🛒	🛒			🛒	
Edinburgh 228	d	04 50											
Glasgow Queen St. 10 226 ⛴	d				08 21			10 37	12 21			18 21	
Westerton 226	d	05 56											
Dalmuir 226	d	06 04			08 39			10 52	12 42			18 38	
Dumbarton Central 226	d				08 48			11 05	12 48			18 47	
Helensburgh Upper	a	06 26			09 03			11 20	13 03			19 02	
	d	06 29			09 06			11 22	13 06			19 04	
Garelochhead	d	06 42			09 17			11 34	13 17			19 16	
Arrochar & Tarbet	d	07 08			09 37			11 54	13 37			19 36	
Ardlui	d	07x22			09 53			12 08	13 53			19 51	
Crianlarich	a	07 43			10 09			12 24	14 09			20 08	
	d	07 44			10 15	10 21	10 21	12 26	14 15	14 21		20 14	20 17
Tyndrum Lower	d				10 24			12 35	14 24			20 23	
Dalmally	d				10 42			12 57	14 42			20 41	
Loch Awe	d				10 47			13 02	14 47			20 46	
Falls of Cruachan §	d												
Taynuilt	d				11 03			13 18	15 03			21 02	
Connel Ferry	d				11 14			13 29	15 14			21 13	
Oban	a				11 27			13 42	15 27			21 26	
Upper Tyndrum	d	07 57				10 32	10 32			14 32			20 28
Bridge of Orchy	d	08 14				10 46	10 46			14 46			20 42
Rannoch	d	08 45				11 08	11 08			15 09			21 07
Corrour	d	08x58				11 20	11 20			15 21			21 19
Tulloch	d	09 18				11 36	11 36			15 38			21 35
Roy Bridge	d	09x29				11 46	11 46			15 48			21 45
Spean Bridge	d	09 37				11 54	11 54			15 56			21 52
Fort William	a	09 54				12 07	12 07			16 09			22 05
	d		08 30	10 18		12 12	12 12			16 19			22 14
Banavie	d		08 36			12 18	12 18			16 25			22 20
Corpach	d		08 42			12 23	12 23			16 30			22 25
Loch Eil Outward Bound	d		08 49	10 37		12 29	12 29			16 36			22 31
Locheilside	d		08x54			12x34	12x34			16x41			22x36
Glenfinnan	d		09 05	11 21		12 46	12 46			16 54			22 47
Lochailort	d		09x20			13x01	13x01			17x10			23x03
Beasdale	d		09x29			13x10	13x10			17x19			23x12
Arisaig	d		09 38	11 59		13 18	13 18			17 27			23 20
Morar	d		09 46			13 26	13 26			17 35			23 28
Mallaig	a		09 53	12 22		13 34	13 34			17 43			23 35

§ Summer station only

A 🛒 to Spean Bridge

B From 1 October until 29 October

Table 227

Sundays
until 25 September

Glasgow Queen Street - Oban, Fort William and Mallaig

		SR ◇ A	SR ◇	WR B	SR ◇	SR ◇		SR ◇	
Edinburgh	228 d	08 10							
Glasgow Queen St. 10 226 ⛴	d		09 55			12 20		18 20	
Westerton	226 d								
Dalmuir	226 d	09u27	10 16			12 34		18 34	
Dumbarton Central	226 d		10 25			12 44		18 44	
Helensburgh Upper	a	09 49	10 37			12 59		18 59	
	d	09 52	10 40			13 06		19 04	
Garelochhead	d	10 03	10 51			13 17		19 16	
Arrochar & Tarbet	d	10 23	11 11			13 37		19 36	
Ardlui	d	10 37	11 27			13 53		19 52	
Crianlarich	a	10 53	11 43			14 09		20 08	
	d	10 56	11 46			14 15	14 21	20 14	20 17
Tyndrum Lower	d	11 04	11 55			14 24		20 23	
Dalmally	d	11 22	12 13			14 42		20 41	
Loch Awe	d	11 27	12 18			14 47		20 46	
Falls of Cruachan §	d	11x32	12x23			14x52		20x51	
Taynuilt	d	11 42	12 41			15 03		21 02	
Connel Ferry	d	11 53	12 52			15 14		21 13	
Oban	a	12 06	13 05			15 27		21 26	
Upper Tyndrum	d						14 32		20 28
Bridge of Orchy	d						14 46		20 45
Rannoch	d						15 09		21 07
Corrour	d						15 21		21 19
Tulloch	d						15 38		21 35
Roy Bridge	d						15 48		21 45
Spean Bridge	d						15 56		21 52
Fort William	a						16 09		22 05
	d			10 18	12 12		16 19		22 14
Banavie	d				12 18		16 25		22 20
Corpach	d				12 23		16 30		22 25
Loch Eil Outward Bound	d			10 37	12 29		16 36		22 31
Locheilside	d				12x34		16x41		22x36
Glenfinnan	d			11c21	12 46		16 54		22 47
Lochailort	d				13x01		17x10		23x03
Beasdale	d				13x10		17x19		23x12
Arisaig	d			11 59	13 18		17 27		23 20
Morar	d				13 27		17 35		23 28
Mallaig	a			12 22	13 35		17 43		23 35

Sundays
2 October to 30 October

		WR C	SR ◇	SR ◇		SR ◇	
Edinburgh	228 d						
Glasgow Queen St. 10 226 ⛴	d			12 20		18 20	
Westerton	226 d						
Dalmuir	226 d			12 34		18 34	
Dumbarton Central	226 d			12 44		18 44	
Helensburgh Upper	a			12 59		18 59	
	d			13 06		19 04	
Garelochhead	d			13 17		19 16	
Arrochar & Tarbet	d			13 37		19 36	
Ardlui	d			13 53		19 52	
Crianlarich	a			14 09		20 08	
	d			14 15	14 21	20 14	20 17
Tyndrum Lower	d			14 24		20 23	
Dalmally	d			14 42		20 41	
Loch Awe	d			14 47		20 46	
Falls of Cruachan §	d						
Taynuilt	d			15 03		21 02	
Connel Ferry	d			15 14		21 13	
Oban	a			15 27		21 26	
Upper Tyndrum	d				14 32		20 28
Bridge of Orchy	d				14 46		20 45
Rannoch	d				15 09		21 07
Corrour	d				15 21		21 19
Tulloch	d				15 38		21 35
Roy Bridge	d				15 48		21 45
Spean Bridge	d				15 56		21 52
Fort William	a				16 09		22 05
	d	10 18	12 12		16 19		22 14
Banavie	d		12 18		16 25		22 20
Corpach	d		12 23		16 30		22 25
Loch Eil Outward Bound	d	10 37	12 29		16 36		22 31
Locheilside	d		12x34		16x41		22x36
Glenfinnan	d	11 21	12 46		16 54		22 47
Lochailort	d		13x01		17x10		23x03
Beasdale	d		13x10		17x19		23x12
Arisaig	d	11 59	13 18		17 27		23 20
Morar	d		13 27		17 35		23 28
Mallaig	a	12 22	13 35		17 43		23 35

§ Summer station only
A from 26 June until 28 August
B not 22 May
C 2 October

Table 227

Mondays to Saturdays

until 24 September

Mallaig, Fort William and Oban - Glasgow Queen Street

Miles	Miles			SR	SR	SR	SR	SR	SR	SR	SR	SR		WR	SR	SR	SR	SR	SR	SR
				MO	MX	SX			SX	SO	SO	SX			SO			FSX		SX
				R	R		◇	◇	◇	◇	◇	◇			◇	◇	◇	◇	◇	R
								A				B					A			
				🛏	🛏		⊼	⊼	⊼	⊼	⊼	⊼			⊼	⊼	⊼	⊼	⊼	🛏
—	0	**Mallaig**	d					06 03	10 10		10 10			14 11			16 05		18 15	
—	3	Morar	d					06 09	10 16		10 16			14 24			16 11		18 21	
—	7½	Arisaig	d					06 19	10 26		10 26			14 39			16 21		18 31	
—	11	Beasdale	d					06x25	10x32		10x32						16x27		18x37	
—	15¾	Lochailort	d					06x34	10x41		10x41						16x36		18x46	
—	25	Glenfinnan	d					06 51	10 59		10 59			15 24			16 53		19 03	
—	31½	Locheilside	d					07x01	11x09		11x09						17x03		19x13	
—	35¼	Loch Eil Outward Bound	d					07 07	11 15		11 15			15 43			17 09		19 19	
—	38¼	Corpach	d					07 13	11 21		11 21						17 15		19 25	
—	39¼	Banavie	d					07 17	11 25		11 25						17 19		19 29	
—	41½	**Fort William**	a					07 25	11 32		11 32			16 03			17 27		19 36	
—	—		d	19p00	19p50			07 42	11 40		11 40						17 37			19 50
—	50¼	Spean Bridge	d	19p20	20p10			07 55	11 55		11 55						17 50			20 10
—	53½	Roy Bridge	d	19b27	20b17			08 02	12 02		12 02						17 57			20x17
—	59¼	Tulloch	d	19p40	20p30			08 13	12 14		12 14						18 08			20 30
—	69¼	Corrour	d	20b01	20b51			08 30	12 31		12 31						18 25			20x51
—	76½	Rannoch	d	20p15	21p06			08 43	12 42		12 42						18 36			21 06
—	92	Bridge of Orchy	d	20c47	21p34			09 03	13 03		13 03						18 56			21 34
—	99¾	Upper Tyndrum	d	21p05	21p52			09 19	13 19		13 19						19 12			21 52
0	—	**Oban**	d				08 11			12 11		12 56			16 11	18 11		18 11		
6¼	—	Connel Ferry	d				08 23			12 23		13 08			16 27	18 23		18 23		
13	—	Taynuilt	d				08 35			12 35		13 20			16 39	18 35		18 35		
18½	—	Falls of Cruachan §	d				08x43			12x43		13x28			16x47	18x43		18x43		
22	—	Loch Awe	d				08 50			12 50		13 35			16 53	18 50		18 50		
24¾	—	Dalmally	d				08 56			12 56		13 41			17 00	18 56		18 56		
36¾	—	Tyndrum Lower	d				09 15			13 15		14 00			17 19	19 15		19 15		
42	104½	**Crianlarich**	a	21p16	22p04		09 29	09 30	13 27	13 29	13 30	14 10			17 28	19 27	19 26	19 27		22 04
—	—																			
—	—		d	21p18	22p05		09 36	09 36	13 36	13 36	13 36	14 12			17 31		19 33			22 05
50¾	113¼	Ardlui	d	21b39	22b26		09 52	09 52	13 52	13 52	13 52	14 28			17 47		19 53			22x26
58¾	121¼	Arrochar & Tarbet	d	21p57	22p44	07 10	10 07	10 07	14 07	14 07	14 07	14 43			18 02		20 08			22 44
69½	132	Garelochhead	d	22p23	23p10	07 30	10 32	10 32	14 27	14 27	14 27	15 03			18 22		20 28			23 10
76¼	138¾	Helensburgh Upper	a	22p35	23p23	07 41	10 42	10 42	14 38	14 38	14 38	15 14			18 33		20 39			23 23
—	—		d	22p37	23p24	07 42	10 44	10 44	14 39	14 39	14 39	15 15			18 34		20 40			23 24
85¼	147¾	Dumbarton Central 226	a			07 56	10 58	10 58	14 52	14 58	14 58	15 28			18 47		20 59			
92½	154¼	Dalmuir 226	a	23p02	23p49		11 07	11 07	15 04	15 07	15 07	15 37			18 56		21 08			23 49
96	157¾	Westerton 226	a	23p11	23p54							15 43								23 54
101½	164¼	**Glasgow Queen St.** 10 226 ⛴	a			08 37	11 30	11 30	15 30	15 30	15 30	16 00			19 20		21 31			
—	—	Edinburgh 228	a	00 13	00 50															00 50

§ Summer station only
A ⊼ from Fort William
B ⊼ from Crianlarich
b Previous night, stops on request
c Previous night, arr. 2041

Mondays to Saturdays

from 26 September

		SR	SR	SR	SR	SR	SR	SR	SR	SR		WR	SR	SR	SR	SR	SR	SR
		MO	MX	SX			SX	SX	SO	SO						FSX		SX
		R	R		◇	◇	◇	◇	◇	◇			◇	◇	◇	◇	◇	R
						A							B		A			
		🛏	🛏		⊼	⊼	⊼	⊼	⊼	⊼			⊼	⊼	⊼	⊼	⊼	🛏
Mallaig	d					06 03		10 10		10 10		14 11			16 05		18 15	
Morar	d					06 09		10 16		10 16		14 24			16 11		18 21	
Arisaig	d					06 19		10 26		10 26		14 39			16 21		18 31	
Beasdale	d					06x25		10x32		10x32					16x27		18x37	
Lochailort	d					06x34		10x41		10x41					16x36		18x46	
Glenfinnan	d					06 51		10 59		10 59		15 24			16 53		19 03	
Locheilside	d					07x01		11x09		11x09					17x03		19x13	
Loch Eil Outward Bound	d					07 07		11 15		11 15		15 43			17 09		19 19	
Corpach	d					07 13		11 21		11 21					17 15		19 25	
Banavie	d					07 17		11 25		11 25					17 19		19 29	
Fort William	a					07 25		11 32		11 32		16 03			17 27		19 36	
	d	19p00	19p50			07 42		11 40		11 40					17 37			19 50
Spean Bridge	d	19p20	20p10			07 55		11 55		11 55					17 50			20 10
Roy Bridge	d	19b27	20b17			08 02		12 02		12 02					17 57			20x17
Tulloch	d	19p40	20p30			08 13		12 14		12 14					18 08			20 30
Corrour	d	20b01	20b51			08 30		12 31		12 31					18 25			20x51
Rannoch	d	20p15	21p06			08 43		12 42		12 42					18 36			21 06
Bridge of Orchy	d	20c47	21p34			09 03		13 03		13 03					18 56			21 34
Upper Tyndrum	d	21p05	21p52			09 19		13 19		13 19					19 12			21 52
Oban	d				08 11		12 11		12 11				16 11	18 11		18 11		
Connel Ferry	d				08 23		12 23		12 23				16 27	18 23		18 23		
Taynuilt	d				08 35		12 35		12 35				16 39	18 35		18 35		
Falls of Cruachan §	d																	
Loch Awe	d				08 50		12 50		12 50				16 53	18 50		18 50		
Dalmally	d				08 56		12 56		12 56				17 00	18 56		18 56		
Tyndrum Lower	d				09 15		13 15		13 15				17 19	19 15		19 15		
Crianlarich	a	21p16	22p04		09 29	09 30	13 29	13 30	13 29	13 30			17 28	19 27	19 26	19 27		22 04
	d	21p18	22p05		09 36		13 36		13 36				17 31		19 33			22 05
Ardlui	d	21b39	22b26		09 52		13 52		13 52				17 47		19 53			22x26
Arrochar & Tarbet	d	21p57	22p44	07 10	10 07		14 07		14 07				18 02		20 08			22 44
Garelochhead	d	22p23	23p10	07 30	10 32		14 27		14 27				18 22		20 28			23 10
Helensburgh Upper	a	22p35	23p23	07 41	10 42		14 38		14 38				18 33		20 39			23 23
	d	22p37	23p24	07 42	10 44		14 39		14 39				18 34		20 40			23 24
Dumbarton Central 226	a			07 56	10 58		14 52		14 58				18 47		20 59			
Dalmuir 226	a	23p02	23p49		11 07		15 04		15 07				18 56		21 08			23 49
Westerton 226	a	23p11	23p54															23 54
Glasgow Queen St. 10 226 ⛴	a			08 37	11 30		15 30		15 30				19 20		21 31			
Edinburgh 228	a	00 13	00 50															00 50

§ Summer station only
A ⊼ from Fort William
B SO from 1 October until 29 October
b Previous night, stops on request
c Previous night, arr. 2041

Table 227

Mallaig, Fort William and Oban - Glasgow Queen Street

Sundays

until 25 September

		SR	SR	WR	SR	SR	SR	SR	SR	SR
									B	
		◇	◇		◇	◇	◇	◇		◇
						A				
		⊤	⊤		⊤		⊤	⊤	☕	⊤
Mallaig	d		10 10	14 11			16 05			18 15
Morar	d		10 16	14 24			16 11			18 21
Arisaig	d		10 26	14 39			16 21			18 31
Beasdale	d		10x32				16x27			18x37
Lochailort	d		10x41				16x36			18x46
Glenfinnan	d		10 59	15 24			16 53			19 03
Locheilside	d		11x09				17x03			19x13
Loch Eil Outward Bound	d		11 15	15 43			17 09			19 19
Corpach	d		11 21				17 15			19 25
Banavie	d		11 25				17 19			19 29
Fort William	a		11 32	16 03			17 27			19 36
	d		11 40				17 37		19 00	
Spean Bridge	d		11 55				17 50		19 20	
Roy Bridge	d		12 02				17 57		19x27	
Tulloch	d		12 14				18 08		19 40	
Corrour	d		12 31				18 25		20x01	
Rannoch	d		12 42				18 36		20 15	
Bridge of Orchy	d		13 03				18 56		20e47	
Upper Tyndrum	d		13 19				19 12		21 05	
Oban	d	12 11			16 10	17 04		18 11		
Connel Ferry	d	12 23			16 26	17 20		18 23		
Taynuilt	d	12 35			16 38	17 31		18 35		
Falls of Cruachan §	d	12x43			16x46	17x39		18x43		
Loch Awe	d	12 50			16 53	17 46		18x49		
Dalmally	d	12 56			16 59	17 52		18 56		
Tyndrum Lower	d	13 15			17 18	18 10		19 15		
Crianlarich	a	13 29	13 30		17 27	18 19	19 26	19 27	21 16	
	d	13 36	13 36		17 30	18 20	19 33		21 18	
Ardlui	d	13 52	13 52		17 46	18x37	19 53		21x39	
Arrochar & Tarbet	d	14 07	14 07		18 01	18 51	20 08		21 57	
Garelochhead	d	14 27	14 27		18 21	19 17	20 28		22 23	
Helensburgh Upper	a	14 38	14 38		18 32	19 27	20 39		22 35	
	d	14 39	14 39		18 33	19 29	20 40		22 37	
Dumbarton Central 226	a	14 53	14 53		18 47		20 53			
Dalmuir 226	a	15 05	15 05		18 56	19s55	21 03		23 02	
Westerton 226	a								23 11	
Glasgow Queen St. 10 226 ⛴	a	15 31	15 31		19 15		21 19			
Edinburgh 228	a					21 09			00 13	

Sundays

2 October to 30 October

		SR	SR	WR	SR	SR	SR	SR
							B	
		◇	◇		◇	◇		◇
		⊤	⊤		⊤	⊤	☕	⊤
Mallaig	d		10 10	14 11	16 05			18 15
Morar	d		10 16	14 24	16 11			18 21
Arisaig	d		10 26	14 39	16 21			18 31
Beasdale	d		10x32		16x27			18x37
Lochailort	d		10x41		16x36			18x46
Glenfinnan	d		10 59	15 24	16 53			19 03
Locheilside	d		11x09		17x03			19x13
Loch Eil Outward Bound	d		11 15	15 43	17 09			19 19
Corpach	d		11 21		17 15			19 25
Banavie	d		11 25		17 19			19 29
Fort William	a		11 32	16 03	17 27			19 36
	d		11 40		17 37		19 00	
Spean Bridge	d		11 55		17 50		19 20	
Roy Bridge	d		12 02		17 57		19x27	
Tulloch	d		12 14		18 08		19 40	
Corrour	d		12 31		18 25		20x01	
Rannoch	d		12 42		18 36		20 15	
Bridge of Orchy	d		13 03		18 56		20 47	
Upper Tyndrum	d		13 19		19 12		21 05	
Oban	d	12 11				18 11		
Connel Ferry	d	12 23				18 23		
Taynuilt	d	12 35				18 35		
Falls of Cruachan §	d							
Loch Awe	d	12 50				18 49		
Dalmally	d	12 56				18 56		
Tyndrum Lower	d	13 15				19 15		
Crianlarich	a	13 29	13 30		19 26	19 27	21 16	
	d	13 36			19 33		21 18	
Ardlui	d	13 52			19c53		21x39	
Arrochar & Tarbet	d	14 07			20 08		21 57	
Garelochhead	d	14 27			20 28		22 23	
Helensburgh Upper	a	14 38			20 39		22 35	
	d	14 39			20 40		22 37	
Dumbarton Central 226	a	14 53			20 53			
Dalmuir 226	a	15 05			21 03		23 02	
Westerton 226	a						23 11	
Glasgow Queen St. 10 226 ⛴	a	15 31			21 19			
Edinburgh 228	a						00 13	

§ Summer station only

A from 26 June until 28 August

SHIPPING SERVICES

Mallaig - Armadale (Skye) and Small Isles

Operated by Caledonian MacBrayne Ltd

Mondays to Saturdays
until 22 October

		ThO	WO	MO	TO G		FO	A	SO B	SX C	
Glasgow Queen St 10 227	d							08 21	08 21	09 07	12 21
Fort William 227	d	08 30	08 30	08 30	08 30	08 30	08 30	12 12	12 12	12 48	16 19
Mallaig 227	a	09 53	09 53	09 53	09 53	09 53	09 53	13 34	13 34	14 09	17 43
Mallaig	d	10 15	10 15	10 15	10 15	10 50	12 40	13 45	14 25	15 10	18 00
Armadale	a					11 20		14 15		15 40	18 30
Eigg	a	11 30		11 30	12 45				15 40		
Muck	a	12 20			11 55				16 25		
Rum	a		11 35	12 45			14 00		19 25		
Canna	a		12 45	13 55			15 10		18 15		

Sundays
until 16 October

Glasgow Queen St 10 227	d						12 20
Fort William 227	d	12 12					16 19
Mallaig 227	a	13 35					17 43
Mallaig	d	14 40					18 00
Armadale	a	15 10					18 30
Eigg	a						
Muck	a						
Rum	a						
Canna	a						

Mondays to Saturdays
until 22 October

			FO	SO E	ThO		TO F	WO		MO	FO
Canna	d			10 15				15 00		14 10	15 25
Rum	d			09 05				16 05		15 20	16 35
Muck	d		10 20	12 00	12 35		13 50				
Eigg	d		11 10	12 50	13 20		13 00			16 35	
Armadale	d	08 50				14 30			17 15		
Mallaig	a	09 20	12 25	14 05	14 35	15 00	15 30	17 25	17 45	17 50	17 55
Mallaig 227	d	10 10	16 05	16 05	16 05	16 05	16 05	18 15	18 15	18 15	18 15
Fort William 227	a	11 32	17 27	17 27	17 27	17 27	17 27	19 36	19 36	19 36	19 36
Glasgow Queen St 10 227	a	15 30	21 31	21 31	21 31	21 31	21 31	00a20	00b20	00a20	00a20

Sundays
until 16 October

												D
Canna	d											
Rum	d											
Muck	d											
Eigg	d											
Armadale	d	09 30					15 20					16 50
Mallaig	a	10 00					15 50					17 20
Mallaig 227	d	10 10					16 05					18 15
Fort William 227	a	11 32					17 27					19 36
Glasgow Queen St 10 227	a	15 31					21 19					

A All Saturdays, also Mondays to Fridays from 26 September
B Sails via Canna
C Until 23 September
D Until 25 September
E Sails from Rum
F Sails from Eigg
G Sails via Muck
a Following day. Change at Fort William and Westerton. Reservations compulsory from Fort William.
b Tuesday to Saturday mornings only. Change at Fort William and Westerton. Reservations compulsory from Fort William.

For details of sailings from 23 October, please telephone Caledonian MacBrayne on 08000 66 5000 or visit www.calmac.co.uk

Table 227B

SHIPPING SERVICES

Mondays to Saturdays

until 22 October

Oban - Craignure (Mull), Lismore, Colonsay, Coll and Tiree

Operated by Caledonian MacBrayne Ltd

	WFO A	SO		MO	ThO B		SO	SX		SO	SX		SO	TO		WO			SO	MFO		SX	FO	
Glasgow Queen St 10 227 d	*18a21*	*18a21*		*18a20*	*18a21*		*08 21*	*08 21*		*10 37*	*08 21*		*10 37*	*08 21*		*12 21*	*12 21*		*12 21*	*12 21*		*12 21*	*18 21*	
Oban 227 a	*21a26*	*21a26*		*21a26*	*21a26*		*11 27*	*11 27*		*13 42*	*11 27*		*13 42*	*11 27*		*15 27*	*15 27*		*15 27*	*15 27*		*15 27*	*21 26*	
Oban d	**05 45**	**07 00**		**08 00**	**08 15**		**11 45**	**11 55**		**14 00**	**14 00**		**14 15**	**14 45**		**15 40**	**16 00**		**17 00**	**17 00**		**17 15**	**22 30**	
Craignure a							**12 31**	**12 41**		**14 46**							**16 46**						**23 16**	
Lismore a											**14 50**		**15 05**						**17 50**			**18 05**		
Colonsay a																**17 55**				**19 20**				
Coll a	**10 15**	**09 40**		**10 55**	**10 55**									**17 25**										
Tiree a	**09 05**	**10 45**		**12 05**	**12 00**									**18 25**										

Sundays

until 16 October

					C				C															
Glasgow Queen St 10 227 d	*18a21*				*09 55*				*09 55*			*12 20*				*12 20*								
Oban 227 a	*21a26*				*13 05*				*13 05*			*15 27*				*15 27*								
Oban d	**09 00**				**14 00**				**15 00**			**16 00**				**17 30**								
Craignure a					**14 46**							**16 46**												
Lismore a									**15 50**															
Colonsay a																**19 50**								
Coll a	**11 55**																							
Tiree a	**13 00**																							

Mondays to Saturdays

until 22 October

	ThSO	SO	TO D		TO E	SX F	SX G		SO	SX F	SX G		WFO	WO	ThO		SO	SO	SO		SX	MO		
Tiree d													**09 20**				**11 15**					**12 25**		
Coll d													**10 20**				**12 20**					**13 35**		
Colonsay d			**07 50**		**07 50**									**11 45**	**11 55**									
Lismore d		**09 00**				**10 00**	**10 00**												**15 15**		**15 00**			
Craignure d	**06 45**								**10 30**	**10 55**	**10 55**							**15 00**					**17 00**	
Oban a	**07 31**	**09 50**	**10 10**		**10 10**	**10 50**	**10 50**		**11 16**	**11 41**	**11 41**		**13 00**	**14 10**	**14 15**		**15 00**	**15 46**	**16 05**		**15 50**	**16 30**	**17 46**	
Oban 227 d	*08 11*	*12 11*	*12 11*		*12 56*	*12 11*	*12 56*		*12 11*	*12 11*	*12 56*		*18 11*	*18 11*	*18 11*		*16 11*	*16 11*	*16 11*		*18 11*	*18 11*	*18 11*	
Glasgow Queen St 10 227 a	*11 30*	*15 30*	*15 30*		*16 00*	*15 30*	*16 00*		*15 30*	*15 30*	*16 00*		*21 31*	*21 31*	*21 31*		*19 20*	*19 20*	*19 20*		*21 31*	*21 31*	*21 31*	

Sundays

until 16 October

				C			C		H	J														
Tiree d													**13 15**											
Coll d													**14 20**											
Colonsay d																								
Lismore d				**12 00**					**16 00**	**16 00**														
Craignure d	**10 55**						**15 00**									**17 00**								
Oban a	**11 41**			**12 50**			**15 46**		**16 50**	**16 50**			**17 15**			**17 46**								
Oban 227 d	*12 11*			*16 10*			*16 10*		*17b04*	*18 11*			*18 11*			*18 11*								
Glasgow Queen St 10 227 a	*15 31*			*19 15*			*19 15*		*20c23*	*21 19*			*21 19*			*21 19*								

A Sails via Tiree
B Sails to Barra arr. 1500
C Until 25 September
D From 27 September
J Until 19 June and from 4 September

E Until 20 September
F From 26 September
G Until 23 September
H 26 June to 28 August

a Previous night
b To Edinburgh arr. 2109
c Change at Dalmuir. Arrive Glasgow Central low level

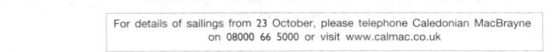

For details of sailings from 23 October, please telephone Caledonian MacBrayne on 08000 66 5000 or visit www.calmac.co.uk

Table 227C

SHIPPING SERVICE

Oban - Castlebay (Barra) and Lochboisdale (South Uist)

Operated by Caledonian MacBrayne Ltd

Mondays to Saturdays

Until 22 October

		WFO	TO A	MSO	ThO A
Glasgow Queen St 10 227	d	*08 21*	*08 21*	*12 21*	*12 21*
Oban 227	a	*11 27*	*11 27*	*15 27*	*15 27*
Oban	d	**13 40**	**13 40**	**15 40**	**15 40**
Castlebay	a	**18 30**	**20 40**	**20 30**	**22 40**
Lochboisdale	a		**18 50**		**20 50**

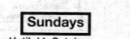

Sundays

Until 16 October

Glasgow Queen St 10 227	d	*12 20*
Oban 227	a	*15 27*
Oban	d	**15 40**
Castlebay	a	**20 30**
Lochboisdale	a	**22 20**

Mondays to Saturdays

Until 22 October

		TO	MO	WFO B
Lochboisdale	d		**07 30**	**08 55**
Castlebay	d	**09 10**	**09 20**	**07 00**
Oban	a	**14 00**	**14 10**	**14 05**
Oban 227	d	*18 11*	*18 11*	*18 11*
Glasgow Queen St 10 227	a	*21 31*	*21 31*	*21 31*

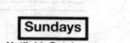

Sundays

Until 16 October

		C	D
Lochboisdale	d		
Castlebay	d	**09 20**	**09 20**
Oban	a	**14 10**	**14 10**
Oban 227	d	*16 10*	*18 11*
Glasgow Queen St 10 227	a	*19 15*	*21 19*

A Sails via Lochboisdale
B Sails from Castlebay
C Until 25 September
D 2, 9 and 16 October only

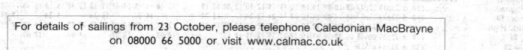

For details of sailings from 23 October, please telephone Caledonian MacBrayne on 08000 66 5000 or visit www.calmac.co.uk

Edinburgh - Falkirk High - Glasgow Queen Street

Miles		SR	SR	SR	SR	SR	SR	SR	SR	SR	SR	SR	SR	SR	SR	SR	SR	SR	SR	SR	SR	SR
		MX	MO	MX			SX				SX	SX	SO	SX								
		1	1	1	1	1	1	1	1	1		1	1		1	1	1	1	1	1	1	1
								🛒	🛒	🛒		🛒	🛒		🛒	🛒	🛒	🛒	🛒	🛒	🛒	🛒
0	**Edinburgh** 10 225,230,242 d	23p00	23p30	23p30	05 55	06 30	06 45	07 00	07 15	07 30		07 45	07 45		08 00	08 15	08 30	08 45	09 00	09 15	09 30	09 45
1¼	Haymarket 225,230,242 d	23p04	23p34	23p34	05 59	06 34	06 49	07 04	07 19	07 34		07 49	07 49		08 04	08 19	08 34	08 49	09 04	09 19	09 34	09 49
17½	Linlithgow 230 d	23p18	23p48	23p48	06 13	06 48	07 04		07 33	07 48	07 59	08 04	08 04			08 33		09 03		09 33		10 03
22¼	Polmont 3 230 d	23p24	23p54	23p54	06 19	06 55		07 21	07 38	07 55					08 22	08 39		09 09		09 39		10 09
25½	**Falkirk High** d	23p29	23p59	23p59	06 24	07 00	07 13	07 26	07 42	08 00	08b11	08 13	08 13		08 26	08 44	08 54	09 14	09 24	09 44	09 54	10 14
35¾	Croy 3 230 a	23p39	00 09	00 09	06 34	07 10	07 23		07 52	08 10				←	08 36		09 03		09 33		10 03	
41	Lenzie 3 230 a	23p44		00 14							08 32	08 25	08 25	08 32								
44	Bishopbriggs 230 a	23p50									→		08 29	08 36								
47¼	**Glasgow Queen Street** 10 230 a	00 01	00 25	00 26	06 49	07 25	07 38	07 50	08 07	08 25		08 40	08 40	08 47	08 55	09 07	09 19	09 36	09 50	10 06	10 19	10 36

	SR	SR	SR	SR	SR	SR	SR	SR	SR	SR	SR	SR	SR	SR	SR	SR	SR	SR	SR	SR	SR	SR
	1	1	1	1	1	1	1	1	1	1	1	1	1	1	1	1	1	1	1	1	1	1
	🛒	🛒	🛒	🛒	🛒	🛒	🛒	🛒	🛒	🛒	🛒	🛒	🛒	🛒	🛒	🛒	🛒	🛒	🛒	🛒	🛒	🛒
Edinburgh 10 225,230,242 d	10 00	10 15	10 30	10 45	11 00	11 15	11 30	11 45	12 00	12 15	12 30	12 45	13 00	13 15	13 30	13 45	14 00	14 15	14 30	14 45	15 00	15 15
Haymarket 225,230,242 d	10 04	10 19	10 34	10 49	11 04	11 19	11 34	11 49	12 04	12 19	12 34	12 49	13 04	13 19	13 34	13 49	14 04	14 19	14 34	14 49	15 04	15 19
Linlithgow 230 d		10 33		11 03		11 33		12 03		12 33		13 03		13 33		14 03		14 33		15 03		15 33
Polmont 3 230 d		10 39		11 09		11 39		12 09		12 39		13 09		13 39		14 09		14 39		15 09		15 39
Falkirk High d	10 24	10 44	10 54	11 14	11 24	11 44	11 54	12 14	12 25	12 44	12 54	13 14	13 24	13 44	13 54	14 14	14 24	14 44	14 54	15 14	15 24	15 44
Croy 3 230 a	10 33		11 03		11 33		12 03		12 34		13 03		13 33		14 03		14 33		15 03		15 33	
Lenzie 3 230 a																						
Bishopbriggs 230 a																						
Glasgow Queen Street 10 230 a	10 49	11 05	11 19	11 37	11 50	12 06	12 20	12 37	12 49	13 05	13 19	13 36	13 49	14 06	14 19	14 36	14 48	15 07	15 22	15 37	15 51	16 07

	SR	SR	SR	SR	SR	SR	SR	SR	SR	SR	SR	SR	SR	SR	SR	SR	SR	SR	SR	SR
													SX	SO						
	1	1	1	1	1	1	1	1	1	1	1	1	1	1	1	1	1	1	1	1
	🛒	🛒	🛒	🛒	🛒	🛒	🛒	🛒	🛒	🛒	🛒	🛒	🛒	🛒	🛒	🛒	🛒			
Edinburgh 10 225,230,242 d	15 30	15 45	16 00	16 15	16 30	16 45	17 00	17 15	17 30	17 45	18 00	18 15	18 30	18 30	18 45	19 00	19 15	19 30	20 00	20 30
Haymarket 225,230,242 d	15 34	15 49	16 04	16 19	16 34	16 49	17 04	17 19	17 34	17 49	18 04	18 19	18 34	18 34	18 49	19 04	19 19	19 34	20 04	20 34
Linlithgow 230 d		16 03		16 33		17 05		17 33		18 03		18 33			19 03		19 33	19 48	20 18	20 48
Polmont 3 230 d		16 09		16 39		17 12		17 39		18 09		18 39			19 09		19 39		20 24	
Falkirk High d	15 54	16 14	16 24	16 44	16 54	17 16	17 24	17 44	17 55	18 14	18 25	18 44	18 55	18 55	19 14	19 24	19 44	19 57	20 29	20 57
Croy 3 230 a	16 03		16 33		17 03		17 34		18 05		18 34		19 04	19 04		19 33		20 07		21 07
Lenzie 3 230 a									18 11											
Bishopbriggs 230 a																				
Glasgow Queen Street 10 230 a	16 19	16 36	16 51	17 07	17 21	17 39	17 51	18 06	18 23	18 37	18 50	19 06	19 20	19 23	19 36	19 49	20 07	20 22	20 51	21 21

	SR	SR	SR	SR	SR	SR
	1	1	1	1	1	1
Edinburgh 10 225,230,242 d	21 00	21 30	22 00	22 30	23 00	23 30
Haymarket 225,230,242 d	21 04	21 34	22 04	22 34	23 04	23 34
Linlithgow 230 d	21 18	21 48	22 18	22 48	23 18	23 48
Polmont 3 230 d	21 24		22 24		23 24	23 54
Falkirk High d	21 29	21 57	22 29	22 57	23 29	23 59
Croy 3 230 a		22 08		23 07	23 39	00 09
Lenzie 3 230 a					23 44	00 14
Bishopbriggs 230 a					23 50	
Glasgow Queen Street 10 230 a	21 51	22 23	22 50	23 22	00 01	00 26

Sundays

	SR	SR	SR	SR	SR	SR	SR	SR	SR	SR	SR	SR	SR	SR	SR	SR	SR	SR	SR	SR	SR	SR
	1	1	1	1	1	1	1	1	1	1	1	1	1	1	1	1	1	1	1	1	1	1
	A	A																				
			🛒		🛒	🛒	🛒	🛒	🛒	🛒	🛒		🛒	🛒	🛒	🛒	🛒		🛒	🛒	🛒	🛒
Edinburgh 10 225,230,242 d	23p00	23p30	08 00	09 00	10 00	11 00	12 00	12 30	13 00	13 30	14 00	14 30	15 00	15 30	16 00	16 30	17 00	17 30	18 00	18 30	19 00	19 30
Haymarket 225,230,242 d	23p04	23p34	08 04	09 04	10 04	11 04	12 04	12 33	13 04	13 34	14 04	14 34	15 04	15 34	16 04	16 34	17 04	17 34	18 04	18 34	19 04	19 34
Linlithgow 230 d	23p18	23p48	08 18	09 18	10 18	11 18	12 18	12 48	13 18	13 48	14 18	14 48	15 18	15 48	16 18	16 48	17 18	17 48	18 18	18 48	19 18	19 48
Polmont 3 230 d	23p24	23p54	08 24	09 24	10 24	11 24	12 24		13 24		14 24		15 24		16 24		17 24		18 24		19 24	
Falkirk High d	23p29	23p59	08 29	09 29	10 29	11 29	12 29	12 57	13 29	13 57	14 29	14 57	15 29	15 57	16 29	16 57	17 29	17 57	18 29	18 57	19 29	19 57
Croy 3 230 a	23p39	00 09	08 39	09 39	10 39	11 39	12 39	13 07		14 07		15 07		16 07		17 07		18 07		19 07		20 07
Lenzie 3 230 a	23p44	00 14																				
Bishopbriggs 230 a	23p50																					
Glasgow Queen Street 10 230 a	00 01	00 26	08 59	10 00	11 00	11 56	12 54	13 23	13 51	14 23	14 51	15 22	15 51	16 22	16 51	17 22	17 52	18 22	18 51	19 22	19 51	20 22

	SR	SR	SR	SR	SR	SR
	1	1	1	1	1	1
Edinburgh 10 225,230,242 d	20 00	20 30	21 00	22 00	23 00	23 30
Haymarket 225,230,242 d	20 04	20 34	21 04	22 04	23 04	23 34
Linlithgow 230 d	20 18	20 48	21 18	22 18	23 18	23 48
Polmont 3 230 d	20 24		21 24	22 24	23 24	23 54
Falkirk High d	20 29	20 57	21 29	22 29	23 29	23 59
Croy 3 230 a		21 07	21 39	22 39	23 39	00 09
Lenzie 3 230 a						
Bishopbriggs 230 a						
Glasgow Queen Street 10 230 a	20 51	21 22	21 55	22 55	23 55	00 25

A not 22 May

b Falkirk Grahamston

c Falkirk Grahamston, arrival time

Glasgow Queen Street - Falkirk High - Edinburgh

Mondays to Saturdays

Miles	Station			SR MO [1]	SR MX [1]	SR [1]	SR SX [1]	SR SO [1]	SR SX [1]	SR [1] (trolley)	SR SX [1] (trolley)	SR SO [1] (trolley)	SR [1] (trolley)	SR [1]	SR [1] (trolley)	SR [1] (trolley)	SR [1] (trolley)	SR [1] (trolley)	SR [1] (trolley)	SR [1] (trolley)	SR [1] (trolley)	SR SO [1]	SR SX [1] (trolley)	SR SX [1] (trolley)
0	**Glasgow Queen Street** [10]	230	d	23p30	23p30	06 00	06 30	06 30	06 45	07 00	07 15	07 15	07 30	07 45	08 00	08 15	08 30	08 45	09 00	09 15	09 30	09 45	09 45	10 00
3¼	Bishopbriggs	230	d																					
6¼	Lenzie [3]	230	d				06 38	06 38		07 08														
11½	Croy [3]	230	d	23p42	23p42			06 43	06 57				07 41		08 11		08 42		09 12		09 42			10 12
21¾	**Falkirk High**		d	23p52	23p52	06 18	06 51	06 51	07 07	07 21	07 33	07 33	07 51	08 04	08 21	08 33	08 52	09 03	09 22	09 33	09 52	10 03	10 03	10 22
25	Polmont [3]	230	a	23p56	23p56	06 23	06 56	06 56		07 26	07 37	07 38		08 09	08 26			09 08		09 38		10 08	10 08	
29¾	Linlithgow	230	a	00 03	00 03	06 29	07 02	07 02	07 14	07 32	07 44	07 44	07 59	08 15		08 41		09 14		09 44		10 14	10 14	
46	Haymarket	225,230,242	a	00s19	00s20	06s45	07s19	07s19	07s31	07s49	08s01	08s01	08s17	08s31	08s45	09s01	09s14	09s30	09s45	10s02	10s12	10s30	10s30	10s44
47¼	**Edinburgh** [10]	225,230,242	a	00 24	00 25	06 50	07 25	07 25	07 37	07 55	08 06	08 06	08 25	08 37	08 52	09 06	09 19	09 36	09 52	10 07	10 17	10 37	10 37	10 49

Station			SR SO [1] (trolley)	SR [1] (trolley)	SR [1] (trolley)	SR [1] (trolley)	SR [1] (trolley)	SR [1] (trolley)	SR [1] (trolley)	SR [1] (trolley)	SR [1] (trolley)	SR [1] (trolley)	SR [1] (trolley)	SR [1] (trolley)	SR [1] (trolley)	SR [1] (trolley)	SR [1] (trolley)	SR [1] (trolley)	SR [1] (trolley)	SR [1] (trolley)	SR [1] (trolley)	SR SX [1] (trolley)	SR SO [1] (trolley)	SR [1] (trolley)
Glasgow Queen Street [10]	230	d	10 00	10 15	10 30	10 45	11 00	11 15	11 30	11 45	12 00	12 15	12 30	12 45	13 00	13 15	13 30	13 45	14 00	14 15	14 30	14 45	14 45	15 00
Bishopbriggs	230	d																						
Lenzie [3]	230	d																						
Croy [3]	230	d	10 12		10 42		11 12		11 42		12 12		12 42		13 12		13 42		14 12		14 42			15 12
Falkirk High		d	10 22	10 33	10 52	11 03	11 22	11 33	11 52	12 04	12 22	12 33	12 52	13 03	13 22	13 33	13 52	14 03	14 22	14 33	14 52	15 03	15 03	15 22
Polmont [3]	230	a		10 38		11 08		11 38		12 08		12 38		13 08		13 38		14 08		14 38		15 08	15 08	
Linlithgow	230	a		10 44		11 14		11 44		12 15		12 44		13 14		13 44		14 14		14 44		15 14	15 14	
Haymarket	225,230,242	a	10s44	11s00	11s15	11s31	11s45	12s00	12s12	12s30	12s44	13s00	13s14	13s30	13s45	14s00	14s11	14s30	14s45	15s00	15s13	15s30	15s30	15s42
Edinburgh [10]	225,230,242	a	10 51	11 05	11 20	11 36	11 51	12 07	12 19	12 36	12 52	13 07	13 19	13 35	13 51	14 05	14 17	14 36	14 50	15 05	15 19	15 35	15 37	15 47

Station			SR [1] (trolley)	SR [1] (trolley)	SR SX [1] (trolley)	SR SO [1] (trolley)	SR SX [1] (trolley)	SR SO [1] (trolley)	SR [1] (trolley)	SR SO [1] (trolley)	SR SX [1] (trolley)	SR SO [1]	SR SX [1] (trolley)	SR SX [1] (trolley)	SR SO [1] (trolley)	SR [1] (trolley)	SR [1] (trolley)	SR [1] (trolley)	SR [1] (trolley)	SR [1] (trolley)	SR [1] (trolley)	SR SX [1] (trolley)	SR SO [1] (trolley)
Glasgow Queen Street [10]	230	d	15 15	15 30	15 45	15 45	16 00	16 00	16 15	16 30	16 30	16 45	16 45	17 00	17 00	17 15	17 30	17 45	18 00	18 15	18 30	18 45	18 45
Bishopbriggs	230	d																					
Lenzie [3]	230	d																					
Croy [3]	230	d		15 42			16 12	16 12		16 42	16 42			17 12	17 12		17 42		18 12		18 42		
Falkirk High		d	15 33	15 52	16 03	16 03	16 22	16 22	16 33	16 52	16 52	17 03	17 03	17 22	17 22	17 33	17 52	18 03	18 22	18 33	18 52	19 03	19 03
Polmont [3]	230	a	15 38		16 08	16 08			16 38			17 08	17 08	17 26	17 26		17 56	18 08		18 38		19 08	19 08
Linlithgow	230	a	15 44		16 13	16 13			16 44			17 14	17 14			17 41	18 03	18 14		18 44		19 14	19 14
Haymarket	225,230,242	a	16s00	16s12	16s30	16s30	16s42	16s47	17s01	17s13	17s16	17s34	17s34	17s45	17s47	18s02	18s19	18s33	18s45	19s01	19s13	19s30	19s34
Edinburgh [10]	225,230,242	a	16 06	16 19	16 35	16 37	16 48	16 52	17 06	17 19	17 22	17 40	17 40	17 50	17 52	18 07	18 24	18 40	18 50	19 07	19 19	19 36	19 39

Station			SR [1] (trolley)	SR [1] (trolley)	SR [1]	SR [1]	SR SX [1]	SR SO [1]	SR [1]	SR [1]	SR [1]	SR [1]	SR [1]	SR [1]
Glasgow Queen Street [10]	230	d	19 00	19 15	19 30	20 00	20 30	20 30	21 00	21 30	22 00	22 30	23 00	23 30
Bishopbriggs	230	d												
Lenzie [3]	230	d												
Croy [3]	230	d	19 12			20 12			21 12		22 12		23 12	23 42
Falkirk High		d	19 22	19 33	19 48	20 22	20 48	20 48	21 22	21 48	22 22	22 48	23 22	23 52
Polmont [3]	230	a		19 38	19 53		20 53	20 53		21 53		22 53	23 26	23 56
Linlithgow	230	a		19 44	19 59	20 29	20 59	20 59	21 29	21 59	22 29	22 59	23 33	00 03
Haymarket	225,230,242	a	19s46	20s00	20s16	20s45	21s15	21s15	21s45	22s18	22s46	23s15	23s49	00s20
Edinburgh [10]	225,230,242	a	19 51	20 07	20 21	20 51	21 20	21 22	21 50	22 23	22 51	23 20	23 55	00 25

Sundays

Station			SR [1] A	SR [1]	SR [1] (trolley)	SR [1] (trolley)	SR [1] (trolley)	SR [1] (trolley)	SR [1] (trolley)	SR [1] (trolley)	SR [1]	SR [1] (trolley)	SR [1] (trolley)	SR [1]	SR [1]	SR [1] (trolley)	SR [1] (trolley)	SR [1] (trolley)	SR [1] (trolley)	SR [1] (trolley)	SR [1] (trolley)	SR [1] (trolley)	SR [1] (trolley)	SR [1]
Glasgow Queen Street [10]	230	d	23p30	07 50	08 30	09 30	10 30	11 30	12 30	13 00	13 30	14 00	14 30	15 00	15 30	16 00	16 30	17 00	17 30	18 00	18 30	19 00	19 30	20 00
Bishopbriggs	230	d	⌇																					
Lenzie [3]	230	d	⌇																					
Croy [3]	230	d	23p42	08 02	08 42	09 42	10 42	11 42	12 42	13 12		14 12		15 12		16 12		17 12		18 12		19 12		20 12
Falkirk High		d	23p52	08 12	08 52	09 52	10 52	11 52	12 52	13 22	13 48	14 22	14 48	15 22	15 48	16 22	16 48	17 22	17 48	18 22	18 48	19 22	19 48	20 22
Polmont [3]	230	a	23p56	08 16	08 56	09 56	10 56	11 56	12 56		13 53		14 53		15 53		16 53		17 53		18 53		19 53	
Linlithgow	230	a	00 03	08 23	09 03	10 03	11 03	12 03	13 02	13 29	13 59	14 29	14 59	15 29	15 59	16 29	16 59	17 29	17 59	18 29	18 59	19 29	19 59	20 29
Haymarket	225,230,242	a	00s20	08 38	09s24	10s23	11s19	12s19	13s21	13s46	14s17	14s47	15s16	15 46	16s18	16s50	17s16	17 47	18s17	18s50	19s16	19s47	20s16	20s46
Edinburgh [10]	225,230,242	a	00 25	08 49	09 29	10 28	11 24	12 24	13 26	13 51	14 22	14 52	15 21	15 51	16 23	16 55	17 21	17 52	18 22	18 55	19 21	19 52	20 21	20 51

Station			SR [1]	SR [1]	SR [1]	SR [1]	SR [1]
Glasgow Queen Street [10]	230	d	20 30	21 00	21 30	22 30	23 30
Bishopbriggs	230	d					
Lenzie [3]	230	d					
Croy [3]	230	d		21 12	21 42	22 42	23 42
Falkirk High		d	20 48	21 22	21 52	22 52	23 52
Polmont [3]	230	a	20 53		21 56	22 56	23 56
Linlithgow	230	a	20 59	21 29	22 03	23 03	00 03
Haymarket	225,230,242	a	21s17	21s46	22s19	23s19	00s19
Edinburgh [10]	225,230,242	a	21 22	21 53	22 24	23 24	00 24

A not 22 May

Edinburgh and Glasgow Queen Street - Perth, Inverness, Dundee, Aberdeen, Dyce and Inverurie

Miles	Miles	Miles	Miles	Miles				SR	SR	SR	SR	SR	SR	SR	SR	SR		XC	SR	SR	SR	SR	SR	SR	SR	SR
								MX	MX	MX	MO															
														R	R											
								◇1	◇1	◇1	◇1	1	◇1			1		◇1	◇1	◇1	1	1	◇1	◇1	◇1	
								A							B					D				A		
														🛏	🛏											
								🛒			🛒									🛒				🛒	🛒	
—	0	—	0	0	**Edinburgh** 10	242	d	19p28	21p40					04 40	04 40				05 30		06 29	07 00		07 28		07 34
—	1¼	—	1¼	1¼	Haymarket	242	d	19p31	21p44										05 33		06 33	07 04		07 31		07 40
—	13¼	—	13¼	—	Inverkeithing	242	d							04s58	04 58				05 46		06 47	07 20				07 53
—	26	—	26	—	Kirkcaldy	242	d		22p12					05s17	05 18				06 02		07 03	07 36		08 02		08 09
—	33¼	—	33¼	—	Markinch		d												06 11		07 12	07 45				08 19
—	39¼	—	39¼	—	Ladybank		d												06 19		07 19	07 53				
—	42¼	—	—	—	Springfield		d																			
—	44½	—	—	—	Cupar		d	20p21											06 25			07 59				
—	—	—	—	—	Leuchars 5		a	20p28	22p33					05s46	05 46				06 32			08 06		08 25		
—	—	—	—	—	St Andrews Bus Station	🚌	a												*07e04*			*08g24*		*08j45*		
—	—	—	—	—	St Andrews Bus Station	🚌	d												*06f00*			*07h40*		*07k55*		
—	51	—	—	—	Leuchars 3		d	20p28	22p34						05 46				06 32			08 06		08 25		
0	—	0	—	—	**Glasgow Queen St.** 10	230 ⛴	d			21p41	21p45									05 56			07 06		07 41	
21	—	21	—	28¼	Larbert	230	d													06 16						
29	—	29	—	36½	Stirling	230	d			22p07	22p11									06 25			07 33		08 07	
34½	—	34½	—	42	Dunblane	230	d				22p17									06 31			07 39		08 15	
46¾	—	46¾	—	54¼	Gleneagles		d				22p28									06 43						
62½	—	62½	57	70¾	**Perth**		a			22p35	22p46									06 59	07 47		08 04		08 40	08 53
—	—	—	—	—			d			22p35	22p46					06 01				07 00	07 47		08 04		08 41	
79¾	—	—	—	—	Invergowrie		d														08 05					
83¾	59¼	—	—	—	**Dundee**		a	20p40	22p48	23p03	23p09			06s08	06 11	06 23		06 40	06 45	07 22	08 13	08 21		08 40	09 03	
87¼	63¼	—	—	—	Broughty Ferry		d																			
89	65	—	—	—	Balmossie		d																			
89¾	65¾	—	—	—	Monifieth		d																			
92¾	68¾	—	—	—	Barry Links		d																			
93½	69½	—	—	—	Golf Street		d																			
94	70	—	—	—	Carnoustie		d			23p15	23p21			06s22					07 03	07 35					09 16	
100¼	76¼	—	—	—	Arbroath		d	20p58	23p05	23p25	23p26			06s31		06 45		06 58	07 10	07 42				08 57	09 23	
114	90	—	—	—	Montrose		d	21p12	23p24	23p41	23p41		06 25	06s47		07 01		07 13	07 23	07 58				09 13	09 38	
124	100	—	—	—	Laurencekirk		d			23p52			06 35						07 35	08 09						
138¼	114¼	—	—	—	Stonehaven		d	21p34	23p46	00 06	00 02		06 49	07s13		07 23		07 34	07 48	08 22				09 34		
146½	122½	—	—	—	Portlethen		d		23p55				06 58						07 59	08 31						
154½	130½	—	—	—	**Aberdeen**		a	21p53	00 08	00 26	00 25		07 13	07 35		07 44		07 55	08 13	08 44				09 52	10 16	
—	—	—	—	—			d	21p55					07 14			07 50				08 50				10 00		
160¾	136¾	—	—	—	Dyce	240 ✈	a	22p04					07 24			08 00				08 59				10 08		
171½	147½	—	—	—	**Inverurie**	240	a	22p16					07 44			08 17								10 22		
—	—	78	72½	86¼	Dunkeld & Birnam		d																08 29			
—	—	91	85½	99¼	Pitlochry		d																08 42			
—	—	97¾	92¼	106	Blair Atholl		d																08 52			
—	—	121	116¼	130¼	Dalwhinnie		d																09 16			
—	—	131¼	126¾	140½	Newtonmore		d																09 27			
—	—	134	129½	143¼	Kingussie		d																09 32			
—	—	145¾	141¼	155	Aviemore		d					07 57											09 44			
—	—	152¾	148¼	162	Carrbridge		d					08 05											09 57			
—	—	180	175	188¾	**Inverness**		a	00 05				08 43	09 40										10 29			

B SX from 4 July until 29 July
e Bus Service. arrives 0713 SO
f Bus Service. departs 0610 SO
g Bus Service. arrives 0830 SO
h Bus Service. departs 0728 SO
j Bus Service. arrives 0700 SO
k Bus Service. departs 0759 SO

Edinburgh and Glasgow Queen Street - Perth, Inverness, Dundee, Aberdeen, Dyce and Inverurie

Station		SR	SR	SR	SR	SR	SR	SR	SR	SR	SR	SR	SR	GR	GR	SR	SR	SR	SR
							SX	SO	SO	SX				SX	SO				
		1	◇1	◇1	◇1	1	◇1	◇1	◇1	◇1		1	◇1	1	1	◇1		1	◇1
			A											C	C				
Edinburgh 10	242 d	08 00	08 28		08 34	09 00	09 28	09 28			09 35	10 00		10 27	10 27		10 35	11 00	11 27
Haymarket	242 d	08 04	08 32		08 39	09 04	09 33	09 33			09 40	10 03		10 32	10 32		10 40	11 04	11 32
Inverkeithing	242 d	08 18				09 17					09 54	10 19		10 47	10 47		10 53	11 17	
Kirkcaldy	242 d	08 34			09 08	09 33					10 10	10 35		11 04	11 04		11 10	11 33	
Markinch	d	08 43			09 17	09 42					10 19	10 44					11 20	11 42	
Ladybank	d	08 51				09 50					10 27	10 51					11 27	11 50	
Springfield	d	08 56																	
Cupar	d	09 00				09 56						10 58						11 56	
Leuchars 5	a	09 07	09 23			10 03		10 23				11 04		11 28	11 28			12 03	12 23
St Andrews Bus Station	a	*09b30*	*09b45*			*10b30*		*10b45*				*11b30*		*11b45*	*11b45*			*12b30*	*12b45*
St Andrews Bus Station	d	*08e47*	*08b55*			*09b40*		*09b55*				*10b40*		*11b10*	*11b10*			*11b40*	*11b55*
Leuchars 3	d	09 07	09 23			10 03		10 23				11 05		11 29	11 29			12 03	12 23
Glasgow Queen St. 10	230 d			08 41					09 41	09 41			10 11			10 41			
Larbert	230 d																		
Stirling	230 d			09 07					10 07	10 07			10 36			11 07			
Dunblane	230 d												10 42						
Gleneagles	d												10 54						
Perth	a			09 36	09 50				10 34	10 34	10 53		11 13			11 37	11 54		
	d			09 36	09 51				10 36	10 36			11 13			11 38			
Invergowrie	d																		
Dundee	a	09 22	09 36	09 59		10 18	10 32	10 35	10 57	10 57		11 20		11 43	11 43	11 59		12 18	12 36
Broughty Ferry	d																		
Balmossie	d																		
Monifieth	d																		
Barry Links	d																		
Golf Street	d																		
Carnoustie	d								11 11	11 11									
Arbroath	d		09 53	10 17			10 50	10 53	11 18	11 18				12 01	12 01	12 17			12 53
Montrose	d			10 31			11 04	11 07	11 34	11 34				12 17	12 17	12 32			
Laurencekirk	d		10 16							11 50						12 43			
Stonehaven	d		10 29	10 53			11 26	11 29		12 04				12 40	12 40				13 27
Portlethen	d			11 02															
Aberdeen	a		10 53	11 17			11 50	11 53	12 14	12 33				13 05	13 05	13 14			13 46
	d		11 04																
Dyce	240 a		11 13																
Inverurie	240 a		11 30																
Dunkeld & Birnam	d												11 34						
Pitlochry	d				10 20								11 47						
Blair Atholl	d												11 57						
Dalwhinnie	d												12 23						
Newtonmore	d																		
Kingussie	d				11 02								12 35						
Aviemore	d				11 15								12 47						
Carrbridge	d												12 55						
Inverness	a				11 54								13 27						

e Bus Service. departs 0840 SO

C From Leeds

b Bus Service

Edinburgh and Glasgow Queen Street - Perth, Inverness, Dundee, Aberdeen, Dyce and Inverurie

			SR	SR	SR	SR	SR	SR	SR	SR	SR	SR	SR	SR	GR	SR	SR	SR	SR	SR
						SO	SX													
			◇1	◇1	1	◇1	◇1	◇1		1	◇1	◇1	◇1	1	1	◇1		1	◇1	◇1
						B	B				B				C				B	
			⚲	⚲		⚲	⚲	⚲			⚲	⚲	⚲		⚲	⚲			⚲	⚲
Edinburgh 10	242	d		11 35	12 00	12 28	12 28		12 35	13 00	13 28		13 35	14 00	14 27		14 35	15 00	15 28	
Haymarket	242	d		11u40	12 05	12 32	12 32		12 40	13 04	13 32		13u40	14 04	14 32		14 40	15 04	15 32	
Inverkeithing	242	d			12 18				12 54	13 17				14 18	14 47		14 53	15 18		
Kirkcaldy	242	d		12u09	12 34				13 10	13 33			14u08	14 34	15 04		15 09	15 34		
Markinch		d		12 18	12 43				13 19	13 42			14 17	14 43			15 19	15 43		
Ladybank		d			12 51					13 50				14 51			15 26	15 53		
Springfield		d																		
Cupar		d			12 57					13 56				14 57				15 59		
Leuchars 5		a			13 04	13 23	13 23			14 03	14 23			15 04	15 28			16 06	16 24	
St Andrews Bus Station	🚌	a			*13b30*	*13b45*	*13b45*			*14b30*	*14b45*			*15b30*	*15b45*			*16b30*	*16b45*	
St Andrews Bus Station	🚌	d			*12b40*	*12b55*	*12b55*			*13b40*	*13b55*			*14b40*	*15b10*			*15e50*	*15b55*	
Leuchars 3		d			13 04	13 23	13 23			14 03	14 23			15 04	15 28			16 06	16 25	
Glasgow Queen St. 10	230	d	11 41					12 41				13 41				14 41				15 41
Larbert	230	d																		
Stirling	230	d	12 07					13 07				14 07				15 07				16 07
Dunblane	230	d																		
Gleneagles		d																		
Perth		a	12 36	12 53				13 35	13 53			14 36	14 53			15 36	15 55			16 36
		d	12 37	12 54				13 36				14 37	14 54			15 36				16 36
Invergowrie		d																		
Dundee		a	12 59		13 19	13 35	13 35	14 00		14 18	14 35	14 59		15 19	15 46	15 59		16 21	16 37	17 00
Broughty Ferry		d																		
Balmossie		d																		
Monifieth		d																		
Barry Links		d																		
Golf Street		d																		
Carnoustie		d	13 12									15 12								17 13
Arbroath		d	13 19			13 53	13 53	14 18			14 53	15 23			16 05	16 20			16 54	17 20
Montrose		d	13 33			14 07	14 07	14 32				15 39			16 21	16 33			17 09	17 33
Laurencekirk		d										15 50							17 20	
Stonehaven		d				14 29	14 29	14 54			15 26				16 44				17 33	17 55
Portlethen		d																		
Aberdeen		a	14 12			14 48	14 53	15 13			15 46	16 20			17 09	17 13			17 53	18 15
		d				14 56	14 56				15 55								17 56	
Dyce	240 ✈	a				15 04	15 04				16 03								18 04	
Inverurie	240	a				15 19	15 19				16 18								18 19	
Dunkeld & Birnam		d		13 11									15 11							
Pitlochry		d		13 24									15 24							
Blair Atholl		d		13 34									15 34							
Dalwhinnie		d											16 01							
Newtonmore		d		14 12																
Kingussie		d		14 17									16 14							
Aviemore		d		14 28									16 27							
Carrbridge		d																		
Inverness		a		15 06									17 05							

e Bus Service. departs 1540 SO
C From London Kings Cross. The Flying Scotsman
b Bus Service

Edinburgh and Glasgow Queen Street - Perth, Inverness, Dundee, Aberdeen, Dyce and Inverurie

			SR	SR		SR		SR	SR	SR	GR	SR	GR			SR				SR	SR	SR	SR	SR		XC
									SX	SO	SO		SX								SO	SX		SX		
				1		◇1		◇1	◇1	◇1	1		1							◇1	◇1	◇1	◇1			◇1
								B			C		D													H
						🛒		🛒	🛒	🛒	🍽🛒		🍽🛒							🛒	🛒	🛒	🛒			
Edinburgh 10	242	d	15 34	15 57				16 29			16 32	16 33	16 33			17 00				17 37			17 42	17 58		18 11
Haymarket	242	d	15 39	16 01				16u33			16 38	16 37	16 38			17 04				17 41			17u46	18 03		18 15
Inverkeithing	242	d	15 53	16 17								16 52				17 22								18 22		18 29
Kirkcaldy	242	d	16 09	16 33								17 08				17 39							18 15	18 40		18 47
Markinch		d	16 18	16 42								17 17				17 48							18 24	18 51		18 57
Ladybank		d	16 27	16 50								17 26				17 56							18 31	18 58		19 04
Springfield		d														18 01										
Cupar		d		16 56				17 17								18 05				18 27				19 05		19 11
Leuchars 5		a		17 03				17 24								18 12				18 33				19 11		19 17
St Andrews Bus Station	🚌	a		*17e34*				*17f49*								*18g35*				*18b55*				*19b29*		*19b37*
St Andrews Bus Station	🚌	d		*16b40*				*16b55*								*17b45*				*18b05*				*18b55*		*18b55*
Leuchars 3		d		17 03				17 24								18 12				18 34				19 12		19 18
Glasgow Queen St. 10	230 🚇	d				16 11			16 41	16 41	17 03		17 11								17 41	17 41	18 11			
Larbert	230	d																								
Stirling	230	d				16 37				17 07	17 19		17 19								18 07	18 14				
Dunblane	230	d				16 48															18 15	18 21				
Gleneagles		d				17 00					17 40		17 39								18 27	18 34				
Perth		a	16 54			17 18			17 36	17 36	18 00	17 54	17 59								18 43	18 51	18 58			
		d				17 18			17 37	17 37	18 00		18 00								18 44	18 53	18 59			
Invergowrie		d																								
Dundee		a		17 18				17 38	17 59	17 59						18 34				18 48	19 06	19 14		19 27		19 32
Broughty Ferry		d						17 47								19 00				←						
Balmossie		d														19 03										
Monifieth		d														19 06										
Barry Links		d														19 10										
Golf Street		d														19 13										
Carnoustie		d						17 55	18 13	18 13						19a17	→				19 27	19 27				
Arbroath		d						18 02	18 20	18 20										19 05	19 34	19 34				19 50
Montrose		d						18 16												19 22	19 48	19 49				20 04
Laurencekirk		d						18 27																		
Stonehaven		d						18 41	18 53	18 53										19 43	20 10	20 11				20 24
Portlethen		d																		19 52						
Aberdeen		a						19 00	19 13	19 13										20 06	20 29	20 32				20 43
		d						19 07																		
Dyce	240 ✈	a						19 16																		
Inverurie	240	a						19 35																		
Dunkeld & Birnam		d				17 37																	19 16			
Pitlochry		d				17 50					18 33		18 32										19 29			
Blair Atholl		d				17 59																				
Dalwhinnie		d																								
Newtonmore		d				18 32																				
Kingussie		d				18 37					19 17		19 16										20 13			
Aviemore		d				18 48					19 29		19 29										20 25			
Carrbridge		d				18 54																				
Inverness		a				19 34					20 11		20 11										21 03			

B 🛒 to Stonehaven
C From London Kings Cross
D From London Kings Cross. The Flying Scotsman
H From Plymouth
b Bus Service
e Bus Service. arrives 1730 SO
f Bus Service. arrives 1745 SO
g Bus Service. arrives 1832 SO

Edinburgh and Glasgow Queen Street - Perth, Inverness, Dundee, Aberdeen, Dyce and Inverurie

		GR	GR	SR	SR	SR	SR	SR	SR	XC	XC	XC	GR	SR	SR	SR	SR
		SO	SX							SX			SX				
		R 1	R 1	◇1		1	◇1	◇1	◇1	◇1	◇1	◇1	R 1	◇1		◇1	◇1
		A	B				C			D	E	F	A				
Edinburgh 10	242 d	18 30	18 30		18 40	19 00	19 28		19 36	20 13	20 15	20 15	20 29		20 44	21 40	
Haymarket	242 d	18 35	18 34		18 45	19 04	19 31		19 40	20 17	20 20	20 20	20 34		20 48	21 44	
Inverkeithing	242 d	18 54	18 54		19 00	19 18			19 54	20 31	20 36	20 36	20 51		21 02		
Kirkcaldy	242 d	19 11	19 11		19 18	19 34			20 10		20 53	20 53	21 08		21 18	22 12	
Markinch	d				19 28	19 43			20 19	21 03	21 03	21 03			21 27		
Ladybank	d				19 35	19 50			20 27	21 11	21 11	21 11			21 35		
Springfield	d																
Cupar	d					19 57	20 21			21 20	21 20	21 20					
Leuchars 5	a	19 38	19 40			20 03	20 28			21 26	21 26	21 27	21 37			22 33	
St Andrews Bus Station	a	*19b59*	*19b59*			*20b29*	*20b51*			*21b59*			*21b59*			*22b59*	
St Andrews Bus Station	d	*19b10*	*19b10*			*19b40*	*20b00*			*21b00*			*21b00*			*22b00*	
Leuchars 3	d	19 38	19 41			20 04	20 28			21 27	21 28	21 28	21 37			22 34	
Glasgow Queen St. 10 230	d			18 41				19 41						20 41			21 41
Larbert	230 d																
Stirling	230 d			19 07				20 07						21 07			22 07
Dunblane	230 d			19 14										21 14			
Gleneagles	d			19 26										21 26			
Perth	a			19 42	20 02			20 36	20 54					21 42	22 01		22 35
	d			19 43				20 36	20 55					21 43			22 35
Invergowrie	d			20 01										22 01			
Dundee	a	19 52	19 55	20 08		20 19	20 40	20 59		21 42	21 44	21 44	21 51	22 07		22 48	23 03
Broughty Ferry	d																
Balmossie	d																
Monifieth	d																
Barry Links	d																
Golf Street	d																
Carnoustie	d																23 15
Arbroath	d	20 10	20 13	20 25			20 58	21 17					22 09	22 25		23 05	23 25
Montrose	d	20 26	20 29	20 40			21 12	21 31					22 25	22 39		23 24	23 41
Laurencekirk	d							21 42									23 52
Stonehaven	d	20 49	20 52				21 34	21 56					22 48	23 01		23 46	00 06
Portlethen	d															23 55	
Aberdeen	a	21 15	21 17	21 19			21 53	22 15					23 14	23 20		00 08	00 26
	d						21 55										
Dyce	240 a						22 04										
Inverurie	240 a						22 16										
Dunkeld & Birnam	d								21 13								
Pitlochry	d								21 26								
Blair Atholl	d								21 35								
Dalwhinnie	d								22 00								
Newtonmore	d								22 11								
Kingussie	d								22 21								
Aviemore	d								22 32								
Carrbridge	d								22 41								
Inverness	a						00 05		23 14								

A From London Kings Cross
B From London Kings Cross. The Flying Scotsman
D From Plymouth
E SO from 17 September. From Plymouth
F SO until 10 September. From Newquay
b Bus Service

Table 229

Sundays

Edinburgh and Glasgow Queen Street - Perth, Inverness, Dundee, Aberdeen, Dyce and Inverurie

			SR	SR	SR	XC	GR	SR	SR	SR	SR	SR	SR	SR	GR	SR	SR	GR	SR	SR	SR
			◇1	◇1	◇1	◇	R 1	◇1	◇1	◇1	◇1	◇1	◇1	◇1	R 1	◇1	◇1	R 1	◇1	◇1	1
			A	B	B										D	E		F			
Edinburgh 10	242	d	19p28	21p40		08 04	09 10		09 25	10 55		12 40		13 50	14 38			16 30	17 05		17 50
Haymarket	242	d	19p31	21p44		08 08	09 14		09 29	10 59		12 44		13 54	14 43			16 35	17 09		17 54
Inverkeithing	242	d				08 25	09 32		09 48	11 15		13 00		14 11	15 01				17 22		18 07
Kirkcaldy	242	d		22p12		08 40	09 49		10 10	11 31		13 16		14 28	15 18				17 38		18 23
Markinch		d																			
Ladybank		d																			
Springfield		d																			
Cupar		d	20p21			08 57															
Leuchars 5		a	20p28	22p33		09 05	10 13			11 54		13 39			15 42				18 01		
St Andrews Bus Station	bus	a				*09b37*	*10b29*			*12b17*		*13b55*			*16b17*				*18b17*		
St Andrews Bus Station	bus	d				*07b55*	*09b50*			*11b35*		*13b15*			*15b15*				*17b35*		
Leuchars 3		d	20p28	22p34		09 06	10 13			11 55		13 40			15 43				18 02		
Glasgow Queen St. 10	230	d			21p41			09 38			11 45		13 45			14 40	15 45			17 45	
Larbert	230	d						10 02								15 00					
Stirling	230	d			22p07			10 12			12 12		14 12			15 09	16 12	17 17		18 12	
Dunblane	230	d						10 18			12 18		14 17			15 16	16 18				
Gleneagles		d						10 30			12 29		14 29			15 28	16 29	17 35			
Perth		a			22p35			10 47	10 52		12 46		14 46	15 12		15 45	16 45	17 53		18 44	19 02
		d			22p35			10 48	10 53		12 47		14 48	15 14		15 46	16 47	17 54		18 45	
Invergowrie		d																			
Dundee		a	20p40	22p48	23p03	09 18	10 27	11 12		12 07	13 10	13 52	15 09		15 57		17 09		18 14	19 08	
Broughty Ferry		d																			
Balmossie		d																			
Monifieth		d																			
Barry Links		d																			
Golf Street		d																			
Carnoustie		d			23p15			11 25												19 21	
Arbroath		d	20p58	23p05	23p25	09 36	10 45	11 29		12 25	13 27	14 10	15 27		16 15		17 27		18 32	19 27	
Montrose		d	21p12	23p24	23p41	09 50	11 01	11 46		12 37	13 42	14 24	15 42		16 31		17 42		18 46	19 42	
Laurencekirk		d			23p52			12 01					15 53							19 55	
Stonehaven		d	21p34	23p46	00 06	10 10	11 24	12 10		12 59	14 03	14 46	16 06		16 54		18 03		19 08	20 06	
Portlethen		d		23p55						13 07									19 16		
Aberdeen		a	21p53	00 08	00 26	10 29	11 52	12 35		13 23	14 23	15 05	16 26		17 19		18 23		19 30	20 29	
		d	21p55																		
Dyce	240 ✈	a	22p04																		
Inverurie	240	a	22p16																		
Dunkeld & Birnam		d							11 11					15 31							
Pitlochry		d							11 25					15 44		16 16		18 27			
Blair Atholl		d							11 34					15 54							
Dalwhinnie		d							12 01					16 19							
Newtonmore		d							12 11					16 29							
Kingussie		d							12 16					16 34		16 59		19c21			
Aviemore		d							12 29					16g48		17 12		19 33			
Carrbridge		d							12 37					17 03							
Inverness		a	00 05						13 09					17 38		17 50		20 19			

A not 22 May
B not 22 May
D From London Kings Cross. The Flying Scotsman
E To Elgin
F From London Kings Cross. The Highland Chieftain
g Arr. 1642
c Arr. 1911
b Bus Service

Table 229

Sundays

Edinburgh and Glasgow Queen Street - Perth, Inverness, Dundee, Aberdeen, Dyce and Inverurie

			SR	XC	GR	SR	SR	SR	SR
			◇1	◇1	R 1	◇1	◇1	◇1	
			A	B	D				
			(catering)		(catering)	(catering)		(catering)	
Edinburgh 10	242	d		18 11	18 42		21 00		23 36
Haymarket	242	d		18 16	18 47		21 05		23 40
Inverkeithing	242	d		18 30	19 02		21 19		23a58
Kirkcaldy	242	d		18 45	19 19		21 35		
Markinch		d		18 54			21 44		
Ladybank		d		19 02			21 50		
Springfield		d							
Cupar		d		19 08			21 58		
Leuchars 5		a		19 14	19 43		22 05		
St Andrews Bus Station	(bus)	a		*19b37*	*19b59*		*22b29*		
St Andrews Bus Station	(bus)	d		*18b30*	*19b15*		*21b30*		
Leuchars 3		d		19 15	19 43		22 05		
Glasgow Queen St. 10	230 (ship)	d	18 10			19 45		21 45	
Larbert	230	d	18 30						
Stirling	230	d	18 39			20 12		22 11	
Dunblane	230	d	18 46			20 17		22 17	
Gleneagles		d	18 58			20 29		22 28	
Perth		a	19 15			20 46		22 46	
		d	19 16			20 47		22 46	
Invergowrie		d							
Dundee		a		19 29	19 57	21 10	22 18	23 09	
Broughty Ferry		d							
Balmossie		d							
Monifieth		d							
Barry Links		d							
Golf Street		d							
Carnoustie		d						23 21	
Arbroath		d		19 47	20 15	21 27	22 38	23 26	
Montrose		d		20 01	20 31	21 42	22 52	23 41	
Laurencekirk		d							
Stonehaven		d		20 24	20 54	22 03	23 14	00 02	
Portlethen		d					23 23		
Aberdeen		a		20 43	21 20	22 24	23 36	00 25	
		d							
Dyce	240 (air)	a							
Inverurie	240	a							
Dunkeld & Birnam		d	19 34						
Pitlochry		d	19 47						
Blair Atholl		d	19 56						
Dalwhinnie		d	20 21						
Newtonmore		d	20 31						
Kingussie		d	20 36						
Aviemore		d	20 50						
Carrbridge		d	20 58						
Inverness		a	21 34						

A To Elgin
B From Plymouth
D From London Kings Cross
b Bus Service

Table 229

Inverurie, Dyce, Aberdeen, Dundee, Inverness and Perth - Glasgow Queen Street and Edinburgh

Miles	Miles	Miles	Miles	Miles	Station		SR MX	XC MX ◇1	SR MO R	SR MX R	SR R A	SR MO 1	SR MSX 1	SR SO 1	SR		SR SX B	SR	SR B	SR SX C	SR	SR	SR SX D	SR SX E	XC SO ◇1 F
—	—	0	0	0	**Inverness**	d																			
—	—	28	28	28	Carrbridge	d																			
—	—	34¾	34¾	34¾	Aviemore	d																			
—	—	46½	46½	46½	Kingussie	d																			
—	—	49¼	49¼	49¼	Newtonmore	d																			
—	—	59½	59½	59½	Dalwhinnie	d																			
—	—	82¾	82¾	82¾	Blair Atholl	d																			
—	—	89½	89½	89½	Pitlochry	d																			
—	—	102½	102½	102½	Dunkeld & Birnam	d																			
0	0	—	—	—	**Inverurie** 240	d																			
10¾	10¾	—	—	—	Dyce 240 ✈	d																			
6¼	6¼	—	—	—	**Aberdeen** 240	a																			
—	—	—	—	—		d		21p31	21p40	21p40	21p40	22p29	22p30	23p22											
14¼	14¼	—	—	—	Portlethen	d							22p40	23p32											
22½	22½	—	—	—	Stonehaven	d		21p49	22g00	22g00	22b00	22p48	22p49	23p41											
36¾	36¾	—	—	—	Laurencekirk	d							23p03	23p55											
46¾	46¾	—	—	—	Montrose	d		22p10	22g25	22g25	22b25	23p11	23p13	00 05											
60½	60½	—	—	—	Arbroath	d		22p26	22g43	22g43	22b43	23p25	23p28	00 20											
66¾	66¾	—	—	—	Carnoustie	d			22g52	22g52	22b52	23p32	23p35	00 27				06 14							
67¼	67¼	—	—	—	Golf Street	d												06 16							
68	68	—	—	—	Barry Links	d												06 18							
71	71	—	—	—	Monifieth	d												06 23							
71¾	71¾	—	—	—	Balmossie	d												06 25							
73¼	73¼	—	—	—	Broughty Ferry	d												06 29							
77½	77½	—	—	—	**Dundee**	a		22p42				23p46	23p50	00 42				06 36							
—	—	—	—	—		d		22p43	23g06	23g06	23b06	23p47	23p51	00 43							05 58	06 05			06 32
81	—	—	—	—	Invergowrie	d							23p57	00 49							06 03				
98¼	—	118	118	118	**Perth**	a						00 09	00 15	01 07							06 20				
—	—	—	—	—		d	22p38								05 16					06 16	06 21				
114	—	133¾	—	133¾	Gleneagles	d									05 33						06 36				
121¼	—	146	—	146	Dunblane 230	d									05 46						06 48				
131¾	—	151½	—	151½	Stirling 230	d									05 53						06 56				
139¾	—	159½	—	159½	Larbert 230	d									06 01						07 04				
160¾	—	180½	—	—	**Glasgow Queen St.** 10 230 ⛴	a									06 34						07 34				
—	85¾	—	—	—	Leuchars 5	a		22p55														06 16			06 44
—	—	—	—	—	St Andrews Bus Station 🚌	a																*07b26*			*07b13*
—	—	—	—	—	St Andrews Bus Station 🚌	d																			*06b10*
—	—	—	—	—	Leuchars 3	d		22p56	23g25	23g25	23b25											06 17			06 46
—	92¼	—	—	—	Cupar	d		23p03														06 25			06 54
—	94½	—	—	—	Springfield	d																		←	
—	97½	—	135¾	—	Ladybank	d	23p01	23p10												06 40		06 32		06 40	07 03
—	103½	—	141	—	Markinch	d	23p10	23p18									05 56		06 24	→		06 40		06 48	07 11
—	110¾	—	149	—	Kirkcaldy 242	d		23p26	23g53	23g53	23b53											06 49			07 21
—	123½	—	161¾	—	Inverkeithing 242	d	23p51	23p42	00u12	00u12	00u12						06 40		07 06			07 12	07 19	07 30	07 38
—	135½	—	173¾	186½	Haymarket 242	a	00 11	23p57									07 02		07 28			07 33	07 39	07 51	07 55
—	136¾	—	175	187¾	**Edinburgh** 10 242	a	00 18	00 05	00 36	00 41	00 41						07 09		07 34			07 38	07 46	07 57	08 01

A TWThO until 16 June, TWThO from 25 October. To London Euston
B To Newcraighall
C To Edinburgh
D From Dunfermline Queen Margaret
E From Perth
F To Plymouth
g Previous night, stops to pick up only
b Bus Service

Inverurie, Dyce, Aberdeen, Dundee, Inverness and Perth - Glasgow Queen Street and Edinburgh

			XC	SR	SR	SR	SR	SR	SR	SR	SR	SR	SR	SR	SR	SR	SR	SR	GR	GR	XC	XC	SR
			SX	SX		SX			SX										SX	SO	SO	SX	
			◇1				◇1	◇1			1	◇1	1	◇1		◇1	1	◇1	R 1	R 1	◇1	◇1	
			A						B					C				C	D	D	E	E	F
							[trolley]					[trolley]		[trolley]		[trolley]		[trolley]	[trolley]	[trolley]			
Inverness		d												04 51		06 47	06 56						
Carrbridge		d															07 28						
Aviemore		d														07 23	07a38						
Kingussie		d														07 35							
Newtonmore		d																					
Dalwhinnie		d																					
Blair Atholl		d									07 12												
Pitlochry		d									07 26					08 15							
Dunkeld & Birnam		d									07 39					08 27							
Inverurie	240	d												06 39				07 14					
Dyce	240 ✈	d												06 52				07 26					
Aberdeen	240	a												07 04				07 37					
		d					05 33	05 56				06 33		07 06				07 40	07 52	07 52	08 20	08 20	
Portlethen		d					05 44					06 43											
Stonehaven		d					05 52	06 12				06 52		07 22				07 56	08 09	08 09	08 38	08 38	
Laurencekirk		d					06 06							07 36									
Montrose		d					06 17	06 34				07 13		07 47				08 18	08 32	08 32	08 59	08 59	
Arbroath		d					06 31	06 48				07 27		08 01				08 32	08 48	08 48	09 15	09 15	
Carnoustie		d						06 55				07 34		08 08				08 39					
Golf Street		d																					
Barry Links		d																					
Monifieth		d																					
Balmossie		d																					
Broughty Ferry		d																					
Dundee		a					06 51	07 06				07 50		08 18				08 53	09 05	09 05	09 31	09 31	
		d	06 32				06 52	07 08		07 20		07 52	08 18	08 20	08 28			08 53	09 06	09 06	09 32	09 32	
Invergowrie		d											08 23										
Perth		a					07 14				07 58	08 12	08 40			08 47		09 15					
		d			06 55	07 03	07 15				08 00	08 12	08 41			08 48		09 15					
Gleneagles		d				07 17	07 30					08 26	08 56										
Dunblane	230	d		07 22		07 29	07 44						09 07										
Stirling	230	d		07 29		07 39	07 53					08 43	09 13					09 44					
Larbert	230	d		07 38		07 48	08 02																
Glasgow Queen St. 10	230 ⇌	a				08 22	08 34					09 15	09 45					10 14					
Leuchars 5		a	06 44					07 20		07 31					08 40				09 20	09 20	09 46	09 46	
St Andrews Bus Station	🚌	a	*07b04*					*08e05*		*08e05*					*09b00*				*09b45*	*09b45*	*10b12*	*10b12*	
St Andrews Bus Station	🚌	d	*06b14*					*07f00*		*07f00*					*08g10*				*08b55*	*08b55*	*09b25*	*09b25*	
Leuchars 3		d	06 46					07 20		07 32					08 40				09 20	09 20	09 47	09 47	
Cupar		d	06 54					07 28		07 39					08 48						09 54	09 54	
Springfield		d								07 44													
Ladybank		d	07 03		07 19					07 49	08 22				08 55						10 01	10 01	
Markinch		d	07 11		07 26					07 56	08 31				09 03						10 08	10 09	
Kirkcaldy	242	d	07 21		07 40			07 48		08 06	08 41				09 12	09 25			09 44	09 44	10 17	10 17	
Inverkeithing	242	d	07 42		07 57					08 30	08 57				09 34				10 01	10 01	10 32	10 32	
Haymarket	242	a	07 59	08 14	08 17			08 19		08 49	09 15			09 26	09 49	09 55			10 19	10 20	10 51	10 52	
Edinburgh 10	242	a	08 05	08 22	08 22			08 25		08 56	09 21			09 33	09 55	10 00			10 25	10 26	10 58	10 58	

A To Plymouth
C [trolley] from Aberdeen
D To London Kings Cross
E To Penzance
b Bus Service
e Bus Service. arrives 0800 SO
f Bus Service. departs 0655 SO
g Bus Service. departs 0814 SO

Table 229

Mondays to Saturdays

Inverurie, Dyce, Aberdeen, Dundee, Inverness and Perth - Glasgow Queen Street and Edinburgh

		SR	SR	GR SX	GR SO	SR	SR		SR	SR	SR	SR	SR	GR SX	GR SO	SR	SR		SR	SR	SR	SR	SR	SR	SR
		■1		▪ ■1	▪ ■1	◇■1	◇■1		■1			◇■1	◇■1	▪ ■1	▪ ■1	■1				◇■1	◇■1	■1		◇■1	◇■1
				A	A					B		C		D	D		B				C		B		
				⊼⊘	⊡⊼	⊼	⊼					⊼	⊼	⊼⊘	⊡⊼					⊼	⊼			⊼	⊼
Inverness	d			07 55	07 55								09 18											10 47	
Carrbridge	d												09 49											11 21	
Aviemore	d			08 29	08 29								10 00											11 33	
Kingussie	d			08 42	08 42								10 13											11 45	
Newtonmore	d												10 17												
Dalwhinnie	d												10 29												
Blair Atholl	d												10 50												
Pitlochry	d			09 23	09 23								11 01											12 27	
Dunkeld & Birnam	d												11 13											12 40	
Inverurie 240	d																				10 38				
Dyce 240 ✈	d											09 08									10 50				
Aberdeen 240	a											09 19									11 01				
	d					08 42	09 07					09 37		09 52	09 52					10 38	11 05				11 42
Portlethen	d																								
Stonehaven	d											09 53		10 09	10 09						11 21				
Laurencekirk	d						09 35														11 35				
Montrose	d					09 18	09 46					10 15		10 32	10 32					11 14	11 46				12 17
Arbroath	d					09 32	10 00					10 29		10 49	10 49					11 28	12 00				12 31
Carnoustie	d					09 39						10 36								11 35					12 38
Golf Street	d																								
Barry Links	d																								
Monifieth	d																								
Balmossie	d																								
Broughty Ferry	d											10 43													
Dundee	a					09 52	10 15					10 52		11 06	11 06					11 49	12 15				12 52
	d	09 41				09 52	10 17		10 35			10 52		11 06	11 06	11 30				11 49	12 16	12 34			12 52
Invergowrie	d																								
Perth	a			09 54	09 54	10 14						11 14	11 33							12 11				12 59	13 14
	d		09 51	09 56	09 56	10 14					11 00	11 14	11 37						12 00	12 11				13 01	13 14
Gleneagles	d			10 13	10 12								11 52												
Dunblane 230	d												12 06												
Stirling 230	d			10 30	10 30	10 43						11 43	12 13							12 43					13 43
Larbert 230	d																								
Glasgow Queen St. 10 230 ⛴	a					11 14						12 15	12 45							13 14					14 14
Leuchars 5	a	09 52					10 28		10 46					11 20	11 20	11 41					12 28	12 46			
St Andrews Bus Station 🚌	a	*10b12*					*10b45*		*11b12*					*11b45*	*11b45*	*12b00*					*12b45*	*13b12*			
St Andrews Bus Station 🚌	d	*09b25*					*10b10*		*10b25*					*10b55*	*10b55*	*11b25*					*12b10*	*12b25*			
Leuchars 3	d	09 53					10 29		10 47					11 20	11 20	11 45					12 28	12 46			
Cupar	d	10 01							10 54							11 53						12 53			
Springfield	d																								
Ladybank	d	10 09	10 14						11 02		11 23					12 00			12 23			13 01			
Markinch	d	10 17	10g33						11 09		11 31					12 08			12 33			13 08		13 31	
Kirkcaldy 242	d	10 26	10 42						11 19		11 41			11 44	11 44	12 17			12 42			13 18		13 41	
Inverkeithing 242	d	10 42	10 59						11 35		11 57			12 01	12 01	12 33			12 58			13 34	13 39		
Haymarket 242	a	11 05	11 19	11 11	11 11		11 23		11 50		12 13			12 19	12 19	12 49			13 14		13 21	13 51	14 01	14 13	
Edinburgh 10 242	a	11 14	11 24	11 17	11 17		11 31		11 55		12 18			12 25	12 25	12 55			13 20		13 26	13 57	14 06	14 19	

A To London Kings Cross. The Highland Chieftain
C ⊼ from Aberdeen
D To London Kings Cross. The Northern Lights
g Arr. 1025
b Bus Service

Inverurie, Dyce, Aberdeen, Dundee, Inverness and Perth - Glasgow Queen Street and Edinburgh

		SR	SR		SR	SR	SR	SR	SR	SR	SR	SR	SR		SR	SR	SR	SR	GR SO	GR SX	SR	SR	SR		SR
		◇1	1				◇1	◇1	1		◇1	◇1	◇1		1			◇1	■ 1	■ 1	◇1		◇1		
		A			B					B						B			C	C					
		trolley					trolley	trolley			trolley	trolley	trolley					trolley	restaurant, trolley	trolley, Ø	trolley		trolley		
Inverness	d										12 47										14 51				
Carrbridge	d																								
Aviemore	d										13 31										15 29				
Kingussie	d										13 43										15 41				
Newtonmore	d										13 48														
Dalwhinnie	d																				15 54				
Blair Atholl	d										14 19														
Pitlochry	d										14 28										16 23				
Dunkeld & Birnam	d										14 41										16 35				
Inverurie	240 d	11 35																							
Dyce	240 ✈ d	11 47																							
Aberdeen	240 a	11 58																							
	d	12 07					12 42	13 06				13 42	14 07					14 39	14 50	14 50			15 33		
Portlethen	d	12 17																							
Stonehaven	d	12 26					12 58	13 22					14 23						15 07	15 07			15 49		
Laurencekirk	d												14 37												
Montrose	d						13 20	13 44				14 17						15 12	15 30	15 30			16 11		
Arbroath	d	13 00					13 34	13 58				14 31	15 00					15 26	15 46	15 46			16 25		
Carnoustie	d											14 38						15 33							
Golf Street	d																								
Barry Links	d																								
Monifieth	d																								
Balmossie	d																								
Broughty Ferry	d																								
Dundee	a	13 15					13 52	14 15				14 52	15 16					15 49	16 03	16 03			16 46		
	d	13 17	13 34				13 54	14 17	14 34			14 52	15 17		15 34			15 49	16 04	16 04			16 47		16 49
Invergowrie	d																						16 53		
Perth	a						14 14				15 00	15 14						16 11			16 54		17 10		
	d					14 00	14 15				15 01	15 14					16 00	16 11			16 55	17 00	17 11		
Gleneagles	d																				17 11		17 26		
Dunblane	230 d																				17 22		17 36		
Stirling	230 d						14 44					15 43						16 43			17 29		17 42		
Larbert	230 d																								
Glasgow Queen St. 10	230 ⇌ a						15 14					16 14						17 18			18 09		18 15		
Leuchars 5	a	13 28	13 45					14 29	14 45				15 28		15 47				16 17	16 17					17 00
St Andrews Bus Station	⇌ a	*13b45*	*14b12*					*14b45*	*15b12*				*15b45*		*16e15*				*16b34*	*16b34*					*17f17*
St Andrews Bus Station	⇌ d	*13b10*	*13b25*					*14b10*	*14b25*				*15b10*		*15b25*				*15b55*	*15b55*					*16b40*
Leuchars 3	d	13 29	13 46					14 29	14 46				15 29		15 48				16 18	16 18					17 01
Cupar	d		13 53						14 53						15 55										17 08
Springfield	d																								
Ladybank	d		14 01			14 21			15 01						16 03		16 23					17 27			17 15
Markinch	d		14 08			14 29			15 08		15 38				16 10		16 31					→			17 22
Kirkcaldy	242 d		14 18			14 39			15 18		15 47				16 20		16 41		16 45	16 45					17 32
Inverkeithing	242 d		14 34			14 55			15 34						16 36		16 57		17 01	17 03					17 55
Haymarket	242 a	14 21	14 49			15 14		15 22	15 50		16 16		16 21		16 51		17 15		17 19	17 21					18 16
Edinburgh 10	242 a	14 27	14 54			15 19		15 29	15 57		16 24		16 28		16 56		17 22		17 26	17 27					18 22

A trolley service from Aberdeen
C To London Kings Cross
b Bus Service
e Bus Service. arrives 1612 SO
f Bus Service. arrives 1730 SO

Inverurie, Dyce, Aberdeen, Dundee, Inverness and Perth - Glasgow Queen Street and Edinburgh

		SR	SR	SR	SR	SR	SR	SR	SR	SR	SR	SR	SR	SR	GR	SR	SR	SR	SR	SR	SR	SR	SR
					SX	SO				SO	SX	SO			SX	SO							
			◇1	1	1		◇1	◇1	1		1		◇1	◇1	R 1	◇1			◇1	◇1			◇1
		A	B		C	C		B							D		E			B	E		
			🛒				🛒	🛒					🛒	🛒	🍴	🛒			🛒	🛒			🛒
Inverness	d												16 53										18 43
Carrbridge	d												17 28										19 14
Aviemore	d												17 36										19g29
Kingussie	d												17 49										19 42
Newtonmore	d												17 53										19 46
Dalwhinnie	d																						19 58
Blair Atholl	d												18 24										20 19
Pitlochry	d												18 34										20 29
Dunkeld & Birnam	d												18 46										20 41
Inverurie 240	d		15 24					16 38												18 43			
Dyce 240 ⇄	d		15 38					16 54	17 05											18 55			
Aberdeen 240	a		15 49					17 05	17 14											19 06			
	d		16 01				16 37	17 07	17 16					17 36	18 16	18 16			18 30	19 09			
Portlethen	d								17 27										18 40				
Stonehaven	d		16 18				16 53		17a37					17 52	18 33	18 33			18 49	19 26			
Laurencekirk	d		16 32					17 38						18 06						19 40			
Montrose	d						17 15	17 49						18 17	18 56	18 56			19 10	19 51			
Arbroath	d		16 55				17 29	18 03						18 31	19 12	19 12			19 24	20 05			
Carnoustie	d		17 02											18 38					19 31				
Golf Street	d																						
Barry Links	d																						
Monifieth	d																						
Balmossie	d																						
Broughty Ferry	d																						
Dundee	a		17 17				17 49	18 18						18 52	19 29	19 29			19 46	20 20			
	d		17 17	17 26			17 51	18 19			18 42	18 42		18 52	19 30	19 30			19 46	20 21		20 42	
Invergowrie	d																						
Perth	a						18 11						19 08	19 14					20 07				21 00
	d				18 00	18 00	18 12			18 28			19 09	19 14				20 00	20 11				21 02
Gleneagles	d																		20 25				
Dunblane 230	d						18 35			18 49													
Stirling 230	d						18 42			18a59				19 43					20 40				
Larbert 230	d																						
Glasgow Queen St. 10 230 ⛴	a						19 16							20 15					21 14				
Leuchars 5	a		17 29	17 38				18 31			18 53	18 53			19 43	19 43				20 33		20 53	
St Andrews Bus Station 🚌	a		*17e49*	*18f02*				*18b55*			*19b14*	*19b12*			*19b55*	*19b55*				*20b59*		*21b15*	
St Andrews Bus Station 🚌	d		*17b10*	*17b17*				*18b05*			*18b25*	*18b25*			*19b10*	*19b10*				*20b00*		*20b30*	
Leuchars 3	d		17 29	17 39				18 31			18 54	18 54			19 44	19 44				20 33		20 54	
Cupar	d			17 46							19 02	19 02										21 01	
Springfield	d	←		17 51																			
Ladybank	d	17 27		17 56	18 23	18 23					19 09	19 09						20 24				21 09	
Markinch	d	17 39		18 03	18 34	18 34					19 17	19 17	19 44					20 32				21 16	21 32
Kirkcaldy 242	d	17 48		18 13	18 44	18 44					19 26	19 26	19 54		20 08	20 08		20 41				21 26	21 42
Inverkeithing 242	d	18 04		18 29	19 00	19 00					19 42	19 42			20 24	20 24		20 59				21 49	
Haymarket 242	a	18 18	18 24	18 43	19 15	19 15		19 27			20 04	20 04	20 24		20 42	20 42		21 15		21 26		22 10	22 13
Edinburgh 10 242	a	18 25	18 32	18 49	19 21	19 21		19 34			20 09	20 09	20 29		20 48	20 48		21 20		21 31		22 16	22 19

A From Perth
B 🛒 from Aberdeen
C To Newcraighall
D To Leeds
g Arr. 1922
b Bus Service
e Bus Service. arrives 1745 SO
f Bus Service. arrives 1800 SO

Table 229

Mondays to Saturdays

Inverurie, Dyce, Aberdeen, Dundee, Inverness and Perth - Glasgow Queen Street and Edinburgh

		SR	SR	SR	SR		SR	SR	XC	SR	XC	SR	SR	SR	SR
									SO		SX	SX		FSX	FO
												🅱	🅱		
		◇■1	◇	◇■1	◇■1			◇■1	◇■1		◇■1			■1	■1
			A				B						C		
												🛏	🛏		
		⚲	⚲									☕	☕		
Inverness	d				20 15										
Carrbridge	d														
Aviemore	d				21 00										
Kingussie	d				21 12										
Newtonmore	d				21 17										
Dalwhinnie	d				21 28										
Blair Atholl	d				21 50										
Pitlochry	d				21 59										
Dunkeld & Birnam	d				22 12										
Inverurie 240	d		19 40												
Dyce 240 ✈	d		19 52												
Aberdeen 240	a		20 03												
	d	19 47	20 05	20 42				21 06	21 17		21 31	21 40	21 40	22 30	23 22
Portlethen	d	19 57												22 40	23 32
Stonehaven	d	20 06	20 21	20 58				21 22	21 35		21 49	22u00	22u00	22 49	23 41
Laurencekirk	d													23 03	23 55
Montrose	d	20 24	20 43	21 20				21 44	21 56		22 10	22u25	22u25	23 13	00 05
Arbroath	d	20 38	20 57	21 34				21 58	22 12		22 26	22u43	22u43	23 28	00 20
Carnoustie	d		21 04									22u52	22u52	23 35	00 27
Golf Street	d														
Barry Links	d														
Monifieth	d														
Balmossie	d														
Broughty Ferry	d														
Dundee	a	20 57	21 15	21 52				22 15	22 28		22 42			23 50	00 42
	d	20 57	21 16	21 52				22 15	22 29		22 43	23u06	23u06	23 51	00 43
Invergowrie	d													23 57	00 49
Perth	a	21 18		22 14	22 29									00 15	01 07
	d	21 18		22 14	22 30					22 38					
Gleneagles	d				22 47										
Dunblane 230	d				22 58										
Stirling 230	d	21 46		22 43	23 05										
Larbert 230	d														
Glasgow Queen St. ■10 230 ⛴	a	22 20		23 15	23 39										
Leuchars ■5	a		21 28					22 27	22 41		22 55				
St Andrews Bus Station 🚌	a		*21b59*					*22b59*	*22b59*		*23b29*				
St Andrews Bus Station 🚌	d		*21b00*					*22b00*	*22b00*		*22b30*				
Leuchars ■3	d		21 28					22 27	22 42		22 56	23u25	23u25		
Cupar	d		21 36					22 34	22 49		23 03				
Springfield	d														
Ladybank	d		21 43					22 42	22 57	23 01	23 10				
Markinch	d		21 51					22 49	23 05	23 10	23 18				
Kirkcaldy 242	d		21 59					22 59	23 14		23 26	23u53	23u53		
Inverkeithing 242	d		22 23					23 23	23 31	23 51	23 42	00u12	00u12		
Haymarket 242	a		22 45					23 43	23 50	00 11	23 57				
Edinburgh ■10 242	a		22 50					23 50	23 55	00 18	00 05	00 41	00 41		

A ⚲ from Aberdeen

C MTWO until 15 June, MTWO from 24 October. To London Euston

b Bus Service

Table 229

Sundays

Inverurie, Dyce, Aberdeen, Dundee, Inverness and Perth - Glasgow Queen Street and Edinburgh

		SR	SR	SR	SR	SR	GR	SR	GR	XC		SR	GR	SR	SR	SR	GR	SR	SR	SR		SR	SR	SR	SR
				1		◇1	R 1		R 1	◇1		◇1	R 1	◇1		◇1	R 1	◇1		◇1		◇1	◇1		◇1
		A					B		C	D			E				E								
						🛒	🍴🛒		🍴🛒			🛒	🍴🛒	🛒		🛒	🍴🛒	🛒		🛒		🛒	🛒		🛒
Inverness	d								09 40					12 30				13 25					16 15		
Carrbridge	d								10 10					13 08									16 46		
Aviemore	d								10 18					13 17				14 02					16 55		
Kingussie	d								10 31					13 30				14 15					17 14		
Newtonmore	d								10 36					13 35											
Dalwhinnie	d													13 46											
Blair Atholl	d								11 08					14 08									17 47		
Pitlochry	d								11 23					14 17				14 54					17 56		
Dunkeld & Birnam	d								11 36					14 30									18 12		
Inverurie	240 d																								
Dyce	240 ✈ d																								
Aberdeen	240 a																								
	d					09 27	09 48			11 12		11 29	11 47			13 27	13 50			15 10		15 30			17 10
Portlethen	d																			15 20					
Stonehaven	d					09 43	10 05			11 29		11 45	12 04			13 43	14 07			15 26		15 46			17 26
Laurencekirk	d					09 57										13 57									
Montrose	d					10 08	10 28			11 50		12 07	12 27			14 07	14 30			15 48		16 08			17 48
Arbroath	d					10 22	10 44			12 06		12 21	12 43			14 22	14 46			16 02		16 22			18 02
Carnoustie	d					10 29														16 09					
Golf Street	d																								
Barry Links	d																								
Monifieth	d																								
Balmossie	d																								
Broughty Ferry	d																								
Dundee	a					10 43	11 01			12 24		12 39	13 00			14 43	15 03			16 23		16 41			18 17
	d		07 25	08 43	09 25	10 43	11 02	11 25		12 25		12 43	13 01		13 25	14 45	15 04		15 25	16 25		16 43		17 25	18 19
Invergowrie	d																								
Perth	a			09 03		11 05			11 58			13 03		14 49		15 06		15 23				17 03	18 29		
	d	22p38		09 03		11 05			11 58			13 05		14 50		15 08		15 25				17 05	18 30		
Gleneagles	d			09 20		11 20			12 14			13 20		15 05		15 21						17 20	18 47		
Dunblane	230 d			09 31		11 31			12 27			13 31		15 16		15 33						17 31	18 58		
Stirling	230 d			09 38		11 38			12 34			13 38		15 22		15 45						17 38	19 05		
Larbert	230 d			09 47										15 31									19 12		
Glasgow Queen St. 10	230 🚇 a			10 15		12 11						14 11		15 56		16 28						18 12	19 37		
Leuchars 5	a		07 36		09 36		11 15	11 36		12 37			13 14		13 37		15 17		15 36	16 36				17 36	18 30
St Andrews Bus Station	🚌 a				*09b55*		*11b55*	*11b55*		*12b57*			*13b37*		*13b55*		*15b37*		*15b55*	*16b55*				*17b55*	*18b55*
St Andrews Bus Station	🚌 d				*09b15*		*10b55*	*11b15*		*12b15*			*12b55*		*13b15*		*14b55*		*15b15*	*16b15*				*17b15*	*18b15*
Leuchars 3	d		07 37		09 37		11 16	11 37		12 38			13 15		13 37		15 18		15 37	16 37				17 37	18 31
Cupar	d		07 44		09 44			11 44		12 45					13 44				15 44					17 44	
Springfield	d																								
Ladybank	d	23p01	07 52		09 52			11 52							13 52				15 52					17 52	
Markinch	d	23p10	07 59		09 59			11 59							13 59				15 59					17 59	
Kirkcaldy	242 d		08 08		10 08		11 40	12 08		13 03			13 39		14 08		15 42	16 03	16 08	17 02				18 07	18 56
Inverkeithing	242 d	23p51	08 30		10 30		11 56	12 30		13 18			13 55		14 30		15 58	16 19	16 30	17 18				18 29	19 12
Haymarket	242 a	00 11	08 52		10 58		12 17	12 58	13 13	13 36			14 18		14 58		16 19	16 35	16 54	17 34				18 52	19 27
Edinburgh 10	242 a	00 18	09 00		11 06		12 25	13 06	13 19	13 42			14 25		15 06		16 25	16 42	16 59	17 41				19 00	19 35

A not 22 May
B To London Kings Cross. The Northern Lights
C To London Kings Cross. The Highland Chieftain
D To Bristol Parkway
E To London Kings Cross
b Bus Service

Table 229

Sundays

Inverurie, Dyce, Aberdeen, Dundee, Inverness and Perth - Glasgow Queen Street and Edinburgh

		SR	SR	SR	SR	SR	SR	XC	SR	SR
									R	
		◇1		◇1	◇1	◇1	◇1	◇1	A	1
									🛏	
		⚮		⚮	⚮	⚮	⚮		⚮	
Inverness	d	15 27			18 30					
Carrbridge	d				19 01					
Aviemore	d				19 09					
Kingussie	d				19 23					
Newtonmore	d				19 27					
Dalwhinnie	d				19 39					
Blair Atholl	d				20 02					
Pitlochry	d				20 11					
Dunkeld & Birnam	d				20 24					
Inverurie 240	d	17 14								
Dyce 240 ✈	d	17 30								
Aberdeen 240	a	17 41								
	d	17 47		19 10		19 35	20 10	21 28	21 40	22 29
Portlethen	d						20 20			
Stonehaven	d	18 04		19 26		19 51	20 26	21 45	22u00	22 48
Laurencekirk	d	18 18								
Montrose	d	18 28		19 48		20 13	20 48	22 06	22u25	23 11
Arbroath	d	18 43		20 02		20 27	21 02	22 22	22u43	23 25
Carnoustie	d			20 09					22u52	23 32
Golf Street	d									
Barry Links	d									
Monifieth	d									
Balmossie	d									
Broughty Ferry	d									
Dundee	a	19 02		20 18		20 42	21 19	22 38		23 46
	d	19 04	19 27	20 20		20 43	21 21	22 39	23u06	23 47
Invergowrie	d									
Perth	a	19 25			20 42	21 04				00 09
	d	19 27			20 46	21 05				
Gleneagles	d					21 20				
Dunblane 230	d					21 31				
Stirling 230	d	19 55				21 38				
Larbert 230	d					21 49				
Glasgow Queen St. 10 230 ⇌	a	20 31				22 15				
Leuchars 5	a		19 38	20 31			21 32	22 51		
St Andrews Bus Station 🚌	a		*19b55*	*20b55*			*21b55*	*23b29*		
St Andrews Bus Station 🚌	d		*19b15*	*20b15*			*21b15*	*22b30*		
Leuchars 3	d		19 39	20 32			21 33	22 52	23u25	
Cupar	d		19 46				21 39	22 59		
Springfield	d									
Ladybank	d		19 54				21 48	23 06		
Markinch	d		20 01				21 54	23 14		
Kirkcaldy 242	d		20 10	20 59	21 25		22 05	23 22	23u53	
Inverkeithing 242	d		20 31	21 15	21 41		22 21	23 38	00u12	
Haymarket 242	a		20 54	21 31	21 57		22 36	23 53		
Edinburgh 10 242	a		21 01	21 36	22 03		22 43	23 58	00 36	

b Bus Service

A To London Euston

Table 229A

Mondays to Saturdays

Leuchars - St Andrews Bus Station - Leuchars

		SR MX	SR MX	SR MX	SR SO	SR SX	SR SX	SR SO	SR SX	SR SO		SR SX	SR SO	SR SX	SR SX	SR SO	SR SO	SR SO	SR SX	SR SX		SR SO	SR	SR SX	SR
Leuchars	d		00 03	00 29											06 53	06 55	07 04			07 05			07 15		
St Andrews Bus Station	a		00 21	00 39											07 04	07 13	07 15			07 23			07 26		
	d	23p50			05 39	05 44	06 00	06 10	06 14	06 29		06 30	06 55	07 00				07 15	07 20			07 25		07 27	07 28
Leuchars	a	00 06			05 57	06 02	06 11	06 21	06 32	06 47		06 41	07 06	07 11				07 33	07 31			07 36		07 45	07 39

		SR SX	SR SX	SR	SR SO	SR SO		SR SX	SR SX	SR	SR SO	SR SX	SR SX	SR	SR SX	SR SO		SR SO	SR SO	SR	SR SX	SR SX	SR	SR	SR
Leuchars	d	07 23				07 49		07 54		08 01		08 13	08 14			08 19		08 23			08 34			08 49	
St Andrews Bus Station	a	07 34				08 00		08 05		08 12		08 24	08 25			08 30		08 34			08 45			09 00	
	d		07 40	07 55	07 59				08 10		08 14			08 25	08 29				08 39	08 40		08 47	08 55		09 10
Leuchars	a		07 51	08 06	08 10				08 21		08 25			08 36	08 40				08 50	08 51		09 02	09 06		09 21

		SR SO		SR SX	SR	SR	SR	SR SX	SR	SR	SR	SR		SR	SR	SR	SR	SR	SR	SR	SR	SR		SR	SR
Leuchars	d	09 01		09 04			09 19	09 21	09 23			09 34			09 49		10 01	10 04			10 19	10 23			
St Andrews Bus Station	a	09 12		09 15			09 30	09 32	09 34			09 45			10 00		10 12	10 15			10 30	10 34			
	d				09 17	09 25				09 39	09 40			09 55		10 10			10 17	10 25				10 39	10 40
Leuchars	a				09 32	09 36				09 50	09 51			10 06		10 21			10 32	10 36				10 50	10 51

		SR	SR	SR	SR	SR	SR	SR		SR	SR	SR	SR	SR	SR	SR	SR	SR		SR	SR	SR	SR	SR	SR
Leuchars	d	10 34		10 49		11 01	11 04				11 19	11 23			11 34		11 49			12 01	12 04			12 19	12 23
St Andrews Bus Station	a	10 45		11 00		11 12	11 15				11 30	11 34			11 45		12 00			12 12	12 15			12 30	12 34
	d		10 55		11 10			11 17		11 25			11 39	11 40		11 55		12 10				12 17	12 25		
Leuchars	a		11 06		11 21			11 32		11 36			11 50	11 51		12 06		12 21				12 32	12 36		

		SR	SR	SR		SR	SR	SR	SR	SR	SR	SR	SR	SR		SR	SR	SR	SR	SR	SR	SR	SR	SR	
Leuchars	d			12 34			12 49		13 01	13 04			13 19	13 23				13 34		13 49		14 01	14 04		
St Andrews Bus Station	a			12 45			13 00		13 12	13 15			13 30	13 34				13 45		14 00		14 12	14 15		
	d	12 39	12 40			12 55		13 10			13 17	13 25				13 39	13 40		13 55		14 10			14 17	
Leuchars	a	12 50	12 51			13 06		13 21			13 32	13 36				13 50	13 51		14 06		14 21			14 32	

		SR	SR	SR	SR	SR	SR	SR	SR	SR		SR	SR	SR SO	SR	SR	SR	SR	SR A	SR		SR B	SR SX	SR	SR
Leuchars	d		14 19	14 23			14 34		14 49			15 01	15 04			15 19	15 23			15 34					15 49
St Andrews Bus Station	a		14 30	14 34			14 45		15 00			15 12	15 15			15 30	15 34			15 45					16 00
	d	14 25			14 39	14 40		14 55		15 10				15 17	15 25			15 39	15 40			15 45	15 50	15 55	
Leuchars	a	14 36			14 50	14 51		15 06		15 21				15 32	15 36			15 50	15 51			15 56	16 01	16 06	

		SR	SR SO	SR	SR SO	SR		SR SX	SR	SR	SR SX	SR	SR	SR	SR	SR		SR	SR	SR SO	SR SX	SR	SR	SR SO	SR SX
Leuchars	d		16 01	16 04					16 19	16 23	16 26			16 34		16 49			17 01	17 04	17 06			17 19	17 23
St Andrews Bus Station	a		16 12	16 15					16 30	16 34	16 37			16 45		17 00			17 12	17 15	17 17			17 30	17 34
	d	16 10			16 17	16 25		16 27				16 39	16 40		16 55			17 10				17 17	17 25		
Leuchars	a	16 21			16 32	16 36		16 42				16 50	16 51		17 06			17 21				17 32	17 36		

		SR		SR SO	SR SO	SR SX	SR SX	SR	SR SO	SR SX	SR	SR SX		SR	SR	SR	SR SO	SR	SR SO	SR	SR SX	SR		SR	SR
Leuchars	d			17 28	17 34	17 37	17 38		17 49	17 51		18 02		18 04			18 21	18 24	18 33		18 40	18 44			
St Andrews Bus Station	a			17 46	17 45	17 55	17 49		18 00	18 02		18 20		18 15			18 32	18 35	18 51		18 58	18 55			
	d	17 45						17 59			18 05				18 17	18 25				18 55				19 09	19 10
Leuchars	a	17 56						18 17			18 16				18 32	18 36				19 06				19 27	19 21

		SR SO	SR	SR C	SR	SR	SR	SR		SR	SR	SR	SR	SR	SR	SR	SR	SR		SR	SR	SR	SR	SR	SR
Leuchars	d	19 01	19 03	19 09	19 18		19 26			19 48		20 03	20 07	20 18				20 33		20 48		21 04	21 18		
St Andrews Bus Station	a	19 12	19 14	19 20	19 29		19 37			19 59		20 21	20 18	20 29				20 51		20 59		21 15	21 29		
	d					19 30		19 40			20 00				20 30	20 39	20 40				21 00			21 30	21 45
Leuchars	a					19 41		19 51			20 11				20 41	20 57	20 51				21 11			21 41	21 56

		SR	SR	SR		SR	SR	SR	SR	SR	SR	SR	SR	SR		SR	SR								
Leuchars	d	21 48		22 03		22 18		22 24			22 48		23 18	23 34			23 48								
St Andrews Bus Station	a	21 59		22 21		22 29		22 35			22 59		23 29	23 45			23 59								
	d		22 00				22 30		22 39	22 45		23 00				23 50									
Leuchars	a		22 11				22 41		22 57	22 56		23 11				00 06									

A SO until 25 June, from 2 July until 15 August, SO from 20 August, also from 10 October until 21 October

B SX until 1 July, SX from 16 August, not from 10 October until 21 October

C SX from 30 May

Table 229A

Sundays

Leuchars - St Andrews Bus Station - Leuchars

		SR	SR	SR	SR	SR	SR	SR	SR	SR		SR	SR	SR	SR	SR	SR	SR	SR	SR		SR	SR	SR	SR
		A					A																		
		🚌	🚌	🚌	🚌	🚌	🚌	🚌	🚌	🚌		🚌	🚌	🚌	🚌	🚌	🚌	🚌	🚌	🚌		🚌	🚌	🚌	🚌
Leuchars	d		00 03	00 29					09 19			09 44	09 48			10 18			10 47	10 48			11 19		11 19
St Andrews Bus Station	a		00 21	00 39					09 37			09 55	09 59			10 29			10 58	10 59			11 30		11 37
	d	23p50			07 55	09 00	09 15	09 30		09 50				10 00	10 15		10 30	10 55				11 15		11 35	
Leuchars	a	00 06			08 13	09 11	09 26	09 41		10 08				10 11	10 26		10 41	11 06				11 26		11 46	

		SR	SR	SR	SR	SR		SR	SR	SR	SR	SR	SR	SR	SR	SR		SR	SR	SR	SR	SR	SR	SR	SR
		🚌	🚌	🚌	🚌	🚌		🚌	🚌	🚌	🚌	🚌	🚌	🚌	🚌	🚌		🚌	🚌	🚌	🚌	🚌	🚌	🚌	🚌
Leuchars	d		11 44		11 46			12 06		12 26		12 46	12 47		13 06			13 19	13 26		13 44		13 46		14 06
St Andrews Bus Station	a		11 55		11 57			12 17		12 37		12 57	12 58		13 17			13 37	13 37		13 55		13 57		14 17
	d	11 50		11 55		12 15			12 35		12 55			13 15		13 35				13 50		13 55		14 15	
Leuchars	a	12 08		12 06		12 26			12 46		13 06			13 26		13 46				14 08		14 06		14 26	

		SR		SR	SR	SR	SR	SR	SR	SR	SR	SR		SR	SR	SR	SR	SR	SR	SR	SR	SR		SR	SR
		🚌		🚌	🚌	🚌	🚌	🚌	🚌	🚌	🚌	🚌		🚌	🚌	🚌	🚌	🚌	🚌	🚌	🚌	🚌		🚌	🚌
Leuchars	d			14 26	14 44		14 46		15 06		15 19	15 26			15 44		15 46		16 06		16 26	16 44			16 46
St Andrews Bus Station	a			14 37	14 55		14 57		15 17		15 37	15 37			15 55		15 57		16 17		16 37	16 55			16 57
	d	14 35				14 55		15 15		15 35				15 50		15 55		16 15		16 35				16 55	
Leuchars	a	14 46				15 06		15 26		15 46				16 08		16 06		16 26		16 46				17 06	

		SR	SR	SR	SR	SR	SR	SR		SR	SR	SR	SR	SR	SR	SR	SR	SR		SR	SR	SR	SR	SR	SR
		🚌	🚌	🚌	🚌	🚌	🚌	🚌		🚌	🚌	🚌	🚌	🚌	🚌	🚌	🚌	🚌		🚌	🚌	🚌	🚌	🚌	🚌
Leuchars	d		17 06		17 19	17 26		17 44		17 46			18 06		18 26	18 44	18 48				19 18		19 19	19 44	19 48
St Andrews Bus Station	a		17 17		17 37	17 37		17 55		17 57			18 17		18 37	18 55	18 59				19 29		19 37	19 55	19 59
	d	17 15		17 35			17 50				18 00	18 15		18 30				19 00		19 15		19 30			
Leuchars	a	17 26		17 46			18 08				18 11	18 26		18 41				19 11		19 26		19 41			

		SR	SR	SR		SR	SR	SR	SR	SR	SR	SR	SR	SR		SR	SR	SR	SR	SR	SR	SR	SR	SR	
		🚌	🚌	🚌		🚌	🚌	🚌	🚌	🚌	🚌	🚌	🚌	🚌		🚌	🚌	🚌	🚌	🚌	🚌	🚌	🚌	🚌	
Leuchars	d					20 18		20 44	20 48			21 18		21 44		21 48	21 49			22 18		22 44	23 18	23 34	
St Andrews Bus Station	a					20 29		20 55	20 59			21 29		21 55		21 59	22 07			22 29		22 55	23 29	23 52	
	d	20 00	20 15	20 20			20 30			21 00	21 15		21 30					22 10	22 15		22 30				
Leuchars	a	20 11	20 26	20 38			20 41			21 11	21 26		21 41					22 28	22 26		22 41				

A not 22 May

Edinburgh, Glasgow Queen Street and Falkirk Grahamston - Stirling, Alloa and Dunblane

Miles	Miles	Miles	Miles	Station		SR MX	SR MO A	SR MX	SR MX A	SR	SR [1] B	SR ◇[1] C ⊥	SR	SR [1] B	SR SO	SR	SR SX [1] B	SR	SR [1] ⊥	SR ◇[1] E
0	0	—	—	**Edinburgh** [10]	d			23p33		05 18	05 55			06 30		06 32	06 45		07 00	
1¼	—	—	—	Haymarket	d			23p37		05 22	05 59			06 34		06 36	06 49		07 04	
3¾	—	—	—	Edinburgh Park	d			23p43		05 27						06 42				
—	17½	—	—	Linlithgow	d			23p55		05 39	06 13			06 48		06 54	07 04			
—	22¼	—	—	Polmont [3]	d			23p59		05 44	06 19			06 55		07 00			07 21	
—	—	0	0	**Glasgow Queen Street** [10]	d	23p18	23p35		23p48			05 56	06 14					06 48	07a50	07 06
—	—	3¼	3¼	Bishopbriggs	d	23p23	23p41		23p53				06 20					06 53		
—	—	6¼	6¼	Lenzie [3]	d	23p29	23p47		23p59				06 25					06 59		
—	—	11½	11½	Croy [3]	d	23p35	23p53		00 05		06a34		06 32	07a10			07a23	07 05		
—	25½	—	—	**Falkirk Grahamston**	d			00 07		05 51						07 07				
—	27	—	—	Camelon	d			00 10		05 54						07 10				
—	28¼	21	21	Larbert	d	23p48	00 05	00 16	00 18	06 00		06 16	06 43			07 15		07 18		
—	36½	29	29	**Stirling**	d	23p59	00 14	00 25	00 30	06 09		06 25	06 51		07 01	07 24		07 40		07 33
—	—	—	35¾	**Alloa**	a	00 11							07 05							
—	40	32½	—	Bridge of Allan	d		00 18	00 29	00 35	06 13					07 05	07 29		07 44		
—	42	34½	—	**Dunblane**	a		00 22	00 36	00 42	06 20		06 31			07 12	07 35		07 52		07 39

Station		SR	SR [1] B ⊥	SR	SR [1] B ⊥	SR ◇[1] F ⊥	SR	SR	SR SX G	SR [1] B ⊥	SR [1] B ⊥	SR	SR [1] ⊥	SR	SR [1] B ⊥	SR ◇[1] F ⊥	SR	SR [1] ⊥	SR
Edinburgh [10]	d	07 03	07 15		07 30		07 33			07 45	08 00	08 03	08 15		08 30		08 31	08 45	
Haymarket	d	07 07	07 19		07 34		07 38			07 49	08 04	08 07	08 19		08 34		08 36	08 49	
Edinburgh Park	d	07 12					07 42					08 13					08 43		
Linlithgow	d	07 24	07 33		07 48		07 54		07 59	08 04		08 25	08 33				08 55	09 03	
Polmont [3]	d	07 30			07 55		08 00				08 22	08 30	08 39				09 01	09 09	
Glasgow Queen Street [10]	d			07 18		07 41		07 48					09a07	08 18		08 41		09a36	08 48
Bishopbriggs	d			07 23				07 53						08 23					08 53
Lenzie [3]	d			07 29				07 59		08a25				08 29					08 59
Croy [3]	d		07a52	07 35	08a10			08 05			08a36			08 35	09a03				09 05
Falkirk Grahamston	d	07 36					08 07		08 11			08 37					09 08		
Camelon	d	07 40					08 10		08a14			08 40					09 11		
Larbert	d	07 46		07 50			08 16	08 18				08 46		08 49			09 16		09 18
Stirling	d	07 55		08 06		08 07	08 25	08 30				08 55		09 00		09a07	09 25		09 30
Alloa	a			08 18										09 13					
Bridge of Allan	d	07 59					08 29	08 35				09 00					09 30		09 35
Dunblane	a	08 08				08 15	08 36	08 43				09 08					09 36		09 43

Station		SR [1] B ⊥	SR	SR [1] ⊥	SR	SR [1] B ⊥	SR ◇[1] F ⊥	SR	SR [1] ⊥	SR	SR [1] B ⊥	SR ◇[1] E ⊥	SR	SR [1] ⊥	SR	SR [1] B ⊥	SR ◇[1] F ⊥	SR	SR [1] ⊥
Edinburgh [10]	d	09 00	09 03	09 15		09 30		09 33	09 45		10 00		10 03	10 15		10 30		10 32	10 45
Haymarket	d	09 04	09 07	09 19		09 34		09 38	09 49		10 04		10 07	10 19		10 34		10 36	10 49
Edinburgh Park	d		09 14					09 43					10 13					10 43	
Linlithgow	d		09 26	09 33				09 55	10 03				10 25	10 33				10 55	11 03
Polmont [3]	d		09 31	09 39				10 00	10 09				10 30	10 39				11 00	11 09
Glasgow Queen Street [10]	d			10a06	09 18		09 41		10a36	09 48		10 11		11a05	10 18		10 41		11a37
Bishopbriggs	d				09 23					09 53					10 23				
Lenzie [3]	d				09 29					09 59					10 29				
Croy [3]	d	09a33			09 35	10a03				10 05	10a33				10 35	11a03			
Falkirk Grahamston	d		09 38					10 08					10 36					11 08	
Camelon	d		09 41					10 11					10 40					11 11	
Larbert	d		09 47		09 48			10 15		10 18			10 46		10 48			11 15	
Stirling	d		09 56		10 00		10a07	10 24		10 42		10 36	10 55		11 00		11a07	11 24	
Alloa	a				10 13										11 13				
Bridge of Allan	d		10 00					10 30		10 47			11 00					11 30	
Dunblane	a		10 07					10 36		10 56		10 42	11 07					11 36	

Station		SR	SR [1] B ⊥	SR	SR [1] ⊥	SR	SR [1] B ⊥	SR ◇[1] F ⊥	SR	SR [1] ⊥	SR	SR [1] B ⊥	SR	SR [1] ⊥	SR	SR [1] B ⊥	SR ◇[1] F ⊥	SR
Edinburgh [10]	d		11 00	11 03	11 15		11 30		11 32	11 45		12 00	12 03	12 15		12 30		12 31
Haymarket	d		11 04	11 08	11 19		11 34		11 36	11 49		12 04	12 08	12 19		12 34		12 36
Edinburgh Park	d			11 13					11 43				12 13					12 43
Linlithgow	d			11 25	11 33				11 55	12 03			12 26	12 33				12 55
Polmont [3]	d			11 31	11 39				12 01	12 09			12 31	12 39				13 01
Glasgow Queen Street [10]	d	10 48			12a06	11 18		11 41		12a37	11 48			13a05	12 18		12 41	
Bishopbriggs	d	10 53				11 23					11 53				12 23			
Lenzie [3]	d	10 59				11 29					11 59				12 29			
Croy [3]	d	11 05	11a33			11 35	12a03				12 05	12a34			12 35	13a03		
Falkirk Grahamston	d			11 38					12 07				12 37					13 07
Camelon	d			11 41					12 10				12 40					13 10
Larbert	d	11 18		11 46		11 48			12 16		12 18		12 47		12 48			13 16
Stirling	d	11 30		11 55		12 00		12a07	12 25		12 30		12 56		13 00		13a07	13 25
Alloa	a					12 13									13 13			
Bridge of Allan	d	11 35		12 00					12 30		12 35		13 00					13 30
Dunblane	a	11 43		12 07					12 36		12 43		13 07					13 36

A To Perth
B To Glasgow Queen Street
C To Dyce
E To Inverness
F To Aberdeen.
G From Kirkcaldy to Glasgow Queen Street

Table 230

Mondays to Saturdays

Edinburgh, Glasgow Queen Street and Falkirk Grahamston - Stirling, Alloa and Dunblane

		SR 1 🍴	SR	SR 1 A 🍴	SR	SR 1 🍴	SR	SR 1 A 🍴				SR ◇1 C 🍴	SR	SR 1 🍴	SR	SR 1 A 🍴	SR	SR 1 🍴		SR	SR 1 A 🍴			SR ◇1 C 🍴	SR
Edinburgh 10	d	12 45		13 00	13 02	13 15		13 30					13 31	13 45		14 00	14 04	14 15			14 30				14 33
Haymarket	d	12 49		13 04	13 06	13 19		13 34					13 36	13 49		14 04	14 07	14 19			14 34				14 36
Edinburgh Park	d				13 14								13 43				14 13								14 43
Linlithgow	d	13 03			13 26	13 33							13 55	14 03			14 25	14 33							14 55
Polmont 3	d	13 09			13 30	13 39							14 00	14 09			14 30	14 39							15 00
Glasgow Queen Street 10 ⛴	d	13a36	12 48			14a06	13 18					13 41		14a36	13 48			15a07		14 18				14 41	
Bishopbriggs	d		12 53				13 25								13 53					14 23					
Lenzie 3	d		12 59				13 31								13 59					14 29					
Croy 3	d		13 05	13a33			13 37	14a03							14 05	14a33				14 35	15a03				
Falkirk Grahamston	d				13 37								14 07				14 37								15 08
Camelon	d				13 40								14 10				14 40								15 11
Larbert	d		13 18		13 46		13 48						14 15		14 16		14 47			14 48					15 15
Stirling	d		13 31		13 55		14 00					14a07	14 24		14 31		14 56			15 00				15a07	15 24
Alloa	a						14 13													15 13					
Bridge of Allan	d		13 35		14 00								14 28		14 36		15 00								15 30
Dunblane	a		13 43		14 07								14 35		14 43		15 07								15 36

		SR 1 🍴	SR	SR 1 A 🍴		SR	SR 1 🍴	SR	SR 1 A 🍴			SR ◇1 C 🍴	SR	SR 1 🍴		SR	SR SX I	SR 1 A 🍴	SR ◇1 D 🍴	SR	SR 1 🍴	SR	SR 1 A 🍴		
Edinburgh 10	d	14 45		15 00		15 03	15 15		15 30				15 31	15 45				16 00		16 04	16 15		16 30		
Haymarket	d	14 49		15 04		15 08	15 19		15 34				15 36	15 49				16 04		16 08	16 19		16 34		
Edinburgh Park	d					15 14							15 43							16 13					
Linlithgow	d	15 03				15 25	15 33						15 55	16 03						16 25	16 33				
Polmont 3	d	15 09				15 30	15 39						16 00	16 09						16 31	16 39				
Glasgow Queen Street 10 ⛴	d	15a37	14 49				16a07	15 18				15 41		16a36		15 48	15 51		16 11		17a07	16 18			
Bishopbriggs	d		14 54					15 23								15 53	15 56					16 24			
Lenzie 3	d		15 00					15 29								15 59	16 08					16 30			
Croy 3	d		15 06	15a33				15 35	16a03							16 05	16 15	16a33				16 36	17a03		
Falkirk Grahamston	d					15 37							16 07				16a33			16 37					
Camelon	d					15 40							16 10							16 40					
Larbert	d		15 18			15 44		15 48					16 16			16 18				16 46		16 49			
Stirling	d		15 30			15 53		16 00				16a07	16 25			16 30			16 37	16 55		17 08			
Alloa	a							16 13														17 20			
Bridge of Allan	d		15 35			15 57							16 29			16 35				17 00					
Dunblane	a		15 43			16 07							16 36			16 43			16 48	17 07					

		SR B	SR SX	SR SO ◇1 C 🍴	GR SO 1 F 🛏🍴	GR SX 1 F 🛏🍴	SR	SR 1 🍴	SR	SR 1 A 🍴		SR SO G	SR SX I	SR SX G	SR	SR 1 🍴	SR	SR A	SR B	SR SO ◇1 C 🍴		SR SX H	SR 1 A 🍴	SR SX ◇1 C 🍴	SR
Edinburgh 10	d				16 32	16 33	16 35	16 45		17 00					17 03	17 15						17 27	17 30		17 32
Haymarket	d				16 38	16 38	16 40	16 49		17 04					17 07	17 19						17 32	17 34		17 35
Edinburgh Park	d						16 46								17 13										17 43
Linlithgow	d						16 58	17 05							17 25	17 33									17 55
Polmont 3	d						17 04	17 12							17 31	17 39									18 00
Glasgow Queen Street 10 ⛴	d	16 22	16 33	16 41				17a39	16 48			17 03	17 03	17 11		18a06	17 18		17 22	17 41				17 41	
Bishopbriggs	d		16 39						16 53			17 08	17 08				17 23								
Lenzie 3	d		16a44						16 59			17 14	17 14				17 29								
Croy 3	d								17 05	17a34		17 19					17 35						18a05		
Falkirk Grahamston	d				17 04	17 04	17 09						17a32		17 37			17 42							18 08
Camelon	d	17a01					17 12								17 40			17a44	18a04						18 11
Larbert	d						17 20		17 23			17 31		17 31	17 46		17 48					17 57			18 15
Stirling	d			17a07	17a19	17a19	17 29		17 35			17 45		17 45	17 55		18 00			18 07		18 06		18 14	18 28
Alloa	a																18 14								18 42
Bridge of Allan	d						17 32		17 40			17 49		17 49	18 00							18 13			
Dunblane	a						17 40		17 47			17 54		17 54	18 08					18 14		18 18		18 21	

A To Glasgow Queen Street
B To Falkirk Grahamston
C To Aberdeen
D To Inverness
F From London Kings Cross to Inverness. **The Highland Chieftan**
G To Perth
H From Newcraighall
I Calls at Camelon

Table 230

Edinburgh, Glasgow Queen Street and Falkirk Grahamston - Stirling, Alloa and Dunblane

		SR ■1 🛒	SR	SR ■1 A 🛒	SR B	SR		SR ■1 🛒	SR			SR C	SR ◇■1 D 🛒	SR	SR ■1 🛒	SR		SR ■1 A 🛒	SR	SR ■1 🛒	SR	SR ■1 A	SR ◇■1 D 🛒		SR
Edinburgh 10	d	17 45		18 00		18 01		18 15						18 34	18 45			19 00	19 03	19 15		19 30			19 33
Haymarket	d	17 49		18 04		18 07		18 19						18 38	18 49			19 04	19 07	19 19		19 34			19 36
Edinburgh Park	d					18 13								18 43					19 13						19 42
Linlithgow	d	18 03				18 25		18 33						18 55	19 03				19 25	19 33		19 48			19 55
Polmont 3	d	18 09				18 30		18 39						19 00	19 09				19 30	19 39					20 01
Glasgow Queen Street 10 ⛴	d	18a37	17 48		18 11			19a06	18 18			18 23	18 41		19a36	18 48				20a07	19 18		19 41		
Bishopbriggs	d		17 53						18 23							18 53					19 23				
Lenzie 3	d		17 59						18 29							18 59					19 29				
Croy 3	d		18 05	18a34					18 35							19 05		19a33			19 35	20a07			
Falkirk Grahamston	d					18 37								19 07					19 37						20 07
Camelon	d					18 40						19a04		19 10					19 40						20 10
Larbert	d		18 19		18 30	18 46			18 50					19 16		19 21			19 45		19 48				20 16
Stirling	d		18 32		18 41	18 55			19 00				19 07	19 25		19 35			19 54		20 00		20a07		20 25
Alloa	a								19 15												20 13				
Bridge of Allan	d		18 37		18 46	18 59								19 29		19 39			20 00						20 30
Dunblane	a		18 44		18 50	19 09							19 14	19 38		19 45			20 08						20 36

		SR			SR ■1	SR	SR	SR ■1 A	SR ◇■1 D	SR	SR	SR ■1				SR	SR ■1 A	SR ◇■1 D	SR B	SR	SR ■1				SR
Edinburgh 10	d				20 00	20 03		20 30		20 33		21 00					21 30		21 33		22 00				
Haymarket	d				20 04	20 07		20 34		20 38		21 04					21 34		21 37		22 04				
Edinburgh Park	d					20 13				20 42									21 43						
Linlithgow	d				20 18	20 25		20 48		20 54		21 18					21 48		21 55		22 18				
Polmont 3	d				20 24	20 30				21 00		21 24							22 00		22 24				
Glasgow Queen Street 10 ⛴	d	19 48			20a51		20 18		20 41		20 48	21a51				21 18		21 41		21 48	22a50				22 18
Bishopbriggs	d	19 54					20 23				20 53					21 23				21 53					22 23
Lenzie 3	d	20 00					20 29				20 59					21 29				21 59					22 29
Croy 3	d	20 06					20 35	21a07			21 05					21 35	22a08			22 05					22 35
Falkirk Grahamston	d					20 37				21 06									22 07						
Camelon	d					20 40				21 09									22 10						
Larbert	d	20 18				20 46	20 48			21 16	21 18					21 48			22 16	22 18					22 47
Stirling	d	20 30				20 55	21 00		21 07	21 25	21 30					22 00		22a07	22 25	22 30					23 01
Alloa	a						21 13									22 13									23 13
Bridge of Allan	d	20 35				20 59				21 29	21 35								22 30	22 35					
Dunblane	a	20 43				21 06			21 14	21 37	21 43								22 34	22 43					

		SR ■1 A	SR	SR B	SR ■1 A			SR		SR ■1 A	SR	SR B
Edinburgh 10	d	22 30	22 33		23 00					23 30	23 33	
Haymarket	d	22 34	22 37		23 04					23 34	23 37	
Edinburgh Park	d		22 43								23 43	
Linlithgow	d	22 48	22 55		23 18					23 48	23 55	
Polmont 3	d		23 00		23 24					23 54	23 59	
Glasgow Queen Street 10 ⛴	d			22 48				23 18				23 48
Bishopbriggs	d			22 53				23 23				23 53
Lenzie 3	d			22 59				23 29				23 59
Croy 3	d	23a07		23 05	23a39			23 35		00a09		00 05
Falkirk Grahamston	d		23 07								00 07	
Camelon	d		23 10								00 10	
Larbert	d		23 16	23 18				23 48			00 16	00 18
Stirling	d		23 25	23 33				23 59			00 25	00 30
Alloa	a							00 11				
Bridge of Allan	d		23 29	23 37							00 29	00 35
Dunblane	a		23 36	23 42							00 36	00 42

Sundays

		SR E	SR E	SR F	SR ■1 A 🛒	SR G	SR G	SR ■1 A	SR G	SR ◇■1 D 🛒		SR	SR G	SR ■1 A 🛒	SR	SR	SR G	SR ■1 A 🛒	SR	SR ◇■1 D		SR	SR G	SR ■1 A 🛒	SR
Edinburgh 10	d		23p33		08 00			09 00				09 33		10 00		10 35		11 00				11 35		12 00	
Haymarket	d		23p37		08 04			09 04				09 36		10 04		10 38		11 04				11 39		12 04	
Edinburgh Park	d		23p43									09 40				10 43						11 43			
Linlithgow	d		23p55		08 18			09 18				09 59		10 18		10 55		11 18				11 55		12 18	
Polmont 3	d		23p59		08 24			09 24				10 05		10 24		11 01		11 24				12 01		12 24	
Glasgow Queen Street 10 ⛴	d	23p18	⌇	23p48		08⌇15	08⌇48		09⌇12	09 38			09⌇47		10 15		10⌇47		11 15	11 45			11⌇48		12 15
Bishopbriggs	d	23p23	⌇	23p53		08⌇21	08⌇54		09⌇18				09⌇53		10 21		10⌇53		11 21				11⌇54		12 21
Lenzie 3	d	23p29	⌇	23p59		08⌇27	09⌇00		09⌇24	09 47			09⌇59		10 27		10⌇59		11 27				12⌇00		12 27
Croy 3	d	23p35	⌇	00⌇05	08a39	08a33	09a06	09a39	09a30				10a05	10a39	10 33		11a05	11a39	11 33				12a06	12a39	12 33
Falkirk Grahamston	d	⌇	00⌇07	⌇								10 11				11 07						12 08			
Camelon	d	⌇	00⌇10	⌇								10 14				11 10						12 10			
Larbert	d	23p48	00⌇16	00⌇18						10 02		10 21			10 45	11 15			11 45			12 15			12 45
Stirling	d	23p59	00⌇25	00⌇30						10 12		10 30			10 55	11 25			11 55	12 12		12 25			12 55
Alloa	a	00⌇11	⌇	⌇											11 07				12 07						13 07
Bridge of Allan	d		00⌇29	00⌇35								10 34				11 30						12 30			
Dunblane	a		00⌇36	00⌇42						10 17		10 41				11 39				12 17		12 38			

A To Glasgow Queen Street
B To Perth
C To Falkirk Grahamston
D To Aberdeen
E not 22 May
F not 22 May. To Perth
G 27 November, 4 December

Table 230

Sundays

Edinburgh, Glasgow Queen Street and Falkirk Grahamston - Stirling, Alloa and Dunblane

		SR	SR	SR	SR	SR		SR	SR	SR	SR	SR	SR	SR	SR	SR		SR	SR	SR	SR	SR	SR	SR	SR
		1			1			1	◇1			1		1	◇1				1		1	◇1			1
		A		B				A	C		B			A	D			B			A	C		B	
		[trolley]			[trolley]			[trolley]	[trolley]			[trolley]			[trolley]				[trolley]		[trolley]	[trolley]			[trolley]
Edinburgh 10	d	12 30	12 35		13 00			13 30		13 36		14 00		14 30		14 36			15 00		15 30		15 35		16 00
Haymarket	d	12 33	12 39		13 04			13 34		13 40		14 04		14 34		14 38			15 04		15 34		15 38		16 04
Edinburgh Park	d		12 43							13 45						14 43							15 43		
Linlithgow	d	12 48	12 55		13 18			13 48		13 57		14 18		14 48		14 55			15 18		15 48		15 55		16 18
Polmont 3	d		13 01		13 24					14 03		14 24				15 01			15 24				16 01		16 24
Glasgow Queen Street 10 ⇌	d			12 47	13a51	13 15			13 45		13 48	14a51	14 15		14 40			14 47	15a51	15 15		15 45		15 48	16a51
Bishopbriggs	d			12 53		13 21					13 54		14 21					14 53		15 21				15 54	
Lenzie 3	d			12 59		13 27					14 00		14 27					14 59		15 27				16 00	
Croy 3	d	13a07		13a05		13 33		14a07			14a06		14 33	15a07				15a05		15 33	16a07			16a06	
Falkirk Grahamston	d		13 08							14 09						15 07							16 07		
Camelon	d		13 10							14 12						15 10							16 10		
Larbert	d		13 15			13 45				14 18			14 45		15 00	15 15				15 45			16 15		
Stirling	d		13 25			13 55			14 12	14 26			14 55		15 09	15 25				15 55		16 12	16 25		
Alloa	a					14 07							15 07							16 07					
Bridge of Allan	d		13 30							14 32						15 30							16 30		
Dunblane	a		13 38						14 17	14 38					15 15	15 38						16 17	16 38		

		SR		SR	GR	SR	SR	SR	SR	SR	SR	SR		SR	SR	SR	SR	SR	SR	SR	SR	SR		SR	SR
					■																				
				1	1			1		1	◇1				1	◇1		1		1		1		◇1	
				A	E		B			A	C			B		D		A				A		C	
				[trolley]	[restaurant] [trolley]			[trolley]			[trolley]				[trolley]	[trolley]		[trolley]		[trolley]		[trolley]		[trolley]	
Edinburgh 10	d			16 30	16 30	16 35		17 00		17 30		17 35			18 00			18 30	18 35	19 00		19 30			19 33
Haymarket	d			16 34	16 35	16 38		17 04		17 34		17 38			18 04			18 34	18 38	19 04		19 34			19 36
Edinburgh Park	d					16 43						17 43							18 43						19 41
Linlithgow	d			16 48		16 55		17 18		17 48		17 55			18 18			18 48	18 55	19 18		19 48			19 55
Polmont 3	d					17 01		17 24				18 01			18 24				19 01	19 24					20 01
Glasgow Queen Street 10 ⇌	d	16 15					16 47	17a52	17 15		17 45			17 48	18a51	18 10	18 16			19a51	19 15			19 45	
Bishopbriggs	d	16 21					16 53		17 21					17 54			18 21				19 21				
Lenzie 3	d	16 27					16 59		17 27					18 00			18 26				19 27				
Croy 3	d	16 33		17a07			17a05		17 33	18a07				18a06			18 33	19a07			19 33	20a07			
Falkirk Grahamston	d				17 02	17 07						18 07							19 07						20 07
Camelon	d					17 10						18 10							19 10						20 10
Larbert	d	16 45				17 15			17 48			18 15				18 30	18 45		19 14		19 45				20 14
Stirling	d	16 55			17a17	17 25			17 57		18a12	18 25				18 39	18 55		19 24		19 55			20 12	20 24
Alloa	a	17 07							18 12								19 07				20 07				
Bridge of Allan	d					17 30						18 30							19 29						20 29
Dunblane	a					17 38						18 38				18 45			19 38					20 17	20 38

		SR	SR	SR	SR	SR	SR	SR		SR	SR	SR	SR	SR	SR	SR
		1		1		1		◇1			1			1	1	
				A		A		C			A		F	A	A	F
								[trolley]								
Edinburgh 10	d	20 00		20 30	20 35	21 00				21 29	22 00		22 34	23 00	23 30	
Haymarket	d	20 04		20 34	20 38	21 04				21 32	22 04		22 39	23 04	23 34	
Edinburgh Park	d				20 43					21 37			22 45			
Linlithgow	d	20 18		20 48	20 55	21 18				21 49	22 18		22 58	23 18	23 48	
Polmont 3	d	20 24			21 01	21 24				21 57	22 24		23 03	23 24	23 54	
Glasgow Queen Street 10 ⇌	d	20a51	20 15				21 15	21 45				22 15				23 35
Bishopbriggs	d		20 21				21 21					22 21				23 41
Lenzie 3	d		20 27				21 27					22 27				23 47
Croy 3	d		20 33	21a07		21a39	21 33				22a39	22 33		23a39	00a09	23 53
Falkirk Grahamston	d				21 07					22 03			23 10			
Camelon	d				21 10					22 06			23 14			
Larbert	d		20 45		21 15		21 45			22 12		22 45	23 19			00 05
Stirling	d		20 55		21 25		21 55	22 11		22 22		22 55	23 28			00 14
Alloa	a		21 07				22 07					23 07				
Bridge of Allan	d				21 30					22 26			23 33			00 18
Dunblane	a				21 38			22 17		22 35			23 37			00 22

A To Glasgow Queen Street
B 27 November, 4 December
C To Aberdeen
D To Elgin
E From London Kings Cross to Inverness. The Highland Chieftain
F To Perth

Dunblane, Alloa and Stirling - Falkirk Grahamston, Glasgow Queen Street and Edinburgh

Miles	Miles	Miles	Miles			SR MX	SR MO [1] B	SR MX [1] B	SR	SR A	SR [1] B	SR SX [1] B	SR	SR SO [1] B	SR	SR SX [1] B	SR [1] B 🚲	SR E	SR SX
0	0	—	—	**Dunblane**	d	23p06			05 21	05 46					06 28			06 48	
2	2	—	—	Bridge of Allan	d	23p09			05 24	05 49					06 31			06 51	
—	—	—	0	**Alloa**	d								06 11						
5½	5½	—	6¾	**Stirling**	d	23p14			05 30	05 53			06 21		06 36			06 56	
13½	13½	—	14¾	Larbert	d	23p23			05 38	06 01			06 29		06 45			07 04	
—	15	—	—	Camelon	d	23p29			05 44						06 51				
—	16½	—	—	**Falkirk Grahamston**	d	23p32			05 47						06 54				
24	—	—	25¼	Croy [3]	d		23p42	23p42		06 12			06 41	06 43		06 57		07 15	
29¼	—	—	30½	Lenzie [3]	d					06 19		06 38	06 48				07 08	07 21	07 34
32¼	—	—	33½	Bishopbriggs	d					06 23			06 52					07 26	07 38
34½	—	—	35¾	**Glasgow Queen Street** [10] ⛴	a					06 34			07 01					07 34	07 47
—	19½	—	—	Polmont [3]	d	23p38	23p56	23p56	05 53		06 23	06 56		06 56	07 02		07 26		
—	24¼	—	—	Linlithgow	d	23p45	00 03	00 03	06 00		06 29	07 03		07 03	07 09	07 14	07 32		
—	38	14¾	—	Edinburgh Park	d	23p58			06 12						07 23				
—	40½	17¼	—	Haymarket	d	00 04	00s19	00s20	06 20		06s45	07s19		07s19	07 28	07s31	07s49		
—	41¾	18½	—	**Edinburgh** [10] 225,242	a	00 09	00 24	00 25	06 24		06 50	07 25		07 25	07 34	07 37	07 55		

		SR	SR [1] B 🚲	SR SX	SR [1] B 🚲	SR A	SR [1] B	SR SX	SR ◇[1] G 🚲	SR [1] B 🚲	SR	SR	SR	SR [1] B 🚲	SR [1] B 🚲	SR [1] B 🚲	SR	SR ◇[1] G 🚲
Dunblane	d			07 22		07 29			07 44		07 58		08 13				08 28	
Bridge of Allan	d			07 25		07 32			07 48		08 01		08 16				08 31	
Alloa	d	07 11						07 39				07 57						
Stirling	d	07 22		07 29		07 39		07 49	07 53		08 07	08 10	08 21				08 36	08 43
Larbert	d	07 30		07 38		07 48		07 58	08 02		08 16	08 19	08 29				08 45	
Camelon	d							08 03			08 20						08 49	
Falkirk Grahamston	d							08 07			08 24						08 54	
Croy [3]	d	07 43			07 41	08 01				08 11		08 32	08 42		08 42			
Lenzie [3]	d	07 50				08 08			08 18			08 37	08 49					
Bishopbriggs	d	07 55				08 13						08 42	08 53					
Glasgow Queen Street [10] ⛴	a	08 04				08 22			08 34			08 52	09 03					09 15
Polmont [3]	d		07 38				08 09	08 16		08 26	08 31					09 08	09 00	
Linlithgow	d		07 44		07 59		08 15	08 23			08 38			08 41		09 14	09 07	
Edinburgh Park	d							08 37			08 51						09 21	
Haymarket	d		08s01	08 15	08s17		08s31	08 44		08s45	08 58			09s01	09s14	09s30	09 30	
Edinburgh [10] 225,242	a		08 06	08 22	08 25		08 37	08 50		08 52	09 03			09 06	09 19	09 36	09 37	

		SR [1] B 🚲	SR	SR	SR [1] E	SR	SR [1] B 🚲	SR [1] B 🚲	SR	SR ◇[1] I 🚲	SR	SR [1] B 🚲	SR SX [1] B 🚲	SR SO [1] B 🚲	SR	SR	SR [1] B 🚲	GR SO [R] [1] J 🚲	GR SX [R] [1] J 🚲	SR [1] B 🚲
Dunblane	d			08 58	09 07	09 13			09 28						09 58	10 13				
Bridge of Allan	d			09 01		09 16			09 31						10 01	10 16				
Alloa	d		08 36								09 41									
Stirling	d		08 51	09 06	09 13	09 21			09 36	09 44	09 51				10 06	10 21		10 30	10 30	
Larbert	d		08 59	09 15		09 29			09 45		09 59				10 15	10 29				
Camelon	d			09 19					09 49						10 19					
Falkirk Grahamston	d			09 24					09 54						10 24			10 45	10 46	
Croy [3]	d	09 12	09 13			09 41		09 42			10 11		10 12	10 12		10 41				10 42
Lenzie [3]	d		09 20			09 48					10 18					10 48				
Bishopbriggs	d		09 24			09 52					10 22					10 52				
Glasgow Queen Street [10] ⛴	a		09 33		09 45	10 03				10 14	10 33					11 01				
Polmont [3]	d			09 30			09 38		10 00			10 08			10 30		10 38			
Linlithgow	d			09 37			09 44		10 07			10 14			10 37		10 44			
Edinburgh Park	d			09 51					10 21						10 51					
Haymarket	d	09s45		10 00			10s02	10s12	10 27			10s30	10s44	10s44	10 59		11s00	11 11	11 11	11s15
Edinburgh [10] 225,242	a	09 52		10 06			10 07	10 17	10 34			10 37	10 49	10 51	11 04		11 05	11 17	11 17	11 20

A From Perth
B From Glasgow Queen Street
D From Dunfermline Queen Margaret
E From Dundee
G From Aberdeen
I From Inverurie
J From Inverness to London Kings Cross. The Highland Chieftain

Dunblane, Alloa and Stirling - Falkirk Grahamston, Glasgow Queen Street and Edinburgh

		SR		SR		SR	SR	SR	SR	SR	SR			SR	SR	SR		SR	SR	SR	SR	SR		SR	SR
				◇1		1	1				1			1		◇1			1	1		◇1			1
				A		C	C				C			C		E			C	C		F			C
				🛒		🛒	🛒				🛒			🛒		🛒			🛒	🛒		🛒			🛒
Dunblane	d	10 28							10 58	11 13					11 28						11 58	12 06		12 13	
Bridge of Allan	d	10 31							11 01	11 16					11 31						12 01			12 16	
Alloa	d							10 36										11 43							
Stirling	d	10 36		10 43				10 51	11 06	11 21					11 36	11 43		11 51			12 06	12 13		12 21	
Larbert	d	10 45						10 59	11 15	11 29					11 45			11 59			12 15			12 29	
Camelon	d	10 49							11 19						11 49						12 19				
Falkirk Grahamston	d	10 54							11 24						11 54						12 24				
Croy 3	d						11 12	11 13		11 41				11 42				12 09		12 12				12 41	
Lenzie 3	d							11 20		11 48								12 17						12 48	
Bishopbriggs	d							11 24		11 52								12 20						12 52	
Glasgow Queen Street 10	a			11 14				11 34		12 03						12 15		12 34				12 45		13 01	
Polmont 3	d	11 00				11 08			11 30		11 38				12 00				12 09		12 30				12 38
Linlithgow	d	11 07				11 14			11 37		11 44				12 07				12 15		12 37				12 44
Edinburgh Park	d	11 21							11 51						12 22						12 51				
Haymarket	d	11 27				11s31	11s45		11 58		12s00			12s12	12 27				12s30	12s44	12 57				13s00
Edinburgh 10 225,242	a	11 32				11 36	11 51		12 02		12 07			12 19	12 34				12 36	12 52	13 03				13 07

			SR		SR	SR		SR		SR	SR	SR	SR	SR		SR		SR		SR		SR	SR	SR	SR
			1			◇1				1	1			1		1				◇1			1	1	
			C			A				C	C			C		C				A			C	C	
			🛒			🛒				🛒	🛒			🛒		🛒				🛒			🛒	🛒	
Dunblane	d				12 28							12 58	13 13					13 28							13 58
Bridge of Allan	d				12 31							13 01	13 16					13 31							14 01
Alloa	d							12 36														13 41			
Stirling	d				12 36	12 43		12 51				13 06	13 21					13 36		13 43		13 51			14 06
Larbert	d				12 45			12 59				13 15	13 29					13 45				13 59			14 15
Camelon	d				12 49							13 19						13 49							14 19
Falkirk Grahamston	d				12 54							13 24						13 54							14 22
Croy 3	d		12 42					13 11			13 12		13 41			13 42						14 11		14 12	
Lenzie 3	d							13 18					13 48									14 18			
Bishopbriggs	d							13 22					13 52									14 22			
Glasgow Queen Street 10	a					13 14		13 33					14 03							14 14		14 33			
Polmont 3	d				13 00					13 08		13 30		13 38				14 00					14 08		14 30
Linlithgow	d				13 07					13 14		13 37		13 44				14 07					14 14		14 37
Edinburgh Park	d				13 21							13 51						14 21							14 51
Haymarket	d		13s14		13 27					13s30	13s45	13 57		14s00		14s11		14 27					14s30	14s45	14 57
Edinburgh 10 225,242	a		13 19		13 32					13 35	13 51	14 02		14 05		14 17		14 34					14 36	14 50	15 02

		SR	SR			SR		SR	SR		SR	SR	SR	SR		SR	SR	SR		SR		SR	SR		
												SX	SO												
			1			1			◇1			1	1	1				1		1			◇1		
			C			C			A			C	C	C				C		C			A		
			🛒			🛒			🛒			🛒	🛒	🛒				🛒		🛒			🛒		
Dunblane	d	14 13						14 28								14 58	15 13					15 28			
Bridge of Allan	d	14 16						14 31								15 01	15 16					15 31			
Alloa	d										14 36														
Stirling	d	14 21						14 36	14 44		14 51					15 06	15 21					15 36	15 43		
Larbert	d	14 29						14 45			14 59					15 15	15 29					15 45			
Camelon	d							14 49								15 19						15 49			
Falkirk Grahamston	d							14 54								15 24						15 54			
Croy 3	d	14 42				14 42					15 11			15 12			15 40			15 42					
Lenzie 3	d	14 48									15 18						15 47								
Bishopbriggs	d	14 53									15 22						15 51								
Glasgow Queen Street 10	a	15 03							15 14		15 34						16 04						16 14		
Polmont 3	d		14 38					15 00				15 08	15 08			15 30		15 38				16 00			
Linlithgow	d		14 44					15 07				15 14	15 14			15 37		15 44				16 07			
Edinburgh Park	d							15 21								15 51						16 21			
Haymarket	d		15s00			15s13		15 27				15s30	15s30	15s42		15 58		16s00		16s12		16 27			
Edinburgh 10 225,242	a		15 05			15 19		15 32				15 35	15 37	15 47		16 04		16 06		16 19		16 33			

		SR	SR	SR	SR	SR	SR	SR	SR				SR	SR	SR	SR			SR			SR	SR	SR	SR
			SX	SO	SX	SO							SO	SX								SX	SO		
			1	1	1	1			1				1	1		◇1			1			1	1		
			C	C	C	C			C				C	C		A			C			C	C		
			🛒	🛒	🛒	🛒			🛒				🛒	🛒		🛒			🛒			🛒	🛒		
Dunblane	d						15 58	16 13							16 28										16 58
Bridge of Allan	d						16 01	16 16							16 31										17 01
Alloa	d	15 41																						16 36	
Stirling	d	15 51					16 06	16 21							16 36	16 43								16 52	17 06
Larbert	d	15 59					16 15	16 29							16 45									17 00	17 15
Camelon	d						16 19								16 49										17 19
Falkirk Grahamston	d						16 24								16 54										17 24
Croy 3	d	16 11			16 12	16 12		16 41					16 42	16 42								17 12	17 12	17 13	
Lenzie 3	d	16 18						16 48																17 19	
Bishopbriggs	d	16 22						16 52																17 24	
Glasgow Queen Street 10	a	16 33						17 03								17 18								17 34	
Polmont 3	d		16 08	16 08			16 30		16 38						17 00				17 09			17 26	17 26		17 30
Linlithgow	d		16 13	16 13			16 37		16 45						17 07				17 14						17 37
Edinburgh Park	d						16 51								17 21										17 50
Haymarket	d		16s30	16s30	16s42	16s47	16 57		17s01				17s13	17s16	17 27				17s34			17s45	17s47		17 58
Edinburgh 10 225,242	a		16 35	16 37	16 48	16 52	17 02		17 06				17 19	17 22	17 35				17 40			17 50	17 52		18 05

A From Aberdeen
C From Glasgow Queen Street
E From Dyce
F From Inverness
G From Inverurie

Dunblane, Alloa and Stirling - Falkirk Grahamston, Glasgow Queen Street and Edinburgh

		SR	SR	SR	SR			SR	SR		SR	SR		SR	SR	SR		SR	SR	SR	SR		SR	SR	SR
																									SX
			◇1	1	1				◇1			1		1				1	1		◇1			◇1	1
			A	B	B				D			B		B				B	B		D			C	B
			🍴	🍴	🍴				🍴			🍴		🍴				🍴	🍴		🍴			🍴	🍴
Dunblane	d	17 13	17 22					17 28	17 36						17 58	18 11				18 28	18 35				
Bridge of Allan	d	17 16						17 31							18 01	18 14				18 31					
Alloa	d										17 41												18 27		
Stirling	d	17 22	17 29					17 36	17 42		17 51				18 06	18 19				18 36	18 42		18 51		
Larbert	d	17 31						17 45			17 59				18 15	18 28				18 45			18 59		
Camelon	d							17 49							18 19					18 49					
Falkirk Grahamston	d							17 54							18 24					18 54					
Croy 3	d	17 42			17 42						18 11			18 12		18 40			18 42				19 11		
Lenzie 3	d	17 49									18 18					18 47							19 18		
Bishopbriggs	d	17 53									18 22					18 51							19 22		
Glasgow Queen Street 10 ⛴	a	18 03	18 09						18 15		18 34					19 03					19 16		19 33		
Polmont 3	d				17 56			18 00				18 08			18 30			18 38		19 00					19 08
Linlithgow	d			17 41	18 03			18 07				18 14			18 37			18 44		19 07					19 14
Edinburgh Park	d							18 21							18 51					19 21					
Haymarket	d			18s02	18s19			18 28				18s33		18s45	18 57			19s01	19s13	19 27				19 28	19s30
Edinburgh 10 225,242	a			18 07	18 24			18 36				18 40		18 50	19 04			19 07	19 19	19 33				19 34	19 36

		SR		SR	SR	SR	SR	SR	SR	SR		SR		SR	SR	SR	SR	SR	SR	SR	SR				SR
		SO															SX	SO							
		1		1			1	1		◇1		1					1	1		◇1					1
		B		B			B	B		D		B					B	B		D					B
		🍴		🍴			🍴			🍴										🍴					
Dunblane	d					19 14			19 28						20 02	20 13			20 28						
Bridge of Allan	d					19 17			19 31						20 05	20 16			20 31						
Alloa	d				18 54									19 43							20 41				
Stirling	d				19 06	19 22			19 36	19 43				19 53	20 10	20 21			20 36	20 40	20 51				
Larbert	d				19 15	19 31			19 45					20 01	20 19	20 29			20 45		20 59				
Camelon	d				19 19				19 49						20 23				20 49						
Falkirk Grahamston	d				19 24				19 54						20 28				20 54						
Croy 3	d			19 12		19 42						20 12		20 13		20 43					21 12				21 12
Lenzie 3	d					19 49								20 20		20 50					21 18				
Bishopbriggs	d					19 53								20 24		20 54					21 23				
Glasgow Queen Street 10 ⛴	a					20 04				20 15				20 34		21 04				21 14	21 34				
Polmont 3	d	19 08			19 30		19 38	19 53	20 00						20 34		20 53	20 53	21 00						
Linlithgow	d	19 14			19 37		19 44	19 59	20 07			20 29			20 41		20 59	20 59	21 07						21 29
Edinburgh Park	d				19 51				20 21						20 54				21 21						
Haymarket	d	19s34		19s46	19 57		20s00	20s16	20 27			20s45			21 00		21s15	21s15	21 27						21s45
Edinburgh 10 225,242	a	19 39		19 51	20 01		20 07	20 21	20 32			20 51			21 06		21 20	21 22	21 31						21 50

		SR	SR	SR	SR	SR	SR	SR			SR	SR	SR	SR	SR	SR	SR			SR	SR				
			SX	SO																					
					◇1	1	1						◇1		1	◇1	1				1				
					D	B	B						D		B	A	B				B				
					🍴																				
Dunblane	d	20 58	21 13	21 13							21 58	22 13				22 58				23 06					
Bridge of Allan	d	21 01	21 16	21 16							22 01	22 16				23 02				23 09					
Alloa	d							21 42						22 41											
Stirling	d	21 06	21 21	21 21	21 46			21 53			22 06	22 21	22 43	22 51		23 05				23 14					
Larbert	d	21 15	21 29	21 29				22 00			22 15	22 29		22 59						23 23					
Camelon	d	21 19									22 19									23 29					
Falkirk Grahamston	d	21 24									22 24									23 32					
Croy 3	d		21 40	21 40			22 12	22 14				22 40		23 12			23 12				23 42				
Lenzie 3	d		21 47	21 47				22 20				22 47		23 19											
Bishopbriggs	d		21 51	21 51				22 25				22 51		23 23											
Glasgow Queen Street 10 ⛴	a		22 03	22 04	22 20			22 34				23 03	23 15	23 34		23 39									
Polmont 3	d	21 30				21 53					22 30				22 53		23 26			23 38	23 56				
Linlithgow	d	21 37				21 59	22 29				22 37				22 59		23 33			23 45	00 03				
Edinburgh Park	d	21 51									22 51									23 58					
Haymarket	d	21 57				22s18	22s46				22 57				23s15		23s49			00 04	00s20				
Edinburgh 10 225,242	a	22 02				22 23	22 51				23 01				23 20		23 55			00 09	00 25				

A From Inverness
B From Glasgow Queen Street
C From Inverurie
D From Aberdeen

Table 230

Sundays

Dunblane, Alloa and Stirling - Falkirk Grahamston, Glasgow Queen Street and Edinburgh

	SR A		SR 1 C	SR 1 D	SR 1 D 🚲	SR E	SR	SR E	SR 1 D 🚲		SR	SR 1 F	SR G	SR E	SR 1 D 🚲	SR	SR	SR E	SR 1 D 🚲		SR	SR ◇1 H 🚲	SR	SR E
Dunblane d	23p06											09 31	09 54				11 01					11 31	12 01	
Bridge of Allan d	23p09												09 58				11 04						12 04	
Alloa d	⌇										09 18					10 18					11 14			
Stirling d	23p14						09 05				09 28	09 38	10 02			10 28	11 10				11 25	11 38	12 10	
Larbert d	23p23						09 13				09 37	09 47	10 11			10 37	11 19				11 34		12 19	
Camelon d	23p29						09 19						10 16				11 24						12 24	
Falkirk Grahamston d	23p32						09 22						10 19				11 27						12 27	
Croy 3 d	⌇		23p42	08 02	08 42	08 49		09 15	09 42		09 48			10 15	10 42	10 48		11 15	11 42		11 45			12 15
Lenzie 3 d	⌇		⌇			08 56		09 22			09 55	10 02		10 22		10 55		11 22			11 52			12 22
Bishopbriggs d	⌇		⌇			09 00		09 26			09 59			10 26		10 59		11 26			11 56			12 26
Glasgow Queen Street 10 ⛴ a	⌇		⌇			09 10		09 35			10 08	10 15		10 35		11 08		11 37			12 05	12 11		12 35
Polmont 3 d	23p38		23p56	08 16	08 56		09 28		09 56				10 25		10 56		11 33		11 56				12 33	
Linlithgow d	23p45		00 03	08 23	09 03		09 35		10 03				10 32		11 03		11 40		12 03				12 40	
Edinburgh Park d	23p58		⌇				09 47						10 45				11 54						12 54	
Haymarket d	00 04		00s20	08 39	09s24		09 59		10s23				10 52		11s19		12 00		12s19				13 00	
Edinburgh 10 225,242 a	00 09		00 25	08 49	09 29		10 04		10 28				10 58		11 24		12 04		12 24				13 04	

	SR	GR 1 I 🚲	SR 1 D 🚲		SR 1 D 🚲		SR	SR E	SR	SR ◇1 H 🚲	SR 1 D	SR 1 D 🚲	SR	SR E	SR		SR 1 D 🚲		SR 1 D	SR	SR E	SR ◇1 K 🚲	SR	SR ◇1 H 🚲
Dunblane d		12 27					13 01			13 31			14 01							15 01		15 16		15 33
Bridge of Allan d							13 04						14 04							15 04				
Alloa d	12 14								13 14						14 14								15 16	
Stirling d	12 25	12 34					13 10		13 25	13 38			14 10		14 25					15 10		15 22	15 26	15 45
Larbert d	12 34						13 19		13 34				14 19		14 34					15 19		15 31	15 34	
Camelon d							13 24						14 24							15 24				
Falkirk Grahamston d		12 50					13 27						14 27							15 27				
Croy 3 d	12 45		12 42		13 12			13 15	13 45			14 12		14 15	14 45				15 12		15 15		15 48	
Lenzie 3 d	12 52							13 22	13 52					14 22	14 52						15 22		15 55	
Bishopbriggs d	12 56							13 26	13 56					14 26	14 56						15 26		15 59	
Glasgow Queen Street 10 ⛴ a	13 05							13 35	14 05	14 11				14 35	15 05						15 35	15 56	16 09	16 28
Polmont 3 d			12 56				13 33				13 53		14 33				14 53			15 33				
Linlithgow d			13 02		13 29		13 40				13 59	14 29	14 40				14 59		15 29	15 40				
Edinburgh Park d							13 54						14 54							15 54				
Haymarket d		13 14	13s21		13s46		14 00				14s17	14s47	15 00				15s16		15 46	16 00				
Edinburgh 10 225,242 a		13 19	13 26		13 51		14 04				14 22	14 52	15 04				15 21		15 51	16 04				

	SR 1 D		SR 1 D 🚲	SR	SR E	SR	SR 1 D 🚲	SR 1 D 🚲	SR E		SR		SR	SR ◇1 H 🚲	SR 1 D 🚲	SR 1 D 🚲	SR	SR E	SR	SR 1 D 🚲			SR 1 D 🚲	SR E
Dunblane d				16 01							17 01			17 31			18 01							
Bridge of Allan d				16 04							17 04						18 04							
Alloa d						16 14							17 14						18 17					
Stirling d				16 10		16 25					17 10		17 25	17 38			18 10		18 27					
Larbert d				16 19		16 34					17 19		17 34				18 19		18 34					
Camelon d				16 24							17 24						18 24							
Falkirk Grahamston d				16 27							17 27						18 27							
Croy 3 d			16 12		16 17	16 45		17 12	17 15				17 45			18 12		18 15	18 47				19 12	19 13
Lenzie 3 d					16 24	16 52			17 22				17 52					18 22	18 54					19 20
Bishopbriggs d					16 28	16 56			17 26				17 56					18 26	18 58					19 24
Glasgow Queen Street 10 ⛴ a					16 37	17 05			17 35				18 05	18 12				18 35	19 08					19 33
Polmont 3 d	15 53			16 33			16 53				17 33				17 53		18 33			18 53				
Linlithgow d	15 59		16 29	16 40			16 59	17 29			17 40				17 59	18 29	18 40			18 59			19 29	
Edinburgh Park d				16 54							17 54						18 54							
Haymarket d	16s18		16s50	17 00			17s16	17 47			18 01				18s17	18s50	19 00			19s16			19s47	
Edinburgh 10 225,242 a	16 23		16 55	17 04			17 21	17 52			18 05				18 22	18 55	19 04			19 21			19 52	

A not 22 May
C not 22 May. From Glasgow Queen Street
D From Glasgow Queen Street
E 27 November, 4 December
F From Dundee
G From Perth
H From Aberdeen
I From Inverness to London Kings Cross. The Highland Chieftain
K From Inverness

	SR ◇1 A 🚲	SR	SR	SR 1 B 🚲	SR ◇1 A 🚲	SR 1 B	SR		SR		SR 1 B		SR 1 B	SR	SR 1 B	SR	SR ◇1 E 🚲		SR	SR 1 B	SR 1 B			
Dunblane d	18 58	19 01					20 01							21 01			21 31		22 01					
Bridge of Allan d		19 04					20 04							21 04					22 04					
Alloa d			19 14						20 14							21 14								
Stirling d	19 05	19 10	19 24		19 55		20 10		20 25					21 10		21 25	21 38		22 10					
Larbert d	19 12	19 19	19 33				20 19		20 34					21 19		21 34	21 49		22 19					
Camelon d		19 24					20 24							21 24					22 24					
Falkirk Grahamston d		19 27					20 27							21 27					22 27					
Croy 3 d			19 44			20 12			20 45				21 12		21 42	21 45				22 42	23 42			
Lenzie 3 d			19 51						20 52							21 52	22 02							
Bishopbriggs d			19 55						20 56							21 56								
Glasgow Queen Street 10 ⛴ a	19 37		20 04		20 31				21 05							22 05	22 15							
Polmont 3 d		19 33		19 53			20 33				20 53			21 33	21 56				22 33	22 56	23 56			
Linlithgow d		19 40		19 59		20 29	20 40				20 59		21 29	21 40	22 03				22 40	23 03	00 03			
Edinburgh Park d		19 54					20 54							21 54					22 54					
Haymarket d		20 00		20s16		20s46	21 00				21s17		21s46	22 00	22s19				23 00	23s19	00s19			
Edinburgh 10 225,242 a		20 04		20 21		20 51	21 06				21 22		21 53	22 05	22 24				23 04	23 24	00 24			

A From Inverness
B From Glasgow Queen Street
D From West Calder
E From Aberdeen

Table 232

Mondays to Saturdays

Glasgow Queen Street - Maryhill and Annieland

Miles				SR SO	SR	SR	SR	SR	SR	SR	SR	SR	SR	SR	SR	SR	SR	SR	SR	SR	SR	SR	SR	SR
0	**Glasgow Queen Street** 10	⛴	d	23p54	06 26	06 56	07 26	07 56	08 26	08 56	09 26	09 56	10 26	10 56	11 26	11 56	12 26	12 56	13 26	13 56	14 26	14 56	15 26	15 56
2¼	Ashfield		d	23p58	06 30	07 00	07 30	08 00	08 30	09 00	09 30	10 00	10 30	11 00	11 30	12 00	12 30	13 00	13 30	14 00	14 30	15 00	15 30	16 00
3	Possilpark & Parkhouse		d	00 01	06 33	07 03	07 33	08 03	08 33	09 03	09 33	10 03	10 33	11 03	11 33	12 03	12 33	13 03	13 33	14 03	14 33	15 03	15 33	16 03
3¼	Gilshochill		d	00 03	06 35	07 05	07 35	08 05	08 35	09 05	09 35	10 05	10 35	11 05	11 35	12 05	12 35	13 05	13 35	14 05	14 35	15 05	15 35	16 05
4¼	Summerston		d	00 06	06 37	07 07	07 37	08 07	08 37	09 07	09 37	10 07	10 37	11 07	11 37	12 07	12 37	13 07	13 37	14 07	14 37	15 07	15 37	16 07
4¾	**Maryhill**		d	00 07	06 39	07 09	07 39	08 09	08 39	09 09	09 39	10 09	10 39	11 09	11 39	12 09	12 39	13 09	13 39	14 09	14 39	15 09	15 39	16 09
5½	Kelvindale		d	00 10	06 41	07 11	07 41	08 11	08 41	09 11	09 41	10 11	10 41	11 11	11 41	12 11	12 41	13 11	13 41	14 11	14 41	15 11	15 41	16 11
6¼	**Anniesland**	226	a	00 14	06 45	07 15	07 46	08 15	08 46	09 15	09 45	10 15	10 45	11 15	11 46	12 15	12 46	13 15	13 45	14 15	14 45	15 15	15 46	16 16

			SR	SR	SR	SR SO	SR SX	SR	SR	SR	SR	SR	SR	SR	SR	SR	SR	SR	SR FO
Glasgow Queen Street 10	⛴	d	16 26	16 56	17 26	17 56	17 56	18 26	18 56	19 26	19 56	20 26	20 56	21 26	21 56	22 26	22 56	23 26	23 54
Ashfield		d	16 30	17 00	17 30	18 00	18 00	18 30	19 00	19 30	20 00	20 30	21 00	21 30	22 00	22 30	23 00	23 30	23 58
Possilpark & Parkhouse		d	16 33	17 03	17 33	18 03	18 03	18 33	19 03	19 33	20 03	20 33	21 03	21 33	22 03	22 33	23 03	23 33	00 01
Gilshochill		d	16 35	17 05	17 35	18 05	18 05	18 35	19 05	19 35	20 05	20 35	21 05	21 35	22 05	22 35	23 05	23 35	00 03
Summerston		d	16 37	17 07	17 37	18 07	18 07	18 37	19 07	19 37	20 07	20 37	21 07	21 37	22 07	22 37	23 07	23 37	00 06
Maryhill		d	16 39	17 09	17 39	18 09	18 09	18 39	19 09	19 39	20 09	20 39	21 09	21 39	22 09	22 39	23 09	23 39	00 07
Kelvindale		d	16 41	17 11	17 41	18 11	18 11	18 41	19 11	19 41	20 11	20 41	21 11	21 41	22 11	22 41	23 11	23 41	00 10
Anniesland	226	a	16 45	17 15	17 45	18 15	18 16	18 46	19 15	19 45	20 15	20 46	21 15	21 46	22 15	22 45	23 15	23 45	00 14

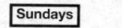

Sundays

from 27 November

			SR A	SR A	SR A	SR A	SR A	SR A	SR A	SR A	SR A	SR A
Glasgow Queen Street 10	⛴	d	08 45	09 58	10 56	11 56	12 55	13 56	14 55	15 57	16 56	17 56
Ashfield		d	08 50	10 01	11 00	12 00	13 01	14 00	15 00	16 00	17 00	18 00
Possilpark & Parkhouse		d	08 53	10 04	11 03	12 03	13 03	14 03	15 03	16 03	17 03	18 03
Gilshochill		d	08 55	10 06	11 05	12 05	13 05	14 05	15 05	16 05	17 05	18 05
Summerston		d	08 57	10 08	11 07	12 07	13 08	14 07	15 07	16 07	17 07	18 07
Maryhill		d	08 59	10 10	11 09	12 09	13 09	14 09	15 09	16 09	17 09	18 09
Kelvindale		d	09 01	10 12	11 11	12 11	13 12	14 11	15 11	16 11	17 11	18 11
Anniesland	226	a	09 04	10 18	11 15	12 15	13 15	14 15	15 14	16 17	17 15	18 15

Anniesland and Maryhill - Glasgow Queen Street

Mondays to Saturdays

Miles				SR	SR	SR	SR	SR SX	SR	SR	SR	SR	SR	SR	SR	SR	SR	SR	SR	SR	SR	SR	SR SO	SR SX
0	**Anniesland**	226	d	06 22	06 52	07 22	07 52		08 24	08 52	09 22	09 52	10 22	10 52	11 22	11 52	12 22	12 52	13 22	13 52	14 22	14 52	15 22	15 22
0¾	Kelvindale		d	06 24	06 54	07 24	07 54		08 26	08 54	09 24	09 54	10 24	10 54	11 24	11 54	12 24	12 54	13 24	13 54	14 24	14 54	15 24	15 24
1½	**Maryhill**		d	06 26	06 56	07 26	07 56	08 17	08 28	08 56	09 26	09 56	10 26	10 56	11 26	11 56	12 26	12 56	13 26	13 56	14 26	14 56	15 26	15 26
2	Summerston		d	06 28	06 58	07 28	07 58		08 30	08 58	09 28	09 58	10 28	10 58	11 28	11 58	12 28	12 58	13 28	13 58	14 28	14 58	15 28	15 28
3	Gilshochill		d	06 30	07 00	07 30	08 00		08 32	09 00	09 30	10 00	10 30	11 00	11 30	12 00	12 30	13 00	13 30	14 00	14 30	15 00	15 30	15 30
3¼	Possilpark & Parkhouse		d	06 32	07 02	07 32	08 02	08 22	08 34	09 02	09 32	10 02	10 32	11 02	11 32	12 02	12 32	13 02	13 32	14 02	14 32	15 02	15 32	15 32
4	Ashfield		d	06 34	07 04	07 34	08 04		08 36	09 04	09 34	10 04	10 34	11 04	11 34	12 04	12 34	13 04	13 34	14 04	14 34	15 04	15 34	15 34
6¼	**Glasgow Queen Street** 10	⛴	a	06 42	07 11	07 41	08 11	08 37	08 44	09 11	09 41	10 11	10 41	11 11	11 41	12 11	12 41	13 11	13 41	14 11	14 41	15 11	15 41	15 44

			SR	SR SO	SR SX	SR	SR	SR SX	SR SO	SR	SR	SR	SR	SR	SR	SR SX	SR SO	SR	SR	SR	SR
Anniesland	226	d	15 52	16 25	16 25	16 54	17 24	17 52	17 52	18 22	18 52	19 22	19 52	20 22	20 52	21 22	21 22	21 52	22 22	22 52	23 22
Kelvindale		d	15 54	16 27	16 27	16 56	17 26	17 54	17 54	18 24	18 54	19 24	19 54	20 24	20 54	21 24	21 24	21 54	22 24	22 54	23 24
Maryhill		d	15 56	16 29	16 29	16 58	17 28	17 56	17 56	18 26	18 56	19 26	19 56	20 26	20 56	21 26	21 26	21 56	22 26	22 56	23 26
Summerston		d	15 58	16 31	16 31	17 00	17 30	17 58	17 58	18 28	18 58	19 28	19 58	20 28	20 58	21 28	21 28	21 58	22 28	22 58	23 28
Gilshochill		d	16 00	16 33	16 33	17 02	17 32	18 00	18 00	18 30	19 00	19 30	20 00	20 30	21 00	21 30	21 30	22 00	22 30	23 00	23 30
Possilpark & Parkhouse		d	16 02	16 35	16 35	17 04	17 34	18 02	18 02	18 32	19 02	19 32	20 02	20 32	21 02	21 32	21 32	22 02	22 32	23 02	23 32
Ashfield		d	16 04	16 38	16 38	17 06	17 36	18 04	18 04	18 34	19 04	19 34	20 04	20 34	21 04	21 34	21 34	22 04	22 34	23 04	23 34
Glasgow Queen Street 10	⛴	a	16 11	16 44	16 48	17 14	17 44	18 12	18 13	18 41	19 11	19 41	20 11	20 41	21 11	21 42	21 44	22 11	22 41	23 11	23 42

Sundays

from 27 November

			SR A	SR A	SR A	SR A	SR A	SR A	SR A	SR A	SR A	SR A
Anniesland	226	d	09 22	10 22	11 22	12 22	13 22	14 22	15 22	16 22	17 22	18 20
Kelvindale		d	09 24	10 24	11 24	12 24	13 24	14 24	15 24	16 24	17 24	18 22
Maryhill		d	09 26	10 26	11 26	12 26	13 26	14 26	15 26	16 26	17 26	18 24
Summerston		d	09 28	10 28	11 28	12 28	13 28	14 28	15 28	16 28	17 28	18 26
Gilshochill		d	09 30	10 30	11 30	12 30	13 30	14 30	15 30	16 30	17 30	18 28
Possilpark & Parkhouse		d	09 32	10 32	11 32	12 32	13 32	14 32	15 32	16 32	17 32	18 30
Ashfield		d	09 34	10 34	11 34	12 34	13 35	14 34	15 35	16 34	17 34	18 32
Glasgow Queen Street 10	⛴	a	09 41	10 41	11 41	12 41	13 41	14 41	15 41	16 41	17 41	18 39

Haymarket and Edinburgh - North Berwick and Dunbar

Miles	Miles			GR A	XC B	SR	SR	SR C	XC B	SR	SR	SR		XC D	SR	SR	SR	XC E	SR	SR	SR	XC E		SR	SR
0	0	**Haymarket** 225,230,242	d		06 57			08 26	08 50					10 54											
1¼	1¼	**Edinburgh** 10 225,230,242	a		07 02			08 33	08 55					10 58											
—	—		d	05 45	07 07	07 14	08 14	08 45	09 08	09 43	10 13	10 43		11 05	11 44	12 11	12 43	13 06	13 43	14 11	14 43	15 08		15 43	16 33
6½	6½	Musselburgh	d			07 20	08 20	08 49		09 47	10 19	10 47			11 48	12 17	12 47		13 47	14 17	14 47			15 47	16 39
8¾	8¾	Wallyford	d			07 24		08 53		09 51		10 51			11 52		12 51		13 51		14 51			15 51	
11	11	Prestonpans	d			07 27		08 56		09 54		10 54			11 55		12 54		13 54		14 54			15 54	
14½	14½	Longniddry	d			07 32		09 01		09 59		10 59			12 00		12 59		13 59		14 59			15 59	
19	19	Drem	d			07 37		09 07		10 05		11 05			12 06		13 05		14 05		15 06			16 05	
—	29¼	**Dunbar**	a	06 05	07 26				09 27		10 38			11 24		12 36		13 26		14 36		15 27			16 58
23½	—	**North Berwick**	a			07 47	08 38	09 18		10 16		11 16			12 17		13 16		14 16		15 16			16 16	

		SR C	XC F	SR	GR G	SR	XC H	SR		GR A	SR	SR	XC I	SR	GR J	SR	SR FX	SR FO		SR
Haymarket 225,230,242	d	16 34		17 05	17 21	17 42	17 54				18 40				20 43					
Edinburgh 10 225,230,242	a	16 39		17 10	17 27	17 46	17 59				18 44				20 48					
	d	16 41	17 08	17 13	17 30	17 48	18 04	18 14		18 30	18 45	19 42	20 05	20 43	21 00	21 44	22 06	23 01		23 08
Musselburgh	d	16 47		17 18		17 54		18 19			18 51	19 46		20 46		21 47	22 12	23 07		23 12
Wallyford	d	16 51		17 22		17 58		18 23			18 56	19 50		20 50		21 51				23 16
Prestonpans	d	16 54		17 26		18 01		18 25			19 00	19 53		20 53		21 54				23 21
Longniddry	d	16 59		17 31		18 06		18 31			19 06	19 58		20 58		21 59				23 26
Drem	d	17 05		17 37		18 11		18 35			19 12	20 03		21 03		22 04				23 31
Dunbar	a		17 27		17 51		18 23			18 50			20 24		21 20		22 41	23 33		
North Berwick	a	17 14		17 48		18 21		18 47			19 20	20 15		21 16		22 17				23 52

Saturdays

until 10 September

		GR A	XC K	SR	SR C	XC L	SR	SR	SR	SR		XC D	SR	SR	SR	SR	XC E	SR	SR	SR		SR	XC E	SR	SR
Haymarket 225,230,242	d		06 57		08 26	08 50						10 52													
Edinburgh 10 225,230,242	a		07 02		08 33	08 54						10 58													
	d	06 20	07 07	07 43	08 40	09 06	09 12	09 43	10 12	10 43		11 05	11 12	11 43	12 12	12 43	13 08	13 12	13 43	14 12		14 43	15 08	15 12	15 43
Musselburgh	d			07 47	08 47		09 15	09 47	10 15	10 47			11 15	11 47	12 15	12 47		13 15	13 47	14 15		14 47		15 15	15 47
Wallyford	d			07 51	08 51		09 19	09 51	10 19	10 51			11 19	11 51	12 19	12 51		13 19	13 51	14 19		14 51		15 19	15 51
Prestonpans	d			07 54	08 54		09 22	09 54	10 22	10 54			11 22	11 54	12 22	12 54		13 22	13 54	14 22		14 54		15 22	15 54
Longniddry	d			07 59	08 59		09 27	09 59	10 27	10 59			11 27	11 59	12 27	12 59		13 27	13 59	14 27		14 59		15 27	15 59
Drem	d			08 05	09 05		09 33	10 05	10 33	11 05			11 33	12 05	12 33	13 05		13 33	14 05	14 33		15 05		15 33	16 05
Dunbar	a	06 40	07 27			09 25						11 24					13 28						15 27		
North Berwick	a			08 16	09 16		09 45	10 16	10 45	11 16			11 45	12 16	12 45	13 16		13 45	14 16	14 45		15 16		15 45	16 16

		SR	SR C	XC M	SR	GR G		SR	XC H	SR	SR	GR N	SR	SR	SR	SR
Haymarket 225,230,242	d		16 34			17 20			17 56							
Edinburgh 10 225,230,242	a		16 39			17 26			18 01							
	d	16 12	16 41	17 08	17 12	17 30		17 43	18 05	18 12	18 40	19 00	19 43	20 43	21 43	23 07
Musselburgh	d	16 15	16 47		17 15			17 47		18 15	18 47		19 47	20 47	21 47	23 11
Wallyford	d	16 19	16 51		17 19			17 51		18 19	18 51		19 51	20 51	21 51	23 15
Prestonpans	d	16 22	16 54		17 22			17 54		18 22	18 54		19 54	20 54	21 54	23 18
Longniddry	d	16 27	16 59		17 27			17 59		18 27	18 59		19 59	20 59	21 59	23 23
Drem	d	16 33	17 05		17 33			18 05		18 33	19 05		20 05	21 05	22 05	23 29
Dunbar	a			17 27		17 50			18 24			19 20				
North Berwick	a	16 45	17 14		17 45			18 16		18 45	19 16		20 16	21 16	22 16	23 50

A To London Kings Cross
B From Glasgow Central to Plymouth. from Edinburgh
C From Glasgow Central
D From Aberdeen to Penzance. from Edinburgh
E To Plymouth
F To Bristol Temple Meads
G From Aberdeen to London Kings Cross
H From Glasgow Central to Birmingham New Street. from Edinburgh
I From Glasgow Central to Newcastle
J From Aberdeen to Leeds
K From Glasgow Central to Paignton. from Edinburgh
L From Glasgow Central to Penzance. from Edinburgh
M To Birmingham New Street
N To Doncaster

Table 238

Haymarket and Edinburgh - North Berwick and Dunbar

Saturdays
from 17 September

			GR	XC	SR	SR	XC	SR	SR	SR	SR		XC	SR	SR	SR	SR	XC	SR	SR	SR		SR	XC	SR	SR
			R 1 A	◇1 B		C	◇1 B						◇1 D					◇1 E						◇1 E		
Haymarket	225,230,242	d		06 54		08 26	08 50						10 52													
Edinburgh 10	225,230,242	a		07 01		08 33	08 54						10 58													
		d	06 20	07 07	07 43	08 40	09 06	09 12	09 43	10 12	10 43		11 05	11 12	11 43	12 12	12 43	13 08	13 12	13 43	14 12		14 43	15 08	15 12	15 43
Musselburgh		d			07 47	08 47		09 15	09 47	10 15	10 47			11 15	11 47	12 15	12 47		13 15	13 47	14 15		14 47		15 15	15 47
Wallyford		d			07 51	08 51		09 19	09 51	10 19	10 51			11 19	11 51	12 19	12 51		13 19	13 51	14 19		14 51		15 19	15 51
Prestonpans		d			07 54	08 54		09 22	09 54	10 22	10 54			11 22	11 54	12 22	12 54		13 22	13 54	14 22		14 54		15 22	15 54
Longniddry		d			07 59	08 59		09 27	09 59	10 27	10 59			11 27	11 59	12 27	12 59		13 27	13 59	14 27		14 59		15 27	15 59
Drem		d			08 05	09 05		09 33	10 05	10 33	11 05			11 33	12 05	12 33	13 05		13 33	14 05	14 33		15 05		15 33	16 05
Dunbar		a	06 40	07 26			09 25						11 24					13 28						15 27		
North Berwick		a			08 16	09 16		09 45	10 16	10 45	11 16			11 45	12 16	12 45	13 16		13 45	14 16	14 45		15 16		15 45	16 16

			SR	SR	XC	SR	GR		SR	XC	SR	SR	GR	SR	SR	SR	SR
				C	◇1 F		R 1 G			◇1 H			R 1 I				
Haymarket	225,230,242	d		16 34			17 20			17 56							
Edinburgh 10	225,230,242	a		16 39			17 26			18 01							
		d	16 12	16 41	17 08	17 12	17 30		17 43	18 05	18 12	18 40	19 00	19 43	20 43	21 43	23 07
Musselburgh		d	16 15	16 47		17 15			17 47		18 15	18 47		19 47	20 47	21 47	23 11
Wallyford		d	16 19	16 51		17 19			17 51		18 19	18 51		19 51	20 51	21 51	23 15
Prestonpans		d	16 22	16 54		17 22			17 54		18 22	18 54		19 54	20 54	21 54	23 18
Longniddry		d	16 27	16 59		17 27			17 59		18 27	18 59		19 59	20 59	21 59	23 23
Drem		d	16 33	17 05		17 33			18 05		18 33	19 05		20 05	21 05	22 05	23 29
Dunbar		a			17 27		17 50			18 24			19 20				
North Berwick		a	16 45	17 14		17 45			18 16		18 45	19 16		20 16	21 16	22 16	23 50

Sundays
until 19 June

			SR	XC	SR	SR	XC	SR	SR	XC	SR		XC	SR	XC	GR	SR	XC	SR	GR	SR	GR	XC	SR	GR	SR
				◇1 J			◇1 B			◇1 K			◇1 K		◇1 F	R 1 A		◇1 H		R 1 A		R 1 L	◇1 M		R 1 N	
Haymarket	225,230,242	d					12 47			14 43			15 51					17 55					19 51			
Edinburgh 10	225,230,242	a					12 52			14 47			15 56					17 59					19 56			
		d	10 33	11 05	11 33	12 33	13 06	13 36	14 33	15 07	15 33		16 05	16 33	17 07	17 30	17 33	18 07	18 33	19 00	19 33	20 00	20 05	20 33	21 00	21 33
Musselburgh		d	10 39		11 39	12 39		13 39	14 39		15 39			16 39			17 39		18 39		19 39			20 39		21 39
Wallyford		d	10 43		11 43	12 43		13 43	14 43		15 43			16 43			17 43		18 43		19 43			20 43		21 43
Prestonpans		d	10 46		11 46	12 46		13 46	14 46		15 46			16 46			17 46		18 46		19 46			20 46		21 46
Longniddry		d	10 51		11 51	12 51		13 51	14 51		15 51			16 51			17 51		18 51		19 51			20 51		21 51
Drem		d	10 56		11 56	12 56		13 57	14 56		15 56			16 56			17 56		18 56		19 56			20 56		21 56
Dunbar		a		11 24			13 25			15 26			16 24		17 26	17 50		18 26		19 20		20 20	20 29		21 20	
North Berwick		a	11 06		12 06	13 06		14 09	15 06		16 06			17 06			18 06		19 06		20 06			21 06		22 06

- **A** To London Kings Cross
- **B** From Glasgow Central to Plymouth. from Edinburgh
- **C** From Glasgow Central
- **D** From Aberdeen to Penzance. from Edinburgh
- **E** To Plymouth
- **F** To Birmingham New Street
- **G** From Aberdeen to London Kings Cross
- **H** From Glasgow Central to Birmingham New Street. from Edinburgh
- **I** To Doncaster
- **J** To Penzance
- **K** From Glasgow Central to Bristol Temple Meads. from Edinburgh
- **L** To Leeds
- **M** From Glasgow Central to Newcastle
- **N** To Newcastle

Sundays
26 June to 31 July

			SR	XC	SR	SR	XC	SR	SR	XC	SR		XC	SR	XC	GR	SR	XC	SR	GR	SR	GR	XC	SR	GR	SR
				◇1 A			◇1 B			◇1 C			◇1 C		◇1 D	R 1 E		◇1 F		R 1 E		R 1 G	◇1 H		R 1 I	
Haymarket	225,230,242	d					12 47			14 43			15 51					17 55					19 51			
Edinburgh 10	225,230,242	a					12 52			14 47			15 56					17 59					19 56			
		d	10 33	11 05	11 33	12 33	13 06	13 36	14 33	15 07	15 33		16 05	16 33	17 07	17 30	17 33	18 07	18 33	19 00	19 33	20 00	20 05	20 33	21 00	21 33
Musselburgh		d	10 39		11 39	12 39		13 39	14 39		15 39			16 39			17 39		18 39		19 39			20 39		21 39
Wallyford		d	10 43		11 43	12 43		13 43	14 43		15 43			16 43			17 43		18 43		19 43			20 43		21 43
Prestonpans		d	10 46		11 46	12 46		13 46	14 46		15 46			16 46			17 46		18 46		19 46			20 46		21 46
Longniddry		d	10 51		11 51	12 51		13 51	14 51		15 51			16 51			17 51		18 51		19 51			20 51		21 51
Drem		d	10 56		11 56	12 56		13 57	14 56		15 56			16 56			17 56		18 56		19 56			20 56		21 56
Dunbar		a		11 24			13 25			15 26			16 24		17 26	17 50		18 26		19 20		20 20	20 29		21 20	
North Berwick		a	11 06		12 06	13 06		14 09	15 06		16 06			17 06			18 06		19 06		20 06			21 06		22 06

Table 238

Sundays

Haymarket and Edinburgh - North Berwick and Dunbar

7 August to 11 September

		SR	XC	SR	SR	XC	SR	SR	XC	SR	XC	SR	XC	GR	SR	XC	SR	GR	SR	GR	XC	SR	GR	SR
														R				R		R			R	
			◇1			◇1			◇1		◇1		◇1	1		◇1		1		1	◇1		1	
			J			B			B		C		D	E		F		E		G	H		I	
			🛒			🛒			🛒		🛒		🛒	□🛒		🛒		□🛒		□🛒			□🛒	
Haymarket 225,230,242	d					12 47			14 43		15 51					17 55					19 51			
Edinburgh 10 225,230,242	a					12 52			14 47		15 56					17 59					19 56			
	d	10 33	11 05	11 33	12 33	13 06	13 36	14 33	15 07	15 33	16 05	16 33	17 07	17 30	17 33	18 07	18 33	19 00	19 33	20 00	20 05	20 33	21 00	21 33
Musselburgh	d	10 39		11 39	12 39		13 39	14 39		15 39		16 39			17 39		18 39		19 39			20 39		21 39
Wallyford	d	10 43		11 43	12 43		13 43	14 43		15 43		16 43			17 43		18 43		19 43			20 43		21 43
Prestonpans	d	10 46		11 46	12 46		13 46	14 46		15 46		16 46			17 46		18 46		19 46			20 46		21 46
Longniddry	d	10 51		11 51	12 51		13 51	14 51		15 51		16 51			17 51		18 51		19 51			20 51		21 51
Drem	d	10 56		11 56	12 56		13 57	14 56		15 56		16 56			17 56		18 56		19 56			20 56		21 56
Dunbar	a		11 24			13 25			15 26		16 24		17 26	17 50		18 26		19 20		20 20	20 29		21 20	
North Berwick	a	11 06		12 06	13 06		14 09	15 06		16 06		17 06			18 06		19 06		20 06			21 06		22 06

Sundays

from 30 October

		SR	XC	SR	SR	XC	SR	SR	XC	SR	XC	SR	XC	GR	SR	XC	SR	GR	SR	GR	XC	SR	GR	SR
														R				R		R			R	
			◇1			◇1			◇1		◇1		◇1	1		◇1		1		1	◇1		1	
			J			B			B		C		D	E		F		E		G	H		I	
			🛒			🛒			🛒		🛒		🛒	□🛒		🛒		□🛒		□🛒			□🛒	
Haymarket 225,230,242	d					12 47			14 43		15 51					17 55					19 51			
Edinburgh 10 225,230,242	a					12 52			14 47		15 56					17 59					19 56			
	d	10 33	11 05	11 33	12 33	13 06	13 36	14 33	15 07	15 33	16 05	16 33	17 07	17 30	17 33	18 07	18 33	19 00	19 33	20 00	20 05	20 33	21 00	21 33
Musselburgh	d	10 39		11 39	12 39		13 39	14 39		15 39		16 39			17 39		18 39		19 39			20 39		21 39
Wallyford	d	10 43		11 43	12 43		13 43	14 43		15 43		16 43			17 43		18 43		19 43			20 43		21 43
Prestonpans	d	10 46		11 46	12 46		13 46	14 46		15 46		16 46			17 46		18 46		19 46			20 46		21 46
Longniddry	d	10 51		11 51	12 51		13 51	14 51		15 51		16 51			17 51		18 51		19 51			20 51		21 51
Drem	d	10 56		11 56	12 56		13 57	14 56		15 56		16 56			17 56		18 56		19 56			20 56		21 56
Dunbar	a		11 24			13 25			15 26		16 24		17 26	17 50		18 26		19 20		20 20	20 29		21 20	
North Berwick	a	11 06		12 06	13 06		14 09	15 06		16 06		17 06			18 06		19 06		20 06			21 06		22 06

A To Penzance
B From Glasgow Central to Plymouth. 🛒 from Edinburgh
C From Glasgow Central to Bristol Temple Meads. 🛒 from Edinburgh
D To Bristol Temple Meads
E To London Kings Cross
F From Glasgow Central to Birmingham New Street. 🛒 from Edinburgh
G To Leeds
H From Glasgow Central to Newcastle
I To Newcastle
J To Plymouth

Table 238

Mondays to Fridays

Dunbar and North Berwick - Edinburgh and Haymarket

Miles	Miles			SR	SR	XC	SR	GR	SR	SR	SR	GR		SR	GR	SR	SR	SR	XC	SR	SR	SR		XC	SR
						◇1		R 1				R 1			R 1				◇1					◇1	
						A		B		A		C			D				E					F	
0	—	**North Berwick**	d	06 07	06 44		07 20			07 56	08 43			09 26		10 26		11 26		12 26		13 26			14 26
—	0	**Dunbar**	d			07 00		07 40				08 54			09 55		10 49		11 37		12 50			13 41	
4½	10¼	Drem	d	06 15	06 51		07 27			08 04	08 51			09 32		10 32		11 32		12 33		13 32			14 32
9	14¾	Longniddry	d	06 21	06 57		07 33			08 10	08 56			09 38		10 38		11 38		12 39		13 38			14 38
12½	18¼	Prestonpans	d	06 26	07 02		07 38		08 07	08 14	09 01			09 43		10 43		11 43		12 44		13 43			14 43
14¾	20½	Wallyford	d	06 29	07 05		07 41		08 10	08 17	09 04			09 46		10 46		11 46		12 47		13 46			14 46
17	22¾	Musselburgh	d	06 33	07 09		07 45		08 13	08 22	09 09			09 49		10 49	11 09	11 49		12 51	13 09	13 50			14 49
22¼	28	**Edinburgh** 10 225,230,242	a	06 40	07 15	07 22	07 55	08 10	08 22	08 32	09 16	09 24		10 00	10 20	11 00	11 15	12 00	12 03	13 00	13 16	14 00		14 10	15 00
—	—		d		07 18	07 26				08 33					10 27										
23½	29¼	**Haymarket** 225,230,242	a		07 22	07 30				08 37					10 31										

		SR	SR	XC	SR	SR	SR	XC		SR	SR	SR	SR	XC	SR	SR	XC	GR		SR
				◇1				◇1						◇1			◇1	R 1		
				F				G		A				H			F	I		
North Berwick	d		15 26		16 26		17 26			17 53	18 26	18 59	19 26		20 26	21 26				22 26
Dunbar	d	15 05		15 41		17 02		17 43						19 44			21 51	22 04		
Drem	d		15 32		16 32		17 32				18 32	19 04	19 33		20 32	21 32				22 32
Longniddry	d		15 38		16 38		17 38				18 38	19 09	19 40		20 38	21 38				22 38
Prestonpans	d		15 43		16 43		17 43				18 43	19 14	19 45		20 43	21 43				22 43
Wallyford	d		15 46		16 46		17 46				18 46	19 17	19 49		20 46	21 46				22 46
Musselburgh	d	15 24	15 49		16 49	17 22	17 49			18 08	18 49	19 21	19 53		20 49	21 49				22 49
Edinburgh 10 225,230,242	a	15 36	16 00	16 05	17 00	17 28	18 00	18 07		18 18	19 00	19 34	20 00	20 09	20 59	21 59	22 16	22 35		23 00
	d					17 28		18 11		18 25				20 13						
Haymarket 225,230,242	a					17 32		18 14		18 27				20 16						

Saturdays

until 10 September

		SR	SR	GR	SR	GR	SR	SR	GR	SR		SR	SR	XC	SR	SR	SR	SR	XC	SR		SR	SR	SR	XC
				R 1		R 1			R 1					◇1					◇1						◇1
				B	A	C			D					E					F						F
North Berwick	d	06 07	07 21		08 21		09 21	09 50		10 21		10 50	11 21		11 50	12 21	12 50	13 21		13 50		14 21	14 50	15 21	
Dunbar	d			07 48		08 55			09 55					11 38					13 38						15 40
Drem	d	06 15	07 28		08 28		09 29	09 57		10 28		10 58	11 28		11 57	12 28	12 57	13 28		13 58		14 28	14 58	15 28	
Longniddry	d	06 21	07 34		08 34		09 34	10 03		10 34		11 03	11 34		12 03	12 34	13 03	13 34		14 03		14 34	15 03	15 34	
Prestonpans	d	06 26	07 39		08 39		09 39	10 08		10 39		11 08	11 39		12 08	12 39	13 08	13 39		14 08		14 39	15 08	15 39	
Wallyford	d	06 29	07 42		08 42		09 42	10 11		10 42		11 11	11 42		12 11	12 42	13 11	13 42		14 11		14 42	15 11	15 42	
Musselburgh	d	06 33	07 46		08 46		09 46	10 15		10 46		11 15	11 46		12 15	12 46	13 15	13 46		14 15		14 46	15 15	15 46	
Edinburgh 10 225,230,242	a	06 40	07 54	08 17	08 53	09 24	09 54	10 23	10 24	10 54		11 23	11 54	12 07	12 23	12 54	13 23	13 54	14 07	14 23		14 54	15 23	15 54	16 04
	d				09 03				10 27																
Haymarket 225,230,242	a				09 05				10 31																

		SR	SR	SR	SR	XC		SR	SR	SR	SR	XC	SR	SR	XC	GR		SR
						◇1						◇1			◇1	R 1		
						G		A				J			F	K		
North Berwick	d	15 50	16 21	16 50	17 21			17 50	18 21	18 50	19 21		20 21	21 21				22 21
Dunbar	d					17 39						19 42			21 50	22 13		
Drem	d	15 58	16 28	16 58	17 28			17 57	18 28	18 58	19 28		20 28	21 28				22 28
Longniddry	d	16 03	16 34	17 03	17 34			18 03	18 34	19 03	19 34		20 34	21 34				22 34
Prestonpans	d	16 08	16 39	17 08	17 39			18 08	18 39	19 08	19 39		20 39	21 39				22 39
Wallyford	d	16 11	16 42	17 11	17 42			18 11	18 42	19 11	19 42		20 42	21 42				22 42
Musselburgh	d	16 15	16 46	17 15	17 46			18 15	18 46	19 15	19 46		20 46	21 46				22 46
Edinburgh 10 225,230,242	a	16 23	16 54	17 23	17 54	18 05		18 23	18 54	19 23	19 54	20 07	20 54	21 54	22 14	22 41		22 54
	d					18 11		18 24				20 15						
Haymarket 225,230,242	a					18 14		18 27				20 19						

A To Glasgow Central
B From Newcastle
C From Doncaster
D From Leeds to Aberdeen
E From Birmingham New Street
F From Plymouth
G From Plymouth to Aberdeen
H From Plymouth to Dundee
I From London Kings Cross.
J From Newquay to Dundee
K From London Kings Cross

Table 238

Saturdays
from 17 September

Dunbar and North Berwick - Edinburgh and Haymarket

		SR	SR	GR	SR	GR	SR	SR	GR	SR		SR	SR	XC	SR	SR	SR	SR	XC	SR		SR	SR	SR	XC
				■ 1		■ 1			■ 1					◇1					◇1						◇1
				A	B	C			D					E					F						F
North Berwick	d	06 07	07 21		08 21		09 21	09 50		10 21		10 50	11 21		11 50	12 21	12 50	13 21		13 50		14 21	14 50	15 21	
Dunbar	d			07 48		08 55			09 55					11 38					13 38						15 40
Drem	d	06 15	07 28		08 28		09 29	09 57		10 28		10 58	11 28		11 57	12 28	12 57	13 28		13 58		14 28	14 58	15 28	
Longniddry	d	06 21	07 34		08 34		09 34	10 03		10 34		11 03	11 34		12 03	12 34	13 03	13 34		14 03		14 34	15 03	15 34	
Prestonpans	d	06 26	07 39		08 39		09 39	10 08		10 39		11 08	11 39		12 08	12 39	13 08	13 39		14 08		14 39	15 08	15 39	
Wallyford	d	06 29	07 42		08 42		09 42	10 11		10 42		11 11	11 42		12 11	12 42	13 11	13 42		14 11		14 42	15 11	15 42	
Musselburgh	d	06 33	07 46		08 46		09 46	10 15		10 46		11 15	11 46		12 15	12 46	13 15	13 46		14 15		14 46	15 15	15 46	
Edinburgh 10 225,230,242	a	06 40	07 54	08 17	08 53	09 24	09 54	10 23	10 24	10 54		11 23	11 54	12 07	12 23	12 54	13 23	13 54	14 07	14 23		14 54	15 23	15 54	16 04
	d				09 03				10 27																
Haymarket 225,230,242	a				09 05				10 31																

		SR	SR	SR	SR	XC		SR	SR	SR	SR	XC	SR	SR	XC	GR		SR
						◇1						◇1			◇1	■ 1		
						G		B				H			F	I		
North Berwick	d	15 50	16 21	16 50	17 21			17 50	18 21	18 50	19 21		20 21	21 21				22 21
Dunbar	d					17 39						19 42			21 50	22 13		
Drem	d	15 58	16 28	16 58	17 28			17 57	18 28	18 58	19 28		20 28	21 28				22 28
Longniddry	d	16 03	16 34	17 03	17 34			18 03	18 34	19 03	19 34		20 34	21 34				22 34
Prestonpans	d	16 08	16 39	17 08	17 39			18 08	18 39	19 08	19 39		20 39	21 39				22 39
Wallyford	d	16 11	16 42	17 11	17 42			18 11	18 42	19 11	19 42		20 42	21 42				22 42
Musselburgh	d	16 15	16 46	17 15	17 46			18 15	18 46	19 15	19 46		20 46	21 46				22 46
Edinburgh 10 225,230,242	a	16 23	16 54	17 23	17 54	18 05		18 23	18 54	19 23	19 54	20 07	20 54	21 54	22 14	22 41		22 54
	d					18 11		18 24				20 15						
Haymarket 225,230,242	a					18 14		18 27				20 19						

Sundays
until 19 June

		SR	GR	SR	SR	GR	SR	SR	XC	SR		SR	XC	SR	SR	XC	SR	GR	SR	XC		SR	GR
			■ 1			■ 1			◇1				◇1			◇1		■ 1		◇1			■ 1
			J			I			E				K			F		L		M			I
North Berwick	d	11 20		12 20	13 24		14 23	15 20		16 20		17 20		18 20	19 20		20 20		21 20			22 20	
Dunbar	d		11 31			13 53			15 41				17 40			19 41		21 02		21 51			23 15
Drem	d	11 27		12 27	13 28		14 27	15 27		16 27		17 27		18 27	19 27		20 27		21 27			22 27	
Longniddry	d	11 33		12 33	13 34		14 33	15 33		16 33		17 33		18 33	19 33		20 33		21 33			22 33	
Prestonpans	d	11 38		12 38	13 39		14 38	15 38		16 38		17 38		18 38	19 38		20 38		21 38			22 38	
Wallyford	d	11 41		12 41	13 42		14 41	15 41		16 41		17 41		18 41	19 41		20 41		21 41			22 41	
Musselburgh	d	11 45		12 45	13 46		14 45	15 45		16 45		17 45		18 45	19 45		20 45		21 45			22 45	
Edinburgh 10 225,230,242	a	11 53	12 01	12 53	13 57	14 23	14 56	15 53	16 06	16 53		17 53	18 07	18 54	19 53	20 05	20 53	21 27	21 53	22 16		22 53	23 46
	d												18 11					21 33					
Haymarket 225,230,242	a												18 14					21 37					

Sundays
26 June to 31 July

		SR	GR	SR	SR	GR	SR	SR	XC	SR		SR	XC	SR	SR	XC	SR	GR	SR	XC		SR	GR
			■ 1			■ 1			◇1				◇1			◇1		■ 1		◇1			■ 1
			J			I			E				K			F		L		F			I
North Berwick	d	11 20		12 20	13 24		14 23	15 20		16 20		17 20		18 20	19 20		20 20		21 20			22 20	
Dunbar	d		11 31			13 53			15 41				17 40			19 41		21 02		21 51			23 15
Drem	d	11 27		12 27	13 28		14 27	15 27		16 27		17 27		18 27	19 27		20 27		21 27			22 27	
Longniddry	d	11 33		12 33	13 34		14 33	15 33		16 33		17 33		18 33	19 33		20 33		21 33			22 33	
Prestonpans	d	11 38		12 38	13 39		14 38	15 38		16 38		17 38		18 38	19 38		20 38		21 38			22 38	
Wallyford	d	11 41		12 41	13 42		14 41	15 41		16 41		17 41		18 41	19 41		20 41		21 41			22 41	
Musselburgh	d	11 45		12 45	13 46		14 45	15 45		16 45		17 45		18 45	19 45		20 45		21 45			22 45	
Edinburgh 10 225,230,242	a	11 53	12 01	12 53	13 57	14 23	14 56	15 53	16 06	16 53		17 53	18 07	18 54	19 53	20 05	20 53	21 27	21 53	22 16		22 53	23 46
	d												18 11					21 33					
Haymarket 225,230,242	a												18 14					21 37					

A From Newcastle
B To Glasgow Central
C From Doncaster
D From Leeds to Aberdeen
E From Birmingham New Street
F From Plymouth
G From Plymouth to Aberdeen
H From Plymouth to Dundee
I From London Kings Cross
J From York
K From Bristol Temple Meads to Aberdeen
L From London Kings Cross to Glasgow Central
M From Penzance

Table 238

Sundays

7 August to 11 September

Dunbar and North Berwick - Edinburgh and Haymarket

			SR	GR	SR	SR	XC	GR	SR	SR	XC	SR	SR	XC	SR	SR	XC	SR	GR	SR	XC	SR	GR
				R 1 A			◇1 B	R 1 C			◇1 D			◇1 E			◇1 F		R 1 G		◇1 H		R 1 C
North Berwick		d	11 20		12 20	13 24			14 23	15 20		16 20	17 20		18 20	19 20		20 20		21 20		22 20	
Dunbar		d		11 31			13 40	13 53			15 41			17 40			19 41		21 02		21 51		23 15
Drem		d	11 27		12 27	13 28			14 27	15 27		16 27	17 27		18 27	19 27		20 27		21 27		22 27	
Longniddry		d	11 33		12 33	13 34			14 33	15 33		16 33	17 33		18 33	19 33		20 33		21 33		22 33	
Prestonpans		d	11 38		12 38	13 39			14 38	15 38		16 38	17 38		18 38	19 38		20 38		21 38		22 38	
Wallyford		d	11 41		12 41	13 42			14 41	15 41		16 41	17 41		18 41	19 41		20 41		21 41		22 41	
Musselburgh		d	11 45		12 45	13 46			14 45	15 45		16 45	17 45		18 45	19 45		20 45		21 45		22 45	
Edinburgh 10	225,230,242	a	11 53	12 01	12 53	13 57	14 07	14 23	14 56	15 53	16 06	16 53	17 53	18 07	18 54	19 53	20 05	20 53	21 27	21 53	22 16	22 53	23 46
		d												18 11					21 33				
Haymarket	225,230,242	a												18 14					21 37				

Sundays

from 30 October

			SR	GR	SR	SR	XC	GR	SR	SR	XC	SR	SR	XC	SR	SR	XC	SR	GR	SR	XC	SR	GR
				R 1 A			◇1 B	R 1 C			◇1 D			◇1 E			◇1 F		R 1 G		◇1 F		R 1 C
North Berwick		d	11 20		12 20	13 24			14 23	15 20		16 20	17 20		18 20	19 20		20 20		21 20		22 20	
Dunbar		d		11 31			13 40	13 53			15 41			17 40			19 41		21 02		21 51		23 15
Drem		d	11 27		12 27	13 28			14 27	15 27		16 27	17 27		18 27	19 27		20 27		21 27		22 27	
Longniddry		d	11 33		12 33	13 34			14 33	15 33		16 33	17 33		18 33	19 33		20 33		21 33		22 33	
Prestonpans		d	11 38		12 38	13 39			14 38	15 38		16 38	17 38		18 38	19 38		20 38		21 38		22 38	
Wallyford		d	11 41		12 41	13 42			14 41	15 41		16 41	17 41		18 41	19 41		20 41		21 41		22 41	
Musselburgh		d	11 45		12 45	13 46			14 45	15 45		16 45	17 45		18 45	19 45		20 45		21 45		22 45	
Edinburgh 10	225,230,242	a	11 53	12 01	12 53	13 57	14 07	14 23	14 56	15 53	16 06	16 53	17 53	18 07	18 54	19 53	20 05	20 53	21 27	21 53	22 16	22 53	23 46
		d												18 11					21 33				
Haymarket	225,230,242	a												18 14					21 37				

A From York
B From Birmingham New Street
C From London Kings Cross
D From Bristol Temple Meads
E From Plymouth to Aberdeen
F From Penzance
G From London Kings Cross to Glasgow Central
H From Newquay

Table 239

Mondays to Saturdays

until 29 October

Inverness - Kyle of Lochalsh, Thurso and Wick

Miles	Miles			SR SO ■	SR ◇■	SR ◇■	SR ◇■ 🍴	SR ◇■	SR ■	SR ◇■ 🍴	SR ◇■ 🍴	SR ■	SR	SR ◇■ 🍴		SR ■	SR FSO ■
—	—	Aberdeen 240	d														
0	0	**Inverness**	d	23p30	07 06	09 00	10 38	11 01	12 16	13 34	13 59	14 39	17 15	17 54		21 09	23 30
10	10	Beauly	d	23p44	07 20	09 14	10 52		12 30	13 48		14 53	17 29	18 08		21 23	23 44
13	13	Muir of Ord	d	23p50	07 29	09 20	10 58	11 18	12 36	13 54	14 16	14 59	17 35	18 14		21 29	23 50
—	—																
18¾	18¾	Dingwall	d	00 02	07 43	09 31	11 07	11 29	12a47	14 03	14 28	15 11	17 46	18 26	18 28	21 40	00 02
—	30½	Garve	d			09 53		11 51		14 25					18 48		
—	36	Lochluichart	d			10x02		11x59		14x33					18x57		
—	40¼	Achanalt	d			10x08		12x05		14x39					19x03		
—	46½	Achnasheen	d			10 19		12 16		14 50					19 16		
—	59¼	Achnashellach	d			10x36		12x34		15x08					19x33		
—	64½	Strathcarron	d			10 46		12 43		15 17					19 44		
—	67	Attadale	d			10x51		12x48		15x23					19x48		
—	72	Stromeferry	d			11 04		13 01		15 35					20 02		
—	75¾	Duncraig	d			11x12		13x09		15x43					20x09		
—	77	Plockton	d			11 16		13 13		15 46					20 13		
—	78½	Duirinish	d			11x19		13x16		15x49					20x16		
—	82¼	**Kyle of Lochalsh**	a			11 28		13 26		15 59					20 26		
28½	—	Alness	d	00x13	07 55		11 20				14 41	15 24	17 59	18 41		21 53	00x13
31½	—	Invergordon	d	00 18	08 00		11 26				14 46	15a29	18 04	18 46		21 58	00 18
40¾	—	Fearn	d	00x29	08 12		11 38				14 58		18 16	18 57		22x09	00x29
44¼	—	Tain	d	00a35	08 18		11 45				15 04		18 22	19 03		22a15	00a35
57¾	—	Ardgay	d		08 33		12 00				15 21		18a38	19 19			
61	—	Culrain	d		08 37		12 06				15x26			19 24			
61½	—	Invershin	d		08x38		12x07							19x25			
67	—	Lairg	d		08 52		12 19				15 44			19 38			
77	—	Rogart	d		09x05		12x32				15x58			19x52			
84½	—	Golspie	d		09 16		12 43				16 08			20 05			
87	—	Dunrobin Castle §	d				12x45				16x11						
90½	—	Brora	d		09 30		12 54				16 19			20 15			
101½	—	Helmsdale	d		09 46		13 09				16 34			20 30			
111	—	Kildonan	d		09x59		13x22				16 46			20x42			
118¼	—	Kinbrace	d		10x08		13x31							20x52			
125¾	—	Forsinard	d		10 22		13 42				17 06			21 03			
134	—	Altnabreac	d		10x32		13x52							21x13			
143	—	Scotscalder	d		10x41		14x01							21x22			
147¼	—	Georgemas Junction	a		10 50		14 12				17 34			21 30			
—	—		d		10 52		14 14				17 36			21 32			
154	—	**Thurso**	a		11 02		14 24				17 46			21 42			
—	—		d		11 04		14 26				17 48			21 44			
160¾	—	Georgemas Junction	d		11 14		14 37				17 59			21 57			
175	—	**Wick**	a		11 32		14 55				18 16			22 14			

Mondays to Saturdays

from 31 October

		SR SO ■	SR ◇■	SR ◇■	SR ◇■ 🍴	SR ◇■	SR ■	SR ◇■ 🍴	SR ◇■ 🍴	SR ■	SR	SR ◇■ 🍴		SR ■	SR FSO ■
Aberdeen 240	d														
Inverness	d	23p30	07 06	09 00	10 38	11 01	12 16	13 34	13 59	14 39	17 15	17 54		21 09	23 30
Beauly	d	23p44	07 20	09 14	10 52		12 30	13 48		14 53	17 29	18 08		21 23	23 44
Muir of Ord	d	23p50	07 29	09 20	10 58	11 18	12 36	13 54	14 16	14 59	17 35	18 14		21 29	23 50
Dingwall	d	00 02	07 43	09 31	11 07	11 29	12a47	14 03	14 28	15 11	17 46	18 26	18 28	21 40	00 02
Garve	d			09 53		11 51		14 25					18 48		
Lochluichart	d			10x02		11x59		14x33					18x57		
Achanalt	d			10x08		12x05		14x39					19x03		
Achnasheen	d			10 19		12 16		14 50					19 16		
Achnashellach	d			10x36		12x34		15x08					19x33		
Strathcarron	d			10 46		12 43		15 17					19 44		
Attadale	d			10x51		12x48		15x23					19x48		
Stromeferry	d			11 04		13 01		15 35					20 02		
Duncraig	d			11x12		13x09		15x43					20x09		
Plockton	d			11 16		13 13		15 46					20 13		
Duirinish	d			11x19		13x16		15x49					20x16		
Kyle of Lochalsh	a			11 28		13 26		15 59					20 26		
Alness	d	00x13	07 55		11 20				14 41	15 24	17 59	18 41		21 53	00x13
Invergordon	d	00 18	08 00		11 26				14 46	15a29	18 04	18 46		21 58	00 18
Fearn	d	00x29	08 12		11 38				14 58		18 16	18 57		22x09	00x29
Tain	d	00a35	08 18		11 45				15 04		18 22	19 03		22a15	00a35
Ardgay	d		08 33		12 00				15 21		18a38	19 19			
Culrain	d		08 37		12 06				15x26			19 24			
Invershin	d		08x38		12x07							19x25			
Lairg	d		08 52		12 19				15 44			19 38			
Rogart	d		09x05		12x32				15x58			19x52			
Golspie	d		09 16		12 43				16 08			20 05			
Dunrobin Castle §	d														
Brora	d		09 30		12 54				16 19			20 15			
Helmsdale	d		09 46		13 09				16 34			20 30			
Kildonan	d		09x59		13x22				16 46			20x42			
Kinbrace	d		10x08		13x31							20x52			
Forsinard	d		10 22		13 42				17 06			21 03			
Altnabreac	d		10x32		13x52							21x13			
Scotscalder	d		10x41		14x01							21x22			
Georgemas Junction	a		10 50		14 12				17 34			21 30			
	d		10 52		14 14				17 36			21 32			
Thurso	a		11 02		14 24				17 46			21 42			
	d		11 04		14 26				17 48			21 44			
Georgemas Junction	d		11 14		14 37				17 59			21 57			
Wick	a		11 32		14 55				18 16			22 14			

§ Summer station only

Table 239

Inverness - Kyle of Lochalsh, Thurso and Wick

Sundays
until 25 September

		SR	SR	SR	SR		SR	SR	SR	SR
		1	1	◇1	1		1	◇1	◇1	1
		A						⊤		
Aberdeen 240	d									
Inverness	d	23p30	10 00	11 11	12 22		15 21	17 55		21 09
Beauly	d	23p44	10 14	11 25	12 36		15 35	18 09		21 23
Muir of Ord	d	23p50	10 20	11 31	12 44		15 43	18 15		21 29
Dingwall	d	00 02	10 32	11 45	12 57		15 54	18 26	18 28	21 40
Garve	d			12 10					18 48	
Lochluichart	d			12x19					18x56	
Achanalt	d			12x25					19x02	
Achnasheen	d			12 36					19 15	
Achnashellach	d			12x53					19x33	
Strathcarron	d			13 03					19 43	
Attadale	d			13x08					19x48	
Stromeferry	d			13 21					20 01	
Duncraig	d			13x29					20x09	
Plockton	d			13 33					20 12	
Duirinish	d			13x36					20x15	
Kyle of Lochalsh	a			13 45					20 26	
Alness	d	00x13	10 44		13x08		16x06	18 41		21 53
Invergordon	d	00 18	10 49		13 13		16a12	18 46		21 58
Fearn	d	00x29	11x00		13x24			18 57		22x09
Tain	d	00a35	11a06		13a30			19 05		22a15
Ardgay	d							19 24		
Culrain	d							19 30		
Invershin	d							19x31		
Lairg	d							19 44		
Rogart	d							19x57		
Golspie	d							20 08		
Dunrobin Castle §	d									
Brora	d							20 18		
Helmsdale	d							20 33		
Kildonan	d							20x45		
Kinbrace	d							20x55		
Forsinard	d							21 06		
Altnabreac	d							21x16		
Scotscalder	d							21x24		
Georgemas Junction	a							21 33		
	d							21 35		
Thurso	a							21 45		
	d							21 47		
Georgemas Junction	d							21 57		
Wick	a							22 14		

Sundays
from 6 November

		SR	SR	SR	SR		SR	SR	SR
		1	1	◇1	1		1	◇1	1
								⊤	
Aberdeen 240	d								
Inverness	d	23p30	10 00	11 11	12 22		15 21	18 00	21 09
Beauly	d	23p44	10 14	11 25	12 36		15 35	18 14	21 23
Muir of Ord	d	23p50	10 20	11 31	12 44		15 43	18 20	21 29
Dingwall	d	00 02	10 32	11 45	12 57		15 54	18 26	21 40
Garve	d			12 10					
Lochluichart	d			12x19					
Achanalt	d			12x25					
Achnasheen	d			12 36					
Achnashellach	d			12x53					
Strathcarron	d			13 03					
Attadale	d			13x08					
Stromeferry	d			13 21					
Duncraig	d			13x29					
Plockton	d			13 33					
Duirinish	d			13x36					
Kyle of Lochalsh	a			13 45					
Alness	d	00x13	10 44		13x08		16x06	18 41	21 53
Invergordon	d	00 18	10 49		13 13		16a12	18 46	21 58
Fearn	d	00x29	11x00		13x24			18 57	22x09
Tain	d	00a35	11a06		13a30			19 03	22a15
Ardgay	d							19 19	
Culrain	d							19 24	
Invershin	d							19x25	
Lairg	d							19 38	
Rogart	d							19x52	
Golspie	d							20 05	
Dunrobin Castle §	d								
Brora	d							20 15	
Helmsdale	d							20 30	
Kildonan	d							20x42	
Kinbrace	d							20x52	
Forsinard	d							21 03	
Altnabreac	d							21x13	
Scotscalder	d							21x22	
Georgemas Junction	a							21 30	
	d							21 32	
Thurso	a							21 42	
	d							21 44	
Georgemas Junction	d							21 54	
Wick	a							22 14	

§ Summer station only

A not 22 May

Table 239

Mondays to Saturdays

until 29 October

Wick, Thurso and Kyle of Lochalsh - Inverness

Miles	Miles			SR	SR	SR	SR	SR	SR	SR	SR	SR	SR	SR	SR	SR	SR
				1	1	◇1	◇1	◇1	1	◇1	1	◇1	◇1	◇1	◇1	1	1
							⊼	⊼				⊏⊼	⊏⊼		⊏⊼		
0	—	**Wick**	d				06 20	08 12				12 36			16 00		
14¼	—	Georgemas Junction	d				06 37	08 29				12 53			16 17		
21	—	**Thurso**	a				06 46	08 38				13 02			16 26		
—	—		d				06 48	08 41				13 05			16 29		
27¾	—	Georgemas Junction	a				06 59	08 50				13 14			16 38		
—	—		d				07 00	08 53				13 17			16 41		
32	—	Scotscalder	d				07x06					13x23			16x47		
41	—	Altnabreac	d				07x15					13x32			16x56		
49¼	—	Forsinard	d				07 27	09 15				13 43			17 07		
56¾	—	Kinbrace	d				07x37					13x53			17x17		
64	—	Kildonan	d				07x48	09 33				14x03			17x25		
73½	—	Helmsdale	d				08 01	09 47				14 18			17 40		
84½	—	Brora	d				08 16	10 03				14 33			17 55		
88	—	Dunrobin Castle §	d					10x08				14x38			18x00		
90½	—	Golspie	d				08 26	10 11				14 42			18 04		
98	—	Rogart	d				08x35	10x19				14x51			18x13		
108	—	Lairg	d		06 34		08 53	10 38				15 08			18 30		
113½	—	Invershin	d		06 43		09x01					15x17			18x39		
114	—	Culrain	d		06 44		09 03					15 20			18 40		
117¼	—	Ardgay	d	06 25	06 51		09 11	10 51				15 25			18 45	19 26	
130¾	—	Tain	d	06 40	07 06		09 26	11 07				15 41			19 03	19 42	22 20
134¼	—	Fearn	d	06 45	07 12		09 31					15 47			19x09	19x47	22x25
143½	—	Invergordon	d	06 58	07 24		09 44	11 26			15 38	15 58			19 21	19 58	22 36
146½	—	Alness	d	07 02	07 28		09 48				15 43	16x03			19x25	20x03	22x41
—	0	**Kyle of Lochalsh**	d			06 21				12 03			14 35	17 15			
—	3¾	Duirinish	d			06x28				12x10			14x42	17x25			
—	5¼	Plockton	d			06 33				12 14			14 47	17 26			
—	6½	Duncraig	d			06x35				12x17			14x49	17x32			
—	10¼	Stromeferry	d			06 44				12 26			14 58	17 38			
—	15¼	Attadale	d			06x56				12x37			15x09	17x52			
—	17¾	Strathcarron	d			07 02				12 45			15 20	17 55			
—	23	Achnashellach	d			07x11				12x54			15x29	18x07			
—	35¾	Achnasheen	d			07 29				13 13			15 48	18 22			
—	42	Achanalt	d			07x39				13x23			15x58	18x35			
—	46¼	Lochluichart	d			07x45				13x29			16x04	18x42			
—	51¾	Garve	d			07 55				13 39			16 14	18 50			
156¼	63½	Dingwall	d	07 16	07 42	08 16	10 04	11 45	12 54	14 04	15 56	16 19	16 37	19 12	19 39	20 16	22 54
162	69¼	Muir of Ord	d	07 28	07 52	08 28	10 13	11 55	13 05	14 16	16 08	16 29	16 46	19 25	19 49	20 25	23 05
164¾	72¼	Beauly	d	07 33	07 57	08 35	10 19		13 11	14 21	16 13	16x34		19 30	19 55	20x29	23x09
175	82¼	**Inverness**	a	07 48	08 12	08 53	10 35	12 13	13 25	14 37	16 28	16 48	17 06	19 49	20 09	20 44	23 24
—	—	Aberdeen 240	a														

Mondays to Saturdays

from 31 October

		SR	SR	SR	SR	SR	SR	SR	SR	SR	SR	SR	SR	SR	SR
		1	1	◇1	◇1	◇1	1	◇1	1	◇1	◇1	◇1	◇1	1	1
					⊼	⊼				⊏⊼	⊏⊼		⊏⊼		
Wick	d				06 20	08 12				12 36			16 00		
Georgemas Junction	d				06 37	08 29				12 53			16 17		
Thurso	a				06 46	08 38				13 02			16 26		
	d				06 48	08 41				13 05			16 29		
Georgemas Junction	a				06 59	08 50				13 14			16 38		
	d				07 00	08 53				13 17			16 41		
Scotscalder	d				07x06					13x23			16x47		
Altnabreac	d				07x15					13x32			16x56		
Forsinard	d				07 27	09 15				13 43			17 07		
Kinbrace	d				07x37					13x53			17x17		
Kildonan	d				07x48	09 33				14x03			17x25		
Helmsdale	d				08 01	09 47				14 18			17 40		
Brora	d				08 16	10 03				14 33			17 55		
Dunrobin Castle §	d														
Golspie	d				08 26	10 11				14 42			18 04		
Rogart	d				08x35	10x19				14x51			18x13		
Lairg	d		06 34		08 53	10 38				15 08			18 30		
Invershin	d		06 43		09x01					15x17			18x39		
Culrain	d		06 44		09 03					15 20			18 40		
Ardgay	d	06 25	06 51		09 11	10 51				15 25			18 45	19 26	
Tain	d	06 40	07 06		09 26	11 07				15 41			19 03	19 42	22 20
Fearn	d	06 45	07 12		09 31					15 47			19x09	19x47	22x25
Invergordon	d	06 58	07 24		09 44	11 26			15 38	15 58			19 21	19 58	22 36
Alness	d	07 02	07 28		09 48				15 43	16x03			19x25	20x03	22x41
Kyle of Lochalsh	d			06 21				12 03			14 35	17 15			
Duirinish	d			06x28				12x10			14x42	17x25			
Plockton	d			06 33				12 14			14 47	17 26			
Duncraig	d			06x35				12x17			14x49	17x32			
Stromeferry	d			06 44				12 26			14 58	17 38			
Attadale	d			06x56				12x37			15x09	17x52			
Strathcarron	d			07 02				12 45			15 20	17 55			
Achnashellach	d			07x11				12x54			15x29	18x07			
Achnasheen	d			07 29				13 13			15 48	18 22			
Achanalt	d			07x39				13x23			15x58	18x35			
Lochluichart	d			07x45				13x29			16x04	18x42			
Garve	d			07 55				13 39			16 14	18 50			
Dingwall	d	07 16	07 42	08 16	10 04	11 45	12 54	14 04	15 56	16 19	16 37	19 12	19 39	20 16	22 54
Muir of Ord	d	07 28	07 52	08 28	10 13	11 55	13 05	14 16	16 08	16 29	16 46	19 25	19 49	20 25	23 05
Beauly	d	07 33	07 57	08 35	10 19		13 11	14 21	16 13	16x34		19 30	19 55	20x29	23x09
Inverness	a	07 48	08 12	08 53	10 35	12 13	13 25	14 37	16 28	16 48	17 06	19 49	20 09	20 44	23 24
Aberdeen 240	a														

§ Summer station only

Table 239

Wick, Thurso and Kyle of Lochalsh - Inverness

Sundays
until 25 September

		SR 1	SR ◇1	SR 1	SR ◇1	SR 1	SR ◇1	SR 1
Wick	d				11 53			
Georgemas Junction	d				12 10			
Thurso	a				12 19			
	d				12 22			
Georgemas Junction	a				12 31			
	d				12 34			
Scotscalder	d				12x40			
Altnabreac	d				12x49			
Forsinard	d				13 00			
Kinbrace	d				13x10			
Kildonan	d				13x20			
Helmsdale	d				13 33			
Brora	d				13 48			
Dunrobin Castle §	d				13x53			
Golspie	d				13 58			
Rogart	d				14x07			
Lairg	d				14 24			
Invershin	d				14x33			
Culrain	d				14x34			
Ardgay	d				14 40			
Tain	d	11 10		14 00	14 55			22 20
Fearn	d	11x15		14x05	15x00			22x25
Invergordon	d	11 26		14 16	15 12	16 19		22 36
Alness	d	11x31		14x21	15x16	16x23		22x41
Kyle of Lochalsh	d		10 34				15 22	
Duirinish	d		10x41				15x29	
Plockton	d		10 46				15 34	
Duncraig	d		10x48				15x36	
Stromeferry	d		10 57				15 45	
Attadale	d		11x09				15x57	
Strathcarron	d		11 15				16 03	
Achnashellach	d		11x24				16x12	
Achnasheen	d		11 40				16 30	
Achanalt	d		11x50				16x40	
Lochluichart	d		11x57				16x47	
Garve	d		12 08				16 56	
Dingwall	d	11 44	12 28	14 36	15 30	16 36	17 18	22 54
Muir of Ord	d	11 55	12 43	14 47	15 42	16 47	17 29	23 05
Beauly	d	12 00	12 48	14x52	15 47	16 52	17 34	23x09
Inverness	a	12 16	13 03	15 07	16 02	17 07	17 49	23 24
Aberdeen 240	a							

Sundays
from 6 November

		SR 1	SR 1	SR ◇1 A	SR 1	SR ◇1	SR 1
Wick	d			11 53			
Georgemas Junction	d			12 10			
Thurso	a			12 19			
	d			12 22			
Georgemas Junction	a			12 31			
	d			12 34			
Scotscalder	d			12x40			
Altnabreac	d			12x49			
Forsinard	d			13 00			
Kinbrace	d			13x10			
Kildonan	d			13x20			
Helmsdale	d			13 33			
Brora	d			13 48			
Dunrobin Castle §	d						
Golspie	d			13 58			
Rogart	d			14x07			
Lairg	d			14 24			
Invershin	d			14x33			
Culrain	d			14x34			
Ardgay	d			14 40			
Tain	d	11 10	14 00	14 55			22 20
Fearn	d	11x15	14x05	15x00			22x25
Invergordon	d	11 26	14 16	15 12	16 19		22 36
Alness	d	11x31	14x21	15x16	16x23		22x41
Kyle of Lochalsh	d					15 22	
Duirinish	d					15x29	
Plockton	d					15 34	
Duncraig	d					15x36	
Stromeferry	d					15 45	
Attadale	d					15x57	
Strathcarron	d					16 03	
Achnashellach	d					16x12	
Achnasheen	d					16 30	
Achanalt	d					16x40	
Lochluichart	d					16x47	
Garve	d					16 56	
Dingwall	d	11 44	14 36	15 30	16 36	17 18	22 54
Muir of Ord	d	11 55	14 47	15 42	16 47	17 29	23 05
Beauly	d	12 00	14x52	15 47	16 52	17 34	23x09
Inverness	a	12 16	15 07	16 02	17 07	17 49	23 24
Aberdeen 240	a						

§ Summer station only

A Dunrobin Castle until 30 October

Scrabster - Stromness (Orkney Isles)

Operated by NorthLink Ferries Ltd

		SO B	SO A	SX	
Inverness	239 d	*07 06*	*07 06*	07 06	*13 59*
Thurso #	239 a	*11c02*	*11a02*	11a02	*17c46*
Scrabster	d	**12 00**	**13 15**	**13 15**	**19 00**
Stromness	a	**13 30**	**14 45**	**14 45**	**20 30**

Mondays to Saturdays

		SX	SO A	SO B	SX	SO A
Stromness	d	**06 30**	**06 30**	**09 00**	**11 00**	**11 00**
Scrabster	a	**08b00**	**08b00**	**10b30**	**12c30**	**12c30**
Thurso #	239 d	*08 41*	*08 41*	*13 05*	*13 05*	*13 05*
Inverness	239 a	*12 13*	*12 13*	*16 48*	*16 48*	*16 48*

Sundays

Stromness	d	**09 00**
Scrabster	a	**10b30**
Thurso #	239 d	*12 22*
Inverness	239 a	*16 02*

A 11 June to 13 August

B Until 4 June and from 20 August

\# A connecting bus service beween Thurso and Scrabster is operated by Stagecoach in the Highlands, from whom details of bus times should be obtained (Tel. 0871 200 22 33).

a Stagecoach in the Highlands bus connection. Departs Princes Street, opposite Miller Academy School (under 5 minute walk).

b Stagecoach in the Highlands bus connection. Arrives Princes Street, opposite Miller Academy School (under 5 minute walk).

c No bus connection available. Passengers must make their own way between Thurso Railway Station and Scrabster Ferry Terminal (2.5 miles). A taxi service is available from Thurso Railway Station.

PASSENGER NOTICE: Please note that NorthLink Ferries requires all passengers aged 16 and over to be in possession of photographic ID at check-in.

THE TALL SHIPS RACES 2011

The above event will take place on Saturday 16 July and as a result there will be a small modification to the sailing schedule on this day. Please telephone 0845 6000 449 or visit www.northlinkferries.co.uk for details.

Table 239B **SHIPPING SERVICES** **Mondays to Saturdays**

until 22 October

Ullapool - Stornoway (Lewis), Uig (Skye), Tarbert (Harris) and Lochmaddy (North Uist)

Operated by Caledonian MacBrayne Ltd

		TTh-SX	TTh-SO	WFO F	SX A	WF-SX H	TThO	SO B	SO C	MFO	SO	WO	WFO F
Edinburgh 10	229 d			09a35	09a35	09a35	09a35	09a35	09a35	09a35	11 35	09a35	15a34
Glasgow Queen St 10	229 d			10 11	10 11	10 11	10 11	10 11	10 11	10 11	11a41	10 11	16 11
Inverness	229 a			13b27	13b27	13b27	13 27	13 27	13 27	13 27	15b06	13 27	19b34
Inverness	239 d	09 00	09 00				13 34	13 34	13 34	13 34		13 34	
Kyle of Lochalsh #	239 a	11c28	11c28				15d59	15d59	15d59	15d59		15d59	
Inverness +	bus d			14 10	15 00	15 00					15 40		20 55
Ullapool +	bus a			15 30	16 20	16 20					17 00		22 15
Ullapool	ship d			16 30	17 35	17 35					18 15		23 00
Stornoway	ship a			19 15	20 20	20 20					21 00		01 45
Uig #	ship d	14 00	14 00				18 00	18 00	18 00	18 00		19 00	
Tarbert	ship a	15 40					19 40	19 40	19 40				
Lochmaddy	ship a		15 45					21 45		19 45		20 45	

Sundays

until 16 October

Edinburgh 10	229 d	09 25
Glasgow Queen St 10	229 d	09a38
Inverness	229 a	13b09
Inverness	239 d	
Kyle of Lochalsh #	239 a	
Inverness +	bus d	15 40
Ullapool +	bus a	17 00
Ullapool	ship d	18 15
Stornoway	ship a	21 00
Uig #	ship d	
Tarbert	ship a	
Lochmaddy	ship a	

Mondays to Saturdays

until 22 October

		MO D	MO E	WFO	WFO F	G	WFX J	TTh-SO	TTh-SO	TTh-SX	WFO F	SX A	WF-SX H	SO
Lochmaddy	ship d	05 30						07 30		11 50				
Tarbert	ship d	07 30	07 30	07 30					11 50					
Uig #	ship a	09e10	09e10	09e10				09e15	13f30	13f35				
Stornoway	ship d				06 00	07 00	07 00				13 00	13 50	13 50	14 30
Ullapool	ship a				08 45	09 45	09 45				15 45	16 35	16 35	17 15
Ullapool	bus d				08 50	09 50	09 50				15 50	16 40	16 40	17 20
Inverness +	bus a				10g10	11g10	11g10				17g10	18g00	18g00	18g40
Kyle of Lochalsh #	239 d	12 03	12 03	12 03				12 03	17 15	17 15				
Inverness	239 a	14 37	14 37	14 37				14 37	19 49	19 49				
Inverness	229 d	14 51	14 51	14 51	10 47	12 47	12 47	14 51	20 15	20 15	18 43	18 43	18 43	20 15
Glasgow Queen St 10	229 a	18 09	18 09	18 09	14a14	16a14	16a14	18 09	23 39	23 39	22a20	22a20	22a20	23 39
Edinburgh 10	229 a	18a25	18a25	18a25	14 19	16 24	16 24	18a25	00h09	00h09	22 19	22 19	22 19	00h09

A Until 17 June and from 29 August
B From 17 September
C Until 10 September
D From 19 September
E Until 12 September
F 22 June to 26 August
G Until 18 June and from 29 August
H 20 June to 25 August
J From 20 June to 27 August
a Change at Perth
b Passengers make their own way between rail station and bus station
c Bus connection dep. Kyle of Lochalsh 1215, Uig arr. 1350
d Bus connection dep. Kyle of Lochalsh 1605, Uig arr. 1745
e Bus connection dep. Uig 0930, Kyle of Lochalsh arr. 1114
f Bus connection dep. Uig 1445, Kyle of Lochalsh arr. 1619
g Passengers make their own way between bus station and rail station
h Change at Stirling

\# Connecting bus service between Uig and Kyle of Lochalsh operated by Scottish Citylink Coaches (Tel. 08705 50 50 50).

\+ Bus station. Connecting bus service between Inverness Bus Station and Ullapool operated by Scottish Citylink Coaches (Tel. 08705 50 50 50).

No Sunday service from Lochmaddy to Uig or Stornoway to Ullapool

For details of sailings from 23 October, please telephone Caledonian MacBrayne on 08000 66 5000 or visit www.calmac.co.uk. For confirmation of Scottish Citylink Coach connections from 3 October, telephone 08705 50 50 50

Table 240

Mondays to Saturdays

Aberdeen and Elgin - Inverness

Miles			SR ◇1 A MX	SR ◇1	SR ◇1	SR ◇1 B	SR 1 C	SR ◇1	SR ◇1 D	SR ◇1 A	SR ◇1 🛒	SR ◇1 A	SR ◇1 🛒
0	**Aberdeen**	d	21p55		06 14	07 14	07 50	08 23	08 50	10 00	10 14	11 04	11 59
6¼	Dyce ✈	d	22p05		06 24	07 31	08 03	08 36	08a59	10 09	10 23	11 16	12 08
17	**Inverurie**	a	22p16		06 37	07 44	08 17	08 48		10 22	10 35	11 30	12 20
—		d	22p17		06 46	07 49		08 48			10 35		12 20
27½	Insch	d	22p29		06 58	08 01		09 03			10 47		12 33
40¾	Huntly	d	22p46		07 19	08 17		09 19			11 03		12 49
53¼	Keith	d	23p00		07 33	08 31		09 33			11 18		13 03
71¼	**Elgin**	d	23p22	07 00	07 58	08 53		09 55			11 42		13 27
83½	Forres	d	23p36	07 14	08 12	09 07		10 11			11 56		13 41
93¼	Nairn	d	23p47	07 27	08 23	09 22		10 22			12 07		13 52
108¼	**Inverness**	a	00 05	07 48	08 41	09 40		10 40			12 25		14 10

Miles			SR 1	SR ◇1 🛒	SR ◇1 A	SR ◇1 🛒	SR ◇1 A	SR 1	SR ◇1 🛒	SR ◇1 A	SR ◇1 🛒	SR ◇1 A
0	**Aberdeen**	d	12 50	13 40	14 56	15 25	15 55	16 43	17 18	17 56	18 20	19 07
6¼	Dyce ✈	d	13 01	13 53	15 05	15 38	16 04	16a52	17 29	18 05	18 29	19 22
17	**Inverurie**	a	13 15	14 05	15 19	15 50	16 18		17 40	18 19	18 41	19 35
—		d		14 05		15 50			17 41		18 41	
27½	Insch	d		14 17		16 02			17 53		18 53	
40¾	Huntly	d		14 33		16 18			18 09		19 09	
53¼	Keith	d		14 47		16 34			18 26		19 24	
71¼	**Elgin**	d		15 11		16 56			18 54		19 46	
83½	Forres	d		15 25		17 10			19 08		20 00	
93¼	Nairn	d		15 41		17 29			19 19		20 15	
108¼	**Inverness**	a		15 59		17 47			19 38		20 33	

		SR ◇1 🛒	SR 1	SR ◇1 A	SR 1
Aberdeen	d	20 11	20 56	21 55	22 50
Dyce ✈	d	20 20	21 05	22 05	22 59
Inverurie	a	20 32	21 19	22 16	23 13
	d	20 32		22 17	
Insch	d	20 44		22 29	
Huntly	d	21 00		22 46	
Keith	d	21 14		23 00	
Elgin	d	21 36		23 22	
Forres	d	21 55		23 36	
Nairn	d	22 06		23 47	
Inverness	a	22 24		00 05	

Sundays

		SR ◇1 E	SR ◇1 🛒	SR ◇1 🛒	SR ◇1 🛒	SR ◇1 🛒	SR ◇1 🛒
Aberdeen	d	21p55	10 00	13 00	15 25	17 18	21 00
Dyce ✈	d	22p05	10 09	13 09	15 34	17 29	21 09
Inverurie	a	22p16	10 21	13 21	15 46	17 41	21 21
	d	22p17	10 21	13 21	15 47	17 41	21 21
Insch	d	22p29	10 33	13 33	15 59	17 53	21 33
Huntly	d	22p46	10 49	13 51	16 15	18 09	21 49
Keith	d	23p00	11 05	14 04	16 35	18 24	22 09
Elgin	d	23p22	11 27	14 26	16 58	18 45	22 31
Forres	d	23p36	11 41	14 40	17 12	19 00	22 45
Nairn	d	23p47	11 52	14 51	17 32	19 11	22 56
Inverness	a	00\05	12 10	15 10	17 50	19 29	23 14

A From Edinburgh
B From Montrose
C From Perth
D From Glasgow Queen Street
E not 22 May. From Edinburgh

Inverness and Elgin - Aberdeen

Mondays to Saturdays

Miles			SR ◇1 A	SR ◇1 B	SR ◇1 🛒	SR 1	SR ◇1 B	SR ◇1	SR ◇1 A	SR ◇1 🛒	SR ◇1 A	SR ◇1 🛒	SR 1
0	**Inverness**	d	04 51		05 57			07 10		09 03		10 58	
15	Nairn	d	05 08		06 14			07 28		09 21		11 15	
24¾	Forres	d	05 19		06 25			07 39		09 37		11 26	
37	**Elgin**	d	05 34		06 42			08 00		09 55		11 42	
55	Keith	d	05 56		07 03			08 21		10 14		12 03	
67½	Huntly	d	06 10		07 19			08 45		10 30		12 17	
80¾	Insch	d	06 26		07 35			09 03		10 49		12 35	
91¼	**Inverurie**	a	06 38		07 48			09 14		11 01		12 47	
—		d	06 39	07 14	07 49	08 22		09 15	10 38	11 01	11 35	12 47	13 38
102	Dyce ✈	d	06 52	07 26	08 03	08 35	09 08	09 27	10 50	11 15	11 47	13 02	13 52
108¼	**Aberdeen**	a	07 04	07 37	08 14	08 46	09 19	09 38	11 01	11 26	11 58	13 13	14 03

Miles			SR ◇1 🛒	SR ◇1 A	SR ◇1 🛒	SR ◇1 A	SR 1 C	SR ◇1 🛒	SR 1	SR ◇1 A	SR ◇1 🛒	SR ◇ A
0	**Inverness**	d	12 42		14 27			15 21			17 11	
15	Nairn	d	12 59		14 44			15 40			17 28	
24¾	Forres	d	13 10		14 55			15 51			17 39	
37	**Elgin**	d	13 28		15 12			16 07			17 58	
55	Keith	d	13 47		15 32			16 28			18 19	
67½	Huntly	d	14 01		15 46			16 47			18 40	
80¾	Insch	d	14 19		16 04			17 04			18 56	
91¼	**Inverurie**	a	14 31		16 18			17 15			19 09	
—		d	14 31	15 24	16 18	16 38		17 16	17 52	18 43	19 09	19 40
102	Dyce ✈	d	14 43	15 38	16 31	16 54	17 05	17 30	18 06	18 55	19 21	19 52
108¼	**Aberdeen**	a	14 54	15 49	16 41	17 05	17 14	17 41	18 17	19 06	19 32	20 03

		SR ◇1	SR ◇1 D	SR 1	SR ◇1
Inverness	d	18 10	19 57		21 20
Nairn	d	18 27	20 14		21 37
Forres	d	18 38	20 25		21 48
Elgin	d	18 55	20a41		22 06
Keith	d	19 16			22 27
Huntly	d	19 37			22 47
Insch	d	19 53			23 03
Inverurie	a	20 05			23 16
	d	20 05		21 24	23 16
Dyce ✈	d	20 21		21 36	23 28
Aberdeen	a	20 32		21 47	23 39

Sundays

		SR ◇1 🛒	SR ◇1 🛒	SR ◇1 B 🛒	SR ◇1 🛒	SR ◇1 E 🛒	SR ◇1 🛒	SR ◇1 E 🛒
Inverness	d	09 55	12 30	15 27	17 12	18 00	21 00	21 42
Nairn	d	10 12	12 47	15 44	17 30	18 17	21 17	21 59
Forres	d	10 23	12 58	15 55	17 41	18 28	21 28	22 10
Elgin	d	10 38	13 13	16 10	17 56	18a44	21 44	22a26
Keith	d	10 59	13 35	16 32	18 18		22 05	
Huntly	d	11 18	13 52	16 46	18 37		22 19	
Insch	d	11 34	14 08	17 02	18 53		22 35	
Inverurie	a	11 47	14 20	17 14	19 05		22 47	
	d	11 47	14 20	17 14	19 05		22 47	
Dyce ✈	d	11 59	14 32	17 30	19 17		22 59	
Aberdeen	a	12 10	14 43	17 41	19 28		23 10	

A To Edinburgh
B To Glasgow Queen Street
C To Stonehaven
D From Kyle Of lochalsh
E From Glasgow Queen Street

Newcraighall and Edinburgh - Dunfermline, Kirkcaldy and Glenrothes with Thornton

Miles	Miles			SR	SR	SR	SR	SR	SR	SR	SR	SR	SR	SR	SR	SR	SR	SR	SR	SR	SR
				MX	SX			SX			SX			SX	SO						
					R	R	◇1			1		1				◇1			1		◇1
					A	B	B		C	D	C	D	C	E	E	G	H	E	D	C	I
0	—	**Newcraighall**	d						06 05					06 57	06 57			07 27		07 59	
0¾	—	Brunstane	d						06 08					07 00	07 00			07 30		08 02	
4¾	0	**Edinburgh** 10	a						06 16					07 07	07 14			07 37		08 09	
—	—		d	23p19	04 40	04 40	05 30	06 09	06 18	06 29	06 33	07 00	07 10	07 18	07 18	07 28	07 34	07 39	08 00	08 11	08 34
6	1¼	Haymarket	d	23p23			05 33	06 13	06 22	06 33	06 37	07 04	07 13	07 22	07 22	07 31	07 40	07 43	08 04	08 14	08 39
9¼	4½	South Gyle	d	23p28				06 18	06 27		06 43		07 18	07 27	07 27			07 48		08 22	
14¼	9½	Dalmeny	d	23p34				06 24	06 33		06 50		07 25	07 34	07 34			07 54		08 28	
16	11¼	North Queensferry	d	23p38				06 28	06 37		06 54		07 28	07 37	07 37			07 58		08 32	
18	13¼	Inverkeithing	d	23p42	04 58	04s58	05 46	06 32	06 41	06 47	06 59	07 20	07 32	07 41	07 41		07 53	08 02	08 18	08 36	
—	14¾	Rosyth	d	23p45					06 44					07 45	07 45					08 39	
—	17	**Dunfermline Town**	d	23p50					06 49					07 50	07 50					08 44	
—	18½	Dunfermline Queen Margaret	d	23p54					06 53					07 53	07 53					08 48	
—	22½	Cowdenbeath	d	23p59					06 59					08 00	08 00					08 54	
—	24¾	Lochgelly	d	00 06					07 05					08 05	08 05					09 00	
—	27	Cardenden	d	00 10					07 09					08 09	08 09					09 04	
19½	—	Dalgety Bay	d					06 35			07 03		07 35					08 05			
22¼	—	Aberdour	d					06 40			07 09		07 40					08 10			
25	—	Burntisland	d					06 44			07 14		07 44					08 14			
27½	—	Kinghorn	d					06 49			07 19		07 49					08 19			
30¾	—	Kirkcaldy	d		05a17	05s17	06a02	06a56		07a02	07 25	07a36	07 54			08a02	08a09	08 24	08a33		09a08
39¾	31¾	Glenrothes With Thornton	a	00 19					07 15		07 33		08 04	08 16	08 16			08 32		09 10	

		SR	SR	SR	SR	SR	SR	SR	SR	SR	SR	GR	GR	SR	SR	SR	SR	SR	SR	SR	SR
												SO	SX								
												R	R								
			1						1			1	1			1				1	
		C	D			H	E	C	D			J	J	H	C	D			C	D	
Newcraighall	d	08 34					09 17			09 47					10 17		10 47		11 17		11 47
Brunstane	d	08 37					09 21			09 50					10 21		10 50		11 21		11 50
Edinburgh 10	a	08 44					09 28			09 57					10 28		10 57		11 29		11 57
	d	08 47	09 00	09 06	09 19	09 35	09 41	09 50	10 00	10 07	10 19	10 27	10 27	10 35	10 38	11 00	11 08	11 20	11 39	12 00	12 06
Haymarket	d	08 51	09 04	09 11	09 23	09 40	09 43	09 54	10 03	10 11	10 23	10 32	10 32	10 40	10 42	11 04	11 12	11 24	11 43	12 05	12 10
South Gyle	d	08 56		09 16	09 28		09 48	10 00		10 16	10 28				10 48		11 17	11 29	11 48		12 15
Dalmeny	d	09 02		09 22	09 34		09 54	10 06		10 22	10 34				10 54		11 23	11 35	11 54		12 21
North Queensferry	d	09 06		09 26	09 38		09 58	10 10		10 26	10 38				10 58		11 27	11 39	11 58		12 25
Inverkeithing	d	09 10	09 17	09 30	09 42	09 54	10 02	10 14	10 19	10 30	10 42	10 47	10 47	10 53	11 02	11 17	11 31	11 43	12 02	12 18	12 29
Rosyth	d	09 13			09 45			10 17			10 45							11 46			
Dunfermline Town	d	09 18			09 50			10 22			10 50							11 51			
Dunfermline Queen Margaret	d	09 22			09 54			10 26			10 54							11 55			
Cowdenbeath	d	09 28			10a03			10 32			11a03							12a04			
Lochgelly	d	09 34						10 38													
Cardenden	d	09 38						10 42													
Dalgety Bay	d			09 33			10 05			10 33					11 05		11 34		12 05		12 32
Aberdour	d			09 38			10 10			10 38					11 10		11 39		12 10		12 37
Burntisland	d			09 42			10 14			10 42					11 14		11 43		12 14		12 41
Kinghorn	d			09 47			10 19			10 47					11 19		11 48		12 19		12 46
Kirkcaldy	d		09a33	09 52		10a09	10 24		10a34	10 52		11a04	11a04	11a10	11 24	11a33	11 53		12 24	12a34	12 51
Glenrothes With Thornton	a	09 44		10 03			10 32	10 48		11 03					11 32		12 04		12 32		13 02

		SR	SR	SR	SR	SR	SR	SR	SR	SR	SR	GR	SR	SR	SR	SR	SR	SR	SR
												R							
					1				1			1			1				
			H	C	D			C	D			K	H	C	D			H	E
Newcraighall	d			12 17		12 47		13 17		13 47				14 17		14 47			15 17
Brunstane	d			12 21		12 50		13 21		13 50				14 21		14 50			15 20
Edinburgh 10	a			12 29		12 57		13 29		13 57				14 28		14 57			15 29
	d	12 18	12 35	12 39	13 00	13 08	13 19	13 39	14 00	14 08	14 18	14 27	14 35	14 39	15 00	15 08	15 20	15 34	15 39
Haymarket	d	12 23	12 40	12 43	13 04	13 12	13 23	13 43	14 04	14 12	14 23	14 32	14 40	14 44	15 04	15 13	15 24	15 39	15 43
South Gyle	d	12 27		12 48		13 17	13 28	13 48		14 17	14 28			14 49		15 18	15 29		15 48
Dalmeny	d	12 34		12 54		13 23	13 34	13 54		14 23	14 34			14 55		15 24	15 35		15 54
North Queensferry	d	12 37		12 58		13 27	13 38	13 58		14 27	14 38			14 59		15 28	15 39		15 58
Inverkeithing	d	12 41	12 54	13 02	13 17	13 31	13 42	14 02	14 18	14 31	14 42	14 47	14 53	15 03	15 18	15 32	15 43	15 53	16 02
Rosyth	d	12 45					13 45				14 45						15 46		
Dunfermline Town	d	12 50					13 50				14 50						15 51		
Dunfermline Queen Margaret	d	12 53					13 54				14 54						15 55		
Cowdenbeath	d	13a03					14a03				15a04						16a04		
Lochgelly	d																		
Cardenden	d																		
Dalgety Bay	d			13 05		13 34		14 05		14 34				15 06		15 35			16 05
Aberdour	d			13 10		13 39		14 10		14 39				15 11		15 40			16 10
Burntisland	d			13 14		13 43		14 14		14 43				15 15		15 44			16 14
Kinghorn	d			13 19		13 48		14 19		14 48				15 20		15 49			16 19
Kirkcaldy	d		13a09	13 24	13a33	13 53		14 24	14a34	14 53		15a03	15a09	15 25	15a34	15 54		16a08	16 24
Glenrothes With Thornton	a			13 32		14 04		14 32		15 04				15 33		16 05			16 32

A From 4 July until 29 July. To Dundee
B To Aberdeen
C To Edinburgh
D To Dundee
E To Newcraighall
F From North Berwick
G To Inverurie
H To Perth
I To Inverness
J From Leeds to Aberdeen
K From London Kings Cross to Aberdeen.

Newcraighall and Edinburgh - Dunfermline, Kirkcaldy and Glenrothes with Thornton

		SR	SR	SR	SR	GR SO	SR	SR	SR	SR	SR	SR	SR SO	SR SX	SR SX	SR	SR SO	SR SX	SR SX
			1			1										◇1			
		A	B	C		D	E	C		G	A				I	L	C	A	B
Newcraighall	d			15 47				16 17				16 47	17 09				17 37	17 37	
Brunstane	d			15 50				16 21				16 50	17 12				17 41	17 40	
Edinburgh 10	a			15 57				16 29				16 57	17 19				17 48	17 54	
	d	15 48	15 57	16 08	16 16	16 32	16 33	16 39	16 49	17 00	17 08	17 13	17 20	17 21	17 28	17 42	17 49	17 55	17 58
Haymarket	d	15 52	16 01	16 12	16 20	16a37	16 37	16 44	16 53	17 04	17 12	17 17	17 25	17 25	17a32	17u46	17 53	17 59	18 03
South Gyle	d	15 57		16 17	16 25			16 49	16 58		17 18	17 22	17 31	17 31			17 58	18 04	
Dalmeny	d	16 03		16 23	16 32			16 56	17 05			17 29	17 38	17 38			18 05	18 10	
North Queensferry	d	16 07		16 27	16 36			17 00	17 09			17 33	17 41	17 41			18 09	18 14	
Inverkeithing	d	16 11	16 17	16 31	16 40		16 52	17 05	17 13	17 22	17 28	17 37	17 47	17 47			18 14	18 18	18 22
Rosyth	d	16 14			16 44				17 17		17 33		17 50	17 50				18 21	
Dunfermline Town	d	16 19			16 49				17 22		17 38		17 55	17 55				18 26	
Dunfermline Queen Margaret	d	16 23			16 52				17 25		17 42		17 59	17 59				18 30	
Cowdenbeath	d	16 29			17a02				17a34		17 49		18 05	18 05				18 36	
Lochgelly	d	16 35									17 55		18 11	18 11				18 42	
Cardenden	d	16 39									17 59		18 15	18a23				18 46	
Dalgety Bay	d			16 34				17 08				17 40					18 17		
Aberdour	d			16 39				17 13				17 45					18 22		
Burntisland	d			16 43				17 17				17 49					18 26		
Kinghorn	d			16 48				17 22				17 54					18 31		
Kirkcaldy	d		16a33	16 53			17a07	17 27		17a37		18a01				18a14	18 36		18a39
Glenrothes With Thornton	a	16 45		17 01				17 35			18 08		18 24				18 44	18 52	

		XC	SR SX	SR SX	SR SO	GR SX	GR SO	SR	SR	SR	SR	SR	SR	SR	SR	XC SX	XC SO	SR	GR SX	SR
		◇1				1	1			1			◇1			◇1	◇1		1	
		M	N	A	A	O	P	E		B			L		B	R	S		P	E
Newcraighall	d			18 03	18 08				18 34			19 06		19 38				20 08		
Brunstane	d			18 06	18 12				18 37			19 09		19 41				20 11		
Edinburgh 10	a			18 13	18 20				18 46			19 16		19 48				20 19		
	d	18 11		18 25	18 25	18 30	18 30	18 40	18 50	19 00	19 09	19 21	19 36	19 50	20 00	20 13	20 15	20 21	20 29	20 44
Haymarket	d	18 15		18 30	18 30	18 34	18 35	18 45	18 54	19 04	19 13	19 26	19 40	19 54	20 04	20 17	20 20	20a26	20 34	20 48
South Gyle	d			18 35	18 35				18 59		19 18	19 30		19 59	20 09					
Dalmeny	d		18 33	18 41	18 41				19 05		19 24	19 37		20 05	20 15					
North Queensferry	d			18 45	18 45				19 09		19 28	19 40		20 09	20 19					
Inverkeithing	d	18 29	18 42	18 49	18 49	18 54	18 54	19 00	19 13	19 18	19 32	19 44	19 54	20 13	20 23	20a30	20 36		20 51	21 02
Rosyth	d			18 52	18 52				19 16			19 48		20 16						
Dunfermline Town	d			18 57	18 57				19 21			19 53		20 21						
Dunfermline Queen Margaret	d			19 01	19 01				19 25			19 56		20 25						
Cowdenbeath	d			19 07	19 07				19 31			20 03		20 31						
Lochgelly	d			19 13	19 13				19 37			20 08		20 37						
Cardenden	d			19 17	19 17				19 41			20 12		20 41						
Dalgety Bay	d		18 45								19 35				20 26					
Aberdour	d		18 51								19 40				20 31					
Burntisland	d		18 54								19 44				20 35					
Kinghorn	d		19 00								19 49				20 40					
Kirkcaldy	d	18a46	19a04			19a11	19a11	19a18		19a33	19a56		20a10		20a44		20a51		21a08	21a17
Glenrothes With Thornton	a			19 23	19 23				19 50			20 22		20 50						

		SR	SR	SR	SR	SR	SR	SR SX	SR SO	SR	SR	SR
				◇1								
			B	K	E	B	E			B		
Newcraighall	d	20 39			21 33			22 37	22 47			23 36
Brunstane	d	20 42			21 36			22 40	22 51			23 39
Edinburgh 10	a	20 49			21 43			22 49	22 58			23 48
	d	20 52	21 07	21 40	21 49	22 09	22 39	22 54	22 59	23 09	23 19	23 48
Haymarket	d	20 56	21 11	21 44	21 53	22 13	22 43	22a58	23a03	23 13	23 23	23a52
South Gyle	d	21 00	21 16		21 58	22 18	22 48			23 18	23 28	
Dalmeny	d	21 07	21 22		22 04	22 24	22 54			23 24	23 34	
North Queensferry	d	21 10	21 26		22 08	22 28	22 58			23 28	23 38	
Inverkeithing	d	21 14	21 30		22 12	22 32	23 02			23 32	23 42	
Rosyth	d	21 17			22 15						23 45	
Dunfermline Town	d	21 23			22 20						23 50	
Dunfermline Queen Margaret	d	21 26			22 24						23 54	
Cowdenbeath	d	21 33			22 30						23 59	
Lochgelly	d	21 38			22 36						00 06	
Cardenden	d	21 42			22 40						00 10	
Dalgety Bay	d		21 33			22 35	23 05			23 35		
Aberdour	d		21 38			22 40	23 10			23 40		
Burntisland	d		21 42			22 44	23 14			23 44		
Kinghorn	d		21 47			22 49	23 19			23 49		
Kirkcaldy	d		21a51	22a12		22a53	23a23			23a53		
Glenrothes With Thornton	a	21 52			22 46						00 19	

A To Edinburgh
B To Dundee
C To Newcraighall
D From London Kings Cross to Inverness
E To Perth
G To Carnoustie
I From Dunbar
K To Aberdeen
L To Inverness
M From Plymouth to Aberdeen
N From Glasgow Queen Street to Markinch
O From London Kings Cross to Aberdeen.
P From London Kings Cross to Aberdeen
Q To Bathgate
R From Plymouth to Dundee
S From Newquay to Dundee

Table 242

Sundays

Newcraighall and Edinburgh - Dunfermline, Kirkcaldy and Glenrothes with Thornton

		SR	XC	GR	SR	SR	SR	SR	SR	SR	SR	SR	SR	SR	SR	SR	SR	GR	SR	SR	SR
			◇	R 1		◇1			◇1				◇1		◇1			R 1			
		A	B	B	C	D	E	E	B	C	E	E	B	C	D	E	E	G	C	E	E
Newcraighall	d																				
Brunstane	d																				
Edinburgh 10	a																				
	d	23p19	08 04	09 10	09 15	09 25	09 55	10 15	10 55	11 15	11 55	12 15	12 40	13 15	13 50	14 00	14 15	14 38	15 15	15 55	16 15
Haymarket	d	23p23	08 08	09 14	09 19	09 29	09 59	10 19	10 59	11 19	11 59	12 19	12 44	13 19	13 54	14 04	14 19	14 43	15 19	15 59	16 19
South Gyle	d	23p28			09 24		10 04	10 24		11 24	12 04	12 24		13 24		14 08	14 24		15 24	16 04	16 24
Dalmeny	d	23p34			09 30		10 10	10 30		11 30	12 12	12 30		13 32		14 11	14 30		15 30	16 10	16 30
North Queensferry	d	23p38			09 34		10 14	10 34		11 34	12 19	12 34		13 36		14 15	14 34		15 34	16 14	16 34
Inverkeithing	d	23p42	08 25	09 32	09 38	09 48	10 18	10 38	11 15	11 38	12 23	12 38	13 00	13 40	14 11	14 22	14 41	15 01	15 38	16 18	16 38
Rosyth	d	23p45					10 23				12 26					14 27				16 21	
Dunfermline Town	d	23p50					10 28				12 31					14 33				16 26	
Dunfermline Queen Margaret	d	23p54					10 33				12 35					14 36				16 30	
Cowdenbeath	d	23p59					10 38				12 41					14 43				16 36	
Lochgelly	d	00 06					10 45				12 47					14 48				16 42	
Cardenden	d	00 10					10 49				12 51					14 52				16 46	
Dalgety Bay	d				09 44			10 44		11 44		12 44		13 46			14 44		15 44		16 41
Aberdour	d				09 49			10 49		11 49		12 49		13 51			14 49		15 49		16 46
Burntisland	d				09 53			10 53		11 53		12 53		13 55			14 53		15 53		16 50
Kinghorn	d				09 58			10 58		11 58		12 58		14 00			14 58		15 58		16 55
Kirkcaldy	d		08a39	09a48	10a03	10a10		11 03	11a31	12a02		13 03	13a16	14a04	14a27		15 03	15a18	16a02		17 00
Glenrothes With Thornton	a	00 19					10 55	11 11			12 57	13 11				15 00	15 14			16 52	17 08

		SR	SR	SR	SR	XC	SR	GR	SR	SR	SR	SR	SR	SR	SR	SR
		◇1		1		◇1		R 1				◇1				
		B	C	I	E	J	E	K	C	E	E	B		E	C	
Newcraighall	d															
Brunstane	d															
Edinburgh 10	a															
	d	17 05	17 15	17 50	17 55	18 11	18 15	18 42	19 15	19 55	20 15	21 00	21 15	21 55	22 25	23 36
Haymarket	d	17 09	17 19	17 54	17 59	18 16	18 19	18 47	19 19	19 59	20 19	21 05	21 19	21 59	22 29	23 40
South Gyle	d		17 24		18 04		18 24		19 24	20 04	20 24		21 24	22 04	22 34	23 45
Dalmeny	d		17 30		18 10		18 30		19 30	20 10	20 30		21 30	22 10	22 40	23 51
North Queensferry	d		17 34		18 14		18 34		19 34	20 14	20 34		21 34	22 14	22 44	23 55
Inverkeithing	d	17 22	17 38	18 07	18 18	18 30	18 38	19 02	19 38	20 18	20 38	21 19	21 38	22 18	22 48	23a58
Rosyth	d				18 21					20 21				22 21		
Dunfermline Town	d				18 26					20 26				22 26		
Dunfermline Queen Margaret	d				18 30					20 30				22 30		
Cowdenbeath	d				18 36					20 36				22 36		
Lochgelly	d				18 42					20 42				22 42		
Cardenden	d				18 46					20 46				22 46		
Dalgety Bay	d		17 41				18 41		19 41		20 41		21 41		22 51	
Aberdour	d		17 46				18 46		19 46		20 46		21 46		22 56	
Burntisland	d		17 50				18 50		19 50		20 50		21 50		23 00	
Kinghorn	d		17 55				18 55		19 55		20 55		21 55		23 05	
Kirkcaldy	d	17a38	17a59	18a23		18a44	19 00	19a18	19a59		21 00	21a34	22a02		23a09	
Glenrothes With Thornton	a				18 52		19 07			20 52	21 09			22 54		

A not 22 May
B To Aberdeen
C To Dundee
D To Inverness
E To Edinburgh
G From London Kings Cross to Aberdeen.
I To Perth
J From Plymouth to Aberdeen
K From London Kings Cross to Aberdeen

Glenrothes with Thornton, Kirkcaldy and Dunfermline - Edinburgh and Newcraighall

Miles	Miles			XC MX ◇1 A	SR MX C	SR MO A	SR MX A	SR	SR E	SR SX C	SR SX F	SR SO C	SR SX	SR F	SR G	SR SX	SR SX C
0	0	Glenrothes With Thornton	d		23p15						06 03			06 30			06 54
7¼	—	**Kirkcaldy**	d	23p26		23b53	23b53			05 53		06 16	06 27		06 49		
10	—	Kinghorn	d							05 58		06 21	06 32		06 54		
12¾	—	Burntisland	d							06 02		06 26	06 36		06 59		
17½	—	Aberdour	d							06 07		06 31	06 41		07 04		
20¼	—	Dalgety Bay	d							06 12		06 36	06 46		07 09		
—	4¾	Cardenden	d		23p23						06 10			06 37			07 01
—	7	Lochgelly	d		23p27						06 14			06 41			07 05
—	9½	Cowdenbeath	d		23p33						06 20			06 47			07 11
—	13½	Dunfermline Queen Margaret	d		23p38						06 26			06 53		07 08	07 17
—	14¾	**Dunfermline Town**	d		23p44						06 30			06 56		07 11	07 20
—	17	Rosyth	d		23p47						06 34			07 00		07 15	07 24
21¾	18½	Inverkeithing	d	23p42	23p51	00u12	00u12			06 16	06 40	06 40	06 49	07 06	07 12	07 19	07 30
23¾	20½	North Queensferry	d		23p55					06 20	06 44	06 44	06 53	07 10		07 24	07 34
25½	22¼	Dalmeny	d		23p58					06 23	06 48	06 48	06 57	07 13	07 19		07 38
30½	27¼	South Gyle	d		00 05					06 29	06 54	06 54	07 03	07 20	07 25	07 32	07 44
33¾	30½	Haymarket	d	23p58	00 12			06 14	06 33	06 40	07 02	07 02	07 12	07 28	07 34	07 40	07 52
35	31¾	**Edinburgh** 10	a	00 05	00 18	00 36	00 41	06 18	06 39	06 46	07 09	07 09	07 16	07 34	07 38	07 46	07 57
—	—		d					06 20	06 41		07 10	07 10		07 38			
39	—	Brunstane	d					06 27	06 48		07 17	07 17		07 45			
39¾	—	**Newcraighall**	a					06 34	06 52		07 21	07 21		07 49			

		SR SX H	XC SO ◇1 I	XC SX ◇1 I	SR SX C	SR SO C	SR C	SR ◇1 A	SR SO J	SR SX	SR SX	SR SX J	SR G	SR J	SR L	SR 1 M	SR L	SR G
Glenrothes With Thornton	d								07 32			07 34		08 04	08 16		08 37	
Kirkcaldy	d	07 13	07 21	07 21			07 40	07 48			07 54		08 06		08 28	08 41		09 12
Kinghorn	d	07 18									07 59		08 11		08 32			09 17
Burntisland	d	07 23									08 04		08 16		08 37			09 22
Aberdour	d	07 28									08 09		08 21		08 42			09 26
Dalgety Bay	d	07 33									08 14		08 26		08 47			09 31
Cardenden	d								07 37	07 36		07 42		08 11			08 45	
Lochgelly	d								07 42	07 42		07 47		08 15			08 49	
Cowdenbeath	d								07 48	07 51		07 57		08 24			08 58	
Dunfermline Queen Margaret	d								07 55	07 57		08 03		08 30			09 03	
Dunfermline Town	d								07 59	08 02		08 07		08 33			09 07	
Rosyth	d								08 02	08 03		08 12		08 37			09 10	
Inverkeithing	d	07 37	07 38	07 42			07 57		08 08	08 10	08 17	08 20	08 30	08 41	08 50	08 57	09 14	09 34
North Queensferry	d								08 12			08 26		08 45	08 54		09 18	
Dalmeny	d	07a42							08 16	08 19	08 24			08 49	08 58		09 22	
South Gyle	d								08 22	08 25	08 30	08 34	08 41	08 55	09 04		09 28	
Haymarket	d		07 56	08 01	08 12	08 12	08 17	08 19	08 28	08 32	08 39	08 45	08 49	09 03	09 12	09 15	09 35	09 50
Edinburgh 10	a		08 01	08 05	08 17	08 17	08 22	08 25	08 37	08 40	08 45	08 53	08 56	09 12	09 17	09 21	09 41	09 55
	d				08 18	08 18			08 47		08 53				09 21		09 51	
Brunstane	d				08 26	08 25			08 53		09 01				09 29		10 00	
Newcraighall	a				08 31	08 31			08 58		09 04				09 33		10 03	

		SR ◇1 N	SR J	GR SX 1 O	GR SO 1 O	SR J	XC SO ◇1 P	XC SX ◇1 P	SR	SR 1 G	GR SO 1 Q	GR SX 1 Q	SR	SR C	SR L	SR J	SR 1 G
Glenrothes With Thornton	d		09 08			09 32							10 23		10 32	10 51	
Kirkcaldy	d	09 25		09 44	09 44		10 17	10 17		10 26			10 32	10 42		11 02	11 19
Kinghorn	d												10 36			11 07	
Burntisland	d												10 41			11 12	
Aberdour	d												10 46			11 16	
Dalgety Bay	d												10 51			11 21	
Cardenden	d		09 16			09 39									10 40		
Lochgelly	d		09 20			09 43									10 44		
Cowdenbeath	d		09 29			09 52			10 21						10 53		
Dunfermline Queen Margaret	d		09 34			09 58			10 26						10 58		
Dunfermline Town	d		09 38			10 01			10 30						11 02		
Rosyth	d		09 41			10 05			10 33						11 05		
Inverkeithing	d		09 46	10 01	10 01	10 09	10 32	10 32	10 37	10 42			10 54	10 59	11 10	11 25	11 35
North Queensferry	d					10 13			10 41				10 58		11 14	11 29	
Dalmeny	d					10 17			10 45				11 02		11 18	11 33	
South Gyle	d					10 23			10 51				11 08		11 24	11 39	
Haymarket	d	09 56	10 04	10 19	10 21	10 30	10 52	10 54	11 01	11 06	11 11	11 11	11 16	11 19	11 34	11 47	11 51
Edinburgh 10	a	10 00	10 13	10 25	10 26	10 36	10 58	10 58	11 07	11 14	11 17	11 17	11 21	11 24	11 38	11 52	11 55
	d		10 21			10 51			11 21						11 51		
Brunstane	d		10 28			11 01			11 29						12 00		
Newcraighall	a		10 35			11 06			11 32						12 03		

A From Aberdeen
C From Perth
F From Markinch
G From Dundee
H To Glasgow Queen Street
I From Dundee to Plymouth
J From Edinburgh
L From Newcraighall
M From Blair Atholl
N From Inverness
O From Aberdeen to London Kings Cross
P From Aberdeen to Penzance
Q From Inverness to London Kings Cross. **The Highland Chieftain**
b Previous night, stops to pick up only

Glenrothes with Thornton, Kirkcaldy and Dunfermline - Edinburgh and Newcraighall

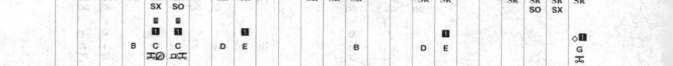

		SR	SR	SR	GR	GR	SR	SR	SR	SR	SR	SR	SR	SR	SR	SR	SR
					SX	SO									SO	SX	
					R 1	R 1		1					1				◇1
				B	C	C	D	E			B	D	E				G
Glenrothes With Thornton	d		11 18				11 48			12 18		12 47			13 18	13 18	
Kirkcaldy	d		11 27	11 41	11 44	11 44	12 00	12 17		12 27	12 42	12 59	13 18		13 26	13 26	13 41
Kinghorn	d		11 31				12 04			12 31		13 03			13 31	13 31	
Burntisland	d		11 36				12 09			12 36		13 08			13 36	13 36	
Aberdour	d		11 41				12 13			12 41		13 13			13 40	13 40	
Dalgety Bay	d		11 46				12 18			12 46		13 18			13 45	13 45	
Cardenden	d																
Lochgelly	d																
Cowdenbeath	d	11 23							12 23					13 23			
Dunfermline Queen Margaret	d	11 28							12 28					13 28			
Dunfermline Town	d	11 32							12 32					13 32			
Rosyth	d	11 35							12 35					13 35			
Inverkeithing	d	11 40	11 49	11 57	12 01	12 01	12 21	12 33	12 39	12 49	12 58	13 21	13 34	13 39	13 49	13 49	
North Queensferry	d	11 44					12 25		12 43	12 53		13 25		13 43	13 53	13 53	
Dalmeny	d	11 48					12 29		12 47	12 57		13 29		13 47	13 57	13 57	
South Gyle	d	11 54	12 00				12 35		12 53	13 03		13 35		13 53	14 03	14 03	
Haymarket	d	12 02	12 08	12 13	12 19	12 19	12 43	12 49	13 02	13 11	13 15	13 43	13 51	14 02	14 10	14 10	14 14
Edinburgh 10	a	12 07	12 13	12 18	12 25	12 25	12 48	12 55	13 07	13 17	13 20	13 48	13 57	14 06	14 16	14 16	14 19
	d		12 20				12 51			13 21		13 51			14 18	14 21	
Brunstane	d		12 28				12 59			13 29		13 58			14 28	14 28	
Newcraighall	a		12 33				13 05			13 33		14 04			14 33	14 33	

		SR	SR	SR	SR	SR	SR	SR	SR	SR	SR	SR	SR	SR
										SO	SX			
			1					1				◇1		1
		D	E			B	D	E				G	D	E
Glenrothes With Thornton	d	13 47			14 18		14 48			15 18	15 18		15 47	
Kirkcaldy	d	13 59	14 18		14 27	14 39	15 00	15 18		15 26	15 26	15 47	15 59	16 20
Kinghorn	d	14 03			14 31		15 05			15 31	15 31		16 03	
Burntisland	d	14 08			14 36		15 10			15 36	15 36		16 08	
Aberdour	d	14 13			14 41		15 14			15 40	15 40		16 13	
Dalgety Bay	d	14 18			14 46		15 19			15 45	15 45		16 18	
Cardenden	d													
Lochgelly	d													
Cowdenbeath	d			14 22					15 23					
Dunfermline Queen Margaret	d			14 27					15 28					
Dunfermline Town	d			14 31					15 32					
Rosyth	d			14 34					15 35					
Inverkeithing	d	14 21	14 34	14 39	14 49	14 55	15 23	15 34	15 39	15 49	15 49		16 21	16 36
North Queensferry	d	14 25		14 43	14 53		15 27		15 43	15 53	15 53		16 25	
Dalmeny	d	14 29		14 47	14 57		15 31		15 47	15 57	15 57		16 29	
South Gyle	d	14 35		14 53	15 03		15 37		15 53	16 03	16 03		16 35	
Haymarket	d	14 43	14 49	14 59	15 11	15 15	15 44	15 50	16 01	16 11	16 14	16 17	16 43	16 52
Edinburgh 10	a	14 48	14 54	15 06	15 16	15 19	15 50	15 57	16 07	16 16	16 18	16 24	16 48	16 56
	d	14 51			15 21		15 51			16 16	16 21		16 51	
Brunstane	d	14 58			15 29		16 00			16 29	16 29		16 58	
Newcraighall	a	15 04			15 33		16 03			16 33	16 33		17 04	

		SR	SR	SR	GR	GR	SR	SR	SR	SR	SR	SR	SR	SR	SR
					SO	SX	SX	SO		SX	SO				
					R 1	R 1									1
				B	J	J	K	K	D	K	K	E	B	K	E
Glenrothes With Thornton	d		16 20				16 32	16 32	16 48	17 01	17 01			17 37	
Kirkcaldy	d		16 29	16 41	16 45	16 45			17 00			17 32	17 48		18 13
Kinghorn	d		16 34						17 05			17 36			
Burntisland	d		16 39						17 10			17 42			
Aberdour	d		16 43						17 14			17 46			
Dalgety Bay	d		16 48						17 19			17 51			
Cardenden	d						16 40	16 40		17 09	17 09			17 44	
Lochgelly	d						16 47	16 47		17 13	17 13			17 48	
Cowdenbeath	d	16 24					16 53	16 53		17 22	17 22			17 57	
Dunfermline Queen Margaret	d	16 29					16 58	16 58		17 27	17 27			18 03	
Dunfermline Town	d	16 33					17 02	17 02		17 31	17 31			18 06	
Rosyth	d	16 36					17 05	17 05		17 34	17 34			18 10	
Inverkeithing	d	16 41	16 52	16 57	17 01	17 03	17 09	17 09	17 23	17 41	17 41	17 55	18 04	18 14	18 29
North Queensferry	d	16 45					17 13	17 13	17 27	17 45	17 45	17 59		18 18	
Dalmeny	d	16 49					17 17	17 17	17 31	17 49	17 49	18 03		18 22	
South Gyle	d	16 55	17 03				17 23	17 23	17 37	17 55	17 55	18 09		18 28	
Haymarket	d	17 03	17 11	17 16	17 20	17 21	17 32	17 32	17 45	18 03	18 03	18 16	18 19	18 35	18 44
Edinburgh 10	a	17 08	17 19	17 22	17 26	17 27	17 38	17 38	17 50	18 08	18 08	18 22	18 25	18 41	18 49
	d		17 21				17 41	17 51		18 17	18 21			18 48	
Brunstane	d		17 29				17 49	17 59		18 25	18 28			18 56	
Newcraighall	a		17 32				17 52	18 03		18 29	18 32			18 59	

B From Perth
C From Aberdeen to London Kings Cross. **The Northern Lights**
D From Edinburgh
E From Dundee
G From Inverness
J From Aberdeen to London Kings Cross
K From Newcraighall

Table 242

Mondays to Saturdays

Glenrothes with Thornton, Kirkcaldy and Dunfermline - Edinburgh and Newcraighall

		SR SO B	SR B	SR SO 1 D	SR F	SR SX H	SR SO H	SR B	SR ◇1 I	GR SX 1 J	SR SO ◇1 K	SR	SR	SR L
Glenrothes With Thornton	d	18 11	18 11		18 44			19 10				20 02		
Kirkcaldy	d	18 23	18 23	18 44		19 26	19 26		19 54	20 08	20 08		20 27	20 41
Kinghorn	d	18 27	18 27										20 32	
Burntisland	d	18 32	18 32										20 37	
Aberdour	d	18 37	18 37										20 41	
Dalgety Bay	d	18 42	18 42										20 46	
Cardenden	d				18 52			19 18				20 09		
Lochgelly	d				18 56			19 22				20 13		
Cowdenbeath	d				19 05			19 31				20 22		
Dunfermline Queen Margaret	d				19 10			19 36				20 27		
Dunfermline Town	d				19 14			19 40				20 31		
Rosyth	d				19 17			19 43				20 34		
Inverkeithing	d	18 45	18 45	19 00	19 21	19 42	19 42	19 47		20 24	20 24	20 39	20 50	20 59
North Queensferry	d	18 49			19 25			19 51				20 43	20 54	
Dalmeny	d	18 53	18 53		19 29			19 55				20 47	20 58	
South Gyle	d	18 59	19 12		19 35			20 01				20 53	21 04	
Haymarket	d	19 08	19 22	19 15	19 43	20 04	20 04	20 10	20 24	20 43	20 43	21 00	21 11	21 16
Edinburgh 10	a	19 13	19 31	19 21	19 48	20 09	20 09	20 14	20 29	20 48	20 48	21 06	21 17	21 20
	d			19 22	19 51			20 16				21 16		
Brunstane	d			19 28	20 00			20 23				21 24		
Newcraighall	a			19 33	20 04			20 27				21 27		

		SR	SR H	SR ◇1 I	SR ◇ E	SR	SR ◇1 K	XC SO ◇1 K	XC SX ◇1 K	SR L	SR SX K
Glenrothes With Thornton	d	21 02				22 02				23 15	
Kirkcaldy	d		21 26	21 42	21 59		22 59	23 14	23 26		23u53
Kinghorn	d		21 30		22 04		23 03				
Burntisland	d		21 36		22 09		23 09				
Aberdour	d		21 40		22 13		23 13				
Dalgety Bay	d		21 45		22 18		23 18				
Cardenden	d	21 09				22 09				23 23	
Lochgelly	d	21 13				22 13				23 27	
Cowdenbeath	d	21 22				22 19				23 33	
Dunfermline Queen Margaret	d	21 27				22 24				23 38	
Dunfermline Town	d	21 31				22 28				23 44	
Rosyth	d	21 34				22 31				23 47	
Inverkeithing	d	21 39	21 49		22 23	22 39	23 23	23 31	23 42	23 51	00u12
North Queensferry	d	21 43	21 53		22 27	22 43	23 27			23 55	
Dalmeny	d	21 47	21 57		22 31	22 47	23 31			23 58	
South Gyle	d	21 53	22 03		22 37	22 53	23 37			00 05	
Haymarket	d	22 00	22 10	22 14	22 46	23 00	23 43	23 51	23 58	00 12	
Edinburgh 10	a	22 06	22 16	22 19	22 50	23 06	23 50	23 55	00 05	00 18	00 41
	d	22 17				23 15					
Brunstane	d	22 25				23 22					
Newcraighall	a	22 28				23 26					

B From Edinburgh
E From Inverurie
F From Newcraighall
H From Dundee
I From Inverness
J From Aberdeen to Leeds
K From Aberdeen
L From Perth

Table 242

Sundays

Glenrothes with Thornton, Kirkcaldy and Dunfermline - Edinburgh and Newcraighall

		SR	SR	SR	SR	SR	GR	SR	XC	SR	SR	GR
							R 1		◇1			R 1
		B	D	D	G	G	I	D	K	G	G	M
Glenrothes With Thornton	d	23p15			10 56	11 11				12 58	13 11	
Kirkcaldy	d		08 08	10 08	11 08		11 40	12 08	13 03	13 10		13 39
Kinghorn	d		08 13	10 13	11 13			12 13		13 15		
Burntisland	d		08 17	10 17	11 17			12 17		13 19		
Aberdour	d		08 22	10 22	11 22			12 22		13 24		
Dalgety Bay	d		08 27	10 27	11 27			12 27		13 29		
Cardenden	d	23p23				11 18					13 19	
Lochgelly	d	23p27				11 22					13 23	
Cowdenbeath	d	23p33				11 30					13 30	
Dunfermline Queen Margaret	d	23p38				11 36					13 36	
Dunfermline Town	d	23p44				11 39					13 39	
Rosyth	d	23p47				11 43					13 43	
Inverkeithing	d	23p51	08 30	10 30	11 30	11 47	11 56	12 30	13 18	13 32	13 47	13 55
North Queensferry	d	23p55	08 34	10 34	11 34	11 51		12 36		13 42	13 51	
Dalmeny	d	23p58	08 38	10 38	11 38	11 56		12 40		13 49	13 56	
South Gyle	d	00 05	08 44	10 44	11 44	12 02		12 46		13 55	14 02	
Haymarket	d	00 12	08 53	10 58	11 58	12 12	12 18	12 58	13 37	14 04	14 10	14 19
Edinburgh 10	a	00 18	09 00	11 06	12 06	12 19	12 25	13 06	13 42	14 08	14 18	14 25
	d											
Brunstane	d											
Newcraighall	a											

		SR	SR	SR	GR	SR	SR	SR	SR	SR	SR	SR	SR	SR
					R 1	◇1		◇1				◇1		
		D	G	G	M	N	D	O	G	G	D	O	G	G
Glenrothes With Thornton	d		15 04	15 14					16 53	17 09			18 53	19 09
Kirkcaldy	d	14 08	15 15		15 42	16 03	16 08	17 02	17 07		18 07	18 56	19 07	
Kinghorn	d	14 13	15 20				16 13		17 12		18 12		19 12	
Burntisland	d	14 17	15 24				16 17		17 16		18 16		19 16	
Aberdour	d	14 22	15 29				16 22		17 21		18 21		19 21	
Dalgety Bay	d	14 27	15 34				16 27		17 26		18 26		19 26	
Cardenden	d			15 21						17 16				19 16
Lochgelly	d			15 25						17 20				19 20
Cowdenbeath	d			15 33						17 28				19 28
Dunfermline Queen Margaret	d			15 39						17 34				19 34
Dunfermline Town	d			15 42						17 37				19 38
Rosyth	d			15 46						17 41				19 41
Inverkeithing	d	14 30	15 37	15 50	15 58	16 19	16 30	17 18	17 29	17 45	18 29	19 12	19 29	19 45
North Queensferry	d	14 34	15 41	15 54			16 34		17 33	17 49	18 33		19 33	19 49
Dalmeny	d	14 38	15 45	16 00			16 38		17 37	17 53	18 37		19 37	19 53
South Gyle	d	14 44	15 51	16 06			16 44		17 43	18 00	18 43		19 43	20 00
Haymarket	d	14 58	15 58	16 16	16 20	16 35	16 55	17 34	17 49	18 09	18 52	19 27	19 52	20 09
Edinburgh 10	a	15 06	16 07	16 21	16 25	16 42	16 59	17 41	17 56	18 14	19 00	19 35	19 56	20 15
	d													
Brunstane	d													
Newcraighall	a													

		SR	SR	SR	SR	SR	SR	SR	SR	XC	SR
			◇1		◇1		◇1			◇1	R
		D	O	G	N	G	O		G	O	O
Glenrothes With Thornton	d			20 54		21 09			22 54		
Kirkcaldy	d	20 10	20 59	21 07	21 25		22 05	22 13	23 06	23 22	23u53
Kinghorn	d	20 15		21 11				22 17	23 10		
Burntisland	d	20 20		21 16				22 22	23 15		
Aberdour	d	20 24		21 20				22 26	23 19		
Dalgety Bay	d	20 29		21 25				22 31	23 24		
Cardenden	d					21 16					
Lochgelly	d					21 20					
Cowdenbeath	d					21 28					
Dunfermline Queen Margaret	d					21 34					
Dunfermline Town	d					21 37					
Rosyth	d					21 41					
Inverkeithing	d	20 31	21 15	21 28	21 41	21 45	22 21	22 34	23 27	23 38	00u12
North Queensferry	d	20 36		21 32		21 49		22 38	23 31		
Dalmeny	d	20 40		21 36		21 53		22 42	23 35		
South Gyle	d	20 46		21 40		22 00		22 48	23 41		
Haymarket	d	20 55	21 31	21 51	21 58	22 09	22 37	22 57	23 50	23 54	
Edinburgh 10	a	21 01	21 36	21 55	22 03	22 13	22 43	23 01	23 56	23 58	00 36
	d										
Brunstane	d										
Newcraighall	a										

B not 22 May. From Perth
D From Dundee
G From Edinburgh
I From Aberdeen to London Kings Cross. The Northern Lights
K From Aberdeen to Bristol Parkway
M From Aberdeen to London Kings Cross
N From Inverness
O From Aberdeen

Sleeper Services

Sleepers enable you to make long distance journeys while having a relaxing night's sleep. You arrive early at your destination, saving a day's travel — or the early morning dash to the airport. Five Sleeper routes link London Euston direct with over 40 stations in Scotland including most principal business and holiday locations. Direct Sleeper services also link Southwest England with London. Customers joining at the starting point of the train may occupy cabins well before departure. At terminating stations customers may vacate cabins up to approximately 0800 on trains which arrive at an earlier time.

Full details of all Sleeper services are given in Tables 400–406.

First Great Western ("Night Riviera Sleeper")

Both single and twin berth cabins are available and feature locking doors, comfortable beds with sheets and blankets, air conditioning, bedside lighting, complimentary toiletries, wash basin with a shaver point and a soft hand towel. Room service facilities, a wake up call, a light breakfast and newspaper are all complimentary.

The trains recently underwent a complete refurbishment to maximise customer comfort. Improvements include a refurbishment of seating areas and berths and the introduction of a hot breakfast offer to set our customers up for the day. All single and twin cabins are available to holders of standard class tickets and large reclining seats are provided throughout seated accommodation, again available to holders of standard class tickets. Customers in most single berths benefit from Volo TV, a new and innovative on-train entertainment service. Customers can choose from 40 different programmes including comedy, drama, documentaries, children's programmes and sport.

There are a number of inclusive Advance fares available that combine travel and accommodation on one ticket. These can be purchased until 1800 hours the day before departure. Holders of Anytime, Off-Peak and Super Off-Peak tickets may upgrade to sleeping accommodation on payment of the applicable single or twin berth supplement. The Lounge Car is provided for the use of customers with a berth. Here you can sit back and relax with a complimentary hot drink, tempt yourself with one of our delicious hot snacks or unwind with something stronger from our well stocked bar - all served at seat by our on-board team. Customers in seated accommodation can purchase refreshments and snacks from the Express Cafe, which is situated in the Lounge Car.

Dogs and pets are not normally allowed in Sleeper cabins. There are special arrangements for guide dogs. Animals may be conveyed if properly labelled and muzzled, and in suitable containers, in the guards van.

ScotRail Caledonian Sleepers

First Class customers receive a toiletry pack and will be woken with a light breakfast accompanied by tea or coffee and a complimentary newspaper. Standard Class customers are served a light morning snack with tea or coffee. Breakfast is available for an additional small supplement and can be ordered after boarding. Customer lounges are available at the following locations - London Euston, Inverness, Carlisle (Lakes Court Hotel) and Edinburgh Waverley. At Glasgow Central customers may use the on-train Lounge Car which is available prior to departure. Full details of the Caledonian Sleeper on-train and station facilities can be found inside the Caledonian Sleeper Guide which is available from principal sleeper departure points.

There are a number of berth inclusive fares available that include travel and accommodation at one all inclusive price. First class travel is in single berth cabins while Standard Class is in twin berth cabins.

The Lounge Car offers a pleasant relaxing atmosphere in which to unwind before a night's rest. Customers can choose from a wide selection of food and drinks including sandwiches, baguettes, snacks and a well stocked bar. At busy times, use of the Lounge Car may be restricted to First Class ticket holders.

Accompanying dogs are only permitted in Sleeper Cabins providing the owner(s) has exclusive use of the cabin and pays the appropriate charge. There are special arrangements for guide dogs. Dogs and pets cannot be conveyed in the guards van. A virtual tour is available via the ScotRail website. Visit www.scotrail.co.uk for details.

Please note that as a result of on-going engineering work some sleeper services may be subject to diversion causing an extension in journey times between Scotland and London. For full details telephone National Rail Enquiries on 08457 48 49 50 (calls may be recorded).

Sleeper Reservations

To book rail tickets and reserve Sleepers, simply visit any main rail station or rail appointed travel agent. Alternatively you can book by phone using most credit/debit cards.

First Great Western Telesales (www.firstgreatwestern.co.uk)	08457 00 01 25
ScotRail Telesales (www.scotrail.co.uk)	08457 55 00 33

For further information about rail tickets or services, call National Rail Enquiries on 08457 48 49 50 (calls may be recorded for training purposes).

48Sleeper Services (continued)

ScotRail Sleeper Services – The Caledonian Sleepers

Operated by ScotRail

Table 400 London and Edinburgh

		Mon–Thu	Fri	Sun
Cabins available from		*2300*	*2300*	*2230*
Edinburgh	d	2340	2340	2315
Carstairs	d	0016*	0016*	2347
Carlisle	d	0141	0141	0112*
Watford Junction ...	a	0619	0627	0623
London Euston ...	a	0643	0650	0646
Vacate cabins by		*0800*	*0800*	*0800*

		Mon–Thu	Fri	Sun
Cabins available from		*2300*	*2300*	*2245*
London Euston ...	d	2350	2350	2327
Watford Junction ...	d	0010*	0010*	2347
Carlisle	a	0516	0516	0504*
Carstairs	a	0620	0621	0620
Edinburgh	a	0716	0715	0716
Vacate cabins by		*0800*	*0800*	*0800*

a Arrival time
d Departure time
R Reservations Compulsory
* Following morning
Services in this table do not run on Saturday nights.
For details of overnight seated services, please refer to Table 65

Table 401 London and Glasgow

		Mon–Thu	Fri	Sun
Cabins available from		*2200*	*2200*	*2200*
Glasgow Central ...	d	2340	2340	2315
Motherwell	d	2356	2356	2331
Carstairs	d	0016*	0016*	2347
Carlisle	d	0141	0141	0112*
Watford Junction ...	a	0619	0627	0623
London Euston ...	a	0643	0650	0646
Vacate cabins by		*0800*	*0800*	*0800*

		Mon–Thu	Fri	Sun
Cabins available from		*2300*	*2300*	*2245*
London Euston ...	d	2350	2350	2327
Watford Junction ...	d	0010*	0010*	2347
Carlisle	a	0516	0516	0504*
Carstairs	a	0620	0621	0620
Motherwell	a	0656	0656	0656
Glasgow Central ...	a	0720	0720	0720
Vacate cabins by		*0800*	*0800*	*0800*

a Arrival time
d Departure time
R Reservations Compulsory
* Following morning
Services in this table do not run on Saturday nights.
For details of overnight seated services, please refer to Table 65

Table 402 London and Aberdeen

		Mon–Thu	Fri	Sun
Cabins available from		*2110*	*2110*	*2050*
Aberdeen	dep	2140	2140	2140
Stonehaven	dep	2200	2200	2200
Montrose	dep	2225	2225	2225
Arbroath	dep	2243	2243	2243
Carnoustie	dep	2252	2252	2252
Dundee	dep	2306	2306	2306
Leuchars for St Andrews•	dep	2325	2325	2325
Kirkcaldy•	dep	2353	2353	2353
Inverkeithing•	dep	0012*	0012*	0012*
Preston	arr	0432	0432	0441
Crewe	arr	0534	0534	0537
London Euston ...	arr	0747	0747	0747
Vacate cabins by		*0800*	*0800*	*0800*

		Mon–Thu	Fri	Sun
Cabins available from		*2030*	*2030*	*2000*
London Euston	dep	2115	2115	2055
Watford Junction	dep	2133	2133	2117
Crewe	dep	2354	2354	2339
Preston	dep	0052*	0052*	0030*
Inverkeithing•	arr	0458	0458	0458
Kirkcaldy•	arr	0517	0517	0517
Leuchars for St Andrews•	arr	0546	0546	0546
Dundee	arr	0608	0608	0608
Carnoustie	arr	0622	0622	0622
Arbroath	arr	0631	0631	0631
Montrose	arr	0647	0647	0647
Stonehaven	arr	0713	0713	0713
Aberdeen	arr	0735	0735	0735
Vacate cabins by		*0800*	*0800*	*0800*

a Arrival time
d Departure time
R Reservations Compulsory
* Following morning
• *Customers may depart from London* or Watford later, and vacate cabins later, by travelling on the London Euston to Edinburgh Sleeper; then by local connecting service from Edinburgh
Services in this table do not run on Saturday nights
For details of overnight seated services, please refer to Table 65

Sleeper Services (continued)

ScotRail Sleeper Services – The Caledonian Sleepers

Operated by ScotRail

Table 403 London and Inverness

			Mon–Thu	Fri	Sun
Cabins available from			*2000*	*2000*	*1945*
Inverness	... ...	**dep**	**2046**	**2046**	**2025**
Aviemore	... ...	**dep**	**2128**	**2128**	**2108**
Kingussie	... ...	**dep**	**2142**	**2142**	**2122**
Newtonmore	... ...	**dep**	**2150**	**2150**	**2129**
Dalwhinnie	... ...	**dep**	**2204**	**2204**	**2143**
Blair Atholl	... ...	**dep**	**2230**	**2230**	**2209**
Pitlochry	... ...	**dep**	**2243**	**2243**	**2222**
Dunkeld & Birnam	...	**dep**	**2258**	**2258**	**2237**
Perth	... ...	**dep**	**2321**	**2321**	**2300**
Gleneagles	... ...	**dep**	**2339**	**2339**	**2318**
Dunblane	... ...	**dep**	**2355**	**2355**	**2334**
Stirling•	... ...	**dep**	**0006***	**0006***	**2345**
Falkirk Grahamston		**dep**	**0023**	**0023**	**0002***
Preston	... ...	**arr**	**0432**	**0432**	**0441**
Crewe	... ...	**arr**	**0534**	**0534**	**0537**
London Euston	... ...	**arr**	**0747**	**0747**	**0747**
Vacate cabins by			*0800*	*0800*	*0800*

			Mon–Thu	Fri	Sun
Cabins available from			*2030*	*2030*	*2000*
London Euston	... ...	**dep**	**2115**	**2115**	**2055**
Watford Junction	... ...	**dep**	**2133**	**2133**	**2117**
Crewe	... ...	**dep**	**2354**	**2354**	**2339**
Preston	... ...	**dep**	**0052***	**0052***	**0030***
Stirling•	... ...	**arr**	**0456**	**0456**	**0456**
Dunblane	... ...	**arr**	**0505**	**0505**	**0505**
Gleneagles	... ...	**arr**	**0520**	**0520**	**0520**
Perth•	... ...	**arr**	**0540**	**0540**	**0540**
Dunkeld & Birnam	...	**arr**	**0601**	**0601**	**0601**
Pitlochry	... ...	**arr**	**0617**	**0617**	**0617**
Blair Atholl	... ...	**arr**	**0629**	**0629**	**0629**
Dalwhinnie	... ...	**arr**	**0700**	**0700**	**0700**
Newtonmore	... ...	**arr**	**0712**	**0712**	**0712**
Kingussie	... ...	**arr**	**0718**	**0718**	**0718**
Aviemore	... ...	**arr**	**0742**	**0742**	**0742**
Inverness	... ...	**arr**	**0831**	**0831**	**0831**
Vacate cabins by			*0835*	*0835*	*0835*

a Arrival time
d Departure time
🅁 Reservations Compulsory
* Following morning
• Customers may depart from London or Watford later, and vacate cabins later, by travelling on the London Euston to Edinburgh Sleeper; then by local connecting service from Edinburgh.

Services in this table do not run on Saturday nights.
For details of overnight seated services, please refer to Table 65

Table 404 London and Fort William

			Mon–Thu	Fri	Sun
Cabins available from			*1920*	*1920*	*1830*
Fort William	... ...	**dep**	**1950**	**1950**	**1900**
Spean Bridge	... ...	**dep**	**2010**	**2010**	**1920**
Roy Bridge	... ...	**dep**	**2017x**	**2017x**	**1927x**
Tulloch	... ...	**dep**	**2030**	**2030**	**1940**
Corrour	... ...	**dep**	**2051x**	**2051x**	**2001x**
Rannoch	... ...	**dep**	**2106**	**2106**	**2015**
Bridge of Orchy	... ...	**dep**	**2134**	**2134**	**2047**
Upper Tyndrum	... ...	**dep**	**2152**	**2152**	**2105**
Crianlarich	... ...	**dep**	**2205**	**2205**	**2118**
Ardlui	... ...	**dep**	**2226x**	**2226x**	**2139x**
Arrochar & Tarbet	... ...	**dep**	**2244**	**2244**	**2157**
Garelochhead	... ...	**dep**	**2310**	**2310**	**2223**
Helensburgh Upper	...	**dep**	**2324**	**2324**	**2237**
Dalmuir	... ...	**dep**	**2351**	**2351**	**2304**
Westerton	... ...	**dep**	**2356**	**2356**	**2313**
Preston	... ...	**arr**	**0432**	**0432**	**0441**
Crewe	... ...	**arr**	**0534**	**0534**	**0537**
London Euston	... ...	**arr**	**0747**	**0747**	**0747**
Vacate cabins by			*0800*	*0800*	*0800*

			Mon–Thu	Fri	Sun
Cabins available from			*2030*	*2030*	*2000*
London Euston	... ...	**dep**	**2115**	**2115**	**2055**
Watford Junction	... ...	**dep**	**2133**	**2133**	**2117**
Crewe	... ...	**dep**	**2354**	**2354**	**2339**
Preston	... ...	**dep**	**0052***	**0052***	**0030***
Westerton	... ...	**arr**	**0555**	**0555**	**0555**
Dalmuir	... ...	**arr**	**0603**	**0603**	**0603**
Helensburgh Upper	...	**arr**	**0626**	**0626**	**0626**
Garelochhead	... ...	**arr**	**0641**	**0641**	**0641**
Arrochar & Tarbet	... ...	**arr**	**0707**	**0707**	**0707**
Ardlui	... ...	**arr**	**0722x**	**0722x**	**0722x**
Crianlarich	... ...	**arr**	**0743**	**0743**	**0743**
Upper Tyndrum	... ...	**arr**	**0755**	**0755**	**0755**
Bridge of Orchy	... ...	**arr**	**0813**	**0813**	**0813**
Rannoch	... ...	**arr**	**0841**	**0841**	**0841**
Corrour	... ...	**arr**	**0858x**	**0858x**	**0858x**
Tulloch	... ...	**arr**	**0917**	**0917**	**0917**
Roy Bridge	... ...	**arr**	**0929x**	**0929x**	**0929x**
Spean Bridge	... ...	**arr**	**0936**	**0936**	**0936**
Fort William	... ...	**arr**	**0954**	**0954**	**0954**
Vacate cabins by			*0956*	*0956*	*0956*

a Arrival time
d Departure time
x Stops on request
🅁 Reservations Compulsory
* Following morning

Services in this table do not run on Saturday nights.
For details of overnight seated services, please refer to Tables 65 and 227.

Sleeper Services (continued)

"Night Riviera" Sleeper

Operated by First Great Western

Table 406 London and Penzance

		Mon-Thu Ⓛ	Fri Ⓛ	Sun Ⓛ
Occupy cabins at Paddington:		*2230*	*2230*	*2230*
London Paddington ...	dep	2345	2345	2350
Reading	dep	0037*	0037*	0037*
Exeter St Davids	arr	0305	0257	0405
Newton Abbot	arr	0432	0320	0455
Plymouth	arr	0513	0401	0535
Liskeard	arr	0614	0614	0654
Bodmin Parkway	arr	0628	0628	0721
Lostwithiel	arr	0635	0635	0728
Par	arr	0642	0642	0736
St Austell	arr	0650	0650	0744
Truro	arr	0709	0709	0803
Redruth	arr	0722	0722	0817
Camborne	arr	0730	0730	0825
Hayle	arr	0739	0739	0834
St Erth	arr	0743	0743	0840
Penzance	arr	0800	0800	0859
Vacate cabins at Penzance by		*0800*	*0800*	*0900*

Ⓛ Sleeper Lounge Car

* Following morning

Services in this table do not run on Saturday nights.

For details of seated services on this route, please refer to Table 135.

		Mon-Fri Ⓛ	Sun Ⓛ
Occupy cabins at Penzance:		*2105*	*2045*
Penzance	dep	2145	2115
St Erth	dep	2155	2125
Camborne	dep	2207	2138
Redruth	dep	2214	2145
Truro	dep	2227	2200
St Austell	dep	2245	2218
Par	dep	2253	-
Bodmin Parkway	dep	2305	2235
Liskeard	dep	2320	2250
Plymouth	dep	2351	2320
Totnes	dep	0019*	2348
Newton Abbot ...	dep	0032	0001*
Exeter St Davids ...	dep	0100	0127
Reading	arr	0400	0417
London Paddington ...	arr	0543	0506
Vacate cabins at Paddington by		*0700*	*0700*

Passenger Representation

Passenger Focus

What is Passenger Focus?

Passenger Focus is the official, independent consumer organisation representing the interests of rail users nationally and bus, coach and tram users across England outside London.

With a strong emphasis on evidence-based campaigning and research, we ensure that we know what is happening on the ground. We use our knowledge to influence decisions on behalf of passengers and we work with the industry, other passenger groups and government to secure journey improvements.

What can Passenger Focus do for me?

We are here to put the interests of rail, bus and coach passengers first. We do this by:

Campaigning for improvements

- we gather research and information, like the National Passenger Survey, where 50,000 passengers give us their views about their rail journeys, so we understand the issues that matter to you
- we work with Government and the industry to ensure that the passenger voice is heard when making decisions about the future
- we focus on a number of key issues:
  - fares and tickets
  - quality and level of services
  - investment in the railway

Providing practical advice

- we provide passengers with advice on how to get the best from the network, explain their rights and help them when things go wrong
- we work with other passenger groups to support them in their work

Resolving complaints

- if you make a complaint and you are unhappy with the response we can take up your complaint with the company involved

Making a complaint

If you have a complaint or comment about any aspect of your rail service, either on the train or at the station, please contact the railway company managing director concerned (contact details are shown on the TOC pages of this timetable).

What should you include in your complaint?

Depending on the nature of your complaint you should include:

- the reason for your complaint
- a description of the inconvenience caused
- which train and which day you travelled on, or which station you used and when
- how many people travelled with you
- your ticket(s) as evidence
- an explanation of the action you would like the company to take to rectify the problem

What next?

If you are not satisfied with the company's response you can contact Passenger Focus or, in the London area, London TravelWatch.

How to get in touch:

Telephone:	0300 123 2350
	0800 - 2000 Monday - Friday 0800 - 1600 at weekends
Address:	Passenger Focus FREEPOST (RRRE-ETTC-LEET) PO BOX 4257 MANCHESTER M60 3AR
Fax:	0161 236 1574
Email:	advice@passengerfocus.org.uk
Website:	www.passengerfocus.org.uk

London TravelWatch

London TravelWatch is the independent, statutory watchdog for transport users in and around London, including all services provided by Transport for London, and represents rail passengers in and around London. We investigate suggestions and complaints from passengers who are dissatisfied with responses received from transport operators.

If your journey is within, or began in, London, please contact:

Telephone:	020 7505 9000 (0900-1700 Monday- Friday)
Address:	London TravelWatch 6 Middle Street LONDON EC1A 7JA
E-mail:	info@londontravelwatch.org.uk
Website:	www.londontravelwatch.org.uk

Compensation

Compensation may be payable under each rail company's Passenger's Charter scheme for poor performance (delays or cancellations). For daily tickets and weekly season tickets a fixed rate usually applies depending on the level of delay which you experience. Compensation is made in National Rail vouchers, as a rule, with a minimum of 20% of the fare for the affected journey leg.

Monthly or longer season tickets compensation can differ between companies. On some it is triggered if performance falls below agreed levels and is paid as discount on renewal. Others offer compensation on a journey-by journey basis like for daily tickets. Always check with the train company which issued your ticket or on which you travel for details of the relevant scheme.

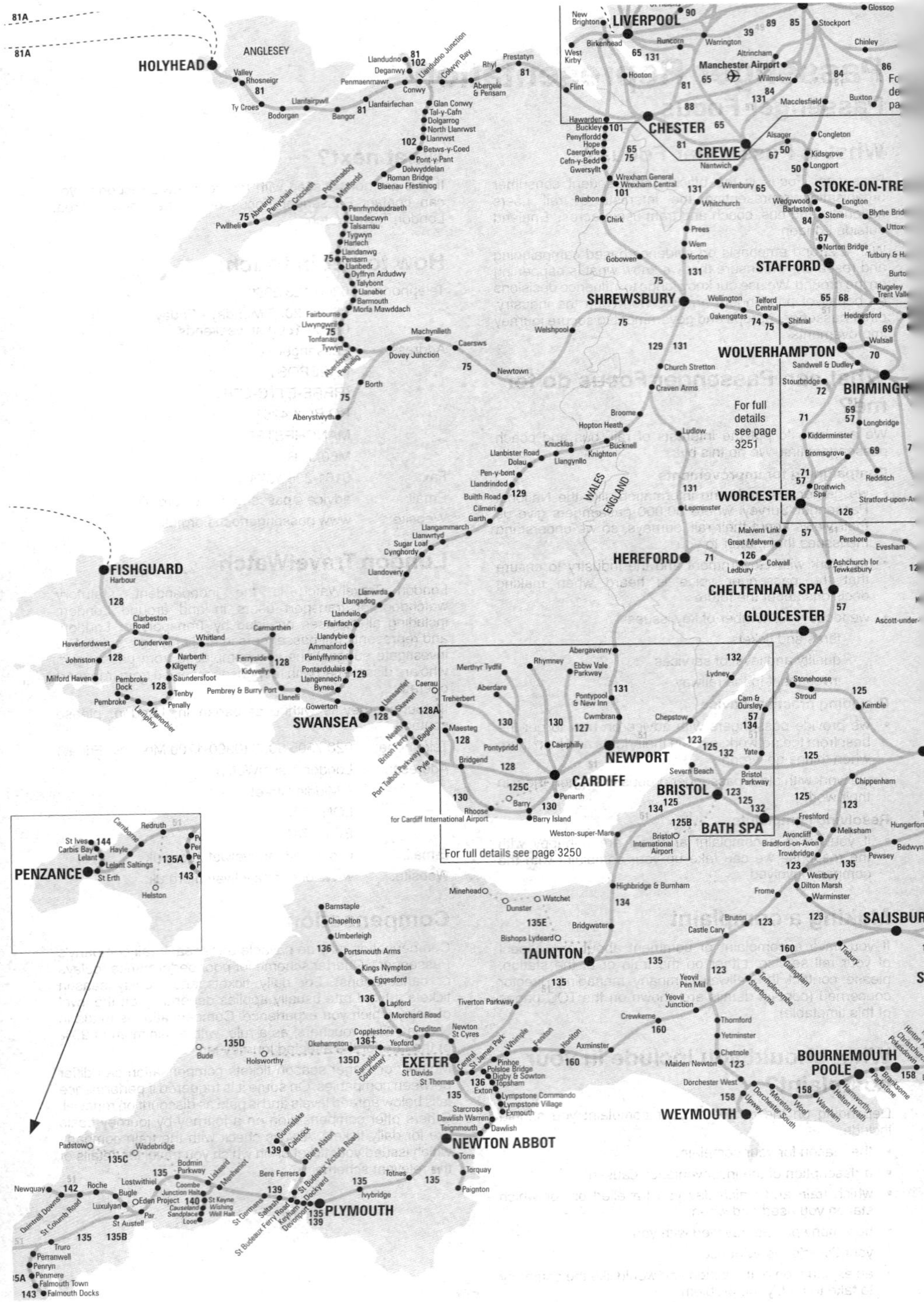
81A
81A
ANGLESEY
HOLYHEAD
Valley
Rhosneigr
Ty Croes
Bodorgan
Llanfairpwll
Bangor
Llanfairfechan
Penmaenmawr
Conwy
Llandudno
Deganwy
Llandudno Junction
Colwyn Bay
Rhyl
Prestatyn
Abergele & Pensarn
Glan Conwy
Tal-y-Cafn
Dolgarrog
North Llanrwst
Llanrwst
Betws-y-Coed
Pont-y-Pant
Dolwyddelan
Roman Bridge
Blaenau Ffestiniog
Pwllheli
Abererch
Penychain
Criccieth
Porthmadog
Minffordd
Penrhyndeudraeth
Llandecwyn
Talsarnau
Tygwyn
Harlech
Llandanwg
Pensarn
Llanbedr
Dyffryn Ardudwy
Talybont
Llanaber
Barmouth
Morfa Mawddach
Fairbourne
Llwyngwril
Tonfanau
Tywyn
Aberdovey
Penhelig
Dovey Junction
Machynlleth
Caersws
Newtown
Borth
Aberystwyth
LIVERPOOL
New Brighton
West Kirby
Birkenhead
Hooton
Flint
Runcorn
Warrington
Altrincham
Manchester Airport
Wilmslow
Macclesfield
Stockport
Glossop
Chinley
Buxton
Hawarden
Buckley
Penyffordd
Hope
Caergwrle
Cefn-y-Bedd
Gwersyllt
CHESTER
CREWE
Alsager
Congleton
Kidsgrove
Longport
Nantwich
Wrenbury
Wrexham General
Wrexham Central
Ruabon
Chirk
Whitchurch
Prees
Wem
Yorton
Gobowen
STOKE-ON-TRENT
Wedgwood
Barlaston
Stone
Longton
Blythe Bridge
Uttoxeter
Norton Bridge
Tutbury & Hatton
STAFFORD
Rugeley Trent Valley
SHREWSBURY
Wellington
Oakengates
Telford Central
Shifnal
Welshpool
Hednesford
Walsall
WOLVERHAMPTON
Sandwell & Dudley
BIRMINGHAM
Stourbridge
Longbridge
Kidderminster
Bromsgrove
Redditch
Droitwich Spa
Stratford-upon-Avon
Church Stretton
Craven Arms
For full details see page 3251
Broome
Hopton Heath
Bucknell
Knighton
Knucklas
Llanbister Road
Dolau
Llangynllo
Pen-y-bont
Llandrindod
Builth Road
Cilmeri
Garth
Llangammarch
Llanwrtyd
Sugar Loaf
Cynghordy
Llandovery
Llanwrda
Llangadog
Llandeilo
Ffairfach
Llandybie
Ammanford
Pantyffynnon
Pontarddulais
Llangennech
Bynea
Ludlow
Leominster
WALES
ENGLAND
WORCESTER
Malvern Link
Great Malvern
Ledbury
Colwall
Pershore
Evesham
HEREFORD
Ashchurch for Tewkesbury
CHELTENHAM SPA
GLOUCESTER
Ascott-under-Wychwood
FISHGUARD
Harbour
Clarbeston Road
Haverfordwest
Clunderwen
Whitland
Carmarthen
Johnston
Milford Haven
Narberth
Kilgetty
Saundersfoot
Pembroke Dock
Pembroke
Lamphey
Manorbier
Penally
Tenby
Ferryside
Kidwelly
Pembrey & Burry Port
Llanelli
Gowerton
SWANSEA
Llansamlet
Skewen
Neath
Briton Ferry
Baglan
Port Talbot Parkway
Pyle
Caerau
Abergavenny
Merthyr Tydfil
Rhymney
Ebbw Vale Parkway
Aberdare
Treherbert
Pontypool & New Inn
Cwmbran
Maesteg
Pontypridd
Caerphilly
Bridgend
NEWPORT
CARDIFF
Penarth
Rhoose
Barry
Barry Island
for Cardiff International Airport
For full details see page 3250
Lydney
Chepstow
Stonehouse
Stroud
Kemble
Cam & Dursley
Yate
Severn Beach
Bristol Parkway
BRISTOL
Chippenham
BATH SPA
Weston-super-Mare
Bristol International Airport
Freshford
Avoncliff
Bradford-on-Avon
Melksham
Trowbridge
Hungerford
Bedwyn
Pewsey
Westbury
Dilton Marsh
Warminster
Frome
SALISBURY
PENZANCE
St Ives
Carbis Bay
Lelant
Lelant Saltings
Hayle
Camborne
Redruth
St Erth
Helston
Minehead
Dunster
Watchet
Bishops Lydeard
Highbridge & Burnham
Bridgwater
TAUNTON
Bruton
Castle Cary
Tisbury
Gillingham
Templecombe
Sherborne
Yeovil Pen Mill
Yeovil Junction
Crewkerne
Thornford
Yetminster
Chetnole
Maiden Newton
Tiverton Parkway
Barnstaple
Chapelton
Umberleigh
Portsmouth Arms
Kings Nympton
Eggesford
Lapford
Morchard Road
Copplestone
Yeoford
Crediton
Newton St Cyres
Okehampton
Sampford Courtenay
Bude
Holsworthy
EXETER
St Davids
Central
St James Park
Whimple
Feniton
Honiton
Axminster
Pinhoe
Polsloe Bridge
Digby & Sowton
Topsham
St Thomas
Exton
Lympstone Commando
Lympstone Village
Exmouth
Starcross
Dawlish Warren
Dawlish
Teignmouth
NEWTON ABBOT
Torre
Torquay
Paignton
Totnes
Ivybridge
Dorchester West
Dorchester South
Upwey
Moreton
Wool
Wareham
Holton Heath
Hamworthy
Parkstone
Branksome
WEYMOUTH
BOURNEMOUTH
POOLE
Pokesdown
Christchurch
Hinton Admiral
New Milton
Lymington
Padstow
Wadebridge
Bodmin Parkway
Newquay
Roche
Lostwithiel
Bugle
Luxulyan
Eden Project
Par
St Austell
Coombe Junction Halt
Causeland
Sandplace
Looe
Liskeard
Menheniot
St Keyne Wishing Well Halt
St Germans
Saltash
St Budeaux Ferry Road
St Budeaux Victoria Road
Keyham
Devonport
Dockyard
Bere Ferrers
Bere Alston
Calstock
Gunnislake
PLYMOUTH
Quintrell Downs
St Columb Road
Truro
Perranwell
Penryn
Penmere
Falmouth Town
Falmouth Docks

Rotherham
Worksop
RETFORD
Gainsborough Central
Gainsborough Lea Road
Market Rasen
Creswell
Whitwell
Chesterfield
Shirebrook
Langwith-Whaley Thorns
Mansfield
Mansfield Woodhouse
Saxilby
LINCOLN
Hykeham
Swinderby
Collingham
Metheringham
Ruskington
Sutton Parkway
Kirkby-in-Ashfield
Newstead
Alfreton
Hucknall
Bulwell
Langley Mill
Belper
Duffield
NOTTINGHAM
Newark Castle
Rolleston
Fiskerton
Bleasby
Thurgarton
Lowdham
Burton Joyce
Carlton
NEWARK
North Gate
Rauceby
Sleaford
Ancaster
Heckington
Swineshead
Hubberts Bridge
Boston
Thorpe Culvert
Wainfleet
Havenhouse
Skegness
Beeston
Attenborough
Spondon
Long Eaton
Netherfield
Radcliffe
Bingham
Aslockton
Elton & Orston
Bottesford
GRANTHAM
Loughborough
Barrow-on-Soar
East Midlands Parkway
Willington
Sileby
Syston
Melton Mowbray
Oakham
Stamford
Spalding
LEICESTER
South Wigston
Narborough
Nuneaton
Hinckley
Market Harborough
Corby
Oundle
PETERBOROUGH
KETTERING
Wellingborough
RUGBY
OVENTRY
Leamington Spa
Wisbech
Whittlesea
March
Manea
Littleport
Ely
Waterbeach
Downham Market
Watlington
KINGS LYNN
Hunstanton
Sandringham
Swaffham
Dereham
Brandon
Lakenheath
Shippea Hill
Thetford
Harling Road
Eccles Road
Attleborough
Spooner Row
Wymondham
NORWICH
Diss
Sheringham
West Runton
Cromer
Roughton Road
Gunton
North Walsham
Worstead
Hoveton & Wroxham
Salhouse
Brundall Gardens
Brundall
Lingwood
Acle
Great Yarmouth
Berney Arms
Haddiscoe
Somerleyton
Oulton Broad North
Oulton Broad South
Lowestoft
Beccles
Brampton
Halesworth
Darsham
Saxmundham
Buckenham
Cantley
Reedham
Long Buckby
NORTHAMPTON
Huntingdon
St. Neots
Bedford
CAMBRIDGE
Newmarket
Bury St Edmunds
Stowmarket
Westerfield
IPSWICH
Felixstowe
Manningtree
HARWICH
Walton-on-the-Naze
Clacton-on-Sea
Sudbury
COLCHESTER
Marks Tey
Braintree
Witham
Chelmsford
STANSTED Airport
Bishops Stortford
Royston
Letchworth
Hitchin
Stevenage
Banbury
Buckingham
MILTON KEYNES
Bletchley
Luton
Bicester
Aylesbury Parkway
Aylesbury
Dunstable
Welwyn Garden City
Hertford
Harlow
OXFORD
Abingdon
Hanborough
Finstock
Combe
Chipping Norton
Moreton-in-Marsh
Princes Risborough
Chinnor
Hemel Hempstead
St Albans
Watford
Amersham
High Wycombe
Didcot Parkway
Henley-on-Thames
Marlow
Maidenhead
Twyford
Slough
Windsor
Heathrow Airport
LONDON
READING
Theale
Aldermaston
Midgham
Thatcham
Newbury
Newbury Racecourse
WINDON
Staines
Ascot
Surbiton
Woking
East Croydon
Oxted
Redhill
Shenfield
Romford
Upminster
Tilbury
Basildon
Wickford
Southminster
SOUTHEND
Shoeburyness
Dartford
Ebbsfleet International
Sheerness-on-Sea
Chatham
Gillingham
Sittingbourne
Faversham
Herne Bay
MARGATE
RAMSGATE
CANTERBURY
Deal
DOVER
FOLKESTONE
ASHFORD
Maidstone
Sevenoaks
Tonbridge
Tunbridge Wells
Basingstoke
Aldershot
Guildford
Dorking
GATWICK Airport
Crawley
East Grinstead
Overton
Whitchurch
Andover
Micheldever
Winchester
Shawford
Eastleigh
Chandlers Ford
Romsey
Mottisfont & Dunbridge
Alton
Haslemere
Horsham
Haywards Heath
Uckfield
Rye
CHANNEL TUNNEL
For full details within this box see other side of sheet
UTHAMPTON
Totton
Southampton Airport Parkway
Ashurst New Forest
Beaulieu Road
Brockenhurst
Sway
Lymington Town
Fareham
Havant
Chichester
WORTHING
Hove
BRIGHTON
Lewes
NEWHAVEN
Seaford
Bexhill
HASTINGS
EASTBOURNE
Littlehampton
Bognor Regis
PORTSMOUTH
See page 3250
Pier Head
Ryde
Esplanade
St Johns Road
Brading
Sandown
Lake
Shanklin
Ventnor
ISLE OF WIGHT
For full details see pages 3246-3247

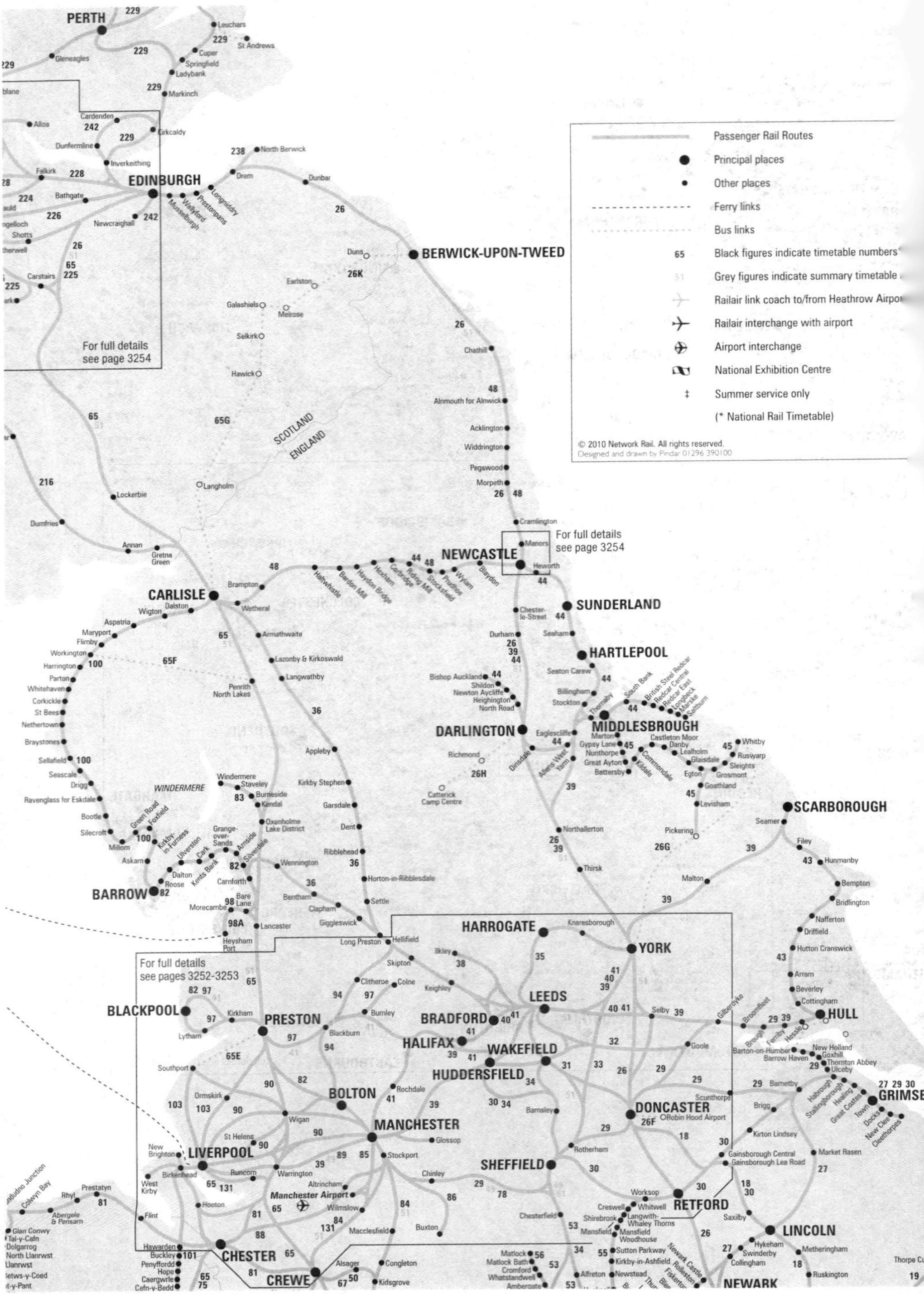
Passenger Rail Routes
Principal places
Other places
Ferry links
Bus links
65 Black figures indicate timetable numbers*
51 Grey figures indicate summary timetable
Railair link coach to/from Heathrow Airport
Railair interchange with airport
Airport interchange
National Exhibition Centre
‡ Summer service only
(* National Rail Timetable)
© 2010 Network Rail. All rights reserved.
Designed and drawn by Pindar 01296 390100
PERTH
Leuchars
St Andrews
Gleneagles
Cupar
Springfield
Ladybank
Markinch
Cardenden
Alloa
Kirkcaldy
Dunfermline
Inverkeithing
North Berwick
Drem
Dunbar
Falkirk
EDINBURGH
Bathgate
Longniddry
Prestonpans
Wallyford
Musselburgh
Newcraighall
Shotts
Carstairs
Duns
BERWICK-UPON-TWEED
Earlston
Galashiels
Melrose
Selkirk
Hawick
For full details see page 3254
SCOTLAND
ENGLAND
Chathill
Alnmouth for Alnwick
Acklington
Widdrington
Pegswood
Morpeth
Langholm
Lockerbie
Dumfries
Annan
Gretna Green
Cramlington
Manors
For full details see page 3254
NEWCASTLE
Heworth
Brampton
Haltwhistle
Bardon Mill
Haydon Bridge
Hexham
Corbridge
Riding Mill
Stocksfield
Prudhoe
Wylam
Blaydon
CARLISLE
Wetheral
Dalston
Wigton
Aspatria
Maryport
Flimby
Workington
Harrington
Parton
Whitehaven
Corkickle
St Bees
Nethertown
Braystones
Sellafield
Seascale
Drigg
Ravenglass for Eskdale
Bootle
Silecroft
Millom
Armathwaite
Lazonby & Kirkoswald
Langwathby
Penrith North Lakes
Appleby
Kirkby Stephen
Garsdale
Dent
Ribblehead
Horton-in-Ribblesdale
Settle
SUNDERLAND
Chester-le-Street
Seaham
Durham
HARTLEPOOL
Seaton Carew
Bishop Auckland
Shildon
Newton Aycliffe
Heighington
North Road
Billingham
Stockton
Thornaby
South Bank
British Steel Redcar
Redcar Central
Redcar East
Longbeck
Marske
Saltburn
MIDDLESBROUGH
DARLINGTON
Eaglescliffe
Marton
Gypsy Lane
Nunthorpe
Great Ayton
Battersby
Castleton Moor
Danby
Lealholm
Glaisdale
Egton
Grosmont
Sleights
Ruswarp
Whitby
Goathland
Levisham
Richmond
Catterick Camp Centre
Dinsdale
Allens West
Yarm
Kildale
Commondale
Northallerton
Thirsk
Pickering
SCARBOROUGH
Seamer
Filey
Hunmanby
Bempton
Bridlington
Malton
Nafferton
Driffield
Hutton Cranswick
Arram
Beverley
Cottingham
WINDERMERE
Windermere
Staveley
Burneside
Kendal
Oxenholme Lake District
Green Road
Foxfield
Kirkby-in-Furness
Askam
Grange-over-Sands
Arnside
Ulverston
Cark
Kents Bank
Silverdale
Dalton
Roose
BARROW
Carnforth
Wennington
Bentham
Clapham
Giggleswick
Bare Lane
Morecambe
Lancaster
Heysham Port
Long Preston
Hellifield
HARROGATE
Knaresborough
YORK
For full details see pages 3252-3253
Ilkley
Skipton
Clitheroe
Colne
Keighley
Burnley
BLACKPOOL
Kirkham
PRESTON
Lytham
Blackburn
LEEDS
BRADFORD
HALIFAX
WAKEFIELD
HUDDERSFIELD
Selby
Gilberdyke
Broomfleet
Brough
Ferriby
Hessle
HULL
Goole
Barton-on-Humber
Barrow Haven
New Holland
Goxhill
Thornton Abbey
Ulceby
Southport
Ormskirk
BOLTON
Rochdale
Wigan
MANCHESTER
Glossop
St Helens
New Brighton
LIVERPOOL
Birkenhead
West Kirby
Runcorn
Warrington
Stockport
Altrincham
Chinley
Manchester Airport
Wilmslow
Macclesfield
Buxton
Hooton
Flint
Barnsley
DONCASTER
Robin Hood Airport
Scunthorpe
Barnetby
Brigg
Habrough
Stallingborough
Healing
Great Coates
Grimsby Town
Grimsby Docks
New Clee
Cleethorpes
GRIMSB
Kirton Lindsey
Market Rasen
Gainsborough Central
Gainsborough Lea Road
Rotherham
SHEFFIELD
Worksop
RETFORD
Saxilby
LINCOLN
Chesterfield
Creswell
Whitwell
Shirebrook
Langwith-Whaley Thorns
Mansfield
Mansfield Woodhouse
Sutton Parkway
Kirkby-in-Ashfield
Newstead
Alfreton
Hykeham
Swinderby
Collingham
Metheringham
Ruskington
Thorpe Culvert
NEWARK
Newark Castle
Rolleston
Fiskerton
Matlock
Matlock Bath
Cromford
Whatstandwell
Ambergate
Llandudno Junction
Colwyn Bay
Rhyl
Prestatyn
Abergele & Pensarn
Glan Conwy
Tal-y-Cafn
Dolgarrog
North Llanrwst
Llanrwst
Betws-y-Coed
Hawarden
Buckley
Penyffordd
Hope
Caergwrle
Cefn-y-Bedd
CHESTER
CREWE
Alsager
Congleton
Kidsgrove

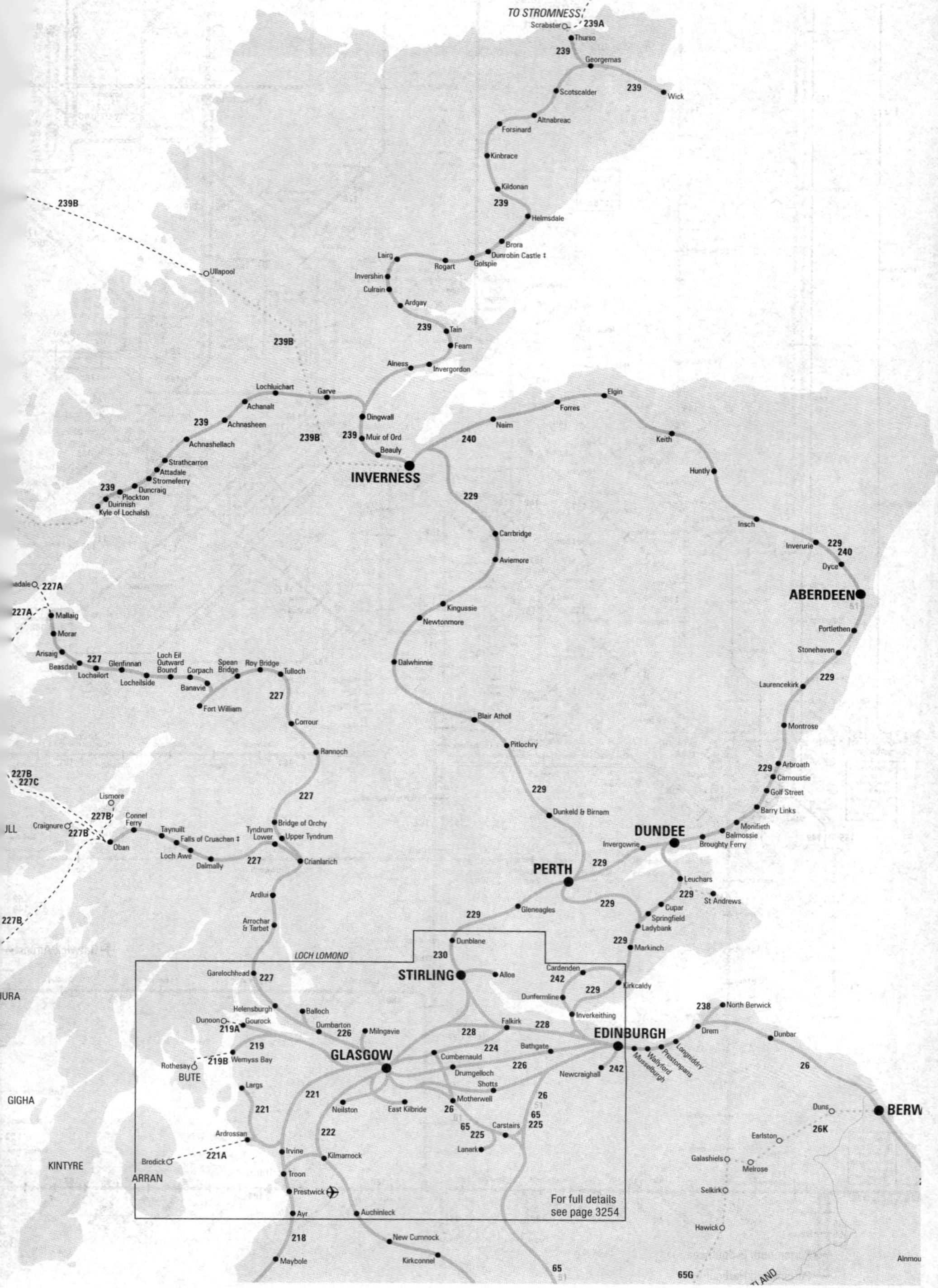
TO STROMNESS
Scrabster
239A
Thurso
239
Georgemas
Wick
Scotscalder
Altnabreac
Forsinard
Kinbrace
Kildonan
Helmsdale
Brora
Dunrobin Castle ‡
Golspie
Rogart
Lairg
Invershin
Culrain
Ardgay
Tain
Fearn
Invergordon
Alness
239B
Ullapool
Lochluichart
Garve
Achanalt
Achnasheen
Achnashellach
Strathcarron
Attadale
Stromeferry
Duncraig
Plockton
Duirinish
Kyle of Lochalsh
Dingwall
Muir of Ord
Beauly
INVERNESS
240
Nairn
Forres
Elgin
Keith
Huntly
Insch
Inverurie
Dyce
ABERDEEN
Portlethen
Stonehaven
Laurencekirk
Montrose
Arbroath
Carnoustie
Golf Street
Barry Links
Monifieth
Balmossie
Broughty Ferry
DUNDEE
Invergowrie
229
Carrbridge
Aviemore
Kingussie
Newtonmore
Dalwhinnie
Blair Atholl
Pitlochry
Dunkeld & Birnam
PERTH
Gleneagles
Leuchars
St Andrews
Cupar
Springfield
Ladybank
Markinch
227A
Mallaig
Morar
Arisaig
Beasdale
Lochailort
227
Glenfinnan
Locheilside
Loch Eil Outward Bound
Corpach
Banavie
Fort William
Spean Bridge
Roy Bridge
Tulloch
Corrour
Rannoch
227B
227C
Lismore
Craignure
Oban
Connel Ferry
Taynuilt
Falls of Cruachan ‡
Loch Awe
Dalmally
Tyndrum Lower
Upper Tyndrum
Bridge of Orchy
Crianlarich
Ardlui
Arrochar & Tarbet
LOCH LOMOND
JURA
Garelochhead
Helensburgh
Balloch
Dunoon
Gourock
219A
219
219B
Wemyss Bay
Rothesay
BUTE
Dumbarton
226
Milngavie
GLASGOW
Dunblane
230
STIRLING
Alloa
Cardenden
242
Dunfermline
Kirkcaldy
Inverkeithing
Falkirk
228
224
Cumbernauld
Bathgate
Drumgelloch
Shotts
EDINBURGH
Newcraighall
Wallyford
Musselburgh
Prestonpans
Longniddry
Drem
238
North Berwick
Dunbar
26
GIGHA
Largs
221
Neilston
East Kilbride
Motherwell
65
225
Carstairs
Lanark
Ardrossan
Irvine
Kilmarnock
222
Brodick
221A
KINTYRE
ARRAN
Troon
Prestwick
Ayr
Auchinleck
218
New Cumnock
Kirkconnel
Maybole
For full details see page 3254
Duns
BERW
26K
Earlston
Galashiels
Melrose
Selkirk
Hawick
65G
Alnmou

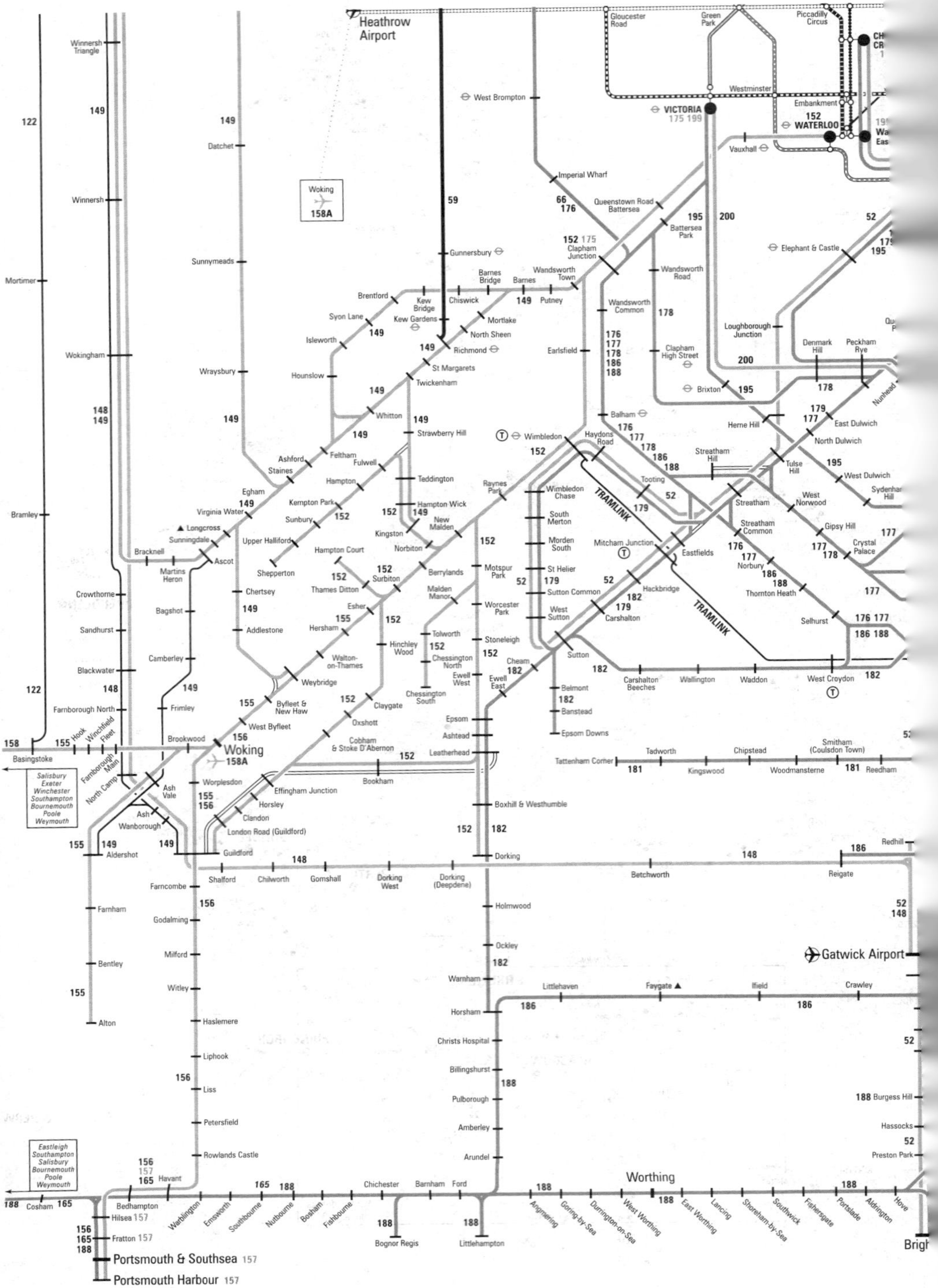

Heathrow Airport
Gloucester Road
Green Park
Piccadilly Circus
Westminster
Embankment
VICTORIA
175 199
152
WATERLOO
Vauxhall
West Brompton
Imperial Wharf
Queenstown Road Battersea
Battersea Park
Clapham Junction
Wandsworth Road
Wandsworth Town
Wandsworth Common
Elephant & Castle
Loughborough Junction
Clapham High Street
Brixton
Denmark Hill
Peckham Rye
Nunhead
Herne Hill
East Dulwich
North Dulwich
Tulse Hill
West Dulwich
Sydenham Hill
West Norwood
Gipsy Hill
Crystal Palace
Streatham Hill
Streatham
Streatham Common
Norbury
Thornton Heath
Selhurst
West Croydon
Balham
Earlsfield
Tooting
Haydons Road
Wimbledon
Wimbledon Chase
South Merton
Morden South
St Helier
Sutton Common
West Sutton
Sutton
Mitcham Junction
Eastfields
Hackbridge
Carshalton
Carshalton Beeches
Wallington
Waddon
TRAMLINK
Belmont
Banstead
Epsom Downs
Tattenham Corner
Tadworth
Kingswood
Chipstead
Woodmansterne
Smitham (Coulsdon Town)
Reedham
Woking
158A
Gunnersbury
Brentford
Kew Bridge
Chiswick
Barnes Bridge
Barnes
Putney
Kew Gardens
Mortlake
North Sheen
Richmond
Syon Lane
Isleworth
Hounslow
St Margarets
Twickenham
Whitton
Strawberry Hill
Feltham
Ashford
Staines
Fulwell
Hampton
Teddington
Hampton Wick
Kempton Park
Sunbury
Upper Halliford
Shepperton
Kingston
Norbiton
New Malden
Raynes Park
Motspur Park
Worcester Park
Stoneleigh
Ewell West
Ewell East
Cheam
Hampton Court
Thames Ditton
Surbiton
Berrylands
Malden Manor
Tolworth
Chessington North
Chessington South
Hinchley Wood
Esher
Hersham
Walton-on-Thames
Weybridge
Byfleet & New Haw
West Byfleet
Claygate
Oxshott
Cobham & Stoke D'Abernon
Epsom
Ashtead
Leatherhead
Bookham
Effingham Junction
Horsley
Clandon
London Road (Guildford)
Guildford
Boxhill & Westhumble
Dorking
Egham
Virginia Water
Longcross
Sunningdale
Ascot
Bracknell
Martins Heron
Bagshot
Camberley
Frimley
Chertsey
Addlestone
Datchet
Sunnymeads
Wraysbury
Winnersh Triangle
Winnersh
Wokingham
Crowthorne
Sandhurst
Blackwater
Farnborough North
Mortimer
Bramley
Basingstoke
Hook
Winchfield
Fleet
Farnborough (Main)
North Camp
Ash Vale
Ash
Wanborough
Aldershot
Brookwood
Worplesdon
Salisbury
Exeter
Winchester
Southampton
Bournemouth
Poole
Weymouth
Shalford
Chilworth
Gomshall
Dorking West
Dorking (Deepdene)
Betchworth
Reigate
Redhill
Farncombe
Godalming
Milford
Witley
Haslemere
Liphook
Liss
Petersfield
Rowlands Castle
Farnham
Bentley
Alton
Holmwood
Ockley
Warnham
Horsham
Littlehaven
Faygate
Ifield
Crawley
Gatwick Airport
Christs Hospital
Billingshurst
Pulborough
Amberley
Arundel
Burgess Hill
Hassocks
Preston Park
Eastleigh
Southampton
Salisbury
Bournemouth
Poole
Weymouth
Cosham
Bedhampton
Havant
Hilsea
Fratton
Portsmouth & Southsea
Portsmouth Harbour
Warblington
Emsworth
Southbourne
Nutbourne
Bosham
Fishbourne
Chichester
Barnham
Ford
Bognor Regis
Littlehampton
Angmering
Goring-by-Sea
Durrington-on-Sea
West Worthing
Worthing
East Worthing
Lancing
Shoreham-by-Sea
Southwick
Fishersgate
Portslade
Aldrington
Hove

Continued on pages 3248-3249

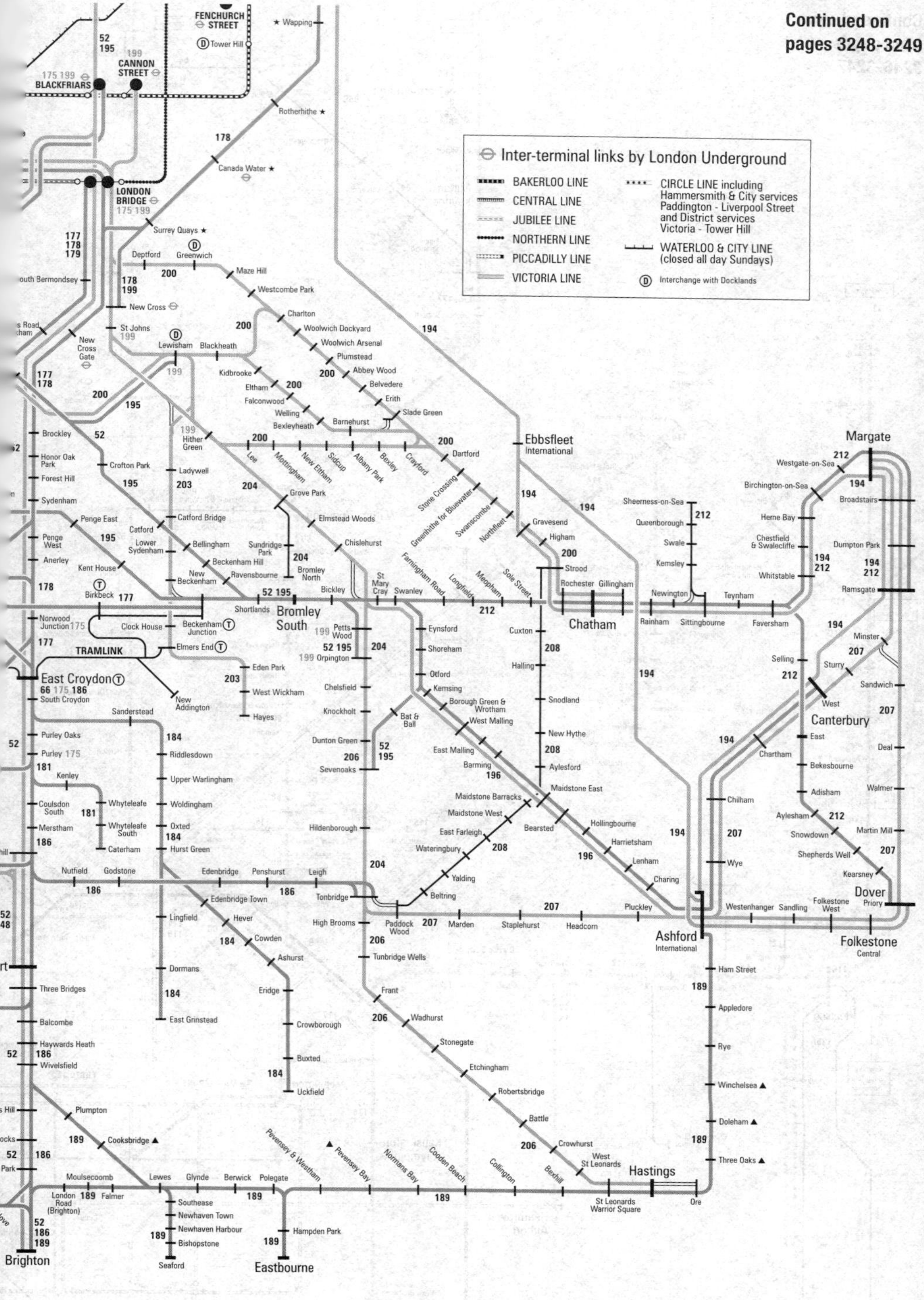

Continued from pages 3246-3247

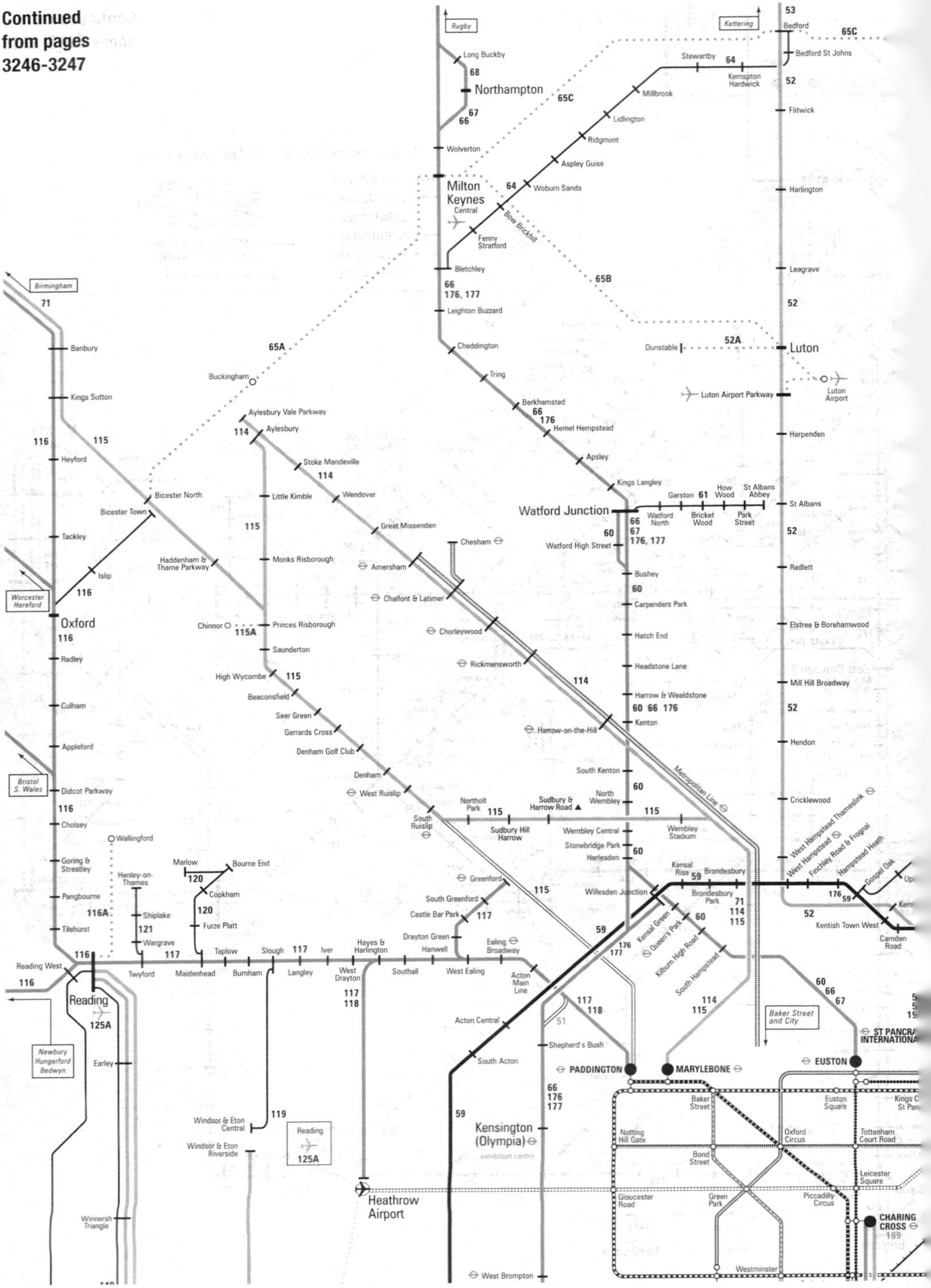

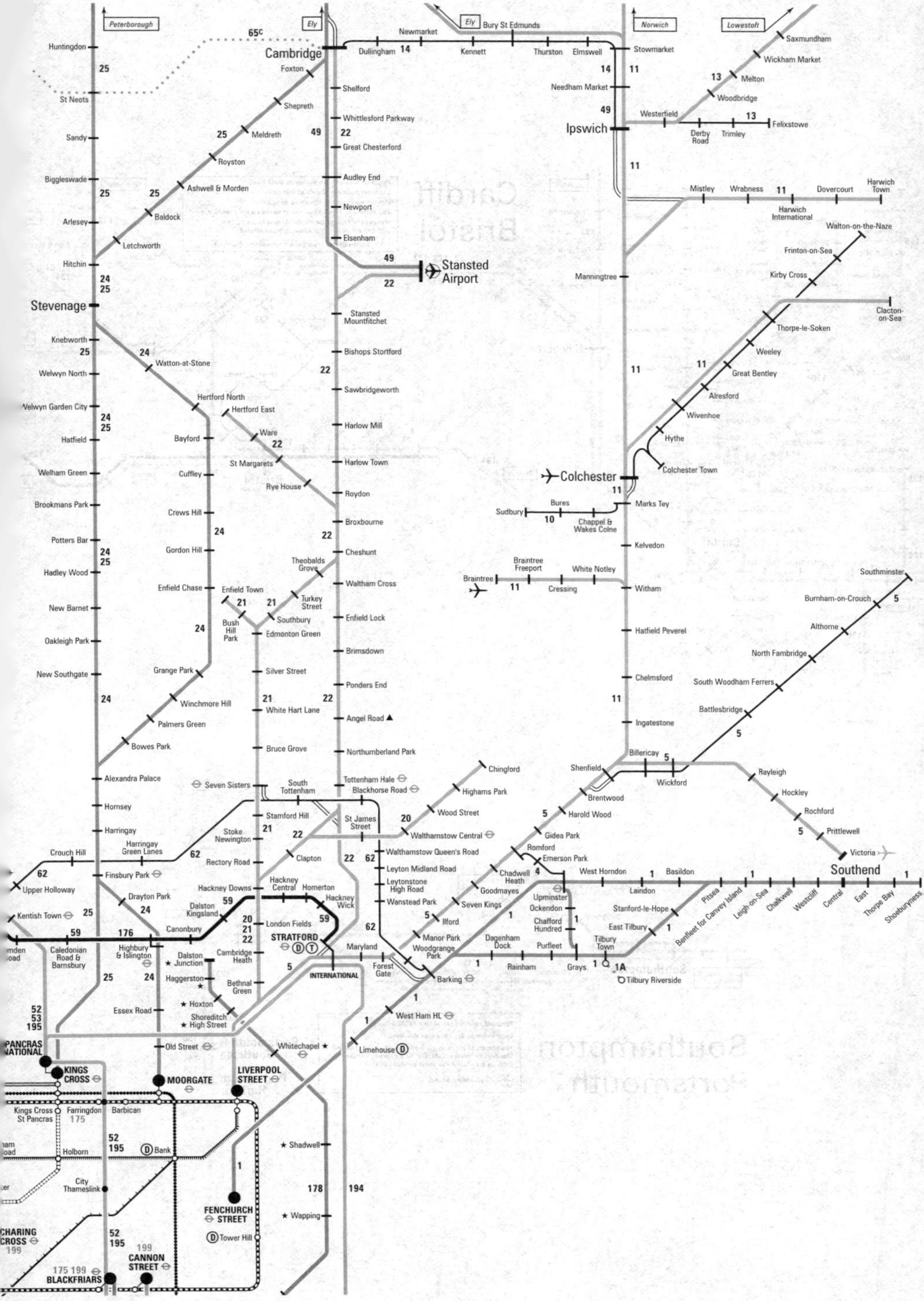

Peterborough
Ely
Ely
Bury St Edmunds
Norwich
Lowestoft
65C
Huntingdon
St Neots
Sandy
Biggleswade
Arlesey
Hitchin
Stevenage
Knebworth
Welwyn North
Welwyn Garden City
Hatfield
Welham Green
Brookmans Park
Potters Bar
Hadley Wood
New Barnet
Oakleigh Park
New Southgate
Alexandra Palace
Hornsey
Harringay
Crouch Hill
Harringay Green Lanes
Finsbury Park
Upper Holloway
Drayton Park
Kentish Town
Caledonian Road & Barnsbury
Highbury & Islington
Canonbury
Dalston Kingsland
Dalston Junction
Haggerston
Hoxton
Shoreditch High Street
Essex Road
Old Street
St Pancras International
Kings Cross
Moorgate
Liverpool Street
Kings Cross St Pancras
Farringdon
Barbican
Holborn
Bank
City Thameslink
Charing Cross
Blackfriars
Cannon Street
Fenchurch Street
Tower Hill
Shadwell
Wapping
Whitechapel
Limehouse
Cambridge
Foxton
Shepreth
Meldreth
Royston
Ashwell & Morden
Baldock
Letchworth
Watton-at-Stone
Hertford North
Hertford East
Bayford
Ware
St Margarets
Rye House
Cuffley
Crews Hill
Gordon Hill
Enfield Chase
Enfield Town
Bush Hill Park
Grange Park
Winchmore Hill
Palmers Green
Bowes Park
Seven Sisters
Stamford Hill
Stoke Newington
Rectory Road
Hackney Downs
London Fields
Cambridge Heath
Bethnal Green
Theobalds Grove
Turkey Street
Southbury
Edmonton Green
Silver Street
White Hart Lane
Bruce Grove
South Tottenham
Clapton
Hackney Central
Homerton
Hackney Wick
Stratford
International
Maryland
Forest Gate
Shelford
Whittlesford Parkway
Great Chesterford
Audley End
Newport
Elsenham
Stansted Airport
Stansted Mountfitchet
Bishops Stortford
Sawbridgeworth
Harlow Mill
Harlow Town
Roydon
Broxbourne
Cheshunt
Waltham Cross
Enfield Lock
Brimsdown
Ponders End
Angel Road
Northumberland Park
Tottenham Hale
Blackhorse Road
St James Street
Walthamstow Central
Walthamstow Queen's Road
Leyton Midland Road
Leytonstone High Road
Wanstead Park
Woodgrange Park
Barking
West Ham HL
Chingford
Highams Park
Wood Street
Newmarket
Dullingham
Kennett
Thurston
Elmswell
Stowmarket
Needham Market
Ipswich
Westerfield
Derby Road
Trimley
Felixstowe
Woodbridge
Melton
Wickham Market
Saxmundham
Mistley
Wrabness
Harwich International
Dovercourt
Harwich Town
Manningtree
Walton-on-the-Naze
Frinton-on-Sea
Kirby Cross
Clacton-on-Sea
Thorpe-le-Soken
Weeley
Great Bentley
Alresford
Wivenhoe
Hythe
Colchester Town
Colchester
Marks Tey
Sudbury
Bures
Chappel & Wakes Colne
Kelvedon
Braintree
Braintree Freeport
Cressing
White Notley
Witham
Hatfield Peverel
Chelmsford
Ingatestone
Shenfield
Billericay
Wickford
Rayleigh
Hockley
Rochford
Prittlewell
Victoria
Southend
Southminster
Burnham-on-Crouch
Althorne
North Fambridge
South Woodham Ferrers
Battlesbridge
Brentwood
Harold Wood
Gidea Park
Romford
Emerson Park
Chadwell Heath
Goodmayes
Seven Kings
Ilford
Manor Park
Upminster
West Horndon
Laindon
Basildon
Pitsea
Benfleet for Canvey Island
Leigh-on-Sea
Chalkwell
Westcliff
Central
East
Thorpe Bay
Shoeburyness
Ockendon
Chafford Hundred
Stanford-le-Hope
East Tilbury
Tilbury Town
Tilbury Riverside
Dagenham Dock
Rainham
Purfleet
Grays

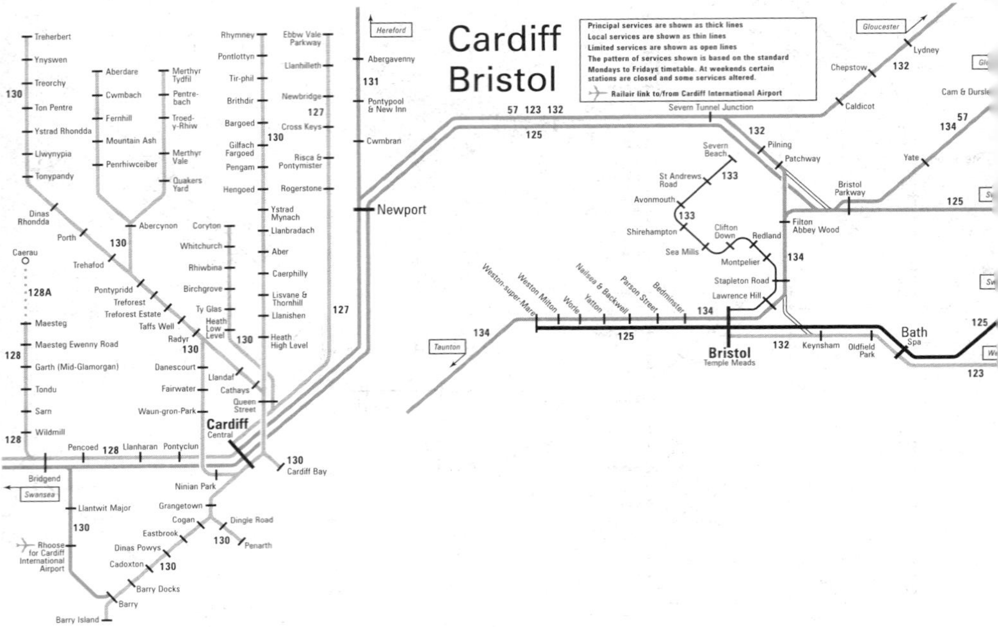
Cardiff
Bristol
Principal services are shown as thick lines
Local services are shown as thin lines
Limited services are shown as open lines
The pattern of services shown is based on the standard Mondays to Fridays timetable. At weekends certain stations are closed and some services altered.
Railair link to/from Cardiff International Airport
Treherbert
Ynyswen
Treorchy
Ton Pentre
Ystrad Rhondda
Llwynypia
Tonypandy
130
Dinas Rhondda
Porth
Trehafod
Aberdare
Cwmbach
Fernhill
Mountain Ash
Penrhiwceiber
Merthyr Tydfil
Pentre-bach
Troed-y-Rhiw
Merthyr Vale
Quakers Yard
Abercynon
130
Pontypridd
Treforest
Treforest Estate
Taffs Well
Radyr
130
Caerau
128A
Maesteg
Maesteg Ewenny Road
Garth (Mid-Glamorgan)
Tondu
Sarn
Wildmill
128
Pencoed
Llanharan
Pontyclun
Bridgend
Swansea
Llantwit Major
130
Rhoose for Cardiff International Airport
Rhymney
Pontlottyn
Tir-phil
Brithdir
Bargoed
Gilfach Fargoed
Pengam
Hengoed
130
Ystrad Mynach
Llanbradach
Aber
Caerphilly
Lisvane & Thornhill
Llanishen
Heath High Level
Coryton
Whitchurch
Rhiwbina
Birchgrove
Ty Glas
Heath Low Level
130
Danescourt
Fairwater
Waun-gron-Park
Llandaf
Cathays
Queen Street
Cardiff
Central
130
Cardiff Bay
Ninian Park
Grangetown
Dingle Road
Penarth
Cogan
Eastbrook
Dinas Powys
Cadoxton
Barry Docks
Barry
Barry Island
Ebbw Vale Parkway
Llanhilleth
Newbridge
127
Cross Keys
Risca & Pontymister
Rogerstone
Hereford
Abergavenny
131
Pontypool & New Inn
Cwmbran
Newport
57 123 132
125
Severn Tunnel Junction
Gloucester
Lydney
Chepstow
132
Caldicot
Cam & Dursley
57
134
Yate
Bristol Parkway
125
Pilning
Patchway
Severn Beach
St Andrews Road
133
Avonmouth
Shirehampton
Sea Mills
Clifton Down
Redland
Montpelier
Filton Abbey Wood
134
Stapleton Road
Lawrence Hill
Weston-super-Mare
Weston Milton
Worle
Yatton
Nailsea & Backwell
Parson Street
Bedminster
134
125
Taunton
Bristol
Temple Meads
132
Keynsham
Oldfield Park
Bath
Spa
125
123

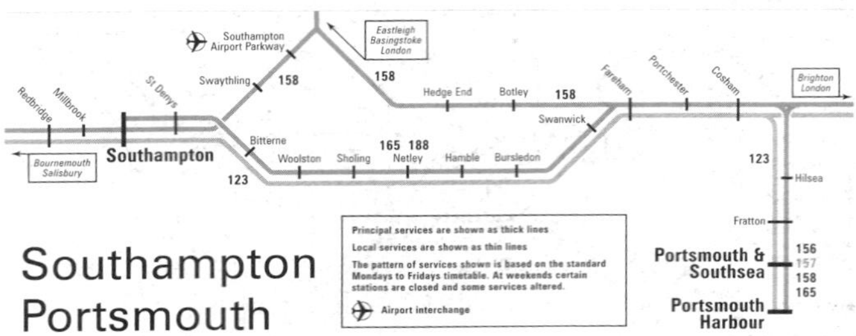
Southampton Airport Parkway
Eastleigh
Basingstoke
London
Swaythling
158
Redbridge
Millbrook
St Denys
Southampton
Bournemouth
Salisbury
Bitterne
Woolston
Sholing
165 188
Netley
Hamble
Bursledon
123
Hedge End
Botley
158
Swanwick
Fareham
Portchester
Cosham
Brighton
London
123
Hilsea
Fratton
Portsmouth & Southsea
156
157
158
165
Portsmouth Harbour
Principal services are shown as thick lines
Local services are shown as thin lines
The pattern of services shown is based on the standard Mondays to Fridays timetable. At weekends certain stations are closed and some services altered.
Airport interchange
Southampton
Portsmouth

Birmingham
West Midlands
Principal services are shown as thick lines
Local services are shown as thin lines
Limited services are shown as open lines
The pattern of services shown is based on the standard Mondays to Fridays timetable. At weekends certain stations are closed and some services altered.
Railair link to/from Birmingham Airport
Tram/Metro Interchange
Shrewsbury
Stafford
Penkridge
68
74
75
Albrighton
Codsall
Bilbrook
Wolverhampton
Coseley
Tipton
66
68
75
Dudley Port
Sandwell & Dudley
Smethwick Galton Bridge
METRO
70
The Hawthorns
Jewellery Quarter
Snow Hill
Smethwick Rolfe Street
New Street
Rugeley Town
Hednesford
Cannock
Landywood
Bloxwich North
Bloxwich
Walsall
Bescot Stadium
Tame Bridge
Hamstead
Perry Barr
Witton
Aston
Duddeston
Lichfield Trent Valley
Lichfield City
Shenstone
69
Blake Street
Butlers Lane
Four Oaks
Sutton Coldfield
Wylde Green
Chester Road
Erdington
Gravelly Hill
67
57
Derby
Tamworth
Wilnecote
Polesworth
Atherstone
49 57
Water Orton
Coleshill Parkway
Nuneaton
Leicester
Adderley Park
Stechford
Lea Hall
Marston Green
Birmingham International for National Exhibition Centre
66 68
Hampton-in-Arden
Berkswell
Tile Hill
Canley
Coventry
Bedworth
Rugby
Birmingham
Small Heath
Tyseley
Acocks Green
Olton
Solihull
Widney Manor
115
Dorridge
Lapworth
Hatton
Warwick Parkway
Warwick
Leamington Spa
116
Banbury
Claverdon
Bearley
Wilmcote
Stratford-upon-Avon
Spring Road
Hall Green
Yardley Wood
Shirley
Whitlocks End
Wythall
Earlswood
The Lakes
Wood End
Danzey
Henley-in-Arden
Wootton Wawen
Bordesley
Moor Street
Five Ways
University
Selly Oak
Bournville
Kings Norton
Northfield
Longbridge
Barnt Green
Langley Green
Rowley Regis
Old Hill
Cradley Heath
Lye
Stourbridge Town
Stourbridge Junction
72
Hagley
Blakedown
Kidderminster
Hartlebury
Droitwich Spa
Hereford
Bromsgrove
Alvechurch
Redditch
Shrub Hill
Foregate Street
Worcester
Great Malvern
Cheltenham Spa
Evesham
126
57
71

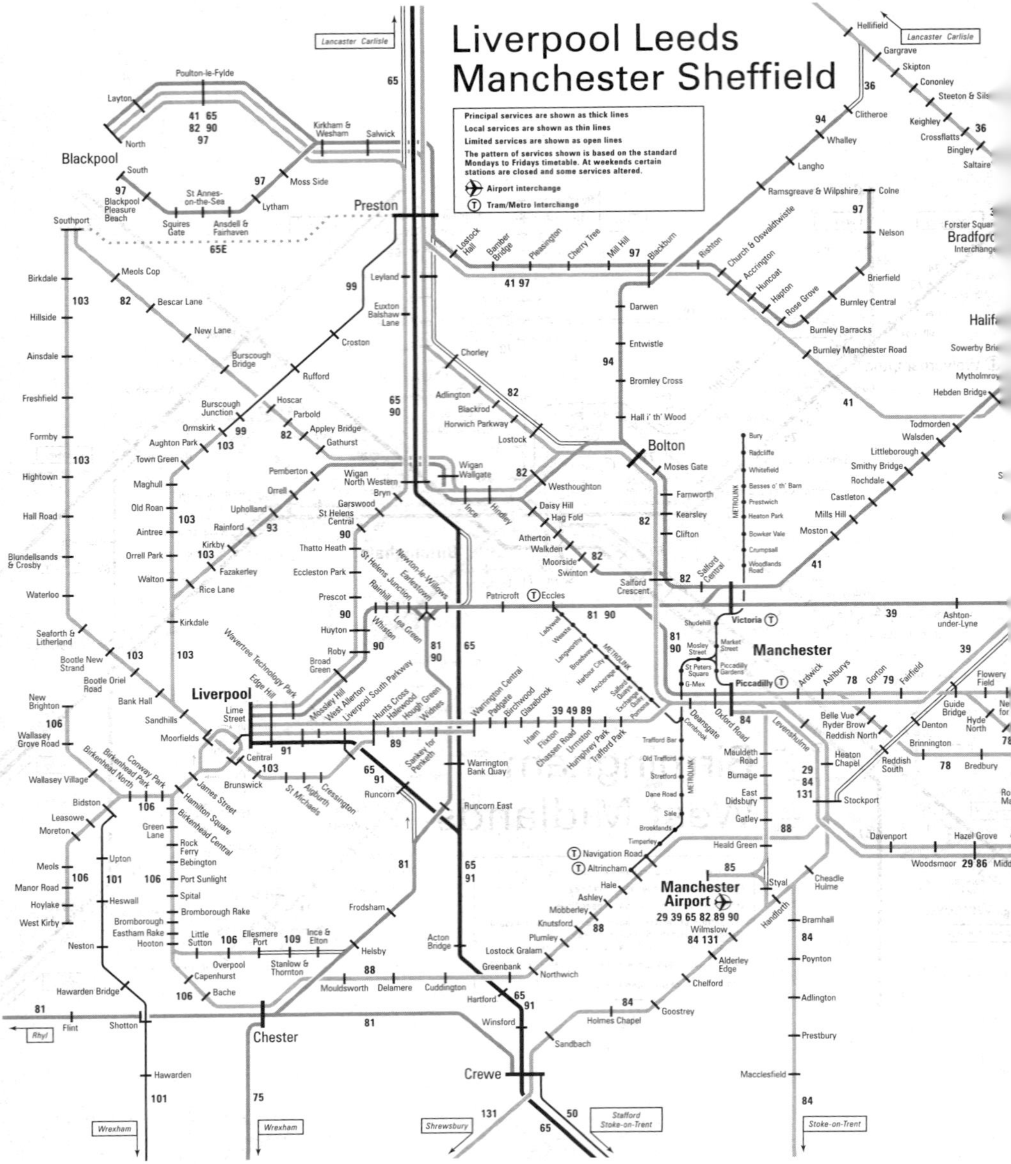
Liverpool Leeds
Manchester Sheffield
Principal services are shown as thick lines
Local services are shown as thin lines
Limited services are shown as open lines
The pattern of services shown is based on the standard Mondays to Fridays timetable. At weekends certain stations are closed and some services altered.
Airport interchange
Tram/Metro interchange
Lancaster Carlisle
Blackpool
Layton
North
South
Poulton-le-Fylde
Kirkham & Wesham
Salwick
Moss Side
Lytham
St Annes-on-the-Sea
Squires Gate
Ansdell & Fairhaven
Blackpool Pleasure Beach
Southport
Preston
Meols Cop
Bescar Lane
New Lane
Burscough Bridge
Birkdale
Hillside
Ainsdale
Freshfield
Formby
Hightown
Hall Road
Blundellsands & Crosby
Waterloo
Seaforth & Litherland
Bootle New Strand
Bootle Oriel Road
Bank Hall
Sandhills
Moorfields
Croston
Rufford
Burscough Junction
Ormskirk
Aughton Park
Town Green
Maghull
Old Roan
Aintree
Orrell Park
Walton
Rice Lane
Kirkdale
Fazakerley
Kirkby
Rainford
Upholland
Orrell
Pemberton
Hoscar
Parbold
Appley Bridge
Gathurst
Leyland
Euxton Balshaw Lane
Chorley
Adlington
Blackrod
Horwich Parkway
Lostock
Bolton
Wigan North Western
Wigan Wallgate
Bryn
Garswood
St Helens Central
Thatto Heath
Eccleston Park
Prescot
Huyton
Roby
Broad Green
Liverpool
Lime Street
Edge Hill
Wavertree Technology Park
Mossley Hill
West Allerton
Liverpool South Parkway
Hunts Cross
Halewood
Hough Green
Widnes
Sankey for Penketh
Warrington Central
Padgate
Birchwood
Glazebrook
Irlam
Flixton
Chassen Road
Urmston
Humphrey Park
Trafford Park
Warrington Bank Quay
Runcorn
Runcorn East
Frodsham
Helsby
Ince & Elton
Ellesmere Port
Stanlow & Thornton
Little Sutton
Overpool
Capenhurst
Bache
Hooton
Eastham Rake
Bromborough
Bromborough Rake
Spital
Port Sunlight
Bebington
Rock Ferry
Green Lane
Birkenhead Central
Hamilton Square
James Street
Central
Brunswick
St Michaels
Aigburth
Cressington
Conway Park
Birkenhead Park
Birkenhead North
Wallasey Village
Wallasey Grove Road
New Brighton
Bidston
Leasowe
Moreton
Meols
Manor Road
Hoylake
West Kirby
Upton
Heswall
Neston
Hawarden Bridge
Shotton
Flint
Rhyl
Hawarden
Wrexham
Chester
Mouldsworth
Delamere
Cuddington
Greenbank
Northwich
Lostock Gralam
Acton Bridge
Hartford
Winsford
Crewe
Shrewsbury
Stafford Stoke-on-Trent
Sandbach
Holmes Chapel
Goostrey
Chelford
Alderley Edge
Wilmslow
Handforth
Manchester Airport
Styal
Heald Green
Gatley
East Didsbury
Burnage
Mauldeth Road
Levenshulme
Heaton Chapel
Stockport
Davenport
Woodsmoor
Hazel Grove
Middlewood
Cheadle Hulme
Bramhall
Poynton
Adlington
Prestbury
Macclesfield
Stoke-on-Trent
Knutsford
Mobberley
Ashley
Hale
Altrincham
Navigation Road
Plumley
Timperley
Brooklands
Sale
Dane Road
Stretford
Old Trafford
Trafford Bar
Cornbrook
Deansgate
Oxford Road
G-Mex
St Peters Square
Mosley Street
Market Street
Piccadilly Gardens
Piccadilly
Shudehill
Victoria
Manchester
Salford Crescent
Salford Central
Patricroft
Eccles
Ladywell
Weaste
Langworthy
Broadway
Harbour City
Anchorage
Salford Quays
Exchange Quay
Pomona
METROLINK
Newton-le-Willows
Earlestown
St Helens Junction
Rainhill
Whiston
Lea Green
Ince
Hindley
Westhoughton
Daisy Hill
Hag Fold
Atherton
Walkden
Moorside
Swinton
Moses Gate
Farnworth
Kearsley
Clifton
Bury
Radcliffe
Whitefield
Besses o' th' Barn
Prestwich
Heaton Park
Bowker Vale
Crumpsall
Woodlands Road
Hall i' th' Wood
Bromley Cross
Entwistle
Darwen
Blackburn
Lostock Hall
Bamber Bridge
Pleasington
Cherry Tree
Mill Hill
Rishton
Church & Oswaldtwistle
Accrington
Huncoat
Hapton
Rose Grove
Burnley Barracks
Burnley Manchester Road
Burnley Central
Brierfield
Nelson
Colne
Ramsgreave & Wilpshire
Langho
Whalley
Clitheroe
Hellifield
Gargrave
Skipton
Cononley
Steeton & Sils
Keighley
Crossflatts
Bingley
Saltaire
Forster Squar
Bradforc
Interchange
Halif
Sowerby Bri
Mytholmroy
Hebden Bridge
Todmorden
Walsden
Littleborough
Smithy Bridge
Rochdale
Castleton
Mills Hill
Moston
Ashton-under-Lyne
Ardwick
Ashburys
Gorton
Fairfield
Flowery Field
Guide Bridge
Hyde North
Belle Vue
Ryder Brow
Reddish North
Denton
Brinnington
Reddish South
Bredbury

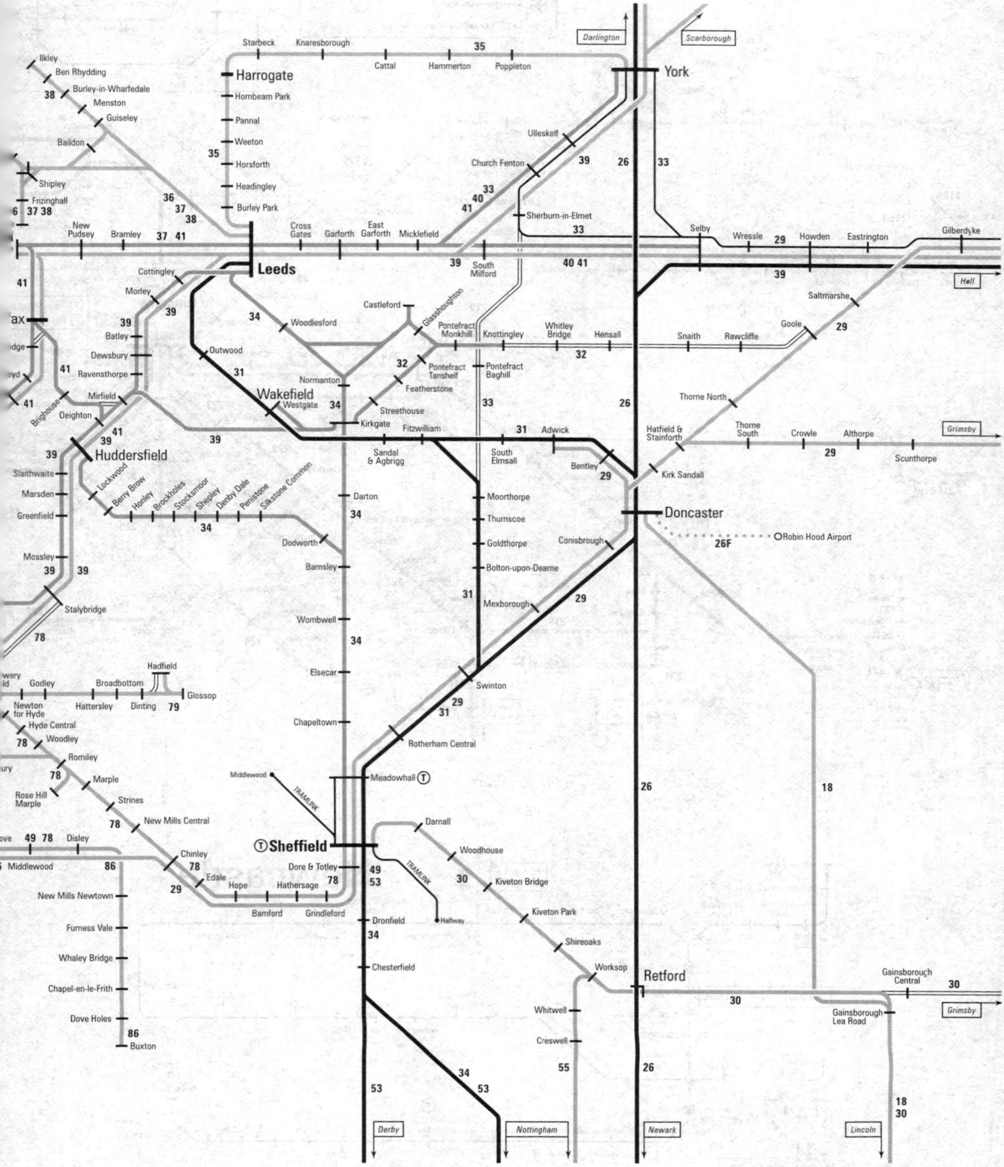
Darlington
Scarborough
York
Starbeck
Knaresborough
35
Cattal
Hammerton
Poppleton
Harrogate
Hornbeam Park
Pannal
Weeton
Horsforth
Headingley
Burley Park
Ilkley
Ben Rhydding
Burley-in-Wharfedale
Menston
Guiseley
Baildon
Shipley
Frizinghall
New Pudsey
Bramley
Cross Gates
Garforth
East Garforth
Micklefield
Leeds
Ulleskelf
Church Fenton
Sherburn-in-Elmet
Selby
Wressle
Howden
Eastrington
Gilberdyke
South Milford
Hull
Saltmarshe
Goole
Cottingley
Morley
Batley
Dewsbury
Ravensthorpe
Mirfield
Deighton
Brighouse
Huddersfield
Woodlesford
Castleford
Glasshoughton
Pontefract Monkhill
Knottingley
Whitley Bridge
Hensall
Snaith
Rawcliffe
Outwood
Normanton
Pontefract Tanshelf
Pontefract Baghill
Featherstone
Wakefield Westgate
Streethouse
Kirkgate
Fitzwilliam
Sandal & Agbrigg
South Elmsall
Adwick
Bentley
Thorne North
Hatfield & Stainforth
Thorne South
Crowle
Althorpe
Grimsby
Scunthorpe
Kirk Sandall
Doncaster
Robin Hood Airport
26F
Slaithwaite
Marsden
Greenfield
Mossley
Stalybridge
Lockwood
Berry Brow
Honley
Brockholes
Stocksmoor
Shepley
Denby Dale
Penistone
Silkstone Common
Darton
Dodworth
Barnsley
Moorthorpe
Thurnscoe
Goldthorpe
Bolton-upon-Dearne
Conisbrough
Mexborough
Wombwell
Elsecar
Swinton
Hadfield
Godley
Broadbottom
Glossop
Newton for Hyde
Hattersley
Dinting
Hyde Central
Woodley
Romiley
Marple
Rose Hill Marple
Strines
New Mills Central
Disley
Chapeltown
Rotherham Central
Meadowhall
Middlewood
TRAMLINK
Sheffield
Darnall
Woodhouse
Kiveton Bridge
Kiveton Park
Shireoaks
Worksop
Retford
Gainsborough Central
Gainsborough Lea Road
Chinley
Edale
Hope
Hathersage
Bamford
Grindleford
Dore & Totley
Dronfield
Chesterfield
Halfway
Middlewood
New Mills Newtown
Furness Vale
Whaley Bridge
Chapel-en-le-Frith
Dove Holes
Buxton
Whitwell
Creswell
Derby
Nottingham
Newark
Lincoln

Glasgow Edinburgh

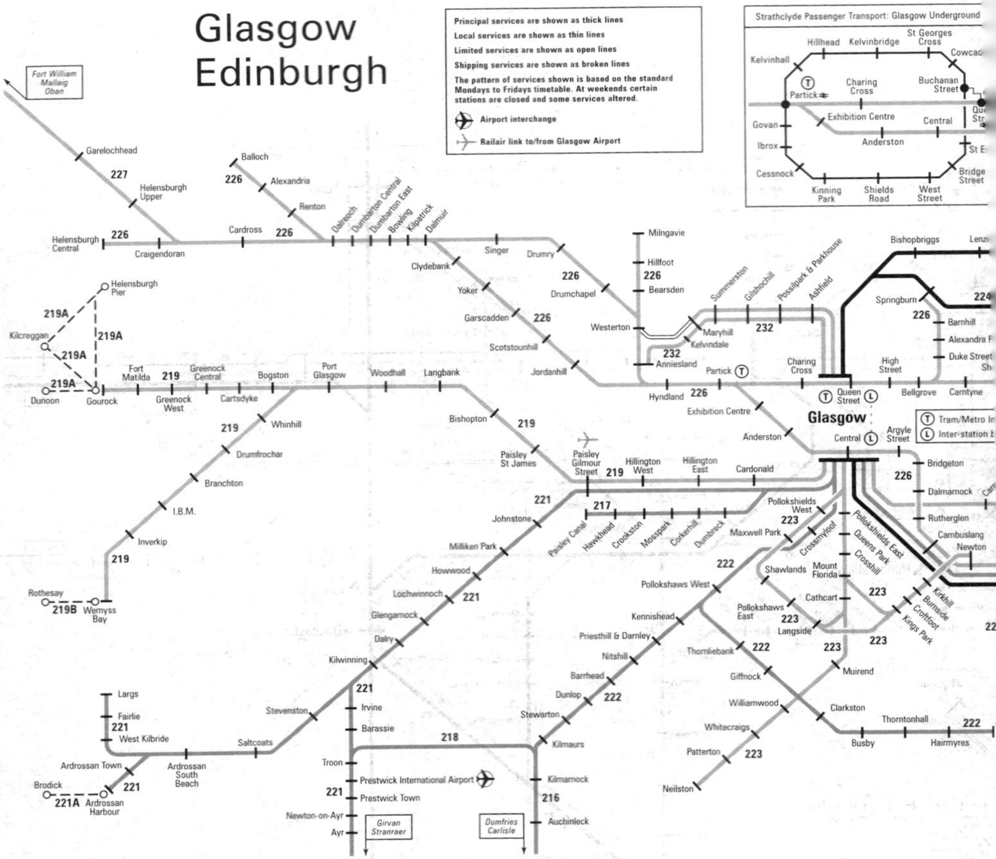

Newcastle

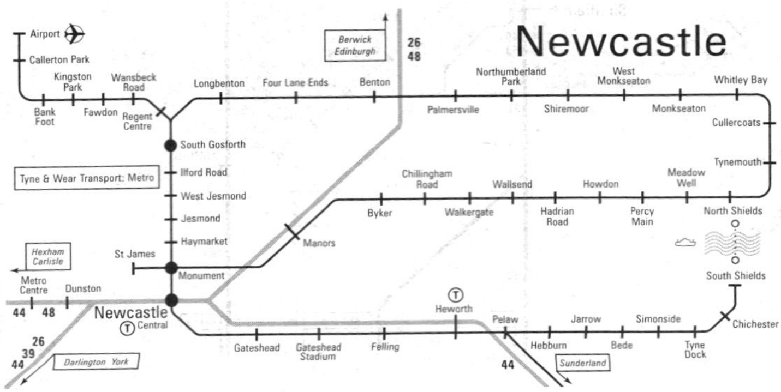

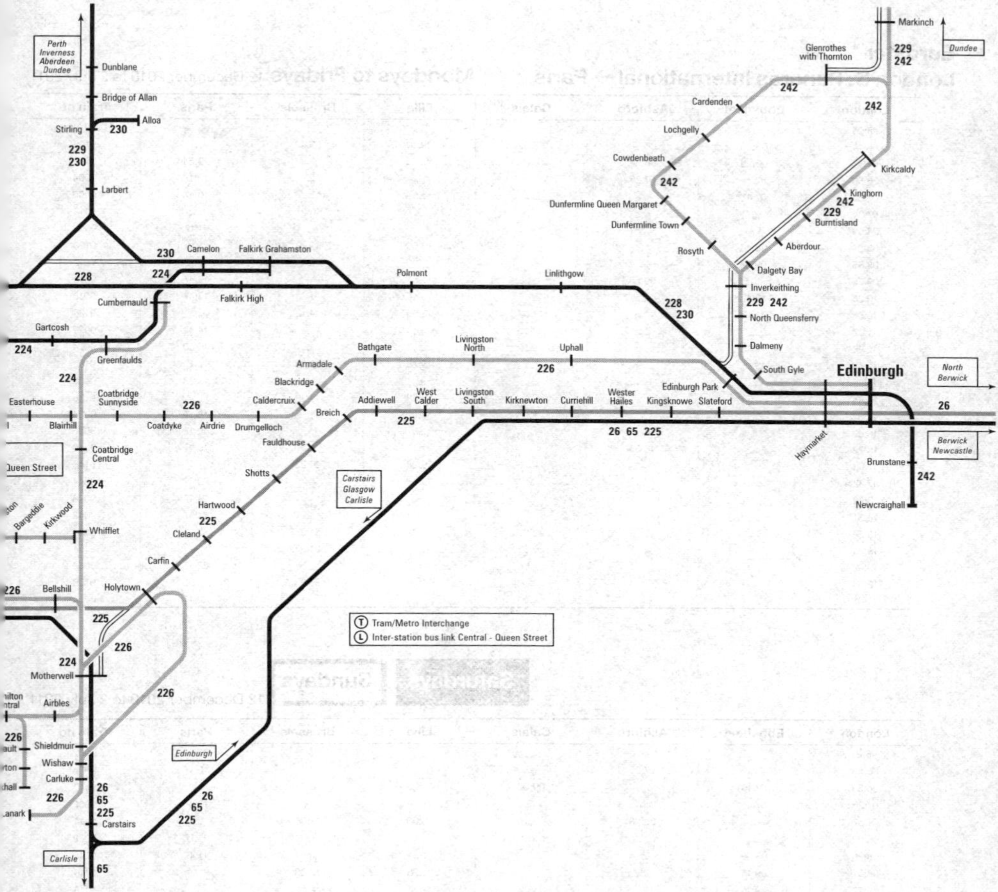

Perth
Inverness
Aberdeen
Dundee
Dunblane
Bridge of Allan
Stirling
Alloa
230
229
230
Larbert
230
Camelon
Falkirk Grahamston
228
224
Polmont
Linlithgow
Falkirk High
Cumbernauld
228
230
Gartcosh
224
Greenfaulds
224
Easterhouse
Blairhill
Coatbridge Sunnyside
Coatdyke
226
Airdrie
Drumgelloch
Caldercruix
Blackridge
Armadale
Bathgate
Livingston North
Uphall
226
Breich
Addiewell
West Calder
Livingston South
Kirknewton
Curriehill
Wester Hailes
Kingsknowe
Slateford
225
26 65 225
Queen Street
Coatbridge Central
224
Fauldhouse
Shotts
Hartwood
225
Cleland
Carfin
Holytown
Bargeddie
Kirkwood
Whifflet
226
Bellshill
225
226
224
Motherwell
226
Airbles
226
Shieldmuir
Wishaw
Carluke
226
Lanark
26
65
225
Carstairs
Carlisle
65
26
65
225
Edinburgh
Carstairs
Glasgow
Carlisle
Tram/Metro Interchange
Inter-station bus link Central - Queen Street
Markinch
Dundee
Glenrothes with Thornton
229
242
242
242
Cardenden
Lochgelly
Cowdenbeath
242
Dunfermline Queen Margaret
Dunfermline Town
Rosyth
Kirkcaldy
Kinghorn
242
229
Burntisland
Aberdour
Dalgety Bay
Inverkeithing
229 242
North Queensferry
Dalmeny
South Gyle
Edinburgh Park
Edinburgh
North Berwick
26
Haymarket
Berwick Newcastle
Brunstane
242
Newcraighall

Eurostar™

London St Pancras International → Paris

Mondays to Fridays 12 December 2010 to 2 July 2011

	London	Ebbsfleet	Ashford	Calais	Lille	Brussels	Paris	Train no
1	05:25	05:42	.....	.....	.....	.....	08:50	9078
	06:19	06:36	06:58	08:32	09:10	09:42	.....	9108
2	06:12	06:29	06:53	.....	.....	.....	09:54	9002
1	06:53	.....	07:25	.....	.....	.....	10:17	9004
	07:22	07:41	.....	.....	.....	.....	10:47	9006
	07:34	.....	.....	.....	.....	10:27	.....	9112
	08:02	.....	.....	.....	.....	.....	11:17	9008
	08:27	08:45	.....	.....	10:58	11:33	.....	9120
1	08:55	09:12	.....	.....	.....	.....	12:17	9012
	09:22	.....	09:55	.....	.....	.....	12:47	9014
	10:25	10:42	.....	.....	.....	.....	13:47	9018
	10:57	11:15	.....	13:02	13:35	14:12	.....	9126
3	11:32	.....	.....	.....	.....	.....	14:47	9022
	12:28	12:45	.....	.....	.....	.....	15:50	9024
	12:58	13:15	.....	.....	15:28	16:05	.....	9132
	14:02	.....	.....	.....	.....	.....	17:23	9030
	14:34	.....	.....	.....	16:58	17:33	.....	9138
	15:02	.....	.....	.....	.....	.....	18:17	9034
	16:02	.....	.....	.....	.....	.....	19:17	9038
	16:22	.....	16.55	.....	.....	.....	19:47	9040
	17:04	.....	.....	.....	19:28	20:03		9148
	17:32	.....	.....	.....	.....	.....	20:47	9044
	18:02	.....	.....	.....	.....	.....	21:17	9046
3	18:31	.....	.....	.....	.....	.....	21:47	9048
4	18:34	.....	.....	20:32	21:02	21:37	.....	9154
3	18:34	.....	.....	20:33	.....	21:33	.....	9154
	19:02	.....	.....	.....	.....	.....	22:17	9050
	19:34	.....	.....	.....	21:58	22:33	.....	9158
	20:02	.....	.....	.....	.....	.....	23:17	9054

Saturdays **Sundays** 12 December 2010 to 2 July 2011

	London	Ebbsfleet	Ashford	Calais	Lille	Brussels	Paris	Train no
7	06:22	.....	.....	.....	.....	.....	09:47	9002
7	06:53	.....	07:25	.....	.....	.....	10:17	9004
7	06:58	07:15	.....	09:02	09:32	10:08	.....	9110
7	07:25	07:41	.....	.....	.....	.....	10:47	9006
7	07:57	.....	08:28	.....	10:33	11:08	.....	9114
7	08:02	.....	.....	.....	.....	.....	11:17	9008
8	08:26	08:42	.....	.....	.....	.....	11:47	9010
7	08:57	09:15	.....	.....	11:28	12:03	.....	9116
8	08:57	09:15	.....	11:02	11:33	12:08	.....	9116
7	09:00	.....	.....	.....	.....	.....	12:17	9012
	09:22	.....	09:55	.....	.....	.....	12:47	9014
8	10:25	10:42	.....	.....	.....	.....	13:47	9018
7	10:25	10:42	.....	.....	.....	.....	13:50	9018
7	10:57	11:15	.....	13:02	13:35	14:12	.....	9126
7	11:25	11:42	.....	.....	.....	.....	14:47	9022
8	11:57	12:15	.....	.....	14:28	15:05	.....	9130
	12:28	12:45	.....	.....	.....	.....	15:50	9024
7	12:58	13:15	.....	.....	15:28	16:05	.....	9132
8	13:02	.....	.....	.....	.....	.....	16:17	9026
	14:02	.....	.....	.....	.....	.....	17:23	9030
8	14:34	.....	.....	.....	16:58	17:33	.....	9138
8	15:02	.....	.....	.....	.....	.....	18:17	9034
	15:32	.....	.....	.....	.....	.....	18:47	9036
	16:04	.....	.....	18:02	18:34	19:11	.....	9144
	16:22	.....	16:55	.....	.....	.....	19:47	9040
8	17:04	.....	.....	.....	19:28	20:03	.....	9148
	17:32	.....	.....	.....	.....	.....	20:47	9044
8	18:02	.....	.....	.....	.....	.....	21:17	9046
8	18:25	.....	18:55	.....	20:55	21:30	.....	9154
	19:02	.....	.....	.....	.....	.....	22:17	9050
7	19:34	.....	.....	.....	21:58	22:33	.....	9158
8	19:34	.....	.....	21:32	22:05	22:39	.....	9158
	20:02	.....	.....	.....	.....	.....	23:17	9054
8	20:32	.....	.....	.....	.....	.....	23:47	9056

Eurostar™

Paris → London St Pancras International

Mondays to Fridays 12 December 2010 to 2 July 2011

	Paris	Brussels	Lille	Calais	Ashford	Ebbsfleet	London	Train no
1	06:43	.....	.....	.....	.....	.....	07:59	9005
	.....	06:51	07:24	07:58	.....	.....	07:56	9109
	07:13	.....	.....	.....	.....	.....	08:28	9007
	08:13	.....	.....	.....	09:06	.....	09:37	9011
	.....	08:29	.....	.....	.....	.....	09:26	9115
	09:13	.....	.....	.....	.....	10:18	10:34	9015
	.....	09:59	10:32	.....	.....	.....	10:56	9121
	10:13	.....	.....	.....	.....	.....	11:28	9019
	11:13	.....	.....	.....	.....	.....	12:29	9023
	.....	12:29	13:02	.....	.....	13:15	13:33	9129
1	12:13	.....	.....	.....	.....	.....	13:28	9027
	13:04	.....	14:02*	.....	.....	14:15	14:31	9031
3	14:13	.....	.....	.....	.....	.....	15:29	9035
	.....	14:29	15:02	.....	.....	.....	15:26	9139
	15:13	.....	.....	.....	16:06	.....	16:37	9039
	.....	15:59	16:32	.....	.....	16:45	17:03	9145
	16:13	.....	.....	.....	.....	17:18	17:34	9043
	17:13	.....	.....	.....	.....	.....	18:29	9047
	.....	17:59	18:32	.....	18:33	.....	19:03	9153
	18:13	.....	.....	.....	.....	19:18	19:34	9051
	18:43	.....	.....	.....	19:36	.....	20:09	9053
	.....	18:50	19:23	19:59	.....	19:45	20:03	9157
	19:13	.....	.....	.....	.....	20:18	20:34	9055
5	.....	19:59	20:32	.....	.....	20:45	21:03	9161
	20:13	.....	.....	.....	.....	.....	21:29	9059
6	.....	20:29	21:02	.....	.....	21:15	21:33	9163
	21:13	.....	.....	.....	.....	22:18	22:34	9063

* Stops at Lille from 6 February

Saturdays Sundays 12 December 2010 to 2 July 2011

	Paris	Brussels	Lille	Calais	Ashford	Ebbsfleet	London	Train no
7	.....	06:51	07:24	07:58	.....	.....	07:56	9109
7	07:13	.....	.....	.....	.....	.....	08:28	9007
7	.....	07:59	.....	08:58	.....	.....	08:56	9113
7	08:13	.....	.....	.....	09:06	.....	09:39	9011
8 9	08:13	.....	.....	.....	09:06	.....	09:36	9011
	09:13	.....	.....	.....	.....	10:18	10:34	9015
	.....	09:29	10:02	.....	.....	.....	10:26	9119
	10:13	.....	.....	.....	.....	.....	11:28	9019
	11:13	.....	.....	.....	.....	.....	12:29	9023
7	.....	11:29	12:02	.....	.....	.....	12:26	9181
8	12:13	.....	.....	.....	.....	.....	13:29	9027
8	.....	12:20	12:53	13:28	.....	13:15	13:33	9129
	13:04	.....	14:02*	.....	.....	14:15	14:31	9031
7	.....	13:49	14:25	14:58	.....	14:45	15:03	9137
	14:13	.....	.....	.....	.....	.....	15:29	9035
8	.....	14:59	15:32	.....	.....	.....	15:56	9141
	15:13	.....	.....	.....	16:06	.....	16:39	9039
	16:13	.....	.....	.....	.....	17:18	17:34	9043
8	16:43	.....	.....	.....	.....	.....	17:59	9045
8	.....	16:49	17:25	17:58	17:33	.....	18:05	9149
7	17:13	.....	.....	.....	.....	.....	18:29	9047
8	17:13	.....	.....	.....	.....	18:18	18:34	9047
8	17:43	.....	.....	.....	.....	.....	18:59	9049
7	.....	17:59	18:32	.....	18:33	.....	19:03	9153
8	.....	17:59	18:32	.....	.....	18:45	19:03	9153
8	18:13	.....	.....	.....	.....	.....	19:29	9051
8 6	.....	18:59	19:32	.....	.....	19:45	20:03	9157
8 5	.....	18:50	19:23	19:59	.....	19:45	20:03	9157
	19:13	.....	.....	.....	.....	20:18	20:34	9055
7	.....	19:59	20:32	.....	.....	20:45	21:03	9161
	20:13	.....	.....	.....	21:06	.....	21:38	9059
8	.....	20:29	21:02	.....	.....	21:15	21:33	9163
8	20:43	.....	.....	.....	.....	.....	21:59	9061
	21:13	.....	.....	.....	.....	.....	22:29	9063

* Stops at Lille from 6 February

1 Runs Mondays and Fridays only from 4 January to 5 February. Runs Monday to Friday at all other times
2 Runs Tuesday to Thursday from 4 January to 5 February only
3 Fridays only
4 Does not run on Fridays
5 Runs from 6 February
6 Runs until 5 February
7 Saturdays only
8 Sundays only
9 From 4 January to 5 February only, arrives in London at 09:37

Variations

Amended Eurostar services may run on and around Public Holidays.
Eurostar timetables are correct at time of going to press.
Times and services are subject to change. For up to date information, please refer to the Eurostar website - www.eurostar.com

London St Pancras International → Disneyland® Resort Paris

Direct daily service

Until 2 July 2011

London	Ebbsfleet	Ashford	Lille	Marne	Train no
09:44	10:04	10:28	12:24	13:31	9074

Marne	Lille	Ashford	Ebbsfleet	London	Train no
19:37	20:38	20:37	20:59	21:19	9057

Does not run on Tuesdays and Saturdays, except from 20 December to 2 January, from 16 to 27 February, from 6 to 24 April, on 30 April and from 31 May to 5 June.

Station key

London	St Pancras International
Ebbsfleet	Ebsfleet International, Kent
Ashford	Ashford International, Kent
Calais	Calais Fréthun
Lille	Lille Europe
Brussels	Brussels-Mid/Zuid
Paris	Gare du Nord
Disneyland® Paris	Marne-la-Vallée (MLV)

London St Pancras International → Paris

From 3-Jul-11 to 10-Dec-11

Notes	Mon	Tue	Wed	Thu	Fri	Sat	Sun	London Dep	Ebbsfleet Dep	Ashford Dep	Calais-Frethun Dep	Lille Dep	Paris Arr	
	●	●	●	●	●			5:25	5:42				8:50	**9078**
						●		6:22					9:47	**9002**
	●	●	●	●	●	●		6:52		7:25			10:17	**9004**
	●	●	●	●	●	●		7:22	7:41				10:47	**9006**
	●	●	●	●	●	●		8:02					11:17	**9008**
							●	8:26	8:42				11:47	**9010**
	●	●	●	●	●			8:55	9:12				12:17	**9012**
						●		9:00					12:17	**9012**
	●	●	●	●	●	●	●	9:22		9:55			12:47	**9014**
1	●	●	●	●	●			10:00					13:17	**9016**
	●	●	●	●	●	●	●	10:25	10:42				13:47	**9018**
2	●	●	●	●	●	●	●	11:01					14:17	**9020**
						●		11:25	11:42				14:47	**9022**
					●			11:32					14:47	**9022**
	●	●	●	●	●	●	●	12:28	12:45				15:50	**9024**
1					●			13:00					16:17	**9026**
							●	13:02					16:17	**9026**
	●	●	●	●	●	●	●	14:02					17:23	**9030**
	●	●	●	●	●		●	15:02					18:17	**9034**
						●	●	15:32					18:47	**9036**
	●	●	●	●	●			16:02					19:17	**9038**
	●	●	●	●	●	●	●	16:22		16:55			19:47	**9040**
3	●	●	●	●	●			17:30					20:47	**9044**
						●	●	17:32					20:47	**9044**
	●	●	●	●	●		●	18:02					21:17	**9046**
					●			18:32					21:47	**9048**
	●	●	●	●	●	●	●	19:02					22:17	**9050**
	●	●	●	●	●	●	●	20:02					23:17	**9054**
							●	20:32					23:47	**9056**

Notes 1 Runs until 26 August 2 Runs until 27 August 3 Runs from 30 August 4 Runs until 29 August

Eurostar™ Paris → London St Pancras International

From 3-Jul-11 to 10-Dec-11

Notes	Mon	Tue	Wed	Thu	Fri	Sat	Sun	Paris *Dep*	Lille *Dep*	Calais-Frethun *Dep*	Ashford *Arr*	Ebbsfleet *Arr*	London *Arr*	
	●	●	●	●	●			06:43					07:59	**9005**
	●	●	●	●	●	●		07:13					08:28	**9007**
	●	●	●	●	●	●	●	08:13			09:06		09:36	**9011**
	●	●	●	●	●	●	●	09:13				10:18	10:34	**9015**
	●	●	●	●	●	●	●	10:13					11:28	**9019**
	●	●	●	●	●	●	●	11:13					12:29	**9023**
1					●			11:43					12:59	**9025**
	●	●	●	●	●		●	12:13					13:29	**9027**
4						●		12:13					13:29	**9027**
	●	●	●	●	●	●	●	13:04	14:06			14:18	14:36	**9031**
2							●	13:43					14:59	**9033**
					●	●	●	14:13					15:29	**9035**
4	●	●	●	●				14:13					15:29	**9035**
1					●			14:43					15:59	**9037**
	●	●	●	●	●	●	●	15:13			16:06		16:36	**9039**
	●	●	●	●	●	●	●	16:13				17:18	17:34	**9043**
							●	16:43					17:59	**9045**
	●	●	●	●	●	●		17:13					18:29	**9047**
							●	17:13				18:18	18:34	**9047**
							●	17:43					18:59	**9049**
	●	●	●	●	●			18:13				19:18	19:34	**9051**
							●	18:13					19:29	**9051**
	●	●	●	●	●			18:43			19:36		20:11	**9053**
	●	●	●	●	●	●	●	19:13				20:18	20:34	**9055**
	●	●	●	●	●			20:13					21:29	**9059**
						●	●	20:13			21:06		21:36	**9059**
							●	20:43					21:59	**9061**
	●	●	●	●	●			21:13				22:18	22:34	**9063**
						●	●	21:13					22:29	**9063**

2 Runs From 30 August 4 Runs until 29 August

[illegible]ancras International → Brussels

From 3-Jul-11 to 10-Dec-11

Notes								London	Ebbsfleet	Ashford	Calais-Frethun	Lille	Bruxelles	
	Mon	Tue	Wed	Thu	Fri	Sat	Sun	*Dep*	*Dep*	*Dep*	*Arr*	*Arr*	*Arr*	
	●	●	●	●	●			06:19	06:36	06:58	08:29	09:07	09:42	**9108**
						●		06:58	07:15		08:59	09:29	10:08	**9110**
	●	●	●	●	●			07:34				09:54	10:33	**9112**
						●		07:57		08:28		10:30	11:08	**9114**
	●	●	●	●	●			08:27	08:45			10:54	11:33	**9120**
						●		08:57	09:15			11:24	12:03	**9116**
							●	08:57	09:15		10:59	11:30	12:08	**9116**
	●	●	●	●	●	●		10:57	11:15		12:59	13:31	14:12	**9126**
							●	11:57	12:15			14:24	15:05	**9130**
	●	●	●	●	●	●		12:57	13:15			15:24	16:05	**9132**
	●	●	●	●	●		●	14:34				16:54	17:33	**9138**
						●	●	16:04			17:59	18:30	19:11	**9144**
	●	●	●	●	●		●	17:04				19:24	20:05	**9148**
	●	●	●	●				18:34			20:29	20:59	21:37	**9154**
					●			18:34			20:29		21:33	**9154**
							●	18:25		18:55		20:51	21:30	**9154**
	●	●	●	●	●	●		19:34				21:54	22:33	**9158**
							●	19:34			21:29	22:01	22:39	**9158**

Eurostar™ Brussels → London St Pancras International

From 3-Jul-11 to 10-Dec-11

Notes							Bruxelles	Lille	Calais-Frethun	Ashford	Ebbsfleet	London	
	Mon	Tue	Wed	Thu	Fri	Sat	Sun	*Dep*	*Dep*	*Dep*	*Dep*	*Dep*	*Arr*	
	●	●	●	●	●	●		06:51	07:28	08:02			07:56	**9109**
	●	●	●	●	●			08:05					08:59	**9113**
						●		07:59		09:02			08:56	**9113**
						●	●	09:29	10:05				10:26	**9119**
	●	●	●	●	●			09:59	10:35				10:56	**9121**
						●		11:29	12:05			12:15	12:33	**9181**
							●	12:20	12:56	13:32		13:15	13:33	**9129**
	●	●	●	●	●			12:29	13:05			13:15	13:33	**9129**
						●		13:49	14:29	15:02		14:45	15:03	**9137**
	●	●	●	●	●			14:29	15:05				15:26	**9139**
							●	14:59	15:35				15:56	**9141**
	●	●	●	●	●			15:59	16:35			16:45	17:03	**9145**
							●	16:49	17:29	18:02	17:33		18:06	**9149**
	●	●	●	●	●	●		17:59	18:35		18:33		19:03	**9153**
							●	17:59	18:35			18:45	19:03	**9153**
	●	●	●	●	●		●	18:50	19:26	20:02		19:45	20:03	**9157**
	●	●	●	●	●			19:59	20:35			20:45	21:09	**9161**
1						●		19:59	20:35			20:45	21:09	**9161**
							●	20:29	21:05			21:15	21:33	**9163**
2						●		20:29	21:05			21:15	21:33	**9163**

Notes 1 Runs from 30 August 2 Runs until 29 August

… International → Disneyland™ Paris Route

From 3-Jul-11 to 10-Dec-11

Notes								London	Ebbsfleet	Ashford	Lille	Marne La Vallée	
	Mon	Tue	Wed	Thu	Fri	Sat	Sun	*Dep*	*Dep*	*Dep*	*Arr*	*Arr*	
	●		●	●	●		●	09:44	10:04	10:28	12:24	13:31	**9074**

Notes								Marne La Vallée	Lille	Ashford	Ebbsfleet	London	
	Mon	Tue	Wed	Thu	Fri	Sat	Sun	*Dep*	*Dep*	*Dep*	*Arr*	*Arr*	
	●		●	●	●		●	19:37		20:37	20:59	21:19	**9057**